A

COMPLETE CONCORDANCE

TO THE

OLD AND NEW TESTAMENT

AND

THE APOCRYPHA.

A

COMPLETE CONCORDANCE

TO THE

OLD AND NEW TESTAMENT

OR A

DICTIONARY AND ALPHABETICAL INDEX TO THE BIBLE

WITH

A COMPLETE TABLE OF PROPER NAMES WITH THEIR MEANINGS IN THE ORIGINAL LANGUAGES,
A CONCORDANCE TO THE PROPER NAMES OF THE OLD AND NEW TESTAMENT,
A CONCORDANCE TO THE APOCRYPHA, AND A COMPENDIUM OF THE HOLY SCRIPTURES,
ETC., ETC.

BY ALEXANDER CRUDEN, M.A.

WITH A MEMOIR
BY WILLIAM YOUNGMAN

FREDERICK WARNE AND CO., LTD.
LONDON AND NEW YORK

PRINTED FOR THE PUBLISHERS
BY
WILLIAM CLOWES AND SONS, LIMITED
LONDON AND BECCLES
1292. 165
PRINTED IN GREAT BRITAIN

TO THE QUEEN*

MADAM,

THIS CONCORDANCE, the work of several years, was begun with a design to promote the study of the Holy Scriptures; and, in pursuance thereof, is now published with many improvements beyond any book of this kind in the *English* language.

Long before this Work was ready for the press, I designed humbly to offer it to your Majesty, and to beg leave to publish it under your royal protection. Your Majesty's illustrious qualities and example in the great scenes of your valuable life, encourage me humbly to beg your countenance to a well-meant attempt for promoting the knowledge of our holy Religion.

The beauty of your person, and the fine accomplishments of your mind, were so celebrated in your father's court, that there was no Prince in the Empire, who had room for such an alliance, that was not ambitious of gaining a Princess of such noble virtues into his Family, either as a Daughter, or as a Consort.

And though the heir to all the dominions of the house of *Austria* was desirous of your alliance, yet you generously declined the prospect of a Crown that was inconsistent with the enjoyment of your Religion. The great Disposer of all things, however, kept in store a reward for such exalted virtue, and by the secret methods of his wisdom hath brought your Majesty to a Crown, as famous for defending and supporting the Protestant Religion, as it is conspicuous for its glory and splendour; which is such a return of Divine Providence as is to be admired with great thankfulness, though without the least surprise, since *He whose kingdom ruleth over all* hath declared, that *such as honour Him, He will honour*.

It was the fame of this heroic constancy that determined his Majesty to desire in marriage a Princess who was now more celebrated for her Christian magnanimity, than for the beauty of her person, which had been so universally admired. We of the *British* nation have reason to rejoice that such a proposal was made and accepted, and that your Majesty, with regard to these two successive treaties, showed as much prudence in your compliance with the one, as piety in your refusal of the other. You no sooner arrived at *Hanover* than you improved the lustre of that court, which was before reckoned among the politest in *Europe*, and increased the happiness of a people, who were before looked upon as the happiest in the Empire. And you immediately became the darling of the Princess *Sophia*, a Princess, justly acknowledged to be one of the most accomplished women of the age in which she lived, who was much pleased with the conversation of one, in whom she saw so lively an image of her own youth.

We daily discover those admirable qualities for which your Majesty was famed in other countries, and rejoice to see them exerted in our Island, where we ourselves are made happy by their influence. We behold the throne of these kingdoms surrounded by your Majesty's royal and numerous Progeny, and hear with pleasure of the great care your Majesty takes to instil early into their minds the principles of Religion, Virtue, and Honour.

Your Majesty is possessed of all those talents which make conversation either delightful or improving. Your fine taste in the elegant arts, and skill in several modern languages, is such, that your discourse is not confined to the ordinary subjects of conversation, but is adapted, with an uncommon grace, to every occasion, and entertains the politest persons of different nations. That agreeable turn which appears in your sentiments upon the most ordinary affairs of life, which is so suitable to the delicacy of your sex, the politeness of your education, and the splendour of your quality, is observed by every one who has the honour to approach you.

But the great regard your Majesty has shown to religion, which diffuses the greatest glory around a human character, encourages me to hope that this Work will meet with your favourable acceptance. May it therefore please your Majesty to take into your royal protection this CONCORDANCE, the design of which is to render the study of the Scriptures more easy. Whatever may be wanting either in the Work or Author, is abundantly supplied by the dignity of the subject; which consideration chiefly encouraged me to presume to offer it to your Majesty, whom God hath exalted to the most eminent station, and blessed with extraordinary endowments of mind, and with a benevolent and beneficent disposition. To whom then can I more properly offer this Work than to your Majesty, who is celebrated both for your inclination and capacity to do good?

May the great GOD continue to multiply his blessings upon the King, your Majesty, and every branch of your Royal Family: May your life be long continued to serve GOD faithfully on earth, and may you reign for ever with Him in heaven, through JESUS CHRIST our Lord. Amen.

These are the sincere prayers of him who is, with the most profound respect,

May it please your Majesty,

Your Majesty's

Most dutiful and

Most obedient servant,

ALEXANDER CRUDEN

London, October, 1737.

* The first Edition of this *Concordance* was dedicated to Queen *Caroline*, and was presented, November 3, 1737, to her Majesty, who departed this life the 20th of that very month.

TO THE KING.

SIRE,

This CONCORDANCE was begun with a design to promote the study and knowledge of the Holy Scriptures, and the method taken therein is deemed by competent judges to be the best towards a complete *Concordance* that hath hitherto appeared in our language. It is acknowledged to be a useful book to private Christians who search the Scriptures, and to be very necessary for all the Preachers of the Gospel. Therefore to whom can this new Edition be more properly offered than to your Majesty, now in the beginning of your reign, having already manifested a great regard to religion, and an earnest concern for promoting it among your subjects?

All other books are of little or no importance in comparison of the Holy Scriptures, which are a revelation from God, and are given as the only rule of faith and practice. If the kings of *Israel* were required not only " to read the law of *Moses* all the days of their life, but also to write out a copy of it with their own hand, that they might learn to fear the Lord their God, and keep all the words of his law;" it may be reasonably expected that Christian Princes should make the glorious Gospel of our Lord and Saviour Jesus Christ their daily study, that it may become their constant guide and rule for the government of their people, as well as for their own salvation.

It hath been often observed, that the most effectual way to a general external reformation is " to make Religion a step to preferment, and Irreligion a bar to it;" because example has a more powerful influence over the minds of men than precept, or even than punishment. The early declarations and strong resolutions which your Majesty was pleased to make at your coming to the throne, " That you would encourage those who are religious, and discourage those that are otherwise," rejoiced the hearts of all who earnestly desire the revival of vital and practical religion, and to see your Majesty's subjects a holy and happy people.

True piety has been in all ages accounted the truest honour; for religion diffuses the greatest glory around a human character, and sweetens and embalms the memory of Princes. A pious Prince, who hath shown a hearty concern for the eternal happiness of his people, as well as for their present protection, will be remembered with great esteem and honour; for the Scripture says, that " the memory of the just is blessed." When they are spoken of, it is with praise and commendation by all good men. All other accomplishments, without true grace and real religion, cannot make the children of men happy, who must all die and rise again, " and appear before the judgment-seat of Christ, to receive according to what they have done in the body, whether good or bad."

The memory of *Hezekiah*, the religious king of *Judah*, is precious: he hath been celebrated in all ages of the Church for his pious zeal in the reformation of his people at the beginning of his reign; for " God honours those that honour him, and they who despise him shall be lightly esteemed." It is said of that pious King, that " he trusted in the Lord God of *Israel*, so that after him there was none like him among all the Kings of *Judah*, nor any that were before him: for he clave to the Lord, and departed not from following him, but kept his commandments, which the Lord commanded *Moses*." *Hezekiah*, like your Majesty, began his reign in his youth, yet his zeal for the worship of God, and for promoting religion among his subjects, carried him through the great difficulties of reforming a people, who had so much degenerated into gross idolatry. May the great God be the guide of your life, and direct and prosper you, that it may be said by the present and future ages, that King George the Third hath been an Hezekiah to our *British Israel*.

I doubt not but your Majesty will pardon my forbearing to enter upon your valuable personal accomplishments: I shall only add that, when it pleased God, the sovereign Lord of life and death, to deprive us of the blessing of your Royal Grandfather King George the Second, the Protector of our Religion and Liberties for many years, it was esteemed a national blessing that God had favoured *Great Britain* with a Prince born and educated among us; who makes the happiness of his People the rule of his government; and without Religion there can be no real happiness for Prince or People.

When your Majesty came to the throne, the loyal and affectionate addresses from your subjects in all parts of the *British* dominions, shewed their great hopes and strong expectations of being happy under your Majesty's government. We of the *British* nation have reason thankfully to remember the appearances of Divine Providence in the preservation of our Religion and Liberties, particularly in settling and establishing the Protestant Succession, and in disappointing from time to time all the contrivances and attempts of its enemies, whether secret or open; and in your Majesty's coming to the throne with the hearts of all your subjects united to you as the heart of one man.

May it please God to bestow his choicest gifts upon your Majesty, upon your Royal Mother the Princess Dowager of *Wales*, and all the Royal Family, and upon your numerous and powerful People. May you be blessed, and made a real blessing, and may your reign be long and prosperous; and after you have been enabled to serve God faithfully here upon earth, may you reign for ever with him in heaven through Jesus Christ. This is the sincere and earnest prayer of him who is, with great humility and profound respect,

May it please your Majesty,

Your Majesty's most dutiful,

And most obedient subject and servant,

ALEXANDER CRUDEN.

London, June 11, 1761.

PREFACE TO THE FIRST EDITION

A CONCORDANCE is a DICTIONARY, or an INDEX, to the BIBLE, wherein all the words used through the inspired writings are arranged alphabetically, and the various places where they occur are referred to, to assist us in finding out passages, and comparing the several significations of the same word. A work of this kind, which tends so much to render the study of the holy Scriptures more easy to all Christians, must be acknowledged to be very useful; for if a good Index to any other book is to be valued, much more ought one to the BIBLE, which is a revelation from GOD, given as the only rule of our faith and practice, and to discover to us the way to eternal life through our Lord JESUS CHRIST.

I do not here propose to treat of the incomparable excellences of that divine book, which is above all commendation, and will be in the highest esteem by all the true members of the church of GOD, whose faith, hope, and comfort are built upon these divine Oracles.

What I shall further do in this Preface, shall be to present the Reader with a short historical account of CONCORDANCES, which will tend to display their great usefulness; and then acquaint him with the method I have followed in this.

Hugo de S. Charo, a preaching Friar of the Dominican order, who was afterwards a Cardinal, was the first who compiled a *Concordance* to the holy Scriptures: he died in the year 1262. He had studied the *Bible* very closely, and for carrying on this great and laborious work the more successfully, we are told he employed five hundred Monks of his order to assist him. He framed an Index of all the declinable words, and referred to the places where they were to be found.

This *Latin Concordance* has been frequently printed with improvements; and since that time works of this sort have been brought to much greater perfection than formerly. At first it was thought sufficient to specify the chapter wherein the word occurred, with these letters *a, b, c, d*, as marks to point out the beginning, the middle, or the end of the chapter. But after *Robert Stephens*, in the year 1545, had divided the chapters of the Bible into verses, the verses likewise began to be numbered, and the letters in the editions of the *Concordances* to be suppressed. And in 1555 this eminent Printer published his fine *Concordance*, wherein the chapters and verses are exactly distinguished.

It could not be thought that when so useful a work as Cardinal *Hugo's* came to be known, men, who carefully studied the Scriptures, would be satisfied that such assistance should be confined only to those who understood *Latin*: accordingly several have been published in various languages, particularly Rabbi *Mordecai Nathan*, otherwise called *Isaac Nathan*, composed an *Hebrew Concordance* in imitation of Cardinal *Hugo's*. He began it in the year 1438, and completed it in 1448, being no less than ten years in finishing it; and besides, as he himself says, he was obliged to employ a great many writers in this work. After printing was invented, it was printed several times: first at *Venice* by *Daniel Bomberg*, in the year 1523, under the title of *Meir Netib*, that is to say, *Which giveth light in the way*; at *Basil* by *Frobenius* in 1581, and at *Rome* in 1621. This was the foundation of that noble work published by *John Buxtorf*, the son, being assisted by his father's papers, at *Basil*, in 1632.

As to the *Greek* text of the New Testament, a *Concordance* was published by *Henry Stephens* at *Geneva* in 1599, and republished in 1624: but a more accurate one was compiled by *Erasmus Schmidius*, and published at *Wittemberg* in 1638, which was republished more correctly at *Leipsic* in 1716, and is reckoned a very complete performance.

A *Greek Concordance* to the *Septuagint Version* of the *Old Testament*, must be owned to be very useful to such as are for comparing the expressions used in it with those of the *New Testament*, and to those who read the *Fathers*. *Conrad Kircher* of *Augsbourg* is celebrated for his *Greek Concordance* of the *Old Testament*, printed at *Francfort* in 1602. This author has inserted the *Hebrew* words in an alphabetical order, and placed under them the *Greek* words to which they answer. But since that time, an excellent *Concordance* to the *Old Testament* has been published at *Amsterdam* in 1718, by the aged and worthy Minister of *Groningen*, M. *Abraham Trommius*, who instead of following the *Hebrew* alphabet with *Kircher* has chosen rather to observe the order of the *Greek* alphabet.

There have been *Concordances* likewise published in various modern languages; in *French* by M. *Gravelin*; in *High Dutch* and *Low Dutch* by several; the most complete one in *Low Dutch* is that begun by M. *Martinitz*, and finished by M. *Trommius* before mentioned. In *English* we have had many. The first was published by Mr. *Marbeck* in 1550, which is dedicated to the pious King *Edward* VI. but this referred only to chapters, not verses. Then Mr. *Cotton* published a pretty large *Concordance*, which has been often printed. Afterwards Mr. *Newman* published one more complete; and lastly, we have had one published under the title of the *Cambridge Concordance*. There have been several abstracts or small *Concordances* published: First by Mr. *Downame*, the next by Mr. *Vavasor Powell*, then by Mr. *John Jackson*, and afterwards by Mr. *Samuel Clarke*. As also other works of this nature have been written by way of a *Dictionary* or *Concordance*, but in a different method, as Mr. *Wilson's Christian Dictionary*, Mr. *Knight's Axiomatical Concordance*, Mr. *Bernard's Thesaurus Biblicus*, and Mr. *Wicken's Concordance*, &c.

Thus it appears that we have had *Concordances* to the BIBLE some centuries ago; and the world has been so sensible of their usefulness, that many of them have been composed and published in different languages. But as there are several in our language, it may be inquired, What occasioned my undertaking this great and laborious work, or what advantages it has above any other hitherto published?

When I first began this work, I designed to compose a useful *Concordance* in *Octavo*; but after I had printed several specimens, I found it necessary to alter my scheme, and to compile one to be printed in this large volume, in order to make those improvements which now render it preferable to any other.

The method is easy and regular, and each text of Scripture is generally contained in one line, whereby the reader may readily find the place he wants, if he remembers any material word. When there are two or more texts of Scripture that are parallel, I have generally mentioned the first that occurs in order in the BIBLE, and have directly added the parallel texts. It is printed with a good letter, though pretty small, which was necessary in order to bring it into this volume, and make it contain *multum in varvo*, much in a little compass; and great care has been taken that the figures referring to the chapters and verses of the BIBLE be exact and correct. When a text is marked with a †, it denotes a marginal reading.

This CONCORDANCE is divided into three *Alphabets*.

The *first Alphabet* contains the *appellative* or *common* words, which is the principal part. It is very full and large, and any text may be found by looking for any material word, whether it be *substantive, adjective, verb*, &c.

In this part, I have given the various SIGNIFICATIONS of the principal words, which, I hope, will be esteemed a useful improvement, there not being any thing of this kind in the other large *Concordances*. By this improvement the Reader will have many texts explained, and difficulties removed; and the meaning of the Scripture may be here known by that which is accounted the best rule of interpreting Scripture, namely, *by comparing one Scripture with another*. There is so large a collection of the various *Significations* of many words in Scripture, as may, perhaps, be not only useful to private Christians, but also to those who preach the Gospel; for hereby many important things may be observed at one view, without the trouble of turning over several volumes; and occasion is sometimes taken to give an account of the *Jewish* customs and ceremonies, by which the Reader is led into the meaning of many passages of Scripture, as may be seen in the words, *Elder, Ephod, Synagogue*, &c.

The *second Alphabet* contains the *Proper Names* in the holy Scriptures, which the Reader will receive with improvements, as in *Abraham, David*, &c. The texts referred to where those names are mentioned, give a short historical account of the remarkable things recorded in Scripture concerning them. To this part is prefixed a *Table*, containing the *Significations* of the words in the original languages from which they are derived.

The *third* and *last Alphabet* is a *Concordance* for those books that are called APOCRYPHAL, which is only added that this work might not be deficient in any thing that is treated of in any other *Concordance;* those books not being of divine Inspiration, nor any part of the Canon of Scripture, and therefore are of no authority in the church of GOD.

I conclude this *Preface*, with praying that GOD, who hath graciously enabled me to bring this large Work to a conclusion, would render it useful to those who seriously and carefully search the Scriptures; and grant that the sacred writings, which are so important and highly worthy of esteem, may meet with all that affection and regard which they deserve. May those who profess to believe the Scriptures to be a *Revelation* from GOD, apply themselves to the reading and study of them; and may they by the Holy Spirit of GOD, who indited the Scriptures, be made *wise to salvation through faith which is in Christ Jesus.* Amen.

A. C.

London, October, 1737.

PREFACE TO THE SECOND EDITION.

As to what respects this NEW EDITION, notwithstanding the great pains taken in the *First*, there was room for improvements. The filling up of the lines to make the text fuller could not so well be done in the manuscript copy, as in the printed. This renders the sentences more complete in many thousands of places: moreover the texts are more distinct in many places by the leading words being distinguished in *Italic characters*. Some texts are added, and some improvements are made in the *Significations* of words, and an historical account is given of some eminent persons under their *Proper Names;* and other things that need not be particularly mentioned.

The labours of many persons to compile *Concordances* to the BIBLE, and their acceptance from time to time by the public, shew their great usefulness. It may be reckoned a good sign that religion is revived in some considerable degree in the present age, by the great demand for *Concordances* and *religious books*. The *First Edition* of several thousands in number has been long sold off, which shews this book's favourable reception from the public; and a demand has been long made for a new Edition. There are few books more necessary to those who study their BIBLES than a *Concordance*, whether private Christians, or Ministers of the Gospel who make the Scripture the standard of their preaching. I was told by an eminent Minister, that the BIBLE and this *Concordance* taught him to preach. This *Dictionary* may be a help, but the Spirit of GOD is the best Teacher, who alone can powerfully and effectually teach and impress the heart with the truths revealed in the Scriptures, and make those who read and study the sacred writings *wise to salvation*.

My great aim and design in this Work is, that it may be the means of propagating among my countrymen, and through all the *British* dominions, the knowledge of GOD through our Lord JESUS CHRIST, and of ourselves, as the same is revealed in the Scriptures; for whose good I heartily wish that it were more complete than it is. For though it be called in the title-page, *A Complete Concordance*, poor sinful man can do nothing absolutely perfect and complete, and therefore the word *complete* is only to be taken in a comparative sense: yet competent judges are of opinion that the method here taken is the best which has appeared in our language towards a *complete Concordance*.

It is hoped that the above-mentioned improvements in this new Edition will serve to recommend the work more and more to the favour of the public. May it please God, by the powerful operations of his Spirit, to make it useful for the spiritual benefit of those who diligently and carefully use it.

A. C.

London, June 11, 1761.

PREFACE TO THE THIRD EDITION.

THE First and Second Editions of this *Concordance* having been well received by the public, seems to shew the great usefulness of such a Dictionary to the BIBLE; for it may be justly said, that if Christians were convinced that *Concordances* tended so much as they really do to promote the study and knowledge of the holy Scriptures, they would be more desirous of having one: and some Ministers have expressed so great an esteem for this *Concordance*, that they have said, "If they could not have another copy, they would not part with it for many pounds." This THIRD EDITION now appears, with some improvements, which it is hoped will engage the continuance of the public approbation this work has already been favoured with. May it please GOD to make it more and more useful, and a blessing to the Church of GOD through our Lord JESUS CHRIST. *Amen.*

A. C.

London, March 24, 1769.

PUBLISHERS' PREFACE.

THE use and great value of a Concordance to the Holy Scriptures is acknowledged by the whole Christian world, since the best and truest interpretation of them must be obtained by the comparison of parallel passages with each other, and these are most quickly found by reference to a good Concordance.

A profitable study of the Bible can scarcely be achieved without one. Bishop Horsley said, "It should be a rule with every one who would read the Holy Scriptures with advantage and improvement, to compare every text which may seem important for the doctrine it may contain, or remarkable for the turn of the expression, with the parallel passages in other parts of Holy Writ; that is, with the passages in which the subject matter is the same, the sense equivalent, or the turn of the expression similar. It is incredible to any one who has not to some degree made the experiment, what a proficiency may be made in that knowledge 'that maketh wise unto salvation,' by studying the Scriptures in this manner without any other commentary or exposition than what the different parts of the Sacred Volume mutually furnish for each other. I will not scruple to assert that the most illiterate Christian, if he can but read his English Bible, and will take the pains to read it in this manner, will not only attain all that practical knowledge that is necessary to his salvation, but by God's blessing he will become learned in everything relating to his religion, in such a degree that he will not be liable to be misled either by the refined arguments or the false assertions of those who endeavour to engraft their own opinions on the Oracles of God."

Of the Concordances hitherto published, Cruden's is allowed to be the best. Its popularity has endured for two centuries, and it is to be found in the study of nearly every Minister of the Word. It ought to be side by side with the Bible in every Christian home. Mr. Spurgeon said, "Be sure you buy a *genuine unabridged Cruden*, and none of the modern substitutes, good as they may be at the price. . . . *You need only one;* have none but the best."

The text of Youngman's has long been recognised as the best; it is that of the present volume, which contains the whole of the Concordance, without any abbreviation. The admirable COLLECTION OF THE NAMES AND TITLES GIVEN TO JESUS CHRIST,—the "*Collection of the Appellations given to the Church of God in the Scriptures,*"—the Compendium of the Holy Bible, and the Contents of each Chapter, which are omitted in most of the cheap editions extant, are retained, being of great value to the Bible student, and making the work as complete as possible.

The full Concordance of the Apocrypha is also given; an alphabetical list of the Proper Names in the Old and New Testaments, with their signification in the original languages; a Concordance of the Proper Names, and a Summary of the Contents of the Bible, complete "a genuine and unabridged Cruden."

NOTE

As this book is a reprint of the original Cruden's Concordance, it will be seen that the letters I and J are together in one section, in alphabetical order, as was the accepted custom when the work was originally compiled. The letter J as known today was the curved initial form of the letter I and was used preceding a vowel.

CONTENTS.

SKETCH

OF

THE LIFE AND CHARACTER

OF

ALEXANDER CRUDEN.

The Sacred Scriptures, of the Old and New Testament, were written and published in the same manner and form as other books of the age and country to which they belong. The prose writings had originally that unbroken flow which distinguishes this species of composition, whilst the poetic parts of the Old Testament were subjected to such arrangements as formed the peculiar quality of Hebrew poesy. The divisions into chapters and verses, which now prevail, were the work of industrious men in later ages, when, in consequence of that strict investigation which the Scriptures had to undergo, for the support or confutation of various disputed points, there arose an eager desire for a verbal examination of their contents, and a consequent necessity for frequent references. It may be, that neither religion nor the Scriptures would have made a worse appearance at the present day, if these changes had never taken place. The breaks made by the chapters frequently occasion a misapprehension of the meaning of the sacred writers, as they sometimes occur in the midst of a chain of reasoning, separating the conclusion from the premises, or both from their application. And as most persons, from the force of habit, continue to read, both in public and private, neither more nor less than a chapter, the errors which are acknowledged to arise from these injudicious divisions, fail of being corrected in practice. Amongst innumerable instances of this kind, the fourth and fifth chapters of the Epistle to the Romans, the fourth and fifth of the Second Epistle to the Corinthians, and the first and second of the Second Epistle of Peter, may be mentioned as illustrations. The division into verses has produced a still more injurious effect. These break the continuity and even surface of the Scriptures into an infinite number of sections, all like electric points, glistening with the fires of controversy; whilst they bring these, apparently distinct and independent propositions, into a state of unnatural prominence. In consequence of these arrangements, all the varieties of sects with which Christendom abounds, are enabled to bring "chapter and verse" for their conflicting and sometimes contradictory statements. Yet, though these distinctions may not have been of advantage to the cause of truth, and to the right understanding of the Scriptures, they have frequently assisted the meditations of the pious Christian, and been found convenient to divines, in the composition of their public discourses. The detached form in which the most important and interesting sentiments appear, gives the memory a firmer hold upon them, and impresses them more strongly on the feelings of the heart. Whether, however, this condition of the Scripture has been for the better or the worse, it has now gained so firm an establishment, as probably to be unalterable; and it forms the basis on which Concordances are constructed, whilst it greatly increases their use and necessity.

The preface to the first edition of Cruden's Concordance, gives an historical account of all that had preceded his own; and states very clearly the advantages of the great work on which he exerted the energies of his mind, and employed the most active portion of his life. The numerous editions which have been published, and the innumerable copies which have been sold, prove its excellence, and its perfect adaptation to the wants of the public. As, however, the value of such a work is greatly dependent on its correctness, much labour has been bestowed in every succeeding edition, to obtain this result. With what degree of success this difficult task has been attended, may be judged from the fact, that in the first fifty pages of the best quarto edition, have been discovered nearly one hundred typographical errors. The publishers of the present edition have exhausted the resources of their art in producing a clear and legible page, and they have adopted every precaution for the attainment of the highest possible degree of accuracy. If defects should still be discovered, their existence will not arise from any deficiency of labour or expense in the execution of the work.

Few of those who consult a Concordance will think of seeking for entertainment from a life of the author; and fewer still would imagine, that a man, who could confine himself for years to such an employment, could be the subject of that waywardness of mind which frequently attends the higher powers of genius, and excites the sympathies of mankind. Yet Alexander Cruden was one of those,

> "Or crazed by care, or crossed by hopeless love,"

who trod the path of life on the verge of that awful abyss, where the hopes and happiness of so many great minds have been ingulfed. And if madness was, in his case, softened into eccentricity, or directed to the correction and amendment of the generation in which he lived, he was probably indebted, for his escape, to that absorption of mind which such a work as this must have occasioned. What would have been to others intolerable drudgery, was a sedative to his agitated mind; and the labour, which would have wasted the energies of a happier man, was the balm of his wounded spirit. Who then was Alexander

Cruden? and what were those sorrows which sought relief in the intensity of mental application, and in unwearied, though often visionary, efforts for the public good?

He is recorded to have been the second son of a worthy citizen, a baillie or alderman of Aberdeen, where he was born in 1701, and educated in the grammar-school of that city. In this school he was the companion of some who afterwards became eminent, amongst whom he is said to have frequently mentioned George Earl Marischal, and James afterwards the celebrated Mareschal Keith.

At the age of nineteen, he took the degree of Master of Arts, at Marischal College, and attended, probably with a view to the ministry, the divinity lectures of the Rev. Mr. Blackwell; but an incident occurred, at this period of his life, which, operating on a sensitive and irritable constitution, blasted his fondest hopes, darkened his fairest prospects, and cast him upon the world with a shattered and distracted mind.

Whilst a student at the university, he had imbibed an ardent affection for the daughter of a minister at Aberdeen. This attachment he prosecuted with his characteristic ardour, but failed of obtaining the success which he desired. The lady was determined against his suit, and the eagerness and obtrusiveness of his applications at last determined her father to close his doors against him. The disappointment overpowered his reason, and his friends were obliged to confine him in a private receptacle for lunatics. The covert of this asylum sheltered him from a heavier calamity; for it was subsequently discovered that this unhappy lady had been the victim of a guilty attachment to one of her brothers. But the wound was incurable, and rankled in his bosom to the close of his earthly career. Many years afterwards, when he was settled in London, his friend Mr. Chalmers, wishing to serve him, offered to introduce him to a merchant near the Royal Exchange, who happened to be a near relation of the young lady. On knocking at the door, Mr. Cruden was astonished to see it opened by the lady herself. He started back with visible signs of wonder and agony, and grasping his friend's hand, exclaimed wildly, "Ah! she has still her fine black eyes." The door to which he had been accidentally led, was that of her youngest brother. No subsequent interview took place, but he never mentioned her without the strongest manifestations of grief and compassion.

In the year 1737, from disappointment in the expected patronage to his Concordance, he was again attacked by his former malady, and was placed in a private asylum at Bethnal Green. On his release, he published a whimsical and satirical pamphlet, describing the hardships to which he had been subjected. He also commenced an action in Westminster Hall against Dr. Munro and others, which was disposed of on July 7th, 1739, by a verdict for the defendants, and exposed him to the taunt of Chief Justice Lee.

He underwent another temporary confinement at Chelsea in 1753, and again endeavoured to avenge himself by publishing an account of those receptacles for the disordered in mind. He also entered into a correspondence with his sister, and some other persons, in which he proposed to them, with great simplicity, a mode by which they might recompense him in a slight degree for the injustice which they had done him. He would have persuaded his friends to submit to imprisonment in Newgate, and to his sister he offered, what appeared to him very mild terms, that she should pay him a fine of £10 to £15, and take her choice of 48 hours' confinement in the prisons of Newgate, Reading, Aylesbury, or that in Windsor Castle.

There is reason to apprehend, that the treatment of the inmates of public and private asylums for lunatics was, at that period, exceedingly improper, harsh, and often cruel. None of the maladies to which our nature is exposed require, in a greater degree, the kindness and sympathy of our fellows; and in none is there so great temptation to the exercise of arbitrary and despotic authority. The unhappy patients are, of necessity, abandoned by their friends, to the sole care and control of professional strangers; and these are, likewise, obliged to delegate their authority to inferior ministers. Sad and bitter must have been the feelings of such as were capable of appreciating the injustice to which they were exposed, and of comparing the stern discipline of a mad-house, with the indulgence and tenderness of domestic intercourse. It cannot therefore be surprising that Mr. Cruden, after his escape, should retain an indignant recollection of his confinement, and seek to expose the evils of those abodes of wretchedness. In later times, the efforts of individuals and of the legislature have been strenuously exerted to redress these evils; and by these, together with the progress of medical science, and of humane and religious principles, the lot of that unhappy portion of our race has, perhaps, received all the amelioration of which it is capable. It is due, however, to the memory of Smollett to remark, that the first impulse to this course of humanity and benevolence was given by him, in that exquisitely pathetic tale, "The Adventures of Sir Launcelot Greaves."

Mr. Cruden, as soon as he was released from his first confinement at Aberdeen, determined to quit the place of his birth, and try his fortune in London, where he arrived in 1722. In the metropolis and its neighbourhood, he obtained successive engagements, as private tutor to young men who were preparing for the university. One of these was at Ware in Hertfordshire. Some unknown cause also led him to the Isle of Man, where he spent several years in similar occupations. He returned to London in 1732, and obtained employment as corrector of the press; in which engagement his knowledge, assiduity, and integrity, obtained him not only the good will of his employers, but also the esteem and patronage of many distinguished persons. By the Lord Mayor and some of the aldermen, and other eminent citizens of London, he was recommended to Sir Robert Walpole, and after a long period of tedious suspense, was, by his influence, appointed, in 1735, bookseller to Queen Caroline, consort of George the Second.

He then began to apply himself seriously to the great work, with which he had been some time occupied, the composition of a CONCORDANCE of the sacred Scriptures, and, through his great diligence, and persevering industry, the first edition was published in 1737. It was dedicated to the Queen, to whom he presented a copy, which met with very gracious acceptance; but all hopes of pecuniary assistance were cut off, by the Queen's death, which happened sixteen days after her majesty's declaration, that "she would not fail to remember the author." This was a heavy stroke upon a poor author, whose little all was embarked in this mighty undertaking; and the disappointment had such an unfavourable effect both on his mind and circumstances, that it brought on his second access of derangement. He was confined, as has been said, at Bethnal Green, whence he contrived to escape, though chained to his bedstead, and, as soon as he was at liberty, published a history of his sufferings, with this characteristic title, "The London citizen exceedingly injured; giving an account of his severe and long confinement at Bethnal Green, for nine weeks and six days; the citizen being sent there in March 1738, by Robert Wightman, a notoriously conceited and whimsical man; where he was chained, handcuffed, strait-waistcoated, and imprisoned; with a history of Wightman's Blind Bench; a sort of court that met at Wightman's room, and unaccountably proceeded to pass decrees in relation to the London citizen," &c. &c. It was on this occasion that he instituted the suit against Wightman the proprietor of the madhouse, and Dr. Munro the physician, and by pleading his own cause insured a verdict for the defendants.

Neither his misfortunes, nor his derangement, however, prevented him from obtaining engagements as corrector of the press; and during fifteen succeeding years he showed the acute state of his mind, by superintending the publication of several editions of the Greek and Roman classics; and manifested the most simple and inoffensive manners, and the most conscientious integrity, in all his undertakings. At last, he unfortunately happened to have some dispute, at his lodgings, with his sister, who had, about a twelvemonth before, married a Mr. Wild; and, through her influence, he was again confined for the space of seventeen days, the shortness of which time seems rather to indicate, that his disorder was not of a very malignant nature. His release was speedily followed by another narrative of adventures, in which he assumed the permanent character of ALEXANDER THE CORRECTOR, the title of which was not less curious than that of his former history: "The adventures of ALEXANDER THE CORRECTOR, wherein is given an account of his being sent to Chelsea, and of his bad usage during the time of his Chelsea campaign, which continued seventeen days, from the 12th to the 29th of September 1753. With an account of the Chelsea academies, or the private places for the confinement of such as are supposed to be deprived of the exercise of their reason. To which is added an account of the prophecies of some pious ministers of the gospel, foretelling that ALEXANDER'S afflictions are designed by Divine Providence to being an introduction, and preparation, to his being a JOSEPH and a prosperous man. With observations on the necessity of a reformation, by executing the laws against swearers, sabbath-breakers, and other offenders." In three parts. It was after the publication of this pamphlet that he made the propositions for indemnity before alluded to.

The remaining portion of his life was passed in a kind of happy and harmless lunacy, which left him sufficiently in possession of his rational faculties, to perform the duties of his arduous occupation, and to exercise himself in the execution of the commission, with which he fancied himself intrusted, to correct the public manners and morals. But, in fulfilling this object, he was not unfrequently led into a course of conduct, which occasioned trouble to his friends and others, and cast a cloud over his name, which, but for this aberration of mind, would have been conspicuous amongst the benefactors of mankind.

Under the impression of this divine commission, he published several tracts, asserting his claims to supernatural communications, and visited Oxford and Cambridge to exhort the idlers of both sexes to a strict observance of the sabbath, under the threat of eternal vengeance. His interference was, as may be supposed, in some cases rather uncourteously received.

But it was in London that his principal attempts were made; and to render them efficient, he thought it desirable that his authority should be recognised by the king in council, and that he should be nominated CORRECTOR OF THE PEOPLE, by act of Parliament. His applications to the higher powers, for this purpose, were supported by testimonials from many ladies, at the head of which was the name of the Lady Mayoress, and those of other ladies of rank. He also made a formal application to His Majesty, for the honour of knighthood, not from personal vanity, but because he thought it would give weight to his endeavours in the "good cause." He gives an amusing account of his interviews with the lords in waiting, secretaries of state, and other great men, for this purpose. Being well known and respected, he was not treated with rudeness; but he complains that he was not attended to, except by EARL PAULETT, who, he says, "always spoke civilly to him; and being goutish in his feet, could not run away from the CORRECTOR, as others were wont to do."

From this same delusion, he offered himself at the general election in 1754, to represent the city of London in Parliament, and his influence was sufficient to induce Mr. Sheriff Chitty to nominate him in the Common Hall. But, though several hands were held up for him, he declined standing a poll, comforting himself with the persuasion that he had the hearts, if not the hands, of the London citizens. His next project was of a more private and personal nature, to pay his addresses to Miss Abney, daughter of Sir Thomas Abney of Newington. This lady he addressed under the name of Elizabeth of Silesia; and he made his suit with such persevering ardour, as must have occasioned no small perplexity to that good family. Among other freaks, he sent round "praying bills" to various congregations, on her going abroad in 1754, that intercession might be made to Almighty God for the safety of herself and attendants. When she returned, he circulated similar forms of thanksgiving. It cost Miss Abney and her attendants some trouble, to free her from such a persevering suitor.

Yet, amidst all these diversions, he still pursued his business with unabated assiduity, and especially the correction of his CONCORDANCE, and the preparing it for a new edition; which was published in 1761, and presented in person by the author to the King, who gave him a donation of £100. He had also the honour of presenting it to Queen Charlotte, and to the Princess Dowager of Wales. At this time, Mr. Cruden was corrector of the press to Mr. Woodfall, in the publication of the Public Advertiser, a paper celebrated by being made the vehicle of the Letters of Junius. Here he had full occupation. At one o'clock in the morning he finished the labours of the office, and at six, he was turning over his Bible, with the most careful attention, for the correction of his CONCORDANCE. In the evening, he again returned to the printing office, near to which he lodged, at "the Flating Mill, over against the Ship, in Ivy Lane." In this round of public and private duty he passed his time tranquilly and happily, embracing every opportunity of performing acts of benevolence to his fellow-creatures; one of which is especially recorded to his honour.

In 1762 one Richard Potter, a poor ignorant sailor, was tried, and convicted, at the Old Bailey, of forging, or uttering knowing it to be forged, a seaman's will. Mr. Cruden was in the court, and was so fully convinced of his being merely the tool of some designing villain, that he determined to interfere in his behalf, and endeavour to move the Royal clemency. For this purpose, he visited him in Newgate, conversed with him on religious subjects, exhorted, instructed, and prayed with him. The man was awakened to a sense of his condition as a sinner, and appeared to be truly converted to God. Encouraged by this success, Mr. Cruden began to take measures for saving his life. By repeated applications to Lord Hallifax, Secretary of State, he obtained a change of the sentence, from death to transportation. As an acknowledgment of his obligations to Lord Hallifax, he presented him with a copy of the second edition of his Concordance, to which he prefixed an elegant manuscript Latin dedication, acknowledging his Lordship's kind interference on behalf of Potter. He published an account of this transaction also, in a quaint yet interesting work, entitled "The history of Richard Potter, &c."

The knowledge which Mr. Cruden obtained, through these visits, of the wicked and degraded state of the felons in Newgate, and the success which had attended his endeavours in the case of Potter, induced him to continue his attempts for the reformation of that prison. He distributed New Testaments and catechisms amongst its inmates, which were accompanied with personal instructions, and the occasional presentation of small rewards to the most docile of his pupils. But the state of the prison at that period, and the total want of discipline which then prevailed, rendered his efforts abortive. They sold his books, and spent the money in drinking. A philanthropist of the present day has cultivated this barren waste with greater success. Uniting female tenderness with the loftiest principles of christian enthusiasm, assisted by the progress of knowledge and humanity, and increased facilities of religious instruction, and aided by the countenance of the wise and good in the higher classes of society, MRS. FRY has been able to accomplish what was denied to Cruden and Howard. Though disappointed in this attempt, he still continued his benevolent exertions in individual instances; and though he might in some cases appear obtrusive, his motives were always kind, and his pleasure was great whenever he could promote the welfare and happiness of his fellow-creatures. One Sunday evening, returning from meeting, he met a man who appeared to be suffering under the extremity of misery, and, on inquiring into his circumstances, learned that the sufferings of his family, through poverty, and other causes, had determined him to destroy himself. By suitable admonitions and consolations, with some pecuniary donation, and promises of future attentions, he restored this unhappy man, to his own great joy, to peace and comfort.

Another evening, he is said to have been accosted by a miserable female, whom he permitted to accompany him to his own door, and then on quitting her, remonstrated with her on the criminal and ruinous course she was pursuing, and earnestly exhorted her to repentance and amendment. The poor girl assured him, with tears, that she would gladly quit her present course of life, but knew not where to go. "It is too late, said he, to talk of this to-night, but, if you remain in the same mind, call on me to-morrow, and I will befriend you." She came to him on the morrow, and declared herself willing to engage in the lowest and most laborious occupation, if she could but disengage herself from that life of infamy. Not knowing where to place her, Mr. Cruden took her to his own house, as assistant to his servant. There she continued till his death, and, by the propriety of her behaviour, manifested the sincerity of her repentance.

In the well known contest which took place between the British government and John Wilkes, in consequence of the publication of No. 45 of the North Briton, Mr. Cruden took a very decided part in the defence of government. He published a pamphlet against Wilkes, and always expressed the utmost abhorrence of his moral and religious character, declaring that such a profligate could not be a patriot. To express, in the most efficacious manner, his dislike, he provided himself with a sponge, and took many a long and tedious walk to efface the badge of party, No. 45, wherever he found it chalked on doors or window-shutters, as well as all other inscriptions offensive to good manners.

In the year 1769, he visited his native city for the last time, where he still maintained his vocation as a public Corrector. He began with giving a couple of lectures, in Latin and English, on the necessity of a general reformation. These were followed by printing, as a hand-bill, the Fourth Commandment, which he distributed every Sunday, to all descriptions of persons. At a considerable expense, he stored his pockets with various religious tracts, which were given to every one who would promise to read them. He was particularly kind and attentive to children, and by his earnest piety, and simple, unaffected benevolence, obtained the general esteem of his townsmen. His efforts to do good, however, still partook of his characteristic eccentricity. "To a young clergyman whom he thought too conceited and *modern*, he very gravely and formally presented a little catechism, used by children in Scotland, called, 'THE MOTHER'S CATECHISM,' *Dedicated to the Young* and Ignorant."

The end of his career was now at hand. After the residence of about a year in Aberdeen, he returned to London, and took lodgings in Camden Street, Islington. His death was marked with something of the peculiarity of his life. No illness or decay indicated his approaching dissolution. He had suffered from a slight attack of asthma, but retired to rest, on his last evening, as usual. In the morning, his maid rang the bell to summon him to breakfast. No answer was returned; and she entered his bed-room, but he was not there. She proceeded to his closet, and found him dead, in the attitude of prayer, kneeling against a chair. Thus lived and thus died Alexander Cruden, who might justly say with Horace,

"Exegi monumentum ære perennius."

He had, amidst the avocations of business, and the disturbance of a deranged intellect, accomplished a work which will live as long as the English Language, and accompany the sacred Scriptures, which are circulated in that language, through all parts of the habitable world. Well may it be said of this pious, benevolent, and industrious man, "He rests from his labours, and his works do follow him."

Mr. Cruden was a Calvinistic dissenter, and firmly maintained his religious opinion. And his religion was not separated from morality, for his was "the faith which worketh by love." He was a member of the church which assembled at Great St. Helen's, under the care of DR. GUISE, whom he used to call "his beloved pastor." On the retirement of DR. GUISE in 1762, he attended the ministry of DR. CONDER, in Moorfields, and, afterwards, that of MR. CRUIKSHANK, in Swallow Street. He still however maintained his connexion with the church at Great St. Helen's, where he received the sacrament of the Lord's Supper on the first Sunday of each month. His death took place November 1, 1770.

As Mr. Cruden never married, he distributed his small property amongst his relations, except a sum which he gave to his native city, to be expended in religious books for the poor. He also founded an exhibition of five pounds per annum to assist in educating a student at Marischal College. His will specified the terms on which this assistance should be enjoyed, one of which was, a perfect acquaintance with Vincent's Catechism.

Besides the works which have been mentioned before, he wrote "An Account of the History and Excellency of the Holy Scriptures" prefixed to a Compendium of the Holy Bible. He also compiled a "Scripture Dictionary," which was published at Aberdeen after his death, in 2 vols. 8vo. He was employed to compile the elaborate verbal index to Bishop Newton's edition of Milton's Works; a work of great labour and talent, and which he is said to have undertaken at the request of Auditor Benson.

On the enlarging and perfecting of his great work, the CONCORDANCE, he employed all the leisure hours of the later periods of his life. The second edition was published in 1761, and dedicated to his late Majesty George the Third. The third appeared in 1769, with the Author's last corrections. The profit of these compensated for the loss upon the first. He received £500 for the second edition, and £300 for the third, with twenty copies printed on fine paper. These sums, with the product of his other labours, supplied his own moderate personal wants, and formed a fund for those labours of love in which his heart delighted.

THE

NAMES AND ORDER

OF ALL THE

BOOKS OF THE OLD AND NEW TESTAMENT,

WITH THE

NUMBER OF THEIR CHAPTERS.

THE BOOKS AND CHAPTERS IN THE OLD TESTAMENT.

	CHAPS.		CHAPS.		CHAPS.
GENESIS	50	II CHRONICLES	36	DANIEL	12
EXODUS	40	EZRA	10	HOSEA	14
LEVITICUS	27	NEHEMIAH	13	JOEL	3
NUMBERS	36	ESTHER	10	AMOS	9
DEUTERONOMY	34	JOB	42	OBADIAH	1
JOSHUA	24	PSALMS	150	JONAH	4
JUDGES	21	PROVERBS	31	MICAH	7
RUTH	4	ECCLESIASTES	12	NAHUM	3
I SAMUEL	31	SOLOMON'S SONG	8	HABAKKUK	3
II SAMUEL	24	ISAIAH	66	ZEPHANIAH	3
I KINGS	22	JEREMIAH	52	HAGGAI	2
II KINGS	25	LAMENTATIONS	5	ZECHARIAH	14
I CHRONICLES	29	EZEKIEL	48	MALACHI	4

THE BOOKS AND CHAPTERS IN THE NEW TESTAMENT.

	CHAPS.		CHAPS.		CHAPS.
MATTHEW	28	EPHESIANS	6	HEBREWS	13
MARK	16	PHILIPPIANS	4	JAMES	5
LUKE	24	COLOSSIANS	4	I PETER	5
JOHN	21	I THESSALONIANS	5	II PETER	3
ACTS	28	II THESSALONIANS	3	I JOHN	5
ROMANS	16	I TIMOTHY	6	II JOHN	1
I CORINTHIANS	16	II TIMOTHY	4	III JOHN	1
II CORINTHIANS	13	TITUS	3	JUDE	1
GALATIANS	6	PHILEMON	1	REVELATION	22

THE BOOKS AND CHAPTERS OF THE APOCRYPHA.

	CHAPS.		CHAPS.		CHAPS.
I ESDRAS	9	WISDOM	19	THE STORY OF SUSANNAH.	
II ESDRAS	16	ECCLESIASTICUS	51	THE IDOL BEL AND THE DRAGON.	
TOBIT	14	BARUCH, WITH THE EPISTLE OF JEREMIAH	6	THE PRAYER OF MANASSES.	
JUDITH	16	THE SONG OF THE THREE CHILDREN.		I MACCABEES	16
THE REST OF ESTHER	6			II MACCABEES	15

A COMPLETE

CONCORDANCE

TO THE

HOLY SCRIPTURES.

ABASE.

JOB 40. 11. behold every one proud, and a. him
Isa. 31. 4. as the lion will not a. himself
Ezek. 21. 26. and a. him that is high
Dan. 4. 37. that walk in pride, is able to a.

ABASED.

Isa. 32. †19. and the city shall be utterly a.
Mat. 23. 12. and whosoever shall exalt himself shall be a. | Luke 14. 11. | 18. 14.
Phil. 4. 12. I know how to be a. and how to abound

ABASING.

2 Cor. 11. 7. have I committed an offence in a. myself

ABATED.

Gen. 8. 3. after 150 days the waters were a. 8. 11.
Lev. 27. 18. it shall be a. from thy estimation
Deut. 34. 7. nor was Moses' natural force a.
Judg. 8. 3. then their anger was a. toward him

ABBA.

Mark 14. 36. a. Father, all things are possible to thee
Rom. 8. 15. the Spirit, whereby we cry, a. Father
Gal. 4. 6. sent Spirit into your hearts, crying, a. Father

ABHOR

Signifies, [1] *To lothe, or detest*, Deut. 32. 19. Job 42. 6. [2] *To despise, or neglect*, Psal. 22. 24. Amos 6. 8. [3] *To reject, or cast off*, Psal. 89. 38.

Lev. 26. 11. and my soul shall not a. you
15. or if your soul a. my judgments
30. I will destroy, and my soul shall a. you
44. nor will I a. them, to destroy them utterly
Deut. 7. 26. thou shalt utterly a. it, a cursed thing
23. 7. shalt not a. an Edomite, not a. an Egyptian
1 Sam. 27. 12. he hath made his people to a. him
Job 9. 31. and mine own clothes shall a. me
30. 10. they a. me, they flee far from me
42. 6. I a. myself, and repent in dust and ashes
Psal. 5. 6. the Lord will a. the bloody man
119. 163. I hate and a. lying, but love thy law
Prov. 24. 24. him people curse, nations shall a. him
Jer. 14. 21. do not a. us for thy name's sake
Amos 5. 10. they a. him that speaketh uprightly
6. 8. I a. the excellency of Jacob, hate his palaces
Mic. 3. 9. hear, ye that a. judgment, and pervert
Rom. 12. 9. a. that which is evil, cleave to good

ABHORRED.

Exod. 5. 21. you have made our savour to be a.
Lev. 20. 23. they committed, and therefore I a. them
26. 43. they despised, their soul a. my statutes
Deut. 32. 19. when the Lord saw it, he a. them
1 Sam. 2. 17. for men a. the offering of the Lord
2 Sam. 16. 21. shall hear, thou art a. of thy father
1 Kings 11. 25. Hadad a. Israel, and reigned over
Job 19. 19. all my inward friends a. me
Psal. 22. 24. nor a. the affliction of the afflicted
78. 59. he was wroth, and greatly a. Israel
89. 38. but thou hast cast off and a. hast been wroth
106. 40. insomuch that he a. his own inheritance
Prov. 22. 14. who is a. of the Lord shall fall therein
Lam. 2. 7. the Lord hath a. his sanctuary
Ezek. 16. 25. thou hast made thy beauty to be a.
Zech. 11. 8. lothed them, and their soul also a. me

ABHORREST.

Isa. 7. 16. the land that thou a. shall be forsaken
Rom. 2. 22. thou that a. idols, dost thou commit

ABHORRETH.

Job 33. 20. so that his life a. bread, and his soul
Psal. 10. 3. blesseth the covetous, whom the Lord a.
36. 4. he deviseth mischief on his bed, he a. not evil
107. 18. their soul a. all manner of meat
Isa. 49. 7. to him whom the nation a. to a servant

ABHORRING.

Isa. 66. 24. and they shall be an a. to all flesh

ABIDE

Signifies, [1] *To stay, or tarry*, Gen. 22. 5. [2] *To dwell or live in a place*, Gen. 29. 19. Psal. 15. 1. [3] *To bear or endure*, Jer. 10. 10. Joel 2. 11. [4] *To be*, Gen. 44. 33. [5] *To continue*, Eccl. 8. 15. John 14. 16. [6] *To wait for*, Acts 20. 23. [7] *To rest*, Prov. 19. 23. [8] *To live*, Phil. 1. 24. [9] *To stand firm*, Psal. 119. 90. 125. 1. [10] *To rule or govern*, Psal. 61. 7.

Gen. 19. 2. but we will a. in the street all night
22. 5. a. you here with the ass, and I and the lad
24. 55. let the damsel a. with us a few days
29. 19. it is better I give her to thee, a. with me
44. 33. let thy servant a. instead of the lad
Exod. 16. 29. a. ye every man in his place
Lev. 8. 35. therefore a. at the door of the tabernacle
19. 13. the wages of him hired shall not a. with thee
Num. 35. 25. shall a. to the death of the high priest
Ruth 2. 8. but a. here fast by my maidens
1 Sam. 1. 22. appear before the Lord, and a. for ever
5. 7. the ark of God of Israel shall not a. with us
22. 23. a. thou with me, fear not, for he that seeks
30. 21. whom they had made to a. at brook Besor
2 Sam. 16. 18. his will I be, and with him will I a.
Job 24. 13. they rebel, nor a. in the paths of the light
38. 40. and a. in the covert to lie in wait
39. 9. will the unicorn be willing to a. by thy crib
Psal. 15. 1. Lord, who shall a. in thy tabernacle?
61. 4. I will a. in thy tabernacle for ever
7. he shall a. before God for ever
91. 1. shall a. under the shadow of the Almighty
Prov. 7. 11. she is loud, her feet a. not in her house
19. 23. and he that hath it shall a. satisfied
Eccl. 8. 15. for that shall a. with him of his labour
Jer. 10. 10. nations not able to a. his indignation
42. 10. if ye a. in this land I will build you
49. 18. no man shall a. there, 33. | 50. 40.
Hos. 3. 3. thou shalt a. for me many days
11. 6. and the sword shall a. on his cities
Joel 2. 11. the day is terrible, who can a. it?
Mic. 5. 4. they shall a. for now shall he be great
Nah. 1. 6. who can a. in the fierceness of his anger?
Mal. 3. 2. but who may a. the day of his coming?
Mat. 10. 11. there a. Mark 6. 10. Luke 9. 4.
Luke 19. 5. for to-day I must a. at thy house
24. 29. a. with us, for it is towards evening
John 12. 46. believes on me, should not a. in dark.
14. 16. give another Comforter that he may a.
15. 4. a. in me and I in you, except ye a. in me, 7.
6. if a man a. not in me, he is cast forth
10. ye shall a. in my love, and a. in his love
Acts 15. 34. it pleased Silas to a. there still
16. 15. come into my house and a. there
20. 23. saying, that bonds and afflictions a. me
27. 31. except these a. in ship, ye cannot be saved
1 Cor. 3. 14. if any man's work a. he shall receive
7. 8. it is good for them if they a. even as I
20. let every man a. in the same calling
40. she is happier if she so a. after my judgment
Phil. 1. 24. to a. in the flesh is more needful for you
25. I know that I shall a. with you all
1 Tim. 1. 3. I besought thee to a. at Ephesus
1 John 2. 24. let that a. in you which ye have heard
27. ye shall a. in him || 28. children a. in him

ABIDETH.

2 Sam. 16. 3. Ziba said, behold he a. at Jerusalem
Psal. 49. 12. man being in honour, a. not, he is
55. 19. God shall hear, even he that a. of old
119. 90. thou hast established the earth, and it a.
125. 1. shall be as mount Zion, which a. for ever
Prov. 15. 31. heareth reproof, a. among the wise
Eccl. 1. 4. another cometh, but the earth a. for ever
Jer. 21. 9. he that a. in this city shall die by sword
John 3. 36. but the wrath of God a. on him
8. 35. the servant a. not, but the son a. for ever
12. 24. except a corn of wheat die, it a. alone
34. we have heard that Christ a. for ever
15. 5. he that a. in me bringeth forth much fruit
1 Cor. 13. 13. now a. faith, hope, charity
2 Tim. 2. 13. if we believe not, yet he a. faithful
Heb. 7. 3. Melchizedec a. a priest continually
1 Pet. 1. 23. by the word of God which a. for ever
1 John 2. 6. he that saith he a. in him ought to walk
10. he that loveth his brother a. in the light
14. ye are strong, and the word of God a. in you
17. but he that doeth the will of God a. for ever
27. the anointing a. in you and teacheth you
3. 6. whosoever a. in him sinneth not
3. 14. that loveth not his brother a. in death
24. and hereby we know that he a. in us
2 John 9. whoso a. not in the doctrine of Christ hath not God, he that a. hath the Father and the Son

ABIDING.

Num. 24. 2. Balaam saw Israel a. in his tents
1 Sam. 26. 19. from a. in the inheritance of the Lord
1 Chron. 29. 15. days as a shadow, there is none a.
Luke 2. 8. there were shepherds a. in the field
John 5. 38. and ye have not his word a. in you
1 John 3. 15. no murderer hath eternal life a. in him

ABJECTS.

Psal. 35. 15. the a. gathered together against me

ABILITY.

Lev. 27. 8. to his a. that vowed, priest shall value
Ezra 2. 69. they gave after their a. to the work
Neh. 5. 8. we after our a. redeemed our brethren
Dan. 1. 4. as had a. to stand in the king's palace
Mat. 25. 15. he gave to each according to his a.
Acts 11. 29. according to his a. determined to send
1 Pet. 4. 11. let him do it as of the a. God giveth

ABLE.

Exod. 18. 21. provide out of all the people a. men
Lev. 14. 22. two pigeons, such as he is a. to get, 31.
Num. 1. 3. all that are a. to go to war, 20, 22, 24, 26, 28, 30, 32, 34, 36, 38, 40, 42, 45. | 26. 2.
13. 30. go up, for we are well a. to overcome it
Deut. 16. 17. every man shall give as he is a.
Josh. 23. 9. no man hath been a. to stand before you
1 Sam. 6. 20. who is a. to stand before this holy God?
1 Kings 3. 9. who is a. to judge so great a people?
2 Chron. 2. 6. but who is a. to build him an house?
20. 6. so that none is a. to withstand thee
25. 9. the Lord is a. to give thee much more
Job 41. 10. who then is a. to stand before me?
Prov. 27. 4. but who is a. to stand before envy?
Ezek. 46. 11. the offering shall be as he is a. to give
Dan. 3. 17. our God whom we serve is a. to deliver
6. 20. thy God is a. to deliver thee from the lions
Mat. 3. 9. God is a. of these stones to raise up children to Abraham, Luke 3. 8.
9. 28. believe ye that I am a. to do this?
10. 28. fear him a. to destroy soul and body in hell
19. 12. he that is a. to receive it, let him receive
20. 22. are ye a. to drink of the cup I shall drink of?
22. 46. no man was a. to answer him a word
Mark 4. 33. spake he, as they were a. to hear it
John 10. 29. no man is a. to pluck them out of my
Acts 15. 10. a yoke our fathers nor we a. to bear
20. 32. word of his grace, a. to build you
25. 5. which among you are a. go down with me?
Rom. 4. 21. he had promised, he was a. to perform
11. 23. for God is a. to graff them in again
14. 4. for God is a. to make him stand
15. 14. ye are a. also to admonish one another
1 Cor. 3. 2. ye were not a. nor yet now are ye a.
10. 13. not suffer to be tempted above that ye are a.
2 Cor. 3. 6. who hath made us a. ministers of new t.
9. 8. God is a. to make all grace abound towards
Eph. 3. 20. to him that is a. to do abundantly above
Phil. 3. 21. he is a. to subdue all things to himself
2 Tim. 1. 12. he is a. to keep that I have committed
3. 7. never a. to come to the knowledge of truth
15. holy scriptures a. to make wise to salvation
Heb. 2. 18. he is a. to succour them that are tempted
5. 7. to him that was a. to save him from death
7. 25. he is a. to save to the uttermost all that come
11. 19. accounting that God was a. to raise him up
Jam. 1. 21. the word which is a. to save your souls
3. 2. is a. also to bridle the whole body
4. 12. there is one lawgiver a. to save and to destroy
Jude 24. to him that is a. to keep you from falling
Rev. 5. 3. no man was a. to open the book nor look
13. 4. who is a. to make war with the beast?
15. 8. no man was a. to enter into the temple

Be ABLE.

Lev. 25. 26. and himself be a. to redeem it
Josh. 1. 5. not any man be a. to stand before thee
Deut. 7. 24. there shall no man be a. to stand, 11. 25.
14. 12. if the Lord be with me I shall be a. to drive
1 Sam. 17. 9. if he be a. to fight with me and kill me
1 Chron. 29. 14. that we should be a. to offer willingly
2 Chron. 32. 14. that your God should be a. to deliver
Isa. 47. 12. if so be thou shalt be a. to profit
Ezek. 33. 12. nor shall the righteous be a. to live
Luke 14. 31. whether he be a. with 10,000 to meet
Rom. 8. 39. be a. to separate us from love of God
1 Cor. 10. 13. that ye may be a. to bear it
Eph. 3. 18. may be a. to comprehend with all saints
6. 11. that ye may be a. to stand against the devil
16. faith, wherewith ye shall be a. to quench
2 Tim. 2. 2. who shall be a. to teach others also
Tit. 1. 9. may be a. by sound doctrine to exhort
2 Pet. 1. 15. that ye may be a. after my decease
Rev. 6. 17. wrath is come, and who shall be a. to stand

Not be ABLE.

2 Kings 18. 29. not be a. to deliver you, Isa. 36. 14.
Psal. 36. 12. cast down, and shall not be a. to rise
Eccl. 8. 17. yet shall he not be a. to find it
Isa. 47. 11. thou shalt not be a. to put it off
Jer. 11. 11. not be a. to escape || 49. 10. not be a. to hide
Ezek. 7. 19. gold shall not be a. to deliver them
Luke 13. 24. seek, not be a. || 21. 15. not be a. to gainsay

Not ABLE.

Lev. 5. 7. and if he be not a. to bring a lamb
Num. 13. 31. we be not a. to go up against the people
14. 16. because the Lord was not a. Deut. 9. 28.
2 Chron. 20. 37. ships were not a. to go to Tarshish
Ezra 10. 13. we are not a. to stand without
Neh. 4. 10. so that we are not a. to build the wall
Psal. 18. 38. wounded that they were not a. to rise
21. 11. device which they are not a. to perform

Ps. 40. 12. hold on me, so that I am *not a.* to look up
Amos 7. 10. the land is *not a.* to bear all his words
Luke 12. 26. if ye be *not a.* to do that thing is least
14. 29. laid foundation, and is *not a.* to finish
John 21. 6. they were *not a.* to draw it for the fishes
Acts 6. 10. and they were *not a.* to resist the wisdom

ABOARD.

Acts 21. 2. a ship sailing, we went *a.* and set forth

ABODE, *Substantive.*

2 Kings 19. 27. but I know thy *a.* Isa. 37. 28.
Ezra 9. †8. to give us a sure *a.* in his holy place
John 14. 23. we will come and make our *a.* with him

ABODE, *Verb.*

Gen. 29. 14. Jacob *a.* with him the space of a month
49. 24. but his bow *a.* in strength, and the arms
Exod. 24. 16. the glory of the Lord *a.* on Sinai
Num. 9. 17. where cloud *a.* Israel pitched, 18, 20.
20. they *a.* in their tents, and journeyed, 22.
11. 35. the people journeyed, and *a.* at Hazeroth
20. 1. the people *a.* in Kadesh, Judg. 11. 17.
22. 8. the princes of Moab, *a.* with Balaam
Deut. 1. 46. so ye *a.* in Kadesh many days
3. 29. we *a.* in the valley || 9. 9. I *a.* in the mount
Josh. 5. 8. they *a.* in their places till they were whole
8. 9. they *a.* between Bethel and Ai, but Joshua
Judg. 5. 17. Gilead *a.* beyond Jordan, Asher continued on the sea-shore, and *a.* in his breaches
19. 4. the Levite *a.* with him three days
20. 47. and *a.* in the rock Rimmon four months
1 Sam. 1. 23. the woman *a.* and gave her son suck
7. 2. while the ark *a.* in Kirjath-jearim, time long
13. 16. Saul and Jonathan *a.* in Gibeah
22. 6. Saul *a.* || 23. 14. David *a.* 25. | 26. 3.
23. 18. David *a.* in wood || 2 Sam. 1. 1. *a.* at Ziklag
2 Sam. 11. 12. Uriah *a.* in Jerusalem that day
15. 8. servant vowed while I *a.* at Geshur
1 Kings 17. 19. he carried him to a loft where he *a.*
Jer. 38. 28. Jeremiah *a.* in the court of the prison
Mat. 17. 22. and while they *a.* in Galilee, Jesus said
Luke 1. 56. Mary *a.* with her about three months
8. 27. nor *a.* in any house, but in the tombs
John 1. 32. I saw the Spirit, and it *a.* upon him
39. they came and *a.* with him that day
7. 9. when he said these words he *a.* in Galilee
8. 44. he was a murderer, and *a.* not in the truth
11. 6. he *a.* two days still in the place where he was
Acts 1. 13. an upper room where *a.* Peter and James
14. 3. long time *a.* they speaking boldly in the
18. 3. Paul *a.* with them and wrought
21. 7. we came and *a.* with the brethren one day
8. we entered the house of Philip and *a.* with him
Gal. 1. 18. I went and *a.* with Peter fifteen days

ABODE *there*, or *there* ABODE.

Deut. 1. 46. according to the days that ye *a. there*
Josh. 2. 22. came to mountain, and *a. there* 3 days
Judg. 21. 2. the people *a. there* till even before God
Ezra 8. 15. and *there a.* we in tents three days
32. we came to Jerusalem and *a. there* three days
John 4. 40. and Jesus *a. there* two days
10. 40. where John at first baptized, and *there a.*
Acts 12. 19. Herod went to Cæsarea, and *there a.*
14. 28. *there* they *a.* long time with the disciples
17. 14. Silas and Timotheus *a. there* still

ABODEST.

Judg. 5. 16. why *a.* thou among the sheepfolds?

ABOLISH

Signifies, [1] *To do away, or make void*, 2 Cor. 3. 13. Ephes. 2. 15. [2] *To destroy*, Isa. 2. 18. 2 Tim. 1. 10.
Isa. 2. 18. and the idols he shall utterly *a.*

ABOLISHED.

Isa. 51. 6. and my righteousness shall not be *a.*
Ezek. 6. 6. and your works may be *a.*
2 Cor. 3. 13. not look to the end of that which is *a.*
Eph. 2. 15. having *a.* in his flesh the enmity
2 Tim. 1. 10. Jesus Christ, who hath *a.* death

ABOMINABLE.

Lev. 7. 21. that shall touch any *a.* unclean thing
11. 43. ye shall not make yourselves *a.* with any
18. 30. commit not any of these *a.* customs
19. 7. if it be eaten on the third day, it is *a.*
20. 25. ye shall not make your souls *a.* by beast
Deut. 14. 3. thou shalt not eat any *a.* thing
1 Chron. 21. 6. for the king's word was *a.* to Joab
2 Chron. 15. 8. Asa put away the *a.* idols from Judah
Job 15. 16. how much more *a.* and filthy is man
Psal. 14. 1. are corrupt, they have done *a.* works
53. 1. corrupt are they, and have done *a.* iniquity
Isa. 14. 19. thou art cast out like an *a.* branch
65. 4. and broth of *a.* things is in their vessels
Jer. 16. 18. filled with carcases of their *a.* things
44. 4. O, do not this *a.* thing that I hate
Ezek. 4. 14. nor came *a.* flesh into my mouth
8. 10. I saw and behold *a.* beasts and idols
16. 52. thy sins committed more *a.* than they
Mic. 6. 10. and the scant measure that is *a.*
Nah. 3. 6. and I will cast *a.* filth on thee
Tit. 1. 16. but in works deny him, being *a.*
1 Pet. 4. 3. when we walked in *a.* idolatries
Rev. 21. 8. fearful, and unbelieving, and the *a.*

ABOMINABLY.

1 Kings 21. 26. Ahab did very *a.* in following idols

ABOMINATION

Signifies, [1] *A thing hateful and detestable*, Gen. 43. 32. Prov. 29. 27. [2] *Sin in general*, Isa. 66. 3. Ezek. 16. 50. [3] *An idol*, 2 Kings 23. 13. Isa. 44. 19. [4] *The Roman army that destroyed the temple and Jewish polity*, Mat. 24. 15. [5] *Evil doctrines and practices*, Rev. 17. 4.
Gen. 43. 32. for that is an *a.* to the Egyptians
46. 34. every shepherd is an *a.* to the Egyptians
Exod. 8. 26. for we shall sacrifice the *a.* of Egyptians
Lev. 7. 18. it shall be an *a.* 11. 41, 42.
11. 10. they shall be an *a.* to you, 12, 20, 23.
18. 22. as with womankind it is *a.* 20. 13.
Deut. 7. 25. it is *a.* to the Lord thy God, 17. 1.
26. nor shalt thou bring an *a.* into thy house
12. 31. every *a.* they have done to their gods
13. 14. that such *a.* is wrought among you, 17. 4.
18. 12. all that do these things are an *a.* 22. 5.
23. 18. both these are an *a.* to the Lord thy God
24. 4. for that is an *a.* before the Lord.
Deut. 25. 16. all that do unrighteously are *a.* to God
27. 15. cursed be the man that maketh *a.* to Lord
1 Sam. 13. 4. Israel was had in *a.* with Philistines
1 Kings 11. 5. Milcom the *a.* of Ammonites, 7.
7. an high place for Chemosh the *a.* of Moab
2 Kings 23. 13. Ashtaroth the *a.* of the Zidonians
Psal. 88. 8. thou hast made me an *a.* to them
Prov. 3. 32. the froward is an *a.* to the Lord
6. 16. yea, seven things are an *a.* to him
8. 7. speak truth, wickedness is an *a.* to my lips
11. 1. a false balance is an *a.* to the Lord
20. they of a froward heart are an *a.* to the Lord
12. 22. lying lips are *a.* to the Lord
13. 19. it is an *a.* to fools to depart from evil
15. 8. the sacrifice of the wicked is an *a.* 21. 27.
9. the way of the wicked is an *a.* to the Lord
26. thoughts of the wicked are an *a.* to the Lord
16. 5. every one that is proud in heart is an *a.*
12. it is an *a.* to kings to commit wickedness
17. 15. they both are an *a.* to the Lord
20. 10. both of them are alike *a.* to the Lord
23. divers weights are an *a.* to the Lord
24. 9. and the scorner is an *a.* to men
28. 9. even his prayer shall be *a.*
29. 27. an unjust man is an *a.* to the just, and he that is upright in the way, is *a.* to the wicked
Isa. 1. 13. incense is an *a.* to me, the new-moons
41. 24. an *a.* is he that chooseth you
44. 19. shall I make the residue thereof an *a.*?
66. 17. eating swine's flesh, and the *a.* and mouse
Jer. 2. 7. ye entered, ye made my heritage an *a.*
6. 15. ashamed when they committed *a.* 8. 12.
32. 35. that they should do this *a.* to cause Judah
Ezek. 16. 50. they were haughty and committed *a.*
18. 12. lift up his eyes to idols and committed *a.*
22. 11. committed *a.* with his neighbour's wife
33. 26. ye stand on your sword and ye work *a.*
Dan. 11. 31. shall place the *a.* that maketh desolate
12. 11. and the *a.* that maketh desolate set up
Mal. 2. 11. an *a.* is committed in Israel and Jerus.
Mat. 24. 15. ye see *a.* of desolation, Mark 13. 14.
Luke 16. 15. esteemed among men is *a.* with God
Rev. 21. 27. shall in no wise enter that worketh *a.*

ABOMINATIONS.

Deut. 18. 9. not learn to do after the *a.* of nations
32. 16. with *a.* provoked they him to anger
1 Kings 14. 24. did according to all *a.* of nations
2 Kings 16. 3. thro' fire according to *a.* 2 Chr. 28. 3.
21. 2. Manasseh did evil in the sight of the Lord after the *a.* of the heathen, 2 Chron. 33. 2.
23. 24. *a.* spied did Josiah put away, 2 Chr. 34. 33.
2 Chron. 36. 8. acts of Jehoiakim and his *a.* he did
14. people transgressed after all *a.* of the heathen
Prov. 26. 25. for there are seven *a.* in his heart
Jer. 44. 22. the Lord could not bear for the *a.*
Ezek. 6. 11. alas for all the evil *a.* of house of Israel
8. 6. seest thou the great *a.* of Israel, but turn thee yet again, and thou shalt see greater *a.* 13, 15.
9. behold the wicked *a.* that they do here
17. is it a light thing to commit *a.* here?
9. 4. that sigh and cry for all the *a.* that be done
11. 18. take away all the *a.* thereof from thence
14. 6. turn away your faces from all your *a.*
16. 2. son of man, cause Jerusalem to know her *a.*
18. 24. when the righteous doth according to all *a.*
20. 4. cause them to know the *a.* of their fathers
7. cast ye away every man the *a.* of his eyes
8. they did not cast away the *a.* of their eyes
22. 2. yea, thou shalt shew her all her *a.*
36. 31. and shall lothe yourselves for all your *a.*
44. 6. O Israel, let it suffice you of all your *a.*
7. they have broken my covenant for all your *a.*
Dan. 9. 27. and for the overspreading of *a.*
Zech. 9. 7. will take his *a.* from between his teeth
Rev. 17. 4. a golden cup in her hand full of *a.*
5. the mother of harlots and *a.* of the earth

***Their* ABOMINATIONS.**

Deut. 20. 18. teach you not to do after all *their a.*
29. 17. and ye have seen *their a.* and their idols
Ezra 9. 1. the people doing according to *their a.*
11. with *their a.* which have filled the land
Isa. 66. 3. and their soul delighteth in *their a.*
Jer. 7. 30. have set *their a.* in the house called, 32. 34.
Ezek. 6. 9. for the evils committed in all *their a.*
7. 20. but they made the images of *their a.*
11. 21. whose heart walketh after *their a.*
12. 16. that they may declare all *their a.*
16. 47. yet hast thou not done after *their a.*
20. 30. and commit ye whoredom after *their a.*
23. 36. yea, declare to them *their a.*
33. 29. the land desolate because of all *their a.*
43. 8. they have defiled my holy name by *their a.*
44. 13. they shall bear their shame and *their a.*
Hos. 9. 10. *their a.* were according as they loved

***These* ABOMINATIONS.**

Lev. 18. 26. ye shall not commit any of *these a.*
27. all *these a.* have the men of the land done
29. whosoever shall commit any of *these a.*
Deut. 18. 12. because of *these a.* the Lord hath driven
2 Kings 21. 11. Manasseh hath done *these a.*
Ezra 9. 14. join in affinity with people of *these a.*
Jer. 7. 10. we are delivered to do all *these a.*
Ezek. 18. 13. he hath done all *these a.* shall surely die

***Thine* or *thy* ABOMINATIONS.**

Jer. 4. 1. if thou wilt put away *thine a.* out of sight
13. 27. I have seen *thine a.* on the hills
Ezek. 5. 9. do what I have not, because of *thine a.*
11. thou hast defiled my sanctuary with *thy a.*
7. 3. I will recompense on thee all *thine a.* 4, 8, 9.
16. 22. in all *thine a.* thou hast not remembered
36. with all the idols of *thine a.* and by the blood
43. not commit this lewdness above all *thine a.*
51. hast multiplied *thine a.* more than they
58. thou hast borne *thine a.* saith the Lord

ABOVE

Signifies, [1] *Aloft, high*, Gen. 6. 16. Prov. 8. 28. [2] *The dignity or excellency of a person or thing*, Psal. 113. 4. Mat. 10. 24. [3] *Beyond*, 2 Cor. 1. 8. [4] *More than*, Gen. 3. 14. | 48. 22. [5] *Upwards*, Exod. 30. 14. Lev. 27. 7. [6] *An higher state or rank*, Num. 16. 3. [7] *Chief in authority and power*, Deut 28. 13. [8] *Heaven, or the highest place*, Job 3. 4. Rom. 10. 6. [9] *Heavenly and spiritual*, Gal. 4. 26. [10] *Things that relate to heaven*, Gal. 4. 26. Col. 3. 1. [11] *God*, Jam. 1. 17.
Gen. 1. 7. from the waters *a.* the firmament
20. and fowl that may fly *a.* the earth
3. 14. the serpent cursed *a.* all cattle, *a.* beast
6. 16. in a cubit shalt thou finish the ark *a.*
7. 17. and the ark was lifted up *a.* the earth
48. 22. given thee one portion *a.* thy brethren
49. 26. prevailed *a.* the blessings of my progenitors
Exod. 25. 22. I will commune from *a.* the mercy-seat
28. 27. *a.* the curious girdle of the ephod, 28.
30. 14. are numbered from twenty years old and *a.*
Lev. 11. 21. which have legs *a.* their feet to leap
27. 7. and if it be from sixty years old and *a.*
Num. 16. 3. lift up yourselves *a.* the congregation
Deut. 17. 20. heart be not lifted up *a.* his brethren
25. 3. lest if he should beat him *a.* these
28. 13. thou shalt be *a.* only, and not be beneath
30. 5. do thee good and multiply thee *a.* thy fathers
Josh. 3. 13. the waters that come down from *a.* 16.
Judg. 5. 24. blessed shall she be *a.* women in the tent
2 Sam. 22. 17. he sent from *a.* Psal. 18. 16.
1 Kings 8. 7. cherubims covered ark *a.* 2 Chr. 5. 8.
2 Kings 25. 28. *a.* the throne of kings, Jer. 52. 32.
1 Chron. 5. 2. for Judah prevailed *a.* his brethren
23. 27. for the Levites were numbered from twenty years old and *a.* Exod. 30. 14.
27. 6. Benaiah was mighty and *a.* the thirty
Neh. 7. 2. Hananiah feared God *a.* many
12. 37. they went up *a.* the house of David
Job 3. 4. let not God regard it from *a.*
18. 16. and *a.* shall his branch be cut off
28. 18. for the price of wisdom is *a.* rubies
31. 2. for what portion of God is there from *a.*?
28. for I should have denied the God that is *a.*
Psal. 10. 5. thy judgments are *a.* out of his sight
18. 48. thou liftest me *a.* those that rise up
27. 6. now shall my head be lifted up *a.* enemies
45. 7. the oil of gladness *a.* thy fellows, Heb. 1. 9
78. 23. though he commanded the clouds from *a.*
119. 127. I love thy commandments *a.* gold
136. 6. that stretched out the earth *a.* the waters
137. 6. if I prefer not Jerusalem *a.* my chief joy
144. 7. send thine hand from *a.* rid me, deliver me
148. 13. his glory is *a.* the earth and heaven
Prov. 8. 28. when he established the clouds *a.*
15. 24. the way of life is *a.* to the wise
31. 10. for her price is far *a.* rubies
Eccl. 3. 19. a man hath no pre-eminence *a.* a beast
Isa. 2. 2. mountains shall be exalted *a.* the hills
6. 2. *a.* it stood the seraphims, each had six wings
7. 11. ask it either in the depth or in the height *a.*
Jer. 15. 8. their widows increased *a.* sand of the seas
Lam. 1. 13. from *a.* hath he sent fire into my bones
Ezek. 1. 26. as appearance of a man *a.* upon it
10. 19. the glory of God was over them *a.* 11. 22.
29. 15. nor exalt itself any more *a.* the nations
Dan. 6. 3. Daniel was preferred *a.* the presidents
11. 36. the king magnify himself *a.* every god
Amos 2. 9. yet I destroyed his fruit from *a.*
Nah. 3. 16. hast multiplied thy merchants *a.* the stars
Mat. 10. 24. disciple not *a.* his master, Luke 6. 40.
John 3. †3. except a man be born from *a.* 7.
6. 13. baskets which remained over and *a.*
8. 23. I am from *a.* ye are of this world
19. 11. except it were given him from *a.*
Acts 4. 22. for the man was *a.* forty years old
26. 13. I saw a light *a.* the brightness of the sun
Rom. 10. 6. that is to bring Christ down from *a.*
14. 5. one man esteemeth one day *a.* another
1 Cor. 4. 6. not to think of men *a.* what is written
10. 13. you to be tempted *a.* that ye are able
15. 6. he was seen of *a.* 500 brethren at once
2 Cor. 1. 8. were pressed out of measure *a.* strength
11. 23. I am more, in stripes *a.* measure
12. 2. *a.* fourteen years ago, whether in body or out
6. lest any man should think of me *a.* that
Gal. 4. 26. but Jerusalem which is *a.* is free
Phil. 2. 9. and given him a name *a.* every name
Col. 3. 1. seek those things which are *a.*
2. set your affection on things *a.* not on earth
Philem. 16. not now as a servant, but *a.* a servant
Heb. 10. 8. *a.* when he said, sacrifice and offering
Jam. 1. 17. every good and perfect gift is from *a.*
3. 15. this wisdom descendeth not from *a.*

ABOVE *all.*

Gen. 3. 14. the serpent is cursed *a. all* cattle
Num. 12. 3. Moses was very meek *a. all* the men
Deut. 7. 14. thou shalt be blessed *a. all* people
10. 15. he chose you *a. all* people, as it is this day
14. 2. chosen thee *a. all* the nations, 26. 19. | 28. 1.
1 Kings 14. 9. done evil *a. all* that were before thee
22. provoked *a. all* that their fathers had done
16. 30. Ahab did evil *a. all* that were before him
2 Kings 21. 11. done wickedly *a. all* the Amorites did
1 Chron. 29. 3. over and *a. all* I have prepared
11. and thou art exalted as head *a. all*
2 Chron. 11. 21. he loved Maacah *a. all* his wives
Neh. 8. 5. for Ezra was *a. all* the people
Esth. 2. 17. king loved Esther *a. all* the women
Psal. 97. 9. thou, Lord art high *a. all* the earth
99. 2. he is high *a. all* people, 113. 4.
138. 2. magnified thy word *a. all* thy name
Prov. 4. †23. keep thy heart *a. all* keeping
Eccl. 2. 7. *a. all* that were in Jerusalem before me
Jer. 17. 9. the heart is deceitful *a. all* things
Ezek. 16. 43. not commit this lewdness *a. all*
31. 5. his height was exalted *a. all* the trees
Dan. 11. 37. for he shall magnify himself *a. all*
Luke 3. 20. Herod added yet this *a. all.*
13. 2. these sinners *a. all* the Galileans, 4.
John 3. 31. he that cometh from heaven is *a. all*
Eph. 1. 21. far *a. all* principality and power
3. 20. *a. all* that we ask || 4. 6. one God *a. all*
6. 16. *a. all* taking the shield of faith to quench
Col. 3. 14. *a. all* these things put on charity
2 Thess. 2. 4. exalteth *a. all* that is called God
Jam. 5. 12. *a. all* things, my brethren, swear not
1 Pet. 4. 8. *a. all* things have fervent charity
3 John 2. I wish *a. all* things that thou prosper

ABOVE all GODS; see GODS. ABOVE heaven; see HEAVEN. Stood ABOVE; see STOOD. ABOVE, me, him, them; see HIM, ME, THEM.

ABOUND.

Prov. 28. 20. the faithful man shall a. with blessings
Isa. 2. † 6. they a. with the children of strangers
Mat. 24. 12. because iniquity shall a. love of many
Rom. 5. 20. the law entered that the offence might a.
6. 1. shall we continue in sin, that grace may a.?
15. 13. that ye may a. in hope through the power
2 Cor. 1. 5. as sufferings a. so consolation abounds
8. 7. as ye a. in every thing, see that ye a.
9. 8. God is able to make all grace a. to you
Phil. 1. 9. I pray that your love may a. more
4. 12. I know how to a. both to a. and suffer
17. but I desire fruit that may a. to your account
18. but I have all and a. I am full
1 Thess. 3. 12. Lord make you to a. in love one
4. 1. so ye would a. more and more
2 Pet. 1. 8. for if these things be in you and a.

ABOUNDED, ETH, ING.

Prov. 8. 24. when no fountains a. with water
29. 22. and a furious man a. in transgression
Rom. 3. 7. for if the truth of God hath more a.
5. 15. grace by Jesus Christ hath a. to many
20. but where sin a. grace did much more a.
1 Cor. 15. 58. always a. in the work of the Lord
2 Cor. 8. 2. deep poverty a. to the riches of liberality
Eph. 1. 8. wherein he hath a. toward us in wisdom
Col. 2. 7. a. therein with thanksgiving
2 Thess. 1. 3. the charity towards each other a.

ABOUT.

Gen. 38. 24. a. three months after was told Judah
41. 25. God shewed Pharaoh what he is a. to do
42. 24. he turned himself a. from them and wept
46. 34. thy servant's trade hath been a. cattle
Exod. 11. 4. a. midnight will I go out into Egypt
13. 18. God led the people a. through the way
19. 23. set bounds a. the mount, and sanctify it
32. 28. there fell that day a. 3000 men
Lev. 6. 5. all that a. which he hath sworn falsely
Num. 16. 24. from a. the tabernacle of Korah
Deut. 32. 10. he led him a. and instructed him
Josh. 10. 13. sun hasted not to go down a. a day
Judg. 17. 2. the silver a. which thou cursedst
Ruth 2. 17. and it was a. an ephah of barley
1 Sam. 1. 20. when the time was come a. Hannah
5. 8. let the ark of God be carried a. to Gath
9. 26. it came to pass, a. the spring of the day
21. 5. women have been kept from us a. three days
2 Sam. 14. 20. to fetch a. this form of speech
1 Kings 2. 15. the kingdom is turned a. and become
22. 36. a. going down of the sun, 2 Chron. 18. 34.
2 Kings 4. 16. a. this season according to the time
2 Chron. 2. 9. the house which I am a. to build
Ezra 10. 15. were employed a. this matter
Job 20. 23. when he is a. to fill his belly
Prov. 3. 3. bind them a. thy neck, 6. 21.
20. 19. he that goeth a. as a tale-bearer
Cant. 7. 2. like a heap of wheat set a. with lilies
Isa. 5. † 2. built a tower, and made a wall a. it
50. 11. that compass yourselves a. with sparks
Jer. 2. 36. why gaddest thou a. so much to change
31. 22. how long wilt thou go a. O thou
41. 14. all the people cast a. and returned
Hos. 7. 2. now their own doings have beset them a.
Mat. 20. 3. he went out a. the third hour
Mark 2. 2. no, not so much as a. the door
12. 1. set an hedge a. it, and digged a place
Luke 2. 49. I must be a. my Father's business
3. 23. Jesus began to be a. thirty years of age
12. 35. let your loins be girded a. and lights
John 3. 25. there arose a question, a. purifying
7. 19. why go ye a. to kill me?
Acts 4. 4. the number of the men was a. 5000
18. 14. and when Paul was a. to open his mouth
27. 30. as they were a. to flee out of the ship
Rom. 4. 19. when he was a. 100 years old
10. 3. going a. to establish their own righteousness
1 Cor. 9. 5. have we not power to lead a. a sister
2 Cor. 4. 10. always bearing a. in the body the dying
Eph. 6. 14. having your loins girt a. with truth
1 Tim. 5. 13. wandering a. from house to house
Heb. 8. 5. when he was a. to make the tabernacle
Rev. 8. 1. silence a. the space of half an hour
10. 4. I was a. to write, and I heard a voice
See GONE, HIM, ME, THEE, THEM, ROUND, STOOD, THIS, TIME, WENT.

ABROAD.

Exod. 12. 46. shalt not carry ought of the flesh a.
Lev. 13. 12. and if a leprosy break out a. in the skin
18. 9. whether she be born at home or a.
Deut. 23. 10. then shall he go a. out of the camp
13. when thou wilt ease thyself a. shalt dig
Judg. 12. 9. took daughters from a. for his sons
2 Kings 4. 3. go, borrow thee vessels a. of neighbours
2 Chron. 29. 16. Levites took it to carry it out a.
31. 5. as soon as the commandment came a.
Esth. 1. 17. this deed of the queen shall come a.
Job 15. 23. he wandereth a. for bread, saying
Psal. 41. 6. when he goeth a. he telleth it
Prov. 5. 16. let thy fountains be dispersed a.
Isa. 44. 24. that spreadeth a. the earth by myself
Jer. 6. 11. I will pour it out on the children a.
Lam. 1. 20. a. the sword bereaveth, at home death
Mark 1. 45. he began to blaze a. the matter.
4. 22. nor kept secret, but that it should come a.
Luke 1. 65. these sayings were noised a. throughout all the hill-country of Judea
2. 17. made known a. the saying about this child
Acts 2. 6. when this was noised a. the multitude
Rom. 5. 5. the love of God is shed a. in our hearts
16. 19. for your obedience is come a. to all men
See CAST, SPREAD, STAND, SCATTER, WENT.

ABSENCE.

Luke 22. 6. to betray him in a. of the multitude
Phil. 2. 12. but now much more in my a. work out

ABSENT.

Gen. 31. 49. when we are a. one from another
1 Cor. 5. 3. for I verily as a. in body, but present in
2 Cor. 5. 6. at home in body are a. from the Lord
2 Cor. 5. 8. willing rather to be a. from the body, pre-
9. whether present or a. we may be accepted [sent
10. 1. but being a. am bold toward you
11. as we are by letters when we are a. such will
13. 2. and being a. now I write to them, 10.
Phil. 1. 27. whether I come, or else be a.
Col. 2. 5. for tho' I be a. in the flesh, yet am I with

ABSTAIN.

Acts 15. 20. that they a. from pollutions of idols
29. that ye a. from meats offered to idols
1 Thess. 4. 3. that ye should a. from fornication
5. 22. a. from all appearance of evil
1 Tim. 4. 3. commanding to a. from meats
1 Pet. 2. 11. a. from fleshly lusts which war against

ABSTINENCE.

Acts 27. 21. after long a. Paul stood forth in midst

ABUNDANCE.

Deut. 28. 47. thou servedst not God for the a. of all
33. 19. they shall suck of the a. of the seas
1 Sam. 1. 16. out of the a. of my complaint
1 Kings 10. 10. came no more such a. of spices
27. as the sycamore-trees for a. 2 Chron. 1. 15.
18. 41. for there is a sound of a. of rain
2 Chron. 9. 9. she gave the king of spices great a.
Job 22. 11. and a. of waters cover thee, 38. 34.
Psal. 72. 7. in his days shall be a. of peace
Eccl. 5. 10. nor he that loveth a. with increase
12. the a. of the rich will not suffer him to sleep
Isa. 7. 22. for a. of milk he shall eat butter
15. 7. therefore the a. they have gotten
47. 9. for the great a. of thy enchantments
60. 5. the a. of the sea shall be converted to thee
66. 11. be delighted with the a. of her glory
Jer. 33. 6. I will reveal to them a. of peace
Ezek. 16. 49. a. of idleness was in her and daughters
26. 10. by reason of the a. of his horses
Zech. 14. 14. gold, silver, and apparel in great a.
Mat. 12. 34. out of the a. of the heart, Luke 6. 45.
13. 12. and he shall have more a. 25. 29.
Mark 12. 44. they cast in of their a. Luke 21. 4.
Rom. 5. 17. more they which receive a. of grace
2 Cor. 8. 2. the a. of their joy abounded to the riches
14. your a. a supply, their a. a supply for want
12. 7. be exalted through the a. of the revelations
Rev. 18. 3. waxed rich through a. of her delicacies

In ABUNDANCE.

2 Sam. 12. 30. David brought spoil of the city in a.
1 Kings 1. 19. Adonijah hath slain oxen in a. 25.
1 Chron. 22. 3. David prepared brass in a. 14.
4. also cedar-trees in a. marble in a. 29. 2.
15. there are workmen with thee in a. hewers
29. 21. they offered sacrifices in a. for all Israel
2 Chron. 2. 9. even to prepare me timber in a.
4. 18. Solomon made all these vessels in great a.
9. 1. Queen of Sheba brought gold in a.
11. 23. Rehoboam gave his sons victuals in a.
14. 15. Asa carried away sheep and camels in a.
15. 9. for they fell to Asa out of Israel in a.
17. 5. all Judah brought presents to Jehoshaphat, and he had riches and honour in a. 18. 1.
18. 2. Ahab killed sheep for Jehoshaphat in a.
20. 25. Jehoshaphat found spoil in a.
24. 11. thus they gathered money in a.
29. 35. and also the burnt-offerings were in a.
31. 5. children of Israel brought in a. first-fruits
32. 5. Hezekiah made darts and shields in a.
29. he provided him cities and possessions in a.
Neh. 9. 25. they took vineyards and fruit-trees in a.
Esth. 1. 7. they gave them royal wine in a.
Job 36. 31. he giveth meat in a.
Psal. 37. 11. delight themselves in a. of peace
52. 7. but trusted in the a. of his riches
105. 30. the land brought forth frogs in a.
Luke 12. 15. man's life consisteth not in a.
2 Cor. 8. 20. that no man blame us in this a.

ABUNDANT.

Exod. 34. 6. Lord God a. in goodness and truth
Prov. 12. † 26. the righteous more a. than neighbour
Isa. 56. 12. shall be as this day and much more a.
Jer. 51. 13. O thou Babylon, a. in treasures
1 Cor. 12. 23. on these we bestow more a. honour
24. having given more a. honour to that part
2 Cor. 4. 15. that the a. grace might redound
7. 15. his inward affection is more a. toward you
9. 12. for the administration is a. by many
11. 23. in labours more a. in stripes above measure
Phil. 1. 26. that your rejoicing may be more a.
1 Tim. 1. 14. the grace of our Lord was exceeding a.
1 Pet. 1. 3. according to his a. mercy hath begotten

ABUNDANTLY.

Gen. 1. 20. let the waters bring forth a. 21.
8. 17. that they may breed a. in the earth
9. 7. multiply, bring forth a. in the earth
Exod. 1. 7. the children of Israel increased a.
8. 3. the river shall bring forth frogs a.
Num. 20. 11. Moses smote and the water came out a.
1 Chron. 12. 40. brought oil, oxen, and sheep a.
22. 5. so David prepared a. before his death
8. thou hast shed blood a. and made great wars
2 Chron. 31. 5. tithe of all things brought they in a.
Job 12. 6. into whose hand God bringeth a.
36. 28. the clouds drop and distil upon man a.
Psal. 36. 8. they shall be a. satisfied with fatness
65. 10. thou waterest the ridges thereof a.
132. 15. I will a. bless her provision
145. 7. shall a. utter the memory of thy goodness
Cant. 5. 1. O friends drink, yea drink a. O beloved
Isa. 15. 3. every one shall howl, weeping a.
35. 2. it shall blossom a. and rejoice with joy
43. † 24. nor hast thou a. moistened with the fat
55. 7. and to our God, for he will a. pardon
John 10. 10. that they might have life more a.
1 Cor. 15. 10. I laboured more a. than they all
2 Cor. 1. 12. conversation, and more a. to you-wards
2. 4. might know the love I have more a. to you
10. 15. shall be enlarged according to our rule a.
12. 15. though the more a. I love you, the less
Eph. 3. 20. to him that is able to do exceeding a.
1 Thess. 2. 17. endeavoured more a. to see your face
Tit. 3. 6. which he shed a. through Jesus Christ
Heb. 6. 17. God willing more a. to shew to the heirs
2 Pet. 1. 11. for so an entrance be ministered to you a.

ABUSE, ED.

Lev. 19. † 20. who lieth with a bond-maid a. by any
Judg. 19. 25. and a. her all the night till morning
1 Sam. 31. 4. lest uncircumcised a. me, 1 Chr. 10. 4.
1 Cor. 9. 18. that I a. not my power in the gospel

ABUSERS, ING.

1 Cor. 6. 9. nor a. of themselves with mankind
7. 31. and they that use this world as not a. it

ACCEPT

Signifies, [1] To receive favourably, Mal. 1. 10, 13. 2 Cor. 11. 4. [2] To take pleasure in, Ezek. 20. 40. [3] To forgive, Gen. 4. 7. Job 42. 9. [4] To respect partially, Job 13. 10. | 32. 21. Prov. 18. 5. [5] To be regarded or valued, 2 Cor. 8. 12. [6] To be beloved or highly esteemed, Luke 4. 24. [7] To be received into grace and favour, Acts 10. 35. Eph. 1. 6.

Gen. 32. 20. peradventure he will a. of me
Exod. 22. 11. and the owner shall a. thereof
Lev. 26. 41. and they a. of the punishment, 43.
Deut. 33. 11. bless and a. the work of his hands
1 Sam. 26. 19. let him a. an offering
2 Sam. 24. 23. Araunah said, the L. thy God a. thee
Job 13. 8. will ye a. his person? will ye contend
10. will reprove if ye do secretly a. persons
32. 21. let me not a. any man's person
42. 8. Job shall pray for you, for him will I a.
Psal. 20. 3. and a. thy burnt-sacrifice
82. 2. and a. the persons of the wicked
119. 108. a. I beseech thee, the free-will-offerings
Prov. 6. † 35. not a. the face of any ransom
18. 5. not good to a. the person of the wicked
Jer. 14. 10. therefore the Lord doth not a. them
12. when offer, I will not a. them, Amos 5. 22.
Ezek. 20. 40. there will I a. them, and require
41. I will a. you with your sweet savour
43. 27. and I will a. you, saith the Lord
Mal. 1. 8. will he be pleased, or a. thy person?
10. nor will I a. an offering at your hand
13. should I a. this of your hands?
Acts 24. 3. we a. it always, and in all places

ACCEPTABLE.

Lev. 22. 20. for it shall not be a. for you
Deut. 33. 24. let Ashur be a. to his brethren
Psal. 19. 14. let the meditation of my heart be a.
69. 13. my prayer is to thee, O Lord, in an a. time
Prov. 10. 32. lips of the righteous know what is a.
21. 3. to do justice and judgment is more a.
Eccl. 12. 10. the preacher sought out a. words
Isa. 49. 8. in an a. time have I heard thee
58. 5. wilt thou call this an a. day to the Lord?
61. 2. to proclaim the a. year of the Lord
Jer. 6. 20. your burnt-offerings are not a.
Dan. 4. 27. O king, let my counsel be a. to thee
Luke 4. 19. to preach the a. year of the Lord
Rom. 12. 1. bodies a living sacrifice, holy, a. to God
2. what is that good and a. will of God
14. 18. is a. to God and approved of men
15. 16. offering up of the Gentiles might be a.
Eph. 5. 10. proving what is a. unto the Lord
Phil. 4. 18. a sacrifice a. well-pleasing to God
1 Tim. 2. 3. for this is a. in the sight of God
5. 4. for that is good and a. before God
1 Pet. 2. 5. sacrifices a. to God by Jesus Christ
20. if ye take it patiently, this is a. with God

ACCEPTABLY.

Heb. 12. 28. whereby we may serve God a.

ACCEPTANCE.

Isa. 60. 7. they shall come up with a. on mine altar

ACCEPTATION.

1 Tim. 1. 15. this is a saying worthy of all a. 4. 9.

ACCEPTED,

Gen. 4. 7. if thou doest well, shalt thou not be a.
19. 21. see, I have a. thee concerning this
Exod. 28. 38. that they may be a. before the Lord
Lev. 1. 4. the offering shall be a. for him, 22. 27.
7. 18. it shall not be a. 19. 7. | 22. 23, 25.
10. 19. should it have been a. in sight of the Lord
22. 21. an offering shall be perfect, to be a.
23. 11. he shall wave the sheaf to be a.
1 Sam. 18. 5. he was a. in the sight of all the people
25. 35. David said, see I have a. thy person
2 Kings 5. † 1. Naaman was a. with his master
Esth. 10. 3. a. of the multitude of his brethren
Job 22. † 8. the a. for countenance dwelt in it
42. 9. the Lord also a. Job
Isa. 56. 7. their sacrifice shall be a. on mine altar
Jer. 37. 20. let my supplication be a. before thee
42. 2. let our supplication be a. before thee
Mal. 2. † 9. but ye have a. faces in the law
Luke 1. † 28. hail, thou that art graciously a.
4. 24. no prophet is a. in his own country
Acts 10. 35. he that worketh righteousness is a.
Rom. 15. 31. my service may be a. of the saints
2 Cor. 5. 9. labour, absent or present, we may be a.
6. 2. heard thee in a time a. now is the a. time
8. 12. it is a. according to that a man hath
17. for indeed he a. the exhortation
11. 4. or another gospel which ye have not a.
Eph. 1. 6. he hath made us a. in the beloved

ACCEPTEST.

Luke 20. 21. neither a. thou the person of any

ACCEPTETH.

Job 34. 19. to him that a. not persons of princes
Eccl. 9. 7. eat with joy, for God now a. thy works
Hos. 8. 13. they sacrifice, but the Lord a. them not
Gal. 2. 6. God a. no man's person

ACCEPTING. See DELIVERANCE.

ACCESS.

Rom. 5. 2. by whom also we have a. by faith
Eph. 2. 18. thro' him we both have a. to the Father
3. 12. in whom we have boldness and a. by faith

ACCOMPANY. See SALVATION.

ACCOMPANIED.

Acts 10. 23. certain brethren from Joppa a. him
11. 12. moreover these six brethren a. me
20. 4. Sopater of Berea a. Paul into Asia
38. and they a. him to the ship

ACCOMPANYING. See ARK of God.

ACCOMPLISH

Signifies, [1] To perform, finish, or fulfil, Jer. 44. 25. Dan. 9. 2. Luke 2. 6. Acts 21. 5. [2] To

yield or condescend to, 1 Kings 5. 9. [3] *Obtained or brought to pass*, Prov. 13. 19.
Lev. 22. 21. offereth a sacrifice to *a.* his vow
1 *Kings* 5. 9. shalt *a.* my desire in giving food
Job 14. 6. till he shall *a.* as an hireling his day
Psal. 64. 6. they *a.* a diligent search
Isa. 55. 11. but it shall *a.* that which I please
Jer. 44. 25. ye will surely *a.* your vows
Ezek. 6. 12. thus will I *a.* my fury upon them
7. 8. now will I *a.* mine anger upon thee
13. 15. thus will I *a.* my wrath upon the wall
20. 8. I will pour out my fury to *a.* my anger, 21.
Dan. 9. 2. that he would *a.* seventy years
Luke 9. 31. which he should *a.* at Jerusalem

ACCOMPLISHED.

2 *Chron.* 36. 22. the word by Jeremiah might be *a.*
Esth. 2. 12. days of purification were *a.* *Luke* 2. 22.
Job 15. 32. it shall be *a.* before his time
Prov. 13. 19. the desire *a.* is sweet to the soul
Isa. 40. 2. cry unto her, that her warfare is *a.*
Jer. 25. 12. when seventy years are *a.* 29. 10.
34. for the days of your dispersions are *a.*
39. 16. my words shall be *a.* before thee
Lam. 4. 11. the Lord hath *a.* his fury
22. the punishment of thine iniquity is *a.*
Ezek. 4. 6. when hast *a.* them, lie on thy right side
5. 13. thus shall mine anger be *a.*
Dan. 11. 36. shall prosper, till the indignation be *a.*
12. 7. *a.* to scatter the power of the holy people
Luke 1. 23. the days of his ministration were *a.*
2. 6. the days were *a.* that she should be delivered
21. when eight days were *a.* for circumcising
12. 50. and how am I straitened till it be *a.*
18. 31. concerning the Son of man, shall be *a.*
22. 37. that is written, must yet be *a.* in me
John 19. 28. knowing that all things were now *a.*
Acts 21. 5. when we had *a.* those days, we departed
1 *Pet.* 5. 9. same afflictions are *a.* in your brethren
ACCOMPLISHING. *See* SERVICE.

ACCOMPLISHMENT.

Acts 21. 26. to signify the *a.* of days of purification

ACCORD.

Lev. 25. 5. groweth of its own *a.* shall not reap
Josh. 9. 2. to fight with Israel with one *a.*
Acts 1. 14. these all continued with one *a.* in prayer
2. 1. they were all with one *a.* in one place
46. they continuing daily with one *a.* in temple
4. 24. they lift up their voice to God with one *a.*
5. 12. were all with one *a.* in Solomon's porch
7. 57. and ran upon Stephen with one *a.*
8. 6. people with one *a.* gave heed to these things
12. 10. the gate opened to them of his own *a.*
20. but they came with one *a.* to him
15. 25. being assembled with one *a.* to send
18. 12. the Jews with one *a.* made insurrection
19. 29. they rushed with one *a.* into the theatre
2 *Cor.* 8. 17. but being more forward of his own *a.*
Phil. 2. 2. being of one *a.* of one mind

ACCORDING.

Gen. 27. 19. I have done *a.* as thou badest me
41. 54. dearth began to come *a.* as Joseph said
Exod. 12. 25. the Lord will give *a.* as he promised
Num. 14. 17. be great, *a.* as thou hast spoken
Deut. 10. 9. his inheritance *a.* as God promised
16. 10. *a.* as the Lord thy God hath blessed thee
1 *Kings* 3. 6. *a.* as he walked before thee in truth
Job 34. 11. and cause every man to find *a.* to his ways, *Jer.* 17. 10. | 21. 14. | 32. 19.
42. 9. went and did *a.* as the Lord commanded
Psal. 7. 8. judge me, O God, *a.* to my righteousness
17. I will praise the Lord *a.* to his righteousness
25. 7. *a.* to thy mercy remember thou me, 51. 1. | 106. 45. | 109. 26. | 119. 124.
28. 4. give them *a.* to their deeds, and *a.* to thee
33. 22. let mercy be on us *a.* as we hope in thee
35. 24. judge me, O God, *a.* to thy righteousness
48. 10. *a.* to thy name, so is thy praise
62. 12. for thou renderest to every man *a.* to his work, *Prov.* 24. 12. 29.
79. 11. *a.* to the greatness of thy power
90. 11. *a.* to thy fear, so is thy wrath
103. 10. nor rewarded us *a.* to our iniquities
119. 25. *a.* to thy word, 28, 41, 58, 65, 76, 107, 116, 154, 169, 170.
159. quicken me *a.* to thy kindness, *Isa.* 63. 7.
150. 2. praise him *a.* to his excellent greatness
Isa. 8. 20. if they speak not *a.* to this word
9. 3. they joy *a.* to the joy in harvest
63. 7. *a.* to all that the Lord has bestowed on us
Jer. 50. 29. recompense her *a.* to her work
Dan. 11. 3. that shall rule, and do *a.* to his will
Hos. 3. 1. *a.* to the love of the Lord toward Israel
12. 2. the Lord will punish Jacob *a.* to his ways
Mic. 7. 15. *a.* to the days of thy coming out of Egypt
Mat. 9. 29. *a.* to your faith be it unto you
16. 27. he will reward every man *a.* to his works, *Rom.* 2. 6. 2 *Tim.* 4. 14. *Rev.* 2. 23.
Luke 12. 47. nor did *a.* to his will, shall be beaten
John 7. 24. judge not *a.* to the appearance
Acts 4. 35. made to every man *a.* as he had need
Rom. 1. 3. made of the seed of David *a.* to the flesh
8. 28. who are the called *a.* to his purpose
12. 6. gifts differing *a.* to the grace given to us
15. 5. to be like-minded *a.* to Christ Jesus
1 *Cor.* 15. 3. Christ died *a.* to the scriptures, 4.
2 *Cor.* 9. 7. every man *a.* as he purposeth in his heart
11. 15. whose end shall be *a.* to their works
Gal. 1. 4. who gave himself *a.* to the will of God
3. 29. Abraham's seed, and heirs *a.* to the promise
Eph. 1. 4. *a.* as he hath chosen us in him, before
5. *a.* to good pleasure || 7. *a.* to riches of his grace
11. being predestinated *a.* to the purpose of him
3. 20. *a.* to the power that worketh in us
Phil. 3. 21. *a.* to the working whereby he is able
4. 19. God shall supply our need *a.* to his riches
2 *Tim.* 1. 9. who hath called us not *a.* to our works
Tit. 3. 5. but *a.* to his mercy he saved us by washing
Heb. 8. 9. not *a.* to the covenant that I made with
1 *Pet.* 1. 3. *a.* to his mercy hath begotten us again
4. 6. but live *a.* to God in the Spirit
2 *Pet.* 1. 3. *a.* as his divine power hath given us
3. 13. we *a.* to his promise look for new heavens
Rev. 20. 12. dead were judged *a.* to their works, 13.
22. 12. I come to give *a.* as his work shall be
ACCORDING *to all*. *See* ALL.

ACCORDING *to that*.

Gen. 27. 8. obey my voice *a. to that* I command
Judg. 11. 36. do to me *a. to that* which proceeded
2 *Kings* 14. 6. slew not *a. to that* which is written
2 *Chron.* 35. 26. *a. to that* which was written
Ezra 6. 13. Tatnai did *a. to that* Darius had sent
Rom. 4. 18. *a. to that* which was spoken, thy seed be
2 *Cor.* 5. 10. *a. to that* he hath done, good or bad
8. 12. *a. to that* a man hath, not *a. to that* he hath not
ACCORDINGLY. *See* REPAY.

ACCOUNT.

Exod. 12. 4. shall make your *a.* for the lamb
2 *Kings* 12. 4. of every one that passeth the *a.*
1 *Chron.* 27. 24. neither was the number put in the *a.*
2 *Chron.* 26. 11. according to the number of their *a.*
Job 33. 13. for he giveth not *a.* of his matters
Psal. 144. 3. or the son of man that thou makest *a.*
Eccl. 7. 27. counting one by one to find out the *a.*
Dan. 6. 2. that the princes might give *a.* to them
Mat. 12. 36. give *a.* thereof in the day of judgment
18. 23. which would take *a.* of his servants
Luke 16. 2. give an *a.* of thy stewardship
Acts 19. 40. whereby we may give an *a.* of this
Rom. 9. † 28. he will finish the *a.*
14. 12. every one shall give *a.* of himself to God
Phil. 4. 17. desire fruit that may abound to your *a.*
Philem. 18. if he oweth thee, put that on mine *a.*
Heb. 13. 17. they watch as they that must give *a.*
1 *Pet.* 4. 5. who shall give *a.* to him that judgeth

ACCOUNT, ED.

Deut. 2. 11. which also were *a.* giants
20. that also was *a.* a land of giants
1 *Kings* 1. 21. I and Solomon shall be *a.* offenders
10. 21. silver was nothing *a.* of, 2 *Chron.* 9. 20.
Psal. 22. 30. be *a.* to the Lord for a generation
Isa. 2. 22. for wherein is he to be *a.* of?
Mark 10. 42. they which are *a.* to rule over Gentiles
Luke 20. 35. be *a.* worthy to obtain that world
22. 24. which of them should be *a.* the greatest
Rom. 8. 36. we are *a.* as sheep for the slaughter
1 *Cor.* 4. 1. let a man so *a.* of us as ministers
Gal. 3. 6. it was *a.* to him for righteousness
2 *Pet.* 3. 15. *a.* that the long-suffering of the Lord

ACCOUNTING.

Heb. 11. 19. *a.* that God was able to raise him up

ACCURSED

Signifies, [1] *Devoted to destruction*, Josh. 6. 17. [2] *Separated from the church*, Rom. 9. 3. [3] *Cursed eternally from God*, 1 Cor. 16. 22. Gal. 1. 8, 9.
Deut. 21. 23. he that is hanged is *a.* of God
Josh. 6. 17. the city shall be *a.* it and all therein
18. in any wise keep from the *a.* thing
7. 1. trespass in the *a.* thing; Achan took of *a.*
11. for they have even taken of the *a.* thing
12. turned their backs, because they were *a.* except ye destroy the *a.* from among you
13. there is an *a.* thing in the midst of thee
15. he that is taken with the *a.* thing
22. 20. did not Achan commit trespass in *a.* thing
1 *Sam.* 3. † 13. his sons made themselves *a.*
1 *Chron.* 2. 7. who transgressed in the thing *a.*
Isa. 65. 20. the sinner an 100 years old shall be *a.*
Rom. 9. 3. for I could wish myself *a.* from Christ
1 *Cor.* 12. 3. no man by the Spirit calleth Jesus *a.*
Gal. 1. 8. preach any other gospel, let him be *a.* 9.

ACCUSATION.

Ezra 4. 6. wrote they to him an *a.* against Judah
Mat. 27. 37. set over his head his *a.* *Mark* 15. 26.
Luke 6. 7. that they might find an *a.* against him
19. 8. if I have taken any thing by false *a.*
John 18. 29. what *a.* bring ye against this man?
Acts 25. 18. they brought no *a.* as I supposed
1 *Tim.* 5. 19. against an elder receive not an *a.*
2 *Pet.* 2. 11. bring not a railing *a.* against them
Jude 9. Michael durst not bring a railing *a.*

ACCUSE.

Prov. 30. 10. *a.* not a servant to his master
Mat. 12. 10. that they might *a.* him, *Mar.* 3. 2. *Luke* 11. 54.
Luke 3. 14. nor *a.* any falsely, and be content
23. 2. and they began to *a.* him, saying
14. touching those things whereof ye *a.* him
John 5. 45. that I will *a.* you to the Father
8. 6. that they might have to *a.* him
Acts 24. 2. Tertullus began to *a.* him, saying
8. take knowledge of all things whereof we *a.*
13. nor can they prove things whereof they *a.* me
25. 5. let them go down with me, and *a.* this man
11. if there be none of those whereof these *a.* me
28. 19. not that I had ought to *a.* my nation of
1 *Pet.* 3. 16. falsely *a.* your good conversation

ACCUSED.

Dan. 3. 8. Chaldeans came near and *a.* the Jews
6. 24. they brought them which had *a.* Daniel
Mat. 27. 12. when he was *a.* he answered nothing
Mark 15. 3. priests *a.* him many things, *Luke* 23. 10.
Luke 16. 1. was *a.* that he had wasted his goods
Acts 22. 30. the certainty wherefore he was *a.*
23. 28. have known the cause wherefore they *a.* him
29. perceived to be *a.* of questions of their law
25. 16. before he which is *a.* have the accusers
26. 2. answer, touching things whereof I am *a.*
7. for which hope's sake I am *a.* of the Jews
Tit. 1. 6. faithful children, not *a.* of riot, or unruly
Rev. 12. 10. accuser, who *a.* them before our God
ACCUSER. *See* CAST *down*.

ACCUSERS.

John 8. 10. woman, where are those thine *a.*?
Acts 23. 30. I gave commandment to his *a.* also
35. I will hear thee when thine *a.* are come
24. 8. commanding his *a.* to come to thee
25. 16. before he have the *a.* face to face
18. against whom, when the *a.* stood up
2 *Tim.* 3. 3. without natural affection, false *a.*
Tit. 2. 3. not false *a.* not given to much wine

ACCUSETH, ING.

John 5. 45. there is one that *a.* you, even Moses
Rom. 2. 15. their thoughts *a.* or excusing

ACCUSTOMED; *see* DO EVIL. ACELDAMA; *see* FIELD.

ACKNOWLEDGE

Signifies, [1] *To own, or confess*, Gen. 38. 26. Psal. 32. 5. [2] *To observe, or take notice of*, Prov. 3. 6. Isa. 33. 13. [3] *To esteem and respect*, Isa. 61. 9. 1 Cor. 16. 18. [4] *To approve of*, 2. Cor. 1. 13. Philem. 6. [5] *To worship, or make profession of*, Dan. 11. 39.
Deut. 1. † 17. ye shall not *a.* faces in judgment
21. 17. he shall *a.* the son of the hated
33. 9. nor did he *a.* his brethren nor children
Psal. 32. 5. I *a.* my sin || 51. 3. I *a.* my transgression
Prov. 3. 6. in all thy ways *a.* him, he shall direct
Isa. 33. 13. ye that are near, *a.* my might
61. 9. all that see them, shall *a.* them
63. 16. thou art our father, tho' Israel *a.* us not
Jer. 3. 13. only *a.* thine iniquity that thou hast
14. 20. we *a.* O Lord, our wickedness
24. 5. so will I *a.* them that are carried away
Dan. 11. 39. with a strange God whom he shall *a.*
Hos. 5. 15. I will go, till they *a.* their offence
1 *Cor.* 14. 37. let him *a.* the things that I write
16. 18. therefore *a.* ye them that are such
2 *Cor.* 1. 13. what you *a.* and I trust shall *a.*

ACKNOWLEDGED.

Gen. 38. 26. Judah *a.* them, and said, she hath been
2 *Cor.* 1. 14. also you have *a.* us in part

ACKNOWLEDGETH.

1 *John* 2. 23. he that *a.* the Son hath the Father

ACKNOWLEDGING.

2 *Tim.* 2. 25. repentance to the *a.* of the truth
Tit. 1. 1. to the *a.* the truth which is after godliness
Philem. 6. by the *a.* every good thing in Christ

ACKNOWLEDGMENT.

Col. 2. 2. to the *a.* of the mystery of God

ACQUAINT, ED, ING.

Job 22. 21. *a.* thyself with him and be at peace
Psal. 139. 3. thou art *a.* with all my ways
Eccl. 2. 3. yet *a.* my heart with wisdom
Isa. 53. 3. a man of sorrows, and *a.* with grief

ACQUAINTANCE.

2 *Kings* 12. 5. let priests take it, every man of his *a.*
7. therefore receive no more money of your *a.*
Job 19. 13. mine *a.* are estranged from me
42. 11. then came all that had been of his *a.*
Psal. 31. 11. I was a reproach and a fear to mine *a.*
55. 13. it was thou, mine equal, and mine *a.*
88. 8. thou hast put away mine *a.* far from me
18. lover put from me, and my *a.* into darkness
Luke 2. 44. they sought him among their *a.*
23. 49. all his *a.* stood afar off, beholding things
Acts 24. 23. he should forbid none of his *a.* to come

ACQUIT.

Job 10. 14. thou wilt not *a.* me from mine iniquity
Nah. 1. 3. the Lord will not at all *a.* the wicked

ACRE, S.

1 *Sam.* 14. 14. 20 men within half an *a.* of land
Isa. 5. 10. ten *a.* of vineyard shall yield one bath

ACT.

Isa. 28. 21. and bring to pass his *a.* his strange *a.*
59. 6. and the *a.* of violence is in their hands
John 8. 4. was taken in adultery, in the very *a.*

ACTS.

Deut. 11. 3. and his *a.* which he did in Egypt
7. your eyes have seen the great *a.* of the Lord
Judg. 5. 11. rehearse the righteous *a.* of the Lord
1 *Sam.* 12. 7. reason of all righteous *a.* of the Lord
2 *Sam.* 23. 20. and Benaiah the son of Jehoiada, who had done many *a.* 1 *Chron.* 11. 22.
1 *Kings* 10. 6. it was a true report I heard of thy *a.*
11. 41. the *a.* of Solomon, are they not written in the book of the *a.* of Solomon? 2 *Chron.* 9. 5.
2 *Kings* 10. 34. the *a.* of Jehu, and all that he did
23. 19. according to all the *a.* he had done
28. the *a.* of Josiah and all that he did are written
1 *Chron.* 29. 29. the *a.* of David, first and last
2 *Chron.* 16. 11. behold the *a.* of Asa, first and last
20. 34. the *a.* of Jehoshaphat, first and last
32. 32. the *a.* of Hezekiah, 2 *Kings* 20. 20.
Esth. 10. 2. all the *a.* of his power and might
Psal. 103. 7. his *a.* to the children of Israel
106. 2. who can utter the mighty *a.* of the Lord?
145. 4. and shall declare thy mighty *a.* 6. 12.
150. 2. praise him for his mighty *a.* praise him

ACTIONS.

1 *Sam.* 2. 3. and by the Lord *a.* are weighed

ACTIVITY.

Gen. 47. 6. if knowest any man of *a.* among them

ADAMANT.

Ezek. 3. 9. as an *a.* have I made thy forehead
Zech. 7. 12. they made their hearts as an *a.* stone

ADD

Signifies, [1] *To join, or put to*, Deut. 4. 2. Acts 2. 41. 2 Pet. 1. 5. [2] *To increase*, Prov. 16. 23. [3] *To give, or bestow*, Gen. 30. 24. Mat. 6. 33. [4] *To make wise by instruction*, Gal. 2. 6. [5] *To utter*, Deut. 5. 22.
Gen. 30. 24. the Lord shall *a.* to me another son
Lev. 5. 16. he shall *a.* a fifth part thereto, 6. 5. | 27. 13, 15, 19, 27, 31. *Num.* 5. 7.
Num. 35. 6. to cities of refuge *a.* forty-two cities
Deut. 4. 2. ye shall not *a.* to the word, 12. 32.
19. 9. thou shalt *a.* three cities more of refuge
29. 19. to *a.* drunkenness to thirst
2 *Sam.* 24. 3. the Lord thy God *a.* to the people
1 *Kings* 12. 11 and now Rehoboam said, I will *a.* to your yoke, 14. 2 *Chron.* 10. 14.
2 *Kings* 20. 6. I *a.* to thy days 15 years, *Isa.* 38. 5.
1 *Chron.* 22. 14. and thou mayest *a.* thereto
2 *Chron.* 28. 13. ye intend to *a.* more to our sins
Psal. 69. 27. *a.* iniquity to their iniquity
Prov. 3. 2. long life and peace shall they *a.* to thee
30. 6. *a.* thou not to his words, lest he reprove thee
Isa. 29. 1. *a.* ye year to year, let them kill sacrifices
30. 1. that they may *a.* sin to sin
Mat. 6. 27. can *a.* one cubit to his stature, *Luke* 12. 25.
Phil. 1. 16. supposing to *a.* affliction to my bonds
2 *Pet.* 1. 5. besides this *a.* to your faith virtue
Rev. 22. 18. if any *a.* God shall *a.* to him plagues

ADDED.

Deut. 5. 22. with a great voice, and he *a.* no more

1 Sam. 12. 19. we have a. to all our sins this evil
Jer. 36. 32. there were a. besides many like words
45. 3. the Lord hath a. grief to my sorrow
Dan. 4. 36. and excellent majesty was a. to me
Mat. 6. 33. all these shall be a. to you, Luke 12. 31.
Luke 3. 20. Herod a. yet this above all, he shut up
19. 11. as they heard, he a. and spake a parable
Acts 2. 41. the same day there were a. 3000 souls
47. and the Lord a. to the church daily such
5. 14. belie ers were the more a. to the Lord
11. 24. and much people was a. to the Lord
Gal. 2. 6. seemed to be somewhat, a. nothing to me
3. 19. the law was a. because of transgressions

ADDETH, ING.

Job 34. 37. for he a. rebellion to his sin
Prov. 10. 22. and he a. no sorrow with it
16. 23. the heart of the wise a. learning to his lips
Gal. 3. 15. no man disannulleth or a. thereto.

ADDER.

Gen. 49. 17. Dan shall be an a. in the path
Psal. 58. 4. they are like the deaf a. that stops
91. 13. thou shalt tread on the lion and a.
140. 3. a. poison is under their lips
Prov. 23. 32. wine at last stingeth like an a.

ADDICTED.

1 Cor. 16. 15. a. themselves to the ministry of saints

ADDITION, S.

1 Kings 7. 29. certain a. were made of thin work
30. undersetters molten at the side of every a.
36. he gra ed cherubims, and a. round about

ADJURE

Signifies, [1] *To bind under the penalty of a fearful curse*, Josh. 6. 26. [2] *To charge earnestly by word or oath*, 1 Kings 22. 16. Mat. 26. 63.
1 Kings 22. 16. the king said, how many times shall I a. thee to tell me nothing, 2 Chron. 18. 15.
Mat. 26. 63. I a. thee by the living God
Mark 5. 7. I a. thee by God, thou torment me not
Acts 19. 13. saying, we a. you by Jesus, whom Paul

ADJURED.

Josh. 6. 26. Joshua a. them at that time
1 Sam. 14. 24. for Saul had a. the people

ADMINISTRATION, S.

1 Cor. 12. 5. there are differences of a.
2 Cor. 9. 12. for the a. of this service supplieth

ADMINISTERED.

2 Cor. 8. 19. a. by us to the glory of the same Lord
20. in this abundance which is a. by us

ADMIRATION.

Jude 16. having men's persons in a.
Rev. 17. 6. I saw her, I wondered with great a.

ADMIRED.

2 Thess. 1. 10. to be a. in all them that believe

ADMONISH, ED.

Eccl. 4. 13. a foolish king, who will no more be a.
12. 12. and further by these, my son, be a.
Jer. 42. 19. know certainly that I have a. you
Acts 27. 9. the fast was now past, Paul a. them
Rom. 15. 14. ye are able also to a. one another
Col. 3. 16. a. one another in psalms and hymns
1 Thess. 5. 12. that are over you in Lord, and a. you
2 Thess. 3. 15. not an enemy, but a. him as a brother
Heb. 8. 5. as Moses was a. of God, when he was

ADMONITION.

1 Cor. 10. 11. they are written for our a.
Eph. 6. 4. bring them up in the a. of the Lord
Tit. 3. 10. after the first and second a. reject

ADO.

Mark 5. 39. he saith, why make ye this a. and weep

ADOPTION

Is an action whereby a man takes a person into his family, in order to make him part of it, acknowledges him for his son, and receives him into the number, and gives him a right to the privileges, of his children. Pharaoh's daughter adopted young Moses, and Mordecai Esther, Exod. 2. 10. Esther 2. 7, 15. *We are not acquainted how far the privileges of adoption extended: but it may be presumed that they were much the same with those mentioned in the Roman laws: The adopted children shared in the estate with the natural children; they assumed the name of the person who adopted them, and became subject to his paternal power who received them into his family. And God doth adopt his children, when he graciously admits strangers and enemies, as all the fallen race of Adam are by nature, into the state and relation of children thro' Jesus Christ; he becoming their Father in him, according to the great promise of the new covenant*, Eph. 2. 11, 12, 13. 1 John 3. 1. Gal. 4. 5. Eph. 1. 5. Jer. 31. 33. 2 Cor. 6. 16. 18. *The adopted are true believers in Christ; they relying upon his blood and surety-righteousness for pardon and reconciliation with God; for* to as many as received him, to them gave he power to become the sons of God, even to them that believe on his name. *They are regenerated by the Spirit, and are* justified freely by grace, through the redemption that is in Jesus Christ, *and are brought through the Spirit's operation to an affectionate obediential frame of spirit towards God as their reconciled Father*, John 1. 12, 13. Rom. 3. 24, 25. Zech. 12. 10. Isa. 63. 18. Gal. 4. 5, 6. Tit. 3. 5, 6. 1 John 2. 29. *Many and great are the privileges of God's adopted children; some of which are, his fatherly protection from temporal and spiritual evils, and his provision of all needful things both for soul and body; his fatherly correction of them; audience and return to their prayers; and a sure title to the heavenly inheritance: for*, if children, then heirs, heirs of God, and joint-heirs with Christ, Rom. 8. 17. Psal. 34. 10. and 121. 7. Heb. 12. 6. 1 John 5. 14, 15. *True believers are said to be put into this state*, [1] *By election*, Eph. 1. 5. [2] *By manifestation and assurance*, Rom. 8. 15. Gal. 4. 5, 6. [3] *By perfect redemption and glory, at the general resurrection*, Rom. 8. 23.
Rom. 8. 15. but ye have received the Spirit of a.
23. waiting for the a. the redemption of our body
9. 4. to whom pertaineth the a. and the glory
Gal. 4. 5. that we might receive the a. of sons
Eph. 1. 5. predestinated us to the a. of children

ADORN, ED, ETH, ING.

Isa. 61. 10. as a bride a. herself with her jewels
Jer. 31. 4. thou shalt be again a. with tabrets
Luke 21. 5. the temple was a. with goodly stones
1 Tim. 2. 9. that women a. in modest apparel
Tit. 2. 10. a. the doctrine of God our Saviour
1 Pet. 3. 3. whose a. let it not be that outward a.
5. women who trusted in God a. themselves
Rev. 21. 2. prepared as a bride a. for her husband

ADVANCED.

1 Sam. 12. 6. it is the Lord that a. Moses and Aaron
Esth. 3. 1. Ahasuerus a. Haman the Agagite
5. 11. Haman told them how he had a. him
10. 2. the greatness whereto the king a. Mordecai

ADVANTAGE, ED, ETH.

Job 35. 3. thou saidst, what a. will it be to thee
Luke 9. 25. what is a man a. if he gain the world
Rom. 3. 1. what a. then hath the Jew, or what
1 Cor. 15. 32. what a. it me if the dead rise not?
2 Cor. 2. 11. lest Satan should get an a. of us
Jude 16. men's persons in admiration, because of a.

ADVENTURE, ED.

Deut. 28. 56. not a. to set the sole of her foot
Judg. 9. 17. my father sought and a. his life far
Acts 19. 31. that he would not a. into the theatre

ADVERSARY.

Exod. 23. 22. I will be an a. to thine adversaries
Num. 22. 22. the angel stood for an a. against Balaam
† 32. behold, I went out to be an a. to thee
1 Sam. 1. 6. and her a. also provoked her sore
29. 4. lest in the battle he be an a. to us
1 Kings 5. 4. there is neither a. nor evil occurrent
11. 14. the Lord stirred up an a. to Solomon, 23.
25. was an a. to Israel all the days of Solomon
Esth. 7. 6. the a. and enemy is this wicked Haman
Job 1. † 6. and the a. came also among them
31. 35. and that my a. had written a book
Psal. 74. 10. how long shall the a. reproach?
109. † 6. let an a. stand at his right hand
Isa. 50. 8. who is mine a. let him come near to me
Lam. 1. 10. the a. hath spread out his hand
2. 4. he stood with his right hand as an a.
4. 12. that the a. should have entered the gates
Amos 3. 11. an a. shall be round about the land
Zech. 3. † 1. shewed me an a. standing to be his a.
Mat. 5. 25. agree with thine a. quickly, lest at any time the a. deliver thee to the judge
Luke 12. 58. when thou goest with thine a.
18. 3. a widow, saying, avenge me of mine a.
1 Tim. 5. 14. give no occasion to the a. to speak
1 Pet. 5. 8. your a. the devil as a roaring lion

ADVERSARIES.

Deut. 32. 27. lest their a. should behave strangely
43. he will render vengeance to his a.
Josh. 5. 13. art thou for us, or for our a.?
1 Sam. 2. 10. the a. of the Lord shall be broken
2 Sam. 19. 22. that ye should this day be a. to me
Ezra 4. 1. when a. of Judah and Benjamin heard
Neh. 4. 11. our a. said, they shall not know
Psal. 38. 20. that render evil for good, are my a.
69. 19. mine a. are all before thee
71. 13. be confounded that are a. to my soul
81. 14. have turned my hand against their a.
89. 42. thou hast set up the right hand of his a.
109. 4. for my love they are my a. but I prayer
20. let this be the reward of my a. from Lord
29. let my a. be clothed with shame
Isa. 1. 24. saith the Lord, I will ease me of my a.
9. 11. the Lord shall set up the a. of Rezin
11. 13. and the a. of Judah shall be cut off
59. 18. he will repay fury to his a.
63. 18. our a. have trodden down thy sanctuary
64. 2. to make thy name known to thine a.
Jer. 30. 16. all thine a. shall go into captivity
46. 10. that he may avenge him of his a.
50. 7. and their a. said, we offend not
Lam. 1. 5. her a. are the chief, her enemies prosper
7. the a. saw her, and did mock her sabbaths
17. that his a. should be round about him
2. 17. he hath set up the horn of thine a.
Mic. 5. 9. thy hand shall be lifted up upon thy a.
Nah. 1. 2. the Lord will take vengeance on his a.
Luke 13. 17. all his a. were ashamed
21. 15. all your a. shall not be able to gainsay
1 Cor. 16. 9. a door is opened, and there are many a.
Phil. 1. 28. and in nothing terrified by your a.
Heb. 10. 27. indignation which shall devour the a.

ADVERSITY, IES.

1 Sam. 10. 19. who himself saved you out of all a.
2 Sam. 4. 9. who redeemed my soul out of all a.
2 Chron. 15. 6. for God did vex them with all a.
Psal. 10. 6. he said in his heart, I shall never be in a.
31. 7. thou hast known my soul in a.
35. 15. but in my a. they rejoiced
94. 13. mayest give him rest from the days of a.
Prov. 17. 17. and a brother is born for a.
24. 10. if thou faint in day of a. thy strength small
Eccl. 7. 14. but in the day of a. consider
Isa. 30. 20. tho' the Lord give you the bread of a.
Heb. 13. 3. remember them which suffer a.

ADVERTISE.

Num. 24. 14. I'll a. thee, what this people shall do
Ruth 4. 4. I thought to a. thee, saying, buy it

ADVICE.

Judg. 19. 30. take a. and speak your minds
20. 7. give here your a. and counsel
1 Sam. 25. 33. blessed be thy a. and blessed be thou
2 Sam. 19. 43. that our a. should not be first had
2 Chron. 10. 9. what a. give ye, that we may answer
14. answered them after the a. of young men
25. 17. king Amaziah took a. and sent to Joash
Prov. 20. 18. and with good a. make war
2 Cor. 8. 10. and herein I give my a.

ADVISE, ED.

2 Sam. 24. 13. a. and see what answer, 1 Chron. 21. 12.
1 Kings 12. 6. how do ye a. that I may answer people
Prov. 13. 10. but with the well a. is wisdom
Acts 27. 12. the more part a. to depart thence also

ADVISEMENT.

1 Chron. 12. 19. the lords upon a. sent him away

ADULTERER, S.

Lev. 20. 10. the a. shall surely be put to death
Job 24. 15. the eye of the a. waiteth for twilight
Psal. 50. 18. thou hast been partaker with a.
Isa. 57. 3. draw near, the seed of a. and the whore
Jer. 9. 2. for they be all a. an assembly of treacherous
23. 10. for the land is full of a. for swearing
Hos. 7. 4. they are all a. as an oven heated
Mal. 3. 5. I will be a swift witness against the a.
Luke 18. 11. I am not as others, extortioners, a.
1 Cor. 6. 9. be not deceived, neither a. shall inherit
Heb. 13. 4. whoremongers and a. God will judge
Jam. 4. 4. ye a. know ye not that the friendship

ADULTERESS, ES.

Lev. 20. 10. the a. shall surely be put to death
Prov. 6. 26. the a. will hunt for the precious life
Ezek. 23. 45. righteous men shall judge them as a.
Hos. 3. 1. go yet, love a woman, yet an a.
Rom. 7. 3. so that she is no a. though she be married

ADULTEROUS.

Prov. 30. 20. such is the way of an a. woman
Mat. 12. 39. an a. generation seeketh a sign, 16. 4.
Mark 8. 38. whoso shall be ashamed in this a.

ADULTERY, IES,

Is twofold, [1] *Natural*, Mat. 5. 28. Mark 10. 11. [2] *Spiritual, which is idolatry*, Jer. 3. 9. Ezek. 23. 37.
Exod. 20. 14. thou shalt not commit a. Deut. 5. 18. Mat. 5. 27 | 19. 18. Rom. 13. 9.
Lev. 20. 10. the man that committeth a. even he that committeth a. shall surely be put to death
Prov. 6. 32. whoso commits a. lacketh understanding
Jer. 3. 8. when backsliding Israel committed a.
9. committed a. with stones and with stocks
5. 7. when I fed them, then they committed a.
7. 9. will ye steal, murder, and commit a.?
13. 27. I have seen thine a. and neighings
23. 14. they commit a. and walk in lies
29. 23. because they have committed a.
Ezek. 16. 32. but as a wife that committeth a.
23. 37. with their idols have they committed a.
43. then said I to her that was old in a.
Hos. 2. 2. put away her a. between her breasts
4. 2. by lying and committing a. they break out
13. and your spouses shall commit a.
14. I'll not punish them when they commit a.
Mat. 5. 28. hath committed a. in his heart
32. whosoever shall marry her that is divorced committeth a. 19. 9. Luke 16. 18.
15. 19. out of the heart proceed a. Mark 7. 21.
Mark 10. 11. whosoever shall put away his wife and marry another, committeth a. Luke 16. 18.
19. do not commit a. Luke 18. 20. Jam. 2. 11.
John 8. 3. brought unto him a woman taken in a. 4.
Rom. 2. 22. sayest, a man should not commit a.
Gal. 5. 19. the works of the flesh are manifest, a.
2 Pet. 2. 14. having eyes full of a. not cease from sin
Rev. 2. 22. I will cast them that commit a. with

ADVOCATE.

1 John 2. 1. we have an a. with the Father, Jesus Christ the righteous

AFAR *joined with* **OFF**

Signifies, [1] *The distance between place and place*, Gen. 37. 18. [2] *To estrange one's self from another*, Psal. 38. 11. [3] *To be absent*, Psal. 10. 1. [4] *To be strangers or not of the visible church*, Eph. 2. 13, 17.
Gen. 22. 4. Abraham saw the place a. off
37. 18. when his brethren saw Joseph a. off
Exod. 24. 1. come up, and worship ye a. off
33. 7. pitch the tabernacle a. off from the camp
Num. 9. 10. be unclean, or be in a journey a. off
2 Kings 4. 25. when the man of God saw her a. off
Ezra 3. 13. shouted, and the noise was heard a. off
Neh. 12. 43. the joy of Jerusalem was heard a. off
Job 36. 3. I will fetch my knowledge from a.
25. a man may see it, a man may behold it a. off
39. 29. seeks her prey, and her eyes behold a. off
Psal. 65. 5. and of them that are a. off on the sea
138. 6. but the proud he knoweth a. off
139. 2. thou understandest my thoughts a. off
Prov. 31. 14. she bringeth her food from a.
Isa. 23. 7. her own feet shall carry her a. off
66. 19. those that escape to the isles a. off
Jer. 23. 23. am I God at hand, and not a God a. off?
30. 10. I will save thee from a. 46. 27.
31. † 3. the Lord appeared from a. unto me
10. and declare it in the isles a. off
49. 30. flee, get you a. off, dwell deep
51. 50. go away, remember the Lord a. off.
Mic. 4. 3. he shall rebuke strong nations a. off
Mat. 26. 58. but Peter followed him a. off, and went in, Mark 14. 54. Luke 22. 54.
27. 55. women beholding a. off, Mark 15. 40.
Mark 5. 6. but when he saw Jesus a. off, he ran
11. 13. and seeing a fig-tree a. off with leaves
Lu. 16. 23. lift up his eyes, and seeth Abraham a. off
Acts 2. 39. the promise is to all that are a. off
Eph. 2. 17. and came and preached peace to you which were a. off, and to them that were nigh
Heb. 11. 13. having seen the promises a. off
2 Pet. 1. 9. is blind, and cannot see a. off
See FAR, STAND, STOOD.

AFFAIRS.

1 Chron. 26. 32. pertaining to God, and a. of the king
Psal. 112. 5. he will guide his a. with discretion
Dan. 2. 49. he set Shadrach over a. of the province
3. 12. Jews whom thou set over a. of the province
Eph. 6. 21. but that ye also may know my a.
22. I have sent, that ye might know our a.
Phil. 1. 27. or be absent, I may hear of your a.
2 Tim. 2. 4. entangleth himself, with the a. of life

AFFECT, ED, ETH.

Lam. 3. 51. mine eye a. my heart, because of all
Acts 14. 2. their minds evil a. against the brethren
Gal. 4. 17. zealously a. you, that ye might a. them
18. it is good to be zealously a. in a good thing

AFFECTION.

1 Chron. 29. 3. have set my a. to the house of God
Rom. 1. 31. without natural a. 2 Tim. 3. 3.
2 Cor. 7. 15. his inward a. is more abundant to you
Col. 3. 2. set your a. on things above, not on things

Col. 3. 5. mortify therefore fornication, inordinate a.

AFFECTIONS.

Rom. 1. 26. for this cause God gave them up to vile a.
Gal. 5. 24. have crucified the flesh with the a.

AFFECTIONATELY.

1 Thess. 2. 8. so being a. desirous of you, willing

AFFECTIONED.

Rom. 12. 10. be kindly a. one to another

AFFINITY.

1 Kings 3. 1. Solomon made a. with Pharaoh
2 Chron. 18. 1. Jehoshaphat joined a. with Ahab
Ezra 9. 14. should we join in a. with the people

AFFIRM

Signifies, [1.] To maintain the truth of a thing, Acts 25. 19. Tit. 3. 8. [2] To teach, 1 Tim. 1. 7.
Rom. 3. 8. and as some a. that we say, let us do evil
1 Tim. 1. 7. what they say, nor whereof they a.
Tit. 3. 8. these things I will that thou a. constantly

AFFIRMED.

Luke 22. 59. about an hour after another a.
Acts 12. 15. but Rhoda constantly a. that it was so
25. 19. and of Jesus, whom Paul a. to be alive

AFFLICT.

Gen. 15. 13. and they shall a. them 400 years
31. 50. if thou shalt a. my daughters, or take
Exod. 1. 11. set over them task masters to a. them
22. 22. ye shall not a. any widow or fatherless
23. if thou a. them in any wise, and they cry
23. † 22. I will a. them that a. thee
Lev. 16. 29. ye shall a. your souls, 31. | 23. 27, 32. Num. 29. 7.
Num. 24. 24. ships from Chittim shall a. Ashur
30. 13. and every binding oath to a. the soul
Judg. 16. 5. that we bind him to a. him
6. wherewith thou mightest be bound to a. thee
19. she began to a. him, and his strength went
2 Sam. 7. 10. nor children of wickedness a. them
1 Kings 11. 39. I will for this a. the seed of David
2 Chron. 6. 26. turn when thou dost a. 1 Kings 8. 35.
Ezra 8. 21. that we might a. ourselves before God
Job 37. 23. touching the Almighty, he will not a.
Psal. 44. 2. how thou didst a. the people, and cast
55. 19. God shall hear and a. them, even he
89. 22. nor the son of wickedness a. him
94. 5. O Lord, they a. thine heritage
143. 12. and destroy all them that a. my soul
Isa. 9. 1. afterward did more grievously a. her
51. 23. put it into the hand of them that a. thee
58. 5. a day for a man to a. his soul?
64. 12. O Lord, wilt thou a. us very sore?
Jer. 31. 28. as I watched to destroy and to a.
Lam. 3. 33. for the Lord doth not a. willingly
Amos 5. 12. they a. the just, they take a bribe
6. 14. they shall a. you from Hemath
Nah. 1. 12. have afflicted, I will a. thee no more
Zeph. 3. 19. behold, I will undo all that a. thee

AFFLICTED.

Exod. 1. 12. the more they a. the more they grew
Lev. 23. 29. the soul that shall not be a. that day
Num. 11. 11. wherefore hast thou a. thy servant?
Deut. 26. 6. the Egyptians a. us and laid on us
Ruth 1. 21. and the Almighty hath a. me
2 Sam. 22. 28. and the a. people thou wilt save
1 Kings 2. 26. a. in all wherein my father was a.
2 Kings 17. 20. the Lord rejected Israel, and a. them
Job 6. 14. to him that is a. pity should be shewed
30. 11. he hath loosed my cord, and a. me
34. 28. and he heareth the cry of the a.
Psal. 9. † 12. he forgetteth not the a.
10. † 12. arise, O Lord, forget not the a.
18. 27. for thou wilt save the a. people
22. 24. nor abhorred the affliction of the a.
25. 16. have mercy on me, for I am desolate and a.
82. 3. do justice to the a. and needy
88. 7. thou hast a. me with all thy waves
15. I am a. and ready to die from my youth
90. 15. according to days wherein thou hast a. us
107. 17. fools, because of their iniquities, are a.
116. 10. I was greatly a. || 119. 67. before I was a.
119. 71. it is good for me that I have been a.
75. and that thou in faithfulness hast a. me
107. I am a. very much, quicken me, O Lord
129. 1. many time have they a. me from youth, 2.
140. 12. Lord will maintain the cause of the a.
Prov. 15. 15. all the days of the a. are evil
22. 22. neither oppress the a. in the gate
26. 28. a lying tongue hateth those that are a.
31. 5. lest they pervert the judgment of the a.
Isa. 9. 1. when at first he lightly a. the land of Zeb.
49. 13. the Lord will have mercy on his a.
51. 21. hear now this, thou a. and drunken
53. 4. did esteem him smitten of God and a.
7. he was oppressed, and was a. yet he opened not
54. 11. O thou a. tossed with tempest, not comforted
58. 3. wherefore have we a. our souls?
10. and if thou satisfy the a. soul, thy light
60. 14. the sons of them that a. thee shall come
63. 9. in all their affliction he was a. and angel
Lam. 1. 4. her priests sigh, her virgins are a.
5. enemies prosper, for the Lord hath a. her
12. my sorrow wherewith the Lord hath a. me
Mic. 4. 6. and I will gather her that I have a.
Nah. 1. 12. tho' I have a. I will afflict no more
Zeph. 3. 12. I will leave in thee an a. people
Mat. 24. 9. they shall deliver you up to be a.
2 Cor. 1. 6. whether we be a. it is for consolation
1 Tim. 5. 10. if she have relieved the a.
Heb. 11. 37. being destitute, a. and tormented
Jam. 4. 9. be a. and mourn, and weep
5. 13. is any among you a.? let him pray

AFFLICTION

Signifies, [1.] Adversity, trouble, or distress, Job 5. 6. [2] Outward oppression, Exod. 3. 7. | 4. 31. [3] Persecution for religion, Mark 4. 17. Heb. 10. 32. [4] Correction from God, Jonah 2. 2.
Gen. 16. 11. because the Lord hath heard thy a.
29. 32. surely the Lord hath looked upon my a.
31. 42. God hath seen mine a. and labour
41. 52. caused me to be fruitful in the land of a.
Exod. 3. 7. I have seen the a. of my people, Acts 7. 34.
17. I will bring you out of the a. of Egypt
4. 31. and that he had looked on their a.
Deut. 16. 3. thou shalt eat even the bread of a. 1 Kings 22. 27. 2 Chron. 18. 26.
26. 7. the Lord heard and looked on our a.
1 Sam. 1. 11. if thou wilt indeed look on my a.
2. † 32. thou shalt see the a. of the tabernacle
2 Sam. 16. 12. it may be the Lord will look on my a.
2 Kings 14. 26. the Lord saw the a. of Israel
2 Chron. 20. 9. cry to thee in our a. thou wilt hear
33. 12. Manasseh was in a. and sought the Lord
Neh. 1. 3. the remnant are in great a. and reproach
9. 9. and didst see the a. of our fathers in Egypt
Job 5. 6. though a. cometh not forth of the dust
10. 15. I am full of confusion, see thou mine a.
30. 16. the days of a. have taken hold on me
27. the days of a. prevented me
36. 8. and if they be holden in cords of a.
15. he delivereth the poor in his a.
21. for this hast thou chosen rather than a.
Psal. 25. 18. look upon my a. and pain, forgive
44. 24. and forgettest our a. and oppression
66. 11. thou laidst a. upon our loins
78. † 42. day when he delivered them from a.
88. 9. mine eye mourneth by reason of a.
106. 44. he regarded their a. when he heard
107. 10. sit in darkness, being bound in a. and iron
39. they are brought low through a. and sorrow
41. yet setteth he the poor on high from a.
119. 50. this is my comfort in my a. thy word
92. I should then have perished in mine a.
153. consider mine a. and deliver me, for I do not
Isa. 30. 20. though the Lord give you water of a.
48. 10. I have chosen thee in the furnace of a.
63. 9. in all their a. he was afflicted, and the angel
Jer. 4. 15. publisheth a. from mount Ephraim
15. 11. to intreat thee well in the time of a.
16. 19. O Lord, my refuge in the day of a.
30. 15. why criest thou for thine a.? thy sorrow
48. 16. Moab's calamity is near, and a. hasteth fast
Lam. 1. 3. Judah is gone into captivity because of a.
7. Jerusalem remembered in the days of her a.
9. had no comforter, O Lord, behold mine a.
3. 1. I am the man that hath seen a. by the rod
19. remembering my a. and my misery
Hos. 5. 15. in their a. they will seek me early
Amos 6. 6. they are not grieved for the a. of Joseph
Obad. 13. thou shouldest not have looked on their a.
Jonah 2. 2. I cried by reason of my a. to the Lord
Nah. 1. 9. a. shall not rise up the second time
Hab. 3. 7. I saw the tents of Cushan in a.
Zech. 1. 15. and they helped forward the a.
8. 10. that went out or came in, because of a.
10. 11. and he shall pass through the sea with a.
Mark 4. 17. when a. ariseth for the word's sake
13. 19. for in those days shall be a. such as
Acts 7. 11. there came a dearth, and great a.
2 Cor. 2. 4. for out of much a. I wrote to you
4. 17. our light a. which is but for a moment
8. 2. how that in a great trial of a.
Phil. 1. 16. supposing to add a. to my bonds
4. 14. that ye communicate with me in my a.
1 Thess. 1. 6. having received the word in much a.
3. 7. we were comforted over you in all our a.
Heb. 11. 25. choosing rather to suffer a. with people
Jam. 1. 27. to visit the fatherless in their a.
5. 10. for an example of suffering a. and of patience

AFFLICTIONS.

Psal. 34. 19. many are the a. of the righteous
132. 1. Lord, remember David, and all his a.
Acts 7. 10. and delivered him out of all his a.
20. 23. saying, that bonds and a. abide me
2 Cor. 6. 4. approving in much patience, in a.
Col. 1. 24. fill up what is behind of the a. of Christ
1 Thess. 3. 3. no man should be moved by these a.
2 Tim. 1. 8. be partakers of the a. of the gospel
3. 11. known the a. which came to me at Antioch
4. 5. but watch in all things, endure a.
Heb. 10. 32. ye endured a great fight of a.
33. whilst ye were made a gazing stock by a.
1 Pet. 5. 9. the same a. accomplished in brethren

AFFORDING.

Psal. 144. 13. our garners full a. all manner of store

AFFRIGHT, ED.

Deut. 7. 21. Thou shalt not be a. at them
2 Chron. 32. 18. they cried with a loud voice to a.
Job 18. 20. as they that went before were a.
39. 22. he mocketh at fear, and is not a.
Isa. 21. 4. my heart panted, fearfulness a. me
Jer. 51. 32. reeds are burnt, and men of war a.
Mark 16. 5. and they were a. Luke 24. 37.
6. he saith, be not a. ye seek Jesus crucified
Rev. 11. 13. and the remnant were a. gave glory

AFOOT.

Mark 6. 33. many ran a. thither out of all cities
Acts 20. 13. Paul minding himself to go a.

AFORE.

2 Kings 20. 4. a. Isaiah was gone out into the court
Psal. 129. 6. which withereth a. it groweth up
Isa. 18. 5. a. the harvest when the bud is perfect
Ezek. 33. 22. a. he that was escaped came
Rom. 1. 2. which he had promised a. by his prophets
9. 23. which he had a. prepared unto glory
Eph. 3. 3. the mystery, as I wrote a. in few words

AFOREHAND.

Mark 14. 8. she is come a. to anoint my body

AFORETIME.

Job 17. 6. me a by-word, and a. I was as a tabret
Isa. 52. 4. my people went down a. into Egypt
Jer. 30. 20. their children also shall be as a.
Dan. 6. 10. he prayed before his God, as he did a.
John 9. 13. they brought him that a. was blind
Rom. 15. 4. for whatsoever things were written a.

AFRAID.

Gen. 42. 35. saw bundles of money, they were a.
Exod. 34. 30. and they were a. to come nigh him
Lev. 26. 6. and none shall make you a. Job 11. 19.
Num. 12. 8. why not a. to speak against Moses?
Deut. 7. 19. do to all the people of whom thou art a.
Judg. 7. 3. proclaim, whosoever is fearful, and a.
1 Sam. 4. 7. the Philistines were a. for they said
18. 29. Saul was yet the more a. of David
2 Sam. 1. 14. how wast thou not a. to destroy
14. 15. because the people have made me a.
2 Sam. 17. 2. I will come on him, and make him a.
22. 5. ungodly men made me a. Psal. 18. 4.
Neh. 6. 9. for they all made us a. saying, their hands
Job 9. 28. I am a. of all my sorrows, I know that
11. 19. shalt lie down, and none shall make thee a.
13. 11. shall not his excellency make you a.
21. and let not thy dread make me a.
15. 24. trouble and anguish shall make him a.
18. 11. terrors shall make him a. on every side
21. 6. even when I remember, I am a. and tremble
23. 15. when I consider, I am a. of him
33. 7. behold, my terror shall not make thee a.
39. 20. canst thou make him a. as a grasshopper?
41. 25. he raiseth up himself, the mighty are a.
Psal. 56. 3. what time I am a. I will trust in thee
65. 8. they that dwell are a. at thy tokens
77. 16. the waters saw thee, and they were a.
83. 15. and make them a. with thy storm
119. 120. and I am a. of thy judgments
Isa. 17. 2. and none shall make them a. Ezek. 34. 28. Mic. 4. 4. Zeph. 3. 13.
33. 14. the sinners in Zion are a. fearfulness hath
41. 5. the ends of the earth were a. and came
57. 11. and of whom hast thou been a. or feared
Jer. 30. 10. be quiet, and none shall make him a.
36. 24. yet they were not a. nor rent garments
38. 19. Zedekiah said, I am a. of the Jews
39. 17. not given to the men, of whom thou art a.
Ezek. 39. 26. and none made them a. Nah. 2. 11.
Dan. 4. 5. I saw a dream, which made me a.
Jonah 1. 5. then the mariners were a. 10.
Hab. 2. 17. made them a. because of men's blood
Mark 5. 15. in his right mind, were a. Luke 8. 35.
9. 32. they understood not, and were a. to ask him
10. 32. and as they followed, they were a.
16. 8. nor said they any thing, for they were a.
Luke 8. 25. and they being a. wondered, saying
Acts 9. 26. but they were all a. of Saul
22. 9. they with me saw the light, and were a.
Gal. 4. 11. I am a. of you, lest I have bestowed
Heb. 11. 23. not a. of the king's commandment
1 Pet. 3. 6. and are not a. with any amazement
2 Pet. 2. 10. they are not a. to speak evil of dignities

Be AFRAID.

Deut. 1. 29. dread not, neither be a. of them, 31. 6.
1 Sam. 23. 3. behold we be a. here in Judah
2 Sam. 22. 46. be a. out of close places, Psal. 18. 45
Neh. 6. 13. was he hired that I should be a.
Job 5. 21. nor shalt thou be a. of destruction
19. 29. be ye a. of the sword, for wrath bringeth
Psal. 27. 1. L. is my strength, of whom shall I be a.?
Isa. 8. 12. nor fear ye their fear, nor be a. 44. 8.
19. 17. that maketh mention, shall be a. in himself
51. 12. thou, that thou shouldest be a. of a man
Rom. 13. 4. if thou do that which is evil, be a.

Not be AFRAID.

Deut. 1. 17. you shall not be a. of the face of man
7. 18. thou shalt not be a. of them, 18. 22.
Psal. 3. 6. I will not be a. of ten thousands of people
56. 11. I will not be a. what man can do to me
91. 5. thou shalt not be a. for the terror by night
112. 7. he shall not be a. of evil tidings, his heart
8. his heart is established, he shall not be a.
Prov. 3. 24. when thou liest down, shalt not be a.
Isa. 12. 2. God my salvation, I will trust and not be a.
31. 4. he will not be a. of their voice, nor abase
Amos 3. 6. a trumpet be blown, and people not be a.
Rom. 13. 3. wilt thou then not be a. of the power?

Be not AFRAID.

Deut. 20. 1. be not a. of them, Josh. 11. 6. Neh. 4. 14. Jer. 10. 5. Ezek. 2. 6. Luke 12. 4.
1 Sam. 28. 13. Saul said be not a. what sawest thou
2 Kings 1. 15. angel said, go down, be not a. of him
Psal. 49. 16. be not a. when one is made rich
Prov. 3. 25. be not a. of sudden fear nor desolation
Isa. 40. 9. lift up thy voice, lift it up, be not a.
Jer. 1. 8. be not a. of their faces, for I am with thee
Ezek. 2. 6. and thou son of man, be not a. of them
Mat. 14. 27. it is I, be not a. Mark 6. 50. John 6. 20.
17. 7. Jesus touched them and said, arise, be not a.
28. 10. be not a. go tell my brethren that they go
Mark 5. 36. saith to the ruler, be not a. only believe
Acts 18. 9. be not a. but speak, and hold not thy peace.
1 Pet. 3. 14. be not a. of their terror, nor be troubled

Sore AFRAID.

Gen. 20. 8. told these things, and men were sore a.
Exod. 14. 10. Egyptians marched, they were sore a.
Num. 22. 3. Moab was sore a. of the people
Josh. 9. 24. therefore we were sore a. of our lives
1 Sam. 17. 24. fled from Goliath, and were sore a.
28. 20. Saul fell along on the earth, and was sore a.
31. 4. his armour bearer was sore a. 1 Chr. 10. 4.
Neh. 2. 2. nothing but sorrow, and was very sore a.
Mark 9. 6. wist not what to say, for they were sore a.
Luke 2. 9. shone about them, and they were sore a.

Was AFRAID.

Gen. 3. 10. I heard thy voice, and I was a.
18. 15. saying, I laughed not, for she was a.
32. 7. then Jacob was greatly a. and distressed
Exod. 3. 6. Moses hid his face, was a. to look on God
Deut. 9. 19. I was a. of the anger and displeasure
Ruth 3. 8. at midnight the man was a. and turned
1 Sam. 18. 12. Saul was a. of David, 15.
21. 1. Ahimelech was a. at the meeting of David
28. 5. Saul saw the host of Philistines, he was a.
2 Sam. 6. 9. David was a. of the Lord, 1 Chr. 13. 12.
1 Chron. 21. 30. David could not go, for he was a.
Job 3. 25. that which I was a. of, is come to me
32. 6. I was a. and durst not shew my opinion
Jer. 26. 21. when Urijah heard it, he was a.
Dan. 8. 17. when he came, was a. and fell on my face
Hab. 3. 2. O Lord, I heard thy speech, and was a.
Mal. 2. 5. he feared me, and was a. before my name
Mat. 2. 22. Joseph was a. to go thither
14. 30. when he saw the wind boisterous, was a.
25. 25. I was a. and hid thy talent in the earth
John 19. 8. when Pilate heard, he was the more a.
Acts 10. 4. when Cornelius looked, he was a.

AFRESH.

Heb. 6. 6. they crucify the Son of God a. and put him

AFTER.

Gen. 18. 12. saying a. I am waxed old, shall I

Gen. 38. 24. about three months a. it was told Judah
Num. 15. 39. that ye seek not a. your own heart
Deut. 6. 14. ye shall not go a. other gods
Josh. 10. 14. no day like that before it, or a. it
1 Sam. 15. 31. Samuel turned again a. Saul
24. 14. a. whom is the king come out? a. a dog
1 Kings 17. 13. and a. make for thee and thy son
Neh. 13. 19. not be opened till a. the sabbath
Job 10. 6. that thou inquirest a. mine iniquity
30. 5. they cried a. them, as a. a thief
Psal. 28. 4. give them a. the work of their hands
Eccl. 1. 11. with those that shall come a.
Isa. 11. 3. he shall not judge a. the sight of eyes
Ezek. 46. 17. a. it shall return to the prince
Hos. 11. 10. they shall walk a. the Lord
Mat. 26. 32. a. I am risen again, I will go before
Mark 16. 14. which had seen him a. he was risen
19. so then a. the Lord had spoken to them
Luke 6. 1. on the second sabbath a. the first
22. 58. and a. a little while another saw him
59. about the space of an hour a. another
23. 26. that he might bear it a. Jesus
John 13. 27. a. the sop Satan entered into him
Acts 5. 7. about the space of three hours a.
Gal. 3. 17. the law which was 430 years a.
2 Pet. 2. 6. to those that a. should live ungodly

AFTER *that*.

Exod. 3. 20. and a. that he will let you go
Deut. 24. 4. shall not take her a. that she is defiled
Judg. 15. 7. I will be avenged, and a. that I will cease
2 Sam. 21. 14. a. that God was intreated for the land
Job 21. 3. a. that I have spoken, mock on
Eccl. 9. 3. and a. that they go to the dead
Jer. 31. 19. a. that I was turned, I repented
Luke 12. 4. a. that have no more that they can do
13. 9. then a. that thou shalt cut it down
15. 4. a. that which is lost, until he find it
Acts 7. 7. a. that shall they come forth and serve me
1 Cor. 15. 6. a. that he was seen of above 500 at once
Rev. 20. 3. and a. that he must be loosed a little

AFTER *this*.

Gen. 23. 19. a. this Abraham buried Sarah his wife
2 Sam. 2. 1. a. this David inquired of the Lord
Acts 15. 16. a. this I will return, and build again

AFTERNOON.

Judg. 19. 8. they tarried till a. and did eat

AFTERWARD, S.

Exod. 11. 1. a. he will let you go hence
Num. 31. 2. a. shalt thou be gathered to thy people
Judg. 7. 11. a. shall thy hands be strengthened
1 Sam. 9. 13. he blessed the sacrifice, a. they eat
24. 5. a. David's heart smote him
Job 18. 2. mark, and a. we will speak
Psal. 73. 24. guide me, and a. receive me to glory
Prov. 20. 17. bread of deceit is sweet, but a.
24. 27. prepare thy work, and a. build thy house
28. 23. a. shall find more favour than he that
29. 11. but a wise man keepeth it in till a.
Hos. 3. 5. a. shall the children of Israel return
Joel 2. 28. a. I will pour out my Spirit upon all
Mat. 4. 2. fasted, he was a. an hungered, Luke 4. 2.
21. 32. ye, when ye had seen it, repented not a.
John 5. 14. a. Jesus findeth him in the temple
13. 36. but thou shalt follow me a.
1 Cor. 15. 23. a. they that are Christ's at his coming
Gal. 3. 23. the faith that should a. be revealed
Heb. 4. 8. would not a. have spoken of another day
12. 11. a. it yieldeth the peaceable fruit of righteous.
17. a. when he would have inherited the blessing
Jude 5. a. destroyed them that believed not

AGAIN.

Gen. 8. 21. I will not a. curse, nor a. smite
15. 16. but they shall come hither a.
30. 31. I will a. feed and keep thy flock
38. 26. Judah knew her a. no more
Exod. 10. 29. said, I will see a. thy face no more
14. 13. ye shall see them a. no more for ever
23. 4. thou shalt surely bring it back to him a.
Num. 32. 15. will yet a. leave them in the wilderness
Josh. 5. 2. and circumcise a. the children of Israel
2 Sam. 16. 19. and a. whom should I serve
1 Kings 17. 22. the soul of the child came into him a.
2 Kings 19. 30. shall yet a. take root downward
Ezra 9. 14. should we a. break thy commandments
Neh. 13. 21. if ye do so a. I will lay hands on you
Job 14. 14. if a man die, shall he live a.?
Psal. 85. 6. wilt thou not revive us a. that thy
107. 39. a. they are minished and brought low
140. 10. into deep pits, that they rise not up a.
Prov. 2. 19. none that go to her return a.
19. 19. if thou deliver him, thou must do it a.
Eccl. 8. 14. a. there be wicked men to whom
Ezek. 26. 21. yet shalt thou never be found a.
Amos 7. 8. I will not a. pass by them, 8. 2.
8. 14. they shall fall, and never rise up a.
Zech. 2. 12. the Lord shall choose Jerusalem a.
John 4. 13. drinketh of this water shall thirst a.
Rom. 8. 15. not received spirit of bondage a. to fear
9. † 20. who art thou that answerest a.?
Phil. 4. 4. rejoice in the Lord, a. I say rejoice
Heb. 1. 5. a. I will be to him a Father, and he shall
2. 13. and a. I will put my trust in him
1 Pet. 1. 3. hath begotten us a. to a lively hope
See BORN, BRING, BROUGHT, COME, TURN, TURNED.

AGAINST.

Gen. 16. 12. his hand will be a. every man
Exod. 7. 15. stand by the river's brink a. he come
Lev. 20. 3. I'll set my face a. that man, Deut. 29. 20.
2 Kings 16. 11. so Urijah made it a. king Ahaz came
19. 22. a. whom hast thou exalted thy voice?
Isa. 40. † 10. the Lord will come a. the strong hand
Jer. 25. 13. which I have pronounced a. it.
Ezek. 13. 20. behold, I am a. your pillows
Mat. 10. 35. to set a man a. his father, Luke 12. 53.
12. 30. he that is not with me, is a. me
Luke 2. 34. for a sign which shall be spoken a.
14. 31. that cometh a. him with 20,000 to
Acts 19. 36. these things cannot be spoken a.
28. 22. this sect is every where spoken a.
See ANOTHER, GOD, HIM, JERUSALEM, ISRAEL, LORD, ME, OVER, THEE, THEM, US, YOU.

AGATE, S.

Exod. 28. 19. third row, an a. an amethyst, 39. 12.
Isa. 54. 12. I will make thy windows of a.
Ezek. 27. 16. Syria occupied in thy fairs with a.

AGE

Signifies, [1] *The whole continuance of a man's life*, Gen. 47. 28. [2] *Times past, present, or to come*, Eph. 2. 7. | 3. 5. [3] *A time apt for conception*, Heb. 11. 11.

Gen. 47. 28. the whole a. of Jacob was 147 years
48. 10. the eyes of Israel were dim for a.
Num. 8. 25. from the a. of 50 years cease waiting
1 Sam. 2. 33. shall die in the flower of their a.
1 Kings 14. 4. Ahijah's eyes were set by reason of a.
1 Chron. 23. 3. Levites numbered from the a. of 30.
24. from the a. of twenty years and upward
2 Chron. 36. 17. or on him that stooped for a.
Job 5. 26. shalt come to thy grave in a full a.
8. 8. inquire, I pray thee, of the former a.
11. 17. thy a. shall be clearer than noon-day
Psal. 39. 5. my a. is as nothing before thee
Isa. 38. 12. my a. is departed and removed
Zech. 8. 4. every man with his staff for a.
Mark 5. 42. she was of the a. of 12 years, Luke 8. 42.
Luke 2. 36. Anna a prophetess was of a great a.
† 52. Jesus increased in wisdom and a.
3. 23. Jesus began to be about 30 years of a.
John 9. 21. he is of a. ask him, 23.
Acts 13. † 36. David had in his own a. served God
1 Cor. 7. 36. if she pass the flower of her a.
14. † 20. in understanding be of a ripe a.
Eph. 4. † 13. till we come to a. of fulness of Christ
Heb. 5. 14. strong meat belongs to them of full a.
11. 11. Sarah was delivered when she was past a.
See OLD, STRICKEN.

AGES.

Psal. 145. † 13. thy kingdom a kingdom of all a.
Isa. 26. † 4. in the Lord Jehovah is the rock of a.
Eph. 2. 7. that in the a. to come he might show
3. 5. which in other a. was not made known
21. to him be glory in the church through all a.
Col. 1. 26. mystery which hath been hid from a.

AGED.

2 Sam. 19. 32. Barzillai was a very a. man
Job 12. 20. he taketh away the understanding of a
15. 10. the grey-headed and very a. men
29. 8. and the a. arose and stood up
32. 9. neither do the a. understand judgment
Jer. 6. 11. the a. with him that is full of days
Tit. 2. 2. that the a. men be sober, grave, sound
3. the a. women, that they be in behaviour
Philem. 9. being such an one as Paul the a.

AGO.

1 Sam. 9. 20. the asses that were lost three days a.
2 Kings 19. 25. thou not heard long a. Isa. 37. 26.
Ezra 5. 11. house that was builded many years a.
Isa. 22. 11. respect to him that fashioned it long a.
Mat. 11. 21. would have repented long a. Luke 10. 13.
Mark 9. 21. how long a. since this came to him?
Acts 10. 30. 4 days a. I was fasting until this hour
15. 7. ye know how that a good while a.
2 Cor. 8. 10. but also to be forward a year a.
9. 2. that Achaia was ready a year a.
12. 2. I knew a man above fourteen years a.

AGONE.

1 Sam. 30. 13. because three days a. I fell sick

AGONY.

Luke 22. 44. being in an a. he prayed more earnestly

AGREE

Signifies, [1] *To bargain with*, Mat. 20. 2, 13. [2] *To approve, or give consent to*, Acts 5. 40. [3] *To be like*, Mark 14. 70. [4] *To conspire, or resolve*, John 9. 22.

AGREE, ED, ETH.

Amos 3. 3. can two walk together except they be a.?
Mat. 5. 25. a. with thine adversary quickly
18. 19. if two of you shall a. on earth, touching
20. 2. when he had a. with labourers for a penny
13. didst thou not a. with me for a penny?
Mark 14. 56. their witness a. not together, 59.
70. art a Galilean, and thy speech a. thereto
Luke 5. 36. taken out of the new, a. not with old
John 9. 22. the Jews had a. already if any man
Acts 5. 9. how is it that ye have a. to tempt
40. and to him they a. and when they had called
15. 15. and to this a. the words of the prophet
23. 20. the Jews have a. to desire thee to bring
28. 25. when they a. not among themselves
1 John 5. 8. spirit, water, blood, these a. in one
Rev. 17. 17. a. to give their kingdom to the beast

AGREEMENT.

2 Kings 18. 31. make an a. by a present, Isa. 36. 16.
Isa. 28. 15. ye have said, with hell are we at a.
18. and your a. with hell shall not stand
Dan. 11. 6. to the king of the north, to make an a.
2 Cor. 6. 16. what a. hath the temple of God with

AGROUND.

Acts 27. 41. two seas met, they ran the ship a.

AGUE.

Lev. 26. 16. I will appoint terror and the burning a.

AH.

Psal. 35. 25. nor say, a. so would we have it
Isa. 1. 4. a. sinful nation, a people laden with iniquity
24. a. I will ease me of mine adversaries
Jer. 1. 6. then said I, a. Lord God, I cannot speak
4. 10. a. Lord God, thou hast deceived this people
14. 13. a. Lord God, the prophets say to them
22. 18. a. brother, a. sister, a. Lord, a. his glory
32. 17. a. Lord, thou hast made the heaven
34. 5. they will lament thee, saying, a. Lord
Ezek. 4. 14. a. Lord, my soul hath not been polluted
9. 8. a. Lord, wilt thou destroy the residue of Israel
11. 13. a. Lord, wilt thou make a full end of the
20. 49. a. Lord, they say of me, doth he not speak
21. 15. a. the sword is made bright, it is wrapt up
Mark 15. 29. a. thou that destroyest the temple

AHA.

Psal. 35. 21. they said, a. our eye hath seen it
40. 15. let them be desolate, that say unto me a.
70. 3. let them be turned back that say a. a.
Isa. 44. 16. a. I am warm, I have seen the fire
Ezek. 25. 3. saidst a. against my sanctuary
26. 2. because Tyrus hath said, a. she is broken
36. 2. a. the ancient places are ours

AIDED.

Judg. 9. 24. a. him in the killing of his brethren

AILED, ETH.

Gen. 21. 17. what a. thee, Hagar? fear not
Judg. 18. 23. they said to Micah, what a. thee?
1 Sam. 11. 5. Saul said, what a. the people to weep?
2 Sam. 14. 5. the king said, what a. 2 Kings 6. 28.
Psal. 114. 5. what a. thee, O sea, that thou fledst?
Isa. 22. 1. what a. thee now, that thou art gone up

AIR.

2 Sam. 21. 10. nor birds of the a. to rest on them
Job 41. 16. that no a. can come between them
Prov. 30. 19. the way of an eagle in the a.
Eccl. 10. 20. a bird of the a. shall carry the voice.
Mat. 8. 20. and the birds of the a. have nests
13. 32. the birds of the a. come and lodge in the branches thereof, Mark 4. 32. Luke 9. 58.
Acts 22. 23. and as they threw dust into the a.
1 Cor. 9. 26. so fight I, not as one that beateth the a.
14. 9. for ye shall speak into the a.
Eph. 2. 2. the prince of the power of the a.
1 Thess. 4. 17. caught up to meet the Lord in the a.
Rev. 9. 2. the sun and the a. were darkened
16. 17. the angel poured out his vial into the a.
See FOWLS.

ALARM.

Num. 10. 5. when ye blow an a, then the camps, 6.
7. you shall blow, but shall not sound an a.
9. and if ye go to war, then ye shall blow an a.
2 Chron. 13. 12. trumpets to cry an a. against you
Isa. 16. † 9. a. is fallen on thy summer fruits
Jer. 4. 19. thou hast heard, O my soul, the a. of war
49. 2. the day is come, I will cause an a. of war
Joel 2. 1. and sound an a. in my holy mountain
Zeph. 1. 16. a day of a. against the fenced cities

ALAS.

Num. 12. 11. Aaron said to Moses, a. my Lord
24. 23. a. who shall live when God doth this?
Josh. 7. 7. Joshua said, a. O Lord, why hast thou
Judg. 6. 22. a. because I have seen an angel
11. 35. a. daughter, thou hast brought me low
1 Kings 13. 30. mourned over him, a. my brother
2 Kings 3. 10. a. that the Lord hath called these
6. 5. he cried, a. master, for it was borrowed
15. servant said, a. my master, how shall we do
Jer. 30. 7. a. for that day is great, none is like it
Ezek. 6. 11. stamp with thy foot, and say a.
Joel 1. 15. a. for the day, for the day of the Lord
Amos 5. 16. they shall say in the highways, a.
Rev. 18. 10. a. a. that great city, Babylon, 16, 19.

ALBEIT.

Ezek. 13. 7. the Lord saith, a. I have not spoken
Philem. 19 a. I say not, how thou owest to me

ALIANT.

Job 19. 15. I am an a. in their sight
Psal. 69. 8. I am an a. to my mother's children

ALIEN, S.

Exod. 18. 3. I have been an a. in a strange land
Deut. 14. 21. or thou mayest sell it to an a
Isa. 61. 5. sons of the a. shall be your plowmen
Lam. 5. 2. and our houses are turned to a.
Eph. 2. 12. a. from the commonwealth of Israel
Heb. 11. 34. who turned to flight the armies of a.

ALIENATE, ED.

Isa. 1. † 4. have forsaken the Lord, they are a.
Ezek. 23. 17. her mind was a. from them
18. my mind was a. from her as from her sister
22. thy lovers from whom thy mind is a. 28.
48. 14. they shall not a. the first fruits of the land
Eph. 4. 18. a. from the life of God thro' ignorance
Col. 1. 21. and you that were sometimes a. enemies

ALIKE

Signifies, [1] *Without any difference*, Rom. 14. 5. [2] *After one and the same manner*, Psal. 33. 15. [3] *Equally troublesome*, Prov. 27. 15.

Deut. 12. 22. unclean and clean eat a. 15. 22.
1 Sam. 30. 24. that tarrieth, they shall part a.
Job 21. 26. they shall lie down a. in the dust
Psal. 33. 15. he fashioneth their hearts a. considers
139. 12. darkness and light are both a. to thee
Prov. 20. 10. both are a. abomination to the Lord
27. 15. dropping and a contentious woman are a.
Eccl. 9. 2. all things come a. to all; one event
11. 6. whether they both shall be a. good
Rom. 14. 5. another esteemeth every day a.

ALIVE

Is taken [1] *Naturally*, Gen. 43. 27. [2] *Supernaturally, being raised from the dead*, Luke 24. 23. [3] *Spiritually, when a person is made alive to God by his special grace, and the powerful operation of his Spirit, working with the word of God*, Luke 15. 24, 32. [4] *Opiniatively, when persons apprehend themselves to be righteous, although in truth they are not*, Rom. 7. 9. [5] *Eternally*, Rev. 1. 18.

Gen. 7. 23. Noah only remained a. and they in ark
12. 12. they will kill me, and save thee a.
50. 20. as it is this day, to save much people a.
Exod. 1. 17. but saved the men-children a. 18.
22. and every daughter ye shall save a.
22. 4. if the theft be found in his hand a.
Lev. 10. 16. he was angry with Aaron's sons left a.
14. 4. command to take two birds a. and clean
16. 10. the scape-goat shall be presented a.
26. 36. are left a. of you, I will send a faintness
Num. 16. 33. they went down a. into the pit
21. 35. smote Og, till there was none left a.
22. 33. I had slain thee, and saved her a.
31. 15. have ye saved all the women a.?
Deut. 4. 4. are a. every one of you this day
5. 3. who are all of us a. here this day
6. 24. that he might preserve us a. at this day
20. 16. shalt save a. nothing that breatheth
32. 39. I kill, and I make a. 1 Sam. 2. 6.
Josh. 2. 13. that ye will save a. my father
6. 25. Joshua saved Rahab the harlot a.
8. 23. and the king of Ai they took a.
14. 10. the Lord hath kept me a. as he said
Judg. 8. 19. if ye had saved them a. I would not
21. 14. gave them wives which they had saved a

1 Sam. 15. 8. he took Agag the king of Amalek a.
27. 9. David left neither man nor woman a.
1 Kings 18. 5. to save the horses and mules a.
20. 18. whether come for peace or war take them a.
21. 15. for Naboth is not a. but dead
2 Kings 5. 7. am I God, to kill and make a.?
7. 4. if they save us a. we shall live
12. when they come out we shall catch them a.
10. 14. he said, take them a. and they took them a.
2 Chron. 25. 12. and other ten thousand left a.
Psal. 30. 3. O Lord, thou hast kept me a. that I
Prov. 1. 12. let us swallow them up a. as the grave
Jer. 49. 11. the fatherless I will preserve a.
Ezek. 13. 18. will ye save the souls a. that come
19. to save the souls a. that should not live
18. 27. doth what is right, he shall save his soul a.
Dan. 5. 19. and whom he would, he kept a.
Hab. 3. † 2. O Lord, preserve a. thy work
Mark 16. 11. when they heard that he was a.
Luke 15. 24. for this my son was dead and is a. 32.
24. 23. they had seen angels who said he was a.
Acts 1. 3. he shewed himself a. after his passion
9. 41. had called the widow, presented her a.
20. 12. and they brought the young man a.
25. 19. Jesus, whom Paul affirmed to be a.
Rom. 6. 11. but a. to God through Christ our Lord
13. to God, as those that are a. from the dead
7. 9. for I was a. without the law once, but when
1 Cor. 15. 22. so in Christ shall all be made a.
1 Thess. 4. 15. that we which are a. and remain, 17.
2 Tim. 2. †26. who are taken a. by him at his will
Rev. 1. 18. and behold I am a. for evermore
2. 8. the first and last, which was dead, and is a.
19. 20. these were both cast a. into a lake of fire
Keep ALIVE; *see* KEEP.
Yet ALIVE.
Gen. 43. 7. asked us, saying, is your father yet a.?
27. is he yet a.? ‖ 28. he is well, he is yet a.
45. 26. they told him, saying, Joseph is yet a. 28.
46. 30. now let me die, because thou art yet a.
Exod. 4. 18. let me go and see whether they be yet a.
Deut. 31. 27. while I am yet a. with you this day
2 Sam. 12. 18. while the child was yet a. 21, 22.
18. 14. while he was yet a. in the midst of the oak
1 Kings 20. 32. is he yet a.? he is my brother
Eccl. 4. 2. more than the living which are yet a.
Ezek. 7. 13. which is sold, altho' they were yet a.
Mat. 27. 63. this deceiver said, while he was yet a.
ALL
Signifies [1] *Every creature*, Prov. 16. 4. Psal. 119. 91. [2] *Every man, or person*, 2 Cor. 5. 10. [3] *Plentiful, or perfect*, Rom. 15. 13. 1 Cor. 13. 2. [4.] *Some of all nations, and degrees*, 1 Tim. 2. 4. Tit. 2. 11. [5] *Many, or the greatest part*, Mat. 3. 5. Phil. 2. 21. [6] *Those that believe*, John 12. 32.
Gen. 20. 7. thou shalt surely die, thou and a. thine
24. 36. to him hath he given a. that he hath
31. 43. Laban said, a. that thou seest is mine
37. 3. Jacob loved Joseph more than a. his children
39. 3. the Lord made a. he did to prosper
42. 11. we are a. one man's sons, we are true men
45. 11. lest thou and a. thou hast come to poverty
48. 15. the God which fed me a. my life long
Exod. 20. 11. made heaven, earth, sea, and a. in them
33. 19. I'll make a. my goodness pass before thee
Num. 19. 14. a. that come into the tent are unclean
23. 13. see the utmost, and shalt not see them a.
Deut. 5. 3. who are a. of us here alive this day
13. six days shalt thou labour and do a. thy work
29. 10. ye stand a. of you before the Lord your God
Josh. 21. 45. failed not, a. came to pass, 23. 14.
1 Sam. 6. 4. one plague was on you a. and your lords
9. 19. I will tell thee a. that is in thine heart
16. 11. Samuel said, are here a. thy children?
30. 8. shalt overtake, and without fail recover a.
2 Sam. 16. 4. thine are a. that pertained to Mephibo.
1 Kings 14. 10. taketh away dung till it be a. gone
16. 25. Omri did worse than a. before him
20. 4. my lord, I am thine, and a. that I have
1 Chron. 7. 3. the sons of Uzzi, a. of them chief men
Ezra 8. 22. wrath is against a. that forsake him
Neh. 9. 6. Lord, thou preservest them a. and hast
Job 16. 2. miserable comforters are ye a.
34. † 13. who hath disposed a. of it
19. for they a. are the work of his hands
Psal. 14. 3. are a. gone aside, a. become filthy
22. 17. I may tell a. my bones, they stare upon me
34. 19. the Lord delivereth him out of them a.
38. 9. Lord, a. my desire is before thee
44. 17. a. this is come upon us, yet have we not
69. 19. mine adversaries are a. before thee
104. 27 these wait a. on thee, that thou mayest give
119. 91. they continue, for a. are thy servants
Prov. 1. 14. cast in thy lot, let us a. have one purse
22. 2. the Lord is the maker of them a.
Eccl. 3. 20. a. are of dust, a. turn to dust again
12. † 13. a. that hath been heard is, fear God
Isa. 64. 9. behold, see, we are a. thy people
Jer. 9. 2. they be a. adulterers, Hos. 7. 4.
Ezek. 7. 16. a. of them mourning, every one for
20. 40. a. of them in the land shall serve me
37. 22. and one king shall be king to them a.
40. 4. son of man, declare a. that thou seest
43. 11. shew them a. the forms, a. the ordinances
Dan. 1. 19. among them a. none found like Daniel
Hos. 5. 2. tho' I have been a rebuker of them a.
Amos 9. 1. and cut them in the head a. of them
Nah. 3. 1. woe to the bloody city, it is a. full of lies
Mal. 2. 10. have we not a. one Father, hath not one
Mat. 5. 18. pass from the law, till a. be fulfilled
13. 56. and his sisters, are they not a. with us?
22. 28. whose wife shall she be, for they a. had her
Mark 12. 33. is more than a. burnt offerings
44. she cast in a. even a. that she had, Luke 21. 4.
Luke 4. 7. if thou worship me, a. shall be thine
6. 10. looking round about on them a. he said
8. 40. for they were a. waiting for him
13. 3. except ye repent, ye shall a. likewise perish
15. 31. he said, son, a. that I have is thine
17. 10. so ye, when ye have done a. say, we are
18. 22. sell a. that thou hast, and distribute to poor

John 1. 16. of his fulness have a. we received
4. 39. woman said, he told me a. that ever I did
13. 10. Jesus saith, ye are clean, but not a.
17. 21. that they a. may be one, as thou art in me
Acts 4. 33. and great grace was upon them a.
10. 33. we are a. here present before the Lord
11. 23. he exhorted them a. to cleave to the Lord
16. 28. do thyself no harm, we are a. here
22. 3. zealous towards God, as ye a. are this day
26. 29. but also a. that hear me this day, were both
27. 35. Paul gave thanks in presence of them a.
Rom. 1. 8. I thank God thro' Jesus Christ for you a.
8. 32. but delivered him up for us a. how shall he
1 Cor. 3. 22. a. are yours, and ye are Christ's
15. 10. but I laboured more abundantly than they a.
Gal. 3. 22. the scripture hath concluded a. under sin
Phil. 4. 18. but I have a. and abound, I am full
2 Thess. 2. 12. that they a. might be damned, who
2 Tim. 3. 11. out of them a. the Lord delivered me
Heb. 1. 14. are they not a. ministering spirits, sent
12. 8. chastisement, whereof a. are partakers
1 Pet. 3. 8. finally, be ye a. of one mind
2 Pet. 3. 9. that a. should come to repentance
1 John 2. 19. manifest that they were not a. of us
Above ALL; *see* ABOVE.
According to ALL.
Gen. 6. 22. Noah did ac. to a. God commanded, 7. 5.
Exod. 31. 11. according to a. the Lord commanded, 36. 1. | 39. 32. 42. | 40. 16. Num. 2. 34. | 8. 20. | 9. 5. | 29. 40. Deut. 1. 3, 41.
Josh. 11. 23. took the land ac. to a. the Lord said
1 Kings 8. 56. given rest ac. to a. that he promised
11. 37. shalt reign ac. to a. that thy soul desireth
22. 53. ac. to a. his father had done, 2 Kings 23. 32. 37. | 24. 9. 19. 2 Chron. 26. 4 | 27. 2.
2 Kings 10. 30. done ac. to a. that was in my heart
18. 3. ac. to a. David his father did, 2 Chron. 29. 2.
1 Chron. 17. 15. ac. to a. these words, ac. to a. this
2 Chron. 2. †16. we will cut wood ac. to a. thy need
Neh. 5. 19. think on me for good, ac. to a. I have done
Jer. 21. 2. deal with us ac. to a. his wondrous works
42. 20. ac. to a. that the Lord shall say, will we do
50. 29. ac. to a. that Babylon hath done, do to her
Ezek. 24. 24. ac. to a. that he hath done, shall ye do
Dan. 9. 16. ac to a. thy righteousness, I beseech thee
After ALL.
Deut. 20. 18. not to do after a. their abominations
2 Chron. 34. 21. have not kept the word to do after a.
Ezra 9. 13. after a. that is come on us for our deeds
Ezek. 16. 23. after a. thy wickedness, wo, wo to thee
Mat. 6. 32. after a. these things do the Gentiles seek
Phil. 2. 26. for he longed after you a. and was full of
At ALL.
Exod. 5. 23. nor hast delivered thy people at a.
22. 23. if thou afflict, and they cry at a. to
Lev. 27. 13. but if he will at a. redeem it
Num. 22. 38. have I now any power at a. to say any
Deut. 8. 19. if thou do at a. forget the Lord
1 Sam. 20. 6. if thy father at a. miss me, then say
1 Kings 9. 6. if ye shall at a. turn from following me
Jer. 11. 12. but they shall not save them at a.
Ezek. 20. 32. cometh in your mind shall not be at a.
Hos. 11. 7. most High, none at a. would exalt him
Mic. 1. 10. weep ye not at a. roll thyself in dust
Nah. 1. 3. Lord will not at a. acquit the wicked
John 19. 11. thou couldst have no power at a.
1 Cor. 16. 12. but his will was not at a. to come
1 John 1. 5. and in him is no darkness at a.
Rev. 18. 21. Babylon shall be found no more at a.
22. the sound shall be heard no more at a. in thee
Before ALL.
Gen. 23. 18. before a. that went in at the gates of city
Lev. 10. 3. before a. the people I will be glorified
2 Chron. 33. 7. Jerusalem which I have chosen bef. a.
Jer. 33. 9. shall be to me an honour before a. nations
Mat. 26. 70. but he denied before them a. saying
Gal. 2. 14. I said to Peter before them a.
1 Tim. 5. 20. them that sin rebuke before a. that
For ALL.
Num. 8. 18. I have taken Levites for a. first-born
Deut. 22. 5. for a. that do so are abomination, 25. 16.
31. 18. hide my face in that day for a. the evils
Psal. 10. 5. as for a. his enemies, he puffeth at them
78. 32. for a. this they sinned still, believed not
116. 12. what render to the Lord for a. his benefits
Eccl. 5. 9. the profit of the earth is for a.
11. 9. for a. these God will bring thee to judgment
Isa. 40. 2. she hath received double for a. her sins
Ezek. 6. 11. alas for a. the evil abominations
20. 43. and ye shall lothe yourselves for a. the evils
Dan. 4. 21. fruit was much, and in it was meat for a.
Luke 3. 19. for a. the evils Herod had done
20. 38. God of the living for a. live unto him
Rom. 3. 23. for a. have sinned and come short of
2 Cor. 5. 14. if one died for a. then were all dead
Phil. 2. 21. for a. seek their own, not the things
1 Tim. 2. 6. who gave himself a ransom for a.
Heb. 8. 11. for a. shall know me, from the least
10. 10. offering of the body of Christ once for a.
From ALL.
Gen. 48. 16. angel who redeemed me from a. evil
Lev. 16. 30. that ye may be clean from a. your sins
Psal. 34. 4. and delivered me from a. my fears
Jer. 16. 15. from a. lands whither he had driven
Dan. 7. 7. it was diverse from a. the beasts before it
Heb. 4. 4. God rested the seventh day from a. works
In ALL.
Gen. 21. 12. in a. that Sarah hath said, hearken
22. God is with thee in a. that thou dost
Deut. 29. 9. that ye may prosper in a. that ye do
Josh. 22. 2. and have obeyed my voice in a. that
2 Sam. 23. 39. mighty men, thirty and seven in a.
1 Kings 2. 3. thou mayest prosper in a. thou dost
26. afflicted in a. my father was afflicted
1 Chron. 2. 6. sons of Zerah, five of them in a
Neh. 9. 33. thou art just in a. that is brought on us
Psal. 10. 4. God is not in a. his thoughts
Prov. 3. 6. in a. thy ways acknowledge him
Isa. 39. 2. nothing in a. his dominions shewed not
63. 9. in a. their afflictions he was afflicted
Jer. 38. 9. have done evil in a. they have done
Ezek. 21. 24. in a. your doings your sins appear

Hos. 12. 8. in a. my labours shall find no iniquity
Acts 27. 37. we were in a. in the ship 276 souls
Rom. 8. 37. in a. these more than conquerors
1 Cor. 12. 6. the same God worketh all in a.
15. 28. put all under, that God may be all in a.
Eph. 1. 23. the fulness of him that filleth all in a.
Col. 3. 11. but Christ is all and in a.
2 Thess. 1. 10. to be admired in a. them that believe
Heb. 13. 4. marriage is honourable in a.
2 Pet. 3. 16. as also in a. his epistles, speaking
ALL *Night*; *see* NIGHT.
Of ALL.
Gen. 6. 2. took them wives of a. which they chose
14. 20. he gave him tithes of a. Heb. 7. 2.
28. 22. of a. thou shalt give me, I will give tenth
Exod. 9. 4. nothing die of a. is children's of Israel
Josh. 8. 35. not a word of a. which Moses command.
Judg. 13. 13. of a. I said to the woman, beware
2 Sam. 16. 21. shall hands of a. with thee be strong
2 Kings 9. 5. and Jehu said, to which of a. us
Esth. 6. 10. let nothing fail of a. thou hast spoken
Job 8. 13. so are the paths of a. that forget God
Eccl. 6. 2. he wanteth nothing of a. he desireth
Ezek. 43. 11. if they be ashamed of a. they have done
Amos 3. 2. you only have I known of a. the families
Mark 9. 35. the same shall be servant of a. 10. 44.
John 6. 39. of a. which hath given me, lose nothing
Acts 10. 36. peace by Jesus Christ, he is Lord of a.
1 Cor. 14. 24. he is convinced of a. judged of a.
Gal. 4. 1. now I say, the heir, though he be l. of a.
Eph. 4. 6. God who is Father of a. above all
Heb. 12. 23. and to God the Judge of a. and to spirits
Jam. 2. 10. offend in one point, he is guilty of a.
On or Upon ALL.
Gen. 39. 5. blessing of the Lord was upon a. he had
Isa. 4. 5. for upon a. the glory shall be a defence
Ezek. 40. 4. set thy heart upon a. that I shall shew
Rom. 3. 22. unto all, and upon a. them that believe
11. 32. that he might have mercy upon a.
Jude 15. to execute judgment upon a. and convince
Rev. 3. 10. the hour of temptation shall come upon a.
Over ALL.
2 Sam. 3. 21. that thou mayest reign over a.
1 Chron. 29. 12. and thou reignest over a. in thy hand
Psal. 103. 19. his kingdom ruleth over a.
Mat. 24. 47. make him ruler over a. Luke 12. 44.
John 17. 2. as thou hast given him power over a.
Rom. 9. 5. who is over a. God blessed for ever
10. 12. the same Lord over a. is rich to all
ALL *these*.
Gen. 15. 10. he took to him a. these and divided
42. 36. Jacob said, a. these things are against me
49. 28. a. these are the twelve tribes of Israel
Exod. 20. 1. God spake a. these words, saying
Job 12. 9. who knoweth not that in a. these
Jer. 9. 26. for a. these nations are uncircumcised
Hab. 2. 6. shall not a. these take up a parable
Mat. 6. 33. a. these shall be added to you, Luke 12. 31.
24. 8. a. these are the beginning of sorrows
Mark 7. 23. a. these evil things come from within
Acts 2. 7. are not a. these which speak Galileans?
1 Cor. 12. 11. a. these worketh that self-same Spirit
Col. 3. 8. but now you put off a. these, anger, wrath
Heb. 11. 13. a. these died in faith, not having received
ALL *this*.
Gen. 41. 39. as God hath shewed thee a. this
Deut. 32. 27. and the Lord hath not done a. this
Judg. 6. 13. why then is a. this befallen us?
1 Sam. 22. 15. thy servant knew nothing of a. this
2 Sam. 14. 19. is not the hand of Joab in a. this?
1 Chron. 28. 19. a. this the Lord made me understand
2 Chron. 21. 18. after a. this the Lord smote him
29. 28. a. this continued till the burnt-offering
Ezra 8. 35. a. this was a burnt-offering to the Lord
Neh. 9. 38. because of a. this we make a covenant
Esth. 5. 13. yet a. this availeth me nothing
Job 1. 22. in a. this Job sinned not, 2. 10.
13. 1. lo, mine eye hath seen a. this
Psal. 44. 17. a. this is come upon us, yet not forgot
78. 32. for a. this they sinned still
Eccl. 7. 23. a. this have I proved by wisdom
8. 9. a. this have I seen, and applied my heart to
9. 1. a. this I considered in my heart, to declare [a. this
Isa. 5. 25. for a. this his anger is not turned away, 9. 12. 17. 21. | 10. 4.
48. 6. thou hast heard, see a. this
Dan. 4. 28. a. this came upon Nebuchadnezzar
5. 22. hast not humbled, tho' thou knewest a. this
7. 16. I came and asked him the truth of a. this
Hos. 7. 10. do not return, nor seek him for a. this
Mic. 1. 5. for the transgression of Jacob is a. this
Mat. 1. 22. a. this was done that the prophets might be fulfilled, 21. 4. | 26. 56.
Luke 16. 26. besides a. this there is a gulf fixed
24. 21. besides a. this to-day is the third day
ALL *that he had*.
Gen. 12. 20. Pharaoh sent him and a. that he had
13. 1. Abram went out of Egypt, and a. that he had
25. 5. and Abraham gave a. that he had to Isaac
31. 21. Jacob fled with a. that he had, and rose up
39. 4. a. that he had he put into Joseph's hand, 6.
5. the blessing of the Lord was on a. that he had
Mat. 18. 25. he sold a. that he had, payment be made
Mark 5. 26. she spent a. that she had, nothing bettered
12. 44. of her want cast in a. that she had, Luke 21. 4.
To or Unto ALL.
Psal. 145. 9. the Lord is good to a. and his mercies
Eccl. 2. 14. one event happeneth to a. them, 9. 3. 11.
9. 2. all things come alike to a. one event to right.
Isa. 36. 6. so is Pharaoh to a. that trust in him
Mark 13. 37. what I say to you, I say unto a. watch
Luke 12. 41. speakest thou this to us, or even to a.?
Acts 2. 39. the promise is to a. that are afar off
4. 16. manifest to a. that dwell in Jerusalem
Rom. 10. 12. the Lord is rich unto a. that call on him
13. 7. render therefore to a. their dues
1 Cor. 9. 19. I made myself a servant unto a.
1 Tim. 4. 15. that thy profiting may appear to a.
With ALL.
Num. 16. 30. with a. that appertain to them

Deut. 6. 5. thou shalt love the Lord *with a.* thy heart, *with a.* thy soul, 11. 13. *Mat.* 22. 37.
2 Chron. 25. 7. *with a.* the children of Ephraim
Prov. 4. 7. *with a.* thy getting, get understanding
Acts 10. 2. that feared God *with a.* his house, 16. 34.
1 Cor. 1. 2. *with a.* that in every place call on Jesus
Phil. 1. 25. I shall abide and continue *with* you *a.*
2. 17. if offered, I joy and rejoice *with* you *a.*

ALL *the while.*

1 Sam. 22. 4. *a. the while* David was in the hold
25. 7. nothing missing *a. the while* they were in Car.
27. 11. so will be his manner *a. the while* he dwell [eth
Job 27. 3. *a. the while* my breath is in me

ALL *ye.*

Isa. 48. 14. *a. ye* assemble yourselves, and hear
50. 11. behold *a. ye* that kindle a fire, that compass
66. 10. be glad with her, *a. ye* that love her
Jer. 29. 20. hear the word, *a. ye* of the captivity
Lam. 1. 12. is it nothing to you, *a. ye* that pass by?
Mat. 11. 28. come to me, *a. ye* that labour and are
23. 8. one is your master; and *a. ye* are brethren
26. 31. *a. ye* shall be offended, *Mark* 14. 27.
Acts 2. 14. *a. ye* that dwell at Jerusalem, hear
See farther other usual Substantives: CONGREGATION, DAY, EARTH, ISRAEL, MEN, PEOPLE, THINGS, &c.

ALLEGING.

Acts 17. 3. *a.* Christ must needs have suffered

ALLEGORY.

Gal. 4. 24. which things are an *a.* for these are

ALLELUIAH.

Rev. 19. 1. I heard a great voice, saying, *a.* 3, 4, 6.

ALLIED.

Neh. 13. 4. Eliashib the priest was *a.* to Tobiah

ALLOW.

Luke 11. 48. that ye *a.* the deeds of your fathers
Acts 24. 15. which they themselves also *a.* that there
Rom. 7. 15. for that which I do, I *a.* not

ALLOWED, ETH.

Rom. 14. 22. himself in that thing which he *a.*
1 Thess. 2. 4. but as we were *a.* of God to be put

ALLOWANCE.

2 Kings 25. 30. his *a.* was a continual *a.* given him
Prov. 30. † 8. feed me with food of my *a.*
Luke 3. † 14. be content with your *a.*

ALLURE.

Hos. 2. 14. I'll *a.* and bring her into the wilderness
2 Pet. 2. 18. they *a.* through the lusts of the flesh

ALMS.

Mat. 6. 1. that ye do not your *a.* before men
2. therefore when thou dost thine *a.* do not sound
4. that thine *a.* may be in secret, and thy Father
Luke 11. 41 give *a.* of such things as you have
12. 33. sell that ye have, and give *a.* provide bags
Acts 3. 2. they laid, to ask *a.* of them that entered
3. who seeing Peter and John, asked an *a.*
10. they knew that it was he which sat for *a.*
10. 2. Cornelius gave much *a.* to the people
4. thine *a.* are come up for a memorial, 31.
24. 17. I came to bring *a.* to my nation and offer.

ALMS-DEEDS.

Acts 9. 36. Dorcas full of *a.-deeds* which she did

ALMIGHTY.

Gen. 17. 1. I am the *a.* God, walk before me
28. 3. God *a.* bless thee, and make thee fruitful
35. 11. I am God *a.* be fruitful and multiply
43. 14. God *a.* give you mercy before the man
48. 3. God *a.* appeared to me at Luz in Canaan
49. 25. by the *a.* who shall bless thee with blessings
Exod. 6. 3. I appeared to Abram by the name God *a.*
Num. 24. 4. which saw the vision of the *a.* 16.
Ruth 1. 20. for the *a.* hath dealt bitterly with me
21. seeing the *a.* hath afflicted me
Job 5. 17. despise not thou the chastening of the *a.*
6. 4. for the arrows of the *a.* are within me
14. but he forsaketh the fear of the *a.*
8. 3. or doth the *a.* pervert justice?
5. and make thy supplication to the *a.*
11. 7. canst thou find out the *a.* to perfection?
13. 3. surely I would speak to the *a.* and desire
15. 25. he strengtheneth himself against the *a.*
21. 15. what is the *a.* that we should serve him?
20. and he shall drink of the wrath of the *a.*
22. 3. is it any pleasure to the *a.* thou art righteous
17. which said, what can the *a.* do for them?
23. if thou return to the *a.* thou shalt be built
25. yea, the *a.* shall be thy defence, thou shalt
26. then shalt thou have thy delight in the *a.*
23. 16. my heart soft, and the *a.* troubleth me
24. 1. why, seeing times are not hid from the *a.*
27. 2. and the *a.* who hath vexed my soul
10. will he delight himself in the *a.?*
11. what is with the *a.* will I not conceal
13. which they shall receive of the *a.*
29. 5. when the *a.* was yet with me
31. 2. what inheritance of the *a.* from on high?
35. my desire is, that the *a.* would answer me
32. 8. inspiration of the *a.* giveth understanding
33. 4. and the breath of the *a.* hath given me life
34. 10. far be it from the *a.* to commit iniquity
12. neither will the *a.* pervert judgment
35. 13. surely the *a.* will not regard vanity
37. 23. touching the *a.* we cannot find him out
40. 2. shall he that contendeth with the *a.* instruct
Psal. 68. 14. when the *a.* scattered kings in it
91. 1. he shall abide under the shadow of the *a.*
Isa. 13. 6. shall come as destruction from the *a.*
Ezek. 1. 24. I heard as the voice of the *a.* 10. 5.
Dan. 11. † 38. for the *a.* God he shall honour
Joel 1. 15. as destruction from the *a.* shall it come
2 Cor. 6. 18. shall be my sons, saith the Lord *a.*
Rev. 1. 8. which is, was, and is to come, the *a.*
4. 8. the Lord God *a.* which was, and is, 11. 17.
15. 3. Lord *a.* just and true are thy ways, 16. 7.
16. 14. the battle of that great day of God *a.*
19. 15. treadeth wine-press of wrath of the *a.* God
21. 22. God *a.* and the Lamb are the temple of it

ALMOND, S.

Gen. 43. 11. carry spices, myrrh, nuts, and *a.*
Exod. 25. 33. made like to *a.* 34. | 37. 19, 20.
Num. 17. 8. the rod of Aaron for Levi yielded *a.*
Eccl. 12. 5. when the *a.* tree shall flourish
Jer. 1. 11. and I said, I see a rod of an *a.* tree

ALMOST.

Exod. 17. 4. they be *a.* ready to stone me
Psal. 73. 2. as for me, my feet were *a.* gone
94. 17. my soul had *a.* dwelt in silence
119. 87. they had *a.* consumed me upon earth
Prov. 5. 14. I was *a.* in all evil in the midst of congre- [gation
Acts 13. 44. came *a.* the whole city together
19. 26. only at Ephesus, but *a.* through all Asia
21. 27. and when the seven days were *a.* ended
26. 28. *a.* thou persuadest me to be a christian
29. were both *a.* and altogether such as I am
Heb. 9. 22. *a.* all things by the law are purged

ALMUG-TREES.

1 Kings 10. 11. brought from Ophir plenty of *a.-trees*
12. made of *a.-tr.* pillars, there came no such *a.-tr.*

ALOES.

Psal. 45. 8. thy garments smell of *a.* and cassia
Prov. 7. 17. I have perfumed my bed with *a.*
Cant. 4. 14. myrrh, *a.* with all the chief spices
John 19. 39. Nicodemus brought a mixture of *a.*

ALOFT.

Prov. 18. † 10. the righteous runneth and is set *a.*

ALONE

Signifies, [1] *One solitary, or by himself,* Lev. 13. 46. Psal. 102. 7. [2] *Only,* Dan. 10. 7. Mat. 4. 4. [3] *To cease from,* Exod. 14. 12.
Gen. 2. 18. it is not good that the man should be *a.*
Exod. 18. 18. art not able to perform it thyself *a.*
24. 2. Moses *a.* shall come near the Lord
Lev. 13. 46. the leper dwell *a.* without the camp
Num. 11. 14. I am not able to bear all this people *a.* *Deut.* 1. 9, 12.
17. that thou bear it not thyself *a.*
23. 9. lo, the people shall dwell *a.* not be reckoned
Deut. 32. 12. so the Lord *a.* did lead him
33. 28. Israel then shall dwell in safety *a.*
Josh. 22. 20. Achan perished not *a.* in his iniquity
2 Sam. 18. 24. behold, a man running *a.* 26.
25. if he be *a.* there is tidings in his mouth
1 Kings 11. 29. they two were *a.* in the field
2 Kings 19. 15. art God *a. Isa.* 37. 16. *Psal.* 86. 10.
1 Chron. 29. 1. Solomon, whom *a.* God hath chosen
Esth. 3. 6. scorn to lay hands on Mordecai *a.*
Job 1. 15. I only am escaped *a.* to tell, 16, 17, 19.
9. 8. God who *a.* spreadeth out the heavens
15. 19. to whom *a.* the earth was given
31. 17. or have I eaten my morsel myself *a.?*
Psal. 83. 18. thou whose name *a.* is Jehovah
102. 7. I watch and am as a sparrow *a.* on housetop
136. 4. to him who *a.* doeth great wonders
148. 13. for his name *a.* is excellent
Eccl. 4. 8. there is one *a.* and there is not a second
10. but wo to him that is *a.* when he falleth
Isa. 2. 11. Lord *a.* shall be exalted in that day, 17.
14. 31. none shall be *a.* in his appointed times
51. 2. for I called him *a.* and blessed him
63. 3. I have trodden the wine-press *a.*
Lam. 3. 28. he sitteth *a.* and keepeth silence
Dan. 10. 7. and I Daniel *a.* saw the vision
Hos. 8. 9. gone to Assyria, a wild ass *a.* by himself
Mat. 4. 4. man shall not live by bread *a. Luke* 4. 4.
14. 23. evening was come, he was *a. Luke* 9. 18.
18. 15. tell his fault between thee and him *a.*
Mark 4. 34. when they were *a.* he expounded
6. 47. ship was in midst of sea, and he *a.* on the land
Luke 5. 21. who can forgive sins but God *a.?*
6. 4. not lawful to eat, but for the priests *a.*
9. 18. it came to pass, as Jesus was *a.* praying
36. when the voice was past, Jesus was found *a.*
10. 40. that my sister hath left me to serve *a.*
John 6. 15. he departed into a mountain *a.*
22. but that his disciples were gone away *a.*
8. 16. for I am not *a.* but I and the Father, 16. 32.
17. 20. neither pray I for these *a.* but for them
Acts 19. 26. ye see and hear that not *a.* at Ephesus
Rom. 4. 23. it was written for his sake *a.*
Gal. 6. 4. he shall have rejoicing in himself *a.*
Heb. 9. 7. went the high-priest *a.* once every year
Jam. 2. 17. faith if it hath not works is dead, being *a.*

Left ALONE.

Gen. 32. 24. Jacob *left a.* and there wrestled a man
42. 38. his brother is dead, and he is *left a.* 44. 20.
Isa. 49. 21. I was *left a.* these where had they been?
Dan. 10. 8. I was *left a.* and saw this great vision
John 8. 9. and Jesus was *left a.* and the woman
29. the Father hath not *left* me *a.* for I do always
Rom. 11. 3. I am *left a.* and they seek my life

Let ALONE.

Exod. 14. 12. *let* us *a.* that we may serve Egyptians
32. 10. *let* me *a.* that my wrath may wax hot
Deut. 9. 14. *let* me *a.* that I may destroy them
Judg. 11. 37. *let* me *a.* two months, that I may go
2 Sam. 16. 11. *let* him *a.* let him curse, L. has bidden
2 Kings 4. 27. *let* her *a.* her soul is vexed in her
Ezra 6. 7. *let* the work of this house of God *a.*
Job 10. 20. and *let* me *a.* that I may take comfort
13. 13. hold your peace, *let* me *a.* that I may speak
Hos. 4. 17. Ephraim is joined to idols, *let* him *a.*
Mat. 15. 14. *let* them *a.* they be blind leaders
Mark 1. 24. *let* us *a.* what have we to do with thee, thou Jesus of Nazareth? *Luke* 4. 34.
14. 6. Jesus said, *let* her *a.* why trouble ye her?
15. 36. *let a.* let us see whether Elias will come
Luke 13. 8. Lord, *let* it *a.* this year also, till I dig
John 11. 48. if we *let* him *a.* all men will believe
12. 7. *let* her *a.* against the day of my burying
Acts 5. 38. refrain from these men, *let* them *a.*

ALONG.

Num. 21. 22. we will go *a.* by the king's highway
1 Sam. 6. 12. the kine went *a.* the highway, lowing
28. 20. then Saul fell all *a.* on the earth
2 Sam. 3. 16. her husband went with her *a.* weeping
16. 13. Shimei went *a.* cursing, and threw stones
Jer. 41. 6. Ishmael went, weeping all *a.* as he went

ALOOF.

Psal. 38. 11. my friends stand *a.* from my sore

ALOUD; *see* CRY, CRIED, SING.

ALPHA.

Rev. 1. 8. I am *a.* and Omega, 11. | 21. 6. | 22. 13.

ALREADY.

Exod. 1. 5. for Joseph was in Egypt *a.*
Eccl. 1. 10. it hath been *a.* of old time, before us
Mal. 2. 2. your blessings, yea, I have cursed them *a.*
Mat. 17. 12. I say unto you, Elias is come *a.*
John 3. 18. he that believeth not is condemned *a.*
1 Cor. 5. 3. but present in spirit, have judged *a.*
Phil. 3. 16. whereto we have *a.* attained
1 Tim. 5. 15. some are *a.* turned aside after Satan
Rev. 2. 25. but that which ye have *a.* hold fast

ALSO.

Gen. 6. 3. strive with man, for that he *a.* is flesh
Num. 16. 10. and seek ye the priesthood *a?*
1 Sam. 14. 44. Saul answered, God do so and more *a.* *2 Sam.* 3. 35. | 19. 13.
2 Kings 7. 4. and if we sit still here, we die *a.*
Psal. 68. 18. gifts, yea, for the rebellious *a.*
Isa. 7. 13. but will ye weary my God *a.?*
Zech. 8. 21. to seek the Lord of hosts I will go *a.*
Mat. 6. 21. there will your heart be *a. Luke* 12. 34.
26. 73. surely thou art *a.* one of them
Mark 1. 38. that I may preach there *a.*
2. 28. Son of man is Lord *a.* of sabbath, *Luke* 6. 5.
Luke 11. 45. thus saying, thou reproachest us *a.*
John 5. 19. what he doth, these *a.* doth the Son
12. 26. where I am, there shall *a.* my servant be
14. 3. that where I am, there ye may be *a.*
Acts 12. 3. he proceeded to take Peter *a.*
Rom. 16. 2. succourer of many, and of myself *a.*
1 Cor. 9. 8. or saith not the law the same *a.*
15. 8. and last of all, he was seen of me *a.*
2 Tim. 1. 5. I am persuaded that in thee *a.*
Jam. 2. 26. faith without works is dead *a.*
1 John 4. 21. that loveth God, love his brother *a.*

ALTAR

Signifies, [1] *A material altar, on which sacrifices were offered,* 1 Kings 13. 1, 2. | 18. 30. [2] *Christ, who is the only christian altar, to whom we bring all our sacrifices and services,* Heb. 13. 10.
Gen. 8. 20. Noah builded an *a.* to the Lord
12. 7. there Abraham built an *a.* to the Lord, 22. 9.
35. 1. Jacob, go to Beth-el, and make there an *a.*
3. up to Beth-el, I will make there an *a.* to God
Exod. 17. 15. Moses built an *a.* Jehovah nissi
20. 24. an *a.* of earth shalt thou make to me
21. 14. shalt take him from mine *a.* that he die
29. 37. sanctify it, it shall be an *a.* most holy
44. I will sanctify the tabernacle and *a.*
30. 27. *a.* of incense, ‖ 40. 10. *a.* of burnt-offering
Lev. 6. 9. the fire of the *a.* shall be burning in it
Num. 7. 84. this was the dedication of the *a.*
18. 3. they shall not come nigh the *a.*
Josh. 22. 34. the children of Gad called the *a.* Ed.
Judg. 6. 25. throw down the *a.* of Baal, and grove
31. because one hath cast down his *a.*
1 Sam. 2. 33. whom I shall not cut off from mine *a.*
2 Sam. 24. 18. go up, rear an *a.* to the Lord
1 Kings 13. 2. he cried against the *a.* O *a.*
18. 30. Elijah repaired the *a.* of the Lord
35. and the water ran round about the *a.*
2 Kings 18. 22. shall worship before this *a. Isa.* 36. 7.
Psal. 26. 6. so will I compass thine *a.* O Lord
43. 4. then will I go to the *a.* of God, to God my joy
Isa. 19. 19. an *a.* to the Lord in the midst of Egypt
27. 9. the stones of the *a.* as chalk-stones
56. 7. their sacrifices be accepted on mine *a.*
Lam. 2. 7. the Lord hath cast off his *a.*
Ezek. 8. 16. between the porch and *a.* 25 men
Joel 1. 13. lament, howl, ye ministers of the *a.*
2. 17. the priests weep between the porch and *a.*
Amos 2. 8. upon clothes laid to pledge by every *a.*
Mal. 1. 7. ye offer polluted bread on mine *a.*
10. nor do kindle fire on mine *a.* for nought
2. 13. covering the *a.* of the Lord with tears
Mat. 5. 23. if thou bring thy gift to the *a.*
23. 10. whoso shall swear by the *a.* it is nothing
35. ye slew between the temple and *a. Luke* 11. 51.
Acts 17. 23. I found an *a.* with this inscription
1 Cor. 9. 13. wait at the *a.* partakers with *a.* 10. 18.
Heb. 7. 13. of which none gave attendance at the *a.*
13. 10. we have an *a.* whereof they have no right
Rev. 6. 9. I saw under the *a.* the souls of them slain
8. 3. should offer it with prayers on the golden *a.*
9. 13. heard a voice from horns of the golden *a.*

See BUILT.

ALTARS.

Exod. 34. 13. shall destroy their *a. Deut.* 7. 5. | 12. 3.
Num. 23. 1. Baalam said, build here seven *a.*
1 Kings 19. 10. Israel have thrown down thine *a.* 14.
2 Chron. 34. 5. burnt the bones of priests on the *a.*
Psal. 84. 3. even thine *a.* O Lord of hosts, my king
Isa. 17. 8. and he shall not look to the *a.* the work
Jer. 17. 1. sin of Judah graven on horns of the *a.*
2. whilst their children remember their *a.*
Ezek. 6. 4. and your *a.* shall be desolate, images be
Hos. 8. 11. made *a.* to sin, *a.* shall be to him to sin
10. 8. thorn and thistle shall come on their *a.*
12. 11. their *a.* are as heaps in the furrows
Amos 3. 14. I will also visit the *a.* of Beth-el
Rom. 11. 3. Lord, they have digged down thine *a.*

ALTER.

Lev. 27. 10. he shall not *a.* it, a good for a bad
Ezra 6. 11. that whosoever shall *a.* this word
12. destroy all that put their hand to *a.* this
Psal. 89. 34. not *a.* the thing gone out of my lips
Prov. 31. † 5. lest they *a.* the judgment of afflicted

ALTERED.

Esth. 1. 19. be not *a.* that Vashti come no more
Luke 9. 29. the fashion of his countenance was *a.*

ALTERETH.

Dan. 6. 8. according to the law which *a.* not, 12.

ALTERING.

Num. 14. † 34. ye shall know my *a.* of purpose

ALTHOUGH.

Exod. 13. 17. *a.* that was near, for God said
2 Sam. 23. 5. *a.* my house be not so with God
Job 2. 3. *a.* thou movedst me against him
Jer. 31. 32. *a.* I was an husband unto them
Ezek. 11. 16. *a.* I have cast them far off
Hab. 3. 17. *a.* the fig-tree shall not blossom
Mark 14. 29. *a.* all shall be offended, yet will not I
Gal. 6. † 1. *a.* a man be overtaken in a fault

ALTOGETHER.

Num. 16. 13. make thyself *a.* a prince over us

Deut. 16. 20. which is a. just shalt thou follow
Psal. 14. 3. they are a. become filthy, Psal. 53. 3.
19. 9. judgments of the Lord are righteous a.
39. 5. every man at his best state is a. vanity
50. 21. that I was a. such an one as thyself
139. 4. but lo, O Lord, thou knowest it a.
Cant. 5. 16. his mouth is sweet, yea, he is a. lovely
John 9. 34. thou wast a. born in sins, dost thou
Acts 26. 29. were almost and a. such as I am
1 Cor. 5. 10. yet not a. with the fornicators
9. 10. or saith he it a. for our sakes?
2 Cor. 4. † 8. perplexed, but not a. without help

ALWAY, ALWAYS,

Signifies, [1] *Continually*, John 8. 29. [2] *Frequently*, Acts 10. 2. [3] *To the end of the world*, Mat. 28. 20. [4.] *During life*, 2 Sam. 9. 10.
Deut. 5. 29. O that they would keep my commands a.
11. 1. thou shalt keep his commandments a.
14. 23. thou mayest learn to fear the Lord a.
Job 7. 16. I lothe it, I would not live a.
27. 10. will he a. call upon God?
Psal. 16. 8. I have set the Lord a. before me
103. 9. he will not a. chide, nor keep his anger
119. 112. inclined to perform thy statutes a.
Prov. 8. 30. I was by him, rejoicing a. before him
Isa. 57. 16. neither will I be a. wroth
Mat. 28. 20. I am with you a. to the end of the world
Mark 14. 7. but me ye have not a. John 12. 8.
John 8. 29. I do a. those things that please him
11. 42. I know that thou hearest me a.
Acts 10. 2. Cornelius prayed to God a.
2 Cor. 2. 14. God, who a. causeth us to triumph
Phil. 1. 4. a. in every prayer of mine for you
20. as a. so now also, Christ shall be magnified
2. 12. as ye have a. obeyed, not in my presence
4. 4. rejoice in the Lord a. and again rejoice
1 Thess. 2. 16. to fill up their sins a. for wrath
2 Pet. 1. 15. to have these a. in remembrance

I AM, I AM *that* I AM.

Exod. 3. 14. *I am that I am* hath sent me to you
Num. 11. 21. the people amongst whom *I am*
Neh. 6. 11. who is there that being as *I am*
Job 9. 32. he is not a man as *I am*, that I should
Psal. 35. 3. say to my soul, *I am* thy salvation
39. 4. that I may know how frail *I am*
50. 7. O Israel, *I am* God, even thy God
143. 12. destroy them, for *I am* thy servant [11.
Isa. 44. 6. *I am* the first, *I am* the last, 48. 12. Rev. 1.
47. 8. *I am*, and none else besides me, Zeph. 2. 15.
58. 9. thou shalt cry, and he shall say, here *I am*
Mat. 16. 13. whom do men say that *I* the Son of man *am*? Mark 8. 27. Luke 9. 18.
Luke 22. 70. art the Son of God, ye say that *I am*
John 6. 35. Jesus said, *I am* the bread of life
8. 12. saying, *I am* the light of the world
58. I say to you, before Abraham was, *I am*
12. 26. where *I am* there shall my servants be
17. 24. I will that they may be with me where *I am*
Acts 26. 29. almost and altogether such as *I am*
27. 23. angel of God, whose *I am*, and whom I serve
1 Cor. 15. 10. by the grace of God *I am* what *I am*
Gal. 4. 12. brethren, be as *I am*, for *I am* as you are
Phil. 4. 11. for I have learned in what state *I am*
Rev. 1. 18. *I am* he that liveth, *I am* alive for ever
19. 10. see thou do it not, *I am* thy fellow-servant

AM I.

Gen. 4. 9. I know not, *am I* my brother's keeper?
30. 2. am I in God's stead, who hath withheld
2 Kings 5. 7. *am I* God, to kill and to make alive?
18. 25. *am I* come up without the Lord, Isa. 36. 10.
Jer. 23. 23. *am I* a God at hand, saith the Lord
Mat. 18. 20. there *am I* in the midst of them
John 7. 33. yet a little while *am I* with you
1 Cor. 9. 1. *am I* not an apostle? *am I* not free?
2 Cor. 12. 10. when I am weak, then *am I* strong

Here AM I, *or Here* I AM. *See* HERE.

AMAZED.

Judg. 20. 41. the men of Benjamin were a.
Job 32. 15. they were a. they answered no more
Isa. 13. 8. they shall be a. one at another
Ezek. 32. 10. I will make many people a. at thee
Mat. 19. 25. the disciples were exceedingly a.
Mark 2. 12. were all a. and glorified God, Luke 5. 26
14. 33. he began to be sore a. and very heavy
Luke 4. 36. all a. and spake among themselves
9. 43. were all a. at the mighty power of God
Acts 9. 21. but all that heard Saul were a.

AMAZEMENT.

Acts 3. 10. filled with a. at what had happened
1 Pet. 3. 6. and are not afraid with any a.

AMBASSADOR.

Prov. 13. 17. but a faithful a. is health
Jer. 49. 14. an a. sent to the heathen, Obad. 1.
Eph. 6. 20. for which I am an a. in bonds

AMBASSADORS.

Josh. 9. 4. went and made as if they had been a.
2 Chron. 32. 31. the business of the a. of Babylon
35. 21. he sent a. what have I to do with thee?
Isa. 18. 2. that sendeth a. by the sea in vessels
30. 4. princes at Zoan, his a. came to Hanes
33. 7. the a. of peace shall weep bitterly
Ezek. 17. 15. he rebelled in sending a. to Egypt
2 Cor. 5. 20. now then we are a. for Christ

AMBASSAGE.

Luke 14. 32. sendeth an a. and desireth conditions

AMBER; *see* COLOUR.

AMBUSH, ES.

Josh. 8. 2. lay thee an a. for the city behind it
Jer. 51. 12. set up the watchmen, prepare the a.

AMBUSHMENT, S.

2 Chron. 13. 13. Jeroboam caused an a. the a. was
20. 22. the Lord set a. against Ammon

AMEN

Signifies, *in Hebrew, true, faithful, certain. It is made use of likewise to affirm any thing, and was an affirmation used often by our Saviour, which is rendered in our translation*, verily, verily; amen, amen, *I say unto you*, John 3. 3, 5. *All the promises of God are* amen *in Christ; that is, certain and firm*, 2 Cor. 1. 20. *Christ himself, the faithful prophet and teacher of his church, is called the* Amen, Rev. 3 14. *In* Isa. 65. 16. *shall bless himself in the God of truth, and swear by the God of truth; which in the Hebrew is*, the God amen. *And it is used in the end of prayer in testimony of an earnest wish, desire, or assurance to be heard*; amen, so be it, so shall it be. *The word* amen *is used in many languages.*
Num. 5. 22. and the woman shall say a. a.
Deut. 27. 15. all the people shall say a. to the end
1 Kings 1. 36. Benaiah answered a. the Lord say so
1 Chron. 16 36. people said a. and praised the Lord
Psal. 41. 13. from everlasting to everlasting; a. and a.
72. 19. earth filled with his glory; a. and a.
89. 52. blessed be the Lord for evermore, a. and a.
106. 48. and let all the people say a.
Jer. 28. 6. even the prophet Jeremiah said a.
Mat. 6. 13. the power and the glory for ever, a.
1 Cor. 14. 16. the room of the unlearned, say a.
2 Cor. 1. 20. the promises in him are yea and a.
Rev. 1. 18. behold, I am alive for evermore, a.
3. 14. write these things, saith the a. the faithful
5. 14. and the four beasts said a. 19. 4.
22. 20. surely I come quickly, a. even so come, Lord [Jesus

AMEND.

Jer. 7. 3. a. ways, and doings, 5. | 26. 13. | 35. 15.
John 4. 52. the hour when he began to a.

AMENDMENT.

Mat. 3. † 8. bring fruits answerable to a. of life

AMENDS.

Lev. 5. 16. he shall make a. for the harm done

AMERCE.

Deut. 22. 19. they shall a. him in 100 shekels

AMETHYST; *see* AGATE *and* JACINTH.

AMIABLE.

Psal. 84. 1. how a. are thy tabernacles, O Lord

AMISS.

2 Chron. 6. 37. we have sinned, we have done a.
Dan. 3. 29. speak any thing a. against the God
Luke 23. 41. but this man hath done nothing a.
Jam. 4. 3. ask and receive not, because ye ask a.

AMONG.

Num. 14. 14. heard that thou, Lord, art a. them
Ezra 10. 18. a. the sons of the priests were found
Neh. 13. 26. yet a. many nations was no king
Job 33. 23. if an interpreter, one a. a thousand
36. 14. and their life is a. the unclean
Eccl. 6. 1. there is an evil common a. men
7. 28. one a. 1000, but a woman a. all those
Cant. 5. 10. the chiefest a. ten thousand
Jer. 5. 26. a. my people are found wicked men
Mic. 7. 2. and there is none upright a. men
Luke 1. 28. blessed art thou a. women
10. 3. I send you forth as lambs a. wolves
John 6. 9. but what are they a. so many?
Col. 1. † 18. a. all he might have the pre-eminence

ANATHEMA.

1 Cor. 16. 22. let him be a. maran-atha

ANCESTORS.

Lev. 26. 45. remember the covenant of their a.

ANCHOR.

Acts 27. 30. as though they would have cast a.
Heb. 6. 19. which hope we have as an a. of the soul

ANCIENT

Signifies, [1] *Old, of former time*, 1 Chron. 4. 22. [2] *Very old men*, Job 12. 12. [3] *Men of former times*, 1 Sam. 24. 13. [4] *Governors, political and ecclesiastical*, Isa. 3. 14. Jer. 19. 1.
Deut. 33. 15. for the chief things of the a. mountains
Judg. 5. 21. that a. river, the river Kishon
2 Kings 19. 25. of a. times, I formed it, Isa. 37. 26.
1 Chron. 4. 22. and these are a. things
Ezra 3. 12. were a. men, and had seen the first house
Job 12. 12. with the a. is wisdom, and in days
Prov. 22. 28. remove not the a. land-mark
Isa. 3. 2. prudent and a. the Lord doth take away
9. 15. the a. and honourable, he is the head
19. 11. how say ye, I am the son of a. kings?
23. 7. whose antiquity is of a. days
44. 7. since I appointed the a. people
47. 6. upon the a. hast thou laid thy yoke
51. 9. awake, O arm of the Lord, as in the a. days
Jer. 18. 15. caused them to stumble from a. paths
Ezek. 9. 6. then they began at the a. men
Dan. 7. 9. the a. of days did sit, whose garment
13. one like the Son of man came to a. of days
22. till the a. of days came, and judgment given

ANCIENTS.

1 Sam. 24. 13. as saith the proverb of the a.
Psal. 119. 100. I understand more than the a.
Isa. 3. 14. Lord will enter into judgment with the a.
24. 23. the Lord shall reign before his a.
Jer. 19. 1. take of a. of the people and a. of priests
Ezek. 7. 26. counsel shall perish from the a.
8. 12. son of man, hast thou seen what the a. do?
27. 9. the a. of Gebal were in thee thy calkers

ANCLE-BONES.

Acts 3. 7. his a.-bones received strength

ANCLES.

2 Sam. 22. † 37. that my a. did not slip, Psal. 18. † 36.
Ezek. 47. 3. the waters were to the a.

ANGEL

Signifies, *A messenger, or bringer of tidings*, and is applied, [1] *To those intellectual and immaterial beings, whom God makes use of as his ministers to execute the orders of providence*, Rev. 22. 8. [2] *To Christ, who is the Mediator and Head of the church*, Zech. 1. 12. Rev. 10. 1. [3] *To ministers of the gospel, who are ambassadors for Christ*, Rev. 2. 1. | 3. 1, 7. [4] *To such whom God employs to execute his judgments*, Rev. 15. 8. | 16. 1. [5] *To devils*, Mat. 25. 41. 1 Cor. 6. 3.
Gen. 22. 11. a. of the Lord said, Abraham, Abraham
24. 7. he shall send his a. before thee, 40.
48. 16. the a. who redeemed me from all evil.
Exod. 23. 20. send a. before thee, 23. | 32. 34. | 33. 2.
Num. 20. 16. sent an a. and brought us out of Egypt
Judg. 13. 19. and the a. did wondrously
2 Sam. 24. 16. the a. stretched out his hand, the a. that destroyed the people, 1 Chron. 21. 15.
17. David spake when he saw the a. that smote
1 Kings 13. 18. a. spake to me by the word of Lord
19. 5. an a. touched Elijah and said arise and eat
1 Chr. 21. 15. God sent an a. to Jerusalem to destroy
20. and Ornan turned back, and saw the a.
27. the Lord commanded the a. and he put up
2 Chron. 32. 21. the Lord sent an a. which cut off
Eccl. 5. 6. nor say before the a. it was an error
Isa. 63. 9. the a. of his presence saved them
Dan. 3. 28. God who hath sent a. and delivered
6. 22. my God hath sent his a. and shut up
Hos. 12. 4. yea, he had power over the a.
Zech. 1. 9. the a. that talked with me said, 4. 5.
13. Lord answered the a. that talked with me
14. the a. that communed with me said
19. I said to the a. that talked, 4. 4. | 5. 10. | 6. 4.
2. 3. the a. that talked went out, and another a.
3. 3. with filthy garments, and stood before the a.
5. 5. the a. that talked with me, went forth
6. 5. the a. answered, these are the four spirits
Mat. 28. 5. the a. answered the woman, fear not
Luke 1. 13. the a. said, fear not, Zacharias
19. the a. answered and said, I am Gabriel
26. in the sixth month the a. Gabriel was sent
30. the a. said to her, fear not, Mary
35. a. answered, Holy Ghost shall come on thee
2. 10. the a. said to the shepherds, fear not
13. suddenly there was with the a. a multitude
21. so named of the a. before he was conceived
22. 43. there appeared an a. strengthening him
John 5. 4. an a. went down at a certain season
12. 29. others said, an a. spake to him
Acts 6. 15. as it had been the face of an a.
7. 35. by hands of the a. that appeared in the bush
38. in the wilderness with the a. which spake
10. 7. when the a. which spake to Cornelius
22. was warned from God by an holy a. to send
11. 13. how he had seen an a. in his house
12. 8. the a. said to Peter, bind on thy sandals
9. that it was true which was done by the a.
10. and forthwith the a. departed from him
11. the Lord hath sent his a. and delivered me
15. Rhoda affirmed, then said they, it is his a.
23. 8. the Sadducees say, neither a. nor spirit
9. if a spirit or an a. hath spoken to him
2 Cor. 11. 14. is transformed into an a. of light
Gal. 1. 8. though we or an a. from heaven preach
Rev. 1. 1. and he signified it by his a. to John
2. 1. unto the a. of the church, 8. 12, 18. | 3. 1, 7, 14.
5. 2. I saw a strong a. proclaiming with loud voice
7. 2. I saw another a. ascending from the east
8. 3. and another a. came and stood at the altar
4. ascended before God out of the a. hand
5. the a. took the censer, and filled it with fire
7. the first a. sounded | 8. second a. | 10. third a.
12. fourth a. | 9. 1. fifth a. | 13. sixth a. sounded
8. 13. I heard an a. flying through midst of heaven
9. 11. which is the a. of the bottomless pit
14. saying to the sixth a. loose the four angels
10. 1. I saw another a. come down, 18. 1. | 20. 1.
5. and the a. which I saw stand on the sea
7. but in the days of the voice of the seventh a.
8. go and take the book in the hand of the a.
10. I took the book || 11. 1. and the a. stood, saying
11. 15. seventh a. sounded, and there were voices
14. 6. I saw another a. fly in the midst of heaven
8. another a. followed, saying, Babylon is
9. third a. followed || 15. another a. came, 17. 18.
19. and the a. thrust in his sickle in the earth
16. 2. a. poured out his vial, 3, 4, 8, 10, 12, 17.
5. and I heard the a. of the waters say
17. 7. the a. said, wherefore didst thou marvel?
18. 21. and mighty a. took up a stone like a great
19. 17. and I saw an a. standing in the sun
21. 17. the measure of a man, that is of the a.
22. 8. fell down to worship before the feet of a.
16. I Jesus have sent mine a. to testify to you

ANGEL *of God.*

Exod. 14. 19. a. of God who went before removed
Judg. 13. 6. like the countenance of an a. of God
1 Sam. 29. 9. art good in my sight, as an a. of God
2 Sam. 14. 17. as an a. of God, so is my lord, 19. 27
20. wise according to the wisdom of an a. of God
Acts 27. 23. stood by me this night the a. of God
Gal. 4. 14. but received me as an a. of God

ANGEL *of the Lord.*

Gen. 16. 7. a. of the L. found Hagar by a fountain
9. the a. of the Lord said to her, 10. 11. | 22. 11.
Num. 22. 32, 35. Judg. 13. 18. 2 Kings 1. 3, 15.
22. 11. a. of the L. called to him out of heaven, 15.
Num. 22. 23. ass saw the a. of the L. standing, 25. 27.
24. a. of the L. stood in a path of the vineyards, 26.
31. Balaam saw a. of the L. standing in the way
34. and Balaam said to a. of the L. I have sinned
35. a. of the L. said to Balaam, go with the men
Judg. 2. 1. a. of the L. came up, 1 Kings 19. 7. Acts 12. 7.
4. when a. of the L. spake these words to Israel
5. 23. curse ye Meroz, said the a. of the Lord
6. 11. came an a. of the L. and sat under an oak
12. a. of L. appeared to Gideon, and said to him
21. the a. of the L. put forth the end of the staff
22. when Gideon perceived he was an a. of the L.
13. 3. a. of the L. appeared to the woman, and said
16. Manoah knew not he was an a. of the L., 21.
20. a. of the L. ascended in the flame of the altar
2 Sam. 24. 16. a. of the L. was by threshing, 1 Ch. 21. 15.
2 Kings 19. 35. a. of L. smote in camp, Isa. 37. 36.
1 Chron. 21. 12. a. of L. destroying throughout coasts
18. a. of the L. commanded Gad to say to David
30. afraid, because of the sword of a. of the Lord
Psal. 34. 7. a. of L. encampeth round them that fear
35. 5. let a. of L. chase them || 6. persecute them
Zech. 1. 11. they answered the a. of the L. that stood
12. a. of L. answered, wilt thou not have mercy
3. 5. a. of L. stood by Joshua || 6. a. of L. protested
12. 8. house of David as the a. of L. before them
Mat. 1. 20. a. of L. appeared in a dream, 2. 13, 19.
24. Joseph did as the a. of the L. had bidden him
28. 2. for the a. of the L. descended from heaven
Luke 1. 11. there appeared to Zacharias an a. of L.
2. 9. a. of L. came upon them, and glory of Lord
Acts 5. 19. a. of L. by night opened the prison-doors
8. 26. a. of the Lord spake to Philip, saying, arise
12. 23. a. of L. smote Herod, because he gave not

ANGELS.
Gen. 19. 1. there came two a. to Sodom at even
15. when the morning arose, the a. hastened Lot
Psal. 8. 5. a little lower than the a. Heb. 2. 7, 9.
68. 17. the chariots of God are thousands of a.
78. 25. man did eat a. food, he sent them meat
49. and trouble, by sending evil a. among them
Mat. 4. 11. a. came and ministered to, Mark 1. 13.
13. 39. end of the world, the reapers are the a.
49. the a. shall come forth and sever the wicked
18. 10. their a. always behold the face of God
24. 36. no man, not the a. in heaven, Mark 13. 32.
25. 31. Son of man, and all the holy a. with him
26. 53. give me more than twelve legions of a.
Mark 8. 38. when the Son of man cometh in the glory of his Father, with the holy a. Luke 9. 26.
12. 25. nor marry, but are as the a. in heaven
Luke 2. 15. as the a. were gone away from them
16. 22. the beggar died, and was carried by the a.
20. 36. nor die, for they are equal unto the a.
24. 23. that they had also seen a vision of a.
John 20. 12. and seeth two a. in white, sitting
Acts 7. 53. who received the law by disposition of a.
Rom. 8. 38. nor life, nor a. able to separate us from
1 Cor. 4. 9. a spectacle to the world, to a. and men
6. 3. know ye not that we shall judge a.?
11. 10. to have power on her head, because of the a.
13. 1. though I speak with tongues of men and a.
Gal. 3. 19. it was rdained by a. in the hand
Col. 2. 18. no man beguile you in worshipping of a.
2 Thess. 1. 7. revealed from heaven with mighty a.
1 Tim. 3. 16. seen of a. preached to the Gentiles
5. 21. I charge thee before God and the elect a.
Heb. 1. 4. being made so much better than the a.
5. to which of the a. said he at any time, 13.
7. of the a. he saith, who maketh his a. spirits
2. 2. if the word spoken by a. was stedfast
5. to the a. hath he not put in subjection
16. he took not on him the nature of a. but seed
12. 22. and to an innumerable company of a.
13. 2. for some have entertained a. unawares
1 Pet. 1. 12. which things the a. desire to look into
3. 22. a. and powers being made subject to him
2 Pet. 2. 4. if God spared not the a. that sinned
11. whereas a. greater in power and might
Jude 6. the a. who kept not their first estate
Rev. 1. 20. seven stars a. of the seven churches
5. 11. the voice of many a. about the throne
7. 1. I saw four a. standing on the four corners
2. and he cried with a loud voice to the four a.
11. all the a. stood round about the throne
8. 13. trumpet of the three a. which are yet to sound
9. 14. loose the four a. which are bound in the river
15. the a. were loosed, which were prepared
14. 10. be tormented in presence of the holy a.
21. 12. twelve gates, and at the gates twelve a.

ANGELS of God.
Gen. 28. 12. a. of God ascend and descend, John 1. 51.
32. 1. Jacob went his way, and a. of God m t him
Mat. 22. 30. but as a. of God in heaven, Mark 12. 25.
Luke 12. 8. him shall the Son confess before a. of God
9. denieth me, shall be denied before the a. of God
15. 10. there is joy in the presence of the a. of God
Heb. 1. 6. let all the a. of God worship him

His ANGELS.
Job 4. 18. and his a. he charged with folly
Psal. 91. 11. give his a. charge, Mat. 4. 6. Luke 4. 10.
103. 20. ye his a. which excel in strength
104. 4. who maketh his a. spirits, Heb. 1. 7.
148. 2. praise ye him all his a. praise ye him
Mat. 13. 41. the Son of man shall send forth his a.
16. 27. come in the glory of his Father with his a.
24. 31. send his a. with a great sound, Mark 13. 27.
25. 41. fire prepared for the devil and his a.
Rev. 3. 5. will confess before my Father and his a.
12. 7. Michael and his a. the dragon and his a.
9. the great dragon was cast out, and his a.

ANGER, Verb.
Rom. 10. 19. by a foolish nation I will a. you

ANGER.
Gen. 27. 45. till thy brother's a. turn away
44. 18. and let not thine a. burn against me
45. † 5. neither let there be a. in your eyes
49. 7. cursed be their a. for it was fierce
Exod. 32. 19. saw the dancing, Moses' a. waxed hot
22. Aaron said, let not the a. of my lord wax hot
Deut. 9. 19. I was afraid of the a. and displeasure
13. 17. Lord may turn from the fierceness of his a.
29. 24. what meaneth the heat of this great a.?
Josh. 7. 26. Lord turned from the fierceness of his a.
Judg. 8. 3. then their a. was abated toward him
Esth. 1. 12. Ahasuerus his a. burned in him
Job 4. † 9. by his a. are they consumed
9. 13. if God will not withdraw his a. the proud
Psal. 21. 9. as a fiery oven in the time of thine a.
30. 5. for his a. endureth but a moment
37. 8. cease from a. and forsake wrath, fret not
38. 3. no soundness in my flesh because of thine a.
69. 24. let thy wrathful a. take hold of them
74. 1. why doth thy a. smoke against the sheep
78. 21. and a. also came up against Israel
38. many a time turned he his a. away
49. he cast on them the fierceness of his a.
50. he made a way to his a. he spared them not
85. 3. hast turned from the fierceness of thine a.
4. and cause thine a. towards us to cease
5. wilt thou draw out thine a. to all generations?
90. 7. for we are consumed by thine a.
11. who knoweth the power of thine a.?
103. 9. nor will he keep his a. for ever, Jer. 3. 5.
Prov. 15. 1. but grievous words stir up a.
19. 11. the discretion of a man deferreth his a.
21. 14. a gift in secret pacifieth a.
22. 8. and the rod of his a. shall fail
27. 4. wrath is cruel, and a. is outrageous
Eccl. 7. 9. a. resteth in the bosom of fools
11. † 10. therefore remove a. from thy heart
Isa. 5. 25. for all this his a. is not turned away, 9. 12, 17, 21. | 10. 4.
7. 4. fear not for the a. of Resin with Syria
10. 5. O Assyrian, the rod of mine a. and staff
25. shall cease, and my a. in their destruction
Isa. 12. 1. though thou wast angry, thine a. is turned
13. 9. the day of the Lord cometh with fierce a.
13. and in the day of his fierce a. Lam. 1. 12.
30. 27. name of the Lord cometh burning with a.
30. the Lord shall show the indignation of his a.
42. 25. therefore he poured on him fury of his a.
48. 9. for my name's sake will I defer mine a.
65. † 5. these are a smoke in mine a.
66. 15. Lord will come to render his a. with fury
Jer. 2. 35. surely his a. shall turn from me
3. 12. I will not cause mine a. to fall on you, I am merciful, and I will not keep mine a. for ever
4. 26. all the cities were broken down by his a.
7. 20. mine a. shall be poured on this place
18. 23. deal with them in the time of thine a.
25. 38. the land is desolate because of his a.
32. 31. city hath been as a provocation of mine a.
36. 7. great is the a. the Lord hath pronounced
42. 18. as mine a. hath been poured on Jerusalem
44. 6. wherefore mine a. was poured forth
49. 37. I will bring evil on them, my fierce a.
Lam. 2. 1. remembered not his footstool in day of a.
6. Lord hath despised in the indignation of his a.
21. thou hast slain them in the day of thine a.
22. in the day of the Lord's a. none escaped
3. 43. thou hast covered with a. and persecuted us
4. 11. he hath poured out his fierce a.
Ezek. 5. 13. thus shall mine a. be accomplished
7. 3. and I will send mine a. upon thee
8. and accomplish mine a. on thee, 20. 8, 21.
25. 14. shall do in Edom, according to mine a.
35. 11. I will even do according to thine a.
Dan. 9. 16. let thine a. be turned away
Hos. 11. 9. will not execute the fierceness of mine a.
14. 4. for mine a. is turned away from him
Amos 1. 11. his a. did tear perpetually, and kept
Jonah 3. 9. if God will turn from his fierce a.
Mic. 7. 18. he retained not his a. for ever
Nah. 1. 6. who can abide the fierceness of his a.?
Hab. 3. 8. was thine a. against the rivers?
Zeph. 3. 8. to pour upon them all my fierce a.
Mark 3. 5. when he had looked on them with a.
Eph. 4. 31. let all a. be put away, Col. 3. 8.

ANGER of the Lord.
Num. 25. 4. fierce a. of the Lord may be turned
32. 14. to augment the a. of the Lord against Israel
Deut. 29. 20. the a. of the Lord shall smoke against
Judg. 2. 14. a. of the Lord against Isr. 20. | 3. 8. | 10. 7.
2 Kings 24. 20. thro' the a. of the Lord it came to pass, Jer. 52. 3.
Jer. 4. 8. the fierce a. of the Lord is not turned away
12. 13. because of the fierce a. of the Lord, 25. 37.
23. 20. the a. of the Lord shall not return, 30. 24.
51. 45. deliver his soul from the fierce a. of the L.
Lam. 4. 16. the a. of the Lord hath divided them
Zeph. 2. 2. before the fierce a. of the L. come on you
3. it may be ye shall be hid in the day of a. of L.

In ANGER.
Gen. 49. 6. for in their a. they slew a man
Exod. 11. 8. he went out from Pharaoh in a.
Deut. 29. 23. which the Lord overthrew in a.
28. the Lord rooted them out of the land in a.
1 Sam. 20. 34. Jonathan rose from the table in a.
2 Chron. 25. 10. they returned home in great a.
Job 9. 5. which overturneth them in his a.
18. 4. he teareth himself in his a.
21. 17. God distributeth sorrows in his a.
35. 15. because it is not so, he hath visited in his a.
Psal. 6. 1. Lord, rebuke me not in thy a. Jer. 10. 24.
7. 6. arise, O Lord, in thine a. lift up thyself
27. 9. put not thy servant away in a.
56. 7. in thine a. cast down the people, O Lord
77. 9. hath he in a. shut up his tender mercies?
Isa. 13. 3. I have also called my mighty ones in a.
14. 6. he that ruled the nations in a.
63. 3. for I will tread them in mine a. 6.
Jer. 21. 5. I will fight against you, even in a.
32. 37. whither I have driven them in mine a.
33. 5. whom I have slain in mine a. and in my fury
Lam. 2. 1. Lord covered Zion with a cloud in his a.
3. he hath cut off in a. all the horn of Israel
3. 66. persecute and destroy them in a.
Ezek. 3. † 14. and I went in hot a.
5. 15. when I shall execute judgments in thee in a.
13. 13. shall be an overflowing shower in mine a.
22. 20. so will I gather you in mine a. and fury
43. 8. wherefore I have consumed them in mine a.
Dan. 11. 20. be destroyed, neither in a. nor in battle
Hos. 13. 11. I gave thee a king in mine a.
Mic. 5. 15. and I will execute vengeance in a.
Hab. 3. 12. thou didst thresh the heathen in a.

ANGER kindled.
Gen. 30. 2. a. of Jacob was kindled against Rachel
Exod. 4. 14. the a. of the Lord was k. against Moses
Num. 11. 1. a. of the L. was k. 10. | 12. 9. | 22. 22.
22. 27. Balaam's a. was k. and he smote the ass
24. 10. Balak's a. was kindled against Balaam
25. 3. the a. of the Lord was kindled against Israel
32. 13. Josh. 7. 1. 2 Sam. 24. 1. 2 Kings 13. 3.
32. 10. the Lord's a. was kindled the same time
Deut. 6. 15. lest the a. of the Lord be k. against thee
7. 4. so will the a. of the Lord be k. against you
29. 27. the a. of the Lord was k. against this land
31. 17. mine a. shall be kindled in that day. Josh. 23. 16.
32. 22. for a fire is kindled in mine a. Jer. 15. 14.
Judg. 9. 30. Zebul's a. was kindled against Gaal
14. 19. Samson's a. k. and he went up to his father's
1 Sam. 11. 6. when Saul heard, his a. was k. greatly
17. 28. Eliab's a. was k. against David, and he said
20. 30. Saul's a. was kindled against Jonathan
2 Sam. 6. 7. a. of L. k. against Uzziah, 1 Chr. 13. 10.
12. 5. David's a. was kindled against the man
2 Kings 23. 26. the wrath wherewith his a. was k.
2 Chron. 25. 10. their a. was kindled against Judah
15. a. of the Lord was kindled against Amaziah
Isa. 5. 25. the a. of the Lord k. against his people
Jer. 17. 4. for ye have kindled a fire in mine a.
Hos. 8. 5. mine a. is kindl. against them, how long
Zech. 10. 3. mine a. was kindl. against the shepherds

Provoke or Provoked to ANGER.
Deut. 4. 25. to provoke him to a. 9. 18. | 31. 29.
2 Kings 17. 17. | 21. 6. | 23. 19. 2 Chr. 33. 6.
32. 16. with abominations provoked they him to a.
21. they have pr. me to a. I will pr. them to a.
Judg. 2. 12. they bowed to them, and pr. the L. to a.
1 Kings 14. 9. made molten images to pr. to a. 15. 30.
15. made their groves pr. the Lord to a. 16. 7, 13.
16. 2. to pr. me to a. with their sins, 2 Kings 17. 11. Jer. 11. 17. | 32. 29, 32. Ezek. 16. 26.
33. Ahab did more to pr. the Lord to a. than all
21. 22. wherewith thou hast provoked me to a.
22. 53. Ahaz pr. to a. the Lord God of Israel
2 Kings 21. 15. they have provoked me to a. since the day
22. 17. forsaken me, that they might provoke me to a. 2 Chron. 34. 25. Jer. 25. 7.
2 Chron. 28. 25. pr. to a. the L. God of his fathers
Neh. 4. 5. have pr. thee to a. before the builders
Psal. 78. 58. pr. him to a. with high places, 106. 29.
Prov. 20. 2. whoso pr. him to a. sinneth against
Isa. 1. 4. they have pr. the Holy One of Israel to a.
65. 3. a people that provoke me to a. continually
Jer. 7. 18. that they may provoke me to a. [pr. to a.
19. do they pr. me to a. ‖ 8. 19. why have they
25. 6. pr. me not to a. ‖ 32. 30. Israel have pr. me to a.
44. 3. their wickedness to pr. me to a. Ezek. 8. 17.
Ezek. 32. † 9. I will provoke to a. the hearts of many
Hos. 12. 14. Ephraim provoked him to a. bitterly
Col. 3. 21. fathers, provoke not your children to a.

Slow to ANGER.
Neh. 9. 17. art a God ready to pardon, slow to a.
Psal. 103. 8. slow to a. plenteous in mercy, 145. 8.
Prov. 15. 18. he that is slow to a. appeaseth strife
16. 32. he that is slow to a. better than the mighty
Joel 2. 13. slow to a. of great kindness, Jonah 4. 2.
Nah. 1. 3. the Lord is slow to a. great in power

ANGERED.
1 Sam. 1. † 6. and her adversary also a. her sore
Psal. 106. 32. they a. him at the waters of strife

ANGLE.
Isa. 19. 8. and all they that cast a. shall lament
Hab. 1. 15. they take up all of them with the a.

ANGRY.
Gen 18. 30. let not the Lord be a. I'll speak, 32.
45. 5. be not a. with yourselves that ye sold me
Lev. 10. 16. and Moses was a. with Eleazar and
Deut. 1. 37. the Lord was a. with me for you, 4. 21.
9. 8. Lord was a. with you to have destroyed you
20. the Lord was very a. with Aaron, I prayed
Judg. 18. 25. lest a. fellows run upon thee
2 Sam. 19. 42. wherefore be ye a. for this matter
1 Kings 8. 46. and thou be a. with them, 2 Ch. 6. 36.
11. 9. and the Lord was a. with Solomon, because
2 Kings 17. 18. therefore the L. was a. with Israel
Ezra 9. 14. wouldst thou not be a. with us till thou
Neh. 5. 6. I was very a. when I heard their cry
Psal. 2. 12. kiss the Son, lest he be a. and ye perish
7. 11. God is a. with the wicked every day
76. 7. who may stand when once thou art a.?
79. 5. how long wilt thou be a.? 80. 4. | 85. 5.
Prov. 14. 17. he that is soon a. dealeth foolishly
21. 19. dwell in wilderness, than with an a. woman
22. 24. make no friendship with an a. man
25. 23. so doth an a. countenance, a backbiting
29. 22. a. man stirreth up strife, and a furious man
Eccl. 5. 6. wherefore should God be a. at thy voice?
7. 9. be not hasty in thy spirit to be a.
Cant. 1. 6. my mother's children were a. with me
Isa. 12. 1. though thou wast a. with me, thine anger
Ezek. 16. 42. I will be quiet, and will be no more a.
Dan. 2. 12. for this cause the kin was a.
Jonah 4. 1. it displeased Jonah, and he was very a.
4. the Lord said, doest thou well to be a.? 9.
9. he said, I do well to be a. even unto death
Mat. 5. 22. whosoever is a. with his brother
Luke 14. 21. the master of the house being a.
15. 28. and he was a. and would not go in
John 7. 23. are ye a. at me because I have made
Eph. 4. 26. be a. and sin not, let not the sun go down
Tit. 1. 7. a bishop must be blameless, not soon a.
Rev. 11. 18. the nations were a. thy wrath is come

ANGUISH.
Gen. 42. 21. guilty, in that we saw the a. of his soul
Exod. 6. 9. but they hearkened not to Moses for a.
Deut. 2. 25. tremble, and be in a. because of thee
2 Sam. 1. 9. slay me, for a. is come upon me
Job 7. 11. I will speak in the a. of my spirit
15. 24. trouble and a. shall make him afraid
Psal. 119. 143. trouble and a. have taken hold on me
Prov. 1. 27. when distress and a. come upon you
Isa. 8. 22. look to the earth, and behold dimness of a.
30. 6. into the land of trouble and a. from whence
Jer. 4. 31. the a. as of her that bringeth forth child
6. 24. a. hath taken hold of us, 49. 24. | 50. 43.
John 16. 21. she remembereth no more her a. for joy
Rom. 2. 9. tribulation and a. upon every soul of man
2 Cor. 2. 4. for out of much a. of heart I wrote to you

ANISE.
Mat. 23. 23. ye pay tithe of mint, a. and cummin

ANOINT
Signifies, [1] *To pour oil upon*, Gen. 28. 18. | 31. 13. [2] *To consecrate and set one apart to an office; anointing being generally practised among the Jews on that occasion, to denote the person's being endued with the gifts and graces of the Spirit*, Exod. 28. 41. [3] *To use spiritual means to get saving knowledge*, Rev. 3. 18. [4] *To smear, or daub*, John 9. 6, 11. [5] *One particularly designed and chosen by God to be the King, Priest, and Prophet of his church, namely, Christ Jesus, who was filled with the Holy Ghost in an extraordinary manner, and thereby consecrated and authorised to be the Messiah*, Psal. 2. 2. | 45. 7. Acts 4. 27. [6] *A king*, Lam. 4. 20.

Touch not mine anointed, Psal. 105. 15. *Hurt not the people consecrated to myself by the gifts and graces of my Spirit, nor those especially among them to whom I familiarly reveal my mind and will, that they may teach others.*

Thou anointest my head with oil, Psal. 23. 5. *Thou bestowest upon me the consolations of thy Spirit.*

The anointing, 1 John 2. 27. *The Spirit of illumination; great knowledge in heavenly things*

Exod. 28. 41. shalt *a.* and consecrate, 30. 30. | 40. 15.
29. 7. take anointing oil and *a.* him, 40. 13.
36. thou shalt *a.* the altar to sanctify it, 40. 10.
30. 26. thou shalt *a.* the tabernacle, 40. 9.
40. 11. thou shalt *a.* the laver and his foot
Lev. 16. 32. and the priest whom he shall *a.*
Deut. 28. 40. but thou shalt not *a.* thyself with oil
Judg. 9. 8. the trees went to *a.* a king over them
15. if in truth ye *a.* me king over you
Ruth 3. 3. wash thyself therefore and *a.* thee
1 Sam. 9. 16. shalt *a.* him to be captain over Israel
15. 1. the Lord sent me to *a.* thee king over Israel
16. 3. thou shalt *a.* him whom I name unto thee
12. the Lord said, arise, *a.* him, this is he
2 Sam. 14. 2. *a.* not thyself with oil, but be as
1 Kings 1. 34. let Zadok *a.* him king over Israel
19. 15. *a.* Hazael king || 16. *a.* Jehu, *a.* Elisha
Isa. 21. 5. arise ye princes, and *a.* the shield
Dan. 9. 24. seal up the vision, and *a.* the most Holy
10. 3. neither did I *a.* myself at all, till weeks
Amos 6. 6. *a.* themselves with the chief ointments
Mic. 6. 15. shalt tread the olives, but not *a.* thee
Mat. 6. 17. when thou fastest *a.* thine head
Mark 14. 8. she is come to *a.* my body to the burying
16. 1. had bought spices that they might *a.* him
Luke 7. 46. my head with oil thou didst not *a.*
Rev. 3. 18. and *a.* thine eyes with eye-salve

ANOINTED.

Exod. 29. 29. garm. be Aaron's sons after him, to *a.*
Lev. 4. 3. if the priest that is *a.* do sin according to
6. 20. the offering of Aaron, when he is *a.*
7. 36. in the day that he *a.* them, by a statute
8. 10. *a.* the tabernacle || 11. *a.* the altar, *Num.* 7. 1.
12. Moses poured oil on Aaron's head, and *a.* him
Num. 3. 3. names of the sons of Aaron which were *a.*
7. 10. the princes offered after it was *a.* 84, 88.
1 Sam. 10. 1. the Lord *a.* thee captain || 15. 17. *a.* Saul
16. 13. *a.* David, 2 *Sam.* 2. 4, 7. | 5. 3, 17. | 12. 7.
2 *Kings* 9. 3, 6, 12. 1 *Chron.* 11. 3. | 14. 8.
2 Sam. 2. 7. the house of Judah have *a.* me king
3. 39. I am this day weak, though *a.* king
12. 20. David arose from the earth, and *a.* himself
23. 1. David the *a.* of the God of Jacob said
Psal. 2. † 6. yet have I *a.* my king on Zion
Isa. 61. 1. the Lord hath *a.* me to preach, *Luke* 4. 18.
Ezek. 28. 14. thou art the *a.* cherub that covers
Luke 7. 38. she kissed his feet and *a.* them
46. but this woman hath *a.* my feet with ointment
John 1. † 41. we found the Messiah, which is the *a.*
9. 6. he *a.* the eyes of the blind man with clay
11. Jesus made clay, and *a.* mine eyes
11. 2. it was that Mary which *a.* the Lord
12. 3. then took Mary ointment and *a.* feet of Jesus
Acts 4. 27. holy child Jesus, whom thou hast *a.*
10. 38. how God *a.* Jesus of Nazareth with holy
2 Cor. 1. 21. he which hath *a.* us is God

ANOINTED *Ones.*

Zech. 4. 14. these are the two *a. ones* which stand

His ANOINTED.

1 Sam. 2. 10. give strength, and exalt horn of *his a.*
12. 3. witness against me before the Lord and *his a.*
5. the Lord and *his a.* is witness this day
2 Sam. 22. 51. sheweth mercy to *his a.* *Psal.* 18. 50.
Psal. 2. 2. against the Lord, and against *his a.*
20. 6. now know I that the Lord saveth *his a.*
28. 8. and he is the saving strength of *his a.*
Isa. 45. 1. thus saith the Lord to *his a.* to Cyrus

Lord's ANOINTED.

1 Sam. 16. 6. surely the *Lord's a.* is before him
24. 6. I should do this to my master, the *Lord's a.*
10. put my hand against my lord, for he is *L. a.*
26. 9. stretch his hand against *L. a.* and be guiltless
16. to die, because ye have not kept the *Lord's a.*
2 Sam. 1. 14. wast thou not afraid to destroy the *L. a.?*
19. 21. put to death because he cursed the *L. a.*
Lam. 4. 20. the *a. of Lord* was taken in their pits

Mine ANOINTED.

1 Sam. 2. 35. he shall walk before *mine a.* for ever
1 Chron. 16. 22. touch not *mine a.* *Psal.* 105. 15.
Psal. 132. 17. I have ordained a lamp for *mine a.*

ANOINTED *with Oil.*

Num. 35. 25. death of high priest *a. with* holy *oil*
2 Sam. 1. 21. as though he had not been *a. with oil*
Psal. 45. 7. God *a.* thee *with oil* of gladness, *Heb.* 1. 9.
89. 20. *with* my holy *oil* have I *a.* him
92. 10. my horn exalt, I shall be *a. with* fresh *oil*

Thine ANOINTED.

2 Chron. 6. 42. O Lord God, turn not away the face of *thine a.* *Psal.* 132. 10.
Psal. 84. 9. behold, O God, look on face of *thine a.*
89. 38. thou hast been wroth with *thine a.*
51. they have reproached the footsteps of *thine a.*
Hab. 3. 13. wentest even for salvation with *thine a.*

ANOINTEDST.

Gen. 31. 13. I am the God of Beth-el where thou *a.*
Psal. 23. 5. *a.* my head with oil, my cup runneth

ANOINTING.

Exod. 40. 15. their *a.* be an everlasting priesthood
Isa. 10. 27. yoke shall be destroyed because of the *a.*
1 John 2. 27. but the *a.* which ye have received of him, as the same *a.* teacheth you all things

ANOINTING *Oil.*

Exod. 37. 29. he made the holy *a. oil* and pure in- [cense
Lev. 8. 12. he poured of the *a. oil* on Aaron's head
10. 7. for the *a. oil* of the Lord is upon you
21. 10. on whose head the *a. oil* was poured
Num. 4. 16. to the office of Eleazar pertaineth *a. oil*
Jam. 5. 14. *a.* him with *oil* in the name of the Lord

ANON.

Mat. 13. 20. heareth, and *a.* with joy receiveth it
Mark 1. 30. mother lay sick, and *a.* they tell him of [her

ANOTHER.

Gen. 4. 25. appointed me *a.* seed instead of Abel
30. 24. the Lord shall add to me *a.* son
43. 7. the man asked us, have ye *a.* brother?
Exod. 22. 9. lost thing, which *a.* challengeth to be his
Lev. 18. † 18. thou shalt not take one wife to *a.*
Num. 14. 24. Caleb, because he had *a.* spirit
Judg. 2. 10. *a.* generation that knew not the Lord
16. 7. then shall I be weak, and be as *a.* man
1 Sam. 10. 6. and shalt be turned into *a.* man
9. and it was so, that God gave him *a.* heart

2 Chron. 20. † 22. and they smote one *a.*
Esth. 1. 19. let the king give her royal estate to *a.*
Job 19. 27. whom mine eyes shall behold and not *a.*
Psal. 109. 8. let *a.* take his office, *Acts* 1. 20.
Prov. 25. 9. and discover not a secret to *a.*
27. 2. let *a.* praise thee, and not thy own mouth
Isa. 42. 8. my glory will I not give to *a.* 48. 11.
44. 5. *a.* shall call himself by the name of Jacob
57. 8. thou hast discovered thyself to *a.* than me
65. 15. and shall call his servants by *a.* name
66. † 17. and purify themselves one after *a.*
Hos. 3. 3. and thou shalt not be for *a.* man.
4. 4. yet let no man strive nor reprove *a.*
Mat. 11. 3. art thou he, or do we look for *a.?*
Mark 14. 19. began to say, is it I? *a.* said, is it I?
Luke 16. 7. then said he to *a.* how much owest thou?
12. if not faithful in that which is *a.* man's
2 Cor. 11. 4. *a.* Jesus, *a.* Spirit, or *a.* gospel
Gal. 1. 7. which is not *a.* but there be some
6. 4. then have rejoicing in himself, and not in *a.*
1 Tim. 6. † 5. gallings one of *a.* destitute of the truth
Heb. 3. 13. exhort one *a.* while called to day 10. 25.
4. 8. he would not have spoken of *a.* day

One ANOTHER, *see* LOVE

One against ANOTHER

1 Sam. 2. 25. if *one* man sin *against a.* the judge shall
Jer. 13. 14. I will dash them *one against a.*
1 Cor. 4. 6. no one of you be puffed up *one against a.*
Jam. 5. 9. grudge not *one against a.* brethren

One for ANOTHER.

1 Cor. 11. 33. when ye come to eat, tarry *one for a.*
12. 25. members should have same care *one for a.*
Jam. 5. 16. pray *one for a.* that ye may be healed.

ANSWER

Signifies, [1] *To reply to a question,* Prov. 26. 4. [2] *To begin to speak, when no question is asked,* Dan. 2. 26. Acts 5. 8. [3] *To witness,* Gen. 30. 33. [4] *To obey,* Isa. 65. 12. Jer. 7. 13. [5] *To grant what one desires in prayer,* Psal. 27. 7. | 86. 7. Isa. 65. 24. [6] *To give account,* Job 9. 3. | 40. 2. [7] *To punish,* Ezek. 14. 7.

Gen. 41. 16. God shall give Pharaoh an *a.* of peace
Deut. 20. 11. if the city make thee an *a.* of peace
2 Sam. 24. 13. see what *a.* I shall return to him
Esth. 4. 15. Esther bade them return Mordecai this *a.*
Job 19. 16. I called my servant, and he gave me no *a.*
32. 3. because they had found no *a.* and condemned
35. 12. there they cry, but none giveth *a.*
Prov. 15. 1. a soft *a.* turneth away wrath
23. a man hath joy by the *a.* of his mouth
16. 1. the *a.* of the tongue is from the Lord
24. 26. shall kiss his lips that giveth a right *a.*
Cant. 5. 6. I called him, but he gave me no *a.*
Mic. 3. 7. cover the lips, for there is no *a.* of God
Luke 20. 26. and they marvelled at his *a.*
John 1. 22. that we may give *a.* to them that sent us
19. 9. whence art thou? Jesus gave him no *a.*
Rom. 11. 4. but what saith the *a.* of God to him?
1 Cor. 9. 3. mine *a.* to them that do examine me is
2 Cor. 1. † 9. but we had the *a.* of death in ourselves
2 Tim. 4. 16. at my first *a.* none stood with me
1 Pet. 3. 15. and be ready to give an *a.* to every
21. but the *a.* of a good conscience towards God

ANSWERS.

Job 21. 34. seeing in your *a.* remaineth falsehood
34. 36. because of his *a.* for wicked men
Luke 2. 47. and all were astonished at his *a.*

ANSWER, *Verb.*

Gen. 30. 33. so shall my righteousness *a.* for me
Deut. 27. 15. all the people shall *a.* and say, amen
1 Kings 18. † 26. they called, saying, O Baal, *a.* us
29. there was neither voice, nor any to *a.*
Job 13. 22. call thou, and I will *a.* and *a.* thou me
23. 5. I would know the words that he would *a.* me
31. 14. when he visiteth, what shall I *a.* him?
33. 12. will *a.* thee, God is greater than man, 35. 4.
40. 2. he that reproveth God, let him *a.*
Psal. 27. 7. have mercy also on me, and *a.* me
65. 5. by terrible things in right, wilt thou *a.* us
86. 7. will call on thee, for thou wilt *a.* me, 38. † 15.
102. 2. in the day when I call *a.* me speedily
108. 6. save with thy right hand, and *a.* me
143. 1. O Lord, in thy faithfulness *a.* me
Prov. 15. 28. heart of the righteous studieth to *a.*
22. 21. that thou mightest *a.* the words of truth
26. 5. *a.* a fool according to his folly, lest he be
Isa. 14. 32. what shall one then *a.* the messengers
50. 2. when I called was there none to *a.?* 66. 4.
58. 9. then shalt thou call, and the Lord will *a.*
Dan. 3. 16. are not careful to *a.* thee in this matter
Joel 2. 19. yea the Lord will *a.* and say to his people
Hab. 2. 1. what I shall *a.* when I am reproved
Mat. 22. 46. no man was able to *a.* him a word
Mark 11. 30. was it from heaven or of men? *a.* me
14. 40. neither wist they what to *a.* him.
Luke 11. 7. and he from within shall *a.* and say
12. 11. how or what thing ye shall *a.* or say
13. 25. he shall *a.* I know you not whence you are
21. 14. not to meditate before what ye shall *a.*
2 Cor. 5. 12. that ye may have somewhat to *a.* them
Col. 4. 6. may know how ye ought to *a.* every man

I will ANSWER.

Job 13. 22. call, *I will a.* 14. 15. *Ps.* 91. 15. *Jer.* 33. 3.
Isa. 65. 24. come to pass, before they call *I will a.*
Ezek. 14. 4. *I* the Lord *will a.* him that cometh, 7.

Not ANSWER.

Gen. 45. 3. Joseph's brethren could *not a.* him
Exod. 23. † 2. shalt *not a.* in a cause to decline
2 Sam. 3. 11. he could *not a.* Abner a word
2 Kings 18. 36. king's command. was, *a. not.* *Isa.* [36. 21.
Job 9. 3. he cannot *a.* him one of a thousand
Prov. 1. 28. they shall call, but I will *not a.*
26. 4. *a. not* a fool according to his folly, lest thou
29. 19. for though he understand, he will *not a.*
Isa. 65. 12. because when I called, ye did *not a.*
Jer. 7. 27. thou shalt call, but they will *not a.* thee
Luke 14. 6. they could *not a.* him again to these
22. 68. if I ask you, you will *not a.* nor let me go

ANSWERABLE.

Exod. 38. 18. *a.* to the hangings of the court
Mat. 3. † 8. bring forth fruit *a.* to amendment

ANSWERED.

Judg. 8. 8. men of Penuel *a.* as the men of Succoth *a.*
1 Sam. 3. 4. the Lord called, and he *a.* here am I, 16.
18. 7. the women *a.* one another as they played
2 Sam. 19. 42. the men of Judah *a.* the men of Israel
1 Kings 2. 30. thus said Joab, and thus he *a.* me
12. 13. the king *a.* people roughly, 2 *Chron.* 10. 13.
18. 26. but there was no voice, nor any that *a.*
2 Chron. 25. 9. the man of God *a.* the Lord is able
Job 11. 2. should not the multitude of words be *a.?*
Ezek. 37. 3. I *a.* O Lord God, thou knowest
Dan. 2. 14. Daniel *a.* with counsel and wisdom
Mic. 6. 5. what Balaam the son of Beor *a.* him
Mat. 27. 12. when he was accused he *a.* nothing, 14.
Mark 14. 61. | 15. 3, 5. *Luke* 23. 9.
Mark 12. 28. perceiving that he had *a.* well
34. when Jesus saw that he *a.* discreetly
Acts 15. 13. after they held their peace, James *a.*
22. 8. I *a.* who art thou, Lord? and he said to me
25. 8. while he *a.* for himself, 26. 1.

ANSWERED, *meant of* GOD.

Gen. 35. 3. who *a.* me in the day of my distress
Exod. 19. 19. Moses spake, and God *a.* him by a voice
1 Sam. 7. † 9. Samuel cried, and the Lord *a.* him
2 Sam. 21. 1. and the Lord *a.* it is for Saul
1 Chron. 21. 26. he *a.* him from heaven by fire
28. when David saw that the Lord had *a.* him
Psal. 81. 7. I *a.* thee in the secret place of thunder
99. 6. they called on the Lord, and he *a.* them
118. 5. the Lord *a.* me, and set me in a large place
Isa. 6. 11. he *a.* till the cities be wasted without
Jer. 23. 35. what hath the Lord *a.* and spoken, 37.
Hab. 2. 2. the Lord *a.* me, write the vision
Zech. 1. 13. the Lord *a.* the angel that talked
Mat. 20. 13. he *a.* one of them and said, friend
25. 26. his lord *a.* and said, thou wicked servant

ANSWERED *not.*

1 Sam. 4. 20. she *a. not,* nor did she regard it
14. 37. but he *a.* him *not* that day, 28. 6.
2 Sam. 22. 42. looked, but *a.* them *not,* *Ps.* 18. 41.
1 Kings 18. 21. and the people *a.* him *not* a word,
2 *Kings* 18. 36. *Isa.* 36. 21.
Jer. 7. 13. and I called you, but ye *a. not,* 35. 17.
Mat. 15. 23. but he *a.* her *not* a word

ANSWERED *and said.*

Exod. 4. 1. Moses *a. and said,* they will not believe
2 Kings 7. 13. one of his servants *a. and said,* let some
Neh. 2. 20. then *a.* I them and said unto them
Job 3. † 2. Job *a. and s.* 6. 1. | 9. 1. | 12. 1. | 16. 1. | 19. 1.
Isa. 21. 9. he *a. and said,* Babylon is fallen, is fallen
Jer. 11. 5. then *a.* I *and said,* so be it, O Lord

ANSWEREDST.

Psal. 99. 8. thou *a.* them, O Lord our God, thou
138. 3. in the day when I cried thou *a.* me

ANSWEREST.

1 Sam. 26. 14. David cried, *a.* thou not, Abner?
Job 16. 3. what emboldeneth thee, that thou *a.?*
Mat. 26. 62. *a.* thou nothing? *Mark* 14. 60. | 15. 4.
John 18. 22. *a.* thou the high-priest so?
Rom. 9. † 20. who art thou that *a.* against God?

ANSWERETH.

1 Sam. 28. 15. God is departed and *a.* me no more
1 Kings 18. 24. let the God that *a.* by fire, be God
Job 12. 4. who calleth on God, and he *a.* him
Prov. 18. 13. that *a.* a matter before he heareth
23. the poor entreat, but the rich *a.* roughly
27. 19. as face *a.* to face, so the heart of man
Eccl. 5. 20. God *a.* him in the joy of his heart
10. 19. wine maketh merry, but money *a.* all things
Mal. 2. † 12. Lord will cut off him that waketh and *a.*
Gal. 4. 25. and *a.* to Jerusalem that now is

ANSWERING.

Luke 23. 40. but the other *a.* rebuked him
Tit. 2. 9. servants be obedient, not *a.* again

ANT, S.

Prov. 6. 6. go to the *a.* thou sluggard, consider
30. 25. the *a.* are a people not strong, yet prepare

ANTIQUITY.

Isa. 23. 7. joyous city, whose *a.* is of ancient days

ANVIL.

Isa. 41. 7. encouraged him that smote the *a.*

ANY.

Exod. 11. 7. against *a.* of the children of Israel
Lev. 4. 2. if a soul shall sin against *a.* of the commandments, 13, 22, 27. | 5. 17.
6. 3. lieth, in *a.* of all these that a man doth
Deut. 32. 39. nor *a.* that can deliver out of my hand
2 Sam. 7. 7. spake I a word with *a.* 1 *Chron.* 17. 6.
9. 1. is there yet *a.* left of the house of Saul?
1 Kings 18. 26. was no voice, nor *a.* that answered
Job 33. 27. he looketh, and if *a.* say, I have sinned
Psal. 4. 6. many say, who will show us *a.* good?
5. † 9. no faithfulness in the mouth of *a.* of them
Prov. 30. 30. a lion turneth not away for *a.*
Isa. 44. 8. there is no God, I know not *a.*
Amos 6. 10. he shall say, is there yet *a.* with thee?
Mark 8. 26. nor go nor tell it to *a.* in the town
11. 25. forgive, if ye have ought against *a.*
Luke 8. 43. had spent all, nor could be healed of *a.*
Acts 9. 2. if he found *a.* of this way, men or women
1 Cor. 6. 12. I will not be brought under power of *a.*
Jam. 1. 5. if *a.* lack wisdom, let him ask of God
2 Pet. 3. 9. not willing that *a.* should perish
2 John 10. if there come *a.* and bring not this doctrine
See FURTHER, GOD, MAN, MORE, THING, TIME, WISE. ANY *while, see* DEAD.

APACE, *see* FLEE, FLED.

APART.

Exod. 13. 12. shalt set *a.* all that open the matrix
Lev. 15. 19. she shall be put *a.* seven days
18. 19. thou shalt not approach, as long as she is *a.*
Neh. 12. † 47. set *a.* holy things to the Levites
Psal. 4. 3. the Lord hath set *a.* him that is godly
Zech. 12. 12. every family *a.* their wives *a.* 14.
Mat. 14. 13. Jesus departed into a desert place *a.*
23. he went up into a mountain *a.* 17. 1. *Luke* 9. 28.
17. 19. then came the disciples to Jesus *a.*
Mark 6. 31. and he said, come ye yourselves *a.*
Jam. 1. 21. wherefore lay *a.* all filthiness

APES, *see* PEACOCKS.

APIECE.

Num. 3. 47. thou shalt take five shekels *a.* by poll

Num. 7. 86. the golden spoons weighing ten shekels a.
17. 6. every one of their princes gave him a rod a.
1 Kings 7. 15. two pillars eighteen cubits high a.
Luke 9. 3. neither take money, nor have two coats a.
John 2. 6. containing two or three firkins a.

APOLLYON, see GREEK.

APOSTLE

Signifies, A messenger sent upon any special errand, Rom. 16. 7. 2 Cor. 8. 23. It is applied, [1] To Christ Jesus; who was sent from heaven to assume our nature, and work out our salvation, with authority to execute his prophetical and all his offices, and to send forth his apostles to publish the gospel, Heb. 3. 1. [2] To a minister immediately sent by Christ to preach the gospel, Mat. 10. 2. Gal. 1. 1.

Rom. 1. 1. Paul called to be an a. 1 Cor. 1. 1.
11. 13. inasmuch as I am the a. of the Gentiles
1 Cor. 9. 1. am I not an a.? am I not free? 2.
15. 9. that am not meet to be called an a.
2 Cor. 1. 1. Paul an a. of Jesus Christ, Eph. 1. 1. Col. 1. 1. 1 Tim. 1. 1. 2 Tim. 1. 1. Gal. 1. 1.
12. 12. the signs of an a. were wrought among you
1 Tim. 2. 7. whereto I am ordained an a. 2 Tim. 1. 11.
Tit. 1. 1. Paul a servant of God, and a. of Christ
Heb. 3. 1. consider the a. and high-priest of our prof.

APOSTLES.

Mat. 10. 2. now the names of the twelve a. are these
Mark 6. 30. the a. gathered themselves together
Luke 6. 13. he chose twelve, whom he named a.
9. 10. the a. when they were returned, told him
11. 49. I will send them prophets and a.
17. 5. the a. said to the Lord, increase our faith
22. 14. he sat down, and the twelve a. with him
24. 10. the women told these things to the a.
Acts 1. 26. he was numbered with the eleven a.
2. 43. many signs were done by the a. 5. 12.
4. 35. laid them down at the a. feet, 37. | 5. 2.
5. 18. laid their hands on the a. and put them
8. 1. were all scattered abroad, except the a.
Rom. 16. 7. who are of note among the a.
1 Cor. 4. 9. God hath set forth us the a. last
12. 28. God hath set first a. || 29. are all a.
15. 9. for I am the least of the a. that am not meet
2 Cor. 11. 5. not a whit behind the chiefest a. 12. 11.
13. such are false a. deceitful workers
Gal. 1. 17. nor went to them that were a. before me
19. but other of the a. saw I none, save James
Eph. 3. 5. as it is now revealed to his holy a.
4. 11. he gave some a. and some prophets
1 Thess. 2. 6. been burdensome as the a. of Christ
2 Pet. 3. 2. of the commandment of us the a. of Lord
Jude 17. the words spoken before of the a.
Rev. 2. 2. them which say they are a. and are not
18. 20. rejoice over her, ye holy a. and prophets

APOSTLESHIP

Signifies, The office of the apostles; which was to preach the gospel, baptize, work miracles, plant and confirm churches, and ordain ministers, Mat. 10. 1. | 28. 19. Acts 14. 23. 1 Cor. 3. 6.

Acts 1. 25. that he may take part of this a.
Rom. 1. 5. by whom we have received grace and a.
1 Cor. 9. 2. the seal of mine a. are ye in the Lord
Gal. 2. 8. wrought effectually in Peter to the a.

APOTHECARY.

Exod. 30. 25. ointment compounded after art of a.
35. a confection after the art of the a. 37. 29.
Eccl. 10. 1. dead flies cause the ointment of the a.

APPARENTLY.

Num. 12. 8. with him will I speak even a. and not

APPAREL.

Judg. 14. †19. Samson slew 30 men, and took a.
2 Sam. 12. 20. David arose and changed his a.
1 Kings 10. 5. queen of Sheba had seen the attendance of his ministers, and their a. 2 Chron. 9. 4.
Isa. 3. 22. the changeable suits of a. and mantles
4. 1. we will eat our own bread and wear our own a.
63. 1. who is this that is glorious in his a.?
Zeph. 1. 8. and all such as are clothed in strange a.
Acts 1. 10. two men stood by them in white a.
20. 33. I have coveted no man's silver or a.
1 Tim. 2. 9. that women adorn themselves in modest a.
Jam. 2. 2. if a man come in goodly a. and a poor
1 Pet. 3. 3. not of wearing gold, or putting on a.
See ROYAL.

APPARELLED.

2 Sam. 13. 18. the king's daughters, virgins, were a.
Luke 7. 25. behold they which are gorgeously a.

APPEAL, ED.

Acts 25. 11. no man deliver me, I a. unto Cesar, 21.
26. 32. been set at liberty, if he had not a. to Cesar
28. 19. I was constrained to a. to Cesar

APPEAR

Signifies, [1] To be in sight, Gen. 1. 9. Heb. 11. 3. [2] To come before, Exod. 34. 23. Acts 22. 30. [3] To be discovered, or laid open, Jer. 13. 26. [4] To present one's self as an advocate, Heb. 9. 24.

Gen. 1. 9. God said, let the dry land a. and it was so
Exod. 23. 15. and none shall a. before me empty, 34. 20. Deut. 16. 16.
17. three times in the year all males shall a.
34. 24. desire thy land, when thou shalt go to a.
Deut. 31. 11. when all Israel is come to a. before L.
Psal. 42. 2. when shall I come and a. before God?
90. 16. let thy work a. to thy servants, and glory
Cant. 2. 12. the flowers a. on the earth, the time of
4. 1. thy hair as a flock of goats that a. 6. 5.
Isa. 1. 12. when ye come to a. before me
Jer. 13. 26. will discover, that thy shame may a.
Ezek. 21. 24. so that in all your doings your sins do a.
Mat. 6. 16. that they may a. to men to fast
23. 28. even so ye outwardly a. righteous to men
24. 30. then shall a. the sign of the Son of man
Luke 11. 44. for ye are as graves which a. not
19. 11. they thought the kingdom of God should a.
Acts 26. 16. of things in which I will a. to thee
Rom. 7. 13. but sin, that it might a. sin, working
2 Cor. 5. 10. we must all a. before the judgment seat
Col. 3. 4. when Christ who is our life shall a. then
1 Tim. 4. 15. that thy profiting may a. to all
Heb. 9. 24. now to a. in the presence of God for us
28. to them shall he a. the second time to salvation
11. 3. were not made of things which do a.
1 Pet. 4. 18. where shall the ungodly and sinner a.?
5. 4. when the chief Shepherd shall a. shall receive
1 John 2. 28. when he shall a. we may have confidence
3. 2. it doth not yet a. what we shall be, but we know that when he shall a. we shall be like him
Rev. 3. 18. the shame of thy nakedness do not a.

APPEAR, referred to GOD.

Lev. 9. 4. for to-day the Lord will a. to you, 6.
16. 2. I will a. in the cloud on the mercy seat
1 Sam. 2. 27. did I plainly a. to the house of thy father
2 Chron. 1. 7. that night did God a. to Solomon
Psal. 102. 16. build up Zion, he shall a. in his glory
Isa. 66. 5. but he shall a. to your joy, they ashamed
Acts 26. 16. of those things in the which I will a.

APPEARANCE.

Num. 9. 15. was on tabernacle as the a. of fire, 16.
1 Sam. 16. 7. for man looketh on the outward a.
Dan. 8. 15. stood before me as the a. of a man, 10. 18.
10. 6. his face as the a. of lightning, his eyes as
John 7. 24. judge not according to the a. but judge
2 Cor. 5. 12. which glory in a. and not in heart
10. † 1. who in outward a. am base among you
7. do ye look on things after the outward a.?
1 Thess. 5. 22. abstain from all a. of evil

APPEARED.

Gen. 12. 7. the L. a. to Abram and said, 17. 1. | 18. 1.
26. 2. the Lord a. to Isaac, and said, go not, 24.
48. 3. Jacob said, God Almighty a. to me at Luz
Exod. 3. 2. angel of the Lord a. in midst of the bush
4. 1. they will say, the Lord hath not a. to thee
6. 3. I a. to Abraham by name of God Almighty
14. 27. the sea returned when the morning a.
2 Sam. 22. 16. and the channels of the sea a.
1 Kings 11. 9. which had a. to Solomon twice
2 Kings 2. 11. behold there a. a chariot of fire
Neh. 4. 21. we laboured in the work till the stars a.
Jer. 31. 3. the Lord hath a. of old to me, saying
Mat. 2. 7. Herod inquired what time the star a.
13. 26. the blade sprung, then a. the tares also
17. 3. there a. to them Moses and Elias, Mark 9. 4.
27. 53. and went into the holy city, and a. to many
Mark 16. 9. Jesus a. first to Mary Magdalene
12. after that he a. in another form to two of them
14. after he a. to the eleven as they sat at meat
Luke 1. 11. there a. to him an angel of the Lord
9. 31. who a. in glory, and spake of his decease
22. 43. there a. an angel to him, strengthening him
24. 34. the Lord is risen indeed, and a. to Simon
Acts 2. 3. there a. to them cloven tongues like fire
7. 2. the God of glory a. to our father Abraham
9. 17. even Jesus, that a. to thee in the way
26. 16. I have a. to thee for this purpose
27. 20. and when neither sun nor stars a.
Tit. 2. 11. the grace of God hath a. to all men
3. 4. after the love of God toward man a.
Heb. 9. 26. in the end hath he a. to put away sin
Rev. 12. 1. there a. a great wonder in heaven, 3.

APPEARETH.

Lev. 13. 43. as the leprosy a. in the skin of the flesh
Deut. 2. 30. that he might deliver him, as a. this
Psal. 46. † 5. God shall help her, when morning a.
84. 7. every one of them in Zion a. before God
Prov. 27. 25. the hay a. and the tender grass
Jer. 6. 1. for evil a. out of the north, and destruction
Mal. 3. 2. and who shall stand when he a.?
Jam. 4. 14. your life is even as a vapour that a.

APPEARING.

1 Tim. 6. 14. keep commandment till a. of our L.
2 Tim. 1. 10. but is now made manifest by the a.
4. 1. who shall judge the quick and dead at his a.
8. but to all them also that love his a.
Tit. 2. 13. looking for glorious a. of the great God
1 Pet. 1. 7. be found to praise at the a. of Jesus

APPEASE.

Gen. 32. 20. I will a. him with the present

APPEASED, ETH.

Esth. 2. 1. Ahasuerus a. he remembered Vashti
Prov. 15. 18. he that is slow to anger a. strife
Acts 19. 35. when the town-clerk had a. the people

APPERTAIN.

Num. 16. 30. earth swallow them, with all that a.
Jer. 10. 7. who would not fear, for to thee doth it a.
See PERTAIN.

APPERTAINED.

Num. 16. 32. and all the men that a. to Korah, 33.

APPERTAINETH, ING.

Lev. 6. 5. and give it to him to whom it a.
Rom. 4. 1. Abraham, our father, as a. to the flesh

APPETITE.

Job 38. 39. wilt thou fill the a. of the young lions?
Prov. 23. 2. to thy throat, if thou be a man given to a.
Eccl. 6. 7. all labour for mouth, yet a. not filled
Isa. 29. 8. but he awaketh, and his soul hath a.
56. † 11. they are strong of a. not satisfied

APPLE of the eye.

Deut. 32. 10. he kept him as the a. of his eye
Psal. 17. 8. keep me as the a. of the eye, hide me
Prov. 7. 2. keep my law as the a. of thine eye
Lam. 2. 18. let not the a. of thine eye cease
Zech. 2. 8. toucheth you, toucheth the a. of his eye

APPLE-TREE.

Cant. 2. 3. as the a.-tree among the trees of the wood
8. 5. I raised thee up under the a.-tree, thy mother
Joel 1. 12. the palm-tree and the a.-tree are withered

APPLES.

Prov. 25. 11. like a. of gold in pictures of silver
Cant. 2. 5. comfort me with a. for I am sick of love
7. 8. breasts as clusters, and smell of thy nose like a.

APPLY.

Psal. 90. 12. that we may a. our hearts to wisdom
Prov. 2. 2. and a. thine heart to understanding
22. 17. hear words, a. thine heart to my knowledge
23. 12. a. thine heart to instruction, and thine ears

APPLIED.

Eccl. 7. 25. I a. my heart to know and seek wisdom
8. 9. I a. my heart to every work that is done
16. when I a. mine heart to know wisdom
Hos. 7. † 6. they have a. their heart like an oven

APPOINT

Signifies, [1] To constitute or ordain, Josh. 20. 9. [2] To assign or allot, Num. 4. 19. [3] To set over, Gen. 41. 34. Lev. 26. 16. [4] To decree, Acts 17. 31. Heb. 9. 27. [5] To purpose or resolve, Acts 20. 13. [6] To promise, Luke 22. 29. [7] To nominate or prefix, Acts 28. 23. [8] To command or order, 2 Sam. 15. 15. [9] To establish or settle, Prov. 8. 29. [10] To set, or place, 2 Kings 10. 24. Neh. 7. 3. [11] To limit, 1 Sam. 13. 11. [12] To ordain or set apart for an office, Acts 6. 3.

Gen. 30. 28. a. me thy wages, and I will give it
41. 34. let Pharaoh a. officers over the land
Lev. 26. 16. I will a. over you terror, consumption
Num. 4. 19. Aaron and his sons a. every one to service
2 Sam. 6. 21. to a. me ruler over the people of Lord
7. 10. I will a. a place for my people Israel, and
Job 14. 13. that thou wouldest a. me a set time
Isa. 26. 1. salvation will God a. for walls and bulwarks
61. 3. to a. them that mourn in Zion, to give
Jer. 15. 3. I will a. over them four kinds, saith Lord
49. 19. and who is a chosen man that I may a. over her? who will a. me the time? 50. 44.
51. 27. will the kingdoms a. a captain against her
Ezek. 21. 19. a. thee two ways || 20. a. a way that
Hos. 1. 11. they shall a. themselves one head
Mat. 24. 51. a. him his portion with the hypocrites
Luke 12. 46. a. him his portion with unbelievers
22. 29. I a. you a kingdom, as my Father unto me
Acts 6. 3. seven men whom we a. over this business

APPOINTED.

Gen. 24. 14. be she that thou hast a. for thy servant
Num. 9. 2. Israel keep the passover in a. seasons, 3.
7. may not offer an offering, but at an a. season
13. because he brought not offering in a. season
Josh. 20. 9. these were the cities a. for refuge
Judg. 20. 38. there was an a. sign between Israel and
1 Sam. 13. 11. thou camest not within the days a.
19. 20. Samuel standing as a. over them, the Spirit
2 Sam. 17. 14. the Lord had a. to defeat the counsel
1 Kings 1. 35. I have a. him to be ruler over Israel
20. 42. let go a man whom I had a. to destruction
Neh. 6. 7. thou hast a. prophets to preach of thee
9. 17. in their rebellion a. a captain to return, but
Job 7. 3. and wearisome nights are a. to me
14. 5. thou hast a. his bounds, that he cannot pass
20. 29. and the heritage a. to him by God
30. 23. to death, and to the house a. for all living
Psal. 44. 11. thou hast given us like sheep a. for meat
78. 5. a. a law in Israel, which he commanded
79. 11. preserve thou those that are a. to die
102. 20. to loose those that are a. to death
Prov. 7. 20. he will come home at the day a.
8. 29. when he a. the foundations of the earth
31. 8. in cause of all such as are a. to destruction
Isa. 1. 14. new-moons and your a. feasts my soul
44. 7. and who, since I a. the ancient people
Jer. 5. 24. he reserveth the a. weeks of the harvest
47. 7. against the sea-shore, there hath he a. it
Ezek. 4. 6. I have a. thee each day for a year
Mic. 6. 9. hear ye the rod, and who hath a. it
Mat. 27. 10. gave for the potter's field, as the L. a.
Luke 3. 13. exact no more than what is a. you
10. 1. after these the Lord a. other seventy
22. 29. to you a kingdom, as my Father hath a. me
Acts 1. 23. they a. two, Joseph and Matthias
17. 31. he hath a. a day in which he will judge
1 Cor. 4. 9. God hath set us apostles last, a. to death
1 Thess. 3. 3. for you know that we are a. thereto
5. 9. God hath not a. us to wrath, but to obtain
2 Tim. 1. 11. whereunto I am a. a preacher, apostle
Tit. 1. 5. and ordain elders in every city, as I a.
Heb. 3. 2. who was faithful to him that a. him
9. 27. and as it is a. to men once to die, but after
1 Pet. 2. 8. disobedient, whereunto also they were a.

APPOINTED time and times.

Gen. 18. 14. at the time a. will I return to thee
Exod. 9. 5. the Lord a. a set time, saying, to-morrow
23. 15. thou shalt eat unleavened bread in time a.
1 Sam. 13. 8. according to the set time Samuel a.
20. 35. Jonathan went into the field at the time a.
2 Sam. 20. 5. tarried longer than the set time a. him
Esth. 9. 27. according to their a. time every year
Job 7. 1. is there not an a. time to man on earth?
14. 14. all the days of my a. time will I wait till
Psal. 81. 3. blow up the trumpet in the time a.
Isa. 14. 31. and none shall be alone in his a. times
40. † 2. cry, that her a. time is accomplished
Jer. 8. 7. the stork in heaven knoweth her a. times
46. 17. Pharaoh, he hath passed the time a.
Dan. 8. 19. for at the time a. the end shall be
10. 1. the thing was true, but the time a. was long
11. 27. for yet the end shall be at the time a.
29. at the time a. shall return, and come south
35. time of the end, because it is yet for a time a.
Hab. 2. 3. the vision is yet for an a. time, wait for it
Acts 17. 26. God hath determined times before a.
Gal. 4. 2. under tutors, until the time a. of the father

APPOINTETH.

Psal. 104. 19. he a. the moon for seasons, the sun
Dan. 5. 21. he a. over it whomsoever he will

APPOINTMENT.

Num. 4. 27. at the a. of Aaron and his sons shall be
Josh. 11. † 5. when kings were assembled by a.
Ezra 6. 9. wheat, salt, according to a. of the priests
2 Sam. 13. 32. by the a. of Absalom this determined
Job 2. 11. they had made an a. together to come

APPREHEND

Signifies, To seize, or take prisoner, Acts 12. 4. That I may apprehend that for which also I am apprehended of Christ Jesus, Phil. 3. 12. That I may obtain that prize, for the obtaining whereof I was laid hold on by Christ, converted and brought into the way of salvation, when I was running on to destruction.

1 Kings 18. † 40. a. the prophets of Baal, and let none
2 Cor. 11. 32. with a garrison desirous to a. me
Phil. 3. 12. I may a. that for which also I am appr.

APPREHENDED.

Acts 12. 4. when he a. Peter, he put him in prison
Phil. 3. 12. for which I am a. of Christ Jesus
13. brethren, I count not myself to have a. but

APPROACH

Signifies, [1] To draw nigh, or come near, 2 Sam. 11.

20. [2] *To draw near to God in the duties of his worship,* Psal. 65. 4. Isa. 58. 2. [3] *To contract marriage with,* Lev. 18. 6. [4] *To hasten, or draw on,* Deut. 31. 14.
Lev. 18. 6. none of you shall a. to any near of kin
21. 17. not a. to offer the bread of his God, 18.
Deut. 20. 3. ye a. this day to battle against enemies
31. 14. behold, thy days a. that thou must die
Job 40. 19. can make his sword to a. to him
Ps. 65. 4. blessed is the man whom thou causest to a.
Jer. 30. 21. he shall a. to me, for who is this that engaged his heart to a. to me, saith the Lord?
1 Tim. 6. 16. dwelling in the light no man can a. unto

APPROACHED.
2 Sam. 11. 20. wherefore a. ye so nigh the city?
1 Kings 20. † 13. there a. a prophet to Ahab
2 Kings 16. 12. the king a. to the altar and offered
Psal. 27. † 2. when my enemies a. they stumbled
Isa. 8. † 3. I a. to the prophetess, she bare a son

APPROACHETH, ING.
Isa. 58. 2. they take delight in a. to God
Luke 12. 33. where no thief a. nor moth corrupteth
Heb. 10. 25. and so much more as ye see the day a.

APPROVE
Signifies, *To like or commend,* Psal. 49. 13.
Approved of God, *Acts* 2. 22. *Demonstrated, and beyond any contradiction proved, to be the Messiah.*
Psal. 49. 13. yet their posterity a. their sayings
1 Cor. 16. 3. whom you shall a. by your letters
Phil. 1. 10. that ye may a. things that are excellent

APPROVED.
Acts 2. 22. Jesus, a man a. of God among you
Rom. 14. 18. is acceptable to God, and a. of men
16. 10. salute Apelles a. in Christ, salute Aristob.
1 Cor. 11. 19. they that are a. may be made manifest
2 Cor. 7. 11. in all things you have a. yourselves
10. 18. not he that commendeth himself is a.
13. 7. not that we should appear a. but that ye
2 Tim. 2. 15. study to show thyself a. unto God

APPROVEST, ETH.
Lam. 3. 36. to subvert a man, the Lord a. not
Rom. 2. 18. a. the things that are more excellent

APPROVING.
2 Cor. 6. 4. but in all things a. ourselves as ministers

APRON, S.
Gen. 3. 7. they sewed fig-leaves together, and made a.
Ruth 3. † 15. bring the a. thou hast, and hold it
Acts 19. 12. from his body were brought to the sick a.

APT.
2 Kings 24. 16. a. for war, king of Babylon brought
1 Tim. 3. 2. a bishop must be a. to teach, 2 Tim. 2. 24

ARCHANGEL.
1 Thess. 4. 16. shall descend with the voice of the a.
Jude 9. Michael the a. when contending with devil

ARCHER, S.
Gen. 21. 20. Ishmael grew and became an a
49. 23. the a. have sorely grieved him, and shot
1 Sam. 31. 3. and the a. hit him, 1 Chron. 10. 3.
Job 16. 13. his a. compass me round about
Isa. 22. 3. thy rulers fled, they are bound by the a.
Jer. 51. 3. against him that bendeth let a. bend bow

ARCHES.
Ezek. 40. 16. there were narrow windows to the a.

ARE
Signifies, [1] *To be of great value and esteem among men,* 1 Cor. 1. 28. [2] *To have authority from,* 1 John 4. 1. [3] *Reputed, judged, esteemed,* 1 Cor. 7. 14. [4] *Represent, or betoken,* Gen. 41. 26, 27. Rev. 1. 20.
Things which are not, 1 *Cor.* 1. 28. *Which are of so small esteem, as if they had no being.*
Gen. 18. 24. for the fifty righteous that a. therein
31. 15. a. we not counted of him strangers?
42. 36. Jacob said, all these things a. against me
Exod. 8. 21. and also the ground whereon they a.
Num. 15. 15. as ye a. so shall the stranger be
Deut. 1. 11. a thousand times so many more as ye a.
1 Kings 8. 8. and there they a. to this day
Job 24. † 24. a. exalted for a while, but a. not
38. 35. that they may go and say to thee, here we a.
Psal. 68. † 26. bless ye God, ye that a. of the fountain
107. 27. they stagger, and a. at their wit's end
Lam. 5. 7. our fathers have sinned, and a. not
Amos 9. 7. a. ye not as children of Ethiopians to me
Nah. 3. 17. the place is not known where they a.
Mat. 2. 18. not be comforted, because they a. not
6. 26. fowls of air, a. ye not much better than they
22. 30. but a. as the angels of God in heaven
Mark 6. 3. and a. not his sisters here with us?
Luke 13. 25. I know not whence you a. 27.
18. 11. God, I thank thee, I am not as other men a.
John 17. 11. given me, that they may be one, as we a.
Rom. 15. 27. and their debtors they a. for if Gentiles
1 Cor. 1. 28. things which a. not, things that a.
2 Cor. 11. 22. a. they Hebrews? a. they Israelites? a. they the seed of Abraham? so am I
Heb. 4. 15. tempted like as we a. yet without sin
Rev. 1. 19. write the things which a. and shall be
4. 11. for thy pleasure they a. and were created
10. 6. created heaven and things which therein a.

ARGUING.
Job 6. 25. but what doth your a. reprove?

ARGUMENTS.
Job 23. 4. I would fill my mouth with a.

ARIGHT.
Psal. 50. 23. to him that ordereth his conversation a.
78. 8. a generation that set not their heart a.
Prov. 4. † 26. all thy ways shall be ordered a.
15. 2. the tongue of the wise useth knowledge a.
23. 31. the wine, when it moveth itself a.
Jer. 8. 6. I hearkened, but they spake not a.

ARISE
Signifies, [1] *To take rise, or proceed from,* Acts 20. 30. [2] *To repent,* Eph. 5. 14. [3] *To be raised and comforted,* Amos 7. 2. *It is likewise a word of encouragement, to excite one to do a thing,* Josh. 1. 2. Acts 22. 16.
Gen. 31. 13. now a. get thee out of this land
35. 1. a. go up to Beth-el, and dwell there
Deut. 13. 1. if there a. among you a prophet
17. 8. then shalt thou a. and get thee up to the
Josh. 1. 2. now therefore a. go over this Jordan

Judg. 5. 12. a. Barak, lead thy captivity captive
2 Sam. 2. 14. let the young men a. and play before us
3. 21. I will a. and gather all Israel to my lord
11. 20. and if so be that the king's wrath a.
1 Kings 3. 12. nor after thee shall any a. like thee
2 Kings 9. 2. make Jehu a. from among his brethren
1 Chron. 22. 16. a. be doing, the Lord be with thee
Neh. 2. 20. therefore we his servants will a. and build
Esth. 1. 18. thus shall there a. too much contempt
4. 14. then shall enlargement a. to the Jews
Job 7. 4. when shall I a. and night be gone?
11. † 17. thy age shall a. above noon-day
25. 3. and upon whom doth not his light a.?
Psal. 3. 7. a. O Lord, save me, O my God, for thou
7. 6. a. O Lord, in thine anger lift up thyself
12. 5. now will I a. saith the Lord, I will set him
44. 26. a. for our help, and redeem us for thy mercy
68. 1. let God a. let his enemies be scattered
88. 10. shall the dead a. and praise thee?
89. 9. when the waves of sea a. thou stillest them
102. 13. thou shalt a. and have mercy on Zion
Prov. 6. 9. when wilt thou a. out of thy sleep?
Cant. 2. 13. a. my love, my fair one, and come away
Isa. 21. 5. a. ye princes, and anoint the shield
26. 19. together with my dead body shall they a.
49. 7. kings shall a. princes shall worship
60. 1. a. shine, for thy light is come, and the glory
2. but the Lord shall a. upon thee, and his glory
Jer. 2. 27. in trouble they will say, a. save us
8. 4. saith the Lord, shall they fall, and not a.?
31. 6. a. ye, let us go up to Zion to the Lord
Lam. 2. 19. a. cry out in the night, pour out thy
Dan. 2. 39. after thee shall a. another kingdom
Amos 7. 2. O Lord, by whom shall Jacob a. for he is, 5.
Mic. 2. 10. a. ye and depart, this is not your rest
4. 13. a. and thresh, O daughter of Zion, I will
7. 8. O mine enemy, when I fall I shall a.
Hab. 2. 19. wo to him that saith to the dumb stone a.
Mal. 4. 2. you that fear shall the Sun of righteousn. a.
Mat. 9. 5. is it easier to say a. and walk? Mark 2. 9.
24. 24. for there shall a. false Christs, false prophets
Mark 5. 41. damsel, I say to thee, a. Luke 8. 54.
Luke 7. 14. Lord said, young man, I say to thee, a.
15. 18. I will a. and go to my father, and say
24. 38. and why do thoughts a. in your hearts?
John 14. 31. even so I do, a. let us go hence
Acts 9. 40. turning to the body said, Tabitha, a.
20. 30. also of your own selves shall men a. speaking
22. 16. why tarriest thou? a. and be baptized
Eph. 5. 14. a. from the dead, and Christ shall give
2 Pet. 1. 19. till the day-star a. in your hearts
See RISE.

ARISETH.
1 Kings 18. 44. behold, there a. a little cloud
Psal. 112. 4. to the upright a. light in darkness
Isa. 2. 19. when he a. to shake terribly the earth, 21.
Mat. 13. 21. when persecution a. Mark 4. 17.
John 7. 52. search, for out of Galilee a. no prophet
Heb. 7. 15. after the similitude of Melchizedec a.
See SUN.

ARK
Signifies, [1] *A chest or coffer to keep things sure or secret,* Exod. 2. 3. [2] *The great vessel in which Noah and his family were preserved during the flood, in length 547 feet,* Gen. 6. 14, 15. Heb. 11. 7. [3] *That chest wherein the two tables of the law, Aaron's rod, and the pot of manna were kept,* Exod. 37. 1. Heb. 9. 4.
The ark of thy strength, *Psal.* 132. 8. *The seat of thy powerful and glorious presence, from whence thou dost put forth and manifest thy strength in behalf of thy people, when they desire and need it.*
Was seen the ark of his testament, *Rev.* 11. 19. *Christ the true* Ark *of our covenant, more known, and the mysteries of religion made more common and familiar than formerly, either under the Old-Testament dispensation, or during the reign of antichrist.*
Gen. 6. 14. make thee an a. of gopher-wood
7. 18. and the a. went on the face of the waters
Exod. 2. 3. she took for him an a. of bulrushes
25. 16. and thou shalt put into the a. the testimony which I shall give thee, 21. | 40. 3, 20.
37. 1. Bezaleel made the a. of shittim-wood
Num. 3. 31. their charge shall be the a. and tables
Josh. 4. 11. a. of L. 6. 12. 1 Sam. 4. 6. | 6. 1. 2 Sam. 6. 9.
1 Sam. 6. 19. he smote because they looked into a.
2 Sam. 11. 11. the a. and Israel abide in tents
1 Kings 2. 26. because thou barest the a. of the Lord
8. 9. was nothing in the a. save the two tables
1 Chron. 6. 31. after that the a. had rest
13. 3. let us bring again the a. of our God to us
9. Uzza put forth his hand to hold the a.
15. 1. David prepared a place for the a. of God
2 Chron. 6. 41. thou and a. of thy strength, Ps. 132. 8.
8. 11. places are holy whereunto the a. hath come
Mat. 24. 38. till Noah entered the a. Luke 17. 27.
Heb. 11. 7. by faith Noah warned of God prep. an a.
1 Pet. 3. 20. God waited while the a. was preparing
Rev. 11. 19. and there was seen in his temple the a.

Before the ARK.
Exod. 40. 5. thou shalt set altar of gold *before the a.*
Josh. 4. 7. waters of Jordan were cut off *before the a.*
7. 6. Joshua fell to the earth on his face *before the a.*
1 Sam. 5. 3. Dagon was fallen on his f. *before the a.*
1 Chr. 16. 37. left *before the a.* Asaph and his brethr.
2 Chr. 5. 6. Solom. and congr. assembled *before the a.*

ARK *of the Covenant.*
Num. 10. 33. a. *of covenant* of Lord went before them
Deut. 31. 26. put book of law inside of *a. of covenant*
Josh. 4. 7. the waters were cut off before *a. of covenant*
Judg. 20. 27. *a. of covenant* of God was there in
1 Sam. 4. 3. let us fetch the *a. of the covenant* of
2 Sam. 15. 24. Levites bearing *a. of covenant* of God
1 Chr. 17. 1. *a. of covenant* remained under curtains
Jer. 3. 16. shall say no more, the *a. of the covenant*
Heb. 9. 4. tabernacle which had the *a. of the covenant*

ARK *of God.*
1 Sam. 3. 3. in the temple where the *a. of God* was
4. 11. the *a. of God* was taken, 17. 22.
6. 3. if ye send away the *a. of God*, send it not empty
2 Sam. 6. 7. there he died before the *a. of God*

2 Sam. 7. 2. but the *a. of God* dwelleth within curtains
15. 25. carry back the *a. of God* into the city
1 Chr. 13. 12. how shall I bring the *a. of God* home
15. 2. none ought to carry the *a. of God* but Levites

ARM
Signifies, [1] *That part of the body so called,* 2 Sam. 1. 10. [2] *Outward strength, and all the instruments of cruelty and mischief used by the wicked,* Psal. 10. 15. [3] *God's infinite power in creating the world,* Jer. 27. 5. | 32. 17. [4] *The mighty power of God making the gospel effectual to the conversion of sinners,* Isa. 53. 1. John 12. 38.
Exod. 15. 16. by greatness of thine a. they shall be
Deut. 33. 20. he teareth the a. with crown of head
1 Sam. 2. 31. behold the days come when I will cut off thy a. and the a. of thy father's house
2 Sam. 1. 10. I took the bracelet that was on his a.
2 Chron. 32. 8. with him is an a. of flesh, with us
Ezra 4. † 23. made them to cease by a. and power
Job 26. 2. savest thou the a. that hath no strength
31. 22. let my a. fall from my shoulder-blade
35. 9. cry out by reason of the a. of the mighty
38. 15. and the high a. shall be broken
40. 9. hast thou an a. like God? or canst thunder
Psal. 10. 15. break thou the a. of the wicked
44. 3. nor did their own a. save them, but thy a.
71. † 18. I have showed thy a. to this generation
77. 15. thou hast with thy a. redeemed thy people
89. 13. thou hast a mighty a. strong is thy hand
21. mine a. also shall strengthen him
98. 1. his holy a. hath gotten him the victory
Cant. 8. 6. set me as a seal on thine a
Isa. 9. 20. they shall eat every man the flesh of his a.
33. 2. be thou their a. every morning, our salvation
40. 10. God will come, and his a. shall rule for him
11. he shall gather the lambs with his a.
51. 5. mine a. shall judge the people, the isles shall wait upon me, and on my a. shall they trust
9. put on strength, O a. of the Lord, awake
52. 10. the Lord hath made bare his holy a.
53. 1. who hath believed our report? and to whom is the a. of the Lord revealed? John 12. 38.
59. 16. therefore his a. brought salvation, 63. 5.
62. 8. Lord hath sworn by the a. of his strength
63. 12. that led them with his glorious a.
Jer. 17. 5. cursed be he that maketh flesh his a.
21. 5. I will fight against you with a strong a.
Ezek. 4. 7. and thine a. shall be uncovered
22. † 6. were in thee to their a. to shed blood
30. 21. I have broken a. of Pharaoh king of Egypt
31. 17. they went down into hell that were his a.
Dan. 11. 6. she shall not retain the power of the a.
Zech. 11. 17. sword be on his a. his a. be dried up
Luke 1. 51. he hath shewed strength with his a.
Acts 13. 17. with an high a. brought he them out

Stretched-out ARM.
Exod. 6. 6. I will redeem you with a *stretched-out a*
Deut. 4. 34. assayed to take nation with *str.-out a.*
5. 15. the Lord thy God brought thee out thence with a *stretched-out a.* 7. 19. | 26. 8. Jer. 32. 21.
11. 2. your children have not seen his *str.-out a.*
2 Chr. 6. 32. stranger is come for thy *stretched-out a.*
Psal. 136. 12. with a *stretched-out a.* for his mercy
Jer. 27. 5. I made earth by my *stretched-out a.* 32. 17.
Ezek. 20. 33. with a *stretched-out a.* will I rule over
34. I will gather you with a *str.-out a.* and fury

ARM-HOLES.
Jer. 38. 12. put these rotten rags under thy *a.-holes*
Ezek. 13. 18. wo to them that sew pillows to *a.-holes*

ARMS.
Gen. 49. 24. the a. of his hands were made strong
Deut. 33. 27. and underneath are the everlasting a.
Judg. 16. 12. he brake them from his a. like thread
2 Sam. 22. 35. he teacheth my hands to war, so that a bow of steel is broken by mine a. Psal. 18. 34.
2 Kings 9. 24. Jehu smote Jehoram between his a
Job 22. 9. the a. of the fatherless have been broken
Psal. 37. 17. the a. of the wicked shall be broken
Prov. 31. 17. she girdeth, and strengtheneth her a.
Isa. 44. 12. and worketh it with strength of his a.
49. 22. they shall bring thy sons in their a.
51. 5. and my a. shall judge the people
Ezek. 13. 20. I will tear them from your a.
30. 22. behold, I will break Pharaoh's a. 24.
24. I will strengthen the a. of king of Babylon, 25.
Dan. 2. 32. his breast and his a. of silver, his belly
10. 6. his a. and feet like to polished brass
11. 15. the a. of the south shall not withstand
22. with the a. of a flood shall they be overflown
31. and a. shall stand on his part, and shall
Hos. 7. 15. I have bound and strengthened their a.
11. 3. taught them to go, taking them by their a.
Mark 9. 36. when he had taken him in his a. he said
10. 16. took them up in his a. put his hands on them
Luke 2. 28. Simeon took Christ in his a. and blessed

ARM, *Verb,*
Is taken, [1] Corporally, *to be furnished with arms for war,* Gen. 14. 14. Num. 31. 5. [2] Spiritually, *to get and exercise those graces and spiritual weapons which are appointed and bestowed by God to defend the soul,* 1 Pet. 4. 1.
Num. 31. 3. a. some of yourselves to the war, and go
1 Pet. 4. 1. a. yourselves with the same mind

ARMED.
Gen. 14. 14. Abram a. his trained servants born in
41. † 40. at thy word shall all my people be a.
Num. 31. 5. of tribe, twelve thousand a. for war
32. 17. but we ourselves will go ready a. 32.
Deut. 3. 18. ye shall pass over a. Josh. 1. 14.
Josh. 4. † 13. about 40,000 a. for war passed over
6. 7. let him that is a. pass on before the ark
2 Chron. 28. 14. so the a. men left the captives
Job 39. 21. he goeth on to meet the a. men
Psal. 78. 9. the children of Ephraim being a.
Prov. 6. 11. and thy want as an a. man, 24. 34.
Luke 11. 21. when a strong man a. keepeth the house

ARMY.
Deut. 11. 4. what he did to the a. of the Egyptians
Judg. 8. 6. that we should give bread to thine a
9. 29. he said, increase thine a. and come out
1 Sam. 4. 12. there ran a man of Benjamin out of a.
17. 21. and the Philistines had put a. against a.

1 Kings 20. 25. number thee an *a.* like the *a.* lost
2 Chron. 20. 21. that they should praise before the *a.*
25. 7. O king, let not the *a.* of Israel go with thee
Neh. 4. 2. he spake before his brethren, and the *a.*
Job 29. 25. sat chief, I dwelt as a king in the *a.*
Psal. 68. † 11. great was the *a.* that published it
Cant. 6. 4. terrible as an *a.* with banners, 10.
Jer. 37. 11. was broken up for fear of Pharaoh's *a.*
Ezek. 29. 18. caused his *a.* to serve a great service
37. 10. there stood up an exceeding great *a.*
Dan. 4. 35. according to his will in the *a.* of heaven
Joel 2. 11. Lord shall utter his voice before his *a.*
25. locust, my great *a.* which I sent among you
Zech. 4. † 6. saying, not by *a.* nor by power
9. 8. will encamp about my house because of the *a.*
Acts 23. 27. then came I with an *a.* and rescued
Rev. 9. 16. the number of the *a.* of horsemen
19. 19. against him that sat on horse and his *a.*
See CHALDEANS.

ARMIES.

Exod. 7. 4. lay hand on Egypt, and bring forth my *a.*
12. 17. same day I brought your *a.* out of Egypt
Num. 33. 1. went forth with their *a.* under Moses
Deut. 20. 9. they shall make captains of the *a.* to lead
1 Sam. 17. 10. said, I defy the *a.* of Israel this day
26. that he should defy the *a.* of the living God
45. come in the name of the God of the *a.* of Israel
Job 25. 3. is there any number of his *a.?*
Psal. 44. 9. thou goest not forth with our *a.*
68. 12. kings of *a.* did flee apace, she that tarried
Cant. 6. 13. as it were the company of two *a.*
Isa. 34. 2. and his fury upon all their *a.*
Dan. 9. † 27. with abominable *a.* make desolate
Mat. 22. 7. he sent forth his *a.* and destroyed
Luke 21. 20. ye see Jerusalem compassed with *a.*
Heb. 11. 34. who turned to flight the *a.* of the aliens
Rev. 19. 14. and the *a.* in heaven followed him
19. the kings of the earth and their *a.* gathered

ARMOUR

Signifies, [1] *Weapons or instruments of war*, 1 Sam. 17. 54. [2] *The strong and powerful lusts of sin, ignorance, error, and profaneness, which are the armour, whereby the devil keeps up his power and dominion in the hearts of men*, Luke 11. 22. [3] *Spoil*, 2 Sam. 2. † 21. [4] *Such graces and spiritual weapons as are for the defence of the soul, and whereby we may be enabled to combat with our spiritual enemies*, Rom. 13. 12. Eph. 6. 11. [5] *A good conscience, which being always attended with uprightness of life, is a defence against all temptations, either from prosperity or adversity*, 2 Cor. 6. 7.

1 Sam. 17. 54. David put Goliath's *a.* in his tent
2 Sam. 2. 21. turn thee aside and take thee his *a.*
1 Kings 22. 38. they washed his *a.* according to
2 Kings 3. 21. they gathered all able to put on *a.*
10. 2. seeing ye have a fenced city also and *a.*
20. 13. Hezekiah shewed his precious things, silver and gold, the house of his *a.* *Isa.* 39. 2.
Job 39. † 21. he goeth on to meet the *a.*
Isa. 22. 8. didst look in that day to *a.* of the house
Luke 11. 22. he taketh his *a.* wherein he trusted
Rom. 13. 12. and let us put on the *a.* of light
2 Cor. 6. 7. approving by the *a.* of righteousness
Eph. 6. 11. put on the *a.* of God to stand ag. devil
13. take to you the whole *a.* of God to withstand

ARMOUR-BEARER.

Judg. 9. 54. Abimelech called his *a.-bearer*, saying
1 Sam. 14. 7. *a.-b.* said, do all that is in thine heart
16. 21. Saul loved David, and he became his *a. b.*
31. 6. Saul died, his three sons, and his *a.-bearer*

ARMOURY.

Cant. 4. 4. like the tower of David builded for an *a.*
Jer. 50. 25. the Lord hath opened his *a.*

AROSE.

Gen. 19. 33. he perceived not when she *a.* 35.
37. 7. and, lo, my sheaf *a.* and stood upright
Exod. 1. 8. now there *a.* up a new king over Egypt who knew not Joseph, *Acts* 7. 18.
Judg. 2. 10. *a.* a generation that knew not the Lord
5. 7. till I Deborah *a.* till I *a.* a mother in Israel
20. 8. all the people *a.* as one man, saying
1 Sam. 9. 26. and they *a.* early, *Isa.* 37. 36.
17. 35. when he *a.* against me, I slew him
2 Kings 23. 25. neither after him *a.* there any like
2 Chron. 36. 16. till the wrath of the Lord *a.*
Job 29. 8. young men hid, aged *a.* and stood up
Psal. 76. 9. when God *a.* to judgment, to save thee
Eccl. 1. 5. the sun hasteth to his place where he *a.*
Dan. 6. 19. the king *a.* early and went to the den
Mat. 2. 14. he *a.* and took the young child, 21.
8. 15. she *a.* and ministered to them, *Luke* 4. 39.
26. he *a.* and rebuked the winds and the sea, and there was a great calm, *Mark* 4. 39. *Luke* 8. 24.
9. 9. and he *a.* and followed him, 19. *Mark* 2. 14.
25. he took her by the hand, and the maid *a.*
27. 52. and many bodies of saints which slept *a.*
Mark 9. 27. but Jesus lifted him up, and he *a.*
Luke 6. 48. when the flood *a.* the stream beat
15. 20. he *a.* and came to his father, he kissed him
Acts 11. 19. the persecution which *a.* about Stephen
19. 23. there *a.* no small stir about that way
23. 7. when he so said there *a.* a dissension, 10.
See ROSE.

AROSE *and went.*

1 Sam. 3. 6. Samuel *a. and went* to Eli, and said, here
23. 16. Jonathan *a. and went* to David into the wood
25. 1. David *a. and went* to the wilderness of Paran
1 Kings 19. 21. Elisha *a. and went* after Elijah
Jonah 3. 3. so Jonah *a. and went* to Nineveh
Acts 9. 39. then Peter *a. and went* with them

ARRAY

Signifies, [1] *To put on apparel*, Esth. 6. 9. Rev. 7. 13. [2] *To put an army in a fit posture to fight*, 2 Sam. 10. 9.

The terrors of God set themselves in array against me, *Job* 6. 4. *His judgments are like a numerous and well-ordered army, under the conduct of an irresistible general, who designs and directs them to invade me on every side.*

Esth. 6. 9. that they may *a.* the man withal
Job 40. 10. and *a.* thyself with glory and beauty
Jer. 43. 12. shall *a.* himself with the land of Egypt
1 Tim. 2. 9. that women adorn, not with costly *a.*

ARRAY.

1 Sam. 4. † 2. they slew of the *a.* in the field
2 Sam. 10. 9. Joab put the choice in *a.* against Syrians
Job 6. 4. the terrors of God set themselves in *a.*
Jer. 50. 14. put yourselves in *a.* against Babylon
See BATTLE.

ARRAYED.

Gen. 41. 42. Pharaoh *a.* Joseph in fine linen
2 Chron. 28. 15. took the captives, with spoil *a.* them
Mat. 6. 29. was not *a.* like one of these, *Luke* 12. 27.
Luke 23. 11. Herod and his men of war *a.* Christ
Acts 12. 21. Herod *a.* in royal apparel sat on his
Rev. 7. 13. what are these that are *a.* in white robes?
17. 4. the woman was *a.* in purple and scarlet colour
19. 8. to her was granted to be *a.* in fine linen

ARRIVED.

Luke 8. 26. they *a.* at the country of the Gadarenes
Acts 20. 15. and the next day we *a.* at Samos

ARROGANCY.

1 Sam. 2. 3. let not *a.* come out of your mouth
Prov. 8. 13. pride and *a.* and the evil way do I hate
Isa. 13. 11. I will cause the *a.* of the proud to cease
Jer. 48. 29. heard pride of Moab, his loftiness, his *a.*

ARROW

Signifies, [1] *A dart used for pleasure or in war*, 1 Sam. 20. 20. Jer. 51. 11. [2] *Inward terrors from God*, Job 6. 4. Psal. 38. 2. [3] *Wicked intentions*, Psal. 11. 2. [4] *Abusive or slanderous words*, Psal. 64. 3. [5] *The judgments of God, such as thunder, lightning, tempests, famine, &c.* 2 Sam. 22. 15. Ezek. 5. 16. Hab. 3. 11. [6] *The word of God, which is sharp and powerful in piercing and turning the hearts of sinners*, Psal. 45. 5.

1 Sam. 20. 36. Jonathan shot an *a.* beyond him
2 Kings 9. 24. and the *a.* went out at his heart
13. 17. *a.* of Lord's deliverance from Syria
19. 32. nor shall he shoot an *a.* there, *Isa.* 37. 33.
Job 34 † 6. my *a.* is incurable without transgression
41. 28. the *a.* cannot make him flee, sling-stones
Psal. 11. 2. they make ready their *a.* on the string
64. 7. with an *a.* suddenly shall they be wounded
91. 5. nor afraid for the *a.* that flieth by day
Prov. 25. 18. that beareth false witness is a sharp *a.*
Jer. 9. 8. their tongue is as an *a.* shot out
Lam. 3. 12. he hath set me as a mark for the *a.*
Zech. 9. 14. and his *a.* shall go forth as lightning

ARROWS.

Num. 24. 8. he shall pierce them thro' with his *a.*
Deut. 32. 23. I will spend mine *a.* upon them
42. I will make mine *a.* drunk with blood
1 Sam. 20. 20. I will shoot three *a.* on the side
2 Sam. 22. 15. the Lord thundered, and he sent out *a.* and scattered them, *Psal.* 18. 14.
2 Kings 13. 15. take bow and *a.* took to him bow and *a.*
18. take the *a.* and smite upon the ground
Job 6. 4. the *a.* of the Almighty are within me
Psal. 7. 13. he ordaineth *a.* against the persecutors
21. 12. shalt make ready thine *a.* against them
38. 2. for thine *a.* stick fast in me, and thy hand
45. 5. thine *a.* are sharp in the heart of enemies
57. 4. sons of men, whose teeth are spears and *a.*
58. 7. when he bendeth his bow to shoot his *a.*
64. 3. bows to shoot their *a.* even bitter words
76. 3. there brake he the *a.* of the bow, the shield
77. 17. clouds poured, thine *a.* also went abroad
120. 4. sharp *a.* of the mighty, with coals of juniper
127. 4. as *a.* are in the hand of a mighty man
144. 6. shoot out thine *a.* and destroy them
Prov. 26. 18. as a mad man who casteth *a.* and death
Isa. 5. 28. whose *a.* are sharp and their bows bent
7. 24. with *a.* and bows shall men come thither
Jer. 50. 9. their *a.* shall be as of an expert man
14. shoot at Babylon, spare no *a.* she hath sinned
51. 11. make bright the *a.* gather the shields
Lam. 3. 13. hath caused the *a.* of his quiver to enter
Ezek. 5. 16. I shall send the evil *a.* of famine
21. 21. he made his *a.* bright, he consulted images
39. 3. I will cause thy *a.* to fall out of thy hand
9. Israel shall go forth, and burn bows and *a.*
Hab. 3. 11. at the light of thine *a.* they went

ART, *Verb.*

Gen. 3. 9. God said to Adam, where *a.* thou?
13. 14. Lord said, look from the place where thou *a.*
24. 23. he said, whose daughter *a.* thou? 47.
27. 24. and he said, *a.* thou my very son Esau?
32. 17. whose *a.* thou? whither goest thou?
39. 9. kept back but thee, because thou *a.* his wife
41. 39. there is none so discreet and wise as thou *a.*
46. 30. now let me die because thou *a.* yet alive
Exod. 4. 26. she said, a bloody husband thou *a.*
Josh. 5. 13. *a.* thou for us, or our adversaries?
Judg. 8. 18. they answered, as thou *a.* so were they
12. 5. the men said to him, *a.* thou an Ephraimite?
13. 11. *a.* thou the man that spakest to the woman?
1 Sam. 19. 3. I will go out and stand by where thou *a.*
1 Kings 13. 18. he said, I am a prophet also as thou *a.*
22. 4. Jehoshaphat said, I am as thou *a.* *2 Kings* 3. 7.
2 Chron. 20. 7. *a.* not thou our God, who didst drive
Job 35. 8. wickedness may hurt a man as thou *a.*
Isa. 14. 10. *a.* thou also become weak as we? *a.* like
Jer. 14. 22. *a.* not thou he, O Lord our God, we
Luke 7. 19. *a.* thou he that should come, or look we
John 1. 49. Rabbi, thou *a.* the Son of God, King of Is.
Acts 21. 38. *a.* not thou that Egyptian made uproar
22. 27. the captain said, tell me, *a.* thou a Roman?
Rev. 11. 17. *a.* and wast, and *a.* to come, 16. 5.

ART, S, *Substantive.*

Exod. 30. 25. an ointm. after the *a.* of the apothecary
2 Chron. 16. 14. divers spices prepared by *a.* of apoth.
Acts 17. 29. the Godhead not like stones graven by *a.*
19. 19. many also of them which used curious *a.*

ARTIFICER.

Gen. 4. 22. Tubal-cain an instructor of every *a.*
Isa. 3. 3. take away the captain and the cunning *a.*

ARTIFICERS.

1 Chron. 29. 5. for all manner of works made by *a.*
2 Chron. 34. 11. to *a.* and builders gave they money

ARTILLERY.

1 Sam. 20. 40. Jonathan gave his *a.* to the lad

AS

Signifies, [1] *Like*, 1 Pet. 3. 8. [2] *While*, Acts 20. 9. [3] *For*, Mat. 6. 12. [4] *Because*, John 15. 12. | 17. 2. [5] *After the manner of*, Job 31. 33. It sheweth, [1] *Likeness in quality, but not in quantity*, Mat. 5. 48. [2] *Equally*, John 5. 23. [3] *The likeness of a thing, but not the truth of that thing*, Mat. 26. 55. [4] *The likeness and truth of a thing*, Heb. 12. 7.

Gen. 2. † 18. I will make him an help *a.* before him
3. 5. ye shall be *a.* gods knowing good and evil
22. behold the man is become *a.* one of us
1 Sam. 16. 7. the Lord seeth not *a.* man seeth
2 Kings 8. 27. he did evil *a.* did the house of Ahab
24. 13. had made in the temple, *a.* the Lord had said
Ezra 10. 12. *a.* thou hast said, so must we do
Psal. 125. 5. *a.* for such *a.* turn aside to crooked ways
Prov. 24. 29. say not, I will do to him *a.* he hath done
Isa. 24. 2. *a.* with the people, *a.* with the servant
Mat. 10. 25. disciple *a.* his master, servant *a.* his Lord
19. 19. shalt love thy neighb. *a.* thyself, *Rom.* 13. 9.
John 1. 14. beheld the glory *a.* of the only-begotten
Acts 7. † 37. the Lord raise up a prophet *a.* myself
51. ye resist H. Ghost, *a.* your fathers did, so do ye
2 Cor. 2. 17. but *a.* of sincerity, but *a.* of God, speak
Gal. 4. 12. brethren, be *a.* I am, for I am *a.* ye are
Col. 2. 6. *a.* ye have received Christ Jesus, so walk

Even AS.

1 Cor. 3. 5. *even a.* the Lord gave to every man
Eph. 5. 33. every one so love his wife *even a.* himself
Col. 3. 13. *even a.* Christ forgave you, so do ye
Rev. 2. 27. *even a.* I received of my Father

ASCEND

Signifies, [1] *To get or climb up*, Josh. 6. 5. [2] *To go up to heaven*, Eph. 4. 9, 10.

Who shall ascend into the hill of the Lord? *Psal.* 24. 3. *Who shall be admitted and accounted a true member of the church, and enjoy the favour and blessing of God?*

No man hath ascended up to heaven, *John* 3. 13. *No man hath attained the perfect knowledge of heavenly things, so as to know the secret will and counsels of God.*

Josh. 6. 5. the people shall *a.* up every man straight
Psal. 24. 3. who shall *a.* into the hill of the Lord, and shall stand in his holy place? *Rom.* 10. 6.
135. 7. he causeth vapours to *a.* *Jer.* 10. 13. | 51. 16.
139. 8. if I *a.* up into heaven, thou art there
Isa. 14. 13. thou hast said, I will *a.* to heaven, 14.
Ezek. 38. 9. thou shalt *a.* and come like a storm
John 6. 62. if ye shall see the Son of man *a.* up
20. 17. I *a.* to my Father, and your Father, my God
Rev. 17. 8. beast shall *a.* out of the bottomless pit

ASCENDED.

Judg. 13. 20. the angel of the Lord *a.* in the flame
Psal. 68. 18. thou hast *a.* up on high, thou hast led
Prov. 30. 4. who hath *a.* up into heaven, or descend.
John 3. 13. no man hath *a.* to heaven, but he that
20. 17. touch me not, I am not yet *a.* to my Father
Acts 2. 34. David is not yet *a.* into the heavens
Eph. 4. 8. when he *a.* up on high, he led captivity cap.
9. now that he *a.* ‖ 10. is the same also that *a.*
Rev. 8. 4. the smoke of the incense *a.* before God
11. 12. they *a.* up to heaven in a cloud, and enemies

ASCENDETH.

Rev. 11. 7. the beast that *a.* out of the bottomless pit
14. 11. the smoke of their torment *a.* for ever

ASCENDING.

Gen. 28. 12. the angels of God *a.* and descending
1 Sam. 28. 13. said, I saw gods *a.* out of the earth
Luke 19. 28. he went before, *a.* up to Jerusalem
John 1. 51. angels of God *a.* and descending on Son
Rev. 7. 2. I saw another angel *a.* from the east

ASCENT.

2 Sam. 15. 30. David went up by the *a.* of Olivet
1 Kings 10. 5. and his *a.* by which he went, *2 Chr.* 9. 4.

ASCRIBE.

Deut. 32. 3. *a.* ye greatness to our God, he is the
Job 36. 3. I will *a.* righteousness to my Maker
Psal. 68. 34. *a.* ye strength to God, his excellency

ASCRIBED.

1 Sam. 18. 8. *a.* to David 10,000, to me *a.* but 1000

ASH.

Isa. 44. 14. he planteth an *a.* the rain doth nourish it

ASHAMED.

Gen. 2. 25. naked, the man and his wife were not *a.*
Judg. 3. 25. and they tarried till they were *a.*
2 Sam. 10. 5. the men were greatly *a.* *1 Chron.* 19. 5.
19. 3. as people being *a.* steal away when they flee
2 Kings 2. 17. and when they urged him till he was *a.*
8. 11. he settled his countenance till he was *a.*
2 Chron. 30. 15. the priests and the Levites were *a.*
Ezra 8. 22. I was *a.* to require of the king a band
9. 6. I am *a.* and blush to lift up my face to thee
Job 6. 20. they came thither, and were *a.*
11. 3. when thou mockest, shall no man make *a.?*
19. 3. ye are not *a.* to make yourselves strange to me
Psal. 34. 5. were lightened, and their faces not *a.*
74. 21. O let not the oppressed return *a.* let poor
Prov. 12. 4. she that maketh *a.* is as rottenness
Isa. 20. 5. shall be *a.* of Ethiopia, their expectation
24. 23. the sun shall be *a.* when the Lord shall reign
30. 5. all *a.* of a people that could not profit them
33. 9. earth mourneth, Lebanon is *a.* and hewn down
Jer. 2. 26. as the thief is *a.* when he is found, so is
6. 15. were they *a.?* they were not at all *a.* 8. 12.
8. 9. the wise men are *a.* they are dismayed
14. 4. plowmen were *a.* they covered their heads
48. 13. Moab shall be *a.* of Chemosh, as Israel was *a.*
Ezek. 16. 27. the daughters of the Philistines are *a.*
32. 30. with terror they are *a.* of their might
Lu. 13. 17. all his adversaries were *a.* and the people
16. 3. what shall I do? I cannot dig, to beg I am *a.*
Rom. 1. 16. I am not *a.* of the gospel of Christ
5. 5. hope maketh not *a.* because the love of God is
6. 21. what fruit in things whereof ye are now *a.?*
2 Cor. 7. 14. if I have boasted any thing, I am not *a.*
2 Tim. 1. 12. I suffer, nevertheless I am not *a.*
16. Onesiphorus was not *a.* of my chain
Heb. 2. 11. he is not *a.* to call them brethren
11. 16. God is not *a.* to be called their God
ASHAMED *and confounded; see* CONFOUNDED

Be ASHAMED.

Gen. 38. 23. let her take it to her, lest we be a.
Psal. 6. 10. let all my enemies be a. and sore vexed
25. 3. yea, let none that wait on thee be a. let them be a. who transgress without cause
31. 1. in thee do I put my trust, let me never be a.
17. let me not be a. let the wicked be a. 35. 26.
69. 6. let not them that wait be a. for my sake
86. 17. they which hate me, may see it and be a.
109. 28. when they arise, let them be a. but let
119. 78. let proud be a. for they dealt perversely
Isa. 1. 29. for they shall be a. of the oaks which ye
23. 4. be thou a. O Zidon, the sea hath spoken
26. 11. they shall see and be a. for their envy
42. 17. they shall be greatly a. that trust in images
44. 9. they see not nor know, that they may be a.
11. all his fellows shall be a. shall be a. together
45. 24. all that are incensed against him shall be a.
65. 13. my servants rejoice, but ye shall be a.
66. 5. shall appear to your joy, and they shall be a.
Jer. 2. 36. thou shalt be a. of Egypt, as a. of Assyria
3. 3. and hadst a whore's forehead, refusedst to be a.
12. 13. and they shall be a. of your revenues
17. 13. O Lord, all that forsake thee shall be a.
20. 11. my persecutors shall stumble and be a.
48. 13. Moab shall be a. of Chemosh, as Israel was
50. 12. your mother that bare you shall be a.
Ezek. 16. 61. shalt remember thy ways, and be a.
43. 10. shew Israel, they may be a. of their iniquities
11. and if they be a. of all that they have done
Hos. 4. 19. they shall be a. because of their sacrifices
10. 6. and Israel shall be a. of his own counsel
Joel 1. 11. be ye a. O ye husbandmen, howl for wheat
2. 26. and my people shall never be a. 27.
Zech. 9. 5. for her expectation shall be a.
13. 4. the prophets every one be a. of his vision
Mark 8. 38. shall be a. of me and my words. Luke 9. 26.
2 Cor. 9. 4. we (that we say not, you) should be a.
Phil. 1. 20. that in nothing I shall be a. but with
2 Thess. 3. 14. no company with him, that he may be a.
Tit. 2. 8. he that is on the contrary part may be a.
1 Pet. 3. 16. may be a. that falsely accuse your good

Not be, or Be not, ASHAMED.

Num. 12. 14. should she not be a. seven days?
Psal. 25. 2. O my God, I trust in thee, let me not be a.
31. 17. let me not be a. O Lord, 119. 116.
37. 19. they shall not be a. in the evil time
119. 6. then shall I not be a. when I have respect to
46. I will speak of thy testimonies, and not be a.
80. let my heart be sound, that I be not a.
127. 5. they shall not be a. but shall speak with
Isa. 29. 22. saith the Lord, Jacob shall not be a.
45. 17. ye shall not be a. world without end
49. 23. they shall not be a. that wait for me
50. 7. my face like a flint, I know I shall not be a.
54. 4. fear not, for thou shalt not be a.
Zeph. 3. 11. in that day shalt thou not be a.
Rom. 9. 33. who believeth on him shall not be a. 10. 11.
2 Cor. 10. 8. for though I boast, I should not be a.
2 Tim. 1. 8. be not therefore a. of testimony of Lord
2. 15. to God, a workman that needeth not be a.
1 Pet. 4. 16. suffer as a Christian, let him not be a.
1 John 2. 28. not be a. before him at his coming

ASHES

Signifies, *The remains of fuel after it has been burned*, 2 Pet. 2. 6. They denote, [1] *The frailty and extreme vileness of man, when compared with his Creator*, Gen. 18. 27. [2] *Deep humiliation*, Esth. 4. 1. Jonah 3. 6.

Gen. 18. 27. to speak, which am but dust and a.
Lev. 6. 10. and the priest shall take up the a.
11. and carry forth the a. without the camp
Num. 19. 9. a man that is clean shall gather the a.
2 Sam. 13. 19. Tamar put a. on her head, and rent
1 Kings 13. 3. altar shall be rent, and a. poured out
20. 38. the prophet disguised himself with a.
Esth. 4. 1. Mordecai put on sackcloth with a.
3. and many lay in sackcloth and a.
Job 2. 8. Job sat down among the a.
13. 12. your remembrances are like to a. your
30. 19. into mire, I am become like dust and a.
42. 6. I abhor myself, and repent in dust and a.
Psal. 20. †3. and turn to a. thy burnt-sacrifice
102. 9. for I have eaten a. like bread, and mingled
147. 16. he scattereth the hoar-frost like a.
Isa. 44. 20. he feedeth on a. a deceived heart turned
58. 5. and to spread sackcloth and a. under him
61. 3. to give them beauty for a. the oil of joy
Jer. 6. 26. O daughter, wallow thyself in a.
Lam. 3. 16. he hath covered me with a.
Ezek. 28. 18. I will bring thee to a. on the earth
Dan. 9. 3. I set my face to seek in sackcloth and a.
Jonah 3. 6. king covered with sackcloth, and sat in a.
Mal. 4. 3. the wicked shall be a. under your feet
Mat. 11. 21. if works were done, they would have repented long ago in sackcloth and a. Luke 10. 13.
Heb. 9. 13. if the a. of an heifer sanctifieth to the
2 Pet. 2. 6. and turning the cities of Sodom into a.

ASIDE.

2 Kings 4. 4. said, thou shalt set a. that which is full
Job 1. †19. came a great wind from a. wilderness
Mark 7. 33. he took him a. from the multitude
John 13. 4. he riseth and laid a. his garment [doth
Heb. 12. 1. let us lay a. every weight, and sin that
See Go, Gone, Turn, Went, Lay.

ASK

Signifies, [1] *To inquire*, Gen. 32. 29. Mark 9. 32. [2] *To require, or demand*, Gen. 34. 12. Dan. 2. 10. [3] *To seek counsel*, Isa. 30. 2. Hag. 2. 11. [4] *To pray*, John 15. 7. Jam. 1. 6. [5] *To expect*, Luke 12. 48. [6] *To salute*, 1 Sam. 25. †5. 2 Sam. 8. †10. [7] *To lay to one's charge*, Psal. 35. †11.

Gen. 32. 29. wherefore dost thou a. after my name?
34. 12. a. me never so much dowry and gift, I give
Deut. 4. 32. for a. now of the days that are past
13. 14. shall a. diligently, and if it be truth
32. 7. a. thy father, and he will shew thee
Josh. 4. 6. when your children a. their fathers, 21.
Judg. 18. 5. a. counsel, we pray thee, of God
1 Sam. 10. †4. and they will a. thee of peace
12. 19. we have added this evil to a. us a king
1 Sam. 25. †5. a. him in name of peace, 2 Sam. 8. †10.
28. 16. why dost thou a. of me, seeing the Lord
2 Sam. 14. 18. hide not from me the thing I a.
1 Kings 3. 5. a. what I shall give thee, 2 Chron. 1. 7.
14. 5. the wife of Jeroboam cometh to a. thee
2 Kings 2. 9. Elijah said, a. what I shall do for thee
2 Chron. 20. 4. Judah gathered to a. help of God
Job 12. 7. a. the beasts, and they shall teach thee
Psal. 2. 8. a. of me, and I will give thee the heathen
Isa. 7. 11. a. thee a sign of Lord, a. it of the depth
12. I will not a. nor will I tempt the Lord
45. 11. saith the Lord, a. me of things to come
58. 2. they a. of me the ordinances of justice
Jer. 6. 16. a. for the old paths, and walk therein
15. 5. who shall go aside, to a. what thou dost
18. 13. a. ye now among the heathen who heard
30. 6. a. and see whether a man doth travail
38. 14. I will a. thee a thing, hide nothing from me
48. 19. a. him that fleeth, and her that escapeth
50. 5. they shall a. the way to Zion with their faces
Lam. 4. 4. the young children a. bread, and no man
Dan. 6. 7. who shall a. a petition of any God, 12.
Hos. 4. 12. my people a. counsel at their stocks
Hag. 2. 11. a. now the priests concerning the law
Zech. 10. 1. a. ye of the Lord rain in time of latter
Mat. 6. 8. what ye have need of, before ye a. him
7. 7. a. and it shall be given you, Luke 11. 9.
9. what man of you, if his son a. bread, Luke 11. 11.
11. shall give good things to them that a. him
14. 7. promised to give her whatsoever she would a.
18. 19. agree touching any thing they shall a.
20. 22. ye know not what ye a. Mark 10. 38.
21. 22. whatsoever ye a. in prayer, believing ye shall
22. 46. nor durst any man a. him more questions, Mark 12. 34. Luke 20. 40.
Mark 6. 22. a. what thou wilt, I will give thee, 23.
9. 32. they were afraid to a. him, Luke 9. 45.
Luke 6. 30. taketh thy goods, a. them not again
11. 13. give the Holy Spirit to them that a. him
12. 48. much committed, of him they will a. more
John 1. 19. when the Jews sent priests to a. him
9. 21. we know not, he is of age, a. him, 23.
11. 22. whatsoever thou wilt a. of God, he will
13. 24. Peter beckoned to him that he should a.
14. 13. whatsoever ye a. in my name, 15. 16.
14. if ye a. any thing in my name I will do it
15. 7. if ye abide in me, a. what ye will, it shall be
16. 19. Jesus knew that they were desirous to a.
23. and in that day ye shall a. me nothing [full
24. a. and ye shall receive, that your joy may be
30. and needest not that any man should a. thee
18. 21. a. them which heard me what I said
Acts 10. 29. I a. therefore for what intent ye sent
1 Cor. 14. 35. let them a. their husbands at home
Eph. 3. 20. to do above all that we can a. or think
Jam. 1. 5. if any lack wisdom, let him a. of God
6. but let him a. in faith, nothing wavering
4. 2. yet ye have not, because ye a. not
3. ye a. and receive not, because ye a. amiss
1 John 3. 22. whatsoever we a. we receive of him
5. 14. if we a. any thing according to his will
15. if we know he heareth us, whatsoever we a.
16. sin a sin which is not unto death, he shall a.
See Counsel.

ASKED.

Gen. 32. 29. Jacob a. him and said, tell me thy name
43. 7. the man a. us straitly of our kindred
Josh. 15. 18. they gave him the city which he a.
Judg. 5. 25. he a. water, she gave him milk
13. 6. but I a. him not whence he was
18. †15. a. him of peace, 1 Sam. 17. †22. | 30. †21.
1 Sam. 1. 17. God grant the petition thou hast a.
†20. she called his name Samuel, that is a. of God
27. the Lord hath given me my petition I a.
1 Kings 3. 11. because thou a. this thing and not a.
2 Kings 2. 10. he said, thou hast a. a hard thing
Ezra 5. 10. we a. their names to certify thee
Job 21. 29. have ye not a. them that go by the way?
Psal. 21. 4. he a. life of thee, thou gavest him
35. †11. they a. me things that I knew not
105. 40. the people a. and he brought quails
Isa. 30. 2. and have not a. at my mouth
41. 28. when I a. of them, could answer a word
65. 1. I am sought of them that a. not for me
Dan. 2. 10. there is no king that a. such things
7. 16. I came and a. him the truth of all this [18.
Mat. 16. 13. he a. his disciples, Mark 8. 27. Luke 9.
22. 23. Sadducees a. him, 35. Mar. 9. 11. | 10. 2. | 12. 18
Luke 18. 40. when come near he a. what wilt thou
John 4. 10. thou wouldest have a. of him
16. 24. hitherto have ye a. nothing in my name
Rom. 10. 20. made manifest to them that a. not

ASKEST.

Judg. 13. 18. why a. thou thus after my name?
John 4. 9. a. drink of me, a woman of Samaria
18. 21. why a. thou me, ask them which heard

ASKETH.

Exod. 13. 14. thy son a. thee in time, Deut. 6. 20.
Mic. 7. 3. prince a. and the judge a. for a reward
Mat. 5. 42. give to him that a. thee, Luke 6. 30.
7. 8. every one that a. receiveth, Luke 11. 10.
John 16. 5. none of you a. me, whither goest thou?
1 Pet. 3. 15. to every one that a. you a reason of hope

ASKING.

1 Sam. 12. 17. may see your wickedness in a. a king
1 Chron. 10. 13. Saul died for a. counsel of a familiar
Psal. 78. 18. tempted God by a. meat for their lust
Luke 2. 46. hearing them, and a. them questions
John 8. 7. they continued a. he lifted up himself
1 Cor. 10. 25. a. no question for conscience, 27.

ASLEEP

Signifies, [1] *To take rest in sleep*, Jonah 1. 5. Mat. 26. 40. [2] *To die*, Acts 7. 60. 2 Pet. 3. 4.

Judg. 4. 21. for Sisera was fast a. and weary
Cant. 7. 9. the lips of those that are a. to speak
Jonah 1. 5. but Jonah lay, and was fast a.
Mat. 8. 24. arose a storm, but he was a. Mark 4. 38.
26. 40. he findeth the disciples a. Mark 14. 40.
Acts 7. 60. when Stephen had said this, he fell a.
1 Cor. 15. 6. part remain, but some are fallen a.
18. then they which are fallen a. in Christ
1 Thess. 4. 13. ignorant concerning them that are a.
1 Th. 4. 15. we alive shall not prevent them that are a.
2 Pet. 3. 4. for since the fathers fell a. all things

ASP, S.

Deut. 32. 33. their wine is the cruel venom of a.
Job 20. 14. his meat is the gall of a. within him
16. he shall suck the poison of a. the viper's tongue
Isa. 11. 8. the child shall play on the hole of the a.
Rom. 3. 13. the poison of a. is under their lips

ASSAULT, ED.

Esth. 8. 11. to cause to perish all that would a. them
Acts 14. 5. when there was an a. made of the Gentiles
17. 5. they a. the house of Jason, and sought to

ASSAY, ED, ING.

Deut. 4. 34. hath God a. to go and take a nation
1 Sam. 17. 39. David a. to go, for he had not proved
Job 4. 2. if we a. to commune with thee, wilt thou
Acts 9. 26. Saul a. to join himself to the disciples
16. 7. they a. to go to Bithynia, but the Spirit
Heb. 11. 29. the Egyptians a. to do, were drowned

ASS. [his a.

Gen. 22. 3. Abraham rose up early, and saddled
5. abide you here with the a. and I and the lad
49. 14. Issachar is a strong a. couching between
Exod. 13. 13. every firstling of an a. redeem with
23. 4. if thou meet thine enemy's a. going astray
12. shalt rest; that thine ox and thine a. may rest
Num. 16. 15. I have not taken one a. from them
22. 23. the a. saw the angel standing, 25. 27.
28. the Lord opened the mouth of the a.
30. the a. said to Balaam, am I not thine a.?
Deut. 22. 10. not plow with an ox and a. together
Josh. 15. 18. and Achsah lighted off her a. Caleb said, what wilt thou? Judg. 1. 14. 1 Sam. 25. 23.
Judg. 15. 16. with the jaw bone of an a. heaps
1 Kings 13. 28. the lion had not torn the a.
2 Kings 6. 25. until an a. head sold for 80 pieces
Job 24. 3. they drive away the a. of the fatherless
Prov. 26. 3. a bridle for the a. and a rod for fool's
Isa. 1. 3. ox his owner, and the a. his master's crib
32. 20. that send forth the feet of the ox and a.
Jer. 22. 19. shall be buried with the burial of an a.
Zech. 9. 9. thy king cometh lowly, riding on an a and on a colt the foal of an a. Mat. 21. 5.
14. 15. and so shall be the plague of the a.
Mat. 21. 2. ye shall find an a. tied, and a colt
Luke 13. 15. doth not each loose his a. on sabbath
14. 5. which of you shall have an a. fallen into pit
John 12. 14. when he had found a young a. sat
2 Pet. 2. 16. the dumb a. speaking forbad madness
See Saddle.

ASS'S COLT.

Gen. 49. 11. binding his a. colt to the choice vine
Job 11. 12. though man be born like a wild a. colt
John 12. 15. thy king cometh sitting on an a. colt

Wild ASS

Job 6. 5. doth the wild a. bray when he hath grass?
39. 5. who hath sent out the wild a. free?
Jer. 2. 24. a wild a. used to the wilderness snuffeth
Hos. 8. 9. they are gone, a wild a. alone by himself

ASSES.

Gen. 12. 16. Abram had he-a. and she-a. and camels
30. 43. Jacob had much cattle, camels, and a.
36. 24. as he fed the a. of Zibeon his father
47. 17. Joseph gave bread in exchange for a.
Judg. 5. 10. speak, ye that ride on white a.
1 Sam. 8. 16. he will take your a. to work
9. 3. the a. of Kish, Saul's father, were lost
20. thy a. that were lost, they are found, 10. 2.
2 Sam. 16. 2. the a. be for the king's household
1 Chron. 27. 30. and over the a. was Jehdeiah
2 Chron. 28. 15. carried the feeble of them upon a.
Ezra 2. 67. a. that went up to Jerusalem, 6720. Neh. 7. 69.
Job 42. 12. for Job had sheep, and a thousand she-a.
Isa. 21. 7. he saw a chariot of a. and of camels
Ezek. 23. 20. whose flesh is as the flesh of a.

Wild ASSES.

Job 24. 5. as wild a. in the desert go they forth
Psal. 104. 11. the wild a. quench their thirst
Isa. 32. 14. the forts shall be a joy of wild a.
Jer. 14. 6. wild a. snuffed up the wind like dragons
Dan. 5. 21. Nebuchadnezzar's dwell. was with w. a.

Young ASSES.

Isa. 30. 6. they will carry their riches on young a.
24. y. a. that ear the ground shall eat provender

ASSEMBLE.

Num. 10. 3. when they blow, the assembly shall a
2 Sam. 20. 4. a. me the men of Judah, and be here
Isa. 11. 12. he shall a. the outcasts of Israel
45. 20. a. yourselves, and come, draw near together
48. 14. all ye a. yourselves and hear
Jer. 4. 5. a. yourselves, and let us go into the cities
8. 14. why do we sit still? a. yourselves, let us
Ezek. 11. 17. I will a. you out of the countries
39. 17. a. yourselves, gather to my sacrifice
Hos. 7. 14. they a. themselves for corn and wine
Joel 2. 16. a. the elders, gather the children
3. 11. a. yourselves and come, all ye heathen
Amos 3. 9. a. yourselves on the mount of Samaria
Mic. 2. 12. I will surely a. O Jacob, all of thee
4. 6. saith the Lord, I will a. her that halteth
Zeph. 3. 8. I'll a. the kingdoms to pour indignation

ASSEMBLED.

Exod. 38. 8. women which a. at the door of the taber.
1 Sam. 2. 22. they lay with the women that a.
1 Chron. 15. 4. David a. the children of Aaron
2 Chron. 30. 13. a. much people to keep the feast
Ezra 9. 4. then a. to me every one that trembled
10. 1. when Ezra had prayed, there a. to him
Neh. 9. 1. the children of Israel a. with fasting
Psal. 48. 4. lo the kings were a. they passed by
Isa. 43. 9. let the people be a. who can declare this
Jer. 5. 7. a. themselves by troops in harlots' houses
Dan. 6. 11. these men a. and found Daniel praying
Mat. 28. 12. when they a. they gave large money
John 20. 19. the disciples a. for fear of the Jews
Acts 1. 4. being a. commanded them not to depart
4. 31. the place was shaken where they were a.
11. 26. a whole year they a. with the church
15. 25. it seemed good to us a. with one accord

ASSEMBLING.

Heb. 10. 25. forsake not the a. yourselves together

ASSEMBLY.

Gen. 28. + 3. that thou mayest be an *a.* of people
49. 6. to their *a.* mine honour be not thou united
Exod. 12. 6. the whole *a.* shall kill it in the even
16. 3. to kill this whole *a.* with hunger
Lev. 4. 13. the thing be hid from the eyes of the *a.*
Num. 10. 2. and make 2 trumpets for calling the *a.*
20. 6. Moses and Aaron went from presence of *a.*
Deut. 9. 10. spake in the mount out of the midst of the fire, in the day of your *a.* 10. 4. | 18. 16.
Judg. 21. 8. none from Jabesh-Gilead to the *a.*
1 *Sam.* 17. 47. all this *a.* shall know the Lord saveth
2 *Chron.* 30. 23. the whole *a.* took counsel to keep
Neh. 5. 7. I set a great *a.* against them
Psal. 22. 16. the *a* of the wicked have inclosed me
89. 7. God is to be feared in the *a.* of the saints
107. 32. praise him in the *a.* of the elders
111. 1. I will praise him in the *a.* of the upright
Prov. 5. 14. I was in all evil in the midst of the *a.*
Jer. 6. 11. I will pour it on the *a.* of young men
9. 2. for they be an *a.* of treacherous men
15. 17. I sat not in the *a.* of the mockers
Lam. 2. 6. he hath destroyed the places of the *a.*
Ezek. 13. 9. they shall not be in the *a.* of my people
23. 24. shall come against Aholibah with an *a.*
Acts 19. 32. the *a.* was confused, and part knew not
39. it shall be determined in a lawful *a.*
41. he had thus spoken, he dismissed the *a.*
Heb. 12. 23. to the general *a.* of the first-born
Jam. 2. 2. if there come to your *a.* a man

Solemn ASSEMBLY.

Lev. 23. 36. on the eighth day it is a *solemn a.* *Num.* 29. 35. *Neh.* 8. 18.
Deut. 16. 8. on the seventh day a *solemn a.* to the Lord
2 *Kin.* 10. 20. Jehu said, proclaim a *solemn a.* for Baal
2 *Chr.* 7. 9. in the eighth day they made a *solemn a.*
Joel 1. 14. sanctify a fast, call a *solemn a.* 2. 15.
Zeph. 3. 18. them that are sorrowful for the *solemn a.*

ASSEMBLIES.

Psal. 86. 14. the *a.* of violent men sought my soul
Eccl. 12. 11. as nails fastened by the masters of *a.*
Isa. 1. 13. the calling of *a.* I cannot away with
4. 5. God will create on her *a.* a cloud and smoke
14. + 31. he shall not be alone in his *a.*
Ezek. 44. 24. they shall keep my laws in all mine *a.*
Amos 5. 21. I will not smell in your solemn *a.*

ASSENT, ED.

2 *Chron.* 18. 12. declare good to the king with one *a.*
Luke 23. + 24. Pilate *a.* it should be as they required
Acts 24. 9. Jews also *a.* that these things were so

ASSIGNED.

Gen. 47. 22. for the priests had a portion *a.* them
Josh. 20. 8. they *a.* Bezer a city of refuge
2 *Sam.* 11. 16. he *a.* Uriah to a place he knew

ASSIST.

Rom. 16. 2. that ye *a.* her in whatsoever business

ASSOCIATE.

Isa. 8. 9. *a.* yourselves, and ye shall be broken in [pieces
Dan. 11. + 6. at the end of years they shall *a.*

AS SOON.

Exod. 9. 29. *a.* as I am gone out of the city
2 *Chron.* 31. 5. *a.* as the commandment came abroad
Psal. 18. 44. *a.* as they hear of me, shall obey me
Isa. 66. 8. *a.* as Zion travailed, she brought forth
Luke 1. 44. *a.* as the voice of thy salutation sounded
8. 6. *a.* as it was sprung up, it withered away
John 18. 6. *a.* as he said, I am he, they went back
Acts 10. 29. therefore came I *a.* as I was sent for
12. 18. *a.* as it was day there was no small stir
Rev. 10. 10. *a.* as I had eaten it, my belly was bitter
12. 4. for to devour the child *a.* as it was born

ASSURANCE.

Deut. 28. 66. thou shalt have none *a.* of thy life
Isa. 32. 17. and the effect of righteousness, *a.*
Acts 17. 31. whereof he hath given *a.* to all men
Col. 2. 2. to all riches of the full *a.* of understanding
1 *Thess.* 1. 5. our gospel came in much *a.*
Heb. 6. 11. to the full *a.* of hope to the end
10. 22. let us draw near in full *a.* of faith

ASSURE.

1 *John* 3. 19. and shall *a.* our hearts before him

ASSURED.

Lev. 27. 19. add the fifth, and it shall be *a.* to him
Jer. 14. 13. I will give you *a.* peace in this place
Rom. 14. + 5. let every one be fully *a.* in his mind
2 *Tim.* 3. 14. continue in things thou hast been *a.*

ASSUREDLY.

1 *Sam.* 28. 1. know *a.* thou shalt go out with me
1 *Kings* 1. 13. *a.* Solomon thy son shall reign, 17, 30.
Jer. 32. 41. I will plant them in this land *a.*
38. 17. if thou *a.* go forth to the king of Babylon
49. 12. they have *a.* drunken, and shalt thou go
Acts 2. 36 let all the house of Israel know *a.*
16. 10. *a.* gathering that the Lord had called us

ASSWAGE, ED.

Gen. 8. 1. over the earth, and the waters were *a.*
Job 16. 5. moving of my lips should *a.* your grief
6. though I speak, yet my grief is not *a.*

ASTONIED.

Ezra 9. 3. plucked off the hair, and sat down *a.*
Job 17. 8. upright men shall be *a.* at this
18. 20. they that come after him shall be *a.*
Ezek. 4. 17. that they may be *a.* one with another
Dan. 3. 24. Nebuchadnezzar was *a.* and rose in haste
4. 19. then Daniel was *a.* for one hour
5. 9. his countenance was changed, his lords *a.*

ASTONISHED.

Lev. 26. 32. and your enemies shall be *a.*
1 *Kings* 9. 8. every one that passeth by shall be *a.* *Jer.* 18. 16. | 19. 8. | 49. 17. | 50. 13.
Job 26. 11. the pillars of heaven tremble and are *a.*
Isa. 52. 14. as many were *a.* at thee, his visage
Jer. 2. 12. be *a.* O ye heavens, at this
4. 9. the heart of the priests shall be *a.*
14. 9. why shouldest thou be as a man *a.*
Ezek. 3. 15. I remained *a.* among them seven days
26. 16. shall tremble at every moment, and be *a.*
28. 19. they that know thee shall be *a.* at thee
8. 27. I Daniel was *a.* at the vision
Mat. 7. 28. the people were *a.* at his doctrine, 22. 33. *Mark* 1. 22. | 6. 2. | 11. 18. *Luke* 4. 32.
Mark 5. 42. they were *a.* with great astonishment
Mark 7. 37. and were beyond measure *a.* 10. 26.
10. 24. the disciples were *a.* at his words
Luke 2. 47. *a.* at his understanding and answers
5. 9. he was *a.* at the draught of fishes
8. 56. her parents were *a.* but he charged them
24. 22. yea, and certain women also made us *a.*
Acts 9. 6. Saul trembling and *a.* said, Lord, what
10. 45. of the circumcision which believed, were *a.*
12. 16. had opened door and saw Peter, they were *a.*
13. 12. the deputy when he saw, believed, being *a.*

ASTONISHMENT.

Deut. 28. 28. the Lord shall smite thee with *a.*
37. thou shalt become an *a.* and a proverb
2 *Chr.* 7. 21. this house shall be an *a.* to every one
29. 8. he hath delivered them to *a.* and hissing
Psal. 60. 3. hast made us to drink the wine of *a.*
Jer. 5. + 30. *a.* is committed in the land
8. 21. I am black, *a.* hath taken hold on me
25. 9. I will make them an *a.* and a hissing, 18.
11. this whole land shall be a desolation and *a.*
29. 18. I'll deliver them to be a curse and an *a.*
42. 18. ye shall be an execration and an *a.* 44. 12.
44. 22. therefore is your land an *a.* and a curse
51. 37. Babylon shall become heaps and an *a.*
Ezek. 4. 16. son of man, behold, they shall drink water by measure, and with *a.* 12. 19.
5. 15. it shall be an *a.* to the nations about thee
23. 33. thou shalt be filled with the cup of *a.*
Zech. 12. 4. I will smite every horse with *a.*

ASTRAY; *see* WENT, GO, GONE.

ASTROLOGERS.

Isa. 47. 13. let now the *a.* the star-gazers, stand
Dan. 1. 20. he found them ten times better than *a.*
2. 27. the secret cannot the *a.* shew to the king
4. 7. then came in the magicians and the *a.*
5. 7 the king cried aloud, to bring in the *a.*

ASUNDER; *see* CLEAVE, CUT, DIVIDE, PUT.

AS WELL.

Lev. 24. 16. *as well* the stranger, as he that is born in
22. one law, *as well* for the stranger, as for your
Deut. 20. 8. lest his brethrens' heart faint, *as well* as
2 *Sam.* 11. 25. the sword devours one *as well* as [another
1 *Chr.* 25. 8. they cast lots, *as well* the small as great
2 *Chr.* 31. 15. to give *as well* to the great as the small
Job 12. 3. but I have understanding *as well* as you
Psal. 87. 7. *as well* the singers as the players shall be
Acts 10. 47. who received the Holy Ghost *as well* as
1 *Cor.* 9. 5. to lead about a sister *as well* as other apos.
Heb. 4. 2. to us the gospel preached *as well* as to them

ATE.

Psal. 106. 28. they *a.* the sacrifices of the dead
Dan. 10. 3. I *a.* no pleasant bread nor flesh
Rev. 10. 10. I took the little book, and *a.* it up

ATHIRST.

Judg. 15. 18. Samson was sore *a.* and called on Lord
Ruth 2. 9. when *a.* go to the vessels and drink
Mat. 25. 44. when saw we thee *a.* or a stranger
Rev. 21. 6. I'll give to him that is *a.* of fountain
22. 17. Spirit and bride say, let him that is *a.* come

ATONEMENT

Signifies, [1] *Reconciliation, or appeasing of anger,* Rom. 5. 1. [2] *A ransom,* Job 33. + 24.
Exod. 29. 33. eat things wherewith *a.* was made
36. thou shalt offer a bullock every day for *a.*
37. seven days thou shalt make *a.* for the altar
30. 10. Aaron once in year shall make *a.* upon it
15. to make an *a.* for your souls, *Lev.* 17. 11.
16. thou shalt take the *a.* money of Israel
32. 30. peradventure I shall make an *a.* for sin
Lev. 1. 4. it shall be accepted for him to make *a.*
4. 20. the priest shall make an *a.* for them, and be forgiven, 26. 31. 35. | 5. 6. | 6. 7. | 12. 8. | 14. 18. *Num.* 15. 25.
8. 34. so the Lord hath commanded to make *a.*
9. 7. make *a.* for thyself and for them, 16. 24.
10. 17. God hath given it you to make *a.* for them
12. 7. make an *a.* for her, and she shall be clean
14. 53. make an *a.* for the house, it shall be clean
16. 10. the scape-goat shall be presented to make *a.*
11. Aaron shall make an *a.* for himself and house
16. he shall make an *a.* for the holy place
17. shall be no man there, when he maketh *a.*
18. he shall go and make *a.* for the altar
27. whose blood was brought in to make *a.*
33. he shall make *a.* for the holy sanctuary
34. everlasting statute to make *a.* once a year
23. 27. tenth day of 7th month shall be a day of *a.*
28. do no work, for it is a day of *a.* to make *a.*
25. 9. in the day of *a.* make the trumpets sound
Num. 8. 21. made *a.* for the Levites to cleanse them
19. given the Levites to make *a.* for Israel
16. 46. go quickly, make *a.* for wrath is gone out
25. 13. Phinehas have it, because he made an *a.*
28. 22. a goat for a sin-offering to make *a.* 30.
29. 5. a kid of the goats to make an *a.* for you
31. 50. ear-rings to make an *a.* for our souls
2 *Sam.* 21. 3. wherewith shall I make the *a.?*
1 *Chron.* 6. 49. Aaron and sons appointed to make *a.*
2 *Chr.* 29. 24. the priests killed them to make an *a.*
Neh. 10. 33. ordinances for offering to make an *a.*
Job 33. + 24. deliver him, I have found an *a.*
Rom. 5. 11. by whom we have now received *a.*

ATTAIN.

Psal. 139. 6. it is high, I cannot *a.* unto it.
Prov. 1. 5. man of understanding shall *a.* to wisdom
Ezek. 46. 7. according as his hand shall *a.* to it
Hos. 8. 5. how long ere they *a.* to innocency ?
Acts 27. 12. if they might *a.* to Phenice
Phil. 3. 11. I might *a.* to the resurrection of the dead

ATTAINED.

Gen. 47. 9. and have not *a.* to the days of my father
Lev. 25. + 26. his hand hath *a.* and found sufficiency
2 *Sam.* 23. 19. howbeit he *a.* not to the first three, 23. 1 *Chron.* 11. 21, 25.
Rom. 9. 30. the Gentiles have *a.* to righteousness
31. Israel hath not *a.* to the law of righteousness
Phil. 3. 12. not as though I had already *a.* or perfect
16. whereto we have already *a.* let us walk
1 *Tim.* 4. 6. good doctrine, whereto thou hast *a.*

ATTEND.

Esth. 4. 5. Hatach whom he appointed to *a.* her
Psal. 17. 1. O Lord, *a.* to my cry, 61. 1. | 142. 6.
55. 2. *a.* to me, hear me, I mourn and make a noise
86. 6. and *a.* to the voice of my supplication
Prov. 4. 1. hear and *a.* to know understanding
20. my son, *a.* to my words, incline thine ear, 7. 24.
5. 1. my son *a.* to my wisdom, and bow thine ear
1 *Cor.* 7. 35. may *a.* on the Lord without distraction

ATTENDANCE.

1 *Kings* 10. 5. saw the *a.* of his ministers, 2 *Chr.* 9. 4.
1 *Tim.* 4. 13. till I come, give *a.* to reading
Heb. 7. 13. of which no man gave *a.* at the altar

ATTENDED.

Job 32. 12. I *a.* to you, none of you convinced Job
Psal. 66. 19. he hath *a.* to the voice of my prayer
Acts 16. 14. she *a.* to the things spoken by Paul

ATTENDING.

Rom. 13. 6. ministers *a.* continually on this very thing

ATTENT.

2 *Chron.* 6. 40. let thine ears be *a.* to the prayer
7. 15. mine ears shall be *a.* to the prayer made

ATTENTIVE.

Neh. 1. 6. let thine ear now be *a.* 11. *Psal.* 130. 2.
8. 3. the ears of the people were *a.* *Luke* 19. 48.

ATTENTIVELY.

Job 37. 2. hear *a.* the noise of his voice and sound

ATTIRE, ED.

Lev. 16. 4. with the linen mitre shall Aaron be *a.*
Prov. 7. 10. met him a woman with *a.* of an harlot
Jer. 2. 32. can a bride forget her *a.?* yet my people
Ezek. 23. 15. exceeding in dyed *a.* on their heads

ATTRIBUTED.

Job 1. + 22. Job sinned not, nor *a.* folly to God

AVAILETH.

Esth. 5. 13. yet all this *a.* me nothing so long as I see
Gal. 5. 6. in Christ circumcision *a.* not, 6. 15.
Jam. 5. 16. the prayer of a righteous man *a.* much

AUDIENCE.

Gen. 23. 13. Abraham spake to Ephron in *a.* of people
Exod. 24. 7. took book of covenant, and read in *a.*
1 *Sam.* 25. 24. let thine handmaid speak in thy *a.*
1 *Chron.* 28. 8. in the *a.* of our God keep and seek
Neh. 13. 1. they read in the book of Moses in the *a.*
Luke 7. 1. ended all his sayings in the *a.* of the people
20. 45. in *a.* of the people he said to his disciples
Acts 13. 16. Israel, and ye that fear God, give *a.*
15. 12. then all the multitude gave *a.* to Barnabas
22. 22. and they gave him *a.* to this word

AVENGE.

Lev. 19. 18. thou shalt not *a.* nor bear grudge
26. 25. that shall *a.* the quarrel of my covenant
Num. 31. 2. *a.* Israel of the Midianites, 3.
Deut. 32. 43. he will *a.* the blood of his servants
1 *Sam.* 24. 12. the Lord judge and *a.* me of thee
2 *Kings* 9. 7. smite the house of Ahab, that I may *a.*
Esth. 8. 13. Jews *a.* themselves on their enemies
Isa. 1. 24. I will *a.* me of mine enemies
Jer. 46. 10. a day of vengeance that he may *a.*
Hos. 1. 4. I will *a.* the blood of Jezreel on Jehu
Luke 18. 3. saying, *a.* me of mine adversary
7. shall not God *a.* his own elect, who cry day
8. I tell you that he will *a.* them speedily
Rom. 12. 19. beloved, *a.* not yourselves, but give
Rev. 6. 10. how long dost thou not *a.* our blood

AVENGED.

Gen. 4. 24. if Cain should be *a.* seven-fold, Lamech
Exod. 21. + 20. and he die, he shall be surely *a.*
Josh. 10. 13. sun and moon stayed till people had *a.*
Judg. 15. 7. though ye have done this, yet I will be *a.*
16. 28. may be *a.* on Philistines for my two eyes
1 *Sam.* 14. 24. that eateth any food, that I may be *a.*
18. 25. an hundred foreskins, to be *a.* of enemies
25. 31. or that my Lord hath *a.* himself
2 *Sam.* 4. 8. the Lord hath *a.* my lord the king
18. 19. how the Lord hath *a.* him of his enemies
31. the Lord hath *a.* thee this day of them
Jer. 5. 9. my soul be *a.* on such a nation, 29. | 9. 9.
Acts 7. 24. Moses *a.* him that was oppressed
Rev. 18. 20. rejoice, for God hath *a.* you on her
19. 2. hath *a.* blood of his servants at her hand

AVENGER.

Num. 35. 12. cities for refuge from the *a.* *Josh.* 20. 3.
Deut. 19. 6. lest the *a.* of blood pursue the slayer
12. the elders deliver him into the hand of the *a.*
Josh. 20. 5. if the *a* of blood pursue after him
9. not die by the hand of the *a.* till he stood
Psal. 8. 2. thou mightest still the enemy and *a.*
44. 16. by reason of the enemy and *a.*
1 *Thess.* 4. 6. because the Lord is the *a.* of all such

AVENGETH.

2 *Sam.* 22. 48. it is God that *a.* me, *Psal.* 18. 47.

AVENGING.

Judg. 5. 2. praise the Lord for the *a.* of Israel
1 *Sam.* 25. 26. Lord hath withholden thee from *a.*
33. blessed be thou who kept me from *a.*

AVERSE.

Mic. 2. 8. pass by securely, as men *a.* from war

AUGMENT.

Num. 32. 14. ye are risen to *a.* the fierce anger

AUNT.

Lev. 18. 14. nor approach to his wife, she is thy *a.*

AVOUCHED.

Deut. 26. 17. hast this day *a.* the Lord to be thy God
18. the Lord hath *a.* thee to be his people

AVOID.

Prov. 4. 15. *a.* it, pass not by it, turn from it
Rom. 16. 17. mark them that cause divisions, and *a.*
1 *Cor.* 7. 2. to *a.* fornication, let every man have his
2 *Tim.* 2. 23. foolish and unlearned questions *a.*
Tit. 3. 9. *a.* foolish questions and genealogies

AVOIDED, ING.

1 *Sam.* 18. 11. David *a.* out of his presence twice
2 *Cor.* 8. 20. *a.* this, that no man should blame us
1 *Tim.* 6. 20. *a.* profane and vain babblings

AUSTERE.

Luke 19. 21. I feared, because thou art an *a.* man

AUTHOR.

Acts 3. + 15. and killed the *a.* of life
1 *Cor.* 14. 33. God is not the *a.* of confusion
Heb. 5. 9. he became the *a.* of eternal salvation
12. 2. looking to Jesus, the *a.* and finisher of faith

AUTHORITY

Signifies, [1] *Power, rule, or dignity,* Prov. 29. 2.

17

Luke 19. 17. [2] *A convincing efficacy and power,* Mat. 7. 29. [3] *A warrant, order, or authentic permission,* Mat. 21. 23. Acts 9. 14.
Esth. 9. 29. Esther and Mordecai wrote with a.
Prov. 29. 2. when righteous are in a. people rejoice
Mat. 7. 29. taught them as one having a. Mark 1. 22.
8. 9. for I am a man under a. and say, Luke 7. 8.
20. 25. they that are great exercise a. Mark 10. 42.
21. 23. by what a. dost thou these? Mark 11. 28.
Mark 1. 27. for with a. commandeth he even the unclean spirits, and they obey him, Luke 4. 36.
13. 34. left his house, and gave a. to his servants
Luke 9. 1. he gave them power and a. over all devils
19. 17. been faithful, have thou a. over ten cities
20. 20. might deliver him to a. of the governor
22. 25. that exercise a. are called benefactors
John 5. 27. hath given him a. to execute judgment
Acts 8. 27. eunuch of great a. under Candace queen
9. 14. here he hath a. to bind, 26. 10, 12.
1 Cor. 15. 24. when he shall have put down all a.
2 Cor. 10. 8. should boast somewhat more of our a.
1 Thess. 2. † 6. when we might have used a.
1 Tim. 2. 2. supplication for kings and all in a.
12. I suffer not a woman to usurp a. over the man
Tit. 2. 15. exhort and rebuke with all a.
1 Pet. 3. 22. angels and a. made subject to him
Rev. 13. 2. the dragon gave him power and great a.

AWAKE

Signifies, [1] *To come out of natural sleep,* Luke 9. 32. [2] *To rouse up out of spiritual sleep, by a vigorous exercise of grace, by leaving off all sinful courses, and setting about the performance of duties required,* Rom. 13. 11. Eph. 5. 14. [3] *To raise from the dead,* Job 14. 12. John 11. 11. [4] *To give present help after it hath long been kept from us, as though God had forgotten us,* Psal. 7. 6. Isa. 51. 9.
Awake not my love till he please, Cant. 2. 7. *Give my beloved Saviour no occasion of offence or departure; neither interrupt that peace I enjoy in him, so long as he is pleased to continue it.*
Judg. 5. 12. a. a. Deborah, a. a. utter a song, arise
Job 8. 6. surely now he would a. for thee
14. 12. till heavens be no more, they shall not a.
19. † 26. I shall a. though this body be destroyed
Psal. 7. 6. a. for me to the judgment, 35. 23.
17. 15. be satisfied when I a. with thy likeness
44. 23. a. why sleepest thou, O Lord, arise
57. 8. a. my glory, I myself will a. early, 108. 2.
59. 4. they prepare, a. to help me, and behold
5. O Lord God, a. to visit all the heathen
Prov. 23. 35. when shall I a. I will seek it yet again
Cant. 2. 7. not a. my love till he please, 3. 5. | 8. 4.
4. 16. a. O north wind, and come, thou south
Isa. 26. 19. a. and sing ye that dwell in the dust
51. 9. a. a. put on strength, O arm of the Lord, a. as in the ancient days, 52. 1.
17. a. a. stand up, O Jerusalem, which hast drunk
Jer. 51. 57. sleep a perpetual sleep, and not a.
Dan. 12. 2. many that sleep in the dust shall a.
Joel 1. 5. a. ye drunkards, weep and howl all ye
Hab. 2. 7. shall they not a. that shall vex thee
19. woe to him that saith to the wood, a.
Zech. 13. 7. a. O sword, against my Shepherd, smite
Mark 4. 38. he was asleep, and they a. him
Luke 9. 32. when they were a. they saw his glory
John 11. 11. I go that I may a. him out of sleep
Rom. 13. 11. it is high time to a. out of sleep
1 Cor. 15. 34. a. to righteousness, and sin not
Eph. 5. 14. a. thou that sleepest, and arise from dead
2 Tim. 2. † 26. may a. themselves out of the snare

AWAKED.

Gen. 28. 16. Jacob a. out of his sleep, and said
Judg. 16. 14. Samson a. and went away with the pin
1 Sam. 26. 12. no man saw it nor knew it, neither a.
1 Kings 18. 27. he sleepeth and must be a.
2 Kings 4. 31. Gehazi told him, the child is not a.
Psal. 3. 5. I a. for the Lord sustained me
78. 65. then the Lord a. as one out of sleep
Jer. 31. 26. upon this I a. and beheld, and my sleep

AWAKEST.

Psal. 73. 20. when thou a. shalt despise their image
Prov. 6. 22. when thou a. it shall talk with thee

AWAKETH, ING.

Psal. 73. 20. as a dream when one a. so, O Lord
Isa. 29. 8. he a. and his soul is empty, a. and is faint
Acts 16. 27. the keeper of the prison a. out of sleep

AWARE.

Cant. 6. 12. or ever I was a. my soul made me like
Jer. 50. 24. art taken, O Babylon, and thou wast not a.
Luke 11. 44. men that walk over them, are not a.

AWAY.

Gen. 15. 11. when fowls came Abram drove them a.
Exod. 8. 28. only ye shall not go very far a.
19. 24. the Lord said to him, a. get thee down
2 Chron. 35. 23. have me a. for I am wounded
Isa. 1. 13. calling of assemblies I cannot a. with
Luke 4. † 34. a. what have we to do with thee
23. 18. a. with this man, release to us Barabbas
John 19. 15. a. with him, a. with him, Acts 21. 36.
Acts 22. 22. a. with such a fellow from the earth

AWE, ETH.

Psal. 4. 4. stand in a. and sin not, commune with
33. 8. inhabitants of the world stand in a. of him
119. 161. my heart standeth in a. of thy word
Prov. 17. † 10. a reproof a. more a wise man

AWL.

Exod. 21. 6. his master shall bore his ear with an a.
Deut. 15. 17. thou shalt take an a. and thrust it

AWOKE.

Gen. 9. 24. Noah a. from his wine, and knew what
41. 4. eat up the fat kine, so Pharaoh a. 7. 21.
Judg. 16. 20. Samson a. out of his sleep and said
1 Kings 3. 15. Solomon a. and behold it was a dream
Mat. 8. 25. his disciples came and a. him, Luke 8. 24.

AX

Signifies, [1] *A carpenter's tool,* Judg. 9. 48. [2] *A human instrument, the king of Assyria,* Isa. 10. 15. [3] *God's vengeance and judgment upon barren and incorrigible sinners,* Mat. 3. 10.
Deut. 19. 5. his hand fetched a stroke with the ax
20. 19. nor destroy the trees by forcing an ax

Judg. 9. 48. Abimelech took an ax in his hand
1 Sam. 13. 20. Israel went down to sharpen his ax
1 Kings 6. 7. neither hammer nor ax was heard
2 Kings 6. 5. the ax-head fell into the water
Isa. 10. 15. shall the ax boast itself against him
Jer. 10. 3. for one cuts a tree with the ax
51. 20. thou art my battle-ax and weapons
Mat. 3. 10. the ax is laid to root of trees, Luke 3. 9.

AXES.

1 Sam. 13. 21. yet they had a file for the a.
2 Sam. 12. 31. he put them under saws and a. of iron, and made them pass through, 1 Chr. 20. 3.
Psal. 74. 5. a man was famous as he lifted up a.
6. they break down the carved work with a.
Jer. 46. 22. and come against her with a. as hewers
Ezek. 26. 9. with a. he shall break down thy tower

AXLE-TREES.

1 Kings 7. 32. the a.-tr. of the wheel join to the base
33. a.-trees, naves, and felloes, were all molten

B.

BABBLER.

Eccl. 10. 11. serpent will bite, and a b. is no better
Acts 17. 18. and some said, what will this b. say?

BABBLING, S.

Prov. 23. 29. who hath contentions? who hath b?
1 Tim. 6. 20. avoiding profane and vain b.
2 Tim. 2. 16. but shun profane and vain b. they

BABE

Signifies, [1] *An infant or child,* Exod. 2. 6. Luke 2. 12. [2] *Such as are weak in faith and knowledge, being ignorant and inconstant, like infants,* 1 Cor. 3. 1. Heb. 5. 13. [3] *Foolish, froward, and unteachable men, incapable of government, for want of understanding, experience, and manners,* Isa. 3. 4.
Exod. 2. 6. saw the child, and behold the b. wept
Luke 1. 41. heard Mary, the b. leaped in her womb
44. the b. leaped in my womb for joy
2. 12. ye shall find b. wrapped in swaddling clothes
16. came and found the b. lying in a manger
Heb. 5. 13. unskilful in the word, for he is a b.

BABES.

Psal. 8. 2. out of the mouth of b. Mat. 21. 16.
17. 14. they leave rest of their substance to their b.
Isa. 3. 4. their princes and b. shall rule over them
Mat. 11. 25. and hast revealed them to b. Luke 10. 21.
Rom. 2. 20. instructor of foolish, a teacher of b.
1 Cor. 3. 1. as to carnal, even as unto b. in Christ
1 Pet. 2. 2. as new-born b. desire the sincere milk of

BACK.

Exod. 18. 2. Zipporah, after he had sent her b.
23. 4. or ass going astray, thou shalt bring it b.
Num. 22. 34. if it please thee, I will get me b.
24. 11. the Lord hath kept thee b. from honour
Josh. 8. 26. Joshua drew not his hand b. till he had
Ruth 2. 6. the Moabitish damsel that came b.
2 Sam. 15. 20. return, and take b. thy brethren
19. 10. why speak ye not of bringing the king b.?
1 Kings 13. 22. but camest b. and hast eaten bread
22. 26. and carry him b. to Amon the governor
2 Chron. 13. 14. when Judah looked b. behold
25. 13. but the soldiers that Amaziah sent b.
Job 26. 9. he holdeth b. the face of his throne
Jer. 46. 5. they are fled apace, and look not b.
Hos. 4. 16. Israel slideth b. as a backsliding heifer
Nah. 2. 8. stand, shall they cry, none shall look b.
Mat. 24. 18. nor let him that is in field return b.
28. 2. angel rolled b. the stone from the door
Luke 8. 37. went into the ship, and returned b. again
9. 62. put his hand to plough, and looking b. is
17. 31. let him likewise not return b.
See DRAW, GO, BRING, KEEP, KEPT, TURN, WENT.

BACK, *Substantive.*

1 Sam. 10. 9. he turned his b. to go from Samuel
1 Kings 14. 9. hast cast me behind thy b. Ezek. 23. 35.
Psal. 21. 12. thou shalt make them turn their b.
129. 3. the plowers plowed on my b. made furrows
Prov. 10. 13. a rod for the b. of him, 19. 29. | 26. 3.
Isa. 38. 17. thou hast cast my sins behind thy b.
50. 6. I gave my b. to the smiters, and my cheeks
Jer. 2. 27. they have turned their b. to thee
18. 17. I will show them the b. and not the face
32. 33. they have turned to me the b. and not face
48. 39. how hath Moab turned the b. with shame
Dan. 7. 6. which had on the b. of it four wings
Rom. 11. 10. not see, and bow down their b. alway

BACK-BONE.

Lev. 3. 9. the rump shall he take off hard by the b.-b.

BACK-PARTS.

Exod. 33. 23. away my hand, thou shalt see my b.-p.

BACKS.

Neh. 9. 26. they cast thy law behind their b.
Ezek. 8. 16. men with their b. towards the temple
10. 12. their whole body and b. full of eyes
See TURNED.

BACKBITERS.

Rom. 1. 30. b. haters of God, despiteful, proud

BACKBITETH.

Psal. 15. 3. he that b. not with his tongue

BACKBITING.

Prov. 25. 23. so an angry countenance, a b. tongue
2 Cor. 12. 20. lest there be debates, strifes, b.

BACKSIDE.

Exod. 3. 1. Moses led the flock to the b. of the desert
26. 12. the half-curtain shall hang over the b.
Rev. 5. 1. on the b. sealed with seven seals

BACKSLIDER.

Prov. 14. 14. b. in heart be filled with his ways

BACKSLIDING, S.

Jer. 2. 19. and thy b. shall reprove thee
3. 6. hast thou seen what b. Israel hath done?
8. causes whereby b. Israel committed adultery
3. 11. the b Israel hath justified herself more
12. return, thou b. Israel, saith the Lord
14. turn, O b. children, saith the Lord, 22.
5. 6. because their transgressions and b. increased
8. 5. this people slidden back by a perpetual b.
14. 7. for our b. are many, we sinned against thee
Jer. 31. 22. how long go about, O b. daughter, 49. 4.
Hos. 4. 16. Israel slideth back, as a b. heifer
11. 7. my people are bent to b. from me
14. 4. I will heal their b. I will love them freely
Zech. 7. † 11. they gave a b. shoulder and stopped

BACKWARD.

Gen. 9. 23. went b. and their faces were b.
49. 17. Dan a serpent, so that his rider shall fall b.
1 Sam. 4. 18. Eli fell from off the seat b. by the gate
2 Kings 20. 10. let the shadow return b. Isa. 38. 8.
Job 23. 8. and b. but I cannot perceive him
Psal. 40. 14. let them be driven b. that wish me evil
70. 2. let them be turned b. that desire my hurt
Isa. 1. 4. they provoked, and are gone away b.
28. 13. that they might go and fall b. be broken
44. 25. that turneth wise men b. and maketh their
59. 14. judgment is turned away b. and justice
Jer. 7. 24. but they went b. and not forward
15. 6. thou art gone b. therefore I will destroy
Lam. 1. 8. Jerusalem sigheth and turneth b.
John 18. 6. they went b. and fell to the ground

BAD.

Gen. 24. 50. we cannot speak to thee b. or good
31. 24. speak not to Jacob good or b. 29.
Lev. 27. 10. a good for a b. or a b. for a good
12. the priest value it, whether it be good or b.
14. estimate the house, whether it be good or b.
33. he shall not search whether it be good or b.
Num. 13. 19. the land they dwell in, if good or b.
24. 13. to do either good or b. of my own mind
2 Sam. 13. 22. Absalom spake neither good nor b.
14. 17. so is my lord the king to discern good or b.
1 Kings 3. 9. a heart that I may discern good and b.
Ezra 4. 12. building the rebellious and b. city
Jer. 24. 2. the figs could not be eaten, they were so b.
Mat. 13. 48. gathered the good but cast the b. away
22. 10. good and b. and the wedding was furnished
2 Cor. 5. 10. that he hath done, whether good or b.

BADNESS.

Gen. 41. 19. never saw in the land of Egypt for b.

BADE, EST.

Gen. 27. 19. I have done according as thou b. me
43. 17. and the man did as Joseph b. and brought
Exod. 16. 24. laid it up till morning as Moses b.
Num. 14. 10. all the congregation b. stone them
Josh. 11. 9. Joshua did to them as the Lord b. him
Ruth 3. 6. to all that her mother-in-law b. her
1 Sam. 24. 10. some b. me kill thee, but I spared
2 Sam. 1. 18. David b. them teach Judah the use
14. 19. for thy servant Joab he b. me, and he put
2 Chron. 10. 12. came on the third day as the king b.
Esth. 4. 15. Esther b. them return this answer
Mat. 16. 12. how he b. them not beware of leaven
Luke 14. 9. and he that b. thee and him, come, 10.
16. a certain man made a supper, and b. many
Acts 11. 12. and the Spirit b. me go with them
18. 21. but b. them farewell, saying, I must keep
22. 24. b. that he should be examined by scourging

BADGERS'-SKINS.

Exod. 25. 5. take of them b.-skins and shittim-wood
26. 14. and a covering for the tent above of b.-skins
35. 7. rams'-skins dyed red, b.-sk. and shittim wood
23. with whom were found skins of rams, and b.-sk.
36. 19. and he made a covering of b.-sk. above that
Num. 4. 10. put it within a covering of b.-skins
Ezek. 16. 10. and I shod thee with b.-skins

BAG

Signifies, *A sack or pouch,* Deut. 25. 13. 1 Sam. 17. 40.
Bags which wax not old, Luke 12. 33. *Heavenly treasures which perish not, as earthly things do.*
Earneth wages to put it into a bag with holes, Hag. 1. 6. *What he gets or labours for, does him no manner of service, but a secret curse consumes it.*
Deut. 25. 13. not have in thy b. divers weights
1 Sam. 17. 40. smooth stones, and put them in a b.
Job 14. 17. my transgression is sealed up in a b.
Prov. 7. 20. he hath taken a b. of money with him
16. 11. all the weights of the b. are his work
Isa. 46. 6. they lavish gold out of the b. and weigh
Mic. 6. 11. and with the b. of deceitful weights
Hag. 1. 6. he earneth wages to put in a b. with holes
John 12. 6. because he was a thief, and had the b.
13. 29. some thought, because Judas had the b.

BAGS.

2 Kings 5. 23. and he bound two talents in two b.
12. 10. they put up in b. and told the money
Luke 12. 33. provide yourselves b. that wax not old

BAKE.

Gen. 19. 3. Lot did b. unleavened bread, they eat
Exod. 16. 23. b. that which you will b. to day
Lev. 24. 5. take flour and b. twelve cakes thereof
26. 26. ten women shall b. your bread in one oven
1 Sam. 28. 24. woman at Endor did b. unleav. bread
2 Sam. 13. 8. Tamar took flour and did b. cakes
Ezek. 4. 12. thou shalt b. it with man's dung
46. 20. the place where they shall b. meat-offering

BAKED.

Exod. 12. 39. they b. unleavened cakes of dough
Num. 11. 8. and b. it in pans, and made cakes of it
1 Chron. 23. 29. and for that which is b. in the pan

BAKE-MEATS.

Gen. 40. 17. all manner of b.-meats for Pharaoh

BAKEN.

Lev. 2. 4. meat-offering b. in the oven, 5, 7. | 7. 9.
6. 17. it shall not be b. with leaven, it is most holy
23. 17. two wave-loaves shall be b. with leaven
1 Kings 19. 6. behold, a cake was b. on the coals

BAKER.

Gen. 40. 1. the butler and b. had offended the king
20. lifted up the head of the chief butler and b.
22. he hanged the b. as Joseph interpreted
41. 10. and put in ward both me and the chief b.
Hos. 7. 4. they are as an oven heated by the b.
6. their b. sleepeth all the night, it burneth

BAKERS.

Gen. 40. 2. was wroth against the chief of the b.
1 Sam. 8. 13. will take your daughters to be b.
Jer. 37. 21. gave Jeremiah bread out of b. street

BAKETH.

Isa. 44. 15. he b. bread, yea he maketh a god

BALD.

Lev. 13. 40. he is b. yet is he clean, 41.

2 Kings 2. 23. go up thou b. head, go up thou b. head
Jer. 16. 6. nor make themselves b. for them
48. 37. every head shall be b. and beard clipt
Ezek. 27. 31. they shall make themselves utterly b.
29. 18. every head was made b. and shoulder peeled
Mic. 1. 16. make thee b. and poll thee for children

BALD-LOCUST.

Lev. 11. 22. ye may eat the b.-locust after his kind

BALDNESS

Signifies, [1] *Want of hair on the head*, Lev. 21. 5.
[2] *A sign of mourning*, Isa. 15. 2. Jer. 47. 5.
Lev. 21. 5. they shall not make b. on their head
Deut. 14. 1. nor make any b. between your eyes
Isa. 3. 24. and instead of well-set hair, b.
15. 2. on all their heads b. and every beard cut
22. 12. the Lord did call to weeping and to b.
Jer. 47. 5. b. is come upon Gaza, Ashkelon cut off
Ezek. 7. 18. and b. on all their heads, Amos 8. 10.
Mic. 1. 16. poll thee, enlarge thy b. as the eagle

BALANCE.

Job 31. 6. let me be weighed in an even b.
Psal. 62. 9. laid in the b. are altogether vanity
Prov. 11. 1. a false b. is abomination, 20. 23.
16. 11. a just weight and b. are the Lord's
Isa. 40. 12. who weighed the hills in a b.?
15. nations counted as the small dust of the b.
46. 6. lavish gold, and weigh silver in the b.

BALANCES.

Lev. 19. 36. just b. a just ephah, Ezek. 45. 10.
Job 6. 2. and my calamity laid in the b. together
Jer. 32. 10. I weighed him the money in the b.
Ezek. 5. 1. take b. to weigh, and divide the hair
Dan. 5. 27. thou art weighed in the b. and wanting
Hos. 12. 7. the b. of deceit are in his hand
Amos 8. 5. and falsifying the b. by deceit
Mic. 6. 11. shall I count them pure with wicked b.?
Rev. 6. 5. he that sat on them had a pair of b.

BALANCINGS.

Job 37. 16. dost thou know the b. of the clouds?

BALL, S.

Isa. 3. † 19. the Lord will take away their sweet b.
22. 18. he will surely turn and toss thee like a b.

BALM.

Gen. 37. 25. Ishmaelites bearing b. and myrrh
43. 11. take in your vessels a little b. and honey
Jer. 8. 22. is there no b. in Gilead? is there no physician?
46. 11. go up to Gilead, and take b. O virgin
51. 8. howl for her, take b. for her pain
Ezek. 27. 17. Judah traded in honey, and oil, and b.

BAND, S,

Signifies, [1] *A company of soldiers*, Acts 10. 1. [2] *Material chains*, Luke 8. 29. Acts 16. 26. [3] *Arguments or instances of love, which might draw and engage persons to their duty*, Hos. 11. 4. [4] *Government and laws, which, like fetters, restrain men from wicked practices*, Psal. 2. 3. Zech. 11. 7, 14. [5] *Faith and love, which attract the soul to Christ*, Col. 2. 19.
Exod. 39. 23. a b. round that it should not rend
Lev. 26. 13. I have broken the b. of your yoke
Judg. 15. 14. and his b. loosed from off his hands
2 Kings 23. 33. Pharaoh put Jehoahaz in b.
Job 38. 9. I made darkness a swaddling b. for it
31. canst bind the Pleiades, or loose the b. of Orion?
39. 5. or who hath loosed the b. of the wild ass?
10. canst thou bind the unicorn with his b.?
Psal. 2. 3. let us break their b. asunder, and cast away
73. 4. for there are no b. in their death
107. 14. and he brake their b. in sunder
Eccl. 7. 26. woman whose heart snares, hands as b.
Isa. 28. 22. be not mockers, lest b. be made strong
52. 2. loose thyself from the b. of thy neck
58. 6. this the fast, to loose the b. of wickedness
Jer. 2. 20. I have broken thy yoke, burst thy b.
Ezek. 3. 25. son of man, they shall put b. on thee
4. 8. and behold I will lay b. upon thee
34. 27. when I have broken the b. of their yoke
Dan. 4. 15. even with a b. of iron and brass, 23.
Hos. 11. 4. I drew them with b. of love, and I was
Zech. 11. 7. I took me two staves, beauty and b.
14. then I cut asunder mine other staff, even b.
Luke 8. 29. he brake b. and was driven of the devil
Acts 16. 26. and every one's b. were loosed
22. 30. the centurion loosed Paul from his b.
Col. 2. 19. the head, from which all the body by b.
See BONDS.

BAND, S.

Gen. 32. 7. Jacob divided the camels into two b.
10. I passed over, and now I am become two b.
1 Sam. 10. 26. and there went with him a b. of men
2 Sam. 4. 2. Saul's son had two men, captains of b.
2 Kings 6. 23. so the b. of Syria came no more
13. 20. and the b. of the Moabites invaded the land
21. as they were burying a man, they spied a b.
24. 2. the Lord sent against him b. of Chaldeans, b.
1 Chron. 7. 4. with them were b. of soldiers for war
12. 18. David made them captains of the b.
21. they helped David against the b. of the rovers
Ezra 8. 22. I was ashamed to require of the king a b.
Job 1. 17. the Chaldeans made out three b. and fell
Psal. 119. 61. the b. of the wicked have robbed me
Prov. 30. 27. the locusts go forth all of them by b.
Ezek. 12. 14. I will scatter all his b. and draw sword
38. 6. Gomer and all his b. Togarmah his b.
22. I will rain upon him and upon his b.
39. 4. fall on mountains of Israel thou and thy b.
Mat. 27. 27. gathered to him whole b. Mark 15. 16.
John 18. 3. Judas having received a b. of men
12. the b. and captain and officers took Jesus
Acts 10. 1. a centurion of the b. called the Italian b.
21. 31. tidings came to the chief captain of the b.
27. 1. to Julius a centurion of Augustus' b.

BANDED.

Acts 23. 12. certain of the Jews b. together

BANK

Signifies, [1] *The side, or brink, of a river*, Gen. 41. 17. [2] *A mount, or heap of earth raised to cover besiegers, while they batter the walls of a city, or shoot at those who defend them*, 2 Sam. 20. 15. [3] *A place where there is a great sum of money taken in, and let out to use*, Luke 19. 23.

Gen. 41. 17. behold I stood on the b. of the river
Deut. 4. 48. from Aroer which is by the b. of the river Arnon, Josh. 12. 2. | 13. 9, 16.
2 Sam. 20. 15. they cast up a b. against the city
2 Kings 2. 13. Elisha stood by the b. of Jordan
19. 32. the king of Assyria not cast a b. Isa. 37. 33.
Ezek. 47. 7. at the b. of the river were many trees
Dan. 12. 5. one on this side of the b. of the river the other on that side of the b. of the river
Luke 19. 23. gavest not thou my money into the b.?

BANKS.

Josh. 3. 15. Jordan overfloweth all his b. 4. 18.
1 Chron. 12. 15. Jordan had overflowed his b.
Isa. 8. 7. the king of Assyria shall go over all his b.
Dan. 8. 16. I heard a man's voice between the b.

BANNER

Signifies, *A standard, or ensign*, Isa. 13. 2.
Thou hast given a banner to them that fear thee, Psal. 60. 4. *An army of men united under one banner, with ability to defend themselves and conquer their enemies; a* banner *being a sign of* victory, *as well as of* battle *and* union.
His banner over me was love, Cant. 2. 4. *The love of Christ displayed, like a banner, in the gospel, conducted, encouraged, and engaged me to come to him.*
Exod. 17. † 15. called the altar, the Lord my b.
Psal. 60. 4. hast given a b. to them that fear thee
Cant. 2. 4. to banquet, and his b. over me was love
Isa. 13. 2. lift ye up a b. on the high mountain

BANNERS.

Psal. 20. 5. in the name of our God we set up our b.
Cant. 6. 4. thou art terrible as an army with b.

BANISHED.

2 Sam. 14. 13. the king doth not fetch home his b.
14. he doth devise means that his b. be not expelled

BANISHMENT.

Ezra 7. 26. whether it be to death or to b.
Lam. 2. 14. have seen false burdens and causes of b.

BANQUET. [5, 8.

Esth. 5. 4. let the king and Haman come to the b.
6. the king said to Esther at the b. of wine, 7. 2.
Job 41. 6. shall the companions make a b. of him?
Amos 6. 7. the b. of them that stretched themselves

BANQUET-HOUSE.

Dan. 5. 10. now the queen came into the b. house

BANQUETING, S.

Cant. 2. 4. he brought me into the b.-house
1 Pet. 4. 3. we walked in lusts, revellings, b.

BAPTISM

Signifies, [1] *The outward ordinance, or sacrament, wherein the washing with water represents the cleansing of the soul from sin by the blood of Christ*, Luke 7. 29. 1 Pet. 3. 21. [2] *Inward spiritual washing, whereby the gifts and graces of the Spirit, signified by the outward sign, are really and actually bestowed*, Mat. 3. 11. [3] *The sufferings of Christ, whereby he was consecrated and prepared for his entrance upon his kingly office*, Mat. 20. 22. Luke 12. 50. [4] *So much of the gospel as John the Baptist taught his disciples when he baptized them*, Acts 18. 25.
Mat. 3. 7. when he saw the Pharisees come to his b.
20. 22. and to be baptized with the b. Mark 10. 38.
21. 25. the b. of John, whence was it, from heaven or of men? Mark 11. 30. Luke 20. 4.
Mark 1. 4. John did baptize in the wilderness, and preach the b. of repentance, Luke 3. 3.
Luke 7. 29. publicans baptized with the b. of John
12. 50. I have a b. to be baptized with, and how am
Acts 1. 22. beginning from the b. of John to that day
10. 37. that word after the b. which John preached
13. 24. John preached the b. of repentance to Israel
18. 25. Apollos knowing only the b. of John
19. 3. were ye baptized? they said, unto John's b.
4. John baptized with the b. of repentance
Rom. 6. 4. we are buried with him by b. into death
Eph. 4. 5. there is one Lord, one faith, one b.
Col. 2. 12. buried with him in b. ye are risen with
Heb. 6. 2. of doctrine of b. and laying on of hands
1 Pet. 3. 21. the like figure whereunto, even b. doth

BAPTIST.

Mat. 3. 1. in those days came John b. preaching
11. 11. among them born of women there hath not risen a greater than John the b. Luke 7. 28.
11. 12. from the days of John the b. till now
14. 2. this is John the b. he is risen from the dead
8. said, give me John the b. head in a charger
16. 14. some say, thou art John the b. Mark 8. 28.
17. 13. understood that he spake of John the b.
Mark 6. 14. John the b. was risen from the dead
25. give me in a charger the head of John the b.
Luke 7. 20. John the b. hath sent us to thee, saying
33. John the b. came neither eating nor drinking
9. 19. they answering said, John the b.

BAPTIZE.

Mat. 3. 11. I b. you with water, he shall b. you with the H. Ghost, Mark 1. 8. Luke 3. 16. John 1. 26.
Mark 1. 4. John did b. in the wilderness, and preach
John 1. 33. he that sent me to b. said unto me
1 Cor. 1. 17. Christ sent me not to b. but to preach

BAPTIZED.

Mat. 3. 6. were b. of him in Jordan, Mark 1. 5.
13. then cometh Jesus to John to be b. of him
14. I have need to be b. of thee, and comest thou
16. Jesus, when he was b. went up out of water
Mark 1. 9. Jesus was b. of John in Jordan
10. 39. the baptism I am b. withal, shall ye be b.
16. 16. he that believeth and is b. shall be saved
Luke 3. 7. said to the multitude that came to be b.
12. then came the publicans to be b. 7. 29.
21. Jesus being b. and praying, heaven was opened
7. 30. Pharisees and lawyers, being not b. of him
John 3. 22. there he tarried with them and b.
23. much water there, and they came and were b.
4. 1. Jesus made and b. more disciples than John
2. though Jesus himself b. not, but his disciples
10. 40. into the place where John at first b.
Acts 1. 5. for John truly b. with water, but ye shall be b. with the Holy Ghost, 11. 16.
2. 38. repent, be b. every one of you in the name of Jesus

Acts 2. 41. they that gladly received his word were b.
8. 12. they were b. both men and women
13. Simon believed also, and when he was b.
16. only they were b. in the name of Jesus
36. here is water, what doth hinder me to be b.?
38. went down Philip and eunuch, and he b. him
9. 18. Saul received sight, and arose and was b.
10. 47. can any forbid, that these should not be b.?
48. Peter commanded them to be b.
16. 15. Lydia when she was b. and her household
33. jailer was b. and all his straightway
18. 8. many of the Corinth. believed, and were b.
19. 3. he said to them, to what then were ye b.?
5. when they heard this they were b.
22. 16. arise, and be b. and wash away thy sins
Rom. 6. 3. were b. into Jesus, were b. into his death
1 Cor. 1. 13. were ye b. in the name of Paul?
14. thank God that I b. none of you, but Crispus
16. I b. household of Stephanas, not b. any other
10. 2. and were all b. to Moses in the cloud
12. 13. for by one Spirit are we all b. into one body
15. 29. else what shall they do who are b. for the dead, why are they b. for the dead?
Gal. 3. 27. as many as have been b. into Christ

BAPTIZEST.

John 1. 25. why b. thou, if thou be not the Christ?

BAPTIZETH.

John 1. 33. the same is he who b. with the H. Ghost
3. 26. behold, the same b. all men come to him

BAPTIZING.

Mat. 28. 19. go ye and teach all nations, b. them
John 1. 28. done beyond Jordan, where John was b.
31. therefore am I come b. with water
3. 23. and John was also b. in Enon, near to Salim

BAR, RED.

Neh. 7. 3. let them shut the doors, and b. them
Cant. 4. † 12. a garden b. is my sister, my spouse

BAR, *Substantive*.

Exod. 26. 28. the middle b. in midst of the boards
36. 33. he made the middle b. to shoot through
Num. 4. 10. and they shall put it upon a b. 12.
Judg. 16. 3. took doors of the city, posts, b. and all
Amos 1. 5. I will break also the b. of Damascus

BARS

Signify, [1] *That by which doors and gates are made fast*, Neh. 3. 3, 6. [2] *That which is made as a rafter to fasten boards unto*, Exod. 26. 26. [3] *Rocks in the sea*, Jonah 2. 6. [4] *The boundary of the waves of the sea*, Job 38. 10.
Exod. 26. 26. thou shalt make b. of shittim-wood for the boards of the tabernacle, 36. 31.
Num. 3. 36. under the charge of the sons of Merari, shall be the boards and b. of the tabernacle, 4. 31.
Deut. 3. 5. all these cities were fenced with gates and b. 1 Kings 4. 13. 2 Chron. 8. 5. | 14. 7
1 Sam. 23. 7. entering into a town that hath b.
Neh. 3. 3. set up locks thereof and b. 6, 13, 14, 15.
Job 17. 16. they shall go down to the b. of the pit
18. † 13. it shall devour the b. of his skin
38. 10. and set b. and doors for the sea
40. 18. Behemoth, his bones are like b. of iron
Psal. 107. 16. and cut b. of iron in sunder, Isa. 45. 2
147. 13. he hath strengthened the b. of thy gates
Prov. 18. 19. contentions are like the b. of a castle
Isa. 43. † 14. I have brought down all their b.
Jer. 49. 31. nation, which have neither gates nor b.
50. † 36. a sword is upon her b. shall be dismayed
51. 30. they have Babylon, her b. are broken
Lam. 2. 9. he hath destroyed and broken her b.
Ezek. 38. 11. and having neither gates nor b.
Jonah 2. 6. the earth with her b. was about me
Nah. 3. 13. gates open, the fire shall devour thy b.

BARBARIAN.

1 Cor. 14. 11. shall be to him a b. and he a b. to me
Col. 3. 11. where there is neither Greek nor Jew, b.

BARBARIANS.

Acts 28. 4. when the b. saw the venomous beast
Rom. 1. 14. I am debtor both to the Greeks and b.

BARBAROUS.

Acts 28. 2. the b. people shewed no little kindness

BARBED.

Job 41. 7. canst thou fill his skin with b. irons

BARBER.

Ezek. 5. 1. son of man, take thee a b. razor

BARE.

Gen. 7. 17. b. the ark, Deut. 31. 9, 25. Josh. 3. 15.
4. 10. | 8. 33. 2 Sam. 6. 13. 1 Chron. 15. 15, 26, 27.
31. 39. that torn by beasts, I b. the loss of it
Exod. 19. 4. and how I b. you on eagle's wings
Deut. 1. 31. thy God b. thee as a man doth bear
Judg. 3. 18. sent the people that b. the present
1 Sam. 14. 1. Jonathan said to the young man that b. his armour, 6. 2 Sam. 18. 15.
1 Kings 5. 15. that b. burdens 70,000, Neh. 4. 17.
1 Chron. 12. 24. of Judah that b. shield, 2 Chr. 14. 8.
Isa. 53. 12. he b. the sin of many, made intercession
63. 9. he b. them all the days of old
Ezek. 12. 7. the stuff I b. upon my shoulder
Mat. 8. 17. saying, himself b. our sicknesses
Luke 7. 14. and they that b. him stood still
John 2. 8. the water made wine, and they b. it
12. 6. had the bag, and b. what was put therein
1 Pet. 2. 24. his own self b. our sins on the tree

BARE.

Gen. 25. 26. Isaac was 60 years, when she b. them
31. 8. then all the cattle b. speckled
38. 5. and he was at Chezib when she b. him
44. 27. ye know that my wife b. me two sons
Exod. 6. 20. Jochebed b. to Amram Moses and Aaron
Judg. 13. 2. Manoah's wife was barren and b. not
2 Sam. 12. 15. struck the child that Uriah's wife b.
1 Kings 1. 6. his mother b. him after Absalom
1 Chron. 4. 9. Jabez, because I b. him with sorrow
Prov. 17. 25. and bitterness to her that b. him
23. 25. and she that b. thee shall rejoice
Cant. 6. 9. she is the choice one of her that b. her
8. 5. there she brought thee forth that b. thee
Isa. 51. 2. and look unto Sarah that b. you
Jer. 16. 3. concerning their mother that b. them
20. 14. let not the day wherein my mother b. me
22. 26. cast thee out, and thy mother that b. thee

Jer. 50. 12. she that b. you shall be ashamed
Luke 11. 27. blessed is the womb that b. thee
23. 29. blessed are the wombs that never b.
BARE fruit.
Luke 8. 8. other sprang up, and b. f. an hundred-fold
Rev. 22. 2. the tree of life b. twelve manner of fruits
BARE rule.
1 Kings 9. 23. the chief officers that b. rule over the people that wrought in the work, 2 Chron. 8. 10.
Neh. 5. 15. their servants b. rule over the people
BARE witness, and record.
Mark 14. 56. many b. false witness against him, 57.
Luke 4. 22. all b. him witness, and wondered
John 1. 15. John b. witness of him, 32, 34.
5. 33. John b. witness to the truth
12. 17. the people that was with him b. record
19. 35. he that saw it b. record, and his record is true
Acts 15. 8. knoweth the hearts, b. them witness
Rev. 1. 2. who b. record of the word of God
BAREST.
1 Kings 2. 26. because thou b. the ark of the Lord
Isa. 63. 19. thou never b. rule over them
John 3. 26. he to whom thou b. witness, baptizeth
BARE, Adjective,
Signifies, [1] Naked, or uncovered, Lev. 13. 45. Isa. 32. 11. [2] Plain, or real, 1 Cor. 15. 37. [3] Deprived of outward comforts, Jer. 49. 10. [4] Violently taken away, Jer. 13. + 22.
Made bare his holy arm, Isa. 52. 10. Hath discovered and put forth his great power, which for a long time seemed to be hid and unemployed.
Lev. 13. 45. his clothes be rent and his head b.
55. whether it be b. within or without
Psal. 137. + 7. make b. make b. to the foundation
Isa. 32. 11. strip ye, make ye b. and gird sackcloth
47. 2. make b. the leg, uncover the thigh, pass
52. 10. the Lord hath made b. his holy arm
Jer. 13. 22. for thine iniquity are thy heels made b.
49. 10. I have made Esau b. I have uncovered his
Ezek. 16. 7. whereas thou wast naked and b.
22. when thou wast naked, and b. and polluted
39. they shall leave thee naked and b. 23. 29.
Joel 1. 7. my fig tree he hath made it clean b.
1 Cor. 15. 37. not that body that shall be, but b. grain
BAREFOOT.
2 Sam. 15. 30. he went b. and the people with him
Isa. 20. 2. Isaiah did so, walking naked and b. 3.
4. led the Egyptians prisoners, naked and b.
BARK.
Isa. 56. 10. they are dumb dogs, they cannot b.
BARKED.
Joel 1. 7. laid my vine waste, and b. the fig-tree
BARLEY.
Exod. 9. 31. the b. was smitten, for b. was in the ear
Lev. 27. 16. an homer of b. seed shall be valued
Num. 5. 15. the tenth part of an ephah of b. meal
Deut. 8. 8. a land of wheat, and b. vines, and fig-trees
Judg. 7. 13. lo a cake of b. bread tumbled into the
Ruth 1. 22. came in the beginning of b. harvest
2. 17. she had gleaned about an ephah of b.
23. so she kept fast to the end of b. harvest
3. 2. behold Boaz winnoweth b. to-night
15. he measured six measures of b. and laid it
2 Sam. 14. 30. Joab's field is near, he hath b. there
17. 28. Barzillai brought beds, b. and flour
21. 9. Saul's sons were hanged in b. harvest
1 Kings 4. 28. b. also and straw for the horses
2 Kings 4. 42. brought the man of God 20 loaves of b.
7. 1. two measures of b. for a shekel, 16, 18.
1 Chron. 11. 13. a parcel of ground full of b.
2 Chron. 2. 10. I will give 20,000 measures of b.
15. wheat, and b. the oil, and wine, let him send
27. 5. Ammon gave 10,000 measures of b.
Job 31. 40. and let cockle grow instead of b.
Isa. 28. 25. the principal wheat, and appointed b.
Jer. 41. 8. we have treasures of wheat and b.
Ezek. 4. 9. take to thee wheat, and b. and beans
12. thou shalt eat it as b. cakes, and bake it
13. 19. will ye pollute me for handfuls of b.
45. 13. sixth part of an ephah of an homer of b.
Hos. 3. 2. bought her for an homer of b. and half
Joel 1. 11. O husbandmen, howl for wheat and b.
John 6. 9. a lad here which hath five b. loaves
6. 13. with the fragments of the five b. loaves
Rev. 6. 6. a voice say, 3 measures of b. for a penny
BARN
Signifies, [1] A repository for any sort of grain, Luke 12. 24. [2] Heaven, Mat. 13. 30.
2 Kings 6. 27. shall I help thee out of the b. floor?
Job 39. 12. and gather thy seed into the b.
Hag. 2. 19. is seed yet in b. vine not brought forth
Mat. 13. 30. but gather the wheat into my b.
Luke 12. 24. which have no store-house nor b.
BARNS.
Deut. 28. + 8. the Lord shall command the blessing upon thee in thy b. and in all thou dost
Prov. 3. 10. so shall thy b. be filled with plenty
Joel 1. 17. the b. are broken down, and withered
Mat. 6. 26. the fowls sow not, nor gather int b.
Luke 12. 18. I will pull down my b. and build
BARREL, S.
1 Kings 17. 12. but a handful of meal in a b. and oil
14. the b. of meal shall not waste, nor oil fail
18. 33. fill four b. with water, and pour it on
BARREN.
Gen. 11. 30. but Sarai was b. she had no child
25. 21. Rebekah was b. ‖ 29. 31. Rachel was b.
Exod. 23. 26. nothing shall cast young nor be b.
Deut. 7. 14. there shall not be male or female b.
Judg. 13. 2. Manoah's wife was b. and bare not, 3.
1 Sam. 2. 5. so that the b. hath born seven
2 Kings 2. 19. the water is naught, and the ground b.
21. shall not be from thence death, or b. land
Job 24. 21. he evil entreateth the b. that bear not
39. 6. I have made the b. land his dwellings
Psal. 113. 9. he maketh the b. woman to keep house
Prov. 30. 16. the grave and b. womb not satisfied
Cant. 4. 2. and none is b. among them, 6. 6.
Isa. 54. 1. sing, O b. thou that didst not bear
Joel 2. 20. and I will drive him into a land b.
Luke 1. 7. had no child, because Elisabeth was b.
36. the sixth month with her, who was called b.

Luke 23. 29. they shall say, blessed are the b. and
Gal. 4. 27. for it is written, rejoice thou b. [wombs
2 Pet. 1. 8. that ye be neither b. nor unfruitful
BARRENNESS.
Psal. 107. 34. he turneth a fruitful land into b.
BASE, S.
1 Kings 7. 27. ten b. four cubits the length of one b.
2 Kings 25. 13. the b. Solomon made, brake they, 16.
Ezra 3. 3. and they set the altar upon his b.
Psal. 104. + 5. founded the earth on her b.
Zech. 5. 11. it shall be set there upon her own b.
BASE, Adjective.
2 Sam. 6. 22. and will be b. in mine own sight
Job 30. 8. yea, they were children of b. men
Isa. 3. 5. and the b. against the honourable
Ezek. 17. 14. that the kingdom might be b.
29. 14. and they shall be there a b. kingdom
Mal. 2. 9. therefore I have made you b.
Acts 17. + 18. some said, what will this b. fellow say
1 Cor. 1. 28. b. things of this world God hath chosen
2 Cor. 10. 1. I, Paul, who in presence am b. among
BASER.
Acts 17. 5. Jews took lewd fellows of the b. sort
BASEST.
Ezek. 29. 15. Pathros shall be the b. of kingdoms
Dan. 4. 17. and setteth up over it the b. of men
BASKET.
Gen. 40. 17. in the b. all manner of bake-meats
Exod. 29. 23. out of the b. of the unleavened bread, Lev. 8. 2, 26. Num. 6. 15, 17.
Lev. 8. 31. the bread in the b. of consecrations
Deut. 26. 4. priest shall take the b. out of thy hand
28. 5. blessed shall be thy b. and thy store
17. cursed shall be thy b. and thy store
Judg. 6. 19. and Gideon put the flesh in a b.
Jer. 24. 2. one b. had very good figs, the other b.
Amos 8. 1. and behold a b. of summer fruit, 2.
Acts 9. 25. the disciples took Saul, and let him down by the wall in a b. 2 Cor. 11. 33.
BASKETS.
Gen. 40. 16. I had three white b. on my head
18. Joseph said, the three b. are three days
2 Kings 10. 7. slew 70, and put their heads in b.
Jer. 6. 9. turn hand as a grape-gatherer into the b.
24. 1. behold, two b. of figs before the temple
Mat. 14. 20. and they took up twelve b. full, Mark 6. 43. Luke 9. 17. John 6. 13.
15. 37. they did all eat, and took of broken meat seven b. full, Mark 8. 8.
16. 9. do ye not remember the five loaves, and how many b. ye took up? 10. Mark 8. 19, 20.
BASON.
Exod. 12. 22. dip it in the blood that is in the b.
1 Chron. 28. 17. gave gold by weight for every b.
John 13. 5. after that he poureth water into a b.
BASONS.
Exod. 24. 6. Moses put half of the blood in b.
2 Sam. 17. 28. Barzillai brought beds and b.
1 Kings 7. 40. Hiram made the lavers and the shovels and the b. 45. | 2 Chron. 4. 8, 11.
Jer. 52. 19. b. and fire-pans the captain took away
BASTARD, S.
Deut. 23. 2. a b. shall not enter into the congregation
Zech. 9. 6. and a b. shall dwell in Ashdod, cut off
Heb. 12. 8. if ye be without chastisement, then are b.
BATH
Was a measure used among the Hebrews, of the same bigness with the Ephah, which contained 60 wine pints, and almost a half; or seven gallons and a half.
Isa. 5. 10. yea, ten acres of vineyard shall yield one b.
Ezek. 45. 10. ye shall have a just ephah, a just b.
11. the ephah and b. shall be of one measure
14. ye shall offer the tenth part of a b.
BATHE.
Lev. 15. 5. shall b. himself in water, 8, 11, 13, 21, 22, 27. | 16. 26, 28. | 17. 15. Num. 19. 7, 8, 19.
17. 16. but if he wash them not, nor b. his flesh
BATHED.
Isa. 34. 5. my sword shall be b. in heaven, behold it
BATHS.
1 Kings 7. 26. molten sea contained 2000 b.
38. one laver containing 40 b. every laver
2 Chron. 2. 10. give thy servants 20,000 b. of wine
4. 5. the sea received and held 3000 b.
Ezra 7. 22. to an hundred b. of wine, 100 b. of oil
Ezek. 45. 14. an homer of ten b. ten b. are an homer
BAT, S.
Lev. 11. 19. lapwing and b. are unclean, Deut. 14. 18.
Isa. 2. 20. shall cast his idols to the moles and b.
BATTLE
Signifies, [1] A general fight, Deut. 20. 3. [2] Victory, Eccl. 9. 11. [3] War, 1 Sam. 17. 13.
Gen. 14. 8. they joined b. 1 Sam. 4. 2. 1 Kings 20. 29.
Num. 32. 27. will pass over before the Lord to b.
Deut. 2. 24. rise up, contend with Sihon in b.
20. 3. O Israel, you approach this day to b.
5. let him return, lest he die in the b. 6, 7.
Josh. 11. 19. of Gibeon, all other they took in b.
Judg. 20. 28. shall I yet again go out to b.?
42. they turned, but the b. overtook them
1 Sam. 14. 22. followed hard after Philistines in b.
17. 20. he came, as the host shouted for the b.
28. for thou art come down to see the b.
47. for the b. is the Lord's, 2 Chron. 20. 15.
26. 10. he shall descend into the b. and perish
28. 1. know that thou shalt go out with me to b.
29. 4. lest in the b. he be an adversary to us
2 Sam. 11. 1. when kings go forth to b. 1 Chron. 20. 1.
15. set Uriah in the forefront of the hottest b.
19. 10. Absalom whom we anointed is dead in b.
1 Kings 8. 44. if thy people go out to b. against enemy
20. 39. thy servant went out into midst of the b.
22. 4. wilt thou go with me to b.? 2 Kings 3. 7.
1 Chron. 5. 20. for they cried to God in the b.
12. 8. of the Gadites, men of war fit for the b.
19. 17. David came upon them, and set b. in array against the Syrians, 2 Chron. 13. 3. | 14. 10.
2 Chron. 25. 8. if thou wilt go, do it, be strong for b.
Job 15. 24. shall prevail, as a king ready to the b.
39. 25. and he smelleth the b. afar off
41. 8. remember the b. do no more

Psal. 18. 39. thou hast girded me with strength to b.
24. 8. the King of glory, the Lord mighty in b.
55. 18. he hath delivered my soul from the b.
76. 3. he brake the shield, the sword, and the b.
89. 43. and hast not made him to stand in the b.
Eccl. 9. 11. race not to the swift, nor b. to the strong
Isa. 9. 5. every b. of the warrior is with noise
13. 4. the Lord mustereth the host of the b.
22. 2. thy slain men are not dead in b.
27. 4. who set briars and thorns against me in b.
28. 6. strength to them that turn the b. to the gate
42. 25. he hath poured on him the strength of the b.
Jer. 8. 6. turned as the horse rusheth into the b.
18. 21. let their young men be slain by sword in b.
46. 3. order buckler and shield, draw near to b.
49. 14. come against her, and rise up to the b.
50. 22. a sound of b. is in land, and destruction
42. put in array, like a man to b. against thee
Ezek. 7. 14. have blown, but none goeth to the b.
13. 5. to stand in the b. in the day of the Lord
Hos. 1. 7. I will not save them by bow nor by b.
2. 18. I will break the bow and b. out of the earth
10. 9. b. in Gibeah did not overtake them
Joel 2. 5. as a strong people set in b. array
Obad. 1. let us rise up against Edom in b.
Zech. 10. 3. made them as his goodly horse in the b.
5. which tread down their enemies in the b.
14. 2. gather all nations against Jerusalem to b.
1 Cor. 14. 8. who shall prepare himself to the b.?
Rev. 9. 7. shapes of locusts like horses prepared to b.
9. sound of chariots of many horses running to b.
16. 14. to gather them to the b. of the great day, 20. 8.
Day of BATTLE.
1 Sam. 13. 22. so it came to pass in the day of b. that
Job 38. 23. I reserved against the day of b. and war
Psal. 78. 9. Ephraim turned back in the day of b.
140. 7. thou hast covered my head in the day of b.
Pro. 21. 31. the horse is prepared against the day of b.
Hos. 10. 14. Shalman spoiled Beth-arbel in day of b.
Amos 1. 14. devour with shouting in the day of b.
Zech. 14. 3. as when he fought in the day of b.
BATTLE-AX, see AX.
BATTLE-BOW.
Zech. 9. 10. and the b.-bow shall be cut off
10. 4. out of him came forth the b.-bow
BATTLES.
1 Sam. 8. 20. may go out before us and fight our b.
18. 17. only be valiant, and fight the Lord's b.
25. 28. my lord fighteth the b. of the Lord
1 Chron. 26. 27. out of the spoils won in b. dedicate
2 Chron. 32. 8. but with us is God, to fight our b.
Isa. 30. 32. and in b. of shakings will he fight with
BATTERED.
2 Sam. 20. 15. the people with Joab b. the wall
BATTERING.
Ezek. 4. 2. and set b. rams against it round about
21. 22. to appoint b. rams against the gates
BATTLEMENT, S.
Deut. 22. 8. thou shalt make a b. for thy roof
Jer. 5. 10. take away her b. they are not the Lord's
BAY.
Zech. 1. + 8. behind him red horses, b. and white
6. 3. in the fourth chariot grizled and b. horses
7. and the b. went forth and sought to go
BAY-TREE.
Psal. 37. 35. wicked spreading like a green b.-tree
BDELLIUM.
Gen. 2. 12. in Havilah there is b. and onyx stone
Num. 11. 7. the colour of manna as the colour of b.
BE
Signifies, [1] To exist or have a being, Rom. 4. 17. [2] To be made or become, Jer. 32. 38. Mat. 19. 5. [3] To be known and apparently seen, Rom. 14. 9. [4] To consecrate and set apart to, Judg. 11. 31.
Gen. 2. 18. it is not good that man should be alone
27. 21. whether thou be my very son Esau, or not
Deut. 10. 5. there they be as the Lord commanded
Judg. 6. 13. if the Lord be with us, why is all this
2 Sam. 18. 32. thine enemies be as that young man is
2 Kings 6. 16. fear not, for they that be with us are more than they that be with them
2 Chr. 36. 23. Lord his God be with him, Ezra 1. 3.
Ezra 6. 6. be ye far from thence, let the work alone
Job 10. 15. if I be wicked, wo to me; if I be righteous
19. 4. and be it indeed that I have erred, mine error
Psal. 139. 24. see if there be any wicked way in me
Cant. 8. 9. if she be a wall, if she be a door
Isa. 8. 13. let him be your fear, let him be your dread
41. 22. let them shew former things what they be
Jer. 36. 19. go hide, and let none know where you be
47. 6. how long will it be ere thou be quiet?
Dan. 12. 13. but go thou thy way till the end be
Hos. 8. 5. how long will it be ere they attain to innoc.?
Mat. 4. 3. if thou be the Son of God, 6. | 27. 40.
7. 13. and many there be that go in thereat
16. 23. for thou savourest not the things that be of God, but those that be of men, Mark 8. 33.
18. 17. let him be to thee as a heathen man or a
19. 9. shall put away, except it be for fornic.
Luke 10. 6. and if the son of peace be there, your
John 3. 9. Nicodemus said, how can these things be?
Acts 19. 2. not heard whether there be any H. Ghost
24. 21. except it be for this one voice that I cried
Rom. 4. 17. who calleth those things which be not as
8. 31. if God be for us, who can be against us?
14. 9. that he might be Lord of the dead and living
1 Cor. 15. 28. under him, that God may be all in all
16. 22. love not, let him be anathema maran atha
2 Cor. 5. + 17. if in Christ let him be a new creature
8. 12. if there be first a willing mind, it is accepted
Gal. 3. 9. they which be of faith are blessed with
4. 12. I beseech you, be as I am, for I am as ye are
5. 10. shall bear his judgment whosoever he be
Phil. 2. 5. let this mind be in you that was in Christ
Heb. 12. 8. but if ye be without chastisement
1 Pet. 2. 3. if so be ye have tasted that L. is gracious
3. 17. for it is better, if the will of God be so
Rev. 18. 22. craftsman, of whatsoever craft he be
22. 11. he that is unjust, let him be unjust still, he who is filthy, let him be filthy still

If it BE.
Gen. 23. 8. *if it be* your mind that I bury my dead
25. 22. and she said, *if it be* so, why am I thus?
Exod. 1. 16. *if it be* a son kill him, *if it be* a daughter
2 *Kings* 10. 15. *if it be*, give me thy hand, and he gave
Zech. 8. 6. *if it be* marvellous in the eyes of remnant
Mat. 14. 28. *if it be* thou, bid me come on the water
Acts 5. 39. *if it be* of God, ye cannot overthrow it
18. 15. but *if it be* a question of words and names
Gal. 3. 4. have ye suffered in vain? *if it be* yet in vain
May BE, *see* MAY. *Peace* BE, *see* PEACE.
Not BE. BE *not*.
Gen. 21. 12. let it *not be* grievous in thy sight
24. 5. if the woman will *not be* willing to follow, 8.
38. 9. Onan knew that the seed should *not be* his
44. 30. I come to my father, and the lad *be not* with
Lev. 26. 13. that ye should *not be* their bond-men
Num. 12. 12. let her *not be* as one dead, of whom
16. 40. that he *be not* as Korah and his company
Josh. 7. 12. neither will I *be* with you any more
Ruth 3. 18. the man will *not be* in rest till finished
2 *Kings* 20. † 19. shall there *not be* peace in my days?
2 *Chron.* 30. 7. *be not* like your fathers, *Zech.* 1. 4.
Psal. 22. 19. *be not* thou far away, 35. 22. | 38. 21. |
Isa. 28. 22. *be ye not* mockers, lest bands [71. 12.
Zech. 8. 11. I will *not be* to the residue of this people
Luke 13. 33. for it can *not be* that a prophet perish
14. 26. hate his life, he can *not be* my disciple, 33.
John 1. 25. if thou *be not* that Christ, nor Elias
Rom. 12. 16. *be not* wise in your own conceits
1 *Cor.* 2. † 5. your faith *not be* in the wisdom of men
9. 2. if I *be not* an apostle unto others, yet to you
14. 20. *be not* children in understanding, but in
2 *Cor.* 6. 14. *be not* unequally yoked together
Gal. 1. 10. I should *not be* the servant of Christ
Eph. 5. 7. *be not* therefore partakers with them
17. *be* ye *not* unwise, but understanding what
Tit. 3. 14. good works, that they *be not* unfruitful
Philem. 14. thy benefit should *not be* of necessity
Heb. 8. 4. if he were on earth, should *not be* a priest
1 *Pet.* 3. 3. let it *not be* that outward adorning of hair
Let there BE.
Gen. 1. 3. *let there be* light | 6. *let there be* a firmament
13. 8. *let there be* no strife between me and thee
26. 28. *let there be* now an oath betwixt us and thee
Exod. 5. 9. *let there be* more work laid on the men
Ezra 5. 17. *let there be* search made in king's treas.
Psal. 69. † 25. *let there be* no dweller in their tents
Shall BE, or *shalt* BE.
Gen. 2. 24. to his wife, and they *shall be* one flesh
4. 7. to thee *shall be* his desire, and thou shalt rule
9. 25. a servant *shall* he *be* to his brethren
26. God of Shem, and Canaan *shall be* his servant
12. 2. I will bless thee, and thou *shalt be* a blessing
15. 5. he said to him, so *shall* thy seed *be*, Rom. 4. 18.
17. 16. Sarah *shall be* a mother of nations
27. 33. I have blessed him, and he *shall be* blessed
28. 21. so I come again, then *shall* L. *be* my God
35. 10. but Israel *shall be* thy name, 1 *Kings* 18. 31.
48. 21. but God *shall be* with you and bring you
49. 10. to him *shall* the gathering of the people *be*
Exod. 4. † 9. the water *shall be* blood on the dry land
16. thou *shalt be* to him instead of God
19. 5. ye *shall be* a peculiar treasure to me
21. 36. pay ox for ox, and the dead *shall be* his own
Lev. 13. 46. without the camp *shall* his habitation *be*
20. 26. ye *shall be* holy to me, ye *shall be* mine
Deut. 28. 44. he *shall be* head, and thou *shalt be* tail
32. 20. hide my face, I see what their end *shall be*
1 *Sam.* 17. 36. this uncircumcised Phil. *shall be* as
1 *Kings* 20. 40. the king said, so *shall* thy judgment *be*
2 *Chron.* 19. 11. the Lord *shall be* with the good
Job 20. 22. in fulness he *shall be* in straits
22. 25. yea, the Almighty *shall be* thy defence
Psal. 128. 2. happy *shalt* thou *be*, it *shall be* well with
141. 5. my prayer also *shall be* in their calamities
Eccl. 1. 9. that which hath been, is that which *shall be*
10. 14. a man cannot tell what *shall be*
11. 3. where the tree falleth, there it *shall be*
Isa. 6. 13. so the holy seed *shall be* the substance
58. 8. the glory of the Lord *shall be* thy rere-ward
Jer. 13. 27. not be made clean, when *shall* it once *be*?
15. 19. thou *shalt be* as my mouth, let them return
32. 5. and there *shall* he *be* till I visit him
33. 9. it *shall be* to me a name of joy, a praise
Ezek. 16. 16. like shall not come, neither *shall be* so
18. 20. wickedness of the wicked *shall be* on him
27. 36. thou *shalt be* a terror, and never *shalt be* more
Dan. 2. 28. what *shall be* in the latter days
8. 19. at the time appointed the end *shall be*, 11. 27.
Hos. 5. 9. have I made known that which *shall be*
Amos 5. 14. so the God of hosts *shall be* with you
Zech. 8. 13. so will I save you, and ye *shall be* a bless.
12. 8. *shall be* as David, house of David *shall be* as
Mal. 3. 12. for ye *shall be* a delightsome land
Mat. 24. 21. this time, no, nor ever *shall be*, *Mark* 13. 19
Mark 9. 19. how long *shall* I *be* with you, *Luke* 9. 41.
John 14. 17. he dwelleth with you, and *shall be* in
19. 24. but cast lots for it, whose it *shall be*
Acts 27. 25. that it *shall be* even as it was told me
1 *Cor.* 15. 37. thou sowest not that body that *shall be*
1 *John* 3. 2. it doth not yet appear what we *shall be*
Rev. 16. 5. O Lord, which art, and wast, and *shalt be*
22. 12. to give every man as his work *shall be*
Shall not, or *shalt not* BE.
Gen. 15. 4. saying, this *shall not be* thine heir
Exod. 22. 25. thou *shalt not be* to him as an usurer
Deut. 28. 13. be above only, thou *shalt not be* beneath
2 *Kings* 2. 10. if thou see me not, it *shall not be* so
Job 7. 21. shalt seek me in morning, but I *shall not be*
8. † 22. the dwelling place of the wicked *shall not be*
Ps. 37. 10. it *sh. n. be*, *Jer.* 48. 30. *Dan.* 11. 29. *Am.* 7.
Hos. 3. 3. thou *shalt not be* for another man [3, 6.
Mat. 16. 22. be it far from thee, this *shall not be* to thee
20. 26. *sh. n. be* so among you, *Mar.* 10. 43. *Luke* 22.
To BE. [26.
Gen. 17. 7. *to be* a God to thee and thy seed after
39. 10. he hearkened not to her *to be* with her
Lev. 22. 33. brought you out *to be* your God, 25. 38.
Prov. 24. 1. neither desire *to be* with them
Eccl. 3. 15. that which is *to be* hath already been
Luke 15. 14. when he spent all, he began *to be* in want

1 *Cor.* 7. 26. I say it is good for a man so *to be*
2 *Cor.* 12. 6. above that which he seeth me *to be*
Phil. 1. 23. having a desire *to be* with Christ
Jam. 3. 10. these things ought not so *to be*
2 *Pet.* 3. 11. what manner of persons ought ye *to be*
Will BE.
Gen. 16. 12. Ishmael *will be* a wild man, his hand *will be* against every man, and every man's ag. him
17. 8. I *will be* their God, *Exod.* 29. 45. *Jer.* 24. 7. | 32. 38. 2 *Cor.* 6. 16.
26. 3. I *will be* with thee, and will bless thee, 31. 3. *Exod.* 3. 12. *Judg.* 6. 16. 1 *Kings* 11. 38.
28. 20. if God *will be* with me, and will keep me
34. 15. if ye *will be* as we be, circumcised
Neh. 4. 12. from all places they *will be* upon you
Psal. 48. 14. he *will be* our guide, even unto death
Jer. 7. 23. obey my voice, I *will be* your God, 30. 22.
Ezek. 11. 16. I *will be* to them as a little sanctuary
20. 32. that ye say, we *will be* as the heathen
Hos. 13. 14. I will redeem them: O death, I *will be* thy plagues, O grave, I *will be* thy destruction
14. 5. I *will be* as the dew to Israel, he shall grow
Joel 3. 16. the Lord *will be* the hope of his people
Zech. 2. 5. I the Lord *will be* to her a wall of fire round about, I *will be* the glory in the midst of her
Mat. 6. 21. where treasure, there *will* your heart *be*
2 *Cor.* 6. 18. I *will be* a Father to you, and ye my
10. 11. such *will* we *be* also indeed, when present
1 *Tim.* 6. 9. they that *will be* rich fall into temptations
Heb. 1. 5. I *will be* to him a Father, he to me a son
8. 10. I *will be* to them a God, they to me a people
Jam. 4. 4. whosoever *will be* a friend of the world
Rev. 21. 7. I *will be* his God, and he shall be my son
BEEN, *see after* BE.

BEACON.
Isa. 30. 17. be left as a *b.* on the top of a mountain

BEAM.
Judg. 16. 14. he went away with the pin of the *b.*
1 *Sam.* 17. 7. and the staff of his spear was like a weaver's *b.* 1 *Chron.* 11. 23. | 20. 5.
2 *Kings* 6. 2. let us go to Jordan, and take thence a *b.*
5. as one was felling a *b.* ax-head fell into water
Hab. 2. 11. the *b.* out of the timber shall answer
Mat. 7. 3. but considerest not the *b.* *Luke* 6. 41, 42.
4. and behold, a *b.* is in thine own eye
5. thou hypocrite, first cast out the *b.* *Luke* 6. 42.

BEAMS.
2 *Chron.* 3. 7. he overlaid the *b.* the posts, and walls
Neh. 2. 8. that he may give timber to make *b.*
Psal. 104. 3. who layeth the *b.* in the waters
Cant. 1. 17. the *b.* of our house are cedar and rafters

BEANS.
2 *Sam.* 17. 28. Barzillai brought *b.* lentiles to David
Ezek. 4. 9. take unto thee wheat, *b.* lentiles, millet

BEAR
Signifies, [1] *To carry*, Jer. 17. 21. Mat. 27. 32. [2] *To suffer, or endure*, 2 Cor. 11. 1. Rev. 2. 2. [3] *To bring forth*, Gen. 18. 13. [4] *To produce, or yield*, Jam. 3. 12. [5] *To uphold, or support*, Psal. 75. 3. | 91. 12. [6] *To be punished for*, Num. 14. 33. [7] *To undergo the care and fatigue of ruling a people*, Deut. 1. 12. [8] *To speak and utter*, Deut. 5. 20. [9] *To tell, or relate*, 2 Sam. 18. 19. [10] *To be answerable in payment for*, 2 Kings 18. 14. [11] *To lay a thing sadly to heart*, Psal. 89. 50. [12] *To give satisfaction for*, Isa. 53. 11. Heb. 9. 28. [13] *To perform, or fully observe*, Acts 15. 10.

To bear the infirmities of the weak, *Rom.* 15. 1. *To comply with their weakness so far as not to use our liberty to their offence, and also to bear with them in their failings through ignorance or weakness, and not to condemn or despise them.*

Gen. 4. 13. my punishment is greater than I can *b.*
13. 6. the land was not able to *b.* them, 36. 7.
43. 9. let me *b.* the blame for ever, 44. 32.
49. 15. Issachar bowed his shoulder to *b.*
Exod. 18. 22. they shall *b.* the burden with thee
25. 27. to *b.* the ark, 27. 7. | 30. 4. | 37. 5. *Deut.* 10. 8. *Josh.* 3. 3, 8, 13, 14. | 4. 16. 2 *Sam.* 15. 24.
28. 12. Aaron shall *b.* their names before the Lord
Lev. 19. 18. thou shalt not *b.* any grudge against
Num. 11. 14. not able to *b.* all this people, *Deut.* 1. 9.
14. 27. how long shall I *b.* with this congregation?
33. children shall *b.* your whoredoms, *Ezek.* 23. 35.
Deut. 1. 31. God bare thee as a man doth *b.* his son
2 *Sam.* 18. 19. let me run and *b.* the king tidings
2 *Kings* 18. 14. which thou puttest on me, I will *b.*
Psal. 75. 3. I *b.* up the pillars of the earth
89. 50. how I do *b.* in my bosom the reproach
91. 12. they shall *b.* thee up, *Mat.* 4. 6. *Luke* 4. 11.
144. † 14. that our oxen be able to *b.* burdens
Prov. 9. 12. if thou scornest, thou alone shalt *b.* it
18. 14. but a wounded spirit who can *b.*?
30. 21. and for four which it cannot *b.*
Isa. 1. 14. your feasts, I am weary to *b.* them
46. 4. I have made and I will *b.* you, even carry
7. they *b.* him upon the shoulder, they carry him
52. 11. be ye clean that *b.* the vessels of the Lord
Jer. 10. 19. truly this is a grief, and I must *b.* it
17. 21. *b.* no burden on the sabbath-day, 27.
31. 19. because I did *b.* the reproach of my youth
44. 22. so that the Lord could no longer *b.*
Lam. 3. 27. it is good to *b.* the yoke in his youth
Ezek. 12. 6. in their sight shalt thou *b.* on shoulders
12. the prince shall *b.* upon his shoulder in twilight
14. 10. they shall *b.* punishment of their iniquity
16. 52. *b.* thou thine own shame for thy sins, 54.
32. 30. and *b.* their shame with them, 36. 7. | 44. 13.
Ezek. 34. 29. nor *b.* the shame of the heathen, 36. 15.
Amos 7. 10. the land is not able to *b.* his words
Mic. 6. 16. ye shall *b.* the reproach of my people
7. 9. I will *b.* the indignation of the Lord, I sinned
Hag. 2. 12. if one *b.* holy flesh in the skirt of his
Zech. 5. 10. whither do these *b.* the ephah?
6. 13. he shall *b.* glory, and shall rule on his throne
Mat. 3. 11. whose shoes I am not worthy to *b.*
27. 32. they found Simon, they compelled him to *b.* his cross, *Mark* 15. 21. *Luke* 23. 26.
Luke 14. 27. and whosoever doth not *b.* his cross
18. 7. avenge his elect, tho' he *b.* long with them?
John 16. 12. many things, but ye cannot *b.* them now

Acts 9. 15. he is a chosen vessel to *b.* my name
15. 10. a yoke, our fathers nor we were able to *b.*
18. 14. O Jews, reason would I should *b.* with you
Rom. 15. 1. we ought to *b.* infirmities of the weak
1 *Cor.* 3. 2. hitherto ye were not able to *b.* it, nor
10. 13. a way to escape, that ye may be able to *b.* it
15. 49. we shall also *b.* the image of the heavenly
2 *Cor.* 11. 1. would to God ye could *b.* with me
4. have not accepted, ye might well *b.* with him
Gal. 6. 2. *b.* one another's burdens, and so fulfil
5. for every man shall *b.* his own burden
17. I *b.* in my body the marks of the Lord Jesus
Heb. 5. † 2. who can reasonably *b.* with the ignorant
Jam. 3. 12. can the fig-tree *b.* olive-berries?
Rev. 2. 2. thou canst not *b.* them that are evil
BEAR *fruit*, *see* FRUIT.

BEAR *iniquity*.
Exod. 28. 38. Aaron may *b.* *iniquity* of holy things
43. Aaron and his sons, that they *b.* not *iniquity*
Lev. 5. 1. he shall *b.* his *iniquity*, 17. | 7. 18. | 17. 16. | 19. 8. | 20. 17.
10. 17. hath given to you to *b.* *iniquity* of the cong.
16. 22. the goat shall *b.* upon him all their *iniquities*
20. 19. they shall *b.* their *iniquity*, *Num.* 18. 23. *Ezek.* 44. 10, 12.
22. 16. or suffer them to *b.* *iniquity* of their trespass
Num. 5. 31. this woman shall *b.* her *iniquity*
14. 34. ye shall *b.* your *iniquity* even forty years
18. 1. Aaron and his sons *b.* *iniquity* of sanctuary
30. 15. after he heard, then he shall *b.* her *iniquity*
Isa. 53. 11. my right. servant shall *b.* their *iniquity*
Ezek. 4. 4. number of days, thou shalt *b.* their *in.* 5, 6.
18. 19. why doth not son *b.* *iniquity* of the father?
20. the son shall not *b.* the *iniquity* of the father

BEAR *judgment*.
Exod. 28. 30. Aaron shall *b.* *judg.* of children of Israel
Gal. 5. 10. he that troubleth you shall *b.* his *judg.*
BEAR *record*, *see* RECORD.

BEAR *rule*.
Esth. 1. 22. every man should *b.* *rule* in his house
Prov. 12. 24. the hand of the diligent shall *b.* *rule*
Jer. 5. 31. the priests *b.* *rule* by their means
Ezek. 19. 11. had strong rods for them that *b.* *rule*
Dan. 2. 39. a kingdom of brass which shall *b.* *rule*

BEAR *sin*.
Lev. 19. † 17. rebuke, that thou *b.* not *sin* for him
20. 20. they shall *b.* their *sin*, they shall die
22. 9. lest they *b.* *sin* for it, and die, therefore
24. 15. whosoever curseth his God, shall *b.* his *sin*
Num. 9. 13. shall be cut off, that man shall *b.* his *sin*
18. 22. not come nigh, lest they *b.* *sin* and die
32. ye shall *b.* no *sin* when ye heaved the best of it
Ezek. 23. 49. and ye shall *b.* the *sin* of your idols
Heb. 9. 28. so Christ was once offered to *b.* *sin*

BEAR *witness*.
Exod. 20. 16. thou shalt not *b.* false *witness* against thy neighb. *Deut.* 5. 20. *Mat.* 19. 18. *Rom.* 13. 9.
1 *Kings* 21. 10. set two men sons of Belial to *b.* *wit.*
Mark 10. 19. do not *b.* false *witness*, *Luke* 18. 20.
Luke 11. 48. truly ye *b.* *wit.* that ye allow the deeds
John 1. 7. the same came for a witness, to *b.* *witness*
8. he was sent to *b.* *witness* of that light
3. 28. ye yourselves *b.* me *witness* that I said
5. 31. if I *b.* *wit.* of myself, my witness is not true
36. same works that I do, *b.* *witness* of me, 10. 25.
8. 18. I am one that *b.* *wit.* of myself, and the Father
15. 27. ye shall also *b.* *wit.* because ye have been
18. 23. if I have spoken evil, *b.* *witness* of the evil
37. for this cause came I, that I should *b.* *witness*
Acts 22. 5. also the high-priest doth *b.* me *witness*
23. 11. so must thou *b.* *witness* also at Rome
1 *John* 1. 2. we have seen it, and *b.* *witness*, and shew
5. 8. and there are three that *b.* *witness* in earth

BEAR.
Gen. 17. 17. and shall Sarah that is 90 years old *b.*?
18. 13. shall I of a surety *b.* a child, which am old
Lev. 12. 5. but if she *b.* a maid child, then unclean
Deut. 28. 57. and towards her children she shall *b.*
Judg. 13. 3. but thou shalt conceive and *b.* a son
1 *Kings* 3. 21. behold, it was not my son that I did *b.*
Cant. 4. 2. sheep, whereof every one *b.* twins, 6. 6.
Isa. 7. 14. a virgin shall conceive and *b.* a son, and
54. 1. sing, O barren, thou that didst not *b.*
Jer. 29. 6. that they may *b.* sons and daughters
Luke 1. 13. thy wife Elisabeth shall *b.* a son
1 *Tim.* 5. 14. younger women marry, *b.* children

BEARERS.
2 *Chron.* 2. 18. he set 70,000 to be *b.* of burdens
34. 13. also they were over the *b.* of burdens
Neh. 4. 10. the strength of the *b.* is decayed

BEAREST.
Judg. 13. 3. behold, thou art barren, and *b.* not
Psal. 106. 4. with the favour thou *b.* to thy people
John 8. 13. thou *b.* record of thyself, thy record
Rom. 11. 18. *b.* not the root, but the root thee
Gal. 4. 27. rejoice thou barren that *b.* note

BEARETH.
Lev. 11. 28. he that *b.* the carcase of them, wash
15. 10. and he that *b.* any of these things
Num. 11. 12. as a nursing father *b.* the child
Deut. 25. 6. the first-born she *b.* shall succeed
29. 18. lest there be among you a root that *b.* gall
23. it is not sown, nor *b.* nor grass groweth
32. 11. as an eagle *b.* her young on her wings
Job 24. 21. evil-entreateth the barren that *b.* not
Cant. 6. 6. whereof every one *b.* twins, none barren
Joel 2. 22. be not afraid, for the tree *b.* her fruit
Mat. 13. 23. which also *b.* fruit, and bringeth forth
John 15. 2. every branch that *b.* not fruit, takes
Rom. 13. 4. for he *b.* not the sword in vain
1 *Cor.* 13. 7. charity *b.* all things, believeth all things
Heb. 6. 8. that which *b.* thorns is rejected

BEARETH *rule*.
Prov. 29. 2. when the wicked *b.* *rule* people mourn

BEARETH *witness*.
Job 16. 8. my leanness rising up *b.* *witness* to my face
Prov. 25. 18. a man that *b.* false *witness* is a maul
John 5. 32. there is another that *b.* *witness* of me
8. 18. and the Father that sent me, *b.* *witness* of me
Rom. 8. 16. the Spirit *b.* *witness* with our spirit
1 *John* 5. 6. and it is the Spirit that *b.* *witness*

BEARING.

Gen. 1. 29. I have given you every herb, *b.* seed
16. 2. the Lord hath restrained me from *b.*
29. 35. she called his name Judah, and left *b.*
37. 25. Ishmaelites with camels *b.* spicery
Num. 10. 17. set forward, *b.* the tabernacle
21. the Kohathites set forward, *b.* the sanctuary
Josh. 3. 3. the priests *b.* the ark, 14. 2 *Sam.* 15. 24.
1 *Sam.* 17. 7. one *b.* a shield went before him
Psal 126. 6. he that goeth forth *b.* precious seed
Mark 14. 13. there shall meet you a man *b.* a pitcher of water, follow him, *Luke* 22. 10.
John 19. 17. he *b.* his cross, went forth to a place
Rom. 2. 15. their conscience also *b.* witness
9. 1. I lie not, my conscience also *b.* me witness
2 *Cor.* 4. 10. *b.* in the body the dying of the L. Jesus
Heb. 2. 4. God also *b.* them witness with signs
13. 13. let us go forth to him, *b.* his reproach
1 *Tim.* 2. 15. she shall be saved in child-*bearing*

BEAR, S.

1 *Sam.* 17. 34. came a lion and a *b.* took a lamb
36. thy servant slew both the lion and the *b.*
2 *Sam.* 17. 8. chafed, as a *b.* robbed of her whelps
2 *Kings* 2. 24. there came forth two she-*b.* and tare
Prov. 17. 12. a *b.* robbed of her whelps meet a man
28. 15. as a roaring lion, and a ranging *b.*
Isa. 11. 7. the cow and *b.* shall feed their young
59. 11. we roar all like *b.* and mourn like doves
Lam. 3. 10. he was to me as a *b.* lying in wait
Dan. 7. 5. another beast, a second like to a *b.*
Hos. 13. 8. I will meet them as a *b.* bereaved
Amos 5. 19. as if a man did flee from a *b.*
Rev. 13. 2. his feet were as the feet of a *b.*

BEARD, S.

Lev. 13. 29. if a man hath a plague on head or *b.*
14. 9. shall shave all his hair off his head and *b.*
19. 27. nor shalt thou mar the corners of *b.* 21. 5.
1 *Sam.* 17. 35. I caught him by his *b.* and slew him
21. 13. David let his spittle fall on his *b.*
2 *Sam.* 10. 5. tarry at Jericho till your *b.* be grown and then return, 1 *Chron.* 19. 5.
19. 24. Mephibosheth trimmed not his *b.*
20. 9. Joab took Amasa by the *b.* to kiss him
Ezra 9. 3. plucked off hair of my head, and of my *b.*
Psal. 133. 2. ran down on the *b.* even Aaron's *b.*
Isa. 7. 20. and it shall also consume the *b.*
15. 2. on all heads baldness, and every *b.* cut off
Jer. 41. 5. fourscore men having their *b.* shaved
48. 37. every head shall be bald, every *b.* clipt
Ezek. 5. 1. cause a razor to pass on thy head and *b.*

BEAST

Signifies, [1] *A brute void of reason*, Prov. 12. 10. [2] *All kind of cattle*, 1 Kings 4. 33. Psal. 8. 7. [3] *Ministers of the gospel, who are full of liveliness and nimbleness, in executing God's commands*, Rev. 4. 6, 8. | 7. 11. [4] *Cruel and unreasonable men, who are led merely by their natural brutish inclinations*, 1 Cor. 15. 32. 2 Pet. 2. 12. [5] *Kingdoms*, Dan. 7. 11. | 8. 4. [6] *Antichrist*, Rev. 13. 2. | 20. 4. [7] *People of several nations*, Dan. 4. 12. 21.

Gen. 1. 24. God said, let the earth bring forth the *b.*
25. God made the *b.* of the earth after his kind
3. 1. the serpent was more subtil than any *b.*
37. 20. some evil *b.* hath devoured him, 33.
Exod. 13. 12. every firstling that cometh of a *b.*
22. 5. put his *b.* and feed in another man's field
10. deliver to his neighbour any *b.* to keep
19. whoso lieth with a *b.* shall be put to death, *Lev.* 18. 23. | 20. 15, 16. *Deut.* 27. 21.
23. 29. the *b.* of the field multiply against thee
Lev. 11. 47. *b.* that may be eaten, and *b.* that may [not
27. 9. if it be a *b.* whereof men bring an offering
Deut. 4. 17. the likeness of any *b.* on the earth
Judg. 20. 48. smote them, as well the men as the *b.*
2 *Chron.* 25. † 18. a *b.* trod down the thistle
Neh. 2. 12. nor any *b.* save the *b.* I rode on
Psal. 68. † 30. rebuke the *b.* of the reeds
73. 22. so ignorant, I was as a *b.* before thee
147. 9. he giveth to the *b.* his food, and to ravens
Prov. 12. 10. a righteous man regards life of his *b.*
Eccl. 3. 19. a man hath no pre-eminence above a *b.*
Isa. 43. 20. the *b.* of the field shall honour me
63. 14. as a *b.* that goeth into the valley
Ezek. 44. 31. dead or torn, whether it be fowl or *b.*
Dan. 4. 16. let a *b.* heart be given to him
7. 11. I beheld even till the *b.* was slain
19. I would know the truth of the fourth *b.*
Hos. 13. † 8. the *b.* of the field shall tear them
Luke 10. 34. set him on his own *b.* and brought him
Acts 28. 5. Paul shook off the *b.* into the fire
Heb. 12. 20. if so much as a *b.* touch the mountain
Rev. 4. 7. first *b.* like a lion, second *b.* third *b.*
6. 3. I heard the second *b.* say, come and see
11. 7. *b.* that ascendeth out of the bottomless pit
13. 1. and I saw a *b.* rise up out of the sea, having
11. I beheld a *b.* coming out of the earth
15. 2. them that had got the victory over the *b.*
16. 13. unclean spirits came out of mouth of the *b.*
17. 8. thou sawest the *b.* that was, and is not, 11.
19. 19. I saw the *b.* and the kings of the earth
20. 10. where the *b.* and false prophet are

Every BEAST.

Gen. 1. 30. to *every b.* I have given green herb for
2. 19. out of the ground God formed *every b.*
20. Adam gave names to *every b.* of the field
3. 14. thou art cursed above *every b.* of the field
7. 2. of *every* clean *b.* take to thee by sevens, 8.
14. they and *every b.* after his kind, and cattle
8. 19. *every b.* after their kinds went out of the ark
20. of *every* clean *b.* and clean fowl he offered
9. 2. dread of you shall be on *every b.* of the earth
5. your blood will I require at hand of *every b.*
10. with *every b.* of earth I establish my covenant
34. 23. shall not *every b.* of theirs be ours?
Lev. 11. 26. the carcases of *every b.* which divideth the hoof, nor cheweth the cud, *Deut.* 14. 6.
Psal. 50. 10. for *every b.* of the forest is mine
104. 11. they give drink to *every b.* of the field
Ezek. 34. 8. my flock became meat to *every b.*
39. 17. son of man, speak to every *b.* of the field

BEAST, joined with *Man.*

Gen. 6. 7. Lord said, I will destroy both *man* and *b.*
Exod. 8. 17. smote dust, it became lice in *man* and *b.*
9. 9. boil breaking with blains upon *man* and *b.* 10.
19. hail shall come down on *man* and *b.* 22, 25
11. 7. not a dog move his tongue against *man* or *b.*
12. 12. and will smite all the first-born in Egypt, both of *man* and *b.* 13. 15. *Psal.* 135. 8.
13. 2. first-born of *man* and *b.* is mine, *Num.* 8. 17.
19. 13. whether *man* or *b.* it shall not live
Lev. 27. 28. no devoted thing of *man* or *b.* shall be
Num. 3. 13. I hallowed to me first-born of *man* and *b.*
31. 26. the prey that was taken, both of *man* and *b.*
Psal. 36. 6. Lord, thou preservest *man* and *b.*
Jer. 7. 20. fury poured on *man* and *b.* 21. 6. | 36. 29.
Ezek. 14. 13, 17, 19, 21. | 25. 13. | 29. 8. *Zeph.* 1. 3.
27. 5. I have made *man* and *b.* that are on ground
31. 27. I will sow Judah with seed of *man* and *b.*
32. 43. ye say, it is desolate without *man* or *b.* 33. 10, 12. | 36. 29. | 51. 62.
50. 3. they shall depart, both *man* and *b.*
Ezek. 36. 11. I will multiply upon you *man* and *b.*
Jonah 3. 7. let not *man* nor *b.* taste any thing

Unclean BEAST.

Lev. 5. 2. or if a soul touch any *unclean b.* 7. 21.
27. 11. if it be *uncl. b.* of which they do not offer, 27.

Wild BEAST.

2 *Kings* 14. 9. there passed by a *wild b.* of Lebanon, and trod down the thistle, 2 *Chron.* 25. 18.
Job 39. 15. forgetteth that *wild b.* may break them
Psal. 80. 13 the *wild b.* of the field doth devour it
Hos. 13. 8. the *wild b.* shall tear them

BEASTS.

Gen. 31. 39. that which was torn of *b.* *Exod.* 22. 31. *Lev.* 7. 24. | 17. 15. | 22. 8.
† 54. then Jacob killed *b.* upon the mount
36. 6. Esau took all his *b.* and his substance
45. 17. lade your *b.* and go to the land of Canaan
Exod. 8. † 21. I will send a mixture of noisome *b.*
11. 5. all the first-born of *b.* shall die
Lev. 11. 2. these *b.* ye shall eat, *Deut.* 14. 4.
3. and chew cud among *b.* shall ye eat, *Deut.* 14. 6.
25. 7. for *b.* shall the increase thereof be meat
26. 6. I will rid evil *b.* out of the land
Num. 20. 8. give the congregation and their *b.* drink
31. 30. of all *b.* give a portion to the Levites
Deut. 32. 24. I will send the teeth of *b.* on them
1 *Kings* 4. † 28. barley for mules, or swift *b.*
33 Solomon spake of *b.* and of fowl, and fishes
18. 5. may find grass, that we lose not all the *b.*
2 *Kings* 3. 17. drink both ye, your cattle and *b.*
Ezra 1. 4. help him with gold, goods, and with *b.*
Job 12. 7. ask the *b.* and they shall teach thee
18. 3. wherefore are we counted as *b.* and vile
37. 8. then the *b.* go into dens, and remain
Psal. 49. 12. man is like the *b.* that perish, 20.
78. † 50. he gave their *b.* to the murrain
104. 20. wherein all the *b.* of the forest creep
25. in the sea, are both small and great *b.*
148 10. *b.* and all cattle, praise the Lord
Prov. 9. 2. wisdom hath killed her *b.*
30. 30. a lion, which is strongest among *b.*
Eccl. 3. 18. they might see that themselves are *b.*
19. that which befalleth men, befalleth *b.*
Isa. 30. 6. the burden of the *b.* of the south
40. 16. nor *b.* thereof for a burnt-offering
46. 1. their idols were on the *b.* and cattle
66. 20. upon swift *b.* to my holy mountain
Jer. 9. 10. the *b.* are fled || 12. 4. the *b.* are consumed
Ezek. 5. 17. I will send on you famine and evil *b.* pestilence, blood, and the sword, 14. 15.
32. 4. I will fill the *b.* of whole earth with thee
13. I will destroy all the *b.* thereof, 34. 25, 28.
Dan. 4. 14. let the *b.* get away from under it
15. let his portion be with the *b.* in the grass
7. 17. these four great *b.* are four kings
8. 4. so that no *b.* might stand before him
Joel 1. 18. how do the *b.* groan, herds perplexed
Amos 5. 22. nor regard the peace-offerings of fat *b.*
Hab. 2. 17. spoil of *b.* which made them afraid
Zeph. 2. 15. become a place for *b.* to lie down in
Zech. 14. 15. so shall be the plague of all the *b.*
Acts 7. 42. O Israel, have ye offered to me slain *b.*?
23. 24. provide them *b.* that ye may set Paul on
Rom. 1. 23. changed into an image made like to *b.*
1 *Cor.* 15. 32. if I have fought with *b.* at Ephesus
Jam. 3. 7. for every kind of *b.* is tamed, but tongue
2 *Pet.* 2. 12. but these as natural brute *b.* speak evil
Jude 10. but what they know naturally as brute *b.*
Rev. 4. 6. four *b.* full of eyes before and behind
8. the four *b.* had each six wings about him
9. when those *b.* give glory and honour to him
5. 6. in midst of the throne and four *b.* stood a Lamb
14. the four *b.* said, Amen, and the 24 elders fell
6. 1. one of the four *b.* saying, come and see, 15. 7.
7. 11. angels stood about the throne and the four *b.*
14. 3. a new song before the throne and four *b.*
19. 4. the 24 elders and four *b.* fell down to worship

BEASTS *of the Earth.*

Deut. 28. 26. carcase shall be meat to all *b. of earth*
1 *Sam.* 17. 46. carcases of Philistines to *b. of earth*
Job 5. 22. nor shalt thou be afraid of the *b. of earth*
35. 11. who teacheth us more than the *b. of earth*
Psal. 79. 2. the flesh of thy saints to the *b. of earth*
Isa. 18. 6. they shall be left to the *b. of the earth*
Jer. 7. 33. the carcases of the people meat for *b. of the earth*, 16. 4. | 19. 7. | 34. 20.
15. 3. I will appoint over them *b. of earth* to devour
Acts 10. 12. all manner of four-footed *b. of earth*, 11. 6.
Rev. 6. 8. kill with hunger and with the *b. of earth*

BEASTS *of the Field.*

Exod. 23. 11. what the poor leave, *b. of field* may eat
Deut. 7. 22. lest the *b. of the field* increase upon thee
1 *Sam.* 17. 44. come, I will give thy flesh to *b. of field*
2 *Sam.* 21. 10. birds by day, nor *b. of the field* by night
Job 5. 23. *b. of the field* shall be at peace with thee
40. 20. mountains, where all the *b. of the field* play
Psal. 8. 7. thou hast put *b. of the field* under his feet
Isa. 56. 9. all ye *b. of the field* come to devour
Jer. 12. 9. assemble all *b. of the field*, come to devour
27. 6. *b of field* have I given him, 28. 14. *Dan.* 2. 38.
Ezek. 29. 5. I have given thee for meat to the *b. of the field*, and to the fowls, 34. 5. | 39. 4.
31. 6. under his branches *b. of the field* bring forth
13. all the *b. of the field* shall be on his branches
38. 20. the *b. of the field* shall shake at my presence
Dan. 4. 12. the *b. of the field* had shadow under it
25. thy dwelling shall be with *b. of the field*, 32.
Hos. 2. 18. make a covenant for them with *b. of field*
4. 3. therefore shall the land mourn with *b. of field*
Joel 1. 20. *b. of field* cry also to thee, for the rivers
2. 22. be not afraid, ye *b. of field*, the pastures spring

Wild BEASTS.

Lev. 26. 22. I will also send *wild b.* among you
1 *Sam.* 17. 46. gave carcases of Philistines to *wild b.*
Psal. 50. 11. and the *wild b.* of the field are mine
Isa. 13. 21. but *wild b.* of the desert shall lie there
22. and the *wild b.* of the islands shall cry
31. 11. the *wild b.* of the desert shall also meet with the *wild b.* of the island, *Jer.* 50. 39.
Mark 1. 13. Christ was there with the *wild b.* and
Acts 10. 12. sheet, wherein were all *wild b.* 11. 6.

BEAT

Signifies, [1] *To smite, or strike*, Deut. 25. 3. Mat. 21. 35. [2] *To bruise, or bray*, Exod. 30. 36. Num. 11. 8. [3] *To batter, or demolish*, Judg. 8. 17. 2 Kings 3. 25. [4] *To get the better of, or overcome*, 2 Kings 13. 25. [5] *To thresh*, Ruth 2. 17. Isa. 28. 27. [6] *To turn or convert one thing into another*, Isa. 2. 4. Joel. 3. 10.

Exod. 30. 36. some of the spices shalt *b.* very small
39. 3. they did *b.* the gold into thin plates
Num. 11. 8. the people *b.* the manna in a mortar
Deut. 25. 3. lest if he exceed and *b.* him above these
Judg. 8. 17. he *b.* down the tower of Penuel
9. 45. Abimelech *b.* down the city, and sowed it
19. 22. certain sons of Belial *b.* at the door
Ruth 2. 17. she *b.* out that she had gleaned
2 *Sam.* 22. 43. then did I *b.* them small, *Psal.* 18. 42.
2 *Kings* 3. 25. the Israelites *b.* down the cities
13. 25. three times did Joash *b.* Benhadad
23. 12. the altars did the king *b.* down, and brake
Psal. 52. † 5. God shall likewise *b.* thee down
89. 23. I will *b.* down his foes before his face
Prov. 23. 14. thou shalt *b.* him with the rod and
Isa. 2. 4. *b.* their swords into plow-shares, *Mic.* 4. 3.
3. 15. what mean ye, that ye *b.* my people
27. 12. the Lord shall *b.* off from the channel
41. 15. thresh the mountains, *b.* them small
Joel 3. 10. *b.* your plow-shares into swords, and your
Jonah 4. 8. the sun *b.* on the head of Jonah
Mic. 4. 13. thou shalt *b.* in pieces many people
Mat. 7. 25. and *b.* on that house, 27. *Luke* 6. 48, 49.
21. 35. the husbandmen took his servants, and *b.* one, *Mark* 12. 3. *Luke* 20. 10, 11.
Mark 4. 37. waves *b.* into the ship, it was now full
Luke 12. 45. and shall begin to *b.* the men-servants
Acts 16. 22. the magistrates commanded to *b.* them
18. 17. the Greeks took Sosthenes and *b.* him
22. 19. I imprisoned and *b.* in every synagogue
27. † 14. there *b.* a wind called Euroclydon

BEATEN.

Exod. 5. 14. the officers of Israel were *b.* 16.
25. 18. cherub of *b.* work, 37. 17, 22. *Num.* 8. 4.
37. 7. made two cherubims *b.* out of one piece
Lev. 2. 14. shalt offer corn *b.* out of full ears
Deut. 25. 2. if the wicked man be worthy to be *b.*
Josh. 8. 15. all Israel made as if were *b.* before them
2 *Sam.* 2. 17. and Abner was *b.* and the men of Israel
2 *Chron.* 15. † 6. nation was *b.* in pieces of nation
34. 7. when he had *b.* graven images to powder
Job 4. † 20. they are *b.* in pieces from morning
Prov. 10. † 8. but a prating fool shall be *b.*
23. 35. they have *b.* me, and I felt it not
Isa. 28. 27. fitches are *b.* out with a staff
30. 31. thro' voice of Lord the Assyrian shall be *b.*
Jer. 46. 5. and their mighty ones are *b.* down
Mic. 1. 7. the graven images shall be *b.* to pieces
Mark 13. 9. in the synagogue ye shall be *b.*
Luke 12. 47. servant who knew and did not shall be *b.*
Acts 5. 40. when they called the apostles and *b.* them
16. 37. they have *b.* us openly uncondemned
2 *Cor.* 11. 25. thrice was I *b.* with rods, once stoned

BEATEN *Gold.*

Num. 8. 4. this work of the candlestick was of *b. gold*
1 *Kings* 10. 16. made two hundred targets of *b. gold*
17. made three hund. shields of *b. gold*, 2 *Chr.* 9. 16.
2 *Chron.* 9. 15. six hundred shekels *b. gold* to a target

BEATEN *Oil.*

Exod. 27. 20. pure *oil b.* for the light, *Lev.* 24. 2.
29. 40. fourth part of an hin of *b. oil*, *Num.* 28. 5.

BEATEST.

Deut. 24. 20. when thou *b.* thy olive tree, shalt not
Prov. 23. 13. for if thou *b.* him with rod, shall not

BEATETH.

1 *Cor.* 9. 26. so fight I, not as one that *b.* the air

BEATING.

1 *Sam.* 14. 16. they went on *b.* down one another
Mark 12. 5. many others, *b.* some, and killing some

BEAUTY

Signifies, [1] *Comeliness, or handsomeness*, 2 Sam. 14. 25. [2] *A chief person, or city*, 2 Sam. 1. 19. Isa. 13. 19. Lam. 2. 1. [3] *Splendour, glory, or dignity*, Lam. 1. 6. Zech. 11. 7. [4] *Joy and gladness*, Isa. 61. 3. [5] *The excellent order of a government, the prosperity, riches, and peace of a country, together with the holiness, purity, and truth of their religion, which were their ornament and glory*, Ezek. 16. 14.

Exod. 28. 2. holy garment for Aaron, for glory and *b.*
2 *Sam.* 1. 19. the *b.* of Israel is slain on high places
14. 25. none so much praised as Absalom for *b.*
1 *Chr.* 16. 29. worship the Lord in the *b.* of holiness, *Psal.* 29. 2. | 96. 9.
2 *Chro.* 20. 21. that should praise the *b.* of holiness
Esth. 1. 11. to show the people and princes her *b.*
Job 40. 10. and array thyself with glory and *b.*
Psal. 27. 4. to behold the *b.* of the Lord, and inquire
39. 11. thou makest his *b.* to consume away
45. 11. so shall the king greatly desire thy *b.*
49. 14. their *b.* shall consume in the grave
50. 2. out of Zion the perfection of *b.* God shined
90. 17. let the *b.* of the Lord our God be on us
96. 6. strength and *b.* are in his sanctuary

Prov. 6. 25. lust not after her *b.* in thy heart
20. 29. the *b.* of old men is the gray head
31. 30. favour is deceitful, and *b.* is vain
Isa. 3. 24. there shall be burning instead of *b.*
4. † 2. branch of the Lord shall be *b.* and glory
13. 19. Babylon the *b.* of the Chaldees' excellency
28. 1. whose glorious *b.* is a fading flower, 4.
5. the Lord will be for a diadem of *b.* to residue
33. 17. thine eyes shall see the King in his *b.*
44. 13. he maketh it according to the *b.* of a man
53. 2. there is no *b.* that we should desire him
61. 3. to give to them that mourn *b.* for ashes
Lam. 1. 6. from Zion all her *b.* is departed
2. 1. and cast down from heaven the *b.* of Israel
15. is this the city men call the perfection of *b.*?
Ezek. 7. 20. as for the *b.* of his ornament he set it
16. 14. thy renown went among the heathen for *b.*
15. but thou didst trust in thine own *b.*
25. thou hast made thy *b.* to be abhorred
27. 3. thou hast said, I am of perfect *b.* 28. 12.
4. thy builders have perfected thy *b.* 11.
28. 7. shall draw swords against the *b.* of thy wisdom
17. thine heart was lifted up because of thy *b.*
31. 8. no tree was like the Assyrian in his *b.*
32. 19. Egypt, whom dost thou pass in *b.*?
Hos. 10. † 11. I passed over on the *b.* of her neck
14. 6. Israel's *b.* shall be as the olive-tree, his smell
Zech. 9. 17. how great is his goodness and his *b.*
11. 7. I took two staves, one I called *b.* 10.

BEAUTIES.

Psal. 110. 3. in the *b.* of holiness, from the womb of

BEAUTIFY.

Ezra 7. 27. put in the king's heart to *b.* Lord's house
Psal. 149. 4. he will *b.* the meek with salvation
Isa. 60. 13. to *b.* the place of my sanctuary

BEAUTIFUL.

Gen. 29. 17. Rachel was *b.* and well-favoured
Deut. 21. 11. seest among the captives a *b.* woman
1 *Sam.* 16. 12. David was of a *b.* countenance
25. 3. Abigail was of a *b.* countenance
2 *Sam.* 11. 2. Bathsheba was very *b.* to look upon
14. † 25. in Israel was not a *b.* man as Absalom
Esth. 2. 7. Esther was fair and *b.* Mordecai took for
Psal. 48. 2. *b.* for situation is mount Zion
Eccl. 3. 11. hath made every thing *b.* in his time
Cant. 6. 4. thou art *b.* O my love, as Tirzah
7. 1. how *b.* are thy feet with shoes, O princess
Isa. 4. 2. in that day shall the branch of Lord be *b.*
52. 1. O Zion, put on thy *b.* garments
7. how *b.* the feet of them that bring, *Rom.* 10. 15.
64. 11. our holy and *b.* house is burnt up
Jer. 13. 20. where is the flock, thy *b.* flock?
48. 17. how is the staff broken, and the *b.* rod
Ezek. 16. 12. I put a *b.* crown upon thine head
13. thou wast exceeding *b.* and didst prosper
23. 42. the Sabeans put *b.* crowns on their heads
Mat. 23. 27. whited sepulchres, which appear *b.*
Acts 3. 2. at the gate of the temple called *b.* 10.

BECAME.

Gen. 2. 7. the breath of life, and man *b.* a living soul
19. 26. Lot's wife looked back and *b.* a pillar of salt
49. 15. Issachar *b.* a servant to tribute
Exod. 4. 3. it *b.* a serpent ‖ 4. *b.* a rod in his hand
36. 13. he coupled it, so it *b.* one tabernacle
1 *Sam.* 25. 37. Nabal's heart died, he *b.* as a stone
1 *Kings* 12. 30. and this thing *b.* a sin, 13. 34.
Dan. 2. 35. the stone *b.* a great mountain, and filled
1 *Cor.* 9. 20. to the Jews I *b.* a Jew, to gain the Jews
Heb. 7. 26. such an High-Priest *b.* us, who is holy
10. 33. whilst ye *b.* companions of them so used
Rev. 16. 3. the sea *b.* as the blood of a dead man

BECAMEST.

1 *Chron.* 17. 22. and thou, Lord, *b.* their God
Ezek. 16. 8. I sware unto thee, and thou *b.* mine

BECAUSE.

Gen. 3. † 1. *b.* God hath said, ye shall not eat
14. said to the serpent, *b.* thou hast done this
Lev. 26. 43. *b.* even *b.* they despised my judgments
Deut. 7. † 12. *b.* ye hearken to these judgments
2 *Sam.* 12. 6. *b.* he did this, *b.* he had no pity
Prov. 1. 24. *b.* I have called, and ye refused
Isa. 7. † 9. do ye not believe, *b.* ye are not stable
Ezek. 13. 10. *b.* even *b.* they seduced my people
36. † 3. *b.* for *b.* they have made you desolate
Mat. 26. 31. all ye shall be offended *b.* of me
Mark 9. 41. give you water, *b.* ye belong to Christ
John 6. 26. ye seek me, not *b.* ye saw the miracles,
but *b.* ye did eat of the loaves, and were filled
8. 43. even *b.* ye cannot hear my word
10. 13. the hireling fleeth, *b.* he is an hireling
14. 19. but ye see me, *b.* I live, ye shall live also
Rom. 8. 10. the Spirit is life *b.* of righteousness
† 11. quicken your mortal bodies *b.* of his Spirit
Eph. 5. 6. *b.* of these cometh the wrath of God
Heb. 4. † 2. not profit, *b.* not united by faith to them
6. 13. *b.* he could swear by no greater, he sware by
1 *John* 3. 14. from death to life, *b.* we love brethren
4. 19. we love him *b.* he first loved us

BECKONED.

Luke 1. 22. Zecharias *b.* and remained speechless
5. 7. they *b.* to their partners in the other ship
John 13. 24. Peter *b.* to him that he should ask
Acts 19. 33. Alexander *b.* with his hand, and would
21. 40. Paul stood on stairs, and *b.* with the hand
24. 10. Paul, after the governor had *b.* answered

BECKONING.

Acts 12. 17. Peter *b.* unto them with the hand
13. 16. Paul stood up, and *b.* with his hand, said

BECOME.

Gen. 3. 22. man is *b.* as one of us, to know good and
17. † 16. I will bless her, and she shall *b.* nations
37. 20. we will see what will *b.* of his dreams
38. † 23. let her take it, lest we *b.* a contempt
Exod. 15. 2. the Lord is my strength, and is *b.* my
salvation, *Psal.* 118. 14. *Isa.* 12. 2.
32. 1. for as for this Moses that brought us up, we
wot not what is *b.* of him, 23. *Acts* 7. 40.
Deut. 27. 9. O Israel, thou art *b.* the people of God
1 *Sam.* 28. 16. seeing the Lord is *b.* thine enemy
Jonah 4. 5. he might see what would *b.* of the city
Mat. 21. 42. the same is *b.* the head of the corner,
Mark 12. 10. *Luke* 20. 17. *Acts* 4. 11.

John 1. 12. he gave power to *b.* the sons of God
2 *Cor.* 5. 17. in Christ, behold, all things are *b.* new
Rev. 11. 15. are *b.* the kingdoms of our Lord

BECOMETH.

Psal. 93. 5. holiness *b.* thy house, O Lord, for ever
Prov. 10. 4. he *b.* poor that dealeth with a slack hand
17. 7. excellent speech *b.* not a fool, much less do
18. a man void of understanding *b.* surety
Eccl. 4. 14. he that is born in his kingdom, *b.* poor
Mat. 3. 15. thus it *b.* us to fulfil all righteousness
13. 22. the deceitfulness of riches choketh the
word, and he *b.* unfruitful, *Mark* 4. 19.
32. greatest among herbs, and *b.* a tree, *Mark* 4. 32.
Rom. 16. 2. that ye receive Phebe our sister as *b.* saints
Eph. 5. 3. covetousness not be once named, as *b.* saints
Phil. 1. 27. let your conversation be as *b.* the gospel
1 *Tim.* 2. 10. as *b.* women professing godliness
Tit. 2. 3. aged women be in behaviour as *b.* holiness

BED

Signifies, [1] *That whereon persons sleep in the night,*
1 Sam. 19. 13. [2] *A couch to rest on in the day,*
2 Sam. 4. 5. [3] *Pain, torment, or tribulation,*
Rev. 2. 22. [4] *The grave, which is as a sleeping*
house, for the righteous, Isa. 57. 2. [5.] *The law-*
ful use of wedlock, Heb. 13. 4.
On my bed, *Cant.* 3. 1. *while I was in a secure or*
slothful frame.
Our bed is green, *Cant.* 1. 16. *The ordinances and*
means of grace, where I enjoy sweet fellowship and
communion with thee, are not only pleasant and
delightful, but also fruitful; and, by the Spirit's
accompanying them, they are made effectual for
the converting of many.
Gen. 47. 31. bowed himself on the *b.* 1 *Kings* 1. 47.
49. 4. wentest up to thy father's *b.* 1 *Chron.* 5. 1.
Exod. 21. 18. and he die not, but keepeth his *b.*
Lev. 15. 4. every *b.* whereon he lieth is unclean, 24.
1 *Sam.* 19. 13. Michal took an image and laid it in *b.*
2 *Sam.* 3. † 31. king David himself followed the *b.*
4. 5. Ish-bosheth who lay on a *b.* at noon
11. 2. in an evening-tide David arose from his *b.*
2 *Kings* 1. 4. shall not come down from that *b.* 6. 16.
4. 10. let us set there for him a *b.* and a table
Job 7. 13. when I say, my *b.* shall comfort me
17. 13. I have made my *b.* in the darkness
33. 15. God speaketh in slumberings upon the *b.*
Psal. 4. 4. commune with your own heart on your *b.*
36. 4. he deviseth mischief on his *b.*
41. 3. thou wilt make all his *b.* in his sickness
63. 6. when I remember thee upon my *b.* and
132. 3. nor go up into my *b.* till I find a place
139. 8. if I make my *b.* in hell, thou art there
Prov. 7. 16. I have decked my *b.* with tapestry, 17.
22. 27. why should he take thy *b.* from under thee?
26. 14. on hinges, so doth the slothful on his *b.*
Cant. 1. 16. fair, yea pleasant, also our *b.* is green
3. 1. by night on my *b.* I sought him whom my soul
7. behold, his *b.* which is Solomon's, valiant men
† 9. Solomon made himself a *b.* wood of Lebanon
Isa. 28. 20. the *b.* is shorter than a man can stretch
57. 7. on a lofty mountain hast thou set thy *b.*
Amos 3. 12. Israel taken out in the corner of a *b.*
Mat. 9. 6. Jesus saith, take up thy *b.* and walk,
Mark 2. 9, 11. *John* 5. 11, 12.
Mark 4. 21. a candle to be put under a *b.* *Luke* 8. 16.
Luke 11. 7. my children are with me in *b.* I cannot
17. 34. two men in one *b.* one taken, the other left
Rev. 2. 22. behold I will cast her into a *b.*

BED *of love.*

Ezek. 23. 17. Babylonians came to her in the *b. of love*

BED *of spices.*

Cant. 5. 13. his cheeks are as a *b. of spices*, as flowers
6. 2. my beloved is gone down to the *b. of spices*

BED *undefiled.*

Heb. 13. 4. marriage is honourable and the *b. undefiled*

BED-CHAMBER.

Exod. 8. 3. frogs come into thy *b.-c.* and on thy bed
2 *Sam.* 4. 7. Ish-bosheth lay in his *b.-c.* they slew him
2 *Kings* 6. 12. telleth the words thou speakest in *b.-c.*
11. 2. hid him and nurse in the *b.-c.* 2 *Chron.* 22. 11.
Eccl. 10. 20. and curse not the rich in thy *b.-c.*

BEDS.

Psal. 149. 5. let the saints sing aloud on their *b.*
Isa. 57. 2. they shall rest in their *b.* each one walking
Hos. 7. 14. not cried when they howled upon their *b.*
Amos 6. 4. lie on *b.* of ivory, and stretch themselves
Mic. 2. 1. wo to them that work evil on their *b.*
Mark 7. † 4. washing of cups, and *b.* brazen vessels

BEDSTEAD.

Deut. 3. 11. king of Bashan, his *b.* was a *b.* of iron

BEE, BEES.

Deut. 1. 44. the Amorites chased you as *b.* in Seir
Judg. 14. 8. a swarm of *b.* in the carcase of the lion
Psal. 118. 12. they compassed me about like *b.*
Isa. 7. 18. the Lord shall hiss for the *b.* in Assyria

BEEN.

1 *Sam.* 10. † 27. Saul was as though he had *b.* deaf
2 *Sam.* 1. 26. very pleasant hast thou *b.* to me
12. 8. if that had *b.* too little, I would have given
Job 3. 13. I should have slept, then had I *b.* at rest
Psal. 27. 9. thou hast *b.* my help, leave me not, 63. 7.
94. 17. unless the L. had *b.* my help, my soul had
Isa. 48. 18. then had thy peace *b.* as a river
49. 21. I was left alone; these, where had they *b.*?
Mat. 23. 30. if we had *b.* in the days of our fathers
28. † 2. behold, there had *b.* a great earthquake
Luke 24. 21. but we trusted that it had *b.* he which
Acts 4. 13. took knowledge they had *b.* with Jesus
Rom. 9. 29. we had *b.* as Sodom, and like Gomorrah
1 *Tim.* 5. 9. a widow, having *b.* the wife of one man
2 *Tim.* 3. † 10. thou hast *b.* a diligent follower of my
2 *Pet.* 2. 21. it had *b.* better not to have known the
1 *John* 2. 19. if they had *b.* of us, no doubt they

Hath BEEN.

Gen. 31. 5. the God of my fathers *hath b.* with me
Deut. 2. 7. the Lord thy God *hath b.* with thee
1 *Sam.* 14. 38. see wherein this sin *hath b.* this day
2 *Chron.* 15. 3. Israel *hath b.* without the true God
Eccl. 3. 15. that which *hath b.* is now, and that
which is to be *hath* already *b.*
Isa. 28. † 10. for precept *hath b.* upon precept
Jer. 22. 21. this *hath b.* thy manner from thy youth

Joel 1. 2. *hath* this *b.* in your days or your fathers?
John 11. 39. for he *hath b.* dead four days
Rom. 11. 34. or who *hath b.* his counsellor?

Have BEEN.

1 *Sam.* 4. 9. not servants to Hebrews as they *have b.*
1 *Chr.* 17. 8. *have b.* with thee whither thou walkedst
Ezra 9. 7. since the days of our fathers *have* we *b.*
Job 10. 19. I should *have b.* as if I had not *b.*
Psal. 25. 6. thy tender mercies *have b.* ever of old
37. 25. *have b.* young, and now old, yet have not seen
42. 3. my tears *have b.* my meat day and night
Isa. 1. 9. should *have b.* as Sodom, *have b.* as Gomorrah
26. 17. so *have* we *b.* in thy sight, O Lord
18. *have b.* with child, *have b.* in pain, as it were
66. 2. all those things *have b.* saith the Lord
Jer. 2. 31. *have* I *b.* a wilderness to Israel?
28. 8. the prophets that *have b.* before me
Hos. 5. 2. though I *have b.* a rebuker of them all
Mal. 2. 9. but *have b.* partial in the law
Mark 8. 2. they *have b.* with me three days
Luke 1. 70. which *have b.* since the world began
John 14. 9. *have* I *b.* so long time with you?
15. 27. because ye *have b.* with me from the begin.
Acts 20. 18. after what manner I *have b.* with you
2 *Cor.* 11. 25. a night and a day I *have b.* in the deep
Gal. 3. 21. righteousness should *have b.* by the law

Not BEEN.

Exod. 9. 18. to rain hail such as hath *not b.* in Egypt
1 *Kings* 3. † 13. *not b.* among the kings like thee
14. 8. yet hast *not b.* as my servant David
Job 3. 16. as an hidden untimely birth I had *not b.*
10. 19. I should have been as tho' I had *not b.*
Psal. 124. 1. if it had *not b.* the Lord on our side, 2.
Eccl. 4. 3. better than both is he that hath *not b.*
Obad. 16. they shall be as though they had *not b.*
Mat. 26. 24. good for that man he had *not b.* born
Luke 16. 11. if therefore ye have *not b.* faithful, 12.

BEETLE.

Lev. 11. 22. these of them ye may eat, the *b.*

BEEVES.

Lev. 22. 19. offer at your own will of the *b.* of sheep
21. whosoever offereth a free-will-offering in *b.*
Num. 31. 28. levy a tribute to the Lord of the *b.*
38. the Lord's tribute of *b.* threescore and twelve

BEFALL.

Gen. 42. 4. lest peradventure mischief *b.* him
38. if mischief *b.* him by the way then, 44. 29.
49. 1. that I may tell you what shall *b.* you in the
last days, *Deut.* 31. 29. *Dan.* 10. 14.
Deut. 31. 17. many evils and troubles shall *b.* them
Psal. 91. 10. there shall no evil *b.* thee, nor plague
Acts 20. 22. not knowing things that shall *b.* me

BEFALLEN.

Lev. 10. 19. and such things have *b.* me
Num. 20. 14. thou knowest all travail that hath *b.* us
Deut. 31. 21. when many troubles are *b.* them
Judg. 6. 13. if Lord be with us, why is all this *b.* us?
1 *Sam.* 20. 26. he thought something had *b.* him
Esth. 6. 13. Haman told every thing that had *b.*
Mat. 8. 33. and what was *b.* to the possessed of devils

BEFALLETH.

Eccl. 3. 19. for that which *b.* the sons of men, *b.*
beasts, even one thing *b.* them

BEFELL.

2 *Sam.* 19. 7. will be worse than all that *b.* thee
Mark 5. 16. told how it *b.* to him that was possessed
Acts 20. 19. *b.* me by the lying in wait of the Jews

BEFORE

Signifies, [1] *In sight of,* Gen. 43. 14. [2] *Rather*
than, 2 Sam. 6. 21. [3] *Free to one's view and*
choice, Gen. 20. 15. [4] *At,* Rev. 3. 9. [5] *Not*
being sent or commissioned by, John 10. 8. [6]
First, (1) *In order of time,* Isa. 43. 13. (2) *In*
order of place, Josh. 8. 10. Luke 22. 47. (3) *In*
order of dignity, John 1. 15, 27.
Gen. 20. 15. behold my land is *b.* thee, dwell where
24. 45. *b.* I had done speaking in my heart
31. 2. his countenance was not toward him as *b.*
43. 14. the Lord give you mercy *b.* the man
48. 20. and he set Ephraim *b.* Manasseh
Exod. 16. 34. Aaron laid it up *b.* the testimony
Num. 6. 12. but the days that were *b.* shall be lost
Josh. 4. 18. Jordan flowed over his banks as *b.*
10. 14. there was no day like that *b.* it, or after it
Judg. 3. 2. at least such as *b.* knew nothing thereof
16. 20. said, I will go as *b.* and shake myself
2 *Sam.* 6. 21. chose me *b.* thy father, and *b.* his house
10. 9. Joab saw the battle was against him *b.* and
behind, 1 *Chron.* 19. 10.
22. † 25. according to my cleanness *b.* his eyes
1 *Kings* 13. 6. the king's hand became as it was *b.*
2 *Chron.* 13. 14. the battle was *b.* and behind
33. 19. Manasseh his trespass *b.* he was humbled
Job 3. 24. for my sighing cometh *b.* I eat
10. 21. *b.* I go, whence I shall not return
42. 10. Lord gave Job twice as much as he had *b.*
Psal. 31. 22. I am cut off from *b.* thine eyes
39. 13. spare me *b.* I go hence and be no more
80. 9. thou preparedst room *b.* it, and didst cause it
119. 67. *b.* I was afflicted I went astray, but now
139. 5. thou hast beset me behind and *b.* and laid
Eccl. 7. 17. why shouldest thou die *b.* thy time?
Isa. 9. 12. Syrians *b.* and the Philistines behind
17. 14. and behold, *b.* the morning he is not
43. 13. *b.* the day was, I am he, and there is none
65. 24. that *b.* they call I will answer and hear
Jer. 1. 5. *b.* I formed thee in the belly, I knew thee
Ezek. 44. 12. they ministered to them *b.* their idols
22. they shall take a widow that had a priest *b.*
Hos. 7. 2. their own doings, they are *b.* my face
Amos 4. 3. every cow at that which is *b.* her
Mal. 2. 5. he feared me, and was afraid *b.* my name
4. 5. I will send Elijah the prophet *b.* the coming
Mat. 1. 18. *b.* they came together, she was with child
6. 8. knoweth what things ye need *b.* ye ask
8. 29. art thou come to torment us *b.* the time
24. 25. behold, I have told you *b.*
Luke 2. 26. not see death *b.* he had seen the Lord
23. 12. for *b.* they were at enmity between them.
John 6. 62. see the Son of man ascend where he was *b.*
7. 51. doth our law judge any man *b.* it hear him?
13. 19. now I tell you *b.* it come, 14. 29.

Acts 2. 31. he seeing this *b.* spake of the resurrection
4. 28. to do thy counsel determined *b.* to be done
10. 41. but to witnesses chosen *b.* of God, to us
2 *Cor.* 8. 10. who have begun *b.* not only to do
Gal. 5. 21. of which I tell you *b.* as I told you
Eph. 3. † 3. as I wrote a little *b.*
Phil. 3. 13. reaching forth to those things that are *b.*
Col. 1. 5. whereof ye heard *b.* in the word of truth
1 *Thess.* 2. 2. but even after that we had suffered *b.*
3. 4. when we were with you, we told you *b.*
1 *Tim.* 1. 13. who was *b.* a blasphemer, a persecutor
Heb. 7. 18. disannulling of the command going *b.*
10. 15. for after that he had said *b.* this is covenant
2 *Pet.* 3. 2. mindful of words spoken *b.* by prophets
17. seeing ye know these things *b.* beware lest
Rev. 3. 9. make them to worship *b.* thy feet
4. 6. were four beasts, full of eyes *b.* and behind

Come BEFORE.

Exod. 22. 9. both parties shall *come b.* the judge
Psal. 100. 2. *come b.* his presence with thanksgiving
Mic. 6. 6. wherewith shall I *come b.* the Lord?
2 *Tim.* 4. 21. do thy diligence to *come b.* winter

BEFORE *the people.*

Gen. 23. 12. Abraham bowed *b. the people* of the land
Exod. 13. 22. nor the pillar of fire from *b. the people*
17. 5. the Lord said to Moses, go on *b. the people*
34. 10. *b.* all *thy people* I will do marvels
Josh. 8. 10. Joshua and elders went *b. the people* to Ai
1 *Sam.* 18. 13. he went out, and came in *b. the people*
Mark 8. 6. gave disciples did set them *b. the people*
Luke 20. 26. not take hold of his words *b. the people*
Rev. 10. 11. thou must prophesy *b.* many *peoples*

BEFORE *whom.*

Gen. 24. 40. Lord *b. whom* I walk will send his angel
48. 15. God *b. whom* my fathers did walk
1 *Kings* 17. 1. Elijah said to Ahab, as the Lord God of Israel liveth, *b. whom* I stand, 18. 15. 2 *Kings* 3. 14. | 5. 16.
Esth. 6. 13. Mordecai *b. whom* thou hast begun to fall
Dan. 7. 8. *b. whom* there were three of the first horns
20. and *b. whom* three fell, even of that horn
Acts 26. 26. the king, *b. whom* also I speak freely
See further, ALL, ARK, GOD, HIM, LORD, ME, MOUNT, STAND, STOOD, THEE, THEM, AS, WENT, YOU.

BEFOREHAND.

Mark 13. 11. take no thought *b.* what to speak
2 *Cor.* 9. 5. go and make up *b.* your bounty
1 *Tim.* 5. 24. some men's sins are open *b.*
25. the good works of some are manifest *b.*
1 *Pet.* 1. 11. testified *b.* the sufferings of Christ

BEFORETIME.

Josh. 20. 5. because he hated him not *b.*
1 *Sam.* 9. 9. *b.* in Israel, when a man went; he who is called a prophet was *b.* called a seer
2 *Sam.* 7. 10. nor afflict them any more as *b.*
2 *Kings* 13. 5. Israel dwelt in their tents as *b.*
Neh. 2. 1. I had not been *b.* sad in his presence
Isa. 41. 26. who hath declared *b.* that we may say
Acts 8. 9. called Simon which *b.* used sorcery

BEGAN.

Gen. 4. 26. then *b.* men to call on the name of Lord
Num. 25. 1. the people *b.* to commit whoredom with
Judg. 20. 31. they *b.* to smite Israel as at other times
1 *Sam.* 14. † 35. that altar he *b.* to build to the Lord
2 *Kings* 10. 32. the Lord *b.* to cut Israel short
2 *Chron.* 20. 22. when they *b.* to sing, the Lord set
31. 7. in the third month they *b.* to lay the heaps
34. 3. while young Josiah *b.* to seek after God
Ezek. 9. 6. then they *b.* at the ancient men
Mat. 4. 17. from that time Jesus *b.* to preach and say
Mark 14. † 72. he *b.* to weep when he thought
Luke 1. 70. which have been since the world *b.*
14. 30. this man *b.* to build and was not able
John 4. 52. inquired the hour when he *b.* to amend
9. 32. since the world *b.* *Acts* 3. 21. *Rom.* 16. 25.
Acts 12. † 1. Herod *b.* to vex certain of the church
2 *Tim.* 1. 9. in Christ before the world *b.* *Tit.* 1. 2.
Heb. 2. 3. salvation at first *b.* to be spoken by the Lord

BEGAT.

Prov. 23. 22. hearken to thy father that *b.* thee
Jer. 16. 3. concerning their fathers that *b.* them
Dan. 11. 6. she shall be given up, and he that *b.* her
Zech. 13. 3. his father and mother that *b.* him
Jam. 1. 18. of his own will *b.* he us with the word
1 *John* 5. 1. every one that loveth him that *b.* loveth

BEGET.

Gen. 17. 20. twelve princes shall he *b.* I will make
Deut. 4. 25. when thou shalt *b.* children, children's
28. 41. thou shalt *b.* sons, but shalt not enjoy them
2 *Kings* 20. 18. of thy sons which thou shalt *b.* shall they take and make eunuchs, *Isa.* 39. 7.
Eccl. 6. 3. if a man *b.* 100 children, and live many
Jer. 29. 6. take wives, and *b.* sons and daughters
Ezek. 18. 10. if he *b.* a son that is a robber
14. if he *b.* a son that seeth all his father's sins

BEGETTEST.

Gen. 48. 6. issue which thou *b.* shall be thine
Isa. 45. 10. that saith to his father, what *b.* thou?

BEGETTETH.

Prov. 17. 21. he that *b.* a fool, doeth it to his sorrow
23. 24. he that *b.* a wise child shall have joy
Eccl. 5. 14. he *b.* a son, and nothing in his hand

BEG.

Psal. 109. 10. let his children be vagabonds and *b.*
Prov. 20. 4. therefore shall the sluggard *b.* in harvest
Luke 16. 3. I cannot dig, to *b.* I am ashamed

BEGGED.

Mat. 27. 58. and *b.* the body of Jesus, *Luke* 23. 52.
John 9. 8. is not this he that sat and *b.*?

BEGGAR.

1 *Sam.* 2. 8. he lifteth the *b.* from the dunghill
Luke 16. 20. and there was a *b.* named Lazarus
22. the *b.* died, and was carried by the angels

BEGGARLY.

Gal. 4. 9. how turn ye again to the *b.* elements

BEGGING.

Psal. 37. 25. I have not seen his seed *b.* bread
Mark 10. 46. Bartimeus sat *b.* *Luke* 18. 35.

BEGIN.

Gen. 11. 6. this they *b.* to do, and now nothing
Deut. 2. 25. this day I *b.* to put the dread of you
Josh. 3. 7. this day will I *b.* to magnify thee
1 *Sam.* 3. 12. when I *b.* I will also make an end
22. 15. did I then *b.* to inquire of God for him?
Neh. 11. 17. Mattaniah to *b.* the thanksgiving
Jer. 25. 29. I *b.* to bring evil on the city called
Ezek. 9. 6. slay old and young, and *b.* at my sanctuary
Hos. 8. † 10. they shall *b.* a little for the burden
Luke 3. 8. and *b.* not to say within yourselves
13. 26. then shall ye *b.* to say, we have eaten
14. 29. all that behold it, *b.* to mock him
21. 28. when these things *b.* to come to pass
2 *Cor.* 3. 1. do we *b.* again to commend ourselves?
1 *Pet.* 4. 17. the time is come, that judgment must *b.* at the house of God, and if it first *b.* at us

BEGINNER.

Heb. 12. † 2. Jesus the *b.* and finisher of our faith

BEGINNING

Signifies, [1] *That which is the first*, Exod. 12. 2. [2] *The creation*, Gen. 1. 1. [3] *At the first*, Prov. 20. 21. Isa. 1. 26. [4] *That which is chief, or most excellent.* Prov. 1. 7. | 9. 10.

I am the beginning and ending, *Rev.* 1. 8. *I am the eternal God, who gave all things a being and beginning.*

Gen. 49. 3. Reuben, thou art the *b.* of my strength
Exod. 12. 2. this month shall be the *b.* of months
Deut. 21. 17. he is the *b.* of his strength, the right
Job 8. 7. tho' thy *b.* was small, yet thy end increase
42. 12. blessed the latter end of Job more than *b.*
Psal. 111. 10. fear of Lord *b.* of wisdom, *Prov.* 9. 10.
Prov. 1. 7. fear of the Lord is the *b.* of knowledge
17. 14. *b.* of strife, as when one letteth out water
Eccl. 7. 8. better is the end of a thing than the *b.*
10. 13. the *b.* of words of his mouth is foolishness
Isa. 64. 4. since *b.* of the world, men have not heard
Mic. 1. 13. is the *b.* of sin to the daughter of Zion
Mat. 24. 8. all these are the *b.* of sorrows, *Mark* 13. 8.
21. tribulation, such as was not since the *b.*
Mark 1. 1. the *b.* of the gospel of Jesus Christ
John 2. 11. this *b.* of miracles did Jesus in Cana
Col. 1. 18. who is the *b.* the first-born from the dead
Heb. 3. 14. if we hold the *b.* of our confidence
6. † 1. leaving the word of the *b.* of Christ
7. 3. having neither *b.* of days, nor end of life
2 *Pet.* 2. 20. the latter end is worse than the *b.*
Rev. 1. 8. I am the *b.* and the ending, 21. 6. | 22. 13.
3. 14. these things saith the *b.* of the creation of God

At the BEGINNING.

Ruth 3. 10. more kindness at latter end, than *at the b.*
1 *Chron.* 17. 9. nor child. of wickedness waste as *at b.*
Prov. 20. 21. an inheritance gotten hastily *at the b.*
Isa. 1. 26. I will restore thy counsellors as *at the b.*
Dan. 9. 23. *at the b.* of thy supplications the command
Mat. 19. 4. which made them, *at b.* made them male
John 16. 4. these things I said not to you *at the b.*
Acts 11. 15. H. Ghost fell on them as on us *at the b.*

From the BEGINNING.

Deut. 11. 12. eyes of L. are on it *from the b.* of year
32. 42. *from the b.* of revenges on the enemy
Psal. 119. 160. word is true *from the b.* and every
Prov. 8. 23. I was set up *from b.* or ever the earth was
Eccl. 3. 11. no man can find work God maketh *from b.*
Isa. 18. 2. go to a people terrible *from the b.* 7.
40. 21. hath it not been told you *from the b.*?
41. 26. who hath declared *from the b.*?
46. 10. declaring the end *from b.* and ancient times
48. 16. I have not spoken in secret *from the b.*
Jer. 17. 12. a glorious high throne *from the b.*
Mat. 19. 8. but *from the b.* it was not so
Luke 1. 2. unto us, which *from b.* were eye-witnesses
John 6. 64. Jesus knew *from the b.* who believed not
8. 25. Jesus saith, even same I said to you *from b.*
44. was a murderer *from b.* and abode not in truth
15. 27. because ye have been with me *from the b.*
Eph. 3. 9. which *from b.* of the world hath been hid
2 *Thess.* 2. 13. God hath *from b.* chosen you to salv.
2 *Pet.* 3. 4. all continue as they were *from the b.*
1 *John* 2. 7. word which ye have heard *from b.* 3. 11.
13. because ye have known him that is *from b.*
3. 8. is of the devil, for the devil sinneth *from the b.*
2 *John* 5. but that which we had *from the b.*

In the BEGINNING.

Gen. 1. 1. *in the b.* God created the heaven and earth
2 *Sam.* 20. † 18. they plainly spake *in b.* ask of Abel
Prov. 8. 22. the L. possessed me *in the b.* of his way
John 1. 1. *in b.* was the Word, Word was with God
2. the same was *in the b.* with God
Phil. 4. 15. ye know that *in the b.* of the gospel
Heb. 1. 10. thou Lord *in the b.* hast laid foundation

BEGINNING.

Mat. 14. 30. *b.* to sink, he cried, Lord, save me
20. 8. give their hire, *b.* from the last to the first
Luke 24. 47. among all nations, *b.* at Jerusalem
John 8. 9. went out, *b.* at the eldest even to the last
Acts 1. 22. *b.* from the baptism of John to that day

BEGINNINGS.

Num. 10. 10. also in the *b.* of your months, 28. 11.
Ezek. 36. 11. I will do better than at your *b.*

BEGINNEST.

Deut. 16. 9. time thou *b.* to put the sickle to corn

BEGOTTEN

Is taken, [1] *Properly and naturally*, Judg. 8. 30. [2] *Supernaturally, thus Isaac was begotten of the dead body and womb of Abraham and Sarah*, Heb. 11. 17. [3] *Spiritually, thus Christians are said to be begotten by such ministers as were instruments of their conversion*, 1 Cor. 4. 15. [4] *Eternally, such only is Christ the only begotten of the Father*, John 1. 14.

Num. 11. 12. have I conceived, have I *b.* them?
Deut. 23. 8. the children *b.* of them shall enter
Judg. 8. 30. Gideon had 70 sons of his body *b.*
Job 38. 28. or who hath *b.* the drops of dew?
Psal. 2. 7. thou art my Son, this day have I *b.* thee, *Acts* 13. 33. *Heb.* 1. 5. | 5. 5.
Isa. 49. 21. thou shalt say, who hath *b.* me these?
Jer. 2. † 27. saying to a stone, thou hast *b.* me
Hos. 5. 7. for they have *b.* strange children
John 1. 14. the glory as of the only *b.* of the Father
18. the only *b.* Son, he hath declared him
3. 16. God so loved, that he gave his only *b.* Son
18. not believed in the name of the only *b.* Son
1 *Cor.* 4. 15. for I have *b.* you through the gospel
Philem. 10. Onesimus, whom I have *b.* in my bonds
Heb. 11. 17. Abraham by faith offered up only *b.* son
1 *Pet.* 1. 3. who hath *b.* us again to a lively hope
1 *John* 4. 9. sent his only *b.* Son, that we might live
5. 1. that begat, loveth him also that is *b.* of him
18. he that is *b.* of God keepeth himself

FIRST-BEGOTTEN.

Heb. 1. 6. when he bringeth in *first-b.* into world
Rev. 1. 5. from Jesus, who is the *first b.* of the dead

BEGUILE.

Col. 2. 4. lest any man *b.* you with enticing words
18. let no man *b.* you of your reward

BEGUILED, ING.

Gen. 3. 13. woman said, serpent *b.* me, and I did eat
29. 25. wherefore then hast thou *b.* me?
Num. 25. 18. they have *b.* you in the matter of Peor
Josh. 9. 22. saying, wherefore have ye *b.* us?
2 *Cor.* 11. 3. but I fear lest as the serpent *b.* Eve
2 *Pet.* 2. 14. cannot cease from sin, *b.* unstable souls

BEGUN.

Num. 16. 46. the plague is *b.* || 47. the plague was *b.*
Deut. 3. 24. thou hast *b.* to shew thy greatness
Esth. 6. 13. before whom thou hast *b.* to fall
9. 23. the Jews undertook to do as they had *b.*
Mat. 18. 24. and when he had *b.* to reckon
2 *Cor.* 8. 6. as he had *b.* so he would also finish
10. this is expedient for you who have *b.* before
Gal. 3. 3. are ye so foolish, having *b.* in the Spirit
Phil. 1. 6. he which hath *b.* a good work in you
1 *Tim.* 5. 11. when they have *b.* to wax wanton

BEHALF.

Exod. 27. 21. a statute on *b.* of the children of Israel
2 *Sam.* 3. 12. Abner sent to David on his *b.*
2 *Chron.* 16. 9. shew himself strong in *b.* of them
Job 36. 2. shew that I have yet to speak on God's *b.*
Dan. 11. 18. but a prince for his own *b.* shall cause
Rom. 16. 19. I am glad therefore on your *b.*
1 *Cor.* 1. 4. I thank my God always on your *b.*
2 *Cor.* 1. 11. thanks may be given by many on our *b.*
5. 12. but give you occasion to glory on our *b.*
Phil. 1. 29. to you it is given in *b.* of Christ, not only
1 *Pet.* 4. 16. let him glorify God on this *b.*

BEHAVE.

Deut. 32. 27. lest adversaries *b.* themselves strangely
1 *Chron.* 19. 13. let us *b.* ourselves valiantly
Job 41. † 33. who *b.* themselves without fear
Psal. 101. 2. I will *b.* wisely in a perfect way
Isa. 3. 5. child shall *b.* himself proudly ag. ancient
42. † 13. the Lord will *b.* himself mightily
1 *Cor.* 13. 5. charity doth not *b.* itself unseemly
1 *Tim.* 3. 15. how thou oughtest to *b.* in house of God

BEHAVED.

1 *Sam.* 18. 5. David *b.* himself wisely, 14, 15, 30.
Psal. 35. 14. I *b.* as though he had been my friend
131. 2. I have *b.* myself as a child that is weaned
Hos. 12. † 3. Jacob *b.* himself princely
Mic. 3. 4. as they have *b.* themselves ill in doings
1 *Thess.* 2. 10. how unblameably we *b.* ourselves
2 *Thess.* 3. 7. *b.* not ourselves disorderly among you

BEHAVETH.

1 *Cor.* 7. 36. if a man think he *b.* uncomely to his

BEHAVIOUR.

1 *Sam.* 21. 13. David changed his *b.* before them
1 *Tim.* 3. 2. a bishop must be sober, of good *b.*
Tit. 2. 3. aged women in *b.* as becometh holiness

BEHEADED.

Deut. 21. 6. elders shall wash hands over the heifer *b.*
2 *Sam.* 4. 7. they smote Ish-bosheth, and *b.* him
Mat. 14. 10. *b.* John, *Mark* 6. 16, 27. *Luke* 9. 9.
Rev. 20. 4. I saw the souls of them that were *b.*

BEHELD.

Num. 21. 9. when he *b.* the serpent of brass, he lived
23. 21. he hath not *b.* iniquity in Jacob
1 *Chron.* 21. 15. as he was destroying, the Lord *b.*
Job 31. 26. if I *b.* the sun when it shined, or moon
Psal. 119. 158. I *b.* transgressors, and was grieved
142. 4. I *b.* but there was no man would know me
Prov. 7. 7. and *b.* among the simple ones, I discerned
Eccl. 8. 17. then I *b.* all the work of God
Isa. 41. 28. I *b.* and there was no man, *Jer.* 4. 25.
Jer. 4. 23. I *b.* the earth, and it was without form
Mark 15. 47. Mary Magdalen, and Mary the mother of Joses, *b.* where he was laid, *Luke* 23. 55.
Luke 10. 18. I *b.* Satan as lightning fall from heaven
19. 41. he *b.* the city, and wept over it
John 1. 14. and we *b.* his glory, the glory as of
Acts 1. 9. while they *b.* Jesus was taken up
17. 23. as I passed by and *b.* your devotions
Rev. 5. 6. I *b.* and lo, in midst of the throne a Lamb
11. 12. they ascended, and their enemies *b.* them

BEHEMOTH.

Job 40. 15. behold now *b.* which I made with thee

BEHIND

Signifies, [1] *Backwards*, Judg. 20. 40. [2] *After*, 2 Sam. 3. 16. [3] *Remaining*, Lev. 25. 51. [4] *Past*, Phil. 3. 13. [5] *Unexpected*, Isa. 30. 21. [6] *Disregarded*, Psal. 50. 17.

Exod. 10. 26. there shall not an hoof be left *b.*
Lev. 25. 51. if there be yet many years *b.* according
Judg. 20. 40. the Benjamites looked *b.* them
1 *Sam.* 30. 9. where those that were left *b.* stayed
2 *Sam.* 3. 16. her husband went weeping *b.* her
1 *Kings* 14. 9. hast cast me *b.* thy back, *Ezek.* 23. 35.
Neh. 4. 16. the rulers were *b.* the house of Judah
9. 26. they rebelled and cast thy law *b.* their backs
Cant. 2. 9. behold, he standeth *b.* our wall, looketh
Isa. 38. 17. thou hast cast all my sins *b.* thy back
Amos 7. † 15. the Lord took me from *b.* the flock
Mark 5. 27. she came in the press *b.* and touched
Luke 2. 43. the child Jesus tarried *b.* in Jerusalem
1 *Cor.* 1. 7. so that ye come *b.* in no gift, waiting for
2 *Cor.* 11. 5. I was not a whit *b.* the chiefest, 12. 11.
Phil. 3. 13. forgetting those things which are *b.*
Col. 1. 24. fill up what is *b.* of afflictions of Christ
See further, BEFORE, HIM, WE, THEE, THEM, US.

BEHOLD

Signifies, [1] *Admiration*, Isa. 7. 14. [2] *Joy and gladness*, Mat. 21. 5. [3] *Obedience*, 1 Sam. 22. † 12. Isa. 6. † 8. [4] *Asseveration*, Gen. 28. 15. [5] *Exhortation to a provident care*, John 19. 27. [6] *Consideration, or observation*,

Luke 24. 39. John 1. 29. [7] *Suddenness, or unexpectedness*, Rev. 16. 15. | 22. 7. [8] *Certainty*, Mat. 23. 38. Luke 1. 20.
Gen. 28. 15. *b.* I am with thee, and will keep thee
31. 51. *b.* this heap, *b.* this pillar I have cast
40. 6. Joseph looked on them, and *b.* they were sad
48. 1. *b.* thy father is sick || 21. Israel said, *b.* I die
Exod. 3. 2. and *b.* the bush burned with fire
16. 4. *b.* I will rain bread from heaven for you
23. 20. *b.* I send an angel before thee to keep thee
24. 8. Moses said, *b.* the blood of the covenant
Num. 20. 16. *b.* we are in Kadesh in the utmost
1 *Sam.* 12. 13. *b.* the king whom ye have chosen
2 *Sam.* 9. 6. and he answered, *b.* thy servant
1 *Kings* 13. 2. *b.* child shall be born to house of Dav.
2 *Kings* 13. 21. that *b.* they spied a band of men
22. 16. *b.* I will bring evil upon this place, and the inhabitants thereof, 2 *Chron.* 34. 24.
2 *Chron.* 20. 11. *b.* I say, how they reward us
Job 1. 12. *b.* all that he hath is in thy power
28. 28. *b.* the fear of the Lord, that is wisdom
33. 12. *b.* in this thou art not just, I will answer
36. 5. *b.* God is mighty, and despiseth not any, 26.
40. 4. *b.* I am vile, what shall I answer thee?
Psal. 33. 18. *b.* eye of the Lord is on them that fear
51. 5. *b.* I was shapen in iniquity, and in sin did
73. 12. *b.* these are the ungodly who prosper in world
78. 20. *b.* he smote the rock, the waters gushed
139. 8. if I make my bed in hell, *b.* thou art there
Cant. 1. 15. *b.* thou art fair, my love, *b.* 16. | 4. 1.
Isa. 7. 14. *b.* a virgin shall conceive, *Mat.* 1. 23.
8. 18. *b.* I and the children whom the Lord, *Heb.* 2. 13.
22. they shall look to the earth, and *b.* trouble
12. 2. *b.* God is my salvation, I will trust, and not
29. 8. a hungry man dreameth, and *b.* he eateth
40. 9. say to the cities of Judah, *b.* your God
41. 27. the first shall say to Zion, *b. b.* them
42. 1. *b.* my servant whom I uphold, mine elect
43. 19. *b.* I will do a new thing, it shall spring
48. 7. lest thou shouldest say, *b.* I knew them
65. 1. I said, *b.* me, *b.* me, to a nation not called by
Jer. 8. 15. we looked for peace, and *b.* trouble 14. 19.
26. 14. *b.* I am in your hands, do with me as seems
Lam. 1. 12. *b.* and see if any sorrow be like my sorrow
Ezek. 36. 9. *b.* I am for you, and will turn to you
Zech. 3. 8. *b.* I will bring my servant the Branch
6. 12. *b.* the man whose name is the Branch
9. 9. *b.* thy King cometh, *Mat.* 21. 5. *John* 12. 15.
Mal. 3. 1. *b.* I will send my messenger, and he shall prepare the way, 4, 5. *Mat.* 11. 10. *Mark* 1. 2.
Mat. 7. 4. and *b.* a beam is in thine own eye
24. 26. *b.* he is in the desert, *b.* he is in the secret
Mark 16. 6. is risen, *b.* the place where they laid him
Luke 24. 39. *b.* my hands and my feet, that it is I
49. *b.* I send the promise of my Father upon you
John 1. 29. *b.* the Lamb of God, which taketh, 36.
47. *b.* an Israelite indeed, in whom is no guile
19. 5. Pilate saith unto them, *b.* the man
Acts 9. 11. Saul of Tarsus, for *b.* he prayeth
2 *Cor.* 6. 9. as dying, and *b.* we live, as chastened
1 *John* 3. 1. *b.* what manner of love the Father
Rev. 3. 20. *b.* I stand at the door and knock
16. 15. *b.* I come as a thief, blessed is he that
22. 7. *b.* I come quickly, blessed is he that keeps, 12.

BEHOLD *it is.*

Gen. 16. 14. *b. it is* between Kadesh and Bered
34. 21. for the land, *b. it is* large enough for them
Exod. 32. 9. and *b. it is* a stiff necked people
Josh. 9. 12. but now *b. it is* dry, it is mouldy
Judg. 18. 9. I have seen the land, *b. it is* very good
Isa. 52. 6. know that I am he that doth speak, *b. it is* I
Ezek. 7. 10. *b.* the day, *b. it is* come, morning is gone
39. 8. *b. it is* come, and it is done, saith the Lord

Now BEHOLD, *or* BEHOLD *now.*

1 *Sam.* 12. 2. *now b.* the king walketh before you
2 *Kings* 18. 21. *now b.* thou trustest on staff of Egypt
Job 16. 19. also *now b.* my witness is in heaven
Jer. 40. 4. *now b.* I loose thee this day from chains
Mat. 26. 65. *now b.* ye have heard his blasphemy
Acts 13. 11. *now b.* the hand of the Lord is on thee
20. 22. *now b.* I go bound in the spirit to Jerusalem
2 *Cor.* 6. 2. *b. now* is the accepted time, *b. now* is day

BEHOLD *it was*, BEHOLD *there was, see* WAS.

BEHOLD, *Verb*,

Signifies, [1] *To look on a thing with our eyes*, Gen. 31. 51. [2] *To think over a thing in our minds*, Lam. 1. 12. Rom. 11. 22.
Num. 12. 8. and the similitude of the Lord shall he *b.*
23. 9. I see him, and from the hills I *b.* him
24. 17. see him, but not now, shall *b.* him, but not nigh
Deut. 3. 27. *b.* it with thine eyes, thou shalt not go
1 *Sam.* 22. † 12. *b.* me, *Isa.* 6. † 8.
Job 19. 27. mine eyes shall *b.* and not another
20. 9. nor shall his place any more *b.* him
23. 9. where he doth work, but I cannot *b.* him
34. 29. when he hideth his face, who can *b.?*
36. 24. that thou magnify his work, which men *b.*
Psal. 11. 4. his eyes *b.* his eye-lids try the children
7. his countenance doth *b.* the upright
17. 2. let thine eyes *b.* the things that are equal
15. I will *b.* thy face in righteousness
27. 4. to *b.* the beauty of the Lord and inquire
37. 37. mark the perfect man, *b.* the upright
46. 8. come, *b.* the works of the Lord
59. 4. they prepare, awake to help me, and *b.*
66. 7. he ruleth for ever, his eyes *b.* the nations
80. 14. look down from heaven, *b.* and visit
91. 8. only with thine eyes shalt thou *b.* and see
102. 19. from heaven did the Lord *b.* the earth
113. 6. he humbleth himself to *b.* the things
119. 18. open thou mine eyes, that I may *b.*
Prov. 23. 33. thine eyes shall *b.* strange women
Eccl. 11. 7. and a pleasant thing it is to *b.* the sun
Isa. 26. 10. he will not *b.* the majesty of the Lord
38. 11. I said, I shall *b.* man no more with the inhab.
41. 23. do good or evil, that we may *b.* it together
63. 15. *b.* from the habitation of thy holiness
Jer. 20. 4. and thine eyes shall *b.* thy terror
29. 32. nor *b.* the good I will do for my people
32. 4. and his eyes shall *b.* his eyes, 34. 3.
42. 2. we are left but a few, as thine eyes do *b.* us
Lam. 1. 18. hear all people, and *b.* my sorrow
La. 3. 50. till the Lord look down and *b.* from heaven
5. 1. O Lord, consider and *b.* our reproach
Ezek. 8. 9. *b.* the wicked abominations they do
28. 17. lay thee before kings that they may *b.*
18. bring thee to ashes in sight of all that *b.*
40. 4. son of man, *b.* with thine eyes, 44. 5.
Dan. 9. 18. open thine eyes, and *b.* our desolation
Obad. † 12. do not *b.* the day of thy brother
Mic. 7. 9. me to light, and I shall *b.* his righteousness
10. she that is my enemy, mine eyes shall *b.* her
Hab. 1. 3. why dost thou cause me to *b.* grievance?
13. thou art of purer eyes than to *b.* evil, canst
Mat. 18. 10. their angels always *b.* face of my Father
Luke 14. 29. all that *b.* it begin to mock him
21. 6. as for these things which ye *b.* the days will
John 17. 24. be with me, that they may *b.* my glory
Acts 7. 31. as he drew near to *b.* it the voice came
32. then Moses trembled, and durst not *b.*
2 *Cor.* 3. 7. Israel could not *b.* the face of Moses
1 *Pet.* 2. 12. your good works which they shall *b.*
3. 2. while they *b.* your chaste conversation
Rev. 17. 8. when they *b.* the beast that was, is not

BEHOLDERS.

Job 31. † 26. God striketh them in the place of *b.*

BEHOLDEST.

Psal. 10. 14. thou *b.* all mischief to requite it
Mat. 7. 3. why *b.* thou the mote? *Luke* 6. 41.
Luke 6. 42. *b.* not the beam that is in thine own eye

BEHOLDETH.

Job 24. 18. he *b.* not the way of the vineyards
Psal. 33. 13. the Lord *b.* all the sons of men
Jam. 1. 24. for he *b.* himself and goeth his way

BEHOLDING.

Psal. 119. 37. turn away mine eyes from *b.* vanity
Prov. 15. 3. Lord in every place, *b.* the evil and good
Eccl. 5. 11. saving the *b.* of them with their eyes
Mat. 27. 55. many women were there, *b. Lu.* 23. 49.
Mark 10. 21. Jesus *b.* him, loved him, and said
Luke 23. 35. people stood *b.* and rulers derided him
48. *b.* things done, smote their breasts and returned
Acts 4. 14. and *b.* man which was healed could say
23. 1. and Paul earnestly *b.* the council, said
2 *Cor.* 3. 18. with open face *b.* as in a glass the glory
Col. 2. 5. with you in spirit, joying, and *b.* your order
Jam. 1. 23. a man *b.* his natural face in a glass

BEHOVED.

Luke 24. 46. and thus it *b.* Christ to suffer and rise
Heb. 2. 17. *b.* him to be made like to his brethren

BEING.

Gen. 24. 27. I *b.* in the way, the Lord led me to house
Exod. 22. 14. the owner thereof not *b.* with it
Lev. 21. 4. he shall not defile himself, *b.* a chief man
Num. 30. 3. vow a vow *b.* in her father's house, 16.
Deut. 32. 31. our enemies themselves *b.* judges
Josh. 9. 23. none of you be freed from *b.* bond-men
1 *Sam.* 15. 23. hath rejected thee from *b.* king, 26.
1 *Kings* 15. 13. Maachah his mother, even her he removed from *b.* queen, 2 *Chron.* 15. 16.
16. 7. in provoking, in *b.* like house of Jeroboam
Neh. 6. 11. who is there that *b.* as I am would flee?
Psal. 49. 12. man *b.* in honour, abideth not, is like
83. 4. come, and let us cut them off from *b.* a nation
Jer. 34. 9. *b.* an Hebrew or Hebrewess go free
Mat. 1. 19. Joseph her husband *b.* a just man
Luke 13. 16. this woman *b.* a daughter of Abraham
16. 23. in hell he lift up his eyes, *b.* in torments
18. † 9. trusted in themselves as *b.* righteous
20. 36. *b.* the children of the resurrection
22. 44. *b.* in an agony, he prayed more earnestly
John 5. 13. Jesus conveyed—multitude *b.* in that place
10. 33. that thou, *b.* a man, makest thyself God
1 *Cor.* 12. 12. all the members *b.* many are one body
Eph. 2. 20. Jesus Christ *b.* the chief corner stone
4. † 15. *b.* sincere in love may grow up into him
Phil. 2. 6. who *b.* in the form of God, thought it not
Heb. 13. 3. as *b.* yourselves also in the body
Rev. 12. 2. she *b.* with child, cried, travailing

BEING.

Psal. 104. 33. I will sing to the Lord, I will sing praise to my God while I have my *b.* 146. 2.
Acts 17. 28. in him we live, move, and have our *b.*

BELCH, ETH.

Psal. 59. 7. behold they *b.* out with their mouth
Prov. 15. † 2. the mouth of fools *b.* out foolishness

BELIEF.

2 *Thess.* 2. 13. sanctification of Spirit, and *b.* of truth

BELIEVE.

Signifies, [1] *To give credit to any thing*, Gen. 45. 26. [2] *To assent barely to gospel truths*, Acts 8. 13. [3] *To receive, depend, and rely upon Christ for life and salvation*, John 1. 12. | 3. 15, 16. Rom. 9. 33. | 10. 4. [4] *To be fully persuaded*, John 6. 69. [5] *To expect, or hope*, Psal 27. 13. [6] *To put confidence in*, 2 Chron. 20. 20. [7] *To know*, John 17. 21. Jam. 2. 19.
Exod. 4. 5. that they may *b.* the Lord hath appeared
19. 9. that they may hear and *b.* thee for ever
Num. 14. 11. how long will it be ere they *b.* me?
2 *Chr.* 20. 20. *b.* in the Lord God, *b.* his prophets
Isa. 43. 10. that ye may know and *b.* me
Mat. 9. 28. *b.* ye that I am able to do this?
18. 6. but whoso shall offend one of these little ones which *b.* in me, *Mark* 9. 42.
21. 32. repented not afterward that ye might *b.* him
27. 42. let him come down, and we will *b.* him
Mark 1. 15. repent ye, and *b.* the gospel
5. 36. he saith, be not afraid, only *b. Luke* 8. 50.
9. 23. if thou canst *b.* all things are possible
24. Lord, I *b.* help mine unbelief, *John* 9. 38.
11. 23. but shall *b.* those things he saith shall come
24. *b.* ye receive them, and ye shall have them
15. 32. let him descend, that we may see and *b.*
16. 17. these signs shall follow them which *b.*
Luke 8. 12. devil taketh away the word, lest they *b.*
13. these have no root, which for a while *b.*
24. 25. O fools, and slow of heart to *b.* all that
John 1. 7. that all men through him might *b.*
12. sons of God, even to them that *b.* on his name
3. 12. how shall ye *b.* if I tell you of heavenly things?
4. 21. woman *b.* me, the hour cometh when ye shall
42. and said, now we *b.* not because of thy saying
5. 44. how can ye *b.* which receive honour one of
John 5. 47. not his writings, how shall ye *b.* my words?
6. 29. work of God, that ye *b.* on him he hath sent
7. 5. for neither did his brethren *b.* in him
39. Spirit, which they that *b.* on him should receive
9. 35. dost thou *b.* on the Son of God?
36. he said, who is he, Lord, that I might *b.* on him
10. 38. *b.* the works, that ye may know and *b.*
11. 15. I was not there, to the intent ye may *b.*
27. I *b.* that thou art the Christ, the Son of God
40. said I not to thee, if wouldst *b.* thou shouldst
42. that they may *b.* that thou hast sent me
48. if we let him alone, all men will *b.* on him
12. 36. while ye have light, *b.* in the light
13. 19. when it is come to pass, ye may *b.* I am he
14. 1. not troubled, ye *b.* in God, *b.* also in me
11. *b.* I am in the Father, or *b.* for the work's sake.
29. that when it is come to pass ye might *b.*
16. 30. by this we *b.* thou camest forth from God
31. Jesus answered them, do ye now *b.?*
17. 20. I pray for them also which shall *b.* on me
21. that the world may *b.* thou hast sent me
19. 35. he knows that he saith true, that ye might *b.*
20. 31. these are written that ye might *b.*
Acts 8. 37. I *b.* that Jesus Christ is the Son of God
13. 39. by him all that *b.* are justified from all things
41. I work a work which you shall in no wise *b.*
15. 7. that the Gentiles by me should hear and *b.*
11. we *b.* thro' grace we shall be saved, as they
16. 31. *b.* on the Lord Jesus, and thou shalt be saved
19. 4. should *b.* on him that should come after him
21. 20. thou seest how many Jews there are which *b.*
25. as touching the Gentiles which *b.* have writ.
27. 25. I *b.* God that it shall be as it was told me
Rom. 3. 22. righteousness of God on all them that *b.*
4. 11. he might be father of all them that *b.*
24. to whom it shall be imputed, if we *b.* on him
6. 8. if dead, we *b.* that we shall also live with him
10. 9. and shalt *b.* in thy heart that God raised him
14. how shall they *b.* in him of whom not heard?
1 *Cor.* 1. 21. by preaching to save them that *b.*
11. 18. I hear there be divisions, and I partly *b.* it
14. 22. tongues are for a sign, not to them that *b.* but prophesying serveth for them which *b.*
2 *Cor.* 4. 13. we also *b.* and therefore speak
Gal. 3. 22. promise might be given to them that *b.*
Eph. 1. 19. the greatness of his power to us who *b.*
Phil. 1. 29. to us it is given not only to *b.* on him
1 *Thess.* 1. 7. ensamples to all that *b.* in Macedonia
2. 10. we behaved ourselves among you that *b.*
13. word which effectually worketh in you that *b.*
4. 14. if we *b.* that Jesus died and rose again
2 *Thess.* 1. 10. come to be admired in all those that *b.*
2. 11. send delusion that they should *b.* a lie
1 *Tim.* 1. 16. for a pattern to them that should *b.*
4. 3. received with thanksgiving of them that *b.*
10. Saviour of all men, especially of those that *b.*
Heb. 10. 39. but of them that *b.* to saving of soul
11. 6. he that cometh to God must *b.* that he is
Jam. 2. 19. the devils also *b.* and tremble
1 *Pet.* 1. 21. who by him do *b.* in God that raised him
2. 7. to you therefore which *b.* he is precious
1 *John* 3. 23. is his commandment that we should *b.*
5. 13. I have written to you that *b.* that ye may *b.*

BELIEVE *not*, or *not* BELIEVE.

Exod. 4. 1. behold, they will *not b.* me, nor hearken
8. it shall come to pass, if they will *not b.* thee, 9.
Deut. 1. 32. yet in this ye did *not b.* the Lord
2 *Kings* 17. 14. like their fathers did *not b.* in Lord
Job 9. 16. yet would I *not b.* that he had hearkened
Prov. 26. 25. when he speaketh fair, *b.* him *not*
Isa. 7. 9. if ye will *not b.* ye shall not be established
Jer. 12. 6. *b. not* them, tho' they speak fair words
Hab. 1. 5. which ye will *not b.* though it be told you
Mat. 21. 25. why then did ye *not b.* him? *Mark* 11. 31.
24. 23. lo, here is Christ, *b.* it *not*, 26. *Mark* 13. 21.
Luke 22. 67. he said, if I tell you, you will *not b.*
John 3. 12. if I told earthly things, and ye *b. not*
4. 48. except ye see signs and wonders ye will *not b.*
5. 38. for whom he hath sent, him ye *b. not*
47. if ye *b. not* his writ. how shall ye *b.* my words?
6. 36. I said to you, ye also have seen me and *b. not*
64. but there are some of you which *b. not*
8. 24. if ye *b. not* that I am he, ye shall die in sins
45. because I tell you the truth, ye *b.* me *not*
46. if I say the truth, why do ye *not b.* me?
10. 26. ye *b. not*, because ye are not of my sheep
37. if I do not the works of my Father, *b.* me *not*
38. if I do, though ye *b. not* me, believe the works
12. 39. they could *not b.* because Isaiah said again
47. if any hear words, and *b. not*, I judge him not
16. 9. reprove of sin, because they *b. not* on me
20. 25. thrust my hand into his side, I will *not b.*
Rom. 3. 3. what if some did *not b.* shall unbelief
15. 31. I may be delivered from them that do *not b.*
1 *Cor.* 10. 27. if any that *b. not* bid you to a feast
14. 22. tongues are for a sign to them that *b. not*
2 *Cor.* 4. 4. hath blinded minds of them that *b. not*
2 *Tim.* 2. 13. if we *b. not*, he abideth faithful
1 *John* 4. 1. *b. not* every spirit, but try the spirits

BELIEVED.

Gen. 15. 6. he *b.* in the Lord, and he counted it for righteousness, *Rom.* 4. 3. *Gal.* 3. 6. *Jam.* 2. 23.
Exod. 4. 31. Aaron spake, and the people *b.*
14. 31. they *b.* the Lord and his servant Moses
1 *Sam.* 27. 12. and Achish *b.* David, saying, he hath
Psal. 27. 13. I had fainted, unless I had *b.* to see
106. 12. then *b.* they his words, they sang his praise
116. 10. I *b.* therefore have I spoken, 2 *Cor.* 4. 13.
119. 66. teach me, for I have *b.* thy commandments
Isa. 53. 1. who hath *b.* our report, to whom arm of the Lord revealed? *John* 12. 38. *Rom.* 10. 16.
Dan. 6. 23. no hurt on him, because he *b.* in his God
Jonah 3. 5. so the people of Nineveh *b.* God
Mat. 8. 13. as thou hast *b.* so be it done to thee
21. 32. but the publicans and harlots *b.* him
Mark 16. 13. went and told it, neither *b.* they them
Luke 1. 1. of those things which are most surely *b.*
45. blessed is she that *b.* for there shall be a perform
John 2. 11. his glory, and his disciples *b.* on him
22. they *b.* the scripture, and the word Jesus had spoken
4. 50. the man *b.* the word that Jesus had spoken
53. the father himself *b.* and his whole house

John 5. 46. had ye *b.* Moses, ye would have *b.* me
7. 48. have any of rulers or Pharisees *b.* on him?
8. 31. then said Jesus to the Jews that *b.* on him
11. 45. who had seen the things Jesus did, *b.* on him
12. 11. many of the Jews went away and *b.* on Jesus
16. 27. the Father loveth you, because you have *b.*
17. 8. and they have *b.* that thou didst send me
20. 8. then went that other disciple, and saw and *b.*
29. thou hast *b.* have not seen, and yet have *b.*
Acts 2. 44. all that *b.* were together, had things
4. 4. many of them which heard the word *b.*
32. multitude of them that *b.* were of one heart
5. † 36. as many as *b.* Theudas were scattered
8. 12. but when they *b.* Philip preaching things
13. then Simon himself *b.* also, and was baptized
10. 45. they of circumcision who *b.* were astonished
11. 17. God gave them like gift as to us who *b.*
21. a great number *b.* and turned to the Lord
13. 12. then deputy *b.* being astonished at doctrine
48. as many as were ordained to eternal life *b.*
14. 1. a multitude of both Jews and Greeks *b.*
23. commended them to the Lord on whom they *b.*
17. 4. some of them *b.* and consorted with Paul
34. howbeit certain men clave to him and *b.*
18. 8. Crispus chief ruler of the synagogue *b.* on L.
27. helped them much which had *b.* thro' grace
19. 2. received ye the Holy Ghost since ye *b.?*
22. 19. I beat in every synagogue them that *b.*
27. 11. the centurion *b.* the master of the ship
28. 24. some *b.* the things spoken, and some *b.* not
Rom. 4. 18. who against hope *b.* in hope, might
13. 11. our salvation is nearer than when we *b.*
1 *Cor.* 3. 5. but ministers by whom ye *b.* as the Lord
15. 2. ye are saved, unless ye have *b.* in vain
11. whether I or they, so we preach, and so ye *b.*
Gal. 2. 16. even we have *b.* in Jesus Christ, that we
Eph. 1. 13. in whom after ye *b.* ye were sealed
2 *Thess.* 1. 10. our testimony among you was *b.*
1 *Tim.* 3. 16. *b.* on in the world, received up into glory
2 *Tim.* 1. 12. for I know whom I have *b.* he is able
Tit. 3. 8. they which have *b.* in God, be careful to
Heb. 4. 3. we which have *b.* do enter into rest
1 *John* 4. 16. we have *b.* the love of God to us

Many BELIEVED.

John 2. 23. at the passover *many b.* in his name
4. 39. *many* of the Samaritans *b.* on him
11. 45. *many* of the Jews which came to Mary *b.* on
12. 42. among the chief rulers also *many b.* on him
Acts 18. 8. *many* of the Corinthians hearing *b.*
19. 18. *many* that *b.* came and confessed their deeds

BELIEVED *not*, or *not* BELIEVED.

Gen. 45. 26. Jacob's heart fainted, he *b.* them *not*
Num. 20. 12. because he *b.* me *not*, to sanctify me
Deut. 9. 23. rebelled, and *b.* him *not*, nor hearkened
1 *Kings* 10. 7. howbeit I *b. not* the words, 2 *Chr.* 9. 6.
Job 29. 24. if I laughed on them, they *b.* it *not*
Psal. 78. 22. because they *b. not* in God, trusted not
32. sinned, and *b. not* for his wondrous works
106. 24. despised the land, they *b. not* his word
Jer. 40. 14. but Gedaliah *b.* them *not*
Lam. 4. 12. inhabitants of world would *not* have *b.*
Mat. 21. 32. John came unto you, and ye *b.* him *not*
Mark 16. 11. when they had heard he was alive *b. not*
14. he upbraided them because they *b. not*
Luke 20. 5. he will say, why then *b.* ye him *not.?*
24. 41. while they *b. not* for joy, and wondered
John 3. 18. condemned already, because he hath *not b.*
6. 64. Jesus knew who they were that *b. not*
10. 25. Jesus answered, I told you, and ye *b. not*
12. 37. had done so many miracles, yet they *b. not*
Acts 9. 26. afraid, and *b. not* that he was a disciple
17. 5. the Jews which *b. not*, moved with envy
19. 9. but when divers were hardened, and *b.* not
Rom. 10. 14. how call on him in whom they have *not b.*
11. 30. for as ye in times past have *not b.* God
31. even so have these also now *not b.*
2 *Thess.* 2. 12. they all might be damned who *b. not*
Heb. 3. 18. not enter into his rest, that *b. not*
11. 31. Rahab perished not with them that *b. not*
Jude 5. Lord afterward destroyed them that *b. not*

BELIEVERS.

Acts 5. 14. *b.* were the more added to the Lord
1 *Tim.* 4. 12. be thou an example of the *b.*

BELIEVEST.

Luke 1. 20. be dumb because thou *b.* not my words
John 1. 50. I saw thee under the fig-tree, *b.* thou?
11. 26. believeth in me, never die, *b.* thou this?
14. 10. *b.* thou not that I am in the Father
Acts 8. 37. if thou *b.* with all thine heart, thou
26. 27. *b.* thou the prophets? I know thou *b.*
Jam. 2. 19. thou *b.* that there is one God, thou dost

BELIEVETH.

Job 15. 22. he *b.* not that he shall return out of
Prov. 14. 15. the simple *b.* every word, but thee
Isa. 28. 16. he that *b.* shall not make haste
Mark 9. 23. all things are possible to him that *b.*
16. 16. he that *b.* and is baptized shall be saved, but he that *b.* not shall be damned
John 3. 15. whoso *b.* in him should not perish, 16.
18. he that *b.* on him is not condemned, but he that *b.* not is condemned already
36. he that *b.* hath everlasting life, 6. 47.
5. 24. *b.* on him that sent me hath everlasting life
6. 35. he that *b.* on me shall never thirst
40. he that seeth the Son and *b.* on him, hath life
7. 38. he that *b.* on me, out of his belly shall flow
11. 25. he that *b.* though he were dead, yet shall live
26. whosoever liveth and *b.* in me shall never die
12. 44. he that *b.* on me, *b.* not on me, but on him
46. whoso *b.* on me, should not abide in darkness
14. 12. he that *b.* on me, the works that I do
Acts 10. 43. who *b.* in him receive remission of sins
Rom. 1. 16. it is the power of God to every one that *b.*
3. 26. and the justifier of him that *b.* on Jesus
4. 5. but to him that worketh not, but *b.* on him
9. 33. whoso *b.* on him shall not be ashamed, 10. 11.
10. 4. Christ is the end of law to every one that *b.*
10. for with the heart man *b.* to righteousness
14. 2. for one *b.* that he may eat all things
1 *Cor.* 7. 12. if any brother hath a wife that *b.* not
13. 7. love *b.* all things, hopeth all things, endureth

1 *Cor.* 14. 24. and there come in one that *b.* not
2 *Cor.* 6. 15. what part hath he that *b.* with infidel
1 *Tim.* 5. 16. if any man that *b.* have widows
1 *Pet.* 2. 6. he that *b.* shall not be confounded
1 *John* 5. 1. whoso *b.* Jesus is the Christ, is of God
5. who is he that overcometh, but he that *b.*
10. he that *b.* on the Son of God; he that *b.* not God, because he *b.* not the record

BELIEVING.

Mat. 21. 22. ask in prayer, *b.* ye shall receive
John 20. 27. said to Thomas, be not faithless, but *b.*
31. that *b.* ye might have life through his name
Acts 16. 34. rejoiced, *b.* in God with all his house
24. 14. *b.* all things which are written in the law
Rom. 15. 13. fill you with all joy and peace in *b.*
1 *Tim.* 6. 2. they that have *b.* masters, not despise
† but rather do them service because they are *b.*
1 *Pet.* 1. 8. yet *b.* ye rejoice with joy unspeakable

BELL, S.

Exod. 28. 33. *b.* of gold betw. pomegranates, 39. 25.
34. a golden *b.* and a pomegranate, 39. 26.
Zech. 14. 20. upon the *b.* of horses, holiness to Lord

BELLOW, *see* BULLS.

BELLOWS.

Jer. 6. 29. the *b.* are burnt, the lead is consumed

BELLY

Signifies, [1] *That part of the body which contains the bowels*, Mat. 15. 17. [2] *The womb*, Jer. 1. 5. [3] *The entrails*, Rev. 10. 9, 10. [4] *The heart*, John 7. 38. [5] *The whole man*, Tit. 1. 12. [6] *Carnal pleasure*, Rom. 16. 18.

Gen. 3. 14. on thy *b.* shalt thou go, and dust eat
Lev. 11. 42. goeth on the *b.* be an abomination
Num. 5. 21. thy thigh to rot, and thy *b.* to swell
25. 8. thrust man of Israel and woman thro' the *b.*
Deut. 28. † 11. plenteous in the fruit of thy *b.*
† 53. and thou shalt eat the fruit of thy *b.*
Judg. 3. 21. the dagger, and thrust it in his *b.*
1 *Kings* 7. 20. had pomegranates over against the *b.*
Job 3. 11. give up ghost when I came out of the *b.*
15. 2. and fill his *b.* with the east wind
35. bring vanity, and their *b.* prepareth deceit
Job 19. † 17. intreated for children's sake of my *b.*
20. 15. God shall cast them out of his *b.*
20. surely he shall not feel quietness in his *b.*
23. when about to fill his *b.* God shall cast fury
32. † 18. the spirit of my *b.* constraineth me
19. behold my *b.* is as wine which hath no vent
Psal. 17. 14. whose *b.* thou fillest with thy hid treas.
22. 10. thou art my God from my mother's *b.*
44. 25. soul bowed down, our *b.* cleaveth to earth
58. † 3. they go astray from the *b.*
132. † 11. of the fruit of thy *b.* I will set on
Prov. 13. 25. but the *b.* of the wicked shall want
18. 8. go into innermost parts of the *b.* 26. 22.
20. a man's *b.* shall be satisfied with fruit
20. 27. searching all the inward parts of the *b.*
30. so do stripes the inward parts of the *b.*
22. † 18. is a pleasant thing, if keep them in thy *b.*
Cant. 5. 14. his *b.* is as bright ivory overlaid with
7. 2. thy *b.* is like an heap of wheat set about with
Isa. 46. 3. which are born by me from the *b.*
Jer. 1. 5. before I formed thee in the *b.* I knew thee
51. 34. he hath filled his *b.* with my delicates
Ezek. 3. 3. he said, son of man, cause thy *b.* to eat
Dan. 2. 32. this image's *b.* and his thighs of brass
Jonah 1. 17. Jonah was in *b.* of the fish, *Mat.* 12. 40.
2. 2. out of the *b.* of hell cried I, and thou heardst
Mic. 6. † 7. fruit of my *b.* for the sin of my soul
Hab. 3. 16. when I heard, my *b.* trembled, my lips
Mat. 15. 17. whatsoever entereth in at the mouth goeth into the *b.* and is cast out, *Mark* 7. 19.
Luke 15. 16. fain have filled his *b.* with the husks
John 7. 38. out of his *b.* shall flow rivers of water
Rom. 16. 18. they serve not our Lord but their own *b.*
1 *Cor.* 6. 13. meats for the *b.* and the *b.* for meats
Phil. 3. 19. whose God is their *b.* and glory in shame
Rev. 10. 9. eat it up, and it shall make thy *b.* bitter
10. as soon as I had eaten it, my *b.* was bitter

BELLIES.

Tit. 1. 12. the Cretians are alway liars, slow *b.*

BELONG.

Gen. 40. 8. do not interpretations *b.* to God?
Lev. 27. 24. in jubilee return to whom it did *b.*
Deut. 29. 29. secret things *b.* to God, revealed *b.*
Psal. 47. 9. for the shields of the earth *b.* to God
68. 20. to our God *b.* the issues from death
Prov. 24. 23. these things also *b.* to the wise
Ezek. 21. † 13. shall they not *b.* to the despising rod?
Dan. 9. 9. to the Lord our God *b.* mercies
Mark 9. 41. in my name, because ye *b.* to Christ
Luke 19. 42. the things which *b.* to thy peace
1 *Cor.* 7. 32. careth for things that *b.* to the Lord

BELONGED, EST.

1 *Sam.* 30. 13. to whom *b.* thou, whence art thou?
1 *Kings* 1. 8. and the mighty men, which *b.* to David
2 *Kings* 7. † 2. a lord which *b.* to the king answered
Luke 23. 7. as he knew he *b.* to Herod's jurisdiction

BELONGETH.

Deut. 32. 35. to me *b.* vengeance and recompense, *Psal.* 94. 1. *Heb.* 10. 30.
Judg. 19. 14. Gibeah which *b.* to Benjamin, 20. 4.
Ezra 10. 4. arise, for this matter *b.* to thee
Psal. 3. 8. salvation *b.* unto the Lord
62. 11. twice have I heard, power *b.* unto God
12. also unto thee, O Lord, *b.* mercy
Dan. 9. 7. O Lord, righteousness *b.* to thee
8. to us *b.* confusion of face, to our kings
Heb. 5. 14. strong meat *b.* to them of full age

BELONGING.

Num. 7. 9. the service of the sanctuary *b.* to them
Ruth 2. 3. to light on a part of a field *b.* to Boaz
Prov. 26. 17. meddleth with strife *b.* not to him
Luke 9. 10. he went into a desert *b.* to Bethsaida

BELOVED

Is applied, [1] *To Christ*, Mat. 3. 17. Mark 1. 11. | 9. 7. [2] *To the church*, Jer. 11. 15. Rom. 9. 25. [3] *To particular saints*, Neh. 13. 26. Dan. 9. 23. [4] *To wife and children*, Deut. 21. 15. Hos. 9. 16. [5] *To the New Jerusalem*, Rev. 20. 9.

Deut. 21. 15. two wives, the one *b.* the other hated
Deut. 33. 12. the *b.* of the Lord shall dwell in safety
2 *Sam.* 12. † 25. Jedidiah, that is *b.* of the Lord
Neh. 13. 26. Solomon, who was *b.* of his God
Psal. 60. 5. that thy *b.* may be delivered, 108. 6.
127. 2. for so he giveth his *b.* sleep
Prov. 4. 3. and only *b.* in the sight of my mother
Cant. 5. 1. eat, O friends, drink abundantly, O *b.*
9. what is thy *b.* more than another *b.?*
6. 1. whither is thy *b.* gone, O thou fairest?
8. 5. who is this that cometh leaning on her *b.?*
Dan. 9. 23. for thou art greatly *b.* 10. 11, 19.
Hos. 3. 1. go yet, love a woman *b.* of her friend
9. 16. I will slay the *b.* fruit of their womb
Acts 15. 25. chosen men with *b.* Barnabas and Paul
Rom. 1. 7. to all that are in Rome, *b.* of God
9. 25. I will call her *b.* which was not *b.*
11. 28. they are *b.* for the Father's sake
16. 12. salute *b.* Persis who laboured much in Lord
Eph. 1. 6. he hath made us accepted in the *b.*
6. 21. Tychicus a *b.* brother and minister, *Col.* 4. 7.
Col. 3. 12. put on as the elect of God, holy and *b.*
4. 9. with Onesimus, a faithful and *b.* brother
14. Luke the *b.* physician and Demas greet you
1 *Thess.* 1. 4. knowing *b.* your election of God
1 *Tim.* 6. 2. do them service, because they are *b.*
Philem. 16. but above a servant, a brother *b.*
Heb. 6. 9. *b.* we are persuaded better things of you
2 *Pet.* 3. 8. *b.* be not ignorant of this one thing
15. even as our *b.* brother Paul hath written
1 *John* 3. 2. *b.* now we are the sons of God, it doth
21. *b.* if our heart condemn us not, then have
4. 1. *b.* believe not every spirit, but try the spirits
7. *b.* let us love one another, for love is of God
11. *b.* if God so loved us, we ought also to love
3 *John* 11. *b.* follow not that which is evil, but good
Jude 20. but ye *b.* building up yourselves in faith
Rev. 20. 9. and they compassed the *b.* city

Dearly BELOVED, *see* DEARLY.

My BELOVED.

Cant. 1. 14. *my b.* is to me a cluster of camphire
16. behold thou art fair, *my b.* yea pleasant
2. 3. as the apple-tree, so is *my b.* among the sons
9. *my b.* is like a roe or a young hart
16. *my b.* is mine, and I am his, he feedeth, 6. 3.
17. turn, *my b.* and be thou like a roe or a hart
4. 16. let *my b.* come into his garden and eat
5. 2. it is the voice of *my b.* that knocketh, 2. 8.
5. I rose up to open to *my b.* || 6. I opened to *my b.*
10. *my b.* is white and ruddy || 16. this is *my b.*
6. 2. *my b.* is gone || 3. I am *my b.* and *my b.* mine, [7. 10.
7. 13. which I have laid up for the, O *my b.*
Isa. 5. 1. a song of *my b.* touching his vineyard
Jer. 11. 15. what hath *my b.* to do in my house
Mat. 3. 17. this is *my b.* Son, 17. 5. *Mark* 1. 11. | 9. 7. *Luke* 3. 22. | 9. 35. 2 *Pet.* 1. 17.
12. 18. behold *my b.* in whom my soul is pleased
Luke 20. 13. I will send *my b.* son, it may be they
Rom. 16. 8. greet Amplias *my b.* in the Lord
1 *Cor.* 4. 14. but as *my b.* sons I warn you
17. I sent Timothy *my b.* son, 2 *Tim.* 1. 2.
Jam. 1. 16. do not err, *my b.* brethren

BELIE, BELIED.

Prov. 30. † 9. lest I be full and *b.* thee
Jer. 5. 12. they have *b.* the Lord, and said, it is not

BEMOAN, ED, ING.

Job 42. 11. they *b.* Job, and comforted him
Jer. 15. 5. who shall *b.* thee, O Jerusalem?
16. 5. neither go to lament, nor *b.* them
22. 10. weep ye not for the dead, nor *b.* him
31. 18. I have surely heard Ephraim *b.* himself
48. 17. all ye that are about him *b.* him
Nah. 3. 7. Nineveh is laid waste, who will *b.* her?

BENCHES.

Ezek. 27. 6. the Ashurites made thy *b.* of ivory

BEND.

Psal. 11. 2. for lo, the wicked *b.* their bow
64. 3. who *b.* their bows to shoot their arrows
Jer. 9. 3. they *b.* their tongue like a bow for lies
46. 9. the Lydians, that handle and *b.* the bow
50. 14. all ye that *b.* the bow shoot at her, 29.
51. 3. against him that bendeth, let the archer *b.*
Ezek. 17. 7. behold this vine did *b.* her roots

BENDETH, ING.

Psal. 58. 7. when he *b.* his bow to shoot arrows
Isa. 60. 14. that afflicted thee shall come *b.* to thee
Jer. 51. 3. against him that *b.* let the archer bend

BENEATH.

Exod. 20. 4. or that is in the earth *b.* *Deut.* 5. 8.
32. 19. he brake the tables *b.* the mount
Deut. 4. 39. on the earth *b.* there is none else
28. 13. thou shalt be above only, and not be *b.*
33. 13. blessed, for the deep that coucheth *b.*
Ezra 9. † 13. hast withheld *b.* our iniquities
Job 18. 16. his roots shall be dried up *b.*
Prov. 15. 24. that he may depart from hell *b.*
Isa. 14. 9. hell from *b.* is moved for thee
51. 6. lift up your eyes, look on the earth *b.*
Jer. 31. 37. if foundations can be searched *b.*
John 8. 23. ye are from *b.* I am from above

BENEFACTORS.

Luke 22. 25. they that exercise authority are called *b.*

BENEFIT.

Jer. 18. 10. repent of good wherewith I *b.* them

BENEFIT, S,

Signifies, [1] *The gifts and favours of God to men*, 2 Chron. 32. 25. Psal. 68. 19. [2] *The favour of God to others*, 2 Cor. 1. 15. Philem. 14. [3] *God's righteous acts*, 1 Sam. 12. † 7. [4] *Salvation*, 1 Tim. 6. 2. [5] *Favour, grace, or spiritual blessings*, Psal. 103. 2. [6] *To profit, or do good*, Jer. 18. 10.

1 *Sam.* 12. † 7. reason with you of all the *b.* of L.
2 *Chr.* 32. 25. Hezekiah rendered not according to *b.*
Psal. 68. 19. Lord who daily loadeth us with *b.*
103. 2. bless the Lord, and forget not all his *b.*
116. 12. what shall I render to Lord for all his *b.?*
2 *Cor.* 1. 15. that you might have a second *b.*
1 *Tim.* 6. 2. faithful and beloved partakers of the *b.*
Philem. 14. that thy *b.* should not be of necessity

BENEVOLENCE.

1 *Cor.* 7. 3. let the husband render to the wife due *b*

BENT.

Psal. 7. 12. he hath *b.* his bow, *Lam.* 2. 4. | 3. 12.
37. 14. have *b.* their bow to cast down the poor
Isa. 5. 28. whose arrows sharp, and all their bows *b.*
21. 15. for they fled from the swords and *b.* bow
Hos. 11. 7. my people are *b.* to backsliding from me
Zech. 9. 13. when I have *b.* Judah for me

BEREAVE.

Deut. 32. † 25. sword and terror shall *b.* young men
Eccl. 4. 8. for whom I labour and *b.* my soul of good
Jer. 15. 7. I will *b.* them of children, 18. 21.
Ezek. 5. 17. send evil beasts, and they shall *b.* thee
14. † 15. if I cause noisome beasts to *b.* the land
36. 12. no more henceforth *b.* them of men, 14.
Hos. 9. 12. bring up children, yet will I *b.* them

BEREAVED.

Gen. 42. 36. Jacob said, me ye have *b.* of my children
43. 14. if I be *b.* of my children, I am *b.*
Ezek. 36. 13. thou land hast *b.* thy nations
Hos. 13. 8. I will meet them as a bear *b.* of her whelps

BEREAVETH.

Lam. 1. 20. abroad the sword *b.* at home is as death

BERRIES.

Isa. 17. 6. two or three *b.* in the top of the bough
Jam. 3. 12. can the fig-tree bear olive *b.* a vine figs?

BERYL.

Dan. 10. 6. his body also was like the *b.* and face
Rev. 21. 20. eighth foundation was *b.* ninth a topaz

BESEECH.

Exod. 33. 18. he said, I *b.* thee show me thy glory
Num. 12. 13. heal her now, O Lord, I *b.* thee
Psal. 80. 14. return, we *b.* thee, O God of hosts
116. 4. O Lord, I *b.* thee, deliver my soul
118. 25. save, I *b.* O Lord, I *b.* thee, send prosperity
119. 108. accept, I *b.* thee, free-will offerings
Jer. 38. 20. obey, I *b.* thee, the voice of the Lord
Amos 7. 2. I said, O Lord God, forgive, I *b.* thee
Jonah 1. 14. they said, we *b.* thee, O Lord, we *b.* thee
4. 3. O Lord, take, I *b.* thee my life from me
Mal. 1. 9. *b.* God, that he will be gracious to us
Luke 8. 28. Jesus, I *b.* thee, torment me not
9. 38. saying, master, I *b.* thee look on my son
Acts 26. 3. wherefore I *b.* thee to hear me patiently
Rom. 12. 1. I *b.* you by the mercies of God
1 *Cor.* 4. 16. I *b.* you, be ye followers of me
2 *Cor.* 2. 8. I *b.* you, confirm your love toward him
5. 20. as though God did *b.* you by us, we pray you
6. 1. we *b.* you receive not the grace of God in vain
10. 1. I Paul *b.* you by the meekness of Christ
Gal. 4. 12. I *b.* you, be as I am, for I am as ye are
Eph. 4. 1. I the prisoner of the Lord *b.* you to walk
Philem. 9. yet for love's sake I rather *b.* thee
10. I *b.* thee for my son Onesimus, whom I have
Heb. 13. 19. but I *b.* you the rather to do this
1 *Pet.* 2. 11. I *b.* you as strangers and pilgrims
2 *John* 5. now I *b.* thee, lady, not as though I wrote
See BRETHREN.

BESEECHING.

Mat. 8. 5. there came a centurion *b.* him, *Luke* 7. 3.
Mark 1. 40. there came a leper to him, *b.* him

BESET.

Judg. 19. 22. sons of Belial *b.* the house round, 20. 5.
Psal. 22. 12. strong bulls of Bashan have *b.* me
139. 5. thou hast *b.* me behind and before
Hos. 7. 2. their own doings have *b.* them about
Heb. 12. 1. lay aside sin which doth so easily *b.* us

BESIDE, BESIDES.

Gen. 19. 12. hast thou here any *b.* bring them out
26. 1. there was a famine *b.* the first famine
Lev. 18. 18. *b.* the other in her life-time
23. 38. *b.* sabbaths, *b.* your gifts, *b.* your vows, *b.* your free-will offerings, which ye give to Lord
Num. 5. 20. man has lain with thee, *b.* thy husband
6. 21. law of Nazarite, *b.* that his hand shall get
11. 6. there is nothing at all *b.* this manna
28. 23. offer these *b.* the burnt-offering, 29. 6.
Deut. 29. 1. *b.* the covenant he made in Horeb
Josh. 22. 19. in building an altar, *b.* the altar, 29.
Judg. 6. 37. if it be dry on all the earth *b.*
11. 34. *b.* her Jephthah had no son nor daughter
1 *Sam.* 19. 3. I will go out and stand *b.* my father
1 *Kings* 10. 13. *b.* that which Solomon gave her
22. 7. not a prophet of the L. *b.* 2 *Chron.* 18. 6.
2 *Kings* 21. 16. *b.* his sin, wherewith he made Judah
Psal. 23. 2. he leadeth me *b.* the still waters
Cant. 1. 8. feed thy kids *b.* the shepherds' tents
Isa. 32. 20. blessed are ye that sow *b.* all waters
56. 8. I will gather others to him *b.* those that
Luke 16. 26. *b.* all this, between us and you a gulf
24. 21. *b.* all this, to-day is the third day since
Philem. 19. thou owest to me thine ownself *b.*

BESIDE.

Mark 3. 21. his friends said, he is *b.* himself
Acts 26. 24. Paul, thou art *b.* thyself, learning
2 *Cor.* 5. 13. whether we be *b.* ourselves, it is to God

BESIEGE.

Deut. 28. 52. he shall *b.* thee in thy gates
1 *Kings* 8. 37. if their enemies *b.* them, 2 *Chr.* 6. 28.
Isa. 21. 2. go up, O Elam, *b.* O Media

BESIEGED.

2 *Kings* 19. 24. with the sole of my feet I have dried up all the rivers of *b.* places, *Isa.* 37. 25.
Eccl. 9. 14. came a great king against it and *b.* it
Isa. 1. 8. the daughter of Zion is left as a *b.* city
Ezek. 6. 12. he that is *b.* shall die by the famine

BESOM.

Isa. 14. 23. I will sweep it with the *b.* of destruction

BESOUGHT.

Gen. 42. 21. when he *b.* us, and we would not hear
Exod. 32. 11. Moses *b.* the Lord, *Deut.* 3. 23.
2 *Sam.* 12. 16. David *b.* God for the child
1 *Kings* 13. 6. and the man of God *b.* the Lord
2 *Kings* 1. 13. third captain fell on his knees and *b.*
13. 4. Jehoahaz *b.* the Lord, the Lord hearkened
2 *Chron* 33. 12. Manasseh in affliction *b.* the Lord
Ezra 8. 23. so we fasted and *b.* our God for this
Esth. 8. 3. *b.* him with tears to put away the mischief
Jer. 26. 19. did not Hezekiah fear, and *b.* the Lord
Mat. 8. 31. so the devils *b.* him, *Mark* 5. 10, 12. *Luke* 8. 31, 32.
34. saw him, they *b.* him to depart, *Luke* 8. 37.
8. † 26. servant *b.* him, Lord, have patience
Mark 5. 23. Jairus *b.* him greatly, *Luke* 8. 41.
John 4. 40. Samaritans *b.* that he would tarry
47. the nobleman of Capernaum *b.* him to come
19. 38. *b.* Pilate that he might take the body
Acts 13. 42. Gentiles *b.* that these words be preached
16. 15. Lydia *b.* us, saying, if ye have judged me
39. magistrates *b.* them, and brought them out
21. 12. we *b.* him not to go up to Jerusalem
2 *Cor.* 12. 8. for this thing I *b.* the Lord thrice

BEST.

Gen. 43. 11. take of the *b.* fruits in the land
47. 6. in *b.* of the land make thy father dwell, 11.
Exod. 22. 5. of *b.* of his own field make restitution
Num. 18. 29. every heave-offering shall be of the *b.*
36. 6. let them marry to whom they think *b.*
Deut. 23. 16. he shall dwell where it likes him *b.*
1 *Sam.* 8. 14. he will take the *b.* of your vineyards
15. 9. Saul and the people spared the *b.* of sheep, 15.
2 *Sam.* 18. 4. what seemeth you *b.* I will do
2 *Kings* 10. 3. look out the *b.* of your master's sons
Psal. 39. 5. every man at his *b.* state is vanity
Cant. 7. 9. the roof of thy mouth like the *b.* wine
Mic. 7. 4. the *b.* of them is as a brier, most upright
Luke 15. 22. bring forth the *b.* robe and put it on
1 *Cor.* 12. 31. but covet earnestly the *b.* gifts

BESTEAD.

Isa. 8. 21. they shall pass thro' it hardly *b.* hungry

BESTIR.

2 *Sam.* 5. 24. when hearest the sound then *b.* thyself

BESTOW.

Exod. 32. 29. that he may *b.* on you a blessing
Deut. 14. 26. *b.* money for what thy soul lusts after
2 *Chron.* 24. 7. the things they did *b.* on Baalim
Ezra 7. 20. which thou shalt have occasion to *b.* it out of the king's treasure-house.
Luke 12. 17. I have no room where to *b.* my fruits
18. and there will I *b.* all my fruits and goods
1 *Cor.* 12. 23. on these we *b.* more abundant honour
13. 3. though I *b.* all my goods to feed the poor

BESTOWED.

2 *Kings* 5. 24. Gehazi *b.* them in the house
1 *Chron.* 29. 25. Lord *b.* on Solomon royal majesty
Isa. 63. 7. according to all the Lord hath *b.* on us
John 4. 38. to reap that whereon ye *b.* no labour
Rom. 16. 6. greet Mary, who *b.* much labour on us
1 *Cor.* 15. 10. his grace *b.* on me was not in vain
2 *Cor.* 1. 11. for the gift *b.* on us by means of many
8. 1. do you to wit of the grace *b.* on the churches
Gal. 4. 11. lest I have *b.* on you labour in vain
1 *John* 3. 1. what manner of love Father *b.* on us

BETAKE.

Isa. 14. † 32. poor of his people *b.* themselves to it

BETHINK.

1 *Kings* 8. 47. if they shall *b.* themselves in the land whither were carried captives, 2 *Chron.* 6. 37.

BETIMES

Signifies, [1] *Early*, Gen. 26. 31. [2] *Seasonably, in due and proper time*, Prov. 13. 24. [3] *Continually, and carefully*, 2 Chron. 36. 15.
Gen. 26. 31. rose up *b.* and sware one to another
2 *Chron.* 36. 15. God sent by his messengers, rising *b.*
Job 8. 5. if thou wouldest seek unto God *b.*
24. 5. as wild asses go they, rising *b.* for prey
Prov. 13. 24. he that loveth him, chasteneth him *b.*

BETRAY.

1 *Chron.* 12. 17. if ye be come to *b.* me to enemies
Mat. 24. 10. and shall *b.* one another and hate
26. 16. from that time he sought opportunity to *b.* him, *Mark* 14. 11. *Luke* 22. 6.
21. I say unto you, that one of you shall *b.* me, *Mark* 14. 18. *John* 13. 21.
46. behold, he is at hand that doth *b.* me
Mark 13. 12. brother shall *b.* brother to death
John 6. 64. Jesus knew who should *b.* him, 13. 11.
13. 2. the devil put into the heart of Judas to *b.* him

BETRAYED.

Mat. 10. 4. Judas Iscariot who *b.* him, *Mark* 3. 19.
17. 22. Son of man shall be *b.* into the hands of men, 20. 18. | 26. 2, 45. *Mark* 14. 41.
26. 24. wo to that man by whom the Son of man is *b.* *Mark* 14. 21. *Luke* 22. 22.
48. he that *b.* gave them a sign, *Mark* 14. 44.
27. 4. I have sinned, in that I *b.* innocent blood
Luke 21. 16. and ye shall be *b.* both by parents and
John 18. 2. Judas which *b.* him knew the place
1 *Cor.* 11. 23. same night he was *b.* he took bread

BETRAYERS.

Acts 7. 52. just One, of whom ye have been the *b.*

BETRAYEST, ETH.

Mark 14. 42. let us go, lo, he that *b.* me is at hand
Luke 22. 21. the hand of him that *b.* is with me
48. Judas, *b.* thou the Son of man with a kiss?
John 21. 20. Lord, which is he that *b.* thee?

BETROTH.

Deut. 28. 30. shalt *b.* a wife, another shall lie with her
Hos. 2. 19. I will *b.* thee to me for ever in righteous.
20. I will *b.* thee to me in faithfulness, shalt know

BETROTHED.

Exod. 21. 8. if she please not her master who *b.* her
22. 16. if a man entice a maid not *b.* *Deut.* 22. 28.
Lev. 19. 20. whosoever lieth with a woman *b.*
Deut. 20. 7. who hath *b.* a wife, and not taken her
22. 23. if a man find a virgin *b.* and lie with her
27. *b.* damsel cried, and there was none to save

BETTER

Signifies, [1] *More valuable, or preferable*, Eccl. 9. 4, 16, 18. [2] *More acceptable*, 1 Sam. 15. 22. [3] *More able*, Dan. 1. 20. [4] *More convenient*, 1 Cor. 7. 38. [5] *More easy*, Mat. 18. 6. [6] *More advantageous*, Phil. 1. 23. [7] *More holy*, 1 Cor. 8. 8. [8] *More safe*, Psal. 118. 8. [9] *More comfortable*, Prov. 15. 16, 17. [10] *More precious*, Prov. 8. 11.

A better hope, *Heb.* 7. 19. *The new covenant, or Christ and his priesthood, and the promises of the gospel depending thereupon; which give hope to lost sinners of obtaining reconciliation with God, and afford more clear and solid grounds to expect the full pardon of their sins, and eternal life, than could be discovered from the dark shadows under the legal dispensation.*

Might obtain a better resurrection, *Heb.* 11. 35. *A resurrection to a far better life than they could have enjoyed on earth; for though they might have been preserved for a while from death now threatened, which was a kind of* resurrection, *yet was it not to be compared with the resurrection to eternal life, glory, bliss, and pleasure, to be enjoyed by them with God in heaven, which would abundantly recompense them for all their sufferings.*

Better sacrifices, *Heb.* 9. 23. *The sacrifice of Christ himself, which is of more value, and comprises all the virtue, benefit, and signification of the legal sacrifices. It is expressed in the* plural *number, both to answer the opposite term, and to set out its excellency; being far above all others, and the very substance of them.*

Gen. 29. 19. *b.* I give her to thee than to another
Exod. 14. 12. *b.* for us to have served the Egyptians
Num. 14. 3. were it not *b.* for us to return to Egypt?
Judg. 8. 2. gleanings of Ephraim *b.* than vintage
11. 25. nor art thou any thing *b.* than Balak
1 *Sam.* 1. 8. am not I *b.* to thee than ten sons?
27. 1. nothing *b.* than to go to the Philistines
1 *Kings* 1. 47. God make the name of k. Solomon *b.*
2. 32. who fell upon two men *b.* than he, and slew
19. 4. Elijah said, I am not *b.* than my fathers
21. 2. I will give thee for it a *b.* vineyard than it
2 *Kings* 5. 12. rivers of Damascus *b.* than Jordan
2 *Chron.* 21. 13. hast slain brethren *b.* than thyself
Psal. 69. 31. this shall please the Lord *b.* than an ox
Eccl. 2. 24. nothing *b.* for a man than to eat and drink
3. 22. there is nothing *b.* than to rejoice in his works
4. 3. *b.* is he than both they, which have not been
9. two are *b.* than one || 6. 11. what is man the *b.*?
7. 10. that the former days were *b.* than these
† 11. wisdom is as good as an inheritance, yea *b.* too
10. 11. the serpent will bite, and a babbler is no *b.*
Isa. 56. 5. give a name *b.* than of sons and daughters
Lam. 4. 9. they that be slain with the sword are *b.*
Ezek. 36. 11. I will settle you, and do *b.* to you
Dan. 1. 20. in all matters he found them ten times *b.*
Hos. 2. 7. then was it *b.* with me than now
Amos 6. 2. be they *b.* than these kingdoms?
Nah. 3. 8. art thou *b.* than populous No?
Mat. 6. 26. behold the fowls of the air, are ye not much *b.* than they? *Luke* 12. 24.
12. 12. how much then is a man *b.* than a sheep?
18. 6. it were *b.* for him that a millstone were hanged about his neck, *Mark* 9. 42. *Luke* 17. 2.
Rom. 3. 9. are we *b.* than they? no, in no wise
1 *Cor.* 7. 38. he that giveth her not in marriage, doth *b.*
8. 8. for neither if we eat are we the *b.*
9. 15. *b.* for me to die, than make my glorying void
11. 17. you come together not for *b.* but for worse
Phil. 2. 3. let each esteem other *b.* than himself
Heb. 1. 4. being made so much *b.* than the angels
6. 9. but beloved, we are persuaded *b.* things of you
7. 7. without contrad. the less is blessed of the *b.*
19. nothing perfect, but bringing in of a *b.* hope did
22. Jesus was made a surety of a *b.* testament
8. 6. by how much also he is the Mediator of a *b.* covenant, established on *b.* promises
9. 23. but heavenly things with *b.* sacrifices
10. 34. in heaven a *b.* and enduring substance
11. 16. they desire a *b.* country, an heavenly
35. that they might obtain a *b.* resurrection
40. God having provided some *b.* thing for us
12. 24. that speaketh *b.* things than that of Abel
2 *Pet.* 2. 21. *b.* for them not to have known the way

BETTER *is.*

Prov. 15. 16. *b.* *is* little with the fear of the Lord
17. *b.* *is* a dinner of herbs where love is, than an ox
16. 8. *b.* *is* a little with righteousness than revenues
16. how much *b.* *is* it to get wisdom than gold
17. 1. *b.* *is* a dry morsel and quietness therewith
19. 1. *b.* *is* the poor that walks in integrity, 28. 6.
27. 10. for *b.* *is* a neighbour that is near, than
Eccl. 4. 6. *b.* *is* an handful with quietness than
13. *b.* *is* a poor wise child than a foolish king
6. 9. *b.* *is* the sight of the eyes than the wandering
7. 8. *b.* *is* the end of a thing than the beginning
Cant. 4. 10. how much *b.* *is* thy love than wine!

Is BETTER, or *is it* BETTER.

Judg. 9. 2. whether *is b.* for you that all reign
18. 19. *is it b.* to be a priest to one, than to a tribe?
Ruth 4. 15. thy daughter *is b.* to thee than seven sons
1 *Sam.* 15. 22. behold, to obey *is b.* than sacrifice
28. given to a neighbour that *is b.* than thou
2 *Sam.* 17. 14. counsel of Hushai the Archite *is b.*
Esth. 1. 19. estate to another that *is b.* than she
Psal. 37. 16. a little a righteous man hath *is b.*
63. 3. thy loving-kindness *is b.* than life
84. 10. a day in thy courts *is b.* than a thousand
119. 72. the law of thy mouth *is b.* to me than gold
Prov. 3. 14. for the merchandise of wisdom *is b.*
8. 11. wisdom *is b.* than rubies, and all things
19. my fruit *is b.* than gold, yea, than fine gold
12. 9. *is b.* than he that honoureth himself
16. 32. that is slow to anger *is b.* than the mighty
19. 22. and a poor man *is b.* than a liar
22. † 1. favour *is b.* than silver and gold
27. 5. open rebuke *is b.* than secret love
Eccl. 6. 3. an untimely birth *is b.* than he
7. 1. a good name *is b.* than precious ointment
3. sorrow *is b.* than laughter, for by the sadness of the countenance the heart *is* made *b.*
8. the patient in spirit *is b.* than the proud in spirit
9. 4. a living dog *is b.* than a dead lion
16. then said I, wisdom *is b.* than strength
18. wisdom *is b.* than weapons of war.
Cant. 1. 2. for thy love *is b.* than wine
Luke 5. 39. for he saith, the old *is b.*
Phil. 1. 23. and to be with Christ, which *is* far *b.*

It is BETTER, or BETTER *it is.*

Gen. 29. 19. *it is b.* I give her to thee than another
2 *Sam.* 18. 3. *it is b.* thou succour us out of the city
Psal. 118. 8. *it is b.* to trust in the Lord than to put, 9.
Prov. 16. 19. *b. it is* to be of an humble spirit
21. 9. *it is b.* to dwell in a corner of the house, 25. 24.
19. *it is b.* to dwell in the wilderness than with
25. 7. *b. it is* that it be said to thee, come up hither
Eccl. 5. 5. *b. it is* that thou shouldest not vow
7. 2. *it is b.* to go to the house of mourning than

Eccl. 7. 5. *it is b.* to hear the rebuke of the wise than
Jonah 4. 3. *it is b.* for me to die than to live, 8.
Mat. 18. 8. *it is b.* for thee to enter into life halt or maimed, than to be cast, 9. *Mark* 9. 43, 45, 47.
1 *Cor.* 7. 9. for *it is b.* to marry than to burn
1 *Pet.* 3. 17. *it is b.* that ye suffer for well doing than [worse

BETTERED.

Mark 5. 26. she was nothing *b.* but rather grew

BETWEEN.

Gen. 1. †4. God divided *b.* light and darkness
†14. to divide *b.* light and darkness
3. 15. I will put enmity *b.* thy seed and her seed
9. 16. the covenant *b.* God and every creature
15. 17. a burning lamp passed *b.* those places
49. 10. nor a lawgiver from *b.* his feet, till Shiloh
Exod 8. 23. I will put a division *b.* my people
12. †6. kill it *b.* the two evenings, *Num.* 9. †3.
13. 9. and it shall be for a sign to thee, and a memorial *b.* thine eyes, 16. *Deut.* 6. 8. | 11. 18.
18. 16. they come, and I judge *b.* one and another
26. 33. the vail shall divide *b.* holy and most holy
Num. 11. 33. while the flesh was *b.* their teeth
28. †4. the other lamb offer *b.* two evenings
Deut. 17. 8. *b.* blood and blood, *b.* plea, *b.* stroke
33. 12. and he shall dwell *b.* his shoulders
Judg. 4. 5. Deborah dwelt *b.* Ramah and Beth-el
1 *Sam.* 7. 14. there was peace *b.* Israel and Amorites
2 *Sam.* 19. 35. discern *b.* good and evil, 1 *Kings* 3. 9.
1 *Kings* 18. 21. how long halt ye *b.* two opinions?
Prov. 18. 18. the lot parteth *b.* the mighty
Jer. 34. 18. they passed *b.* parts of the calf, 19.
Ezek. 34. 17. I judge *b.* cattle and cattle, *b.* rams
Hos. 2. 2. and her adulteries from *b.* her breasts
Joel 2. 17. the priests weep *b.* the porch and altar
Zech. 11. 14. break the brotherhood *b.* Judah
Mat. 23. 35. ye slew *b.* the temple and the altar
John 3. 25. a question *b.* John's disciples and Jews
Acts 13. †42. might be preached the sabbath *b.*
Rom. 10. 12. no difference *b.* the Jew and Greek
1 *Cor.* 7. 34. there is difference *b.* a wife and a virgin
1 *Tim.* 2. 5. there is one Mediator *b.* God and men

BETWIXT.

Job 36. 32. not to shine by the cloud that cometh *b.*
Cant. 1. 13. he shall lie all night *b.* my breasts
Phil. 1. 23. I am in a strait *b.* two, having a desire

BEWAIL.

Lev. 10. 6. *b.* the burning the Lord hath kindled
Deut. 21. 13. and *b.* her father and mother a month
Judg. 11. 37. that I may go and *b.* my virginity, 38.
Isa. 16. 9. I will *b.* with the weeping of Jazer
2 *Cor.* 12. 21. that I shall *b.* many who have sinned
Rev. 18. 9. shall *b.* her, when they see the smoke

BEWAILED, ETH.

Jer. 4. 31. the daughter of Zion that *b.* herself
Luke 8. 52. and all wept, and *b.* her, but he said
23. 27. of women also who *b.* and lamented him

BEWARE

Signifies, [1] *To take care,* Prov. 19. 25. [2] *To have a singular and special regard to,* Exod. 23. 21.
We must beware, [1] *Of forgetting God,* Deut. 6. 12. | 8. 11. [2] *Of evil thoughts,* Deut. 15. 9. [3] *Of things forbidden,* Judg. 13. 4, 13. [4] *Of dangers foretold,* 2 Kings 6. 9. Job 36. 18. [5] *Of God's wrath,* Acts 13. 40. [6] *Of false teachers,* Mat. 7. 15. | 16. 6, 11. [7] *Of men,* Mat. 10. 17. [8] *Of evil workers,* Phil. 3. 2. [9] *Of the error of the wicked,* 2 Pet. 3. 17. [10] *Of covetousness,* Luke 12. 15. | 20. 46.
Gen. 24. 6. *b.* that thou bring not my son thither
Exod. 23. 21. *b.* of him, and obey his voice
Deut. 6. 12. then *b.* lest thou forget the Lord, 8. 11.
15. 9. *b.* there be not a wicked thought in thy heart
Judg. 13. 4. *b.* I pray thee, and drink no wine, 13.
2 *Sam.* 18. 12. *b.* that none touch the young man
2 *Kings* 6. 9. saying *b.* that thou pass not such a place
Job 36. 18. *b.* lest he take thee away with his stroke
Prov. 19. 25. smite a scorner, and the simple will *b.*
Isa. 36. 18. *b.* lest Hezekiah persuade you, saying
Mat. 7. 15. *b.* of false prophets || 10. 17. *b.* of men
16. 6. take heed and *b.* of the leaven of the Pharisees, 11. *Mark* 8. 15. *Luke* 12. 1.
Mark 12. 38. *b.* of the scribes, *Luke* 20. 46.
Luke 12. 15. take heed and *b.* of covetousness
Acts 13. 40. *b.* lest that come which is spoken
Phil. 3. 2. *b.* of dogs, *b.* of evil workers, *b.* of concision
Col. 2. 8. *b.* lest any man spoil you thro' philosophy
2 *Pet.* 3. 17. *b.* lest ye also, being led away with [error

BEWITCHED.

Acts 8. 9. Simon *b.* the people of Samaria, 11.
Gal. 3. 1. O foolish Galatians, who hath *b.* you?

BEWRAY.

Isa. 16. 3. hide the outcasts, *b.* not him that wandereth

BEWRAYETH.

Prov. 27. 16. the ointment of his right hand *b.* itself
29. 24. he heareth cursing, and *b.* it not
Mat. 26. 73. thou art one of them, thy speech *b.* thee

BEYOND.

Num. 22. 18. Balaam said, I cannot go *b.* the word of the Lord my God, to do less or more, 24. 13.
Deut. 30. 13. nor is it *b.* the sea, that shouldest say
1 *Sam.* 20. 22. the arrows are *b.* thee, 36. 37.
2 *Sam.* 10. 16. *b.* the river, 1 *Kings* 14. 15. 1 *Chron.* 19. 16. *Ezra* 4. 17, 20. | 6. 6, 8. | 7. 21, 25. *Neh.* 2. 7, 9. *Isa.* 7. 20. | 18. 1. *Zeph.* 3. 10.
2 *Chron.* 20. 2. multitude from *b.* the sea, *Jer.* 25. 22.
Mark 6. 51. they were amazed *b.* measure, 7. 37.
2 *Cor.* 8. 3. and *b.* their power they were willing
10. 14. for we stretch not *b.* our measure
Gal. 1. 13. *b.* measure I persecuted the church of God
1 *Thess.* 4. 6. that no man go *b.* and defraud his brother

BEYOND *Jordan.* *See* JORDAN.

BIBBER. *See* WINE.

BID

Signifies, [1] *To invite,* Mat. 22. 9. Luke 14. 12. [2] *To command,* Mat. 14. 28. [3] *To wish,* 2 John 10. [4] *To sanctify, or prepare,* Zeph. 1. †7.
Josh. 6. 10. till the day I *b.* you shout, then shout
1 *Sam.* 9. 27. said, *b.* the servant pass on before us
2 *Sam.* 2. 26. how long ere *b.* the people return from
2 *Kings* 4. 24. slack not riding for me except I *b.* thee
5. 13. if the prophet had *b.* thee do a great thing
10. 5. we will do all that thou shalt *b.* us
Jonah 3. 2. preach to it the preaching that I *b.* thee
Zeph. 1. 7. for the Lord hath *b.* his guests
Mat. 14. 28. *b.* me come to thee on the water
22. 9. as many as ye shall find *b.* to the marriage
23. 3. what they *b.* you observe, that observe and do
Luke 9. 61. let me first *b.* them farewell at home
10. 40. *b.* her therefore that she help me
14. 12. lest they also *b.* thee again, and a recompence
1 *Cor.* 10. 27. if any that believe not *b.* you to a feast
2 *John* 10. receive him not, nor *b.* him God speed

BIDDEN.

1 *Sam.* 9. 13. and afterwards they eat that be *b.*
2 *Sam.* 16. 11. let him curse, for the Lord hath *b.*
Mat. 1. 24. then Joseph did as the angel had *b.* him
22. 3. and sent to call them that were *b.* to wedding
4. tell them who are *b.* I have prepared my dinner
8. but they who were *b.* were not worthy
Luke 7. 39. when the Pharisee who had *b.* him saw it
14. 7. he put forth a parable to those who were *b.*
8. when thou art *b.* lest a more honourable man be *b.*
10. when thou art *b.* go and sit in the lowest room
24. none of those men *b.* shall taste of my supper

BIDDETH, BIDDING.

1 *Sam.* 22. 14. goeth at thy *b.* and is honourable
2 *John* 11. he that *b.* him God speed, is partaker

BIDE.

Rom. 11. 23. if they *b.* not still in unbelief, be grafted

BIER.

2 *Sam.* 3. 31. king David himself followed the *b.*
Luke 7. 14. he came and touched the *b.* and said

BILL.

Luke 16. 6. take thy *b.* and write, 50. || 7. take thy *b.*
See DIVORCE.

BILLOWS.

Psal. 42. 7. all thy *b.* are gone over me, *Jonah* 2. 3.

BIND

Signifies, [1] *To tie up, or fasten together,* Gen. 37. 7. Deut. 14. 25. [2] *To bind with chains,* Mark 5. 3. Acts 12. 6. [3] *To keep fast, or sure,* Prov. 3. 3. | 6. 21. [4] *To engage by vow, or promise,* Num. 30. 2, 9, 13. [5] *To confirm, or ratify,* Mat. 16. 19. [6] *Judicially to declare or pronounce a person's sins unpardoned, according to the directions of God's word, and to inflict any church censure upon him for the same,* Mat. 16. 19. | 18. 18. [7] *To distress, or trouble,* Luke 13. 16. [8] *To restrain,* Job 28. 11. [9] *To be under a marriage tie, or obligation to perform the duties incumbent on a person in that relation,* Rom. 7. 2. 1 Cor. 7. 39. [10] *Powerfully to persuade, influence, or constrain,* Acts 20. 22.
They bind heavy burdens on men, *Mat.* 23. 4. *They impose many strict injunctions, over and above what the law requires, and severely exact obedience thereto from others.*
Exod. 28. 28. they shall *b.* the breast-plate by rings
Num. 30. 2. if a man swear an oath to *b.* his soul
Deut. 6. 8. thou shalt *b.* them for a sign on thy hand
14. 25. shalt *b.* up the money, and go to the place
Josh. 2. 18. thou shalt *b.* this line in the window
Judg. 15. 10. to *b.* Samson are we come up
12. they said, we are come down to *b.* thee
13. no, but we will *b.* thee fast, and deliver thee
16. 5. that we may *b.* Samson to afflict him
Job 31. 36. I will *b.* it as a crown to me
34. †17. shall even he that hateth right *b.*?
38. 31. canst *b.* the sweet influences of Pleiades?
39. 10. canst thou *b.* the unicorn with his band?
40. 13. hide them, and *b.* their faces in secret
41. 5. wilt thou *b.* Leviathan for thy maidens?
Psal. 105. 22. to *b.* his princes at his pleasure
118. 27. *b.* the sacrifice with cords to the altar
149. 8. to *b.* their kings with chains, and nobles
Prov. 3. 3. *b.* them about thy neck, write them
6. 21. *b.* them continually upon thine heart
7. 3. *b.* them on thy fingers, write them on thy heart
Isa. 8. 16. *b.* up the testimony, seal the law
49. 18. and *b.* them on thee as a bride doth
61. 1. he hath sent me to *b.* up the broken hearted
Ezek. 34. 16. I will *b.* up what was broken
Dan. 3. 20. he commanded most mighty men to *b.*
Hos. 6. 1. he hath smitten us, and will *b.* us up
10. 10. when they *b.* themselves in two furrows
Mic. 1. 13. *b.* the chariot to the swift beast
Mat. 12. 29. except he first *b.* the strong man, and then he will spoil his house, *Mark* 3. 27.
13. 30. *b.* the tares in bundles to burn them
16. 19. whatsoever thou shalt *b.* on earth, 18. 18.
22. 13. *b.* him hand and foot, take and cast him
23. 4. *b.* heavy burdens grievous to be borne
Mark 5. 3. no man could *b.* him with chains
Acts 9. 14. authority to *b.* all that call on thy name
12. 8. angel said, gird thyself, *b.* on thy sandals
21. 11. so shall the Jews *b.* the man that owneth

BINDETH.

Job 5. 18. he maketh sore and *b.* up, he woundeth
26. 8. he *b.* up the waters in his thick clouds
28. 11. he *b.* the floods from overflowing
30. 18. it *b.* me about as the collar of my coat
36. 13. hypocrites, they cry not when he *b.* them
Psal. 129. 7. nor he that *b.* sheaves, his bosom
147. 3. he healeth the broken in heart, and *b.* up
Prov. 26. 8. as he that *b.* a stone in a sling, so is he
Isa. 30. 26. in day Lord *b.* up breach of his people

BINDING.

Gen. 37. 7. we were *b.* sheaves in field, my sheaf arose
49. 11. *b.* his foal to the vine, and his ass's colt
Num. 30. 13. every *b.* oath to afflict the soul
Acts 22. 4. *b.* and delivering into prisons men

BIRD

Signifies, [1] *A fowl, small or large,* Jam. 3. 7. [2] Cyrus, *who came swiftly from* Persia *to destroy* Babylon, Isa. 46. 11. [3] *The* Chaldeans, *or other neighbours that persecuted and afflicted the* Jews, Jer. 12. 9. [4] *The polluted and corrupt inhabitants of* Babylon, Rev. 18. 2.
Gen. 7. 14. every *b.* of every sort went into the ark
Lev. 14. 52. shall cleanse the house with the living *b.*
Job 41. 5. wilt thou play with him as with a *b.*?
Psal. 11. 1. to my soul, flee as a *b.* to your mountain
124. 7. our soul is escaped as a *b.* out of the snare
Prov. 1. 17. in vain the net is spread in sight of any *b.*
6. 5. and as a *b.* from the hand of the fowler
7. 23. as a *b.* hasteth to the snare, knows not
26. 2. as the *b.* by wandering, so the curse causeless
27. 8. as a *b.* that wandereth from her nest, so a man
Eccl. 10. 20. the *b.* of the air shall tell the matter
12. 4. he shall rise up at the voice of the *b.*
Isa. 16. 2. as a wandering *b.* cast out of her nest
46. 11. calling a ravenous *b.* from the east
Jer. 12. 9. my heritage is to me as a speckled *b.*
Lam. 3. 52. mine enemies chased me like a *b.*
Hos. 9. 11. their glory shall fly away like a *b.*
11. 11. they shall tremble as a *b.* out of Egypt
Amos 3. 5. can a *b.* fall where no gin is for him?
Rev. 18. 2. a cage of every unclean and hateful *b.*

BIRDS.

Gen. 15. 10. but the *b.* divided he not
40. 17. the *b.* did eat them out of the basket
19. the *b.* shall eat thy flesh from off thee
Lev. 14. 4. priest shall command to take two *b.* alive
Deut. 14. 11. of all clean *b.* ye shall eat
2 *Sam.* 21. 10. suffered not the *b.* to rest by day
Psal. 104. 17. where the *b.* make their nests
148. †10. praise the Lord, ye *b.* of wing
Eccl. 9. 12. as *b.* that are caught in the snare
Cant. 2. 12. the time of the singing of *b.* is come
Isa. 31. 5. as *b.* flying, so will L. defend Jerusalem
Jer. 4. 25. and all the *b.* of the heaven were fled
5. 27. as a cage full of *b.* so are their houses
12. 4. the beasts are consumed and the *b.*
9. the *b.* round about are against her, come ye
Ezek. 39. 4. I will give thee to the ravenous *b.*
Dan. 4. 33. his nails were grown like *b.* claws
Mat. 8. 20. holes, and the *b.* of the air have nests, *Luke* 9. 58.
13. 32. the *b.* lodge in the branches thereof
Rom. 1. 23. into an image like to *b.* and beasts
1 *Cor.* 15. 39. another of fishes, another of *b.*
Jam. 3. 7. every kind of beasts and *b.* is tamed

BIRTH

Is, [1] *Natural,* Exod. 28. 10. [2] *Abortive, or untimely,* Job 3. 16. Psal. 58. 8. Eccl. 6. 3. [3] *Supernatural, as was the birth of Christ,* Mat. 1. 18. Luke 1. 14. [4] *Figurative, for heavy anguish and distress,* 2 Kings 19. 3. Isa. 37. 3. [5] *For deliverance at hand,* Isa. 66. 9. [6] *For a natural state in sin,* Ezek. 16. 3. [7] *For regeneration,* Tit. 3. 5. [8] *For earnest desire for the good of souls,* Gal. 4. 19.
The children are come to the birth, 2 *Kings* 19. 3. *We have begun a happy reformation, but are hindered by this insolent* Assyrian, *from bringing it to perfection.*
Thy birth is of the land of Canaan; *Ezek.* 16. 3. *Thy root whence thou didst spring, the rock whence thou wast cut, the place where thou grewest up, the company and commerce thou didst use, all were of the land of* Canaan; *thy original is no better than the worst of nations, thou hast their vicious nature, manners, and practices, and art as vile and obnoxious to my curse as they are.*
2 *Kings* 19. 3. children are come to the *b.* *Isa.* 37. 3.
Job 3. 16. as an hidden untimely *b.* I had not been
Psal. 58. 8. let them pass like the untimely *b.*
Eccl. 6. 3. an untimely *b.* is better than he
7. 1. day of death is better than day of one's *b.*
Isa. 66. 9. shall I bring to the *b.* not cause to bring
Ezek. 16. 3. thy *b.* and nativity is of Canaan
Hos. 9. 11. glory of Ephraim shall fly from the *b.*
Mat. 1. 18. the *b.* of Jesus Christ was on this wise
Luke 1. 14. and many shall rejoice at his *b.*
John 9. 1. he saw a man who was blind from his *b.*
Gal. 4. 19. my children, of whom I travail in *b.*
Rev. 12. 2. and she cried, travailing in *b.* and passed

BIRTH-DAY.

Gen. 40. 20. the third day, which was Pharaoh's *b.-d.*
Mat. 14. 6. when Herod's *b.-d.* was kept, *Mark* 6. 21.

BIRTH-RIGHT.

Gen. 25. 31. Jacob said, sell me this day thy *b.-right*
33. and he sware, and sold his *b.-right* to Jacob
34. thus Esau despised his *b.-right*
27. 36. took away my *b.-right*, and now my blessing
43. 33. sat, the first-born according to his *b.-right*
1 *Chron.* 5. 1. Reuben's *b.-r.* given to sons of Joseph
Heb. 12. 16. Esau for one morsel sold his *b.-right*

BISHOP, S,

Signifies, [1] *Spiritual overseers that have the charge of souls, to instruct and rule them by the word,* 1 Tim. 3. 1, 2. Acts 20. 28. [2] *Christ himself,* 1 Pet. 2. 25.
Phil. 1. 1. to all saints at Philippi, with *b.* and deacons
1 *Tim.* 3. 1. if a man desire the office of a *b.*
2. a *b.* then must be blameless, *Tit.* 1. 7.
1 *Pet.* 2. 25. now returned to the *b.* of your souls

BISHOPRIC.

Acts 1. 20. and his *b.* let another take

BIT, S.

Psal. 32. 9. whose mouth must be held in with *b.*
Jam. 3. 3. behold we put *b.* in the horses' mouths

BIT.

Num. 21. 6. Lord sent fiery serpents, they *b.* people
Amos 5. 19. leaned on a wall, and a serpent *b.* him

BITE.

Eccl. 10. 8. breaketh an hedge, a serpent shall *b.* him
11. the serpent will *b.* without enchantment
Jer. 8. 17. I will send serpents, and they shall *b.* you
Amos 9. 3. I will command serpent, and he shall *b.*
Mic. 3. 5. the prophets that *b.* with the teeth
Hab. 2. 7. shall they not rise up that shall *b.* thee?
Gal. 5. 15. but if ye *b.* and devour one another

BITETH.

Gen. 49. 17. Dan an adder, that *b.* the horse-heels
Prov. 23. 32. at the last it *b.* like a serpent

BITTEN.

Num. 21. 8. every one that is *b.* when he looks on
9. came to pass, that if a serpent had *b.* any man

BITTER.

Gen. 27. 34. Esau cried with an exceeding *b.* cry
Exod. 1. 14. the Egyptians made their lives *b.*
12. 8. with *b.* herbs shall ye eat it, *Num.* 9. 11.
15. 23. not drink of the waters, for they were *b.*
Deut. 32. 24. shall be devoured with *b.* destruction

Deut. 32. 32. are grapes of gall, their clusters are b.
Judg. 18. † 25. lest fellows b. of soul run on thee
Ruth 1. † 20. call me not Naomi, but b.
1 Sam. 1. † 10. Hannah was b. of soul and prayed
22. † 2. every one b. of soul gathered to him
30. † 6. spake of stoning, the peoples' soul was b.
2 Sam. 17. † 8. fa her's men be mighty, and b. of soul
2 Kings 4. † 27. let her alone, her soul is b. in her
14. 26. Lord saw affliction of Israel that it was b.
Esth. 4. 1. Mordecai cried with loud voice and b. cry
Job 3. † 5. terrify it, as those who have a b. day
20. and why is life given to the b. in soul?
13. 26. thou writest b. things against me
23. 2. even to-day is my complaint b.
27. † 2. the Almighty who hath made my soul b.
Psal. 64. 3. to shoot their arrows, even b. words
Prov. 5. 4. but her end is b. as wormwood
27. 7. to the hungry soul every b. thing is sweet
31. † 6. give wine to those that are b. of soul
Eccl. 7. 26. I find more b. than death the woman
Isa. 5. 20. that put b. for sweet, and sweet for b.
22. † 4. look from me, I will be b. in weeping
24. 9. strong drink shall be b. to them that drink
Jer. 2. 19. it is an evil thing and b. that thou
4. 18. this is thy wickedness, because it is b.
6. 26. make most b. lamentation as for a son
31. 15. a voice was heard in Ramah, b. weeping
Ezek. 3. † 14. Spirit took me away, and I went b.
27. 31. shall weep for thee with b. wailing
Amos 8. 10. and the end thereof, as a b. day
Hab. 1. 6. Chaldeans, that b. and hasty nation.
Col. 3. 19. love your wives, be not b. against them
Jam. 3. 14. if ye have b. envying and strife
Rev. 8. 11. men died of waters because made b.
10. 9. eat it up, and it shall make thy belly b.
10. as soon as I had eaten it, my belly was b.

BITTER-WATER.

Num. 5. 18. the b.-water that causeth the curse
Jam. 3. 11. doth a fountain send sweet w. and b.?

BITTERLY.

Judg. 5. 23. curse ye b. the inhabitants thereof
Ruth 1. 20. the Almighty hath dealt b. with me
Isa. 22. 4. look away from me, I will weep b.
33. 7. the ambassadors of peace shall weep b.
Ezek. 27. 30. the pilots of Tyre shall cry b.
Hos. 12. 14. Ephraim provoked him most b.
Zeph. 1. 14. the mighty man shall cry b.
Mat. 26. 75. Peter went out, wept b. Luke 22. 62.

BITTERN.

Isa. 14. 23. make it a possession for the b. 34. 11.
Zeph. 2. 14. the b. shall lodge in the upper lintels

BITTERNESS

Signifies, [1] *That which is opposed to sweetness*, Exod. 15. 23. [2] *Deep sorrow and heaviness of spirit*, Job 7. 11. Prov. 14. 10. [3] *A thing most pernicious, or that produces dreadful effects*, 2 Sam. 2. 26. [4] *Violent inward displeasure against others*, Eph. 4. 31. [5] *Great impiety*, Acts 8. 23.
The gall of bitterness, Acts 8. 23. *In a state most offensive and distasteful to God; under the power of corruption, hypocrisy, and ambition.*
A root of bitterness, Heb. 12. 15. *Any scandalous sin, dangerous error, or schism, tending to draw persons to apostasy, the end whereof will be bitter.*

Gen. 26. † 35. which were b. of spirit to Isaac
Exod. 15. † 23. the name of it was called b.
Ruth 1. † 13. I have much b. for your sake
1 Sam. 1. 10. Hannah was in b. of soul and prayed
15. 32. surely the b. of death is past
2 Sam. 2. 26. the sword will be b. in the latter end
Job 7. 11. I will complain in the b. of my soul
9. 18. to take my breath, but filleth me with b.
10. 1. I will speak in the b. of my soul
21. 25. another dieth in the b. of his soul
Prov. 14. 10. the heart knoweth his own b.
17. 25. a foolish son is b. to her that bare him
Isa. 38. 15. go softly all my life in b. of my soul
17. behold, for peace I had great b.
Lam. 1. 4. her virgins are afflicted, and she is in b.
3. 15. he hath filled me with b. he hath made
Ezek. 3. 14. Spirit took me away, and I went in b.
21. 6. and with b. sigh before their eyes
27. 31. they shall weep for thee with b.
Hos. 12. † 14. Ephraim provoked him with b.
Zech. 12. 10. be in b. for him as one that is in b. for
Acts 8. 23. I perceive thou art in the gall of b.
Rom. 3. 14. whose mouth is full of cursing and b.
Eph. 4. 31. let all b. be put away from you
Heb. 12. 15. lest any root of b. springing up

BLACK

Signifies, *The colour so call.d, which is opposite to white*, Mat. 5. 36.
It is applied, [1] *To the church, whose outward beauty is often eclipsed by reason of infirmities, scandals, reproaches, and persecutions*, Cant. 1. 5. [2] *To the Jews, whose countenance changed and turned black, like persons ready to be strangled, being struck with terror at the approach of God's judgments*, Joel 2. 6. Nah. 2. 10. [3] *To hell, the place of extreme darkness, horror, and misery*, Jude 13.

Lev. 13. 31. and that there is no b. hair in it
37. and there is b. hair grown up therein
1 Kings 18. 45. the heaven was b. with clouds
Job 30. 30. my skin is b. upon me, my bones burnt
Prov. 7. 9. in the evening, in the b. and dark night
Cant. 1. 5. I am b. but comely, O daughters of Jerus.
6. look not upon me, because I am b.
5. 11. his locks are bushy and b. as a raven
Jer. 4. 28. for this the heavens shall be b.
8. 21. for the hurt of my people I am hurt, I am b.
14. 2. the gates thereof languish, they are b.
Lam. 5. 10. our skin was b. like an oven
Ezek. 31. † 15. I caused Lebanon to be b. for him
Zech. 6. 2. in the second chariot b. horses
6. b. horses go forth into the north country
Mal. 3. † 14. what profit that we walked in b.?
Mat. 5. 36. canst not make one hair white or b.
Rev. 6. 5. and I beheld, and lo a b. horse
12. the sun became b. as sackcloth of hair

BLACKER.

Lam. 4. 8. their visage is b. than a coal

BLACKISH.

Job 6. 16. which are b. by reason of the ice

BLACKNESS.

Job 3. 5. let the b. of the day terrify it
Isa. 50. 3. I clothe the heavens with b.
Lam. 4. † 8. their visage is darker than b.
Joel 2. 6. all faces shall gather b. Nah. 2. 10.
Heb. 12. 18. ye are not come to b. and darkness
Jude 13. to whom is reserved b. of darkness

BLADE.

Judg. 3. 22. the haft also went in after the b.
Job 31. 22. then let my arm fall from my shoulder-b.
Mat. 13. 26. when the b. was sprung up, Mark 4. 28.

BLAINS.

Exod. 9. 9. a boil breaking forth with b. 10.

BLAME.

Gen. 43. 9. then let me bear the b. for ever, 44. 32.
2 Cor. 8. 20. avoiding that no man should b. us
Eph. 1. 4. holy and without b. before him in love

BLAMED.

2 Cor. 6. 3. no offence, that the ministry be not b.
Gal. 2. 11. withstood him, because he was to be b.

BLAMELESS.

Gen. 44. 10. he shall be my servant, ye shall be b.
Josh. 2. 17. we will be b. of this thine oath
Judg. 15. 3. now shall I be more b. than Philistines
Mat. 12. 5. the priests profane sabbath, and are b.
Luke 1. 6. walking in ordinances of the Lord b.
1 Cor. 1. 8. that ye may be b. in the day of the Lord
Phil. 2. 15. that ye may be b. and harmless
3. 6. touching the righteousness in the law b.
1 Thess. 5. 23. spirit, soul, and body, be preserved b.
1 Tim. 3. 2. a bishop then must be b. Tit. 1. 7.
10. use the office of a deacon, being found b.
5. 7. give in charge, that they may be b.
Tit. 1. 6. if any be b. the husband of one wife
2 Pet. 3. 14. ye may be found without spot and b.

BLASPHEME

Signifies, [1] *To speak evil of God*, Rom. 2. 24, Tit. 2. 5. [2] *To rail against and deny the work of the Holy Spirit out of malice*, Mat. 12. 31.

2 Sam. 12. 14. occasion to enemies of the Lord to b.
1 Kings 21. 10. thou didst b. God and the king, 13.
Psal. 74. 10. shall the enemy b. thy name for ever?
Mark 3. 28. wherewith soever they shall b.
29. but he that shall b. against the Holy Ghost
Acts 26. 11. and I compelled them to b.
1 Tim. 1. 20. that they may learn not to b.
Jam. 2. 7. do not they b. that worthy name
Rev. 13. 6. to b. his name and his tabernacle

BLASPHEMED.

Lev. 24. 11. the Israelitish woman's son b.
2 Kings 19. 6. with which the servants of the king of Assyria have b. me, 22. Isa. 37. 6, 23.
Psal. 74. 18. the foolish people have b. thy name
Isa. 52. 5. my name continually every day is b.
65. 7. have burnt incense, and b. me on the hills
Ezek. 20. 27. in this your fathers have b. me
Acts 18. 6. when they opposed themselves and b.
Rom. 2. 24. for the name of God is b. through you
1 Tim. 6. 1. name of God and his doctrine be not b.
Tit. 2. 5. that the word of God be not b.
Rev. 16. 9. men were scorched with heat, and b.
11. b. the God of heaven because of their pains
21. men b. God because of the plague of hail

BLASPHEMEST, ETH.

Lev. 24. 16. whoso b. the Lord, be put to death
Psal. 44. 16. for the voice of him that b.
Mat. 9. 3. certain of the scribes said, this man b.
John 10. 36. whom the Father sanctified, thou b.

BLASPHEMING.

Acts 13. 45. spoken of Paul, contradicting and b.

BLASPHEMER, S.

Acts 19. 37. which are not b. of your goddess
1 Tim. 1. 13. who was before a b. and a persecutor
2 Tim. 3. 2. in the last days men shall be b.

BLASPHEMY.

2 Kings 19. 3. this day is a day of b. Isa. 37. 3.
Mat. 12. 31. all manner of b. shall be forgiven, but b. against the Holy Ghost shall not be forgiven
26. 65. he hath spoken b. behold, now ye have heard his b. Mark 14. 64.
Mark 7. 22. out of the heart of men proceed b.
John 10. 33. we stone thee not, but for b.
Col. 3. 8. but now you also put off malice, b.
Rev. 2. 9. I know b. of them that say they are Jews
13. 1. and upon his heads is the name of b.
6. and he opened his mouth in b. against God

BLASPHEMIES.

Ezek. 35. 12. know that I have heard all thy b.
Mat. 15. 19. out of the heart proceed thefts, b.
Mark 2. 7. why doth this man thus speak b.?
3. 28. and b. wherewith they shall blaspheme
Luke 5. 21. who is this which speaketh b.?
Rev. 13. 5. was a mouth given him speaking b.

BLASPHEMOUS.

Acts 6. 11. we have heard him speak b. words
13. this man ceaseth not to speak b. words

BLASPHEMOUSLY.

Luke 22. 65. many other things b. spake they

BLAST

Signifies, [1] *Wind and frosts that immediately follow rain, and are very destructive to fruits*, Gen. 41. 6. 1 Kings 8. 37. [2] *A blowing in horns*, Josh. 6. 5. [3] *God's anger and power*, Exod. 15. 8. 2 Sam. 22. 16. Job 4. 9. [4] *A violent, sudden, and terrible stroke sent by God upon the wicked*, 2 Kings 19. 7. [5] *The furious temptations of men and the devil*, Isa. 25. 4.

Exod. 15. 8. with b. of thy nostrils the waters were
Josh. 6. 5. when they make a long b. with horns
2 Sam. 22. 16. at rebuke of the Lord, at the b. of the breath of his nostrils, Psal. 18. 15.
2 Kings 19. 7. I'll send a b. on Sennacherib, Isa. 37. 7.
Job 4. 9. by the b. of God they perish
Isa. 25. 4. when the b. of the terrible is as a storm

BLASTED.

Gen. 41. 6. thin ears b. with the east wind, 23. 27.
2 Kings 19. 26. as corn b. before grown, Isa. 37. 27.

BLASTING.

Deut. 28. 22. the Lord shall smite thee with b.
1 Kings 8. 37. if there be b. mildew, 2 Chron. 6. 28.
Amos 4. 9. I have smitten you with b. and mildew
Hag. 2. 17. I smote you with b. and mildew

BLAZE.

Mark 1. 45. he began to b. abroad the matter

BLEATING, S.

Judg. 5. 16. abodest in sheepfolds to hear b. of flocks
1 Sam. 15. 14. what meaneth this b. of the sheep?

BLEMISH.

Exod. 12. 5. lamb shall be without b. a male of first year, Lev. 9. 3. | 14. 10. | 23. 12. Num. 6. 14.
29. 1. take a young bullock and two rams without b. Lev. 5. 15, 18. | 6. 6. | 9. 2. Ezek. 46. 4.
Lev. 1. 3. offer a male without b. 10. | 4. 23. | 22. 19.
3. 1. whether male or female without b. 6.
4. 3. a bullock without b. Deut. 17. 1. Ezek. 45. 18.
28. he shall bring a kid, a female without b.
21. 17. he that hath b. shall not approach, 21. 23.
22. 20. but whatsoever hath a b. that shall ye not offer, it shall not be acceptable, Deut. 15. 21.
21. in peace offering and free-will offering no b.
24. 19. if a man cause a b. in his neighbour
20. as he hath caused a b. in a man, so shall it be
Num. 19. 2. they bring a red heifer without b.
29. 2. one bullock, one ram, seven lambs without b.
2 Sam. 14. 25. there was no b. in Absalom
Dan. 1. 4. children in whom was no b.
Eph. 5. 27. that it should be holy and without b.
1 Pet. 1. 19. as of a lamb without b. and spot

BLEMISHES.

Lev. 22. 25. b. in them, they shall not be accepted
2 Pet. 2. 13. spots they are and b. sporting

BLESS

Is referred, I. *To God; and* signifies, [1] *To bestow plenty of temporal good things upon a person, and make his affairs prosperous and successful*, Gen. 30. 27. | 39. 5. [2] *To bestow both temporal and spiritual blessings upon a person*, Gen. 12. 2. | 24. 35. Eph. 1. 3. [3] *To make one perfectly happy in the full enjoyment of himself in heaven*, Rev. 14. 13. [4] *To consecrate and set apart any thing for an holy and sacred use*, Gen. 2. 3. Exod. 20. 11. [5] *To give power of procreation and fruitfulness, so as the creatures might multiply their kind*, Gen. 1. 22. [6] *To endue one with an heroic spirit, singular valour, miraculous strength of body, and all other gifts and graces necessary to his calling*, Judg. 13. 24. II. *To Christ; and* signifies, [1] *To give thanks to God the Father in a special manner, and pray for his blessing, thereby paying the homage of his human nature to his Father*, Mat. 14. 19. Mark 6. 41. [2] *To commend others to God in prayer, as he was man*, Mark 10. 16. [3] *Powerfully and effectually to work on men for their conversion, so as to save them from their sins*, Acts 3. 26. III. *To men; and* signifies, [1] *To extol and praise God for the infinite excellencies and perfections of his nature*, Psal. 104. 1. | 148. 1, 2. [2] *To give thanks to God for his mercies and benefits to us*, Psal. 16. 7. | 103. 1, 2. [3] *To pronounce a solemn, extraordinary, and prophetical benediction upon a person, whereby the holy patriarchs, by God's appointment, and with his concurrence, did declare and constitute one of their sons as heir, not only of their inheritance, but of the promises and blessings of the covenant which God made with them and their fathers; both praying for, and foretelling, those blessings which God would confer upon them*, Gen. 27. 4, 25, 30. [4] *To salute persons, to wish them peace and prosperity*, Gen. 47. 7. 1 Sam. 13. † 10. Psal. 129. 8. [5] *To pray to God in behalf of others, that he may bestow his blessing upon them*, Num. 6. 23, 24. 2 Sam. 6. 18. Luke 6. 28. [6] *To account and reckon oneself happy in having God for his God*, Isa. 65. 16. Jer. 4. 2. [7] *To applaud oneself as a wise and happy person, taking outward prosperity for an argument of God's love and favour*, Psal. 49. 18. [8] *To flatter oneself with the hopes of impunity, as if God did not take notice of sin, and either could not, or would not, punish sinners*, Deut. 29. 19.

God hath promised to bless, [1] *Such as put their trust in him*, Psal. 2. 12. [2] *Such as fear him, and walk in his ways*, Psal. 128. 1. [3] *Such as God chooses and causes to draw nigh to him in the duties of his worship*, Psal. 65. 4. [4] *Such as have the saving knowledge of Jesus Christ wrought in them by the Spirit of God*, Mat. 16. 17. [5] *Such as mourn for their sins and spiritual wants*, Mat. 5. 4. [6] *Such as are humble and lowly in mind, affection, and conversation, who are sensible of their lost and undone condition in themselves, and of their own inability to help themselves*, Mat. 5. 3. [7] *Such as are gentle, patient, and quiet-spirited; who murmur not against God, but submit to all his corrections; and who quarrel not with, nor revenge themselves of, those that wrong them*, Mat. 5. 5. [8] *Such as hunger and thirst after Christ and his benefits; after freedom from sin, and holiness of life*, Mat. 5. 6. [9] *Such who, being inwardly affected with the miseries of others, do relieve them according to their ability*, Mat. 5. 7. [10] *Such as love and labour for peace among all that are at odds, whether with God, with themselves, or one with another*, Mat. 5. 9. [11] *Such as are sincere, whose hearts and course of life agree with their profession*, Psal. 119. 1. [12] *Such as do not associate themselves with the wicked, nor follow their evil instigations or examples*, Psal. 1. 1. [13] *Such whose transgressions are forgiven, whose sin is pardoned*, Psal. 32. 1. [14] *Such as do not censure or condemn a person under sickness or affliction, as if he was wicked or hated of God, but pity and relieve him*, Psal. 41. 1.

BLESS, *God being agent.*

Gen. 12. 2. the Lord said, I will b. thee, 26. 3, 24.
3. I will b. them that bless thee, and curse him
17. 16. I will b. her, and give thee a son of her

Gen. 22. 17. in blessing I will b. thee, Heb. 6. 14.
28. 3. God almighty b. thee, and multiply thee
32. 26. I will not let thee go, except thou b. me
48. 16. b. the lads, and let my name be named
49. 25. by the Almighty who shall b. thee
Exod. 20. 24. I will come to thee, and I will b. thee
23. 25. he shall b. thy bread and thy water
Num. 6. 24. the Lord b. thee and keep thee
27. put my name on Israel, and I will b. them
24. 1. saw that it pleased the Lord to b. Israel
Deut. 1. 11. and b. you as he hath promised you
7. 13. he will b. thee, b. the fruit of thy womb
14. 29. that the Lord may b. thee, 23. 20. | 24. 19.
15. 4. shall be no poor, for the Lord shall b. thee
10. for this thing the Lord thy God shall b. thee
18. the Lord thy God shall b. thee in all, 30. 16.
16. 15. because the Lord shall b. thee in all
26. 15. look down and b. thy people Israel
28. 8. he shall b. thee in the land he giveth
12. and to b. all the work of thine hand
33. 11. b. Lord, his substance, and accept
Ruth 2. 4. saying, the Lord b. thee, Jer. 31. 23.
2 Sam. 7. 29. therefore now let it please thee to b.
the house of thy servant, 1 Chron. 17. 27.
1 Chron. 4. 10. O that thou wouldest b. me indeed
Psal. 5. 12. thou, Lord, wilt b. the righteous
28. 9. save thy people, b. thine inheritance
29. 11. the Lord will b. his people with peace
67. 1. God, even our own God, shall b. us, 6, 7.
115. 12. the Lord will b. us, he will b. the house
of Israel, he will b. the house of Aaron
13. he will b. them that fear the Lord
128. 5. the Lord shall b. thee out of Zion
132. 15. I will abundantly b. her provision
134. 3. the Lord b. thee out of Zion
Isa. 19. 25. whom the Lord of hosts shall b.
Hag. 2. 19. from this day will I b. you
Acts 3. 26. sent him to b. you in turning you

BLESS, *God being the object.*

Deut. 8. 10. art full, then thou shalt b. the Lord
Judg. 5. 9. b. ye the Lord, Psal. 103. 21. | 134. 1.
1 Chron. 29. 20. David said, now b. Lord your God
Neh. 9. 5. stand up and b. Lord for ever and ever
Psal. 16. 7. I will b. Lord who hath given me counsel
26. 12. in the congregations will I b. the Lord
34. 1. I will b. the Lord at all times
63. 4. thus will I b. thee while I live
66. 8. O b. our God, make his praise to be heard
68. 26. b. ye God in the congregations, even
96. 2. sing to the Lord, b. his name, shew forth
100. 4. be thankful to him, b. his name, 103. 1.
103. 1. b. the Lord, O my soul, 2. 22. | 104. 1, 35.
20. b. the Lord, ye his angels || 21. b. ye his hosts
22. b. the Lord all his works in all places
115. 18. we will b. the Lord from this time
134. 2. lift up your hands, and b. the Lord
135. 19. b. the Lord, O house of Israel, b. the
Lord, O house of Aaron
20. O Levi, ye that fear the Lord, b. the Lord
145. 1. I will b. thy name for ever and ever
2. every day will I b. thee, and praise thy name
10. O Lord, thy saints shall b. thee
21. let all flesh b. his holy name for ever
Jam. 3. 9. therewith b. we God, even the Father

BLESS, *man agent and object.*

Gen. 27. 4. my soul may b. thee before I die, 25.
31. b. me, even me also, O my father, 38.
48. 9. bring them to me, and I will b. them
20. in thee shall Israel b. saying, God make thee
Exod. 12. 32. take flocks and begone, and b. me also
Num. 6. 23. on this wise ye shall b. Israel
23. 20. I have received commandment to b.
25. neither curse them nor b. them at all
Deut. 10. 8. the Lord separated Levi to b. 21. 5.
24. 13. sleep in his own raiment, and b. thee
27. 12. these shall stand on mount Gerizim, to b.
29. 19. heareth words of this curse, he b. himself
Josh. 8. 33. as Moses commanded they should b.
1 Sam. 9. 13. because he doth b. the sacrifice
13. †10. Saul went to meet Samuel to b. him
2 Sam. 6. 20. then David returned to b. his household, 1 Chron. 16. 43.
8. 10. Toi sent Joram his son to b. David
21. 3. that ye may b. the inheritance of the Lord
1 Kings 1. 47. servants came to b. our Lord k. David
1 Chron. 23. 13. and to b. in his name for ever
Psal. 62. 4. they b. with their mouths, but curse
109. 28. let them curse, but b. thou
129. 8. we b. you in the name of the Lord
Prov. 30. 11. there is a generation that curseth their
father, and doth not b. their mother
Isa. 65. 16. shall b. himself in the God of truth
Jer. 4. 2. the nations shall b. themselves in him
Mat. 5. 44. b. them that curse you, Luke 6. 28.
Rom. 12. 14. b. those persecute you, b. and curse not
1 Cor. 4. 12. being reviled we b. being persecuted
14. 16. else when thou shalt b. with the spirit

BLESS.

1 Cor. 10. 16. the cup of blessing which we b.

BLESSED, *man agent and object.*

Gen. 14. 19. Melchisedek b. Abram, and said, b. be
24. 60. they b. Rebekah, and said unto her
27. 23. so Isaac b. Jacob, and said, 27.
29. and b. be he that blesseth thee
33. I have b. him, yea, and he shall be b.
41. the blessing wherewith his father b. him
28. 1. Isaac called Jacob, b. him, and charged him
6. as he b. him he gave him a charge, Heb. 11. 20.
30. 13. for the daughters will call me b.
31. 55. kissed his sons and daughters, and b. them
47. 7. Jacob b. Pharaoh, 10. || 48. 15. he b. Joseph
48. 20. Jacob b. Manasseh and Ephraim, Heb. 11. 21.
49. 28. Jacob b. his sons, every one he b.
Exod. 39. 43. and Moses b. them, Deut. 33. 1.
Lev. 9. 22. Aaron lift up his hands and b. them
23. Moses and Aaron b. the people
Num. 22. 6. I wot that he whom thou blessest is b.
23. 11. thou hast b. them altogether, 24. 10.
Deut. 33. 20. b. be he that enlargeth Gad
24. let Asher be b. with children
Josh. 14. 13. Joshua b. Caleb, and gave him Hebron
22. 6. Joshua b. them, and sent them away, 7.
Josh. 24. 10. therefore Balaam b. you still
Judg. 5. 24. b. above women shall Jael be
Ruth 2. 19. b. be he that took knowledge of thee
1 Sam. 2. 20. Eli b. Elkanah and his wife Hannah
25. 33. b. be thy advice, and b. be thou who kept
26. 25. Saul said, b. be thou, my son David
2 Sam. 6. 18. David b. the people, 1 Chron. 16. 2.
13. 25. howbeit he would not go, but b. him
19. 39. the king kissed Barzillai, and b. him
1 Kings 2. 45. and king Solomon shall be b.
8. 14. king Solomon b. all the congregation, 55.
66. congregation b. Solomon, 2 Chron. 6. 3.
2 Chron. 30. 27. priests and Levites b. the people
Neh. 11. 2. people b. all that willingly offered
Job 29. 11. when the ear heard me, it b. me
31. 20. if his loins have not b. me
Psal. 49. 18. while he lived he b. his soul
72. 17. men shall be b. in him, nations call him b.
118. 26. b. be he that cometh in name of the Lord,
we have b. you out of house of the Lord
Prov. 31. 28. her children arise, and call her b.
Eccl. 10. 17. b. art thou, O land, when thy king
Cant. 6. 9. the daughters saw her, and b. her
Isa. 66. 3. that burneth incense, as if he b. an idol
Jer. 20. 14. let not the day my mother bare me be b.
Mal. 3. 12. and all nations shall call you b.
Mark 11. 10. b. be the kingdom of our father
Luke 1. 48. all generations shall call me b.
2. 34. Simeon b. them, and said to Mary
Acts 20. 35. it is more b. to give than to receive
Tit. 2. 13. looking for that b. hope and appearing
Heb. 7. 1. Melchisedek met Abraham and b. him, 6.
7. without contradiction the less is b. of the better

BLESSED, *God the agent.*

Gen. 1. 22. God b. them, saying, be fruitful, 28. | 5. 2.
2. 3. and God b. the seventh day, Exod. 20. 11.
9. 1. and God b. Noah and his sons, and said to them
12. 3. in thee shall all families be b. 18. 18. | 22.
18. | 26. 4. | 28. 14. Acts 3. 25. Gal. 3. 8.
17. 20. I have b. Ishmael || 24. 1. Lord b. Abraham
24. 31. and he said, come in thou b. of the Lord
25. 11. after death of Abraham, God b. Isaac, 26. 12.
26. 29. thou art now the b. of the Lord
27. 27. the smell of a field which the Lord hath b.
30. 27. that the Lord hath b. me for thy sake
30. the Lord hath b. thee since my coming
32. 29. and he b. Jacob there, 35. 9. | 48. 3.
39. 5. that the Lord b. the Egyptian's house
Num. 22. 12. shalt not curse, for the people are b.
23. 20. he hath b. and I cannot reverse it
Deut. 2. 7. thy God hath b. thee, 12. 7. | 15. 14. | 16.
7. 14. thou shalt be b. above all people [10.
14. 24. if place be too far, when the Lord hath b.
28. 3. b. shalt thou be in the city, b. in the field
4. b. shall be fruit of thy body || 5. b. thy basket
33. 13. of Joseph he said, b. of the Lord be his
Josh. 17. 14. forasmuch as the Lord hath b. me
Judg. 13. 24. Samson grew, and the Lord b. him
17. 2. b. be thou of Lord, Ruth 3. 10. 1 Sam. 15. 13.
Ruth 2. 20. b. be he of the Lord who hath not
3. 10. b. be thou of the Lord, my daughter
1 Sam. 23. 21. b. be ye of the Lord, 2 Sam. 2. 5.
2 Sam. 6. 11. the Lord b. Obed-edom, and all his
household, 12. 1 Chron. 13. 14. | 26. 5.
7. 29. the house of thy servant be b. for ever
1 Chron. 17. 27. blessest, O Lord, and it shall be b.
2 Chron. 31. 10. the Lord hath b. his people
Job 1. 10. thou hast b. the work of his hands
42. 12. the Lord b. the latter end of Job
Psal. 21. 6. for thou hast made him most b.
33. 12. b. is the nation whose God is the Lord
37. 22. for such as be b. of him shall inherit
26. he is merciful and lendeth, and his seed is b.
41. 2. the Lord will keep him, and he shall be b.
45. 2. therefore God hath b. thee for ever
89. 15. b. is the people that know the joyful sound
112. 2. the generation of the upright shall be b.
115. 15. you are b. of the Lord who made heaven
119. 1. b. are the undefiled in the way
128. 1. b. is every one that feareth the Lord
4. thus shall the man be b. that feareth the Lord
147. 13. he hath b. thy children within thee
Prov. 5. 18. let thy fountain be b. and rejoice
10. 7. the memory of the just is b.
20. 7. the just man's children are b. after him
21. but the end thereof shall not be b.
22. 9. he that hath a bountiful eye shall be b.
Isa. 19. 25. saying, b. be Egypt my people
51. 2. for I called him alone and b. him
61. 9. they are the seed the Lord hath b. 65. 23.
Mat. 5. 3. b. are the poor in spirit || 5. b. are the meek
7. b. are the merciful || 8. b. are the pure in heart
9. b. are the peace-makers || 10. b. are persecuted
13. 16. b. are your eyes, for they see, Luke 10. 23.
14. 19. he b. and brake, and gave the loaves, 26. 26.
Mark 6. 41. | 14. 22. Luke 9. 16. | 24. 30.
16. 17. Jesus said, b. art thou, Simon Bar-jona
24. 46. b. is that servant, Luke 12. 43.
25. 34. come, ye b. of my Father, inherit kingdom
Mark 10. 16. took them up in his arms, and b. them
14. 61. thou art Christ, the Son of the b.
Luke 1. 28. b. art thou among women, 42.
45. b. is she that believed || 6. 20. b. be ye poor
11. 27. b. is the womb that bare thee, and paps
12. 37. b. are those servants whom the Lord when
he cometh shall find watching, 38.
14. 14. thou shalt be b. they cannot recompense
19. 38. b. be the King that cometh in name of Lord
23. 29. b. are the barren that never bare
24. 50. he b. them || 51. while he b. them
Gal. 3. 9. they are b. with faithful Abraham
Eph. 1. 3. who hath b. us with spiritual blessings
Jam. 1. 25. this man shall be b. in his deed
Rev. 14. 13. b. are the dead that die in the Lord

BLESSED, *God the object.*

Gen. 9. 26. he said, b. be the Lord, 24. 27. Exod.
18. 10. Ruth 4. 14. 1 Sam. 25. 32, 39. 2 Sam.
18. 28. 1 Kings 1. 48. | 5. 7. | 8. 15, 56. | 10. 9.
1 Chron. 16. 36. 2 Chron. 2. 12. | 6. 4. | 9. 8.
Ezra 7. 27. Psal. 28. 6. | 31. 21. | 41. 13. | 68.
19. | 72. 18. | 89. 52. | 106. 48. | 124. 6. | 135.
21. | 144. 1. Zech. 11. 5. Luke 1. 68.
Gen. 14. 20. b. be most high God who delivered
Josh. 22. 33. and the children of Israel b. God
2 Sam. 22. 47. and b. be my rock, Psal. 18. 46.
1 Chr. 29. 10. David b. the Lord, b. thou, O Lord
20. all the congregation b. the Lord God
2 Chron. 20. 26. for there they b. the Lord
31. 8. when they saw the heaps, they b. the Lord
Neh. 8. 6. and Ezra b. the Lord, the great God
9. 5. b. be thy glorious name, Psal. 72. 19.
Job 1. 21. b. be the name of the Lord, Psal. 113. 2.
Psal. 66. 20. b. be God, 68. 35. 2 Cor. 1. 3.
119. 12. b. art thou, O Lord, teach me thy statutes
Ezek. 3. 12. saying, b. be the glory of the Lord
Dan. 2. 19. Daniel b. the God of heaven, 20.
4. 34. Nebuchadnezzar b. the most High
Luke 2. 28. took him in his arms and b. God
John 12. 13. b. is the King of Israel that cometh
Rom. 1. 25. than the Creator, who is b. for ever
9. 5. Christ, who is over all, God b. for ever
2 Cor. 11. 31. is b. for evermore, knoweth I lie not
Eph. 1. 3. b. be the Father of our Lord, 1 Pet. 1. 3.
1 Tim. 1. 11. the glorious gospel of the b. God
6. 15. who is the b. and only Potentate

BLESSED *are they.*

Psal. 2. 12. b. are they that put their trust in him
84. 4. b. are they that dwell in thy house
106. 3. b. are they that keep judgment at all times
119. 2. b. are they that keep his testimonies
Prov. 8. 32. for b. are they that keep my ways
Isa. 30. 18. b. are they that wait for him
Mat. 5. 4. b. are they that mourn, shall be comforted
6. b. are they who hunger || 10. who are persecuted
Luke 11. 28. yea, rather b. are they that hear the word
John 20. 29. b. are they that have not seen, believed
Rom. 4. 7. b. are they whose iniquities are forgiven
Rev. 19. 9. b. are they who are called to the marriage
supper
22. 14. b. are they that do his commandments

BLESSED *are ye.*

Isa. 32. 20. b. are ye that sow beside all waters
Mat. 5. 11. b. are ye when men shall revile you
Luke 6. 21. b. are ye that hunger now, ye shall be
filled; b. are ye that weep now, for ye shall laugh
22. b. are ye when men shall hate you

BLESSED *is he.*

Num. 24. 9. b. is he that blesseth thee, and cursed
Psal. 32. 1. b. is he whose transgression is forgiven
41. 1. b. is he that considereth the poor
Dan. 12. 12. b. is he that waiteth, cometh to days
Mat. 11. 6. and b. is he whosoever shall not be
offended in me, Luke 7. 23.
21. 9. b. is he that cometh in the name of the Lord,
23. 39. Mark 11. 9. Luke 13. 35.
Luke 14. 15. b. is he that shall eat bread in kingdom
Rev. 1. 3. b. is he that readeth, and they that hear
16. 15. b. is he that watcheth, and keepeth
20. 6. b. is he that hath part in the first resurrection
22. 7. b. is he that keepeth sayings of the prophecy

BLESSED *is the man.*

Psal. 1. 1. b. is the man that walketh not in counsel
32. 2. b. is the man to whom the Lord imputeth
not iniquity, Rom. 4. 8.
34. 8. b. is man that trusteth in him, 84. 12. Jer. 17. 7.
40. 4. b. is the man that maketh the Lord his trust
65. 4. b. is the man whom thou choosest, and causest
84. 5. b. is the man whose strength is in thee
94. 12. b. is the man whom thou chastenest, O Lord
112. 1. b. is the man that feareth Lord, that delights
Prov. 8. 34. b. is the man that heareth me, watching
Isa. 56. 2. b. is the man that doth this, and son of man
Jam. 1. 12. b. is the man that endureth temptation

BLESSEDNESS.

Rom. 4. 6. even as David describeth the b.
9. cometh this b. on the circumcision only?
Gal. 4. 15. where is then the b. ye spake of?

BLESSEST.

Num. 22. 6. I wot that he whom thou b. is blessed
1 Chr. 17. 27. thou b. O Lord, and it shall be blessed
Psal. 65. 10. thou b. the springing thereof

BLESSETH.

Gen. 27. 29. blessed is he that b. thee, Num. 24. 9.
Deut. 15. 6. thy God b. thee as he promised
Psal. 10. 3. b. covetous whom the Lord abhorreth
107. 38. he b. them so that they are multiplied
Prov. 3. 33. but he b. the habitation of the just
27. 14. he that b. his friend with a loud voice
Isa. 65. 16. he who b. himself in the earth

BLESSING

Signifies, [1] *The favour, kindness, and goodness of God, making what his people do to succeed and prosper,* Psal. 3. 8. [2] *All good things, gifts, graces, and privileges, which God bestows upon his people, whether spiritual or temporal, whether they respect the soul, or the body, this present life, or that which is to come,* Deut. 28. 2. Psal. 24. 5. Isa. 44. 3. Eph. 1. 3. [3] *The means of conveying a blessing to others,* Isa. 19. 24. *Thus the Jews are called a* Blessing, *because Christ was to be born of them, and the gospel-church and ordinances were first established among them, and by them conveyed to the Gentiles.* [4] *Wishing, praying for, and endeavouring the good of our enemies,* 1 Pet. 3. 9. [5] *Alms, bounty, or liberality,* 2 Cor. 9. †5. [6] *A gift, or present,* Gen. 33. 11. 2 Kings 5. 15.

Thou shalt be a blessing, Gen. 12. 2. *Thou shalt be a means of conveying blessedness,* [1] *To thy posterity, who shall be blessed for thy sake.* [2] *To thy friends and servants, who shall be blessed by thy instruction and example.* [3] *To all the world, by being the progenitor of* Christ, *and an eminent pattern of faith and holiness to all.*

Leave a blessing behind him, Joel 2. 14. *Reserve some of the fruits of the earth from the common destruction, for their support, and his own worship.*

The blessing of Abraham, Gal. 3. 14. *The blessing conferred on Abraham, namely, justification and reconciliation with God, through faith in the blood of Christ.*

Gen. 12. 2. I will bless thee, thou shalt be a b.
22. 17. that in b. I will bless thee, Heb. 6. 14.
27. 12. I shall bring a curse on me, and not a b.
35. thy brother hath taken away thy b.

Gen. 27. 38. Esau said, hast thou but one b. my father?
28. 4. God give thee the b. of Abraham
33. 11. take, I pray thee, my b. that is brought
39. 5. the b. of the Lord was on all that he had
49. 28. every one according to his b. he blessed
Exod. 32. 29. then he may bestow on you a b.
Lev. 25. 21. then will I command my b. on you
Deut. 11. 26. behold, I set before you a b. 30. 19.
27. a b. if ye obey the commandments of the Lord
29. thou shalt put the b. on mount Gerizim
12. 15. according to the b. of the Lord, 16. 17.
23. 5. the Lord turned the curse into a b.
28. 8. Lord shall command a b. on store house
33. 1. this is the b. wherewith Moses blessed, 7.
16. let the b. come upon the head of Joseph
23. Naphtali full with the b. of the Lord
Josh. 15. 19. answered, give me a b. Judg. 1. 15.
1 Sam. 25. 27. this b. thy handmaid hath brought
30. † 26. behold a b. for you from the spoil
2 Sam. 7. 29. with thy b. let my house be blessed
2 Kings 5. 15. I pray thee take a b. of thy servant
18. † 31. make with me a b. and come out to me, and eat of his own vine, Isa. 36. 16.
Neh. 9. 5. which is exalted above all b. and praise
13. 2. our God turned the curse into a b.
Job 29. 13. the b. of him that was ready to perish
Psal. 3. 8. thy b. is upon thy people
24. 5. he shall receive the b. from the Lord
109. 17. as he delighted not in b. let it be far
129. 8. the b. of the Lord be upon you
133. 3. there Lord commanded the b. even life
Prov. 10. 22. the b. of the Lord maketh rich
11. 11. by the b. of the upright the city is exalted
† 25. the soul of b. shall be made fat
26. but a b. on the head of him that selleth it
24. 25. a good b. shall come on them that rebuke
Isa. 19. 24. even a b. in the midst of the land
44. 3. and I will pour my b. on thy offspring
65. 8. destroy it not, for a b. is in it
Ezek. 34. 26. I will make them and the places about my hill a b. there shall be showers of b.
44. 30. he may cause the b. to rest in thy house
Joel 2. 14. if he will leave a b. behind him
Zech. 8. 13. I will save you, and ye shall be a b.
Mal. 3. 10. open heaven, and pour you out a b.
Luke 24. 53. in the temple praising and b. God
Rom. 15. 29. in the fulness of the b. of the gospel
1 Cor. 10. 16. the cup of b. which we bless
Gal. 3. 14. that the b. of Abraham might come
2 Cor. 9. 5. make up beforehand your b.
Heb. 6. 7. for the earth receiveth b. from God
12. 17. when he would have inherited the b.
Jam. 3. 10. of the same mouth proceed b. and cursing
1 Pet. 3. 9. but contrariwise b. knowing that ye are thereunto called, that ye should inherit a b.
Rev. 5. 12. worthy to receive honour, glory, b.
13. b. to him that sitteth on the throne
7. 12. b. and glory to our God for ever and ever

BLESSINGS.

Gen. 49. 25. Almighty who shall bless thee with b. of heaven above, b. of the deep, b. of the breasts
26. b. of thy father prevailed above the b. of my
Deut. 28. 2. all these b. shall come on thee, if [hearken
Josh. 8. 34. afterwards he read the b. and cursings
Psal. 21. 3. for thou preventest him with the b.
† 6. thou hast set him to be b. for e er
Prov. 10. 6. b. are upon the head of the just
28. 20. a faithful man shall abound with b.
Mal. 2. 2. I will send a curse, and will curse your b.
Eph. 1. 3. who hath blessed us with all spiritual b.

BLEW, *Verb.*

Josh. 6. 8. priests passed on before the Lord and b.
Judg. 3. 27. Ehud b. a trumpet in the mount
6. 34. Spirit come on Gideon, and he b. a trumpet
7. 19. they b. the trumpets and brake, 20, 22.
1 Sam. 13. 3. Saul b. saying, let the Hebrews hear
2 Sam. 2. 28. Joab b. a trumpet, 18. 16. | 20. 22.
20. 1. Sheba a Benjamite b. a trumpet and said
1 Kings 1. 39. they b. the trumpet, people said, God save king Solomon, 2 Kings 9. 13. | 11. 14.
Mat. 7. 25. winds b. and beat on that house, 27.
John 6. 18. the sea arose by a great wind that b.
Acts 27. 13. when the south-wind b. 28. 13.

BLIND

Signifies, [1] *Such as are deprived of natural sight,* John 9. 1. Acts 13. 11. [2] *Such whose judgments are so corrupted by taking of gifts, that they cannot or will not discern between right and wrong,* Exod. 23. 8. Deut. 16. 19. [3] *Such as are wilfully and obstinately ignorant, in matters that concern salvation,* Mat. 15. 14. [4] *Such as through simplicity and ignorance are easily misled and seduced by the pernicious counsel of others,* Deut. 27. 18. Mat. 15. 14.

It is applied, [1] *To ignorant ministers,* Isa. 56. 10. [2] *To deceitful teachers, who are blinded by their own interest against any conviction,* Isa. 42. 19. Mat. 23. 16. [3] *To an ignorant people,* Mat. 15. 14. Rom. 2. 19. [4] *To such as reject the knowledge and faith of Christ, notwithstanding the clear discoveries of the way of salvation in the gospel,* 2 Cor. 4. 4. [5] *To such as live in hatred,* 1 John 2. 11. [6] *To such as are self-conceited, being puffed up with an high opinion of their qualifications and attainments,* Rev. 3. 17.

Exod. 4. 11. who maketh the seeing or the b.?
Lev. 19. 14. not put a stumbling-block before b.
21. 18. a b. or lame man shall not offer
22. 22. not offer the b. to the Lord, Deut. 15. 21.
Deut. 27. 18. cursed that maketh the b. to wander
28. 29. grope at noon-day, as b. gropeth in darkness
2 Sam. 5. 6. except thou take away the b. and lame
8. smiteth the lame and b. hated of David, the b. and the lame shall not come into house
Job 29. 15. I was eyes to the b. feet to the lame
Psal. 146. 8. the Lord openeth the eyes of the b.
Isa. 29. 18. the eyes of the b. shall see, 35. 5.
42. 7. give thee for a light to open the b. eyes
16. I will bring the b. by a way they knew not
18. hear, ye deaf, look, ye b. that ye may see

Isa. 42. 19. who is b. but my servant? who is b. as he that is perfect, and b. as the Lord's servant?
43. 8. bring forth the b. people that have eyes
56. 10. his watchmen are b. they are all ignorant
59. 10. we grope for the wall like the b.
Jer. 31. 8. I will gather with them the b. and lame
Lam. 4. 14. they wandered as b. men in the streets
Zeph. 1. 17. that they shall walk like b. men
Mal. 1. 8. if ye offer the b. for sacrifice is it not evil?
Mat. 9. 27. two b. men followed him, crying, 20. 30.
11. 5. the b. receive their sight, 12. 22. Luke 7. 22.
15. 14. they be b. leaders of the b. if the b. lead the b. both shall fall into the ditch, Luke 6. 39.
23. 16. wo to you, ye b. guides, which say
17. ye fools and b. whether is greater, 19.
26. thou b. Pharisee, cleanse first within
Mark 8. 23. and he took the b. man by the hand
10. 46. b. Bartimeus sat by the way side begging
Luke 4. 18. to preach recovery of sight to the b.
7. 21. to many that were b. he gave sight
14. 13. when thou makest a feast, call the b.
John 5. 3. in these lay a great multitude of b.
9. 1. he saw a man that was b. from his birth
39. that they which see might be made b.
40. are we b. also? || 41. if ye were b.
10. 21. can a devil open the eyes of the b.?
Acts 13. 11. thou shalt be b. not seeing the sun
Rom. 2. 19. art confident thou art a guide to the b.
2 Pet. 1. 9. but he that lacketh these things is b.
Rev. 3. 17. and knowest not that thou art b.

BLIND, *Verb.*

Deut. 16. 19. a gift doth b. the eyes of the wise
1 Sam. 12. 3. of whom received I a bribe to b.

BLINDED, ETH.

Exod. 23. 8. take no gift, for a gift b. the wise
Jer. 52. † 11. then he b. the eyes of Zedekiah
John 12. 40. he hath b. their eyes, and hardened
Rom. 11. 7. election hath obtained, the rest are b.
2 Cor. 3. 14. but their minds were b.
4. 4. in whom god of this world hath b. the minds
1 John 2. 11. because darkness hath b. his eyes

BLINDFOLDED.

Luke 22. 64. when they had b. him, they struck

BLINDNESS.

Gen. 19. 11. smote the men at the door with b.
Deut. 28. 28. the Lord shall smite thee with b.
2 Kings 6. 18. Elisha prayed, smite this people, I pray thee, with b. and he smote them with b.
Zech. 12. 4. I will smite every horse with b.
Mark 3. † 5. being grieved for their b. of heart
Rom. 11. 25. b. in part has happened to Israel
Eph. 4. 18. because of the b. of their heart

BLOCK. *See* STUMBLING.

BLOOD

Signifies, [1] *A warm red liquor or humour circulating through the whole body,* Exod. 29. 12. [2] *Death, slaughter, or murder, together with the guilt following upon it,* Gen. 4. 10. Mat. 27. 24. [3] *The punishment or vengeance due for the shedding of blood,* Mat. 27. 25. [4] *That which was bought or purchased with the price of blood,* Acts 1. 19. [5] *Wealth, goods, or money got by taking away the lives of the innocent, and then seizing upon their estates,* Nah. 3. 10. Hab. 2. 12. [6] *The guilt and punishment of sin,* Acts 18. 6. [7] *Fallen nature,* Ezek. 16. 6. John 1. 13. [8] *The first man Adam, who was the root or stock from which all mankind descended,* Acts 17. 26. [9] *Human reason or wisdom,* Mat. 16. 17. [10] *The juice of grapes,* Gen. 49. 11. [11] *A sacramental symbol and representation of the blood of Christ,* Mat. 26. 28. [12] *The death and sufferings of Christ,* Rom. 3. 25. | 5. 9. Eph. 1. 7.

The blood of the covenant, Heb. 10. 29. *The blood of Christ, whereby the new covenant or testament was confirmed and ratified.*

Where mark'd with † it is in the Original BLOODS.

Gen. 4. † 10. the voice of thy brother's b. crieth
9. 4. the life which is the b. shall you not eat
5. surely your b. of your lives will I require
37. 31. they killed a kid and dipped the coat in b.
Exod. 4. 9. water shall become b. on the dry land
7. 17. and the waters shall be turned into b.
12. 13. the b. shall be for a token, when I see b.
23. 18. shalt not offer the b. with leaven, 34. 25.
29. 21. thou shalt take of the b. upon the altar
Lev. 10. 18. the b. of it was not brought in
15. 19. and if the issue in her flesh shall be b.
17. 4. b. shall be imputed unto that man
11. for it is the b. that maketh an atonement
19. 16. not stand against the b. of thy neighbour
Num. 23. 24. and drink the b. of the slain
35. 33. not cleansed but by the b. of him that shed it
Deut. 17. 8. matter between b. and b. 2 Chron. 19. 10.
21. 8. and the b. shall be forgiven them
22. 8. make a battlement, that thou bring not b.
32. 43. he will avenge the b. of his servants
Judg. 9. 24. and their b. be laid upon Abimelech
1 Sam. 26. 20. let not my b. fall to the earth
2 Sam. 1. 16. David said, thy b. be upon thy head
22. from the b. of the slain, from the fat
3. † 28. I and my kingdom guiltless from the b.
16. † 7. come out, come out, thou man of b.
8. the Lord hath returned upon thee all the b.
20. 12. Amasa wallowed in b. in the highway
23. 17. is not this the b. of the men? 1 Chr. 11. 19.
1 Kings 2. 5. and put the b. of war on his girdle
37. thy b. shall be on thy own head, Ezek. 33. 4.
18. 28. till the b. gushed out upon them
2 Kings 3. 22. the Moabites saw the waters red as b.
23. they said, this is b. the kings are surely slain
9. † 26. I have seen the b. of Naboth, b. of his sons
Job 16. 18. O earth, cover not thou my b.
39. 30. the eagles' young ones also suck up b.
Psal. 30. 9. what profit is there in my b.?
50. 13. or will I drink the b. of goats?
58. 10. righteous wash his feet in the b. of wicked
68. 23. foot may be dipped in the b. of thy enemy
72. 14. precious shall their b. be in his sight
Prov. 28. 17. that doth violence to the b. of any
Isa. 1. † 15. your hands are full of b.

Isa. 4. 4. the Lord shall purge the b. of Jerusalem
9. 5. with noise, and garments rolled in b. wash ye
15. 9. the waters of Dimon shall be full of b.
26. † 21. the earth shall disclose her b.
33. † 15. that stoppeth his ear from hearing b.
34. 3. the mountains shall be melted with their b.
Jer. 2. 34. is found the b. of the poor innocents
18. 21. pour out their b. by the force of the sword
48. 10. cursed be he that keepeth his sword from b.
51. 35. my b. be on the inhabitants of Chaldea
Lam. 4. 14. they have polluted themselves with b.
Ezek. 5. 17. pestilence and b. pass through thee
9. 9. the land is full of b. and the city is full of
14. 19. or if I pour out my fury upon it in b.
16. 6. I said to thee when thou wast in thy b. live
† 9. I thoroughly washed away thy b. from thee
38. I will give thee b. in fury and jealousy
18. 10. if he beget a son that is a shedder of b.
† 13. he shall die, his b. shall be upon him
19. 10. thy mother is like a vine in thy b.
21. 32. thy b. shall be in the midst of the land, 22. 13.
22. 3. the city sheddeth b. in the midst of it
23. 37. and b. is in their hands, 45.
24. 8. I have set her b. on the top of a rock
28. 23. for I will send b. into her streets
32. 6. I will also water with thy b. the land
35. 6. saith the Lord, I will prepare thee to b, thou hast not hated b. even b. shall pursue thee
44. 7. when ye offer my bread, the fat and the b. 15.
Hos. 1. 4. for yet I will avenge the b. of Jezreel
4. † 2. they break out, and b. toucheth b.
Joel 2. 30. b. fire, and pillars of smoke, Acts 2. 19.
31. the moon shall be turned into b. Acts 2. 20.
3. 21. I will cleanse their b. that I have not cleansed
Zeph. 1. 17. their b. shall be poured out as dust
Mat. 9. 20. behold a woman diseased with an issue of b. twelve years, Mark 5. 25. Luke 8. 43.
16. 17. flesh and b. hath not revealed it to thee
23. 30. not partakers in the b. of the prophets
35. from the b. of righteous Abel, Luke 11. 51.
26. 28. my b. of the new testament, Mark 14. 24.
27. 6. not to put into treasury, because it is price of b.
8. was called the field of b. to this day, Acts 1. 19.
24. I am innocent of the b. of this just person
Lu. 13. 1. whose b. Pilate had mingled with sacrifices
22. 20. the new testament in my b. 1 Cor. 11. 25.
44 his sweat was as great drops of b. falling
John 1. 13. which were born not of b. nor flesh
6. 54. who eateth my flesh and drinketh my b. 56.
55. my flesh is meat, and my b. is drink indeed
19. 34. forthwith came thereout b. and water
Acts 5. 28. ye intend to bring this man's b. on us
15. 20. that they abstain from b. 29. | 21. 25.
17. 26. and hath made of one b. all nations
18. 6. your b. be on your own heads, I am clean
20. 26. I am pure from the b. of all men
1 Cor. 11. 27. guilty of the body and b. of the Lord
15. 50. flesh and b. cannot inherit the kingdom
Eph. 6. 12. we wrestle not against flesh and b.
Col. 1. 20. having made peace thro' b. of his cross
Heb. 2. 14. the children are partakers of flesh and b.
9. 7. not without b. which he offered for himself
12. nor by the b. of goats, but by his own b.
13. if the b. of bulls and goats sanctifieth
20. this is the b. of the testament God enjoined
22. without shedding of b. there is no remission
10. 19. to enter into the holiest by the b. of Jesus
11. 28. he kept the passover, and sprinkling of b.
12. 4. ye have not yet resisted unto b. striving
24. to the b. of sprinkling that speaketh better
13. 11. whose b. is brought into the sanctuary
1 Pet. 1. 2. and sprinkling of the b. of Jesus Christ
1 John 1. 7. the b. of Jesus Christ cleanseth us from
5. 6. this is he that came by water and b.
8. three in earth, the Spirit, the water, and b.
Rev. 5. 9. thou hast redeemed us to God by thy b.
6. 10. how long dost thou not avenge our b.?
12. the sun was black, and the moon became as b.
7. 14. made them white in the b. of the Lamb
8. 8. the third part of the sea became b. 16. 3.
11. 6. have power to turn the waters into b.
12. 11. they overcame him by the b. of the Lamb
14. 20. and b. came out of the wine-press
16. 6. and thou hast given them b. to drink
18. 24. in her was found the b. of the prophets
19. 2. he hath avenged the b. of his servants
13. he was clothed with a vesture dipped in b.

See AVENGER, REVENGER.

BLOOD *be upon.*

Lev. 20. 9. that curseth his father, his b. *be upon* him
11. incest || 13. sodomy, their b. *be upon* them
16. bestiality || 27. wizard, their b. *be upon* them
Deut. 19. 10. innocent b. shed, and so *be upon* thee
Ezek. 18. 13. done abominations, his b. *be upon* him
33. 5. took not warning, his b. shall *be upon* him

BLOOD, with *bullock.*

Exod. 29. 12. take b. of *bullock,* Lev. 4. 5. | 16. 14, 18.
Lev. 4. 7. pour b. of *bullock* at bottom of the altar
16. 15. do with that as he did with b. of the *bullock*
Isa. 1. 11. I delight not in b. of *bullocks* or of lambs

BLOOD *of Christ.*

1 Cor. 10. 16. is it not communion of the b. *of Christ?*
Eph. 2. 13. were far off, are made nigh by b. *of Christ*
Heb. 9. 14. how much more shall b. *of Christ* purge?
1 Pet. 1. 19. but with precious b. *of Christ* as of a lamb
1 John 1. 7. the b. *of Christ* cleanseth us from all sin

BLOOD *of the Covenant.*

Exod. 24. 8. Moses said, behold the b. *of the covenant*
Zech. 9. 11. as for thee also by the b. *of covenant*
Heb. 10. 29. hath counted b. *of cov.* an unholy thing
13. 20. through the b. *of the* everlasting *covenant*

BLOOD, with *eat.*

Lev. 3. 17. a statute that ye *eat* neither fat nor b.
7. 26. ye shall *eat* no manner of b. of fowl or beast, 27. | 17. 14. Deut. 12. 16, 23. | 15. 23.
27. that *eateth* b. that soul shall be cut off, 17. 10.
1 Sam. 14. 32. the people did *eat* them with the b.
Ezek. 33. 25. ye *eat* with b. and lift up your eyes

For BLOOD.

Num. 35. 33. not pollute land, *for* b. it defileth land
2 Sam. 3. 27. he died *for* the b. of Asahel his brother
2 Chron. 24. 25. *for* the b. of the sons of Jehoiada

Psal. 9. 12. when he maketh inquisition for b.
Prov. 1. 11. they say, come let us lay wait for b. 18.
12. 6. the words of wicked are to lie in wait for b.
Mic. 7. 2. they all lie in wait for b. they hunt

His BLOOD.

Gen. 37. 26. if we slay our brother and conceal his b.
42. 22. therefore behold his b. is required
Josh. 2. 19. his b. shall be upon his head
2 Sam. 4. 11. shall I not require his b. of your hand?
1 Kings 2. 32. Lord shall return his b. on his head
Ezek. 3. 18. shall die in his iniquity, but his b. will
I require at thy hand, 20. | 33. 4, 6, 8.
Hos. 12. 14. therefore shall he leave his b. on him
Zech. 9. †7. take away his b. out of his mouth
Mat. 27. 25. his b. be on us and our children
Acts 20. 28. church he hath purchased with his b.
Rom. 3. 25. a propitiation through faith in his b.
5. 9. much more being now justified by his b.
Eph. 1. 7. we have redemption thro' his b. Col. 1. 14.
Heb. 9. 12. but by his own b. he entered in once
13. 12. that he might sanctify the people with his b.
Rev. 1. 5. and washed us from our sins in his b.

Innocent BLOOD.

Deut. 19. 10. that innocent b. be not shed in the land
13. thou shalt put away guilt of innocent b. 21. 9.
21. 8. lay not innocent b. to thy people's charge
1 Sam. 19. 5. wilt thou sin against innocent b. to slay
1 Kings 2. 31. take away innocent b. that Joab shed
2 Kings 21. 16. Manasseh shed innocent b. 24. 4.
Psal. 94. 21. they gather and condemn innocent b.
106. 38. shed innocent b. even b. of sons and daugh.
Prov. 6. 17. Lord hateth hands that shed innocent b.
Isa. 59. 7. and they make haste to shed innocent b.
Jer. 7. 6. if ye oppress not, shed not innocent b. 22. 3.
22. 17. thine eyes and heart are to shed innocent b.
26. 15. ye shall surely bring innoc. b. on yourselves
Joel 3. 19. because they have shed innocent b. in land
Jonah 1. 14. O Lord, we beseech, lay not on us innoc. b.
Mat. 27. 4. I sinned in that I have betrayed innoc. b.

Shed BLOOD.

Gen. 9. 6. who sheddeth man's b. by man his b. be shed
37. 22. Reuben said to them, shed no b.
Exod. 22. 2. there shall no b. be shed for him
3. if the sun be risen upon him, b. be shed for him
Lev. 17. 4. he hath shed b. that man shall be cut off
Num. 35. 33. land not cleansed of b. shed but by b.
Deut. 21. 7. our hands have not shed this b.
1 Sam. 25. 26. withholden from coming to shed b.
1 Kings 2. 5. whom he slew and shed b. of war in peace
1 Chron. 22. 8. because thou hast shed b. much b. 28. 3.
Psal. 79. 3. their b. shed like water round Jerusalem
10. known by revenging b. of thy servants shed
Prov. 1. 16. they make haste to shed b. Rom. 3. 15.
Lam. 4. 13. prophets that have shed the b. of the just
Ezek. 16. 38. judge thee as women that shed b. 23. 45.
22. 4. art become guilty in thy b. thou hast shed
6. the princes in thee to their power to shed b.
23. 45. after the manner of women that shed b.
33. 25. ye shed b. and shall ye possess the land?
35. 5. because thou hast shed b. of children of Israel
36. 18. poured fury on them for the b. they shed
Mat. 23. 35. on you come all the righteous b. shed
Mark 14. 24. this is my b. which is shed, Luke 22. 20.
Luke 11. 50. b. of all the prophets which was shed
Acts 22. 20. when the b. of Stephen was shed
Rev. 16. 6. for they have shed the b. of the saints

Sprinkle BLOOD.

Exod. 29. 16. take the ram's b. and sprinkle it on altar
20. shalt sprinkle b. on altar round about, Lev.
1. 5, 11. | 3. 2, 8, 13. | 7. 2. | 17. 6. Num.
18. 17.
Lev. 4. 6. priest sp. b. seven times, 17. | 16. 14, 19.
5. 9. sprinkle b. of sin offering on side of the altar
7. 14. it shall be the priest's that sprinkle the b.
Num. 19. 4. sprinkle of the b. before the tabernacle
2 Kings 16. 15. sprinkle on it the b. of burnt-offering
Ezek. 43. 18. when make an altar to spr. b. thereon

BLOOD sprinkled.

Exod. 24. 6. half of b. Moses sp. on altar, Lev. 8. 19, 24.
8. Moses took the b. and sprinkled on the people
Lev. 6. 27. when there is sprinkled b. on any garment
8. 30. Moses took of the b. and sprinkled on Aaron
9. 12. Aaron's sons presented him b. he sprinkled, 18.
2 Kings 9. 33. some of Athaliah's b. sprinkled on wall
16. 13. Ahaz sprinkled the b. of his peace offering
2 Chron. 29. 22. sprinkled the b. of bullocks, 30. 16.
35. 11. the priests sprinkled the b. from their hands
Isa. 63. 3. their b. shall be sprinkled on my garment
Heb. 9. 21. he sprinkled with b. the tabernacle

With BLOOD.

Exod. 30. 10. Aaron shall make atonement with b.
Lev. 14. 52. cleanse the house with b. of the bird
19. 26. ye shall not eat any thing with b.
1 Kings 2. 9. his hoary head bring thou down with b.
Psal. 106. 38. and the land was polluted with b.
Isa. 34. 6. sword of Lord filled with b. made fat with b
7. and their land shall be soaked with b.
49. 26. they shall be drunken with their own b.
59. 3. for your hands are defiled with b.
Jer. 19. 4. filled this place with the b. of innocents
46. 10. it shall be made drunk with their b.
Lam. 4. 14. they have polluted themselves with b.
Ezek. 38. 22. I will plead against him with b.
Hos. 6. 8. Gilead is a city polluted with b.
Mic. 3. 10. they build up Zion with b. and Jerusalem
Hab. 2. 12. wo to him that buildeth a town with b.
Gal. 1. 16. immediately I conferred not with b.
Heb. 9. 22. all things are by the law purged with b.
Rev. 8. 7. followed hail and fire, mingled with b.
17. 6. saw the woman drunken with b. of the saints

BLOOD-GUILTINESS.

Psal. 51. 14. deliver me from b.-guiltiness, O God

BLOOD-THIRSTY.

Prov. 29. 10. the b.-thirsty hate the upright

BLOODY.

Exod. 4. 25. surely a b. husband art thou to me, 26.
2 Sam. 16. 7. Shimei said, come out, thou b. man
21. 1. the famine is for Saul, and his b. house
Psal. 5. 6. the Lord will abhor the b. man
26. 9. gather not my life with b. men
55. 23. b. men shall not live out half their days
59. 2. deliver me, and save me from b. men

Psal. 139. 19. depart from me therefore, ye b. men
Ezek. 7. 23. for the land is full of b. crimes
22. 2. son of man, wilt thou judge the b. city?
24. 6. wo to the b. city, 9. Nah. 3. 1.
Acts 28. 8. father of Publius lay sick of a b. flux

BLOOMED.

Num. 17. 8. Aaron's rod b. blossoms and almonds

BLOSSOM

Signifies, [1] *A flower of a tree or plant*, Gen. 40.
10. [2] *To put forth into flowers or blossoms*,
Num. 17. 5. Hab. 3. 17. [3] *To increase,
flourish, and prosper*, Isa. 27. 6. | 35. 1, 2.
Their root shall be as rottenness, and their blossom
shall go up as dust, Isa. 5. 24. that is, *Utter
destruction shall seize upon them; they shall be
destroyed both root and branch.*
The rod hath blossomed, Ezek. 7. 10. *The instrument that God will make use of for your correction
is ready made and prepared.*
Gen. 40. 10. her b. shot forth, and the clusters
Isa. 5. 24. and their b. shall go up as dust

BLOSSOM, ED.

Num. 17. 5. the man's rod whom I choose shall b.
Isa. 27. 6. Israel shall b. and bud, and fill the world
35. 1. the desert shall rejoice and b. as the rose
2. it shall b. abundantly and rejoice with joy
Ezek. 7. 10. the rod hath b. pride hath budded
Hos. 14. †5. and he shall b. as the lily
Hab. 3. 17. altho' the fig tree shall not b. nor fruit

BLOT

Signifies, [1] *Censure, scorn, or reproach*, Prov. 9. 7.
[2] *Unjust gain, which is a blemish, scandal, and
disgrace to a person*, Job 31. 7.
Blot me out of thy book, Exod. 32. 32. *Blot me
out of the book of life, out of the catalogue or
number of those that shall be saved; let me die
rather than see the evil that shall come to this
people, if thou do not forgive them. Wherein
Moses does not express what he thought might
be done, but rather wisheth, if it were possible,
that God would accept of him as a sacrifice in
their stead, and by his utter destruction and
annihilation prevent so great a mischief to them;
In which he was a type of Christ, who laid
down his life, and was made a curse for us*,
Gal. 3. 13.
That I may blot out their name from under heaven,
Deut. 9. 14. *That I may utterly destroy and
consume them, and make their name to be forgotten among men.*
Blot out my transgressions, Psal. 51. 1. *Sins
are compared to debts*, Mat. 6. 12. *which are
written in the creditor's book, and crossed or
blotted out when they are paid. Men's sins are
written in the book of God's remembrance or accounts, out of which all men shall be judged
hereafter*, Rev. 20. 12. *and when sin is pardoned,
it is said to be blotted out*, Isa. 44. 22. *and not
to be found any more, though it should be sought
for*, Jer. 50. 20.
Deut. 32. †5. their b. is not of his children
Job 31. 7. if any b. hath cleaved to my hands
Prov. 9. 7. that rebuketh the wicked, getteth a b.

BLOT out.

Gen. 7. †4. every living thing will I b. out
Exod. 32. 32. and if not, b. me out of thy book
33. whosoever hath sinned, him will I b. out
Num. 5. 23. shall b. them out with bitter water
Deut. 9. 14. let me alone that I may b. out their name
25. 19. shall b. out the remembrance of Amalek
29. 20. the Lord shall b. out his name from under h.
2 Kings 14. 27. said not, that he would b. out Israel
Psal. 51. 1. have mercy, O God, b. out transgress.
9. hide my sins, and b. out all mine iniquities
Jer. 18. 23. nor b. out their sin from thy sight
Rev. 3. 5. I will not b. his name out of book of life

BLOTTED.

Neh. 4. 5. let not their sin be b. out from before thee
Psal. 69. 28. let them be b. out of book of the living
109. 13. posterity cut off, let their name be b. out
14. let not the sin of his mother be b. out
Isa. 44. 22. I have b. out as a thick cloud
Acts 3. 19. repent, that your sins may be b. out

BLOTTETH, ING.

Isa. 43. 25. I am he that b. out thy transgressions
Col. 2. 14. b. out the hand-writing of ordinances

BLOW

Signifies, *A stroke, calamity, or judgment, such as
sword, or famine, which God inflicts upon a people
for their sins*, Jer. 14. 17.
Awake, O north wind, and blow upon my garden,
&c. Cant. 4. 16. *Let the Holy Spirit in his
several operations, both convincing and mortifying,
and also comforting, stir up and quicken my heart
and soul, that the graces that are in me may be
quickened and exercised.*
The wind bloweth where it listeth; so is every
man that is born of the Spirit, John 3. 8. *As
there are many things in nature, particularly the
wind, which are evident in their effects, yet no
man can give a clear and full account of them,
man's reason cannot reach to know from whence
the wind rises, from how great a distance it comes,
or how far it goes; so is this spiritual change
wrought freely, where, in whom, when, and in
what measure, the Spirit pleases; and also powerfully, so as to make an evident, sensible change;
though the manner thereof be incomprehensible, it
is known by the effects.*
I did blow upon it, Hag. 1. 9. *I did blast it,
that it did you no good.*
A fire not blown, Job 20. 26. *Some heavy judgment that comes no man knows how.*
Psal. 39. 10. I am consumed by the b. of thy hand
Jer. 14. 17. people is broken with a grievous b.

BLOW, Verb.

Exod. 15. 10. thou didst b. with thy wind
Num. 10. 5. when ye b. an alarm, camps shall go, 6.
9. then ye shall b. an alarm with trumpets
Judg. 7. 18. when I b. with a trumpet, then b. ye
Psal. 78. 26. he caused an east-wind to b. in heaven
147. 18. causeth his wind to b. and waters flow

Cant. 4. 16. come, thou south, b. upon my garden
Isa. 40. 24. he shall also b. upon them, shall wither
Ezek. 21. 31. I will b. against thee, 22. 21.
Hos. 5. 8. b. ye the cornet in Gibeah, cry aloud
Hag. 1. 9. when ye brought it, I did b. upon it
Luke 12. 55. when ye see the south-wind b.
Rev. 7. 1. that wind should not b. on the earth
See TRUMPET.

BLOWETH.

Isa. 40. 7. because the Spirit of the Lord b. on it
54. 16. I have created the smith that b. the coals
John 3. 8. the wind b. where it listeth, thou hearest

BLOWN.

Job 20. 26. a fire not b. shall consume him
Mal. 1. †13. whereas ye might have b. it away

BLUE.

Exod. 25. 4. b. purple, scarlet, 26. 1, 31, 36. | 27. 16.
28. 31. make the robe of the ephod of b. 39. 22.
39. 3. they cut gold into wires to work it in the b.
Num. 15. 38. put on the fringes a ribband of b.
2 Chron. 2. 7. send a man cunning to work in b. 14.
Esth. 1. 6. b. hangings, a pavement of b. marble
8. 15. Mordecai went in royal apparel of b.
Ezek. 23. 6. the Assyrians were clothed with b.
See PURPLE, CLOTH, LACE, LOOPS.

BLUENESS.

Prov. 20. 30. b. of a wound cleanseth away evil

BLUNT.

Eccl. 10. 10. if iron be b. and he do not whet it

BLUSH.

Ezra 9. 6. I b. to lift up my face to thee, my God
Jer. 6. 15. not ashamed, nor could they b. 8. 12.

BOAR.

Psal. 80. 13. b. out of the wood doth waste it

BOARD, S.

Exod. 26. 29. shalt overlay b. with gold, 36. 34.
27. 8. hollow with b. shalt thou make it, 36. 34.
36. 30. under every b. were two sockets
Num. 3. 36. under custody of Merari shall be b.
Cant. 8. 9. we will inclose her with b. of cedar
Acts 27. 44. the rest, some on b. came to land

BOAST, Substantive.

Psal. 34. 2. my soul shall make her b. in the Lord
Rom. 2. 17. art a Jew, and makest thy b. of God
23. thou that makest thy b. of the law

BOAST, Verb.

1 Kings 20. 11. not b. as he that putteth it off
2 Chron. 25. 19. thine heart lifteth thee up to b.
Psal. 44. 8. in God we b. all the day long
49. 6. and b. themselves in their riches
94. 4. the workers of iniquity b. themselves
97. 7. confounded be they that b. of idols
Prov. 27. 1. b. not thyself of to-morrow
Isa. 10. 15. shall the ax b. itself against him that
61. 6. in their glory shall you b. yourselves
Rom. 11. 18. b. not against branches, if thou b.
2 Cor. 9. 2. for which I b. to them of Macedonia
10. 8. for though I should b. somewhat more
13. we will not b. of things without our measure
16. and not to b. in another man's line
11. 16. receive me that I may b. myself a little
Eph. 2. 9. not of works, lest any man should b.

BOASTED.

Ezek. 35. 13. with mouth ye have b. against me
2 Cor. 7. 14. if I have b. any thing to him

BOASTERS.

Rom. 1. 30. proud, b. inventors of evil things
2 Tim. 3. 2. covetous, b. proud, blasphemers

BOASTEST, ETH.

Psal. 10. 3. the wicked b. of his heart's desire
52. 1. why b. thou thyself in mischief?
Prov. 20. 14. when he is gone his way, then he b.
25. 14. whoso b. himself of a false gift
Jam. 3. 5. tongue a little member, and b. great things

BOASTING, Participle.

Acts 5. 36. rose Theudas, b. himself to be somebody
2 Cor. 10. 15. not b. of things without our measure

BOASTING, Substantive.

Rom. 3. 27. where is b. then? it is excluded
2 Cor. 7. 14. even so our b. before Titus is found truth
8. 24. shew ye to them the proof of our b.
9. 3. lest our b. of you should be in vain in this behalf
4. we should be ashamed in this same confident b.
11. 10. no man shall stop me of this b. in Achaia
17. but as it were foolishly in this confidence of b.
Jam. 4. 16. but now ye rejoice in your b.

BOAT, S.

John 6. 22. the people saw there was no other b.
there, and that Jesus went not into the b.
23. there came other b. from Tiberias
Acts 27. 16. had much work to come by the b.
30. when they had let down the b. into the sea
32. the soldiers cut off the ropes of the b.

BODY

Signifies, [1] *The material part of man*, 1 Cor. 15.
44. [2] *The whole man*, Rom. 6. 12. | 12. 1.
[3] *The substance of a shadow, or ceremony*,
Col. 2. 17. [4] *The church of God firmly
united to Christ and among themselves, by the
Spirit, faith, love, sacraments, word, and ministry,
which, like the veins and arteries in the body,
serve to join them with Christ, and among themselves, and also to convey influence and nourishment from the head to every particular member
of this mystical body*, 1 Cor. 10. 17. Eph.
4. 16. Col. 1. 18. [5] *The human nature of
Christ*, Heb. 10. 5. [6] *The unrenewed part of
man, such as the sensitive powers, carnal affections, and sinful inclinations*, 1 Cor. 9. 27.
This is my body, Mat. 26. 26. *This bread is a
sign or representation, and is hereafter to be a
memorial also, of my body, and of my sufferings
in it; and also a seal and pledge, whereby I
make over to you all the benefits I have purchased
thereby: Or, This taking and eating is a holy
rite of commemorating my death, and a means
of making all worthy receivers partakers of the
benefits thereof.*
The body of this death, Rom. 7. 24. *The corruption of nature, acting chiefly by the body, which
tends to, and binds me over to, death.*
Exod. 24. 10. as the b. of heaven in its clearness

1 *Sam.* 31. 12. took the *b.* of Saul, 1 *Chron.* 10. 12.
Job 19. 17. for the childrens' sake of my own *b.*
26. though after my skin worms destroy this *b.*
20. 25. it is drawn and cometh out of the *b.*
Psal. 139. † 15. my *b.* was not hid from thee
Prov. 5. 11. when thy flesh and *b.* are consumed
Isa. 10. 18. and shall consume both soul and *b.*
51. 23. and thou hast laid thy *b.* as the ground
Ezek. 10. 12. their whole *b.* was full of eyes
Dan. 7. 15. I was grieved in spirit in midst of my *b.*
Mat. 5. 29. that thy whole *b.* be cast into hell, 30.
6. 22. the light of the *b.* is the eye, *Luke* 11. 34.
thy *b.* shall be full of light. *Luke* 11. 34, 36.
23. thy whole *b.* shall be full of darkness
25. take no thought for your *b.* *Luke* 12. 22.
and the *b.* more than raiment, *Luke* 12. 23.
10. 28. fear not them that kill the *b.* *Luke* 12. 4.
14. 12. John's disciples came and took up the *b.*
26. 12. she hath poured this ointment on my *b.*
26. Jesus took bread and said, take, eat, this is my
b. *Mark* 14. 22. *Luke* 22. 19. 1 *Cor.* 11. 24.
27. 58. Joseph of Arimathea went to Pilate, and
begged the *b.* of Jesus, *Mark* 15. 43. *Luke* 23. 52.
Mark 5. 29. she felt in her *b.* that she was healed
14. 8. she is come aforehand to anoint my *b.*
51. having a linen cloth cast about his *b.*
15. 45. Pilate gave the *b.* to Joseph, *Mat.* 27. 58.
Luke 17. 37. where the *b.* is, thither the eagles
24. 3. they found not the *b.* of the Lord Jesus
John 20. 12. where the *b.* of Jesus had lain
Rom. 6. 6. that the *b.* of sin may be destroyed
7. 4. become dead to the law by the *b.* of Christ
24. who shall deliver me from the *b.* of this death
8. 10. Christ in you, the *b.* is dead because of sin
13. if ye thro' the Spirit mortify deeds of the *b.*
23. for the adoption, the redemption of our *b.*
1 *Cor.* 6. 13. now the *b.* is not for fornication, but for
the Lord, and the Lord for the *b.*
18. every sin a man doth is without the *b.*
6. 19. your *b.* is the temple of the Holy Ghost
7. 4. the wife hath no power of her own *b.*
9. 27. but I keep under my *b.* and bring it to subjec.
10. 16. the communion of the *b.* of Christ
11. 27. be guilty of the *b.* and blood of the Lord
29. eats damnation, not discerning the Lord's *b.*
12. 14. for the *b.* is not one member, but many
15. is it therefore not of the *b.*? 16.
17. if whole *b.* were an eye, where were hearing?
19. where were the *b.*? ‖ 20. yet but one *b.*
27. now ye are the *b.* of Christ, and members
13. 3. tho' I give my *b.* to be burned, and have not
15. 35. and with what *b.* do the dead come?
37. thou sowest not that *b.* that shall be
38. but God giveth it a *b.* as it hath pleased him
44. it is sown a natural *b.* raised a spiritual *b.*
2 *Cor.* 5. 8. willing rather to be absent from the *b.*
Eph. 3. 6. Gentiles be fellow-heirs of the same *b.*
4. 12. for the edifying of the *b.* of Christ
16. from whom the whole *b.* fitly joined together
5. 23. and he is the Saviour of the *b.*
Phil. 3. 21. who shall change our vile *b.* that it may
Col. 1. 18. he is the head of the *b.* the church
2. 11. in putting off the *b.* of the sins of the flesh
17. which are a shadow, but the *b.* is of Christ
19. from which the *b.* by joints and bands
23. a shew of wisdom in neglecting of the *b.*
1 *Thess.* 5. 23. I pray your soul and *b.* be preserved
Heb. 10. 5. but a *b.* hast thou prepared me
10. through the offering of the *b.* of Jesus
Jam. 2. 16. give not things are needful to the *b.*
26. as the *b.* without the Spirit is dead, so faith
3. 2. and is able also to bridle the whole *b.*
3. and we turn about their whole *b.*
6. the tongue defileth the whole *b.* and sets on fire
Jude 9. Michael disputed about the *b.* of Moses

Dead BODY.

Lev. 21. 11. nor shall ye go in to any *dead b.* *Num.* 6. 6.
Num. 9. 6. certain men were defiled by a *dead b.* 7.
10. any of you be unclean by a *dead b.* *Hag.* 2. 13.
19. 11. he that toucheth *dead b.* be unclean, 16.
2 *Kings* 8. 5. how he had restored a *dead b.* to life
Isa. 26. 19. with my *dead b.* shall they arise
Jer. 26. 23. and cast his *dead b.* into the graves
36. 30. his *dead b.* shall be cast out in the day

Fruit of the BODY.

Deut. 28. 4. blessed shall be the *fruit of thy b.*
11. make thee plenteous in the *fruit of thy b.* 30. 9.
18. cursed shall be the *fruit of thy b.* and of thy land
53. thou shalt eat the *fruit of thy b.* in the siege
Psal. 132. 11. *fruit of thy b.* will I set on thy throne
Mic. 6. 7. shall I give *fruit of my b.* for sin of my soul

His BODY.

Exod. 21. † 3. if he came in with *his b.* he shall go
Deut. 21. 23. *his b.* not remain all night on the tree
Judg. 8. 30. Gideon had 70 sons of *his b.* begotten
1 *Sam.* 31. 10. fastened *his b.* to wall of Bethshan
Dan. 4. 33. *his b.* wet with the dew of heaven, 5. 21.
7. 11. till beast was slain, and *his b.* destroyed
10. 6. *his b.* also was like the beryl
Luke 23. 55. the women beheld how *his b.* was laid
24. 23. when they found not *his b.* they came
John 2. 21. but he spake of the temple of *his b.*
Acts 19. 12. from *his b.* were brought to the sick
Rom. 4. 19. he considered not *his b.* now dead
1 *Cor.* 6. 18. commits fornication sinneth against *his b.*
7. 4. the husband hath not power of *his* own *b.*
2 *Cor.* 5. 10. may receive the things done in *his b.*
Eph. 1. 23. which is *his b.* fulness of him that fills
Phil. 3. 21. may be fashioned like to *his* glorious *b.*
Col. 1. 24. for *his b.* sake, which is the church
1 *Pet.* 2. 24. who bare our sins in *his b.* on the tree

In BODY.

Lam. 4. 7. they were more ruddy *in b.* than rubies
Rom. 6. 12. let not sin reign *in* your mortal *b.*
1 *Cor.* 5. 3. I verily as absent *in b.* have judged
6. 20. therefore glorify God *in* your *b.* and spirit
7. 34. that she may be holy *in b.* and in spirit
12. 18. God hath set members every one *in* the *b.*
25. that there should be no schism *in* the *b.*
2 *Cor.* 4. 10. bearing about *in* the *b.* the dying of our
Ld. that life of Jesus might be manifest *in* our *b.*
5. 6. knowing that whilst we are at home *in b.*
2 *Cor.* 12. 2. whether *in b.* or whether out of the *b.*
Gal. 6. 17. I bear *in b.* the marks of the Lord Jesus
Phil. 1. 20. Christ shall be magnified *in* my *b.*
Col. 1. 22. reconciled *in b.* of his flesh thro' death
Heb. 13. 3. as being yourselves also *in* the *b.*

One BODY.

Rom. 12. 4. as we have many members in *one b.*
5. we being many are *one b.* in Christ, 1 *Cor.* 10. 17.
1 *Cor.* 6. 16. he that is joined to an harlot, is *one b.*
12. 12. as the *b.* is *one*, and hath many members
13. we are baptized into *one b.* whether Jews
20. now are they many members, yet but *one b.*
Eph. 2. 16. he might reconcile both to God in *one b.*
4. 4. there is *one b.* and one Spirit, as ye are called
Col. 3. 15. to which ye are also called in *one b.*

BODIES.

Gen. 47. 18. not ought left, but our *b.* and lands
1 *Sam.* 31. 12. took *b.* of Saul's sons, 1 *Chr.* 10. 12.
Neh. 9. 37. they have dominion over our *b.* and cattle
Job 13. 12. your *b.* are like unto *b.* of clay
Ezek. 1. 11. two wings covered their *b.* 23.
Dan. 3. 27. on whose *b.* the fire had no power
28. yielded their *b.* that they might not serve
Mat. 27. 52. many *b.* of saints which slept, arose
John 19. 31. the *b.* should not remain on the cross
Rom. 1. 24. gave them up to dishonour their own *b.*
8. 11. shall quicken your mortal *b.* by his Spirit
12. 1. that ye present your *b.* a living sacrifice
1 *Cor.* 6. 15. your *b.* are members of Christ
15. 40. there are celestial *b.* and *b.* terrestrial
Eph. 5. 28. to love their wives as their own *b.*
Heb. 10. 22. and our *b.* washed with pure water
13. 11. the *b.* of beasts, whose blood is brought
Rev. 18. † 13. the merchandise of *b.* and souls

Dead BODIES.

2 *Chron.* 20. 24. behold they were *dead b.* fallen
25. they found *dead b.* precious jewels
Psal. 79. 2. *dead b.* of thy servants given to be meat
110. 6. he shall fill the places with the *dead b.*
Jer. 31. 40. whole valley of *dead b.* shall be holy
33. 5. but it is to fill them with *dead b.* of men
34. 20. their *dead b.* shall be for meat to the fowls
41. 9. the pit wherein Ishmael cast *dead b.* of men
Amos 8. 3. shall be many *dead b.* in every place
Rev. 11. 8. their *dead b.* shall lie in the street of city
9. nations see their *dead b.* three days and an half,
nor suffer their *dead b.* to be put in graves

BODILY.

Luke 3. 22. the Holy Ghost descended in a *b.* shape
2 *Cor.* 10. 10. but his *b.* presence is weak
Col. 2. 9. in him all the fulness of the Godhead *b.*
1 *Tim.* 4. 8. for *b.* exercise profiteth little

BOIL.

Lev. 8. 31. *b.* the flesh at the door of the tabernacle
Job 41. 31. he maketh the deep to *b.* like a pot
Isa. 64. 2. the fire causeth the waters to *b.*
Ezek. 24. 5. burn the bones, and make it *b.* well
46. 20. the place where the priests shall *b.* 24.

BOILED.

1 *Kings* 19. 21. he took a yoke of oxen and *b.* them
2 *Kings* 6. 29. so we *b.* my son and did eat him
Job 30. 27. my bowels *b.* and rested not

BOILETH, ING.

Psal. 45. † 1. my heart *b.* up a good matter
Ezek. 46. 23. made with *b.* places under the rows

BOISTEROUS.

Mat. 14. 30. when he saw the wind *b.* he was afraid

BOLD.

Prov. 28. 1. but the righteous are *b.* as a lion
Acts 13. 46. Paul and Barnabas waxed *b.*
Rom. 10. 20. Esaias is very *b.* and saith, I was found
2 *Cor.* 10. 1. but being absent, am *b.* towards you
2. I may not be *b.* wherewith I think to be *b.*
11. 21. howbeit, wherein any is *b.* I am *b.* also
Phil. 1. 14. by my bonds, are much more *b.* to speak
1 *Thess.* 2. 2. we were *b.* in our God to speak to you
Philem. 8. though I might be much *b.* in Christ

BOLDLY.

Gen. 34. 25. Simeon and Levi came on the city *b.*
Mark 15. 43. Joseph came, and went in *b.* to Pilate
John 7. 26. he speaketh *b.* and they say nothing
Acts 9. 27. how he preached *b.* at Damascus
29. he spake *b.* in the name of the Lord Jesus
14. 3. long time abode they, speaking *b.* in the Lord
18. 26. Apollos began to speak *b.* in the synagogue
19. 8. spake *b.* for the space of three months
Rom. 15. 15. I have written the more *b.* to you
Eph. 6. 19. given me, that I may open my mouth *b.*
20. that I may speak *b.* as I ought to speak
Heb. 4. 16. let us come *b.* to the throne of grace
13. 6. that we may *b.* say, the Lord is my helper

BOLDNESS.

Eccl. 8. 1. and the *b.* of his face shall be changed
Acts 4. 13. when they saw the *b.* of Peter and John
29. that with all *b.* they may speak thy word
31. and they spake the word of God with *b.*
2 *Cor.* 3. † 12. we use great *b.* of speech
7. 4. great is my *b.* of speech toward you
Eph. 3. 12. in whom we have *b.* and access by faith
Phil. 1. 20. but that with all *b.* as always, so now
1 *Tim.* 3. 13. they purchase great *b.* in the faith
Heb. 10. 19. having *b.* to enter into the holiest
1 *John* 4. 17. that we may have *b.* in judgment

BOLLED.

Exod. 9. 31. barley was in the ear, and the flax *b.*

BOLSTER.

1 *Sam.* 19. 13. a pillow of goats' hair for his *b.* 16.
26. 7. spear at his *b.* 11. 12. ‖ 16. water at his *b.*

BOLT, ED.

2 *Sam.* 13. 17. *b.* the door ‖ 18. he *b.* the door

BOND

Signifies, [1] *An obligation, or vow*, Num. 30. 5, 14.
[2] *Sufferings for Christ and his gospel*, Heb. 13. 3.
Thou hast loosed my bonds, *Psal.* 116. 16. *Thou hast rescued me from mine enemies, whose captive and vassal I was, and therefore hast a just right and title to me and to my service.*
He looseth the bonds of kings, *Job* 12. 18. *He deprives them of that majesty, power, and authority, which should keep their subjects in awe, and wherewith they bind them to obedience.*
Charity is the bond of perfectness, *Col.* 3. 14. *Love to our neighbour, flowing from love to God, is the chief means to a perfect union among all the members of the church, and to make their gifts and graces subservient to the good of one another.*
Num. 30. 2. or swear to bind his soul with a *b.*
3. if a woman vow and bind herself by a *b.*
4. and her father hear her vow and her *b.*
Ezek. 20. 37. I will bring you into *b.* of covenant
Luke 13. 16. be loosed from his *b.* on the sabbath
Acts 8. 23. thou art in the *b.* of iniquity
Eph. 4. 3. the unity of the Spirit, in the *b.* of peace
Col. 3. 14. put on charity, the *b.* of perfectness

BOND.

1 *Cor.* 12. 13. baptized into one body, *b.* or free
See FREE.

BONDS.

Num. 30. 5. not any of her vows or *b.* shall stand
7. *b.* wherewith she bound her soul shall stand
14. he establisheth all her *b.* which are on her
Job 12. 18. he looseth the *b.* of kings
Psal. 116. 16. O Lord, thou hast loosed my *b.*
Jer. 5. 5. have broken the yoke, and burst the *b.*
27. 2. make thee *b.* and yokes, and put on thy neck
30. 8. I will break his yoke, and burst thy *b.*
Nah. 1. 13. and I will burst thy *b.* in sunder
Acts 20. 23. that *b.* and afflictions abide me
23. 29. done nothing worthy of death or *b.* 26. 31.
25. 14. there is a certain man left in *b.* by Felix
26. 29. altogether such as I am, except these *b.*
Eph. 6. 20. for which I am an ambassador in *b.*
Phil. 1. 7. in *b.* ye are all partakers of my grace
13. so that my *b.* in Christ are manifest
14. the brethren waxing confident by my *b.*
16. supposing to add affliction to my *b.*
Col. 4. 3. for which I am in *b.* ‖ 18. remember my *b.*
2 *Tim.* 2. 9. wherein I suffer trouble, even to *b.*
Philem. 10. whom I have begotten in my *b.*
13. have ministered to me in the *b.* of the gospel
Heb. 10. 34. ye had compassion of me in my *b.*
11. 36. others had trial of *b.* and imprisonment
13. 3. remember them that are in *b.* as bound

BONDAGE

Signifies, [1] *Outward slavery and oppressions*, Exod. 6. 5. Ezra 9. 8, 9. [2] *Spiritual subjection to sin and Satan*, Heb. 2. 15. [3] *Subjection to the yoke of the ceremonial law*, Gal. 2. 4. | 4. 9. [4] *Servile fear*, Rom. 8. 15. [5] *Corruption and death*, Rom. 8. 21.
The one gendereth to bondage, *Gal.* 4. 24. *Begets children to bondage; that is, They who adhered to the old covenant, or legal dispensation, by* Moses, *were not thereby freed from their bondage to sin, Satan, and God's wrath*, Gal. 3. 10. *and were of a servile, mercenary disposition, doing what they did in God's service, not from love, but slavish fear*, Rom. 8. 15. *and thinking to merit heaven by their works.*
Exod. 1. 14. made their lives bitter with hard *b.*
2. 23. and Israel sighed by reason of the *b.* and
they cried to God by reason of the *b.*
6. 6. and I will rid you out of their *b.*
9. but they hearkened not to Moses for cruel *b.*
13. 3. day in which ye came out of the house of *b.*
14. Lord brought us out of the house of *b.* 20. 2.
Deut. 5. 6. | 6. 12. | 8. 14. | 13. 5, 10.
Josh. 24. 17. *Judg.* 6. 8.
Deut. 26. 6. the Egyptians laid upon us hard *b.*
Neh. 5. 5. we bring into *b.* our sons and daughters,
some of our daughters are brought unto *b.*
18. because the *b.* was heavy on this people
9. 17. they appointed a captain to return to *b.*
Isa. 14. 3. Lord shall give thee rest from thy hard *b.*
Rom. 8. 15. ye have not received the spirit of *b.*
21. shall be delivered from the *b.* of corruption
Gal. 4. 24. from mount Sinai, which gendereth to *b.*
5. 1. be not entangled again with the yoke of *b.*
Heb. 2. 15. were all their lifetime subject to *b.*

In, into, or *under* BONDAGE.

Exod. 6. 5. Israel, whom the Egyptians keep *in b.*
Ezra 9. 8. and give us a little reviving *in* our *b.*
9. our God hath not forsaken us *in* our *b.*
John 8. 33. we were never *in b.* to any man
Acts 7. 6. and that they should bring them *into b.*
7. and the nation to whom they shall be *in b.*
1 *Cor.* 7. 15. a brother or sister is not *under b.*
2 *Cor.* 11. 20. ye suffer, if a man bring you *into b.*
Gal. 2. 4. that they might bring us *into b.*
4. 3. were *in b.* under the elements of the world
9. whereunto ye desire again to be *in b.*
25. answereth to Jerusalem, which is *in b.*
2 *Pet.* 2. 19. of the same is he brought *into b.*

BOND-MAN.

Gen. 44. 33. let me abide instead of the lad a *b.*
Deut. 15. 15. remember thou wast a *b.* in Egypt,
and the Lord redeemed thee, 16. 12. | 24. 18, 22.
Rev. 6. 15. every *b.* hid themselves in the dens

BOND-MAID, S.

Lev. 19. 20. whoso lieth with a *b.* betrothed
25. 44. thy *b.* shall be of the heathen, buy ye *b.*
Gal. 4. 22. one by a *b.* the other by a free-woman

BOND-MEN.

Gen. 43. 18. he may take us for *b.* and our asses
44. 9. let him die, and we will be my lord's *b.*
Lev. 25. 42. they shall not be sold as *b.*
44. *b.* shall be of the heathen, of them buy *b.*
46. they shall be your *b.* for ever
26. 13. that ye should not be their *b.*
Deut. 6. † 12. beware, lest thou forget the Lord,
who brought thee out of the house of *b.* 13. † 10.
21. then say to thy son, we were Pharaoh's *b.*
7. 8. and redeemed you out of the house of *b.*
28. 68. there ye shall be sold for *b.* and bond-women
Josh. 9. 23. none of you be freed from being *b.*
1 *Kings* 9. 22. but of Israel Solomon made no *b.*
2 *Kings* 4. 1. is come to take my two sons to be *b.*
2 *Chron.* 28. 10. to keep the children of Judah for *b.*
Ezra 9. 9. we were *b.* yet God hath not forsaken
Esth. 7. 4. if we had been sold for *b.* and bond-women
Jer. 34. 13. I brought them out of the house of *b.*

BOND-SERVANT.

Lev. 25. 39. shalt not compel him to serve as a *b.*

BOND-SERVICE.

1 *Kings* 9. 21. Solomon did levy a tribute of *b*

BOND-WOMAN.
Gen. 21. 10. cast out this b. and her son, for the son of the b. shall not be heir, Gal. 4. 30.
12. let it not grieve thee because of the b.
13. of the son of the b. will I make a nation
Gal. 4. 23. son of the b. was born after the flesh
31. we are not children of the b. but the free
BOND-WOMEN, See BOND-MEN.
BONE
Signifies, [1] *That part of the body white and hard, affording support to the whole fabric*, Job 10. 11. [2] *The dead body*, 1 Kings 13. 31. [3] *The whole man*, Job 20. 11. Psal. 35. 10.
The bones which thou hast broken, Psal. 51. 8. *My heart, which hath been sorely wounded and terrified by the dreadful message sent by* Nathan, *and by the dismal sentence of thy law, denounced against such sinners as I am.*
This is bone of my bones, and flesh of my flesh, Gen. 2. 23. *God hath provided me a meet help and wife, not out of the brute creatures, but of mine own body, and of the same nature with myself.*
We are members of his flesh and bones, Eph. 5. 30. *All that grace and glory which the church hath is from Christ*, 1 Cor. 1. 30. Eph. 2. 10. *(as the woman was taken out of the man*, Gen. 2. 23.) *and she has the same graces and glory that Christ hath*, John 1. 16. | 17. 22.
Gen. 2. 23. this is b. of my bones, and flesh of my flesh
29. 14. surely thou art my b. and my flesh
Exod. 12. 46. neither shall ye break a b. Num. 9. 12.
Num. 19. 16. toucheth a b. of a man, be unclean
Judg. 9. 2. remember that I am your b. and flesh
2 Sam. 5. 1. behold we are thy b. 1 Chron. 11. 1.
19. 13. art thou not of my b. and of my flesh?
Job 2. 5. touch his b. and flesh, and he will curse
19. 20. my b. cleaveth to my skin, and to my flesh
31. 22. let my arm be broken from the b.
Prov. 25. 15. a soft tongue breaketh the b.
Ezek. 37. 7. the bones came together, b. to his b.
39. 15. when any seeth a man's b. then set up
John 19. 36. a b. of him shall not be broken
BONES.
Exod. 13. 19. Moses took the b. of Joseph with
Josh. 24. 32. the b. of Joseph buried in Shechem
Judg. 19. 29. divided his concubine with her b.
2 Sam. 21. 12. took the b. of Saul, b. of Jonathan
14. b. of Saul and Jonathan buried in Zelah
1 Kings 13. 2. men's b. shall be burnt upon thee
2 Kings 13. 21. touched the b. of Elisha, he revived
23. 14. he filled the places with the b. of men
16. and took the b. out of the sepulchres
20. and he burnt men's b. upon the altars
2 Chron. 34. 5. he burnt the b. of the priests
Job 10. 11. thou hast fenced me with b. and sinews
Psal. 51. 8. the b. thou hast broken may rejoice
53. 5. God scattereth the b. of him that encampeth
141. 7. our b. are scattered at the grave's mouth
Prov. 3. 8. fear Lord, it shall be marrow to thy b.
14. 30. but envy the rottenness of the b.
15. 30. a good report maketh the b. fat
16. 24. pleasant words are health to the b.
17. 22. but a broken spirit drieth the b.
Eccl. 11. 5. nor how the b. do grow in the womb
Isa. 58. 11. the Lord shall make fat thy b.
66. 14. your b. shall flourish like an herb
Jer. 8. 1. bring the b. of the kings, and b. of the priests, b. of prophets, and b. of inhabitants
Ezek. 6. 5. I will scatter your b. about your altars
24. 4. fill it with the choice b. || 5. burn b. 10.
37. 1. valley full of b. || 3. can these b. live?
4. prophesy upon these b. and say, O ye dry b.
11. these b. are house of Israel, our b. are dried
Amos 2. 1. because he burnt b. of the king of Edom
6. 10. that burneth him, to bring out the b.
Zeph. 3. 3. they gnaw not the b. till the morrow
Mat. 23. 27. but are within full of dead men's b.
Luke 24. 39. for a spirit hath not flesh and b.
His BONES.
1 Kings 13. 31. when I am dead lay my b. beside his b.
2 Kings 23. 18. let no man move his b. so they let his b.
Job 20. 11. his b. are full of the sin of his youth
21. 24. his b. are moistened with marrow
33. 19. the multitude of his b. with strong pain
21. and his b. that were not seen, stick out
40. 18. his b. as pieces of brass, his b. as iron
Psal. 34. 20. he keepeth all his b. not one is broken
109. 18. so let it come like oil into his b.
Prov. 12. 4. makes ashamed is as rottenness in his b.
Jer. 50. 17. Nebuchadnezzar hath broken his b.
Eph. 5. 30. we are members of his flesh and of his b.
Heb. 11. 22. and gave command concerning his b.
My BONES.
Gen. 50. 25. ye shall carry up my b. Exod. 13. 19.
2 Sam. 19. 12. ye are my b. and my flesh
1 Kings 13. 31. when I am dead, my b. beside his b.
Job 4. 14. trembling made all my b. to shake
7. † 15. my soul chooseth death rather than my b.
30. 17. my b. are pierced in me in the night
30. my skin is black, and my b. burnt with heat
Psal. 6. 2. O Lord, heal me, for my b. are vexed
22. 14. all my b. are out of joint || 17. I may tell my b.
31. 10. my b. are consumed || 32. 3. my b. waxed old
35. 10. all my b. shall say, Lord, who is like to thee
38. 3. neither is there any rest in my b.
42. 10. as with a sword in my b. enemies reproach
102. 3. days consumed, my b. are burnt as an hearth
5. by reason of groaning my b. cleave to my skin
Isa. 38. 13. as a lion so will he break all my b.
Jer. 20. 9. as a burning fire shut up in my b.
23. 9. my heart is broken, all my b. shake
Lam. 1. 13. he hath sent fire into my b.
3. 4. my flesh he made old, he hath broken my b.
Hab. 3. 16. rottenness entered into my b.
Their BONES.
Num. 24. 8. Israel shall break their b. and pierce
1 Sam. 31. 13. took their b. and buried them at Jabesh
1 Chr. 10. 12. buried their b. under an oak at Jabesh
Lam. 4. 8. their skin cleaveth to their b.
Ezek. 32. 27. their iniquity shall be on their b.
Dan. 6. 24. the lions brake all their b. in pieces

Mic. 3. 2. pluck off their skin and flesh from their b.
3. they break their b. and chop them in pieces
BONNETS.
Exod. 28. 40. for Aaron's sons thou shalt make b.
29. 9. thou shalt put the b. on them, Lev. 8. 13.
39. 28. they made goodly b. of fine linen
Isa. 3. 20. the Lord will take away the b.
Ezek. 44. 18. they shall have linen b. on their heads
BOOK
Signifies, [1] *A register wherein things are written*, Gen. 5. 1. Esth. 6. 1. [2] *The holy scriptures*, Psal. 40. 7. Rev. 22. 19. [3] *The consciences of men*, Dan. 7. 10. Rev. 20. 12. [4] *God's counsel and purpose*, Psal. 139. 16. [5] *His omniscience, or careful remembrance of the services and afflictions of his people*, Psal. 56. 8. Mal. 3. 16. [6] *His election to life eternal*, Rev. 21. 27.
Exod. 17. 14. write this for a memorial in a b.
32. 32. if wilt not forgive, blot me out of thy b.
33. who hath sinned, him will I blot out of my b.
Num. 5. 23. the priest shall write these curses in a b.
21. 14. it is said in the b. of the wars of the Lord
Deut. 17. 18. shall write him a copy of this law in a b.
31. 24. made an end of writing this law in a b.
Josh. 10. 13. written in the b. of Jasher, 2 Sam. 1. 18.
18. 9. the men described it into seven parts in a b.
1 Sam. 10. 25. Samuel told, and wrote it in a b.
1 Kings 11. 41. written in the b. of acts of Solomon
2 Kings 22. 8. Hilkiah gave the b. to Shaphan
10. Hilkiah delivered me a b. 2 Chron. 34. 15, 18.
16. I'll bring evil, even all the words of the b.
23. 24. might perform the words written in the b.
1 Chron. 9. 1. were written in the b. of the kings
29. 29. are written in the b. of Samuel the seer
2 Chron. 9. 29. acts of Solomon in the b. of Nathan
12. 15. acts of Rehoboam in the b. of Shemaiah
20. 34. the acts of Jehoshaphat in the b. of Jehu
34. 16. Shaphan carried the b. to the king
21. concerning the words of the b. that is found
24. all the curses that are written in the b.
Ezra 4. 15. search may be made in b. of records
Neh. 8. 5. Ezra opened the b. in the sight of all
Esth. 9. 32. of Purim, and it was written in the b.
Job 19. 23. oh that they were printed in a b.
31. 35. that mine adversary had written a b.
Psal. 40. 7. in the volume of thy b. Heb. 10. 7.
56. 8. put thou my tears, are they not in thy b.?
69. 28. let them be blotted out of b. of the living
139. 16. in thy b. all my members were written
Isa. 29. 11. as the words of a b. that is sealed
12. the b. is delivered to him that is not learned
18. the deaf shall hear the words of the b.
30. 8. now go and note it in a b. that it may be
34. 16. seek ye out of the b. of the Lord, and read
Jer. 30. 2. write the words I have spoken in a b.
32. † 10. I wrote in the b. the evidence
12. witnesses that subscribed the b. of the purchase
36. 2. take a roll of a b. || 10. read in the b.
45. 1. written the words in a b. from Jeremiah
51. 60. so Jeremiah wrote in a b. all the evil
Ezek. 2. 9. and lo, a roll of a b. was therein
Dan. 12. 1. every one found written in the b.
4. O Daniel, shut up the words, and seal the b.
Nah. 1. 1. the b. of the vision of Nahum
Mal. 3. 16. a b. of remembrance was written
Mat. 1. 1. the b. of the generation of Jesus
Luke 3. 4. as it is written in the b. of Esaias
4. 17. there was delivered to Jesus the b. of the prophet Esaias, and when he had opened the b.
20. he closed the b. and gave it to the minister
20. 42. in the b. of the Psalms, Acts 1. 20.
Acts 7. 42. it is written in the b. of the prophets
Heb. 9. 19. he sprinkled the b. and the people
Rev. 1. 11. what thou seest, write in a b.
5. 1. a b. written within, on the backside sealed
2. who is worthy to open the b. and to loose seals?
3. and no man was able to open the b.
10. 2. and he had in his hand a little b. open
8. go and take the little b. which is open
9. give me the little b. || 10. I took the little b.
20. 12. another b. was opened, the b. of life
22. 19. if any take away from the words of the b.
See COVENANT.
BOOK *of the Law*.
Deut. 28. 61. every plague not written in b. of the law
29. 21. according to the curses in this b. of the law
30. 10. to keep his statutes written in this b. of law
31. 26. take this b. of the law and put it in the ark
Josh. 1. 8. this b. of the law shall not depart out of
8. 31. written in b. of law of Moses, 2 Kings 14. 6.
2 Kings 22. 8. I have found b. of the law in the house
Neh. 8. 8. so they read in the b. of the law distinctly
Gal. 3. 10. that are written in b. of law to do them
BOOK *of Life*.
Phil. 4. 3. whose names are written in the b. of life
Rev. 3. 5. I will not blot his name out of b. of life
13. 8. names are not written in the b. of life, 17. 8.
20. 12. another b. opened, which is the b. of life
15. was not found written in the b. of life was cast
21. 27. which are written in the Lamb's b. of life
22. 19. shall take away his part out of the b. of life
BOOK *of Moses*.
2 Chron. 25. 4. but did as it is written in b. of Moses
35. 12. to offer as it is written in the b. of Moses
Ezra 6. 18. set priests, as it is written in b. of Moses
Neh. 13. 1. on that day they read in the b. of Moses
Mark 12. 26. have ye not read in the b. of Moses?
This BOOK.
Gen. 5. 1. this is the b. of the generation of Adam
Deut. 28. 58. do all written in this b. 2 Chron. 34. 21.
29. 20. the curses that are written in this b. 27.
2 Kings 22. 13. inquire concerning the words of this b. fathers have not hearkened to the words of this b.
23. 3. to perform the words written in this b.
Jer. 25. 13. I'll bring all that is written in this b.
51. 63. when hast made an end of reading this b.
John 20. 30. signs which are not written in this b.
Rev. 22. 7. the sayings of the prophecy of this b.
9. of them which keep the sayings of this b.
10. seal not the sayings of the prophecy of this b.
18. heareth the words of the prophecy of this b. if any add, add to him plagues written in this b.

Rev. 22. 19. his part from the things written in [this b.
BOOKS.
Ezra 6. 1. search was made in the house of the b.
Eccl. 12. 12. of making many b. there is no end
Dan. 7. 10. and the b. were opened, Rev. 20. 12.
9. 2. I understood by b. the number of years
John 21. 25. the world could not contain the b.
Acts 19. 19. many brought their b. and burned them
2 Tim. 4. 13. bring the b. especially the parchments
Rev. 20. 12. dead judged out of things written in b.
BOOTH.
Job 27. 18. as a b. that the keeper maketh
Jonah 4. 5. Jonah went and made him a b.
BOOTHS.
Gen. 33. 17. and Jacob made b. for his cattle
† therefore the name of the place is called b.
Lev. 23. 42. ye shall dwell in b. seven days
43. I made the children of Israel dwell in b.
Neh. 8. 14. Israel should dwell in b. || 16. made b.
BOOTY, IES.
Num. 31. 32. b. the rest of the prey, 675,000 sheep
Jer. 49. 32. and their camels shall be a b.
Hab. 2. 7. thou shalt be for b. unto them
Zeph. 1. 13. therefore their goods shall become a b.
BORDER.
Gen. 49. 13. Zebulun his b. shall be to Zidon
Exod. 19. 12. or touch the b. of the mount
Num. 21. 23. not suffer Israel to pass thro' his b.
34. 8. from Hor ye shall point out your b.
35. 26. if the slayer shall come without the b.
Deut. 12. 20. when the Lord shall enlarge thy b.
Josh. 22. 25. the Lord hath made Jordan a b.
24. 30. and they buried Joshua in the b. of his inheritance in mount Ephraim, Judg. 2. 9.
2 Sam. 8. 3. smote him as he went to recover his b.
1 Kings 4. 21. and Solomon reigned over all kingdoms unto the b. of Egypt, 2 Chron. 9. 26.
2 Kings 3. 21. all that were able stood in the b.
Psal. 78. 54. brought them to the b. of his sanctuary
Prov. 15. 25. he will establish the b. of the widow
Isa. 28. † 25. cast in wheat and rye in their b.
37. 24. I will enter into the height of his b.
Jer. 31. 17. thy children come again to their b.
Ezek. 11. 10. I will judge you in the b. of Israel, 11.
47. 13. this shall be the b. whereby ye inherit
Joel 3. 6. might remove them from their b.
Amos 1. 13. that they might enlarge their b.
6. 2. or their b. greater than your b.
Obad. 7. the men have brought thee even to the b.
Zeph. 2. 8. and magnified themselves against their b.
Mal. 1. 4. they shall call them the b. of wickedness
5. Lord will be magnified from the b. of Israel
See EAST, SOUTH.
BORDER.
Exod. 25. 25. make to it a b. of an hand-breadth, make a golden crown to the b. round about
Mark 6. 56. touch, if it were but the b. of his garm.
Luke 8. 44. came behind, and touched b. of his garm.
BORDER, *Verb*.
Zech. 9. 2. and Hamath also shall b. thereby
BORDERS.
Gen. 23. 17. the trees in all the b. were made sure
Exod. 16. 35. till they come to the b. of Canaan
34. 24. I will cast out nations, and enlarge thy b.
Num. 20. 17. until we have passed thy b. 21. 22.
2 Kings 19. 23. I will enter the lodgings of his b.
Psal. 74. 17. thou hast set the b. of the earth
147. 14. he maketh peace in thy b. filleth thee
Isa. 15. † 5. my heart shall cry out to the b.
54. 12. I will make thy b. of pleasant stones
Jer. 15. 13. that for all thy sins, even in all thy b.
Ezek. 45. 1. this shall be holy in all the b.
Mic. 5. 6. when he treadeth within our b.
Mat. 4. 13. in the b. of Zabulon and Nephthalim
BORDERS.
Num. 15. 38. fringes in b. on fringe of b. a ribband
1 Kings 7. 28. they had b. and b. were between ledges
2 Kings 16. 17. Ahaz cut off the b. of the bases
Cant. 1. 11. we will make the b. of gold with studs
Mat. 23. 5. and enlarge the b. of their garments
BORE.
Exod. 21. 6. his master shall b. his ear through
Num. 16. † 14. wilt thou b. out eyes of these men?
Job 40. † 21. will any b. his nose with a gin?
41. 2. canst thou b. his jaw through with a thorn?
BORED.
Judg. 16. † 21. the Philistines b. out his eyes
2 Kings 12. 9. Jehoiada took a chest and b. a hole
BORN
Is taken, [1] Naturally, *for being brought into the world*, Gen. 30. 22. Job 1. 2. [2] Supernaturally, *thus the mighty and miraculous power of God was seen in the production of* Isaac, *enabling* Abraham *to beget*, and Sarah *to conceive and bear him, when both their bodies were as dead*, Gen. 17. 17. Rom. 4. 19. Heb. 11. 11. [3] Carnally, *so was* Ishmael *born, according to the ordinary course of nature, and not by promise, as* Isaac *was*, Gal. 4. 23, 29. [4] Spiritually, *such as are regenerated and renewed by the power and grace of the Spirit of God, in the ministry of the word, and so are made like God, by partaking of a divine nature*, John 1. 13. | 3. 5, 6. 2 Pet. 1. 4. 1 John 3. 9.
BORN *again*. [be b. a.
John 3. 3. except a man be b. a. 5. || 7. ye must
1 Pet. 1. 23. being b. again, not of corruptible seed
See FIRST-BORN, WITNESS.
BORN, *for brought forth*.
Gen. 17. 17. a child b. to him 100 years old, 21. 5.
21. 7. I have b. him a son in his old age
24. 15. Rebekah came, who was b. to Bethuel
29. 34. because I have b. him three sons
30. 20. because I have b. him six sons
31. 43. what do to the children which they have b.
Exod. 1. 22. every son b. ye shall cast into the river
Lev. 12. 7. this is the law of her that hath b. a male
19. 34. the stranger shall be as one b. among you
23. 42. all that are Israelites b. shall dwell in booths
Num. 15. 29. one law for him that is b. and stranger
Josh. 5. 5. b. in the wilderness had not circumcised
8. 33. as well the stranger, as he that was b.

Judg. 13. 8. what do to the child that shall be b.
18. 29. called city after the name of Dan b. to Isr.
Ruth 4. 15. for thy daughter-in-law hath b. him
1 Sam. 2. 5. so that the barren hath b. seven
4. 20. the women said, fear not, thou hast b. a son
2 Sam. 12. 14. the child b. to thee shall surely die
1 Kings 13. 2. a child shall be b. to the house of [David
1 Chron. 7. 21. the men of Gath b. in that land slew
20. † 6. he also was b. to the giant
22. 9. behold a son shall be b. to thee
Job 3. 3. let the day perish wherein I was b.
5. 7. yet man is b. to trouble, as sparks fly upward
11. 12. though man be b. like a wild ass's colt
15. 7. art thou the first man that was b.?
38. 21. knowest thou it, because thou wast then b.?
Psal. 22. 31. shall declare to a people that shall be b.
58. 3. they go astray as soon as they be b.
78. 6. even the children that should be b.
87. 4. this man was b. there, 6. ‖ 5. that man b.
Prov. 17. 17. a brother is b. for adversity
Eccl. 3. 2. a time to be b. ‖ 4. 14. b. in his kingdom
Isa. 9. 6. for unto us a child is b. to us a son is given
66. 8. or shall a nation be b. at once?
Jer. 15. 9. she that hath b. seven languisheth
10. wo is me, that thou hast b. me a man of strife
16. 3. concerning sons and daughters b. in this place
20. 14. cursed be the day wherein I was b.
22. 26. where ye were not b. there shall ye die
Ezek. 16. 4. in the day thou wast b. thy navel not cut
5. to the lothing of thy person in day thou wast b.
20. hast taken thy sons whom thou hast b. to me
Hos. 2. 3. lest I set her as in the day that she was b.
Mat. 2. 2. where is he that is b. king of the Jews?
4. Herod demanded where Christ should be b.
19. 12. there are some eunuchs which were so b.
26. 24. good if he had not been b. Mark 14. 21.
Luke 1. 35. that holy thing that shall be b. of thee
2. 11. to you is b. this day in the city of David
John 3. 4. how can a man be b. when he is old?
5. except a man be b. of water and of the Spirit
6. that of flesh is flesh, that b. of Spirit is spirit
8. so is every one that is b. of the Spirit
8. 41. they said to him, we be not b. of fornication
9. 2. master, who did sin, that he was b. blind?
34. wast altogether b. in sins, and dost teach us?
16. 21. for joy that a man is b. into the world
18. 37. to this end was I b. and for this cause
Acts 2. 8. hear in our own tongue wherein we were b.
7. 20. in which time Moses was b. and was fair
18. 2. Paul found a Jew named Aquila b. in Pontus
24. a Jew named Apollos b. at Alexandria
22. 3. I am a Jew b. in Tarsus ‖ 28. I was free b.
Rom. 9. 11. for the children being not yet b.
1 Cor. 15. 8. seen of me, as of one b. out of due time
Gal. 4. 23. of bond-woman, was b. after the flesh, 29.
Heb. 11. 23. by faith Moses when b. was hid
1 Pet. 2. 2. as new b. babes desire sincere milk of word
1 John 2. 29. that doth righteousness, is b. of him
Rev. 12. 4. to devour the child as soon as it was b.

BORN of God.

John 1. 13. which were b. not of blood, but of God
1 John 3. 9. b. of God doth not commit sin, because b.
4. 7. every one that loveth is b. of God, and knoweth
5. 1. who believeth that Jesus is Christ is b. of God
4. whatsoever is b. of God overcometh the world
18. whosoever is b. of God sinneth not

BORN in the house.

Gen. 14. 14. armed his trained servants b. in his house
15. 3. to me no seed, one b. in my house is my heir
17. 12. b. in the house shall be circumcised, 13, 23, 27.
Lev. 22. 11. b. in the priest's house eat of his meat
Eccl. 2. 7. I had servants b. in my house

BORN in the land.

Exod. 12. 19. no leaven, whether stranger or b. in land
48. the stranger shall be as one b. in the land
Lev. 24. 16. b. in land that blasphemeth put to death
Num. 9. 14. one ordinance for stranger and b. in land
15. 30. doth ought presumptuously, whether b. in l.

BORN of a woman, or women.

Job 14. 1. man that is b. of a woman is of few days
15. 14. that is b. of a w. that he should be righteous?
25. 4. how can he be clean that is b. of a woman?
Mat. 11. 11. among them that are b. of a w. Luke 7. 28.

BORN.

Gen. 50. † 23. children of Machir b. on Joseph's knees
Exod. 25. 14. that the ark may be b. with them
28. that the table may be b. with them
Judg. 16. 29. the pillars on which the house was b. up
Isa. 46. 3. which are b. by me from the belly
66. 12. ye shall be b. upon her sides and be dandled
Jer. 10. 5. they must be b. because they cannot go
Amos 5. 26. ye have b. the tabernacle of Moloch
Mark 2. 3. bringing one sick of palsy, was b. of four
John 20. 15. if thou hast b. him hence tell me
Acts 21. 35. so it was that he was b. of the soldiers
1 Cor. 15. 49. as we have b. the image of the earthly

BORNE.

Job 34. 31. to be said to God, I have b. chastisement
Psal. 55. 12. it was not an enemy, then I could have b.
69. 7. because for thy sake I have b. reproach
Isa. 53. 4. surely he hath b. griefs, carried sorrows
Lam. 3. 28. because he hath b. it upon him
5. 7. fathers sinned, and we have b. their iniquities
Ezek. 16. 58. thou hast b. thy lewdness and abomin.
32. 24. they have b. their shame, 36. 6. ‖ 39. 26.
Mat. 20. 12. which have b. burden and heat of day
23. 4. heavy burdens, grievous to be b. Luke 11. 46.
Rev. 2. 3. hast b. and hast patience, and not fainted

BORROW.

Exod. 3. 22. every woman shall b. of neighbour, 11. 2.
22. 14. if a man b. ought, and it be hurt or die
Deut. 15. 6. thou shalt lend, but shalt not b. 28. 12.
2 Kings 4. 3. Elisha said, go b. vessels abro., b. not few
Mat. 5. 42. him that would b. of thee, turn not away

BORROWED.

Exod. 12. 35. they b. of Egyptians jewels of silver
2 Kings 6. 5. he cried, alas, master, for it was b.
Neh. 5. 4. we have b. money for the king's tribute

BORROWER.

Prov. 22. 7. and the b. is servant to the lender
Isa. 24. 2. as with the lender, so with the b.

BORROWETH.

Psal. 37. 21. the wicked b. and payeth not again

BOSOM

Signifies, [1] *That part of the body which incloses the heart*, Exod. 4. 6. [2] *The arms*, Psal. 129. 7.

The son which is in the bosom of the Father, John 1. 18. *who is one with the Father, entirely beloved by him, and intimately acquainted with all his counsels and will.*

Render into their bosom, Psal. 79. 12. *Punish them sensibly, so as it may come home to them, and fall heavily upon them in their own persons.*

He shall carry them in his bosom, Isa. 40. 11. *He shall perform all the offices of a tender and faithful shepherd toward his people, carrying himself with great wisdom, condescension, and compassion to every one of them, according to their several capacities and infirmities.*

Abraham's bosom, Luke 16. 23. *Lazarus was in a place of rest, where he had communion with the saints, and enjoyed the same felicity with Abraham the friend of God; and this place was* heaven.

Gen. 16. 5. Sarai said, I have given my maid into
Exod. 4. 6. put now thy hand into thy b. 7. [thy b.
Num. 11. 12. that shouldst say, carry them in thy b.
Deut. 13. 6. if the wife of thy b. entice thee secretly
28. 54. his eye evil toward the wife of his b.
56. her eye evil toward the husband of her b.
Ruth 4. 16. Naomi took the child and laid it in her b.
2 Sam. 12. 3. drank of his cup, and lay in his b.
8. I gave thee thy master's wives into thy b.
1 Kings 1. 2. a young virgin, let her lie in thy b.
3. 20. she arose and took my son, and laid it in her b. and laid her dead child in my b.
17. 19. Elijah took him out of her b.
22. † 35. the blood ran into the b. of the chariot
Job 19. † 27. though my reins be consumed in my b.
31. 33. by hiding mine iniquity in my b.
Psal. 35. 13. my prayer returned into my own b.
74. 11. pluck thy right hand out of thy b.
79. 12. and render seven-fold into their b.
89. 50. how I do bear in my b. the reproach of all
129. 7. nor he that bindeth sheaves, his b.
Prov. 5. 20. wilt thou embrace the b. of a stranger?
6. 27. can a man take fire in his b.?
17. 23. a wicked man taketh a gift out of the b.
19. 24. a slothful man hideth his hand in b. 26. 15.
21. 14. a reward in the b. pacifieth wrath
Eccl. 7. 9. for anger resteth in the b. of fools
Isa. 40. 11. he shall carry the lambs in his b.
49. † 22. they shall bring thy sons in their b.
65. 6. will recompense, even recomp. into their b.
7. I will measure their former work into their b.
Jer. 32. 18. iniquity of fathers into the b. of childr.
Lam. 2. 12. their soul was poured into mother's b.
Ezek. 43. † 13. b. of the altar shall be a cubit
Mic. 7. 5. keep from her that lieth in thy b.
Luke 6. 38. good measure men give into your b.
16. 22. was carried by the angels into Abraham's b.
23. seeth Abraham, and Lazarus in his b.
John 1. 18. which is in the b. of the Father
13. 23. now there was leaning on Jesus' b. a disciple

BOSSES.

Job 15. 26. upon the thick b. of his bucklers

BOTCH.

Deut. 28. 27. Lord will smite thee with the b. 35.

BOTH.

Gen. 2. 25. were b. naked ‖ 3. 7. the eyes of b. opened
19. 36. thus were b. the daughters of Lot with child
21. 27. and b. of them made a covenant
22. 8. so they went b. of them together
27. 45. why should I be deprived of you b. in one day?
31. 37. that they may judge betwixt us b.
Exod. 22. 9. cause of b. shall come before judges
11. then shall an oath of the Lord be between b.
Lev. 20. 11. b. of them surely be put to death, their blood shall be upon them, 12. Deut. 22. 22.
Num. 12. 5. called Aaron and Miriam, they b. came
25. 8. Phinehas went after and thrust b. through
Deut. 19. 17. b. the men shall stand before the Lord
1 Sam. 2. 34. in one day they shall die b. of them
9. 26. went out b. of them, he and Samuel, abroad
20. 42. forasmuch as we have sworn b. of us
Job 9. 33. any days-man that might lay his hand on b.
Prov. 17. 15. b. are abomination to the Lord, 20. 10.
20. 12. the Lord hath made even b. of them
24. 22. and who knoweth the ruin of them b.?
Eccl. 4. 3. better than b. is he that hath not been
Isa. 1. 31. they shall b. burn together, none quench
7. 16. the land shall be forsaken of b. her kings
Jer. 46. 12. and they are fallen b. together
Ezek. 21. 19. b. twain shall come forth of one land
23. 13. then I saw that they b. took one way
Mic. 7. 3. that they may do evil with b. hands
Zech. 6. 13. counsel of peace shall be between
9. † 15. they shall fill b. the bowls [them b.
Mat. 15. 14. b. shall fall into the ditch, Luke 6. 39.
Luke 7. 42. nothing to pay, frankly forgave them b.
Acts 23. 8. nor angel nor spirit, but Pharis. confess b.
Eph. 2. 14. he is our peace, who hath made b. one
16. he might reconcile b. unto God by the cross
2 Pet. 3. 1. in b. I stir up your pure minds
Rev. 19. 20. b. were cast alive into the lake of fire

BOTTLE

Signifies, [1] *A vessel to contain liquids*, Gen. 21. 14. Josh. 9. 4. [2] *The inhabitants of* Jerusalem, *whom God threatened to fill with the wine of terror and astonishment for their sins*, Jer. 13. 12. [3] *The clouds in which the rain is kept, as in bottles, out of which God poureth it when he sees fit*, Job 38. 37.

Put my tears in thy bottle, Psal. 56. 8. *Regard and consider all my troubles, which have caused so much grief to me, and deliver me from them.*

Gen. 21. 14. took a b. of water and gave it Hagar
15. water was spent in the b. ‖ 19. she filled the b.
Judg. 4. 19. she opened a b. of milk and covered him
1 Sam. 1. 24. Hannah took a b. of wine, brought him
10. 3. shall meet another carrying a b. of wine
16. 20. Jesse took a b. of wine and sent to Saul
2 Sam. 16. 1. Ziba brought to David a b. of wine
Psal. 56. 8. put thou my tears into thy b. are they not
119. 83. I am become like a b. in the smoke
Isa. 30. † 14. he shall break it as the b. of potters
Jer. 13. 12. every b. shall be filled with wine
19. 1. get a potter's earthen b. ‖ 10. break the b.
Hab. 2. 15. puttest thy b. to him and makest drunken

BOTTLES.

Josh. 9. 4. the Gibeonites took wine b. and rent
13. these b. of wine which we filled were new
1 Sam. 25. 18. Abigail took two b. of wine, five sheep
Job 32. 19. my belly ready to burst like new b.
38. 37. or who can stay the b. of heaven?
Jer. 48. 12. shall empty his vessels, and break b.
Hos. 7. 5. the prince made him sick with b. of wine
Mat. 9. 17. neither do men put new wine into old b. else the b. break, Mark 2. 22. Luke 5. 37, 38.

BOTTOM.

Exod. 15. 5. they sank into the b. as a stone
29. 12. thou shalt pour blood beside the b. of the altar, Lev. 4. 7, 18, 25, 30. | 5. 9. | 8. 15. | 9. 9.
Job 36. 30. behold, God covereth the b. of the sea
Cant. 3. 10. he made the b. thereof of gold
Ezek. 36. † 4. thus saith the Lord to hills and b.
Dan. 6. 24. or ever they came at the b. of the den
Amos 9. 3. tho' they be hid from my sight in the b.
Jonah 2. 6. I went down to the b. of the mountains
Zech. 1. 8. he stood among myrtle-trees in the b.
Mat. 27. 51. vail rent from top to b. Mark 15. 38.

BOTTOMLESS.

Rev. 9. 1. to him was given the key of the b. pit
2. he opened the b. pit, and there arose smoke
11. had a king, which is the angel of the b. pit
11. 7. the beast that ascendeth out of the b. pit
17. 8. the beast shall ascend out of the b. pit
20. 1. an angel having the key of the b. pit
3. and cast him into the b. pit, and shut him up

BOUGH.

Gen. 49. 22. Joseph is a fruitful b. even a fruitful b. by a well, whose branches run over the wall
Judg. 9. 48. Abimelech cut down a b. from the trees
49. the people cut down every man his b.
Isa. 10. 33. the Lord shall lop the b. with terror
17. 6. two or three berries in top of uppermost b.
9. in that day his strong cities be as a forsaken b.

BOUGHS.

Lev. 23. 40. b. of goodly trees, b. of thick trees
Deut. 24. 20. thou shalt not go over the b. again
2 Sam. 18. 9. the mule went under the b. of an oak
Job 14. 9. and brought forth b. like a plant
Psal. 80. 10. the b. were like the goodly cedar-trees
11. she sent out her b. to the sea, branches to river
Cant. 7. 8. I will take hold of the b. thereof
Isa. 27. 11. when the b. thereof are withered
30. † 17. till ye be left as a tree bereft of b.
Ezek. 17. 23. it shall bring forth b. and bear fruit
31. 3. his top was among the thick b. 14.
6. the fowls made their nests in his b. Dan. 4. 12.

BOUGHT.

1 Sam. 25. † 29. in the midst of the b. of a sling

BOUGHT.

Gen. 17. 12. circumcised every man-child born in house b. with his money, 13, 23, 27. Exod. 12. 44.
33. 19. Jacob b. a parcel of a field, Josh. 24. 32.
39. 1. Potiphar b. Joseph of the Ishmaelites
47. 14. Joseph gathered money for the corn they b.
20. Joseph b. all the land of Egypt, 23.
49. 30. which Abraham b. 50. 13. Acts 7. 16.
Lev. 25. 28. shall remain in the hand of him that b. it
30. shall be established for ever to him that b. it
50. he shall reckon with him that b. him
25. 51. give out of the money that he was b. for
27. 22. sanctify to the Lord a field that he b.
24. in jubilee return to him of whom it was b.
Deut. 32. 6. is not he thy father that b. thee?
Ruth 4. 9. I have b. all that was Elimelech's
2 Sam. 12. 3. one little ewe-lamb which he had b.
24. 24. so David b. the threshing-floor and oxen
1 Kings 16. 24. Omri b. the hill Samaria of Shemer
Neh. 5. 16. I continued in work, nor b. we any land
Jer. 32. 9. I b. the field of Hanameel my uncle's son
43. and fields shall be b. in this land
Hos. 3. 2. so I b. her to me for 15 pieces of silver
Mat. 13. 46. he sold all that he had, and b. that field
21. 12. Jesus cast out all them that sold and b. in the temple, Mark 11. 15. Luke 19. 45.
27. 7. took counsel and b. with them potters' field
† 9. whom they b. of the children of Israel
Mark 15. 46. Joseph b. fine linen and took him down
16. 1. had b. sweet spices to come and anoint him
Luke 14. 18. I have b. a piece of ground, and go see it
19. I have b. five yoke of oxen, I go to prove them
17. 28. they did eat, they drank, they b. and sold
1 Cor. 6. 20. for ye are b. with a price, 7. 23.
2 Pet. 2. 1. even denying the Lord that b. them
Rev. 14. † 4. these were b. from among men

BOUND, actively.

Gen. 22. 9. b. Isaac his son, and laid him on the altar
38. 28. the midwife b. on his hand a scarlet thread
42. 24. took Simeon and b. him before them
Lev. 8. 7. he b. the ephod with the curious girdle
† 13. he b. bonnets on Aaron's sons
Num. 30. 4. she had b. her soul, 5, 6, 7, 8, 9, 10, 11.
Josh. 2. 21. she b. a scarlet line in the window
Judg. 15. 13. they b. Samson with two new cords
16. 8. b. with withs ‖ 12. ropes ‖ 21. fetters
2 Kings 5. 23. he b. two talents of silver in two bags
17. 4. he shut up Hoshea and b. him in prison
25. 7. they b. Zedekiah with fetters of brass
2 Chron. 33. 11. b. Manasseh ‖ 36. 6. b. Jehoiakim
Prov. 30. 4. who hath b. the waters in a garment
Hos. 7. 15. tho' I have b. and strengthened their arms
Mat. 14. 3. Herod b. John and put in pris. Mark 6. 17.
27. 2. they had b. Jesus, Mark 15. 1. John 18. 12.
Luke 13. 16. this daughter whom Satan hath b.
Acts 21. 11. Agabus b. his own hands and feet
22. 25. as they b. Paul with thongs he said, 29.
23. 12. b. themselves under a curse, 14, 21.
Rev. 20. 2. he b. Satan a thousand years

BOUND, passively.

Gen. 39. 20. a place where the king's prisoners are b.
40. 3. into the prison where Joseph was b.

Gen.40.5. the butler and baker which were *b.* in pris.
42. † 16. ye shall be *b.* in prison to prove your words
19. let one of your brethren be *b.* in prison
Num. 19. 15. vessel which hath no cover *b.* on it
Judg. 16. 6. wherewith thou mightest be *b.* 10, 13.
1 *Sam.* 25. 29. the soul of my lord shall be *b.*
2 *Sam.* 3. 34. thy hands were not *b.* nor feet
Job 36. 8. and if they be *b.* in fetters and holden
Psal. 107. 10. being *b.* in affliction and iron
Prov. 22. 15. foolishness is *b.* in the heart of a child
Isa. 22. 3. are *b.* by the archers, all are *b.* together
61. 1. the opening of the prison to them that are *b.*
Lam. 1. 14. the yoke of my transgressions is *b.*
Dan. 3. 21. *b.* in their coats ‖ 23. fell down *b.*
24. did not we cast three men *b.* into the furnace?
Mat. 16. 19. bind on earth, be *b.* in heaven, 18. 18.
23. † 18. he that sweareth by the gift, he is *b.*
Mark 15. 7. lay *b.* with them that made insurrection
John 11. 44. *b.* hand and foot, his face was *b.*
18. 24. Annas had sent him *b.* to Caiaphas, † 13.
Acts 9. 2. that he might bring them *b.* 21. ‖ 22. 5.
12. 6. Peter *b.* with chains ‖ 24. 27. left Paul *b.*
20. 22. behold I go *b.* in the Spirit to Jerusalem
21. 13. I am ready not to be *b.* only, but to die
Rom. 7. 2. is *b.* by the law to her husband, 1 *Cor.* 7. 39.
1 *Cor.* 7. 27. art thou *b.* unto a wife, seek not to be
2 *Thess.* 1. 3. we are *b.* to thank God always, 2. 13.
2 *Tim.* 2. 9. but the word of God is not *b.*
Heb. 13. 3. them that are in bonds, as *b.* with them
Rev. 9. 14. loose the angels *b.* in the river Euphrates

BOUND *with chains.*

2 *Chr.* 33. † 11. Manasseh *b.*- ‖ 36. † 6. Jehoiakim *b.*-
Psal. 68. 6. God bringeth out those which are *b. w. c.*
Jer. 39. 7. *b.* Zedekiah- 52. 11. ‖ 40. 1. Jeremiah *b.*-
Nah. 3. 10. all her great men were *b. with chains*
Mark 5. 4. because he had been often *b. with chains*
Luke 8. 29. he was kept *b. with chains,* in fetters
Acts 21. 33. commanded Paul to be *b. with* two *chains*
28. 20. for hope of Israel I am *b. with* this *chain*

BOUND *up.*

Gen. 44. 30. his life is *b. up* in the lad's life
2 *Sam.* 20. † 3. they were *b. up* living in widowhood
2 *Kings* 12. † 10. which *b. up* silver in bags
Isa. 1. 6. they have not been closed neither *b. up*
Jer. 30. 13. none to plead, that thou mayest be *b. up*
Ezek. 30. 21. it shall not be *b. up* to be healed
34. 4. nor have ye *b. up* that which was broken
Hos. 4. 19. the wind hath *b.* her *up* in her wings
13. 12. the iniquity of Ephraim is *b. up*
Luke 10. 34. he *b. up* his wounds, pouring in oil

BOUND, *Substantive.*

Gen. 49. 26. to the utmost *b.* of the everlasting hills
Job 38. 20. thou shouldest take it to the *b.* thereof
Psal. 104. 9. to waters set a *b.* that they may not pass
Prov. 22. † 28. remove not the ancient *b.* 23. † 10.
Jer. 5. 22. have placed the sand for the *b.* of the sea
Ezek. 40. † 12. the *b.* before the little chambers
Hos. 5. 10. the princes like them that remove the *b.*

BOUNDS.

Exod. 19. 12. thou shalt set *b.* to the people round
23. set *b.* about the mount, and sanctify it
23. 31. I will set thy *b.* from the Red sea to sea of
Deut. 32. 8. he set the *b.* of the people by number
Job 14. 5. hast appointed his *b.* that he cannot pass
26. 10. he hath compassed the waters with *b.*
Isa. 10. 13. I have removed the *b.* of the people
Acts 17. 26. hast determined the *b.* of their habitation

BOUNTY.

1 *Kings* 3. † 6. thou hast shewed to David great *b.*
10. 13. which Solomon gave her of his royal *b.*
Prov. 20. † 6. most men will proclaim their own *b.*
2 *Cor.* 9. 5. and make up beforehand your *b.* that the same might be ready as a matter of *b.*

BOUNTIFUL.

Psal. 145. † 17. the Lord is *b.* in all his works
Prov. 22. 9. he that hath a *b.* eye shall be blessed
Isa. 32. 5. nor shall the churl be said to be *b.*

BOUNTIFULNESS.

2 *Cor.* 9. 11. being enriched in every thing to all *b.*

BOUNTIFULLY.

Psal. 13. 6. because he hath dealt *b.* with me
116. 7. for the Lord hath dealt *b.* with thee
119. 17. deal *b.* with thy servant that I may live
142. 7. for thou shalt deal *b.* with me
2 *Cor.* 9. 6. he which soweth *b.* shall reap *b.*

BOW

Signifies, [1] *An instrument for shooting arrows,* Gen. 27. 3. 2 Kings 9. 24. [2] *The whole furniture for war,* Psal. 44. 6. [3] *Strength,* Job 29. 20. [4] *The rain-bow, the sign of God's covenant in the cloud, which, though naturally a sign of rain, yet by God's appointment was turned into an assurance, that there should be no more such overflowing rain as then had been,* Gen. 9. 13, 14. [5] *His promise and help,* Hab. 3. 9. [6] *Faith and patience,* Gen. 49. 24.

If he turn not, he hath bent his bow, *Psal.* 7. 12. *If he leave not his wicked course, then God hath prepared, and will speedily execute his judgments on him.*

His bow abode in strength, *Gen.* 49. 24. *His innocence, patience, temperance, his faith and hope in God, continued firm, whereby he resisted and vanquished all the temptations and difficulties he met with, so that his enemies could neither defile nor destroy him.*

Gen. 9. 13. I do set my *b.* in the cloud for a token
14. that the *b.* shall be seen in the cloud, 16.
27. 3. take, I pray thee, thy quiver and thy *b.*
48. 22. I took of the Amorite with my sword and *b.*
49. 24. his *b.* abode in strength, and arms of hands
Josh. 24. 12. but not with thy sword nor thy *b.*
1 *Sam.* 18. 4. Jonathan gave David his sword, *b.*
2 *Sam.* 1. 18. bade them teach Judah the use of the *b.*
22. the *b.* of Jonathan turned not back
1 *Kings* 22. 34. a certain man drew a *b.* at a venture and smote the king of Israel, 2 *Chron.* 18. 33.
2 *Kings* 6. 22. smite those taken with sword and *b.*
9. 24. Jehu drew a *b.* with his full strength
13. 15. take *b.* and arrows, he took *b.* and arrows
16. put thy hand upon the *b.* he put his hand
1 *Chron.* 5. 18. valiant men, able to shoot with *b.*
1 *Chr.* 12. 2. armed with *b.* and shooting arr. out of *b.*
Job 29. 20. my *b.* was renewed in my hand
Psal. 44. 6. I will not trust in my *b.* nor sword
46. 9. he breaketh the *b.* and cutteth the spear
76. 3. there brake he the arrows of the *b.*
78. 57. they were turned aside like a deceitful *b.*
Isa. 41. 2. he gave them as stubble to his *b.*
66. 19. that escape to the nations that draw the *b.*
Jer. 6. 23. they shall lay hold on *b.* and spear
49. 35. behold, I will break the *b.* of Elam
50. 42. they shall hold the *b.* and the lance
Lam. 2. 4. he hath bent his *b.* like an enemy
Ezek. 1. 28. as the appearance of the *b.* in the cloud
39. 3. I will smite thy *b.* out of thy left hand
Hos. 1. 5. I will break *b.* of Israel in valley of Jezreel
7. I will not save them by *b.* nor by sword
2. 18. I will break the *b.* and the sword
7. 16. not to most High, they are like a deceitful *b.*
Amos 2. 15. he that handleth *b.* not deliver himself
Hab. 3. 9. thy *b.* was made quite naked, thy word
Zech. 9. 13. when I filled the *b.* with Ephraim
Rev. 6. 2. he that sat on the white horse had a *b.*

See Bend, Bent, Battle-Bow.

BOW-SHOT.

Gen. 21. 16. sat over against him as it were a *b.*

BOWS.

1 *Sam.* 2. 4. the *b.* of the mighty are broken
31. † 3. and men with *b.* hit him, 1 *Chron.* 10. 3.
1 *Chron.* 12. 2. they were armed with *b.* and could use
2 *Chron.* 14. 8. army out of Benjamin that drew *b.*
26. 14. Uzziah prepared for them *b.* and slings
Neh. 4. 13. I even set the people with their *b.*
16. the other half of them held both spears and *b.*
Psal. 37. 15. and their *b.* shall be broken
Isa. 7. 24. with arrows and *b.* shall men come
13. 18. their *b.* shall dash young men to pieces
21. † 17. the number of *b.* shall be diminished
Jer. 51. 56. every one of their *b.* is broken
Ezek. 39. 9. they shall burn the *b.* and the arrows

BOW.

Josh. 23. 7. neither make mention, nor serve, nor *b.* yourselves to their gods, 2 *Kings* 17. 35.
2 *Kings* 5. 18. I *b.* myself in the house of Rimmon
Job 39. 3. they *b.* themselves, they bring forth
Psal. 22. 29. all that go down to the dust, shall *b.*
72. 9. that dwell in wilderness shall *b.* before him
78. † 31. wrath of G. made to *b.* down chosen men
144. 5. *b.* thy heavens, O Lord, and come down
Prov. 5. 1. and *b.* thine ear to my understanding
14. 19. evil *b.* before the good, wicked at gates of
Eccl. 12. 3. the strong men shall *b.* themselves
Mic. 6. 6. and *b.* myself before the high God?
Hab. 3. 6. the perpetual hills did *b.* his ways everlast.
Eph. 3. 14. for this cause I *b.* my knees to the Father

BOW *down.*

Gen. 27. 29. nations *b. down,* mother's sons *b. down*
37. 10. shall I, thy mother, and brethren *b. down*
49. 8. father's children shall *b. down* before me
Exod. 11. 8. these thy servants shall *b. down* to me
20. 5. shalt not *b. down* thyself to them, *Deut.* 5. 9.
23. 24. thou shalt not *b. down* to their gods
Lev. 26. 1. neither set up any image to *b. down* to it
Judg. 2. 19. in following other gods to *b. down*
2 *Kings* 5. 18. when I *b. down* in house of Rimmon
19. 16. L. *b. down* thine ear, and hear, *Psal.* 86. 1.
Job 31. 10. and let others *b. down* upon her
Psal. 31. 2. *b. down* thine ear to me, *Prov.* 22. 17.
95. 6. O come, let us worship and *b. down,* let us kneel
Isa. 10. 4. without me they *b. down* under prisoners
46. 2. they stoop, they *b. down* together, they could
49. 23. kings and queens shall *b. down* to thee
51. 23. have said, *b. down* that we may go over
58. 5. is it to *b. down* his head as a bulrush
60. 14. they that despised thee shall *b. down*
65. 12. ye shall all *b. down* to the slaughter
Rom. 11. 10. eyes darkened, *b. down* their back alway

BOW *knee.*

Gen. 41. 43. and they cried before him, *b.* the *knee*
Isa. 45. 23. to me every *knee* shall *b.* *Rom.* 14. 11.
Eph. 3. 14. I *b.* my *knee* to Father of our Lord Jesus
Phil. 2. 10. at the name of Jesus every *knee* shall *b.*

BOWED.

Gen. 33. 6. the handmaidens and their children *b.*
7. Leah also with her children *b.* Rachel *b.*
43. 26. Joseph's brethren *b.* themselves to him
49. 15. Issachar *b.* his shoulder to bear, became a
Josh. 23. 16. transgressed the covenant, served other gods, and *b.* yourselves to them, *Judg.* 2. 12, 17.
Judg. 5. 27. at her feet he *b.* where he *b.* he fell
Ruth 2. 10. she fell on her face and *b.* herself
1 *Sam.* 4. 19. Phinehas's wife *b.* herself and travailed
20. 41. David *b.* himself ‖ 25. 23. Abigail *b.* 41.
2 *Sam.* 19. 14. David *b.* the heart of the men of Judah
22. 10. he *b.* heavens and came down, *Psal.* 18. 9.
1 *Kings* 1. 16. Bath-sheba *b.* and did obeisance, 31.
19. 18. knees which have not *b.* to Baal, *Rom.* 11. 4.
2 *Kings* 1. † 13. the third captain *b.* before Elijah
2. 15. the sons of the prophets *b.* before Elisha
4. 37. *b.* herself to ground, and took up her son
2 *Chron.* 7. 3. *b.* themselves upon the pavement
29. 29. the king and all present *b.* themselves
Esth. 3. 2. *b.* to Haman ‖ 5. Mordecai *b.* not
Lam. 3. † 20. and my soul is *b.* in me
Mat. 27. 29. *b.* the knee before him, and mocked
Luke 13. 11. a spirit of infirmity, and was *b.*

BOWED *down.*

Gen. 23. 12. Abraham *b. down* before the people
42. 6. Joseph's brethren came and *b. down,* 43. 28.
Num. 25. 2. people did eat, and *b. down* to their gods
Judg. 7. 6. rest of the people *b. down* on their knees
2 *Kings* 9. † 24. Joram *b. down* in his chariot
2 *Chr.* 25. 14. set them up to be his gods, and *b. down*
Psal. 35. 14. I *b. down* heavily as one that mourneth
38. 6. I am *b. down* greatly, I go mourning all day
42. † 5. why art thou *b. down,* O my soul? hope in God
44. 25. our soul is *b. down* to the dust, our belly
57. 6. my soul is *b. down,* they have digged a pit
145. 14. raiseth up all those that be *b. down,* 146. 8.
Isa. 2. 11. the haughtiness of men shall be *b. down*
17. and the loftiness of man shall be *b. down*
21. 3. I was *b. down* at the hearing of it
Luke 24. 5. they were afraid and *b. down* their faces

BOWED *head.*

Gen. 24. 26. man *b.* his *head* and worshipped, 48.
43. 28. they *b.* their *heads* and made obeisance
Exod. 4. 31. then they *b.* their *heads* and worshipped, 12. 27. *Neh.* 8. 6.
34. 8. Moses made haste and *b.* his *head* to earth
Num. 22. 31. Balaam *b.* his *head* and fell flat on face
† Balaam *b.* down his *head,* and *b.* himself
1 *Chron.* 29. 20. *b.* down their *heads* and worshipped
2 *Chr.* 20. 18. Jehoshaphat *b.* his *head* to the ground
29. 30. they sang praises and *b.* their *heads*
John 19. 30. Jesus *b.* his *head* and gave up the ghost

BOWED *himself.*

Gen. 18. 2. Abraham *b. h.* 23. 7, 12. ‖ 19. 1. Lot *b. h.*
33. 3. Jacob *b. himself,* 47. 31. ‖ 48. 12. Joseph *b. h.*
Judg. 16. 30. Samson *b. himself* with all his might
1 *Sam.* 24. 8. David stooped to Saul and *b. himself*
28. 14. Saul perceived it was Samuel and *b. himself*
2 *Sam.* 9. 8. Mephibosheth *b. himself* to David
14. 22. Joab *b. hims.* to David ‖ 33. Absalom *b. hims.*
18. 21. and Cushi *b. himself* to Joab, and ran
24. 20. Araunah *b. h.* before the king, 1 *Chr.* 21. 21.
1 *Kings* 1. 23. Nathan *b. h.* ‖ 47. the king *b. h.* on bed
53. Adonijah came and *b. himself* to king Solomon
2. 19. Solomon rose and *b. himself* to his mother

BOWETH.

Judg. 7. 5. every one that *b.* on his knees to drink
Isa. 2. 9. the mean man *b.* ‖ 46. 1. Bel *b.* down

BOWING.

Gen. 24. 52. Eliezer *b.* himself to the earth
Job 4. † 4. thou hast strengthened the *b.* knees
Psal. 17. 11. set their eyes, *b.* down to the earth
62. 3. as a *b.* wall shall ye be, and a tottering fence
Mark 15. 19. they did spit upon him, *b.* their knees

BOWMEN.

Jer. 4. 29. the city shall flee from the noise of the *b.*

BOWELS

Signifies, [1] *The entrails,* Job 20. 14. Acts 1. 18. [2] *The heart,* 2 Cor. 6. 12. Philem. 7. [3] *The womb,* Gen. 25. 23. [4] *Pity, or compassion,* Isa. 63. 15. Jer. 31. 20. [5] *One greatly beloved, whom a person loves as his own soul,* Philem. 12. [6] *Tender mercies,* Psal. 25. † 6. Prov. 12. † 10.

Gen. 15. 4. out of thine own *b.* shall be thy heir
25. 23. two manner of people shall be from thy *b.*
43. 30. for his *b.* did yearn upon his brother
Num. 5. 22. this water shall go into thy *b.*
2 *Sam.* 7. 12. thy seed which proceed out of thy *b.*
16. 11. behold my son which came forth of my *b.*
20. 10. Joab shed out Amasa's *b.* to the ground
1 *Kings* 3. 26. for her *b.* yearned upon her son
2 *Chron.* 21. 15. great sickness by disease of thy *b.*
18. Lord smote him in his *b.* ‖ 19. his *b.* fell out
32. 21. they that came forth of his own *b.* slew him
Job 20. 14. yet his meat in his *b.* is turned
30. 27. my *b.* boiled, and rested not
Psal. 22. 14. it is melted in the midst of my *b.*
25. † 6. remember, O Lord, thy *b.* and kindnesses
40. † 8. thy law is in the midst of my *b.*
71. 6. art he that took me out of my mother's *b.*
109. 18. let it come into his *b.* like water
Prov. 12. † 10. the *b.* of the wicked are cruel
Cant. 5. 4. and my *b.* were moved for him
Isa. 16. 11. my *b.* shall sound like an harp
48. 19. the offspring of thy *b.* like the gravel
49. 1. from the *b.* of my mother he made mention
63. 15. where is the sounding of thy *b.* and mercies?
Jer. 4. 19. my *b.* my *b.* I am pained at my heart
31. 20. therefore my *b.* are troubled for him
Lam. 1. 20. behold, O Lord, my *b.* are troubled, 2. 11.
Ezek. 3. 3. fill thy *b.* with this roll I give thee
7. 19. not satisfy their souls, nor fill their *b.*
Jonah 1. † 17. Jonah was in the *b.* of the fish
Luke 1. † 78. through the *b.* of the mercy of our God
Acts 1. 18. Judas burst, and all his *b.* gushed out
2 *Cor.* 6. 12. ye are straitened in your own *b.*
7. † 15. Titus, his *b.* are more abundant
Phil. 1. 8. I long after you in the *b.* of Christ
2. 1. if consol. in Chr. if there be any *b.* and mercies
Col. 3. 12. put on *b.* of mercies, kindness, meekness
Philem. 7. the *b.* of the saints are refreshed by thee
12. therefore receive him that is my own *b.*
20. yea, brother, refresh my *b.* in the Lord
1 *John* 3. 17. and shutteth up his *b.* of compassion

BOWL.

Num. 7. 85. each *b.* weighing seventy shekels
Judg. 6. 38. and wringed the dew, a *b.* full of water
Eccl. 12. 6. or ever the golden *b.* be broken
Zech. 4. 2. a candlestick of gold with a *b.* on it
3. two olive trees, one on the right side of the *b.*

BOWLS.

Exod. 25. 29. thou shalt make *b.* to cover, 37. 16.
Num. 4. 7. spread a cloth of blue, dishes and *b.* † 14.
1 *Kings* 7. 50. *b.* and snuffers of pure gold, 1 *Chr.* 28. 17.
2 *Chron.* 4. † 8. Solomon made an 100 *b.* of gold
Amos 6. 6. that drink wine in *b.* but not grieved for
Zech. 9. 15. shall be filled like *b.* as corners of altar
14. 20. the pots in the Lord's house shall be like *b.*

BOX.

2 *Kings* 9. 1. take this *b.* of oil in thine hand, 3.
Mat. 26. 7. having an alabaster *b.* *Mark* 14. 3.
Mark 14. 3. she brake the *b.* and poured, *Luke* 7. 37.

BOX-TREE.

Isa. 41. 19. I will set in the desert the pine and *b.*
60. 13. the glory of Lebanon shall come, the *b.*

BOY, S.

Gen. 25. 27. the *b.* grew, and Esau was a hunter
Joel 3. 3. they have given a *b.* for a harlot
Zech. 8. 5. streets shall be full of *b.* and girls playing

BOYL, or BOIL, S.

Exod. 9. 9. it shall be a *b.* with blains on man
10. it became a *b.* breaking forth with blains
11. the magicians could not stand, because of the *b.*
Lev. 13. 18. the flesh also in which was a *b.*
2 *Kings* 20. 7. took figs and laid on the *b.* *Isa.* 38. 21.
Job 2. 7. so Satan smote Job with sore *b.*

BRACELET, S.

Gen. 24. 30. when he saw *b.* on his sister's hands
38. 18. thy signet, thy *b.* and thy staff, 25.
Exod. 35. 22. were willing, brought *b.* *Num.* 31. 50.
2 *Sam.* 1. 10. the *b.* on his arm I have brought
Isa. 3. 19. I will take away the chains, *b.*

Ezek. 16. 11. and I put *b.* upon thine hands

BRAKE.

Exod. 9. 25. the hail *b.* every tree of the field
32. 3. the people *b.* off the golden ear-rings
19. he cast the tables and *b.* them, *Deut.* 9. 17.
Judg. 7. 19. they *b.* pitchers in their hands, 20.
9. 53. cast a piece of millstone to *b.* his scull
16. 9. *b.* the withs as a thread ‖ 12. *b.* new ropes
1 *Sam.* 4. 18. Eli fell backward and his neck *b.*
2 *Sam.* 23. 16. three mighty men *b.* thro',1 *Chr.* 11. 18.
1 *Kings* 19. 11. a strong wind *b.* in pieces the rocks
2 *Kings* 11. 18. Baal's images *b.* they in pieces
18. 4. *b.* images, *b.* brazen serpent Moses had made
23. 14. Josiah *b.* the images, 2 *Chron.* 34. 4.
2 *Chron.* 21. 17. Arabians came and *b.* into Judah
31. † 5. as soon as the commandment *b.* forth
Job 29. † 17. I *b.* the jaws of the wicked
38. 8. who shut up the sea when it *b.* forth?
10. and *b.* up for it my decreed place, and set bars
Psal. 76. 3. there *b.* he the arrows of the bow
105. 16. moreover, he *b.* the whole staff of bread
33. he smote their vines, *b.* trees of their coast
106. 29. and the plague *b.* in upon them
107. 14. out of darkness he *b.* their bands in sunder
Isa. 59. † 5. as if there *b.* out a viper
Jer. 28. 10. took the yoke from Jeremiah and *b.* it
31. 32. my covenant they *b.* tho' I was a husband
Ezek. 17. 16. whose oath he despised, and cov. he *b.*
Dan. 2. 1. spirit troubled and sleep *b.* from him
34. smote the image on his feet, and *b.* them, 45.
6. 24. the lions *b.* all their bones in pieces
7. 7. the fourth beast devoured and *b.* in pieces
8. 7. goat smote the ram, and *b.* his two horns
Mat. 14. 19. he blessed and *b.* and gave the loaves
15. 36. | 26. 26. *Mark* 6. 41. | 8. 6. | 14. 22. *Luke*
9. 16. | 22. 19. | 24. 30. 1 *Cor.* 11. 24.
Mark 8. 19. when I *b.* the five loaves among 5000
14. 3. she *b.* the box, and poured it on his head
Luke 5. 6. their net *b.* ‖ 8. 29. he *b.* the bands
John 19. 32. the soldiers *b.* the legs of the first
33. and saw that he was dead, they *b.* not his legs

BRAKE *down.*

2 *Kings* 10. 27. *b. down* image of Baal, 2 *Chr.* 23. 17.
11. 18. people went and *b. down* the house of Baal
14. 13. king of Israel *b. down* wall of Jerusalem
2 *Chron.* 25. 23. | 36. 19. *Jer.* 39. 8. | 52. 14.
23. 7. he *b. down* the houses of the Sodomites
8. he *b. down* high places ‖ 12. *b. down* altars, 15.
2 *Chron.* 14. 3. Asa *b. down* images, cut down groves
26. 6. Uzziah *b.* down the wall of Gath
34. 4. they *b. down* the altars of Baalim

BRAKEST. [10. 2.

Exod. 34. 1. words in the first table thou *b. Deut.*
Psal. 74. 13. thou *b.* the heads of the dragons, 14.
Isa. 9. † 4. when thou *b.* the yoke of his burden
Ezek. 29. 7. when they leaned on thee, thou *b.*

BRAMBLE, S.

Judg. 9. 14. then said all the tre s to the *b.*
15. the *b.* said, let fire come out of the *b.*
Isa. 34. 13. nettles and *b.* shall come up in fortresses
Luke 6. 44. nor of a *b.*-bush gather they grapes

BRANCH

Signifies, *The bough of a tree,* Psal. 104. 12.
To which are compared, [1] Jesus Christ *the Messiah, who was born of the royal house of* David, *at that time when it was in an afflicted and contemptible condition, like a tree cut down, and whereof nothing is left but a stump or root under ground,* Isa. 11. 1. Jer. 23. 5. Zech. 3. 8. | 6. 12. [2] *True believers who are ingrafted into Christ the true vine; who is the root, fountain, and head of influence, whence his people and members derive life, grace, fruitfulness, and all good; as fruitful branches derive continual influence from the vine,* John 15. 5. [3] *Earthly kings descended of royal ancestors, as branches spring from the root,* Ezek. 17. 3. Dan. 11. 7. [4] *Children or posterity,* Job 8. 16. | 15. 32.

Exod. 25. 33. a knop and a flower in one *b.* 37. 19.
Num. 13. 23. cut down a *b.* with one cluster of grapes
Job 8. 16. his *b.* shooteth forth in his garden
14. 7. and the tender *b.* thereof will not cease
15. 32. and his *b.* shall not be green
18. 16. and above shall his *b.* be cut off
29. 19. and the dew lay all night upon my *b.*
Psal. 80. 15. the *b.* thou madest strong for thyself
Prov. 11. 28. the righteous shall flourish as a *b.*
Isa. 4. 2. in that day shall *b.* of the Lord be beautiful
9. 14. the Lord will cut off *b.* and root in one day
11. 1. and a *b.* shall grow out of his roots
14. 19. thou art cast out like an abominable *b.*
17. 9. strong cities shall be as an uppermost *b.* left
19. 15. nor any work which *b.* or rush may do
25. 5. the *b.* of terrible ones shall be brought low
60. 21. the *b.* of my planting, the work of my hands
Jer. 23. 5. I will raise to David a righteous *b.*
33. 15. I will cause the *b.* of righteousness grow
Ezek. 8. 17. and lo, they put the *b.* to their nose
15. 2. what is the vine tree more than the *b.?*
17. 3. an eagle came, and took the highest *b.* 22.
Dan. 11. 7. out of a *b.* of her roots shall one stand
Zech. 3. 8. I will bring forth my servant the *b.*
6. 12. behold the man whose name is the *b.*
Mal. 4. 1. it shall leave them neither root nor *b.*
Mat. 24. 32. when his *b.* is yet tender, *Mark* 13. 28.
Luke 1. † 78. the *b.* from on high hath visited
John 15. 2. every *b.* that beareth not, *b.* that beareth
4. as the *b.* cannot bear fruit itself, except it abide
6. if he abide not in me, he is cast forth as a *b.*

BRANCHES.

Gen. 40. 10. and in the vine were three *b.*
12. Joseph said, the three *b.* are three days
49. 22. a bough, whose *b.* run over the wall
Exod. 25. 32. six *b.* come out of the sides of the candlestick, three *b.* out of one side, 37. 18, 21.
Lev. 23. 40. shall take *b.* of palm trees, *Neh.* 8. 15.
Job 15. 30. the flame shall dry up his *b.*
Psal. 80. 11. she sent out her *b.* to the river
104. 12. the fowls which sing among the *b.*
Isa. 16. 8. Moab's *b.* are stretched out
17. 6. four or five in the outmost fruitful *b.* thereof

Isa. 18. 5. he shall take away and cut down the *b.*
27. 10. there shall he lie and consume the *b.*
30. † 17. till ye be left as a tree bereft of *b.*
Jer. 11. 16. and the *b.* of it are broken
Ezek. 17. 6. became a spreading vine whose *b.* turned
19. 10. she was fruitful and full of *b.*
14. fire is gone out of a rod of her *b.*
31. 8. the chesnut-trees not like the Assyrian's *b.*
36. 8. O mountains of Israel, ye shall shoot *b.*
Dan. 4. 14. hew down the tree, cut off his *b.*
Hos. 11. 6. the sword shall consume Ephraim's *b.*
14. 6. his *b.* shall spread, and his beauty as olive
Joel 1. 7. my vine waste, *b.* thereof are made white
Neh. 2. 2. the emptiers have marred their vine *b.*
Zech. 4. 12. I said, what be these two olive *b.?*
Mat. 13. 32. the birds lodge in the *b. Luke* 13. 19.
21. 8. others cut down *b. Mark* 11. 8. *John* 12. 13.
Mark 4. 32. greater than all herbs, shooteth out *b.*
John 15. 5. I am the vine, ye are the *b.*
Rom. 11. 16. if the root be holy, so are the *b.*
17. if some of the *b.* be broken off, 19.
18. boast not against the *b.* but if thou boast
21. for if God spared not the natural *b.* take heed

BRAND, S.

Judg. 15. 5. and when he had set the *b.* on fire
Zech. 3. 2. is not this a *b.* plucked out of the fire?

BRANDISH.

Ezek. 32. 10. when I shall *b.* my sword before them?

BRASS

Is a sort of metal, Exod. 31. 4. *and* denotes, [1] *A people impudent in sin,* Isa. 48. 4. Jer. 6. 28. Ezek. 22. 18. [2] *The infinite power of Christ,* Rev. 1. 15.
A kingdom of brass, *Dan.* 2. 39. *The Grecian monarchy under* Alexander *the* Great, *said to be of* brass, *because of their many wars, and frequent use of arms, which were generally made of* brass.
I will make thy hoofs brass, *Mic.* 4. 13. *I will give thee strength to tread under foot, and break the power of thine enemies into pieces, that it shall never be repaired. It is a* metaphor, *taken from their manner of threshing corn, which was by the treading of oxen, whose hoofs were shod with iron or brass,* Deut. 25. 4. Hos. 10. 11.
Mountains of brass, *Zech.* 6. 1. denote *the immoveable decrees of God, his steady execution of his counsels, and the insuperable restraints that are upon all empires and counsels, which God keeps within the barriers of such impregnable mountains, that not one can start till he open the way.*

Exod. 25. 3. the offering, take gold, silver, *b.* 35. 5.
26. 11. make taches of *b.* 36. 18. | 30. 18. laver of *b.*
37. thou shalt cast five sockets of *b.* for them, 27. 10, 17, 18. | 36. 38. | 38. 11, 17, 19.
27. 2. shall overlay the altar with *b.* 6. | 38. 2.
4. net-work of *b.* | 19. pins of the court of *b.*
31. 4. to work in gold, silver, and *b.* 35. 32.
38. 5. rings of *b.* ‖ 6. overlaid the staves with *b.*
29. the *b.* of the offering was seventy talents
39. 39. the brasen altar and his grate of *b.*
Num. 21. 9. made a serpent of *b.* and put it on a pole, when he beheld the serpent of *b.* he lived
Deut. 8. 9. out of whose hills thou mayest dig *b.*
28. 23. the heaven over thy head shall be *b.*
Judg. 16. 21. Samson bound with fetters of *b.*
1 *Sam.* 17. 5. Goliath had an helmet of *b.* 38.
6. and he had greaves of *b.* on his legs
2 *Sam.* 8. 8. king David took much *b.* 1 *Chr.* 18. 8.
1 *Kings* 7. 14. Hiram was a worker in *b.*
15. for he cast two pillars of *b.* 2 *Kings* 25. 13.
16. chapiters of *b.* 2 *Kings* 25. 17. *Jer.* 52. 22.
27. bases of *b.* ‖ 30. plates ‖ 38. lavers, 2 *Chr.* 4. 16.
45. the pots and shovels were of bright *b.*
47. weight of the *b.* was not found, 2 *Chron.* 4. 18.
2 *Kings* 25. 7. bound Zedekiah with fetters of *b.*
13. carried the *b.* to Babylon, *Jer.* 52. 17.
1 *Chron.* 15. 19. to sound with cymbals of *b.*
22. 3. David prepared *b.* in abundance, 29. 7.
29. 2. I have prepared the *b.* for things of *b.*
2 *Chron.* 12. 10. Rehoboam made shields of *b.*
Job 6. 12. the strength of stones, or is my flesh *b.?*
40. 18. his bones are as strong pieces of *b.*
41. 27. Leviathan esteemeth *b.* as rotten wood
Psal. 107. 16. he hath broken the gates of *b.*
Isa. 45. 2. I will break in pieces the gates of *b.*
60. 17. for wood I will bring *b.* for *b.* gold
Ezek. 24. 11. that the *b.* of it may be hot and burn
Dan. 2. 32. his belly and his thighs were of *b.*
39. shall arise another third kingdom of *b.*
7. 19. the fourth beast, whose nails were of *b.*
10. 6. his feet like in colour to polished *b.*
Mic. 4. 13. will make thine horn iron, and hoofs *b.*
Zech. 6. 1. the mountains were mountains of *b.*
Mat. 10. 9. provide neither gold nor silver, nor *b.*
1 *Cor.* 13. 1. I am become as sounding *b.* or cymbal
Rev. 1. 15. and his feet like to fine *b.* 2. 18.
9. 20. that they should not worship idols of *b.*

Iron and BRASS.

Gen. 4. 22. Tubal-cain, instructor in *b. and iron*
Lev. 26. 19. I'll make your heaven *iron,* your earth *b.*
Num. 31. 22. *b. and iron* which may abide the fire
Deut. 33. 25. thy shoes shall be *iron and b.* as thy days
Josh. 22. 8. return with *b. and iron,* and much raiment
1 *Chron.* 22. 14. prep. *b. and iron* without weight, 16.
2 *Chron.* 2. 7. a cunning man to work in *b. and iron*
14. sent a cunning man to work in *b. and iron*
24. 12. hired such as wrought in *iron and b.* to mend
Job 28. 2. *iron* taken out of the earth, *and b.*
Isa. 48. 4. and thy neck is an *iron* sinew, *and* brow *b.*
60. 17. for *b.* I will bring gold, for *iron* silver
Jer. 6. 28. they are *b. and iron, Ezek.* 22. 18.
Ezek. 22. 20. as they gather *iron and b.* into furnaces
Dan. 2. 35. then was *iron,* clay, *b.* brok. to pieces, 45.
4. 15. with a band of *iron and b.* in tender grass, 23.
5. 4. they praised gods of silver, *b. and iron,* wood

Vessels of BRASS.

Exod. 27. 3. make all *vessels of b.* ‖ 38. 3. made *v. of b.*
Josh. 6. 19. all *vessels of b.* are consecrated to the L.
24. *vessels of b.* and iron they put into the treasury
2 *Sam.* 8. 10. Joram brought *vessels of b.* 1 *Ch.* 18. 10.
2 *Kings* 25. 14. *vessels of b.* took they away, *Jer.* 52. 18.
16. which Solomon had ma e, the *b. of* all these *vessels* was without weight, *Jer.* 52. 20.

Ezra 8. † 27. two *vessels of* yellow or shining *b.*
Ezek. 27. 13. they traded in *vessels of b. Rev.* 18. 12.

BRAZEN.

Exod. 27. 4. make. *b.* rings ‖ 35. 16. *b.* grate, 38. 4.
38. † 8. *b.* glasses ‖ 10. their *b.* sockets twenty
Lev. 6. 28. the sin-offering sodden in a *b.* pot
Num. 16. 39. *b.* censers ‖ 1 *Kings* 4. 13. *b.* bars
1 *Kings* 7. 30. *b.* wheels ‖ 14. 27. made *b.* shields
2 *Kings* 16. 17. *b.* oxen ‖ 18. 4. brake the *b.* serpent
25. 13. the *b.* sea did Chaldees break, *Jer.* 52. 17.
2 *Chron.* 6. 13. Solomon had made a *b.* scaffold
Job 6. † 12. strength of stones, or is my flesh *b.?*
Jer. 1. 18. I have made thee this day *b.* walls
15. 20. I will make thee a fenced *b.* wall
52. 20. the *b.* bulls ‖ *Mark* 7. 4. *b.* vessels

See ALTAR.

BRAVERY.

Isa. 3. 18. the Lord will take away their *b.*

BRAWLER, S.

1 *Tim.* 3. 3. a bishop must be no *b.* ‖ *Tit.* 3. 2. to be [no *b.*

BRAWLING, S.

Prov. 25. 24. with *b.* woman in wide house, 21. 19.
Jam. 4. † 1. from whence come wars and *b.?*

BRAY, ED, ETH.

Job 6. 5. doth the wild ass *b.* when he hath grass?
30. 7. among the bushes they *b.* they were gathered
Psal. 42. † 1. as the hart *b.* after the water-brooks
Prov. 27. 22. tho' thou shouldest *b.* a fool in a mortar

BREACH

Signifies, [1] *The ruin of a wall made by warlike engines,* Ezek. 26. 10. [2] *The altering, or not performing, of one's promise,* Num. 14. 34. [3] *A fracture, or bruise,* Lev. 24. 20. [4] *Decayed or ruined places,* Isa. 58. 12. [5] *Judgment, or punishment,* 2 Sam. 6. 8. [6] *Confusions and animosities,* Psal. 60. 2.
Had not Moses stood in the breach, *Psal.* 106. 23. *God had made an hedge, or wall, about them; but they had made a gap or breach in it, by their sins, at which God, who was now justly become their enemy, might enter to destroy them; which he would have done, had not* Moses *interceded for them.*

Gen. 38. 29. the midwife said, this *b.* be upon thee † therefore his name was called a *b.*
Lev. 24. 20. *b.* for *b.* eye for eye, tooth for tooth
Num. 14. 34. ye shall know my *b.* of promise
Judg. 21. 15. the Lord had made a *b.* in the tribes
2 *Sam.* 5. 20. broken forth as the *b.* of waters
6. 8. Lord made a *b.* on Uzzah, 1 *Chron.* 13. 11.
2 *Kings* 12. 5. wheresoever any *b.* shall be found
1 *Chron.* 15. 13. the Lord our God made a *b.* on us
Neh. 6. 1. builded the wall, and there was no *b.*
Job 16. 14. he breaketh me with *b.* upon *b.*
Psal. 106. 23. had not Moses stood in the *b.*
Prov. 15. 4. but perverseness is a *b.* in the spirit
Isa. 7. 6. let us make a *b.* therein for us, and set a king
30. 13. this iniquity shall be to you as a *b.*
26. in the day that the Lord bindeth up the *b.*
58. 12. thou shalt be called the repairer of the *b.*
Jer. 6. † 14. they have healed the *b.* slightly
14. 17. daughter of my people is broken with a *b.*
17. † 18. break them with a double *b.* [thee?
Lam. 2. 13. thy *b.* is great like sea, who can heal
Ezek. 26. 10. enter into a city wherein is made a *b.*
Dan. 9. † 25. the *b.* built in troublous times
Amos 6. † 6. not grieved for the *b.* of Joseph

BREACHES.

Judg. 5. 17. Asher continued and abode in his *b.*
2 *Sam.* 5. † 20. called place, plain of *b.* 1 *Chr.* 14. 11.
1 *Kings* 11. 27. repaired the *b.* of the city of David
2 *Kings* 12. 5. let them repair the *b.* of the house
6. the priests had not repaired the *b.* of the house
12. to masons to repair *b.* of house of Lord, 22. 5.
Neh. 4. 7. that the *b.* began to be stopped, were wroth
Psal. 60. 2. heal the *b.* thereof for it shaketh
Isa. 22. 9. ye have seen the *b.* of the city of David
Ezek. 13. † 5. ye have not gone up to the *b.*
Amos 4. 3. and ye shall go out at the *b.*
6. 11. Lord will smite the great house with *b.*
9. 11. and I will close up the *b.* thereof

BREAD

Signifies, [1] *Natural food, or that eatable made of corn,* Gen. 3. 19. | 49. 20. [2] *All things necessary for this life,* Mat. 6. 11. [3] *Manna wherewith God fed the children of Israel in the wilderness,* Neh. 9. 15. John 6. 31.
To bread are compared, (1) *Jesus Christ, who is the true food for the soul, and both the author and matter of spiritual life,* John 6. 41, 51. (2) *The gospel, and ordinances and privileges thereof,* Prov. 9. 5. (3) *The* Canaanites, *who were destroyed by the* Israelites *as easily as men eat up their bread, or common food,* Num. 14. 9.
We are one bread, 1 *Cor.* 10. 17. *We are joined together into one mystical body, and declare ourselves to be so, by our fellowship together in the ordinance of the Lord's supper; for the bread we there eat is one bread, and the wine we drink is one wine; though the one be composed of many grains of corn, and the other made up of many particular grapes.*
Children's bread, *Mat.* 15. 26. *The publication of the gospel, and working miracles, which belonged to the* Jews, *who were God's peculiar people.*
Shew bread, 1 *Sam.* 21. 6. *The* Hebrew *signifies* Bread of faces, *or of the face. They thus called the loaves of bread, that the priest of the week put every sabbath day upon the golden table which was in the* Sanctum *before the Lord. They were twelve in number, and represented the twelve tribes of* Israel. *Every loaf must have been of a considerable bigness, since they used two tenth deals of flour for each, which are about six pints,* Lev. 24. 5, 6, 7. *They served them up hot on the sabbath-day in the presence of the Lord, and at the same time took away the stale ones, which had been exposed for the whole week, and which could not be eaten but by the priests alone. If, in an extraordinary case,* David *thought he might eat of them, nothing but urgent necessity could exempt him from sin,* 1 Sam. 21. 4, 5. Mat. 12. 4.

Gen. 14. 18. the king of Salem brought forth *b.*

Gen. 18. 5. and I will fetch a morsel of b.
21. 14. Abraham took b. and gave to Hagar
25. 34. then Jacob gave Esau b. and pottage
27. 17. she gave savoury meat and b. to Jacob
41. 54. in the land of Egypt there was b.
55. the people cried to Pharaoh for b.
43. 31. set on b. || 45. 23. b. for his father
47. 12. Joseph nourished his father's house with b.
15. give us b. || 17. gave them b. for horses
19. buy us and our land for b. that we may live
49. 20. out of Asher his b. shall be fat
Exod. 16. 4. I will rain b. from heaven for you
8. and in the morning b. to the full, 12.
29. he giveth on the sixth day the b. of two days
32. they may see the b. wherewith I fed you
23. 25. he shall bless thy b. and thy water
29. 32. and the b. in the basket by the door
34. if ought of the b. remain unto the morning
40. 23. he set the b. in order upon the table
Lev. 8. 26. he took a cake of oiled b. and a wafer
32. what remaineth of the b. ye shall burn
21. 6. the b. of their God they do offer, 8, 17, 21, 22.
22. 25. nor from a stranger shall ye offer b.
23. 18. ye shall offer with the b. seven lambs
26. 26. ten women shall bake your b. in one oven
Num. 4. 7. and the continual b. shall be thereon
14. 9. the people of the land, they are b. for us
21. 5. no b. nor water, our soul lotheth this light b.
28. 2. my b. for my sacrifices shall ye observe
Deut. 8. 3. that he might make thee know that man doth not live by b. only, Mat. 4. 4. Luke 4. 4.
23. 4. they met you not with b. and water
29. 6. ye have not eaten b. nor drunk water
Josh. 9. 5. all b. of their provision was dry and mouldy
12. this our b. we took hot for our provision
Judg. 7. 13. a cake of barley b. tumbled into the host
8. 6. that we should give b. to thy army, 15.
19. 5. comfort thy heart with a morsel of b.
19. and there is b. and wine also for me
Ruth 1. 6. Lord visited his people in giving them b.
1 Sam. 2. 5. they hired out themselves for b.
36. shall come and crouch to him for a morsel of b.
9. 7. for the b. is spent in our vessels, not a present
16. 20. Jesse took an ass laden with b. and bottle
21. 4. but there is hallowed b. || 5. b. is common
6. priest gave him hallowed b. to put hot b. in day
22. 13. thou hast given him b. and a sword
25. 11. shall I take my b. and my water to give
28. 22. let me set a morsel of b. before thee
30. 11. they found an Egyptian and gave him b.
2 Sam. 3. 29. let not fail from Joab one that lacketh b.
35. if I taste b. or ought else till the sun be down
6. 19. he dealt to every one a cake of b. and piece of
1 Kings 4. † 22. Solomon's b. for one day was thirty
13. 22. but camest back and hast eaten b. and drunk
23. after he had eaten b. and after he had drunk
17. 6. ravens brought b. and flesh in evening
11. bring me, I pray thee, a morsel of b.
18. 4. and fed them with b. and water, 13.
2 Kings 4. 42. and brought the man of God b.
18. 32. till I take you to a land of b. Isa. 36. 17.
1 Chr. 12. 40. they of Zabulon brought b. on asses
Neh. 5. 14. have not eaten the b. of the governor
9. 15. and gavest them b. from heaven for hunger
13. 2. because they met not Israel with b. and water
Job 15. 23. wandereth abroad for b. saying, where is it
22. 7. thou hast withholden b. from the hungry
27. 14. his offspring shall not be satisfied with b.
28. 5. as for the earth, out of it cometh b.
33. 20. his life abhorreth b. and soul dainty meat
Psal. 37. 25. nor have I seen his seed begging b.
78. 20. can he give b.? || 102. 9. eaten ashes like b.
80. 5. thou feedest them with the b. of tears
104. 15. and b. which strengtheneth man's heart
105. 40. and satisfied them with the b. of heaven
109. 10. let them seek their b. out of desolate places
132. 15. I will satisfy her poor with b.
Prov. 9. 17. stolen waters sweet, b. eat. secret is pleas.
12. 9. he that is despised and hath a servant is better than he that honoureth himself and lacketh b.
11. tilleth land shall be satisfied with b. 28. 19.
20. 13. open thine eyes, thou shalt be satisfied with b.
17. b. of deceit is sweet to a man, but afterward
22. 9. for he giveth of his b. to the poor
31. 27. she eateth not the b. of idleness
Eccl. 9. 11. I saw race is not to swift, nor b. to wise
11. 1. cast thy b. upon the waters, for shalt find it
Isa. 3. 1. Lord doth take away the whole stay of b.
7. for in my house is neither b. nor clothing
21. 14. they prevented with their b. him that fled
30. 20. though the Lord give you the b. of adversity
33. 16. his b. shall be given him, his waters be sure
44. 15. he baketh b. on the coals thereof, 19.
51. 14. should not die, nor that his b. should fail
55. 2. why spend money for that which is not b.?
10. that it may give seed to the sower, b. to eater
58. 7. is it not to deal thy b. to the hungry?
Jer. 11. † 19. let us destroy the stalk with his b.
42. 14. we shall see no war, nor have hunger of b.
44. † 17. for then had we plenty of b.
Lam. 1. 11. all her people sigh, they seek b.
4. 4. young children ask b. no man breaks it them
5. 6. given hand to Egyptians to be satisfied with b.
9. we gat our b. with the peril of our lives
Ezek. 4. 15. thou shalt prepare thy b. therewith
17. that they may want b. and water and consume
16. 49. pride, fulness of b. and abundance of idleness
18. 7. but hath given his b. to the hungry, 16.
44. 7. brought strangers when ye offer my b.
Hos. 2. 5. I will go after my lovers that give me b.
9. 4. their sacrifices shall be as the b. of mourners
Amos 4. 6. given you want of b. in all your places
8. 11. not a famine of b. but of hearing the word
Hag. 2. 12. if one with his skirt do touch b. or wine
Mal. 1. 7. ye offer polluted b. upon mine altar
Mat. 4. 3. command these stones be made b. Luke 4. 3.
6. 11. give us this day our daily b. Luke 11. 11.
7. 9. if his son ask b. will he give him a stone?
15. 26. not meet to take the children's b. Mark 7. 27.
33. whence should we have so much b.? Mark 8. 4.
16. 5. they had forgotten to take b. Mark 8. 14.
11. that I spake it not to you concerning b.

Mat. 16. 12. he bade them not beware of leaven of b.
26. 26. Jesus took b. and blessed it, Mark 14. 22.
Luke 7. 33. John Baptist came neither eating b.
9. 3. take nothing for your journey, neither b.
15. 17. servants of my father's have b. enough
22. 19. took b. gave thanks and brake it, 24. 30.
24. 35. how he was known of them in breaking b.
John 6. 5. two hundred penny-worth of b. is not suff.
32. Moses gave you not that b. from heaven, my Father giveth you the true b. from heaven
33. the b. of God is he || 34. Lord, give us this b.
35. Jesus said to them, I am the b. of life, 48.
41. I am the b. which came down, 50, 58.
58. he that eateth of this b. shall live for ever
13. 18. he that eateth b. with me hath lift his heel
21. 9. they saw a fire and fish laid thereon and b.
13. Jesus then taketh b. and giveth them
Acts 2. 42. they continued in breaking of b.
46. and breaking b. from house to house
20. 7. when the disciples came to break b.
11. when he had broken b. and eaten, and talked
27. 35. he took b. and gave thanks to God
1 Cor. 10. 16. b. we break, is it not the communion
17. for we being many are one b. and one body
11. 23. have received of Lord, that the Lord Jesus, the same night in which he was betrayed, took b.
2 Cor. 9. 10. both minister b. to your food
See Affliction.

BREAD-CORN.

Isa. 28. 28. b.-corn is bruised, because he will not b.

BREAD, with eat.

Gen. 3. 19. in the sweat of thy face shalt thou eat b.
28. 20. if Lord will give me b. to eat and raiment
31. 54. Jacob called his brethren to eat b.
37. 25. Joseph's brethren sat down to eat b.
39. 6. knew not ought he had, save the b. he did eat
43. 25. they heard that they should eat b. there
32. Egyptians might not eat b. with the Hebrews
Exod. 2. 20. where is he? call him that he may eat b.
16. 3. and when we did eat b. to the full
15. this is the b. the Lord hath given you to eat
18. 12. came to eat b. with Moses' father-in-law
34. 28. he did not eat b. forty days, Deut. 9. 9, 18.
Lev. 8. 31. there eat it, with the b. in the basket
21. 22. he shall eat the b. of his God, both of holy
23. 14. ye shall neither eat b. nor parched corn
26. 5. and ye shall eat your b. to the full and dwell
Num. 15. 19. when ye eat the b. of the land
Deut. 8. 9. thou shalt eat b. without scarceness
Judg. 13. 16. tho' thou detain me, I will not eat thy b.
Ruth 2. 14. at meal-time come thou, and eat b.
2 Sam. 9. 7. thou shalt eat b. at my table, 10.
12. 17. neither did he eat b. with them
20. set b. and he did eat || 21. didst rise and eat b.
16. 2. and summer fruit for young men to eat
1 Kings 13. 8. nor will I eat b. nor drink water, 16.
9. charged me by the Lord, saying, eat no b.
15. then said he, come home with me and eat b.
21. 7. arise, eat b. let thy heart be merry
2 Kings 4. 8. Shunamite constrained Elisha to eat b.
6. 22. set b. and water, they may eat and drink
23. 9. but they did eat of the unleavened b.
25. 29. did eat b. continually before him, Jer 52. 33.
Job 42. 11. and did eat b. with Job in his house
Psal. 14. 4. who eat up my people, as they eat b. 53. 4.
41. 9. who did eat of my b. hath lifted up his heel
78. † 25. every one did eat the b. of the mighty
102. 4. my heart smitten, so that I forget to eat my b.
127. 2. vain to sit up late, to eat the b. of sorrows
Prov. 4. 17. for they eat the b. of wickedness
9. 5. come, eat of my b. and drink of the wine
23. 6. eat not the b. of him that hath an evil eye
25. 21. if thy enemy hunger, give him b. to eat
Eccl. 9. 7. go thy way, eat thy b. with joy
Isa. 4. 1. we will eat our b. and wear our apparel
Jer. 5. 17. they shall eat up thy harvest and thy b.
41. 1. there they did eat b. together in Mizpah
Ezek. 4. 13. thus shall they eat their defiled b.
16. they shall eat b. by weight and with care
12. 18. eat b. with quaking || 19. eat b. with care
24. 17. cover not thy lips, and eat not b. of men, 22.
44. 3. prince sit in it to eat b. before the Lord
Amos 7. 12. flee into Judah, there eat b. and prophesy
Obad. 7. they that eat thy b. have laid a wound
Mat. 15. 2. wash not their hands when they eat b.
Mark 3. 20. that they could not so much as eat b.
6. 36. and buy b. for they have nothing to eat
7. 2. saw disciples eat b. with defiled hands, 5.
Luke 14. 1. to Pharisee's house to eat b. on sabbath
15. blessed is he that shall eat b. in kingd. of God
John 6. 5. whence shall we buy b. that these may eat?
23. nigh to the place where they did eat b.
31. he gave them b. from heaven to eat
51. if any man eat of this b. he shall live for ever
1 Cor. 11. 26. for as often as ye eat this b. and drink
27. whosoever shall eat this b. and drink this cup
2 Thess. 3. 8. did we eat any man's b. for nought?
12. that with quietness they work and eat b.

Leavened BREAD.

Exod. 12. 15. who eateth leav. b. that soul be cut off
13. 3. there shall no leavened b. be eaten
7. there shall no leav. b. be seen, Deut. 16. 3, 4.
Exod. 23. 18. not offer blood of my sacr. with leav. b.
Lev. 7. 13. he shall offer for his offering leavened b.

Loaf or Loaves of BREAD.

Exod. 29. 23. one loaf of b. with ram of consecration
Judg. 8. 5. give loaf of b. to people that follow me
1 Sam. 10. 3. another carrying three loaves of b.
4. they will salute, and give thee two loaves of b.
21. 3. give me five loaves of b. in my hand
2 Sam. 16. 1. and upon asses two hundred loaves of b.
1 Chr. 16. 3. he dealt to every one of Israel a loaf of b.

No BREAD.

Gen. 47. 13. there was no b. in all the land
Num. 21. 5. there is no b. and our soul loatheth
1 Sam. 21. 4. there is no common b. under my hand
6. for there was no b. there, but shew-bread
28. 20. Saul had eaten no b. all the day nor night
30. 12. the Egyptian had eaten no b. three days
1 Kings 13. 9. eat no b. nor drink water, 17. 22.
21. 4. turned away his face, and would eat no b.
5. why is thy spirit so sad, that thou eatest no b.?

2 Kings 25. 3. there was no b. for the people, Jer. 52. 6.
Ezra 10. 6. when he came thither, he did eat no b.
Jer. 38. 9. for there is no more b. in the city
Dan. 10. 3. I ate no pleasant b. nor came flesh
Mat. 16. 7. reasoned among themselves, saying, it is because we have taken no b. 8. Mark 8. 16, 17.
Mark 6. 8. take no scrip, no b. no money in purse

Piece or Pieces of BREAD.

1 Sam. 2. 36. put me, I pray, that I may eat a piece of b.
Prov. 6. 26. for by means of a whorish woman a man is brought to a piece of b.
28. 21. for a piece of b. that man will transgress
Jer. 37. 21 to give Jeremiah daily a piece of b.
Ezek. 13. 19. and will ye pollute me for pieces of b.?

Shew-Bread; see Shew.

Staff of BREAD.

Lev. 26. 26. when I have broken staff of your b.
Psal. 105. 16. moreover, he brake whole staff of b.
Ezek. 4. 16. I will break staff of b. 5. 16. | 14. 13.

Unleavened BREAD.

Gen. 19. 3. Lot did bake unleavened b. they did eat
Exod. 12. 18. eat passover with unleav. b. Num. 9. 11.
15. seven days eat unleavened b. 13. 6, 7. | 23. 15. | 34. 18. Lev. 23. 6. Num. 28. 17. Deut. 16. 3.
18. on fourteenth day of month eat unleavened b.
20. in all your habitations shall ye eat unleav. b.
29. 2. take unleavened b. to hallow the priests
Lev. 6. 16. meat offering ye shall eat with unleav. b.
Num. 6. 15. wafers of unleavened b. anointed with oil
Deut. 16. 8. six days thou shalt eat unleavened b.
1 Sam. 28. 24. witch of Endor did bake unleav. b.
2 Kings 23. 9. did eat unleav. b. among their brethren
Ezek. 45. 21. on 14th day passover of unl. b. be eaten
Mark 14. 12. first day of unl. b. when they killed
Luke 22. 7. then came the days of unl. b. Acts 12. 3.
Acts 20. 6. after the days of unleavened b. we sailed
1 Cor. 5. 8. but with the unleavened b. of sincerity
See Basket, Feast.

BREADTH.

Gen. 6. 15. the fashion of the ark, the b. fifty cubits
13. 17. arise, walk thro' the land in the b. of it
Exod. 27. 18. b. of the court fifty cubits every where
28. 16. breast-plate, a span the b. thereof, 39. 9.
38. 1. he made the altar, five cubits the b. thereof
Deut. 2. 5. not give of their land, so much as a foot b.
Judg. 20. 16. could sling stones at an hair's b.
1 Kings 6. 2. the b. of the Lord's house was twenty cubits, the length threescore cubits, 2 Chron. 3. 3.
7. 6. the b. of the porch was thirty cubits
2 Chron. 4. 1. the b. of the altar was twenty cubits
Ezra 6. 3. the b. of the Lord's house sixty cubits
Job 37. 10. and the b. of the waters is straitened
38. 18. hast thou perceived the b. of the earth?
Isa. 8. 8. his wings shall fill the b. of thy land
Ezek. 40. 5. the b. of the building || 11. b. of the entry
13. the b. of the gate, 20, 48. || 49. b. of the porch
41. 1. the b. of the tabernacle || 2. b. of the door, 3.
5. b. of side chambers || 7. b. of house was upward
11. the b. of place left || 14. b. of face of the house
45. 1. the b. of the holy portion of the land
Dan. 3. 1. the b. of the image was six cubits
Hab. 1. 6. which shall march thro' the b. of the land
Zech. 2. 2. to measure Jerusalem, to see the b.
5. 2. I see a flying roll, the b. thereof ten cubits
Eph. 3. 18. what is the b. and length and depth
Rev. 20. 9. they went up on the b. of the earth
21. 16. the length of the city is as large as the b.

BREAK.

2 Sam. 2. 32. Joab came to Hebron at b. of day
Acts 20. 11. he talked a long while till b. of day

BREAK

Signifies, [1] To dash to pieces, Exod. 34. 13. [2] To make void, or of none effect, 1 Kings 15. 19. [3] To punish, or afflict, Job 13. 25. [4] To disunite and sever, Zech. 11. 14. [5] To pant, or faint, Psal. 119. 20. [6] To take away, Psal. 105. 16. [7] To weaken, Psal. 10. 15. [8] To plough, Jer. 4. 3. [9] To cause great sorrow of heart, Acts 21. 13. [10] To shine, or appear, Cant. 2. 17. [11] To profane, Psal. 89. † 31.

Gen. 19. 9. they came near to b. the door
27. 40. thou shalt b. his yoke from off thy neck
Exod. 12. 46. nor shall ye b. a bone, Num. 9. 12.
13. 13. then thou shalt b. his neck, 34. 20.
34. 13. but ye shall b. their images, and cut down
Lev. 11. 33. every earthen vessel unclean ye shall b.
26. 19. I will b. the pride of your power
Num. 24. 8. Israel shall b. their bones, pierce them
30. 2. if a man vow, he shall not b. his word
32. † 7. wherefore b. ye the heart of Israel?
Deut. 12. 3. ye shall b. their pillars, and burn groves
1 Sam. 25. 10. b. away every man from his master
1 Kings 15. 19. b. thy league with Baasha, 2 Chr. 16. 3.
Ezra 9. 14. should we again b. thy commandments
Job 13. 25. wilt thou b. a leaf driven to and fro?
39. 15. forgetteth that the wild beast may b. them
Psal. 2. 3. let us b. their bands asunder
9. thou shalt b. them with a rod of iron
10. 15. b. thou the arm of the wicked
58. 6. b. their teeth, O God, in their mouth
74. † 8. they said in their hearts, let us b. them
89. 31. if they b. my statutes and keep not my com.
104. † 11. the wild asses b. their thirst
141. 5. shall be an oil which shall not b. my head
Cant. 2. 17. until day b. and shadows flee away, 4. 6
Isa. 14. 25. I will b. the Assyrian in my land
28. 24. b. the clods || 28. not b. it with a wheel
30. 14. b. it as the breaking of a potter's vessel
38. 13. as a lion so will he b. all my bones
42. 3. a bruised reed will he not b. Mat. 12. 20.
58. 6. is not this the fast, that ye b. every yoke?
Jer. 15. 12. shall iron b. the northern iron and steel?
16. † 7. neither shall men b. bread for them
17. † 18. b. them with a double breach
19. 10. b. the bottle, so will I b. this people, 11.
28. 4. I will b. yoke of king of Babylon, 11. | 30. 8.
43. 13. he shall b. the images of Beth-shemesh
48. 12. I will send wanderers and b. Moab's bottles
49. 35. saith the Lord, I will b. the bow of Elam
Ezek. 4. 16. I will b. the staff of bread, 5. 16. | 14. 13.
16. 38. judge thee as women that b. wedlock

Ezek. 23. 34. thou shalt *b.* the sherds thereof
29. 7. when they took hold of thee thou didst *b.*
30. 18. when I shall *b.* the yokes of Egypt
22. and I will *b.* Pharaoh's arms, 24.
Hos. 1. 5. I will *b.* the bow of Israel in Jezreel
2. 18. I will *b.* the bow, the sword and battle
10. 11. Judah shall plow, and Jacob shall *b.* his clods
Joel 2. 7. they shall march and not *b.* their ranks
Amos 1. 5. I will *b.* the bar of Damascus
Mic. 3. 3. who flay their skin, and *b.* their bones
Nah. 1. 13. now will I *b.* his yoke from off thee
Zech. 11. 14. that I might *b.* the brotherhood
Mat. 5. 19. *b.* one of these least commandments
9. 17. else the bottles *b.* and the wine runneth
Acts 20. 7. the disciples came together to *b.* bread
21. 13. what mean ye to weep and to *b.* my heart?
1 *Cor.* 10. 16. the bread which we *b.* is it not

BREAK *covenant.*

Lev. 26. 15. but that ye *b.* my *c.* || 44. I will not *b.* my *c.*
Deut. 31. 16. this people will *b.* my *cov.* I made, 20.
Judg. 2. 1. I said, I will never *b.* my *cov.* with you
Psal. 89. 34. my *c.* will I not *b.* nor alter the thing
Jer. 14. 21. remember, *b.* not thy *covenant* with us
33. 20. if ye can *b.* my *cov.* of the day and night
Ezek. 17. 15. shall he *b.* *covenant* and be delivered?
Zech. 11. 10. that I might *b.* my *cov.* which I made

BREAK *down.*

Exod. 23. 24. quite *b.* *down* their images, *Deut.* 7. 5.
Lev. 14. 45. and he shall *b.* *down* house, the stones
Deut. 12. † 3. ye shall *b.* *down* their altars
Judg. 8. 9. when I come again, I will *b.* *down* tower
Neh. 4. 3. if a fox go up, he shall *b.* *down* stone wall
Psal. 74. 6. now they *b.* *down* the carved work
Eccl. 3. 3. a time to *b.* *down* and a time to build
Isa. 5. 5. I will *b.* *down* the wall of the vineyard
Jer. 31. 28. as I have watched over them to *b.* *down*
45. 4. that which I have built will I *b.* *down*
Ezek. 13. 14. so will I *b.* *down* wall ye have daubed
16. 39. they shall *b.* *down* thy high places
26. 4. they shall *b.* *down* the towers of Tyrus
12. and they shall *b.* *down* thy walls
Hos. 10. 2. he shall *b.* *down* their altars, and spoil

BREAK *forth.*

Exod. 19. 22. lest the Lord *b.* *forth* upon them, 24.
Isa. 14. 7. they *b.* *f.* into sing. 44. 23. | 49. 13. | 54. 1.
52. 9. *b.* *forth* into joy, sing together, ye waste places
54. 3. for thou shalt *b.* *forth* on the right hand
55. 12. hills shall *b.* *forth* before you into singing
58. 8. then shall thy light *b.* *forth* as the morning
Jer. 1. 14. out of the north an evil shall *b.* *forth*
Gal. 4. 27. *b.* *forth* and cry, thou that travailest not

BREAK *off.*

Gen. 27. 40. thou shalt *b.* his yoke *off* thy neck
Exod. 32. 2. *b.* *off* the golden ear rings, 24.
Dan. 4. 27. O king, *b.* *off* thy sins by righteousness

BREAK *out.*

Exod. 22. 6. if fire *b.* *out* || *Lev.* 13. 12. if leprosy *b.* *out*
Lev. 14. 43. if the plague come again and *b.* *out*
Psal. 58. 6. *b.* *out* the great teeth of the young lion
Isa. 35. 6. in the wilderness shall waters *b.* *out*
Hos. 4. 2. they *b.* *out*, and blood toucheth blood
Amos 5. 6. lest he *b.* *out* like fire in the house of Joseph

BREAK *in pieces.*

2 *Kings* 25. 13. Chaldeans *b.* *in pieces* pillars of brass
Job 19. 2. how long will ye *b.* me *in pieces* with words?
34. 24. shall *b.* *in pieces* mighty men without number
Psal. 72. 4. he shall *b.* *in pieces* the oppressor
94. 5. they *b.* *in pieces* thy people, O Lord
Isa. 45. 2. I will *b.* *in pieces* the gates of brass
Jer. 1. † 17. lest I *b.* thee *in pieces* before them
51. 20. with thee will I *b.* *in pieces* the nations
21. with thee *b.* *in pieces* horse and rider, chariot
22. with thee *b.* *in p.* man, woman, old and young
Dan. 2. 40. shall it *b.* *in p.* and bruise kingdoms, 44.
7. 23. the fourth beast shall *b.* *in pieces* whole earth

BREAK *through.*

Exod. 19. 21. lest they *b.* *thro'* to the Lord to gaze
24. let not the priests and people *b.* *through*
2 *Kings* 3. 26. to *b.* *through* to the king of Edom
Mat. 6. 19. thieves *b.* *thro'* || 20. thieves *b.* not *thro'*

BREAK *up.*

2 *Chron.* 32. † 1. Sennacherib thought to *b.* them *up*
Jer. 4. 3. *b.* *up* your fallow ground, *Hos.* 10. 12.

BREAKER.

Ezek. 18. † 10. if he beget a son, a *b.* up of a house
Mic. 2. 13. *b.* is come up || *Rom.* 2. 25. if a *b.* of law

BREAKERS.

Rom. 1. 31. without understanding, covenant-*b.*

BREAKEST.

Psal. 48. 7. thou *b.* ships of Tarshish with east-wind

BREAKETH.

Gen. 32. 26. he said, let me go, for the day *b.*
Job 9. 17. for he *b.* me with tempest and multiplies
12. 14. he *b.* down, and it cannot be built again
16. 14. he *b.* me with breach upon breach
28. 4. the flood *b.* out from the inhabitants
Psal. 10. † 10. he *b.* himself, that the poor may fall
29. 5. *b.* the cedars || 46. 9. he *b.* the bow
119. 20. my soul *b.* for the longing that it hath
Prov. 25. 15. and a soft tongue *b.* the bone
Eccl. 10. 8. whoso *b.* an hedge, a serpent shall bite
Isa. 59. 5. which is crushed *b.* out into a viper
Jer. 19. 11. as one *b.* a potter's vessel, not made whole
23. 29. is not my word like a hammer that *b.* rock?
Lam. 4. 4. children ask bread, and no man *b.* it
Dan. 2. 40. forasmuch as iron *b.* in pieces all these

BREAKING.

Gen. 32. 24. there wrestled a man till the *b.* of day
Exod. 9. 9. shall be a boyl *b.* forth with blains, 10.
22. 2. if a thief be found *b.* up, and be smitten
Judg. 7. † 15. Gideon heard the dream, and *b.* thereof
2 *Kings* 11. † 6. keep the watch of the house from *b.* up
1 *Chron.* 14. 11. on enemies, like *b.* forth of waters
Job 30. 14. came upon me as a wide *b.* in of waters
41. 25. by reason of *b.* they purify themselves
Psal. 144. 14. that there be no *b.* in nor going out
Isa. 22. 5. *b.* down walls, and of crying to mount.
30. 13. whose *b.* cometh suddenly at an instant
14. shall break it as the *b.* of the potter's vessel
Ezek. 16. 59. despised the oath in *b.* covenant, 17. 18.
21. 6. sigh, son of man, with *b.* of thy loins
Hos. 13. 13. not stay long in place of *b.* forth of chil.
Luke 24. 35. he was known of them in *b.* of bread
John 7. † 23. without *b.* the law of Moses
Acts 2. 42. they continued in *b.* of bread and prayers
46. in the temple, *b.* bread from house to house
Rom. 2. 23. through *b.* the law, dishonourest God

BREAST.

Exod. 29. 26. take the *b.* of the ram of consecration
27. shall sanctify the *b.* of the wave offering
Lev. 7. 30. *b.* may be waved, the fat with the *b.*
31. but the *b.* shall be Aaron's and his sons'
34. the wave-*b.* and heave-shoulder have I taken
8. 29. Moses took the *b.* and waved it for an offering
10. 14. the wave-*b.* shall ye eat in a clean place
Num. 6. 20. is holy to the priest, with the wave-*b.*
18. 18. as wave-*b.* and right shoulder are thine
Job 24. 9. they pluck the fatherless from the *b.*
Isa. 60. 16. thou shalt suck the *b.* of kings
Lam. 4. 3. even the sea monsters draw out the *b.*
Dan. 2. 32. head of gold, his *b.* and his arms of
Luke 18. 13. the publican smote upon his *b.* saying
John 13. 25. he then lying on Jesus' *b.* saith, 21. 20.

BREASTS.

Gen. 49. 25. bless with blessings of the *b.* and womb
Lev. 9. 20. put fat on the *b.* || 21. *b.* Aaron waved
Job 3. 12. or why the *b.* that I should suck
21. 24. his *b.* full of milk, and his bones moistened
Psal. 22. 9. make me hope when I was on mother's *b.*
Prov. 5. 19. let her *b.* satisfy thee at all times
Cant. 1. 13. he shall lie all night betwixt my *b.*
4. 5. thy two *b.* are like two young roes, 7. 3.
7. 7. thy *b.* are like to clusters of grapes
8. thy *b.* shall be as clusters of the vine
8. 1. my brother that sucked the *b.* of my mother
8. we have a little sister, and she hath no *b.*
10. I am a wall, and my *b.* like towers
Isa. 28. 9. are weaned from the milk drawn from *b.*
66. 11. be satisfied with the *b.* of her consolations
Ezek. 16. 7. thy *b.* are fashioned, and hair grown
23. 3. there were their *b.* pressed, there they bruised
8. and they bruised the *b.* of her virginity
34. and thou shalt pluck off thine own *b.*
Hos. 2. 2. put away her adulteries from betw. her *b.*
9. 14. give them a miscarrying womb and dry *b.*
Joel 2. 16. and gather those that suck the *b.*
Nah. 2. 7. as with voice of doves tabring on their *b.*
Luke 23. 48. the people smote their *b.* and returned
Rev. 15. 6. having their *b.* girded with golden girdles

BREAST-PLATE

Was *a piece of embroidery of about ten inches square, of very rich work, which the high-priest of the* Jews *wore upon his breast, and which was set with four rows of precious stones, upon every one of which was engraven the name of one of the tribes of* Israel: *It was double, or made of two pieces folded one upon the other, like a kind of purse, or bag, that it might the better support the precious stones, and that it might receive the* Urim *and* Thummim, *Lev.* 8. 8. *It was called the* Breast-plate of judgment, *Exod.* 28. 15. *because from thence the* Israelites *were to expect and receive their judgment, and the mind of God in all those weighty and momentous matters of war and peace, wherein they consulted God for direction.*

Breast-plate *is likewise a piece of defensive armour,* Rev. 9. 9. *In which sense, faith and love are called* Breast-plates; 1 *Thess.* 5. 8. Faith *is a defensive grace; not only as it assents to the doctrine of the gospel as true, but also as it doth depend upon God's faithfulness and all-sufficiency to perform his promises, and apply them to our souls for our support and comfort.* Love, *when it worketh, will defend against the persecutions, afflictions, and temptations of the world,* Cant. 8. 7. *Slavish fear will overcome us, if we want love to defend against it, when true religion is under disgrace, and persecuted in the world,* 1 John 4. 18. Love *will defend against apostacy, and so help us to persevere to the coming of* Christ; *and love, being seated in the heart, is fitly compared to a* Breast-plate *that encompasseth the heart.*

Exod. 25. 7. and stones to be set in the *b.* 35. 9.
28. 4. shall make a *b.* and ephod, 15. | 39. 8.
22. thou shalt make upon the *b.* chains at the end
23. put rings on two ends of the *b.* 26. | 39. 16.
28. they shall bind the *b.* by the rings, 39. 21.
29. Aaron shall bear the names of Israel in *b.*
30. put in *b.* of judgment the Urim, *Lev.* 8. 8.
1 *Kings* 22. † 34. smote Ahab between joints and *b.*
Isa. 59. 17. he put on righteousness as a *b.*
Eph. 6. 14. having on the *b.* of righteousness
1 *Thess.* 5. 8. putting on the *b.* of faith and love
Rev. 9. 9. they had *b.* as it were *b.* of iron
17. having *b.* of fire, of jacinth, and brimstone

BREATH

Signifies, [1] *The air received and discharged by our bodies, by the dilatation and compression of the lungs,* Job 9. 18. [2] *The life,* Psal. 146. 4. Dan. 5. 23. [3] *God's powerful word,* Psal. 33. 6. Isa. 11. 4. [4] *His anger,* Job 4. 9. Isa. 30. 33.

Gen. 2. 7. God breathed into his nostrils the *b.* of life
6. 17. to destroy all flesh wherein is the *b.* of life
7. 15. entered two and two wherein is the *b.* of life
22. all in whose nostrils was *b.* of life died
Josh. 11. † 11. he destroyed, there was not any *b.*
2 *Sam.* 22. 16. foundations of the world discovered at the blast of the *b.* of his nostrils, *Psal.* 18. 15.
1 *Kings* 17. 17. and there was no *b.* left in him
Job 4. 9. by the *b.* of his nostrils are they consumed
9. 18. he will not suffer me to take my *b.*
11. † 20. their hope shall be as a puff of *b.*
12. 10. in whose hand is the *b.* of all mankind
15. 30. by the *b.* of his mouth shall he go away
17. 1. my *b.* is corrupt, my days are extinct
19. 17. my *b.* is strange to my wife, tho' I entreated
27. 3. all the while my *b.* is in me, and Sp. of God
33. 4. the *b.* of the Almighty hath given me life
34. 14. if he gather to himself his Spirit and *b.*
37. 10. by the *b.* of God frost is given
41. 21. his *b.* kindleth coals, and a flame goeth
Psal. 33. 6. all of them made by the *b.* of his mouth
104. 29. thou takest away their *b.* they die
135. 17. nor is there any *b.* in their mouths
146. 4. his *b.* goeth forth, he returneth to earth
150. 6. let every thing that hath *b.* praise the Lord
Eccl. 3. 19. yea, they have all one *b.* all is vanity
Isa. 2. 22. cease from man, whose *b.* is in his nostrils
11. 4. with *b.* of his lips will he slay the wicked
30. 28. and his *b.* as an overflowing stream reach
33. *b.* of the Lord like a stream of brimstone
33. 11. your *b.* as fire shall devour you
42. 5. he that giveth *b.* to the people upon it
Jer. 10. 14. and there is no *b.* in them, 51. 17.
Lam. 4. 20. the *b.* of our nostrils, the anointed of L.
Ezek. 37. 5. I will cause *b.* to enter into you, shall live
6. I will cover you with skin, and put *b.* in you
8. there was no *b.* in them || 9. and say, come, O *b.*
10. and the *b.* came into them and they lived
Dan. 5. 23. the God in whose hand thy *b.* is
10. 17. no strength, neither is there *b.* left in me
Hab. 2. 19. there is no *b.* at all in midst of the image
Acts 17. 25. seeing he giveth to all life and *b.*
Jam. 2. † 26. the body without *b.* is dead
Rev. 13. † 15. he had power to give *b.* to the image

BREATHE

Signifies, [1] *To draw breath naturally, as man and beast do,* Josh. 10. 40. [2] *To infuse the soul into the body,* Gen. 2. 7. [3] *To live, breathing or respiration being a sign of life,* Josh. 11. 11. [4] *To inspire with the gifts and graces of the Holy Ghost,* John 20. 22.

Josh. 11. 11. there was not any left to *b.* 14.
Job 31. † 39. caused soul of the owners to *b.* out
Ps. 27. 12. witnesses risen, and such as *b.* out cruelty
Cant. 4. † 6. till the day *b.* and shadows flee away
Ezek. 37. 9. come, O breath, and *b.* on these slain

BREATHED.

Gen. 2. 7. God *b.* into man's nostrils the *b.* of life
Josh. 10. 40. but utterly destroyed all that *b.*
1 *Kings* 15. 29. he left not to Jeroboam any that *b.*
John 20. 22. he *b.* on them, and saith, receive ye

BREATHETH, ING.

Deut. 20. 16. thou shalt save alive nothing that *b.*
Lam. 3. 56. hide not thine ear at my *b.* at my cry
Acts 9. 1. Saul yet *b.* out threatenings and slaughter

BRED.

Exod. 16. 20. some left, and it *b.* worms and stank

BREECHES.

Exod. 28. 42. thou shalt make them linen *b.* 39. 28.
Lev. 6. 10. the priest shall put on his linen *b.*
16. 4. he shall have the linen *b.* on his flesh
Ezek. 44. 18. they shall have linen *b.* on their loins

BREED.

Gen. 8. 17. that they may *b.* abundantly on the earth

BREED.

Deut. 32. 14. rams of the *b.* of Bashan and goats

BREEDING.

Zeph. 2. 9. as Sodom, even *b.* of nettles and salt-pits

BRETHREN.

Men are so called, [1] *By being the sons of one father and mother, or of either of them,* Gen. 42. 13. [2] *By community of nature, or habitation,* Gen. 19. 7. [3] *By natural affinity, or by being kinsmen,* Gen. 13. 8. [4] *By regeneration, and profession of the same faith and religion,* Col. 1. 2. [5] *By adoption,* John 20. 17. [6] *By office,* 1 Chron. 25. 9. 2 Cor. 8. 23.

Gen. 13. 8. let there be no strife, for we be *b.*
19. 7. Lot said, I pray you, *b.* do not so wickedly
24. 27. Lord led me to the house of my master's *b.*
34. 11. Shechem said to her father and to her *b.*
25. Dinah's *b.* took each man his sword and slew
42. 3. Joseph's ten *b.* went down to buy corn
6. *b.* came and bowed || 13. we are twelve *b.* 32.
45. 16. Joseph's *b.* are come || 49. 5. are *b.* of cruelty
50. 15. Joseph's *b.* saw their father was dead
Num. 27. 4. give us a possession among the *b.*
7. give us a possession among our father's *b.*
10. if he have no *b.* give it to his father's *b.*
11. if his father have no *b.* ye shall give to kinsmen
Deut. 25. 5. if *b.* dwell together and one of them die
Josh. 6. 23. Rahab brought out her father and *b.*
17. 4. he gave them an inheritance among the *b.*
Judg. 9. 1. Abimelech went to his mother's *b.*
3. his mother's *b.* spake of him to men of Shechem
2 *Kings* 10. 13. they answered, we are *b.* of Ahaziah
1 *Chron.* 12. 2. there came to David of Saul's *b.*
26. 7. sons of Shemaiah, whose *b.* were strong men
27. 18. of Judah, Elihu, one of the *b.* of David
2 *Chron.* 21. 2. he had *b.* the sons of Jehoshaphat
22. 8. when Jehu found the *b.* of Ahaziah
Psal. 133. 1. pleasant for *b.* to dwell together in unity
Prov. 6. 19. and him that soweth discord among *b.*
17. 2. shall have part of the inheritance among *b.*
19. 7. all the *b.* of the poor do hate him
Amos 1. † 9. remembered not the covenant of *b.*
Mat. 4. 18. Jesus saw two *b.* || 21. saw other two *b.*
19. 29. every one that hath forsaken houses, *b.*
20. 24. were moved with indignation against two *b.*
22. 25. there were with us seven *b.* *Mark* 12. 20.
23. 8. one is your Master, even Christ, all ye are *b.*
Mark 10. 29. no man hath left house or *b.* father, mother, wife, or children, for my sake, *Luke* 18. 29.
30. shall receive an hundred-fold, houses, *b.*
Luke 14. 26. if any come, and hate not children *b.*
16. 28. for I have five *b.* that he may testify to them
21. 16. ye shall be betrayed by parents and *b.*
John 21. 23. this saying went abroad among the *b.*
Acts 3. 17. *b.* I wot that through ignorance ye did it
6. 3. wherefore *b.* look out among you seven men
7. 26. sirs, ye are *b.* || 9. 30. which when the *b.* knew
10. 23. certain *b.* from Joppa accompanied him
11. 12. moreover these six *b.* accompanied me
29. they determined to send relief to the *b.*
12. 17. go shew these things to James and to the *b.*
14. 2. made their minds evil-affected against the *b.*
15. 1. certain men from Judea taught the *b.*
3. and they caused great joy to all the *b.*
15. 22. Barsabas and Silas chief among the *b.*
23. apostles and elders and *b.* send greeting to the *b.* which are of the Gentiles in Antioch
32. exhorted the *b.* with many words, 1 *Thess.* 5. 14.

*Acts*15.33.were let go in peace from the *b.* to apostles
40. being recommended by the *b.* to grace of God
16. 2. Timotheus was well reported of by the *b.*
40. when they had seen the *b.* they comforted
17. 6. they drew Jason and certain *b.* to the rulers
10. the *b.* immediately sent away Paul, 14.
18. 18. Paul then took his leave of the *b.*
27. the *b.* wrote exhorting to receive Apollos
20. 32. now *b.* I commend you to God and his grace
21. 7. we came to Ptolemais and saluted the *b.*
17. were come to Jerusalem, *b.* received us gladly
22. 5. from whom also I received letters to the *b.*
23. 5. I wist not, *b.* that he was the high-priest
28. 14. where we found *b.* and were desired to tarry
15. when the *b.* heard of us, they came to meet us
21. nor any of the *b.* that came spake harm of thee
Rom. 1. 13. now I would not have you ignorant, *b.*
11. 25. 1 *Cor.* 10. 1. | 12. 1. 1 *Thess.* 4. 13.
7. 1. know ye not, *b.* that the law hath dominion
8. 12. *b.* we are debtors, not to the flesh, to live
29. that he might be the first-born among many *b.*
10. 1. *b.* my prayer to God for Isr. is, may be saved
12. 1. I beseech you therefore, *b.* by the mercies of God, 15. 30. | 16. 17. 1 *Cor.* 1. 10. | 16. 15. *Gal.* 4. 12. *Heb.* 13. 22.
+ 10. be kindly affectioned in love of the *b.*
16. 14. salute the *b.* which are with them, *Col.* 4. 15.
1 *Cor.* 1. 26. for ye see your calling, *b.* how that
2. 1. and I, *b.* when I came to you, came not with
3. 1. I, *b.* could not speak to you as to spiritual
4. 6. these things, *b.* I have in a figure transferred
7. 29. but this I say, *b.* the time is short, 15. 50.
8.12. when ye sin so against the *b.* ye sin against Ch.
9. 5. and as the *b.* of the Lord and Cephas
11. 2. now I praise you, *b.* that ye remember me
14. 26. how is it, *b.* when ye come together
15. 6. after he was seen of above 500 *b.* at once
58. therefore my beloved, *b.* be stedfast, *Jam.* 2. 5.
16. 11. for I look for him with the *b.*
12. I desired him to come to you with the *b.*
20. all the *b.* greet you, *Phil.* 4. 21.
2 *Cor.* 9. 3. yet have I sent the *b.* lest our boasting
5. I thought it necessary to exhort the *b.*
11. 9. the *b.* which came from Macedonia supplied
26. I have been in perils among false *b.*
13.11.finally *b.* farewell, be perfect, of good comfort
Gal. 1. 2. all *b.* that are with me to the churches
2. 4. because of false *b.* unawares brought in
Eph. 6. 23. peace be to the *b.* and love with faith
Phil. 1. 14. many of the *b.* waxing confident
Col. 1. 2. to the saints and faithful *b.* in Christ
1 *Thess.*4.1. we beseech you *b.*10.‖5. 12. 2 *Thess.* 2. 1.
10. indeed ye do it towards all *b.* in Macedonia
5. 25. *b.* pray for us, 2 *Thess.* 3. 1.
26. greet all the *b.* with an holy kiss
27. that this epistle be read to all the holy *b.*
1 *Tim.* 4. 6. put the *b.* in remembrance of these things
5. 1. intreat him as a father, and younger men as *b.*
6. 2. let them not despise them because they are *b.*
Heb. 2. 11. he is not ashamed to call them *b.*
3. 1. holy *b.* partakers, consider the Apostle
1 *Pet.* 1. 22. unto unfeigned love of the *b.*
3.8. be of one mind, love as *b.* be pitiful, be courteous
1 *John* 3. 14. from death to life, because we love *b.*
16. we ought to lay down our lives for the *b.*
3 *John* 3. rejoiced greatly when *b.* testified of truth
5 whatsoever thou doest to the *b.* and to strangers
10. neither doth he himself receive the *b.*

His BRETHREN.

Gen. 9. 22. and Ham told *his* two *b.* without
25. Canaan, a servant of servants shall be to *his b.*
16. 12. he shall dwell in presence of *his b.* 25. 18.
27. 37. *his b.* have I given to him for servants
37. 2. Joseph was feeding the flock with *his b.*
5. Joseph dreamed a dream and told it *his b.*
11. *his b.* envied him, his father observed the saying
30. Reuben returned to *his b.* and said, child is not
38. 11. for he said, lest he die also as *his b.* did
44. 33. and let the lad go up with *his b.*
47. 12. Joseph nourished his father and *his b.*
49. 26. that was separate from *his b. Deut.* 33. 16.
Exod. 1. 6. Joseph died, *his b.* and all that generation
2. 11. Moses went out to *his b.* and looked on their burdens, and spied an Egypt. smiting one of *his b.*
Lev. 21. 10. and he that is high-priest among *his b.*
25. 48. after he is sold, one of *his b.* may redeem him
Num. 25. 6. brought to *his b.* a Midianitish woman
27. 9. then shall ye give his inheritance to *his b.*
Deut. 10. 9. Levi hath no part with *his b.*
17. 20. that his heart be not lifted up above *his b.*
18. 7. he shall minister as all *his b.* the Levites do
20. 8. lest *his b.* heart faint as well as his heart
24. 7. if a man be found stealing any of *his b.*
33. 9. nor did he acknowledge *his b.* nor knew
24. let Asher be blessed and acceptable to *his b.*
Judg. 9. 5. Abimelech slew *his b.* being 70 persons
26. Gaal came with *his b.* and went to Shechem
56. which he did to his father in slaying *his* 70 *b.*
11. 3. Jephthah fled from *his b.* and dwelt in Tob
Ruth 4. 10. name of the dead be not cut off from *his b.*
1 *Sam.* 16. 13. Samuel anointed him in midst of *his b.*
22. 1. when *his b.* and father's house heard it
2 *Kings* 9. 2. make him rise up from among *his b.*
1 *Chron.* 4. 9. Jabez more honourable than *his b.*
5. 2. for Judah prevailed above *his b.*
7. 22. Ephraim mourned, *his b.* came to comfort him
25. 9. with *his b.* and sons were twelve
[*So to the end of the chapter.*]
2 *Chr.* 21. 4. Jehoram slew all *his b.* with the sword
Esth. 10. 3. Mordecai the Jew was accepted of *his b.*
Hos. 13. 15. though he be fruitful among *his b.*
Mic. 5. 3. the remnant of *his b.* shall return to Israel
Mat. 12. 46. his mother and *his b.* stood without, desiring to speak with him, *Mark* 3. 31. *Luke* 8. 19.
John 7. 5. for neither did *his b.* believe in him
Acts 7. 13. Joseph was made known to *his b.*
23. it came into Moses' heart to visit *his b.*
25. for he supposed *his b.* would have understood
1 *Cor.* 6. 5. not one able to judge between *his b.*
Heb. 2. 17. it behoved him to be made like to *his b.*

Men and BRETHREN.

Acts 1. 16. *men and b.* this scripture must be fulfilled
Acts 2. 29. *m. and b.* let me freely speak to you of D.
37. Peter and rest, *men and b.* what shall we do?
7. 2. and he said, *men, b.* and fathers, hearken
13. 15. *men and b.* if ye have any word of exhortation
26. *men and b.* children of the stock of Abraham
38. be it known to you, *men and b.* thro' this man
15. 7. *men and b.* ye know G. made choice among us
13. James answered, *men and b.* hearken unto me
22. 1. *men b.* and fathers, hear my defence
23. 1. *men and b.* I have lived in all good conscience
6. *men and b.* I am a Pharisee, the son of a Pharisee
28. 17. *men and b.* tho' I have committed nothing

My BRETHREN.

Gen. 29. 4. Jacob said to them, *my b.* whence be ye?
31. 37. set it here before *my b.* and thy brethren
37. 16. I seek *my b.* tell me where they feed flocks
46. 31. *my b.* and father's house are come to me, 47. 1.
Exod. 4. 18. let me go and return to *my b.* in Egypt
Josh. 2. 13. they will save alive my father and *my b.*
14. 8. *my b.* made the heart of the people melt
Judg. 8. 19. Gideon said, they were *my b.*
19. 23. *my b.* I pray you, do not so wickedly
1 *Sam.* 20. 29. let me get away, I pray, and see *my b.*
30. 23. then David said, ye shall not do so, *my b.*
2 *Sam.* 19. 12. ye are *my b.* my bones, and my flesh
1 *Chr.* 28. 2. David said, hear me, *my b.* and people
Neh. 1. 2. Hanani, one of *my b.* came and men
4. 23. I nor *my b.* nor guard put off our clothes
5. 10. I and *my b.* might exact of them money
14. I and *my b.* have not eaten bread of governor
Job 6. 15. *my b.* have dealt deceitfully
19. 13. he hath put *my b.* far from me, and acquaint.
*Psa.*22.22. I will declare thy name to *my b. Heb.*2.12.
69. 8. I am become a stranger to *my b.* an alien
122. 8. for *my b.* and companions' sake, I will say
*Mat.*12.48. he said to him, who are *my b. Mark* 3. 33.
49. behold my mother and *my b. Mark* 3. 34.
25. 40. ye have done it to the least of these *my b.*
28. 10. go tell *my b.* that they go into Galilee
Luke 8. 21. *my b.* are these which hear word of God
John 20. 17. go to *my b.* and say to them, I ascend
Rom. 9. 3. myself were accursed from Christ for *my b.*
Jam. 5. 10. take *my b.* the prophets who have spoken
12. but above all things, *my b.* swear not

Our BRETHREN.

Gen. 31. 32. before *our b.* discern what is thine, take
Num. 20. 3. when *our b.* died before the Lord
Deut. 1. 28. *our b.* have discouraged our hearts
2 *Sam.* 19. 41. why have *our b.* stolen thee away?
1 *Chr.* 13. 2. let us send abroad to *our b.* every where
Neh. 5. 5. yet now our flesh is as the flesh of *our b.*
8. after our ability have redeemed *our b.* the Jews
Acts 15. 36. let us go again visit *our b.* in every city
2 *Cor.* 8. 23. or *our b.* be inquired of, are messengers
Rev. 12. 10. for the accuser of *our b.* is cast down

Their BRETHREN.

Num. 8. 26. but shall minister with *their b.* in taber.
Deut. 18. 2. Levites have no inherit. among *their b.*
18. I will raise a prophet from among *their b.*
Judg. 20. 13. not hearken to the voice of *their b.*
21. 22. when *their b.* come to us to complain
2 *Sam.* 2. 26. bid people return from following *their b.*
2 *Kings* 23. 9. did eat unleav. bread among *their b.*
1 *Chr.* 8. 32. these dwelt with *their b.* in Jerus. 9. 38.
12. 32. all *their b.* were at their commandment
39. drinking, for *their b.* had prepared for them
2 *Chr.* 28. 15. brought them to *their b.* to Jericho
Neh. 5. 1. was a great cry against *their b.* the Jews
13. 13. their office was to distribute to *their b.*
Job 42. 15. father gave them inherit. among *their b.*
Jer. 41. 8. for he slew them not among *their b.*
Heb. 7. 5. to take tithes of people, that is of *their b.*
Rev. 6. 11. till *their b.* should be killed as they were

Thy BRETHREN.

Gen. 27. 29. be lord over *thy b.* let mother's sons bow
31. 37. set it before *thy b.* that they may judge
37. 10. I and *thy b.* come to bow ourselves to thee
13. do not *thy b.* feed the flock in Shechem?
14. whether it be well with *thy b.* and the flocks
48. 22. I have given to thee one portion above *thy b.*
49. 8. thou art he whom *thy b.* shall praise
Deut. 15. 7. if a poor man of *thy b.* be within gates
17. 15. from among *thy b.* shalt thou set king over
18. 15. I will raise up a prophet of *thy b.* like to me
24. 14. not oppress the poor of *thy b.* or stranger
Josh. 2. 18. thou shalt bring *thy b.* home unto thee
Judg. 14. 3. no woman among daughters of *thy b.*
1 *Sam.* 17. 17. take for *thy b.* run to camp to *thy b.*
18. look how *thy b.* fare, and take their pledge
2 *Sam.* 15. 20. return, take back *thy b.* with thee
2 *Chron.* 21. 13. hast slain *thy b.* better than thyself
Jer. 12. 6. *thy b.* have dealt treacherously with thee
Ezek. 11. 15. *thy b.* even *thy b.* men of thy kindred
Mat. 12. 47. behold, thy mother and *thy b.* stand without, *Mark* 3. 32. *Luke* 8. 20.
Luke 14. 12. call not *thy b.* lest they bid thee again
22. 32. when thou art converted, strengthen *thy b.*
Rev. 19. 10. see thou do it not, I am of *thy b.* 22. 9.

Your BRETHREN.

Gen. 42. 19. let one of *your b.* be bound in prison
33. leave one of *your b.* here with me
Lev. 10. 4. carry *your b.* from before the sanctuary
6. let *your b.* bewail the burning the Lord kindled
25. 46. over *your b.* ye shall not rule with rigour
Num. 18. 6. behold I have taken *your b.* the Levites
32. 6. shall *your b.* go to war and shall ye sit here?
Deut. 1. 16. hear the causes between *your b.*
3. 18. pass over armed before *your b. Josh.* 1. 14.
20. till Lord hath given rest to *your b. Josh.* 1. 15.
Josh. 22. 3. ye have not left *your b.* these many days
4. and now the Lord hath given rest to *your b.*
8. divide the spoil of your enemies with *your b.*
1 *Kings* 12. 24. not fight against *your b.* 2 *Chr.* 11. 4.
2 *Chron.* 19. 10. what cause shall come to you of *your b.* and so wrath come upon you and *your b.*
28. 11. deliver captives ye have taken of *your b.*
30. 7. be not ye like *your b.* which trespassed
9. if ye turn, *your b.* shall find compassion
Neh. 4. 14. and fight for *your b.* your sons and wives
5. 8. will you even sell *your b.* or shall they be sold?
Isa. 66. 5. *your b.* that hated you, that cast you out
20. they shall bring *your b.* for an offering to Lord
Jer. 7. 15. cast you out as I have cast out all *your b.*
Hos. 2. 1. say to *your b.* Ammi, to sisters, Ruhamah
Mat. 5. 47. if ye salute *your b.* only, what do you more
Acts 3. 22. a prophet shall Lord raise of *your b.* 7. 37.
1 *Cor.* 6. 8. ye do wrong and defraud and that *your b.*
1 *Pet.* 5. 9. same afflictions accomplished in *your b.*

BRIBE, S.

1 *Sam.* 8. 3. Samuel's sons took *b.* and perverted judg
12. 3. of whose hand have I received any *b.*?
Psal. 26. 10. and their right hand is full of *b.*
Isa. 33. 15. that shaketh his hands from holding *b.*
Amos 5. 12. they take a *b.* and turn aside the poor

BRIBERY.

Job 15. 34. fire shall consume the tabernacles of *b.*

BRICK.

Gen. 11. 3. let us make *b.* they had *b.* for stone
Exod. 1. 14. they made their lives bitter in *b.*
5. 7. no more give the people straw to make *b.* 16.
Isa. 65. 3. and burneth incense on altars of *b.*

BRICKS.

Exod. 5. 8. the tale of *b.* you shall lay upon them
18. yet shall ye deliver the tale of *b.* 19.
Isa. 9. 10. the *b.* are fallen down, but we will build

BRICK-KILN.

2 *Sam.* 12. 31. and made them pass through the *b.*
Jer. 43. 9. hide great stones in the clay in the *b.*
Nah. 3. 14. tread the mortar, make strong the *b.*

BRIDE.

Isa. 49. 18. and bind them on thee, as a *b.* doth
61. 10. as a *b.* adorneth herself with jewels
62. 5. as the bridegroom rejoiceth over the *b.*
Jer. 2. 32. or can a *b.* forget her attire?
7. 34. cause to cease the voice of the *b.* 16. 9. | 25. 10.
33. 11. shall be heard in this place voice of the *b.*
Joel 2. 16. and let the *b.* go out of her closet
John 3. 29. he that hath the *b.* is the bridegroom
Rev. 18. 23. voice of the *b.* heard no more in thee
21. 2. prepared as a *b.* adorned for her husband
9. I will shew thee the *b.* the Lamb's wife
22. 17. and the Spirit and the *b.* say, Come

BRIDE-CHAMBER.

Mat. 9. 15. can the children of the *b.* mourn?
Mark 2. 19. can the children of the *b.* fast? *Luke* 5. 34.

BRIDEGROOM.

Psal. 19. 5. as a *b.* coming out of his chamber
Isa. 61. 10. as a *b.* decketh himself with ornaments
62. 5. as *b.* rejoiceth over bride, so God over thee,
Mat. 9. 15. can children of bride-chamber mourn while *b.* is with them? *Mark* 2. 19. *Luke* 5. 34.
25. 1. ten virgins went forth to meet the *b.*
5. while the *b.* tarried ‖ 6. cry made, *b.* cometh, 10.
John 2. 9. the governor of the feast called the *b.*
3. 29. he that hath the bride is the *b.* but the friend of the *b.* rejoiceth greatly because of the *b.* voice
See BRIDE.

BRIDLE

Is taken, [1] Properly, *for the reins or bit whereby horses, mules, &c. are kept in, and made to go which pace and which way their riders please,* Psal. 32. 9. [2] Figuratively, (1) *For those restraints of law, humanity, or modesty, whereby people are kept in awe,* Job 30. 11. and (2) *For the restraining power and providence of God,* 2 Kings 19. 28. Isa. 30. 28.

2 *Kings* 19. 28. I will put my *b.* in thy lips, *Isa.* 37 29.
Job 30. 11. they have let loose the *b.* before me
41. 13. who can come to him with his double *b.*?
Psal. 32. 9. whose mouth must be held in with a *b.*?
39. 1. I will keep my mouth with a *b.*
Prov. 26. 3. a *b.* for the ass, a rod for the fool's back
Isa. 30. 28. there shall be a *b.* in jaws of the people
Zech. 14. + 20. on the *b.* holiness to the Lord
Jam. 1. 26. if any seem religious and *b.* not his tongue
3. 2. and able also to *b.* the whole body
Rev. 14. 20. blood came out of wine-press to horse *b.*

BRIEFLY.

Rom. 13. 9. it is *b.* comprehended in this saying
1 *Pet.* 5. 12. by Sylvanus a brother I have written *b.*

BRIER

Is *a prickly hurtful sort of plant,* Isa. 5. 6. To which are compared, [1] *An enemy, the Assyrian army, that molested the children of Israel,* Isa. 10. 17. [2] *Mischievous and hurtful persons,* Ezek. 28. 24. [3] *Sins, lusts, and corruptions, which spring from a stony and unregenerated heart,* Heb. 6. 8.

Isa. 55. 13. instead of the *b.* come up the myrtle-tree
Ezek. 28. 24. shall be no more a pricking *b.* to Israel
Mic. 7. 4. the best of them is as a *b.*

BRIERS.

Judg. 8. 7. then I will tear your flesh with *b.*
16. he took the elders of the city and *b.*
Isa. 5. 6. there shall come up *b.* and thorns
7. 23. it shall even be for *b.* and thorns
24. because all land shall become *b.* and thorns
25. not come thither the fear of *b.* and thorns
9. 18. wickedness shall devour the *b.* and thorns
10. 17. it shall devour his *b.* and thorns in one day
27. 4. would set *b.* and thorns against me in battle
32. 13. on the land shall come up *b.* and thorns
Ezek. 2. 6. son of man, tho' *b.* and thorns be with thee
Heb. 6. 8. that which beareth *b.* and thorns is rejected

BRIGANDINE.

Jer. 46. 4. furbish the spears and put on the *b.*
51. 3. against him that lifteth up himself in his *b.*

BRIGHT.

Lev. 13. 2. when a man shall have a *b.* spot, 24, 38.
4. if the *b.* spot be white in the skin of his flesh
23. if *b.* spot stay in his place and spread not, 28.
14. 56. this is the law for a scab and for a *b.* spot
1 *Kings* 7. 45. all the vessels Hiram made for the house of the Lord were of *b.* brass, 2 *Chron.* 4. 16.
Job 37. 11. he scattereth his *b.* cloud
21. now men see not the *b.* light in the clouds
Cant. 5. 14. belly is as *b.* ivory overlaid with sapphires
Jer. 51. 11. make *b.* the arrows, gather the shields
Ezek. 1. 13. the fire was *b.* and out of fire lightning
21. 15. the sword is made *b.* it is wrapt up
21. for the king of Babylon made his arrows *b.*
27. 19. *b.* iron and cassia were in thy market
32. 8. *b.* lights I will make dark over thee
Nah. 3. 3. the horseman lifteth up the *b.* sword

Zech. 10. 1. so the Lord shall make b. clouds
Mat. 17. 5. behold a b. cloud overshadowed them
Luke 11. 36. as when the b. shining of a candle
Acts 10. 30. a man stood before me in b. clothing
Rev. 22. 16. I am the b. and morning star

BRIGHTNESS

Signifies, [1] *Light or lucidness*, Isa. 59. 9. Amos 5. 20. [2] *Natural form or beauty*, Dan. 4. 36. [3] *Royal dignity, glory, and splendour*, Ezek. 28. 7.

2 Sam. 22. 13. through the b. before him were coals of fire kindled, Psal. 18. 12.
Job 31. 26. or beheld the moon walking in b.
Psal. 89. † 44. thou madest his b. to cease
Isa. 59. 9. we wait for b. but we walk in darkness
60. 3. and kings shall come to the b. of thy rising
19. nor for b. shall the moon give light to thee
62. 1. till the righteousness thereof go forth as b.
66. † 11. be delighted with the b. of her glory
Ezek. 1. 4. and a fire and a b. was about it, 27.
28. so was the appearance of b. round about
8. 2. as the appearance of b. as the colour of amber
10. 4. the court was full of b. of the Lord's glory
28. 7. behold, strangers shall defile thy b.
17. thou hast corrupted by reason of thy b.
Dan. 2. 31. this great image, whose b. was excellent
4. 36. my honour and b. returned unto me
5. † 6. then the king's b. was changed, †9.
12. 3. the wise shall shine as the b. of the firmament
Amos 5. 20. day of Lord shall be very dark and no b.
Hab. 3. 4. his b. was as the light, he had horns
Acts 26. 13. light from heaven above b. of the sun
2 Thess. 2. 8. shall destroy with the b. of his coming
Heb. 1. 3. who being the b. of his glory and image

BRIM.

Josh. 3. 15. feet of the priest dipped in b. of water
1 Kings 7. 26. b. wrought like b. of a cup, 2 Chr. 4. 5.
2 Chron. 4. 2. he made a molten sea from b. to b.
John 2. 7. and they filled them up to the b.

BRIMSTONE.

Gen. 19. 24. rained on Gom. b. and fire, Luke 17. 29.
Deut. 29. 23. the whole land thereof is b. and salt
Job 18. 15. b. shall be scattered on his habitation
Psal. 11. 6. upon wicked he shall rain snares, fire and b. and an horrible tempest, Ezek. 38. 22.
Isa. 30. 33. breath of the Lord like a stream of b.
34. 9. and the dust thereof turned into b.
Rev. 9. 17. out of their mouths issued fire and b.
18. the third part of men was killed by the b.
14. 10. he shall be tormented with fire and b.
19. 20. cast into a lake of fire, burning with b. 20. 10.
Rev. 21. 8. whoremongers, and all liars, shall have their part in lake which burneth with fire and b.

BRING.

Gen. 6. 17. I do b. a flood of waters on the earth
19. two of every sort shalt thou b. into the ark
9. 14. when I b. a cloud over earth, the bow seen
18. 16. Abraham did b. them on their way
19. Lord may b. on Abraham what he hath spoken
27. 4. and b. it to me that I may eat, 25.
5. b. me venison ‖ 12. I shall b. a curse on me
42. 20. b. your youngest brother to me, 34.
37. if I b. him not to thee, 43. 9. | 44. 32.
43. 16. b. these men home, slay and make ready
45. 19. take waggons and b. your father, and come
48. 9. b. them, I pray, to me, and I will bless them
Exod. 10. 4. else to morrow I will b. the locusts
11. 1. yet will I b. one plague more on Pharaoh
13. 5. it shall be when the Lord shall b. thee, 11.
18. 19. that thou mayest b. the causes to God
21. 6. his master shall b. him to the judges
22. 13. if it be torn in pieces, b. it for witness
23. 4. thou shalt surely b. it back to him again
19. first of first-fruits of thy land shalt b. 34. 26.
20. I will send an Angel to b. thee into the place
35. 5. whoso is of a willing heart, let him b.
36. 5. the people b. much more than enough
Lev. 5. 7. if he be not able to b. a lamb, 11. | 12. 8.
8. and he shall b. them to the priest, 12.
16. 12. shall b. fire and incense within the vail
17. 5. that Israel may b. their sacrifices to the L.
Num. 8. 9. and thou shalt b. the Levites, 10.
14. 8. if the Lord delight in us, then he will b. us
16. because the L. was not able to b. Deut. 9. 28.
24. my servant Caleb, him will I b. into the land
16. 17. b. before the Lord every man his censer
20. 12. ye shall not b. this congregation into land
32. 5. give this land, and b. us not over Jordan
Deut. 1. 17. the cause too hard for you b. it to me
7. 1. when the Lord shall b. thee into the land
21. 12. then thou shalt b. her home to thy house
22. 2. then thou shalt b. it unto thine own house
30. 12. b. it to us, that we may hear and do, 13.
33. 7. hear, Lord, and b. Judah to his people
1 Sam. 1. 22. till child be weaned, then I will b. him
9. 7. then said Saul, what shall we b. the man?
23. b. the portion I gave thee, of which I said
11. 12. b. the men, that we may put them to death
20. 8. for why shouldest thou b. me to thy father?
2 Sam. 3. 12. my hand with thee, to b. Israel to thee
13. except thou b. Michal when thou comest
14. 10. whosoever saith aught to thee, b. him to me
19. 11. why are ye last to b. the king back?
1 Kings 3. 24. and the king said, b. me a sword
8. 32. the wicked, to b. his way on his head
† 47. if b. back to their heart, 2 Chron. 6. † 37.
13. 18. b. him back with thee to thine house
17. 11. b. me a morsel of bread in thine hand
20. 33. then he said, go ye b. him
2 Kings 2. 20. b. me a new cruse, and put salt
4. 6. b. yet a vessel ‖ 41. b. meal and cast it
6. 19. I will b. you to the man whom ye seek
1 Chron. 13. † 3. let us b. about the ark of our God
16. 29. b. an offering and come before him
21. 2. b. the number of them to me, that I may
2 Chron. 31. 10. since the people began to b. offerings
Neh. 13. 18. did not our God b. this evil on us?
Job 6. 22. did I say b. unto me, or give a reward
10. 9. wilt thou b. me into the dust again?
14. 4. who can b. a clean thing out of an unclean?
18. 14. it shall b. him to the king of terrors
30. 23. for I know thou wilt b. me to death

Job 33. 30. to b. back his soul from the pit
Psal. 43. 3. let them b. me to thy holy hill
60. 9. who will b. me into strong city? 108. 10.
72. 3. the mountains shall b. peace to the people
94. 23. he shall b. on them their own iniquity
Prov. 29. 8. scornful men b. a city into a snare
Eccl. 3. 22. who shall b. him to see what shall be?
11. 9. know that God will b. thee into judgment
12. 14. God shall b. every work into judgment
Cant. 8. 2. I would b. thee into my mother's house
Isa. 7. 17. Lord shall b. on thee and my people
14. 2. the people shall b. them to their place
15. 9. for I will b. more upon Dimon, lions on him
16. † 3. b. counsel, execute judgment, make thy
25. 12. shall he b. to the ground, even to the
45. 21. tell ye and b. them near, let them take
46. 13. I b. near my righteousness, it not be far off
56. 7. even them will I b. to my holy mountain
58. 7. and that thou b. the poor to thy house
60. 17. for brass I will b. gold, for iron b. silver
66. 4. I will b. their fears upon them
Jer. 3. 14. I will take you and b. you to Zion
10. 24. not in anger, lest thou b. me to nothing
11. 8. I will b. on them all the words of this cov.
17. 18. b. upon them day of evil and destroy them
31. 8. I will b. them from the north country
32. 42. so I will b. on them all the good promised
33. 6. behold I will b. it health and cure
11. them that shall b. sacrifice of praise into house
49. 5. behold, I will b. a fear upon thee
Lam. 1. † 16. that should b. back my soul is far
Ezek. 6. 3. I, even I, will b. a sword upon you
11. 9. I will b. you out of the midst thereof
20. 15. that I would not b. them into the land
21. 29. I will b. on the necks of them that are slain
23. 22. I will b. them against thee on every side
34. 13. I will b. them to their land, 36. 24. | 37. 21.
38. 17. that I would b. thee against them
Hos. 2. 14. I will allure and b. her to wilderness
Amos 4. 1. b. and let us drink ‖ 4. b. your sacrifices
Mic. 1. 15. yet will I b. an heir to thee
Zech. 8. 8. I will b. them, and they shall dwell
Mal. 1. † 7. ye b. polluted bread to mine altar
3. 10. b. all the tithes into the store-house
Mat. 2. 13. be thou there till I b. thee word
5. 23. therefore if thou b. thy gift to the altar
17. 17. b. him hither to me, Mark 9. 19.
21. 2. ye shall find an ass and a colt, loose them and b. them to me, Mark 11. 2. Luke 19. 30.
Mark 7. 32. and they b. to him one that was deaf
Luke 2. 10. for I b. you good tidings of great joy
8. 14. choked with cares, and b. no fruit to perfect.
12. 11. when they b. you unto the synagogues
John 10. 16. other sheep, them also I must b.
14. 26. and b. all things to your remembrance
18. 29. Pilate said, what accusation b. you?
21. 10. b. of the fish which ye have now caught
Acts 5. 28. ye intend to b. this man's blood on us
7. 6. that they should b. them into bondage
9. 2. he might b. them bound to Jerusalem, 21.
22. 5. I went to Damascus to b. them bound
23. 10. commanded to b. Paul into the castle
17. b. this young man to the chief captain
1 Cor. 1. 19. I will b. to nothing the understanding
28. things that are not, b. to nought things that are
4. 17. shall b. you into remembrance of my ways
9. 27. keep under my body, I b. it into subjection
16. 6. that ye may b. me on my journey whither I go
2 Cor. 11. 20. ye suffer, if a man b. you into bondage
Gal. 3. 24. our schoolmaster to b. us to Christ
1 Thess. 4. 14. them that sleep will God b. with him
2 Tim. 4. 11. take Mark and b. him with thee
1 Pet. 3. 18. suffered that he might b. us to God
2 John 10. if any come and b. not this doctrine
3 John 6. whom if thou b. forward on their journey
Rev. 21. 24. and kings do b. their glory to it
26. they shall b. the glory of nations into it
See Home, Hither.

BRING again.

Gen. 24. 5. must I b. thy son again to the land
6. beware thou, that thou b. not my son again, 8.
28. 15. I will b. thee again into this land, 48. 21.
37. 14. if well with brethren, and b. word again
42. 37. deliver him, and I'll b. him to thee again
Exod. 23. 4. shalt surely b. it back to him again
Num. 17. 10. b. Aaron's rod again before testimony
22. 8. lodge this night, and I'll b. you word again
Deut. 1. 22. b. us word again what way we must go
22. 1. in any case b. them again to thy brother
28. 68. the Lord shall b. thee into Egypt again
Judg. 11. 9. if ye b. me home again to fight
19. 3. her husband arose, and went to b. her again
2 Sam. 12. 23. can I b. him again, I shall go to him
14. 21. b. the young man Absalom again
15. 8. if the Lord shall b. me again to Jerusalem
25. he will b. me again and shew me it [6. 25.
1 Kings 8. 34. forgive and b. them again, 2 Chron.
12. 21. he assembled Judah against Isr. to b. kingdom again to Rehoboam, 2 Chron. 11. 1.
1 Chron 13. 3. let us b. again the ark of our God
21. 12. advise what word I shall b. again to him
2 Chron. 24. 19. he sent prophets to b. them again
Neh. 9. 29. that mightest b. them again to thy law
Psal. 68. 22. Lord said, I will b. again from Bashan, I will b. again my people from the depths of sea
Prov. 19. 24. not so much as b. it to his mouth again
26. 15. grieveth him to b. it again to his mouth
Isa. 38. 8. I will b. again the shadow of the degrees
46. 8. b. it again to mind, O ye transgressors
49. 5. saith the Lord, to b. Jacob again to him
52. 8. shall see when the Lord shall b. again Zion
Jer. 12. 15. I will return and b. them again, 50. 19.
15. 19. if thou wilt return, then will I b. thee again
16. 15. I will b. them ag. to their land, 24. 6. | 32. 37.
23. 3. I will b. them again into their folds
28. 3. in two years I will b. again the vessels
4. I will b. again to this place Jeconiah, 6.
30. 3. I will b. again captivity of my people Isr. and Judah, 18. [31. 23. Ezek. 39. 25. Amos 9. 14.
48. 47. yet will I b. again the captivity of Moab
49. 6. b. again the captivity of Ammon ‖ 39. of Elam
Ezek. 16. 53. when I b. ag. their captivity, I will b. a.

Ezek. 29. 14. I will b. again the captivity of Egypt
34. 16. I will b. again that which was driven
Zeph. 3. 20. at that time I will b. you again
Zech. 10. 6. I will b. them again to place them
10. I will b. them again out of land of Egypt
Mat. 2. 8. b. me word again that I may worship
See Captivity.

BRING down.

Gen. 42. 38. b. down my grey hairs, 44. 29, 31.
43. 7. he would say, b. your brother down, 44. 21.
45. 13. ye shall haste and b. down my father
Deut. 9. 3. he shall b. them down before thy face
Judg. 7. 4. b. them down to the water, and I will try
1 Sam. 30. 15. canst b. me down, I will b. thee down
2 Sam. 22. 28. eyes on the haughty to b. them down
1 Kings 1. 33. Solomon b. him down to Gihon
2. 9. his hoary head b. thou down with blood
Psal. 18. 27. wilt save afflicted, b. down high looks
55. 23. shalt b. them down to pit of destruction
Isa. 25. 5. thou shalt b. down the noise of strangers
11. he shall b. down their pride together with spoils
12. the high fort of thy walls shall he b. down
63. 6. I will b. down their strength to the earth
Jer. 49. 16. I will b. thee down from thence, Obad. 4.
51. 40. I will b. them down like lambs to slaughter
Ezek. 26. 20. when I shall b. thee down with them
28. 8. they shall b. thee down to pit, and shalt die
Hos. 7. 12. I will b. them down as fowls of heaven
Joel 3. 2. b. them down to the valley of Jehoshaphat
† 11. the Lord shall b. down thy mighty ones
Amos 3. 11. he shall b. down thy strength from thee
9. 2. tho' climb to heaven, thence will b. them down
Obad. 3. saith in his heart, who shall b. me down?
Acts 23. 15. that he b. him down to you to-morrow
20. the Jews desire thou wouldest b. down Paul
Rom. 10. 6. that is, to b. Christ down from above
See Evil.

BRING forth.

Gen. 1. 11. let earth b. forth, 24. ‖ 20. waters b. forth
3. 16. in sorrow thou shalt b. forth children
18. thorns and thistles shall it b. forth to thee
8. 17. b. forth every living thing that is with thee
9. 7. b. forth abundantly in the earth and multiply
38. 24. Judah said, b. her forth, and let her be burnt
Exod. 3. 10. that thou mayest b. forth my people Israel
11. who am I, that I should b. forth Israel?
7. 4. that I may b. forth my armies and people
8. 3. the river shall b. forth frogs abundantly
18. magicians did so to b. forth lice, but could not
Lev. 24. 14. b. forth him that hath cursed, 23.
25. 21. it shall b. forth fruit for three years
26. 10. ye shall eat and b. forth old, because of new
Num. 20. 8 shalt b. forth to them water out of rock
Deut. 14. 28. thou shalt b. forth all tithe of increase
17. 5. then shalt thou b. forth that man or woman
22. 15. b. forth the tokens of the damsel's virginity
Josh. 2. 3. b. forth the men that are come to thee
Judg. 6. 18. till I come and b. forth my present
19. 22. b. forth the man that came to thy house
2 Kings 10. 22. b. forth vestments for the worshippers
19. 3. and there is no strength to b. forth, Isa. 37. 3.
23. 4. to b. forth all the vessels were made for Baal
Ezra 1. 8. those did Cyrus b. forth by Mithredath
10. † 3. make a covenant to b. forth our wives
Job 14. 9. it will bud and b. forth boughs like a plant
15. 35. they conceive mischief, and b. forth vanity
38. 32. canst thou b. forth Mazzaroth in his season?
39. 1. knowest thou when wild goats b. forth? 2, 3.
40. 20. surely the mountains b. him forth food
Psal. 25. † 15. he shall b. forth my feet out of the net
37. 6. he shall b. forth thy righteousness as light
92. 14. they shall still b. forth fruit in old age
104. 14. that he may b. forth food out of the earth
144. 13. that our sheep may b. forth thousands
Prov. 8. † 35. whoso findeth me shall b. forth favour
27. 1. thou knowest not what a day may b. forth
Isa. 5. 2. he looked that it should b. forth grapes, 4.
23. 4. saying, I travail not, nor b. forth children
33. 11. ye shall conceive chaff, and b. forth stubble
41. 21. b. forth your strong reasons, saith the King
22. let them b. forth and show what shall happen
42. 1. he shall b. forth judgment to the Gentiles
3. he shall b. forth judgment unto truth
43. 8. b. forth blind people that have eyes, and deaf
9. let them b. forth their witnesses, that they may
45. 8. let earth open, and let them b. forth salvation
55. 10. watereth the earth, and maketh it b. forth
59. 4. they conceive mischief, and b. forth iniquity
65. 9. I will b. forth a seed out of Jacob
23. not labour in vain, nor b. forth for trouble
66. 8. shall the earth be made to b. forth in one day?
9. shall I bring to birth, and not cause to b. forth?
Jer. 12. 2. they grow, yea, they b. forth fruit
51. 44. I'll b. forth out of mouth what he swallowed
Ezek. 12. 4. thou shalt b. forth thy stuff by day
17. 23. and it shall b. forth boughs and bear fruit
20. 6. to b. them forth of the land of Egypt
38. I will b. them forth out of the country
28. 18. therefore will I b. forth a fire in the midst of
38. 4. I will b. thee forth, thy army and horsemen
47. 12. shall b. forth new fruit according to months
Hos. 9. 13. but Ephraim shall b. forth his children
16. tho' they b. forth, yet will I slay beloved fruit
Mic. 4. 10. be in pain and labour to b. forth, O Zion
7. 9. he will b. me forth to the light
Zeph. 2. 2. before the decree b. forth, the day pass
Zech. 3. 8. I will b. forth my servant the Branch
4. 7. shall b. forth the head-stone with shoutings
5. 4. b. forth a curse, and it shall enter the house
Mat. 1. 23. behold, a virgin shall b. forth a son, 21.
3. 8. b. forth fruit meet for repentance, Luke 3. 8.
7. 18. good tree cannot b. forth evil fruit, Luke 6. 43.
Mark 4. 20. b. forth fruit, some 30 fold, some sixty
Luke 1. 31. b. f. a son, and shalt call his name Jesus
8. 15. having heard word, keep it, and b. forth fruit
15. 22. b. forth the best robe and put it on him
John 15. 2. purgeth, that it may b. forth more fruit
16. I ordained you, that you should b. forth fruit
19. 4. I b. him forth to you that ye may know
Acts 12. 4. after Easter to b. him forth to the people
Rom. 7. 4. that we should b. forth fruit unto God

Rom. 7. 5. motions of sin to *b. forth* fruit unto death

BRING *in*.

Exod. 6. 8. I will *b.* you *in* unto the land I did swear
15. 17. shall *b. in* and plant them in the mountain
16. 5. on the sixth day prepare that they *b. in*
23. 23. my Angel shall go before and *b.* thee *in*
Num. 14. 31. your little ones, them will I *b. in*
2 *Chron.* 24. 9. they made proclamation to *b. in* to the Lord the collection Moses laid on Israel
28. 13. ye shall not *b. in* the captives hither
Jer. 17. 24. *b. in* no burden on the sabbath-day
Dan. 2. 24. *b.* me *in* before the king, and I will shew
5. 7. the king cried to *b. in* the astrologers
9. 24. to *b. in* everlasting righteousness
Hag. 1. 6. ye have sown much and *b. in* little
Luke 5. 18. sought means to *b.* him *in* and lay him
14. 21. *b. in* hither the poor, the maimed and halt
2 *Pet.* 2. 1. who privily *b. in* damnable heresies

BRING *out*.

Gen. 19. 5. *b.* them *out* to us that we may know, 8. 12.
40. 14. make mention, and *b.* me *out* of this house
50. 24. God will visit and *b.* you *out* of this land
Exod. 6. 6. I will *b.* you *out* from under the burden
13. gave them a charge to *b.* the children of Israel *out* of Egypt, 26. 27. | 7. 5. | 12. 51. *Jer.* 31. 32.
32. 12. for mischief did he *b.* them *out* to slay them
Deut. 21. 19. lay hold and *b.* him *out* to the elders
22. 21. *b. out* the damsel || 24. *b.* both *out* to the gate
24. 11. shall *b. out* the pledge abroad unto thee
Josh. 6. 22. *b. out* thence Rahab and all she hath
10. 22. *b. out* those five kings out of the cave
Judg. 6. 30. *b. out* thy son that he may die
19. 24. them I will *b. out*, and humble ye them
Psal. 25. 17. O *b.* thou me *out* of my distresses
142. 7. *b.* my soul *out* of prison, that I may praise
143. 11. O Lord, *b.* my soul *out* of trouble
Isa. 42. 7. to *b. out* the prisoners from the prison
Jer. 8. 1. shall *b. out* the bones of the kings of Judah
38. 23. *b. out* all thy wives and children to Chaldeans
Ezek. 11. 7. but I will *b.* you forth *out* of midst of it
20. 34. I will *b.* you *out* from the people, 34. 13.
41. accept you, when I *b.* you *out* from the people
24. 6. *b.* it *out* piece by piece, let no lot fall
Amos 6. 10. that burneth him to *b. out* the bones
Acts 17. 5. sought to *b.* them *out* to the people

BRING *to pass*.

Gen. 41. 32. the dream, God will shortly *b.* it *to pass*
50. 20. to *b. to pass* as at this day, to save people alive
Psal. 37. 5. trust in him, and he shall *b.* it *to pass*
Isa. 28. 21. and *b. to pass* his act, his strange act
46. 11. I have spoken, I will also *b.* it *to pass*

BRING *up*.

Gen. 46. 4. and I will also surely *b.* thee *up* again
Exod. 3. 8. and to *b.* them *up* out of that land
17. I have said, I will *b.* you *up* out of affliction
33. 12. see, thou sayest to me, *b. up* this people
Num. 14. 37. men that *b. up* evil report on the land
20. 25. *b. up* Aaron and his son to mount Hor
Deut. 22. 14. *b. up* an evil name on her, and say
Judg. 6. 13. did not the Lord *b.* us *up* from Egypt
1 *Sam.* 19. 15. *b.* him *up* in the bed, that I may slay
28. 11. whom shall I *b. up*, he said, *b.* me *up* Samuel
2 *Sam.* 2. 3. his men did David *b. up* every man
6. 2. to *b. up* from thence the ark of God, 1 *Kings* 8. 1, 4. 1 *Chron.* 13. 6. | 15. 3, 12, 14, 25. 2 *Chron.* 5. 2, 5.
1 *Chron.* 17. 5. since I did *b. up* Israel to this day
Ezra 1. 11. did Sheshbazzar *b. up* with them
Neh. 10. 38. shall *b. up* tithes to the house of God
Isa. 23. 4. I travail not, nor *b.* forth children, nor do I nourish *up* young men, nor *b. up* virgins
Jer. 27. 22. then will I *b.* them *up* and restore
Ezek. 16. 40. shall *b. up* a company against thee
23. 46. I will *b. up* a company upon them
26. 19. when I shall *b. up* the deep upon thee
29. 4. will *b.* thee *up* out of the midst of thy rivers
32. 3. a company shall *b.* thee *up* in my net
37. 6. I will *b. up* flesh on you, and cover you
Hos. 9. 12. though they *b. up* children, I will bereave
Amos 8. 10. I will *b. up* sackcloth upon all loins
Rom. 10. 7. to *b. up* Christ again from the dead
Eph. 6. 4. *b.* them *up* in the nurture of the Lord

BRINGERS.

2 *Kings* 10. 5. the *b. up* of children sent to Jehu

BRINGEST.

Job 14. 3. and *b.* me into judgment with thee
Isa. 40. 9. O Jerus. that *b.* good tidings, lift up voice
Acts 17. 20. for thou *b.* strange things to our ears

BRINGETH.

Exod. 6. 7. who *b.* you out from under the burden
Lev. 11. 45. I am the Lord that *b.* you out of Egypt
17. 4. *b.* it not to the door of the tabernacle, 9.
Deut. 8. 7. the Lord *b.* thee into a good land
1 *Sam.* 2. 6. he *b.* down to the grave, and *b.* up
7. Lord maketh poor, he *b.* low, and lifteth up
2 *Sam.* 22. 48. that *b.* down the people under me
49. and that *b.* me forth from mine enemies
Job 12. 6. into whose hand God *b.* abundantly
22. he *b.* out to light the shadow of death
19. 29. wrath *b.* the punishments of the sword
28. 11. the thing that is hid *b.* he forth to light
Psal. 1. 3. that *b.* forth his fruit in his season
14. 7. when the Lord *b.* back the captivity, 53. 6.
33. 10. Ld. *b.* the counsel of the heathen to nought
37. 7. the man who *b.* wicked devices to pass
68. 6. he *b.* out them that are bound with chains
107. 28. and *b.* them out of their distresses
30. so he *b.* them to their desired haven
135. 7. *b.* wind out of treasuries, *Jer.* 10. 13. | 51. 16.
Prov. 10. 31. the mouth of the just *b.* forth wisdom
16. 30. moving his lips he *b.* evil to pass
18. 16. a man's gift *b.* him before great men
19. 26. is a son that causeth shame, and *b.* reproach
20. 26. a wise king *b.* the wheel over them
21. 27. much more when he *b.* it with a wicked
29. 15. but a child left, *b.* his mother to shame
21. he that delicately *b.* up his servant from a child
25. the fear of man *b.* a snare, but whoso trusts
30. 33. *b.* forth butter, *b.* blood, *b.* forth strife
31. 14. like ships, she *b.* her food from afar
Eccl. 2. 6. to water the wood that *b.* forth trees
Isa. 8. 7. Lord *b.* on them the waters of the river

Isa. 26. 5. *b.* down them that dwell on high, *b.* to dust
40. 23. that *b.* the princes to nothing, he makes
26. that *b.* out their host by number
43. 17. which *b.* forth the chariot and horse
54. 16. the smith that *b.* forth an instrument
61. 11. for as the earth *b.* forth her bud
Jer. 4. 31. anguish of her that *b.* forth her first child
Ezek. 29. 16. which *b.* iniquity to remembrance
Hos. 10. 1. Israel *b.* forth fruit to himself
Hag. 1. 11. drought on that which ground *b.* forth
Mat. 3. 10. every tree that *b.* not forth good fruit is hewn down, and cast into fire, 7. 19. *Luke* 3. 9.
7. 17. even so every good tree *b.* forth good fruit
12. 35. a good man out of heart *b.* forth good things, and an evil man *b.* forth evil things, *Luke* 6. 45.
13. 23. *b.* forth some an hundred fold, some sixty
52. who *b.* out of his treasure things new and old
17. 1. Jesus *b.* them up into an high mountain
Mark 4. 28. the earth *b.* forth fruit of herself
Luke 6. 43. a good tree *b.* not forth corrupt fruit
John 12. 24. if it die, it *b.* forth much fruit, 15. 5.
Col. 1. 6. gospel *b.* forth fruit, as it doth also in you
Tit. 2. 11. the grace of God that *b.* salvation
Heb. 1. 6. *b.* in the first-begotten into the world
6. 7. the earth *b.* forth herbs meet for them
Jam. 1. 15. lust *b.* forth sin, and sin *b.* forth death

See TIDINGS.

BRINGING.

Exod. 12. 42. to be much observed for *b.* them out
36. 6. so the people were restrained from *b.*
Num. 5. 15. an offering *b.* iniquity to remembrance
14. 36. by *b.* up a slander upon the land
2 *Sam.* 19. 10. speak ye not of *b.* the king back, 43.
1 *Kings* 10. 22. navy *b.* gold and silver, 2 *Chro.* 9. 21.
2 *Kings* 21. 12. I am *b.* such evil on Jerusalem
Neh. 13. 15. some on the sabbath *b.* in sheaves
Psal. 126. 6. rejoicing, *b.* his sheaves with him
Jer. 17. 26. *b.* burnt offerings, *b.* sacrifices of praise
Ezek. 20. 9. I made myself known in *b.* them out
Dan. 9. 12. his word by *b.* upon us great evil
Mat. 21. 43. to a nation *b.* forth the fruit thereof
Mark 2. 3. *b.* one sick of the palsy borne of four
Luke 24. 1. *b.* the spices which they prepared
Acts 5. 16. a multitude *b.* sick folks
Rom. 7. 23. *b.* me into captivity to the law of sin
2 *Cor.* 10. 5. and *b.* into captivity every thought
Heb. 2. 10. in *b.* many sons unto glory to make capt.
7. 19. but the *b.* in of a better hope did
2 *Pet.* 2. 5. *b.* in the flood on the world of ungodly

BRINK.

Gen. 41. 3. stood by the other kine on the *b.* of river
Exod. 2. 3. laid the ark in flags by the river's *b.*
7. 15. shalt stand by the river's *b.* when he comes
Deut. 2. 36. from Aroer by the *b.* of the river
Josh. 3. 8. when ye are come to the *b.* of Jordan
Ezek. 47. 6. he caused me return to the *b.* of the river

BROAD.

Num. 16. 38. make censers, *b.* plates for covering
39. make *b.* plates for the covering of the altar
Neh. 3. 8. Uzziel and Hananiah repaired, and they fortified Jerusalem to the *b.* wall, 12. 38.
7. † 4. the city was *b.* in spaces, the people few
Job 36. 16. removed out of the strait into a *b.* place
Psal. 119. 96. thy commandment is exceeding *b.*
Cant. 3. 2. and in the *b.* ways I will seek him
Isa. 33. 21. the Lord will be a place of *b.* rivers
Jer. 5. 1. know and seek in the *b.* places thereof
51. 58. the *b.* walls of Babylon shall be broken
Nah. 2. 4. the chariots shall justle in the *b.* ways
Mat. 7. 13. *b.* is the way that leadeth to destruction
23. 5. they make *b.* their phylacteries and enlarge

BROADER.

Job 11. 9. the measure thereof is *b.* than the sea

BROIDERED.

Exod. 28. 4. make a robe, a *b.* coat, a mitre, a girdle
Ezek. 16. 10. I clothed thee also with *b.* work
13. and thy raiment was of silk and *b.* work
18. tookest thy *b.* garments and coveredst them
26. 16. the princes shall put off their *b.* garments
27. 7. linen with *b.* work from Egypt to be thy sail
16. they occupied in thy fairs with *b.* work
24. thy merchants in blue clothes and *b.* work
1 *Tim.* 2. 9. that women adorn, not with *b.* hair

BROILED.

Luke 24. 42. they gave him a piece of a *b.* fish

BROKEN.

Gen. 17. 14. he hath *b.* my covenant, *Psal.* 55. 20. *Isa.* 24. 5. | 33. 8. *Jer.* 11. 10.
Lev. 6. 28. earthen vessel wherein sodden, shall be *b.*
15. 12. the vessel that he touched shall be *b.*
21. 19. or a man that is *b.* footed, or *b.* handed
20. that hath his stones *b.* let him not offer
22. 22. blind, *b.* or maimed, ye shall not offer, 24.
26. 13. and I have *b.* the bands of your yoke
26. when I have *b.* the staff of your bread
Num. 15. 31. because he hath *b.* his commandment
Judg. 5. 22. then were the horse-hoofs *b.* by prancings
16. 9. he brake the withs, as a thread of tow is *b.*
1 *Sam.* 2. 4. the bows of the mighty men are *b.*
2 *Sam.* 22. 35. that a bow of steel is *b.* *Psal.* 18. 34.
1 *Kings* 22. 48. the ships were *b.* at Ezion geber
1 *Chron.* 14. 11. God hath *b.* in upon mine enemies
2 *Chron.* 20. 37. Lord hath *b.* thy works, ships *b.*
32. 5. also he built up all the wall that was *b.*
Job 4. 10. the teeth of the young lions are *b.*
7. 5. my skin is *b.* and become loathsome
16. 12. I was at ease, but he hath *b.* me asunder
22. 9. the arms of the fatherless have been *b.*
24. 20. and wickedness shall be *b.* as a tree
31. 22. and let mine arm be *b.* from the bone
38. 15. and the high arm shall be *b.*
Psal. 3. 7. thou hast *b.* the teeth of the ungodly
31. 12. I am forgotten, I am like a *b.* vessel
34. 18. the Lord is nigh them of a *b.* heart, 51. 17.
20. he keepeth his bones, not one of them is *b.*
37. 15. their bows shall be *b.* || 17. arms shall be *b.*
38. 8. I am feeble and sore *b.* I have roared
44. 19. tho' thou hast *b.* us in the place of dragons
51. 8. that the bones thou hast *b.* may rejoice
17. the sacrifices of God are a *b.* spirit, a contrite
60. † 1. thou hast cast us off, thou hast *b.* us
2. hast made the earth to tremble, thou hast *b.* it

Psal. 69. 20. reproach hath *b.* my heart, and I am full
107. 16. for he hath *b.* the gates of brass and bars
109. 16. that he might even slay the *b.* in heart
124. 7. the snare is *b.* and we are escaped
147. 3. he healeth the *b.* in heart, and bindeth up
Prov. 6. 15. suddenly shall he be *b.* without remedy
11. † 15. that is surety for a stranger, shall be sore *b.*
13. † 20. a companion of fools shall be *b.*
15. 13. but by sorrow of the heart the spirit is *b.*
17. 22. but a *b.* spirit drieth the bones
25. 19. is like a *b.* tooth and a foot out of joint
Eccl. 4. 12. and a threefold cord is not quickly *b.*
12. 6. or the golden bowl be *b.* or pitcher be *b.*
Isa. 5. 27. nor the latchet of their shoes be *b.*
7. 8. within sixty-five years shall Ephraim be *b.*
8. 15. many among them shall fall and be *b.*
9. 4. for thou hast *b.* the yoke of his burden
14. 5. the Lord hath *b.* the staff of the wicked
29. because the rod of him that smote thee is *b.*
19. 10. they shall be *b.* in the purposes thereof
21. 9. all graven images he hath *b.* to the ground
28. 13. that they might fall backward and be *b.*
33. 8. he hath *b.* the covenant, he regardeth no man
20. nor shall any of the cords thereof be *b.*
36. 6. lo, thou trustest in the staff of this *b.* reed
42. † 4. he shall not fail nor be *b.* till he have set
Jer. 2. 13. hewed out *b.* cisterns that hold no water
16. the children have *b.* the crown of thy head
20. of old I have *b.* thy yoke, and burst bands
5. 5. these have *b.* thy yoke, and burst thy bonds
10. 20. all my cords are *b.* my children gone
11. 16. kindled a fire, and the branches of it are *b.*
14. 17. for the virgin daughter of my people is *b.*
22. 28. is this man Coniah a despised *b.* idol?
23. 9. mine heart is *b.* because of the prophets
28. 2. I have *b.* the yoke of the king of Babylon
13. Hananiah, thou hast *b.* the yokes of wood
33. 21. then may also my covenant be *b.* with David
48. 17. how is the strong staff *b.* and beautiful rod?
25. the arm of Moab is *b.* saith the Lord
38. for I have *b.* Moab like a vessel, wherein is no
50. 17. this Nebuchadnezzar hath *b.* Israel's bones
23. the hammer of whole earth cut asunder and *b.*
51. 56. Babylon, every one of their bows is *b.*
58. the broad walls of Babylon shall be utterly *b.*
Lam. 2. 9. he hath destroyed and *b.* her bars
3. 4. hath *b.* my bones || 16. he hath *b.* my teeth
Ezek. 6. 4. your altars, and your images shall be *b.* 6.
9. because I am *b.* with their whorish heart
17. 19. and my covenant that he hath *b.*
19. 12. her strong rods were *b.* and withered
26. 2. aha, she is *b.* that was the gates of the people
27. 26. the east-wind hath *b.* thee in the seas
34. the time when thou shalt be *b.* by the seas
30. 21. I have *b.* the arm of Pharaoh king of Egypt
22. I will break the strong and that which was *b.*
31. 12. his boughs are *b.* by all the rivers of land
32. 28. be *b.* in the midst of the uncircumcised
34. 4. nor have ye bound up that which was *b.*
16. and I will bind up that which was *b.*
27. when I have *b.* the bands of their yoke
44. 7. and they have *b.* my covenant
Dan. 2. 42. so kingdom partly strong, and partly *b.*
8. 8. when he was strong, the great horn was *b.*
22. now that being *b.* whereas four stood up for it
25. but he shall be *b.* without hand
11. 4. his kingdom shall be *b.* and shall be divided
22. with the arms of a flood be overflown and *b.*
Hos. 5. 11. Ephraim is oppressed and *b.* in judgment
Jonah 1. 4. so that the ship was like to be *b.*
Zech. 11. 11. and it was *b.* in that day, and so poor
16. a shepherd shall not heal that which is *b.*
Mat. 15. 37. took up of the *b.* meat, *Mark* 8. 8.
21. 44. fall on this stone, shall be *b.* *Luke* 20. 18.
Luke 12. 39. not have suffered his house to be *b.*
John 5. 18. because he had not only *b.* the sabbath
7. 23. that the law of Moses should not be *b.*
10. 35. word of God came, and scripture cannot be *b.*
19. 31. Jews besought Pilate their legs might be *b.*
36. scripture fulfilled, a bone of him shall not be *b.*
21. 11. for all so many, yet was not the net *b.*
Acts 20. 11. had *b.* bread and talked a long while
27. 35. gave thanks, when he had *b.* it he began to
41. but the hinder part was *b.* with the waves
1 *Cor.* 11. 24. this is my body which is *b.* for you
Rev. 2. 27. as vessels of a potter shall they be *b.*

BROKEN *down*.

Lev. 11. 35. oven or ranges *b. d.* for they are unclean
1 *Kings* 18. 30. repaired altar of Lord that was *b. d.*
2 *Kings* 11. 6. keep the watch, that it be not *b. down*
2 *Chron.* 33. 3. built high places Hezekiah had *b. d.*
34. 7. Josiah had *b. down* the altars and groves
Neh. 1. 3. the wall of Jerusalem is *b. d.* gates burnt
2. 13. and I viewed the walls which were *b. down*
Psal. 80. 12. why hast thou then *b. down* her hedges?
89. 40. thou hast *b. down* all his hedges
Prov. 24. 31. the stone wall thereof was *b. down*
25. 28. hath no rule over his spirit, like a city *b. d.*
Isa. 16. 8. have *b. down* the principal plants thereof
22. 10. the houses have ye *b. d.* to fortify the wall
24. 10. city of confusion is *b. d.* every house shut
19. the earth is utterly *b. down*, it is dissolved
Jer. 4. 26. cities were *b. d.* || 48. 20. Moab *b. d.* 39.
Ezek. 30. 4. and her foundations shall be *b. down*
Joel 1. 17. the barns are *b. down*, the corn withered
Eph. 2. 14. Christ hath *b. d.* middle wall between us

BROKEN *forth*.

Gen. 30. † 30. and it is now *b. forth* to a multitude
38. 29. how hast thou *b. forth?* breach be on thee
2 *Sam.* 5. 20. the Lord hath *b. forth* on mine enemies

BROKEN *in*.

1 *Chron.* 14. 11. God hath *b. in* on mine enemies

BROKEN *off*.

Job 17. 11. my days are past, my purposes are *b. off*
Isa. 27. 11. when boughs withered, shall be *b. off*
Rom. 11. 17. and if some of the branches be *b. off*
20. because of unbelief they were *b. off*, 19.

BROKEN *out*.

Lev. 13. 20. plague of leprosy *b. out* of the boyl, 25.

BROKEN *in*, or *to*, *pieces*.

1 *Sam.* 2. 10. adversaries of Lord shall be *b. to pieces*
2 *Chron.* 25. 12. cast them from rock, were *b. in pieces*

Psal. 89.10. thou hast b. Rahab in pieces as one slain
Isa. 8. 9. associate ye people, ye shall be b. in pieces
30. 14. break it as a potter's vessel that is b. in pieces
Jer. 50.2. Merodach is b. in pieces, her images b. in p.
Dan. 2. 35. brass, silver, gold, b. to pieces together
Hos. 8. 6. but the calf of Samaria shall be b. in pieces
Mark 5. 4. had been bound, and fetters been b. in p.

BROKEN up.

Gen. 7. 11. all the fountains of the great deep b. up
2 Kings 25. 4. city Jerusalem b. up Jer. 39. 2. | 52. 7.
2 Chr. 24. 7. sons of Athaliah had b. up house of God
Prov. 3. 20. by his knowledge the depths are b. up
Jer. 37. 11. when the army of Chaldeans was b. up
Mic. 2. 13. they have b. up and passed the gate
Mat. 24. 43. not have suffered his house to be b. up
Mark 2. 4. when they had b. roof up they let down
Acts 13. 43. when the congregation was b. up

BROKEN-HEARTED.

Isa. 61. 1. Lord sent me to bind up the b.-hearted
Luke 4. 18. to heal b.-hearted, to preach deliverance

BROOD.

Luke 13. 34. as a hen gathers her b. under her wings

BROOK.

Gen. 32. 23. he took them and sent them over the b.
Lev. 23. 40. take willows of the b. and rejoice
Num. 13. 23. came to b. Eshcol and cut a branch
24. called, b. Eshcol because of cluster of grapes
Deut. 2. 13. get over the b. Zered, went over b. 14.
9. 21. and I cast the dust thereof into the b.
1 Sam. 17. 40. chose five smooth stones out of the b.
30. 9. David and 600 men came to the b. Besor
2 Sam. 15. 23. the king passed over the b. Kidron
17. 20. they be gone over the b. of water
1 Kings 2. 37. be on the day thou passest over the b.
15. 13. idol burnt by the b. Kidron, 2 Chr. 15. 16.
17. 3. get hence, hide thyself by the b. Cherith, 5.
6. the ravens brought bread, he drank of the b.
18. 40. Elijah brought them to the b. Kishon
2 Kings 23. 6. he burnt the grove at the b. Kidron
12. cast dust into the b. Kidron, 2 Chron. 30. 14.
2 Chron. 20. 16. ye shall find them at end of the b.
29. 16. the Levites carried it to the b. Kidron
32. 4. much people gathered and stopt the b.
Neh. 2. 15. went up by the b. and viewed the wall
Job 6. 15. my brethren dealt deceitfully as a b.
40. 22. the willows of the b. compass him about
Psal. 83. 9. do to them as to Jabin at the b. Kison
110. 7. he shall drink of the b. in the way, therefore
Prov. 18. 4. well-spring of wisdom as a flowing b.
30. † 17. the ravens of the b. shall pick it out
Isa. 15. 7. shall carry away to the b. of the willows
Jer. 31. 40. all fields to b. Kidron be holy to Lord
John 18. 1. went with his disciples over b. Cedron

BROOKS.

Num. 21. 14. what he did in Redsea and b. of Arnon
15. and at the stream of the b. that goeth to Ar
Deut. 8. 7. to a land of b. of water and fountains
2 Sam. 23. 30. of the b. of Gaash, 1 Chron. 11. 32.
1 Kings 18. 5. Ahab said, go unto all b. of water
Job 6. 15. and as the stream of b. they pass away
20. 17. he shall not see the b. of honey and butter
22. 24. then shalt lay up gold as stones of the b.
Psal. 42. 1. as the hart panteth after the water-b.
Isa. 19. 6. b. of defence shall be emptied and dried up
7. the paper-reeds by the b. by the mouth of the b.
and every thing sown by the b. shall wither
8. all they that cast angle into the b. shall lament

BROTH.

Judg. 6. 19. Gideon put the b. in a pot, brought it
20. the angel said, pour out the b. and he did so
Isa. 65. 4. b. of abominable things is in their vessels

BROTHER.

See Signification on BRETHREN.

Gen. 9. 5. at hand of every man's b. will I require life
24. 29. Rebekah had a b. whose name was Laban
53. gave also to her b. and mother precious things
29. 12. Jacob told Rachel he was her father's b.
43. 6, 7. why dealt ye so ill with me, as to tell ye
had a b. the man asked, have ye another b.? 44. 19.
Deut. 25. 5. her husband's b. shall go in to her
Judg. 9. 24. their blood laid on Abimelech their b.
21. 6. Israel repented them for Benjamin their b.
Job 1. 13. were eating in their elder b. house, 18.
30. 29. I am a b. to dragons, a companion to owls
Prov. 17. 17. and a b. is born for adversity
18. 9. he that is slothful is b. to him that is a waster
19. a b. offended is harder to be won than a city
24. there is a friend that sticketh closer than a b.
27. 10. better a neighbour near than a b. far off
Eccl. 4. 8. yea, he hath neither child nor b.
Jer. 9. 4. trust not in any b. for every b. will supplant
Ezek. 44. 25. for b. they may defile themselves
Mal. 1. 2. was not Esau Jacob's b.? saith the Lord
Mat. 10. 21. b. shall deliver up the b. Mark 13. 12.
Mark 12. 19. if a man's b. die and leave, Luke 20. 28.
John 11. 2. Mary, whose b. Lazarus was sick
19. Jews came to comfort them concern. their b.
Acts 9. 17. b. Saul, receive thy sight, 22. 13.
12. 2. he killed James the b. of John with the sword
21. 20. thou seest, b. how many thousands believe
Rom. 16. 23. and Quartus a b. saluteth you
1 Cor. 5. 11. if any man called a b. be a fornicator
6. 6. b. goeth to law with b. before unbelievers
7. 12. if any b. hath a wife that believeth not
15. a b. or sister is not under bondage in such cases
8. 11. thro' thy knowledge shall the weak b. perish
2 Cor. 8. 18. and we have sent with him the b.
2 Thess. 3. 6. that ye withdraw from every b.
15. count not an enemy, but admonish him as a b.
Philem. 7. bowels of saints are refreshed by thee, b.
16. but above a servant, a b. beloved to me

His BROTHER.

Gen. 25. 26. and after that came his b. out
38. 9. lest that he should give seed to his b.
42. 38. his b. is dead, and he is left alone, 44. 20.
Exod. 32. 27. slay every man his b. and companion
Lev. 21. 2. for his father or his b. he may be defiled
Num. 6. 7. shall not make himself unclean for his b.
Deut. 15. 2. not exact it of his neighbour or his b.
19. 19. as he had thought to have done to his b.
25. 6. the first born shall succeed in name of his b.
28. 54. his eye shall be evil toward his b.

Judg. 9. 21. Jotham fled for fear of Abimelech his b.
2 Sam. 3. 27. smote him for blood of Asahel his b.
1 Kings 1. 10. but Solomon his b. he called not
Neh. 5. 7. you exact usury every one of his b.
Psal. 49. 7. none can by any means redeem his b.
Isa. 3. 6. when a man shall take hold of his b.
9. 19. people be as fuel, no man shall spare his b.
19. 2. they shall fight every one against his b.
41. 6. every one said to his b. be of good courage
Jer. 13. † 14. I will dash a man against his b.
31. 34. teach no more every man his b. Heb. 8. 11.
34. 9. that none serve himself of a Jew his b.
14. let ye go every man his b. an Hebrew
17. in proclaiming liberty every one to his b.
Ezek. 18. 18. because he spoiled his b. by violence
33. 30. speak every one to his b. saying, come
Hos. 12. 3. Jacob took his b. by the heel in the womb
Amos 1. 11. because he did pursue his b. with sword
Mic. 7. 2. they hunt every man his b. with a net
Hag. 2. 22. every one by the sword of his b.
Zech. 7. 9. and shew mercy every man to his b.
10. let none imagine evil against his b. in heart
Mal. 2. 10. why deal treacherously against his b.?
Mat. 5. 22. whoso is angry and sayeth Raca to his b.
18. 35. my Father do also to you if ye from your
hearts forgive not every one his b. their trespasses
22. 24. raise seed to his b. Mark 12. 19. Luke 20. 28.
25. having no issue, left his wife to his b.
John 1. 41. he findeth his b. Simon, and saith to him
Rom. 14. 13. or an occasion to fall in his b. way
1 Thess. 4. 6. that no man defraud his b. in any matter
Jam. 4. 11. speaketh evil of his b. and judgeth his b.
1 John 2. 9. in the light, and hateth his b. 11.
10. he that loveth his b. abideth in the light
3. 10. neither he that loveth not his b. 14.
12. not as Cain, who was of that wicked one, and
slew his b. because his b. works were righteous
15. whoso hateth his b. is a murderer, 4. 20.
1 John 4. 21. he who loveth God love his b. also
5. 16. if any see his b. sin a sin not to death

My BROTHER.

Gen. 4. 9. Cain said, I know not, am I my b. keeper?
20. 5. herself said, he is my b. 13. 1 Kings 20. 32.
27. 41. Esau said, then will I slay my b. Jacob
29. 15. Laban said to Jacob, because thou art my b.
Judg. 20. 23. to battle against Benjamin my b. 28.
2 Sam. 1. 26. distressed for thee, my b. Jonathan
13. 12. nay my b. do not force me, do not this
1 Kings 13. 30. they mourned, saying, alas my b.
Psal. 35. 14. I behaved as though he had been my b.
Cant. 8. 1. O that thou wert as my b. that sucked
Jer. 22. 18. they shall not lament, saying, ah my b.
Mat. 12. 50. same is my b. and sister, Mark 3. 35.
18. 21. Lord, how oft shall my b. sin against me?
Luke 12. 13. speak to my b. that he divide inherit.
John 11. 21. if hadst been here, my b. had not died
1 Cor. 8. 13. if meat make my b. to offend, eat no flesh
2 Cor. 2. 13. because I found not Titus my b.

Our BROTHER.

Gen. 37. 26. what profit is it if we slay our b.?
27. for he is our b. and our flesh, Judg. 9. 3.
42. 21. we are verily guilty concerning our b.
43. 4. if thou wilt send our b. with us, we will go
2 Cor. 8. 22. and we have sent with them our b.
Philem. 1. and Timothy our b. to Philemon

Thy BROTHER.

Gen. 4. 9. Lord said to Cain, where is Abel thy b.?
10. the voice of thy b. blood crieth unto me
27. 40. live by thy sword, and shalt serve thy b.
38. 8. go in to thy b. wife and raise up seed to thy b.
Exod. 4. 14. is not Aaron the Levite thy b.?
28. 1. take to thee Aaron thy b. and his sons
Lev. 19. 17. thou shalt not hate thy b. in thine heart
25. 36. fear thy God that thy b. may live with thee
Num. 27. 13. Aaron thy b. was gathered, Deut. 32. 50.
Deut. 13. 6. if thy b. entice thee secretly, saying
15. 14. open thy hand wide to thy b. to thy poor
12. if thy b. an Hebrew be sold to thee and serve
22. 1. in any case bring them again to thy b.
3. in like manner with all lost things of thy b.
23. 7. not abhor an Edomite, for he is thy b.
19. thou shalt not lend upon usury to thy b.
2 Sam. 2. 22. how hold up my face to Joab thy b.?
13. 20. hold thy peace, my sister, he is thy b.
1 Kings 20. 33. and they said, thy b. Benhadad
Job 22. 6. hast taken a pledge from thy b. for nought
Psal. 50. 20. thou sittest and speakest against thy b.
Prov. 27. 10. nor go into thy b. house in calamity
Obad. 10. for thy violence against thy b. Jacob
12. shouldest not have looked on the day of thy b.
Mat. 5. 23. rememberest that thy b. hath ought against
24. first be reconciled to thy b. then offer thy gift
7. 3. beholdest mote in thy b. eye, 5. Luke 6. 41, 42.
18. 15. if thy b. trespass, hast gained thy b. Luke 17. 3.
John 11. 23. Jesus saith, thy b. shall rise again
Rom. 14. 10. but why dost thou judge thy b.? or why
dost thou set at nought thy b.?

Your BROTHER.

Gen. 42. 34. bring your b. so will I deliver you y. b.
43. 3. not see my face, except your b. be with you
13. take your b. arise, and go again unto the man
45. 4. I am Joseph your b. whom ye sold into Egypt
Judg. 9. 18. Abimelech king, because he is your b.
Rev. 1. 9. John, who also am your b. and companion

BROTHERHOOD.

Zech. 11. 14. might break b. between Judah and Is.
1 Pet. 2. 17. love the b. fear God, honour the king

BROTHERLY.

Amos 1. 9. they remembered not the b. covenant
Rom. 12. 10. be kindly affectioned, with b. love
1 Thess. 4. 9. as touching b. love, ye need not that I
Heb. 13. 1. let b. love continue
2 Pet. 1. 7. to godliness b. kindness, and to b. kindn.

BROUGHT.

Gen. 20. 9. hast b. on me and my kingdom a great sin
27. 20. because the Lord thy God b. it to me
31. 39. that torn of beasts I b. not to thee
43. 26. they b. him the present in their hand
Exod. 9. 19. every beast in field not b. home shall die
10. 13. Lord b. east-wind, the east-wind b. locusts
18. 26. the hard causes they b. to Moses
19. 4. how I bare you and b. you to myself

Exod. 32. 1. the man that b. us up out of Egypt, 23
21. that thou hast b. so great a sin on them
35. 23. they that had purple and scarlet b. them
Lev. 13. 2. he shall be b. to Aaron the priest, 9.
23. 14. till ye have b. an offering to your God
24. 11. they b. the blasphemer to Moses
Num. 6. 13. he shall be b. to the door of tabernacle
9. 13. because b. not the offering in his season
14. 3. wherefore hath the Lord b. us to this land?
16. 10. and he hath b. thee near to him
27. 5. Moses b. their cause before the Lord
31. 50. we have therefore b. an oblation for Lord
32. 17. till we have b. them to their place
Deut. 5. 15. the Lord thy God b. thee out thence
26. 10. I have b. the first-fruits of the land
13. I have b. away the hallowed things
Josh. 7. 14. in the morning ye shall be b.
23. they took and b. them to Joshua
24. they b. them to the valley of Achor
24. 7. Lord b. the sea upon them and covered them
Judg. 2. 1. I have b. you unto the land I sware
16. 18. the Philistines b. money in their hand
18. 3. who b. thee hither? and what makest thou
1 Sam. 1. 24. she b. Samuel to the house of the Lord
25. they slew a bullock, and b. the child to Eli
10. 27. they despised him, and b. him no presents
21. 14. wherefore then have ye b. him to me?
25. 35. David received what Abigail had b. him
30. 11. they found and b. an Egyptian to David
2 Sam. 1. 10. crown and bracelet, b. them to my lord
7. 18. who am I, O Lord God? what is my house,
that thou hast b. me hitherto? 1 Chron. 17. 16.
1 Kings 9. 9. Lord b. on them this evil, 2 Chro. 7. 22.
10. 25. they b. each his present, 2 Chron. 9. 24.
17. 20. hast thou also b. evil upon the widow?
22. 37. so the king died, and was b. to Samaria
2 Kings 5. 20. spared Naaman, in not receiv. what
he b.
17. 4. Hoshea b. no presents to the king of Assyria
27. carry thither the priest ye b. from thence
20. 11. he b. the shadow ten degrees backward
24. 16. craftsmen the king b. captive to Babylon
1 Chron. 11. 19. with jeopardy of lives they b. it
14. 17. the Lord b. fear of him on all nations
2 Chr. 13. 18. the children of Israel were b. under
17. 5. all Judah b. to Jehoshaphat presents
22. 9. b. Ahaziah to Jehu, and when had slain
28. 5. the king of Syria b. Israel to Damascus
15. b. captives to Jericho to their brethren
32. 23. many b. gifts to the Lord to Jerusalem
Ezra 8. 18. they b. us a man of understanding
10. † 10. ye have b. back strange wives
Neh. 4. 15. God had b. their counsel to nought
8. 16. the people b. them and made them booths
9. 33. thou art just in all that is b. upon us
13. 12. Judah b. tithe of corn and new wine
Esth. 6. 8. let the royal apparel be b. the king usetl
9. 11. number of slain in Shushan b. to the king
Job 4. 12. now a thing was secretly b. to me
21. 32. yet shall he be b. to the grave and tomb
Psal. 35. 4. let them be b. to confusion, 26.
45. 15. with gladness and rejoic. shall they be b
71. 24. they are b. to shame that seek my hurt
Prov. 6. 26. a man is b. to a piece of bread
Cant. 2. 4. he b. me to the banqueting-house
Isa. 15. 1. Ar. b. Kir of Moab is b. to silence
23. 13. b. the land of the Chaldæans to ruin
29. 20. for the terrible one is b. to nought
43. 23. thou hast not b. small cattle to me, 24.
48. 15. yea, I have called him, I have b. him
53. 7. he is b. as a lamb to the slaughter
59. 16. therefore his arm b. salvation, 63. 5.
60. 11. and that their kings may be b.
62. 9. they that b. it shall drink it in the courts
Jer. 11. 19. as an ox that is b. to the slaughter
15. 8. I have b. on them a spoiler at noon-day
32. 42. as I have b. all this evil on this people
40. 3. now Lord hath b. it and done as he said
Ezek. 14. 22. be comforted concerning the evil I b.
23. 8. nor left she her whoredoms b. from Egypt
29. 5. thou shalt not be b. together nor gathered
40. 4. that I might shew them, art thou b. hither
47. 3. he b. me through the waters to the ancles, 4.
Dan. 6. 18. nor instruments of music b. before him
7. 13. b. him near before the ancient of days
9. 14. Lord watched on the evil, and b. it on us
11. 6. she be given up, and they that b. her
Hag. 1. 9. when ye b. it home I did blow on it
Mal. 1. 13. ye b. what was torn, and lame, and sick
Mat. 10. 18. ye shall be b. before kings for my sake,
for a test. against them, Mark 13. 9. Luke 21. 12.
12. 25. kingdom is b. to desolation, Luke 11. 17.
14. 11. she b. John Baptist's head to her mother
17. 16. I b. him to thy disciples, could not cure him
18. 24. one was b. that owed him 10,000 talents
19. 13. were b. to him little children, Mark 10. 13.
Mark 4. 21. a candle b. to be put under a bushel
6. 27. the king commanded his head to be b.
10. 13. the disciples rebuked those that b. them
Luke 2. 22. b. him to Jerusalem to present him
7. 37. a woman b. an alabaster box of ointment
10. 34. b. him to an inn and took care of him
John 7. 45. they said, why have ye not b. him?
Acts 5. 21. and sent to the prison to have them b.
9. 27. Barnabas b. him to the apostles, and declared
15. 3. and being b. on their way by the church
16. 16. who b. her masters gain by soothsaying
20. b. them to the magistrates, saying, those men
19. 12. from his body were b. to the sick, aprons
19. b. their books, and burned them before all men
24. Demetrius b. no small gain to the craftsmen
37. ye b. hither these men, no robbers of churches
20. 12. and they b. the young man alive
21. 5. they all b. us on our way, with wives
25. 6. the next day commanded Paul to be b.
27. 24. fear not, Paul, thou must be b. before Cesar
Rom. 15. 24. to be b. on my way thither by you
1 Cor. 6. 12. I will not be b. under the power of any
2 Cor. 1. 16. of you to be b. on my way to Judea
2 Tim. 1. 10. hath b. life and immortality to light
1 Pet. 1. 13. for the grace that is to be b. to you
2 Pet. 2. 19. of the same is he b. in bondage

BROUGHT *again*.
Gen.14.16. Abram *b. again* his brother Lot and goods
43. 12. and the money that was *b. again* in sacks
Exod. 10. 8. Moses and Aaron *b. again* to Pharaoh
15. 19. Lord *b. again* the waters of the sea on them
Deut. 1. 25. *b.* us word *ag.* and said, it is a good land
Josh. 14. 7. I *b.* him word *ag.* as it was in my heart
Ruth 1. 21. the Lord hath *b.* me home *ag.* empty
1 Sam. 6. 21. the Philistines *b. ag.* ark of the Lord
2 Sam. 3. 26. *b. ag.* Abner from the well of Sirah
2 Kings 22. 9. Shaphan the scribe came and *b.* the king word *ag.* 20. 1 Kings 20. 9. 2 Chron. 34. 28.
2 Chr. 33. 13. Lord *b.* Manasseh *again* to Jerusalem
Neh. 13. 9. thither *b.* I *ag.* the vessels of the house
Jer. 27. 16. the vessels shall shortly be *b. again*
Ezek. 34. 4. ye have not *b. again* what was driven
39. 27. when I have *b.* them *ag.* from the people
Mat. 27. 3. repented and *b. ag.* 30 pieces of silver
Heb. 13. 20. God of peace that *b. ag.* from the dead

BROUGHT *back*.
Gen. 14. 16. Abram *b. back* all the goods and Lot
Num. 13. 26. *b. back* word to them and congregation
1 Kings 13. 23. for the prophet whom he had *b. back*
2 Chr. 19. 4. Jehoshaphat *b.* them *back* to the Lord
Psal. 85. 1. thou hast *b. back* the captivity of Jacob
Ezek. 38. 8. come into land *b. back* from the sword

BROUGHT *down*.
Gen. 39. 1. and Joseph was *b. down* into Egypt
Judg. 7. 5. he *b. down* the people to the waters
16. 21. the Philistines *b. down* Samson to Gaza
1 Sam. 30. 16. when he had *b.* him *d.* they were spread
1 Kings 1. 53. they *b.* Adonijah *down* from the altar
17. 23. Elijah *b.* the child *d.* out of the chamber
18. 40. *b.* them *d.* to brook Kishon and slew them
Psal. 20. 8. they are *b. d.* and fallen, but we are risen
107. 12. he *b. down* their heart with labour
Isa. 5. 15. and the mean man shall be *b. down*
14. 11. thy pomp is *b. down* to the grave
15. thou shalt be *b. down* to hell, to sides of pit
29. 4. thou shalt be *b. d.* and speak out of ground
43. 14. for your sake I have *b. d.* all the nobles
Lam. 2. 2. he hath *b.* them *down* to the ground
Ezek. 17. 24. I the Lord have *b. d.* the high tree
31. 18. shall be *b. down* with the trees of Eden
Zech. 10. 11. the pride of Assyria shall be *b. down*
Mat. 11. 23. thou Capernaum be *b. down* to hell
Acts 9. 30. the brethren *b.* him *down* to Cesarea

BROUGHT *forth*.
Gen. 1. 12. the earth *b. forth* grass and herbs
21. waters *b. forth* abundantly after their kind
14. 18. the king of Salem *b. forth* bread and wine
15. 5. the Lord *b. forth* Abram abroad, and said
19. 16. angels *b.* Lot *forth*, and set him without city
24. 53. the servant *b. forth* jewels of silver and gold
38. 25. when *b. forth*, she sent to her father-in-law
41. 47. in plenteous years earth *b. forth* by handfuls
Exod. 3. 12. when thou hast *b. forth* the people
16. 3. for ye have *b.* us *forth* into the wilderness
29. 46. shall know I am the Lord who *b.* them *forth* out of the land of Egypt, Lev. 25. 38. | 26. 13, 45.
Num. 17. 8. Aaron's rod *b. forth* buds, and bloomed
20. 16. sent an angel, and *b.* us *forth* out of Egypt
24. 8. God *b.* him *forth* out of Egypt, he hath strength
Deut. 6. 12. lest forget Lord who *b.* thee *forth*, 8. 14.
8. 15. who *b. forth* water out of the rock of flint
9. 12. thy people thou *b. f.* have corrupted thems.
26. 8. the Lord *b.* us *forth* with a mighty hand
29. 25. the covenant he made when he *b.* them *forth*
33. 14. for precious fruits *b. forth* by the sun
Josh. 10. 23. *b. forth* those five kings out of the cave
Judg. 5. 25. she *b. forth* butter in a lordly dish
6. 8. I *b.* you *forth* out of the house of bondage
1 Sam. 12. 8. sent Moses, who *b. forth* your fathers
2 Sam. 22. 20. *b.* me *f.* into large place, Psal. 18. 19.
1 Kings 9. 9. they forsook the Lord who *b. f.* their fathers out of the land of Egypt, 2 Chr. 7. 22.
2 Kings 10. 22. *b. forth* vestments for worshippers
11. 12. *b. forth* the king's son, and put the crown on
Job 10. 18. wherefore hast *b.* me *forth* out of womb
21. 30. the wicked shall be *b. forth* to day of wrath
Psal. 7. 14. conceived mischief, and *b. f.* falsehood
90. 2. before the mountains were *b. forth*, art God
105. 30. their land *b. forth* frogs in abundance
43. he *b. forth* his people with joy and gladness
Prov. 8. 24. when there were no depths, I was *b. f.*
25. before the hills was I *b. forth*
Cant. 8. 5. there thy mother *b.* thee *forth*, she *b. forth*
Isa. 5. 2. he looked for grapes, and it *b. f.* wild grapes
26. 18. *b. forth* wind || 45. 10. what hast thou *b. f.*?
51. 18. to guide her among sons, she hath *b. forth*
66. 7. before she travailed, she *b. f.* before her pain
8. for as soon as Zion travailed, she *b. f.* children
Jer. 2. 27. saying to a stone, thou hast *b.* me *forth*
11. 4. I commanded in the day I *b.* them *f.* 34. 13.
17. † 11. gathereth young which he hath not *b. forth*
20. 3. Pashur *b. forth* Jeremiah out of the stocks
32. 21. hast *b. forth* thy people Israel with signs
50. 25. Lord *b. f.* the weapons of his indignation
51. 10. the Lord hath *b. forth* our righteousness
Ezek. 12. 7. I *b. forth* my stuff by day in their sight
14. 22. a remnant *b. forth*, both sons and daughters
20. 22. the heathen in whose sight I *b.* them *forth*
Mic. 5. 3. till time she which travaileth hath *b. forth*
Hag. 2. 19. and the olive-tree hath not *b. forth*
Mat. 1. 25. till she had *b. forth* her first-born son
13. 8. fell in good ground, and *b. f.* fruit, Mark 4. 8.
Luke 1. 57. now Elisabeth's time came, she *b. f.* a son
2. 7. she *b. f.* her first-born son and wrapped him
12. 16. the ground of a rich man *b. forth* plentifully
John 19. 13. when Pilate heard that, he *b. f.* Jesus
Acts 5. 19. opened the prison doors and *b.* them *forth*
12. 6. when Herod would have *b.* him *forth*
25. 17. I commanded the man to be *b. forth*
Jam. 5. 18. he prayed, and the earth *b. forth* her fruit
Rev. 12. 5. she *b. forth* a man-child, who was to rule
13. the dragon persecuted the woman which *b. f.*

BROUGHT *in*.
Gen. 39. 14. he hath *b. in* an Hebrew to mock us
47. 7. Joseph *b. in* Jacob his father, Jacob blessed
Lev. 10. 18. blood was not *b. in* within holy place
16. 27. the bullock and goat, whose blood was *b. in*
Num. 12. 15. they journeyed not till Miriam was *b. in*
Deut. 9. 4. for my righteousness the Lord *b.* me *in*
11. 29. when the Lord hath *b.* thee *in* to the land
2 Sam. 3. 22. Joab *b. in* a great spoil with him
6. 17. they *b. in* the ark of the Lord, 1 Kings 8. 6.
Neh. 13. 19. no burden *b. in* on the sabbath-day
Psal. 78. 26. by his power he *b. in* the south wind
Dan. 5. 13. then was Daniel *b. in* before the king
Mat. 14. 11. John's head was *b. in* in a charger
Acts 7. 45. *b. in* with Jesus into possession of Gentiles
Gal. 2. 4. false brethren *b. in* to spy our liberty
Heb. 9. † 16. must be *b. in* the death of the testator

BROUGHT *into*.
Num. 16. 14. not *b.* us *into* a land that floweth
Deut. 6. 10. when the Lord hath *b.* thee *into*, 31. 20.
1 Sam. 5. 2. *b.* the ark *into* Dagon's house and set it
9. 22. *b.* them *into* the parlour, and made them sit
20. 8. *b.* thy servant *into* a covenant with thee
2 Kings 12. 16. sin-money not *b. into* house of Lord
Psal. 22. 15. hast *b.* me *into* the dust of death
Cant. 1. 4. the king hath *b.* me *into* his chambers
Jer. 2. 7. I *b.* you *into* a plentiful country to eat
Lam. 3. 2. hath *b.* me *into* darkness, but not light
Ezek. 27. 26. thy rowers have *b.* thee *into* waters
44. 7. ye have *b. into* my sanctuary strangers
Acts 9. 8. they led him and *b.* him *into* Damascus
21. 28. *b.* Greeks *into* the temple, and polluted it
1 Tim. 6. 7. for we *b.* nothing *into* this world
Heb. 13. 11. whose blood is *b. into* the sanctuary

BROUGHT *low*.
Judg. 11. 35. daughter, thou hast *b.* me very *low*
2 Chron. 28. 19. Lord *b.* Judah *low*, because of Ahaz
Job 14. 21. they are *b. low*, but he perceiveth it not
24. 24. wicked are gone and *b. low*, they are taken
Psal. 79. 8. let mercies prevent us, for we are *b. low*
106. 43. and were *b. low* for their iniquity
107. 39. they are *b. low*, thro' oppression and sorrow
116. 6. I was *b. low*, and he helped me
142. 6. attend to my cry, for I am *b.* very *low*
Eccl. 12. 4. all daughters of music shall be *b. low*
Isa. 2. 12. upon every one lifted up, he shall be *b. low*
25. 5. the branch of the terrible ones shall be *b. low*
Luke 3. 5. every mountain and hill *b. low*, Isa. 40. 4.

BROUGHT *out*.
Gen. 15. 7. that *b.* thee *out* of Ur of the Chaldees
41. 14. they *b.* him hastily *out* of the dungeon
43. 23. and he *b.* Simeon *out* unto them
Exod. 13. 3. for by strength of hand the Lord *b.* you *out* from this place, 9, 14, 16. Deut. 6. 21.
20. 2. I am the Lord thy God, which *b.* thee *out*, Lev. 19. 36. Num. 15. 41. Deut. 5. 6. Psal. 81. 10.
Lev. 23. 43. when I *b.* them *out* of Egypt, 1 Kings 8. 21.
Deut. 5. 15. remember that Lord *b.* thee *out* thence
9. 28. *b.* them *out* to slay them in the wilderness
Josh. 6. 23. young men *b. out* Rahab and all she had
24. 5. plagued Egypt, and afterward I *b.* you *out*
2 Sam. 13. 18. servant *b.* her *out*, and bolted the door
2 Kings 23. 6. he *b. out* the grove from house of Lord
1 Chron. 20. 3. he *b. out* the people that were in it
2 Chron. 23. 11. then they *b. out* the king's son
29. 16. priests *b. out* all uncleanness they found
Psal. 78. 16. he *b.* streams also *out* of the rock
80. 8. thou hast *b.* a vine *out* of Egypt
107. 14. he *b.* them *out* of darkness, and brake
136. 11. and *b. out* Israel from among them
Jer. 7. 22. in the day I *b.* them *out* of Egypt
Dan. 5. 13. whom the king my father *b. out* of Jewry
Hos. 12. 13. by a prophet the Lord *b.* Israel *out*
Acts 7. 40. this Moses, which *b.* us *out* of Egypt
12. 17. declared how the Lord *b.* him *out* of prison
13. 17. with an high arm *b.* them *out* of Egypt
16. 30. *b. out*, and said, what must I do to be saved?
39. they came and besought them, and *b.* them *out*

BROUGHT *to pass*.
2 Kings 19. 25. now have I *b.* it *to pass*, Isa. 37. 26.
Ezek. 21. 7. it cometh, and shall be *b. to pass*
1 Cor. 15. 54. then shall be *b. to pass* the saying

BROUGHT *up*.
Exod. 17. 3. wherefore hast thou *b.* us *up*? Num. 21. 5.
32. 1. as for Moses, the man that *b.* us *up*, 23.
4. these thy gods which *b.* thee *up*, 8. 1 Kings 12. 28.
33. 1. thou and the people which thou hast *b. up*
Num. 13. 32. they *b. up* an evil report of the land
16. 13. is it a small thing that thou hast *b.* us *up*?
20. 4. why have ye *b. up* the congregation of Lord?
Deut. 20. 1. the Lord is with thee, which *b.* thee *up*
22. 19. because he *b. up* an evil name on a virgin
Josh. 24. 17. he it is that *b.* us *up* and our fathers
32. bones of Joseph *b. up*, they buried in Shechem
Judg. 6. 8. I *b.* you *up* from Egypt, 1 Sam. 10. 18.
15. 13. *b.* Samson *up* || 16. 31. *b.* him *up* and buried
16. 8. the lords *b. up* to her seven green withs
1 Sam. 2. 14. all the flesh-hook *b. up* the priest took
8. 8. since the day I *b.* them *up*, 2 Sam. 7. 6. 1 Chron. 17. 5.
12. 6. Lord that *b.* your fathers *up* out of Egypt
2 Sam. 6. 12. David went and *b. up* the ark of God, 15. 1 Kings 8. 4. 1 Chr. 15. 28. 2 Chr. 1. 4.
21. 8. *b. up* for Adriel || 13. *b. up* the bones of Saul
2 Kings 10. 1. to them that *b. up* Ahab's children, 6.
17. 7. Israel sinned against Lord who *b.* them *up*
36. the Lord who *b.* you *up*, him fear and worship
25. 6. *b. up* Zedekiah to king of Babylon, Jer. 39. 5.
2 Chr. 8. 11. Solomon *b. up* the daughter of Pharaoh
10. 8. counsel with young men *b. up* with him, 10.
Ezra 1. 11. all these vessels *b. up* from Babylon
4. 2. Esar-haddon king of Assur *b.* us *up* hither
Neh. 9. 18. this is thy God that *b.* thee *up* out of Egypt
Esth. 2. 7. Mordecai *b. up* Esther his uncle's daughter
20. like as when she was *b. up* with him
Job 31. 18. from my youth he was *b. up* with me
Psal. 30. 3. thou hast *b. up* my soul from the grave
40. 2. he *b.* me *up* out of an horrible pit
Prov. 8. 30. then I was by him, as one *b. up* with him
Isa. 1. 2. I have nourished and *b. up* children
49. 21. who hath *b. up* these? where had they been?
51. 18. none to guide her of all the sons she *b. up*
63. 11. where is he that *b.* them *up*? Jer. 2. 6.
Jer. 11. 7. I protested in the day I *b.* them *up*
16. 14. the Lord that *b. up* Israel out of Egypt, 23. 7.
15. the Lord that *b. up* Israel from the north, 23. 8.
Lam. 2. 22. those I *b. up* hath my enemy consumed
Lam. 4. 5. that were *b. up* in scarlet embrace dungh.
Ezek. 19. 3. she *b. up* one of her whelps, a young lion
31. † 4. the deep *b.* him up on high with her rivers
37. 13. when I have *b.* you *up* out of your graves
Amos 2. 10. I *b.* you *up*, 3. 1. | 9. 7. Mic. 6. 4.
Jonah 2. 6. yet hast *b. up* my life from corruption
Nah. 2. 7. she shall be *b. up*, and her maids lead her
Luke 4. 16. to Nazareth, where she had been *b. up*
Acts 13. 1. had been *b. up* with Herod the tetrarch
22. 3. yet *b. up* in this city at the feet of Gamaliel
1 Tim. 5. 10. a widow, if she have *b. up* children

BROUGHTEST.
Exod. 32. 7. thy people thou *b.* out have corrupted
Num. 14. 13. thou *b.* up this people in thy might
Deut. 9. 28. lest the land whence thou *b.* us out say
29. thy inheritance thou *b.* out, 1 Kings 8. 51.
2 Sam. 5. 2. wast he that *b.* in Israel, 1 Chron. 11. 2.
1 Kings 8. 53. when thou *b.* our fathers out of Egypt
Neh. 9. 7. *b.* him forth out of Ur of the Chaldees
15. thou *b.* forth water for them out of the rock
23. *b.* them into the land thou hadst promised
Psal. 66. 11. thou *b.* us into the net, thou laid'st
12. but thou *b.* us out into a wealthy place

BROW.
Isa. 48. 4. thy neck is an iron sinew, and thy *b.* brass
Luke 4. 29. they led him to the *b.* of the hill

BROWN.
Gen. 30. 32. all *b.* cattle among the sheep, 35. 40.
33. every one that is not *b.* shall be accounted stolen

BRUISE, *Substantive.*
Isa. 53. † 5. and with his *b.* we are healed
Jer. 6. † 14. they healed the *b.* of my people slightly
30. 12. thus saith the Lord, thy *b.* is incurable
Nah. 3. 19. there is no healing of thy *b.* wound griev.

BRUISES.
Isa. 1. 6. no soundness, but wounds, and *b.* and sores
Ezek. 47. † 12. the leaf thereof for *b.* and sores

BRUISE
Signifies, [1] *To crush, injure, or oppress*, Gen. 3. 15. Dan. 2. 40. [2] *To punish, chastise, or correct*, Isa. 53. 10. It is spoken, (1) Corporally, *of the body*, Luke 9. 39. (2) Spiritually, *of doubts and troubles*, Mat. 12. 20. (3) Morally, *of corruptions*, Isa. 1. 6. (4) Politically, *of a weak decaying nation*, 2 Kings 18. 21.

A bruised reed shall he not break, Isa. 42. 3. *Christ will not deal roughly and rigorously with those that come to him, but will use all gentleness and tenderness to them; passing by their greatest sins, bearing with their present infirmities, cherishing and encouraging the smallest beginnings of grace, and comforting and healing wounded consciences.*

To bruise the teats, Ezek. 23. 3, 21. *To commit bodily whoredom; or idolatry, which is spiritual whoredom.*

Gen. 3. 15. it shall *b.* thy head, thou shalt *b.* his heel
Isa. 28. 28. nor will he *b.* it with his horsemen
53. 10. yet it pleased the Lord to *b.* him
Dan. 2. 40. as iron shall it break in pieces and *b.*
Rom. 16. 20. the God of peace shall *b.* Satan shortly

BRUISED.
Lev. 22. 24. ye shall not offer to the Lord what is *b.*
2 Kings 18. 21. trustest on the staff of this *b.* reed
Isa. 42. 3. a *b.* reed shall he not break, Mat. 12. 20.
53. 5. he was *b.* for our iniquities, the chastisement
Ezek. 23. 3. there they *b.* the teats of their virginity
8. and they *b.* the breasts of her virginity
Luke 4. 18. sent me to set at liberty them that are *b.*

BRUISING.
Ezek. 23. 21. in *b.* thy teats by the Egyptians
Luke 9. 39. the spirit *b.* him, hardly departeth from

BRUIT.
Jer. 10. 22. behold, the noise of the *b.* is come
Nah. 3. 19. all that hear the *b.* of thee, shall clap

BRUTE; *see* BEASTS.

BRUTISH.
Psal. 49. 10. the fool and the *b.* person perish
92. 6. a *b.* man knoweth not, nor a fool understand
94. 8. understand, ye *b.* among the people
Prov. 12. 1. but he that hateth reproof is *b.*
30. 2. surely I am more *b.* than any man
Isa. 19. 11. the princes of Zoan are fools, the counsel of the wise counsellors of Pharaoh is become *b.*
Jer. 10. 8. they are altogether *b.* and foolish
14. every man is *b.* 51. 17. || 21. pastors are *b.*
Ezek. 21. 31. deliver thee into the hand of *b.* men

BUCKET, S.
Num. 24. 7. he shall pour the water out of his *b.*
Isa. 40. 15. the nations are as a drop of a *b.* and dust

BUCKLER
Is *a piece of defensive armour*, 1 Chron. 5. 18. *God is often called the* Buckler, *or* Shield, *of his people*, Psal. 18. 2. Prov. 2. 7. *He will protect and save them from that mischief and ruin which will befal all wicked men. And in* Cant. 4. 4. *the faith of the church, or of believers, whereby they are united to Christ, is compared to* the tower of *David*, whereon hang a thousand bucklers; *nothing, how strong and invincible faith is, which furnishes with weapons out of Christ's fulness, and abundantly defends from all spiritual enemies*, Eph. 6. 16.

2 Sam. 22. 31. a *b.* to all that trust in him, Ps. 18. 30.
1 Chron. 5. 18. men able to bear *b.* and sword
12. 8. Gadites that could handle shield and *b.*
Psal. 18. 2. Lord is my God, my *b.* my high tower
35. 2. take hold of shield and *b.* stand up for help
91. 4. his truth shall be thy shield and *b.*
Prov. 2. 7. he is a *b.* to them that walk uprightly
Jer. 46. 3. order ye the *b.* and shield, and draw near
Ezek. 23. 24. shall set against the *b.* shield, and helmet
26. 8. he shall lift up the *b.* against thee

BUCKLERS.
2 Chr. 23. 9. Jehoiada delivered spears, *b.* and shields
Job 15. 26. runneth upon the thick bosses of his *b.*
Cant. 4. 4. whereon there hanged a thousand *b.*
Ezek. 38. 4. a great company with *b.* and shields
39. 9. they shall set on fire shields, *b.* and bows

BUD, *Substantive.*
Job 38. 27. cause the *b.* of the tender herb to spring
Isa. 18. 5. afore the harvest, when the *b.* is perfect
61. 11. for as the earth bringeth forth her *b.*

Ezek. 16. 7. caused thee to multiply as *b.* of the field
Hos. 8. 7. *b.* shall yield no meal, stranger swallow it

BUD, *Verb.*

Gen. 3. † 18. thistles shall it cause to *b.* to thee
Job 14. 9. yet through the scent of water it will *b.*
Psal. 132. 17. I will make the horn of David to *b.*
Cant. 7. 12. let us see if the pomegranates *b.* forth
Isa. 27. 6. Israel shall blossom and *b.* and fill the world
55. 10. maketh the earth to bring forth and *b.*
Ezek. 29. 21. cause the horn of Israel to *b.* forth

BUDS.

Num. 17. 8. Aaron's rod brought forth *b.* and bloomed

BUDDED.

Gen. 40. 10. the vine was as though it *b.* and shot [forth
Num. 17. 8. Aaron's rod for the house of Levi *b.*
Cant. 6. 11. to see whether the pomegranates *b.*
Ezek. 7. 10. the rod hath blossomed, pride hath *b.*
Heb. 9. 4. the ark wherein was Aaron's rod that *b.*

BUFFET.

2 *Cor.* 12. 7. the messenger of Satan to *b.* me

BUFFETED.

Mat. 26. 67. spit in his face and *b.* him, *Mark* 14. 65.
1 *Cor.* 4. 11. even to this present hour we are *b.*
1 *Pet.* 2. 20. if when ye be *b.* for your faults

BUILD

Signifies, [1] *To erect, or make houses, &c.* Deut. 28. 30. [2] *To strengthen and increase knowledge, faith, love, and all other graces,* Acts 20. 32. [3] *To cement and knit together spiritually; thus believers are united to Christ by faith, and among themselves by love,* Eph. 2. 22. [4] *To preserve, bless, and prosper,* Psal. 127. 1. Jer. 24. 6. [5] *To settle and establish,* 1 Sam. 2. 35.

Who did build the house of Israel, *Ruth* 4. 11. *Who did increase his family by a numerous progeny.*

I will build up thy throne, *Psal.* 89. 4. *I will perpetuate the kingdom to thy posterity.*

Shall build the old wastes, *Isa.* 61. 4. *The Gentiles, who have been long destitute of the true knowledge of God, and like a wilderness overgrown with briers and thorns, shall be brought, by the ministry of the word, to know and serve the true God.*

BUILD, referred to *God.*

1 *Sam.* 2. 35. I will raise up a priest, and will *b.* him a sure house, 2 *Sam.* 7. 27. 1 *Kings* 11. 38.
1 *Chron.* 17. 10. that the Lord will *b.* thee an house
25. hast told that thou wilt *b.* him an house
Psal. 28. 5. he shall destroy, and not *b.* them up
51. 18. do good to Sion, *b.* the walls of Jerusalem
69. 35. for God will *b.* the cities of Judah
89. 4. and *b.* up thy throne to all generations
102. 16. when Lord shall *b.* up Zion, will appear
127. 1. except Lord *b.* house, they labour in vain
147. 2. Lord doth *b.* up Jerusalem, gathers outcasts
Jer. 18. 9. I speak concerning a nation to *b.* it
24. 6. I will *b.* and not pull them down, 31. 28.
31. 4. again I will *b.* thee, O virgin of Israel
33. 7. I will *b.* Judah and Israel as at the first
42. 10. if ye will abide in this land I will *b.* you
Ezek. 36. 36. that I the Lord *b.* the ruined places
Amos 9. 11. I will *b.* it as in the days of old
Mat. 16. 18. on this rock will I *b.* my church
26. 61. I am able to *b.* it in three days *Mark* 14. 58.
Acts 15. 16. I will *b.* again the tabernacle of David

BUILD *altars.*

Exod. 20. 25. shalt not *b.* an *altar* of hewn stone
Num. 23. 1. Balaam said, *b.* me here seven *altars,* 29.
Deut. 27. 5. there thou shalt *b.* an *altar* to the Lord
6. thou shalt *b.* *altar* of the Lord of whole stones
Josh. 22. 29. God forbid, we rebel and *b.* an *altar*
See BEGAN.

BUILD, joined with *house.*

Deut. 25. 9. man that will not *b.* his brother's *house*
28. 30. shalt *b.* an *house,* not dwell in it, *Zeph.* 1. 13.
Ruth 4. 11. which two did *b.* the *house* of Israel
2 *Sam.* 7. 5. shalt thou *b.* me an *house* to dwell in?
7. spake I, saying, why *b.* ye not me an *h.* of cedar?
13. thy seed shall *b.* an *house* for my name, 1 *Kings* 5. 5. | 8. 19. 1 *Chr.* 17. 12. | 22. 10.
1 *Kings* 2. 36. *b.* thee an *h.* in Jerusalem, and dwell
5. 3. David could not *b.* an *h.* for wars about him
5. I purpose to *b.* an *h.* to the Lord, 2 *Chr.* 2. 1.
8. 16. I chose no city to *b.* an *house,* 2 *Chron.* 6. 5.
17. it was in heart of David my father to *b.* an *h.* for God of Israel, 1 *Chr.* 28. 2. 2 *Chr.* 6. 7.
1 *Chr.* 17. 12. he shall *b.* me an *house,* 2 *Chr.* 6. 9.
22. 8. shalt not *b.* an *h.* because thou shed blood
11. my son, *b.* the *h.* of Lord, as he said of thee
28. 6. Solomon shall *b.* my *house* and my courts
2 *Chr.* 2. 4. behold, I *b.* an *house* to the Lord my God
5. the *house* I *b.* is great, for great is our God
6. who is able to *b.* him an *house?* that I should *b.* an *house*
36. 23. he hath charged me to *b.* him an *h.* *Ezra* 1. 2.
Ezra 1. 3. go to Jerusalem and *b.* the *house* of Lord
5. 3. who hath commanded you to *b.* this *house?* 9.
6. 7. let the governor of the Jews *b.* this *house*
Psal. 127. 1. they labour in vain that *b.* the *house*
Prov. 24. 27. prepare, and afterwards *b.* thy *house*
Isa. 65. 21. they shall *b.* *houses* and inhabit them
66. 1. where is the *house* that ye *b.* unto me?
Jer. 22. 14. I will *b.* me a wide *h.* and large chambers
29. 5. *b.* *houses* and dwell in them, and plant, 28.
35. 7. neither shall ye *b.* *house* nor sow seed
Ezek. 11. 3. which say, it is not near, let us *b.* *houses*
28. 26. they shall dwell safely, and shall *b.* *houses*
Hag. 1. 8. go to the mountain, bring wood, *b.* *house*
Zech. 5. 11. to *b.* it an *house* in the land of Shinar
Acts 7. 49. what *house* will ye *b.* me, saith the Lord?

BUILD.

Gen. 11. 4. go to, let us *b.* us a city and a tower
8. and they left off to *b.* the city
Num. 32. 16. we will *b.* sheep folds for our cattle
24. *b.* cities for your little ones, and folds for sheep
Deut. 20. 20. thou shalt *b.* bulwarks against the city
1 *Kings* 9. 19. all the cities of store, and that which Solomon desired to *b.* in Jerusalem, 2 *Chr.* 8. 6.
24. Pharaoh's daughter came up, then did *b.* Millo
11. 7. Solomon did *b.* an high place for Chemosh
16. 34. in Ahab's days Hiel the Bethelite *b.* Jericho

1 *Chr.* 22. 19. *b.* ye the sanctuary of the Lord God
29. 19. give to Solomon an heart to *b.* the palace
2 *Chron.* 14. 7. let us *b.* these cities and make walls
Ezra 4. 2. let us *b.* with you, we seek your God
5. † 4. what are the men that *b.* this building?
Neh. 2. 17. let us *b.* the wall ‖ 18. let us rise and *b.*
20. therefore we his servants will rise and *b.*
4. 3. which they *b.* if a fox go up he shall break down
10. so that we are not able to *b.* the wall
Eccl. 3. 3. a time to break down, and a time to *b.* up
Cant. 8. 9. if she be a wall, we will *b.* upon her
Isa. 9. 10. the bricks are fallen, but we will *b.*
45. 13. I have raised him up, he shall *b.* my city
58. 12. they shall *b.* the old waste places, 61. 4.
60. 10. the sons of strangers shall *b.* up thy walls
65. 22. they shall not *b.* and another inhabit
Jer. 1. 10. have set thee over nations to *b.* and plant
Ezek. 4. 2. lay siege, *b.* a fort against it, 21. 22.
39. † 15. then shall ye *b.* up a sign by the bone
Dan. 9. 25. to restore and *b.* Jerusalem to Messiah
Amos 9. 11. I will *b.* it as in the days of old
14. Israel shall *b.* the waste cities and inhabit them
Mic. 3. 10. they *b.* up Zion with blood and Jerus.
Zech. 6. 12. he shall *b.* the temple of the Lord, 13.
15. that are far off shall *b.* in the temple of Lord
9. 3. Tyrus did *b.* herself a strong hold, heaped silver
Mal. 1. 4. they shall *b.* but I will throw down
Mat. 23. 29. ye *b.* tombs of prophets, *Luke* 11. 47, 48.
Luke 12. 18. I will pull down my barns and *b.* greater
14. 28. which of you intending to *b.* a tower?
30. this man began to *b.* and not able to finish
Acts 20. 32. to the word of his grace, able to *b.* you up
Rom. 15. 20. lest I *b.* on another man's foundation
1 *Cor.* 3. 12. if any *b.* on this foundation, gold, silver
Gal. 2. 18. if I *b.* again the things which I destroyed

BUILDED.

Gen. 2. † 22. of the rib the Lord *b.* a woman
4. 17. Cain *b.* a city, and called it Enoch
8. 20. Noah *b.* an altar to the Lord, and offered
10. 11. Asher *b.* Nineveh, Rehoboth, and Caleb
11. 5. Ld. came to see the tower children of men *b.*
12. 7. Abram *b.* an altar to the Lord, 13. 18.
16. † 2. it may be I may be *b.* by her, 30. † 3.
26. 25. Isaac *b.* an altar ‖ *Exod.* 24. 4. Moses *b.*
Josh. 22. 16. in that ye have *b.* you an altar
1 *Kings* 8. 27. how much less this house I have *b.* 43.
15. 22. the stones wherewith Baasha had *b.*
2 *Kings* 23. 13. Solomon had *b.* for Ashtoreth
1 *Chron.* 22. 5. the house to be *b.* must be magnifical
Ezra 4. 1. when the adversaries heard that they *b.*
13. be it known, that if this city be *b.* 16.
21. give commandment that this city be not *b.*
5. 8. we went to the house of great God which is *b.*
11. we build the house that was *b.* many years ago
15. let the house of God be *b.* in his place, 6. 3.
6. 14. elders of the Jews *b.* and they prospered
Neh. 4. 18. every one had his sword girded, and so *b.*
Job 20. 19. he hath taken away an house he *b.* not
Psal. 122. 3. Jerusalem is *b.* a city that is compact
Prov. 9. 1. Wisdom hath *b.* her house, hewn out pill.
24. 3. through wisdom is an house *b.* and established
Eccl. 2. 4. I *b.* me houses, I planted vineyards
Cant. 4. 4. thy neck like tower of D. *b.* for armoury
Jer. 30. 18. the city shall be *b.* on her own heap
Lam. 3. 5. he hath *b.* against me, and compassed me
Ezek. 36. 10. and the wastes shall be *b.* 33.
Luke 17. 28. they bought, they sold, they planted, [they *b.*
Eph. 2. 22. in whom ye are *b.* together for habitat.
Heb. 3. 3. he who *b.* the house hath more honour
4. every house is *b.* by some man, he that built

BUILDEDST.

Deut. 6. 10. to give thee goodly cities thou *b.* not

BUILDER, S,

Is spoken, [1] *Of such as erect houses, &c.* 2 Kings 22. 6. [2] *Of God, the great Architect, who created the heavens and the earth, and all things in them,* Heb. 11. 10. [3] *Of faithful ministers of the gospel, who like wise master-builders ought first to lay the foundation, and then build upon it; first to acquaint such as they have the charge of, with the fundamentals of religion, showing them that Christ is the only way to salvation, and then to make their superstructure upon this foundation,* 1 Cor. 3. 10.

1 *Kings* 5. 18. Solomon's and Hiram's *b.* did hew
2 *Kings* 12. 11. laid money out to the *b.* that wrought
22. 6. give it to carpenters and *b.* 2 *Chr.* 34. 11.
Ezra 3. 10. when *b.* laid foundation of the temple
Neh. 4. 5. have provoked thee to anger before the *b.*
Psal. 118. 22. stone which *b.* refus. become head-stone, *Mat.* 21. 42. *Mark* 12. 10. *Luke* 20. 17. *Acts* 4. 11.
127. † 1. they labour in vain that are *b.* in it
Ezek. 27. 4. thy *b.* have perfected thy beauty
1 *Cor.* 3. 10. as a wise master-*b.* I have laid foundation
Heb. 11. 10. looked for a city whose *b.* and maker is G.
1 *Pet.* 2. 7. the stone which the *b.* disallowed

BUILDEST.

Deut. 22. 8. when thou *b.* a new house, make battlem.
Neh. 6. 6. for which cause thou *b.* the wall
Ezek. 16. 31. in that thou *b.* thine eminent place
Mat. 27. 40. thou that destroyest the temple and *b.* it in three days, save thyself, *Mark* 15. 29.

BUILDETH.

Josh. 6. 26. cursed be the man that *b.* this city
Job 27. 18. he *b.* his house as a moth, as a booth
Prov. 14. 1. every wise woman *b.* her house, but fool.
Jer. 22. 13. woe to him that *b.* by unrighteousness
Hos. 8. 14. Israel hath forgotten Maker, *b.* temples
Amos 9. 6. it is he that *b.* his stories in the heavens
Hab. 2. 12. woe to him that *b.* a town with blood
1 *Cor.* 3. 10. I laid the foundation, another *b.* thereon

BUILDING.

Josh. 22. 19. but rebel not against L. in *b.* an altar
1 *Kings* 3. 1. till he made an end of *b.* his own house
6. 7. no tool of iron heard in the house while *b.*
38. so was Solomon seven years in *b.* it
7. 1. Solomon was *b.* his own house thirteen years
2 *Chron.* 16. 6. the stones wherewith Baasha was *b.*
Ezra 4. 12. *b.* the rebellious and the bad city
Ezek. 17. 17. by *b.* forts to cut off many persons
John 2. 20. this temple was forty-six years in *b.*

Jude 20. *b.* up yourselves on your most holy faith

BUILDING, *Substantive.*

1 *Kings* 9. 1. when Solomon finished *b.* house of L.
15. 21. he left off *b.* of Ramah, 2 *Chron.* 16. 5.
1 *Chron.* 28. 2. and had made ready for the *b.*
2 *Chron.* 3. 3. Solomon was instructed for the *b.*
Ezra 5. 4. the names of the men that make this *b.*
6. 8. what ye shall do for the *b.* of this house of God
Eccl. 10. 18. by much slothfulness the *b.* decayeth
Ezek. 40. 5. he measured the breadth of the *b.* 41. 15.
46. 23. there was a row of *b.* round about in them
1 *Cor.* 3. 9. ye are God's husbandry, ye are God's *b.*
2 *Cor.* 5. 1. we have a *b.* of God, an house not made
Eph. 2. 21. in whom all the *b.* fitly framed together
Heb. 9. 11. an high-priest by a tabernacle not of this *b.*
Rev. 21. 18. *b.* of wall was of jasper, city pure gold

BUILDINGS.

Mat. 24. 1. disciples came to shew him *b.* of temple
Mark 13. 1. Master, see what *b.* are here, 2.

BUILT.

Deut. 13. 16. it shall be an heap and not be *b.* again
1 *Kings* 22. 39. the cities that Ahab *b.* are written
2 *Chr.* 14. 7. rest on every side, so they *b.* and pros.
20. 8. they have *b.* thee a sanctuary therein
26. 9. Uzziah *b.* towers in Jerusalem, 10.
27. 4. Jotham *b.* in the forests castles and towers
Job 3. 14. who *b.* desolate places for themselves
12. 14. he breaketh down, and it cannot be *b.* again
22. 23. if thou return to Almighty, shalt be *b.* up
Psal. 78. 69. he *b.* his sanctuary like high palaces
89. 2. I have said, mercy shall be *b.* up for ever
Isa. 5. 2. he *b.* a tower in the midst of his vineyard
44. 26. saith to the cities of Judah, ye shall be *b.*
28. saying to Jerusalem, thou shalt be *b.*
Jer. 12. 16. shall they be *b.* in midst of my people
31. 4. thou shalt be *b.* O virgin of Israel
32. 31. as a provocation from the day they *b.* it
45. 4. that which I have *b.* will I break down
Ezek. 16. 24. thou hast *b.* to thee an eminent place
25. hast *b.* thy high place at every head of way
26. 14. thou shalt be *b.* no more, saith the Lord G.
Dan. 4. 30. is not this great Babylon I have *b.*?
9. 25. the street shall be *b.* again and the wall
Zech. 8. 9. let hands be strong, that temple be *b.*
Mat. 21. 33. dig. a wine-press, *b.* a tower, *Mark* 12. 1.
Luke 7. 5. the centurion hath *b.* us a synagogue
1 *Cor.* 3. 14. if work abide which he hath *b.* thereon
Eph. 2. 20. are *b.* on the foundation of the apostles
Col. 2. 7. rooted and *b.* in him, established in faith
Heb 3. 4. but he that *b.* all things is God

BUILT *altar.*

Gen. 33. † 20. Jacob *b.* an *altar,* El-elohe-Israel
Exod. 17. 15. Moses *b.* *a.* 24. 4. ‖ 32. 5. Aaron *b.* *a.*
Josh. 8. 30. Joshua *b.* an *a.* ‖ 22. 10. half tribe *b.* *a.*
Judg. 6. 24. Gideon *b.* an *a.* ‖ 21. 4. people *b.* an *a.*
1 *Sam.* 7. 17. Samuel *b.* *altar* ‖ 14. 35. Saul *b.* *altar*
2 *Sam.* 24. 25. David *b.* an *altar* to the Lord
1 *Kings* 9. 25. Solomon offered on the *altar* he *b.*
18. 32. with stones Elisha *b.* *altar* in name of Lord
2 *Kings* 16. 11. Urijah the priest *b.* an *altar*

BUILT *altars.*

Num. 23. 14. Balak *b.* seven *altars,* and offered
2 *Kings* 21. 4. he *b.* *altars* in the house of the Lord
5. *b.* *a.* for all the host of heaven, 2 *Chron.* 33. 5.
2 *Chron.* 33. 15. took away *a.* he had *b.* in the mount

BUILT *city.*

Num. 21. 27. let the *city* of Sihon be *b.* and prepared
Josh. 19. 50. Joshua *b.* the *city* and dwelt therein
Judg. 18. 28. Danites *b.* *c.* ‖ 1 *Kings* 16. 24. Omri *b.* *c.*
1 *Chron.* 11. 8. David *b.* *c.* round about from Millo
Isa. 25. 2. a palace to be no *c.* it shall never be *b.*
Jer. 31. 38. days come, the *c.* shall be *b.* to the Lord
Luke 4. 29. to brow of the hill whereon *city* was *b.*

BUILT *cities.*

Exod. 1. 11. they *b.* for Pharaoh treasure-*cities.*
Josh. 24. 13. I have given you *cities* which ye *b.* not
1 *Kings* 15. 23. the *cities* which Asa *b.* are written
2 *Chron.* 8. 2. *cities* Huram had restored, Solomon *b.*
11. 5. Rehoboam *b.* *cities* for defence in Judah
14. 6. Asa *b.* fenced *c.* in Judah, the land had rest
17. 12. Jehoshaphat *b.* castles and *cities* of store
26. 6. Uzziah *b.* *cities* about Ashdod, and among
27. 4. Jotham *b.* *cities* in the mountains of Judah
Isa. 44. 26. saith to the *cities* of Judah, ye shall be *b.*

BUILT *house,* or *houses.*

Deut. 8. 12. when thou hast *b.* goodly *h.* and dwelt
20. 5. what man is there that hath *b.* a new *house?*
1 *Kings* 3. 2. there was no *h.* *b.* to the name of Lord
6. 9. Solomon *b.* *h.* 14. ‖ 8. 13. I have *b.* thee an *h.*
8. 20. and have *b.* an *h.* for the name of the Lord
44. toward *house* I have *b.* 48. 2 *Chron.* 6. 34, 38.
11. 38. build thee a sure *house,* as I *b.* for David
1 *Chr.* 17. 6. saying, why have ye not *b.* me an *h.*?
2 *Chr.* 6. 18. how much less this *house* I have *b.*?
Amos 5. 11. ye have *b.* *houses* of hewn stone
Hag. 1. 2. the time that the Lord's *h.* should be *b.*
Zech. 1. 16. my *h.* shall be *b.* in it, saith the Lord
Mat. 7. 24. wise man *b.* his *h.* on a rock, *Luke* 6. 48.
26. foolish man which *b.* his *h.* on sand, *Luke* 6. 49.
Acts 7. 47. but Solomon *b.* him an *house*
1 *Pet.* 2. 5. ye also are *b.* up a spiritual *h.* an holy

BUILT *high places.*

1 *Kings* 14. 23. Judah *b.* *high p.* images, and groves
2 *Kings* 17. 9. children of Israel *b.* *high p.* in cities
21. 3. Manasseh *b.* up again *high p.* 2 *Chron.* 33. 3.
Jer. 7. 31. *b.* *high p.* of Tophet ‖ 19. 5. of Baal, 32. 35.

BUILT *wall,* or *walls.*

1 *Kings* 6. 15. Solomon *b.* the *walls* of house within
2 *Chr.* 27. 3. and on the *walls* of Ophel he *b.* much
32. 5. Hezekiah *b.* up the *wall* that was broken
33. 14. Manasseh *b.* a *wall* without city of David
Neh. 4. 6. so *b.* we the *wall* ‖ 7. 1. when *wall* was *b.*
Ezek. 13. 10. one *b.* up the *wall,* another daubed it
Dan. 9. 25. the street shall be *b.* again and the *wall*
Mic. 7. 11. in the day that thy *walls* are to be *b.*

BULL

Signifies, [1] *The beast so called,* Job 21. 10. [2] *Pillars in the shape of bulls,* Jer. 52. 20. [3] *Wicked, violent, and furious enemies,* Psal. 22. 12. [4] *The eighth month of the year, which answers to our October,* 1 Kings 6. 38.

Job 21. 10. their *b.* gendereth and faileth not

Isa. 51. 20. thy sons lie as a wild b. in a net

BULLS.

Gen. 32. 15. Jacob took ten b. as a present to Esau
Psal. 22. 12. many b. have compassed me, strong b.
50. 13. will I eat flesh of b. or drink blood of goats
68. 30. rebuke the multitude of the b.
Isa. 34. 7. bullocks with the b. shall come down
Jer. 50. 11. because ye bellow as b. O destroyers
52. 20. twelve brasen b. under the bases with calves
Heb. 9. 13. if the blood of b. and goats sanctifieth
10. 4. it is not possible blood of b. take away sins

BULLOCK.

Exod. 29. 3. shalt bring them in the basket with the b.
11. shalt kill the b. before Lord, Lev. 1. 5. | 9. 18.
Lev. 4. 4. bring the b. to the door of the tabernacle
Num. 15. 9. bring with the b. a meat offering, 29. 37.
Deut. 17. 1. not sacrifice to Lord any b. with blemish
33. 17. his glory is like the firstling of a b.
Judg. 6. 25. take the young b. the second b. 26.
1 Kings 18. 23. and let them choose one b. 25.
33. Elijah cut b. in pieces, and laid him on wood
Psal. 50. 9. I will take no b. out of thine house
69. 31. better than a b. that hath horns and hoofs
Isa. 65. 25. the lion shall eat straw like the b.
Jer. 31. 18. as a b. unaccustomed to the yoke

BULLOCK, with sin offering.

Exod. 29. 36. offer every day a b. for a sin offering
Lev. 16. 6. shall offer his b. of the sin offering
Ezek. 45. 22. shall prepare a b. for a sin offering
See Blood.

Young BULLOCK.

Lev. 4. 3. if priest sin, bring a young b. Ezek. 43. 19.
14. congregation shall offer a y. b. Num. 15. 24.
16. 3. Aaron come into holy place with a young b.
Num. 7. 15. one young b. one ram, one lamb, 21, 27, 33, 39, 45, 51, 57, 63, 69, 75, 81.
2 Chron. 13. 9. to consecrate himself with a young b.
Ezek. 45. 18. take a young b. and cleanse the sanc.
46. 6. in the day of the new moon a young b.

BULLOCKS.

Num. 29. 23. on the fourth day ten b. two rams
1 Chron. 29. 21. they offered a thousand b. for Israel
Ezra 6. 17. they offered at the dedication 100 b.
Psal. 51. 19. then shall they offer b. on thy altar
66. 15. I will offer unto thee b. with goats
Isa. 1. 11. I delight not in the blood of b. or lambs
34. 7. the b. with the bulls shall come down
Jer. 46. 21. her hired men are like fatted b.
50. 27. slay all her b. let them go down to slaughter
Ezek. 39. 18. ye shall drink the blood of goats, of b.
Hos. 12. 11. are vanity, they sacrifice b. in Gilgal
See Seven.

BULRUSH, ES.

Exod. 2. 3. she took for him an ark of b. and daubed
Isa. 18. 2. send ambassadors by the sea in vessels of b.
58. 5. is it to bow down his head like a b.?

BULWARKS.

Deut. 20. 20. thou shalt build b. against the city
2 Chron. 26. 15. Uzziah made engines on the b.
Psal. 48. 13. mark well her b. consider her palaces
Eccl. 9. 14. a great king came and built b. against it
Isa. 26. 1. salvation will G. appoint for walls and b.

BUNCH, ES.

Exod. 12. 22. take a b. of hyssop and dip it in blood
2 Sam. 16. 1. Ziba met him with 100 b. of raisins
1 Chr. 12. 40. Zebulun brought b. of raisins and wine
Isa. 30. 6. will carry their treasures upon b. of camels

BUNDLE, S.

Gen. 42. 35. every man's b. of money in his sack
1 Sam. 25. 29. the soul of my lord bound in b. of life
Cant. 1. 13. a b. of myrrh is my well-beloved to me
Isa. 58. † 6. this is the fast, to undo b. of the yoke
Amos 9. † 6. hath founded his b. in the earth
Mat. 13. 30. bind the tares in b. to burn them
Acts 28. 3. when Paul had gathered a b. of sticks

BURDEN

Signifies, [1] *A load, or weight of any thing, as much as a man, horse, &c. can well carry,* 2 Kings 5. 17. Jer. 17. 27. [2] *Labour and servitude,* Exod. 2. 11. Psal. 81. 6. [3] *A burdensome prophecy, a heavy doom, or a prophecy delivered in heavy and threatening words,* Isa. 13. 1. Nah. 1. 1. [4] *Afflictions, crosses, cares, or fears,* Psal. 55. 22. [5] *Imperfections, failings, and infirmities, with which persons are loaded or grieved,* Gal. 6. 2. [6] *Toil and fatigue,* Mat. 20. 12. [7] *Tribute, or taxes,* Hos. 8. 10. [8] *The office of a magistrate,* Exod. 18. 22. [9] *Human traditions, or strict injunctions over and above what the law requires,* Mat. 23. 4. [10] *Sin, which is the greatest slavery and burden,* Psal. 38. 4. Heb. 12. 1. [11] *The lading, or cargo of a ship,* Acts 21. 3.

The doctrine, or commands of Christ are called a burden, Mat. 11. 30. *Nothing makes them so, but our corruption, which flows from the depravity of our nature; to the unrenewed person they are a grievous burden: yet this burden is* light, (1) *In comparison of the service of sin, the covenant of works, and the ceremonial law.* (2) *To them that love God,* 1 John 5. 3. (3) *To such as are regenerated, so far as they are renewed,* Rom. 7. 22. *It is light to such, because,* (1) *The law is written in their hearts,* Psal. 37. 31. (2) *They are endued with faith,* Mark 9. 23. (3) *They are strengthened, and enabled by Christ,* Phil. 4. 13.

Exod. 18. 22. shall bear the b. with thee, Num. 11. 17.
23. 5. the ass of him that hateth thee lying under b.
Num. 4. 19. Aaron shall appoint each to his b.
11. 11. thou layest the b. of all this people on me
Deut. 1. 12. how can I myself alone bear your b.?
2 Sam. 15. 33. then thou shalt be a b. to me
19. 35. why should thy servant be a b. to my lord?
1 Kings 11. † 28. Jeroboam ruler over b. of Joseph
2 Kings 5. 17. to thy servant two mules' b. of earth
8. 9. Hazael brought forty camels' b. to Elisha
2 Chr. 35. 3. it shall not be a b. on your shoulders
Neh. 13. 19. no b. be brought in on the sabbath
Job 7. 20. as a mark, so that I am a b. to myself
Psal. 38. 4. iniquit. as a b. they are too heavy for me
55. 22. cast thy b. on the Lord, he will sustain thee
Psal. 81. 6. I removed his shoulder from the b.
Eccl. 12. 5. and the grasshopper shall be a b.
Isa. 9. 4. for thou hast broken the yoke of his b.
10. 27. his b. shall be taken from off thy shoulder
14. 25. his b. depart from off their shoulders
30. 27. name of the Lord, the b. thereof is heavy
46. 1. your carriages are a b. to the weary beast
Jer. 17. 21. bear no b. on the sabbath-day, 22, 27.
Zeph. 3. 18. to whom the reproach of it was a b.
Mat. 11. 30. my yoke is easy, and my b. is light
20. 12. which have borne the b. and heat of the day
Acts 15. 28. seemed good to lay on you no greater b.
21. 3. for there the ship was to unlade her b.
Rev. 2. 24. I will put upon you none other b.

BURDEN.

2 Kings 9. 25. the Lord laid this b. upon him
Isa. 13. 1. the b. of Babylon which Isaiah did see
14. 28. the year king Ahaz died, was this b.
15. 1. the b. of Moab || 17. 1. the b. of Damascus
19. 1. the b. of Egypt || 23. 1. the b. of Tyre
21. 1. the b. of the desert of the sea, as whirlwinds
11. the b. of Dumah || 13. the b. upon Arabia
22. 1. the b. of the valley of vision, what aileth
25. the b. that was upon it shall be cut off
30. 6. the b. of the beasts of the south
46. 2. they could not deliver the b. are gone into
Jer. 23. 33. what is the b. of the Lord? what b.?
36. the b. of the Lord shall ye mention no more
38. but sith ye say, the b. of the Lord
Ezek. 12. 10. this b. concerneth the prince in Jerus.
Hos. 8. 10. sorrow a little for the b. of the king of pr.
Nah. 1. 1. the b. of Nineveh, the book of the vision
Hab. 1. 1. b. which Habakkuk the prophet did see
Zech. 9. 1. the b. of the word of the Lord in Hadrach
12. 1. the b. of the word of the Lord for Israel
Mal. 1. 1. the b. of the word of the Lord to Israel
Gal. 6. 5. for every man shall bear his own b.

BURDEN, ED.

Zech. 12. 3. all that b. themselves be cut in pieces
2 Cor. 5. 4. in this tabernacle we groan being b.
8. 13. I mean not that others be eased, and you b.
12. 16. but be it so, I did not b. you, caught with

BURDENS.

Gen. 49. 14. Issachar couching down between two b.
Exod. 1. 11. task-masters to afflict them with their b.
2. 11. Moses went out and looked on their b.
5. 4. the king of Egypt said, get you to your b.
5. you make them rest from their b.
6. 6. I will bring you from the b. of Egyptians, 7.
Num. 4. 27. ye shall appoint to them all their b.
Neh. 4. 10. the strength of the bearers of b. decayed
17. they that bare b. with other hand held a weap.
13. 15. all manner of b. brought in on the sabbath
Isa. 58. 6. this is the fast, to undo the heavy b.
Lam. 2. 14. the prophets have seen for thee false b.
Amos 5. 11. ye take from the poor b. of wheat
Mat. 23. 4. they bind heavy b. Luke 11. 46.
Gal. 6. 2. bear ye one another's b. and so fulfil

BURDENSOME.

Zech. 12. 3. I will make Jerusalem a b. stone
2 Cor. 11. 9. I have kept myself from being b. to you
12. 13. except it be that I myself was not b. to you
14. the third time I come, I will not be b. to you
1 Thess. 2. 6. when we might have been b. as apostles

BURIAL.

Eccl. 6. 3. and also that he have no b.
Isa. 14. 20. thou shalt not be joined with them in b.
Jer. 22. 19. he shall be buried with the b. of an ass
Mat. 26. 12. poured ointment, she did it for my b.
Acts 8. 2. devout men carried Stephen to his b.

BURY

Signifies, *To inter a dead body,* Gen. 23. 4.

To be buried with Christ in baptism, Rom. 6. 4. *To have communion with him in his death and burial.* Baptism *doth not only represent our mortification and death to sin, by which we have communion with Christ in his death; but also our progress and perseverance in mortification, by which we have communion with him in his* burial *also;* burial *implies a continuing under* death, *so is* mortification *a continual dying to sin.*

Gen. 23. 4. that I may b. my dead out of my sight
6. in choice of our sepulchres b. thy dead, 11, 15.
47. 29. b. me not, I pray thee, in Egypt, 49. 29.
50. 5. let me go and b. my father, I will come again
6. go up and b. thy father, as he made thee swear
Deut. 21. 23. thou shalt in any wise b. him that day
1 Kings 2. 31. go and fall upon Joab and b. him
11. 15. when Joab was gone up to b. the slain
13. 29. the old prophet came to mourn and b. him
31. when I am dead, b. me in the sepulchre
14. 13. Israel shall mourn for him and b. him
2 Kings 9. 10. and there shall be none to b. Jezebel
34. go see now this cursed woman, and b. her
35. they went to b. her, but found only the scull
Psal. 79. 3. and there was none to b. them
Jer. 7. 32. for they shall b. in Tophet, 19. 11.
14. 16. and they shall have none to b. them
Ezek. 39. 11. there shall they b. Gog and his multitude
13. yea, all the people of the land shall b. them
Hos. 9. 6. Egypt gather up, Memphis shall b. them
Mat. 8. 21. suffer me to go b. my father, Luke 9. 59.
22. and let the dead b. their dead, Luke 9. 60.
27. 7. bought the potter's field to b. strangers in
John 19. 40. as the manner of the Jews is to b.

BURIED.

Gen 25. 10. there was Abraham b. and Sarah his [wife
49. 31. there they b. Abraham and Sarah his wife, Isaac and Rebekah his wife, and there I b. Leah
Num. 11. 34. there they b. the people that lusted
20. 1. Miriam died there, and was b. there
33. 4. for the Egyptians b. all their first-born
Deut. 10. 6. there Aaron died, and there he was b.
Josh. 24. 32. the bones of Joseph b. they in Shechem
Ruth 1. 17. where diest will I die, and there will be b.
2 Sam. 4. 12. they took head of Ish-bosheth and b. it
21. 14. bones of Saul and Jonathan they b. in Zelah
1 Kings 13. 31. bury me where the man of God is b.
Eccl. 8. 10. and so I saw the wicked b.
Jer. 8. 2. not be gathered nor b. 16. 6. | 20. 6. | 25.
16. 4. they shall not be lamented nor b. [33.
22. 19. he shall be b. with the burial of an ass
Ezek. 39. 15. set up a sign, till buriers have b. it
Mat. 14. 12. his disciples took the body and b. it
Luke 16. 22. the rich man also died and was b.
Acts 2. 29. the patriarch David is both dead and b.
5. 9. the feet of them which b. thy husband
10. carrying her forth, b. her by her husband
Rom. 6. 4. we are b. with him by baptism into death
1 Cor. 15. 4. that he was b. and rose again third day
Col. 2. 12. b. with him in baptism, wherein are risen

BURIED him.

Deut. 34. 6. he b. him in a valley, in the land of Moab
2 Sam. 2. 5. blessed be ye that have b. Saul
1 Kings 14. 18. they b. him, all Israel mourned him
2 Chron. 21. 20. they b. Jehoram in the city of David
24. 16. b. Jehoiada in city of David, among kings
25. they b. him not in the sepulchres of the kings
Acts 5. 6. the young men carried him out and b. him

BURIED in.

Gen. 15. 15. and thou shalt be b. in a good old age
1 Kings 2. 10. David was b. in city of David
34. Joab b. in his own house in the wilderness
2 Kings 21. 18. Manasseh was b. in garden of his house
26. Amon was b. in sepulchre, in garden of Uzzah
Job 27. 15. those that remain shall be b. in death

BURIED with his fathers.

1 Kings 14. 31. Rehoboam || 15. 24. Asa b. with his f.
22. 50. Jehoshaphat || 2 Kings 8. 24. Joram b. with f.
12. 21. Joash b. with f. || 14. 20. Amaziah b. with f.
15. 7. Azariah || 38. Jotham || 16. 20. Ahaz b. with f.

BURIERS.

Ezek. 39. 15. shall set up a sign till b. have buried

BURYING.

Gen. 23. 4. a possess. of a b. place, 9. | 49. 30. | 50. 13.
Judg. 16. 31. buried Samson in b. place of Manoah
2 Kin. 13. 21. as they were b. a man, they spied a band
Ezek. 39. 12. seven months shall Israel be b. of them
Mark 14. 8. she is come to anoint my body to the b.
John 12. 7. against day of my b. hath she kept this

BURN

Signifies, [1] *To consume, or destroy with fire,* Josh. 11. 13. [2] *To be inflamed with just anger and indignation,* Lam. 2. 3. [3] *To be perpetually haunted with violent, lustful desires,* 1 Cor. 7. 9. [4] *To be filled with a holy zeal for the glory of God, and the good of others,* 2 Cor. 11. 29.

The bush burned, and was not consumed, Exod. 3. 2. *This represented the condition of the church and people of Israel, who were then in the fire of affliction; yet so as that God was present with them, and that they should not be consumed in it, whereof this vision was a pledge.*

The spirit of burning, Isa. 4. 4. *The Holy Spirit of God, who is compared to fire,* Mat. 3. 11. *because he doth burn up and consume the dross which is in the church, and in the minds and hearts of men, and inflames the souls of believers with love to God, and zeal for his glory.*

Gen. 44. 18. Judah said, let not thine anger b.
Exod. 27. 20. command that they bring pure olive oil to cause the lamp to b. alway, Lev. 24. 2.
29. 13. shalt take caul, liver, and kidneys, and b. upon the altar, 18. 25. Lev. 1. 9, 15. | 2. 2, 9, 16. | 3. 5, 11, 16. | 5. 12. | 6. 15. | 9. 17. Num. 5. 26.
Lev. 4. 19. priest shall take fat, and b. upon the altar, 26. 31. | 7. 31. | 16. 25. | 17. 6. Num. 18. 17.
Num. 19. 5. one shall b. the heifer in his sight
Josh. 11. 13. save Hazor only, that did Joshua b.
1 Sam. 2. 16. let them not fail to b. the fat presently
2 Chron. 2. 6. save only to b. sacrifice before them
13. 11. and they b. to the Lord every morning
Isa. 1. 31. they shall both b. together, none quench
10. 17. it shall b. and devour his thorns and briers
27. 4. I would go through them and b. them together
40. 16. Lebanon is not sufficient to b. nor the beasts
44. 15. then shall it be for a man to b. he will take
Jer. 7. 20. my fury shall b. and not be quenched
34. 5. so shall they b. odours for thee, and lament
36. 25. that the king would not b. the roll
Ezek. 24. 5. b. also the bones under it, make it boil
11. that the brass of it may be hot, and may b.
39. 9. they shall set on fire and b. the weapons
43. 21. he shall b. bullock in the appointed place
Nah. 2. 13. I will b. her chariots in the smoke
Mal. 4. 1. the day cometh that shall b. as an oven
Mat. 13. 30. bind the tares in bundles to b. them
Luke 3. 17. but chaff he will b. with fire unquenchable
24. 32. they said, did not our heart b. within us?
1 Cor. 7. 9. for it is better to marry than to b.
2 Cor. 11. 29. who is offended, and I b. not?

BURN, joined with fire.

Exod. 12. 10. that which remaineth of it till morning ye shall b. with fire, 29. 34. Lev. 8. 32.
Lev. 13. 57. b. that wherein the plague is with fire
16. 27. b. with fire their skins, flesh, and dung
Deut. 5. 23. for the mountain did b. with fire
7. 5. b. their images with fire, 25. || 12. 3. b. groves
32. 22. a fire shall b. to the lowest hell, Jer. 17. 4.
Josh. 11. 6. thou shalt b. their chariots with fire
Judg. 9. 52. went to the tower to b. it with fire
12. 1. will b. thine house with f. || 14. 15. b. thee f.
Psal. 79. 5. how long shall thy jealousy b. like fire?
89. 46. how long, Lord, shall thy wrath b. like fire?
Isa. 47. 14. shall be as stubble, the fire shall b. them
Jer. 4. 4. my fury come forth like fire and b. 21. 12.
7. 31. to b. sons and daughters in the fire, 19. 5.
21. 10. Nebuchadnezzar shall b. this city with f. 32. 29. | 34. 2, 22. | 37. 8, 10. | 38. 18.
Ezek. 5. 2. b. with fire a third part in midst of city
16. 41. they b. thine houses with fire, 23. 47.
Mat. 3. 12. he will gather his wheat, but he will b. up the chaff with unquenchable fire, Luke 3. 17.
Rev. 17. 16. shall eat her flesh, and b. her with fire

BURN incense.

Exod. 30. 1. thou shalt make an altar to b. incense on
7. Aaron shall b. thereon sweet inc. every morn. 8.
1 Kings 13. 1. Jeroboam stood by the altar to b. inc.
2 Kings 18. 4. the children of Israel did b. inc. to it
1 Chron. 23. 13. he and his sons for ever to b. inc.
2 Chron. 2. 4. I build an house to b. sweet incense
13. 11. b. every morning sweet incense to the Lord
26. 16. Uzziah went into temple to b. incense, 19.
28. 25. in Judah Ahaz made high places to b. inc.

2 Chr. 20. 11. my sons, Lord hath chosen you to b. in.
32. 12. worship before one altar, and b. inc. on it
Jer. 7. 9. will ye steal and b. incense to Baal? 11. 13.
44. 17. we will b. incense to the queen of heaven
Hos. 4. 13. they b. incense upon the hills under oaks
Hab. 1. 16. therefore they b. incense to their drag
Luke 1. 9. Zacharias his lot was to b. inc. in temple

BURNED.

Exod. 3. 2. bush b. with fire, and was not consumed
3. I will turn and see why the bush is not b.
Deut. 9. 15. I came down, and mount b. with fire
32. † 22. a fire kindled and hath b. to lowest hell
Josh. 7. 25. b. them with fire, after they stoned them
2 Chron. 25. 14. Amaziah b. incense to the gods
34. 25. have forsaken me, and b. incense to gods
Esth. 1. 12. the king was wroth, and anger b. in him
Psal. 39. 3. while I was musing the fire b.
Isa. 24. 6. therefore the inhabitants of the earth are b.
42. 25. it b. him, yet he laid it not to heart
Lam. 2. 3. he b. against Jacob like a flaming fire
John 15. 6. withered branches are gathered and b.
Acts 19. 19. many brought their books and b. them
Rom. 1. 27. b. in their lust one towards another
1 Cor. 13. 3. and though I give my body to be b.
Heb. 6. 8. is rejected, whose end is to be b.
12. 18. for ye are not come to the mount that b.
Rev. 1. 15. his feet like brass, as if b. in a furnace
16. † 9. and men were b. with great heat

BURNETH.

Lev. 16. 28. he that b. them shall wash his clothes
and bathe his flesh in water, Num. 19. 8.
Psal. 46. 9. he breaketh the bow and b. chariot in fire
83. 14. as the fire b. wood, and as the flame setteth
97. 3. a fire b. up his enemies round about
Isa. 9. 18. for wickedness b. as the fire
44. 16. he b. part thereof in fire, he warms himself
62. 1. the salvation thereof as a lamp that b.
64. 2. as when the melting fire b. the fire causeth
65. 5. these are a smoke and fire that b. all the day
66. 3. he that b. incense, as if he blessed an idol
Jer. 48. 35. cause to cease that b. incense to his gods
Joel 2. 3. a fire before them, behind them a flame b.
Rev. 21. 8. shall have part in lake which b. with fire

BURNING.

Gen. 15. 17. a b. lamp passed between the pieces
Lev. 6. 9. the fire of the altar shall be b. in it, 12, 13.
26. 16. I will appoint over you the b. ague
Deut. 28. 22. Lord shall smite thee with extreme b.
32. 24. they shall be devoured with b. heat
Job 5. † 7. as sons of the b. coal lift up to fly
41. 19. of his mouth go b. lamps, sparks of fire
Psal. 11. † 6. on wicked he shall reign a b. tempest
140. 10. let b. coals fall upon them, cast into fire
Prov. 16. 27. in his lips there is as a b. fire
26. 21. as coals are to b. coals, and wood to fire
23. b. lips and a wicked heart are like a potsherd
Isa. 30. 27. name of Lord cometh far, b. with anger
34. 9. the land thereof shall become b. pitch
Jer. 20. 9. his word was in my heart as a b. fire
Ezek. 1. 13. their appearance was like b. coals
21. † 31. I will deliver into the hand of b. men
Dan. 3. 6. shall be cast into midst of a b. furnace, 11.
17. is able to deliver us from the b. furnace
20. to cast them into the b. fiery furnace, 21, 23.
26. Nebuchadnezzar came near the b. furnace
7. 9. his throne like flame, his wheels were as b. fire
Hab. 3. 5. and b. coals went forth at his feet
Luke 12. 35. let your loins be girded, and lights b.
John 5. 35. John was a b. and a shining light
Rev. 4. 5. there were seven lamps b. before throne
8. 8. and as it were a great mountain b. with fire
10. there fell a great star b. as it were a lamp
19. 20. they both were cast alive into a lake b.

BURNING.

Gen. 11. † 3. and let us burn the bricks to a b.
Exod. 21. 25. b. for b. wound for wound, stripe for
Lev. 10. 6. bewail the b. which the Lord kindled
13. 28. if the spot stay, it is a rising of the b.
Num. 11 † 3. he called the name of the place a b.
Deut. 29. 23. the wole land is brimstone, salt, and b.
2 Chron. 16. 14. they made a very great b. for him
21. 19. people made no b. like the b. of his fathers
Isa. 3. 24. there shall be b. instead of beauty
4. 4. purged blood of Jerusalem by the spirit of b.
9. 5. but this shall be with b. and fuel of fire
10. 16. under his glory, kindle b. like b. of fire
32. † 13. b. shall come upon all houses of joy
33. 12. the people shall be as the b. of lime
Amos 4. 11. even as a firebrand plucked out of the b.
Rev. 18. 9. when they shall see the smoke of her b.

BURNINGS.

Josh. 11. † 8. they chased them to the b. of waters
Isa. 33. 14. who shall dwell with everlasting b.?
Jer. 34. 5. with b. of thy fathers the former kings

BURNISHED.

Ezek. 1. 7. they sparkled like the colour of b. brass

BURNT.

Gen. 38. 24. Judah said, bring her forth, let her be b.
Lev. 2. 12. but they shall not be b. on the altar
6. 22. meat offering shall be wholly b. 23. | 8. 21.
10. 16. Moses sought the goat, and it was b.
Num. 16. 39. Eleazar the priest took the brazen
censers, wherewith they that were b. had offered
Deut. 32. 24. shall be b. with hunger, and devoured
1 Sam. 2. 15. before they b. fat, priest's servant came
2 Sam. 5. 21. David and his men b. their images
1 Kings 13. 2. mens' bones shall be b. upon thee
15. 13. Asa b. her idol by the brook, 2 Chr. 15. 16.
2 Kings 23. 6. he b. the grove at the brook Kidron
15. she b. the high place, and stampt it small
16. he took bones out of sepulchres and b. them
25. 9. b. the house of L. 2 Chr. 36. 19. Jer. 52. 13.
Job 30. 30. and my bones are b. with heat
Psal. 102. 3. my skin black, bones are b. as an hearth
Prov. 6. 27. take fire, and his clothes not be b.
28. can one go on coals and his feet not be b.
Jer. 2. 15. his cities are b. || 6. 29. the bellows are b.
36. 28. in the roll which Jehoiakim hath b.
51. 25. and I will make thee a b. mountain
Ezek. 20. 47. and all faces shall be b. therein
24. 10. kindle the fire, and let the bones be b.
Joel 1. 19. the flame hath b. all the trees of the field
Amos 2. 1. because he b. the bones of king of Edom
Nah. 1. 5. and the earth is b. at his presence
1 Cor. 3. 15. if any man's work be b. shall suffer loss
Heb. 13. 11. those beasts are b. without the camp

BURNT, joined with fire.

Exod. 32. 20. he b. the calf in the fire, Deut. 9. 21.
Lev. 6. 30. the sin offering shall be b. in the fire
7. 17. but the remainder of the flesh of the sacrifice
on the third day shall be b. with fire, 19. 6.
20. 14. if a man take a wife and her mother, they
shall be b. with fire, both he and they
21. 9. if the daughter of any priest profane herself
by playing the whore, she shall be b. with fire
Num. 11. 1. the fire of the Lord b. among them, 3.
Deut. 4. 11. ye came near, the mountain b. with fire
12. 31. their sons and daughters they b. in the fire
Josh. 6. 24. they b. Jericho with fire and all therein
7. 15. it shall be, he that is taken with the accursed
thing shall be b. with fire, he and all he hath
11. 9. Joshua b. their chariots with fire
11. and he took Hazor and b. it with fire
Judg. 15. 6. they b. her and her father with fire
14. the cords became as flax that was b. with fire
18. 27. they came to Laish and b. it with fire
1 Sam. 30. 1. the Amalekites b. Ziklag with fire
2 Sam. 23. 7. they shall be utterly b. with fire
1 Kings 9. 16. for Pharaoh had b. Gezer with fire
16. 18. Zimri b. the king's house with fire
2 Kings 1. 14. fire from heaven b. up the two captains
17. 31. the Sepharvites b. their children with fire
23. 11. and b. the chariots of the sun with fire
25. 9. every great man's house b. he with fire
1 Chron. 14. 12. their gods were b. with fire
2 Chron. 28. 3. Ahaz b. his children in the fire
Neh. 1. 3. the gates thereof are b. with fire, 2. 17.
Psal. 80. 16. it is b. with fire, it is cut down
Isa. 1. 7. your cities are b. with fire
43. 2. when walkest thro' fire thou shalt not be b.
64. 11. our holy and beautiful house is b. with fire
Jer. 38. 17. this city shall not be b. with fire
23. thou shalt cause this city to be b. with fire
49. 2. and her daughters shall be b. with fire
51. 32. and the reeds they have b. with fire
58. Babylon's high gates shall be b. with fire
Mic. 1. 7. the hires thereof shall be b. with the fire
Rev. 18. 8. she shall be utterly b. with fire

BURNT incense.

Exod. 40. 27. b. sweet inc. thereon, as commanded
1 Kings 3. 3. only Solomon b. inc. in high places
9. 25. Solomon b. inc. upon the altar before Lord
12. 33. Jeroboam offered on the altar and b. inc.
22. 43. people b. inc. 2 Kings 12. 3. | 14. 4. | 15. 4, 35.
2 Kings 16. 4. Ahaz b. inc. in high places, 2 Chr. 28. 3, 4.
2 Chron. 29. 7. put out lamps and have not b. inc.
Isa. 65. 7. which have b. inc. on the mountains
Jer. 18. 15. my people have b. inc. to vanity
44. 15. men which knew that their wives had b. inc.
Hos. 2. 13. the days wherein she b. inc. to them
11. 2. they sacrificed and b. inc. to graven images

BURNT OFFERING.

Gen. 22. 7. but where is the lamb for a b. offering?
8. my son, God will provide a lamb for a b. off.
13. he offered him for a b.-offering instead of Isaac
Exod. 18. 12. and Jethro took a b. offering for God
29. 18. the ram is a b. offering unto the Lord
Lev. 1. 4. he shall put his hand on head of b. offering
4. 29. he shall slay the sin-offering in the place of
the b. offering, 33. | 6. 25. | 7. 2. | 14. 13.
6. 9. saying, this is the law of the b. offering, 7. 37.
7. 8. the priest shall have the skin of the b. offering
9. 2. take thee a ram for a b. off. 16. 3, 5. | 23. 18.
5. take a calf and a lamb for b. off. 12. 6. | 23. 12.
Num. 7. 15. one lamb of the first year for a b. off.
21, 27, 33, 39, 51, 57, 63, 69, 75, 81.
Ezek 45. 15.
23. 3. stand by thy b. offering and I will go, 15.
28. 10. this is the b. offering of every sabbath
13. for a b.-off. of a sweet savour unto the Lord
14. this is the b.-offering of every month
29. 6. beside the meat-offering and the daily b. off.
Josh. 22. 26. to build us an altar not for a b. offering
Judg. 13. 23. not have received a b. off. at our hands
1 Sam. 7. 10. as Samuel was offering up a b. offering
13. 12. I forced myself and offered a b. offering
2 Kings 3. 27. offered him for a b. off. on the wall
2 Chr. 7. 1. fire came down and consumed the b. off.
29. 24. the b. offering should be made for all Israel
Psal. 40. 6. b. offerings hast thou not required
51. 16. for thou delightest not in b. offering
19. shalt be pleased with b. off. and whole b. off.
Isa. 40. 16. nor the beasts thereof for a b. offering
61. 8. for I the Lord hate robbery for b. offering
Ezek. 44. 11. they shall slay the b. off. and sacrifice
45. 17. prince shall prepare the b. off. for Israel
46. 2. the priest shall prepare the prince's b. off.
13. thou shalt daily prepare a b. off. to the Lord

Continual BURNT OFFERING.

Exod. 29. 42. a continual b. offering, Num. 28. 3.
6, 10, 15, 24, 31. | 29. 11, 16, 19, 22. Ezra
3. 5. Neh. 10. 33. Ezek. 46. 15.

Offer BURNT OFFERING.

Gen. 22. 2. take Isaac and offer him there for a b. off.
Lev. 9. 7. go to the altar and offer thy b. offering
Num. 28. 11. in beginnings of months offer a b. off.
23. ye shall offer these besides the b. offering
Judg. 11. 31. I will offer it up for a b. offering
13. 16. if thou offer a b.-off. offer it to the Lord
1 Sam. 6. 14. and offered the kine for a b. offering
7. 9. Samuel offered a sucking lamb for a b. offering
2 Kings 5. 17. will henceforth offer neither b. offering
2 Chron. 29. 27. Hezekiah commanded to offer b. off.
Job 42. 8. and offer up for yourselves a b. offering
Ezek. 46. 4. b. offering the prince shall offer in sab.

BURNT OFFERINGS.

Gen. 8. 20. Noah offered b. offerings on the altar
Exod. 10. 25. also give us sacrifices and b. offerings
20. 24. and shalt sacrifice thereon thy b. offerings
Num. 10. 10. blow with trumpets over your b. off.
Deut. 12. 6. thither bring your b. offerings, 11, 14, 27.
Josh. 22. 27. do the service of the Lord with b. off.
1 Sam. 15. 22. hath Lord as great delight in b. off.
1 Kings 3. 15. Solomon stood and offered b. offerings
1 Kings 8. 64. middle of court, there he offered b. off.
1 Chron. 29. 21. they offered b. offerings to the Lord
2 Chron. 2. 4. behold, I build an house for b. off.
7. 7. brazen altar was not able to receive b. off.
29. 7. have not offered b.-off. in the holy place
34. the priests could not slay all the b. offerings
30. 15. Levites were ashamed, brought b. off.
35. 14. sons of Aaron busied in offering b. off.
Ezra 3. 4. offered the daily b. offerings by number
6. 9. that which they have need of for b. offerings
Job 1. 5. offered b. offerings according to the number
Psal. 50. 8. I will not reprove thee for thy b. off.
66. 13. I will go into thy house with b. offerings
Isa. 1. 11. I am full of the b. offerings of rams
43. 23. nor brought me small cattle of thy b. off.
56. 7. their b. off. shall be accepted on mine altar
Jer. 6. 20. your b. offerings are not acceptable
7. 21. put your b. offerings to your sacrifices
22. spake not to your fathers concerning b. off.
17. 26. shall come from the south bringing b. off.
19. 5. to burn their sons for b. offerings to Baal
Ezek. 45. 17. be the prince's part to give b. offerings
Hos. 6. 6. the knowledge of God more than b. off.
Mic. 6. 6. shall I come before him with b. offerings?
Mark 12. 33. to love neighbour is more than b. off.
Heb. 10. 6. in b. off. for sin thou hast had no pleasure

Offer BURNT OFFERINGS.

1 Sam. 10. 8. I will come down to thee to offer b. off.
2 Sam. 24. 24. nor will I offer b. offerings of that
which doth cost me nothing, 1 Chron. 21. 24.
1 Kings 3. 4. a thousand b. off. did Solomon offer
9. 25. three times a year did Solomon offer b. off.
Ezra 3. 2. Jeshua builded the altar to offer b. off.
Jer. 33. 18. Levites not want a man to offer b. off.
Ezek. 43. 18. in the day they make it to offer b. off.
Amos 5. 22. though ye offer me b. off. I will not accept

BURNT SACRIFICE.

Exod. 30. 9. offer no strange incense, nor b. s. thereon
Lev. 1. 9. the priest shall burn all to be a b. s. 3. 5.
Num. 23. 6. lo, he stood by his b. s. and the princes
Deut. 33. 10. shall put whole b. s. on thine altar
2 Sam. 24. 22. behold, here be oxen for b. sacrifice
1 Kings 18. 38. fire fell and consumed the b. sacrifice
2 Kings 16. 15. on the great altar burn the king's b. s.
Psal. 20. 3. remember thy offerings, accept thy b. s.

BURNT SACRIFICES.

1 Chron. 23. 31. to offer all b. s. in the sabbaths
2 Chron. 13. 11. burn morning and evening b. s.
Psal. 66. 15. I will offer to thee b. s. of fatlings

BURNT up.

Judg. 15. 5. the foxes b. up the shocks and corn
2 Kings 1. 14. fire came down, and b. up the two capt.
Job 1. 16. the fire of God hath b. up the sheep
Psal. 74. 8. they have b. up all the synagogues
106. 18. fire was kindled, flame b. up the wicked
Isa. 3. † 14. for ye have b. up the vineyard
64. 11. our holy and beautiful house is b. up
Jer. 9. 10. b. up that none can pass thro' them, 12.
Mat. 22. 7. the king sent and b. up their city
2 Pet. 3. 10. earth and works therein shall be b. up
Rev. 8. 7. they were cast on the earth, and the third
part of trees was b. up and all green grass was b. up

BURST.

Job 32. 19. it is ready to b. like new bottles
Prov. 3. 10. thy presses shall b. with new wine
Jer. 2. 20. I have b. thy bands, 5. 5. | 30. 8. Nah. 1. 13.
Mark 2. 22. else new wine doth b. bottles, Luke 5. 37.
Acts 1. 18. he b. asunder in midst, bowels gushed out

BURSTING.

Isa. 30. 14. not be found in the b. of it a sherd

BUSH, ES.

Exod. 3. 2. in a flame of fire in the b. Acts 7. 30.
4. God called to him out of the midst of the b.
Deut. 33. 16. the good-will of him that dwelt in b.
Job 30. 4. who cut up mallows by the b. for meat
7. among the b. they brayed, under the nettles
Isa. 7. 19. they shall come and rest upon all b.
Mark 12. 26. how in the b. God spake to him
Luke 6. 44. nor of a bramble b. gather they grapes
20. 37. that dead are raised, Moses shewed at the b.
Acts 7. 35. the angel which appeared in the b.

BUSHEL.

Mat. 5. 15. nor do men light a candle and put it under
a b. but on a candlestick, Mark 4. 21. Luke 11. 33.

BUSHY.

Cant. 5. 11. his locks are b. and black as a raven

BUSY-BODY, IES.

2 Thess. 3. 11. but some of you are b.-b. 1 Tim. 5. 13.
1 Pet. 4. 15. but let none of you suffer as a b.-body

BUSY, IED.

1 Kings 20. 40. as thy servant was b. here and there
2 Chron. 35. 14. the sons of Aaron b. in offering

BUSINESS.

Gen. 39. 11. Joseph went into house to do his b.
Deut. 24. 5. nor shall he be charged with any b.
Josh. 2. 14. our life for yours, if ye utter not our b.
20. if thou utter this our b. we will be quit
Judg. 18. 7. they had no b. with any man, 28.
1 Sam. 10. † 2. thy father hath left the b. of the asses
20. 19. didst hide thyself when the b. was in hand
21. 2. let no man know any thing of the b.
8. because the king's b. required haste
25. † 2. there was a man whose b. was in Carmel
2 Chron. 13. 10. and the Levites wait on their b.
29. † 15. gathered their brethren in b. of the Lord
32. 31. in the b. of the ambassadors God left him
Neh. 13. 30. I appointed every man in his b.
Esth. 3. 9. to them that have the charge of the b.
9. † 3. those that did the king's b. helped the Jews
Psal. 107. 23. they that do b. in great waters
Prov. 18. † 1. he that intermeddleth in every b
22. 29. seest thou a man diligent in his b.?
Eccl. 5. 3. a dream cometh through multitude of b.
Dan. 8. 27. afterwards I rose, and did the king's b.
Luke 2. 49. wist ye not I must be about Father's b?
Acts 6. 3. whom we may appoint over this b.
Rom. 12. 11. not slothful in b. fervent in spirit
16. 2. assist her in what b. she hath need of you
1 Thess. 4. 11. that ye study to do your own b.

BUT.

1 Sam. 20. 3. there is b. a step between me and death
2 Kings 7. 4. and if they kill us, we shall b. die

Psal. 115. 5. mouths b. speak not; eyes b. see not
6. have ears b. hear not; noses b. smell not
7. have hands b. handle not; feet b. walk not
Mat. 24. 36. b. of that day and hour knoweth no man
37. b. as the days of Noe were, so shall the coming
Mark 5. 28. she said, if I may touch b. his clothes
1 Cor. 4. 19. I will know not the speech, b. the power
6. 11. b. ye are washed || 7. 10. yet not I, b. the Lord
12. 4. b. the same Spirit || 5. b. the same Lord
6. b. it is the same God which worketh all in all
2 Cor. 2. 5. he hath not grieved me b. in part
4. 17. our light affliction, which is b. for a moment
Gal. 1. 12. b. by the revelation of Jesus Christ
But *the end*. *See* End.

BUTTER.

Gen. 18. 8. Abraham took b. and milk, and the calf
Deut. 32. 14. b. of kine, milk of sheep, fat of lambs
Judg. 5. 25. she brought forth b. in a lordly dish
2 Sam. 17. 29. Barzillai brought honey and b. for Da.
Job 20. 17. shall not see the brooks of honey and b.
29. 6. when I washed my steps with b. rock poured
Psal. 55. 21. words of his mouth smoother than b.
Prov. 30. 33. churning of milk bringeth forth b.
Isa. 7. 15. b. and honey shall he eat, 22.

BUTLER, S.

Gen. 40. 1. the b. of the king of Egypt offended
9. the chief b. told his dream to Joseph
21. he restored his chief b. to his butlership
41. 9. the chief b. said, I remember my faults

BUTTOCKS.

2 Sam. 10. 4. cut off garments to their b. 1 Chron. 19. 4.
Isa. 20. 4. with b. uncovered to the shame of Egypt

BUY

Signifies, [1] *To procure any commodity by price,* 2 Sam. 24. 21. [2] *To receive, by such ways and means as God has directed, those spiritual blessings which are freely offered in the gospel, even Christ and all his benefits,* Isa. 55. 1. Rev. 3. 18.

Gen. 42. 2. get you down to Egypt and b. for us
7. said, from land of Canaan to b. food, 43. 20.
47. 19. b. us and our land for bread, we be servants
Exod. 21. 2. if thou b. an Hebrew servant
Lev. 22. 11. if the priests b. any soul with money
25. 15. after the jubilee b. of thy neighbour
44. of them shall ye b. bondmen and maids, 45.
Deut. 2. 6. ye shall b. meat of them for money
28. 68. ye shall be sold, and no man shall b. you
Ruth 4. 4. b. it before the inhabitants, before elders
5. thou must b. it also of Ruth the Moabitess
2 Sam. 24. 21. David said, to b. the threshing-floor, and build an altar to the Lord, 24. 1 Chr. 21. 24.
2 Kings 12. 12. gave it to masons to b. timber, 22. 6.
Neh. 10. 31. we would not b. it on the sabbath
Isa. 55. 1. come, b. and eat, b. wine and milk
Jer. 32. 7. b. thee my field that is in Anathoth
44. men shall b. fields for money and subscribe
Mat. 14. 15. may b. themselves victuals, Mark 6. 36.
25. 9. go to them that sell, and b. for yourselves
10. while they went to b. the bridegroom came
Mark 6. 37. shall we go and b. 200 pennyworth?
Luke 9. 13. except we b. meat for all this people
22. 36. let him sell his garment and b. one
John 4. 8. his disciples were gone to b. meat
6. 5. whence shall we b. bread that these may eat?
13. 29. b. those things that we have need of
1 Cor. 7. 30. they that b. as tho' they possessed not
Jam. 4. 13. and we will b. and sell, and get gain
Rev. 3. 18. I counsel thee to b. of me gold tried in fire
13. 17. no man b. or sell, save he that had the mark

BUY *corn.*

Gen. 41. 57. all countries came to Joseph to b. corn
42. 3. Joseph's brethren went down to b. corn
Neh. 5. 3. we have mortgaged our lands to b. corn

BUY *poor.*

Amos 8. 6. that we may b. the poor for silver

BUY *truth.*

Prov. 23. 23. b. the truth and sell it not, also wisdom

BUYER.

Prov. 20. 14. it is naught, it is naught, saith the b.
Isa. 24. 2. as with the b. so with the seller
Ezek. 7. 12. let not the b. rejoice, nor seller mourn

BUYEST.

Lev. 25. 14. and if thou sell ought, or b. ought
Ruth 4. 5. what day thou b. the field of Naomi

BUYETH.

Prov. 31. 16. she considereth a field, and b. it
Mat. 13. 44. he selleth all he hath, and b. that field
Rev. 18. 11. no man b. her merchandise any more

BY *and* **BY.**

Mat. 13. 21. when persecution, b. and b. is offended
Mark 6. 25. give me b. and b. in a charger the head
Luke 17. 7. will say to him b. and b. sit down to meat
21. 9. come to pass, but the end is not b. and b.

BY-WAYS.

Judg. 5. 6. and the travellers walked through b.

BY-WORD. [tions

Deut. 28. 37. thou shalt become a b. among all na-
1 Kings 9. 7. Israel shall be a b. among all the people
2 Chron. 7. 20. make this house a proverb and a b.
Job 17. 6. he hath made me a b. of the people
30. 9. and now am I their song, yea, I am their b.
Psal. 44. 14. thou makest us a b. among the heathen
Joel 2. †17. why heath. should use a b. against them?

C.

CABINS.

Jer. 37. 16. when Jeremiah was entered into the c.

CAGE.

Jer. 5. 27. as a c. is full of birds, so are their houses full of deceit, therefore they are become great
Rev. 18. 2. Babylon is a c. of every unclean bird

CAKE, S.

Exod. 12. 39. they baked unleavened c. of the dough
Lev. 7. 12. with sacrifice of thanksgiving, unleav. c.
24. 5. take fine flour, and bake twelve c. thereof
Num. 15. 20. offer up a c. of the first of your dough
Judg. 7. 13. and lo, a c. tumbled into host of Midian
2 Sam. 6. 19. David dealt to every one a c. of bread
13. 6. make me a couple of c. in my sight to eat
1 Kings 17. 12. as the Lord liveth, I have not a c.
17. 13. make me a little c. first, and bring it
19. 6. there was a c. baken on coals, a cruse of water
Jer. 7. 18. to make c. to the queen of heaven, 44. 19.
Ezek. 4. 12. and thou shalt eat it as barley c.
Hos. 7. 8. Ephraim is a c. not turned
See Figs, Unleavened.

CALAMITY, IES.

Deut. 32. 35. for the day of their c. is at hand
2 Sam. 22. 19. prevented me in day of c. Ps. 18. 18.
Job 6. 2. and my c. laid in the balances together
30. 13. they set forward my c. they have no helper
Psal. 57. 1. my refuge until these c. be overpast
141. 5. for yet my prayer also shall be in their c.
Prov. 1. 26. I will laugh at your c. I will mock
6. 15. therefore his c. shall come suddenly
17. 5. he that is glad at c. shall not be unpunished
19. 13. a foolish son is the c. of his father
24. 22. for their c. shall rise suddenly
27. 10. nor go into thy brother's house in day of c.
Jer. 18. 17. I will shew them the back in day of c.
46. 21. the day of their c. was come upon them
48. 16. the c. of Moab is near to come, hasteth
49. 8. for I will bring the c. of Esau upon him
32. and I will bring their c. from all sides thereof
Ezek. 35. 5. hast shed blood of Isr. in day of their c.
Obad. 13. on their substance in the day of their c.

CALAMUS.

Exod. 30. 23. take of sweet c. 250 shekels
Cant. 4. 14. spikenard, saffron, c. and cinnamon
Ezek. 27. 19. c. was in the market of Tyrus

CALDRON.

1 Sam. 2. 14. he struck it into the pan, c. or pot
Job 41. 20. goeth smoke, as out of a seething c.
Ezek. 11. 3. this city is the c. and we the flesh, 7.
11. this city shall not be your c. nor ye the flesh
Mic. 3. 3. they chop them as flesh within the c.

CALDRONS.

2 Chron. 35. 13. holy offerings sod they in pots and c.
Jer. 52. 18. c. also and spoons took they away, 19.

CALF.

Gen. 18. 7. Abraham fetched a c. tender and good
Exod. 32. 4. after he had made it a molten c.
20. Moses burnt c. and strawed it on the water
Lev. 9. 2. take thee a young c. for a sin offering
3. take a c. and a lamb for a burnt-offering
Deut. 9. 16. ye had sinned against the Lord, and had made you a molten c. Neh. 9. 18. Psal. 106. 19.
Job 21. 10. their cow calveth and casteth not her c.
Psal. 29. 6. he maketh them also to skip like a c.
Isa. 11. 6. the c. and the young lion together
27. 10. there shall the c. feed, and there lie down
Jer. 34. 18. when they cut the c. in twain and passed
Ezek. 1. 7. their feet were like the sole of a c. foot
Hos. 8. 5. thy c. O Samaria, hath cast thee off
6. the c. of Samaria shall be broken in pieces
Luke 15. 23. and bring hither the fatted c. and kill it
27. thy father hath killed the fatted c. 30.
Acts 7. 41. and they made a c. in those days
Rev. 4. 7. and the second beast was like a c.

CALKERS.

Ezek. 27. 9. ancients of Gebal were in thee thy c.
27. thy c. shall fall into the midst of the seas

CALL

Signifies, [1] *To name,* Gen. 1. 5. | 5. 2. [2] *To appoint and qualify a person for some work and service,* Exod. 31. 2. Isa. 22. 20. [3] *To cause, by a powerful word, those things to exist, which had no being before,* Rom. 4. 17. [4] *To invite, warn, and exhort, by the dispensations of Providence,* Isa. 22. 12. [5] *To cause to grow,* Ezek. 36. 29. [6] *To invite sinners to repentance, either by the ministry of the word, by awful dispensations of Providence, by the motions of the Holy Spirit, or by their own consciences,* Prov. 1. 24. Mat. 22. 14. [7] *To bring persons, by the preaching of the word and effectual operation of the Spirit, to know, believe, and obey, the gospel,* Rom. 8. 28, 30. [8] *To own and acknowledge,* Heb. 2. 11. [9] *To worship,* Gen. 4. 26. Acts 9. 14. [10] *To pray to,* Psal. 50. 15. Jonah 1. 6. [11] *To appeal to,* 2 Cor. 1. 23. [12] *To proclaim,* Joel 1. 14. | 2. 15. [13] *To reckon, or account,* Mal. 3. 15. Acts 10. 15. [14] *To be,* Luke 1. 32. *where it is said of Christ,* Thou shalt be called the Son of the Highest; *that is, Thou shalt really be, and be acknowledged, the true, eternal, and essential Son of God.*

Gen. 2. 19. to Adam, to see what he would c. them
Exod. 2. 7. c. to thee a nurse of the Hebrew women
20. where is he? c. him that he may eat bread
Num. 16. 12. Moses sent to c. Dathan and Abiram
22. 20. if the men c. thee, rise up and go with them
Deut. 4. 7. as God is in all things we c. on him for
26. I c. heaven and earth to witness against you this day, shall not pro. your days, 30. 19. | 31. 28.
Judg. 16. 25. c. for Samson that he may make us sport
21. 13. they sent to c. peaceably unto them
1 Sam. 3. 6. here am I, for thou didst c. me, 8.
16. 3. c. Jesse to the sacrifice, and I will shew thee
22. 11. then king sent to c. Ahimelech the priest
2 Sam. 17. 5. then said Absalom, c. now Hushai
1 Kings 1. 28. c. Bathsheba || 32. c. Zadok and Nathan
8. 52. hearken to them in all they c. for unto thee
17. 18. art come to me to c. my sin to remembrance?
18. 24. and c. ye on the name of your gods, 25.
2 Kings 4. 12. Elisha said, c. this Shunammite
10. 19. c. unto me all the prophets of Baal
Job 5. 1. c. now if there be any that will answer
13. 22. then c. thou, and I will answer, 14. 15.
Psal. 4. 1. hear when I c. O God of my righteousness
3. the Lord will hear when I c. unto him
14. 4. who eat up my people, and c. not upon Lord
20. 9. save, Lord, let the king hear us when we c.
49. 11. they c. their lands after their own names
77. 6. I c. to remembrance my song in the night
86. 5. and plenteous in mercy to all that c. on thee
99. 6. Samuel among them that c. on his name
102. 2. in the day when I c. answer me speedily
145. 18. the Lord is nigh all them that c. on him
Prov. 8. 4. to you, O men, I c. my voice to sons of men
9. 15. to c. passengers who go right on their ways
31. 28. her children arise, and c. her blessed
Isa. 3. †12. O my people, they who c. thee blessed cause thee to err, and destroy thy paths, 9. †16.
5. 20. woe to them that c. evil good, and good evil
22. 12. in that day did the Lord c. to weeping
45. 3. I the Lord which c. thee by thy name
48. 2. for they c. themselves of the holy city
13. when I c. to them they stand up together
55. 6. c. ye upon him while he is near
58. 5. wilt thou c. this a fast to the Lord?
13. c. the sabbath a delight, holy of the Lord
65. 15. and c. his servants by another name
24. it shall come, that before they c. I will answer
Jer. 9. 17. consider and c. for the mourning women
33. 3. c. unto me, and I will answer thee
Lam. 2. 15. is this city men c. perfection of beauty?
Hos. 1. 4. the Lord said, c. his name Jezreel
6. God said unto him, c. her name Lo-ruhamah
9. c. his name Lo-ammi, for ye are not my people
7. 11. they c. to Egypt, they go to Assyria
Joel 1. 14. sanctify a fast c. solemn assembly, 2. 15.
Jonah 1. 6. O sleeper, arise, c. upon thy God
Zech. 3. 10. ye shall c. every man his neighbour
Mal. 3. 15. now we c. proud happy, they that work
Mat. 9. 13. I am not come to c. the righteous, but sinners to repentance, Mark 2. 17. Luke 5. 32.
20. 8. c. the labourers and give them their hire
22. 3. sent his servants to c. them that were bidden
43. how then doth David in spirit c. him Lord?
23. 9. c. no man your father upon the earth
Luke 6. 46. why c. ye me L. and do not things I say?
14. 13. when thou makest a feast c. the poor
John 4. 16. go c. thy husband, and come hither
13. 13. ye c. me Master and Lord, and ye say well
Acts 9. 14. to bind all that c. on thy name
19. 13. to c. over them which had evil spirits
24. 14. that after the way which they c. heresy
Rom. 10. 12. same Lord is rich to all that c. on him
2 Cor. 1. 23. I c. God for a record upon my soul
2 Tim. 1. 5. when I c. to remembrance the faith
2. 22. follow peace with them that c. on the Lord
Heb. 2. 11. he is not ashamed to c. them brethren
10. 32. but c. to remembrance the former days
Jam. 5. 14. let him c. the elders of the church
1 Pet. 1. 17. if ye c. on the Father who judgeth

CALL *on the name of the Lord.*

Gen. 4. 26. then began men to c. upon name of the L.
1 Kings 18. 24. I will c. on name of L. Psal. 116. 17.
2 Kings 5. 11. he will come out and c. on name of L.
1 Chr. 16. 8. c. upon his name, Psal. 105. 1. Isa. 12. 4.
Joel 2. 32. whosoever shall c. on the name of the L. shall be delivered, Acts 2. 21. Rom. 10. 13.
Zeph. 3. 9. that they may all c. upon name of the L.
1 Cor. 1. 2. that in every place c. on the name of L.

Not **CALL.**

Gen. 17. 15. shall not c. her name Sarai, but Sarah
Judg. 12. 1. and didst not c. us to go with thee
Ruth 1. 20. she said, c. me not Naomi, c. me Mara
Psal. 14. 4. and they c. not upon the Lord
Isa. 31. 2. yet he will not c. back his words
Jer. 10. 25. upon families that c. not upon thy name
Luke 14. 12. c. not thy friends, nor thy brethren
John 15. 15. henceforth I c. you not servants
Acts 10. 15. that c. not thou common, 11. 9.
28. God hath shewed me n. to c. any man common

Shall, or shalt **CALL.**

Gen. 17. 19. and thou shalt c. his name Isaac
Deut. 25. 8. then the elders of his city shall c. him
30. 1. thou shalt c. them to mind among the nations
33. 19. they shall c. the people to the mountain
Job 14. 15. thou shalt c. and I will answer thee
Psal. 50. 4. he shall c. to the heavens from above
72. 17. blessed in him, all nations shall c. him blessed
Isa. 7. 14. shall c. his name Emmanuel, Mat. 1. 23.
34. 12. they shall c. the nobles to the kingdom
41. 25. from rising of sun shall he c. on my name
44. 5. another shall c. himself by the name of Jacob
7. and who, as I, shall c. and shall declare it?
55. 5. thou shalt c. a nation that thou knowest not
58. 9. then shalt thou c. and the Lord shall answer
60. 14. they shall c. thee the city of the Lord
18. shalt c. thy walls salvation, and gates praise
61. 6. men shall c. you the ministers of our God
62. 12. they shall c. them the holy people, redeemed
Jer. 3. 17. they shall c. Jerusalem the throne of L.
19. shalt c. me, my father, shalt not turn away
6. 30. reprobate silver shall men c. them
7. 27. shalt c. to them, but they will not answer thee
Hos. 2. 16. and thou shalt c. me no more Baali
Joel 2. 32. in the remnant whom the Lord shall c.
Amos 5. 16. they shall c. husbandman to mourning
Zech. 13. 9. shall c. on my name and I will hear them
Mal. 1. 4. they shall c. them the border of wickedness
3. 12. and all nations shall c. you blessed
Mat. 1. 21. thou shalt c. his name Jesus, shall save
10. 25. how much more shall c. them of household?
Luke 1. 13. and thou shalt c. his name John
48. behold, all generations shall c. me blessed
Acts 2. 39. as many as the Lord our God shall c.
Rom. 10. 14. how then shall they c. on him in whom

Will **CALL.**

Gen. 24. 57. we will c. the damsel and inquire at her
30. 13. for the daughters will c. me blessed
1 Sam. 12. 17. I will c. unto Lord, and he shall send
2 Sam. 22. 4. I will c. on the Lord, Psal. 18. 3.
Job 27. 10. will the hypocrite always c. on God?
Psal. 55. 16. as for me, I will c. upon God, 86. 7
80. 18. quicken us, and we will c. on thy name
116. 2. therefore will I c. on him as long as I
Isa. 22. 20. that I will c. my servant Eliakim
Jer. 1. 15. I will c. all the families of the north
25. 29. for I will c. for a sword, Ezek. 38. 21.
Ezek. 21. 23. he will c. to remembrance the iniquity
36. 29. I will c. for the corn, and will increase it
Acts 24. 25. a convenient season I will c. for thee
Rom. 9. 25. I will c. them my people which were not

CALL *upon me.* [liver

Psal. 50. 15. c. upon me in day of trouble, I will de-
91. 15. he shall c. upon me, and I will answer him
Prov. 1. 28. shall c. upon me, but I will not answer
Jer. 29. 12. shall ye c. upon me, and I will hearken

CALLED.

Gen. 11. 9. therefore is the name of it c. Babel

Gen. 21. 17. the angel of God c. to Hagar out of hea.
22. 11. the angel c. to Abraham out of heaven
35. 10. thy name shall not be c. any more Jacob
18. c. him Ben-oni, but his father c. him Benjamin
39. 14. she c. to the men of her house, and spake
Exod. 1. 18. the king of Egypt c. for the midwives
8. 8. Phar. c. for M. 25. | 9. 27. | 10. 16, 24. | 12. 31.
Num. 13. 16. Moses c. Oshea son of Nun, Jehoshua
Deut. 5. 1. Moses c. all Israel and said to them, 29. 2.
15. 2. not exact it, because it is c. the Lord's release
28. 10. shall see thou art c. by name of the Lord
Josh. 21. + 9. gave these cities here c. by name
Judg. 12. + 1. the men of Ephraim were c. together
14. 15. have ye c. us to take what we have?
15. 17. he cast away the jaw-bone, and c. the place
18. Samson was sore athirst, and c. on the Lord
+ 19. he c. it the well of him that c. or cried
16. 28. Samson c. to the Lord and said, O Lord
1 Sam. 9. 9. that is now c. a prophet, was c. a seer
2 Sam. 6. 2. whose name is c. by the name of the Ld.
12. 28. lest I take city, and it be c. after my name
18. 26. the watchman c. to the porter, and said
21. 2. the king c. the Gibeonites, and said to them
1 Kings 1. 9. Adonijah c. all his brethren, 19. 25.
18. 3. Ahab c. Obadiah, who was the governor
26. they c. on the name of Baal from morning
2 Kings 4. 22. she c. to her husband and said, send me
7. 10. they came and c. to the porter of the city
1 Chron. 4. 10. and Jabez c. on the God of Israel
13. 6. bring the ark of God, whose name is c. on it
21. 26. David c. on the Lord, he answered him
Esth. 2. 14. came no more, except she were c. by name
4. 11. who is not c. I have not been c. to come
Job 17. + 14. I have c. to corruption, my father
Ps. 53. 4. eat up my people, they have not c. upon G.
79. 6. the kingdoms that have not c. on thy name
Isa. 31. 4. a mult. of shepherds is c. forth against him
43. 22. but thou hast not c. on me, O Jacob
48. 1. O Jacob, ye that are c. by the name of Israel
12. hearken unto me, O Jacob, and Israel my c.
61. 3. that they might be c. trees of righteousness
Jer. 7. 32. that it shall no more be c. Tophet
Lam. 1. 21. thou wilt bring day that thou hast c.
2. 22. thou hast c. as a solemn day my terrors
Ezek. 20. 29. and the name thereof is c. Bamah
Dan. 5. 12. now let Daniel be c. and he will shew
Mat. 1. 16. of whom was born Jesus, who is c. Christ
10. 2. the first Simon, who is c. Peter
13. 55. they said, is not his mother c. Mary?
18. 2. and Jesus c. a little child unto him
20. 16. for many be c. but few chosen, 22. 14.
32. and Jesus stood still, and c. them, and said
23. 8. be not ye c. Rabbi, one is your Master, 10.
26. 14. one of the twelve c. Judas Iscariot
27. 17. or shall I release Jesus, c. Christ? 22.
Mark 10. 49. Jesus commanded him to be c.
14. 72. Peter c. to mind the word that Jesus said
Luke 1. 61. none of thy kindred is c. by this name
62. they made signs how he would have him c.
15. 19. I am no more worthy to be c. thy son, 21.
19. 15. he commanded the servants to be c.
23. 33. when come to the place that is c. Calvary
John 1. 48. before that Philip c. thee I saw thee
4. 25. I know Messiah cometh, who is c. Christ
9. 11. a man c. Jesus made clay and anoint. my eyes
Acts 9. 11. go into the street c. Straight, for one c. Saul
11. 26. disciples were c. Christians first at Antioch
13. 7. who c. for Barnabas and Saul, desired to hear
9. then Saul, c. Paul, filled with the Holy Ghost
15. 17. all the Gentiles on whom my name is c.
19. 40. to be c. in question for this day's upr ar
23. 6. I am c. in question by you this day, 24. 21.
18. Paul the prisoner c. and prayed me to bring
Rom. 1. 1. Paul c. to be an apostle, 1 Cor. 1. 1.
6. among whom are ye also the c. of Jesus
7. to them that are c. to be saints, 1 Cor. 1. 2.
2. 17. thou art c. a Jew, and restest in the law
8. 28. who are the c. according to his purpose
1 Cor. 1. 9. by whom ye were c. to the fellowship
24. to them which are c. both Jews and Greeks
26. not many mighty, not many noble, are c.
5. 11. if any man c. a brother be a fornicator
7. 18. is any man c. being circumcised? is any c.
21. art thou c. being a servant? care not for it
24. let every man wherein he is c. therein abide
Gal. 1. 6. so soon removed from him that c. you
5. 13. for, brethren, ye have been c. to liberty
Eph. 2. 11. who are c. uncircumcision by that c.
4. 1. walk worthy of vocation wherewith ye are c.
4. even as ye are c. in one hope of your calling
Col. 3. 15. to the which ye are c. in one body
4. 11. Jesus, which is c. Justus, saluteth you
2 Thess. 2. 4. who exalteth above all that is c. God
1 Tim. 6. 12. eternal life, whereto thou art c.
20. avoiding oppositions of science, falsely so c.
Heb. 3. 13. but exhort daily while it is c. to day
9. 2. the tabernacle which is c. the sanctuary
15. they that are c. might receive the promise
11. 16. God is not ashamed to be c. their God
24. Moses refused to be c. son of Pharaoh's daugh.
Jam. 2. 7. blaspheme that name by which ye are c.
1 Pet. 2. 9. of him who hath c. you out of darkness
21. for hereunto were ye c. because Christ suffered
3. 9. knowing that ye are thereunto c. to inherit
2 Pet. 1. 3. that hath c. us to glory and virtue
1 John 3. 1. that we should be c. the sons of God
Jude 1. to sanctified, preserved in Jesus Christ, and c.
Rev. 8. 11. the name of the star is c. wormwood
11. 8. city which spiritually is c. Sodom and Egypt
12. 9. that old serpent c. the Devil, and Satan
17. 14. they that are with him, are c. and chosen
19. 9. blessed that are c. to the marriage supper

CALLED, joined with *God*, or *Lord*.

Gen. 1. 5. God c. light day, darkness he c. night
8. and God c. the firmament, heaven
10. God c. dry land earth, the waters c. he seas
5. 2. God blessed them, and c. their name Adam
Exod. 3. 4. God c. to him out of the midst of the bush
19. 3. the Lord c. to him out of the mountain
20. the Lord c. Moses up to the top of the mount
35. 30. see, the Lord hath c. my name Bezaleel
Num. 12. 5. and the Lord c. Aaron and Miriam
1 Sam. 3. 4. the Lord c. Samuel, 6, 8, 10.
2 Kings 3. 10. alas, Lord hath c. these three kings, 13.
8. 1. for the Lord hath c. for a famine on the land
Psal. 50. 1. Lord hath c. the earth from rising of sun
Isa. 41. 2. the Lord raised, and c. him to his foot
42. 6. I the Lord have c. thee in righteousness
49. 1. the Lord hath c. me from the womb
54. 6. the Lord hath c. thee as a woman forsaken
Jer. 11. 16. Lord c. thy name a green olive-tree
20. 3. the Lord hath not c. thy name Pashur
Amos 7. 4. the Lord God c. to contend by fire
Acts 16. 10. gathering that the Lord had c. us
1 Cor. 7. 15. but God hath c. us to peace
17. as the Lord hath c. every one, so let him walk
Gal. 1. 15. it pleased God, who c. me by his grace
1 Thess. 2. 12. who c. you to his kingdom and glory
4. 7. for God hath not c. us to uncleanness
2 Thess. 2. 14. whereunto God c. you by our gospel
2 Tim. 1. 9. who hath c. us with a holy calling
Heb. 5. 4. but he that is c. of God, as was Aaron
10. c. of God an high-priest after order of Melchis.
1 Pet. 5. 10. the God of all grace, who hath c. us

He CALLED.

Gen. 21. 31. wherefore he c. that place Beer-sheba
26. 18. he c. their names as his father called them
35. 10. thy name is Jacob, he c. his name Israel
Exod. 24. 16. the Lord c. to Moses out of the cloud
Judg. 6. 32. on that day he c. him Jerubbaal
2 Sam. 1. 7. when he looked he saw me and c. to me
13. 17. then he c. his servant that ministered to him
1 Kings 1. 10. but Solom. his brother he c. not, 19, 26.
9. 13. he c. them land of Cabul to this day
2 Kings 4. 36. and he c. to Gehazi, so he c. her
18. 4. he brake brazen serpent, he c. it Nehushtan
Psal. 105. 16. he c. for a famine on the land
Jer. 42. 8. then c. he Johanan and all the captains
Lam. 1. 15. he hath c. an assembly against me
Ezek. 9. 3. he c. to the man clothed with linen
Mat. 10. 1. he c. the twelve || 15. 10. he c. multitude
Mark 1. 20. straightway he c. them and they left
Luke 13. 12. when Jesus saw her, he c. her to him
John 10. 35. if he c. them gods, to whom the word
Acts 9. 41. when he had c. the saints and widows
10. 23. then c. he them in, and lodged them
16. 29. then he c. for a light, and sprang in
19. 25. whom he c. together with the workmen
23. 23. he c. unto him two centurions, saying
Rom. 8. 30. them he also c. whom he c. he justified
9. 24. even us whom he hath c. not of Jews only
1 Pet. 1. 15. but as he which hath c. you is holy

See CALLED *the name*.

I CALLED, or, *I have* CALLED.

Num. 24. 10. I c. thee to curse mine enemies
Judg. 12. 2. when I c. you, ye delivered me not
1 Sam. 3. 5. Eli said, I c. not, lie down again, 6.
28. 15. I have c. thee, thou mayest make known to me
2 Sam. 22. 7. in my distress I c. Psal. 18. 6. | 118. 5.
Neh. 5. 12. I c. the priests, and took an oath of them
Job 9. 16. if I had c. and he had answered me
19. 16. I c. my servant, and he gave me no answer
Psal. 17. 6. I have c. on thee, for thou wilt hear
31. 17. let me not be ashamed, for I have c. upon thee
88. 9. Lord, I have c. daily upon thee
116. 4. then c. I upon the name of the Lord
Prov. 1. 24. because I have c. and ye refused
Cant. 5. 6. I c. him, but he gave me no answer
Isa. 13. 3. I have c. my mighty ones for mine anger
41. 9. I have c. thee from the chief men thereof
43. 1. I c. thee by thy name, thou art mine, 45. 4.
48. 15. yea, I have c. him, I have brought him
50. 2. when I c. was there none to answer?
51. 2. for I c. him alone, and blessed him
65. 12. when I c. ye did not answer, Jer. 7. 13.
66. 4. because when I c. none did answer
Jer. 35. 17. because I have c. to them, but they not
Lam. 1. 19. I c. for my lovers, but they deceived me
3. 55. I c. on thy name out of the low dungeon
57. thou drewest near in the day I c. upon thee
Hos. 11. 1. then I c. my Son out of Egypt, Mat. 2. 15.
Hag. 1. 11. and I c. for a drought upon the land
Zech. 11. 7. one I c. Beauty, the other I c. Bands
John 15. 15. not servants, but I have c. you friends
Acts 13. 2. for the work whereto I have c. them
28. 20. for this cause have I c. for you to see

CALLED *by my name*.

2 Chron. 7. 14. my people who are c. by my n. humble
Isa. 43. 7. bring, even every one that is c. by my n.
65. 1. behold, to a nation that was not c. by my n.
Jer. 7. 10. house c. by my n. 11, 14, 30. | 32. 34. | 34. 15.
25. 29. to bring evil on the city which is c. by my n.
Amos 9. 12. remnant of heathen which are c. by my n.

CALLED *by thy name*.

1 Kings 8. 43. house I builded is c. by thy n. 2 Ch. 6. 33.
Isa. 4. 1. let us be c. by thy n. to take away our reproach
43. 1. I have c. thee by thy n. thou art mine, 45. 4.
63. 19. we are thine, they were not c. by thy n.
Jer. 14. 9. O Lord, we are c. by thy n. leave us not
15. 16. for I am c. by thy n. O Lord God of hosts
Dan. 9. 18. and behold the city which is c. by thy n.
19. defer not, for thy city and people are c. by thy n.

CALLED *his name*.

Gen. 35. 10. thy name is Jacob, he c. his n. Israel
18. she c. his n. Benoni, but his father Benjamin
1 Chron. 4. 9. his mother c. his n. Jabez, saying
7. 16. she c. his n. Peresh || 23. and he c. his n. Beriah
Mat. 1. 25. her first born son, and he c. his n. Jesus
Rev. 19. 13. and his name is c. the Word of God

CALLED *the name*.

Gen. 28. 19. c. the n. of the place Beth-el, 35. 15.
Exod. 16. 31. and Israel c. the n. thereof Manna
17. 7. he c. the n. of the place Massah and Meribah
15. Moses c. the n. of the altar JEHOVAH-nissi
Judg. 15. 19. Samson c. the n. thereof En-hakkore
2 Sam. 5. 20. c. the n. of that place Baal-perazim
1 Kings 7. 21. c. the n. thereof Jachin, 2 Chr. 3. 17.
Job 42. 14. and he c. the n. of the first Jemima

Sent and CALLED.

Gen. 27. 42. she sent and c. Jacob her younger son
31. 4. Jacob sent and c. Rachel and Leah to the field
41. 14. then Pharaoh sent and c. Joseph
Josh. 24. 9. Balak sent and c. Balaam to curse you
Judg. 4. 6. she sent and c. Barak out of Kadesh
Judg. 16. 18. she sent and c. the lords of Philistines
2 Sam. 12. 25. he sent and c. his name Jedidiah
1 Kings 2. 36. the king sent and c. for Shimei, 42.
12. 3. they sent and c. Jeroboam, 2 Chron. 10. 3.
Esth. 5. 10. Haman sent and c. for his friends
Acts 20. 17. he sent to Ephesus, and c. the elders

Shall be CALLED.

Gen. 2. 23. shall be c. woman, because taken out of man
17. 5. thy name shall be c. Abraham, for a father
21. 12. hearken to Sarah's voice, for in Isaac shall thy seed be c. Rom. 9. 7. Heb. 11. 18
32. 28. name shall be c. no more Jacob, but Israel
48. 6. thy issue shall be c. after their brethren
Deut. 25. 10. his name shall be c. in Israel, house of
Prov. 16. 21. the wise in heart shall be c. prudent
24. 8. deviseth evil, shall be c. a mischievous person
Isa. 4. 3. that remaineth in Jerusalem shall be c. holy
9. 6. and his name shall be c. Wonderful, Counsellor
19. 18. one shall be c. the city of destruction
32. 5. the vile person shall no more be c. liberal
35. 8. and a way, and it shall be c. way of holiness
54. 5. the God of the whole earth shall he be c.
56. 7. house shall be c. house of prayer, Mat. 21. 13.
Jer. 7. 32. it shall no more be c. Tophet, 19. 6.
23. 6. he shall be c. Lord our Righteousness, 33. 16.
Zech. 8. 3. Jerusalem shall be c. a city of truth
Mat. 1. + 23. and his name shall be c. Emmanuel
2. 23. it might be fulfilled, shall be c. a Nazarene
5. 9. peace-makers shall be c. the children of God
19. he shall be c. the least in the kingdom of heaven
Luke 1. 32. and he shall be c. the Son of the Highest
35. also that holy thing shall be c. the Son of God
60. his mother said, not so; but he shall be c. John
2. 23. every male shall be c. holy to the Lord
Rom. 7. 3. if she be married, shall be c. an adulteress
9. 26. they shall be c. the children of God

Shalt be CALLED.

Isa. 1. 26. thou shalt be c. the city of righteousness
47. 1. thou shalt be c. no more tender and delicate
5. thou shalt no more be c. lady of kingdoms
58. 12. thou shalt be c. the repairer of the breach
62. 2. shalt be c. by a new name, Lord shall name
4. thou shalt be c. Hephzi-bah, thy land Beulah
12. thou shalt be c. sought for, a city not forsaken
Luke 1. 76. thou shalt be c. Prophet of the Highest
John 1. 42. thou shalt be c. Cephas, which is, a stone

They CALLED.

Gen. 19. 5. they c. Lot, and said, where are the men?
Num. 25. 2. they c. the people to the sacrifices
Judg. 16. 25. they c. for Samson out of the prison
Esth. 9. 26. they c. these days Purim, after Pur
Psal. 99. 6. they c. upon the Lord, and he answered
Jer. 12. 6. they have c. a multitude after thee
30. 17. because they c. thee an outcast, saying
Hos. 11. 2. as they c. to them, so they went from them
7. though they c. them to the most High
Mat. 10. 25. if they have c. the master Beelzebub
Luke 1. 59. they c. him Zacharias, after his father
John 9. 18. they c. parents of him that received sight
24. then again they c. the man that was blind
Acts 4. 18. they c. them, and commanded not to speak
5. 40. when they had c. the apostles, and beaten
14. 12. they c. Barnabas, Jupiter; Paul, Mercurius

Was CALLED.

Deut. 3. 13. which was c. the land of giants
Judg. 6. + 34. and Abiezer was c. after him
2 Chron. 20. 26. place was c. the valley of Berachah
Ezra 2. 61. and was c. after their name, Neh. 7. 63.
Isa. 48. 8. wast c. a transgressor from the womb
Dan. 10. 1. whose name was c. Belteshazzar
Mat. 26. 3. the high priest, who was c. Caiaphas
27. 8. was c. the field of blood, unto this day
Luke 1. 36. sixth month with her who was c. barren
2. 21. his name was c. JESUS, so named of the angel
John 2. 2. Jesus was c. and his disciples to marriage
Acts 13. 1. in the church Simeon, that was c. Niger
24. 2. and when he was c. forth, Tertullus began
28. 1. they knew that the island was c. Melita
1 Cor. 7. 20. abide in the calling wherein he was c.
Heb. 11. 8. Abraham when he was c. obeyed
Jam. 2. 23. and he was c. the friend of God
Rev. 19. 11. he that sat on him was c. Faithful

CALLEDST, CALLEST.

Judg. 8. 1. that thou c. us not when thou wentest
1 Sam. 3. 5. and he said, here am I, for thou c. me
Psal. 81. 7. thou c. in trouble, and I delivered thee
Ezek. 23. 21. c. to remembrance lewdness of youth
Mat. 19. 17. why c. thou me good? there is none good but God, Mark 10. 18. Luke 18. 19.

CALLETH.

1 Kings 8. 43. hear thou in heaven, do according to all that the stranger c. to thee for, 2 Chr. 6. 33.
Job 12. 4. who c. on God, and he answered him
Psal. 42. 7. deep c. unto deep at the noise of thy
147. 4. he c. them all by their names, Isa. 40. 26.
Prov. 18. 6. a fool's mouth c. for strokes
Isa. 21. 11. he c. to me out of Seir, watchman
59. 4. none c. for justice, nor any pleadeth
64. 7. and there is none that c. on thy name
Hos. 7. 7. there is none among them that c. to me
Amos 5. 8. that c. for the waters of the sea, 9. 6.
Mat. 27. 47. this man c. for Elias, Mark 15. 35.
Mark 3. 13. c. to him whom he would, they came
6. 7. c. to him the twelve, and began to send them
8. 1. Jesus c. his disciples, and saith to them
10. 49. be of good comfort, arise, he c. thee
12. 37. if David therefore c. him Lord, Luke 20. 44.
Luke 15. 6. he c. together his friends and her neighbours
9. she c. her friends and her neighbours
20. 37. when he c. the Lord, the God of Abraham
John 10. 3. and he c. his own sheep by name
11. 28. the master is come and c. for thee
Rom. 4. 17. c. things which be not, as tho' they were
9. 11. purpose of election might stand of him that c.
1 Cor. 12. 3. no man by the Spirit c. Jesus accursed
Gal. 5. 8. persuasion cometh not of him that c. you
1 Thess. 5. 24. faithful is he that c. you, who will do it
Rev. 2. 20. Jezebel, that c. herself a prophetess

CALLING

Signifies, [1] *Any lawful employment, or way of living*, 1 Cor. 7. 20. [2] *That effectual calling, whereby sinners savingly believe, and obey the*

gospel, Phil. 3. 14. Heb. 3. 1. [3] The state of glory, and blessedness in heaven, to which believers are called, 2 Thess. 1. 11.
Num. 10. 2. use trumpets for the c. of the assembly
Isa. 1. 13. the c. of assemblies I cannot away with
Ezek. 23. 19. in c. to remembrance her youth
Rom. 11. 29. the c. of God without repentance
1 Cor. 1. 26. for ye see your c. brethren not many
7. 20. let every man abide in same c. wherein called
Eph. 1. 18. may know what is the hope of his c.
4. 4. as ye are called in one hope of your c.
Phil. 3. 14. for the prize of the high c. of God
2 Thess. 1. 11. that God count you worthy of this c.
2 Tim. 1. 9. who hath called us with any holy c.
Heb. 3. 1. partakers of the heavenly c. consider
2 Pet. 1. 10. to make your c. and election sure

CALLING, *Participle.*

Isa. 41. 4. c. the generations from the beginning
46. 11. c. a ravenous bird from the east
Mat. 11. 16. and c. to their fellows, Luke 7. 32.
Mark 11. 21. Peter, c. to remembrance, saith
Acts 7. 59. they stoned Stephen c. upon God
22. 16. wash away thy sins, c. on name of the Lord
1 Pet. 3. 6. Sarah obeyed Abraham, c. him Lord

CALM.

Psal. 107. 29. he maketh the storm a c.
Jonah 1. 11. that the sea may be c. unto us
12. cast me forth, so shall the sea be c. to you
Mat. 8. 26. there was a great c. Mark 4. 39. Luke 8. 24.

CALVE, ED, ETH.

Job 21. 10. their cow c. and casteth not her calf
39. 1. canst thou mark when the hinds do c.?
Psal. 29. 9. the voice of the Lord maketh hinds to c.
Jer. 14. 5. the hind c. in the field, and forsook it

CALVES.

1 Sam. 6. 7. and bring their c. home from them
1 Kings 12. 28. the king made two c. of gold
32. sacrificing to the c. that he had made
2 Kings 10. 29. Jehu departed not from the golden c.
2 Chron. 11. 15. he ordained him priests, for the c.
13. 8. and there are with you golden c.
Psal. 68. 30. rebuke the bulls with the c. of people
Hos. 10. 5. shall fear, because of the c. of Beth-aven
13. 2. let the men that sacrifice kiss the c.
14. 2. so will we render the c. of our lips
Amos 6. 4. and eat c. out of the midst of the stall
Mic. 6. 6. shall I come with c. of a year old?
Mal. 4. 2. ye shall grow up as c. of the stall
Heb. 9. 12. nor by blood of goats and c. but own blood
19. took blood of c. and sprinkled book and people

CAME.

Gen. 10. 14. out of whom c. Philistim, 1 Chron. 1. 12.
19. 1. two angels c. to Sodom at even, Lot sat in gate
20. 3. God c. to Abimelech in a dream by night
27. 35. brother c. with subtilty and taken blessing
31. 24. God c. to Laban the Syrian in dream by night
32. 6. c. to thy brother Esau, he cometh to meet thee
39. 16. she laid up his garment until his lord c. home
Num. 13. 27. c. to the land whither thou sentest us
19. 2. a red heifer, upon which never c. yoke
22. 9. God c. to Balaam at night, and said, 20.
24. 2. Sp. of God c. on him, Judg. 3. 10. 1 Sam. 10. 10.
Deut. 1. 19. and we c. to Kadesh-barnea
33. 2. the Lord c. from Sinai, and rose up from Seir
Josh. 15. 18. as she c. to him she moved, Judg. 1. 14.
Judg. 5. 19. kings c. and fought, kings of Canaan
7. 13. the cake of bread c. to a tent and smote it
9. 25. they robbed all that c. along that way by them
57. upon them c. curse of Jotham son of Jerubb.
11. 18. but c. not within the border of Moab
13. 10. the man that c. to me the other day
11. Manoah arose and c. to the man, and said
19. 22. bring forth the man that c. into thy house
20. 48. Israel smote Benjamin, all that c. to hand
Ruth 2. 6. it is the Moabitish damsel that c. back
1 Sam. 2. 13. custom was, the priest's servant, c. 15.
14. so they did to all Israelites that c. thither
27. there c. a man of God to Eli, and said to him
4. 1. and the word of Samuel c. to all Israel
7. 13. they c. no more into the coast of Israel
9. 15. Lord told Samuel in his ear before Saul c.
10. 14. when we saw asses no where, c. to Samuel
13. 8. but Samuel c. not to Gilgal, people scattered
17. 34. there c. a lion and a bear, and took a lamb
2 Sam. 2. 4. men of Judah c. and anointed David king
3. 25. thou knowest Abner, that c. to deceive thee
13. 30. while in the way the tidings c. to David
36. behold, king's sons c. and wept, the king wept
15. 2. when any c. to king for judgment, Absalom
16. 15. Absalom and Ahithophel c. to Jerusalem
20. 12. saw every one that c. by him stood still
1 Kings 1. 42. while he spake, Jonat. son of Abiath. c.
4. 34. c. of all people to hear wisdom of Solomon
10. 10. there c. no more such spices as these
12. there c. no such almug-trees to this day
12. 12. Jerob. and all the people c. 2 Chron. 10. 12.
13. 10. he returned not by the way he c. to Bethel
19. 9. he c. thither to a cave and lodged there
20. 43. the king of Israel c. heavy to Samaria
2 Kings 4. 11. it fell on a day that he c. thither
27. when she c. to the man of God to the hill
5. 15. Naaman c. and stood before Elisha
6. 23. the bands of Syria c. no more into Israel
32. but ere messenger c. to him, he said to elders
8. 14. Hazael departed from Elisha, c. to his master
9. 11. wherefore c. this mad fellow to thee?
10. 12. Jehu arose, departed, and c. to Samaria
21. all worshippers of Baal c. house of Baal full
17. 28. one of the priests c. and dwelt in Beth-el
19. 33. by the way that he c. shall he return
24. 3. at the command of the Lord c. this on Judah
1 Chron. 4. 41. these c. in the days of Hezekiah
5. 2. Judah prevailed, of him c. the chief ruler
7. 22. Ephraim's brethren c. to comfort him
12. 1. now these are they that c. to Dav. day by day
22. there c. to David to help him a great host
2 Chron. 11. 14. the Levites left all and c. to Judah
12. 11. the guard c. and fetched the shields
14. 14. for the fear of the Lord c. upon them
22. 1. the band of men that c. with the Arabians
24. 18. wrath c. on Judah and Jerusalem for trespass
25. 20. Amaziah would not hear, for it c. of God
30. 11. divers humbled thems. and c. to Jerus.
31. 5. and as soon as commandment c. abroad
Ezra 2. 2. which c. with Zerubbabel, Mordecai
5. 5. not cause to cease till the matter c. to Darius
Neh. 7. 73. when seventh month c. were in their cities
Esth. 1. 17. Vashti to be brought in, but she c. not
2. 13. then thus c. every maiden to the king
4. 2. Mordecai c. even before the king's gate
8. 17. whither the king's decree c. Jews had joy
Job 3. †25. I feared a fear, and it c. upon me
26. I was not in safety, nor had rest, yet trouble c.
29. 13. the blessing of him ready to perish c. on him
30. 26. I looked for good, evil c. darkness c.
Psal. 18. 6. my cry c. before me, even to his ears
27. 2. when my foes c. upon me they stumbled
78. 31. wrath of God c. upon them, and slew them
105. 19. until time that his word c. word tried them
31. he spake, and there c. divers sorts of flies
34. he spake, and locusts c. and caterpillars
Eccl. 5. 15. to go as he c. and take nothing, 16.
Isa. 20. 1. in the year that Tartan c. to Ashdod
30. 4. and his ambassadors c. to Hanes
41. 5. ends of earth were afraid, drew near and c.
Jer. 7. 31. nor c. it into my mind, 19. 5. | 32. 35.
8. 15. we looked for peace, but no good c.
44. 21. incense you burnt, c. it not into his mind?
Ezek. 4. 14. nor c. there abominable flesh into mouth
17. 3. c. to Lebanon, and took the highest branch
33. 22. afore he that was escaped c. opened mouth
37. 7. the bones c. together, bone to his bone
10. breath c. into them, they lived and stood up
43. 2. the glory of God of Israel c. from the east
Dan. 2. †29. thoughts c. up into thy mind on thy bed
4. 28. all this c. on the king Nebuchadnezzar
7. 13. one like Son of Man c. with clouds of heaven
22. till the ancient of days c. and judgment given
Amos 6. 1. to whom the house of Israel c.
Jonah 3. 6. for word c. to the king of Nineveh
Hab. 3. 3. God c. from Teman, and the Holy One
Hag. 1. 9. ye looked for much, and lo it c. to little
2. 16. when one c. to the press-fat to draw out
Zech. 7. 12. c. a great wrath from the Lord of hosts
14. 16. of all the nations that c. against Jerusalem
Mat. 2. 1. there c. wise men from the east to Jerus.
9. till it c. and stood over where the child was
3. 1. in those days c. John the Baptist preaching
7. 25. and the rains descended, and the floods c. 27.
9. 1. he passed over and c. into his own city
20. a woman c. behind, touched hem of his garm.
28. come into the house, the blind men c. to Jesus
20. 28. Son of man c. not to be ministered to
21. 28. c. to the first and said, son, go work to-day
30. he c. to the second, and said likewise
32. John c. to you in the way of righteousness
25. 10. they went to buy, the bridegroom c.
36. I was in prison, and ye c. to me
26. 49. forthwith he c. to Jesus and kissed him
60. though false witnesses c. yet found they none
28. 13. his disciples c. by night, and stole him away
Mark 3. 8. heard what great things he did, c. to him
9. 21. how long is it ago since this c. to him?
12. 28. one of the scribes c. and asked him
42. c. a certain poor widow threw two mites
Luke 1. 57. now Elisabeth's full time c. to be deliv.
9. 34. there c. a cloud and overshadowed them
35. and there c. a voice out of the cloud, saying,
15. 17. when he c. to himself, he said, how many
20. and he arose and c. to his father
John 1. 7. the same c. to bear witness of the light
11. he c. to his own, and his own received him not
17. but grace and truth c. by Jesus Christ
3. 2. the same c. to Jesus by night, 7. 50. | 19. 39.
23. and they c. and were baptized
4. 27. upon this c. his disciples, and marvelled that
10. 35. if he called gods to whom word of God c.
12. 30. the voice c. not because of me, but for you
20. 19. at even c. Jesus, and stood in the midst
Acts 8. 40. preached in all cities, till he c. to Cesarea
9. 21. c. hither for that intent, to bring them bound
10. 45. as many as c. with Peter were astonished
11. 5. the vessel descended, and it c. even to me
23. when he c. and had seen the grace of God
19. 18. and many that believed c. and confessed
28. 21. nor brethren that c. spake any harm of thee
Rom. 5. 18. judgment c. the free gift c. on all men
7. 9. when the commandment c. sin revived
9. 5. of whom, as concerning the flesh, Christ c.
1 Cor. 15. 21. since by man c. death, by man c. also
Gal. 2. 12. for before that certain c. from James
3. 23. before faith c. we were kept under the law
Eph. 2. 17. and c. and preached peace to you afar off
1 Thess. 1. 5. our gospel c. not in word only but in
1 Tim. 1. 15. that Christ c. to save sinners [power
2 Tim. 3. 11. persecutions which c. to me at Antioch
2 Pet. 1. 17. when there c. such a voice to him
18. this voice which c. from heaven we heard
21. prophecy c. not in old time by the will of man
1 John 5. 6. this is he that c. by water and blood
3 John 3. when brethren c. and testified of the truth
Rev. 16. 19. and great Babylon c. in remembrance

See Spirit of the LORD.

CAME *again.*

Judg. 13. 9. angel c. again to the woman as she sat
15. 19. his spirit c. again to him, 1 Sam. 30. 12.
21. 14. and Benjamin c. again at that time
1 Kings 17. 22. the soul of the child c. into him again
19. 7. the angel of the Lord c. again the second time
2 Kings 5. 14. his flesh c. again like the flesh of a child
7. 8. lepers c. again, and entered into another tent
Ezra 2. 1. these c. again to Judah and Jerus. Neh. 7. 6.
Esth. 6. 12. Mordecai c. again to the king's gate
Dan. 10. 18. c. again and touched me one like a man
Zech. 4. 1. the angel c. again and waked me
Luke 8. 55. her spirit c. ag. and she arose straightway
John 8. 2. and early he c. again into the temple

CAME *down.*

Gen. 11. 5. Lord c. down to see the city and tower
15. 11. when the fowls c. down on the carcases
43. 20. O Sir, we c. down at first to buy food
Exod. 19. 20. the Lord c. down upon mount Sinai
34. 29. when Moses c. down from mount Sinai
Lev. 9. 22. and Aaron c. down from offering
Num. 11. 25. the Lord c. down in a cloud, 12. 5.
14. 45. then Amalekites c. down and smote them
Judg. 5. 14. out of Machir c. down the governors
2 Sam. 22. 10. bowed heavens and c. down, Psal. 18. 9
2 Kings 1. 10. there c. down fire from heaven, 12, 14.
1 Chron. 7. 21. men of Gath c. d. to take their cattle
2 Chron. 7. 1. made an end of praying, fire c. d. 3.
Lam. 1. 9. therefore she c. down wonderfully
Dan. 4. 13. an holy one c. down from heaven
Mic. 1. 12. evil c. down from the Lord to the gate
Mat. 17. 9. as they c. d. from mountain, Mark 9. 9.
Luke 10. 31. there c. down a certain priest that way
19. 6. he made haste and c. down and received him
John 3. 13. he that c. down from heaven, Son of Man
6. 38. I c. d. from heaven, not to do mine own will
41. the bread which c. down from heaven, 51, 58.
Acts 15. 1. men which c. down from Judea taught
21. 10. there c. down from Judea a certain prophet
Rev. 20. 9. fire c. d. from God and devoured them

CAME *forth.*

Exod. 13. 8. Lord did to me when I c. f. out of Egypt
Num. 11. 20. wept, saying, why c. f. out of Egypt?
12. 5. Aaron and Miriam, they both c. forth
Deut. 23. 4. met you not with water when ye c. f.
Josh. 9. 12. our bread hot on day we c. forth to you
Judg. 14. 14. he said to them, out of the eater c. f. meat, and out of the strong c. f. sweetness
2 Sam. 16. 5. Shimei c. f. and cursed as he came
11. son which c. f. of my bowels seeketh my life
1 Kings 22. 21. c. f. a spirit, and stood before Lord
2 Kings 2. 23. c. f. little children and mocked him
24. c. forth two she-bears and tare 42 children
21. 15. their fathers c. f. out of Egypt, Jer 7. 25.
2 Chron. 32. 21. that c. forth of his bowels slew him
Prov. 7. 15. therefore c. I forth to meet thee
Eccl. 5. 15. as he c. forth naked, shall he return
Jer. 20. 18. wherefore c. I forth out of the womb?
Dan. 3. 26. they c. forth of the midst of the fire
5. 5. c. forth fingers and wrote on plaster of wall
7. 10. a fiery stream c. forth from before him
8. 9. out of one of them c. forth a little horn
9. 23. the command c. f. and I am come to shew
Zech. 10. 4. out of him c. forth the corner, the nail
Mark 1. 38. that I may preach, for therefore c. I f.
John 11. 44. and he that was dead c. forth bound
16. 28. I c. forth from the Father into the world
19. 5. Jesus c. forth wearing the crown of thorns

I CAME.

Gen. 24. 42. and I c. this day to the well, and said
30. 30. for it was little thou hadst before I c.
48. 5. which were born before I c. into Egypt
7. when I c. from Padan, Rachel died by me
Exod. 5. 23. since I c. to speak to Pharaoh in thy name
Deut. 22. 14. when I c. to her found her not a maid
Judg. 20. 4. Levite said, I c. into Gibeah of Benj.
1 Kings 10. 7. I believed not till I c. 2 Chron. 9. 6.
Neh. 6. 10. afterwards I c. to the house of Shemaiah
13. 6. I c. to the king and obtained leave
7. I c. to Jerusalem and understood of the evil
Isa. 50. 2. wherefore, when I c. was there no man
Ezek. 3. 15. then I c. to them of the captivity
43. 3. when I c. to destroy the city
Mat. 10. 34. I c. not to send peace, but a sword
Mark 2. 17. I c. not to call the righteous, Luke 5. 32.
John 8. 14. I know whence I c. and whither I go
42. I c. from God, nor c. I of myself, he sent me
12. 27. but for this cause I c. to this hour
47. for I c. not to judge the world, but to save
18. 37. for this cause c. I into the world, that I bear
Acts 10. 29. therefore c. I as soon as I was sent for
20. 18. ye know from the first day I c. into Asia
22. 11. being led by the hand, I c. into Damascus
23. 27. then c. I with an army and rescued him
24. 17. I c. to bring alms to my nation, and offerings
1 Cor. 2. 1. when I c. to you I c. not with excellency
2 Cor. 1. 23. that to spare you I c. not as yet to Corinth
2. 3. lest when I c. I should have sorrow from them
12. when I c. to Troas to preach Christ's gospel
Gal. 1. 21. afterwards I c. into the regions of Syria

CAME *in.*

Gen. 6. 4. the sons of God c. in to daughters of men
19. 5. where are the men that c. in to thee this night?
38. 18. Judah c. in unto her, and she conceived
39. 14. he c. in to lie with me, and I cried loud
Exod. 21. 3. if he c. in by himself, he shall go out
Josh. 6. 1. none went out, and none c. in to Jericho
1 Sam. 18. 13. went out and c. in before the people, 16.
2 Sam. 11. 4. she c. in to him, and he lay with her
1 Kings 14. 6. as she c. in at the door, Ahijah said
2 Chron. 15. 5. no peace to him that c. in, Zech. 8. 10.
Esth. 2. 14. she c. in to the king no more except
Jer. 32. 23. and they c. in and possessed it
37. 4. now Jeremiah c. in and went out among people
Ezek. 46. 9. not return by way of the gate he c. in
Dan. 4. 7. then c. in the magicians, the Chaldeans, 5. 8.
8. but at the last Daniel c. in before me
Jonah 2. 7. my prayer c. in to thy holy temple
Mat. 22. 11. when the king c. in to see the guests
Luke 1. 28. the angel c. in to Mary, and said, hail
7. 45. but this woman since I c. in kissed my feet
Acts 5. 7. his wife not knowing what was done c. in
10. the young men c. in and found her dead
Gal. 2. 4. who c. in privily to spy out our liberty

CAME *near.*

Gen. 19. 9. they pressed, and c. near to break the door
Exod. 14. 20. the one c. not near the other all night
40. 32. when they c. n. to the altar, they washed
Num. 31. 48. officers and captains c. near to Moses
36. 1. the chief of Joseph c. near before Moses
Deut. 1. 22. ye c. near to me every one of you, 5. 23.
Josh. 10. 24. c. near and put your feet on the necks
17. 4. they c. near before Eleazar the priest, 21. 1.
1 Kings 18. 36. at the time of the offering of the evening sacrifice, Elijah c. near and said
2 Kings 4. 27. Gehazi c. near to thrust her away
2 Chron. 18. 23. Zedekiah c. n. and smote Micaiah
Jer. 42. 1. from the least even to the greatest c. near
Dan. 3. 8. Chaldeans c. near and accused the Jews
26. Nebuchadnezzar c. near to the furnace
Acts 9. 3. he c. near to Damascus, there shined light

CAME *nigh.*

Exod. 32. 19. as soon as he c. nigh he saw the calf

Exod. 34. 32. afterward all children of Israel *c. nigh*
2 *Sam* 15. 5. when any *c. nigh* to do him obeisance
Mat. 15. 29. Jesus *c. nigh* to the sea of Galilee
Mark 11. 1. when they *c. nigh* to Jerusalem
Luke 7. 12. when he *c. nigh* to the gate of the city

CAME *over.*

Josh. 4. 22. Israel *c. over* this Jordan on dry land
Judg. 19. 10. the Levite *c. over* against Jebus
Mark 5. 1. they *c. over* to the other side of the sea

CAME *out.*

Gen. 24. 15. behold Rebekah *c. out* with her pitcher
25. 25. first *c. out* red, all over like a hairy garment
38. 28. the midwife said, this *c. out* first
46. 26. all the souls which *c. out* of his loins
Exod. 13. 3. remember the day in which ye *c. out,* 4.
Lev. 9. 24. a fire *c. out* from the Lord, *Num.* 16. 35.
Num. 12. 4. the L. spake suddenly, they three *c. out*
16. 27. Dathan and Abiram *c. out* and stood
20. 11. he smote rock, and water *c. out* abundantly
Deut. 11. 10. not as land of Egypt whence ye *c. out*
Josh. 5. 4. all that *c. out* were circumcised, 5.
6. till all that *c. out* of Egypt were consumed
Judg. 4. 22. Jael *c. out* to meet him, and said, come
1 *Sam.* 4. 16. the man said to Eli, I am he that *c. out* of the army, I fled to-day out of the army
21. 5. about these three days since I *c. out*
2 *Sam.* 2. 23. the spear *c. out* behind him, and he fell
6. 20. Michael *c. out* to meet David, and said
11. 23. the men prevailed against us, and *c. out*
18. 4. and all the people *c. out* by hundreds and by
1 *Kings* 8. 9. when the Lord made a covenant with Israel, when they *c. out* of Egypt, 2 *Chron.* 5. 10.
20. 19. these young men princes of provinces *c. out*
2 *Chron.* 20. 10. not Israel invade, when they *c. out*
Job 1. 21. naked *c.* I *out* of my mother's womb
3. 11. why died I not from the womb? why did I not give up the ghost when I *c. out* of the belly?
Jer. 17. 16. that which *c. out* of my lips was right
Ezek. 1. 4. a whirlwind *c. out* of the north, a cloud
Hab. 3. 14. they *c. out* as a whirlwind to scatter me
Zech. 5. 9. *c. out* two women, and wind in their wings
Mat. 8. 34. the whole city *c. out* to meet Jesus
12. 44. return to house whence I *c. out, Luke* 11. 24.
27. 32. as they *c. out* they found Simon of Cyrene
53. and *c. out* of the graves after his resurrection
Mark 1. 26. unclean spirit had cried, he *c. out,* 9. 26.
6. 34. when he *c. out,* he saw much people
9. 7. a voice *c. out* of the cloud, saying, this is my
Luke 1. 22. when he *c. out* he could not speak to them
4. 35. and he *c. out* of him, and hurt him not
15. 28. therefore *c. out* his father, and entreated
John 16. 27. because ye believed I *c. out* from God
17. 8. they have known that I *c. out* from thee
19. 34. his side, forthwith *c. out* blood and water
Acts 8. 7. for unclean spirits *c. out* of many possessed
16. 18. and the spirit *c. out* the same hour
1 *Cor.* 14. 36. *c.* word of God *out* from you, or to you
Heb. 3. 16. not all that *c. out* of Egypt by Moses
Rev. 7. 14. these *c. out* of great tribulation and washed
14. 15. another angel *c. out* of the temple, 17.
18. another angel *c. out* from the altar
15. 6. the seven angels *c. out* of the temple
19. 5. a voice *c. out* of the throne, praise our God

CAME *to pass.*

Exod. 12. 41. and it *c. to pass* at the end of 430 years, even the self-same day it *c. to pass,* 51.
Deut. 2. 16. so it *c. to pass,* 1 *Sam.* 13. 22. 2 *Kings* 15. 12. *Esth.* 2. 8. *Acts* 27. 44.
Josh. 17. 13. it *c. to pass* when Israel grew strong
21. 45. there failed not any thing; all *c. to pass*
Judg. 13. 20. for it *c. to pass,* 1 *Kings* 11. 4, 15.
15. 1. it *c. to pass,* 2 *Kings* 3. 5. *Neh.* 2. 1. | 4. 1, 7. 6. 1 | 7. 1. *Jer.* 35. 11.
1 *Sam.* 1. 20. it *c. to pass* when the time was come
10. 9. and all those signs *c. to pass* that day
16. 23. it *c. to pass* when the evil spirit from God
2 *Sam.* 2. 1. it *c. to pass* after this, 8. 1. | 10. 1. 2 *Kings* 6. 24. 2 *Chron.* 20. 1.
2 *Kings* 8. 15. and it *c. to pass* on the morrow, 1 *Chron.* 10. 8. *Jer.* 20. 3. *Acts* 4. 5.
Isa. 48. 3. I did them suddenly, and they *c. to pass*
5. before it *c. to pass* I shewed it thee
1 *Thess.* 3. 4. even as it *c. to pass* and ye know

Then CAME.

Exod. 17. 8. *then c.* Amalek and fought with Israel
Num. 27. 1. *then c.* the daughters of Zelophehad
1 *Sam.* 21. 1. *then c.* David to Ahimelech the priest
2 *Sam.* 5. 1. *then c.* all the tribes to David to Hebron
24. 6. *then* they *c.* to Gilead, and numbered people
2 *Kin.* 18. 37. *then c.* Eliakim and Shebna, *Isa.* 36. 22.
2 *Chron.* 1. 13. *then c.* Solomon from his journey
12. 5. *then c.* Shemaiah the prophet to Rehoboam
Ezra 5. 16. *then c.* Sheshbazzar, and laid foundation
Neh. 1. 2. *then* Hanani one of my brethren *c.*
2. 9. *then* I *c.* to the governors beyond the river
Job 30. 26. when I looked for good, *then* evil *c.*
Jer. 19. 14. *then c.* Jeremiah from Tophet, whither
38. 27. *then c.* all the princes to Jeremiah
Ezek. 14. 1. *then c.* certain of the elders of Israel
23. 39. *then* they *c.* the same day into my sanctuary
Mat. 9. 14. *then c.* to him the disciples of John
15. 1. *then c.* to Jesus scribes and Pharisees, saying
12. *then c.* his disciples, and said to him, 17. 19.
25. *then c.* she, and worshipped him, *Mark* 7. 25.
18. 21. *then c.* Peter to him, and said, Lord, how oft
20. 20. *then c.* the mother of Zebedee's children
26. 50. *then c.* they, and laid hands on Jesus
Luke 3. 12. *then c.* also publicans to be baptized
22. 7. *then c.* the day of unleavened bread
John 7. 45. *then c.* the officers to the chief priests
12. 28. *then* there *c.* a voice from heaven, saying
20. 26. *then c.* Jesus, the doors being shut, and stood

They CAME, or CAME *they.*

Gen. 11. 31. *they c.* to Haran and dwelt there
12. 5. and into the land of Canaan *they c.*
22. 9. *they c.* to the place which God told them of
Exod. 16. 35. till *they c.* to a land inhabited
19. 1. same day *c. they* into the wilderness of Sinai
2 *Sam.* 4. 7. when *they c.* he lay on bed, they slew him
1 *Kings* 1. 32. Zadok and Nathan, *they c.* before king
2. 7. so *they c.* to me, when I fled from Absalom
13. 25. *they c.* and told it in city, where old prophet
2 *Kings* 2. 4. I will not leave, so *they c.* to Jericho
6. 4. when *they c.* to Jordan, they cut down wood
20. 14. these men whence *c. they* to thee, *Isa.* 39. 3.
2 *Chron.* 20. 4. out of all Juda *they c.* to seek Lord
29. 17. on eighth day *c. they* to the porch of Lord
Ezra 2. 68. some when *they c.* offered freely
Neh. 13. 21. from that time forth *c. they* no more
Job 6. 20. *they c.* thither and were ashamed
30. 14. *they c.* upon me as a wide breaking in
Psal. 88. 17. *they c.* round about me like water
Jer. 14. 3. *they c.* to the pits and found no water
43. 7. thus *c. they* even to Tahpanhes
Ezek. 23. 40. a messenger was sent, lo *they c.*
Dan. 2. 2. *they c.* and stood before the king
6. 24. or ever *they c.* at the bottom of the den
Mat. 1. 18. before *they c.* together she was found
14. 34. *they c.* into the land of Gennesaret
18. 31. *they c.* and told their Lord all, *Luke* 14. 21.
26. 73. after a while *c. they* that stood by
Mark 1. 45. *they c.* to him from every quarter
3. 13. he called whom he would, and *they c.* to him
Luke 2. 16. *they c.* with haste and found Mary
24. 23. *they c.* saying, that they had seen a vision
John 12. 9. and *they c.* not for Jesus' sake only
Acts 8. 36. *they c.* unto a certain water, eunuch said
12. 10. *they c.* to the iron gate which opened
20. *they c.* with one accord and desired peace
17. 13. *they c.* thither also and stirred up the people
23. 14. *they c.* to the chief priests and elders
33. who when *they c.* to Cesarea, presented Paul
Rev. 7. 13. what are these, and whence *c. they?*

Word of the Lord CAME.

Gen. 15. 1. *word of Lord c.* to Abraham in a vision, 4.
1 *Sam.* 15. 10. *word of Lord c.* to Samuel, saying
2 *Sam.* 24. 11. *c.* the *word of Lord* to Gad, David's
1 *Kings* 6. 11. *word of Lord c.* to Solomon, saying
16. 1. *word of L. c.* to Jehu against Baasha, saying, 7.
17. 2. the *word of Lord c.* unto Elijah, 8. | 18. 1. | 19. 9. | 21. 17, 28.
18. 31. whom *word of L. c.* saying, Israel thy name
2 *Kings* 20. 4. the *word of L. c.* to Isaiah, *Isa.* 38. 4.
1 *Chr.* 17. 3. *word of L. c.* to Nathan || 22. 8. to David
2 *Ch.* 11. 2. *w. of L. c.* to Shemaiah, 12. 7. | 1 *Kings* 12. 22.
Jer. 1. 2. *word of the Lord c.* to Jeremiah, 4. | 2. 1. | 14. 1. | 29. 30. | 33. 1. 19, *Dan.* 9. 2.
Ezek. 1. 3. *word of L. c.* expressly to Ezekiel, 3. 16.
Hos. 1. 1. *word of L. c.* to Hosea || *Joel* 1. 1. *c.* to Joel
Jonah 1. 1. *w. of L. c.* to Jonah, 3. 1.
Mic. 1. 1. *w. of L. c.* to Micah
Zeph. 1. 1. *w. of L. c.* to Zeph. || *Hag.* 1. 1. *c.* by Haggai
Zech. 1. 1. to Zechariah || 7. 4. *c.* of hosts to me, 8. 1.

CAMEL.

Gen. 24. 64. Rebekah saw Isaac, lighted off the *c.*
Lev. 11. 4. these ye shall not eat, the *c. Deut.* 14. 7.
1 *Sam.* 15. 3. but slay infant, ox, and *c.* and ass
Zech. 14. 15. so shall be the plague of the *c.* and ass
Mat. 19. 24. it is easier for a *c.* to go thro' the eye of a needle, *Mark* 10. 25. *Luke* 18. 25.
23. 24. which strain at a gnat and swallow a *c.*

CAMELEON.

Lev. 11. 30. these shall be unclean, the *c.* the lizard

CAMELS.

Gen. 12. 16. Abram had sheep, oxen, she asses, and *c.*
24. 19. I will draw water for thy *c.* also, 44.
30. 43. Jacob had much cattle, asses, and *c.*
31. 34. Rachel put them in the *c.* furniture
37. 25. Ishmaelites came with their *c.* bearing
Exod. 9. 3. hand of the Lord on the *c.* and the oxen
Judg. 6. 5. they and their *c.* without number, 7. 12.
8. 21. took away ornaments on their *c.* necks, 26.
1 *Sam.* 27. 9. David took away *c.* and the apparel
30. 17. save 400 young men who rode on *c.* and fled
1 *Kings* 10. 2. came to Jerusalem with *c.* 2 *Chr.* 9. 1.
2 *Kings* 8. 9. Hazael took a present forty *c.* burden
1 *Chron.* 5. 21. the Reubenites took away of *c.* 50,000
12. 40. they of Zebulun brought bread on *c.*
27. 30. over the *c.* also was Obil the Ishmaelite
Ezra 2. 67. their *c.* were 435. *Neh.* 7. 69.
Esth. 8. 10. he sent letters by post on mules, *c.* 14.
Job 1. 3. his substance also was three thousand *c.*
17. the Chaldeans fell on the *c.* and carried them
Isa. 21. 7. he saw a chariot of asses and of *c.*
30. 6. will carry their treasures on the bunches of *c.*
60. 6. the multitude of *c.* shall cover thee
Jer. 49. 29. they shall take to themselves their *c.*
32. their *c.* shall be a booty, and their cattle
Ezek. 25. 5. I will make Rabbah a stable for *c.*
Mat. 3. 4. John had raiment of *c. hair, Mark* 1. 6.

CAMEST.

Gen. 16. 8. Hagar, Sarai's maid, whence *c.* thou?
24. 5. bring again to the land from whence thou *c.*
27. 33. and I have eaten of all before thou *c.*
Exod. 23. 15. for in it thou *c.* out from Egypt, 34. 18.
Num. 22. 37. wherefore *c.* thou not unto me?
Deut. 2. 37. to the land of Ammon thou *c.* not
16. 3. remember the day thou *c.* thou in haste
1 *Sam.* 13. 11. thou *c.* not within the days appointed
17. 28. Eliab said, why *c.* thou down hither?
2 *Sam.* 11. 10. *c.* thou not from thy journey?
15. 20. whereas thou *c.* but yesterday, should I
1 *Kings* 13. 9. not return by the way thou *c.* 17.
14. art thou the man of God that *c.* from Judah?
2 *Kings* 19. 28. I will turn thee back by the way by which thou *c. Isa.* 37. 29.
Neh. 9. 13. thou *c.* down also on mount Sinai
Isa. 64. 3. thou *c.* down the mountains flowed
Jer. 1. 5. before thou *c.* forth, I sanctified thee
Ezek. 32. 2. and thou *c.* forth with thy rivers
Mat. 22. 12. friend, how *c.* thou in hither not having
John 6. 25. they said, Rabbi, when *c.* thou hither?
16. 30. we believe that thou *c.* forth from God
Acts 9. 17. Jesus appeared to thee in way, as thou *c.*

CAMP.

Exod. 14. 19. the angel of Lord went before the *c.*
16. 13. at even the quails came up and covered *c.*
32. 17. there is a noise of war in the *c.*
27. go thro' the *c.* and slay every man his brother
36. 6. they caused it to be proclaimed thro' the *c.*
Lev. 17. 3. what man killeth any goat in the *c.?*
24. 10. they strove together in the *c.*
Num. 1. 52. Israel shall pitch every one by his own *c.*
2. 3. on the east side shall the *c.* of Judah pitch
Num. 4. 5. when *c.* setteth forward, Aaron shall come
15. as the *c.* is to set forward, after that the sons
11. 1. consumed them in the utmost parts of the *c.*
26. Eldad and Medad prophesied in the *c.*
Deut. 23. 10. he shall not come within the *c.*
14. the Lord walked in the midst of thy *c.*
Josh. 6. 18. and make the *c.* of Israel a curse
Judg. 7. 17. when I come to the outside of the *c.*
13. 25. Spirit of God began to move him in the *c.*
21. 8. there came none to the *c.* from Jabesh
12. young virgins, they brought them to the *c.*
1 *Sam.* 4. 6. the noise of this great shout in the *c.*
13. †23. the standing *c.* of the Philistines went
17. 17. and run to the *c.* to thy brethren
1 *Kings* 16. 16. all Israel made Omri king in the *c.*
2 *Kings* 6. 8. in such and such a place shall be my *c.*
7. 7. they left the *c.* as it was, and fled for life
8. and when these lepers came to the *c.*
19. 35. the angel of the Lord smote in the *c.* of Assyrians, 185,000, *Isa.* 37. 36.
2 *Chron.* 22. 1. the band came with the Arabians to *c.*
Psal. 78. 28. let it fall in the midst of their *c.*
106. 16. they envied Moses also in the *c.*
Ezek. 4. 2. lay siege, set the *c.* also against it
Joel 2. 11. for his *c.* is very great, for he is strong
Rev. 20. 9. compassed the *c.* of the saints about

Into the CAMP.

Lev. 14. 8. after that he shall come *into c.* 16. 26, 28.
Num. 11. 30. Moses gat him *into c.* he and elders
Deut. 23. 11. sun is down, he shall come *into c.* again
1 *Sam.* 4. 7. the Philistines said, God is come *into c.*

Out of the CAMP.

Exod. 19. 17. Moses brought forth people *out of the c.*
Lev. 10. 4. come near, carry your brethren *out of c.*
14. 3. the priest shall go forth *out of the c.* and look
17. 3. what man soever killeth a goat *out of the c.*
24. 23. should bring him that had cursed *out of c.*
Num. 5. 2. command they put every leper *out of c.*
12. 14. let Miriam be shut *out of the c.* seven days
14. 44. the ark and Moses departed not *out of c.*
Deut. 23. 10. unclean person shall go abroad *out of c.*
1 *Sam.* 13. 17. spoilers came *out of c.* of Philistines
2 *Sam.* 1. 2. behold, a man came *out of c.* from Saul
3. he said to him, *out of c.* of Israel am I escaped

Round about the CAMP.

Num. 11. 31. quails fell, spread them *round ab. c.* 32.
Judg. 7. 21. stood every man in place *round ab. c.*

Without the CAMP.

Exod. 29. 14. the flesh of the bullock shalt thou burn *without the c. Lev.* 8. 17. | 9. 11. | 16. 27.
33. 7. pitched tabern. sought Lord, went *without c.*
Lev. 6. 11. and shall carry forth ashes *without the c.*
13. 46. that hath the plague shall dwell *without c.*
Num. 5. 3. every leper shall be put out *without the c.*
15. 35. gatherer of sticks shall be stoned *without c.*
19. 3. bring the red heifer *without c.* and slay her
31. 19. and do ye abide *without the c.* seven days
Deut. 23. 12. thou shalt have a place also *without c.*
Josh. 6. 23. Rahab left her kindred *without the c.*
Heb. 13. 11. bodies of those beasts are burnt *without c.*
13. let us go forth to him *without c.* bearing his

CAMP.

Isa. 29. 3. I will *c.* against thee round about
Jer. 50. 29. all ye that bend the bow *c.* against it
Nah. 3. 17. which *c.* in the hedges in the cold day

CAMPED.

Exod. 19. 2. and there Israel *c.* before the mount

CAMPS.

Gen. 32. †2. he called the name of that place two *c.*
Num. 5. 3. leper put out, that they defile not their *c.*
10. 2. make two trumpets for journeying of the *c.*
Amos 4. 10. I have made stink of your *c.* to come up

CAMPHIRE.

Cant. 1. 14. my beloved is to me as a cluster of *c.*
4. 13. thy plants are an orchard of *c.* with spikenard

CAN.

Gen. 41. 38. Phara. said, *c.* we find such a one as this?
Deut. 31. 2. I *c.* no more go out and come in
2 *Sam.* 12. 23. he is dead, *c.* I bring him back again?
19. 35. *c.* I discern, *c.* I hear voice of singing-men?
Job 6. 6. *c.* that which is unsavoury be eaten?
8. 11. *c.* the rush grow without mire? *c.* the flag?
22. 2. *c.* a man be profitable to God?
13. *c.* he judge through the dark cloud?
36. 29. *c.* any understand the spreading of clouds?
Psal. 78. 19. they said, *c.* God furnish a table?
20. *c.* he give bread also? *c.* he provide flesh?
89. 6. who *c.* be compared? *c.* be likened to Lord?
Prov. 6. 27. *c.* a man take fire in his bosom?
28. *c.* one go on hot coals and not be burnt?
Isa. 46. 7. one shall cry, yet *c.* he not answer
49. 15. *c.* a woman forget her sucking child?
Jer. 2. 32. *c.* a maid forget her ornaments, or a bride
23. 24. *c.* any hide himself in secret places that I
Amos 3. 3. *c.* two walk together except they be agreed?
5. *c.* a bird fall in a snare where no gin is for him?
8. Lord God hath spoken, who *c.* but prophesy?
Mat. 19. 25. who *c.* be saved? *Mark* 10. 26. *Luke* 18. 26.
27. 65. go your way, make it as sure as you *c.*
Mark 2. 19. *c.* the children of bride-chamber fast?
9. 29. this kind *c.* come forth but by prayer
10. 38. *c.* ye drink of the cup that I drink of?
Luke 6. 39. spake a parable, *c.* the blind lead blind?
John 1. 46. *c.* any good come out of Nazareth?
6. 60. this is an hard saying, who *c.* hear it
10. 21. *c.* a devil open the eyes of the blind?
15. 4. no more *c.* ye, except ye abide in me
Acts 10. 47. *c.* any man forbid water, that these
Rom. 8. 7. mind is not subject to law, nor indeed *c.* be
Jam. 2. 14. and have not works, *c.* faith save him?
3. 12. *c.* the fig-tree bear olive-berries? a vine figs?

How CAN.

Deut. 1. 12. *how c.* I alone bear your cumbrance?
1 *Sam.* 16. 2. *how c.* I go, if Saul hear, he will kill me
Esth. 8. 6. *how c.* I endure to see evil or destruction
Job 25. 4. *how c.* a man be justified with God?
Prov. 20. 24. *how c.* a man understand his way?
Eccl. 4. 11. but *how c.* one be warm alone?
Jer. 47. 7. *how c.* it be quiet seeing Lord given charge
† *how canst* thou be quiet seeing Lord given charge
Mat. 12. 34. *how c.* ye being evil speak good things?
John 3. 4. *how c.* a man be born when he is old?

John 3. 9. Nicodemus said, h. can these things be?
6. 52. how c. this man give us his flesh to eat?
14. 5. Thomas said, Lord, how c. we know the way?
Acts 8. 31. how c. I, except some man guide me?

CANNOT.

Isa. 1. 13. the calling of assemblies I c. away with
29. 11. read this; he saith, I c. for it is sealed
Jer. 5. 22. yet the waves c. prevail, c. pass over
18. 6. c. I do with you as this potter, saith Lord?
Dan. 2. 27. secret king demanded, c. astrologers shew
Mat. 16. 3. c. ye discern the signs of the times?
Luke 13. 33. it c. be that a prophet perish out of Jerus.
16. 26. which would pass from hence to you c.
1 Cor. 11. † 20. ye c. eat the Lord's supper
Heb. 9. 5. of which we c. now speak particularly

CANST.

Exod. 33. 20. thou c. not see my face and live
Deut. 28. 27. with itch, whereof thou c. not be healed
Job 33. 5. if thou c. answer me, set thy words in order
Mat. 8. 2. Lord, if thou wilt, thou c. make me clean
Mark 9. 22. if thou c. do any thing, have compassion
Acts 21. 37. chief captain said, c. thou speak Greek?

CANDLE

Is *a long roll or cylinder made of tallow, wax, &c. for giving light*, Jer. 25. 10. Luke 15. 8.
To which are compared, [1] *The reasonable soul, which is as a light set up in man by God, and as his deputy to observe and judge our actions, and to inform and direct us*, Prov. 20. 27. [2] *Ministers, or the gifts and graces which God bestows on men, which are not given them only for their own sakes, but for the good of others also; as when men light a candle, they are not to hide it under a bushel, but to put it on a candlestick that it may communicate its light to all in the house*, Mat. 5. 15. [3] *The favour and blessing of God, which both direct and comfort the soul*, Job 29. 3.
They need no candle, *Rev.* 22. 5. Light, *in its metaphorical notion, signifies*, knowledge, *or* comfort: *The saints in heaven shall have no need of any created beings to help them to either of these; God and Christ shall there fill their souls with knowledge and joy not to be expressed.*

Job 18. 6. his c. shall be put out with him
21. 17. how oft is the c. of the wicked put out?
29. 3. when his c. shined upon my head
Psal. 18. 28. for thou wilt light my c. the Lord my G.
Prov. 20. 27. the spirit of man is the c. of the Lord
24. 20. the c. of the wicked shall be put out
31. 18. her c. goeth not out by night
Jer. 25. 10. and from them the light of the c.
Mat. 5. 15. nor do men light a c. and put it under a bushel, Mark 4. 21. Luke 8. 16. | 11. 33.
Luke 11. 36. when bright shining of a c. giveth light
15. 8. doth not she light a c. and sweep the house
Rev. 18. 23. light of a c. shine no more in thee
22. 5. and they need no c. nor light of the sun

CANDLES.

Zeph. 1. 12. I will search Jerusalem with c.

CANDLESTICK.

In Exod. 25. 31, 32, &c. *we read of the* candlestick *of gold with six branches, which* Moses *made by the command of God to be put into the tabernacle: It was of hammered gold, a talent in weight: It had one foot of the same metal, and a stock with the branches adorned at equal distances with six flowers like lilies, with as many bowls and knops placed alternately: Upon the stock and six branches of the candlestick were the golden lamps which were immoveable, wherein there was put oil and cotton. It was placed on the south side in the holy place, and served to illuminate the altar of perfume, and the table of shew-bread, which were in the same place.*
The seven golden candlesticks represent the church, Rev. 1. 20. *enlightened by the Spirit of God with his seven-fold, or various operations*, Rev. 1. 4. *And a* candlestick *may be an emblem of the church, which has not the light it shews from itself, but only holds it forth from Christ.*

Exod. 25. 31. make c. of pure gold, 37. 17. Num. 8. 4.
33. six branches that came out of the c. 37. 19.
34. in the c. shall be four bowls, 37. 20.
26. 35. thou shalt set the c. over against the table
40. 24. put the c. in the tent of the congregation
Lev. 24. 4. he shall order the lamps on the c.
Num. 3. 31. their charge shall be the ark and c.
4. 9. shall take a cloth and cover the c. of the light
8. 2. the lamps shall give light over against the c.
2 Kings 4. 10. let us set for him there a bed, a table, a c.
1 Chr. 28. 15. lamps of gold, by weight for every c.
2 Chr. 13. 11. also set they in order the c. of gold
Dan. 5. 5. and wrote over against the c. on plaister
Zech. 4. 2. I looked, and behold a c. all of gold
11. two olive-trees on the right side of the c.
Mat. 5. 15. but on a c. and it giveth light to all in the house, Luke 8. 16. | 11. 33.
Mark 4. 21. is a candle brought not to be set on a c.?
Heb. 9. 2. the first, wherein was the c. and the table
Rev. 2. 5. repent, else I will come and remove thy c.

CANDLESTICKS.

1 Kings 7. 49. made the c. of pure gold, 2 Chron. 4. 7.
1 Chron. 28. 15. even the weight for the c. of gold
Jer. 52. 19. he took away the c. spoons, and cups
Rev. 11. 4. the two c. standing before the Lord
See SEVEN.

CANE.

Isa. 43. 24. hast bought me no sweet c. with money
Jer. 6. 20. and the sweet c. from a far country

CANKER, ED.

2 Tim. 2. 17. and their word will eat as doth a c.
Jam. 5. 3. your gold and silver is c. and the rust

CANKER-WORM.

Joel 1. 4. hath c. eaten, and what c. left, 2. 25.
Nah. 3. 15. shall eat thee like c. make thyself as c.
16. the c. spoileth, and fleeth away

CAPTAIN

Is a name applied, [1] *To the king, or prince of a people*, 1 Sam. 9. 16. [2] *To a chief marshal*, Gen. 37. † 36. [3] *To a general, or commander in an army*, Gen. 26. 26. 2 Sam. 5. 8. [4] *To the head of a family, or tribe*, Num. 2. 3. [5] *To the governor of a province*, Hag. 1. † 1. [6] *To such as have the command of a company, consisting sometimes of more, sometimes of fewer, men*, Deut. 1. 15.
Christ Jesus *is called the* Captain of salvation, *Heb.* 2. 10. *He is the author and guide, or leader to salvation. He by his sufferings and death merited salvation for his people; by his word and Spirit fits them for it; he vanquishes all opposers of it; and puts them finally into the actual possession of it in heaven.*

Gen 37. 36. sold Joseph to Potiphar, c. of the guard
40. 4. c. of the guard charged Joseph with them
Num. 2. 3. Nahshon, c. of the children of Israel
5. Nethaneel, c. of the children of Issachar
14. 4. let us make a c. and return, Neh. 9. 17.
Josh. 5. 14. but as c. of the host of the Lord I come
15. the c. of the Lord's host said to Joshua
Judg. 4. 2. c. of Jabin's host was Sisera. 7. 1 Sam. 12. 9.
11. 6. they said to Jephthah, come and be our c.
11. the people made him head and c. over them
1 Sam. 9. 16. shalt anoint him c. over my people, 10. 1.
13. 14. Lord commanded him to be c. over his people
17. 18. carry these ten cheeses to the c. of thousand
22. 2. and David became a c. over them
2 Sam. 5. 2. thou shalt feed, and be a c. over Israel
8. he shall be chief and c. 1 Chron. 11. 6.
19. 13. if thou be not c. of host in room of Joab
23. 19. Abishai was therefore their c.
1 Kings 16. 16. Israel made Omri, c. of the host, king
2 Kings 1. 9. the king sent a c. with his fifty
11. he sent to him another c. with his fifty, 13.
4. 13. wouldest thou be spoken for to the c. of host?
5. 1. Naaman, c. of the host of the king of Syria
9. 5. he said, I have an errand to thee, O c.
15. 25. but Pekah, a c. of his, conspired against him
18. 24. will turn away the face of one c. Isa. 36. 9.
20. 5. and tell Hezekiah the c. of my people
25. 8. came Nebuzar-adan, c. of guard, Jer. 52. 12.
† 19. took away scribe of c. of host, Jer. 52. † 25.
1 Chron. 11. 21. more honourable, for he was their c.
19. 18. killed Shophach c. of the host, 2 Sam. 10. 18.
27. 5. the third c. Benaiah || 7. fourth c. Asahel
8. the fifth c. Shamhuth || 9. the sixth c. Ira
2 Chron. 13. 12. God himself is with us for our c.
Isa. 3. 3. the Lord doth take away the c. of fifty
Jer. 37. 13. a c. of the ward Irijah took Jeremiah
40. 2. the c. of the guard took Jeremiah, and said
5. c. gave victuals and a reward, and let him go
51. 27. call together, appoint a c. against her
Hag. 1. † 1. word came to Zerubbabel, c. of Judah
John 18. 12. then the band and the c. took Jesus
Acts 5. 26. then the c. with officers went and brought
Heb. 2. 10. to make c. of their salvation perfect thro'

CAPTAINS.

Exod. 15. 4. his chosen c. also are drowned in Red sea
Num. 31. 14. Moses was wroth with c. of thousands
Deut. 1. 15. I made wise men c. over thousands
20. 9. shall make c. of the army to lead the people
1 Sam. 8. 12. he will appoint him c. over thousands
22. 7. will son of Jesse make you all c. of thousands?
2 Sam. 18. 5. when the king gave all the c. charge
23. 8. that sat in the seat chief among the c.
† 13. the three c. came to the cave of Adullam
1 Kings 2. 5. thou knowest what Joab did to the c.
9. 22. they were his princes, and c. and rulers
20. 24. take kings away, and put c. in their rooms
22. 33. when the c. perceived that he was not the king of Israel, they turned back, 2 Chron. 18. 32.
2 Kings 11. 15. Jehoiada commanded c. of hundreds
1 Chron. 4. 42. having for c. Pelatiah and Neariah
11. 15. now three of the 30 c. went down to David
12. 34. of Naphtali a thousand c. and with them
2 Chron. 21. 9. Jehoram smote the Edomites and c.
33. 11. Lord brought on them the c. of the host
Neh. 2. 9. the king had sent c. of the army with me
Job 39. 25. the thunder of the c. and the shouting
Jer. 13. 21. for thou hast taught them to be c.
51. 23. with thee will I break in pieces c. and rulers
57. I will make drunk her c. and her rulers
Ezek. 21. 22. c. to open the mouth in the slaughter
23. 6. c. and rulers all desirable young men, 12, 23.
Dan. 3. 27. the c. saw these men on whose bodies
6. 7. the c. have consulted to establish a statute
Nah. 3. 17. and thy c. as the great grasshoppers
Mark 6. 21. Herod on birth-day made supper to his c.
Luke 22. 4. Judas went and communed with the c.
Rev. 19. 18. may eat the flesh of c. and mighty men

CAPTIVE.

Gen. 14. 14. heard that his brother was taken c.
34. 29. their wives took they c. and spoiled all
Exod. 12. 29. unto the first-born of the c. in dungeon
Deut. 21. 10. and thou hast taken them c.
2 Kings 5. 2. and had brought away c. a little maid
6. 22. smite those thou hast taken c. with thy
Isa. 49. 21. I am desolate, a c. and removing to and fro
24. or shall the lawful c. be delivered?
51. 14. the c. exile hasteneth, that he may be loosed
52. 2. loose thyself, O c. daughter of Zion
Amos 6. 7. they shall go c. with the first that go c.
2 Tim. 2. 26. who are taken c. by him at his will

Carry or carried CAPTIVE, *or* CAPTIVES.

Gen. 31. 26. carried away my daughters as c. taken
Num. 24. 22. until Ashur shall carry thee away c.
1 Kings 8. 46. that they carry them away c. 2 Ch. 6. 36.
47. if they bethink themselves in the land whither they were carried c. 2 Chron. 6. 37.
2 Kings 15. 29. Tiglath-pileser carried them c. to
16. 9. he carried the people of Damascus c. to Kir
1 Chron. 5. 6. whom the king of Assyria carried c.
2 Chron. 25. 12. other 10,000 did Judah carry c.
28. 5. they carried away a great multitude c.
8. Israel carried c. of their brethren 200,000
Psal. 106. 46. be pitied of those that carried them c.
137. 3. they that carried us c. required of us a song
Jer. 13. 17. because the Lord's flock is carried c.
19. Judah shall be wholly carried away c.
20. 4. he shall carry them c. to Babylon, and slay
24. 5. I will acknowledge them that are carried c.
27. 20. took not when he carried c. Jeconiah
29. 4. saith the Lord to all that are carried c.
Jer. 29. 14. I will bring you again into the place whence I caused you to be carried away c.
40. 1. Judah which were carried away c. 52. 27.
7. of them that were not carried c. to Babylon
41. 10. Ishmael carried away c. all the residue
43. 12. shall carry the Egyptians c. and array himself
52. 29. Neb. carried c. from Jerusalem 832 persons
30. carried away c. of the Jews 745 persons
Lam. 4. † 22. he will carry thee c. for thy sins
Ezek. 6. 9. nations, whither they shall be carried c.
Dan. 11. 8. and shall also carry c. into Egypt
Amos 1. 6. because they carried c. the captivity
Obad. 11. in the day that strangers carried c. his

Carrying CAPTIVE.

Jer. 1. 3. to the carrying away of Jerusalem c.

Lead, or led, CAPTIVE.

Judg. 5. 12. lead thy captivity c. thou son of Abinoam
1 Kings 8. 48. in land of their enemies who led them c.
2 Chron. 30. 9. compassion before them that lead c.
Psal. 68. 18. thou hast led captivity c. Eph. 4. 8.
Jer. 22. 12. die in place whither they led him c.
Amos 7. 11. Israel shall be led c. out of their land
Nah. 2. 7. Huzzab shall be led c. her maids shall lead
Luke 21. 24. shall be led away c. into all nations
2 Tim. 3. 6. lead c. silly women laden with sins

CAPTIVES.

Num. 31. 9. Israel took all the women of Midian c.
12. they brought the c. || 19. purify your c.
Deut. 21. 11. seest among the c. a beautiful woman
32. 42. mine arrows drunk with the blood of the c.
1 Sam. 30. 5. David's two wives were taken c.
2 Kings 24. 14. he carried from Jerusalem 10,000 c.
2 Chron. 28. 11. hear me, and deliver the c. again
13. and said, ye shall not bring in the c. hither
Isa. 14. 2. shall take them c. whose c. they were
20. 4. lead away the Ethiopians c. young and old
45. 13. he shall let go my c. not for price nor reward
49. 25. the c. of the mighty shall be taken away
61. 1. to proclaim liberty to the c. Luke 4. 18.
Jer. 48. 46. thy sons and daughters are taken c.
50. 33. and all that took them c. held them fast
Ezek. 1. 1. as I was among the c. by the river Chebar
16. 53. I will bring again the captivity of thy c.
Dan. 2. 25. I have found a man of the c. of Judah

CAPTIVITY.

God generally punished the vices and infidelities of his people by different captivities or servitudes whereinto he permitted them to fall. After the deliverance of the Israelites *out of* Egypt, *there are reckoned six bondages or captivities during the government of Judges: The first under* Chushan-rishathaim, *king of* Mesopotamia, *which continued about eight years*, Judg. 3. 8. *The second under* Eglon, *king of* Moab, *from which they were delivered by* Ehud, *Judg.* 3. 14, 15. *The third under the* Philistines, *out of which they were rescued by* Shamgar, *Judg.* 3. 31. *The fourth under* Jabin, *king of* Hazor, *from which they were delivered by* Deborah *and* Barak, *Judg.* 4. 22, 23. *The fifth under the* Midianites, *from which* Gideon *freed them*, Judg. 6. 2, 12. *The sixth under the* Ammonites *and* Philistines, *during the judicatures of* Jephthah, Ibzan, Elon, Abdon, Eli, Samson, Samuel.
The greatest and most remarkable captivities of the Hebrews, *were those of* Judah *and* Israel, *which happened under the kings of each of these kingdoms.*
Tiglath-pileser, *king of* Assyria, *in the year of the world* 3264, *took several cities belonging to the kingdom of* Israel, *and carried away a great number of captives, principally from the tribes of* Reuben, Gad, *and the half tribe of* Manasseh, 2 *Kings* 15. 29. *Next to him* Shalmaneser *took and destroyed* Samaria, *after a siege of three years, in* 3283, *and transplanted the tribes which had been spared by* Tiglath-pileser, *to the provinces beyond the* Euphrates, 2 *Kings* 18. 9, 10, 11. *And it is generally believed that there was no return from this captivity, and that the ten tribes never came back again after their dispersion.*
As to the captivities of Judah; *in the fifth year of* Rehoboam, *son of* Solomon, Shishak, *king of* Egypt, *came up against* Jerusalem *with a numerous army, and sacked the city, took away the treasures out of the house of the Lord, and out of the house of the king*, 2 Chron. 12. 2.
Afterwards, in the reign of Hezekiah, Sennacherib, *king of* Assyria, *sent a great army and laid close siege to it. Upon this* Hezekiah *fortified and repaired it*, 2 Chron. 32. 5. *and the hand of the Lord being with him, for he was a pious good king, the Assyrians, after a time, were forced to raise the siege, not being able to take the city, yet after this, it was taken and plundered three several times by* Nebuchadnezzar *king of* Babylon; first, *in the reign of* Jehoiakim; again, *in that of* Jehoiachin, *his son; and a third time, in that of* Zedekiah, *his brother; when he burnt the whole city, and carried away all the people to* Babylon, *where they remained seventy years*, Jer. 25. 12.
Upon their being permitted to return by Cyrus, *king of* Persia, *after they had remained in captivity seventy years*, Zerubbabel *rebuilt the temple, and* Nehemiah *the city; and* Ezra *the priest and scribe restored the law. And thus they stood, till the time of* Antiochus Epiphanes, *who plundered the city, burned the law, and profaned the temple.*
But all was soon after set right again by the valorous conduct of Judas Maccabeus; *and they continued in a flourishing condition for many years; till* Hyrcanus *and* Aristobulus, *two brothers, contending about the crown*, Pompey, *who at that time was at the head of the* Roman *army in* Syria, *took advantage of this dissension, and seized the city; which* Antigonus, *the son of* Aristobulus, *by the assistance of the* Parthians, *soon after recovered.*
From him it was presently after taken by the first Herod, *who, by the favour of the* Romans, *and the assistance of their Proconsul of* Syria, *was declared king thereof.*

Thenceforward it continued in subjection sometimes to the Herods, *but mostly to governors sent from* Rome, *till about forty years after the* Jews *had crucified* Christ, *because of the rebellious disposition of its inhabitants, it was, together with the temple, utterly destroyed and levelled with the ground, by* Titus, *the son of* Vespasian Cæsar. *After which, the* Jews *never attempted more to return to it.*

It is said, Job 42. 10. that the Lord turned the captivity of Job, *that is, he brought him out of that state of bondage in which he had been so long held by Satan and his own spirit, and out of all his distresses and miseries.*

In Eph. 4. 8. He led captivity captive. *He led them captive who had led others into captivity,* Our Lord Jesus Christ, *the head of the church by his ascension and victory over death, Satan and sin, conquered and triumphed over them and all our spiritual enemies.*

Num. 21. 29. he hath given his daughters into *c.*
Deut. 21. 13. she shall put the raiment of *c.* from her
30. 3. Lord will turn thy *c.* and have compassion
Judg. 18. 30. till the day of the *c.* of the land
2 *Kings* 24. 15. those carried he into *c.* to Babylon
25. 27. in thirty-seventh year of the *c. Jer.* 52. 31.
1 *Chr.* 5. 22. they dwelt in their steads until the *c.*
6. 15. Jehozadak went into *c.* when the Lord carried
2 *Chron.* 6. 37. if they pray to thee in the land of *c.*
38. if they return to thee in the land of their *c.*
29. 9. our sons and our wives are in *c.* for this
Ezra 9. 7. have been delivered to *c.* and to a spoil
Neh. 1. 2. the Jews which were left of the *c.*
4. 4. give them for a prey in the land of their *c.*
Esth. 2. 6. Mordecai carried away with the *c.*
Job 42. 10. and the Lord turned the *c.* of Job
Psal. 14. 7. when the Lord bringeth back the *c.* 85. 1.
78. 61. and delivered his strength into *c.*
126. 1. when the Lord turned again the *c.* of Zion
4. turn again our *c.* O Lord, as streams in south
Isa. 5. 13. therefore my people are gone into *c.*
20. † 4. so Assyria shall lead away the *c.* of Egypt
22. 17. Lord will carry thee away with a mighty *c.*
46. 2. but themselves are gone into *c.*
49. † 25. *c.* of the mighty shall be taken away
Jer. 15. 2. such as are for the *c.* to the *c.* 43. 11.
24. † 5. as good figs, so will I acknowledge the *c.*
29. 14. I will turn away your *c.* saith the Lord, 30. 3. | 32. 44. | 33. 7, 11, 26.
20. hear ye, all ye of the *c.* || 28. this *c.* is long
22. shall be taken up a curse by all the *c.* of Judah
31. send to all them of the *c.* saying, thus saith Lord
30. 10. and thy seed from the land of their *c.* 46. 27.
48. 11. Moab is at ease, nor hath he gone into *c.*
† 46. woe to thee, O Moab, thy sons are taken into *c.*
Lam. 1. 3. Judah is gone into *c.* because of affliction
5. her children are gone into *c.* before the enemy
2. 14. they have not discovered, to turn away thy *c.*
4. 22. he will no more carry thee away into *c.*
Ezek. 1. 2. was the fifth year of Jehoiachin's *c.*
3. 11. get to them of the *c.* and speak to them
15. then I came to them of the *c.* 11. 24.
11. 25. I spake to them of the *c.* all things
12. 7. I brought forth my stuff, as stuff for *c.*
16. 53. when I shall bring again their *c.* the *c.* of Sodom, and the *c.* of Samaria, and her daugh.
25. 3. when they went into *c.* thou saidst, Aha
33. 21. in the twelfth year of the *c.* one escaped
39. 23. that the house of Israel went into *c.*
40. 1. in the five and twentieth year of our *c.*
Dan. 6. 13. Daniel which is of the *c.* of Judah
11. 33. shall fall by *c.* and by spoil many days
Hos. 6. 11. when I returned the *c.* of my people
Amos 4. † 10. slain young men with *c.* of your horses
Obad. 20. the *c.* of this host, the *c.* of Jerusalem
Mic. 1. 16. for they are gone into *c.* from thee
Nah. 3. 10. No went into *c.* her children dashed
Hab. 1. † 7. from them shall proceed the *c.* of these
9. and they shall gather the *c.* as the sand
Zeph. 2. 7. the Lord shall turn away their *c.* 3. 20.
Zech. 6. 10. take of them of the *c.* even of Heldai
Rom. 7. 23. and bringing me into *c.* to the law of sin
2 *Cor.* 10. 5. bringing into *c.* every thought to obed.
See CAPTIVE.

Bring CAPTIVITY.

Ezra 1. 11. he did *bring* up with them of the *c.*
Psal. 53. 6. when God *bringeth* back *c.* of his people
Jer. 30. 18. I will *bring* again the *c.* of Jacob's tents
31. 23. when I shall *bring* again their *c.*
48. 47. yet will I *bring* again the *c.* of Moab
49. 6. I will *bring* again the *c.* of Ammon
39. I will *bring* again the *c.* of Elam, saith the L.
Ezek. 29. 14. I will *bring* again the *c.* of Egypt
39. 25. now will I *bring* again the *c.* of Jacob
Joel 3. 1. when I *bring* again the *c.* of Judah
Amos 9. 14. I will *bring* again the *c.* of my people

Children of CAPTIVITY.

Ezra 4. 1. heard that *childr. of c.* builded the temple
6. 16. the rest of *children of c.* kept the dedication
19. the *child. of c.* kept passover on the 14th day
20. killed passover for *children of c.* and brethren
10. 7. they made proclamation to the *children of c.*
16. the *children of c.* did so, and all were separated
Dan. 5. 13. Daniel which art of *childr. of c.* of Judah

Go into CAPTIVITY.

Deut. 28. 41. thy sons and daughters shall *go into c.*
Jer. 20. 6. thou and all in thine house shall *go in. c.*
22. 22. eat thy pastors and thy lovers shall *go in. c.*
30. 16. adversaries, every one of them shall *go in. c.*
46. 19. O daughter, furnish thyself to *go into c.*
48. 7. Chemosh *go into c.* || 49. 3. their kings *go into c.*
Ezek. 12. 4. shalt go forth, as they that *go into c.*
30. 17. and these cities shall *go into c.*
18. as for Egypt her daughters shall *go into c.*
Amos 1. 5. the people of Syria shall *go into c.* unto Kir
15. their king shall *go into c.* he and his princes
5. 5. for Gilgal shall surely *go into c.* and Beth-el
27. therefore will I cause you to *go into c.* beyond
7. 17. Israel shall surely *go into c.* forth of his land
9. 4. and though they *go into c.* before their enemies
Zech. 14. 2. and half of the city shall *go into c.*
Rev. 13. 10. he that leadeth into *c.* shall *go into c.*

Out of CAPTIVITY.

Ezra 2. 1. now these went up *out of c. Neh.* 7. 6.
3. 8. all that were come up *out of c. Neh.* 8. 17.
6. 21. the children of Israel which were come again *out of c.* kept the feast with joy
8. 35. were come *out of c.* offered to God of Israel

CARBUNCLE, S.

Exod. 28. 17. the first row shall be a *c.* 39. 10.
Isa. 54. 12. and I will make thy gates of *c.*
Ezek. 28. 13. the topaz and *c.* were thy covering

CARCASE.

Lev. 5. 2. touch *c.* of unclean thing, is unclean
7. † 24. fat of the *c.* may be used, but not eaten
11. 8. their *c.* ye shall not touch, *Deut.* 14. 8.
17. † 15. every soul that eateth a *c.* shall wash
Deut. 28. 26. thy *c.* shall be meat unto fowls of air
Josh. 8. 29. that they should take his *c.* down
Judg. 14. 8. to see the *c.* of the lion, honey in the *c.*
1 *Kings* 13. 22. thy *c.* shall not come to the sepulchre
24. his *c.* cast in the way, a lion stood by the *c.*
2 *Kings* 9. 37. the *c.* of Jezebel shall be as dung
Isa. 14. 19. cast out as a *c.* trodden under feet
Mat. 24. 28. where the *c.* is, there will the eagles be

CARCASES.

Gen. 15. 11. when the fowls came down on the *c.*
Lev. 11. 11. ye shall have their *c.* in abomination, 26.
26. 30. I will cast your *c.* on the *c.* of your idols
Num. 14. 29. your *c.* shall fall in the wilderness
1 *Sam.* 17. 46. I will give the *c.* of the Philistines
Isa. 5. 25. their *c.* were torn in midst of the streets
34. 3. their stink shall come up out of their *c.*
66. 24. look on *c.* of them that have transgressed
Jer. 7. 33. and the *c.* of this people shall be meat for the fowls of heaven, 16. 4. | 19. 7.
16. 18. they have filled mine inheritance with the *c.*
Ezek. 6. 5. I will lay the *c.* of Israel before idols
43. 7. my name no more defile by *c.* of their kings
9. let them put the *c.* of their kings far from me
Nah. 3. 3. and there is a great number of *c.*
Heb. 3. 17. grieved with them whose *c.* fell in wild.

CARE

Is applied, [1] *To God,* (1) *In general, in respect of his care for all his creatures,* Mat. 6. 26, 30. 1 Cor. 9. 9. (2) *In particular, in respect of the godly,* 1 Pet. 5. 7. [11] *To men, and is either lawful,* (1) *When they endeavour to please God, to mourn for their sins, and amend what has been amiss in their conduct,* 2 Cor. 7. 11. (2) *When they are concerned and solicitous about the welfare of others, and the salvation of their souls,* 2 Cor. 7. 12. Phil. 2. 20. (3) *When they moderately take thought for the things of this present life, resigning themselves at the same time to the will and providence of God,* 1 Pet. 5. 7. *Or unlawful,* (1) *When they are careful about things that are not in any case warrantable, as to make provision for the flesh, to fulfil the lusts thereof,* Rom. 13. 14. (2) *When they have a perplexing, distrustful care about things which in their own nature are lawful and warrantable, as for one to be so diligent in his particular calling as to be careless of the worship of God, or to distrust his providence,* Mat. 13. 22. Luke 10. 41.

We are not careful to answer thee in this matter, *Dan.* 3. 16. *The case is so plain, that it admits no dispute, or deliberation; it requires no answer at all, at least in words, but rather in deeds of constancy and courage on our parts.*

1 *Sam.* 10. 2. thy father hath left the *c.* of the asses
2 *Kings* 4. 13. hast been careful for us with all this *c.*
Jer. 49. 31. the nation that dwelleth without *c.*
Ezek. 4. 16. shall eat bread by weight and with *c.*
Mat. 13. 22. the *c.* of this world chokes the word
Luke 10. 34. he took *c.* of him || 35. take *c.* of him
1 *Cor.* 9. 9. doth God take *c.* for oxen?
12. 25. should have the same *c.* one for another
2 *Cor.* 7. 12. but that our *c.* for you might appear
8. 16. put the same earnest *c.* in Titus for you
11. 28. besides the *c.* of all the churches
1 *Tim.* 3. 5. how shall he take *c.* of the church of God
1 *Pet.* 5. 7. casting your *c.* on him, for he careth for

CARE, ED.

2 *Sam.* 18. 3. for if we flee, they will not *c.* for us
Psal. 142. 4. refuge failed, no man *c.* for my soul
Luke 10. 40. dost thou not *c.* that my sister left me?
John 12. 6. this he said, not that he *c.* for the poor
Acts 18. 17. and Gallio *c.* for none of those things
1 *Cor.* 7. 21. art called being a servant, *c.* not for it
Phil. 2. 20. who will naturally *c.* for your state

CAREFUL.

2 *Kings* 4. 13. behold thou hast been *c.* for us with
Jer. 17. 8. and shall not be *c.* in the year of drought
Dan. 3. 16. O Nebuch. we are not *c.* to answer thee
Luke 10. 41. Martha, thou art *c.* about many things
12. † 29. live not in *c.* suspense
Phil. 4. 6. *c.* for nothing, but by prayer let requests
10. wherein ye were *c.* but lacked opportunity
Tit. 3. 8. they might be *c.* to maintain good works

CAREFULLY.

Deut. 15. 5. if thou *c.* hearken unto the Lord
2 *Chron.* 36. † 15. sending his messengers *c.*
Mic. 1. 12. for the inhabitant of Maroth waiteth *c.*
Phil. 2. 28. I sent him therefore the more *c.*
Heb. 12. 17. though he sought it *c.* with tears

CAREFULNESS.

Ezek. 12. 18. drink thy water with trembling and *c.*
19. they shall eat their bread with *c.* and drink
1 *Cor.* 7. 32. but I would have you without *c.*
2 *Cor.* 7. 11. what *c.* it wrought in you, what clearing

CARELESS.

Judg. 18. 7. the five men saw how they dwelt *c.*
Isa. 32. 9. hear my voice, ye *c.* daughters, give ear
10. shall be troubled, ye *c.* women || 11. ye *c.* ones
Ezek. 30. 9. to make the *c.* Ethiopians afraid

CARELESSLY.

Isa. 47. 8. hear now this, thou that dwellest *c.*
Ezek. 39. 6. send a fire among them that dwell *c.*
Zeph. 2. 15. this is the rejoicing city that dwelt *c.*

CARES.

Mark 4. 19. the *c.* of this world choke the word
Luke 8. 14. and they are choked with *c.* and riches
21. 34. lest be overcharged with the *c.* of this life

CAREST, ETH, ING.

Deut. 11. 12. a land which the Lord thy God *c.* for
1 *Sam.* 9. 5. lest my father leave *c.* for the asses
Mat. 22. 16. thou art true, nor *c.* thou for any man
Mark 4. 38. Master, *c.* thou not that we perish?
12. 14. know thou art true, and *c.* for no man
John 10. 13. because an hireling *c.* not for the sheep
1 *Cor.* 7. 32. that is unmarried *c.* for the things, 34.
33. that is married, *c.* for things of the world, 34.
1 *Pet.* 5. 7. casting your care on him, for he *c.* for you

CARNAL

Signifies, *Belonging to the flesh, fleshly,* or *sensual.* This word is applied, [1] *To such as are in a natural unregenerated state, who are enemies to God, and given to sensual pleasures,* John 3. 6. Rom. 8. 7. [2] *To one who is in part renewed by the grace of God, yet so as that there are remainders of sin and corruption, which oppose and war against this gracious principle,* Rom. 7. 14. *Such a one is carnal,* in part, *in regard of the remainders of corruption;* and comparatively, *in respect of the purity of the law of God.* [3] *To the ceremonial law, which consisted of such rites, ceremonies, and ordinances, as only related to the body and the purifying of the flesh, but did not reach the soul,* Heb. 9. 10. [4] *To worldly things, such as silver and gold, and other things needful for the sustentation of the body,* Rom. 15. 27. 1 Cor. 9. 11.

Rom. 7. 14. law is spiritual, but I am *c.* sold under
8. 7. because the *c.* mind is enmity against God
15. 27. duty is to minister to them in *c.* things
1 *Cor.* 3. 1. but as unto *c.* even to babes in Christ
3. for ye are yet *c.* || 4. are ye not *c.*?
9. 11. is it a great thing if we reap your *c.* things?
2 *Cor.* 10. 4. the weapons of our warfare are not *c.*
Heb. 7. 16. made not after the law of a *c.* command.
9. 10. which stood in *c.* ordinances imposed on them

CARNALLY.

Lev. 18. 20. shalt not lie *c.* with thy neighbour's wife
19. 20. whosoever lieth *c.* with a bond-maid
Num. 5. 13. and a man lie with her *c.* and it be hid
Rom. 8. 6. for to be *c.* minded is death, but to be sp.

CARPENTER, S.

2 *Sam.* 5. 11. Hiram sent *c.* to David, 1 *Chron.* 14. 1.
2 *Kings* 12. 11. they laid it out to *c.* and builders
2 *Chron.* 24. 12. they hired *c.* to repair, *Ezra* 3. 7.
Isa. 41. 7. so the *c.* encouraged the goldsmith
44. 13. the *c.* stretcheth out his rule, he marketh
Jer. 24. 1. the *c.* and smiths he carried away, 29. 2.
Zech. 1. 20. and the Lord shewed me four *c.*
Mat. 13. 55. they said, is not this the *c.* son?
Mark 6. 3. is not this the *c.* the son of Mary?

CARRIAGE, S.

Num. 4. † 24. this is the *c.* of the Gershonites
Judg. 18. 21. the Danites, and the *c.* before them
1 *Sam.* 17. † 20. David came to the place of the *c.*
22. David left his *c.* with the keeper of the *c.*
Isa. 10. 28. at Michmash he hath laid up his *c.*
46. 1. your *c.* were heavy laden, they are a burd.
Acts 21. 15. we took up our *c.* went up to Jerusalem

CARRY

Signifies, [1] *To bear, or remove.* 2 Sam. 15. 29. [2] *To protect and keep safely,* Isa. 46. 3, 4. [3] *To lead, or drive,* Gen. 31. 18. [4] *To make to ride,* 1 Chron. 13. † 7.

Gen. 37. 25. Ishmaelites going to *c.* spicery to Egypt
42. 19. go ye, *c.* corn for the famine of your houses
43. 11. *c.* the man a present, a little balm, honey
12. the money brought, *c.* it again in your hand
44. 1. fill the sacks with as much as they can *c.*
45. 27. he saw waggons Joseph sent to *c.* him, 46. 5
50. 25. ye shall *c.* up my bones, *Exod.* 13. 19.
Exod. 33. 15. thy presence go not, *c.* us not up hence
Lev. 10. 4. *c.* your brethren out of the camp
Num. 11. 12. should say, *c.* them in thy bosom
Deut. 14. 24. so that thou art not able to *c.* it
Josh. 4. 3. *c.* the twelve stones over with you
1 *Sam.* 17. 18. *c.* these ten cheeses to the captain
20. 40. Jonathan said, go, *c.* them to the city
2 *Sam.* 19. 18. a ferry-boat to *c.* over king's house.
1 *Kings* 18. 12. the Spirit of the Lord shall *c.* thee
2 *Kings* 4. 19. his father said, *c.* him to his mother
9. 2. and *c.* Jehu to an inner chamber
17. 27. saying, *c.* thither one of the priests
1 *Chron.* 10. 9. sent to the Philistines to *c.* tidings
15. 2. none ought to *c.* the ark but the Levites
23. 26. the Levites shall no more *c.* the tabernacle
2 *Chr.* 2. 16. thou shalt *c.* the wood up to Jerusalem
36. 6. bound him to *c.* him to Babylon, *Jer.* 39. 7.
Ezra 5. 15. *c.* these vessels into the temple at Jerus.
7. 15. *c.* the silver and gold freely offered to God of
Eccl. 10. 20. a bird of the air shall *c.* the voice
Isa. 23. 7. her own feet shall *c.* her afar off to sojourn
30. 6. they will *c.* their riches on young asses
40. 11. he shall *c.* the lambs in his bosom
46. 4. and even to hoary hairs will I *c.* you
7. they *c.* him and set him in his place
Jer. 20. 5. will I take them and *c.* them to Babylon
39. 14. that Gedaliah should *c.* Jeremiah home
Ezek. 22. 9. in thee are men *c.* tales to shed blood
Mark 6. 55. and began to *c.* about in beds the sick
11. 16. not suffer any to *c.* a vessel thro' the temple
Luke 10. 4. *c.* neither purse, nor scrip, nor shoes
John 5. 10. it is not lawful for thee to *c.* thy bed
21. 18. and *c.* thee whither thou wouldest not

CARRY *away.*

2 *Kings* 18. 11. king of Assyria did *c. away* Israel
25. 11. the fugitives did Nebuzar-adan *c. away*
2 *Chron.* 20. 25. found more than they could *c. away*
Job 15. 12. why doth thine heart *c.* thee *away*?
Psal. 49. 17. when he dieth he shall *c.* nothing *away*
Eccl. 5. 15. nothing left which he may *c. a.* in hand
Isa. 5. 29. they shall *c.* the prey *away* safe
15. 7. which they have laid up shall they *c. away*
22. 17. behold the Lord will *c.* thee *away*
41. 16. fan them, and wind shall *c.* them *away*, 57. 13.
Lam. 4. 22. he will no more *c.* thee *away*, O Zion
Ezek. 38. 13. art thou come to *c. away* silver?
Acts 7. 43. and I will *c.* you *away* beyond Babylon
See CAPTIVE.

CARRY *back.*

2 *Sam.* 15. 25. *c. back* the ark of God into the city

1 Kings 22. 26. c. Micaiah b. to Amon, 2 Chr. 18. 25.

CARRY forth.

Exod. 12. 46. shalt not c. forth aught of the passover
14. 11. dealt thus with us to c. us f. out of Egypt
Lev. 4. 12. even the whole bullock shall he c. f. 21.
6. 11. c. f. ashes without the camp, 14. 45. ‖ 16. 27.
2 Chr. 29. 5. c. forth the filthiness out of holy place
Jer. 17. 22. nor c. forth a burden on the sabbath-day
Ezek. 12. 6. in their sight, c. it forth in the twilight

CARRY out.

Gen. 47. 30. Jacob said, thou shalt c. me out of Egypt
Deut. 28. 38. shall c. much seed out, gather little in
1 Kings 21. 10. then c. him out and stone him
22. 34. he said, c. me out of the host, 2 Chr. 18. 33.
2 Chron. 29. 16. c. it out abroad into brook Kidron
Ezek. 12. 5. dig through the wall, and c. out thereby
Acts 5. 9. the feet at the door, and shall c. thee out
1 Tim. 6. 7. it is certain we can c. nothing out

CARRIED.

Gen. 46. 5. the sons of Israel c. Jacob, 50. 13.
Lev. 10. 5. c. them in their coats out of the camp
Josh. 4. 8. they c. the stones over with them
Judg. 16. 3. he c. them up to the top of an hill
1 Sam. 5. 8. let the ark of God be c. unto Gath
2 Sam. 6. 10. David c. the ark aside, 1 Chr. 13. 13.
15. 29. Abiathar c. the ark of God to Jerusalem
1 Kings 17. 19. he c. him into a loft and laid him
21. 13. they c. Naboth forth and stoned him
2 Kings 7. 8. and c. thence silver and gold and hid it
9. 28. his servants c. him in a chariot, 23. 30.
20. 17. that which thy fathers have laid up in store shall be c. to Babylon, Isa. 39. 6.
23. 4. c. the ashes of the vessels to Beth-el
24. 13. he c. out thence all the treasures
25. 7. they bound Zedekiah and c. him to Babylon
2 Chron. 24. 11. c. the chest to his place again
28. 15. and c. all the feeble of them upon asses
33. 11. who took and c. Manasseh to Babylon
34. 16. Shaphan c. the book to the king
36. 4. Necho took and c. Jehoahaz to Egypt
Job 5. 13. the counsel of the froward is c. headlong
10. 19. I should have been c. from the womb
Psal. 46. 2. tho' the mountains be c. into the sea
Isa. 46. 3. remnant of Israel which are c. from womb
49. 22. thy daughters shall be c. on thy shoulders
53. 4. surely he hath borne our griefs, c. our sorrows
63. 9. he bare and c. them all the days of old
Jer. 27. 22. be c. into Babylon, 28. 3. | 52. 11, 17.
Ezek. 17. 4. he c. twigs into a land of traffic
37. 1. and c. me out in the Spirit of the Lord
Dan. 1. 2. which he c. into the land of Shinar
Hos. 10. 6. it shall be also c. into Assyria for a present
12. 1. make a covenant, and oil is c. into Egypt
Joel 3. 5. and ye have c. into your temples
Luke 7. 12. behold, there was a dead man c. out
16. 22. and the beggar was c. by the angels
24. 51. was parted from them, and c. up into heaven
Acts 3. 2. one lame from his mother's womb was c.
5. 6. young men c. Ananias out and buried him
7. 16. our fathers were c. over into Sychem
8. 2. devout men c. Stephen to his burial
21. 34. commanded him to be c. into the castle
Eph. 4. 14. and c. about with every wind of doctrine
Heb. 13. 9. be not c. about with divers doctrines
2 Pet. 2. 17. clouds that are c. with a tempest
Jude 12. clouds without water, c. about of winds

See CAPTIVE.

CARRIED away.

Gen. 31. 18. Jacob c. away all his cattle and goods
26. hath c. away my daughters as captives
1 Sam. 30. 2. slew not any, but c. them away, 18.
2 Kings 17. 6. c. Israel away into Assyria, 23.
11. heathen whom the Lord c. away before them
28. then one of the priests, whom they had c. away
24. 14. c. away all Jerusalem and all the princes
15. c. away Jehoiachin to Babylon and his wives
25. 21. so Judah was c. away out of their land
1 Chron. 5. 26. Tilgath-pilneser c. away Reubenites
6. 15. when the Lord c. away Judah and Jerusalem
9. 1. who were c. away for their transgression
2 Chron. 12. 9. Shishak c. away the shields of gold
14. 13. Asa and the people c. a. much spoil, 21. 17.
15. they c. away sheep and camels in abundance
Ezra 2. 1. these that had been c. away, Neh. 7. 6.
9. 4. transgression of those that had been c. a. 10. 6.
10. 8. separated from congregation of those c. away
Job 1. 17. fell upon the camels, and c. them away
Jer. 29. 4. whom I have caused to be c. away captive
Dan. 2. 35. iron, gold broken, and winds c. them a.
Nah. 3. 10. No was c. away into captivity
Mat. 1. 11. about time they were c. away to Babylon
Mark 15. 1. c. Jesus a. and delivered him to Pilate
1 Cor. 12. 2. were Gentiles c. a. to those dumb idols
Gal. 2. 13. Barnabas was c. away with dissimulation
Rev. 12. 15. might cause her to be c. away of the flood
17. 3. so he c. me away in the Spirit, 21. 10.

CARRIEST, ETH, ING.

Gen. 45. † 23. ten asses c. the good things of Egypt
1 Sam. 10. 3. one c. three kids, c. three loaves of bread
Job 21. 18. are as chaff that the storm c. away
27. 21. the east wind c. the rich man away
Psal. 78. 9. Ephraim c. bows, turned back in battle
90. 5. thou c. them away as with a flood
Mat. 1. 17. till the c. into Babylon, from the c.
Acts 5. 10. they c. her and buried her by her husband
Rev. 17. 7. the mystery of the beast that c. her

CART.

1 Sam. 6. 7. make a new c. and tie the kine to the c.
2 Sam. 6. 3. they set the ark on a new c. and brought
1 Chron. 13. 7. and Uzza and Ahio drave the c.
Isa. 28. 28. nor break corn with the wheel of the c.
Amos 2. 13. as a c. is pressed that is full of sheaves

CART-ROPE.

Isa. 5. 18. woe to them that draw sin as with a c.-rope

CART-WHEEL.

Isa. 28. 27. nor is c.-wheel turned about on cummin

CARVED, ING, INGS.

Exod. 31. 5. Bezaleel in c. of timber, 35. 33.
Judg. 18. 18. men went and fetched the c. image
1 Kings 6. 18. the cedar of the house within was c.
29. he c. all the walls of house round about, 32.
2 Chron. 33. 7. he set a c. image in the house of God
2 Chron. 33. 22. Amon sacrificed to all the c. images
34. 3. Josiah purged Judah from the c. images
4. he cut down the c. images, and brake in pieces
Psal. 74. 6. they break down the c. work at once
Prov. 7. 16. I have decked my bed with c. work

CASE, S.

Exod. 5. 19. officers did see that they were in evil c.
Deut. 19. 4. this is the c. of the slayer who shall flee
22. 1. thou shalt in any c. bring them again
24. 13. in any c. thou shalt deliver the pledge
Psal. 144. 15. happy that people that is in such a c.
Jer. 2. † 25. but thou saidst, is the c. desperate?
12. † 1. yet let me reason the c. with thee
Mat. 5. 20. ye shall in no c. enter the kingdom
19. 10. if the c. of the man be so with his wife
John 5. 6. and had been now long time in that c.
1 Cor. 7. 15. is not under bondage in such c.

CASEMENT.

Prov. 7. 6. at the window I looked through my c.

CASSIA

Is *a sweet spice mentioned by* Moses *as an ingredient in the composition of the holy oil, which was to be made use of for anointing the sacred vessels of the tabernacle*, Ex. 30. 24. *The* Hebrew *calls it* Kidda; *and the* Septuagint Iris. *This aromatic is said to be the bark of a tree very like cinnamon, and grows in the* Indies *without cultivation.*

Exod. 30. 24. take of c. 500 shekels for the oil
Psal. 45. 8. all thy garments smell of aloes and c.
Ezek. 27. 19. c. and calamus were in thy market

CAST.

Luke 22. 41. he was withdrawn about a stone's c.

CAST

Signifies, [1] *To fling, or throw*, Dan. 3. 6. [2] *To miscarry, or bring forth before the time*, Gen. 31. 38. Exod. 23. 26. [3] *To melt, make, or frame*, Exod. 25. 12.

They cast him out, John 9. 34. *They put him out of the synagogue, or excommunicated him.*

Thou hast cast me behind thy back, 1 Kings 14. 9. *Thou hast despised, disregarded, and forsaken me, and my commands and worship, as men do things which they cast behind their backs.*

Exod. 38. 27. of talents of the silver were c. sockets
Job 18. 8. for he is c. into a net by his own feet
Psal. 22. 10. I was c. upon thee from the womb
76. 6. chariot and horse are c. into a dead sleep
140. 10. let him be c. into the fire, into pits
Prov. 16. 33. the lot is c. into the lap, but the
Isa. 25. 7. the face of the covering c. over all people
Jer. 22. 28. are c. into a land which they know not
38. 11. and took thence old c. clouts and rags
12. put now these old c. clouts under thy arm
Ezek. 15. 4. the vine-tree is c. into the fire for fuel
Dan. 3. 6. be c. into the midst of a fiery furnace
21. these were c. into the midst of the furnace
6. 7. he shall be c. into the den of lions, 16.
Jonah 2. 4. then I said, I am c. out of thy sight
Mat. 4. 12. Jesus heard that John was c. into prison
5. 25. deliver thee to judge, and be c. into prison
29. not that thy whole body be c. into hell, 30.
6. 30. and to-morrow is c. into the oven, Luke 12. 28.
21. 21. say to mountain, be thou c. into the sea
Mark 9. 42. better he were c. into the sea, Luke 17. 2.
45. having two eyes, feet, to be c. into hell, 47.
Luke 3. 9. hewn down, c. into the fire, Mat. 3. 10. | 7. 19.
23. 19. and for murder was c. into prison, 25.
John 3. 24. for John was not yet c. into prison
Acts 27. 26. howbeit, we must be c. on a certain island
Rev. 8. 7. hail and fire were c. on the earth
8. a mountain burning was c. into the sea
12. 13. dragon saw that he was c. unto the earth
19. 20. these both were c. alive into the lake
20. 10. the devil was c. into the lake of fire
14. death and hell were c. into the lake of fire
15. not found in the book of life, c. into the lake

CAST.

Gen. 21. 15. Hagar c. the child under a shrub
31. 38. thy she goats have not c. their young
37. 20. let us slay him, and c. him into some pit
39. 7. his master's wife c. her eyes upon Joseph
Exod. 1. 22. every son ye shall c. into the river
4. 3. said, c. it, and he c. the rod on the ground
25. Zipporah c. the foreskin at his feet
10. 19. took locusts and c. them into the Red sea
15. 4. Pharaoh's chariots he c. into the sea
25. when he had c. the tree into the waters
22. 31. not eat flesh torn of beasts, c. it to the dogs
23. 26. there shall nothing c. their young, nor be
25. 12. shall c. four rings of gold, 37. 3, 13. | 38. 5.
32. 19. Moses c. tables out of his hand, and brake
24. I c. into the fire, there came out this calf
Num. 19. 6. priest c. cedar wood into midst of burning
35. 22. c. any thing on him without laying wait
23. seeing him not, and c. it on him that he die
Deut. 29. 28. the Lord c. them into another land
Josh. 8. 29. c. king of Ai at the gate of the city
10. 27. c. them into the cave wherein had been hid
Judg. 8. 25. c. every one the ear-rings of his prey
9. † 17. for my father c. his life far
53. a woman c. a piece of millstone, 2 Sam. 11. 21.
1 Sam. 18. 11. Saul c. the javelin, 20. 33.
2 Sam. 16. 6. Shimei c. stones at David and his serv.
13. Shimei cursed, and threw stones and c. dust
18. 17. they c. Absalom into a great pit in the wood
20. 12. Joab's man c. a cloth upon Amasa
1 Kings 7. 46. in plain of Jordan c. them, 2 Chr. 4. 17.
14. 9. and thou hast c. me behind thy back
19. 19. Elijah c. his mantle upon Elisha
2 Kings 2. 16. lest the Spirit c. him on some mountain
21. he went to spring and c. the salt in there
3. 25. on every good piece of land c. each his stone
4. 41. then bring meal, and he c. it into the pot
6. 6. he c. in the stick, and the iron swam
9. 25. c. him in the portion of field of Naboth, 26.
13. 21. c. the man into the sepulchre of Elisha
23. neither c. he them from his presence as yet
19. 18. have c. their gods into the fire, Isa. 37. 19.
32. nor c. a bank against it, Isa. 37. 33.
Neh. 9. 26. and c. thy law behind their backs
Esth. 3. 7. they c. Pur, that is, the lot, before Haman
Esth. 9. 24. Haman had c. Pur, that is, the lot
Job 20. 23. God shall c. the fury of his wrath on him
27. 22. God shall c. upon him and not spare
29. † 17. I c. the spoil out of his teeth
30. 19. he hath c. me into the mire and am become
40. 11. c. abroad the rage of thy wrath
Psal. 55. 3. they c. iniquity on me, and hate me
22. c. thy burden on the Lord, he shall sustain thee
74. 7. they have c. fire into thy sanctuary
78. 49. he c. on them the fierceness of his wrath
Prov. 1. 14. c. in thy lot among us, let us all have
Eccl. 11. 1. c. thy bread on the waters, for shalt find
Isa. 2. 20. a man shall c. his idols to the bats
38. 17. thou hast c. all my sins behind thy back
Jer. 26. 23. c. Urijah's body into the graves of people
36. 23. c. it into the fire that was on the hearth
38. 6. they c. Jeremiah into the dungeon, 9.
41. 7. Ishmael slew, and c. them into the pit
Lam. 3. 53. cut off my life, and c. a stone upon me
Ezek. 7. 19. they shall c. their silver in the streets
11. 16. altho' I have c. them far off among heathen
23. 35. because thou hast c. me behind thy back
28. 17. I will c. thee to the ground, I will lay thee
Dan. 3. 20. and to c. them into the fiery furnace
24. did not we c. three men bound into the fire?
6. 24. c. them into the den of lions, their children
Jonah 2. 3. for thou hadst c. me into the deep
Mic. 4. 7. I will make her c. off, a strong nation
7. 19. thou wilt c. all their sins into the sea
Nah. 3. 6. I will c. abominable filth on thee
Zech. 5. 8. c. it into the ephah, c. the weight
11. 13. c. it to the potter, c. them to the potter
Mal. 3. 11. nor vine c. her fruit before time in field
Mat. 3. 10. is hewn down and c. into the fire, 7. 19.
5. 29. pluck it out and c. it from thee, 30. | 18. 8, 9.
7. 6. nor c. your pearls before swine, lest they
15. 26. children's bread, and c. it to dogs, Mark 7. 27.
17. 27. c. an hook, and take up fish first cometh up
18. 30. c. him into prison, till he pay the debt
22. 13. c. him into outer darkness, 25. 30.
27. 44. the thieves c. the same in his teeth
Mark 9. 22. oft-times it hath c. him into the fire
11. 7. c. their garments on him, Luke 19. 35.
12. 4. another servant, and at him they c. stones
41. c. money into the treasury, Luke 21. 4.
43. this poor widow hath c. more in than all, 44.
Luke 12. 5. who hath power to c. into hell, fear him
19. 43. thy enemies shall c. a trench about thee
John 8. 7. let him first c. a stone at her
21. 7. Peter did c. himself into the sea
Acts 12. 8. c. thy garment about thee, follow me
16. 23. they c. Paul and Silas into prison
27. 43. who could swim c. themselves first into sea
1 Cor. 7. 35. not that I may c. a snare upon you
Rev. 2. 10. devil should c. some of you into prison
14. who taught Balak to c. a stumbling-block
22. I will c. her into a bed, and them that commit
4. 10. the elders c. their crowns before the throne
18. 21. like a mill-stone, and c. it into the sea

CAST away.

Lev. 26. 44. I will not c. them away nor abhor them
Judg. 15. 17. c. away the jaw-bone out of his hand
2 Sam. 1. 21. the shield of the mighty is c. away
2 Kings 7. 15. vessels the Syrians had c. away in haste
2 Chron. 29. 19. vessels Ahaz in his reign did c. away
Job 8. 4. have c. them away for their transgression
20. behold God will not c. away a perfect man
Psal. 2. 3. let us c. away their cords from us
51. 11. me not away from thy presence
Eccl. 3. 5. a time to c. away stones, and gather, 6.
Isa. 5. 24. because they have c. away the law
30. 22. shall c. them away as a menstruous cloth
31. 7. every man shall c. away his idols of silver
41. 9. I have chosen thee, and not c. thee away
Jer. 7. 29. cut thy hair, and c. it away, O Jerusalem
33. 26. then will I c. away the seed of Jacob
Ezek. 18. 31. c. away from you all your transgressions
20. 7. c. away every man abominations of his eyes
8. they did not c. away the abominations of eyes
Hos. 9. 17. my God will c. them away, because
Mat. 13. 48. gathered the good, but c. the bad away
Luke 9. 25. if a man lose himself, or be c. away
Rom. 11. 1. hath God c. away his people, God forbid
2. God hath not c. away his people, he foreknew
Heb. 10. 35. c. not away your confidence which hath

CAST-AWAY.

1 Cor. 9. 27. lest that I myself should be a cast-away

CAST down.

Exod. 7. 10. Aaron c. down his rod ‖ 12. they c. down
Josh. 10. 11. Lord c. down great stones upon them
Judg. 6. 28. altar of Baal was c. down and the grove
1 Kings 18. 42. Elijah c. himself down on the earth
2 Chron. 25. 8. God hath power to help and c. down
12. and c. them down from the top of the rock
Neh. 6. 16. they were c. down in their own eyes
Job 18. 7. his own counsel shall c. him down
22. 29. when men are c. down, then say, lifting up
29. 24. light of my countenance they c. not down
41. 9. shall not one be c. down at the sight of him?
Psal. 17. 13. O Lord, disappoint him, c. him down
36. 12. they are c. down and shall not be able to rise
37. 14. bent their bow to c. d. poor and needy
24. though he fall, he shall not be utterly c. down
42. 5. why art thou c. down, O my soul, 11. | 43. 5.
6. O my God, my soul is c. down within me
56. 7. in thine anger c. down the people, O Lord
62. 4. consult to c. him down from his excellency
89. 44. thou hast c. his throne down to the ground
102. 10. thou hast lifted me up, and c. me down
Prov. 7. 26. for she hath c. down many wounded
Isa. 28. 2. the Lord shall c. down with his hand
Jer. 6. 15. time I visit, they shall be c. down, 8. 12.
Lam. 2. 1. c. down to the earth the beauty of Israel
Ezek. 6. 4. I will c. down your slain before your idols
19. 12. thy mother was c. down to the ground
31. 16. when I c. the Assyrian down to hell
32. 18. wail for Egypt, and c. her d. and daughters
Dan. 7. 9. I beheld till the thrones were c. down
8. 7. the he-goat c. down the ram to the ground
10. it c. down some of the host, and of the stars
11. sanctuary was c. d. ‖ 12. c. d. truth to ground
11. 12. he shall c. down many ten thousands

Mat. 4. 6. if thou Son of God, *c.* thyself *d. Luke* 4. 9.
15. 30. *c.* them *down* at Jesus' feet, and he healed
27. 5. he *c. down* the pieces of silver in the temple
Luke 4. 29. they might *c.* Jesus *down* headlong
2 *Cor.* 4. 9. we are *c. down*, but not destroyed
7. 6. God that comforteth those that are *c. down*
2 *Pet.* 2. 4. but *c.* the angels *down* to hell
Rev. 12. 10. the accuser of our brethren is *c. down*

CAST *forth.*

Neh. 13. 8. I *c. f.* all the household stuff of Tobias
Psal. 144. 6. *c. forth* lightning, and scatter them
Jer. 22. 19. Jehoiakim *c. forth* beyond the gates
Ezek. 32. 4. I will *c.* thee *forth* upon the open field
Hos. 14. 5. he shall *c. forth* his roots as Lebanon
Jonah 1. † 4. the Lord will *c. forth* a great wind
5. mariners *c. f.* the wares in ship into the sea
12. *c.* me *f.* into the sea, so shall the sea be calm
15. they took Jonah and *c.* him *forth* in o the sea
Mark 7. 26. would *c. forth* devil out of her daughter
John 15. 6. he is *c. forth* as a branch and withered

CAST *lots.*

Lev. 16. 8. Aaron shall *c. lots* on the two goats
Josh. 18. 10. Joshua *c. lots* for them in Shiloh
1 *Sam.* 14. 42. *c. lots* between me and Jonathan
1 *Chron.* 26. 13. they *c. lots* as well small as great
Psal. 22. 18. they part my garments and *c. lots* upon my vesture, *Mat.* 27. 35. *John* 19. 24.
Isa. 34. 17. he hath *c.* the *lot* for them
Joel 3. 3. and they have *c. lots* for my people
Obad. 11. in the day foreigners *c. lots* upon Jerus.
Jonah 1. 7. come and let us *c. lots* that we may know
Nah. 3. 10. and they *c. lots* for her honourable men

CAST *off.*

2 *Kings* 23. 27. I will *c. off* this city Jerusalem
1 *Chron.* 28. 9. if forsake, he will *c.* thee *off* for ever
2 *Chr.* 11. 14. for Jeroboam and sons had *c.* them *off*
Job 15. 33. and shall *c. off* his flower as the olive
Psal. 43. 2. why dost thou *c.* me *off?* why go I?
44. 9. thou hast *c. off.* 60. 1, 10. | 89. 38. | 108. 11.
23. awake, O Lord, arise, *c.* us not *off* for ever
71. 9. *c.* me not *off* in the time of old age
74. 1. O God, why hast thou *c.* us *off* for ever?
77. 7. will the Lord *c. off* for ever?
94. 14. Lord will not *c. off* his people, *Lam.* 3. 31.
Jer. 28. 16. I will *c.* Hananiah *off* from the earth
31. 37. I will *c. off* the seed of Israel, 33. 24.
Lam. 2. 7. the Lord hath *c. off* his altar, abhorred
Hos. 8. 3. Israel hath *c. off* the thing that is good
5. thy calf, O Samaria, hath *c.* thee *off*
Amos 1. 11. because Edom did *c. off* all pity
Zech. 10. 6. shall be as though I had not *c.* them *off*
Acts 22. 23. as they cried and *c. off* their clothes
Rom. 13. 12. let us *c. off* the works of darkness
1 *Tim.* 5. 12. because they have *c. off* their first faith

CAST *out.*

Gen. 21. 10. *c. out* this bondwoman and her son
Exod. 34. 24. I will *c. out* the nations before thee
Lev. 18. 24. nations are defiled which I *c. out* before you, 20. 23. *Deut.* 7. 1.
Deut. 9. 17. I *c.* the two tables *out* of my two hands
Josh. 13. 12. these did Moses smite, and *c.* them *out*
2 *Sam.* 20. 22. they *c. out* Sheba's head to Joab
1 *Kings* 9. 7. this house will I *c. out*, 2 *Chron.* 7. 20.
21. 26. as did the Amorites, whom the Lord *c. out* before the children of Israel, 2 *Kings* 16. 3.
2 *Kings* 10. 25. the captains *c.* them *out* and went
17. 20. till he had *c.* them *out* of his sight, 24. 20.
2 *Chron.* 13. 9. have ye not *c. out* priests of the Lord
20. 11. to come to *c.* us *out* of thy possession
Neh. 1. 9. if ye turn, though there were of you *c. out*
Job 20. 15. God shall *c.* them *out* of his belly
39. 3. they bow themselves, they *c. out* their sorrows
Psal. 5. 10. *c.* them *out* in their transgressions
18. 42. I did *c.* them *out* as the dirt in the streets
44. 2. how thou didst afflict people and *c.* them *out*
60. 8. over Edom will I *c. out* my shoe, 108. 9.
78. 55. he *c. out* the heathen before them, 80. 8.
Prov. 22. 10. *c. out* the scorner, and contention go out
Isa. 14. 19. but thou art *c. out* of thy grave, like an
16. 2. as a wandering bird *c. out* of the nest
26. 19. and the earth shall *c. out* the dead
34. 3. their slain also shall be *c. out* and stink come
58. 7. that thou bring the poor that are *c. out*
66. 5. brethren that *c.* you *out* for my name's sake
Jer. 7. 15. I will *c.* you *out* of my sight, as I have *c. out*
9. 19. because our dwellings have *c.* us *out*
15. 1. *c.* them *out* of my sight, 23. 39. | 52. 3.
16. 13. therefore will I *c.* you *out* of this land
22. 26. I will *c.* thee *out*, and thy mother that bare
36. 30. his dead body shall be *c. out* in the day
51. 34. Nebuchadnezzar hath *c.* me *out*
Ezek. 16. 5. but thou wast *c. out* in the open field
28. 16. will *c.* thee as profane *out* of mount. of God
Amos 8. 8. the land shall be *c. out* and drowned
Mic. 2. 9. the women of my people have ye *c. out*
Zeph. 3. 15. the Lord hath *c. out* thine enemy
Zech. 1. 21. to *c. out* the horns of the Gentiles
9. 4. the Lord will *c.* her *out*, and smite her power
Mat. 5. 13. salt unsavoury to be *c. out*, *Luke* 14. 35.
7. 5. hypocrite, first *c. out* the beam, *Luke* 6. 42.
22. Lord, have we not in thy name *c. out* devils?
8. 12. the children of the kingdom shall be *c. out*
16. and he *c. out* the spirits with his word
31. if thou *c.* us *out*, suffer us to go into swine
9. 33. when the devil was *c. out* the dumb spake
10. 1. gave them power against spirits to *c.* them *out*
8. heal the sick, raise the dead, *c. out* devils
12. 24. not *c. out* devils but by Beelzeb. *Luke* 11. 18.
26. if Satan *c. out* Satan, divided against himself
28. but if I by the Spirit of God *c. out* devils
15. 17. goeth into belly, and is *c. out* into draught
17. 19. why could not we *c.* him *out?* *Mark* 9. 28.
21. 12. *c. out* all that sold, *Mark* 11. 15. *Luke* 19. 45.
39. *c.* him *out* of vineyard, *Mark* 12. 8. *Luke* 20. 15.
Mark 1. 34. healed and *c. out* many devils, 39. | 6. 13.
3. 15. and have power to heal and *c. out* devils
23. he said to them, how can Satan *c. out* Satan?
16. 9. Magdalene, *out* of whom he had *c.* seven devils
17. in my name shall they *c. out* devils
Luke 6. 22. *c. out* your name as evil, for Son of man
11. 20. if I with the finger of God *c. out* devils
13. 32. I *c. out* devils, and do cures to-day and

Luke 20. 12. they wounded him also, and *c.* him *out*
John 6. 37. him that cometh I will in no wise *c. out*
9. 34. dost thou teach us? and they *c.* him *out*
12. 31. now shall the prince of this world be *c. out*
Acts 7. 19. so that they *c. out* their young children
21. when Moses was *c. out* Pharaoh's daughter took
58. they *c.* Stephen *out* of the city and stoned him
27. 19. third day we *c. out* the tackling of the ship
29. *c.* four anchors *out* ‖ 38. *c. out* wheat into sea
Gal. 4. 30. *c. out* the bondwoman and her son
Rev. 12. 9. and the great dragon was *c. out*, the devil
15. the serpent *c. out* of his mouth waters, 16.

Lord CAST *out.*

1 *Kings* 14. 24. which the *Lord c. out* before children of Israel, 2 *Kings* 16. 3. 2 *Chron.* 28. 3. | 33. 2.
2 *Kings* 17. 8. the *Lord c. out* before Israel, 21. 2.
Zech. 9. 4. behold, the *Lord* will *c.* her *out* and smite

CAST *up.*

2 *Sam.* 20. 15. they *c. up* a bank against the city
Isa. 57. 14. *c.* ye *up*, prepare the way, 62. 10.
20. troubled sea, whose waters *c. up* mire and dirt
Jer. 18. 15. to walk in paths, in a way not *c. up*
50. 26. *c.* her *up* as heaps, and destroy her utterly
Lam. 2. 10. *c. up* dust on their heads, *Ezek.* 27. 30.
Dan. 11. 15. king of the north shall *c. up* a mount

CASTEST, ETH.

Job 15. 4. yea, thou *c.* off fear and restrainest [prayer
21. 10. their cow calveth and *c.* not her calf
Psal. 50. 17. seeing thou *c.* my words behind thee
73. 18. thou *c.* them down into destruction
88. 14. why *c.* thou off my soul? why hidest face?
147. 6. the Lord *c.* the wicked down to the ground
17. he *c.* forth his ice like morsels, who can stand
Prov. 10. 3. he *c.* away the substance of the wicked
19. 15. slothfulness *c.* into a deep sleep, an idle soul
21. 22. *c.* down the strength of the confidence
26. 18. as a madman *c.* fire-brands, arrows, and death
Jer. 6. 7. as a fountain so she *c.* out her wickedness
Hos. 9. † 14. give them a womb that *c.* the fruit
Mat. 9. 34. he *c.* out devils, *Mark* 3. 22. *Luke* 11. 15.
1 *John* 4. 18. no fear in love, but perfect love *c.* fear
3 *John* 10. and *c.* them out of the church
Rev. 6. 13. even as a fig-tree *c.* her untimely figs

CASTING.

2 *Sam.* 8. 2. he smote Moab, *c.* them down to ground
1 *Kings* 7. 37. the bases, all of them had one *c.*
Ezra 10. 1. weeping and *c.* himself down before house
Job 6. 21. ye see my *c.* down, and are afraid
Psal. 74. 7. by *c.* down dwelling-place of thy name
89. 39. and profaned his crown by *c.* it to the ground
Mic. 6. 14. and thy *c.* down shall be in midst of thee
Mat. 4. 18. Peter and Andrew *c.* a net into the sea
27. 35. parted his garments, *c.* lots, *Mark* 15. 24.
Mark 9. 38. we saw one *c.* out devils, *Luke* 9. 49.
Luke 21. 1. he saw the rich men *c.* their gifts into
2. he saw also a poor widow *c.* in two mites
Rom. 11. 15. if *c.* away of them be the reconciling
2 *Cor.* 10. 5. *c.* down imaginations and every thing
1 *Pet.* 5. 7. *c.* all your care on him, for he careth for

CASTLE.

1 *Chron.* 11. 5. David took *c.* of Zion, city of David
7. David dwelt in the *c.* the city of David
Prov. 18. 19. their contentions are like bars of a *c.*
Acts 21. 34. the chief captain commanded Paul to be carried into the *c.* 37. | 22. 24. | 23. 10.
23. 16. he went and entered into the *c.* and told Paul

CASTLES.

Gen. 25. 16. names of Ishmael's sons by their *c.*
Num. 31. 10. they burnt their goodly *c.* with fire
1 *Chron.* 6. 54. these the priests' *c.* in their coasts
27. 25. over treasures, and in *c.* Jehonathan
2 *Chron.* 17. 12. Jehoshaphat built in Judah *c.*
27. 4. Jotham in the forest built *c.* and towers

CASTOR: *see* SIGN.

CATCH.

Exod. 22. 6. if fire break out and *c.* in thorns
Judg. 21. 21. and *c.* you every man his wife
1 *Kings* 20. 33. now the men did hastily *c.* it
2 *Kings* 7. 12. we shall *c.* them alive, and get into city
Psal. 10. 9. in wait to *c.* the poor, he doth *c.* the poor
35. 8. let his net that he hath hid *c.* himself
109. 11. let the extortioner *c.* all he hath
Jer. 5. 26. they lay wait, they set a trap, they *c.* men
Ezek. 19. 3. and it learned to *c.* the prey, 6.
Hab. 1. 15. they *c.* them in their net and gather
Mark 12. 13. send Herodians to *c.* him in his words
Luke 5. 10. from henceforth thou shalt see men
11. 54. seeking to *c.* something out of his mouth

CATCHETH, ING.

Lev. 17. 13. who *c.* any beast or fowl may be eaten
Ezek. 1. † 4. a fire *c.* itself, and brightness
Mat. 13. 19. the devil *c.* away what was sown
John 10. 12. the wolf *c.* and scattereth the sheep

CATERPILLER, S.

1 *Kings* 8. 37. if there be any *c.* 2 *Chron.* 6. 28.
Psal. 78. 46. he gave their increase to the *c.*
105. 34. he spake, and *c.* came without number
Isa. 33. 4. your spoil like the gathering of the *c.*
Jer. 51. 14. I will fill thee with men as with *c.*
27. cause the horses come up as the rough *c.*
Joel 1. 4. what canker-worm left hath the *c.* eaten
2. 25. I will restore the ears the *c.* hath eaten

CATTLE.

Gen. 1. 25. God made the *c.* after their kind
3. 14. Lord God said, thou art cursed above all *c.*
7. 21. all flesh died, both of fowl and *c.* and beast
8. 1. God remembered Noah, and *c.* with him in ark
9. 10. I establish my covenant with fowls, *c.*
13. 2. Abram was very rich in *c.* silver, and gold
30. 40. Jacob put them not to Laban's *c.*
31. 9. God hath taken away the *c.* of our father
43. these *c.* are my *c.* and all thou seest is mine
34. 5. his sons were with the *c.* in the field
46. 32. for their trade hath been to feed *c.*
47. 6. then make them rulers over my *c.*
17. Joseph gave bread in exchange for *c.*
Exod. 9. 4. shall sever betw. *c.* of Isr. and *c.* of Egypt
20. made his servants and *c.* flee into the houses
12. 29. Lord smote all the first-born of the *c.*
Lev. 1. 2. ye shall bring your offering of the *c.*
Num. 3. 41. take *c.* of the Levites instead of all
20. 19. if I and my *c.* drink, I will pay for it

Num. 32. 4. is a land for *c.* and thy servants have *c.*
Deut. 2. 35. the *c.* we took for a prey, 3. 7.
Josh. 8. 2. only the *c.* shall ye take for a prey
27. only the *c.* Israel took for a prey, 11. 14.
1 *Kings* 1. 9. Adonijah slew oxen and *c.* 19, 25.
1 *Chron.* 28. † 1. David assembled stewards over *c.*
Job 1. † 3. his *c.* also was seven thousand sheep
† 10. his *c.* was increased in the land
36. 33. the *c.* also concerning the vapour
Psal. 50. 10. the *c.* upon a thousand hills is mine
104. 14. he causeth the grass to grow for the *c.*
148. 10. beasts and all *c.* praise the Lord
Eccl. 2. 7. had great possessions of great and small *c.*
Isa. 7. 25. and for the treading of lesser *c.*
43. 23. thou hast not brought me the small *c.*
46. 1. their idols were upon the beasts and the *c.*
Jer. 9. 10. nor can men hear the voice of the *c.*
Ezek. 34. 17. I judge between *c.* and *c.* 20, 22.
Hag. 1. 11. I called for a drought upon land and *c.*
Zech. 2. 4. for the multitude of men and *c.* therein
13. 5. men taught me to keep *c.* from my youth
Luke 17. 7. having servant feeding *c.* will say to him
John 4. 12. Jacob, his children drank, and his *c.*

Much CATTLE.

Gen. 30. 43. Jacob increased and had *much c.*
Exod. 12. 38. Israel went out of Egypt with *much c.*
Deut. 3. 19. for I know that ye have *much c.*
Josh. 22. 8. return to your tents with very *much c.*
2 *Chron.* 26. 10. Uzziah had *much c.* in the plains
Jonah 4. 11. spare Nineveh, wherein is *much c.*

Our CATTLE.

Exod. 10. 26. *our c.* also shall go with us
17. 3. to kill us, our children, and *our c.* with thirst
Num. 20. 4. that we and *our c.* should die there
32. 16. we will build sheepfolds here for *our c.*
26. all *our c.* shall be there in the cities of Gilead
Josh. 21. 2. give us cities with suburbs for *our c.*
Neh. 9. 37. have dominion over our bodies and *our c.*
10. 36. to bring also first-born of our sons and *our c.*

Their CATTLE.

Gen. 34. 23. shall not *their c.* and substance be ours
Num. 31. 9. slew Midianites, and took spoil of *their c.*
35. 3. the suburbs shall be for *their c. Josh.* 14. 4.
Judg. 6. 5. the Midianites came up with *their c.*
1 *Sam.* 23. 5. David fought, and brought away *their c.*
1 *Chron.* 5. 9. because *their c.* were multiplied
7. 21. because they came down to take away *their c.*
Psal. 78. 48. he gave up *their c.* also to the hail
107. 38. he suffered not *their c.* to decrease
Jer. 49. 32. their camels a booty, *their c.* a spoil

Thy CATTLE.

Gen. 30. 29. thou knowest how *thy c.* was with me
31. 41. I served thee six years for *thy c.*
Exod. 9. 3. hand of the Lord is on *thy c.* in the field
19. send therefore now and gather *thy c.*
20. 10. servant nor *thy c.* do any work, *Deut.* 5. 14.
34. 19. every firstling among *thy c.* is mine
Lev. 19. 19. let not *thy c.* gender with a diverse kind
25. 7. sabbath of the land shall be meat for *thy c.*
Deut. 11. 15. I will send grass in fields for *thy c.*
28. 4. blessed shall be the fruit of *thy c.* 11. | 30. 9.
51. he shall eat the fruit of *thy c.* and thy land
Isa. 30. 23. that day shall *thy c.* feed in large pastures

Your CATTLE.

Gen. 47. 16. give *your c.* give you for *your c.*
Lev. 26. 22. if ye will not hearken, will destroy *y. c.*
Deut. 3. 19. *your c.* shall abide in cities, *Josh.* 1. 14.
7. 14. male nor female shall be barren among *y. c.*
2 *Kings* 3. 17. that ye may drink, both ye and *y. c.*

CAUGHT.

Gen. 22. 13. behold, behind him a ram *c.* by horns
39. 12. she *c.* him by garment, saying, lie with me
Exod. 4. 4. put forth his hand, and *c.* the serpent
Num. 31. 32. rest of the prey the men of war had *c.*
Judg. 1. 6. *c.* Adoni-bezek, and cut off his thumbs
8. 14. *c.* a young man of the men of Succoth, and said
15. 4. Samson went and *c.* three hundred foxes
21. 23. took wives of them danced, whom they *c.*
1 *Sam.* 17. 35. I *c.* him by his beard and slew him
2 *Sam.* 2. 16. and they *c.* every one his fellow
18. 9. Absalom's head *c.* hold of the oak
1 *Kings* 1. 50. and Adonijah *c.* hold on the altar
2. 28. Joab *c.* hold on the horns of the altar
11. 30. Ahijah *c.* the new garment and rent it
2 *Kings* 4. 27. the Shunammite *c.* Elisha by the feet
2 *Chron.* 22. 9. they *c.* Ahaziah and brought him
Prov. 7. 13. so she *c.* him, and kissed him, and said
Jer. 50. 24. O Babylon, thou art found and also *c.*
Mat. 14. 31. Jesus *c.* Peter, and said unto him
21. 39. the husbandmen *c.* him and cast him out
Mark 12. 3. they *c.* the servant and beat him
Luke 8. 29. oftentimes it *c.* him, and he was bound
John 21. 3. they went, and that night *c.* nothing
Acts 6. 12. they came upon Stephen and *c.* him
8. 39. the Spirit of the Lord *c.* away Philip
16. 19. they *c.* Paul and Silas, and drew them
26. 21. for these causes the Jews *c.* me in the temple
27. 15. when the ship was *c.* we let her drive
2 *Cor.* 12. 2. I knew a man *c.* up to the third heaven
4. how he was *c.* up into paradise, and heard words
16. being crafty, I *c.* you with guile
1 *Thess.* 4. 17. we shall be *c.* up together with them
Rev. 12. 5. her child was *c.* up to God, to his throne

CAUL, S.

Exod. 29. 13. the *c.* that is above the liver, 22. *Lev.* 3. 4, 10, 15. | 4. 9. | 7. 4. | 8. 16, 25. | 9. 10, 19.
Isa. 3. 18. the Lord will take away their *c.* and tires
Hos. 13. 8. will rend the *c.* of their heart and devour

CAUSE

Signifies, [1] *A ground, reason, or motive,* 1 Sam. 17. 29. [2] *A suit, action, or controversy,* Exod. 22. 9. Isa. 1. 23. [3] *Sake, or account,* 2 Cor. 7. 12.

Exod. 22. 9. the *c.* of both shall come before judges
23. 2. nor speak in a *c.* to decline after many
3. nor shalt thou countenance a poor man in his *c.*
6. nor wrest the judgment of the poor in his *c.*
Num. 16. 11. for which *c.* thou and all thy company are gathered together against the Lord
27. 5. Moses brought their *c.* before the Lord
Deut. 1. 17. the *c.* that is too hard for you, bring
Josh. 20. 4. the manslayer shall declare his *c.*

1 *Sam.* 17. 29. and David said, is there not a *c.?*
25. 39. Lord hath pleaded the *c.* of my reproach
2 *Sam.* 13. 16. there is no *c.* this evil is greater than
15. 4. that hath any suit or *c.* might come to me
1 *Kings* 8. 45. maintain their *c.* 49, 59. 2 *Ch.* 6. 35, 39.
11. 27. this was the *c.* that he lift up his hand
12. 15. for the *c.* was from the Lord, 2 *Chr.* 10. 15.
1 *Chr.* 21. 3. why will he be a *c.* of trespass to Israel?
2 *Chron.* 19. 10. what *c.* shall come of your brethren
Ezra 4. 15. for which *c.* this city was destroyed
Neh. 6. 6. for which *c.* thou buildest the wall
Job 5. 8. and unto God will I commit my *c.*
13. 18. behold now, I have ordered my *c.*
23. 4. I would order my *c.* before him, and fill
29. 16. the *c.* which I knew not, I searched out
31. 13. if I did despise the *c.* of my man-servant
Psal. 9. 4. for thou hast maintained my *c.*
35. 23. awake to my *c.* my God and my Lord
27. let them be glad that favour my righteous *c.*
140. 12. I know that the Lord will maintain the *c.*
Prov. 18. 17. he that is first in his own *c.* seems just
25. 9. debate thy *c.* with thy neighbour himself
29. 7. the righteous considereth the *c.* of the poor
31. 8. open thy mouth for the dumb in the *c.*
Eccl. 7. 10. say not thou, what is the *c.* that
Isa. 1. 23. nor doth *c.* of the widow come to them
41. 21. produce your *c.* saith the Lord, bring
50. † 8. who is the master of my *c.* let him come
51. 22. God that pleadeth the *c.* of his people
Jer. 5. 28. they judge not the *c.* of the fatherless
11. 20. for to thee have I revealed my *c.*
20. 12. Lord, unto thee have I opened my *c.*
22. 16. he judged the *c.* of the poor and needy
Lam. 3. 36. to subvert in a *c.* the Ld. approveth not
59. Lord, thou hast seen my wrong, judge my *c.*
Jonah 1. 7. that he may know for whose *c.* 8.
Mat. 5. 32. his wife, saving for the *c.* of fornication
19. 3. for a man to put away his wife for every *c.*
Luke 8. 47. declared for what *c.* she touched him
23. 22. I have found no *c.* of death in him
Acts 10. 21. what is the *c.* wherefore ye are come?
13. 28. though they found no *c.* of death in him
25. 14. Festus declared Paul's *c.* to the king
28. 18. because there was no *c.* of death in me
2 *Cor.* 4. 16. for which *c.* we faint not, but though
5. 13. or whether we be sober, it is for your *c.*
7. 12. I did it not for his *c.* that had done wrong
Phil. 2. 18. for the same *c.* also do ye joy with me
2 *Tim.* 1. 12. for which *c.* I suffer these things
Heb. 2. 11. for which *c.* he is not ashamed to call
1 *Pet.* 2. † 23. committed his *c.* to him that judgeth

Plead CAUSE.

1 *Sam.* 24. 15. the Lord be judge, and *plead* my *c.*
Psal. 35. 1. | 43. 1. | 119. 154.
Psal. 74. 22. arise, O God, *plead* thine own *c.*
Prov. 22. 23. for the Lord will *plead* their *c.*
23. 11. he shall *plead* their *c.* with thee
31. 9. open thy mouth, *plead* the *c.* of poor, needy
Jer. 30. 13. there is none to *plead* thy *c.*
50. 34. the Lord shall thoroughly *plead* their *c.*
51. 36. behold, I will *plead* thy *c.* and take veng.
Mic. 7. 9. until he *plead* my *c.* and execute

For this CAUSE.

Exod. 9. 16. *for this c.* have I raised up Pharaoh
2 *Chron.* 32. 20. *for this c.* Hezekiah and Isaiah pray.
Dan. 2. 12. *for this c.* the king was angry and furious
Mat. 19. 5. *for this c.* shall a man leave father and
mother, and cleave to wife, *Mark* 10. 7. *Eph.* 5. 31.
John 12. 27. but *for this c.* came I unto this hour
18. 37. and *for this c.* came I into the world
Rom. 1. 26. *for this c.* G. gave them up to vile affect.
13. 6. *for this c.* pay ye tribute also
15. 9. *for this c.* I will conf. to thee among the gent.
1 *Cor.* 11. 30. *for this c.* many are weak and sickly
Eph. 3. 14. *for this c.* I bow my knees to the Father
1 *Thess.* 2. 13. *for this c.* thank God without ceasing
2 *Thess.* 2. 11. *for this c.* G. shall send strong delusion
1 *Tim.* 1. 16. howbeit, *for this c.* I obtained mercy
Heb. 9. 15. *for this c.* he is the mediator of new testa.
1 *Pet.* 4. 6. *for this c.* was the gospel preach. to them

Without CAUSE.

1 *Sam.* 19. 5. wilt thou sin, to slay David *without* a *c.?*
Job 2. 3. thou movedst me to destroy him *without* a *c.*
9. 17. he multiplieth my wounds *without c.*
Psal. 7. 4. I delivered him that *w. c.* is my enemy
25. 3. let them be ashamed that transgress *w. c.*
35. 7. *w. c.* they hid for me a net, digged a pit *w. c.*
19. that hate me *without c.* 69. 4. *John* 15. 25.
109. 3. and they fought against me *without* a *c.*
119. 78. the proud dealt perversely with me *w.* a *c.*
161. princes have persecuted me *without c.*
Prov. 1. 11. let us lurk for the innocent *without c.*
3. 30. strive not with a man *w. c.* if he have done
23. 29. who hath sorrow, who hath wounds, *w. c.*
24. 28. be not witness against neighbour *without c.*
Isa. 52. 4. the Assyrian oppressed them *without c.*
Lam. 3. 52. mine enemies chased me sore *without c.*
Ezek. 14. 23. have not done *w. c.* all I have done
Mat. 5. 22. whoso is angry with his brother *w. c.*

CAUSE.

Gen. 7. 4. I will *c.* it rain on the earth forty days
45. 1. he cried, *c.* every man to go out from me
Exod. 8. 5. *c.* frogs to come up on the land of Egypt
21. 19. and shall *c.* him to be thoroughly healed
Lev. 19. 29. thy daughter, to *c.* her to be a whore
26. 16. consume the eyes, and *c.* sorrow of heart
Num. 8. † 7. *c.* a razor to pass over the Levites
16. 5. who is holy, the Lord will *c.* him to come
Deut. 1. 38. encourage him, for he shall *c.* Israel to
inherit it, 3. 28. | 31. 7. *Josh.* 1. † 6.
12. 11. God shall choose to *c.* his name to dwell
24. 4. and thou shalt not *c.* the land to sin which
28. † 61. them will Lord *c.* to ascend till destroyed
Judg. 6. † 11. Gideon threshed wheat to *c.* it flee
2 *Sam* 13. 13. whither shall I *c.* my shame to go?
1 *Kings* 8. 31. an oath laid on him to *c.* him swear
2 *Kings* 19. 7. will *c.* him to fall by sword, *Isa.* 37. 7.
Neh. 13. 26. him did outlandish women *c.* to sin
Esth. 3. 13. *c.* to perish all the Jews, 7. † 4. | 8. 11.
5. 5. *c.* Haman make haste to do as Esther said
6. † 9. *c.* him to ride on horseback through the city
Job 6. 24. *c.* me to understand wherein I have erred
Job 6. † 27. yea, ye *c.* to fall upon the fatherless
34. 11. *c.* to every man to find according to his ways
38. † 37. who can *c.* to lie down the bottles of heaven
Psal. 10. 17. thou wilt *c.* thine ear to hear
67. 1. and *c.* his face to shine upon us, 80. 3, 7, 19.
76. 8. thou didst *c.* judgm. to be heard from heav.
90. † 12. we may *c.* our hearts to come to wisdom
143. 8. *c.* me to hear, *c.* me to know the way
Prov. 4. 16. sleep taken away, unless *c.* some to fall
19. † 18. let not thy soul spare to *c.* him to die
23. † 5. wilt *c.* thine eyes to flee on what is not?
Eccl. 5. 6. suffer not thy mouth to *c.* thy flesh to sin
Cant. 8. 13. hearken to thy voice, *c.* me to hear it
Isa. 3. 12. they who lead thee *c.* thee to err, 9. 16.
27. 6. he shall *c.* them of Jacob to take root
28. 12. this is the rest ye may *c.* the weary to rest
30. 30. the Lord *c.* his glorious voice to be heard
42. 2. nor *c.* his voice to be heard in the streets
58. 14. I will *c.* thee to ride upon the high places
61. 11. so Lord will *c.* righteousness to spring forth
66. 9. shall I bring to birth, and not *c.* bring forth?
Jer. 3. 12. I will not *c.* mine anger to fall on you
7. 3. I will *c.* you to dwell in this place, 7.
12. † 9. *c.* beasts of the field to come and devour
13. 16. give glory to the Lord before he *c.* darkness
15. 11. I will *c.* the enemy to entreat thee well
23. 27. who think to *c.* my people forget thy na.
25. † 10. I will *c.* to perish the voice of mirth
31. 2. even Israel, when I went to *c.* him to rest
9. I will *c.* them to walk by the rivers of waters
32. 44. I will *c.* their captivity to return, 33. 26.
Lam. 3. 32. though he *c.* grief, yet will have com.
Ezek. 20. 37. I will *c.* you to pass under the rod
24. 8. that it might *c.* fury to come to vengeance
34. 15. I will *c.* them to lie down, saith the Lord
36. 12. I will *c.* men to walk on you, even Israel
Dan. 8. 25. he shall *c.* craft to prosper in his hand
9. 17. O our God, *c.* thy face to shine on sanctuary
† 18. we do not *c.* to fall our supplication
11. † 32. shall he *c.* to dissemble by flatteries
Hos. 4. † 9. I will *c.* to return for their ways
Joel 3. 11. thither *c.* thy mighty ones come down
Amos 6. 3. and *c.* the seat of violence to come near
8. 9. I will *c.* sun to go down at noon and darken
9. † 9. *c.* to move Israel among all nations
Nah. 2. † 8. stand, but none shall *c.* them to turn
Hab. 1. 3. why dost thou *c.* me to behold grievance?
Mat. 5. † 29. if thy right eye *c.* thee to offend
6. † 2. *c.* not a trumpet to be sounded
10. 21. children rise up against parents and *c.* them
to be put to death, *Mark* 13. 12. *Luke* 21. 16.
Rom. 16. 17. mark them who *c.* divisions and offences
Col. 4. 16. *c.* that it be read in church of Laodiceans

CAUSE *to cease.* *See* CEASE.

CAUSED.

Gen. 2. 21. God *c.* a deep sleep to fall on Adam
20. 13. God *c.* me to wander from my fathers
Exod. 14. 21. the Lord *c.* the sea to go back
Num. 31. 16. these *c.* Israel to commit whoredom
Deut. 34. 4. this is the land, I have *c.* thee to see it
2 *Sam.* 7. 11. *c.* thee to rest from thine enemies
22. † 40. hast thou *c.* to bow, *Psal.* 18. † 39.
1 *Kings* 2. 19. *c.* a seat to be set for the king's mother
2 *Chr.* 34. 32. he *c.* all present in Jerus. to stand it
Ezra 1. † 1. Cyrus *c.* a voice to pass thro' his kingdom
6. 12. the God that hath *c.* his name to dwell
Neh. 8. 7. Levites *c.* people to understand the law, 8.
Esth. 5. † 10. Haman sent and *c.* his friends to come
14. Haman *c.* the gallows to be made
Job 31. 16. if I have *c.* eyes of the widow to fail
Psal. 66. 12. thou hast *c.* men to ride over our heads
78. 13. he divided the sea, and *c.* them to pass thro'
26. he *c.* an east wind to blow in the heaven
119. 49. word on which thou hast *c.* me to hope
Prov. 7. 21. with fair speech she *c.* him to yield
Isa. 6. † 7. *c.* it to touch my mouth, and said to
19. 14. they have *c.* Egypt to err in every work
43. 23. I have not *c.* thee to serve with an offering
47. † 10. thy wisdom *c.* thee to turn away
63. 14. the Spirit of the Lord *c.* him to rest
Jer. 3. † 18. to the land I *c.* your fathers possess
12. 14. which I have *c.* my people Israel to inherit
13. 11. I have *c.* to cleave to me house of Israel
29. 31. Shemaiah *c.* you to trust in a lie
32. 23. therefore thou hast *c.* all this evil to come
34. 11. after they *c.* the servants to return, 16.
48. 4. her little ones have *c.* a cry to be heard
Ezek. 16. 7. I have *c.* thee to multiply as the bud
24. 13. till I have *c.* my fury to rest on thee
29. 18. Nebuch. *c.* his army to serve against Tyrus
32. 23. which *c.* terror in the land, 24, 25, 26.
Dan. 9. 21. Gabriel being *c.* to fly swiftly, touched
Hos. 4. 12. the spirit of whoredoms *c.* them to err
Amos 2. 4. and their lies *c.* them to err, after which
4. 7. I *c.* to rain on one city, I *c.* not to rain on
Zech. 3. 4. I have *c.* thine iniquity to pass from thee
Mal. 2. 8. ye have *c.* many to stumble at the law
John 11. 37. have *c.* this man should not have died
Acts 15. 3. they *c.* great joy to all the brethren
2 *Cor.* 2. 5. but if any have *c.* grief, hath grieved part
Rev. 13. 16. *c.* all to receive a mark in their right-hand

CAUSES.

Exod. 18. 19. that thou mayest bring *c.* to God
26. the hard *c.* they brought to Moses
Deut. 1. 16. hear the *c.* between your brethren
Jer. 3. 8. all the *c.* whereby backsliding Israel
Lam. 2. 14. but have seen for thee *c.* of banishment
3. 58. O Lord, thou hast pleaded the *c.* of my soul
Acts 26. 21. for these *c.* the Jews caught me in temple

CAUSEST.

Job 30. 22. thou *c.* me to ride on the wind
Psal. 65. 4. blessed is man thou *c.* approach to thee

CAUSETH.

Num. 5. 18. the water that *c.* the curse, 19, 22, 24, 27.
Job 12. 24. he *c.* them to wander in a wilderness
where there is no way, *Psal.* 107. 40.
20. 3. the spirit of understanding *c.* me to answer
37. 13. he *c.* it to come hither for correction
Psal. 104. 14. he *c.* the grass to grow for the cattle
135. 7. he *c.* vapours to ascend, *Jer.* 10. 13. | 51. 16.
147. 18. *c.* his wind to blow, and the waters flow
Prov. 10. 5. is a son that *c.* shame, 17. 2. | 19. 26.
Prov. 10. † 17. he that refuseth reproof *c.* to err
17. 2. a wise servant shall rule over a son *c.* shame
19. 27. cease to hear the instruction that *c.* to err
28. 10. whoso *c.* righteous to go astray in evil way
Isa. 64. 2. the fire *c.* the waters to boil, to make
Ezek. 44. 18. not gird with any thing that *c.* sweat
Dan. 11. † 20. one that *c.* an exacter of the kingdom
Mat. 5. 32. put away wife *c.* her to commit adultery
2 *Cor.* 2. 14. thanks be to God, who *c.* us to triumph
9. 11. which *c.* through us thanksgiving to God
Rev. 13. 12. *c.* the earth to worship the first beast

CAUSEWAY.

1 *Chron.* 26. 16. lot came forth by the *c.* of going up
18. at Parbar westward four at the *c.* and two
Prov. 15. † 19. way of righteous raised up as a *c*
Isa. 7. † 3. go up in the *c.* of the fuller's field

CAUSING.

2 *Kings* 2. † 19. the ground *c.* to miscarry
Cant. 7. 9. *c.* the lips of those asleep to speak
Isa. 30. 28. a bridle in the jaws *c.* them to err
Jer. 29. 10. in *c.* you to return to this place
33. 12. shepherds *c.* their flocks to lie down
Ezek. 39. † 28. know I am the Lord *c.* them to be led

CAUSELESS.

1 *Sam.* 25. 31. either that thou hast shed blood *c.*
Prov. 26. 2. so the curse *c.* shall not come

CAVE, S.

Gen. 19. 30. Lot dwelt in a *c.* he and his daughters
23. 17. field and *c.* made sure to Abraham, 20.
19. Abraham buried Sarah in the *c.* of the field
49. 29. bury me with my father in *c.* of Ephron
Josh. 10. 16. these five kings fled and hid in a *c.* 17.
Judg. 6. 2. because of the Midianites Israel made *c.*
1 *Sam.* 13. 6. Israel did hide themselves in *c.* in rocks
22. 1. David escaped to the *c.* of Adullam
24. 10. Lord delivered thee into my hand in the *c.*
2 *Sam.* 23. 13. came to David to the *c.* of Adullam
1 *Kings* 18. 4. the prophets hid by fifty in a *c.* 13.
19. 9. Elijah came to a *c.* and lodged there
Isa. 2. 19. they shall go into *c.* for fear of the Lord
Ezek. 33. 27. they shall die that be in the *c.*
John 11. 38. the grave, it was a *c.* a stone lay upon it
Heb. 11. 38. they wandered in dens and *c.* of earth

CEASE

Signifies, [1] *To leave off, or give over,* 1 Sam. 7.
8. Isa. 33. 1. [2] *To be utterly forgotten,* Deut.
32. 26. [3] *To be quiet,* Judg. 15. 7. [4] *To be
wanting,* Deut. 15. 11. [5] *To be removed by
death, or otherwise,* Lam. 5. 14. [6] *Not to lean
to, or depend on,* Prov. 23. 4. [7] *To abstain
from,* Psal. 37. 8. Isa. 1. 16.

Gen. 8. 22. and day and night shall not *c.*
Exod. 9. 29. as I am gone the thunder shall *c.*
23. † 5. would *c.* to leave thy business for him
Num. 8. 25. from the age of fifty years shall *c.*
11. 25. seventy elders prophesied, and did not *c.*
17. 5. I will make to *c.* the murmurings
Deut. 15. 11. the poor shall never *c.* out of the land
32. 26. I would make remembrance of them to *c*
Josh. 22. 25. so make our children *c.* from fearing L.
Judg. 15. 7. yet will I be avenged, after I will *c.*
20. 28. shall I yet again go to battle, or shall I *c.?*
1 *Sam.* 7. 8. *c.* not to cry to Lord our God for us
2 *Kings* 23. † 5. caused to *c.* the idolatrous priests
2 *Chron.* 16. 5. when Baasha heard it, let his work *c.*
Ezra 4. 23. made them to *c.* by force and power
6. † 8. that they be not made to *c.*
Neh. 6. 3. why should the work *c.* while I come?
Job 3. 17. there the wicked *c.* from troubling
10. 20. my days few, *c.* then, let me alone
14. 7. that the tender branch thereof will not *c.*
Psal. 37. 8. *c.* from anger, and forsake wrath
46. 9. he maketh wars to *c.* to the end of the earth
89. 44. thou hast made his glory to *c.* and cast
119. † 119. thou causest the wicked to *c.*
Prov. 19. 27. *c.* to hear instruction that causeth to err
20. 3. it is an honour for a man to *c.* from strife
22. 10. cast scorner, yea strife and reproach shall *c.*
23. 4. labour to be rich, *c.* from thy wisdom
Eccl. 12. 3. the grinders *c.* because they are few
Isa. 1. 16. *c.* to do evil ‖ 2. 22. *c.* ye from man
10. 25. yet a little while and indignation shall *c.*
16. 10. I have made their vintage shouting to *c.*
17. 3. the fortress also shall *c.* from Ephraim
21. 2. all the sighing thereof have I made to *c.*
33. 1. when thou shalt *c.* to spoil, shalt be spoiled
Jer. 14. 17. let tears run down and let them not *c.*
17. 8. leaf green, nor shall *c.* from yielding fruit
31. 36. then the seed of Israel shall *c.*
Lam. 2. 18. let not the apple of thine eye *c.*
Ezek. 6. 6. that your idols may be broken and *c.*
7. 24. I will make the pomp of the strong to *c.*
12. 23. saith the Lord, I will make this proverb *c.*
23. 27. thus will I make thy lewdness to *c.*
30. 10. I will make the multitude of Egypt to *c.*
18. the pomp of her strength shall *c.* 33. 28.
Hos. 7. † 4. raiser will *c.* from raising
Amos 7. 5. O Lord God, *c.* by whom shall Jacob arise
Acts 13. 10. will not *c.* to pervert the right ways
1 *Cor.* 13. 8. whether they be tongues, they shall *c.*
Eph. 1. 16. I *c.* not to give thanks for you
Col. 1. 9. we do not *c.* to pray for you to be filled
2 *Pet.* 2. 14. having eyes that cannot *c.* from sin

Cause to CEASE.

Lev. 26. † 6. I will *cause to c.* evil beasts, *Ezek.* 34. 25.
Ruth 4. † 14. not *caused to c.* to thee a kinsman
2 *Kings* 23. † 5. *cause to c.* the idolatrous priests
Ezra 4. 21. *cause* these men *to c.* city be not built
5. 5. the eye of their God on them, they could not
cause them *to c.* till matter came to Darius
Neh. 4. 11. slay them and *cause* the work *to c.*
Psal. 85. 4. *cause* thine anger toward us *to c.*
Prov. 18. 18. the lot *causeth* contentions *to c.*
Isa. 13. 11. I will *cause* the arrogancy of proud *to c.*
30. 11. *cause* the holy One of Israel *to c.* before us
Jer. 7. 34. *cause* mirth *to c.* from the cities of Judah
36. 29. *cause to c.* man and beast, *Hos.* 2. 11.
48. 35. I will *cause to c.* in Moab him that offereth
Ezek. 16. 41. *cause* thee *to c.* from playing harlot
23. 48. thus will I *cause* lewdness *to c.*
26. 13. I will *cause* the noise of thy songs *to c.*
30. 13. I will *cause* their images *to c.* out of Noph

Ezek. 34. 10. *cause* them *to c.* from feeding the flock
Dan. 9. 27. he shall *cause* the oblation *to c.*
11. 18. *cause* the reproach offered by him *to c.*
Hos. 1. 4. will *cause to c.* kingdom of house of Israel

CEASED.

Gen. 18. 11. it *c.* to be with Sarai after manner of
Exod. 9. 33. thunders and hail *c.* and rain was not
34. when Pharaoh saw that the thunders *c.*
Josh. 5. 12. the manna *c.* on the morrow after
Judg. 2. 19. they *c.* not from their own doings
5. 7. the inhabitants of villages *c.* they *c.* in Israel
1 *Sam.* 2. 5. and they that were hungry *c.*
25. 9. they spake in the name of David and *c.*
Ezra 4. 24. then *c.* the work of the house of God
Job 32. 1. so these three men *c.* to answer Job
Psal. 35. 15. they did tear me and *c.* not
77. 2. my sore ran in the night and *c.* not
Isa. 14. 4. how hath the oppressor *c.* golden city *c.*
Lam. 5. 14. the elders have *c.* from the gate
15. the joy of our heart is *c.* our dance is turned
Jonah 1. 15. they took up Jonah, sea *c.* from raging
Mat. 14. 32. the wind *c.* *Mark* 4. 39. | 6. 51.
Luke 7. 45. this woman hath not *c.* to kiss my feet
11. 1. as he was praying in a place, when he *c.*
Acts 5. 42. they *c.* not to teach and preach Jesus
20. 1. after the uproar was *c.* Paul called disciples
31. by space of three years I *c.* not to warn every
21. 14. when he would not be persuaded we *c.*
Gal. 5. 11. then is the offence of the cross *c.*
Heb. 4. 10. he also hath *c.* from his own works
10. 2. for then they would not have *c.* to be offer.
1 *Pet.* 4. 1. who suffered in flesh, hath *c.* from sin

CEASETH.

Psal. 12. 1. help, Lord, for the godly man *c.*
49. 8. redempt. of soul precious, and it *c.* for ever
Prov. 26. 20. so where there is no tale-bearer strife *c.*
Isa. 16. 4. the extortioner is at an end, the spoiler *c.*
24. 8. the mirth of tabrets *c.* joy of the harp *c.*
33. 8. high-ways lie waste, the way-faring man *c.*
Lam. 3. 49. mine eye trickleth down and *c.* not
Hos. 7. 4. *c.* from raising after he kneaded dough
Acts 6. 13. this man *c.* not speak blasphemous words

CEASING.

Exod. 21. † 19. he shall pay for the *c.* of his time
1 *Sam.* 12. 23. I should sin in *c.* to pray for you
Isa. 6. † 9. hear ye without *c.* but understand not
Acts 12. 5. but prayer was made without *c.* for him
Rom. 1. 9. without *c.* I make mention, 1 *Thess.* 1. 3.
1 *Thess.* 2. 13. for this we thank God without *c.*
5. 17. pray without *c.* in every thing give thanks
2 *Tim.* 1. 3. without *c.* I have remembrance of thee

CEDAR.

This tree is much celebrated in the scriptures: It shoots out its branches at ten or twelve feet from the ground: Its branches are large, and at a distance from one another; its leaves are something like those of rosemary; it is always green, and distils a kind of gum, to which different effects are attributed: The wood of it is incorruptible, beautiful, solid, and inclining to a brown colour; it bears a small apple, like that of the pine. They made use of this wood not only for the beams and planks which covered edifices, and served for ceilings to apartments, but they placed them likewise in the substance of their walls, and so disposed them and the stone together, that there were three rows of stone and one of cedar wood, 1 Kings 6. 36. *By the* cedar *of* Lebanon, *the king of* Israel *may be understood,* 2 Kings 14. 9. *Hereunto also the felicity and growth of the faithful is compared,* Psal. 92. 12.

2 *Sam.* 7. 2. king said, I dwell in an house of *c.*
7. saying, why build ye not me an house of *c.*?
1 *Kings* 4. 33. he spake from the *c.* to the hyssop
5. 8. I will do all thy desire concerning *c.*
2 *Kings* 14. 9. the thistle sent to the *c.* 2 *Chr.* 25. 18.
Job 40. 17. Behemoth moveth his tail like a *c.*
Psal. 92. 12. the righteous shall grow like a *c.*
Cant. 1. 17. the beams of our house are *c.*
8. 9. we will inclose her with boards of *c.*
Isa. 41. 19. I will plant in the wilderness the *c.*
Jer. 22. 14. it is ceiled with *c.* painted with vermil.
15. because thou closest thyself in *c.*
Ezek. 17. 3. a great eagle took highest branch of *c.*
22. I will take of the highest branch of the *c.*
23. it shall bear fruit and be a goodly *c.*
27. 24. chests made of *c.* among the merchandise
31. 3. the Assyrian was a *c.* in Lebanon
Zeph. 2. 14. for he shall uncover the *c.* work
Zech. 11. 2. howl, fir-tree, for the *c.* is fallen

CEDAR-TREES.

Num. 24. 6. Israel's tabernacles are *c.* beside waters
2 *Sam.* 5. 11. Hiram sent *c.* to David and carpenters
1 *Kings* 5. 6. that they hew me *c.* out of Lebanon
10. so Hiram gave Solomon *c.* and fir-trees, 9. 11.
2 *Kings* 19. 23. I will cut down the tall *c.* thereof
1 *Chron.* 22. 4. David prepared *c.* in abundance
2 *Chron.* 1. 15. *c.* made he as the sycamore, 9. 27.
2. 8. send me *c.* and fir-trees out of Lebanon
Ezra 3. 7. gave money to bring *c.* from Lebanon

CEDAR-WOOD.

Lev. 14. 4. take *c.* and hyssop, 6, 49, 51, 52.
Num. 19. 6. the priest shall take *c.* and hyssop
1 *Chron.* 22. 4. they brought much *c.* to David

CEDARS.

1 *Kings* 10. 27. *c.* made he to be as sycamore trees
1 *Chr.* 17. 1. David said, I dwell in an house of *c.*
2 *Chr.* 2. 3. didst send David *c.* to build an house
Psal. 29. 5. the voice of the Lord breaketh the *c.*
80. 10. the boughs thereof were like goodly *c.*
148. 9. praise him also *c.* and fruitful trees
Cant. 5. 15. his countenance excellent as the *c.*
Isa. 9. 10. we will change the sycamores into *c.*
37. 24. I will cut down the tall *c.* thereof
44. 14. he heweth him down *c.* and taketh oak
Jer. 22. 7. they shall cut down thy choice *c.*
23. O Lebanon, that makest thy nest in the *c.*
Ezek 31. 8. *c.* in garden of God could not hide him
Amos 2. 9. Amorites height as the height of *c.*
Zech. 11. 1. O Lebanon, that fire may devour thy *c.*

CEDARS *of Lebanon.*

Judg. 9. 15. fire out of the bramble devour *c. of Leb.*
Psal. 104. 16. the *c. of Leb.* which he hath planted
Isa. 2. 13. day of the Lord upon all the *c. of Leb.*
14. 8. *c. of Leb.* rejoice at thee, saying, since thou
Ezek. 27. 5. *c.* from *Leb.* to make masts for thee

CELEBRATE.

Lev. 23. 32. from even to even shall *c.* your sabbath
41. a statute, ye shall *c.* it in the seventh month
Isa. 38. 18. for the grave cannot, death cannot *c.* thee

CELESTIAL.

1 *Cor.* 15. 40. are *c.* bodies, glory of the *c.* is one

CELLARS.

1 *Chron.* 27. 28. and over the *c.* of oil was Joash

CENSER, S.

Lev. 10. 1. sons of Aaron took either of them *c.*
16. 12. he shall take a *c.* full of burning coals
Num. 4. 14. they shall put upon it vessels, even *c.*
16. 6. this do, take ye *c.* || 17. every man his *c.*
39. Eleazar the priest took the brasen *c.*
1 *Kings* 7. 50. made *c.* of pure gold, 2 *Chr.* 4. 22.
2 *Chron.* 26. 19. Uzziah had a *c.* in his hand to burn
Ezek. 8. 11. with every man his *c.* in his hand
Heb. 9. 4. the holiest had the golden *c.* and the ark
Rev. 8. 3. the angel came, having a golden *c.*
5. the angel took the *c.* and filled it with fire

CENSURE.

2 *Cor.* 2. † 6. sufficient to such a man is this *c.*

CENTURION, S.

Mat. 8. 5. there unto him a *c.* beseeching him
8. *c.* said, Lord, I am not worthy thou shouldest
27. 54. when the *c.* saw the earthquake [come
Luke 7. 2. *c.* servant, who was dear to him, was sick
23. 47. now when the *c.* saw what was done
Acts 10. 1. Cornelius was a *c.* of the Italian band
22. Cornelius the *c.* a just man that feareth God
21. 32. who immediately took *c.* and ran down
22. 26. when the *c.* heard that, he went and told
23. 17. then Paul called one of the *c.* to him
23. he called to him two *c.* saying, make ready
24. 23. and he commanded a *c.* to keep Paul [band
27. 1. delivered Paul to Julius a *c.* of Augustus'
11. the *c.* believed the master more than Paul
43. *c.* willing to save Paul, kept them from purp.
28. 16. the *c.* delivered the prisoners to the captain

CEREMONIES.

Num. 9. 3. shall keep passover according to all the *c.*
Heb. 9. † 1. the first covenant had also *c.*

A CERTAIN *Man. See* MAN.

CERTAIN.

Exod. 16. 4. ye shall gather a *c.* rate every day
Num. 16. 2. Korah rose with *c.* of children of Isr.
Deut. 13. 13. *c.* men the children of Belial are gone
25. 2. the wicked man be beaten by a *c.* number
2 *Chron.* 8. 13. after a *c.* rate every day offering
Neh. 1. 2. Hanani came, he and *c.* men of Judah
4. I mourned *c.* days, and fasted, and prayed
11. 23. a *c.* portion should be for singers every day
13. 25. I smote *c.* of them, and plucked off hair
Jer. 41. 5. there came *c.* from Shechem, from Shiloh
52. 15. the captain carried away *c.* of poor people
Dan. 8. 27. I Daniel fainted and was sick *c.* days
11. 13. the king of north shall come after *c.* years
Mat. 18. 23. kingd. of heav. likened to *c.* king, 22. 2.
20. 20. she and her sons desiring a *c.* thing of him
Mark 12. 42. there came a *c.* poor widow, *Luke* 21. 2.
14. 57. arose *c.* and bare false witness against him
Luke 5. 12. it came to pass when he was in a *c.* city
8. 20. told him by *c.* thy mother stands to see thee
10. 38. as he went into a *c.* village, 17. 12.
11. 27. a *c.* woman lifted up her voice and said
37. a *c.* Pharisee besought him to dine with him
18. 9. this parable to *c.* who trusted in themselves
23. 19. who for a *c.* sedition and for murder
24. 22. *c.* women also made us astonished, who were
24. *c.* of them with us went to the sepulchre
John 5. 4. an angel went down at a *c.* season
Acts 9. 19. Saul was *c.* days with the disciples
10. 48. they prayed Peter to tarry *c.* days
12. 1. Herod the king to vex *c.* of the church
15. 24. *c.* which went from us have troubled us
17. 28. as *c.* of your own poets have said, for we
Rom. 15. 26. to make a *c.* contribution for saints at
Gal. 2. 12. for before that *c.* came from James
Heb. 2. 6. but one in a *c.* place testified, what is man
4. 4. he spake in a *c.* place of 7th day on this wise
7. he limiteth a *c.* day, saying in David, to day
10. 27. but a *c.* fearful looking for of judgment
Jude 4. for there are *c.* men crept in unawares

CERTAIN.

Deut. 13. 14. if it be truth, and the thing *c.* 17. 4.
1 *Kings* 2. 37. know for *c.* thou shalt surely die, 42.
Jer. 26. 15. know for *c.* if ye put me to death
Dan. 2. 45. the dream is *c.* and interpretation sure
Acts 25. 26. I have no *c.* thing to write to my lord
1 *Cor.* 4. 11. we have no *c.* dwelling-place
1 *Tim.* 6. 7. it is *c.* we can carry nothing out

CERTAINLY.

Gen. 18. 10. he said, I will *c.* return to thee
26. 28. we saw *c.* the Lord was with thee
43. 7. could we *c.* know, he would say, bring your
44. 15. wot ye not such a man as I can *c.* divine
50. 15. will *c.* requite us all the evil we did to him
Exod. 3. 12. *c.* I will be with thee, this be a token
22. 4. if theft be *c.* found in his hand alive
Lev. 5. 19. he hath *c.* trespassed against the Lord
24. 16. all the congregation shall *c.* stone him
Josh. 9. 24. because it was *c.* told thy servants
Judg. 14. 12. if ye can *c.* declare the riddle to me
1 *Sam.* 20. 3. thy father *c.* knoweth I have found
9. if I knew *c.* evil were determined by my father
23. 10. *c.* heard that Saul will come to Keilah
25. 28. Lord will *c.* make my lord a sure house
1 *Kings* 1. 30. even so will I *c.* do this day
2 *Kings* 8. 10. go, say to him, thou mayest *c.* recover
2 *Chr.* 18. 27. Micaiah said, if thou *c.* return in peace
Prov. 23. 5. for riches *c.* make themselves wings
Jer. 8. 8. we are wise, lo, *c.* in vain made he it
13. 12. do we not *c.* know every bottle be filled
25. 28. thus saith the Lord, ye shall *c.* drink
36. 29. king of Babylon shall *c.* destroy this land
40. 14. dost thou *c.* know that Baal is sent
42. 19. know *c.* I have admonished you this day
22. *c.* ye shall die by the sword and by famine
Jer. 44. 17. *c.* do what thing goeth out of our mouth
Lam. 2. 16. *c.* this is the day that we looked for
Dan. 11. 10. one shall *c.* come and overflow, 13.
Zech. 11. † 11. poor *c.* knew it was word of the Lord
Luke 23. 47. saying, *c.* this was a righteous man

CERTAINTY.

Josh. 23. 13. know for *c.* Lord will no more drive
1 *Sam.* 23. 23. come ye again to me with the *c.*
Prov. 22. 21. make known the *c.* of words of truth
Dan. 2. 8. I know of *c.* ye would gain the time
Luke 1. 4. thou mightest know the *c.* of those things
Acts 21. 34. he could not know the *c.* for tumult
22. 30. because he would have known the *c.* why

CERTIFY, IED.

2 *Sam.* 15. 28. till there come word from you to *c.* me
Ezra 4. 14. therefore have we sent and *c.* the king
16. we *c.* the king, that if this city be built again
5. 10. we asked their names also to *c.* thee
7. 24. we *c.* you to impose no toll on the Levites
Esth. 2. 22. Esther *c.* king thereof in Mordecai's name
Gal. 1. 11. I *c.* you gospel I preached, not after man

CHAFED.

2 *Sam.* 17. 18. they be *c.* in their minds as bear robbed

CHAFF

Is *the refuse of winnowed corn, which is barren, light, and apt to be driven to and fro with the wind,* Psal. 1. 4. To which are compared, (1) *False doctrine, or men's dreams and inventions,* Jer. 23. 28. (2) *Fruitless plots and designs,* Isa. 33. 11. (3) *Hypocrites and ungodly persons, who are vile, barren, and inconstant, like chaff,* Mat. 3. 12.

Job 21. 18. wicked as *c.* that storm carrieth away
Psal. 1. 4. like the *c.* which the wind driveth away
35. 5. let them be as *c.* before the wind
Isa. 5. 24. as flame consumeth the *c.* so their root
17. 13. the nations shall be chased as the *c.*
29. 5. terrible ones shall be as *c.* that passeth away
33. 11. ye shall conceive *c.* and bring forth stubble
41. 15. thresh mountains, and make the hills as *c.*
Jer. 23. 28. what is the *c.* to the wheat? saith Lord
Dan. 2. 35. became like the *c.* of the threshing floor
Hos. 13. 3. as the *c.* which is driven with whirlwind
Zeph. 2. 2. before the decree, before day pass as *c.*
Mat. 3. 12. will burn up the *c.* with fire, *Luke* 3. 17.

CHAIN

Signifies, [1] *Links of iron, gold, or silver, one within another, which were,* (1) *Sacred, those made by the command of God, for the breastplate worn by the high-priest,* Exod. 39. 15, 17, 18. (2) *Idolatrous, such as were made for idols, or images,* Isa. 40. 19. (3) *Common, wherewith prisoners were chained,* Acts 12. 7. [II] *Bondage, or affliction,* Lam. 3. 7. [III] *Severe laws for the curbing of all open impiety,* Rev. 20. 1.

Gen. 41. 42. gold *c.* about his neck, *Dan.* 5. 7, 16, 29.
Psal. 73. 6. pride compasseth them about as a *c.*
Cant. 4. 9. have ravished me with one *c.* of thy neck
Lam. 3. 7. hedged me about, hath made my *c.* heavy
Ezek. 7. 23. make a *c.* land is full of bloody crimes
16. 11. I put bracelets, and a *c.* on thy neck
Acts 28. 20. for hope of Israel I am bound with this *c.*
Eph. 6. † 20. for which I am ambassador in a *c.*
2 *Tim.* 1. 16. Onesiphorus was not ashamed of my *c.*
Rev. 20. 1. an angel and a great *c.* in his hand

CHAIN-WORK.

1 *Kings* 7. 17. wreaths of *c.* for chapiters of pillars

CHAINS.

Exod. 28. 14. fasten the wreathen *c.* to ouches, 24.
39. 15. they made on breast-plate *c.* at the ends
Num. 31. 50. for atonement, *c.* and bracelets, rings
Judg. 8. 26. besides the *c.* about their camels' necks
1 *Kings* 6. 21. by the *c.* of gold before the oracle
Psal. 149. 8. to bind their kings with *c.* and nobles
Prov. 1. 9. instruction shall be *c.* about thy neck
Cant. 1. 10. thy neck comely with *c.* of gold
Isa. 3. 19. the Lord will take away thy *c.*
40. 19. goldsmith with gold, and casteth silver *c.*
45. 14. they shall come after thee in *c.* come over
Jer. 40. 4. I loose thee this day from thy *c.*
Ezek. 19. 4. they brought him with *c.* into Egypt
9. they put him in ward in *c.* and brought him
Mark 5. 3. no man could bind him, no not with *c.*
4. the *c.* had been oft plucked asunder by him
Acts 12. 7. Peter's *c.* fell off from his hands
2 *Pet.* 2. 4. to hell, delivered them into *c.* of darkn.
Jude 6. he hath reserved in everlasting *c.* under dark.
See BOUND.

CHALCEDONY.

Rev. 21. 19. the third foundation was a *c.*

CHALK-STONES.

Isa. 27. 9. he maketh all the *stones* of the altar *c.*

CHALLENGETH.

Exod. 22. 9. any lost thing another *c.* to be his

CHAMBER

Signifies, [1] *An apartment, or room in a house,* Gen. 43. 30. Dan. 6. 10. [2] *The clouds,* Psal. 104. 13. [3] *An upper room, or an apartment wherein people generally eat, where the disciples did eat the passover, and did partake of the Lord's supper, and where afterwards they assembled for divine worship,* Acts 1. 13. | 20. 8.

The chambers of the south, *Job* 9. 9. *Those stars and constellations which are towards the southern pole; so called, because they are for the most part hid and shut up, as chambers commonly are, from these parts of the world, and do not rise or appear to us till the beginning of summer, when they raise winds and tempests, as astronomers observe.*

The king hath brought me into his chambers, *Cant.* 1. 4. *Christ the King of his church has vouchsafed unto me most intimate and familiar fellowship with himself in his ordinances.*

Enter thou into thy chambers, *Isa.* 26. 20. *Fly to God by faith, prayer, and repentance, for protection, depend upon his providence, lay hold upon his promises, and make use of his attributes. He alludes to the common practice of men, who, when there are storms or dangers abroad, betake themselves to their own chambers or houses for safety; or, as some think, to that history,* Exod.

9. 19, 20. *or to that command*, of not going out of their houses, *Exod.* 12. 22. *or to the like charge given to* Rahab, *Josh.* 2. 19.
Gen. 43. 30. Joseph entered into his c. and wept
Judg. 15. 1. I will go in to my wife into the c.
16. 9. there were liers in wait abiding in the c. 12.
2 Sam. 13. 10. bring meat into the c. that I may eat
2 Kings 4. 11. Elisha turned into the c. and lay there
Neh. 13. 5. he prepared for Tobiah a great c.
8. cast forth all the household stuff out of the c.
Job 37. † 9. out of the c. cometh the whirlwind
Psal. 19. 5. as a bridegroom cometh out of his c.
Cant. 3. 4. into the c. of her that conceived me
Jer. 36. 10. read the book in the c. of Gemariah
20. laid up the roll in c. of Elishama the scribe
Ezek. 40. 45. c. whose prospect toward the south
46. c. whose prospect toward the north for priests
Dan. 6. 10. his windows being open in his c. to Jerus.
Joel 2. 16. let the bridegroom go forth of his c.
BED-CHAMBER; *See* BED. GUARD-CHAMBER; *See* GUARD.

Guest-CHAMBER.
Mark 14. 14. say, where is the *guest-c.* Luke 22. 11.

Inner CHAMBER.
1 Kings 20. 30. Benhadad fled, and came into *inner* c.
22. 25. shalt go into *inner* c. to hide, 2 Chr. 18. 24.
2 Kings 9. 2. carry Jehu into *inner* c. and take the box

Little CHAMBER.
2 Kings 4. 10. let us make a *little* c. on the wall
Ezek. 40. 7. *little* c. was one reed long and one broad
13. measured the gate from the roof of one *lit.* c.

Side CHAMBER, S.
Ezek. 41. 5. the breadth of every *side-c.* four cubits
6. the *side* c. were three, one over another
9. thickness of wall for *side-c.* without, five cubits

Upper CHAMBER.
2 Kings 1. 2. Ahaz fell thro' a lattice in his *upper* c.
23. 12. altars in top of the *upper* c. Josiah beat down
Acts 9. 37. washed, and laid Dorcas in an *upper* c.
39. brought Peter, when come into the *upper* c.
20. 8. many lights in *upper* c. where were gathered

CHAMBERS.
Deut. 32. † 25. sword without, terror from the c.
1 Kings 6. 5. against wall of the house he built c.
1 Chron. 9. 26. chief porters were over the c. 23. 28.
2 Chron. 31. 11. Hezekiah commanded to prepare c.
Ezra 8. 29. keep them till ye weigh them in the c.
Neh. 13. 9. I commanded, and they cleansed the c.
Job 9. 9. which maketh the c. of the south
Psal. 104. 3. who layeth beams of his c. in the waters
13. he watereth the hills from his c. earth satisfied
105. 30. land brought forth frogs in c. of their king
Prov. 7. 27. way to hell going down to c. of death
24. 4. by knowledge c. shall be filled with riches
Cant. 1. 4. the king hath brought me into his c.
Isa. 26. 20. enter thou into thy c. and shut thy doors
Jer. 22. 13. woe to him that buildeth his c. by wrong
14. I will build me a wide house, and large c.
Jer. 35. 2. bring the Rechabites into one of the c.
Ezek. 8. 12. every man in the c. of his imagery
21. 14. the sword which entereth into their privy c.
42. 13. they be holy c. where priests shall eat
Mat. 24. 26. behold, he is in the secret c. believe not

Upper-CHAMBERS.
2 Chr. 3. 9. and he overlaid the *upper* c. with gold
Ezek. 42. 5. the *upper* c. were shorter for galleries

CHAMBERING.
Rom. 13. 13. walk not in c. and wantonness

CHAMBERLAIN, S.
2 Kings 9. † 32. looked out to Jehu two or three c.
23. 11. by the chamber of Nathan-melech the c.
Esth. 1. 10. the seven c. that served the king
2. 15. but what Hegai the king's c. appointed
21. two of king's c. were wroth, and sought to lay
Acts 12. 20. Blastus the king's c. their friend
Rom. 16. 23. Erastus, c. of the city, saluteth you

CHAMOIS.
Deut. 14. 5. these ye shall eat, wild ox and the c.

CHAMPAIGN.
Duet. 11. 30. who dwell in the c. over against Gilgal
Ezek. 37. † 2. many bones in the open c.

CHAMPION.
1 Sam. 17. 4. there went out a c. out of the camp
51. when the Philistines saw their c. was dead

CHANCE.
Deut. 22. 6. if a bird's nest c. to be before thee
1 Cor. 15. 37. it may c. of wheat or other grain

CHANCE.
1 Sam. 6. 9. it was a c. that happened to us
2 Sam. 1. 6. as I happened by c. on mount Gilboa
Eccl. 9. 11. but time and c. happeneth to them all
Luke 10. 31. by c. a priest came down that way

CHANCETH.
Deut. 23. 10. uncleanness that c. him by night

CHANCELLOR.
Ezra 4. 8. Rehum c. wrote a letter to Artaxerxes, 9.
17. then the king sent answer to Rehum the c.

CHANGEABLE.
Isa. 3. 22. Lord take away the c. suits of apparel

CHANGE, S.
Lev. 27. 33. both it and the c. thereof shall be holy
Judg. 14. 12. I will give you thirty c. of raiment
13. you shall give me thirty c. of raiment
Job 11. † 10. if he make a c. who can hinder?
14. 14. all my days will I wait till my c. come
Prov. 24. 21. meddle not with them given to c.
Zech. 3. 4. I will clothe thee with c. of raiment
Heb. 7. 12. there is made of necessity a c. of the law

CHANGE, *Verb.*
Gen. 35. 2. be clean and c. your garments
Lev. 27. 10. he shall not c. it || 33. nor c. it, if he c.
Job 17. 12. they c. the night into day, light is short
Psal 102. 26. as a vesture shalt thou c. them
Isa. 9. 10. but we will c. them into cedars
40. † 31. that wait on the Lord shall c. strength
Jer. 2. 36. why gaddest thou so much to c. thy way?
13. 23. can Ethiopian c. his skin, or leopard spots?
Dan. 7. 25. he shall think to c. times and laws
Hos. 4. 7. I will c. their glory into shame
Hab. 1. 11. then shall his mind c. and pass over
Mal. 3. 6. for I am the Lord, I c. not, therefore
Acts 6. 14. and shall c. the customs delivered
Rom. 1. 26. their women did c. the natural use
Gal. 4. 20. I desire to be present, and c. my voice
Phil. 3. 21. Christ, who shall c. our vile body
Heb. 12. † 17. be found no way to c. his mind

CHANGED, ETH.
Gen. 31. 7. your father c. my wages ten times, 41.
41. 14. Joseph c. his raiment and came in to Pharaoh
Lev. 13. 16. if raw flesh turn and be c. to white
55. if the plague have not c. his colour
1 Sam. 21. 13. he c. his behaviour before them
2 Sam. 12. 20. Dav. c. his apparel, came to house of L.
2 Kings 24. 17. k. of Babylon c. his name to Zedek.
25. 29. c. his prison-garments, Jer. 52. 33.
Esth. 2. † 9. he c. her and maids to the best place
Job 29. † 20. my bow was c. in my hand
30. 18. great force of my disease is my garment c.
Psal. 15. 4. he sweareth to his hurt, and c. not
102. 26. as a vesture they shall be c. Heb. 1. 12.
106. 20. thus they c. their glory into an ox
Eccl. 8. 1. the boldness of his face shall be c.
Isa. 24. 5. c. the ordinance, broken the covenant
Jer. 2. 11. c. their gods, my people have c. their glory
48. 11. his taste remained, and his scent is not c.
Lam. 4. 1. gold dim, how is the most fine gold c.!
Ezek. 5. 6. she hath c. my judgments into wickedn.
Dan. 2. 9. prepar. lying to speak, till the time be c.
21. he c. the times and seasons, removeth kings
3. 19. form of his visage was c. against Shadrach
27. nor were their coats c. nor smell of fire passed
4. 16. let his heart be c. from man's, and let a beast's
6. 8. sign writing that it be not c. according to law
15. that no decree the king established may be c.
17. that the purpose might not be c. about Daniel
Mic. 2. 4. he hath c. the portion of my people
Acts 28. 6. the barbarians c. their minds, and said
Rom. 1. 23. c. the glory of the uncorruptible God
25. who c. the truth of God into a lie
1 Cor. 15. 51. not all sleep, but we shall all be c. 52.
2 Cor. 3. 18. c. into same image from glory to glory
Heb. 7. 12. for priesthood being c. a change of law

CHANGEST, ED, *countenance.*
Job 14. 20. thou c. his *countenance*, sendest him away
Dan. 5. 6. the king's *countenance* was c. in him, 9.
10. nor let thy *count.* be c. || 7. 28. my *count.* c. in me

CHANGERS.
Prov. 24. † 21. fear Lord and king, meddle not with c.
Mat. 21. 12. Jesus went to temple and overthrew tables of money-c. Mark 11. 15. John 2. 14, 15.

CHANGES.
Gen. 45. 22. to each he gave c. to Benjamin five c.
2 Kings 5. 5. he took with him ten c. of raiment
22. give them, I pray thee, two c. of garments
23. bound two c. of garments, and laid them
Job 10. 17. c. and war are against me
Psal. 55. 19. because they have no c. they fear not

CHANGING.
Ruth 4. 7. this was manner in Israel concerning c.

CHANNEL, S.
2 Sam. 22. 16. c. of the sea appeared, Psal. 18. 15.
Job 31. † 22. let my arm be broken from c. bone
Isa. 8. 7. he shall come up over all his c. and banks
27. 12. the Lord shall beat off from c. of the river

CHAPITER, S.
Exod. 36. 38. he overlaid their c. with gold, 38. 28.
38. 17. the overlaying of their c. were silver, 19.
1 Kings 7. 16. made two c. of brass, 2 Chron. 4. 12, 13.
2 Kings 25. 17. the c. upon it was brass, Jer. 52. 22.
Amos 9. † 1. smite the c. of the door that posts shake
Zeph. 2. † 14. the bittern shall lodge in the c.

CHAPMEN.
2 Chr. 9. 14. besides what c. and merchants brought

CHAPEL.
Amos 7. 13. it is the king's c. and the king's court

CHAPT.
Jer. 14. 4. because ground is c. there was no rain

CHARASHIM.
1 Chron. 4. 14. Joab the father of the valley of c.

CHARGE
Signifies, [1] *To command*, Exod. 1. 22. [2] *To prohibit, or interdict*, Gen. 28. 1. [3] *To adjure, or bind by a solemn oath*, 1 Sam. 14. 27. [4] *To load, or burden*, Deut. 24. 5. 1 Tim. 5. 16. [5] *To exhort*, 1 Thess. 2. 11. [6] *An office, or employ*, Num. 8. 26.
To lay any thing to one's charge, *is to accuse him of it, and prosecute and punish him for it*, Psal. 35. 11.
To have the charge of any thing, *to be intrusted with it, or to have the oversight and management of it*, Acts 8. 27.
Gen. 26. 5. Abraham kept my c. and my statutes
28. 6. Isaac gave Jacob a c. saying, not take a wife
Exod. 6. 13. the Lord gave Moses and Aaron a c.
Num. 4. 31. this is the c. of their burden in tabern.
8. 26. thus shalt do to the Levites, touching their c.
9. 19. then Israel kept the c. of the Lord, 23.
27. 23. Moses gave Joshua a c. Deut. 31. 23.
Deut. 21. 8. lay not innocent blood to people's c.
Josh. 22. 3. Reubenites have kept c. of the Lord
2 Sam. 17. † 23. Ahithophel gave c. concerning
18. 5. the king gave c. concerning Absalom
1 Kings 11. 28. Jeroboam made ruler over all the c.
2 Kings 7. 17. the lord to have the c. of the gate
1 Chron. 9. 27. because the c. was upon them
26. † 30. of Hebronites 1700 over the c.
2 Chr. 30. 17. Levites had the c. of killing passovers
Neh. 7. 2. I gave Hanani c. over Jerusalem
Esth. 3. 9. of those that had c. of the business
Job 34. 13. who hath given him a c. over the earth?
Psal. 35. 11. they laid to my c. things I knew not
109. † 8. let another take his c. Acts 1. † 20.
Jer. 39. 11. king of Bab. gave c. concerning Jeremiah
47. 7. Lord hath given it a c. against Ashkelon
Ezek. 9. 1. cause them that have c. over the city
44. 8. ye have not kept the c. of my holy things
15. the priests that kept the c. of my sanctuary
48. 11. priests kept my c. who went not astray
Acts 7. 60. Lord, lay not this sin to their c.
8. 27. an eunuch, who had c. of all her treasure
12. † 25. when Barnabas and Saul fulfilled their c.
16. 24. received such a c. thrust them into prison
23. 29. nothing laid to his c. worthy of death
Rom. 8. 33. who shall lay any thing to c. of God's elect
1 Cor. 9. 18. make the gospel of Christ without c.
1 Tim. 1. 18. this c. I commit to thee, son Timothy
2 Tim. 4. 16. I pray it may not be laid to their c.
See KEEP.

Give CHARGE.
Num. 27. 19. and *give* Joshua a c. in their sight
Deut. 31. 14. call Joshua that I may *give* him a c.
2 Sam. 14. 8. go, and I will *give* c. concerning thee
2 Kings 20. † 1. *give* c. concerning house, Isa. 38. † 1
1 Chron. 22. 12. only the L. *give* thee wisdom and c.
Psal. 91. 11. *give* his angels c. Mat. 4. 6. Luke 4. 10.
Isa. 10. 6. will I *give* him a c. to take the spoil
1 Tim. 5. 7. these things *give* in c. that they be
6. 13. I *give* thee c. in sight of God, who quickeneth

CHARGE.
Exod. 19. 21. the Lord said, go down, c. the people
Num. 5. 19. the priest shall c. her by an oath
Deut. 3. 28. but c. Joshua and encourage him
Neh. 10. 32. to c. ourselves yearly with third part
Esth. 4. 8. c. Esther that she go in to the king
Cant. 2. 7. I c. you, O ye daughters, 3. 5. | 5. 8. | 8. 4.
5. 9. what is thy beloved, that thou dost so c. us?
Mark 9. 25. I c. thee come out and enter no more
1 Thess. 5. 27. I c. you that this epistle be read
1 Tim. 1. 3. c. that they teach no other doctrine
5. 21. I c. thee before God and Jes. Christ, 2 Tim. 4. 1.
6. 17. c. them that are rich in this world, that they

CHARGEABLE.
2 Sam. 13. 25. let us not all go, lest we be c. to thee
Neh. 5. 15. the former governors were c. to people
2 Cor. 11. 9. when with you, I was c. to no man
1 Thess. 2. 9. because we would not be c. to any of you
2 Thess. 3. 8. that we might not be c. to any of you

CHARGED.
Gen. 26. 11. Abimelech c. his people, saying
28. 1. Isaac called Jacob, and c. him, and said
40. 4. captain of the guard, c. Joseph with them
49. 29. Jacob c. his sons, and said to them, I am
50. † 16. they c. a messenger to Joseph
Exod. 1. 22. Pharaoh c. all his people, saying
Deut. 1. 16. I c. your judges at that time, saying
24. 5. nor shall he be c. with any business, but free
27. 11. Moses c. the people the same day, saying
1 Sam. 14. 27. Jonathan heard not when Saul c. peop.
2 Sam. 18. 12. for in our hearing the king c. thee
1 Kings 2. 1. David c. Solomon his son, saying, I go
43. the commandment that I have c. thee with
13. 9. so was it c. me by the word of the Lord
2 Chron. 36. 23. Lord c. me to build house, Ezra 1. 2.
Neh. 13. 19. c. they not be opened till after sabbath
Esth. 2. 10. not shewed people, as Mordecai c. her, 20.
Job 1. 22. Job sinned not, nor c. God foolishly
4. 18. and his angels he c. with folly
Jer. 32. 13. I c. Baruch before them, saying
35. 8. have obeyed Jonadab in all that he hath c. us
Mat. 9. 30. Jesus straitly c. them, saying, see that no man know it, Mark 5. 43. Luke 9. 21.
12. 16. Jesus c. not to make him known, Mark 3. 12.
Mark 7. 36. c. not to tell, 8. 30. | 9. 9. Luke 5. 14. | 8. 56.
10. 48. many c. him that he should hold his peace
Rom. 3. † 9. we have c. Jews and Gentiles under sin
1 Thess. 2. 11. we c. every one of you as a father
1 Tim. 5. 16. and let not church be c. that it may

CHARGEDST.
Exod. 19. 23. thou c. us, saying, set bounds about

CHARGER, S.
Num. 7. 13. his offering was one silver c. 19, 25, 31, 37, 43, 49, 61, 67, 73, 79.
84. this was the dedication of the altar, twelve c.
85. each c. of silver weighing 130 shekels
Ezra 1. 9. this is number of them, one thousand c.
Mat. 14. 8. give John Bapt. head in a c. Mark 6. 25.

CHARGES.
2 Chron. 8. 14. he appointed the Levites to their c.
31. 17. from 20 years in their c. by courses
35. 2. he set priests in their c. and encouraged them
Acts 21. 24. them take, and be at c. with them
1 Cor. 9. 7. who goeth a warfare at his own c.?

CHARGEST.
2 Sam. 3. 8. thou c. me to-day with a fault

CHARGING.
Acts 16. 23. c. the jailor to keep them safely
2 Tim. 2. 14. c. that they strive not about words

CHARIOT
Signifies, [1] *A sort of light coach*, Gen. 46. 29. [2] *Chariots of war, out of which some of the ancients fought; they were armed with javelins and scythes in several places, which tore every thing they met with to pieces*, Exod 14. 7. Josh. 11. 4. [3] *Hosts, or armies*, Psal. 68. 17. [4] *Human or worldly things, wherein men repose their confidence*, Psal. 20. 7.
Elijah *is called the* chariot of Israel and horsemen thereof, 2 Kings 2. 12. *that is, By his example, his counsels, his prayers, and power with God, he did more for the defence and preservation of* Israel, *than all their chariots and horses, and other warlike provisions.*
Solomon made a chariot of the wood of Lebanon, Cant. 3. 9. Christ, *of whom* Solomon *was a type, established for the glory of his grace the new covenant, or the gospel, whereby believers are carried to heaven; which is of an everlasting nature,* Heb. 13. 20. Rev. 14. 6.
Gen. 41. 43. he made him to ride in the second c.
Exod. 14. 25. the Lord took off their c. wheels
1 Kings 7. 33. the wheels like the work of a c. wheel
18. 44. prepare thy c. and get thee down
20. 25. number thee c. for c. and we will fight
33. he caused him to come up into the c.
22. 35. the blood ran into the midst of the c.
38. one washed the c. in the pool of Samaria
2 Kings 2. 11. there appeared a c. of fire and horses
12. cried, my father, the c. of Israel, 13. 14.
5. 21. he lighted from the c. to meet Gehazi
9. 16. Jehu rode in a c. || 27. smite him in the c.
28. servants carried him in a c. to Jerus. 23. 30.
1 Chron. 28. 18. gave gold for the pattern of the c.
2 Chron. 35. 24. his servants took him out of the c.
Psal. 46. 9. he burneth the c. in the fire
76. 6. c. and horse are cast into a dead sleep

Cant. 3. 9. made a c. of the wood of Lebanon
Isa. 21. 7. he saw a c. with horsemen, a c. of asses
9. here cometh a c. of men with horsemen
43. 17. who bringeth forth the c. and horse
Jer. 51. 21. will I break in pieces the c. and rider
Mic. 1. 13. bind the c. to the swift beast
Zech. 6. 2. first c. red horses, second c. black horses
9. 10. I will cut off the c. from Ephraim
Acts 8. 29. said, go near and join thyself to this c.
38. he commanded the c. to stand still
His CHARIOT.
Gen. 46. 29. Joseph made ready his c. and went
Exod. 14. 6. Pharaoh made ready his c. and took
Judg. 4. 15. Sisera lighted off his c. and fled away
5. 28. why is his c. so long in coming? why tarry
1 Kings 12. 18. king made speed to his c. 2 Chr. 10. 18.
22. 34. he said to the driver of his c. turn thy hand
35. Ahab was stayed up in his c. and died at even
2 Kings 5. 9. Naaman came with his c. and stood
26. when the man turned again from his c.
9. 21. his c. was made ready, went out each in his c.
24. smote Jehoram, and he sunk down in his c.
10. 16. so they made him to ride in his c.
Psal. 104. 3. who maketh the clouds his c.
Jer. 4. 13. his c. shall be as a whirlwind
Acts 8. 28. sitting in his c. read Esaias the prophet
CHARIOT-CITIES.
2 Chron. 1. 14. horsemen which he placed in c.-cities
8. 6. Solomon built c.-cities, and store cities
9. 25. bestowed in the c.-cities and with the king
CHARIOT-HORSES.
2 Sam. 8. 4. David houghed all c.-horses, 1 Chr. 18. 4.
2 Kings 7. 14. they took therefore two c.-horses
CHARIOT-MAN.
2 Chr. 18. 33. he said to the c.-man, turn thy hand
CHARIOTS.
Gen. 50. 9. there went up with Joseph c. and horse.
Exod. 14. 7. Pharaoh took 600 c. and all the c.
17. I will get honour upon his c. and horsemen
28. the waters covered all the c. and all the host
15. 4. Pharaoh's c. and host hath he cast into sea
19. for the horse of Pharaoh went in with his c.
Josh. 17. 16. have c. of iron, 18. Judg. 1. 19. | 4. 3.
Judg. 4. 15. Lord discomfited Sisera and all his c.
5. 28. she cried, why tarry the wheels of his c.?
1 Sam. 8. 11. the king will appoint them for his c.
13. 5. Philistines, to fight against Israel, 30,000 c.
2 Sam. 1. 6. the c. and horsemen followed after Saul
10. 18. David slew the men of 700 c. of Syrians
1 Kings 10. 26. Solomon had 1400 c. 12,000 horsemen
16. 9. Zimri captain of half his c. conspired
22. 32 when the captains of the c. saw Jehoshaphat
2 Kings 13. 7. left but ten c. and fifty horsemen
18. 24. how put thy trust on Egypt for c. Isa. 36. 9.
Psal. 68. 17. the c. of God are twenty thousand
Cant. 6. 12. my soul like the c. of Ammi nadib
Isa. 2. 7. full of horses, nor is any end of their c.
22. 18. c. of thy glory be the shame of thy lord
31. 1. woe to them that trust in c. because many
37. 24. by the multitude of my c. am I come up
66. 15. behold the Lord will come with fire and c.
like a whirlwind, Jer. 4. 13. Dan. 11. 40.
Jer. 47. 3. at rushing of his c. fathers not look back
Ezek. 23. 24. they shall come against thee with c.
26. 10. thy walls shall shake at the noise of the c.
Joel 2. 5. like the noise of the c. shall they leap
Mic. 5. 10. I will cut off horses, and destroy thy c.
Nah. 2. 3. the c. shall be with flaming torches
4. the c. shall rage in streets and justle one another
13. I am against, and I will burn her c. in smoke
Hag. 2. 22. I will overthrow the c. and those ride
Rev. 9. 9. the sound of their wings as the sound of c.
CHARIOTS, with horses.
Exod. 14. 9. all the horses and c. of Pharaoh, 23.
Deut. 11. 4. what he did to their horses and c.
20. 1. when thou seest horses and c. fear not
Josh. 11. 6. thou shalt hough their horses, burn c.
9. Joshua houghed horses, burnt their c. with fire
2 Sam. 15. 1. Absalom prepared horses and c.
1 Kings 20. 1. against Samaria with c. and horses
2 Kings 6. 17. the mountain was full of c. and horses
7. 6. the Syrians to hear a noise of horses and c.
10. 2. are with you c. and horses, a fenced city
Psal. 20. 7. some trust in c. and some in horses
Cant. 1. 9. compared thee to horses in Pharaoh's c.
Isa. 66. 20. bring your brethren on horses and in c.
Jer. 17. 25. shall enter princes riding in c. 22. 4.
46. 9. come up, ye horses, and rage, ye c.
50. 37. a sword is upon their horses and their c.
Ezek. 26. 7. upon Tyrus Nebuchad. with h. and c.
39. 20. shall be filled at my table with horses and c.
Nah. 3. 2. noise of prancing horses and jumping c.
Hab. 3. 8. didst ride on thy horses and c. of salvation
Rev. 18. 13. no man buys their horses and c.
CHARITABLY.
Rom. 14. 15. brother grieved, now walkest not c.
CHARITY
Is a principle of prevailing love to God and good will to men, which effectually inclines one endued with it to glorify God, and to do good to others; to be patient, slow to anger, and ready to put up with wrongs; to show kindness to all, and seek the good of others, though with prejudice to himself. A person endued therewith does not interpret doubtful things to the worst sense, but the best; is sorry for the sins of others, but rejoices when any one does well, and is apt to bear with their failings and infirmities; and lastly, this grace is never lost, but goes with us into another world, and is exercised there, 1 Cor. 13. 1, 4, &c.
Rom. 14. †15. now walkest thou not according to c.
1 Cor. 8. 1. knowledge puffeth up, but c. edifieth
13. 1. speak with tongues, and have not, c. 2, 3.
4. c. suffereth long, and is kind, c. envieth not
13. faith, hope, c. but the greatest of these is c.
14. 1. follow after c. and desire spiritual gifts
16. 14. let all your things be done with c.
Col. 3. 14. above all these things put on c.
1 Thess. 3. 6. brought good tidings of your faith and c.
2 Thess. 1. 3. c. towards each other aboundeth
1 Tim. 1. 5. now the end of the commandment is c.
2. 15. be saved if they continue in faith and c.

1 Tim. 4. 12. be an example in c. in spirit, in faith
2 Tim. 2. 22. follow righteousness, faith, c. peace
3. 10. hast fully known my doctrine, life, faith, c.
Tit. 2. 2. aged men be sober, sound in faith, in c.
1 Pet. 4. 8. have fervent c. for c. shall cover sins
5. 14. greet ye one another with a kiss of c.
2 Pet. 1. 7. and to brotherly kindness c.
3 John 6. strangers who have borne witness of thy c.
Jude 12. these are spots in your feasts of c.
Rev. 2. 19. I know thy works, and c. and service
CHARMED.
Jer. 8. 17. I will send serpents which will not be c.
CHARMER, S.
Deut. 18. 11. there shall not be found among you a c.
Psal. 58. 5. not hearken to the voice of c. charming
† not hearken to c. be the c. never so cunning
CHASE.
Lev. 26. 7. ye shall c. your enemies, and they fall
8. and five of you shall c. an hundred
36. and the sound of a shaking leaf shall c. them
Deut. 32. 30. how should one c. 1000. Josh 23. 10.
Psal. 35. 5. let the angel of the Lord c. them
CHASED, ETH, ING.
Deut. 1. 44. and the Amorites c. you as bees do
Judg. 9. 40. Abimelech c. him, he fled before him
20. 43. they inclosed Benjamites and c. them
1 Sam. 17. 53. Israel returned from c. the Philistines
Neh. 13. 28. therefore I c. him from me
Job 18. 18. he shall be c. out of the world
20. 8. he shall be c. away as a vision of the night
Prov. 19. 26. and he that c. away his mother
Isa. 13. 14. it shall be as the c. roe, as a sheep that
17. 13. they shall be c. as the chaff before the wind
Lam. 3. 52. mine enemies c. me sore like a bird
1 Thess. 2. †15. killed their prophets, and c. us out
CHASTE.
2 Cor. 11. 2. that I may present you as a c. virgin
Tit. 2. 5. that the young women be c. obedient
1 Pet. 3. 2. while they behold your c. conversation
CHASTEN
Signifies, [1] To correct in love, Psal. 118. 18. Heb. 12. 5, 6. [2] To punish in justice, Lev. 26. 28. [3] To humble oneself before God by fasting and prayer, Dan. 10. 12.
The chastisement of our peace was upon him, Isa. 53. 5. That punishment by which our peace, that is, our reconciliation to God, and salvation or happiness, were to be purchased, was laid upon Christ, by God's justice, with his own consent.
2 Sam. 7. 14. I will c. him with the rod of men
Psal. 6. 1. nor c. me in thy hot displeasure, 38. 1.
Prov. 19. 18. c. thy son while there is hope, spare
Dan. 10. 12. thou didst c. thyself before thy God
Rev. 3. 19. as many as I love I rebuke and c.
CHASTENED.
Deut. 21. 18. they have c. him, he will not hearken
Job 33. 19. he is c. also with pain on his bed
Psal. 69. 10. I wept, and c. my soul with fasting
73. 14. all day been plagued, and c. every morning
118. 18. Lord hath c. me sore, he hath not given
Hos. 7. †15. though I have c. they imagine mischief
1 Cor. 11. 32. we are c. that we be not condemned
2 Cor. 6. 9. as dying, yet live, as c. and not killed
Heb. 12. 10. for they verily for a few days c. us
CHASTENEST, ETH, ING.
Deut. 8. 5. as a man c. his son, so the Lord c. thee
Job 5. 17. happy whom God correcteth; despise not thou c. of Almighty, Prov. 3. 11. Heb. 12. 5.
Psal. 94. 12. blessed is the man whom thou c.
Prov. 13. 24. but he that loveth him c. betimes
Isa. 26. 16. poured out a prayer when c. was on them
Heb. 12. 6. for whom the Lord loveth he c.
7. if ye endure c. what son whom father c. not?
11. no c. for present seems to be joyous, but griev.
CHASTISE.
Lev. 26. 28. I will c. you seven times for your sins
Deut. 22. 18. elders shall take the man and c. him
1 Kings 12. 11. I will add to your yoke, I will c. you with scorpions, 14. 2 Chron. 10. 11, 14.
Hos. 7. 12. I will c. them as their congregation heard
10. 10. it is my desire that I should c. them
Luke 23. 16. I will c. him, and release him, 22.
CHASTISED, ETH.
1 Kings 12. 11. did lade with heavy yoke; father hath c. you with whips, 14. 2 Chron. 10. 11, 14.
Ps. 94. 10. he that c. heathen, shall not he correct?
Jer. 31. 18. hast c. me, and I was c. turn thou me
CHASTISEMENT.
Deut. 11. 2. your children who have not seen the c.
Job 34. 31. I have borne c. I will not offend more
Psal. 73. †14. my c. was every morning
Isa. 53. 5. the c. of our peace was upon him
Jer. 30. 14. have wounded with the c. of a cruel one
Heb. 12. 8. if without c. then are ye bastards, not sons
CHANT.
Amos 6. 5. they c. to the sound of the viol, and invent
CHATTER.
Isa. 38. 14. like a crane or swallow, so did I c.
CHAWS.
Ezek. 29. 4. but I will put hooks in thy c. 38. 4.
CHEARFUL; see CHEERFUL.
CHECK.
Job 20. 3. I have heard the c. of my reproach
CHECKER-WORK.
1 Kings 7. 17. Hiram made nets of c.-w. and wreaths
CHEEK.
1 Kings 22. 24. Zedekiah smote Micaiah on the c. said, which way Spirit of Lord, 2 Chron. 18. 23.
Job 16. 10. have smitten me on the c. reproachfully
Lam. 3. 30. he giveth his c. to him that smiteth him
Mic. 5. 1. shall smite the judge with a rod on the c.
Luke 6. 29. to him smiteth one c. offer also the other
Right CHEEK.
Mat. 5. 39. smite thee on thy right c. turn the other
CHEEK-BONE.
Psal. 3. 7. hast smitten all mine enemies on c.-bone
CHEEKS.
Deut. 18. 3. shall give to priest the two c. and maw
Cant. 1. 10. thy c. are comely with rows of jewels
5. 13. his c. are as a bed of spices, as sweet flowers
Isa. 50. 6. I gave my c. to them that plucked off hair
Lam. 1. 2. she weepeth, and her tears are on her c.

CHEEK-TEETH.
Joel 1. 6. nation come up, hath c.-teeth of a great lion
CHEER.
Deut. 24. 5. and shall c. up his wife he hath taken
Eccl. 11. 9. let thy heart c. thee in days of thy youth
CHEER.
Prov. 17. †1. than a house full of good c. with strife
Mat. 9. 2. son, be of good c. thy sins be forgiven thee
14. 27. be of good c. it is I, be not afraid, Mark 6. 50.
John 16. 33. be of good c. I have overcome world
Acts 23. 11. stood by him and said, be of good c.
27. 22. and now I exhort you to be of good c.
25. wherefore, sirs, be of good c. for I believe God
36. then were they all of good c. and took meat
CHEERETH.
Judg. 9. 13. leave my wine, which c. God and man
CHEERFUL.
Prov. 15. 13. merry heart maketh a c. countenance
Zech. 8. 19. shall be to house of Judah joy and c. f.
9. 17. corn shall make young men c. and new wine
2 Cor. 9. 7. or of necessity, for G. loveth a c. giver
CHEERFULNESS.
Rom. 12. 8. he that sheweth mercy with c.
CHEERFULLY.
Acts 24. 10. I do the more c. answer for myself
CHEESE, S.
1 Sam. 17. 18. carry these ten c. to the captain
2 Sam. 17. 29. Barzillai brought sheep and c. to D.
Job 10. 10. hast thou not curdled me like c.?
CHERISH.
1 Kings 1. 2. let her c. him, and lie in thy bosom
CHERISHED.
1 Kings 1. 4. the damsel was fair, and c. the king
CHERISHETH.
Eph. 5. 29. c. his own flesh, as the Lord the church
1 Thess. 2. 7. were gentle, even as a nurse c. children
CHERUB.
This word in the Hebrew signifies fulness of knowledge; and angels are so called from their exquisite knowledge, and were therefore used for the punishment of man, who sinned by affecting divine knowledge, Gen. 3. 24. There is but an obscure description given us in scripture of these cherubims, which Moses placed upon the ark of the covenant, Exod. 25. 18. as well as of those which God posted at the entrance of that delightful garden out of which he had driven Adam and Eve. But it is probable that both one and the other had a human figure, since it is said of those which were placed at the entrance of Paradise, that they had their station there assigned them, to guard the entrance to it, and held a flaming sword in their hands. And Ezekiel compares the king of Tyre to the cherub that covered the ark of the covenant, Ezek. 28. 14. that is, he was like to this cherub, glittering all over with gold and glory. Moses says, that two cherubims covered the mercy-seat with their wings extended on both sides, and looked one to another, having their faces turned toward the mercy-seat which covered the ark. God is supposed to sit on the mercy-seat, whose face the angels in heaven always behold, and upon whom their eyes are fixed to observe and receive his commands, and towards Christ, the true Propitiatory, which mystery they desire to look into, 1 Pet. 1. 12. not envying mankind their near and happy relation to him, but taking pleasure in the contemplation of it. Moses likewise calls those representations which were made in embroideries upon the veils of the tabernacle, cherubims of cunning work, Exod. 26. 1.
Exod. 25. 19. make one c. on one end, and the other c. on the other end, 37. 8.
2 Sam. 22. 11. he rode upon a c. Psal. 18. 10.
1 Kings 6. 25. and the other c. was ten cubits
26. the height of one c. ten cubits, so of the other
Ezek. 9. 3. the glory of God was gone up from the c. to the threshold of the house, 10. 4.
10. 7. and one c. stretched forth his hand from the
14. first face was the face of a c. second of a man
28. 14. thou art the anointed c. that covereth
16. and I will destroy thee, O covering c.
41. 18. between a c. and a c. every c. had two faces
CHERUBIMS.
Gen. 3. 24. he placed at the east of the garden c.
Exod. 25. 18. thou shalt make two c. of gold
26. 1. the tabernacle of c. of cunning work, 31.
37. 7. he made two c. of beaten gold of one piece
1 Kings 6. 23. within the oracle he made two c.
25. both the c. were of one measure and one size
28. and he overlaid the c. with gold
8. 7. the c. covered the ark, 2 Chr. 5. 8. Heb. 9. 5.
2 Chr. 3. 10. in the most holy place he made two c.
Ezek. 10. 5. the sound of the c. wings was heard
16. when the c. went, the wheels went by them
19. c. lift up their wings and mounted, 11. 22.
Between the CHERUBIMS.
Exod. 25. 22. will meet thee from between the two c
Num. 7. 89. from between the two c. he spake to him
1 Sam. 4. 4. the ark of Lord which dwelleth between the c. 2 Sam. 6. 2. 2 Kings 19. 15. Isa. 37. 16.
Psal. 80. 1. that dwelleth between the c. shine forth
99. 1. he sitteth between the c. let earth be moved
Ezek. 10. 2. fill with coals of fire from between the c.
7. hand from between c. to fire that was between c.
CHESNUT-TREE, S.
Gen. 30. 37. and Jacob took him rods of c.-tree
Ezek. 31. 8. the c.-trees were not like his branches
CHEST, S.
2 Kings 12. 9. Jehoiada took c. and bored hole in lid
2 Chr. 24. 8. at king's commandment they made c.
11. high-priest's officer came, and emptied the c.
Ezek. 27. 24. thy merchants in c. of rich apparel
CHEW.
Lev. 11. 4. not eat of them that c. the cud, Deut. 14. 7.
CHEWED.
Num. 11. 33. ere the flesh was c. wrath was kindled
CHEWETH.
Lev. 11. 4. because he c. the cud, 5, 6. Deut. 14. 6.
7. yet the swine c. not the cud, Deut. 14. 8.
CHICKENS.
Mat. 23. 37. gathered even as a hen gathereth her c

CHIDE.

Exod. 17. 2. the people did c. why c. you with me?
Judg. 8. 1. the men of Ephraim did c. with Gideon
Psal. 103. 9. he will not always c. nor keep anger

CHIDING.

Exod. 17. 7. called Meribah, because of c. of Israel

CHIEF

Signifies, [1] *The principal person of a family congregation, tribe, army, &c.* Num. 3. 30. Deut. 1. 15. 1 Sam. 14. 38. 2 Sam. 5. 8. [2] *The best, or most valuable,* 1 Sam. 15. 21. [3] *The highest, or uppermost,* Mat. 23. 6. [4] *The dearest, or most familiar,* Prov. 16. 28. [5] *The greatest,* Psal. 137. 6. [6] *Most in esteem and reputation,* Luke 14. 1. 2 Cor. 12. 11. [7] *Most forward and active,* Ezra 9. 2. [8] *Most remarkable and wonderful,* Job 40. 19.

Gen. 37. † 36. they sold Joseph to a c. marshal
40. 9. the c. butler told his dream to Joseph
21. he restored the c. butler to his butlership again
22. but hanged the c. baker as Joseph interpreted
Num. 3. 32. Eleazar shall be c. over c. of Levites
Deut. 1. 15. I took the c. of your tribes, wise men
1 Sam. 15. 21. the people took the c. of the things
2 Sam. 23. 18. Abishai brother of Joab c. among three
1 Kings 9. 23. these were the c. of the officers
1 Chron. 5. 2. for of Judah came the c. ruler
11. 6. whosoever smiteth the Jebusites first shall be c. and captain, Joab went first and was c.
18. 17. the sons of David were c. about the king
26. 10. tho' not first-born his father made him c.
Ezra 9. 2. the rulers have been c. in this trespass
Neh. 11. 3. these are c. of the province that dwelt
Job 12. 24. he taketh away heart of c. of people
29. 25. I chose out their way, and sat c. dwelt as
40. 19. behemoth is the c. of the ways of God
Psal. 78. 51. he smote c. of their strength, 105. 36.
137. 6. if I prefer not Jerusalem above my c. joy
Prov. 1. 21. Wisdom crieth in c. place of concourse
8. † 26. nor had made c. part of the dust of the world
16. 28. a whisperer separateth c. friends
Cant. 4. 14. an orchard with all the c. spices
Isa. 14. 9. he stirreth up the c. ones of the earth
Jer. 13. 21. thou hast taught them as c. over thee
31. 7. sing and shout among the c. of the nations
50. † 36. a sword is upon their c. stays, shall dote
51. † 59. this Seraiah was a c. chamberlain
Lam. 1. 5. her adversaries are the c. enemies prosper
Ezek. 4. † 2. set c. leaders against Jerusalem round
20. † 40. there will I require c. of your oblations
44. † 30. c. of the first fruits shall be the priest's
Dan. 2. † 14. Daniel answer. Arioch the c. marshal
11. 41. the c. of children of Ammon shall escape
Amos 6. 1. which are named c. of the nations
6. drunk and anoint themselves with c. ointments
Mat. 20. 27. whosoever will be c. among you, let
23. 6. they love the uppermost rooms at feasts and c. seats in the synagogues, Mark 12. 39.
Mark 6. 21. Herod made a supper to his c. estates
Luke 11. 15. casteth out devils thro' c. of the devils
14. 1. he went into house of one of the c. Pharisees
7. he marked how they chose the c. rooms, 20. 46.
22. 26. and he that is c. as he that doth serve
John 12. 42. among c. rulers many believed on him
Acts 14. 12. because Paul was the c. speaker
17. 4. some believed, and of c. women not a few
Eph. 2. 20. Jesus Christ the c. corner-stone, 1 Pet. 2. 6.
1 Tim. 1. 15. Jesus came to save sinners of whom I c.
1 Pet. 5. 4. when c. Shepherd shall appear, shall receive

CHIEF *captain.*

2 Sam. 5. 8. who smiteth he shall be c. and captain
Acts 21. 31. tidings came to the c. captain of band
32. when they saw the c. captain they left beating
23. 17. Paul said, bring this young man to c. captain
24. 7. c. captain Lysias came upon us, took him
22. c. captain shall come, I will know uttermost

CHIEF *captains.*

2 Sam. 23. 8. Adino the Tachmonite sat c. among capt.
1 Chron. 27. 3. c. of all the captains for first month
2 Chron. 8. 9. but Israel were c. of Solomon's capt.
Acts 25. 23. when Agrippa was entered with c. capt.
Rev. 6. 15. rich men and c. captains hid themselves

CHIEF *fathers.*

Num. 31. 26. thou and the c. fathers of congregation
1 Chron. 9. 34. these c. fathers of Levites were chief
24. 31. the c. fathers of the priests and Levites
26. 32. were 2700 c. fathers David made rulers
2 Chron. 26. 12. whole number of c. fathers of mighty
Ezra 1. 5. then rose up the c. of the fathers of Judah
Neh. 7. 70. the c. of the fathers gave to the work, 71.

CHIEF *house.*

Num. 3. 24. the c. of house of Gershonites, Eliasaph
30. the c. of house of the Kohathites, Elizaphan
35. c. of the house of the Merarites, was Zuriel
25. 14. Zimri was of a c. house among Simeonites
15. name of woman was Cozbi, of a c. h. in Midian
Josh. 22. 14. out of each c. house a prince was sent

CHIEF *man,* or *men.*

Lev. 21. 4. not defile himself, being a c. man
1 Chron. 7. 3. the sons of Uzzi, all of them c. men
24. 4. more c. men of Eleazar than of Ithamar
Ezra 5. 10. the names of the men that were c.
7. 28. I gathered together c. men to go up with me
Isa. 41. 9. I called thee from the c. men thereof
Acts 13. 50. but the Jews stirred up the c. men
15. 22. Judas and Silas, c. men among brethren
28. 7. were possessions of the c. man of the island

CHIEF *priest.*

2 Kings 25. 18. the capt. took Seraiah the c. priest
1 Chron. 27. 5. Benaiah a c. priest was third capt.
29. 22. and anointed Zadok to be c. priest
2 Chron. 19. 11. Amariah c. p. is over you in matters
26. 20. and Azariah the c. priest looked on him

CHIEF *priests.*

Ezra 8. 24. then I separated twelve of c. of priests
10. 5. made the c. priests and all Israel to swear
Neh. 12. 7. these were c. priests in days of Joshua
Mat. 16. 21. and suffer many things of the c. priests
26. 47. a multitude with staves from the c. priests
27. 12. when he was accused of c. priests, Mark 15. 3.
41. c. priests mocking with scribes, Mark 15. 31.
Mark 14. 1. c. priests sought to take him and put him to death, 55. Mat. 26. 59. Luke 9. 22. | 22. 2.
Luke 23. 23. voices of them and c. priests prevailed
John 7. 32. c. priests sent officers to take him, 18. 3.
19. 15. c. priests answered, we have no king but Cesar
Acts 9. 14. he hath authority from c. priests, 26. 10.
22. 30. commanded the c. p. and council to appear

CHIEF *prince,* or *princes.*

1 Chron. 5. † 2. and of Judah came the c. prince
7. 40. were children of Asher, c. of the princes
Ezek. 38. 2. Gog c. prince of Meshech, 3. | 39. 1.
Dan. 10. 13. Michael one of the c. princes came

CHIEF *singer,* or *singers.*

Neh. 12. 46. in days of David were c. of the singers
Hab. 3. 19. to the c. singer on my instruments

CHIEFEST.

1 Sam. 2. 29. to make yourselves fat with c. offerings
9. 22. Samuel made them sit in the c. place
21. 7. Doeg an Edomite, c. of the herd-men to Saul
2 Chr. 32. 33. Hezekiah buried in c. of sepulchres
Cant. 5. 10. my beloved is the c. among 10,000
Mark 10. 44. who will be c. shall be servant of all
2 Cor. 11. 5. not a whit behind c. of apostles, 12. 11.

CHIEFLY.

Rom. 3. 2. c. because to them were commit. oracles
Phil. 4. 22. c. they that are of Cesar's household
2 Pet. 2. 10. but c. them that walk after the flesh

CHILD

Signifies, [1] *One young in years,* 1 Sam. 1. 22. [2] *One weak in knowledge,* Isa. 10. 19. 1 Cor. 13. 11. [3] *Such as are young in grace,* 1 John 2. 13. [4] *Such as are humble and docile,* Mat. 18. 3, 4. [5] *Whatsoever is dear to a person,* Jer. 15. 7.

CHILD, CHILDREN, or SONS, *are taken different ways in Scripture. The descendants of a man, how remote soever they may be, are called* sons, *or* children. *For example:* the children of Edom, the children of Moab, the children of Israel. *These expressions,* the children of light, the children of darkness, *are used to signify those who follow light, and those who remain in darkness:* the children of the kingdom, *those who belong to the kingdom. Persons who are almost of age, are often called* children. *For example:* Joseph *is called a* child *though he was at least sixteen years old,* Gen. 37. 30. *and* Benjamin *of the age of above thirty, is still called* a little child, Gen. 44. 20. *Likewise men of full age have often the name of* children *given them,* Isa. 65. 20. The child shall die an hundred years old; that is, *men shall die at the age of an hundred years; there shall be no more untimely deaths seen.*

CHILDREN, *or* Sons of God. *By this name angels are sometimes described, as,* Job 1. 6. | 2. 1. There was a day when the sons of God came to present themselves before the Lord. *Good men, in opposition to the wicked, are likewise called by this name; the children of* Seth's *family in opposition to the race of* Cain, Gen. 6. 2. The sons of God saw the daughters of men. *Judges and magistrates are likewise termed* children of God, Psal. 82. 6. I have said, ye are gods; and all of you are the children of the Most High.

In the New Testament, believers are commonly called the children of God, *by virtue of their adoption, and the prerogatives which* Christ *purchased for them by the merits of his death and sufferings.* John 1. 12. He hath given us power to become the sons of God: *and elsewhere; see* Rom. 8. 14. Gal. 3. 26.

CHILDREN, *or* Sons of men. *This name is given to the men of* Cain's *family, who lived before the deluge; and in particular to the giants, those violent and corrupt men, who before the deluge had corrupted their ways, and drew down the most terrible effects of God's anger upon the earth. Afterwards the impious, the wicked* Israelites *were called the* sons of men, Psal. 4. 2. O ye sons of men, how long will ye love vanity? See Psal. 12. 1. | 57. 4. *But very often, by* sons of men, *mankind are to be understood, without any odious notion, as,* Psal. 8. 4. What is the son of man, that thou visitest him? Psal. 11. 4. | 145. 12.

Gen. 21. 15. Hagar cast the c. under one of the shrubs
16. she said, let me not see the death of the c.
37. 30. the c. is not, and I, whither shall I go?
42. 22. spake I not, do not sin against the c.?
Exod. 2. 8. the maid went, and called the c. mother
22. 22. ye shall not afflict any fatherless c.
Judg. 11. 34. Jephthah's daughter was his only c.
13. 8. and teach us what we shall do to the c.
1 Sam. 1. 25. and they brought the c. to Eli
3. 8. Eli perceived the Lord had called the c.
2 Sam. 12. 14. the c. that is born to thee shall die
15. Lord struck the c. that Uriah's wife bare
16. David therefore besought God for the c.
19. David perceived that the c. was dead
1 Kings 3. 25. he said, divide the living c. in two
14. 3. he shall tell thee, what shall become of the c.
17. 22. the soul of the c. came into him again
2 Kings 4. 31. he told him, the c. is not awaked
35. the c. sneezed, and the c. opened his eyes
Prov. 23. 13. withhold not correction from the c.
Eccl. 4. 8. yea, he hath neither c. nor brother
15. with second c. that shall stand up in his stead
Isa. 3. 5. the c. shall behave himself proudly
7. 16. for before the c. shall know to refuse the evil
8. 4. before the c. shall know to cry, my father
11. 8. the weaned c. put his hand on cockatrice den
65. 20. the c. shall die an hundred years old
Jer. 4. 31. as of her that bringeth forth her first c.
31. 20. is Ephraim my son? is he a pleasant c.?
44. 7. to cut off from you man, woman, and c.
Mat. 10. 21. the father shall deliver the c. to death
17. 18. the c. was cured from that very hour
23. 15. ye make him twofold more the c. of hell
Luke 1. 59. on eighth day they came to circumcise c.
66. saying, what manner of c. shall this be?
76. thou c. shalt be called Prophet of the Highest
80. the c. grew, and waxed strong in spirit, 2. 40.
Luke 2. 27. when the parents brought in the c. Jesus
9. 38. Master, look on my son, he is my only c.
42. Jesus healed c. and delivered him to his father
John 4. 49. sir, come down ere my c. die
16. 21. but as soon as she is delivered of the c.
Acts 4. 27. of a truth against thy holy c. Jesus
30. that signs may be done by name of thy c. Jesus
13. 10. Saul said, thou c. of the devil, thou enemy
Rev. 12. 4. to devour her c. as soon as it was born
5. her c. was caught up to God and to his throne

A CHILD.

Gen. 18. 13. shall I of a surety bear a c. who am old?
44. 20. a father, and a c. of his old age, a little one
Exod. 2. 2. she saw he was a goodly c. Heb. 11. 23.
1 Sam. 2. 18. Samuel, a c. girded with a linen ephod
1 Kings 3. 17. was delivered of a c. with her in house
13. 2. a c. shall be born to house of David, Josiah
Job 33. 25. his flesh shall be fresher than a c.
Psal. 131. 2. I quieted myself as a c. as a weaned c.
Prov. 20. 11. even a c. is known by his doings
22. 6. train up a c. in the way he should go
15. foolishness is bound in the heart of a c.
29. 15. but a c. left to himself bringeth to shame
21. he that bringeth up his servant from a c.
Eccl. 4. 13. better is a wise c. than a foolish king
10. 16. woe to thee, O land, when thy king is a c.
Isa. 9. 6. for to us a c. is born, to us a son is given
10. 19. trees shall be few, that a c. may write them
Jer. 1. 6. behold I cannot speak, for I am a c. 7.
20. 15. tidings, saying, a man c. is born to thee
Hos. 11. 1. when Israel was a c. then I loved him
Mark 9. 21. how long since this came? he said of a c.
36. took a c. and set him in the midst, Luke 9. 47.
1 Cor. 13. 11. when I was a c. I spake as a c. I understood as a c. I thought as a c.
Gal. 4. 1. I say, the heir as long as he is a c. differs not
2 Tim. 3. 15. from a c. hast known holy scriptures
Heb. 11. 11. Sarah delivered of a c. when past age
Rev. 12. 5. she brought forth a man c. who was to rule all nations with a rod of iron

Little CHILD.

Gen. 47. † 12. nourish. his father's house as a little c.
1 Kings 3. 7. am a little c. I know not how to go out
11. 17. Hadad fled into Egypt, being yet a little c.
2 Kings 5. 14. came again like the flesh of a little c.
Isa. 11. 6. and a little c. shall lead them
Mat. 18. 2. Jesus called a little c. to him, and set him
5. who shall receive one such little c. in my name
Mark 10. 15. whosoever shall not receive the kingdom of God as a little c. shall not enter it, Luke 18. 17.

No CHILD.

Gen. 11. 30. but Sarai was barren, she had no c.
Lev. 22. 13. but if the priest's daughter have no c.
Deut. 25. 5. if one brother die, and have no c.
2 Sam. 6. 23. Michal had no c. to the day of death
2 Kings 4. 14. Gehazi answered, verily she hath no c.
Luke 1. 7. they had no c. because Elisabeth was [barren
Acts 7. 5. promised to him when as yet he had no c.

Sucking CHILD.

Num. 11. 12. as a nursing father beareth sucking c.
Isa. 11. 8. sucking c. shall play on the hole of the asp
49. 15. can a woman forget her s. c.? yea, they may
Lam. 4. 4. tongue of the suck. c. cleaveth to the roof

This CHILD.

Exod. 2. 9. take this c. and nurse him for me
Luke 2. 17. saying, which was told concerning this c.
34. this c. is set for fall and rising of many in Israel
9. 48. whoso shall receive this c. my name, receives

With CHILD.

Gen. 16. 11. the angel said, Hagar, thou art with c.
19. 36. daught. of Lot were with c. by their father
38. 24. Tamar thy daughter is with c. by whoredom
25. by the man whose these are am I with c.
Exod. 21. 22. if men strive and hurt a woman with c.
1 Sam. 4. 19. his daughter, Phinehas' wife, was with c.
2 Sam. 11. 5. Bath-sheba sent and said, I am with c.
2 Kings 8. 12. wilt rip up their women with c. 15. 16.
Eccl. 11. 5. bones grow in womb of her that is with c.
Isa. 26. 17. like a woman with c. that draweth near
18. we have been with c. we have been in pain
54. 1. sing, O barren, that didst not travail with c.
Jer. 30. 6. see whether a man doth travail with c.
31. 8. I will bring forth from north woman with c.
Hos. 13. 16. their women with c. shall be ripped up
Amos 1. 13. because they ripped up the wom. with c.
Mat. 1. 18. she was found with c. of the Holy Ghost
23. a virgin shall be with c. and bring forth a son
24. 19. woe to them that are with c. and to them give suck in those days, Mark 13. 17. Luke 21. 23.
Luke 2. 5. to be taxed with Mary, being great with c.
1 Thess. 5. 3. as travail upon a woman with c.
Rev. 12. 2. and she being with c. cried, travailing

Young CHILD.

1 Sam. 1. 24. she brought him, and the c. was young
Mat. 2. 8. go and search diligently for the young c.
13. take the young c. and his mother, and flee
14. he took the young c. and his mother by night

CHILD-BEARING.

1 Tim. 2. 15. notwithstand. she shall be saved in c.-b.

CHILDHOOD.

1 Sam. 12. 2. I have walked before you from my c.
Job 33. † 25. his flesh shall be fresher than c.
Eccl. 11. 10. for c. and youth are vanity

CHILDISH.

1 Cor. 13. 11. when a man, I put away c. things

CHILDLESS.

Gen. 15. 2. what wilt thou give me, seeing I go c.?
Lev. 20. 20. they shall bear their sin, they shall die c.
1 Sam. 15. 33. Samuel said, as thy sword hath made women c. so shall thy mother be c. among women
Jer. 22. 30. saith the Lord, write you this man c.
Luke 20. 30. the second took her to wife, and died c.

CHILDREN.

Gen. 3. 16. in sorrow shalt thou bring forth c.
16. 2. it may be that I may obtain c. by her
25. 22. the c. struggled together within her
29. † 1. Jacob came into the land of the c. of the east
30. 1. Rachael said to Jacob, give me c. or I die
33. 5. the c. which God hath given thy servant
49. 8. thy father's c. shall bow down before thee
Exod. 12. 37. journeyed about 600,000 men, besides c

Exod. 20.5. a jealous God, visiting the iniquity of the fathers upon the c. 34. 7. Num. 14. 18. Deut. 5. 9.
21. 4. the wife and her c. shall be her master's
Num. 13. 28. and we saw the c. of Anak there
17. † 10. for a token against the c. of rebellion
26. 11. notwithstanding the c. of Korah died not
Deut. 2. 9. I have given Ar to the c. of Lot, 19.
9. 2. who can stand before the c. of Anak?
13. 13. the c. of Belial are gone out from you
14. 1. ye are the c. of the Lord your God
21. 15. have born him c. both beloved and hated
23. 8. the c. begotten of them shall enter into cong.
24. 16. the fathers shall not be put to death for the c. nor the c. for the fathers, 2 Chron. 25. 4.
32. 20. they are c. in whom there is no faith
33. 24. of Asher he said, let Asher be blessed c.
Josh. 22. 9. c. of Reuben and Gad, half tribe of Manasseh, returned and built there an altar, 10, 11.
Judg. 4. 6. take 10,000 men of the c. of Naphtali
8. 18. each one resembled the c. of a king
14. 16. thou hast put forth a riddle to c. of people
20. 13. now deliver us the men, the c. of Belial
1 Sam. 2. 5. she that hath many c. is waxed feeble
10. 27. c. of Belial said, how shall this man save us?
2 Sam. 3. † 34. as a man falleth before c. of iniquity
7. 10. neither shall the c. of wickedness afflict them any more as before-time, 1 Chron. 17. 9.
1 Kings 21. 13. there came in two men, c. of Belial
2 Kings 2. 24. two she bears came and tare 42 c.
9. 1. Elisha called one of the c. of the prophets
10. 13. to salute the c. of the king, c. of the queen
14. 6. but the c. of murderers he slew not, as is written in the law of Moses, 2 Chron. 25. 4.
17. 34. nor do as Lord commanded the c. of Jacob
19. 3. for the c. are come to the birth, Isa. 37. 3.
1 Chron. 2. 30. but Seled died without c.
32. and Jether died without c.
4. 27. but Shimei's brethren had not many c.
16. 13. O ye c. of Jacob his chosen, Psal. 105. 6.
2 Chron. 13. 7. gathered to Jeroboam c. of Belial
25. 7. the Lord is not with all the c. of Ephraim
11. Amaziah smote of the c. of Seir 10,000
Ezra 2. 1. these are c. of the province, Neh. 7. 6.
10. 44. some had wives by whom they had c.
Neh. 9. 23. the c. multipliedst thou as stars of heav.
Job 19. 17. I intreated for the c. sake of my body
30. 8. they were c. of fools, yea, c. of base men
41. 34. he is a king over all the c. of pride
Psal. 17. 14. they are full of c. and leave the rest
34. 11. come ye c. hearken to me, I will teach you
69. 8. I am become an alien to my mother's c.
72. 4. he shall save the c. of the needy
78. 6. the c. which should be born might know
82. 6. and all of you are c. of the most High
83. 8. they have holpen the c. of Lot. Selah
102. 28. the c. of thy servants shall continue
113. 9. makes the barren to be a joyful mother of c.
127. 3. lo c. are an heritage of the Lord
4. as arrows in the hand, so are the c. of youth
137. 7. remember, O Lord, the c. of Edom
148. 12. let old men and c. praise the Lord
149. 2. let the c. of Zion be joyful in their king
Prov. 4. 1. hear, ye c. instruction, 5. 7. | 7. 24. | 8. 32.
17. 6. and the glory of c. are their fathers
31. 28. her c. arise up and call her blessed
Eccl. 6. 3. if a man beget 100 c. and live years
Cant. 1. 6. my mother's c. were angry with me
Isa. 1. 2. I have brought up c. and they rebelled
4. ah sinful nation, c. that are corrupters
2. 6. they please themselves in the c. of strangers
3. 4. and I will give c. to be their princes, and babes
12. as for my people, c. are their oppressors
8. 18. I and c. whom Lord hath given me, Heb. 2. 13.
13. 18. shall have no pity, their eye not spare c.
21. 17. mighty men of c. of Kedar be diminished
23. 4. saying, I travail not, nor bring forth c.
30. 1. woe to the rebellious c. saith the Lord
9. lying c. c. that will not hear the law of the L.
38. 19. father to the c. make known thy truth
47. 8. neither shall I know the loss of c.
9. come in one day the loss of c. and widowhood
49. 20. the c. which thou shalt have, shall say
54. 1. sing, O barren, for more are c. of the desolate than c. of the married wife, Gal. 4. 27.
57. 4. are ye not c. of transgression, a seed of falseh.
5. slaying the c. in the valleys under clifts of rocks
63. 8. they are my people, c. that will not lie
66. 8. as soon as Zion travailed, she brought forth c.
Jer. 3. 14. turn, O backsliding c. saith the Lord, 22.
19. I said, how shall I put thee among the c.?
4. 22. for my people is foolish, they are sottish c.
6. 11. I will pour it out upon the c. abroad
7. 18. the c. gather wood, the fathers kindle the fire
9. 21. for death entered to cut off c. from without
15. 7. I will fan them, I will bereave them of c.
31. 15. Rachel weeping for her c. Mat. 2. 18.
29. the c. teeth are set on edge, Ezek. 18. 2.
48. † 45. shall devour the crown of the c. of noise
Lam. 2. 20. shall the women eat c. of a span long?
5. 13. young men to grind, c. fell under the wood
Ezek. 2. 4. for they are impudent c. and stiff hearted
20. 21. the c. rebelled against me, they walked
23. † 17. c. of Babel came to her into bed of love
33. 30. the c. still are talking against thee by walls
44. † 7. brought into my sanctuary c. of a stranger
47. 22. to strangers that shall beget c. among you
Dan. 1. 4. c. in whom was no blemish, but skilful
15. their countenances fairer and fatter than all c.
17. as for these four c. God gave them knowledge
2. † 25. found a man of the c. of the captivity
12. 1. Michael shall stand for the c. of thy people
Hos. 1. 2. take unto thee c. of whoredoms
2. 4. I will not have mercy on her c. for they be c.
10. 9. the battle against the c. of iniquity did not
14. the mother was dashed in pieces upon her c.
11. 10. then the c. shall tremble from the west
13. 13. not stay long in place of breaking forth of c.
Joel 2. 16. gather c. and those that suck the breasts
23. be glad then ye c. of Zion, and rejoice in Lord
Amos 9. 7. are ye not as c. of the Ethiopians to me?
Mic. 1. 16. make bald, and poll thee for delicate c.
Zeph. 1. 8. I will punish the princes and king's c.

Mal. 4. 6. he shall turn the heart of fathers to the c. and the heart of c. to their fathers, Luke 1. 17.
Mat. 2. 16. Herod slew all the c. in Bethlehem
3. 9. able of these stones to raise up c. Luke 3. 8.
5. 45. that ye may be the c. of your Father in heav.
8. 12. but the c. of the kingdom shall be cast out
9. 15. Jesus said, can c. of bride-cham. mourn while bridegroom with them? Mark 2. 19. Luke 5. 34.
10. 21. c. shall rise against parents, Mark 13. 12.
11. 19. but Wisdom is justified of her c. Luke 7. 35.
13. 38. the good seed are the c. of the kingdom, but the tares are the c. of the wicked one
15. 26. not meet to take the c. bread, Mark 7. 27.
17. 26. Jesus saith to him, then are the c. free
19. 29. forsaken wife or c. for my sake, Mark 10. 29.
20. 20. then came the mother of Zebedee's c.
21. 15. priests and scribes saw the c. crying in temp.
Mat. 23. 31. ye are c. of them that killed prophets
Mark 7. 27. Jesus said to her, let the c. first be filled
28. the dogs under the table eat of the c. crumbs
9. 37. shall receive one of such c. in my name, 41.
Luke 6. 35. be great, ye shall be the c. of the High.
16. 8. for c. of this world are wiser than c. of light
20. 29. the first took a wife and died without c.
34. the c. of this world marry, and are given in
John 8. 39. if ye were Abraham's c. would do works
21. 5. Jesus saith to them, c. have ye any meat?
Acts 3. 25. ye are the c. of the prophets and covenant
Rom. 8. 17. if c. then heirs, heirs of God, joint-heirs
9. 7. because the seed of Abraham are they all c.
11. for c. being not yet born, nor done good or evil
1 Cor. 14. 20. be not c. in understanding, in malice c.
2 Cor. 12. 14. for the c. ought not to lay up for the parents, but the parents for the c.
Gal. 3. 7. of faith, the same are the c. of Abraham
4. 3. so we, when we were c. were in bondage
25. Jerusalem, which is in bondage with her c.
31. we are not c. of bond-woman, but of the free
Eph. 1. 5. having predestinated us to adoption of c.
2. 2. the spirit that worketh in c. of disobedience
3. were by nature c. of wrath, even as others
4. 14. we be henceforth no more c. tossed to and fro
5. 1. be ye therefore followers of God as dear c.
6. wrath cometh on c. of disobedience, Col. 3. 6.
6. 1. c. obey your parents in the Lord, Col. 3. 20.
1 Tim. 5. 4. but if any widow have c. or nephews
10. if she hath brought up c. if she hath lodged
14. I will that the younger women marry, bear c.
Heb. 2. 14. as the c. are partakers of flesh and blood
12. 5. exhortation which speaketh to you as to c.
1 Pet. 1. 14. as obedient c. not fashioning by lusts
2 Pet. 2. 14. having eyes full of adultery, cursed c.
1 John 3. 10. c. of God manifest, and c. of the devil
2 John 1. the elder to the elect lady and her c.
13. the c. of thy elect sister greet thee
Rev. 2. 23. I will kill her c. with death, churches
See AMMON, CAPTIVITY.

CHILDREN of Benjamin.

Num. 1. 36. of the c. of B. by their genealogy 35,400
Judg. 1. 21. c. of B. did not drive out the Jebusites
20. 13. the c. of B. would not hearken to brethren
2 Sam. 2. 25. c. of B. gathered together after Abner
1 Chr. 9. 3. in Jerusalem dwelt of c. of B. Neh. 11. 4.
12. 16. there came of c. of B. to the hold to David
Jer. 6. 1. O ye c. of Benj. gather yourselves to flee

Children's CHILDREN.

Gen. 45. 10. shalt be near to me, thou and thy ch. c.
Exod. 34. 7. visiting iniquity of fathers on childr. c.
Deut. 4. 25. when thou shalt beget c. and childr. c.
2 Kings 17. 41. served images both their c. and ch. c.
Psal. 103. 17. and his righteousness unto childr. c.
128. 6. shalt see thy childr. c. and peace on Israel
Prov. 13. 22. leaveth an inheritance to his childr. c.
17. 6. childr. c. are crown of old men, glory of c.
Jer. 2. 9. and with your children's c. will I plead
Ezek. 37. 25. shall dwell, and their childr. c. for ever

Fatherless CHILDREN.

Psal. 109. 12. nor let there be any to favour father. c.
Jer. 49. 11. leave thy father. c. I will preserve them

CHILDREN of God.

Mat. 5. 9. peace-makers shall be called the c. of G.
Luke 20. 36. are the c. of G. being c. of resurrection
John 11. 52. should gather together in one c. of God
Rom. 8. 16. beareth witness that we are the c. of G.
21. delivered into the glorious liberty of c. of God
9. 8. the c. of the flesh, these are not the c. of God
26. there shall they be called c. of the living God
Gal. 3. 26. ye are all c. of God by faith in Christ
1 John 3. 10. c. of God manifest, and c. of the devil
5. 2. by this we know that we love the c. of God

His CHILDREN.

Gen. 18. 19. I know Abraham will command his c.
37. 3. Israel loved Joseph more than all his c.
Deut. 17. 20. may prolong his days, he and his c.
32. 5. corrupted, their spot is not the spot of his c.
† they are not his c. that is their blot
33. 9. neither acknowledge, nor knew his own c.
1 Sam. 30. 22. save to every man his wife and his c.
2 Sam. 12. 3. a little ewe-lamb, it grew up with his c.
2 Kings 8. 19. to give him always a light, and to his c.
2 Chr. 28. 3. burnt his c. in fire after the heathen
33. 6. he caused his c. to pass thro' the fire
Job 5. 4. his c. are far from safety, and are crushed
17. 5. even the eyes of his c. shall fail
20. 10. his c. shall seek to please the poor
21. 19. God layeth up his iniquity for his c.
27. 14. if his c. be multiplied, it is for the sword
Psal. 89. 30. if his c. forsake my law, and walk not
103. 13. like as a father pitieth his c. so Lord pities
109. 9. let his c. be fatherless, his wife a widow
10. let his c. be vagabonds, and beg bread
Prov. 14. 26. his c. shall have a place of refuge
20. 7. the just man, his c. are blessed after him
Isa. 14. 21. prepare slaughter for his c. for iniquity of
29. 23. when he seeth his c. in the midst of him
Hos. 9. 13. but Ephraim shall bring forth his c.
John 4. 12. his c. and cattle drank thereof
1 Thess. 2. 11. we charged you as a father doth his c.
1 Tim. 3. 4. having his c. in subjection with gravity

CHILDREN of Israel.

Gen. 50. 25. Joseph took an oath of the c. of Israel
Exod. 1. 7. the c. of Israel were fruitful and increased

Exod. 1. 12. they were grieved because of c. of Isr.
2. 23. c. of Is. sighed || 25. God looked on c. of Isr.
4. 31. when they heard Lord had visited c. of Isr.
6. 5. I have also heard the groaning of the c. of Is.
13. to bring c. of Isr. out of Egypt, 26, 27. | 12. 51.
9. 4. shall nothing die of all that is the c. of Israel
12. 37. c. of Isr. journeyed about 600,000 on foot
29. 43. and there I will meet with the c. of Israel
31. 17. it is a sign between me and c. of Is. for ever
Lev. 17. 13. whosoever he be, c. of Isr. or stranger
25. 55. for to me the c. of Israel are servants
Num. 14. 10. glory of Lord appeared before c. of Is.
Josh. 7. 12. c. of Isr. could not stand before enemies
1 Sam. 11. 8. when numbered c. of Isr. were 300,000
2 Sam. 21. 2. the Gibeonites were not of c. of Isr.
2 Kings 17. 24. and placed them instead of c. of Is.
Neh. 8. 17. to that day had not the c. of Is. done so
Psal. 103. 7. he made known his acts to c. of Isr.
148. 14. even of the c. of Isr. a people near to him
Isa. 27. 12. shall be gathered one by one, O ye c. of Is.
Ezek. 44. 15. when c. of Israel went astray, 48. 11.
Amos 2. 11. is it not even thus, O ye c. of Israel?
4. 5. this liketh you, O ye c. of Isr. saith the Lord
Luke 1. 16. many of the c. of Isr. shall turn to Lord
Acts 7. 23. to visit his brethren the c. of Israel
37. this is that Moses which said to the c. of Israel
9. 15. chosen to bear my name before the c. of Isr.
10. 36. word God sent to c. of Isr. preaching peace
Rom. 9. 27. though number of c. of Is. be as the sand
2 Cor. 3. 7. c. of Isr. could not behold face of Moses
Heb. 11. 22. made mention of departing of c. of Is.
Rev. 2. 14. to cast a stumbling-block before c. of Is.
7. 4. sealed 144,000 of all the tribes of the c. of Is.
21. 12. the names of the twelve tribes of the c. of Is.

CHILDREN of Judah.

Num. 1. 26. of the c. of Judah by their generations
Josh. 14. 6. c. of Judah came to Joshua to Gilgal
2 Sam. 1. 18. bade teach c. of Jud. the use of the bow
2 Chr. 13. 18. c. of J. prevailed, because they relied
25. 12. other 10,000 did c. of J. carry away captive
28. 10. now ye purpose to keep under the c. of Jud.
Jer. 32. 32. because of all the evil of the c. of Jud.
50. 4. they and the c. of Judah going and weeping
33. Israel and c. of Jud. were oppressed together
Joel 3. 19. for the violence against the c. of Judah

CHILDREN of light.

Luke 16. 8. c. of this world are wiser than c. of light
John 12. 36. believe, that ye may be the c. of light
Eph. 5. 8. but now are light in Lord, walk as c. of l.
1 Thess. 5. 5. ye are all c. of light, and child. of day

Little CHILDREN.

Num. 16. 27. little c. stood in the door of their tents
2 Kings 2. 23. came forth little c. and mocked him
Esth. 3. 13. in one day to destroy little c. and women
Ezek. 9. 6. slay utterly maids, little c. and women
Mat. 18. 3. except converted, and become as little c.
19. 13. then were there brought to him little c.
14. suffer little c. to come, Mark 10. 14. Luke 18. 16.
John 13. 33. little c. yet a little while I am with you
Gal. 4. 19. my little c. of whom I travail in birth
1 John 2. 1. my little c. I write to you, 12, 13.
4. 4. are of God, little c. and have overcome world
5. 21. little c. keep yourselves from idols

CHILDREN of men.

Gen. 11. 5. to see the tower which c. of men built
1 Sam. 26. 19. if they be c. of men, cursed be they
2 Sam. 7. 14. I'll chastise him with stripes of c. of m.
1 Kings 8. 39. knowest hearts of c. of m. 2 Chr. 6. 30.
Psal. 11. 4. eyes behold, his eyelids try the c. of m.
12. 1. for the faithful fail from among c. of men
14. 2. looked down from heaven upon c. of m. 53. 2.
36. 7. the c. of men put their trust under shadow
45. 2. thou art fairer than c. of m. grace is poured
90. 3. turnest man, and sayest, return ye c. of m.
107. 8. his wonderful works to c. of m. 15, 21, 31.
115. 16. the earth hath he given to the c. of men
Prov. 15. 11. how much more then hearts of c. of m.
Lam. 3. 33. he doth not afflict, nor grieve c. of m.
Dan. 2. 38. wherever c. of men dwell hath he given

Men-CHILDREN.

Exod. 1. 17. the midwives saved the men-c. alive, 18.
34. 23. all the men-c. shall appear before the Lord
Josh. 17. 2. these were the male-c. of Manasseh

Men, Women, and CHILDREN.

Deut. 3. 6. in Bashan we destroyed m. women, and c.
31. 12. gather m. women, and c. to hear and learn
1 Sam. 22. 19. smote Nob, m. w. and c. and sucklings
Ezra 10. 1. a great congregat. of men, women, and c.
Jer. 40. 7. had committed to Gedaliah m. w. and c.
Mat. 14. 21. and they that had eaten were about 5000 men, beside women and c. 15. 38.

My CHILDREN.

Gen. 30. 26. give me my wives and my c. for whom
31. 43. these c. are my c. these cattle my cattle
42. 36. Jacob said, me ye have bereaved of my c.
43. 14. if I be bereaved of my c. I am bereaved
Exod. 13. 15. but the first-born of my c. I redeem
21. 5. I love my master, wife, and my c. I'll not go
1 Kings 20. 7. he sent to me for my wives and my c.
Job 29. 5. that I were as when my c. were about me
Isa. 49. 21. seeing I have lost my c. and am desol.
Jer. 10. 20. my c. are gone forth of me, and are not
Lam. 1. 16. my c. are desolate, the enemy prevailed
Ezek. 16. 21. is it small that thou hast slain my c.?
Luke 11. 7. trouble me not, my c. are with me in bed
2 Cor. 6. 13. I speak as to my c. be ye enlarged.
3 John 4. joy to hear that my c. walk in the truth

No CHILDREN.

Gen. 16. 1. now Sarai Abram's wife bare him no c.
30. 1. when Rachel saw that she bare Jacob no c.
Num. 3. 4. Nadab and Abihu died, and had no c.
1 Sam. 1. 2. Peninnah had, but Hannah had no c.
Mat. 22. 24. if any man die having no c. Mark 12. 19
Luke 20. 31. the seven took her, and left no c.

Our CHILDREN.

Gen. 31. 16. all the riches are ours and our c.
Exod. 17. 3. to kill us, and our c. and our cattle
Num. 14. 3. that our wives and our c. be a prey
Deut. 29. 29. belong to us and to our c. for ever
Josh 22. 24. your c. might speak to our c. saying
25. your c. make our c. cease from fearing Lord
Neh. 5. 5. as the flesh of brethren, our c. as their c.

Mat. 27. 25. and said, his blood be on us and on our c.

CHILDREN of promise.

Rom. 9. 8. but the c. of prom. are counted for the seed
Gal. 4. 28. we, brethren, as Isaac was, are c. of p.

Strange CHILDREN.

Neh. 9. †2. Israel separated themselves from str. c.
Psal. 144. 7. rid and deliver me from strange c. 11.
Hos. 5. 7. for they have begotten strange c.

Their CHILDREN.

Gen. 31. 43. what can I do to daughters or their c.
Deut. 4. 10. and that they may teach their c.
5. 29. that it might be well with their c. for ever
31. 13. that their c. may learn to fear the Lord
Josh. 5. 7. and their c. them Joshua circumcised
1 Kings 9. 21. of their c. did Solomon levy a tribute
2 Kings 8. 12. thou wilt dash their c. and rip women
17. 31. burnt their c. in the fire to the gods
41. their c. served images as did their fathers
2 Chron. 20. 13. before Lord with wives and their c.
25. 4. he slew not their c. but did as it is written
Neh. 9. 23. their c. thou multipliedst as stars of heav.
13. 24. their c. spake half in the speech of Ashdod
Job 21. 11. send their little ones, their c. dance
24. 5. the wilderness yieldeth food for their c.
Psal. 78. 4. we will not hide them from their c.
6. should arise and declare them to their c.
90. 16. and let thy glory appear to their c.
132. 12. their c. shall sit on thy throne for ever
Isa. 13. 16. their c. shall be dashed to pieces before
Jer. 17. 2. whilst their c. remember their altars
18. 21. therefore deliver up their c. to the famine
30. 20. their c. also shall be as aforetime
32. 18. the iniquity of fathers into bosom of their c.
39. for good of them and of their c. after them
47. 3. the fathers shall not look back to their c.
Lam. 4. 10. the hands of women have sodden their c.
Ezek. 20. 18. I said to their c. in the wilderness
23. 39. when they had slain their c. to idols
37. 25. they and their c. shall dwell therein
Dan. 6. 24. cast them and their c. into den of lions
Hos. 9. 12. tho' bring up their c. yet I will bereave
Joel 1. 3. let your c. tell their c. and their c. another
Mic. 2. 9. from their c. have ye taken away my glory
Zech. 10. 7. yea, their c. shall see it and be glad
9. they shall live with their c. and turn again
Acts 13. 33. God hath fulfilled the same to us their c.
1 Tim. 3. 12. the deacons rule their c. and houses well
Tit. 2. 4. young women to love husbands and their c.

Thy CHILDREN.

Exod. 13. 13. the first-born among thy c. redeem
Deut. 4. 40. go well with thy c. after thee, 12. 25, 28.
6. 7. thou shalt teach them diligently to thy c.
30. 2. thou and thy c. shall obey with all thine heart
Josh. 14. 9. the land be thine and thy c. for ever
1 Sam. 16. 11. Samuel said, are here all thy c.?
1 Kings 2. 4. if thy c. take heed to their way to walk
8. 25. so that thy c. take heed, 2 Chron. 6. 16.
20. 3. saith, thy wives also and thy c. are mine
2 Kings 4. 7. live thou and thy c. of the rest
10. 30. thy c. of fourth generation shall sit on throne
2 Chron. 21. 14. Lord will smite thy people and c.
Job 8. 4. if thy c. have sinned against him, he cast
Psal. 45. 16. instead of thy fathers shall be thy c.
73. 15. should offend against generation of thy c.
128. 3. thy c. like olive-plants round about thy table
132. 12. if thy c. will keep my covenant and test.
147. 13. he hath blessed thy c. within thee
Isa. 49. 17. thy c. shall make haste, thy destroyers
25. I will contend, and I will save thy c.
54. 13. and all thy c. shall be taught of the Lord, and great shall be the peace of thy c.
Jer. 5. 7. thy c. have forsaken me, and sworn by them
31. 17. there is hope that thy c. shall come again
38. 23. they shall bring out thy c. to the Chaldeans
Ezek. 16. 36. by blood of thy c. thou didst give them
Hos. 4. 6. forgotten the law, I will also forget thy c.
Mat. 23. 37. how often would I have gathered thy c. as a hen gathereth her chickens! Luke 13. 34.
Luke 19. 44. they shall lay thy c. within thee
2 John 4. that I found of thy c. walking in truth

Your CHILDREN.

Exod. 12. 26. when your c. shall say unto you
22. 24. wives be widows, and your c. be fatherless
Lev. 25. 46. take them as inheritance for your c.
26. 22. said, wild beasts shall rob you of your c.
Num. 14. 33. your c. shall wander in the wilderness
Deut. 1. 39. your c. shall go in thither and possess
11. 2. I speak not with your c. who have not known
19. these my words, ye shall teach them your c.
21. that days of your c. be multiplied in the land
29. 22. the generation to come of your c. shall say
32. 46. which ye shall command your c. to observe
Josh. 4. 6. when your c. ask their fathers, 21.
22. then ye shall let your c. know, saying, Israel
1 Kings 9. 6. if your c. turn from following me
1 Chron. 28. 8. for an inherit. to your c. Ezra 9. 12.
2 Chron. 30. 9. your c. shall find compassion before
Psal. 115. 14. the Lord shall increase you and your c.
Jer. 2. 30. in vain have I smitten your c.
Mat. 7. 11. to give good gifts to your c. Luke 11. 13.
12. 27. by whom do your c. cast them out?
Luke 23. 28. but weep for yourselves and your c.
Acts 2. 39. for the promise is to you and your c.
1 Cor. 7. 14. else were your c. unclean, but now holy
Eph. 6. 4. provoke not your c. to wrath, Col. 3. 21.

Young CHILDREN.

Job 19. 18. yea, young c. despised me, they spake
Lam. 4. 4. the young c. ask bread, no man breaketh
Nah. 3. 10. her young c. were dashed in pieces
Mark 10. 13. brought young c. to him to touch them
Acts 7. 19. so that they cast out their young c.

CHIMNEY.

Hos. 13. 3. they shall be as smoke out of the c.

CHODE.

Gen. 31. 36. Jacob was wroth, and c. with Laban
Num. 20. 3. the people c. with Moses and spake

CHOICE.

Gen. 23. 6. in c. of our sepulchres bury thy dead
49. 11. binding his ass's colt to the c. vine
Deut. 12. 11. thither shall bring all your c. vows
1 Sam. 9. 2. Saul a c. young man and a goodly
2 Sam. 10. 9. he chose of c. of Israel, 1 Chr. 19. 10.
2 Kings 19. 23. cut down the c. fir-trees, Isa. 37. 24.
2 Chron. 25. 5. he found them 300,000 c. men
Neh. 5. 18. now prepared for me daily six c. sheep
Prov. 8. 10. and knowledge rather than c. gold
19. and my revenue is better than c. silver
10. 20. the tongue of the just is as c. silver
Cant. 6. 9. she is the c. one of her that bare her
Jer. 22. 7. they shall cut down thy c. cedars
48. †15. the c. of Moab are gone down to slaughter
Ezek. 23. †7. committed whored. with c. of Asher
24. 4. set on a pot, fill it with the c. bones
5. take the c. of the flock and burn the bones
Acts 15. 7. God made c. among us, that the Gentiles

CHOICEST.

Isa. 5. 2. and planted the vineyard with the c. vine
22. 7. thy c. valley shall be full of chariots

CHOKE.

Mat. 13. 22. the care of this world and the deceitfulness of riches c. the word, Mark 4. 19.

CHOKED.

Mat. 13. 7. thorns c. them, Mark 4. 7. Luke 8. 7.
Mark 5. 13. and were c. in the sea, Luke 8. 33.
Luke 8. 14. go forth and are c. with cares and riches

CHOLER.

Dan. 8. 7. an he-goat moved with c. smote the ram
11. 11. the king of the south shall be moved with c.

CHOP.

Mic. 3. 3. break their bones and c. them in pieces

CHOOSE

Signifies, [1] *To select, or make choice of*, Exod. 17. 9. Psal. 25. 12. [2] *To renew a choice, or to choose again*, Isa. 14. 1. | 48. 10. [3] *To follow, imitate, or practise*, Prov. 3. 31.

It is spoken, (I) *Of persons, as,* [1] *Of* Christ, *who was chosen and set apart from eternity by God the Father for the office of Mediator*, Isa. 42. 1. [2] *Of such whom God from all eternity elected and separated from among the children of men, to deliver them from sin and hell, and by his Spirit working in them to unite them by faith to Christ, the Head of the church, and to sanctify and save them by him*, Mark 13. 20. Eph. 1. 4. [3] *Of the* Jews, *who were set apart as God's peculiar people*, Deut. 7. 6. Psal. 105. 6. [4] *Of persons chosen to office*, John 6. 70. (II) *Of things*, Isa. 58. 6. (III) *Of places*, 2 Chr. 6. 38.

CHOOSE, *as an act of God.*

Num. 16. 7. the man the Lord doth c. shall be holy
17. 5. the man's rod whom I shall c. shall blossom
Deut. 7. 7. the Lord did not c. you because more
12. 5. the place which Lord shall c. 11, 14, 18, 26. | 14. 23, 24, 25. | 15. 20. | 16. 2, 6, 7, 15, 16. | 17. 8, 10. | 18. 6. | 26. 2. | 31. 11. Josh. 9. 27.
17. 15. shall set him king, whom the Lord shall c.
1 Sam. 2. 28. did I c. him out of all tribes of Israel
2 Sam. 16. 18. whom the Lord and his people c.
21. 6. will hang them in Gibeah whom Lord did c.
1 Kings 14. 21. the city which the Lord did c.
Neh. 9. 7. thou art the God who didst c. Abram
Psal. 25. 12. him shall he teach in way he shall c.
47. 4. he shall c. our inheritance for us
Isa. 14. 1. for the Lord will yet c. Israel
49. 7. the Holy One of Israel, he shall c. thee
66. 4. I also will c. their delusions, and bring fears
Zech. 1. 17. the Lord will yet c. Jerusalem, 2. 12.

CHOOSE.

Exod. 17. 9. c. us out men, and go out, fight with
Deut. 23. 16. he shall dwell in that place he shall c
30. 19. therefore c. life, that thou and seed may live
Josh. 24. 15. c. this day whom you will serve
1 Sam. 17. 8. c. you a man for you, let him come
2 Sam. 17. 1. let me c. 12,000 men, and I will pursue
19. †38. what thou shalt c. that will I do for thee
24. 12. I offer thee c. one of them, 1 Chr. 21. 10.
1 Kings 18. 23. let them c. one bullock, 25.
Job 9. 14. c. out my words to reason with him
34. 4. let us c. to us judgment, let us know
33. whether thou refuse, or whether thou c.
Ps. 84. †10. I would c. rather to sit at the threshold
Prov. 1. 29. and did not c. the fear of the Lord
3. 31. the oppressor, and c. none of his ways
Isa. 7. 15. may know to refuse evil, and c. good, 16.
56. 4. to the eunuchs that c. things that please me
65. 12. and did c. that wherein I delighted not
Ezek. 21. 19. c. a place, c. it at the head of the way
Phil. 1. 22. yet what I shall c. I wot not

CHOOSEST, ETH, ING.

Job 7. 15. so that my soul c. strangling and death
15. 5. and thou c. the tongue of the crafty
Psal. 65. 4. blessed is the man whom thou c.
Isa. 40. 20. he c. a tree that will not rot
41. 24. an abomination is he that c. you
Heb. 11. 25. c. rather to suffer affliction with people

CHOSE.

Gen. 6. 2. they took them wives of all which they c.
13. 11. then Lot c. him all the plain of Jordan
Exod. 18. 25. Moses c. able men, and made heads
Deut. 4. 37. he c. their seed after them, 10. 15.
Josh. 8. 3. Joshua c. 30,000 mighty men of valour
Judg. 5. 8. they c. new gods, then was war in gates
2 Sam. 6. 21. the Lord who c. me before thy father
1 Kings 8. 16. I c. no city out of all the tribes of Isr. to build an house for my name, 2 Chr. 6. 5.
1 Chr. 28. 4. the Lord c. me before all the house of
Job 29. 25. I c. out their way and sat chief
Psal 78. 67. and c. not the tribe of Ephraim
68. but c. the tribe of Judah, the mount Zion
70. he c. David also his servant, and took him
Isa. 66. 4. and c. that in which I delighted not
Ezek. 20. 5. say to them, in the day when I c. Israel
Luke 6. 13. of his disciples he c. twelve apostles
14. 7. when he marked how they c. chief rooms
Acts 6. 5. c. Stephen a man full of faith and H. Ghost
13. 17. God of this people Israel c. our fathers
15. 40. Paul c. Silas and departed, being recommend.

CHOSEN.

Exod. 15. 4. his c. captains are drowned in the sea
Num. 16. 5. him whom he hath c. cause to come
Josh. 24. 22. ye have c. you the Lord to serve him
Judg. 10. 14. go and cry to the gods ye have c.
1 Sam. 8. 18. because of the king ye have c. 12. 13.
20. 30. I know that thou hast c. the son of Jesse
1 Kings 3. 8. hast c. a great people, cannot be number.
8. 44. the city thou hast c. 48. 2 Chron. 6. 34, 38.
1 Chron. 16. 13. ye children of Jacob his c. ones
Job 36. 21. this hast thou c. rather than affliction
Psal. 33. 12. people he hath c. for his inheritance
89. 3. I have made a covenant with my c.
19. I have exalted one c. out of the people
105. 6. seed of Abraham, ye child. of Jacob his c
43. he brought forth his c. with gladness
106. 5. that I may see the good of thy c.
23. had not Moses his c. stood before him
Prov. 16. 16. understand. rather to be c. than silver
22. 1. a good name is rather to be c. than riches
Isa. 43. 20. to give drink to my people, my c.
65. 15. shall leave your name a curse to my c.
66. 3. yea, they have c. their own ways
Jer. 8. 3. and death shall be c. rather than life
49. 19. who is a c. man that I may appoint, 50. 44.
Mat. 20. 16. many be called, but few c. 22. 14.
Mark 13. 20. for his elect's sake whom he hath c.
Luke 10. 42. and Mary hath c. that good part
Acts 1. 24. shew whether of these two thou hast c.
9. 15. go thy way, for he is a c. vessel to me
Rom. 16. 13. salute Rufus, c. in the Lord
2 Cor. 8. 19. who was c. of the churches to travel
1 Tim. 5. †9. let not a widow be c. into the number
2 Tim. 2. 4. please him who hath c. him to be a soldier
1 Pet. 2. 9. ye are a c. generation, a royal priesth.
Rev. 17. 14. they are called, c. and faithful

CHOSEN *of God.*

Luke 23. 35. if he be the Christ, the c. of God
Acts 10. 41. but to witnesses c. before of God
1 Pet. 2. 4. a living stone, c. of God and precious

God hath CHOSEN.

Deut. 12. 21. God hath c. to put name there, 16. 11.
21. 5. them God hath c. to minister unto him
1 Chron. 29. 1. Solomon whom God hath c. is young
Acts 22. 14. the God of our fathers hath c. thee
1 Cor. 1. 27. God hath c. foolish things, God hath c. weak things
28. things despised God hath c. and things that are
2 Thess. 2. 13. God from the beginning hath c. you
Jam. 2. 5. hath not God c. the poor of this world

I have CHOSEN.

1 Kings 11. 13. for David's sake and Jerusalem's sake I have c. 2 Kings 21. 7. | 23. 27. 2 Chr. 6. 6.
32. the city which I have c. out of all the tribes
Neh. 1. 9. bring them to place I have c. to set name
Psal. 119. 30. I have c. the way of truth, 173.
Isa. 41. 8. Jacob whom I have c. the seed of Abrah.
9. I have c. thee, and not cast thee away
43. 10. my servant whom I have c. Mat. 12. 18.
44. 1. Israel whom I have c. ‖ 2. Jesurun I have c.
48. 10. I have c. thee in the furnace of affliction
58. 5. is not this the fast that I have c.? 6.
Hag. 2. 23. I have c. thee, saith the Lord of hosts
John 13. 18. speak not of all, I know whom I have c.
15. 16. ye have not c. me, but I have c. you
19. but I have c. you out of the world, therefore

Lord hath CHOSEN.

Deut. 7. 6. Lord hath c. thee a special people, 14. 2.
18. 5. the Lord hath c. him out of all the tribes
1 Sam. 10. 24. see him whom Lord hath c. none like
16. 8. and he said, neither hath the Lord c. this
10. Samuel said, the Lord hath not c. these
1 Chron. 15. 2. for them the Lord hath c. to carry ark
28. 4. Lord hath c. Judah ruler, and house of fath.
5. Lord hath c. Solomon to sit to build an house, 10.
2 Chron. 29. 11. Lord hath c. you to stand to serve him
Psal. 105. 26. he sent Aaron whom he had c.
132. 13. Lord hath c. Zion ‖ 135. 4. Lord hath c. Jacob
Jer. 33. 24. the two families which the Lord hath c.
Zech. 3. 2. Lord that hath c. Jerusalem rebuke thee
Eph. 1. 4. according as he hath c. us in him

CHOSEN *men.*

Judg. 20. 16. seven hundred c. men left-handed
1 Kings 12. 21. of Judah 180,000 c. men, 2 Chr. 11. 1.
2 Chron. 13. 3. Abijah set the battle in array with 400,000 c. men, Jeroboam with 800,000 c. men
Psal. 78. 31. wrath smote down the c. men of Israel
Acts 15. 22. to send c. men of their company, 25.

CHRIST.

The anointed of God; the same with the Hebrew *Messiah*, Psal. 45. 7. Isa. 61. 1. *The eternal Son of God, the second Person of the glorious Trinity*, Mat. 28. 19. 1 John 5. 8. *In his divine nature he is equal with the Father, and over all, God blessed for ever; but in his human nature, subordinate and inferior to the Father, being like to men in all things, sin excepted. Both natures are united in the person of* Christ, *that he might be our prophet, priest, and king, and the author of a complete, perfect, all-sufficient, and eternal salvation. He ever lives to intercede for all that come to him*, Heb. 7. 25.

In Christ *all the types, prophecies, and promises centre. He is the most suitable object for the sinner to look to, trust in, and expect all his hopes, joys, and consolations from, as by him alone life and salvation are procured. He is the head of principalities and powers, the brightness of his Father's glory; and the express image of his person*, Heb. 1. 3. *the glory of all worlds, and the refulgent luminary of the universe*, John 1. 9. *the inexhaustible fountain of all the treasures of nature, grace, and glory*, Jer. 2. 13. *and the matchless, incomparable Redeemer of all that come to him*, John 6. 37. Christ *was the grand subject of all the apostles' ministry*, Acts 8. 5. *and, indeed, a sermon without* Christ *is like a cloud without water, or a shadow without substance. One moment's communion with* Christ *is of more worth than ten thousand worlds; his person most glorious, and he is altogether lovely*, Cant. 5. 16.

The ancient Hebrews, *being instructed by the prophets, had very clear notions of the* Messiah: *but they were changed by little and little, so that when* Christ *appeared in* Judea, *they had entertained a very wrong notion of the* Messias, *expecting a temporal monarch and conqueror, that should bring the whole world under subjection. From whence it came to pass, that they were much scandalized at the outward appearance, the humility and seeming weakness, of our Saviour, which hindered them from acknowledging him as the* Christ *whom they expected.*

The ancient prophets had foretold, that the Messias *should be God and Man, exalted and abased, Master and Servant, Priest and Victim, King and Subject, mortal, and a Conqueror of death, rich and poor, a King, a Conqueror, glorious, yet a man of griefs, involved in our infirmities, in a state of great humiliation. All these seeming contrarieties were to be reconciled in the person of the* Messiah, *as they did really meet in the person of* Christ. *It was known that the* Messiah *was to be born of a virgin, of the tribe of* Judah, *of the race of* David, *in the village of* Beth-lehem: *that he was to continue for ever, that his name should be continued as long as the sun, that he was the great Prophet promised in the law, that he was both the Son and Lord of* David, *that he was to perform great miracles, that he should restore all things, that he should die and rise again, that* Elias *should be the forerunner of his appearance, that a proof of his coming should be, the cure of the lepers, life restored to the dead, and the gospel preached to the poor: that he should not destroy the law, but should perfect and fulfil it; that he should be a stone of offence, and a stumbling-block, against which many should bruise themselves; that he should suffer oppositions and contradictions, and that a strange people should come and submit themselves to his discipline.*

When Christ *appeared, these notions of him were still common among the* Jews. *Our Saviour herein appeals even to themselves, and asks them if these were not the characters of the* Messiah, *and if they do not see the completion of them in himself. The evangelists take care to put them in mind of them, to prove thereby, that* Jesus *is the* Christ *whom they expected. The Evangelist* Luke *says, that our Saviour entering into a synagogue at* Nazareth, *there opened the book of the prophet* Isaiah *where he read,* The Spirit of the Lord is upon me, because he hath anointed me to preach the gospel to the poor, *Luke* 4. 18. *After which he shewed them that this prophecy was accomplished in his person. And* St. Peter *and the other believers being assembled together,* Acts 4. 24, 25, *&c. say to God, from* Psal. 2. 1, 2, Why did the heathen rage, *&c. and apply this prophecy to* Christ, *verse* 27. *And in* Acts 10. 38. Peter, *speaking to* Cornelius *the centurion, and to those that were with him, tells them that the Lord had sent peace to men, by* Jesus Christ whom God had anointed with the Holy Ghost and with power. *So that when* Christ, *or his disciples, are said to be anointed, it is to be understood of the spiritual and internal unction of grace and of the Holy Ghost, of which the outward and sensible unction, with which they anciently anointed kings, priests, and prophets, was but the figure and symbol. See* MESSIAH.

Christ *is taken for the* mystical body of Christ, *both himself the Head, and the church as his members, which make but one body,* 1 Cor. 12. 12. *Likewise for the doctrine of Christ, or the rule of life prescribed by him,* Eph. 4. 20. *And for the Spirit, and spiritual gifts and graces of Christ,* Rom. 8. 10.

Mat. 2. 4. he demanded where *C.* should be born
16. 16. thou art *C.* the Son of the living God
23. 8. for one is your Master, even *C.* 10.
24. 5. many shall come, saying, I am *C.* and shall deceive many, *Mark* 13. 6. *Luke* 21. 8.
26. 68. prophesy to us, thou *C.* who smote thee?
Mark 9. 41. in my name because ye belong to *C.*
15. 32. let *C.* descend now from the cross
Luke 2. 26. should not die, before he had seen *C.*
4. 41. the devils, they knew that he was *C.*
23. 35. save himself, if he be *C.* the chosen of God
39. saying, if thou be *C.* save thyself and us
24. 26. ought not *C.* to have suffered these
46. thus it behoved *C.* to suffer and rise from dead
John 4. 25. the Messias cometh, which is called *C.*
7. 27. when *C.* cometh no man knoweth
31. when *C.* cometh, will he do more miracles?
41. but some said, shall *C.* come out of Galilee?
42. said, that *C.* cometh of the seed of David
9. 22. that if any man did confess that he was *C.*
12. 34. we have heard that *C.* abideth for ever
Acts 2. 30. he would raise up *C.* to sit on his throne
36. God hath made that Jesus both Lord and *C.*
3. 18. God had before shewed that *C.* should suffer
8. 5. Philip went and preached *C.* to them
9. 20. and straightway he preached *C.* in synago.
17. 3. alleging that *C.* must needs have suffered
26. 23. that *C.* should suffer, and rise first from d.
Rom. 5. 6. in due time *C.* died for the ungodly
8. in that while we were yet sinners *C.* died for us
6. 4. like as *C.* was raised up from the dead by
9. knowing that *C.* being raised, dieth no more
7. 4. ye are become dead to law by the body of *C.*
8. 9. if any have not Spirit of *C.* he is none of his
10. if *C.* be in you, the body is dead because of sin
11. he that raised up *C.* from dead shall quicken
9. 3. I could wish myself were accursed from *C.*
5. of whom *C.* came, who is over all, God blessed
10. 4. *C.* is the end of the law for righteousness
6. that is, to bring up *C.* down from above
7. that is, to bring *C.* again from the dead
14. 9. for to this end *C.* died, and rose, and revived
15. destroy not him with meat for whom *C.* died
18. for he that in these things serveth *C.* is accept.
15. 3. for even *C.* pleased not himself, but reproach.
7. as *C.* also received us, to the glory of God
18. of things which *C.* hath not wrought by me
20. I strived to preach, not where *C.* was named
16. 5. Epenetus the first-fruits of Achaia to *C.*
1 *Cor.* 1. 23. but we preach *C.* crucified, to the Jews
24. *C.* the power of God, and the wisdom of God
3. 23. and ye are *C.* and *C.* is God's

1 *Cor.* 5. 7. even *C.* our passover is sacrificed for us
8. 11. the weak brother perish, for whom *C.* died
9. 21. but under the law to *C.* that I might gain
10. 4. all drank of that rock, and that rock was *C.*
9. nor let us tempt *C.* as some of them also tempted
15. 3. I delivered to you, how *C.* died for our sins
12. if *C.* be preached that he rose from the dead
16. if the dead rise not, then is not *C.* raised
17. and if *C.* be not raised, your faith is vain
23. every man in his own order, *C.* the first-fruits
2 *Cor.* 3. 4. such trust have we thro' *C.* to God-ward
5. 16. yea, tho' we have known *C.* after the flesh
6. 15. and what concord hath *C.* with Belial?
11. 2. I may present you as a chaste virgin to *C.*
Gal. 2. 20. I live, yet not I, but *C.* liveth in me
21. if right. come by law, then *C.* died in vain
3. 13. *C.* hath redeemed us from the curse of the law
24. the law was our schoolmaster, to bring us to *C.*
29. if ye be *C.* then are Abraham's seed, and heirs
4. 7. if a son, then an heir of God through *C.*
19. of whom I travail, till *C.* be formed in you
5. 1. the liberty wherewith *C.* hath made us free
2. if ye be circumcised, *C.* shall profit you nothing
4. *C.* is become of no effect unto you, if justified by law
24. that are *C.* have crucified the flesh with affect.
Eph. 2. 12. at that time ye were without *C.*
3. 17. that *C.* may dwell in your hearts by faith
4. 15. may grow in him which is the head, even *C.*
20. but ye have not so learned *C.*
5. 2. as *C.* also loved us, and hath given himself for
14. arise from the dead, and *C.* shall give thee light
23. husband is the head of the wife, as *C.* is the head of the church
24. as the church is subject to *C.* so let wives be
25. love your wives, as *C.* also loved the church
32. but I speak concerning *C.* and the church
6. 5. obedient, in singleness of your heart as to *C.*
Phil. 1. 15. some indeed preach *C.* of envy and strife
16. the one preach *C.* of contention, not sincerely
18. *C.* is preached, and I therein do rejoice
20. so now *C.* shall be magnified in my body
3. 8. I count them but dung, that I may win *C.*
4. 13. I can do all through *C.* who strengtheneth me
Col. 2. 8. after rudiments of world, and not after *C.*
3. 1. where *C.* sitteth on the right hand of God
4. when *C.* who is our life shall appear, then shall
11. bond nor free, but *C.* is all and in all
13. even as *C.* forgave you, so also do ye
24. receive the reward, for ye serve the Lord *C.*
Heb. 3. 6. but *C.* as a son over his own house
5. 5. so also *C.* glorified not himself to be an high pr.
9. 11. but *C.* being come an high priest of good
24. *C.* not entered into holy places made with hands
28. *C.* was once offered to bear the sins of many
1 *Pet.* 2. 21. because *C.* also suffered for us, an exam.
3. 18. *C.* hath once suffered for sins, just for unjust
4. 1. as *C.* suffered for us in the flesh, arm yourselves
Rev. 11. 15. the kingdoms of our Lord and his *C.*
12. 10. now is come kingd. of G. power of his *C.*

Against CHRIST.

Acts 4. 26. kings and rulers gathered *against* his *C.*
1 *Cor.* 8. 12. when ye sin against the brethren ye sin *against C.*
1 *Tim.* 5. 11. wax wanton *against C.* they will marry

By CHRIST.

2 *Cor.* 1. 5. so our consolation aboundeth *by C.*
Gal. 2. 17. but if while we seek to be justified *by C.*
Eph. 3. 21. to him be glory in church *by C.* Jesus

For CHRIST.

1 *Cor.* 1. 17. *for C.* sent me not to baptize, but to
4. 10. we are fools *for C.* sake, but ye are wise in *C.*
2 *Cor.* 5. 20. now we are ambassadors *for C.* we pray
12. 10. I take pleasure in distresses *for C.* sake
Eph. 4. 32. as God *for C.* sake hath forgiven you
Phil. 3. 7 gain to me, those I counted loss *for C.*
2 *Thess.* 3. 5. L. direct to the patient waiting *for C*
Heb. 11. †26. esteeming reproach *for C.* greater rich.

Jesus with CHRIST.

Mat. 1. 16. was born *Jesus*, who is called *C.* 27. 17, 22.
John 1. 17. but grace and truth came by *Jesus C.*
17. 3. know thee, and *Jesus C.* whom thou sent
Acts 2. 38. be baptized in the name of *Jesus C.*
3. 6. in the name of *Jesus C.* rise up and walk
20. shall send *Jesus C.* who was preached to you
4. 10. by the name of *Jesus C.* doth this man stand
5. 42. and daily they ceased not to preach *Jesus C.*
8. 12. when they believed Philip preaching things concerning name of *Jesus C.* they were baptized
37. I believe that *Jesus C.* is the Son of God
9. 34. Eneas, *Jesus C.* maketh thee whole, arise
10. 36. preaching peace by *Jesus C.* he is Lord of all
16. 18. I command thee in the name of *J. C.* come out
17. 3. and that this *Jesus* I preach to you is *C.*
18. 5. Paul testified to the Jews that *Jesus* was *C.*
28. shewing by the scriptures that *Jesus* was *C.*
19. 4. that they should believe on *C. Jesus*
Rom. 1. 1. Paul a servant of *Jesus C.* *Phil.* 1. 1.
3. concerning his Son *Jesus C.* our Lord, of seed
6. among whom are ye the called of *Jesus C.*
8. I thank my God through *Jesus C.* for you all
2. 16. shall judge the secrets of men by *Jesus C.*
3. 22. righteousness, which is by faith of *Jesus C.*
24. justified through the redemption in *Jesus C.*
5. 15. gift by grace, which is by one man *Jesus C.*
17. shall much more reign in life by one *Jesus C.*
6. 3. so many as were baptized into *Jesus C.*
8. 1. no condemnation to them that are in *C. Jesus*
2. the Spirit of life in *C. Jesus* hath made me free
16. 3. Priscilla and Aquila, my helpers in *C. Jesus*
1 *Cor.* 1. 1. Paul apostle of *J. C.* 2 *Cor.* 1. 1. *Eph.* 1. 1.
2. with all that call on the name of *Jesus C.*
4. for the grace of God given you by *Jesus C.*
30. but of him are ye in *C. Jesus*, who is made to
2. 2. not to know any thing, save *Jesus C.* crucified
4. 15. for in *C. J.* have I begotten you thro' gospel
2 *Cor.* 4. 6. the knowledge of God in face of *J. C.*
5. 18. hath reconciled us to himself by *Jesus C.*
13. 5. know ye not, how that *Jesus C.* is in you
Gal. 2. 16. a man is justified by the faith of *Jesus C.*
3. 14. blessing come on the Gentiles thro' *Jesus C.*
28. male nor female, for ye are all one in *C. Jesus*

Gal. 4. 14. ye received me as an angel, even as *C. J.*
Eph. 2. 6. made us sit in heavenly places in *C. Jesus*
20. *Jesus C.* being the chief corner-stone
Phil. 1. 8. I long after you in the bowels of *Jesus C.*
2. 5. mind be in you, which was also in *C. Jesus*
11. *Jesus C.* is Lord, to the glory of God the F.
21. all seek not the things which are *Jesus C.*
3. 8. I count all loss for the excellency of *C. Jesus*
12. for which also I am apprehended of *C. Jesus*
4. 19. according to his riches in glory by *C. Jesus*
Col. 2. 6. as ye have received *C. J.* so walk ye in him
1 *Tim.* 1. 15. that *C. Jesus* came to save sinners
2. 5. mediator between God and men, man *C. Jesus*
6. 13. before *C. J.* who witnessed a good confession
2 *Tim.* 1. 9. according to his grace given us in *C. J*
13. in faith and love, which is in *C. Jesus*
Philem. 1. Paul a prisoner of *Jesus C.* 9. 23.
Heb. 13. 8. *J. C.* the same yesterday, and for ever
1 *John* 1. 7. blood of *Jesus C.* cleanseth from all sin
2. 1. we have an advocate, *Jesus C.* the righteous
5. 6. this is he that came by water and blood, *J. C*
20. we are in him, even in his Son *Jesus C.*

Lord Jesus CHRIST.

Acts 11. 17. as to us who believed on the *L. J. C.*
15. 11. thro' the grace of *L. J. C.* we shall be saved
16. 31. believe on the *L. J. C.* thou shalt be saved
20. 21. testifying faith toward our *Lord Jesus C.*
Rom. 5. 1. we have peace with God, thro' *L. J. C*
11. we also joy in God, thro' our *Lord Jesus C.*
6. 23. gift of God is eternal life thro' our *L. J. C.*
8. 39. separate from love of God in *C. Jesus* our *L.*
13. 14. put ye on *L. J. C.* and make not provision
16. 20. grace of *L. J. C.* be with you, 24. 2 *Cor.* 13. 14. *Gal.* 6. 18. 2 *Thess.* 3. 18. *Rev.* 22. 21.
1 *Cor.* 1. 7. waiting for the coming of *Lord Jesus C.*
8. 6. but to us one *L. J. C.* by whom are all things
15. 57. God giveth us the victory thro' our *L. J. C.*
16. 22. if any man love not the *Lord Jesus C.*
2 *Cor.* 1. 2. grace and peace from God, and from the *L. J. C.* *Gal.* 1. 3. *Eph.* 1. 2. *Col.* 1. 2.
8. 9. for ye know the grace of our *Lord Jesus C.*
Gal. 6. 14. glory save in the cross of our *L. J. C.*
Eph. 1. 3. blessed be the Father of our *Lord Jesus C.*
17. God of our *L. J. C.* give you spirit of wisdom
1 *Thess.* 1. 3. your patience of hope in our *L. J. C.*
2. 19. ye are our joy in presence of our *Lord J. C.*
3. 13. may establish you at coming of our *L. J. C.*
5. 23. be preserved unto coming of our *L. J. C.*
2 *Thess.* 2. 1. we beseech you by coming of *L. J. C.*
16. now our *L. J. C.* hath given us consolation
1 *Tim.* 5. 21. I charge thee bef. *L. J. C.* 2 *Tim.* 4. 1.
2 *Tim.* 4. 22. the *L. J. C.* be with thy spirit, amen
2 *Pet.* 1. 11. an entrance into kingdom of *L. J. C.*
3. 18. grow in grace and in knowledge of *L. J. C.*

In CHRIST.

Acts 24. 24. heard him concerning the faith *in C.*
Rom. 9. 1. I say the truth *in C.* I lie not, my cons.
12. 5. so we being many are one body *in C.*
16. 7. are of note, who also were *in C.* before me
9. salute Urbane, our helper *in C.* and Stachys
10. salute Apelles approved *in C.* salute Aristo.
1 *Cor.* 3. 1. I speak to you, even as unto babes *in C.*
4. 10. we are fools, but ye are wise *in C.*
15. tho' ye have 10,000 instruct. *in C.* not many
15. 18. they that are fallen asleep *in C.* are perish.
19. if in this life only we have hope *in C.*
22. even so *in C.* shall all be made alive
2 *Cor.* 1. 21. he which stablisheth us with you *in C.*
2. 14. God who causeth us to triumph *in C.*
17. as of God, in the sight of God speak we *in C.*
3. 14. vail untaken away, vail is done away *in C.*
5. 17. if any man be *in C.* he is a new creature
19. that God was *in C.* reconciling the world
20. we pray you *in C.* stead, be reconciled to G.
12. 2. I knew a man *in C.* above fourteen years ago
19. we speak before God, *in C.* we do all things
Gal. 1. 22. unknown to the churches of Judea *in C.*
3. 17. the covenant confirmed before of God *in C.*
27. as many as have been baptized *into C.*
Eph. 1. 3. blessed us with spiritual blessings *in C.*
10. he might gather in one all things *in C.*
12. should be to his glory, who first trusted *in C.*
20. which he wrought *in C.* when he raised him
3. 6. partakers of his promise *in C.* by the gospel
Phil. 1. 13. so that my bonds *in C.* are manifest in
2. 1. if there be any consolation *in C.* if comfort
Col. 2. 5. beholding stedfastness of your faith *in C.*
1 *Thess.* 4. 16. and the dead *in C.* shall rise first
1 *Tim.* 2. 7. I speak the truth *in C.* and lie not
1 *Pet.* 3. 16. accuse your good conversation *in C.*

Is CHRIST.

Mat. 24. 23. if any say, lo, here *is C.* *Mark* 13. 21.
Mark 12. 35. that *C. is* the son of David, *Luke* 20. 41.
Luke 2. 11. is born a Saviour which *is C.* the Lord
23. 2. saying, that he himself *is C.* a king
John 7. 41. others said, this *is* the *C.* some said
Acts 9. 22. Saul increased, proving this *is* very *C.*
17. 3. that this Jesus whom I preach to you *is C.*
Rom. 8. 34. it *is C.* that died, yea rather risen again
1 *Cor.* 1. 13. *is C.* divided? was Paul crucified for
7. 22. he that is called, being free, *is C.* servant
11. 3. know that the head of every man *is C.*
12. 12. members being many are one body, so *is C.*
15. 13. if dead rise not, then *is C.* not risen, 16.
20. but now *is C.* risen from the dead, and first
2 *Cor.* 10. 7. if any man trust that he *is C.*
Gal. 2. 17. *is* therefore *C.* the minister of sin?
3. 16. but as of one, and to thy seed, which *is C.*
Phil. 1. 21. for to me to live *is C.* but to die is gain
Col. 1. 27. which *is C.* in you, the hope of glory

Of CHRIST.

Mat. 11. 2. John heard in prison the works *of C.*
22. 42. what think you *of C.*? whose son is he?
Rom. 8. 9. if any man have not the Spirit *of C.*
35. who shall separate us from the love *of C.*?
14. 10. we shall all stand before judgment seat *of C.*
1 *Cor.* 1. 17. lest cross *of C.* be made of none effect
2. 16. but we have the mind *of C.*
6. 15. know ye not your bodies are members *of C.*
10. 16. cup, is it not the communion of blood *of C.* the bread, is it not the communion of body *of C.*
11. 1. be ye followers of me, even as I also am *of C.*

1 *Cor.* 11. 3. head of woman is man, head *of C.* is God
12. 27. now ye are the body *of C.* and members
2 *Cor.* 1. 5. as the sufferings of *C.* abound in us
2. 10. for you forgave I it in the person *of C.*
15. for we are to God a sweet savour *of C.*
3. 3. ye are the epistle *of C.* ministered by us
4. 4. lest the light of the glorious gospel *of C.* shine
5. 14. for the love *of C.* constraineth us, because
8. 23. or our brethren, they are the glory *of C.*
10. 1. beseech by the meekness and gentleness *of C.*
5. bringing every thought to the obedience *of C.*
11. 10. as the truth *of C.* is in me, none shall stop
12. 9. power *of C.* may rest on me, *Rev.* 12. 10.
13. 3. since ye seek a proof *of C.* speaking in me
Gal. 1. 10. if pleased men, should not be serv. *of C.*
2. 16. that we might be justified by the faith *of C.*
6. 12. lest suffer persecution for the cross *of C.*
Eph. 2. 13. ye are made nigh by the blood *of C.*
3. 4. understand my knowled. in the mystery *of C.*
8. should preach the unsearchable riches *of C.*
19. know the love of *C.* which passeth knowledge
4. 7. according to the measure of the gift *of C.*
5. 5. hath any inheritance in the kingdom *of C.*
6. 6. as servants *of C.* doing the will of God
Phil. 1. 10. be without offence till the day *of C.*
29. for to you it is given in behalf *of C.* to believe
2. 16. that I may rejoice in the day *of C.*
30. for the work *of C.* he was nigh to death
3. 18. they are the enemies of the cross *of C.*
Col. 1. 24. fill up what is behind of afflictions *of C.*
2. 2. mystery of God, and of the Father, and *of C.*
17. are a shadow of things, but the body is *of C.*
3. 16. let the word *of C.* dwell in you richly
4. 3. open to us a door, to speak the mystery *of C.*
2 *Thess.* 3. † 5. Lord direct you into the patience *of C.*
2 *Tim.* 2. 19. every one that nameth the name *of C.*
Heb. 3. 14. for we are made partakers *of C.* if we hold
9. 14. how much more blood *of C.* purge conscien.
11. 26. reproach *of C.* greater riches than treasur.
1 *Pet.* 1. 11. what time the Spirit *of C.* did signify
19. ye are redeemed with the precious blood *of C.*
4. 13. as ye are partakers *of C.* sufferings, that when
14. if ye be reproached for the name *of C.*
Rev. 20. 6. they shall be priests of God and *of C.*

That CHRIST.

John 1. 25. if be not *that C.* nor Elias, nor prophet
6. 69. we are sure thou art *that C.* the Son of God

The CHRIST.

Mat. 16. 20. saying, tell no man that he was *the C.*
26. 63. I adjure thee, tell whether thou be *the C.*
Mark 8. 29. Peter saith unto him, thou art *the C.*
14. 61. art thou *the C.* the Son of the Blessed?
Luke 3. 15. mused of John, whether he were *the C.*
9. 20. Peter said, thou art *the C.* of God
22. 67. scribes, saying, art thou *the C.?* tell us
John 1. 20. but he confessed, I am not *the C.*
41. we have found the Messias, which is *the C.*
3. 28. I said, I am not *the C.* but sent before him
4. 29. see a man who told me all, is not this *the C.?*
42. we know that this is indeed *the C.* 7. 26.
7. 41. others said, this is *the C.* but some said
10. 24. if thou be *the C.* tell us plainly
11. 27. I believe thou art *the C.* the Son of God
20. 31. that ye might believe that Jesus is *the C.*
1 *John* 2. 22. but he that denieth that Jesus is *the C.*
5. 1. whoso believeth Jesus is *the C.* is born of God

With CHRIST.

Rom. 6. 8. if we be dead *with C.* we shall also live
8. 17. if children, then joint-heirs *with C.*
Gal. 2. 20. I am crucified *with C.* I live, *C.* liveth
Eph. 2. 5. God hath quickened us together *with C.*
Phil. 1. 23. having a desire to depart and be *with C.*
Col. 2. 20. if ye be dead *with C.* from the world
3. 1. if ye be risen *with C.* seek the things above
3. ye are dead, and your life is hid *with C.* in G.
Rev. 20. 4. and they reigned *with C.* 1000 years

CHRISTIAN, S.

Acts 11. 26. disciples were first called *c.* at Antioch
26. 28. almost thou persuadest me to be a *c.*
1 *Pet.* 4. 16. yet if any man suffer as a *c.* not be asha.

CHRISTS.

Mat. 24. 24. there shall arise false *c.* *Mark* 13. 22.

CHRONICLES.

1 *Kings* 14. 19. rest of acts of Jeroboam are in the *c.*
1 *Chron.* 27. 24. nor number put in the account of *c.*
Esth. 6. 1. to bring the book of the records of *c.*
See BOOK.

CHRYSOLITE.

Rev. 21. 20. seventh foundation of the city was a *c.*

CHRYSOPRASUS.

Rev. 21. 20. tenth foundation of the city was a *c.*

CHURCH

Signifies, [1] *A religious assembly selected and called out of the world by the doctrine of the gospel, to worship the true God in Christ, according to his word,* 1 Cor. 1. 2. Rev. 2. 7. [2] *All the elect of God, of what nation soever, from the beginning to the end of the world, who make but one body, whereof Jesus Christ is the Head,* Col. 1. 18. [3] *The faithful of some one family, together with such christians as were wont to assemble with them for solemn worship,* Rom. 16. 5. Col. 4. 15. Philem. 2. [4] *The faithful of some one province,* 2 Thess. 1. 1. [5] *The governors, or representatives of the church,* Mat. 18. 17. Tell it to the church; *that is, to such rulers, to whom the censures of the church do of right belong, that by them it may be communicated to the whole society.* [6] *A multitude of people assembled together, whether good or bad,* Acts 19. 37. [7] *The congregation of the* Jews, *which was formerly the church and people of God,* Acts 7. 38.

Mat. 16. 18. and upon this rock I will build my *c.*
18. 17. tell it to the *c.* if he neglect to hear the *c.*
Acts 2. 47. Lord added to *c.* daily such sh. be saved
5. 11. and great fear came on all the *c.* and as many
8. 1. was a great persecution against the *c.* at Jeru.
11. 26. they assembled themselves with the *c.*
14. 23. when they had ordained elders in every *c.*
27. when they had gathered the *c.* together
15. 3. being brought on their way by the *c.*
Acts 15. 22. it pleased elders with the whole *c.* to send
18. 22. when he had gone up and saluted the *c.*
Rom. 16. 5. greet the *c.* that is in their house
1 *Cor.* 4. 17. as I teach every where, in every *c.*
14. 4. but he that prophesieth edifieth the *c.*
5. except interpret that the *c.* may receive edify.
23. if the *c.* be come together into one place
16. 19. salute you, with *c.* that is in their house
Eph. 1. 22. gave him to be head over all to the *c.*
3. 10. might be known by the *c.* the wisdom of God
5. 24. as the *c.* is subject to Christ, so let wives
25. as Christ loved the *c.* and gave himself for it
27. that he might present to himself a glorious *c.*
29. but cherisheth it, even as the Lord the *c.*
32. but I speak concerning Christ and the *c.*
Phil. 3. 6. concerning zeal, persecuting the *c.*
4. 15. no *c.* communicated with me, but ye only
Col. 1. 18. and he is the head of the body the *c.*
24. for his body's sake, which is the *c.*
4. 15. salute the *c.* which is in Nymphas' house
1 *Tim.* 5. 16. and let not the *c.* be charged
Philem. 2. Paul a prisoner, to the *c.* in thy house
Heb. 12. 23. to the *c.* of the first-born in heaven
1 *Pet.* 5. 13. the *c.* at Babylon elected saluteth you
3 *John* 6. borne witness of thy charity before the *c.*
9. I wrote unto *c.* but Diotrephes receiveth us not

In the CHURCH.

Acts 7. 38. this is he that was *in the c.* in wilderness
13. 1. there were prophets *in the c.* at Antioch
1 *Cor.* 6. 4. to judge who are least esteemed *in the c.*
11. 18. first of all when ye come together *in the c.*
12. 28. God hath set some *in the c.* first apostles
14. 19. yet *in the c.* I had rather speak five words
28. let him keep silence *in the c.* and speak to God
35. it is a shame for women to speak *in the c.*
Eph. 3. 21. to him be glory *in the c.* by Christ Jesus
Col. 4. 16. cause it to be read *in the c.* of Laodicea

Of the CHURCH.

Acts 8. 3. as for Saul, he made havock *of the c.*
11. 22. tidings from Antioch came to ears *of the c.*
12. 1. at that time Herod vexed certain *of the c.*
5. prayer was made *of the c.* unto God for Peter
15. 4. they were received *of the c.* and elders
20. 17. Paul sent and called the elders *of the c.*
Rom. 16. 1. Phebe our sister, a servant *of the c.*
23. Gaius mine host and *of the* whole *c.* saluteth
1 *Cor.* 14. 12. may excel to the edifying *of the c.*
Eph. 5. 23. even as Christ is the head *of the c.*
Heb. 2. 12. in midst *of the c.* I will sing praise
Jam. 5. 14. let him call for the elders *of the c.*
3 *John* 10. Diotrephes casteth them out *of the c.*
Rev. 2. 1. to the angel *of the c.* of Ephesus, write
8. *c.* in Smyrna ‖ 12. Pergamus ‖ 18. Thyatira
3. 1. *c.* of Sardis ‖ 7. Philadelphia ‖ 14. Laodicea

CHURCH *of God.*

Acts 20. 28. feed the *c. of God* which he purchased
1 *Cor.* 1. 2. to the *c. of God* which is at Corinth
10. 32. give none offence to the *c. of God*
11. 22. or despise ye the *c. of God* and shame them
15. 9. because I persecuted *c. of God, Gal.* 1. 13.
1 *Tim.* 3. 5. how shall he take care of the *c. of God?*

CHURCHES.

Acts 9. 31. then had the *c.* rest through all Judea
15. 41. Paul went through Syria confirming the *c.*
16. 5. so were the *c.* established in the faith
19. 37. these men who are neither robbers of *c.*
Rom. 16. 4. to whom all *c.* of Gentiles give thanks
16. salute one another, the *c.* of Christ salute you
1 *Cor.* 7. 17. so let him walk, so ordain I in all *c.*
11. 16. we have no such custom, neither *c.* of Christ
14. 33. but author of peace as in all *c.* of the saints
34. let your women keep silence in the *c.*
16. 1. as I have given order to *c.* of Galatia so do ye
19. *c.* of Asia salute you; Aquila and Priscilla
2 *Cor.* 8. 1. of the grace bestowed on *c.* of Macedonia
19. but who was chosen of the *c.* to travel with us
23. brethren, they are the messengers of the *c.*
11. 8. I robbed other *c.* taking wages of them
28. cometh upon me daily the care of all the *c.*
12. 13. what is it wherein ye were inferior to *c.?*
Gal. 1. 22. were unknown by face to *c.* of Judea
1 *Thess.* 2. 14. ye became followers of the *c.* of God
2 *Thess.* 1. 4. so that we ourselves glory in you in *c.*
Rev. 1. 4. John to the seven *c.* in Asia, grace to you
11. send it to the seven *c.* which are in Asia
20. the seven stars are the angels of the seven *c.*
and the seven candlesticks are the seven *c.*
2. 7. he that hath an ear, let him hear what Spirit
saith unto the *c.* 11, 17, 29. | 3. 6, 13, 22.
23. *c.* know I am he which searcheth the reins
22. 16. I Jesus sent to testify these things in the *c.*

CHURL.

Isa. 32. 5. nor shall the *c.* be said to be bountiful
7. the instruments also of the *c.* are evil

CHURLISH.

1 *Sam.* 25. 3. man Nabal was *c.* and evil in his doings

CHURNING.

Prov. 30. 33. surely the *c.* of milk bringeth butter

CIELED.

2 *Chron.* 3. 5. he *c.* the greater house with fir-tree
Jer. 22. 14. it is *c.* with cedar and painted with ver.
Hag. 1. 4. is it time for you to dwell in your *c.* houses?

CIELING.

1 *Kings* 6. 15. he built walls of the house with *c.*
Ezek. 41. † 16. over-against the door *c.* with wood

CINNAMON.

Exod. 30. 23. take of sweet *c.* half so much
Prov. 7. 17. I have perfumed my bed with aloes and *c.*
Cant. 4. 14. thy plants are an orch. of calamus and *c.*
Rev. 18. 13. no man buyeth her merchandise of *c.*

CIRCLE.

Prov. 8. † 27. when he set a *c.* on face of the depth
Isa. 40. 22. it is he that sitteth on the *c.* of the earth

CIRCUIT, S.

1 *Sam.* 7. 16. he went from year to year in *c.* to Bethel
Job 22. 14. and he walketh in the *c.* of heaven
Psal. 19. 6. and his *c.* from the ends of the earth
Eccl. 1. 6. wind returneth again according to his *c.*

CIRCUMCISE.

Gen. 17. 11. ye shall *c.* the flesh of your foreskins
Deut. 10. 16. *c.* therefore the foreskin of your heart
30. 6. the Lord thy God will *c.* thine heart
Josh. 5. 2. and *c.* again children of Israel second time
4. and this is the cause why Joshua did *c.*
Jer. 4. 4. *c.* yourselves to the Lord, and take away
Luke 1. 59. on eighth day they came to *c.* the child
John 7. 22. and ye on the sabbath-day *c.* a man
Acts 15. 5. saying, it was needful to *c.* them
21. 21. that they ought not to *c.* their children

CIRCUMCISED.

Gen. 17. 10. every man-child among you shall be *c.*
14. whose flesh is not *c.* that soul shall be cut off
23. and Abraham *c.* the flesh of their foreskin
26. in that day Abrah. was *c.* and Ishmael his son
34. 15. if as we be, that every male of you be *c.*
24. and every male was *c.* *Exod.* 12. 48.
Josh. 5. 3. Joshua *c.* children of Israel at the hill
7. because they had not *c.* them by the way
† 8. when the people had made an end to be *c.*
Jer. 9. 25. will punish all *c.* with the uncircumcised
Acts 15. 1. except ye be *c.* ye cannot be saved, 24.
16. 3. Paul *c.* Timothy because of the Jews
Rom. 4. 11. be father of all that believe, though not *c*
1 *Cor.* 7. 18. is any man called being *c.* let him not
become uncircum. in uncircum. not become *c.*
Gal. 2. 3. neither was Titus compelled to be *c.*
5. 2. if ye be *c.* Christ shall profit you nothing
6. 12. they constrain you to be *c.* lest they suffer
13. for they that are *c.* kept not the law
Phil. 3. 5. *c.* the eighth day, of the stock of Israel
Col. 2. 11. in whom also ye are *c.* with circumcision

CIRCUMCISING.

Josh. 5. 8. when they had done *c.* all the people
Luke 2. 21. when eight days accomplished for *c.* child

CIRCUMCISION.

This term is taken from the Latin, circumcidere, *which signifies to cut all round, because the Jews, who circumcised their children, cut off the little skin or prepuce after that manner, which covers the nut of the penis, or natural part. God enjoined* Abraham *to use circumcision, as a sign of that covenant which he had entered into with him,* Gen. 17. 10, 11, &c. *This was a sign, evidence, and assurance, both of the blessing promised by that God who appointed this ordinance, particularly that he would give them* Christ, *the promised seed, out of the loins of* Abraham, *and in him accept of them for his peculiar people, pardon their sins, and cleanse them from their natural corruption, signified by the cutting off of their foreskins: and also of men's obligation to the duties required;* namely, *to believe in this* Messiah, *to put off the old man, and serve him as new creatures; which is signified by his acceptance of, and submission to, the ordinance.*

Circumcision *is likewise put for the* Jews, *who were circumcised, as* uncircumcision *is put for the uncircumcised Gentiles,* Gal. 2. 7, 8, 9. *And for such as are spiritually circumcised, who are the true spiritual seed of* Abraham, *who have the thing signified by that sign, or ceremony, and perform that which circumcision was designed to engage unto,* Phil. 3. 3.

John 7. 22. Moses therefore gave unto you *c.*
23. if a man on the sabbath-day receive *c.* are ye
Rom. 2. 25. for *c.* profiteth, if thou keep the law; if
thou break the law, thy *c.* is made uncircumcision
28. nor is that *c.* which is outward in the flesh
29. and *c.* is that of the heart, in the spirit
3. 30. one God, who shall justify the *c.* by faith
4. 9. cometh this blessedness then on the *c.* only?
10. how was it reckoned, when he was in *c.?* not in *c.*
1 *Cor.* 7. 19. *c.* is the keeping of the commandments
Gal. 2. 9. and that they should go unto the *c.*
5. 6. for in Jesus Christ neither *c.* availeth, 6. 15.
11. and I, brethren, if I yet preach *c.* why do I yet
Eph. 2. 11. by that which is called the *c.* in the flesh
Phil. 3. 3. we are the *c.* which worship G. in spirit
Col. 2. 11. with *c.* without hands, by *c.* of Christ
3. 11. there is neither *c.* nor uncircum. but Chr. is

Of CIRCUMCISION.

Exod. 4. 26. a bloody husband art thou, because *of c.*
Acts 7. 8. he gave Abraham the covenant *of c.*
10. 45. they *of c.* which believed were astonished
11. 2. they that were *of* the *c.* contended with Peter
Rom. 3. 1. what profit is there *of c.?* much every way
4. 11. he received the sign *of c.* a seal of righteousn.
12. a father *of c.* to them who are not *of* the *c.*
15. 8. Jesus Chr. was a minister *of c.* for truth of G.
Gal. 2. 7. as the gospel *of c.* was committed to Peter
8. he that wrought in Peter to apostleship *of* the *c.*
Col. 4. 11. Marcus and Justus, who are *of c.* sal. you
Tit. 1. 10. for there many unruly, especially they *of c.*

CIRCUMSPECT.

Exod. 23. 13. in all things that I have said to you, be *c.*

CIRCUMSPECTLY.

Eph. 5. 15. see that ye walk *c.* not as fools but as wise

CISTERN

Signifies, [1] *A vessel of lead to hold water for household uses,* 2 Kings 18. 31. [2] *Any thing that persons put their trust in besides God, whether in idols, powerful neighbours and allies, friends, traditions, merits, &c. which are but broken cisterns,* Jer. 2. 13. [3] *The left ventricle of the heart,* Eccl. 12. 6.

2 *Kings* 18. 31. drink ye every one waters of his *c.*
Prov. 5. 15. drink waters out of thine own *c.*
Eccl. 12. 6. or the wheel broken at the *c.*
Isa. 36. 16. drink every one the waters of his own *c.*

CISTERNS.

2 *Chron.* 26. † 10. Uzziah cut out many *c.*
Neh. 9. † 25. possessed houses full of goods and *c.*
Jer. 2. 13. my people have hewed out *c.* broken *c.*

CITY

Signifies, [1] *A walled town for people to dwell in,* Josh. 6. 3. [2] *The inhabitants of cities,* Gen. 35. 5. Isa. 14. 31. Jer. 26. 2. [3] *The church of God upon earth,* Cant. 3. 2, 3. Rev. 11. 2. [4] *The church triumphant all united in glory,* Rev. 21. 2. | 22. 19. [5] *Heaven, the eternal inheritance of all believers,* Heb. 11. 10, 16. [6] *That wherein a man puts his trust and confidence,* Prov. 10. 15.

Gen. 4. 17. Cain builded a *c.* and called it Enoch

Gen. 11. 4. let us build us a c. and a tower, whose top
5. Lord came down to see the c. and the tower
8. Ld. scattered them, and they left off to build c.
18. 26. if I find in Sod. fifty righteous within the c.
28. wilt thou destroy all the c. for lack of five?
24. 13. the daughters of the c. come to draw water
34. 24. hearkened all that went out of the gate of c.
25. came upon the c. boldly, and slew the males
Num. 21. 28. a flame is gone out from c. of Sihon
22. † 39. Balaam came to a c. of streets
Deut. 2. 36. there was not one c. too strong for us
3. 4. there was not a c. we took not from them
13. 15. shalt surely smite the inhabitants of that c.
21. 3. c. next to slain man shall take a heifer, 6.
Josh. 3. 16. on an heap very far from the c. Adam
6. 3. ye shall compass c. and go round six days, 7.
24. they burnt the c. with fire, and all therein,
Deut. 13. 16. Josh. 8. 8, 19. Judg. 1. 8. | 18. 27.
8. 2. lay thee an ambush for the c. behind it
17. they left the c. open, and pursued after Isr.
20. the smoke of the c. ascended up to heaven
11. 19. was not a c. made peace, save the Hivites
Josh. 15. 13. to Caleb the c. of Arba, which c. is Heb.
19. 50. they gave Joshua the c. which he asked
20. 4. he shall stand at the entry of the gate of c.
Judg. 6. 27. because he feared the men of the c.
8. 17. and Gideon slew the men of the c.
9. 45. and beat down the c. and sowed it with salt
51. all they of the c. fled, and shut it to them
20. 40. the flame of the c. ascended up to heaven
Ruth 1. 19. that all the c. was moved about them
3. 11. for all the c. of my people know that thou
1 Sam. 1. 3. this man went out of c. yearly to wors.
4. 13. when the man told it, all the c. cried out
5. 11. there was a deadly destruction thro' all the c.
8. 22. Samuel said to Israel, go ye every man to his
c. 1 Kings 22. 36. Ezra 2. 1. Neh. 7. 6.
28. 3. Israel buried him in Ramah, his own c.
2 Sam. 12. 1. two men in one c. one rich, other poor
15. 2. then Absalom called, of what c. art thou?
19. 37. I may die in mine own c. and be buried
20. 19. seekest to destroy a c. and mother in Israel
1 Kings 1. 45. rejoicing, so that the c. rang again
11. 32. for Jerusalem's sake, c. I have chosen, 36.
2 Kings 6. 19. neither is this the c. follow me
11. 20. the people rejoiced, and the c. was in quiet
24. 10. the c. Jerusalem was besieged, 25. 2.
2 Chr. 15. 6. was destroyed of c. for G. did vex them
19. 5. and he set judges in the land c. by c.
30. 10. so the posts passed from c. to c.
32. 18. to trouble them that they might take the c.
Ezra 4. 12. the Jews are building the rebellious c.
Neh. 2. 3. why not sad, when the c. lieth waste, 5.
11. 9. Judah son of Senuah was second over the c.
Esth. 3. 15. but the c. Shushan was perplexed
8. 15. the c. of Shushan rejoiced and was glad
Psal. 48. 2. the c. of the great king, Mat. 5. 35.
59. 6. and they go round about the c. 14.
72. 16. they of c. shall flourish like grass of earth
107. 4. they wandered, they found no c. to dwell in
122. 3. Jerusalem is builded as a c. compact
127. 1. except Lord keep the c. watchmen in vain
Prov. 8. 3. Wisdom crieth at the entry of the c.
10. 15. rich man's wealth is his strong c. 18. 11.
11. 10. when it goeth well with the righteous, the
c. rejoiceth, and shouting when wicked perish
11. by blessing of the upright the c. is exalted
16. 32. ruleth his spirit, than he that taketh a c.
25. 28. is like a c. broken down without walls
29. 8. scornful men bring a c. into a snare
Eccl. 9. 14. there was a little c. and few men in it
15. and the poor wise man delivered the c.
Isa. 1. 26. called c. of righteousness, faithful c. 21.
14. 31. howl, O gate, cry, O c. whole Palestina
17. 1. Damascus is taken away from being a c.
19. 2. shall fight c. against c. kingd. against kingd.
24. 10. the c. of confusion is broken down
25. 2. thou hast made of a c. an heap, to be no c.
33. 20. look on Zion, the c. of our solemnities
60. 14. they shall call thee the c. of the Lord
62. 12. thou shalt be called a c. not forsaken
Jer. 3. 14. I will take you one of a c. two of a tribe
4. 29. whole c. shall flee from noise of horsemen
19. 12. thus will I do, even make this c. as Tophet
25. 29. to bring evil on the c. called by my name
32. 24. they are come to the c. and the c. is given
39. 2. the c. was broken up, men of war fled, 52. 7.
46. 8. I will destroy the c. and the inhabitants
49. 25. how is the c. of praise not left, the c. of joy
Lam. 1. 1. how doth c. sit solitary, full of people?
2. 15. is this c. that men called perfection of beauty?
Ezek. 4. 1. pourtray on it the c. even Jerusalem
7. 23. make a chain, for the c. is full of violence
9. 1. cause them that have charge over the c.
4. go thro' the midst of c. Jerusalem, set a mark
9. land full of blood, the c. is full of perverseness
10. 2. and scatter the coals of fire over the c.
27. 32. what c. is like Tyrus in midst of the sea?
33. 21. one came to me, saying, the c. is smitten
48. 35. name of the c. shall be, the Lord is there
Dan. 9. 18. behold the c. called by thy name, 19.
Hos. 6. 8. Gilead a c. of them that work iniquity
Amos 4. 7. I caused to rain on one c. not on another
5. 3. the c. that went out by a thousand shall leave
Mic. 6. 9. Lord's voice crieth to the c. hear the rod
Hab. 2. 12. woe to him that stablisheth a c. by iniq.
Zeph. 3. 1. woe to filthy and polluted, oppressing c.
Zech. 8. 3. Jerusalem shall be called a c. of truth
5. streets of the c. shall be full of boys and girls
14. 2. the c. shall be taken and the houses rifled, the
residue of people shall not be cut off from the c.
Mat. 5. 14. a c. that is set on a hill cannot be hid
35. nor by Jerusalem, for it is the c. of great king
8. 34. behold, the whole c. came out to meet Jesus
10. 11. into whatsoever c. ye shall enter, inquire
15. than for that c. Mark 6. 11. Luke 10. 12.
21. 10. all the c. was moved, saying, who is this?
22. 7. the king sent and burnt up their c.
23. 34. and persecute them from c. to c.
Mark 1. 33. all the c. was gathered together at door
5. 14. they that fed swine told it in c. Luke 8. 34.
Luke 2. 3. went to be taxed, every one to his own c.
Luke 7. 12. and much people of the c. was with her
19. 41. he beheld the c. and wept over it
23. 51. Joseph was of Arimathea, a c. of the Jews
John 4. 39. many of that c. believed on him
Acts 8. 8. and there was great joy in that c.
13. 44. came together almost the whole c. to hear
16. 12. we were abiding in that c. certain days
17. 5. and set all the c. in an uproar and assaulted
19. 29. the whole c. was filled with confusion
21. 30. all the c. was moved, and the people ran
Heb. 11. 10. he looked for a c. that hath foundations
16. for he hath prepared for them a c.
12. 22. ye are come to the c. of the living God
13. 14. for here we have no continuing c. but seek
Jam. 4. 13. we will go into such a c. buy and sell
Rev. 20. 9. they went and compassed the beloved c.
21. 14. the wall of the c. had twelve foundations
18. the c. was pure gold, like to clear glass
23. the c. had no need of the sun nor moon

Bloody CITY.

Ezek. 22. 2. son of man, wilt thou judge the bloody c.?
24. 6. woe to the bloody c. to the pot, 9. Nah. 3. 1.

Defenced CITY.

Isa. 25. 2. thou hast made of a defenced c. a ruin
27. 10. yet the defenced c. shall be desolate
Jer. 1. 18. I have made thee this day a defenced c.

CITY of David.

2 Sam. 5. 9. called it the c. of David, 1 Chr. 11. 7.
6. 10. would not remove the ark into c. of David
12. brought up the ark into the c. of David, 16.
1 Kings 2. 10. David was buried in the c. of David
3. 1. Solomon brought her into the c. of David
8. 1. bring the ark out of c. of David, 2 Chr. 5. 2.
11. 43. Solomon buried in c. of D. 2 Chr. 9. 31.
14. 31. Rehoboam buried in c. of D. 2 Chr. 12. 16.
15. 8. they buried Abijam in c. of D. 2 Chr. 14. 1.
22. 50. Jehoshaphat buried in c. of D. 2 Chr. 21. 1.
2 Kings 8. 24. Joram buried in c. of D. 2 Chr. 21. 20.
9. 28. Ahaziah was buried in the c. of David
12. 21. Jehoash buried in c. of D. 2 Chron. 24. 25.
14. 20. Amaziah || 15. 7. Azariah buried in c. of D.
15. 38. Jothan was buried in c. of D. 2 Chr. 27. 9.
16. 20. Ahaz was buried in the c. of David
2 Chron. 24. 16. they buried Jehoiada in the c. of D.
Isa. 22. 9. seen the breaches of the c. of David
29. 1. woe to Ariel, the c. where David dwelt
Luke 2. 4. Joseph also went into the c. of David
11. to you is born in the c. of David a Saviour

Elders with CITY.

Deut. 19. 12. the elders of his c. shall fetch him
21. 6. the elders of that c. next to the slain man
20. say to the elders of his c. our son is stubborn
22. 17. spread the cloth before the elders of the c.
25. 8. then the elders of his c. shall call him
Josh. 20. 4. declare his cause to the elders of that c.
Judg. 8. 16. Gideon took the elders of the c.
Ruth 4. 2. Boaz took ten men of the elders of the c.
Ezra 10. 14. and with them the elders of every c.

Every CITY.

Judg. 20. 48. smote as well the men of every c.
2 Kings 3. 19. ye shall smite every fenced c.
2 Chron. 11. 12. in every c. Rehoboam put shields
28. 25. in every c. of Judah he made high places
31. 19. of sons of Aaron which were in every c.
Jer. 4. 29. every c. shall be forsaken, not a man dwell
48. 8. and the spoiler shall come upon every c.
Mat. 12. 25. and every c. divided against itself
Luke 10. 1. sent them two and two into every c.
Acts 15. 21. hath in every c. them that preach him
36. let us go and visit our brethren in every c.
20. 23. the Holy Ghost witnesseth in every c. that
Tit. 1. 5. that thou shouldst ordain elders in every c.

Fenced CITY.

2 Kings 10. 2. with you a fenced c. also and armour
17. 9. from the tower of watchmen to the fenced c.
2 Chron. 11. 23. he dispersed of all his children thro'
Judah and Benjamin unto every fenced c.

CITY of God.

Psal. 46. 4. the streams shall make glad the c. of G.
48. 1. Lord greatly to be praised in c. of our God
8. the c. of God, God will establish it for ever
87. 3. glorious things spoken of thee, O c. of God
Heb. 12. 22. ye are come to the c. of the living God
Rev. 3. 12. write on him the name of c. of my God

Great CITY.

Gen. 10. 12. Ashur builded Resen, same is a great c.
Josh. 10. 2. feared, because Gibeon was a great c.
Neh. 7. 4. now the c. was large and great, but people
Jer. 22. 8. why hath Lord done thus to this great c.?
Jonah 1. 2. arise, go to Nineveh, that great c. 3. 2.
3. 3. now Nineveh was an exceeding great c.
4. 11. should I not spare Nineveh, that great c.?
Rev. 11. 8. dead bodies lie in the street of the great c.
14. 8. Babylon fallen, that great c. 18. 10, 16, 19, 21.
16. 19. the great c. was divided into three parts
17. 18. the woman thou sawest, is that great c.
21. 10. he shewed me that great c. holy Jerusalem

Holy CITY.

Neh. 11. 1. cast lots to dwell in Jerusalem the holy c.
18. all the Levites of the holy c. were 284
Isa. 48. 2. they call themselves of the holy c.
52. 1. put on thy beautiful garments, O holy c.
Dan. 9. 24. seventy weeks determined on thy holy c.
Mat. 4. 5. the devil taketh him up into the holy c.
27. 53. went into the holy c. and appeared to many
Rev. 11. 2. the holy c. shall they tread under foot
21. 2. I John saw the holy c. coming down from God
22. 19. God shall take his part out of the holy c.

In, or Into, the CITY.

Gen. 19. 12. whatsoever thou hast in the c. bring
Deut. 20. 14. all that is in the c. take to thyself
28. 3. blessed shalt thou be in the c. and in the field
16. cursed shalt thou be in the c. and in the field
Josh. 6. 20. so that the people went into the c.
21. they utterly destroyed all that was in the c.
8. 19. they entered into the c. and set it on fire
Judg. 1. 24. shew us the entrance into the c.
8. 27. Gideon put the ephod in his c. in Ophrah
1 Sam. 4. 13. when the man came into the c. and told
2 Sam. 15. 25. carry back the ark of God into the c.
27. return into the c. and your sons with you
1 Kings 13. 25. and they came and told it in the c.
1 Kin. 14. 11. that dieth of Jeroboam in the c. dogs eat
12. arise, and when thy feet enter into the c.
16. 4. that dieth of Baasha in the c. shall dogs eat
20. 30. came into the c. into an inner chamber
21. 24. that dieth of Ahab, in the c. dogs eat
2 Kings 7. 4. if we say, we will enter into the c.
12. we shall catch them, and get into the c.
20. 20. how Hezekiah brought water into the c.
25. 3. famine prevailed in the c. there was no bread
Psal. 31. 21. blessed be the Lord, for he hath shewed
me his marvellous kindness in a strong c.
55. 9. I have seen violence and strife in the c.
Prov. 1. 21. in the c. Wisdom uttereth her words
Eccl. 7. 19. than ten mighty men which are in the c.
8. 10. and the wicked were forgotten in the c.
Isa. 24. 12. in the c. is left desolation and gate smitten
Jer. 14. 18. if I enter into the c. then behold sick
38. 9. like to die, for there is no more bread in the c.
52. 6. famine was sore in the c. there was no bread
Lam. 1. 19. my elders gave up the ghost in the c.
Ezek. 7. 15. in the c. famine shall devour him
9. 7. and they went forth and slew in the c.
Hos. 11. 9. and I will not enter into the c.
Joel 2. 9. they shall run to and fro in the c. on the wall
Amos 3. 6. shall a trumpet be blown in the c. shall
there be evil in a c. and Lord hath not done it?
7. 17. thy wife shall be an harlot in the c. thy sons
Jonah 3. 4. and Jonah began to enter into the c.
Mat. 9. 1. he passed over and came into his own c.
10. 5. into any c. of the Samaritans enter not
10. 11. and into whatsoever c. ye shall enter
26. 18. go into the c. to such a man, and say to him
28. 11. behold, some of the watch came into the c.
Mark 14. 13. he saith, go into the c. Acts 9. 6.
Luke 2. 3. all went to be taxed, every one into his c.
7. 37. a woman in the c. which was a sinner
18. 2. there was in a c. a judge, who feared not G.
3. there was a widow in that c. and she came
22. 10. behold, when ye are entered into the c.
24. 49. but tarry ye in the c. of Jerusalem
John 4. 8. his disciples were gone into the c.
Acts 11. 5. I was in the c. of Joppa, praying
14. 20. howbeit, he rose up and came into the c.
21. 29. had seen Trophimus with him in the c.
24. 12. neither in the synagogues nor in the c.
2 Cor. 11. 26. I have been in perils in the c. in the sea
Rev. 22. 14. and may enter thro' the gates into the c.

CITY of the Lord.

Psal. 101. 8. I will destroy the wicked, that I may
cut off all the wicked doers from the c. of the Lord
Isa. 60. 14. they shall call thee the c. of the Lord

Out of the CITY.

Gen. 44. 4. when they were gone out of the c.
Exod. 9. 29. Moses said, as soon as I am gone out of c.
33. and Moses went out of the c. from Pharaoh
Lev. 14. 45. he shall carry them forth out of the c.
Josh. 8. 22. the other side issued out of the c. against
Judg. 1. 24. the spies saw a man come out of the c.
2 Sam. 18. 3. better thou succour us out of the c.
20. 16. then cried a wise woman out of the c.
1 Kings 21. 13. they carried Naboth out of the c.
2 Kings 7. 12. when they come out of the c. we shall
9. 15. Jehu said, let none escape out of the c.
1 Chron. 20. 2. he brought much spoil out of the c.
2 Chron. 33. 15. Josiah cast the idols out of the c.
Job 24. 12. men groan from out of the c. the soul
Jer. 39. 4. Zedekiah went out of the c. 52. 7.
Ezek. 48. 30. these are the goings out of the c.
Mic. 4. 10. now shalt thou go forth out of the c.
Mat. 21. 17. he left them, and went out of the c.
Mark 11. 19. when even was come, went out of the c.
Luke 4. 29. they rose and thrust him out of the c.
9. 5. when ye go out of that c. shake off the dust
John 4. 30. then they went out of the c. and came
Acts 7. 58. cast Stephen out of the c. and stoned him
14. 19. having stoned Paul, drew him out of the c.
16. 13. and on the sabbath we went out of the c.
21. 5. they brought us, till we were out of the c.

CITY of refuge.

Num. 35. 25. shall restore him to the c. of refuge
26. if come without border of the c. of refuge, 27.
28. he should have remained in the c. of refuge
32. for him that is fled to the c. of refuge
Josh. 21. 13. they gave Hebron to be a c. of refuge
21. Shechem || 27. Golan || 32. Kedesh || 38. Ramoth
1 Chron. 6. 57. to sons of Aaron, Hebron a c. of refuge

This CITY.

Gen. 19. 14. Lot said, up, for Ld. will destroy this c.
20. behold now, this c. is near to flee unto
21. and he said, I will not overthrow this c.
Josh. 6. 26. cursed be he that buildeth this c. Jericho
Judg. 19. 11. come, and let us turn in unto this c.
1 Sam. 9. 6. there is in this c. a man of God
2 Kings 2. 19. the situation of this c. is pleasant
18. 30. this c. shall not be delivered, Isa. 36. 15.
19. 32. shall not come into this c. 33. Isa. 37. 34.
34. I will defend this c. 20. 6. Isa. 37. 35. | 38. 6.
23. 27. I will cast off this c. Jerusalem I have chosen
2 Chron. 6. 34. they pray to thee toward this c.
Ezra 4. 13. that if this c. be builded again, 16.
15. know that this c. is a rebellious city.
Neh. 13. 18. did not God bring evil upon this c.?
Jer. 6. 6. this is the c. to be visited, is oppression
17. 25. Jerusalem, and this c. shall remain for ever
19. 8. I will make this c. desolate, and an hissing
11. even so will I break this people and this c.
15. I will bring upon this c. and towns all the evil
20. 5. I will deliver all the strength of this c.
21. 9. he that abideth in this c. shall die by the sword
10. I set my face against this c. for evil and not good
22. 8. why hath the Lord done thus unto this c.?
26. 6. I will make this c. a curse to nations of earth
15. ye shall bring innocent blood on this c.
27. 17. wherefore should this c. be laid waste?
32. 3. I will give this c. to Chaldeans, 28. | 34. 2.
31. this c. hath been to me as a provocation
33. 5. for wickedness I have hid my face from this c.
34. 22. command and cause them to return to this c.
38. 17. this c. shall not be burnt with fire
23. thou shalt cause this c. to be burnt with fire
39. 16. I will bring my words on this c. for evil
Ezek. 11. 2. these men give wicked counsel in this c.

*Ezek.*11.3. *this c.* is the caldron, and we be the flesh, 7.
11. *this c.* shall not be your caldron, nor ye the flesh
Mat. 10. 23. when they persecute you in *this c.* flee
Acts 18. 10. for I have much people in *this c.*
22. 3. I was brought up in *this c.* at feet of Gamaliel
Without CITY.
Gen. 19. 16. and the men set him *without* the *c.*
Lev. 14. 40. into an unclean place *without* the *c.* 41.
Num. 35. 5. ye shall measure from *without* the *c.*
2 *Chron.* 32. 3. to stop the fountains *without* the *c.*
*Rev.*14.20. the wine-press was trodden *without* the *c.*
CITIES.
Gen. 19. 29. when God destroyed the *c.* of the plain
35. 5. terror of God was upon the *c.* round about
41. 48. Joseph laid up the food in the *c.*
47. 21. as for the people, he removed them to the *c.*
Lev. 25. 32. the *c.* of the Levites may be redeemed
Num. 13. 19. what *c.* they be that they dwell in
35. 8. every one shall give of his *c.* to the Levites
Deut. 2. 37. nor camest thou to *c.* in the mountains
3. 12. *c.* thereof gave I to Reubenites and Gadites
19. abide in your *c.* which I have given you
6. 10. into the land to give thee great and goodly *c.*
19. 5. he shall flee to one of these *c.* and live
Josh. 9. 17. Israel came to their *c.* on the third day
10. 19. suffer them not to enter into their *c.*
11. 13. as for the *c.* that stood still in their strength
18. 9. described it by *c.* into seven parts in a book
Judg. 12. 7. Jephthah was buried in one of the *c.*
20.48. men of Israel set fire on all the *c.* they came to
21. 23. they repaired the *c.* and dwelt in them
1 *Sam.* 31. 7. the Israelites forsook the *c.* and fled
2 *Sam.* 10. 12. for the *c.* of our God, 1 *Chron.* 19. 13.
1 *Kings* 9. 12. Hiram came from Tyre to see the *c.*
13. what *c.* are these that thou hast given me?
20. 34. the *c.* my father took I will restore
1 *Chron.* 2. 22. Jair had 23 *c.* in the land of Gilead
4. 31. these were their *c.* to the reign of David
2 *Chron.* 34. 6. and so did he in the *c.* of Manasseh
Ezra 3. 1. when the seventh month was come, and
the Israelites were in their *c.* *Neh.* 7. 73.
Neh. 11. 1. and nine parts to dwell in other *c.*
Job 15. 28. dwelleth in desolate *c.* and houses no man
Psal. 9. 6. O enemy, thou hast destroyed *c.*
Isa. 6. 11. he answered, till *c.* be wasted, and houses
14. 21. nor fill the face of the world with *c.*
19. 18. in that day shall five *c.* in the land of Egypt
33. 8. he hath despised the *c.* he regardeth no man
64. 10. thy holy *c.* are a wildern. Zion is a wildern.
Jer. 2. 15. they made his land waste, his *c.* are burnt
28. according to the number of thy *c.* 11. 13.
13. 19. *c.* of south be shut up, and none shall open
20. 16. that man be as the *c.* which Lord overthrew
31. 21. turn again, O virgin of Israel, to these thy *c.*
49. 13. all the *c.* thereof shall be perpetual wastes
50. 32. I will kindle fire in his *c.* it shall devour
Ezek. 26. 19. like the *c.* that are not inhabited
30. 17. and these *c.* shall go into captivity
35. 9. thy *c.* shall not return, know that I am Lord
Hos. 8.14. I will send fire upon his *c.* it shall devour
11. 6. the sword shall abide on his *c.* and consume
Amos 4. 8. two or three *c.* wand. unto one for water
Mic. 5. 11. and I will cut off the *c.* of thy land
14. pluck up groves, so will I destroy thy *c.*
Zeph. 3. 6. their *c.* are destroyed, there is no man
*Zech.*1.17. my *c.* by prosper. shall yet spread abroad
Mat. 10. 23. shall not have gone over the *c.* of Israel
11. 1. he departed to teach and preach in their *c.*
Acts 26. 11. I persecuted them even to strange *c.*
2 *Pet.* 2. 6. turning *c.* of Sodom and Gomor. to ashes
Jude 7. and *c.* about them in like manner an example
Rev. 16.19. and the *c.* of the nations fell and Babylon
All CITIES.
Num. 21. 25. and Israel took *all* these *c.* and dwelt in
c. of Amorites, *Deut.* 2. 34. | 3. 4. *Josh.* 10. 39.
31. 10. they burnt *all* their *c.* *Judg.* 20. 48.
Num. 35. 7. *all* the *c.* of the Levites shall be 48 *c.*
Deut. 20. 15. thus do to *all c.* afar off from thee
Josh. 11. 12. *all* the *c.* of the kings utterly destroy.
21. 19. *all* the *c.* of the children of Aaron were 13 *c.*
33. *all* the *c.* of the Gershonites were 13 *c.*
40. *all* the *c.* of children of Merari by lot 12 *c.*
41. *all* the *c.* of the Levites were 48 *c.*
1 *Sam.* 18. 6. the women came out of *all c.* of Israel
2 *Sam.* 12. 31. thus did he to *all c.* of the Ammon.
24. 7. they came to *all* the *c.* of the Hivites
1 *Kings* 22. 39. *all c.* Ahab built are written in book
2 *Chron.* 14. 14. Asa smote *all* the *c.* about Gerar
Neh. 10. 37. have tithes in *all* the *c.* of our tillage
Jer. 4. 26. *all* the *c.* thereof were broken down
33. 12. in *all c.* thereof an habitation of shepherds
Hos. 13. 10. any that may save thee in *all* thy *c.*
Acts 8. 40. preached in *all c.* till he came to Cesarea
Defenced CITIES.
Isa. 36.1. Sennacherib cometh against the *defenced c.*
37. 26. that shouldest be to lay waste the *defenced c.*
Jer. 4. 5. assemble, let us go into the *defenced c.* 8.14.
34. 7. for these *defenced c.* remained of Judah
Fenced CITIES.
Num. 32. 17. little ones shall dwell in the *fenced c.*
Deut. 3. 5. all these *c.* were *fenced* with high walls
9. 1. to possess *c. fenced* up to heaven, *Josh.* 14. 12.
Josh. 10. 20. the rest of them entered into *fenced c.*
2 *Sam.* 20. 6. lest he get him *fenced c.* and escape us
2 *Chr.* 12. 4. Shishak took the *fenced c.* of Judah
14. 6. Asa built *fenced c.* in Judah, land had rest
17. 2. Jehoshaphat placed forces in the *fenced c.*
19. 5. set judges through all the *fenced c.* of Judah
21. 3. Jehoshaphat gave his sons *fenced c.* in Judah
Jer. 5. 17. they shall impoverish thy *fenced c.*
Dan. 11. 15. k. of the north take the most *fenced c.*
Hos. 8. 14. and Judah hath multiplied *fenced c.*
Zeph. 1. 16. a day of an alarm against the *fenced c.*
CITIES *of Judah.*
2 *Sam.* 2. 1. shall I go up to any of the *c. of Judah?*
2 *Kings* 23. 5. that burnt incense in the *c. of Judah*
1 *Chr.* 6. 57. to sons of Aaron they gave the *c. of J.*
2 *Chr.* 17. 7. to teach in *c. of J.* || 13. business in *c. of J.*
19. 5. set judges in the *c. of Judah*, city by city
23. 2. gather the Levites out of all the *c. of Judah*
31. 6. Israel in the *c. of Judah* brought tithes
33. 14. and put captains of war in the *c. of Judah*

Neh. 11. 3. in *c. of Jud.* each dwelt in his possession
Psal. 69. 35. God will save Zion, and b. *c. of Judah*
Isa. 40. 9. say to the *c. of Judah*, behold your God
44. 26. and that saith to *c. of Judah*, ye shall be built
Jer. 1. 15. the families of the north against *c. of Jud.*
4. 16. give out their voice against the *c. of Judah*
7. 17. seest thou not what they do in the *c. of Jud.*
9. 11. I will make *c. of J.* desolate, 10. 22. | 34. 22.
11. 12. then shall *c. of Jud.* go and cry to the gods
32. 44. buy fields, and take witness in the *c. of J.*
33. 10. without man and beast, even in the *c. of J.*
13. in *c. of Judah* shall flocks pass under the hands
44. 6. my fury and anger was kindled in *c. of Jud.*
21. the incense that he burnt in the *c. of Judah*
Lam. 5. 11. they ravished the maids in the *c. of Jud.*
Zech. 1. 12. wilt thou not have mercy on the *c. of J.*
CITIES *of refuge.*
Num. 35. 6. there shall be six *c. for refuge*, 13, 14.
11. ye shall appoint for you *c. of refuge*, *Josh.* 20. 2.
1 *Chr.* 6. 67. they gave to sons of Kohath of *c. of ref.*
Six CITIES.
Num. 35. 6. *six c.* shall ye have for refuge, 13, 15.
Josh. 15. 59. in the mountains of Judah *six c.*
CITIES with *Suburbs.*
Lev. 25. 34. the *suburbs* of their *c.* may not be sold
Num. 35. 2. shall give to Levites *suburbs* for the *c.*
Josh. 21. 3. Israel gave to Levites *c.* and *suburbs*
41. the *c.* of Levites forty-eight with their *suburbs*
CITIES with *Villages.*
1 *Sam.* 6. 18. of fenced *c.* and of country *villages*
1 *Chron.* 27. 25. over store-houses in *c.* and *villages*
Mat. 9. 35. Jesus went about all the *c.* and *villages*
teaching and preaching the gospel, *Luke* 13. 22.
Mark 6. 56. whithers. he entered into *villages* or *c.*
CITIES with *waste.*
Lev. 26. 31. and I will make your *c. waste*, 33.
Isa. 61. 4. they shall repair the *waste c.* desolations
Jer. 4. 7. thy *c.* shall be laid *waste* without inhabitants
Ezek. 6. 6. in all your dwellings your *c.* shall be *w.*
19. 7. laid *w.* their *c.* || 35. 4. I will lay thy *c. w.*
36. 35. *waste c.* are become fenced and inhabited
38. so shall the *waste c.* be filled with flocks of men
Amos 9. 14. and they shall build thy *waste c.*
Your CITIES.
Isa. 1. 7. *your c.* are burnt with fire, land desolate
Jer. 40. 10. and dwell in *your c.* that ye have taken
Amos 4. 6. have given cleanness of teeth in all *your c.*
CITIZEN, S.
Luke 15. 15. the prodigal joined himself to a *c.*
19. 14. his *c.* hated him, and sent after him
Acts 21. 39. I am of Tarsus, a *c.* of no mean city
Eph. 2. 19. but fellow-*c.* with saints and household
CLAD.
1 *Kings* 11. 29. Jeroboam *c.* himself with a new garm.
Isa. 59. 17. for clothing was *c.* with zeal as a cloke
CLAMOROUS.
Prov. 9. 19. a foolish woman is *c.* she is simple
CLAMOUR.
Eph. 4. 31. all anger and *c.* be put away from you
CLAP.
Job 27. 23. men shall *c.* hands at him, and hiss him
Psal. 47. 1. *c.* your hands, all ye people, shout to G.
98. 8. let floods *c.* their hands, let hills be joyful
Isa. 55. 12. the trees of the field shall *c.* their hands
Lam. 2. 15. all that pass by *c.* their hands at thee
Nah. 3. 19. that bear fruit of thee shall *c.* their hands
CLAPPED.
Ezek. 25. 6. because thou hast *c.* thine hands
CLAPPETH.
Job 34. 37. he *c.* his hands among us, multip. words
CLAPT.
2 *Kings* 11. 12. *c.* their hands, and said, God save [king
CLAVE.
Gen. 22. 3. Abraham *c.* the wood for burnt-offering
Num. 16. 31. the ground *c.* asunder under them
Judg. 15. 19. God *c.* an hollow place in the jaw
1 *Sam.* 6. 14. they *c.* wood of the cart and offered
Ps. 78. 15. he *c.* the rocks in wilderness, *Isa.* 48. 21.
CLAVE.
Gen. 34. 3. Shechem his soul *c.* to Dinah, Jac. daugh.
Ruth 1. 14. but Ruth *c.* to her mother-in-law
2 *Sam.* 20. 2. the men of Judah *c.* to their king
23. 10. he smote till his hand *c.* to the sword
1 *Kings* 11. 2. Solomon *c.* to these in love
2 *Kings* 18. 6. for Hezekiah *c.* to Lord, departed not
Neh. 10. 29. they *c.* to their brethren, their nobles
Acts 17. 34. certain men *c.* to Paul and believed
CLAWS.
Deut. 14. 6. beast that cleaveth the cleft into two *c.*
Dan. 4. 33. his nails were grown like birds' *c.*
Zech. 11. 16. he shall tear their *c.* in pieces
CLAY.
Job 4. 19. much less them that dwell in houses of *c.*
10. 9. remember thou hast made me as the *c.*
13. 12. your bodies are like to bodies of *c.*
27. 16. though he prepare raiment as the *c.*
33. 6. I also am formed out of the *c.*
38. 14. it is turned as *c.* to the seal, they stand
Psal. 40. 2. he brought me up out of the miry *c.*
Isa. 29. 16. shall be esteemed as the potter's *c.*
41. 25. on princes, as the potter treadeth the *c.*
45. 9. shall the *c.* say to him that fashioneth it?
64. 8. we are *c.* thou our potter, work of thy hand
Jer. 18. 4. the vessel that he made of *c.* was marred
6. as *c.* is in the potter's hand, so are ye in mine
43. 9. take great stones, hide them in the *c.*
Dan. 2. 33. his feet part of iron, part of *c.* 34, 42.
35. then was the *c.* broken in pieces, 45.
41. thou sawest the feet and toes part of potter's *c.*
Nah. 3. 14. go into *c.* and tread the mortar
Hab. 2. 6. woe to him that ladeth himself with *c.*
John 9. 6. he spat on the ground, made *c.* of spittle,
and anointed the eyes of the blind man with *c.*
15. he put *c.* on mine eyes, I washed, and do see
Rom. 9. 21. hath not the potter power over the *c.?*
CLAY-GROUND.
1 *Kings* 7. 46. cast vessels in *c.-g.* 2 *Chron.* 4. 17.
CLEAN.
Lev. 23. 22. thou shalt not make *c.* riddance in field
Josh. 3. 17. the people passed *c.* over Jordan, 4. 1, 11.
Psal. 77. 8. is his mercy *c.* gone for ever? his promise
Isa. 24. 19. the earth is *c.* dissolved, is moved

Joel 1. 7. he hath made it *c.* bare, and cast it away
Zech. 11.17. his arm shall be *c.* dried up, and right eye
2 *Pet.* 2. 18. were *c.* escaped them that live in error
CLEAN, *Adjective,*
Signifies, [1] *That which is free from filth, or ceremonially pure,* Lev. 10. 14. [2] *One who is free from the guilt of sin, by the blood of Christ,* Psal. 51. 7. [3] *One who is delivered from the power of sin, by sanctifying grace,* John 13. 10. [4] *That which may be lawfully used,* Luke 11. 41. [5] *Guiltless, or innocent,* Acts 18. 6. [6] *Cured,* 2 Kings 5. 12. [7] *Empty,* Prov. 14. 4
The fear of the Lord is clean, *Psal.* 19. 9. *The holy law of God, which works a due fear of God, and teaches men how to worship him, is sincere, not adulterated with any mixture of vanity, falsehood, or vice; not requiring or allowing any wickedness, but cleansing from it.*
Gen. 7. 2. of every *c.* beast thou shalt take by sevens
8. 20. Noah took of every *c.* beast and *c.* fowl
35. 2. Jacob said, be *c.* and change your garments
Lev. 4. 12. carry the bullock unto a *c.* place, 6. 11.
7. 19. the flesh, all that be *c.* shall eat thereof
10. 10. that ye may put difference between *c.* and
unclean, 11. 47. | 20. 25. *Ezek.* 22. 26. | 44. 23.
14. the wave-breast eat in a *c.* place, *Num.* 19. 9.
16. 30. that ye may be *c.* from your sins before L.
22. 4. he shall not eat of holy things till he be *c.*
Num. 19. 12. purify, on seventh day he shall be *c.*
18. a *c.* person shall take hyssop and dip in water
Deut. 12. 15. unclean and *c.* may eat thereof, 15. 22.
1 *Sam.* 20. 26. he is not *c.* surely he is not *c.*
2 *Kings* 5. 10. thy flesh come again, and thou be *c.* 14.
12. may not I wash in them and be *c.?*
13. when he saith to thee, wash and be *c.*
Job 11. 4. for thou hast said, I am *c.* in thine eyes
14. 4. who can bring a *c.* thing out of an unclean
15. 14. what is man that he should be *c.?*
15. yea, the heavens are not *c.* in his sight
25. 4. how can he be *c.* that is born of a woman?
33. 9. I am *c.* without transgres. nor iniquity in me
Prov. 16. 2. the ways of a man are *c.* in his own eyes
Eccl. 9. 2. all things come alike to the *c* and unclean
Isa. 1. 16. wash ye, make you *c.* put away evil
28. 8. all tables full, so that there is no place *c.*
30. 24. oxen and young asses shall eat *c.* provender
52. 11. be ye *c.* that bare the vessels of the Lord
66. 20. bring an offering in a *c.* vessel to house of L.
Jer. 13. 27. O Jerusalem, wilt thou not be made *c.?*
Ezek. 36. 25. then will I sprinkle *c.* water on you
Mat. 8. 2. a leper came, saying, Lord, if thou wilt,
thou canst make me *c.* *Mark* 1. 40. *Luke* 5. 12.
3. I will, be thou *c.* *Mark* 1. 41. *Luke* 5. 13.
23. 25. for ye make *c.* the outside, *Luke* 11. 39.
Luke 11. 41. behold, all things are *c.* unto you
John 13. 11. therefore said he, ye are not all *c.*
15. 3. now ye are *c.* thro' word I have spoken to you
Acts 18. 6. your blood be on your own heads, I am *c.*
Rev. 19. 8. she be arrayed in fine linen, *c.* white, 14.
CLEAN *hands.*
Job 9. 30. if I make my *hands* ever so *c.*
17. 9. he that hath *c. hands* shall be stronger
Psal. 24. 4. he that hath *c. hands* and a pure heart
CLEAN *heart.*
Psal. 51. 10. create in me a *c. heart,* O God, renew
73. 1. God is good to Isr. and such as are of a *c. h.*
Prov. 20. 9. who can say, I have made my *heart c.?*
Is CLEAN.
Lev. 13. 13. he *is c,* 17, 37, 39. || 40. yet *is* he *c.* 41.
15. 8. that hath the issue spit on him that *is c.*
Num. 9. 13. a man that *is c.* not on a journey, 19. 9.
Psal. 19. 9. fear of the Lord *is c.* enduring for ever
Prov. 14. 4. where no oxen are, the crib *is c.*
John 13. 10. to wash his feet, but *is c.* every whit
Pronounce CLEAN.
Lev. 13. 6. the priest shall *pronounce* him *c.* 14. 7.
Shall be CLEAN.
Lev. 11. 36. a fountain wherein is water *shall be c.*
12. 8. she *c.* 15. 28. || 13. 58. it *c.* 14. 53. *Num.* 31. 23.
14. 9. he shall wash his flesh in water, he *shall be c.*
20. | 15. 13. | 17. 15. | 22. 7. *Num.* 19. 12, 19.
Num. 31. 24. and ye *shall be c.* *Ezek.* 36. 25.
Psal. 51. 7. purge me with hyssop, and I *shall be c.*
CLEANNESS.
2 *Sam.* 22. 21. according to the *c.* of my hands hath
the Lord recompensed me, *Psal.* 18. 20.
25. according to my *c.* in his eye sight, *Psal.* 18. 24.
Amos 4. 6. I also have given you *c.* of teeth in cities
CLEANSE.
Exod. 29. 36. thou shalt *c.* the altar, *Lev.* 16. 19.
Lev. 14. 49. shalt take to *c.* the house, two birds, 52.
Num. 8. 6. take the Levites and *c.* them
2 *Chron.* 29. 15. to *c.* the house of the Lord, 16.
Neh. 13. 22. that the Levites should *c.* themselves
Psal. 19. 12. *c.* thou me from secret faults
51. 2. wash me thoroughly, and *c.* me from my sin
119. 9. wherewith shall a young man *c.* his way?
Jer. 4. 11. a dry wind not to fan nor to *c.*
33. 8. I will *c.* them from iniquity, *Ezek.* 37. 23.
Ezek. 36. 25. from all your idols will I *c.* you
39. 12. burying, that they may *c.* the land, 16.
43. 20. thus shalt thou *c.* and purge it
45. 18. take a young bullock, and *c.* the sanctuary
Joel 3. 21. I will *c.* their blood I have not cleansed
Mat. 10. 8. heal the sick, *c.* lepers, raise the dead
23. 26. *c.* first that which is within the cup
2 *Cor.* 7. 1. let us *c.* ourselves from all filthiness of flesh
Eph. 5. 26. might *c.* it with the washing of water
Jam. 4. 8. *c.* your hands, ye sinners, purify hearts
1 *John* 1. 9. to *c.* us from all unrighteousness
CLEANSED.
Lev. 11. 32. be unclean until even, so shall it be *c.*
12. 7. she shall be *c.* from the issue of her blood
14. 4. to take for him that is to be *c.* 19, 31.
14. the ear of him that is to be *c.* 17, 18, 25, 28.
Num. 35. 33. the land cannot be *c.* of the blood
Josh. 22. 17. from which we are not *c.* till this day
2 *Chron.* 29. 18. we have *c.* all the house of the L.
30. 18. for many had not *c.* themselves, yet did eat
19. that prepareth his heart, though he be not *c.*
34. 5. Josiah *c.* Judah and Jerusalem
Neh. 13. 9. I commanded, and they *c.* the chambers

Neh. 13. 30. thus I *c.* them from all strangers
Job 35. 3. what profit, if I be *c.* from my sin?
Psal. 73. 13. verily I have *c.* my heart in vain
Isa. 3. † 26. she being *c.* shall sit on the ground
Ezek. 22. 24. thou art the land that is not *c.*
44. 26. after he is *c.* reckon to him seven days
Dan. 8. 14. then shall the sanctuary be *c.*
Joel 3. 21. cleanse their blood I have not *c.*
Mat. 8. 3. immediately his leprosy was *c.*
11. 5. the lepers are *c.* the deaf hear, *Luke* 7. 22.
Mark 1. 42. the leprosy departed, and he was *c.*
Luke 4. 27. none was *c.* save Naaman the Syrian
7. 22. the lepers *c.* the deaf hear, the dead raised
17. 14. that as the lepers went they were *c.*
17. were not ten *c.* but where are the nine?
Acts 10. 15. the voice spake, what G. hath *c.* 11. 9.

CLEANSETH.

Job 37. 21. but the wind passeth and *c.* them
Prov. 20. 30. blueness of a wound *c.* away evil
1 *John* 1. 7. blood of Jesus Christ *c.* us from all sin

CLEANSING.

Lev. 13. 7. hath been seen of the priest for his *c.*
Num. 6. 9. shave his head in the day of his *c.*
Mark 1. 44. go and offer for thy *c.* *Luke* 5. 14.

CLEAR.

Gen. 24. 8. thou shalt be *c.* from this my oath, 41.
44. 16. or how shall we *c.* ourselves?
Exod. 34. 7. and that will by no means *c.* the guilty
2 *Sam.* 23. 4. as tender grass, by *c.* shining after rain
Psal. 51. 4. mightest be *c.* when thou judgest
Eccl. 3. † 18. that they might *c.* God, and see
Cant. 6. 10. fair as moon, *c.* as the sun, as an army
Isa. 18. 4. in my dwelling-place like a *c.* heat on herbs
Amos 8. 9. I will darken the earth in a *c.* day
Zech. 14. 6. the light shall not be *c.* nor dark
2 *Cor.* 7. 11. ye have approved yourselves to be *c.*
Rev. 21. 11. her light was *c.* as crystal, 22. 1.
18. the city was pure gold like to *c.* glass

CLEARER.

Job 11. 17. thine age shall be *c.* than the noon-day

CLEARING.

Num. 14. 18. and by no means *c.* the guilty
2 *Cor.* 7. 11. what *c.* of yourselves it wrought

CLEARLY.

Job 33. 3. my lips shall utter knowledge *c.*
Mat. 7. 5. see *c.* to pull out the mote, *Luke* 6. 42.
Mark 8. 25. was restored, and saw every man *c.*
Rom. 1. 20. things from creation are *c.* seen

CLEARNESS.

Exod. 24. 10. and as the body of heaven in his *c.*

CLEAVE.

Lev. 1. 17. he shall *c.* it with the wings thereof
Psal. 74. 15. thou didst *c.* the fountain and the flood
Hab. 3. 9. thou didst *c.* the earth with rivers
Zech. 14. 4. the mount shall *c.* in the midst thereof

CLEAVE, *Verb.*

Gen. 2. 24. a man shall leave father and mother, and shall *c.* to his wife, *Mat.* 19. 5. *Mark* 10. 7.
Deut. 4. 4. ye that did *c.* to the Lord your God
10. 20. him serve, to him shalt thou *c.* and swear by his name, 11. 22. | 13. 4. | 30. 20. *Josh.* 22. 5.
13. 17. shall *c.* nought of cursed thing to thy hand
Josh. 23. 8. but *c.* to the Lord your God
† if you will *c.* to the Lord your God
2 *Kings* 5. 27. the leprosy of Naaman shall *c.* to thee
Job 38. 38. and the clods *c.* fast together
Psal. 101. 3. I hate the work, it shall not *c.* to me
102. 5. by my groaning my bones *c.* to my skin
137. 6. let my tongue *c.* to the roof of my mouth
Isa. 14. 1. they shall *c.* to the house of Jacob
Jer. 13. 11. so have I caused to *c.* to me Israel
42. † 16. the famine whereof ye were afraid shall *c.* after you in Egypt, and there ye shall die
Ezek. 3. 26. I will make thy tongue *c.* to the roof
Dan. 2. 43. but they shall not *c.* one to another
11. 34. many shall *c.* to them with flatteries
Acts 11. 23. with purpose of heart *c.* to the Lord
Rom. 12. 9. abhor evil, *c.* to that which is good

CLEAVED.

2 *Kings* 3. 3. Jehoram *c.* to Jeroboam's sins
Job 29. 10. their tongue *c.* to the roof of their mouth
31. 7. and if any blot have *c.* to my hands

CLEAVETH.

Job 19. 20. my bone *c.* to my skin and to my flesh
Psal. 22. 15. strength dried up, my tongue *c.* to jaws
41. 8. an evil disease, say they, *c.* fast to him
44. 25. our soul bowed down, our belly *c.* to earth
119. 25. my soul *c.* to the dust, quicken me
Jer. 13. 11. as the girdle *c.* to the loins of a man
Lam. 4. 4. the tongue of sucking child *c.* to the roof
8. their skin *c.* to their bones, it is withered
Luke 10. 11. the dust of your city which *c.* on us

CLEAVETH.

Deut. 14. 6. beast that *c.* the cleft into two claws
Job 16. 13. he *c.* my reins asunder, and spareth not
Psal. 141. 7. when one cutteth and *c.* wood on earth
Eccl. 10. 9. that *c.* wood shall be endangered thereby

CLEFT.

Deut. 14. 6. that cleaveth the *c.* into two claws
Mic. 1. 4. the valley shall be *c.* as wax before the fire

CLEFTS.

Cant. 2. 14. O my dove, that art in *c.* of the rocks
Isa. 2. 21. to go into the *c.* of the rocks for fear
Jer. 49. 16. O thou that dwellest in the *c.* *Obad.* 3.
Amos. 6. 11. he will smite the little house with *c.*

CLEMENCY.

Acts 24. 4. that thou hear us of thy *c.* a few words

CLERK.

Acts 19. 35. when town *c.* had appeased the people

CLIFT, S.

Exod. 33. 22. I will put thee in a *c.* of the rock
2 *Chron.* 20. 16. they come up by the *c.* of Ziz
Job 30. 6. to dwell in the *c.* of the valleys
Isa. 57. 5. slaying children in valleys under *c.* of rocks

CLIMB, ED, ETH.

1 *Sam.* 14. 13. Jonathan *c.* up upon his hands
Jer. 4. 29. they shall *c.* up upon the rocks
Joel 2. 7. they shall *c.* the wall like men of war
9. they shall *c.* up upon the houses, shall enter
Amos 9. 2. they *c.* up to heaven, thence bring them
Luke 19. 4. Zaccheus *c.* up into a sycamore-tree
John 10. 1. but *c.* up some other way, is a thief

CLIPT.

Jer. 48. 37. every head be bald, every beard be *c.*

CLODS.

Job 7. 5. my flesh is clothed with *c.* of dust
21. 33. the *c.* of the valley shall be sweet to him
38. 38. and the *c.* cleave fast together
Isa. 28. 24. doth plowman break *c.* of his ground?
Hos. 10. 11. Judah shall plow, Jacob shall break his *c.*
Joel 1. 17. seed is rotten under their *c.* the garners

CLOKE.

Isa. 59. 17. he was clad with zeal as a *c.*
Mat. 5. 40. if take thy coat, let him have thy *c.* also
Luke 6. 29. him that taketh thy *c.* forbid not to take
John 15. 22. now they have no *c.* for their sin
1 *Thess.* 2. 5. nor used we a *c.* of covetousness
2 *Tim.* 4. 13. the *c.* I left at Troas bring with thee
1 *Pet.* 2. 16. not using liberty for a *c.* of malicious.

CLOSE.

Num. 5. 13. and it be kept *c.* from her husband
2 *Sam.* 22. 46. be afraid out of *c.* places, *Psal.* 18. 45.
1 *Chron.* 12. 1. while David yet kept himself *c.*
Job 28. 21. and kept *c.* from the fowls of the air
41. 15. his scales shut up together as with a *c.* seal
Jer. 42. 16. famine follow *c.* after you into Egypt
Dan. 8. 7. and I saw him come *c.* to the ram
Amos 9. 11. and *c.* up the breaches thereof
Luke 9. 36. they kept it *c.* and told no man in those
Acts 27. 13. loosing thence, they sailed *c.* by Crete

CLOSED.

Gen. 2. 21. Lord *c.* up the flesh instead thereof
20. 18. the Lord had fast *c.* up all the wombs
Num. 16. 33. the earth *c.* upon them, they perished
Judg. 3. 22. and the fat *c.* upon the blade, so that he
Isa. 1. 6. they have not been *c.* nor bound up
29. 10. for the Lord hath *c.* your eyes
Dan. 12. 9. for the words are *c.* up and sealed
Jonah 2. 5. the depth *c.* me round about, weeds wrapt
Mat. 13. 15. their eyes they have *c.* *Acts* 28. 27.
Luke 4. 20. he *c.* book, and gave it to the minister

CLOSER. [a brother

Prov. 18. 24. there is a friend that sticketh *c.* than

CLOSEST.

Jer. 22. 15. thou reign, because *c.* thyself in cedar

CLOSET, S.

Joel 2. 16. let the bride go out of her *c.*
Mat. 6. 6. when thou prayest, enter into thy *c.*
Luke 12. 3. what ye have spoken in the ear in *c.*

CLOTH.

Num. 4. 8. they shall spread on them a *c.* of scarlet
12. take instruments and put them in a *c.* of blue
Deut. 22. 17. shall spread the *c.* before the elders
1 *Sam.* 19. 13. Michal covered the image with a *c.*
21. 9. the sword of Goliath, it is wrapt in a *c.*
2 *Sam.* 20. 12. removed Amasa, and cast a *c.* on him
2 *Kings* 8. 15. Hazael took a thick *c.* and dipt it
Isa. 30. 22. shall cast them away as a menstruous *c.*
Mat. 9. 16. putteth a piece of new *c.* *Mark* 2. 21.
27. 59. taken the body, he wrapped it in a linen *c.*
Mark 14. 51. having a linen *c.* about his body

CLOTHE.

Exod. 40. 14. shalt bring his sons and *c.* with coats
Esth. 4. 4. she sent raiment to *c.* Mordecai
Psal. 132. 16. I will *c.* her priests with salvation
18. his enemies will I *c.* with shame, but on hims.
Prov. 23. 21. drowsiness shall *c.* a man with rags
Isa. 22. 21. I will *c.* him with thy robe and strength.
49. 18. thou shalt surely *c.* thee with them all
50. 3. I *c.* the heavens with blackness, and make
Ezek. 26. 16. shall *c.* themselves with trembling
34. 3. ye eat the fat, and *c.* you with the wool
Hag. 1. 6. ye *c.* you, but there is none warm
Zech. 3. 4. I will *c.* thee with change of raiment
Mat. 6. 30. if God so *c.* grass of field, shall he not much more *c.* you, O ye of little faith? *Luke* 12. 28.

CLOTHED.

Gen. 3. 21. L. God made coats of skins and *c.* them
Lev. 8. 7. Moses *c.* Aaron with robe, and put ephod
Judg. 6. † 34. the Spirit of the Lord *c.* Gideon
1 *Sam.* 17. † 5. Goliath was *c.* with a coat of mail
† 38. Saul *c.* David with his clothes
2 *Sam.* 1. 24. weep over Saul who *c.* you with scar.
1 *Chron.* 12. † 18. then the Spirit *c.* Amasai
21. 16. David and Isr. who were *c.* with sackcloth
2 *Chron.* 6. 41. let thy priests be *c.* with salvation
18. 9. the king of Isr. and Judah *c.* in robes sat
24. † 20. the Spirit of God *c.* Zachariah
28. 15. spoil *c.* all that were naked among them
Esth. 4. 2. none enter king's gate *c.* with sackcloth
Job 7. 5. my flesh is *c.* with worms and clods
10. 11. thou hast *c.* me with skin and flesh
29. 14. I put on righteousness and it *c.* me
39. 19. hast thou *c.* his neck with thunder?
Psal. 35. 26. let them be *c.* with shame, 109. 29.
65. 13. the pastures are *c.* with flocks, the valleys
93. 1. Lord is *c.* with majesty, Lord is *c.* with
104. 1. thou art *c.* with honour and majesty
109. 18. as he *c.* hims. with cursing as with garm.
132. 9. let thy priests be *c.* with righteousness
Prov. 31. 21. for all her househ. are *c.* with scarlet
Isa. 61. 10. he hath *c.* me with garments of salvation
Ezek. 16. 10. I *c.* thee also with broidered work
Dan. 5. 29. they *c.* Daniel with scarlet and a chain
Zeph. 1. 8. all such as are *c.* with strange apparel
Zech. 3. 3. Joshua was *c.* with filthy garments
Mat. 11. 8. a man *c.* in soft raiment, *Luke* 7. 25.
25. 36. nak. and ye *c.* me || 43. nak. and ye *c.* me not
Mark 1. 6. John was *c.* with camel's hair and girdle
5. 15. they see him sitting, and *c.* *Luke* 8. 35.
15. 17. and they *c.* Jesus with purple, and platted
Luke 16. 19. a certain rich man *c.* in purple and linen
2 *Cor.* 5. 2. desiring to be *c.* upon with our house
3. if so be that being *c.* we shall not be found naked
1 *Pet.* 5. 5. and be *c.* with humility, G. resists proud
Rev. 3. 18. white raiment, that thou mayest be *c.*
10. 1. I saw another mighty angel *c.* with a cloud
11. 3. the two witnesses shall prophesy *c.* in sackcl.
12. 1. there appeared a woman *c.* with the sun
19. 13. he was *c.* with a vesture dipt in blood

CLOTHED, with *linen.*

Ezek. 9. 2. one man among them was *c.* with *linen*
44. 17. they shall be *c.* with *linen* garments
Dan. 10. 5. behold a certain man *c.* with *linen*
Dan. 12. 6. one said to the man *c.* in *linen*, how long
Rev. 15. 6. *c.* in pure and white *linen*, 18. 16. | 19. 14.

Shall be CLOTHED.

Job 8. 22. they that hate thee *shall be c.* with shame
Ezek. 7. 27. the prince *shall be c.* with desolation
Dan. 5. 7. read this writing, *shall be c.* with scarlet
Mat. 6. 31. or wherewithal *shall* we *be c.?*
Rev. 3. 5. he that overcometh *shall be c.* 4. 4.

CLOTHES.

Gen. 49. 11. he washed his *c.* in the blood of grapes
Exod. 12. 34. their troughs bound up in their *c.*
35. 19. the *c.* of service to do service, 39. 1, 41.
Lev. 10. 6. nor rend your *c.* lest ye die, 21. 10.
Deut. 29. 5. your *c.* are not waxen old, *Neh.* 9. 21.
Ruth 3. † 4. lift up the *c.* that are at his feet
1 *Sam.* 19. 24. Saul stript off his *c.* and prophesied
1 *Kings* 1. 1. covered k. David with *c.* but no heat
2 *Kings* 2. 12. he took hold of his own *c.* and rent
2 *Chron.* 34. 27. thou didst rend thy *c.* and weep
Neh. 4. 23. I nor brethren, none of us put off our *c*
Job 9. 31. and my own *c.* shall abhor me
22. † 6. thou hast stripped the *c.* off the naked
Prov. 6. 27. take fire, and his *c.* not be burnt?
Ezek. 16. 39. shall strip thee also of thy *c.* 23. 26.
Mat. 24. 18. nor let him return back to take his *c.*
Mark 5. 28. if I touch but his *c.* I shall be whole
15. 20. took off purple, and put his own *c.* on him
Luke 2. 7. and wrapped him in swaddling *c.* 12.
8. 27. a man that ware no *c.* nor abode in any house
19. 36. as he went they spread their *c.* in the way
24. 12. he beheld the linen *c.* laid, *John* 20. 5.
John 11. 44. came bound hand and foot with grave *c*
19. 40. took body of Jesus, and wound it in linen *c.*
20. 7. the napkin not lying with the linen *c.*
Acts 7. 58. witnesses laid down their *c.* at Saul's feet
22. 23. as they cried out and cast off their *c.*

Rent CLOTHES.

Gen. 37. 29. Reuben || 34. Jacob *rent* his *c.*
44. 13. Joseph's brethren *rent* their *c.* and returned
Num. 14. 6. Joshua and Caleb *rent* their *c.*
Josh. 7. 6. Joshua || *Judg.* 11. 35. Jephthah *rent* his *c.*
2 *Sam.* 3. 31. *rent* your *c.* gird you with sackcloth
1 *Kings* 21. 27. Ahab || 2 *Kings* 5. 8. king of Israel *rent* his *c.* 6. 30.
2 *Kings* 11. 14. Athaliah *rent* her *c.* 2 *Chr.* 23. 13.
19. 1. when Hezekiah heard he *rent* his *c.* *Isa.* 37. 1.
Esth. 4. 1. when Mordecai perceived, he *rent* his *c.*
Mat. 26. 65. high priest *rent* his *c.* *Mark* 14. 63.
Acts 14. 14. apost. Barnabas and Paul *rent* their *c.*
16. 22. and the magistrates *rent* off their *c.*

CLOTHES *rent.*

Lev. 13. 45. the leper's *c.* shall be *rent*, his head bare
1 *Sam.* 4. 12. a man came to Shiloh with his *c.* *rent*
2 *Sam.* 1. 2. came a man from Saul with his *c.* *rent*
13. 31. all his servants stood with their *c.* *rent*
2 *Kings* 18. 37. to Hezekiah with *c.* *rent*, *Isa.* 36. 22.
Jer. 41. 5. men came to Mizpeh with their *c.* *rent*

Wash CLOTHES.

Exod. 19. 10. let them *wash* their *c.* *Num.* 8. 7.
Lev. 11. 25. shall *wash* his *c.* 40. | 13. 6. | 14. 8, 9, 47. | 15. 5, 8, 11, 22. | 16. 26, 28. *Num.* 19. 10, 19.
Num. 19. 7. then the priest shall *wash* his *c.* 8, 19.
31. 24. ye shall *wash* your *c.* on the seventh day

Washed CLOTHES.

Exod. 19. 14. and the people *washed* their *c.*
Num. 8. 21. Levites purified and *washed* their *c.*
2 *Sam.* 19. 24. Mephibosheth *washed* not his *c.*

CLOTHEST.

Jer. 4. 30. though thou *c.* thyself with crimson

CLOTHING.

Job 22. 6. thou hast stripped the naked of their *c.*
24. 7. they cause the naked to lodge without *c.*
10. they cause him to go naked without *c.*
31. 19. if I have seen any perish for want of *c.*
Psal. 35. 13. but as for me, my *c.* was sackcloth
45. 13. king's daughter, her *c.* is of wrought gold
Prov. 27. 26. the lambs are for thy *c.* and goats
31. 22. the virtuous woman's *c.* is silk and purple
25. strength and honour are her *c.* she shall rejoice
Isa. 3. 6. saying, thou hast *c.* be thou our ruler
7. for in my house is neither bread nor *c.*
23. 18. her merchandise shall be for durable *c.*
59. 17. he put on the garments of vengeance for *c.*
Jer. 10. 9. blue and purple is their *c.* are the work
Mat. 7. 15. in sheep's *c.* || 11. 8. that wear soft *c.*
Mark 12. 38. the scribes that love to go in long *c.*
Acts 10. 30. a man stood before me in bright *c*
James 2. 3. respect to him that weareth the gay *c.*

CLOUD

Signifies, [1] *A congeries chiefly of watery particles, drawn or sent out of the earth in vapours, into the middle region of the air,* 2 Sam. 22. 12. [2] *The heavens,* Psal. 36. 5. | 68. 34. [3] *A great number,* Heb. 12. 1. [4] *A fog, or mist,* Hos. 6. 4.

The scripture represents the clouds as conservatories of water, or rain, which are scattered upon the earth at God's command, Job 26. 8. He bindeth up the waters in his thick clouds. *God confines the waters in the clouds, as in a bottle; he scatters them afterwards upon the earth, as it were through a watering-pot.* Job *speaking of the matter of the Chaos, which covered the whole earth at the beginning of the world, says, that God had hemmed in the sea, or the waters, as it were with a cloud, and covered it with darkness, as a child is wrapped up in swaddling-clothes,* Job 38. 9. *When the sacred writers speak of the second coming of* Christ, *they describe him to us as descending upon the* clouds, *encompassed with all his majesty,* Mat. 24. 30. Rev. 1. 7. *The prophet* Isaiah, *speaking of the conversion of the Gentiles, compares their flocking into the church to the flight or quick motion of a* cloud; *noting that they should come in great multitudes, and with great speed and eagerness,* Isa. 60. 8. St. Peter *compares seducers to* clouds that are carried with a tempest, 2 Pet. 2. 17. *By which comparison he sets forth both the inconstancy of these seducers, that, like clouds driven with the wind, they are tossed to and fro from one doctrine to another; and likewise their de-*

ceitfulness, that they make a shew of what they have not, as clouds do of rain, and yet are scattered without yielding any. And Solomon *compares the infirmities of old age, which arise successively one after another, to* clouds returning after rain, *Eccl.* 12. 2.

When the Israelites *departed out of* Egypt, *God gave them a pillar of cloud to direct them in their march. This pillar was commonly in the front of the* Israelitish *army; but when they were come to the Red sea, and the Egyptian army appeared to them, the pillar of cloud which stood before the camp of* Israel, *placed itself between that and the camp of the* Egyptians, *so that the* Egyptians *could not come near the* Israelites *all night,* Exod. 14. 19, 20. *But in the morning about break of day, seeing the cloud moving on toward the sea, and following the* Israelites *who had passed through its channel, which was left dry for them in the night time, the* Egyptians *resolved upon pursuing them, and were all covered with the waters of the Red sea, which returned upon them and destroyed them. This cloud continued always from that time to attend the* Israelites *in the wilderness. It was clear and bright during the night, in order to give them light when it grew dark; and in the day-time it was thick and gloomy, the better to defend them from the excessive heats of the* Arabian *deserts, through which they performed their journey.*

The same cloud by its motions gave likewise the signal to the Israelites, *either to encamp or to decamp; so that where that stayed, the people stayed till it rose again; then they broke up their camp, and followed it till it stopped. It was called a* Pillar, *by reason of its form, which was high and elevated, as it were a pile and heap of fogs. This cloud not only enlightened the* Israelites, *but also protected them, and was a continual pledge of God's presence, power, and protection. To this the prophet* Isaiah *alludes, when he says,* The Lord will create upon every dwelling-place of mount Zion, and upon her assemblies, a cloud and smoke by day, and the shining of a flaming fire by night, *Isa.* 4. 5. *that is, That God would be the director, protector, and glory, of his church.*

Gen. 9. 13. I do set my bow in the *c.* for a token
14. that the bow shall be seen in the *c.* 16.
Exod. 14. 20. it was a *c.* and darkness to them
16. 10. behold, the glory of the L. appeared in the *c.*
19. 9. Lord said, lo, I come unto thee in a thick *c.*
24. 15. Moses went up, and a *c.* covered the mount
16. and the *c.* covered it six days, and seventh day God called to Moses out of the midst of the *c.*
18. Moses went into the midst of the *c.*
34. 5. the Lord descended in the *c.* *Num.* 11. 25.
40. 34. a *c.* covered the tent of the congregation
38. the *c.* of Lord was on the tabernacle by day
Lev. 16. 2. I will appear in the *c.* on mercy-seat
Num. 9. 19. when the *c.* tarried long on tabernacle
10. 34. the *c.* of the Lord was upon them by day
1 *Kings* 8. 10. priests came out of holy place, the *c.* filled house of Lord, 2 *Chron.* 5. 13. *Ezek.* 10. 4.
18. 44. there ariseth a little *c.* like a man's hand
Job 3. 5. that day be darkness, let a *c.* dwell upon it
22. 13. how God know? can he judge thro' dark *c.?*
30. 15. and my welfare passeth away as a *c.*
38. 9. when I made the *c.* the garment thereof
Psal. 78. 14. in the day-time he led them with a *c.*
105. 39. he spread a *c.* for a covering, and fire to
Prov. 16. 15. his favour is as a *c.* of the latter rain
Isa. 4. 5. Lord will create on her assemblies a *c.*
18. 4. like a sea of dew in the heat of harvest
19. 1. behold, the Lord rideth upon a swift *c.*
44. 22. I have blotted out as a thick *c.* thy transgressions, and as a *c.* thy sins, return, I have redeem. thee
60. 8. who are these that flee as a *c.* as the doves?
Lam. 2. 1. covered the daughter of Zion with a *c.*
3. 44. thou hast covered thyself with a *c.*
Ezek. 1. 4. a great *c.* and a fire infolding itself
28. as the appearance of the bow that is in the *c.*
8. 11. and a thick *c.* of incense went up
10. 4. and the house was filled with the *c.*
30. 18. as for her, a *c.* shall cover her, her daughters
32. 7. I will cover the sun with a *c.* and the moon
38. 9. thou shalt be like a *c.* to cover the land, 16.
Mat. 17. 5. *c.* overshadowed, *Mark* 9. 7. *Luke* 9. 34. behold, a voice out of the *c.* said, *Luke* 9. 35.
Luke 12. 54. when ye see a *c.* rise out of the west
21. 27. shall see the Son of Man coming in a *c.*
Acts 1. 9. a *c.* received him out of their sight
1 *Cor.* 10. 1. all our fathers were under the *c.*
2. and were all baptized to Moses in the *c.*
Rev. 10. 1. a mighty angel came clothed with a *c.*
11. 12. they ascended up to heaven in a *c.*
14. 14. white *c.* and upon the *c.* one sat, 15, 16.

CLOUD *abode.*

Exod. 40. 35. because the *c.* *abode* thereon
Num. 9. 17. where *c.* *abode* there pitched their tents
18. as long as *c.* *abode* they rested in the tents

Morning CLOUD.

Hos. 6. 4. for your goodness is as a *morning c.*
13. 3. they shall be as the *morning c.* and early dew

Pillar of CLOUD.

Exod. 13. 21. went before them by day in a *p. of c.*
22. he took not away the *p. of c.* by day, nor fire
14. 24. Lord looked on Egyptians thro' *pillar of c.*
Num. 12. 5. L. came down in *pillar of c.* and stood
Deut. 31. 15. L. appeared in *p. of c.* and *p. of c.* stood
Neh. 9. 19. the *pillar of c.* departed not from them

CLOUD *taken up.*

Exod. 40. 36. when the *c.* was *taken up*, *Num.* 9. 17.
3. if the *c.* were not *taken up*, they journeyed not
Num. 9. 17. *c.* was *taken up* from tabernacle, 10. 11.

White CLOUD.

Rev. 14. 14. behold a *white c.* and on the *c.* one sat

CLOUD *of witnesses.*

Heb. 12. 1. we are compassed with so great a *c. of w.*

CLOUDS.

Deut. 4. 11. with darkness, *c.* and thick darkness
Judg. 5. 4. heavens dropped, *c.* also dropped water
2 *Sam.* 22. 12. about him thick *c.* of the skies
2 *Sam.* 23. 4. he shall be as a morning without *c.*
1 *Kings* 18. 45. the heaven was black with *c.*
Job 20. 6. though his head reach to the *c.*
22. 14. thick *c.* are a covering that he seeth not
26. 8. he bindeth up the waters in his thick *c.*
36. 29. can any understand the spreadings of the *c.?*
37. 16. knowest thou the balancings of the *c.?*
38. 37. who can number the *c.* in wisdom?
Psal. 36. 5. thy faithfulness reacheth to the *c.*
57. 10. and thy truth reacheth to the *c.* 108. 4.
68. 34. and his strength is in the *c.*
77. 17. *c.* poured out water, skies sent out a sound
78. 23. tho' he had commanded the *c.* from above
97. 2. *c.* and darkness are round about him
104. 3. *c.* his chariot ‖ 147. 8. covers heaven with *c.*
Prov. 3. 20. and the *c.* dropped down the dew
8. 28. when he established the *c.* above
25. 14. is like *c.* and wind without rain
Eccl. 11. 4. he that regardeth the *c.* shall not reap
12. 2. nor the *c.* return after the rain
Isa. 5. 6. I will command the *c.* that they rain not
14. 14. I will ascend above the height of the *c.*
Jer. 4. 13. behold he shall come up as *c.* and chariots
Dan. 7. 13. Son of Man came with the *c.* of heaven
Joel 2. 2. a day of *c.* and darkness, *Zeph.* 1. 15.
Nah. 1. 3. and the *c.* are the dust of his feet
Zech. 10. 1. so the Lord shall make bright *c.*
Mat. 24. 30. they shall see the Son of Man coming in the *c.* with power, 26. 64. *Mark* 13. 26. | 14. 62.
1 *Thess.* 4. 17. shall be caught up with them in *c.*
2 *Pet.* 2. 17. they are *c.* carried with a tempest
Jude 12. *c.* they are without water, carried about
Rev. 1. 7. behold he cometh with *c.* every eye shall see

CLOUDY.

Exod. 33. 9. the *c.* pillar descended, and stood at door
10. all the people saw the *c.* pillar stand at door
Neh. 9. 12. thou leddest them in the day by *c.* pillar
Psal. 99. 7. he spake to them in the *c.* pillar
Ezek. 30. 3. the day of the Lord is near, a *c.* day
34. 12. they have been scattered in the *c.* day

CLOVEN.

Lev. 11. 3. whatsoever is *c.*-footed that shall ye eat
7. tho' the swine be *c.*-footed he is unclean
26. not *c.*-footed are unclean to you, *Deut.* 14. 7.
Acts 2. 3. there appeared to them *c.* tongues

CLOUTED.

Josh. 9. 5. they took old shoes and *c.* on their feet

CLOUTS.

Jer. 38. 11. Ebed-melech took old cast *c.* and rags
12. put these old cast *c.* under thine arm-holes

CLUSTER.

Num. 13. 23. cut from Eshcol a branch with one *c.*
Cant. 1. 14. my beloved is as a *c.* of camphire
Isa. 65. 8. as new wine is found in the *c.* so will I do
Mic. 7. 1. woe is me, there is no *c.* to eat

CLUSTERS.

Gen. 40. 10. the *c.* thereof brought forth ripe grapes
Deut. 32. 32. grapes are grapes of gall, their *c.* bitter
1 *Sam.* 25. 18. Abigail brought 100 *c.* of raisins
30. 12. they gave the Egyptian two *c.* of raisins
Cant. 7. 7. thy breasts like two *c.* of grapes, 8.
Rev. 14. 18. gather the *c.* of the vine of the earth

COAL.

2 *Sam.* 14. 7. so shall quench my *c.* which is left
Isa. 6. 6. seraphim having a live *c.* in his hand
47. 14. there shall not be a *c.* to warm at
Lam. 4. 8. their visage is blacker than a *c.*

COALS.

Lev. 16. 12. he shall take a censer full of burning *c.*
Deut. 32. † 24. shall be devoured with burning *c.*
1 *Kings* 19. 6. a cake baken on the *c.* and a cruse
Job 41. 21. his breath kindleth *c.* and a flame goeth
Psal. 18. 8. there went fire, *c.* were kindled by it
12. thick clouds passed, hail-stones and *c.* of fire
120. 4. sharp arrows of mighty with *c.* of juniper
140. 10. let burning *c.* fall on them, let them
Prov. 6. 28. can one go on hot *c.* and not be burnt?
25. 22. thou shalt heap *c.* of fire, *Rom.* 12. 20.
26. 21. as *c.* are to burning *c.* and wood to fire
Cant. 8. 6. the *c.* thereof are *c.* of fire, which hath
Isa. 44. 12. the smith with tongs worketh in the *c.*
19. I have baked bread upon the *c.* thereof
54. 16. I created the smith that bloweth the *c.*
Ezek. 1. 13. their appearance was like burning *c.*
10. 2. go in and fill thine hand with *c.* of fire
24. 11. then set it empty on the *c.* thereof
Hab. 3. 5. burning *c.* went forth at his feet
John 18. 18. the servants who had made a fire of *c.*
21. 9. they saw a fire of *c.* and fish laid thereon

COAST.

Exod. 10. 4. I will bring the locusts into thy *c.*
Num. 24. 24. ships shall come from *c.* of Chittim
Deut. 11. 24. to the uttermost sea shall your *c.* be
19. 8. if the Lord thy God enlarge thy *c.*
Josh. 1. 4. going down of the sun shall be your *c.*
18. 5. Judah shall abide in their *c.* on the south
Judg. 11. 20. Sihon trusted not Israel to pass his *c.*
1 *Sam.* 6. 9. if it go up by the way of his own *c.*
7. 13. they came no more into the *c.* of Israel
17. † 1. the Philistines pitched in *c.* of Dammim
27. 1. to seek me any more in any *c.* of Israel
30. 14. we made an invasion on the *c.* of Judah
2 *Kings* 14. 25. Jeroboam restored the *c.* of Israel
1 *Chron.* 4. 10. wouldest bless me, and enlarge my *c.*
Zeph. 2. 7. the *c.* shall be for the remnant of Judah

Sea COAST.

Ezek. 25. 16. I will destroy the remnant of the sea *c.*
Zeph. 2. 5. woe to the inhabitants of the sea *c.*
6. the sea *c.* shall be dwellings for the shepherds
Mat. 4. 13. Jesus dwelt in Capernaum upon the sea *c.*
Luke 6. 17. multitude from sea *c.* came to hear

South COAST.

Josh. 15. 1. Zin the uttermost part of the south *c.*
4. were at the sea, this shall be your south *c.*
18. 19. at south end of Jordan; this was the south *c.*

COASTS.

Exod. 10. 14. the locusts rested in all the *c.* of Egypt
19. remained not one locust in all the *c.* of Egypt
Deut. 2. 4. to pass through the *c.* of your brethren
16. 4. no leavened bread be seen in all thy *c.*
19. 3. thou shalt divide the *c.* of thy land
Josh. 18. 5. Joseph shall abide in their *c.* on north
Judg. 18. 2. Dan sent five men from their *c.*
19. 29. sent his concubine into all the *c.* of Israel
1 *Sam.* 7. 14. the *c.* thereof did Israel deliver out of
11. 3. may send messengers into all *c.* of Israel, 7.
2 *Sam.* 21. 5. be destroyed from the *c.* of Israel
1 *Chron.* 21. 12. angel of Lord destroying thro' all *c.*
2 *Chron.* 11. 13. resorted to him out of all their *c.*
Psal. 105. 31. there came lice in all their *c.*
33. he smote their vines, and brake trees of their *c.*
Jer. 25. 32. a great whirlwind be raised from the *c.*
Ezek. 33. 2. if the people take a man of their *c.*
Joel 3. 4. what to do with me, all *c.* of Palestine?
Mat. 2. 16. Herod sent and slew children in all the *c.*
8. 34. he would depart out of their *c.* *Mark* 5. 17.
15. 21. then Jesus depart. into *c.* of Tyre and Sidon
Mark 7. 31. departing from the *c.* of Tyre and Sidon
Acts 13. 50. expelled Paul and Barnabas out of *c.*

COAT.

Gen. 37. 3. Jacob made Joseph a *c.* of many colours
32. they sent the *c.* of many colours, and said, this have we found, know whether it be thy son's *c.*
Exod. 28. 4. make for Aaron a robe and broidered *c.*
29. 5. and thou shalt put upon Aaron the *c.*
Lev. 8. 7. he put upon him the *c.* and girded him
16. 4. he shall put on the holy linen *c.*
1 *Sam.* 2. 19. his mother made Samuel a little *c.*
17. 5. Goliath was armed with a *c.* of mail, 38.
2 *Sam.* 15. 32. Hushai met David with his *c.* rent
Job 30. 18. it bindeth me about as collar of my *c.*
Cant. 5. 3. I have put off my *c.* how shall I put it on?
Mat. 5. 40. if any sue thee, and take away thy *c.*
Luke 6. 29. thy cloke, forbid not to take thy *c.* also
John 19. 23. now the *c.* was without seam, woven
21. 7. Peter girt his fisher's *c.* unto him, cast hims.

COATS.

Gen. 3. 21. God made *c.* of skins, and clothed them
Exod. 28. 40. for Aaron's sons thou shalt make *c.*
29. 8. bring his sons, and put *c.* on them, 40. 14.
Lev. 8. 13. Moses put *c.* upon Aaron's sons
10. 5. they carried them in their *c.* out of the camp
Dan. 3. 21. then these men were bound in their *c.*
27. nor were their *c.* changed, nor smell of fire
Mat. 10. 10. neither provide two *c.* nor shoes, nor
Mark 6. 9. shod with sandals, and put not on two *c.*
Luke 3. 11. he that hath two *c.* let him impart to him
Acts 9. 39. shewing the *c.* which Dorcas made

COCKLE.

Job 31. 40. and let *c.* grow instead of barley

COCKATRICE, S.

Prov. 23. † 32. at last it stingeth like a *c.*
Isa. 11. 8. weaned child put his hand on the *c.* den
14. 29. out of serpent's root shall come forth a *c.*
59. 5. they hatch *c.* eggs, weave the spider's web
Jer. 8. 17. I will send serpents, *c.* among you

COCK.

Mat. 26. 34. this night before *c.* crow, thou shalt deny me thrice, 75. *Mark* 14. 30, 72. *Luke* 22. 34, 61.
74. immediately *c.* crew, *Luke* 22. 60. *John* 18. 27.
Mark 13. 35. if the master cometh at *c.* crowing
14. 68. he went out into porch, and the *c.* crew, 72.
John 13. 38. verily, verily, I say to thee, the *c.* shall not crow till thou hast denied me thrice

COFFER.

1 *Sam.* 6. 8. and put the jewels of gold in a *c.*
11. they laid ark and *c.* with mice of gold on cart
15. the Levites took down the *c.* with the ark
Ezra 6. † 2. there was found in a *c.* a roll

COFFIN.

Gen. 50. 26. Joseph was put in a *c.* in Egypt
Luke 7. † 14. he came and touched the *c.* and said

COGITATIONS.

Dan. 7. 28. as for me, my *c.* much troubled me

COLD.

Gen. 8. 22. *c.* and heat, day and night shall not cease
Job 24. 7. the naked have no covering in the *c.*
37. 9. and *c.* cometh out of the north
Psal. 147. 17. who can stand before his *c.?*
Prov. 20. 4. the sluggard will not plow by reason of *c.*
25. 13. as *c.* of snow in the time of harvest, so is
20. that taketh away a garment in *c.* weather
25. as *c.* waters to a thirsty soul, so is good news
Jer. 18. 14. shall the *c.* flowing waters be forsaken?
Nah. 3. 17. which camp in the hedges in the *c.* day
Mat. 10. 42. give to little ones a cup of *c.* water
24. 12. iniquity abound, love of many shall wax *c.*
John 18. 18. servants had made a fire, for it was *c.*
Acts 28. 2. they received us, because of the *c.*
2 *Cor.* 11. 27. in fastings often, in *c.* and nakedness
Rev. 3. 15. that thou art neither *c.* nor hot, 16.

COLLAR, S.

Judg. 8. 26. golden ear-rings from Midian, beside *c.*
Job 30. 18. my disease bindeth me as *c.* of my coat

COLLECTION.

2 *Chron.* 24. 6. to bring in out of Judah the *c.* 9.
1 *Cor.* 16. 1. now concerning the *c.* for the saints

COLLEGE.

2 *Kings* 22. 14. Huldah dwelt in *c.* 2 *Chron.* 34. 22.

COLLOPS.

Job 15. 27. because he maketh *c.* of fat on his flanks

COLONY.

Acts 16. 12. Philippi, chief city of Macedonia, and *c.*

COLOUR.

Lev. 13. 55. if the plague have not changed his *c.*
Num. 11. 7. the *c.* thereof as the *c.* of bdellium
Esth. 1. † 6. alabaster and stone of blue *c.*
Prov. 23. 31. when the wine giveth his *c.* in the cup
Ezek. 1. 4. out of the midst thereof as the *c.* of amber
7. sparkled like *c.* of burnished brass, *Dan.* 10. 6.
1. 16. the wheels like unto *c.* of a beryl, 10. 9.
22. the firmament was as the *c.* of the crystal
Rev. 17. 4. woman was arrayed in purple and scarlet *c.*

COLOURED.

Rev. 17. 3. I saw a woman sit on a scarlet *c.* beast

COLOURS.

Gen. 37. 3. Jacob made a coat of many *c.* for Joseph
Judg. 5. 30. to Sisera a prey of divers *c.* meet for
2 *Sam.* 13. 18. Tamar had a garment of divers *c*
1 *Chron.* 29. 2. I have prepared stones of divers *c.*
Isa. 54. 11. I will lay thy stones with fair *c.*
Ezek. 16. 16. deckedst thy high places with divers *c.*
17. 3. an eagle with divers *c.* came to Lebanon

COLOUR.
Acts 27. 30. under *c.* as tho' they would cast anchor
COLT, S.
Gen. 32. 15. thirty milch camels with their *c.* forty
49. 11. binding his ass's *c.* to the choice vine
Judg. 10. 4. Jair had 30 sons that rode on 30 ass's *c.*
12. 14. Abdon's sons and nephews rode on 70 ass's *c.*
Job 11. 12. though man be born like a wild ass's *c.*
Zech. 9. 9. riding upon a *c.* *Mat.* 21. 5. *John* 12. 15.
Mat. 21. 2. Jesus sent two disciples, saying, go, ye shall find ass tied, *c.* with her, *Mark* 11. 2. *Luke* 19. 30.
7. brought ass and *c.* and set thereon, *Mark* 11. 7.
Mark 11. 5. what do you loosing the *c.?* *Luke* 19. 33.
Luke 19. 35. cast garm. on *c.* and set Jesus thereon
COME
Signifies, [1] *To draw nigh, or approach,* Exod. 34. 3. [2] *To proceed from,* 1 Chron. 29. 14. [3] *To befall,* Ezra 9. 13. Job 4. 5. [4] *To believe,* John 5. 40. | 6. 37. [5] *To attain to,* Acts 26. 7. [6] *To join with,* Proverbs 1. 11. [7] *To touch,* Ezek. 44. 25. [8] *To be married to,* Dan. 11. 6. [9] *To lie carnally with,* Gen. 38. 16. [10] *To invade,* Gen. 34. 25. [11] *To arise,* Num. 24. 7.
Gen. 6. 20. two of every sort shall *c.* to keep alive
7. 1. *c.* thou, and all thy house into the ark
8. † 9. he caused her to *c.* to him into the ark
19. 32. *c.* let us make our father drink wine
26. 27. wherefore *c.* ye to me, seeing ye hate me?
31. 44. *c.* let us make a covenant, I and thou
37. 10. *c.* let us slay him, and cast into some pit
41. † 21. when they had *c.* to inward parts of them
42. 7. he said to them, whence *c.* ye? *Josh.* 9. 8.
45. 19. take waggons, bring your father and *c.*
49. 10. sceptre not depart from Judah till Shiloh *c.*
Exod. 19. 9. lo, I *c.* to thee in a thick cloud
20. 24. where I record my name I will *c.* and bless
23. 27. destroy all people to whom thou shalt *c.*
Num. 10. 29. *c.* thou with us, we will do thee good
22. 6. *c.* I pray thee, curse me this people, 11.
24. 19. out of Jacob shall *c.* he that shall have dominion, and shall destroy him that remaineth of city
Deut. 18. 6. if a Levite *c.* and *c.* with desire of mind
28. 2. all these blessings shall *c.* on thee, overtake
15. all these curses *c.* on thee, overtake thee, 45.
Judg. 13. 5. no razor *c.* on his head, 1 *Sam.* 1. 11.
1 *Sam.* 2. 34. that shall *c.* on thy two sons in one day
9. 13. for the people will not eat till he *c.* because
10. 8. seven days thou shalt tarry, till I *c.* to thee
17. 45. but I *c.* to thee in the name of the Lord
20. 21. then *c.* thou, for there is peace to thee
2 *Sam.* 6. 9. how shall the ark of the Lord *c.* to me?
15. † 2. when any *c.* to the king for judgment
17. 2. I will *c.* on him while he is weary and weak
19. 33. *c.* thou over with me and I will feed thee
1 *Kings* 8. 31. and the oath *c.* before thine altar
20. 33. observe, if any thing would *c.* from him
22. 27. feed this fellow until I *c.* in peace
2 *Kings* 5. 8. let him *c.* now to me, he shall know
6. † 19. this is not the way, *c.* ye after me
18. 32. till I *c.* and take you away, *Isa.* 36. 17.
1 *Chron.* 29. 12. both riches and honour *c.* of thee
14. all things *c.* of thee, and of thine have we
2 *Chron.* 8. 11. holy, whereto the ark of Lord hath *c.*
Esth. 1. 12. queen Vashti refused to *c.* at king's com.
5. † 10. Haman caused his friends to *c.*
8. 6. how endure to see evil *c.* to my people?
Job 3. 7. let no joyful voice *c.* therein
13. 13. that I may speak, let *c.* on me what will
14. 14. all my time will I wait till my change *c.*
21. his sons *c.* to honour, and he knoweth it not
37. 13. he caused it to *c.* for correction on land
38. 11. hitherto shalt thou *c.* but no further
Psal. 40. 7. then said I, lo, I *c.* *Heb.* 10. 7, 9.
42. 2. when shall I *c.* and appear before God?
50. 3. our God shall *c.* and not keep silence
65. 2. that hearest prayer, unto thee shall all flesh *c.*
80. 2. stir up thy strength, and *c.* and save us
86. 9. all nations shall *c.* and worship thee
90. † 12. we may cause our heart to *c.* to wisdom
101. 2. O when wilt thou *c.* unto me, I will walk
109. 17. as he loved cursing, so let it *c.* unto him
119. 41. let thy mercies *c.* unto me, O Lord, 77.
Prov. 6. 11. so shall thy poverty *c.* as one, 24. 34.
10. 24. the fear of the wicked shall *c.* upon him
26. 2. so the curse causeless shall not *c.*
Eccl. 9. 2. all things *c.* alike to all, there is one event
Cant. 2. 10. rise up, my love, and *c.* away, 13.
4. 8. *c.* with me from Lebanon, my spouse, with me
16. and *c.* thou south, blow upon my garden
Isa. 5. 19. let the counsel of the holy One of Israel *c.*
13. 5. they *c.* from a far country, even the Lord
6. the day of the Lord, it shall *c.* as destruction
21. 12. if ye will inquire, inquire ye; return, *c.*
26. 20. *c.* my people, enter into thy chambers
27. 6. cause them that *c.* of Jacob to take root
35. 4. your God will *c.* with vengeance, he will *c.*
40. 10. the Lord will *c.* with a strong hand
41. 25. I have raised up one, and he shall *c.*
44. 7. I appointed things coming, and shall *c.*
45. 20. assemble yourselves, and *c.* draw near
24. even to him shall men *c.* and all that are
51. 11. the redeemed shall *c.* with singing to Zion
55. 1. *c.* ye to the waters, *c.* ye, buy, *c.* buy wine
3. *c.* unto me, hear, and your soul shall live
59. 20. and the Redeemer shall *c.* to Zion
60. 3. and the Gentiles shall *c.* to thy light, 5.
66. 15. behold, Lord will *c.* with fire and chariots
Jer. 2. 31. why, say they, we will *c.* no more to thee
3. 22. behold, we *c.* to thee, for thou art our God
9. 17. call the mourning women, that they may *c.*
13. 22. wherefore *c.* these things upon me?
17. 15. where is the word of the Lord? let it *c.*
27. 7. shall serve him till the very time of his land *c.*
31. 9. they shall *c.* with weeping and with supplic.
38. 25. if the princes hear, and *c.* to thee, and say
40. 4. if it seem good to *c.* if it seem ill to *c.* forbear
46. 18. and as Carmel by the sea, so shall he *c.*
49. 4. that trusted, saying, who shall *c.* unto me?
Lam. 1. 4. ways of Zion mourn, none *c.* to solemn [feasts
22. let all their wickedness *c.* before thee
Ezek. 12. 16. declare abominations whither they *c.*
Ezek. 13. 18. will ye save souls alive that *c.* to you?
21. 19. two ways that the sword may *c.* 20. | 32. 11.
27. shall be no more, till he *c.* whose right it is
33. 3. when he seeth the sword *c.* on the land, 6.
31. they *c.* to thee as the people cometh
33. lo it will *c.* then shall know that a prophet
36. 8. to my people Israel, they are at hand to *c.*
Hos. 6. 1. *c.* let us return to the Ld. for he hath torn
3. and he shall *c.* to us, as the rain to the earth
10. 12. it is time to seek the Lord till he *c.* and rain
Joel 1. 15. day of the Lord, as a destruction shall it *c.*
2. 31. before the terrible day of the Lord *c.*
Jonah 1. 7. *c.* let us cast lots, that we may know
Mic. 4. 8. to thee shall it *c.* the kingdom shall *c.*
Hab. 2. 3. because it will surely *c.* and not tarry
Zeph. 2. 2. before the fierce anger of Lord *c.* on you
Zech. 1. 21. then said I, what *c.* these to do?
14. 5. God shall *c.* and all the saints with thee
Mal. 3. 1. the Lord ye seek shall *c.* to his temple
4. 6. lest I *c.* and smite the earth with a curse
Mat. 2. 6. for out of thee shall *c.* a Governor
5. 24. first be reconciled, then *c.* and offer thy gift
6. 10. thy kingdom *c.* thy will be done, *Luke* 11. 2.
7. 15. false prophets *c.* to you in sheep's clothing
8. 7. Jesus saith to him, I will *c.* and heal him
8. I am not worthy thou shouldest *c.* under my roof
9. and to another, *c.* and he cometh, *Luke* 7. 8.
11. many shall *c.* from east and west, and sit down
11. 3. art thou he that should *c.?* *Luke* 7. 19, 20.
28. *c.* all ye that labour and are heavy lad n
16. 24. if any man will *c.* after me, let him deny
17. 10. why say the scribes, Elias must first *c.?* 11.
19. 21. go, sell that thou hast, and *c.* *Luke* 18. 22.
Mat. 22. 4. all things are ready *c.* unto the marriage
24. 14. gospel shall be preached, then shall end *c.*
42. ye know not what hour your Lord doth *c.*
25. 34. *c.* ye blessed of my father, inherit kingdom
Mark 8. 34. if any will *c.* after me, *Luke* 9. 23. | 14. 27.
10. 14. suffer little children to *c.* to me, *Luke* 18. 16.
21. and *c.* take up the cross, and follow me
12. 7. this is the heir, *c.* let us kill him, *Luke* 20. 14.
Luke 10. 1. every place whither he himself would *c.*
13. 7. three years I *c.* seeking fruit on this fig-tree
14. there are six days, in them *c.* and be healed
17. 20. when the kingdom of God should *c.*
19. 13. he said unto them, occupy till I *c.*
20. 16. he shall *c.* and destroy these husbandmen
22. 18. fruit of vine, till kingdom of God shall *c.*
John 1. 39. he saith unto them, *c.* and see
3. 26. the same baptizeth, and all men *c.* to him
5. 14. sin no more, lest a worse thing *c.* to thee
40. ye will not *c.* to me, that ye might have life
6. 37. all that the Father giveth me shall *c.* to me
44. no man can *c.* to me except F. draw him, 65.
7. 34. and where I am, thither ye cannot *c.*
37. if any man thirst, let him *c.* to me and drink
8. 14. ye cannot tell whence I *c.* and whither I go
13. 19. now I tell you before it *c.* that when it is *c.*
14. 18. I will not leave you comfortless, I will *c.*
23. and we will *c.* unto him, and make our abode
17. 11. but these are in the world, I *c.* to thee, 13.
21. 22. if I will he tarry till I *c.* what to thee? 23.
Acts 1. 11. this J. shall so *c.* as ye have seen him go
2. 20. before that great and notable day of Lord *c.*
3. 19. sins blotted out, when times of refreshing *c.*
7. 34. and now *c.* I will send thee into Egypt
8. 24. pray that none of these things *c.* upon me
9. 38. that he would not delay to *c.* to them
13. 40. lest that *c.* on you that is spoken in proph.
16. 9. saying, *c.* over into Macedonia, and help us
19. 4. believe on him that should *c.* after him
24. 23. should forbid no acquaintance to *c.* to him
26. 7. to which promise our twelve tribes hope to *c.*
22. no other than proph. and Moses say should *c.*
Rom. 3. 8. that we say, let us do evil, that good *c.*
9. 9. the word of promise, at this time will I *c.*
1 *Cor.* 4. 5. judge nothing till the Lord *c.* who will
11. 26. ye do shew the Lord's death till he *c.*
34. the rest will I set in order when I *c.*
15. 35. the dead, and with what body do they *c.?*
16. 2. that there be no gatherings when I *c.*
10. if Timothy *c.* see he be with you without fear
12. as to Apollos, I desired him to *c.* to you
2 *Cor.* 1. 15. I was minded to *c.* to you before
12. 20. for I fear, lest when I *c.* I shall not find you such as I would, and be to you as you would not
Gal. 2. 21. if righteousness *c.* by the law, then is
3. 14. the blessing of Abraham might *c.* on Gentiles
19. it was added, till the seed should *c.* to whom
2 *Thess.* 1. 10. when he shall *c.* to be glorified in saints
2. 3. not *c.* except there *c.* a falling away first
1 *Tim.* 4. 8. the life that now is, and of that to *c.*
13. till I *c.* give attendance to reading, to doctrine
2 *Tim.* 3. 1. in last days perilous times shall *c.*
4. 3. time will *c.* will not endure sound doctrine
Tit. 3. 12. be diligent to *c.* to me to Nicopolis
Heb. 4. 16. let us *c.* boldly to the throne of grace
7. 25. he is able to save them that *c.* to God by him
10. 37. he that shall *c.* will *c.* and not tarry
Jam. 4. 1. whence *c.* wars, *c.* they not of your lusts?
5. 1. weep for your miseries that shall *c.* on you
2 *Pet.* 3. 9. but that all should *c.* to repentance
10. day of L. will *c.* as a thief, *Rev.* 3. 3. | 16. 15.
1 *John* 2. 18. as ye have heard, antichrist shall *c.*
3 *John* 10. if I *c.* I will remember his deeds
Rev. 2. 5. repent, or else I will *c.* to thee quickly
25. that which ye have already, hold fast till I *c.*
3. 11. behold, I *c.* quickly, hold that fast, 22. 7, 20.
6. 1. one of the four beasts, saying, *c.* and see, 3, 5, 7.
18. 10. for in one hour is thy judgment *c.*
22. 17. and let him that is athirst *c.* whoever will
COME *again.*
Gen. 28. 21. so that I *c. again* to my father's house
Exod. 14. 26. that waters may *c. again* on Egyptians
Lev. 14. 43. if the plague *c. again* and break out
Judg. 8. 9. when I *c. again* in peace I will break down
13. 8. let man of God *c. again* to us, and teach us
1 *Kings* 2. 41. Shimei had gone to Gath, and was *c. a.*
12. 5. depart for 3 days, and then *c. a.* 2 *Chr.* 10. 5.
17. 21. O Lord, I pray, let this child's soul *c. again*
Ezra 6. 21. children of Israel *c. again, Neh.* 8. 17.
Psal. 126. 6. he shall *c. again* with rejoicing
Prov. 3. 28. say not to thy neighbour, go and *c. again*
Jer. 37. 8. the Chaldeans shall *c. again* and fight
Lam. 1. † 11. given for meat to make their soul *c. a.*
Luke 10. 35. when I *c. again* I will repay thee
John 14. 3. I will *c. again* and receive you to myself
28. ye have heard how I said, I go away and *c. a.*
2 *Cor.* 2. 1. that I would not *c. again* in heaviness
12. 21. lest, when I *c. again,* God will humble me
13. 2. I write, that if I *c. again* I will not spare
COME *down.*
Gen. 45. 9. thus saith Joseph, *c. d.* to me, tarry not
Exod. 3. 8. I am *c. d.* to deliver and bring them up
19. 11. the Lord will *c. down* on mount Sinai
Num. 11. 17. I will *c. d.* and talk with thee there
Deut. 28. 24. from heaven it shall *c. down* on thee
Judg. 7. 24. saying, *c. down* against the Midianites
15. 12. they said, we are *c. down* to bind thee
1 *Sam.* 6. 21. *c. down* and fetch the ark up to you
23. 11. will Saul *c. d.?* the Lord said, he will *c. d*
20. *c. down,* according to the desire of thy soul
2 *Kings* 1. 4. thou shalt not *c. d.* from that bed, 6, 16.
9. thou man of God, *c. d.* ‖ 10. let fire *c. d.* 11, 12.
Neh. 6. 3. I am doing a great work, I cannot *c. down*
Psal. 7. 16. his dealing shall *c. down* on his own pate
72. 6. he shall *c. down* like rain on mown grass
144. 5. bow the heavens, O Lord, and *c. down*
Isa. 34. 5. my sword, it shall *c. down* on Idumea
47. 1. *c. down,* sit in the dust, O virgin daughter
64. 1. oh, that thou wouldest *c. down* that mount,
Jer. 13. 18. your principalities shall *c. down*
21. 13. which say, who shall *c. down* against us?
48. 18. *c. down* from thy glory, and sit in thirst
Ezek. 26. 16. the princes of the sea shall *c. down*
27. 29. all pilots shall *c. down* from their ships
30. 6. the pride of her power shall *c. down*
Dan. 5. † 20. hardened in pride, he was made to *c. d.*
Joel 3. 11. cause thy mighty ones to *c. down*
Mat. 24. 17. not *c. d.* to take any thing out of house
27. 40. *c. down* from the cross, 42. *Mark* 15. 30.
Luke 9. 54. wilt thou that we command fire to *c. d.?*
19. 5. Jesus said, Zaccheus, make haste and *c. d.*
John 4. 49. saith, Sir, *c. down* ere my child die
Acts 14. 11. the gods are *c. down* to us like men
Rev. 12. 12. devil is *c. down* to you, having wrath
13. 13. maketh fire *c. down* from heaven on earth
20. 1. angel *c. d.* having the key of bottomless pit
COME *forth.*
Gen. 15. 4. he that shall *c. forth* out of thy bowels
1 *Sam.* 14. 11. Hebrews *c. forth* out of their holes
1 *Kings* 2. 30. Benaiah said, thus saith the k. *c. f.*
2 *Kings* 10. 25. go in and slay them, let none *c. f.*
Job 23. 10. when tried, I shall *c. forth* as gold
Psal. 17. 2. let my sentence *c. f.* from thy presence
88. 8. I am shut up, and I cannot *c. forth*
Eccl. 7. 18. that feareth God shall *c. f.* of them all
Isa. 11. 1. shall *c. f.* a rod out of the stem of Jesse
48. 1. and art *c. forth* out of the waters of Judah
Jer. 4. 4. lest my fury *c. forth* like fire and burn
37. 5. Pharaoh's army was *c. forth* out of Egypt, 7.
46. 9. let mighty men *c. forth,* the Ethiopians
48. 45. a fire shall *c. forth* out of Heshbon
Ezek. 21. 19. both twain shall *c. f.* out of one land
Dan. 3. 26. ye servants of the most high God, *c. f.*
9. 22. O Daniel, I am *c. forth* to give thee skill
Joel 3. 18. a fountain shall *c. forth* of house of Lord
Mic. 5. 2. out of thee shall *c. f.* that is to be ruler
Zech. 2. 6. *c. f.* and flee from the land of the north
Mat. 13. 49. angels shall *c. forth* and sever wicked
15. 18. *c. forth* from the heart, and defile the man
Mark 9. 29. this kind *c. forth* by nothing but prayer
Luke 12. 37. and will *c. forth* and serve them
John 5. 29. shall *c. forth,* they that have done good
11. 43. he cried with a loud voice, Lazarus, *c. forth*
Acts 7. 7. after that they shall *c. forth* and serve me
COME *hither.*
Gen. 15. 16. in the fourth generation shall *c. hither*
Judg. 16. 2. it was told Gazites, Samson is *c. hither*
Ruth 2. 14. at meal-time *c.* thou *hither* and eat
1 *Sam.* 10. 22. they inquired if the man should *c. h.*
16. 11. we will not sit down till he *c. hither*
2 *Sam.* 14. 32. *c. h.* that I may send thee to the king
20. 16. say to Joab, *c. h.* that I may speak with thee
2 *Kings* 8. 7. told Ben-hadad, the man of G. is *c. h.*
Prov. 25. 7. better it be said to thee, *c.* up *hither*
Dan. 3. 26. ye servants of G. *c.* forth and *c. hither*
Mat. 8. 29. art thou *c. h.* to torment us before time?
John 4. 15. that I thirst not, neither *c. h.* to draw
16. Jesus saith, call thy husband and *c. hither*
Acts 17. 6. that have turned the world are *c. hither*
Rev. 4. 1. voice said, *c.* up *h.* 11. 12. | 17. 1. | 21. 9.
COME *in,* or *into.*
Gen. 6. 18. thou shalt *c. into* the ark, and thy sons
19. 31. there is not a man in the earth to *c. in* to us
24. 31. and he said, *c. in* thou blessed of the Lord
Exod. 12. 23. Lord will not suffer destroyer to *c. in*
28. 43. when they *c. in* unto the tabernacle
Lev. 16. 26. he shall bathe his flesh, and afterward shall *c. into* the camp, 28. *Num.* 19. 7. | 31. 24.
Num. 27. 21. and at his word they shall *c. in*
Deut. 31. 2. I can no more go out nor *c. in*
Josh. 14. 11. so is my strength to go out and *c. in*
23. † 1. Joshua waxed old, and *c. into* days
1 *Kings* 1. 14. I will *c. in* after thee and confirm
3. 7. I am a child, I know not how to go out or *c. in*
14. 6. he said *c. in* thou wife of Jeroboam
15. 17. he might not suffer any to go out or *c. in*
2 *Kings* 4. 4. when *c. in* shut the door upon thee
11. 9. they took each his men to *c. in* and go out
2 *Chron.* 1. 10. go out and *c. in* before this people
16. 1. that he might let none go out or *c. in* to Asa
23. 6. none *c. into* the house of the L. save priests
Neh. 2. 7. convey me over, till I *c. into* Judah
Esth. 5. 12. Esther let no man *c. in* with the king
6. 5. and the king said, let Haman *c. in*
Psal. 24. 7. and the King of glory shall *c. in,* 9
69. 1. for the waters are *c. in* unto my soul
96. 8. bring an offering and *c. into* his courts
109. 18. so let it *c. into* his bowels like water
Cant. 4. 16. let my beloved *c. into* his garden
Isa. 19. 1. behold, the Lord shall *c. into* Egypt
23. the Assyrian shall *c. into* Egypt, Egyptian
24. 10. every house shut up, that no man *c. in*

Isa. 59. 19. when the enemy shall c. in like a flood
Jer. 17. 19. gate, whereby the kings of Judah c. in
51. 50. and let Jerusalem c. into your mind
51. for strangers are c. into the sanctuaries
Ezek. 11. 5. I know things that c. into your mind
38. 10. at the same time shall things c. into thy mind
Mic. 5. 5. when the Assyrian shall c. into our land
Mat. 10. 12. when ye c. into an house, salute it
16. 27. Son of man shall c. in glory of his Father
24. 5. for many shall c. in my name, saying, I am
Christ, and deceive many, Mark 13. 6. Luke 21. 8.
25. 31. when the Son of man shall c. in his glory
Luke 11. 33. they which c. in may see the light
12. 38. c. in the second watch, or c. in the third
46. will c. in a day when he looketh not for him
14. 23. go out, and compel them to c. in, that my
16. 28. lest they c. into this place of torment
John 5. 43. I am c. in my Father's name, ye receive
me not, if another c. in his own name ye receive
6. 14. prophet that should c. into the world, 11. 27.
Acts 16. 15. Lydia, saying, c. into house, abide there
Rom. 11. 25. till the fulness of Gentiles be c. in
1 Cor. 14. 23. there c. in those that are unlearned
24. if there c. in one that believeth not
Jam. 2. 2. there c. in also a poor man in vile raiment
Rev. 3. 20. I will c. in to him, and sup with him

COME *near*.

Gen. 12. 11. Abram was c. near to enter into Egypt
20. 4. but Abimelech had not c. near her
Exod. 12. 48. then let him c. near and keep it
16. 9. say unto Israel, c. near before the Lord
28. 43. or when they c. near to the altar, 30. 20.
Num. 16. 5. and will cause him to c. near to him
40. that no stranger c. near to offer incense
Josh. 10. 24. c. near, put your feet on the necks
1 Sam. 10. 20. had caused all the tribes to c. near
Psal. 32. 9. be held in, lest they c. near unto thee
119. 169. let my cry c. near before thee
Isa. 41. 1. let us c. near together to judgment
† 21. cause to c. near your cause, saith the L.
48. 16. c. ye near unto me, hear ye this
50. 8. who is mine adversary? let him c. near me
Ezek. 18. 6. nor hath c. near to a menstruous woman
40. 46. which c. near to the Lord to minister to him
44. 15. they shall c. near to me to minister to me
16. they shall c. near to my table to minister to me
Amos 6. 3. which cause the seat of violence to c. near
Mal. 3. 5. and I will c. near to you to judgment
Luke 19. 41. when he was c. near he beheld the city
Acts 23. 15. and we, or he c. near, are ready to kill him

COME *nigh*.

Exod. 34. 30. but they were afraid to c. nigh him
Lev. 10. 3. I will be sanctified in all that c. nigh me
21. 21. no man that hath blemish shall c. nigh, 23.
Num. 18. 4. a stranger shall not c. nigh to you
Deut. 20. 2. when ye are c. nigh to battle, the priest
Luke 10. 9. kingdom of God is c. nigh unto you, 11.

COME *not*.

Exod. 19. 15. be ready, c. not at your wives
24. 2. but they shall not c. nigh, nor the people
Num. 14. 30. ye shall not c. into the land I sware
16. 12. Dathan and Abiram said, we will not c. up, 14.
Deut. 23. 10. unclean shall not c. within the camp
Josh. 3. 4. c. not near unto the ark, that ye may
23. 7. that ye c. not among these nations
Judg. 16. 17. there hath not c. a razor on mine head
2 Sam. 14. 29. Absalom sent for Joab, but he would
not c. he sent the second time, he would not c.
1 Kings 13. 22. carcase not c. to sepulchre of fathers
2 Kings 19. 32. king of Assyria shall not c. into this
city, nor shoot arrow there, 33. Isa. 37. 33, 34.
2 Chron. 35. 21. I c. not against thee this day
Ezra 10. 8. whosoever would not c. within three days
Neh. 13. 1. Moabite not c. into congregation for ever
Job 3. 6. let it not c. into the number of the months
13. 16. for an hypocrite shall not c. before him
Psal. 32. 6. in floods they shall not c. nigh to him
69. 27. let them not c. into thy righteousness
91. 7. thousands shall fall, but it shall not c. nigh thee
132. 3. I will not c. into the tabernacle of my house
Prov. 5. 8. c. not nigh the door of her house
Isa. 7. 17. Lord shall bring days that have not c.
25. there shall not c. the fear of briars and thorns
28. 15. the overflowing scourge shall not c. to me
32. 10. vintage shall fail, the gathering shall not c.
54. 14. far from terror, for it shall not c. near thee
65. 5. which say, stand by thyself, c. not near me
Jer. 37. 19. saying, the king of Babylon shall not c.
Ezek. 16. 16. like things shall not c. nor shall it be so
44. 13. they shall not c. near to me to do office
Hos. 4. 15. c. not ye unto Gilgal, nor go to Beth-
9. 4. their soul shall not c. into house of the Lord
Zech. 14. 18. and if the family of Egypt c. not
Mat. 22. 3. sent to call, and they would not c.
Mark 2. 4. they could not c. nigh for press, Luke 8. 19.
Luke 14. 20. I have married a wife, I cannot c.
John 5. 24. and shall not c. into condemnation
40. ye will not c. to me that ye might have life
7. 34. where I am, thither ye cannot c. 36.
11. 56. think ye that he will not c. to the feast?
15. 22. if I had not c. they had not had sin
16. 7. if I go not away, the Comforter will not c.
1 Cor. 4. 18. as though I would not c. to you

COME *out*.

Gen. 15. 14. afterward shall c. out with great sub-[stance
17. 6. and kings shall c. out of thee, 35. 11.
24. 13. the daughters of city c. out to draw water
Lev. 16. 17. till he c. out and have made atonement
Num. 11. 20. shall eat till it c. out at your nostrils
12. 4. c. out ye three unto tabernacle of congregat.
20. 18. lest I c. out against thee with the sword
22. 5. there is a people c. out of Egypt, 11.
33. 38. Aaron died fortieth year after Israel c. out
Deut. 28. 7. c. out one way, and flee seven ways
Judg. 9. 15. if not, let fire c. out of the bramble
29. he said, increase thine army and c. out
1 Sam. 2. 3. let not arrogancy c. out of your mouth
11. 3. to-morrow we will c. out unto thee, 10.
24. 14. after whom is the king of Israel c. out?
2 Sam. 16. 7. c. out, c. out, thou bloody man
1 Kings 6. 1. in the 480th year after Isr. were c. out
20. 17. saying, there are men c. out of Samaria
2 Kings 5. 11. he will c. out to me, and lay his hand
18. 31. make an agreement and c. out, Isa. 36. 16.
19. 9. behold, he is c. out to fight against thee
Psal. 14. 7. O that salvation were c. out of Zion!
68. 31. princes shall c. out of Egypt, Ethiopia
Prov. 12. 13. but the just shall c. out of trouble
Isa. 34. 3. their stink shall c. out of their carcases
Nah. 1. 11. there is one c. out that imagineth evil
Mat. 5. 26. by no means c. out till thou hast paid
26. 55. are ye c. out as against a thief with swords
and staves to take me? Mark 14. 48. Luke 22. 52.
Mark 1. 25. hold thy peace, c. out of him, Luke 4. 35.
5. 8. said, c. out, thou unclean spirit, Luke 8. 29.
John 1. 46. can any good thing c. out of Nazareth?
7. 41. some said, shall Christ c. out of Galilee?
Acts 16. 18. in the name of Jesus to c. out of her
Rom. 11. 26. there shall c. out of Zion the Deliverer
2 Cor. 6. 17. wherefore c. out from among them
Heb. 7. 5. though they c. out of the loins of Abraham
Rev. 16. 13. saw spirits c. out of the mouth of dragon
18. 4. a voice saying, c. out of her, my people

COME *to pass*.

Exod. 4. 8. it shall c. to pass if they will not believe, 9.
Num. 11. 23. whether my word shall c. to pass or not
17. 5. c. to pass the man's rod I choose shall blossom
Deut. 7. 12. shall c. to pass if ye heark. 11. 13. | 28. 1.
13. 2. and the sign or the wonder c. to pass
Josh. 23. 14. all are c. to pass, no good thing failed
Judg. 13. 12. Manoah said, let thy words c. to pass
17. when thy sayings c. to pass we may do honour
21. 3. O Lord, why is this c. to pass in Israel, that
1 Kings 13. 32. the saying shall surely c. to pass
Isa. 7. 7. it shall not stand, nor shall it c. to pass
14. 24. as I have thought, so shall it c. to pass
42. 9. behold, the former things are c. to pass
Jer. 17. 24. it shall c. to pass if ye diligently hearken
32. 24. what thou hast spoken is c. to pass
Ezek. 12. 25. the word that I speak shall c. to pass
24. 14. I have spoken, it shall c. to pass, I will do it
Dan. 2. 29. maketh known to thee what shall c. to p.
Hos. 1. 5. c. to pass that I will break the bow of Isr.
Joel 2. 32. c. to pass that whosoever shall call on L.
Amos 8. 9. c. to p. I will cause sun to go down at noon
Zech. 6. 15. this shall c. to p. if ye diligently obey
7. 13. therefore it is c. to pass, that as he cried
Mat. 24. 6. all these things must c. to pass, end not yet
Mark 11. 23. things which he saith shall c. to pass
13. 29. when ye shall see these c. to p. Luke 21. 31.
Luke 2. 15. and see this thing which is c. to pass
21. 7. what sign when these things shall c. to p. 28.
24. 12. wondering in himself at what was c. to pass
18. hast not known the things which are c. to pass
John 13. 19. when it is c. to p. ye may believe, 14. 29.
Acts 3. 23. c. to p. that every soul that will not hear
Rev. 1. 1. to shew things must shortly c. to p. 22. 6.

COME *short*.

Rom. 3. 23. all have sinned and c. short of glory of G.
Heb. 4. 1. lest any of you should seem to c. short of it

COME *together*.

Job 9. 32. and we should c. together in judgment
19. 12. his troops c. together against me and encamp
Jer. 3. 18. shall c. together out of land of the north
50. 4. Isr. and Jud. shall c. together, going and weep.
Acts 1. 6. when they were c. together, 28. 17.
10. 27. he found many that were c. together
19. 32. knew not wherefore they were c. together
21. 22. the multitude must needs c. together
1 Cor. 7. 5. c. together again, that Sat. tempt you not
11. 17. you c. together, not for better but for worse
18. when ye c. together in church, 20. 33. | 14. 26.
34. that ye c. not together to condemnation
14. 23. if whole church be c. together to one place

COME *up*.

Exod. 19. 13. trumpet sound they shall c. up to mount
24. thou shalt c. up, thou and Aaron with thee
24. 12. c. up to me into the mount, and be there
33. 5. I will c. up into midst of thee in a moment
34. 2. and c. up in the morning to mount Sinai
3. no man shall c. up with thee nor be seen
Num. 20. 5. why have ye made us c. up out Egypt?
Josh. 4. 16. that the priests c. up out of Jordan, 17, 18.
10. 4. c. up to me, and help me to smite Gibeon
6. c. up to us quickly, save us, and help us
Judg. 1. 3. Judah said, c. up with me into my lot
15. 10. Judah said, why are ye c. up against us?
16. 18. Delilah sent, saying, c. up this once
1 Sam. 14. 10. if they say, c. up to us, we will go up
17. 25. said, have ye seen this man that is c. up?
1 Kings 1. 35. then ye shall c. up after him, that he
20. 22. the king of Syria will c. up against thee
2 Kings 16. 7. c. up and save me from king of Syria
18. 25. am I now c. up without L. Isa. 36. 10.
2 Chr. 20. 16. behold, they c. up by the cliff of Ziz
Job 7. 9. that goeth to the grave, shall c. up no more
Prov. 25. 7. better that it be said, c. up hither
Isa. 5. 6. but there shall c. up briers and thorns
8. 7. and he shall c. up over all his channels
14. 8. since laid down no fellow is c. up against us
60. 7. they shall c. up with accept. on mine altar
Jer. 9. 21. for death is c. up into our windows
49. 19. behold, he shall c. up like a lion, 50. 44.
22. behold, he shall c. up and fly as the eagle
51. 27. cause the horses to c. up as caterpillars
42. the sea is c. up upon Babylon, she is covered
Lam. 1. 14. are wreathed, and c. up upon my neck
Ezek. 24. 8. that it might cause fury to c. up to take
37. 12. and cause you to c. up out of your graves
38. 16. thou shalt c. up against my people Israel
47. † 12. on the bank shall c. up all trees
Hos. 1. 11. and they shall c. up out of the land
10. 8. the thistle shall c. up on their altars
13. 15. the wind of Lord shall c. up from wildern.
Joel 2. 20. his stink and ill savour shall c. up
3. 9. let all men of war draw near, let them c. up
12. let heathen c. up to the valley of Jehoshaphat
Amos 4. 10. I made the stink of your camps to c. up
Obad. 21. saviours shall c. up on mount Zion to judge
Jonah 1. 2. their wickedness is c. up before me
4. 6. the Lord made a gourd to c. up over Jonah
Mic. 2. 13. the breaker is c. up before them
Nah. 2. 1. he that dasheth in pieces is c. up
Zech. 14. 17. it shall be, that whoso will not c. up
Zech. 14. 18. if the family of Egypt go not up, c. not
Acts 8. 31. he desired Phil. to c. up and sit with him
39. when they were c. up out of the water
10. 4. Cornelius, thy alms are c. up before God
Rev. 4. 1. c. up hither, and I will shew thee, 11. 12.

COME, *Passive*.

Gen. 6. 13. the end of all flesh is c. before me
18. 5. for therefore are ye c. to your servant
21. according to the cry which is c. to me
42. 21. therefore is this distress c. upon us
Exod. 3. 9. cry of the children of Israel is c. to me
20. 20. fear not, for God is c. to prove you
Num. 22. 11. there is a people c. out of Egypt
Deut. 31. 11. when all Isr. is c. to appear before L.
Josh. 5. 14. as captain of the host of Lord am I c.
Judg. 16. 2. it was told, Samson is c. hither
1 Sam. 4. 7. for they said, God is c. into the camp
9. 16. looked on my peop. because their cry is c. to me
2 Sam. 1. 9. slay me, for anguish is c. upon me
19. 11. the speech of all Israel is c. to the king
2 Kings 4. 1. the creditor is c. to take my sons
5. 6. when this letter is c. to thee, I sent Naaman
8. 7. told him, saying, the man of God is c. hither
Ezra 9. 13. and after all that is c. upon us
Job 3. 25. the thing I greatly feared is c. 4. 5.
Psal. 44. 17. all this is c. upon us, yet we have not
53. 6. O that the salvation of Israel were c.
55. 5. fearfulness and trembling are c. upon me
69. 2. I am c. into deep waters, floods overflow me
102. 13. time to favour Zion, yea the set time is c.
Isa. 10. 28. he is c. to Aiath, he is passed to Migron
56. 1. for my salvat. is near to c. and my righteous.
60. 1. arise, shine, for thy light is c. and glory of L.
63. 4. and the year of my redeemed is c.
Jer. 40. 3. have sinned, therefore this is c. upon you
47. 5. baldness is c. on Gaza, Ashkelon is cut off
50. 27. woe to them, for their day is c. the time of
31. thy day is c. the time that I will visit thee
51. 13. that dwellest on many waters, thy end is c.
Lam. 4. 18. our days are fulfilled, our end is c.
5. 1. remember, O Lord, what is c. upon us
Ezek. 7. 2. an end, the end is c. upon the land, 6.
5. thus saith L. an evil, an only evil, behold is c.
7. the morn. is c. upon thee, O thou that dwellest
10. behold the day, behold, it is c. 39. 8.
17. 12. the king of Babylon is c. to Jerusalem
21. 25. thou wicked prince whose day is c. 29.
Dan. 9. 13. as it is written, all this evil is c. on us
Amos 8. 2. the end is c. on my people of Israel
Mic. 1. 9. he is c. to gate of my people, to Jerusalem
Mat. 3. 7. who warned you to flee from wrath to c.?
12. 28. the kingdom of God is c. unto you
44. when he is c. he findeth it empty, swept
18. 11. Son of man is c. to save that which was lost
Mark 1. 24. art thou c. to destroy us? Luke 4. 34.
4. 29. he puts in the sickle, because the harvest is c.
14. 8. she is c. aforehand to anoint my body
41. sleep on now, it is enough, the hour is c.
Luke 7. 34. the Son of man is c. eating and drink.
15. 27. thy brother is c. father hath killed fatted calf
19. 9. this day is salvation c. to this house
10. the Son of man is c. to seek and to save lost
John 3. 19. that light is c. into the world, men loved
4. 25. when he is c. he will tell us all things
11. 28. the Master is c. and calleth for thee
12. 23. the hour is c. Son of man be glorified, 17. 1.
15. 26. when the Comforter is c. whom I will send
16. 8. when he is c. he will reprove the world of sin
13. when the Spirit of truth is c. he will guide
21. a woman hath sorrow because her hour is c.
Rom. 11. 11. salvation is c. unto the Gentiles
16. 19. for your obedience is c. abroad among all
1 Cor. 13. 10. when that which is perfect is c. then
Gal. 3. 25. but after that faith is c. we are no longer
Col. 1. 6. which gospel is c. to you, as it is in all world
1 John 4. 2. that Jesus Christ is c. in the flesh
3. every spirit that confesseth not that Jesus Christ
is c. in the flesh is not of God, 2 John 7.
5. 20. we know that the Son of God is c. and given
Rev. 6. 17. for the great day of his wrath is c.
11. 18. and thy wrath is c. and time of the dead
12. 10. now is c. salvat. and strength, and king. of G.
14. 7. fear God, for the hour of his judgment is c.
18. 17. in one hour, so great riches is c. to nought
19. 7. for marriage of the Lamb is c. and his wife

I am COME, *or am I* COME.

Exod. 18. 6. I thy father in law am c. to thee
Num. 22. 38. Balaam said, lo I am c. to thee
Deut. 26. 3. I am c. into the country the Lord sware
1 Sam. 16. 2. I am c. to sacrifice to the Lord, 5.
2 Sam. 14. 15. now that I am c. to speak of this thing
32. to say, wherefore am I c. from Geshur?
19. 20. I am c. first to meet my lord the king
Ps. 69. 2. I am c. into deep waters where the floods
Eccl. 1. 16. I communed, lo, I am c. to great estate
Cant. 5. 1. I am c. into my gar. my sister, my spouse
Dan. 9. 23. and I am c. to shew thee, 10. 14.
10. 12. thy words were heard, I am c. for thy w.
Mat. 5. 17. think not I am c. to destroy the law
9. 13. I am not c. to call the righteous but sinners
10. 34. think not that I am c. to send peace on earth
35. I am c. to set a man at variance against father
Luke 12. 51. suppose ye that I am c. to give peace
John 1. 31. therefore am I c. baptizing with water
5. 43. I am c. in my Father's name, ye receive me not
7. 28. I am not c. of myself, he that sent me is true
9. 39. Jesus said, for judgm. I am c. into this world
10. 10. I am c. that they might have life, and abund.
12. 46. I am c. a light into the world, whoso believes
16. 28. I am c. into the world, again I leave world

COME, joined with *time*.

Gen. 30. 33. shall my righteous. answer in time to c.
Exod. 13. 14. when thy son asketh thee in time to c.
saying, what is this? Deut. 6. 20. Josh. 4. 6, 21.
Josh. 22. 24. in time to c. your childr. might speak, 28.
1 Sam. 1. 20. time was c. after Hannah conceived
Psal. 102. 13. time to favour Zion, the set time is c.
Prov. 31. 25. she shall rejoice in time to c.
Cant. 2. 12. time of singing of birds is c. voice of turtle
Isa. 13. 22. her time is near to c. her days shall not
30. 8. note in a book that it may be for time to c.
42. 23. who will hearken and hear for time to c.

Ezek. 7. 7. the time is c. the day of trouble is near
Hag. 1. 2. the time is not c. the Lord's house be built
Luke 9. 51. the time was c. he should be received up
Gal. 4. 4. but when the fulness of time was c.
1 Tim. 6. 19. laying up good foundation against time to c.
1 Pet. 4. 17. the time is c. that judgm. must begin

Yet COME.

Deut. 12. 9. for ye are not as yet c. to rest L. giveth
John 2. 4. Jesus saith, woman, my hour is not yet c.
7. 6. Jesus said to them, my time is not yet c. 8.
30. because his hour was not yet c. 8. 20.
11. 30. Jesus was not yet c. into the town
Rev. 17. 10. five are fallen, the other is not yet c.

COMELY.

1 Sam. 16. 18. David, a son of Jesse, a c. person
Job 41. 12. I will not conceal his c. proportion
Psal. 33. 1. praise is c. for the upright, 147. 1.
Prov. 30. 29. yea, four are c. in going
Eccl. 5. 18. it is c. for one to eat, drink, and enjoy
Cant. 1. 5. I am black but c. O daughters of Jerus.
10. thy cheeks are c. with rows of jewels
2. 14. thy voice is sweet, and thy countenance is c.
4. 3. thy lips are like scarlet, thy speech is c.
6. 4. thou art c. O my love, as Jerusalem, terrible as
Isa. 4. 2. fruit of the earth shall be excellent and c.
Jer. 6. 2. I likened daughter of Zion to a c. woman
1 Cor. 7. 35. but I speak for that which is c.
11. 13. is it c. that a woman pray to God uncovered?
12. 24. for our c. parts have no need, but God

COMELINESS.

Isa. 53. 2. he hath no form nor c. nor beauty, that
Ezek. 16. 14. for it was perfect through my c.
27. 10. they of Persia and Lud set forth thy c.
Dan. 10. 8. my c. was turned in me into corruption
1 Cor. 12. 23. our uncomely parts have more abund. c.

COMERS.

Heb. 10. 1. can never make the c. thereunto perfect

COMEST.

Gen. 10. 19. was from Sidon as thou c. to Gerar
13. 10. like the land of Egypt, as thou c. to Zoar
24. 41. when thou c. to my kindred, if they give not
Deut. 2. 19. thou c. nigh the children of Ammon
20. 10. when thou c. nigh to city to fight against it
28. 6. blessed shalt thou be when thou c. in
19. cursed shalt thou be when thou c. in
Judg. 17. 9. Micah said to Levite, whence c. thou?
19. 17. the old man said to Levite, whence c. thou?
1 Sam. 16. 4. and said, c. thou peaceably? 1 Kin. 2. 13.
17. 43. am I a dog, that thou c. to me with staves?
45. thou c. to me with a sword and with a spear
2 Sam. 3. 13. bring Michal when thou c. to see me
1 Kings 19. 15. when thou c. anoint Hazael to be king
2 Kings 5. 25. Elisha said, whence c. thou, Gehazi?
Job 1. 7. whence c. thou? Satan answered, 2. 2.
Jer. 51. 61. when thou c. to Babylon and shalt see
Jonah 1. 8. what thy occupation? whence c. thou?
Mat. 3. 14. to be baptized of thee, and c. thou to me?
Luke 23. 42. rememb. me when c. into thy kingdom

COMETH.

Gen. 37. 19. they said, behold this dreamer c.
Lev. 11. 34. on which such water c. is unclean
Deut. 18. 8. beside what c. of sale of his patrimony
23. 13. turn backward cover that which c. from thee
1 Sam. 4. 3. when ark c. among us, it may save us
9. 6. all that the man of God saith c. surely to pass
20. 27. wherefore c. not the son of Jesse to meat?
29. therefore he c. not to the king's table
1 Kings 14. 5. for when she c. in will feign herself
2 Kings 9. 18. came to them, but he c. not again, 20.
11. 8. be ye with the king as he c. in, 2 Chr. 23. 7.
Job 3. 21. which long for death, and it c. not
28. 20. whence c. wisdom, where understanding?
Psal. 30. 5. weeping for night, but joy c. in morning
62. 1. my soul waiteth on God, from him c. my salv.
75. 6. promotion c. not from the east nor west
96. 13. before Lord, for he c. to judge the earth
118. 26. blessed is he that c. in name of the Lord
121. 1. my eyes to hills, from whence c. my help
2. my help c. from the Lord who made heaven
Prov. 1. 26. I will mock when your fear c.
27. when your destruction c. as a whirlwind
11. 2. when pride c. then c. shame, but with lowly
18. 3. when the wicked c. then c. contempt
Eccl. 6. 4. he c. in with vanity, departeth in darkness
11. 8. if a man live many years, all that c. is vanity
Cant. 2. 8. he c. leaping upon the mountains
Isa. 13. 9. the day of the Lord c. with wrath
30. 13. whose breaking c. suddenly at an instant
27. the name of the Lord c. from far, burning
44. † 19. fall down to that which c. on a tree
62. 11. say ye to Zion, behold, thy salvation c.
63. 1. who is this that c. from Edom, from Bozra?
Jer. 17. 6. like heathen, he shall not see when good c.
8. and shall not see when heat c. but her leaf
43. 11. when he c. he shall smite the land of Egypt
Lam. 3. 37. who is he that saith, and it c. to pass
5. † 4. our water for money, our wood c. for price
Ezek. 14. 4. and c. to a prophet to inquire, 7.
20. 32. that which c. in your mind shall not be
21. 7. for the tidings, because it c. behold it c.
24. 24. when this c. you shall know I am the Lord
33. 31. they come to thee as the people c. and sit
33. when this c. to pass, then shall they know
47. 9. every thing shall live whither the rivers c.
Dan. 11. 16. that c. against him shall do exploits
12. 12. blessed is he that c. to the 1335 days
Hos. 7. 1. the thief c. in, and the troop of robbers
Joel 2. 1. day of the L. c. Zech. 14. 1. 1 Thess. 5. 2.
Mic. 5. 6. deliver us from the Assyrian when he c.
Mal. 4. 1. the day c. that shall burn, day that c.
Mat. 3. 11. he that c. after me is might. than I, whose shoes not worthy to bear, Mark 1. 7. Luke 3. 16.
5. 37. whatsoever is more than these c. of evil
8. 9. I say to another, come, and he c. Luke 7. 8.
13. 19. then c. the wicked one, and catcheth away
21. 5. behold, thy king c. unto thee, John 12. 15.
9. blessed is he that c. in name of Lord, hosanna in the highest, Mark 11. 9. Luke 13. 35. | 19. 38.
25. 19. after a long time lord of those servants c.
Mark 6. 48. he c. to them walking on the sea
8. 38. be ashamed when he c. in glory of his Father
9. 12. Elias c. first, and restoreth all things
14. 43. while he spake c. Judas one of the twelve
Luke 6. 47. whoso c. to me, and heareth my sayings
12. 37. the Lord when he c. shall find watching
40. Son of man c. at an hour when ye think not
43. his lord, when he c. shall find so doing
55. ye say, there will be heat, and it c. to pass
17. 20. kingdom of God c. not with observation
18. 8. Son of man c. shall he find faith on earth?
John 3. 8. but thou canst not tell whence it c.
20. nor c. to the light, lest his deeds be reproved
21. he that doth the truth, c. to the light
4. 21. woman, believe me, the hour c. 23. | 16. 32.
6. 35. he that c. to me shall never hunger, 37.
45. man that hath learned of the Father c. to me
7. 27. when Christ c. no man knoweth, 31.
42. said, that Christ c. of the seed of David
9. 4. the night c. when no man can work
14. 6. no man c. to the Father but by me
16. 2. the time c. that whosoever killeth you
25. the time c. I shall no more speak in proverbs
32. the hour c. that ye shall be scattered
Acts 10. 32. who when he c. shall speak to thee
Rom. 4. 9. c. this blessedness on the circumcision only
10. 17. so then, faith c. by hearing, hearing by word
1 Cor. 15. 24. then c. the end, when he shall have
2 Cor. 11. 28. besides that which c. on me daily
Eph. 5. 6. for these things c. the wrath of God upon the children of disobedience, Col. 3. 6.
1 Thess. 5. 2. day of the Lord so c. as a thief in night
Heb. 11. 6. he that c. to God must believe that he is
Jude 14. the Lord c. with 10,000 of his saints
Rev. 1. 7. he c. with clouds, every eye shall see him
17. 10. when he c. he must continue a short space

COMETH down.

Isa. 55. 10. as the rain c. down from heaven
John 6. 33. bread of God is he which c. down, 50.
James 1. 17. every good and perfect gift c. down
Rev. 3. 12. new Jerusalem which c. down from God

COMETH forth.

Gen. 24. 43. when the virgin c. forth to draw water
Exod. 4. 14. also behold he c. forth to meet thee
8. 20. before Pharaoh, lo, he c. forth to the water
Judg. 11. 31. whatsoever c. forth of the doors
1 Sam. 11. 7. whosoever c. not forth after Saul
Job 5. 6. though affliction c. not forth of the dust
14. 2. he c. forth like a flower, and is cut down
Isa. 28. 29. this also c. forth from the Lord
Ezek. 33. 30. hear what words c. forth from Lord
Mic. 1. 3. behold the Lord c. forth out of his place

COMETH nigh.

Num. 1. 51. Levites set up tabernacle, the stranger that c. nigh shall be put to death, 3. 10, 38. | 18. 7.

COMETH out.

Exod. 28. 35. be heard when he c. out that he die not
Num. 12. 12. flesh is half consumed when he c. out
Deut. 28. 57. her eye evil toward young that c. out
1 Kings 8. 41. a stranger that c. out of a far country
Job 20. 25. it is drawn, and c. out of the body
37. 22. fair weather c. out of the north, with God is
Cant. 3. 6. who is this that c. out of the wilderness?
Isa. 26. 21. the Lord c. out of his place to punish
42. 5. spread forth earth, and that which c. out of it
Jer. 46. 20. destruction cometh, it c. out of the north
Ezek. 4. 12. shall bake it with dung that c. out of man
Mat. 15. 11. but that which c. out of the mouth, this defileth a man, Mark 7. 20.
24. 27. for as the lightning c. out of the east

COMETH up.

1 Sam. 28. 14. and she said, an old man c. up covered
Cant. 8. 5. who is this that c. up from wilderness?
Isa. 24. 18. and he that c. up out of midst of the pit
Jer. 46. 7. who is this that c. up as a flood?
50. 3. out of north there c. up a nation against her
Hab. 3. 16. when he c. up to people, will invade them
Mat. 17. 27. cast an hook, take up the fish first c. up

COMFORT, Substantive.

Job 6. 10. then should I yet have c. yea, I would
10. 20. let me alone, that I may take c. a little
Psal. 119. 50. this is my c. in my affliction, thy word
76. let thy merciful kindness be for my c.
Isa. 57. 6. should I receive c. in these?
Ezek. 16. 54. in that thou art a c. to them
Mat. 9. 22. daughter, be of good c. Luke 8. 48.
Mark 10. 49. be of good c. rise, he calleth thee
Acts 9. 31. walking in the c. of the Holy Ghost
Rom. 15. 4. through patience and c. of the scriptures
1 Cor. 14. 3. speaketh to men to exhortation and c.
2 Cor. 1. 3. blessed be God, even the God of all c.
4. by the c. wherewith we are comforted of God
7. 4. great is my glorying of you, I am filled with c.
13. therefore we were comforted in your c.
13. 11. brethren, be perfect, be of good c.
Phil. 2. 1. if there be therefore any c. of love
19. that I also may be of good c. when I know
Col. 4. 11. these only, which have been a c. to me

COMFORT, Verb.

Gen. 5. 29. this same shall c. us concerning our work
18. 5. c. ye your hearts, after that you shall pass on
27. 42. Esau as touching thee doth c. himself
37. 35. all his sons and daughters rose up to c. him
Judg. 19. 5. c. thy heart with a morsel of bread, 8.
2 Sam. 10. 2. David sent to c. him, 1 Chron. 19. 2.
1 Chron. 7. 22. and his brethren came to c. him
19. 2. servants of David came to Hanun to c. him
Job 2. 11. his friends came to mourn with and c. him
7. 13. when I say, my bed shall c. me, my couch
9. 27. if I say, I will forget, I will c. myself
21. 34. how then c. ye in vain, seeing in answers
Psal. 23. 4. thy rod and thy staff, they c. me
71. 21. thou shalt increase and c. me on every side
119. † 76. let thy merciful kindness c. me
82. my eyes fail, saying, when wilt thou c. me?
Cant. 2. 5. c. me with apples, for I am sick of love
Isa. 22. 4. look away from me, labour not to c. me
40. 1. c. ye, c. ye my people, saith your God
51. 3. Lord shall c. Zion, he will c. her waste places
19. two things are come, by whom shall I c. thee?
61. 2. he hath sent me to c. all that mourn
66. 13. so will I c. you, ye shall be in Jerusalem
Jer. 8. 18. when I would c. myself, heart is faint in me
16. 7. nor shall men tear to c. them for the dead
31. 13. I will c. them, make rejoice from sorrow
Lam. 1. 2. among lovers she hath none to c. her, 17
21. they heard that I sigh, there is none to c. me
2. 13. what shall I equal to thee, that I may c. thee?
Ezek. 14. 23. they shall c. you when ye see their ways
Zech. 1. 17. Lord shall yet c. Zion, and choose Jerus.
10. 2. diviners told false dreams, they c. in vain
John 11. 19. to c. them concerning their brother
2 Cor. 1. 4. that ye may be able to c. them who
2. 7. ye ought rather to forgive and c. him
Eph. 6. 22. and that he might c. your hearts
Col. 4. 8. he might know your estates, c. your hearts
1 Thess. 3. 2. to c. you concerning your faith
4. 18. wherefore c. one another with these words
5. 11. wherefore c. yourselves together and edify
14. c. the feeble-minded, support the weak
2 Thess. 2. 17. now our Lord Jesus c. your hearts

COMFORTABLE.

2 Sam. 14. 17. the word of my Lord shall now be c.
Zech. 1. 13. Lord answered the angel with c. words

COMFORTABLY.

2 Sam. 19. 7. go forth and speak c. to thy servants
2 Chron. 30. 22. he spake c. to all the Levites
32. 6. he set captains over the people, and spake c.
Isa. 40. 2. speak ye c. to Jerusalem, cry to her
Hos. 2. 14. I will allure her, and speak c. to her

COMFORTED.

Gen. 24. 67. Isaac was c. after his mother's death
37. 35. Jac. refus. to be c. for he said, I go to grave
38. 12. Jud. was c. and went up to his sheep shear.
50. 21. Joseph c. his brethren, and spake kindly
Ruth 2. 13. let me find fav. for that thou hast c. me
2 Sam. 12. 24. David c. Bath-sheba his wife
13. 39. for he was c. concerning Amnon
Job 42. 11. all his brethren c. him over all the evil
Psal. 77. 2. my sore ran, my soul refused to be c.
86. 17. because thou, Lord, hast holpen me and c. me
119. 52. I remembered thy judgments, have c. mys.
Isa. 49. 13. for God hath c. his people, 52. 9.
54. 11. oh, thou afflicted, tossed, and not c.
66. 13. and ye shall be c. in Jerusalem
Jer. 31. 15. Rachel weeping, refus. to be c. for child.
Ezek. 5. 13. I will cause fury to rest, I will be c.
14. 22. ye shall be c. concerning all the evil
31. 16. all that drink water be c. in parts of earth
32. 31. Pharaoh shall see them, and shall be c.
Mat. 2. 18. would not be c. because they were not
5. 4. bless. are they that mourn, for they shall be c.
Luke 16. 25. now he is c. and thou art tormented
John 11. 31. the Jews which c. her, saw Mary rise
Acts 16. 40. when they had seen brethren, c. them
20. 12. brought young man alive, were not a lit. c.
Rom. 1. 12. that I may be c. together with you
1 Cor. 14. 31. that all may learn, and all may be c.
2 Cor. 1. 4. the comfort wherewith we are c. of G.
7. 6. God c. us by the coming of Titus
7. the consolation wherewith he was c. in you
13. therefore we were c. in your comfort
Col. 2. 2. that their hearts might be c. being knit
1 Thess. 2. 11. ye know how he exhorted and c. you
3. 7. we were c. over you in all our affliction

COMFORTEDST.

Isa. 12. 1. thine anger is turned away, and thou c. me

COMFORTER, S.

2 Sam. 10. 3. that he hath sent c. to thee, 1 Chr. 19. 3
Job 16. 2. heard many things, miserable c. are ye all
Psal. 69. 20. I looked for c. but found none
Eccl. 4. 1. tears of the oppressed, and they had no c.
Lam. 1. 9. she came down wonderfully, she had no c
16. c. that should relieve my soul is far from me
Nah. 3. 7. whence shall I seek c. for thee?
John 14. 16. he shall give you another C. to abide
26. but the C. which is Holy Ghost, shall teach
15. 26. when the C. is come || 16. 7. C. will not come

COMFORTETH.

Job 29. 25. I dwelt, as one that c. the mourners
Isa. 51. 12. I, even I, am he that c. you, who art thou
66. 13. as one whom mother c. will I comfort you
2 Cor. 1. 4. who c. us in all our tribulations
7. 6. God that c. those that are cast down

COMFORTLESS.

John 14. 18. I will not leave you c. will come to you

COMFORTS.

Psal. 94. 19. of my thoughts, thy c. delight my soul
Isa. 57. 18. I will lead him also, and restore c. to him

COMING.

Gen. 30. 30. the Lord hath blessed thee since my c.
43. † 20. O sir, c. down we came to buy food
Lev. 14. † 48. if the priest c. in shall come and look
Num. 22. 16. let nothing hinder thee from c.
Judg. 5. 28. why is his chariot so long in c.?
1 Sam. 16. 4. elders of the town tremble at his c.
29. 6. thy going and c. in with me since day of c.
2 Sam. 3. 25. to know thy going out and thy c. in
2 Kings 13. 20. invaded the land at c. in of the year
19. 27. I know thy going out and c. in, Isa. 37. 28.
Psal. 37. 13. for he seeth that his day is c.
121. 8. Lord shall preserve thy going out and c. in
Isa. 14. 9. hell is moved for thee to meet thee at c.
44. 7. the things that are c. let them shew to them
Jer. 8. 7. and swallow observe the time of their c.
Dan. 4. 23. saw an holy one c. down from heaven
Mic. 7. 15. accord. to the days of the c. out of Egypt
Mal. 3. 2. who may abide the day of his c.?
4. 5. before the c. of the great day of the Lord
Mat. 16. 28. till they see Son of man c. in his kingd.
24. 3. tell us what shall be the sign of thy c.?
27. so shall the c. of the Son of man be, 37, 39.
30. when they shall see the Son of man c. in clouds, 26. 64. Mark 13. 26. | 14. 62. Luke 21. 27
48. shall say, my Lord delayeth his c. Luke 12. 45
25. 27. at my c. have received my own, Luke 19. 23
Mark 6. 31. for there were many c. and going
Luke 9. 42. as he was yet c. the devil tare him
18. 5. lest by her continual c. she weary me
John 5. 7. while I am c. another steppeth before me
25. the hour is c. 28. || 10. 12. seeth the wolf c.
Acts 1. † 8. receive the power of the Holy Ghost c
7. 52. shewed before of the c. of the just one
9. 28. he was with them c. in and going out
10. 25. as Peter was c. in Cornelius met him
13. 24. when John had preached before his c.

1 Cor. 1. 7. waiting for the c. of our Lord Jesus
15. 23. afterward they that are Christ's at his c.
16. 17. I am glad of c. of Stephanus and Fortunatus
2 Cor. 7. 6. God comforted us by the c. of Titus
7. not by his c. only, but by the consolation
Phil. 1. 26. be more abundant by my c. to you again
1 Thess. 2. 19. are not ye our rejoicing at our Ld's c.
3. 13. hearts unblameable at the c. of our Lord
4. 15. we who remain to the c. of our Lord
5. 23. preserved blameless to the c. of our Lord
2 Thess. 2. 1. we beseech you by the c. of our Lord
8. and shall destroy with the brightness of his c.
9. even him whose c. is after the working of Satan
Jam. 5. 7. be patient, brethren, to the c. of the Lord
8. for the c. of the Lord draweth nigh
1 Pet. 2. 4. to whom c. as unto a living stone
2 Pet. 1. 16. make known power and c. of our Lord J.
3. 4. saying, where is the promise of his c.?
12. looking and hasting to the c. of the day of God
1 John 2. 28. not be ashamed before him at his c.
Rev. 13. 11. beheld another beast c. up out of earth
21. 2. new Jerusalem c. down from God out of hea- [ven

COMINGS.

Ezek. 43. 11. shew them the goings out and c. in

COMMAND.

2 Sam. 23. † 23. David set Benaiah at his c.
Job 39. 27. doth the eagle mount up at thy c.?

COMMAND

Is referred, (I) To God, *whose command extendeth to the earth*, Psal. 33. 9. *To the heavens*, Psal. 148. 5. *To his people*, Exod. 34. 11. *To the adversaries of the church*, Lam. 1. 17. *To the clouds*, Isaiah 5. 6. *To serpents*, Amos 9. 3. *To unclean spirits*, Mark 1. 27. It signifies, [1] *His authority and power over his creatures*, Psal. 148. 5. [2] *His will and readiness to help his own children in their distress*, Psal. 42. 8. [3] *To require due obedience to his laws*, Deut. 11. 22. [4] *To procure, or work*, Psal. 44. 4. [5] *To enable and incline*, Job 36. 10. [6] *To restrain*, Isa. 5. 6. [7] *To appoint, or establish firmly*, Psalm. 111. 9. [8] *To stir up by his providence*, Isa. 13. 3. [9] *To give, or bestow*, Lev. 25. 21. *This word comprehendeth* instruction, prediction, exhortation, *and* consolation, Mat. 11. 1. compared with Mat. 10. 6, 17, 26, 40.

(II) To man, *as parents commanding their children*, Gen. 18. 19. | 50. 16. *Governors their officers*, Joshua 1. 10. *Kings their subjects*, 2 Chron. 14, 4. *Pastors their people*, 2 Thess. 3. 4, 6.

Gen. 18. 19. Abrah. will c. his child. and household
Exod. 8. 27. we will sacrifice as God shall c. us
18. 23. if thou do this thing, and God c. thee so
Num. 9. 8. I will hear what the Lord will c.
36. 6. this is the thing which the Lord doth c.
Deut. 28. 8. the Lord shall c. the blessing on thee
32. 46. ye shall c. your children to observe to do
Josh. 11. 15. so did Moses c. Joshua, and so he did
Psal. 42. 8. the Lord will c. his loving-kindness
44. 4. art my king, O God, c. deliverance for Jacob
Isa. 45. 11. concerning the work of my hands, c. me
Jer. 27. 4. c. them to say to their masters
Lam. 1. 10. heathen didst c. they should not enter
Mat. 4. 3. c. these stones be made bread, Luke 4. 3.
19. 7. why did Moses c. to give writing of divorcem.
27. 64. c. therefore that sepulchre be made sure
Mark 10. 3. he said to them, what did Moses c. you
Luke 8. 31. that he would not c. them to go into deep
9. 54. wilt thou we c. fire to come down from heaven
Acts 5. 28. saying, did not we straitly c. you
15. 5. and to c. them to keep the law of Moses
2 Thess. 3. 4. ye both do and will do things we c. you
6. we c. you, brethren, in name of our Lord Jesus
12. that are such we c. and exhort by our Ld. Jesus
1 Tim. 4. 11. these things c. and teach

I COMMAND.

Exod. 7. 2. shall speak all that I c. thee, Jer. 1. 7, 17.
34. 11. observe thou what I c. thee, Deut. 12. 28.
Lev. 25. 21. then I will c. my blessing upon you
Deut. 4. 2. ye shall not add to the word I c. you
7. 11. shalt keep command. I c. thee this day, to do them, 8. 11. | 10. 13. | 11. 8, 27. | 13. 18. | 30. 8.
21. 18. therefore I c. thee to do this thing, 22.
30. 16. I c. thee this day to love the Lord thy God
Isa. 5. 6. I will c. the clouds that they rain not
Jer. 11. 4. obey my voice, and do all which I c. you
34. 22. behold, I will c. saith the Lord, and cause
Amos 9. 3. thence will I c. serpent, he shall bite them
4. thence I c. the sword, and it shall slay them
9. I will c. and I will sift the house of Israel
John 15. 14. ye are my friends, if ye do what I c. you
17. these things I c. you, that ye love one another
Acts 16. 18. I c. thee in the name of Jesus Christ
1 Cor. 7. 10. to the married I c. yet not I, but Lord

COMMANDED.

Gen. 45. 19. now thou art c. this do ye, take waggons
50. 12. Joseph's sons did to him as he c. them
Exod. 1. 17. midwives did not as king of Egypt c.
Lev. 10. 13. eat it in the holy place, for so I am c.
Deut. 1. 18. I c. you at that time all things, 3. 18, 21.
Josh. 4. 8. the children of Israel did as Joshua c.
8. 8. set the city on fire, see I have c. you
22. 2. ye have obeyed my voice in all I c. you
Judg. 13. 14. all that I c. her, let her observe
1 Sam. 20. 29. my brother, he hath c. me to be there
21. 2. David said, the king c. me a business, and said
2 Sam. 13. 28. then kill Amnon, have not I c. you
21. 14. they performed all that the king c.
2 Kings 11. 9. according to all that Jehoiada priest c.
16. 16. thus did according to all that king Ahaz c.
1 Chron. 21. 17. is it not I c. people to be numbered
2 Chron. 8. 14. for so had David the man of God c.
14. 4. Asa c. Judah to seek L. God of their fathers
32. 12. Hezekiah || 33. 16. Manasseh c. Judah
Neh. 13. 19. I c. that the gates should be shut
22. I c. Levites to cleanse themselves, keep gates
Esth. 3. 2. for the king had so c. concerning Haman
12. was written according to all that Haman c.
4. 17. Mordecai did according as Esther c. him
8. 9. written according to all that Mordecai c.
Job 38. 12. hast thou c. the morning since thy days?

Isa. 48. 5. say, my molten image hath c. them
Jer. 35. 6. Jonadab our father c. us, 10, 14, 16, 18.
Ezek. 12. 7. and I did so as I was c. 37. 7.
Dan. 3. 4. cried, to you it is c. O people, nations
19. he c. that they should heat the furnace
6. 16. then the king c. and they brought Daniel
24. the king c. and they brought those men
Amos 2. 12. c. the prophets, saying, prophesy not
Mat. 14. 9. he c. it to be given her, Mark 6. 27.
19. he c. multitude to sit down, 15. 35. Mark 6. 39.
18. 25. his lord c. him to be sold, and all he had
21. 6. the disciples went and did as Jesus c. them
28. 20. teaching to observe all things I have c. you
Luke 9. 21. he c. them to tell no man that thing
Acts 10. 48. he c. them to be baptized in the name
25. 6. the next day Festus c. Paul to be brought
1 Cor. 14. 34. but are c. to be under obedience
1 Thess. 4. 11. work with your hands as we c. you
2 Thess. 3. 10. we c. you that if any would not work
Heb. 12. 20. they could not endure that which was c.
Rev. 9. 4. it was c. them not to hurt the grass

God COMMANDED.

Gen. 2. 16. God c. man to eat freely of every tree
6. 22. according to all that God c. him, so did he
7. 9. there went into the ark as God had c. Noah, 16. | 21. 4. Deut. 20. 17. Josh. 10. 40.
Deut. 5. 15. God c. thee to keep the sabbath-day
5. 32. observe to do as the Lord your God c. you
33. walk in all the ways the L. your God c. you
6. 1. which L. your God c. to teach you, 20. | 13. 5.
26. 16. this day the Lord thy God c. thee to keep
Judg. 4. 6. hath not Lord G. c. to go toward Tabor?
1 Chron. 14. 16. David therefore did as God c. him
2 Chr. 35. 21. God c. me, make haste, forbear thou
Ezra 7. 23. whatsoever is c. by the God of heaven
Psal. 68. 28. thy G. hath c. thy strength, strengthen
Mat. 15. 4. for God c. saying, honour thy father
Acts 10. 33. to hear all things that are c. thee of G.
2 Cor. 4. 6. G. who c. light to shine out of darkness

Lord COMMANDED.

Gen. 7. 5. Noah did according to all the Lord c.
Exod. 7. 6. Moses and Aaron did as the Lord c. them, 10, 20. | 12. 28, 50. Num. 17. 11.
16. 16. this is the thing Ld. c. 32. | 35. 4. Num. 30. 1.
34. as the Lord c. Moses, 34. 4. | 39. 1, 5, 7, &c. 40. 19, &c. Lev. 8. 9. | 9. 10.
Lev. 8. 4. Moses did as L. c. him, Num. 20. 27. | 27. 11.
Num. 36. 2. Lord c. my lord to give land to Israel
Deut. 6. 24. the Lord c. us to do all these statutes
9. 16. had turned aside out of the way Lord c. you
10. 5. the tables, there they be as the Lord c. me
1 Sam. 13. 14. L. c. him to be captain over people
2 Sam. 17. † 14. L. c. to defeat counsel of Ahithophel
24. 19. and David went up, as the Lord c.
1 Chr. 21. 27. L. c. the angel, he put up his sword
24. 19. the orderings as L. God of Israel c. him
Psal. 106. 34. concerning whom the Lord c. them
133. 3. for there the Lord c. the blessing, even life
Jer. 13. 5. I hid it by Euphrates, as the Lord c. me
Lam. 1. 17. the Lord hath c. concerning Jacob
Acts 13. 46, 47. we turn to Gentiles, so hath the L. c.

Lord or God COMMANDED, *implicitly*.

Gen. 3. 11. eaten of the tree I c. not to eat, 17.
Exod. 23. 15. as I c. thee in the time appointed
Lev. 7. 38. in the day he c. the children of Israel
10. 1. offered strange fire which he c. them not
Deut. 17. 3. hath served other gods, which I have not c. 18. 20. Jer. 19. 5. | 23. 32. | 29. 23.
Josh. 1. 9. have not I c. thee? be strong and of cour.
7. 11. transgressed my covenant I c. Judg. 2. 20.
13. 6. divide thou it by lot, as I have c. thee
2 Sam. 7. 7. whom I c. to feed my people, 1 Chr. 17. 6.
11. since the time that I c. judges, 1 Chr. 17. 10.
1 Kings 11. 10. had c. him concerning this thing
17. 4. I have c. the ravens to feed thee there
9. I have c. a widow woman there to sustain thee
1 Ch. 16. 15. be mindful of his covenant, the word which he c. to a thousand generations, Ps. 105. 8.
40. that it is written in the law, which he c. Israel
Psal. 7. 6. awake to the judgment that thou hast c.
33. 9. he spake and it was done, he c. and it stood fast
111. 9. hath c. his covenant for ever, holy is his name
119. 4. thou hast c. us to keep thy precepts diligently
138. thy testimonies that thou hast c. are righteous
148. 5. for the Lord c. and they were created
Isa. 13. 3. I have c. my sanctified ones, I have called
34. 16. for my mouth it hath c. and his spirit
45. 12. the heavens and all their host have I c.
Jer. 7. 23. but this thing c. I them, obey my voice
31. which I c. them not, 19. 5. | 32. 35.
11. 8. all words of covenant which I c. them to do
17. 22. but hallow the sabbath, as I c. your fathers
50. 21. do according to all that I have c. thee
Lam. 2. 17. his word that he had c. in days of old
Ezek. 9. 11. I have done as thou hast c. me
24. 18. I did in the morning as I was c. 37. 10.
Zech. 1. 6. my words which I c. did they not take
Mal. 4. 4. remember the law which I c. in Horeb
Luke 14. 22. Lord, it is done as thou hast c. and room
Acts 10. 42. he c. us to preach to the people

Moses COMMANDED.

Num. 16. 47. Aaron took as Moses had c. and ran
Deut. 31. 29. turn aside from the way I have c. you
33. 4. Moses c. us a law, even the inheritance
Josh. 1. 7. observe to do according to all Moses c.
22. 2. ye have kept all that Moses c. you
1 Chr. 15. 15. Moses c. according to word of the L.
Mat. 8. 4. offer the gift that Moses c. for a testimony
Mark 1. 44. offer for thy cleans. those things which Moses c. for a testimony to them, Luke 5. 14.
John 8. 5. Moses in law c. that such should be stoned

COMMANDEDST.

Neh. 1. 7. which thou c. thy servant Moses, 8.
9. 14. thou c. them precepts, statutes, and laws
Jer. 32. 23. they have done nothing that thou c.

COMMANDER.

Isa. 55. 4. given him for a leader and c. to people

COMMANDEST.

Josh. 1. 16. all that thou c. us we will do
18. whoso will not hearken in all that thou c.
Jer. 32. 23. have done nothing of all thou c. them
Acts 23. 3. c. me to be smitten contrary to the law

COMMANDETH.

Num. 32. 25. thy servants will do as my lord c.
Job 9. 7. God, who c. the sun, and it riseth not
36. 10. he c. that they return from iniquity
32. he covereth the light, and c. it not to shine
37. 12. that they may do whatever he c. them
Psal. 107. 25. he c. and raiseth the stormy wind
Lam. 3. 37. who saith, it cometh, when Ld. c. it not?
Amos 6. 11. Lord c. and he will smite great house
Mark 1. 27. he c. the unclean spirits, Luke 4. 36.
Luke 8. 25. he c. the winds, and they obey him
Acts 17. 30. now c. all men every where to repent

COMMANDING.

Gen. 49. 33. Jacob made an end of c. his sons
Mat. 11. 1. Jesus made an end of c. his disciples
Acts 24. 8. c. his accusers to come to thee
1 Tim. 4. 3. c. to abstain from meats God created

COMMANDMENT.

Exod. 34. 32. he gave them in c. all Lord had spoken
Num. 15. 31. broken his c. that soul shall be cut off
23. 20. behold, I have received c. to bless
27. 14. ye rebelled against my c. in the desert
Deut. 30. 11. this c. I command thee this day
1 Kings 2. 43. why hast thou not kept the c. I charged
2 Kings 18. 36. king's c. was, ans. not, Isa. 36. 21.
1 Chron. 12. 32. all their brethren were at their c.
28. 21. all the people will be wholly at thy c.
2 Chron. 8. 13. offering according to the c. of Moses
† 14. so was the c. of David the man of God
19. 10. what cause shall come between law and c.
30. 12. one heart to do the c. of king and princes
31. 5. and as soon as the c. came abroad, Israel
Ezra 8. 17. I sent them with c. to Iddo the chief
10. 3. of those that tremble at the c. of God
Neh. 11. 23. it was the king's c. concerning them
13. † 5. wine and oil, which was the c. of Levites
Esth. 1. 12. Vashti refused to come at the king's c.
2. 20. Esther did the c. of Mordecai, like as when
3. 3. why transgressest thou the king's c.?
9. 1. when king's c. drew nigh to be put in execution
Job 23. 12. nor gone back from the c. of his lips
Psal. 119. 96. but thy c. is exceeding broad
147. 15. he sendeth forth his c. upon earth
Prov. 6. 23. the c. is a lamp, and the law is light
8. 29. that the waters should not pass his c.
13. 13. he that feareth the c. shall be rewarded
19. 16. he that keepeth the c. keepeth his soul
Eccl. 8. 5. whoso keepeth c. shall feel no evil thing
Jer. 35. 14. but they obey their father Jonadab's c.
Dan. 3. 22. because the king's c. was urgent
9. 23. the c. came forth, and I am come to shew
Hos. 5. 11. because he willingly walked after the c.
Mal. 2. 1. now, O ye priests, this c. is for you
4. ye shall know that I have sent this c. to you
Mat. 15. 3. why do ye transgress the c. of God?
6. thus have ye made the c. of God of no effect
22. 36. Master, which is the great c. in the law?
38. this is the first and great c. Mark 12. 30.
Mark 7. 8. for laying aside the c. of God, ye hold
9. he said, full well ye reject the c. of God
12. 31. there is no other c. greater than these
Luke 15. 29. nor transgressed I at any time thy c.
23. 56. rested the sabbath-day according to the c.
John 10. 18. this c. have I received of my Father
12. 49. he gave me a c. what I should say
50. I know that his c. is life everlasting
14. 31. as the Father gave me c. even so I do
15. 12. my c. that ye love one another, 1 John 3. 23.
Acts 15. 24. to whom we gave no such c.
17. 15. receiving a c. to Silas to come to him
23. 30. and gave c. to his accusers also to say
25. 23. at Festus' c. Paul was brought forth
Rom. 7. 8. but sin taking occasion by the c. 11.
9. when the c. came, sin revived, and I died
10. c. which was ordained to life, I found to death
12. and the c. is holy, and just, and good
13. that sin by c. might become exceeding sinful
13. 9. if there be any other c. it is briefly in this
16. 26. according to the c. of the everlasting God
1 Cor. 7. 6. I speak this by permission, not of c.
2 Cor. 8. 8. I speak not by c. but by occasion of
Eph. 6. 2. which is the first c. with promise
1 Tim. 1. 1. by the c. of God our Saviour, Tit. 1. 3.
5. the end of the c. is charity, out of a pure heart
Heb. 7. 16. who is made not after law of a carnal c.
18. there is a disannulling of the c. going before
11. 22. Joseph gave c. concerning his bones
23. Moses hid, they were not afraid of the king's c.
2 Pet. 2. 21. to turn from holy c. delivered to them
3. 2. mindful of c. of us the apostles of the Lord
1 John 2. 7. but an old c. which ye have heard
3. † 11. this is the c. ye heard from the beginning
23. this is his c. that we should believe on the name
4. 21. this c. have we from him, he who loveth God
2 John 4. as we have received a c. from the Father
6. this is the c. that as ye have heard from beginn.

Give or given COMMANDMENT.

Exod. 25. 22. things which I will give thee in c.
Deut. 1. 3. the Lord had given him in c. unto them
Ezra 4. 21. give c. to cease till another c. be given
Psal. 71. 3. hast given c. to save me, thou my rock
Isa. 23. 11. the Lord hath given c. against the city
Nah. 1. 14. the Lord hath given c. concerning thee
John 11. 57. given c. if any knew where he were

Keep COMMANDMENT, *see* KEEP.

COMMANDMENT *of the Lord*.

Exod. 17. 1. journ. c. of L. Num. 9. 18, 20. | 10. 13.
Num. 3. 39. Moses and Aaron numbered at c. of L.
24. 13. I cannot go beyond the c. of L. to do good
33. 38. Aaron went up to Hor at c. of Lord and died
Josh. 22. 3. ye have kept charge of c. of L. your God
1 Sam. 12. 14. and not rebel against the c. of Lord
15. if ye will not obey, but rebel against c. of L.
13. 13. thou hast not kept the c. of Lord thy God
15. 13. Saul said, I have performed the c. of Lord
24. I have transgressed the c. of L. and thy word
2 Sam. 12. 9. wherefore hast thou despised c. of L.
2 Kings 24. 3. at the c. of Lord came this on Judah
2 Chron. 29. 25. for so was c. of L. by his prophets
Psal. 19. 8. the c. of L. is pure, enlightening the eyes
1 Cor. 7. 25. concerning virgins I have no c. of L.

New COMMANDMENT.

John 13. 34. a *new c.* I give unto you, that ye love
1 *John* 2. 7. brethren, I write no *new c.* unto you
8. a *new c.* I write unto you, which is true in him
2 *John* 5. not as though I wrote a *new c.* unto thee

Rebelled against the COMMANDMENT.

Num. 27. 14. ye *rebelled ag.* my *c.* in the des. of Zin
Deut. 1. 26. but ye *rebel. ag. c.* of L. your God, 43.
9. 23. then ye *rebel. ag. c.* of L. and believed not
Lam. 1. 18. L. is righteous, I have *rebelled ag.* his *c.*

COMMANDMENTS.

Gen. 26. 5. because that Abraham kept my *c.*
Exod. 15. 26. and if thou wilt give ear to his *c.*
34. 28. wrote on tables the ten *c. Deut.* 4. 13. | 10. 4.
Lev. 4. 13. have done somewhat ag. any of the *c.* 27.
5. 17. commit sin forbidden by the *c.* of the Lord
27. 34. these are the *c.* the Lord commanded
Num. 15. 39. remember all the *c.* of the Lord
Deut. 8. 11. in not keeping *c.* which I command thee
11. 13. if you shall hearken to *c.* 28. 13. *Judg.* 3. 4.
27. if ye will obey the *c.* of the Lord your God
28. if ye will not obey the *c.* of the Lord your G.
1 *Sam.* 15. 11. Saul hath not performed my *c.*
1 *Kings* 11. 34. because he hath kept my *c.* and stat.
14. 8. David who kept my *c.* and followed me
18. 18. in that ye have forsaken the *c.* of the Lord
2 *Kings* 17. 16. and they left all the *c.* of the Lord
19. Judah kept not the *c.* of the Lord their God
18. 6. but kept his *c.* which he commanded Moses
2 *Chron.* 7. 19. if ye forsake my *c.* I set before you
24. 20. why transgress ye the *c.* of the Lord?
Ezra 9. 10. O our God, for we have forsaken thy *c.*
14. should we again break thy *c.* and join in affin.
Psal. 89. 31. if they keep not my *c.* then will I visit
111. 7. his works are verity, all his *c.* are sure
112. 1. blessed is he that delight. greatly in his *c.*
119. 10. O let me not wander from thy *c.*
19. I am a stranger, hide not thy *c.* from me
35. make me to go in the path of thy *c.*
47. I will delight in thy *c.* which I have loved
66. teach me, for I have believed thy *c.*
73. give understanding, that I may learn thy *c.*
86. all thy *c.* are faith. ‖ 151. all thy *c.* are truth
98. thou through thy *c.* hast made me wiser than
127. I love thy *c.* ‖ 131. I longed for thy *c.*
143. thy *c.* are my delights ‖ 172. *c.* righteous.
166. I have done thy *c.* ‖ 176. not forget thy *c.*
Prov. 2. 1. if thou wilt hide my *c.* with thee
7. 1. keep my words and lay up my *c.* with thee
10. 8. the wise in heart will receive *c.*
Isa. 48. 18. O that thou hadst hearkened to my *c.*
Mat. 5. 19. whoso shall break one of these least *c.*
15. 9. teach. for doctrines the *c.* of men, *Mark* 7. 7.
22. 40. on these two *c.* hang all the law and proph.
Mark 10. 19. thou knowest the *c. Luke* 18. 20.
12. 29. the first of all the *c.* is, hear O Isr. the L.
Luke 1. 6. walking in all the *c.* of the L. blameless
John 14. 21. he that hath my *c.* and keepeth them
15. 10. if keep my *c.* as I have kept my Father's *c.*
1 *Cor.* 7. 19. is nothing, but keeping the *c.* of God
14. 37. things I write you, are the *c.* of the Lord
Col. 2. 22. after the *c.* and doctrines of men
1 *Thess.* 4. 2. for ye know what *c.* we gave you by L.
1 *John* 2. 4. he that keepeth not his *c.* is a liar
3. 24. he that keepeth his *c.* dwelleth in him
2 *John* 6. this is love, that we walk after his *c.*

Do COMMANDMENTS.

Num. 15. 40. *do* all my *c.* and be holy to your God
Deut. 6. 25. obs. to *do* all *c.* 15. 5. | 28. 1, 15. | 30. 8.
1 *Chron.* 28. 7. if he be constant to *do* my *c.*
Psal. 103. 18. those that remember his *c.* to *do* them
111. 10. understanding have they that *do* his *c.*
Rev. 22. 14. blessed are they that *do* his *c.*

Not do COMMANDMENTS.

Lev. 26. 14. but if ye will *not do* all these *c.*
15. so that ye will *not do* all my *c.* but break coven.

Keep COMMANDMENTS, *see* KEEP.

COMMEND

Signifies, [1] *To extol, or praise,* 2 Cor. 3. 1. | 5. 12. [2] *To commit, or give in charge,* Luke 23. 46. [3] *To render more illustrious and commendable,* Rom. 3. 5. [4] *To make or render one more acceptable,* 1 Cor. 8. 8.

Luke 23. 46. Father, into thy hands I *c.* my spirit
Acts 20. 32. and now, brethren, I *c.* you to God
Rom. 3. 5. if our unrighteousness *c.* righteous. of God
16. 1. I *c.* unto you Phebe our sister, a servant
2 *Cor.* 3. 1. do we begin again to *c.* ourselves?
5. 12. for we *c.* not ourselves again to you
10. 12. or compare ourselves with some that *c.*

COMMENDATION.

2 *Cor.* 3. 1. or need we, as some others, epistles of *c.*?

COMMENDED.

Gen. 12. 15. the princes *c.* Sarai before Pharaoh
Prov. 12. 8. a man shall be *c.* accord. to his wisdom
Eccl. 8. 15. then I *c.* mirth, because a man hath
Luke 16. 8. the Lord *c.* the unjust steward, because
Acts 14. 23. *c.* them to the L. on whom they believed
2 *Cor.* 12. 11. I ought to have been *c.* of you

COMMENDETH.

Rom. 5. 8. but God *c.* his love towards us, in that
1 *Cor.* 8. 8. but meat *c.* us not to God
2 *Cor.* 10. 18. not he that *c.* is approved, but whom L.

COMMENDING.

2 *Cor.* 4. 2. *c.* ourselves to every man's conscience
6. † 4. in all *c.* ourselves as the ministers of God

COMMISSION, S.

Ezra 8. 36. and they delivered the king's *c.*
Acts 26. 12. as I went with *c.* from the chief priest

COMMIT.

Exod. 20. 14. thou shalt not *c.* adultery, *Deut.* 5. 18. *Mat.* 5. 27. | 19. 18. *Rom.* 13. 9.
Lev. 5. 17. if sin, and *c.* any of these things forbidden
18. 26. not *c.* any of these abominations, 30.
29. who shall *c.* any of these abominations
Num. 5. 6. if a man or woman *c.* any sin that men *c.*
Deut. 19. 20. *c.* no more any such evil among you
Judg. 13. † 1. added to *c.* evil in the sight of the Lord
2 *Chron.* 21. 11. caused Jerusalem to *c.* fornication
Job 5. 8. unto God would I *c.* my cause
Psal. 31. 5. into thine hand I *c.* my spirit
37. 5. *c.* thy way to the Lord, trust also in him
Prov. 16. 3. *c.* thy works unto the Lord, thy thoughts
12. an abomination to kings to *c.* wickedness
Isa. 22. 21. I will *c.* thy government into his hand
Jer. 37. 21. *c.* Jeremiah to the court of prison
44. 7. why *c.* ye this great evil against your souls?
Ezek. 8. 17. *c.* abominations which they *c.* here
16. 43. and thou shalt not *c.* this lewdness
22. 9. in the midst of thee they *c.* lewdness
Hos. 6. 9. the priests murder, they *c.* lewdness
7. 1. for they *c.* falsehood, and the thief cometh
Luke 12. 48. and did *c.* things worthy of stripes
16. 11. who will *c.* to your trust the true riches?
John 2. 24. Jesus did not *c.* himself to them
Rom. 1. 32. who *c.* such things are worthy of death
2. 2. is against them which *c.* such things
22. that abhorrest idols, dost thou *c.* sacrilege?
1 *Cor.* 10. 8. neither let us *c.* fornication
1 *Tim.* 1. 18. this charge I *c.* to thee, son Timothy
2 *Tim.* 2. 2. the same *c.* thou to faithful men
Jam. 2. 9. if ye have respect to persons ye *c.* sin
1 *Pet.* 4. 19. *c.* the keeping of their souls to him
1 *John* 3. 9. whoso is born of God doth not *c.* sin
Rev. 2. 14. who taught Israel to *c.* fornication
20. to teach and seduce my servants to *c.* fornication

See ADULTERY.

COMMIT *iniquity.*

2 *Sam.* 7. 14. if he *c. iniquity* I will chasten him
Job 34. 10. Almighty, that he should *c. iniquity*
Jer. 9. 5. they weary themselves to *c. iniquity*
Ezek. 3. 20. turn from righteousn. and *c. in.* 33. 13.

COMMIT *trespass.*

Lev. 5. 15. if a soul *c.* a *trespass* through ignorance
Num. 5. 12. if a man's wife go aside and *c. trespass*
31. 16. caused Israel to *c. trespass* against the Lord
Josh. 22. 20. Achan *c.* a *trespass* in the accurs. thing

COMMIT *whoredom,* or *whoredoms.*

Lev. 20. 5. I will cut off that *c. whor.* with Molech
Num. 25. 1. to *c. whor.* with the daughters of Moab
Ezek. 16. 17. and thou didst *c. whor.* with images
34. whereas none followeth thee to *c. whoredom*
20. 30. *c.* ye *whoredom* after their abominations?
23. 43. will they *c. w.* with her, and she with them
Hos. 4. 10. they shall *c. whoredoms* and not increase
13. therefore your daughters shall *c. whor.* 14.

COMMITTED.

Gen. 39. 8. he hath *c.* all that he hath to my hand
22. the keeper *c.* to Joseph all the prisoners
Lev. 4. 35. priest make atonement for sin he hath *c.*
18. 30. these abominable customs which were *c.*
20. 23. they *c.* these things, and I abhorred them
Num. 15. 24. if aught be *c.* by ignorance
Deut. 17. 5. bring forth that man or woman that *c.*
21. 22. if a man have *c.* a sin worthy of death
Judg. 20. 6. they have *c.* folly and lewdness in Israel
1 *Kings* 8. 47. we have sinned, we have *c.* wickedn.
14. 22. they provoked him with sins, they *c.*
27. brasen shields *c.* he to the guard, 2 *Chr.* 12. 10.
1 *Chr.* 10. 13. Saul died for his transgression he *c.*
Jer. 2. 13. for my people have *c.* two evils
5. 30. a wonderful and horrible thing is *c.* in land
16. 10. what is our sin that we have *c.* against Lord
44. 3. which they have *c.* to provoke to anger, 9.
Ezek. 16. 26. thou hast *c.* fornication with Egypt
51. nor hath Samaria *c.* half of thy sins
18. 21. turn from all his sins he hath *c.* 22, 28.
20. 43. shall lothe yourselves for evils ye have *c.*
23. 3. they *c.* whoredoms in Egypt in their youth
7. thus she *c.* whoredoms with them
33. 16. none of the sins he *c.* shall be mentioned
Hos. 1. 2. for the land hath *c.* great whoredom
4. 18. they have *c.* whoredom continually
Mark 15. 7. who had *c.* murder in the insurrection
Luke 12. 48. and to whom men have *c.* much, of him
John 5. 22. Father hath *c.* all judgment to the Son
Acts 8. 3. haling men and women, *c.* them to prison
25. 11. if I have *c.* any thing worthy of death
25. had found he had *c.* nothing worthy of death
27. 40. they *c.* themselves to the sea and loosed
28. 17. though I have *c.* nothing against the people
Rom. 3. 2. because to them were *c.* the oracles of God
1 *Cor.* 9. 17. dispensation of gospel is *c.* to me, *Tit.* 1. 3.
10. 8. nor let us commit fornic. as some of them *c.*
2 *Cor.* 5. 19. hath *c.* to us the word of reconciliation
12. 21. and lasciviousness which they have *c.*
Gal. 2. 7. gospel of the uncircumcision was *c.* to me as gospel of circumcision to Peter, 1 *Tim.* 1. 11.
1 *Tim.* 6. 20. O Timothy, keep what is *c.* to thee
2 *Tim.* 1. 12. he is able to keep that which I *c.* to him
Jam. 5. 15. if he have *c.* sins, they shall be forgiven
1 *Pet.* 2. 23. *c.* himself to him that judgeth righteously
Jude 15. of all their ungodly deeds which they have *c.*
Rev. 17. 2. with whom kings have *c.* fornic. 18. 3, 9.

See ABOMINATIONS.

COMMITTED *iniquity.*

Psal. 106. 6. we have *c. iniq.* we have done wickedly
Ezek. 33. 13. for his *iniq.* he hath *c.* he shall die, 18.
Dan. 9. 5. we have *c. iniquity* and done foolishly

COMMITTED *trespass.*

Lev. 5. 7. bring for his *trespass* he *c.* two turtle-doves
Josh. 7. 1. Israel *c.* a *trespass* in the accursed thing
22. 16. what *trespass* is this ye have *c.* against God?
31. because ye have not *c.* this *trespass* against L.
Ezek. 15. 8. because they have *c.* a *trespass,* I will
20. 27. in that they *c.* a *trespass* against me

COMMITTEST, ETH, ING.

Psal. 10. 14. the poor *c.* himself to thee, thou helper
Ezek. 8. 6. the great abominations that Israel *c.* here
33. 15. walk in statutes of life without *c.* iniquity
Hos. 4. 2. by lying, killing, stealing, and *c.* adultery
5. 3. for now, O Ephraim, thou *c.* whoredom
John 8. 34. whosoever *c.* sin is the servant of sin
1 *Cor.* 6. 18. but he that *c.* fornic. sinneth against
1 *John* 3. 4. whoso *c.* sin transgresseth also the law
8. he that *c.* sin is of the devil, for the devil sinneth

COMMODIOUS.

Acts 27. 12. the haven was not *c.* to winter in

COMMON.

By common, *is meant that which is ordinary, or usual; as a* common death, *Num.* 16. 29. a common evil, *Eccl.* 6. 1. *Sometimes that which is ceremonially unclean,* Acts 11. 9. *To eat with* common hands, that is, *without washing one's hands,* Mark 7. 2. Common bread, that is, *unhallowed bread,* 1 Sam. 21. 4. *It is said,* Acts 2. 44. That such as believed had all things common: that is, *as to use, but not as to title.* Moses *calls a vineyard* common, *or* profane: What man is he that hath planted a vineyard, and hath not yet made it common? *Deut.* 20. † 6. *If there be such an one, he may return to his house; because the first fruits of trees and vines were reckoned unclean, or rather were consecrated to the Lord, and the owner was not allowed to touch them, till after the fourth year,* Lev. 19. 24, 25.

See PROFANE.

Num. 16. 29. if these men die the *c.* death of all men
Deut. 20. † 6. planted a vineyard, and not made it *c.*
28. † 30. shall plant, and not use it as *c.* meat
1 *Sam.* 21. 4. there is no *c.* bread under my hand
5. the vessels holy, and the bread is in manner *c.*
Eccl. 6. 1. there is an evil, and it is *c.* among men
Jer. 31. 5. the planters shall eat them as *c.* things
Ezek. 23. 42. men of *c.* sort were brought Sabeans
Mat. 27. 27. the soldiers took Jesus into the *c.* hall
Mark 7. † 2. the disciples eat bread with *c.* hands
Acts 2. 44. believers had all things *c.* 4. 32.
5. 18. and put the apostles in the *c.* prison
10. 14. I have never eaten any thing that is *c.* 11. 8.
15. what God hath cleansed call not thou *c.* 11. 9.
28. that I should not call any thing *c.* or unclean
Rom. 14. † 14. there is nothing *c.* of itself; but to him that esteemeth any thing to be *c.*
1 *Cor.* 10. 13. no temptation taken you but *c.* to men
Tit. 1. 4. to Titus my own son, after the *c.* faith
Jude 3. diligence to write to you of the *c.* salvation

COMMON *people.*

Lev. 4. 27. if any of the *c. people* sin thro' ignorance
Jer. 26. 23. cast his dead body into the graves of *c. p.*
Mark 12. 37. and the *c. people* heard him gladly

COMMON-WEALTH.

Eph. 2. 12. being aliens from the *c.-wealth* of Israel

COMMONLY; *see* REPORTED.

COMMOTION, S.

2 *Chron.* 29. † 8. Lord hath delivered them to great *c.*
Jer. 10. 22. a great *c.* out of the north country
Luke 21. 9. when ye hear of *c.* be not terrified

COMMUNE.

Exod. 25. 22. and there I will meet and *c.* with thee
1 *Sam.* 18. 22. *c.* with David secretly, and say, behold
19. 3. and I will *c.* with my father of thee
Job 4. 2. if we essay to *c.* with thee, wilt be grieved?
Psal. 4. 4. *c.* with your own heart on your bed, be still
64. 5. they *c.* of laying snares privily, they say
77. 6. in the night I *c.* with mine own heart

COMMUNED.

Gen. 23. 8. Abraham *c.* ‖ 34. 6. Hamor *c.* with Jac. 8.
42. 24. Joseph *c.* ‖ *Judg.* 9. 1. Abimelech *c.*
1 *Sam.* 9. 25. Samuel *c.* ‖ 25. 39. David *c.* with Abigail
1 *Kings* 10. 2. the queen of Sheba *c.* with Solomon of all that was in her heart, 2 *Chron.* 9. 1.
2 *Kings* 22. 14. they *c.* with Huldah the prophetess
Eccl. 1. 16. I *c.* with mine own heart, saying, lo
Dan. 1. 19. and king *c.* with them, none like Daniel
Zech. 1. 14. the angel that *c.* with me said unto me
Luke 6. 11. they *c.* what they might do to Jesus
22. 4. Judas *c.* to betray Jesus unto them
24. 15. that while they *c.* Jesus himself drew near
Acts 24. 26. Felix sent and *c.* the oftener with Paul

COMMUNICATE.

Gal. 6. 6. let him that is taught *c.* to him that teacheth
Phil. 4. 14. that ye did *c.* with my affliction
1 *Tim.* 6. 18. that they do good, be willing to *c.*
Heb. 13. 16. but to do good and to *c.* forget not

COMMUNICATED.

Gal. 2. 2. I *c.* to them that gospel which I preach
Phil. 4. 15. no church *c.* with me but ye only

COMMUNICATION, S.

2 *Sam.* 3. 17. Abner had *c.* with the elders of Israel
2 *Kings* 9. 11. he said, ye know the man and his *c.*
Mat. 5. 37. but let your *c.* be yea, yea, nay, nay
Luke 24. 17. what manner of *c.* are these ye have?
1 *Cor.* 15. 33. evil *c.* corrupt good manners
Eph. 4. 29. no corrupt *c.* proceed out of your mouth, *Col.* 3. 8.
Philem. 6. that *c.* of thy faith may become effectual

COMMUNING.

Gen. 18. 33. the Lord left *c.* with Abraham
Exod. 31. 18. when he had made an end of *c.* on Sinai

COMMUNION.

This word signifies fellowship, concord, or agreement, 2 Cor. 6. 14. What communion hath light with darkness? *Such as are enlightened by the word and spirit of God can have no profitable, agreeable, or comfortable converse with such as are in darkness or ignorance.* Communion *is likewise taken for a sacrament, or sacred sign of our spiritual fellowship with Christ,* 1 Cor. 10. 16. The cup of blessing, is it not the communion of the blood of Christ? *Our drinking of the wine in the cup, is a religious action, whereby and wherein Christ communicates himself and his grace to us, and we communicate our souls to him; so that Christ, and believers in that action, have a mutual communion one with another. Believers have communion with Christ by election in him; by their kindred with his humanity; and by a participation of his Spirit. They have communion* with the Father and the Son, 1 John 1. 3. *They partake of all those blessings that God the Father has promised to those that are in covenant with him; and also of all those privileges which Christ has purchased for his members; such as, pardon, reconciliation, adoption, sanctification, &c.*

The Communion of saints: *That fellowship which the saints have with Christ, and all his benefits by faith, and among themselves by love,* 1 John 1. 3. *This Communion is both active and passive;* that is, *it consists both in doing good to, and receiving good from, one another. There be divers sorts of it, as,* (1) *Fellowship in doctrine, or belief,* Acts 2. 42. Gal. 2. 9. (2) *In exhortation,* Heb. 10. 24, 25. (3) *In consolation,* Eph. 5. 19.

1 Thess. 4. 18. (4) *In humility, or submission*, Rom. 12. 10. Eph. 5. 21. (5) *In love*, Rom. 12. 10. (6) *In pity*, Rom. 12. 16. (7) *In prayer*, Eph. 6. 18, 19. (8) *In helping and relieving one another*, Acts 4. 32, 34, 35.
1 *Cor.* 10. 16. *c.* of the blood of Christ, *c.* of the body of Christ
2 *Cor.* 6. 14. what *c.* hath light with darkness?
13. 14. the *c.* of the Holy Ghost be with you all

COMPACT.

Psal. 122. 3. Jerusalem is a city *c.* together

COMPACTED.

Eph. 4. 16. from whom whole body fitly joined and *c.*

COMPANY.

Gen. 30. † 11. Leah called his name Gad, a *c.*
32. 8. if Esau come to the one *c.* and smite it
21. and himself lodged that night in the *c.*
35. 11. a *c.* of nations shall be of thee, kings come
Num. 16. 6. take ye censers, Korah and all his *c.*
16. be thou and all thy *c.* before the Lord
40. no stranger offer, that he be not as Korah and *c.*
22. 4. now shall this *c.* lick up all that are round
26. 9. who strove in the *c.* of Korah, 27. 3.
Judg. 9. 37. another *c.* come along by the plain
18. 23. what ails thee, thou comest with such a *c.*?
1 *Sam.* 10. 5. thou shalt meet a *c.* of prophets
19. 20. they saw the *c.* of prophets prophesying
30. 15. canst thou bring me down to this *c.*?
2 *Kings* 5. 15. he and all his *c.* came to Elisha
9. 17. he spied the *c.* of Jehu, and said, I see a *c.*
2 *Chron.* 24. 24. the Syrians came with a small *c.*
Job 16. 7. thou hast made desolate all my *c.*
34. 8. goeth in *c.* with the workers of iniquity
Psal. 55. 14. we walked to the house of God in *c.*
68. † 27. the princes of Judah with their *c.*
30. rebuke the *c.* of spearmen, the bulls, the calves
84. † 7. they go from *c.* to *c.* every one in Zion
106. 17. the earth covered the *c.* of Abiram
18. and a fire was kindled in their *c.*
Prov. 24. † 19. keep not *c.* with the wicked
29. 3. that keepeth *c.* with harlots, spendeth
Cant. 1. 9. to a *c.* of horses in Pharaoh's chariots
6. 13. as it were the *c.* of two armies
Ezek. 16. 40. they shall bring up a *c.* against thee
23. 46. saith the Lord, I will bring up a *c.* on them
32. 22. Ashur is there and all her *c.* his graves
38. 7. prepare for thyself, thou and all thy *c.*
Hos. 6. 9. so the *c.* of priests murder in the way
Luke 2. 44. supposing him to have been in *c.*
6. 17. he came down and the *c.* of his disciples
22. when they separate you from their *c.*
9. 14. make them sit down by fifties in a *c.*
38. a man of the *c.* cried out, saying, Master
24. 22. a woman of our *c.* made us astonished
Acts 4. 23. being let go, they went to their own *c.*
10. 28. unlawful for a man that is a Jew to keep *c.*
15. 22. to send chosen men of their *c.* to Antioch
17. 5. Jews gathered a *c.* and set city on an uproar
21. 8. next day we that were of Paul's *c.* departed
Rom. 15. 24. if first I be somewhat filled with your *c.*
1 *Cor.* 5. 11. not to keep *c.* with a fornicator, a drunk.
2 *Thess.* 3. 14. note that man, and have no *c.* with him
Heb. 12. 22. are come to an innumerable *c.* of angels
Rev. 18. 17. all *c.* in ships and sailors stood afar off

Great COMPANY.

Gen. 50. 9. there went up with Joseph a *great c.*
2 *Chron.* 9. 1. the queen of Sheba came with a *great c.*
20. 12. we have no might against this *great c.*
Psal. 68. 11. *great* was the *c.* of those that published
Jer. 31. 8. a *great c.* shall return thither
Ezek. 17. 17. nor shall Pharaoh with his *great c.*
John 6. 5. saw a *great c.* come to him, he saith
Acts 6. 7. a *great c.* of priests obedient to the faith

COMPANY.

1 *Cor.* 5. 9. I wrote not to *c.* with fornicators

COMPANIED.

Acts 1. 21. of these men which have *c.* with us

COMPANIES.

Judg. 7. 16. he divided the 300 men into three *c.*
20. and the three *c.* blew the trumpets
9. 34. they laid wait against Shechem in four *c.*
43. the people he divided them into three *c.*
1 *Sam.* 11. 11. Saul put the people in three *c.*
13. 17. the spoilers came out of camp in three *c.*
2 *Kings* 5. 2. the Syrians had gone out by *c.*
11. † 7. two *c.* of you shall keep the watch
Neh. 12. 31. two great *c.* of them gave thanks, 40.
Job 6. 19. the *c.* of Sheba waited for them
Isa. 21. 13. O ye travelling *c.* of Dedanim
57. 13. when thou criest, let thy *c.* deliver thee
Mark 6. 39. to make all sit down by *c.* on green grass

COMPANION.

Exod. 32. 27. go thro' camp and slay every man his *c.*
Judg. 14. 20. Samson's wife was given to his *c.* 15. 6.
1 *Chron.* 27. 33. Hushai the Archite was king's *c.*
Job 30. 29. I am a brother to dragons, a *c.* to owls
Psal. 119. 63. I am a *c.* to all them that fear thee
Prov. 13. 20. but a *c.* of fools shall be destroyed
28. 7. but a *c.* of riotous men shameth his father
24. the same is the *c.* of a destroyer
Cant. 1. † 15. thou art fair, my *c.* thou art fair
Mal. 2. 14. yet she is thy *c.* wife of thy covenant
Phil. 2. 25. Epaphroditus my brother and *c.* in labour
Rev. 1. 9. I John, your brother and *c.* in tribulation

COMPANIONS.

Judg. 11. 38. with her *c.* and bewailed her virginity
14. 11. they brought thirty *c.* to be with him
Job 35. 4. I will answer thee and thy *c.* with thee
41. 6. shall the *c.* make a banquet of him
Psal. 45. 14. her *c.* shall be brought unto thee
122. 8. for my *c.* sake I will say, peace be in thee
Cant. 1. 7. that turneth aside by the flocks of thy *c.*
8. 13. the *c.* hearken to thy voice, cause me to hear
Isa. 1. 23. thy princes are rebellious and *c.* of thieves
Ezek. 37. 16. write on it for Judah and Israel his *c.*
Dan. 2. 17. he made the thing known to his *c.*
Acts 19. 29. having caught Paul's *c.* in travel
Heb. 10. 33. ye became *c.* of them that were so used

COMPARABLE.

Lam. 4. 2. the precious sons of Zion *c.* to fine gold

COMPARE, ED, ING.

Psal. 89. 6. who in heaven can be *c.* to the Lord?
Prov. 3. 15. are not to be *c.* to wisdom, 8. 11.
Cant. 1. 9. I have *c.* thee, O my love, to a company
Isa. 40. 18. or what likeness will ye *c.* to him?
46. 5. to whom will ye *c.* me, that we may be like?
Rom. 8. 18. are not worthy to be *c.* with the glory
1 *Cor.* 2. 13. *c.* spiritual things with spiritual
2 *Cor.* 10. 12. *c.* ourselves with some that commend, and *c.* themselves amongst themselves, are not wise

COMPARISON.

Judg. 8. 2. what have I done now in *c.* of you? 3.
Hag. 2. 3. is it not in your eyes in *c.* of it as nothing?
Mark 4. 30. or with what *c.* shall we compare it?

COMPASS, *Substantive*.

Exod. 27. 5. shall put the net under the *c.* of altar
38. 4. he made a grate of net-work under the *c.*
2 *Sam.* 5. 23. but fetch a *c.* behind them and come
2 *Kings* 3. 9. they fetched a *c.* of seven days' journey
Prov. 8. 27. when he set a *c.* on the face of the earth
Isa. 44. 13. he marketh the image out with the *c.*
Acts 28. 13. from thence we fetched a *c.* to Rhegium

COMPASS, *Verb*.

Num. 21. 4. they journeyed to *c.* the land of Edom
Josh. 6. 3. ye shall *c.* the city, all ye men of war
4. and the seventh day *c.* the city seven times
2 *Sam.* 24. † 2. *c.* the tribes of Israel and number
2 *Kings* 11. 8. *c.* the king round about, 2 *Chr.* 23. 7.
Job 16. 13. his archers *c.* me round about, he cleav.
40. 22. the willows of the brook *c.* him about
Psal. 5. 12. with favour wilt thou *c.* him as a shield
7. 7. the congregation of the people *c.* thee about
17. 9. from my deadly enemies who *c.* me about
26. 6. wash my hands, so will I *c.* thine altar, O L.
32. 7. shalt *c.* me about with songs of deliverance
10. trusteth in the Lord, mercy shall *c.* him about
49. 5. the iniquity of my heels shall *c.* me about
140. 9. as for the head of those that *c.* me about
142. 7. the righteous shall *c.* me about, for shalt deal
Prov. 4. † 9. she shall *c.* thee with a crown of glory
Isa. 50. 11. that *c.* yourselves about with sparks
Jer. 31. 22. a new thing, a woman shall *c.* a man
Hab. 1. 4. for the wicked doth *c.* about the righteous
Mat. 23. 15. woe to you, for ye *c.* sea and land
Luke 19. 43. thine enemies shall *c.* thee round

COMPASSED.

Gen. 19. 4. the men of Sodom *c.* the house round
Deut. 2. 1. and we *c.* mount Seir many days
Josh. 6. 11. so the ark of the Lord *c.* the city
Judg. 11. 18. then they *c.* land of Edom and Moab
16. 2. they *c.* Samson in, and laid wait all night
1 *Sam.* 23. 26. Saul and his men *c.* D. and his men
2 *Sam.* 22. 5. waves of death *c.* me, *Ps.* 18. 4. | 116. 3.
2 *Kings* 6. 15. beheld an host *c.* the city with horses
2 *Chron.* 21. 9. smote the Edomites which *c.* him in
Job 19. 6. know that God hath *c.* me with his net
26. 10. he hath *c.* the waters with bounds
Psal. 17. 11. they have now *c.* us in our steps
22. 12. many bulls *c.* me || 16. for dogs have *c.* me
Eccl. 7. † 25. I and my heart *c.* to know wisdom
Lam. 3. 5. he hath *c.* me with gall and travail
Zech. 14. † 10. all the land shall be *c.* as a plain
Luke 21. 20. when ye shall see Jerus. *c.* with armies
Heb. 5. 2. for that he himself also is *c.* with infirmity

COMPASSED *about*.

Deut. 32. † 10. in howling wilderness he *c.* them *about*
2 *Sam.* 18. 15. ten young men *c.* Absalom *about*
22. 6. the sorrows of hell *c.* me *about*, *Psal.* 18. 5.
2 *Kings* 6. 14. Syrians came by night and *c.* city *a.*
8. 21. Joram smote Edomites which *c.* him *about*
2 *Chron.* 18. 31. they *c. about* Jehoshaphat to fight
Psal. 40. 12. innumerable evils have *c.* me *about*
88. 17. they *c.* me *a.* together, 109. 3. | 118. 11, 12.
118. 10. all nations *c.* me *about*, but in the name
Jonah 2. 3. floods *c.* me *a.* thy billows passed over me
Heb. 11. 30. walls of Jericho fell, after *c. a.* 7 days
12. 1. *c. about* with such a cloud of witnesses
Rev. 20. 9. they went up and *c.* camp of saints *ab.*

COMPASSEST, ETH.

Gen. 2. 11. *c.* Havilah || 13. *c.* the land of Ethiopia
Psal. 73. 6. therefore pride *c.* them about as a chain
139. 3. thou *c.* my path and my lying down
Hos. 11. 12. Ephraim *c.* me about with lies, and Isr.

COMPASSION.

1 *Kings* 8. 50. give them *c.* before them who carry
2 *Chr.* 30. 9. your children shall find *c.* before them
Mat. 9. 36. Jesus moved with *c.* 14. 14. *Mark* 6. 34.
18. 27. the lord of that servant was moved with *c.*
Mark 1. 41. Jesus moved with *c.* put forth his hand
1 *Pet.* 3. 8. be of one mind, having *c.* one of another
1 *John* 3. 17. shutteth up his bowels of *c.* from him

Full of COMPASSION.

Psal. 78. 38. he being *full of c.* forgave their iniquity
86. 15. thou art a *G. f. of c.* 111. 4. | 112. 4. | 145. 8.

Have or *had* COMPASSION.

Exod. 2. 6. the babe wept, and she *had c.* on him
Deut. 13. 17. the Lord may turn and *have c.* on thee
30. 3. then the Lord thy God will *have c.* on thee
1 *Sam.* 23. 21. blessed be ye of L. for ye *have c.* on me
1 *Kings* 8. 50. that they may *have c.* on them
2 *Kings* 13. 23. Lord was gracious and *had c.* on them
2 *Chron.* 36. 15. because he *had c.* on his people
17. Chaldees *had* no *c.* on young man or maiden
Isa. 49. 15. that she should not *have c.* on son of womb
Jer. 12. 15. I will return and *have c.* on them
Lam. 3. 32. yet will he *have c.* *Mic.* 7. 19.
Mat. 15. 32. I *have c.* on the multitude, *Mark* 8. 2.
18. 33. also have *had c.* on thy fellow servant
20. 34. so Jes. *had c.* on them and touched their eyes
Mark 5. 19. how the Lord hath *had c.* on thee
9. 22. if thou canst, *have c.* on us, and help us
Luke 7. 13. when the Lord saw her, he *had c.* on her
10. 33. the Samaritan saw him, he *had c.* on him
15. 20. father *had c.* and ran and fell on his neck
Rom. 9. 15. I will *have c.* on whom I will *have c.*
Heb. 5. 2. who can *have c.* on the ignorant, and them
10. 34. for ye *had c.* of me in my bonds
Jude 22. of some *have c.* making a difference

COMPASSIONS.

Lam. 3. 22. are not consumed, because his *c.* fail not
Zech. 7. 9. shew mercy and *c.* every man to brother

COMPEL.

Lev. 25. 39. not *c.* him to serve as a bond-servant
Mat. 5. 41. *c.* thee to go a mile, go with him twain
Mark 15. 21. they *c.* one Simon to bear his cross
Luke 14. 23. go into highways, *c.* them to come in

COMPELLED, EST.

1 *Sam.* 28. 23. his servants with the woman *c.* Saul
2 *Chron.* 21. 11. moreover Jehoram *c.* Judah thereto
Mat. 27. 32. Simon, him they *c.* to bear his cross
Acts 26. 11. and I *c.* them to blaspheme and persecut.
2 *Cor.* 12. 11. I am a fool in glorying, ye have *c.* me
Gal. 2. 3. nor Titus a Greek was *c.* to be circumcised
14. why *c.* thou the Gentiles to live as the Jews?

COMPLAIN, ED, ING.

Num. 11. 1. the people *c.* it displeased the Lord
Judg. 21. 22. or their brethren came to us to *c.*
Job 7. 11. I will *c.* in the bitterness of my soul
31. 38. that the furrows likewise thereof *c.*
Psal. 77. 3. I *c.* and my spirit was overwhelmed
144. 14. that there be no *c.* in our streets
Lam. 3. 39. wherefore doth a living man *c.*? a man

COMPLAINERS.

Num. 11. † 1. when people were *c.* it displeased Lord
Jude 16. these are murmurers, *c.* walking after lusts

COMPLAINT, S.

1 *Sam.* 1. 16. out of abundance of my *c.* have I spoken
Job 7. 13. when I say, my couch shall ease my *c.*
9. 27. if I say, I will forget my *c.* I will leave off
10. 1. I will leave my *c.* on myself, I will speak
21. 4. as for me, is my *c.* to man? and if it were so
23. 2. even to-day is my *c.* bitter, my stroke heavier
Psal. 55. 2. I mourn in my *c.* and make a noise
142. 2. I poured out my *c.* before him, and trouble
Acts 25. 7. laid *c.* against Paul, they could not prove
Col. 3. † 13. if any man have a *c.* against any

COMPLETE.

Lev. 23. 15. ye shall count, seven sabbaths shall be *c.*
Col. 2. 10. ye are *c.* in him who is the head of all
4. 12. that ye may stand *c.* in all the will of God

COMPOSITION.

Exod. 30. 32. nor make any like it after the *c.* 37.

COMPOUND, ETH.

Exod. 30. 25. an ointment *c.* after art of apothecary
33. whosoever *c.* any thing like it, or putteth any

COMPREHEND.

Job 37. 5. great things doth he which we cannot *c.*
Eph. 3. 18. may be able to *c.* with saints the breadth

COMPREHENDED.

Isa. 40. 12. hath *c.* the dust of the earth in a measure
John 1. 5. light shined, and the darkness *c.* it not
Rom. 13. 9. is briefly *c.* in this saying, thou shalt love

CONCEAL, ED, ETH.

Gen. 37. 26. if we slay our brother and *c.* his blood
Deut. 13. 8. not spare, neither shalt thou *c.* him
Job 6. 10. I have not *c.* the words of the holy One
27. 11. what is with the Almighty will I not *c.*
41. 12. I will not *c.* his parts nor his proportion
Psal. 40. 10. I have not *c.* thy loving-kind. and truth
Prov. 11. 13. he that is of a faithful spirit *c.* the matter
12. 23. a prudent man *c.* knowledge, heart of fools
25. 2. it is the glory of God to *c.* a thing
Jer. 50. 2. declare ye, publish and *c.* not

CONCEIT, S.

Prov. 18. 11. rich man's wealth as an high wall in *c.*
26. 5. answer a fool, lest he be wise in his own *c.*
12. seest thou a man wise in his own *c.*? more hope
16. sluggard is wiser in his own *c.* than seven men
28. 11. the rich man is wise in his own *c.*
Rom. 11. 25. lest ye should be wise in your own *c.*
12. 16. be not wise in your own *c.*

CONCEIVE, ING.

Gen. 30. 38. they should *c.* when they came to drink
Num. 5. 28. then she shall be free, and shall *c.* seed
Judg. 13. 3. shalt *c.* and bear a son, 5, 7. *Luke* 1. 31.
Job 15. 35. they *c.* mischief, bring vanity, *Isa.* 59. 4.
Psal. 51. 5. and in sin did my mother *c.* me
Isa. 7. 14. a virgin shall *c.* and bear a son
33. 11. shall *c.* chaff || 59. 13. *c.* words of falsehood
Ezek. 38. † 10. thou shalt *c.* a mischievous purpose
Heb. 11. 11. Sarah received strength to *c.* seed

CONCEIVED.

Gen. 4. 1. Eve *c.* and bare Cain || 17. Cain's wife *c.*
16. 4. Hagar *c.* || 21. 2. Sarah *c.* and bare Isaac
25. 21. Rebekah his wife *c.* || 29. 32. Leah *c.* 33.
30. 5. Bilhah *c.* || 23. Rachael *c.* and bare a son
39. the flocks *c.* 31. 10. || 38. 3. Shuah *c.* 4, 5.
38. 18. Tamar *c.* || *Exod.* 2. 2. Jochebed *c.* and bare
Lev. 12. 2. have *c.* seed, and born a man child
Num. 11. 12. Moses said, have I *c.* all this people?
1 *Sam.* 1. 20. Hannah *c.* and bare a son, Samuel, 2. 21.
2 *Sam.* 11. 5. Bathsheba *c.* sent and told David
2 *Kings* 4. 17. Shunamite *c.* || *Isa.* 8. 3. prophetess *c.*
Job 3. 3. it was said, there is a man child *c.*
Psal. 7. 14. *c.* mischief, brought forth falsehood
Cant. 3. 4. into the chamber of her that *c.* me
Jer. 49. 30. and hath *c.* a purpose against you
Hos. 1. 3. Gomer which *c.* and bare him
2. 5. she that *c.* them hath done shamefully
Mat. 1. 20. that which is *c.* in her is of the H. Ghost
Luke 1. 36. Elisabeth hath *c.* a son in her old age
2. 21. was so named before he was *c.* in womb
Acts 5. 4. why hast thou *c.* this thing in thine heart?
Rom. 9. 10. when Rebekah had *c.*
Jam. 1. 15. when lust hath *c.* it brings forth sin

CONCEPTION.

Gen. 3. 16. I will greatly multiply thy sorrow and *c.*
Ruth 4. 13. the Lord gave her *c.* and she bare a son
Hos. 9. 11. their glory shall flee from the birth and *c.*

CONCERN, ETH.

Ezek. 12. 10. say to them, this burden *c.* the prince
Acts 28. 31. teaching things which *c.* the L. J. C.
2 *Cor.* 11. 30. glory in things which *c.* my infirmities

CONCERNING.

Gen. 19. 21. I have accepted thee *c.* this thing
Exod. 6. 8. *c.* which I did swear to give, *Num.* 14. 30.
Lev. 4. 26. priest make atonem. for him *c.* sin, 5. 6.
6. 3. hath found what was lost, and lieth *c.* it
Num. 10. 29. the Lord hath spoken good *c.* Israel
1 *Kings* 11. 10. had commanded him *c.* this thing
2 *Kings* 20. † 1. give charge *c.* thy house, *Isa.* 38. † 1.
Neh. 1. 2. I asked them *c.* the Jews that escaped
Psal. 90. 13. repent thee *c.* thy servants, 135. 14.
Eccl. 7. 10. for thou dost not inquire wisely *c.* this
Isa. 5. † 20. woe to them that say *c.* evil, it is good
30. 7. shall help in vain, theref. have I cried *c.* this

Isa. 45. 11. ask me c. my sons, and c. work of hands
Jer. 16. 3. thus saith the Lord c. sons, c. daughters born in this place, c. their mothers, c. their fathers
27. 19. c. the pillars, c. the sea, c. bases, c. vessels
Ezek. 14. 22. shall be comforted c. evil, even c. all
21. 28. thus saith the Lord God c. the Ammonites
47. 14. c. which I have lifted up my hand to give
Dan. 2. 18. would desire mercies of G. c. this secret
6. 17. that purpose might not be changed c. Daniel
Mat. 16. 11. that I spake it not to you c. bread
Mark 5. 16. they that saw, told also c. the swine
Luke 24. 27. he expounded the things c. himself
Acts 13. 34. as c. that he raised him up from dead
28. 22. as c. this sect, we know it is spoken against
Rom. 9. 5. of whom as c. flesh Christ came, who is G.
11. 28. as c. the gospel, are enemies for your sake
16. 19. you wise to what is good, and simple c. evil
2 Cor. 11. 21. I speak as c. reproach, as though weak
Eph. 5. 32. but I speak c. Christ and the church
Phil. 4. 15. as c. giving and receiving, but ye only
1 Tim. 6. 21. some professing have erred c. the faith
2 Tim. 2. 18. who c. the truth have erred, saying
3. 8. men of corrupt minds, reprobates c. the faith
1 Pet. 4. 12. think it not strange c. the fiery trial
See HIM, ME, THEE, THEM, US, YOU.

CONCISION.

Beware of the concision, *Phil.* 3. 2. that is, *such who under pretence of maintaining circumcision, which is now no longer a seal of God's covenant, and so is no better than a mere cutting or slashing of the flesh, do prove destroyers and renders of the church.*
Joel 3. † 14. multitudes in the valley of c.
Phil. 3. 2. beware of dogs, beware of the c.

CONCLUDE.

Rom. 3. 28. we c. a man is justified by faith without

CONCLUDED.

Acts 21. 25. as touching the Gentiles, we have c.
Rom. 11. 32. for God hath c. them all in unbelief
Gal. 3. 22. but the scripture hath c. all under sin

CONCLUSION.

Eccl. 12. 13. let us hear the c. of the whole matter

CONCORD.

2 Cor. 6. 15. and what c. hath Christ with Belial?

CONCOURSE.

Prov. 1. 21. she crieth in the chief place of c.
Acts 19. 40. whereby we may give account of this c.

CONCUBINE.

This term in scripture signifies a wife of the second rank, who was inferior to the matron, or mistress of the house. The chief wives differed from the concubines, (1) In that they were taken into fellowship with their husbands by solemn stipulation, and with consent and solemn rejoicing of friends. (2) They brought with them dowries to their husbands. (3) They had the government of their families under and with their husbands. (4) The inheritance belonged to the children brought forth by them. Though the children of concubines *did not inherit their father's estate, yet the father in his life-time might provide for them, and make presents to them: Thus* Sarah *was* Abraham's *wife, of whom he had* Isaac, *the heir of all his wealth: But he had besides two* concubines, *namely,* Hagar *and* Keturah; *of these he had other children, whom he distinguished from* Isaac, *and made presents to them. As polygamy was sometimes practised by the patriarchs and among the* Jews, *either by God's permission, who could rightly dispense with his own laws when and where he pleased; or by their mistake about the lawfulness of it; as this was their practice, it was a common thing to see one, two, or many wives, in a family; and besides these several concubines.* David *had seven wives, and ten concubines,* 2 Sam. 3. 2, 3, 4, 5. | 20. 3. Solomon *had seven hundred wives, who all lived in the quality of queens, and three hundred concubines; and his wives turned away his heart,* 1 Kings 11. 3. Rehoboam *his son had eighteen wives, and sixty concubines,* 2 Chron. 11. 21. *But ever since the abrogation of polygamy by our Lord* Jesus Christ, *and the reduction of marriage to its primitive institution, the abuse of concubines has been condemned and forbidden among Christians.*
Judg. 19. 2. his c. played the whore against him
29. he laid hold on his c. and divided her
20. 4. I came into Gibeah, I and my c. to lodge
2 Sam. 3. 7. why hast thou gone in to my father's c.?
21. 11. what Rizpah the c. of Saul had done

CONCUBINES.

Gen. 25. 6. to sons of the c. Abraham gave gifts
2 Sam. 5. 13. David took him more c. and wives
16. 22. Absalom went in to father's c. in sight of Isr.
19. 5. have saved thy life, and the lives of thy c.
20. 3. the king put his c. in ward and fed them
1 Kings 11. 3. and Solomon had three hundred c.
2 Chron. 11. 21. for Rehoboam took threescore c.
Esth. 2. 14. to custody of Shaashgaz who kept the c.
Cant. 6. 8. there are 60 queens and 80 c. and virgins
9. yea, the queens and the c. and they praised her
Dan. 5. 3. the king and his c. drank in them, 23.

CONCUPISCENCE

Signifies, [1] *Sinful lusts, the depravity of our nature, or that original concupiscence which is the fountain from whence all particular lusts do flow, the furnace from which all sinful motions, as so many sparks, do continually arise,* Rom. 7. † 7. Jam. 1. 14. [2] *Actual motions and inclinations to sin, springing from this natural concupiscence,* Rom. 7. 8.
Rom. 7. † 7. I had not known c. except law had said
8. sin wrought in me all manner of c.
Col. 3. 5. mortify members, evil c. and covetousness
1 Thess. 4. 5. not in the lust of c. as the Gentiles

CONDEMNATION

Signifies, [1] *A declaring guilty, or pronouncing the sentence of punishment upon any malefactor by some judge,* John 8. 10. [2] *That which aggravates one's sin and punishment, or that which is the reason, the evidence, and great cause of condemnation,* John 3. 19. [3] *The punishment itself, whereunto one is adjudged and condemned,* 1 Cor. 11. 32. [4] *A censuring other men's persons, purposes, words, or actions, either rashly, unjustly, or uncharitably,* Luke 6. 37. [5] *A witnessing against and convicting persons of their wickedness and faults by the good example and conduct of others; thus the* Ninevites *shall condemn the obstinate* Jews, Mat. 12. 41. *because the former repented at the preaching of* Jonas, *but the others shewed no signs of repentance, notwithstanding our Saviour preached and did many mighty works among them.*
God condemned sin in the flesh, *Rom.* 8. 3. *He adjudged it to destruction, passed sentence upon it, and accordingly punished it by the sufferings of his Son in the flesh; and thereby declared openly before all the world, by these sufferings of his Son, how abominable sin was to him, and how contrary to his nature.*
Christ, *being no civil judge or magistrate, did not condemn the woman taken in adultery to a civil punishment: Neither did he acquit her, for that would have been making void the law of God: He only performs the office of a minister, and speaks to her as the Mediator and Saviour of men, in calling her to repentance and reformation,* John 8. 10, 11.
The manner of passing sentence upon persons, varied in most countries. The Jews, *by a simple pronunciation of the sentence, as* Thou N. art just; Thou N. art guilty; *both absolved and condemned them. The* Romans *gave sentence, by casting in tables into a certain box or urn prepared for the purpose. If they absolved any, they wrote the letter* A *in the table, it being the first letter of* Absolvo; *if they condemned any, they wrote the letter* C, *the first of* Condemno. *Among the* Grecians, *condemnation was signified by giving a black stone; Absolution by giving a white stone: To this last there seemeth to be an allusion,* Rev. 2. 17. To him that overcometh I will give a white stone: that is, *I will absolve and acquit him in the day of judgment.*
Luke 23. 40. seeing thou art in the same c.
John 3. 19. this is the c. that light is come into world
5. 24. he that believeth shall not come into c.
Rom. 5. 16. for the judgment was by one to c.
18. as by one, judgment came upon all men to c.
8. 1. there is no c. to them who are in Christ Jesus
1 Cor. 11. 34. that ye come not together to c.
2 Cor. 3. 9. if the ministration of c. be glorious
1 Tim. 3. 6. lest he fall into the c. of the devil
Jam. 3. 1. knowing we shall receive the greater c.
5. 12. let your nay be nay, lest ye fall into c.
Jude 4. who were of old ordained to this c.

CONDEMN.

Exod. 22. 9. whom the judges shall c. he shall pay
Deut. 25. 1. judges may judge them, and c. the wick.
Job 9. 20. if I justify myself, my mouth shall c. me
10. 2. I will say to G. do not c. me, shew me why
34. 17. and wilt thou c. him that is most just?
40. 8. wilt thou c. me, that thou mayest be righte.
Psal. 37. 33. not leave him, nor c. him when judged
94. 21. and they c. the innocent blood
109. 31. to save him from those that c. his soul
Prov. 12. 2. a man of wicked devices will he c.
Isa. 50. 9. L. will help me, who is he that shall c. me?
54. 17. every tongue that shall rise ag. thee shall c.
Mat. 12. 41. and shall c. it because, *Luke* 11. 32.
42. queen of the south shall rise up in judgment and c. it, *Luke* 11. 31.
20. 18. they shall c. him to death, *Mark* 10. 33.
Luke 6. 37. c. not, and ye shall not be condemned
John 3. 17. God sent not his Son to c. the world
8. 11. neither do I c. thee, go and sin no more
2 Cor. 7. 3. I speak not this to c. you, for I said
1 John 3. 20. if our heart c. us, God is greater than
21. if our heart c. us not, then have we confidence

CONDEMNED.

2 Chron. 36. 3. and c. the land in 100 talents of silver
Job 32. 3. they found no answer, yet had c. Job
Psal. 109. 7. when he shall be judged, let him be c.
Amos 2. 8. drink the wine of c. in house of their god
Mat. 12. 7. ye would not have c. the guiltless
37. and by thy words thou shalt be c.
27. 3. Judas, when he saw that he was c. repented
Mark 14. 64. they all c. him to be guilty of death
Luke 24. 20. how the rulers delivered him to be c.
John 3. 18. he that believeth on him is not c. but he that believeth not is c. already, because not believed
8. 10. Jesus said, woman, hath no man c. thee?
Rom. 8. 3. sending his Son, for sin c. sin in flesh
1 Cor. 11. 32. we should not be c. with the world
Tit. 2. 8. sincerity, sound speech that cannot be c.
3. 11. sinneth, being c. of himself is subverted
Heb. 11. 7. and ark, by the which he c. the world
Jam. 5. 6. ye have c. and killed just, not resist you
9. judge not one another, brethren, lest ye be c.
2 Pet. 2. 6. God c. them with an overthrow

CONDEMNEST, ETH, ING.

1 Kings 8. 32. and judge thy servants, c. the wicked
Job 15. 6. thine own mouth c. thee, and not I
Prov. 17. 15. he that c. the just, is abomination to Ld.
Acts 13. 27. they have fulfilled them in c. him
Rom. 2. 1. wherein judgest another thou c. thyself
8. 34. it is God that justifieth, who is he that c.?
14. 22. that c. not himself in that thing he alloweth

CONDESCEND.

Rom. 12. 16. not high things, but c. to men of low

CONDITION, S.

1 Sam. 11. 2. on this c. I will make a coven. with you
Dan. 11. † 17. set his face to enter with equal c.
Luke 14. 32. he sendeth and desireth c. of peace

CONDUCT, ED.

2 Sam. 19. 15. Judah came to c. king over Jordan, 31.
40. all the people of Judah c. the king and Israel
Acts 17. 15. they that c. Paul brought him to Athens
1 Cor. 16. 11. but c. him forth in peace to come to me

CONDUIT.

2 Kings 18. 17. they came and stood by c. *Isa.* 36. 2.
20. 20. Hezekiah, how he made a pool and a c.
Isa. 7. 3. go forth to meet Ahaz at the end of the c.
Ezek. 31. † 4. sent out her c. to the trees of the field

CONFECTION.

Exod. 30. 35. shalt make a c. after art of apothecary

CONFECTIONARIES.

1 Sam. 8. 13. he will take your daughters to be c.

CONFEDERACY.

Isa. 8. 12. say ye not, a c. to whom people say, a c.
Obad. 7. all men of thy c. brought thee to the border

CONFEDERATE.

Gen. 14. 13. and these were c. with Abram
Psal. 83. 5. have consulted, they are c. against thee
Isa. 7. 2. it was told, Syria is c. with Ephraim

CONFERENCE.

Gal. 2. 6. for they in c. added nothing to me

CONFERRED.

1 Kings 1. 7. Adonijah c. with Joab and Abiathar
Acts 4. 15. they c. among thems. what do to these men
25. 12. Festus, when he had c. with the council
Gal. 1. 16. immediately I c. not with flesh and blood

CONFESS

Signifies, [1] *Publicly to own and acknowledge as his own: Thus Christ will confess the faithful in the day of judgment,* Luke 12. 8. [2] *To own and profess the truths of Christ, and to obey his commandments, and that in spite of all opposition and danger from enemies,* Mat. 10. 32. Whosoever shall confess me before men. [3] *To utter, or speak forth the praises of God, or to give him thanks,* Heb. 13. † 15. Offer to God the fruit of your lips, confessing his name; *that is, acknowledge his benefits, and give him thanks for them.* [4] *To own, and lay open our sins and offences, either unto God, in private, or public confessions; or to our neighbour whom we have wronged: or to some godly persons, at whose hands we look to receive comfort and spiritual instruction; or to the whole congregation, when our fault is public,* Psal. 32. 5. Mat. 3. 6. Jam. 5. 16. 1 John 1. 9. [5] *To acknowledge a crime before a judge,* Josh. 7. 19. [6] *To own and profess the gospel of Christ, and pay obedience to it,* Luke 12. 8. We are to make confession, (1) *To God, whom we have offended, who knows our sins, can pardon us, or else will punish us if we refuse to confess,* Psal. 32. 5. Prov. 28. 13. (2) *To our neighbour hurt by us, who otherwise complaining to God, shall have him to revenge his quarrel; and thus man can and ought to forgive so much of the offence as is done against him, if his adversary repent and confess, and seek pardon,* Mat. 5. 23, 24. Luke 17. 4. (3) *To the minister of God, or to some godly person, that, pitying the sinner's case, can and will give him spiritual advice against his sin, and pray for him,* Job 33. 23.
Confession *to God is made by a man for himself,* Psal. 32. 5. *A father for his children,* Job 1. 5. *A magistrate for those under his authority,* Neh. 1. 6. *And must be with knowledge of sin,* Jer. 2. 23. *Consideration of that which is done* Jer. 8. 6. *Humiliation,* 2 Chron. 7. 14. *Accepting of punishment for sin,* Lev. 26. 41. *A particularizing of sins,* Lev. 5. 5. 1 Sam. 12. 19. *Prayer,* Exod. 32. 32. *And forsaking of sin,* Prov. 28. 13.
Lev. 5. 5. he shall c. that he hath sinned in that thing
16. 21. Aaron shall c. over live goat all the iniquit.
26. 40. if they shall c. their iniquity and fathers'
Num. 5. 7. they shall c. their sins they have done
1 Kings 8. 33. Isr. c. thy name and pray, *2 Chr.* 6. 24.
35. c. thy name and turn from sin, *2 Chron.* 6. 26.
Neh. 1. 6. and c. the sins of the children of Israel
Job 40. 14. I will c. that thy hand can save thee
Psal. 18. † 49. I will c. to thee among the heathen
32. 5. I said, I will c. my transgressions to the Lord
Mat. 10. 32. whosoever shall c. me before men, him will I c. before my Father in heaven, *Luke* 12. 8.
John 9. 22. if any man did c. that he was Christ
12. 42. rulers did not c. him, lest be put out of synag.
Acts 23. 8. say no resurrection, but Pharisees c. both
24. 14. this I c. that after the way they call heresy
Rom. 10. 9. shalt c. with thy mouth the Lord Jesus
14. 11. every knee bow, every tongue shall c. to G.
15. 9. I will c. to thee among the Gentiles and sing
Phil. 2. 11. that every tongue shall c. Jesus is Lord
Jam. 5. 16. c. your faults one to another and pray
1 John 1. 9. if we c. our sins, he is faithful to forgive
4. 15. whoso shall c. that Jesus is the Son of God
2 John 7. who c. not that Jesus Chr. is come in flesh
Rev. 3. 5. but I will c. his name before my Father

CONFESSED, ETH, ING.

Ezra 10. 1. when Ezra had c. weeping and casting
Neh. 9. 2. Isr. stood and c. their sins, a fourth part c.
Prov. 28. 13. but whoso c. and forsaketh them shall
Dan. 9. 20. while c. my sin and the sin of my people
Mat. 3. 6. were baptized of him in Jordan, c. their sins
John 1. 20. John c. that I am not the Christ
Acts 19. 18. many came and c. and shewed their deeds
Heb. 11. 13. these c. that they were strangers on earth
13. † 15. the fruit of our lips, c. to his name
1 John 4. 2. every spirit that c. Christ is come in flesh
3. every spirit that c. not that Jesus Christ is come

CONFESSION.

Josh. 7. 19. give glory to God and make c. to him
2 Chr. 30. 22. offering peace-offerings and making c.
Ezra 10. 11. now therefore make c. to the Ld. God
Dan. 9. 4. I prayed to the Ld. my God and made c.
Rom. 10. 10. with the mouth c. is made to salvation
1 Tim. 6. 13. who before Pilate witnessed a good c.

CONFIDENCE

Signifies, [1] *Assurance,* 2 Cor. 8. 22. [2] *Boldness, or courageousness,* Acts 28. 31. [3] *Trust, or hope,* Job 4. 6. [4] *That wherein one trusteth,* Jer. 48. 13. [5] *Succour, or help,* 2 Kings 18. 19. [6] *Safety, or security,* Ezek. 28. 26. [7] *A due resolution,* 2 Cor. 10. 2. [8] *A free and bold profession of Christ and the gospel,* Heb. 10. 35. [9] *A well-grounded persuasion of audience and acceptance,* Eph. 3. 12.
Judg. 9. 26. men of Shechem put their c. in Gaal
2 Kings 18. 19. thus saith the great king of Assyria what c. is this wherein thou trustest? *Isa.* 36. 4.

Job 4. 6. is not this thy fear, thy c. thy hope?
18. 14. his c. shall be rooted out of his tabernacle
31. 24. if I have said to fine gold, thou art my c.
Psal. 65. 5. who art the c. of all ends of the earth
118. 8. better to trust in Ld. than to put c. in man
9. better to trust in Lord than to put c. in princes
Prov. 3. 26. for Ld. shall be thy c. and keep thy foot
14. 26. in the fear of the Lord is strong c.
21. 22. casteth down the strength of the c. thereof
25. 19. c. in an unfaithful man is like a broken tooth
Isa. 30. 15. in quietn. and c. shall be your strength
Jer. 48. 13. as Isr. was ashamed of Beth-el their c.
Ezek. 28. 26. plant viney. they shall dwell with c.
29. 16. Egypt shall be no more the c. of h. of Isr.
Mic. 7. 5. trust not a friend, put ye not c. in a guide
Acts 28. 31. preaching the kingd. of God with all c.
2 Cor. 1. 15. in this c. I was minded to come before
2. 3. having c. in you all, that my joy is joy of you
7. 16. I rejoice that I have c. in you in all things
8. 22. diligent on the great c. which I have in you
10. 2. with that c. wherewith I think to be bold
11. 17. but as it were foolishly in this c. of boast.
Gal. 5. 10. I have c. in you through the Lord
Eph. 3. 12. in whom access with c. by faith in him
Phil. 1. 25. having this c. I shall abide with you all
3. 3. we rejoice in Chr. Jes. and have no c. in flesh
4. though I might also have c. in flesh, if any other
2 Thess. 3. 4. we have c. in the Lord touching you
Philem. 21. having c. in thy obedience, I wrote to you
Heb. 3. 6. if we hold fast the c. and hope to the end
14. if we hold beginning of our c. stedfast to end
10. 35. cast not away therefore your c. which hath
11. †1. faith is the c. of things hoped for
1 John 2. 28. when he shall appear, we may have c.
3. 21. if heart condemn not, then have c. toward G.
5. 14. and this is the c. that we have in him

CONFIDENCES.

Jer. 2. 37. the Lord hath rejected thy c. not prosper

CONFIDENT.

Psal. 27. 3. though war should rise, in this will I be c.
Prov. 14. 16. but the fool rageth and is c.
Rom. 2. 19. art c. thou thyself art a guide of the blind
2 Cor. 5. 6. therefore we are always c. knowing
8. we are c. willing rather to be absent from body
9. 4. we should be ashamed in this same c. boasting
Phil. 1. 6. being c. of this very thing, who hath begun
14. many of the brethren waxing c. by my bonds

CONFIDENTLY.

1 Kings 4. †25. Judah and Isr. dwelt c. under vine
Psal. 16. †9. my flesh shall dwell c. in hope
Ezek. 38. †11. I will go to them that dwell c.
39. †6. I will send a fire among them that dwell c.
Luke 22. 59. another c. affirmed, this fellow was with

CONFIRMATION.

Phil. 1. 7. in defence and c. of the gospel partakers
Heb. 6. 16. an oath of c. is to them an end of all strife

CONFIRM

Signifies, [1] *To strengthen, settle, or establish,* 1 Chron. 14. 2. Acts 14. 22. [2] *To give new assurance of the truth and certainty of any thing,* 1 Kings 1. 14. 2 Cor. 2. 8. [3] *To ratify, or make sure,* Ruth 4. 7. [4] *To refresh,* Psalm 68. 9. [5] *To continue to perform,* Deut. 27. 26. [6] *To fulfil, accomplish, or make good,* Rom. 15. 8. To confirm the promises made to the fathers. *To make it evidently appear unto men, that God who promised to send his Son unto the* Jews, *was faithful and true, because in the fulness of time he did send him. The promises of God are in themselves most firm and stable, as heaven and earth, so they are immoveable and constant: they are said to be confirmed in respect of men, whose faith, being weak and full of doubts, had need to be helped and strengthened; not God's promises, but men's belief is feeble.*

Confirmation *is a work of the Spirit of God, strengthening faint and weak minds in faith and obedience unto the end,* 1 Pet. 5. 10. The God of all grace confirm and strengthen you. *God confirmeth as the author or efficient cause of strength; the word, sacraments, and ministers, confirm as instruments or helps,* Luke 22. 32. When converted, strengthen thy brethren. *And a man confirms himself when he takes heart and courage to himself in a good cause, upon hope and confidence of God's help,* 1 Cor. 16. 13. But David encouraged himself in the Lord his God, 1 Sam. 30. 6.

Ruth 4. 7. this was the manner for to c. all things
1 Kings 1. 14. I will come in after and c. thy words
2 Kings 15. 19. to c. the kingdom in his hand
Esth. 9. 29. Esth. wrote to c. second letter of Purim
31. to c. these days of Purim in their times
Psal. 68. 9. didst c. thine inheritance when weary
Isa. 35. 3 strengthen weak hands and c. feeble knees
Ezek. 13. 6. to hope that they would c. the word
Dan. 9. 27. he shall c. the covenant for one week
11. 1. even I stood to c. and to strengthen him
Rom. 15. 8. to c. the promises made to the fathers
1 Cor. 1. 8. who shall also c. you to the end
2 Cor. 2. 8. that ye would c. your love toward him

CONFIRMED.

2 Sam. 7. 24. thou hast c. to thyself thy people Isr.
2 Kings 14. 5. as soon as the kingdom was c. he slew
1 Chron 14. 2. Lord had c. him king over Israel
16. 17. and hath c. the same to Jacob, Ps. 105. 10.
2 Chron. 25. †3. when the kingdom was c. he slew
Esth. 9. 32. Esther c. these matters of Purim
Dan. 9. 12. hath c. his words which he spake ag. us
Acts 15. 32. exhorted the brethren and c. them
1 Cor. 1. 6. the testimony of Christ was c. in you
Gal. 3. 15. yet if it be c. no man disannulleth it
17. the covenant that was c. before of God
Heb. 2. 3. was c. to us by them that heard him
6. 17. immutability of counsel, he c. it by an oath

CONFIRMETH, ING.

Num. 30. 14. bonds which are on her, he c. them
Deut. 27. 26. cursed be he that c. not all the words
Isa. 44. 26. that c. the word of his servant
Mark 16. 20. preached, c. word with signs following
Acts 14. 22. c. souls of the disciples, exhorting them
15. 41. went thro' Syria and Cilicia c. the churches

CONFISCATION.

Ezra 7. 26. let judgm. be executed to c. or imprison.

CONFLICT.

Psal. 39. †10. I am consumed by the c. of thine hand
Phil. 1. 30. having the same c. which ye saw in me
Col. 2. 1. that ye knew what great c. I have for you

CONFORMABLE.

Phil. 3. 10. may know him, being made c. to his death

CONFORMED.

Rom. 8. 29. predestinate to be c. to image of his Son
12. 2. be not c. to this world, but be ye transformed

CONFOUND

Signifies, [1] *To disorder, mingle, or jumble together,* Gen. 11. 7. [2] *To baffle, or confute,* Acts 9. 22. [3] *To be ashamed by reason of some disappointment,* Job 6. 20. [4] *To destroy, or break in pieces,* Jer. 1. 17. Zech. 10. 5. [5] *To be amazed, astonished, or troubled in mind,* Acts 2. 6. *It is said,* 1 Pet. 2. 6. He that believeth shall not be confounded; *that is, he shall not be disappointed of his expectation of salvation; the scripture referred to by the apostle is,* Isa. 28. 16. He that believeth shall not make haste: *that is, he shall not hastily and greedily catch at any way of escaping his danger, whether it be right or wrong: but shall patiently wait upon God for deliverance and salvation in his way.*

Gen. 11. 7. let us go down and c. their language, 9.
Jer. 1. 17. be not dismayed, lest I c. thee before them
1 Cor. 1. 27. to c. the wise, to c. things that are mighty

CONFOUNDED.

2 Kings 19. 26. the inhabitants were c. Isa. 37. 27.
Job 6. 20. they were c. because they had hoped
Psal. 35. 4. let them be c. that seek after my soul
69. 6. let not those that seek thee be c. for my sake
71. 13. let them be c. that are adversaries to my soul
24. for they are c. that seek my hurt
83. 17. let them be c. and troubled for ever
97. 7. c. be all they that serve graven images
129. 5. let them all be c. turned back that hate Zion
Isa. 1. 29. shall be c. for gardens that ye have chosen
19. 9. they that weave net-works shall be c.
37. 27. their inhabitants were dismayed and c.
Jer. 9. 19. greatly c. because we have forsaken land
10. 14. every founder is c. by graven image, 51. 17.
17. 18. let them be c. that persecute me, let not me
46. 24. daughter of Egypt c. ‖ 48. 20. Moab is c.
49. 23. Hamath is c. ‖ 50. 2. Babylon taken, Bel c.
50. 12. your mother shall be sore c. be ashamed
51. 47. Babylon, her whole land shall be c.
51. we are c. because we have heard reproach
Ezek. 16. 52. be thou c. and bear thy shame, 54, 63.
Mic. 7. 16. nations shall see and be c. at their might
Zech. 10. 5. and the riders on horses shall be c.
Acts 2. 6. the multitude came together and were c.
9. 22. Saul c. the Jews who dwelt at Damascus

Ashamed and CONFOUNDED.

Psal. 40. 14. *as. and c.* that seek after my soul, 70. 2.
Isa. 24. 23. the moon shall be c. *and* the sun *ashamed*
41. 11. incensed against thee shall be *ashamed and c.*
45. 16. idol-makers shall be *ash. and c.* all of them
54. 4. thou shalt not be *ashamed,* neither be thou c.
Jer. 14. 3. nobles and little ones were *ashamed and c.*
15. 9. that hath born seven hath been *ashamed and c.*
22. 22. surely then shalt thou be *ashamed and c.*
31. 19. I was *ashamed,* yea *and c.* because I did bear
Ezek. 36. 32. be *ashamed and c.* for your own ways
Mic. 3. 7. then shall seers be *ashamed and* diviners c.

Not CONFOUNDED.

Psal. 22. 5. our fathers trusted, and were *not* c.
Isa. 45. 17. *not* ashamed nor c. world without end
50. 7. God will help, therefore shall I *not* be c.
1 Pet. 2. 6. he that believeth on him shall *not* be c.

CONFUSED.

Isa. 9. 5. for every battle of warrior is with c. noise
Acts 19. 32. some cried, for the assembly was c.

CONFUSION.

Gen. 11. †9. therefore is the name of it called c.
Lev. 18. 23. a beast to lie down thereto, it is c.
20. 12. surely be put to death, they have wrought c.
1 Sam. 20. 30. hast chosen David to thy c. and to c.
Ezra 9. 7. been delivered to c. of face, as at this day
Job 10. 15. I am full of c. therefore see mine afflict.
Psal. 35. 4. let them be brought to c. devise my hurt
44. 15. my c. is continually before me and shame
70. 2. let them be put to c. that desire my hurt
71. 1. O Lord, let me never be put to c.
109. 29. let them cover themselves with their own c.
Isa. 24. 10. the city of c. is broken down
30. 3. and the trust in the shadow of Egypt your c.
34. 11. he shall stretch out upon it the line of c.
41. 29. their molten images are wind and c.
45. 16. makers of idols shall go to c. together
61. 7. for c. they shall rejoice in their portion
Jer. 3. 25. we lie in shame and our c. covereth us
7. 19. do they not provoke thems. to c. of their faces
20. 11. their everlasting c. shall never be forgotten
Dan. 9. 7. but to us belongeth c. of faces, 8.
Acts 19. 29. the whole city was filled with c.
1 Cor. 14. 33. for God is not author of c. but peace
Jam. 3. 16. for where envying and strife is, there is c.

CONGEALED.

Exod. 15. 8. the depths were c. in heart of the sea

CONGRATULATE.

1 Chron. 18. 10. to inquire of his welfare and c. him

CONGREGATION.

Lev. 4. 21. it is a sin offering for the c.
10. 17. God hath given it you to bear iniquity of c.
16. 33. he shall make an atonement for all the c.
Num. 1. 16. these were the renowned of the c.
10. 7. but when c. is to be gathered you shall blow
14. 27. how long shall I bear with this evil c.?
15. 15. one ordinance shall be for c. and stranger
16. 21. separate yourselves from c. that I may cons.
45. get you up from among this c. that I may cons.
47. Aaron took and ran into the midst of the c.
19. 20. that soul shall be cut off from among the c.
27. 16. let the Lord set a man over the c.
35. 12. cities of refuge that manslayer die not, till he stand before the c. for judgment, Josh. 20. 6.
Josh. 9. 27. made them drawers of water for the c.
Judg. 20. 1. the c. was gathered as one man from Dan
Judg. 21. 5. that came not up with the c. to the Lord
1 Kings 12. 20. they sent and called Jerob. to the c.
2 Chr. 30. 24. Hezekiah did give to c. 1000 bullocks
Ezra 10. 8. and himself separated from the c.
Neh. 13. 1. the Moabite should not come into the c.
Job 15. 34. for the c. of hypocrites shall be desolate
30. 28. I stood up and I cried in the c.
Psal. 1. 5. nor sinners in the c. of the righteous
22. 22. in the midst of the c. will I praise thee
26. 5. I have hated the c. of evil doers
58. 1. do ye indeed speak righteousness, O c.?
74. 2. remember thy c. thou hast purchased of old
19. forget not the c. of thy poor for ever
75. 2. when I receive the c. I will judge uprightly
82. 1. God standeth in the c. of the mighty
89. 5. thy faithfulness also in the c. of the saints
107. 32. let them exalt him also in c. of the people
111. 1. I will praise the L. in the assembly and c.
Prov. 5. 14. I was almost in all evil in midst of c.
21. 16. the men shall remain in the c. of the dead
Isa. 14. 13. I will sit upon the mount of the c.
Jer. 6. 18. and know, O c. what is among them
30. 20. their c. shall be established before me
Lam. 1. 10. that they should not enter into thy c.
Hos. 7. 12. I will chastise them as their c. hath heard
Joel 2. 16. gather the people, sanctify the c.
Acts 13. 43. now when the c. was broken up

All the CONGREGATION.

Lev. 8. 3. gather *all the c.* together to door of tabern.
16. 17. make atonement for *all the c.* of Israel
24. 14. let *all the c.* stone him, 16. Num. 15. 35.
Num. 14. 10. *all the c.* bade stone them with stones
16. 3. seeing *all the c.* are holy, every one of them
22. shall one sin, wilt thou be wroth with *all c.?*
20. 27. they went up in sight of *all the c.* 25. 6.
27. 19. set him before Eleazar and *all the c.* 22.
Josh. 8. 35. which Joshua read not before *all the c*
9. 18. *all the c.* murmured against the princes
22. 20. wrath fell on *all the c.* of Israel
1 Kings 8. 14. the king blessed *all the c.* of Isr. 55.
1 Chron. 29. 20. *all the c.* blessed the Lord God
2 Chron. 23. 3. *all the c.* made a covenant with the k.
29. 28. *all the c.* worshipped and the singers sang
Neh. 5. 13. *all the c.* said, amen, and praised the L.
8. 17. *all the c.* that were come again made booths

Elders of the CONGREGATION.

Lev. 4. 15. *elders of the c.* shall lay their hands
Judg. 21. 16. *eld. of c.* said, how shall we do for [wives?

Great CONGREGATION.

1 Kings 8. 65. at that time Solomon held a feast, all Israel with him, a *great c.* 2 Chron. 7. 8. ‖ 30. 13.
Ezra 10. 1. assembled to him out of Israel a *great c.*
Psal. 22. 25. my praise shall be of thee in the *great c.*
35. 18. I will give thee thanks in the *great c.*
40. 9. I have preached righteousness in the *great c.*
10. I have not concealed thy truth from *great c.*

CONGREGATION *of Israel.*

Exod. 12. 6. *c. of Israel* shall kill it in the evening
19. that soul shall be cut off from the *c. of Israel*
47. all the *c. of Israel* shall keep the passover
Lev. 4. 13. if whole *c. of Isr.* sin through ignorance
Num. 16. 9. Lord hath separated you from *c. of Isr.*
2 Chron. 5. 6. Solom. and *c. of Isr.* sacrificed sheep
24. 6. according to the commandment of *c. of Isr.*

CONGREGATION *of the Lord.* [*L.?*

Num. 16. 3. why lift you yourselves above *c. of the*
27. 17. *c. of L.* not as sheep that have no shepherd
31. 16. was a plague among *c. of the L. Josh.* 22. 17.
Deut. 23. 1. shall not enter into the *c. of the L.* 2, 3.
1 Chron. 28. 8. in sight of *c. of L.* keep commandm.
Mic. 2. 5. that shall cast a cord by lot in the *c. of L.*

Tabernacle of the CONGREGATION.

Exod. 29. 10. bullock brought before the *tab. of c.*
44. I will sanctify *t. of c.* ‖ 30. 26. anoint *t. of c.*
33. 7. called it the *t. of c.* went out to the *t. of c.*
Lev. 3. 8. kill it bef. *t. of c.* 13. ‖ 4. 5. bring it to *t. of c.*
10. 7. ye shall not go out from the door of *t. of c.*
9. drink no wine when ye go into the *tab. of c.*
16. 16. so do for *t. of c.* ‖ 33. atonement for *t. of c.*
Num. 4. 3. work of the *t. of c.* 23, 25, 30, 35, 39, 43.
8. 9. thou shalt bring the Levites before *tab. of c.*
12. 4. Lord spake, come out ye three to *tab. of c.*
14. 10. glory of the Lord appeared in the *tab. of c.*
17. 4. lay up in *t. of c.* ‖ 18. 4. keep charge of *t. of c.*
25. 6. Israel weeping before the door of *tab. of c.*
Deut. 31. 14. present yourselves in *tabern. of the c.*
Josh. 18. 1. at Shiloh, and set up the *tab. of c.* there
1 Kings 8. 4. they brought up *tab. of c.* 2 Chr. 5. 5.
2 Chron. 1. 3. for there was the *tab. of c.* of God

See Door.

Tent of the CONGREGATION.

Exod. 39. 32. *t. of c.* finished ‖ 40. 2. set up *t. of c.*
40. 22. table in *t. of c.* ‖ 24. candlestick in *t. of c.*
26. and he put the golden altar in the *tent of the c.*
34. then a cloud covered the *tent of the c.*
35. Moses was not able to enter into the *tent of c.*

Whole CONGREGATION.

Exod. 16. 2. the *whole c.* of Israel murmured
Num. 3. 7. they shall keep the charge of the *w. c.*
Josh. 22. 18. to-morrow he will be wroth with *w. c.*
Judg. 21. 13. the *whole c.* sent to speak to Benjamin
2 Chr. 6. 3. the king blessed the *whole c.* of Israel
Ezra 2. 64. the *whole c.* was 42,360. Neh. 7. 66.
Prov. 26. 26. wickedness be shewed before *whole c.*

CONGREGATIONS.

Psal. 26. 12. in the c. will I bless the Lord
68. 26. bless ye God in the c. even the Lord
74. 4. thine enemies roar in the midst of thy c.

CONQUER.

Rev. 6. 2. he went forth conquering and to c.

CONQUERORS.

Rom. 8. 37. in all these things we are more than c.

CONSCIENCE

Is *the testimony and secret judgment of the soul, which gives its approbation to actions that it thinks good, or reproaches itself with those which it believes to be evil: Or, it is a particular knowledge which we have with us of our own deeds, good or evil, arising out of the general knowledge of the mind, which shows us what is good, or evil; and* Conscience tells us when we have done the one or the other, Rom. 2. 15. *It is either,* (I) Good, 1 Tim. 1. 5. *And this is called,* [1] A conscience void of offence toward God and men; *which does not accuse a person for any wilful offence, either against God or men,* Acts 24. 16. [2] A conscience bearing a person witness in the Holy Ghost, *that is, by the conduct and guidance of the Holy Ghost, who cannot lie,* Rom. 9. 1. [3] Pure and good, *being purified by the blood of Christ,* Heb. 9. 14. 1 Tim. 3. 9. [4] Purged from dead works; *that is, freed from that sentence of death which it receives by reason of sin,* Heb. 9. 14. [5] *A conscience not troubled with a sense of guilt,* Heb. 10. 2. [6] *A conscience checking and condemning persons, when they have gone against their light, and approving and justifying them, when they have conformed to it,* Rom. 2. 15. Or, (II) Evil, Heb. 10. 22. *when it is defiled with vicious habits, so that it does not perform its office aright. It is called,* [1] A conscience seared with a hot iron; *that is, quite extinct and cut off, or utterly hardened, which has lost all sense and feeling,* 1 Tim. 4. 2. [2] A defiled conscience; *when it is blinded and perverted, so that it cannot judge of its own actions,* Tit. 1. 15. *This* evil conscience *is sometimes quiet, sometimes stirring and troubled: It accuseth when it should excuse, and excuseth when it should accuse. The* conscience *also even of the best, is now and then* erroneous *and* doubtful.

The apostle Paul *permits the faithful to go and eat at the houses of the Gentiles, if they were invited thither, and to partake of every thing which was served up at their tables, without making particular inquiries out of any scrupulosity of conscience;* asking no question for conscience' sake, 1 Cor. 10. 27, &c. *But if any one says to them, this has been sacrificed to idols; do not eat of it, says he, for his sake who gave you this information; and likewise lest ye wound not your own, but another's, conscience:* Conscience, I say, not thine own, but of the other. *If he who gives you this notice is a* Christian, *and notwithstanding the information so given you forbear not to eat: he will condemn you in his heart, or will eat of it after your example against his own conscience, and so the guilt of his sin will be imputed to you. If he is an* Heathen, *who thus advertises you, and he sees you eat of it, he will conceive a contempt for you and your religion. In another place the same Apostle requires Christians to be submissive to secular power,* not only for wrath, but also for conscience' sake, *Rom.* 13. 5. *that is, not only for fear of punishment from the magistrate, but more especially out of conscience of duty, both to God, who is the ordainer of him to that special ministry, under himself; and to the magistrate, whose due it is, in respect of his office.*

Eccl. 10. † 20. curse not the king, no not in thy *c.*
John 8. 9. being convicted by their own *c.* went out
Acts 23. 1. Paul said, I have lived in all good *c.*
24. 16. to have a *c.* void of offence toward God and toward men
Rom. 2. 15. their *c.* also bearing witness, and thoughts
9. 1. my *c.* bearing me witness in the Holy Ghost
13. 5. ye must be subject also for *c.* sake
1 *Cor.* 8. 7. for some with *c.* of the idol to this hour eat it, and their *c.* being weak is defiled
10. shall not the weak *c.* be emboldened to eat?
12. but when ye wound their weak *c.* ye sin against Christ
10. 25. that eat, asking no question for *c.* sake, 27.
28. eat not, for his sake that shewed it, for *c.* sake
29. *c.* I say, not thine own, but of the other
2 *Cor.* 1. 12. our rejoicing is this, testimony of our *c.*
4. 2. commending yourselves to every man's *c.*
1 *Tim.* 1. 5. out of a pure heart, and of a good *c.*
19. war a warfare, holding faith and a good *c.*
3. 9. holding the mystery of faith in a pure *c.*
4. 2. having their *c.* seared with a hot iron
2 *Tim.* 1. 3. I thank God, whom I serve with *c.*
Tit. 1. 15. but even their mind and *c.* is defiled
Heb. 9. 9. make perfect, as pertaining to the *c.*
14. purge *c.* from dead works to serve living God
10. 2. worshippers should have had no more *c.* of sins
22. having our hearts sprinkled from an evil *c.*
13. 18. we trust we have a good *c.* in all things
1 *Pet.* 2. 19. if a man for *c.* toward God endure grief
3. 16. having a good *c.* as they speak evil of you
21. but the answer of a good *c.* towards God

CONSCIENCES.

2 *Cor.* 5. 11. I trust also are made manifest in your *c.*

CONSECRATE.

To consecrate, is to offer or devote any thing to God's worship and service. In the Old Testament, *God ordained that all the first-born, both of man and beast, should be consecrated,* Exod. 13. 2, 12, 15. *He consecrated the whole race of* Israel *particularly to his worship,* Exod. 19. 6. *And likewise he devoted the tribe of* Levi, *and the family of* Aaron, *in a more especial manner to his service,* Num. 1. 49. | 3. 12. *Besides these consecrations, which God thus ordained by his own absolute and sovereign authority, there were others which depended on the good will of men, who consecrated themselves, or the things belonging to them, or the persons depending on them, to the service of God, for ever, or for a time only.* Hannah, Samuel's *mother, offered her son to the Lord, to serve all his life-time in the tabernacle,* 1 Sam. 1. 11, 22. *Some of the* Nazarites *consecrated themselves to the Lord only for a certain time,* Num. 6. 13. *And the* Hebrews *sometimes devoted their fields, or cattle, to the Lord; after which they were no longer in their power,* Lev. 27. 28. *In the* New Testament *all the faithful are consecrated to the Lord;* they are a chosen generation, a royal priesthood, an holy nation, a peculiar people, 1 *Pet.* 2. 9.

Exod. 28. 3. *c.* Aaron || 41. anoint and *c.* Aaron's sons
29. 9. thou shalt *c.* Aaron and his sons, 30. 30.
Exod. 29. 35. seven days shalt thou *c.* them, *Lev.* 8. 33.
32. 29. Moses said, *c.* yourselves this day to the L.
Num. 6. 12. shall *c.* to L. the days of his separation
1 *Chron.* 29. 5. to *c.* his service this day to the Lord
2 *Chron.* 13. 9. to *c.* himself with a young bullock
Ezek. 43. 26. purge altar, and they shall *c.* themselves
Mic. 4. 13. I will *c.* their gain to Lord and substance

CONSECRATED.

Num. 3. 3. the sons of Aaron, whom he *c.* to minister
Josh. 6. 19. vessels of brass and iron, are *c.* to the L.
Judg. 17. 5. Micah *c.* one of his sons for his priest, 12.
1 *Kings* 13. 33. whosoever would, Jeroboam *c.* him
2 *Chr.* 29. 31. now ye have *c.* yourselves to the L.
31. 6. the tithe of holy things which were *c.* to L.
Ezra 3. 5. of all the set feasts of Lord that were *c.*
Heb. 7. 28. maketh the Son, who is *c.* for evermore
10. 20. by a new and living way which he hath *c.*

CONSECRATED.

2 *Chr.* 29. 33. *c.* things were 600 oxen, 3000 sheep

CONSECRATION, S.

Exod. 29. 22. shalt take of ram, for it is a ram of *c.*
34. if ought of the flesh of the *c.* remain
Lev. 7. 37. this is the law of the *c.* and sacrifice
8. 28. they were *c.* for a sweet savour to the Lord
31. eat it with the bread that is in the basket of *c.*
33. till the days of your *c.* be at an end
Num. 6. 7. because the *c.* of his G. is upon his head
9. and he hath defiled the head of his *c.*

CONSENT, ED, ING.

Gen. 34. 15. but in this will we *c.* unto you
23. only let us *c.* to them, they will dwell with us
Deut. 13. 8. shalt not *c.* to him, nor hearken to him
Judg. 11. 17. sent to king of Moab, but would not *c.*
1 *Kings* 20. 8. elders said, hearken not to him nor *c.*
2 *Kings* 12. 8. the priests *c.* to receive no more mon.
Psal. 50. 18. when sawest a thief, thou *c.* with him
Prov. 1. 10. if sinners entice thee, *c.* thou not
Dan. 1. 14. so he *c.* to them, and proved them ten days
Luke 23. 51. the same had not *c.* to the deed of them
Acts 8. 1. and Saul was *c.* to Stephen's death, 22. 20.
18. 20. desired to tarry longer with them, he *c.* not
Rom. 1. † 32. not only do the same, but *c.* with them
7. 16. what I would not, I *c.* to law that it is good
1 *Tim.* 6. 3. if any man *c.* not to wholesome words

CONSENT.

1 *Sam.* 11. 7. and they came out with one *c.*
Psal. 83. 5. they have consulted together with one *c.*
Hos. 6. 9. so the company of the priests murder by *c.*
Zeph. 3. 9. may all call on L. to serve with one *c.*
Luke 14. 18. all with one *c.* began to make excuse
1 *Cor.* 7. 5. one another, except it be with *c.* for a time

CONSIDER

Signifies, [1] *To think of, or meditate upon,* 2 Tim. 2. 7. [2] *To view, mark, or observe,* Lev. 13. 13. [3] *To resolve, or determine,* Judg. 18. 14. [4] *To wonder and admire at,* Job 37. 14. [5] *To pity, comfort, or relieve,* Psal. 41. 1. [6] *To remember, or call to mind,* 1 Sam. 12. 24.

Lev. 13. 13. then the priest shall *c.* the leprosy
Deut. 4. 39. know this day and *c.* it in thine heart
32. 29. O that they were wise to *c.* their latter end
Judg. 18. 14. now therefore *c.* what ye have to do
1 *Sam.* 12. 24. *c.* how great things hath done for you
25. 17. therefore know and *c.* what thou wilt do
Job 11. 11. he seeth also, will he not then *c.* it?
23. 15. when I *c.* I am afraid of him
34. 27. turned back and would not *c.* of his ways
37. 14. stand still and *c.* the wondrous works of God
Psal. 5. 1. *c.* my meditation || 9. 13. *c.* my trouble
8. 3. when I *c.* the heavens, the work of thy fingers
13. 3. *c.* and hear, 45. 10. || 25. 19. *c.* my enemies
37. 10. shalt diligently *c.* his place, it shall not be
48. 13. *c.* her palaces, that ye may tell it to gener.
50. 22. now *c.* this, ye that forget God, lest I tear
64. 9. for they shall wisely *c.* of his doing
119. 95. but I will *c.* thy testimonies
153. *c.* mine affliction, and deliver me, I forget not
159. *c.* how I love thy precepts, quicken me, O Lord
Prov. 6. 6. go to the ant, *c.* her ways, and be wise
23. 1. with a ruler *c.* diligently what is before thee
24. 12. doth not he that pondereth the heart *c.* it?
Eccl. 5. 1. for they *c.* not that they do evil
7. 13. *c.* the work of God, who can make straight
14. in prosperity be joyful, but in day of adver. *c.*
Isa. 1. 3. Israel doth not know, my people doth not *c.*
5. 12. neither *c.* the operation of his hands
14. 16. shall narrowly look upon thee and *c.* thee
18. 4. and I will *c.* in my dwelling-place
41. 20. that they may see, and know, and *c.*
43. 18. remember ye not, nor *c.* the things of old
52. 15. what they had not heard shall they *c.*
Jer. 2. 10. *c.* and see if there be such a thing
23. 20. in the latter days ye shall *c.* it, 30. 24.
Lam. 2. 20. O Lord, *c.* to whom thou hast done this
5. 1. O Lord, *c.* and behold our reproach
Ezek. 12. 3. it may be they will *c.* though they be a rebellious house
Dan. 9. 23. understand the matter, and *c.* the vision
Hos. 7. 2. they *c.* not in their hearts that I remember
Hag. 1. 5. thus saith the Lord, *c.* your ways, 7.
2. 15. I pray you, *c.* from this day and upward, 18.
Mat. 6. 28. *c.* the lilies of the field, *Luke* 12. 27.
Luke 12. 24. *c.* the ravens, they neither sow nor reap
John 11. 50. nor *c.* it is expedient for us that one die
Acts 15. 6. the elders came to *c.* of this matter
2 *Tim.* 2. 7. *c.* and the Lord give thee understanding
Heb. 3. 1. brethren, *c.* the Apostle and High-priest
7. 4. now *c.* how great this man was, unto whom
10. 24. let us *c.* one another to provoke to love
12. 3. *c.* him that endured contradiction of sinners

CONSIDERED, EST.

1 *Kings* 3. 21. when I *c.* in morning, it was not my son
5. 8. I have *c.* things which thou sentest to me for
Job 1. 8. hast thou *c.* my servant Job? 2. 3.
Psal. 31. 7. I will be glad, for thou hast *c.* my trouble
Prov. 24. 32. then I saw and *c.* it well
Eccl. 4. 1. I *c.* all the oppressions that are done
4. again I *c.* all travail and every right work
9. 1. for all this I *c.* in my heart to declare this
Jer. 33. 24. *c.* not what this people have spoken
Dan. 7. 8. I *c.* the horns, and behold there came up
Mat. 7. 3. *c.* not the beam that is in thine own eye
Mark 6. 52. they *c.* not the miracle of the loaves
Acts 12. 12. when Peter had *c.* the thing, he came
Rom. 4. 19. he *c.* not his own body now dead

CONSIDERETH, ING.

Ps. 33. 15. fashion. hearts alike, he *c.* all their works
41. 1. blessed is he that *c.* the poor, Lord will deliver
Prov. 21. 12. righteous man *c.* house of the wicked
† 29. but as for the upright, he *c.* his way
28. 22. and *c.* not that poverty shall come on him
29. 7. the righteous *c.* the cause of the poor
31. 16. she *c.* a field, and buyeth it, plants vineyards
Isa. 44. 19. none *c.* in his heart to say, I have burnt
57. 1. none *c.* that the righteous is taken away
Ezek. 18. 14. and *c.* and doth not such like, 28.
Dan. 8. 5. as I was *c.* behold an he goat came
Gal. 6. 1. *c.* thyself, lest thou also be tempted
Heb. 13. 7. *c.* the end of their conversation

CONSIST, ETH.

Luke 12. 15. a man's life *c.* not in the abundance
Col. 1. 17. he is before all things, by him all things *c.*

CONSOLATION

Is *that inward spiritual refreshing and strengthening of the heart, by the consideration and experience of God's gracious promises in Christ,* 2 Cor. 1. 5. *The Holy Ghost is the worker of comfort, and is therefore called the* Comforter, John 16. 7. *The promises of the word are the grounds of comfort,* 1 Thess. 4. 18.; *and godly ministers and the faithful, are the helpers of our comfort and consolation,* 2 Cor. 7. 6, 7.

Waiting for the consolation of Israel, *Luke* 2. 25. *He waited for Christ to comfort them against their troubles both spiritual and outward. The prophets used to comfort the people of God among the* Jews, *against all their sad tidings they brought them, with the prophecies of the coming and kingdom of Christ,* Isa. 66. 12, 13. *Herein* Simeon *shewed the truth of his piety and devotion, that he believed, and waited for the coming of Christ.*

Jer. 16. 7. nor shall men give them the cup of *c.*
Luke 2. 25. Simeon, waiting for the *c.* of Israel
6. 24. woe to you rich, for ye have received your *c.*
Acts 4. 36. which is, being interpreted, the son of *c.*
15. 31. which when read, they rejoiced for the *c.*
Rom. 15. 5. the God of *c.* grant you to be like-minded
2 *Cor.* 1. 5. so our *c.* also aboundeth by Christ
6. afflicted, for your *c.* and sal. comf. for your *c.*
7. of sufferings, so shall ye be partakers of the *c.*
7. 7. but by the *c.* wherewith he was comforted
Phil. 2. 1. if there be any *c.* in Christ, fulfil ye my joy
2 *Thess.* 2. 16. who hath given us everlasting *c.*
Philem. 7. we have great joy and *c.* in thy love
Heb. 6. 18. we might have a strong *c.* who have fled

CONSOLATIONS.

Job 15. 11. are the *c.* of God small with thee?
21. 2. hear my speech, and let this be your *c.*
Isa. 66. 11. and be satisfied with the breasts of her *c.*

CONSORTED.

Acts 17. 4. some of them *c.* with Paul and Silas

CONSPIRACY.

2 *Sam.* 15. 12. and Absalom's *c.* was strong
2 *Kings* 12. 20. his serv. made a *c.* and slew Joash
14. 19. they made a *c.* ag. Amaziah, 2 *Chr.* 25. 27.
15. 15. acts of Shallum and his *c.* which he made
30. Hoshea made a *c.* against Pekah
17. 4. the king of Assyria found *c.* in Hoshea
Jer. 11. 9. a *c.* is found among the men of Judah
Ezek. 22. 25. is a *c.* of her prophets in midst thereof
Acts 23. 13. more than forty who had made this *c.*

CONSPIRATORS.

2 *Sam.* 15. 31. Ahithophel is among *c.* with Absalom

CONSPIRED.

Gen. 37. 18. they *c.* against Joseph to slay him
1 *Sam.* 22. 8. that all of you have *c.* against me
13. why have ye *c.* ag. me, thou and son of Jesse
1 *Kings* 15. 27. Baasha son of Ahijah *c.* ag. Nadab
16. 9. Zimri *c.* against Elah and slew him, 16.
2 *Kings* 9. 14. Jehu son of Nimshi *c.* against Joram
10. 9. I *c.* against my master and slew him
15. 10. Shallum *c.* against Zachariah, and smote him
25. Pekah *c.* against Pekahiah, and smote him
21. 23. the servants of Amon *c.* against him
24. slew all that *c.* against Amon, 2 *Chr.* 33. 25.
2 *Chron.* 24. 21. and they *c.* against Jehoiada
25. the servants of Joash *c.* against him, 26.
Neh. 4. 8. *c.* all of them together, and come and fight
Amos 7. 10. Amos hath *c.* against thee in Israel

CONSTANT, LY.

1 *Chron.* 28. 7. if he be *c.* to do my commandments
Ezra 9. † 8. to give us a *c.* abode in his holy place
Psal. 51. † 10. and renew a *c.* spirit within me
Prov. 21. 28. but the man that heareth, speaketh *c.*
Acts 12. 15. Rhoda *c.* affirmed that it was even so
Tit. 3. 8. these things I will that thou affirm *c.*

CONSTELLATIONS.

2 *Kings* 23. † 5. put down those that burnt incense to *c.*
Isa. 13. 10. the *c.* thereof shall not give their light

CONSTRAIN.

Gal. 6. 12. they *c.* you to be circumcised, only lest

CONSTRAINED, ETH.

2 *Kings* 4. 8. the woman of Shunem *c.* him to eat bread
Job 32. 18. full of matter, the spirit within me *c.* me
Mat. 14. 22. Jesus *c.* his disciples, *Mark* 6. 45.
Luke 24. 29. but they *c.* him, saying, abide with us
Acts 16. 15. Lydia *c.* us to come into her house
28. 19. I was *c.* to appeal to Cæsar
2 *Cor.* 5. 14. for love of Chr. *c.* us, because we judge

CONSTRAINT.

1 *Pet.* 5. 2. taking oversight, not by *c.* but willingly

CONSULT.

Psal. 62. 4. only *c.* to cast him down from excellency

CONSULTATION.

Mark 15. 1. the chief priests held a *c.* with the elders

CONSULTED.

1 *Kings* 12. 6. Rehoboam *c.* with the old men, 8.
1 *Chr.* 13. 1. Dav. *c.* with the captains of thousands
2 *Chron.* 20. 21. Jehoshaphat *c.* with the people
Neh. 5. 7. I *c.* with myself, and rebuked the nobles
Psal. 83. 3. they have *c.* against thy hidden ones
5. for they have *c.* together with one consent
Ezek. 21. 21. the king of Babylon *c.* with images

Dan. 6. 7. all the presidents and captains c. together
Mic. 6. 5. remember what Balak king of Moab c.
Hab. 2. 10. hast c. shame to thy house, by cutting off
Mat. 26. 4. c. that they might take Jesus and kill
John 12. 10. chief priests c. to put Lazarus to death

CONSULTER.

Deut. 18. 11. not found among you a c. with spirits

CONSULTETH.

Luke 14. 31. c. whether he be able with 10,000 to meet

CONSUME

Signifies, [1] *To waste, destroy, and bring to utter ruin, and desolation,* Exod. 32. 10. [2] *To spend, or squander away,* Jam. 4. 3. [3] *To vanish away,* Job 7. 9. [4] *To make or cause to pass away,* Psal. 78. 33. [5] *To burn up,* Luke 9. 54. [6] *To melt away,* Jer. 6. 29. [7] *To crush,* Esth. 9. † 24.

Gen. 41. 30. and the famine shall c. the land
Exod. 33. 3. lest I c. thee in the way, 5.
Lev. 26. 16. the burning ague that shall c. the eyes
Deut. 5. 25. for this great fire will c. us
7. 16. thou shalt c. all people which Lord God shall
28. 38. gather but little, for locust shall c. it, 42.
32. 22. a fire kindled in mine anger shall c. earth
Josh. 24. 20. will c. you after he hath done you good
1 Sam. 2. 33. the man of thine shall be to c. thine eyes
2 Kings 1. 10. let fire c. thee and thy fifty, 12.
Job 15. 34. fire shall c. the tabernacles of bribery
20. 26. a fire not blown shall c. him
24. 19. drought and heat c. the snow-waters
Psal. 37. 20. shall c. into smoke shall they c. away
39. 11. makest his beauty to c. away like a moth
49. 14. their beauty shall c. in the grave
78. 33. therefore their days did he c. in vanity
Isa. 7. 20. and it shall also c. the beard
10. 18. and shall c. the glory of his forest and field
27. 10. there shall the calf c. the branches
Jer. 49. 27. fire shall c. the palaces of Ben-hadad
Ezek. 4. 17. and c. away for their iniquity
13. 13. and great hail-stones in my fury to c. it
21. 28. the sword is drawn, it is furbished to c.
22. 15. I will c. thy filthiness out of thee
24. 10. kindle the fire, c. the flesh, and spice it well
35. 12. they are desolate, they are given us to c.
Dan. 2. 44. it shall c. all these kingdoms and stand
Hos. 11. 6. and the sword shall c. his branches
Zeph. 1. 2. I will c. all things from off the land
3. I will c. man and beast, I will c. fowls of heaven
Zech. 5. 4. it shall remain in his house and c. it
14. 12. their flesh, eyes, tongue shall c. away
2 Thess. 2. 8. that wicked one, whom the Lord shall c.
Jam. 4. 3. ye ask that ye may c. it on your lusts

CONSUME *them.*

Exod. 32. 10. wrath wax hot, that I may c. them, 12.
Num. 16. 21. that I may c. them in a moment, 45.
Deut. 7. 22. thou mayest not c. them at once
1 Sam. 15. † 18. destroy Amalekites till thou c. them
2 Chron. 18. † 10. push Syria till thou c. them
Neh. 9. 31. thou didst not utterly c. them
Esth. 9. † 24. Haman had cast the lot to c. them
Psal. 59. 13. c. th. in wrath, c. th. that they may not be
Jer. 8. 13. I will surely c. them, saith the Lord
14. 12. but I will c. them by the sword and famine
Ezek. 20. 13. I would pour fury on them to c. them
Luke 9. 54. fire to come and c. them, as Elias did

CONSUMED.

Gen. 19. 15. lest thou be c. in the iniquity of the city
17. escape to the mountain, lest thou be c.
31. 40. thus I was, in the day the drought c. me
Exod. 3. 2. behold the bush burned, and was not c.
15. 7. sentest thy wrath, which c. them as stubble
22. 6. if the corn or the field be c. therewith
Lev. 9. 24. and c. upon the altar the burnt-offering
Num. 11. 1. c. them in uttermost parts of the camp
12. 12. let her not be as one of whom flesh is half c.
16. 26. depart lest ye be c. in all their sins
35. there came out fire and c. the 250 men
21. 28. a fire is gone out, it hath c. Ar of Moab
25. 11. that I c. not the children of Israel
32. 13. till the generation that had done evil was c.
Deut. 2. 16. when the men of war were c. and dead
Judg. 6. 21. there rose fire out of rock and c. flesh
1 Sam. 27. † 1. I shall one day be c. by hand of Saul
2 Sam. 13. † 39. the soul of David was c. to go forth
21. 5. the man that c. us, and devised against us
1 Kings 18. 38. then the fire of the Lord fell and c. the sacrifice, and licked up the water, 2 Chr. 7. 1.
2 Kings 1. 10. and fire c. him and his fifty, 12.
2 Chron. 8. 8. whom the children of Israel c. not
Neh. 2. 3. the gates thereof are c. with fire, 13.
Job 1. 16. the fire of God hath c. sheep and servants
4. 9. by the breath of his nostrils are they c.
6. 17. the snow and the ice are c. out of their place
7. 9. as the cloud is c. and vanisheth away
19. 27. my reins c. ‖ 33. 21. his flesh is c. away
Psal. 6. 7. mine eyes c. 31. 9. ‖ 10. my bones c. 102. 3,
39. 10. I am c. by the blow of thine hand
64. † 6. we are c. by that which they searched
71. 13. let them be confounded and c. that are
73. 19. they are utterly c. with terrors
78. 63. fire c. their young men, maidens not given
90. 7. for we are c. by thine anger and thy wrath
104. 35. let the sinners be c. out of the earth
119. 87. they had almost c. me upon the earth
139. my zeal hath c. me, because mine enemies
Prov. 5. 11. when thy flesh and thy body are c.
22. † 8. with the rod of his anger he shall be c.
Isa. 16. 4. the oppressors are c. out of the land
29. 20. scorner is c. and all that watch for iniquity
64. 7. thou hast c. us, because of our iniquities
Jer. 5. 3. hast c. them, but they refused correction
6. 29. the lead is c. ‖ 12. 4. the beasts are c.
20. 18. that my days should be c. with shame
36. 23. till all the roll was c. in the fire on hearth
44. 18. we have been c. by sword and famine
Lam. 2. 22. those I swaddled hath mine enemy c.
3. 22. it is of the Lord's mercies we are not c.
Ezek. 19. 12. her rods broken, fire c. them, 22. 31.
24. 11. on the coals, that the scum of it may be c.
43. 8. wherefore I have c. them in mine anger
Mal. 3. 6. therefore the sons of Jacob are not c.
Gal. 5. 15. take heed ye be not c. one of another

Shall be CONSUMED.

Num. 14. 35. in this wilderness shall they be c.
17. 13. shall die, shall we be c. with dying?
1 Sam. 12. 25. ye shall be c. both ye and your kin
Isa. 1. 28. they that forsake the Lord shall be c.
66. 17. eating swine's flesh, shall be c. together: they that eat swine's flesh shall be c.
Jer. 14. 15. by famine shall those prophets be c.
16. 4. they shall be c. by the sword, 44. 12, 27.
Ezek. 5. 12. with famine shall they be c. in the midst
13. 14. it shall fall, ye shall be c. in the midst thereof
34. 29. they shall be no more c. with hunger
47. 12. leaf not fade, nor shall the fruit thereof be c.
Dan. 11. 16. land which by his hand shall be c.

CONSUMED, with *till,* or *until.*

Deut. 2. 15. to destroy, until they were c. Josh. 5. 6.
28. 21. pestilence cleave to thee, until he have c. thee
Josh. 10. 20. an end of slaying them till they were c.
1 Sam. 15. 18. and fight against them until they be c.
2 Sam. 22. 38. I have pursued my enemies, and I turned not again until I had c. them, Psal. 18. 37.
1 Kings 22. 11. shalt push the Syrians until thou have c. them, 2 Kings 13. 17, 19. 2 Chr. 18. 10.
Ezra 9. 14. be angry with us till thou hadst c. us
Jer. 9. 16. and I will send a sword after them till I have c. them, 24. 10. | 27. 8. | 49. 37.

CONSUMETH, ING.

Deut. 4. 24. the Lord thy G. is a c. fire, Heb. 12. 29.
9. 3. the Lord goeth over before thee as a c. fire
Job 13. 28. he c. as a garment that is moth-eaten
22. 20. but the remnant of them the fire c.
31. 12. for it is a fire that c. to destruction
Isa. 5. 24. as the fire the stubble, and as the flame c. chaff

CONSUMMATION.

Dan. 9. 27. shall make it desolate, even until the c.

CONSUMPTION.

Lev. 26. 16. I will appoint over you terror, c.
Deut. 28. 22. the Lord shall smite thee with a c.
Judg. 20. † 40. the whole c. of the city ascended up
Isa. 10. 22. the c. decreed shall overflow with right.
23. for the Lord God of hosts shall make a c.
28. 22. for I have heard from the L. G. of hosts a c.

CONTAIN.

1 Kings 8. 27. behold the heaven and heaven of heavens cannot c. thee, 2 Chron. 2. 6. | 6. 18.
Ezek. 45. 11. bath may c. tenth part of an homer
John 21. 25. the world could not c. the books written
1 Cor. 7. 9. but if they cannot c. let them marry

CONTAINED, ETH, ING.

Ezek. 23. 32. drink of thy sister's cup, it c. much
John 2. 6. six water-pots c. 2 or 3 firkins a piece
Rom. 2. 14. do by nature the things c. in the law
Eph. 2. 15. having abolished the law c. in ordinances
1 Pet. 2. 6. wheref. it is c. in scripture, behold I lay

CONTEMN, ED, ETH.

Psal. 10. 13. wherefore do the wicked c. God?
15. 4. in whose eyes a vile person is c. but honours
107. 11. they c. the counsel of the most High
Cant. 8. 7. if give his substance for love, it would be c.
Isa. 16. 14. glory of Moab shall be c. with great mult.
Ezek. 21. 10. it c. the rod of my son, as every tree
13. and what if the sword c. even the rod?

CONTEMPT.

Gen. 38. † 23. let her take it lest we become a c.
Esth. 1. 18. thus shall there arise too much c.
Job 12. 21. he poureth c. on princes, Psal. 107. 40.
31. 34. or did the c. of families terrify me?
Psal. 119. 22. remove from me reproach and c.
123. 3. for we are exceedingly filled with c.
4. our soul is filled with the c. of the proud
Prov. 18. 3. when the wicked cometh, then cometh c.
Isa. 23. 9. to bring into c. all the honourable of earth
Dan. 12. 2. some shall awake to everlasting c.

CONTEMPTIBLE.

Mal. 1. 7. in that ye say, the table of the Lord is c.
12. even his meat is c. ‖ 2. 9. I also made you c.
2 Cor. 10. 10. his presence is weak, his speech c.

CONTEMPTUOUSLY.

Psal. 31. 18. which speak c. against the righteous

CONTEND

Signifies, [1] *To strive,* Jer. 18. 19. [2] *To dispute,* Acts 11. 2. [3] *To debate, or plead,* Job 9. 3. | 40. 2. [4] *To fight,* Deut. 2. 9. [5] *To reprove sharply,* Neh. 13. 11. [6] *To endeavour to convince a person of, and reclaim him from his evil way,* Prov. 29. 9. [7] *To punish,* Amos 7. 4. Earnestly to contend for the faith, Jude 3. *strenuously to maintain and defend the apostolical doctrine, by constancy in the faith, zeal for the truth, holiness of life, mutual exhortation, prayer, suffering for the gospel, &c. withstanding all such heretics as would impugn and corrupt the doctrines revealed in the gospel.*

Deut. 2. 9. neither c. with Moabites in battle, 24.
Job 9. 3. if c. he cannot answer him one of a thousand
13. 8. will ye accept his person, and c. for God?
Prov. 28. 4. such as keep the law c. with them
Eccl. 6. 10. nor may he c. with him that is mightier
Isa. 49. 25. I will c. with them that c. with thee
50. 8. he is near that justifieth, who will c. with me?
57. 16. I will not c. for ever, nor will I be wroth
Jer. 12. 5. then how canst thou c. with horses?
18. 19. hearken to voice of them that c. with me
Amos 7. 4. behold the Lord God called to c. by fire
Mic. 6. 1. hear ye, arise, c. thou before the mount
Jude 3. should earnestly c. for faith deliv. to saints

CONTENDED.

Neh. 13. 11. then c. I with the rulers and said, 17.
25. I c. with them, and cursed them, and smote
Job 31. 13. if I despised my servants when they c.
Isa. 41. 12. thou shalt not find them that c. with thee
Acts 11. 2. they of the circumcision c. with him

CONTENDEST.

Job 10. 2. shew me wherefore thou c. with me

CONTENDETH.

Job 40. 2. shall he that c. with Almighty instruct
Prov. 29. 9. if a wise man c. with a foolish man

CONTENDING.

Jude 9. c. with devil, he disputed about body of Moses

CONTENT.

Gen. 37. 27. let us sell him, and his brethren were c.
Exod. 2. 21. Moses was c. to dwell with the man
Lev. 10. 20. when Moses heard that he was c.
Josh. 7. 7. would to G. we had been c. dwelt on other
Judg. 17. 11. Levite was c. to dwell with Micah
19. 6. be c. I pray thee, and tarry all night
2 Kings 5. 23. Naaman said, be c. take two talents
6. 3. one said, be c. and go with thy servants
Job 6. 28. now therefore be c. look upon me
Prov. 6. 35. nor will he rest c. though thou givest gifts
Mark 15. 15. Pilate willing to c. people released Bar.
Luke 3. 14. nor accuse falsely, be c. with your wages
Phil. 4. 11. I have learned in every state to be c.
1 Tim. 6. 8. having food and raiment, let us be c.
Heb. 13. 5. and be c. with such things as ye have
3 John 10. and not c. with prating against us

CONTENTION.

Gen. 26. † 20. he called the name of the well c.
Psal. 95. † 8. harden not your heart, as in the c.
Prov. 13. 10. only by pride cometh c. but wisdom with
17. 14. leave off c. before it be meddled with
18. 6. a fool's lips enter into c. and his mouth calls
22. 10. cast out the scorner, and c. shall go out
Isa. 41. † 12. thou shalt not find the men of thy c.
Jer. 15. 10. woe is me, thou hast borne me a man of c
Hab. 1. 3. and there are that raise up strife and c.
Acts 15. 39. the c. was so sharp between them
Phil. 1. 16. the one preach Christ of c. not sincerely
1 Thess. 2. 2. to speak the gospel of God with much c.

CONTENTIONS.

Prov. 18. 18. the lot causeth c. to cease, and parteth
19. and their c. are like the bars of a castle
19. 13. c. of a wife are a continual dropping, 27. 15.
21. † 9. than with a woman of c. in a wide house
23. 29. who hath woe? who hath c.? hath babbling?
1 Cor. 1. 11. I hear that there are c. among you
Tit. 3. 9. avoid c. and strivings about the law

CONTENTIOUS.

Prov. 21. 19. than with a c. and angry woman
26. 21. as wood to fire, so is a c. man to kindle strife
27. 15. a continual dropping and a c. woman alike
Rom. 2. 8. but to them that are c. and do not obey
1 Cor. 11. 16. but if any man seem to be c. no custom

CONTENTMENT.

1 Tim. 6. 6. but godliness with c. is great gain

CONTINUAL.

Exod. 29. 42. this shall be a c. burnt-offering
Num. 4. 7. and the c. bread shall be thereon
2 Chron. 2. 4. I build an house for the c. shew-bread
Prov. 15. 15. that is of a merry heart hath a c. feast
Isa. 14. 6. he who smote the people with a c. stroke
Jer. 48. 5. for in the going up c. weeping shall go up
52. 34. there was a c. diet given him, 2 Kings 25. 30.
Ezek. 39. 14. shall sever out men of c. employment
Luke 18. 5. lest by her c. coming she weary me
Rom. 9. 2. that I have c. sorrow in my heart

See BURNT-OFFERINGS.

CONTINUALLY.

Gen. 6. 5. every imagination of his heart was evil c.
Exod. 28. 30. upon his heart before the Lord c.
29. 38. two lambs of the first year, day by day c.
Lev. 24. 2. bring oil olive to cause lamps to burn c.
1 Sam. 18. 29. and Saul became David's enemy c.
2 Sam. 9. 7. thou shalt eat bread at my table c.
2 Kings 25. 29. Jehoiachin eat bread, c. Jer. 52. 33.
1 Chron. 16. 11. seek the Lord, seek his face c.
2 Chron. 12. 15. was between Jerob. and Rehob. c.
36. † 15. sent to them, rising up c. and sending them
Job 1. 5. sent and sanctified his sons, thus did Job c.
Psal. 34. 1. his praise shall be c. in my mouth, 71. 6.
35. 27. say c. the Lord be magnified, 40. 16. | 70. 4.
38. 17. ready to halt and my sorrow is c. before me
40. 11. let thy loving-kindness and truth c. preserve
42. 3. while they c. say to me, where is thy God?
44. 15. my confusion is c. before me, and shame
50. 8. thy burnt-offerings to have been c. before me
52. 1. O mighty man, goodness of God endureth c.
71. 3. my habitation, whereunto I may c. resort
6. I have been holden up, my praise shall be c.
14. I will hope c. and praise thee more and more
73. 23. I am c. with thee, thou hast holden me
74. 23. the tumult of those that rise up increaseth c.
109. 15. let them be before the Lord c. to cut off
119. 44. so shall I keep thy law c. for ever and ever
109. my soul is c. in my hand, yet do I not forget
117. and I will have respect to thy statutes c.
140. 2. c. are they gathered together for war
Prov. 6. 14. he deviseth mischief c. he soweth discord
21. bind them c. on thy heart, and tie them
Isa. 21. 8. I stand c. upon the watch-tower in day-time
49. 16. I have graven thee, walls are c. before me
51. 13. and hast feared c. every day, because of f.
52. 5. my name c. every day is blasphemed
58. 11. and the Lord shall guide thee c. and satisfy
60. 11. therefore thy gates shall be open c.
65. 3. a people that provoketh me to anger c.
Jer. 6. 7. before me c. is grief and wounds
Ezek. 46. 14. a meat-offering c. to the Lord
Dan. 6. 16. thy God whom thou servest c. 20.
Hos. 4. 18. they have committed whoredom c.
12. 6. keep mercy, and wait on thy God c.
Obad. 16. so shall all the heathen drink c.
Nah. 3. 19. for hath not thy wickedness passed c.?
Hab. 1. 17. shall they not spare c. to slay the nations?
Zech. 8. † 21. let us go c. and pray before the Lord
Luke 24. 53. were c. in the temple, praising God
Acts 6. 4. we will give ourselves c. to prayer
10. 7. a soldier of them that waited on Cornelius c.
Rom. 13. 6. attending c. upon this very thing
Heb. 7. 3. like the Son of God, abideth a priest c.
10. 1. with those sacrifices offered year by year c.
13. 15. by him let us offer the sacrifice of praise c.

CONTINUANCE.

Deut. 28. 59. even great plagues and of long c.
Ps. 139. 16. my members which in c. were fashion.
Isa. 64. 5. in those is c. and we shall be saved
Ezek. 39. † 14. they shall sever out men of c.
Dan. 1. † 10. faces worse liking than children of c.
Rom. 2. 7. by patient c. in well doing seek for glory

CONTINUE.

Exod. 21. 21. if he c. a day or two, not be punished
Lev. 12. 4. c. in the blood of her purifying, 5.
1 Sam. 12. 14. c. following the Lord your God
13. 14. but now thy kingdom shall not c.

2 Sam. 7. 29. that it may c. for ever before thee
1 Kings 2. 4. the Lord may c. his word that he spake
Job 15. 29. not be rich, nor shall his substance c.
17. 2. doth not mine eye c. in their provocation?
Psal. 36. 10. O c. thy loving-kindness unto them
49. 11. thought that their houses shall c. for ever
72. † 17. shall be as a son to c. his father's name
102. 28. the children of thy servants shall c.
119. 91. they c. according to thine ordinances
Isa. 5. 11. that c. till night, till wine inflame them
65. † 22. and mine elect shall make them c. long
Jer. 32. 14. that the evidences may c. many days
Dan. 11. 8. c. more years than the king of the north
Mat. 15. 32. because they c. with me three days
John 8. 31. if ye c. in my word, then are ye disciples
15. 9. so have I loved you, c. ye in my love
Acts 13. 43. persuaded to c. in the grace of God
14. 22. confirming and exhorting them to c. in faith
26. 22. having obtained help of God, I c. unto day
Rom. 6. 1. shall we c. in sin that grace may abound
11. 22. towards thee goodness, if thou c. in goodness
Gal. 2. 5. that the truth of gospel might c. with you
Phil. 1. 25. I know that I shall c. with you all
Col. 1. 23. if ye c. in the faith, and be not moved
4. 2. c. in prayer, and watch with thanksgiving
1 Tim. 2. 15. if they c. in faith, charity, and holiness
4. 16. take heed to thy doctrine, c. in them
2 Tim. 3. 14. c. in the things which thou hast learned
Heb. 7. 23. priests not suffered to c. by reason of death
13. 1. let brotherly love c. entertain strangers
Jam. 4. 13. and c. there a year, and buy and sell
2 Pet. 3. 4. since the fathers all things c. as they were
1 John 2. 24. ye shall c. in the Son and Father
Rev. 13. 5. power was given him to c. 42 months
17. 10. when he cometh, he must c. a short space

CONTINUED.

Gen. 40. 4. he served them, and c. a season in ward
1 Sam. 1. 12. as she c. praying before the Lord
2 Chron. 29. 28. c. till burnt offering was finished
Neh. 5. 16. yea, also I c. in the work of this wall
Psal. 72. 17. his name shall be c. as long as the sun
Jer. 31. † 32. should I have c. an husband to them
Dan. 1. 21. Daniel c. to first year of king Cyrus
Mat. 20. † 12. these last have c. one hour only
Luke 6. 12. he c. all night in prayer to God
22. 28. ye are they that c. with me in temptation
Acts 1. 14. these all c. with one accord in prayer
2. 42. they c. stedfastly in the apostles' doctrine
8. 13. Simon himself c. with Philip, and wondered
12. 16. but Peter c. knocking, when they had opened
20. 7. Paul preached and c. his speech till midnight
Heb. 8. 9. because they c. not in my covenant
1 John 2. 19. they would no doubt have c. with us

CONTINUETH, ING.

Job 14. 2. he fleeth also as a shadow, and c. not
Jer. 30. 23. a c. whirlwind, it shall fall on wicked
Acts 2. 46. they c. daily with one accord in temple
Rom. 12. 12. rejoicing in hope, c. instant in prayer
Gal. 3. 10. cursed that c. not in all things, in the law
1 Tim. 5. 5. she that is a widow c. in supplications
Heb. 7. 24. but this man, because he c. ever, hath an
13. 14. for here we have no c. city, but we seek
Jam. 1. 25. looketh into the perfect law, and c. in it

CONTRADICTING.

Acts 13. 45. filled with envy, c. and blaspheming

CONTRADICTION.

Heb. 7. 7. without c. the less is blessed of the better
12. 3. consider him that endured such c. of sinners

CONTRARY.

Lev. 26. 21. and if ye walk c. to me, 23, 27, 40.
24. then will I also walk c. to you, 28, 41.
Esth. 9. 1. though it was turned to the c. Jews had rule
Ezek. 16. 34. the c. is in thee, therefore thou art c.
Mat. 14. 24. the ship was tossed, for the wind was c.
Acts 17. 7. these all do c. to the decrees of Cæsar
18. 13. persuaded men to worship God c. to the law
23. 3. commandest me to be smitten c. to the law
26. 9. to do many things c. to the name of Jesus
Rom. 11. 24. graffed c. to nature into a good olive-tree
16. 17. c. to the doctrine which ye have learned
Gal. 5. 17. and these are c. the one to the other
Col. 2. 14. the hand-writing which was c. to us
1 Thess. 2. 15. please not God, and are c. to all men
1 Tim. 1. 10. if any thing that is c. to sound doctrine
Tit. 2. 8. that he of the c. part may be ashamed

CONTRARIWISE.

2 Cor. 2. 7. c. ye ought rather to forgive him
Gal. 2. 7. c. when they saw the gospel was committed
1 Pet. 3. 9. not rendering railing, but c. blessing

CONTRIBUTION.

Rom. 15. 26. to make c. for the poor saints at Jerus.

CONTRITE.

They are of a contrite spirit, *whose hearts are truly and deeply humbled under a sense of their sin and guilt, and God's displeasure following upon it; whose proud and self-willed hearts are subdued, and made obedient to God's will, and submissive to his providence, being willing to accept of reconciliation with God upon any terms,* Psal. 34. 18. | 51. 17. Isa. 66. 2. *This is opposed to the* stony heart, *that is insensible of the burden of sin, stubborn and rebellious against God, impenitent and incorrigible.*

Psal. 34. 18. he saveth such as be of a c. spirit
51. 17. a c. heart, O God, thou wilt not despise
Isa. 57. 15. with him also that is of a c. and humble spirit, to revive the heart of the c. ones
66. 2. that is of a c. spirit and trembleth at my word

CONTROVERSY.

Deut. 17. 8. being matters of c. within thy gates
19. 17. men between whom the c. is shall stand
21. 5. by their word shall every c. be tried
25. 1. if there be a c. between men, and they come
2 Sam. 15. 2. when any man that had a c. came
2 Chron. 19. 8. Jehoshaphat set the Levites for c.
Isa. 34. 8. the year of recompences for the c. of Zion
Jer. 25. 31. the Lord hath a c. with the nations
Ezek. 44. 24. in c. they shall stand in judgment
Hos. 4. 1. the Lord hath a c. with inhabitants of land
12. 2. the Lord hath also a c. with Judah
Mic. 6. 2. the Lord hath a c. with his people
1 Tim. 3. 16. without c. great is the mystery of godl.

CONVENIENT.

Prov. 30. 8. feed me with food c. for me
Jer. 40. 4. it seemeth good and c. for thee to go, 5.
Mark 6. 21. and when a c. day was come Herod made
Acts 24. 25. when I have a c. season will call for thee
Rom. 1. 28. to do those things which are not c.
1 Cor. 16. 12. will come when he shall have c. time
Eph. 5. 4. talking, nor jesting, which are not c.
Philem. 8. might be bold to enjoin that which is c.

CONVENIENTLY.

Mark 14. 11. Judas sought how he might c. betray

CONVERSANT.

Josh. 8. 35. and strangers were c. among them
1 Sam. 25. 15. as long as we were c. with them

CONVERSATION.

Psal. 37. 14. to slay such as be of upright c.
50. 23. to him that ordereth his c. aright shew salv.
2 Cor. 1. 12. in godly sincerity we have had our c.
Gal. 1. 13. ye have heard of my c. in time past
Eph. 2. 3. among whom we had our c. in times past
4. 22. that ye put off concerning the former c.
Phil. 1. 27. only let your c. be as becometh gospel
3. 20. for our c. is in heaven, whence we look
1 Tim. 4. 12. be an example of believers in c. in purity
Heb. 13. 5. let your c. be without covetousness
7. whose faith follow, considering end of their c.
Jam. 3. 13. let him shew out of a good c. his works
1 Pet. 1. 15. so be ye holy in all manner of c.
18. not redeemed with corrup. things from vain c.
2. 12. having your c. honest among the Gentiles
3. 1. they also may be won by the c. of the wives
2. while they behold your chaste c. with fear
16. be ashamed that falsely accuse your good c.
2 Pet. 2. 7. Lot vexed with the filthy c. of wicked
3. 11. ought ye to be, in all holy c. and godliness

CONVERSION

Is the turning, or total change of a sinner from his sins to God, Psal. 51. 13. And sinners shall be converted unto thee. *God is the author of this change, who by his Spirit puts repentance, faith, love, and every grace, into the soul,* Jer. 31. 18. Turn thou me. John 6. 44. No man can come unto me except the Father draw him. *The word of God is a means or instrument of conversion,* Psal. 19. 7. The law of the Lord is perfect, converting the soul. *Ministers, by the preaching of the gospel, are also instrumental in this change.* 1 Cor. 4. 15. In Christ Jesus I have begotten you through the gospel. *And particular Christians, by private admonitions and exhortations, are sometimes a means of this change,* Jam. 5. 19, 20. *Regeneration is the infusion of grace into the soul; conversion is the exercise of grace.* Draw me, I will run, Cant. 1. 4. *Converts are new creatures,* 2 Cor. 5. 17.; *being formed in the image of Christ,* Rom. 8. 29. *and made holy in part here, and shall have a perfection of it after death,* 1 John 3. 2. Rev. 21. 27.

Acts 15. 3. declaring the c. of the Gentiles caused joy

CONVERT, ED.

Psal. 51. 13. and sinners shall be c. unto thee
Isa. 6. 10. lest they understand, and c. and be healed
60. 5. the abundance of the sea shall be c. to thee
Mat. 13. 15. be c. and I should heal them, Mark 4. 12.
18. 3. except ye be c. and become as children
Luke 22. 32. when c. strengthen thy brethren
John 12. 40. be c. and I heal them, Acts 28. 27.
Acts 3. 19. repent ye therefore, and be c. that sins
Jam. 5. 19. do err from the truth, and one c. him

CONVERTETH, ING.

Psal. 19. 7. the law of the Lord is perfect, c. the soul
Jam. 5. 20. that he who c. a sinner from the error

CONVERTS.

Isa. 1. 27. her c. shall be redeemed with righteous.

CONVEY, ED.

1 Kings 5. 9. and I will c. them by sea in floats
Neh. 2. 7. that they may c. me over till I come
John 5. 13. for Jesus had c. himself away

CONVICTED.

John 8. 9. being c. by their own conscience went out

CONVINCE, ED, ETH.

Job 32. 12. there is none of you that c. Job
John 8. 46. which of you c. me of sin?
16. † 8. when he is come he will c. the world of sin
Acts 18. 28. for he mightily c. the Jews, shewing
1 Cor. 14. 24. he is c. of all, he is judged of all
Tit. 1. 9. that he may be able to c. gainsayers
Jam. 2. 9. and are c. of the law as transgressors
Jude 15. to c. all that are ungodly among them

CONVOCATION, S.

Exod. 12. 16. in the first day there shall be an holy c. Lev. 23. 7, 24, 35. Num. 28. 18. | 29. 1.
Lev. 23. 2. ye shall proclaim to be holy c. 4. 21, 37.
3. the seventh day as an holy c. 8. Num. 28. 25.
27. tenth day 7th month an holy c. Num. 29. 7.
36. on the eighth day shall be an holy c. to you
Num. 28. 26. the day of first-fruits shall have holy c.
29. 12. on fifteenth day of seventh month an holy c.

CONEY, IES.

Lev. 11. 5. and the c. because he cheweth cud, but divideth not hoof, is unclean to you, Deut. 14. 7.
Psal. 104. 18. the rocks are a refuge for the c.
Prov. 30. 26. c. are but a feeble folk, make houses

COOK, S.

Gen. 40. † 17. in uppermost basket was work of a c.
1 Sam. 8. 13. he will take your daughters to be c.
9. 23. Samuel said to c. bring portion I gave thee
24. c. took up the shoulder and set it before Saul

COOL, *Substantive.*

Gen. 3. 8. walking in the garden in the c. of the day

COOL, *Adjective.*

Prov. 17. † 27. a man of understanding is of a c. spirit

COOL, *Verb.*

Luke 16. 24. dip tip of his finger and c. my tongue

COPIED.

Prov. 25. 1. men of Hezekiah king of Judah c. out

COPING.

1 Kings 7. 9. costly stones from the foundation to c.

COPPER.

Ezra 8. 27. two vessels of fine c. precious as gold

COPPER-SMITH.

2 Tim. 4. 14. Alexander the c.-s. did me much evil

COPULATION.

Lev. 15. 16. if any man's seed of c. go out
17. skin whereon is seed of c. shall be washed
18. with whom man shall lie with seed of c.

COPY.

Deut. 17. 18. write him a c. of this law in a book
Josh. 8. 32. he wrote on stones a c. of law of Moses
Ezra 4. 11. this is c. of a letter sent to him, 5. 6.
23. c. of Artaxerxes' letter was read before Rehum
7. 11. this is c. of the letter Artaxerxes gave Ezra
Esth. 3. 14. c. of a writing for a commandment, 8. 13.
4. 8. Mordecai gave Hatach a c. of the writing

COR.

Ezek. 45. 14. offer a tenth part of a bath out of the c.

CORAL.

Job 28. 18. no mention shall be made of c. or pearls
Ezek. 27. 16. Syria was thy merchant in c. and agate

CORBAN.

Mark 7. 11. it is c. that is to say, a gift, shall be free

CORD.

The cords of the wicked *are the snares with which they catch weak and unwary people,* Psal. 129. 4. The cords of sin, Prov. 5. 22. *are the consequences of crimes and bad habits. Sin never goes unpunished; and the bad habits which are contracted, are, as it were, indissoluble bands, from which it is almost impossible to get free.* Let us cast away their cords from us, Psal. 2. 3. *Let us cast off their government, and free ourselves from subjection to their laws, which like fetters restrain us from our purposes.* To draw iniquity with cords of vanity, Isa. 5. 18. *that is, to spare no cost nor pains in the pursuit of sin. These* cords of vanity *may signify worldly vanities and pleasures, profit or preferment, by which, as by cords, the devil withdraws persons from God and his laws, and the way to heaven, and leads them down to the bottomless pit: Or, those vain and deceitful arguments and pretences, whereby sinners generally draw themselves to sin, as hope of impunity and the like.* I drew them with the cords of a man, Hos. 11. 4. *I used all fair and gentle means, such as are fitted to man's temper, as he is a reasonable creature, to allure them to obedience: I found them backward and unapt to lead, I therefore in my pity laid my hand on them, and as a father or friend drew them gently to me.* To stretch a line or cord about a city, Lam. 2. 8. *signifies to ruin, to destroy it utterly, to level it with the ground. The cords extended in setting up tents, do likewise furnish several metaphors, denoting either the stability or ruin of a place or people, according as they are said to be extended or loose,* Isa. 33. 20. Jer. 10. 20.

Josh. 2. 15. Rahab let spies down by a c. thro' win-[dow
Job 30. 11. he hath loosed my c. and afflicted me
41. 1. canst draw out leviathan's tongue with a c.?
Eccl. 4. 12. a threefold c. is not quickly broken
12. 6. or ever the silver c. be loosed, or golden bowl
Isa. 54. 2. spare not, lengthen c. strengthen stakes
Mic. 2. 5. a c. by lot in congregation of the Lord

CORDS.

Exod. 35. 18. the pins of the court and their c.
Judg. 15. 13. they bound Samson with new c.
Job 36. 8. if they be holden in c. of affliction
Psal. 2. 3. let us cast away their c. from us
118. 27. bind the sacr. with c. to horns of altar
129. 4. he hath cut asunder the c. of the wicked
140. 5. the proud have hid a snare and c. for me
Prov. 5. 22. he shall be holden with the c. of his sins
Isa. 5. 18. woe to them that draw iniquity with c.
33. 20. nor shall any of the c. thereof be broken
Jer. 10. 20. tabernacle is spoiled, all my c. broken
38. 6. and they let down Jeremiah with c.
13. so they drew up Jeremiah with c. took him
Ezek. 27. 24. in chests of rich apparel bound with c
Hos. 11. 4. I drew them with the c. of a man
John 2. 15. when he had made a scourge of small c.

CORIANDER.

Exod. 16. 31. manna was like c. seed, Num. 11. 7.

CORMORANT.

Lev. 11. 17. ye shall have in abomination the little owl, and the c. and the great owl, Deut. 14. 17.
Isa. 34. 11. but the c. shall possess it, Zeph. 2. 14.

CORN.

Gen. 41. 57. all countries came to Joseph to buy c.
42. 2. Jacob heard there was c. in Egypt, Acts 7. 12.
19. go ye, carry c. for the famine of your houses
Exod. 22. 6. so that the stacks of c. be consumed
Lev. 2. 16. priest shall burn part of beaten c. thereof
23. 14. ye shall eat neither bread nor parched c.
Num. 18. 27. as tho' it were the c. of threshing floor
Deut. 16. 9. as thou beginnest to put the sickle to c.
25. 4. thou shalt not muzzle the ox when he treadeth out the c. 1 Cor. 9. 9. 1 Tim. 5. 18.
Josh. 5. 11. they did eat of the old c. of the land, 12.
Ruth 2. 14. he reached her parched c. and she did eat
3. 7. Boaz went to lie down at end of the heap of c.
1 Sam. 17. 17. take for breth. an ephah of parched c.
25. 18. Abigail took five measures of parched c.
2 Sam. 17. 28. they brought parched c. and beans
2 Kings 19. 26. they were as blasted c. Isa. 37. 27.
Neh. 5. 2. we take up c. for them, that we may eat
Job 5. 26. as a shock of c. cometh in in his season
24. 6. they reap every one his c. in the field
39. 4. their young ones they grow up with c.
Psal. 65. 9. preparest them c. when thou providest
13. the valleys also are covered over with c.
72. 16. there shall be a handful of c. in the earth
78. 24. and had given them of the c. of heaven
Prov. 11. 26. that withholdeth c. people shall curse
Isa. 17. 5. when the harvest-man gathereth the c.
62. 8. I will no more give thy c. to thine enemies
Ezek. 36. 29. I will call for the c. and will increase
Hos. 2. 9. I will take away my c. in the time thereof
10. 11. Ephraim loveth to tread out the c.
14. 7. they shall revive as the c. and grow as the vine
Joel 1. 10. for the c. is wasted, new wine is dried up
1. 17. barns are broken down, for c. is withered
Amos 8. 5. the new moon be gone that we may sell c
9. 9. I will sift Israel like as c. is sifted in a sieve
Mark 4. 28. after that the full c. in the ear

John 12. 24. except a *c.* of wheat fall into ground
Ears of CORN.
Gen. 41. 5. seven *ears of c.* came up upon one stalk
Lev. 2. 14. shalt offer green *ears of c.* dried by the fire
Ruth 2. 2. let me go and glean *ears of c.* after him
2 *Kings* 4. 42. brought full *ears of c.* in husk thereof
Job 24. 24. they are cut off as the tops of the *ears of c.*
Mat. 12. 1. to pluck *ears of c.* *Mark* 2. 23. *Luke* 6. 1.
CORN-FIELDS.
Mark 2. 23. came to pass, that he went through *c.-fields* on the sabbath-day, *Mat.* 12. 1. *Luke* 6. 1.
CORN-FLOOR.
Isa. 21. 10. O my threshing, and the *c.* of my *floor*
Hos. 9. 1. thou hast loved a reward on every *c.-floor*
Standing CORN.
Exod. 22. 6. so that the *standing c.* be consumed
Deut. 23. 25. come into *standing c.* of thy neighbour
Judg. 15. 5. let foxes go into *standing c.* burn up *st. c.*
CORN *and wine.*
Gen. 27. 28. God give thee plenty of *c. and wine*
37. with *c. and wine* have I sustained him
Deut. 7. 13. he will also bless thy *c. and wine*
11. 14. that mayest gather in thy *c. and wine* and oil
12. 17. mayest not eat tithe of thy *c. and w.* 14. 23.
16. 13. after thou hast gathered in thy *c. and wine*
18. 4. give him first-fruit of thy *c. and w.* and oil
28. 51. which shall not leave thee *c. and w.* or oil
33. 28. Jacob shall be upon a land of *c. and wine*
2 *Kings* 18. 32. to a land of *c. and wine*, *Isa.* 36. 17.
2 *Chron.* 31. 5. Isr. brought first fruits of *c. and w.*
32. 28. store-houses for increase of *c. wine*, and oil
Neh. 5. 11. restore the 100th part of *c. wine*, and oil
10. 39. bring offering of *c.* of new *wine*, 13. 5, 12.
Psal. 4. 7. than in time their *c. and wine* increased
Lam. 2. 12. say to their mothers, where is *c. and wine?*
Hos. 2. 8. she knew not that I gave her *c. w.* and oil
22. the earth shall hear the *c. and wine* and the oil
7. 14. they assemble themselves for *c. and wine*
Joel 2. 19. behold, I will send you *c. and w.* and oil
Hag. 1. 11. I called for drought on *c. and* new *wine*
Zech. 9. 17. *c.* make men cheerful, *and w.* the maids
CORNER.
Lev. 21. 5. shall they shave off the *c.* of their beard
2 *Chron.* 28. 24. he made altars in every *c.* of Jerus.
Prov. 7. 8. passing through the street near her *c.*
12. she is without, and lieth in wait at every *c.*
21. 9. better to dwell in *c.* of the house-top, 25. 24.
Isa. 30. 20. yet thy teachers not be removed into a *c.*
Jer. 48. 45. a flame shall devour the *c.* of Moab
51. 26. they shall not take of thee a stone for a *c.*
Ezek. 46. 21. in every *c.* of court there was a court
Amos 3. 12. that dwell in Samaria in the *c.* of a bed
Zech. 10. 4. out of him came forth the *c.* and nail
Mat. 21. 42. the stone the builders rejected, the same is become the head of the *c.* *Psal.* 118. 22. *Mark* 12. 10. *Luke* 20. 17. *Acts* 4. 11. 1 *Pet.* 2. 7.
Acts 26. 26. for this thing was not done in a *c.*
CORNER GATE.
2 *Kings* 14. 13. from gate of Ephraim to the *c. gate*
2 *Chron.* 26. 9. built towers at Jerusalem at *c. gate*
Jer. 31. 38. city shall be built from tower to *gate* of *c.*
Zech. 14. 10. land shall be inhabited to the *c. gate*
CORNER STONE.
Job 38. 6. or who laid the *c.-stone* thereof?
Psal. 118. 22. is become the head *stone* of the *c.*
144. 12. that our daughters may be as *c. stones*
Isa. 28. 16. in Zion a precious *c. stone*, 1 *Pet.* 2. 6.
Eph. 2. 20. Christ himself being the chief *c. stone*
CORNERS.
Exod. 25. 12. put rings in four *c.* of ark, two on one side, and two on the other, 26. | 27. 4. | 37. 13.
27. 2. make the horns upon the four *c.* 38. 2.
Lev. 19. 9. shalt not reap the *c.* of your field, 23. 22.
27. ye shall not round *c.* of your heads nor beard
Num. 24. 17. a sceptre shall smite the *c.* of Moab
Deut. 32. 26. I said, I will scatter them into *c.*
1 *Sam.* 14. †38. draw near, ye *c.* of the people
Neh. 9. 22. moreover thou didst divide them into *c.*
Job 1. 19. a great wind smote the four *c.* of the house
Isa. 11. 12. gather dispersed of Judah from four *c.*
Jer. 9. 25, 26. I will punish circumcised with uncircumcised, all that are in utterm. *c.* 25. 23. | 49. 32.
Ezek. 7. 2. the end is come upon four *c.* of the land
45. 19. put blood upon the four *c.* of settle of altar
Zeph. 3. †6. their *c.* are desolate, their streets waste
Zech. 9. †15. shall be filled as the *c.* of the altars
Mat. 6. 5. they love to pray in the *c.* of the streets
Acts 10. 11. a great sheet knit at four *c.* 11. 5.
Rev. 7. 1. four angels standing on four *c.* of the earth
CORNET.
Exod. 19. †13. when the *c.* soundeth long, come up
1 *Chron.* 15. 28. brought up the ark with sound of *c.*
Psal. 98. 6. with sound of the *c.* make a joyful noise
150. †3. praise him with the sound of the *c.*
Dan. 3. 5. at what time ye hear the sound of *c.* 15.
10. made decree. even man shall hear sound of *c.*
Hos. 5. 8. blow ye the *c.* in Gibeah, and the trumpet
Joel 2. †1. blow ye the *c.* in Zion, and sound alarm
CORNETS.
2 *Sam.* 6. 5. David played before the Lord on *c.*
2 *Chron.* 15. 14. sware to the Lord shouting with *c.*
CORPSE, S.
2 *Kings* 19. 35. behold they were all dead *c.* *Isa.* 37. 36.
Nah. 3. 3. there is no end of *c.* they stumble on *c.*
Mark 6. 29. disciples took John's *c.* and laid in tomb
CORPULENT.
Jer. 50. †11. because ye are grown *c.* as a heifer
CORRECT.
Psal. 39. 11. when thou dost *c.* man for iniquity
94. 10. he that chastiseth heathen, shall not he *c.?*
Prov. 29. 17. *c.* thy son, and he shall give thee rest
Jer. 2. 19. thine own wickedness shall *c.* thee
10. 24. O L. *c.* me, but with judgment, not in anger
30. 11. but I will *c.* thee in measure, 46. 28.
CORRECTED, ETH.
Job 5. 17. behold, happy is the man whom God *c.*
Prov. 3. 12. for whom the Lord loveth, he *c.*
29. 19. a servant will not be *c.* by words
Heb. 12. 9. we have had fathers of our flesh which *c.*
CORRECTION.
Job 37. 13. rain to come, whether for *c.* or mercy
Prov. 3. 11. my son, despise not nor be weary of his *c.*
Prov. 7. 22. he goeth as a fool to the *c.* of the stocks
15. 10. *c.* is grievous to him that forsaketh the way
†32. he that refuseth *c.* despiseth his own soul
22. 15. but the rod of *c.* shall drive it from him
23. 13. withhold not *c.* from the child
Jer. 2. 30. your children they received no *c.*
5. 3. but they have refused to receive *c.*
7. 28. this is a nation that receiveth not *c.*
Hos. 5. †2. though I have been a *c.* of them all
Hab. 1. 12. O God, thou hast established them for *c.*
Zeph. 3. 2. she obeyed not, she received not *c.*
2 *Tim.* 3. 16. the scripture is profitable for *c.*
CORRUPT
Signifies, [1] *To consume*, Mat. 6. 19. [2] *To defile, or pollute*, Exod. 32. 7. [3] *To mar, spoil, or infect*, 1 Cor. 15. 33. [4] *To entice, or allure*, 2 Cor. 11. 3. [5] *To break, or make void*, Mal. 2. 8. [6] *To cause to dissemble*, Dan. 11. †32. [7] *Vicious and unsound, wholly biassed by carnal interest and corrupt affections*, 1 Tim. 6. 5. 2 Tim. 3. 8. [8] *Filthy and unsavoury*, corrupt communication, *Eph.* 4. 29.; *that is, such communication as proceeds from corruption in the speaker, and tends to infect and corrupt the minds or manners of the hearers.* [9] *Deceitful*, Dan. 2. 9.
Corruption *sometimes signifies rottenness or putrefaction, such as our bodies are subject to in the grave*, Psal. 16. 10. Thou wilt not suffer thine holy One to see corruption; 1 *Cor.* 15. 42. It is sown in corruption: *Like seed it is laid in the earth, subject to rottenness. It likewise signifies the infectious and poisonous nature of sin, which spiritually wastes the soul, being contrary to that integrity and soundness in which we were created.* Eph. 4. 22. Put off the old man which is corrupt; *that is, labour to mortify and subdue that corruption of nature which has infected the whole man, both soul and body, and which daily grows worse and more corrupt by the fulfilling of its lusts. The apostle* Peter, *speaking of seducers, says, that* they are the servants of corruption, 2 *Pet.* 2. 19. *They are slaves to their lusts, and under the power and dominion of sin. The mount of* Olives *is called* the mount of corruption, 2 *Kings* 23. 13. *because* Solomon *built thereon temples to the gods of the* Ammonites, *and of the* Moabites, *to gratify his wives, who were natives of these nations.*
Gen. 6. 11. the earth also was *c.* before God, 12.
Judg. 2. †19. when the judge was dead they were *c.*
Job 17. 1. my breath is *c.* my days are extinct
Ps. 14. 1. they are *c.* none doth good, 53. 1. | 73. 8.
38. 5. my wounds stink, and are *c.* because of folly
Prov. 25. 26. as a troubled fountain and *c.* spring
Ezek. 20. 44. not according to your *c.* doings, O Israel
23. 11. she was more *c.* in her inordinate love than
Dan. 2. 9. ye have prepared lying and *c.* words
Mal. 1. 14. cursed that sacrificeth to Lord a *c.* thing
Mat. 7. 17. a *c.* tree bringeth forth evil fruit
18. nor can a *c.* tree bring good fruit, *Luke* 6. 43.
12. 33. or else make the tree *c.* and his fruit *c.*
Eph. 4. 22. put off the old man which is *c.*
29. let no *c.* communication proceed out of mouth
1 *Tim.* 6. 5. perverse disputings of men of *c.* minds
2 *Tim.* 3. 8. these resist the truth, men of *c.* minds
CORRUPT.
Deut. 4. 16. take heed lest ye *c.* yourselves, 25.
31. 29. after my death ye will *c.* yourselves
Dan. 11. †17. give him the daughter of women to *c.*
32. such as do wickedly shall he *c.* by flatteries
Mal. 2. 3. behold I will *c.* your seed, spread dung
Mat. 6. 19. on earth, where moth and rust doth *c.*
20. treasures, where neither moth nor rust doth *c.*
1 *Cor.* 15. 33. evil communications *c.* good manners
2 *Cor.* 2. 17. we are not as many that *c.* the word
Jude 10. in those things they *c.* themselves
Rev. 11. †18. shouldest destroy them that *c.* earth
19. 2. great whore did *c.* earth with her fornications
CORRUPTED, ETH.
Gen. 6. 12. for all flesh had *c.* his way upon the earth
Exod. 8. 24. the land was *c.* by reason of the flies
32. 7. Lord said to Moses, get thee down, for thy people have *c.* themselves, *Deut.* 9. 12. | 32. 5.
Judg. 2. 19. *c.* themselves more than their fathers
Ezek. 16. 47. thou wast *c.* more than they in ways
28. 17. thou hast *c.* thy wisdom by thy brightness
Hos. 9. 9. have deeply *c.* thems. as in days of Gibeah
Amos 1. †11. pursued broth. and *c.* his compassions
Zeph. 3. 7. they rose early and *c.* all their doings
Mal. 2. 8. ye have *c.* the covenant of Levi, saith Lord
Luke 12. 33. where no thief approacheth, nor moth *c.*
2 *Cor.* 7. 2. we have wronged no man, have *c.* no man
11. 3. lest your minds be *c.* from simplicity in Christ
Jam. 5. 1, 2. go to ye rich men, your riches are *c.*
CORRUPTERS.
Isa. 1. 4. ah sinful nation, children that are *c.*
Jer. 6. 28. they are brass and iron, they are all *c.*
CORRUPTIBLE.
Rom. 1. 23. changed to an image made like to *c.* man
1 *Cor.* 9. 25. now they do it to obtain a *c.* crown
15. 53. for this *c.* must put on incorruption
1 *Pet.* 1. 18. ye were not redeemed with *c.* things
23. being born again, not of *c.* seed but incorrupt.
3. 4. but let it be in that which is not *c.* meek spirit
CORRUPTING.
Dan. 11. 17. give him the daughter of women *c.* her
CORRUPTION.
Lev. 22. 25. because their *c.* is in them, and blemishes
2 *Kings* 23. 13. on the right hand of the mount of *c.*
Job 17. 14. I have said to *c.* thou art my father
Psal. 16. 10. not leave my soul, nor wilt thou suffer thine holy One to see *c.* *Acts* 2. 27 | 13. 35.
49. 9. that he should live for ever, and not see *c.*
Isa. 38. 17. thou hast delivered it from the pit of *c.*
Dan. 10. 8. for my comeliness was turned in me to *c.*
Jonah 2. 6. yet hast thou brought up my life from *c.*
Acts 2. 31. soul not left in hell, nor his flesh did see *c.*
13. 34. he raised him up, no more to return to *c.*
36. David was laid to his fathers and saw *c.*
37. but he whom God raised again saw no *c.*
Rom. 8. 21. shall be delivered from the bondage of *c.*
1 *Cor.* 15. 42. it is sown in *c.* raised in incorruption
50. neither doth *c.* inherit incorruption
Gal. 6. 8. that soweth to the flesh, shall of flesh reap *c.*
2 *Pet.* 1. 4. escaped the *c.* that is in world thro' lust
2. 12. and shall utterly perish in their own *c.*
19. they themselves are the servants of *c.*
CORRUPTLY.
2 *Chron.* 27. 2. and the people did yet *c.*
Neh. 1. 7. we have dealt very *c.* against thee
COST.
2 *Sam.* 19. 42. have we eaten at all of the king's *c?*
24. 24. nor offer to G. of that which *c.* me nothing
1 *Chr.* 21. 24. nor offer burnt-offerings without *c.*
Luke 14. 28. sitteth not down first, and counteth *c.*
COSTLINESS.
Rev. 18. 19. all that had ships made rich by her *c.*
COSTLY.
1 *Kings* 5. 17. they brought *c.* stones, hewed stones
7. 9. all these were of *c.* stones by the measures
10. foundation was of *c.* stones, even great stones
11. and above were *c.* stones and cedars
John 12. 3. Mary took a pound of spikenard, very *c.*
1 *Tim.* 2. 9. that women adorn thems. not with *c.* array
COTES.
2 *Chron.* 32. 28. Hezekiah made *c.* for flocks
COTTAGE, S.
Isa. 1. 8. daugh. of Zion is left as a *c.* in a vineyard
24. 20. the earth shall be removed like a *c.*
Zeph. 2. 6. the sea-coast shall be *c.* for shepherds
COUCH, ES.
Gen. 49. 4. Reuben defiled it and went up to my *c.*
Job 7. 13. I say, my *c.* shall ease my complaint
Psal. 6. 6. all night I water my *c.* with my tears
Amos 3. 12. Israel be taken out in Damascus in a *c.*
6. 4. that stretch themselves upon their *c.*
Luke 5. 19. let him down through tiling with his *c.*
24. arise, take up thy *c.* and go to thy house
Acts 5. 15. they laid sick folk on beds and *c.*
COUCH.
Job 38. 40. when they *c.* in dens, and abide in covert
COUCHED.
Gen. 49. 9. Judah *c.* as a lion, and as an old lion
Num. 24. 9. he *c.* he lay down as a lion, as great lion
COUCHETH.
Deut. 33. 13. for dew, and for deep that *c.* beneath
COUCHING.
Gen. 49. 14. Issachar *c.* down between two burdens
Ezek. 25. 5. will make Ammonites a *c.* place for flocks
COVENANT
Is *a mutual agreement between two or more parties*, Gen. 21. 32. *There is*, [1] *A covenant of works, the terms whereof are, Do and live; sin and die*, Gen. 2. 17. Isa. 1. 19, 20. *which covenant was broken by our first parents sinning against God, in eating the forbidden fruit, and the covenant being made with* Adam *as a public person, not only for himself but for his posterity, all mankind, descending from him by ordinary generation, sinned in him, and fell with him in their first transgression*, Rom. 5. 12—20. [2] *The covenant of redemption, and salvation by grace, entered into by the sacred Three, in behalf of elect sinners, on whom grace and glory were settled for ever, in* Christ, *their covenant-head*, Psal. 89. 3, 28. Eph. 1. 3, 4. 2 Tim. 1. 9. *This covenant is*, (1) *The fruit of the sovereign love and good will of God*, John 3. 16. Col. 1. 19. (2) *Sure*, Isa. 55. 3. (3) *It is everlasting*, Isa. 61. 8. (4) *Absolute*, Jer. 32. 38, 40. (5) *A covenant filled with all spiritual blessings to true believers in* Christ, Eph. 1. 5. (6) *Called new*, Heb. 8. 6, 8. *not in respect of its date, it being made from everlasting, but in the manner of its dispensation and manifestation: Not that it differed in substance from the* old, *for therein* Christ *was promised, his death and sufferings shadowed forth by the legal sacrifices; and such as were saved under the* Old Testament, *were so only by faith in the blood of the* Messiah *that was to come;* Gal. 4. 3. Abraham believed God, and it was counted to him for righteousness; *he believed in a special manner the promise of the covenant concerning Christ, in whom believers of all nations should be blessed*, Gen. 12. 3. *But this testament or* covenant *is called* new, *in regard of the manner of its dispensation; being ratified afresh by the blood and actual sufferings of* Christ; *being freed from those rites or ceremonies wherewith it was formerly administered; as it contains a more full and clear revelation of the mysteries of religion; as it is attended with a larger measure of the gifts and graces of the Spirit; and as it is never to wax old or be abolished.* (2) *For circumcision, which was the sign or seal of the old covenant*, Gen. 17. 9, 13. (3) *For the duties of the covenant;* Psal. 25. 14. He will shew them his covenant: *He will reveal to them, and make them understand the duties, and bestow upon them the blessings of the covenant.* (4) *For the laws or conditions required of men by the covenant; or the precepts of God, which are the testimonies or witnesses of God's will and of man's duty*, Psal. 25. 10. (5) *For the decalogue, or ten commandments, which contain the articles of the covenant*, Deut. 4. 13. (6) *For the law, religion, and people, of the* Jews, *who were in covenant with God*, Dan. 11. 28. (7) *For the vow, promise, or engagement, whereby a man and woman mutually bind themselves to each other in marriage; and this is called* the covenant of God, *Prov.* 2. 17. *because God is the institutor of that society and mutual obligation; and because God is called to be the witness and judge of that solemn promise and covenant, and the avenger of the transgression of it.*
Gen. 9. 12. this is the token of the *c.* 13, 17. | 17. 11.
17. 4. as for me, behold, my *c.* is with thee
13. my *c.* shall be in your flesh for an everlasting *c.*
14. that soul be cut off, he hath broken my *c.*
Exod. 31. 16. keep the sabbath for a perpetual *c.*
34. 28. he wrote upon the tables the words of the *c.*
Lev. 26. 15. ye do not my comm. but ye break my *c.*
Num. 25. 12. behold, I give to him my *c.* of peace

Num. 25. 13. even the c. of an everlasting priesthood
Deut. 4. 13. and he declared unto you his c.
23. lest ye forget the c. of the Lord your God
31. Lord will not forget the c. of thy fathers
9. 9. when I was gone to receive the tables of the c.
11. the Lord gave me the tables of the c.
15. the two tables of the c. were in my two hands
29. 1. these are the words of the c. which L. comm.
12. thou shouldest enter into c. with the Lord
21. according to all the curses of the c. in this book
25. because ye have forsaken the c. of the Lord
31. 20. they will provoke me, and break my c.
Judg. 2. 1. I said, I will never break my c. with you
1 Sam. 20. 8. hast brought thy servant into c. of Lord
1 Kings 19. 10. for Israel have forsaken thy c. 14.
20. 34. Ahab said, I will send thee away with this c.
2 Kings 13. 23. because of his c. with Abraham
23. 3. to perform words of the c. written in book
and all the people stood to the c. 2 Chron. 34. 31.
1 Chron. 16. 15. be ye mindful always of his c.
2 Chron. 15. 12. they entered into c. to seek Ld. God
Neh. 13. 29. they have defiled the c. of priesthood
Psal. 25. 14. that fear him, he will shew them his c.
44. 17. neither have we dealt falsely in thy c.
50. 16. that thou shouldest take my c. in thy mouth
55. 20. he put forth his hands, he hath broken c.
74. 20. have respect to the c. for dark places of earth
78. 37. heart not right, nor were they stedfast in c.
89. 28. mercy keep and c. shall stand fast with him
34. my c. will I not break, nor alter the thing gone
39. thou hast made void the c. of thy servant
111. 5. he will ever be mindful of his c.
9. commanded his c. for ever, holy is his name
Prov. 2. 17. and forgetteth the c. of her God
Isa. 28. 18. your c. with death shall be disannulled
33. 8. he hath broken the c. he hath despised cities
42. 6. and give thee for a c. of the people, 49. 8.
54. 10. nor shall the c. of my peace be removed
56. 4. the eunuchs that take hold of my c. 6.
59. 21. as for me, this is my c. with them
Jer. 11. 2. hear ye the words of this c. 6.
3. cursed be the man that obeyeth not words of c.
14. 21. remember, break not thy c. with us
22. 9. because they have forsaken the c. of the Ld.
31. 32. which my c. they brake, saith the Lord
33. 20. if you can break my c. of day and c. of night
21. then may c. be broken with David my servant
25. if my c. be not with day and night
34. 10. the people which had entered into c. heard
18. who have not performed the words of this c.
50. 5. let us join to the Lord in a perpetual c.
Ezek. 16. 8. I sware and entered into a c. with thee
59. hast despised oath in breaking the c. 17. 18.
61. give them to thee for daughters, not by thy c.
17. 15. or shall he break the c. and be delivered?
16. whose oath he despised, whose c. he brake
19. my c. he hath broken, it will I recompense
20. 37. I will bring you into the bond of the c.
44. 7. they have broken my c. because of abominat.
Dan. 9. 27. shall confirm c. with many for one week
11. 22. shall be broken, yea also the prince of the c.
28. and his heart shall be against the holy c.
30. he shall have indignation against the holy c.
32. such as do wickedly against c. shall be corrupt
Hos. 10. 4. spoken words, swearing falsely in making c.
Zech. 11. 10. that I might break my c. I had made
Mal. 2. 4. that my c. might be with Levi, saith Ld. 5.
8. ye have corrupted c. of Levi, saith Ld. of hosts
10. by profaning the c. of our fathers
14. yet she is thy companion, and the wife of thy c.
3. 1. even messenger of the c. whom ye delight in
Acts 3. 25. ye are children of the c. God made with
7. 8. and he gave him the c. of circumcision
Rom. 1. 31. without understanding, c. breakers
11. 27. this is my c. when I take away their sins
Gal. 3. 15. though it be man's c. yet if confirmed
17. that the c. was confirmed before of God
Heb. 8. 6. he is Mediator of a better c. established
7. if that first c. had been faultless, then no place
9. they continued in my c. and I regarded them not
9. 1. then verily the first c. had also ordinances
4. Aaron's rod that budded, and tables of the c.
See Ark, Blood, Break.

Book of the COVENANT.
Exod. 24. 7. Moses took the *book of the c.* and read
2 Kings 23. 2. Josiah read in their ears all the words
of the *book of the c.* found, 2 Chron. 34. 30.
21. keep the passover, as it is written in *book of c.*

Establish COVENANT.
Gen. 6. 18. with thee will I *estab.* my c. and sons, 9. 9.
17. 7. I will *estab.* my c. between me and Abraham
19. *estab.* c. with Isaac and his seed after him, 21.
Exod. 6. 4. I have *estab.* my c. with them to give land
Lev. 26. 9. I will multiply and *estab.* my c. with you
Deut. 8. 18. that he may *estab.* his c. which he sware
Ezek. 16. 60. I will *estab.* to thee an everlasting c.
62. I will *estab.* my c. with thee, thou shalt know

Everlasting COVENANT.
Gen. 9. 16. that I may remember the *everlast.* c.
17. 13. it shall be in your flesh for an *everlast.* c.
19. I will establish my c. with Isaac for an *everl.* c.
Lev. 24. 8. being taken from Israel by an *everlast.* c.
2 Sam. 23. 5. yet he hath made with me an *everl.* c.
1 Chr. 16. 17. confirmed the same to Jacob for a
law, and to Israel for an *everlast.* c. Psal. 105. 10.
Isa. 24. 5. because they have broken the *everlast.* c.
55. 3. I will make *ever.* c. with you, 61. 8. Jer. 32. 40.
Ezek. 37. 26. it shall be an *everlast.* c. with them
Heb. 13. 20. through the blood of the *everlast.* c.

Keep, keepest, keepeth, or kept COVENANT.
Gen. 17. 9. thou shalt *keep* my c. thou and thy seed
10. this is my c. which ye shall *keep* between me
Exod. 19. 5. if ye will obey my voice and *keep* my c.
Deut. 7. 9. he is G. faithful God, who *keepeth* c. 12.
1 Kings 8. 23. 2 Chron. 6. 14. Neh. 1. 5. | 9. 32.
29. 9. *keep* therefore the words of this c. and do them
33. 9. they have observed thy word, *kept* thy c.
1 Kings 11. 11. thou hast not *kept* my c. Psal. 78. 10.
Psal. 25. 10. mer. and truth to such as *keep* c. 103. 18.
132. 12. if thy children will *keep* my c. and testim.
Ezek. 17. 14. by *keeping* of his c. it might stand
Dan. 9. 4. *keeping* c. and mercy to them that love him

Made COVENANT.
Gen. 15. 18. same day the L. *made* a c. with Abram
21. 27. Abraham and Abimelech *made* a c. 32.
Exod. 34. 27. I have *made* a c. with thee and Israel
Deut. 5. 2. L. our G. *made* a c. with us in Horeb
3. L. *made* not this c. with our fathers, Heb. 8. 9.
29. 1. beside the c. he *made* with them in Horeb
31. 16. will break my c. I have *made* with them
Josh. 24. 25. Joshua *made* a c. with people that day
1 Sam. 18. 3. Jonathan and David *made* a c. 23. 18.
20. 16. Jonathan *made* a c. with the house of David
1 Kings 8. 9. L. *made* a c. with Israel, 2 Chr. 6. 11.
21. ark wherein is c. of the L. which he *made*
20. 34. Ahab *made* a c. with Ben-hadad
2 Kings 11. 4. Jehoiada *made* a c. with the rulers
17. *made* a c. between the Lord and the king
17. 15. Israel rejected his c. he *made* with fathers
35. with whom the L. had *made* a c. and charged
38. the c. *made* with you ye shall not forget
23. 3. Josiah *made* a c. before Lord, 2 Chr. 34. 31.
1 Chr. 11. 3. David *made* a c. with elders in Hebron
16. 16. be ye mindful even of the c. which he *made*
with Abraham, Neh. 9. 8. Psal. 105. 9.
2 Chron. 21. 7. because of c. he had *made* with David
23. 3. all the congregation *made* a c. with king Joash
Job 31. 1. I *made* a c. with mine eyes, why then
Psal. 50. 5. that have *made* a c. with me by sacrifice
89. 3. have *made* a c. with my chosen, I have sworn
Isa. 28. 15. ye said, ye have *made* a c. with death
57. 8. enlarged thy bed, and *made* a c. with them
Jer. 11. 10. broke the c. I *made* with their fathers
31. 32. not according to the c. I *made* with fathers
34. 8. after Zedekiah had *made* a c. with people, 15.
13. saith the Lord, I *made* a c. with your fathers
15. ye had *made* a c. before me in house called
18. performed not the words of the c. ye had *made*
Ezek. 17. 13. and *made* a c. with him, and taken oath

Make COVENANT.
Gen. 17. 2. I will *make* my c. between me and thee
26. 28. let us *make* a c. with thee, 31. 44. Ezra 10. 3.
Exod. 23. 32. thou shalt *make* no c. Deut. 7. 2.
34. 10. behold I *make* a c. before all thy people
12. lest thou *make* a c. with the inhabitants, 15.
Deut. 29. 14. nor with you only do I *make* this c.
1 Sam. 11. 1. *make* a c. with us, and we will serve
2. on this condition will I *make* a c. with you
2 Chron. 29. 10. now it is in my heart to *make* a c.
Neh. 9. 38. and we *make* a sure c. and write it
Job 41. 4. will he *make* a c. with thee?
Jer. 31. 33. this is c. I will *make*, Heb. 8. 10. | 10. 16.
Ezek. 34. 25. I will *m.* with them a c. of peace, 37. 26.
Hos. 2. 18. I will *make* a c. for them with the beasts
12. 1. and they do *make* a c. with the Assyrians

New COVENANT.
Jer. 31. 31. I will make a *new* c. with Isr. Heb. 8. 8.
Heb. 8. 13. a *new* c. he hath made the first old
12. 24. and to Jesus the Mediator of the *new* c.

Remember COVENANT.
Gen. 9. 15. I will *rem.* my c. Lev. 26. 42. Ezek. 16. 60.
Exod. 6. 5, 6. I have *rememb.* my c. wherefore say
Lev. 26. 45. for their sakes *rem.* c. of their ancestors
Psal. 105. 8. he hath *rem.* his c. for ever, 106. 45.
Amos 1. 9. because they *rem.* not the brotherly c.
Luke 1. 72. mercy promised, and to *rem.* his holy c.

COVENANT *of Salt.*
Lev. 2. 13. the *salt of* c. of thy God to be lacking
Num. 18. 19. it is a c. *of salt* for ever before Lord
2 Chron. 13. 5. to David and his sons by a c. *of salt*

Transgressed COVENANT.
Deut. 17. 2. hath wrought wickedness in *trans.* his c.
Josh. 7. 11. they have also *transgressed* my c.
15. because he *t.* c. of L. Judg. 2. 20. 2 Kings 18. 12.
23. 16. when ye have *transgressed* c. of the Lord
Jer. 34. 18. and I will give the men that *trans.* my c.
Hos. 6. 7. but they like men have *transgressed* the c.
8. 1. because they have *trans.* my c. and trespassed

COVENANTED.
2 Chron. 7. 18. according as I have c. with David
Hag. 2. 5. according to the word that I c. with you
Mat. 26. 15. they c. with him for thirty pieces of silver
Luke 22. 5. were glad, and c. to give him money

COVENANTS.
Rom. 9. 4. to whom pertaineth the glory and the c.
Gal. 4. 24. these are the two c. one from mount Sinai
Eph. 2. 12. and strangers from the c. of promise

COVER

Signifies, [1] *To hide*, Prov. 12. 16. [2] *To clothe*, 1 Sam. 28. 14. [3] *To protect and defend*, Psal. 91. 4. [4] *To pardon, or forgive*, Psal. 32. 1. Rom. 4. 7. [5] *To vail*, 1 Cor. 11. 6. [6] *To inclose*, Exod. 29. 13. [7] *Not to confess*, Prov. 28. 13.

Violence covereth the mouth of the wicked, *Prov.* 10. 6. *Their violent unjust courses shall bring down God's judgments upon them whereby they shall be so convinced of their former injurious practices, that they shall have nothing to say for themselves, their mouths shall be stopped.*

To cover the feet, *Judg.* 3. 24. *and* 1 Sam. 24. 3. *This phrase is commonly understood in both these places, of easing nature; because the men not wearing breeches as we do, but long coats, they did in that act cover their feet. But others expound it, of composing one's self to take a little sleep or rest, as was very usual to do in the day-time in those hot countries,* 2 Sam. 4. 5. *and when they did so in a cool place, they used to cover their feet, as appears from* Ruth 3. 7. *And this exposition seems best to agree with the history in both places where this phrase is found. For the servants of* Ehud *staying so long for their lord, seems to imply, that they judged him gone to sleep, which might take up a considerable time, rather than to that other work, which takes up but a little time. And if* Saul *was asleep in the cave, then it is not strange that he neither heard* David *and his men talking of him, nor perceived when* David *cut off the skirt of his robe.*

Exod. 10. 5. the locusts shall c. the face of the earth
21. 33. if a man shall dig a pit and not c. it
28. 42. make linen breeches to c. nakedness
33. 22. I will c. thee with my hand while I pass
40. 3. thou shalt c. the ark with the vail
Lev. 16. 13. cloud of incense may c. the mercy-seat
17. 13. pour out the blood, and c. it with dust
Num. 22. 5. behold they c. the face of the earth
Deut. 23. 13. and c. that which cometh from thee
33. 12. the Lord shall c. him all the day long
1 Sam. 24. 3. and Saul went in to c. his feet
Neh. 4. 5. c. not their iniquity, let not their sin
Job 16. 18. O earth, c. not thou my blood, let my cry
21. 26. shall lie down in dust, worms shall c. them
22. 11. the abundance of waters c. thee, 38. 34.
40. 22. the shady trees c. him with their shadow
Psal. 91. 4. he shall c. thee with his feathers
104. 9. that they turn not again to c. the earth
109. 29. c. themselves with their own confusion
139. 11. if I say, surely the darkness shall c. me
140. 9. let the mischief of their lips c. them
Isa. 11. 9. as the waters c. the sea, Hab. 2. 14.
14. 11. is spread under thee, the worms c. thee
22. 17. behold, the Lord will surely c. thee
26. 21. the earth shall no more c. her slain
30. 1. that c. with a covering, but not of my Spirit
58. 7. when thou seest the naked, that thou c. him
59. 6. neither c. themselves with their works
60. 2. for behold the darkness shall c. the earth
6. the multitude of camels shall c. thee
Jer. 46. 8. I will go up, and will c. the earth
Ezek. 7. 18. horror shall c. them, shame on all faces
12. 6. thou shalt c. thy face that thou see not
12. he shall c. his face that he see not the ground
24. 7. poured it not on ground to c. it with dust
17. c. not thy lips, and eat not the bread of men
22. ye shall not c. your lips, nor eat bread of men
26. 10. abund. of his horses, their dust shall c. thee
19. and when great waters shall c. thee
30. 18. as for her, a cloud shall c. her and daught.
32. 7. I will c. the heaven, I will c. the sun
37. 6. I will c. you with skin, and put breath in you
38. 9. thou shalt be like a cloud to c. the land, 16.
Hos. 2. 9. recover my flax given to c. her nakedness
10. 8. shall say to the mountains, c. us, Luke 23. 30.
Obad. 10. for thy violence shame shall c. thee
Mic. 3. 7. yea, they shall all c. their lips, no answer
7. 10. and shame shall c. her that said to me
Hab. 2. 17. the violence of Lebanon shall c. thee
Mark 14. 65. some began to spit on him and c. his face
1 Cor. 11. 7. a man ought not to c. his head
1 Pet. 4. 8. for charity shall c. the multitude of sins

COVERED.
Gen. 7. 19. the mountains were c. with waters, 20.
9. 23. they c. the nakedness of their father
24. 65. Rebekah took a vail and c. herself
38. 14. Tamar c. her with a vail, sat in open place
Exod. 8. 6. the frogs came up and c. land of Egypt
14. 28. the waters c. the chariots and horsemen
15. 5. the depths c. them, they sank as a stone
10. the sea c. them, they sank as lead, Josh. 24. 7.
16. 13. at even the quails came up and c. the camp
24. 15. Moses went up, a cloud c. the mount, 16.
37. 9. c. with their wings over the mercy-seat
40. 21. the vail c. the ark of the testimony
34. a cloud c. the tent of the congregation
Lev. 13. 13. behold, if the leprosy have c. all his flesh
Num. 4. 20. to see when the holy things are c.
9. 15. the cloud c. the tabernacle, 16. | 16. 42.
Deut. 32. 15. art waxen fat, thou art c. with fatness
Judg. 4. 18. Jael c. him with a mantle, 19.
1 Sam. 19. 13. Michal c. the pillow with a cloth
28. 14. an old man cometh up c. with a mantle
1 Kin. 1. 1. c. king David with clothes, but no heat
8. 7. cherubims c. ark, 1 Chron. 28. 18. 2 Chr. 5. 8.
2 Kings 19. 1. king Hezekiah heard it, he rent his
clothes, and c. himself with sackcloth, Isa. 37. 1.
2 Chr. 3. †6. Solomon c. house with precious stones
Job 23. 17. nor c. he the darkness from my face
31. 33. if I c. my transgressions as Adam
Psal 44. 15. the shame of my face hath c. me
19. tho' thou hast c. us with the shadow of death
55. † 5. are come upon me, and horror hath c. me
65. 13. the valleys also are c. over with corn
68. 13. shall be as the wings of a dove c. with silver
71. 13. let them be c. with reproach that seek
78. †53. but the sea c. their enemies, 106. † 11.
89. 45. glory to cease, thou hast c. him with shame
106. 17. the earth c. the company of Abiram
139. 13. thou hast c. me in my mother's womb
Prov. 26. 23. like a potsherd c. with silver dross
26. whose hatred is c. by deceit, his wickedness
Eccl. 6. 4. his name shall be c. with darkness
Isa. 6. 2. with twain he c. his face, he c. his feet
22. † 17. the Lord who c. with excellent covering
25. †7. will destroy the covering c. over all people
29. 10. and your rulers the seers hath he c.
51. 16. I have c. thee in the shadow of my hand
61. 10. he c. me with the robe of righteousness
Jer. 51. 42. she is c. with the multitude of waves
Lam. 2. 1. c. the daughter of Zion with a cloud
3. 16. broken my teeth, he hath c. me with ashes
43. thou hast c. with anger, and persecuted us
44. thou hast c. thyself with a cloud, that prayer
Ezek. 1. 11. and two wings c. their bodies, 23.
16. 8. I spread my skirt, and c. thy nakedness
10. I girded thee with linen, I c. thee with silk
18. 7. and hath c. the naked with a garment, 16.
24. 8. top of a rock, that her blood should not be c.
27. 7. blue and purple was that which c. thee
31. 15. I c. the deep for him, and I restrained
37. 8. the flesh came up, and skin c. them above
Jonah 3. 6. the king of Nineveh c. with sackcloth
8. let man and beast be c. with sackcloth
Hab. 3. 3. God came, his glory c. the heavens
Mat. 8. 24. the ship was c. with the waves
10. 26. there is nothing c. that shall not be revealed,
and hid that shall not be known, Luke 12. 2.
1 Cor. 11. 6. if the woman be not c. let her be shorn

COVERED *face.*
Gen. 38. 15. because Tamar had c. her *face*
Exod. 10. 15. the locusts c. the *face* of whole earth
2 Sam. 19. 4. but David c. his *face*, and cried
Esth. 7. 8. as the word went they c. Haman's *face*
Psal. 60. 7. because shame hath c. my *face*

Prov. 24. 31. nettles had c. the face thereof
Isa. 6. 2. with twain he c. his face, and with twain
Jer. 51. 51. heard reproach, shame hath c. our faces

Head COVERED.

2 Sam. 15. 30. David and every man had his head c.
Esth. 6. 12. Haman went mourning, his head c.
Psal. 140. 7. hast c. my head in the day of battle
Jer. 14. 3. were confounded, and c. their heads, 4.
1 Cor. 11. 4. every man praying, having his head c.

COVERED sin, or sins.

Psal. 32. 1. blessed is he whose sin is c. Rom. 4. 7.
85. 2. thou hast c. all their sins, Selah

COVEREDST.

Psal. 104. 6. thou c. it with the deep as a garment
Ezek. 16. 18. tookest broidered garments and c. them

COVERER.

Nah. 2. †5. shall make haste, and c. shall be prepared

COVEREST.

Deut. 22. 12. vesture, wherewith thou c. thyself
Psal. 5. † 11. shout for joy, because thou c. them
104. 2. who c. thyself with light as with a garment

COVERETH.

Exod. 29. 13. thou shalt take all the fat that c. the inwards, 22. Lev. 3. 3, 9, 14. | 4. 8. | 7. 3. | 9. 19.
Num. 22. 11. a people which c. the face of the earth
Judg. 3. 24. surely he c. his feet in his chamber
Job 9. 24. he c. the faces of the judges thereof
15. 27. because he c. his face with his fatness
36. 30. behold, he c. the bottom of the sea
32. with clouds he c. light, commands not to shine
Ps. 73. 6. pride as a chain, violence c. them as a gar.
84. † 6. through valley of Baca, rain also c. the pools
109. 19. be to him as the garment which c. him
147. 8. who c. the heavens with clouds, prep. rain
Prov. 10. 6. violence c. the mouth of the wicked, 11.
12. love c. all sins || 12. 16. a prudent man c. shame
17. 9. he that c. a transgression seeketh love
28. 13. he that c. his sins shall not prosper
Jer. 3. 25. we lie down in shame, our confusion c. us
Ezek. 28. 14. thou art the anointed cherub that c.
Mal. 2. 16. for one c. violence with his garment
Luke 8. 16. when he lighted candle c. it with a vessel

COVERING.

Gen. 8. 13. Noah removed the c. of the ark
20. 16. behold, he is to thee a c. of the eyes
Exod. 22. 27. for that is his c. raiment for his skin
Lev. 13. 45. the leper shall put a c. on his upper lip
Num. 19. 15. every vessel which hath no c. bound on
2 Sam. 17. 19. woman spread a c. over well's mouth
Job 22. 14. thick clouds are a c. to him, he seeth not
24. 7. that the naked have no c. in the cold
26. 6. naked before him, destruction hath no c.
31. 19. if I have seen any poor without c.
Psal. 105. 39. he spread a cloud for c. and fire
Cant. 3. 10. he made the c. of it of purple
Isa. 4. † 5. for upon all the glory shall be a c.
22. 8. and he discovered the c. of Judah
† 17. who covered thee with an excellent c.
25. 7. destroy the face of the c. cast over all people
28. 20. the c. narrower than he can wrap hims. in
30. 1. that cover with a c. but not of my Spirit
22. ye shall defile the c. of thy graven images
50. 3. I clothe heavens, and make sackc. their c.
Ezek. 28. 13. every precious stone was thy c. sardius
1 Cor. 11. † 10. a woman ought to have a c.
15. glory to her, for her hair is given her for a c.

See BADGERS skins.

COVERING.

Exod. 25. 20. c. the mercy-seat with their wings
Num. 4. 5. Aaron shall take down the c. vail
Ezek. 28. 16. I will destroy thee, O c. cherub
Mal. 2. 13. I have done c. altar of the Lord with tears

COVERINGS.

Prov. 7. 16. decked my bed with c. of tapestry
31. 22. she maketh herself c. of tapestry

COVERS.

Exod. 25. 29. make c. || 37. 16. he made his c.
Num. 4. 7. put thereon c. to cover withal

COVERT

Signifies, [1] *An umbrage, or shady place,* 1 Sam. 25. 20. [2] *A thicket for wild beasts,* Job 38. 40. [3] *Something made to shelter the people from the weather on the sabbath; or some costly chair of state, wherein the kings of* Judah *used to hear the priests expound the law on the sabbath,* 2 Kings 16. 18. [4] Christ Jesus, the *saints' shelter, defence, or refuge,* Isa. 32. 2.

1 Sam. 25. 20. Abigail came down by c. of the hill
2 Kings 16. 18. the c. for the sabbath Ahaz took down
Job 38. 40. when lions abide in the c. to lie in wait
40. 21. behemoth lieth in the c. of the reed
Psal. 61. 4. I will trust in the c. of thy wings
Isa. 4. 6. a tabernacle for a c. from storm and rain
16. 4. be thou a c. to them from the face of spoiler
32. 2. a man shall be a c. from the tempest
Jer. 25. 38. he hath forsaken his c. as a lion

COVET.

This word is sometimes taken in a good sense, as in 1 Cor. 12. 31. Covet earnestly the best gifts. *This covetousness is good and commendable, when spiritual blessings are earnestly desired and sought after. But most commonly it is taken in a bad sense, for an eager and immoderate desire after earthly things,* Josh. 7. 21. Prov. 21. 26. Covetousness *is called* idolatry, *Col.* 3. 5. *because the covetous man places that love, delight, and confidence in riches, which are due to God alone. This sin is condemned in all sorts of persons, and is expressly forbidden by the tenth commandment,* Thou shalt not covet, *Exod.* 20. 17. *Such as are addicted to this sin, are hated of God,* Psal. 10. 3. *They are cruel and oppressive,* Mi . 2. 2. *The riches they are so eager in the pursuit of, prove but poison to kill them, and thus they are miserable,* Job 20. 15, 16, 17. Prov. 1. 19. *The inordinate love of wealth does likewise betray men to manifold sins, and exposes them to manifold sufferings; both from themselves, in denying themselves the comfort of their estates; and from others, as extortioners, thieves, and the like,* Deut. 16. 19. Eccl. 4. 8. Mat. 26 15. 1 Tim. 6. 10.

Exod. 20. 17. thou shalt not c. thy neighbour's house, wife, nor servant, Deut. 5. 21. Rom. 7. 7. | 13. 9.
Mic. 2. 2. they c. fields and take them by violence
1 Cor. 12. 31. but c. earnestly the best gifts
14. 39. c. to prophesy, and forbid not to speak

COVETED.

Josh. 7. 21. Achan said, then I c. them, took them
Acts 20. 33. I have c. no man's silver or gold
1 Tim. 6. 10. which while some c. after they erred

COVETETH.

Prov. 21. 26. he c. greedily all the day long
Hab. 2. 9. woe to him that c. an evil covetousness

COVETOUS.

Psal. 10. 3. the wicked blesseth c. whom Ld. abhors
Luke 16. 14. Pharisees who were c. heard these things
1 Cor. 5. 10. yet not altogether with the c.
11. if any brother be c. with such not to eat
6. 10. nor c. shall inherit king. of God, Eph. 5. 5.
1 Tim. 3. 3. a bishop then must not be c.
2 Tim. 3. 2. in the last times men shall be c. boasters
2 Pet. 2. 14. an heart exercised with c. practices

COVETOUSNESS.

Exod. 18. 21. provide able men, men hating c.
Psal. 119. 36. incline not my heart to c.
Prov. 28. 16. he that hateth c. shall prolong his days
Isa. 57. 17. for the iniquity of his c. was I wroth
Jer. 6. 13. every one is given to c. 8. 10.
22. 17. thy eyes and heart are not but for thy c.
51. 13. thine end is come, and the measure of thy c.
Ezek. 33. 31. but their heart goeth after their c.
Hab. 2. 9. woe to him that coveteth an evil c.
Mark 7. 22. out of the heart proceedeth c.
Luke 12. 15. he said, take heed, and beware of c.
Rom. 1. 29. being filled with all c. fornication
2 Cor. 9. 5. as a matter of bounty, and not of c.
Eph. 5. 3. but c. let it not be once named among you
Col. 3. 5. mortify your memb. and c. which is idolatry
1 Thess. 2. 5. nor at any time used we a cloke of c.
Heb. 13. 5. let your conversation be without c.
2 Pet. 2. 3. thro' c. shall they make merchand. of you

COULD.

Gen. 27. 1. when Isaac was old, so that he c. not see
Exod. 8. 18. did so to bring forth lice, but c. not
1 Sam. 3. 2. Eli's eyes began to wax dim, he c. not see
1 Kings 14. 4. Ahijah c. not see his eyes were set
2 Kings 3. 26. to break to king of Edom, but c. not
1 Chron. 21. 30. but David c. not go before it
2 Chron. 13. 7. Rehoboam c. not withstand them
Psal. 37. 36. yea, I sought him, but he c. not be found
Isa. 5. 4. what c. have been done more to vineyard?
Jer. 15. 1. my mind c. not be toward this people
Jonah 1. 13. men rowed to bring it to land, but c. not
Mark 6. 19. therefore Herodias had a quarrel against John, and would have killed him, but she c. not
9. 18. cast him out, and they c. not, Luke 9. 40.
14. 8. she hath done what she c. she is come
John 21. 25. the world c. not contain the books
Acts 13. 39. from which ye c. not be justified by law

COULDEST.

Jer. 3. 5. and hast done evil things as thou c.
Ezek. 16. 28. and yet thou c. not be satisfied

COULTER, S.

1 Sam. 13. 20. Israel went to sharpen each his c.
21. they had a file for their c. and the forks

COUNCIL.

2 Sam. 23. † 23. David set Benaiah over his c.
Mat. 5. 22. shall say, Raca, shall be in danger of c.
26. 59. the c. sought false witness, Mark 14. 55.
Mark 15. 1. whole c. bound Jes. and carried him away
Luke 22. 66. the elders led Jesus into their c.
John 11. 47. the chief priests gathered a c. Acts 5. 21.
Acts 4. 15. had commanded them to go out of the c.
5. 27. they brought and set them before the c.
34. then stood there up one in the c. a Pharisee
41. and they departed from the c. rejoicing
6. 12. caught Stephen, and brought him to the c.
15. all in the c. looking on him, saw his face
22. 30. he commanded all their c. to appear
23. 15. ye with the c. signify to the chief captain
24. 20. any evil in me, while I stood before the c.

COUNCILS.

Mat. 10. 17. they will deliver you up to c. Mark 13. 9.

COUNSEL

Signifies, [1] *Advice,* Prov. 20. 18. Dan. 4. 27. [2] *God's purpose and decree,* Acts 4. 28. [3] *The directions of his word, the motions of his Spirit, and the kindness of his providence,* Psal. 73. 24. [4] *His will or doctrine concerning the way of salvation,* Luke 7. 30. Acts 20. 27. [5] *The designs, thoughts, and most secret resolutions,* 1 Cor. 4. 5.

Christ Jesus *is called* Counsellor, *Isa.* 9. 6. [1] *On account of his infinite wisdom,* Col. 2. 3. [2] *On account of his willingness to instruct and give counsel to men; as also, to plead their cause before his throne,* Rev. 3. 18. 1 John 2. 1.

Exod. 18. 19. hearken to me, I will give thee c.
Num. 27. 21. before Eleazar, who shall ask c. for him
31. 16. these caused Israel thro' the c. of Balaam, to commit trespass against L. in the matter of Peor
Deut. 32. 28. are a nation void of c. nor is understand.
Josh. 9. 14. asked not c. at the mouth of the Lord
Judg. 20. 7. behold, give here your advice and c.
2 Sam. 15. 31. turn c. of Ahithophel into foolishness
16. 23. so was all the c. of Ahithophel with David
17. 14. the Lord defeated the good c. of Ahithophel
20. 18. saying, they shall surely ask c. at Abel
1 Kings 1. 12. let me, I pray thee, give thee c.
12. 8. forsook the c. of old men, 13. 2 Chr. 10. 8, 13.
2 Kings 6. 8. king of Syria took c. with his servants
18. 20. I have c. and strength for war, Isa. 36. 5.
1 Chron. 10. 13. so Saul died for asking c. of one
2 Chron. 22. 5. Ahaziah walked after their c.
25. 16. king said, art thou made of the king's c.?
30. 2. the king had taken c. to keep the passover
23. the assembly took c. to keep other seven days
Ezra 10. 3. according to the c. of my lord, and those
8. according to the c. of the princes and elders
Neh. 4. 15. God had brought their c. to nought
Job 5. 13. the c. of the froward is carried headlong
10. 3. and should shine upon the c. of the wicked
12. 13. wisdom and strength he hath c. and underst.

Job 21. 16. the c. of the wicked is far from me [22. 18.
38. 2. who is this that darkeneth c. by words?
42. 3. who is he that hideth c. without knowledge?
Psal. 1. 1. that walketh not in the c. of the ungodly
14. 6. you have shamed the c. of the poor
16. 7. I will bless the Lord, who hath given me c.
20. 4. the Lord grant thee, and fulfil all thy c.
31. 13. while they took c. together against me
33. 10. Lord brings the c. of the heath. to nought
55. 14. we took sweet c. together, and walked
64. 2. hide me from the secret c. of the wicked
68. 27. the princes of Judah and their c.
73. 24. thou shalt guide me with thy c. afterward
83. 3. they have taken crafty c. against thy people
106. 13. they waited not for his c. but lusted
43. but they provoked him with their c.
107. 11. they contemned the c. of the Most High
Prov. 8. 14. c. is mine, sound wisdom, I am underst.
11. 14. where no c. is, the people fall, but in multit.
12. 15. but he that hearkeneth unto c. is wise
15. 22. without c. purposes are disappointed
19. 20. hear c. and receive instruction, that thou
20. 5. c. in the heart of man is like deep water
18. every purpose is established by c. and with
21. 30. there is no wisdom nor c. against the L.
24. 6. for by wise c. thou shalt make thy war
27. 9. so doth the sweetness of a friend by hearty c.
Isa. 5. 19. let the c. of the Holy One draw nigh
7. 5. they have taken evil c. against thee, saying
11. 2. spirit of c. and might shall rest upon him
19. 3. and I will destroy the c. of Egypt
11. the c. of counsellors of Phar. is become brutish
23. 8. who hath taken this c. against Tyre?
28. 29. from the Lord, who is wonderful in c.
29. 15. that seek deep to hide c. from the Lord
40. † 13. who being of his c. hath taught him?
14. with whom took he c.? who instructed him?
44. 26. and performeth the c. of his messengers
Jer. 18. 18. nor shall c. perish from the wise
23. thou knowest all their c. against me to slay me
19. 7. I will make void c. of Judah and Jerusalem
32. 19. mighty God, great in c. mighty in work
38. 15. if I give thee c. wilt not thou hearken to me
49. 7. is c. perished from prudent? is wisd. vanished?
30. the king of Babylon hath taken c. against you
Ezek. 7. 26. and c. shall perish from the ancients
11. 2. and that give wicked c. in this city
13. † 9. they shall not be in the c. of my people
Dan. 2. 14. David answered with c. and wisdom
Hos. 4. 12. my people ask c. at their stocks and staff
Mic. 4. 12. neither understand they his c.
Zech. 6. 13. the c. of peace shall be between them both
Mat. 12. 14. the Pharisees held a c. against him
27. 7. they took c. and bought the potter's field
28. 12. when they had taken c. they gave money
Mark 3. 6. they took c. against Jesus, John 11. 53.
Luke 23. 51. he had not consented to the c. of them
John 18. 14. now Caiaphas was he who gave c.
Acts 4. 28. what thy c. determined before to be done
5. 33. when they heard, they took c. to slay them
38. if this c. be of men, it will come to nought
9. 23. after that the Jews took c. to kill him
27. 42. the soldiers' c. was to kill the prisoners
Eph. 1. 11. who worketh after the c. of his own will
Heb. 6. 17. to shew the immutability of his c.

COUNSEL of God or Lord.

Judg. 18. 5. they said, ask c. we pray thee, of God
20. 18. the children of Israel asked c. of God, 23.
1 Sam. 14. 37. Saul asked c. of God, shall I go down?
Psal. 33. 11. the c. of the Lord standeth, Prov. 19. 21.
Isa. 19. 17. because of the c. of the Lord of hosts
Jer. 23. 18. who hath stood in the c. of the Lord?
49. 20. therefore hear the c. of the Lord, 50. 45.
Luke 7. 30. the lawyers rejected the c. of God
Acts 2. 23. him delivered by the determinate c. of G.
20. 27. not ashamed to declare to you all c. of God

My COUNSEL.

2 Chron. 25. 16. and hast not hearkened to my c.
Job 29. 21. men waited and kept silence at my c.
Psal. 119. † 24. thy testimonies are the men of my c.
Prov. 1. 25. but ye have set at nought all my c.
30. they would none of my c. they despised my
Isa. 46. 10. my c. shall stand, and I will do all
11. man that executeth my c. from a far country
Jer. 23. 22. but if they had stood in my c.
Dan. 4. 27. O king, let my c. be acceptable to thee

Own COUNSEL.

Job 18. 7. and his own c. shall cast him down
Hos. 10. 6. Israel shall be ashamed of his own c.

Take COUNSEL.

Neh. 6. 7. come now, and let us take c. together
Psal. 2. 2. rulers take c. against Lord and Anointed
13. 2. how long shall I take c. in my soul?
71. 10. that wait for my soul, take c. together
Isa. 8. 10. take c. and it shall come to nought
16. 3. take c. execute judgment, make thy shadow
30. 1. woe to children that take c. but not of me
45. 21. tell ye, yea let them take c. together

COUNSEL, ED.

2 Sam. 16. 23. which Ahithophel c. in those days
17. † 7. that Ahithophel hath c. is not good
11. I c. that all Israel be gathered unto thee
15. thus and thus Ahithophel c. and thus I c. 21.
2 Chron. 25. † 16. God hath c. to destroy thee
Job 26. 3. how hast thou c. him that hath no wisdom?
Psal. 32. † 8. I will c. thee, mine eyes shall be on thee
Eccl. 8. 2. I c. thee to keep the king's commandment
Rev. 3. 18. I c. thee to buy of me gold tried in fire

COUNSELLOR.

2 Sam. 15. 12. Ahithophel, David's c. 1 Chr. 27. 33.
1 Chron. 26. 14. for Zechariah his son, a wise c.
27. 32. Jonathan, David's uncle, was a c. a scribe
2 Chron. 22. 3. Athaliah was his c. to do wickedly
Isa. 3. 3. Lord taketh away the c. and artificer
9. 6. his name shall be called Wonderful, C.
40. 13. or who being his c. hath taught him
41. 28. for I beheld, and there was no man, no c.
Mic. 4. 9. is there no king in thee? is thy c. perished
Nah. 1. 11. there is come out of thee a wicked c.
Mark 15. 43. Joseph an honourable c. Luke 23. 50.
Rom. 11. 34. who known mind of L. who been his c.?

COUNSELLORS.
2 *Chr.* 22. 4. they were his *c.* after his father's death
Ezra 4. 5. they hired *c.* against them, to frustrate
7. 14. as thou art sent of the king, and his seven *c.*
28. extended mercy to me before the king and *c.*
8. 25. gold, which the king and his *c.* had offered
Job 3. 14. been at rest with kings and *c.* of the earth
12. 17. leadeth *c.* away spoiled, makes judges fools
Psal. 119. 24. thy testimonies are my delight and *c.*
Prov. 11. 14. in the multitude of *c.* is safety, 24. 6.
12. 20. deceit in heart, but to the *c.* of peace is joy
15. 22. in the multitude of *c.* they are established
Isa. 1. 26. I will restore thy *c.* as at the beginning
19. 11. counsel of wise *c.* of Pharaoh is brutish
Dan. 3. 24. said to his *c.* did we not cast three men?
27. the king's *c.* being gathered, saw these men
4. 36. my *c.* and my lords sought unto me
6. 7. all the *c.* and the captains have consulted

COUNSELS.
Job 37. 12. and it is turned round about by his *c.*
Psal. 5. 10. O God, let them fall by their own *c.*
81. 12. and they walked in their own *c.*
Prov. 1. 5. man of understand. shall attain to wise *c.*
12. 5. but the *c.* of the wicked are deceit
22. 20. have not I written excellent things in *c.?*
Isa. 25. 1. thy *c.* of old are faithfulness and truth
47. 13. are wearied in the multitude of thy *c.*
Jer. 7. 24. walked in the *c.* of their evil heart
Hos. 11. 6. devour them, because of their own *c.*
Mic. 6. 16. ye walk in the *c.* of the house of Ahab
1 *Cor.* 4. 5. will make manifest the *c.* of the heart

COUNT.
Exod. 12. 4. shall make your *c.* for the lamb

COUNT, *Verb.*
Lev. 23. 15. *c.* from the morrow after the sabbath
25. 27. let him *c.* the years of the sale, 52.
Num. 23. 10. who can *c.* the dust of Jacob?
1 *Sam.* 1. 16. *c.* not me for a daughter of Belial
Job 19. 15. and my maids *c.* me for a stranger
31. 4. doth not he see my ways, *c.* all my steps?
Psal. 87. 6. the Lord shall *c.* when he writeth
139. 18. if I *c.* them, they are more than the sand
22. I hate them, I *c.* them mine enemies
Mic. 6. 11. shall I *c.* them pure with wicked balances
Acts 20. 24. neither *c.* I my life dear to myself
Phil. 3. 8. I *c.* all things loss, and do *c.* them but dung
13. I *c.* not myself to have apprehended, but this
2 *Thess.* 1. 11. God would *c.* you worthy of this calling
3. 15. *c.* him not as an enemy, but admonish him
1 *Tim.* 6. 1. *c.* their masters worthy of all honour
Philem. 17. if thou *c.* me a partner, receive him
Jam. 1. 2. *c.* it joy when ye fall into temptations
5. 11. behold, we *c.* them happy which endure
2 *Pet.* 2. 13. as they that *c.* it pleasure to riot in day
3. 9. Lord is not slack, as some men *c.* slackness
Rev. 13. 18. let him *c.* the number of the beast

COUNTED.
Gen. 15. 6. Abram believed, and he *c.* it to him for righteousness, *Ps.* 106. 31. *Rom.* 4. 3. *Gal.* 3. 6.
30. 33. the sheep that shall be *c.* stolen with me
31. 15. are we not *c.* of him strangers? sold us
1 *Kings* 3. 8. that cannot be numbered or *c.* for mult.
1 *Chron.* 21. 6. but Levi and Benjamin *c.* he not
Neh. 13. 13. for they were *c.* faithful, office was
Job 18. 3. wherefore we are *c.* as beasts and vile
41. 29. darts are *c.* as stubble, laugheth at shaking
Psal. 44. 22. we are *c.* as sheep for the slaughter
88. 4. I am *c.* with them that go down to the pit
Prov. 17. 28. even a fool, when he holdeth his peace is *c.* wise, and he that shutteth his lips is a man
27. 14. rising early, it shall be *c.* a curse to him
Isa. 5. 28. their horses' hoofs shall be *c.* like flint
32. 15. and the fruitful field be *c.* for a forest
33. 18. where is he that *c.* the towers?
40. 15. the nations are *c.* as small dust of balance
17. all nations are *c.* to him less than nothing
Hos. 8. 12. but they were *c.* as a strange thing
Mat. 14. 5. they *c.* him as a prophet, *Mark* 11. 32.
Luke 21. 36. be *c.* worthy to escape these things
Acts 5. 41. rejoicing that they were *c.* worthy
19. 19. they burned their books, and *c.* the price
Rom. 2. 26. uncircumcision be *c.* for circumcision
4. 5. to him believeth, his faith is *c.* for righteous.
9. 8. but the children of promise are *c.* for the seed
Phil. 3. 7. what were gain, those I *c.* loss for Christ
2 *Thess.* 1. 5. be *c.* worthy of the kingdom of God
1 *Tim.* 1. 12. enabled me, for that he *c.* me faithful
5. 17. let elders be *c.* worthy of double honour
Heb. 3. 3. this man was *c.* worthy of more glory
7. 6. he whose descent is not *c.* from them
10. 29. hath *c.* blood of the covenant unholy thing
See ACCOUNTED.

COUNTETH, ING.
Job 19. 11. he *c.* me as one of his enemies, 33. 10.
Eccl. 7. 27. *c.* one by one, to find out the account
Luke 14. 28. sitteth not down first, and *c.* the cost

COUNTENANCE
Signifies, [1] *The face, or visage,* 1 Sam. 16. 7. [2] *Love, favour, and affection,* Gen. 31. 5. [3] *Brightness, festivity, or alacrity,* Dan. 5. 6. [4] *God's love and favour, manifested by the graces and benefits which he bestows upon his people,* Psal. 4. 6. *Because men by their* countenance *discover their anger, or love; hence it is that when it is attributed to God, who is said sometimes to* lift up the light of his countenance *upon his people, at other times to* hide his face, *or* countenance, *it signifies either his grace and favour, or his anger, or displeasure.*
Gen. 4. 5. Cain was very wroth, and his *c.* fell
24. † 16. the damsel was good of *c.* a virgin
31. 2. Jacob beheld the *c.* of Laban, and behold
5. I see your father's *c.* that it is not toward me
Num. 6. 26. the Lord lift up his *c.* upon thee
Deut. 28. 50. Lord will bring a nation of fierce *c.*
Judg. 13. 6. his *c.* was like the *c.* of an angel
1 *Sam.* 1. 18. Hannah, her *c.* was no more sad
16. 7. look not on his *c.* or the height of his stature
12. now David was of a beautiful *c.* 17. 42.
25. 3. Abigail ‖ 2 *Sam.* 14. 27. Tamar of a fair *c.*
2 *Sam.* 23. † 21. he slew an Egyptian, a man of *c.*
2 *Kings* 5. † 1. Naaman was a man lifted up in *c.*
2 *Kings* 8. 11. he settled his *c.* stedfastly on Hazael
Neh. 2. 2. why is thy *c.* sad, seeing thou art not sick?
3. why should not my *c.* be sad, when the city
Job 14. 20. thou changest his *c.* and sendest him away
29. 24. and the light of my *c.* they cast not down
Psal. 4. 6. Lord, lift up the light of thy *c.* upon us
10. 4. the wicked, thro' pride of *c.* will not seek G.
11. 7. righteous Ld. his *c.* doth behold the upright
21. 6. thou hast made him glad with thy *c.*
42. 5. I shall yet praise him for the help of his *c.*
11. who is the health of my *c.* and my God, 43. 5.
44. 3. but the light of thy *c.* did save them
80. 16. they perish at the rebuke of thy *c.*
89. 15. shall walk, O Lord, in the light of thy *c.*
90. 8. hast set our secret sins in the light of thy *c.*
Prov. 15. 13. a merry heart maketh a cheerful *c.*
16. 15. in the light of the king's *c.* is life
25. 23. so doth the angry *c.* a backbiting tongue
27. 17. so a man sharpeneth the *c.* of his friend
Eccl. 7. 3. by sadness of *c.* the heart is made better
Cant. 2. 14. let me see thy *c.* thy *c.* is comely
5. 15. his *c.* is as Lebanon, excellent as cedars
Isa. 3. † 3. Lord doth take away man eminent in *c.*
9. the shew of their *c.* doth witness against them
Ezek. 27. 35. they shall be troubled in their *c.*
Dan. 5. 6. then king's *c.* was changed, and thoughts
8. 23. a king of fierce *c.* shall stand up
Mat. 6. 16. be not as the hypocrites, of a sad *c.*
28. 3. his *c.* was like lightning, *Luke* 9. 29.
Acts 2. 28. shalt make me full of joy with thy *c.*
2 *Cor.* 3. 7. could not behold Moses for glory of his *c.*
Rev. 1. 16. and his *c.* was as the sun shineth
See CHANGED.

COUNTENANCE.
Exod. 23. 3. nor shalt thou *c.* a poor man in his cause

COUNTENANCES.
Dan. 1. 13. then let our *c.* be looked upon before thee
15. their *c.* appeared fairer and fatter in flesh

COUNTERVAIL.
Esth. 7. 4. though enemy could not *c.* king's damage

COUNTRY.
Gen. 19. 28. and lo, the smoke of the *c.* went up
24. 4. but thou shalt go to my *c.* and my kindred
29. 26. Laban said, it must not be so done in our *c.*
30. 25. send me away, that I may go to my *c.*
34. 2. Shechem the prince of the *c.* saw her
42. 33. the man, the Lord of the *c.* said unto us
Num. 15. 13. all born in the *c.* shall do these things
32. 4. the *c.* which the Lord smote before Israel
Deut. 26. 3. I am come into the *c.* L. sware to give
Josh. 2. 2. there came men to search out the *c.* 3.
7. 2. Joshua sent, saying, go up and view the *c.*
Judg. 11. 21. Israel possessed the land of that *c.*
16. 24. our enemy and the destroyer of our *c.*
Ruth 1. 2. and they came into the *c.* of Moab
22. who returned out of the *c.* of Moab
2 *Sam.* 15. 23. all thy *c.* wept with a loud voice
21. 14. bones of Saul buried they in *c.* of Benjamin
1 *Kings* 20. 27. but the Syrians filled the *c.*
2 *Kings* 3. 20. and the *c.* was filled with water
Isa. 1. 7. your *c.* is desolate, your cities burnt with fire
20. † 6. the inhabitants of this *c.* shall say
22. 18. he will toss thee like a ball in a large *c.*
Jer. 22. 10. he shall not return, nor see his native *c.*
31. 8. behold I will bring them from the north *c.*
48. 21. and judgment is come upon the plain *c.*
50. 9. cause an assembly to come from the north *c.*
51. † 49. at Babylon fall the slain of all the *c.*
Ezek. 20. 38. I will bring them forth out of the *c.*
25. 9. glory of the *c.* Bethjeshi-moth, Baal-meon
47. 22. they shall be to you as born in the *c.*
Jonah 4. 2. my saying, when I was yet in my *c.*
Mic. 1. † 11. the inhabitant of *c.* of flocks came not
Mat. 9. 31. they spread abroad his fame in all that *c.*
Mark 5. 10. that he would not send them out of *c.*
14. told it in the city, and in the *c.* *Luke* 8. 34.
Luke 15. 15. he joined himself to a citizen of that *c.*
Acts 12. 20. because their *c.* was nourished by k.'s *c.*
27. 27. shipmen deemed they drew near to some *c.*
Heb. 11. 9. sojourned in land of prom. as in strange *c.*
14. they declare plainly that they seek a *c.*
15. and truly if they had been mindful of that *c.*
16. now they desire a better *c.* that is an heavenly

Far COUNTRY.
Josh. 9. 6. they said, we be come from a *far c.* 9.
1 *Kings* 8. 41. out of a *far c.* for thy sake, 2 *Chr.* 6. 32.
2 *Kings* 20. 14. Hezekiah said, they are come from a *far c.* even from Babylon, *Isa.* 39. 3.
Prov. 25. 25. so is good news from a *far c.*
Isa. 13. 5. from a *far c.* to destroy the whole land
46. 11. man that executeth my counsel from *far c.*
Jer. 4. 16. publish, that watchers come from a *far c.*
8. 19. because of them that dwell in a *far c.*
Mat. 21. 33. househd. went into a *far c.* *Mark* 12. 1.
25. 14. kingd. of heaven is as a man trav. into *far c.*
Luke 15. 13. younger son took his journey into *far c.*

Own COUNTRY.
Lev. 16. 29. whether one of your *o. c.* 17. 15. ‖ 24. 22.
1 *Kings* 10. 13. she turned and went to her *own c.*
11. 21. let me depart, that I may go to my *own c.*
22. 36. a proclamation every man to his *own c.*
Jer. 51. 9. let us go every one into his *own c.*
Mat. 2. 12. they departed into their *own c.*
13. 57. save in his *own c.* *Mark* 6. 4. *Luke* 4. 24.
Mark 6. 1. he went thence and came into his *own c.*
John 4. 44. a prophet hath no honour in his *own c.*

Thy COUNTRY.
Gen. 12. 1. Abram, get thee out of *thy c.* *Acts* 7. 3.
32. 9. return to *thy c.* and to thy kind. I will deal
Num. 20. 17. let us pass, I pray thee, thro' *thy c.*
Jonah 1. 8. what is *thy c.?* of what people art thou?
Luke 4. 23. heard done in Capern. do here in *thy c.*

COUNTRY VILLAGES.
1 *Sam.* 6. 18. both of fenced cities and *c. villages*

COUNTRYMEN.
2 *Cor.* 11. 26. in journeying, in perils by mine own *c.*
1 *Thess.* 2. 14. ye have suffered like things of your *c.*

COUNTRIES.
Gen. 26. 3. to thee and thy seed will I give these *c.* 4.
41. 57. all *c.* came into Egypt to Joseph to buy corn
2 *Kings* 18. 35. who among all *c.* that have delivered
1 *Chr.* 22. 5. house of fame and glory throughout *c.*
2 *Chron.* 20. 29. the fear of God was on all those *c.*
Ezra 3. 3. fear on them, because of people of those *c.*
4. 20. mighty kings who have ruled over all *c.*
Psal. 110. 6. he shall wound the heads over many *c.*
Isa. 8. 9. and give ear all ye of far *c.* gird yourselves
Jer. 23. 3. I will gather the remnant of my flock out of all *c.* and bring them again, 8. ‖ 32. 37.
28. 8. the prophets prophesied against many *c.*
Ezek. 5. 5. I have set Jerusalem in midst of the *c.*
6. she hath changed my statutes more than the *c.*
6. 8. when ye shall be scattered through the *c.*
11. 16. tho' I have scattered them among the *c.* yet I will be to them as a little sanctuary in the *c.*
17. I will assemble you out of the *c.* 20. 34, 41.
22. 4. I have made thee a mocking to all *c.*
25. 7. I will cause thee to perish out of the *c.*
29. 12. I will disperse them through the *c.* 36. 19.
35. 10. thou hast said, these two *c.* shall be mine
Dan. 11. 40. he shall enter into the *c.* and overflow
41. many *c.* shall be overthrown, but these escape
42. he shall stretch forth his hand upon the *c.*
Zech. 10. 9. and they shall remember me in far *c.*
Luke 21. 21. let not them that are in the *c.* enter

COUPLE.
2 *Sam.* 13. 6. let Tamar make me a *c.* of cakes
16. 1. Ziba met David with a *c.* of asses saddled
Isa. 21. 7. he saw a chariot with a *c.* of horsemen, 9.

COUPLE, *Verb.*
Exod. 26. 6. thou shalt *c.* the curtains with taches, 9.
11. shalt make taches to *c.* tent together, 36. 18.
39. 4. made shoulder-pieces to *c.* ephod together

COUPLED, ETH.
Exod. 26. 3. the five curtains be *c.* 36. 10, 13, 16.
10. in the edge of the curtain which *c.* the second
24. the two boards shall be *c.* together, 36. 29.
39. 4. by the two edges was it *c.* together
1 *Pet.* 3. 2. your chaste conversation *c.* with fear

COUPLING.
Exod. 26. 4. make loops from selvedge in *c.* 36. 11.
4. likewise make in *c.* of the second, 36. 11, 12.
10. one curtain that is outmost in the *c.* 36. 17.
28. 27. over-against the other *c.* thereof, 39. 20.

COUPLINGS.
2 *Chr.* 34. 11. to buy hewn stone and timber for *c.*

COURAGE.
Josh. 2. 11. nor did there remain any more *c.* in any
2 *Chron.* 15. 8. he took *c.* and put away the idols
19. † 11. take *c.* and do, and Lord be with the good
Isa. 44. † 14. which he taketh *c.* for himself
Dan. 11. 25. shall stir up his *c.* ag. king of south
Acts 28. 15. when Paul saw thanked God, took *c.*

Good COURAGE.
Num. 13. 20. be ye of *good c.* and bring the fruit
Deut. 31. 6. be strong, and of *good c.* fear not, 7, 23. *Josh.* 1. 6, 9, 18. ‖ 10. 25. 1 *Chron.* 22. 13. ‖ 28. 20.
2 *Sam.* 10. 12. be of *good c.* let us play the men, 1 *Chron.* 19. 13. *Ezra* 10. 4. *Isa.* 41. 6.
Psal. 27. 14. wait on Lord, be of *good c.* and he shall strengthen thine heart, wait on Lord, 31. 24.

COURAGEOUS.
Josh. 1. 7. be thou strong and *c.* 23. 6. 2 *Chr.* 32. 7.
2 *Sam.* 13. 28. fear not, be *c.* and be valiant
Amos 2. 16. he that is *c.* among migh. shall flee away

COURAGEOUSLY.
2 *Chr.* 19. 11. deal *c.* and L. shall be with the good

COURSE
Signifies, [1] *That race which is prescribed us to run and follow,* 2 Tim. 4. 7. [2] *Order or turn,* 2 Chron. 5. 11. [3] *Manner or way,* Eph. 2. 2. [4] *Progress and success,* 2 Thess. 3. 1. [5] *A voyage,* Acts 21. 7. [6] *The gospel-ministry,* Acts 13. 25.
1 *Chron.* 27. 1. the chief fathers of every *c.* 24,000.
2 *Chron.* 5. 11. the priests did not then wait by *c.*
Ezra 3. 11. they sung together by *c.* in praising
Psal. 82. 5. all the foundations of earth are out of *c.*
Jer. 8. 6. every one turned to his *c.* as the horse
23. 10. their *c.* is evil, and their force is not right
Luke 1. 5. Zacharias was of the *c.* of Abiah
8. while he executed in the order of his *c.*
Acts 13. 25. and as John fulfilled his *c.* he said
16. 11. came with straight *c.* to Samothracia, 21. 1.
20. 24. that I might finish my *c.* with joy
21. 7. when we had finished our *c.* from Tyre
1 *Cor.* 14. 27. or at most by three, and that by *c.*
2 *Thess.* 3. 1. that word of the Lord may have free *c.*
2 *Tim.* 4. 7. I have finished my *c.* kept the faith
Jam. 3. 6. the tongue setteth on fire the *c.* of nature
WATER-COURSE. *See* WATER.

COURSES.
Judg. 5. 20. the stars in their *c.* fought against Sisera
1 *Chron.* 23. 6. David divided the Levites into *c.*
2 *Chron.* 8. 14. Solomon appointed the *c.* of the priests
23. 8. for Jehoiada the priest dismissed not the *c.*
31. 2. Hezekiah appointed the *c.* of the priests
35. 10. and the Levites stood in their *c.*
Ezra 6. 18. they set the Levites in their *c.* for service

COURT,
In Hebrew Chazer, *is an entrance into a palace or house,* Esth. 6. 4, 5. *The great* courts *belonging to the temple were three; the first called the* court of the Gentiles, *because the* Gentiles *were allowed to enter so far, and no farther. The second called the* court of Israel, *because all the* Israelites, *if purified, had a right of admission. The third* court *was that of the* Priests, *where the altar of burnt offerings stood, and where the* Priests *and* Levites *exercised their ministry.* It signifies *the church of Christ,* Zech. 3. 7. Also *the false church,* Rev. 11. 2.
Exod. 27. 9. thou shalt make the *c.* of the tabern. shall be hangings for the *c.* 35. 17. ‖ 38. 9. ‖ 39. 40.
12. breadth of the *c.* 13. ‖ 18. length of the *c.*
19. all the pins of the *c.* 35. 18. ‖ 38. 20, 31.
40. 8. and thou shalt set up the *c.* round about
Lev. 6. 16. in the *c.* of the tabernacle shall eat it, 26
2 *Sam.* 17. 18. a man which had a well in his *c.*
2 *Kings* 20. 4. afore Isaiah was gone into middle *c.*
2 *Chron.* 20. 5. Jehoshaphat stood before the new *c.*
24. 21. they stoned Zechariah in *c.* of Lord's house
29. 16. brought out the uncleanness into the *c.*
Esth. 5. 1. Esther stood in the inner *c.* of king's house

Esth. 6. 4. and the king said, who is in the *c.?*
5. servants said, behold Haman standeth in the *c.*
Isa. 34. 13. habitation of dragons, and a *c.* for owls
35. † 7. shall be a *c.* for reeds and rushes
Jer. 19. 14. Jeremiah stood in the *c.* of Lord's house
26. 2. stand in the *c.* of the Lord's house and speak
32. 2. and Jeremiah the prophet was shut up in the *c.* of the prison, 33. 1. | 39. 15.
38. 6. they cast Jeremiah into the dungeon in the *c.*
Ezek. 8. 7. he brought me to the door of the *c.* 16.
10. 3. the man went in, the cloud filled the inner *c.*
40. 17. he brought me into outward *c.* 42. 1. | 46. 21.
28. he brought me to the inner *c.* and measured
43. 5. the Spirit brought me into the inner *c.*
45. 19. put blood upon the gate of the inner *c.*
46. 21. in every corner of the *c.* there was a *c.*
Amos 7. 13. king's chapel, and it is the king's *c.*
Acts 16. † 19. they drew Paul and Silas into the *c.*
17. † 22. Paul stood in midst of *c.* of the Areopagites
19. † 38. the *c.* days are kept, there are deputies
Phil. 1. † 13. my bonds are manifest in Cæsar's *c.*
Rev. 11. 2. the *c.* without the temple, leave out

COURTS.

2 *Kings* 21. 5. Manasseh built altars for all the host of heaven in the two *c.* 2 *Chron.* 33. 5.
23. 12. altars in the two *c.* Josiah brake down
1 *Chron.* 23. 28. their office was to wait in the *c.*
28. 6. Solomon shall build my house and my *c.*
12. David gave Solomon the pattern of the *c.*
2 *Chron.* 23. 5. all the people shall be in the *c.*
Psal. 65. 4. approach to thee, that he dwell in thy *c.*
84. 2. my soul fainteth for the *c.* of the Lord
92. 13. they shall flourish in the *c.* of our God
96. 8. bring an offering and come into his *c.*
100. 4. enter into his *c.* with praise, be thankful to
116. 19. pay my vows in the *c.* of the Lord's house
135. 2. ye that stand in the *c.* of the house of God
Isa. 1. 12. who hath required this to tread my *c.?*
62. 9. they shall drink it in the *c.* of my holiness
Ezek. 9. 7. and fill the *c.* with the slain, go ye forth
Zech. 3. 7. thou shalt judge my house, and keep my *c*
Luke 7. 25. they that live delicately are in king's *c.*

COURTEOUS.

1 *Pet.* 3. 8. love as brethren, be pitiful, be *c.*

COURTEOUSLY.

Acts 27. 3. Julius *c.* entreated Paul and gave liberty
28. 7. Publius received us and lodged us 3 days *c.*

COURTIER.

John 4. † 46. there was a certain *c.* whose son was

COUSIN.

Luke 1. 36. thy *c.* Elisabeth hath conceived a son

COUSINS.

Luke 1. 58. her neighbours and *c.* heard how L.

COW.

Lev. 22. 28. whether *c.* or ewe, ye shall not kill it
Num. 18. 17. firstling of a *c.* thou shalt not redeem
Job 21. 10. their *c.* calveth, and casteth not her calf
Isa. 7. 21. a man nourish a young *c.* and two sheep
11. 7. and the *c.* and the bear shall feed, lion eat
Ezek. 4. 15. I have given thee *c.* dung for man's
Amos 4. 3. every *c.* at that which is before her

CRACKLING.

Eccl. 7. 6. as *c.* of thorns under a pot, so is laughter

CRACKNELS.

1 *Kings* 14. 3. take with thee ten loaves and *c.*

CRAFT.

Dan. 8. 25. thro' his policy shall cause *c.* to prosper
Mark 14. 1. take him by *c.* and put him to death
Acts 18. 3. because he was of the same *c.* abode with
19. 25. ye know that by this *c.* we have wealth
27. so that not only this our *c.* is in danger
Rev. 18. 22. no craftsman, of whatsoever *c.* he be

CRAFTILY.

Judg. 9. † 31. he sent messengers to Abimelech *c.*

CRAFTINESS.

Job 5. 13. he taketh the wise in their *c.* 1 *Cor.* 3. 19.
Luke 20. 23. but he perceived their *c.* and said
2 *Cor.* 4. 2. not walking in *c.* nor handling the word
Eph. 4. 14. we be no more carried by cunning *c.*

CRAFTY.

Job 5. 12. he disappointeth the devices of the *c.*
15. 5. and thou choosest the tongue of the *c.*
Psal. 83. 3. have taken *c.* counsel against thy people
2 *Cor.* 12. 16. being *c.* I caught you with guile

CRAFTSMAN.

Deut. 27. 15. the work of the hands of the *c.*
Rev. 18. 22. no *c.* shall be found any more in thee

CRAFTSMEN.

2 *Kings* 24. 14. carried away all the *c.* and smiths, 16.
1 *Chron.* 4. 14. of Charashim, for they were *c.*
Neh. 11. 35. Lod and Ono, the valley of *c.*
Hos. 13. 2. molten images, all of it the work of *c.*
Acts 19. 24. Demetrius brought no small gain to *c.*
38. if the *c.* have a matter against any man

CRAG.

Job 39. 28. the eagle abideth on the *c.* of the rock

CRANE.

Isa. 38. 14. like a *c.* or swallow so did I chatter
Jer. 8. 7. *c.* and swallow observe the time of coming

CRASHING.

Zeph. 1. 10. there shall be a great *c.* from the hills

CRAVED.

Mark 15. 43. Joseph went in, and *c.* the body of Jesus

CRAVETH.

Prov. 16. 26. labours for himself, his mouth *c.* it

CREATE

Signifies, [1] *To make out of nothing, to bring being out of non-entity,* Gen. 1. 1. [2] *To change the form, state, and situation of matter, which is wholly indisposed for such a change, and requires as great power as to make out of nothing,* Gen. 1. 21. | 2. 19. [3] *To give and work grace where it is not,* Eph. 2. 10. [4] *To cleanse the heart more and more from its natural corruption by the power of sanctifying grace,* Psal. 51. 10.

Num. 16. † 30. but if the Lord *c.* a creature
Psal. 51. 10 *c.* in me a clean heart, O God, renew
Isa. 4. 5. *c.* on every dwelling place of Zion a cloud
45. 7. I form the light and *c.* darkness, I *c.* evil
57. 19. I *c.* the fruit of the lips, peace to him
65. 17. behold, I *c.* new heavens and a new earth
18. be glad and rejoice for ever in that which I *c.*

CREATED.

Gen. 1. 1. in the beginning God *c.* heaven and earth
21. God *c.* great whales and every living creature
27. so God *c.* man in his own image, in the image of God, male and female *c.* he them, 5. 2.
2. 3. in it he had rested from all he *c.* and made
6. 7. Lord said, I will destroy man whom I have *c.*
Deut. 4. 32. since the day God *c.* man on the earth
Psal. 89. 12. the north and south thou hast *c.* them
102. 18. people which shall be *c.* shall praise Lord
104. 30. thou sendest forth thy Spirit, they are *c.*
148. 5. for he commanded, and they were *c.*
Isa. 40. 26. behold who hath *c.* these things
41. 20. and the holy One of Israel hath *c.* it
42. 5. saith the Lord, he that *c.* the heavens
43. 1. the L. that *c.* thee, O Jacob, and formed thee
7. have *c.* him for my glory, yea, I have made him
45. 8. let the earth open, I the Lord have *c.* it
12. I have made the earth, and *c.* man upon it
18. he hath established it, he *c.* it not in vain
48. 7. they are *c.* now, and not from the beginning
54. 16. I have *c.* the smith, I have *c.* the waster
Jer. 31. 22. for the Lord hath *c.* a new thing in earth
Ezek. 21. 30. I will judge thee where thou wast *c.*
28. 13. prepared in the day that thou wast *c.*
15. wast perfect from the day that thou wast *c.*
Mal. 2. 10. have one father, hath not one God *c.* us?
Mark 13. 19. from beginning of creat. which God *c.*
1 *Cor.* 11. 9. neither was the man *c.* for the woman
Eph. 2. 10. we are his workmanship *c.* in Christ Jesus
3. 9. hid in God, who *c.* all things by Jesus Christ
4. 24. the new man, after God *c.* in righteousness
Col. 1. 16. for by him were all things *c.* in heaven all things were *c.* by him, and for him
3. 10. new man after the image of him that *c.* him
1 *Tim.* 4. 3. from meats, which God *c.* to be received
Rev. 4. 11. thou art worthy, for thou hast *c.* all things, and for thy pleasure they are, and were *c.*
10. 6. who *c.* heaven and the things that therein are

CREATETH.

Amos 4. 13. he that *c.* the wind, the Lord is his name

CREATION.

Mark. 10. 6. from the *c.* God made male and female
13. 19. as was not from the beginning of the *c.*
Rom. 1. 20. things of him from the *c.* are clearly seen
8. 22. for we know that the whole *c.* groaneth
2 *Pet.* 3. 4. things continue as they were from the *c.*
Rev. 3. 14. the Amen, the beginning of the *c.* of God

CREATOR.

Eccl. 12. 1. remember thy *c.* in the days of thy youth
Isa. 40. 28. the Lord, the *c.* of the ends of the earth
43. 15. I am the Lord, the *c.* of Israel, your king
Rom. 1. 25. who served the creature more than the *c.*
1 *Pet.* 4. 19. to him in well-doing as to a faithful *c.*

CREATURE.

Gen. 1. 20. let waters bring forth the moving *c.*
Lev. 11. 46. this is the law of every *c.* that moveth
Num. 16. † 30. if the Lord create a new *c.*
Mark 16. 15. preach the gospel to every *c.* *Col.* 1. 23.
Rom. 8. 19. the earnest expectation of the *c.* waiteth
20. for the *c.* was made subject to vanity
21. the *c.* shall be delivered from the bondage
† 22. that every *c.* groaneth and travaileth in pain
39. nor any *c.* shall be able to separate us
2 *Cor.* 5. 17. if any man be in Christ, he is a new *c.*
Gal. 6. 15. nor uncircumcision, but a new *c.*
Col. 1. 15. who is the first-born of every *c.*
1 *Tim.* 4. 4. for every *c.* of God is good, if it be
Heb. 4. 13. nor is there any *c.* that is not manifest
Rev. 5. 13. every *c.* in heaven heard I, saying, blessing

Living CREATURE.

Gen. 1. 21. and God created every *living c.*
24. God said, let the earth bring forth the *living c.*
2. 19. whatsoever Adam called every *living c.*
9. 10. establish my covenant with every *living c.*
12. the token between me and every *living c.* 15.
Lev. 11. 46. the law of every *living c.* that moveth
Ezek. 1. 20. spirit of *living c.* was within, 21. | 10. 17.
10. 15. the *living c.* that I saw by river Chebar, 20.

CREATURES.

Isa. 13. 21. their houses shall be full of doleful *c.*
Jam. 1. 18. should be a kind of first-fruits of his *c.*
Rev. 8. 9. a third part of the *c.* in the sea died

Living CREATURES.

Ezek. 1. 5. came the likeness of four *living c.*
13. it went up and down among the *living c.*
14. *living c.* ran, and returned as lightning
15. as I beheld *living c.* one wheel by *living c.*
19. when the *living c.* went, the wheels went
3. 13. I heard noise of the wings of the *living c.*

CREDITOR.

Deut. 15. 2. every *c.* that lendeth shall release it
1 *Sam.* 22. † 2. every one that had a *c.* went to David
2 *Kings* 4. 1. *c.* is come to take my two sons bond.
4. † 7. he said, go, sell the oil, and pay the *c.*
Luke 7. 41. there was a certain *c.* who had two debtors

CREDITORS.

Isa. 50. 1. to which of my *c.* have I sold you

CREEK, S.

Judg. 5. † 17. Asher continued on the *c.* and abode
Acts 27. 39. they discovered a certain *c.* with a shore

CREEP.

Lev. 11. 31. these are uncl. to you among all that *c.*
Psal. 104. 20. all the beasts of the forest do *c.* forth
2 *Tim.* 3. 6. of this sort are they who *c.* into houses

CREEPETH.

Gen. 1. 25. G. made every thing that *c.* on earth, 26.
† 28. have dominion over every liv. thing that *c.*
30. have given to every thing that *c.* herb for
7. 8. every thing that *c.* went in two and two, 14.
21. all flesh died of every thing that *c.* on earth
8. 17. bring forth with thee every thing that *c.*
19. whatsoever *c.* on the earth went out of ark
Lev. 11. 41. every creeping thing that *c.* on the earth shall be an abomination, 43, 44. | 20. 25.
Deut. 4. 18. likeness of any thing that *c.* on ground
Psal. 69. † 34. let every thing that *c.* praise him

CREEPING.

Gen. 1. † 20. let waters bring forth *c.* creature
26. let them have dominion over every *c.* thing
7. 14. every *c.* thing after his kind went into ark
Lev. 5. 2. touch the carcase of unclean *c.* things
Lev. 11. 21. yet these may ye eat, of every *c.* thing
Gen. 22. 5. or whosoever toucheth any *c.* thing
Deut. 14. 19. every *c.* thing that flieth is unclean
1 *Kings* 4. 33. spake of beasts, *c.* things, and fishes
Psal. 104. 25. in the sea are *c.* things innumerable
148. 10. all cattle, *c.* things praise the Lord
Ezek. 8. 10. form of *c.* things pourtrayed on wall
38. 20. all *c.* things shall shake at my presence
Hos. 2. 18. I will make a covenant with the *c.* things
Mic. 7. † 17. move out of their holes like *c.* things
Hab. 1. 14. and maketh men as the *c.* things
Acts 10. 12. Peter saw *c.* things and fowls, 11. 6.
Rom. 1. 23. into an image made like to *c.* things

CREPT.

Jude 4. for there are certain men *c.* in unawares

CREW.

Mat. 26. 74. I know not the man, and immediately the cock *c.* *Mark* 14. 68. *Luke* 22. 60.
Mark 14. 72. the second time the cock *c.* *John* 18. 27.

CRIB.

Job 39. 9. will the unicorn abide by thy *c.?*
Prov. 14. 4. where no oxen are the *c.* is clean
Isa. 1. 3. and the ass knoweth his master's *c.*

CRIED, *See* after CRY.

CRIME, S.

Job 31. 11. this is an heinous *c.* yea it is an iniquity
Ezek. 7. 23. for the land is full of bloody *c.* and the
Acts 25. 16. to answer concerning *c.* laid against him
27. and not to signify the *c.* laid against him

CRIMSON.

Some think that it is the same with scarlet; *others that it is of a deeper dye. In the* Hebrew *it is called* Tolahat Shani; *that is,* the double worm, *or* the worm Shani; *as if* Shani *were the proper name of this worm: In the* Arabic *it is called,* Kermes, *or* Karmes; *whence comes the word* crimson, *because they made use of these little worms to dye this colour. The* Kermes *is a small round shell, membranous, thin, smooth, and shining; of a reddish brown colour, mixed with a whitish ash colour, about a quarter of an inch diameter, generally divided into two equal cavities, the greatest of which is full of a vast number of little oval eggs, very red, or vermilion; and the smaller cavity is full of a kind of liquor, which is red likewise, and not much different from blood. This cod, or shell, grows upon a kind of green oak, that grows only to the height of a shrub. These shrubs are found in* Palestine, *in* Provence, *in* Languedoc, *in* Spain, *and elsewhere. They loosen these cods, or shells, from the leaves to which they are fastened, and the worms of which they are full come out of the hole made by taking them from the leaf; they separate these little animals from the shells with a sieve, and put them together by pressing them lightly, and make them into balls of the bigness of a pullet's egg.*

2 *Chron.* 2. 7. send a man cunning to work in *c.* 14.
3. 14. he made the vail of blue, *c.* and fine linen
Isa. 1. 18. though your sins be red like *c.* they shall be
Jer. 4. 30. though thou clothest thyself with *c.*

CRIPPLE.

Acts 14. 8. being a *c.* from his mother's womb

CRISPING-PINS.

Isa. 3. 22. Lord will take away the mantles and *c.*

CROOK-BACKED.

Lev. 21. 20. a man that is *c.* shall not approach

CROOKED.

Deut. 32. 5. they are a perverse and *c.* generation
Judg. 5. † 6. the travellers walked through *c.* ways
Job 26. 13. his hand hath formed the *c.* serpent
Ps. 125. 5. as for such as turn aside to their *c.* ways
Prov. 2. 15. whose ways are *c.* and they froward
Eccl. 1. 15. what is *c.* cannot be made straight, 7. 13.
Isa. 27. 1. shall punish Leviathan, that *c.* serpent
40. 4. *c.* shall be made straight, 42. 16. *Luke* 3. 5.
45. 2. I will go and make the *c.* places straight
59. 8. no judgment, they have made them *c.* paths
Lam. 3. 9. he inclosed, he hath made my paths *c.*
Phil. 2. 15. the sons of God, in midst of a *c.* nation

CROP.

Lev. 1. 16. shall pluck away his *c.* with his feathers

CROP, *Verb.*

Ezek. 17. 22. I will *c.* off from the top of his twigs

CROPPED.

Ezek. 17. 4. he *c.* off the top of his young twigs

CROSS.

By the word cross is understood a gibbet made of two pieces of wood put across; whether they cross with right angles at the top as a T, *or in the middle of their length like an* X. *The cross was the punishment of the vilest slaves, and was called a* servile punishment: *This punishment our Saviour underwent,* Mat. 27. 35. Phil. 2. 8. *This penalty was so common among the* Romans, *that pains, afflictions, troubles, and unprosperous affairs were called* crosses; *and the verb* cruciare *was used for all sorts of chastisements, and pains of body and mind.* See PUNISHMENT.

Our Saviour says often in his gospel, that he who would be his disciple, must take up his cross and follow him, *Mat.* 16. 24. *He must submit readily to whatsoever afflictions God lays upon him, or any suffering that befalls him in the service of God, even to death itself.* Cross *is taken for the whole of Christ's sufferings, from his birth to his death, but especially those upon the tree,* Eph. 2. 16. Heb. 12. 2. *And for the doctrine of the gospel;* that is, *of salvation through Christ crucified,* 1 Cor. 1. 18. *False teachers, who pressed the observation of the law of* Moses, *as necessary to salvation, besides faith in Christ, are called* enemies of the cross of Christ, *Phil.* 3. 18. *because by such doctrine they did really oppose and undermine the power and merit of Christ's passion, and sought to avoid persecution, which they would have been exposed to, had they preached salvation only by Christ crucified, as the apostle Paul was,* Gal. 5. 11.

To crucify, *is not only taken for putting to death on a cross,* Mat. 27. 35. *but also for subduing and mortifying sin; for breaking the*

strength and suppressing the motions and breakings out of corrupt nature, Gal. 5. 24. They that are Christ's have crucified the flesh. Christ's death on the cross has not only merited reconciliation with God, but is also made effectual to mortify and subdue the lusts of the flesh, Gal. 2. 20. I am crucified with Christ. It is said of them, who for some time have made profession of religion, and afterwards turn apostates, that they crucify to themselves the Son of God afresh, Heb. 6. 6. that is, They shew themselves to be of the same opinion with those that did crucify Christ, and would do it again, were it in their power.
The apostle tells the Galatians, that Jesus Christ had been evidently set forth crucified among them, Gal. 3. 1. They had been as fully and clearly informed of the nature and design of Christ's sufferings, as if all had been transacted in their sight.
Mat. 10. 38. he that taketh not his c. Luke 14. 27.
16. 24. let him deny himself, take up his c. and follow me, Mark 8. 34. | 10. 21. Luke 9. 23.
27. 32. they found Simon, him they compelled to bear his c. Mark 15. 21. Luke 23. 26.
40. saying, if thou be the Son of God, come down from the c. 42. Mark 15. 30, 32.
John 19. 17. he bearing his c. went forth to a place
19. Pilate wrote a title, and put it on the c.
25. there stood by the c. of Jesus his mother
31. bodies should not remain on the c. on sabbath
1 Cor. 1. 17. lest c. of Christ be made of none effect
18. preaching of the c. is to them foolishness
Gal. 5. 11. then is the offence of the c. ceased
6. 12. lest they suffer persecution for the c. of Chr.
14. God forbid that I should glory, save in the c.
Eph. 2. 16. reconcile both in one body by the c.
Phil. 2. 8. he became obedient to the death of the c.
3. 18. that they are enemies of the c. of Christ
Col. 1. 20. having made peace thro' the blood of c.
2. 14. and took it out of the way, nailing it to his c.
Heb. 12. 2. for the joy set before him, endured the c.

CROSS-WAY.
Obad. 14. nor shouldest thou have stood in the c.

CROUCH.
1 Sam. 2. 36. shall come and c. to him for a piece

CROUCHETH.
Psal. 10. 10. he c. and humbleth himself, that poor

CROW, CROWING. See COCK.

CROWN
Is properly taken for a cap of state worn on the heads of sovereign princes, 1 Chron. 20. 2. But in a figurative sense it signifies honour, splendour, or dignity, Lam. 5. 16. The crown is fallen from our head. And the apostle says of the Philippians, that they were his joy and crown, Phil. 4. 1. They were his honour and glory, the great ornament of his ministry, by means whereof they had been converted to Christ. It is used likewise for reward, because conquerors in the public games were crowned, 1 Cor. 9. 25. They do it to obtain a corruptible crown, but we an incorruptible: that is, the wrestlers in those games which are practised among you, contend in order to obtain a wreath, or garland, of flowers, herbs, or leaves, of laurel, olive, and the like; but we Christians strive for an inheritance incorruptible, undefiled, and that fadeth not away, reserved in heaven for us. St. John, speaking of Christ governing the affairs of his church, says, that on his head were many crowns, Rev. 19. 12. noting his absolute sovereignty, and many triumphs. A crown is a sign of victory, Rev. 4. 4.
The high-priest among the Jews wore a crown, which girt about his mitre, or the lower part of his bonnet, and was tied behind his head. On the forepart was a plate of gold, with these words engraven on it, Holiness to the Lord, Exod. 28. 36. | 29. 6. New married men and women wore crowns upon their wedding-day, Cant. 3. 11. The spouse invites her companions to see king Solomon with the crown wherewith his mother crowned him in the day of his espousals; and alluding to this custom, it is said, Ezek. 16. 12. that when God entered into covenant with the Jewish nation, he put a beautiful crown upon their head.
Exod. 25. 25. shalt make a golden c. to the border
29. 6. and put the holy c. upon the mitre
30. 4. make golden rings to it under the c. 37. 27.
39. 30. made the plate of the c. of pure gold
Lev. 8. 9. upon his forefront he put the holy c.
21. 12. the c. of the anointing oil is upon him
2 Kings 11. 12. put the c. upon Joash, 2 Chr. 23. 11.
Esth. 1. 11. to bring Vashti with the c. royal
Job 31. 36. surely I would bind it as a c. to me
Psal. 89. 39. thou hast profaned his c. by casting it
132. 18. but upon himself shall his c. flourish
Prov. 4. 9. a c. of glory shall she deliver to thee
12. 4. a virtuous woman is a c. to her husband
14. 24. the c. of the wise is their riches
16. 31. the hoary head is a c. of glory if found in
17. 6. children's children are the c. of old men
27. 24. doth the c. endure to every generation?
Cant. 3. 11. go forth, behold king Solomon with c.
Isa. 28. 1. woe to the c. of pride, to the drunkards
5. that day Lord of hosts shall be for a c. of glory
62. 3. thou shalt also be a c. of glory in the hand of
Jer. 13. 18. the c. of your glory shall come down
Ezek. 21. 26. remove the diadem, take off the c.
Zech. 9. 16. they shall be as the stones of a c. lifted
John 19. 5. Jesus wearing a c. of thorns, and purple
1 Cor. 9. 25. they do it to obtain a corruptible c.
Phil. 4. 1. dearly belov. and longed for, my joy and c.
1 Thess. 2. 19. for what is our hope, or c. of rejoicing
2 Tim. 4. 8. there is laid up for me a c. of righteous.
Jam. 1. 12. he shall receive c. of life Lord promised
1 Pet. 5. 4. ye shall receive a c. of glory fadeth not
Rev. 2. 10. faithful to death, I will give a c. of life
3. 11. hold that fast, that no man take thy c.
6. 2. a c. given to him, and went forth conquering

CROWN of gold.
Exod. 25. 11. thou shalt make upon it a c. of gold round about, 24. | 30. 3. | 37. 2, 11, 12, 26.
Esth. 8. 15. Mordecai went out with a great c. [of gold
Psal. 21. 3. thou settest a c. of pure gold on his head

CROWN, with head.
Gen. 49. 26. they shall be on the c. of Joseph's head
Deut. 33. 20. teareth the arm with the c. of the head
2 Sam. 1. 10. I took the c. that was upon his head
12. 30. took king's c. from his head, 1 Chr. 20. 2.
14. 25. from the sole even to c. of his head, Job 2. 7.
Esth. 2. 17. the king set the royal c. on her head
6. 8. the c. royal which is set upon his head
Job 19. 9. he hath taken the c. from my head
Isa. 3. 17. Lord will smite with a scab the c. of head
Jer. 2. 16. have broken the c. of thy head
48. 45. the c. of the head of the tumultuous ones
Lam. 5. 16. the c. is fallen from our head, woe to us
Ezek. 16. 12. I put a beautiful c. on thine head
Mat. 27. 29. they platted a c. of thorns, and put it on his head, Mark 15. 17. John 19. 2.
Rev. 12. 1. and upon her head a c. of twelve stars
14. 14. having on his head a golden c. and a sickle

CROWN, Verb.
Psal. 5. † 12. with favour wilt thou c. him, as with

CROWNED.
Psal. 8. 5. thou hast c. him with glory and honour
Prov. 14. 18. the prudent are c. with knowledge
Cant. 3. 11. the crown wherewith his mother c. him
Nah. 3. 17. thy c. are as locusts, and thy captains
2 Tim. 2. 5. he is not c. except he strive lawfully
Heb. 2. 9. we see Jesus c. with glory and honour

CROWNEDST.
Heb. 2. 7. thou c. him with glory and honour

CROWNEST.
Psal. 65. 11. thou c. the year with thy goodness

CROWNETH.
Psal. 103. 4. who c. thee with loving-kindness

CROWNING.
Isa. 23. 8. taken counsel against Tyre the c. city

CROWNS.
1 Chron. 2. † 54. the c. of the house of Joab
Ezek. 23. 42. which put beautiful c. on their heads
Zech. 6. 11. make c. || 14. the c. shall be to Helem
Rev. 4. 4. the elders had on their heads c. of gold
10. and they cast their c. before the throne, saying
9. 7. on the locusts' heads were c. like gold
12. 3. a red dragon having seven c. on his heads
13. 1. a beast rise up, having upon his horns ten c.
19. 12. and on his head were many c.

CRUCIFY.
Mat. 20. 19. shall deliver him to Gentiles to c. him
23. 34. some of them ye shall kill, and c. and scourge
27. 31. they led him away to c. him, Mark 15. 20.
Mark 15. 13. and they cried out again, c. him, 14.
27. and with him they c. two thieves, the one
Luke 23. 21. they cried, c. him, c. him, John 19. 6, 15.
Heb. 6. 6. they c. to themselves the Son of God afresh

CRUCIFIED.
Mat. 26. 2. Son of man is betrayed to be c. Luke 24. 7.
27. 22. they all said unto him, let him be c. 23.
26. Pilate delivered him to be c. John 19. 16.
35. c. him and parted his garments, John 19. 23.
38. then were there two thieves c. with him, 44. Mark 15. 32. Luke 23. 33. John 19. 18.
28. 5. I know ye seek Jesus who was c. Mark 16. 6.
John 19. 20. for the place where Jesus was c. 41.
Acts 2. 23. by wicked hands ye have c. and slain
36. made Jesus, whom ye c. Lord and C. 4. 10.
Rom. 6. 6. knowing that our old man is c. with him
1 Cor. 1. 13. is Christ divided? was Paul c. for you?
23. we preach C. c. unto the Jews a stumbling
2. 2. know any thing, save Jesus C. and him c.
8. they would not have c. the Lord of glory
2 Cor. 13. 4. for tho' he was c. through weakness, yet
Gal. 2. 20. I am c. with Christ, nevertheless, I live
3. 1. Christ hath been set forth, c. among you
5. 24. they that are Christ's have c. the flesh with
6. 14. by whom the world is c. to me, I to world
Rev. 11. 8. and Egypt, where also our Lord was c.

CRUEL.
Gen. 49. 7. cursed be their wrath, for it was c.
Exod. 6. 9. but they hearkened not for c. bondage
Deut. 32. 33. their wine is the c. venom of asps
Job 30. 21. thou art become c. to me, thou opposest
Psal. 25. 19. mine enemies hate me with c. hatred
71. 4. deliver me out of the hand of the c. man
Prov. 5. 9. lest thou give thy years to the c.
11. 17. but he that is c. troubleth his own flesh
12. 10. but the tender mercies of the wicked are c.
17. 11. a c. messenger shall be sent against him
27. 4. wrath is c. || Cant. 8. 6. jealousy is c.
Isa. 13. 9. behold, the day of the Lord cometh, c.
19. 4. the Egyptians will I give over to a c. lord
Jer. 6. 23. they are c. and have no mercy, 50. 42.
30. 14. wounded with chastisement of a c. one
Lam. 4. 3. the daughter of my people is become c.
Heb. 11. 36. others had trial of c. mockings

CRUELLY.
Ezek. 18. 18. because he c. oppressed, he shall die

CRUELTY.
Gen. 49. 5. instruments of c. are in their habitations
Judg. 9. 24. the c. done to the sons of Jerubbaal
Psal. 27. 12. such as breathe out c. are risen up
74. 20. dark places are full of the habitations of c.
Prov. 27. † 4. wrath is c. anger is outrageous
Ezek. 34. 4. with force and c. have ye ruled them

CRUMBS.
Mat. 15. 27. yet the dogs eat of the c. which fall from their master's table, Mark 7. 28.
Luke 16. 21. to be fed with c. which fell from rich

CRUSE.
1 Sam. 26. 11. take spear and c. of water let us go
12. so David took the spear and the c. 16.
1 Kings 14. 3. take with thee a c. of honey and go
17. 12. she said, I have but a little oil in a c.
14. nor c. of oil fail, till the Lord send rain, 16.
19. 6. Elijah had a c. of water at his head
2 Kings 2. 20. bring me a new c. and put salt therein

CRUSH.
Job 39. 15. ostrich forgetteth her foot may c. them
Lam. 1. 15. assembly against me to c. my young men
3. 34. to c. under his feet all the prisoners of earth
Amos 4. 1. ye kine of Bashan which c. the needy

CRUSHED, CRUSHT.
Lev. 22. 24. ye shall not offer to the Lord what is c.
Num. 22. 25. the ass c. Balaam's foot against wall
Deut. 28. 33. shalt be only oppressed and c. alway
Judg. 10. † 8. the Philistines c. the children of Isr.
2 Chr. 16. † 10. Asa c. some of the people same time
Job 4. 19. in the dust, which are c. before the moth
5. 4. his children far from safety are c. in the gate
20. † 19. because he hath c. and forsaken the poor
34. † 25. he overturneth them, so that they are c.
Isa. 59. 5. that which is c. breaketh out into a viper
Jer. 51. 34. Nebuchadnezzar the king hath c. me

CRY
Is taken for a loud extending of the voice, Eccl. 9. 17. Mat. 21. 15. Also for weeping, mourning, and lamentation, Exod. 11. 6. | 12. 30. In the Psalms, and elsewhere, it is often put for fervent and earnest prayer, either with the voice, or in the heart only, Psal. 17. 1. Attend unto my cry. Exod. 14. 15. God says to Moses, Wherefore criest thou unto me? Though as yet Moses had said nothing. To cry, likewise signifies, to call to God for vengeance, Gen. 4. 10. Sins are said to cry, when they are gross, manifest, and impudent, and such as highly provoke God to anger; thus the cry of the sins and irregularities of Sodom ascended up to heaven, and called for vengeance, Gen. 18. 20. I looked for righteousness, but behold a cry, Isa. 5. 7. The cry of the oppressed, praying for help from men, and vengeance from God upon their oppressors. The prophets, by prosopopeias, frequently make beasts, trees, mountains, lands, and cities, to speak. The young ravens cry, and speak their wants to God after their manner, Psal. 147. 9. See Isa. 15. 4. | 34. 14. Joel 1. 20.
Gen. 18. 21. according to the c. which is come up
Exod. 2. 23. and their c. came up unto God, 3. 9.
3. 7. I have heard their c. I know their sorrows
Num. 16. 34. and all Israel fled at the c. of them
Judg. 4. † 13. Sisera gathered by c. all his chariots
1 Sam. 5. 12. the c. of the city went up to heaven
9. 16. because their c. is come up unto me
2 Sam. 22. 7. and my c. did enter into his ears
1 Kings 8. 28. to hearken to the c. and to the prayer which thy servant prayeth, 2 Chron. 6. 19
Neh. 5. 6. I was angry when I heard their c.
9. 9. thou heardest their c. by the Red sea
Esth. 4. 1. Mordecai cried with a loud and bitter c
9. 31. the matters of their fastings and their c.
Job 16. 18. O earth, let my c. have no place
34. 28. so that they cause the c. of the poor to come to him, he heareth the c. of the afflicted
Psal. 5. 2. hearken to voice of my c. my King, my G.
9. 12. he forgetteth not the c. of the humble
17. 1. hear the right, O Lord, attend unto my c.
18. 6. my c. came before him, even into his ears
34. 15. and his ears are open to their c.
39. 12. hear my prayer, O Lord, give ear to my c.
40. 1. he inclined unto me, and heard my c.
88. 2. God of my salv. incline thine ear unto my c.
102. 1. hear, O Lord, and let my c. come unto thee
106. 44. he regarded, when he heard their c.
119. 169. let my c. come near before thee, O Lord
142. 6. attend to my c. I am brought very low
Prov. 21. 13. who stoppeth his ears at the c. of poor
Eccl. 9. 17. more than the c. of him that ruleth
Isa. 5. 7. he looked for righteousness, behold a c.
15. 5. they shall raise up a c. of destruction
8. the c. is gone round about the borders of Moab
30. 19. he will be gracious at the voice of thy c.
43. 14. the Chaldeans, whose c. is in the ships
Jer. 7. 16. nor lift up c. nor prayer for them, 11. 14
8. 19. behold the voice of the c. of my people
14. 2. and the c. of Jerusalem is gone up
18. 22. let a c. be heard from their houses
25. 36. the c. of the shepherds shall be heard
46. 12. and thy c. hath filled the land
48. 4. her little ones have caused a c. to be heard
5. the enemies have heard a c. of destruction
49. 21. the earth is moved at the c. of Edom
50. 46. the c. is heard at the taking of Babylon
51. 54. a sound of a c. cometh from Babylon
Lam. 3. 56. hast heard, hide not thine ear at my c.
Ezek. 27. 28. the suburbs shake at the c. of pilots
Zeph. 1. 10. there shall be a c. from the fish gate
Mat. 25. 6. at midnight there was a c. made, behold

Great CRY.
Gen. 18. 20. because the c. of Sodom is great, 19. 13.
27. 34. Esau cried with a great and bitter c.
Exod. 11. 6. there shall be a great c. through Egypt
12. 30. Pharaoh rose, there was a great c. in Egypt
Neh. 5. 1. was great c. of the people and their wives
Acts 23. 9. when he so said, there arose a great c.

Hear CRY.
Exod. 22. 23. if they c. I will surely hear their c.
Job 27. 9. will God hear his c. when trouble comes
Psal. 61. 1. hear my c. O God, attend to my prayer
145. 19. he also will hear their c. and save them
Jer. 20. 16. let him hear the c. in the morning

Not hear CRY.
Jer. 14. 12. when they fast, I will not hear their c.

CRIES.
Jam. 5. 4. the c. of them that reaped are entered

CRY, Verb.
Exod. 5. 8. for they are idle, therefore they c.
22. 23. if thou afflict them, and they c. unto me
32. 18. neither is it the voice of them that c.
Lev. 13. 45. shall cover his upper lip, and c. unclean
Judg. 10. 14. go c. to the gods ye have chosen
2 Sam. 19. 28. what right have I yet to c. to the king
2 Kings 8. 3. she went to c. for her house and land
2 Chron. 20. 9. and c. in our affliction, thou wilt hear
Job 30. 20. I c. unto thee, and thou dost not hear
24. though they c. in his destruction
35. 9. they make the oppressed to c. they c. out
12. there they c. but none giveth answer, because
36. 13. they c. not when he bindeth them
38. 41. when his young ones c. to God, they wander
Psal. 22. 2. I c. in the day time, thou hearest not
27. 7. hear, O Lord, when I c. with my voice, 28. 2.
28. 1. to thee will I c. O Lord, my rock, 2.
34. 17. the righteous c. and the Lord heareth

Psa.56.9. when I *c*. then shall mine enemies turn back
57. 2. I will *c*. to God most high, that performeth
61. 2. from the end of the earth will I *c*. unto thee
86. 3. be merciful to me, O Lord, for I *c*. to thee
89. 26. he shall *c*. unto me, thou art my father
141. 1. Lord, I *c*. unto thee, make haste unto me
147. 9. he giveth food to young ravens which *c*.
Prov. 8. 1. doth not wisdom *c*. and understanding
21. 13. he also shall *c*. but shall not be heard
Isa. 8. 4. before the child shall know to *c*. my father
10. † 30. *c*. shrill with thy voice, O daugh. of Gallim
13. 22. the wild beasts of the island shall *c*.
14. 31. *c*. O city, thou Palestina, art dissolved
15. 4. and Heshbon shall *c*. and Elealeh
33. 7. behold their valiant ones shall *c*. without
34. 14. and the satyr shall *c*. to his fellow
40. 2. *c*. to Jerusalem, her warfare accomplished
6. the voice said, *c*. and he said, what shall I *c*.?
42. 2. he shall not *c*. nor cause his voice to be heard
13. he shall *c*. yea, prevail against his enemies
14. now will I *c*. like a travailing woman
46. 7. one shall *c*. to him, yet can he not answer
58. 9. thou shalt *c*. and he shall say, here I am
65. 14. but ye shall *c*. for sorrow of heart, and howl
Jer. 2. 2. go and *c*. in the ears of Jerusalem
3. 4. wilt thou not from this time *c*. unto me
4. 5. blow ye the trumpet in the land, *c*. gather
11. 11. though they *c*. to me, I will not hearken
12. *c*. to the gods to whom they offer incense
14. for I will not hear when they *c*. *Ezek*. 8. 18.
22. 20. go up to Lebanon, and *c*. from the passages
25. 34. howl ye shepherds and *c*. 48. 20. *Ezek*. 21. 12.
31. 6. the watchmen on mount Ephraim shall *c*.
Lam. 3. 8. when I *c*. and shout, he shutteth out my
Ezek. 9. 4. that *c*. for all the abominations done in
24. 17. forbear to *c*. make no mourning for dead
26. 15. the isles shake, when the wounded *c*.
27. 30. and they shall *c*. bitterly for Tyrus
Hos. 8. 2. Israel shall *c*. unto me, we know thee
Joel 1. 19. O Lord, to thee will I *c*. for the fire
20. the beasts of the field *c*. also unto thee
Jonah 3. 8. let man and beast *c*. mightily unto God
Mic. 3. 5. prophets bite with their teeth, and *c*. peace
Nah. 2. 8. stand, shall they *c*. but none look back
Zeph. 1. 14. the mighty men shall *c*. bitterly
Zech. 1. 14. the angel said unto me, *c*. thou, saying
Mat. 12. 19. he shall not strive, nor *c*. nor shall any
Luke 18. 7. shall not God avenge his elect, who *c*. day
Rom. 8. 15. the Spirit, whereby we *c*. Abba, Father
Gal. 4. 27. break forth and *c*. thou that travailest not

CRY *against*.

Deut. 15. 9. and he *c*. to the Lord *against* thee, 24. 15.
2 *Chron*. 13. 12. his priests to *c*. alarm *against* you
Job 31. 38. if my land *c*. *against* me, or the furrows
Jonah 1. 2. arise, go to Nineveh, and *c*. *against* it

CRY *aloud*.

1 *Kings* 18. 27. Elijah said, *c*. *aloud*, for he is a god
Job 19. 7. I *c*. *aloud*, but there is no judgment
Psal. 55. 17. at noon will I pray and *c*. *aloud*
Isa. 24. 14. they shall *c*. *aloud* from the sea
54. 1. sing, break forth into singing, and *c*. *aloud*
58. 1. *c*. *aloud*, spare not, lift up thy voice like a
Hos. 5. 8. trumpet in Ramah, *c*. *aloud* at Beth-aven
Mic. 4. 9. why dost thou *c*. *aloud*? is there no king

CRY *to the Lord*.

1 *Sam*. 7. 8. cease not to *c*. unto the *Lord* for us
Psal. 107. 19. they *c*. *to the Lord* in trouble, 28.
Isa. 19. 20. they shall *c*. *to Ld*. because of oppressors
Joel 1. 14. sanctify ye a fast, and *c*. *to the Lord*
Mic. 3. 4. shall *c*. *to the Lord*, but he will not hear

CRY *out*.

1 *Sam*. 2. † 24. ye make the Lord's people to *c*. *out*
4. † 19. Phinehas' wife was with child, near to *c*. *out*
8. 18. ye shall *c*. *out* that day, because of your k.
Job 19. 7. I *c*. *out* of wrong, but I am not heard
35. 9. they *c*. *out* by reason of the arm of mighty
Isa. 12. 6. *c*. *out* and shout, thou inhabitant of Zion
15. 4. the armed soldiers of Moab shall *c*. *out*
5. my heart shall *c*. *out* for Moab, his fugitives
29. 9. stay yourselves and wonder, *c*. *out* and cry
Jer. 48. 31. I will howl and *c*. *out* for all Moab
Lam. 2. 19. arise, *c*. *out* in the night, in the watches
Amos 3. 4. will a young lion *c*. *out* of his den?
Hab. 1. 2. I *c*. *out* to thee, but thou wilt not save
2. 11. for the stone shall *c*. *out* of the wall
Mark 10. 47. he began to *c*. *out* and say, have mercy
Luke 19. 40. the stones would immediately *c*. *out*

CRIED.

Gen. 27. 34. Esau *c*. with a great and bitter cry
39. 15. he heard that I lifted up my voice and *c*.
41. 43. and they *c*. before him, bow the knee
55. people *c*. to Pharaoh for bread, go to Joseph
45. 1. he *c*. cause every man to go out from me
Exod. 5. 15. the officers came and *c*. to Pharaoh
Num. 11. 2. the people *c*. to Moses, and he prayed
Deut. 22. 24. stone them, the damsel, bec. she *c*. not
27. the damsel *c*. and there was none to save her
Judg. 5. 28. Sisera's mother *c*. through the lattice
7. 21. and all the host ran and *c*. and fled
10. 12. and ye *c*. to me, and I delivered you
15. † 19. called the name the well of him that *c*.
1 *Sam*. 14. † 20. Saul and the people were *c*. together
17. 8. he stood and *c*. to the armies of Israel
20. 37. Jonathan *c*. after the lad, and said, 38.
2 *Sam*. 20. 16. then *c*. a wise woman out of the city
22. 7. I *c*. to my God, and he did hear my voice
1 *Kings* 13. 2. he *c*. ag. the altar in Beth-el, 4. 32.
18. 28. and they *c*. aloud, and cut themselves
2 *Kings* 2. 12. Elisha saw it, and *c*. my father, my
3. † 21. all the Moabites were *c*. together
6. 5. he *c*. alas, master, for it was borrowed
8. 5. the woman *c*. to the king for her house
11. 14. and Athaliah *c*. treason, treason
1 *Chron*. 5. 20. they *c*. to God in the battle, and he
2 *Chron*. 32. 20. Isaiah prayed and *c*. to heaven
Neh. 9. 27. when they *c*. to thee thou heardest, 28.
Job 17. † 14. I have *c*. to corruption, my father
29. 12. because I delivered the poor that *c*.
30. 5. they *c*. after them, as after a thief
Psal. 18. 6. in my distress I *c*. unto my God
41. they *c*. but there was none to save them
22. 5. they *c*. to thee and were delivered

Psal. 22. 24. but when he *c*. unto him he heard
30. 2. O Lord my God, I *c*. to thee, and hast healed
8. I *c*. to thee, O Lord, and made supplication
31. 22. heardest my supplications when I *c*. to thee
34. 6. this poor man *c*. and the Lord heard him
66. 17. I *c*. unto him with my mouth, 77. 1.
88. 1. O Lord, I have *c*. day and night before thee
13. unto thee have I *c*. O Lord, in the morning
119. 145. I *c*. with my whole heart, hear me
130. 1. out of the depths have I *c*. to thee, O Lord
138. 3. in the day when I *c*. thou answeredst me
Isa. 6. 4. the posts moved at the voice of him that *c*.
30. 7. therefore I *c*. concerning this, their strength
Jer. 4. 20. destruction upon destruction is *c*. for land
12. † 6. thy brethren *c*. after thee fully
Ezek. 9. 8. that I fell on my face and *c*. and said
10. 13. it was *c*. to them in my hearing, O wheel
Dan. 6. 20. he *c*. with a lamentable voice, O Dan.
Hos. 7. 14. they have not *c*. to me with their heart
Jonah 1. 5. the mariners *c*. every man to his god
2. 2. I *c*. by reason of mine affliction, to the Lord,
and he heard me; out of the belly of hell *c*. I
Zech. 7. 13. that as he *c*. and they would not hear, so
they *c*. and I would not hear, saith L. of hosts
Mat. 14. 30. Peter *c*. saying, Lord, save me
20. 31. but they *c*. the more, saying, have mercy on
us, O Lord, *Mark* 10. 48. *Luke* 18. 39.
Mark 9. 26. the spirit *c*. and rent him sore
John 7. 37. Jesus *c*. if any man thirst, let him come
Acts 19. 32. some *c*. one thing, some another, 21. 34.
22. 24. might know wheref. they *c*. so against him
Rev. 10. 3. when he *c*. seven thunders uttered voices
12. 2. and she being with child, *c*. travailing in
14. 18. *c*. with a loud cry to him that had sickle
18. 2. he *c*. mightily with a strong voice, saying
18. *c*. when they saw the smoke of her burning
19. they *c*. weeping and wailing saying, alas, alas

CRIED *to the Lord*.

Ex. 8. 12. Moses *c*. *to L*. 15. 25. | 17. 4. *Num*. 12. 13.
14. 10. Isr. *c*. *to L*. *Judg*. 3. 9, 15. | 4. 3. | 6. 7. | 10. 10.
Num. 20. 16. when we *c*. *to L*. he heard, *Deut*. 26. 7.
Josh. 24. 7. when they *c*. *to the L*. he put darkness
1 *Sam*. 7. 9. Sam. *c*. *to L*. 15. 11. ‖ 1 *Kings* 17. 20.
Elijah, 21.
2 *Kings* 20. 11. Isa. *c*. *to L*. 2 *Chr*. 14. 11. Asa *c*. *to L*.
2 *Chr*. 13. 14. they *c*. *to L*. *Ps*. 107. 6, 13. *Jon*. 1. 14.
Psal. 3. 4. I *c*. *to L*. with my voice, 120. 1. | 142. 1.
Lam. 2. 18. their heart *c*. *to L*. O daughter of Zion

CRIED *with a loud voice*.

1 *Sam*. 28. 12. woman at En-dor *c*. *with a loud voice*
2 *Sam*. 19. 4. David *c*. *with loud voice*, O Absalom, my
2 *Kings* 18. 28. Rabshakeh *c*. *with l. v*. *Isa*. 36. 13.
Neh. 9. 4. Lev. *c*. *with l. v*. ‖ *Ezek*. 11. 13. Ezek. *c*.
Mat. 27. 46. about ninth hour Jesus *c*. *with a l. voice*,
50. *Mark* 15. 34, 37. *Luke* 23. 46. *John* 11. 43.
Mark 1. 26. evil spir. *c*. *with l. v*. ‖ *Acts* 16. 28. Paul *c*.
Acts 7. 57. Steph. enemies *c*. *with l. v*. | 60. Steph. *c*.
Rev. 6. 10. they *c*. *with loud v*. saying, how long, O
7. 2. the angel *c*. *with a loud voice*, 10. 3. | 19. 17.
10. mult. stood before Lamb *c*. *with a loud voice*

CRIED *out*.

1 *Sam*. 4. 13. all the city *c*. *out* ‖ 5. 10. Ekronites *c*. *out*
1 *Kings* 22. 32. Jehoshaphat *c*. *out*, 2 *Chron*. 18. 31.
2 *Kings* 4. 40. they *c*. *out*, there is death in the pot
Jer. 20. 8. I *c*. *out*, I cried, violence and spoil
Mat. 8. 29. behold, the spirits *c*. *out*, *Luke* 4. 33.
14. 26. the disciples *c*. *out* for fear, *Mark* 6. 49.
20. 30. the blind men *c*. *out*, have mercy upon us
Mark 1. 23. the man with an unclean spirit *c*. out
9. 24. the father of the child *c*. *out*, *Luke* 9. 38.
15. 13. and they *c*. *out* again, crucify him, *Mat*. 27.
23. *Luke* 23. 18. *John* 19. 6.
Acts 19. 28. they *c*. *out*, saying, great is Diana, 34.
22. 23. as they *c*. *out*, and threw dust in the air
23. 6. Paul *c*. *out* in the council, I am a Pharisee

CRIEST, ETH.

Gen. 4. 10. the voice of thy brother's blood *c*. to me
Exod. 14. 15. wherefore *c*. thou to me? speak to
22. 27. when he *c*. unto me, that I will hear
1 *Sam*. 26. 14. who art thou that *c*. to the king?
Job 24. 12. and the soul of the wounded *c*. out
Psal. 72. 12. he shall deliver the needy when he *c*.
84. 2. my heart and flesh *c*. out for the living God
Prov. 1. 20. wisdom *c*. without, 8. 3. | 9. 3.
2. 3. yea, if thou *c*. after knowledge, and liftest
Isa. 26. 17. like as a woman that *c*. out in her pangs
40. 3. the voice of him that *c*. in the wilderness
57. 13. when thou *c*. let companies deliver thee
Jer. 12. 8. my heritage *c*. out against me
30. 15. why *c*. thou for thine affliction?
Mic. 6. 9. Lord's voice *c*. to the city, hear the rod
Mat. 15. 23. send her away, for she *c*. after us
Luke 9. 39. he suddenly *c*. out, and it teareth him
Rom. 9. 27. Esaias also *c*. concerning Israel, though
Jam. 5. 4. behold, the hire of the labourers *c*.

CRYING.

1 *Sam*. 4. 14. when Eli heard the noise of the *c*.
2 *Sam*. 13. 19. Tamar put ashes, and went on *c*.
Job 39. 7. nor regardeth he the *c*. of the driver
Prov. 19. 18. and let not thy soul spare for his *c*.
30. 15. the horse-leech hath two daughters *c*. give
Isa. 22. 5. it is a day of *c*. to the mountains
24. 11. there is a *c*. for wine in the streets
65. 19. voice of *c*. shall be no more heard in her
Jer. 48. 3. a voice of *c*. shall be from Horonaim
Zech. 4. 7. shall bring forth the head-stone with *c*.
Mal. 2. 13. covering the altar of the Lord with *c*.
Mat. 3. 3. voice of one *c*. in the wilderness, prepare,
Mark 1. 3. *Luke* 3. 4. *John* 1. 23.
21. 15. and saw the children *c*. in the temple
Luke 4. 41. devils *c*. thou art Christ, the Son of God
Acts 8. 7. for unclean spirits *c*. came out of many
14. 14. they ran in among the people, *c*. out
21. 28. laid hands on him, *c*. out, men of Israel
36. the multitude followed, *c*. away with him
Gal. 4. 6. Spirit into your hearts, *c*. Abba Father
Heb. 5. 7. he offered up prayers with strong *c*.
Rev. 21. 4. there will be no more death nor *c*.

CRYSTAL.

Job 28. 17. the gold and the *c*. cannot equal it
Ezek. 1. 22. firmament was as colour of terrible *c*.
Rev. 4. 6. there was a sea of glass like unto *c*.

Rev. 21. 11. the light of the great city was clear as *c*.
22. 1. a pure river of water of life, clear as *c*.

CUBIT

Is *the distance from the elbow bending inwards to the extremity of the middle finger: this is called* a common cubit, *the cubit of a man, containing a foot and a half, or half a yard*, Deut. 3. 11. *There is likewise the* sacred cubit, *which is a full yard, and contains two* common cubits. *There is mention made of both these sorts of cubits, in* 1 Kings 7. 15. *and* 2 Chron. 3. 15. *In the former the two columns of brass which were in* Solomon's *temple, are said to be eighteen cubits high; and in the* Chronicles, *thirty-five cubits; which is double the other. Some are of opinion, that the* cubit *which* Noah *made use of when he built the ark, was equal to six* common cubits; *they call this a* geometrical cubit.

Gen. 6. 16. in a *c*. shalt thou finish the ark above
Deut. 3. 11. the breadth of it, after the *c*. of a man
1 *Kings* 7. 24. the knops compassing it, ten in a *c*.
2 *Chron*. 4. 3. ten in a *c*. compassing the sea about
Ezek. 43. 13. the *c*. is a *c*. and an hand-breadth
Mat. 6. 27. can add one *c*. to his stature, *Luke* 12. 25.

CUBITS.

Gen. 6. 15. length of the ark 300 *c*. breadth 50 *c*.
7. 20. fifteen *c*. upward did the waters prevail
Exod. 25. 10. two *c*. and a half the length of the ark
1 *Sam*. 17. 4. Goliath's height six *c*. and a span
1 *Kings* 6. 2. length of the house 60 *c*. breadth 20.
23. each of the cherubims was ten *c*. high
7. 38. and every laver was four *c*. high
2 *Kings* 14. 13. Jehoash brake down the wall of Jerusalem, 400 *c*. 2 *Chron*. 25. 23.
Ezra 6. 3. the height 60 *c*. the breadth 60 *c*.
Esth. 5. 14. let a gallows be made fifty *c*. high, 7. 9.
Ezek. 40. 23. he measured from gate to gate 100 *c*.
47. the court 100 *c*. ‖ 43. 17. the settle 14 *c*.
41. 2. and the breadth of the door was ten *c*.
9. the thickness of the wall was five *c*.
43. 16. and the altar shall be twelve *c*. long
Dan. 3. 1. the height of the image was 60 *c*.
Zech. 5. 2. the length of the flying roll is 20 *c*.
John 21. 8. they were from land as it were 200 *c*.
Rev. 21. 17. He measured the wall of the city 144 *c*.

CUCKOW.

Lev. 11. 16. *c*. have in abomination, *Deut*. 14. 15.

CUCUMBERS.

Num. 11. 5. we remember the *c*. and the melons
Isa. 1. 8. Zion is left as a lodge in a garden of *c*.

CUD; *see* CHEW *and* CHEWETH.

CUMBERED.

Luke 10. 40. Martha was *c*. about much serving

CUMBERETH.

Luke 13. 7. cut it down, why *c*. it the ground?

CUMBRANCE.

Deut. 1. 12. how can I myself alone bear your *c*.?

CUMMIN.

Isa. 28. 25. doth he not scatter the *c*. and cast in
27. nor is a cart-wheel turned about upon the *c*.
but the *c*. is beaten out with a rod
Mat. 23. 23. woe to you scribes, ye pay tithe of *c*.

CUNNING.

Gen. 25. 27. the boys grew, and Esau was a *c*. hunter
Exod. 26. 1. with cherubims of *c*. work, 36. 8.
28. 15. thou shalt make the breastplate of *c*. work
31. 4. to devise *c*. works in gold and silver
38. 23. Aholiab a *c*. workman and embroiderer
39. 8. he made the breast-plate of *c*. work
1 *Sam*. 16. 16. a man who is a *c*. player on an harp
18. I have seen a son of Jesse that is *c*. in playing
1 *Chron*. 25. 7. all that were *c*. in songs, were 288
2 *Chron*. 2. 7. send me a man *c*. to work in gold
13. I have sent a *c*. man of Huram my father's
Psal. 58. † 5. not hearken, be the charmer never so *c*.
137. 5. if I forget, let my right hand forget her *c*.
Prov. 19. † 25. and the simple will be *c*.
Cant. 7. 1. thy joints, the work of a *c*. workman
Isa. 3. 3. I will take away the *c*. artificer
40. 20. he seeketh to him a *c*. workman to prepare
Jer. 9. 17. send for *c*. women that they may come
10. 9. they are all the work of *c*. men
Dan. 1. 4. children well favoured, *c*. in knowledge
Hos. 6. † 8. Gilead is a city *c*. for blood
Eph. 4. 14. and carried about by *c*. craftiness, whereby

CUNNINGLY.

2 *Pet*. 1. 16. we have not followed *c*. devised fables

CUP.

This word is taken in Scripture in a proper and in a figurative sense. In a proper sense it signifies a material cup, which people drink out of at meals, Gen. 40. 13. *In the figurative sense it is taken*, (1) *For the wine in the cup*, 1 Cor. 11. 27. (2) *For those sufferings and afflictions which God sends upon a person or people: To drink of this cup, signifies to undergo and endure those sufferings*: Isa. 51. 17. Stand up, O Jerusalem, which hast drunk at the hand of the Lord the cup of his fury. *Psal*. 75. 8. In the hand of the Lord there is a cup, the dregs thereof all the wicked of the earth shall wring them out, and drink them. *In these and the like passages God is compared to the master of a feast, who then used to distribute portions of meats or drinks to the several guests, as he thought fit. Our Saviour prays*, Mat. 26. 39. Let this cup pass from me. *Let me be freed from these sufferings both in my soul and body: And he tells his disciples*, Mat. 20. 23. That they should indeed drink of his cup; *that is, They should taste of inward afflictions and desertions, and have their share of outward sufferings for the gospel, as well as himself*. (3) *For God's blessings and favours*, Psal. 23. 5.

Babylon *is called a golden cup*, Jer. 51. 7. *because of her great riches and plenty. And it is said of the woman arrayed in purple, or of the antichristian church, that* she had a golden cup in her hand, *Rev*. 17. 4. *which may denote the enticing means, and specious pretences, which she uses to allure people to idolatry, particularly by sensuality, luxury, and affluence*.

I will take the cup of salvation, *Psal*. 116. 13.

will offer the sacrifice of thanksgiving unto God. It denotes joy and thanksgiving, and is a phrase taken from the common practice of the Jews in their thank offerings, in which a feast was made of the remainder of their sacrifices, and the offerers, together with the priest, did eat and drink before the Lord: and, among other rites, the master of the feast took a cup of wine into his hand, and solemnly blessed God for it, and for the mercy which was then acknowledged; and then gave it to all the guests, of which every one did drink in his turn, 1 Chron. 16. 2, 3. *To which custom it is supposed that our blessed Lord alludes in the institution of the cup, which also is called* the cup of blessing, 1 *Cor.* 10. 16.

Gen. 40. 11. and Pharaoh's *c.* was in mine hand
44. 2. put my *c.* the silver *c.* in the sack's mouth
2 *Sam.* 12. 3. it drank of his own *c.* and lay in bosom
1 *Kings* 7. 26. wrought like brim of a *c.* 2 *Chr.* 4. 5.
Psal. 11. 6. this shall be the portion of their *c.*
16. 5. the Lord is the portion of my *c.* thou
23. 5. thou anointest my head, my *c.* runneth over
73. 10. waters of a full *c.* are wrung out to them
75. 8. in the hand of the Lord there is a *c.*
116. 13. I will take the *c.* of salvation and call on
Prov. 23. 31. when it giveth its colour in the *c.*
Isa. 51. 17. which hast drunk at the hand of the Lord the *c.* the dregs of the *c.* of trembling
22. taken out of thy hand the *c.* of trembling
Jer. 16. 7. nor shall men give them *c.* of consolation
25. 15. take the wine-*c.* of his fury at my hand
17. then took I the *c.* at the Lord's hand
28. if they refuse to take the *c.* at thine hand
49. 12. whose judgment was not to drink the *c.*
51. 7. Babylon hath been a golden *c.* in the hand
Lam. 4. 21. the *c.* also shall pass through to thee
Ezek. 23. 31. I will give her *c.* into thine hand
32. thou shalt drink of thy sister's *c.* deep and large
Hab. 2. 16. *c.* of the Lord's right hand shall be turned
Zech. 12. 2. I will make Jerusalem a *c.* of trembling
Mat. 10. 42. give a *c.* of cold water only, *Mark* 9. 41.
20. 22. are ye able to drink of *c.*? *Mark* 10. 38.
23. ye shall drink indeed of my *c.* *Mark* 10. 39.
23. 25. for you make clean the outside of the *c.*
26. cleanse first what is within the *c.* and platter
26. 27. and he took the *c.* and gave thanks, *Mark* 14. 23. *Luke* 22. 17, 20. 1 *Cor.* 11. 25.
39. O my Father, if it be possible, let this *c.* pass from me, *Mark* 14. 36. *Luke* 22. 42.
42. if this *c.* may not pass away from me
Luke 22. 20. this *c.* is the new testament in my blood, 1 *Cor.* 11. 25.
John 18. 11. the *c.* which my Father hath given me
1 *Cor.* 10. 16. the *c.* of blessing we bless, is it not the
21. ye cannot drink the *c.* of Lord and *c.* of devils
11. 26. as often as ye drink of this *c.* ye do shew
27. and drink this *c.* of the Lord unworthily
Rev. 14. 10. poured without mixture into the *c.*
16. 19. to give unto her the *c.* of his wrath
17. 4. the woman having a golden *c.* in her hand
18. 6. in the *c.* she filled, fill to her double

CUP-BEARER.

Neh. 1. 11. for I was the king's *cup-bearer*

CUP-BEARERS.

1 *Kings* 10. 5. queen of Sheba saw *c.-b.* 2 *Chr.* 9. 4.

CUPS.

2 *Sam.* 17. †28. Barzillai brought beds and *c.*
1 *Chron.* 28. 17. David gave pure gold for the *c.*
Isa. 22. 24. shall hang on Eliakim the vessels of *c.*
Jer. 35. 5. and I set pots full of wine and *c.*
52. 19. the Chaldeans took away spoons and *c.*
Mark 7. 4. as the washing of *c.* and pots, 8.

CURDLED.

Job 10. 10. hast not thou *c.* me like cheese?

CURE.

Jer. 33. 6. behold I will bring it health and *c.*
46. †11. daughter of Egypt, no *c.* shall be to thee

CURE, ED.

Jer. 33. 6. I will *c.* them and will reveal peace
46. 11. O daughter of Egypt, thou shalt not be *c.*
Hos. 5. 13. yet could he not *c.* you of your wound
Mat. 17. 16. thy disciples, they could not *c.* him
18. the child was *c.* from that very hour
Luke 7. 21. in that same hour he *c.* many
9. 1. he gave them power to *c.* diseases
John 5. 10. the Jews said to him that was *c.*

CURES.

Luke 13. 32. I cast out devils, I do *c.* to-day and

CURIOUS.

Exod. 28. 8. *c.* girdle, 27, 28. | 29. 5. | 39. 5. *Lev.* 8. 7.
35. 32. and to devise *c.* works, to work in gold
Acts 19. 19. many of them that used *c.* arts brought

CURIOUSLY.

Psal. 139. 15. and *c.* wrought in the lowest parts

CURLED.

Cant. 5. †11. his locks are *c.* and black as a raven

CURRENT.

Gen. 23. 16. *c.* money with the merchant

CURSE.

To curse, *signifies to imprecate, to call down mischief upon, or to wish evil to:* Noah *cursed his grandson* Canaan, *Gen.* 9. 25. Cursed be *Canaan; may he be hateful to God, abhorred by men, and miserable in his person and posterity.* Jacob *cursed the fury of his two sons* Simeon and Levi, *who massacred the* Shechemites, *and plundered their city,* Gen. 49. 7. Moses *enjoins the people of* Israel *to denounce curses against the violators of the law,* Deut. 27. 15, 16, *&c. And* Joshua *cursed him who should undertake to build* Jericho, *Josh.* 6. 26. *These* curses *were either ordained by God himself, or pronounced by men abounding with the Spirit; or were predictions of what evil should happen to a person, or people, uttered in the terms of imprecations, which had their accomplishment: They were not the effects of passion, impatience, or revenge, and therefore were not such as God condemns in his law, and in his word.* For example: *he ordains that no one shall presume to curse his father or his mother upon pain of death,* Exod. 21. 17. *He shall not wish any mischief to befall them, nor use any kind of malicious reviling speeches, which argue a contempt of his parents. He ordains that no one curse the prince of his people,* Exod. 22. 28. *or one that is deaf,* Lev. 19. 14. *In the gospel, our Saviour pronounces those of his disciples to be blessed, who are loaded with curses, and requires them to bless those that curse them, to render blessing for cursing,* Mat. 5. 11. Luke 6. 28. Rom. 12. 14. *God denounced his curse against the serpent which seduced* Eve, *and against the earth, which thenceforth was to produce briers and thorns: it should produce both fewer and worse fruits, and that with more trouble of men's minds and labour of their bodies,* Gen. 3. 14, 17. *He cursed* Cain *also, who had imbrued his hands in his brother* Abel's *blood,* Gen. 4. 11. *He was devoted to destruction, cast out from God's presence and the communion of the church, and the society of his kindred and acquaintance, and wandered from one country to another by reason of the trouble and perplexity of his conscience. The divine maledictions are not merely imprecations, impotent and fruitless desires; they carry their effects with them, and are attended with all the miseries denounced by God.*

Gen. 27. 12. I shall bring a *c.* on me, not a blessing
13. his mother said, upon me be thy *c.* my son
Num. 5. 18. and the priest have in his hand the bitter water that causeth the *c.* 19, 22, 24, 27.
27. the woman shall be a *c.* among her people
Deut. 11. 26. I set before you a blessing and *c.* 30. 1.
28. a *c.* if ye will not obey the commandments
29. and shalt put the *c.* upon mount Ebal
21. †23. he that is hanged is the *c.* of God
23. 5. God turned the *c.* into a blessing, *Neh.* 13. 2.
29. 19. when he heareth the words of this *c.*
Josh. 6. 18. and make the camp of Israel a *c.*
Judg. 9. 57. on them came the *c.* of Jotham
1 *Kings* 2. 8. who cursed me with a grievous *c.*
2 *Kings* 22. 19. that they should become a *c.*
Neh. 10. 29. they entered into a *c.* and into an oath
Job 31. 30. nor to sin by wishing a *c.* to his soul
Prov. 3. 33. the *c.* of Lord is in the house of wicked
26. 2. so the *c.* causeless shall not come
27. 14. rising early it shall be counted a *c.* to him
28. 27. that hideth his eyes shall have many a *c.*
Isa. 24. 6. therefore hath the *c.* devoured the earth
34. 5. it shall come down on the people of my *c.*
43. 28. therefore I have given Jacob to the *c.*
65. 15. shall leave your name for a *c.* to my chosen
Jer. 24. 9. I will deliver them to be a taunt and a *c.* 25. 18. | 29. 18. | 42. 18. | 44. 8, 12.
26. 6. I will make this city a *c.* to all nations
44. 22. therefore is your land a *c.* at this day
49. 13. I have sworn that Bozrah shall become a *c.*
Lam. 3. 65. give them sorrow, they *c.* unto them
Dan. 9. 11. therefore the *c.* is poured upon us
Zech. 5. 3. this is the *c.* that goeth forth over earth
8. 13. that as we were a *c.* among the heathen
Mal. 2. 2. if ye will not hear, I will send a *c.* on you
3. 9. ye are cursed with a *c.* for ye have robbed me
4. 6. lest I come and smite the earth with a *c.*
Acts 23. 12. and bound themselves under a *c.* 14.
Gal. 3. 10. as are of the works of law, are under *c.*
13. Chr. redeemed us from the *c.* being made a *c.*
Rev. 22. 3. shall be no more *c.* but throne of God

CURSE, *Verb.*

Gen. 8. 21. the Lord said, I will not *c.* the ground
12. 3. and I will *c.* him that curseth thee
Exod. 22. 28. thou shalt not *c.* the ruler of thy peo.
Lev. 19. 14. thou shalt not *c.* the deaf, nor put a
Num. 22. 6. come, I pray thee, *c.* me this peo. 17.
11. Balak said, come now, *c.* me them, 23. 7, 13.
12. God said to Balaam, thou shalt not *c.* people
23. 8. how shall I *c.* whom God hath not cursed?
11. I took thee to *c.* mine enemies, 24. 10.
25. neither *c.* them at all, nor bless them at all
Deut. 23. 4. they hired Balaam to *c.* thee, *Neh.* 13. 2.
27. 13. and these shall stand on mount Ebal to *c.*
Josh. 24. 9. Balak king of Moab called Balaam to *c.*
Judg. 5. 23. *c.* Meroz, said the angel, *c.* ye bitterly
2 *Sam.* 16. 9. why should this dead dog *c.* the king?
10. let him *c.* because L. hath said, *c.* David, 11.
Job 1. 11. and he will *c.* thee to thy face, 2. 5.
2. 9. then said his wife to him, *c.* God and die
3. 8. let them *c.* it that *c.* the day, who are ready
Psal. 62. 4. they bless with mouth but *c.* inwardly
109. 28. let them *c.* but bless thou, when they
Prov. 11. 26. withholdeth corn, people shall *c.* him
24. 24. him shall the people *c.* nations abhor him
30. 10. accuse not a servant to master, lest he *c.*
Eccl. 7. 21. lest thou hear thy servant *c.* thee
10. 20. *c.* not the king in thought, *c.* not the rich
Isa. 8. 21. *c.* their king and God, and look upward
Jer. 15. 10. yet every one of them doth *c.* me
Mal. 2. 2. I will *c.* your blessings, I have cursed
Mat. 5. 44. bless them that *c.* you, *Luke* 6. 28.
26. 74. he began to *c.* and to swear, *Mark* 14. 71.
Rom. 12. 14. which persecute you; bless and *c.* not
Jam. 3. 9. therewith *c.* we men, which are made

CURSED.

Gen. 3. 14. the serpent *c.* ‖ 17. *c.* is the ground
4. 11. Cain *c.* ‖ 9. 25. Noah said, *c.* be Canaan
5. 29. because of ground which the Lord hath *c.*
27. 29. *c.* be every one that curseth, *Num.* 24. 9.
49. 7. *c.* be their anger, for it was fierce and cruel
Lev. 20. 9. he hath *c.* his father or his mother
24. 11. blasphemed the name of the Lord and *c.*
14. saying, bring forth him that hath *c.* 23.
Num. 22. 6. I wot that he whom thou cursest is *c.*
Deut. 27. 15. *c.* be he, 16, 17, 18, 19, 20, 21, 22, 23, 24, 25, 26.
28. 16. *c.* shalt thou be in the city, *c.* in the field
17. *c.* shall be thy basket and thy store
18. *c.* shall be the fruit of thy body and land
19. *c.* when thou comest in, when thou goest out
Josh. 6. 26. *c.* be the man that buildeth Jericho
9. 23. now therefore ye Gibeonites are *c.* none of
Judg. 9. 27. they did eat and drink, and *c.* Abimelech
21. 18. *c.* be he that giveth a wife to Benjamin
1 *Sam.* 14. 24. *c.* that eateth food till evening, 28.
1 *Sam.* 17. 43. and the Philistine *c.* David by his gods
26. 19. but if men, *c.* be they before the Lord
2 *Sam.* 16. 5. Shimei came forth, and *c.* still, 7. 13.
19. 21. for this, because he *c.* the Lord's anointed
1 *Kings* 2. 8. Shimei who *c.* me with a grievous curse
2 *Kings* 2. 24. and *c.* them in the name of the Lord
9. 34. go see now this *c.* woman, and bury her
Neh. 13. 25. I contended with them, and *c.* them
Job 1. 5. it may be my sons have sinned and *c.* God
3. 1. then Job opened his mouth and *c.* his day
5. 3. foolish taking root, suddenly I *c.* his habitation
24. 18. their portion is *c.* in the earth
Psal. 37. 22. they that be *c.* of him shall be cut off
119. 21. thou hast rebuked the proud that are *c.*
Eccl. 7. 22. knoweth thyself likewise hast *c.* others
Jer. 11. 3. *c.* be the man obeyeth not this covenant
17. 5. *c.* be the man that trusteth in man
20. 14. *c.* be the day wherein I was born
15. *c.* be the man who brought tidings to my father
48. 10. *c.* be he that doeth the Lord's work deceitfully, *c.* that keepeth back his sword from blood
Mal. 1. 14. but *c.* be the deceiver, who hath a male
2. 2. yea, I have *c.* your blessings already, because
3. 9. ye are *c.* with a curse, for ye have robbed me
Mat. 25. 41. he shall say, depart from me, ye *c.*
John 7. 49. people who knoweth not the law, are *c.*
Gal. 3. 10. *c.* is every one that continueth not in all
13. *c.* is every one that hangeth on a tree
2 *Pet.* 2. 14. *c.* children, who have forsaken the way

CURSED *thing.*

Deut. 7. 26. lest thou be a *c. thing,* for it is a *c. thing*
13. 17. shall cleave nought of the *c. t.* to thy hand

CURSEDST.

Judg. 17. 2. silver taken from thee, which thou *c.*
Mark 11. 21. the fig-tree thou *c.* is withered away

CURSES.

Num. 5. 23. the priest shall write these *c.* in a book
Deut. 28. 15. that all these *c.* shall come on thee, 45.
29. 20. all the *c.* that are written in this book shall lie upon him, 27. 2 *Chron.* 34. 24.
21. according to all the *c.* of the covenant in book
30. 7. Lord thy God will put these *c.* on thy enemies

CURSETH.

Exod. 21. 17. he that *c.* his father or his mother shall surely be put to death, *Lev.* 20. 9. *Prov.* 20. 20.
Lev. 24. 15. whosoever *c.* his God shall bear his sin
Prov. 30. 11. a generation that *c.* their father
Mat. 15. 4. honour father and mother, he that *c.* father or mother, let him die death, *Mark* 7. 10.

CURSING.

Num. 5. 21. priest charge woman with an oath of *c.*
Deut. 27. †13. these shall stand for a *c.* on Ebal
28. 20. the Lord shall send upon thee *c.* in all thou
Deut. 30. 19. I have set before you blessing and *c.*
2 *Sam.* 16. 12. Lord will requite me good for his *c.*
Psal. 10. 7. his mouth is full of *c.* *Rom.* 3. 14.
59. 12. and for *c.* and lying which they speak
109. 17. as he loved *c.* so let it come unto him
18. as he clothed himself with *c.* as a garment
Prov. 29. 24. he heareth *c.* and bewrayeth it not
Jer. 23. †10. for because of *c.* the land mourneth
Heb. 6. 8. earth which beareth thorns is nigh to *c.*
Jam. 3. 10. out of the same mouth blessing and *c.*

CURSINGS.

Josh. 8. 34. he read all the blessings and *c.*

CURTAIN.

Psal. 104. 2. who coverest thyself with light, who stretchest out the heavens like a *c.* *Isa.* 40. 22.

CURTAINS.

Exod. 26. 1. make tabernacle with ten *c.* 2. | 36. 9.
Num. 4. 25. the Gershonites shall bear the *c.* of tab.
2 *Sam.* 7. 2. ark of God dwelleth within *c.* 1 *Chr.* 17. 1.
Cant. 1. 5. but I am comely as the *c.* of Solomon
Isa. 54. 2. let them stretch forth *c.* of thy habitation
Jer. 4. 20. my tents spoiled, and my *c.* in a moment
10. 20. none to stretch my tent, and set up my *c.*
49. 29. they shall take to themselves their *c.* and
Hab. 3. 7. the *c.* of the land of Midian did tremble

CUSTODY.

Num. 3. 36. under *c.* of the sons of Merari, boards
Esth. 2. 3. gather fair virgins to the *c.* of Hege, 8.
14. to the *c.* of Shaashgaz the king's chamberlain

CUSTOM

Signifies, [1] *Manner, or way,* Luke 4. 16. [2] *That which has been established by long use, and the consent of ancestors,* Judg. 11. 39. John 18. 39. [3] *A duty paid to the king or prince upon the importation or exportation of commodities,* Rom. 13. 7. [4] *The way of women, namely, the natural disease for which they used to be put apart,* Gen. 31. 35.

Gen. 31. 35. for the *c.* of women is upon me
Judg. 11. 39. and it was a *c.* in Israel
1 *Sam.* 2. 13. the priests' *c.* with the people was
Ezra 3. 4. according to the *c.* *Jer.* 32. 11.
4. 13. then will they not pay toll, tribute, and *c.*
20. been mighty kings, and *c.* was paid to them
7. 24. shall not be lawful to impose *c.* on priests
Psal. 119. †132. be merciful according to the *c.*
Mat. 9. 9. Jesus passed forth, and saw Matthew sitting at the receipt of *c.* *Mark* 2. 14. *Luke* 5. 27.
17. 25. of whom do the kings of the earth take *c.*?
Luke 1. 9. according to the *c.* of the priest's office
2. 27. to do for him after the *c.* of the law
42. went to Jerusalem after the *c.* of the feast
4. 16. as Jesus' *c.* was, he went into the synagogue
John 18. 39. ye have a *c.* that I should release one
Rom. 13. 7. render therefore *c.* to whom *c.* is due
1 *Cor.* 11. 16. we have no such *c.* nor the churches

CUSTOMS.

Lev. 18. 30. commit none of these abominable *c.*
Jer. 10. 3. for the *c.* of the people are vain
Acts 6. 14. shall change the *c.* Moses delivered us
16. 21. teach *c.* which are not lawful to receive
21. 21. that they ought not to walk after the *c.*
26. 3. I know thee to be expert in all *c.* and quest.
28. 17. tho' I committed nothing against the *c.*

CUT.

Lev. 22. 24. ye shall not offer to the Lord what is *c.*
Ezek. 16. 4. when born thy navel was not *c.*
Acts 5. 33. when they heard that, they were *c.* 7. 54.

CUT.

Exod. 39. 3. and *c.* it in wires to work it in the blue

Lev. 1. 6. shall *c.* the burnt-offering into pieces, 12.
8. 20. he *c.* the ram into pieces, *Exod.* 29. 17.
Deut. 14. 1. ye shall not *c.* yourselves nor make
Judg. 20. 6. I took my concubine and *c.* her in [pieces
1 *Kings* 18. 23. and *c.* the bullock in pieces, 33.
28. they *c.* themselves after their manner with
2 *Kings* 24. 13. he *c.* in pieces all the vessels of gold Solomon had made in temple, 2 *Chron.* 28. 24.
1 *Chron.* 20. 3. the people, he *c.* them with saws
2 *Chron.* 2. 8. thy servants can skill to *c.* timber, 10.
Psal. 58. 7. he bendeth, let them be as *c.* in pieces
107. 16. *c.* the bars of iron in sunder, *Isa.* 45. 2.
Isa. 9. † 20. he shall *c.* on the right and be hungry
51. 9. art thou not it that hath *c.* Rahab?
Jer. 16. 6. nor lament, nor *c.* themselves for them
34. 18. when they *c.* the calf in twain, and passed
36. 23. he *c.* the roll with the penknife, and cast
41. 5. their clothes rent, and having *c.* themselves
47. 5. how long wilt thou *c.* thyself?
Dan. 2. 5. if ye will not, ye shall be *c.* in pieces
3. 29. who speak against God shall be *c.* in pieces
Amos 9. 1. and *c.* them in the head, all of them
Hab. 3. † 16. he will *c.* them with his troops
Zech. 12. 3. that burden themselves with it shall be *c.*
Acts 27. † 40. and when they had *c.* the anchors

CUT *asunder.*

Psal. 129. 4. he hath *c. asunder* cords of the wicked
Jer. 50. 23. hammer of the whole earth *c. asunder*
Zech. 11. 10. I took staff Beauty, and *c.* it *asunder*
14. then I *c. asunder* my other staff, even Bands
Mat. 24. 51. and shall *c.* him *asunder*, *Luke* 12. 46.

CUT *down.*

Exod. 34. 13. but ye shall *c. down* their groves
Lev. 26. 30. I will *c. down* your images, and cast
Num. 13. 23. and *c. down* from thence a branch, 24.
Deut. 7. 5. ye shall break down their images, and *c. down* their groves, 2 *Kings* 18. 4. | 23. 14.
20. 19. trees for meat thou shalt not *c. down*
20. the trees not for meat thou shalt *c. down*
Judg. 6. 25. and *c. down* the grove that is by it
2 *Kings* 19. 23. I will *c. down* cedars, *Isa.* 37. 24.
2 *Chr.* 15. 16. and Asa *c. d.* her idol, and stamped it
34. 7. Josiah *c. down* all the idols in the land
Job 8. 12. while in his greenness, and not *c. down*
14. 2. cometh forth like a flower, and is *c. down*
7. for there is hope of a tree if it be *c. down*
22. 16. the wicked were *c. down* out of time
20. whereas our substance is not *c. down*
Psal. 37. 2. they shall soon be *c. down* like grass
80. 16. branch is burnt, it is *c. down*, they perish
90. 6. in the evening it is *c. down*, and withereth
Isa. 9. 10. sycamores are *c. down*, but we will build
14. 12. how art thou *c. down* to the ground
22. 25. the nail shall be removed and *c. down*
Jer. 22. 7. they shall *c. down* thy choice cedars
25. 37. the peaceable habitations are *c. down*
48. 2. also thou shalt be *c. down*, O madmen
Ezek. 6. 6. that your images may be *c. down*
Nah. 1. 12. though many, yet thus shall they be *c. d.*
Zeph. 1. 11. for all the merchant-people are *c. down*
Mat. 21. 8. others *c. down* branches, *Mark* 11. 8.
Luke 13. 7. *c.* it *d.* why cumbereth it the ground?
9. then after that thou shalt *c.* it *down*

CUT *off.*

Gen. 9. 11. neither shall all flesh be *c. off*
17. 14. the uncircumcised child shall be *c. off*
41. † 36. that the land be not *c. off* through famine
Exod. 4. 25. and *c. off* the fore-skin of her son
8. † 9. to *c. off* the frogs from thee, and thy houses
12. 15. that soul shall be *c. off* from Israel, 19. | 31. 14. *Num.* 15. 30, 31. | 19. 13.
23. 23. Angel go before, and I will *c.* them *off*
30. 33. shall be *c. off* from his people, 38. *Lev.* 7. 20, 21, 25, 27. | 17. 4, 9. | 19. 8. | 23. 29. *Num.* 9. 13.
Lev. 17. 10. I will *c.* him *off* from among his people, 18. 29. | 20. 3, 6, 18. *Num.* 19. 20
14. whosoever eateth blood shall be *c. off*
20. 17. shall be *c. off* in the sight of their people
22. 3. that soul shall be *c. off* from my presence
25. † 23. land shall not be sold to be quite *c. off*
Num. 4. 18. *c.* ye not *off* the tribe of Kohathites
15. 31. that soul shall utterly be *c. off*, his iniquity
Deut. 12. 29. when thy God shall *c. off* nations
19. 1. when God hath *c. off* the nations, *Josh.* 23. 4.
23. 1. or hath his privy member *c. off* shall not
25. 12. then thou shalt *c. off* her hand, pity not
Josh. 3. 13. that the waters of Jordan shall be *c. off* from the waters that come down, 16. | 4. 7
7. 9. and shall *c. off* our name from the earth
9. † 23. not be *c. off* from you from being bondmen
11. 21. at that time Joshua *c. off* the Anakims
Judg. 1. 6. and *c. off* his thumbs, and his great toes
21. 6. there is one tribe *c. off* from Israel this day
Ruth 4. 10. that the name of the dead be not *c. off*
1 *Sam.* 2. 31. days come that I will *c. off* thine arm
33. man whom I shall not *c. off* from mine altar
5. 4. the palms of Dagon's hands were *c. off*
17. 51. David ran and *c. off* Goliath's head
20. 15. thou shalt not *c. off* thy kindness from my house, 24. 21. no, not when the Lord hath *c. off* the enemies of David from the face of the earth
24. 4. David *c. off* the skirt of Saul's robe, 5.
† 7. so David *c. off* his servants with these words
11. for in that I *c. off* the skirt of thy robe
28. 9. knowest how Saul hath *c. off* the wizards
31. 9. and they *c. off* Saul's head, and stripped off
2 *Sam.* 4. 12. they slew them and *c. off* their hands
10. 4. Hanun took David's servants, and *c. off* their garments in the middle, 1 *Chr.* 19. 4.
20. 22. and they *c. off* the head of Sheba
21. † 5. the man that consumed us and *c.* us *off*
1 *Kings* 8. † 25. not be *c. off* to thee a man in my sight
9. 7. then will I *c. off* Israel out of the land
11. 16. till he had *c. off* every male in Edom
13. 34. even to *c. off* Jeroboam's house, 14. 14.
14. 10. I will *c. off* from Jeroboam him that pisseth
18. 4. when Jezebel *c. off* the prophets of the Lord
21. 21. behold, I will *c. off* from Ahab him that pisseth against the wall, 2 *Kings* 9. 8.
2 *Kings* 16. 17. Ahaz *c. off* the borders of the bases

2 *Kings* 18. 16. Hezekiah *c. off* the gold from the doors
1 *Chr.* 17. 8. have *c. off* thine enemies before thee
2 *Chr.* 22. 7. Lord anointed to *c. off* house of Ahab
32. 21. the angel to *c. off* all mighty men of valour
Job 4. 7. or where were the righteous *c. off?*
6. 9. that he would let loose his hand, and *c.* me *off*
8. 14. whose hope shall be *c. off*, and whose trust
10. † 1. my soul is *c. off* while I live, I will leave my
11. 10. if he *c. off*, then who can hinder him?
14. † 10. man dieth, and is *c. off*, and where is he?
18. 16. and above shall his branch be *c. off*
21. 21. when number of his months is *c. off* in midst
23. 17. because I was not *c. off* before the darkness
24. 24. they are *c. off* as the tops of ears of corn
36. 20. when people are *c. off* in their place
Psal. 12. 3. the Lord shall *c. off* all flattering lips
31. † 17. let the wicked be *c. off* for the graves
22. I said, I am *c. off* from before thine eyes
34. 16. to *c. off* remembrance of them from earth
37. 9. for evil doers shall be *c. off*, but those who
22. they that be cursed of him shall be *c. off*
28. but the seed of the wicked shall be *c. off*
34. when the wicked are *c. off*, thou shalt see it
38. the end of the wicked shall be *c. off*
54. 5. he shall reward, *c.* them *off* in thy truth
75. 10. all the horns of the wicked will I *c. off*
76. 12. he shall *c. off* the spirit of princes
83. 4. they said, come, and let us *c.* them *off*
88. 5. and they are *c. off* from thy hand
16. wrath goeth over me, terrors have *c.* me *off*
94. 23. he shall *c.* them *off* in their wickedness
101. 5. that slandereth his neighbour will I *c. off*
8. that I may *c. off* all wicked doers from the city of the Lord
109. 13. let his posterity be *c. off* and blotted out
15. that the Lord may *c. off* the memory of them
118. † 10. in the name of the Lord I will *c.* them *off*
119. † 139. my zeal hath *c.* me *off*, because
143. 12. and of thy mercy *c. off* mine enemies
Prov. 2. 22. but the wicked shall be *c. off* from earth
23. 18. thy expectation shall not be *c. off*, 24. 14.
Isa. 6. † 5. then said I, woe is me, for I am *c. off*
9. 14. the Lord will *c. off* from Israel head and tail
10. 7. to destroy and *c. off* nations not a few
11. 13. the adversaries of Judah shall be *c. off*
14. 22. I will *c. off* from Babylon the name
15. † 1. Moab is *c. off* ‖ 2. and every beard *c. off*
22. 25. burden that was upon it shall be *c. off*
29. 20. all that watch for iniquity are *c. off*
38. 12. he will *c.* me *off* with pining sickness
48. 9. my praise will refrain, that I *c.* thee not *off*
19. his name should not have been *c. off*
53. 8. he was *c. off* out of the land of the living
55. 13. shall be for a sign that shall not be *c. off*
66. 3. that sacrificeth, as if he *c. off* a dog's neck
Jer. 7. 28. truth is perished and *c. off* from mouth
29. *c. off* thine hair, O Jerusalem, cast it away
9. 21. to *c. off* the children without, and young men
11. 19. let us *c.* him *off* from the land of the living
44. 7. to *c. off* from you man and woman out of Jud.
8. that ye might *c.* yourselves *off* and be a curse
44. 11. set my face against you to *c. off* Judah
46. † 28. yet will I not utterly *c.* thee *off*
47. 4. to *c. off* from Tyrus ‖ 5. Ashkelon is *c. off*
48. 2. come, let us *c.* it *off* from being a nation
25. the horn of Moab is *c. off*, his arm is broken
49. 26. all the men of war shall be *c. off*, 50. 30.
50. 16. *c. off* the sower from Babylon, and him that
51. 6. flee out, and be not *c. off* in her iniquity
62. thou hast spoken against this place to *c.* it *off*
Lam. 2. 3. *c. off* in his anger the horn of Israel
3. 53. they have *c. off* my life in the dungeon
Ezek. 14. 8. and I will *c.* him *off* from my people
13. *c. off* man and beast, 17, 19, 21. | 25. 13. | 29. 8.
17. 9. shall he not *c. off* fruit thereof, that it wither?
17. and building forts to *c. off* many persons
21. 3. I will *c. off* the righteous and the wicked, 4.
25. 7. behold, I will *c.* thee *off* from the people
16. I will *c. off* the Cherethims, and destroy the remnant of the sea-coasts
30. 15. and I will *c. off* the multitude of No
31. 12. terrible of the nations have *c.* him *off*
35. 7. I will *c. off* from Seir him that passeth out
37. 11. our hope is lost, we are *c. off* for our parts
Dan. 4. 14. hew down the tree, *c. off* his branches
9. 26. Messiah shall be *c. off*, but not for himself
Hos. 4. † 5. *c. off* thy mother | † 6. people are *c. off*
8. 4. they have made idols, that they may be *c. off*
10. 7. Samaria, her king is *c. off* as the foam, 15.
Joel 1. 5. the new wine is *c. off* from your mouth, 9.
16. is not the meat *c. off* before our eyes?
Amos 1. 5. I will *c. off* the inhabitant from Aven
8. I will *c. off* the inhabitant from Ashdod
2. 3. I will *c. off* the judge from the midst thereof
3. 14. the horns of the altar shall be *c. off*
Obad. 5. if robbers by night, how art thou *c. off*
9. every one of Esau may be *c. off* by slaughter
10. and thou shalt be *c. off* for ever
14. nor stand to *c. off those* of his that did escape
Mic. 5. 9. and all thine enemies shall be *c. off*
10. horses ‖ 11. cities ‖ 12. witchcrafts *c. off*
13. thy graven images will I *c. off*, *Nah.* 1. 14.
Nah. 1. 15. for the wicked is utterly *c. off*
2. 13. and I will *c. off* thy prey from the earth
3. 15. the sword shall *c.* thee *off*, it shall eat
Hab. 3. 17. tho' the flock shall be *c. off* from the fold
Zeph. 1. 3. I will *c. off* man from off the land
4. *c. off* remn. of Baal ‖ 11. that bear silver *c. off*
3. 6. I have *c. off* the nations, towers are desolate
7. so their dwelling should not be *c. off*
Zech. 5. 3. for every one that stealeth as on this side, and every one that sweareth, shall be *c. off*
9. 6. I will *c. off* the pride of the Philistines
10. and I will *c. off* the chariot from Ephraim
11. 8. three shepherds also I *c. off* in one month
9. and that, that is to be *c. off*, let it be *c. off*
13. 2. I will *c. off* the names of idols out of land
8. two parts in the land shall be *c. off* and die
14. 2. the residue of the people shall not be *c. off*
Mal. 2. 12. Lord will *c. off* the man that doeth this

Mat. 5. 30. if thy right hand offend thee, *c.* it *off*, 18. 8. *Mark* 9. 43, 45.
Mark 14. 47. *c. off* ear, *Luke* 22. 50. *John* 18. 10, 26.
Acts 27. 32. the soldiers *c. off* the ropes of the boat
Rom. 11. 22. otherwise thou shalt also be *c. off*
2 *Cor.* 11. 12. that I may *c. off* occasion from them
Gal. 5. 12. I would they were *c. off* that trouble you

CUT *out.*

2 *Chron.* 26. † 10. Uzziah *c. out* many cisterns
Job 33. † 6. I also am *c. out* of the clay
Prov. 10. 31. the froward tongue shall be *c. out*
Dan. 2. 34. a stone was *c. out* without hands, 45.
Rom. 11. 24. for if thou wert *c. out* of the olive tree

CUT *short.*

2 *Kings* 10. 32. the Lord began to *c.* Israel *short*
Rom. 9. 28. will finish and *c.* it *short* in righteousness

CUT *up.*

Job 30. 4. who *c. up* mallows by the bushes
Isa. 33. 12. as thorns *c. up* shall they be burnt

CUTTEST, ETH.

Deut. 24. 19. when thou *c.* down thine harvest
Job 28. 10. he *c.* out rivers among the rocks
Psal. 29. † 7. the voice of the Lord *c.* flames of fire
46. 9. he breaketh bow, and *c.* the spear in sunder
141. 7. as when one *c.* and cleaveth wood on earth
Prov. 26. 6. sendeth message by fool, *c.* off the feet
Jer. 10. 3. for one *c.* a tree out of the forest with axe
22. 14. build chambers and *c.* him out windows

CUTTING.

Exod. 31. 5. and in *c.* of stones to set them, 35. 33.
Lev. 25. † 23. the land shall not be sold for *c.* of
Deut. 24. † 1. let him write her a bill of *c.* off
Isa. 38. 10. I said in the *c.* of my days, I shall go
Jer. 30. † 23. a *c.* whirlwind, it shall fall with pain
Ezek. 7. † 25. *c.* off cometh, they shall seek peace
16. † 3. thy *c.* out is of the land of Canaan
Hab. 2. 10. consulted shame by *c.* off many people
Mark 5. 5. tombs, crying and *c.* himself with stones

CUTTINGS.

Lev. 19. 28. ye shall not make any *c.* for dead, 21. 5.
Jer. 48. 37. upon all the hands shall be *c.* and on
Jonah 2. † 6. I went down to the *c.* of the mount

CYMBAL.

1 *Cor.* 13. 1. I am become as sounding brass, or a [tinkling *c.*

CYMBALS.

2 *Sam.* 6. 5. played on cornets and *c.* 1 *Chr.* 13. 8.
1 *Chron.* 15. 16. harps and *c.* sounding, 16. 42.
16. 5. but Asaph made a sound with *c.*
25. 6. these were under the hands of their father for song in the house of the Lord with *c.*
2 *Chron.* 5. 13. they lift up their voice with *c.*
29. 25. he set Levites in house of the Lord with *c.*
Ezra 3. 10. the sons of Asaph with *c.* *Neh.* 12. 27.
Psal. 150. 5. praise him upon loud-sounding *c.*

CYPRESS.

Cant. 1. † 14. my beloved is to me as a cluster of *c.*
4. † 13. with pleasant fruits, *c.* with spikenard
Isa. 44. 14. he taketh the *c.* and the oak

D.

DAGGER.

Judg. 3. 16. Ehud made him a *d.* with two edges
21. he took the *d.* from his right thigh
22. that he could not draw the *d.* out of his belly

DAILY; *see after* DAYS.

DAINTY, TIES.

Gen. 49. 20. Asher shall yield royal *d.*
Job 33. 20. and his soul abhorreth *d.* meat
Psal. 141. 4. and let me not eat of their *d.*
Prov. 23. 3. be not desirous of his *d.* for they are
6. an evil eye, neither desire thou his *d.* meats
Hab. 1. † 16. their portion is fat, their meat *d.*
Rev. 18. 14. all things which were *d.* are departed

DALE.

Gen. 14. 17. valley of Shaveh, which is the king's *d.*
2 *Sam.* 18. 18. a pillar which is in the king's *d.*

DAMAGE.

Ezra 4. 22. why should *d.* grow to the hurt of kings
Esth. 7. 4. enemy could not countervail the king's *d.*
Prov. 26. 6. cutteth off the feet, and drinketh *d.*
Dan. 6. 2. and the king should have no *d.*
Acts 27. 10. voyage will be with hurt and much *d.*
2 *Cor.* 7. 9. that ye might receive *d.* by us in nothing

DAM.

Exod. 22. 30. seven days it shall be with his *d.* on the eighth shall give it me, *Lev.* 22. 27.
Deut. 22. 6. thou shalt not take the *d.* with young
7. but thou shalt in any wise let the *d.* go

DAMNABLE.

2 *Pet.* 2. 1. who privily shall bring in *d.* heresies

DAMNATION.

Mat. 23. 14. therefore ye shall receive the greater *d.* *Mark* 12. 40. *Luke* 20. 47.
33. ye serpents, how can ye escape the *d.* of hell?
Mark 3. 29. but is in danger of eternal *d.*
John 5. 29. have done evil to the resurrection of *d.*
Rom. 3. 8. evil, that good may come whose *d.* is just
13. 2. they shall receive to themselves *d.*
1 *Cor.* 11. 29. he eateth and drinketh *d.* to himself
1 *Tim.* 5. 12. having *d.* because have cast off first faith
2 *Pet.* 2. 3. lingereth not, and their *d.* slumbereth not

DAMNED.

Mark 16. 16. but he that believeth not shall be *d.*
Rom. 14. 23. and he that doubteth is *d.* if he eat
2 *Thess.* 2. 12. that all might be *d.* who believed not

DAMSEL.

Gen. 24. 55. her mother said, let the *d.* abide few days
34. 3. and he loved the *d.* and spake kindly to *d.*
12. ask never so much, but give me the *d.* to wife
Deut. 22. 15. bring forth tokens of the *d.* virginity
20. but if the tokens be not found for the *d.*
21. they shall bring out the *d.* and stone her
24. the *d.* because she cried not, being in the city
26. there is in the *d.* no sin worthy of death
29. shall give the *d.* father fifty shekels of silver
Judg. 5. 30. divided to every man a *d.* or two
19. 4. the *d.* father retained him, and he abode
Ruth 2. 5. then Boaz said, whose *d.* is this?
6. it is Moabitish *d.* that came back with Naomi
1 *Kings* 1. † 2. he sought for the king a young *d.*

1 Kings 1. 4. and d. was very fair, and cherished him
Mat. 14. 11. John Baptist's head was brought in a charger, and given to the d. Mark 6. 28.
26. 69. a d. came to Peter, saying, John 18. 17.
Mark 5. 39. the d. is not dead, but sleepeth
40. he taketh the father and mother of the d. and entereth in where the d. was lying
Acts 12. 13. a d. came to hearken, named Rhoda
16. 16. a certain d. possessed with a spirit, met us

DAMSELS.

Gen. 24. 61. Rebekah arose and her d. and rode
1 Sam. 25. 42. Abigail rode with five d. of hers
Psal. 68. 25. amongst them were the d. playing

DANCE.

Psal. 149. 3. let them praise him in the d. 150. 4.
Jer. 31. 13. the virgins shall rejoice in the d.
Lam. 5. 15. our d. is turned into mourning

DANCE.

Judg. 21. 21. if the daughters of Shiloh come to d.
Job 21. 11. send forth little ones, their children d.
Eccl. 3. 4. a time to mourn, and a time to d.
Isa. 13. 21. owls dwell there, satyrs shall d. there

DANCED.

Judg. 21. 23. according to their number that d.
2 Sam. 6. 14. and David d. before the Lord
Mat. 11. 17. have piped, and ye have not d. Luke 7. 32.
14. 6. the daughter of Herodias d. Mark 6. 22.

DANCES.

Exod. 15. 20. the women went after her with d.
Judg. 11. 34. daughter came to meet him with d.
1 Sam. 21. 11. did they not sing of him in d. 29. 5.
Jer. 31. 4. thou shalt go forth in the d. of them

DANCING.

Exod. 32. 19. he came nigh, he saw the calf and d.
1 Sam. 18. 6. the women came out singing and d.
30. 16. were spread on all the earth, eating and d.
2 Sam. 6. 16. she saw king David d. 1 Chr. 15. 29.
Psal. 30. 11. thou hast turned my mourning into d.
Luke 15. 25. as he came he heard music and d.

DANDLED.

Isa. 66. 12. and ye shall be d. upon her knees

DANGER.

Mat. 5. 21. shall be in d. of the judgment
22. shall be in d. of council, in d. of hell-fire
Mark 3. 29. but is in d. of eternal damnation
Acts 19. 27. not only this our craft is in d. but temple
40. in d. to be called in question for this uproar

DANGEROUS.

Acts 27. 9. and when sailing was now d. because

DARE.

Job 41. 10. none is so fierce that d. stir him up
Rom. 5. 7. for a good man some would even d. to die
15. 18. for I will not d. to speak of any thing
1 Cor. 6. 1. d. any of you go to law before the unjust?
2 Cor. 10. 12. we d. not make ourselves of the number

DARK.

Gen. 15. 17. when the sun went down, and it was d.
Exod. 9. † 32. for the wheat and the rye were d.
Lev. 13. 6. if the plague be d. 21, 26, 28, 56.
Num. 12. 8. speak apparently, and not in d. speeches
Josh. 2. 5. when it was d. the men went out
2 Sam. 22. 12. about him d. waters, Psal. 18. 11.
Neh. 13. 19. the gates of Jerusalem began to be d.
Job 3. 9. let the stars of the twilight thereof be d.
12. 25. they grope in the d. without light
18. 6. the light shall be d. in his tabernacle
22. 13. can he judge through the d. cloud?
24. 16. in the d. they dig thro' houses, which they
30. † 3. want and famine they were d. as night
Psal. 35. 6. let their way be d. and slippery
49. 4. I will open my d. saying on the harp
74. 20. d. places of the earth are full of cruelty
78. 2. in parables, I will utter d. sayings of old
88. 12. shall thy wonders be known in the d.?
105. 28. he sent darkness and made it d.
Prov. 1. 6. the words of the wise and their d. sayings
7. 9. in the twilight, in the black and d. night
Isa. 5. † 30. it shall be d. in the destruction thereof
29. 15. and their works are in the d. and they say
45. 19. I have not spoken in a d. place of the earth
Jer. 13. 16. your feet stumble on the d. mountains
Lam. 3. 6. he hath set me in d. places, as they that
Ezek. 8. 12. what the house of Israel do in the d.
32. 7. and I will make the stars thereof d.
8. the bright lights of heaven will I make d.
34. 12. have been scattered in the cloudy and d. day
Dan. 8. 23. a king understanding d. sentences shall
Joel 2. 10. the sun and the moon shall be d.
Amos 5. 8. seek him that maketh the day d. 20.
Mic. 3. 6. it shall be d. to you, the day shall be d.
Zech. 14. 6. the light shall not be clear, nor d.
Luke 11. 36. if thy body be light, having no part d.
John 6. 17. went over the sea, and it was now d.
20. 1. Mary came early, when it was yet d.
2 Pet. 1. 19. as to a light that shineth in a d. place

DARKEN.

Amos 8. 9. and I will d. the earth in the clear day

DARKLY.

1 Cor. 13. 12. for now we see through a glass d.

DARKENED.

Exod. 10. 15. for they covered, so that the land was d.
Psal. 69. 23. let their eyes be d. Rom. 11. 10.
Eccl. 12. 2. while sun, moon, or the stars be not d.
3. those that look out of the windows be d.
Isa. 5. 30. light is d. in the heavens thereof
9. 19. the land is d. || 13. 10. the sun d. Joel 3. 15.
24. 11. all joy is d. the mirth of the land gone
Ezek. 30. 18. at Tehaphnehes the day shall be d.
Zech. 11. 17. his right eye shall be utterly d.
Mat. 24. 29. then shall the sun be d. Mark 13. 24.
Luke 23. 45. and the sun was d. and vail was rent
Rom. 1. 21. and their foolish heart was d.
Eph. 4. 18. having the understanding d. alienated
Rev. 8. 12. so as the third part of them was d.
9. 2. and the sun and the air were d.

DARKENETH.

Job 38. 2. who is this that d. counsel by words?
Psal. 139. † 12. yea, the darkness d. not from thee

DARKISH.

Lev. 13. 39. if the bright spots in skin be d. white

DARKNESS

Signifies, [1] *The privation or want of natural light*, Mat. 27. 45. [2] *Hell, the place of eternal misery, confusion, and horror, called* outer darkness, Mat. 22. 13. [3] *Ignorance and unbelief, which is the want of spiritual light*, John 3. 19. [4] *The minds of men, which, since the fall, are full of ignorance and error*, John 1. 5. [5] *A private or secret place, where but few persons are present*, Mat. 10. 27. What I tell you in darkness; that is, *in parables, and in private between ourselves.* [6] *Great distress, perplexity, and calamity*, Isa. 8. 22. Joel 2. 2. [7] *Sin, or impurity*, 1 John 1. 5.

The land of darkness *is the grave*, Job 10. 21, 22. Such as sit in darkness and in the shadow of death, Psal. 107. 10. *such as are in a disconsolate and forlorn condition, shut up in prisons, or dungeons. The* children of light, *set in opposition to* the children of darkness, *means the righteous in opposition to the wicked; the faithful in opposition to the incredulous and infidels*, 2 Cor. 6. 14. *Our Saviour calls the exercise of Satan's power*, the power of darkness, Luke 22. 53. But this is your hour, and the power of darkness; *this is the time wherein power is given to the devil, and his instruments, to execute their designs against me.* The power of darkness, *is likewise taken for the dominion of sin, and slavery to the devil, under which all unregenerated persons are*, Col. 1. 13.

Gen. 1. 2. and d. was upon the face of the deep
5. the light day, and the d. he called night
18. God set them to divide the light from the d.
15. 12. an horror of great d. fell upon Abram
Exod. 10. 21. that there may be d. over Egypt
22. there was a thick d. in all Egypt three days
14. 20. it was a cloud and d. to them, but light
20. 21. and Moses drew near unto the thick d.
Deut. 4. 11. the mountain burnt with thick d.
5. 22. these words the Lord spake out of thick d.
Josh. 24. 7. he put d. between you and the Egyptians
2 Sam. 22. 10. d. was under his feet, Psal. 18. 9.
12. he made d. his pavilions round about him
29. the Lord will enlighten my d. Psal. 18. 28.
Job 3. 5. let d. and the shadow of death stain it
6. as for that night, let d. seize upon it
5. 14. they meet with d. in the day time
10. 22. a land of d. as d. itself, without any order
19. 8. and he hath set d. in my paths
20. 26. all d. shall be hid in his secret places
22. 11. or d. that thou canst not see
23. 17. because I was not cut off before the d. neither hath he covered the d. from my face
28. 3. he setteth an end to d. the stones of d.
34. 22. no d. where workers of iniquity may hide
37. 19. we cannot order our speech by reason of d.
38. 9. when I made thick d. a swaddling-band
19. and as for d. where is the place thereof?
Psal. 18. 11. he made d. his secret place
35. † 6. let their way be d. and slipperiness
88. 18. and hast put mine acquaintance into d.
97. 2. clouds and d. are round about him
104. 20. thou makest d. and it is night
105. 28. he sent d. and made it dark
139. 11. if I say, surely the d. shall cover me
12. yea, the d. hideth not from thee
Prov. 2. 13. leave paths to walk in the ways of d.
4. 19. the way of the wicked is as d. they know not
Eccl. 6. 4. his name shall be covered with d.
Isa. 5. 30. and if one look to the land, behold d.
8. 22. they shall look, and behold trouble and d.
45. 3. I will give thee the treasures of d.
47. 5. get thee into d. O daughter of Chaldeans
60. 2. for behold, the d. shall cover the earth, and gross d. the people, but Lord shall arise on thee
Jer. 13. 16. before he cause d. and make gross d.
Ezek. 32. 8. I will set d. upon thy land, saith Lord
Joel 2. 2. a day of d. of clouds and of thick d.
31. the sun shall be turned into d. Acts 2. 20.
Amos 4. 13. he that maketh the morning d.
Nah. 1. 8. and d. shall pursue his enemies
Mat. 6. 23. thy whole body full of d. Luke 11. 34.
8. 12. be cast out into outer d. 22. 13. | 25. 30.
27. 45. from sixth hour there was d. Mark 15. 33.
Luke 22. 53. this is your hour and the power of d.
23. 44. and there was d. over all the earth
Acts 13. 11. there fell on him a mist and a d.
Eph. 5. 11. have no fellowship with the works of d.
6. 12. against the rulers of the d. of this world
Col. 1. 13. who hath delivered us from power of d.
1 Thess. 5. 5. we are not of the night nor of d.
Heb. 12. 18. ye are not come to blackness and d.
2 Pet. 2. 4. and delivered them into chains of d.
17. to whom the mist of d. is reserved for ever
1 John 2. 11. because that d. hath blinded his eyes
Jude 6. hath reserved in everlasting chains under d.
13. to whom is reserved the blackn. of d. for ever
Rev. 16. 10. and his kingdom was full of d.

DARKNESS, with day.

Job 3. 4. let that day be d. let not God regard it
15. 23. he knoweth that the day of d. is at hand
Eccl. 11. 8. yet let him remember the days of d.
Isa. 58. 10. then shall thy d. be as the noon-day
Joel 2. 2. a day of d. and gloominess, Zeph. 1. 15.
Amos 5. 20. shall not the day of the Lord be d.?

In DARKNESS.

Deut. 28. 29. thou shalt grope as the blind in d.
1 Sam. 2. 9. and the wicked shall be silent in d.
1 Kings 8. 12. Solomon spake, the Lord said that he would dwell in the thick d. 2 Chr. 6. 1.
Job 17. 13. I have made my bed in the d.
Psal. 11. † 2. they may in d. shoot at the upright
82. 5. they know not, they walk on in d.
88. 6. thou hast laid me in d. in the deeps
91. 6. nor for the pestilence that walketh in d.
107. 10. such as sit in d. and the shadow of death
143. 3. the enemy hath made me to dwell in d.
Prov. 20. 20. his lamp shall be put out in obscure d.
Eccl. 2. 14. but the fool walketh in d.
5. 17. he eateth in d. || 6. 4. he departeth in d.
Isa. 42. 7. bring them that sit in d. out of prison h.
49. 9. to them that are in d. shew yourselves
59. 9. we wait for light, but we walk in d.
Jer. 23. 12. their ways shall be as slippery ways in d.
Dan. 2. 22. he knoweth what is in the d. and light
John 8. 12. he that followeth me shall not walk in d.
12. 35. for he that walketh in d. knoweth not
46. whosoever believeth me, should not abide in d.
1 Thess. 5. 4. but ye, brethren, are not in d.
1 John 1. 6. and walk in d. we lie and do not truth
2. 9. hateth his brother, is in d. even till now
11. hateth his brother, is in d. walketh in d.

Land of DARKNESS.

Job 10. 21. before I go even to the land of d.
22. a land of d. as d. itself, and shadow of death
Jer. 2. 31. have I been to Israel a land of d.?

DARKNESS, with light.

Gen. 1. 4. and God divided the light from the d.
18. two great lights to divide the light from d
Job 10. 22. a land where the light is as d.
17. 12. the light is short because of d.
18. 18. he shall be driven from light into d.
26. † 10. until the end of light with d.
29. 3. when by his light I walked through d.
30. 26. when I waited for light, there came d.
Psal. 112. 4. to upright there ariseth light in d.
139. 12. the d. and light are both alike to thee
Eccl. 2. 13. wisdom excels as far as light excelleth d.
Isa. 5. 20. that put d. for light, and light for d.
9. 2. the people that walked in d. have seen a great light, upon them hath light shined, Mat. 4. 16.
42. 16. I will make d. light before them
45. 7. I form light and create d. I make peace
50. 10. that walketh in d. and hath no light
Jer. 13. 16. while ye look for light, he make it gross d.
Lam. 3. 2. he brought me into d. but not into light
Amos 5. 18. the day of the Lord is d. and not light
Mic. 7. 8. when I sit in d. the Lord shall be a light
Mat. 6. 23. light in thee be d. how great is that d.!
10. 27. what I tell in d. speak in light, Luke 12. 3.
Luke 1. 79. light to them that sit in d. Rom. 2. 19.
11. 35. that the light which is in thee be not d.
John 1. 5. light shineth in d. d. comprehended it not
3. 19. and men loved d. rather than light
12. 35. walk while ye have light, lest d. come
Acts 26. 18. and to turn them from d. to light
Rom. 13. 12. cast off the works of d. put on light
1 Cor. 4. 5. to bring to light the hidden things of d.
2 Cor. 4. 6. who commanded light to shine out of d.
6. 14. what communion hath light with d.?
1 Pet. 2. 9. called you out of d. into marvellous light
1 John 1. 5. God is light, and in him is no d. at all
2. 8. d. is past, and the true light now shineth

Out of DARKNESS.

Deut. 5. 22. when ye heard the voice out of the d.
Job 12. 22. he discovereth deep things out of d.
15. 22. believeth not that he shall return out of d.
30. he shall not depart out of d. the flame dry up
Psal. 107. 14. he brought them out of d. and shadow
Isa. 29. 18. the eyes of the blind shall see out of d.

DARLING.

Psal. 22. 20. deliver my d. from power of the dog
35. 17. Lord, rescue my d. from the lions

DART, S.

2 Sam. 18. 14. Joab took three d. in his hand
2 Chron. 32. 5. Hezekiah made d. and shields
Job 41. 26. the spear nor the d. cannot hold
29. d. are counted as stubble, he laugheth at
Prov. 7. 23. till a d. strike through his liver
Joel 2. † 8. when they fall on d. not be wounded
Eph. 6. 16. to quench the fiery d. of the wicked
Heb. 12. 20. it shall be thrust through with a d.

DASH.

2 Kings 8. 12. and thou wilt d. their children
Psal. 2. 9. lest d. them in pieces like a potter's vessel
91. 12. they shall bear thee up, lest thou d. thy foot against a stone, Mat. 4. 6. Luke 4. 11.
Isa. 13. 18. their bows shall d. the young men
Jer. 13. 14. I will d. them one against another

DASHED.

Exod. 15. 6. thy right hand, O Lord, hath d. in pieces
Isa. 13. 16. their children also shall be d. in pieces before their eyes, Hos. 13. 16. Nah. 3. 10.
Hos. 10. 14. the mother was d. upon her children

DASHETH.

Psal. 137. 9. that d. thy little ones against the stones

DATES.

2 Chron. 31. † 5. the children of Israel brought d.

DAUB, ED, ING.

Exod. 2. 3. she d. the ark with slime and pitch
Ezek. 13. 10. others d. it with untempered mortar
11. say to them which d. it, that it shall fall
12. where is the d. wherewith ye have d. it?
14. so will I break down the wall ye have d.
22. 28. her prophets have d. them with mortar

DAUGHTER

Signifies, [1] *A female child*, Gen. 34. 1. [2] *A sister*, Gen. 34. 17. [3] *A niece, or brother's daughter*, Exod. 2. 21. [4] *A daughter-in-law, or son's wife*, Ruth 3. 18. [5] *The women that dwell in a country*, Gen. 34. 1. [6] *The inhabitants of a city or country, both men and women*, Isa. 16. 2. Mat. 21. 5. [7] *Posterity, lineage, or offspring*, Luke 1. 5. [8] *The lungs, and other organs of singing, called* the daughters of music, Eccl. 12. 4. [9] *The branches of trees*, Gen. 49. † 22. [10] *The church of God*, Psal. 45. 9, 10. Cant. 5. 8.

Gen. 20. 12. is d. of my father, not d. of my mother
24. 23. whose d. art thou? tell me, I pray thee, 47.
48. to take my master's brother's d. to his son
34. 7. he had wrought folly in lying with Jacob's d.
8. soul of my son Shechem longeth for your d.
17. then will we take our d. and we will be gone
19. because he had delight in Jacob's d.
Exod. 1. 16. but if it be a d. then she shall live
21. 31. whether he have gored a son or a d.
Lev. 12. 6. when the days are fulfilled for a d.
14. † 10. to take an ewe lamb, the d. of her year
18. 17. nor shalt thou take her daughter's d.
21. 9. the d. of any priest, if she profane herself
22. 12. if the priest's d. be married to a stranger
13. if the priest's d. be a widow or divorced
Num. 27. 9. if he have no d. give his inheritance
36. 8. every d. that possesseth an inheritance

Deut. 27. 22. cursed be he that lieth with his sister, the d. of his father or the d. of his mother
28. 56. her eye shall be evil towards her d.
Judg. 11. 34. Jephthah's d. came out to meet him
40. to lament Jephthah's d. four days in a year
1 Sam. 1. 16. count not thy handmaid a d. of Belial
18. 19. when Saul's d. should have been given
2 Sam. 12. 3. little ewe lamb was unto him as a d.
1 Kings 3. 1. Solomon took Pharaoh's d.
11. 1. loved many women with the d. of Pharaoh
2 Kings 8. 18. the d. of Ahab was Jehoram's wife
9. 34. go bury Jezebel, for she is a king's d.
1 Chron. 2. 49. and the d. of Caleb was Achsah
Esth. 2. 7. he took his uncle's d. for his own d.
Psal. 45. 10. hearken, O d. and consider, and incline
13. the king's d. is all glorious within
Cant. 7. 1. how beautiful with shoes, O prince's d.
Jer. 31. 22. how long go about, backsliding d. 49. 4.
46. 19. O d. dwelling in Egypt, furnish thyself
48. 18. thou d. that dost inhabit Dibon, come down
Ezek. 14. 16. neither deliver son nor d. 18, 20.
16. 44. saying, as is the mother, so is her d.
45. thou art thy mother's d. that loatheth
27. † 6. the d. of the Ashurites made thy benches
44. 25. for son or d. they may defile themselves
Dan. 11. 6. the king's d. of the south shall come
17. shall give him the d. of women corrupting
Hos. 1. 6. and she conceived again, and bare a d.
Mic. 5. 1. gather thyself in troops, O d. of troops
7. 6. d. riseth up against her mother, daughter-in-law against her mother, Mat. 10. 35. Luke 12. 53.
Zeph. 3. 10. the d. of my dispersed shall bring
Mal. 2. 11. hath married the d. of a strange god
Mat. 9. 22. Jesus said, d. be of good comf. thy faith hath made thee whole, Mark 5. 34. Luke 8. 48.
10. 37. he that loveth son or d. more than me
14. 6. the d. of Herodias danced before them
15. 28. her d. was made whole from that hour
Mark 7. 26. he would cast forth devil out of her d.
Luke 8. 42. he had one only d. about 12 years of age
13. 16. ought not this woman, being d. of Abraham
Acts 7. 21. Pharaoh's d. took him up and nourished
Heb. 11. 24. Moses refused to be son of Pharaoh's d.

DAUGHTER of Babylon.

Psal. 137. 8. O d. of Babylon, who art to be destroyed
Isa. 47. 1. O d. of Babylon, sit on the ground
Jer. 50. 42. to battle against thee, O d. of Babylon
51. 33. d. of Babylon is like a threshing floor
Zech. 2. 7. O Zion, that dwellest with d. of Babylon

DAUGHTER of the Chaldeans.

Isa. 47. 1. there is no throne, O d. of the Chaldeans
5. get thee into darkness, O d. of the Chaldeans

DAUGHTER of Edom.

Lam. 4. 21. rejoice and be glad, O d. of Edom
22. he will visit thine iniquity, O d. of Edom

DAUGHTER of Egypt.

Jer. 46. 11. go into Gilead, O virgin, d. of Egypt
24. the d. of Egypt shall be confounded

DAUGHTER of Gallim.

Isa 10. 30. lift up thy voice, O d. of Gallim

His DAUGHTER.

Gen. 29. 6. Rachael his d. cometh with the sheep
Exod. 21. 7. if a man sell his d. to be a servant
Lev. 21. 2. for his son or his d. he may be defiled
Num. 27. 8. shall cause inheritance to pass to his d.
30. 16. the statutes between the father and his d.
Deut. 7. 3. nor his d. shalt thou take to thy son
18. 10. there shall not be found one that maketh his d. to pass through the fire, 2 Kings 23. 10.
Judg. 21. 1. not any of us give his d. to Benjamin
1 Sam. 17. 25. king will enrich and give him his d.

DAUGHTER of Jerusalem.

2 Kings 19. 21. the daughter of Zion, the d. of Jerus. hath shaken her head at thee, Isa. 37. 22.
Lam. 2. 13. what thing shall I liken to thee, O d. of Jerusalem, O daughter of Zion, to comfort thee?
15. they wag their head at the d. of Jerusalem
Mic. 4. 8. the kingdom shall come to d. of Jerusalem
Zeph. 3. 14. rejoice with all the heart, O d. of Jerus.
Zech. 9. 9. shout, O d. of Jerus. thy King cometh

DAUGHTER of Judah.

Lam. 1. 15. the Lord hath trodden the d. of Judah
2. 2. he hath thrown down strong holds of d. of Judah
5. he hath increased in d. of Judah mourning

DAUGHTER-IN-LAW.

Gen. 38. 16. he knew not that she was his d.-in-law
24. Tamar thy d.-in-law hath played the harlot
Lev. 18. 15. not uncover nakedness of thy d.-in-law
20. 12. if a man lie with his d.-in law both shall die
Ruth 1. 22. Naomi returned, and Ruth her d.-in-law
4. 15. d.-in-law which loveth thee, hath born him
1 Sam. 4. 19. d.-in-law Phinehas' wife was with child
Ezek. 22. 11. another lewdly defileth his d.-in-law
Mic. 7. 6. for the d.-in-law riseth up against the mother-in-law, Mat. 10. 35. Luke 12. 53.

My DAUGHTER.

Deut. 22. 16. I gave my d. to this man to wife
17. these are the tokens of my d. virginity
Josh. 15. 16. to him will I give my d. Judg. 1. 12.
Judg. 11. 35. alas, my d. thou hast brought me low
19. 24. behold, here is my d. a maiden
Ruth 2. 2. and she said unto her, go, my d.
3. 10. he said, blessed be thou of the Lord, my d.
16. her mother said, who art thou, my d.?
18. sit still, my d. till thou know the matter
Mat. 9. 18. a ruler, saying, my d. is even now dead
15. 22. my d. is grievously vexed with a devil
Mark 5. 23. my little d. lieth at the point of death

DAUGHTER of my people.

Isa. 22. 4. because of the spoiling of the d. of my p.
Jer. 4. 11. a dry wind toward d. of my p. not to fan
6. 14. healed the heart of d. of my p. slightly, 8. 11.
26. O d. of my people, gird thee with sackcloth
8. 19. behold, the voice of the cry of the d. of my p.
21. for hurt of d. of my p. am I hurt, I am black
22. why is not health of the d. of my p. recovered
9. 1. that I might weep for slain of the d. of my p.
7. I will try them, for how shall I do for d. of my p.
14. 17. virgin d. of my p. is broken with a breach
Lam. 2. 11. for the destruction of d. of my p. 3. 48.
4. 3. the d. of my p. is become cruel, like ostriches
6. the iniquity of the d. of my p. is greater than

Lam. 4. 10. were their meat in destruction of d. of my p.

DAUGHTER of Tarshish.

Isa. 23. 10. pass through as a river, O d. of Tarshish

Thy DAUGHTER.

Gen. 29. 18. I will serve 7 years for thy younger d.
Exod. 20. 10. nor thy son, nor thy d. Deut. 5. 14.
Lev. 18. 10. the nakedness of thy daughter's d.
19. 29. do not prostitute thy d. to be a whore
Deut. 7. 3. thy d. shalt thou not give to his son
12. 18. thou shalt rejoice and thy d. 16. 11, 14.
13. 6. if thy son or thy d. entice thee, saying
22. 17. saying, I found not thy d. a maid
2 Kings 14. 9. give thy d. to my son, 2 Chron. 25. 18.
Mark 5. 35. certain who said, thy d. is dead, Luke 8. 49.
7. 29. go thy way, the devil is gone out of thy d.

DAUGHTER of Tyre.

Psal. 45. 12. d. of Tyre shall be there with a gift

DAUGHTER of Zidon.

Isa. 23. 12. O thou oppressed virgin, d. of Zidon

DAUGHTER of Zion.

2 Kings 19. 21. d. of Z. hath despised thee, Isa. 37. 22.
Psal. 9. 14. thy praise in the gates of the d. of Zion
Isa. 1. 8. d. of Zion left as a cottage in vineyard
4. 4. have washed away the filth of the d. of Zion
10. 32. shake against mount of d. of Zion, 16. 1.
52. 2. loose thyself, O captive d. of Zion
62. 11. say to the d. of Zion, thy salvation cometh
Jer. 4. 31. I have heard the voice of the d. of Zion
6. 2. I have likened d. of Zion to a comely woman
23. as men of war against thee, O d. of Zion
Lam. 1. 6. from the d. of Zion beauty is departed
2. 1. Lord covereth the d. of Zion with a cloud
4. and slew in the tabernacle of the d. of Zion
8. Lord purposed to destroy the wall of d. of Zion
10. the elders of d. of Zion sit on the ground
13. what shall I equal to thee, O d. of Zion?
18. O wall of the d. of Zion, let tears run down
4. 22. punishment is accomplished, O d. of Zion
Mic. 1. 13. the beginning of sin to the d. of Zion
4. 8. O tower, the strong hold of the d. of Zion
10. be in pain, labour to bring forth, O d. of Zion
13. arise and thresh, O d. of Zion, I will make
Zeph. 3. 14. sing, O d. of Zion, shout O Israel
Zech. 2. 10. sing and rejoice, O d. of Zion, 9. 9.
Mat. 21. 5. tell ye the d. of Zion, thy king cometh
John 12. 15. fear not, d. of Zion, thy king cometh

DAUGHTER of Zur.

Num. 25. 15. the woman was Cozbi the d. of Zur

DAUGHTERS.

Gen. 6. 1. and when d. were born to them
2. the sons of God saw the d. of men, and took
6. 4. the sons of God came in unto the d. of men
19. 14. Lot spake to them which married his d.
36. both the d. of Lot with child by their father
24. 3. take not a wife of d. of Canaan, 37. | 28. 1, 6.
13. the d. of the city came out to draw water
27. 46. weary of my life because of the d. of Heth
30. 13. happy am I, for the d. will call me blessed
31. 26. thou hast carried away my d. as captives
43. these d. are my d. || 50. if thou afflict my d.
34. 1. Dinah went out to see the d. of the land
9. give your d. to us, and take our d. unto you
16. then will we give our d. to you, and take d.
49. † 22. Joseph is a bough whose d. run over
Exod. 2. 16. the priest of Midian had seven d.
21. 9. he shall deal with her after the manner of d.
34. 16. their d. go a whoring after their gods
Lev. 26. 29. the flesh of your d. shall ye eat
Num. 21. † 25. dwelt in Heshbon and d. thereof
26. 33. names of d. of Zelophehad, 27. 1. Josh. 17. 3.
27. 7. the d. of Zelophehad speak right
36. 10. even so did the d. of Zelophehad
Deut. 23. 17. shall be no whore of the d. of Israel
Judg. 3. 6. they took their d. to be their wives
21. 7. we will not give them of our d. to wives
18. howbeit, we may not give them wives of our d.
Ruth 1. 11. turn again, my d. why will ye go? 12.
13. nay, my d. it grieveth me for your sakes
1 Sam. 8. 13. take your d. to be confectionaries
2 Sam. 13. 18. were king's d. virgins apparelled
Neh. 3. 12. next repaired Shallum, he and his d.
5. 5. our d. are brought into bondage already
7. 63. took one of d. of Barzillai to wife, Ezra 2. 61.
10. 30. not give our d. to the people of the land
Job 42. 15. no women were so fair as the d. of Job
Psal. 45. 9. king's d. among thy honourable women
144. 12. that our d. may be as corner stones
Prov. 31. 29. many d. have done virtuously, but thou
Cant. 2. 2. as the lily, so is my love among the d.
6. 9. the d. saw her and blessed her, yea the queens
Isa. 13. † 21. d. of the owl dwell there, 34. † 13.
32. 9. hear my voice, ye careless d. give ear
43. † 20. the d. of the owl shall honour me
60. 4. and thy d. shall be nursed at thy side
Jer. 9. 20. O ye women, teach your d. wailing
29. 6. give your d. to husbands, that they may bear
49. 2. and her d. shall be burnt with fire
3. cry, ye d. of Rabbah, gird ye with sackcloth
Lam. 3. 51. because of all the d. of my city
Ezek. 13. 17. set thy face against the d. of thy peo.
16. † 31. in thy d. is thine eminent place
46. sister Samaria, and her d. Sodom, and her d.
49. abundance of idleness was in her and in her d.
53. when I bring back the captivity of her d.
55. when thy sister Sodom and d. shall return
61. and I will give them unto thee for d.
23. 2. there were two women, the d. of one mother
26. 6. her d. shall be slain in the field, 8.
30. 18. and her d. shall go into captivity
32. 16. the d. of the nations shall lament her
Hos. 4. 13. therefore your d. shall commit whoredom
14. I will not punish your d. when they commit
Mic. 1. † 8. make a mourning as the d. of the owl
Luke 1. 5. and his wife was of the d. of Aaron
Acts 21. 9. the same man had four d. virgins
1 Pet. 3. 6. whose d. ye are as long as ye do well

DAUGHTERS of Jerusalem.

Cant. 1. 5. I am black, but comely, O d. of Jerus.
2. 7. I charge you, O d. of Jerus. 3. 5. | 5. 8. | 8. 4.
3. 10. paved with love for the d. of Jerusalem
5. 16. this is my beloved, O d. of Jerusalem
Luke 23. 28. d. of Jerusalem, weep not for me

DAUGHTERS of Israel.

Deut. 23. 17. there shall be no whore of d. of Israel
Judg. 11. 40. d. of Israel went yearly to lament
2 Sam. 1. 24. ye d. of Israel, weep over Saul, who

DAUGHTERS of Judah.

Psal. 48. 11. let the d. of Judah be glad, because
97. 8. Zion heard, and the d. of Judah rejoiced

DAUGHTERS-IN-LAW.

Ruth 1. 6. then she arose with her d.-in-law, 7.
8. Naomi said to her two d.-in-law, go return

DAUGHTERS of Moab.

Num. 25. 1. Isr. committed whoredom with d. of M.
Isa. 16. 2. so the d. of M. shall be at fords of Arnon

DAUGHTERS of music.

Eccl. 12. 4. the d. of music shall be brought low

DAUGHTERS of the Philistines.

Judg. 14. 1. Samson saw a woman of the d. of Phil.
2. I have seen a woman of d. of Phil. get her for me
2 Sam. 1. 20. publish it not lest the d. of the Philistines rejoice
Ezek. 16. 27. I have delivered thee to the d. of Phil.
57. the d. of Phil. which despise thee round about

DAUGHTERS of Shiloh.

Judg. 21. 21. if the d. of Shiloh come out to dance, catch ye every man a wife of the d. of Shiloh

DAUGHTERS, joined with Sons.

Gen. 5. 4. he begat sons and d. 7, 10, 13, 16. | 11. 11.
19. 12. thy sons and d. bring out of this place
31. 28. not suffered me to kiss my sons and d.
55. he kissed his sons and d. and blessed them
37. 35. all his sons and d. rose to comfort him
Exod. 3. 22. ye shall put them on your sons and d.
10. 9. with our sons and with our d. will we go
21. 4. and she have born him sons or d.
32. 2. ear-rings of your sons and d. bring to me
34. 16. and thou take of their d. to thy sons
Lev. 10. 14. thou, thy sons and d. with thee, shall eat in the holy place, Num. 18. 11, 19.
Num. 21. 29. given his sons and d. into captivity
26. 33. Zelophehad had no sons, but d. Josh. 17. 3.
Deut. 12. 12. ye and your sons and d. rejoice
31. their sons and d. they have burnt in the fire, 2 Kings 17. 17. Jer. 7. 31. | 32. 35.
28. 32. thy sons and d. given to another people
41. beget sons and d. but shalt not enjoy them
53. thou shalt eat the flesh of thy sons and d.
32. 19. because of provoking of his sons and d.
Josh. 7. 24. they brought Achan, his sons and d.
17. 6. d. of Manasseh had inheritance among sons
Judg. 3. 6. they gave their d. to their sons
12. 9. Ibzan took in thirty d. for his sons
1 Sam. 1. 4. he gave Peninnah, her sons and d. portions
2. 21. so Hannah bare three sons and two d.
30. 3. their sons and d. were taken captives
6. grieved, every man for his sons and for his d.
19. there was nothing lacking, neither sons nor d.
2 Sam. 5. 13. and there were yet sons and d. born to David, 1 Chron. 14. 3.
19. 5. which saved the lives of thy sons and of thy d.
1 Chr. 2. 34. now Sheshan had no sons but d.
4. 27. Shimei had sixteen sons and six d.
23. 22. Eleazar died, and had no sons but d.
25. 5. God gave Heman fourteen sons and three d.
2 Chron. 11. 21. Rehoboam had 28 sons and 60 d.
13. 21. Abijah begat 22 sons and 16 d.
24. 3. Jehoiada took wives and begat sons and d.
28. 8. carried captive 200,000 women, sons and d.
29. 9. our sons d. and wives are in captivity for this
31. 18. to the genealogy of their sons and d.
Ezra 9. 2. have taken of their d. for their sons
12. give not your d. to their sons, Neh. 13. 25.
Neh. 4. 14. and fight for your sons, d. and your wives
5. 2. that said, we, our sons and our d. are many
5. we bring into bondage our sons and our d.
10. 28. their sons and d. clave to their brethren
Job 1. 2. there were born to Job 7 s. and 3 d. 42. 13.
13. a day when his sons and d. were eating, 18.
Psal. 106. 37. they sac. their sons and d. to devils
38. and shed even the blood of their sons and d.
Isa. 43. 6. bring my s. from far, and my d. from the
49. 22. bring thy sons in their arms, and thy d.
56. 5. will I give a name better than of s. and d.
Jer. 3. 24. shame hath devoured their sons and d.
5. 17. eat that which thy sons and d. should eat
11. 22. their sons and their d. shall die by famine
14. 16. they shall have none to bury their s. and d.
16. 2. neither shalt thou have s. nor d. in this place
3. saith the Lord concerning the sons and d.
19. 9. I will cause them eat the flesh of s. and d.
29. 6. take ye wives and beget sons and d.
35. 8. we, our sons and our d. drink no wine
48. 46. thy sons and thy d. are taken captives
Ezek. 14. 16. they shall deliver neither sons nor d. 18.
22. left a remnant brought forth, both sons and d.
16. 20. taken thy sons and d. and sacrificed them
23. 4. and they were mine, and bare sons and d.
10. they took her sons and d. and slew her, 25.
47. they shall slay their sons and d. and burn up
24. 21. your sons and d. fall by the sword, Amos 7. 17.
25. when I take from them their sons and d.
Joel 2. 28. your sons and d. prophesy, Acts 2. 17.
3. 8. I will sell your sons and d. to Judah
2 Cor. 6. 18. ye shall be my sons and d. saith the Lord

DAUGHTERS of Syria.

Ezek. 16. 57. time of thy reproach of the d. of Syria

Two DAUGHTERS.

Gen. 19. 8. I have two d. let me bring them out to you
15. take thy wife and thy two d. which are here
30. Lot dwelt in a cave, he and his two d.
29. 16. Laban had two d. Leah and Rachel
31. 41. I served thee fourteen years for thy two d.
Ruth 1. 7. Naomi went out with her two d.
1 Sam. 2. 21. Hannah conceived and bare two d.
14. 49. Saul's two d. were Merab and Michal
Prov. 30. 15. the horseleech hath two d. crying

DAUGHTERS of the uncircumcised.

2 Sam. 1. 20. publish it not, lest d. of the unc. triumph

DAUGHTERS of Zion.

Cant. 3. 11. go forth, O ye d. of Zion, and behold
Isa. 3. 16. because the d. of Zion are haughty
17. smite with a scab the head of the d. of Zion
4. 4. have washed away the filth of the d. of Zion

DAWN, ING.

Josh. 6. 15. they rose about the *d.* of the day
Judg. 19. 26. then came the woman in the *d.* of day
Job 3. 9. neither let it see the *d.* of the day
7. 4. I am full of tossings to the *d.* of the day
Psal. 119. 147. I prevented the *d.* of the morning
Mat. 28. 1. as it began to *d.* towards the first day
2 *Pet.* 1. 19. till the day *d.* and the day-star arise in

DAY.

The day *is distinguished into* natural, civil, *and* artificial. *The* natural *or* solar day, *is the duration of four and twenty hours. The* artificial day, *is the time of the sun's continuance above the horizon, which is unequal, according to different times and seasons, by reason of the obliquity of the sphere.* God called the light day, *that is, the artificial day.* The evening and the morning were the first day, *namely, natural,* Gen. 1. 5. The civil day, *is that, the beginning and end whereof is determined by the common custom of any nation. The* Hebrews *began their civil and ecclesiastical day from one evening to another.* From even unto even shall ye celebrate your sabbath, *Lev.* 23. 32. *The* Babylonians *reckoned their days from one sun-rising to another; the* Italians *from one sun-set to another; some from noon to noon; and others from midnight to midnight.*

This day, *or* to-day, *does not only signify the particular day on which one is speaking, but likewise any indefinite time.* Thou art to pass over Jordan this day, *Deut.* 9. 1. *that is, in a short time after this, the word* day *being often put for* time, *as in* Gen. 2. 4, 17. In the day when God made the earth and the heavens: in the day thou eatest thereof thou shalt surely die, *that is, at the time when thou eatest thereof.* To-day, if ye will hear his voice, *Heb.* 3. 15.; *that is, in this present season of grace, while you enjoy the means of grace.* The night is far spent, the day is at hand, *Rom.* 13. 12. *The time of heathenish ignorance and profaneness is in a great measure over; and the time of gospel-light and saving knowledge is begun among us.* The day of Jerusalem, *is the time of its calamity and destruction,* Psal. 137. 7. Abraham desired to see my day, *says our Saviour,* John 8. 56. *He desired to have a prospect of the time of my coming in the flesh.* One man esteemeth one day above another, *Rom.* 14. 5. *He thinks that the* Jewish *festivals are holier than other days, and still to be observed.* He seeth that his day is coming, *Psal.* 37. 13. *The time appointed by God for his punishment, or destruction.* This day have I begotten thee, *Psal.* 2. 7. *that is, from all eternity, in which there is no succession, no* yesterday, *no* to-morrow, *but it is all as one continued day or moment, without change or flux.* Or, this day, *may refer to the manifestation of* Christ's *eternal sonship in time; either in his birth and life, when his being the Son of God was demonstrated by the testimony of the angel,* Luke 1. 32. *And of God the Father,* Mat. 3. 17. | 17. 5. *But chiefly at his resurrection, by which* he was declared to be the Son of God with power, *Rom.* 1. 4. In one day, *that is, suddenly and unexpectedly,* Rev. 18. 8. *The Christian sabbath is called the* Lord's day, *Rev.* 1. 10. *as the sacrament is called the* Lord's supper, 1 *Cor.* 11. 20. *because* Christ *instituted it, or, because the end of its institution was the remembrance of Christ's resurrection, at the end of the Lord's supper was the commemoration of his death; or, because it is employed in his worship and service. The day of judgment is likewise called the* Lord's day, 1 *Thess.* 5. 2. *It is his by* destination, *because thereon he has appointed to judge the world; but the sabbath is his* by consecration, choice, *and* institution.

Gen. 1. 5. God called the light *d.* and darkness night
32. 26. he said, let me go, for the *d.* breaketh
Exod. 21. 21. if he continue a *d.* or two, he shall
40. 37. journeyed not, till the *d.* it was taken up
Lev. 23. 37. feasts of Lord, every thing upon his *d.*
Num. 3. 13. on the *d.* I smote the first-born in Egypt
7. 11. each prince shall offer his offering on his *d.*
14. 34. each *d.* for a year shall bear your iniquities
30. 8. if her husband disallow her on the *d.* 12.
Deut. 4. 10. the *d.* thou stoodest before L. in Horeb
15. ye saw no manner of similitude on the *d.*
9. 7. from the *d.* thou didst depart out of Egypt
24. have been rebellious from the *d.* I knew you
24. 15. at his *d.* thou shalt give him his hire
Josh. 6. 10. till the *d.* I bid you shout, then shout
9. 12. on the *d.* we came forth to go to you
10. 13. the sun hasted not down about a whole *d.*
14. was no *d.* like that before or after it
Judg. 16. 2. when it is *d.* we shall kill Samson
19. † 8. and they tarried till the *d.* declined
30. from the *d.* that Israel came out of Egypt
Ruth 4. 5. what *d.* thou buyest the field of Naomi
1 *Sam.* 9. 15. the Lord told Samuel a *d.* before
24. 4. behold the *d.* of which the Lord said
26. 10. smite him, or his *d.* shall come to die
2 *Sam.* 3. 35. while it was yet *d. Jer.* 15. 9.
13. 32. from the *d.* he forced his sister Tamar
19. 24. from the *d.* the king departed, till the *d.*
1 *Kings* 2. 37. that on the *d.* thou goest out, 42.
8. † 59. maintain the thing of a *d.* in his *d.*
17. 14. till the *d.* that the Lord sendeth rain
2 *Kings* 4. 8. it fell on a *d.* that Elisha passed, 11, 18.
Neh. 4. 2. he said, will they make an end in a *d.*?
22. in the night a guard, and labour on the *d.*
Esth. 9. 17. and made it a *d.* of feasting, 18, 19.
Job 1. 4. feasted in their houses, every one his *d.*
6. there was a *d.* when the sons of God, 13. | 2. 1.
3. 3. let the *d.* perish wherein I was born
14. 6. he may rest, till he shall accomplish his *d.*
18. 20. they shall be astonied at his *d.*
19. 25. he shall stand at latter *d.* upon the earth
21. 30. the wicked is reserved to *d.* of destruction
Psal. 19. 2. *d.* unto *d.* uttereth speech, and night
Psal. 37. 13. for he seeth that his *d.* is coming
78. 42. nor remembered *d.* when he delivered them
84. 10. a *d.* in thy courts is better than a thousand
119. 164. seven times a *d.* do I praise thee
Prov. 4. 18. that shineth more and more to perfect *d.*
7. 20. he will come home at the *d.* appointed
27. 1. thou knowest not what a *d.* may bring forth
Cant. 2. 17. till *d.* break, and shadows flee away, 4. 6.
Isa. 7. 17. from the *d.* that Ephraim departed
30. † 8. that it may be for the latter *d.* for ever
43. 13. yea, before the *d.* was, I am he
58. 5. a *d.* for a man to afflict his soul? wilt thou call this a fast, an acceptable *d.* to the Lord?
61. 2. and the *d.* of vengeance of our God, 63. 4.
Jer. 12. 3. prepare them for the *d.* of slaughter
27. 22. there shall they be till the *d.* I visit them
32. 31. from the *d.* they built it, even to this *d.*
36. 2. from the *d.* I spake to thee, even to this *d.*
38. 28. till the *d.* that Jerusalem was taken
47. 4. because of the *d.* that cometh to spoil
50. 27. woe unto them, for their *d.* is come
Ezek. 4. 6. I have appointed thee each *d.* for a year
7. 10. behold the *d.* behold it is come, the morning
21. 25. thou wicked prince, whose *d.* is come, 29.
28. 15. from the *d.* that thou wast created
30. 2. woe worth the *d.* ‖ 3. for the *d.* is near
18. at Tehaphnehes also the *d.* shall be darkened
Dan. 6. 10. maketh petition three times a *d.* 13.
Hos. 9. 5. what will ye do in the solemn *d.*?
Joel 2. 2. a *d.* of darkness and of gloominess
Amos 5. 8. seek him that maketh the *d.* dark
8. 10. I will make the end thereof as a bitter *d.*
Mic. 3. 6. and the *d.* shall be dark over them
7. 4. the *d.* of thy watchmen, and thy visitation
Zeph. 2. 2. before the decree, the *d.* pass as the chaff
3. 8. till the *d.* that I rise up to the prey
Zech. 4. 10. for who hath despised *d.* of small things?
Mal. 3. 2. but who may abide the *d.* of his coming?
4. 1. the *d.* cometh that shall burn as an oven
Mat. 24. 38. marrying and giving in marriage, till the *d.* that Noe entered into the ark, *Luke* 17. 27.
50. the Lord of that servant shall come in a *d.* when he looketh not for him, *Luke* 12. 46.
25. 13. ye neither know the *d.* nor the hour
Mark 1. 35. rising up a great while before *d.* went out
Luke 1. 20. dumb till the *d.* these things be performed
80. child grew till the *d.* of his shewing unto Israel
17. 4. trespass seven times in a *d.* and turn again
24. so shall also the Son of man be in his *d.*
John 6. 39. but should raise it again at the last *d.*
40. I will raise him up at the last *d.* 44, 54.
8. 56. your father Abraham rejoiced to see my *d.*
9. 4. I must work the work of him while it is *d.*
Acts 1. 2. until the *d.* in which he was taken up
12. 21. on a set *d.* Herod sat upon his throne
16. 35. and when it was *d.* 23. 12. | 27. 39.
17. 31. because he hath appointed a *d.* in which
27. 29. they cast four anchors, and wished for *d.*
Rom. 2. 5. but treasurest wrath against the *d.* of wrath
13. 12. *d.* is at hand, let us therefore cast off works
14. 6. he that regardeth a *d.* regardeth it to the Lord
1 *Cor.* 3. 13. for the *d.* shall declare it, because it shall
4. † 3. should be judged of you or of man's *d.*
2 *Cor.* 6. 2. behold, now is the *d.* of salvation
Eph. 4. 30. ye are sealed to the *d.* of redemption
Phil. 1. 6. will perform it until the *d.* of Jesus Christ
1 *Thess.* 5. 5. ye are all the children of the *d.*
8. but let us who are of the *d.* be sober, putting on
Heb. 4. 7. again he limiteth a certain *d.* saying, to-d.
8. would he not afterward spoken of another *d.*?
10. 25. the more as ye see the *d.* approaching
2 *Pet.* 1. 19. till the *d.* dawn, and the day-star arise
3. 12. hasting to the coming of the *d.* of God
Rev. 9. 15. which were prepared for an hour and a *d.*
See Atonement, Battle, Calamity, Darkness, Evil, Holy, Last.

All the DAY.

Psal. 25. 5. teach me, for on thee do I wait *all the d.*
71. 15. my mouth shew forth thy salvation *all the d.*
89. 16. in thy name shall they rejoice *all the d.*
102. 8. mine enemies reproach me *all the d.*
119. 97. thy law is my meditation *all the d.*
Isa. 28. 24. doth the ploughman plough *all the d.* to sow
65. 2. I have spread out my hands *all the d.*
5. these are a smoke, a fire that burneth *all the d.*
Lam. 1. 13. hath made me desolate and faint *all the d.*
3. 3. he turneth his hand against me *all the d.*
14. I was a derision to my people *all the d.*
62. thou hast heard their device aga. me *all the d.*
Mat. 20. 6. why stand ye here *all the d.* idle?

All the DAY *long.*

Deut. 28. 32. fail with longing for them *all the d. long*
33. 12. the Lord shall cover him *all the d. long*
Psal. 32. 3. through my roaring *all the d. long*
35. 28. shall speak of thy praise *all the d. long*
38. 6. I am troubled, I go mourning *all the d. long*
12. they imagine deceits *all the d. long*
44. 8. in God we boast *all the d. long*, and praise
22. for thy sake we are killed *all the d. long*
71. 24. shall talk of thy righteousness *all the d. long*
73. 14. for *all the d. long* have I been plagued
Prov. 21. 26. he coveteth greedily *all the d. long*
23. 17. be in the fear of the Lord *all the d. long*
Rom. 10. 21. *all the d. long* I stretched forth my hands

DAY *of death.*

Gen. 27. 2. I am old, I know not the *d. of* my *death*
Judg. 13. 7. child be a Nazarite to *d. of* his *death*
1 *Sam.* 15. 35. Sam. came not to see Saul till *d. of death*
2 *Sam.* 6. 23. Michal had no child till *d. of death*
20. 3. concubines were shut up to *d. of* their *death*
2 *Kings* 15. 5. Uzziah the king was a leper to the *d.* of his *death*, 2 *Chron.* 26. 21.
Eccl. 7. 1. the *d. of death* better than *d.* of one's birth
8. 8. neither hath he power in the *d. of death*
Jer. 52. 11. put him in prison till the *d. of* his *death*
34. every day a portion, till the *d. of* his *death*

By DAY, and *Day by day.*

Gen. 39. 10. as she spake to Joseph *d. by d.*
Exod. 13. 21. the Lord went before them *by d.*
22. he took not away the pillar of the cloud *by d.*
29. 38. thou shalt offer two lambs of the first year *d. by d.* continually, *Num.* 28. † 3.
Exod. 40. 38. for the cloud of the Lord was upon the tabernacle *by d.* and fire by night, *Num.* 9. 16.
Num. 10. 34. the cloud of the Lord was on them *by d.* 14. 14. *Deut.* 1. 33. *Neh.* 9. 19.
Judg. 6. 27. because he could not do it *by d.*
2 *Sam.* 21. 10. nor birds of air to rest on them *by d.*
1 *Chron.* 12. 22. *d. by d.* there came to help David
2 *Chron.* 21. 15. by reason of the sickness *d. by d.*
24. 11. thus they did *d. by d.* and gathered money
30. 21. the priests praised the Lord *d. by d.*
Ezra 6. 9. let it be given *d. by d.* without fail
Neh. 8. 18. *d. by d.* he read in the law of God
Psal. 91. 5. nor the arrow that flieth *by d.*
121. 6. the sun shall not smite thee *by d.*
136. 8. the sun to rule *by d.* for his mercy endureth
Isa. 60. 19. the sun shall be no more thy light *by d.*
Jer. 31. 35. who giveth the sun for a light *by d.*
Ezek. 12. 3. and remove *by d.* in their sight
7. I did so, I brought forth my stuff *by d.*
Luke 11. 3. give us *d. by d.* our daily bread
2 *Cor.* 4. 16. the inward man is renewed *d. by d.*
Rev. 21. 25. the gates of it shall not be shut *by d.*

Every DAY.

Gen. 6. † 5. the thoughts of his heart evil *every d.*
Exod. 16. 4. go out and gather a certain rate *every d.*
29. 36. thou shalt offer a bullock *every d.*
1 *Sam.* 23. 14. and Saul sought David *every d.*
2 *Sam.* 13. 37. David mourned for his son *every d.*
2 *Kings* 25. 30. given him a daily rate for *every d.*
1 *Chron.* 16. 37. minister, as *every d.* work required
2 *Chron.* 8. 13. even after a certain rate *every d.*
14. as the duty of *every d.* required, *Ezra* 3. 4.
Neh. 11. 23. a portion for singers, due for *every d.*
12. 47. and the porters *every d.* his portion
Esth. 2. 11. Mordecai walked *every d.* before court
Psal. 7. 11. God is angry with the wicked *every d.*
56. 5. *every d.* they wrest my words, their thoughts
145. 2. *every d.* will I bless thee and praise thy name
Isa. 51. 13. and hast feared continually *every d.*
52. 5. and my name *every d.* is blasphemed
Ezek. 43. 25. seven days prepare *every d.* a goat
Luke 16. 19. rich man fared sumptuously *every d.*
Rom. 14. 5. another esteemeth *every d.* alike

Feast DAY.

Psal. 81. 3. blow trumpet on our solemn *feast d.*
Mat. 26. 5. they said, not on the *feast d. Mark* 14. 2.
John 2. 23. in *feast d.* many believed in his name

First DAY.

Gen. 1. 5. the evening and morning were *first d.*
8. 5. on the *first d.* of the month the mountains were seen, 13. *Exod.* 40. 2, 17. *Lev.* 23. 24.
Exod. 12. 15. the *first d.* ye shall put away leaven, whoso eateth from *first d.* to seventh
16. in the *first d.* shall be an holy convocation, *Lev.* 23. 7, 35. *Num.* 28. 18. | 29. 1.
Lev. 23. 39. on the *first d.* shall be a sabbath
40. shall take on *first d.* boughs of goodly trees
Num. 1. 1. the Lord spake to Moses on the *first d.*
18. they assembled the congregation on the *first d.*
33. 38. on the *first d.* Aaron went up to mount Hor
Deut. 16. 4. the flesh sacrificed *first d.* not remain
2 *Chron.* 29. 17. they began on *first d.* to sanctify
Ezra 3. 6. from the *first d.* began they to offer
7. 9. on the *first d.* began he to go up from Babylon, and on the *first d.* came he to Jerusalem
10. 16. sat down on *first d.* of the tenth month
17. by *first d.* of first month they made an end
Neh. 8. 2. Ezra brought the law on *first d.* of month
18. from *first* unto last *d.* he read in the law of God
Ezek. 26. 1. in the *first d.* the word of the Lord came, 29. 17. | 31. 1. | 32. 1. *Hag.* 1. 1.
45. 18. in *first d.* of the month shalt offer a bullock
Dan. 10. 12. from the *first d.* thou didst set thy heart
Mat. 26. 17. *first d.* of unleavened bread, *Mark* 14. 12.
Acts 20. 18. ye know from *first d.* I came into Asia
Phil. 1. 5. for your fellowship from *first d.* till now
See Week.

Second DAY.

Gen. 1. 8. the evening and morning were *second d.*
Exod. 2. 13. and when he went out the *second d.*
Num. 7. 18. on the *second d.* Nethaneel did offer
29. 17. on the *second d.* offer twelve young bullocks
Josh. 6. 14. the *second d.* they compassed city once
10. 32. took Lachish on the *second d.* and smote it
Judg. 20. 24. Israel came against Benjamin *second d.*
1 *Sam.* 20. 34. Jonathan did eat no meat *second d.*
2 *Chron.* 3. 2. he began to build *second d.* of the month
Neh. 8. 13. on the *second d.* were gathered together
Esth. 7. 2. the king said to Esther the *second d.*
Jer. 41. 4. the *second d.* after he had slain Gedaliah
Ezek. 43. 22. on the *second d.* thou shalt offer a kid

Third DAY.

Gen. 1. 13. evening and morning were the *third d.*
22. 4. on *third d.* Abraham saw the place afar off
31. 22. it was told Laban on *third d.* Jacob was fled
34. 25. on *third d.* when they were sore, two sons
Exod. 4. † 10. nor since the *third d. Josh.* 3. † 4.
19. 11. be ready against the *third d.* for the *third d.* Lord will come down on mount Sinai, 15.
Lev. 7. 17. the remainder of the flesh of sacrifice on the *third d.* shall be burnt with fire, 19. 6.
Num. 19. 12. shall purify himself on *third d.* 31. 19.
19. the clean person sprinkle unclean on *third d.*
29. 20. on the *third d.* eleven bullocks, two rams
Deut. 19. † 4. hated not from yesterday *third d.* 6.
Josh. 9. 17. Israel came to their cities on the *third d.*
Judg. 20. 30. Israel went against Benj. the *third d.*
1 *Sam.* 4. † 7. not such a thing yesterday or *third d.*
19. † 7. was in his presence as yesterday or *third d.*
2 *Sam.* 3. † 17. ye sought Dav. yesterday and *third d.*
1 *Kings* 12. 12. came to Rehob. *third d.* 2 *Chr.* 10. 12.
2 *Kings* 13. † 5. Isr. dwelt as yesterday and *third d.*
20. 5. on the *third d.* go up to the house of Lord, 8.
1 *Chron.* 11. † 2. on *third d.* wast he that leddest out
Ezra 6. 15. the house was finished on the *third d.*
Esth. 5. 1. on the *third d.* Esther put on royal apparel
Hos. 6. 2. in the *third d.* he will raise us up and live
Mat. 16. 21. suffer, and be killed, and be raised again the *third d.* 17. 23. *Luke* 9. 22.
20. 19. and the *third d.* he shall rise again, *Mark* 9. 31. | 10. 34. *Luke* 18. 33. | 24. 7, 46.
27. 64. the sepulchre be made sure till the *third d.*

Luke 13. 32. and the *third d.* I shall be perfected
24. 21. to-day is the *third d.* since all these things
John 2. 1. on the *third d.* there was a marriage in Cana
Acts 27. 19. the *third d.* we cast out tackling of ship
1 Cor. 15. 4. and that he rose again the *third d.*

Fourth DAY.

Gen. 1. 19. evening and morning were the *fourth d.*
Num. 29. 23. on the *fourth d.* ten bullocks, two rams
2 Chron. 20. 26. on the *fourth d.* they assembled
Ezra 8. 33. on *fourth d.* was silver and gold weighed
Zech. 7. 1. word came to Zechariah on the *fourth d.*

Fifth DAY.

Gen. 1. 23. the evening and morning were the *fifth d.*
Num. 29. 26. on the *fifth d.* nine bullocks, two rams
Ezek. 1. 1. in the *fifth d.* of the month, 2. | 8. 1.
33. 21. in the *fifth d.* one came unto me, saying

Sixth DAY.

Gen. 1. 31. evening and morning were the *sixth d.*
Exod. 16. 5. on the *sixth d.* gather twice as much, 22.
29. giveth you on the *sixth d.* the bread of two days
Num. 7. 42. on the *sixth d.* Eliasaph offered
29. 29. on the *sixth d.* eight bullocks, two rams

Seventh DAY.

Gen. 2. 2. on the *seventh d.* God ended his work
3. and God blessed the *seventh d.* Exod. 20. 11.
Exod. 12. 15. eateth leaven from first d. to *seventh d.*
16. on the *seventh d.* shall be an holy convocation, Lev. 23. 8. Num. 28. 25.
13. 6. and in the *seventh d.* shall be a feast
16. 26. six days gather it, but the *seventh d.* is the sabbath, 20. 10. Lev. 23. 3. Deut. 5. 14.
27. there went out some of the *seventh d.*
29. let no man go out of his place on the *seventh d.*
24. 16. on the *seventh d.* he called unto Moses
31. 17. on the *seventh d.* God rested, Heb. 4. 4.
34. 21. on *seventh d.* thou shalt rest, in earing-time
35. 2. on *seventh d.* there shall be a holy d. to you
Lev. 13. 5. the priest shall look on him the *seventh d.* 6, 27, 32, 34, 51. | 14. 39.
14. 9. the *seventh d.* he shall shave it, Num. 6. 9.
Num. 19. 12. on the *seventh d.* he shall be clean
19. on the *seventh d.* purify himself, 31. 19.
31. 24. ye shall wash your clothes on the *seventh d.*
Deut. 16. 8. on the *seventh d.* a solemn assembly
Josh. 6. 4. on *seventh d.* compass city seven times, 15.
Judg. 14. 15. on *seventh d.* they said to Samson's wife
17. on the *seventh d.* he told her, because she
2 Sam. 12. 18. on the *seventh d.* the child died
1 Kings 20. 29. on the *seventh d.* battle was joined
2 Kings 25. 8. on the *seventh d.* came Nebuzar-adan
Esth. 1. 10. on *seventh d.* when Ahasuerus was merry
Ezek. 30. 20. in the *seventh d.* the word came
45. 20. and so do the *seventh d.* of the month
Heb. 4. 4. he spake of the *seventh d.* on this wise, God did rest the *seventh d.* from all his works

Eighth DAY.

Exod. 22. 30. on the *eighth d.* thou shalt give it me
Lev. 9. 1. on the *eighth d.* Moses called Aaron
12. 3. on *eighth d.* flesh of foreskin be circumcised
14. 10. on the *eighth d.* he shall take two he-lambs
23. bring two turtles on *eighth d.* 15. 14. Num. 6. 10.
22. 27. from the *eighth d.* it shall be accepted
23. 36. on the *eighth d.* shall be an holy convoca.
39. and on the *eighth d.* shall be a sabbath
Num. 29. 35. on the *eighth d.* ye shall have a solemn assembly, 2 Chron. 7. 9. Neh. 8. 18.
Ezek. 43. 27. on *eighth d.* priests make burnt-offerings
Luke 1. 59. that on the *eighth d.* they came to circumcise the child, Acts 7. 8. Phil. 3. 5.

Ninth DAY.

Lev. 23. 32. shall afflict your souls in the *ninth d.*
2 Kings 25. 3. on *ninth d.* famine was sore, Jer. 52. 6.
Jer. 39. 2. the *ninth d.* the city was broken up

Tenth DAY.

Exod. 12. 3. the *tenth d.* of this month take a lamb
Lev. 16. 29. on the *tenth d.* of the month ye shall afflict your souls, 23. 27. Num. 29. 7.
25. 9. on *tenth d.* the trumpet of jubilee shall sound
Josh. 4. 19. people came out of Jordan on *tenth d.*
2 Kings 25. 1. on the *tenth d.* Nebuchadnezzar came against Jerusalem, Jer. 52. 4. Ezek. 24. 1.
Jer. 52. 12. on the *tenth d.* Neb. burnt house of Ld.
Ezek. 20. 1. on *tenth d.* the elders came to inquire
40. 1. on *tenth d.* the hand of the Lord was upon

Eleventh DAY.

Num. 7. 72. on the *eleventh d.* Pagiel of Asher offered

Twelfth DAY.

Num. 7. 78. on *twelfth d.* Ahira of Naphtali offered
Ezra 8. 31. departed on *twelfth d.* to go to Jerusalem
Ezek. 29. 1. on *twelfth d.* the word came to Ezekiel

Thirteenth DAY.

Esth. 3. 12. king's scribes were called on *thirteenth d.*
13. to destroy all Jews on *thirteenth d.* 8. 12. | 9. 1.
9. 17. on the *thirteenth d.* of month Adar they rested
18. the Jews at Shushan assemb. on *thirteenth d.*

Fourteenth DAY.

Exod. 12. 6. ye shall keep the lamb till *fourteenth d.*
18. on *fourteenth d.* ye shall eat unleavened bread
Lev. 23. 5. in the *fourteenth d.* is the Lord's passover Num. 9. 3, 5. | 28. 16. Josh. 5. 10. 2 Chr. 30. 15. | 35. 1. Ezra 6. 19. Ezek. 45. 21.
Num. 9. 11. on *fourteenth d.* at even they shall eat it
Esth. 9. 15. Jews gathered together on *fourteenth d.*
17. and on the *fourteenth d.* of the same rested they
Acts 27. 33. this is *fourteenth d.* ye continued fasting

Fifteenth DAY.

Exod. 16. 1. came to wildern. of Sinai on *fifteenth d.*
Lev. 23. 6. and on *fifteenth d.* is feast, Num. 28. 17.
34. the *fifteenth d.* of the seventh month, 39. Num. 29. 12. Ezek. 45. 25.
Num. 33. 3. departed from Rameses on *fifteenth d.*
1 Kings 12. 32. he ordained a feast on *fifteenth d.* 33.
Esth. 9. 18. the Jews on *fifteenth d.* rested yearly, 21.
Ezek. 32. 17. on *fifteenth d.* word of L. came to Ezek.

Sixteenth DAY.

2 Chr. 29. 17. and in *sixteenth d.* they made an end

Seventeenth DAY.

Gen. 7. 11. on *seventeenth d.* were fount. broken up
8. 4. ark rested on *seventeenth d.* on mount Ararat

Twentieth DAY.

Num. 10. 11. on *twentieth d.* the cloud was taken up
Ezra 10. 9. on *twentieth d.* people sat in the streets

Twenty-first DAY.

Exod. 12. 18. eat unleaven. bread till *twenty-first d.*
Hag. 2. 1. in *twenty-first d.* came the word to Haggai

Twenty-third DAY.

2 Chron. 7. 10. *t. t. d.* Solomon sent people to tents
Esth. 8. 9. on *t.-t. d.* written as Mordecai commanded

Twenty-fourth DAY.

Neh. 9. 1. on *t.-fourth d.* Isr. assembled with fast.
Dan. 10. 4. on *t.-fourth d.* I was by river Hiddekel
Hag. 1. 15. in *t.-fourth d.* Ld. stirred up Zerubbabel
2. 10. in the *t.-fourth d.* word came to Haggai, 20.
18. consider from the *t.-fourth d.* of nine month
Zech. 1. 7. on the *t.-fourth d.* came word to Zechariah

Twenty-fifth DAY.

Neh. 6. 15. the wall was finish. in the *twenty-fifth d.*
Jer. 52. 31. on *t.-fifth d.* Evil-merodach lifted head

Twenty-seventh DAY.

Gen. 8. 14. on the *t.-seventh d.* was the earth dried
2 Kings 25. 27. on *t.-s. d.* Evil-merodach lifted head

Good DAY.

1 Sam. 25. 8. we come in a *good d.* give to David
Esth. 8. 17. Jews had gladness and a *good d.* 9. 19.
9. 22. was turned from mourning into a *good d.*

Great DAY.

Jer. 30. 7. alas, that *d.* is *great*, none is like it
Hos. 1. 11. for *great* shall be the *d.* of Jezreel
Joel 2. 11. the *d.* of the Lord is *great* and terrible
31. sun to darkness, moon to blood, before the *g.* and terrible *d.* of the Lord come, Acts 2. 20.
Zeph. 1. 14. the *great d.* of the Lord is near
Mal. 4. 5. before the coming of *great d.* of the Lord
John 7. 37. that *great d.* of the feast, Jesus cried
Jude 6. reserved unto the judgment of the *great d.*
Rev. 6. 17. for the *great d.* of his wrath is come
16. 14. to gather to the battle of the *great d.*

In the DAY.

Gen. 2. 4. *in the d.* that the Lord made the earth
17. *in the d.* thou eatest thereof thou shalt die
3. 5. *in the d.* ye eat, your eyes shall be opened
31. 40. thus I was, *in the d.* drought consumed me
35. 3. who answered me *in the d.* of my distress
Exod. 32. 34. nevertheless *in the d.* when I visit
Lev. 6. 5. *in the d.* of his trespass-offering
20. offer *in the d.* when he is anointed, 7. 36.
7. 35. *in the d.* he presented them to minister
14. 2. law of leper *in the d.* of his cleans. Num. 6. 9.
† 57. *in the d.* of the clean and unclean
Num. 28. 26. also *in the d.* of the first-fruits
30. 5. if her father disallow *in the d.* he heareth
7. husband held his peace *in the d.* he heard it
Josh. 10. 12. *in the d.* L. delivered up the Amorites
14. 11. as strong as I was *in the d.* Moses sent me
1 Sam. 20. † 19. where thou didst hide *in the d.*
21. 6. put hot bread *in the d.* it was taken away
2 Sam. 22. 1. *in the d.* the Lord had delivered him
1 Kings 2. 8. who cursed me *in the d.* that I fled
Neh. 13. 15. *in the d.* wherein they sold victuals
Esth. 9. 1. *in the d.* the enemies of the Jews hoped
Job 20. 28. his goods flow away *in the d.* of wrath
Psal. 95. 8. as *in the d.* of temptation, Heb. 3. 8.
102. 2. hide not thy face *in the d.* of trouble, *in the d.* when I call, answer me speedily
110. 3. thy people be willing *in the d.* of thy power
5. shall strike through kings *in the d.* of his wrath
137. 7. remember Edom *in the d.* of Jerusalem
138. 3. *in the d.* when I cried, thou answeredst me
Prov. 6. 34. he will not spare *in the d.* of vengeance
11. 4. riches profit not *in the d.* of wrath
24. 10. if thou faint *in the d.* of adversity
Eccl. 7. 14. *in the d.* of prosperity be joyful, but *in the d.* of adversity consider
8. 8. neither hath he power *in the d.* of death
12. 3. *in the d.* when the keepers shall tremble
Cant. 3. 11. crowned him *in the d.* of his espousals, and *in the d.* of the gladness of his heart
8. 8. *in the d.* when she shall be spoken for
Isa. 9. 4. broken the yoke as *in the d.* of Midian
10. 3. what will ye do *in the d.* of visitation?
11. 16. *in the d.* he came out of Egypt, Hos. 2. 15.
13. 13. shall remove *in the d.* of his fierce anger
17. 11. *in the d.* shalt thou make thy plant grow *in the d.* of grief and desperate sorrow
30. 25. *in the d.* of great slaughter, when the towers
26. *in the d.* that the Lord bindeth up the breach
58. 3. *in the d.* of your fast you find pleasure
Jer. 16. 19. O Lord, my refuge *in the d.* of affliction
17. 17. thou art my hope *in the d.* of evil
18. 17. shew back and not face *in the d.* of calamity
36. 30. his dead body shall be cast out *in the d.*
Lam. 1. 12. afflicted me *in the d.* of his fierce anger
2. 1. remembered not his footstool *in the d.* of anger
3. 57. thou drewest near *in the d.* that I called
Ezek. 7. 19. gold not deliver them *in the d.* of wrath
16. 4. thy nativity *in the d.* thou wast born, 5.
56. Sodom not mentioned *in the d.* of thy pride
27. 27. they shall fall *in the d.* of thy ruin
30. 9. great pain came on them as *in the d.* of Egypt
32. 10. every man for his life *in the d.* of thy fall
33. 12. *in the d.* he turneth from his wickedness, not able to live *in the d.* that he sinneth
Hos. 2. 3. lest I set her as *in the d.* she was born
4. 5. therefore shalt thou fall *in the d.* and prophet
Amos 1. 14. with a tempest *in the d.* of a whirlwind
8. 9. I will darken the earth *in the* clear *d.*
Obad. 11. *in the d.* thou stoodest on the other side
12. nor rejoiced *in the d.* of their destruction
14. those of his that did remain *in the d.* of dist.
Mal. 4. 3. *in the d.* that I shall do this, saith Lord
Luke 17. 30. *in the d.* when the Son is revealed
John 11. 9. if any walk *in the d.* he stumbleth not
Rom. 2. 16. *in d.* when G. shall judge secrets of men
13. 13. let us walk honestly as *in the d.*
1 Cor. 1. 8. may be blameless *in the d.* of our Lord
2 Cor. 6. 2. *in the d.* of salvation I succoured thee
Phil. 2. 16. that I may rejoice *in the d.* of Christ
Heb. 8. 9. *in the d.* when I took them by the hand
1 Pet. 2. 12. may glorify God *in the d.* of visitation

DAY *of Judgment.*

Mat. 10. 15. it shall be more tolerable for Sodom in the *d. of judgment*, 11. 24. Mark 6. 11.
11. 22. more tolerable for Tyre and Sidon at *d. of j.*
12. 36. shall give account thereof in *d. of judgment*
2 Pet. 2. 9. and to reserve the unjust to *d. of judg.*
3. 7. are reserved unto fire against the *d. of judg.*
1 John 4. 17. we may have boldness in the *d. of j.*

DAY *of the Lord.*

Isa. 2. 12. *d. of the L.* shall be on every one proud
13. 6. *d. of the L.* is at hand, Joel 1. 15. Zeph. 1. 7.
9. the *d. of the L.* cometh, Joel 2. 1. Zech. 14. 1.
34. 8. for it is the *d. of the Lord's* vengeance
Jer. 46. 10. this is the *d. of the Lord* God of hosts
Lam. 2. 22. in the *d. of the Lord's* anger none escaped
Ezek. 13. 5. to stand in battle in the *d. of the Lord*
30. 3. the *d. of the L.* is near, Joel 3. 14. Obad. 15.
Amos 5. 18. woe to you that desire the *d. of the L.*
Zeph. 1. 8. in *d. of the L.'s* sacrifice I will punish
18. shall deliver them in the *d. of the L.'s* wrath
2. 2. before the *d. of the L.'s* anger come on you
3. ye shall be hid in the *d. of the Lord's* anger
Mal. 4. 5. before the coming of the *d. of the Lord*
1 Cor. 5. 5. spirit may be saved in *d. of the Lord*
2 Cor. 1. 14. as ye are ours in the *d. of the Lord*
1 Thess. 5. 2. *d. of L.* cometh as a thief, 2 Pet. 3. 10.
Rev. 1. 10. I was in the Spirit on *the Lord's d.*
See Great DAY.

One DAY.

Gen. 27. 45. why deprived of you both in *one d.?*
Lev. 22. 28. not kill it and her young in *one d.*
Num. 11. 19. ye shall not eat *one d.* or two days
1 Sam. 2. 34. in *one d.* they shall die both of them
27. 1. I shall *one d.* perish by the hand of Saul
1 Kings 4. 22. Solomon's provision for *one d.* was
20. 29. Israel slew of Syrians 100,000 in *one d.*
2 Chr. 28. 6. Pekah slew in Judah 120,000 in *one d.*
Ezra 10. 13. neither is this the work of *one d.*
Esth. 3. 13. kill children and women in *one d.* 8. 12.
Isa. 9. 14. Lord cut off branch and rush in *one d.*
10. 17. shall devour his thorns and briers in *one d.*
47. 9. two things shall come to thee in *one d.*
66. 8. shall earth be made to bring forth in *one d.?*
Zech. 3. 9. remove the iniquity of land in *one d.*
14. 7. it shall be *one d.* which shall be known
Acts 21. 7. we abode with the brethren *one d.*
28. 13. and after *one d.* the south wind blew
Rom. 14. 5. one esteemeth *one d.* above another
1 Cor. 10. 8. fell in *one d.* twenty-three thousand
2 Pet. 3. 8. *one d.* with the Lord as a thousand years
Rev. 18. 8. therefore her plagues come in *one d.*

DAY, joined with *night.*

Gen. 1. 14. lights to divide *d.* from the *night*
18. to rule over the *d.* and over the *night*
8. 22. cold and heat, *d.* and *night*, shall not cease
31. 39. I bare loss, whether stolen by *d.* or *night*
Exod. 10. 13. Lord brought an east wind *d.* and *night*
13. 21. to give them light to go by *d.* and *night*
Lev. 8. 35. abide at door of tabernacle *d.* and *night*
Num. 11. 32. people stood up that *d.* and all *night*
Deut. 28. 66. and thou shalt fear *d.* and *night*
Josh. 1. 8. this book of the law not depart, but thou shalt meditate therein *d.* and *night*, Psal. 1. 2.
1 Sam. 19. 24. lay naked all that *d.* and that *night*
1 Kings 8. 29. that thine eyes might be opened toward this house *night* and *d.* 2 Chr. 6. 20.
Neh. 1. 6. which I pray before thee *d.* and *night*
4. 9. and set a watch against them *d.* and *night*
Esth. 4. 16. neither eat nor drink *night* or *d.*
Job 17. 12. they change the *night* into *d.*
26. 10. till the *d.* and *night* come to an end
Psal. 32. 4. *d.* and *night* thy hand was heavy on me
42. 3. my tears have been my meat *d.* and *night*
55. 10. *d.* and *night* they go about it on the walls
74. 16. the *d.* is thine, the *night* also is thine
88. 1. O Lord, I have cried *d.* and *night* before thee
139. 12. but the *night* shineth as the *d.*
Eccl. 8. 16. that neither *d.* nor *night* seeth sleep
Isa. 4. 5. smoke by *d.* and flaming fire by *night*
27. 3. I the Lord will keep it *d.* and *night*
34. 10. it shall not be quenched *d.* nor *night*
38. 12. with pining sickness from *d.* to *night*
13. from *d.* to *night* wilt thou make an end of me
60. 11. gates, they shall not be shut *d.* nor *night*
62. 6. watchmen never hold their peace *d.* nor *night*
Jer. 9. 1. that I might weep *d.* and *night* for slain
14. 17. eyes run down tears *d.* and *night*, Lam. 2. 18.
16. 13. and there serve other gods *d.* and *night*
33. 20. that there should not be *d.* nor *night*
Zech. 14. 7. day known to the Lord, not *d.* nor *night*
Mark 4. 27. and should sleep and rise *night* and *d.*
5. 5. *d.* and *night* he was in the mountains
14. 30. this *d.* even this *night*, before the cock crow
Luke 2. 37. with fastings and prayers *night* and *d.*
18. 7. his elect, which cry *d.* and *night* to him
Acts 9. 24. watched gates *night* and *d.* to kill him
20. 31. cease not to warn every one *night* and *d.*
26. 7. our tribes instantly serving God *d.* and *night*
2 Cor. 11. 25. thrice I suffered shipwreck, a *d.* and *n.*
1 Thess. 2. 9. labouring *d.* and *n.* because would not
3. 10. *night* and *d.* praying exceedingly, 1 Tim. 5. 5.
2 Thess. 3. 8. but wrought with labour *night* and *d.*
2 Tim. 1. 3. without ceasing I have remembrance of thee in my prayers *night* and *d.*
Rev. 4. 8. and they rest not *d.* and *night*, saying
7. 15. and serve him *d.* and *night* in his temple
8. 12. *d.* shone not for a third part, and the *night*
12. 10. who accused them before God *d.* and *night*
14. 11. they have no rest *d.* nor *night*, who worship
20. 10. be tormented *d.* and *night* for ever and ever

Sabbath-DAY.

Exod. 16. 26. the seventh *d.* is the *sabbath*, 20. 10.
20. 8. remember the *sabbath-d.* to keep it holy, Deut. 5. 12.
11. Lord blessed the *sabbath d.* and hallowed it
31. 15. whosoever doth any work on *sabbath-d.*
35. 3. ye shall kindle no fire on the *sabbath-d.*
Num. 15. 32. a man that gathered sticks on *sabbath d.*
28. 9. offer on the *sabbath-d.* two lambs of first year
Deut. 5. 15. God commanded to keep the *sabbath-d.*
Neh. 10. 31. if the people sell victuals on *sabbath-d.*
13. 15. burdens brought to Jerusalem on *sabbath d.*
17. evil that ye do, and profane the *sabbath-d.*
19. should no burden be brought in on *sabbath-d.*
22. Levites keep the gates to sanctify *sabbath-d.*
Jer. 17. 21. and bear no burden on the *sabbath-d.*
22. nor carry forth a burden on the *sabbath-d.*

Ezek. 46. 4. the prince shall offer in the *sabbath-d.*
Mat. 12. 1. Jesus went on the *sabbath-d.* through the corn, and disciples were an hungered, *Mark* 2. 23.
8. for the Son of man is Lord of the *sabbath-d.*
11. if it fall into a pit on *sabbath-d. Luke* 14. 5.
24. 20. pray that your flight be not on *sabbath-d.*
Mark 2. 24. why do they on *s.-d.* that is not lawful?
3. 2. whether he would heal on *sab.-d. Luke* 6. 7.
6. 2. he went into the synagogue on the *sabbath-d. Luke* 4. 16. *Acts* 13. 14.
Luke 13. 16. be loosed from this bond on *sabbath-d.*
14. 1. as he went to eat bread on the *sabbath-d.*
23. 56. prepared spices, and rested the *sabbath-d.*
John 5. 10. it is *sabbath-d.* it is not lawful to carry
16. because he had done these things on *sabbath-d.*
7. 22. and ye on the *sabbath-d.* circumcise a man
9. 14. it was the *sabbath-d.* when Jesus made clay
19. 31. bodies not remain on the cross on *sabbath-d.*
Acts 13. 27. which are read every *sabbath d.* 15. 21.
44. next *sabbath-d.* came almost the whole city

Same DAY.

Gen. 7. 11. the *same d.* were the fountains broken up
13. the self-*same d.* entered Noah into the ark
15. 18. in that *same d.* the Lord made a covenant
Exod. 12. 17. the *same d.* I brought your armies, 51.
Lev. 7. 15. flesh eaten the *same d.* 16. | 19. 6. | 22. 30.
23. 14. ye shall eat no parched corn till *same d.*
28. and ye shall do no work in that *same d.*
29. that shall not be afflicted in that *same d.*
Num. 6. 11. priest shall hallow his head that *same d.*
Deut. 32. 48. the Lord spake to Moses that *same d.*
1 *Kings* 8. 64. *same d.* king hallowed middle court
13. 3. and he gave a sign the *same d.* saying
Ezek. 23. 38. have defiled my sanctuary, *same d.* 39.
24. 2. write thee the name of this *same d.* king of Babylon set himself against Jerusalem this *same d.*
Zeph. 1. 9. the *same d.* also will I punish those
Zech. 6. 10. take of them, and come the *same d.*
Luke 17. 29. but the *same d.* Lot went out of Sodom
23. 12. the *same d.* Pilate and Herod made friends
John 5. 9. and on the *same d.* was the sabbath
20. 19. *same d.* at evening Jesus stood in midst
Acts 1. 22. unto the *same d.* that he was taken up
2. 41. the *s. d.* were added to church 3,000 souls

Since the DAY.

Exod. 10. 6. *since the d.* they were on the earth
Deut. 4. 32. *since the d.* that God created man
1 *Sam.* 8. 8. *since the d.* that I brought them up out of Egypt to this day, 1 *Kings* 8. 16. 1 *Chron.* 17. 5.
2 *Kings* 8. 6. *since the d.* that she left the land
Jer. 7. 25. *since the d.* your fathers came forth
Col. 1. 6. as in you, *since the d.* ye heard of it
9. *since the d.* we heard it, do not cease to pray

That DAY.

Exod. 8. 22. I will sever in *that d.* land of Goshen
10. 13. Lord brought east wind on land all *that d.*
28. *that d.* thou seest my face, thou shalt die
13. 8. thou shalt shew thy son in *that d.* saying
14. 30. thus the L. saved Israel *that d.* out of hand
32. 28. there fell of the people *that d.* 3,000
Lev. 16. 30. *that d.* shall the priest make atonement
Num. 9. 6. they could not keep the passover *that d.*
30. 14. because he held his peace in *that d.*
Deut. 1. 39. your children in *that d.* had no knowledge
21. 23. thou shalt in any wise bury him *that d.*
31. 18. I will surely hide my face in *that d.*
Josh. 6. 15. only *that d.* they compassed the city
14. 12. heardest in *that d.* how Anakims were there
Judg. 20. 26. Israel fasted *that d.* 1 *Sam.* 7. 6.
1 *Sam.* 8. 18. and ye shall cry out in *that d.* and the Lord will not hear you in *that d.*
9. 24. so Saul did eat with Samuel *that d.*
10. 9. and all those signs came to pass *that d.*
12. 18. the Lord sent thunder and rain *that d.*
14. 23. so the Lord saved Israel *that d.*
37. Saul asked, but he answered him not *that d.*
16. 13. Spirit of Lord came on David from *that d.*
18. 9. Saul eyed David from *that d.* and forward
2 *Sam.* 6. 9. David was afraid of the Lord *that d.*
11. 12. so Uriah abode in Jerusalem *that d.*
1 *Kings* 14. 14. cut off the house of Jeroboam *that d.*
2 *Chron.* 15. + 11. offered *that d.* of spoil 700 oxen
18. 24. behold, thou shalt see on *that d.*
Neh. 8. 17. to *that d.* Israel had not done so
Esth. 3. 14. they should be ready against *that d.* 8. 13.
Job 3. 4. let *that d.* be darkness, let not G. regard it
Psal. 146. 4. in *that* very *d.* his thoughts perish
Prov. 12. + 16. a fool's wrath is in *that d.* known
Isa. 2. 11. Lord alone shall be exalted in *that d.* 17.
10. 32. as yet shall he remain at Nob *that d.*
19. 21. Egyptians shall know the Lord in *that d.*
24. 21. in *that d.* the Lord shall punish the host
26. 1. in *that d.* shall this song be sung in Judah
29. 18. in *that d.* shall the deaf hear the words
52. 6. they shall know in *that d.* that I am he
Jer. 39. + 10. Nebuz. gave them vineyards in *that d.*
16. they shall be accomplished in *that d.*
17. but I will deliver thee in *that d.* saith the L.
Ezek. 29. 21. in *that d.* Israel shall be exalted
38. 19. in *that d.* there shall be a great shaking
39. 22. know I am the Lord from *that d.* forward
48. 35. the name of the city from *that d.* shall be
Hos. 2. 18. and in *that d.* will I make a covenant
Joel 3. 18. in *that d.* mountains shall drop new wine
Amos 2. 16. he shall flee away naked in *that d.*
8. 3. the songs of the temple be howlings in *that d.*
Obad. 8. shall I not in *that d.* destroy the wise men?
Zeph. 1. 15. *that d.* is a day of wrath of trouble
Zech. 2. 11. nations be joined to the Lord in *that d.*
9. 16. Lord their God shall save them in *that d.*
11. 11. my covenant it was broken in *that d.*
12. 8. the feeble at *that d.* shall be as David
11. in *that d.* shall there be a great mourning
13. 1. in *that d.* there shall be a fountain opened
14. 4. his feet shall stand *that d.* on the mount
9. in *that d.* shall there be one Lord, his name one
Mal. 3. 17. in *that d.* when I make up my jewels
Mat. 7. 22. many will say to me in *that d.* Lord
24. 36. but of *that d.* knoweth no man, *Mark* 13. 32.
26. 29. till *that d.* I drink it new, *Mark* 14. 25.
Luke 6. 23. rejoice ye in *that d.* and leap for joy
10. 12. be more tolerable in that *d.* for Sodom

Luke 21. 34. and so *that d.* come on you unawares
23. 54. and that *d.* was the preparation and sabbath
John 1. 39. they came and abode with him *that d.*
11. 53. from *that d.* they took counsel together
14. 20. at *that d.* ye shall know I am in the Father
16. 23. and in *that d.* ye shall ask me nothing
26. at *that d.* ye shall ask in my name
1 *Thess.* 5. 4. *that d.* should overtake you as a thief
2 *Thess.* 1. 10. our testimony was believed in *that d.*
2. 3. *that d.* shall not come, except there come
2 *Tim.* 1. 12. I have committed to him against *that d.*
18. he may find mercy of the Lord in *that d.*
4. 8. the crown the Lord shall give me at *that d.*

This DAY.

Gen. 4. 14. thou hast driven me out *this d.* from earth
24. 12. I pray thee send me good speed *this d.*
25. 31. he said, sell me *this d.* thy birth-right
33. swear to me *this d.* and he sware unto him
41. 9. I do remember my faults *this d.*
48. 15. God who fed me all my life long to *this d.*
Exod. 12. 14. *this d.* shall be for a memorial
17. therefore observe *this d.* in your generations
13. 3. remember *this d.* in which ye came out, 4.
Deut. 1. 10. you are *this d.* as the stars of heaven
2. 25. *this d.* will I begin to put the dread of thee
4. 4. are alive every one of you *this d.* 5. 3.
5. 24. seen *this d.* that God doth talk with man
6. 24. as it is at *this d.* 8. 18. *Ezra* 9. 7.
7. 11. the statutes which I commanded thee *this d.* 4. 40. | 6. 6. | 8. 1, 11. | 10. 13. | 30. 2, 8.
8. 19. I testify against you *this d.* ye shall perish
11. 8. commandments which I command you *this d.* 13, 27, 28. | 13. 18. | 15. 5. | 19. 9. | 27. 1, 4.
32. statutes which I set before you *this d.*
12. 8. not do after all things ye do here *this d.*
26. 17. avouched *this d.* the Lord to be thy God
27. 9. *this d.* thou art become the people of the L.
29. 4. hath not given you ears to hear to *this d.*
10. ye stand *this d.* all of you before the Lord
18. whose heart turneth away *this d.* from the L.
30. 15. I set before thee *this d.* life and death, 19.
16. I command thee *this d.* to love the Lord
31. 27. while I am yet alive with you *this d.*
34. 6. no man knoweth his sepulchre to *this d.*
Josh. 3. 7. *this d.* will I begin to magnify thee
4. 9. the twelve stones are there unto *this d.*
7. 25. the Lord shall trouble thee *this d.*
14. 10. and now I am *this d.* eighty-five years old
11. I am as strong *this d.* as when Moses sent me
22. 16. to turn away *this d.* from following Lord
17. from which we are not cleansed till *this d.*
22. if it be in rebellion, save us not *this d.*
23. 8. cleave to the Ld. as ye have done unto *this d.*
24. 15. choose you *this d.* whom ye will serve
Judg. 1. 26. Luz is the name thereof unto *this d.*
10. 15. deliver us only, we pray thee, *this d.*
19. 30. since Israel came up out of the land of Egypt to *this d.* 1 *Sam.* 8. 8. 2 *Sam.* 7. 6. 2 *Kings* 21. 15. 1 *Chron.* 17. 5. *Jer.* 7. 25.
Ruth 4. 9. Boaz said, ye are witnesses *this d.* 10.
1 *Sam.* 10. 19. ye have *this d.* rejected your God
11. 13. there shall not a man be put to death *this d.*
14. 45. Jonathan hath wrought with God *this d.*
15. 28. Lord hath rent kingdom from thee *this d.*
17. 10. I defy the armies of Israel *this d.*
18. 21. thou shalt *this d.* be my son-in-law
21. 5. though it were sanctified *this d.* in the vessel
22. 8. my servant to lie in wait as at *this d.* 13.
25. 32. the Ld. which sent thee *this d.* to meet me
33. who kept me *this d.* from coming to shed blood
26. 21. my soul was precious in thine eyes *this d.*
24. as thy life was much set by *this d.* in my eyes
30. 25. made it an ordinance for Israel to *this d.*
2 *Sam.* 3. 39. I am *this d.* weak, though anoint. king
4. 3. Beerothites were sojourners unto *this d.*
1 *Kings* 8. 61. to keep his commands as at *this d.*
2 *Kings* 7. 9. *this d.* is a day of good tidings
17. 34. unto *this d.* do after former manners, 41.
2 *Chron.* 5. 9. and there it is unto *this d.*
35. 21. I come not against thee *this d.* but against
Neh. 9. 36. behold, we are servants *this d.*
Psal. 2. 7. the Lord said, thou art my Son, *this d.* have I begotten thee, *Acts* 13. 33. *Heb.* 1. 5.
118. 24. *this* is the *d.* which the Lord hath made
119. 91. they continue *this d.* according to thy
Prov. 7. 14. *this d.* have I paid my vows
22. 19. I have made known to thee *this d.*
Isa. 38. 19. the living praise thee, as I do *this d.*
56. 12. and to-morrow shall be as *this d.* and much
Jer. 25. 18. hissing and a curse, as at *this d.* 44. 22.
35. 14. for to *this d.* they drink none, but obey
36. 2. from the days of Josiah even to *this d.*
44. 10. they are not humbled even unto *this d.*
Lam. 2. 16. certainly *this* is the *d.* that we looked for
Ezek. 39. 8. *this* is the *d.* whereof I have spoken
Dan. 9. 7. to us confusion of faces, as at *this d.*
Hag. 2. 15. consider from *this d.* and forward, 18.
19. from *this d.* will I bless you
Mat. 6. 11. give us *this d.* our daily bread
11. 23. Sodom would have remained to *this d.*
27. 8. was called the field of blood to *this d.*
19. I have suffered many things *this d.* in a dream
28. 15. is reported among the Jews to *this d.*
Luke 2. 11. for to you is born *this d.* a Saviour
4. 21. *this d.* is this scripture fulfilled in your ears
19. 9. *this d.* is salvation come to this house
42. if thou hadst known, at least in *this* thy *d.*
22. 34. cock not crow *this d.* before thou deny me
Acts 2. 29. his sepulchre is with us to *this d.*
22. 3. zealous toward God, as ye are all *this d.*
23. 1. in good conscience before God till *this d.*
24. 21. I am called in question by you *this d.*
26. 22. I continue unto *this d.* witnessing to small
29. I would all that hear me *this d.* were as I am
Rom. 11. 8. that they should not hear unto *this d.*
2 *Cor.* 3. 14. till *this d.* remaineth the vail, 15.

To DAY.

Gen. 21. 26. neither yet heard I of it but *to d.*
30. 32. I will pass through all thy flock *to d.*
40. 7. wherefore look ye so sadly *to d.?*
Exod. 2. 18. how is it that ye are come so soon *to d.?*
14. 13. salvation which he will shew you *to d.*

Exod. 16. 23. bake that which you will bake *to d.*
32. 29. consecrate yourselves *to d.* to the Lord
Lev. 9. 4. for *to d.* the Lord will appear to you
Deut. 15. 15. I command thee this thing *to d.*
29. 13. that he may establish thee *to d.* for a people
1 *Sam.* 4. 3. wherefore hath Lord smitten us *to d.?*
9. + 13. get you up, for *to d.* ye shall find him
+ 27. stand still *to d.* that I may shew thee
11. 13. *to d.* Lord wrought salvation in Israel
24. 10. behold, how that the Lord had delivered thee *to d.* into mine hand in the cave, 26. 23.
2 *Sam.* 6. 20. how glorious was the king *to d.!*
13. 4. why art thou lean from day *to d.?*
16. 3. *to d.* shall the house of Israel restore me
1 *Kings* 18. 15. I will shew myself to him *to d.*
22. 5. inquire at word of Lord *to d.* 2 *Chr.* 18. 4.
2 *Kings* 4. 23. wherefore wilt thou go to him *to d.?*
6. 28. give thy son that we may eat him *to d.*
1 *Chron.* 16. 23. sing to Lord all the earth, shew forth from day *to d.* his salvation, *Psal.* 96. 2.
Esth. 3. 7. they cast the lot from day *to d.*
Job 23. 2. even *to d.* is my complaint bitter
Psal. 95. 7. he is our God, we his pasture, *to d.* if ye will hear his voice, *Heb.* 3. 7, 15. | 4. 7.
Jer. 34. + 15. ye were *to d.* turned, and had done right
Zech. 9. 12. *to d.* do I declare, that I will render
Mat. 6. 30. the grass of the field, which *to d.* is, and to-morrow is cast into the oven, *Luke* 12. 28.
21. 28. said, son, go work *to d.* in my vineyard
Luke 5. 26. we have seen strange things *to d.*
13. 32. behold, I do cures *to d.* and to-morrow
33. I must walk *to d.* and the day following
19. 5. for *to d.* I must abide at thy house
23. 43. *to d.* shalt thou be with me in paradise
24. 21. besides all this, *to d.* is the third day
Heb. 3. 13. exhort daily, while it is called *to d.*
5. 5. thou art my Son, *to d.* have I begotten thee
13. 8. Jesus Christ, same yesterd. *to d.* and for ever
Jam. 4. 13. ye that say, *to d.* or morrow, we will go
2 *Pet.* 2. 8. Lot vexed his righteous soul from day *to d.*

DAY *of trouble.*

2 *Kings* 19. 3. this day is a *d. of trouble*, *Isa.* 37. 3.
Psal. 20. 1. Lord hear thee in the *d. of trouble*
50. 15. and call upon me in the *d. of trouble*
59. 16. hast been my refuge in the *d. of trouble*
77. 2. in the *d. of trouble* I sought the Lord
86. 7. in the *d. of trouble* I will call on thee
Isa. 22. 5. it is a *d. of trouble*, and of treading down
Jer. 51. 2. in the *d. of trouble* they shall be ag. her
Ezek. 7. 7. the time is come, *d. of trouble* is near
Nah. 1. 7. Lord is a strong hold in *d. of trouble*
Hab. 3. 16. that I might rest in the *d. of trouble*
Zeph. 1. 15. that day is a *d. of trouble* and distress

DAY-TIME.

Job 5. 14. they meet with darkness in the *d.-time*
24. 16. dig thro' houses they marked in the *d.-time*
Psal. 22. 2. I cry in the *d.-time*, but thou hearest not
42. 8. Lord command his loving-kindness in *d. time*
78. 14. in the *d.-time* also he led them with a cloud
Isa. 4. 6. shall be a tabernacle for a shadow in *d. time*
21. 8. I stand on the watch-tower in the *d.-time*
Luke 21. 37. in *d.-time* he was teaching in temple
2 *Pet.* 2. 13. that count it pleasure to riot in *d. time*

DAYS.

Gen. 4. + 3. at end of *d.* Cain brought an offering
8. 3. after 150 *d.* the waters were abated
24. + 1. and Abraham was old and gone into *d.*
27. 41. *d.* of mourning for my father are at hand
29. + 14. and Jacob abode with him a month of *d.*
47. 9. the *d.* of my pilgrimage are 130 years
+ 28. the *d.* of the years of his life were 147 years
50. 4. when the *d.* of his mourning were past
Num. 11. + 20. ye shall eat of it a month of *d.*
14. 34. after the number of *d.* ye searched the land
Deut. 4. 32. for ask now of the *d.* that are past
10. 10. and I stayed in the mount forty *d.*
Josh. 23. + 1. Joshua waxed old and come into *d.*
Judg. 11. + 4. after *d.* children of Ammon made war
1 *Sam.* 13. 11. Samuel came not within *d.* appointed
18. 26. and the *d.* were not expired, wherefore
27. + 7. David dwelt with Philistines a year of *d.*
29. 3. which hath been with me these *d.*
1 *Kings* 2. 11. the *d.* David reigned over Israel
3. 2. no house was built to the Lord till those *d.*
14. 20. *d.* that Jeroboam reigned were 22 years
30. war between Rehoboam and Jerob. all their *d.*
15. 16. between Asa and Baasha all their *d.* 32.
2 *Kings* 10. + 36. *d.* that Jehu reigned were 28 years
13. 3. into the hand of Benhadad all their *d.*
15. + 13. and Shallum reigned a month of *d.*
18. 4. to those *d.* Israel did burn incense to it
23. 22. from *d.* of the judges, not such a passover
1 *Chron.* 23. 1. when David was old and full of *d.*
29. 15. our *d.* are on earth as a shadow, *Job* 8. 9.
28. he died full of *d.* riches and honour
2 *Chron.* 24. 15. Jehoiada was old and full of *d.*
Ezra 4. 2. since the *d.* Esar-haddon brought us up
9. 7. since *d.* of our fathers have we been in trespass
Neh. 1. 4. I wept and mourned certain *d.*
8. 17. since *d.* of Jeshua, son of Nun, unto that day
Esth. 9. 22. as the *d.* whereon the Jews rested
26. they called these *d.* Purim, after Pur
28. and that these *d.* should be rememb. and kept
Job 3. 6. let it not be joined to the *d.* of the year
7. 1. are not his *d.* also like the *d.* of an hireling?
12. 12. and in length of *d.* understanding
21. 13. they spend their *d.* in wealth, and go down
30. + 1. but now they that are of fewer *d.* than I
16. the *d.* of affliction have taken hold on me
27. the *d.* of affliction prevented me
32. + 4. Elihu waited, for they were elder for *d.*
7. I said, *d.* should speak, and years teach wisdom
33. 25. he shall return to the *d.* of his youth
36. 11. they shall spend their *d.* in prosperity
42. 17. so Job died, being old and full of *d.*
Psal. 21. 4. thou gavest him length of *d.* for ever
23. + 6. dwell in the Lord's house to length of *d.*
37. 18. the Lord knoweth the *d.* of the upright
44. 1. told us what work thou didst in their *d.*
55. 23. deceitful men not live out half their *d.*
61. + 6. thou shalt add *d.* to the *d.* of the king
77. 5. I have considered the *d.* of old, the years

Psal. 78. 33. therefore their d. did he consume in
89. 29. and his throne as the d. of heaven
45. the d. of his youth hast thou shortened
90. 9. all our d. are passed away in thy wrath
10. the d. of our years are threescore and ten
12. so teach us to number our d. that we may apply
14. that we may rejoice and be glad all our d.
91. † 16. with length of d. will I satisfy him
93. † 5. holiness becometh thy house to length of d.
94. 13. mayest give him rest from the d. of adversity
119. 84. how many are the d. of thy servant?
139. † 16. written, what d. they should be fash.
143. 5. I remember the d. of old, I meditate
Prov. 3. 2. for length of d. shall they add to thee
16. length of d. is in her right hand
Eccl. 5. 20. not much remember the d. of his life
7. 10. the cause that the former d. were better
8. 15. that shall abide with him the d. of his life
11. 8. let him remember the d. of darkness
12. 1. while the evil d. come not, nor the years
Isa. 23. 7. whose antiquity is of ancient d.
15. seventy years, according to the d. of one king
60. 20. the d. of thy mourning shall be ended
65. 20. shall be no more thence an infant of d.
22. as the d. of a tree are the d. of my people
Jer. 2. 32. have forgotten me d. without number
6. 11. the aged, with him that is full of d.
28. † 3. in two years of d. will I bring again
31. 33. after those d. I will put my law in their
32. † 39. one heart, that they may fear me all d.
36. 2. from the d. of Josiah even to this day
Lam. 4. 18. our d. are fulfilled, our end is come
Ezek. 4. 4. according to the number of the d. 5, 9.
12. 23. the d. are at hand, and effect of every vision
16. 22. not remembered the d. of thy youth, 43.
Dan. 8. 14. unto 2300 d. sanctuary be cleansed
10. † 2. I was mourning three weeks of d.
12. 11. abomination set up, there shall be 1290 d.
12. blessed is he that waiteth to the 1335 d.
Hos. 2. 13. I will visit on her the d. of Baalim
9. 7. d. of visitation, d. of recompence are come
10. 9. thou hast sinned from the d. of Gibeah
Amos 4. † 4. bring tithes after three years of d.
5. † 21. and I will not smell your holy d.
Mic. 5. † 2. have been from the d. of eternity
7. 15. according to the d. of thy coming out
Hag. 2. 16. since those d. were, when one came to
Zech. 8. † 4. with his staff for multitude of d.
9. ye that hear in these d. these words
10. before these d. there was no hire for man
11. I will not be as in former d. saith the Lord
15. so have I thought in these d. to do well
Mal. 3. 7. from d. of our fathers ye are gone away
Mat. 11. 12. from d. of John the Baptist till now
24. 22. and except those d. should be shortened, no
flesh should be saved, Mark 13. 20.
37. as d. of Noe, so shall the coming of the Son be
Luke 1. 24. after those d. Elisabeth conceived
21. 22. for these be the d. of vengeance
Acts 3. 24. have likewise foretold of these d.
5. 36. for before these d. rose up Theudas
11. 27. in these d. came prophets to Antioch
12. 3. then were the d. of unleavened bread
19. † 38. if matter against any court d. are kept
20. 6. we sailed after the d. of unleavened bread
21. 38. which before these d. madest an uproar
Gal. 4. 10. ye observed d. and months and times
Eph. 5. 16. redeeming time, because the d. are evil
Heb. 7. 3. neither beginning of d. nor end of life
10. 32. but call to remembrance the former d.
1 Pet. 3. 10. he that would see good d. let him ref.
Rev. 11. 3. shall prophesy 1260 d. in sackcloth
12. 6. that they should feed her there 1260 d.
See DAVID, LAST, OLD, JOURNEY.

All the DAYS.

Gen. 3. 14. dust shalt thou eat all the d. of thy life
5. 5. all the d. Adam lived were 930 years
8. all d. of Seth 912 years || 11. of Enos 905 years
14. d. of Cainan 910 years || 23. Enoch 365 years
27. all the d. of Methuselah were 969 years
9. 29. all the d. of Noah were 950 years
Lev. 13. 46. all the d. wherein the plague shall be
15. 25. all the d. of her issue shall be unclean, 26.
Num. 6. 4. all the d. of his separation, 5, 6, 8.
Deut. 4. 9. lest they depart from thy heart all the d.
10. to fear me all the d. they live, 1 Kings 8. 40.
12. 1. to possess it all the d. ye live on the earth
Josh 4. † 24. that you might fear the Lord all the d.
24. 31. and Israel served the Lord all the d. of
Joshua and all the d. of the elders, Judg. 2. 7.
Judg. 2. 18. delivered them all the d. of the judge
1 Sam. 1. 11. I will give him to Lord all d. of his life
7. 13. against Philistines all the d. of Samuel
15. Samuel judged Israel all the d. of his life
1 Kings 4. 25. dwelt safely all the d. of Solomon
11. 25. Rezon was advers. all the d. of Solomon
2 Kings 13. 22. Hazael oppressed Israel all the d. of
23. 22. nor in all the d. of the kings of Israel
2 Chron. 24. 2. all the d. of Jehoiada the priest, 14.
Ezra 4. 5. to frustrate their purposes all d. of Cyrus
Job 1. † 5. thus did Job all the d.
14. 14. all the d. of my appointed time will I wait
Psal. 23. 6. mercy shall follow me all d. of my life
27. 4. dwell in house of Lord all the d. of my life
Prov. 15. 15. all the d. of the afflicted are evil
31. 12. do him good, not evil, all the d. of her life
Luke 1. 75. in holiness before him all the d. of our life
See His LIFE, Thy LIFE.

DAYS come.

Isa. 7. 17. shall bring on thee d. that have not come
Jer. 23. 5. behold the d. come, 7. | 30. 3. | 31. 27,31,38.
Amos 4. 2. the d. come that he will take you away
Mat. 9. 15. the d. shall come when the bridegroom
shall be taken from them, Mark 2. 20. Luke 5. 35.
Luke 17. 22. the d. come when ye shall desire to see
19. 43. the d. come thy enemies shall cast a trench
21. 6. the d. come in which there shall not be left
Heb. 8. 8. d. come when I will make a new covenant

Few DAYS.

Gen. 24. 55. let the damsel abide with us a few d.
27. 44. tarry a few d. till thy brother's fury turn
29. 20. and they seemed to him but a few d.
Gen. 47. 9. few and evil are the d. of my pilgrimage
Num. 9. 20. when the cloud was a few d. on tabern.
Job 14. 1. man that is born of a woman is of few d.
32. † 6. Elihu said, I am of few d. and ye are old
Psal. 109. 8. let his d. be few, and let another
Dan. 11. 20. within few d. he shall be destroyed
Heb. 12. 10. they verily for a few d. chastened us

His DAYS.

Gen. 6. 3. yet his d. shall be 120 years
10. 25. in his d. was the earth divided, 1 Chr. 1. 19.
Deut. 22. 19. may not put her away all his d. 29.
1 Kings 1. † 6. had not displeased him from his d.
15. 14. Asa was perfect all his d. 2 Chron. 15. 17.
16. 34. in his d. did Hiel build Jericho
21. 29. I will not bring the evil in his d.
2 Kings 8. 20. in his d. Edom revolted, 2 Chr. 21. 8.
12. 2. Jehoash did what was right all his d.
15. 18. he departed not all his d. from the sins
1 Chron. 22. 9. and quietness to Israel in his d.
2 Chron. 34. 33. all his d. they departed not from
Job 14. 5. seeing his d. are determined, his months
15. 20. wicked man travaileth with pain all his d.
24. 1. why do they that know him not see his d.?
Psal. 72. 7. in his d. shall the righteous flourish
103. 15. as for man, his d. are as grass, as flower
144. 4. his d. are as a shadow that passeth away
Prov. 28. 16. that hateth covetousness prolong his d.
Eccl. 2. 23. for all his d. are sorrows, his travail
5. 17. all his d. also he eateth in darkness
8. 12. and though his d. be prolonged, yet I know
13. the wicked shall not prolong his d.
Isa. 65. 20. nor old man that hath not filled his d.
Jer. 17. 11. shall leave them in the midst of his d.
22. 30. write a man that shall not prosper in his d.
23. 6. in his d. Judah shall be saved, Israel dwell

In the DAYS.

Gen. 30. 14. Reuben went in the d. of wheat-harvest
Judg. 5. 6. in the d. of Shamgar, in the d. of Jael
8. 28. was in quietness 40 years in the d. of Gideon
1 Sam. 17. 12. went for an old man in the d. of Saul
2 Sam. 21. 1. there was a famine in the d. of David
9. they were put to death in the d. of harvest, in
the first d. in beginning of barley-harvest
1 Kings 10. 21. silver was nothing accounted of in
the d. of Solomon, 2 Chron. 9. 20.
22. 46. Sodomites which remained in the d. of Asa
1 Chron. 4. 41. these came in the d. of Hezekiah
13. 3. we inquired not at it in the d. of Saul
2 Chron. 26. 5. he sought God in the d. of Zechariah
32. 26. came not on them in the d. of Hezekiah
Job 29. 2. as in the d. when God preserved me
4. as I was in the d. of my youth, when the secret
Psal. 37. 19. in the d. of famine shall be satisfied
49. 5. wherefore should I fear in the d. of evil?
Eccl. 2. 16. in the d. to come shall be forgotten
11. 9. let thy heart cheer thee in the d. of youth
12. 1. remember thy Creator in the d. of youth
Jer. 26. 18. Micah prophesied in the d. of Hezekiah
Lam. 1. 7. Jerus. remembered in the d. of her afflict.
Ezek. 16. 60. I will remember my covenant in the d.
22. 14. or hands be strong in the d. I shall deal
Dan. 2. 44. in the d. of these kings shall God set up
5. 11. in the d. of thy father, light was found in him
Hos. 2. 15. she shall sing as in the d. of her youth
9. 9. have deeply corrupted as in the d. of Gibeah
12. 9. to dwell, as in the d. of the solemn feast
Joel 1. 2. hath this been in the d. of your fathers?
Mat. 2. 1. when Jesus was born in the d. of Herod
23. 30. if we had been in the d. of our fathers
24. 38. for as in the d. that were before the flood
Mark 2. 26. into the house of God in d. of Abiathar
Luke 1. 25. thus hath Lord dealt with me in the d.
4. 25. many widows were in the d. of Elias
17. 26. as in the d. of Noe || 28. in the d. of Lot
Acts 5. 37. rose up Judas in the d. of the taxing
11. 28. came to pass in the d. of Claudius Cæsar
Heb. 5. 7. who in the d. of his flesh, when he offered
1 Pet. 3. 20. long-suffer. G. waited in the d. of Noah
Rev. 10. 7. in the d. of the voice of seventh angel
11. 6. that it rain not in the d. of their prophecy

In those DAYS.

Gen. 6. 4. there were giants in the earth in those d.
Deut. 17. 9. come to the judge in those d. 19. 17.
26. 3. go to the priest that shall be in those d.
Judg. 17. 6. in those d. there was no king in Israel,
18. 1. | 21. 25.
20. 27. for the ark of God was there in those d.
1 Sam. 3. 1. the word of L. was precious in those d.
2 Sam. 16. 23. which he counselled in those d.
2 Kings 20. 1. in those d. was Hezekiah sick unto
death, 2 Chron. 32. 24. Isa. 38. 1.
Jer. 33. 16. in those d. shall Judah be saved
50. 4. in those d. Israel shall go and seek God
20. in those d. iniq. shall be sought for, and none
Joel 2. 29. in those d. will pour out my Spirit on the
servants and on the handmaids, Acts 2. 18.
Mat. 24. 19. woe to them that give suck in those d.
Mark 13. 17. Luke 21. 23.
Luke 1. 39. and Mary arose in those d. and went
20. 1. on one of those d. as he taught the people
Acts 7. 41. they made a calf in those d. and offered
Rev. 2. 13. hast not denied my faith in those d.
9. 6. in those d. shall men seek death and not find it

Latter DAYS.

Num. 24. 14. people do to thy people in the latter d.
Deut. 4. 30. in latter d. if thou turn to the Lord
31. 29. and evil will befall you in the latter d.
Jer. 23. 20. in latter d. consider it perfectly, 30. 24.
48. 47. yet will I bring again the captivity of Moab
in the latter d. saith the Lord
49. 39. the captivity of Elam in the latter d.
Ezek. 38. 16. come against my people in the latter d.
Dan. 2. 28. maketh known what shall be in latter d.
10. 14. what shall befall thy people in the latter d.
Hos. 3. 5. and shall fear the Lord in the latter d.

Many DAYS.

Gen. 37. 34. Israel mourned for his son many d.
47. † 8. how many are the d. of thy life?
Josh. 22. 3. nor left your brethren these many d.
2 Sam. 19. † 34. Barzillai said to the king, how many
d. are the years of my life?
1 Kings 2. 38. Shimei dwelt at Jerusalem many d.
1 Kings 3. † 11. and hast not asked for thyself many d.
17. 15. she, and he, and her house, did eat many d.
1 Chron. 7. 22. and Ephraim mourned many d.
Psal. 34. 12. what man is he that loveth many d.?
119. 84. how many are the d. of thy servant?
Eccl. 6. 3. so that the d. of his years be many
11. 1. for thou shalt find it after many d.
Isa. 24. 22. after m. d. shall they be visited, Ezek. 38. 8
32. 10. many d. and years shall ye be troubled
Jer. 32. 14. they may continue many d. 35. 7.
37. 16. Jeremiah had remained there many d.
Ezek. 12. 27. the vision that he seeth is for many d.
Dan. 8. 26. | 10. 14.
Dan. 11. 33. shall fall by captivity and spoil many d.
Hos. 3. 3. thou shalt abide for me many d.
4. Israel shall abide many d. without a king
Luke 15. 13. not many d. after, younger son gather.
John 2. 12. they continued there not many d.
Acts 1. 5. ye shall be baptized not many d. hence
13. 31. he was seen many d. of them which came
16. 18. this did she many d. Paul being grieved
27. 20. nor sun nor stars in many d. appeared

My DAYS.

Gen. 29. 21. give me my wife, for my d. are fulfilled
2 Kings 20. 19. good if peace and truth be in my d.
Job 7. 6. my d. are swifter than a weaver's shuttle
16. let me alone, for my d. are vanity
9. 25. now my d. are swifter than a post, they flee
10. 20. are not my d. few, cease then, and let alone
17. 1. my d. are extinct, graves are ready for me
11. my d. are past, my purposes are broken
27. † 6. my heart shall not reproach me for my d.
29. 18. I shall multiply my d. as the sand
Psal. 39. 4. know mine end, and the measure of my d.
5. thou hast made my d. as an hand-breadth
102. 3. for my d. are consumed like smoke
11. my d. are like a shadow that declineth
23. he weakened my strength, he shortened my d.
24. take me not away in the midst of my d.
116. † 2. therefore will I call upon him in my d.
Isa. 38. 10. I said, in the cutting off of my d.
39. 8. there shall be peace and truth in my d.
Jer. 20. 18. my d. shall be consumed with shame

Now-a-DAYS.

1 Sam. 25. 10. be many servants now-a-d. break away

Prolong, ed, eth, DAYS.

Deut. 4. 26. shall not prolong your d. on it, 30. 18.
40. and that thou mayest prolong thy d. 22. 7.
5. 16. and that thy d. may be prolonged, 6. 2.
33. that ye may prolong your d. in the land, 11. 9.
17. 20. to the end that he may prolong his d.
32. 47. ye shall prolong your d. in the land
Prov. 10. 27. the fear of the Lord prolongeth d.
28. 16. hateth covetousness, shall prolong his d.
Eccl. 8. 12. though a sinner's d. be prolonged, yet
13. neither shall the wicked prolong his d.
Isa. 13. 22. and her d. shall not be prolonged
53. 10. see his seed, he shall prolong his d.
Ezek. 12. 22. the d. are prolonged, vision faileth

Sabbath-DAYS.

Mat. 12. 5. how on the sabbath-d. the priests profane
10. is it lawful to heal on the sabbath-d.?
12. it is lawful to do well on the sabbath-d.?
Mark 3. 4. lawful to do good on sabbath-d. Luke 6. 9.
Luke 4. 31. he came and taught them on sabbath-d.
6. 2. which is not lawful to do on the sabbath-d.
Acts 17. 2. three sabbath-d. reasoned with them
Col. 2. 16. judge you in respect of sabbath-d.

Thy DAYS.

Exod. 20. 12. honour thy father and thy mother, that
thy d. may be long on land L. thy G. giveth thee
23. 26. the number of thy d. I will fulfil
Deut. 12. † 19. forsake not the Levite all thy d.
23. 6. shall not seek their prosperity all thy d.
25. 15. that thy d. may be lengthened in land God
30. 20. he is thy life, and the length of thy d.
31. 14. thy d. approach that thou must die
33. 25. and as thy d. so shall thy strength be
1 Sam. 25. 28. evil not found with thee all thy d.
2 Sam. 7. 12. and when thy d. be fulfilled
1 Kings 3. 13. shall not be any like thee all thy d.
14. walk in my ways, then I will lengthen thy d.
11. 12. in thy d. I will not do it, for David's sake
2 Kings 20. 6. I will add to thy d. 15 years, Isa. 38. 5.
1 Chron. 17. 11. when thy d. be expired, that thou go
Job 10. 5. are thy d. as the days of man, are thy years
38. 12. hast thou commanded morning since thy d.
21. because the number of thy d. is great
Prov. 9. 11. for by me thy d. shall be multiplied
Ezek. 22. 4. thou hast caused thy d. to draw near

Two DAYS.

Exod. 16. 29. on the sixth day the bread of two d.
Num. 9. 22. whether it were two d. or a month
11. 19. ye shall not eat one, nor two d. nor five
2 Sam. 1. 1. and David had abode two d. in Ziklag
Ezra 10. 13. nor is this a work of one day or two d.
Esth. 9. 27. that they would keep these two d.
Hos. 6. 2. after two d. will he revive us, third day
Mat. 26. 2. after two d. is the feast, Mark 14. 1.
John 4. 40. and he abode there two d.
43. now after two d. he departed thence
11. 6. he abode two d. still in the same place

Three DAYS.

Gen. 40. 12. Joseph said, three branches are three d.
13. within three d. shall Phar. lift up thy head, 19.
18. Joseph said, the three baskets are three d.
42. 17. he put them altogether into ward three d.
Exod. 3. 18. let us go three d. journey into wilderness
to sacrifice to Lord our God, 5. 3. | 8. 27. | 15. 22.
10. 22. there was a thick darkness in Egypt three d.
23. nor rose any from his place for three d.
Josh. 1. 11. within three d. ye shall pass over Jordan
2. 16. and hide yourselves there three d. 22.
Judg. 19. 4. and he abode with him three d.
1 Sam. 9. 20. thy asses that were lost three d. ago
21. 5. women have been kept from us these three d.
30. 12. he had eaten no bread three d. and nights
13. master left me, because three d. agone I fell sick
2 Sam. 20. 4. assemble the men of Judah in three d.
24. 13. there be three d. pestilence, 1 Chr. 21. 12.
1 Kings 12. 5. depart for three d. 2 Chron. 10. 5.
2 Kings 2. 17. sought him three d. but found him not

2 *Chron.* 20. 25. were *three d.* gathering the spoil
Ezra 8. 15. there we abode in tents *three d.*
10. 8. whosoever would not come in *three d.* 9.
Esth. 4. 16. and neither eat nor drink *three d.*
Jonah 1. 17. Lord prepared a fish, Jonah was in belly of the fish *three d.* and three nights, *Mat.* 12. 40.
Mat. 15.32. I have compassion on multitude because they continue with me now *three d. Mark* 8. 2.
26. 61. to destroy temple of God, and to build it in *three d.* 27. 40. *Mark* 14. 58. | 15. 29. *John* 2. 19.
27. 63. after *three d.* I will rise again, *Mark* 8. 31.
Luke 2. 46. after *three d.* found him in the temple
Acts 9. 9. Saul was *three d.* without sight, eat nor drink
28. 7. Publius lodged us *three d.* courteously
Rev. 11. 9. see their dead bodies *three d.* and an half
11. after *three d.* and an half, spirit of life entered

Four DAYS.

Judg. 11. 40. lament daughter of Jephthah *four d.*
John 11. 17. Lazarus had lain in the grave *four d.*
39. he stinketh, for he hath been dead *four d.*
Acts 10. 30. *four d.* ago I was fasting to this hour

Five DAYS.

Num. 11. 19. nor *five d.* nor ten d. nor twenty d.
Acts 20. 6. we came to them to Troas in *five d.*
24. 1. after *five d.* Ananias the high priest descend.

Six DAYS.

Exod. 16. 26. *six d.* ye shall gather it, but on sabbath
20. 9. keep sabbath holy, *six d.* shalt thou labour and do all thy work, 23. 12. | 34. 21. *Deut.* 5. 13.
11. in *six d.* Lord made heaven and earth, 31. 17.
24. 16. the cloud covered mount Sinai *six d.*
31. 15. *six d.* may work be done, 35. 2. *Lev.* 23. 3.
Deut. 16. 8. *six d.* shalt thou eat unleavened bread
Josh. 6. 3. go round city, thus shalt thou do *six d.*
14. they compassed city once, so they did *six d.*
Ezek. 46. 1. gate shall be shut the *six* working *d.*
Luke 13. 14. *six d.* in which men ought to work
John 12. 1. Jesus *six d.* before passover came to Beth.

Seven DAYS.

Gen. 7. 4. yet *seven d.* I will cause it to rain on earth
8. 10. and Noah stayed yet other *seven d.* 12.
50. 10. Joseph mourned for his father *seven d.*
Exod. 12. 15. *seven d.* ye shall eat unleavened bread, 13. 6, 7. | 23. 15. | 34. 18. *Lev.* 23. 6. *Num.* 28. 17. *Deut.* 16. 3.
19. *seven d.* shall no leaven be found, *Deut.* 16. 4.
22. 30. *seven d.* it shall be with the dam, *Lev.* 22. 27.
29. 30. the priest shall put them on *seven d.*
35. *seven d.* shalt thou consecrate them, *Lev.* 8. 33.
37. *seven d.* shalt make an atonement for the altar
Lev. 12. 2. a man child, she shall be unclean *seven d.*
13. 5. if the plague be at a stay, then the priest shall shut him up *seven d.* more, 21. 26, 33, 50, 54.
14. 8. he shall tarry abroad out of his tent *seven d.*
15. 19. have an issue, she shall be put apart *seven d.*
23. 8. shall offer an offering by fire to Ld. *seven d.*
39. also when fruit gathered in, ye shall keep a feast to the Lord *seven d.* 40, 41. *Num.* 29, 12.
Num. 12. 14. should Miriam not be ashamed *sev. d.?*
19. 14. all in the tent shall be unclean *seven d.*
Deut. 16. 13. observe the feast of tabernacles *seven d.*
Judg. 14. 12. if ye can declare it to me within *seven d.*
17. and she wept before him the *seven d.*
1 *Sam.* 10. 8. *seven d.* shalt thou tarry till I come
11. 3. the elders said, give us *seven d.* respite
13. 8. he tarried *seven d.* according to the time
31. 13. and they fasted *seven d.* 1 *Chron.* 10. 12.
1 *Kings* 8. 65. Solom. held a feast before L. *seven d.*
16. 15. Zimri did reign *seven d.* in Tirzah
2 *Chron.* 7. 9. they kept dedication of altar *seven d.*
30. 21. the children of Israel kept the feast of unleavened bread *seven d.* 35. 17. *Ezra* 6. 22.
23. assembly took counsel to keep other *seven d.*
Esth. 1. 5. a feast both to great and small *seven d.*
Isa. 30. 26. light of the sun, as the light of *seven d.*
Ezek. 3. 15. I remained there astonished *seven d.*
43. 26. *seven d.* shall they purge the altar, purify
Heb. 11. 30. fell, after they were compassed *seven d.*

Eight DAYS.

Gen. 17. 12. *eight d.* old shall be circumcised, 21. 4.
2 *Chron.* 29. 17. sanctify house of the Ld. in *eight d.*
Luke 2. 21. when *eight d.* were accomplished for the
John 20. 26. after *eight d.* Jesus came and stood in [midst

Ten DAYS.

Num. 11. 19. ye shall not eat *ten d.* nor twenty d.
1 *Sam.* 25. 38. *ten d.* after the Lord smote Nabal
Neh. 5. 18. once in *ten d.* store of all sorts of wine
Jer. 42. 7. after *ten d.* the word of the Lord came
Dan. 1. 12. prove thy servants, I pray thee, *ten d.*
15. at the end of *ten d.* their countenances fairer
Acts 25. 6. when he had tarried more than *ten d.*
Rev. 2. 10. but ye shall have tribulation *ten d.*

Eleven DAYS.

Deut. 1. 2. *eleven d.* journey betw. Horeb and Kadesh

Twelve DAYS.

Acts 24. 11. there are but *twelve d.* since I went up

Fourteen DAYS.

1 *Kings* 8. 65. Solomon held a feast *fourteen d.*

Fifteen DAYS.

Gal. 1. 18. I went and abode with Peter *fifteen d.*

Twenty DAYS.

Num. 11. 19. ye shall not eat flesh *twenty d.*

Twenty-one DAYS.

Dan. 10. 13. prince of Pers. withstood me *twenty-one* [d.

Thirty DAYS.

Num. 20. 29. they mourned for Aaron *thirty d.*
Deut. 34. 8. Israel wept for Moses *thirty d.*
Esth. 4. 11. not been called to the king these *thirty d.*
Dan. 6. 7. whosoever shall ask petition for *thirty d.* [12.

Thirty-three DAYS.

Lev. 12. 4. in the blood of her purify. *thirty-three d.*

Forty DAYS.

Gen. 7. 4. I will cause it to rain on the earth *forty d.*
50. 3. *forty d.* were fulfilled for embalming him
Exod. 24. 18. Moses was in the mount *forty d.* and *forty* nights, 34. 28. *Deut.* 9. 9. | 10. 10.
Num. 13. 25. they returned after *forty d.* 14. 34.
Deut. 9. 25. I fell down before the Lord *forty d.*
1 *Kings* 19. 8. went in strength of that meat *forty d.*
Ezek. 4. 6. shalt bear the iniquity of Judah *forty d.*
Jonah 3. 4. yet *forty d.* and Nineveh be overthrown
Mat. 4. 2. when he had fasted *forty d.* and *forty* nights
Mark 1. 13. Jesus was *forty d.* in the wilderness tempted of Satan, was with wild beasts, *Luke* 4. 2.
Acts 1. 3. being seen of them *forty d.* and speaking

Fifty-two DAYS.

Neh. 6. 15. so the wall was finished in *fifty-two d.*

Your DAYS.

Deut. 11. 21. that *your d.* may be multiplied
Jer. 16. 9. I will cause to cease in *your d.* mirth
35. 7. but all *your d.* ye shall dwell in tents
Ezek. 12. 25. in *y. d.* will I say word, and perform it
Joel 1. 2. hath this been in *your d.* or d. of fathers?
Hab. 1. 5. I will work a work in *your d. Acts* 13. 41.

DAILY.

Exod. 16. 5. twice as much as they gathered *d.*
Num. 4. 16. the *d.* meat-offering, *Ezek.* 46. 13.
28. 24. after this manner ye shall offer *d.*
29. 6. beside the *d.* burnt-offering, *Ezra* 3. 4.
Judg. 16. 16. when she pressed him *d.* with her words
2 *Kings* 25. 30. allowance was a *d.* rate for every day
Neh. 5. 18. now that which was prepared for me *d.*
Esth. 3. 4. when they spake *d.* hearkened not to them
Psal. 13. 2. having sorrow in my heart *d.* how long
42. 10. while they say *d.* to me, where is thy God?
56. 1. be merciful, he fighting *d.* oppresseth me
2. mine enemies would *d.* swallow me up
61. 8. I will sing, that I may *d.* perform my vows
68. 19. blessed be the Lord who *d.* loadeth us
72. 15. he shall live and *d.* shall he be praised
74. 22. how the foolish man reproacheth thee *d.*
86. 3. I cry to thee *d.* || 88. 9. I called *d.* upon thee
88. 17. they came round about me *d.* like water
Prov. 8. 30. and I was *d.* his delight, rejoicing in
34. that heareth me, watching *d.* at my gates
Isa. 58. 2. yet they seek me *d.* and delight to know
Jer. 7. 25. *d.* rising up early and sending them
20. 7. I am in derision *d.* every one mocketh, 8.
Ezek. 30. 16. and Noph shall have distresses *d.*
Dan. 1. 5. the king appointed them a *d.* provision
8. 11. he magnified himself, and by him the *d.* sacrifice was taken away, 11. 31. | 12. 11.
Hos. 12. 1. Ephraim *d.* increaseth lies and desolation
Mat. 6. 11. give us this day our *d.* bread, *Luke* 11. 3.
26. 55. I sat *d.* with you teaching in the temple, *Mark* 14. 49. *Luke* 19. 47. | 22. 53.
Luke 9. 23. let him take up his cross *d.* and follow me
Acts 2. 46. continuing *d.* with one accord in temple
47. Lord added to the church *d.* such to be saved
6. 1. widows were neglected in the *d.* ministration
16. 5. the churches increased in number *d.*
17. 11. the noble Bereans searched the scriptures *d.*
1 *Cor.* 15. 31. I die *d.* || *Heb.* 3. 13. but exhort *d.*
Heb. 7. 27. who needeth not *d.* to offer sacrifice
Jam. 2. 15. if a sister be naked, and destitute of *d.* food

DAYS-MAN.

Job 9. 33. neither is there any *d.* betwixt us

DAY-*spring.*

Job 38. 12. caused the *d. spring* to know his place
Luke 1. 78. whereby *d.-spring* from on high visited us

DAY-*star.*

2 *Pet.* 1. 19. and the *d.-star* arise in your hearts

DEACON, S.

Phil. 1. 1. to the saints with the bishops and *d.*
1 *Tim.* 3. 8. the *d.* must be grave, not double-tongued
10. then let them use the office of a *d.* 13.
12. let the *d.* be the husbands of one wife

DEAD

Signifies, [1] *One whose soul is separated from his body, either by a natural or violent death,* Ruth 1. 8. Job 1. 19. [2] *Such as are in a state of spiritual death, being void of grace, lying under the power of sin, and as unable to do any thing that is spiritually good, or to convert and raise themselves, as a dead body is to quicken itself,* Eph. 2. 1. 1 Tim. 5. 6. [3] *Such as have no being at all, but are extinct, both body and soul;* Mat. 22. 32. God is not the God of the dead, *that is, of such as are finally and irrecoverably perished, without any possibility of living again, as the Sadduces thought;* but he is the God of the living; *that is, of such whose souls do live and are in being, and whose bodies, though now dead, shall be made alive again.* [4] *Such as were like dead persons, as the* Jews, *who seemed to be lost in* Babylon, *of whom there was no more hope that they should return and live in their own land, than that a dead man should rise to life.* Isa. 26. 19. Thy dead men shall live. [5] *One very near to death, as good as dead,* Gen. 20. 3. Thou art but a dead man, *says God to Abimelech: Thou deservest a present and untimely death; and if thou proceedest in thy intended wickedness, it shall be inflicted upon thee.* [6] *Dead idols or images,* Isa. 8. 19. [7] *Impotent or unable for generation, according to the course of nature,* Rom. 4. 19. [8] *Such as are decayed in grace,* Rev. 3. 1. [9] *Free from sin, and the law, as to expectation of eternal life thereby,* Gal. 2. 19. [10] *The state of the dead.* Rom. 8. 11. [11] *The resurrection of the dead,* 1 Cor. 15. 29.

Gen. 20. 3. God said to Abim. thou art but a *d.* man
23. 3. and Abraham stood up from before his *d.*
Exod. 4. 19. the men are *d.* which sought thy life
9. 7. there was not one of the Israelites' cattle *d.*
12. 30. was not a house where there was not one *d.*
33. the Egyptians said, we be all *d.* men
14. 30. Israel saw the Egyptians *d.* on the shore
21. 34. and the *d.* beast shall be his, 36.
35. and the *d.* ox also they shall divide
Lev. 22. 4. toucheth any thing unclean by the *d.*
Num. 5. 2. and whosoever is defiled by the *d.*
12. 12. let her not be as one *d.* of whom the flesh is
16. 48. he stood between the *d.* and the living
Deut. 25. 5. the wife of the *d.* not marry a stranger
Judg. 3. 25. behold, their lord was fallen down *d.*
4. 22. when he came in, behold, Sisera lay *d.*
16. 30. *d.* Samson slew at his death were more than
Ruth 1. 8. as ye have dealt with *d.* and with me
4. 5. to raise up name of the *d.* on his inheritance
1 *Sam.* 4. 17. thy sons Hophni and Phinehas are *d.*
19. that her father-in-law and husband were *d.*
24. 14. dost thou pursue? after a *d.* dog, after a flea?
1 *Sam.* 31. 7. Saul and his sons were *d.* 1 *Chr.* 10. 7.
2 *Sam.* 9. 8. shouldest look on such a *d.* dog as I am
13. 33. to think that all the king's sons are *d.*
16. 9. why should this *d.* dog curse my lord the king
19. 28. all of my father's house were but *d.* men
1 *Kings* 3. 22. living mine, and the *d.* is thy son, 23.
13. 31. when I am *d.* bury me in the sepulchre
21. 15. arise, for Naboth is not alive but *d.*
Job 1. 19. house fell on young men, and they are *d.*
26. 5. *d.* things are formed from under the waters
Psal. 31. 12. I am forgotten as a *d.* man out of mind
76. 6. the chariot and horse are cast into *d.* sleep
88. 5. free among the *d.* like slain that lie in grave
10. wilt thou show wonders to the *d.?*
106. 28. and they ate the sacrifices of the *d.*
115. 17. the *d.* praise not the Lord, neither any
143. 3. in darkness, as those that have been long *d.*
Prov. 2. 18. house inclineth, and her paths unto the *d.*
9. 18. but he knoweth not that the *d.* are there
21. 16. shall remain in the congregation of the *d.*
Eccl. 4. 2. I praised the *d.* which are already *d.*
9. 3. and after that they go to the *d.*
4. for a living dog is better than a *d.* lion
5. the *d.* know not any thing, neither have they
10. 1. *d.* flies cause the ointment of the apothecary
Isa. 8. 19. seek to their God, for the living to the *d.*
14. 9. it stirreth up the *d.* for thee, the chief ones
22. 2. not slain with the sword, nor *d.* in battle
26. 14. they are *d.* shall not live, they are deceased
19. thy *d.* men shall live, with my *d.* body
59. 10. we are in desolate places as *d.* men
Lam. 3. 6. in dark places, as they that be *d.* of old
Ezek. 44. 25. they shall come at no *d.* person to defile
Mat. 2. 20. are *d.* that sought the young child's life
8. 22. follow me, and let the *d.* bury their *d.*
9. 24. he said to them, give place, for the maid is not *d.* but sleepeth, *Mark* 5. 39. *Luke* 8. 52.
10. 8. heal the sick, raise the *d.* cast out devils
11. 5. the deaf hear, *d.* are raised up, *Luke* 7. 22.
22. 31. touching the resurr. of the *d. Mark* 12. 26.
32. God is not the God of the *d.* but of the living, *Mark* 12. 27. *Luke* 20. 38.
23. 27. but are within full of *d.* men's bones
28. 4. for fear the keepers became as *d.* men
Mark 9. 26. he was as one *d.* many said, he is *d.*
15. 44. Pilate marvelled if he were already *d.*
Luke 7. 12. behold, there was a *d.* man carried out
10. 30. and departed, leaving him half *d.*
24. 5. said, why seek ye the living among the *d.?*
John 5. 21. for as the Father raiseth up the *d.*
25. when the *d.* shall hear voice of the Son of God
6. 49. your fathers did eat manna, and are *d.* 58.
11. 25. that believeth, tho' he were *d.* shall he live
Acts 2. 29. the patriarch David is both *d.* and buried
5. 10. the young men came in and found her *d.*
10. 42. testify that it is he who was ordained of God to be the judge of quick and *d.* 2 *Tim.* 4. 1.
14. 19. drew him out, supposing he had been *d.*
20. 9. Eutychus fell down, and was taken up *d.*
26. 8. why incredible that God should raise the *d.?*
28. 6. have swollen or fallen down *d.* suddenly
Rom. 4. 17. even God who quickeneth the *d.*
19. he considered not his own body now *d.*
5. 15. for if through the offence of one many be *d.*
6. 2. we that are *d.* to sin, live any longer therein?
8. if we be *d.* with Christ, we believe that we
11. reckon ye yourselves to be *d.* to sin, but alive
7. 2. but if the husband be *d.* 3. 1 *Cor.* 7. 39.
4. ye also are become *d.* to the law, *Gal.* 2. 19.
14. 9. that he might be lord both of *d.* and living
1 *Cor.* 15. 15. if so be that the *d.* rise not
35. but some man will say, how are the *d.* raised?
52. and the *d.* shall be raised incorruptible
2 *Cor.* 1. 9. but trust in God who raiseth the *d.*
5. 14. that if one died for all, then were all *d.*
Eph. 2. 1. were *d.* in trespasses and sins, 5. *Col.* 2. 13.
Col. 2. 20. if ye be *d.* with Christ, 2 *Tim.* 2. 11.
3. 3. ye are *d.* and your life is hid with Christ in G.
1 *Thess.* 4. 16. and the *d.* in Christ shall rise first
Heb. 6. 1. the foundation of repentance from *d.* works
9. 14. blood of Chr. purge conscience from *d.* works
17. a testament is of force after men are *d.*
11. 4. and by it he being *d.* yet speaketh
12. sprang there even of one, and him as good as *d.*
35. women received their *d.* raised to life again
1 *Pet.* 2. 24. we being *d.* to sin should live to righteousness
4. 5. who is ready to judge the quick and the *d.*
6. the gospel was preached to them that are *d.*
Jude 12. twice *d.* plucked up by the roots
Rev. 1. 5. Jesus, who is the first-begotten of the *d.*
17. when I saw him, I fell at his feet as *d.*
3. 1. thou hast a name that thou livest, and art *d.*
14. 13. blessed are the *d.* who die in the Lord
16. 3. the sea became as the blood of a *d.* man
20. 5. but the rest of the *d.* lived not again
12. saw the *d.* stand before G.; the *d.* were judged out of those things written in the books
13. sea gave up *d.* which were in it, death and hell

See BODY, BURY, CARCASE, CORPSE, RESURRECTION.

For the DEAD.

Lev. 19. 28. ye shall not make cuttings *for the d.*
21. 1. there shall none be defiled *for the d.*
Deut. 14. 1. ye shall not make any baldness *for the d.*
26. 14. I have not given ought thereof *for the d.*
2 *Sam.* 14. 2. as a woman that had mourned *for the d.*
Jer. 16. 7. not tear to comfort them *for the d.*
22. 10. weep ye not *for the d.* nor bemoan him
Ezek. 24. 17. forbear, make no mourning *for the d.*
1 *Cor.* 15. 29. what shall they do who are baptized *for the d.* why are they also baptized *for the d.?*

From the DEAD.

Mat. 14. 2. John Baptist, he is risen *from the d.*
Mark 9. 10. what the rising *from the d.* should mean
Luke 16. 30. nay, but if one went to them *from the d.*
31. not be persuaded, though one rose *from the d.*
24. 46. to rise *from the d.* the third day, *John* 20. 9.
Acts 10. 41. drink with him after he rose *from the d.*
26. 23. be the first that should rise *from the d.*
Rom. 6. 13. as those that are alive *from the d.*
10. 7. that is, to bring up Christ again *from the d.*

Rom. 11. 15. receiving of them be but life from the d.
1 Cor. 15. 12. if Chr. be preached that rose from the d.
Eph. 5. 14. arise from the d. Christ shall give thee
Col. 1. 18. who is the first-born from the d. [light
Heb. 11. 19. God was able to raise him from the d.
13. 20. brought again from the d. our Lord Jesus
See Raised, Risen.

Is DEAD.

Gen. 42. 38. for his brother is d. and he left, 44. 20.
Deut. 25. 6. in the name of his brother that is d.
Josh. 1. 2. Moses my servant is d. arise, go over
Judg. 20. 5. my concubine they forced that she is d.
2 Sam. 2. 7. Saul is d. 4. 10. ‖ 11. 21. Uriah is d. 24.
12. 18. the child is d. 19. ‖ 13. 32. Amnon only is d.
14. 5. I am a widow and my husb. is d. 2 Kings 4. 1.
18. 20. no tidings because the king's son is d.
19. 10. Absalom is d. ‖ 1 Kings 21. 14. Naboth is d.
Ezek. 44. 31. priests shall not eat that is d. of itself
Mat. 9. 18. my daughter is d. Mark 5. 35. Luke 8. 49.
Mark 9. 26. insomuch that many said, he is d.
John 8. 52. Abraham is d. and the prophets, 53.
11. 14. then said Jesus plainly, Lazarus is d.
Rom. 6. 7. for he that is d. is freed from sin
8. 10. if Christ be in you, body is d. because of sin
Gal. 2. 21. if righteous. by law, Christ is d. in vain
1 Tim. 5. 6. liveth in pleasure, is d. while she liveth
Jam. 2. 17. faith, if it hath not works is d. 20.
26. for as the body without the spirit is d. so faith

Was DEAD.

Judg. 2. 19. when the judge was d. they returned
9. 55. when men of Israel saw Abimelech was d.
1 Sam. 17. 51. Philistines saw their champion was d.
25. 39. when David heard that Nabal was d.
31. 5. armour-bearer saw Saul was d. 1 Chr. 10. 5.
2 Sam. 4. 1. Saul's son heard that Abner was d.
11. 26. Bathsheba heard her husband was d.
12. 19. David perceived that the child was d.
13. 39. comforted for Amnon, seeing he was d.
1 Kings 3. 21. to give my child suck, behold, it was d.
11. 21. when Hadad heard that Joab was d.
21. 15. when Jezebel heard that Naboth was d.
2 Kings 3. 5. when Ahab was d. Moab rebelled
4. 32. behold, the child was d. and laid on his bed
11. 1. Athaliah saw her son was d. 2 Chron. 22. 10.
Mat. 2. 19. but when Herod was d. behold an angel
Luke 7. 15. he that was d. sat up and began to speak
8. 53. laughed to scorn, knowing that she was d.
15. 24. this my son was d. and is alive again
32. for this thy brother was d. and is alive again
John 11. 39. Martha, the sister of him that was d.
44. and he that was d. came forth bound
19. 33. saw that Jesus was d. brake not his legs
Acts 25. 19. questions of one Jesus who was d.
Rom. 7. 8. for without the law sin was d.
Rev. 1. 18. I am he that liveth, and was d. behold

DEADLY.

1 Sam. 5. 11. was a d. destruction throughout city
Psal. 17. 9. deliver me from d. enemies who compass
Ezek. 30. 24. with groanings of a d. wounded man
Mark 16. 18. if drink d. thing, it shall not hurt them
Jam. 3. 8. tongue is an unruly evil, full of d. poison
Rev. 13. 3. and his d. wound was healed, 12.

DEADNESS.

Rom. 4. 19. neither yet the d. of Sarah's womb

DEAF.

Exod. 4. 11. or who maketh the d. or the seeing?
Lev. 19. 14. thou shalt not curse the d. nor put
1 Sam. 10. † 27. Saul was as though he had been d.
Psal. 38. 13. but I as a d. man heard not, I was dumb
58. 4. they are like the d. adder that stoppeth
Isa. 29. 18. in that day shall the d. hear the words
35. 5. and the ears of the d. shall be unstopped
42. 18. hear, ye d. look, ye blind, that ye may see
19. who is d. as my messenger that I sent?
43. 8. bring forth blind, and the d. that have ears
Mic. 7. 16. their ears shall be d. shall lick the dust
Mat. 11. 5. the d. hear, dead are raised, Luke 7. 22.
Mark 7. 32. they brought to him one that was d.
37. he maketh the d. to hear, the dumb to speak
9. 25. thou dumb and d. spirit, come out of him

DEAL.

Gen. 19. 9. now will we d. worse with thee than
24. 49. now if you will d. truly with my master
32. 9. Lord said, return, and I will d. well with thee
34. 31. should he d. with our sister as an harlot?
Exod. 1. 10. come on, let us d. wisely with them
21. 9. d. with her after the manner of daughters
23. 11. in like manner d. with thy vineyard
Lev. 19. 11. ye shall not steal, nor d. falsely, nor lie
Num. 11. 15. if thou d. thus with me, kill me
Deut. 7. 5. but thus shall ye d. with them, ye shall
2 Chron. 2. 3. Solomon sent to Huram, as thou didst
d. with David my father, even so d. with me
Job 42. 8. lest I d. with you after your folly
Psal. 75. 4. I said to the fools, d. not foolishly
119. 17. d. bountifully with thy servant, 142. 7.
124. d. with thy servant according to thy mercy
Prov. 12. 22. but they that d. truly are his delight
Isa. 26. 10. in land of uprightness he will d. unjustly
52. 13. behold, my servant shall d. prudently
58. 7. is it not to d. thy bread to the hungry?
Jer. 18. 23. d. thus with them in time of thine anger
21. 2. if so be that the Lord d. with us according
Ezek. 8. 18. therefore will I also d. in fury, my eye
16. 59. I will d. with thee as thou hast done
22. 14. or hands be strong in days I d. with thee
23. 25. and they shall d. furiously with thee
31. 11. he shall surely d. with him, I have driven
Dan. 1. 13. and as thou seest d. with thy servants
5. † 20. his mind was hardened to d. proudly
11. 7. and shall d. against them and shall prevail
2 Cor. 2. † 17. d. deceitfully with the word of God
See Treacherously.

DEAL.

Exod. 29. 40. a tenth d. of flour mingled with oil,
Lev. 14. 21. Num. 15. 4. | 29. 4.
Num. 28. 13. a several tenth d. 21. 29. | 29. 10, 15.
Mark 7. 36. so much more a great d. they published
10. 48. he cried the more a great d. Son of David

DEALS.

Lev. 14. 10. the priest shall take three tenth d. of
fine flour for a meat-offering, Num. 15. 9.
Lev. 23. 13. two tenth d. for a meat-offer. Num. 28. 9.
17. shall bring two wave-loaves of two tenth d.
24. 5. two tenth d. shall be in one cake
Num. 15. 6. for a ram for a meat offering, two
tenth d. of flour, 28. 20, 28. | 29. 3, 9, 14.
28. 20. three tenth d. to a bullock, 28. | 29. 3, 9, 14.

DEALER.

Isa. 21. 2. the treacherous d. dealeth treacherously

DEALERS.

Isa. 24. 16. treacherous d. have dealt treacherously

DEALEST.

Exod. 5. 15. wherefore d. thus with thy servants?
Isa. 33. 1. woe to thee that spoilest and d. treach.

DEALETH.

Judg. 18. 4. thus and thus d. Micah with me
1 Sam. 23. 22. it was told me that he d. subtilly
Prov. 10. 4. he becometh poor that d. with slack hand
13. 16. every prudent man d. with knowledge
14. 17. he that is soon angry d. foolishly
21. 24. scorner is his name, who d. in proud wrath
Isa. 21. 2. the treacherous dealer d. treacherously
Jer. 6. 13. is given to covetousness, from the prophet
even to the priest every one d. falsely, 8. 10.
Heb. 12. 7. God d. with you as sons, for what son

DEALING, S.

Lev. 6. † 2. if a soul sin, and lie to his neighbour in d.
1 Sam. 2. 23. I hear of your evil d. by all this people
Ps. 7. 16. his violent d. shall come down on his pate
John 4. 9. the Jews have no d. with the Samaritans

DEALT.

Gen. 16. 6. when Sarai d. hardly with her, she fled
33. 11. because God hath d. graciously with me
43. 6. wherefore d. ye so ill with me, as to tell
Exod. 1. 20. therefore God d. well with midwives
14. 11. wherefore hast thou d. thus with us, to carry
18. 11. for in the thing wherein they d. proudly
21. 8. seeing he hath d. deceitfully with her
Judg. 9. 16. if ye have d. well with Jerubbaal
19. if ye have d. truly, rejoice in Abimelech
Ruth 1. 8. as ye have d. with the dead, and with me
20. the Almighty hath d. bitterly with me
1 Sam. 14. † 33. Saul said, ye have d. treacherously
24. 18. how that thou hast d. well with me
25. 31. when the Lord shall have d. well with thee
2 Sam. 6. 19. he d. among the people, 1 Chr. 16. 3.
2 Kings 12. 15. for they d. faithfully, 22. 7.
21. 6. Manasseh d. with familiar spirits and wizards
1 Chr. 20. 3. so d. David with the cities of Ammon
2 Chr. 6. 37. we have done amiss, and d. wickedly
11. 23. Rehob. d. wisely, and dispersed children
33. 6. Manas. d. with a familiar spirit and wizards
Neh. 1. 7. we have d. very corruptly against thee
9. 10. thou knewest that they d. proudly, 16, 29.
Job 6. 15. my breth. have d. deceitfully, as a brook
Psal. 13. 6. the Lord hath d. bountifully with me
44. 17. nor have we d. falsely in thy covenant
78. 57. and d. unfaithfully like their fathers
103. 10. he hath not d. with us after our sins
116. 7. the Lord hath d. bountifully with thee
119. 65. thou hast d. well with servant, according
78. they d. perversely with me without a cause
147. 20. he hath not d. so with any nation
Isa. 24. 16. the treacherous dealers have d. very treacherously, Jer. 3. 20. | 5. 11. | 12. 6. Lam. 1. 2.
Ezek. 22. 7. in thee have they d. by oppression
25. 12. because that Edom hath d. against Judah
15. because the Philistines have d. by revenge
Hos. 5. 7. they have d. treacherously against the L.
6. 7. there have they d. treacherously against me
Joel 2. 26. name of your G. that hath d. wondrously
Zech. 1. 6. as the L. thought, so hath he d. with us
Mal. 2. 11. Jud. hath d. treacherously and abominat.
14. against whom thou hast d. treacherously
Luke 1. 25. thus hath the Lord d. with me in days
2. 48. son, why hast thou thus d. with us?
Acts 7. 19. the same d. subtilly with our kindred
25. 24. the multitude of the Jews have d. with me
Rom. 12. 3. according as God hath d. to every man

DEAR.

Jer. 15. † 7. I will bereave them of what is d.
31. 20. is Eph. my d. son, is he a pleasant child?
Luke 7. 2. a centurion's servant, who was d. to him
Acts 20. 24. neither count I my life d. to myself
Eph. 5. 1. be ye followers of God as d. children
Phil. 2. † 20. I have no man so d. to me
Col. 1. 7. ye learned of Epaphras, our d. fellow-serv.
13. hath translated us into kingdom of his d. Son
1 Thess. 2. 8. our own souls, because ye were d. to us

DEARLY beloved.

Jer. 12. 7. I have given d. b. of my soul to enemies
Rom. 12. 19. d. beloved, avenge not yourselves
1 Cor. 10. 14. my d. beloved, Phil. 4. 1. 2 Tim. 1. 2.
2 Cor. 7. 1. d. beloved, 12. 19. Phil. 4. 1. 1 Pet. 2. 11.
Philem. 1. Paul, unto Philemon, our d. beloved.

DEARTH.

Gen. 41. 54. d. began to come, d. was in all the lands
2 Kings 4. 38. and there was a d. in the land
2 Chron. 6. 28. if there be a d. in the land, or mildew
Neh. 5. 3. we might buy corn because of the d.
Jer. 14. 1. word came to Jeremiah concerning the d.
Acts 7. 11. there came a d. over all the land of
[Egypt
11. 28. Agabus signified, there should be a great d.

DEATH

Signifies, [1] *The separation of the soul from the body*, Gen. 25. 11. *This is* temporal death. [2] *A separation of soul and body from God's favour in this life, which is the state of all unregenerated and unrenewed persons, who are without the light of knowledge, and the quickening power of grace*, Luke 1. 79. *This is* spiritual death. [3] *The perpetual separation of the whole man from God's heavenly presence and glory, to be tormented for ever with the devil and his angels*, Rev. 2. 11. *This is the* second death, *or* eternal death. *To all these kinds of* death, *Adam made himself and his posterity liable, by transgressing the commandment of God in eating the forbidden fruit*, Gen. 2. 17. [4] *Some poisonous deadly thing*, 2 Kings 4. 40. [5] *Imminent dangers of death*, 2 Cor. 11. 23. [6] *The pestilence of contagious diseases.* Jer. 15. 2.

By the gates of death, *the grave is signified, and the state of the dead after this life*, Job 38. 17. Have the gates of death been opened unto thee? *Hast thou seen, or dost thou perfectly know, the place and state of the dead; the depths and bowels of that earth, in which the generality of dead men are buried; or the several ways and methods of death; or the states and conditions of men after death? And the* Psalmist *says*, Thou liftest me up from the gates of death, Psal. 9. 13. *Thou didst bring me back from the brink or mouth of the grave, into which I was ready to drop, being as near death as a man is to the city, that is come to the very gates of it.* By the instruments of death, *dangerous and deadly weapons are meant*, Psal. 7. 13. Love is strong as death, Cant. 8. 6. *The spiritual love of the church to Christ is strong as death, which overcomes the strongest man*, Psal. 89. 48.

Gen. 21. 16. let me not see the d. of the child
24. 67. Isaac was comforted after his mother's d.
25. 11. after the d. of Abraham God blessed Isaac
27. 7. that I may eat, and bless thee before my d.
10. that he may bless thee before his d.
Exod. 10. 17. that he may take from me this d. only
Num. 16. 29. if these men die common d. of all men
23. 10. let me die d. of righteous, and my last end
35. 25. the slayer shall abide in it unto the d. of
the high priest, 28. 32. Josh. 20. 6.
31. no satisfaction for life of murderer guilty of d.
Deut. 30. 15. I have set before you this day life
and good, d. and evil, Jer. 21. 8.
31. 27. how much more will ye rebel after my d.!
29. I know after my d. ye will corrupt yourselves
33. 1. Moses blessed Isr. before his d. the man of G.
Judg. 5. 18. that jeoparded their lives to the d.
16. 16. she urged him that his soul was vexed to d.
30. dead which he slew at his d. were more than
Ruth 1. 17. Ruth said, if ought but d. part thee and me
2. 11. all thou hast done since d. of thy husband
1 Sam. 4. 20. about time of her d. the women said
15. 32. Agag said, surely the bitterness of d. is past
20. 3. there is but a step between me and d.
22. 22. I have occasioned d. of thy father's house
26. † 16. ye are sons of d. ye kept not your master
2 Sam. 1. 23. and in their d. they were not divided
15. 21. in d. or life, there will thy servant be
19. † 28. all my father's house were but men of d.
22. 5. when the waves of d. compassed me, floods of
ungodly made me afraid, Psal. 18. 4. | 116. 3.
6. the snares of d. prevented me, Psal. 18. 5.
1 Kings 11. 40. Jeroboam was in Egypt till d. of Sol.
2 Kings 2. 21. shall not be any more d. or barren land
4. 40. O thou man of God, d. is in the pot
1 Chron. 22. 5. so David prepared before his d.
2 Chron. 22. 4. his counsellors after d. of his father
32. 33. all Judah did Hezekiah honour at his d.
Ezra 7. 26. whether it be to d. or to banishment
Job 3. 21. which long for d. but it cometh not
7. 15. so that my soul chooseth d. rather than life
18. 13. the first-born of d. shall devour his strength
27. 15. that remain of him shall be buried in d.
28. 22. destruction and d. say, we have heard fame
30. 23. I know that thou wilt bring me to d.
Psal. 6. 5. in d. there is no remembrance of thee
7. 13. hath prepared for him the instruments of d.
13. 3. lighten mine eyes, lest I sleep the sleep of d.
22. 15. thou hast brought me into the dust of d.
48. 14. God will be our guide, even unto d.
49. 14. and laid in the grave, d. shall feed on them
55. 4. and the terrors of d. are fallen upon me
15. let d. seize on them, and let them go down
73. 4. for there are no bands in their d. strength
79. † 11. reserve the children of d.
89. 48. what man that liveth, and shall not see d.?
102. 20. to loose those that are appointed to d.
116. 15. precious in sight of Lord is d. of his saints
118. 18. but he hath not given me over unto d.
Prov. 2. 18. her house inclineth to d. paths to dead
5. 5. her feet go down to d. steps take hold on hell
7. 27. to hell going down to the chambers of d.
8. 36. all they that hate me love d.
11. 19. that pursueth evil, pursueth it to his own d.
12. 28. in the path-ways thereof there is no d.
13. 14. to depart from the snares of d. 14. 27.
14. 32. but the righteous hath hope in his d.
16. 14. the wrath of a king is as messengers of d.
18. 21. d. and life are in the power of the tongue
21. 6. vanity tossed to and fro of them that seek d.
24. 11. forbear to deliver them that are drawn to d.
26. 18. as a mad man who casteth arrows and d.
Eccl. 7. 26. I find more bitter than d. the woman
Cant. 8. 6. for love is strong as d. jealousy cruel as
Isa. 25. 8. he will swallow up d. in victory
38. 18. for d. cannot celebrate thee
53. 9. and with the rich in his d. because he
12. because he poured out his soul unto d.
Jer. 8. 3. and d. shall be chosen rather than life
9. 21. for d. is come up to our windows
15. 2. tell them such as are for d. to d. 43. 11.
18. † 23. thou knowest all their counsel for d.
26. † 11. the judgment of d. is for this man
Lam. 1. 20. abroad the sword, at home there is as d.
Ezek. 18. 32. saith the L. God, I have no pleasure
in the d. of the wicked, 33. 11.
31. 14. for they are all delivered unto d.
Hos. 13. 14. O d. I will be thy plagues, O grave
Jonah 4. 9. I do well to be angry even unto d.
Hab. 2. 5. who is as d. and cannot be satisfied
Mat. 2. 15. and was there till the d. of Herod
10. 21. brother deliver brother to d. Mark 13. 12.
15. 4. honour father and mother, he that curseth
father or mother, let him die the d. Mark 7. 10.
16. 28. some here shall not taste of d. till they see
the Son of Man coming, Mark 9. 1. Luke 9. 27.
20. 18. they shall condemn him to d. Mark 10. 33
26. 38. my soul is sorrowful to d. Mark 14. 34.
66. they said, he is guilty of d. Mark 14. 64.
Mark 5. 23. my daughter lieth at the point of d.
Luke 2. 26. should not see d. before he had seen C.
22. 33. I will go with thee both to prison and d.
23. 22. I have found no cause of d. in him

John 4. 47. heal his son for he was at the point of *d*.
8. 51. if a man keep my saying, shall never see *d*. 52.
11. 4. Jesus said, this sickness is not unto *d*.
13. howbeit, Jesus spake of his *d*.
12. 33. he said, signifying what *d*. should die, 18. 32.
21. 19. signifying by what *d*. he should glorify God
Acts 2. 24. raised up, having loosed the pains of *d*.
8. 1. Saul was consenting to his *d*. 22. 20.
13. 28. though they found no cause of *d*. in him
22. 4. and I persecuted this way unto the *d*.
28. 18. because there was no cause of *d*. in me
Rom. 5. 10. we were reconciled to G. by the *d*. of his
Son, much more be saved by his life, *Col*. 1. 22.
12. and *d*. by sin, and so *d*. passed upon all men
14. *d*. reigned from Adam to Moses over them, 17.
21. as sin hath reigned to *d*. even so might grace
6. 3. know ye not, that so many of us as were baptized into Jesus Christ, were baptized into his *d*.?
4. we are buried with him by baptism into *d*.
5. for if we have been planted in likeness of his *d*.
9. dieth no more, *d*. hath no dominion over him
16. his servants ye are, whether of sin unto *d*.
21. now ashamed, for end of those things is *d*.
23. for the wages of sin is *d*. but the gift of God
7. 5. motions of sin did work to bring fruit to *d*.
10. the commandment of life I found to be to *d*.
13. was then that which is good made *d*. to me?
24. who shall deliver me from the body of this *d*.?
8. 2. hath made me free from the law of sin and *d*.
6. to be carnal. mind. is *d*. but spirit. life and peace
38. nor *d*. nor life shall separate us from love of G.
1 *Cor*. 3. 22. whether world, life, or *d*. all are yours
4. 9. G. set forth apostles, as it were appointed to *d*.
11. 26. ye do show the Lord's *d*. till he come
15. 21. for since by man came *d*. by man came also
26. the last enemy that shall be destroyed is *d*.
54. saying written, *d*. is swallowed up in victory
55. O *d*. where is thy sting! ‖ 56. sting of *d*. is sin
2 *Cor*. 1. 9. but we had the sentence of *d*. in ourselves
10. who delivered us from so great a *d*. doth deliver
2. 16. to the one we are the savour of *d*. unto *d*.
3. 7. if the ministration of *d*. was glorious
4. 11. we are always delivered to *d*. for Jesus' sake
12. so then *d*. worketh in us, but life in you
7. 10. but the sorrow of the world worketh *d*.
Phil. 1. 20. Chr. magnified, whether by life or by *d*.
2. 8. he became obedient unto *d*. even *d*. of the cross
27. Epaphroditus was nigh to *d*. but G. had mercy
30. because for work of Christ he was nigh to *d*.
3. 10. know him, being made conformable to his *d*.
2 *Tim*. 1. 10. our Lord, who hath abolished *d*.
Heb. 2. 9. but we see Jesus, for the suffering of *d*. crowned, that he should taste *d*. for every man
14. thro' *d*. might destroy him that had power of *d*.
15. and deliver them who through fear of *d*. were
7. 23. were not suffered to continue, by reason of *d*.
9. 15. that by means of *d*. for the redemption of
16. there must of necessity be the *d*. of the testator
11. 5. Enoch was translated, that he should not see *d*.
Jam. 1. 15. sin when finished bringeth forth *d*.
1 *John* 3. 14. that loveth not his brother abideth in *d*.
5. 16. there is a sin unto *d*. ‖ 17. a sin not unto *d*.
Rev. 1. 18. and I have the keys of hell and of *d*.
2. 10. be faithful unto *d*. I will give thee a crown
11. that overcomes shall not be hurt of second *d*.
6. 8. and his name that sat on him was *d*. and hell
9. 6. men shall seek *d*. and *d*. shall flee from them
12. 11. and they loved not their lives to the *d*.
13. 3. saw one of his heads as it were wounded to *d*.
18. 8. her plagues shall come one day, *d*. mourning
20. 6. on such the second *d*. hath no power
13. and *d*. and hell delivered up the dead in them
14. *d*. and hell cast into lake, this is the second *d*.
21. 4. and there shall be no more *d*. nor sorrow

See DAY.

From DEATH.

Josh. 2. 13. Rahab's sisters, deliver our lives *from d*.
Job 5. 20. in famine he shall redeem thee *from d*.
Psal. 33. 19. to deliver their soul *from d*. keep alive
56. 13. thou hast delivered my soul *from d*. 116. 8.
68. 20. to the Lord belong the issues *from d*.
78. 50. he spared not their soul *from d*. but gave
Prov. 10. 2. righteousness delivereth *from d*. 11. 4.
Hos. 13. 14. I will redeem thee *from d*. O death
John 5. 24. but is passed *from d*. to life, 1 *John* 3. 14.
Heb. 5. 7. to him that was able to save him *from d*.
Jam. 5. 20. know that he shall save a soul *from d*.

Gates of DEATH.

Job 38. 17. have the *gates of d*. been opened to thee?
Psal. 9. 13. thou that liftest me up from *gates of d*.
107. 18. and they draw near to the *gates of d*.

Put to DEATH.

Gen. 26. 11. that toucheth this man shall be *put to d*.
Exod. 21. 29. ox stoned, his owner also be *put to d*.
35. 2. whosoever work on sabbath, shall be *put to d*.
Lev. 19. 20. shall not be *put to d*. because not free
20. 11. both of them shall surely be *put to d*.
24. 21. that killeth shall be *put to d*. *Num*. 35. 30.
Num. 1. 51. Levites shall set up tabernacles, stranger that cometh nigh shall be *put to d*. 3. 10, 38. | 18. 7.
Deut. 13. 5. that dreamer of dreams shall be *put to d*.
9. thy hand shall be first on him to *put to d*. 17. 7.
17. 6. at the mouth of one witness not be *put to d*.
21. 22. he be *put to d*. and thou hang him on a tree
24. 16. fathers shall not be *put to d*. for children, nor children *put to d*. for fathers, 2 *Kings* 14. 6.
Josh. 1. 18. rebel against thy commandm. be *put to d*.
Judg. 6. 31. he that pleadeth for Baal be *put to d*.
20. 13. that we may *put* them *to d*. 1 *Sam*. 11. 12.
1 *Sam*. 11. 13. not a man be *put to d*. 2 *Sam*. 19. 22.
2 *Sam*. 8. 2. with two lines measured he to *put to d*.
19. 21. shall not Shimei be *put to d*. for this?
21. 9. were *put to d*. in the days of barley-harvest
1 *Kings* 2. 8. I sware saying, I will not *put* thee *to d*.
24. Adonijah shall be *put to d*. this day
26. but I will not at this time *put* thee *to d*.
2 *Chron*. 15. 13. not seek the Lord should be *put to d*.
23. 7. cometh into the house, shall be *put to d*.
Esth. 4. 11. there is one law of his to *put* him *to d*.
Jer. 18. 21. wives be widows, their men be *put to d*.
26. 15. know for certain, that if ye *put* me *to d*.
19. did king and all Judah *put* him at all *to d*.?
Jer. 26. 21. king Jehoiakim sought to *put* Urijah *to d*.
38. 4. we beseech thee, let this man be *put to d*.
15. Jer. said, wilt thou not surely *put* me *to d*.?
16. the king sware, I will not *put* thee *to d*. 25.
43. 3. hands of Chald. that they might *put* us *to d*.
52. 27. smote them and *put* them *to d*. in Riblah
Mat. 10. 21. childr. shall rise up ag. parents, cause them to be *put to d*. *Mark* 13. 12. *Luke* 21. 16.
14. 5. when he would *put* him *to d*. he fear. mult.
26. 59. the chief priests sought false witness against Jesus to *put* him *to d*. 27. 1. *Mark* 14. 55.
Mark 14. 1. how to take him by craft and *put to d*.
Luke 18. 33. they shall scourge and *put* him *to d*.
23. 32. there were two malefact. led to be *put to d*.
John 11. 53. they took counsel to *put* him *to d*.
12. 10. that they might *put* Lazarus also *to d*.
18. 31. it is not lawful for us to *put* any man *to d*.
Acts 12. 19. Herod command. keepers to be *put to d*.
26. 10. when they were *put to d*. I gave voice ag. them
1 *Pet*. 3. 18. *put to d*. in flesh, but quickened by Spirit

See SURELY.

Shadow of DEATH.

Job 3. 5. let darkness and the *shadow of d*. stain it
10. 21. to land of darkness and the *shadow of d*. 22.
12. 22. and bringeth out to light the *shadow of d*.
16. 16. and on my eye-lids is the *shadow of d*.
24. 17. morning is to them even as *shadow of d*.
28. 3. he searcheth out darkness and *shadow of d*.
34. 22. is no *shadow of d*. where sinners may hide
38. 17. or hast thou seen doors of the *shadow of d*.?
Psal. 23. 4. tho' I walk thro' valley of *shadow of d*.
44. 19. tho' thou hast covered us with *shadow of d*.
107. 10. such as sit in darkness, and *shadow of d*.
14. brought them out of darkn. and *shadow of d*.
Isa. 9. 2. that dwell in the land of the *shadow of d*.
Jer. 2. 6. that brought us thro' land of *shadow of d*.
13. 16. ye look for light, he turn it into *shadow of d*.
Amos 5. 8. turneth *shadow of d*. into the morning
Mat. 4. 16. peo. that sat in region and *shadow of d*.
Luke 1. 79. give light to them that sit in *shadow of d*.

Ways of DEATH.

Prov. 14. 12. the end thereof are *ways of d*. 16. 25.

With DEATH.

Isa. 28. 15. we have made a covenant *with d*.
18. your covenant *with d*. shall be disannulled
Rev. 2. 23. and I will kill her children *with d*.
6. 8. and power was given to them to kill *with d*.

Worthy of DEATH.

Deut. 17. 6. that is *worthy of d*. shall be put to *d*.
19. 6. slay him, whereas he was not *worthy of d*.
21. 22. a man have committed a sin *worthy of d*.
22. 26. there is in the damsel no sin *worthy of d*.
1 *Kings* 2. 26. said to Abiathar, thou art *worthy of d*.
Luke 23. 15. lo, nothing *worthy of d*. is done to him
Acts 23. 29. nothing laid to his charge *worthy of d*.
25. 11. if I have committed any thing *worthy of d*.
25. found he had committed nothing *worthy of d*.
26. 31. this man doth nothing *worthy of d*.
Rom. 1. 32. who commit such things are *worthy of d*.

DEATHS.

Jer. 16. 4. they shall die of grievous *d*. not be buried
Ezek. 28. 8. shalt die *d*. of them that are slain in seas
10. thou shalt die the *d*. of the uncircumcised
2 *Cor*. 11. 23. in prisons more frequent, in *d*. oft

DEBASE.

Isa. 57. 9. and didst *d*. thyself even unto hell

DEBATE, *Verb*.

Prov. 25. 9. *d*. thy cause with thy neighbour himself
Isa. 27. 8. in measure, thou wilt *d*. with it, he stayeth

DEBATE, S.

Isa. 58. 4. behold, ye fast for strife and *d*. and to smite
Rom. 1. 29. full of envy, murder, *d*. deceit, malignity
2 *Cor*. 12. 20. I fear lest there be *d*. wraths, strifes

DEBT

Is *what is due by one man to another*, Neh. 10. 31. Sins *are by resemblance called* debts, *Mat*. 6. 12. *As a debt obliges the debtor to payment, so sin doth the sinner to punishment. And as the creditor hath a right to exact the payment from the debtor, so God hath a right to inflict punishment on the guilty. Thus men are debtors to God, by trespassing against him; and to their neighbours, when they wrong, injure, or offend them*, Mat. 6. 12. *The apostle* Paul *says*, Rom. 1. 14. I am a debtor both to the *Greeks* and *barbarians*. *I am bound by my office to preach the gospel to all nations, whether more civilized, or more rude. And speaking of such as looked upon circumcision as necessary to their justification and salvation, he says*, I testify to every man that is circumcised, that he is a debtor to do the whole law, *Gal*. 5. 3. *He obliges himself to keep the whole law, as the condition of life, and so virtually disclaims all pardon by* Christ.

1 *Sam*. 22. 2. every one that was in *d*. went to David
2 *Kings* 4. 7. he said, go, sell the oil, pay thy *d*. and live
Neh. 10. 31. we would leave the exaction of every *d*.
Mat. 18. 27. loosed him, and forgave him the *d*.
30. went and cast into prison till he should pay *d*.
32. his lord said, I forgave thee all that *d*.
Rom. 4. 4. reward is not reckoned of grace but *d*.

DEBTOR.

Ezek. 18. 7. but hath restored to the *d*. his pledge
Mat. 23. 16. shall swear by gold of the temple is a *d*.
† 18. whoso sweareth by the gift, he is the *d*.
Rom. 1. 14. I am *d*. to the Greeks and barbarians
Gal. 5. 3. that he is a *d*. to do the whole law

DEBTORS.

Mat. 6. 12. forgive us our debts, as we forgive our *d*.
Luke 7. 41. a certain creditor had two *d*.
13. † 4. think ye that they were *d*. above all men?
16. 5. he called every one of his lord's *d*.
Rom. 8. 12. therefore, brethren, we are *d*. not to flesh
15. 27. it pleased them verily, and their *d*. they are

DEBTS.

Prov. 22. 26. be not of them that are sureties for *d*.
Mat. 6. 12. forgive us our *d*. as we forgive our debtors

DECAY.

Lev. 25. 35. if thy brother be poor and fallen in *d*.
Rom. 11. † 12. *d*. of them the riches of the Gentiles

DECAYED.

Neh. 4. 10. the strength of the bearers of burdens *d*.
Isa. 44. 26. I will raise up the *d*. places thereof

DECAYETH.

Job 14. 11. and as the flood *d*. and drieth up
Eccl. 10. 18. by much slothfulness the building *d*.
Heb. 8. 13. that which *d*. is ready to vanish away

DECEASE.

Luke 9. 31. and spake of his *d*. at Jerusalem
2 *Pet*. 1. 15. after my *d*. to have in remembrance

DECEASED.

Isa. 26. 14. they are *d*. they shall not rise
Mat. 22. 25. first, when he had married a wife, *d*.

DECEIT

Signifies, [1] *Guile or fraud*, Psal. 10. 7. | 36. 3. [2] *Deceitful persons*, Jer. 9. 6. [3] *Deluding messages, dreams, and lies, of false teachers, whereby they please the humours, and comply with the lusts, of sinful persons*, Isa. 30. 10. Jer. 8. 5. [4] *Goods gotten by oppression, false accusation, and deceit*, Jer. 5. 27. Zeph. 1. 9. [5] *Devices or fair pretences to deceive*, Psal. 38. 12.

They handle the word of God deceitfully, 2 Cor. 4. 2. *who mingle it with their own inventions, or passions of pride, covetousness, &c. or wrest it according to men's pleasures*.

Job 15. 35. and their belly prepareth *d*.
27. 4. my lips not speak, nor my tongue utter *d*.
31. 5. or if my foot hath hasted to *d*.
Psal. 5. † 6. the Lord will abhor the man of *d*.
10. 7. his mouth is full of cursing, *d*. and fraud
36. 3. the words of his mouth are iniquity and *d*.
43. † 1. O deliver me from the man of *d*.
50. 19. thy mouth to evil, thy tongue frameth *d*.
55. 11. *d*. and guile depart not from her streets
† 23. men of *d*. shall not live half their days
72. 14. he shall redeem their soul from *d*. and viol.
101. 7. he that worketh *d*. not dwell in my house
109. † 2. the mouth of *d*. is opened against me
119. 118. trodden them that err, their *d*. is falseh.
Prov. 11. † 1. balances of *d*. are abomination to Lord
12. 5. but the counsels of the wicked are *d*.
17. but a false witness sheweth forth *d*.
20. *d*. is in the heart of them that imagine evil
14. 8. but the folly of fools is *d*.
20. 17. bread of *d*. is sweet to a man, but afterwards
† 23. and balances of *d*. are not good
26. 24. he that hateth, layeth up *d*. within him
26. whose hatred is covered by *d*. his wickedness
Isa. 53. 9. neither was any *d*. in his mouth
Jer. 5. 27. cage full of birds, so are houses full of *d*.
8. 5. they hold fast *d*. they refuse to return
9. 6. thro' *d*. they refuse to know me, saith the L.
8. tongue is as an arrow shot out, it speaketh *d*.
14. 14. they prophesy the *d*. of their heart
23. 26. they are prophets of *d*. of their own heart
42. † 20. you have used *d*. against your souls
Ezek. 22. † 7. in thee have they dealt by *d*.
† 29. the people of the land have used *d*.
Hos. 11. 12. the house of Isr. compasseth me with *d*.
12. 7. the balances of *d*. are in his hands
Amos 8. 5. and falsifying the balances by *d*.
Zeph. 1. 9. who fill their masters' houses with *d*.
Mark 7. 22. out of the heart of men proceed *d*.
Rom. 1. 29. full of murder, debate, *d*. malignity
3. 13. with their tongues they have used *d*.
Col. 2. 8. lest any man spoil you thro' vain philos. *d*.
1 *Thess*. 2. 3. for our exhortation was not of *d*.

DECEITFUL.

Ps. 5. 6. the Lord will abhor the bloody and *d*. man
35. 20. they devise *d*. matters ag. them quiet in land
43. 1. O deliver me from the *d*. and unjust man
52. 4. lovest devouring words, O thou *d*. tongue
55. 23. bloody and *d*. men shall not live half their *d*.
78. 57. they were turned aside like a *d*. bow
109. 2. the mouth of the *d*. are opened against me
120. 2. deliver my soul from a *d*. tongue
Prov. 11. 18. the wicked worketh a *d*. work
12. † 24. but the *d*. shall be under tribute
14. 25. but a *d*. witness speaketh lies
23. 3. not desirous of dainties for they are *d*. meat
27. 6. but the kisses of an enemy are *d*.
29. 13. the poor and the *d*. man meet together
31. 30. favour is *d*. and beauty is vain, but a woman
Jer. 17. 9. the heart is *d*. above all things and wicked
Hos. 7. 16. return not to most High, are like a *d*. bow
Mic. 6. 11. and with the bag of *d*. weights
12. and their tongue is *d*. in their mouth
Zeph. 3. 13. nor shall a *d*. tongue be found in mouth
2 *Cor*. 11. 13. such are false apostles, *d*. workers
Eph. 4. 22. old man corrupt according to the *d*. lusts

DECEITFULLY.

Gen. 34. 13. sons answered Hamor and Shechem *d*.
Exod. 8. 29. let not Pharaoh deal *d*. any more
21. 8. seeing he hath dealt *d*. with her
Lev. 6. 4. or the thing which he hath *d*. gotten
Job 6. 15. my brethren have dealt *d*. as a brook
13. 7. will ye talk wickedly or *d*. for God?
Psal. 24. 4. hath not lift up his soul nor sworn *d*.
52. 2. thy tongue like a sharp razor, working *d*.
Jer. 48. 10. cursed that doth work of the Lord *d*.
Dan. 11. 23. after the league made, he shall work *d*.
2 *Cor*. 2. † 17. not as many that deal *d*. with word
4. 2. not in craftiness, nor handling word of God *d*.

DECEITFULNESS.

Mat. 13. 22. the care of this world, and the *d*. of riches choke the word, *Mark* 4. 19.
Heb. 3. 13. lest any be hardened thro' the *d*. of sin

DECEITS.

Psal. 38. 12. seek my hurt, and imagine *d*. all day
Isa. 30. 10. speak to us smooth things, prophesy *d*.
33. † 15. he that despiseth the gain of *d*.

DECEIVE

Signifies, [1] *To beguile, cheat, or cozen*, Gen. 31. 7. Lev. 6. 2. [2] *To mislead, subdue, or corrupt*, Deut. 11. 16. Isa. 44. 20. [3] *To allure, delude, or entice*, Job 31. 9.

I the Lord have deceived that prophet, *Ezek*. 14. 9. *I have given him up to the delusions of his own heart, and justly left him in his blindness, that he shall not discern his own self-deceivings: Or, when such a prophet promiseth good, and thinks that he concurrence of all second causes tend to it, I will disappoint and frustrate*.

O Lord, thou hast deceived me, and I was deceived, *Jer.* 20. 7. that is, *Thou hast persuaded me to undertake this office, contrary to my own inclinations, and hast disappointed me of that comfort and satisfaction therein that I expected.*
2 *Sam.* 3. 25. thou knowest Abner came to *d.* thee
1 *Kings* 22. † 20. the Lord said, who shall *d.* Ahab?
2 *Kings* 4. 28. she said, did not I say, do not *d.* me?
18. 29. saith king, let not Hezekiah *d.* you, not able to deliver you, 2 *Chron.* 32. 15. *Isa.* 36. 14.
19. 10. let not thy God *d.* thee, saying, *Isa.* 37. 10.
Prov. 24. 28. be not a witness, and *d.* not with lips
Isa. 58. † 11. like a spring whose waters *d.* not
Jer. 9. 5. they will *d.* every one his neighbour
29. 8. your diviners that be in midst of you *d.* you
37. 9. thus saith the Lord, *d.* not yourselves
Hos. 12. † 7. he is a merchant, he loveth to *d.*
Zech. 13. 4. neither wear a rough garment to *d.*
Mat. 24. 4. take heed that no man *d.* you, *Mark* 13. 5.
5. saying, I am Christ, *d.* many, 11. *Mark* 13. 6.
24. that, if possible, they shall *d.* the very elect
Acts 5. † 3. why hath Satan filled thy heart to *d.?*
Rom. 16. 18. by fair speeches *d.* the hearts of simple
1 *Cor.* 3. 18. let no man *d.* himself, if any man seems
Eph. 4. 14. craftiness whereby they lie in wait to *d.*
5. 6. let no man *d.* you, 2 *Thess.* 2. 3. 1 *John* 3. 7.
1 *John* 1. 8. if we say we have no sin, we *d.* ourselves
Rev. 20. 3. that he should *d.* the nations no more
8. go to *d.* nations in four quarters of the earth

DECEIVABLENESS.

2 *Thess.* 2. 10. and with all *d.* of unrighteousness

DECEIVED.

Gen. 31. 7. father hath *d.* me and changed my wages
Lev. 6. 2. or if a soul sin, or hath *d.* his neighbour
Deut. 11. 16. take heed that your heart be not *d.*
1 *Sam.* 19. 17. why hast thou *d.* me so? 28. 12.
2 *Sam.* 19. 26. my lord, O king, my servant *d.* me
Job 12. 16. the *d.* and the deceiver are his
15. 31. let not him that is *d.* trust in vanity
31. 9. if mine heart have been *d.* by a woman
Isa. 19. 13. the princes of Noph are *d.* seduced Egypt
44. 20. a *d.* heart hath turned him aside that cannot
Jer. 4. 10. surely thou hast greatly *d.* this people
20. 7. O Lord, thou hast *d.* me, and I was *d.*
49. 16. thy terribleness hath *d.* thee and pride of heart
Lam. 1. 19. I called for my lovers, but they *d.* me
Ezek. 14. 9. if the prophet be *d.* I have *d.* him
Obad. 3. the pride of thine heart hath *d.* thee
7. men that were at peace with thee have *d.* thee
Luke 21. 8. he said, take heed that ye be not *d.*
John 7. 47. the Pharisees answered, are ye also *d.?*
Rom. 7. 11. for sin taking occasion by comm. *d.* me
1 *Cor.* 6. 9. be not *d.* 15. 33. *Gal.* 6. 7.
1 *Tim.* 2. 14. Adam was not *d.* but woman being *d.*
2 *Tim.* 3. 13. wax worse and worse, deceiv. and being *d.*
Tit. 3. 3. we were foolish *d.* serving divers lusts
Rev. 18. 23. by thy sorceries all nations were *d.*
19. 20. he *d.* them that had received mark of beast
20. 10. devil that *d.* them was cast into lake of fire

DECEIVER.

Gen. 27. 12. and I shall seem to my father as a *d.*
Job 12. 16. the deceived and the *d.* are his
Mal. 1. 14. cursed be *d.* who hath in his flock a male
Mat. 27. 63. rememb. that that *d.* said, after 3 days
2 *John* 7. confess not Jes. this is a *d.* and an antichrist

DECEIVERS.

2 *Cor.* 6. 8. by evil and good report, as *d.* and yet true
Tit. 1. 10. many *d.* especially of the circumcision
2 *John* 7. for many *d.* are entered into the world

DECEIVETH.

2 *Kings* 18. † 32. hearken not to Hezekiah when he *d.*
Prov. 26. 19. so is the man that *d.* his neighbour
John 7. 12. others said, nay, but he *d.* the people
Gal. 6. 3. to be something when nothing, he *d.* hims.
Jam. 1. 26. *d.* his own heart, this man's relig. is vain
Rev. 12. 9. that old serpent, called the devil, which *d.*
13. 14. and *d.* them that dwell on the earth

DECEIVING.

Isa. 3. † 16. daughters of Zion *d.* with their eyes
2 *Tim.* 3. 13. evil men wax worse, *d.* and being deceiv.
Jam. 1. 22. and not hearers only *d.* your own selves

DECEIVINGS.

2 *Pet.* 2. 13. sporting themselves with their own *d.*

DECENTLY.

Rom. 13. † 13. let us walk *d.* as in day, not in rioting
1 *Cor.* 14. 40. let all things be done *d.* and in order

DECIDED.

1 *Kings* 20. 40. the king said, thyself hast *d.* it

DECISION.

Joel 3. 14. multitudes in valley of *d.* for day of Lord

DECK.

Job 40. 10. *d.* thyself now with majesty and excell.
Jer. 10. 4. they *d.* it with silver and with gold

DECKED.

Prov. 7. 16. I have *d.* my bed with cover. of tapestry
Isa. 63. † 1. who is this that is *d.* in his apparel?
Ezek. 16. 11. I *d.* thee also with ornaments
13. thou wast thus *d.* with gold and silver
Hos. 2. 13. and she *d.* herself with her ear-rings
Rev. 17. 4. the woman was arrayed and *d.* with gold
18. 16. alas, alas, that great city that was *d.*

DECKEDST.

Ezek. 16. 16. didst take garm. and *d.* high-places
23. 40. didst wash and *d.* thyself with ornaments

DECKEST, ETH.

Isa. 61. 10. as a bridegroom *d.* himself with ornam.
Jer. 4. 30. tho' thou *d.* thee with ornaments of gold

DECLARE.

Gen. 41. 24. there was none that could *d.* it to me
Deut. 1. 5. in land of Moab began Moses to *d.* this law
Josh. 20. 4. shall *d.* his cause in ears of elders of city
Judg. 14. 12. if ye can *d.* it me within the seven days
1 *Kings* 22. 13. prophets *d.* good to king, 2 *Ch.* 18. 12.
1 *Chron.* 16. 24. *d.* his glory among the heathen, his marvellous works among all nations, *Psal.* 96. 3.
Esth. 4. 8. to shew the copy and *d.* it to Esther
Job 12. 8. the fishes of the sea shall *d.* unto thee
21. 31. who shall *d.* his way to his face?
28. 27. then did he see it, and *d.* it, he prepared it
31. 37. I would *d.* to him the number of my steps
38. 4. found. of earth, *d.* if thou hast understanding
18. the breadth of earth, *d.* if thou knowest it all

Job 40. 7. I will demand of thee, *d.* thou to me, 42. 4.
Psal. 9. 11. *d.* among the people his doings
19. 1. the heavens *d.* the glory of God
22. 31. shall come and *d.* his righteous. 50. 6. | 97. 6.
30. 9. shall dust praise thee, shall it *d.* thy truth?
40. 5. if I would *d.* and speak of them, they are more
50. 16. what hast thou to do to *d.* my statutes?
64. 9. all men shall fear and *d.* the work of God
73. 28. my trust in L. that I may *d.* all thy works
75. 1. thy name is near thy wondrous works *d.*
78. 6. should arise and *d.* them to their children
102. 21. to *d.* the name of the Lord in Zion
107. 22. and *d.* his works with rejoicing
118. 17. but live and *d.* the works of the Lord
145. 4. one generation shall *d.* thy mighty acts
Eccl. 9. 1. I considered in my heart even to *d.* all this
Isa. 3. 9. they *d.* their sin as Sodom, they hide not
12. 4. shall ye say, *d.* his doings among the people
21. 6. set a watchman, let him *d.* what he seeth
41. 22. or let them *d.* to us things for to come
42. 9. and new things do I *d.* before they spring
12. and let them *d.* his praise in the islands
43. 9. who among them can *d.* this, and shew us?
26. *d.* thou that thou mayest be justified
44. 7. and who, as I, shall call, and shall *d.* it?
45. 19. I the Lord *d.* things that are right
48. 6. see all this, and will not ye *d.* it?
53. 8. who shall *d.* his generation? *Acts* 8. 33.
66. 19. they shall *d.* my glory among the Gentiles
Jer. 5. 20. *d.* this in house of Jacob, publish in Judah
9. 12. the Lord hath spoken, that he may *d.* it
31. 10. and *d.* it in the isles afar off, and say
38. 15. if I *d.* it to thee, wilt thou not put to death?
25. *d.* unto us what thou hast said to the king
42. 20. what G. shall say, *d.* to us, and we will do it
50. 28. *d.* in Zion the vengeance of the L. our G.
51. 10. let us *d.* in Zion the work of the L. our G.
Ezek. 12. 16. may *d.* all their abominations, 23. 36.
40. 4. *d.* all that thou seest to the house of Israel
Dan. 4. 18. O Belteshazzar, *d.* the interpretation
Mic. 3. 8. to *d.* to Jacob his transgression, and Israel
Zech. 9. 12. even to-day do I *d.* that I will render
Mat. 13. 36. *d.* unto us the parable of tares of field
15. 15. then said Peter, *d.* unto us this parable
Acts 13. 32. and we *d.* unto you glad tidings
41. shall in no wise believe, tho' a man *d.* it to you
17. 23. whom ye ignorantly worship, him *d.* I to you
20. 27. not shunned to *d.* to you the counsel of God
Rom. 3. 25. set forth to *d.* his righteousness, 26.
1 *Cor.* 3. 13. work be manifest, the day shall *d.* it
11. 17. in this that I *d.* to you, I praise you not
15. 1. I *d.* unto you the gospel which I preached
Col. 4. 7. all my state shall Tychicus *d.* to you
Heb. 11. 14. they that say such things *d.* plainly that
1 *John* 1. 3. that which we have seen *d.* we to you
5. this then is the message which we *d.* unto you

I will DECLARE.

Job 15. 17. and that which I have seen *I will d.*
Psal. 2. 7. *I will d.* the decree, the Lord hath said
22. 22. *I will d.* thy name to brethren, *Heb.* 2. 12.
38. 18. *I will d.* mine iniquity, I will be sorry for sin
66. 16. *I will d.* what he hath done for my soul
75. 9. but *I will d.* for ever, I will sing praises to G.
145. 6. speak of thy acts, *I will d.* thy greatness
Isa. 57. 12. *I will d.* thy righteousness and thy works
Jer. 42. 4. *I will d.* it, I will keep nothing back
John 17. 26. have declared thy name, and *will d.* it

DECLARE *ye.*

Isa. 48. 20. with a voice of singing *d. ye*, tell this
Jer. 4. 5. *d. ye* in Judah, and publish in Jerusalem
46. 14. *d. ye* in Egypt, and publish in Migdol
50. 2. *d. ye* among the nations, publish, conceal not
Mic. 1. 10. *d. ye* it not at Gath, weep ye not at all

DECLARATION.

Esth. 10. 2. the *d.* of the greatness of Mordecai
Job 13. 17. and hear my *d.* with your ears
Luke 1. 1. taken in hand to set forth in order a *d.*
2 *Cor.* 8. 19. and to the *d.* of your ready mind

DECLARED.

Exod. 9. 16. I raised thee, that my name may be *d.*
Lev. 23. 44. Moses *d.* to the children of Israel
Num. 1. 18. they *d.* their pedigrees by their poll
15. 34. put him in ward, because it was not *d.*
Deut. 4. 13. and he *d.* to you his covenant
2 *Sam.* 19. 6. for thou hast *d.* this day that thou
Neh. 8. 12. understood words that were *d.* to them
Job 26. 3. how hast thou plentifully *d.* thing as it is
Psal. 40. 10. I have *d.* thy faithfulness and salvation
71. 17. hitherto have I *d.* thy wondrous works
77. 14. thou hast *d.* thy strength among the people
88. 11. shall thy loving-kindness be *d.* in the grave
119. 13. with my lips have I *d.* all the judgments
26. I have *d.* my ways, and thou heardest me
Isa. 21. 2. a grievous vision is *d.* unto me
10. that which I heard of God have I *d.* unto you
41. 26. who hath *d.* from the beginning, 45. 21.
43. 12. I have *d.* and have saved, 44. 8. | 48. 5.
48. 3. I have *d.* former things from the beginning
14. which among them hath *d.* these things?
Jer. 36. 13. Micaiah *d.* all the words he heard
42. 21. and now I have this day *d.* it to you
Luke 8. 47. she *d.* to him before all the people
John 1. 18. no man hath seen God, the Son *d.* him
17. 26. I have *d.* to them thy name and will declare
Acts 9. 27. he *d.* to them how he had seen the Lord
10. 8. when he had *d.* all these things to them
12. 17. he *d.* how L. had brought him out of prison
15. 4. *d.* all things that God had done with them
14. Simeon hath *d.* how God at first did visit
25. 14. Festus *d.* Paul's cause to the king, saying
Rom. 1. 4. and *d.* to be the Son of God with power
9. 17. that my name might be *d.* through the earth
1 *Cor.* 1. 11. for it hath been *d.* to me of you
2 *Cor.* 3. 3. ye are manifestly *d.* to be the epistle of C.
Col. 1. 8. who also *d.* to us your love in the Spirit
Rev. 10. 7. the mystery of God be finished as he *d.*

DECLARETH, ING.

Isa. 41. 26. yea, there is none that *d.* that heareth
46. 10. *d.* the end from the beginning, and from
Jer. 4. 15. a voice *d.* from Dan, publisheth affliction
Hos. 4. 12. my people, their staff *d.* unto them
Amos 4. 13. lo, he that *d.* to man what is his thought

Acts 15. 3. *d.* the conversion of the Gentiles
12. *d.* what miracles God had wrought by them
1 *Cor.* 2. 1. *d.* to you the testimony of God

DECLINE.

Exod. 23. 2. nor speak in a cause, to *d.* after many
Deut. 17. 11. thou shalt not *d.* from the sentence
Psal. 119. 157. yet do I not *d.* from thy testimonies
Prov. 4. 5. neither *d.* from the words of my mouth
7. 25. let not thine heart *d.* to her ways, go not astray

DECLINED, ETH.

Judg. 19. † 8. they tarried till the day *d.*
2 *Chr.* 34. 2. *d.* neither to the right-hand nor left
Job 23. 11. his way have I kept and not *d.*
Psal. 44. 18. nor have our steps *d.* from thy way
102. 11. my days are like a shadow that *d.*
109. 23. I am gone like the shadow when it *d.*
119. 51. yet have I not *d.* from thy law

DECREASE.

Ps. 107. 38. blesseth them and suffer not cattle to *d.*
John 3. 30. he must increase, but I must *d.*

DECREASED, ING.

Gen. 8. 5. the waters *d.* continually till tenth month
† the waters were in going and *d.* till tenth month

DECREE.

2 *Chron.* 30. 5. so they established a *d.* to make procl.
Ezra 4. † 21. make a *d.* to cause these men to cease
5. 13. king Cyrus made a *d.* to build this house, 17.
6. 1. Darius made a *d.* 12. ‖ 7. 21. Artaxerxes a *d.*
Esth. 3. 15. the *d.* was given in Shushan, 9. 14.
9. 32. *d.* of Esther confirmed these matters of Purim
Job 20. † 29. and the heritage of his *d.* from God
28. 26. when he made a *d.* for the rain, and a way
38. † 10. and established my *d.* upon it, and set bars
Psal. 2. 7. I will declare the *d.* the Lord hath said
148. 6. he hath made a *d.* which shall not pass
Prov. 8. 29. when he gave to sea his *d.* waters not pass
Jer. 5. 22. for the bound of the sea by a perpetual *d.*
Dan. 2. 9. if ye will not, there is but one *d.* for you
4. 17. this matter is by the *d.* of the watchers
24. and this is the *d.* of the most High
6. 8. now, O king, establish the *d.* and sign writing
13. Daniel regardeth not thee, nor a *d.* hast signed
26. I make a *d.* that in every dominion men fear
Jonah 3. 7. proclaimed by the *d.* of king and nobles
Mic. 7. 11. in that day shall the *d.* be far removed
Zeph. 2. 2. before the *d.* bring forth, before day pass
Luke 2. 1. there went out a *d.* from Cæsar Augustus

DECREE.

Job 22. 28. thou shalt also *d.* a thing, and it shall be
Prov. 8. 15. by me kings reign, and princes *d.* justice
Isa. 10. 1. woe to them that *d.* unrighteous decrees

DECREED.

Esth. 2. 1. he remembered what was *d.* ag. Vashti
9. 31. as they had *d.* for themselves and their seed
Job 38. 10. and brake up for it my *d.* place, set bars
Isa. 10. 22. consumption *d.* shall overflow with right.
1 *Cor.* 7. 37. hath so *d.* in his heart, that he will keep

DECREES.

Isa. 10. 1. woe to them that decree unrighteous *d.*
Acts 16. 4. they delivered them the *d.* to keep
17. 7. these do contrary to the *d.* of Cæsar, saying

DEDICATE.

Deut. 20. 5. lest he die and another man *d.* it
2 *Sam.* 8. 11. which also David did *d.* to the Lord
1 *Chron.* 26. 27. out of spoils they did *d.* to maintain
2 *Chr.* 2. 4. behold I build an house to *d.* it to God

DEDICATED.

Deut. 20. 5. hath built a new house and hath not *d.* it
Judg. 17. 3. I had wholly *d.* the silver to the Lord
1 *Kings* 7. 51. Solom. brought in things which David his father had *d.* 1 *Chron.* 18. 11. 2 *Chron.* 5. 1.
8. 63. the king and Israel *d.* the house, 2 *Chr.* 7. 5.
15. 15. Asa brought in the things his fathers had *d.* and things which himself had *d.* 2 *Chr.* 15. 18.
2 *Kings* 12. 4. all the money of the *d.* things brought
18. the things the kings of Judah had *d.*
1 *Chron.* 26. 20. over the treasures of *d.* things, 26.
26. what the captains of the hosts had *d.*
28. and all that Samuel, Saul, and Joab had *d.*
28. 12. the pattern of the treasures of *d.* things
2 *Chr.* 24. 7. the *d.* things did bestow upon Baalim
31. 12. and brought in the *d.* things faithfully
Ezek. 44. 29. every *d.* thing in Israel shall be theirs
Heb. 9. 18. nor the first testament *d.* without blood

DEDICATING.

Num. 7. 10. the princes offered for *d.* of the altar
11. each prince on his day for *d.* of the altar

DEDICATION.

Num. 7. 84. this was the *d.* of the altar, 88.
2 *Chron.* 7. 9. for they kept the *d.* of the altar
Ezra 6. 16. childr. of captivity kept the *d.* with joy
17. and offered at the *d.* of this house of God
Neh. 12. 27. at the *d.* of the wall of Jerusalem
Dan. 3. 2. come to *d.* of the image the king set up, 3.
John 10. 22. it was at Jerusalem the feast of the *d.*

DEED.

Gen. 44. 15. Joseph said, what *d.* is this ye have done.
Exod. 9. 16. in very *d.* for this cause I raised thee up
Judg. 19. 30. all said, there was no such *d.* done
1 *Sam.* 25. 34. in very *d.* except thou hadst hasted
26. 4. David understood Saul was come in very *d.*
2 *Sam.* 12. 14. by this *d.* hast given great occasion
Esth. 1. 17. for this *d.* of queen shall come abroad
Ps. 137. † 8. happy that recompenseth thy *d.* to us
Prov. 19. † 17. his *d.* will he pay him again
Luke 23. 51. Joseph had not consented to *d.* of them
24. 19. Jesus who was a prophet mighty in *d.*
Acts 4. 9. if we this day be examined of the good *d.*
Rom. 15. 18. to make Gent. obedient by word and *d*
1 *Cor.* 5. 2. that hath done this *d.* be taken away
3. concerning him that hath so done this *d.*
Col. 3. 17. whatever ye do in word or *d.* do all in name
Jam. 1. 25. this man shall be blessed in his *d.*
1 *John* 3. 18. let us not love in word, but in *d.*

DEEDS.

Gen. 20. 9. hast done *d.* that ought not to be done
1 *Chron.* 11. † 22. son of a man of Kabzeel, great of *d.*
16. 8. make known his *d.* am. people, *Psal.* 105. 1.
2 *Chron.* 35. 27. his *d.* first and last, are written
Ezra 9. 13. after all is come upon us for our evil *d.*
Neh. 6. 19. also they reported his good *d.* before me
13. 14. wipe not out my good *d.* that I have done

Psal. 28. 4. gave them according to their *d.*
Isa. 59. 18. according to their *d.* he will repay
Jer. 5. 28. they overpass the *d.* of the wicked
25. 14. will recompense them according to their *d.*
Luke 11. 48. that ye allow the *d.* of your fathers
23. 41. we receive the due reward of our *d.*
John 3.19. loved darkness, because their *d.*were evil
20. to the light, lest his *d.* should be reproved
21. that his *d.* may be made manifest, that they
8. 41. Jesus saith, ye do the *d.* of your father
Acts 7. 22. Moses was mighty in word and in *d.*
9. 36. Dorcas was full of alms-*d.* which she did
19. 18. many confessed, and shewed their *d.*
24. 2. seeing by thy providence worthy *d.* are done
Rom. 2. 6. render to every man according to his *d.*
3. 20. by the *d.* of the law shall no flesh be justified
28. is justified by faith without the *d.* of the law
8. 13. if ye mortify the *d.* of the body ye shall live
2 *Cor.* 12. 12. were wrought in signs and mighty *d.*
Col. 3. 9. ye have put off the old man with his *d.*
2 *Pet.* 2. 8. Lot vexed his soul with their unlawful *d.*
2 *John* 11. for he is partaker of his evil *d.*
3 *John* 10. I will remember his *d.* which he doth
Jude 15. to convince them of their ungodly *d.*
Rev. 2. 6. thou hatest the *d.* of the Nicolaitans
22. great tribulation, except they repent of their *d.*
16. 11. and they repented not of their *d.*

DEEMED.

Acts 27. 27. the shipmen *d.* that they drew near

DEEP

Signifies, [1] *That which is a great way from the surface to the bottom*, Ezek. 32. 24. [2] *The sea*, Job 41. 31. [3] *Any great and imminent danger*, Psal. 69. 15. [4] *Strange, or unknown*, Isa. 33. 19. [5] *Hidden, or secret*, Job 12. 22. Dan. 2. 22. [6] *Inconceivable, or incomprehensible*, Psal. 92. 5. [7] *Hell*, Luke 8. 31. Rev. 20. 3. [8] *The* Chaldean, *or* Nebuchadnezzar's, *army*, Ezek. 26. 19.

A wise man's words are compared to deep waters, *Prov.* 18. 4. *They are full of deep wisdom and prudent counsels. And the apostle says*, Rom. 8. 39. *that* neither height nor depth shall be able to separate us from the love of God. *Neither the most exalted height, a prospect of advancement in the highest station, nor the lowest degree of adversity and distress.*

To revolt, or sin deeply, *denotes a long habit of crimes, and obstinate course of idolatry; or else a profound and very great iniquity, a crime that has taken deep root in the soul by long and inveterate custom;* they have deeply corrupted themselves as in the days of *Gibeah*, Hos. 9. 9. *They have carried on their wickedness to such a pitch, as to imitate the ancient crimes of the inhabitants of* Gibeah, *which are recorded in* Judg. 19. 22, &c. *And* Isaiah *says*, Turn ye unto him from whom the children of *Israel* have deeply revolted, *namely, by neglecting and forsaking him, and seeking to* Egypt *for help*, Isa. 31. 6.

Gen. 1. 2. and darkness was upon the face of the *d.*
7. 11. the fountains of the *d.* were broken up
8. 2. the fountains also of the *d.* were stopped
49. 25. who shall bless thee with blessings of the *d.*
Deut. 33. 13. and for the *d.* that coucheth beneath
Job 38. 30. and the face of the *d.* is frozen
41. 31. he maketh the *d.* to boil like a pot
32. one would think the *d.* to be hoary
Psal. 36. 6. thy judgments are a great *d.*
42. 7. *d.* calleth to *d.* at noise of thy water-spouts
69. 15. neither let the *d.* swallow me up
104. 6. thou coveredst it with the *d.* as with garm.
107. 24. and these see his wonders in the *d.*
Prov. 8. 28. he strengtheus the fountains of the *d.*
Isa. 44. 27. that saith to the *d.* be dry, I will dry
51. 10. thou not it which dried waters of great *d.?*
63. 13. that led them through the *d.* as an horse
Ezek. 26. 19. when I shall bring up the *d.* on thee
31. 4. the *d.* set him on high with her rivers
15. I covered the *d.* for him, I restrained floods
Amos 7. 4. it devoured great *d.* and did eat up a part
Jonah 2. 3. for thou hadst cast me into the *d.*
Hab. 3. 10. the *d.* uttered his voice, and lift up hands
Luke 5. 4. launch out in the *d.*and let down your nets
8. 31. would not command them to go into the *d.*
Rom. 10. 7. or who shall descend into the *d.?*
2 *Cor.* 11. 25. a night and day I have been in the *d.*

DEEP, *Adjective.*

Job 12. 22. he discovereth *d.* things out of darkness
Psal. 64. 6. the inward thought and the heart is *d.*
69. 2. I sink in *d.* mire, where is no standing, I am come into *d.* waters, where floods overflow me
14. let me be delivered out of the *d.* waters
80. 9. and thou didst cause it to take *d.* root
92. 5. O Lord, thy thoughts are very *d.*
95. 4. in his hand are the *d.* places of the earth
135. 6. that did he in the seas and all *d.* places
140. 10. them be cast into *d.* pits that they rise not
Prov. 18. 4. words of a man's mouth are as *d.* waters
20. 5. counsel in the heart of man is like *d.* waters
22. 14. the mouth of strange women is a *d.* pit
23. 27. for a whore is a *d.* ditch, and a narrow pit
Eccl. 7. 24. and exceeding *d.* who can find it out?
Isa. 7. † 11. ask thee a sign, make thy petition *d.*
29. 15. woe to them that seek *d.* to hide their couns.
30. 33. he hath made Tophet *d.* and large
Jer. 49. 8. turn back, dwell *d.* O inhabit. of Dedan
Ezek. 3. † 5. not sent to a people *d.* of lips, † 6.
23. 32. shalt drink of thy sister's cup *d.* and large
32. 14. then will I make their waters *d.*
34. 18. and to have drunk of the *d.* waters
Dan. 2. 22. he revealeth the *d.* and secret things
Luke 6. 48. digged *d.* and laid foundation on a rock
John 4. 11. hast nothing to draw, and the well is *d.*
1 *Cor.* 2. 10. the Spirit searcheth the *d.* things of God
2 *Cor.* 8. 2. how their *d.* poverty abounded to riches

DEEP *sleep.*

Gen. 2. 21. God caused a *d. sleep* to fall on Adam
15. 12. a *d. sleep* fell on Abram, and great darkness
1 *Sam.* 26. 12. because a *d. sleep* was fallen on them
Job 4. 13. when *d. sleep* falleth on men, 33. 15.
Prov. 19. 15. slothfulness casteth into *d. sleep*
Isa. 29. 10. L. poured out on you spirit of *d. sleep*
Dan. 8. 18. I was in a *d. sleep* on my face, 10. 9.
Acts 20. 9. Eutychus being fallen into *d. sleep*

DEEPER.

Lev. 13. 3. the plague in sight be *d.* than skin, 25. 30.
4. if the bright spot in sight be not *d.* 31, 32, 34.
Job 11. 8. it is *d.* than hell, what canst thou know?
Isa. 33. 19. a people of *d.* speech than canst perceive

DEEPLY.

Isa. 31. 6. the children of Israel have *d.* revolted
Hos. 9. 9. they have *d.* corrupt. themselves as in days
Mark 8. 12. Jesus sighed *d.* in his spirit, and saith

DEEPNESS.

Mat. 13. 5. sprung up, because they had no *d.* of earth

DEEPS.

Neh. 9. 11. their persecutors thou threwest into the *d.*
Psal. 88. 6. thou hast laid me in the pit, in the *d.*
148. 7. praise the Lord, ye dragons and all *d.*
Zech. 10. 11. all the *d.* of the river shall dry up

DEER.

Deut. 14. 5. ye shall eat the fallow *d.* and wild goat
1 *Kings* 4. 23. Solom. had fallow *d.* and fatted fowl

DEFAMED.

1 *Cor.* 4. 13. being *d.* we intreat, are made offscouring

DEFAMING.

Jer. 20. 10. for I heard *d.* of many, fear on every side

DEFEAT.

2 *Sam.* 15. 34. *d.* the counsel of Ahithophel, 17. 14.

DEFENCE.

Num. 14. 9. their *d.* is depart. from them, L. with us
2 *Chron.* 11. 5. Rehoboam built cities for *d.* of Jud.
Job 22. 25. yea, the Almighty shall be thy *d.*
Psal. 7. 10. my *d.* is of G. which saveth the upright
31. 2. be thou for an house of *d.* to save me
59. 9. I will wait upon thee, for G. is my *d.* 17.
16. thou hast been my *d.* and refuge in trouble
62. 2. God is my *d.* I shall not be greatly moved, 6.
89. 18. for Lord is our *d.* holy One of Israel our king
94. 22. Lord is my *d.* and God rock of my refuge
Eccl. 7. 12. for wisdom is a *d.* and money is a *d.*
Isa. 4. 5. for upon all the glory shall be a *d.*
19. 6. the brooks of *d.* shall be emptied and dried
33. 16. his place of *d.* shall be the munitions of rocks
Nah. 2. 5. and the *d.* shall be prepared
Acts 19. 33. would have made his *d.* to the people
22. 1. hear my *d.* which I make now unto you
Phil. 1. 7. in my bonds and in the *d.* of the gospel
17. knowing that I am set for the *d.* of the gospel

DEFENCED.

Zech. 11. † 2. for the *d.* forest is come down
See City, Cities.

DEFEND.

Judg. 10. 1. Tola son of Puah arose to *d.* Israel
2 *Kings* 19. 34. I will *d.* city, 20. 6. *Isa.* 37. 35. | 38. 6.
Psal. 20. 1. the name of the God of Jacob *d.* thee
59. 1. *d.* me from them that rise up against me
82. 3. *d.* the poor and fatherless, do justice to needy
Isa. 31. 5. so will the Lord of hosts *d.* Jerusalem
Zech. 9. 15. the Lord of hosts shall *d.* them
12. 8. in that day shall Lord *d.* inhabitants of Jerus.

DEFENDED.

2 *Sam.* 23. 12. Shammah stood and *d.* the ground
Acts 7. 24. he *d.* him and avenged the oppressed

DEFENDEST.

Psal. 5. 11. ever shout for joy, because thou *d.* them

DEFENDING.

Isa. 31. 5. *d.* Jerus. he will deliver and preserve it

DEFER.

Eccl. 5. 4. when thou vowest a vow, *d.* not to pay it
Isa. 48. 9. for my name's sake will I *d.* mine anger
Dan. 9. 19. *d.* not for thine own sake, O my God

DEFERRED.

Gen. 34. 19. the young man *d.* not to do the thing
Prov. 13. 12. hope *d.* maketh the heart sick
Acts 24. 22. when Felix heard these he *d.* them

DEFERRETH.

Prov. 19. 11. the discretion of a man *d.* his anger

DEFY.

Num. 23. 7. come, curse me Jacob, and *d.* Israel
8. how shall I *d.* whom the Lord hath not defied?
1 *Sam.* 17. 10. I *d.* the armies of Israel this day
25. is come up, surely to *d.* Israel is he come up
26. that he should *d.* the armies of the living God

DEFIED.

Num. 23. 8. how shall I defy whom Lord hath not *d.?*
1 *Sam.* 17. 36. he hath *d.* the armies of the living God
45. the God of Israel whom thou hast *d.*
2 *Sam.* 21. 21. when he *d.* Israel, Jonathan, son of Shimeah, brother of David, slew him, 1 *Chr.* 20. 7.
23. 9. when they *d.* Philistines gathered to battle

DEFILE.

Man is defiled, *or* polluted, *either inwardly, by sin*, 1 Cor. 8. 7. Tit. 1. 15. Heb. 12. 15. *or outwardly and ceremonially, as by the plague of leprosy*, Lev. 13. 46. *or by touching a dead body*, Num. 5. 2. *Both inwardly and outwardly, by following the abominations of the heathen*, Lev. 18. 24. *By seeking after wizards*, Lev. 19. 31. *By idols*, Ezek. 20. 7. *By unnatural uncleanness*, 1 Tim. 1. 10. *By the unruliness of the tongue, which involves men in the guilt of sin, and fills the world with contentions and combustions, when it is not kept under government*, Jam. 3. 6.

Man is also said to defile *others.* Shechem *defiled* Dinah, *the daughter of* Jacob; *he humbled, he debauched her, or lay carnally with her*, Gen. 34. 13. *And such as commit adultery*, defile their neighbours' wives, *Ezek.* 18. 11. *Those that gave their seed to* Molech, *are said to* defile God's sanctuary, *Lev.* 20. 3.; *because such persons, to screen their idolatry, came into his sanctuary as others did; or, because by these actions they did pronounce and declare to all men, that they esteemed the sanctuary and service of God abominable and vile, by preferring such odious and pernicious idolatry before it.*

Lev. 11. 44. nor shall ye *d.* yourselves, 18. 24.
15. 31. when they *d.* my tabernacle among them
18. 20. to *d.* thyself with thy neighbour's wife
23. neither lie with any beast to *d.* thyself
28. that the land spue not you out when ye *d.* it
20. 3. given his seed to Molech, to *d.* my sanctuary
Lev. 21. 4. he shall not *d.* himself, being a chief man
11. nor *d.* himself for his father or his mother
22. 8. he shall not eat to *d.* himself therewith
Num. 5. 3. put out, that they *d.* not their camps
35. 34. *d.* not the land which ye shall inhabit
2 *Kings* 23. 13. the high places did the king *d.*
Cant. 5. 3. have washed my feet, how shall I *d.* them?
Isa. 30. 22. shall *d.* the covering of thy graven images
Jer. 32. 34. in the house called by my name to *d.* it
Ezek. 7. 22. for robbers shall enter into it and *d.* it
9. 7. *d.* the house, fill the courts with the slain
20. 7. *d.* not yourselves with idols of Egypt, 18.
22. 3. maketh idols against herself to *d.* herself
28. 7. and they shall *d.* thy brightness
33. 26. ye *d.* every man his neighbour's wife
37. 23. nor shall they *d.* themselves any more
43. 7. and my name shall Israel no more *d.*
44. 25. shall come at no dead person to *d.* themselves
Dan. 1. 8. would not *d.* himself with the king's meat
Mat. 15. 18. and they *d.* the man, *Mark* 7. 15, 23.
1 *Cor.* 3. 17. if any man *d.* the temple of God
1 *Tim.* 1. 10. the law is for them that *d.* themselves
Jude 8. likewise these filthy dreamers *d.* the flesh

DEFILED.

Gen. 34. 2. Shechem lay with Dinah, and *d.* her
5. Jacob heard that he had *d.* Dinah his daughter
13. because he had *d.* Dinah their sister, 27.
Lev. 5. 3. what uncleanness a man shall be *d.* with
11. 43. unclean, that ye should be *d.* thereby
13. 46. while the plague is in him he shall be *d.*
15. 32. this is the law of him that is *d.* by his seed
18. 24. in all these things the nations are *d.*
25. the land is *d.* I do visit iniquity on it, 27.
19. 31. nor seek after wizards to be *d.* by them
21. 1. there shall none be *d.* for the dead
3. for his sister a virgin, for her may he be *d.*
Num. 5. 2. put out whosoever is *d.* by the dead
13. and if she be *d.* 27. || 14. if she be not *d.* 28.
6. 9. and he hath *d.* the head of his consecration
12. days be lost, because his separation was *d.*
9. 6. men who were *d.* by the dead body of a man, 7.
19. 20. because he hath *d.* the sanctuary of Lord
Deut. 21. 23. bury him, that thy land be not *d.*
22. 9. lest the fruit of thy vineyard be *d.*
24. 4. former husband may not take her after *d.*
2 *Kings* 23. 8. Josiah *d.* high places || 10. *d.* Topheth
1 *Chron.* 5. 1. forasmuch as he *d.* his father's bed
Neh. 13. 29. because they have *d.* the priesthood
Job 16. 15. I have *d.* my horn in the dust
Psal. 74. 7. *d.* the dwelling-place of thy name, 79. 1.
106. 39. thus were they *d.* with their own works
Isa. 24. 5. the earth is *d.* under inhabitants thereof
59. 3. for your hands are *d.* with blood, and fingers
Jer. 2. 7. but when ye entered, ye *d.* my land
3. 9. through lightness of her whoredom she *d.* land
16. 18. because they have *d.* my land, they filled
19. 13. the houses of the kings of Judah shall be *d.*
Ezek. 4. 13. thus shall Israel eat their *d.* bread
5. 11. surely because thou hast *d.* my sanctuary
7. 24. I will make, their holy places shall be *d.*
18. 6. neither hath *d.* his neighbour's wife, 15.
11. and hath even *d.* his neighbour's wife
20. 43. all your doings wherein ye have been *d.*
22. 4. and hast *d.* thyself in thy idols, 23. 7.
11. another hath lewdly *d.* his daughter-in-law
23. 13. I saw that she was *d.* both took one way
17. the Babylonians *d.* her with their whoredom
38. they have *d.* my sanctuary in the same day
28. 18. thou hast *d.* thy sanctuaries by thy iniqui.
36. 17. they *d.* it by their own way and doings
43. 8. they have *d.* my holy name by abominations
Hos. 5. 3. whoredom of Ephraim, and Isr. is *d.* 6. 10.
Mic. 4. 11. many nations that say, let her be *d.*
Mark 7. 2. the disciples eat bread with *d.* hands
John 18. 28. they went not in, lest they should be *d.*
1 *Cor.* 8. 7. and their conscience being weak is *d.*
Tit. 1. 15. but to them that are *d.* and unbelieving is nothing pure, even their mind and conscience *d.*
Heb. 12. 15. trouble you, and thereby many be *d.*
Rev. 3. 4. a few who have not *d.* their garments
14. 4. these are they who are not *d.* with women

DEFILEDST.

Gen. 49. 4. wentest up to father's bed, then *d.* thou it

DEFILETH.

Exod. 31. 14. that *d.* sabbath, surely be put to death
Num. 19. 13. purifieth not himself, *d.* the tabernacle
35. 33. shalt not pollute the land, blood *d.* the land
Mat. 15. 11. not that which goeth into the mouth *d.*
20. to eat with unwashen hands *d.* not a man
Mark 7. 20. what cometh out of man that *d.* man
Jam. 3. 6. so is the tongue, that it *d.* the whole body
Rev. 21. 27. in no wise enter any thing that *d.*

DEFRAUD.

Lev. 19. 13. thou shalt not *d.* thy neighbour
Mic. 2. † 2. so they *d.* a man and his house
Mal. 3. † 5. against those that *d.* the hireling
Mark 10. 19. do not bear false witness, *d.* not
1 *Cor.* 6. 8. nay you do wrong, and *d.* your brethren
7. 5. *d.* not, except it be with consent for a time
1 *Thess.* 4. 6. that no man *d.* his brother in any mat.

DEFRAUDED.

1 *Sam.* 12. 3. whom have I *d.?* whom have I oppress.
4. they said, thou hast not *d.* nor oppressed us
1 *Cor.* 6. 7. why do not rather suffer yours. to be *d.*
2 *Cor.* 7. 2. we have wrong. no man, have *d.* no man

DEGENERATE.

Jer. 2. 21. how art thou turned into the *d.* plant!

DEGREE, S.

Psalms, or Songs of degrees: *This title is given to fifteen* Psalms, *which are the* 120*th, and all that follow to the* 134*th, inclusive. The* Hebrew *text calls them*, A song of ascents. Junius *and* Tremellius *translate the* Hebrew *by*, A song of excellences, *or* An excellent song; *because of the excellent matter of them, as eminent persons are called* men of high degree, 1 *Chron.* 17. 17. *Some call them* Psalms of elevation; *because, say they, they were sung with an exalted voice, or because at every* Psalm *the voice was raised. But the common translation, or*, Psalms of degrees, *has more generally obtained. Some interpreters think that they were so called, because they were sung* *upon the fifteen steps of the temple; but they are not agreed about the place where these fifteen steps were. Others think they were so called, because they were sung in a gallery, which they say, was in the court of* Israel, *where sometimes the* Levites *read the law. But others are of opinion that the most probable reason why they are called* songs of degrees, *or of* ascent, *is, because they were composed and sung by the* Jews *on the occasion of their deliverance from the captivity of* Babylon, *whether it were to implore this deliverance from God, or to return thanks for it after it had happened. All these* Psalms *have some relation to this great event. And the scripture commonly applies the phrase,* to ascend, *or* go up, *to express this return,* Ezra 1. 3, 5, 11. | 7. 6, 7, 9. *because* Babylon *was situated in a plain and* Jerusalem *in a mountainous country. And although one of the* Psalms *is ascribed to* David, *and another to* Solomon, *yet they also, as well as the rest, might have been used on this occasion, though they were composed by* David *and* Solomon *upon other occasions.*

The apostle Paul *says,* That such as have used the office of a deacon well, purchase to themselves a good degree, 1 *Tim.* 3. 13. *They gain great honour, respect, and reputation.*

2 *Kings* 20. 9. or backward ten *d.* 10, 11. *Isa.* 38. 8.
† 11. by which it had gone down in *d.* of Ahaz
1 *Chron.* 15. 18. brethren of second *d.* with them
17. 17. according to the state of a man of high *d.*
Psal. 62. 9. men of low *d.* vanity, men of high *d.* a lie
Luke 1. 52. he hath exalted them of low *d.*
1 *Tim.* 3. 13. they purchase to themselves a good *d.*
Jam. 1. 9. let brother of low *d.* rejoice he is exalted

DELAY, ED, ETH.

Exod. 22. 29. thou shalt not *d.* to offer the first-fruits
32. 1. the people saw that Moses *d.* to come down
Psal. 119. 60. *d.* not to keep thy commandments
Mat. 24. 48. my lord *d.* his coming, *Luke* 12. 45.
Acts 9. 38. that he would not *d.* to come to them

DELAY, *Substantive.*

Acts 25. 17. without any *d.* I sat on the judgment-seat

DELECTABLE.

Isa. 44. 9. and their *d.* things shall not profit

DELICACIES.

Rev. 18. 3. the merchants are rich through her *d.*

DELICATE.

Deut. 28. 54. the *d.* man or woman among you, 56.
Isa. 47. 1. thou shalt no more be called tender and *d.*
Jer. 6. 2. likened Zion to a comely and *d.* woman
Mic. 1. 16. make thee bald for thy *d.* children

DELICATES.

Jer. 51. 34. he hath filled his belly with my *d.*

DELICATELY.

1 *Sam.* 15. 32. bring Agag, and Agag came to him *d.*
Prov. 29. 21. he that *d.* bringeth up his servant
Lam. 4. 5. they that did feed *d.* are desolate in streets
Luke 7. 25. they that live *d.* are in kings' courts
1 *Tim.* 5. † 6. she that liveth *d.* is dead while she liv.

DELICATENESS.

Deut. 28. 56. to set her foot on the ground for *d.*

DELICIOUSLY.

Rev. 18. 7. how she glorified herself and lived *d.* 9.

DELIGHT, *Substantive.*

Gen. 34. 19. Shechem had *d.* in Jacob's daughter
Deut. 10. 15. L. had a *d.* in thy fathers to love them
21. 14. and it shall be if thou have no *d.* in her
1 *Sam.* 15. 22. hath the L. as great *d.* in offerings?
18. 22. and say, behold, the king hath *d.* in thee
2 *Sam.* 15. 26. if he thus say, I have no *d.* in thee
Job 22. 26. then shalt thou have *d.* in the Almighty
Psal. 1. 2. but his *d.* is in the law of the Lord
16. 3. and to the excellent, in whom is all my *d.*
27. † 4. to behold the *d.* of the Lord and inquire
119. 24. thy testimonies also are my *d.* and counsel
77. that I may live, for thy law is my *d.* 174.
Prov. 8. 30. I was daily his *d.* rejoicing always in the
11. 1. but a just weight is the Lord's *d.*
20. such as are upright in their way are his *d.*
12. 22. but they that deal truly are his *d.*
15. 8. but the prayer of the upright is his *d.*
16. 13. righteous lips are the *d.* of kings
18. 2. a fool hath no *d.* in understanding
19. 10. *d.* is not seemly for a fool, much less for
24. 25. but to them that rebuke him shall be *d.*
29. 17. yea, he shall give *d.* unto thy soul
Eccl. 12. † 10. preacher sought to find out words of *d.*
Cant. 2. 3. I sat under his shadow with great *d.*
Isa. 58. 2. they take *d.* in approaching to God
13. if thou call the sabbath a *d.* the holy of Lord
62. † 4. thou shalt be called, my *d.* is in her
Jer. 6. 10. they have no *d.* in the word of the Lord
Dan. 11. † 41. he shall enter into the land of *d.*
† 45. shall plant tabernacle in the mount of *d.*

DELIGHT, *Verb.*

Num. 14. 8. if L. *d.* in us, will bring us into this land
2 *Sam.* 24. 3. why should the king *d.* in this thing?
Job 27. 10. will he *d.* himself in the Almighty?
34. 9. that he should *d.* himself with God
Psal. 22. † 8. let him deliver him, if he *d.* in him
37. 4. *d.* thyself also in the Lord, he shall give
11. the meek shall *d.* in the abundance of peace
40. 8. I *d.* to do thy will, O my God, thy law is
49 † 13. yet their posterity *d.* in their mouth
62. 4. they *d.* in lies ‖ 68. 30. the people that *d.* in war
94. 19. in mult. of thoughts thy comforts *d.* soul
119. 16. I will *d.* myself in thy statutes, 35.
47. *d.* in thy commandments ‖ 70. I *d.* in thy law
Prov. 1. 22. how long will scorners *d.* in scorning?
2. 14. and *d.* in the frowardness of the wicked
Eccl. 2. † 24. than that he *d.* his senses in good
Isa. 1. 11. I *d.* not in the blood of bullocks
13. 17. and as for gold, they shall not *d.* in it
55. 2. and let your soul *d.* itself in fatness
58. 2. yet they seek me, and *d.* to know my ways
14. then shalt thou *d.* thyself in the Lord
Jer. 9. 24. in these things I *d.* saith the Lord
Mal. 3. 1. messenger of the covenant whom ye *d.* in
Rom. 7. 22. I *d.* in the law of God after inward man

DELIGHTED.

1 *Sam.* 19. 2. Jonathan *d.* much in David
2 *Sam.* 22. 20. because he *d.* in me, *Psal.* 18. 19.
1 *Kings* 10. 9. the L. who *d.* in thee, 2 *Chr.* 9. 8.
Neh. 9. 25. and *d.* themselves in thy great goodness
Esth. 2. 14. she came no more, except king *d.* in her
Psal. 22. 8. let him deliver him, seeing he *d.* in him
109. 17. as he *d.* not in blessing, let it be far from
Cant. 2. † 3. I *d.* and sat down under his shadow
Isa. 65. 12. did choose that wherein I *d.* not, 66. 4.
66. 11. be *d.* with the abundance of her glory

DELIGHTEST.

Psal. 51. 16. not sacrifice, thou *d.* not in burnt-offer.

DELIGHTETH.

Esth. 6. 6. whom the king *d.* to honour, 7, 9, 11.
Psal. 37. 23. are ordered by L. and he *d.* in his way
112. 1. that *d.* greatly in his commandments
147. 10. he *d.* not in the strength of the horse
Prov. 3. 12. as a father the son in whom he *d.*
Isa. 42. 1. behold mine elect, in whom my soul *d.*
62. 4. called Hephzi-bah, for the Lord *d.* in thee
66. 3. and their soul *d.* in their abominations
Mic. 7. 18. retaineth not anger, because *d.* in mercy
Mal. 2. 17. when ye say, G. *d.* in them that do evil

DELIGHTS.

2 *Sam.* 1. 24. who clothed you in scarlet with other *d.*
Psal. 119. 92. unless thy law had been my *d.*
143. yet thy commandments are my *d.*
Prov. 8. 31. my *d.* were with the sons of men
Eccl. 2. 8. I gat me men-singers, and the *d.* of men
Cant. 7. 6. how pleasant art thou, O love, for *d.*

DELIGHTSOME.

Mal. 3. 12. ye shall be a *d.* land, saith the Lord

DELIVER.

Gen. 40. 13. thou shalt *d.* Pharaoh's cup into his hand
Exod. 5. 18. yet shall he *d.* the tale of bricks
22. 7. if a man shall *d.* unto his neighbour, 10.
26. thou shalt *d.* it by that the sun goeth down
23. 31. I will *d.* the inhabitants of the land
Num. 21. 2. if thou wilt indeed *d.* this people
35. 25. the congregation shall *d.* the slayer out of
Deut. 7. 24. he shall *d.* their kings into thy hand
23. 15. thou shalt not *d.* to his master the servant
25. 11. to *d.* her husband out of the hand of him
32. 39. any that can *d.* out of my hand, *Isa.* 43. 13.
Josh. 2. 13. that ye will *d.* our lives from death
8. 7. for your God will *d.* it into your hand
20. 5. they shall not *d.* the slayer into his hand
Judg. 7. 7. and *d.* the Midianites into thine hand
10. † 1. after Abimelech arose Tola to *d.* Israel
11. 30. if thou shalt without fail *d.* the Ammonites
13. 5. Samson shall begin to *d.* Israel from Philist.
1 *Sam.* 7. 14. the coasts thereof did Israel *d.*
12. 21. after things which cannot profit nor *d.*
23. 4. I will *d.* the Philistines, 2 *Sam.* 5. 19.
24. 4. I will *d.* thine enemy into thine hand
28. 19. the Lord will *d.* Israel to the Philistines
2 *Sam.* 14. 16. the king will hear to *d.* his handmaid
20. † 6. lest Sheba *d.* himself from our eyes
1 *Kings* 18. 9. thou wouldest *d.* thy servant to Ahab
20. 13. I will *d.* this multitude into thy hand, 28.
22. 6. they said, go up, for the Lord shall *d.* it into the king's hand, 12. 15. 2 *Chron.* 18. 5, 11.
2 *Kings* 3. 18. he will *d.* the Moabites into your hand
12. 7. but *d.* it for the breaches of the house
18. 35. that Lord should *d.* Jerusalem, *Isa.* 36. 20.
22. 5. let them *d.* it into the hand of the workmen
2 *Chron.* 25. 15. who could not *d.* their own people
28. 11. now hear me and *d.* the captives again
32. 13. were gods of nations able to *d.* their lands?
14. that your God should be able to *d.* you, 17.
Ezra 7. 19. those *d.* thou before the God of Jerusalem
Job 10. 7. there is none can *d.* out of thy hand
22. 30. he shall *d.* the island of the innocent
33. 28. he will *d.* his soul from going into the pit
Ps. 6. 4. *d.* my soul, 17. 13. | 22. 20. | 116. 4. | 120. 2.
7. 2. rending it while there is none to *d.* 50. 22.
33. 17. nor shall he *d.* any by his great strength
19. to *d.* their soul from death, and to keep alive
56. 13. wilt not thou *d.* my feet from falling?
72. 12. for he shall *d.* the needy when he crieth
74. 19. O *d.* not the soul of thy turtle-dove
82. 4. *d.* the poor and needy out of hand of wicked
89. 48. shall he *d.* his soul from hand of the grave?
Prov. 4. 9. a crown of glory shall she *d.* to thee
6. 3. do this now, my son, and *d.* thyself
23. 14. beat him, thou shalt *d.* his soul from hell
Eccl. 8. 8. nor shall wickedness *d.* those given to it
Isa. 5. 29. shall carry it away safe, and none shall *d.* it
29. 11. which men *d.* to one that is learned
31. 5. defending also he will *d.* it, and passing over
44. 20. he cannot *d.* his soul, nor say, is there not
46. 2. they stoop, they could not *d.* the burden
47. 14. they shall not *d.* themselves from the flame
50. 2. is my hand shortened? have I no power to *d.*?
Jer. 15. 9. the residue of them will I *d.* to the sword
18. 21. therefore *d.* up their children to the famine
20. 5. moreover I will *d.* all strength of this city
21. 7. afterwards I will *d.* Zedekiah from the sword
22. 3. *d.* the spoiled out of the hand of the oppressor
43. 11. he shall *d.* such as are for death to death
51. 6. flee out of Bab. *d.* every man his soul, 45.
Ezek. 13. 21. I will *d.* my people out of your [hand, 23.
14. 14. they should *d.* but their own souls, 20.
16. shall *d.* neither sons nor daughters, 18. 20.
33. 5. he that taketh warning shall *d.* his soul
34. 10. for I will *d.* my flock from their mouth
Dan. 3. 29. there is no other god can *d.* after this sort
8. 4. nor was there any that could *d.* from the ram
7. none that could *d.* the ram out of his hand
Hos. 2. 10. none shall *d.* her out of mine hand
Amos 2. 14. neither shall the mighty *d.* himself
15. he that is swift of foot shall not *d.* himself
6. 8. I will *d.* the city with all that is therein
Mic. 5. 8. who teareth in pieces and none can *d.*
6. 14. and thou shalt take hold, but shalt not *d.*
Zech. 2. 7. *d.* thyself, O Zion, that dwellest with
11. 6. I will *d.* every one into his neighbour's hand
Mat. 10. 21. the brother shall *d.* the brother to death
Acts 25. 16. not manner of Romans to *d.* man to die
1 *Cor.* 5. 5. *d.* such one to Sat. for destruct. of flesh
2 *Cor.* 1. 10. who delivered us from death, and doth *d.*
2 *Pet.* 2. 9. the Lord knoweth how to *d.* the godly

DELIVER *him.*

Gen. 37. 22. rid him, to *d. him* to his father again
42. 37. *d. him* into my hand, I will bring him to thee
Exod. 21. 13. but God will *d. him* into his hand
Deut. 2. 30. that he might *d. him* into thy hand
3. 2. I will *d. him* and his people into thy hand
19. 12. *d. him* into the hand of the avenger of blood
24. 13. in any case thou shalt *d. him* the pledge
Judg. 4. 7. I will draw Sisera and *d. him* into thy hand
1 *Sam.* 23. 20. our part shall be to *d. him* into thy hand
2 *Sam.* 14. 7. said, *d. him* that smote his brother
20. 21. *d. him* and I will depart from the city
Job 33. 24. *d. him* from going down to the pit
Psal. 22. 8. that he would *d. him*, let him *d. him*
41. 1. the Lord will *d. him* in time of trouble
2. thou wilt not *d. him* to the will of his enemies
71. 11. and take him, for there is none to *d. him*
91. 14. hath set his love on me, theref. will I *d. him*
15. I will be with him, will *d. him*, and honour him
Prov. 19. 19. if thou *d. him*, thou must do it again
Jer. 21. 12. *d. him* that is spoiled from the oppress.
Ezek. 33. 12. righteous. of righteous shall not *d. him*
Dan. 6. 14. the king set his heart on Dan. to *d. him*
Jonah 4. 6. might be a shadow to *d. him* from grief
Mat. 20. 19. and shall *d. him* to Gentiles to crucify him, *Mark* 10. 33. *Luke* 20. 20. *Acts* 21. 11.
26. 15. what will ye give, and I will *d. him* to you
27. 43. let him *d. him* now, if he will have him

DELIVER *me.*

Gen. 32. 11. *d. me* I pray thee from the hand of Esau
1 *Sam.* 17. 37. he will *d. me* out of hand of Goliath
23. 11. will the men of Keilah *d. me* up? 12.
24. 15. the Ld. be judge, and *d. me* out of thy hand
26. 24. and let him *d. me* out of all tribulation
30. 15. nor *d. me* into the hands of my master
2 *Sam.* 3. 14. Da. sent, saying, *d. me* my wife Michal
1 *Kings* 20. 5. thou shalt *d. me.* thy silver and gold
Job 6. 23. *d. me* from enemies, *Ps.* 31. 15. | 59. 1.
Psal. 7. 1. O Lord, save me from them and *d. me*
25. 20. keep my soul, and *d. me*, for I trust in thee
27. 12. *d. me* not over to the will of mine enemies
31. 2. bow down thine ear to me, *d. me* speedily
39. 8. *d. me* from my transgressions, make me not
40. 13. be pleased to *d. me* ‖ 70. 1. make haste to *d. me*
43. 1. O *d. me* from the deceitful and unjust man
51. 14. *d. me* from blood-guiltiness, O God
59. 2. *d. me* from the workers of iniquity, save me
69. 14. *d. me* out of the mire, and let me not sink
18. draw nigh to my soul, and redeem it, *d. me*
71. 2. *d. me* in thy righteousness, cause me. 31. 1.
4. *d. me*, O my God, out of hand of the wicked
109. 21. because thy mercy is good *d.* thou *me*
119. 134. *d. me* from the oppression of man
153. consider mine affliction, and *d. me.*
154. plead my cause, and *d. me*, quicken me
170. *d. me* according to thy word
140. 1. *d. me* O Ld. from the evil man, preserve me
142. 6. *d. me* from my persecutors, for they are
143. 9. *d. me* from mine enemies, I flee unto thee
144. 7. rid me, and *d. me* out of great waters
11. *d. me* from the hand of strange children
Isa. 44. 17. he saith, *d. me*, for thou art my God
Jer. 38. 19. I am afraid of the Jews, lest they *d. me*
Acts 25. 11. no man may *d. me* to them, I appeal
Rom. 7. 24. who shall *d. me* from the body of death?
2 *Tim.* 4. 18. the Ld. shall *d. me* from every evil work

DELIVER *thee.*

Deut. 7. 16. the people which the Lord shall *d. thee.*
23. 14. Ld. walketh in midst of thy camp to *d. thee*
Judg. 15. 12. to bind thee, that we may *d. thee*, 13.
1 *Sam.* 17. 46. the Lord will *d. thee* into mine hand
23. 12. and the Lord said, they will *d. thee* up
2 *Kings* 18. 23. I will *d. thee* two thousand horses
20. 6. and I will *d. thee* and this city, *Isa.* 38. 6.
Job 5. 19. he shall *d. thee* in six troubles, in seven
36. 18. beware, then a great ransom cannot *d. thee*
Ps. 50. 15. I will *d.* thee, and thou shalt glorify me
91. 3. he shall *d. thee* from the snare of the fowler
Prov. 2. 12. to *d. thee* from the way of the evil man
16. to *d. thee* from the strange woman, the stranger
Isa. 57. 13. when thou criest, let thy companies *d. thee*
Jer. 1. 8. I am with thee to *d. thee*, 19. | 15. 20, 21.
38. 20. but Jeremiah said, they shall not *d. thee*
39. 17. I will *d. thee* in that day, saith the Lord
18. I will surely *d. thee*, thou shalt not fall by sword
Ezek. 21. 31. *d. thee* into the hand of brutish men
23. 28. I will *d. thee* to them whom thou hatest
25. 4. I will *d. thee* to men of the east for a possession
7. I will *d. thee* for a spoil to the heathen
Dan. 6. 16. thy God whom thou servest will *d. thee*
20. is thy God able to *d. thee* from the lions?
Hos. 11. 8. how shall I *d. thee*, Israel, how shall I
Mat. 5. 25. judge *d. thee* to the officer, *Luke* 12. 58.

DELIVER *them.*

Exod. 3. 8. I am come down to *d. them*, *Acts* 7. 34.
Deut. 7. 2. when the Lord thy God shall *d. them*, 23.
Josh. 11. 6. to-morrow will I *d. them* up all slain
Judg. 11. 9. and if the Lord *d. them* before me
20. 28. to-morrow I will *d. them* into thine hand
1 *Sam.* 14. 37. wilt thou *d. t.* 2 *Sam.* 5. 19. 1 *Chr.* 14. 10.
1 *Kings* 8. 46. and *d. t.* to the enemy, 2 *Kings* 21. 14.
2 *Kings* 3. 10. to *d. them* into the hand of Moab, 13.
1 *Chron.* 14. 10. L. said, I will *d. them* into thy hand
2 *Chron.* 6. 36. and *d. th.* over before their enemies
25. 20. for it came of God, that he might *d. them*
Neh. 9. 28. and many times didst thou *d. them*
Job 5. 4. crushed, neither is there any to *d. them*
Psal. 22. 4. they trusted, and thou didst *d. them*
37. 40. the Lord shall help them, and *d. them*
106. 43. many times did he *d. them* they provoked
Prov. 11. 6. the righteousness of upright shall *d. them*
12. 6. the mouth of the upright shall *d. them*
24. 11. forbear to *d. them* that are drawn to death
Isa. 19. 20. he shall send a Saviour and *d. them*
Jer. 24. 9. I will *d. them* to be removed, 29. 18.
29. 21. *d. th.* into hand of Nebuchadrezzar, 46. 26.
Ezek. 7. 19. their gold shall not *d. them*, *Zeph.* 1. 18.
34. 12. so will I seek and *d. them* out of all places
Amos 1. 6. they carried away to *d. them* up to Edom
Zech. 11. 6. out of their hand I will not *d. them*
Acts 7. 25. that God by his hand would *d. them*
Heb. 2. 15. and *d. them* who through fear of death

DELIVER *us*.
Deut. 1. 27. to *d. us* into hand of Amorites, Josh. 7.7.
Judg. 10. 15. *d. us* only, we pray thee, this day
20. 13. *d. us* the men, the children of Belial
1 Sam. 4. 8. woe to us, who shall *d. us* out of hand
12. 10. but now *d. us* out of hand of our enemies
2 Kings 18. 30. the L. will *d. us*, 32. Isa. 36. 15, 18.
1 Chron. 16. 35. save and *d. us* from the heathen
2 Chron. 32. 11. saying, the L. our God shall *d. us*
Psal. 79. 9. and *d. us*, and purge away our sins
Jer. 43. 3. to *d. us* into the hand of the Chaldeans
Lam. 5. 8. none that doth *d. us* out of their hand
Dan. 3. 17. our God is able to *d. us* and will *d. us*
Mic. 5. 6. thus shall he *d. us* from the Assyrians
Mat. 6. 13. but *d. us* from evil, Luke 11. 4.
2 Cor. 1. 10. in whom we trust that he will yet *d. us*
Gal. 1. 4. that he might *d. us* from this evil world
DELIVER *you*.
Gen. 42. 34. so will I *d. y.* your brother, shall traffic
Lev. 26. 26. they shall *d. you* your bread by weight
Judg. 10. 11. did not I *d. you* from the Egyptians?
13. ye have forsaken me, I will *d. you* no more
14. let them *d. you* in the time of tribulation
1 Sam. 7. 3. he will *d. you* from the Philistines
2 Kings 17. 39. he shall *d. y.* from all your enemies
18. 29. shall not be able to *d. you* out of his hand
2 Chron. 32. 14. be able to *d. you* out of mine hand
Isa. 36. 14. Hezekiah shall not be able to *d. you*
46. 4. I will bear, I will carry, and will *d. you*
Ezek. 11. 9. I will *d. you* into hands of strangers
Dan. 3. 15. who is that God that shall *d. you?*
Mat. 10. 17. for they will *d. you* up, Mark 13. 9.
19. but when they *d. you* up, 24. 9. Mark 13. 11.
DELIVERANCE.
Gen. 45. 7. G. sent me to save your lives by a great *d.*
Judg. 15. 18. thou hast given this great *d.*
1 Sam. 11. † 9. to-morrow ye shall have *d.*
2 Sam. 19. † 2. the *d.* was turned into mourning
2 Kings 5. 1. by him the Lord had given *d.* to Syria
13. 17. the arrow of the Lord's *d.* of *d.* from Syria
1 Chron. 11. 14. the Lord saved them by a great *d.*
2 Chron. 12. 7. but I will grant them some *d.*
Ezra 9. 13. and hast given us such *d.* as this
Esth. 4. 14. then shall there *d.* arise to the Jews
Psal. 18. 50. great *d.* giveth he to his king, to David
32. 7. thou shalt compass me about with songs of *d.*
Isa. 26. 18. we have not wrought any *d.* in the earth
Joel 2. 32. in Zion and in Jerusalem shall be *d.*
Obad. 17. but upon mount Zion shall be *d.*
Luke 4. 18. he sent me to preach *d.* to the captives
Heb. 11. 35. others were tortured, not accepting *d.*
DELIVERANCES.
Psal. 44. 4. thou art my King, command *d.* for Jacob
DELIVERED.
Gen. 9. 2. on every beast, into your hand are they *d.*
14. 20. God who *d.* thine enemies into thy hand
25. 24. when her days to be *d.* were fulfilled
Exod. 1. 19. are *d.* ere the midwives come to them
5. 23. neither hast thou *d.* thy people at all
12. 27. he smote the Egyptians, and *d.* our houses
18. 10. who hath *d.* people from under Egypt
Deut. 2. 36. the Lord our God *d.* all unto us
3. 3. God *d.* into our hands the king of Bashan
9. 10. the Lord *d.* unto me two tables of stone
31. 9. and Moses *d.* the law unto the priests
Josh. 21. 44. the Ld. *d.* their enemies into their hand
Judg. 1. 4. he *d.* the Canaanites into their hand
3. 31. after him was Shamgar, he also *d.* Israel
5. 11. they that are *d.* from the noise of archers
8. 7. when L. hath *d.* Zebah and Zalmunna
11. 21. the Lord *d.* Sihon into the hand of Israel
16. 23. our god hath *d.* Samson our enemy, 24.
1 Sam. 4. 19. Phinehas' wife was near to be *d.*
17. 35. I smote him and *d.* it out of his mouth
30. 23. who *d.* the company that came against us
2 Sam. 21. 6. let seven of Saul's sons be *d.* to us
1 Kings 3. 17. and I was *d.* of a child with her
18. third day after I was *d.* this woman was *d.*
2 Kings 19. 11. and shalt thou be *d.?* Isa. 37. 11.
1 Chr. 11. 14. *d.* that parcel and slew Philistines
16. 7. then on that day David *d.* this psalm
2 Chr. 23. 9. Jehoiada *d.* to the captains shields
34. 9. they *d.* money was brought into house of G.
15. and Hilkiah *d.* the book to Shaphan
Ezra 5. 14. the vessels were *d.* to Sheshbazzar
8. 36. and they *d.* the king's commissions
Job 22. 30. it is *d.* by the pureness of thine hands
23. 7. so should I be *d.* for ever from my judge
29. 12. because I *d.* the poor that cried, and fatherless
Psal. 22. 5. they cried to thee, and were *d.*
33. 16. a mighty man is not *d.* by much strength
55. 18. he hath *d.* my soul in peace from battle
56. 13. hast *d.* my soul from death, 86. 13 | 116. 8.
60. 5. that thy beloved may be *d.* 108. 6.
69. 14. let me be *d.* from them that hate me
78. 61. and *d.* his strength into captivity
Prov 11. 8. the righteous is *d.* out of trouble
9. but through knowledge shall the just be *d.*
21. but the seed of the righteous shall be *d.*
28. 26. but whoso walketh wisely shall be *d.*
Eccl. 9. 15. poor wise man by wisdom he *d.* the city
Isa. 20. 6. for help to be *d.* from the king of Assyria
29. 12. the book is *d.* to him that is not learned
36. 19. and have they *d.* Samaria out of my hand?
38. 17. thou hast *d.* it from the pit of corruption
49. 24. or shall the lawful captive be *d.?*
25. and the prey of the terrible shall be *d.*
66. 7. before pain came, she was *d.* of a man-child
Jer. 7. 10. we are *d.* to do all these abominations
20. 13. for he hath *d.* the soul of the poor
32. 16. now when I had *d.* the evidence to Baruch
Ezek. 3. 19. but thou hast *d.* thy soul, 21. | 33. 9.
14. 16. as I live, they only shall be *d.* 18.
17. 15. or shall he break the covenant and be *d.?*
31. 14. for they are all *d.* unto death to the earth
32. 20. she is *d.* to the sword, draw her multitudes
Dan. 3. 28. and *d.* his servants that trusted in him
6. 27. who *d.* Daniel from the power of the lions
12. 1. at that time thy people shall be *d.*
Joel 2. 32. shall call on name of the Lord shall be *d.*
Amos 9. 1. and he that escapeth shall not be *d.*
Mic. 4. 10. go to Babylon, there shalt thou be *d.*

Hab. 2. 9. that he may be *d.* from the power of evil.
Mal. 3. 15. yea, they that tempt God are even *d.*
Mat. 11. 27. all things are *d.* to me of my Father, no man knoweth Son but the Father, Luke 10. 22.
27. 58. Pilate commanded the body to be *d.*
Mark 7. 13. thro' your tradition which ye have *d.*
10. 33. the Son of man shall be *d.* to the chief priests
15. 15. released Barabbas, and *d.* Jesus, Luke 23. 25.
Luke 1. 57. time came that she should be *d.* 2. 6.
4. 6. that is *d.* to me, and to whom I will, I give it
17. there was *d.* to him the book of Esaias
9. 44. Son of man shall be *d.* into hands of men
12. 58. give diligence that thou mayest be *d.*
18. 32. for he shall be *d.* unto the Gentiles
John 16. 21. but as soon as she is *d.* of the child
18. 36. that I should not be *d.* to the Jews
Acts 2. 23. him being *d.* by the counsel of God
15. 30. Judas and Silas came to Ant. and *d.* epistle
23. 33. and they *d.* the epistle to the governor
27. 1. they *d.* Paul to one Julius, a centurion
28. 17. yet was I *d.* prisoner from Jerusalem
Rom. 4. 25. was *d.* for our offences and raised again
7. 6. now we are *d.* from the law, that being dead
8. 21. the creature itself shall be *d.* from corruption
15. 31. I may be *d.* from them that do not believe
2 Cor. 4. 11. are alway *d.* to death for Jesus' sake
2 Thess. 3. 2. we may be *d.* from unreasonable men
1 Tim. 1. 20. whom I have *d.* to Satan, that they learn
2 Tim. 4. 17. I was *d.* out of the mouth of the lion
Heb. 11. 11. by faith Sarah was *d.* of a child
2 Pet. 2. 7. and *d.* just Lot, vexed with the filthy
21. to turn from the commandment *d.* to them
Jude 3. for the faith which was once *d.* to the saints
Rev. 12. 2. travailing in birth, and pained to be *d.*
4. before the woman which was ready to be *d.*
See HAND, HANDS.
DELIVERED *him*.
Gen. 37. 21. Reuben *d. him* out of their hands
Lev. 6. 2. in that which was *d. him* to keep, 4.
Deut. 2. 33. the Lord our God *d. him* before us
1 Kings 13. 26. therefore the Lord *d. him* to the lion
17. 23. and Elijah *d. him* unto his mother
Psal. 7. 4. yea, I have *d. him* that is mine enemy
Mat. 18. 34. his Lord *d. him* to the tormentors
27. 2. and *d. him* to Pontius Pilate, Mark 15. 1.
18. that for envy they had *d. him*, Mark 15. 10.
26. he *d. him* to be crucified, John 19. 16.
Luke 7. 15. and Jesus *d. him* to his mother
9. 42. Jesus healed the child, and *d. him* to his father
24. 20. how our rulers *d. him* to be condemned
John 18. 30. we would not have *d. him* to thee
Acts 7. 10. God *d. him* out of all his afflictions
12. 4. Herod *d. him* to four quaternions of soldiers
DELIVERED *me*.
Exod. 18. 4. God *d. me* from the sword of Pharaoh
Judg. 12. 3. and when I saw that ye *d. me* not
1 Sam. 17. 37. the Lord that *d. me* from the lion
2 Sam. 22. 18. he *d. me* from my strong enemy
20. he *d. me* because delighted in me, Psal. 18. 19.
49. thou hast *d. me* from violent man, Psal. 18. 48.
2 Kings 22. 10. Hilkiah the priest hath *d. me* a book
Job 16. 11. God hath *d. me* to the ungodly
Psal. 18. 17. he *d. me* from my strong enemies
43. hast *d. me* from the strivings of the people
34. 4. the Lord heard, and *d. me* from all my fears
54. 7. for he hath *d. me* out of all trouble
John 19. 11. he that *d. me* to thee hath greater sin
2 Tim. 3. 11. but out of them all the Lord *d. me*
DELIVERED *thee*.
1 Sam. 24. 10. the Lord *d. thee* to-day into my hand
2 Sam. 12. 7. and I *d. thee* out of the hand of Saul
Psal. 81. 7. thou calledst in trouble, and I *d. thee*
Ezek. 16. 27. I *d. thee* to will of them that hate thee
John 18. 35. the chief priests *d. thee* unto me
DELIVERED *them*.
Exod. 18. 8. Moses told how the Lord *d. them*
Deut 5. 22. in tables of stone, and *d. them* to me
Judg. 3. 9. Lord raised up a deliverer, who *d. them*
2 Kings 19. 12. gods of nations *d. them*, Isa. 37. 12.
2 Chr. 29. 8. hath *d. them* to trouble, to astonishment
Psal. 78. 42. when he *d. them* from the enemy
107. 6. and he *d. them* out of their distresses
20. and he *d. them* from their destructions
Isa. 34. 2. he hath *d. them* to the slaughter
Ezek. 16. 21. *d. them* to cause them to pass thro' fire
Mat. 25. 14. called servants, and *d.* to *them* his goods
Luke 1. 2. even as they *d. them* to us eye-witnesses
19. 13. he *d. them* ten pounds, and said, occupy till
Acts 16. 4. they *d. them* the decrees for to keep
1 Cor. 11. 2. keep ordinances, as I *d. them* to you
2 Pet. 2. 4. and *d. them* into chains of darkness
DELIVERED *up*.
Num. 21. 3. and the Lord *d. up* the Canaanites
Josh. 10. 12. when the Ld. *d. up* Amorites before Isr.
2 Sam. 18. 28. *d. up* the men that lift up their hand
Amos 1. 9. because they *d. up* the captivity to Edom
Obad. 14. nor shouldest have *d. up* those that remain
Mat. 4. † 12. heard that John was *d. up* into prison
Acts 3. 13. hath glorified his Son whom ye *d. up*
Rom. 8. 32. spared not his Son, but *d.* him *up* for us
1 Cor. 15. 24. when he shall have *d. up* the kingdom
Rev. 20. 13. death and hell *d. up* the dead in them
DELIVERED *us*.
Exod. 2. 19. an Egyptian *d. us* from the shepherds
Acts 6. 14. change the customs which Moses *d. us*
2 Cor. 1. 10. who *d. us* from so great a death
Col. 1. 13. hath *d. us* from the power of darkness
1 Thess. 1. 10. Jesus, who *d. us* from wrath to come
DELIVERED *you*.
Rom. 6. 17. ye obeyed the doctrine which was *d. you*
1 Cor. 11. 23. I received that which I *d. you*, 15. 3.
DELIVEREDST, EST.
Neh. 9. 27. thou *d.* them to enemies who vexed
Psal. 35. 10. who *d.* poor from him that spoileth him
Mic. 6. 14. what thou *d.* will I give up to the sword
Mat. 25. 20. Lord, thou *d.* unto me five talents
22. and said, Lord, thou *d.* unto me two talents
DELIVERER.
Judg. 3. 9. the Lord raised up a *d.* to Israel, 15.
18. 28. there was no *d.* 2 Sam. 14. † 6. Psal. 7. † 2.
2 Sam. 22. 2. the Lord is my rock and *d.* Psal. 18. 2.
Psal. 40. 17. thou art my help and my *d.* 70. 5.

Psal. 144. 2. my fortress, my high tower, and my *d.*
Acts 7. 35. the same did God send to be a *d.*
Rom. 11. 26. there shall come out of Sion the *d.*
DELIVERETH.
Job 36. 15. he *d.* the poor in his affliction, opens ears
Psal. 18. 48. he *d.* me from mine enemies
34. 7. about them that fear him, and *d.* them
17. the Lord *d.* them out of all their troubles, 19.
97. 10. he *d.* them out of the hand of the wicked
144. 10. who *d.* David from the hurtful sword
Prov. 10. 2. righteousness *d.* from death, 11. 4.
14. 25. a true witness *d.* souls, but a deceitful
31. 24. and she *d.* girdles unto the merchant
Isa. 42. 22. they are for a prey, and none *d.*
Dan. 6. 27. God *d.* and rescueth, and worketh signs
Amos 3. † 12. as shepherd *d.* out of mouth of lion
DELIVERING.
Exod. 5. † 23. *d.* thou hast not delivered thy people
Luke 21. 12. *d.* you up to synagogues and into prisons
Acts 22. 4. *d.* into prisons both men and women
26. 17. *d.* thee from the people and the Gentiles
DELIVERY.
Isa. 26. 17. that draweth near the time of her *d*
DELUSION.
2 Thess. 2. 11. God shall send them strong *d.*
DELUSIONS.
Isa. 66. 4. I also will choose their *d.* and bring fears
DEMAND.
Dan. 4. 17. the *d.* by the word of the holy ones
DEMAND, ED.
Exod. 5. 14. *d.* why have ye not fulfilled your task?
2 Sam. 11. 7. David *d.* of Uriah how Joab did
Job 38. 3. I will *d.* of thee, answer thou, 40. 7. | 42. 4.
Dan. 2. 27. the secret which the king hath *d.*
Mat. 2. 4. he *d.* where Christ should be born
Luke 3. 14. the soldiers *d.* of him, what shall we do
17. 20. and when he was *d.* of the Pharisees
Acts. 21. 33. the chief captain *d.* who he was
DEMONSTRATION.
1 Cor. 2. 4. but in *d.* of the Spirit, and of power
DEN, S.
Judg. 6. 2. the children of Israel made them *d.*
Job 37. 8. then the beasts go into *d.* and remain
38. 40. when they couch in their *d.* and abide
Psal. 10. 9. he lieth in wait as a lion in his *d.*
104. 22. they lay themselves down in their *d.*
Cant. 4. 8. look from Shenir, from the lions' *d.*
Isa. 11. 8. shall put his hand on the cockatrice' *d.*
32. 14. the towers shall be for *d.* for ever
Jer. 7. 11. is this house become a *d.* of robbers?
9. 11. I will make Jerusalem a *d.* of dragons
10. 22. to make the cities of Judah a *d.* of dragons
Dan. 6. 7. he shall be cast into the *d.* of lions, 12.
16. and they cast him into the *d.* of lions
19. the king arose and went in haste to the *d.*
23. they should take Daniel up out of the *d.*
24. and they cast them into the *d.* of lions
Amos 3. 4. will a young lion cry out of his *d.?*
Nah. 2. 12. the lion filled his *d.* with ravin
Mat. 21. 13. my house be called house of prayer, but ye have made it a *d.* of thieves, Mark 11. 17.
Heb. 11. 38. they wandered in deserts and in *d.*
Rev. 6. 15. bondman and freeman hid themsel. in *d.*
DENY.
Josh. 24. 27. be a witness, lest ye *d.* your God
1 Kings 2. 16. I ask of thee, *d.* me not, Prov. 30. 7.
Job 8. 18. if he destroy him, then it shall *d.* him
Prov. 30. 9. lest I be full and *d.* thee, and say
Mat. 10. 33. whosoever shall *d.* me, him will I *d.*
16. 24. let him *d.* himself, Mark 8. 34. Luke 9. 23.
26. 34. Jesus said to him, before the cock crow thou shalt *d.* me thrice, 75. Mark 14. 30, 72.
35. die with thee, yet will I not *d.* thee, Mark 14. 31.
Luke 20. 27. which *d.* there is any resurrection
2 Tim. 2. 12. if we *d.* him, he also will *d.* us
13. yet he abideth faithful, he cannot *d.* himself
Tit. 1. 16. that know God, but in works they *d.* him
DENIED.
Gen. 18. 15. Sarah *d.* saying, I laughed not
1 Kings 20. 7. he sent to me, and I *d.* him not
Job 31. 28. for I should have *d.* God that is above
Mat. 26. 70. Peter *d.* before them all, saying, I know not, 72. Mark 14. 70. Luke 22. 57. John 18. 25, 27.
Luke 8. 45. when all *d.* that they touched him
12. 9. who denies shall be *d.* before the angels of G.
John 1. 20. John confessed, and *d.* not, I am not Chr.
13. 38. shall not crow, till thou hast *d.* me thrice
Acts 3. 13. whom ye *d.* in the presence of Pilate
14. but ye *d.* the holy One and the just
1 Tim. 5. 8. he hath *d.* the faith, and is worse than
Rev. 2. 13. holdest fast my name, and not *d.* my faith
3. 8. hast kept my word, and hast not *d.* my name
DENIETH, ING.
Luke 12. 9. but he that *d.* me before men, be denied
2 Tim. 3. 5. having a form of godliness, but *d.* power
Tit. 2. 12. teaching us, that *d.* ungodliness and lusts
2 Pet. 2. 1. even *d.* the Lord that bought them
1 John 2. 22. is a liar, that *d.* Jesus is the Christ
23. who *d.* the Son, the same hath not the Father
Jude 4. *d.* the only Lord God, and our Lord Jesus
DENOUNCE.
Deut. 30. 18. I *d.* this day, that ye shall surely perish
DEPART.
Gen. 13. 9. if thou *d.* to the right hand, I will go
Exod. 18. 27. Moses let his father-in-law *d.*
33. 1. *d.* thou and the people thou hast brought up
Num. 10. 30. I will *d.* to mine own land and kindred
Deut. 9. 7. from the day thou didst *d.* out of Egypt
Josh. 24. 28. so Joshua let the people *d.* to inheritance
Judg. 19. 5. the Levite rose up to *d.* 7, 8, 9.
1 Sam. 22. 5. and God said, abide not in the hold, *d.*
29. 10. as soon as ye be up and have light, *d.*
11. David and his men rose up to *d.* in the morn.
30. 22. that they may lead them away and *d.*
2 Sam. 11. 12. and to-morrow I will let thee *d.*
15. 14. make speed to *d.* lest he overtake us
1 Kings 12. 5. *d.* for three days, then come ag. to me
Job 20. 28. the increase of his house shall *d.*
Isa. 11. 13. the envy also of Ephraim shall *d.*
52. 11. *d.* ye, *d.* ye, go out from thence, Lam. 4. 15
54. 10. for the mountains shall *d.* and the hills
Jer. 50. 3. they shall *d.* both man and beast

Mic. 2. 10. arise ye, and *d.* this is not your rest
Zech. 10. 11. the sceptre of Egypt shall *d.* away
Mat. 8. 34. would *d.* out of their coasts, *Mark* 5. 17.
10. 14. when ye *d.* out of that house or city, shake off the dust of your feet, *Mark* 6. 11. *Luke* 9. 4.
Luke 2. 29. now lettest thou thy servant *d.* in peace
13. 31. *d.* hence, for Herod will kill thee
21. 21. let them which are in the midst *d.* out of it
John 7. 3. they said, *d.* hence and go into Judea
13. 1. when Jesus knew he should *d.* out of world
16. 7. but if I *d.* I will send him unto you
Acts 16. 36. now therefore *d.* and go in peace
39. and desired them to *d.* out of the city
20. 7. Paul preach. to them ready to *d.* on morrow
22. 21. *d.* for I will send thee to the Gentiles
25. 4. that he himself would *d.* shortly thither
27. 12. the more part advised to *d.* thence also
1 *Cor.* 7. 11. but if she *d.* let her remain unmarried
15. but if the unbelieving *d.* let him *d.*
Phil. 1. 23. a desire to *d.* and to be with Christ
Jam. 2. 16. say to them, *d.* in peace, be ye clothed

DEPART *from.*

Exod. 8. 11. and the frogs shall *d. from* thee
29. that the swarms of flies may *d. from* Pharaoh
21. 22. hurt a woman, so that her fruit *d. from* her
Lev. 25. 41. and then shall he *d. from* thee
Num. 16. 26. *d. from* the tents of these wicked men
Deut. 4. 9. take heed, lest they *d. from* thy heart
Judg. 7. 3. who is fearful, let him *d. from* Gilead
1 *Sam.* 15. 6. *d. from* the Amalekites, lest I destroy
2 *Sam.* 12. 10. the sword shall never *d. from* thy house
20. 21. deliver Sheba, and I will *d. from* the city
1 *Kings* 15. 19. that he may *d. from* me, 2 *Chr.* 16. 3.
2 *Chr.* 18. 31. and God moved them to *d. from* him
Job 21. 14. they say to God, *d. from* us, 22. 17.
28. 28. and to *d. from* evil is understanding
Psal. 6. 8. *d. from* me, all ye workers of iniquity, *Mat.* 7. 23. *Luke* 13. 27.
34. 14. *d. from* evil, and do good, 37. 27.
101. 4. a froward heart shall *d. from* me
119. 115. *d. from* me, ye evil doers, for I will keep
139. 19. *d. from* me therefore, ye bloody men
Prov. 3. 7. fear the Lord, and *d. from* evil
13. 14. to *d. from* the snares of death, 14. 27.
19. but it is abomination to fools to *d. from* evil
15. 24. that he may *d. from* hell beneath
16. 6. by the fear of the Lord men *d. from* evil
17. the highway of the upright is to *d. from* evil
Isa. 14. 25. his burden *d. from* off their shoulders
Jer. 6. 8. be instructed, lest my soul *d. from* thee
17. 13. that *d. from* me shall be written in the earth
31. 36. if those ordinances *d. from* before me
37. 9. the Chaldeans shall surely *d. from* us
Ezek. 16. 42. my jealousy shall *d. from* thee
Hos. 9. 12. woe also to them when I *d. from* them
Mat. 25. 41. *d. from* me ye cursed, into everlast. fire
Mark 6. 10. there abide, till ye *d. from* that place
Luke 5. 8. *d. from* me, for I am a sinful man, O Lord
8. 37. Gadarenes besought him to *d. from* them
Acts 1. 4. that they should not *d. from* Jerusalem
18. 2. commanded all the Jews to *d. from* Rome
1 *Cor.* 7. 10. let not the wife *d. from* her husband
2 *Cor.* 12. 8. I besought Lord that it might *d. from* me
1 *Tim.* 4. 1. in latter times some shall *d. from* the faith
2 *Tim.* 2. 19. that nameth Christ *d. from* iniquity

Not DEPART.

Gen. 49. 10. the sceptre shall *not d.* from Judah
Josh. 1. 8. this book of the law shall *not d.* meditate
Judg. 6. 18. *d. not* hence, I pray thee, till I come
2 *Sam.* 7. 15. but my mercy shall *not d.* from him
22. 23. as for his statutes, I did *not d.* from them
2 *Chron.* 35. 15. they might *not d.* from their service
Job 7. 19. how long wilt thou *not d.* from me?
15. 30. he shall *not d.* out of darkness, the flame
Psal. 55. 11. deceit and guile *d. not* from her streets
Prov. 3. 21. let them *not d.* from thine eyes, 4. 21.
5. 7. hear me, and *d. not* from words of my mouth
17. 13. evil for good, evil shall *not d.* from his house
22. 6. when he is old he will *not d.* from it
27. 22. yet will *not* his foolishness *d.* from him
Isa. 54. 10. but my kindness shall *not d.* from thee
59. 21. my cov. my Spirit, and words, shall *not d.*
Jer. 32. 40. put my fear, that they shall *not d.* from me
37. 9. the Chaldeans, for they shall *not d.*
Mat. 14. 16. they need *not d.* give ye them to eat
Luke 4. 42. stayed him, that should *not d.* from them
12. 59. thou shalt *not d.* thence, till thou hast paid

DEPARTED.

Gen. 12. 4. so Abraham *d.* as the Lord had spoken
14. 12. they took Lot and *d.* || 21. 14. Hagar *d.*
24. 10. Eliezer *d.* || 26. 17. Isaac *d.* || 31. 55. Laban *d.*
37. 17. and the man said, they are *d.* hence
42. 26. they laded their asses with corn, and *d.*
45. 24. he sent his brethren away, and they *d.*
Num. 12. 9. anger of the L. was kindled, and he *d.*
22. 7. and the elders of Moab and Midian *d.*
Josh. 2. 21. she sent the spies away, and they *d.*
Judg. 9. 55. *d.* every man to his place, 2 *Sam.* 6. 19.
18. 7. then the five men *d.* and came to Laish, 21.
19. 10. the Levite *d.* || 21. 24. Israel *d.* thence
1 *Sam.* 6. 6. did they not let Israel go, and they *d.*?
20. 42. David *d.* 22. 1. 5. || 2 *Sam.* 12. 15. so Nath. *d.*
2 *Sam.* 19. 24. nor washed from the day the king *d.*
1 *Kings* 12. 5. and the people *d.* 2 *Chron.* 10. 5.
14. 17. and Jeroboam's wife arose and *d.* to Tirza
19. 19. Elijah *d.* and found Elisha, 2 *Kings* 1. 4.
20. 9. the messengers *d.* and brought word again
38. so the prophet *d.* and waited for the king
2 *Kings* 5. 5. Naam. *d.* || 10. 12. Jehu arose and *d.* 15.
19. 36. so Sennacherib *d.* and went, *Isa.* 37. 37.
1 *Chr.* 16. 43. all people *d.* every man to his house
21. 4. wherefore Joab *d.* and went through Israel
2 *Chr.* 21. 20. Jehoram *d.* without being desired
Psal. 105. 38. Egypt was glad when they *d.*
Isa. 38. 12. mine age is *d.* and removed from me
Jer. 41. 10. Ishmael *d.* to go over to the Ammonites
Lam. 1. 6. from daughter of Zion all her beauty is *d.*
Mat. 2. 9. when had heard the king, wise men *d.* 12.
14. Joseph and Mary arose, and *d.* into Egypt
4. 12. Jesus *d.* 9. 27. | 11. 1 | 12. 9. | 13. 53. | 14. 13. | 15. 21, 29. | 16. 4. | 19. 15.
27. 5. Judas *d.* || *Luke* 1. 23. Zacharias *d.* to his house

Mark 1. 35. Jesus *d.* 6. 46. | 8. 13. *Luke* 4. 42. *John* 4. 3, 43. | 6. 15. | 12. 36.
Luke 5. 25. he *d.* to his own house, glorifying God
7. 24. when the messengers of John were *d.*
8. 35. the man out of whom the devils were *d.*
10. 30. the thieves wounded him and *d.*
35. on the morrow when the Samaritan *d.*
John 5. 15. the man *d.* and told the Jews it was Jesus
Acts 10. 7. when the angel *d.* || 11. 25. Barnabas *d.*
12. 17. Peter *d.* || 13. 4. they *d.* to Seleucia
14. 20. Paul *d.* || 15. 39. Paul and Barnabas *d.* asunder
16. 40. Paul and Silas *d.* || 18. 7. Paul *d.* 23. | 20. 1, 11.
21. 5. we *d.* and went our way, 8. | 28. 10, 11.
28. 29. when he said these words, the Jews *d.*
2 *Tim.* 4. 10. Demas forsaken me, is *d.* to Thessalonica
Philem. 15. for perhaps he therefore *d.* for a season
Rev. 6. 14. and the heaven *d.* as a scroll rolled

DEPARTED *from.*

Gen. 26. 31. they arose and *d. from* Isaac in peace
31. 40. thus was I, my sleep *d. from* mine eyes
Exod. 19. 2. they were *d. f.* Rephidim, *Num.* 33. 15.
35. 20. all Israel *d. from* the presence of Moses
Lev. 13. 58. if the plague be *d. from* them, then
Num. 10. 33. they *d. from* the mount of the Lord
12. 10. the cloud *d. from* off the tabernacle
14. 9. their defence is *d. from* them, fear not
33. 3. they *d. from* Rameses | 6. *d. from* Succoth
8. *d. from* Pi-hahiroth || 13. *d. from* Dophkah
All their departures set down to verse 49.
Deut. 1. 19. and when we *d. from* Horeb, we went
Judg. 16. 20. he wist not that Lord was *d. f.* him
1 *Sam.* 4. 21. saying, the glory is *d. from* Israel, 22.
10. 2. when thou art *d. from* me, thou shalt find
15. 6. Kenites *d. from* among the Amalekites
16. 14. the Spirit of the Lord *d. from* Saul, 18. 12.
23. was refreshed, and the evil Spirit *d. from* him
28. 15. God is *d. from* me, and answereth me not
16. ask of me, seeing the Lord is *d. from* thee
1 *Kings* 20. 36. as soon as thou art *d. from* me
2 *Kings* 3. 27. they *d. from* him to their own land
5. 19. so he *d. from* Elisha a little way, 8. 14.
19. 8. Sennacherib *d. from* Lachish, *Isa.* 37. 8.
2 *Chron.* 24. 25. and when they were *d. from* him
Ezra 8. 31. then we *d. from* the river of Ahava
Psal. 18. 21. and have not wickedly *d. from* my G.
Isa. 7. 17. from the day that Ephraim *d. from* Jud.
Jer. 29. 2. and the smiths were *d. from* Jerusalem
37. 5. the Chaldeans heard they *d. from* Jerusalem
Ezek. 6. 9. their whorish heart which hath *d. from* me
10. 18. the glory of the Lord *d. from* the threshold
Dan. 4. 31. O king, the kingdom is *d. from* thee
Hos. 10. 5. for the glory of Samaria is *d. from* it
Mat. 15. 29. and Jesus *d. from* thence, and came
19. 1. had finished these sayings, he *d. from* Galilee
20. 29. as they *d. from* Jericho, a multitude followed
24. 1. Jesus went out and *d. from* the temple
28. 8. they *d.* quickly *from* the sepulchre
Mark 1. 42. the leprosy *d. from* him, *Luke* 5. 13.
Luke 1. 38. and the angel *d. from* Mary
4. 13. the devil *d. from* him for a season
9. 33. as they *d. from* him, Peter said to Jesus
Acts 5. 41. they *d. from* the presence of the council
12. 10. and forthwith the angel *d. from* him
13. 14. they came when they had *d. from* Perga
15. 38. John *d. from* them from Pamphylia
17. 33. Paul *d. from* them, 18. 1. | 19. 9. *Phil.* 4. 15.
19. 12. diseases *d. from* them, and evil spirits went out
Rev. 18. 14. and the fruits that thy soul lusted after are *d. from* thee, and all things dainty are *d.*

DEPARTED *not from.*

2 *Sam.* 22. 22. I have *not d. from* my G. *Psal.* 18. 21.
2 *Kings* 3. 3. he *d. not therefrom*, 13. 2.
10. 29. Jehu *d. not from* the sins of Jeroboam, who made Israel to sin, to wit, golden calves, 31. | 13. 6, 11. | 14. 24. | 15. 9, 18. | 17. 22.
18. 6. Hezekiah *d. not from* following the Lord
2 *Chr.* 8. 15. *d. not from* commandment of the king
20. 32. Jehoshaphat *d. not from* the way of Asa
34. 33. they *d. not from* following the Lord
Neh. 9. 19. the cloud *d. not from* them by day
Psal. 119. 102. I have *not d. from* thy judgments
Luke 2. 37. Anna *d. not from* the temp. but served God

DEPARTED *out.*

Gen. 12. 4. was 75 years old when he *d. out* of Haran
Deut. 24. 2. and when she is *d. out* of his house
Judg. 6. 21. angel of the Lord *d. out* of his sight
17. 8. the Levite *d. out* of Beth-lehem-judah
1 *Sam.* 23. 13. David and his men *d. out* of Keilah
2 *Sam.* 11. 8. and Uriah *d. out* of the king's house
Mal. 2. 8. ye are *d. out* of the way, ye have corrupt.
Mat. 17. 18. rebuked the devil, and he *d. out* of him

DEPARTED *not out.*

Exod. 33. 11. Joshua *d. not out* of the tabernacle
Num. 14. 44. the ark and Mos. *d. not out* of the camp

DEPARTETH.

Job 27. 21. the wind carrieth him away, and he *d.*
Prov. 11. †22. so is a fair wom. who *d.* from discret.
14. 16. a wise man feareth, and *d.* from evil
Eccl. 6. 4. he cometh in with vanity, and *d.* in dark.
Isa. 59. 15. he that *d.* from evil maketh hims. a prey
Jer. 3. 20. as a wife treacherously *d.* from her husb.
17. 5. cursed be the man whose heart *d.* from L.
Nah. 3. 1. woe to the bloody city, the prey *d.* not
Luke 9. 39. and bruising him, hardly *d.* from him

DEPARTING.

Gen. 35. 18. as her soul was in *d.* she called his name
Exod. 16. 1. after their *d.* out of the land of Egypt
Isa. 59. 13. in lying and *d.* away from our God
Dan. 9. 5. we have sinned, by *d.* from thy precepts, 11.
Hos. 1. 2. have committed whoredom *d.* from Lord
Mark 6. 33. the people saw them *d.* and knew him
7. 31. and *d.* from the coast of Tyre and Sidon
Acts 13. 13. John *d.* from them, returned to Jerus.
20. 29. I know after my *d.* shall wolves enter in
Heb. 3. 12. an evil heart, in *d.* from the living God
11. 22. Joseph made mention of the *d.* of Israel

DEPARTURE.

Ezek. 26. 18. the isles shall be troubled at thy *d.*
2 *Tim.* 4. 6. and the time of my *d.* is at hand

DEPEND.

Job 22. † 2. doth his good success *d.* thereon

DEPOSED.

Dan. 5. 20. he was *d.* from his kingly throne

DEPRIVED.

Gen. 27. 45. why should I be *d.* of both in one day
Job 39. 17. because God hath *d.* her of wisdom
Isa. 38. 10. I am *d.* of the residue of my years

DEPRIVING.

Psal. 35. † 12. me evil for good, to the *d.* of my soul

DEPTH.

Job 28. 14. the *d.* saith, it is not in me, and sea saith
38. 16. or hast thou walked in search of the *d.*?
Psal. 33. 7. he layeth up the *d.* in store-houses
69. † 2. I sink in the mire of *d.* where there is no
Prov. 8. 27. when he set a compass on face of the *d.*
25. 3. heaven for height, and the earth for *d.*
Isa. 7. 11. ask it either in the *d.* or in the height
Jonah 2. 5. the *d.* closed me round about, weeds wrapt
Mat. 18. 6. better he were drowned in the *d.* of the sea
Mark 4. 5. because it had no *d.* of earth, it withered
Rom. 8. 39. nor *d.* separate us from the love of God
11. 33. O the *d.* of the riches both of the wisdom
Eph. 3. 18. what is breadth and *d.* of love of Christ

DEPTHS.

Exod. 15. 5. the *d.* have covered them, they sank
8. the *d.* were congealed in the heart of the sea
Deut. 8. 7. the *d.* that spring out of valleys and hills
Psal. 68. 22. bring my people from the *d.* of the sea
71. 20. shall bring me up from the *d.* of the earth
77. 16. the waters were afraid, the *d.* were troubled
78. 15. he gave them drink as out of the great *d.*
106. 9. he led them thro' the *d.* as thro' wilderness
107. 26. they mount up, they go down again to *d.*
130. 1. out of the *d.* have I cried to thee, O Lord
Prov. 3. 20. by his knowledge the *d.* are broken up
8. 24. when there were no *d.* I was brought forth
9. 18. and that her guests are in the *d.* of hell
Isa. 51. 10. that hath made the *d.* of the sea a way
Ezek. 27. 34. thou shalt be broken in *d.* of waters
Mic. 7. 19. will cast their sins into the *d.* of the sea
Rev. 2. 24. which have not known the *d.* of Satan

DEPUTED.

2 *Sam.* 15. 3. but there is no man *d.* of the king

DEPUTY.

1 *Kings* 22. 47. was no king in Edom, a *d.* was king
Acts 13. 7. a sorcerer Barjesus who was with the *d.*
8. seeking to turn away the *d.* from the faith
18. 12. and when Gallio was the *d.* of Achaia

DEPUTIES.

Esth. 8. 9. it was written to *d.* and rulers of provinces
9. 3. and the *d.* and officers helped the Jews
Acts 19. 38. there are *d.* let them implead one another

DERIDE.

Hab. 1. 10. they shall *d.* every strong hold, heap dust

DERIDED.

Luke 16. 14. Pharisees heard these things, and *d.* him
23. 35. the rulers also with the people *d.* him

DERISION.

Job 30. 1. that are younger than I, have me in *d.*
Psal. 2. 4. the Lord shall have them in *d.*
44. 13. a *d.* to them that are round about us, 79. 4.
59. 8. thou shalt have all the heathen in *d.*
119. 51. the proud have had me greatly in *d.*
Jer. 20. 7. I am in *d.* daily || 8. was made a *d.* daily
48. 26. and Moab also shall be in *d.* 39.
27. for was not Israel a *d.* unto thee?
Lam. 3. 14. I was a *d.* to my people and song all day
Ezek. 23. 32. thou shalt drink, and be had in *d.*
36. 4. to cities which became a *d.* to the heathen
Hos. 7. 16. this shall be their *d.* in the land of Egypt

DESCEND.

Num. 34. 11. the border shall *d.* and reach to sea
1 *Sam.* 26. 10. he shall *d.* into battle and perish
Psal. 49. 17. his glory shall not *d.* after him
65. † 10. thou causest rain *d.* into the furrows
104. † 8. the mountains to ascend, the valleys *d.* 10.
Ezek. 26. 20. with them that *d.* into the pit, 31. 16.
Mark 15. 32. let Christ *d.* now from the cross
Acts 11. 5. I saw vision, certain vessel *d.* great sheet
Rom. 10. 7. or who shall *d.* into the deep?
1 *Thess.* 4. 16. Ld. shall *d.* from heaven with a shou

DESCENDED.

Exod. 19. 18. because the Lord *d.* on Sinai in fire
33. 9. the cloudy pillar *d.* || 34. 5. *d.* in a cloud
Deut. 9. 21. the brook that *d.* out of the mount
Josh. 2. 23. so the two men *d.* from the mountain
Psal. 133. 3. as dew that *d.* on mountains of Zion
Prov. 30. 4. who hath ascended up to heaven, or *d.*
Mat. 7. 25. the rain *d.* and the floods came, 27.
28. 2. for the angel of the Lord *d.* from heaven
Luke 3. 22. the Holy Ghost *d.* in a bodily shape
Acts 24. 1. Ananias the high-priest *d.* with the elders
Eph. 4. 10. he that *d.* is the same that ascended

DESCENDETH.

Jam. 3. 15. this wisdom *d.* not from above but sensual

DESCENDING.

Gen. 28. 12. top of ladder reached to heaven, and the angels of God ascending and *d.* *John* 1. 51.
Isa. 15. † 3. every one shall howl *d.* into weeping
Mat. 3. 16. he saw the Spirit of God *d.* *Mark* 1. 10.
John 1. 32. I saw Spirit *d.* from heaven like a dove
33. on whom thou shalt see Spirit *d.* and remaining
Acts 10. 11. a vessel *d.* as it had been a great sheet
Rev. 21. 10. that great city *d.* out of heaven from G

DESCENT.

Mic. 1. † 4. as waters that are poured down a *d.*
Luke 19. 37. when come nigh at *d.* of mount Olives
Heb. 7. 3. Melchisedec without father, mother, and *d.*
6. but he whose *d.* is not counted from them

DESCRIBE, ED, ETH.

Josh. 18. 4. they shall go through land and *d.* it, 6, 8.
8. Joshua charged them that went to *d.* the land
9. and they *d.* it by cities into seven parts in a book
Judg. 8. 14. he *d.* to him the princes of Succoth
Rom. 4. 6. even as David also *d.* blessedn. of the man
10. 5. for Moses *d.* the righteousness of the law

DESCRIPTION.

Josh. 18. 6. and ye shall bring the d. hither to me

DESCRY.

Judg. 1. 23. the house of Joseph sent to *d.* Bethel.

DESERT.

Exod. 3. 1. he led his flock to the backside of the *d.*
5. 3. let us go three days' journey into the *d.*

Exod. 19. 2. and they were come to the d. of Sinai
23. 31. I will set thy bounds from d. to the river
Num. 20. 1. then Israel came into the d. of Zin
27. 14. for ye rebelled against me in the d. of Zin
33. 16. and they removed from the d. of Sinai
2 Chron. 26. 10. Uzziah built towers in the d.
Job 24. 5. as wild asses in the d. go they forth
Psal. 75. † 6. promotion cometh not from the d.
78. 40. how oft did they grieve him in the d.?
102. 6. I am like a pelican, an owl of the d.
106. 14. but lusted and tempted God in the d.
Isa. 13. 21. but wild beasts of d. shall lie there, their houses full of doleful creatures, 34. 14. Jer. 50. 39.
21. 1. as whirlwinds, so it cometh from the d.
35. 1. the d. shall rejoice || 6. streams in the d.
40. 3. make straight in d. a high-way for our God
41. 19. I will set in d. the fir-tree and the pine
43. 19. I will even make rivers in the d. 20.
51. 3. will make her d. like the garden of the Lord
Jer. 17. 6. for he shall be like the heath in the d.
25. 24. people that dwell in d. shall drink after them
50. 12. Chaldea shall be a dry land and a d.
Ezek. 47. 8. these waters go down into the d.
Mat. 24. 26. if they say, behold, he is in the d.
John 6. 31. our fathers did eat manna in the d.
Acts 8. 26. from Jerusalem to Gaza, which is d.

DESERT *land*.

Deut. 32. 10. he found him in a d. *land*, he led him
Prov. 21. † 19. better dwell in the *land* of the d.

DESERT *place*.

Mark 6. 31. come ye yourselves into a d. *place*
32. depart. into a d. *place*, Mat. 14. 13. Luke 4. 42.
35. this is a d. *place*, Mat. 14. 15. Luke 9. 12.
Luke 9. 10. he went aside privately into a d. *place*

DESERTS.

Isa. 48. 21. thirsted not when he led them through d.
Jer. 2. 6. the Lord that led us through a land of d.
5. † 6. a wolf of the d. shall spoil them
Ezek. 13. 4. thy prophets are like foxes in the d.
Luke 1. 80. John was in the d. till his shewing to Isr.
Heb. 11. 38. they wandered in d. and in mountains

DESERT.

Psal. 28. 4. after work of hands, render them their d.

DESERTS.

Ezek. 7. 27. according to their d. will I judge them

DESERVE.

Ezra 9. 13. hast punished less than our iniquities d.

DESERVETH.

Job 11. 6. God exacteth less than thy iniquity d.

DESERVING.

Judg. 9. 16. done to him according to d. of his hands

DESIRE

Signifies, [1] *Longing, or wishing*, 1 Sam. 23. 20. [2] *The prayer, request, or longing of the soul, for some spiritual or bodily good things, whereof it feels a want*, Psal. 145. 19. [3] *Love, or affection*, Cant. 7. 10. Dan. 11. 37. [4] *Hope, or expectation*, 1 Sam. 9. 20. [5] *An inclination to, or delight in, the pleasures of life*, Eccl. 12. 5. [6] *A wife*, called the desire of the eyes, Ezek. 24. 16. [7] *Sinful lusts and affections*, Eph. 2. 3.

Thy desire shall be to thy husband, and he shall rule over thee, Gen. 3. 16. *Thy desires or requests shall be referred, or submitted, to thy husband's will and pleasure, to grant or deny them, as he sees fit. Thou shalt be obliged to such a subjection, as shall be many times against thy will, and be uneasy to thee.*

Gen. 3. † 6. saw that the tree was a d. to the eyes
16. thy d. shall be to thy husband, he shall rule
4. 7. to thee shall be his d. thou shalt rule over him
Deut. 18. 6. and come with all the d. of his mind
21. 11. and hast a d. to her, to have her to wife
1 Sam. 9. 20. and on whom is all the d. of Israel?
23. 20. come down accord. to all the d. of thy soul
2 Sam. 23. 5. this is all my salvation, and all my d.
1 Kings 5. 8. I will do all thy d. concerning timber
9. thou shalt accomplish my d. in giving food
10. according to all Solomon's d. 9. 11.
9. 1. Solomon had finished building, and all his d.
† 19. the d. of Solomon which he desired
10. 13. king Solomon gave to the queen of Sheba all her d. whatsoever she asked, 2 Chron. 9. 12.
2 Chron. 15. 15. and sought him with their whole d.
21. † 20. Jehoram departed without d.
32. † 27. he made treasures for instruments of d.
36. † 10. he took the vessels of d. to Babylon
Job 9. † 26. my days are passed away as ships of d.
14. 15. thou wilt have a d. to work of thine hands
31. 16. if I have withheld the poor from their d.
35. my d. is that the Almighty would answer me
33. † 20. so that his soul abhorreth meat of d.
34. 36. my d. is that Job may be tried to the end
Psal. 10. 3. the wicked boasteth of his heart's d.
17. Lord, thou hast heard the d. of the humble
21. 2. thou hast given his heart's d. not withheld
38. 9. Lord, all my d. is before thee, my groan.
54. 7. eye hath seen his d. on mine enemies, 92. 11.
59. 10. God shall let me see my d. on mine enemies
78. 29. were filled, for he gave them their own d.
92. 11. mine ears shall hear my d. of the wicked
106. † 24. yea, they despised a land of d.
112. 8. not afraid, till he see his d. on his enemies
10. the d. of the wicked shall perish
118. 7. therefore shall I see my d. on them hate me
145. 16. thou satisfiest the d. of every living thing
19. he will fulfil the d. of them that fear him
Prov. 10. 24. the d. of righteous shall be granted
11. 23. the d. of the righteous is only good
13. 12. but when d. cometh, it is a tree of life
19. the d. accomplished is sweet to the soul
19. 22. the d. of a man is his kindness
21. 25. the d. of the slothful killeth him
Eccl. 6. 9. the sight of the eyes than wandering of d.
12. 5. d. shall fail, because man goeth to long home
Cant. 7. 10. my beloved's, and his d. is toward me
Isa. 2. † 16. the day of the Lord on all pictures of d.
26. 8. the d. of our soul is to thy name, and to
32. † 12. they shall lament for the fields of d.
Jer. 2. 24. snuffeth up wind at the d. of her heart
3. † 19. how shall I give thee a land of d.!
Jer. 12. † 10. they made my portion of d. a wildern.
25. † 34. you shall sail like a vessel of d.
44. 14. the land to which you have a d. to return
Ezek. 24. 16. I will take from thee the d. of thy eyes
21. I will profane the d. of your eyes, 25.
26. † 12. they shall destroy houses of thy d.
Dan. 11. † 8. carry into Egypt vessels of their d.
37. neither shall he regard the d. of women
Hos. 10. 10. it is my d. I should chastise them
13. † 15. shall spoil the treasure of vessels of d.
Amos 5. † 11. ye have planted vineyards of d.
Mic. 7. 3. the great man uttereth his mischievous d.
Nah. 2. † 9. none end of all the vessels of d.
Hab. 2. 5. who enlargeth his d. as hell, is as death
Hag. 2. 7. and the d. of all nations shall come
Zech. 7. † 14. they laid the land of d. desolate
Luke 22. 15. he said, with d. I have desired to eat
Rom. 10. 1. my heart's d. to G. for Isr. is to be saved
15. 23. having a great d. these many years to come
2 Cor. 7. 7. when he told us your earnest d. towards
11. what fear, what vehement d. yea what zeal
Phil. 1. 23. I am in a strait, having a d. to depart
1 Thess. 2. 17. to see your face with great d.

DESIRE, *Verb*.

Exod. 10. 11. serve the Lord, for that ye did d.
34. 24. neither shall any man d. thy land
Deut. 5. 21. nor shalt thou d. thy neighbour's wife
7. 25. thou shalt not d. the silver or gold on them
Judg. 8. 24. Gideon said, I would d. a request of you
1 Kings 2. 20. I d. one small petition of thee
2 Kings 4. 28. she said, did I d. a son of my lord?
Neh. 1. 11. thy servants who d. to fear thy name
Job 13. 3. surely I d. to reason with God
21. 14. for we d. not the knowledge of thy ways
33. 32. speak, for I d. to justify thee
36. 20. d. not the night when people are cut off
Psal. 40. 6. sacrifice and offering thou didst not d.
45. 11. so shall the king greatly d. thy beauty
65. † 9. after thou hadst made it to d. rain
70. 2. let them be put to confusion that d. my hurt
73. 25. there is none on earth I d. besides thee
Prov. 3. 15. all thou canst d. are not to be compared
23. 6. neither d. thou his dainty meats
24. 1. against evil men, nor d. to be with them
Isa. 53. 2. there is no beauty that we should d. him
Jer. 22. 27. the land whereunto they d. to return
42. 22. ye shall die in the place whither ye d. to go
Dan. 2. 18. I would d. mercies of the G. of heaven
Amos 5. 18. woe to you that d. the day of the Lord
Mark 9. 35. he saith, if any man d. to be first
10. 35. shouldest do for us whatsoever we shall d.
11. 24. what things soever ye d. when ye pray
15. 8. began to d. him to do as he had ever done
Luke 17. 22. when ye shall d. to see one of the days
20. 46. the scribes which d. to walk in long robes
Acts 23. 20. the Jews have agreed to d. thee to bring
28. 22. we d. to hear of thee what thou thinkest
1 Cor. 14. 1. follow after charity, and d. spirit. gifts
2 Cor. 11. 12. cut off from them which d. occasion
12. 6. tho' I would d. to glory, I shall not be a fool
Gal. 4. 9. whereunto ye d. again to be in bondage
20. I d. to be present with you now, and to change
21. tell me, ye that d. to be under the law
6. 12. as many as d. to make a fair shew in the flesh
13. but d. to have you circumcised, that they may
Eph. 3. 13. wherefore I d. that ye faint not
Phil. 4. 17. not because I d. a gift, but I d. fruit
Col. 1. 9. to d. ye may be filled with knowledge
1 Tim. 2. † 1. I d. supplications be made for all men
3. 1. if a man d. the office of a bishop, a good work
Heb. 6. 11. we d. every one of you to shew diligence
11. 16. but now they d. a better country, that is
Jam. 4. 2. ye kill, ye d. to have, and cannot obtain
1 Pet. 1. 12. which things the angels d. to look into
2. 2. as new-born babes d. the sincere milk of word
Rev. 9. 6. men shall d. to die, and death shall flee

DESIRABLE.

Gen. 27. † 15. Rebekah took d. raiment of son Esau
1 Kings 20. † 6. d. in thy eyes, they shall take away
Ezra 8. † 27. two vessels of copper d. as gold
Isa. 44. † 9. and their d. things shall not profit
Lam. 1. † 7. Jerusalem remembered all her d. things
† 10. hath spread his hand upon her d. things
2. † 4. he stood and slew all the d. of the eye
Ezek. 23. 6. all of them d. young men, 12. 23.
Joel 3. † 5. carried into your temples my d. things

DESIRED.

Gen. 3. 6. and a tree to be d. to make one wise
1 Sam. 12. 13. and behold the king whom ye d.
1 Kings 9. 19. the desire which Solomon d. 2 Chr. 8. 6.
2 Chron. 11. 23. and Rehoboam d. many wives
Esth. 2. 13. whatsoever she d. was given her
Job 20. 20. he shall not save of that which he d.
Psal. 19. 10. more to be d. are they than gold
27. 4. one thing I d. of the L. that I may dwell
39. † 11. that which is to be d. in him to melt away
107. 30. so he bringeth them to their d. haven
132. 13. he hath d. Zion for his habitation
14. my rest, here will I dwell, for I have d.
Prov. 8. 11. all that may be d. not to be compared
21. 20. there is a treasure to be d. and oil in dwell.
Eccl. 2. 10. what my eyes d. I kept not from them
Isa. 1. 29. shall be ashamed of the oaks ye have d.
26. 9. with my soul have I d. thee in the night
Jer. 17. 16. nor have I d. woeful day, thou knowest
Dan. 2. 16. Daniel went and d. of the king time
23. hast made known unto me what we d. of thee
11. † 38. he shall honour God with things d.
Hos. 6. 6. for I d. mercy and not sacrifice
Mic. 7. 1. no cluster, my soul d. the first-ripe fruit
Zeph. 2. 1. gather together, O nation not d.
Mat. 13. 17. many righteous men have d. to see those
16. 1. the Pharisees d. he would shew a sign
Mark 15. 6. one prisoner whom they d. Luke 23. 25.
Luke 7. 36. one of the Pharisees d. Jesus to eat
9. 9. but who is this, and he d. to see him
10. 24. many kings have d. to see those things
22. 15. I have d. to eat this passover with you
31. Satan hath d. to have you to sift you as wheat
23. 25. and he released to them him whom they d.
Acts 3. 14. and d. a murderer to be granted unto you
7. 46. and d. to find a tabern. for the G. of Jacob
Acts 8. 31. the eunuch d. Philip to come into chariot
9. 2. Paul d. of the high-priest letters to Damascus
12. 20. having made Blastus their friend, d. peace
13. 7. Sergius Paulus d. to hear the word of God
21. afterward they d. a king, God gave them Saul
28. yet d. they Pilate that he should be slain
16. 39. and d. them to depart out of the city
25. 3. d. favour against Paul that he would send
1 Cor. 16. 12. I greatly d. him to come to you
2 Cor. 8. 6. insomuch that we d. Titus to finish in you
12. 18. I d. Titus, and with him I sent a brother
1 John 5. 15. we know we have the petitions we d.

DESIREDST.

Deut. 18. 16. according to all that thou d. of God
Mat. 18. 32. I forgave thee, because thou d. me

DESIRES.

Gen. 6. † 5. all the d. of his heart are only evil
Psal. 37. 4. he shall give thee the d. of thy heart
140. 8. grant not, O Lord, the d. of the wicked
Dan. 9. † 23. for thou art a man of d. 10. † 11.
10. † 3. I ate no bread of d. neither came flesh
Hos. 9. † 16. yet will I slay the d. of their womb
Eph. 2. 3. fulfilling the d. of the flesh and mind

DESIREST.

Psal. 51. 6. thou d. truth in the inward parts
16. thou d. not sacrifice, else would I give it

DESIRETH.

Deut. 14. 26. bestow it for whatsoever thy soul d.
1 Sam. 2. 16. then take as much as thy soul d.
18. 25. say to David, the king d. not any dowry
20. 4. what thy soul d. I will do, 1 Kings 11. 37.
2 Sam. 3. 21. mayest reign over all that thy heart d.
Job 7. 2. as a servant earnestly d. the shadow
23. 13. what his soul d. even that he doth
Psal. 17. † 12. is as a lion that d. to ravin
34. 12. what man is he that d. life and loveth days
68. 16. this is the hill which God d. to dwell in
Prov. 12. 12. the wicked d. the net of evil men
13. 4. the soul of the sluggard d. and hath not
21. 10. the soul of the wicked d. evil
Eccl. 6. 2. he wanteth nothing of all that he d.
Luke 5. 39. having drunk old wine straightway d. new
14. 32. he sendeth and d. conditions of peace
1 Tim. 3. 1. the office of a bishop, he d. a good work

DESIRING.

Mat. 12. 46. his brethren d. to speak with him, 47.
20. 20. worshipping and d. a certain thing of him
Luke 8. 20. thy breth. stand without d. to see thee
16. 21. d. to be fed with the crumbs which fell
Acts 25. 15. d. to have judgment against him
2 Cor. 5. 2. d. to be clothed upon with our house
1 Thess. 3. 6. d. greatly to see us as we to see you
1 Tim. 1. 7. d. to be teachers of the law
2 Tim. 1. 4. greatly d. to see thee, being mindful

DESIROUS.

Prov. 23. 3. be not d. of his dainties, for they are
Zeph. 2. † 1. gather together, O nation not d.
Luke 23. 8. Herod was d. to see him of a long season
John 16. 19. Jesus knew they were d. to ask him
2 Cor. 11. 32. with a garrison d. to apprehend me
Gal. 5. 26. let us not be d. of vain-glory, envying
1 Thess. 2. 8. so being affectionately d. of you

DESOLATE.

2 Sam. 13. 20. Tamar remain. d. in Absalom's house
Job 15. 28. he dwelleth in d. cities and in houses
16. 7. thou hast made d. all my company
30. 3. the wilderness in former time d. and waste
38. 27. to satisfy the d. and waste ground
Psal. 25. 16. turn and have mercy on me, for I am d.
40. 15. let them be d. for a reward of their shame
69. 25. let their habitation be d. let none dwell
143. 4. therefore my heart within me is d.
Isa. 1. 7. your country is d. your cities burnt
3. 26. she being d. shall sit upon the ground
7. 19. they shall rest all of them in d. valleys
13. 22. the beast shall cry in their d. houses
24. 6. and they that dwell therein are d.
49. 8. to cause to inherit the d. heritages
21. seeing I have lost my children, and am d.
54. 1. more are the children of the d. Gal. 4. 27.
3. and make the d. cities to be inhabited
Jer. 2. 12. be ye very d. saith the Lord
6. 8. lest I make thee d. a land not inhabited
9. † 10. the habitations of the wilderness are d.
11. I will make the cities of Judah d. without an inhabitant, 10. 22. | 33. 10. | 44. 6.
10. 25. they have made his habitation d.
12. 11. they made it d. and being d. it mourneth
19. 8. I will make this city d. and an hissing
32. 43. it is d. without man or beast, 33. 12.
49. 20. he shall make their habitations d. 50. 45.
Lam. 1. 4. all her gates are d. her priests sigh
13. he hath made me d. and faint all day, 3. 11.
16. my children are d. the enemy prevailed
4. 5. they that did feed delicately are d. in the street
5. 18. because of the mountain of Zion which is d.
Ezek. 6. 6. that your altars may be made d.
19. 7. he knew their d. palaces, and he laid waste
20. 26. that I might make them d. to the end
25. 13. I will make Edom d. from Teman
26. 19. when I shall make thee a d. city
29. 12. in the midst of the countries that are d.
30. 14. I will make Pathros d. and will set fire
35. 3. O mount Seir, I will make thee most d. 7.
12. they are d. they are given us to consume
35. 14. when earth rejoiceth, I will make thee d.
15. as thou didst rejoice, because it was d.
36. 3. because they have made you d. and swallowed
4. thus saith the Lord to the hills and d. wastes
35. the d. cities are become fenced and inhabited
36. know that I the Lord plant that that was d.
Dan. 9. 17. to shine on thy sanctuary that is d.
27. for the abominations he shall make it d.
11. 31. the abomination that maketh d. 12. 11.
Hos. 2. † 12. I will make d. her vines and fig-trees
13. 16. Samaria shall become d. for she rebelled
Joel 1. 17. the garners are laid d. barns are broken
18. yea the flocks of sheep are made d.
Mic. 1. 7. and all the idols thereof will I lay d.
6. 13. in making thee d. because of thy sins
Zeph. 3. 6. their towers are d. their streets waste
Mat. 23. 38. your house is left to you d. Luke 13. 35.

Acts 1. 20. it is written, let his habitation be *d.*
1 *Tim.* 5. 5. now she that is a widow indeed and *d.*
Rev. 17. 16. these shall hate the whore, and make *d.*
18. 19. for in one hour is she made *d.*

Land DESOLATE.

Gen. 47. 19. give us seed that the *land* be not *d.*
Exod. 23. 29. lest the *land* become *d.* beast mul iply
Lev. 26. 34. then shall the *land* enjoy her sabbaths as long as it lieth *d.* 35, 43. 2 *Chron.* 36. 21.
Isa. 6. 11. he said, until the *land* be utterly *d.*
13. 9. the day of the Lord cometh to lay the *land d.*
62. 4. nor shall thy *land* any more be termed *d.*
Jer. 4. 7. he is gone forth to make thy *land d.*
27. the Lord said, the whole *land* shall be *d.*
7. 34. to cease voice of mirth, for the *land* shall be *d.*
12. 11. they made it *d.* the whole *land* is made *d.*
18. 16. to make their *land d.* and a perpetual hissing
25. 38. for their *land* is *d.* because of his anger
32. 43. in this *land* whereof ye say it is *d.*
50. 3. a nation which shall make her *land d.*
Ezek. 6. 14. and make the *land d.* yea more *d.*
12. 19. her *land* may be *d.* from all that is therein
20. the cities laid waste, and the *land* shall be *d.*
14. 16. but the *land* shall be *d.* *Mic.* 7. 13.
15. 8. and I will make the *land d.* saith the Lord
19. 7. the *land* was *d.* and the fulness thereof
29. 9. the *land* of Egypt shall be *d.* they shall know that I am the Lord, 10. 12. | 30. 7. | 32. 15.
33. 28. for I will lay the *land* most *d.* pomp cease
29. that I am L. when I have laid the *land* most *d.*
36. 34. the *d. land* shall be tilled, whereas it lay *d.*
35. the *land* that was *d.* is like the garden of Eden
Joel 2. 20. I will drive him to a *land* barren and *d.*
Zech. 7. 14. *land* was *d.* for they laid pleasant *land d.*

DESOLATE *places.*

Job 3. 14. which built *d. places* for themselves
Psal. 109. 10. let them seek bread also out of *d. places*
Isa. 49. 19. thy waste and *d. places* shall be too narrow
59. 10. we stumble, we are in *d. places* as dead men
Ezek. 6. 6. cities laid waste, and high *places* shall be *d.*
26. 20. when I shall set thee in *places d.* of old
38. 12. to turn thine hand upon the *d. places*
Amos 7. 9. the high *places* of Isaac shall be *d.*
Mal. 1. 4. we will return, and build the *d. places*

Shall be, or *shalt be* DESOLATE.

Lev. 26. 22. wild beasts, and your highways *shall be d.*
33. your land *shall be d.* and your cities waste
Job 15. 34. for congregation of hypocrites *shall be d.*
Psal. 34. 21. they that hate the righteous *shall be d.*
22. none of them that trust in him *shall be d.*
Isa. 5. 9. of a truth many houses *shall be d.*
15. 6. for waters of Nimrim *shall be d. Jer.* 48. 34.
27. 10. yet the defenced city *shall be d.* and forsaken
Jer. 26. 9. this city *shall be d.* without inhabitant
33. 10. in this place which ye say *shall be d.*
46. 19. Noph *shall be d.* without an inhabitant
48. 9. Moab, for the cities thereof *shall be d.*
49. 2. Rabbah of Ammonites *shall be* a *d.* heap
50. 13. but Babylon *shall be* wholly *d.*
51. 26. thou *shalt be d.* for ever, saith the Lord
Ezek. 6. 4. your altars *shall be d.* your images broken
29. 12. the cities of Egypt *shall be d.* forty years
33. 28. and the mountains of Israel *shall be d.*
35. 4. behold, O mount Seir, thou *shalt be d.* 15.
Hos. 5. 9. Ephraim *shall be d.* in the day of rebuke

DESOLATE *wilderness.*

Jer. 12. 10. made my pleasant portion a *d. wilderness*
Joel 2. 3. and behind them it is a *d. wilderness*
3. 19. Egypt and Edom shall be a *d. wilderness*

DESOLATION.

Lev. 26. 31. I will bring your sanctuaries to *d.*
32. and I will bring the land into *d.* and your enemies which dwell therein shall be astonished
Josh. 8. 28. Joshua made Ai a *d.* unto this day
2 *Kings* 22. 19. that they should become a *d.* and curse
2 *Chron.* 30. 7. who gave them to *d.* as ye see
Job 30. 14. in the *d.* they rolled themselves upon me
Psal. 73. 19. are they brought to *d.* in a moment
Prov. 1. 27. when your fear cometh as *d.* and destruc.
3. 25. be not afraid of the *d.* of the wicked
Isa. 6. † 11. till the land be desolate with *d.*
17. 9. in that day there shall be *d.*
24. 12. in the city is left *d.* the gate is smitten
47. 11. and *d.* shall come upon thee suddenly
51. 19. these two things are come unto thee, *d.*
64. 10. Zion is a wilderness, Jerusalem a *d.*
Jer. 9. † 11. I will make cities of Judah a *d.* 34. 22.
22. 5. I swear that this house shall become a *d.*
25. 11. and this whole land shall be a *d.* and aston.
18. to make Jerusalem and Judah a *d.* and aston.
† 38. forsaken his covert, for their land is *d.*
44. 2. and behold, this day they are *d.* none dwells
22. therefore is your land a *d.* and a curse
49. 13. Bozra a *d.* ‖ 17. Edom a *d.* ‖ 33. Hazor a *d.*
50. 23. how is Bab. become a *d.* among nations!
51. 29. to make the land of Babylon a *d.*
43. her cities are a *d.* a dry land, and a wilderness
Lam. 3. 47. fear and a snare is come on us, *d.*
Ezek. 7. 27. the prince shall be clothed with *d.*
23. 33. thou shalt be filled with the cup of *d.*
33. † 28. for I will lay the land *d.* and *d.*
35. † 7. thus will I make mount Seir *d.* and *d.*
Dan. 8. 13. concerning the transgression of *d.*
Hos. 12. 1. Ephraim daily increaseth lies and *d.*
Joel 3. 19. Egypt and Edom shall be a *d.* for viol.
Mic. 6. 16. that I should make thee a *d.* and hissing
Zeph. 1. 13. goods a booty, houses shall become a *d.*
15. that day is a day of wrath, wasteness, and *d.*
2. 4. Ashkelon shall be a *d.* ‖ 9. Moab a perpetual *d.*
13. and he will make Nineveh a *d.* and wilderness
14. *d.* shall be in thresholds, uncover cedar-work
15. how is Nineveh become a *d.* for beasts!
Mat. 12. 25. Jesus knowing thoughts, saith, every king. divided ag. itself is brought to *d. Luke* 11. 17.
24. 15. see the abomination of *d. Mark* 13. 14.
Luke 21. 20. then know that the *d.* thereof is nigh

DESOLATIONS.

Ezra 9. 9. give a reviving, and to repair *d.* thereof
Psal. 46. 8. what *d.* he hath made in the earth
74. 3. lift up thy feet to the perpetual *d.*
Isa. 15. † 6. for the waters of Nimrim shall be *d.* the hay is withered away, *Jer.* 48. † 34.
49. † 6. be my servant to restore the *d.* of Israel
61. 4. shall build the old wastes, they shall raise up the former *d.* the *d.* of many generations
Jer. 25. 9. I will make these nations perpetual *d.*
12. make the land of the Chaldeans perpetual *d.*
51. † 26. Babylon shall be everlasting *d.* † 62.
Ezek. 35. 9. I will make mount Seir perpetual *d.*
Dan. 9. 2. accomplish seventy years in *d.* of Jerus.
18. O my God, open thine eyes, and behold our *d.*
26. to the end of the war *d.* are determined

DESPAIR.

2 *Cor.* 4. 8. we are perplexed, but not in *d.*

DESPAIR.

1 *Sam.* 27. 1. and Saul shall *d.* of me, to seek me
Eccl. 2. 20. I went about to cause my heart to *d.*

DESPAIRED.

2 *Cor.* 1. 8. insomuch that we *d.* even of life

DESPERATE.

Job 6. 26. reprove the speeches of one that is *d.*
Isa. 17. 11. in the day of grief and of *d.* sorrow
Jer. 2. † 25. but thou saidst, is the case *d.?*

DESPERATELY.

Jer. 17. 9. heart of man is deceitful, and *d.* wicked

DESPISE.

Lev. 26. 15. and if ye shall *d.* my statutes
1 *Sam.* 2. 30. that *d.* me shall be lightly esteemed
2 *Sam.* 19. 43. Israel said, why then did ye *d.* us?
Esth. 1. 17. so that they shall *d.* their husbands
Job 5. 17. happy whom God correcteth, *d.* not thou chastening of the Almighty, *Prov.* 3. 11. *Heb.* 12. 5.
9. 21. though I were perfect, I would *d.* my life
10. 3. that thou shouldest *d.* the work of thine hands
31. 13. if I did *d.* the cause of my man servant
Psal. 51. 17. a contrite heart, O G. thou wilt not *d.*
73. 20. thou awakest, thou shalt *d.* their image
102. 17. and he will not *d.* their prayer
Prov. 1. 7. but fools *d.* wisdom and instruction
3. 11. my son, *d.* not chastening of L. *Heb.* 12. 5.
6. 30. men do not *d.* a thief, if he steal to satisfy
23. 9. a fool will *d.* the wisdom of thy words
22. and *d.* not thy mother when she is old
Isa. 18. † 2. whose land the rivers *d.*
30. 12. because ye *d.* this word, and trust in oppres.
Jer. 4. 30. thy lovers will *d.* thee, they will seek
23. 17. they say still to them that *d.* me
Lam. 1. 8. all that honoured her, *d.* her, because
Ezek. 16. 57. daughters of Philistines which *d.* thee
28. 26. executed judgm. on all those that *d.* them
Amos 5. 21. I hate, I *d.* your feast-days, will not smell
Mal. 1. 6. unto you, O priests, that *d.* my name
Mat. 6. 24. hold to one, and *d.* the other, *Luke* 16. 13.
18. 10. that ye *d.* not one of these little ones
Rom. 14. 3. let not him that eateth, *d.* him eateth not
1 *Cor.* 11. 22. or *d.* ye the church of God and shame
16. 11. let no man therefore *d.* him, conduct him
1 *Thess.* 5. 20. *d.* not prophesyings, prove all things
1 *Tim.* 4. 12. let none *d.* thy youth, be an example
6. 2. let them not *d.* them, because they are brethr.
Tit. 2. 15. speak and exhort, let no man *d.* thee
2 *Pet.* 2. 10. chiefly them that *d.* government
Jude 8. *d.* dominion, and speak evil of dignities

DESPISED.

Gen. 16. 4. Hagar's mistress was *d.* in her eyes
5. saw she had conceived, I was *d.* in her eyes
25. 34. thus Esau *d.* his birth-right
Lev. 26. 43. because they *d.* my judgments
Num. 11. 20. because that ye have *d.* the Lord
14. 31. they shall know the land that ye have *d.*
15. 31. because he *d.* the word of the Lord
Deut. 32. † 19. and when the Lord saw it, he *d.* them
Judg. 9. 38. is not this the people thou hast *d.?*
1 *Sam.* 10. 27. they *d.* him and brought no presents
2 *Sam.* 6. 16. she *d.* him in her heart, 1 *Chr.* 15. 29.
12. 9. why hast thou *d.* the commandment of Lord?
10. because thou hast *d.* me, taken wife of Uriah
2 *Kings* 19. 21. the virgin the daughter of Zion hath *d.* thee, and laughed thee to scorn, *Isa.* 37. 22.
2 *Chron.* 36. 16. but they mocked and *d.* his words
Neh. 2. 19. they laughed us to scorn and *d.* us
4. 4. hear, O our God, for we are *d.* and turn
Job 12. 5. he is as a lamp *d.* of him that is at ease
19. 18. yea, young children *d.* me, I arose
Psal. 22. 6. but I am *d.* of the people, *Isa.* 53. 3.
24. he hath not *d.* the affliction of the afflicted
53. 5. put them to shame, because G. hath *d.* them
106. 24. yea, they *d.* the pleasant land, believ. not
119. 141. I am small and *d.* yet do not I forget
Prov. 1. 30. they *d.* all my reproof, therefore
5. 12. and thou say, how hath my heart *d.* reproof?
12. 8. he that is of a perverse heart shall be *d.*
9. he that is *d.* and hath a servant, is better
Eccl. 9. 16. yet the poor man's wisdom is *d.*
Cant. 8. 1. I would kiss thee, yea I should not be *d.*
Isa. 5. 24. and *d.* the word of the holy One of Israel
33. 8. he hath *d.* the cities, he regardeth no man
53. 3. he is *d.* and rejected of men, and acquainted with grief, he was *d.* and we esteemed him not
60. 14. all they that *d.* thee shall bow down
Jer. 22. 28. is this man Coniah a *d.* broken idol
33. 24. thus they have *d.* my people, to be no more
49. 15. I will make thee small and *d.* among men
Lam. 2. 6. he hath *d.* in the indignation of his anger
Ezek. 16. 59. which hast *d.* the oath, 17. 16, 18, 19.
20. 13. they *d.* my judgments, which if a man do
16. because they *d.* my judgments, and walked
24. but had *d.* my statutes, and had polluted
22. 8. thou hast *d.* mine holy things, and profaned
Amos 2. 4. because they *d.* the law of the Lord
Obad. 2. I made thee small, thou art greatly *d.*
Zech. 4. 10. for who hath *d.* the day of small things?
Mal. 1. 6. ye say, wherein have we *d.* thy name?
Luke 18. 9. they were righteous, and *d.* others
Acts 19. 27. that the temple of Diana should be *d.*
1 *Cor.* 1. 28. the things which are *d.* hath God chosen
4. 10. ye are honourable, but we are *d.*
Gal. 4. 14. my temptation in my flesh ye *d.* not
Heb. 10. 28. that *d.* Moses' law, died without mercy
Jam. 2. 6. but ye have *d.* the poor, do not rich men

DESPISERS.

Acts 13. 41. behold, ye *d.* and wonder, and perish
2 *Tim.* 3. 3. incontinent, fierce, *d.* of those are good

DESPISEST.

Rom. 2. 4. or *d.* thou the riches of his goodness?

DESPISETH.

Job 36. 5. behold, God is mighty, and *d.* not any
Psal. 69. 33. for the Lord *d.* not his prisoners
Prov. 11. 12. that is void of wisdom *d.* his neighbour
13. 13. whoso *d.* the word shall be destroyed
14. 2. but he that is perverse in his ways *d.* him
21. he that *d.* his neighbour sinneth, but he that
15. 5. a fool *d.* his father's instruction, but he that
20. a wise son, but a foolish man *d.* his mother
32. he that refuseth instruction *d.* his own soul
19. 16. but he that *d.* his ways shall die
30. 17. the eye that *d.* to obey his mother, ravens
Isa. 33. 15. he that *d.* the gain of oppressions
49. 7. thus saith the Lord to him whom man *d.*
Ezek. 21. † 10. it is the rod of my son, it *d.* every tree
Luke 10. 16. *d.* you, *d.* me; *d.* me, *d.* him that sent me
1 *Thess.* 4. 8. he therefore that *d.* *d.* not man but God

DESPISING.

Ezek. 21. † 13. shall not they belong to the *d.* rod?
Heb. 12. 2. who endured the cross, *d.* the shame

DESPITE.

Neh. 4. † 4. hear, O our God, for we are a *d.*
Ezek. 25. 6. with thy *d.* against the land of Judah
Heb. 10. 29. and hath done *d.* to the Spirit of grace

DESPITEFUL.

Ezek. 25. 15. have taken vengeance with a *d.* heart
36. 5. with *d.* minds to cast it out for a prey
Rom. 1. 30. haters of God, *d.* proud, boasters

DESPITEFULLY.

Mat. 5. 44. pray for them that *d.* use you, *Luke* 6. 28.
Acts 14. 5. an assault was made to use them *d.*

DESTITUTE.

Gen 24. 27. who hath not left *d.* my master of mercy
Psal. 102. 17. he will regard the prayer of the *d.*
141. 8. in thee is my trust, leave not my soul *d.*
Prov. 11. † 12. *d.* of heart, despiseth his neighbour
15. 21. folly is joy to him that is *d.* of wisdom
Ezek. 32. 15. shall be *d.* of that whereof it was full
1 *Tim.* 6. 5. men of corrupt minds, *d.* of the truth
Heb. 11. 37. wandered, being *d.* afflicted, tormented
Jam. 2. 15. if a brother or sister be naked and *d.*

DESTROY.

To destroy, *signifies to pull down, or ruin a city, or building, levelling it with the ground,* Gen. 19. 14. The Lord will destroy this city, *Exod.* 34. 13. Ye shall destroy their altars; that is, *ye shall not leave one stone upon another, as our Saviour speaks in* Luke 21. 6. Also it signifies, *to take away a thing quite, so as it be no more; in this sense Christ is said to destroy sin,* Rom. 6. 6. That the body of sin might be destroyed; *that is, that it might be weakened and subdued more and more, until it be quite taken out of our nature. Sometimes it signifies to bring persons into irrecoverable and utter ruin and misery; thus God destroys the wicked,* Psal. 37. 38. The transgressors shall be destroyed together: *and* Job 21. 30. The wicked is reserved to the day of destruction. *God preserves the wicked from the common calamities of this life, only to destroy them, and display his vengeance against them. It is taken for punishing transgressors by death, as magistrates do,* Psal. 101. 8. I will early destroy all the wicked of the land, *says* David. *I will set about this work upon the first opportunity, as soon as I am seated on the throne, that so I may both prevent all that mischief which otherwise they might do; and hinder the infection of others by their evil example; and discourage and deter all my subjects from the like practices. The apostle* Paul *says,* Rom. 14. 15. Destroy not him with thy meat, for whom Christ died. *To edify, signifies to build up, strengthen, and encourage believers in their faith and profession, by endeavouring to make them more wise, holy, and humble, and to live more to the glory of God.* On the contrary, *to* destroy, *implies a doing of that which may tend to the destruction of a weak believer, by drawing him to act against his conscience in the use of things indifferent, or by giving him so great an offence as may alienate his mind from the christian profession. The evil spirits say to our Saviour,* Mark 1. 24. Art thou come to destroy us? that is, either, *art thou come to dispossess us:* or, *art thou come to execute the final judgment upon us, and to command us to our chains, before the day of judgment? And Christ by his death is said* to destroy him that had the power of death, that is, the devil, *Heb.* 2. 14. *The devil is said* to have the power of death, *because he induces men to commit sin that meritoriously renders them liable to death; because he inspires them with furious thoughts, and inflames their passions, from whence proceed strifes and wars, that efficiently cause death; because he is many times the executioner of God's wrath, and inflicts death upon rebellious and incorrigible sinners; hence says the* Psalmist, *That* God cast upon the *Egyptians* the fierceness of his anger, wrath, indignation, and trouble, by sending *evil angels* among them, *Psal.* 78. 49. *He is likewise so called, because he makes death more formidable to sinners, by heightening their guilty fears of God's tribunal; and this title may also signify his tormenting sinners with unrelenting cruelty in hell, which is the second death. These penal evils which Satan brings upon mankind, are upon the account of our disobedience; and his mighty power in temptation is from our inward corruption. The* Lord Jesus *by his death hath taken away the guilt and power of sin: the guilt, in enduring the curse of the law, thereby satisfying the injured justice of God; and the power of it,* by crucifying our old man with him, that the body of sin might be destroyed, *Rom.* 6. 6. *And thus our Saviour by his death destroys the cruel tyranny of the devil.*

Destruction *is taken for a temporal death,* Psal. 90. 3. Thou turnest man to destruction. *For mortification,* 1 Cor. 5. 5. To deliver such an

one to Satan, for the destruction of the flesh. For damnation, 2 Pet. 2. 1. And bring upon themselves swift destruction. Also for hell, the place where the wicked are eternally tormented, Mat. 7. 13. Broad is the way that leadeth to destruction. For extirpation, or utter rooting out, Esth. 8. 6. How can I endure to see the destruction of my kindred? For a consuming plague, Psal. 91. 6. The destruction that wasteth at noon-day. And for a corrupting, painful, and deadly disease, 1 Sam. 5. 9. Destroy signifies to afflict, Job 2. 3. to destroy him without cause.
Gen. 18. 23. wilt thou d. the righteous with wicked?
24. wilt thou d. and not spare the place?
28. wilt thou d. all the city for lack of five?
19. 13. we will d. this place || 14. d. this city
Exod. 15. 9. draw my sword, my hand shall d. them
34. 13. but ye shall d. their altars, Deut. 7. 5.
Lev. 26. 22. I will send beasts to d. your cattle
Num. 24. 17. and shall d. all the children of Sheth
32. 15. and ye shall d. all this people
33. 52. shall d. their pictures and molten images
Deut. 6. 15. lest the anger of the Lord thy G. d. thee
7. 23. L. shall d. them with a mighty destruction
24. thou shalt d. their name from under heaven
9. 3. he shall d. them, and bring them down
14. let me alone, that I may d. them and blot
25. because the Lord had said he would d. you
20. 20. the trees that are not for meat thou shalt d.
31. 3. the Lord thy God he will d. these nations
32. 25. shall d. both the young man and virgin
33. 27. shall thrust out enemy, and say, d. them
Josh. 7. 12. except ye d. accursed from among you
1 Sam. 15. 6. depart, lest I d. you with them
2 Sam. 14. 7. and we will d. the heir also
11. she said, that thou wouldest not suffer the revengers to d. any more, lest they d. my son
16. that would d. me and my son together
20. 20. far be it from me I should swallow or d.
22. 41. I might d. them that hate me, Psal. 18. 40.
1 Kings 16. 12. thus did Zimri d. the house of Baasha
2 Kings 10. 19. he might d. the worshippers of Baal
18. 25. go against this land, and d. it, Isa. 36. 10.
Ezra 6. 12. d. kings that shall put to their hand
Esth. 7. † 4. for we are sold, that they should d.
Job 8. 18. if he d. him from his place, it shall deny
10. 8. thine hands made me, yet thou dost d. me
19. 26. though after my skin, worms d. this body
Psal. 5. 6. thou shalt d. them that speak leasing
10. d. them, O God, let them fall by their counsels
21. 10. their fruit shalt thou d. from the earth
28. 5. he shall d. them, and not build them up
52. 5. God shall likewise d. thee for ever
55. 9. d. O Lord, and divide their tongues
69. 4. they that would d. me are mighty
74. 8. they said, let us d. them together
127. † 5. they shall d. the enemies in the gate
143. 12. and d. all them that afflict my soul
144. 6. shoot out thine arrows and d. them
145. 20. but all the wicked will he d.
Prov. 1. 32. the prosperity of fools shall d. them
11. 3. the perverseness of transgressors shall d. them
15. 25. the Lord will d. the house of the proud
21. 7. the robberies of the wicked shall d. them
Eccl. 5. 6. why should G. d. the work of thine hands?
7. 16. nor over-wise, why shouldest thou d. thyself?
Isa. 3. 12. and they d. the way of thy paths
11. 9. nor d. in all my holy mountain, 65. 25.
13. 9. and he shall d. the sinners thereof out of it
25. 7. he will d. in this mountain the face
Jer. 5. 10. go ye up upon her walls and d.
6. 5. let us go by night and d. her palaces
11. 19. let us d. the tree with the fruit thereof
12. 17. I will pluck up and d. that nation
13. 14. I will not spare nor have mercy, but d. them
15. 6. will stretch my hand against thee and d. thee
17. 18. and d. them with double destruction
23. 1. woe to pastors that d. the sheep of my pasture
36. 29. the king of Babylon shall d. this land
48. 18. and he shall d. thy strong holds
49. 9. if thieves by night they will d. till have
51. 3. spare ye not, d. ye utterly all her host
Lam. 3. 66. persecute and d. them in anger
Ezek. 9. 8. wilt thou d. all the residue of Israel?
25. 16. and d. the remnant of the sea-coast
26. 4. and they shall d. the walls of Tyrus
12. and they shall d. thy pleasant houses
Dan. 2. † 18. that they should not d. Daniel
4. 23. saying, hew the tree down and d. it
8. 24. he shall d. wonderfully, and d. the mighty
25. and by peace shall he d. many
9. 26. the people shall d. the city and the sanctuary
11. 26. they that feed on his meat shall d. him
Obad. 8. shall I not d. the wise men out of Edom?
Mic. 2. 10. because it is polluted, it shall d. you
Zeph. 2. 13. stretch hand against north, and d. Assy.
Mat. 12. 14. they might d. him, Mark 3. 6. | 11. 18.
21. 41. he will miserably d. those wicked men
27. 20. that they should ask Barabbas, and d. Jesus
Mark 12. 9. he will d. the husbandmen, Luke 20. 16.
John 2. 19. Jesus said to them, d. this temple
Acts 6. 14. this Jesus of Nazareth shall d. this place
1 Cor. 3. † 17. if any man d. the temple of God, him shall God d. for the temple of God is holy
6. 13. but God shall d. both it and them
2 Thess. 2. 8. shall d. with brightness of his coming
Heb. 2. 14. might d. him that had the power of death
1 John 3. 8. that he might d. the works of the devil
Rev. 11. 18. shouldest d. them which d. the earth

I will, or will I DESTROY.

Gen. 6. 7. I will d. man whom I have created
13. and behold, I will d. them with the earth
7. 4. and every living substance will I d.
Exod. 23. 27. and I will d. all the people to whom
Lev. 23. 30. the same soul will I d. from his people
26. 30. and I will d. your high places, Ezek. 6. 3.
Psal. 101. 8. I will early d. all the wicked of land
118. 10. in the name of the L. will I d. them, 11, 12.
Isa. 19. 3. and I will d. the counsel thereof
42. 14. I will cry, I will d. and devour at once
Jer. 15. 7. I will d. my people, since they return not
46. 8. I will d. the city, and the inhabitants thereof
Jer. 49. 38. I will d. from thence the king and princes
51. 20. my battle-axe, with thee will I d. kingdoms
Ezek. 14. 9. I the Lord will d. that prophet
25. 7. behold, I will d. thee, and thou shalt know that I am the Lord, 28. 16. Zeph. 2. 5.
30. 13. thus saith the Lord, I will d. the idols
32. 13. I will d. also all the beasts thereof
34. 16. but I will d. the fat and the strong
Hos. 2. 12. I will d. her vines and her fig-trees
4. 5. thou shalt fall, and I will d. thy mother
Amos 9. 8. and I will d. the sinful kingdom
Mic. 5. 10. I will d. thy chariots || 14. d. thy cities
Hag. 2. 22. I will d. the strength of the kingdoms
Mark 14. 58. we heard him say, I will d. this temple
1 Cor. 1. 19. I will d. the wisdom of the wise

Not DESTROY.

Gen. 18. 28. if I find forty-five I will not d. it
31. he said, I will not d. it for twenty's sake
32. he said, I will not d. Sodom for ten's sake
Deut. 4. 31. he will not forsake thee, not d. thee
9. 26. d. not thy people and thine inheritance
10. 10. and the Lord would not d. thee
20. 19. thou shalt not d. the trees thereof
1 Sam. 24. 21. swear that thou wilt not d. my name
26. 9. and David said to Abishai, d. him not
2 Kings 8. 19. would not d. Judah for David's sake
13. 23. would not d. them, nor cast them out
2 Chron. 12. 7. therefore I will not d. them
12. that the Lord would not d. him altogether
21. 7. the Lord would not d. the house of David
35. 21. forbear from God that he d. thee not
Psal. 106. 34. they did not d. the nations of whom
Isa. 65. 8. d. it not for a blessing is in it; so will I do for my servant's sake, that I may not d. them all
Ezek. 22. 30. stand in the gap, that I should not d. it
Dan. 2. 24. d. not the wise men of Babylon, bring me
Mal. 3. 11. he shall not d. fruits of your ground
Rom. 14. 15. d. not him with thy meat for whom
20. for meat d. not the work of God

To DESTROY.

Gen. 6. 17. I do bring a flood of waters to d. all flesh
9. 11. nor shall there be any more a flood to d. 15.
19. 13. and the Lord hath sent us to d. it
Exod. 8. 9. intreat for thee to d. the frogs from thee
12. 13. the plague shall not be on you to d. you
Deut. 1. 27. brought us out of Egypt to deliver us into the hand of the Amorites to d. us, Josh. 7. 7.
2. 15. hand of Ld. to d. them from among the host
7. 10. repayeth them that hate him to d. them
9. 19. the Lord was wroth against you to d. you
28. 63. so the Lord will rejoice over you to d. you
Josh. 9. 24. and to d. all the inhabitants of the land
22. 33. to d. the land where Reubenites dwelt
Judg. 6. 5. the Midianites entered to d. the land
1 Sam. 23. 10. Saul seeketh to d. the city for my sake
26. 15. came in one of the people to d. the king
2 Sam. 1. 14. not afraid to d. the Lord's anointed
14. 11. not suffer the revengers of blood to d.
20. 19. thou seekest to d. a city and a mother
24. 16. stretched out his hand on Jerusalem to d. it
1 Kings 13. 34. sin to the house of Jeroboam to d. it
2 Kings 24. 2. and sent them against Judah to d. it
1 Chr. 21. 15. God sent an angel to Jerusalem to d.
2 Chron. 25. 16. God hath determined to d. thee
Esth. 3. 6. Haman sought to d. Jews, 13. | 4. 7, 8. | 9. 24
† 9. let it be written to d. them, and I will pay
Job 2. 3. thou movedst me to d. him without cause
6. 9. even that it would please God to d. me
Psal. 40. 14. that seek after my soul to d. it, 63. 9.
119. 95. the wicked have waited for me to d. me
Isa. 10. 7. but it is in his heart to d. and cut off
13. 5. they come from far to d. the whole land
23. 11. the Lord hath given a commandment to d.
32. 7. he deviseth wicked devices to d. the poor
51. 13. as if the oppressor were ready to d.
54. 16. behold, I have created the waster to d.
Jer. 1. 10. I have set thee to d. 18. 7. | 31. 28.
15. 3. I will appoint the beasts of the earth to d.
51. 11. his device is against Babylon to d. it
Lam. 2. 8. the Lord hath purposed to d. the wall
Ezek. 5. 16. famine, which I will send to d. you
22. 27. and to d. souls, to get dishonest gain
25. 15. with a despiteful heart to d. it for old hatred
30. 11. the nations shall be brought to d. the land
43. 3. the vision I saw when I came to d. the city
Dan. 2. 12. to d. all the wise men of Babylon, 24.
7. 26. and to d. his dominion unto the end
11. 44. he shall go forth with great fury to d.
Hos. 11. 9. I will not return to d. Ephraim, I am G.
Zech. 12. 9. that I will seek to d. all the nations
Mat. 2. 13. Herod will seek young child to d. him
5. 17. think not that I am come to d. the law or the prophets, I am not come to d. but to fulfil
10. 28. rather fear him who is able to d. both
26. 61. this fellow said, I am able to d. the temple
Mark 1. 24. art thou come to d. us? Luke 4. 34.
Luke 6. 9. is it lawful on sab. days to save life or to d.
9. 56. the Son of man is not come to d. men's lives
19. 47. the chief of the people sought to d. him
John 10. 10. the thief cometh not but to d.
Jam. 4. 12. there is one law-giv. able to save and to d.

DESTROYED.

Gen. 13. 10. before the Ld. d. Sodom and Gomorrah
19. 29. when God d. the cities of the plain
Exod. 8. † 24. the land was d. by the swarm of flies
10. 7. knowest thou not yet that Egypt is d.?
Deut. 2. 21. but the Lord d. them before them, 4. 3. | 11. 4. 2 Kings 21. 9. 2 Chron. 33. 9.
7. 23. with a mighty destruction, till they be d.
24. no man be able to stand till thou have d.
9. 8. the Lord was angry with you to have d. you
12. 30. after that they be d. from before thee
28. 20. until thou be d. 24, 45, 51, 61.
48. shall put a yoke on thy neck till he have d.
Josh. 24. 8. and I d. them from before you
Judg. 5. † 27. where he bowed, there he fell down d.
20. 21. Benjamin d. of Isr. 22,000 men that day, 25.
35. children of Israel d. 25,100 of Benjamin, 42.
2 Sam. 21. 5. man that devised that we should be d.
24. 16. he said to the angel that d. 1 Chron. 21. 15.
1 Kings 15. 13. Asa d. her idol and burnt it
2 Kings 3. † 23. this is blood, the kings are surely d.
2 Kings 10. 28. thus Jehu d. Baal out of Israel
11. 1. Athaliah arose and d. all the seed royal
19. 18. therefore they have d. them, Isa. 37. 19.
1 Chron. 5. 25. the people whom God d. before them
2 Chron. 14. 13. for they were d. before the Lord
15. 6. nation was d. of nation, city of city
34. 11. the houses which the kings of Judah had d.
Ezra 4. 15. for which cause was this city d.
6. † 11. whoso alters this word let him be d.
Esth. 3. 9. let it be written, that they may be d.
Job 19. 10. he hath d. me on every side, and I am gone
† 26. though this body be d. yet shall I see God
Psal. 9. 5. thou hast d. the wicked || 6. hast d. cities
73. 27. thou hast d. all them that go a whoring
78. 45. he sent frogs among them, which d. them
47. he d. their vines with hail, and sycamore-trees
137. 8. O daughter of Babylon, who art to be d.
Prov. 13. 23. there is that is d. for want of judgment
Isa. 14. 20. because thou hast d. land, and slain peo.
26. 14. therefore hast thou visited and d. them
Jer. 12. 10. many pastors have d. my vineyard
48. 4. Moab is d. || 51. 8. Babylon is suddenly d.
51. 55. Lord hath d. out of Babylon the great voice
Lam. 2. 5. the Lord hath d. his strong holds
6. he hath d. his places of the assembly
9. he hath d. and broken her bars, her king
Ezek. 27. 32. Tyrus, like the d. in the midst of sea
43. † 3. to prophesy that the city should be d.
Dan. 7. 11. the beast was slain, and his body d.
Hos. 13. 9. O Isr. thou hast d. thyself, but in me help
Amos 2. 9. yet d. I the Amorite, I d. his fruit
Mat. 22. 7. he sent his armies and d. those murderers
Luke 17. 27. and the flood came, and d. them all
29. it rained fire from heaven and d. them all
Acts 9. 21. is not this he that d. them that called
13. 19. when he had d. seven nations in Chanaan
19. 27. and her magnificence should be d.
Rom. 6. 6. that the body of sin might be d.
1 Cor. 10. 9. d. of serpents || 10. d. of the destroyer
Gal. 1. 23. now preacheth the faith which once he d.
2. 18. if I build again the things which I d.
Heb. 11. 28. lest he that d. the first-born touch them
2 Pet. 2. 12. as natural brute beasts made to be d.
Jude 5. the L. afterward d. them that believed not
Rev. 8. 9. and the third part of the ships were d.

Are DESTROYED.

Judg. 21. 16. the women are d. out of Benjamin
Job 4. 20. they are d. from morning to night
34. 25. he overturneth them so that they are d.
Isa. 9. 16. and they that are led of them are d.
Jer. 22. 20. and cry, for all thy lovers are d.
Hos. 4. 6. my people are d. for lack of knowledge
Zeph. 3. 6. their cities are d. there is no inhabitant

Not DESTROYED.

2 Chron. 20. 10. but they d. them not, Psal. 78. 38.
Dan. 7. 14. his kingdom which shall not be d.
2 Cor. 4. 9. but not forsaken; cast down, but not d.

Shall be DESTROYED.

Gen. 34. 30. and I shall be d. I and my house
Esth. 4. 14. thou and thy father's house shall be d.
Psal. 37. 38. but the transgressors shall be d. together
92. 7. it is that they shall be d. for ever
Prov. 13. 13. whoso despiseth the word shall be d.
20. but a companion of fools shall be d.
29. 1. he that hardeneth his neck shall be d.
Isa. 10. 27. the yoke shall be d. because of anointing
Jer. 48. 8. the valley shall perish, the plain shall be d.
Ezek. 30. 8. and when all her helpers shall be d.
Dan. 2. 44. a kingdom which shall never be d. 6. 26.
11. 20. but within few days he shall be d.
Hos. 10. 8. places of Aven, the sin of Isr. shall be d.
Acts 3. 23. he that will not hear shall be d.
1 Cor. 15. 26. the last enemy that shall be d. is death

Utterly DESTROYED.

Exod. 22. 20. he that sacrificeth to any god, save unto the Lord only, he shall be utterly d.
Num. 21. 3. they utterly d. the Canaanites
Deut. 2. 34. we utterly d. Sihon and his people
3. 6. we utterly d. the cities of Og, Josh. 2. 10.
4. 26. if ye corrupt yourselves, ye shall be utterly d.
Josh. 6. 21. Jericho || 8. 26. Ai utterly d. 10. 1.
10. 28. Makkedah || 35. Eglon || 37. Hebron ut. d.
39. Debir || 40. he utterly d. all that breathed
11. 12. Joshua utterly d. them with cities, 21.
Judg. 1. 17. Judah and Simeon utterly d. Zephath
1 Sam. 15. 8. Saul utterly d. all the people
9. he would not utterly d. the best of the sheep
15. to sacrifice, and the rest we have utterly d.
20. he said, I have utterly d. the Amalekites
21. things which should have been utterly d.
1 Chron. 4. 41. the inhabitants of Gedor utterly d.
2 Chron. 31. 1. Hezekiah utterly d. the images
32. 14. gods those nations my father utterly d.
Isa. 34. 2. the Lord hath utterly d. all nations

DESTROYER.

Exod. 12. 23. will not suffer d. to come into houses
Judg. 16. 24. hath delivered the d. of our country
Job 15. 21. in prosperity the d. shall come
Psal. 17. 4. I have kept me from paths of the d.
Prov. 28. 24. the same is the companion of a d.
Jer. 4. 7. the d. of the Gentiles is on his way
50. † 9. their arrows shall be as of a mighty d.
1 Cor. 10. 10. and were destroyed of the d.
Rev. 9. † 11. king over them hath his name a d.

DESTROYERS.

Job 33. 22. and his life draweth near to the d.
Isa. 49. 17. thy d. shall go forth of thee
Jer. 22. 7. and I will prepare d. against thee
50. 11. because ye rejoiced, O d. of my heritage

DESTROYEST, ETH.

Deut. 8. 20. as the nations which the Lord d.
Job 9. 22. he d. the perfect and the wicked
12. 23. he increaseth the nations, and d. them
14. 19. and thou d. the hope of man
Psal. 18. † 47. it is God that d. people under me
Prov. 6. 32. he that doth it, d. his own soul
11. 9. an hypocrite with his mouth d. his neighbour
31. 3. give not thy ways to that which d. kings
Eccl. 7. 7. oppress. maketh mad, and a gift d. heart
9. 18. wisd. better than war, sinner d. much good
Jer. 51. 25. O mountain, which d. all the earth
Mat. 27. 40. thou that d. the temple, Mark 15. 29.

DESTROYING.
1 Chron. 21. 12. the angel of the Lord d. thro' Israel
15. and as he was d. the Lord repented him
Prov. 28. † 24. the same is the companion of man d.
Isa. 28. 2. the Lord hath a strong one, as a d. storm
Jer. 2. 30. your sword devoured like a d. lion
13. † 14. I will not have mercy from d. them
51. 1. I will raise against Babylon a d. wind
25. I am against thee, O d. mountain, said Lord
Lam. 2. 8. he hath not withdrawn his hand from d.
Ezek. 9. 1. every man with his d. weapon in his hand
20. 17. mine eye spared them from d. them
See UTTERLY.
DESTRUCTION.
Exod. 12. † 13. plague shall not be on you for a d.
Num. 21. † 3. and he called that place, utter d.
24. † 20. but his latter end shall be even to d.
Deut. 7. 23. L. shall destroy them with a mighty d.
32. 24. they shall be devoured with bitter d.
1 Sam. 5. 9. L. was against the city with a great d.
11. for there was a deadly d. through the city
1 Kings 20. 42. a man whom I appointed to utter d.
2 Chron. 20. † 23. one helped for the d. of another
22. 4. for they were his counsellors to his d.
7. d. of Ahaziah was of God, by coming to Joram
26. 16. when strong, his heart was lifted up to his d.
Esth. 8. 6. how endure to see the d. of my kindred?
9. 5. the Jews smote their enemies with d.
Job 5. 21. neither shalt thou be afraid of d.
22. at d. and famine thou shalt laugh
18. 12. and d. shall be ready at his side
21. 17. and how oft cometh their d. upon them?
20. his eyes shall see his d. and he shall drink
30. the wicked is reserved to the day of d.
26. 6. hell naked before him, d. hath no covering
28. 22. d. and death say, we have heard the fame
30. 12. they raise against me the ways of their d.
24. not stretch out his hand, tho' they cry in his d.
31. 3. is not d. to the wicked? and punishment to
12. for it is a fire that consumeth to d.
23. for d. from God was a terror to me
29. if I rejoiced at the d. of him that hated me
Psal. 35. 8. let d. come upon him unawares, and his net catch himself, into that very d. let him fall
55. 23. thou shalt bring them down to the pit of d.
73. 18. surely thou castedst them down into d.
88. 11. or thy faithfulness be declared in d.?
90. 3. thou turnest man to d. and sayest, return ye
91. 6. nor for the d. that wasteth at noon-day
103. 4. who redeemeth thy life from d. who crowns
Prov. 1. 27. when your d. cometh as a whirlwind
10. 14. but the mouth of the foolish is near d.
15. the d. of the poor is their poverty
29. d. shall be to the workers of iniquity, 21. 15.
13. 3. but he that openeth wide his lips shall have d.
14. 28. the want of people is the d. of the prince
15. 11. hell and d. are before the Lord
16. 18. pride goeth before d. and a haughty spirit
17. 19. and he that exalteth his gate seeketh d.
18. 7. a fool's mouth is his d. and his lips a snare
12. before d. the heart of man is haughty
19. † 18. and let not thy soul spare to his d.
24. 2. for their heart studieth d. and lips talk
27. 20. hell and d. are never full, so the eyes of man
31. 8. in the cause of such as are appointed to d.
Isa. 1. 28. d. of transgressors and sinners together
10. 25. and mine anger shall cease in their d.
13. 6. it shall come as a d. from the Almighty
14. 23. I will sweep Babylon with the besom of d.
15. 5. in the way they shall raise up a cry of d.
19. 18. one shall be called the city of d.
24. 12. and the gate is smitten with d.
49. 19. the land of thy d. shall be too narrow
51. 19. desolation and d. are come unto thee
59. 7. wasting and d. are in their paths
60. 18. d. shall no more be heard in thy borders
Jer. 4. 6. I will bring from the north a great d. 6. 1.
20. d. upon d. is cried, for the land is spoiled
17. 18. and destroy them with double d.
46. 20. d. cometh, it cometh out of the north
48. 3. a voice from Horonaim, spoiling and d.
5. the enemies have heard a cry of d.
50. 22. a sound of great d. is in the land
51. 54. great d. from the land of the Chaldeans
Lam. 2. 11. for d. of the daughter of my people, 3. 48.
3. 47. desolation and d. is come upon us
4. 10. in the d. of the daughter of my people
Ezek. 5. 16. when I will send famine for their d.
7. 25. d. cometh, and they shall seek peace
9. † 6. slay to d. old and young, maids and children
32. 9. when I bring thy d. among the nations
Hos. 7. 13. d. to them, because they have transgressed
9. 6. for lo, they are gone, because of d.
13. 14. O grave, I will be thy d. repentance hid
Joel 1. 15. as a d. from the Almighty it shall come
Obad. 12. neither rejoiced in the day of their d.
Mic. 2. 10. it shall destroy you with a sore d.
Zech. 14. 11. and there shall be no more utter d.
Mat. 7. 13. broad is the way that leadeth to d.
Rom. 3. 16. d. and misery are in their ways
9. 22. endured the vessels of wrath fitted to d.
1 Cor. 5. 5. to deliver to Satan for d. of the flesh
2 Cor. 10. 8. hath given us not for your d. 13. 10.
Phil. 3. 19. for many walk whose end is d.
1 Thess. 5. 3. then sudden d. cometh upon them
2 Thess. 1. 9. who shall be punished with everlast. d.
1 Tim. 6. 9. into many lusts which drown men in d.
2 Pet. 2. 1. and bring on themselves swift d.
3. 16. which the unstable wrest to their own d.
DESTRUCTIONS.
Psal. 9. 6. O enemy, d. are come to a perpetual end
35. 17. Lord, rescue my soul from their d.
107. 20. he delivereth them from their d.
Isa. 5. † 30. when light, it shall be dark in the d.
DETAIN, ED.
Judg. 13. 15. let us d. thee till we have made ready
16. though thou d. me, I will not eat of thy bread
1 Sam. 21. 7. Doeg was that day d. before the Lord
DETERMINATE.
Acts 2. 23. him delivered by the d. counsel of God
DETERMINATION.
Zeph. 3. 8. for my d. is to gather the nations

DETERMINE.
Exod. 21. 22. and he shall pay as the judges d.
DETERMINED.
1 Sam. 20. 7. then be sure that evil is d. by him
9. if I knew that evil were d. by my father
33. Jonathan knew that it was d. of his father
25. 17. for evil is d. ag. our master and household
2 Sam. 13. 32. for by Absalom this hath been d.
2 Chr. 2. 1. Solomon d. to build a house for Lord
25. 16. I know that God hath d. to destroy thee
Esth. 7. 7. he saw that there was evil d. against him
Job 14. 5. seeing his days are d. number of months
Isa. 10. 23. a consumption d. in all the land, 28. 22.
19. 17. counsel of Lord which hath d. against it
Dan. 9. 24. seventy weeks are d. on thy people
26. and to the end of the war desolations are d.
27. and that d. shall be poured upon the desolate
11. 36. for that, that is d. shall be done
Luke 22. 22. the Son of man goeth as it was d.
Acts 3. 13. when Pilate was d. to let him go
4. 28. to do what thy counsel d. before to be done
11. 29. the disciples d. to send relief to brethren
15. 2. d. that Paul and Barnabas go to Jerusalem
37. and Barnabas d. to take with them John
17. 26. and hath d. the times before appointed
19. 39. it shall be d. in a lawful assembly
20. 16. for Paul had d. to sail by Ephesus
25. 25. I have d. to send Paul to Augustus
27. 1. when it was d. that we should sail into Italy
Rom. 1. † 4. and d. to be the Son of God with power
1 Cor. 2. 2. I d. not to know any thing save Jesus
5. † 3. but present in spirit I have d. already
2 Cor. 2. 1. but I d. this with myself, that I would
Tit. 3. 12. to Nicopolis, for I have d. there to winter
DETEST.
Deut. 7. 26. but thou shalt utterly d. and abhor it
DETESTABLE.
Jer. 16. 18. they defiled my land with d. things
Ezek. 5. 11. hast defiled sanctuary with thy d. things
7. 20. they made images of their d. things therein
11. 18. they shall take away all the d. things
21. whose heart walketh after their d. things
37. 23. nor shall any more defile with their d. things
DEVICE.
2 Chr. 2. 14. to find out every d. shall be put to him
Esth. 8. 3. to put away his d. that he had devised
† 5. let it be written to reverse the d. by Haman
9. 25. his wicked d. should return upon his own head
Psal. 21. 11. they imagined a mischievous d.
140. 8. O Lord, further not his wicked d.
Eccl. 9. 10. there is no work nor d. in the grave
Jer. 18. 11. behold, I devise a d. against you
51. 11. for his d. is against Babylon to destroy it
Lam. 3. 62. and their d. against me all the day
Acts 17. 29. is like to stone graven by man's d.
DEVICES.
Job 5. 12. he disappointeth the d. of the crafty
11. † 3. should thy d. make men hold their peace?
21. 27. d. which ye wrongfully imagine against me
Ps. 10. 2. let them be taken in the d. they imagined
33. 10. he maketh the d. of the people of none effect
37. 7. for the man who bringeth wicked d. to pass
Prov. 1. 31. and be filled with their own d.
12. 2. but a man of wicked d. will he condemn
19. 21. there are many d. in a man's heart
Isa. 32. 7. he deviseth wicked d. to destroy the poor
66. † 4. I also will choose their d. and bring fears
Jer. 11. 19. that they had devised d. against me
18. 12. no hope, but we will walk after our own d.
18. come and let us devise d. against Jeremiah
Dan. 11. 24. yea, and he shall forecast his d. for a time
25. for they shall forecast d. against him
2 Cor. 2. 11. for we are not ignorant of his d.
DEVIL.
A most wicked angel, the implacable enemy and tempter of the human race, especially believers, whom he desires to devour, 1 Pet. 5. 8. *He is called* Abaddon *in Hebrew,* Apollyon *in Greek, that is, destroyer.*—Rev. 9. 11. *Angel of the bottomless pit.—Prince of the world,* John 12. 31.—*Prince of darkness,* Eph. 6. 12.—*A roaring Lion, and an Adversary,* 1 Pet. 5. 8.—*A sinner from the beginning,* 1 John 3. 8.—*Beelzebub,* Mat. 12. 24.—*Accuser,* Rev. 12. 10.—*Belial,* 2 Cor. 6. 15.—*Deceiver,* Rev. 20. 10. —*Dragon,* Rev. 12. 7.—*Liar,* John 8. 44.—*Leviathan,* Isa. 27. 1.—*Lucifer,* Isa. 14. 12.—*Murderer,* John 8. 44.—*Serpent,* Isa. 27. 1.—*Satan,* Job 2. 6.—*Tormenter,* Mat. 18. 34.—*The god of this world,* 2 Cor. 4. 4.
He is compared to a Dog, Psal. 22. 16.—*Fowls,* Mat. 13. 4.—*A Fowler,* Psal. 91. 3.—*Lightning,* Luke 10. 18.—*Locusts,* Rev. 9. 3.—*A Wolf,* John 10. 12.—*An Adder,* Psal. 91. 13.
These names are given to the prince of the Devils, who, perhaps, was the first and leader in that grand rebellion against God, whereby they all fell into a rooted enmity against holiness, and into endless horror, blackness, and despair, Jude 6.
Devil is put for, [1] *Idols,* Psal. 106. 37. 2 Chron. 11. 15. [2] *A wicked man,* John 6. 70. [3] *Persecutors,* Rev. 2. 10.
This word comes from the Greek, Diabolos, *which signifies a* Calumniator, *or* Accuser, *who* accuseth us before God day and night, *Rev.* 12. 9, 10. *Hence he is called,* The accuser of the brethren, *Rev.* 12. 10. *He hath cast off all obedience to God; and likewise called* Belial, *which is an* Hebrew *word, and signifies one who is good for nothing, a libertine, one that is extremely wicked.* 2 Cor. 6. 15. What concord hath *Christ* with *Belial? Also* Satan, *which signifies an* Adversary, *or an* Accuser, *in a court of justice.* Job 2. 1. Satan came also among them. *He is likewise called the* Old Serpent, *Rev.* 12. 9. *Because he conveyed himself into the serpent, when he tempted* Eve; *and in respect of his serpentine disposition; his poison is always ready, as in a fountain; and runneth continually as in full streams, both against* Christ *and against all his members for his sake: He is also crafty, wise, and subtle, as a* serpent; *concerning whose subtilty, see* SERPENT.

The most subtle of these spirits contrived a temptation, which might be most taking and dangerous to man in his exalted and happy state: He attempts him with art, by propounding the lure of knowledge and pleasure, to inveigle the spiritual and sensitive appetites at once. And that he might the better succeed, he addressed the woman, the weakest and most liable to seduction. He hides himself in the body of a serpent, which before sin was not terrible unto her, and by this instrument insinuates his temptation. He first allured with the hopes of impunity, Ye shall not die; *then he promised an universal knowledge of* good *and* evil. *By these pretences he ruined innocence itself. For the woman, deceived by these specious allectives, swallowed the poison of the serpent; and, having tasted death, she persuaded her husband, by the same motives, to despise the law of their Creator. Thus sin entered, and brought confusion into the world.*
Man, since his fall, is under the tyranny and slavery of Satan, who is called the god of this world, 2 Cor. 4. 4. *because he rules in wicked men. His old enmity and hatred against the souls of men continues: It is another hell to him to see them restored to the favour of God, and his glorious image re-engraven on them. He is a jealous jailer, and, if possible, will not lose any of his captives. The Scripture represents him as a strong and subtle adversary;* a roaring lion that goes about seeking whom he may devour, 1 *Pet.* 5. 8. *His title, the* Tempter, Mat. 4. 3. *implies his constant practice. He bribes some with profit, and allures others with pleasure. He is surprisingly subtle; his strength is superior to ours: his malice is deadly; his activity and diligence are equal to his malice; and he has a mighty number of principalities and powers under his command.*
Sometimes devil *is taken for a wicked man, a libertine, a treacherous person,* John 6. 70. Have not I chosen you twelve, and one of you is a devil? *It is taken also for idols,* 2 Chron. 11. 15. *so called, because the* devil *is eminently served in the worship of them; and the spirits which were supposed to inhabit them, were evil spirits or devils: and because in and by them the* devil *oftentimes manifested himself to men, and gave them answers, and received their worship. Their worship is an invention of the devil; for what other deity besides the devil could require human victims, like those that were sacrificed to* Moloch? Devil *is likewise taken for persecutors, those instruments which he makes use of in executing his wicked designs against the godly,* Rev. 2. 10.
Lest he fall into the condemnation of the devil, 1 Tim. 3. 6. *Lest he become guilty of the sin for which the devil was condemned, and so receive the same punishment which was inflicted upon him.*
Mat. 4. 1. Jesus was led to be tempted of the d.
5. d. taketh him up to holy city ‖ 11. d. leaveth him
8. the d. taketh him up to an high mountain
9. 32. a dumb man possessed with a d. 12. 22.
11. 18. and they say he hath a d. Luke 7. 33.
13. 39. the enemy that sowed them is the d.
15. 22. my daughter is grievously vexed with a d.
17. 18. Jesus rebuked d. he departed out of him
25. 41. fire, prepared for the d. and his angels
Mark 5. 15. him that was possessed with the d. 16, 18.
7. 29. the d. is gone out of thy daughter, 30.
Luke 4. 2. Jesus being forty days tempted of the d.
3. the d. said to him, 6. ‖ 5. the d. taking him up
13. when the d. had ended all the temptation
33. a man which had a spirit of an unclean d.
35. and when the d. had thrown him in the midst
8. 12. then cometh the d. and taketh away the word
29. was driven of the d. into the wilderness
9. 42. as he was coming the d. threw him down
11. 14. casting out a d. when the d. was gone out
John 6. 70. chosen twelve, and one of you is a d.
7. 20. the people said, thou hast a d. 8. 48.
8. 44. ye are of your father d. and his lusts will do
49. I have not a d. ‖ 52. we know that thou hast a d.
10. 20. many of them said, he hath a d.
21. these are not the words of him that hath a d.
13. 2. the d. having put into the heart of Judas
Acts 10. 38. healing all that were oppressed of d.
13. 10. O full of all mischief, thou child of the d.
Eph. 4. 27. neither give place to the d.
6. 11. may be able to stand against the wiles of the d.
1 Tim. 3. 6. he fall into the condemnation of the d.
7. lest he fall into reproach, and snare of the d.
2 Tim. 2. 26. may recov. themselves out of snare of d.
Heb. 2. 14. had the power of death, that is the d.
Jam. 4. 7. resist the d. and he will flee from you
1 Pet. 5. 8. watch, because your adversary the d.
1 John 3. 8. he that committeth sin is of the d. that he might destroy the works of the d.
10. in this the children of the d. are manifest
Jude 9. Michael, when contending with the d.
Rev. 2. 10. the d. shall cast some into prison
12. 9. the old serpent called the d. and Satan
12. for the d. is come down to you having power
20. 2. that old serpent, which is the d. and Satan
10. d. that deceived them was cast into lake of fire
DEVILISH.
Jam. 3. 15. this wisdom is earthly, sensual, d.
DEVILS.
Lev. 17. 7. shall no more offer their sacrifices to d.
Deut. 32. 17. they sacrificed to d. not to God
2 Chron. 11. 15. he ordained him priest for the d.
Ps. 106. 37. sacrificed their sons and daughters to d.
Mat. 4. 24. brought him those which were possessed with d. 8. 16, 28, 33. Mark 1. 32. Luke 8. 36.
8. 31. so the d. besought him saying, Mark 5. 12.
Mark 9. 38. Master, we saw one casting out d. in thy name, and he followeth not us, Luke 9. 49.
16. 17. in my name shall they cast out d.
Luke 4. 41. and d. also came out of many, saying
8. 2. Mary Magdalene, out of whom went seven d.
36. by what means he that was possessed of d.
9. 1. he gave them power and authority over all d.
10. 17. Lord, even the d. are subject to us
13. 32. go and tell that fox, behold, I cast out d.

1 Cor. 10. 20. Gentiles sacrificed to d. and not to G.
I would not ye should have fellowship with d.
21. ye cannot drink the cup of the Lord and cup
of d. of the Lord's table and of the table of d.
1 Tim. 4. 1. some giving heed to doctrines of d.
Jam. 2. 19. the d. also believe and tremble
Rev. 9. 20. that they should not worship d. and idols
16. 14. for they are spirits of d. working miracles
18. 2. Babylon is become the habitation of d.
See Cast.

DEVISE.

Exod. 31. 4. d. cunning works in gold silver, 35. 35.
35. 32. to d. curious works in gold, silver, and brass
2 Sam. 14. 14. yet doth he d. means that his banished
Psal. 35. 4. be brought to confusion, that d. my hurt
20. but they d. deceitful matters against them
41. 7. against me do they d. my hurt
Prov. 3. 29. d. not evil against thy neighbour
14. 22. do they not err that d. evil? but mercy
and truth shall be to them that d. good
16. 30. he shutteth his eyes to d. froward things
Jer. 18. 11. behold, I d. a device against you
18. come and let us d. devices against Jeremiah
Ezek. 11. 2. these are the men that d. mischief
Mic. 2. 1. woe to them that d. iniquity and work evil
3. behold, against this family do I d. an evil

DEVISED.

2 Sam. 21. 5. man that consumed us d. against us
1 Kings 12. 33. month which he d. of his own heart
Esth. 8. 3. his devise that he had d. against the Jews
5. let it be written to reverse letters d. by Haman
Psal. 31. 13. they d. to take away my life
Jer. 11. 19. knew not that they had d. devices against
48. 2. in Heshbon they have d. evil against it
51. 12. the L. hath both d. and done, Lam. 2. 17.
2 Pet. 1. 16. we have not followed cunningly d. fables

DEVISETH.

Psal. 36. 4. he d. mischief on his bed, abhors not evil
52. 2. thy tongue d. mischiefs like a sharp razor
Prov. 6. 14. he d. mischief continually, soweth discord
18. an heart that d. wicked imaginations
16. 9. man's heart d. his way, L. directeth steps
24. 8. d. to do evil shall be called mischievous
Isa. 32. 7. he d. wicked devices to destroy the poor
8. but the liberal d. liberal things, and shall stand

DEVOTE.

Lev. 27. 28. thing that a man shall d. to the Lord

DEVOTED.

Lev. 27. 21. shall be holy to the Lord, as a field d.
28. no d. thing sold, every d. thing is most holy
Num. 18. 14. every thing d. in Israel shall be thine
Deut. 13. † 17. there shall cleave nothing of d. thing
Josh. 6. † 17. the city shall be d. even it and all in it
Ezra 10. † 8. all his substance shall be d.
Psal. 119. 38. word to thy servant, who is d. thy fear
Ezek. 44. † 29. every d. thing shall be theirs

DEVOTIONS.

Acts 17. 23. for as I passed by and beheld your d.

DEVOUR

Signifies, [1] *To eat up, or swallow down greedily*, Gen. 37. 20. [2] *To waste, or spend riotously*, Luke 15. 30. [3] *By cunning pretences to defraud others of that which is theirs*, Mat. 23. 14. [4] *With cruel fierceness to tear, and spoil spiritually the souls and bodies of men, as a lion devours his prey*, 1 Pet. 5. 8. The devil walketh about, seeking whom he may devour. [5] *To kill, or destroy*, 2 Sam. 18. 8. [6] *To convert to one's own private use that which is dedicated unto God*, Prov. 20. 25.

Gen. 49. 27. in the morning he shall d. the prey
Deut. 32. 42. arrows with blood, and sword d. flesh
2 Sam. 2. 26. Abner said, shall the sword d. for ever?
18. † 8. and the wood multiplied to d. the people
2 Chron. 7. 13. if I command the locusts to d.
Job 18. 13. first-born of death shall d. his strength
Psal. 80. 13. the wild beasts of the field doth d. it
Prov. 30. 14. and their jaw teeth as knives to d.
Isa. 1. 7. your land strangers d. it in your presence
9. 12. they shall d. Israel with open mouth
18. for wickedness shall d. the briers and thorns
31. 8. the sword, not of a mean man, shall d. him
42. 14. I will cry, I will destroy and d. at once
56. 9. all ye beasts of the field come to d. yea, all
ye beasts in the forest, Jer. 12. 9. | 15. 3.
Jer. 2. 3. that d. Israel shall offend, evil come on them
12. 12. the sword of the Lord shall d. 46. 10, 14.
30. 16. and all that d. thee shall be devoured
48. 45. a flame shall d. the corner of Moab
Ezek. 7. 15. famine and pestilence shall d. him
34. 28. neither shall the beasts of the land d.
35. † 12. the mountains, they are given us to d.
36. 14. therefore shalt thou d. men no more
Dan. 7. 5. arise d. much flesh, || 23. d. whole earth
Hos. 5. 7. now shall a month d. them with portions
11. 6. and the sword shall d. his branches
13. 8. there will I d. them like a lion, shall tear them
Amos 1. 4. fire shall d. the palaces, 7. 10, 12.
Obad. 18. they shall kindle in them, and d. them
Nah. 2. 13. the sword shall d. the young lions
Hab. 3. 14. their rejoicing was as to d. poor secretly
Zech. 9. 15. they shall d. and subdue with stones
12. 6. they shall d. all the people round about
Mat. 23. 14. woe unto you, hypocrites, for ye d.
widows' houses, Mark 12. 40. Luke 20. 47.
2 Cor. 11. 20. for ye suffer, if a man d. you
Gal. 5. 15. but if ye bite and d. one another
Heb. 10. 27. indignat. which shall d. the adversaries
1 Pet. 5. 8. walketh about, seeking whom he may d.
Rev. 12. 4. to d. her child as soon as it was born

Fire DEVOUR.

Judg. 9. 15. let fire d. the cedars of Lebanon
20. let fire d. the men of Shechem, and Abimelech
Psal. 21. 9. shall swallow up, and fire shall d. them
50. 3. God shall come, a fire shall d. before him
Isa. 26. 11. yea, the fire of thine enem. shall d. them
33. 11. stubble, your breath as fire shall d. you
Ezek. 15. 7. and another fire shall d. them
23. 37. to pass for them through the fire to d. them
Amos 5. 6. lest he break out like fire and d. it
Nah. 3. 13. the gates open, the fire shall d. thy bars
15. there shall the fire d. thee, sword cut thee off

Zech. 11. 1. O Lebanon, that fire may d. thy cedars

It shall DEVOUR.

Job 18. 13. it shall d. the strength of his skin
Isa. 10. 17. it shall burn and d. his thorns and briers
Jer. 5. 14. I will make my words fire, it shall d. them
17. 27. I will kindle a fire and it shall d. the palaces
of Jerusalem, and not be quenched, Amos 2. 5.
21. 14. it shall d. all things round about, 50. 32.
Ezek. 20. 47. and it shall d. every green tree
28. 18. it shall d. and I will bring thee to ashes
Hos. 8. 14. and it shall d. the palaces of Judah
Amos 1. 14. it shall d. the palaces of Rabbah
2. 2. send a fire, it shall d. the palaces of Kirioth

DEVOURED.

Gen. 31. 15. he hath sold us, and quite d. our money
37. 20. will say, some evil beast hath d. him, 33.
41. 7. the seven thin ears d. the seven rank, 24.
Lev. 10. 2. there went fire from the L. and d. them
Num. 26. 10. what time the fire d. 250 men
Deut. 31. 17. I will hide my face, they shall be d.
32. 24. they shall be d. with burning heat
2 Sam. 18. 8. the wood d. more than the sword d.
22. 9. and fire out of his mouth d. Psal. 18. 8.
Psal. 78. 45. he sent divers sorts of flies which d. them
79. 7. for they have d. Jacob, and laid waste his
105. 35. the locusts d. the fruit of their ground
Isa. 1. 20. if rebel, ye shall be d. with the sword
24. 6. therefore hath the curse d. the earth
Jer. 2. 30. your sword hath d. the prophets
3. 24. for shame hath d. the labour of our fathers
8. 16. for they are come, and have d. the land
10. 25. for they have eaten up Jacob, and d. him
30. 16. all they that devour thee shall be d.
50. 7. all that found them have d. them
17. first, the king of Assyria hath d. him
51. 34. Nebuchadrezzar king of Babylon d. me
Lam. 4. 11. it hath d. the foundations thereof
Ezek. 15. 5. how much less when the fire hath d. it
16. 20. hast sacrificed thy sons to them to be d.
19. 3. it learned to catch the prey, it d. men, 6.
14. fire is gone out, which hath d. her fruit
22. 25. like a roaring lion, they have d. souls
23. 25. and thy residue shall be d. by the fire
33. 27. I will give to the beasts to be d. 39. 4.
Dan. 7. 7. it d. and brake in pieces, and stamped, 19.
Hos. 7. 7. they are hot, and have d. their judges
9. strangers have d. his strength, he knoweth it not
Joel 1. 19. for fire hath d. the pastures, 20.
Amos 4. 9. your fig-trees, the palmer-worm d. them
7. 4. to contend by fire, and it d. the great deep
Nah. 1. 10. they shall be d. as stubble fully dry
Zeph. 1. 18. land shall be d. by the fire of his jealousy
3. 8. all the earth shall be d. with fire of my jealousy
Zech. 9. 4. and Tyrus shall be d. with fire
Mat. 13. 4. fowls came and d. them, Mark 4. 4.
Luke 8. 5.
Luke 15. 30. this thy son who hath d. thy living
Rev. 20. 9. fire came down from God and d. them

DEVOURER.

Mal. 3. 11. I will rebuke the d. for your sakes

DEVOUREST.

Ezek. 36. 13. because they say, thou land d. up men

DEVOURETH.

2 Sam. 11. 25. the sword d. one as well as another
Prov. 19. 28. the mouth of the wicked d. iniquity
20. 25. a snare to the man who d. that which is holy
Isa. 5. 24. as fire d. stubble, and flame chaff, Joel 2. 5.
Lam. 2. 3. like a flaming fire which d. round about
Ezek. 15. 4. behold, the fire d. both the ends of it
Joel 2. 3. a fire d. before them, behind them a flame
Hab. 1. 13. the wicked d. man that is more righteous
Rev. 11. 5. if any hurt them, fire d. their enemies

DEVOURING.

Exod. 24. 17. his appearance was like d. fire on mount
Psal. 52. 4. thou lovest all d. words, O tongue
Isa. 29. 6. thou shalt be visited with d. fire, 30. 30.
30. 27. and his tongue is as a d. fire.
33. 14. who among us shall dwell with the d. fire?

DEVOUT.

Luke 2. 25. Simeon was just and d. waiting for consol.
Acts 2. 5. there were at Jerusalem Jews, d. men
8. 2. d. men carried Stephen to his burial lament.
10. 2. Cornelius was a d. man || 7. a d. soldier
13. 50. but the Jews stirred up the d. women
17. 4. of the d. Greeks a great multitude believed
17. Paul disputed with the Jews and d. persons
22. 12. Ananias a d. man, according to the law

DEW

Is *a small rain, which falling on the ground in the morning, doth keep it moist, and make it fruitful. In warm countries, and in places where it rains but seldom, the night-dews supply in some sort the want of rain. And therefore the bestowing of it is a blessing from God.* Deut. 33. 13. Blessed of the Lord be Joseph's land for the *dew*; *and the withholding of it is a curse:* 2 Sam. 1. 21. Ye mountains of Gilboa, let there be no *dew* on you. Hushai *compares an army sallying upon the enemy to the* dew *descending on the ground*, 2 Sam. 17. 12. *God promises to* be as the *dew* unto Israel, Hos. 14. 5. *Though they were as withered and dying grass, yet he would refresh and strengthen them: By bestowing upon them his grace and Spirit, he would make them fruitful and flourishing. This comparison of God's visitation of his people to* dew, *is remarkable in several places of Scripture.* Isa. 26. 19. Thy *dew* is as the *dew* of herbs; *Or, thy* dew *is a bright* dew, *a* dew *of light and dawn. The prophet there speaks of the captivity of* Babylon, *as of a state of death:* Thy dead men shall live; *but God's visitation of his people, his favour and blessing, would recover them in some sort to life and light, would make them revive and flourish again. Heavenly doctrine, or the word of God, is likewise compared to* dew, *Deut.* 32. 2. My speech shall distil as the dew: *My doctrine shall have the same effect upon your hearts, as the* dew *has upon the earth; it shall make them soft, pliable, and fruitful. The prophet* Hosea, *speaking of the goodness of hypocrites, compares it to the* early *dew* that soon goeth away, *that is soon exhaled by the heat of the sun,* Hos. 6. 4. *Brotherly love, or the communion of saints, is compared to the* dew *which falls upon the hill of* Hermon, *and refreshes and makes it fruitful,* Psal. 133. 3. *As the drops of* dew *are innumerable, and as they fall suddenly and secretly without being perceived: In allusion to these qualities of the* dew, *such as were converted to* Christ *in the earliest gospel times are compared to it,* Psal. 110. 3. Thou hast the *dew* of thy youth. *It is said,* Cant. 5. 2. My head is filled with *dew*, and my locks with the drops of the night. Christ *here alludes to the custom of lovers, who often and willingly suffer such inconveniences for their hopes and desires of enjoying their beloved, and signifies his sufferings for the church's good: elsewhere, for a man* to be wet with the *dew* of heaven *is a sign of misery,* Dan. 4. 25. *So* drops, *or* droppings, *signify troubles,* Amos 6. † 11. *But* dew *and* rain *upon the land make it fruitful; so is* Christ *by his doctrine to his church,* Deut. 32. 2.

Gen. 27. 28. God give thee of the d. of heaven, 39.
Exod. 16. 13. in the morning d. lay round the host
14. and when the d. that lay was gone up
Num. 11. 9. when the d. fell on the camp in night
Deut. 32. 2. my speech shall distil as d. as small rain
33. 13. blessed is Joseph's land for d. and for deep
28. also his heaven shall drop down d.
Judg. 6. 37. Gideon said, if d. be on the fleece only
39. on ground let there be d. || 40. there was d.
2 Sam. 1. 21. let there be no d. nor rain upon you
17. 12. we will light on him as the d. falleth
1 Kings 17. 1. there shall not be d. nor rain these years
Job 29. 19. the d. lay all night on my branch
38. 28. or who hath begotten the drops of d.?
Psal. 110. 3. thou hast the d. of thy youth
133. 3. as the d. of Hermon, and as the d. that
Prov. 3. 20. and the clouds drop down the d.
19. 12. but his favour is as d. upon the grass
Cant. 5. 2. open to me, for my head is filled with d.
Isa. 18. 4. like a cloud of d. in the heat of harvest
26. 19. for thy d. is as the d. of herbs, earth cast out
Dan. 4. 15. let it be wet with the d. of heaven, 23.
25. they shall wet thee with the d. of heaven
33. and his body was wet with the d. 5. 21.
Hos. 6. 4. goodness is as early d. it goeth away, 13. 3.
14. 5. I will be as d. to Israel, he shall grow as lily
Mic. 5. 7. Jacob shall be as the d. from the Lord
Hag. 1. 10. the heaven over you is stayed from d.
Zech. 8. 12. and the heavens shall give their d.

DIADEM.

Job 29. 14. my judgment was as a robe and a d.
Isa. 28. 5. and for a d. of beauty to residue of his peo.
62. 3. and a royal d. in the hand of thy God
Ezek. 21. 26. remove the d. take off the crown

DIAL.

2 Kings 20. 11. gone down in the d. of Ahaz, Isa. 38. 8.

DIAMOND.

Exod. 28. 18. and the second row a d. 39. 11.
Jer. 17. 1. sin of Judah is written with point of a d.
Ezek. 28. 13. the d. the beryl, was covering of Tyrus

DID.

1 Sam. 30. † 21. David asked them how they d.
1 Kings 11. 25. besides the mischief that Hadad d.
2 Kings 18. 3. d. right according to all that David d.
Neh. 2. 16. knew not whither I went or what I d.
Esth. 2. 11. Mordecai walked to know how Esther d.
Mat. 12. 3. have ye not read what David d.?
21. 15. when they saw wonderful things that he d.
Mark 3. 8. they heard what great things he d.
John 2. 23. they saw miracles which he d. 6. 2, 14.
4. 29. who told me all things that ever I d. 39.
9. 26. then said they, what d. he to thee?
15. 24. done the works which none other man d.
Acts 3. 17. thro' ignorance ye d. it, as d. your rulers
26. 10. which thing I also d. in Jerusalem
2 Cor. 8. 5. and this they d. not as we hoped
1 Pet. 2. 22. who d. no sin, nor was guile found

DID joined with *as*.

Gen. 21. 1. the Lord d. to Sarah as he had spoken
43. 17. the man d. as Joseph bade, and brought men
50. 12. his sons d. to him as he commanded them
Exod. 7. 6. d. as the Lord commanded, 10, 20. | 12.
28, 50. | 39. 32. Lev. 8. 4. | 16. 34. | 24. 23.
Num. 1. 54. | 2. 34. | 20. 27. 27. 22. | 31. 31.
Lev. 4. 20. as he d. with the bullock, 16. 15.
Num. 23. 2. Balak d. as Balaam had spoken, 30.
Deut. 2. 12. as Israel d. to the land of his possession
22. as he d. to children of Esau || 3. 6. as d. to Sihon
Josh. 4. 18. waters flowed over banks, as they d. before
23. as the Lord your God d. to the Red sea
10. 28. d. to king of Makkedah, as he d. to Jericho
11. 9. Joshua d. to them as the Lord bade him
Judg. 6. 27. Gideon d. as the Lord said to him
15. 11. as they d. to me, so I have done to them
2 Sam. 3. 36. as what the king d. pleased the people
5. 25. and David d. so as the Lord commanded him
1 Kings 21. 11. elders d. as Jezebel had sent to them
26. Ahab d. according as d. the Amorites
2 Kings 8. 18. Jehoram, as d. the house of Ahab
17. 11. as d. the heathen which the Lord carried
41. as d. their fathers, so do they to this day
1 Chron. 14. 16. David d. as God commanded him
2 Chr. 25. 4. d. as it is written in the law of Moses
Isa. 58. 2. seek me as a nation that d. righteousness
Dan. 6. 10. Daniel gave thanks as he d. aforetime
Mat. 1. 24. Joseph d. as the angel had bidden him
21. 6. and d. as Jesus commanded them, 26. 19.
28. 15. took money, so watch d. as they were taught
Luke 9. 54. and consume them even as Elias d.
Acts 3. 17. thro' ignorance ye did it, as d. your rulers
7. 51. ye resist H. Ghost, as your fathers d. so do ye
11. 17. God gave them the like gift, as he d. to us
Heb. 4. 10. ceased from his works, as God d. from his

DID joined with *evil*.

Gen. 50. 15. he will requite us the evil we d. him
17. forgive thy brethren, for they d. to thee evil
Judg. 2. 11. d. evil in the sight of the Lord, 3. 7, 12.
| 4. 1. | 6. 1. | 10. 6. | 13. 1. 1 Kings 14. 22. | 15.
26, 34. | 16. 7, 30. 2 Kings 8. 27. | 13. 2, 11. | 14.
24. | 15. 9, 18, 24, 28. | 17. 2. 2 Chron. 22. 4.

1 Kings 11. 6. Solomon d. evil in sight of the Lord
2 Kings 21. 2. Manasseh d. evil, 2 Chron. 33. 2.
23. 32. Jehoahaz d. evil || 37. Jehoiakim d. evil
24. 9. Jehoiachim d. evil || 19. Zedekiah d. evil
2 Chr. 12. 14. Rehoboam d. e. || 33. 22. Amon d. e.
Neh. 9. 28. but after they had rest, they d. evil
13. 7. understood the e. that Eliashib d. for Tobiah
Isa. 65. 12. not hear, but d. e. before mine eyes, 66. 4.
2 Tim. 4. 14. Alexander copper smith d. me much e.

DID *not.*

Exod. 1. 17. midwives d. not as king commanded
2 Kings 16. 2. Ahaz d. n. what was right, 2. Chr. 28. 1.
Neh. 13. 18. d. not your fathers thus, and d. not our G. bring all this evil upon us and upon this city?
Jer. 11. 8. commanded to do, but they d. them not
Jonah 3. 10. God repented of the evil, and d. it not
Mat. 13. 58. he d. not many mighty works there
25. 45. d. it not to one of these, ye d. it not to me
John 8. 40. ye seek to kill me, this d. not Abraham
2 Cor. 7. 12. I d. it not for his cause had done wrong

DID *so.*

Gen. 6. 22. thus did Noah, as G. command. so d. he
29. 28. Jacob d. so, and fulfilled her week
42. 20. bring your youngest brother, and they d. so
Exod. 7. 6. as the Lord commanded so d. they, 10. | 12. 28, 50. | 39, 32. | 40. 16. Num. 1. 54.
22. magicians d. so, 8. 7, 18. || 24. Lord d. so
17. 6. Moses d. so, || 10. Josh. || Num. 8. 3. Aaron d. so
Num. 36. 10. so d. the daughters of Zelophehad
Josh. 6. 14. they compassed the city, so they d. six d.
11. 15. so d. Moses command, and so d. Joshua
Judg. 2. 17. they d. not so || 6. 40. G. d. so that night
1 Sam. 1. 7. as he d. so year by year, when she went
2. 14. so they d. in Shiloh to all the Israelites
27. 11. so d. David, and so will be his manner
1 Kings 12. 32. so d. he in Beth el, sacrificing
14. 4. Jeroboam's wife d. so, and went to Shiloh
Ezra 6. 13. so they d. || Neh. 5. 15. but so d. not I
Isa. 20. 2. Isaiah d. so, walking naked and barefoot
Jer. 38. 12. Jeremiah d. so || Ezek. 12. 7. and I d. so
Mat. 9. 19. Jesus arose, and so d. his disciples
Luke 6. 10. stretch forth thy hand, and he d. so
26. so d. their fathers to the false prophets
John 18. 15. followed Jesus, and so d. another discip.
Acts 19. 14. there were seven sons of Sceva who d. so

Thus DID.

Gen. 42. 25. to fill their sacks, thus d. he unto them
Exod. 36. 29. thus d. he to both of them in corners
40. 16. thus d. Moses, according as Ld. commanded
Num. 32. 8. thus d. your fathers when I sent them
2 Sam. 12. 31. thus d. he to all the cities of Ammon
2 Kings 16. 16. thus d. Urijah the priest, according
2 Chr. 24. 11. thus they d. day by day, and gathered
31. 20. thus d. Hezekiah throughout all Judah
Neh. 13. 18. d. not your fathers thus, and did not G.
Job 1. 5. sanctified them, thus d. Job continually

DIDST.

Gen. 20. 6. thou d. this in the integrity of thy heart
Num. 21. 34. shalt do as thou d. to Sihon, Deut. 3. 2.
Josh. 8. 2. shalt do as thou d. to Jericho and her king
2 Sam. 12. 12. for thou d. it secretly, but I will do
13. 16. is greater than the other that thou d. to me
1 Kings 2. 44. that thou d. to David my father
8. 18. d. well that it was in thy heart, 2 Chron. 6. 8.
Neh. 9. 17. thy wonders that thou d. among them
Psal. 39. 9. I was dumb, because thou d. it
44. 1. fathers told us what work thou d. in their days
137. † 8. recompenseth the deed which thou d. to us
Isa. 64. 3. when d. terrible things not looked for
Acts 7. 28. wilt thou kill me as thou d. Egyptian?

DIDRACHMA

Is a Greek word, *signifying a piece of money of two drachms in value. A Didrachm was worth about fourteen-pence* English; *two* Didrachms, *two shillings and fourpence, which made an* Hebrew *shekel. The* Jews *were by the law obliged to pay every one a half shekel to the temple. It is said in* Mat. 17. 24. *that they that received the tribute or capitation of two drachms or half a shekel, came and demanded it of our Saviour; and that he, having sent* Peter *to fish in the lake, told him, that the first fish he should take, would have a piece of money in its mouth, of four drachms in value; that he should take it, and give it to the receivers of this tribute for both of them.*

DIE.

See on DEAD *and* DEATH.

Gen. 6. 17. every thing that is in the earth shall d.
33. 13. if men over-drive them, all the flock will d.
41. 9. let him d. || 22. his father would d.
46. 30. now let me d. || 47. 29. that Israel must d.
Exod. 7. 18. the fish that is in the river shall d.
9. 4. nothing shall d. that is the children's of Israel
10. 28. the day thou seest my face thou shalt d.
11. 5. all the first-born in land of Egypt shall d.
28. 43. when they come to the altar to minister, that they bear not iniquity, and d. Lev. 22. 9.
Lev. 11. 39. if any beast of which ye may eat d.
20. 20. they shall bear sin, they shall d. childless
Num. 4. 15. shall not touch holy thing, lest they d.
20. when holy things are covered, lest they d.
6. 9. if any man d. very suddenly by him
14. 35. in this wilderness, and there they shall d.
16. 29. if these d. the common death of all men
17. 13. who cometh near tabernacle shall d. 18. 22.
18. 3. not come near, neither they, nor you also d.
20. 26. strip Aaron, and he shall d. on mount Hor
23. 10. let me d. the death of the righteous
27. 8. speak, saying, if a man d. and have no son
Deut. 17. 5. shalt stone them that they d. 22. 21, 24.
12. that man shall d. || 18. 20. prophet shall d.
22. 22. both shall d. || 25. the man only shall d.
24. 3. if the latter husband d. || 7. that thief shall d.
25. 5. if one d. and have no children, Mark 12. 19.
31. 14. to Moses, thy days approach that thou d.
32. 50. behold land of Canaan, and d. in the mount
Judg. 16. 30. Samson said let me d. with Philistines
1 Sam. 2. 33. all the increase of thy house shall d.
34. thy two sons, in one day they shall d. both
14. 45. the people said to Saul, shall Jonathan d.?
2 Sam. 18. 3. nor if half of us d. will they care
1 Kings 14. 12. when thy feet enter city, child shall d.

2 Kings 20. 1. thou shalt d. and not live, Isa. 38. 1.
2 Chron. 25. 4. fathers not d. for the children, but every man shall d. for his own sin, Jer. 31. 30.
Job 2. 9. then his wife said to him, curse God and d.
4. 21. excellency goeth away, they d. without wisd.
12. 2. ye are the people, wisdom shall d. with you
14. 8. though the stock thereof d. in the ground
14. a man d. shall he live again? all my days wait
34. 20. in a moment shall they d. people be troubled
36. 12. if obey not, they shall d. without knowledge
14. they d. in youth, their life is among unclean
Ps. 49. 10. for he seeth that wise men d. also the fool
104. 29. thou takest away their breath, they d.
Prov. 10. 21. but fools d. for want of wisdom
Eccl. 7. 17. why shouldest thou d. before time?
9. 5. living know they shall d. but dead know not
Isa. 22. 18. a ball in large country, there thou shalt d.
51. 6. they that dwell therein shall d. in like manner
12. that shouldest be afraid of a man that shall d.
65. 20. for the child shall d. a hundred years old
Jer. 11. 22. I will punish them, young men shall d. by sword, their sons and daught. shall d. by fam.
16. 4. they shall d. of grievous deaths, not lamented
6. both the great and the small shall d. in this land
28. 16. thus saith Lord, this year thou shalt d.
34. 5. but thou shalt d. in peace, and with burnings
Ezek. 18. 4. the soul that sinneth, it shall d. 20.
28. 8. thou shalt d. deaths of them that are slain
10. thou shalt d. the deaths of the uncircumcised
33. 8. that wicked man shall d. in his iniquity
27. they in the caves shall d. of the pestilence
Amos 2. 2. Moab shall d. with tumult, with shouting
6. 9. if there be ten men in one house they shall d.
7. 11. Amos saith, Jeroboam shall d. by the sword
17. saith the Lord, thou shalt d. in a polluted land
9. 10. the sinners of my people shall d. by the sword
Zech. 11. 9. then said I, that that dieth, let it d.
13. 8. saith Lord, two parts shall be cut off and d.
Mat. 15. 4. honour father and mother, he that curseth father or mother, let him d. the death, Mark 7. 10.
22. 24. if a man d. having no seed, Luke 20. 28.
Luke 20. 36. nor can they d. any more, equal to angels
John 4. 49. he saith, sir, come down ere my child d.
11. 50. that one man d. for the people, 18. 14.
51. prophesied that Jesus should d. for that nation
12. 24. except a corn of wheat d. but if it d. it brings
Rom. 5. 7. scarcely for a righteous man will one d.
1 Cor. 15. 22. for as in Adam all d. so in Christ shall
36. what thou sowest is not quickened except it d.
Heb. 7. 8. and here men that d. receive tithes
Rev. 14. 13. blessed are the dead that d. in the Lord

He DIE.

Gen. 38. 11. for he said, lest he d. as his brethren did
44. 31. when he seeth the lad is not with us, he will d.
Exod. 21. 12. he that smiteth a man, so that he d.
14. shall take him from mine altar, that he may d.
20. smite his servant, and he d. under his hand
22. 2. if a thief be found and smitten that he d.
Num. 35. 16. if he smite him so that he d. 20, 21, 23.
Deut. 13. 10. | 19. 5, 11. | 21. 21.
17. wherewith he may d. 18. 23. Deut. 19. 12.
Deut. 20. 5. let him return, lest he d. in battle, 6. 7.
Judg. 6. 30. bring out thy son that he may d.
2 Sam. 11. 15. retire from him that he may d.
1 Kings 1. 52. if wickedness be in him, he shall d.
2. 1. the days of David drew nigh that he should d.
19. 4. Elijah requested for himself that he might d.
21. 10. carry out and stone him that he may d.
Psal. 41. 5. when shall he d. and his name perish?
Prov. 5. 23. he shall d. without instruction, go astray
15. 10. and he that hateth reproof shall d.
19. 16. but he that despiseth his ways shall d.
Jer. 22. 12. he shall d. whither they led him captive
38. 10. take up Jerem. out of dungeon before he d.
Ezek. 3. 19. if thou warn the wicked, he shall d. in his iniquity, 20. | 18. 18, 24, 26. | 33. 9, 13, 18.
12. 13. he shall not see it, though he shall d. there
17. 16. in the midst of Babylon he shall d.
John 12. 33. signifying what death he should d. 18. 32.

I DIE.

Gen. 19. 19. lest some evil take me, and I d.
26. 9. Isaac said, because I said, lest I d. for her
27. 4. that my soul may bless thee before I d.
30. 1. Rachel said, give me children, or else I d.
45. 28. I will go and see him before I d.
48. 21. Israel said to Joseph, behold, I d.
50. 5. lo, I d. || 24. Joseph said to his brethren I d.
Deut. 4. 22. but I must d. in this land, I must not go
Judg. 15. 18. now shall I d. for thirst, and fall into
Ruth 1. 17. where thou diest will I d. and be buried
1 Sam. 14. 43. I did but taste, and lo, I must d.
2 Sam. 19. 37. that I may d. in mine own city
1 Kings 2. 30. he said, nay, but I will d. here
Job 27. 5. that I sh. justify you; till I d. not remove
29. 18. then I said, I shall d. in my nest and multiply
Prov. 30. 7. two things, deny me them not before I d.
Jer. 37. 20. cause me not to return, lest I d. there
Mat. 26. 35. tho' I should d. with thee, Mark 14. 31.
1 Cor. 15. 31. I protest by your rejoicing, I d. daily

Not DIE.

Gen. 42. 2. that we may live and not d. 43. 8. | 47. 19.
20. so shall your words be verified, ye shall not d.
Exod. 21. 18. and he d. not, but keepeth his bed
28. 35. his sound shall be heard, that he d. not
30. 20. shall wash with water, that they d. not, 21.
Lev. 8. 35. keep the charge of the Lord that ye d. not
15. 31. that they d. not, Num. 4. 19. | 17. 10.
16. 2. that he come not at all times, that he d. not
13. the cloud cover the mercy-seat, that he d. not
Num. 35. 12. that the manslayer, d. not, Josh. 20. 9.
Deut. 18. 16. nor let me see this fire, that I d. not
33. 6. let Reuben live and n. d. let not his men be few
Judg. 6. 23. peace be to thee, fear not, thou shalt n. d. 1 Sam. 20. 2. 2 Sam. 12. 13. | 19. 23. Jer. 38. 24.
1 Sam. 12. 19. pray to the L. for us, that we d. not
20. 14. shew me the kindness of the L. that I d. not
2 Kings 18. 32. take you, that ye may live and not d.
2 Chron. 25. 4. fathers shall not d. for the children
Psal. 118. 17. I shall not d. but live, and declare
Prov. 23. 13. if thou beatest him with rod, he shall not d. Ezek. 18. 17, 21, 28. | 33. 15. John 21. 23.
Isa. 51. 14. and that he should not d. in the pit

Isa. 66. 24. their worm shall not d. nor fire quenched
Jer. 11. 21. that thou d. not by our hand
34. 4. Zedekiah, thou shalt not d. by the sword
Ezek. 13. 19. to slay the souls that should not d.
Hab. 1. 12. we shall not d. L. thou hast ordained
John 6. 50. that a man may eat thereof, and not d.
21. 23. saying that that disciple should not d.

Surely DIE.

Gen. 2. 17. thou shalt surely d. 20. 7. 1 Sam. 14. 44. | 22. 16. 1 Kings 2. 37, 42. Jer. 26. 8. Ezek. 3. 18. | 33. 8, 14.
3. 4. the serpent said, ye shall not surely d.
Num. 26. 65. the L. had said, they shall surely d.
Judg. 13. 22. we shall surely d. because we have seen
1 Sam. 14. 39. tho' in Jonath. my son, he shall surely d. 20. 31. 2 Sam. 12. 5. 2 Kings 8. 10. Ezek. 18. 13.
2 Sam. 12. 14. the child born to thee shall surely d.
2 Kings 1. 4. not come down, but shall surely d. 6. 16.

To DIE.

Gen. 25. 32. Esau said, behold, I am at the point to d.
Ex. d. 14. 11. to d. in the wilderness, Num. 21. 5.
Num. 18. † 22. come nigh, lest they bear sin to d.
35. 30. not testify against any, to cause him to d.
† 31. no satisfaction for him who is faulty to d.
Josh. 2. † 14. our life instead of you to d.
1 Sam. 26. 10. L. smite him, or his day shall come to d.
16. ye are worthy to d. because ye kept not
28. 9. layest a snare for my life, to cause me to d.
2 Chron. 32. 11. to give yourselves to d. by famine
Psal. 79. 11. preserve those that are appointed to d.
88. 15. I am afflicted and ready to d. from youth
Prov. 19. † 18. soul not spare, to cause him to d.
Eccl. 3. 2. a time to be born, and a time to d.
Jer. 26. 11. is worthy to d. || 16. not worthy to d.
38. 9. he is like to d. for hunger in the place
26. to return to Jonathan's house to d. there
Jonah 4. 3. for it is better for me to d. than to live, 8.
8. Jonah fainted, and wished in himself to d.
Luke 7. 2. the centurion's servant was ready to d.
John 19. 7. have a law, and by our law he ought to d.
Acts 21. 13. I am ready also to d. at Jerusalem
25. 11. if worthy of death I refuse not to d.
16. not the manner of Romans to deliver any to d.
Rom. 5. 7. for a good man some would even dare to d.
1 Cor. 9. 15. for it were better for me to d. than
2 Cor. 7. 3. you are in our hearts to d. and live
Phil. 1. 21. for me to live is Christ, and to d. is gain
Heb. 9. 27. as it is appointed to men once to d. but
Rev. 3. 2. things that remain, that are ready to d.
9. 6. men shall desire to d. and death shall flee

We DIE.

Gen. 47. 15. why should we d. in thy presence? 19.
Exod. 14. 12. than that we should d. in the wilderness
20. 19. let not God speak, lest we d. Deut. 5. 25.
Num. 17. 12. behold, we d. we perish, we all perish
20. 4. that we and our cattle should d. there
1 Sam. 12. 19. pray for thy servants, that we d. not
2 Sam. 14. 14. for we must needs d. and are as water
1 Kings 17. 12. I dress it, that we may eat it and d.
2 Kings 7. 3. they said, why sit we here till we d.? 4. and if they kill us, we shall but d.
Isa. 22. 13. for to-morrow we shall d. 1 Cor. 15. 32.
John 11. 16. let us go that we may d. with him
Rom. 14. 8. and whether we d. we d. unto the Lord

Ye DIE.

Gen. 3. 3. neither shall ye touch it, lest ye d.
Lev. 10. 6. neither rend your clothes, lest ye d.
7. ye shall not go out from the door, lest ye d.
Num. 18. 32. nor pollute holy things, lest ye d.
Psal. 82. 7. but ye shall d. like men, and fall like one
Isa. 22. 14. surely this iniqui. not be purged till ye d.
Jer. 22. 26. anoth. country, there shall ye d. 42. 16.
27. 13. for why will ye d.? Ezek. 18. 31. | 33. 11.
42. 22. know that ye shall d. by the sword
John 8. 21. shall seek me, and ye shall d. in sins, 24.
Rom. 8. 13. if ye live after the flesh ye shall d.

DIED.

Gen. 7. 21. all flesh d. 22. || 11. 28. and Haran d.
11. 32. Terah d. || 23. 2. Sarah d. || 25. 8. Abraham d.
25. 17. Ishmael d. || 35. 8. Deborah the nurse d.
35. 18. Rachel d. 19. | 48. 7. || 35. 29. Isaac d.
36. 33. Belah d. || 34. Jobab d. || 35. Husham d.
36. Hadad d. || 1 Chr. 1. 51. || 36. 37. Samlah d.
38. Saul d. || 39. Baal-hanan son of Achbor d.
38. 12. Judah's wife d. || 46. 12. Er, Onan d. Canaan
50. 16. Jacob d. || 26. Joseph d. Exod. 1. 6.
Exod. 2. 23. the king of Egypt d. || 7. 21. the fish d.
8. 13. the frogs d. || 9. 6. the cattle of Egypt d.
16. 3. would to God we had d. by the hand of the Lord in Egypt, Num. 14. 2. | 20. 3. | 26. 10.
Lev. 10. 2. Nadab and Abihu d. before the Lord, 16. 1. Num. 3. 4. | 26. 61. 1 Chron. 24. 2.
Num. 14. 37. the searchers of the land d. by plague
20. 28. Aaron d. 33, 38, 39. Deut. 10. 6. | 32. 50.
16. 49. now they that d. beside them that d.
20. 1. Miriam d. || 21. 6. much people of Israel d.
25. 9. those that d. in the plague were 24,000
26. 11. notwithstand. the children of Korah d. not
27. 3. daughters of Zelophehad said, our father d. in wilderness, but d. in his own sin, and had no sons
Deut. 34. 5. Moses d. || 7. he was 120 years when he d.
Josh. 5. 4. even all the men of war d. by the way
10. 11. they were more which d. with hailstones
24. 29. Joshua the son of Nun d. Judg. 2. 8.
33. Eleazar the son of Aaron d. 1 Chron. 23. 22.
Judg. 1. 7. Adonibezek d. || 3. 11. Othniel d.
8. 32. Gideon d. || 10. 2. Tola d. || 5. Jair d.
9. 49. all the men of the tower of Shechem d.
12. 7. Jephthah judged Israel six years, then d.
10. Ibzan d. || 12. Elon d. || 15. Abdon d.
Ruth 1. 3. Elimelech d. || 5. Mahlon, Chilion d.
1 Sam. 4. † 11. Eli's sons, Hophni and Phinehas, d.
5. 12. that d. not were smitten with the emerods
25. 1. Samuel d. || 37. Nabal's heart d. within him
31. 5. Saul was dead, his armour-bearer fell on his sword and d. with him, 6. 1 Chron. 10. 5, 13.
2 Sam. 2. 23. Asahel d. || 3. 33. d. Abner as a fool
6. 7. there he d. before the Lord, 1 Chron. 13. 10.
10. 1. king of child. of Ammon d. 1 Chr. 19. 1.
18. Shobach d. || 11. 17. Uriah the Hittite d.
12. 18. on seventh day child d. feared to tell David
17. 23. Ahithophel hanged himself and d.

2 Sam. 18. 33. would to God I had *d.* for thee, O Abs.
19. 6. and all we had *d.* this day, it had pleased thee
24. 15. there *d.* of people, even from Dan to Beersh.
1 Kings 3. 19. this woman's child *d.* in the night
14. 17. when she came to the threshold the child *d.*
16. 18. Zimri *d.* ‖ 22. Tibni *d.* ‖ 22. 35. Ahab *d.* 37.
2 Kings 4. 20. he sat on her knees till noon and then *d.*
9. 27. Ahaziah fled to Megiddo and *d.* there
13. 14. Elisha *d.* 20. ‖ 24. Hazael king of Syria *d.*
23. 34. Jehoahaz came to Egypt and *d.* there
1 Chron. 2. 30. but Seled *d.* without children
32. and Jether *d.* ‖ *2 Chron.* 16. 13. Asa *d.*
2 Chron. 24. 15. Jehoiada was full of days when he *d.*
22. when he *d.* he said, the Lord look on it
Job 3. 11. why *d.* I not from the womb?
42. 17. so Job *d.* being old and full of days
Isa. 6. 1. in the year that king Uzziah *d.* I saw Lord
14. 28. in the year that king Ahaz *d.* was this burd.
Jer. 28. 17. Hananiah *d.* ‖ *Ezek.* 11. 13. Pelatiah *d.*
Ezek. 24. 18. I spake in morn. and at even my wife *d.*
Hos. 13. 1. but when he offended in Baal, he *d.*
Mat. 22. 27. seven brethren deceased, and last of all the wom. *d.* also, *Mark* 12. 22. *Luke* 20. 32.
Luke 16. 22. the beggar *d.* the rich man also *d.*
John 11. 21. if had been here, my brother not *d.* 32.
37. caused that even this man should not have *d.*
Acts 9. 37. in those days Dorcas was sick and *d.*
Rom. 5. 6. in due time Christ *d.* for the ungodly, 8.
7. 9. sin revived and I. *d.* ‖ 8. 34. it is Christ that *d.*
14. 9. for to this end Christ both *d.* rose and revived
15. but if thy brother be grieved, destroy not him with thy meat for whom Christ *d.* *1 Cor.* 8. 11.
1 Cor. 15. 3. how that Christ *d.* for our sins
2 Cor. 5. 14. if one *d.* for all, then were all dead
15. should live to him who *d.* for them and rose ag.
1 Thess. 4. 14. if we believe that Jesus *d.* and rose ag.
5. 10. who *d.* for us that we should live with him
Heb. 10. 28. he that despised Moses' law *d.* without
11. 13. these *d.* in faith, not having received prom.
22. by faith Joseph when he *d.* made mention of
Rev. 8. 9. third part of creatures which had life *d.*
11. many men *d.* of waters that were made bitter
16. 3. and every living soul *d.* in the sea

And he, So he, That he DIED.

Gen. 5. 5. the days of Adam were 930 years *and he d.*
9. 29. Noah's days were 950 years, *and he d.*
Judg. 4. 21. Jael smote nail into his temple, *so he d.*
1 Sam. 4. 18. Eli's neck brake *and he d.* for he was old
14. 45. so the people rescued Jonathan *that he d.* not
25. 38. that the Lord smote Nabal *that he d.*
2 Sam. 11. 21. smote Abimelech *that he d.* in Thebez
1 Kings 12. 18. stoned Adoram *that he d.* *2 Chr.* 10. 18.
2 Kings 1. 17. *so he d.* according to the word of Lord
7. 17. people trod on him in the gate *and he d.* 20.
8. 15. he spread a cloth on his face, *so that he d.*
2 Chr. 13. 20. the Lord struck Jeroboam *and he d.*
21. 19. Jehoram's bowels fell out, *so he d.*
Luke 20. 29. *and he d.* without children, 30.
Acts 7. 15. Jacob *d.* in Egypt, *he and* our fathers
Rom. 6. 10. for in *that he d. he d.* unto sin once
2 Cor. 5. 15. *that he d.* for all, that they who live

DIEST.

Ruth 1. 17. where thou *d.* will I die and there be bur.

DIET.

Jer. 52. 34. for *d.* there was a continual *d.* given him

DIETH.

Lev. 7. 24. fat of beast that *d.* of itself shall not eat
22. 8. what *d.* of itself shall not eat, *Deut.* 14. 21.
Num. 16. † 29. if these men die as every man *d.*
19. 14. when a man *d.* in a tent all shall be unclean
2 Sam. 3. 33. the king said, died Abner as a fool *d.*?
1 Kings 14. 11. him that *d.* in the city shall dogs eat
16. 4. *d.* in the field fowls of the air eat, 21. 24.
Job 14. 10. man *d.* and wasteth away, gives up ghost
21. 23. one *d.* in his full strength, being at ease
25. another *d.* in the bitterness of his soul
36. † 14. their soul *d.* in youth, life among unclean
Psal. 49. 17. when he *d.* he shall carry nothing away
Prov. 11. 7. when a wicked man *d.* his expectation perish
Eccl. 2. 16. and how *d.* the wise man? as the fool?
3. 19. as the one *d.* so *d.* the other, all one breath
Isa. 50. 2. their fish stinketh and *d.* for thirst
59. 5. he that eateth of their eggs *d.* what is crushed
Ezek. 4. 14. nor eaten that which *d.* of itself
18. 26. committeth iniquity, and *d.* in them
32. I have no pleasure in the death of him that *d.*
Zech. 11. 9. then said I, that that *d.* let it die
Mark 9. 44. where their worm *d.* not, 46, 48.
Rom. 6. 9. Christ being raised from dead *d.* no more
14. 7. none of us liveth and no man *d.* to himself

DYED.

Exod. 25. 5. take of them rams'-skins *d.* red, and shittim-wood, 26. 14. | 35. 7. | 36. 19. | 39. 34.
Isa. 63. 1. cometh with *d.* garments from Bozrah
Ezek. 23. 15. exceeding in *d.* attire upon their heads
Nah. 2. † 3. the valiant men are *d.* in scarlet

DYING.

Gen. 2. † 17. when thou eatest, *d.* thou shalt die
Num. 17. 13. shall we be consumed with *d.*?
Mark 12. 20. and the first *d.* left no seed
Luke 8. 42. Jairus's only daughter lay a *d.*
2 Cor. 4. 10. bearing in the body the *d.* of Lord Jesus
6. 9. as *d.* and behold we live, as chastened and not
Heb. 11. 21. by faith, Jacob when *d.* blessed sons of

DIFFER.

Rom. 2. † 18. and thou triest the things that *d.*
1 Cor. 4. 7. who maketh thee to *d.* from another?
Phil. 1. † 10. that ye may try the things that *d.*

DIFFERENCE.

Exod. 11. 7. Lord put a *d.* between Egyptians and Is.
Lev. 10. 10. may put a *d.* between holy and unholy
11. 47. to make a *d.* between unclean and clean
20. 25. put a *d.* between clean beasts and unclean
Ezek. 22. 26. they have put no *d.* they shewed no *d.*
44. 23. they shall teach my people the *d.* betw. holy
Acts 15. 9. and put no *d.* between us and them
Rom. 3. 22. on them that believe, for there is no *d.*
10. 12. there is no *d.* between the Jew and Greek
14. † 23. he that putteth a *d.* between meats
1 Cor. 7. 34. there is *d.* between a wife and a virgin
Jude 22. of some have compassion making a *d.*

DIFFERENCES.

1 Cor. 12. 5. there are *d.* of administrations

DIFFERETH.

1 Cor. 15. 41. one star *d.* from another in glory
Gal. 4. 1. heir when a child *d.* nothing from a servant

DIFFERING.

Rom. 12. 6. gifts *d.* according to the grace given

DIFFICULT.

Zech. 8. † 6. if it be *d.* in the eyes of this people

DIG.

Exod. 21. 33. if a man *d.* a pit, and not cover it
Deut. 8. 9. out of whose hills thou mayest *d.* brass
23. 13. thou shalt have a paddle, and *d.* therewith
Job 3. 21. *d.* for it more than for hid treasures
6. 27. and ye *d.* a pit for your friend
11. 18. thou shalt *d.* about thee, take rest in safety
24. 16. in the dark they *d.* through houses marked
39. † 21. his feet *d.* in the valley
Ezek. 8. 8. he said, son of man, *d.* now in the wall
12. 5. *d.* thou through the wall in their sight, 12.
Amos 9. 2. though they *d.* into hell, tho' they climb
Luke 13. 8. Lord, let it alone, till I shall *d.* about it
16. 3. I cannot *d.* to beg I am ashamed

DIGGED.

Gen. 21. 30. may be a witness that I have *d.* this well
26. 15. the wells his father's servants had *d.* 18.
19. Isaac's servants *d.* in the valley, 21, 22, 25.
32. and told Isaac of the well that they had *d.*
49. 6. for in their self-will they *d.* down a wall
50. 5. in my grave which I had *d.* for me bury me
Exod. 7. 24. all the Egyptians *d.* for water to drink
Num. 21. 18. the princes *d.* the well, the nobles *d.*
Deut. 6. 11. wells *d.* thou diggedst not, *Neh.* 9. 25.
2 Kings 19. 24. I have *d.* and drunk strange waters, and dried up all the rivers of places, *Isa.* 37. 25.
2 Chron. 16. † 14. sepulchres he had *d.* for himself
26. 10. Uzziah *d.* many wells for his cattle
Psal. 7. 15. made a pit and *d.* it, and is fallen, 57. 6.
35. 7. without cause they *d.* a pit for my soul
40. † 6. mine ears hast thou *d.* offering not required
94. 13. till the pit be *d.* for the wicked
119. 85. proud have *d.* pits for me not after thy law
Isa. 5. 6. it shall not be pruned nor *d.* come up briers
7. 25. and on all hills that be *d.* with the mattock
51. 1. look to the hole of the pit whence ye are *d.*
Jer. 13. 7. then I went to Euphrates and *d.*
18. 20. they have *d.* a pit for my soul, 22.
Ezek. 8. 8. and when I had *d.* in the wall
Jonah 1. † 13. the men *d.* hard to bring it to land
Mat. 21. 33. hedged it, and *d.* a wine-press in it
25. 18. *d.* in the earth, and hid his lord's money
Luke 6. 48. who *d.* and laid the foundation on a rock
Rom. 11. 3. Lord they have *d.* down thine altars

DIGGEDST.

Deut. 6. 11. and wells digged which thou *d.* not

DIGGETH.

Prov. 16. 27. an ungodly man *d.* up evil, fire in lips
26. 27. whoso *d.* a pit shall fall therein, *Eccl.* 10. 8.

DIGGING.

Jer. 2. † 34. I have not found it by *d.* but on all these

DIGNITY.

Gen. 49. 3. Reuben, thou art the excellency of *d.*
Esth. 6. 3. what *d.* hath been done to Mordecai?
Eccl. 10. 6. folly is set in great *d.* and the rich sit in
Hab. 1. 7. their *d.* shall proceed of themselves

DIGNITIES.

2 Pet. 2. 10. are not afraid to speak evil of *d.* *Jude* 8.

DILIGENCE.

Prov. 4. 23. keep thy heart with all *d.* for issues of life
Luke 12. 58. as thou art in the way, give *d.* to be
Rom. 12. 8. that ruleth with *d.* mercy with cheerfuln.
2 Cor. 8. 7. therefore as ye abound in faith and all *d.*
2 Tim. 4. 9. do thy *d.* to come shortly to me, 21.
Heb. 6. 11. that every one of you shew the same *d.*
2 Pet. 1. 5. giving all *d.* to add to your faith virtue
10. brethren, give *d.* to make your calling sure
Jude 3. when I gave all *d.* to write to you of salva.

DILIGENT.

Deut. 19. 18. the judges shall make *d.* inquisition
Josh. 22. 5. take *d.* heed to do the commandment
Psal. 64. 6. search iniquity, accomplish a *d.* search
77. 6. with my heart and my spirit made *d.* search
Prov. 10. 4. but the hand of the *d.* maketh rich
12. 24. the hand of the *d.* shall bear rule
27. but the substance of a *d.* man is precious
13. 4. but the soul of the *d.* shall be made fat
21. 5. thoughts of *d.* tend only to plenty
22. 29. seest thou a man *d.* in his business?
27. 23. be thou *d.* to know the state of thy flock
2 Cor. 8. 22. whom we have oftentimes proved *d.* but now much more *d.* upon the confidence in you
2 Tim. 3. † 10. but thou hast been a *d.* follower
Tit. 3. 12. be *d.* to come unto me to Nicopolis
2 Pet. 3. 14. be *d.* that ye be found of him in peace

DILIGENTLY.

Exod. 15. 26. if thou wilt *d.* hearken to the voice of the Lord thy God, *Deut.* 11. 13. | 28. 1. *Jer.* 17. 24.
Lev. 10. 16. Moses *d.* sought the goat of sin-offering
Deut. 4. 9. only take heed and keep thy soul *d.*
6. 7. thou shalt teach them *d.* to thy children
17. you shall *d.* keep the commandments, 11. 22.
13. 14. make search, and ask *d.* and if it be truth
24. 8. take heed that thou observe *d.* and do
1 Sam. 20. † 19. then thou shalt go down *d.* and come
1 Kings 20. 33. now the men did *d.* observe whether
Ezra 7. 23. let it be *d.* done for the house of God
Job 13. 17. hear *d.* my speech and declaration, 21. 2.
Psal. 37. 10. thou shalt *d.* consider his place, it shall not be
119. 4. hast commanded us to keep thy precepts *d.*
Prov. 7. 15. I came forth *d.* to seek thy face
11. 27. he that *d.* seeketh good, procureth favour
23. 1. consider *d.* what is before thee
Isa. 21. 7. he hearkened *d.* with much heed
55. 2. hearken *d.* to me, and eat that which is good
Jer. 2. 10. consider *d.* see if there be such a thing
12. 16. if they will *d.* learn the ways of my people
Zech. 6. 15. if ye will *d.* obey the voice of the Lord
Mat. 2. 7. he inquired *d.* when the star appeared
8. Herod said, go and search *d.* for the young child
16. which he had *d.* inquired of the wise men
Mark 7. † 3. except they wash hands *d.* they eat not
Luke 15. 8. sweep house and seek *d.* till she find it
Acts 18. 25. he taught *d.* the things of the Lord
1 Tim. 5. 10. if she have *d.* followed every good work
2 Tim. 1. 17. in Rome he sought me *d.* and found me
Tit. 3. 13. bring Zenas the lawyer and Apollos on their journey *d.* that nothing be wanting to them
Heb. 11. 6. a rewarder of them that *d.* seek him
12. 15. looking *d.* lest any man fail of grace of God
1 Pet. 1. 10. of which the prophets searched *d.*

DIMINISH, ED.

Exod. 5. 8. you shall not *d.* ought thereof, they be idle
11. not ought of your work shall be *d.* 19.
21. 10. her duty of marriage shall he not *d.*
30. † 15. the rich shall not multiply, the poor not *d*
Lev. 25. 16. according to the years thou shalt *d.*
Num. 26. † 54. to few *d.* his inheritance, 33. † 54.
Deut. 4. 2. nor shall you *d.* ought from it, 12. 32.
Prov. 13. 11. wealth gotten by vanity shall be *d.*
Isa. 21. 17. the mighty men of Kedar shall be *d.*
Jer. 10. † 24. correct not in anger, lest thou *d.* me
26. 2. speak what I command thee, *d.* not a word
29. 6. that ye may be increased and not *d.*
48. † 37. every head bald, and every beard *d.*
Ezek. 5. 11. hast defiled, therefore will I also *d.* thee
16. 27. behold, I have *d.* thine ordinary food
29. 15. I will *d.* them, they shall no more rule

DIMINISHING.

Rom. 11. 12. *d.* of them be the riches of the Gentiles

DIM.

Gen. 27. 1. when Isaac was old and his eyes *d.*
48. 10. now the eyes of Israel were *d.* for age
Deut. 34. 7. Moses' eye was not *d.* nor force abated
1 Sam. 3. 2. Eli's eyes began to wax *d.* 4. 15.
Job 17. 7. mine eye also is *d.* by reason of sorrow
Isa. 32. 3. the eyes of them that see shall not be *d.*
Lam. 4. 1. how is gold become *d.*! fine gold changed
5. 17. for these things our eyes are *d.* our heart faint

DIMNESS.

Isa. 8. 22. and behold trouble darkness *d.* of anguish
9. 1. *d.* shall not be such as was in her vexation

DINE, D.

Gen. 43. 16. for these men shall *d.* with me at noon
Luke 11. 37. a Pharisee besought him to *d.* with him
John 21. 12. Jesus saith to them, come and *d.*
15. so when they had *d.* Jesus saith to Simon

DINNER.

Prov. 15. 17. better is a *d.* of herbs where love is
Mat. 22. 4. behold, I have prepared my *d.* my oxen
Luke 11. 38. that he had not first washed before *d.*
14. 12. when makest a *d.* or supper, call not friends

DIP.

Exod. 12. 22. *d.* it in the blood that is in the basin
Lev. 4. 6. the priest shall *d.* his finger, 17. 14, 16.
14. 6. *d.* the cedar wood and the living bird, 51.
Num. 19. 18. clean person should *d.* hyssop in water
Deut. 33. 24. Moses said, let Asher *d.* his foot in oil
Ruth 2. 14. Boaz said to Ruth, *d.* morsel in vinegar
Luke 16. 24. send Lazarus that he may *d.* his finger

DIPPED, ETH.

Gen. 37. 31. and they *d.* the coat in the blood
Josh. 3. 15. the priests' feet were *d.* in brim of water
2 Kings 5. 14. Naaman *d.* in Jordan seven times
Psal. 68. 23. that thy foot may be *d.* in blood
Mat. 26. 23. he that *d.* his hand with me in the dish, the same shall betray me, *Mark* 14. 20.
John 13. 26. to whom I give a sop, when I have *d.* it; when he had *d.* the sop, he gave it to Judas

DIPT.

Lev. 9. 9. Aaron *d.* his finger in the blood
1 Sam. 14. 27. he *d.* the end of rod in an honey-comb
2 Kings 8. 15. Hazael took a cloth and *d.* it in water
Rev. 19. 13. was clothed with a vesture *d.* in blood

DIRECT.

Gen. 46. 28. he sent Judah to *d.* his face to Goshen
Psal. 5. 3. in the morning will I *d.* my prayer
Prov. 3. 6. acknowledge him, he shall *d.* thy paths
11. 5. the righteousness of the perfect shall *d.*
Eccl. 10. 10. but wisdom is profitable to *d.*
Isa. 45. 13. have raised him up, I will *d.* all his ways
61. 8. I will *d.* their work in truth and make
Jer. 10. 23. it is not in man that walketh to *d.* his steps
1 Thess. 3. 11. our L. Jesus Christ *d.* our way to you
2 Thess. 3. 5. Lord *d.* your hearts into the love of G.

DIRECTED.

Job 32. 14. he hath not *d.* his words against me
Psal. 119. 5. O that my ways were *d.* to keep stat.
141. † 2. let my prayer be *d.* as incense, and lifting
Isa. 40. 13. who hath *d.* the Spirit of the Lord?

DIRECTETH.

Job 37. 3. he *d.* it under the whole heaven
Prov. 16. 9. his ways, but the Lord *d.* his steps
21. 29. as for the upright he *d.* his way

DIRECTION.

Num. 21. 18. princes judged it by *d.* of the lawgiver
Psal. 19. † 4. their *d.* is gone out through the earth

DIRECTLY.

Num. 19. 4. sprinkle blood *d.* before the tabernacle
Ezek. 42. 12. even the way *d.* before the wall

DIRT.

Judg. 3. 22. the fat closed, and the *d.* came out
Psal. 18. 42. I did cast them out as *d.* in the streets
Isa. 57. 20. whose waters cast up mire and *d.*

DISALLOW, ED.

Num. 30. 5. because her father *d.* her
8. but if her husband *d.* her ‖ 11. he *d.* her not
1 Pet. 2. 4. *d.* indeed of men, but chosen of God
7. the stone which the builders *d.* is made head

DISANNUL.

Job 40. 8. wilt thou also *d.* my judgment?
Isa. 14. 27. Lord hath purposed who shall *d.* it?
Gal. 3. 17. this covenant the law cannot *d.*

DISANNULLED.

Isa. 28. 18. your covenant with death shall be *d.*

DISANNULLETH.

Gal. 3. 15. covenant no man *d.* or addeth thereto

DISANNULLING.

Heb. 7. 18. there is a *d.* of the commandment

DISAPPOINT.

Psal. 17. 13. arise, O Lord, *d.* him, cast him down

DISAPPOINTED.

Prov. 15. 22. without counsel purposes are *d.*

DISAPPOINTETH.

Job 5. 12. he *d.* the devices of the crafty

DISCERN.

Discerning of spirit *is one of the gifts of God, mentioned by the apostle* Paul, 1 Cor. 12. 10. *It consists in discerning among those who say they are inspired by God, whether they are animated or inspired by a good or evil spirit, whether they are true or false prophets. This gift was of very great importance, both in the Old Testament, wherein it is found that false prophets often rose up, and seducers who deceived the people; and also in the New, in the primitive ages of the church, when supernatural gifts were common; when the messenger of* Satan *was sometimes transformed into an angel of light, and false apostles, under the outward appearance of sheep, concealed the sentiments of ravening wolves. Wherefore the evangelist cautioned believers, saying,* Believe not every spirit, but try the spirits, whether they be of God, 1 John 4. 1. *See in* Deut. 18. 20, 21, 22. *the marks which are given by God to distinguish true from false prophets.*

Gen. 31. 32. *d.* thou what is thine with me, and take it
38. 25. she said, *d.* I pray thee, whose are these
2 *Sam.* 14. 17. so is my lord the king to *d.* good and bad
19. 35. and can I *d.* between good and evil?
1 *Kings* 3. 9. that I may *d.* between good and bad
11. thou hast asked understanding to *d.* judgment
Ezra 3. 13. the people could not *d.* the noise of joy
Job 4. 16. but I could not *d* the form thereof
6. 30. cannot my taste *d.* perverse things?
Ezek. 44. 23. cause them *d.* betw. unclean and clean
Jonah 4. 11. cannot *d.* between right hand and left
Mal. 3. 18. *d.* between the righteous and the wicked
Mat. 16. 3. ye can *d.* the face of the sky, *Luke* 12. 56.
Heb. 5. 14. their senses exercised to *d.* good and evil

DISCERNED, ETH.

Gen. 27. 23. he *d.* him not, his hands were hairy
1 *Kings* 20. 41. and the king of Israel *d.* him
Neh. 13. †24. they *d.* not to speak in Jews' language
Prov. 7. 7. I *d.* among the youth a young man
Eccl. 8. 5. a wise man *d.* time and judgment
Rom. 14. †23. that *d.* between meats is damned, if eat
1 *Cor.* 2. 14. nor know, because they are spiritually *d.*
†15. he that is spiritual *d.* all things, yet he himself is *d.* of no man, for who hath known

DISCERNING.

1 *Cor.* 11. 29. eateth unworthily, not *d.* Lord's body
12. 10. to another is given *d.* of spirits, to another

DISCERNER.

Heb. 4. 12. word is a *d.* of the thoughts of the heart

DISCHARGE, D.

1 *Kings* 5. 9. and will cause them to be *d.* there
Eccl. 8. 8. day of death, there is no *d.* in that war

DISCIPLE.

The word disciple, *absolutely taken, signifies in the New Testament, a believer,* a christian, *a scholar, a follower of* Christ, *or his apostles; as in* Acts 6. 1. When the number of the *disciples* was multiplied, there arose a murmuring of the *Grecians* against the *Hebrews,* because their widows were neglected in the daily ministration. *And in* Acts 9. 1. *Saul* yet breathing out threatenings and slaughter against the *disciples* of the Lord, *that is, against the* followers of Christ.

The name of disciple *is often set down for that of* apostle; *particularly in the Gospel,* Mat. 5. 1. | 8. 23. | 10. 1. *but in other places the apostles are distinguished from disciples. The apostles were chosen particularly by* Christ *out of the number of his disciples, to be the stewards of his most secret mysteries, and the principal ministers for propagating and establishing the christian religion. They were twelve in number,* Mat. 10. 2. Luke 6. 13.

But the disciples *who followed our Saviour from the beginning, and are called simply* disciples, *were seventy in number. The precepts and admonitions which our Saviour gave them, when he sent them to preach in the cities of* Judea, *are recorded in* Luke 10. *from the beginning to verse* 17.

Mat. 10. 24. *d.* is not above his master, *Luke* 6. 40.
25. enough for the *d.* that he be as his master
42. whoso shall give a cup of cold water to a *d.*
27. 57. Joseph of Arimathea himself was Jesus' *d.*
John 9. 28. thou art his *d.* we are Moses' disciples
18. 15. and so did another *d.* that *d.* was known
16. then went out that other *d.* that was known
19. 26. the *d.* standing by, whom Jesus loved
27. then saith he to that *d.* behold thy mother, and from that hour that *d.* took her to his own home
38. being a *d.* but secretly, for fear of the Jews
20. 2. the other *d.* whom Jesus loved, 21. 7, 20.
3. Peter went forth, and that other *d.* and came
4. the other *d.* did outrun Peter, and came first
8. then went in also that other *d.* and he saw
21. 23. this saying, that that *d.* should not die
24. this is the *d.* which testifieth these things
Acts 9. 10. there was a certain *d.* at Damascus
26. but they believed not that he was a *d.*
36. now there was at Joppa a *d.* named Tabitha
16. 1. a certain *d.* was there, named Timotheus
21. 16. an old *d.* with whom we should lodge

My DISCIPLE.

Luke 14. 26. if he hate not his life, cannot be *my d.*
27. whoso doth not bear his cross, cannot be *my d.*
33. that forsaketh not all, he cannot be *my d.*

DISCIPLES.

Mat. 9. 14. then came to him the *d.* of John, saying
10. 1. when he had called unto him his twelve *d.*
11. 1. he had made an end of commanding his *d.*
14. 26. when the *d.* saw him walking on the sea
17. 6. when the *d.* heard it, they fell on their face
19. 13. and the *d.* rebuked them, *Mark* 10. 13.
20. 17. Jesus took the twelve *d.* apart in the way
21. 1. Jesus sent two *d.* saying, go into the village
22. 16. the Pharisees sent unto him their *d.*
26. 26. Jesus took bread, and gave it to the *d.*
35. I will not deny thee, likewise also said the *d.*
56. then all the *d.* forsook him, and fled
Mark 2. 18. why do the *d.* of John and of the Pharisees fast, but thy *d.* fast not? *Luke* 5. 33.
8. 14. now the *d.* had forgotten to take bread
Luke 19. 37. the *d.* began to rejoice and praise G.
John 3. 25. between some of John's *d.* and the Jews
4. 1. that Jesus baptized more *d.* than John
9. 28. thou art his disciple, but we are Moses' *d.*
13. 5. he began to wash the *d.* feet, and to wipe them
18. 17. art not thou also one of this man's *d.?*
20. 18. Mary told the *d.* that she had seen the Lord
Acts 9. 1. Saul breathing out slaughter against the *d.*
26. Saul essayed to join himself to the *d.*
11. 26. the *d.* were called Christians first in Antioch
19. 1. Paul came to Ephesus, and finding certain *d.*
30. Paul would have entered, *d.* suffered him not
20. 7. first day of week *d.* came together break bread
30. men speaking, to draw away *d.* after them

His DISCIPLES.

Mat. 8. 25. *his d.* came and awoke him, saying
9. 19. Jesus arose and followed, and so did *his d.*
28. 7. go, and tell *his d.* he is risen from the dead
13. say ye, *his d.* came by night and stole him
Mark 10. 10. in the house *his d.* asked him again
Luke 5. 30. the Pharisees murmured against *his d.*
6. 20. he lifted up his eyes on *his d.* and said
11. 1. teach us to pray, as John taught *his d.*
John 2. 11. his glory, and *his d.* believed on him
4. 2. though Jesus himself baptized not, but *his d.*
27. upon this came *his d.* and marvelled that he
6. 3. up to a mountain, and there he sat with *his d.*
22. but that *his d.* were gone away alone
9. 27. why would ye hear it again? will ye be *his d.*
11. 12. then said *his d.* L. if he sleep shall do well
18. 1. he went with *his d.* over the brook Cedron
2. for Jesus often resorted thither with *his d.*
20. 26. again, *his d.* were within, Thomas with them

Of his DISCIPLES.

Mat. 11. 2. when John had heard works of Christ, he sent two *of his d. Mark* 11. 1. | 14. 13. *Luke* 19. 29.
Mark 7. 2. some *of his d.* eat with unwashen hands
John 6. 66. from that time many *of his d.* went back
18. 19. the high priest asked Jesus *of his d.*
25. art not thou also one *of his d.?* he denied
21. 12. none *of his d.* durst ask him, who art thou?

To his DISCIPLES.

Mat. 14. 19. blessed, and gave the loaves *to his d.*
Mark 4. 34. he expounded all things *to his d.*
Luke 10. 23. he turned himself *to his d.* and said
John 21. 14. third time Jesus shewed himself *to his d.*

My DISCIPLES.

Isa. 8. 16. bind up testimony, seal law among *my d.*
Mat. 26. 18. master saith, I will keep the passover at thy house with *my d. Mark* 14. 14. *Luke* 22. 11.
John 8. 31. then are ye *my d.* indeed, 13. 35.
15. 8. that ye bear much fruit, so shall ye be *my d.*

Thy DISCIPLES.

Mat. 9. 14. why do we fast, *thy d.* fast not, *Mark* 2. 18.
12. 2. *thy d.* do that which is not lawful on sabbath
15. 2. why do *thy d.* transgress the tradition?
17. 16. I brought him to *thy d.* they could not cure
Mark 7. 5. why walk not *thy d.* according to tradit.
9. 18. I spake to *thy d.* to cast him out, *Luke* 9. 40.
Luke 19. 39. the Pharisees said, Master, rebuke *thy d.*
John 7. 3. that *thy d.* may see the works thou doest

DISCIPLINE.

Job 36. 10. he openeth also their ears to *d.* and com.

DISCLOSE.

Isa. 26. 21. behold, the earth also shall *d.* her blood

DISCOMFITED.

Exod. 17. 13. Joshua *d.* Amalek and his people
Num. 14. 45. smote and *d.* them, even to Hormah
Josh. 10. 10. Lord *d.* them before Isr. and slew them
Judg. 4. 15. the Lord *d.* Sisera and his chariots
8. 12. Gideon pursued them, and *d.* all the host
1 *Sam.* 7. 10. thundered on the Philistines, and *d.* them
2 *Sam.* 22. 15. lightning, and *d.* them, *Psal.* 18. 14.
Isa. 31. 8. shall flee, and his young men shall be *d.*

DISCOMFITURE.

1 *Sam.* 14. 20. and there was a very great *d.*

DISCONTENTED.

1 *Sam.* 22. 2. every one that was *d.* gathered to Dav.

DISCONTINUE.

Jer. 17. 4. and thou shalt *d.* from mine heritage

DISCORD.

Prov. 6. 14. he deviseth mischief, he soweth *d.*
19. and him that soweth *d.* among brethren

DISCOVER.

Deut. 22. 30. a man shall not *d.* his father's skirt
1 *Sam.* 14. 8. and we will *d.* ourselves to them
Job 41. 13. who can *d.* the face of his garment?
Prov. 18. 2. but that his heart may *d.* itself
25. 9. thy cause, and *d.* not a secret to another
Isa. 3. 17. the Lord will *d.* their secret parts
Jer. 13. 26. I will *d.* thy skirts on thy face, *Nah.* 3. 5.
Lam. 4. 22. O daughter of Edom, he will *d.* thy sins
Ezek. 16. 37. I will *d.* thy nakedness to them
Hos. 2. 10. I will *d.* her lewdness in sight of lovers
Mic. 1. 6. the stones, I will *d.* the foundation thereof

DISCOVERED.

Exod. 20. 26. that thy nakedness be not *d.* thereon
Lev. 20. 18. he hath *d.* her fountain, she uncovered
1 *Sam.* 14. 11. both *d.* themselves to the garrison
22. 6. when Saul heard that David was *d.* and men
2 *Sam.* 22. 16. the foundations of the world were *d.* at the rebuking of the Lord, *Psal.* 18. 15.
Isa. 22. 8. and he *d.* the covering of Judah
57. 8. for thou hast *d.* thyself to another than me
Jer. 13. 22. for thine iniquity are thy skirts *d.*
Lam. 2. 14. and they have not *d.* thine iniquity
Ezek. 13. 14. so that foundation thereof shall be *d.*
16. 36. thy nakedness *d.* through thy whoredoms
57. before thy wickedness was *d.* as at the time
21. 24. saith Lord, in that your transgressions are *d.*
22. 10. in thee have they *d.* their father's nakedness
23. 10. these *d.* nakedness, they took her sons
18. she *d.* her whoredoms, and *d.* her nakedness
29. the nakedness of thy whoredoms shall be *d.*
Hos. 7. 1. then the iniquity of Ephraim was *d.*
Acts 21. 3. now when we had *d.* Cyprus, we left
27. 39. but they *d.* a certain creek with a shore

DISCOVERETH.

Job 12. 22. he *d.* deep things out of darkness
Psal. 29. 9. the voice of the Lord *d.* the forest

DISCOVERING.

Hab. 3. 13. by *d.* the foundation to the neck

DISCOURAGE.

Num. 32. 7. why *d.* ye the hearts of the people?

DISCOURAGED.

Num. 21. 4. the soul of the people was much *d.*
32. 9. they *d.* the heart of the children of Israel
Deut. 1. 21. go and possess it, fear not, nor be *d.*
28. our brethren have *d.* our heart, saying
Isa. 42. 4. he shall not fail nor be *d.* till he set
Col. 3. 21. provoke not your children, lest they be *d*

DISCREET.

Gen. 41. 33. let Pharaoh look out a man *d.* and wise
39. there is none so *d.* and wise as thou art
Tit. 2. 5. that the aged teach young women to be *d*
†6. young men likewise exhort to be *d.*

DISCREETLY.

Mark 12. 34. when Jesus saw that he answered *d.*

DISCRETION.

Psal. 112. 5. he will guide his affairs with *d.*
Prov. 1. 4. to the young man knowledge and *d.*
2. 11. *d.* shall preserve thee, understand. keep thee
3. 21. my son, keep sound wisdom and *d.*
5. 2. thou mayest regard *d.* and keep knowledge
11. 22. so is a fair woman who is without *d.*
19. 11. the *d.* of a man deferreth his anger
Isa. 28. 26. for his God doth instruct him to *d.*
Jer. 10. 12. he stretched out the heavens by his *d.*

DISDAINED.

1 *Sam.* 17. 42. when Goliath saw David, he *d.* him
Job 30. 1. whose fathers I would *d.* to set with dogs

DISEASE.

Diseases *and death are the consequences and effects of sin; this is the idea which we have of them from Scripture. The ancient* Hebrews, *who were very little versed in the study of natural philosophy, and not much accustomed to recur to physical causes, and consult physicians, when they were sick, imputed their diseases generally to evil spirits, the executioners of divine vengeance. If their infirmities appeared to be beyond what was usual, and the causes of them were not known to them, they did not fail to say, that it was a blow from the avenging hand of God; to him the wisest and most religious had recourse for cure; and king* Asa *is blamed for placing his confidence in physicians, when he had a very painful fit of the gout in his feet, and for not applying himself to the Lord,* 2 Chron. 16. 12. In his disease he sought not to the Lord, but to the physicians. Job's *friends immediately ascribed all the distempers with which that holy man was afflicted, to God's justice,* Job 4. 7, 8. *Leprosies, which were so common among the* Jews, *were treated as diseases sent by God; the priests were the persons who judged of the nature and qualities of this evil, shut up the diseased, and declared that they were healed, or had their leprosy upon them; and after their recovery they offered sacrifices, as it were to expiate for their faults.* Miriam, Gehazi, *and king* Uzziah, *were smitten suddenly with a leprosy; the first as a punishment for her detracting discourses; the second for his avarice; and the third for his presumption.* Num. 12. 10. 2 Kings 5. 27. 2 Chron. 26. 21.

In the New Testament, *the cause of many diseases is attributed to the devil. It is said there, that the devil had bound the woman, who had been bowed down for eighteen years,* Luke 13. 16. Ought not this woman, being a daughter of *Abraham,* whom *Satan* hath bound, lo, these eighteen years, to be loosed from this bond on the sabbath day? *In* verse 11. *the same person is mentioned,* as having a spirit of infirmity, *that is, a sore disease inflicted by the devil. We are told of a dumb devil, and of another that could scarce speak,* Mark 9. 17. Luke 11. 14. *that is to say, which caused these infirmities in those who were possessed by them: and whenever* Christ *or his apostles had a mind to restore these indisposed persons to their health, they began with casting out the devils; for the cure immediately followed.*

The apostle Paul *attributes the death and diseases of many to their communicating unworthily,* 1 Cor. 11. 30. For this cause many are weak and sickly among you, and many sleep. *The same apostle ascribes the infirmities wherewith he was afflicted, to an evil angel,* 2 Cor. 12. 7. There was given me a thorn in the flesh, the messenger of *Satan* to buffet me. *It was the destroying angel that made such havoc of* Sennacherib's *army,* 2 Kings 19. 35. *It was the avenging angel that drew his sword against the people, and smote them with the pestilence, as a punishment for* David's *sin,* 1 Chron. 21. 15, 16. *No sooner had* Abimelech, *king of* Gerar, *taken* Sarah, *the wife of* Abraham, *forcibly away, but he was threatened with death,* Gen. 20. 3, 4. Er *and* Onan, *the sons of* Judah, *were carried off by unknown diseases, for having committed actions of an infamous and detestable nature,* Gen. 38. 7, 10. *And the* Philistines *were smitten with an ignominious disease, for not treating the ark with that respect that it deserved,* 1 Sam. 5. 12. *There are a great number of diseases recorded in Scripture, which were sent by God in the way of punishment for sins.*

The diseases of Egypt, *from which God promised to defend his people,* Exod. 15. 26; *and which he threatens, in case of their disobedience, to inflict upon them,* Deut. 28. 60. *These* diseases *are either the plagues with which God afflicted* Egypt *before the departure of the* Israelites, *or the diseases which were most common in the country, such as blindness, ulcers in the legs, consumptions, and the leprosy, called* Elephantiasis, *which was peculiar to this country, as* Pliny *observes,* Ægypti peculiare hoc malum *Elephantiasis.*

2 *Kings* 1. 2. inquire, whether if I shall recov. of *d.*
8. 8. saying, shall I recover of this *d.?* 9.
2 *Chr.* 16. 12. Asa diseased till his *d.* was exceeding great, yet in his *d.* he sought not to the Lord
21. 15. shall have great sickness by *d.* of thy bowels
18. the Lord smote him with an incurable *d.*

Job 30. 18. by force of my d. is my garment changed
Psal. 38. 7. my loins are filled with a loathsome d.
41. 8. an evil d. say they, cleaveth fast to him
Eccl. 6. 2. this is vanity, and it is an evil d.
Mat. 4. 23. healing all manner of d. 9. 35. | 10. 1.
John 5. 4. was made whole of whatsoever d. he had

DISEASES.
Exod. 15. 26. put none of these d. on you, Deut. 7. 15.
Deut. 28. 60. he will bring on thee all the d. of Egypt
2 Chr. 21. 19. his bowels fell out, he died of sore d.
24. 25. for they left him in great d. his servants
Psal. 103. 3. bless the Lord, who healeth all thy d.
Hab. 3. † 5. and burning d. went forth at his feet
Mat. 4. 24. brought to him all sick people that were taken with divers d. Mark 1. 34. Luke 4. 40.
Luke 9. 1. gave them power over devils, and cure d.
Acts 19. 12. and the d. departed from them
28. 9. others which had d. in the island, came

DISEASED.
1 Kings 15. 23. Asa was d. in his feet, 2 Chr. 16. 12.
Ezek. 34. 4. d. have ye not strengthened nor healed
21. because ye have push. the d. with your horns
Mat. 9. 20. a woman d. with an issue of blood
14. 35. they brought all that were d. Mark 1. 32.
John 6. 2. saw miracles he did on them that were d.

DISFIGURE.
Mat. 6. 16. be not as hypocrites, for they d. their faces

DISGRACE.
Jer. 14. 21. do not d. the throne of thy glory

DISGUISE, ED.
1 Sam. 28. 8. and Saul d. himself, and he went
1 Kings 14. 2. Jeroboam said, arise, and d. thyself
20. 38. one of the sons of the prophets d. himself
22. 30. Ahab the king of Israel said, I will d. myself, and he d. himself, 2 Chron. 18. 29.
2 Chron. 35. 22. Josiah d. himself to fight with him

DISGUISETH.
Job 24. 15. the adulterer also waiteth and d. his face

DISH, ES.
Exod. 25. 29. thou shalt make the d. thereof, 37. 16.
Num. 4. 7. and put thereon the d. and the spoons
Judg. 5. 25. she brought forth butter in a lordly d.
2 Kings 21. 13. as a man wipeth a d. turning it
Mat. 26. 23. dippeth with me in the d. Mark 14. 20.

DISHONEST; *see* GAIN.

DISHONESTY.
2 Cor. 4. 2. have renounced the hidden things of d.

DISHONOUR.
Ezra 4. 14. was not meet for us to see the king's d.
Psal. 35. 26. be clothed with shame and d. 71. 13.
69. 19. thou hast known my shame and my d.
Prov. 6. 33. a wound and d. shall he get
Rom. 9. 21. make one vessel to honour, another to d.
1 Cor. 15. 43. it is sown in d. it is raised in glory
2 Cor. 6. 8. by honour and d. by evil and good report
2 Tim. 2. 20. are vessels, some to honour, some to d.

DISHONOUR, EST, ETH.
Mic. 7. 6. for the son d. father, daughter ag. mother
John 8. 49. I honour my Father, and ye d. me
Rom. 1. 24. to d. their own bodies between themselves
2. 23. through breaking of the law, d. thou God?
1 Cor. 11. 4. man d. his head || 5. woman d. her head

DISINHERIT.
Num. 14. 12. I will d. them, and make of thee a greater

DISJOINTED.
Jer. 6. † 8. be instructed, lest my soul be d. from thee
Ezek. 23. † 17. and her mind was d. from them

DISMAYED.
Deut. 31. 8. he will not fail nor forsake thee, fear not, nor be d. Josh. 1. 9. | 8. 1. | 10. 25. 1 Chr. 22. 13. | 28. 20. 2 Chron. 20. 15, 17. | 32. 7.
1 Sam. 17. 11. they were d. 2 Kings 19. 26. Isa. 37. 27.
Isa. 21. 3. I was bowed down, d. at the seeing of it
41. 10. fear not, be not d. Jer. 1. 17. | 10. 2. | 23. 4. | 30. 10. | 46. 27. Ezek. 2. 6. | 3. 9.
23. that we may be d. and behold it together
Jer. 8. 9. the wise men are d. and taken, 10. 2.
17. 18. let them be d. but let not me be d.
46. 5. wherefore have I seen them d. turned back?
48. 1. Misgab is d. || 49. 37. cause Elam to be d.
50. 36. the mighty men of Babylon shall be d.
Obad. 9. thy mighty men, O Teman, shall be d.

DISMAYING.
Jer. 48. 39. Moab shall be a d. to all about him
Ezek. 32. † 23. caused d. in the land of the living

DISMISSED.
2 Chr. 23. 8. Jehoiada the priest d. not the courses
Acts 15. 30. when they were d. they came to Antioch
19. 41. when he had thus spoken, he d. assembly

DISOBEDIENCE.
Rom. 5. 19. by one man's d. many were made sinners
2 Cor. 10. 6. having in readiness to revenge all d.
Eph. 2. 2. the spirit that worketh in children of d.
5. 6. wrath of God on the children of d. Col. 3. 6.
Heb. 2. 2. every d. received a just recompence of rew.
4. † 11. lest any fall by the same example of d.

DISOBEDIENT.
1 Kings 13. 26. man of God, who was d. to the word
Neh. 9. 26. they were d. and rebelled against me
Luke 1. 17. turn the d. to the wisdom of the just
Acts 26. 19. I was not d. to the heavenly vision
Rom. 1. 30. boasters, d. to parents, 2 Tim. 3. 2.
10. 21. I stretched forth my hands to a d. people
15. † 31. that I may be delivered from d. in Judea
1 Tim. 1. 9. the law was made for the lawless and d.
Tit. 1. 16. deny him, being abominable and d.
3. 3. for we ourselves also were sometimes d.
Heb. 11. † 31. Rahab perished not with the d.
1 Pet. 2. 7. but to them which be d. the stone which
8. to them who stumble at the word, being d.
3. 20. to spirits in prison, which sometime were d.

DISOBEYED.
1 Kings 13. 21. as thou hast d. the mouth of the L.

DISORDERLY.
1 Thess. 5. 14. brethren, warn them that are d.
2 Thess. 3. 6. withdraw from a brother who walks d.
7. we behaved not ourselves d. among you
11. there are some who walk among you d.

DISPATCH.
Ezek. 23. 47. they shall d. them with their swords

DISPATCHED.
Ezra 10. † 14. let them come, till the matter be d.

DISPENSATION.
1 Cor. 9. 17. a d. of the gospel is committed to me
Eph. 1. 10. in the d. of the fulness of times
3. 2. ye have heard of the d. of the grace of God
Col. 1. 25. a minister according to the d. of God

DISPERSE.
1 Sam. 14. 34. Saul said, d. yourselves among people
Prov. 15. 7. the lips of the wise d. knowledge
Ezek. 12. 15. when I shall scatter them and d. them in the countries, 20. 23. | 29. 12. | 30. 23, 26.
22. 15. and I will d. thee in the countries

DISPERSED.
2 Chron. 11. 23. Rehoboam d. of all his children
Esth. 3. 8. there is a certain people d. among people
Psal. 112. 9. he hath d. he hath given, 2 Cor. 9. 9.
Prov. 5. 16. let thy fountains be d. abroad
Isa. 11. 12. he shall gather together the d. of Judah
Ezek. 36. 19. they were d. through the countries
Zeph. 3. 10. the daughter of my d. shall bring
John 7. 35. will he go to the d. among the Gentiles?
Acts 5. 37. and as many as obeyed him were d.

DISPERSER.
Nah. 2. † 1. the d. is come before thy face

DISPERSIONS.
Jer. 25. 34. the days of your d. are accomplished

DISPLAYED.
Ps. 60. 4. thou hast given a banner that it may be d.

DISPLEASE.
Gen. 31. 35. let it not d. my lord that I cannot rise
Num. 22. 34. if it d. thee, I will get me back again
1 Sam. 29. 7. return, that thou d. not the lords
2 Sam. 11. 25. say to Joab, let not this d. thee
Prov. 24. 18. lest the Lord see it, and it d. him

DISPLEASED.
Gen. 38. 10. the thing which he did d. the Lord
48. 17. laid right hand on head of Ephraim, it d.
Num. 11. 1. the people complained, it d. the Lord
10. anger of the L. was kindled, Moses also was d.
1 Sam. 8. 6. but the thing d. Samuel, when they said
18. 8. then Saul was very wroth, and the saying d.
2 Sam. 6. 8. and David was d. because the Lord had made a breach upon Uzzah, 1 Chron. 13. 11.
11. 27. the thing David had done d. the Lord
1 Kings 1. 6. his father had not d. him at any time
20. 43. the king of Israel went to his house d. 21. 4.
1 Chron. 21. 7. and God was d. with this thing
Psal. 60. 1. thou hast been d. O turn thyself to us
Isa. 59. 15. it d. him that there was no judgment
Dan. 6. 14. the king was sore d. with himself
Jonah 4. 1. but it d. Jonah exceedingly, was angry
Hab. 3. 8. was the Lord d. against the rivers?
Zech. 1. 2. the Lord hath been sore d. with fathers
15. I am very sore d. with heathen at ease; for I was but a little d. they helped forward affliction
Mat. 21. 15. when the scribes saw, they were d.
Mark 10. 14. when Jesus saw it, he was much d.
41. they began to be much d. with James and John
Acts 12. 20. Herod was highly d. with them of Tyre

DISPLEASING.
1 Kings 9. † 13. he called them land of d. to this day

DISPLEASURE.
Deut. 9. 19. for I was afraid of the hot d. of the Ld.
Judg. 15. 3. be more blameless, though I do them a d.
Psal. 2. 5. then shall he vex them in his sore d.
6. 1. neither chasten me in thy hot d. 38. 1.
Zech. 1. † 2. Lord hath been with d. displeased

DISPOSED.
Job 34. 13. or who hath d. the whole world?
37. 15. dost thou know when God d. them?
Acts 18. 27. when he was d. to pass into Achaia
1 Cor. 10. 27. bid you to a feast and ye be d. to go

DISPOSETH.
Psal 50. † 23. to him that d. his way aright

DISPOSING.
Prov. 16. 33. the whole d. thereof is of the Lord

DISPOSINGS.
Prov. 16. † 1. the d. of the heart in man is of the L.

DISPOSITION.
Acts 7. 53. who received the law by the d. of angels

DISPOSSESS, ED.
Num. 32. 39. the children of Machir d. the Amorite
33. 53. ye shall d. the inhabitants of the land
Deut. 7. 17. if thou shalt say, how can I d. them?
Judg. 11. 23. Ld. God of Isr. hath d. the Amorites

DISPUTATION.
Acts 15. 2. Paul and Barnabas had no small d.

DISPUTATIONS.
Rom. 14. 1. him receive, but not to doubtful d.

DISPUTE.
Job 23. 7. there the righteous might d. with him

DISPUTED.
Mark 9. 33. what was it that ye d. by the way?
34. for they had d. who should be the greatest
Acts 9. 29. Saul d. against the Grecians, went to slay
17. 17. Paul d. in the synagogue with the Jews
Jude 9. Michael d. about the body of Moses, durst

DISPUTER.
1 Cor. 1. 20. where is the d. of this world?

DISPUTEST.
Rom. 9. † 20. who art thou that d. with God?

DISPUTING.
Acts 6. 9. and them of Asia d. with Stephen
15. 7. when there had been much d. Peter rose up
19. 8. d. and persuading the things of God, 9.
24. 12. they neither found me d. with any man

DISPUTINGS.
Phil. 2. 14. do all things without murmurings and d.
1 Tim. 6. 5. perverse d. of men of corrupt minds

DISQUIET.
Jer. 50. 34. and d. the inhabitants of Babylon

DISQUIETED.
1 Sam. 28. 15. why hast thou d. me to bring me up?
Psal. 39. 6. surely they are d. in vain, heaps up riches
42. 5. why art thou cast down, O my soul? why art thou d. within me? 11. | 43. 5.
Prov. 30. 21. for three things the earth is d.

DISQUIETNESS.
Psal. 38. 8. I have roared by reason of d. of my heart

DISSEMBLED.
Josh. 7. 11. they have also stolen and d. also
Jer. 42. 20. for ye d. in your hearts, when ye sent
Gal. 2. 13. the other Jews d. likewise with him

DISSEMBLERS.
Psal. 26. 4. with vain persons, nor will I go in with d.

DISSEMBLETH.
Prov. 26. 24. e that hateth d. with his lips

DISSENSION.
Acts 15. 2. Paul and Barnabas had no small d.
23. 7. there arose a d. between the Pharisees and the Sadducees
10. when there arose a great d. the chief captain

DISSIMULATION.
Rom. 12. 9. let love be without d. abhor evil
Gal. 2. 13. Barnabas was carried away with their d.

DISSOLVE.
Dan. 5. 16. I have heard that thou canst d. doubts

DISSOLVED.
Psal. 75. 3. earth and all inhabitants thereof are d.
Isa. 14. 31. cry, O city, thou whole Palestina art d.
24. 19. the earth is clean d. the earth is moved
34. 4. and all the host of heaven shall be d.
Nah. 2. 6. gates opened, and the palace shall be d.
2 Cor. 5. 1. if our house of this tabernacle were d.
2 Pet. 3. 11. seeing that all these things shall be d.
12. wherein the heavens being on fire shall be d.

DISSOLVEST.
Job 30. 22. and thou d. my substance
Psal. 65. † 10. thou d. the earth with showers

DISSOLVING.
Dan. 5. 12. and d. of doubts was found in Daniel

DISTAFF.
Prov. 31. 19. to the spindle, and her hands hold the d.

DISTANCES.
Isa. 33. † 17. they shall behold the land of far d.

DISTANT.
Exod. 36. 22. one board had two tenons equally d.

DISTIL.
Deut. 32. 2. my speech shall d. as dew, as small rain
Job 36. 28. the clouds d. on man abundantly

DISTINCTION.
1 Cor. 14. 7. except they give a d. in the sounds

DISTINGUISHETH.
1 Cor. 4. † 7. for who d. thee from another?

DISTINCTLY.
Neh. 8. 8. they read in the book of the law of God d.

DISTRACTED.
Psal. 88. 15. while I suffer thy terrors, I am d.

DISTRACTION.
1 Cor. 7. 35. you may attend on the Lord without d.

DISTRESS.
Gen. 35. 3. God who answered me in day of my d.
42. 21. therefore is this d. come upon us
Judg. 11. 7. ye come to me now, when ye are in d.
1 Sam. 22. 2. every one that was in d. came to David
2 Sam. 22. 7. in my d. I called on the Lord, and cried to my God, Psal. 18. 6. | 118. 5. | 120. 1.
1 Kings 1. 29. that redeemed my soul out of all d.
2 Chron. 28. 22. in his d. Ahaz trespassed more
Neh. 2. 17. I said, ye see the d. that we are in
9. 37. they have dominion and we are in great d.
Psal. 4. 1. thou hast enlarged me when I was d.
Prov. 1. 27. I will mock when d. cometh upon you
Isa. 5. † 30. if one look to the land, behold d.
25. 4. thou hast been a strength to the needy in d.
53. † 8. he was taken away by d. and judgment
Lam. 1. 20. behold, O Lord, for I am in d.
Obad. 12. nor shouldest spoken proudly in day of d.
14. nor shouldest delivered up those in day of d.
Zeph. 1. 15. that day is a day of trouble and d.
17. I will bring d. upon men, they shall walk
Luke 21. 23. there shall be great d. in the land
25. on the earth d. of nations, with perplexity
Rom. 8. 35. shall d. separate us from love of Christ?
1 Cor. 7. 26. that this is good for the present d.
1 Thess. 3. 7. we were comforted over you in our d.

DISTRESS, ED.
Gen. 32. 7. then Jacob was greatly afraid and d.
Num. 22. 3. Moab was d. || Judg. 2. 15. Isr. d. 10. 9.
Deut. 2. 9. d. not the Moabites || 19. Ammonites
28. 53. wherewith enemies shall d. thee, 55, 57.
1 Sam. 13. 6. for people were d. did hide themselves
14. 24. men of Israel were d. || 28. 15. Saul was d.
30. 6. David was greatly d. for the people spake
2 Sam. 1. 26. I am d. for thee, my brother Jonathan
2 Chr. 28. 20. king of Assyria came and d. Ahaz
Isa. 29. 2. yet I will d. Ariel, there shall be sorrow
7. that d. her shall be as a dream of night vision
Jer. 10. 18. I will d. the inhabitants of the land
2 Cor. 4. 8. we are troubled on every side, yet not d.

DISTRESSES.
Psal. 25. 17. O bring thou me out of my d.
107. 6. and he delivered them out of their d.
13. and he saved them out of their d. 19.
28. and he bringeth them out of their d.
Ezek. 30. 16. and Noph shall have d. daily
2 Cor. 6. 4. approving ourselves in necessities, in d.
12. 10. I take pleasure in d. for Christ's sake

DISTRIBUTE.
Josh. 13. 32. which Moses did d. for inherit. in Moab
2 Chr. 31. 14. Kore to d. the oblations of the Lord
Neh. 13. 13. their office was to d. to their brethren
Luke 18. 22. sell all thou hast, and d. to the poor
Eph. 4. † 28. he may have to d. to him that needeth
1 Tim. 6. 18. charge the rich to be ready to d.

DISTRIBUTED.
Josh. 14. 1. Eleazar and Joshua d. for inheritance
1 Chr. 24. 3. David d. them, both Zadok and Ahimelech according to their offices, 2 Chr. 23. 18.
John 6. 11. Jesus gave thanks and d. to the disciples
1 Cor. 7. 17. but as God hath d. to every man
2 Cor. 10. 13. according to the rule G. hath d. to us

DISTRIBUTETH, ING.
Job 21. 17. God d. sorrows in his anger
Rom. 12. 13. d. to the necessity of the saints, given

DISTRIBUTION.
Acts 4. 35. d. was made to every one as he had need
2 Cor. 9. 13. for your liberal d. to them and all men
Heb. 2. † 4. God bearing witness, with d. of H. Ghost

DITCH.
1 Kings 21. † 23. the dogs eat Jezebel by d. of Jezreel
Job 9. 31. yet shalt thou plunge me in the d.
Psal. 7. 15. he is fallen into the d. which he made
Prov. 23. 27. a whore is a deep d. and strange woman
Isa. 22. 11. ye made a d. between the two walls

Dan. 9. † 25. and the *d.* even in troublous times
Mat. 15. 14. both shall fall into the *d.* *Luke* 6. 39.

DITCHES.

2 *Kings* 3. 16. thus saith L. make this valley full of *d.*

DIVERS.

Lev. 19. 19. nor let thy cattle gender with *d.* kinds
Deut. 22. 9. not sow thy vineyard with *d.* kinds
11. thou shalt not wear a garment of *d.* sorts
25. 13. thou shalt not have in thy bag *d.* weights
25. 14. in thy house *d.* measures, great and small
Judg. 5. 30. to Sisera a prey of *d.* colours, a prey of *d.* colours of needle work, on both sides
2 *Sam.* 13. 18. Tamar had a garm. of *d.* colours, 19.
1 *Chr.* 29. 2. prepared glistering stones of *d.* colours
2 *Chron.* 16. 14. they laid Asa in the bed which was filled with odours and *d.* kinds of spices
21. 4. Jehoram slew *d.* of the princes of Israel
30. 11. *d.* of Asher humbled themselves
Esth. 1. 7. the vessels being *d.* one from another
3. 8. their laws are *d.* from all people
Psal. 78. 45. he sent *d.* sorts of flies among them
105. 31. he spake, there came *d.* sorts of flies
Prov. 20. 10. *d.* weights and *d.* measures abomination
23. *d.* weights are an abomination to the Lord
Eccl. 5. 7. there are also *d.* vanities; but fear thou G.
Ezek. 16. 16. thou deckest high places with *d.* colours
17. 3. great eagle had *d.* colours, came to Lebanon
Dan. 7. 3. great beasts came up, *d.* one from another
7. a fourth beast *d.* from all the beasts, 19.
23. *d.* from all kingdoms ‖ 24. *d.* from the first
Mat. 4. 24. they brought to Jesus sick people taken with *d.* diseases, *Mark* 1. 34. *Luke* 4. 40.
24. 7. there shall be famines, pestilences, and earthquakes in *d.* places, *Mark* 13. 8. *Luke* 21. 11.
Mark 8. 3. for *d.* of them came from far
Acts 19. 9. for when *d.* were hardened, believed not
1 *Cor.* 12. 10. to another *d.* kinds of tongues
2 *Tim.* 3. 6. captive silly women led away with *d.* lusts
Tit. 3. 3. deceived, serving *d.* lusts and pleasures
Heb. 1. 1. who in *d.* manners spake in time past
2. 4. G. bearing witness with signs and *d.* miracles
9. 10. stood in *d.* washings ‖ 13. 9. *d.* doctrines
Jam. 1. 2. count it joy when fall into *d.* temptations

DIVERSITIES.

1 *Cor.* 12. 4. *d.* of gifts ‖ 6. *d.* of operations
28. God hath set in the church *d.* of tongues

DIVIDE.

Gen. 1. 6. and let the firmament *d.* the waters
14. be lights, to *d.* the day from the night, 18.
49. 27. and at night he shall *d.* the spoil
Exod. 14. 16. stretch thy hand over the sea, and *d.* it
21. 35. *d.* the money of it, *d.* the dead ox
26. 33. vail shall *d.* between holy and most holy
Lev. 1. 17. cleave it, but not *d.* it asunder, 5. 8.
11. 4. not eat of them that *d.* the hoof, 7. *Deut.* 14. 7.
Num. 31. 27. and *d.* the prey into two parts
33. 54. ye shall *d.* the land by lot, 34. 17, 18, 29.
Deut. 19. 3. *d.* the coasts of thy land into three parts
Josh. 1. 6. *d.* for an inheritance, 13. 6, 7. | 18. 5.
22. 8. *d.* the spoil of your enemies with brethren
2 *Sam.* 19. 29. I said, thou and Ziba *d.* the land
1 *Kings* 3. 25. *d.* the living child in two, 26.
Neh. 9. 11. and thou didst *d.* the sea, *Psal.* 74. 13.
22. and thou didst *d.* them into corners
Job 27. 17. the innocent shall *d.* the silver
Psal. 55. 9. destroy, O Lord, and *d.* their tongues
Prov. 16. 19. than to *d.* the spoil with the proud
Isa. 9. 3. as men rejoice when they *d.* the spoil
53. 12. he shall *d.* the spoil with the strong
Ezek. 5. 1. take the balances and *d.* the hair
45. 1. ye shall *d.* the land by lot, 47. 21, 22.
48. 29. this is the land which ye shall *d.*
Dan. 11. 39. and he shall *d.* the land for gain
Luke 12. 13. that he *d.* the inheritance with me
22. 17. take this, and *d.* it among yourselves

I will DIVIDE.

Gen. 49. 7. *I will d.* them in Jacob and scatter in Isr.
Exod. 15. 9. the enemy said, *I will d.* the spoil
Psal. 60. 6. *I will d.* Shechem, and mete out, 108. 7.
Isa. 53. 12. therefore *will I d.* him a portion

DIVIDED.

Gen. 1. 4. God *d.* the light ‖ 7. God *d.* the waters
10. 5. by these were the isles of the Gentiles *d.*
25. in his days was the earth *d.* 1 *Chron.* 1. 19.
32. by these were the nations *d.* after the flood
14. 15. and Abram *d.* himself against them
15. 10. Abram *d.* them in midst, the birds *d.* he not
32. 7. Jacob *d.* the people that was with him
33. 1. he *d.* the children to Leah and Rachel
Exod. 14. 21. the sea dry land, and waters were *d.*
Num. 26. 53. to these the land shall be *d.* for inherit.
56. by lot shall the possession of the land be *d.*
31. 42. which Moses *d.* from men that warred
Deut. 4. 19. which the Lord thy God hath *d.*
29. † 26. gods who had not *d.* to them any portion
32. 8. when the most High *d.* to the nations
Josh. 14. 5. they *d.* the land, 18. 10. | 19. 51. | 23. 4.
Judg. 5. 30. have they not *d.* the prey, to every man
7. 16. he *d.* the 300 men into three companies
9. 43. Abimelech *d.* them into three companies
19. 29. Levite *d.* her with her bones into 12 pieces
2 *Sam.* 1. 23. and in their death they were not *d.*
1 *Kings* 16. 21. then were the people of Israel *d.*
18. 6. Ahab and Obadiah *d.* the land between them
2 *Kings* 2. 8. the waters were *d.* hither and thither
1 *Chr.* 23. 6. Dav. *d.* them into courses among Lev.
24. 4. chief men, thus were they *d.* by lot, 5.
2 *Chron.* 35. 13. they *d.* other offerings speedily
Job 38. 25. who hath *d.* a water-course for waters?
Psal. 68. 12. she that tarried at home *d.* the spoil
78. 13. he *d.* the sea, and caused them to pass
55. *d.* them an inheritance by line, *Acts* 13. 19.
136. 13. to him which *d.* the red Sea into parts
Isa. 33. 23. then is the prey of a great spoil *d.*
34. 17. his hand hath *d.* it to them by line
51. 15. I am the Lord thy God that *d.* the sea
Lam. 4. 16. the anger of the Lord hath *d.* them
Ezek. 1. † 11. their wings were *d.* above
37. 22. nor shall they be *d.* into two kingdoms
Dan. 2. 41. kingdom shall be *d.* but strength of iron
5. 28. thy kingdom is *d.* and given to the Medes
11. 4. his kingdom shall be *d.* toward the four winds

Hos. 10. 2. their heart is *d.* now shall be found faulty
Amos 1. † 13. because they *d.* the mountains
7. 17. thy land shall be *d.* by line shalt die
Mic. 2. 4. turning away, he hath *d.* our fields
Zech. 14. 1. thy spoil shall be *d.* in the midst
Mat. 12. 25. every kingdom or house *d.* against itself shall not stand, *Mark* 3. 24, 25. *Luke* 11. 17.
26. he is *d.* ag. himself, *Mark* 3. 26. *Luke* 11. 18.
Mark 6. 41. the two fishes *d.* he among them
Luke 12. 52. there shall be five in one house *d.*
53. the father shall be *d.* against the son, and son
15. 12. and he *d.* unto them his living
Acts 14. 4. the multitude of the city was *d.* 23. 7.
1 *Cor.* 1. 13. is Christ *d.*? was Paul crucified for you?
Rev. 16. 19. the great city was *d.* into three parts

DIVIDER.

Luke 12. 14. he said, man, who made me a *d.* over [you?

DIVIDETH.

Lev. 11. 4. cheweth the cud, but *d.* not the hoof, 5, 6.
26. the carcases of every beast which *d.* the hoof
Deut. 14. 8. the swine, because it *d.* the hoof
Job 26. 12. he *d.* the sea with his power
Psal. 29. 7. the voice of the Lord *d.* the flames
Jer. 31. 35. which *d.* the sea when the waves roar
Mat. 25. 32. as a shepherd *d.* his sheep from the goats
Luke 11. 22. taketh his armour, and *d.* his spoils

DIVIDING.

Josh. 19. 49. they had made an end of *d.* the land
51. so they made an end of *d.* the country
Isa. 63. 12. led them *d.* the water before them
Dan. 7. 25. until a time, and times, and a *d.* of time
1 *Cor.* 12. 11. *d.* to every man severally as he will
2 *Tim.* 2. 15. a workman rightly *d.* the word of truth
Heb. 4. 12. piercing to the *d.* asunder of the joints

DIVINATION.

The eastern people, and particularly the Israelites, *were always very fond of* divinations, *magic, and the curious arts of interpreting dreams, and inquiring by unlawful methods into the knowledge of what was to come: this was a consequence of their timorous and superstitious genius. When* Moses *published the law of God, this evil was and had been for some time very common in* Egypt, *and the neighbouring countries; and to cure the* Israelites *of their inclination to consult diviners, fortune-tellers, augurs, and interpreters of dreams, &c. he promised them from God that the Spirit of prophecy should not depart from among them; and forbade them, under very severe penalties, to consult diviners, astrologers, and other persons of this kind. He commanded them to be stoned, who pretended to have a familiar spirit, or the spirit of* divination, *Lev.* 20. 27. *And in* Deut. 18. 9, 10, 11, 15. *he says,* When thou art come into the land which the Lord thy God giveth thee, thou shalt not learn to do after the abominations of those nations. There shall not be found among you any one that maketh his son or his daughter to pass through the fire, or that useth *divination,* or an observer of times, or an enchanter, or a witch: Or a charmer, or a consulter with familiar spirits, or a wizard, or a necromancer. God will raise up unto thee a *Prophet,* from the midst of thee, of thy brethren, like unto me; unto him ye shall hearken. *The writings of the prophets are full of invectives against the* Israelites, *who consulted diviners, and against the false prophets, who set up to foretell things future, and by this means seduced the people,* Jer. 14. 14. Ezek. 13. 6, 7.

There were several sorts of divinations, *namely, by water, fire, earth, air; by the flight of birds, and their singing; by lots, by dreams, by the staff, or wand, by the entrails of victims, and by cups. The heathens used many divinations, being excited thereto by distrust of God, and the temptations of the devil, who had a great hand in many of their answers,* Acts 16. 16.

Joseph's *cup, mentioned in* Gen. 44. 5. *which was concealed in* Benjamin's *sack, the younger brother of this patriarch, is the subject of many different conjectures, founded on the words of* Joseph's *officer,* Is not this the cup in which my lord drinketh, and whereby he divineth? *Some question whether* Joseph *did indeed make use of this cup in foretelling what was to come: whether his people believed so, or whether this was said by them, according to the common opinion of the* Egyptians, *who held* Joseph *for a great magician; or whether they said so to intimidate* Joseph's *brethren, making them believe, that* Joseph, *whom as yet they knew not to be their brother, was a man very expert in the art of divining, and had discovered the theft which they had committed, by virtue of this art.*

All these several opinions have their defenders. It is certain, that the ancients had a sort of divination by cups. The eastern people say, that old king Giamschid, *who is the* Solomon *of the* Persians, *and* Alexander *the Great, had cups, by means whereof they knew things natural, and sometimes even supernatural. The ancients speak of certain divining cups full of wine, or other liquors, which were poured out with ceremony from the side where the handle was, and that from thence they drew presages of what was to come.* Pliny *speaks of divinations with water and basins, in lib.* xxx. *cap.* 2. *The manner of divining by the goblet was this: Little plates of gold, or silver, or some precious stones, with certain characters engraved upon them, were thrown into it; and after some invocations, and superstitious ceremonies, the demon was consulted. He answered in several ways; sometimes by articulate sounds; sometimes he made the characters in the goblet appear upon the superficies of the water, and formed his answer by the order in which they stood. Sometimes he traced the images of the person on whose account he was interrogated. At other times a ring was fastened to a thread, and held suspended over the water in the cup: the ring, by its different percussions, showed the several things which were inquired after.*

But as to Joseph, *it is not to be believed that he used his cup in divinations: he was too wise and religious to practise any thing so vain, and so contrary to religion, as* divinations, *of what nature soever they might be. He was certainly very skilful in the science of foretelling things to come; but this knowledge was not acquired; it was no curious and diabolical art, but some supernatural faculty which God had communicated to him, whereby he procured that high consideration he was in throughout* Egypt. *It is not incredible that the* Egyptians, *and perhaps some of his own people, might think him to be truly a magician, and might have spoken of him according to this prejudice; but it does not follow, that he used a cup in divining. The* Hebrew *text of* Genesis *will bear another construction,* Is not this the cup wherein my lord drinks, and searches for so carefully? *Or,* Is not this the cup wherein my lord drinks, and by which he has tried you? *He will try whether you are as acknowledging as you ought to be, for the particular favours he has shewn you. This cup will serve to give a proof of your ingratitude and infidelity.*

Divination by the wand *is taken notice of in* Ezek. 21. 21, 22. *and in* Hos. 4. 12. The king of *Babylon* stood at the parting of the way, to use divination; he made his arrows bright. *Either writing on these arrows the names of cities and countries, then putting them into a quiver, and mixing them, and thence drawing them out, and concluding according as the names were, which were on the arrows: Or, by shooting the arrows, and judging by their flight; or casting them up in the air, and divining by their fall. In the same passage,* divination by the entrails of victims *is taken notice of;* He consulted with images, he looked into the liver. *From the position and colour of the liver, they used to judge of future prosperous or unprosperous events.*

Num. 22. 7. with the rewards of *d.* in their hand
23. 23. neither is there any *d.* against Israel
Deut. 18. 10. or that useth *d.* 2 *Kings* 17. 17.
1 *Sam.* 15. † 23. rebellion is as the sin of *d.*
Prov. 16. † 10. *d.* is in the lips of the king
Jer. 14. 14. they prophesy unto you visions and *d.*
Ezek. 12. 24. nor flattering *d.* in Israel
13. 6. they have seen vanity, and lying *d.*
7. and have ye not spoken a lying *d.*?
21. 21. the king of Babylon stood to use *d.*
22. at his right hand was the *d.* for Jerusalem
23. it shall be to them as a false *d.* in their sight
Acts 16. 16. a damsel possessed with a spirit of *d.*

DIVINATIONS.

Ezek. 13. 23. ye shall see no more divine *d.*

DIVINE.

Gen. 44. 15. wot ye not that such a man as I can *d.*?
1 *Sam.* 28. 8. *d.* to me by the familiar spirit
Ezek. 13. 9. my hand on the prophets that *d.* lies
23. ye shall see no more vanity, or *d.* divinations
21. 29. whiles they *d.* a lie unto thee to bring thee
Mic. 3. 6. it shall be dark to you, that ye shall not *d.*
11. and the prophets thereof *d.* for money

DIVINE, *Adjective.*

Prov. 16. 10. a *d.* sentence is in the lips of the king
Heb. 9. 1. first covenant had ordinances of *d.* service
2 *Pet.* 1. 3. as his *d.* power hath given to us all things
4. that ye might be partakers of the *d.* nature

DIVINER, S.

Deut. 18. 14. for these nations hearkened to *d.*
Josh. 13. † 22. Balaam the *d.* did Israel slay
1 *Sam.* 6. 2. the Philistines called for the *d.*
Isa. 44. 25. that turneth, that maketh *d.* mad
Jer. 27. 9. therefore hearken not to your *d.*
29. 8. let not your prophets and *d.* deceive you
Mic. 3. 7. seers be ashamed, and the *d.* confounded
Zech. 10. 2. the *d.* have seen a lie, told false dreams

DIVINETH.

Gen. 44. 5. is not this it whereby indeed he *d.*?

DIVINING.

Ezek. 22. 28. seeing vanity, and *d.* lies to them
Mic. 3. † 6. it shall be dark unto you from *d.*

DIVISION.

Exod. 8. 23. I will put a *d.* between my people
1 *Chron.* 1. † 19. the name of Eber's son was Peleg, *d.*
2 *Chron.* 35. 5. according to the *d.* of the Levites
Cant. 2. † 17. as a hart on the mountains of *d.*
Luke 12. 51. I tell you, nay, but rather *d.*
John 7. 43. so there was a *d.* among the people, because of him, 9. 16. | 10. 19.
1 *Cor.* 12. † 25. there should be no *d.* in the body

DIVISIONS.

Josh. 11. 23. gave the land to Israel, according to their *d.* 12. 7. | 18. 10. 2 *Chron.* 35. 5, 12.
Judg. 5. 15. for the *d.* of Reuben, there were great thoughts of heart, 16.
1 *Sam.* 23. † 28. called the place the rock of *d.*
1 *Chron.* 23. † 6. David divided them into *d.*
24. 1. these are the *d.* of the sons of Aaron
26. 1. concerning the *d.* of the porters, 12, 19.
Ezra 6. 18. they set the priests in their *d.* *Neh.* 11. 36.
Rom. 16. 17. mark them which cause *d.* and offences
1 *Cor.* 1. 10. that there be no *d.* among you
3. 3. whereas there is among you strife and *d.*
11. 18. I hear that there be *d.* among you

DIVORCE

Is *the dissolution of marriage, or a separation of husband and wife.* Moses *tolerated* divorces: *His words on this subject are in* Deut. 24. 1, 2, 3, 4. When a man hath taken a wife and married her, and it come to pass that she find no favour in his eyes, because he hath found some uncleanness in her; then let him write her a bill of divorcement, &c. *Commentators are much divided concerning the sense of these words,* because he hath found some uncleanness, *or, as the* Hebrew *has it,* matter of nakedness, in her.

The school of Shammah, *who lived a little before our Saviour, taught, that a man could not lawfully be divorced from his wife, unless he had found her guilty of some action which was really infamous, and contrary to the rules of virtue.*

But the school of Hillel, *who was* Shammah's *disciple, taught, on the contrary, that the least reasons were sufficient to authorize a man to put away his wife; for example, if she did not dress his meat well, or if he found any other woman whom he liked better. He translated* Moses' *text thus:* If he hath found any thing in her, or an uncleanness. Akiba, *he affirmed, that it was sufficient cause for a man to put away his wife, if she were not agreeable to her husband. After this manner he explained the text of* Moses: If she find no favour in his eyes: *this was the first reason; the second was,* If he find any uncleanness in her. Josephus *and* Philo *shew sufficiently, that in their time the* Jews *believed* divorce *to be lawful upon very trivial causes. But nothing can justify such a procedure but adultery, whereby the marriage relation is radically dissolved,* Mat. 5. 32.

That the Pharisees *explained this toleration of* Moses *in the like extensive manner, may be gathered from the question they put to our Saviour,* Mat. 19. 3. Is it lawful for a man to put away his wife for every cause? *This they proposed to our Saviour, trying if they could get any thing from him to his prejudice. Had he answered in the affirmative, he had contradicted what he formerly delivered on this head,* Mat. 5. 32. *Had he denied, they would have accused him for contradicting the law of* Moses, *Deut.* 24. 1. *Our Saviour answered neither yea nor nay, but gave them a fair occasion to answer themselves, and tacitly charged them with ignorance and corruption of the law of God. He referred them to the first institution of marriage, in* Gen. 1. 27. | 2. 24. Have ye not read, that he who made them at the beginning, made them male and female? and said, For this cause shall a man leave father and mother, and shall cleave to his wife, and they twain shall be one flesh. Wherefore they are no more twain, but one flesh. What therefore God hath joined together, let no man put asunder. *From hence he leaves them to conclude, whether it was probable that* Moses, *whom they so reverenced, and who was so faithful in the house of God as a servant, did give them a liberty to put asunder those whom God had joined together. Or whether they had not put an interpretation upon the law of* Moses, *which it could not bear, in consistency with the law of God. Our Saviour adds,* that *Moses,* because of the hardness of your hearts, suffered you to put away your wives; but from the beginning it was not so; *that is,* Moses *gave you no positive command in the case: he could not make a law directly opposite to the law of God. But seeing your wicked and malicious disposition, that you would turn away your wives without any just and warrantable cause, and to restrain your extravagances of cruelty to your wives, or disorderly turning them off upon any occasion, he made a judicial, political, or civil law, whereby, upon reason of state, namely, to prevent a greater civil mischief, he did so far allow of it, as to exempt them that did it from any civil punishment; but still it was a transgression of the moral law, and so a sin against God. After which our Saviour determines on this question, according to the original law of God, and limits the permission of divorce to the single case of adultery:* And I say unto you, Whosoever shall put away his wife, *except it be for fornication,* and shall marry another, committeth adultery, and whoso marrieth her that is put away, doth commit adultery. *In the case of* adultery, *the marriage covenant being broken, the marriage bond is fundamentally dissolved, and it lies in the power of the party wronged to prosecute it to a formal dissolution, by* divorce; *and then the wronged party is at liberty to marry again.*

Jer. 3. 8. I had put her away, and given a bill of *d.*

DIVORCED.

Lev. 21. 14. high-priest shall not take a *d.* woman
22. 13. but if the priest's daughter be a widow or *d.*
Num. 30. 9. every vow of her that is *d.* shall stand
Mat. 5. 32. whosoever shall marry her that is *d.*

DIVORCEMENT.

Deut. 24. 1. then let him write her a bill of *d.* 3.
Isa. 50. 1. where is the bill of your mother's *d.?*
Mark 10. 4. Moses suffered to write a bill of *d.*
See WRITING.

DO.

Gen. 16. 6. Abram said, *do* to her as it pleaseth thee
18. 25. shall not the Judge of all the earth *do* right?
31. 16. now then what God hath said to thee, *do*
32. 12. thou saidst, I will surely *do* thee good
41. 25. G. hath shewed what he is about to *do*, 28.
Exod. 4. 15. and I will teach you what ye shall *do*
12. † 47. all the congregation shall *do* it
15. 26. if thou wilt *do* that which is right, and keep his statutes, *Deut.* 6. 18. | 12. 25. | 13. 18. | 21. 9.
18. 20. and shew them the work that they must *do*
19. 8. all that the Lord hath spoken we will *do*
20. 9. six days *do* all thy work, 23. 12. *Deut.* 5. 13.
29. 35. thus shalt thou *do* to Aaron and his sons
Lev. 18. 4. ye shall *do* my judgments, and keep my ordinances, 19. 37. | 20. 22. *Ezek.* 36. 27.
5. which if man *do*, *Neh.* 9. 29. *Ezek.* 20. 11, 13, 21.
25. 18. ye shall *do* my statutes and keep my judgments, 20. 8. | 22. 31. *Deut.* 17. 19. | 26. 16.
Num. 22. 20. word I say to thee, that shalt thou *do*
24. 14. what this people shall *do* to thy people
32. 25. thy servants will *do* as my lord commandeth
Deut. 5. † 1. that ye may learn, and keep to *do* them
7. 11. keep the commandments to *do* them, 11. 22.
17. 10. shalt *do* according to the sentence, 11.
19. 19. then shall ye *do* to him as he thought to *do*
20. 15. thus shalt thou *do* to all the cities
27. 26. all the words of this law to *do* them
30. 12. that we may hear it and *do* it, 13.
31. 4. the Lord shall *do* to them as he did to Sihon
32. 6. *do* ye thus requite the L. O foolish people
Josh. 6. 3. round the city, thus shalt thou *do* six days
Josh. 7. 9. and what wilt thou *do* to thy great name?
10. 25. thus shall the Lord *do* to your enemies
22. 24. what have ye to *do* with the God of Israel?
23. 6. to *do* all that is written in the book of the law of Moses, that ye turn not aside therefrom, 1 *Chron.* 16. 40. 2 *Chron.* 34. 21.
Judg. 7. 17. it shall be, that as I *do* so shall ye *do*
8. 3. what was I able to *do* in comparison of you?
10. 15. *do* to us whatsoever seemeth good to thee
18. 14. consider therefore what ye have to *do*
18. then said the priest unto them, what *do* ye?
Ruth 3. 4. he will tell thee what thou shalt *do*
1 *Sam.* 16. 3. I will shew thee what thou shalt *do*
22. 3. till I know what God will *do* for me
26. 25. thou shalt *do* great things, and still prevail
2 *Sam.* 3. 18. now then *do* it, the Lord hath spoken
15. 4. oh that I were judge, I would *do* him justice
26. here I am, let him *do* to me as seemeth good
21. † 4. it is not silver, we have to *do* with Saul
24. 12. that I may *do* it to thee, 1 *Chron.* 21. 10.
1 *Kings* 2. 6. *do* therefore according to thy wisdom
31. *do* as he hath said, and fall upon him
8. 32. then hear, and *do*, and judge thy servants
39. hear in heaven, forgive, and *do*, 2 *Chr.* 6. 23.
11. 33. *do* that is right in mine eyes, 38. | 14. 8.
18. 34. *do* it the second time, *do* it the third time
2 *Kings* 9. 18. what hast thou to *do* with peace? 19.
17. 34. to this day they *do* after the former manners
20. 9. the Lord will *do* as he hath spoken
1 *Chron.* 4. † 10. that thou wouldest *do* me from evil
17. 2. Nathan said, *do* all that is in thine heart
23. let thing be established and *do* as thou hast said
21. 8. *do* away the iniquity of thy servant
2 *Chron.* 9. 8. thee king, to *do* judgment and justice
19. 6. said to the judges, take heed what ye *do*
7. wherefore now take heed and *do* it
9. thus shall ye *do* in the fear of the Lord
20. 12. we have no might, nor know we what to *do*
25. 8. if thou wilt go, *do* it, be strong for battle
Ezra 4. 2. for we seek your God, as ye *do*
7. 10. to seek the law of the Lord, and *do* it
18. that *do* after the will of your God
Neh. 2. 12. what God hath put in my heart to *do*
5. 12. they should *do* according to this promise
9. 24. that they might *do* with them as they would
Job 7. 20. I have sinned, what shall I *do* to thee?
11. 8. it is high as heaven, what canst thou *do?*
13. 20. only *do* not two things unto me
Psal. 40. 8. I delight to *do* thy will, O my God
50. 16. what hast thou to *do* to declare my statutes
83. 9. *do* unto them as unto the Midianites
109. 21. but *do* thou for me, O God the Lord
119. † 112. I have inclined my heart to *do*
132. as thou usest to *do* to those that love thy name
143. 10. teach me to *do* thy will, thou art my God
Prov. 3. 27. it is in the power of thy hand to *do* it
Eccl. 9. 10. *do* it with thy might, there is no work
Isa. 10. 3. what will ye *do* in the day of visitation?
28. 21. that he may *do* his work, his strange work
45. 7. I the Lord *do* all these things
Jer. 2. 18. what hast thou to *do* in the way of Egypt? what hast thou to *do* in the way of Assyria?
4. 30. when thou art spoiled, what wilt thou *do?*
5. 31. and what will ye *do* in the end thereof?
7. 17. seest thou not what they *do* in cities of Jud.
11. 4. saying, obey my voice, and *do* them
15. what hath my beloved to *do* in mine house?
12. 5. how wilt thou *do* in the swelling of Jordan?
14. 7. O Lord, *do* thou it for thy name's sake
39. 12. *do* to him, even as he shall say to thee
42. 3. and may shew the thing that we may *do*
50. 15. as she hath done, *do* unto her, 29.
Lam. 1. 22. *do* unto them as thou hast done unto me
Ezek. 8. 6. son of man, seest thou what they *do?*
16. 5. no eye pitied thee, to *do* any of these to thee
18. 5. but if a man be just, and *do* that which is lawful and right, 21. | 33. 14, 19.
24. 22. and ye shall *do* as I have done, 24.
31. † 11. in doing he shall *do* unto him
36. 37. I will be inquired of to *do* it for them
Dan. 9. 19. O Lord, hearken and *do*, defer not
11. 3. he shall *do* according to his will, 16. 36.
39. thus shall he *do* in the most strong holds
Hos. 9. 5. what will ye *do* in the solemn day?
10. 3. what then should a king *do* to us?
Joel 3. 4. what have ye to *do* with me, O Tyre?
Amos 3. † 6. and shall not the Lord *do* somewhat
7. the Lord will *do* nothing, but he revealeth
Jonah 4. 9. I *do* well to be angry, even unto death
Mic. 6. 8. but to *do* justly, and to love mercy
Zech. 1. 21. then said I, what come these to *do?*
8. 16. these are the things that ye shall *do*
Mat. 5. 19. but whosoever shall *do* and teach them
47. brethren only, what *do* ye more than others?
8. 29. behold, they cried out, saying, what have we to *do* with thee? *Mark* 1. 24. *Luke* 4. 34.
12. 50. for whosoever shall *do* the will of my Father who is in heaven, *Mark* 3. 35.
20. 15. lawful to *do* what I will with mine own
32. what will ye that I shall *do* to you? *Mark* 10. 36.
21. 24. I will ask, if ye tell me, I will tell you by what authority I *do* these things, *Mark* 11. 29.
27. he said, neither tell I you by what authority I *do* these things, *Mark* 11. 33. *Luke* 20. 8.
40. when lord of vineyard cometh, what will he *do* to those husbandmen? *Mark* 12. 9. *Luke* 20. 15.
23. 5. all their works they *do* to be seen of men
27. 19. have nothing to *do* with that just man
Mark 7. 8. many other such like things, ye *do*, 13.
12. ye suffer him no more to *do* for father or mother
11. 28. who gave thee authority to *do* these things?
Luke 4. 23. what have heard done, *do* in thy country
6. 2. why *do* ye that which is not lawful to *do?*
11. they communed what they might *do* to Jesus
31. as ye would that men should *do* to you, *do* ye
8. 21. these who hear the word of God and *do* it
16. 4. I am resolved what to *do* when I am put out
17. 10. have done that which was our duty to *do*
19. 48. and could not find what they might *do*
23. 31. if they *do* these things in a green tree
34. forgive them, they know not what they *do*
John 2. 5. whatsoever he saith to you, *do* it
John 4. 34. my meat is to *do* will of him that sent me
5. 30. I can of mine own self *do* nothing
36. the works that I *do* bear witness of me
6. 6. for he himself knew what he would *do*
28. what shall we *do? Acts* 2. 37. | 16. 30.
7. 4. if thou *do* these things shew thyself to world
17. if any man will *do* his will, he shall know
8. 29. I *do* always those things that please him
39. ye would *do* the works of Abraham
9. 33. if he were not of God, he could *do* nothing
10. 25. the works that I *do* in my Father's name
11. 47. chief priests and Pharisees said, what *do* we?
13. 7. what I *do* thou knowest not now
15. that ye should *do* as I have done to you
17. if ye know these, happy are ye if ye *do* them
14. 12. the works that I *do* shall he *do* also
14. if ye ask any thing in my name, I will *do* it
15. 14. my friends, if ye *do* whatever I command you
21. these things will they *do* unto you, 16. 3.
17. 4. the work which thou gavest me to *do*
21. 21. Lord, and what shall this man *do?*
Acts 1. 1. of all that Jesus began to *do* and teach
4. 28. to *do* whatsoever thy counsel determined
9. 6. he said, Lord, what wilt thou have me to *do?*
10. 6. he shall tell thee what thou oughtest to *do*
14. 15. saying, sirs, why *do* ye these things?
15. 36. visit our brethren, and see how they *do*
16. 28. *do* thyself no harm, for we are all here
17. 7. these *do* contrary to the decrees of Cesar
Rom. 1. 32. not only *do* the same but have pleasure
2. 14. *do* by nature the things contained in the law
7. 15. for that which I *do* I allow not, what I would that *do* I not, but what I hate that *do* I
16. if I *do* that which I would not, I consent not
17. then it is no more I that *do* it, but sin, 20.
12. 8. that giveth, let him *do* it with simplicity
1 *Cor.* 7. 36. let him *do* what he will, he sinneth not
10. 31. whatsoever ye do, *do* all to the glory of G.
16. 10. he worketh the work of the Ld. as I also *do*
2 *Cor.* 8. 10. not only to *do*, but also to be forward
13. 7. that ye should *do* that which is honest
Gal. 2. 10. the same which I also was forward to *do*
14. not as *do* the Jews, to live as *do* the Jews
3. 10. written in the book of the law to *do* them
5. 21. they which *do* such things shall not inherit
Eph. 6. 9. masters, *do* the same things to servants
21. that ye may know my affairs, and how I *do*
Phil. 2. 13. God worketh both to will and to *do*
4. 9. the things ye have heard and seen in me, *do*
Col. 3. 17. whatsoever ye *do* in word or deed, *do* all in the name of the Lord Jesus, giving thanks
23. whatsoever ye *do*, *do* it heartily, as to the L.
1 *Thess.* 3. 12. in love, even as we *do* towards you
4. 10. indeed ye *do* it towards all the brethren
5. 6. therefore let us not sleep as *do* others
11. and edify one another, even as also ye *do*
24. faithful is he that calleth, who also will *do* it
2 *Thess.* 3. 4. that ye both *do* and will *do* the things
2 *Tim.* 4. 5. *do* the work of an evangelist, make proof
9. *do* thy diligence to come shortly to me, 21.
Philem. 21. knowing thou wilt *do* more than I say
Heb. 4. 13. to eyes of him with whom we have to *do*
10. 7. then said I, lo, I come to *do* thy will, O G. 9.
13. 6. I will not fear what man shall *do* to me
21. make you perfect in every work, to *do* his will
1 *Pet.* 4. 11. let him *do* it as of the ability God giveth
2 *Pet.* 1. 10. if ye *do* these, ye shall never fall
3. 16. wrest, as they *do* also other scriptures
1 *John* 1. 6. we lie, and *do* not the truth
3. 22. *do* those things that are pleasing in his sight
Rev. 2. 5. and repent, and *do* the first works

Can or canst DO.

Gen. 31. 43. what *can* I *do* to these my daughters
Deut. 3. 24. none *can do* according to thy works
1 *Sam.* 28. 2. shalt know what thy servant *can do*
Job 15. 3. speeches wherewith he *can do* no good
22. 17. and what *can* the Almighty *do* for them?
42. 2. I know that thou *canst do* every thing
Psal. 11. 3. found. destroyed, what *can* righteous *do?*
56. 4. I will not fear what flesh *can do* to me, 11.
118. 6. I will not fear what man *can do* to me
Eccl. 2. 12. what *can* man *do* that cometh after king?
Jer. 38. 5. that *can do* any thing against you
Mark 9. 22. if *canst do* any thing, have comp. on us
Luke 12. 4. after that have no more they *can do*
John 3. 2. for no man *can do* these miracles thou dost
5. 19. the Son *can do* nothing of himself, 30.
15. 5. for without me ye *can do* nothing
2 *Cor.* 13. 8. we *can do* nothing against the truth
Phil. 4. 13. I *can do* all things thro' Ch. strengthen. me
See DO COMMANDMENTS.

DO with *evil.*

Exod. 23. 2. thou shalt not follow a multitude to *do e.*
Lev. 5. 4. if a soul swear to *do evil* or good, or do good
Deut. 4. 25. shall *do evil* in the sight of the Lord
31. 29. because ye will *do evil* in sight of the Lord
1 *Sam.* 20. 13. if it please my father to *do* thee *evil*
2 *Sam.* 12. 9. why despised L. to *do evil* in his sight
2 *Kings* 8. 12. because I know the *evil* thou wilt *do*
17. 17. sold themselves to *do evil* in sight of Lord
21. 9. Manasseh seduced them to *do* more *evil*
Neh. 9. † 28. they returned to *do evil* before thee
Psal. 34. 16. the face of L. against them that *do evil*
37. 8. fret not thyself in any wise to *do evil*
Prov. 2. 14. who rejoice to *do evil*, and delight in
24. 8. he that deviseth to *do evil* shall be called
Eccl. 5. 1. for they consider not that they *do evil*
8. 11. the heart of men fully set in them to *do evil*
12. though a sinner *do evil* an hundred times
Isa. 1. 16. wash ye, make you clean, cease to *do evil*
41. 23. *do* good or *evil*, that we may be dismayed
Jer. 4. 22. my peo. are wise to *do evil*, but to do good
10. 5. be not afraid, for they cannot *do evil*
13. 23. then may ye that are accustomed to *do evil*
18. 10. if it *do evil* in my sight, that it obey not
Ezek. 6. 10. that I would *do* this *evil* unto them
Mic. 7. 3. that they may *do evil* with both hands
Zeph. 1. 12. say, Ld. not do good, nor will he *do evil*
Mark 3. 4. is it lawful to do good or *do evil? Luke* 6. 9.
Rom. 3. 8. that we say, let us *do evil* that good may
13. 4. but if thou *do* that which is *evil*, be afraid
2 *Cor.* 13. 7. now I pray to God that ye *do* no *evil*

1 Pet. 3. 12. face of Lord is against them that do evil
DO joined with good.
Gen. 19. 8. do ye to them as is good in your eyes
27. 46. Rebekah said, what g. shall my life do me?
Lev. 5. 4. if a soul swear, pronouncing to do good
Num. 10. 29. come with us, and we will do thee good
24. 13. to do either good or bad of my own mind
Deut. 1. 14. thing thou hast spoken is g. for us to do
8. 16. prove thee, to do thee good at the latter end
28. 63. the Lord rejoiced over you to do you good
30. 5. and he will do thee good, and multiply thee
Judg. 17. 13. now know I the Lord will do me good
19. 24. do with them what seemeth good to you
1 Sam. 1. 23. Elkanah said to Hannah, do what seemeth thee good, 14. 36, 40. 2 Sam. 19. 27, 37.
3. 18. Eli said, it is the Lord, let him do what seemeth him good, 2 Sam. 10. 12.
2 Kings 10. 5. do that which is good in thine eyes
1 Chron. 19. 13. let the L. do what is good in his sight
21. 23. lest the king do that which is good in his eyes
Neh. 5. 9. also I said, it is not good that ye do
Psal. 34. 14. do good, 37. 3, 27. | 51. 18. | 125. 4. Mat. 5. 44. Luke 6. 9, 35.
36. 3. he hath left off to be wise and to do good
Prov. 31. 12. she will do him good and not evil
Eccl. 3. 12. but for a man to do good in his life
Isa. 41. 23. yea do good or do evil, that we may be
Jer. 4. 22. but to do good they have no knowledge
10. 5. cannot do evil, nor is it in them to do good
13. 23. then may ye do good that are accustomed
26. 14. do with me as seemeth good and meet to you
29. 32. nor behold the good I will do for my people
32. 40. I will not turn away from them to do them g.
41. I will rejoice over them to do them good
33. 9. which shall hear all the good I do to them
Mic. 2. 7. do not my words do good to the upright
Zeph. 1. 12. that say, the Lord will not do good
Mark 3. 4. Jesus saith to them, is it lawful to do good on the sabbath-days, or to do evil? Luke 6. 9.
14. 7. the poor, when ye will, ye may do them good
Luke 6. 33. if ye do good to them that do good to you
Rom. 7. 19. for the good that I would, I do not
21. when I would do good evil is present with me
13. 3. do what is good, and thou shalt have praise
Gal. 6. 10. let us do good to all men, especially to them
1 Tim. 6. 18. charge the rich, that they do good
Heb. 13. 16. to do good and communicate, forget not
Jam. 4. 17. that knoweth to do good, and doth it not
1 Pet. 3. 11. let him eschew evil, and do good
Have I to DO.
2 Sam. 16. 10. what have I to do with you? 19. 22.
1 Kings 17. 18. what have I to do with thee? 2 Kings 3. 13. 2 Chron. 35. 21. Mark 5. 7. Luke 8. 28. John 2. 4.
Hos. 14. 8. what have I to do any more with idols?
1 Cor. 5. 12. what have I to do to judge them without
I shall, or I will DO; or will I, shall I DO.
Gen. 27. 37. what shall I do now to thee, my son?
47. 30. and he said, I will do as thou hast said
Exod. 3. 20. which I will do in the midst thereof
6. 1. thou shalt see what I will do to Pharaoh
17. 4. Moses cried, what shall I do to this people?
34. 10. I will do marvels, shall see work of the Lord, for it is a terrible thing that I will do with thee
Num. 14. 35. I will surely do it to this congregation
22. 17. I will do whatsoever thou sayest to me
33. 56. I shall do to you as I thought to do to them
Ruth 3. 5. she said, all thou sayest to me I will do
11. I will do to thee all that thou requirest
13. then will I do the part of a kinsman to thee
1 Sam. 3. 11. behold, I will do a thing in Israel
10. 2. sorroweth, saying, what shall I do for my son
20. 4. thy soul desireth, I will do it for thee
28. 15. mayest make known to me what I shall do
2 Sam. 12. 12. but I will do this thing before Israel
18. 4. what seemeth you best I will do, 19. 38.
21. 3. said to Gibeonites, what shall I do for you?
4. what you shall say, that will I do for you
1 Kings 5. 8. I will do all thy desire for timber of
20. 9. all thou didst send for at first, I will do
2 Kings 2. 9. Elijah said, ask what I shall do for thee
4. 2. Elisha said to her, what shall I do for thee?
Esth. 5. 8. I will do to-morrow as the king hath said
Job 7. 20. what shall I do to thee, O thou preserver
31. 14. what then shall I do when God riseth up
34. 32. if I have done iniquity, I will do no more
Prov. 24. 29. I will do so to him as he hath done
Isa. 5. 5. I will tell what I will do to my vineyard
42. 16. these things will I do, and not forsake them
43. 19. I will do a new thing, now it shall spring
46. 10. my counsel stand, I will do all my pleasure
11. I have purposed it, I will also do it
48. 11. even for mine own sake will I do it
Jer. 7. 14. therefore will I do unto this house called
9. 7. how shall I do for daughter of my people?
19. 12. thus will I do to this place, saith the Lord
25. 6. provoke me not, and I will do you no hurt
29. 32. the good that I will do for my people
51. 47. I will do judgment on the graven images
Ezek. 5. 9. I will do in thee what I have not done
7. 27. I will do unto them after their way
22. 14. I have spoken, and will do it, 24. 14. | 36. 36.
35. 11. I will even do according to thine anger
36. 11. I will do better to you than at the beginning
Hos. 6. 4. O Ephraim, what shall I do unto thee?
Amos 4. 12. thus will I do unto thee, O Israel
Mat. 19. 16. Master, what good thing shall I do?
27. 22. Pilate saith, what shall I do with Jesus?
Luke 12. 17. what shall I do, because I have no room
16. 3. what shall I do? 20. 13. Acts 22. 10.
John 14. 13. whatever ye shall ask, that will I do
14. if ye shall ask any thing in my name I w. do it
2 Cor. 11. 12. but what I do, that I will do
Philem. 14. without thy mind would I do nothing
See JUDGMENT.
Must DO.
Exod. 18. 20. shalt shew the work that they must do
Num. 23. 26. all the Lord speaketh, that I must do
Prov. 19. 19. if thou deliver, thou must do it again
Acts 16. 30. jailer said, what must I do to be saved?
DO joined with no, or not.
Gen. 18. 29. he said, I will not do it for forty's sake
Gen. 18. 30. he said, I will not do if I find thirty there
19. 22. I cannot do any thing till thou come thither
34. 19. the young man deferred not to do the thing
Exod. 20. 10. is the sabbath of the Lord thy God, in it thou shalt not do any work, Lev. 23. 31.
21. 11. and if he do not these three unto her
23. 24. thou shalt not do after their works
Lev. 16. 29. ye shall afflict your souls and do no work, 23. 3, 28. Deut. 15. 19. Jer. 17. 24.
18. 3. and after their doings ye shall not do
19. 15. do no unrighteousness in judgment, 35.
23. 7. ye shall do no servile work therein, 8, 21, 25, 35, 36. Num. 28. 18, 25, 26.
26. 14. but if ye will not do my commandments, 15.
Num. 8. 26. from age of fifty years shall do no service
23. 19. hath he said, and shall he not do it?
29. 7. ye shall not do any work, Deut. 5. 14. | 16. 8.
Deut. 12. 8. shall not do after all the things we do here
13. 11. shall do no more any such wickedness as this
17. 13. shall fear and do no more presumptuously
Judg. 6. 27. feared, that he could not do it by day
19. 23. my brethren, I pray you, do not this folly
24. but to this man do not so vile a thing
Ruth 3. 13. if he will not do the part of a kinsman
1 Sam. 26. 21. return, I will no more do thee harm
1 Kings 11. 12. in thy days I will not do it for David
2 Kings 7. 9. lepers said one to anoth. we do not well
17. 15. Lord charged they should not do like them
18. 12. and would not hear them, nor do them
Ezra 7. 26. whoso will not do the law of thy God
Job 13. 20. only do not two things unto me
34. 12. yea, surely God will not do wickedly
41. 8. remember the battle, do no more
Psal. 119. 3. they do no iniqui. they walk in his ways
Jer. 18. 6. O Isr. cannot I do with you as this potter?
22. 3. do no wrong, do no violence to the stranger
42. 5. the L. be a true witness, if we do not
Ezek. 5. 9. I will not do any more the like
23. 48. may be taught not to do after your lewdness
33. 31. hear thy words, but they will not do them
32. hear thy words, but they do them not
Zeph. 3. 5. the just Lord, he will not do iniquity
13. the remnant of Israel shall not do iniquity
Mat. 5. 46. do not even the publicans the same? 47.
6. 1. take heed ye do not your alms before men
2. when dost alms sound not a trumpet before thee
12. 2. do that which is not lawful to do on sabbath
19. 18. Jesus said, thou shalt do no murder
20. 13. he said, friend, I do thee no wrong
23. 3. do not after their works, they say and do not
Mark 6. 5. and he could there do no mighty work
Luke 6. 46. and do not the things which I say
John 6. 38. I came down not to do mine own will
10. 37. if I do not the works of my Father
Rom. 7. 15. for what I would, that do I not, 19.
8. 3. for what the law could not do, in that weak
Gal. 5. 17. ye cannot do the things that ye would
1 John 1. 6. we lie, and do not the truth
Rev. 19. 10. he said to me, see thou do it not, 22. 9.
Observe with DO.
Deut. 5. 32. ye shall observe to do as L. commanded you, 8. 1. | 11. 32. | 12. 1. | 24. 8. 2 Kings 17. 37.
6. 3. observe to do, 12. 32. | 28. 13, 15, 58. | 31. 12. | 32. 46.
25. if we observe to do these commandments
15. 5. to observe to do all these commandments
16. 12. and thou shalt observe and do these statutes
17. 10. shalt observe to do as they inform thee
Josh. 1. 7. that thou mayest observe to do all the law
2 Kings 21. 8. if they will observe to do according to
Neh. 10. 29. entered into an oath to observe and do
Ezek. 37. 24. they shall observe and do them
Mat. 23. 3. what they bid you, that observe and do
Will we DO. We will DO.
Exod. 19. 8. all the L. hath said we will do, 24. 3, 7.
Num. 10. 32. the same goodness will we do to thee
Deut. 5. 27. and we will hear it and do it
Josh. 1. 16. all that thou commandest us we will do
Judg. 20. 9. the thing which we will do to Gibeah
2 Kings 10. 5. we will do all that thou shalt bid us
Jer. 18. 12. we will every one do the imagination
42. 20. so declare unto us, and we will do it
44. 17. we will certainly do whatever proceedeth
Shall we DO. We shall DO.
Judg. 13. 8. teach us what we shall do to the child
12. how shall order, how shall we do unto him?
21. 7. how shall we do for wives for them? 16.
1 Sam. 5. 8. what shall we do with the ark of God?
6. 2. what shall we do to the ark of the Lord?
2 Sam. 16. 20. give couns. among you what we shall do
17. 6. shall we do after his saying? speak thou
2 Kings 6. 15. said, alas my master, how shall we do?
2 Chr. 25. 9. what shall we do for the 100 talents?
Esth. 1. 15. what shall we do to the queen Vashti?
Psal. 60. 12. thro' God we shall do valiantly, 108. 13.
Cant. 8. 8. what shall we do for our sister in the day?
Jonah 1. 11. they said, what shall we do to thee?
Luke 3. 10. people asked, what shall we do? 12. 14.
John 6. 28. what shall we do that we might work?
Acts 2. 37. men and brethren, what shall we do?
4. 16. saying, what shall we do to these men?
DO joined with so.
Gen. 18. 5. they said, so do as thou hast said
19. 7. I pray you, do not so wickedly, Judg. 19. 23.
44. 17. Joseph said, God forbid that I should do so
Exod. 8. 26. Moses said, it is not meet so to do
Lev. 4. 20. so shall he do, 16. 16. Num. 9. 14. | 15. 14.
8. 34. so the Lord hath commanded to do
Num. 14. 28. so will I do, 32. 31. Isa. 65. 8. Ezek. 35. 15.
15. 12. so shall he do to every one accord. to number
22. 30. was I ever wont to do so unto thee?
32. 23. if ye will not do so ye have sinned ag. L.
Deut. 3. 21. so shall the Lord do to all the kings
12. 4. ye shall not do so to the Lord your God, 31.
30. how did these nations serve their gods? so I do
18. 14. Lord thy G. hath not suffered thee so to do
22. 3. and so shalt thou do with his raiment
5. all that do so are abomination to Lord thy God
Judg. 7. 17. it shall be, that as I do, so shall ye do
11. 10. if we do not so according to thy words
14. 10. for so used the young men to do
19. 24. but to this man do not so vile a thing
Ruth 1. 17. the Lord do so to me, 1 Sam. 14. 44.
1 Sam. 3. 17. God do so to thee and more also
8. 8. have served other gods, so do they also to thee
20. 13. Lord do so and much more to Jonathan
25. 22. so and more also do G. to enemies of David
30. 23. David said, ye shall not do so, my brethren
2 Sam. 3. 9. so do God to Abner, even so I do to him
35. God do so to me, and more also, 19. 13
1 Kings 2. 23. | 20. 10. 2 Kings 6. 31
9. 11. then said Ziba, so shall thy servant do
1 Kings 1. 30. even so will I certainly do this day
2. 38. as the king hath said, so will thy servant do
19. 2. so let the gods do to me, and more also
22. 22. he said, go forth, and do so, 2 Chron. 18. 21
2 Kings 17. 41. as did their fathers, so do they to-day
1 Chr. 13. 4. all congregation said they would do so
Ezra 10. 12. as thou hast said, so must we do
Neh. 5. 12. they said, so will we do as thou sayest
6. 13. that I should be afraid, and do so, and sin
13. 21. if ye do so again, I will lay hands on you
Esth. 6. 10. and do even so to Mordecai the Jew
7. 5. who and where is he durst presume to do so?
Job 13. 9. as one man mocketh, do ye so mock him?
Prov. 20. 30. so do stripes the inward parts of belly
24. 29. say not, I will do so to him as he hath done
Isa. 10. 11. shall I so do to Jerusalem and her idols?
Jer. 28. 6. the Lord do so, the Lord perform words
Ezek. 45. 20. so thou shalt do seventh day of month
Dan. 11. 30. so shall he do, he shall even return
Hos. 10. 15. so shall Beth-el do to you, because of your
Mat. 5. 47. do not even the publicans so?
7. 12. men should do to you, do ye even so to them
18. 35. so shall my heavenly Father do unto you
John 14. 31. as Father gave commandment, so I do
Acts 7. 51. as your fathers did, so do ye
1 Cor. 16. 1. as I have given order, even so do ye
Col. 3. 13. even as Christ forgave you, so do ye
1 Tim. 1. 4. than edifying, which is in faith, so do
Jam. 2. 12. so do ye, as they that shall be judged
DO joined with this.
Gen. 11. 6. people is one, and this they begin to do
39. 9. can I do this great wicked. and sin ag. God
41. 34. let Pharaoh do this, let him appoint officers
42. 18. Joseph said, this do and live, I fear God
43. 11. if it must be so now, do this, 45. 17, 19.
Lev. 26. 16. I will do this to you, I will appoint terror
Num. 16. 6. this do, take you censers, Korah and all
Josh. 9. 20. this we will do to the Gibeonites
Judg. 19. 23. my brethren, I pray, do not this folly
2 Sam. 13. 12. my brother, do not thou this folly
23. 17. be it far from me that I should do this
2 Kings 19. 31. the zeal of L. shall do this, Isa. 37. 32.
2 Chron. 19. 10. this do, and ye shall not trespass
Ezra 4. 22. take heed that ye fail not to do this
Prov. 6. 3. do this now, my son, deliver thyself
Isa. 38. 19. the living praise thee, as I do this day
Jer. 32. 35. that they should do this abomination
Ezek. 6. 10. that I would do this evil to them
36. 22. I do not this for your sakes, O Israel, 32.
Amos 4. 12. and because I will do this to thee
Mal. 4. 3. in day that I shall do this, saith the Lord
Mat. 8. 9. to my servant, do th. he doeth it, Luke 7. 8.
9. 28. believe ye that I am able to do this?
21. 21. if ye have faith, ye shall not only do this
Mark 11. 3. if any say to you, why do ye this?
Luke 7. 4. he was worthy for whom he should do this
10. 28. he said to him, this do, and thou shalt live
12. 18. he said, this will I do, I will pull down
22. 19. this do in remembr. of me, 1 Cor. 11. 24, 25.
Acts 21. 23. do therefore this that we say to thee
1 Cor. 9. 17. for if I d. t. thing willingly, have reward
23. and this I do for the gospel's sake
Heb. 6. 3. and this will we do if God permit
13. 19. but I beseech you the rather to do this
Jam. 4. 15. if the Lord will, we will do this or that
See THIS, THING.
DO well.
Isa. 1. 17. learn to do well, seek judgment
Jonah 4. 9. I do well to be angry, even to death
Zech. 8. 15. to do well to Jerusalem and Judah
Mat. 12. 12. it is lawful to do well on sabbath-days
John 11. 12. Lord, if he sleep, he shall do well
Acts 15. 29. if ye keep yourselves, ye shall do well
Jam. 2. 8. if ye fulfil the royal law, ye do well
1 Pet. 2. 14. for the praise of them that do well
20. but if when ye do well and suffer for it
3. 6. whose daughters ye are as long as ye do well
2 Pet. 1. 19. whereto ye do well that ye take heed
3 John 6. whom if thou bring, thou shalt do well
DOER.
Gen. 39. 22. what they did there, he was the d. of it
2 Sam. 3. 39. the Lord shall reward the d. of evil
Psal. 31. 23. Ld. plentifully rewardeth the proud d.
Prov. 17. 4. a wicked d. giveth heed to false lips
Isa. 9. 17. for every one is an hypocrite and evil d.
2 Tim. 2. 9. wherein I suffer trouble as an evil d.
Jam. 1. 23. if any be a hearer, and not a d. of word
25. he being not a forgetful hearer, but a d.
4. 11. thou art not a d. of the law, but a judge
1 Pet. 4. 15. let none of you suffer as an evil d.
DOERS.
2 Kings 22. 5. let them give it to the d. of the work
Psal. 101. 8. that I may cut off all wicked d.
Rom. 2. 13. but the d. of the law shall be justified
Jam. 1. 22. be ye d. of the word, not hearers only
EVIL-DOER, DOERS; see EVIL.
DOST.
Gen. 4. 7. if thou d. well, and if thou d. not well
21. 22. God is with thee in all that thou d.
Exod. 18. 17. the thing that thou d. is not good
Deut. 12. 28. when thou d. which is good and right
15. 18. God shall bless thee in all that thou d.
2 Sam. 3. 25. Abner came to know all that thou d.
1 Kings 2. 3. that thou mayest prosper in all thou d.
19. 9. he said, what d. thou here, Elijah? 13.
20. 22. go, and mark, and see what thou d.
Job 9. 12. who will say to him, what d. thou?
35. 6. if thou sinnest, what d. thou against him?
Psal. 49. 18. praise thee, when thou d. well to thyself
77. 14. thou art the God that d. wonders
86. 10. for thou art great, and d. wondrous things
119. 68. thou art good, and d. good, teach me

Eccl. 8. 4. or say to him, what *d.* thou? *Dan.* 4. 35.
Jer. 11. 15. when thou *d.* evil, then thou rejoicest
15. 5. who shall go aside to ask how thou *d.*?
Ezek. 12. 9. the rebellious house said, what *d.* thou
16. 30. weak heart, seeing thou *d.* all these things
24. 19. tell what these are to us, that thou *d.* so
Jonah 4. 4. Lord said, *d.* thou well to be angry? 9.
Mat. 6. 2. therefore when thou *d.* thine alms, 3.
21. 23. the priests and elders said, by what authority *d.* thou these things? *Mark* 11. 28. *Luke* 20. 2.
John 2. 18. what sign seeing that thou *d.* these things?
3. 2. no man can do these miracles that thou *d.*
7. 3. that thy disciples may see the works thou *d.*
13. 27. Jesus said to him, that thou *d.* do quickly
Acts 22. 26. saying, take heed what thou *d.*
Rom. 2. 1. thou that judgest, *d.* the same things, 3.
Jam. 2. 19. thou believest on God, thou *d.* well
3 *John* 5. thou *d.* faithfully what thou *d.* to brethren

DOTH.

Gen. 31. 12. I have seen all that Laban *d.* to thee
Exod. 31. 14. for whosoever *d.* any work therein that soul shall be cut off, 15. *Lev.* 23. 30.
Lev. 6. 3. in any of all these that a man *d.* sinning
Num. 15. † 29. one law for him that *d.* thro' ignorance
24. 23. alas, who shall live when God *d.* this!
Job 5. 9. to God who *d.* great things and unsearchable, 9, 10. | 37. 5. *Psal.* 72. 18. | 136. 4.
23. 13. what his soul desireth, even that he *d.*
Psal. 1. 3. leaf not wither, whatsoever he *d.* prosper
14. 1. there is none *d.* good, 3. | 53. 1, 3. *Rom.* 3. 12.
15. 5. he that *d.* these things, shall never be moved
106. 3. blessed is he that *d.* righteous. at all times
118. 15. right hand of the Lord *d.* valiantly, 16.
Prov. 6. 32. he that *d.* it, destroyeth his own soul
11. 17. the merciful man *d.* good to his own soul
17. 22. a merry heart *d.* good like a medicine
Eccl. 2. 2. and I said of mirth, what *d.* it?
3. 14. whatsoever God *d.* it shall be for ever, and God *d.* it that men should fear before him
7. 20. there is not a man *d.* good and sinneth not
8. 3. for he *d.* whatsoever pleaseth him
Isa. 56. 2. blessed is the man *d.* this, and son of man
Ezek. 17. 15. shall he escape that *d.* such things?
18. 10. that *d.* the like to any one of these things
11. and that *d.* not any of those duties
27. and *d.* that which is lawful and right
Dan. 4. 35. *d.* accord. to will in heaven and earth
9. 14. for the Lord our God is righteous in all he *d.*
Amos 9. 12. are called, saith the Lord that *d.* this
Mal. 2. 12. Lord will cut off the man that *d.* this
Mat. 6. 3. let not left hand know what thy right *d.*
7. 21. but he that *d.* will of my Father in heaven
24. whoso heareth these sayings, and *d.* them
26. every one that heareth and *d.* not, *Luke* 6. 49.
8. 9. to my servant, do this, and he *d.* it, *Luke* 7. 8.
John 3. 20. every one that *d.* evil, hateth the light
21. but he that *d.* truth cometh to the light
5. 19. what things soever he *d.* these *d.* the Son
7. 51. before it hear him and know what he *d.*
9. 31. but if any man *d.* his will, him he heareth
15. 15. the servant knoweth not what his lord *d.*
16. 2. killeth you, will think he *d.* God service
Rom. 2. 9. anguish upon every soul of man that *d.* evil
10. 5. righteousness of law, that the man that *d.* these things shall live by them, *Gal.* 3. 12.
13. 4. to execute wrath upon him that *d.* evil
1 *Cor.* 6. 18. every sin a man *d.* is without the body
7. 37. decreed that he will keep his virgin, *d.* well
38. so then he that giveth her in marriage *d.* well
Gal. 3. 5. *d.* he it by works of the law, or by faith?
Eph. 6. 8. whatsoever good thing any man *d.*
Col. 1. 6. bringeth forth fruit, as it *d.* also in you
3. 25. but he that *d.* wrong, shall receive for wrong
1 *Thess.* 2. 11. exhorted as a father *d.* his children
Jam. 4. 17. that knoweth to do good, and *d.* it not
1 *John* 2. 17. he that *d.* will of God abideth for ever
29. that *d.* righteousness is born of him, 3. 7.
3 *John* 10. I will remember his deeds which he *d.*
11. but he that *d.* evil hath not seen God
Rev. 13. 13. and he *d.* great wonders, he maketh fire

DOCTOR.

Acts 5. 34. then stood up Gamaliel, a *d.* of the law

DOCTORS.

Luke 2. 46. they found Jesus sitting in midst of the *d.*
5. 17. there were Pharisees and *d.* of law sitting by

DOCTRINE

Signifies, [1] *Knowledge, or learning,* Isa. 28. 9. [2] *A tenet, or opinion,* Mat. 16. 12. [3] *The truths of the gospel in general,* Tit. 2. 10. [4] *Instruction, information, and confirmation, in the truths of the gospel,* 2 Tim. 3. 16. [5] *The manner of teaching, with the matter also,* Mat. 7. 28. [6] *The act of teaching,* Mark 4. 2. [7] *Divine institutions,* Mat. 15. 9.

The doctrine of *Balaam,* Rev. 2. 14. *The history of* Balaam *is recorded in* Numbers, *chapters* 22, 23, 24. *He was sent for by* Balak, *king of* Moab, *to come and curse* Israel; *and finding that God restrained him, and turned him from cursing to pronouncing blessings upon them, he instructed* Balak *at last, how to lay a stumbling-block before them, to make them to fall: He told* Balak *and the* Midianites, *that if they would secure themselves from the attempts that the* Hebrews *might make against them, and obtain some advantage over them, they should engage them in idolatry and whoredom; that then they would be forsaken by their God, and would become a prey to their enemies: the young women of* Moab *invited the* Israelites *to the feasts of* Baal-peor; *and after they had persuaded them to embrace idolatry, they seduced them to impurity. This doctrine is the same with what is called* the doctrine of the *Nicolaitans,* Rev. 2. 15. *This sect took their name from* Nicolas, *one of the seven first deacons, of whom mention is made in* Acts 6. 5. *He plunged himself into irregularities, as it is said, and gave beginning not only to this sect, but also to that of the* Gnostics, *and to several others, who, following the bent of their passions, invented many different sorts of crimes and wickednesses. Among these* Nicolaitans, *adulteries, and the use of meats offered to idols, were held as indifferent things.* St. Austin says, Hæres, 5. *that they have their women in common, and make no scruple to conform to all the pagan superstitions.*

Psal. 19. † 7. the *d.* of the Lord is perfect
Isa. 28. 9. whom shall he make to understand *d.*
† 19. it shall be a vexation to understand *d.*
29. 24. and they that murmured shall learn *d.*
53. † 1. to him who hath believed our *d.* or to whom arm
Jer. 10. 8. brutish, the stock is a *d.* of vanities
Mat. 7. 28. the people were astonished at his *d.* 22. 33. *Mark* 1. 22. | 11. 18. *Luke* 4. 32.
16. 12. beware of the *d.* of the Pharisees
Mark 1. 27. people amazed, saying, what new *d.*
4. 2. he taught and said to them in his *d.* 12. 38.
John 7. 17. if do his will, he shall know of the *d.*
18. 19. the high priest then asked Jesus of his *d.*
Acts 2. 42. they continued in the apostles' *d.*
5. 28. ye have filled Jerusalem with your *d.*
13. 12. being astonished at the *d.* of the Lord
17. 19. saying, may we know what this new *d.* is?
Rom. 6. 17. but ye have obeyed that form of *d.*
16. 17. contrary to the *d.* which ye have learned
1 *Cor.* 14. 6. except I shall speak to you by *d.*
26. every one of you hath a *d.* a tongue
Eph. 4. 14. carried about with every wind of *d.*
1 *Tim.* 1. 3. charge that they teach no other *d.*
4. 13. till I come, give attendance to reading, to *d.*
16. take heed to thyself, and to thy *d.*
5. 17. especially they who labour in the word and *d.*
6. 1. the name of G. and his *d.* be not blasphemed
3. and to the *d.* which is according to godliness
2 *Tim.* 3. 16. all scripture is profitable for *d.*
4. 2. rebuke, exhort, with all longsuffering and *d.*
Tit. 2. 7. in *d.* shewing incorruptness, gravity
10. that they may adorn the *d.* of G. our Saviour
Heb. 6. 1. leaving the principles of the *d.* of Christ
2. of the *d.* of baptisms, and of laying on of hands
2 *John* 9. whoso abideth not in the *d.* of Christ; he that abideth in *d.* of Christ hath Father and Son
Rev. 2. 14. thou hast them that hold *d.* of Balaam
15. that hold *d.* of the Nicolaitans, which I hate

Good DOCTRINE.

Prov. 4. 2. I give you *good d.* forsake not my law
1 *Tim.* 4. 6. nourished up in the words of *good d.*

My DOCTRINE.

Deut. 32. 2. *my d.* shall drop as the rain, my speech
Job 11. 4. *my d.* is pure, and I am clean in thine eyes
John 7. 16. *my d.* is not mine, but his that sent me
2 *Tim.* 3. 10. but thou hast fully known *my d.*

Sound DOCTRINE.

1 *Tim.* 1. 10. any thing that is contrary to *sound d.*
2 *Tim.* 4. 3. when they will not endure *sound d.*
Tit. 1. 9. by *sound d.* to exhort and convince
2. 1. but speak things which become *sound d.*

This DOCTRINE.

2 *John* 10. if there come any and bring not *this d.*
Rev. 2. 24. and to as many as have not *this d.*

DOCTRINES.

Mat. 15. 9. for *d.* the commandm. of men, *Mark* 7. 7.
Col. 2. 22. after the commandments and *d.* of men
1 *Tim.* 4. 1. from the faith, giving heed to *d.* of devils
Heb. 13. 9. be not carried about with strange *d.*

DOG

Is *a domestic animal well known. By the law it was declared unclean, and was very much despised among the* Jews: *the most offensive expression they could use, was to compare a man to a* dead dog. David *in order to make* Saul *sensible, that the unjust persecution which he carried on against him, did himself no honour, said to him,* After whom is the king of Israel come out? after whom dost thou pursue? after a *dead dog,* 1 Sam. 24. 14.

The name of dog *is sometimes put for one who has lost all modesty; for one who prostitutes himself by committing any abominable action, such as sodomy. In this manner several understand the injunction delivered by* Moses, *of not offering in the tabernacle of the Lord* the hire of a whore or the price of a dog, *Deut.* 23. 18. *And* Christ *excludes* dogs, sorcerers, whoremongers, murderers, *and* idolaters, *from the kingdom of heaven,* Rev. 22. 15. *The apostle* Paul *calls the false apostles* dogs, *by reason of their impudence and greedy love of sordid gain,* Phil. 3. 2. Solomon *and the apostle* Peter *compare sinners who continually relapse into their sins,* to dogs *returning to their vomit,* Prov. 26. 11. 2 Pet. 2. 22. Dog *or* dogs, *is put for,* [1] *The devil,* Psal. 22. 20. [2] *Persecutors,* Psal. 22. 16. [3] *False teachers,* Isa. 56. 11. Phil. 3. 2. [4] *Unholy men,* Mat. 7. 6. [5] *The Gentiles,* Mat. 15. 27.

Exod. 11. 7. but against Israel shall not a *d.* move
Deut. 23. 18. not bring price of a *d.* into house of L.
Judg. 7. 5. every one that lappeth as a *d.* lappeth
1 *Sam.* 17. 43. Philistine said to David, am I a *d.*?
24. 14. after whom dost thou pursue? after a *d.*?
2 *Sam.* 3. 8. then Abner said, am I a *dog's* head?
9. 8. thou shouldest look upon such a dead *d.* as I am
16. 9. why should this dead *d.* curse my lord?
2 *Kings* 8. 13. Hazael said, but what is thy serv. a *d.*
Psal. 22. 20. my darling from the power of the *d.*
59. 6. at evening they make a noise like a *d.* 14.
Prov. 26. 11. as a *d.* returneth to his vomit, so a fool returneth to his folly, 2 *Pet.* 2. 22.
17. is like one that taketh a *d.* by the ears
Eccl. 9. 4. a living *d.* is better than a dead lion
Isa. 66. 3. sacrificeth, as if he cut off a *dog's* neck

DOGS.

Exod. 22. 31. nor eat flesh torn of beasts, ye shall cast it to the *d.* *Mat.* 15. 26. *Mark* 7. 27.
1 *Kings* 14. 11. shall the *d.* eat, 16. 4. | 21. 24.
21. 19. thus saith the Lord, in the place where *d.* licked the blood of Naboth, shall *d.* lick thy blood
23. the *d.* shall eat Jezebel, 2 *Kings* 9. 10, 36.
22. 38. and the *d.* licked up Ahab's blood
Job 30. 1. disdained to have set with *d.* of my flock
Psal 22. 16. for *d.* have compassed me, they pierced
68. 23. and the tongue of thy *d.* in the same
Isa. 56. 10. they are all dumb *d.* ‖ 11. greedy *d.*
Jer. 15. 3. the sword to slay, and the *d.* to tear
Mat. 7. 6. give not that which is holy unto *d.*
15. 27. yet the *d.* eat of the crumbs, *Mark* 7. 28.
Luke 16. 21. the *d.* came and licked his sores
Phil. 3. 2. beware of *d.* beware of evil workers
Rev. 22. 15. for without are *d.* and sorcerers

DOING.

Gen. 31. 28. thou hast done foolishly in so *d.*
44. 5. is not this it? ye have done evil in so *d.*
Exod. 15. 11. like thee, fearful in praises, *d.* wonders
Num. 20. 19. I will only, without *d.* any thing else
Deut. 9. 18. because ye sinned in *d.* wickedly
1 *Kings* 16. 19. he sinned in *d.* evil, 2 *Kings* 21. 16.
22. 43. *d.* that which was right, 2 *Chron.* 20. 32.
1 *Chron.* 22. 16. arise, and be *d.* Lord be with thee
Neh. 6. 3. I am *d.* a great work, I cannot come down
Job 32. 22. in so *d.* my Maker would take me away
Psal. 64. 9. they shall wisely consider of his *d.*
66. 5. he is terrible in *d.* toward children of men
118. 23. this is the Lord's *d.* it is marvellous in our eyes, *Mat.* 21. 42. *Mark* 12. 11.
Isa. 56. 2. and keepeth his hand from *d.* any evil
58. 13. from *d.* thy pleasure on my holy day, and
Jer. 32. † 19. great in counsel, and mighty in *d.*
Ezek. 31. † 11. in *d.* he shall do unto him
Mat. 24. 46. his Lord shall find so *d.* *Luke* 12. 43.
Acts 10. 38. Jesus, who went about *d.* good
24. 20. if they have found any evil *d.* in me
Rom. 12. 20. for in so *d.* thou shalt heap coals of fire
2 *Cor.* 8. 11. now therefore perform the *d.* of it
Eph. 6. 6. as the servants of Christ, *d.* the will of God from the heart
1 *Tim.* 4. 16. in *d.* this thou shalt save thyself and them
5. 21. observe these things, *d.* nothing by partiality
Heb. 13. † 21. *d.* in you what is well-pleasing in sight
Jam. 1. † 25. this man shall be blessed in his *d.*

Well-DOING.

Rom. 2. 7. by patient continuance in *well-d.*
Gal. 6. 9. let us not be weary in *well-d.* 2 *Thess.* 3. 13.
1 *Pet.* 2. 15. with *well-d.* ye may put to silence
3. 17. for it is better that ye suffer for *well-d.*
4. 19. commit their souls unto him in *well-d.* as to

DOINGS.

Lev. 18. 3. after the *d.* of Egypt, and after the *d.* of Canaan, whither I bring you, shall ye not do
Deut. 28. 20. because of the wickedness of thy *d.*
Judg. 2. 19. they ceased not from their own *d.*
1 *Sam.* 25. 3. Nabal was churlish and evil in his *d.*
2 *Chron.* 17. 4. and walked not after the *d.* of Israel
Ps. 9. 11. declare among the people his *d.* *Isa.* 12. 4.
77. 12. I will meditate of thy works, talk of thy *d.*
Prov. 20. 11. even a child is known by his *d.*
Isa. 1. 16. wash ye, put away the evil of your *d.*
3. 8. because their tongue and *d.* are against the L.
10. for they shall eat the fruit of their *d.*
Jer. 4. 4. lest my fury come and burn, because of the evil of your *d.* 21. 12. | 26. 3. | 44. 22.
18. thy *d.* have procured these things to thee
7. 3. amend your ways and *d.* 5. | 26. 13. | 35. 15.
11. 18. then thou shewedst me their *d.*
17. 10. according to the fruit of his *d.* 21. 14.
18. 11. return, and make your ways and *d.* good
23. 2. I will visit upon you the evil of your *d.*
22. and from the evil of their *d.* 25. 5. *Zech.* 1. 4.
32. 19. to give according to the fruit of his *d.*
Ezek. 14. 22. ye shall see their way and their *d.*
20. 43. there shall ye remember your *d.* and your
44. nor accord. to your wicked ways, corrupt *d.*
21. 24. so that in all your *d.* your sins do appear
24. 14. according to thy *d.* shall they judge
36. 17. they defiled it by their own way and *d.*
19. and according to their *d.* I judged them
31. shall remember your *d.* that were not good
Hos. 4. 9. I will punish and reward them their *d.*
5. 4. they will not frame their *d.* to turn to their G.
7. 2. now their own *d.* have set them about
9. 15. for the wickedness of their *d.* I will drive
12. 2. according to his *d.* will he recompense
Mic. 2. 7. O house of Jacob, are these his *d.*?
3. 4. as they have behaved themselves ill in their *d.*
7. 13. land shall be desolate for the fruit of their *d.*
Zeph. 3. 7. but they rose early, corrupted all their *d.*
11. shalt thou not be ashamed for all thy *d.*?
Zech. 1. 6. according to our *d.* so hath dealt with us

DOLEFUL.

Isa. 13. 21. their houses full of *d.* creatures
Mic. 2. 4. in that day shall lament with a *d.* lamentat.

DOMINION

Signifies, [1] *Power,* Neh. 9. 28. Rom. 6. 9. [2] *Persons ruled over,* Psal. 114. 2. [3] *Kings and kingdoms,* Dan. 6. 26. | 7. 27. [4] *Angels,* Eph. 1. 21. Col. 1. 16. [5] *Magistrates,* 2 Pet. 2. † 10. Jude 8. [6] *The universal and unlimited authority and government of* God, Psal. 72. 8. | 145. 13. Dan. 4. 3, 22, 34. | 7. 14.

Gen. 1. 26. have *d.* over the fish of the sea, 28.
27. 40. and when thou shalt have the *d.* shalt break
37. 8. or shalt thou indeed have *d.* over us?
Num. 24. 19. out of Jacob come he that shall have *d.*
Judg. 5. 13. he made him have *d.* over the nobles
14. 4. at that time the Philistines had *d.* over Israel
1 *Kings* 4. 24. Solomon had *d.* over all the region
9. 19. to build in the land of his *d.* 2 *Chron.* 8. 6.
2 *Kings* 20. 13. there was nothing in his house or in all his *d.* that Hezekiah shewed not, *Isa.* 39. 2.
1 *Chron.* 4. 22. men of Chozeba who had *d.* in Moab
18. 3. as he went to stablish his *d.* by the river
2 *Chron.* 21. 8. the Edomites from under Judah's *d.*
32. † 9. Sennacherib and all his *d.* with him
Neh. 9. 28. so that they had the *d.* over them
37. also they have *d.* over our bodies and cattle
Job 25. 2. *d.* and fear are with him, he maketh peace
38. 33. canst thou set the *d.* thereof in the earth?
Psal. 8. 6. to have *d.* over the works of thy hands
19. 13. from sins, let them not have *d.* over me
49. 14. the upright shall have *d.* over them
72. 8. he shall have *d.* also from sea to sea
103. 22. bless the Lord in all places of his *d.*
114. 2. Judah was his sanctuary, and Israel his *d.*
119. 133. let not any iniquity have *d.* over me
145. 13. thy *d.* endureth through all generations
Isa. 26. 13. other lords besides thee had *d.* over us

Jer. 2. † 31. wherefore say my people, we have *d.?*
Dan. 4. 3. his *d.* is from generation to generation
22. thy *d.* reacheth to the end of the earth
34. most High, whose *d.* is an everlasting *d.* 7. 14.
6. 26. that in every *d.* of my kingdom men tremble
and fear before the God of Daniel, and his
d. shall be even unto the end
7. 6. the beast had four heads, and *d.* was given to it
12. the rest of the beasts had their *d.* taken away
14. there was given him *d.* and glory, a kingdom
26. they shall take away his *d.* to consume it
27. the *d.* shall be given to the saints of most High
11. 3. a mighty king that shall rule with great *d.* 5.
4. not according to his *d.* which he ruled
Mic. 4. 8. to thee shall it come even the first *d.*
Zech. 9. 10. his *d.* shall be from sea to sea
Mat. 20. 25. the princes of the Gentiles exercise *d.*
Rom. 6. 9. raised, death hath no more *d.* over him
14. for sin shall not have *d.* over you, under grace
7. 1. law hath *d.* over a man as long as he liveth
2 *Cor.* 1. 24 not that we have *d.* over your faith
Eph. 1. 21. above all power, might, and *d.* every name
1 *Pet.* 4. 11. that God may be glorified, to whom be
praise and *d.* for ever and ever, 5. 11. *Rev.* 1. 6.
2 *Pet.* 2. † 10. but them that despise *d.* *Jude* 8.
Jude 25. to the only wise God be *d.* and power

DOMINIONS.

Dan. 7. 27. and all *d.* shall serve and obey him
Col. 1. 16. whether they be thrones, or *d.* or powers

DONE.

Gen. 9. 24. Noah knew what his younger son had *d.*
18. 21. they have *d.* according to the cry of it
24. 66. the servant told Isaac all that he had *d.*
26. 29. as we have *d.* to thee nothing but good
29. 26. Laban said, it must not be *d.* in our country
34. 7. wrought folly, which ought not to be *d.*
44. 5. ye have *d.* evil in so doing
15. Joseph said, what deed is this ye have *d.?*
Exod. 1. 18. he said, why have ye *d.* this thing?
2. 4. his sister stood to wit, what would be *d.* to him
12. 16. no manner of work shall be *d.* in them,
save what must be eat, that only may be *d.* of you
13. 8. this is *d.* because of that the Lord did to me
18. 1. Jethro heard of all that God had *d.* for Moses
9. the goodness which the Lord had *d.* to Israel
21. 31. according to this judgment shall it be *d.*
31. 15. six days may work be *d.* 35. 2. *Lev.* 23. 3.
39. 43. they had *d.* it as the Lord had commanded,
even so had they *d.* it, and Moses blessed them
Lev. 5. 17. and commit things forbidden to be *d.*
8. 5. the Lord commanded to be *d.* *Deut.* 26. 14.
11. 32. what vessel it be, wherein any work is *d.*
18. 27. these abominations have the men of land *d.*
24. 20. eye for eye, so shall it be *d.* to him again
Num. 5. 7. they shall confess their sin they have *d.*
12. 11. wherein we have *d.* foolishly and sinned
15. 34. it was not declared what should be *d.* to him
22. 2. Balak saw all that Israel had *d.* to Amorites
27. 4. why should name of our father be *d.* away?
32. 13. all that had *d.* evil in sight of L. were cons.
Deut. 10. 21. he is thy God that hath *d.* for thee
25. 9. so shall it be *d.* to that man will not build up
29. 24. nations say, wherefore hath the Ld. *d.* thus
to this land? 1 *Kings* 9. 8. 2 *Chron.* 7. 21.
Josh. 10. 32. as he had *d.* also to Libnah, 39.
35. he had *d.* to Lachish ‖ 37. he had *d.* to Eglon
22. 24. if we have not rather *d.* it for fear of this
24. 31. had known all that he had *d.* for Israel
Judg. 2. 10. who knew not works he had *d.* for Israel
3. 12. because they had *d.* evil in sight of the Lord
9. 16. if ye have *d.* truly and sincerely, and have *d.*
to Jerubbaal according to deserving of his hands
24. cruelty *d.* to the seventy sons of Jerubbaal
19. 30. there was no such deed *d.* nor seen
Ruth 3. 16. told her all that the man had *d.* to her
1 *Sam.* 4. 16. and he said, what is there *d.* my son?
11. 7. cometh not forth, so shall it be *d.* to his oxen
17. 26. what shall be *d.* to the man that killeth him?
27. so shall it be *d.* to the man that killeth him
25. 30. when the Lord shall have *d.* to my lord
28. 17. the Lord hath *d.* as he spake, *Ezek.* 12. 28.
2 *Sam.* 11. 27. thing David had *d.* displeased the L.
13. 12. no such thing ought to be *d.* in Israel
24. 17. what have they *d.?* 1 *Chron.* 21. 17.
1 *Kings* 8. 66. goodness the Lord hath *d.* for David
14. 22. above all that their fathers had *d.*
19. 1. Ahab told Jezebel all that Elijah had *d.*
22. 53. provoked the Lord according to all that his
father had *d.* 2 *Kings* 15. 3, 9, 34. | 23. 32.
2 *Kings* 4. 13. he said, what is to be *d.* for thee?
8. 4. tell me all the great things Elisha hath *d.*
10. 10. for the Lord hath *d.* that which he spake
by his servant Elijah, *Isa.* 38. 15. *Jer.* 40. 3.
19. 11. thou hast heard what the kings of Assyria
have *d.* to all lands, 2 *Chron.* 32. 13. *Isa.* 37. 11.
21. 15. because they have *d.* evil, 2 *Chron.* 29. 6.
23. 19. all the acts that he had *d.* in Bethel
2 *Chron* 24. 16. because he had *d.* good in Israel
29. 36. rejoiced, for the thing was *d.* suddenly
32. 25. rendered not according to benefit *d.* to him
31. who sent to inquire of the wonder that was *d.*
Ezra 6. 12. made a decree, let it be *d.* with speed
9. 1. when these things were *d.* the princes came
Neh. 6. 8. there are no such things *d.* as thou sayest
9. 33. we have *d.* wickedly, *Ps.* 106. 6. *Dan.* 9. 5, 15.
Esth. 2. 1. he rememb. Vashti, and what she had *d.*
4. 1. Mordecai perceived all was *d.* rent his clothes
6. 6. the king said, what shall be *d.* to the man?
9. thus shall it be *d.* to the man the king honours
Job 21. 31. who shall repay him what he hath *d.?*
34. 29. whether it be *d.* ag. a nation or a man only
Psal. 33. 9. he spake and it was *d.* he commanded
71. 19. he hath *d.* great things, 106. 21. | 126. 2, 3.
120. 3. what shall be *d.* to thee, false tongue?
Prov. 3. 30. strive not if he have *d.* thee no harm
4. 16. they sleep not, except they have *d.* mischief
Eccl. 1. 9. that which is *d.* is that which shall be *d.*
14. have seen the works are *d.* under sun, 4. 1, 3.
2. 12. even that which hath been already *d.*
Isa. 3. † 11. the reward of his hands shall be *d.* to him
41. 4. who hath wrought and *d.* it? I the Lord
44. 23. sing, O heavens, for the Lord hath *d.* it

Isa. 48. 5. lest thou shouldest say, my idol hath *d.*
them
Jer. 3. 6. hast seen what backsliding Israel hath *d.*
5. 13. prophets wind, thus shall it be *d.* unto them
7. 13. because ye have *d.* all these works, saith L.
30. for children of Judah have *d.* evil in my sight
31. 15. were turned, and had *d.* right in my sight
35. 10. have *d.* all that Jonadab commanded, 18.
38. 9. these men have *d.* evil to Jeremiah prophet
44. 17. as we have *d.* we and our fathers, kings
48. 19. ask him that fleeth, and say, what is *d.*
50. 15. vengeance as she hath *d.* do unto her, 29.
51. 35. the violence *d.* to me and to my flesh
Lam. 2. 17. Lord hath *d.* that which he had devised
Ezek. 23. 39. thus have they *d.* in midst of my house
39. 8. it is come, it is *d.* saith the Lord God
43. 11. if they be ashamed of all that they have *d.*
44. 14. and for all that shall be *d.* therein
Dan. 11. 36. for that that is determined shall be *d.*
Zeph. 3. 4. the priests have *d.* violence to the law
Mat. 6. 10. thy will be *d.* 26. 42. *Luke* 11. 2. | 22. 42.
8. 13. as thou hast believed, so be it *d.* to thee
11. 21. if the mighty works which were *d.* in you
had been *d.* in Tyre and Sidon, *Luke* 10. 13.
18. 19. any thing they ask, it shall be *d.* for them
31. when his fellow-servants saw what was *d.*
21. 21. be thou cast into the sea, it shall be *d.*
23. 23. these ought ye to have *d.* *Luke* 11. 42.
25. 21. well *d.* good and faithful servant, 23.
40. inasmuch as ye have *d.* it to one of the least of
these my brethren, ye have *d.* it to me
27. 54. saw those things that were *d.* 28. 11.
Mark 5. 14. went out to see what was *d.* *Luke* 8. 35.
19. go home to thy friends, tell what great things
the Lord hath *d.* for thee, 20. *Luke* 8. 39.
33. the woman knowing what was *d.* in her
6. 30. they told him what they had *d.* and taught
9. 13. they have *d.* to him whatsoever they listed
13. 30. shall not pass till all these things be *d.*
15. 8. desire him to do, as he had ever *d.* to them
Luke 1. 49. he that is mighty hath *d.* great things
3. 19. being reproved for the evils Herod had *d.*
8. 56. he charged them to tell no man what was *d.*
9. 10. the apostles told him all that they had *d.*
14. 22. Lord, it is *d.* as thou hast commanded
17. 10. ye, when ye shall have *d.* all those things,
we have *d.* that which was our duty to do
23. 31. if in a green tree, what shall be *d.* in dry?
47. now when the centurion saw what was *d.*
24. 21. the third day since these things were *d.*
John 5. 29. they that have *d.* good to resurrection of
life; they that have *d.* evil, to damnation
15. 7. ask what ye will, and it shall be *d.* unto you
19. 36. these things were *d.* that the Scripture be
Acts 2. 43. many signs were *d.* by the apostles
4. 9. of the good deed *d.* to the impotent man
16. a notable miracle hath been *d.* by them
21. all men glorified God for that which was *d.*
28. what thy counsel determined before to be *d.*
5. 7. his wife, not knowing what was *d.* came in
12. 9. he wist not that it was true which was *d.*
14. 27. they rehearsed all that God had *d.* 15. 4.
21. 14. saying, the will of the Lord be *d.*
33. the chief captain demanded what he had *d.*
Rom. 9. 11. neither having *d.* any good or evil
1 *Cor.* 9. 15. nor that it should be *d.* unto me
13. 10. that which is in part shall be *d.* away
14. 26. let all things be *d.* to edifying
40. be *d.* decently ‖ 16. 14. be *d.* with charity
2 *Cor.* 3. 7. which glory was to be *d.* away
14. Old Testament, which vail is *d.* away in Christ
5. 10. may receive the things *d.* in his body, according to that he hath *d.* whether good or bad
Eph. 5. 12. things which are *d.* of them in secret
6. 13. able to withstand, and having *d.* all to stand
Phil. 2. 3. let nothing be *d.* thro' strife or vain-glory
4. 14. ye have well *d.* that ye did communicate
Col. 4. 9. will make known all things that are *d.*
Tit. 3. 5. not by works of righteousness we have *d.*
Heb. 10. 29. and hath *d.* despite to the Spirit of grace
Rev. 16. 17. came a voice, saying, it is *d.* 21. 6.
22. 6. to shew the things which must shortly be *d.*

Have I DONE.

Gen. 20. 5. in innocency of my hands *have I d.* this
40. 15. and here also *have I d.* nothing to put me
Num. 22. 28. what *have I d?* 1 *Kings* 19. 20. *Mic.* 6. 3.
Josh. 7. 20. I have sinned, thus and thus *have I d.*
Judg. 8. 2. he said, what *h. I* now *d.?* 1 *Sam.* 17. 29.
1 *Sam.* 20. 1. what *have I d.?* 26. 18. | 29. 8. *Jer.* 8. 6.
Ezek. 39. 24. accord. to their transgress. *h. I, d.* them
Acts 25. 10. to the Jews *have I d.* no wrong

He hath DONE, or, *hath he* DONE.

Exod. 5. 23. *he hath d.* evil to this people
Lev. 5. 16. make amends for the harm *he hath d.*
8. 34. as *he hath d.* so the Lord commanded to do
19. 21. atonement for his sin which *he hath d.*
24. 19. as *he hath d.* so shall it be done to him
Josh. 24. 20. consume you, after *he hath d.* you good
Judg. 15. 10. to do to him as *he hath d.* to us
1 *Sam.* 6. 9. then *he hath d.* us this great evil
12. 24. consider how great things *he hath d.* for you
20. 32. why shall he be slain? what *hath he d.?*
1 *Chron.* 16. 12. remember his marvellous works
that *he hath d.* *Psal.* 78. 4. | 98. 1. | 105. 5.
Psal. 66. 16. I will declare what *he hath d.* for soul
115. 3. our God *hath d.* whatsoever *he* pleased
Prov. 24. 29. I will do so to him as *he hath d.* to me
Isa. 12. 5. sing to L. for *he hath d.* excellent things
Ezek. 3. 20. righteousness which *he hath d.* 18. 24.
17. 18. *he hath d.* these things, he shall not escape
18. 13. *he hath d.* all these abominations
14. that seeth his father's sins which *he hath d.*
22. in righteousness that *he hath d.* he shall live
24. 24. according to all that *he hath d.* shall ye do
33. 16. *he hath d.* that which is lawful and right
Joel 2. 20. because *he hath d.* great things
Mat. 27. 23. and the governor said, why, what evil
hath he d.? *Mark* 15. 14. *Luke* 23. 22.
Mark 7. 37. saying, *he hath d.* all things well
Acts 9. 13. much evil *hath he d.* to thy saints
2 *Cor.* 5. 10. may receive according to that *he hath d.*
Col. 3. 25. receive for the wrong which *he hath d.*

I have DONE.

Gen. 8. 21. nor will I smite every thing as *I have d.*
21. 23. according to the kindness *I have d.* thee
27. 19. I am Esau, *I have d.* as thou badest me
28. 15. till *I have d.* that which I have spoken
30. 26. thou knowest my service *I have d.* thee
Exod. 10. 2. my signs which *I have d.* among them
Josh. 24. 7. your eyes have seen what *I have d.*
Judg. 1. 7. as *I have d.* so God hath requited me
9. † 48. what *I have d.* make haste, do as *I have d.*
15. 11. as they did to me, so *have I d.* to them
2 *Sam.* 14. 21. behold now *I have d.* this thing
24. 10. David said, I have sinned greatly in that
I have d. *I have d.* very foolishly, 1 *Chr.* 21. 8.
17. I have sinned, and *I have d.* wickedly
1 *Kings* 3. 12. behold, *I have d.* accord. to thy word
2 *Kings* 19. 25. hast thou not heard, how *I have d.* it?
Neh. 13. 14. that *I have d.* for the house of my God
Job 34. 32. if *I have d.* iniquity, I will do no more
Psal. 7. 3. O Lord, my God, if *I have d.* this
119. 121. *I have d.* judgment and justice, leave not
Prov. 30. 20. and saith, *I have d.* no wickedness
Isa. 10. 11. shall I not, as *I have d.* to Samaria, so do
13. by the strength of my hand *I have d.* it
33. 13. hear ye that are far off what *I have d.*
37. 26. hast thou not heard how *I have d.* it?
Jer. 42. 10. I repent of the evil *I have d.* to you
Ezek. 9. 11. *I have d.* as thou hast commanded me
12. 11. as *I have d.* so shall it be done to them
14. 23. ye shall know that *I have* not *d.* without
cause, all that *I have d.* in it, saith the Lord
24. 22. ye shall do as *I have d.* ye shall not cover
Dan. 6. 22. before thee, O king, *have I d.* no hurt
Zech. 7. 3. weep, as *I have d.* these so many years
John 7. 21. *I have d.* one work, and ye all marvel
13. 12. so after he had washed their feet, he said
to them, know ye what *I have d.* to you?
15. that ye should do as *I have d.* to you

Hast thou DONE.

Gen. 4. 10. he said, what *hast thou d.?* 31. 26. *Num.*
23. 11. 1 *Sam.* 13. 11. 2 *Sam.* 3. 24. *John* 18. 35.
20. 9. what *hast thou d.* to us? *Judg.* 15. 11.
2 *Sam.* 7. 21. according to thy heart *hast thou d.*
16. 10. who shall say, wherefore *hast thou d.* so?
1 *Kings* 1. 6. in saying, why *hast thou d.* so?
1 *Chr.* 17. 19. O Lord, *hast thou d.* all this greatness
Psal. 50. 21. these things *hast thou d.* I kept silence
Jonah 1. 10. the men said, why *hast thou d.* this?

Thou hast DONE.

Gen. 3. 13. what is this that *thou hast d.?* 12.
18. | 26. 10. | 29. 25. *Judg.* 8. † 1. | 15.
11. 2 *Sam.* 12. 21.
14. because *thou hast d.* this, 22. 16. 2 *Chr.* 25. 16.
20. 9. *thou hast d.* deeds which ought not to be done
27. 45. he forget that which *thou hast d.* to him
31. 28. *thou hast* now *d.* foolishly in so doing,
1 *Sam* 13. 13. 2 *Chron.* 16. 9.
Josh. 7. 19. tell me what *thou hast d.* 1 *Sam.* 14. 43.
Ruth 2. 11. it hath been shewed me all *thou hast d.*
1 *Sam.* 24. 19. for that *thou hast d.* to me this day
26. 16. the thing is not good that *thou hast d.*
1 *Kings* 14. 9. but *thou hast d.* evil above all bef. thee
2 *Kings* 2. † 10. he said, *thou hast d.* hard in asking
10. 30. because *thou hast d.* well in executing
23. 17. *thou hast d.* against the altar of Beth-el
Neh. 9. 33. for *thou hast d.* right, but we wickedly
Psal. 40. 5. thy wonderful works which *thou hast d.*
52. 9. I will praise thee, because *thou hast d.* it
109. 27. that they may know that *thou hast d.* it
Prov. 30. 32. if *thou hast d.* foolishly in lifting up
Isa. 25. 1. exalt thee, for *thou hast d.* wonder. works
Jer. 2. 23. see thy way, know what *thou hast d.*
3. 5. behold, *thou hast* spoken and *d.* evil things
Lam. 1. 21. they are glad that *thou hast d.* it
22. do unto them as *thou hast d.* unto me
2. 20. O Lord, consider to whom *thou hast d.* this
Ezek. 16. 48. Sodom hath not done as *thou hast d.*
51. in all thy abominations which *thou hast d.*
59. I will even deal with thee as *thou hast d.*
63. when I am pacified for all that *thou hast d.*
Obad. 15. as *thou hast d.* it shall be done to thee
Jonah 1. 14. O Lord, *thou hast d.* as it pleaseth thee
Acts 10. 33. *thou hast d.* well that thou art come

Not DONE.

Gen. 20. 9. hast done deeds that ought *not* to be *d.*
34. 7. which thing ought *not* to be *d.*
Exod. 34. 10. marvels, such as have *not* been *d.*
Lev. 4. 2. concern. things which ought *not* to be *d.* 13.
Num. 16. 28. I have *not d.* them of mine own mind
Deut. 32. 27. lest they say, Lord hath *not d.* all this
Judg. 16. † 11. ropes wherewith work *not* been *d.*
2 *Sam.* 17. † 23. Ahithophel saw his counsel *not d.*
2 *Kings* 5. 13. if proph. wouldest thou *not* have *d* it?
2 *Chron.* 30. 5. they had *not d.* it of a long time
Neh. 6. 9. weakened from the work, that it be *not d.*
8. 17. from the days of Joshua, Isr. had *not d.* so
Esth. 1. 16. Vashti had *not d.* wrong to the king only
Isa. 5. 4. what could been done, that I have *not d.*
46. 10. declaring the things that are *not* yet *d.*
Jer. 3. 16. neither shall that be *d.* any more
Ezek. 5. 9. I will do in thee that I have *not d.*
Dan. 9. 12. for under the whole heaven hath *not*
been *d.* as hath been done upon Jerusalem
11. 24. do that which his fathers have *not d.*
Amos 3. 6. shall evil be in city, and L. hath *not d.* it?
John 15. 24. if I had *not d.* among them the works
Acts 14. 18. scarce restrained they had *n. d.* sacrifice
26. 26. for this thing was *not d.* in a corner

DONE with *this.*

Gen. 21. 26. I wot not who hath *d. this* thing
42. 28. what is *this* that God hath *d.* to us?
44. 15. what deed is *this* that ye have *d.?*
Exod. 1. 18. why have ye *d. this* thing, and saved
13. 8. *this* is *d.* because of that which the Lord did
14. 5. and they said, why have we *d. this?*
Josh. 9. 24. we were sore afraid, and have *d. this?*
23. 8. but cleave to Lord, as ye have *d.* to *this* day
Judg. 2. 2. ye have not obeyed, why have ye *d. this?*
6. 29. they said, who hath *d. this* thing? 15. 6.
11. 37. she said, let *this* thing be *d.* for me
15. 7. though ye have *d. this,* yet will I be avenged
20. 12. what wickedness is *this* that is *d.* among you

1 *Sam.* 12. 20. ye have *d.* all *this* wickedness
28. 18. therefore hath the Lord *d. this* thing
2 *Sam.* 2. 6. because ye have *d. this* thing
12. 5. the man that hath *d. this* thing shall die
14. 20. hath thy servant Joab *d. this* thing?
21. king said, behold now, I have *d. this* thing
1 *Kings* 1. 27. is *this* thing *d.* by my Lord the king?
11. 11. Lord said, forasmuch as *this* is *d.* of thee
2 *Chron.* 11. 4. return, for *this* thing is *d.* of men
Psal. 7. 3. O Lord, my God, if I have *d. this*
22. 31. they shall declare that he hath *d. this*
51. 4. I have sinned, and *d. this* evil in thy sight
Isa. 41. 20. that the hand of the Lord hath *d. this*
Ezek. 23. 38. moreover, *this* they have *d.* unto me
Mal. 2. 13. *this* have ye *d.* again, covering the altar
Mat. 1. 22. now all *this* was *d.* 21. 4. | 26. 56.
13. 28. he said to them, an enemy hath *d. this*
21. 21. not only do *this* which is *d.* to the fig-tree
26. 13. *this* that this woman hath *d. Mark* 14. 9.
Mark 5. 32. to see her that had *d. this* thing
Luke 5. 6. when they had *d. this* they inclosed
23. 41. but *this* man hath *d.* nothing amiss
John 7. 31. miracles than these *this* man hath *d.?*
12. 18. for they heard he had *d. this* miracle
Acts 4. 7. by what power or name have ye *d. this?*
10. 16. *this* was *d.* thrice, vessel received, 11. 10.
28. 9. so when *this* was *d.* others also came
1 *Cor.* 5. 2. not mourned that he hath *d. this* deed, 3.

DOOR

Properly *signifies the entrance into a house,* Gen. 19. 9. *It is likewise taken in a metaphorical sense: Our Saviour says,* John 10. 9. I am the *door;* by me if any man enter in he shall be saved. *I am the only way whereby lost sinners may come to God, and obtain salvation: The only way of entrance and admission both into the church militant and triumphant is by me; for none, but such as have a true and a lively faith in me, wrought in their soul by my Spirit, can be true members of my church here, much less members of the glorious church in heaven. It is said, in* Rev. 3. 20. Behold, I stand at the *door,* and knock. *I stand at the door of sinners' hearts, in the gospel dispensation, inviting them to repent, and turn from their evil ways. There is likewise mention made of* the door of mercy, *or the time or season of grace.* Mat. 25. 10. They that were ready went in with him to the marriage, and the *door* was shut, *Luke* 13. 25. When once the master of the house is risen up, and hath shut to the *door,* &c. *By these parabolical expressions our Saviour intimates, that there is a determinate time, wherein sinners must, if ever, accept of the offers of grace and salvation, which if they slip, they will not be able to obtain of God an entrance into the kingdom of heaven;* the door *of mercy and grace, the* door *of heaven and glory, will be shut against them. In* Acts 14. 27. *we read of the* door *of faith;* God had opened the *door* of faith to the Gentiles; *He had caused the gospel to be preached unto them, whereby they were brought to believe in Christ, and to become members of his church.*

The apostle Paul *writing to the* Corinthians, *and telling them of the special opportunity which God had given him of doing much good by the gospel, uses this expression,* A door is opened unto me, 1 *Cor.* 16. 9. 2 *Cor.* 2. 12. *And the same apostle speaks of a* door *of utterance;* That God would open unto us a door of utterance, *that is, would afford us an opportunity, and vouchsafe ability and courage, to preach the gospel,* Col. 4. 3. To lie at the door; To be at the door? To stand before the door; *are phrases denoting that a person or thing is near at hand,* Gen. 4. 7. Mat. 24. 33. Jam. 5. 9. *God promises to give his people, upon their repentance,* The valley of *Achor* for a door of hope, *Hos.* 2. 15. Achor *was a valley in the territory of* Jericho, *and in the tribe of* Benjamin, *on the very entrance into the land of* Canaan: *The Israelites, fatigued and discouraged with marching and encamping for forty years in the wilderness, and coming to this valley, began to entertain hopes of enjoying the promised land; in allusion to this, God promises his people, by* Hosea, *that he would give them some beginnings of mercy and favour, as the earnests and pledges of future blessings.*

Gen. 4. 7. if thou dost not well, sin lieth at the *d.*
19. 9. they pressed, and came near to break the *d.*
Exod. 12. 23. the Lord also will pass over the *d.*
21. 6. his master shall bring him to the *d.*
Deut. 15. 17. shall thrust it through his ear to the *d.*
2 *Sam.* 13. 17. put her from me, bolt the *d.* after her
18. brought her out, and he bolted the *d.* after her
2 *Kings* 4. 15. when he called, she stood in the *d.*
9. 3. then open the *d.* and flee, and tarry not
Esth. 2. 21. of those which kept the *d.* 6. 2.
Job 31. 9. if I have laid wait at my neighbour's *d.*
34. did I fear, that I went not out of the *d.?*
Psal. 141. 3. O Lord, keep the *d.* of my lips
Prov. 26. 14. as the *d.* turneth upon his hinges
Cant. 5. 4. he put in his hand by the hole of the *d.*
8. 9. if she be a *d.* we will inclose her with boards
Ezek. 8. 3. brought me to the *d.* of the inner gate, 7.
8. when I had digged in the wall, behold a *d.*
10. 19. every one stood at the *d.* of the east-gate
11. 1. behold, at the *d.* of the gate, twenty-five men
41. 2. the breadth of the *d.* was ten cubits
46. 3. the people shall worship at the *d.* of this gate
Dan. 3. † 26. Nebuchad. came to the *d.* of the furnace
Hos. 2. 15. will give valley of Achor for a *d.* of hope
Amos 9. 1. he said, smite the lintel of the *d.*
Mat. 27. 60. he rolled a great stone to the *d.* of the sepulchre, and departed, *Mark* 15. 46.
28. 2. the angel rolled the stone from the *d.*
Mark 1. 33. all the city was gathered at the *d.*
2. 2. was no room, no not so much as about the *d.*
16. 3. who shall roll us the stone from the *d.?*
John 10. 1. he that entereth not by the *d.* is a thief
2. that entereth in by the *d.* ‖ 7. I am the *d.* 9.
John 18. 16. but Peter stood at the *d.* without
17. then saith the damsel that kept the *d.* to Peter
Acts 5. 9. feet of them are at the *d.* to carry thee out
12. 13. as Peter knocked at the *d.* of the gate
16. when they had opened the *d.* and saw him
14. 27. how he had opened the *d.* of faith to Gentiles
1 *Cor.* 16. 9. a great *d.* and effectual is opened
2 *Cor.* 2. 12. a *d.* was opened to me of the Lord
Col. 4. 3. that God would open a *d.* of utterance
Jam. 5. 9. the judge standeth before the *d.*
Rev. 3. 8. I set before thee an open *d.* none can shut
20. I stand at *d.* and knock, if any man open the *d.*
4. 1. I looked, and behold a *d.* was open in heaven

DOOR, with *house.*

Gen. 19. 11. smote them that were at *d.* of the *house*
43. 19. they communed at the *d.* of the *house*
Exod. 12. 22. none of you go out at the *d.* of his *house*
Lev. 14. 38. the priest shall go to the *d.* of the *house*
Deut. 22. 21. bring damsel to *d.* of her father's *house*
Judg. 19. 26. fell down at *d.* of the man's *house,* 27.
2 *Sam.* 11. 9. Uriah slept at *d.* of the king's *house*
2 *Kings* 5. 9. Naaman stood at *d.* of *house* of Elisha
Neh. 3. 20. unto the *d.* of the *house* of Eliashib
21. Merimoth repaired from the *d.* of the *house*
Prov. 5. 8. and come not nigh the *d.* of her *house*
9. 14. for she sitteth at the *d.* of her *house* on a seat
Jer. 26. † 10. the princes sat at *d.* of the Lord's *house*
36. † 10. Baruch read at the *d.* of the Lord's *house*
Ezek. 8. 14. he brought me to *d.* of Lord's *h.* 47. 1.

DOOR, with *shut.*

Gen. 19. 6. Lot *shut* the *d.* ‖ 10. angels *shut* the *d.*
2 *Kings* 4. 4. when come in shalt *shut d.* upon thee
5. she *shut d.* upon her ‖ 21. she *shut d.* on him
33. he went in, and *shut* the *d.* on them twain
6. 32. *shut* the *d.* and hold him fast at the *d.*
Mat. 6. 6. and when thou hast *shut* thy *d.* pray to
25. 10. the *d.* was shut ‖ *Luke* 11. 7. the *d.* is now *shut*
Luke 13. 25. master risen, and hath *shut* to the *d.*
Rev. 3. 8. set before thee an open *d.* no man can *shut*

DOOR, with *tabernacle.*

Exod. 29. 4. thou shalt bring to *d.* of the *tabernacle,* 40. 12. *Lev.* 4. 4. | 8. 3, 4. | 12. 6. *Num.* 6. 10.
11. shalt kill bullock by the *d.* of the *tabernacle,* 32. | 40. 29. *Lev.* 1. 5. *Num.* 27. 2.
42. burnt-offering at the *d.* of the *tabernacle,* 33. 9, 10. | 38. 8. | 40. 28. *Lev.* 1. 3. | 3. 2. | 4. 7, 18.
40. 6. before the *d.* of the *tabernacle, Num.* 25. 6.
Lev. 8. 31. at the *d.* of the *tabernacle,* 35. | 14. 11. | 16. 7. | 17. 6. *Num.* 6. 18. | 10. 3. *Josh.* 19. 51.
33. ye shall not go out of the *d.* of the *tabernacle*
10. 7. ye shall not go out from the *d.* of the *tabern.*
14. 23. unto the *d.* of the *tabernacle,* 15. 14, 29. | 19. 21. *Num.* 16. 18, 19, 50. | 20. 6.
17. 4. bringeth it not to the *d.* of the *tabernacle,* 9.
Num. 12. 5. stood in the *d.* of the *tabernacle,* 16. 18.
Deut 31. 15. a pillar of cloud stood over *d.* of *tabernacle.*
1 *Chron.* 9. 21. Zechariah was porter of *d.* of *tabern.*

DOOR, joined with *tent.*

Gen. 18. 1. Abraham sat in the *tent d.* in heat of d.
2. he ran to meet them from the *tent d.* and bowed
10. Sarah heard it in the *tent d.* behind him
Exod. 33. 8. the people stood every man at his *tent d.*
10. the people worshipped, every man in his *tent d.*
Num. 11. 10. weeping, every man in the *d.* of his *tent*
16. 27. Dathan and Abiram stood in *d.* of their *tents*
Judg. 4. 20. he said, stand in the *d.* of the *tent*

DOOR-KEEPER.

Ps. 84. 10. I had rather be a *d. keeper* in house of G.
Jer. 35. 4. the chamber of Maaseiah, *keeper* of the *d.*

DOOR-KEEPERS.

2 *Kings* 22. 4. which *keepers* of the *d.* have gathered
23. 4. the *keepers* of the *d.* to bring the vessels
25. 18. the captain of the guard took the chief priest and the three *keepers* of the *d. Jer.* 52. 24.
1 *Chr.* 15. 23. Berechiah, Elkanah, were *d.-keepers*
24. Obed-edom and Jehiah *d.-keepers* for the ark
Esth. 6. 2. the *keepers* of the *d.* sought to lay hand

DOOR-POST.

Exod. 21. 6. his master shall bring him to the *d.-post*
Ezek. 41. 3. he measured the *post* of the *d.* two cubits

DOOR-POSTS.

Exod. 12. 7. strike blood on upper *d.-posts* of houses
Deut. 11. 20. shall write them on *d.-posts* of thy house
Isa. 6. 4. the *posts* of the *d.* moved at the voice
Ezek. 41. 16. he measured the *d.-posts* and windows

DOORS.

Josh. 2. 19. whosoever shall go out of the *d.*
Judg. 3. 24. the *d.* of the parlour were locked
25. he opened not the *d.* of the parlour
11. 31. what cometh forth of the *d.* I will offer it
16. 3. Samson took the *d.* of the gate of the city
19. 27. her lord rose up, and opened the *d.*
1 *Sam.* 3. 15. Samuel opened the *d.* of the house
21. 13. David scrabbled on the *d.* of the gate
2 *Kings* 18. 16. Hezekiah cut off the gold from the *d.*
2 *Chron.* 23. 4. of the Levites be porters of the *d.*
29. 3. Hezekiah opened the *d.* of the house
Neh. 3. 1. and they set up the *d.* of it, 3. | 7. 1.
Job 31. 32. but I opened my *d.* to the traveller
38. 10. when I set bars and *d.* to the sea
17. hast thou seen the *d.* of the shadow of death?
41. 14. who can open the *d.* of his face?
Psal. 24. 7. be ye lifted up, ye everlasting *d.* 9.
78. 23. though he had opened the *d.* of heaven
Prov. 8. 3. Wisdom crieth at the coming in at the *d.*
34. heareth me, waiting at the posts of my *d.*
Isa. 57. 8. behind *d.* hast thou set up remembrance
Ezek. 33. 30. still talking in the *d.* of the houses
Mic. 7. 5. keep the *d.* of thy mouth from her
Zech. 11. 1. open thy *d.* O Lebanon, that the fire
Mat. 24. 33. know it is near, at the *d. Mark* 13. 29.
Acts 5. 19. the angel by night opened the prison *d.*
23. and the keepers standing before the *d.*
16. 26. immediately all the *d.* were opened
27. keeper awaking, and seeing the prison *d.* open

Shut DOORS.

Judg. 3. 23. Ehud *shut* the *d.* of the parlour
2 *Chron.* 28. 24. Ahaz *shut* up the *d.* of Lord's house
29. 7. our fathers have *shut* the *d.* of the porch
Neh. 6. 10. and let us *shut* the *d.* of the temple
7. 3. let them *shut* the *d.* and bar them
Job 3. 10. because *shut* not up *d.* of mother's womb
38. 8. or who *shut* up the sea with *d.?*
Eccl. 12. 4. the *d.* shall be *shut* in the streets
Isa. 26. 20. enter, and *shut* thy *d.* about thee
Mal. 1. 10. who that would *shut* the *d.* for nought?
John 20. 19. when the *d.* were *shut* Jesus came, 26.
Acts 21. 30. and forthwith the *d.* were shut

DOTE.

Jer. 50. 36. a sword is on liars, and they shall *d.*

DOTED.

Ezek. 23. 5. Aholah *d.* on her lovers the Assyrians,
7. committed whoredoms with all on whom she *d.*
9. into hand of Assyrians, on whom she *d.* 12.
16. as soon as she saw them, she *d.* upon them
20. for she *d.* upon their paramours, whose flesh

DOTING.

1 *Tim.* 6. 4. *d.* about questions and strifes of words

DOUBLE.

Double *commonly signifies twice as much,* Gen. 43. 12. Take double money, *that is, twice as much money.* A double garment *may mean a lined habit, such as the high-priest's breast-plate was,* Exod. 39. 9. *or a complete habit or suit of clothes, a cloke and tunic,* Judg. 17. † 10. Dwell with me, and I will give thee a double suit of apparel, *or* an order of garments. Double *sometimes signifies abundance, as much as answers one's design,* Isa. 40. 2. She hath received of the Lord's hand double for all her sins. *They have received punishment, though not so much as their sins deserved, yet abundantly sufficient to answer God's design, which was to humble and reform them, and to warn others by their example. See* Jer. 16. 18. | 17. 18. 1 Tim. 5. 17. A double heart, a double tongue, double mind, *are opposite to a simple, honest, sincere heart; a true tongue; a just, faithful, sincere mind,* Psal. 12. 2. 1 Tim. 3. 8. Jam. 1. 8.

Gen. 43. 12. and take *d.* money in your hand
15. and they took *d.* money in their hand
Exod. 22. 4. if theft be found, he shall restore *d.*
7. if found, let him pay *d.* ‖ 9. he shall pay *d.*
39. 9. they made the breast-plate *d.* a span was
Deut. 15. 18. been worth a *d.* hired servant to thee
21. 17. by giving him a *d.* portion of all he hath
Judg. 17. † 10. I will give thee a *d.* suit of apparel
1 *Sam.* 1. † 5. to Hannah he gave *d.* portion
2 *Kings* 2. 9. let a *d.* portion of thy spirit be on me
1 *Chron.* 12. 33. they were not of a *d.* heart
Job 11. 6. that they are *d.* to that which is
41. 13. who can come to him with his *d.* bridle?
42. † 10. also the Lord added to Job unto the *d.*
Psal. 12. 2. and with a *d.* heart do they speak
Prov. 31. † 21. her household clothed with *d.* garm.
Isa. 40. 2. she hath received *d.* for all her sins
61. 7. for your shame you shall have *d.* therefore in their land they shall possess the *d.*
Jer. 16. 18. I will recompense their sin *d.*
17. 18. and destroy them with *d.* destruction
Zech. 9. 12. I declare, that I will render *d.* to thee
1 *Tim.* 3. 8. deacons must be grave, not *d.*-tongued
5. 17. rule well, be counted worthy of *d.* honour
Rev. 18. 6. *d.* unto her, *d.* according to her works, in the cup which she hath filled, fill to her *d.*

DOUBLE, *Verb.*

Exod. 26. 9. thou shalt *d.* sixth curtain of tabernacle
Rev. 18. 6. reward her, and *d.* unto her *d.*

DOUBLE-MINDED.

Jam. 1. 8. a *d.-minded* man is unstable in his ways
4. 8. and purify your hearts, ye *d.-minded*

DOUBLED.

Gen. 41. 32. the dream was *d.* to Pharaoh twice
Exod. 28. 16. four-square it shall be, being *d.*
39. 9. a span was the breadth thereof, being *d.*
2 *Sam.* 20. † 10. Joab *d.* not his stroke to Amasa
Ezek. 21. 14. let the sword be *d.* the third time

DOUBT.

Gen. 37. 33. Joseph is without *d.* rent in pieces
Deut. 28. 66. thy life shall hang in *d.* before thee
Job 12. 2. no *d.* but ye are the people, wisd. shall die
Luke 11. 20. no *d.* the kingdom of G. is come on you
Acts 2. 12. were in *d.* saying, what meaneth this?
28. 4. they said, no *d.* this man is a murderer
1 *Cor.* 9. 10. for our sakes, no *d.* this is written
Gal. 4. 20. to change my voice for I stand in *d.* of you
1 *John* 2. 19. would no *d.* have continued with us

DOUBTS.

Dan. 5. 12. dissolving of *d.* was found in Daniel
16. I have heard that thou canst dissolve *d.*

DOUBT.

Mat. 14. 31. Jesus said, wherefore didst thou *d.?*
21. 21. I say unto you, if ye have faith, and *d.* not
Mark 11. 23. shall not *d.* in his heart, but believe
John 10. 24. how long dost thou make us to *d.?*

DOUBTED.

Mat. 28. 17. they worshipped him, but some *d.*
Acts 5. 24. they *d.* whereunto this would grow
10. 17. now while Peter *d.* in himself of the vision
25. 20. because I *d.* of such manner of questions

DOUBTETH.

Rom. 14. 23. he that *d.* is damned if he eat

DOUBTFUL.

Luke 12. 29. neither be ye of a *d.* mind
Acts 25. † 20. because I was *d.* how to inquire
Rom. 14. 1. receive you, but not to *d.* disputations

DOUBTING.

John 13. 22. they looked, *d.* of whom he spake
Acts 10. 20. go with them, nothing *d.* 11. 12.
1 *Tim.* 2. 8. that men pray without wrath and *d.*

DOUBTLESS.

Num. 14. 30. *d.* ye shall not come into the land
2 *Sam.* 5. 19. I will *d.* deliver the Philistines
Psal. 126. 6. he shall *d.* come again, rejoicing
Isa. 63. 16. *d.* thou art our Father, thou, O Lord
1 *Cor.* 9. 2. if not to others, yet *d.* I am to you
2 *Cor.* 12. 1. it is not expedient for me *d.* to glory
Phil. 3. 8. yea *d.* I count all things but loss for Christ

DOVE

Is a tame bird, which by the law of Moses was declared to be pure. The law ordained that when any woman went to the temple after lying-in, she should offer to the Lord a lamb, a dove, or turtle, or else a pigeon, or a young turtle, Lev. 12. 6, 8. The lamb was offered as a burnt-offering, the pigeon for a sin-offering. Or if the person could not afford a lamb, then instead of it she offered two pigeons, or two turtles. The Virgin Mary, to comply with this law, offered two pigeons, or two turtles, because she was poor, Luke 2. 24. And as it was difficult for all those who came from remote places, to bring doves with them, the priests gave permission for the selling of these birds in the courts of that holy place, which our Saviour could not endure; and having entered into the temple, he made a scourge, and drove out those who traded there in pigeons, Mark 11. 15.

The dove is the symbol of simplicity and innocency. The Holy Spirit appeared at the baptism of our Saviour in the form of a dove, Mat. 3. 16. to signify what Christ is, (1) In his own nature to them that come to him, namely, meek, harmless, loving. (2) In the execution of his office, even He by whom the Father is pacified, and who brings the good tidings of the assuaging the deluge of wrath, as the dove did of the retiring of the waters to Noah. (3) What he is in the operations of his Spirit upon his people, that they are made meek, harmless, and lowly as doves. Christ recommends to his disciples the wisdom of the serpent, and the harmlessness of the dove, Mat. 10. 16. The prophet Hosea compares the Israelites to a silly dove without heart, or understanding, Hos. 7. 11. The dove is a defenceless creature, without gall, or cunning, exposed to the pursuit of men and beasts; which is able neither to protect itself nor its young, nor to take precaution against those who have designs upon its life and liberty. Thus the Israelites, notwithstanding the chastisements with which God afflicted them, and the captivities to which he had reduced them, still relapsed into their irregularities, and exposed themselves again to the same calamities. The dove, when absent from its mate, sits solitary, and coos, or mourns; in allusion to which are these expressions, Isa. 38. 14. I did mourn as a dove. And chap. 59. 11. We mourn sore like doves. Nah. 2. 7. Her maids shall lead her as with the voice of doves. The spouse, or church, in the Canticles is compared often to a dove, by reason of her dove-like temper and disposition, because she is chaste, mild, harmless, and faithful: also by reason of her dove-like condition, she being weak, and exposed to persecution, and given to mourning, and subject to many fears, as doves are, Cant. 2. 14. | 5. 2.

It is further observed of the dove; that the male and female love each other, and keep faithful one towards the other; and, if any breach happen between them, they are presently reconciled, manifesting the same by their embracing each other. They love men's dwelling-houses, and to be in their company; and, being carried from home, will return many miles to their own houses; for which reason some make use of them to carry letters, by tying them about their necks, which their friends at home untie and read, and are thereby acquainted with their mind. The dove is an enemy to carrion or ordure, and feedeth upon the purest seed or grain, and loveth neatness and pure waters. It quickly forgets injuries, as the spoiling its nest, taking away its young, &c. It is very fruitful, having young ones almost every month. Its feathers are of divers colours, which, according to the variety of its postures, and of the light shining upon it, look like silver or gold, as the Psalmist observes, Psal. 68. 13.

It is said in 2 Kings 6. 25. that during the siege of Samaria, in the reign of Ahab, king of Israel, the famine was so great, that the fourth part of a cab of doves' dung was sold for five shekels. A cab held two pints and something over. Five shekels made about twelve shillings sterling. Some think that it is not incredible that they did really eat doves' dung, seeing a famine hath constrained people to eat things as improper and unfit for nourishment as this, as is implied, Isa. 36. 12. Josephus and Theodoret were of opinion, that this doves' dung was bought instead of salt. The Rabbins affirm, that it was not the dung of pigeons, but the corn in their crops, which they brought back well filled out of the fields, whither, during the siege, they went to feed. Others suppose the dove's belly, her guts and inwards, to be meant here.

The several species of the dove, are the wood-pigeon, the tame pigeon, the ring-dove or turtle, the Picaipinima, and the St. Thomas's pigeon. The three first often occur in the Bible, under the names of the pigeon and turtle-dove, and the two last are natives of America; the Picaipinima being the grey and black dove, with a white breast; and the St. Thomas's pigeon being the Columba, with yellow legs.

Gen. 8. 8. Noah sent forth a *d.* from him, 10. 12.
9. the *d.* found no rest for the sole of her foot
11. the *d.* came in to him in the evening
15. 9. he said to him, take a turtle-*d.* *Lev.* 12. 6.
Psal. 55. 6. Oh! that I had wings like a *d.*
68. 13. ye shall be as the wings of a *d.* covered
74. 19. O deliver not the soul of thy turtle-*d.*
Cant. 1. 15. thou art fair, thou hast *d.* eyes, 4. 1.
2. 14. O my *d.* let me see thy countenance
5. 2. open to me, my sister, my love, my *d.*
6. 9. my *d.* my undefiled is but one, she is
Isa. 38. 14. I did mourn as a *d.* mine eyes fail
Jer. 48. 28. dwell in the rock and be like the *d.*
Hos. 7. 11. Ephraim also is like a silly *d.*
11. 11. they shall tremble as a *d.* out of Assyria
Mat. 3. 16. Jesus saw the Spirit of God descending like a *d.* *Mark* 1. 10. *Luke* 3. 22. *John* 1. 32.

DOVES.

Kings 6. 25. the fourth part of a cab of *d.* dung

Cant. 5. 12. his eyes are as the eyes of *d.*
Isa. 59. 11. we roar like bears, we mourn sore like *d.*
60. 8. that flee as the *d.* to their windows
Ezek. 7. 16. they shall be like the *d.* of the valleys
Nah. 2. 7. lead her as with the voice of *d.* tabering
Mat. 10. 16. be wise as serpents, harmless as *d.*
21. 12. the seats of them that sold *d.* *Mark* 11. 15.
John 2. 14. found in the temple those that sold *d.*
16. said unto them that sold *d.* take these hence

Turtle-DOVES.

Lev. 14. 22. he shall take two *turtle-d.* or pigeons
Luke 2. 24. offer sacrifice of two *turtle-d.* or pigeons

DOUGH.

Exod. 8. † 3. the frogs shall come into thy *d.*
12. † 34. the people took their *d.* before it was leavened, their *d.* being bound up in their clothes
39. they baked unleavened cakes of the *d.*
Num. 15. 20. offer a cake of the first of your *d.* 21.
Deut. 28. † 5. blessed shall be thy basket and *d.*
Neh. 10. 37. should bring the first-fruits of our *d.*
Jer. 7. 18. women knead their *d.* to bake cakes
Ezek. 44. 30. give the priests the first of your *d.*
Hos. 7. 4. after he hath kneaded the *d.* till leavened

DOWN.

Lev. 22. 7. when the sun is *d.* *Deut.* 23. 11.
Josh. 8. 29. as soon as sun was *d.* Josh. commanded to take the king of Ai's carcase *d.* from the tree
2 *Sam.* 3. 35. if I taste aught till the sun be *d.*
Job 1. 7. and from walking up and *d.* in it, 2. 2.
Psal. 59. 15. let them wander up and *d.* for meat
109. 23. I am tossed up and *d.* as the locust
Ezek. 28. 14. hast walked up and *d.* in midst of stones
Zech. 10. 12. they shall walk up and *d.* in his name
Acts 27. 27. as we were driven up and *d.* in Adria
Rev. 1. 13. clothed with a garment *d.* to the foot

DOWN-SITTING.

Psal. 139. 2. thou knowest my *d.* and up-rising

DOWNWARD.

2 *Kings* 19. 30. shall again take root *d.* *Isa.* 37. 31.
Eccl. 3. 21. the spirit of the beast that goeth *d.*
Ezek. 1. 27. the appearance of his loins *d.* 8. 2.

DOWRY.

Gen. 30. 20. God hath endued me with a good *d.*
34. 12. ask me never so much *d.* and gift
Exod. 22. 17. pay according to the *d.* of virgins
1 *Sam.* 18. 25. the king desireth not any *d.*

DRAG.

Hab. 1. 16. they burn incense to their *d.*

DRAGS.

Hab. 1. 15. they gather them in their *d.*

DRAGGING.

John 21. 8. came in little ship, *d.* the net with fishes

DRAGON.

This word answers generally to the Hebrew, Thannim, or Thannin, which signifies a large fish, a sea-dragon. By comparing the different passages where the word tannin, or tannim, is to be met with, it signifies sometimes large river or sea fishes, and at other times venomous and land serpents, and more particularly the crocodile and whale, Gen. 1. 21. Job 7. 12. Isa. 34. 13. Ezek. 29. 3. | 32. 2.

As to the dragons which are talked of, and are often mentioned in books, they are for the most part only old serpents grown with age to a prodigious size. Some are described with wings, feet, claws, crests, and heads of different figures. There is no question but there are winged serpents; Moses speaks of them under the name of Zeraph, Num. 21. 6. Real Dragons, by Solinus's account of them, have a small mouth, and cannot bite; or if they do, their biting is not venomous. The Egyptians call them good geniuses, and keep them tame in their houses. But these were not the dragons spoken of by the prophets; these were dangerous creatures, mischievous, deadly, and wild.

As serpents, dragons, and venomous beasts, hide themselves in uninhabited places, in the ruins of cities and in rubbish; for this reason, where there is mention of the ruin of a city, the ravaging of a province, or of a land reduced to a wilderness, it is said to be a dwelling for dragons, Isa. 13. 22. | 34. 13. Jer. 9. 11.

This word is taken in Scripture for the devil, Rev. 12. 9. so called for his great strength, and bloody cruelty against the saints. It is also taken for cruel tyrants, as Pharaoh, Psal. 74. 13. Ezek. 29. 3. And for any hurtful thing, Ps. 91. 13.

Psal. 91. 13. the *d.* shalt thou trample under foot
Isa. 27. 1. he shall slay the *d.* that is in the sea
51. 9. that hath cut Rahab, and wounded the *d.*
Jer. 51. 34. Nebuch. hath swallowed me up like a *d.*
Ezek. 29. 3. Pharaoh, the great *d.* that lieth
Rev. 12. 3. another wonder, behold, a great red *d.*
4. the *d.* stood ‖ 7. *d.* fought ‖ 9. *d.* was cast out, 13.
16. the flood which the *d.* cast out of his mouth
17. and the *d.* was wroth with the woman
13. 2. the *d.* gave him his power and his seat
4. they worshipped the *d.* ‖ 11. he spake as a *d.*
16. 13. like frogs came out of the mouth of the *d.*
20. 2. he laid hold on the *d.* that old serpent

DRAGON-*well.*

Neh. 2. 13. I went out, even before the *d.-well*

DRAGONS.

Deut. 32. 33. their wine is the poison of *d.*
Job 30. 29. I am a brother to *d.* and a companion
Psal. 44. 19. thou hast sore broken us in place of *d.*
74. 13. thou breakest the heads of *d.* in the waters
148. 7. praise Lord from earth, ye *d.* and all deeps
Isa. 13. 22. and *d.* in their pleasant palaces
34. 13. it shall be an habitation for *d.* 35. 7.
43. 20. the *d.* and the owls shall honour me
Jer. 9. 11. I will make Jerusalem a den of *d.*
10. 22. to make the cities of Judah a den of *d.*
14. 6. they snuffed up the wind like *d.*
49. 33. Hazor ‖ 51. 37. Babylon a dwelling for *d.*
Mic. 1. 8. I will make a wailing like the *d.*
Mal. 1. 3. I laid his heritage waste for *d.* of wilderness

DRAMS.

1 *Chron.* 29. 7. they gave of gold ten thousand *d.*
Ezra 2. 69. they gave 61,000 *d.* of gold
Ezra 8. 27. also twenty basins of gold, of a thousand *d.*
Neh. 7. 70. gave to the treasure a thousand *d.* of gold
71. gave twenty thousand *d.* of gold, 72.

DRANK.

Gen. 9. 21. Noah *d.* of the wine and was drunken
24. 46. I *d.* and she made the camels drink also
27. 25. and he brought him wine, and he *d.*
43. † 34. they *d.* largely, were merry with him
Num. 20. 11. the congregation *d.* and their beasts
Deut. 32. 38. and *d.* the wine of their drink-offerings
1 *Sam.* 30. 12. nor *d.* water three days and three nights
2 *Sam.* 12. 3. eat of his own meat, and *d.* of his own cup
1 *Kings* 13. 19. did eat bread in his house, and *d.* water
17. 6. brought bread and flesh, and he *d.* of the brook
Dan. 1. 5. the king appointed of the wine which he *d.*
8. that he would not defile himself with wine he *d.*
5. 1. Belshazzar *d.* wine before the thousand
3. his wives and his concubines *d.* in them
4. they *d.* wine, and praised the gods of gold
Mark 14. 23. he gave to them, and they all *d.* of it
Luke 17. 27. they eat, they *d.* they married, 28.
John 4. 12. than our father Jacob who *d.* thereof
1 *Cor.* 10. 4. for they *d.* of that spiritual rock

DRAVE.

Exod. 14. 25. chariot-wheels, they *d.* them heavily
Josh. 16. 10. they *d.* not out the Canaanites in Gezer
24. 12. and *d.* them out from before you, *Judg.* 6. 9.
18. the Lord *d.* out before us all the people
Judg. 1. 19. Judah *d.* out inhabitants of the mountain
1 *Sam.* 30. 20. which they *d.* before other cattle
2 *Sam.* 6. 3. Uzzah and Ahio *d.* the cart, 1 *Chr.* 13. 7.
2 *Kings* 16. 6. at that time Rezin *d.* Jews from Elath
18. 21. Jeroboam *d.* Israel from following the Ld.
Acts 7. 45. whom God *d.* out before our fathers
18. 16. Gallio *d.* them from the judgment-seat

See DROVE.

DRAUGHT.

Mat. 15. 17. and is cast out in the *d.* *Mark* 7. 19.
Luke 5. 4. launch out and let down your nets for a *d.*
9. for he was astonished at the *d.* of the fishes

DRAUGHT-HOUSE.

2 *Kings* 10. 27. they made Baal's house a *d.* to this day

DRAW.

Gen. 24. 44. and I will also *d.* for thy camels
Exod. 15. 9. the enemy said, I will *d.* my sword
Judg. 4. 6. *d.* toward mount Tabor, and take with thee
7. I will *d.* to thee Sisera, captain of Jabin's army
5. † 14. out of Zebulun they that *d.* with the pen
9. 54. Abimelech said, *d.* thy sword and slay me, 1 *Sam.* 31. 4. 1 *Chron.* 10. 4.
20. 32. *d.* them from the city to the high-ways
2 *Sam.* 17. 13. we will *d.* that city into the river
Job 21. 33. and every man shall *d.* after him
Psal. 28. 3. *d.* me not away with the wicked
Eccl. 2. † 3. I sought to *d.* my flesh with wine
Cant. 1. 4. *d.* me, we will run after thee
Isa. 5. 18. woe to those *d.* iniq. with cords of vanity
66. 19. send those to the nations that *d.* the bow
Ezek. 21. 3. I will *d.* my sword out of his sheath
28. 7. and strangers shall *d.* their swords
30. 11. they shall *d.* their swords against Egypt
32. 20. *d.* her, and all her multitudes
John 4. 11. thou hast nothing to *d.* with, well is deep
15. water that I thirst not, nor come hither to *d.*
6. 44. except the Father which hath sent me *d.* him
12. 32. if I be lifted up from earth, *d.* all men to me
21. 6. and now they were not able to *d.* it
Acts 20. 30. to *d.* away disciples after them
Jam. 2. 6. and *d.* you before the judgment-seats

DRAW *back.*

Ezek. 39. † 2. I will *d.* thee *back* with a hook
Heb. 10. 38. just shall live by faith, but if any *d. back*
39. we are not of them who *d. back* to perdition

DRAW *near.*

Judg. 19. 13. let us *d. near* to one of these cities
1 *Sam.* 14. 36. said the priest, let us *d. near* to God
38. Saul said, *d.* ye *near* hither all the chief
Psal. 73. 28. it is good for me to *d. near* to God
107. 18. they *d. near* to the gates of death
Isa. 29. 13. this people *d. near* with their lips but heart
45. 20. *d. near,* ye that are escaped of the nations
57. 3. *d. near* hither, ye sons of the sorceress
Jer. 30. 21. and I will cause him to *d. near* to me
46. 3. order the buckler, and *d. near* to battle
Ezek. 9. 1. that have charge over the city to *d. near*
22. 4. thou hast caused thy days to *d. near*
Joel 3. 9. wake up, let all the men of war *d. near*
Heb. 10. 22. let us *d. near* with a true heart, in full

DRAW *nigh.*

Exod. 3. 5. he said, *d.* not *nigh* hither, put off shoes
Psal. 69. 18. *d. nigh* to my soul, and redeem it
119. 150. they *d. nigh* that follow mischief
Eccl. 12. 1. nor years *d. nigh* when thou shalt say
Isa. 5. 19. let the counsel of the holy One *d. nigh*
Heb. 7. 19. by the which we *d. nigh* unto God
Jam. 4. 8. *d. nigh* to God, he will *d. nigh* to you

DRAW *out.*

Exod. 12. 21. *d. out* and take you a lamb, and kill
Lev. 26. 33. I will *d. out* a sword after you
Judg. 3. 22. he could not *d.* the dagger *out* of his belly
Job 41. 1. canst thou *d. out* leviathan with an hook?
Psal. 35. 3. *d. out* also the spear, and stop the way
36. † 10. *d. out* at length thy loving-kindness
85. 5. wilt thou *d. out* thine anger to all generations?
Prov. 20. 5. a man of understanding will *d.* it *out*
Isa. 57. 4. against whom do ye *d. out* the tongue?
58. 10. if thou *d. out* thy soul to the hungry
Jer. 49. 20. the least of the flock *d.* them *out,* 50. 45.
Lam. 4. 3. even the sea-monsters *d. out* the breast
Ezek. 5. 2. a third part shall scatter in the wind, and I will *d. out* a sword after them, 12. | 12. 14.
Hag. 2. 16. when one came to *d. out* fifty vessels
John 2. 8. *d. out* now, and bear to the governor

DRAW *up.*

Job 40. 23. he trusteth that he can *d. up* Jordan

DRAW joined with *water.*

Gen. 24. 11. the time that women go out to *d. w.* 43.
13. and the daughters come out to *d. water*
20. Rebekah ran again to the well to *d. water*
1 *Sam.* 9. 11. found young maidens going to *d. water*
Isa. 12. 3. with joy shall ye *d. water* of wells of salv.
Nah. 3. 14. *d.* thee *waters* for the siege, fortify

John 4. 7. cometh a woman of Samaria to d. water

DRAWN.

Exod. 2. † 10. and she called his name d. out
Num. 22. 23. the ass saw the angel, and his sword d. in his hand, 31. Josh. 5. 13. 1 Chron. 21. 16.
Deut. 21. 3. an heifer, which hath not d. in yoke
30. 17. but shalt be d. away, and worship gods
Josh. 8. 6. till we have d. them from the city
16. they were d. away from the city, Judg. 20. 31.
Ruth 2. 9. drank of that which young men have d.
Job 20. 25. it is d. and cometh out of the body
Psal. 37. 14. the wicked have d. out the sword
55. 21. words softer than oil yet were they d. swords
Prov. 24. 11. to deliver them that are d. to death
Isa. 21. 15. for they fled from the d. swords
28. 9. and them that are d. from the breasts
Jer. 22. 19. d. and cast forth beyond the gates
31. 3. with loving-kindness have I d. thee
Lam. 2. 3. he hath d. back his right hand from
Ezek. 21. 5. I the Lord have d. my sword, 28.
Acts 11. 10. all were d. up again to heaven
Jam. 1. 14. when he is d. away of his own lusts

DRAWER.

Deut. 29. 11. from the hewer of wood to d. of water

DRAWERS.

Josh. 9. 21. be d. of water to the congregation, 27.
23. and d. of water for the house of my God

DRAWETH.

Deut. 25. 11. the wife of the one d. near to deliver
Judg. 19. 9. now the day d. towards evening
Job 24. 22. he d. also the mighty with his power
33. 22. yea his soul d. near to the grave
Psal. 10. 9. catch the poor when he d. him into his net
88. 3. and my life d. nigh unto the grave
Prov. 3. † 13. happy man that d. out understanding
Isa. 26. 17. that d. near the time of her delivery
Ezek. 7. 12. the time is come, the day d. near
Amos 9. † 13. overtaketh him that d. forth seed
Mat. 15. 8. this people d. nigh with their lips
Luke 21. 8. saying, I am Christ, and the time d. near
28. then look up, for your redemption d. nigh
Jam. 5. 8. for the coming of the Lord d. nigh

DRAWING.

Judg. 5. 11. are delivered in the places of d. water
8. † 10. there fell 120,000 every one d. sword
John 6. 19. they see Jesus d. nigh to the ship

DREAD.

Gen. 9. 2. the d. of you shall be on every beast
Exod. 15. 16. fear and d. shall fall upon them
Deut. 2. 25. this day will I begin to put the d. of thee and fear of thee upon the nations, 11. 25.
Job 13. 11. shall not his d. fall upon you?
21. and let not thy d. make me afraid
Isa. 8. 13. let him be your fear, let him be your d.

DREAD.

Deut. 1. 29. I said to you, d. not, nor be afraid
1 Chr. 22. 13. be strong, d. not, nor be dismayed

DREADFUL.

Gen. 28. 17. Jacob said, how d. is this place!
Job 15. 21. a d. sound in his ears, in prosperity
Ezek. 1. 18. as for their rings, they were d.
Dan. 7. 7. behold, a fourth beast, d. and terrible, 19.
9. 4. and I said, O Lord, the great and d. God
Hab. 1. 7. the Chaldeans are terrible and d.
Mal. 1. 14. my name is d. among the heathen
4. 5. the coming of the great and d. day of the Lord

DREAM.

By this word are to be understood those vain images, which are formed in the imagination while we are asleep, Job 20. 8. He shall fly away as a *dream,* and shall not be found; yea, he shall be chased away as a vision of the night. *The eastern people, and in particular the* Jews, *had a very great regard to dreams; they observed them, and applied to those who pretended to explain them. We see the antiquity of this custom among the* Egyptians, *in the history of* Pharaoh's *butler and baker, and in* Pharaoh *himself,* Gen. 40. 5, 8. | 41. 15. Nebuchadnezzar *is an instance of the same among the* Chaldeans, *Dan.* 2. 1, 2, 3, *&c. God had very expressly forbidden his people to observe dreams, and to consult those who took upon them to explain them. He condemned any one to death who pretended to have prophetic dreams, and to foretell what was to come, though what he should so foretell were to come to pass, if after this he would engage the people in idolatry,* Deut. 13. 1, 2, 3, &c. *But they were not forbid, when they thought they had any significative dream, to address themselves to the prophets of the Lord, or to the high-priest dressed in his ephod, in order to have it explained.*

Wherefore in that very place, wherein God forbid the Hebrews *to consult diviners, magicians, and interpreters of dreams, he tells them,* The people whose land ye are going to possess, consult soothsayers and diviners; but ye have not been so taught. The Lord shall raise up from the midst of you, and among your brethren, a prophet like unto me, him ye shall consult and hearken to, *Deut.* 18. 14, 15. *The* Israelites *therefore were to address themselves to God and his prophets, to learn the explanation of their dreams, and the prediction of things to come.* Saul, *a little before the battle of* Gilboa, *consulted a woman with a familiar spirit,* because the Lord had departed from him, and would not answer him, *and discover the success of this war to him,* neither by dreams, nor by Urim, nor by prophets, 1 *Sam.* 28. 6, 15.

And we find that the Lord did indeed sometimes discover his will in dreams, *and raised up persons to explain them. He informed* Abimelech *in a* dream, *that* Sarah *was the wife of* Abraham, *Gen.* 20. 3, 6. *He shewed* Jacob *the mysterious ladder in a* dream, *Gen.* 28. 12, 13, 14. Joseph *was favoured very early with* prophetic dreams, *the signification whereof was easily discovered by* Jacob *his father,* Gen. 37. 4, 5, 6, &c. *The* dreams *of the butler and the baker belonging to the king of* Egypt, *were explained by* Joseph, *as well as those of* Pharaoh, *Gen.* 40. 12, 18. | 41. 25. *And the Lord expressly declares, that he would sometimes thus reveal himself,* Num. 12. 6. If there be a prophet among you, I the Lord will make myself known unto him in a vision, and will speak unto him in a *dream. In the New Testament, we read that* the angel of the Lord appeared unto *Joseph* in a dream *several times,* Mat. 1. 20. | 2. 19, 22. *And it is among the signs and effects of the promulgation of the gospel, prophetically said;* It shall come to pass, that I will pour out my Spirit upon all flesh; your sons and your daughters shall prophesy, your old men shall dream dreams; your young men shall see visions, *Joel* 2. 28. *The prophet* Jeremiah *exclaims against the false prophets, who pretended to have dreams,* Jer. 23. 25, 28, 29. *Dreams are,* (1) *Natural,* Eccl. 5. 7. (2) *Divine,* Gen. 28. 12. (3) *Diabolical and sinful,* Deut. 13. 1, 2. Jer. 23. 32.

Gen. 20. 3. God came to Abimelech in a d. 6.
31. 10. Jacob saw in a d. the rams which leaped
11. the angel of God spake to Jacob in a d.
24. God came to Laban the Syrian in a d.
37. 5. Joseph dreamed a d. and told it, 9, 10.
40. 5. butler and baker dreamed a d. both of them
41. 7. awoke, and behold, it was a d. 1 Kings 3. 15.
12. did interpret to each man according to his d.
25. Joseph said, the d. of Pharaoh is one, 26.
32. for that the d. was doubled unto Pharaoh
Num. 12. 6. I the Lord will speak to him in a d.
Judg. 7. 13. a man that told a d. to his fellow
15. when Gideon heard the telling of the d.
1 Kings 3. 5. the Lord appeared to Solomon in a d.
Job 20. 8. he shall fly away as a d. and not be found
33. 15. in a d. he openeth the ears of men
Psal. 73. 20. as a d. when one awaketh, so, O Lord
Eccl. 5. 3. for a d. cometh through much business
Isa. 29. 7. nations that fight against Ariel be as a d.
Jer. 23. 28. prophet that hath a d. let him tell a d.
Dan. 2. 3. my spirit was troubled to know the d.
4. tell thy servants the d. || 6. if ye shew the d.
36. this is the d. and we will tell the interpretation
4. 19. my lord, the d. be to them that hate thee
7. 1. Daniel had a d. then he wrote the d.
Mat. 1. 20. the angel of the Lord appeared to Joseph in a d. saying, fear not to take Mary, 2. 13, 19.
2. 12. and being warned of God in a d. 22.
27. 19. I have suffered many things in a d.

DREAM, *Verb.*

Psal. 126. 1. we were like them that d.
Joel 2. 28. your old men d. dreams, Acts 2. 17.

DREAMED.

Gen. 28. 12. Jacob d. || 37. 5. Joseph d. a dream
40. 5. the officers d. || 41. 1. Pharaoh d. 15.
42. 9. Joseph remembered the dreams which he d.
Jer. 23. 25. the prophets said, I have d. I have d.
29. 8. to your dreams which you cause to be d.
Dan. 2. 1. Nebuchad. d. dreams, spirit was troubled
3. the king said to them, I have d. a dream

DREAMER.

Gen. 37. 19. they said, behold, this d. cometh
Deut. 13. 1. if a d. of dreams arise among you
3. thou shalt not hearken to that d. of dreams
5. that prophet or d. of dreams shall be put to death
Jer. 29. † 24. thus spake to Shemaiah the d.

DREAMERS.

Jer. 27. 9. therefore hearken not to diviners nor d.
Jude 8. those filthy d. defile flesh, despise dominion

DREAMS.

Gen. 37. 8. they hated Joseph the more for his d.
20. we shall see what will become of his d.
41. 12. an Hebrew, and he interpreted our d.
42. 9. Joseph remembered the d. he dreamed
1 Sam. 28. 6. the Lord answered him not by d. 15.
Job 7. 14. then thou scarest me with d. and terrifiest
Eccl. 5. 7. in multitude of d. are divers vanities
Jer. 23. 27. to forget my name with their d.
32. I am against them that prophesy false d.
27. † 9. nor hearken to your d. 29. 8.
Dan. 1. 17. Daniel had understanding in d. 5. 12.
Zech. 10. 2. the diviners have told false d.

DREAMING.

Isa. 56. † 10. his watchmen are d. talking in sleep

DREAMETH.

Isa. 29. 8. when a hungry man d. a thirsty man d.

DREGS.

Psal. 75. 8. the d. thereof the wicked shall drink out
Isa. 51. 17. thou hast drunken the d. of the cup, 22.

DRESS.

Gen. 2. 15. God put the man into the garden to d. it
18. 7. gave it to a young man, and he hasted to d. it
Deut. 21. † 12. shave her head, and d. her nails
28. 39. thou shalt plant vineyards, and d. them
2 Sam. 12. 4. to d. of his own for the way-faring man
13. 5. let Tamar d. the meat in my sight
7. go to Amnon's house, and d. him meat
1 Kings 17. 12. that I may d. it for me and my son
18. 23. I will d. the other bullock and lay it on wood
25. Elijah said, d. it first, for ye are many

DRESSED.

Gen. 18. 8. Abraham took the calf which he had d.
Lev. 7. 9. all that is d. in the frying-pan be the priest's
1 Sam. 25. 18. Abigail took five sheep ready d.
2 Sam. 12. 4. but took the poor man's lamb and d. it
19. 24. Mephibosheth, son of Saul, had not d. his feet
1 Kings 18. 26. they d. it, and called on Baal
Heb. 6. 7. bringeth herbs for them by whom it is d.

DRESSER.

Luke 13. 7. then said he to the d. of the vineyard

DRESSETH.

Exod. 30. 7. when he d. the lamps, he shall burn

DREW.

Gen. 24. 20. Rebekah d. water for his camels, 45.
37. 28. they d. and lifted up Joseph out of the pit
38. 29. it came to pass, Zarah d. back his hand
Exod. 2. 10. because I d. him out of the water
16. Jethro's daughters came and d. water
19. an Egyptian d. water enough for us
Josh. 8. 26. for Joshua d. not his hand back
Judg. 8. 10. there fell 120,000 men that d. sword
20. but the youth d. not his sword, for he feared
Judg. 20. 2. the chief of Israel 400,000 that d. sword
15. of Benjamin numbered 26,000 that d. sword
25. all these d. the sword, 35.
37. liers in wait d. themselves along, and smote
46. fell of Benjamin 25,000 that d. the sword
Ruth 4. 8. buy it for thee, so he d. off his shoe
1 Sam. 7. 6. Israel gathered to Mizpeh, and d. water
17. 51. David d. Goliath's sword out of the sheath
2 Sam. 22. 17. he sent from above, he took me, he d. me out of many waters, Psal. 18. 16.
23. 16. the three mighty men d. water of the well of Bethlehem, 1 Chron. 11. 18.
24. 9. there were in Israel 800,000 that d. the sword
1 Kings 22. 34. certain man d. a bow, 2 Chr. 18. 33.
2 Kings 3. 26. king of Moab took 700 that d. sword
9. 24. Jehu d. a bow with his full strength
1 Chr. 19. 16. they sent and d. forth the Syrians
21. 5. Israel were eleven hundred thousand men that d. sword, Judah was 470,000 that d. sword
2 Chron. 5. 9. d. out staves of the ark, 1 Kings 8. 8.
14. 8. of Benjamin that d. bows, 280,000
Jer. 38. 13. they d. up Jeremiah with cords
Hos. 11. 4. I d. them with cords of a man
Mat. 13. 48. when full, they d. to shore, Mark 6. 53.
26. 51. Peter d. his sword, Mark 14. 47. John 18. 10.
Luke 23. 54. the preparation, and the sabbath d. on
John 2. 9. the servants which d. the water knew
21. 11. and d. the net to land full of fishes
Acts 5. 37. and d. away much people after him
14. 19. stoned Paul and d. him out of the city
16. 19. and d. Paul and Silas into the market-place
27. the jailer d. his sword, and would have killed
17. 6. they d. Jason and certain brethren
19. 33. they d. Alexander out of the multitude
21. 30. they took Paul and d. him out of the temple
Rev. 12. 4. his tail d. the third part of the stars

DREW *near,* or *nigh.*

Gen. 18. 23. Abraham d. near and said, wilt thou
47. 29. the time d. nigh that Israel must die
Exod. 14. 10. when Pharaoh d. nigh Israel cried
20. 21. Moses d. near to the thick darkness
Lev. 9. 5. the congregation d. near before the Lord
Josh. 8. 11. all the people d. nigh before Ai
1 Sam. 7. 10. the Philistines d. near to battle
9. 18. Saul d. near to Samuel in the gate
17. 16. Goliath d. n. morning and evening, 41, 48.
40. David d. near to Goliath the Philistine
2 Sam. 10. 13. Joab d. nigh against the Syrians
18. 25. Ahimaaz came apace and d. near
Esth. 5. 2. Esther d. near and touched the sceptre
9. 1. the king's decree d. near to be put in execution
Zeph. 3. 2. she trusted not, she d. not near to her God
Mat. 21. 1. and when they d. nigh to Jerusalem
34. when the time of the fruit d. near, he sent
Luke 15. 1. then d. near the publicans to hear him
25. elder son came, and as he d. nigh to the house
22. 1. now the feast of unleavened bread d. nigh
47. and Judas d. near to Jesus to kiss him
24. 15. Jesus himself d. near, and went with them
28. they d. nigh to the village where they went
Acts 7. 17. when the time of the promise d. nigh
31. as he d. near to behold it, the voice came
10. 9. as they d. nigh to the city, Peter went
27. 27. deemed that they d. near some country

DREWEST.

Lam. 3. 57. thou d. near in the day that I called

DRIED. *See after* DRY.

DRINK.

Gen. 21. 19. Hagar filled bottle, and gave the lad d.
24. 14. I will give thy camels d. also, 46.
Lev. 11. 34. all d. that may be drunk in such vessel
Num. 20. 8. thou shalt give the congregation d.
Judg. 4. 19. she gave Sisera d. and covered him
Ezra 3. 7. they gave meat and d. to them of Zidon
Esth. 1. 7. they gave them d. in vessels of gold
Psal. 78. 15. he gave them d. as out of great depths
102. 9. for I have mingled my d. with weeping
104. 11. they gave d. to every beast of the field
Isa. 32. 6. he will cause the d. of the thirsty to fail
43. 20. rivers, to give d. to my people, my chosen
Dan. 1. † 5. the king appointed them of his d. 10.
Hos. 2. 5. go after my lovers that give me my d.
4. 18. their d. is sour, they have committed
Hab. 2. 15. woe to him that giveth his neighbour d.
Hag. 1. 6. ye drink, but ye are not filled with d.
Mat. 25. 35. I was thirsty, and ye gave me d.
37. gave thee d. || 42. thirsty, and ye gave me no d.
John 4. 9. that thou, being a Jew, askest d. of me
6. 55. my flesh is meat indeed, my blood is d. indeed
Rom. 12. 20. if thine enemy thirst, give him d.
14. 17. the kingdom of God is not meat and d.
1 Cor. 10. 4. and did all drink the same spiritual d.
Col. 2. 16. let no man judge you in meat or in d.

Strong DRINK.

Lev. 10. 9. do not drink strong d. when ye go in
Num. 6. 3. Nazarite separate himself from strong d.
Deut. 14. 26. shalt bestow that money for strong d.
29. 6. nor have ye drunk strong d. these forty years
Judg. 13. 4. Manoah's wife not drink strong d. 7. 14.
1 Sam. 1. 15. I drunk neither wine nor strong d.
Psal. 69. † 12. I was the song of drinkers of strong d.
Prov. 20. 1. wine is a mocker, strong d. is raging
31. 4. it is not for princes to drink strong d.
6. give strong d. to him that is ready to perish
Isa. 5. 11. that they may follow str. d. woe to them
22. woe to men of strength to mingle strong d.
24. 9. strong d. shall be bitter to them that drink it
28. 7. but they also have erred through strong d. and they are out of the way through strong d.
29. 9. they stagger, but not with strong d.
56. 12. come ye, we will fill ourselves with strong d.
Mic. 2. 11. will prophesy to thee of wine and str. d.
Luke 1. 15. John shall not drink wine nor strong d.

DRINK-*offering.*

Gen. 35. 14. Jacob poured a d. offering on the pillar
Exod. 29. 40. an hin of oil, and the fourth part of an hin of wine for a d. offering, Num. 15. 5.
41. shalt do thereto according to the d. offering
30. 9. nor shall ye pour d. offering thereon
Lev. 23. 13. and the d. offering shall be of wine
Num. 6. 17. the priest shall offer also his d. offering
15. 7. for a d. offer. a third part of an hin of wine

Num. 15. 10. bring for a *d. offering* half an hin of wine
24. his *d. offering* according to the manner
28. 10. besides the continual *d. off.* 15, 24. | 29. 16.
Isa. 57. 6. to them hast thou poured a *d. offering*
65. 11. that furnish the *d. offering* to that number
Joel 1. 9. the *d. off.* is cut off from the house of L.
13. the *d. off.* is withholden from house of God
2. 14. if he will return and leave a *d. offering*

DRINK *offerings.*

Lev. 23. 18. they shall be for a burnt offering with *d. offerings*, 37. *Num.* 6. 15. | 28. 31. | 29. 11, 18, 19, 21, 24, 30, 33, 37, 39.
Num. 28. 14. their *d. off.* shall be half an hin of wine
Deut. 32. 38. and drank the wine of their *d. offer.*
1 *Chr.* 29. 21. offered with their *d. off.* 2 *Chr.* 29. 35.
Ezra 7. 17. buy speedily meat-offerings and *d. off.*
Psal. 16. 4. their *d. offer.* of blood will I not offer
Jer. 7. 18. and to pour out *d. offerings* to other gods to provoke me to anger, 19. 13. | 32. 29.
44. 17. pour out *d. off.* to queen of heaven, 18, 19, 25.
Ezek. 20. 28. there they poured out their *d. offer.*
45. 17. prince's part to give *d. offerings* in the feasts

DRINK.

To drink *signifies to drink liquor moderately, for the satisfying of thirst,* Num. 6. 3. Ruth 2. 9. *Sometimes it signifies to drink plentifully, liberally, and largely, so as to be merry, but not to excess or drunkenness: Thus it is said,* Gen. 43. 34. *that* Joseph's *brethren* drank and were merry with him: *The* Hebrew *word here used often signifies to drink to excess; but it is not to be supposed that* Jacob's *sons should forget themselves so far upon this occasion, as to be wanting in that decency and respect which they owed to one so considerable as* Joseph, *whom as yet they knew not to be their brother. And in* John 2. 10. Every man at the beginning doth set forth good wine; and when men have well drunk, then that which is worse; but thou hast kept the good wine until now. *It is incredible that our Saviour waited till the guests were drunk, in order to perform the miracle which he wrought at* Cana *in their favour. And in* 1 Cor. 11. 21. One is hungry, and another is drunken, *that is, One wants, and the other abounds: The poor Christians were hungry, while the richer sort had too much, and fared liberally.* To drink, *in other parts of Scripture, is often taken in an odious sense, for drinking to excess, for being intoxicated with liquor:* Gen. 9. 21. *Noah* drank of the wine, and was drunken, and he was uncovered in his tent. Lot's *two daughters made their father drink to excess, and both proved with child by him,* Gen. 19. 32, 33, &c.

Our Saviour says in the gospel, If any man thirst, let him come unto me and drink, *John* 7. 37. *If any man have a desire after spiritual blessings, let him come unto me by faith, and he shall partake largely of my refreshing grace. And he tells the woman of* Samaria, *John* 4. 14. Whosoever drinketh of the water that I shall give him shall never thirst. *Whosoever partakes of the graces of the Holy Spirit, which I have to bestow, and do offer in the gospel, he shall never desire and pursue worldly things as his chief happiness. It is said,* Job 15. 16. *That the* wicked drinketh iniquity like water. *Besides his natural proneness to sin, he has contracted habits and customs of sinning, so that he sinneth as readily, greedily, and delightfully, as men used to drink up water, especially in those hot countries. And* Elihu *says,* Job 34. 7. What man is like *Job,* who drinketh up scorning like water? *Who with greediness and delight breaks forth into scornful and contemptuous expressions, not only against his friends, but in some sort even against God himself, whom he insolently charges with rigorous dealing.* Rab-shakeh *says, that* Hezekiah *designed to persuade the* Jews *into a resolution of holding out the siege of* Jerusalem, *that so he might reduce them to the necessity of* drinking their own urine; *that is, of exposing themselves to the utmost extremities of a siege,* 2 Kings 18. 27. Solomon *exhorts his disciple,* Prov. 5. 15. to drink water out of his own cistern; *that is, to content himself with the lawful pleasures of marriage, without thinking on that which was prohibited by the law.* To eat and drink *is used in* Eccl. 5. 18. *to signify people's enjoying themselves, using the good things of this life liberally and decently; and not with penuriousness, which is base and dishonourable:* It is good and comely for one to eat and drink, and to enjoy the good of all his labour. *It is said in* Mat. 11. 18, 19. *John* came neither eating nor drinking; *that is, he did not live in the common and ordinary manner, as other men did, but used a mean and peculiar diet:* but the Son of man came eating and drinking; *using such a diet as other men did, and conversing freely and sociably with all sorts.*

Sennacherib *says in* 2 Kings 19. 24. Isa. 37. 25. I have digged and drunk strange waters, and with the sole of my feet have I dried up all the rivers of besieged places. *I have brought water to places where there was none before, to supply my army: and I have drunk up the water belonging to the people through whose country I have marched my armies; I have exhausted their wells and their cisterns. The prophet* Jeremiah *upbraids the* Jews *with having had recourse to* Egypt *for muddy water, to drink; and with having addressed themselves to the* Assyrians, *that they might drink the water of their river; that is, with having sought for the water of* Nile *in* Egypt, *and the water of* Euphrates *in* Assyria; *thereby describing the assistance of these two people, which the* Jews *sought for,* Jer. 2. 18.

To drink blood, *signifies to be satiated with slaughter,* Ezek. 39. 18. Ye shall drink the blood of the princes of the earth; *ye shall put them to death.* David *refused to drink the water which the three valiant men of his army went and procured for him at the hazard of their lives; saying,* God forbid that I should drink the blood of these men; *but* he poured it out unto the Lord, *as a kind of drink-offering, and acknowledgment of God's goodness in preserving the lives of his captains in so dangerous an enterprise,* 2 Sam. 23. 16, 17. To buy water to drink, *and* to drink water by measure, *denote the utmost scarcity and extreme desolation,* Lam. 5. 4. Ezek. 4. 11.

God's judgments are often in scripture expressed under the notion of a cup of strong and intoxicating drink: and the suffering or enduring of these, is set out under the notion of drinking such a cup. See CUP. In the hand of the Lord there is a cup, and the wine is red, the dregs thereof all the wicked of the earth shall drink them, *Psal.* 75. 8. Thou hast made us to drink the wine of astonishment, *Psal.* 60. 3. *Thou hast filled us with horror and astonishment, as if we had drunk some poisonous wine.* Stand up, O *Jerusalem,* which hast drunk at the hand of the Lord the cup of his fury: Hear now this, thou afflicted and drunken, but not with wine, *Isa.* 51. 17, 21. I will fill the kings, the priests, the prophets, and all the inhabitants of *Jerusalem,* with drunkenness, *Jer.* 13. 13. *that is, with the wine of terror and astonishment, by reason of those grievous calamities that shall come upon them, and which will put them to their wit's end. And in* Ezek. 23. 33. Thou shalt be filled with drunkenness and sorrow. *See* Obad. 16. Rev. 14. 10.

Drink is put for, (1) *The blood of Christ,* John 6. 55. (2) *Spiritual delight,* Cant. 8. 2. (3) *Afflictions,* Mat. 20. 23. (4) *The wrath of God,* Job 21. 20. Rev. 14. 10. (5) *Greedy desire,* Job 15. 16.

Gen. 24. 14. let me *d.* 17, 45. ‖ 18. *d.* my lord, 46.
30. 38. he set rods when the flocks came to *d.*
Exod. 15. 24. people murmured, what shall we *d.*
32. 20. Moses made the children of Israel *d.* of it
Lev. 10. 9. do not *d.* wine nor strong *d.* lest ye die
Num. 6. 3. neither shall he *d.* liquor of grapes
Judg. 7. 5. that boweth down on his knees to *d.*
Ruth 2. 9. when athirst, go to the vessels and *d.*
2 *Sam.* 23. 16. three mighty men drew water, but David would not *d.* thereof, 17. 1 *Chr.* 11. 18, 19.
1 *Kings* 17. 4. that thou shalt *d.* of the brook
Esth. 3. 15. the king and Haman sat down to *d.*
7. †1. the king and Haman came to *d.* with Esther
Job 21. 20. he shall *d.* the wrath of the Almighty
Ps. 36. 8. make them *d.* of the river of thy pleasures
60. 3. made us to *d.* the wine of astonishment
69. 21. in my thirst they gave me vinegar to *d.*
75. 8. the wicked of the earth shall *d.* them
78. 44. their rivers into blood, they could not *d.*
80. 5. thou gavest them tears to *d.*
110. 7. he shall *d.* of the brook in the way
Prov. 4. 17. for they *d.* the wine of violence
31. 5. lest they *d.* and forget the law, and pervert
7. let him *d.* and forget his poverty
Cant. 5. 1. *d.* yea, *d.* abundantly, O beloved
Isa. 24. 9. strong drink bitter to them that *d.* it
51. 22. thou shalt no more *d.* it again
62. 9. they shall *d.* it in the courts of my holiness
65. 13. my servants shall *d.* but ye shall be thirsty
Jer. 16. 7. nor give the cup of consolation to *d.*
23. 15. and make them *d.* the water of gall
25. 15. cause nations, to whom I send thee, to *d.* it
16. and they shall *d.* and be moved, and be mad
17. then I took the cup, and made all nations to *d.*
27. *d.* ye, and be drunken, and spue, and fall
28. thus saith the Lord, ye shall certainly *d.*
35. 14. to this day they *d.* none, but obey father's
49. 12. they whose judgment was not to *d.* of the cup, shalt not go unpunished, shalt surely *d.* of it
Ezek. 4. 11. *d.* by measure, from time to time shalt *d.*
23. 32. thou shalt *d.* of sister's cup deep and large
34. 19. they *d.* that which ye have fouled
Dan. 5. 2. that his concubines might *d.* therein
Amos 4. 1. say to their masters, bring, and let us *d.*
Obad. 16. so shall all the heathen *d.* continually, yea, they shall *d.* and shall swallow down
Hab. 2. 16. *d.* thou, let thy foreskin be uncovered
Hag. 1. 6. ye *d.* but ye are not filled with drink
Zech. 9. 15. and they shall *d.* and make a noise
Mat. 10. 42. whoso shall give to *d.* to one of these
20. 22. are ye able to *d.* of the cup that I shall *d.* of, and be baptized with the baptism? *Mark* 10. 38.
23. ye shall *d.* indeed of my cup, *Mark* 10. 39.
26. 27. he gave them the cup, saying, *d.* ye all of it
29. I say, I will not *d.* henceforth till that day when I *d.* it new with you, *Mark* 14. 25. *Luke* 22. 18.
42. if cup may not pass except I *d.* thy will be done
27. 34. gave him vinegar to *d.* mingled with gall
48. one filled a spunge with vinegar, and put it on a reed, and gave him to *d. Mark* 15. 36.
Mark 16. 18. if they *d.* any deadly thing, not hurt
John 4. 10. who it is that saith to thee, give me to *d.*
7. 37. if any man thirst, let him come to me and *d.*
18. 11. cup my father hath given me, shall I not *d.*?
1 *Cor.* 10. 4. and did all *d.* the same spiritual drink
21. ye cannot *d.* the cup of the Lord and of devils
11. 25. this do, as oft as ye *d.* in remembrance of me
12. 13. and have been all made to *d.* into one spirit

DRINK *water,* or *waters.*

Gen. 24. 43. give me a little *water* of thy pitcher to *d.*
Exod. 7. 18. shall lothe to *d. water* of the river, 21.
24. digged round about the river for *water* to *d.*
15. 23. they could not *d.* of the *waters* of Marah
17. 1. there was no *water* for the people to *d.*
6. shall come *water* out of it, that they may *d.*
Num. 5. 24. cause woman to *d.* bitter *water,* 26, 27.
20. 5. neither is there any *water* to *d.* 33. 14.
17. nor will we *d.* of the *water* of the wells, 21. 22.
Deut. 2. 6. buy *water* for money, that ye may *d.* 28.
Judg. 4. 19. give me a little *water* to *d.* I am thirsty
7. 6. the rest bowed upon their knees to *d. water*
1 *Sam.* 30. 11. and they made the Egyptian *d. water*
2 *Sam.* 23. 15. David said, give me to *d.* of the *water* of the well of Beth-lehem, 1 *Chron.* 11. 17.
1 *Kings* 13. 8. nor will I eat bread, nor *d. water,* 9.
17. 10. fetch a little *water* in a vessel that I may *d.*
2 *Kings* 3. 17. valley filled with *water* that ye may *d.*
18. 31. *d.* every one *waters* of his cistern, *Isa.* 36. 16.
Job 22. 7. thou hast not given *water* to weary to *d.*
Prov. 5. 15. *d. waters* out of thine own cistern
25. 21. if thy enemy be thirsty, give him *water* to *d.*
Jer. 2. 18. to *d.* the *waters* of Sihor, waters of river
8. 14. Lord hath given us *water* of gall to *d.* 9. 15.
Ezek. 4. 11. thou shalt *d. water* by measure, 16.
12. 18. son of man, *d.* thy *water* with trembling
19. they shall *d.* their *water* with astonishment
31. 14. all their trees that *d. water,* 16.
Dan. 1. 12. give us pulse to eat, and *water* to *d.*
Amos 4. 8. wandered to *d. water,* were not satisfied
Jonah 3. 7. let them not feed nor *d. water*
Mark 9. 41. who shall give you a cup of *water* to *d.*
John 4. 7. Jesus saith to her, give me *water* to *d.*
1 *Tim.* 5. 23. *d.* no longer *water,* but use a little wine

DRINK, with *wine.*

Gen. 19. 32. let us make our father *d. wine,* 34.
33. and they made their father *d. wine,* 35.
Lev. 10. 9. nor *d. wine* when ye go into tabernacle
Num. 6. 3. the Nazarite shall *d.* no vinegar of *wine*
20. after that the Nazarite may *d. wine*
Deut. 28. 39. thou shalt plant vineyards, but shalt not *d.* of the wine, nor gather the grapes, *Amos* 5. 11.
Judg. 13. 4. Manoah's wife might *d.* no *wine,* 7, 14.
2 *Sam.* 16. 2. the *wine,* that such as be faint may *d.*
Psal. 60. 3. hast made us *d.* the *wine* of astonishment
Prov. 4. 17. for they *d.* the *wine* of violence
9. 5. and *d.* of the *wine* which I have mingled
31. 4. it is not for kings, O Lemuel, to *d. wine*
Eccl. 9. 7. go and *d.* thy *wine* with a merry heart
Cant. 8. 2. I would cause thee to *d.* of spiced *wine*
Isa. 5. 22. woe to them that are mighty to *d. wine*
24. 9. they shall not *d. wine* with a song
62. 8. the sons of the stranger shall not *d.* thy *wine*
Jer. 35. 2. go and give the Rechabites *wine* to *d.*
6. we will *d.* no *wine,* ye shall *d.* no *wine* for ever
Ezek. 44. 21. neither shall any priest *d. wine* when
Dan. 1. 16. took away the *wine* that they should *d.*
Joel 3. 3. they have sold a girl for *wine* to *d.*
Amos 2. 8. they *d.* the *wine* of the condemned
12. but ye gave the Nazarites *wine* to *d.*
6. 6. that *d. wine* in bowls, and anoint themselves
9. 14. shall plant vineyards, and *d. wine* thereof
Mic. 6. 15. but shall not *d. wine, Zeph.* 1. 13.
Mark 15. 23. gave him to *d. wine,* mingled with myrrh
Luke 1. 15. John shall *d.* neither *wine* nor strong
Rom. 14. 21. it is not good to eat flesh or *d. wine*
Rev. 14. 8. she made all nations *d.* of the *wine*
10. same shall *d.* of the *wine* of the wrath of God

DRINKERS.

Psal. 69. † 12. the song of the *d.* of strong drink
Joel 1. 5. awake, and howl, all ye *d.* of wine

DRINKS.

Heb. 9. 10. which stood only in meats, and *d.* and divers washings

DRINKETH.

Gen. 44. 5. is not this it in which my lord *d.*?
Deut. 11. 11. the land *d.* water of the rain of heaven
Job 6. 4. the poison whereof *d.* up my spirit
15. 16. how filthy is man, who *d.* iniq. like water!
34. 7. like Job who *d.* up scorning like water
40. 23. behold, he *d.* up a river, and hasteth not
Prov. 26. 6. he that sendeth by a fool *d.* damage
Isa. 29. 8. he *d.* but he awaketh, and he is faint
44. 12. the smith, he *d.* no water and is faint
Mark 2. 16. how is it that he *d.* with publicans?
John 4. 13. whosoever *d.* of this water shall thirst
14. whosoever *d.* of water that I shall give him
6. 54. whoso *d.* my blood, hath eternal life
56. that *d.* my blood dwelleth in me, and I in him
1 *Cor.* 11. 29. he that *d.* unworthily *d.* damnation
Heb. 6. 7. for the earth which *d.* in the rain

DRINKING.

Gen. 24. 19. water for camels till they have done *d.*
22. as camels had done *d.* the man took an ear-ring
Ruth 3. 3. till Boaz have done eating and *d.*
1 *Sam.* 30. 16. they were eating and *d.* and dancing
1 *Kings* 4. 20. Judah and Israel were many, *d.*
10. 21. Solomon's *d.* vessels of gold, 2 *Chr.* 9. 20.
16. 9. Elah was *d.* ‖ 20. 12. Benhadad was *d.* 16.
1 *Chron.* 12. 39. with David three days eating and *d.*
Esth. 1. 8. *d.* was according to the law, none compel
Job 1. 13. his sons and daughters were *d.* 18.
Isa. 22. 13. and behold, eating flesh, and *d.* wine
Mat. 11. 18. for John came neither eating nor *d.* and they say, he hath a devil, *Luke* 7. 33.
19. Son of man came eating and *d. Luke* 7. 34.
24. 38. they were eating and *d.* till the flood came
Luke 10. 7. eating and *d.* such things as they give
Col. 2. † 16. let no man judge you for eating or *d.*

DRIVE.

Exod. 6. 1. with a strong hand shall he *d.* them out
23. 28. will send hornets, which shall *d.* out Hivite
29. I will not *d.* them out before thee in one year
30. by little and little I will *d.* them out before
31. and thou shalt *d.* them out before thee
33. 2. I will *d.* out the Canaanite, the Amorite
34. 11. behold I *d.* out before thee the Amorite
Num. 22. 6. that I may *d.* them out of the land
11. I may be able to overcome and *d.* them out
33. 52. then shall ye *d.* out all the inhabitants
55. but if ye will not *d.* out the inhabitants
Deut. 4. 38. to *d.* out nations from before thee, greater and mightier than thee, 9. 4, 5. *Josh.* 3. 10.
9. 3. so shalt thou *d.* them out and destroy them
11. 23. then will the Lord *d.* out these nations
18. 12. Lord thy God doth *d.* them out before thee
Josh. 13. 6. them will I *d.* out from before Israel
14. 12. then I shall be able to *d.* them out, as L. said
15. 63. the children of Judah could not *d.* them out
17. 12. the children of Manasseh could not *d.* out
13. but did not utterly *d.* them out, *Judg.* 1. 28.
18. for thou shalt *d.* out the Canaanites
23. 5. the Lord shall *d.* them out of your sight
13. the Lord will no more *d.* out, *Judg.* 2. 3, 21.
Judg. 1. 19. Judah could not *d.* inhabitants o. mount

Judg. 1. 21. Benjamin did not d. out the Jebusites
27. Manasseh d. || 29. Ephraim || 30. Zebulun
31. Asher || 33. Naphtali did not d. out
11. 24. whom the Lord our God shall d. out
2 Kings 4. 24. d. go forward, slack not riding for me
2 Chron. 20. 7. who didst d. out the inhabitants
Job 18. 11. terrors shall make afraid, and d. to feet
† 18. he shall d. him from light into darkness
24. 3. they d. away the ass of the fatherless
Psal. 44. 2. how thou didst d. out the heathen
68. 2. as smoke is driven away, so d. them away
Prov. 22. 15. but rod of correction shall d. it away
Isa. 22. 19. and I will d. thee from thy station
Jer. 24. 9. to be a curse whither I shall d. them
27. 10. that I should d. you out, and ye perish, 15.
46. 15. they stood not, because Lord did d. them
Ezek. 4. 13. among Gentiles, whither I will d. them
Dan. 4. 25. and they shall d. thee from men, 32.
Hos. 9. 15. I will d. them out of my house
Joel 2. 20. I will d. the northern army into a land
Zeph. 2. 4. they shall d. out Ashdod at noon-day
Acts 27. 15. the ship was caught, we let her d.
Gal. 5. †7. ye did run well, who did d. you back?

DRIVEN.

Gen. 4. 14. behold, thou hast d. me out this day
Exod. 10. 11. they were d. from Pharaoh's presence
22. 10. the beast be d. away, no man seeing it
Lev. 26. † 36. sound of a d. leaf shall chase them
Num. 32. 21. till he have d. out enemies before him
Deut. 4. 19. lest thou shouldest be d. to worship them
30. 1. whither the Lord thy God hath d. thee
4. if any of them be d. out to the utmost parts
Josh. 23. 9. the Lord hath d. out great nations
1 Sam. 26. 19. for they have d. me out this day
Job 6. 13. and is wisdom d. quite from me?
13. 25. wilt thou break a leaf d. to and fro?
18. 18. he shall be d. from light into darkness
30. 5. they were d. forth from among men
Psal. 40. 14. let them be d. backward that wish evil
68. 2. as smoke is d. away, so drive them away
114. 3. sea saw it and fled, Jordan was d. back, 5.
Prov. 14. 32. wicked is d. away in his wickedness
Eccl. 3. † 15. God requireth that which is d. away
Isa. 8. 22. and they shall be d. to darkness
19. 7. every thing sown by the brooks be d. away
41. 2. he gave them as d. stubble to his bow
Jer. 8. 3. who remain in all the places whither I have d. them, 23. 3, 8. | 29. 14, 18. | 32. 37.
16. 15. from all the lands whither he had d. them
23. 2. ye have d. them away, and have not visited
12. they shall be d. on and fall therein
40. 12. out of all places whither they were d. 43. 5.
46. 28. a full end of nations whither I have d. thee
49. 5. ye shall be d. out every man right forth
50. 17. Israel, the lions have d. him away
Ezek. 31. 11. I have d. him out for his wickedness
34. 4. nor brought again, which was d. away, 16.
Dan. 4. 33. and he was d. from men, 5. 21.
9. 7. thro' all countries whither thou hast d. them
Hos. 13. 3. as the chaff that is d. with the whirlwind
Mic. 4. 6. I will gather her that was d. Zeph. 3. 19.
Luke 8. 29. he was d. of the devil into the wilderness
Acts 27. 17. they strake sail, and so were d.
27. we were d. up and down in Adria at midnight
Jam. 1. 6. is like a wave of the sea d. with the wind
3. 4. the ships though great are d. of fierce winds

DRIVER.

1 Kings 22. 34. Ahab said to the d. of his chariot
Job 39. 7. nor regardeth the crying of the d.

DRIVETH.

2 Kings 9. 20. driving is like Jehu, for he d. furiously
Psal. 1. 4. ungodly like chaff which wind d. away
Prov. 25. 23. the north wind d. away rain
Mark 1. 12. the spirit d. him into the wilderness

DRIVING.

Judg. 2. 23. Lord left without d. them out hastily
2 Kings 9. 20. and the d. is like the d. of Jehu
1 Chron. 17. 21 by d. out nations before thy people

DROMEDARY

Is *a sort of camel; It is called* Dromedary *from the* Greek, δρεμω, *I run, by reason of its running very swiftly.* Dromedaries *are smaller than common camels, slenderer, and more nimble. Upon their backs they have a kind of natural saddle, which is composed of a great deal of hair, that stands up, and forms as it were a large bunch. In eastern countries, when persons would go any where with speed, they generally make use of* Dromedaries. *It is said that they can go an hundred miles in a day with them; nay, some affirm, that there are some which will travel an hundred and fifty miles in a day.*

There *are two sorts of* dromedaries, *one of a larger kind, with two bunches upon its back; the other lesser, with only one. Both are very common in the western parts of* Asia, *such as* Syria, *and* Arabia. *That which hath but one bunch upon its back, is more commonly called* camel; *the other is named* dromedary. *They are both capable of very great fatigues; their hair is soft, and shorn, but about the middle of their backs, camels have a little eminence covered with hair, a foot high upon their bunch; and dromedaries have two bunches, and two eminences of hair, which, however, are very small; and if it be rightly considered,* dromedaries *and* camels *are no more hunch-backed than other animals. They have no fingers and fore-teeth; they have no horn upon their feet, for they are only covered with a fleshy skin. It is said, that when they drink, they disturb the water with their feet: some believe they do this to make the water heavier, that it may continue longer in their stomachs. They are said to drink a great deal, and keep it a long time, against their being thirsty afterwards; nay, some will have it that travellers upon pressing necessities open their stomachs, take out the water contained in them, and satisfy their thirst with it: The stomach of these creatures is composed of four ventricles, and in the second there are several mouths which open a passage into about twenty cavities made like sacks, that serve them for conservatories of water.*

Jer. 2. 23. thou art a swift d. traversing her ways

DROMEDARIES.

1 Kings 4. 28. they brought barley and straw for d.
Esth. 8. 10. and sent letters by riders on young d.
Isa. 60. 6. d. of Midian and Ephah shall cover thee

DROP.

Isa. 40. 15. the nations are as the d. of a bucket

DROP, Verb.

Deut. 32. 2. my doctrine shall d. as the rain
33. 28. also heavens shall d. down dew, Prov. 3. 20.
Job 36. 28. which clouds do d. and distil upon man
Psal. 65. 11. crownest year, and thy paths d. fatness
12. they d. on the pastures of the wilderness
Prov. 5. 3. lips of a strange woman d. as honey-comb
Cant. 4. 11. thy lips, my spouse, d. as the honey-comb
Isa. 45. 8. d. down, ye heavens, from above
Ezek. 20. 46. d. thy word toward south, and prophesy
21. 2. d. thy word toward holy places and prophesy
Joel 3. 18. the mountains shall d. down new wine, and the hills shall flow with milk, Amos 9. 13.
Amos 7. 16. d. not thy word against the house of Isaac
Mic. 2. † 6. d. not, say they to them that prophesy

DROPPED.

Judg. 5. 4. the heavens d. the clouds also d. water
1 Sam. 14. 26. were come into wood, behold honey d.
2 Sam. 21. 10. till water d. on them out of heaven
Job 29. 22. and my speech d. upon them
Psal. 68. 8. the heavens also d. at the presence of God
Cant. 5. 5. my hands d. with myrrh, and fingers

DROPPETH.

Psal. 119. † 28. my soul d. for heaviness, strengthen
Eccl. 10. 18. through idleness the house d. through

DROPPING, S.

Prov. 19. 13. a foolish son is calamity, and the contentions of a wife are a continual d. 27. 15.
Cant. 5. 13. his lips d. sweet-smelling myrrh
Amos 6. † 11. I will smite the great house with d.

DROPS.

Job 36. 27. he maketh small the d. of water
38. 28. or who hath begotten the d. of the dew?
Cant. 5. 2. and my locks with the d. of the night
Luke 22. 44. his sweat was as great d. of blood

DROPSY.

Luke 14. 2. there was a man before him, who had d.

DROSS.

Psal. 119. 119. thou puttest away the wicked like d.
Prov. 25. 4. take away the d. from the silver
26. 23. are like a potsherd covered with silver d.
Isa. 1. 22. silver is become d. wine mixed with water
25. I will purely purge away thy d. and thy tin
Ezek. 22. 18. house of Israel is to me become d. 19.

DROVE, S.

Gen. 32. 16. every d. by themselves, and said, pass over before me, and put a space betwixt d. and d.
19. so commanded he all that followed the d.
33. 8. what meanest thou by all this d. which I met?

DROVE, Verb.

Gen. 3. 24. so God d. out the man, and he placed at the east of the garden of Eden cherubims
15. 11. when the fowls came, Abram d. them away
Exod. 2. 17. the shepherds came and d. them away
Num. 21. 32. they d. out the Amorites that were there
Josh. 15. 14. Caleb d. thence the sons of Anak
1 Chr. 8. 13. who d. away the inhabitants of Gath
Hab. 3. 6. he beheld, and d. asunder the nations
John 2. 15. he d. them all out of the temple

DROUGHT.

Gen. 31. 40. thus I was, in the day d. consumed me
Deut. 8. 15. wherein were fiery serpents and d.
28. † 22. the Lord shall smite thee with the d.
Job 24. 19. d. and heat consume the snow waters
Psal. 32. 4. my moisture is turned into d. of summer
Isa. 58. 11. the Lord shall satisfy thy soul in d.
Jer. 2. 6. the Lord that brought us thro' a land of d.
17. 8. and shall not be careful in the year of d.
50. 38. a d. is upon her waters, they shall be dried
Hos. 13. 5. I did know thee in the land of great d.
Hag. 1. 11. and I called for a d. upon the land

DROWN.

Cant. 8. 7. cannot quench love, nor can floods d. it
1 Tim. 6. 9. into foolish lusts, that d. men in perdition

DROWNED.

Exod. 15. 4. his chosen captains are d. in the Red sea
Amos 8. 8. it shall be d. as by flood of Egypt, 9. 5.
Mat. 18. 6. better he were d. in the midst of the sea
Heb. 11. 29. which the Egyptians assaying to do, [were d.

DROWSINESS.

Prov. 23. 21. and d. shall clothe a man with rags

DRUNK.

Lev. 11. 34. all drink that may be d. shall be [unclean
Deut. 29. 6. have not eaten bread, nor d. wine
32. 42. I will make mine arrows d. with blood
Judg. 15. 19. when Samson had d. Spirit came again
Ruth 3. 7. when Boaz had eaten and d. he went to lie
1 Sam. 1. 9. Hannah rose up after they d. in Shiloh
15. I have d. neither wine nor strong drink
2 Sam. 11. 13. David made Uriah d. and he went out
1 Kings 13. 22. and hast eaten bread and d. water
16. 9. as Elah was in Tirzah, drinking himself d.
20. 16. Benhadad was drinking himself d. in pavil.
2 Kings 6. 23. they had eaten and d. he sent them away
19. 24. have digged and d. strange waters, Isa. 37. 25.
Cant. 5. 1. I have d. my wine with my milk
Isa. 43. † 24. nor hast thou made me d. with the fat
51. 17. which hast d. the cup of his fury
63. 6. and I will make them d. in my fury
Jer. 46. 10. sword shall be made d. with their blood
51. 57. I will make d. her princes and her wise men
Ezek. 34. 18. and to have d. of the deep waters
Dan. 5. 23. thou and thy concubines have d. in them
Obad. 16. as ye have d. upon my holy mountain
Luke 5. 39. no man having d. old wine desires new
13. 26. we have eaten and d. in thy presence
John 2. 10. when men have well d. then worse
Eph. 5. 18. be not d. with wine wherein is excess
Rev. 17. 2. made d. with the wine of her fornication
18. 3. for all nations have d. of the wine of wrath

DRUNKARD.

Deut. 21. 20. this our son is a glutton and a d.
Prov. 23. 21. for d. and glutton shall come to poverty
26. 9. as a thorn goeth up into the hand of a d.
Isa. 24. 20. the earth shall reel to and fro like a d.
1 Cor. 5. 11. with a brother a fornicator or a d. eat not

DRUNKARDS.

Psal. 69. 12. and I was the song of the d.
Isa. 28. 1. woe to pride, to the d. of Ephraim, 3.
Ezek. 23. † 42. d. were brought from the wilderness
Joel 1. 5. awake, ye d. and weep, howl, ye drinkers
Nah. 1. 10. and while they are drunken as d.
1 Cor. 6. 10. nor d. shall inherit the kingdom of God

See on Drink.

DRUNKEN.

Gen. 9. 21. Noah was d. and he was uncovered
Deut. 29. † 19. to add the d. to the thirsty
1 Sam. 1. 13. Eli thought Hannah had been d.
14. Eli said to her, how long wilt thou be d.?
25. 36. Nabal's heart was merry, for he was very d.
Job 12. 25. to stagger like a d. man, Psal. 107. 27.
Isa. 19. 14. as a d. man staggereth in his vomit
29. 9. they are d. but not with wine, 51. 21.
34. † 7. and their land shall be d. with blood
49. 26. they shall be d. with their own blood
51. 17. thou hast d. the dregs of cup of trembling
Jer. 23. 9. my bones shake, I am like a d. man
25. 27. be d. and spue, and fall, and rise no more
48. 26. make ye him d. for he magnified himself
49. 12. behold, they have assuredly d. and art thou
51. 7. Babylon a golden cup that made all earth d.
39. I will make them d. that they may sleep
Lam. 3. 15. he hath made me d. with wormwood
4. 21. O Edom, thou shalt be d. Nah. 3. 11.
5. 4. we have d. water for money, wood is sold
Ezek. 39. 19. ye shall drink blood till ye be d.
Nah. 1. 10. and while they are d. as drunkards
Hab. 2. 15. his neighbour, and makest him d. also
Mat. 24. 49. shall begin to smite his fellow-servants and to eat and drink with the d. Luke 12. 45
Luke 17. 8. make ready, serve till I have eaten and d
Acts 2. 15. for these are not d. as ye suppose
1 Cor. 11. 21. one is hungry, and another is d.
1 Thess. 5. 7. they that be d. are d. in the night
Rev. 17. 6. I saw the woman d. with blood of saints

DRUNKENNESS.

Deut. 29. 19. I walk in imaginat. to add d. to thirst
Eccl. 10. 17. princes eat for strength, and not for d.
Jer. 13. 13. will fill inhabitants of Jerusalem with d.
Ezek. 23. 33. thou shalt be filled with d. and sorrow
Luke 21. 34. lest your hearts be overcharged with d.
Rom. 13. 13. let us walk, not in rioting and d.
Gal. 5. 21. the works of the flesh are murders, d.

DRY.

By the words annexed to DRY, *the meaning is obvious. It is spoken of land, ground, provision, waters, trees, and other things. The prophet* Isaiah *speaking of the* Messiah *says,* He shall grow up as a root out of a dry ground, *Isa.* 53. 2. *Which prophecy respects our Saviour's mean original, either as he sprang of the* Jewish *nation, which, about the time of his appearing in the world, was poor, despised, and enslaved. Or, by the* dry ground, *may be understood the royal family of* David, *which, at that time, was poor, decayed, and contemptible. The same prophet says,* chap. 56. 3. Neither let the eunuch say, behold I am a dry tree. *The Lord, by his prophet, does here encourage the eunuch, who, being excluded* from the congregation of the Lord, *Deut.* 23. 1. *and also by reason of his barrenness, which was often threatened as a curse, and was a matter of reproach among the* Jews, *might be ready to think that he was cast out of God's covenant, and cut off from his people, to whom the blessing of a numerous posterity was promised. Yet he is desired not to be discouraged on these accounts, and assured that God would accept of him, notwithstanding his barrenness, and his being excluded from the participation of church-privileges.*

When our Saviour was led away to be crucified, he tells the Jews, *Luke* 23. 31. If they do these things in a green tree, what shall be done in the dry? *If such evils befall me, who have deserved no such thing, but rather to be cherished and kindly entreated; what will befall you, who are fitted for destruction, like dry wood for the fire? The prophets sometimes compare a barren and unfruitful people to a* dry land. *Isa.* 41. 18. I will make the *dry land* springs of water. *I will make the* Jews *and* Gentiles, *who are like a dry and barren wilderness, to become fruitful. In other places, when judgments are threatened upon a land, it is said to be made* a wilderness, a dry land, a desert, *Jer.* 50. 12.

Lev. 7. 10. meat-offering mingled with oil and d.
13. 30. it is d. scald, a leprosy on the head
Josh. 9. 5. bread of provision was d. and mouldy, 12.
Judg. 6. 37. and it be d. on all the earth beside
39. Gideon said, let it now be d. only on the fleece
Job 13. 25. wilt thou pursue the d. stubble?
Psal. 105. 41. they ran in d. places like a river
Prov. 17. 1. better is a d. morsel and quietness
Isa. 25. 5. as the heat in a d. place, even the heat
32. 2. a man shall be as rivers of water in a d. place
44. 27. that saith to the deep, be d. I will dry up
56. 3. neither let the eunuch say, I am a d. tree
Jer. 4. 11. a d. wind, not to fan, nor to cleanse
51. 36. I will dry up, and make her springs d.
Ezek. 17. 24. that have made the d. tree flourish
20. 47. it shall devour every d. tree in thee
30. 12. I will make the rivers d. and sell the land
37. 2. the bones were very d. || 4. O ye d. bones
Hos. 9. 14. give them, O L. give them d. breasts
13. 15. his spring shall become d. fountain dried up
Nah. 1. 4. he rebuketh the sea, and maketh it d.
10. they shall be devoured as stubble fully d.
Zeph. 2. 13. will make Nineveh d. like a wilderness
Mat. 12. 43. he walketh thro' d. places, Luke 11. 24.
Luke 23. 31. if in green tree what shall be done in d.?

DRY *ground*.

Gen. 8. 13. behold the face of the ground was d.
Exod. 14. 16. Isr. shall go on d. ground in the sea, 22.

Josh. 3. 17. the priests that bore the ark stood firm on d. ground in Jordan, Israel passed on d. ground
2 Kings 2. 8. Elijah and Elisha went over on d. g.
Psal. 107. 33. he turneth water-springs into d. ground
35. he turneth d. ground into water-springs
Isa. 44. 3. I will pour floods upon the d. ground
53. 2. he shall grow as a root out of a d. ground
Ezek. 19. 13. she is planted in a d. and thirsty ground
See LAND.

DRY, *Verb.*

Job 12. 15. he withholdeth the waters and they d. up
15. 30. the flame shall d. up his branches
Isa. 42. 15. I will d. up herbs, I will d. up the pools
44. 27. I will d. up thy rivers || 50. 2. I d. up the sea
Jer. 51. 36. saith the Lord, I will d. up her sea
Zech. 10. 11. the deeps of the river shall d. up

DRIED.

Gen. 8. 7. until waters were d. up from earth, 13.
14. on the twenty-seventh day was the earth d.
Lev. 2. 14. shalt offer green ears of corn d. by fire
Num. 6. 3. nor shall he eat moist grapes or d.
11. 6. our soul is d. away, there is nothing at all
Josh. 2. 10. have heard how the Lord d. up Red sea
4. 23. the Lord your God d. up waters of Jordan, as Lord did Red sea, which he d. up from before us
5. 1. heard the Lord had d. up the waters of Jordan
Judg. 16. 7. bind me with withs that were never d.
1 Kings 13. 4. and Jeroboam's hand d. up
17. 7. the brook d. because there had been no rain
2 Kings 19. 24. and with the sole of my feet have I d. all the rivers of besieged places, Isa. 37. 25.
Job 18. 16. his roots shall be d. up beneath
28. 4. they are d. up, they are gone away
Psal. 22. 15. my strength is d. up like a potsherd
69. 3. my throat is d. mine eyes fail while I wait
106. 9. he rebuked the Red sea, and it was d. up
Isa. 5. 13. and their multitude d. up with thirst
19. 5. the river shall be wasted and d. up
6. the brooks of defence shall be emptied and d. up
51. 10. art thou not it which hath d. the sea?
Jer. 23. 10. pleasant places of wilderness are d. up
50. 38. upon her waters and they shall be d. up
Ezek. 17. 24. shall know that I have d. up green tree
19. 12. and the east wind d. up her fruit
37. 11. they say, our bones are d. and hope is lost
Hos. 9. 16. their root is d. up, they shall bear no fruit
13. 15. and his fountain shall be d. up
Joel 1. 10. the new wine is d. up, the oil languisheth
12. the vine is d. up || 20. rivers of water are d. up
Zech. 11. 17. his arm shall be clean d. up
Mark 5. 29. the fountain of her blood was d. up
11. 20. they saw the fig-tree d. up from the roots
Rev. 14. † 15. for the harvest of the earth is d.
16. 12. the water of Euphrates was d. up

DRIEDST.

Psal. 74. 15. the flood, thou d. up mighty rivers

DRIETH.

Job 14. 11. and as the flood decayeth and d. up
Prov. 17. 22. but a broken spirit d. the bones
Nah. 1. 4. L. makes the sea dry, and d. up all rivers

DRY-SHOD.

Isa. 11. 15. shall smite river, and make men go d.-sh.

DUE.

Lev. 10. 13. because it is thy d. and thy son's d. 14.
Deut. 18. 3. this shall be the priest's d. from people
1 Chr. 15. 13. we sought him not after the d. order
16. 29. the glory d. to his name, Psal. 29. 2. | 96. 8.
Neh. 11. 23. a portion for singers, d. for every day
Prov. 3. 27. withhold not from them to whom it is d.
Mat. 18. 34. till he should pay all that was d. to him
Luke 23. 41. we receive the d. reward of our deeds
Rom. 13. 7. render tribute to whom tribute is d.

DUE *benevolence.*

1 Cor. 7. 3. let the husband render to the wife d. b.

DUE *season.*

Lev. 26. 4. I will give you rain in d. s. Deut. 11. 14.
Num. 28. 2. observe to offer to me in their d. season
Psal. 104. 27. give them their meat in d. s. 145. 15.
Prov. 15. 23. a word spoken in d. s. how good is it!
Eccl. 10. 17. when thy princes eat in d. season
Mat. 24. 45. to give them meat in d. s. Luke 12. 42.
Gal. 6. 9. in d. season we shall reap if we faint not

DUE *time.*

Deut. 32. 35. their foot shall slide in d. time
Rom. 5. 6. in d. time Christ died for the ungodly
1 Cor. 15. 8. seen of me, as of one born out of d. time
1 Tim. 2. 6. a ransom, to be testified in d. time
Tit. 1. 3. but hath in d. time manifested his word
1 Pet. 5. 6. that he may exalt you in d. time

DUES.

Rom. 13. 7. render therefore to all their d. tribute

DUKE.

Gen. 36. 40. d. Alvah, d. Jetheth, 1 Chron. 1. 51.

DUKES.

Gen. 36. 15. these were d. of the sons of Esau, 19.
21. these are the d. of the Horites, 29.
Exod. 15. 15. then the d. of Edom shall be amazed
Josh. 13. 21. Hur, and Reba, which were d. of Sihon

DULCIMER.

Dan. 3. 5. flute, d. and all kinds of music, 10, 15.

DULL.

Mat. 13. 15. this people's heart is waxed gross, and their ears are d. of hearing, Isa. 6. 9. Acts 28. 27.
Heb. 5. 11. hard to utter, seeing ye are d. of hearing

DUMB

Is taken, (1) *For one that cannot speak for want of natural ability;* Exod. 4. 11. Who maketh the dumb, or deaf, or blind? have not I the Lord? (2) *For one that cannot speak to, and teach others, for lack of grace and knowledge;* Isa. 56. 10. His watchmen are ignorant, they are dumb dogs, they cannot bark. (3) *For one that will not speak, though he can, being submissive and silent under the dispensations of God's providence;* Psal. 39. 9. I was dumb, I opened not my mouth, because thou didst it. (4) *For such as cannot speak in their own cause, either through ignorance and infirmity, or because of the dread of their more potent adversaries, or of the majesty of him that sits in judgment;* Prov. 31. 8. Open thy mouth for the dumb in the cause of all such as are appointed to destruction. (5) *For one that is made speechless by a divine ecstasy;* Dan. 10. 15. When he had spoken such words, I became dumb. A dumb, or deaf spirit, *is a spirit that makes those persons deaf, or dumb, whom he possesses,* Mark 9. 17, 25.

Exod. 4. 11. or who maketh the d. or deaf, or blind?
Psal. 38. 13. I was as a d. man, that openeth not his mouth
39. 2. I was d. with silence, I held my peace, 9.
Prov. 31. 8. open thy mouth for the d. in cause of all
Isa. 35. 6. and the tongue of the d. shall sing
53. 7. and as a sheep before her shearers is d.
56. 10. his watchmen are blind, they are all d. dogs
Ezek. 3. 26. be d. and shalt not be to them a reprover
24. 27. thou shalt speak, and be no more d.
33. 22. my mouth was opened, and I was no more d.
Dan. 10. 15. I set my face to the ground, I became d.
Hab. 2. 18. trusteth therein, to make him d. idols
19. woe to him that saith to the d. stone, arise
Mat. 9. 32. they brought to him a d. man, possessed
33. devil was cast out, the d. spake, Luke 11. 14.
12. 22. one blind and d. and he healed him
15. 30. having with them those that were blind, d.
31. the multitude wondered, when they saw the d. speak, and the blind to see, Mark 7. 37.
Mark 9. 17. brought my son who hath a d. spirit
25. thou d. spirit, I charge thee come out of him
Luke 1. 20. behold, thou shalt be d. until the day that
Acts 8. 32. and like a lamb d. before his shearer
1 Cor. 12. 2. carried away to these d. idols, even as
2 Pet. 2. 16. the d. ass speaking with man's voice

DUNG.

By dung *is represented any thing that is nauseous, or loathsome, as the carcases of the dead,* Jer. 8. 2. | 9. 22. The wicked man, *says Job,* shall perish for ever, like his own dung, *Job* 20. 7. *which men cast away with contempt and abhorrence.* To spread dung upon the face, *expresses the greatest contempt, undervalue, and scorn.* Mal. 2. 3. I will spread dung upon your faces, even the dung of your solemn feasts. *I will pour disgrace and contempt upon you, and reject your persons and sacrifices, with as much contempt as if I took the dung of those sacrifices, and threw it in your faces. The apostle* Paul *says,* Phil. 3. 8. I count all things but dung, that I may win Christ. *All things, without* Christ, *are as dung, utterly insufficient to procure our pardon and acceptance with God.*

DOVE'S DUNG; *see on* DOVE.

Exod. 29. 14. but the flesh, skin, and d. shalt thou burn, Lev. 4. 11. | 8. 17. | 16. 27. Num. 19. 5.
1 Kings 14. 10. take away, as a man taketh away d.
2 Kings 6. 25. the fourth part of a cab of doves' d.
9. 37. carcase of Jezebel shall be as d. in the field
18. 27. that they may eat their own d. Isa. 36. 12.
Job 20. 7. yet he shall perish for ever like his own d.
Psal. 83. 10. they became as d. for the earth
Isa. 5. † 25. their carcases were as d. Jer. 9. 22.
Jer. 8. 2. they shall be for d. on the face of the earth
16. 4. they shall be as d. || 25. 33. they shall be d.
Ezek. 4. 12. bake it with d. that cometh from man
15. lo, I have given thee cow's d. for man's d.
Zeph. 1. 17. and their flesh shall be as the d.
Mal. 2. 3. I will corrupt your seed, and spread d. on your faces, even the d. of your solemn feasts
Phil. 3. 8. I do count all things but d. to win Christ

DUNG, *Verb.*

Luke 13. 8. let it alone, till I dig about it, and d. it

DUNG-*gate.*

Neh. 3. 13. Hanun repaired valley-gate to the d.-gate
14. but the d.-g. repaired Malchia son of Rechab
12. 31. one company went on wall toward d.-gate

DUNGHILL.

1 Sam. 2. 8. he lifteth up beggar from d. Ps. 113. 7.
Ezra 6. 11. let his house be made a d. for this
Isa. 25. 10. even as straw is trodden down for the d.
Dan. 2. 5. and your houses shall be made a d.
3. 29. their houses shall be made a d. because
Luke 14. 35. unsavoury salt is not fit for land or d.

DUNGHILLS.

Lam. 4. 5. were brought up in scarlet, embrace d.

DUNGY.

Deut. 29. † 17. ye have seen d. gods, wood and stone

DUNG-*port.*

Neh. 2. 13. Nehemiah went to the d.-port and viewed

DUNGEON.

Gen. 40. 15. that they should put me into the d.
41. 14. they brought Joseph hastily out of the d.
Exod. 12. 29. to the first-born of the captive in d.
Isa. 24. † 22. shall be gathered as prisoners in the d.
Jer. 37. 16. when Jeremiah was entered into the d.
38. 6. they cast him into d. was no water in d. 9.
10. take up Jeremiah out of the d. before he die
11. let them down by cords into the d. to Jeremiah
13. so they drew up Jeremiah out of the d.
Lam. 3. 53. they have cut off my life in the d.
55. I called on thy name, O Lord, out of the d.

DURABLE.

Prov. 8. 18. yea, d. riches and righteous. are with me
Isa. 23. 18. her merchandise shall be for d. clothing

DURETH.

Mat. 13. 21. hath not root in himself, d. for a while

DURST.

Esth. 7. 5. he that d. presume in his heart to do so
Job 32. 6. afraid, I d. not shew you mine opinion
Mat. 22. 46. no man able to answer him, nor d. ask any more questions, Mark 12. 34. Luke 20. 40.
John 21. 12. none of disciples d. ask, who art thou?
Acts 5. 13. and of the rest d. no man join to them
7. 32. then Moses trembled, and d. not behold
Jude 9. he d. not bring ag. him a railing accusation

DUST.

The Hebrews, *when they mourned, put* dust *or* ashes *upon their heads,* Josh. 7. 6. *Joshua* and the elders of *Israel* put dust upon their heads. *In their afflictions they sat down in the dust, and threw themselves with their faces upon the ground.* Lam. 3. 29. He putteth his mouth in the dust, if so be there may be hope. *Isa.* 47. 1. Come down and sit in the dust, O virgin daughter of *Babylon*, sit on the ground. *In* Acts 22. 23. *some of the* Jews, *in the height of their rage,* threw dust into the air, *as it were to shew that they would reduce to powder the apostle* Paul, *whom they had taken in the temple.* *The* dust *denotes likewise the grave and death,* Gen. 3. 19. Dust thou art, and to dust thou shalt return. *Job* 7. 21. For now shall I sleep in the dust, *Psal.* 22. 15. Thou hast brought me into the dust of death. *The* dust *signifies likewise a multitude.* Gen. 13. 16. I will make thy seed as the dust of the earth. *And* Balaam, *upon the sight of the* Israelitish *camp, says,* Who can count the dust of *Jacob?* Num. 23. 10. *This vast multitude of the* Israelites, *who are as numerous as the dust. And in* Psal. 78. 27. He rained flesh also upon them as dust: *a great multitude of quails as if they were* dust.

Dust *signifies a most low and miserable condition.* 1 Sam. 2. 8. God raiseth up the poor out of the dust. *Nah.* 3. 18. Thy nobles shall dwell in the dust: *They shall be reduced to a mean condition. Our Saviour commands his disciples to* shake the dust off their feet against those who would not hearken to them, nor receive them, *Mat.* 10. 14. *Luke* 9. 5. *to shew thereby, that they desire to have no commerce with them; that they abhor every thing belonging to them; and that they give them up to their misery and hardness.* Dust *signifies earthly things,* Amos 2. 7.

Gen. 3. 14. d. shalt thou eat all the days of thy life
19. d. thou art, and unto d. shalt thou return
13. 16. so that if a man can number the d. of earth
18. 27. to speak to Lord, who am but d. and ashes
Exod. 8. 16. say to Aaron, smite the d. of the land
17. for Aaron smote the d. of the earth
9. 9. it shall become small d. in all the land
Lev. 14. 41. shall pour out the d. they scrape off
17. 13. pour out the blood, and cover it with d.
Num. 19. † 17. take of the d. of the burnt heifer
23. 10. who can count the d. of Jacob?
Deut. 9. 21. I cast the d. into brook, 2 Kings 23. 12.
28. 24. Lord shall make the rain of thy land d.
Josh. 7. 6. and the elders put d. on their heads
2 Sam. 16. 13. Shimei cursed David, and cast d.
1 Kings 18. 38. the fire of the Lord consumed the d.
20. 10. if the d. of Samaria shall suffice for handfuls
2 Chron. 34. 4. Josiah made d. of the images
Job 2. 12. they sprinkled d. upon their heads
7. 5. my flesh is clothed with worms and clods of d.
10. 9. and wilt thou bring me into d. again?
28. † 2. iron is taken out of d. and brass molten
6. as for the earth, it hath d. of gold
34. 15. all flesh perish, man shall turn again to d.
38. 38. when the d. groweth into hardness
42. 6. I abhor myself, and repent in d. and ashes
Psal. 22. 15. thou hast brought me into the d.
30. 9. shall d. praise thee, shall it declare thy truth?
72. 9. and his enemies shall lick the d.
78. 27. he rained flesh also upon them as d.
102. 14. thy servants favour the d. thereof
103. 14. he remembereth that we are d.
Eccl. 12. 7. then shall the d. return to the earth
Isa. 2. † 19. go into the caves of the d. for fear
34. 7. their d. shall be made fat with fatness
9. the d. thereof shall be turned into brimstone
40. 12. who hath comprehended the d. of earth?
49. 23. they shall lick up the d. of thy feet
52. 2. shake thyself from the d. O Jerusalem
65. 25. and d. shall be the serpent's meat
Lam. 2. 10. have cast d. on their heads, Ezek. 27. 30.
Ezek. 24. 7. she poured it not, to cover it with d.
26. 4. I will also scrape her d. from her
10. by his horses, their d. shall cover thee
Amos 2. 7. that pant after the d. of the earth
Mic. 7. 17. they shall lick the d. like a serpent
Nah. 1. 3. and the clouds are the d. of his feet
Hab. 1. 10. for they shall heap d. and take it
Mat. 10. 14. when ye depart out of that city, shake off the d. of your feet, Mark 6. 11. Luke 9. 5.
Luke 10. 11. even the d. of your city we do wipe off
Acts 13. 51. they shook off the d. of their feet
22. 23. and as they threw d. into the air
Rev. 18. 19. they cast d. on their heads, and cried

***As the* DUST.**

Gen. 13. 16. I will give thee the land, and make thy seed as the d. of the earth, 28. 14. 2 Chron. 1. 9.
Deut. 9. 21 I stamped the calf small as the d.
2 Sam. 22. 43. I beat them as small as d. Ps. 18. 42.
Job 22. 24. then shalt thou lay up gold as the d.
27. 16. though he heap up silver as the d.
Isa. 5. 24. and their blossom shall go up as d.
40. 15. the nations as the small d. of the balance
41. 2. he gave them as the d. to his sword
Zeph. 1. 17. their blood shall be poured out as d.
Zech. 9. 3. and Tyrus heaped up silver as the d.

***In the* DUST.**

Job 4. 19. on them, whose foundation is in the d.
7. 21. now shall I sleep in the d. thou shalt seek
16. 15. and I have defiled my horn in the d.
17. 16. when our rest together is in the d.
20. 11. which shall lie down with him in the d.
21. 26. they shall lie down alike in the d.
39. 14. leaveth eggs, and warmeth them in the d.
40. 13. hide them in the d. together, and bind
Psal. 7. 5. let the enemy lay mine honour in the d.
Isa. 2. 10. hide thee in the d. for fear of the Lord
26. 19. awake and sing, ye that dwell in the d.
47. 1. come down and sit in the d. O virgin
Lam. 3. 29. he putteth his mouth in the d. if so be
Dan. 12. 2. many that sleep in the d. shall awake
Mic. 1. 10. weep not at all, roll thyself in the d.
Nah. 3. 18. thy nobles shall dwell in the d.

***Like the* DUST.**

2 Kings 13. 7. make them like the d. by threshing
Isa. 29. 5. the multitude of thy strangers be like d.

***Of the* DUST.**

Gen. 2. 7. Lord formed man of the d. of the ground
Num. 5. 17. priest shall take of the d. in the tabern.
Deut. 32. 24. I will send poison of serpents of the d.

1 Sam. 2. 8. he raiseth poor out of the d. Psal. 113. 7.
1 Kings 16. 2. I exalted thee out of the d. and made
Job 5. 6. affliction cometh not forth of the d.
14. 19. washest away things that grow out of the d.
Prov. 8. 26. nor highest part of the d. of the world
Eccl. 3. 20. all go to one place, all are of the d.
Isa. 29. 4. thy speech shall be low out of the d.

To the DUST.

Psal. 22. 29. all that go down to the d. shall bow
44. 25. for our soul is bowed down to the d.
104. 29. they die and return to their d.
119. 25. my soul cleaveth to the d. quicken me
Eccl. 3. 20. all are of the d. and turn to d. again
Isa. 25. 12. he shall bring the fortress to the d.
26. 5. he bringeth the lofty city even to the d.

DUSTED.

2 Sam. 16. † 13. Shimei threw stones and d. with dust

DUTY.

Exod. 21. 10. her d. of marriage shall he not diminish
Deut. 25. 5. shall perform d. of a husband's brother
7. will not perform the d. of my husband's brother
2 Chron. 8. 14. as d. of every day required, Ezra 3. 4.
Eccl. 12. 13. for this is the whole d. of man
Luke 17. 10. we have done that which was our d. to do
Rom. 15. 27. their d. is to minister in carnal things

DUTIES.

Ezek. 18. 11. if he beget a son that doth not those d.

DWARF.

Lev. 21. 20. a d. shall not come nigh to offer offerings

DWELL.

To dwell *signifies to abide in, to inhabit, to have a fixed residence in a place*, Num. 33. 53. Psal. 78. 55. *Sometimes it is taken for sojourning*, Heb. 11. 9. *where it is said*, that *Abraham* dwelt in tabernacles; *that is, sojourned: for he had no fixed abode in the land of* Canaan. It is spoken, [1] Of God, *who is said* to dwell in the heavens, *Psal.* 123. 1. *He hath a certain and glorious place where he resideth, even the highest heavens, where he is clothed with infinite power and majesty, and from whence he beholdeth and governeth this lower world and all that is in it. His gracious presence with his people on earth is signified by* dwelling with them. *Psal.* 9. 11. Sing praises to the Lord who dwelleth in Zion: *where the ark was, which was the symbol of his special and gracious presence. And in* Isa. 57. 15. I dwell with him that is of a contrite and humble spirit.

[2] *Of* Christ, *signifying*, (1) *His manifestation in the flesh.* John 1. 14. The WORD was made flesh, and dwelt among us (2) *His spiritual abode in every faithful soul.* Eph. 3. 17. That Christ may dwell in your hearts by faith. *Christ dwells in his people by his merit to justify them; by his grace and Spirit to renew and purify them; by his power to keep them; by his wisdom to lead and instruct them; and by his communion and compassion to share with them in all their troubles.*

[3] *Of the* Holy Ghost, *who dwells in the soul by his gracious operations, working faith, love, and other graces therein.* Rom. 8. 9. But ye are not in the flesh, but in the Spirit, if so be that the Spirit of God dwell in you.

[4] *Of the* word of God, *which may be said to* dwell *in a person, when it is diligently studied, firmly believed, and carefully practised*, Col. 3. 16. Let the word of God dwell richly in you in all wisdom.

[5] *Of* Satan, *who dwells in wicked men, when he fills them with further degrees of error, malice, blasphemy, impenitence, and blindness; thereby making them highly wicked, and worse and worse daily.* Mat. 12. 45.

[6] *Of* the godly, *who are said to dwell in God*, 1 John 3. 24. *They have most intimate union and communion with God in* Christ.

Gen. 9. 27. Japhet shall d. in the tents of Shem
16. 12. he shall d. in the presence of his brethren
19. 30. Lot went up, for he feared to d. in Zoar
20. 15. behold my land, d. where it pleaseth thee
24. 3. daughters of Canaanites, amongst whom I d.
34. 10. land before you, d. and trade you therein
16. we will d. with you, and become one people
35. 1. arise, go up to Beth-el, and d. there
Exod. 2. 21. Moses was content to d. with the man
25. 8. that I may d. amongst them, 29. 46.
29. 45. I will d. amongst the children of Israel
Lev. 13. 46. the unclean shall d. alone
23. 42. ye shall d. in booths, 43. Neh. 8. 14.
Num. 5. 3. their camps, in the midst whereof I d.
23. 9. lo, the people shall d. alone, not be reckoned
32. 17. our little ones shall d. in fenced cities
35. 2. that they give to the Levites, cities to d. in, and suburbs round, 3. Josh. 14. 4. | 21. 2.
34. I the Lord d. among the children of Israel
Deut. 12. 11. to cause his name d. there, Ezra 6. 12.
23. 16. the servant escaped shall d. with thee
33. 12. he shall d. between his shoulders
Josh. 9. 7. peradventure ye d. among us, 22.
20. 6. he shall d. in that city, till he stand before
24. 13. cities ye built not, and ye d. in them
Judg. 9. 41. that Gaal should not d. in Shechem
17. 10. Micah said to the Levite, d. with me
1 Sam. 27. 5. that I may d. there, for why should thy servant d. in the royal city with thee?
1 Kings 6. 13. I will d. among the children of Israel
8. 12. he would d. in thick darkness, 2 Chr. 6. 1.
17. 9. get thee to Zarephath, and d. there
2 Kings 4. 13. she answered, I d. among mine own people
17. 27. let them go and d. there, let him teach
Ezra 10. † 10. ye have caused to d. strange wives, to increase the trespass of Israel, Neh. 13. † 23.
Job 3. 5. let a cloud d. upon it, let blackness of day
11. 14. let not wickedness d. in thy tabernacle
18. 15. shall d. in his tabernacle, because none of his
30. 6. to d. in the clifts of the valleys, in caves
Psal. 5. 4. neither shall evil d. with thee
15. 1. Lord, who shall d. in thy holy hill?
16. † 9. my flesh shall d. in confidence
25. 13. his soul shall d. at ease, and seed inherit
37. 27. depart from evil, and d. for evermore
65. 4. to approach, that he may d. in thy courts
8. they also that d. in the uttermost parts of earth
68. 16. this is the hill which God desireth to d. in, yea the Lord will d. in it for ever and ever
18. that the Lord might d. among them
69. 35. will build Judah that they may d. there
72. 9. they that d. in the wilderness shall bow
78. 55. and made Israel to d. in their tents
84. 10. than to d. in the tents of wickedness
101. 6. on the faithful, that they may d. with me
107. 4. they wandered, they found no city to d. in
36. and there he maketh the hungry to d.
113. † 5. like the Lord who exalteth himself to d.
120. 5. woe is me, that I d. in the tents of Kedar
132. 14. my rest, here will I d. for I have desired it
139. 9. if I d. in uttermost parts of the sea
140. 13. the upright shall d. in thy presence
143. 3. he hath made me to d. in darkness
Prov. 1. 33. whoso hearkeneth to me shall d. safely
8. 12. I wisdom d. with prudence and find out
21. † 7. robbery of the wicked shall d. with them
19. it is better to d. in wilderness, than with
Isa. 6. 5. I d. in midst of a people of unclean lips
11. 6. the wolf also shall d. with the lamb
13. 21. owls shall d. there, satyrs shall dance there
16. 4. let mine outcasts d. with thee, Moab
23. 18. merchandise for them that d. before the Ld.
24. 6. they that d. therein are desolate
26. 5. he bringeth down them that d. on high
19. awake and sing, ye that d. in the dust
30. 19. the people shall d. in Zion at Jerusalem
32. 16. then judgment shall d. in the wilderness
18. my people d. in a peaceful habitation
33. 14. who among us shall d. with devouring fire? who shall d. with everlasting burnings?
16. he shall d. on high, his place of defence
24. the people that d. therein shall be forgiven
34. 11. the owl and the raven shall d. in it
40. 22. he spreadeth them out as a tent to d. in
49. 20. give place to me that I may d.
58. 12. shall be called the restorer of paths to d. in
65. 9. and my servants shall d. there
Jer. 29. 32. Shemaiah shall not have a man to d.
31. 24. there shall d. in Judah husbandmen
35. 7. but all your days ye shall d. in tents
40. 5. and d. with him among the people
10. I will d. at Mizpeh to serve the Chaldeans
42. 14. we will go into Egypt, and there will we d.
44. 14. they have a desire to return to d. there
49. 8. flee ye, d. deep, O inhabitants of Dedan
18. nor shall a son of man d. in it, 33. | 50. 40.
31. which d. alone || 51. 1. that d. in midst of them
Ezek. 2. 6. and thou dost d. among scorpions
16. 46. she and her daughters d. at thy left hand
43. 7. where I will d. in the midst of Israel for ever, 9. Zech. 2. 10, 11.
Hos. 12. 9. I will make thee to d. in tabernacles
14. 7. they that d. under his shadow shall return
Joel 3. 20. but Judah shall d. for ever, and Jerusal.
Amos 3. 12. Isr. shall be taken out that d. in Samaria
Mic. 4. 10. thou shalt d. in the field, go to Babylon
7. 14. the flock which d. solitarily in the wood
Nah. 3. 18. O Assyria, thy nobles shall d. in dust
Hag. 1. 4. is it time to d. in your ceiled houses?
Zech. 8. 4. old men and women shall d. in Jerusal.
9. 6. and a bastard shall d. in Ashdod
14. 11. shall be inhabited, and men shall d. in it
Mat. 12. 45. they enter in and d. there, Luke 11. 26.
Luke 21. 35. as a snare shall it come on all them that d. on face of the whole earth, Acts 17. 26.
Acts 7. 4. he removed into land wherein ye now d.
28. 16. Paul was suffered to d. by himself
Rom. 8. 9. if so be the Spirit of God d. in you, 11.
1 Cor. 7. 12. and she be pleased to d. with him
2 Cor. 6. 16. as God hath said, I will d. in them
Eph. 3. 17. that Christ may d. in your hearts by faith
Col. 1. 19. Father that in him should all fulness d.
3. 16. let the word of Christ d. in you richly
1 Pet. 3. 7. likewise, ye husbands, d. with them
1 John 4. 13. hereby know we that we d. in him
Rev. 7. 15. he that sitteth on the throne shall d.
12. 12. rejoice, ye heavens, and ye that d. in them
13. 6. and against them that d. in heaven
21. 3. is with men, and he will d. with them

DWELL, with *earth.*

1 Kings 8. 27. will God d. on earth? 2 Chr. 6. 18.
Dan. 4. 1. languages that d. in all the earth, 6. 25.
Rev. 3. 10. to try them that d. on the earth
6. 10. avenge our blood on them that d. on earth
11. 10. they that d. on the earth shall rejoice
13. 8. all that d. on the earth shall worship
14. and deceiveth them that d. on the earth
14. 6. to preach to them that d. on the earth
17. 8. they that d. on the earth shall wonder

DWELL, with *house.*

Deut. 28. 30. shalt build an house, and shalt not d. therein, plant vineyard, not gather, Amos 5. 11.
2 Sam. 7. 2. I d. in a house of cedar, 1 Chr. 17. 1.
5. shall build me an house to d. in, 1 Chr. 17. 1.
1 Kings 2. 36. build house in Jerusalem and d. there
3. 17. O my lord, I and this woman d. in one house
8. 13. I have surely built thee an house to d. in
2 Chron. 8. 11. my wife shall not d. in house of David
Job 4. 19. much less them that d. in houses of clay
19. 15. they that d. in my house count me a stranger
Psal. 23. 6. I will d. in the house of the Lord for ever
27. 4. that I may d. in the house of the Lord
84. 4. blessed are they that d. in thy house
101. 7. worketh deceit, shall not d. in my house
113. † 9. he maketh the barren to d. in an house
Prov. 21. 9. better d. in the corner of a house, 25. 24.
Jer. 20. 6. all that d. in thy house go to captivity
29. 5. build ye houses, and d. in them, 28.
35. 9. not to build houses for us to d. in, nor vineyard

DWELL, with *Jerusalem.*

1 Chr. 23. 25. that ye may d. in Jerusalem for ever
Neh. 11. 1. to bring one of ten to d. in Jerusalem
2. willingly offered themselves to d. at Jerusalem
Jer. 33. 16. Judah saved, and Jerusalem shall d. safe.
35. 11. for fear of Chaldeans so we d. at Jerusal.
Zech. 8. 3. and I will d. in the midst of Jerusalem
8. and they shall d. in the midst of Jerusalem
Acts 2. 14. and all ye that d. at Jerusalem
4. 16. is manifest to all them that d. in Jerusalem
13. 27. they that d. at Jerusal. have condemned him

DWELL, with *land.*

Gen. 24. 37. of the Canaanites in whose land I d.
26. 2. d. in the land which I shall tell thee of
34. 21. let them d. in the land, and trade therein
45. 10. and thou shalt d. in the land of Goshen
46. 34. that ye may d. in the land of Goshen
47. 6. in the land of Goshen let them d.
Exod. 8. 22. the land of Goshen, in which my people d.
23. 33. they shall not d. in thy land, lest they
Lev. 25. 18. and ye shall d. in the land in safety
26. 5. ye shall eat and d. in your land safely
Num. 13. 19. and what the land is that they d. in
35. 34. defile not the land wherein I d.
Deut. 12. 10. d. in the land which the L. giveth you
30. 20. that thou mayest d. in the land Lord sware
Josh. 17. 12. could not drive them out, but the Canaanites would d. in that land, Judg. 1. 27.
24. 15. the gods in whose land ye d. Judg. 6. 10.
2 Kings 25. 24. fear not, d. in land, Jer. 25. 5. | 40. 9.
Psal. 37. 3. do good, so shalt thou d. in the land
68. 6. but the rebellious d. in a dry land
85. 9. salvation near, that glory may d. in our land
Prov. 2. 21. for the upright shall d. in the land
Isa. 9. 2. that d. in land of the shadow of death
Jer. 23. 8. they shall d. in their own land, 27. 11.
24. 8. that d. in the land of Egypt, 44. 1, 8, 13, 26.
35. 15. ye shall d. in the land, Ezek. 36. 28. | 37. 25.
42. 13. if ye say, we will not d. in this land
43. 4. obeyed not L. to d. in the land of Judah, 5.
50. 3. make the land desolate, none shall d. therein
Ezek. 28. 25. then shall they d. in their land
38. 12. the people that d. in the midst of the land
Hos. 9. 3. they shall not d. in the Lord's land
Hab. 2. 8. for the violence of land, and all that d. 17.
Zeph. 1. 18. make a riddance of all that d. in the land

DWELL, with *place.*

Exod. 15. 17. in the place thou hast made to d. in
1 Sam. 12. 8. and made them to d. in this place
2 Sam. 7. 10. they may d. in a place of their own
2 Kings 6. 1. behold the place where we d. is strait
2. let us make us a place where we may d.
1 Chron. 17. 9. and they shall d. in their place
Isa. 57. 15. I d. in the high and holy place
Jer. 7. 3. I will cause you to d. in this place, 7.

DWELL *safely.*

Prov. 1. 33. whoso hearkeneth to me shall d. safely
Jer. 23. 6. in his days Judah shall be saved and Israel shall d. safely, Ezek. 28. 26. | 34. 25, 28. | 38. 8.
32. 37. and I will cause them to d. safely
Ezek. 38. 11. I will go to them at rest that d. safely

DWELL *in safety.*

Lev. 25. 18. keep my judgments and do them, and ye shall d. in the land in safety, 19. Deut. 12. 10.
Deut. 33. 12. beloved of the Lord shall d. in safety
28. Israel then shall d. in safety alone
Psal. 4. 8. thou, Lord, only makest me to d. in safety

DWELL *therein.*

Lev. 27. 32. enemies which d. therein be astonished
Num. 14. 30. the land I sware to make you d. therein
33. 53. and ye shall d. therein, Deut. 11. 31.
Psal. 24. 1. the world and they that d. therein
37. 29. the righteous shall d. therein for ever
69. 36. they that love his name shall d. therein
107. 34. for wickedn. of them that d. th. Jer. 12. 4.
Isa. 24. 6. they that d. th. are desolate, Amos 9. 5.
33. 24. people that d. therein are forgiven iniquity
34. 17. from generat. to generat. shall they d. therein
51. 6. they that d. therein shall die in like manner
Jer. 4. 29. city forsaken, and not a man d. therein
8. 16. devoured the city, and all that d. therein
12. 4. for the wickedness of them that d. therein
47. 2. overflow the land and them that d. therein
48. 9. the cities desolate without any to d. therein
50. 39. the wild beasts and the owls shall d. therein
Ezek. 12. 19. the violence of them that d. therein
32. 15. when I shall smite them that d. therein
37. 25. they and their children shall d. therein
Mic. 7. 13. desolate, because of them that d. therein
Nah. 1. 5. yea, the world is burnt, and all that d. th.
Acts 1. 20. his habitation, let no man d. therein

DWELL *together.*

Gen. 13. 6. that they might d. together, their substance was great, so that they could not d. together
36. 7. riches more than that they might d. together
Deut. 25. 5. if brethren d. together, and one die
Psal. 133. 1. for brethren to d. together in unity

DWELLED.

Gen. 13. 7. the Perizzite d. then in the land
12. Abram d. in the land of Canaan, Lot d. in the cities of the plain, and pitched toward Sodom
20. 1. and Abraham d. between Kadesh and Shur
Ruth 1. 4. and they d. there about ten years
1 Sam. 12. 11. God delivered you, and ye d. safe

DWELLER.

Psal. 69. † 25. let there not be a d. in their tents

DWELLERS.

Isa. 18. 3. ye d. on earth, see ye, when he lifteth up
Acts 1. 19. it was known to the d. at Jerusalem
2. 9. the d. in Mesopotamia, we do hear them speak

DWELLEST.

Deut. 12. 29. thou succeedest them and d. in their land
2 Kings 19. 15. O Lord God of Israel, which d. between the cherubims, Psal. 80. 1. Isa. 37. 16.
Psal. 123. 1. O thou that d. in the heavens
Cant. 8. 13. thou that d. in the gardens
Isa. 10. 24. O my people that d. in Zion, be not afraid
47. 8. hear now this, thou that d. carelessly
Jer. 49. 16. O thou that d. in the clefts, Obad. 3.
51. 13. O thou that d. upon many waters
Lam. 4. 21. O daughter of Edom, that d. in land of Uz
Ezek. 7. 7. thou that d. in the land, time is come
12. 2. thou d. in the midst of a rebellious house
Mic. 1. † 11. pass ye away, thou that d. fairly

Zech. 2. 7. that *d.* with the daughter of Babylon
John 1. 38. they said, Master, where *d.* thou?
Rev. 2. 13. I know thy works, and where thou *d.*

DWELLETH.

Lev. 16. † 16. the tabernacle that *d.* among them
19. 34. but the stranger that *d.* with you shall be
25. 39. if thy brother that *d.* by thee be poor, 47.
Deut. 33. 20. God *d.* as a lion, and teareth the arm
Josh. 6. 25. Rahab *d.* in Israel even to this day
22. 19. wherein the Lord's tabernacle *d.*
1 *Sam.* 4. 4. the ark of covenant of Lord, who *d.* between cherubims, 2 *Sam.* 6. 2. 1 *Chron.* 13. 6.
2 *Sam.* 7. 2. but the ark *d.* within curtains
1 *Chron.* 23. † 25. the Lord *d.* in Jerusalem for ever
Job 15. 28. he *d.* in desolate cities and in houses
38. 19. where is the way where light *d.*?
39. 28. she *d.* and abideth on the rock
Psal. 9. 11. sing praises to the Lord who *d.* in Zion
26. 8. Lord, I loved the place where thine honour *d.*
91. 1. he that *d.* in the secret place of the most High
113. 5. who is like the Lord our G. who *d.* on high?
135. 21. blessed be the Lord who *d.* at Jerusalem
Prov. 3. 29. seeing he *d.* securely by thee
Isa. 8. 18. from the Lord, who *d.* in mount Zion
33. 5. the Lord is exalted, for he *d.* on high
Jer. 44. 2. are a desolation, and no man *d.* therein
49. 31. the wealthy nation that *d.* without care
Lam. 1. 3. Judah, she *d.* among the heathen
Ezek. 16. 46. thy younger sister *d.* at thy right hand
17. 16. where the king *d.* that made him king
Dan. 2. 22. he revealeth, and the light *d.* with him
Hos. 4. 3. the land shall mourn, and every one that *d.* therein shall mourn, *Amos* 8. 8.
Joel 3. 21. I will cleanse their blood, for L. *d.* in Zion
Mat. 23. 21. sweareth by it and him that *d.* therein
John 6. 56. drinketh my blood, *d.* in me, and I in him
14. 10. the Father that *d.* in me, he doeth the works
17. the Spirit, for he *d.* in you, and shall be in you
Acts 7. 48. *d.* not in temples made with hands, 17. 24.
Rom. 7. 17. it is no more I, but sin that *d.* in me, 20.
18. I know that in my flesh *d.* no good thing
8. 11. shall quicken, by his Spirit that *d.* in you
1 *Cor.* 3. 16. and that the Spirit of God *d.* in you
Col. 2. 9. in him *d.* the fulness of Godhead bodily
2 *Tim.* 1. 14. keep by the Holy Ghost which *d.* in us
Jam. 4. 5. the spirit that *d.* in us lusteth to envy
2 *Pet.* 3. 13. a new earth wherein *d.* righteousness
1 *John* 3. 17. how *d.* the love of God in him?
24. that keepeth his commandments, *d.* in him
4. 12. if we love one another, God *d.* in us
15. confess that Jesus is Son of God, God *d.* in him
16. he that *d.* in love, *d.* in God, and God in him
2 *John* 2. for the truth's sake which *d.* in us
Rev. 2. 13. was slain among you, where Satan *d.*

DWELLING, *Substantive.*

Gen. 27. 39. thy *d.* shall be the fatness of the earth
2 *Kings* 17. 25. at the beginning of their *d.* there
2 *Chr.* 6. 2. I have built a place for thy *d.* for ever
Ps. 49. 14. shall consume in the grave from their *d.*
91. 10. nor shall any plague come nigh thy *d.*
Prov. 21. 20. there is oil in the *d.* of the wise
24. 15. lay not wait against the *d.* of the righteous
Jer. 49. 33. Hazor shall be a *d.* for dragons and desolation
Dan. 2. 11. the gods, whose *d.* is not with flesh
4. 25. thy *d.* shall be with the beasts, 32. | 5. 21.
Nah. 2. 11. where is the *d.* of the lions?
Mark 5. 3. who had his *d.* among the tombs

DWELLING.

Gen. 25. 27. Jacob was a plain man, *d.* in tents
30. † 20. and she called his name, *d.*
Lev. 25. 29. if a man sell a *d.* house in a city
Num. 24. 21. and he said, strong is thy *d.* place
1 *Kings* 8. 30. hear thou in heaven thy *d.* place, when heard forgive, 39, 43, 49. 2 *Chron.* 6. 21, 30, 39.
2 *Chr.* 30. 27. their prayer came up to his holy *d.*
36. 15. the Lord had compassion on his *d.* place
Job 8. 22. the *d.* place of the wicked come to nought
21. 28. where are the *d.* places of the wicked?
Psal. 49. 11. and their *d.* places to all generations
52. 5. God shall pluck thee out of thy *d.*
74. 7. by casting down the *d.* place of thy name
76. 2. in Salem his tabernacle, his *d.* place in Zion
79. 7. for they have laid waste his *d.* place
90. 1. Lord thou hast been our *d.* place in all generations
Isa. 4. 5. the Lord will create on every *d.* place
18. 4. and I will consider in my *d.* place
Jer. 6. † 2. I likened Zion to a woman *d.* at home
30. 18. and I will have mercy on his *d.* places
46. 19. O thou daughter *d.* in Egypt, furnish thyself
51. 30. have burnt their *d.* places, bars are broken
37. Babylon shall become a *d.* place for dragons
Ezek. 6. 6. in all your *d.* places the cities laid waste
37. 23. I will save them out of all their *d.* places
38. 11. all of them *d.* without walls, bars, nor gates
Joel 3. 17. that I am the Lord your God *d.* in Zion
Hab. 1. 6. to possess the *d.* places that are not theirs
Zeph. 3. 7. so their *d.* should not be cut off
Acts 2. 5. there were *d.* at Jerus. Jews, devout men
19. 17. was known to the Greeks, *d.* at Ephesus
1 *Cor.* 4. 11. are naked, and have no certain *d.* place
1 *Tim.* 6. 16. *d.* in the light no man can approach
Heb. 11. 9. *d.* in tabernacles with Isaac and Jacob
2 *Pet.* 2. 8. Lot, that righteous man, *d.* among them

DWELLINGS.

Exod. 10. 23. all the children of Isr. had light in *d.*
Lev. 3. 17. it shall be a perpetual statute throughout all your *d.* 23. 14. *Num.* 35. 29.
7. 26. ye shall eat no blood in any of your *d.*
23. 3. ye shall do no work in all your *d.* 31.
Job 18. 19. shall not have any remaining in his *d.*
21. surely such are the *d.* of the wicked
39. 6. I have made the barren land his *d.*
Psal. 55. 15. for wickedness is in their *d.*
87. 2. gates of Zion, more than all the *d.* of Jacob
Isa. 32. 18. my people shall dwell in sure *d.*
Jer. 9. 19. because our *d.* have cast us out
Ezek. 25. 4. men of the east make their *d.* in thee
Zeph. 2. 6. the sea coast shall be *d.* for shepherds

DWELT.

Gen. 11. 2. and they *d.* there, 31. | 26. 17. 2 *Kings* 16. 6. 1 *Chron.* 4. 43. 2 *Chron.* 28. 18.
23. 10. Ephron *d.* among the children of Heth
Lev. 18. 3. the doings of Egypt wherein ye *d.* not do
Num. 31. 10. wherein they *d.* 2 *Kings* 17. 29.
1 *Kings* 13. 11. *d.* an old prophet in Beth-el, 25.
Job 29. 25. and I *d.* as a king in the army
Psal. 74. 2. this mount Zion wherein thou hast *d.*
Isa. 29. 1. woe to Ariel, the city where David *d.*
Jer. 2. 6. led us through a land where no man *d.*
39. 14. so Jeremiah *d.* among the people
Ezek. 3. 15. that *d.* by the river of Chebar
31. 6. under his shadow *d.* great nations, 17.
37. 25. the land wherein your fathers have *d.*
Dan. 4. 21. under which the beasts of the field *d.*
Zeph. 2. 15. this is the rejoicing city that *d.* carelessly
Luke 1. 65. fear came on all that *d.* round about
John 1. 14. the word was made flesh and *d.* among us
39. they came and saw where he *d.* and abode
Acts 13. 17. when they *d.* as strangers in Egypt
22. 12. Ananias having good report of all that *d.*
28. 30. Paul *d.* two years in his own hired house
Rev. 11. 10. tormented them that *d.* on the earth

DWELT *at.*

Gen. 22. 19. and Abraham *d. at* Beer-sheba
Num. 21. 34. Amor. which *d. at* Heshbon, *Deut.* 3. 2.
Judg. 9. 41. and Abimelech *d. at* Arumah
1 *Kings* 15. 18. Benhadad *d. at* Damasc. 2 *Ch.* 16. 2.
2 *Kings* 19. 36. Sennacher. *d. at* Nineveh, *Isa.* 37. 37.
1 *Chr.* 2. 55. families of the scribes which *d. at* Jabez
9. 34. these fathers of the Levites *d. at* Jerusalem
Acts 9. 22. Saul confounded Jews that *d. at* Damas.
32. Peter came to the saints who *d. at* Lydda

DWELT *in.*

Num. 20. 15. and we have *d. in* Egypt a long time
21. 31. thus Israel *d. in* the land of the Amorites
Deut. 2. 12. *d. in* their stead, 21, 22, 23. 1 *Chr.* 5. 22.
33. 16. the good will of him that *d. in* the bush
Judg. 8. 11. by the way of them that *d. in* tents
29. Jerubbaal went and *d. in* his own house
1 *Sam.* 19. 18. David and Samuel *d. in* Naioth
31. 7. Philistines came and *d. in* them, 1 *Chr.* 10. 7.
2 *Sam.* 7. 6. whereas I have not *d. in* any house since I brought Israel out of Egypt, 1 *Chron.* 17. 5.
9. 12. all that *d. in* the house of Ziba were servants
14. 28. Absalom *d.* two full years *in* Jerusalem
1 *Kings* 2. 38. Shimei *d. in* Jerusalem many days
12. 2. Jerob. was fled from Solomon, *d.* in Egypt
2 *Kings* 13. 5. Israel *d. in* their tents as aforetime
15. 5. Ahaziah *d. in* a several house, 2 *Chr.* 26. 21.
22. 14. Huldah the prophetess, wife of Shallum, *d. in* Jerusalem, in the college, 2 *Chron.* 34. 22.
1 *Chron.* 4. 41. these came and *d. in* their rooms
5. 10. the Hagarites fell, and they *d. in* their tents
8. 28. were chief men, these *d. in* Jerusalem
11. 7. and David *d. in* the castle, 2 *Sam.* 5. 9.
Ezra 2. 70. the priests, the Levites, and the Nethinims, *d. in* their cities, *Neh.* 3. 26. | 11. 21.
Neh. 7. 73. Nethinims and all Israel *d. in* their cities
Job 22. 8. and the honourable men *d. in* it
Psal. 94. 17. my soul had almost *d. in* silence
Isa. 13. 20. shall never be inhabited, nor shall it be *d. in* from generation to generation, *Jer.* 50. 39.
Jer. 35. 10. but we have *d. in* tents, and obeyed
41. 17. they *d. in* the habitation of Chimham
Ezek. 36. 17. when Israel *d. in* their own land
39. 26. when *d.* safely *in* their land, none made afraid
Dan. 4. 12. the fowls of the heaven *d. in* the boughs
Mat. 2. 23. Joseph *d. in* a city called Nazareth
4. 13. Jesus came and *d. in* Capernaum
Luke 13. 4. were sinners above all that *d. in* Jer.
Acts 7. 2. before Abraham *d. in* Charran, 4.
19. 10. all they who *d. in* Asia heard word of Jesus
2 *Tim.* 1. 5. which *d.* first *in* thy grandmother Lois

DWELT *therein.*

Num. 32. 40. he gave Gilead to Machir, he *d. therein*
Deut. 2. 10. Emims *d. th.* || 20. giants *d. th.* in old time
1 *Kings* 11. 24. Rezon went to Damascus and *d. th.*
12. 25. Jeroboam built Shechem, and *d. therein*
Neh. 13. 16. there *d.* men of Tyre also *therein*
Psal. 68. 10. thy congregation hath *d. therein*

DWELT *with.*

Ruth 2. 23. and Ruth *d. with* her mother-in-law
1 *Sam.* 22. 4. his father and mother *d. w.* k. of Moab
1 *Chron.* 4. 23. there they *d. with* king for his work
8. 32. these also *d. with* their brethren, 9. 38.
Psal. 120. 6. my soul hath long *d. with* him that
Jer. 40. 6. Jeremiah *d. with* him among the people

E.

EACH.

Gen. 15. 10. Abraham laid *e.* piece against another
34. 25. Simeon and Levi took *e.* man his sword
40. 5. *e.* man his dream, || 45. 22. *e.* changes of raim.
Exod. 18. 7. and they asked *e.* other of their welfare
30. 34. of *e.* shall there be a like weight
Num. 1. 44. *e.* one was for the house of his fathers
7. 3. and they brought for *e.* one an ox
16. 17. thou also and Aaron *e.* of you his censer
Josh. 22. 14. of *e.* chief house a prince, *e.* one was head
Judg. 8. 18. *e.* one resembled the children of a king
21. 22. because we reserved not to *e.* man his wife
Ruth 1. 9. grant that they may find rest *e.* of you
1 *Kings* 4. 7. *e.* man his month in a year made prov.
22. 10. and the kings *e.* sat on his throne
2 *Kings* 15. 20. he exacted of *e.* man fifty shekels
Psal. 85. 10. righteousness and peace kissed *e.* other
Isa. 2. 20. they made *e.* one for himself to worship
6. 2. stood the seraphims, *e.* one had six wings
35. 7. where *e.* lay, shall be grass, reeds, and rushes
57. 2. *e.* one walking in his uprightness
Ezek. 4. 6. I have appointed thee *e.* day for a year
Luke 13. 15. doth not *e.* on sabbath loose his ox or ass
Acts 2. 3. cloven tongues sat upon *e.* of them
Phil. 2. 3. let *e.* esteem other better than himself
2 *Thess.* 1. 3. charity toward *e.* other aboundeth
Rev. 4. 8. the four beasts had *e.* of them six wings

EAGLE

Is *a bird of prey, whereof there is frequent mention in scripture. It is declared in* Lev. 11. 13. *to be unclean, as are all other birds of its species; as the sea-eagle, and the eagle named* Ossifrage, *because it breaks the bones in order to extract the marrow. The hawk and vulture may also be reckoned as different species of eagles.*

It is said that when an eagle sees its young ones so well-grown, as to venture upon flying, it hovers over their nest, flutters with its wings, and excites them to imitate it, and take their flight; and when it sees them weary or fearful, it takes them upon its back, and carries them so, that the fowlers cannot hurt the young without piercing through the body of the old one. In allusion to this, it is said, Exod. 19. 4. *That God delivered his people out of* Egypt, *and bore them* upon eagles' wings; *and in* Deut. 32. 11. *That the Lord took upon himself the care of his people; that he led them out of* Egypt, *and set them at liberty; as an eagle takes its young out of the nest, to teach them how to fly, by gently fluttering about them.*

It is of great courage, so as to set on harts and great beasts. And has no less subtilty in taking them; for having filled its wings with sand and dust, it sitteth on their horns, and by its wings shaketh it in their eyes, whereby they become an easy prey. It flieth very high, Prov. 30. 19. *yet, in the twinkling of an eye, seizeth on its prey, whether on the earth, or in the sea. It buildeth its nest very high in the tops of rocks,* Job 39. 27. *It goeth forth to prey about noon, when men are gone home out of the fields.*

It hath a little eye, but a very quick sight, and discerns its prey afar off, and beholds the sun with open eyes. Such of her young as through weakness of sight cannot behold the sun it rejects as unnatural. It liveth long, nor dieth of age or sickness, say some, but of hunger; for by age, its bill grows so hooked, that it cannot feed. It preys not on small birds, but on geese, hares, harts, serpents, and dead carcases. It is said, that it preserves its nest from poison, by having therein a precious stone named Aetites, *(without which it is thought the eagle cannot lay her eggs, and which some use to prevent abortion, and helps delivery in women, by tying it above or below the navel,) and keepeth it clean by the frequent use of the herb* maiden-hair. *Unless it be very hungry, it devoureth not the whole prey, but leaveth part of it for other birds, which follow it. Its feathers or quills are said to consume other quills, that lie near them. Between the eagle and dragon there is constant enmity, the eagle seeking to kill it, and the dragon breaks all the* eagle's eggs *it can find; and hearing the noise of the eagle in the air, speedeth to its den, and there hides himself. To provoke its young ones to fly, it flutters over them and takes them on its wings,* Deut. 32. 11. Isa. 40. 31. *and if they attempt not to fly, it beats them with its bill, and gives them no food. Being exceedingly hot and dry, it soon waxeth angry, nor keepeth, but shuns society with others. Some eagles prey in the air, some in the sea, wherein they can from on high perceive the smallest fish, and some on the land.* The eagle *moulters and loses its feathers yearly, at which seasons it is very feeble. It is said,* Psal. 103. 5. Thy youth is renewed like the eagle's; *that is, thy bodily health and strength continue vigorous and lively, as the* eagle's *doth, even till old age.*

In Micah 1. 16. *it is said,* Enlarge thy baldness as the eagle: *This signifies, that they to whom the prophet addresses himself, should cut off their hair in time of mourning, should be naked and stripped like an eagle when it moults its feathers. It is said that the eagle, at that season, casts almost all its feathers, and falls into a languishing condition, so as neither to be able to hunt after prey as usual, nor create terror in other birds.*

Our Saviour, in Mat. 24. 28. *says,* Wheresoever the carcase is, there will the eagles be gathered together. Job *says of the eagle, chap.* 39. 30. Where the slain are, there is she. *Naturalists observe, that the common sort of eagles eat no carrion, but that there is a particular species which does: that there is not one of any kind but what eats raw flesh, though not indifferently of all sorts, nor that of any creature which dies of itself, but such only as is fresh and lately killed. What Job says concerning the eagle is to be understood in a literal sense: but our Saviour makes an allegory of it, and says, that wherever there are* Jews, *who deal unfaithfully with God, there will be also* Romans, *who bore the eagle in their standards, to execute God's vengeance upon them.*

As the eagle generally flies most swiftly, especially when hunger and the sight of prey quicken its motion: in this sense the days of men are compared to it. Job 9. 26. My days are passed away as the *eagle*, that hasteth to the prey. *So are riches;* Prov. 23. 5. Riches certainly make themselves wings, they fly away as an eagle towards heaven. *As also the persecutors of the church;* Lam. 4. 19. Our persecutors are swifter than the eagles of the heaven. *The kings of* Babylon *and* Egypt *are also compared to an* eagle, *Ezek.* 17. 3, 7.

Lev. 11. 13. the *e.* have in abomination, *Deut.* 14. 12.
Deut. 28. 49. a nation as swift as the *e.* flieth
32. 11. as an *e.* stirreth up her nest, fluttereth over
Job 9. 26. as the *e.* that hasteth to the prey
39. 27. doth the *e.* mount up at thy command?
Prov. 23. 5. riches fly away as an *e.* towards heaven
30. 19. the way of an *e.* in the air is wonderful
Jer. 48. 40. behold, he shall fly as an *e.* over Moab
49. 16. tho' thou shouldest make thy nest high as *e.*
Ezek. 1. 10. they four also had the face of an *e.* 10. 14.
17. 3. a great *e.* with great wings came, 7.

Dan. 4. 33. his hairs were grown like e. feathers
7. 4. the first beast was like a lion, and had e. wings
Hos. 8. 1. as an e. against the house of the Lord
Obad. 4. tho' thou exalt thyself as e. bring thee down
Mic. 1. 16. enlarge thy baldness as the e.
Hab. 1. 8. the Chaldeans shall fly as the e.
Rev. 4. 7. the fourth beast was like a flying e.
12. 14. to the woman were given wings of a great e.

EAGLES.

Exod. 19. 4. ye have seen how I bare you on e. wings
2 Sam. 1. 23. were swifter than e. stronger than lions
Psal. 103. 5. thy youth is renewed like the e.
Prov. 30. 17. and the young e. shall eat it
Isa. 40. 31. they shall mount up with wings as e.
Jer. 4. 13. his horses are swifter than e.
Lam. 4. 19. our persecutors are swifter than the e.
Mat. 24. 28. there will e. be gathered, Luke 17. 37.

EAR.

The ear is the instrument or organ of hearing, Eccl. 1. 8. *The Lord says to* Isaiah, Make the hearts of this people fat, and make their ears heavy, Isa. 6. 10.; *that is, tell them that I will suffer them to harden their hearts, and stop their ears against my word. The scripture sometimes says that the prophets do what they foretell only. The same prophet, speaking of himself, says,* The Lord hath opened mine ear, and I was not rebellious, Isa. 50. 5. *He has given me his orders, and I obey without contradiction. And speaking to the Jews,* Thou heardest not, yea, thou knewest not, yea, from that time that thine ear was not opened, Isa. 48. 8. *Thou hast never heard any mention made of what I am going to tell thee.* Uncircumcised ears, Jer. 6. 10. *are ears deaf to the word of God:* Their ear is uncircumcised; *overgrown, as it were, with a thick skin; their hearts are filled with obstinacy and impenitency, which make them incapable of entertaining any good counsel.* What ye hear in the ear, that preach ye upon the house-tops, Mat. 10. 27. *Declare that every where, and publicly, which I have revealed to you in private.* He that hath ears to hear, let him hear, Mat. 11. 15. *He that hath his ears opened, that hath a mind enabled by God to believe what I say, let him make use of these abilities to understand and consider it.* Ear *is figuratively, and after the manner of men, applied to God, denoting his readiness to hear and answer the prayers of his people,* Psal. 34. 15. | 116. 2. His ears are open unto their cry. Because he hath inclined his ear unto me, therefore will I call upon him as long as I live.

To uncover the ear *is an* Hebraism, *whereby is meant, to show, or reveal something to a person.* 1 Sam. 20. † 2. My father will do nothing either great or small, but that he will *uncover mine ear; that is,* he will shew it me. *The servant who renounced the privilege of being freed from servitude in the sabbatical year, had his* ear *pierced with an awl: this was performed in the presence of the judges, that it might appear that this was his own free choice, and that he was not overawed, or compelled thereto by his master; and likewise that the agreement being so publicly and solemnly confirmed, might be irrevocable: His ear was bored at his master's door; which was a mark of servitude and bondage, and did represent his settled and perpetual obligation to abide in that house, and there to hear and obey his master's commands,* Exod. 21. 6. Deut. 15. 16, 17.

The Psalmist *speaking in the person of the* Messiah, *says to God,* Sacrifice and offering thou didst not desire, mine ears hast thou opened. *The Hebrew reads,* Mine ears hast thou digged; *thou hast opened them and made them attentive; thou hast given me ears to hear, and obey thy precepts: Or, otherwise, thou hast pierced them, as those servants were used, who chose to remain with their masters after the sabbatical year; thou hast fitted, inclined, and obliged me to thy service. The Septuagint, whom the Apostle follows,* Heb. 10. 5. *read this passage,* A body hast thou prepared me: *Wherein, though the words differ, the sense is the same. That Christ might become God's servant for ever, which was signified* by boring of the ear, *God the Father by his Spirit did furnish him with an human nature, that so he might perform that piece of service which* God *required, namely, the offering up himself a bloody sacrifice for sin, to which he was obedient.* Phil. 2. 8. Being found in fashion as a man, he became obedient unto death, even the death of the cross. *Thus were his ears bored, which could not be, if he had not been clothed with a body.*

Exod. 21. 6. his master shall bore his e. Deut. 15. 17.
1 Sam. 9. 15. the Lord hath told Samuel in his e.
20. † 2. but that he will uncover mine e.
† 12. if I send not to thee and uncover thine e.
22. † 8. there is none that uncovereth mine e.
2 Sam. 7. † 27. thou, O Lord, hast opened the e.
2 Kings 19. 16. bow down thine e. Ps. 31. 2. | 86. 1.
1 Chr. 17. † 25. hast revealed the e. of thy servant
Neh. 1. 6. let thine e. be attentive, and eyes open, 11.
Job 4. 12. and mine e. received a little thereof
12. 11. doth not the e. try words? 34. 3.
13. 1. mine e. hath heard and understood it
29. 11. when the e. heard me, then it blessed me
21. to me men gave e. waited, and kept silence
32. 11. behold, I gave e. to your reasons
36. 10. he openeth also their e. to discipline
42. 5. I have heard of thee by the hearing of the e.
Psal. 10. 17. thou wilt cause thine e. to hear
18. † 44. at the hearing of the e. they shall obey
31. 2. bow down thine e. to me, deliver me speedily
58. 4. like the deaf adder that stoppeth her e.
77. 1. I cried unto God, and he gave e. unto me
94. 9. he that planted the e. shall he not hear?
116. 2. because he hath inclined his e. unto me
Prov. 5. 1. and bow thine e. to my understanding
5. 13. nor inclined my e. to them that instructed
15. 31. the e. that heareth the reproof of life
17. 4. and a liar giveth e. to a naughty tongue
18. 15. the e. of the wise seeketh knowledge
20. 12. the hearing e. the seeing eye, Ld. made both
22. 17. bow thine e. hear the words of the wise
25. 12. so is a wise reprover on an obedient e.
28. 9. he that turneth away his e. from hearing
Eccl. 1. 8. nor is the e. filled with hearing
Isa. 48. 8. from that time that thine e. was not opened
50. 4. he wakeneth my e. to hear as the learned
5. Lord hath opened mine e. and I was not rebellious
59. 1. nor is his e. heavy that it cannot hear
64. 4. men have not heard, nor perceived by the e.
Jer. 6. 10. behold their e. is uncircumcised
7. 24. they hearkened not, nor inclined their e. 26.
| 11. 8. | 17. 23. | 25. 4. | 34. 14. | 44. 5.
9. 20. let your e. receive the word of the Lord
35. 15. but ye have not inclined your e.
Lam. 3. 56. hide not thine e. at my breathing
Amos 3. 12. taketh from the lion a piece of an e.
Mat. 10. 27. what ye hear in the e. that preach
26. 51. and smote off his e. Mark 14. 47.
Luke 12. 3. that which ye have spoken in the e.
22. 51. and he touched his e. and healed him
John 18. 26. the servant whose e. Peter cut off
1 Cor. 2. 9. is written, eye hath not seen, nor e. heard
12. 16. if the e. shall say, because I am not the eye
Rev. 2. 7. he that hath an e. let him hear what Spirit saith to churches, 11, 17, 29. | 3. 6, 13, 22. | 13. 9.

Incline EAR.

Ps. 17. 6. O God, *incline* thine e. to me, and hear my speech, 71. 2. | 88. 2. Isa. 37. 17. Dan. 9. 18.
45. 10. O daughter, consider, and *incline* thine e.
49. 4. I will *incline* mine e. to a parable
Prov. 2. 2. so that thou *incline* thine e. to wisdom
4. 20. my son, *incline* thine e. to my sayings
Isa. 55. 3. *incline* your e. and come unto me

Give EAR.

Exod. 15. 26. if wilt *give* e. to his commandments
Deut. 1. 45. but the Lord would not hearken nor *give* e. to your voice, 2 Chron. 24. 19. Neh. 9. 30.
32. 1. *give* e. O heavens, and I will speak
Judg. 5. 3. hear, O ye kings, *give* e. O ye princes
Job 34. 2. *give* e. to me, ye that have knowledge
Psal. 5. 1. *give* e. to my words, O Lord, 54. 2.
17. 1. *give* e. unto my prayer, 55. 1. | 86. 6.
39. 12. hear my prayer, *give* e. to my cry, 141. 1.
49. 1. *give* e. all ye inhabitants of the world
78. 1. *give* e. O my people || 80. 1. *give* e. shepherd
84. 8. hear my prayer, *give* e. O God of Jacob
143. 1. O Lord, *give* e. to my supplications
Isa. 1. 2. *give* e. O earth, for the Lord hath spoken
10. *give* e. to the law of our God, ye people
8. 9. *give* e. all ye of far countries, gird yourselves
28. 23. *give* ye e. and hear my voice, hearken
32. 9. ye careless daughters, *give* e. to my speech
42. 23. who among you will *give* e. to this?
51. 4. hearken and *give* e. to me, O my nation
Jer. 13. 15. *give* e. be not proud, the L. hath spoken
Hos. 5. 1. and *give* ye e. O house of the king
Joel 1. 2. *give* e. all ye inhabitants of the land

Right EAR.

Exod. 29. 20. upon the tip of the *right* e. of his sons, Lev. 8. 23, 24. | 14. 14, 17, 25, 28.
Luke 22. 50. one cut off his *right* e. John 18. 10.

EAR.

Exod. 9. 31. for barley was in the e. and flax bolled
Mark 4. 28. then the e. the full corn in the e.

EAR.

1 Sam. 8. 12. the king will set them to e. the ground
Isa. 30. 24. the oxen that e. the ground shall eat

EARED.

Deut. 21. 4. to a rough valley neither e. nor sown

EARING.

Gen. 45. 6. in which shall be neither e. nor harvest
Exod. 34. 21. in e. time and harvest thou shalt rest

EARLY.

Gen. 19. 2. ye shall rise e. and go on your way
Judg. 7. 3. whoso is fearful, let him depart e.
19. 9. and to-morrow get you e. on your way
2 Kings 6. 15. servant of the man of G. was risen e.
Psal. 46. 5. God shall help her, and that right e.
57. 8. awake up, I myself will awake e. 108. 2.
63. 1. thou art my God, e. will I seek thee
78. 34. they returned and enquired e. after God
90. 14. O satisfy us e. with thy mercy that we may
101. 8. I will e. destroy all the wicked of the land
Prov. 1. 28. they shall seek me e. but not find me
8. 17. those that seek me e. shall find me
Cant. 7. 12. let us get up e. to the vineyards
Isa. 26. 9. with my spirit will I seek thee e.
Hos. 5. 15. in their affliction they will seek me e.
6. 4. and as the e. dew it goeth away, 13. 3.
Luke 24. 22. women who were e. at the sepulchre
John 18. 28. they led Jesus to the hall, and it was e.
20. 1. the first day cometh Mary Magdalene e.
Jam. 5. 7. till he receive the e. and latter rain
See Arose, Rise, Risen, Rising, Rose, Morning.

EAR-RING.

Gen. 24. 22. that the man took a golden e.
30. when Laban saw e. and bracelets on his [sister's hands
47. I put the e. upon her face, and the bracelets
Job 42. 11. every one gave Job an e. of gold
Prov. 25. 12. as an e. of gold, so is a wise reprover

EAR-RINGS.

Gen. 35. 4. they gave to Jacob all their e.
Exod. 32. 2. break off the golden e. and bring to me
35. 22. they brought e. for their offerings
Num. 31. 50. we have brought e. to make atonement
Judg. 8. 24. give every man the e. of his prey
Isa. 3. 20. the Lord will take away the e.
Ezek. 16. 12. and I put e. in thine ears
Hos. 2. 13. and she decked herself with her e.

EARS.

Gen. 23. † 10. Ephron answered in the e. of children
44. 18. let me speak a word in my lord's e.
50. 4. speak, I pray you, in the e. of Pharaoh
Exod. 10. 2. thou mayest tell it in the e. of thy son
17. 14 and rehearse it in the e. of Joshua
Num. 11. † 1. it was evil in the e. of the Lord
18. for you have wept in the e. of the Lord
Deut. 31. 30. Moses spake in the e. of the congre- [gation
Josh. 20. 4. declare his cause in the e. of the elders
Judg. 9. 2. in the e. of the men of Shechem, 3.
1 Sam. 3. 11. at which both the e. of every one that heareth it shall tingle, 2 Kings 21. 12. Jer. 19. 3.
8. 21. he rehearseth them in the e. of the Lord
25. † 24. let thine handmaid speak in thine e.
2 Sam. 7. 22. nor any god beside thee, according to all that we have heard with our e. 1 Chron. 17. 20.
22. 7. and my cry did enter into his e.
Job 15. 21. a dreadful sound is in his e. in prosperity
28. 22. we have heard the fame thereof with our e.
33. 16. then he openeth the e. of men, and sealeth
Psal. 18. 6. and my cry came even into his e.
34. 15. and his e. are opened to their cry
44. 1. we have heard with our e. O God
115. 6. they have e. but hear not, 135. 17.
Prov. 21. 13. whoso stoppeth his e. at cry of the poor
23. 9. speak not in the e. of a fool, he will despise
26. 17. like one that taketh a dog by the e.
Isa. 11. 3. nor reprove after the hearing of his e.
32. 3. the e. of them that hear shall hearken
33. 15. that stoppeth his e. from hearing of blood
35. 5. and the e. of the deaf shall be unstopped
42. 20. opening the e. but he heareth not
43. 8. bring forth the blind and deaf that have e.
Jer. 2. 2. go, and cry in the e. of Jerusalem
5. 21. O people, which have e. and hear not
29. 29. Zephaniah read in the e. of Jeremiah
36. 15. sit down now, and read it in our e.
21. Jehudi read it in the e. of the king and princes
Mat. 28. 14. if this come to the governor's e.
Mark 7. 33. he put his fingers into his e. and spit
35. and straightway his e. were opened
8. 18. having e. hear ye not? do ye not remember?
Acts 7. 51. ye uncircumcised in heart and e. resist
11. 22. tidings came to the e. of the church
17. 20. thou bringest strange things to our e.
Rom. 11. 8. hath given e. that they should not hear
2 Tim. 4. 3. they heap teachers, having itching e.
Jam. 5. 4. are entered into e. of the Lord of sabaoth
1 Pet. 3. 12. and his e. are open to their prayers

EARS *to hear.*

Deut. 29. 4. the Lord hath not given you e. *to hear*
Ezek. 12. 2. they have e. *to hear*, and hear not
Mat. 11. 15. he that hath e. *to hear*, let him hear 13. 9, 43. Mark 4. 9, 23. | 7. 16. Luke 8. 8. | 14. 35.

Mine EARS.

Num. 14. 28. as ye have spoken in *mine* e. I will do
Judg. 17. 2. the silver thou spakest of in *mine* e.
1 Sam. 15. 14. this bleating of sheep in *mine* e.?
2 Kings 19. 28. tumult come into *mine* e. Isa. 37. 29
2 Chron. 7. 15. and *mine* e. attent to the prayer
Job 33. † 8. surely thou hast spoken in *mine* e.
Psal. 40. 6. *mine* e. hast thou opened, burnt-offering
92. 11. *mine* e. shall hear my desire of the wicked
Isa. 5. 9. in *mine* e. said the Lord of hosts
22. 14. it was revealed in *mine* e. by the Lord
Ezek. 8. 18. tho' they cry in *mine* e. with loud voice
9. 1. he cried also in *mine* e. with a loud voice
Luke 1. 44. thy salutation sounded in *mine* e.

EARS *of the people.*

Exod. 11. 2. speak now in the e. *of the people*
Deut. 32. 44. Moses spake in the e. *of the people*
Judg. 7. 3. go to, proclaim in the e. *of the people*
1 Sam. 11. 4. told the tidings in the e. *of the people*
2 Kings 18. 26. talk not in the e. *of people*, Isa. 36. 11.
Neh. 8. 3. e. *of the people* were attentive to the law
13. † 1. on that day they read in the e. *of the people*, Jer. 28. 7. | 36. 6, 10, 13, 14.

Their EARS.

Gen. 20. 8. Abimelech told these things in *their* e.
35. 4. gave Jacob ear-rings which were in *their* e.
Exod. 32. 3. people brake off the ear-rings in *their* e.
Deut. 31. 28. I may speak these words in *their* e.
2 Kings 23. 2. read in *their* e. 2 Chr. 34. 30. Jer. 36. 15.
Job 36. 15. he openeth *their* e. in oppression
Isa. 6. 10. make heart fat, *their* e. heavy, lest they hear with *their* e. Mat. 13. 15. Acts 28. 27
Mic. 7. 16. the nations shall see, *their* e. shall be deaf
Zech. 7. 11. but they stopped *their* e. Acts 7. 57.
2 Tim. 4. 4. they shall turn away *their* e. from truth

Thine EARS.

1 Sam. 25. † 24. let thine handmaid speak in *thine* e.
2 Chron. 6. 40. let *thine* e. be attent to the prayer
Psal. 10. 17. thou wilt cause *thine* e. to hear
130. 2. let *thine* e. be attentive to the voice
Prov. 23. 12. apply *thine* e. to words of knowledge
Isa. 30. 21. *thine* e. shall hear a word behind thee
49. 20. the children shall say again in *thine* e.
Jer. 28. 7. hear this word that I speak in *thine* e.
Ezek. 3. 10. and hear with *thine* e. 40. 4. | 44. 5.
16. 12. I put ear-rings in *thine* e. and a crown
23. 25. they shall take away thy nose and *thine* e.
24. 26. to cause thee to hear with *thine* e.

Your EARS.

Deut. 5. 1. hear the statutes which I speak in *your* e.
Job 13. 17. hear my declaration with *your* e.
Psal. 78. 1. incline *your* e. to the words of my mouth
Jer. 26. 11. as ye have heard with *your* e.
15. Lord sent me to speak these words in *your* e.
Mat. 13. 16. but blessed are *your* e. for they hear
Luke 4. 21. this scripture is fulfilled in *your* e.
9. 44. let these sayings sink down in *your* e.

EARS.

Gen. 41. 5. behold, seven e. of corn came up, 22.
Lev. 2. 14. shalt offer for a meat offering green e.
23. 14. not eat green e. till ye bring an offering
Deut. 23. 25. mayest pluck the e. with thine hand
Ruth 2. 2. let me go and glean e. of corn after him
2 Kings 4. 42. brought the man of G. full e. of corn
Job 24. 24. the wicked cut off as tops of e. of corn
Isa. 17. 5. the glory of Jacob, as when one reapeth e.
Mat. 12. 1. his disciples were an hungered, and began to pluck the e. of corn, Mark 2. 23. Luke 6. 1.
See Seven.

EARNEST.

The apostle Paul *speaks of* the earnest of the

Spirit, 2 Cor. 1. 22. the first-fruits of the Spirit, Rom. 8. 23 *and of* being sealed by the Spirit, Eph. 1. 13. *These phrases signify the assurance which the Spirit of adoption does give believers of their inheritance in heaven. For as the* first-fruits *were pledges to the* Jews *of the ensuing crop: and as he that receives* earnest, *is sure to have the full sum paid him, or the full bargain made good, when the person that gives it is honest and faithful: So the graces wrought in the soul by the Spirit of God, such as love, joy, peace, &c. are pledges of that abundance and fulness of joy and felicity, which believers shall partake of in heaven. Yet these graces and comforts which the godly enjoy here, are but* first-fruits *in regard of their* order; *they precede the full harvest: And in regard of their* quantity, *they are but an handful in comparison of the whole* seal *and* earnest: *though they both imply assurance, yet they differ thus;* sealing *especially refers to the understanding;* earnest *to the affections. Though the* seal *assures us, yet it is not part of the inheritance; but the* earnest *so assures us, that it gives a part of the inheritance; It works that joy in the heart, which is a foretaste of heaven, and which the saints are filled with there.*

2 Cor. 1. 22. hath given the e. of the Spirit, 5. 5.
Eph. 1. 14. which is the e. of our inheritance

EARNEST.

Prov. 27. †6. but the kisses of an enemy are e.
Acts 12. †5. e. prayer was made to God for him
Rom. 8. 19. the e. expectation of the creature waiteth
2 Cor. 7. 7. when he told us your e. desire
8. 16. which put the same e. care into Titus
Phil. 1. 20. according to my e. expectation and hope
Heb. 2. 1. we ought to give the more e. heed to things

EARNESTLY.

Num. 22. 37. did I not e. send to thee to call thee?
1 Sam. 20. 6. David e. asked leave of me, 28.
Neh. 3. 20. Baruch e. repaired the other piece
13. †6. and after certain days I e. requested
Job 7. 2. as a servant e. desireth the shadow
Jer. 11. 7. for I e. protested to your fathers
31. 20. I do e. remember him still
Mic. 7. 3. they may do evil with both hands e.
Luke 22. 44. being in an agony he prayed more e.
56. but a certain maid e. looked upon Peter
Acts 3. 12. men of Israel, why look ye so e. on us?
23. 1. Paul e. beholding council, said, I have lived
1 Cor. 12. 31. but covet e. the best gifts
2 Cor. 5. 2. in this we groan, e. desiring to be clothed
Jam. 5. 17. Elias prayed e. that it might not rain
Jude 3. that ye should e. contend for the faith

EARNETH.

Hag. 1. 6. he that e. wages, e. to put it in a bag

EARTH,

Is taken (1) *For that gross and terrestrial element which sustains and nourishes us,* Gen. 1. 10. God called the dry land, earth. *In this sense it is taken in those passages, where the* earth *is said to yield fruit, to be barren, watered, &c.* (2) *For all that rude matter which was created in the beginning.* Gen. 1. 1. God created the heaven and the earth; *that is, the matter of all sensible beings.* (3) *By the* earth *is meant the terraqueous globe, the earth and all that it contains, men, animals, plants, metals, waters, fish, &c.* Psal. 24. 1. The earth is the Lord's and the fulness thereof. (4) *The earth is often taken for those who inhabit it,* Gen. 6. 13. | 11. 1. The earth is filled with violence, The whole earth was of one language. Psal. 96. 1. Sing unto the Lord, all the earth. (5) *Sometimes* the whole earth, *or* all the kingdoms of the earth, *signifies no more than the whole empire of* Chaldea *and* Assyria. *Ezra* 1. 2. The Lord God of heaven hath given me all the kingdoms of the earth. Earth *is taken for* Canaan, *or the land of the* Jews; *Rom.* 9. 28. A short work will the Lord make upon the earth. *He will bring a sudden destruction upon that land and people. And in* Mat. 9. 26. Mark 15. 33. Luke 4. 25. *the word which is translated* land, *is in the* Greek, *earth.*

A man of the earth, *Gen.* 9. † 20. Noah was a man of the earth, *a husbandman, or one who tilled the ground. In* Psal. 10. 18. the man of the earth *signifies a mortal, earthly-minded man, who was made of the dust, and must return to the dust.* Earth, *in the moral sense of it, is set in opposition to heaven; things earthly and carnal, to things heavenly and spiritual.* John 3. 31. He that is of the earth is earthly, and speaketh of the earth: he that cometh from heaven is above all. *Col.* 3. 1, 2. If ye then be risen with Christ, seek those things which are above, and set not your affections on things on the earth. *The terrestrial man is set in opposition to the heavenly,* 1 Cor. 15. 47, 48. The first man is of the earth, earthy, the second man is the Lord from heaven. Adam, *the first public person and head of the old covenant, was formed of the earth; he was mortal and corruptible: But* Christ, *the second public person, and head of the new covenant, is of a heavenly descent, and has a divine as well as a human nature. In like manner the earthly house is set in opposition to the heavenly;* 2 Cor. 5. 1. If our earthly house of this tabernacle were dissolved, we have a building of God, an house not made with hands, eternal in the heavens. *If this bodily frame of nature were taken to pieces by death, there is a state of glory provided by God for the separate soul to pass unto.*

Gen. 1. 2. and the e was without form and void
10. and God called the dry land e.
11. and God said, let the e. bring forth grass, 24.
12. and the e. brought forth grass and herb
28. be fruitful, replenish the e. and subdue it, 9. 1.
6. 11. the e. also was corrupt before God
7. 17. and the ark was lifted up above the e.
8. 14. in the second month was the e. dried
22. while e. remaineth, seed-time shall not cease
9. 13. for a token of a covenant between me and e.
10. 25. in his days was the e. divided, 1 Chr. 1. 19.
18. 18. and all the nations of the e. shall be blessed in him, 22. 18. | 26. 4. | 28. 14.
27. 28. God give thee of the fatness of the e.
41. 47. in plenteous years e. brought forth handfuls
Exod. 8. 22. I am the Lord in the midst of the e.
9. 29. that thou mayest know that the e. is the Lord's, Deut. 10. 14. Psal. 24. 1. 1 Cor. 10. 26.
10. 5. that one cannot be able to see the e.
15. 12. stretchest thy hand, e. swallowed them
20. 24. an altar of e. thou shalt make unto me
Num. 16. 30. if the e. open her mouth and swallow
32. and the e. opened her mouth and swallowed them up and their houses, 26. 10. Psal. 106. 17.
34. they said, lest the e. swallow us up also
Deut. 28. 1. Lord will set thee above all nations of e.
23. the e. that is under thee shall be iron
32. 1. and hear, O e. the words of my mouth
13. he made him ride on the high places of the e.
22. a fire shall consume the e. with her increase
1 Sam. 2. 8. for the pillars of the e. are the Lord's
4. 5. Israel shouted, so that the e. rang again
14. 15. they also trembled, and the e. quaked
2 Sam. 1. 2. a man came with e. on his head, 15. 32.
22. 8. then the e. shook and trembled, Psal. 18. 7.
1 Kings 1. 40. so that the e. rent with the sound
2 Kings 5. 17. to thy servant two mules' burden of e.
1 Chron. 16. 31. and let the e. rejoice, Psal. 96. 11.
33. at the presence of the Lord, because God cometh to judge the e. Psal. 96. 13. | 98. 9.
Ezra 5. 11. the servants of the God of heaven and e.
Neh. 9. 6. thou hast made the e. Isa. 45. 12.
Job 5. 25. and thy offspring as the grass of the e.
9. 6. which shaketh the e. out of her place
24. the e. is given into the hand of the wicked
11. 9. the measure thereof is longer than the e.
12. 15. he sendeth waters and they overturn the e.
15. 19. to whom alone the e. was given
16. 18. O e. cover not thou my blood, let my cry
18. 4. shall the e. be forsaken for thee?
20. 27. and the e. shall rise up against him
22. 8. but as for the mighty man, he had the e.
24. 4. the poor of the e. hide themselves
26. 7. he hangeth the e. upon nothing
30. 6. to dwell in the caves of the e. and in rocks
8. children of base men, they were viler than the e.
34. 13. who hath given him a charge over the e.?
37. 17. when he quieteth the e. by the south-wind
38. 4. when I laid the foundations of the e.
18. hast thou perceived the breadth of the e.?
Psal. 2. 8. give thee the uttermost parts of the e.
10. be instructed, ye judges of the e.
10. 18. that the man of the e. may no more oppress
12. 6. pure words, as silver tried in a furnace of e.
25. 13. and his seed shall inherit the e.
33. 5. the e. is full of the goodness of the Lord
14. he looketh on all the inhabitants of the e.
37. 9. that wait on Lord shall inherit the e. 11, 22.
46. 2. we will not fear though the e. be removed
6. he uttered his voice, the e. melted
47. 9. for the shields of the e. belong unto God
48. 2. the joy of the whole e. is mount Zion
60. 2. thou hast made the e. to tremble
63. 9. shall go into the lower parts of the e.
65. 8. that dwell in the uttermost parts of the e.
9. thou visitest the e. and waterest it
67. 6. then shall e. yield her increase, Ezek. 34. 27.
68. 8. the e. shook, the heavens also dropped
32. sing unto God, ye kingdoms of the e.
71. 20. shalt bring me up from the depths of the e.
72. 6. shall come down as showers that water the e.
73. 9. and their tongue walketh through the e.
75. 3. the e. and all the inhabitants thereof are dissolved, I bear up its pillars, Isa. 24. 19.
8. the wicked of the e. shall wring them out
76. 8. the e. feared || 77. 18. the e. trembled, 97. 4.
9. when God arose to save the meek of the e.
78. 69. like the e. which he hath established for ever
82. 8. arise, O God, judge the e. thou shalt inherit
90. 2. or ever thou hadst formed the e.
97. 1. the Lord reigneth, let the e. rejoice
99. 1. the Lord reigneth, let the e. be moved
102. 25. of old hast thou laid the foundation of the e. 104. 5. Prov. 8. 29. Isa. 48. 13.
104. 13. the e. is satisfied with the fruit of thy works
24. O Lord, the e. is full of thy riches
114. 7. tremble, O e. at the presence of the Lord
115. 16. the e. hath he given to the children of men
119. 64. the e. O Lord, is full of thy mercy
90. thou hast established the e. and it abideth
147. 8. who prepareth rain for the e.
148. 13. his glory is above the e. and the heaven
Prov. 3. 19. the Lord hath founded the e. Isa. 24. 1.
8. 23. I was set up from everlasting, or ever e. was
26. as yet he had not made the e. nor fields
25. 3. e. for depth and heart of kings is unsearchable
30. 16. the e. that is not filled with water
21. for three things the e. is disquieted, for four
Eccl. 1. 4. but the e. abideth for ever
5. 9. moreover, the profit of the e. is for all
Isa. 4. 2. the fruit of the e. shall be excellent
11. 4. that smiteth the e. with the rod of his mouth
9. e. shall be full of the knowledge of the Lord
13. 13. the e. shall remove out of her place
14. 16. is this the man that made the e. to tremble?
24. 4. the e. mourneth and fadeth away, 33. 9.
5. the e. is defiled under the inhabitants thereof
24. 19. e. is utterly broken down, the e. is dissolved
20. e. shall reel || 26. 19. e. shall cast out the dead
26. 21. the e. also shall disclose her blood
34. 1. let the e. hear, and all that is therein
40. 22. it is he that sitteth on the circle of the e.
28. the Creator of the ends of the e. fainteth not
44. 24. that spread abroad the e. by myself
45. 8. let the e. open || 12. I have made the e.
22. look to me and be ye saved, all ends of the e.
49. 13. sing, O heavens, and be joyful, O e.
51. 6. look on the e. the e. shall wax old
66. 1. thus saith the Lord, the e. is my footstool
8. shall the e. be made to bring forth in one day?
Jer. 4. 23. I beheld the e. it was without form
28. for this shall the e. mourn, heavens be black
6. 19. hear, O e. I will bring evil on this peopl
10. 10. at his wrath the e. shall tremble
22. 29. O e. e. e. hear the word of the Lord, write ye this man childless, Mic. 1. 2
46. 8. Egypt saith, I will go up and cover the e.
49. 21. the e. is moved at the noise, 50. 46.
51. 15. he hath made the e. by his power
Ezek. 7. 21. I will give it to the wicked of the e.
9. 9. they say, the Lord hath forsaken the e.
43. 2. and the e. shined with his glory
Hos. 2. 22. the e. shall hear the corn and the wine
Joel 2. 10. the e. shall quake before them
Amos 8. 9. I will darken the e. in the clear day
Jonah 2. 6. the e. with her bars was about me
Mic. 6. 2. hear, ye strong foundations of the e.
7. 17. they shall move out like worms of the e.
Nah. 1. 5. the e. is burnt up at his presence
Hab. 2. 14. the e. filled with knowledge of the L.
3. 3. and the e. was full of his praise
9. thou didst cleave the e. with rivers
Hag. 1. 10. the e. is stayed from her fruit
Zech. 1. 10. sent to walk to and fro thro' the e. 6. 7.
4. 10. the eyes of the Lord which run thro' the e.
Mal. 4. 6. lest I smite the e. with a curse
Mat. 5. 5. blessed are meek, for they shall inherit e.
35. swear not by the e. it is God's footstool
13. 5. where they had not much e. Mark 4. 5.
Mark 4. 28. for the e. bringeth forth fruit of herself
John 3. 31. he that is of the e. is earthly, and speaketh of the e. he that cometh from heaven is above all
1 Cor. 15. 47. the first man is of the e. earthy
2 Tim. 2. 20. but also vessels of wood and of e.
Heb. 6. 7. the e. which drinketh in the rain
12. 26. whose voice then shook the e. but now
Jam. 5. 7. waiteth for the precious fruit of the e.
18. and the e. brought forth her fruit
2 Pet. 3. 10. the e. and works therein shall be burnt up
Rev. 7. 3. hurt not the e. nor sea, nor the trees
11. 4. olive trees standing before the God of the e.
6. have power to smite the e. with all plagues
12. 16. the e. opened and swallowed up the flood
13. 12. causeth the e. to worship the first beast
18. 1. and the e. was lightened with his glory
19. 2. the great whore, which did corrupt the e.
20. 11. from whose face the e. fled away

See BEASTS, DUST, ENDS, FACE, KINGS, HEAVEN, PEOPLE, WHOLE.

All the EARTH.

Gen. 1. 26. let them have dominion over *all the e.*
7. 3. to keep seed alive on the face of *all the e.*
11. 9. there confound the language of *all the e.*
18. 25. shall not the Judge of *all the e.* do right?
19. 31. to come in to us after manner of *all the e.*
Exod. 9. 14. there is none like me in *all the e.*
16. my name declared thro' *all the e.* Rom. 9. 17.
19. 5. a peculiar treasure; for *all the e.* is mine
34. 10. such as have not been done in *all the e.*
Num. 14. 21. *all the e.* shall be filled with glory
Josh. 3. 11. the Lord of *all the e.* 13. Zech. 6. 5.
23. 14. I am going the way of *all the e.* 1 Kings 2. 2.
Judg. 6. 37. and if it be dry on *all the e.* beside
1 Sam. 17. 46. that *all the e.* may know there is a God
1 Kings 10. 24. *all the e.* sought to Solomon to hear
2 Kings 5. 15. no God in *all the e.* but in Israel
1 Chr. 16. 14. judgm. are in *all the e.* Psal. 105. 7
23. sing to the Lord, *all the e.* Psal. 96. 1.
30. fear before him, *all the e.* Psal. 33. 8. | 96. 9.
Psal. 8. 1. excellent is thy name in *all the e.* 9.
45. 16. whom thou mayest make princes in *all the e.*
47. 2. L. is a great king over *all the e.* 7. Zech. 14. 9.
57. 5. let thy glory be above *all the e.* 11. | 108. 5.
66. †1. make a joyful noise *all the e.* 98. 4. | 100. †1.
4. *all the e.* shall worship thee, and sing to thee
83. 18. that thou art most high over *all the e.* 97. 9.
Isa. 10. 14. so have I gathered *all the e.* none moved
12. 5. done excellent things, this is known in *all e.*
25. 8. take the rebuke of his people, from *all the e.*
Jer. 26. 6. I will make this city a curse to *all the e.*
33. 9. it shall be an honour before *all the e.*
51. 7. a golden cup that made *all the e.* drunken
25. O mountain, which destroyest *all the e.*
49. so at Babylon shall fall the slain of *all the e.*
Dan. 2. 39. a kingdom shall bear rule over *all the e.*
Hab. 2. 20. let *all the e.* keep silence before him
Zeph. 3. 8. *all the e.* shall be devoured with fire
Zech. 1. 11. *all the e.* sitteth still and is at rest
Luke 23. 44. there was a darkness over *all the e.*
Rom. 10. 18. their sound went into *all the e.*
Rev. 5. 6. seven Spirits of God sent forth into *all e.*

From the EARTH.

Gen. 2. 6. but there went up a mist *from the e.*
4. 11. and now art thou cursed *from the e.*
6. †13. behold, I will destroy them *from the e.*
7. 23. and they were destroyed *from the e.*
8. 11. Noah knew waters were abated *from the e.*
Exod. 9. 15. thou shalt be cut off *from the e.* Josh. 7. 9. Psal. 109. 15. Prov. 2. 22. Nah. 2. 13.
1 Sam. 28. 23. Saul arose *from the e.* and sat on bed
2 Sam. 4. 11. shall I not take you away *from the e.?*
12. 17. the elders went to raise him *from the e.*
20. David arose *from the e.* and washed himself
Job 18. 17. his remembrance shall perish *from the e.*
Psal. 21. 10. shalt destroy their fruit *from the e.*
34. 16. cut off remembrance of them *from the e.*
148. 7. praise L. *from the e.* ye dragons and deeps
Prov. 30. 14. as knives to devour poor *from the e.*
Jer. 10. 11. even they shall perish *from the e.*
Ezek. 1. 19. living creatures were lift up *from e.* 21.
Dan. 7. 4. and it was lifted up *from the e.*
Amos 3. 5. shall one take up a snare *from the e.*
John 12. 32. and I, if I be lifted up *from the e.*
Acts 8. 33. for his life is taken *from the e.*
9. 8. Saul arose *from the e.* and he saw no man
22. 22. said, away with such a fellow *from the e.*
Rev. 6. 4. power given him to take peace *from the e.*
14. 3. but 144,000 which were redeemed *from the e.*

In the EARTH.

Gen. 1. 22. and let fowl multiply *in the e.*
4. 12. a vagabond shalt thou be *in the e.* 14.
6. 5. the wickedness of man was great *in the e.*
10. 8. Nimrod began to be a mighty one *in the e.*
19. 31. not a man *in the e.* to come in unto us

Gen. 45. 7. sent me, to preserve a posterity in the e.
Exod. 20. 4. or that is in the e. beneath, or water
Josh. 7. 21. and behold they are hid in the e.
Judg. 18. 10. no want of any thing that is in the e.
2 Sam. 7. 9. a great name, like to the name of the great men that are in the e. 1 Chron. 17. 8.
23. what nation in e. like Israel? 1 Chr. 17. 21.
14. 20. to know all things that are in the e.
1 Chron. 29. 11. for all that is in the e. is thine
2 Chron. 6. 14. there is no God like thee in the e.
Job 1. 7. from going to and fro in the e. 2. 2.
8. that there is none like him in the e. 2. 3.
14. 8. though the root thereof wax old in the e.
24. 18. their portion is cursed in the e.
39. 14. ostrich, which leaveth her eggs in the e.
Psal. 16. 3. but to the saints that are in the e.
46. 8. what desolations he hath made in the e.
10. be still, I will be exalted in the e.
58. 11. verily he is a God that judgeth in the e.
72. 16. there shall be a handful of corn in the e.
119. 19. I am a stranger in the e. hide not thy com.
140. 11. let not an evil speaker be established in e.
Prov. 11. 31. the righteous be recompensed in the e.
Isa. 26. 9. for when thy judgments are in the e.
18. we have not wrought deliverance in the e.
40. 24. their stock shall not take root in the e.
42. 4. till he have set judgment in the e.
62. 7. till he make Jerusalem a praise in the e.
65. 16. shall bless in God of truth, who blesseth himself in the e. and he that sweareth in the e.
Jer. 17. 13. that forsake thee, be written in the e.
31. 22. the Lord hath created a new thing in the e.
Hos. 2. 23. and I will sow her unto me in the e.
Joel 2. 30. and I will shew wonders in the e.
Amos 5. 7. ye who leave off righteousness in the e.
Mat. 25. 18. he went and digged in the e. and hid
25. I was afraid, and hid thy talent in the e.
Mark 4. 31. it is like a grain of mustard seed, when it is sown in the e. is less than all seeds in the e.
1 John 5. 8. there are three that bear witness in the e.

On, or upon, the EARTH.

Gen. 6. 6. repented that he had made man on the e.
12. God looked upon the e. behold it was corrupt
7. 4. I will cause it to rain upon the e. forty days
12. the rain was upon the e. forty days, 17.
8. 17. be fruitful and multiply upon the e.
19. 23. sun was risen upon the e. when Lot entered
28. 12. and behold a ladder set upon the e.
Exod. 10. 6. since the day they were upon the e.
Lev. 11. 29. things that creep upon the e. 42, 44.
Deut. 4. 10. all days they live upon the e. 12. 1, 19.
36. upon the e. he shewed thee his great fire
12. 16. ye shall pour it upon the e. as water, 24.
2 Sam. 12. 16. David lay all night upon the e.
14. 7. not leave name nor remainder upon the e.
1 Kings 8. 27. but will God indeed dwell on the e.? heaven cannot contain thee, 2 Chron. 6. 18.
17. 14. till the day the Lord sends rain upon the e.
1 Chron. 29. 15. our days on e. as a shadow, Job 8. 9.
Job 7. 1. is there not an appointed time to man on e.?
19. 25. he shall stand at the latter day upon the e.
20. 4. knowest not since man was placed on the e.
37. 6. for he saith to the snow, be thou on the e.
41. 33. on e. there is not his like, leviathan made
Psal. 7. 5. let the enemy tread down my life on the e.
41. 2. and he shall be blessed upon the e.
67. 2. that thy way may be known upon the e.
73. 25. there is none upon e. I desire besides thee
112. 2. his seed shall be mighty upon the e.
Prov. 30. 24. four things that are little upon the e.
Eccl. 7. 20. for there is not a just man upon the e.
10. 7. and princes walking as servants upon the e.
11. 2. knowest not what evil shall be done upon e.
3. the clouds empty themselves upon the e.
Cant. 2. 12. flowers appear on the e. time of singing
Isa. 28. 22. a consumption determined upon the e.
51. 6. lift up your eyes, and look upon the e.
Jer. 9. 3. are not valiant for the truth upon the e.
Lam. 2. 11. eyes fail, my liver is poured upon the e.
Dan. 2. 10. not a man on the e. can shew the matter
Amos 3. 5. can a bird fall in a snare upon the e.
9. 9. yet shall not the least grain fall upon the e.
Mat. 6. 19. lay not up for yours. treasures upon e.
9. 6. may know that the Son of man hath power on e. to forgive sins, Mark 2. 10. Luke 5. 24.
10. 34. think not I am come to send peace on e.
16. 19. whatsoever thou shalt bind on e. 18. 18.
18. 19. I say, that if two of you shall agree on e.
23. 9. and call no man your father upon the e.
35. all the righteous blood shed upon the e.
Mark 9. 3. so as no fuller on e. can white them
Luke 2. 14. glory to God in the highest, on e. peace
6. 49. like a man that built an house upon the e.
12. 49. I am come to send fire on the e.
51. suppose ye that I am come to give peace on e.?
18. 8. the Son cometh, shall he find faith on e.?
21. 26. for the things which are coming on the e.
John 17. 4. I have glorified thee on the e.
Rom. 9. 28. a short work will the Lord make on the e.
Col. 3. 2. set your affection not on things on the e.
5. mortify your members which are upon the e.
Heb. 8. 4. if he were on e. he should not be a priest
11. 13. and confessed they were strangers on the e.
12. 25. who refused him that spake on e.
Jam. 5. 5. ye have lived in pleasure on the e.
17. it rained not on the e. for three years
Rev. 3. 10. to try them that dwell upon the e.
5. 10. made us kings and priests, we shall reign on e.
6. 10. avenge our blood on them that dwell on the e.
7. 1. that the wind should not blow on the e.
8. 7. hail, and fire, and they were cast upon the e.
10. 8. in hand of angel which standeth upon the e.
11. 10. dwell on the e. 13. 8, 14. | 14. 6. | 17. 8.
14. 16. and he thrust in his sickle on the e.
16. 2. the first poured out his vial upon the e.
18. 24. the blood of all that were slain upon the e.

Out of the EARTH.

1 Sam. 28. 13. I saw gods ascending out of the e.
2 Sam. 23. 4. as tender grass springing out of the e.
Job 8. 19. and out of the e. shall others grow
28. 2. iron is taken out of the e. and brass molten
5. as for the e. out of it cometh bread
Psal. 85. 11. truth shall spring out of the e.
104. 14. that he may bring food out of the e.
35. let the sinners be consumed out of the e.
Dan. 7. 17. four kings, which shall arise out of the e.
Hos. 2. 18. I will break the battle out of the e.
Mic. 7. 2. the good man is perished out of the e.
Rev. 13. 11. another beast coming up out of the e.

To, or unto, the EARTH.

Gen. 24. 52. he worshipped, bowing himself to the e.
37. 10. to bow down ourselves to thee, to the e.
42. 6. they bowed themselves to the e. 43. 26.
48. 12. he bowed himself with his face to the e.
Josh. 5. 14. Joshua fell on his face to the e. 7. 6.
1 Sam. 5. 3. Dagon was fallen on his face to the e.
17. 49. Goliath fell on his face to the e.
24. 8. David stooped with his face to the e.
25. 41. she bowed herself to the e. 1 Kings 1. 31.
26. 8. let me smite him, I pray thee, to the e.
20. therefore let not my blood fall to the e.
2 Sam. 1. 2. when he came to David he fell to the e.
14. 11. not one hair shall fall to the e. 1 Kings 1. 52.
2 Kings 10. 10. fall to the e. nothing of the word of L.
2 Chron. 20. 24. were dead bodies fallen to the e.
Job 12. 8. or speak to the e. it shall teach thee
Psal. 17. 11. set their eyes, bowing down to the e.
44. 25. for our belly cleaveth unto the e.
50. 4. he shall call to the e. that he may judge
146. 4. his breath goeth forth, he returneth to the e.
Eccl. 3. 21. the spirit of beast that goeth to the e.
12. 7. then shall the dust return to the e.
Isa. 8. 22. and they shall look unto the e.
63. 6. I will bring down their strength to the e.
Jer. 15. 10. a man of contention to the whole e.
Hos. 6. 3. as the latter and former rain to the e.
Luke 24. 5. and bowed down their faces to the e.
Acts 9. 4. Saul fell to the e. and heard a voice
10. 11. as a great sheet, and let down to the e.
26. 14. and when we were all fallen to the e.
Rev. 6. 13. and the stars of heaven fell to the e.
12. 4. drew the stars, and did not cast them to the e.
13. when the dragon saw he was cast unto the e.

EARTHEN.

Lev. 6. 28. the e. vessel wherein it was sodden
11. 33. the e. vessel whereinto any of them falleth
14. 5. one of the birds killed in an e. vessel, 50.
Num. 5. 17. priest shall take holy water in e. vessel
2 Sam. 17. 28. brought beds, basins, and e. vessels
Jer. 19. 1. go and get a potter's e. bottle
32. 14. put these evidences in an e. vessel
Lam. 4. 2. how are they esteemed as e. pitchers
2 Cor. 4. 7. we have this treasure in e. vessels

EARTHLY.

John 3. 12. if I have told you e. things, believe not
31. he that is of the earth is e. speaks of earth
2 Cor. 5. 1. if our e. house of tabern. were dissolved
Phil. 3. 19. many walk, who mind e. things
Jam. 3. 15. this wisdom is e. sensual, devilish

EARTHY.

1 Cor. 15. 47. the first man is of the earth, e.
48. as is the e. such are they also that are e.
49. and as we have borne the image of the e.

EARTHQUAKE.

The Scripture speaks of several natural earthquakes. One of the most remarkable, is that which was in the twenty-seventh year of Uzziah, king of Judah. There is mention of this earthquake in Amos 1. 1. and in Zech. 14. 5. Josephus says, that this earthquake was so violent, as to divide a mountain in halves, which lay to the west of Jerusalem, and moved one part of it from its place four furlongs, or five hundred paces.

Another very memorable earthquake, was that at the time of our Saviour's crucifixion, Mat. 27. 51. Many have been of opinion, that this motion was perceived by all the world. Others maintain, that it was sensible only in Judea, or even in the temple, the gates whereof were shaken, and the vail rent asunder. It must have been attended with very terrible circumstances, since the centurion, and they who were with him, were so affected with it, and were induced by it to acknowledge the injustice of our Saviour's condemnation, Mat. 27. 54.

An earthquake is a great shaking or trembling of the earth, or of some parts of it, Amos 1. 1. Great alterations and changes are expressed in Scripture by a shaking of the earth, Heb. 12. 26. The delivering of the Israelites out of Egypt is called a moving, or shaking, of the earth, Psal. 68. 8. And an extraordinary and unexpected alteration in the state of affairs, civil or ecclesiastical, is represented by a great earthquake, Rev. 6. 12. and 16. 18.

1 Kings 19. 11. after the wind, an e. Ld. was not in e.
12. after the e. a fire, the Lord was not in the fire
Isa. 29. 6. thou shalt be visited of the Lord with e.
Amos 1. 1. which he saw two years before the e.
Zech. 14. 5. like as ye fled from before the e.
Mat. 27. 54. now when the centurion saw the e.
28. 2. behold, there was a great e. the angel of the Lord came, Acts 16. 26. Rev. 6. 12. | 11. 13.
Rev. 8. 5. there were thunderings and an e. 11. 19.
16. 18. a great e. so mighty an e. and so great

EARTHQUAKES.

Mat. 24. 7. there shall be famines, pestilences, and e. in divers places, Mark 13. 8. Luke 21. 11.

EASE.

Deut. 28. 65. among nations shalt thou find no e.
Judg. 20. 43. they trod the Benjamites down with e.
Job 12. 5. in the thought of him that is at e.
16. 12. I was at e. || 21. 23. dieth, being wholly at e.
Ps. 25. 13. his soul shall dwell at e. his seed inherit
123. 4. with the scorning of those that are at e.
Prov. 1. † 32. the e. of the simple shall slay them
Isa. 32. 9. rise up, ye women that are at e.
11. tremble, ye women that are at e. be troubled
Jer. 46. 27. Jacob shall return, and be in rest, at e.
48. 11. Moab hath been at e. from his youth
49. † 31. get you up to the nation that is at e.
Ezek. 23. 42. a voice of a multitude being at e.
Amos 6. 1. woe to them that are at e. in Zion
Zech. 1. 15. I am sore displeased with heathen at e.
Luke 12. 19. take thine e. eat, drink, and be merry

EASE.

Deut. 23. 13. when thou wilt e. thyself abroad
2 Chron. 10. 4. e. thou somewhat the yoke, 9.
Job 7. 13. my couch shall e. my complaint
Isa. 1. 24. ah, I will e. me of mine adversaries
38. † 14. O Lord, I am oppressed, e. me

EASED.

Job 16. 6. and though I forbear, what am I e.?
2 Cor. 8. 13. that other men be e. and ye burdened

EASEMENT.

Judg. 3. † 24. he doeth his e. in his summer chamber

EASIER.

Exod. 18. 22. so shall it be e. for thyself, shall bear
Mat. 9. 5. whether is e. to say, thy sins be forgiven thee, or to say, arise, Mark 2. 9. Luke 5. 23.
19. 24. it is e. for camel to go thro' the eye of needle, than a rich man, Mark 10. 25. Luke 18. 25.
Luke 16. 17. it is e. for heaven and earth to pass

EASILY.

1 Cor. 13. 5. charity is not e. provoked, thinks no evil
Heb. 12. 1. lay aside the sin which doth so e. beset us

EAST.

The Hebrews express the east, west, north, and south, by words which signify, before, behind, left, and right, according to the situation of a man with his face turned towards the east. By the east they describe frequently not only Arabia Deserta, and the lands of Moab and Ammon, which lay to the east of Palestine; but Assyria likewise, Mesopotamia, Babylonia, and Chaldea, which lie rather to the north than to the east of Judea. It is said, in Gen. 11. 1, 2. that the sons of Noah having but one language, departed from the east, and came into the land of Shinar. Hereupon some difficulties have been raised: for the land of Shinar is not to the west of Armenia, where the ark rested; and Armenia does not lie to the east of Babylonia, where the land of Shinar was. On the contrary, it is to the north of this country. Interpreters and commentators, to disengage themselves out of these perplexities, have imagined different explanations of this passage.

Some, by the Hebrew word, Kedem, or East, have understood the country which was afterwards peopled by Kedemah, the youngest son of Ishmael. Others, that Kedem was used for, At the beginning; and that Moses intended to describe the particular time at which the first men departed after the deluge, in order to spread themselves into different countries. Others, that Moses spoke according to the custom of the Assyrians, who called all the provinces of their empire which were situated beyond the Tigris, Kedem, or East; and those on this side the same river, the West, or Arab. Others, instead of, they departed or journeyed from the east, translate, they departed to go towards the east.

Calmet says, that it appears to him from a great number of places in the Old and even in the New Testament, that the sacred writers called the provinces which were beyond the Tigris and Euphrates, even Mesopotamia, Armenia, and Persia, Kedem, or the East. Moses, who had been bred up in Egypt, and lived long in Arabia, in this likewise might probably follow the custom of the country. It is certain, says he, that Babylonia, Chaldea, Susiana, Persia, and a part of Mesopotamia, as well as the rivers of Euphrates and Tigris, for the greatest part of their course, are to the east of Palestine, Egypt, and Arabia.

He adds, that it is farther certain, that the people who came from Armenia, Syria, Media, and Upper Mesopotamia, entered Palestine and Egypt from the east side, which was sufficient for the Hebrews to say, that these people lay to the east with respect to them. He proves by the following passages, that these countries were known among the Hebrews by the name of East. In Num. 23. 7. Balaam says, that Balak, king of Moab, had brought him from the mountains of the east; that is, from Pethor upon the Euphrates. Isaiah says, ch. 41. 2. that Abraham came from the east into the land of Canaan: And it is known that he came from Mesopotamia and Chaldea. The same prophet says, that Cyrus should come from the east against Babylon, Isa. 46. 11. He places Syria to the east of Judea. St. Matthew says, that the wise men, who came to worship Christ, set out from the east, Mat. 2. 1.

All this, says he, demonstrates, that in the scripture style, the East is often used for the provinces which lie to the north of Judea and Egypt, from whence, however, people generally enter Palestine by the way only of Damascus, which is to the north-east of this country.

The East is the first of the four cardinal points of the horizon, where the sun is seen to rise when in the equinoctial.

Gen. 3. 24. God placed at the e. of the garden of Eden
12. 8. Abraham removed to a mountain on the e.
13. 11. Lot chose the plain, and journeyed e.
28. 14. thou shalt spread abroad to the west and e.
29. 1. came into the land of the people of the e.
Num. 3. 38. but those that encamp toward the e.
23. 7. Balak hath brought me out of the e.
Judg. 6. 3. the children of the e. came up against them, 33. | 7. 12. | 8. 10. 1 Kings 4. 30.
1 Kings 7. 25. three looking toward the e. 2 Chr. 4. 4.
1 Chron. 9. 24. the porters toward the e. west, north
12. 15. they put to flight them toward the e.
Job 1. 3. the greatest of all the men of the e.
Psal. 75. 6. promotion cometh not from e. nor west
103. 12. as far as the e. is from the west
107. 3. he gathered them from the e. and west
Isa. 2. 6. because they be replenished from the e.
11. 14. they shall spoil them of the e. Jer. 49. 28.
41. 2. who raised up the righteous man from the e.
43. 5. I will bring thy seed from the e. Zech. 8. 7.
46. 11. calling a ravenous bird from the e. the man
Ezek. 8. 16. men 25, with their faces towards the e.

Ezek. 25. 4. I will deliver thee to the men of the e. 10.
40. 6. then came he to the gate which looketh toward the e. 22. | 43. 1. | 44. 1. | 46. 1, 12.
43. 2. the glory of God came from the way of the e.
47. 8. these waters issue out toward the e. country
48. 10. toward the e. ten thousand in breadth
17. the suburbs of the city toward the e. 250.
Dan. 8. 9. the horn waxed great toward the e.
11. 44. tidings out of the e. shall trouble him
Joel 2. 20. I will drive him toward the e. sea
Amos 8. 12. they shall wander from north to e.
Zech. 14. 4. the mount shall cleave toward the e.
Mat. 2. 1. there came wise men from the e.
2. for we have seen his star in the e. 9.
8. 11. many come from e. and west, Luke 13. 29.
24. 27. as lightning cometh out of the e.
Rev. 7. 2. another angel ascending from the e.
16. 12. the way of kings of e. might be prepared
21. 13. on the e. three gates, on the north three

EAST BORDER.

Num. 34. 10. and ye shall point out your e. border
Josh. 4. 19. encamped in the e. border of Jericho
15. 5. the e. border was the salt sea to end of Jordan
Ezek. 45. 7. from the west border to the e. border
48. 21. of the oblation toward the e. border

EASTER.

Acts 12. 4. intending after e. to bring him forth

EAST GATE.

Neh. 3. 29. Shemaiah, the keeper of the e. gate
Jer. 19. 2. which is by the entry of the e. gate
Ezek. 10. 19. every one stood at the door of the e. g.
11. 1. the Spirit brought me unto the e. gate

EAST SIDE.

Exod. 27. 13. the breadth of the court on the e. side
Num. 2. 3. and on the e. side shall Judah pitch
Josh. 7. 2. to Ai, which is on the e. side of Bethel
16. 5. the border of their inheritance on the e. side
Judg. 11. 18. came by e. side of the land of Moab
Ezek. 11. 23. the mountain on the e. side of the city
42. 16. he measured the e. side with the reed
48. 2. from the e. side even unto the west side, 3, 4, 5, 6, 7, 8, 23, 24, 25, 26, 27.
Jonah 4. 5. Jonah sat on the e. side of the city

EASTWARD.

Gen. 13. 14. lift up thine eyes e. and look, Deut. 3. 27.
2 Kings 13. 17. open the window e. and he opened it
1 Chr. 26. 17. e. were six Levites, northward four
Ezek. 47. 3. the man with the line went forth e.

EAST WIND.

Gen. 41. 6. thin ears, blasted with the e. wind, 23, 27.
Exod. 10. 13. the Lord brought an e. wind, 14. 21.
Job 15. 2. and fill his belly with the e. wind
27. 21. e. wind carrieth him away, he departeth
38. 24. which scattereth the e. wind upon the earth
Psal. 48. 7. thou breakest the ships with an e. wind
78. 26. he caused an e. wind to blow in heaven
Isa. 27. 8. he stayeth his rough wind in day of e. w.
Jer. 18. 17. I will scatter them as with an e. wind
Ezek. 17. 10. wither, when the e. wind toucheth it
19. 12. and the e. wind drieth up her fruit
27. 26. the e. wind hath broken thee in the seas
Hos. 12. 1. Ephraim followeth after the e. wind
13. 15. though he be fruitful, an e. wind shall come
Jonah 4. 8. God prepared a vehement e. wind
Hab. 1. 9. their faces shall sup up as the e. wind

EASY.

Prov. 14. 6. knowledge is e. to him that understands
Mat. 11. 30. my yoke is e. my burden is light
1 Cor. 14. 9. except ye utter words e. to be understood
Jam. 3. 17. wisdom from above is e. to be intreated

EAT.

To eat signifies, [1] To chew meat with the teeth to make it fit to enter the stomach, Gen. 27. 4. [2] To enjoy, Isa. 1. 19. [3] To waste, or consume, Eccl. 5. 11. [4] To oppress and undo, Psal. 14. 4. [5] To believe, John 6. 56. [6] To have fellowship with, 1 Cor. 5. 11. [7] To feed on God's word, Isa. 55. 1. [8] To feast, Isa. 22. 13. [9] To do the will of God with delight, John 4. 32. It is said in Ezek. 3. 1. Son of man, eat that thou findest, eat this roll. Read attentively, meditate throughly, impress the things upon thy soul deeply. So in Jer. 15. 16. Thy words were found, and I did eat them.

In John 6. 53, 56. our Saviour says, Except ye eat the flesh of the Son of man, and drink his blood, ye have no life in you. Except ye partake of those benefits which I purchased by my sufferings in my human nature, ye have no spiritual life, nor communion with God, but continue in your sins, and shall not partake of eternal life. Again: He that eateth my flesh, and drinketh my blood, dwelleth in me, and I in him. There is an intimate union and communion between us, he having a constant dependence upon me for life, which is his dwelling in me; and I giving out a constant influence and quickening virtue to make him live, which is my dwelling in him. And in John 4. 32. he says, I have meat to eat which ye know not of. I have something to do which I prefer before bodily food, namely, to bring these Samaritans to believe in and own me for the true Messiah.

The Psalmist says, Psal. 69. 9. The zeal of thine house hath eaten me up: That fervent passion which I have for thy house, and service, and glory, and people, hath enhausted my natural moisture and vital spirits. The Apostle charges the Corinthians not to eat with a brother that is a fornicator, or covetous, or an idolater: not to entertain any unnecessary familiarity with them, 1 Cor. 5. 11. Hosea, speaking of the priests, says, They eat up the sin of my people, Hos. 4. 8. They feast upon, and pamper themselves with, those sacrifices which my people offer for their sins, and are greedy after them, and do neither desire nor endeavour to reclaim the people, lest thereby their gain should be diminished.

The ancient Hebrews did not eat indifferently with all sorts of persons; they would have polluted and dishonoured themselves in their own opinion, if they had eaten with people of another religion, or of a profession that was odious and in disrepute. In the patriarch Joseph's time they neither ate with the Egyptians, nor the Egyptians with them, Gen. 43. 32. In our Saviour's time they did not eat with the Samaritans: For the Jews have no dealings with the Samaritans, John 4. 9. And the Jews were very much scandalized to see that Christ made no scruple of eating with publicans and sinners: Why eateth your Master with publicans and sinners? Mat. 9. 11. As there were several sorts of meats, the use whereof was not allowed them, they could not conveniently eat with those who partook of them, for fear of contracting some pollution by touching them, or lest by accident any part of them should fall upon them. Before they sit down to table, they are very careful to wash their hands: they speak of this practice as a ceremony that is essential and strictly obliging.

Gen. 2. 16. of every tree thou mayest freely e.
3. 5. in the day ye e. your eyes shall be opened
6. Eve took and did e. || 12. and I did e. 13.
14. and dust shalt thou e. all the days of thy life
17. in sorrow shalt thou e. of it all days of thy life
18. 8. he stood by the angels, and they did e. 19. 3.
27. 4. savoury meat, bring it to me, that I may e.
31. 46. and they did e. there upon the heap
40. 17. the birds did e. them out of the basket
43. † 16. these men shall e. with me at noon
32. for the Egyptians did e. by themselves
Exod. 10. 5. the locusts shall e. every tree that grow.
12. the locusts may e. every herb of the land
12. 8. roast with fire, with bitter herbs they shall e. it
16. no work done, save that which every man e.
43. no stranger shall e. thereof, 48. Lev. 22. 13.
44. when circumcised, then shall he e. thereof
16. 25. e. that to day, for to day is a sabbath to L.
35. the children of Israel did e. manna forty years, till came to borders of Canaan, John 6. 31, 49, 58.
23. 11. that the poor of thy people may e.
29. 32. Aaron and sons shall e. Lev. 6. 16. | 8. 31.
34. 15. one call thee, and thou e. of his sacrifice
Lev. 6. 18. males shall e. it, 29. | 7. 6. Num. 18. 10.
26. the priest that offereth it for sin shall e. it
7. 19. all that be clean shall e. thereof, Num. 18. 11.
24. any other use, but ye shall in no wise e. of it
10. 12. e. it without leaven beside the altar
11. 21. yet these ye may e. 22. Deut. 14. 20.
24. 9. Aaron and his sons shall e. in the holy place
25. 20. if ye say, what shall we e. the seventh year
26. 16. shall sow in vain, your enemies shall e. it
Num. 11. 5. we remember the fish we did e. freely
13. weep, saying, give us flesh, that we may e.
23. 24. he shall not lie down till he e. of the prey
25. 2. the peo. did e. of their sacrifices, and bowed
Deut. 2. 6. ye shall buy meat of them that ye may e.
12. 15. e. in thy gates, 21. | 15. 22. | 26. 12.
15. the unclean and clean may e. 22. | 15. 22.
18. thou must e. before the Lord, 14. 26. | 15. 20.
20. shalt say, I will e. flesh, thou mayest e. flesh
14. 21. give it to the stranger that he may e.
20. 6. lest he die, and another man e. of it
23. 24. then thou mayest e. grapes thy fill
28. 39. not gather grapes, for worms shall e. them
53. shall e. fruit of thine own body, Lam. 2. 20.
32. 38. which did e. the fat of their sacrifices
Josh. 5. 11. they did e. of the old corn of the land
24. 13. of the vineyards ye planted not do ye e.
Judg. 19. 8. they tarried, and did e. both of them
1 Sam. 1. 18. Hannah did e. and was no more sad
9. 13. and afterwards they e. that be bidden
14. 34. and e. and sin not against the Lord
20. 34. Jonathan did e. no meat the second day
28. 22. and e. that thou mayest have strength
2 Sam. 9. 11. he shall e. at my table, 1 Kings 2. 7.
1 Kings 14. 11. him that dieth of Jeroboam shall the dogs e. 16. 4. | 21. 23. 2 Kings 9. 10, 36.
17. 12. for me and my son, that we may e. and die
19. 5. the angel said, arise and e. Acts 10. 13. | 11. 7.
2 Kings 4. 43. they shall e. and leave thereof
44. they did e. and left thereof, according to word
6. 28. this woman said, give thy son that we may e. him to-day, and we will e. my son to-morrow
29. so we boiled my son, and did e. him
18. 31. ye e. every man of his own vine, Isa. 36. 16.
2 Chron. 30. 18. yet did they e. the passover
Ezra 6. 21. and the children of Israel did e.
Neh. 5. 2. take up corn, that we may e. and live
9. 25. so they did e. and were filled, Psal. 78. 29.
Job 3. 24. for my sighing cometh before I e.
31. 8. then let me sow, and let another e.
Psal. 22. 26. the meek shall e. and be satisfied
29. all they that be fat on earth shall e.
50. 13. will I e. the flesh of bulls, or drink blood
78. 25. man did e. angels' food, he sent them meat
128. 2. thou shalt e. the labour of thine hands
Prov. 1. 31. e. the fruit of their own way, Isa. 3. 10.
13. 2. but the soul of transgressors shall e. violence
18. 21. and they that love it shall e. the fruit
24. 13. my son, e. thou honey, because it is good
27. 18. whoso keepeth fig-tree shall e. fruit thereof
30. 17. the eye, and the young eagles shall e. it
Eccl. 2. 25. for who can e. or hasten more than I?
5. 11. goods increase they are increased that e. them
12. sleep is sweet, whether he e. little or much
10. 16. and thy princes e. in the morning
17. blessed, when thy princes e. in due season
Cant. 4. † 1. as a flock of goats that e. of Gilead
16. come into his garden and e. his pleasant fruits
Isa. 4. 1. we will e. our own bread, and wear our own apparel
7. 15. butter and honey shall he e. that he may know
22. butter and honey shall every one e. that is left
9. 20. e. on the left hand, e. the flesh of his arm
11. 7. the lion shall e. straw like the ox, 65. 25.
30. 24. oxen and asses shall e. clean provender
37. 30. sow ye and reap, plant vineyards, and e. the fruit thereof, 65. 21. Jer. 29. 5, 28.
51. 8. and the worm shall e. them like wool
55. 1. come ye, buy and e. yea, come, buy wine
2. hearken to me, and e. that which is good
62. 9. they that have gathered it shall e. it
Isa. 65. 4. a people which e. swine's flesh and broth
13. my servants shall e. but ye shall be hungry
22. they shall not plant and another e.
Jer. 15. 16. thy words were found, and I did e. them
19. 9. shall e. every one the flesh of his friend in the siege and straitness
Ezek. 2. 8. open thy mouth and e. that I give thee
3. 1. son of man, e. that thou findest, e. this roll
4. 10. e. by weight || 5. 10. fathers shall e. sons
16. 13. thou didst e. fine flour, and honey, and oil
22. 9. and in thee they e. upon the mountains
34. 3. ye e. the fat, and clothe you with the wool
Dan. 4. 33. Nebuchadnezzar did e. grass as oxen
Hos. 4. 10. for they shall e. and not have enough, they shall not increase, Mic. 6. 14. Hag. 1. 6.
9. 3. they shall e. unclean things in Assyria
4. all that e. thereof shall be polluted
Amos 6. 4. that e. the lambs out of the flock
Mic. 3. 3. who also e. the flesh of my people
Zech. 11. 9. let the rest e. every one flesh of another
16. but he shall e. the flesh of the fat and tear
Mat. 12. 4. how David did e. the shew-bread
14. 20. did all e. and were filled, took up fragments, 15. 37. Mark 6. 42. | 8. 8. Luke 9. 17.
15. 27. yet the dogs e. of the crumbs, Mark 7. 28.
38. they that did e. were 4000, beside women
26. 21. and as they did e. he said, Mark 14. 18, 22.
26. Jesus took bread, brake it, and said, take, e. this is my body, Mark 14. 22. 1 Cor. 11. 24.
Mark 2. 16. when they saw him e. with publicans
6. 44. they that did e. were above 5000 men
11. 14. no man e. fruit of thee hereafter for ever
14. 12. where go and prepare that thou mayest e. the passover? 14. Luke 22. 8, 11. John 18. 28.
Luke 6. 1. and did e. rubbing them in their hands
7. 36. one desired him that he would e. with him
10. 8. e. such things as are set before you
15. 23. kill fatted calf, let us e. and be merry
24. 43. he took it, and did e. before them
John 4. 31. disciples prayed him, saying, Master, e.
6. 26. because ye did e. of loaves and were filled
50. that a man may e. thereof and not die
53. except ye e. the flesh of the Son of man
Acts 2. 46. they did e. their meat with gladness
11. 3. thou wentest in and didst e. with them
23. 14. we will e. nothing till we have slain Paul
Rom. 14. 2. one believeth he may e. all things
23. he that doubteth is damned if he e.
1 Cor. 8. 7. for some e. it as a thing offered to an idol
8. neither if we e. are we the better, if we e. not
13. I will e. no flesh while the world standeth
10. 3. and did all e. the same spiritual meat
18. who e. of the sacrifices, partakers of the altar
25. whatsoever is sold in the shambles, that e.
27. e. asking no question for conscience sake
11. 34. if any man hunger, let him e. at home
2 Thess. 3. 10. if any work not, neither should he e.
2 Tim. 2. 17. their word will e. as doth a canker
Jam. 5. 3. and shall e. your flesh as it were fire
Rev. 17. 16. shall e. her flesh, and burn her with fire
19. 18. that ye may e. flesh of kings and captains
See BLOOD, BREAD, FAT.

EAT, with drink.

Gen. 24. 54. and they did e. and drink, 26. 30. Exod. 24. 11. Judg. 9. 27. | 19. 4.
Exod. 32. 6. sat down to e. and drink, 1 Cor. 10. 7.
34. 28. nor e. bread, nor drink water, Deut. 9. 9, 18.
1 Sam. 30. 11. Egyptians did e. bread and drink water
2 Sam. 11. 11. shall I go to my house to e. and drink?
12. 3. it did e. of his meat and drink of his cup
19. 35. can thy servant taste what I e. or drink?
1 Kings 1. 25. they e. and drink before Adonijah
13. 8. I will not e. bread nor drink water, 9, 17, 22.
16. neither will I e. bread nor drink water
18. 41. Elijah said, get thee up, e. and drink
2 Kings 6. 22. set bread, that they may e. and drink
7. 8. they went into one tent and did e. and drink
18. 27. e. own dung and drink piss, Isa. 36. 12.
1 Chr. 29. 22. and did e. and drink before the Lord
2 Chron. 28. 15. and gave them to e. and to drink
Ezra 10. 6. Ezra did e. no bread nor drink water
Neh. 8. 10. go your way, e. the fat and drink sweet
Esth. 4. 16. fast for me, nor e. nor drink three days
Job 1. 4. called sisters to e. and drink with them
Prov. 23. 7. so is he, e. and drink saith he to thee
Eccl. 2. 24. there is nothing better than that he should e. and drink, 3. 13. | 5. 18. | 8. 15.
Cant. 5. 1. e. O friends, yea, drink abundantly
Isa. 21. 5. e. drink, ye princes, anoint the shield
22. 13. behold joy and gladness, let us e. and drink, for to-morrow we shall die, 1 Cor. 15. 32.
Jer. 22. 15. did not thy father e. and drink?
Ezek. 25. 4. shall e. thy fruit and drink thy milk
39. 17. that ye may e. flesh and drink blood
Dan. 1. 12. give us pulse to e. and water to drink
Zech. 7. 6. when ye did e. and when ye did drink
Mat. 6. 25. what shall e. or drink, 31. Luke 12. 29
24. 49. to e. and drink with drunken, Luke 12. 45.
Luke 5. 30. why do ye e. and d. with publicans?
33. John's disciples fast, but thy disciples e. and d.
12. 19. take thine ease, e. drink, and be merry
17. 8. and afterward thou shalt e. and drink
27. they did e. they drank, they married, 28.
22. 30. that ye may e. and drink at my table
Acts 9. 9. Saul three days did neither e. nor drink
23. 12. e. nor drink till they had killed Paul, 21.
Rom. 14. 21. neither to e. flesh nor drink wine
1 Cor. 9. 4. have we not power to e. and to drink?
10. 31. wheth. therefore ye e. or drink, or whatever
11. 22. have ye not houses to e. and drink in?
26. as oft as ye e. this bread and drink this cup
27. whosoever shall e. and drink unworthily
28. and so let him e. and drink of that cup

He did EAT.

Gen. 3. 6. Eve gave to her husband, and he did e.
25. 28. loved Esau, because he did e. of his venison
27. 25. he brought it near to Isaac, and he did e.
39. 6. he knew not ought, save the bread he did e.
1 Sam. 30. 11. gave the Egyptian bread, and he did e.
2 Sam. 9. 13. he did e. continually at his table
12. 20. they set bread before him, and he did e.
Mark 1. 6. John did e. locusts and wild honey

Luke 4. 2. and in those days he did e. nothing
Gal. 2. 12. for before he did e. with the Gentiles

EAT not.

Gen. 2. 17. but of the tree of the knowledge of good
and evil, thou shalt not e. of it, 3. 1, 3.
3. 11. whereof I commanded thee not to e. 17.
9. 4. the blood thereof shall you not e. Lev. 19. 26.
Deut. 12. 16, 23, 24, 25. | 15. 23.
24. 33. I will not e. till I have told my errand
32. 32. the children of Israel e. not of the sinew
43. 32. the Egyptians might not e. with the Hebrews
Exod. 12. 9. e. not of it raw, nor sodden at all
45. a foreigner shall not e. thereof, 29. 33.
Lev. 11. 4. these shall ye not e. Deut. 14. 3, 7.
22. 4. a leper not e. of the holy things, 6, 10, 12.
8. that torn he shall not e. to defile himself
Num. 11. 19. ye shall not e. one day, or two days
Deut. 14. 21. ye shall not e. of any thing that dieth
of itself, shalt give it to stranger, Ezek. 44. 31.
28. 31. ox be slain, and thou shalt not e. thereof
Judg. 13. 4. and e. not any unclean thing, 7, 14.
1 Sam. 1. 7. therefore she wept, and did not e.
9. 13. for the people will not e. till he come
28. 23. Saul refused, and said, I will not e.
2 Kings 4. 40. and they could not e. thereof
7. 2. shalt see it with thy eyes, but not e. thereof, 19.
Ezra 2. 63. not e. of most holy things, Neh. 7. 65.
Psal. 141. 4. and let me not e. of their dainties
Prov. 23. 6. e. not bread of him that hath an evil eye
Ezek. 24. 17. cover not lips, and e. not bread of men
Mark 7. 3. Jews, except they wash, they e. not, 4.
Luke 22. 16. I will not e. thereof, until fulfilled
1 Cor. 5. 11. with such an one no not to e.
8. 8. neither if we e. not are we the worse
10. 28. e. not, for his sake that shewed it

Shall ye EAT.

Exod. 12. 11. thus shall ye e. it, with loins girded
15. seven days shall ye e. unleavened bread, 20.
22. 31. nor shall ye e. any flesh torn of beasts
Lev. 10. 14. wave breast shall ye e. in a clean place
11. 3. cheweth the cud, that shall ye e. Deut. 14. 4, 6.
9. these shall ye e. of all that are in the waters
19. 25. in the fifth year shall ye e. of the fruit
26. 29. the flesh of your daughters shall ye e.
Deut. 14. 9. all that have fins and scales shall ye e.

Ye shall EAT.

Gen. 45. 18. and ye shall e. the fat of the land
Exod. 12. 11. ye shall e. it in haste, Lord's passover
18. first month at even ye shall e. unleav. bread
16. 12. saying, at even ye shall e. flesh, and in morn.
Lev. 7. 23. ye shall e. no manner of fat, 24.
26. ye shall e. no manner of blood, 17. 14.
10. 13. and ye shall e. it in the holy place
23. 14. ye shall e. neither bread nor parched corn
25. 12. ye shall e. the increase thereof out of the field
19. ye shall e. your fill, and dwell in safety
22. ye shall e. of the old store, 26. 10.
26. 26. and ye shall e. and not be satisfied
29. ye shall e. the flesh of your sons and daughters
Num. 11. 18. the Lord will give flesh, and ye shall e.
18. 31. and ye shall e. in every place, and households
Deut. 12. 7. there ye shall e. before Lord your God
14. 11. of all clean birds ye shall e.
1 Sam. 9. 19. go up, for ye shall e. with me to-day
2 Kings 19. 29. this shall be a sign, ye shall e. this
year such things as grow themselves, Isa. 37. 30.
Isa. 1. 19. if obedient, ye shall e. the good of the land
61. 6. ye shall e. the riches of the Gent. in their glory
Ezek. 39. 19. and ye shall e. fat till ye be full
Joel. 2. 26. ye shall e. in plenty, and be satisfied
Luke 12. 22. take no thought what ye shall e. nor put

To EAT.

Exod. 16. 8. Lord shall give you in evening flesh to e.
Num. 11. 4. said, who shall give us flesh to e.? 18.
Deut. 12. 20. because thy soul longeth to e. flesh
18. 8. they shall have like portions to e.
1 Sam. 9. 13. before he go to the high place to e.
20. 24. the king sat him down to e. meat
2 Sam. 3. 35. the people came to cause David to e.
9. 10. that thy master's son may have food to e.
13. 9. poured before him, but he refused to e.
16. 2. and summer-fruit for the young men to e.
17. 29. for the people that were with him to e.
2 Kings 4. 40. so they poured out for the men to e.
2 Chron. 31. 10. we have had enough to e. and left
Neh. 9. 36. land thou gavest, to e. the fruit thereof
Psal. 78. 24. and had rained manna on them to e.
Prov. 23. 1. when thou sittest to e. with a ruler
25. 27. it is not good to e. much honey
Eccl. 5. 19. hath given him power to e. thereof
6. 2. yet God giveth him not power to e. thereof
Isa. 23. 18. shall be for them to e. sufficiently
Jer. 19. 9. cause them to e. the flesh of their sons
Ezek. 3. 2. and he caused me to e. that roll
3. he said, son of man, cause thy belly to e.
Dan. 4. 25. they shall make thee to e. grass, 32.
Mic. 7. 1. woe is me, there is no cluster to e.
Hab. 1. 8. they shall flee as eagle that hasteth to e.
Mat. 12. 1. they began to pluck ears of corn, and to e.
4. not lawful for him to e. Mark 2. 26. Luke 6. 4.
14. 16. give ye them to e. Mark 6. 37. Luke 9. 13.
15. 20. to e. with unwashen hands defileth not
32. the multitude have nothing to e. Mark 8. 1, 2.
26. 17. where wilt that we prepare to e. passover?
Mark 5. 43. that something should be given her to e.
6. 31. and they had no leisure so much as to e.
Luke 22. 15. I have desired to e. this passover
John 4. 32. I have meat to e. that ye know not of
33. hath any man brought him aught to e.?
6. 52. how can this man give us his flesh to e.?
Acts 27. 35. when he had broken it, he began to e.
1 Cor. 8. 10. emboldened to e. things offered to idols
11. 20. when ye come, this is not to e. Lord's supper
33. brethren, when ye come together to e.
Heb. 13. 10. an altar whereof they have no right to e.
Rev. 2. 7. will I give to e. of the tree of life in midst
14. to e. things sacrificed unto idols, 20.
17. I will give to e. of hidden manna, a white stone

EAT up.

Gen. 41. 4. the lean did e. up the seven fat kine, 20.
Lev. 26. 38. land of your enemies shall e. you up
Num. 24. 8. he shall e. up the nations his enemies
Deut. 28. 33. a nation thou knowest not shall e. up
Psal. 27. 2. my enemies came on me to e. up my flesh
105. 35. did e. up all the herbs in their land
Isa. 50. 9. the moth shall e. them up, 51. 8.
Jer. 5. 17. they shall e. up thine harvest and thy
bread, e. up thy flocks, e. up thy vines and fig-trees
22. 22. the wind shall e. up all thy pastures
Hos. 4. 8. they e. up the sin of my people
Amos 7. 4. it devoured the deep, and did e. up a part
Mic. 5. †6. they shall e. up the land of Assyria
Nah. 3. 15. it shall e. thee up like the canker-worm
Rev. 10. 9. angel said to me, take it, and e. it up

EATEN.

Gen. 3. 11. hast thou e. of tree whereof shouldest not?
14. 24. save that which the young men have e.
31. 38. the rams of thy flock have I not e.
41. 21. when they had e. them up, it could not be
known that they had e. them, but were ill-favoured
Exod. 12. 46. in one house shall it be e.
13. 3. there shall no leavened bread be e. 7.
21. 28. ox shall be stoned, his flesh shall not be e.
22. 5. if a man cause a field or vineyard to be e.
29. 34. it shall not be e. because it is holy
Lev. 6. 16. it shall be e. in the holy place, 26. | 7. 6.
23. it shall be wholly burnt, it shall not be e. 7. 19.
30. no sin offering shall be e. it shall be burnt
7. 15. shall be e. the same day it is offered, 16.
18. if the sacrifice of peace offering be e.
10. 17. why have ye not e. the sin offering?
18. ye should indeed have e. it in the holy place
19. if I had e. the sin offering to day
11. 13. they shall not be e. 41. Deut. 14. 19.
19. 6. it shall be e. the same day ye offer, 22. 30.
7. and if it be e. at all on the third day
Num. 28. 17. unleavened bread be e. Ezek. 45. 21.
Deut. 6. 11. to give vineyards thou plantedst not,
when thou shalt have e. and be full, 8. 10, 12.
12. 22. even as the roebuck and the hart is e.
20. 6. hath planted a vineyard, and hath not e. of it
26. 14. I have not e. thereof in my mourning
29. 6. ye have not e. bread nor drunk wine
31. 20. when they shall have e. and be filled
Josh. 5. 12. after they had e. of the old corn
Ruth 3. 7. when Boaz had e. and drunk, he went
1 Sam. 14. 30. if haply the people had e. freely
28. 20. for he had e. no bread all the day
30. 12. when he had e. his spirit came again
2 Sam. 19. 42. have we e. at all of the king's cost?
1 Kings 13. 22. but camest back, and hast e. bread
28. the lion had not e. the carcase, nor torn the ass
Neh. 5. 14. have not e. the bread of the governor
Job 6. 6. that is unsavoury be e. without salt
31. 17. or have e. my morsel myself alone
39. if I have e. the fruits thereof without money
Ps. 69. 9. for the zeal of thine house hath e. me up,
and reproaches are fallen upon me, John 2. 17.
102. 9. I have e. ashes like bread, mingled my drink
Prov. 9. 17. and bread e. in secret is pleasant
23. 8. the morsel that thou hast e. shalt thou vomit
Cant. 5. 1. I have e. my honey-comb with my honey
Isa. 3. 14. for ye have e. up the vineyard spoil of poor,
Jer. 10. 25. they have e. up Jacob, and devoured him
24. 2. figs which could not be e. 3. 8. | 29. 17.
31. 29. fathers have e. sour grapes, Ezek. 18. 2.
Ezek. 4. 14. I have not e. that which dieth of itself
18. 6. and hath not e. upon the mountains, 15.
11. but even hath e. upon the mountains
Hos. 10. 13. ye have e. the fruit of lies
Joel 1. 4. that locust hath left, canker-worm e. 2. 25.
Mat. 14. 21. and they that had e. Mark 8. 9.
Luke 13. 26. we have e. and drunk in thy presence
17. 8. till I have e. afterward thou shalt e.
John 6. 13. which remained to them that had e.
Acts 10. 10. he became hungry, and would have e.
14. Lord, I have never e. any thing common
12. 23. he was e. of worms, and gave up the ghost
20. 11. when he had broken bread and e. departed
27. 38. when they had e. enough they lightened
Rev. 10. 10. as soon as I had e. it, my belly was bitter

EATER.

Judg. 14. 14. he said, out of the e. came forth meat
Isa. 55. 10. that it may give bread to the e.
Nah. 3. 12. they shall fall into the mouth of the e.

EATERS.

Prov. 23. 20. be not among riotous e. of flesh

EATEST.

Gen. 2. 17. in the day thou e. thou shalt surely die
1 Sam. 1. 8. then said Elkanah, why e. thou not?
1 Kings 21. 5. why spirit so sad that thou e. no bread?

EATETH.

Exod. 12. 15. who e. leavened bread be cut off, 19.
Lev. 7. 18. the soul that e. 20, 25, 27. | 17. 10, 15.
19. 8. every one that e. shall bear his iniquity
Num. 13. 32. a land that e. up the inhabitants
1 Sam. 14. 24. cursed be the man that e. 28.
Job 5. 5. whose harvest the hungry e. up
21. 25. and another never e. with pleasure
40. 15. behemoth which I made, he e. grass as an ox
Psal. 106. 20. the similitude of an ox that e. grass
Prov. 13. 25. the righteous e. to satisfying of his soul
30. 20. she e. and wipeth her mouth, and saith
31. 27. and she e. not the bread of idleness
Eccl. 4. 5. the fool foldeth hands and e. his own flesh
5. 17. all his days also he e. in darkness
6. 2. but a stranger e. it, this is vanity, evil disease
Isa. 28. 4. while it is yet in his hand he e. it up
29. 8. behold, he e. but awaketh, and is hungry
44. 16. and with part thereof he e. flesh, roasteth
59. 5. he that e. of their eggs dieth
Jer. 31. 30. every man that e. the sour grape
Mat. 9. 11. Pharisees said, why e. your master with
publicans and sinners? Mark 2. 16. Luke 15. 2.
Mark 14. 18. Jesus said, verily, one of you who e.
with me, shall betray me, John 13. 18.
John 6. 54. whoso e. my flesh hath eternal life
56. he that e. my flesh dwelleth in me, I in him
57. so he that e. me, even he shall live by me
58. he that e. of this bread, shall live for ever
Rom. 14. 2. another who is weak e. herbs
3. let not him that e. despise him that e. not
6. that e. to the Lord, that e. not, to the Lord e. not
20. it is evil for that man who e. with offence
Rom. 14. 23. damned if he eat, because e. not of faith
1 Cor. 9. 7. who planteth a vineyard, and e. not of
fruit thereof? and e. not of the milk of the flock
11. 29. he that e. unworthily, e. damnation to hims.

EATING.

Gen. 2. †16. of every tree e. thou shalt eat, but of tree
Exod. 12. 4. take a lamb according to the number of
souls, every man according to his e. 16. 16, 18, 21.
Judg. 14. 9. Samson took thereof, and went on e.
1 Sam. 14. 34. sin not against the L. in e. with blood
30. 16. they were spread abroad on all the earth e.
1 Kings 1. 41. Adonijah's guests made an end of e.
2 Kings 4. 40. as they were e. of pottage, cried out
Job 20. 23. and shall rain it upon him while he is e.
Isa. 66. 17. e. swine's flesh, and the abomination
Amos 7. 2. when they had made an end of e. grass
Mat. 26. 26 as they were e. Jesus took bread
Acts 1. † 4. and e. with them, commanded them
1 Cor. 8. 4. concerning e. of things sacrificed to idols
11. 21. in e. every one taketh his own supper
See DRINKING.

ECHO.

Ezek. 7. † 7. and not the e. of the mountains

EDGE.

Exod. 13. 20. Etham in e. of wilderness, Num. 33. 6.
26. 10. make fifty loops in the e. of one curtain
Eccl. 10. 10. be blunt, and he do not whet the e.
Luke 4. † 29. they led Jesus to the e. of the hill
See TEETH.

EDGE of the sword.

Gen. 34. 26. and they slew Hamor with the e. of sword
Exod. 17. 13. discomfited Amalek with the e. of sw.
Num. 21. 24. and Israel smote Sihon with e. of sword
Josh. 6. 21. they utterly destroyed all with e. of sword
8. 24. the Israelites smote Ai with the e. of sword
Judg. 4. 15. Sisera with e. of s. || 21. 10. Jabesh-gilead
Job 1. 15. Joab's servants slain with e. of sword, 17.
Psal. 89. 43. thou hast also turned the e. of the sword
Jer. 21. 7. Nebuchadnezzar smite them with e. of s.
Luke 21. 24. the Jews shall fall by the e. of sword
Heb. 11. 34. who thro' faith escaped the e. of sword

EDGED.

Psal. 149. 6. and a two-e. sword in their hand
Prov. 5. 4. but her end is sharp as a two-e. sword
Heb. 4. 12. word of God sharper than a two-e. sword
Rev. 1. 16. out of mouth went a sharp two-e. sword

EDGES.

Exod. 28. 7. joined at the two e. thereof, 39. 4.
Judg. 3. 16. Ehud's dagger had two e. length a cubit
Rev. 2. 12. who hath the sharp sword with two e.

EDIFICATION.

Rom. 15. 2. let every one please his neighbour to e.
1 Cor. 14. 3. that prophesieth speaketh to men to e.
2 Cor. 10. 8. which the Lord hath given us for e.
13. 10. power which the Lord hath given me to e.

EDIFY.

Rom. 14. 19. things wherewith one may e. another
1 Cor. 10. 23. all things are lawful, but e. not
Eph. 4. † 29. that which is good to e. profitably
1 Thess. 5. 11. e. one another, even as also ye do

EDIFIED.

Acts 9. 31. the churches had rest, and were e.
1 Cor. 8. † 10. conscience of him that is weak be e.
14. 17. givest thanks well, but the other is not e.

EDIFIETH.

1 Cor. 8. 1. knowledge puffeth up, but charity e.
14. 4. he that speaks in an unknown tongue e. himself; but he that prophesieth e. the church

EDIFYING.

1 Cor. 14. 5. that the church may receive e.
12. seek that ye may excel to the e. of the church
14. 26. let all things be done to e.
2 Cor. 12. 19. but we do all things for your e.
Eph. 4. 12. for the e. of the body of Christ
16. increase of the body, to the e. of itself in love
29. but that which is good to the use of e.
1 Tim. 1. 4. which minister questions rather than e.

EFFECT, Substantive.

Num. 30. 8. her husband shall make her vow of no e.
2 Chron. 34. 22. and they spake to her to that e.
Psal. 33. 10. makes the devices of people of none e.
Isa. 32. 17. the e. of righteousness, quietness
Ezek. 12. 23. days are at hand, and e. of every vision
Mat. 15. 6. make commandment of God of none e.
Mark 7. 13. making the word of God of none e.
Rom. 3. 3. unbelief make the faith of God without e.?
4. 14. the promise made of none e. Gal. 3. 17.
9. 6. not as though the word hath taken none e.
1 Cor. 1. 17. lest the cross of Christ be of none e.
Gal. 5. 4. Christ is become of no e. to you, who are

EFFECT, Verb.

Jer. 48. 30. it shall not be so, his lies shall not so e. it

EFFECTED.

2 Chr. 7. 11. Solomon prosperously e. all in his heart

EFFECTUAL.

1 Cor. 16. 9. for a great door and e. is opened to me
2 Cor. 1. 6. which is e. in enduring same sufferings
Eph. 3. 7. by the e. working of his power given me
4. 16. according to the e. working in the measure
Philem. 6. that thy faith may become e. by good thing
Jam. 5. 16. the e. prayer of a righteous man availeth

EFFECTUALLY.

Gal. 2. 8. for he that wrought e. in Peter, same in me
1 Thess. 2. 13. the word e. worketh in you that believe

EFFEMINATE.

1 Cor. 6. 9. nor e. shall inherit the kingdom of God

EGG.

Job 6. 6. is there any taste in the white of an e.?
Luke 11. 12. if he ask an e. will offer him a scorpion.

EGGS.

Deut. 22. 6. whether young ones or e. and the dam
sitting on the young or e. shall not take the dam
Job 39. 14. the ostrich leaveth her e. in the earth
Isa. 10. 14. one gathereth e. that are left, I gathered
59. 5. they hatch cockatrice's e. he that eateth e.
Jer. 17. 11. as partridge sitteth on e. and hatcheth

EIGHT.

Gen. 17. 12. he that is e. days old shall be circumcised, every man child, 21. 4. Luke 2. 21.
22. 23. these e. Milcah did bear to Nahor
Exod. 26. 25. they shall be e. boards, and sockets silver
Num. 7. 8. Moses gave 4 waggons, e. oxen to Merari

Num. 29. 29. on the sixth day *e.* bullocks, two rams
Judg. 3.8. Israel served Chushan-rishathaim *e.* years
12. 14. Abdon, the son of Hillel, judged Isr. *e.* years
1 *Sam.* 17. 12. Jesse the Ephrathite had *e.* sons
1 *Kings* 7. 10. foundation was of stones of *e.* cubits
2 *Kings* 8. 17. Jehoram reigned *e.* years in Jerusalem
22. 1. Josiah was *e.* years old when he began to reign, and reigned thirty-one, 2 *Chr.* 34. 1.
1 *Chron.* 24. 4. *e.* among the sons of Ithamar
2 *Chron.* 29. 17. they sanctified house of L. in *e.* days
Eccl. 11. 2. give a portion to seven, and also to *e.*
Jer. 41. 15. but Ishmael escaped with *e.* men
Ezek. 40. 31. the going up had *e.* steps, 34, 37.
41. *e.* tables, whereon they slew their sacrifices
Mic. 5. 5. raise ag. him 7 shepherds, *e.* principal men
Luke 9. 28. about an *e.* days after these sayings, Peter
John 20. 26. after *e.* days his disciples were within
Acts 9. 33. Eneas, who had kept his bed *e.* years
1 *Pet.* 3. 20. wherein *e.* souls were saved by water

EIGHTH.

Lev. 25. 22. and ye shall sow the *e.* year and eat
1 *Kings* 6. 38. in Bul, which is *e.* month, house finished
12. 32. Jeroboam ordained a feast in the *e.* month
1 *Chron.* 24. 10. the *e.* lot came forth to Abijah
25. 15. the *e.* to Jeshaiah ‖ 26. 5. Peulthaia the *e.*
27. 11. the *e.* captain for the *e.* month, Sibbecai
Zech. 1. 1. in *e.* month the word came to Zechariah
2 *Pet.* 2. 5. but saved Noah the *e.* person, a preacher
Rev. 17. 11. beast that was, is not, even he is the *e.*
21. 20. the *e.* foundation was a beryl, ninth a topaz
See DAY, DAYS.

EIGHT *hundred.*

Gen. 5. 4. Adam lived after he begat Seth *e. h.* years
5. 19. Jared lived after he begat Enoch *e. h.* years
2 *Sam.* 23. 8. Adino slew *e. hundred* at one time
2 *Chron.* 13. 3. Jeroboam set in array *e. h.* thousand

EIGHTEEN.

Judg. 3. 14. Isr. served Eglon king of Moab *e.* years
10. 8. Ammon vexed and oppressed Israel *e.* years
1 *Kings* 7. 15. for he cast two pillars of brass *e.* cubits high apiece, 2 *Kings* 25. 17. *Jer.* 52. 21.
1 *Chron.* 26. 9. Meshelemiah had sons and brethren *e.*
2 *Chron.* 11. 21. for Rehoboam took *e.* wives
Luke 13. 4. or those *e.* on whom tower in Siloam fell
16. whom Satan hath bound, lo, these *e.* years

EIGHTEEN *thousand.*

Judg. 20. 25. Benjamin destroyed of Israel *e. thous.*
44. there fell of Benjamin *e. thous.* men of valour
1 *Chr.* 12. 31. of the half tribe of Manasseh, *e. th.*
18. 12. Abishai slew of the Edomites *e. thousand*
29. 7. the princes gave of brass *e. thousand* talents
Ezek. 48. 35. the city round was *e. thous.* measures

EIGHTEENTH.

1 *Kings* 15. 1. in *e.* year of Jeroboam, 2 *Chr.* 13. 1.
2 *Kings* 3. 1. Jehoram reigned the *e.* year of Jehosh.
22. 3. in the *e.* year of king Josiah, the king sent Shaphan, 23. 23. 2 *Chron.* 34. 8. | 35. 19.
1 *Chron.* 24. 15. the *e.* lot came forth to Aphses
25. 25. the *e.* to Hanani, he, his sons, his brethren
Jer. 32. 1. was *e.* year of Nebuchadnezzar, 52. 29.

EITHER.

Gen. 31. 24. speak not to Jacob *e.* good or bad, 29.
Lev. 10. 1. Nadab and Abihu took *e.* of them his censer, and offered strange fire before the Lord
Deut. 17. 3. hath worship. other gods, *e.* sun or moon
28. 51. a nation shall not leave thee *e.* corn or wine
1 *Kings* 18. 27. *e.* he is talking, or pursuing, or in
Eccl. 11. 6. whether shall prosper, *e.* this or that
Isa. 7. 11. ask a sign *e.* in the depth or height above
Mat. 6. 24. no man can serve two masters, for *e.* he will hate the one, and love the other, *Luke* 16. 13.
12. 33. *e.* make the tree good, and his fruit good
Luke 6. 42. *e.* how canst thou say to thy brother
15. 8. *e.* what woman having ten pieces of silver
John 19. 18. crucified, on *e.* side one, Jesus in midst
1 *Cor.* 14. 6. except I speak to you *e.* by revelation
Jam. 3. 12. *e.* can a vine, my brethren, bear figs?
Rev. 22. 2. of *e.* side the river there was tree of life

ELDER.

The Elders *among the* Hebrews *were the magistrates, heads, or rulers of the people. Even while they were slaves to the* Egyptians, *they had among themselves some order and government, and had doubtless some whom they owned as their teachers and rulers, as heads of tribes and families; hence, when the Lord sent* Moses *to bring the children of* Israel *out of* Egypt, *he says,* Exod. 3. 16. Go and gather the elders of *Israel* together, and say unto them, the Lord hath visited you, and seen what is done to you in *Egypt. These* elders *were men of experience, wisdom, and gravity, and of authority among the people.*

But the first institution of courts of judicature, was in the wilderness; when Jethro *brought back* Zipporah *to* Moses, *who was then encamped at the foot of mount* Sinai. Moses *having related all that the Lord had done for the* Israelites, Jethro *blessed God for it, offered burnt offerings, and peace offerings, and did eat with* Moses, Aaron, *and the* elders *of* Israel, *before the Lord. The next day,* Moses *taking his seat in order to judge* Israel, *continued from morning to evening employed in this manner.* Jethro *remonstrated to him, that this was a fatigue above his strength to undergo, and would be tiresome both to himself and the people; that therefore he should choose some men of firmness and fortitude, who feared God, and hated covetousness, that they might share with him in the weight of government; that the cognizance of lesser affairs should be referred to them; and those of more consequence should be reserved to himself.* Moses *submitted to this advice, and chose certain men of merit out of all* Israel, *whom he appointed to have rule over the people; some over a thousand, others over an hundred, fifty, and ten. They administered justice to the people; and when any thing of greater difficulty than ordinary occurred, they referred it to* Moses, Exod. 18. 1, 2, 3, &c. *The commission given to these judges is recorded in* Deut. 1. 16, 17.

Afterwards, we have the particular appointment of God concerning this, Num. 11. 11, 12, 13, &c. Moses, *being discouraged by the continual murmurings of the* Israelites, *addressed himself to God, and desired to be relieved from some part of the burden of government. Then the Lord said to him,* Gather unto me seventy men, of the *elders* of *Israel,* whom thou knowest to be the *elders* of the people, and officers over them; and bring them to the tabernacle of the congregation, that they may stand there with thee. And I will come down and talk with thee there; and I will take of the spirit which is upon thee, and will put it upon them, and they shall bear the burden of the people with thee, that thou bear it not thyself alone. *These elders, which composed the* Senate *belonging to all the tribes in general, sat with the* Leader, Judge, *or* King, *who presided in this court. Thus we read,* Deut. 27. 1. *Moses,* with the *elders* of *Israel,* commanded the people, saying, &c. *And, afterwards, the* elders *of the congregation consult how to supply the remainder of the* Benjamites *with wives,* Judg. 21. 16. *And the elders of* Israel gathered themselves together, and came to *Samuel* to *Ramah,* 1 Sam. 8. 4. *We read of these* elders *continually, to the time of the captivity: And we find them again after the return,* Ezra 10. 7, 8. A proclamation was made throughout *Judah* and *Jerusalem* unto all the children of the captivity, according to the counsel of the princes and *elders.*

Besides these, there were likewise elders *belonging to every several city. These elders are mentioned by* Moses *in the law; where several things are required to be done by* the elders of the city, *Deut.* 19. 12. | 21. 3, 19. Boaz *appealed to* ten men of the elders of the city of *Beth-lehem-judah,* Ruth 4. 2. *And we read, after the captivity, of* the elders of every city, *Ezra* 10. 14.

The Rabbins *and interpreters give the following account of courts of judicature among the* Jews.

(I) *There were three judges in every city, who had the cognizance of lesser faults: Matters concerning* loss, gain, *and* restitution, *were pleaded before them. These three judges had a right only to condemn criminals to be whipt: The parties named their judges: one of the parties chose his judge; the other named a second; and these two judges took a third, with whom they decided causes. This tribunal was consulted about the intercalation of months.*

(II) *There was another court composed of three and twenty judges, who decided matters of importance, and of a more criminal nature, and their sentences were such as generally affected the lives of persons: no causes being brought before them, but such as deserved the penalty of death. Some say, that they could only sentence to death by the sword.*

(III) *Their great council, or* Sanhedrim, *which consisted of seventy senators, and which had the cognizance of the most important affairs of state and religion, and of those which concerned the king, or high-priest. It was intended as a court of appeal, if there should be occasion, from any of the inferior courts. Some think that our Saviour alludes to these two last courts, when he says,* Mat. 5. 22. Whosoever is angry with his brother, without a cause, shall be in danger of the judgment; and whosoever shall say to his brother, *Raca,* shall be in danger of the council; but whosoever shall say, *Thou fool,* shall be in danger of hell-fire. *Some interpreters suppose that our Lord proportions the punishments in the next world, according to the different sentences which were usual in the different courts of judicature at* Jerusalem. *Therefore they say,* the judgment *means that court where the judges were three and twenty, and who could only sentence to death by* the sword: *The* council *alludes to the court where the seventy elders sat, which was the* great Sanhedrim, *and could punish* by stoning to death: *And that, by* hell-fire, *the* burning *of the greatest malefactors in the valley of* Hinnom *is implied.*

As to the Sanhedrim, *it was limited to the place where the ark of God stood. The* Jews *say, that in the time of* Moses *this council was held at the door of the tabernacle of the testimony. As soon as the people were in possession of the land of promise, the* Sanhedrim *followed the tabernacle. It was kept successively at* Gilgal, *at* Shiloh, *at* Kirjath-jearim, *at* Nob, *at* Gibeon, *in the house of* Obededom; *and lastly, it was settled at* Jerusalem, *till the* Babylonish *captivity. During the captivity it was kept up at* Babylon. *After the return from* Babylon, *it continued at* Jerusalem, *to the time of the* Sicarii, *or* Assassins; *these were certain robbers, who appeared in* Judea *some time before the war of the* Jews *against the* Romans. *They were called* Sicarii, *from* Sica, *a dagger; because they carried daggers secretly about them, so as not to be perceived, and mixing themselves with the multitude of people that came to the great feast at* Jerusalem, *they stabbed whom they thought fit; and then were commonly the first to cry out murder, as* Josephus *relates. The* Jews, *finding that these profligate wretches, whose number increased every day, sometimes escaped punishment by the favour of the president, or judges, removed the* Sanhedrim *to* Hamoth, *which were certain abodes situated, as the* Rabbins *say, upon the mountain of the temple. Afterwards they removed to* Jamnia; *thence to* Jericho, *to* Uzzah, *to* Sepharvaim, *to* Bethsanim, *to* Sephoris, *last of all to* Tiberias, *where they continued to the time of their utter extinction. This is the account the* Jews *give of the* Sanhedrim.

What the scripture says of this court is found in Deut. 17. 8, 9, 10, 11, 12, 13. If there arise a matter too hard for thee in judgment *(speaking to the inferior magistrates)* between blood and blood, between plea and plea, and between stroke and stroke, being matters of controversy within thy gates; then shalt thou arise, and get thee up into the place which the Lord thy God shall choose. And thou shalt come unto the priests, the Levites, and unto the judge that shall be in those days, and enquire; and they shall shew thee the sentence of judgment. And thou shalt do according to the sentence, which they of that place which the Lord shall choose, shall shew thee, &c. *By this it appears that the chief* Conductor, Judge, King, High priest, *or whoever was at the head of their affairs, was to be the president of this court. The rest of the judges seem to have consisted chiefly of the priests and Levites, though there were among them wise and learned men of other tribes, as is acknowledged by the* Jewish *and most other writers.*

In process of time, as their kings came to be idolatrous, this ordinance, among others, was neglected. For we find Jehoshaphat *restoring it, at the same time as he did the courts in every city,* 2 Chron. 19. 8, 9, 10, 11. *In this passage we find, that, if the cause was of a* spiritual *or* ecclesiastical *nature, the* High-priest *was the chief judge; if otherwise,* a chief justice, *who sat in behalf of the king:* And, behold, *Amariah,* the chief-priest, is over you in all matters of the Lord; and *Zebadiah,* the ruler of the house of *Judah,* for all the king's matters.

Some think it probable, that in causes ecclesiastical, *the* court *was made up of the* High-priest, *and the chief-priests, or Heads of the four and twenty courses only: and that in matters purely temporal, the supreme magistrate, with the* princes, elders, *and* scribes, *who were doctors of the law, either by himself, or his deputy, took cognizance. And that, where any one was accused of crimes relating to religion and state both, the judges, in each of these faculties, sat to hear the cause. So, at the trial of our blessed Lord,* Joseph of Arimathea, a rich man and a counsellor, *probably one of the* seventy elders, *was one of them who sat as judges; but did not join in the sentence of condemnation;* He consented not to the counsel and deed of them, *Luke* 23. 51.

This council, *at their return from the captivity, was restored, with the rest of their commonwealth, as the prophet* Ezekiel *foretold it should,* Ezek. 44. 23, 24. The priests, the Levites, shall teach my people the difference between the unclean and the clean. And, in controversy, they shall stand in judgment; and they shall judge it according to my judgments.

Some are of opinion, that the origin of the Sanhedrim *is by no means to be depended upon; for the council of the seventy elders established by* Moses, *was not what the* Jews *understand by the name of* Sanhedrim. *Besides, say they, we cannot perceive that this establishment subsisted either under* Joshua, *the Judges, or the Kings. We find nothing of it after the captivity, till the time of the* Maccabees. *Only we are certain, that this Senate was in being in the time of our Saviour, and when the Evangelists wrote their gospels, since they are mentioned in their writings: But then their authority was much lessened; for after the banishment of* Archelaus, *the* Romans, *having reduced* Judea *into a province, assumed the power of life and death to themselves alone: So that this council could proceed no farther than to* condemnation: *For* execution, *they were to apply to the* Roman *Governor.*

The places where the Hebrews *held their courts of judicature were, generally, one of the gates of the city. See* GATE. *As the merits of every cause were to turn upon the evidence given; see what rules the law lays down in reference thereunto in* Deut. 17. 6. | 19. 15. *and what is said in relation to false witnesses,* Deut. 19. 16, 17, 18, 19. *It was likewise a part of their law, that no man should be condemned without being brought to a fair trial, and hearing what he had to say for himself. And therefore* Nicodemus *says to the* chief priests *and* Pharisees, Doth our law judge any man before it hear him, and know what he doeth? *John* 7. 51.

The method of proceeding in the Sanhedrim, *is said to be this: They who had a mind to implead any one, applied either to the* king, *or the* high-priest, *or whosoever filled the post of* Chief Justice, *and informed against him. Upon this, proper officers were sent to take him up; and if occasion required, a detachment from the temple-guard went along with them. The person thus taken was examined by the Justice, and then committed, either to prison, or to the custody of the officer of the guard, till his trial came on.*

When the court sat, those who brought the information against the criminal, did it in these words: This man, *having done so or so,* is worthy to die. *And they who were to defend him, answered,* This man is not worthy to die; *for he has only done so or so. And when the pleadings on both sides were finished, the Judges gave their opinions singly, whether he was guilty or not: And according to the majority of votes, one way or the other, the culprit was acquitted or condemned.*

Of the manner of laying the indictment, and giving in the answer, we have an instance in the case of Jeremiah; *who was informed against for prophesying the destruction of both the city and temple of* Jerusalem, *in case the* Jews *continued to neglect the observance of God's law,* Jer. 26. 8, 9, 10, &c. *See the form of condemnation in* Mat. 26. 65, 66.

Elder, *in the New Testament, is a general name, comprehending under it all such as have any ecclesiastical function, as apostles, pastors, teachers, or other church officers,* 1 Tim. 5. 17. Tit. 1. 5. *The apostle* Peter *calls himself an* elder. The elders that are among you I exhort, who also am an *elder,* 1 Pet. 5. 1.

Gen. 10. 21. Shem the brother of Japhet the e.
25. 23. the e. shall serve the younger, Rom. 9. 12.
1 Sam. 18. 17. behold, my e. daughter Merab
1 Kings 2. 22. ask the kingdom, he is mine e. brother
Job 15. 10. very aged men, much e. than thy father
32. 4. Elihu waited, because they were e. than he
Ezek. 16. 46. thy e. sister is Samaria, younger Sodom
23. 4. the names of them were Aholah the e.
Luke 15. 25. his e. son was in the field, heard music
1 Tim. 5. 2. intreat the e. women as mothers
1 Pet. 5. 5. ye younger, submit yourselves to the e.

ELDER for *ruler*.

1 Tim. 5. 1. rebuke not an e. but intreat him as father
19. against an e. receive not an accusat. but before
1 Pet. 5. 1. the elders I exhort, who am also an e.
2 John 1. the e. to the elect lady and her children
3 John 1. the e. unto well-beloved Gaius whom I love

ELDERS.

Gen. 50. 7. the e. of his house went up with him
Lev. 4. 15. the e. of congreg. shall lay their hands
Num. 11. 25. L. gave of the Spirit to the seventy e.
Deut. 25. 7. go up to the gate to the e. and say
29. 10. ye stand before the L. your e. and officers
31. 28. gather to me all e. of your tribes and officers
32. 7. ask thy father and e. and they will tell thee
Josh. 24. 31. Israel served the Lord all the days of Joshua, and of e. that overlived Joshua, Judg. 2. 7.
Judg. 8. 14. he described to him the e. of Succoth
1 Sam. 16. 4. e. of the town trembled at his coming
30. 26. he sent of the spoil to the e. of Judah
1 Kings. 20. 8. all the e. said to him, hearken not
21. 11. the e. did as Jezebel had sent to them
2 Kings 6. 32. Elisha sat in house, and e. sat with him
10. 1. Jehu wrote letters and sent to e. of Jezreel
19. 2. Hezekiah sent the e. of the priests covered with sackcloth to Isaiah the prophet, Isa. 37. 2.
Ezra 5. 5. the eye of their God was upon the e.
6. 14. the e. of the Jews builded and prospered
10. 8. according to the counsel of the princes and e.
Psal. 107. 32. praise him in the assembly of the e.
Prov. 31. 23. her husband is known among the e.
Lam. 1. 19. my priests and e. gave up the ghost in city
2. 10. e. of Zion sit upon the ground and keep silence
4. 16. respected not priests, favoured not e. 5. 12.
5. 14. e. have ceased from gate, young m. from music
Ezek. 8. 1. and the e. of Judah sat before me
Joel 1. 14. sanctify a fast, gather the e. 2. 16.
Mat. 15. 2. why transgress the tradition of the e.?
16. 21. must suffer many things of the e. 27. 12.
26. 59. the e. sought false witness against Jesus
27. 20. chief priests and e. persuaded the multitude
41. the chief priests mocking with the e. said
28. 12. and when they were assembled with the e.
Mark 7. 3. the Jews holding the tradition of the e.
8. 31. must suffer and be rejected of the e. Luke 9. 22.
14. 43. with Judas a great multitude from the e.
15. 1. chief priests held a consultation with the e.
Luke 22. 52. Jesus said unto the captains and e.
Acts 4. 5. their rulers and e. were gathered together
23. they reported all that the e. had said to them
6. 12. they stirred up the people and the e.
11. 30. sent it to the e. by Barnabas and Saul
14. 23. when they ordained e. in every church
15. 4. they were received of the church and of the e.
6. the apostles and e. came together to consider
23. the apostles, e. and brethren, send greeting
16. 4. they delivered the decrees ordained of the e.
20. 17. he sent and called the e. of the church
22. 5. all the estate of the e. bear me witness
24. 1. Ananias the priest descended with the e.
25. 15. about whom the e. of Jews informed me
1 Tim. 5. 17. let e. that rule well be counted worthy
Tit. 1. 5. that thou shouldest ordain e. in every city
Heb. 11. 2. by faith the e. obtained a good report
Jam. 5. 14. let him call for the e. of the church
1 Pet. 5. 1. the e. which are among you, I exhort
Rev. 4. 4. upon the seats I saw 24. e. sitting, clothed
10. the 24 e. fall before him, 5. 8, 14. | 11. 16. | 19. 4.
5. 5. and one of the e. saith unto me, weep not
6. and lo, in the midst of the e. stood a Lamb
11. I heard the voice of many angels about the e.
7. 11. all angels stood about the e. and four beasts
13. one of the e. ans. saying to me, what are these?
14. 3. they sung a new song before the throne and e.

ELDERS, with *city*.

Deut. 19. 12. the e. of his city shall fetch him thence
21. 3. e. of that city shall take and bring the heifer
6. e. of that city shall wash their hands over heifer
21. 19. shall bring their son to the e. of his city
22. 15. bring tokens of virginity to the e. of the city
25. 8. the e. of his city shall call and speak to him
Josh. 20. 4. shall declare his cause to e. of that city
Judg. 8. 16. he took the e. of the city and thorns
Ruth 4. 2. Boaz took ten men of the e. of the city
Ezra 10. 14. and with them the e. of every city

ELDERS *of Israel*.

Exod. 3. 16. go and gather the e. of Israel together
12. 21. Moses called for all the e. of Israel
17. 5. and take with thee of the e. of Israel
18. 12. the e. of Israel came to eat with Jethro
24. 1. seventy of the e. of Israel, 9. Num. 11. 16.
Deut. 27. 1. the e. of Israel commanded the people
31. 9. Moses delivered this law to the e. of Israel
Josh. 7. 6. the e. of Israel put dust on their heads
2 Sam. 5. 3. so all the e. of Israel came to the king at Hebron, 1 Kings 8. 3. 2 Chron. 5. 4.
17. 4. the saying pleased all the e. of Israel
15. thus did Ahithophel counsel the e. of Israel
1 Chr. 11. 3. e. of Israel came to the king to Hebron
21. 16. David and e. of Israel fell upon their faces
Ezek. 14. 1. then came the e. of Israel unto me
20. 1. the e. of Israel came to inquire of the Lord
Acts 4. 8. ye rulers of the people, and e. of Israel

ELDERS, with *people*.

Exod. 19. 7. Moses called for the e. of the people
Num. 11. 16. whom thou knowest to be e. of the peo.
24. Moses gathered 70 men of the e. of the people
Ruth 4. 4. buy it before the e. of my people
1 Sam. 15. 30. honour me before the e. of my people
Mat. 21. 23. the e. of the people came, Luke 22. 66.
26. 47. with a multitude from e. of the people
27. 1. e. of the people took counsel against Jesus
Acts 6. 12. they stirred up the people and the e.

ELDEST.

Gen. 24. 2. Abraham said to his e. servant of his house
27. 1. Isaac called Esau his e. son, and said, my son
44. 12. and he searched, and began at the e.
Num. 1. 20. Reuben, Israel's e. son, 26. 5.
1 Sam. 17. 13. the three e. sons of Jesse followed, 14.
28. Eliab his e. brother heard David speak
2 Kings 3. 27. he took his e. son and offered him
2 Chron. 22. 1. for the band of men had slain all the e.
Job 1. 13. drinking in their e. brother's house, 18.
John 8. 9. they went out one by one, beginning at e.

ELECT,

Or Chosen, *is spoken*, [1] *Of* Christ, *who was chosen and set apart from eternity by God the Father to the great work of redemption and mediation*, Isa. 42. 1. Mat. 12. 18. [2] *Of good angels, whom God chose from among the rest to eternal life and happiness:* I charge thee before the elect angels, 1 Tim. 5. 21. [3] *Of the* Israelites, *who were God's chosen and peculiar people*, Isa. 65. 9, 22. [4] *Of such as are chosen by God in Christ to eternal life and salvation out of all the nations upon earth*, Tit. 1. 1. *This election is,* [1] *An act of distinguishing love*, Deut. 7. 8. [2] *Of divine sovereignty irrespective of any goodness in the objects of it*, Rom. 9. 11, 12, 16. [3] *Eternal*, Eph. 1. 4. 2 Thess. 2. 13. [4] *Absolute, and irrevocable*, Rom. 9. 11. 2 Tim. 2. 19. [5] *Personal, that is, of a certain number of persons*, Mat. 20. 23. 2 Tim. 2. 19. [6] *Of some of the chief of sinners*, 1 Tim. 1. 15. [7] *It is in Christ*, Eph. 1. 4. [8] *It is to sanctification and holiness as the means, and eternal glory as the end*, Eph. 1. 4. 1 Thess. 5. 9.

Isa. 42. 1. behold mine e. in whom my soul delighteth
45. 4. Israel mine e. I have called thee by thy name
65. 9. mine e. shall inherit it, and my servants
22. mine e. shall long enjoy work of their hands
Mat. 24. 22. no flesh should be saved, but for the e. sake those days shall be shortened, Mark 13. 20.
24. if possible deceive the very e. Mark 13. 22.
31. shall send his angels, and they shall gather together his e. from the four winds, Mark 13. 27.
Luke 18. 7. and shall not God avenge his own e.?
Rom. 8. 33. who shall lay any thing to charge of G. e.?
Col. 3. 12. put on as the e. of God bowels of mercies
1 Tim. 5. 21. I charge thee before the e. angels
2 Tim. 2. 10. I endure al. things for the e. sake
Tit. 1. 1. an apostle according to the faith of G.'s e.
1 Pet. 1. 2. e. according to foreknowledge of God
2. 6. I lay in Sion a chief corner-stone, e. precious
2 John 1. the elder to the e. lady, and her children
13. the children of thy e. sister greet thee

ELECTED.

1 Pet. 5. 13. church at Babylon e. together with you

ELECTION.

Rom. 9. 11. purpose of G. according to e. might stand
11. 5. there is a remnant according to the e. of grace
7. the e. hath obtained it, the rest were blinded
28. but as touching the e. they are beloved
1 Thess. 1. 4. knowing, brethren, your e. of God
2 Pet. 1. 10. all dilig. to make your calling and e. sure

ELEGANTLY.

Isa. 32. † 4. the tongue of stammerers shall speak e.

ELEMENTS.

Gal. 4. 3. we were in bondage under e. of the world
9. how turn ye again to the weak and beggarly e.
Col. 2. † 8. after the e. of the world, not after Christ
† 20. dead with Christ from the e. of the world
2 Pet. 3. 10. the e. shall melt with fervent heat, 12.

ELEPHANT.

The elephant *is the largest of all four-footed beasts. They who have studied the nature of the elephant with most accuracy, tell many extraordinary things of the sagacity, faithfulness, prudence, and even understanding of this creature.* Pliny *says of this animal:* Maximum animal est Elephas, proximumque humanis sensibus: quippe intellectus illis sermonis patrii, &c. *Hist. Nat. lib.* 8. *It has been often observed to do such things as are much above the capacity of other beasts.* The Hebrews *seem generally to have described it under the name of* Behemoth, *which signifies in general*, beasts of service. *The word* Elephas *may be derived from* Aleph, *which signifies*, to instruct, *by reason of the docility of this animal; or from* Eleph, *which signifies* a head, or captain; *because the elephant is, as it were, the head of all other terrestrial animals.*

The Lord, speaking to Job, *describes the* elephant *or* Behemoth, *Job* 40. *from verse* 15. *to the end of the chapter. It is there said, that* he eateth grass as an ox. *This agrees well with what historians relate of the* elephant. *He does not feed upon carrion, and is not at all wild; hay, herbs, and legumens, are his nourishment, as they are of our tame beasts.*

His bones are as strong pieces of brass, and his small bones like bars of iron. *These hyperbolical expressions shew the extraordinary strength of the* elephant; *with one stroke of his trunk he kills a camel or an horse. An* elephant, *it is said, has been seen to draw two cast cannons five hundred paces with his teeth; they were fastened together with cables, and weighed each three thousand pounds. And there is mention in the* Maccabees *of an* elephant *in* Antiochus's *army, which carried two and thirty armed men. They were all in a tower made of very solid wood, upon the* elephant's *back, and the tower was bound with a very strong chain under the* elephant's *belly.*

He is the chief of the ways of God. *He is a remarkable piece of the creation among four-footed beasts. He exceeds all others in size, strength, docility, address, fidelity, agility, long life,* modesty *and* pudicity; *for, it is said, that he never covers the female as long as any one appears in sight. The scripture adds, that* God, who made him, can make his sword to approach unto him. *Though he be so strong and terrible, yet God can easily subdue and destroy him: or,* God hath put his sword into his hands, *hath trusted him with his arms; the* elephant *is terrible when provoked. His arms are his* trunk *and his* teeth. *His teeth are the ivory, so well known in* Europe.

Surely the mountains bring him forth grass, where all the beasts of the field play. Elephants *are the gentlest of animals; they never use their strength but when they are compelled to it. They are not of that sort of animals which create terror in others: If he passes through a herd of other beasts, he puts them gently out of his way with his trunk to make room for him; He feeds in the fields and meadows, and the weakest and tamest animals play with impunity before him.*

He lieth under the shady trees, in the covert of the reeds and fens. *This also agrees well with the* elephant, *according to the account that historians give of him.* Ælian *says, that he may be called an animal of the marshes, because he lives along waters, and in moist places. He sometimes plunges himself into rivers in such a manner, that no more of him is to be seen than the end of his trunk: In the summer time he covers himself with mud, to avoid the heat.*

He drinketh up a river, and hasteth not: he trusteth that he can draw up *Jordan* into his mouth. *This also may be fitly applied to the* elephant; *he drinks a great deal, and large draughts, as if he were to swallow up a river, and as if* Jordan *were scarcely sufficient to satisfy his thirst: he is not afraid when he drinks, but does it leisurely, and takes time to disturb the water which he drinketh. The Scripture adds,* He taketh it with his eyes, his nose pierceth through snares. *When he sees the waters of a river, he trusteth that he can drink them all up:* his eye is bigger than his belly, *as is commonly said. He thrusteth his snout also into the river, and if there be any snares laid for other creatures, he breaks them to pieces. But others translate this verse,* Can any man take him in his eyes, or pierce his nose with snares or gins? *Can he be taken openly and by force? Surely no. His force or strength is too great for man to resist or overcome. Others thus,* He is taken by the eyes as a fish is taken by a hook. *Serpents attack* elephants *principally in the eyes, as* Pliny *observes. The same author says, that there are serpents in the* Ganges, *sixty yards long, who take* elephants *by the trunk as they are drinking, drag them along, and drown them in the waters,* Plin. *lib.* 8. *cap.* 12.

Some understand by Behemoth, *a creature called* hippopotamus, *or the* sea-horse; *which is an amphibious creature, and lives and preys both in the water and on land. This animal, say they, was well known to Job and his friends, as being frequent in the adjacent parts: and the description here given of the* Behemoth, *is very applicable to the* hippopotamus.

1 Kings 10. † 22. navy bringing e. teeth, 2 Chr. 9. 21.
Job 40. † 15. behold the e. which I have made

ELEVATION.

Judg. 20. † 38. they should make great e. with smoke

ELEVEN.

Gen. 32. 22. Jacob took his e. sons and passed over
37. 9. sun, moon, and e. stars, made obeisance to me
Exod. 26. 7. curtains of goats' hair, e. curt. shalt make
8. the e. curtains shall be all of one measure
36. 14. e. curtains he made ‖ 15. e. of one size
Num. 29. 20. on the third day e. bullocks, two rams
Deut. 1. 2. there are e. days' journey from Horeb
Josh. 15. 51. e. cities with their villages
Judg. 16. 5. we will give thee e. hund. pieces of silv.
17. 2. I took the e. hundred shekels of silver
3. when he restored e. hund. shekels to his mother
2 Kings 23. 36. Jehoiakim twenty-five years old, he reigned e. years in Jerusalem, 2 Chr. 36. 5.
24. 18. Zedekiah e. years, 2 Chr. 36. 11. Jer. 52. 1.
Mat. 28. 16. then the e. disciples went away to Galilee
Mark 16. 14. afterward he appeared to the e.
Luke 24. 9. they told all these things to the e. and rest
33. and they found the e. gathered together
Acts 1. 26. and he was numbered with the e. apostles
2. 14. but Peter standing up with the e. said to them

ELEVENTH.

1 Kings 6. 38. in the e. year was the house finished
2 Kings 9. 29. in the e. year of Joram began Ahaziah
25. 2. the city of Jerusalem was besieged to the e. year of king Zedekiah, Jer. 52. 5.
1 Chron. 24. 12. the e. lot came forth to Eliashib
25. 18. the e. to Azareel, he, his sons, and brethren
27. 14. the e. captain for the e. month, Benaiah
Jer. 1. 3. Jeremiah prophesied in e. year of Zedekiah
39. 2. in the e. year the city was broken up
Ezek. 26. 1. word of the Lord came to Ezekiel in the e. year, in first day of the month, 30. 20. | 31. 1.
Mat. 20. 6. and about the e. hour he went out
9. they came that were hired about the e. hour
Rev. 21. 20. e. foundation of the city was a jacinth

ELOQUENT.

Exod. 4. 10. Moses said, O my Lord, I am not e.
Prov. 1. † 6. to understand a proverb and an e. speech
Isa. 3. 3. the Lord doth take away the e. orator
Acts 18. 24. a certain Jew named Apollos, an e. man

ELSE.

Gen. 30. 1. she said, give me children or e. I die
Num. 20. 19. I will without doing any thing e. go
Deut. 4. 35. thou mightest know that the Lord he is God, there is none e. 39. 1 Kings 8. 60. Isa. 45. 5, 6, 14, 18, 21, 22. | 46. 9. Joel 2. 27.
Josh. 23. 12. e. if ye do in any wise go back and cleave
Judg. 7. 14. this is nothing e. save sword of Gideon
2 Sam. 3. 35. if I taste ought e. till the sun be down
1 Chr. 21. 12. or e. three days sword of the Lord
2 Chr. 23. 7. whoso e. cometh in, shall be put to death
Neh. 2. 2. this is nothing e. but sorrow of heart
Psal. 51. 16. desirest not sacrifice, e. would I give it
Eccl. 2. 25. who e. can hasten hereunto more than I?
Isa. 47. 8. that sayest, I am, none e. besides me, 10.

John 14. 11. or *e.* believe me for the work's sake
Acts 17. 21. spent time in nothing *e.* but tell or hear
Rom. 2. 15. accusing or *e.* excusing one another
1 *Cor.* 7. 14. *e.* were your child. unclean, but now holy
14. 16. *e.* when thou shalt bless with the Spirit
Rev. 2. 5. repent, or *e.* I will come to thee quickly, 16.

EMBALM.

Gen. 50. 2. Joseph comm. physicians to *e.* his father

EMBALMED.

Gen. 50. 2. and the physicians *e.* Israel
3. for so are fulfilled the days of those that are *e.*
26. they *e.* Joseph, put him in a coffin in Egypt

EMBOLDENED.

1 *Cor.* 8. 10. the conscience of him that is weak be *e.*

EMBOLDENETH.

Job 16. 3. what *e.* thee that thou answerest?

EMBRACE.

2 *Kings* 4. 16. about this season thou shalt *e.* a son
Job 24. 8. they *e.* the rock for want of a shelter
Prov. 4. 8. shall bring to honor, when thou dost *e.* her
5. 20. why wilt thou *e.* the bosom of a stranger?
Eccl. 3. 5. a time to *e.* and refrain from embracing
Cant. 2. 6. and his right hand doth *e.* me, 8. 3.
Lam. 4. 5. that were brought up in scarlet *e.* dunghills

EMBRACED.

Gen. 29. 13. Laban *e.* Jacob and kissed him
33. 4. Esau ran and *e.* Jacob and kissed him
48. 10. Jacob kissed and *e.* Joseph's sons
Acts 20. 1. Paul *e.* disciples and departed to Maced.
Heb. 11. 13. having seen and *e.* the promises

EMBRACING.

Eccl. 3. 5. a time to embrace and a time to refrain *e.*
Acts 20. 10. Paul *e.* Eutychus, said, trouble not yours.

EMBROIDER.

Exod. 28. 39. thou shalt *e.* the coat of fine linen

EMBROIDERER.

Exod. 35. 35. to work all manner of work of the *e.*
38. 23. with him was Aholiab, an *e.* in blue

EMERALD, S.

Exod. 28. 18. the second row shall be an *e.* 39. 11.
Ezek. 27. 16. Syria occupied in thy fairs with *e.*
28. 13. every precious stone thy covering, the *e.*
Rev. 4. 3. there was a rainbow in sight like unto an *e.*
21. 19. the fourth foundation of the city was an *e.*

EMERODS.

Deut. 28. 27. the Lord will smite thee with the *e.*
1 *Sam.* 5. 6. Lord smote them of Ashdod with the *e.*
9. men of the city had *e.* in their secret parts
12. the men that died not were smitten with *e.*
6. 4. they answered, five golden *e.* and five mice, 17.
5. shall make images of your *e.* and your mice, 11.

EMINENT.

Job 22. † 8. and the *e.* man dwelt in the earth
Isa. 3. † 3. doth take away the *e.* in countenance
Ezek. 16. 24. thou hast built to thee an *e.* place, 31.
39. they shall throw down thine *e.* place
17. 22. I will plant it on an high and *e.* mountain
1 *Tim.* 2. † 2. pray for kings and all that are in *e.* place

EMMANUEL,

Or Immanuel, *is a* Hebrew *word, which signifies* God with us. Isaiah, *in that prophecy, wherein he declares to* Ahaz *the birth of the* Messiah, *who was to be born of a virgin, says, This child shall be called, and really be,* Emmanuel, *that is,* God with us, *Isa.* 7. 14. *He repeats the same thing while he is speaking of the enemy's army, which, like a torrent, was to overflow* Judea, *in which* Christ *was to be born, to live and die;* The stretching out of his wings shall fill the breadth of thy land, O Emmanuel, *Isa.* 8. 8. Matthew *says, that this prophecy was accomplished in the birth of* Christ, *born of the virgin* Mary, *in whom the two natures, divine and human, were united; and so in this sense he was really* Emmanuel, *or* God with us, *Mat.* 1. 23.
Isa. 7. 14. and shall call his name *Em. Mat.* 1. 23.
8. 8. he shall fill the breadth of thy land, O *Em.*

EMPIRE.

Esth. 1. 20. shall be published throughout all his *e.*

EMPLOY.

Deut. 20. 19. for the tree is man's life, to *e.* in siege

EMPLOYED.

Deut. 20. † 19. O man, the tree is to be *e.* in the siege
1 *Chron.* 9. 33. these singers were *e.* day and night
Ezra 10. 15. Jonat. and Jahaziah *e.* about this matter

EMPLOYMENT.

Ezek. 39. 14. shall sever out men of continual *e.*

EMPTY.

Gen. 31. 42. surely thou hadst sent me away now *e.*
37. 24. the pit was *e.* there was no water in it
41. 27. the seven *e.* ears blasted with the east wind
Exod. 3. 21. that when ye go, ye shall not go *e.*
23. 15. in mouth Abib camest from Egypt, none shall appear before me *e.* 34. 20. *Deut.* 16. 16.
Deut. 15. 13. thou shalt not let him go away *e.*
Judg. 7. 16. he put in every man's hand *e.* pitchers
Ruth 1. 21. the Lord hath brought me home *e.*
3. 17. for he said, go not *e.* to thy mother-in-law
1 *Sam.* 6. 3. they said, send not the ark away *e.*
20. 18. be missed, because thy seat will be *e.* 25, 27.
2 *Sam.* 1. 22. the sword of Saul returned not *e.*
2 *Kings* 4. 3. go, borrow thee *e.* vessels, not a few
Neh. 5. † 13. even thus be he shaken out and *e.*
Job 11. † 12. for *e.* man would be wise, tho' born like
22. 9. thou hast sent widows away *e.* and the arms
26. 7. he stretcheth out the north over the *e.* place
Isa. 24. 1. the Lord maketh the earth *e.* and waste
29. 8. a hungry man awaketh, and his soul is *e.*
32. 6. to make *e.* the soul of the hungry
Jer. 14. 3. they returned with their vessels *e.*
51. 34. the king of Babylon made me an *e.* vessel
Ezek. 24. 11. then set it *e.* upon the coals thereof
Hos. 10. 1. Isr. is an *e.* vine, he bringeth forth fruit
Nah. 2. 10. Nineveh is *e.* and void, and waste
Mat. 12. 44. and when he is come, he findeth it *e.*
Mark 12. 3. they caught him and beat him, and sent him away *e.* *Luke* 20. 10, 11.
Luke 1. 53. and the rich he hath sent *e.* away

EMPTY, *Verb.*

Lev. 14. 36. priest command that they *e.* the house
Eccl. 11. 3. the clouds *e.* themselves on the earth
Jer. 48. 12. and send wanderers shall *e.* his vessels

Jer. 51. 2. fanners that shall fan her and *e.* her land
Hab. 1. 17. shall they therefore *e.* their net, not spare
Zech. 4. 12. which *e.* the golden oil out of themselv.
Mal. 3. † 10. if I will not *e.* you out a blessing

EMPTIED.

Gen. 24. 20. Rebekah hasted and *e.* her pitcher
42. 35. it came to pass as they *e.* their sacks
2 *Chron.* 24. 11. the high priest's officer *e.* the chest
Neh. 5. 13. even thus be he shaken out and *e.*
Isa. 3. † 26. she being *e.* shall sit on the ground
19. † 3. spirit of Egy. shall be *e.* in the midst thereof
6. and the brooks of defence shall be *e.*
24. 3. the land shall be utterly *e.* and spoiled
Jer. 48. 11. Moab not been *e.* from vessel to vessel
Nah. 2. 2. for the emptiers have *e.* them out

EMPTIERS.

Nah. 2. 2. for the *e.* have emptied them out

EMPTINESS.

Isa. 34. 11. he shall stretch out upon it the stones of *e*

EMPTYING.

Hos. 10. † 1. a vine *e.* the fruit which it giveth

EMULATION.

Rom. 11. 14. if I may provoke to *e.* my brethren

EMULATIONS.

Gal. 5. 20. the works of the flesh are *e.* wrath, strife

ENABLED.

1 *Tim.* 1. 12. I thank Christ Jesus who hath *e.* me

ENCAMP.

Exod. 14. 2. that they *e.* before Pi-hahiroth
Num. 1. 50. the Levites shall *e.* about the tabernacle
2. 17. as they *e.* so shall they set forward
3. 38. but those that *e.* before the tabernacle
10. 31. thou knowest how we are to *e.* in wilderness
2 *Sam.* 12. 28. *e.* against Rabbah, and take it
Job 19. 12. his troops come and *e.* about my tabernacle
Psal. 27. 3. though an host should *e.* against me
Zech. 9. 8. I will *e.* about mine house for the army

ENCAMPED.

Exod. 13. 20. *e.* in Etham ‖ 15. 27. *e.* by the waters
18. 5. where Moses *e.* at the mount of God
Num. 33. 10. from Elim they *e.* by the Red-sea
11. from Red-sea, and *e.* in the wilderness of Sin
Josh. 4. 19. people came up and *e.* in Gilgal, 5. 10.
10. 5. the kings of the Amorites *e.* before Gibeon
Judg. 6. 4. the Midianites *e.* against Israel
9. 50. Abimelech *e.* against Thebez and took it
10. 17. the children of Ammon *e.* in Gilead and Israel assembled themselves and *e.* at Mizpeh
1 *Sam.* 11. 1. Nahash *e.* against Jabesh-Gilead
13. 16. but the Philistines *e.* in Michmash
2 *Sam.* 11. 11. the servants are *e.* in the open fields
1 *Kings* 16. 15. the people *e.* against Gibbethon, 16.
1 *Chron.* 11. 15. the Philistines, *e.* in the valley
2 *Chr.* 32. 1. Sennacherib *e.* against the fenced cities

ENCAMPETH.

Psal. 34. 7. angel of the Lord *e.* round about ther
53. 5. hath scattered bones of him that *e.* agst. thee

ENCAMPING.

Exod. 14. 9. Egyptians overtook them *e.* by the sea
2 *Kings* 6. † 8. saying, in such a place shall be my *e.*

ENCLINE, ENCLOSE; *see* INCLINE, INCLOSE.

ENCOUNTERED.

Acts 17. 18. then certain philosophers *e.* him

ENCOURAGE.

Deut. 1. 38. *e.* him, he shall cause to inherit it, 3. 28.
2 *Sam.* 11. 25. thus say to Joab, and *e.* thou him
Psal. 64. 5. they *e.* themselves in an evil matter

ENCOURAGED.

1 *Sam.* 30. 6. David *e.* himself in the Lord his God
2 *Chr.* 17. † 6. his heart was *e.* in ways of the Lord
31. 4. that the priests and Levites might be *e.*
35. 2. Josiah *e.* them to the service of the Lord
Isa. 41. 7. so the carpenter *e.* the goldsmith

END.

The end *signifies the extremity or utmost part of a thing,* as the end of a rod, 1 *Sam.* 14. 27. The *end* of an heap of corn, *Ruth* 3. 7. The *ends* of the earth, *that is, The extremities, or most remote parts of the world,* Job 37. 3. ‖ 38. 13. *or the people inhabiting those parts,* 1 Sam. 2. 10. The Lord shall judge the ends of the earth, *He shall condemn and punish the* Philistines, *who dwelt in the utmost borders of the land of* Canaan, *upon the sea-coast. And in* Psalm 98. 3. All the ends of the earth have seen the salvation of our God; *that is, All the inhabitants of the earth from one end to the other.* End *is taken for the conclusion, the sum or substance of a discourse,* Eccl. 12. † 13. Let us hear the conclusion of the whole matter; *or,* the end of the matter. *It is also taken for destruction,* Gen. 6. 13. The end of all flesh is come before me. *I am resolved to destroy man and beast. And in* Amos 8. 2. The end is come upon my people of *Israel: The time of their utter and final overthrow. And in* Mat. 24. 6. *our Saviour prophesying of the destruction of* Jerusalem, *and of the temple, says to his disciples,* Ye shall hear of wars, and rumours of wars, see that ye be not troubled, for all these things must come to pass, but the end is not yet. *The destruction of* Jerusalem *is not presently: Or, though God shall bring remarkable judgments upon that place and people, yet he will not utterly destroy them: Or by* end *here may be understood,* the day of judgment, *or the time of* Christ's *second coming.*

In Rev. 21. 6. Christ *says,* I am the beginning and the end: *I made all things at first, and I will bring all to that perfection and happiness I have promised. And it is said,* Rom. 10. 4. *Christ* is the end of the law for righteousness to every one that believeth; *that is, The law was given for this end, that sinners being thereby brought to the knowledge of their sins, and their lost and undone estate, by reason thereof, should fly to* Christ *and his righteousness for refuge. Or,* Christ *is the perfection and consummation of the law. He perfected the* ceremonial law, *as he was the Substance, whereof all the ceremonies of the law were shadows; they all referred to him as their scope and end. He perfected also the* moral law, *both by his active obedience, fulfilling all the righteousness thereof; and by his passive obedience, bearing the curse and punishment of the law which was due to us.*

The end of the commandment is charity, *or* love, 1 *Tim.* 1. 5. *We truly accomplish the law by fulfilling the precept of love; for* love is the fulfilling of the law, *Rom.* 13. 10. *The main scope and design both of law and gospel, is to produce a pure, ardent love of God, and of men, for his sake. There is also mention of* the end of faith, 1 *Pet.* 1. 9. Receiving the end of your faith, even the salvation of your souls; *that is, receiving that which is the scope or mark to which faith tends, or which is the reward of faith, namely, the assurance of the salvation of your souls.* To endure to the end, *Mat.* 10. 22. *is to fight against sin and temptations as long as one lives, and constantly to adhere to* Christ, *in spite of all persecutions for his sake.* End *is also taken for* reward *or* wages, *Rom.* 6. 21. For the end of those things is death. *Eternal death is the reward or wages of sin.*

Gen. 6. 13. the *e.* of all flesh is come before me
47. 21. from one *e.* of Egypt even to the other *e.*
Exod. 23. 16. the feast of in-gathering which is in the *e.* of year, when gathered out of field, 34. 22.
25. 19. make one cherub on the one *e.* and the other cherub on the other *e.* even of mercy-seat
Deut. 28. 64. Lord scatter from one *e.* of the earth
32. 20. Lord said, I will see what their *e.* shall be
Judg. 6. 21. the angel put forth the *e.* of his staff
19. 9. behold, the day groweth to an *e.* lodge here
1 *Sam.* 14. 27. Jonathan put forth the *e.* of the rod
2 *Kings* 10. 21. the house of Baal was full from one *e.*
21. 16. filled Jerusalem with blood from one *e.*
2 *Chron.* 21. 19. after the *e.* of two years, his bowels
Ezra 9. 11. filled with unclean from one *e.* to another
Job 6. 11. what is my *e.* that I should prolong my life?
16. 3. shall vain words have *e.*? or what emboldens
26. 10. till the day and night come to an *e.*
28. 3. he setteth an *e.* to darkness, and searcheth
Psal. 7. 9. the wickedness of the wicked come to an *e.*
9. 6. destructions are come to a perpetual *e.*
19. 6. his going forth is from the *e.* of heaven
37. 37. upright man, for the *e.* of that man is peace
38. the *e.* of the wicked shall be cut off
39. 4. make me know *e.* ‖ 73. 17. I understood their *e.*
61. 2. from the *e.* of the earth will I cry to thee
102. 27. thou art the same, and thy years have no *e.*
119. 96. I have seen an *e.* of all perfection
Prov. 5. 4. her *e.* is bitter ‖ 23. 18. there is an *e.*
14. 12. but the *e.* thereof are the ways of death
25. 8. lest thou know not what to do in the *e.*
Eccl. 4. 8. yet there is no *e.* of all his labour
16. there is no *e.* of all the people before them
7. 2. the *e.* of all men ‖ 8. better the *e.* of a thing
10. 13. the *e.* of his talk is mischievous madness
12. 12. of making many books there is no *e.*
† 13. let us hear the *e.* of the whole matter
Isa. 2. 7. land full of gold, nor is there any *e.* of their treasures, nor is there any *e.* of their chariots
9. 7. of his government there shall be no *e.*
13. 5. they come from the *e.* of heaven to destroy
16. 4. for the extortioner is at an *e.* spoiler ceaseth
23. 15. after *e.* of 70 years Tyre shall sing, 17.
42. 10. sing his praise from the *e.* of the earth
45. 17. shall not be confounded world without *e.*
46. 10. declaring the *e.* from the beginning
Jer. 5. 31. what will you do in the *e.* thereof?
12. 12. for the sword of the Lord shall devour from one *e.* to the other *e.* of the land, 25. 33.
17. 11. gets riches, and at his *e.* he shall be a fool
29. 11. I think to give you an expected *e.*
31. 17. there is hope in thine *e.* saith the Lord
44. 27. be consumed, till there be an *e.* of them
50. † 26. came against Babylon from the *e.*
51. 13. O thou that dwellest, thine *e.* is come
31. to shew that his city is taken at one *e.*
Lam. 4. 18. our *e.* is near, for our *e.* is come
Ezek. 7. 2. an *e.* the *e.* is come on the land, 3, 6.
21. 25. when iniquity shall have an *e.* 29. ‖ 35. 5.
Dan. 7. 28. hitherto is the *e.* of the matter
8. 17. at the time of *e.* shall be the vision
19. at the time appointed the *e.* shall be, 11. 27.
9. 26. the *e.* thereof shall be with a flood, and to *e.*
11. 6. and in the *e.* of years they shall join
35. to purge them even to the time of the *e.*
40. at time of the *e.* king of south shall push him
45. yet he shall come to his *e.* and none help
12. 4. seal the book even to the time of the *e.*
8. O Lord, what shall be the *e.* of these things?
9. words are closed up, till the time of the *e.*
13. but go thou thy way till the *e.* be, shalt rest
Amos 3. 15. the great houses shall have an *e.*
5. 18. to what *e.* is it for you to desire the day?
8. 2. the *e.* is come upon my people of Israel
10. I will make the *e.* thereof as a bitter day
Nah. 2. 9. for there is none *e.* of the store
3. 3. and there is none *e.* of their corpses
Mat. 13. 39. the harvest is the *e.* of the world
24. 3. what shall be the sign of the *e.* of the world?
14. the gospel be preached, then shall the *e.* come
31. gather from one *e.* of heaven to the other
26. 58. but Peter went in and sat to see the *e.*
28. 1. in the *e.* of the sabbath came Mary to see
Mark 3. 26. he cannot stand, but hath an *e.*
Luke 1. 33. of his kingdom there shall be no *e.*
18. 1. he spake a parable to them, to this *e.*
22. 37. the things concerning me have an *e.*
John 18. 37. sayest I am a king, to this *e.* was I born
Rom. 6. 21. for the *e.* of those things is death
22. ye have fruit to holiness, the *e.* everlasting life
10. 4. Christ is the *e.* of the law for righteousness
14. 9. to this *e.* Christ both died, rose, and revived
2 *Cor.* 2. 9. for to this *e.* also did I write to know
11. 15. whose *e.* shall be according to their works
Eph. 3. 21. to him be glory world without *e.*
Phil. 3. 19. many walk, whose *e.* is destruction
1 *Tim.* 1. 5. the *e.* of the commandment is charity
Heb. 6. 8. nigh to cursing, whose *e.* is to be burned

Heb. 6. 16. and an oath is to them an *e.* of all strife
7. 3. having neither beginning nor *e.* of life
9. 26. but now once in the *e.* hath he appeared
13. 7. considering the *e.* of their conversation
Jam. 5. 11. and ye have seen the *e.* of the Lord
1 *Pet.* 1. 9. receiving *e.* of your faith, even salvation
4. 17. what shall be the *e.* of them obey not gospel?
Rev. 21. 6. I am Alpha and Omega, the beginning
and the *e.* will give to him athirst, 22. 13.

At the END.

Gen. 4. † 3. *at the e.* of days Cain brought offering
8. 6. *at the e.* of forty days Noah opened window
41. 1. *at the e.* of two years Pharaoh dreamed
Exod. 12. 41. *at the e.* of 430 years, Lord's hosts went
Lev. 8. 33. the days of consecration be *at* an *e.*
Deut. 9. 11. *at the e.* of 40 days and 40 nights
14. 28. *at the e.* of three years bring the tithe
15. 1. *at the e.* of every seventh year a release
31. 10. *at the e.* of every seventh year read this law
Josh. 9. 16. *at the e.* of three days after the league
Judg. 11. 39. *at the e.* of two months she returned
Ruth 3. 7. Boaz lay down *at the e.* of the heap
2 *Sam.* 14. 26. *at the e.* of every year he polled it
24. 8. Joab came to Jerus. *at the e.* of nine months
1 *Kings* 2. 39. *at the e.* of 3 years two of Shimei's ser.
17. † 7. *at the e.* of days the brook dried up
2 *Kings* 8. 3. *at the e.* of 7 years the woman returned
18. 10. *at the e.* of three years they took Samaria
2 *Chron.* 18. † 2. *at the e.* of years Jehoshaphat went
20. 16. ye shall find them *at the e.* of the brook
24. 23. *at the e.* of the year the host of Syria came
Neh. 13. † 6. *at the e.* of days I obtained leave
Psal. 107. 27. they stagger, and are *at* their wit's *e.*
Isa. 7. 3. go to meet Ahaz *at the e.* of the conduit
Jer. 34. 14. *at the e.* of seven years let go every serv.
Ezek. 3. 16. *at the e.* of seven days word of L. came
Dan. 1. 5. *at the e.* they might stand before the king
4. 29. *at the e.* of 12 months he walked in palace
11. † 13. *at the e.* of times shall come with an army
12. 13. thou shalt stand in the lot *at the e.* of days
Hab. 2. 3. but *at the e.* it shall speak, and not lie
Mat. 13. 40. so shall it be in *the e.* of this world

But the END.

Prov. 14. 12. a way that seems right to a man, *but
the e.* thereof are the ways of death, 16. 25.
20. 21. *but the e.* thereof shall not be blessed
Mat. 24. 6. *but the e.* is not yet, *Mark* 13. 7. *Luke* 21. 9.
1 *Pet.* 4. 7. *but the e.* of all things is at hand

Last END.

Num. 23. 10. and let my *last e.* be like his
Jer. 12. 4. they said, he shall not see our *last e.*
Lam. 1. 9. she remembereth not her *last e.*
Dan. 8. 19. make thee know what shall be in the *last e.*

Latter END.

Num. 24. 20. his *latter e.* shall be that he perish
Deut. 8. 16. to do thee good at thy *latter e.*
32. 29. that they would consider their *latter e.*
Ruth 3. 10. shewed more kindness in the *latter e.*
2 *Sam.* 2. 26. it will be bitterness in the *latter e.*
Job 8. 7. yet thy *latter e.* should greatly increase
42. 12. the Lord blessed the *latter e.* of Job more
Prov. 19. 20. that thou mayest be wise in thy *latter e.*
Isa. 41. 22. consider them, and know the *latter e.*
47. 7. neither didst remember the *latter e.* of it
2 *Pet.* 2. 20. the *latter e.* is worse than the beginning

Made an END.

Gen. 27. 30. as Isaac had *made an e.* of blessing
49. 33. Jacob *made an e.* of commanding his sons
Lev. 16. 20. *made an e.* of reconciling the holy place
Num. 4. 15. *made an e.* of covering the sanctuary
16. 31. had *made an e.* of speaking, *Deut.* 20. 9.
Deut. 26. 12. hast *made an e.* of tithing the tithes
31. 24. when Moses had *made an e.* of writing
32. 45. *made an e.* of speaking, *Judg.* 15. 17.
1 *Sam.* 18. 1. | 24. 16. 2 *Sam.* 13. 36. 1 *Kings*
1. 41. | 3. 1. *Jer.* 26. 8. | 43. 1. | 51. 63.
Josh. 5. † 8. they had *made an e.* of circumcising
8. 24. Israel had *made an e.* of slaying, 10. 20.
19. 49. they *made an e.* of dividing the land, 51.
Judg. 3. 18. he had *made an e.* to offer, 1 *Sam.* 13. 10.
1 *Sam.* 10. 13. he had *made an e.* of prophesying
2 *Sam.* 11. 19. when thou hast *made an e.* of telling
1 *Kings* 7. 40. Hiram *made an e.* of doing the work
8. 54. Solomon *made an e.* of praying, 2 *Chr.* 7. 1.
2 *Kings* 10. 25. as soon as he had *made an e.* of
offering, 1 *Chron.* 16. 2. 2 *Chron.* 29. 29.
2 *Chr.* 20. 23. *made an e.* of the inhabitants of Seir
24. 10. cast into the chest, till they had *made an e.*
Ezra 10. 17. *made an e.* with all that had strange wives
Ezek. 42. 15. *made an e.* of measuring inner house
43. 23. when thou hast *made an e.* of cleansing it
Amos 7. 2. they *made an e.* of eating the grass
Mat. 11. 1. *made an e.* of commanding his disciples

Make an END.

1 *Sam.* 3. 12. when I begin, I will also *make an e.*
2 *Chr.* 31. † 1. brake the images, until to *make an e.*
Neh. 4. 2. feeble Jews, will they *make an e.* in a day
Job 18. 2. how long ere you *make an e.* of words?
Isa. 33. 1. thou shalt *make an e.* to deal treacherously
38. 12. to-night wilt thou *make an e.* of me, 13.
Ezek. 20. 17. eye spared, nor did I *make an e.* of them
Dan. 9. 24. seventy weeks, to *make an e.* of sins
Nah. 1. 8. he will *make an* utter *e.* of the place, 9.
Zeph. 1. † 2. by taking away, I will *make an e?*

Make a full END.

Jer. 4. 27. the whole land shall be desolate, yet will
I not *make a full e.* 5. 18. | 30. 11. | 46. 28.
5. 10. go ye up and destroy, but *make* not *a full e.*
Ezek. 11. 13. ah Lord, wilt thou *make a full e.?*

To the END.

Exod. 8. 22. I will sever land of Goshen, *to the e.* thou
mayest know that I am the Lord, *Ezek.* 20. 26.
Lev. 17. 5. *to the e.* Israel may bring sacrifices
Deut. 15. † 4. *to the e.* there be no poor among you
17. 16. *to the e.* that he should multiply horses
20. *to the e.* that he may prolong his days
Psal. 19. 4. their words *to the e.* of the world
30. 12. *to the e.* my glory may sing praise to thee
119. 112. to perform thy statutes even *to the e.*
Eccl. 3. 11. can find out from beginning *to the e.*
7. 14. *to the e.* man should find nothing after him
Isa. 48. 20. utter it even *to the e.* of the earth
Isa. 49. 6. mayest be my salvation *to the e.* of earth
Jer. 3. 5. his anger, will he keep it *to the e.?*
Ezek. 31. 14. *to the e.* that none of the trees exalt
Dan. 4. 11. sight thereof *to the e.* of all the earth
22. thy dominion reacheth *to the e.* of the earth
12. 6. how long shall be *to the e.* of these wonders?
Obad. 9. *to the e.* that every one may be cut off
Mat. 10. 22. but he that endureth *to the e.* shall be
saved, 24. 13. *Mark* 13. 13.
Acts 7. 19. cast out, *to the e.* they might not live
Rom. 1. 11. *to the e.* you may be established
4. 16. *to the e.* the promise might be sure to seed
2 *Cor.* 1. 13. I trust you shall acknowledge *to the e.*
3. 13. look *to the e.* of that which is abolished
1 *Thess.* 3. 13. *to the e.* he may establish your hearts
1 *Pet.* 1. 13. wherefore be sober, and hope *to the e.*

Unto the END.

Deut. 11. 12. from beginning *unto the e.* of the year
Josh. 15. 5. the east border was *unto the e.* of Jordan
Ruth 2. 23. to glean *unto the e.* of barley harvest
Job 34. 36. my desire is Job may be tried *unto the e.*
Psal. 46. 9. maketh wars to cease *unto the e.* of earth
119. 33. teach me, and I shall keep it *unto the e.*
Isa. 62. 11. L. hath proclaimed *unto the e.* of earth
Jer. 1. 3. it came *unto the e.* of the eleventh year
Dan. 6. 26. his dominion shall be even *unto the e.*
7. 26. to destroy his dominion *unto the e.*
9. 26. and *unto the e.* of the war desolations
Mat. 28. 20. I am with you alway, even *unto the e.*
John 13. 1. having loved, he loved them *unto the e.*
1 *Cor.* 1. 8. who shall also confirm you *unto the e.*
Heb. 3. 6. if we hold fast the confidence *unto the e.*
14. if we hold the beginning stedfast *unto the e.*
6. 11. to the full assurance of hope *unto the e.*
Rev. 2. 26. he that keepeth my works *unto the e.*

END.

Mat. 10. † 23. ye shall not *e.* the cities of Israel

ENDAMAGE.

Ezra 4. 13. so thou shalt *e.* the revenue of kings

ENDANGER.

Dan. 1. 10. ye shall make me *e.* my head to the king

ENDANGERED.

Eccl. 10. 9. he that cleaveth wood shall be *e.* thereby

ENDED.

Gen. 2. 2. on the seventh day God *e.* his work
41. 53. the seven years of plenteousness were *e.*
Deut. 31. 30. he spake the words till they were *e.*
34. 8. the days of mourning for Moses were *e.*
2 *Sam.* 20. 18. ask counsel, and so they *e.* the matter
Esth. 9. † 28. nor memorial be *e.* from their seed
Job 31. 40. the words of Job are *e.*
Ps. 72. 20. prayers of David, the son of Jesse are *e.*
Isa. 60. 20. the days of thy mourning shall be *e.*
Jer. 8. 20. the harvest is past, the summer is *e.*
Mat. 7. 28. when Jesus had *e.* these sayings
Luke 4. 2. when forty days were *e.* he hungered
13. when the devil had *e.* all the temptation
John 13. 2. supper being *e.* the devil having now put

ENDETH.

Isa. 24. 8. the noise of them that rejoice *e.*

ENDING.

1 *Sam.* 3. † 12. I will perform beginning and *e.*
Rev. 1. 8. I am the beginning and *e.* saith the L.

ENDLESS.

1 *Tim.* 1. 4. neither give heed to *e.* genealogies
Heb. 7. 16. who is made after the power of an *e.* life

ENDEAVOUR.

2 *Cor.* 5. † 9. we *e.* that we may be accepted of him
2 *Pet.* 1. 15. I will *e.* that you may be able after

ENDEAVOURED.

Acts 16. 10. we *e.* to go into Macedonia, gathering
1 *Thess.* 2. 17. we *e.* to see your face with great desire

ENDEAVOURING.

Eph. 4. 3. *e.* to keep the unity of the Spirit in bond

ENDEAVOURS.

Psal. 28. 4. according to the wickedness of their *e.*

ENDOW.

Exod. 22. 16. he shall surely *e.* her to be his wife

ENDS.

Deut. 33. 17. shall push the people to *e.* of the earth
1 *Sam.* 2. 10. the Lord shall judge the *e.* of the earth
1 *Kings* 8. 8. the *e.* of staves were seen, 2 *Chr.* 5. 9.
2 *Kings* 10. † 32. L. began to cut off the *e.* of Israel
Job 28. 24. for he looketh to the *e.* of the earth
37. 3. he directeth his lightning to *e.* of the earth
38. 13. it might take hold of the *e.* of the earth
Psal. 19. 6. and his circuit to the *e.* of it
22. 27. all the *e.* of the world shall remember
48. 10. so is thy praise to the *e.* of the earth
59. 13. God ruleth in Jacob to the *e.* of the earth
65. 5. the confidence of all the *e.* of the earth
67. 7. all the *e.* of the earth shall fear him
98. 3. the *e.* of earth have seen the salvation of God
135. 7. the Lord causeth the vapours to ascend from
the *e.* of the earth, *Jer.* 10. 13. | 51. 16.
Prov. 17. 24. eyes of a fool are in the *e.* of the earth
30. 4. who hath established all the *e.* of the earth?
Isa. 40. 28. the Lord, the creator of the *e.* of the earth
41. 5. the *e.* of the earth were afraid, drew near
9. whom I have taken from the *e.* of the earth
43. 6. bring my daughters from the *e.* of the earth
45. 22. look to me and be saved, all *e.* of the earth
52. 10. all the *e.* shall see the salvation of God
Jer. 16. 19. Gentiles shall come from *e.* of the earth
25. 31. a noise shall come to the *e.* of the earth
Ezek. 15. 4. the fire devoureth both the *e.* of it
Mic. 5. 4. now shall he be great to *e.* of the earth
Zech. 9. 10. his dominion to the *e.* of the earth
Acts 13. 47. thou be for salvation to *e.* of the earth
Rom. 10. 18. and their words to the *e.* of the world
1 *Cor.* 10. 11. on whom the *e.* of the world are come

ENDUED.

Gen. 30. 20. God hath *e.* me with a good dowry
2 *Chron.* 2. 12. to David a wise son, *e.* with prudence
13. have sent a cunning man, *e.* with understanding
Luke 24. 49. till ye be *e.* with power from on high
Jam. 3. 13. who is wise and *e.* with knowledge

ENDURE.

Gen. 33. 14. and as the children be able to *e.*
Exod. 18. 23. then thou shalt be able to *e.*
Esth. 8. 6. for how can I *e.* to see evil and destruction
Job 8. 15. he shall hold it fast, but it shall not *e.*
Job 31. 23. by reason of his highness I could not *e.*
Psal. 9. 7. the L. shall *e.* for ever, he hath prepared
his throne for judgment, 102. 12, 26. | 104. 31.
30. 5. weeping may *e.* for a night, but joy cometh
72. 5. they shall fear thee as long as sun and moon *e.*
17. his name shall *e.* for ever, as long as the sun
89. 29. his seed will I make to *e.* for ever, 36.
Prov. 27. 24. doth the crown *e.* to every generation?
Ezek. 22. 14. can thy heart *e.* or thy hands be strong?
Mat. 24. 13. he that shall *e.* to the end, *Mark* 13. 13.
Mark 4. 17. having no root, and so *e.* but for a time
2 *Thess.* 1. 4. in all your tribulations that ye *e.*
2 *Tim.* 2. 3. thou therefore *e.* hardness as a soldier
10. therefore I *e.* all things for the elects' sake
4. 3. when they will not *e.* sound doctrine
5. but watch thou in all things, *e.* afflictions
Heb. 12. 7. if ye *e.* chastening, G. dealeth with you
20. they could not *e.* what was commanded
Jam. 5. 11. behold, we count them happy who *e.*
1 *Pet.* 2. 19. if a man for conscience *e.* grief

ENDURED.

Psal. 81. 15. their time should have *e.* for ever
Rom. 9. 22. if God *e.* with much long-suffering
2 *Tim.* 3. 11. hast known what persecutions I *e.*
Heb. 6. 15. after he had patiently *e.* he obtained pro
10. 32. ye *e.* a great fight of afflictions
11. 27. for Moses *e.* as seeing him who is invisible
12. 2. he *e.* the cross ‖ 3. he *e.* such contradiction

ENDURETH.

Psal. 15. † 3. nor *e.* reproach against his neighbour
30. 5. for his anger *e.* but a moment, favour is life
52. 1. the goodness of God *e.* continually
72. 7. abundance of peace so long as the moon *e.*
100. 5. and his truth *e.* to all generations
145. 13. thy dominion *e.* through all generations
Mat. 10. 22. he that *e.* to the end shall be saved
John 6. 27. but for that meat which *e.* unto life
1 *Cor.* 13. 7. charity hopeth all things, *e.* all things
Jam. 1. 12. blessed is the man that *e.* temptation

ENDURETH *for ever.*

1 *Chron.* 16. 34. for his mercy *e. for ever,* 41.
2 *Chron.* 5. 13. | 7. 3, 6. | 20. 21. *Ezra* 3. 11.
Psal. 106. 1. | 107. 1. | 118. 1, 2, 3, 4. | 136.
1, 2, 3, *&c.* | 138. 8. *Jer.* 33. 11.
Psal. 111. 3. his righteousness *e. for ever,* 112. 3, 9.
111. 10. his praise *e. for ever* ‖ 117. 2. his truth *e.*
119. 160. every one of thy judgments *e. for ever*
135. 13. thy name, O Lord, *e. for ever,* thy mem.
1 *Pet.* 1. 25. but the word of the Lord *e. for ever*

ENDURING.

Psal. 19. 9. the fear of the Lord is clean, *e.* for ever
2 *Cor.* 1. 6. is effectual in *e.* the same sufferings
Heb. 10. 34. have in heaven a better and *e.* substance

ENEMY.

Exod. 15. 6. thy right hand hath dashed in pieces *e.*
9. the *e.* said, I will pursue, I will overtake
23. 22. then I will be an *e.* to thine enemies
Num. 10. 9. and if you go to war against the *e.*
35. 23. and was not his *e.* nor sought his harm
Deut. 32. 27. were it not I feared the wrath of the *e.*
42. from the beginning of revenges upon the *e.*
33. 27. he shall thrust out the *e.* before thee
Judg. 16. 23. our god hath delivered our *e.* into, 24.
1 *Sam.* 2. 32. thou shalt see an *e.* in my habitation
18. 29. Saul became David's *e.* continually
24. 19. if a man find his *e.* will he let him go?
1 *Kings* 8. 33. when thy people be smitten down
before *e.* because sinned ag. thee, 2 *Chron.* 6. 24.
46. if they sin, and thou deliver them to the *e.*
2 *Chron.* 25. 8. G. shall make thee fall before the *e.*
Esth. 7. 4. the *e.* could not countervail the damage
6. Esther said, the *e.* is this wicked Haman
Job 33. 10. behold, he counteth me for his *e.*
Psal. 7. 5. let the *e.* persecute my soul and take it
8. 2. thou mightest still the *e.* and the avenger
9. 6. O thou *e.* destructions are come to an end
42. 9. why go I mourning because of the *e.?* 43. 2.
44. 10. thou makest us to turn back from the *e.*
55. 3. I mourn, because of the voice of the *e.*
12. for it was not an *e.* that reproached me
61. 3. thou hast been a strong tower from the *e.*
64. 1. preserve my life from fear of the *e.*
74. 3. even all that the *e.* hath done wickedly
10. shall the *e.* blaspheme thy name for ever?
18. remember the *e.* hath reproached, O Lord
78. 42. remembered not when he delivered from *e.*
89. 22. the *e.* shall not exact upon him
143. 3. for the *e.* hath persecuted my soul
Prov. 27. 6. but the kisses of an *e.* are deceitful
Isa. 59. 19. when the *e.* shall come in like a flood
63. 10. therefore he was turned to be their *e.*
Jer. 6. 25. the sword of the *e.* is on every side
15. 11. I will cause the *e.* to entreat thee well
18. 17. I will scatter them with east-wind before *e.*
30. 14. I have wounded thee with wound of an *e.*
Lam. 1. 5. are gone into captivity before the *e.*
9. behold, for the *e.* hath magnified himself
16. my children are desolate, because *e.* prevailed
2. 3. he hath drawn back his hand before the *e.*
4. he hath bent his bow like an *e.* he stood
5. the Lord was as an *e.* he hath swallowed up
4. 12. that the *e.* should have entered the gates
Ezek. 36. 2. because the *e.* had said against you, aha
Hos. 8. 3. Israel, the *e.* shall pursue him
Mic. 2. 8. even of late my people is risen up as an *e.*
Nah. 3. 11. thou shalt seek strength because of *e.*
Mat. 13. 25. his *e.* came, sowed tares, went his way
28. he said unto them, an *e.* hath done this
39. the *e.* that sowed them is the devil
Luke 10. 19. to tread over all the power of the *e.*
Acts 13. 10. child of devil, thou *e.* of all righteousn.
1 *Cor.* 15. 26. the last *e.* to be destroyed is death
Gal. 4. 16. am I become your *e.* because I tell truth?
2 *Thess.* 3. 15. count him not as an *e.* but admonish
Jam. 4. 4. a friend of the world is the *e.* of God

Hand of the ENEMY.

Lev. 26. 25. I will send the pestilence, and ye shall
be delivered into the *hand of the e.* *Neh.* 9. 27
Ezra 8. 31. he delivered us from the *hand of the e.*
Psal. 31. 8. hast not shut me up into *hand of the e.*
78. 61. he delivered his glory into the *e.* *hand*
106. 10. redeemed from the *hand of the e.* 107. 2.

Lam. 1. 7. her people fell into the *hand of the e.*
2. 7. hath given into the *hand of the e.* the walls

Mine ENEMY.

1 *Sam.* 19. 17. why hast thou sent away *mine e.?*
2 *Sam.* 22. 18. delivered me from *my e. Psal.* 18. 17.
1 *Kings* 21. 20. hast thou found me, O *mine e.?*
Job 16. 9. *mine e.* sharpeneth his eyes upon me
27. 7. let *mine e.* be as wicked, and he that riseth
Psal. 7. 4. yea, I delivered him that is *mine e.*
13. 2. how long shall *mine e.* be exalted over me?
4. lest *mine e.* say, I have prevailed against him
41. 11. because *mine e.* doth not triumph over me
Lam. 2. 22. those I swaddled hath *mine e.* consumed
Mic. 7. 8. rejoice not against me, O *mine e.*
10. then she that is *mine e.* shall see it, and shame

Thine ENEMY.

Exod. 23. 4. if thou meet *thine e.* ox or his ass
Deut. 28. 57. *thine e.* shall distress thee in thy gates
1 *Sam.* 24. 4. deliver *thine e.* into thy hand, 26. 8.
28. 16. seeing the Lord is become *thine e.*
2 *Sam.* 4. 8. behold the head of Ish-bosheth *thine e.*
Job 13. 24. wherefore holdest thou me for *thine e.?*
Prov. 24. 17. rejoice not when *thine e.* falleth
25. 21. if *thine e.* hunger, give bread, *Rom.* 12. 20.
Lam. 2. 17. hath caused *thine e.* to rejoice over thee
Zeph. 3. 15. the Lord hath cast out *thine e.*
Mat. 5. 43. it hath been said, thou shalt hate *thine e.*

ENEMIES.

1 *Sam.* 18. 25. to be avenged of the king's *e.*
20. 15. when the Lord hath cut off the *e.* of David
16. the Lord require it at the hand of David's *e.*
25. 22. so and more do God to the *e.* of David
30. 26. behold a present of the spoil of *e.* of Lord
2 *Sam.* 12. 14. given occasion to *e.* to blaspheme
18. 32. the *e.* of my lord be as that young man is
2 *Chr.* 20. 29. Lord fought against the *e.* of Israel
Esth. 9. 1. the *e.* of the Jews hoped to have power
Job 6. 23. or deliver me from the *e.* hand
Psal. 17. 9. hide me from my deadly *e.* who compass
37. 20. the *e.* of the Lord shall be as fat of lambs
45. 5. thine arrows are sharp in heart of king's *e.*
78. 61. he delivered his glory into the *e.* hand
127. 5. they shall speak with the *e.* in the gate
Jer. 12. 7. have given beloved into hands of her *e.*
48. 5. the *e.* have heard a cry of destruction
Lam. 1. 2. all her friends are become her *e.*
5. her adversaries are the chief, her *e.* prosper
Mic. 7. 6. a man's *e.* are the men of his own house
Rom. 5. 10. if when we were *e.* we were reconciled
11. 28. as concerning the gospel, they are *e.*
1 *Cor.* 15. 25. till he hath put all *e.* under his feet
Phil. 3. 18. they are the *e.* of the cross of Christ
Col. 1. 21. were *e.* in your mind by wicked works

His ENEMIES.

Gen. 22. 17. thy seed shall possess the gate of *his e.*
Num. 24. 8. he shall eat up the nations *his e.*
32. 21. till he hath driven out *his e.* before him
Deut. 33. 7. be thou an help to him from *his e.*
2 *Sam.* 7. 1. the Lord hath given him rest from *his e.*
18. 19. how the Lord hath avenged him of *his e.*
22. 1. hast delivered him out of hand of all *his e.*
1 *Chron.* 22. 9. I will give him rest from all *his e.*
Job 19. 11. he counteth me as one of *his e.*
Psal. 10. 5. as for all *his e.* he puffeth at them
41. 2. thou wilt not deliver him to the will of *his e.*
68. 1. let God arise, let *his e.* be scattered
21. but God shall wound the head of *his e.*
72. 9. and *his e.* shall lick the dust
78. 66. and he smote *his e.* in the hinder parts
89. 42. thou hast made all *his e.* to rejoice
97. 3. a fire burneth up *his e.* round about
112. 8. until he see his desire upon *his e.*
132. 18. *his e.* will I clothe with shame
Prov. 16. 7. he maketh *his e.* to be at peace with him
Isa. 9. 11. the Lord shall join *his e.* together
42. 13. he shall cry, he shall prevail against *his e.*
59. 18. he will repay recompence to *his e.*
66. 6. a voice that rendereth recompence to *his e.*
14. his indignation be known towards *his e.*
Jer. 44. 30. will give Pharaoh into hand of *his e.*
Nah. 1. 2. and he reserveth wrath for *his e.*
8. and darkness shall pursue *his e.*
Heb. 10. 13. expecting till *his e.* be made his footstool

Mine ENEMIES.

Num. 23. 11. I took thee to curse *mine e.* 24. 10.
Deut. 32. 41. I will render vengeance to *mine e.*
1 *Sam.* 2. 1. my mouth is enlarged over *mine e.*
14. 24. that I may be avenged on *mine e.*
2 *Sam.* 5. 20. the Lord hath broken forth upon *mine e.* as the breach of waters, 1 *Chr.* 14. 11.
22. 4. so shall I be saved from *mine e. Psal.* 18. 3.
38. I have pursued *mine e. Psal.* 18. 37.
41. hast given me the necks of *mine e. Ps.* 18. 40.
49. and that bringeth me forth from *mine e.*
1 *Chr.* 12. 17. if ye be come to betray me to *mine e.*
Psal. 3. 7. save me, for thou hast smitten all *mine e.*
5. 8. lead me, O Lord, because of *mine e.*
6. 7. mine eye waxeth old because of all *mine e.*
10. let all *mine e.* be ashamed and sore vexed
7. 6. arise, O Lord, because of the rage of *mine e.*
9. 3. when *mine e.* are turned, they shall fall
18. 48. he delivereth me from *mine e.*
23. 5. thou preparest a table in presence of *mine e.*
25. 2. let not *mine e.* triumph over me, 35. 19.
19. consider *mine e.* for they are many
27. 2. when *mine e.* came upon me to eat my flesh
6. now shall mine head be lifted up above *mine e.*
11. lead me in a plain path, because of *mine e.*
12. deliver me not over to the will of *mine e.*
31. 11. I was a reproach among all *mine e.*
15. deliver me from the hand of *mine e.*
38. 19. but *mine e.* are lively, and they are strong
41. 5. *mine e.* speak evil of me; when shall he die
42. 10. *mine e.* reproach me all the day, 102. 8.
54. 5. he shall reward evil to *mine e.* cut them off
7. eye hath seen his desire upon *mine e.* 59. 10.
56. 2. *mine e.* would swallow me up, they be many
9. when I cry, then shall *mine e.* turn back
59. 1. deliver me from *mine e.* O my God, 143. 9.
69. 4. they being *mine e.* wrongfully are mighty
18. draw nigh, deliver me because of *mine e.*
71. 10. *mine e.* speak against me, they lay wait

Ps. 92. 11. mine eye shall see my desire on *mine e.*
119. 98. thou hast made me wiser than *mine e.*
139. because *mine e.* have forgotten thy word
157. many are *mine e.* yet do I not decline
138. 7. stretch forth thy hand against *mine e.*
139. 22. I hate them, I count them *mine e.*
143. 12. of thy mercy cut off *mine e.* and destroy
Isa. 1. 24. saith the Lord, I will avenge me of *mine e.*
Lam. 1. 21. all *mine e.* have heard of my trouble
3. 52. *mine e.* chased me sore like a bird without
Luke 19. 27. those *mine e.* bring hither and slay them

Our ENEMIES.

Exod. 1. 10. they join also to *our e.* and fight
Deut. 32. 31. *our e.* themselves being judges
1 *Sam.* 4. 3. it may save us out of hand of *our e.*
12. 10. but deliver us out of the hand of *our e.*
2 *Sam.* 19. 9. saved us out of hand of *our e. Ps.* 44. 7.
Neh. 5. 9. because of the reproach of *our e.*
6. 1. when rest of *our e.* heard I had builded, 16.
Psal. 44. 5. through thee will we push down *our e.*
60. 12. he it is shall tread down *our e.* 108. 13.
80. 6. and *our e.* laugh among themselves
136. 24. and hath redeemed us from *our e.*
Lam. 3. 46. *our e.* have opened their mouths
Luke 1. 71. that we should be saved from *our e.*
74. being delivered out of the hands of *our e.*

Their ENEMIES.

Exod. 32. 25. had made them naked amongst *their e.*
Lev. 26. 36. send faintness in the land of *their e.*
44. yet when they be in the land of *their e.*
Josh. 7. 8. Israel turneth backs before *their e.* 12.
21. 44. there stood not a man of *their e.* before them, the Lord delivered all *their e.* into their hand
23. 1. had given rest from *their e. Esth.* 9. 16.
Judg. 2. 14. sold them into the hand of *their e.*
18. delivered them out of hand of *their e.* 8. 34.
2 *Kings* 21. 14. deliver them into the hand of *their e.* and be a prey, 2 *Chr.* 6. 36. | 25. 20. *Neh.* 9. 27.
Psal. 78. 53. but the sea overwhelmed *their e.*
81. 14. I should soon have subdued *their e.*
105. 24. and made them stronger than *their e.*
106. 11. the waters covered *their e.* not one was left
42. *their e.* oppressed them, he delivered them
Jer. 15. 9. I will deliver to the sword before *their e.*
19. 7. to fall by the sword before *their e.* 20. 4.
9. wherewith *their e.* shall straiten them
20. 5. all treasures of kings of Judah will give into hands of *their e.* 34. 20, 21. | 21. 7. *Ezek.* 39. 23.
Ezek. 39. 27. gathered them out of *their e.* lands
Amos 9. 4. tho' they go into captivity before *their e.*
Zech. 10. 5. mighty men, which tread down *their e.*
Rev. 11. 5. if any hurt, fire devoureth *their e.*
12. they ascended, and *their e.* beheld them

Thine ENEMIES.

Gen. 14. 20. who delivered *thine e.* into thy hand
49. 8. thy hand shall be in the neck of *thine e.*
Exod. 23. 22. then I will be an enemy to *thine e.*
27. I will make *thine e.* to turn their backs to thee
Num. 10. 35. rise, Lord, let *thine e.* be scattered
Deut. 6. 19. to cast out all *thine e.* from before thee
20. 1. when thou goest against *thine e.* 21. 10.
28. 53. wherewith *thine e.* shall distress thee, 55, 57.
33. 29. *thine e.* shall be found liars to thee
Josh. 7. 13. thou canst not stand before *thine e.*
Judg. 5. 31. so let all *thine e.* perish, O Lord
11. 36. hath taken vengeance for thee of *thine e.*
1 *Sam.* 25. 26. now let *thine e.* be as Nabal
29. the souls of *thine e.* shall he sling out
2 *Sam.* 7. 9. I have cut off all *thine e.* 1 *Chr.* 17. 8.
19. 6. in that lovest *thine e.* and hatest thy friends
24. 13. or flee three months before *thine e.*
1 *Kings* 3. 11. nor asked life of *thine e.* 2 *Chr.* 1. 11.
1 *Chr.* 21. 12. while the sword of *thine e.* overtaketh
Psal. 8. 2. hast ordained strength because of *thine e.*
21. 8. thine hand shall find out all *thine e.*
66. 3. through thy power shall *thine e.* submit
68. 23. thy foot may be dipped in blood of *thine e.*
74. 4. *thine e.* roar || 83. 2. *thine e.* make a tumult
23. forget not the voice of *thine e.* the tumult
89. 10. thou hast scattered *thine e.* with thy arm
51. wherewith *thine e.* have reproached, O Lord
92. 9. lo, *thine e.* O Lord, *thine e.* shall perish
110. 1. till I make *thine e.* thy footstool, *Mat.* 22. 44. *Mark* 12. 36. *Luke* 20. 43. *Heb.* 1. 13.
2. rule thou in the midst of *thine e.*
139. 20. and *thine e.* take thy name in vain
Isa. 26. 11. the fire of *thine e.* shall devour them
62. 8. no more give thy corn to be meat for *thine e.*
Jer. 15. 14. I will make thee to pass with *thine e.*
Lam. 2. 16. *thine e.* have opened their mouth
Dan. 4. 19. and the interpretation be to *thine e.*
Mic. 4. 10. Lord shall redeem thee from *thine e.*
5. 9. and all *thine e.* shall be cut off
† 14. pluck up groves, so will I destroy *thine e.*
Nah. 3. 13. thy gate shall be set open to *thine e.*
Luke 19. 43. *thine e.* shall cast a trench about thee

Your ENEMIES.

Lev. 26. 7. ye shall chase *your e.* they shall fall
8. *your e.* shall fall before you by the sword
16. ye shall sow in vain, for *your e.* shall eat it
17. and ye shall be slain before *your e.*
37. shall have no power to stand before *your e.*
Num 10. 9. ye shall be saved from *your e.*
14. 42. be not smitten before *your e. Deut.* 1. 42.
Deut 12. 10. he giveth you rest from all *your e.*
20. 3. ye approach to battle against *your e.*
4. the Lord goeth to fight for you against *your e.*
28. 68. and there ye shall be sold to *your e.*
Josh. 10. 25. thus shall the Lord do to all *your e.*
22. 8. divide the spoil of *your e.* with your brethren
1 *Sam.* 12. 11. the Lord delivered you out of hand of *your e.* and ye dwelled safe, 2 *Kings* 17. 39.
Mat. 5. 44 but I say, love *your e. Luke* 6. 27, 35.

ENFLAME; *see* INFLAME.

ENGAGED.

Jer. 30. 21. who is this that *e.* his heart to approach?

ENGINE, S.

2 *Chron.* 26. 15. Uzziah made in Jerusalem *e.*
Jer. 6. † 6. pour out the *e.* of shot, *Ezek.* 26. † 8.
32. † 24. behold the *e.* of shot, they are come
Ezek. 26. 9. he shall set *e.* of war against thy walls

ENGRAFTED.

Jam. 1. 21. receive with meekness the *e.* word

ENGRAVE.

Exod. 28. 11. like a signet shalt *e.* the two stones
Zech. 3. 9. behold, I will *e.* the graving thereof

ENGRAVEN.

2 *Cor.* 3. 7. the ministration of death *e.* in stones

ENGRAVER.

Exod. 28. 11. with the work of an *e.* in stone
35. 35. to work all manner of work of the *e.*
38. 23. Aholiab, of the tribe of Dan, an *e.*

ENGRAVINGS.

Exod. 28. 11. like *e.* of a signet, 21, 36. | 39. 14, 30.

ENJOY.

Lev. 26. 34. the land shall *e.* her sabbaths, 43.
Num. 36. 8. that Israel may *e.* inheritance of fathers
Deut. 28. 41. thou shalt beget sons, but not *e.* them
Josh. 1. 15. then shall return to the land and *e.* it
Job 7. † 7. mine eye shall no more *e.* good
Eccl. 2. 1. *e.* pleasure, behold this also is vanity
24. he should make his soul *e.* good, 3. 13. | 5. 18.
9. † 9. *e.* life with the wife whom thou lovest
Isa. 65. 22. mine elect shall long *e.* work of hands
Acts 24. 2. seeing by thee we *e.* great quietness
1 *Tim.* 6. 17. God, who giveth us all things to *e.*
Heb. 11. 25. than *e.* the pleasures of sin for a season

ENJOYED.

2 *Chron.* 36. 21. till the land *e.* her sabbaths

ENJOIN.

Philem. 8. to *e.* thee that which is convenient

ENJOINED.

Esth. 9. 31. to confirm days of Purim as Esth. had *e.*
Job 36. 23. who hath *e.* him his ways?
Heb. 9. 20. blood of testament God hath *e.* to you

ENLARGE.

This word principally signifies the dilatation or expanding of the heart, which happens on occasions of prosperity and joy, opposite to that contraction and oppression of the heart which happens in adversity. Psal. 4. 1. Thou hast enlarged me when I was in distress. 2 Cor. 6. 11. O ye *Corinthians*, our mouth is open unto you, our heart is enlarged. *Our mouth is open to speak freely to you, and to communicate to you the whole will and counsel of God: Our heart is enlarged both by the love that we have towards you, and by the rejoicing that we have in you.* To enlarge *is used likewise for extending one's limits, and carrying one's conquests into a foreign country.* Gen. 9. 27. God shall enlarge *Japhet. God shall give him a large inheritance, and increase his posterity. Or otherwise:* God shall persuade *Japhet, namely, to dwell in the tents of* Shem, *where God dwelleth; he shall bring him to faith and obedience; so that this may be a prophecy of the calling of the* Gentiles, *the posterity of* Japhet. *Also in* Exod. 34. 24. For I will cast out the nations before thee, and enlarge thy borders.

My mouth is enlarged, *says* Hannah, 1 *Sam.* 2. 1. *It is opened wide to pour forth abundant praises to God; and to give a full answer to all the reproaches of my adversaries; whereas before it was shut through grief and confusion.* Thou hast enlarged thy bed, *Isa.* 57. 8. *Thou hast multiplied thine idols and altars. The same prophet says,* chap. 5. 14. Hell hath enlarged herself, and opened her mouth without measure. *The grave hath opened its mouth; it is ready to swallow up a vast number of the dead; it desires no more than to devour, and absorb such as shall die by this famine, or otherwise.*

Enlargement, *Heb.* Respiration, *Esth.* 4. 14. Then shall their enlargement arise to the *Jews* from another place. *They were so filled with grief and terror arising from their present danger, as that they could scarce breathe, as Job speaks,* Job 9. 18. *but their grief and sorrow should be removed, and then should they have a breathing-time, a time of sweet refreshment.*

Gen. 9. 27. G. shall *e.* Japhet, he shall dwell in tents
Exod. 34. 24. I will cast out nations and *e.* borders
Deut. 12. 20. when the Lord shall *e.* thy border
19. 8. if the Lord *e.* thy coast as he hath sworn
1 *Chr.* 4. 10. O that wouldest bless me, and *e.* coast
Psal. 119. 32. when thou shalt *e.* my heart
Isa. 54. 2. *e.* the place of thy tent and stretch forth
Amos 1. 13. that they might *e.* their border
Mic. 1. 16. make bald, *e.* thy baldness as the eagle
Mat. 23. 5. and *e.* the borders of their garments

ENLARGED.

1 *Sam.* 2. 1. my mouth is *e.* over mine enemies
2 *Sam.* 22. 37. thou hast *e.* my steps, *Psal* 18. 36.
Psal. 4. 1. thou hast *e.* me when I was in distress
25. 17. the troubles of my heart are *e.* O bring me
Isa. 5. 14. therefore hell hath *e.* hers. opened mouth
57. 8. thou hast *e.* thy bed, and made a covenant
60. 5. and thine heart shall fear and be *e.*
2 *Cor.* 6. 11. O ye Corinthians, our heart is *e.*
13. for a recompence in the same, be ye also *e.*
10. 15. having hope, that we shall be *e.* by you

ENLARGETH.

Deut. 33. 20. he said, blessed be he that *e.* Gad
Job 12. 23. he *e.* the nations, and straiteneth them
Hab. 2. 5. who *e.* his desire as hell, and is as death

ENLARGEMENT.

Esth. 4. 14. then *e.* shall arise from another place

ENLARGING.

Ezek. 41. 7. and there was an *e.* and a winding

ENLIGHTEN.

Psal. 18. 28. the Lord my God will *e.* my darkness

ENLIGHTENED.

1 *Sam.* 14. 27. and Jonathan's eyes were *e.* 29.
Job 33. 30. to be *e.* with the light of the living
Psal. 97. 4. his lightnings *e.* the world, earth saw
Isa. 60. † 1. arise, be *e.* for thy light cometh
Eph. 1. 18. the eyes of your understanding being *e.*
Heb. 6. 4. it is impossible for those who were once *e.*

ENLIGHTENING.

Psal. 19. 8. commandment of Ld. is pure, *e.* the eyes

ENMITY.

Gen. 3. 15. I will put *e.* between thee and the woman
Num. 35. 21. or in *e.* smite him with his hand

Num. 35.22. but if he thrust him suddenly without *e.*
Luke 23.12. for before they were at *e.* betw. thems.
Rom. 8. 7. the carnal mind is *e.* against God
Eph. 2. 15. having abolished in his flesh the *e.*
16. by the cross, having slain the *e.* thereby
Jam. 4. 4. the friendship of the world is *e.* with G.

ENOUGH.

Gen. 24. 25. we have straw and provender *e.*
33. 9. and Esau said, I have *e.* my brother
11. take, I pray, my blessing, because I have *e.*
34. 21. the land, behold it is large *e.* for them
45. 28. Israel said, it is *e.* Joseph is yet alive
Exod. 9. 28. entreat the Lord, for it is *e.* that
36. 5. the people bring much more than *e.* for work
Deut. 1. 6. ye have dwelt long *e.* in this mount
2. 3. ye have compassed this mountain long *e.*
Josh. 17. 16. they said, the hill is not *e.* for us
2 *Sam.* 24. 16. it is *e.* stay thine hand, 1 *Kings* 19. 4.
1 *Chron.* 21. 15. *Mark* 14. 41. *Luke* 22. 38.
2 *Chr.* 31. 10. we have had *e.* to eat and have left
Prov. 27. 27. thou shalt have goats' milk *e.* for food
28. 19. he that tilleth land have plenty, but he that followeth after vain persons have poverty *e.*
30. 15. yea, four things say not, it is *e.*
16. and the fire that saith not, it is *e.*
Isa. 56. 11. greedy dogs, which can never have *e.*
Jer. 49. 9. they will destroy till they have *e.*
Hos. 4. 10. for they shall eat, and not have *e.*
Obad. 5. would they not have stolen till they had *e.*
Nah. 2. 12. the lion did tear *e.* for his whelps
Hag. 1. 6. ye eat, but ye have not *e.* ye drink, but not
Mal. 3. 10. there shall not be room *e.* to receive it
Mat. 10. 25. it is *e.* for the disciple to be as his master
25. 9. not so, lest there be not *e.* for us and you
Luke 15.17. hired servants have bread *e.* and to spare
Acts 27.38. when they had eaten *e.* lightened the ship

ENQUIRE.

To enquire *signifies to ask,* Acts 9. 11. Enquire in the house of *Judas* for one *Saul of Tarsus. And* Gen. 24. 57. We will call the damsel, and enquire at her mouth: *We will ask her whether she be willing to depart so very soon, and understand her mind by her words or answer. Sometimes it signifies to pray,* Ezek. 36. 37. *And also to examine or search narrowly into a thing.* Deut. 17. 4. And if thou hast enquired diligently, and behold it be true. *Sometimes it is taken for saluting a person, and asking him of his welfare,* 1 Chron. 18. 10. *Tou* sent *Hadoram* his son to salute king *David,* to ask of his welfare. *But this word is most commonly used for asking counsel and direction from God.* Rebekah, *finding the two children with which she was big struggling together in her womb, and giving her some uneasiness,* went to enquire of the Lord, *Gen.* 25. 22. *Either she put up ardent prayers immediately to God, that he would reveal his mind to her herein: Or she consulted God immediately by her father* Abraham, *or by some other godly patriarch yet surviving, by whom God used to manifest his mind and will to others, when he thought fit. As to the different ways of consulting God under the Old Testament, see the word* ORACLE.

Gen. 24. 57. we will call the damsel, and *e.* at her
25. 22. Rebekah went to *e.* of the Lord
Exod. 18. 15. the people come to me to *e.* of God
Deut. 12. 30. and that thou *e.* not after their gods
13. 14. then shalt thou *e.* and make search
17. 9. thou shalt come unto the judge and *e.*
Judg. 4. 20. when any man doth come and *e.* of thee
1 *Sam.* 9. 9. beforetime when a man went to *e.* of God
22. 15. did I then begin to *e.* of God for him?
28. 7. seek me a woman, that I may *e.* of her
1 *Kings* 22. 5. Jehoshaphat said, *e.* I pray thee, at the word of the Lord to day, 2 *Chron.* 18. 4.
7. none besides, that we may *e.* of, 2 *Chron.* 18. 6.
2 *Kings* 1. 2. go, *e.* of Baal-zebub the god of Ekron
3. 11. is there not here a prophet to *e.* by him?
8. 8. go meet the man, and *e.* of the Lord by him
16. 15. the brazen altar shall be for me to *e.* by
22. 13. go ye, *e.* of the Lord for me, 2 *Chr.* 34. 21.
18. the king which sent you to *e.* 2 *Chr.* 34. 26.
1 *Chron.* 10. 13. that had a familiar spirit, to *e.* of it
18. 10. Tou sent to David to *e.* of his welfare
21. 30. David could not go before it to *e.* of God
Ezra 7. 14. are sent to *e.* concerning Judah and [Jerusalem
Job 8. 8. for *e.* I pray thee of the former age
Psal. 27. 4. beauty of the L. and to *e.* in his temple
Eccl. 7. 10. thou dost not *e.* wisely concerning this
Isa. 21. 12. if ye will *e. e.* ye, return, come
Jer. 21. 2. *e.* I pray thee, of the Lord for us
37. 7. the king of Judah that sent you to *e.* of me
Ezek. 14. 7. and cometh to a prophet to *e.* of him
20. 1. the elders of Israel came to *e.* of the Lord
3. thus saith the Lord, are ye come to *e.* of me?
Mat. 10. 11. *e.* who in it is worthy, and there abide
Luke 22. 23. to *e.* among themselves, *John* 16. 19.
Acts 9. 11. *e.* for Saul ‖ 25. † 20. doubtful how to *e.*
19. 39. but if ye *e.* concerning other matters
23. 15. as though ye would *e.* something more, 20.
2 *Cor.* 8. 23. whether any do *e.* of Titus my partner

ENQUIRED.

Deut. 17. 4. thou hast heard of it, and *e.* diligently
Judg. 20. 27. the children of Israel *e.* of the Lord
1 *Sam.* 10. 22. therefore they *e.* of the Lord further
22. 10. and he *e.* of the Lord for him, 13.
23. 2. therefore David *e.* of the Lord, 4. | 30. 8. 2 *Sam.* 2. 1. | 5. 19, 23. | 21. 1. 1 *Chr.* 14. 10, 14
28. 6. when Saul *e.* the Lord answered him not
2 *Sam.* 11. 3. David sent and *e.* after the woman
16. 23. as if a man had *e.* at the oracle of God
1 *Chron.* 10. 14. Saul *e.* not of the Lord he slew him
13. 3. for we *e.* not at the ark in the days of Saul
Psal. 78. 34. they returned and *e.* early after God
Ezek. 14. 3. should I be *e.* of at all by them?
20. 3. as I live, saith Lord, I will not be *e.* of by you
31. shall I be *e.* of by you, O house of Israel? as I live, saith Lord God, I will not be *e.* of by you
36. 37. I will yet for this be *e.* of by Israel
Dan. 1. 20. in all matters that the king *e.* of them

Zeph. 1. 6. those that have not *e.* for the Lord
Mat. 2. 7. Herod *e.* of the wise men diligently, 16.
John 4. 52. then *e.* he the hour he began to amend
2 *Cor.* 8. 23. or our brethren be *e.* of. are messengers
1 *Pet.* 1. 10. of which salvation the prophets *e.*

ENQUIREST.

Job 10. 6. that thou *e.* after mine iniquity and sin

ENQUIRY.

Prov. 20. 25. and after vows to make *e.*
Acts 10. 17. the men had made *e.* for Simon's house

ENRAGED.

Prov. 26. † 17. is *e.* with strife belonging not to him

ENRICH.

1 *Sam.* 17. 25. the king will *e.* him with great riches
Ezek. 27. 33. thou didst *e.* the kings of the earth

ENRICHED.

1 *Cor.* 1. 5. that in every thing ye are *e.* by him
2 *Cor.* 9. 11. being *e.* in every thing to all bountifuln.

ENRICHEST.

Psal. 65. 9. thou greatly *e.* it with the river of God

ENROLLED.

Luke 2. † 1. a decree that all the world should be *e.*
Heb. 12. † 23. church of the first-born *e.* in heaven

ENSAMPLE.

Phil. 3. 17. be followers, as ye have us for an *e.*
2 *Thess.* 3. 9. but to make ourselves an *e.* to you
2 *Pet.* 2. 6 an *e.* to those that should live ungodly

ENSAMPLES.

1 *Cor.* 10 11. these things happened to them for *e.*
1 *Thess.* 1. 7. so that ye were *e.* to all that believe
1 *Pet.* 5. 3. not as lords, but being *e.* to the flock

ENSIGN.

Ensigns *are warlike banners, monuments, or trophies of victory.* Psal. 74. 4. Thine enemies set up their ensigns for signs. *And the prophet* Isaiah, *threatening the Israelites with an invasion, tells them,* That God would lift up an ensign to the nations from far, *Isa.* 5. 26. *He would, by his providence, bring the* Assyrians, *or the* Chaldeans, *against the* Jews; *he would, as it were, invite them to list themselves under his colours, as generals use to lift up their standards for the raising of armies. The same prophet says,* That there shall be a *root of Jesse,* which shall stand for an *ensign* of the people, and to it shall the *Gentiles* seek, *Isa.* 11. 10. *that is, That* Christ *the* Messiah *growing upon the root of* Jesse, *should mount up, and be advanced, by the preaching of the gospel, to a great height, so as to become a visible and eminent* ensign, *which the* Gentiles, *as well as the* Jews, *may discern; to whom they should repair by faith, and in whom they should put their trust.*

Isa. 5. 26. he will lift up an *e.* to the nations from far
11. 10. which shall stand for an *e.* to the people
12. and he shall set up an *e.* for the nations
18. 3. dwellers, see ye, when he lifteth up an *e.*
30. 17. till ye be left as an *e.* on an hill
31. 9. his princes shall be afraid of the *e.* saith L.
Zech. 9. 16. as the stones of a crown lifted as an *e.*

ENSIGNS.

Psal. 74. 4. they set up their *e.* for signs

ENSNARE.

Psal. 12. † 5. I will set in safety from him would *e.*

ENSNARED.

Job 34. 30. hypocrite reign not, lest the people be *e.*

ENSUE.

1 *Pet.* 3. 11. let him do good, seek peace, and *e.* it

ENTANGLE; *see* INTANGLE.

ENTER.

Judg. 18. 9. not slothful to *e.* to possess the land
Ezek. 44. 3. prince shall *e.* by the porch, 46. 2, 8.
Dan. 11. 17. shall also set his face to *e.* with strength
24. he shall *e.* peaceably on the fattest places
Heb. 4. 6. it remaineth that some must *e.* therein

ENTER *in,* or *into.*

Gen. 12. 11. Abram was come near to *e. into* Egypt
Exod. 40. 35. Moses was not able to *e. into* the tent
Num. 4. 23. all that *e. in* to perform the service
5. 24. the water that causeth the curse shall *e. into* the woman, and become bitter, 27.
Deut. 23. 8. children shall *e. into* the congregation
29. 12. that thou shouldest *e. into* covenant with L.
Josh. 10. 19. suffer them not to *e. into* their cities
2 *Sam.* 22. 7. and my cry did *e. into* his ears
1 *Kings* 14. 12. when thy feet *e. into* city, child die
22. 30. I will disguise myself and *e. into* the battle
2 *Kings* 7. 4. if we *e. into* the city, then the famine
11. 5. a third part of you that *e. in* on sabbath
19. 23. and I will *e. into* lodgings of his borders, and into the forest of Carmel, *Isa.* 37. 24.
2 *Chron.* 23. 19. that none unclean should *e. in*
30. 8. *e. into* his sanctuary, which he sanctified
Neh. 2. 8. and for the house that I shall *e. into*
Esth. 4. 2. for none might *e. into* the king's gate
Job 22. 4. will he *e.* with thee *into* judgment?
34. 23. that he should *e. into* judgment with God
Ps. 37. 15. their sword shall *e. into* their own heart
45. 15. they shall *e. into* the king's palace
100. 4. *e. into* his gates with thanksgiving
118. 20. the gate *into* which the righteous shall *e.*
Prov. 18. 6. a fool's lips *e. into* contention
Isa. 2. 10. *e. into* the rock, and hide thee in the dust
3. 14. the L. will *e. into* judgment with ancients
26. 2. that the righteous nation may *e. in*
20. come, my people, *e.* thou *into* thy chambers
57. 2. he shall *e. into* peace, they shall rest in beds
Jer. 7. 2. that *e. in* at these gates, 17. 20. | 22. 2.
8. 14. and let us *e. into* the defenced cities
14. 18. if I *e. into* the city, behold famine
17. 25. there shall *e. into* the gates kings, 22. 4.
21. 13. or who shall *e. into* our habitations?
41. 17. they departed to go to *e. into* Egypt
42. 15. if ye set your faces to *e. into* Egypt
Lam. 3. 13. hath caused arrows to *e. into* my reins
Ezek. 7. 22. robbers shall *e. into* it and defile it
13. 9. nor shall they *e. into* the land of Israel
26. 10. when he shall *e. into* thy gates, as men *e. into* a city wherein is made a breach
37. 5. behold, I will cause breath to *e. into* you
42. 14. when the priests *e. therein,* then not go out
44. 2. this gate be shut, no man shall *e. in* by it
16. they shall *e. into* my sanctuary, and come near

Ezek. 44. 17. when they *e. in* at gates of inner court
Dan. 11. 7. shall *e. into* the fortress of king of north
40. he shall *e. into* the countries and overflow
41. he shall *e.* also *into* the glorious land
Joel 2. 9. like a thief they shall *e. in* at the windows
Amos 5. 5. seek not Beth-el, nor *e. into* Gilgal
Jonah 3. 4. and Jonah began to *e. into* the city
Zech. 5. 4. flying roll shall *e. into* the house of thief
Mat. 5. 20. in no case *e. into* kingdom of heaven
6. 6. when thou prayest, *e. into* thy closet
7. 13. *e. in* at the strait gate, *Luke* 13. 24.
21. not every one that saith, Lord, shall *e. in*
10. 11. *into* what city ye shall *e. Luke* 10. 8, 10.
12. 29. *e. into* a strong man's house, *Mark* 3. 27.
45. and they *e. in* and dwell there, *Luke* 11. 26.
18. 8. it is better for thee to *e. into* life halt or maimed, rather than be cast into everlasting fire, *Mark* 9. 43, 45, 47.
19. 17. if thou wilt *e. into* life, keep the commands
23. a rich man shall hardly *e. into* the kingdom
24. than for a rich man to *e. into* the kingdom of God, *Mark* 10. 25. *Luke* 18. 25
25. 21. well done, *e. into* the joy of thy Lord
Mark 1. 45. could no more openly *e. into* the city
5. 12. that we may *e. into* the swine, 9. *Luke* 8. 32.
6. 10. what house ye *e. into, Luke* 9. 4 | 10. 5.
9. 25. come out of him, and *e.* no more *into* him
14. 38. lest ye *e. into* temptation, *Luke* 22. 46.
Luke 8. 16. that they which *e. in* may see light
13. 24. many will seek to *e. in* and shall not be able
24. 26. to have suffered, and to *e. into* his glory?
John 3. 4. can he *e. into* his mother's womb again?
5. he cannot *e. into* the kingdom of God
10. 9. by me if any man *e. in,* he shall be saved
Acts 14. 22. through tribulation *e. into* the kingdom
20. 29. grievous wolves shall *e. in* among you
Heb. 4. 3. do *e. into* rest, if they shall *e. into* rest, 5.
11. let us labour therefore to *e. into* that rest
10. 19. boldness to *e. into* holiest by blood of Jesus
Rev. 15. 8. no man was able to *e. into* the temple
21. 27. in no wise *e. into* it any thing that defileth
22. 14. may *e. in* through the gates into the city

ENTER *not.*

Psal. 143. 2. *e. not* into judgment with thy servant
Prov. 4. 14. *e. not* into the path of the wicked
23. 10. *e. not* into the fields of the fatherless
Jer. 16. 5. *e. not* into the house of mourning
Mat. 10. 5. into any city of the Samaritans *e. not*
26. 41. that ye *e. not* into temptation, *Luke* 22. 40.

Not ENTER.

Num. 20. 24. for Aaron shall *not e.* into the land
Deut. 23. 1. shall *not e.* into the congregation, 2, 3.
2 *Chron.* 7. 2. the priests could *not e.* into the house
Psal. 95. 11. that they should *not e.* into my rest
Isa. 59. 14. truth is fallen, and equity *cannot e.*
Lam. 1. 10. they should *not e.* into thy congregation
Ezek. 20. 38. they shall *not e.* into the land
44. 9. *nor* uncircumcised *e.* into my sanctuary
Hos. 11. 9. and I will *not e.* into the city
Mat. 18. 3. ye shall *not e.* into kingdom of heaven
Mark 10. 15. he shall *not e.* therein, *Luke* 18. 17.
Heb. 3. 11. they shall *not e.* into my rest, 18.
19. we see they could *not e.* because of unbelief
See KINGDOM.

ENTRANCE.

Judg. 1. 24. they said, shew us the *e.* into the city
25. when he shewed them the *e.* they smote it
1 *Kings* 18. 46. he ran before Ahab to *e.* of Jezreel
22. 10. the two kings sat in the *e.* of Samaria
2 *Chron.* 12. 10. that kept the *e.* of the king's house
Psal. 119. 130. the *e.* of thy words giveth light
1 *Thess.* 2. 1. yourselves know our *e.* in unto you
2 *Pet.* 1. 11. so an *e.* shall be ministered to you

ENTERED.

Gen. 7. 13. the self-same day *e.* Noah and his sons
19. 3. the angels turned in, and *e.* into his house
23. the sun was risen when Lot *e.* into Zoar
43. 30. Joseph *e.* into his chamber and wept there
Exod. 33. 9. as Moses *e.* into the tabernacle
Josh. 2. 3. bring the men that are *e.* into thy house
Judg. 6. 5. and they *e.* into the land to destroy it
9. 46. they *e.* into an hold of the god Berith
1 *Kings* 1. † 1. now king David was *e.* into days
2 *Kings* 7. 8. *e.* into another tent, and took thence
9. 31. as Jehu *e.* in at the gate, Jezebel said
2 *Chron.* 12. 11. when the king *e.* into the house
15. 12. they *e.* into a covenant to seek the Lord
27. 2. Jotham *e.* not into the temple of the Lord
Neh. 10. 29. they *e.* into a curse, and into an oath
Job 38. 16. hast thou *e.* into the springs of the sea?
22. hast thou *e.* into the treasures of the snow?
Jer. 2. 7. but when ye *e.* ye defiled my land
9. 21. for death is *e.* into our windows and palaces
34. 10. the people which had *e.* into covenant
37. 16. when Jeremiah was *e.* into the dungeon
Lam. 1. 10. the heathen *e.* into her sanctuary
4. 12. that the enemy should have *e.* the gates
Ezek. 2. 2. spirit *e.* into me when he spake, 3. 24
16. 8. yea, I sware and *e.* into a covenant with thee
36. 20. and when they *e.* unto the heathen
44. 2. because the God of Israel hath *e.* in by it
Obad. 11. in the day that foreigners *e.* into his gates
13. thou shouldest not have *e.* into the gate
Hab. 3. 16. rottenness *e.* into my bones, I trembled
Mat. 8. 5. when Jesus was *e.* into Capernaum
9. 1. and he *e.* into a ship and passed over
12. 4. how he *e.* into the house of God and did eat
24. 38. day that Noah *e.* into the ark, *Luke* 17. 27.
Mark 5. 13. the unclean spirits went out and *e.* into the swine, and were choked in the sea, *Luke* 8. 33.
6. 56. whithersoever he *e.* they laid the sick
Luke 1. 40. Mary *e.* into the house of Zacharias
7. 44. I *e.* thine house, thou gavest me no water
9. 34. and they feared as they *e.* into the cloud
11. 52. woe to lawyers, ye *e.* not in yourselves
22. 3. then *e.* Satan into Judas, *John* 13. 27.
10. when ye are *e.* the city there shall meet you
John 4. 38. and ye are *e.* into their labours
18. 1. where was a garden, into the which he *e.*
33. then Pilate *e.* into the judgment-hall
Acts 9. 17. Ananias *e.* and putting his hands on Saul
11. 8. nothing unclean hath *e.* into my mouth

Acts 23. 16. he *e.* into the castle and told Paul, went
25. 23. Agrippa was *e.* into the place of hearing
28. 8. to whom Paul *e.* in, and prayed, and healed
Rom. 5. 12. sin *e.* into the world ‖ 20. the law *e.*
1 *Cor.* 2. 9. neither have *e.* into the heart of man
Heb. 4. 6. they *e.* not in because of unbelief
10. for he that is *e.* into his rest, hath ceased
6. 20. whither the forerunner is for us *e.* even Jes.
9. 12. he *e.* in once into the holy place, 24.
Jam. 5. 4. are *e.* into the ears of the L. of sabaoth
2 *John* 7. many deceivers are *e.* into the world
Rev. 11. 11. Spirit of life from God *e.* into them

ENTERETH.

Num. 4. 30. number every one that *e.* into the service to do work of the tabernacle, 35, 39, 43.
2 *Chr.* 31. 16. to every one that *e.* house of the L.
Prov. 2. 10. when wisdom *e.* into thine heart
17. 10. a reproof *e.* more into a wise man than
Ezek. 21. 14. the sword *e.* into their privy chambers
46. 9. he that *e.* in by the way of the north gate
Mat. 15. 17. whatsoever *e.* in at the mouth, goeth into the belly, and is cast out, *Mark* 7. 18.
Mark 5. 40. and *e.* in where the damsel was lying
Luke 22. 10. follow him into house where he *e.* in
John 10. 1. *e.* not by the door into the sheepfold
2. he that *e.* in by the door, is the shepherd
Heb. 6. 19. and which *e.* into that within the vail
9. 25. as the high-priest *e.* every year with blood

ENTERING.

Josh. 8. 29. cast it at the *e.* of the gate of the city
20. 4. shall stand at the *e.* of the gate of the city
Judg. 9. 35. Gaal stood in the *e.* of the gate of city
44. Abimelech stood in the *e.* of the gate of city
18. 16. the 600 men of Dan stood by the *e.* of the gate
17. and the priest stood in the *e.* of the gate
1 *Sam.* 23. 7. by *e.* into a town that hath gates, bars
2 *Sam.* 10. 8. put the battle in array at *e.* in of gate
1 *Kings* 6. 31. for the *e.* of the oracle he made doors
19. 13. Elijah stood in the *e.* in of the cave
2 *Kings* 7. 3. four leprous men at the *e.* of the gate
10. 8. lay the heads in two heaps at *e.* of the gate
23. 8. that were in the *e.* of the gate of Joshua
2 *Chr.* 18. 9. kings sat at *e.* of the gate of Samaria
Isa. 23. 1. so that there is no house, no *e.* in
Jer. 1. 15. set thrones at the *e.* of the gates, 17. 27.
Ezek. 44. 5. mark well the *e.* in of the house
Mat. 23. 13. for ye neither go in yourselves, nor suffer ye them that are *e.* to go in, *Luke* 11. 52.
Mark 4. 19. the lusts of other things *e.* in choke
7. 15. nothing without *e.* into him can defile him
16. 5. *e.* into the sepulchre they saw a young man
Luke 19. 30. at your *e.* ye shall find a colt tied
Acts 8. 3. Saul *e.* into every house, and haling men
1 *Thess.* 1. 9. what manner of *e.* in we had to you
Heb. 4. 1. a promise left us of *e.* into his rest

See HAMATH.

ENTERINGS.

Ezek. 26. † 10. according to the *e.* of a city broken

ENTERPRISE.

Job 5. 12. their hands cannot perform their *e.*

ENTERTAIN.

Heb. 13. 2. be not forgetful to *e.* strangers

ENTERTAINED.

Heb. 13. 2. for thereby some have *e.* angels

ENTICE

Signifies, [1] *To persuade, or allure,* Judg. 14. 15. | 16. 5. 2 Chron. 18. 20. [2] *To deceive,* Jer. 20. 10. Jam. 1. 14. It is referred, (1) *To* Satan *seducing false prophets, by inspiring them with lies,* 2 Chron. 18. 20. (2) *To a man cunningly insinuating himself into a maid's affections, in order to gain her consent to lie with him, either by his persuasions, promise of marriage, or reward,* Exod. 22. 16.

(3) *To* notorious sinners, *such as thieves, robbers, murderers, or oppressors, who endeavour to allure others by fair pretences to associate themselves with them,* Prov. 1. 10. | 16. 29.

(4) *To a man's own* lust *and* concupiscence, *which may promise him pleasure in sin, and may thus allure him to the commission of it, more than any temptation which he may have from without,* Jam. 1. 14.

(5) *To* false *and* treacherous *friends, the enemies of God's people, who watch for an advantage against the godly; thus* Jeremiah *complains,* chap. 20. 10. All my familiars watched for my halting, saying, peradventure he will be enticed; *namely, to utter something which we may lay hold on to accuse him for.*

(6) *To* the heart *allured with the sight of outward objects.* Job 31. 26, 27. If I beheld the sun when it shined, and my heart hath been secretly enticed; *that is, inwardly moved to esteem either the sun or moon as deities, or secretly to adore or worship them.*

(7) *To* false teachers, *who are said to deceive and seduce others,* by enticing words, *by erroneous philosophical notions and fancies mingled with the gospel,* 1 Cor. 2. 4. Col. 2. 4.

(8) *To* unfaithful wives, *flattering their husbands with a purpose to deceive,* Judg. 14. 15. | 16. 5.

Exod. 22. 16. if a man *e.* a maid not betrothed
Deut. 13. 6. if thy wife *e.* thee secretly, saying
Judg. 14. 15. *e.* husband, that he may declare riddle
16. 5. the lords said to Delilah, *e.* him and see
2 *Chr.* 18. 19. the Lord said, who shall *e.* Ahab?
20. I will *e.* him ‖ 21. thou shalt *e.* him and prevail
Prov. 1. 10. if sinners *e.* thee, consent thou not

ENTICED.

Job 31. 27. if my heart hath been secretly *e.*
Jer. 20. † 7. thou hast deceived me, and I was *e.*
10. peradventure he will be *e.* we shall prevail
Jam. 1. 14. is tempted when drawn away and *e.*

ENTICETH.

Prov. 16. 29. a violent man *e.* his neighbour
20. † 19. meddle not with him that *e.* with lips

ENTICING.

1 *Cor.* 2. 4. my preaching was not with *e.* words
Col. 2. 4. lest any man beguile you with *e.* words

ENTIRE.

Amos 1. † 6. carried them with an *e.* captivity
Jam. 1. 4. that ye be perfect and *e.* wanting nothing

ENTRY.

2 *Kings* 16. 18. k.'s *e.* without turned he from house
1 *Chron.* 9. 19. their fathers were keepers of the *e.*
2 *Chron.* 4. 22. doors of *e.* of the house were of gold
Prov. 8. 3. wisdom crieth at the gates, at *e.* of the city
Jer. 38. 14. Zedekiah took Jeremiah into the third *e.*
43. 9. hide the stones at the *e.* of Pharaoh's house
Ezek. 8. 5. this image of jealousy in the *e.*

ENTRIES.

Ezek. 40. 38. the chambers and *e.* were by the posts

ENVY

Is *an evil affection of the heart which makes men grieve and fret at the good and prosperity of others,* Psal. 73. 3. Rachel *envied* Leah, *because of her fruitfulness,* Gen. 30. 1. Joseph *was envied of his brethren, because his father loved him,* Gen. 37. 11. *The* Jews *envied* Paul *and* Barnabas, *because they preached* Christ, Acts 13. 45. Envy *at the good of others, and malice, wishing them evil, as one observes, is a deep pollution of spirit. This absolutely alienates men from the nature and life of God: for the clearest conception we have of the Deity is, that he is good, and does good. This is not only contrary to supernatural grace, but to natural conscience, and turns a man into a devil. This vice is immediately attended with its punishment: The envious man is his own tormentor.* Envy slayeth the silly one, *Job* 5. 2. Envy is the rottenness of the bones, *Prov.* 14. 30. *Besides, this stops the descent of divine blessings, and turns the petitions of the envious into imprecations against themselves.*

The spirit that dwelleth in us lusteth to envy, *Jam.* 4. 5. *According as spirit is taken, either for the Spirit of God, or for the human spirit, or natural corruption; the sense of these words may be, either,* (1) *The Spirit of God that dwelleth in us, teacheth us better things than strife and envy; for it lusteth against envy, that is, makes us lust against it, carries out our hearts to hate and resist it: The* Greek *preposition* προς, *here Englished* to, *often signifies* against, *as in* Luke 20. 19. Eph. 6. 11. *Or,* (2) *Our natural corruption, excited and inflamed by the devil, strongly inclines us to envy, and consequently to other wickedness.*

Job 5. 2. wrath killeth, and *e.* slayeth the silly one
Prov. 14. 30. *e.* is the rottenness of the bones
27. 4. but who is able to stand before *e.*?
Eccl. 4. † 4. this the *e.* of man from his neighbour
9. 6. their love, their hatred, and *e.* is now perished
Isa. 11. 13. the *e.* also of Ephraim shall depart
26. 11. they shall see and be ashamed for their *e.*
Ezek. 35. 11. I will even do according to thine *e.*
Mat. 27. 18. for *e.* they delivered him, *Mark* 15. 10.
Acts. 5. † 17. rose up, and were filled with *e.*
7. 9. the patriarchs moved with *e.* sold Joseph
13. 45. Jews filled with *e.* spake against those things
17. 5. the Jews which believed not, moved with *e.*
Rom. 1. 29. full of *e.* murder, debate, deceit
Phil. 1. 15. some indeed preach Christ, even of *e.*
1 *Tim.* 6. 4. whereof cometh *e.* strife, railings
Tit. 3. 3. we were foolish, living in malice and *e.*
Jam. 4. 5. the spirit that dwelleth in us lusteth to *e.*

ENVY.

Prov. 3. 31. *e.* thou not oppressor, choose not his ways
23. 17. let not thine heart *e.* sinners, be in fear of L.
Isa. 11. 13. Ephraim not *e.* Judah, Judah not vex

ENVIED.

Gen. 26. 14. and the Philistines *e.* Isaac
30. 1. Rachel *e.* her sister, and said unto Jacob
37. 11. Joseph's breth. *e.* him, his father observed
Psal. 106. 16. they *e.* Moses also in the camp
Eccl. 4. 4. for this a man is *e.* of his neighbour
Ezek. 31. 9. the trees in the garden of God *e.* him

ENVIES.

1 *Pet.* 2. 1. laying aside all malice, guile, and *e.*

ENVIEST.

Num. 11. 29. Moses said, *e.* thou for my sake?

ENVIETH.

1 *Cor.* 13. 4. charity suffereth long, and *e.* not

ENVYING.

Rom. 13. 13. let us walk honestly, not in strife and *e.*
1 *Cor.* 3. 3. whereas there is among you *e.* and strife
Gal. 5. 26. provoking one another, *e.* one another
Jam. 3. 14. but if ye have bitter *e.* and strife in hearts
16. where *e.* is, there is confusion, every evil work

ENVYINGS.

2 *Cor.* 12. 20. I fear lest there be debates, *e.* wraths
Gal. 5. 21. the works of the flesh are *e.* murders

ENVIOUS.

Psal. 37. 1. nor be *e.* against the workers of iniquity
73. 3. for I was *e.* at the foolish, when I saw
Prov. 24. 1. be not thou *e.* against evil men
19. fret not, neither be thou *e.* at the wicked

ENVIRON.

Josh. 7. 9. the Canaanites shall hear and *e.* us round

EPHAH

Is *an* Hebrew *measure of the same capacity with the* Bath, *containing ten* homers. *See* BATH, *and* HOMER.

Exod. 16. 36. an homer is the tenth part of an *e.*
Lev. 5. 11. the tenth part of an *e.* of flour, 6. 20.
19. 36. ye shall have a just *e.* *Ezek.* 45. 10.
Num. 5. 15. the tenth part of an *e.* of barley-meal
Judg. 6. 19. made unleavened cakes of an *e.* of flour
Ruth 2. 17. and it was about an *e.* of barley
1 *Sam.* 17. 17. take now an *e.* of this parched corn
Isa. 5. 10. the seed of an homer shall yield an *e.*
Ezek. 45. 11. the *e.* and baths shall be of one measure
46. 5. and an hin of oil to an *e.* 7, 11.
Amos 8. 5. making the *e.* small, and the shekel great
Zech. 5. 6. he said, this is an *e.* that goeth forth
8. and he cast it into the midst of the *e.*

See PART.

EPHOD

Was a sort of ornament, or upper garment, worn by the Hebrew *priests. There were two sorts of ephods, one of plain linen for the priests, and another embroidered for the high-priest. That for the high-priest was composed of gold, blue, purple, crimson, and twisted cotton; that is, it was a very rich composition of different colours. Upon that part of the* ephod, *which came upon the two shoulders of the high-priest, were two large precious stones, upon which were engraven the names of the twelve tribes of* Israel, *upon each stone six names,* Exod. 28. 4, 5, 6. &c.

There, where the ephod crossed the high-priest's breast, was a square ornament, called the breast plate, *wherein twelve precious stones were set, with the names of the twelve tribes of* Israel *engraved on them, one on each stone. The upper side of the breast plate was fastened by chains of gold to that part of the* ephod *which was on the shoulder; and the lower side of it, by blue laces, to the girdle of the* ephod: *for which purpose it had four rings of gold, at the four corners; that being all fitly joined together, it might appear like one entire garment,* Exod. 39. 21. *and accordingly, the whole was sometimes called and understood by the single word* Ephod, 1 *Sam.* 30. 7. *Hos.* 3. 4.

The Ephod *worn by common priests, which was of linen only, was of the same extent and use, but neither so rich, nor so much adorned. This garment was worn sometimes by those who, strictly speaking, were not priests; as by* Samuel *in the tabernacle, when he was but a child,* 1 Sam. 2. 18. *and by* David *when he brought the ark from the house of* Obed-Edom *to* Jerusalem, 2 *Sam.* 6. 14. *But, as both these were holy occasions, it is probable the* Ephod *was properly an holy robe; and never worn by any, but those who served in some holy employment.*

Some affirm that the Jewish *kings had a right to wear the* Ephod, *and to consult the Lord by* Urim *and* Thummim. *They ground their opinion principally on what is said concerning* David, 1 *Sam.* 30. 7. *when he came to* Ziklag, *and found that the* Amalekites *had pillaged the city, and carried away his and his people's wives, he said to* Abiathar *the high-priest,* Bring me hither the *Ephod,* and *Abiathar* brought thither the *Ephod* to *David. What follows* verse 8. *favours this opinion.* And *David* enquired at the Lord, saying, Shall I pursue after this troop? And he answered him, Pursue.

But the generality of commentators are of opinion, that neither David, Saul, *nor* Joshua, *nor any other prince of* Israel, *dressed themselves in the high priest's* Ephod, *in order to consult God of themselves, and that the passage now related signifies no more than,* Put on *the Ephod,* and consult the Lord for me. Grotius *believes, the high priest turned the* Ephod, *or breast plate, towards* David, *that he might see with his own eyes, what God should answer to him by the stones upon the breast plate.*

Exod. 25. 7. stones to be set in the *e.* 35. 9, 27.
28. 4. they shall make an *e.* and a robe, 6.
8. curious girdle of *e.* 27, 28. | 39. 5, 20. *Lev.* 8. 7.
12. put them on the shoulders of the *e.* 25.
15. make it after the work of the *e.* 39. 8.
31. shalt make the robe of the *e.* of blue, 39. 22.
39. 2. he made the *e.* of gold, blue, and purple
Lev. 8. 7. he put the *e.* upon him, and girded him
Judg. 8. 27. and Gideon made an *e.* thereof
17. 5. the man Micah made an *e.* and teraphim
18. 14. that there is in these houses an *e.* and teraph.
1 *Sam.* 2. 18. Samuel was girded with a linen *e.*
28. did I choose him to wear an *e.* before me?
14. 3. and Ahiah the Lord's priest wearing an *e.*
21. 9. the sword is wrapt in a cloth behind the *e.*
22. 18. Doeg slew 85 persons that did wear an *e.*
23. 6. Abimelech fled with an *e.* in his hand
9. David said, bring hither the *e.* 30. 7.
2 *Sam.* 6. 14. David danced before the Lord, and was girded with a linen *e.* 1 *Chron.* 15. 27.
Hos. 3. 4. Israel shall abide many days without an *e.*

EPISTLE

Is a *letter or writing, whereby one person communicates his mind to another at a distance; thus* David *communicated his mind to* Joab *in a letter which he sent by the hand of* Uriah, 2 *Sam.* 11. 14. *The holy Apostles likewise communicated to the church by* epistles *the mind and will of God, according as the Holy Spirit inspired and directed them; which inspired* epistles *make a part of the Canon of the holy Scriptures. And the whole word of God may be called his* epistle, *because therein he has declared and revealed his mind and will to mankind.*

The apostle Paul *writing to the* Corinthians, *says,* Ye are our epistle written in our hearts, known and read of all men. Forasmuch as ye are manifestly declared to be the epistle of Christ ministered by us, written not with ink, but with the Spirit of the living God, not in tables of stone, but in fleshly tables of the heart, 2 *Cor.* 3. 2, 3. *that is, You are my epistle of commendation; your conversion to Christianity is a real commendation of my ministry, and a demonstration of its efficacy: You are written in my heart; I have a hearty affection for you: Nor are you only taken notice of by me as a famous church, but all Christians look upon you as a church, to the planting and watering of which God hath blessed my labours. And it appears that ye are our epistle, in that it is evident that* Christ *has written his law in your hearts, by my ministry, which was made effectual to this end by the Holy Ghost.*

Acts 15. 30. they delivered the *e.* 23. 33.
Rom. 16. 22. I Tertius who wrote this *e.* salute you
1 *Cor.* 5. 9. I wrote to you in an *e.* not to company
2 *Cor.* 3. 2. ye are our *e.* written in our hearts
3. as ye are declared to be the *e.* of Christ
7. 8. I perceive that the same *e.* made you sorry
Col. 4. 16. when this *e.* is read amongst you, likewise read the *e.* from Laodicea
1 *Thess.* 5. 27. this *e.* be read to all the brethren
2 *Thess.* 2. 15. been taught whether by word or our *e.*
3. 14. if any man obey not our word by this *e.*
17. which is the token in every *e.* so I write

2 *Pet.* 3. 1. this second *e.* I now write unto you
EPISTLES.
2 *Cor.* 3. 1. or need we *e.* of commendation to you
2 *Pet.* 3. 16. as also in all his *e.* speaking in them
EQUAL.
Esth. 3. † 8. it is not *e.* for the king to suffer them
Psal. 17. 2. thine eyes behold the things that are *e.*
55. 13. but it was thou, a man, mine *e.* my guide
Prov. 26. 7. the legs of the lame are not *e.*
Isa. 40. 25. to whom then shall I be *e.?* 46. 5.
Lam. 2. 13. what shall I *e.* to thee, O virgin daughter
Ezek. 18. 25. yet ye say, the way of the Lord is not *e.* hear, is not my way *e.?* 29. | 33. 17, 20.
29. O house of Israel, are not my ways *e.?*
33. 17. but as for them, their way is not *e.*
Dan. 5. † 21. he made his heart *e.* with the beasts
Mat. 20. 12. and thou hast made them *e.* to us
Luke 20. 36. for they are *e.* to angels, childr. of God
John 5. 18. making himself *e.* with God
Phil. 2. 6. he thought it not robbery to be *e.* with G.
Col. 4. 1. masters, give your servants what is *e.*
Rev. 21. 16. the breadth and height of the city are *e.*
EQUAL.
Job 28. 17. the gold and the crystal cannot *e.* it
19. the topaz of Ethiopia shall not *e.* it
EQUALITY.
2 *Cor.* 8. 14. but by an *e.* that there may be an *e.*
EQUALLETH.
2 *Sam.* 22. † 34. he *e.* my feet with hinds' feet
EQUALLY.
Exod. 36. 22. one board had two tenons *e.* distant
EQUALS.
Gal. 1. 14. I profited above many my *e.* in my nation
EQUITY.
Psal. 98. 9. he shall judge the people with *e.*
99. 4. thou dost establish *e.* thou executest judgment
Prov. 1. 3. to receive the instruction of wisdom and *e.*
2. 9. then shalt thou understand judgment and *e.*
17. 26. it is not good to strike princes for *e.*
Eccl. 2. 21. there is a man whose labour is in *e.*
Isa. 11. 4. reprove with *e.* for the meek of the earth
56. † 1. thus saith the Lord, keep *e.* and do justice
59. 14. truth is fallen in street, and *e.* cannot enter
Mic. 3. 9. hear this, ye that pervert all *e.*
Mal. 2. 6. he walked with me in peace and *e.*
ERE.
Exod. 1. 19. they are delivered *e.* the midwives come
Num. 14. 11. how long will it be *e.* they believe me?
Job 18. 2. how long *e.* you make an end of words?
Jer. 47. 6. O sword, how long *e.* thou be quiet?
Hos. 8. 5. how long *e.* they attain to innocency?
John 4. 49. Sir, come down *e.* my child die
ERECTED.
Gen. 33. 20. Jacob *e.* there an altar, El-Elohe Israel
ERRAND.
Gen. 24. 33. I will not eat till I have told mine *e.*
Judg. 3. 19. I have a secret *e.* unto thee, O king
2 *Kings* 9. 5. he said, I have an *e.* to thee, O capt.
ERR.
2 *Chron.* 33. 9. so Manasseh made Judah to *e.*
Job 5. † 24. thou shalt visit thy habitation, and not *e.*
Psal. 95. 10. a people that do *e.* in their heart
119. 21. which do *e.* from thy commandments
118. hast trodden them that *e.* from thy statutes
Prov. 5. † 19. and *e.* thou always in her love
10. † 17. he that refuseth reproof, causeth to *e.*
14. 22. do they not *e.* that devise evil?
19. 27. cease to hear instruction that causeth to *e.*
Isa. 3. 12. O my people, they which lead thee cause thee to *e.* and destroy thy paths, 9. 16.
19. 14. and they have caused Egypt to *e.*
28. 7. they *e.* in vision, they stumble in judgment
30. 28. there shall be a bridle causing them to *e.*
35. 8. the wayfaring men shall not *e.* therein
63. 17. why hast thou made us to *e.* from thy ways?
Jer. 23. 13. the prophets prophesied in Baal, and caused my people Israel to *e.* *Mic.* 3. 5.
Hos. 4. 12. spirit of whoredom hath caused them to *e.*
Amos 2. 4. and their lies caused them to *e.*
Mat. 22. 29. Jesus said, ye do *e.* not knowing the scriptures nor power of God, *Mark* 12. 24, 27.
Heb. 3. 10. they do always *e.* in their hearts
Jam. 1. 16. do not *e.* my beloved brethren
5. 19. brethren, if any of you do *e.* from the truth
ERRED.
Lev. 5. 18. concerning ignorance wherein he *e.*
Num. 15. 22. ye have *e.* and not observed these com.
1 *Sam.* 26. 21. behold, I have *e.* exceedingly
Job 6. 24. cause me to understand wherein I have *e.*
19. 4. be it indeed that I have *e.* mine err. remaineth
Psal. 119. 110. yet I *e.* not from thy precepts
Isa. 28. 7. but they also have *e.* thro' wine and thro' strong drink, the priest and the prophet have *e.*
29. 24. they also that *e.* in spirit shall come
1 *Tim.* 6. 10. some coveted they have *e.* from the faith
21. some professing have *e.* concerning the faith
2 *Tim.* 2. 18. who concerning the truth have *e.*
ERRETH.
Prov. 10. 17. but he that refuseth reproof *e.*
Ezek. 45. 20. so shalt thou do for every one that *e.*
ERROR
Signifies, [1] *A mistake, or oversight,* Eccl. 5. 6. [2] *False doctrine, which is not agreeable to the word of God,* 1 John 4. 6. [3] *Sins of all sorts,* Psal. 19. 12. Heb. 9. 7. [4] *Idols,* Jer. 10. 15. [5] *Sins against nature,* Rom. 1. 27. [6] *Unfaithfulness in an office,* Dan. 6. 4.
The error of *Balaam,* Jude 11. *is covetousness, to which the persons of whom the apostle speaks were excessively addicted, and for the sake of filthy lucre did corrupt the doctrine of* Christ; *as* Balaam, *for the sake of gain, taught* Balak *to entice the children of* Israel *to commit fornication, and to eat things sacrificed unto idols.*
Job, *speaking to his friends, says,* Be it indeed that I have erred, mine error remaineth with myself, *Job* 19. 4. *If my opinion in this point be faulty and erroneous, as you pretend it is, it is likely to continue; I see no cause from your reasons to change my judgment. Or, if I have sinned, you see I suffer deeply for my sins, and therefore deserve your pity and help, rather than your reproaches, whereby you add affliction to the afflicted.*
Num. 35. † 11. the slayer that killeth any by *e.*
2 *Sam.* 6. 7. anger kindled, G. smote Uzzah for his *e.*
Job 19. 4. if erred mine *e.* remaineth with myself
Eccl. 5. 6. neither say thou that it was an *e.*
10. 5. there is an evil which I have seen as an *e.*
Isa. 32. 6. and to utter *e.* against the Lord
Dan. 3. † 29. who speak *e.* against God of Shadrach
4. † 27. if it may be a healing of thine *e.*
6. 4. neither was there any *e.* found in him
Mat. 27. 64. the last *e.* shall be worse than the first
Rom. 1. 27. receiving that recompence of their *e.*
Jam. 5. 20. converteth the sinner from *e.* of his way
2 *Pet.* 2. 18. were escaped from them who live in *e.*
3. 17. ye being led away with the *e.* of the wicked
1 *John* 4. 6. hereby know we the spirit of *e.*
Jude 11. they have ran greedily after *e.* of Balaam
ERRORS.
Ps. 19. 12. who can understand his *e.?* cleanse me
Jer. 10. 15. they are vanity, the work of *e.* 51. 18.
Heb. 9. 7. which he offered for the *e.* of the people
ESCAPE.
Gen. 19. 17. *e.* for thy life, *e.* to the mountain
20. O let me *e.* ‖ 22. haste thee, *e.* thither
32. 8. the other company which is left shall *e.*
Josh. 8. 22. they let none of them remain or *e.*
1 *Sam.* 27. 1. *e.* into the land of the Philistines
2 *Sam.* 15. 14. let us flee, for we shall not else *e.*
20. 6. lest Sheba get him fenced cities and *e.* us
1 *Kings* 18. 40. let none of them *e.* 2 *Kings* 9. 15.
2 *Kings* 10. 24. if any of the men I have brought *e.*
19. 31. they that *e.* out of mount Zion, *Isa.* 37. 32.
23. † 18. they let his bones *e.* with bones of prophet
Ezra 9. 8. grace been shewn, to leave us a remn. to *e.*
Esth. 4. 13. think not thou shalt *e.* in king's house
Job 11. 20. but the wicked shall not *e.* their hope fail
Ps. 56. 7. shall they *e.* by iniquity? cast down people
71. 2. deliver me in thy right. and cause me to *e.*
141. 10. let the wicked fall, whilst I withal *e.*
Prov. 19. 5. he that speaketh lies shall not *e.*
Eccl. 7. 26. whoso pleaseth God shall *e.* from her
Isa. 20. 6. we flee for help, and how shall we *e.*
66. 19. I will send those that *e.* to the nations
Jer. 11. 11. bring evil on them shall not be able to *e.*
25. 35. nor the principal of the flock to *e.*
32. 4. Zedekiah shall not *e.* 34. 3. | 38. 18, 23.
42. 17. none that go into Egypt shall *e.* 44. 14.
44. 14. none shall return but such as shall *e.*
28. yet a small number that *e.* the sword
46. 6. let not the swift flee, nor mighty man *e.*
48. 8. the spoiler shall come, no city shall *e.*
50. 28. voice of them that flee and *e.* out of Babylon
29. let none thereof *e.* recompense her according
Ezek. 6. 8. may have some that shall *e.* the sword
9. and they that *e.* of you shall remember me
7. 16. they that *e.* shall *e.* and be like doves
17. 15. shall he *e.* that doth such things?
18. hath done all these things, he shall not *e.*
Dan. 11. 41. but these shall *e.* out of his hand
42. and the land of Egypt shall not *e.*
Joel 2. 3. yea, and nothing shall *e.* them
Obad. 14. to cut off those of his that did *e.*
† 17. but on mount Zion shall be they that *e.*
Mat. 23. 33. how can ye *e.* the damnation of hell?
Luke 21. 36. be accounted worthy to *e.* these things
Acts 27. 42. counsel to kill the prisoners, lest any *e.*
Rom. 2. 3. that thou shalt *e.* the judgment of God?
1 *Cor.* 10. 13. but will also make a way to *e.*
1 *Thess.* 5. 3. sudden destruction, and they shall not *e.*
Heb. 2. 3. how shall we *e.* if we neglect so great salva.
12. 25. much more shall not we *e.* if we turn away
ESCAPE.
Psal. 55. 8. I would hasten my *e.* from the storm
ESCAPED.
Gen. 14. 13. there came one that had *e.* and told
Exod. 10. 5. the locust eat the residue of what is *e.*
Num. 21. 29. hath given his sons that *e.* into captivity
Deut. 23. 15. not deliver servant *e.* from his master
Judg. 3. 26. and Ehud *e.* while they tarried
29. there *e.* not a man of them, 1 *Sam.* 30. 17.
21. 17. must be an inheritance for them that be *e.*
1 *Sam.* 14. 41. Saul and Jonath. taken, but people *e.*
19. 10. David fled and *e.* that night, 12, 18.
2 *Sam.* 1. 3. out of the camp of Israel am I *e.*
4. 6. and Rachab and Baanah his brother *e.*
1 *Kings* 20. 20. Ben-hadad the king *e.* on an horse
2 *Kings* 19. 30. the remnant that is *e.* of Judah shall take root and bear fruit, *Isa.* 37. 31.
1 *Chron.* 4. 43. they smote the rest that were *e.*
2 *Chron.* 16. 7. therefore is the host of Syria *e.*
30. 6. and he will return to you that are *e.*
Ezra 9. 15. for we remain yet *e.* as it is this day
Neh. 1. 2. I asked concerning the Jews that had *e.*
Job 1. 15. I only am *e.* to tell thee, 16, 17, 19.
19. 20. and I am *e.* with the skin of my teeth
Psal. 124. 7. our soul is *e.* as a bird out of the snare of the fowlers, the snare is broken and we are *e.*
Isa. 4. 2. shall be comely for them that are *e.* of Israel
10. 20. the remnant and such as are *e.* of Jacob
45. 20. draw near, ye that are *e.* of the nations
Jer. 41. 15. but Ishmael the son of Nethaniah *e.*
51. 50. ye that have *e.* remember the Lord afar off
Lam. 2. 22. so that none in that day *e.* nor remained
Ezek. 24. 27. thy mouth be opened to him that is *e.*
33. 21. that one that had *e.* came unto me, 22.
John 10. 39. but he *e.* out of their hands
Acts 27. 44. so it came to pass, they *e.* all safe to land
28. 4. though he *e.* the sea, yet vengeance suffers not
2 *Cor.* 11. 33. I was let down and *e.* his hands
Heb. 11. 34. through faith *e.* the edge of the sword
12. 25. if they *e.* not who refused him that spake
2 *Pet.* 1. 4. *e.* the corruption that is in the world
2. 18. allure thro' lusts of flesh those that were cleane.
20. after they have *e.* the pollutions of the world
ESCAPER.
2 *Kings* 9. † 15. let no *e.* go out of the city to tell
ESCAPETH.
1 *Kings* 19. 17. him that *e.* the sword of Hazael shall Jehu slay; him that *e.* Jehu shall Elisha slay
Isa. 15. 9. bring lions upon him that *e.* of Moab
Jer. 48. 19. ask her that *e.* and say, what is done?
Ezek. 24. 26. he that *e.* in that day shall come to thee
Amos 9. 1. he that *e.* of them shall not be delivered
ESCAPING.
2 *Kings* 19. † 30. the *e.* of the house of Judah that remaineth shall again take root, *Isa.* 37. † 31.
2 *Chr.* 20. † 24. they were dead, there was not an *e.*
Ezra 9. 14. so that there should be no remnant nor *e.*
Isa. 4. † 2. the branch be comely for the *e.* of Isr.
37. † 32. the *e.* shall go forth out of mount Zion
Jer. 25. † 35. and *e.* from the principal of the flock
ESCHEW.
1 *Pet.* 3. 11. let him *e.* evil and do good, seek peace
ESCHEWED, ETH.
Job 1. 1. one that feared God and *e.* evil, 8. | 2. 3.
ESPECIALLY *and* SPECIALLY.
Deut. 4. 10. *s.* the day thou stoodest before the Lord
Psal. 31. 11. a reproach *e.* among my neighbours
Acts 25. 26. and *s.* before thee, O king Agrippa
26. 3. *e.* because I know thee to be expert
Gal. 6. 10. *e.* to them of the household of faith
1 *Tim.* 4. 10. the Saviour *s.* of those that believe
5. 8. provide, *s.* for them of his own house
17. *e.* they who labour in word and doctrine
2 *Tim.* 4. 13. the cloke bring, but *e.* the parchments
Tit. 1. 10. deceivers, *s.* they of the circumcision
Philem. 16. above a servant, brother beloved, *s.* to me
ESPY.
Josh. 14. 7. Moses sent me to *e.* out the land
Jer. 48. 19. stand by way, and *e.* ask him that fleeth
ESPIED.
Gen. 42. 27. he *e.* his money in his sack's mouth
Ezek. 20. 6. into a land that I had *e.* for them
See SPY, SPIED.
ESPOUSALS.
Cant. 3. 11. his mother crowned him in day of his *e.*
Jer. 2. 2. I remember thee, the love of thine *e.*
ESPOUSED.
Espousing, *or* betrothing, *was a promise of marriage made by two persons each to other, at such a distance of time afterwards. This was done either by a formal writing or contract in presence of witnesses. Or without writing, by the man's giving a piece of silver to the bride before witnesses, and saying to her,* Receive this piece of silver as a pledge that at such a time you shall become my spouse. *After the marriage was thus contracted, the young people had the liberty of seeing each other, which was not allowed them before.*
We read, Mat. 1. 18. *that* when *Mary* was espoused to *Joseph,* before they came together, she was found with child of the Holy Ghost. *God would have his son to be born of a betrothed virgin,* (1) *That he might not be under the reproach of illegitimacy.* (2) *That his mother might not be subjected to the punishment of the judicial law.* (3) *That by the genealogy of* Joseph, *of whose kindred* Mary *was, her pedigree might also be shewed.* (4) *That* Christ *might have a guardian in his infancy.*
The union of believers with Christ *is expressed under the notion of a marriage,* Isa. 54. 5. *Hence the apostle tells the* Corinthians, I have espoused you to one husband, that I may present you a chaste virgin to *Christ,* 2 Cor. 11. 2. *The* husband *is* Christ, *Mat.* 25. 6. *The* virgin bride *are all true believers. The contract, or marriage-covenant, is made in this life, in making of which faithful ministers are instrumental;* I have espoused you, *says the apostle. But the marriage is celebrated in the other world, where believers have uninterrupted communion with God in Christ, Rev.* 19. 7.
2 *Sam.* 3. 14. deliver me my wife Michal whom I *e.*
Mat. 1. 18. when his mother Mary was *e.* to Joseph
Luke 1. 27. to a virgin *e.* to a man named Joseph
2. 5. Joseph went to be taxed with Mary his *e.* wife
2 *Cor.* 11. 2. for I have *e.* you to one husband
ESTABLISH *and* STABLISH
Signifies, [1] *To fix, or settle,* 1 Kings 9. 5. [2] *To confirm,* Num. 30. 13. Rom. 1. 11. [3] *To perform, or make good,* Psal. 119. 38. [4] *To ordain, or appoint,* Hab. 1. 12. [5] *To accomplish and bring to a good issue,* Prov. 20. 18. [6] *To set up one thing in the room of another.* Rom. 10. 3. [7] *To ratify,* Heb. 10. 9.
The Lord shall establish thee an holy people unto himself, *Deut.* 28. 9. *He shall confirm and establish his covenant with thee, by which he separated thee to himself as an holy and peculiar people, and shall publicly own thee for such.*
Establish thou the work of our hands, *Psal.* 90. 17. *that is, Direct us in, and give success to, all our undertakings and endeavours: carry them on, by thy continual aid and blessing, unto perfection.*
Gen. 6. 18. but with thee will I *e.* my covenant, 9. 9. | 17. 7. *Lev.* 26. 9. *Ezek.* 16. 62.
17. 19. I will *e.* my covenant with him, 21.
Num. 30. 13. every vow, her husband may *e.* it
Deut. 8. 18. that he may *e.* his covenant he sware
28. 9. the L. shall *e.* thee an holy people to himself
29. 13. that he may *e.* thee to-day for a people
1 *Sam.* 1. 23. only the L. *e.* his word, 2 *Sam.* 7. 25.
2 *Sam.* 7. 12. I will set up thy seed after thee, I will *e.* his kingdom, 13. 1 *Chr.* 17. 11. | 22. 10. | 28. 7.
1 *Kings* 7. † 21. he set up and called the name of the right pillar, he shall *e.* 2 *Chron.* 3. † 17.
9. 5. I will *e.* the throne of thy kingdom
15. 4. to set up his son after him, and to *e.* Jerusalem
1 *Chron.* 17. 12. and I will *s.* his throne for ever
18. 3. as he went to *s.* his dominion by Euphrates
29. † 18. O Lord God, *s.* their heart unto thee
2 *Chron.* 7. 18. then will I *s.* throne of thy kingdom
9. 8. because God loved Israel to *e.* them for ever
Esth. 9. 21. to *s.* among them the days of Purim
Job 36. 7. yea he doth *e.* them for ever, are exalted
Psal. 7. 9. but *e.* the just ‖ 48. 8. God will *e.* it
10. † 17. thou wilt *e.* the heart of the humble
87. 5. and the Highest himself shall *e.* her
89. 2. thy faithfulness shalt thou *e.* in the heavens
4. thy seed will I *e.* for ever, and build thy throne

Psal. 90. 17. *e.* thou the work of our hands, *e.* thou it
99. 4. thou dost *e.* equity, thou executest judgment
119. 38. *s.* thy word to thy servant, who is devoted
Prov. 15. 25. he will *e.* the border of the widow
Isa. 9. 7. to *e.* it with judgment and with justice
49. 8. give thee for a covenant to *e.* the earth
62. 7. till he *e.* and make Jerusalem a praise
Jer. 33. 2. the lord that formed it, to *e.* it
Ezek. 16. 60. I will *e.* an everlasting covenant
Dan. 6. 7. have consulted to *e.* a royal statute
8. O king, *e.* the decree, and sign the writing
11. 14. shall exalt themselves to *e.* the vision
Amos 5. 15. love the good, and *e.* judgment in the gate
Rom. 3. 31. do we make void? yea, we *e.* the law
10. 3. going about to *e.* their own righteousness
16. 25. now to him that is of power to *s.* you
1 *Thess.* 3. 2. we sent Timothy our brother to *e.* you
13. to the end he may *s.* your hearts unblameable
2 *Thess.* 2. 17. *s.* you in every good word and work
3. 3. the Lord shall *s.* you, and keep you from evil
Heb. 10. 9. takes away first, that he may *e.* second
Jam. 5. 8. be ye also patient, *s.* your hearts
1 *Pet.* 5. 10. the God of all grace *s.* settle you

ESTABLISHED, STABLISHED.

Gen. 9. 17. the token of the covenant which I have *e.*
41. 32. it is because the thing is *e.* by God
Exod. 6. 4. I have also *e.* my covenant with them
15. 17. in the sanctuary which thy hands have *e.*
Deut. 32. 6. hath he not made thee, and *e.* thee?
1 *Sam.* 3. 20. Samuel was *e.* a prophet of the Lord
13. 13. now would the Lord have *e.* thy kingdom
20. 31. thou shalt not be *e.* nor thy kingdom
2 *Sam.* 5. 12. David perceived that the L. had *e.* him
7. 26. Lord is God over Israel, let the house of thy servant David be *e.* for ever, 1 *Chron.* 17. 24.
1 *Kings* 2. 12. and his kingdom was *e.* greatly
24. as the Lord liveth, which hath *e.* me
46. the kingdom was *e.* in the hand of Solomon
1 *Chron.* 17. 23. let the thing be *e.* for ever, 24.
2 *Chron.* 1. 9. now, O Lord God, let thy promise be *e.*
12. 1. when Rehoboam had *e.* the kingdom
17. 5 the Lord *s.* the kingdom in his hand
25. 3. when the kingdom was *e.* to him, he slew
27. † 6. Jotham *e.* his ways before the Lord
30. 5. so they *e.* a decree to keep the passover
Job 21. 8. their seed is *e.* in their sight with them
38. † 10. when I *e.* my decree upon it, and set bars
Psal. 24. 2. for he hath *e.* it upon the floods
37. † 23. the steps of a good man are *e.* by the Lord
40. 2. he set my feet on a rock, and *e.* my goings
78. 5. he *e.* a testimony in Jacob, and law in Israel
69. the earth he hath *e.* for ever, 119. 90.
93. 1. the world is *e.* ‖ 2. thy throne is *e.* of old
101. † 7. he that telleth lies shall not be *e.*
111. † 8. his commandments are *s.* for ever
112. 8. his heart is *e.* he shall not be afraid
140. 11. let not an evil speaker be *e.* in the earth
148. 6. he hath *s.* the waters for ever and ever
Prov. 3. 19. Lord, by understand. hath *e.* the heavens
4. 26. ponder thy paths, and let all thy ways be *e.*
8. 28. when he *e.* the clouds above, when he
12. 3. man shall not be *e.* by wickedness
15. 22. in multitude of counsellors they are *e.*
16. 12. for the throne is *e.* by righteousness
20. 18. every purpose is *e.* by counsel, with advice
24. 3. and by understanding is an house *e.*
30. 4. who hath *e.* all the ends of the earth
Isa. 7. 9. if ye will not believe, ye shall not be *e.*
16. 5. and in mercy shall the throne be *e.*
45. 18. God that made the earth, he hath *e.* it
Jer. 10. 12. he *e.* the world by his wisdom, 51. 15.
Dan. 4. 36. I was *e.* in my kingdom, and majesty
Hab. 1. 12. O mighty God, thou *e.* them for correct.
Mat. 18. 16. mouth of two witnesses every word be *e.*
Acts 16. 5. so were the churches *e.* in the faith
Rom. 1. 11. impart some gift, to end you may be *e.*
Col. 2. 7. built up in him, and *s.* in the faith
Heb. 8. 6. which was *e.* upon better promises
13. 9. it is good that the heart be *e.* with grace
2 *Pet.* 1. 12. though ye be *e.* in the present truth

Shall be ESTABLISHED.

Lev. 25. 30. house *shall be e.* for ever, 2 *Sam.* 7. 16.
Deut. 19. 15. at the mouth of two or three witnesses *shall* the matter *be e.* 2 *Cor.* 13. 1.
1 *Sam.* 24. 20. the kingdom *shall be e.* in thine hand
2 *Sam.* 7. 16. thine house, thy kingdom, and thy throne, *shall be e.* for ever, 1 *Kings* 2. 45.
1 *Chr.* 17. 14. I will settle him in my kingdom, and his throne *shall be e.* for evermore, *Psal.* 89. 37.
2 *Chr.* 20. 20. believe in Lord God, so *shall* ye *be e.*
Job 22. 28. thou shalt decree, and it *shall be e.*
Psal. 89. 21. with whom my hand *shall be e.*
96. 10. the world *shall be e.* before thee
102. 28. and their seed *shall be e.* before thee
Prov. 12. 19. the lip of truth *shall be e.* for ever
16. 3. commit thy works, and thy thoughts *shall be e.*
25. 5. his throne *shall be e.* for ever, 29. 14.
Isa. 2. 2. mountain of the Lord's house *shall be e.*
16. 5. and in mercy *shall* the throne *be e.*
32. † 8. and by liberal things *shall* he *be e.*
54. 14. in righteousness *shalt* thou *be e.*
Jer. 30. 20. their congregation *shall be e.* before me
Mic. 4. 1. mountain of house of the Lord *shall be e.*
Zech. 5. 11. to build it an house, and it *shall be e.*

ESTABLISHETH.

Num. 30. 14. he *e.* all her vows, or all her bonds
Prov. 29. 4. the king by judgment *e.* the land
Dan. 6. 15. no decree the king *e.* may be changed
Hab. 2. 12. woe to him that *e.* a city by iniquity
2 *Cor.* 1. 21. now he which *e.* us with you in Christ

ESTABLISHMENT.

2 *Chron.* 32. 1. after the *e.* Sennacherib came
Psal. 89. † 14. justice and judgment are the *e.* of thy throne, mercy and truth before thee, 97. † 2.

ESTATE, STATE.

Gen. 43. 7. the man asked us straitly of our *s.*
1 *Chron.* 17. 17. to the *e.* of a man of high degree
2 *Chron.* 24. 13. they set the house of God in his *s.*
Esth. 1. 7. according to the *s.* of the king
19. let the king give her royal *e.* to another
2. 18. gave gifts according to the *s.* of the king
Job 22. † 20. whereas our *e.* is not cut down
Psal. 39. 5. every man at his best *s.* altogether vanity
136. 23. who remembered us in our low *e.*
Prov. 27. 23. be diligent to know the *s.* of thy flocks
28. 2. by a man of knowledge *s.* shall be prolonged
Eccl. 1. 16. saying, lo, I am come to great *e.*
3. 18. concerning the *e.* of the sons of men
Isa. 22. 19. from thy *s.* shall he pull thee down
Ezek. 16. 55. Samaria shall return to her former *e.*
Dan. 11. 7. one shall stand up in his *e.* 21.
20. then shall stand up in his *e.* a raiser of taxes
38. but in his *e.* shall he honour the God of forces
Mat. 12. 45. seven other spirits enter, the last *s.* of that man is worse than the first, *Luke* 11. 26.
Luke 1. 48. hath regarded low *e.* of his handmaiden
Acts 22. 5. all *e.* of the elders doth bear witness
Rom. 12. 16. but condescend to men of low *e.*
Phil. 2. 19. I may be of comfort when I know your *s.*
20. like-minded, will naturally care for your *s.*
4. 11. learned in whatsoever *s.* I am to be content
Col. 4. 7. all my *s.* shall Tychicus declare to you
8. whom I sent, that he might know your *e.*
Jude 6. the angels which kept not their first *e.*

ESTATES.

Ezek. 36. 11. I will settle you after your old *e.*
Mark 6. 21. Herod made a supper to his chief *e.*

ESTEEM.

Job 36. 19. will he *e.* thy riches? no not gold
Psal. 119. 128. I *e.* all thy precepts to be right
Isa. 53. 4. we did *e.* him smitten of God, afflicted
Phil. 2. 3. let each *e.* other better than themselves
1 *Thess.* 5. 13. to *e.* them highly for their work's sake
1 *Pet.* 2. † 17. *e.* all men, love the brotherhood

ESTEEMED.

Deut. 32. 15. and lightly *e.* the rock of his salvation
1 *Sam.* 2. 30. they that despise me shall be lightly *e.*
18. 23. seeing I am a poor man and lightly *e.*
Job 23. 12. I have *e.* the words of his mouth more
Prov. 17. 28. shutteth his lips is *e.* a man of understanding
Isa. 29. 16. your turning shall be *e.* as the potters' clay
17. the fruitful field shall be *e.* as a forest
53. 3. he was despised, and we *e.* him not
Lam. 4. 2. how are they *e.* as earthen pitchers
Luke 16. 15. highly *e.* among men, abominable to G.
1 *Cor.* 6. 4. set them to judge who are least *e.*

ESTEEMETH.

Job 41. 27. he *e.* iron as straw, brass as rotten wood
Rom. 14. 5. one *e.* one day above another: another *e.* every day alike
14. but to him that *e.* any thing to be unclean

ESTEEMING.

Heb. 11. 26. *e.* the reproach of Christ greater riches

ESTIMATE.

Lev. 27. 14. the priest shall *e.* it, whether it be good or bad, as the priest shall *e.* it, so shall it stand

ESTIMATION.

Lev. 5. 15. bring a ram with thy *e.* by shekels of silver
27. 2. the persons shall be for the Lord, by thy *e.*
3. thy *e.* shall be of the male from 20 years, 5.
This word found often in this Chapter.
Num. 18. 16. from a month old, according to thy *e.*
2 *Kings* 12. † 4. the money of the souls of his *e.*

ESTIMATIONS.

Lev. 27. 25. all thy *e.* according to the shekel

ESTRANGED.

Job 19. 13. mine acquaintance are *e.* from me
Psal. 58. 3. the wicked are *e.* from the womb
78. 30. they were not *e.* from their lust
Jer. 19. 4. because they have *e.* this place, and burnt
Ezek. 14. 5. because they are all *e.* from me thro' idols

ETERNAL.

The words eternal, everlasting, for ever, *are sometimes taken for a long time, and are not always to be understood strictly; for example, it is said,* Gen. 17. 8. I will give to thee and to thy seed the land of *Canaan,* for an *everlasting* possession. *And in* chap. 13. 15. I will give it to thee, and to thy seed for ever; *that is, for a long space of time. And in* Gen. 49. 26. *we find* everlasting hills, *so called to denote their antiquity, stability, and duration; and this expression is used to shew the long continuance and durableness of* Joseph's *blessing. God promises a throne to* David, *an eternal kingdom, a posterity that will never be extinguished; that is, that his and his sons' empire will be of a very long duration,* 2 Sam. 7. 16. 1 Chron. 17. 14. *that it will be even eternal, if hereby the kingdom of the* Messiah *be understood. Thus,* Thou shalt be our guide from this time forth even for ever, *that is, during our whole life. And in many other places of Scripture, and in particular, when the word* for ever *is applied to the* Jewish *rites and privileges, it commonly signifies no more than during the standing of that commonwealth, or until the coming of the* Messiah, *Exod.* 12. 14, 17. *Num.* 10. 8.
Eternity, *when God is the subject in question, always denotes a real eternity.* Exod. 15. 18. The Lord shall reign for ever and ever. *Deut.* 32. 40. I lift up my hand to heaven, and say, I live for ever. *Deut.* 33. 27. The eternal God is thy refuge. *The blessed will enjoy eternal life and happiness, and reprobates be cast into eternal fire; the happiness of the one, and misery of the other, will never have an end,* Mat. 25. 46. *The Son of God is eternal in the highest sense, without beginning, without end,* 1 Tim. 1. 17. *He is called* a priest for ever after the order of *Melchizedek,* Psal. 110. 4. *His gospel,* the everlasting gospel. *Rev.* 14. 6. *The same gospel that was from the beginning, and besides which, there neither is, nor ever shall be, any other doctrine of salvation revealed, while the world endureth. The redemption which he has procured for us, is an* eternal redemption, *Heb.* 9. 12. *Its virtue is of perpetual continuance; such as are redeemed from the guilt and punishment of sin, are so for ever. The Covenant, or New Testament, which he confirmed by his blood,* is an everlasting covenant, *Heb.* 13. 20. *It is a covenant never to be changed, as the former was: Everlasting life is promised in it; and it is of eternal efficacy. The glory and reward which he hath merited for us, is an* eternal weight of glory, 2 *Cor.* 4. 17. Everlasting habitations, *or* tents, *Luke* 16. 9. *are the habitations appointed by God in heaven for the predestinated, those chosen to salvation* through sanctification of the Spirit, and belief of the truth.
Deut. 33. 27. the *e.* G. is thy refuge, and underneath
Isa. 60. 15. I will make thee an *e.* excellency
Mark 3. 29. but is in danger of *e.* damnation
Rom. 1. 20. that are made, even his *e.* power and
2 *Cor.* 4. 17. worketh for us an *e.* weight of glory
18. but the things which are not seen are *e.*
5. 1. we have an house *e.* in the heavens
Eph. 3. 11. according to the *e.* purpose in Christ
1 *Tim.* 1. 17. unto the King *e.* be honour and glory
2 *Tim.* 2. 10. they may obtain salvation with *e.* glory
Heb. 5. 9. he became the author of *e.* salvation
6. 2. the doctrine of baptisms, and of *e.* judgment
9. 12. having obtained *e.* redemption for us
14. who thro' the *e.* Spirit offered himself to God
15. might receive the promise of *e.* inheritance
1 *Pet.* 5. 10. G. called us unto his *e.* glory by Ch. Je.
Jude 7. an example, suffering the vengeance of *e.* fire

ETERNAL *life.*

Mat. 19. 16. what shall I do that I may have *e. life?*
25. 46. but the righteous shall go into *life e.*
Mark 10. 17. good Master, what shall I do, that I may inherit *e. life? Luke* 10. 25. | 18. 18.
30. he shall receive in the world to come *e. life*
John 3. 15. believeth in him should have *e. life*
4. 36. and gathereth fruit unto *life e.*
5. 39. search scriptures, for in them ye have *e. life*
6. 54. whoso drinketh my blood hath *e. life*
68. to whom shall we go? thou hast words of *e. life*
10. 28. I give unto my sheep *e. life* never perish
12. 25. that hateth his life, shall keep it to *e. life*
17. 2. he should give *e. life* to as many as given him
3. this is *life e.* that they might know thee and Son
Acts 13. 48. many as were ordained to *e. life* believed
Rom. 2. 7. to them who seek for glory *e. life*
5. 21. even so might grace reign to *e. life* by Jesus
6. 23. but the gift of G. is *e. life* thro' Jesus Christ
1 *Tim.* 6. 12. O man of God, lay hold on *e. life,* 19.
Tit. 1. 2. in hope of *e. life,* which God promised
3. 7. be made heirs according to the hope of *e. life*
1 *John* 1. 2. *e. life* which was with the Father
2. 25. this is the promise he promised, even *e. life*
3. 15. no murderer hath *e. life* abiding in him
5. 11. the record that God hath given to us *e. life*
13. that ye may know that ye have *e. life*
20. this is the true God, and *e. life*
Jude 21. looking for the mercy of Lord unto *e. life*

ETERNITY.

1 *Sam.* 15. † 29. also the *e.* of Israel will not lie
Isa. 57. 15. the high and lofty One that inhabiteth *e.*
Jer. 10. † 10. the Lord is the true God, King of *e.*
Mic. 5. † 2. whose goings have been from days of *e.*

EVANGELIST.

Acts 21. 8. we entered into the house of Philip the
2 *Tim.* 4. 5. but watch thou, do the work of an *e.*

EVANGELISTS.

Eph. 4. 11. he gave some apostles and some *e.*

EVEN.

Gen. 19. 1. there came two angels to Sodom at *e.*
Exod. 12. 18. on fourteenth day of the month at *e.*
16. 6. Moses said, at *e.* then shall ye know that Lord
12. at *e.* eat flesh ‖ 13. at *e.* the quails came
18. 14. the people stand by thee from morning to *e.*
30. 8. and when Aaron lighteth the lamps at *e.*
Lev. 11. 24. shall be unclean until *e.* 25, 27, 28, 31, 39, 40. | 14. 46. | 15. 5, 6, 7, *&c.* | 17. 15. | 22. 6. | *Num.* 19. 7, 8, 10, 21, 22.
23. 5. the fourteenth day of first month, at *e.* is the Lord's passover, *Num.* 9. 3. *Deut.* 16. 6.
Num. 9. 11. the 14th day of the second month at *e.*
21. when the cloud abode from *e.* to morning
19. 19. bathe himself in water, shall be clean at *e.*
Deut. 28. 67. thou shalt say, would God it were *e.*
Judg. 20. 23. they wept before the Lord till *e.*
26. they wept and fasted till *e.* 2 *Sam.* 1. 12.
21. 2. the people abode till *e.* before God, and wept
Ruth 2. 17. so Ruth gleaned in the field until *e.*
1 *Sam.* 20. 5. I may hide myself unto third day at *e.*
1 *Kings* 22. 35. Ahab died at *e.* 2 *Chron.* 18. 34.
1 *Chr.* 23. 30. praise the Lord every morning and *e.*
Ezek. 12. 4. thou shalt go forth at *e.* in their sight
7. in the *e.* I digged thro' the wall with my hand
24. 18. I spake to people, and at *e.* my wife died
Mat. 8. 16. when the *e.* was come, 20. 8. | 26. 20. | 27. 57. *Mark* 4. 35. | 6. 47. | 11. 19. | 15. 42.
Mark 1. 32. at *e.* they brought to him the diseased
13. 35. at *e.* at midnight, or at cock-crowing
John 6. 16. when *e.* was come, disciples went down

EVEN.

1 *Kings* 1. 48. sit on my throne, mine eyes *e.* seeing it
Prov. 22. 19. I made known to thee, *e.* to thee
Isa. 44. 28. *e.* saying to Jerusal. thou shalt be built
56. 5. *e.* to them will I give a name better than
Ezek. 20. 11. which if a man do, he shall *e.* live
21. 13. what if the sword contemn *e.* the rod
Rom. 8. 23. *e.* we ourselves groan within ourselves
1 *Cor.* 11. 14. doth not *e.* nature itself teach you?
15. 24. deliver. up the kingd. to God, *e.* the Father
2 *Cor.* 1. 3. blessed be God, *e.* the Father of our Ld.
10. 13. hath distributed a measure to reach *e.* to you
Phil. 2. 8. obedient to death, *e.* the death of the cross

EVEN.

Exod. 27. 5. that the net may be *e.* to midst of altar
Job 31. 6. let me be weighed in an *e.* balance
Psal. 26. 12. my foot standeth in an *e.* place
Cant. 4. 2. teeth like a flock of sheep that are *e.* shorn
Luke 19. 44. enemies shall lay thee *e.* with the ground

EVENING.

Gen. 8. 11. and the dove came in to him in the *e.*
30. 16. Jacob came out of the field in the *e.*
Exod. 12. 6. assembly of Israel shall kill it in the *e.*
Deut. 23. 11. but when *e.* cometh, shall wash hims.
Josh. 10. 26. they were hanging on the trees until *e.*
Judg. 19. 9. now the day draweth towards *e.*
1 *Sam.* 14. 24. cursed be the man that eateth till *e.*

1 *Sam.* 30. 17. David smote them to *e.* of next day
Esth. 2. 14. in the *e.* she went, and on the morrow
Job 7. † 4. when shall I rise, and the *e.* be measured?
Psal. 59. 6. they return at *e.* they make a noise
14. at *e.* let them return and make a noise
90. 6. in the *e.* it is cut down and withereth
104. 23. man goeth forth to his labour until the *e.*
Prov. 7. 9. he went the way to her house in the *e.*
Eccl. 11. 6. in the *e.* withhold not thine hand
Jer. 6. 4. the shadows of the *e.* are stretched out
Ezek. 33. 22. the hand of Lord was on me in the *e.*
46. 2. but the gate shall not be shut till the *e.*
Zeph. 2. 7. in Ashkelon shall they lie down in the *e.*
Mat. 14. 23. when *e.* was come, he was there alone
16. 2. when it is *e.* ye say, it will be fair weather
Mark 14. 17. in the *e.* he cometh with the twelve
Luke 24. 29. abide with us, for it is towards *e.*
John 20. 19. the same day at *e.* came Jesus and stood

EVENING, with *morning.*

Gen. 1. 5. the *e.* and *morning* were the first day
8. the second day || 13. third day || 19. fourth day
23. the fifth day || 31. were the sixth day
Exod. 18. 13. people stood by Moses from *morn.* to *e.*
27. 21. shall order it from *e.* to *morn.* *Lev.* 24. 3.
1 *Sam.* 17. 16. Philistine drew near *morning* and *e.*
1 *Kings* 17. 6. brought him bread *morning* and *e.*
1 *Chr.* 16. 40. to offer burnt-offerings *morning* and *e.* 2 *Chr.* 2. 4. | 13. 11. | 31. 3. *Ezra* 3. 3.
Job 4. 20. they are destroyed from *morning* to *e.*
Psal. 30. † 5. weeping in the *e.* joy in the *morning*
55. 17. *e.* and *morning*, and at noon, will I pray
65. 8. the out-goings of *morning* and *e.* to rejoice
Dan. 8. † 14. to 2300 *e. morning* sanctuary cleans.
26. the vision of the *e.* and *morning* is true
Acts 28. 23. persuading them from *morning* to *e.*

EVENING, *Adjective.*

1 *Kings* 18. 29. they prophesied till the *e.* sacrifice
36. at the time of the offering of the *e.* sacrifice
2 *Kings* 16. 15. on great altar burn *e.* meat-offering
Ezra 9. 4. I sat astonished until the *e.* sacrifice
5. at *e.* sacrifice I arose from my heaviness
Psal. 141. 2. let my prayer be as the *e.* sacrifice
Dan. 9. 21. touched me about the time of *e.* oblation
Hab. 1. 8. and are more fierce than the *e.* wolves
Zeph. 3. 3. her judges are *e.* wolves, they gnaw not
Zech. 14. 7. come to pass, that at *e.* time shall be light

EVENINGS.

Exod. 12. † 6. shall kill it between the two *e.*
Num. 9. † 3. keep the passover between the two *e.*
28. † 4. offer the other lamb between the two *e.*
Jer. 5. 6. and a wolf of the *e.* shall spoil them

EVENT.

Eccl. 2. 14. one *e.* happeneth to them all, 9. 3.
9. 2. there is one *e.* to the righteous and wicked

EVEN-TIDE, *or* EVENING-TIDE.

Gen. 24. 63. Isaac went out to meditate at the *e.*
Josh. 7. 6. Joshua fell on his face till the *e.*
8. 29. and the king of Ai he hanged on a tree till *e.*
2 *Sam.* 11. 2. in an *e.* David walked on the top
Isa. 17. 14. behold, at *e.* trouble, and before
Mark 11. 11. now the *e.* was come, Jesus went out
Acts 4. 3. they put them in hold, for it was now *e.*

EVER.

Lev. 6. 13. the fire shall *e.* be burning on the altar
Num. 22. 30. hast ridden on, *e.* since I was thine
Deut. 4. 33. did *e.* people hear the voice of God?
19. 9. to love God, and to walk *e.* in his ways
Judg. 11. 25. did *e.* fight against Israel?
1 *Kings* 5. 1. for Hiram was *e.* a lover of David
Job 4. 7. remember, who *e.* perished, being innocent?
Ps. 5. 11. those that trust, let them *e.* shout for joy
25. 6. thy tender mercies have been *e.* of old
15. mine eyes are *e.* towards Lord, shall pluck
37. 26. he is *e.* merciful, and lendeth, seed blessed
51. 3. my transgressions and my sin is *e.* before me
90. 2. or *e.* thou hadst formed earth, *Prov.* 8. 23.
111. 5. he will *e.* be mindful of his covenant
119. 98. thy commandments are *e.* with me
Cant. 6. 12. or *e.* I was aware, my soul made me like
Isa. 28. 28. because he will not *e.* be threshing it
33. 20. not one of the stakes shall *e.* be removed
Dan. 6. 24. or *e.* they came at the bottom of the den
Joel 2. 2. hath not been *e.* the like nor any more
Mat. 24. 21. such as was not, no, nor *e.* shall be
Mark 15. 8. to desire him to do as he had *e.* done
Luke 15. 31. and he said, son, thou art *e.* with me
John 4. 29. a man told me all things that *e.* I did, 39.
8. 35. servant abideth not, but the Son abideth *e.*
10. 8. all that *e.* came before me are thieves
18. 20. I *e.* taught in the synagogue and temple
Acts 23. 15. we, or *e.* he come, are ready to kill him
Eph. 5. 29. for no man *e.* yet hated his own flesh
1 *Thess.* 4. 17. and so shall we *e.* be with the Lord
5. 15. but *e.* follow that which is good
2 *Tim.* 3. 7. *e.* learning, and never able to come
Heb. 7. 24. but this man, because he continueth *e.*
25. seeing *e.* liveth to make intercession for them
Jude 25. to God our Saviour be glory, now and *e.*
See ENDURETH.

For EVER.

See *Signification* on ETERNAL.

Gen. 13. 15. to thee will I give it and thy seed *for e.*
43. 9. then let me bear the blame *for e.* 44. 32.
Exod. 3. 15. this is my name *for e.* and my memorial
12. 14. keep it a feast by an ordinance *for e.* 17.
24. an ordinance to thee, and to thy sons *for e.*
14. 13. ye shall see them again no more *for e.*
19. 9. that the people may believe thee *for e.*
21. 6. bore his ear, and he shall serve him *for e.*
31. 17. it is a sign between me and Israel *for e.*
32. 13. give this land, and they shall inherit it *for e.*
Lev. 25. 23. the land shall not be sold *for e.* is mine
30. the house shall be established *for e.* to him
46. they shall be your bondmen *for e.*
Num. 10. 8. for an ordinance *for e.* 15. 15. | 18. 8.
18. 19. it is a covenant of salt *for e.* unto thee
24. 20. he said, Amalek shall perish *for e.*
24. shall afflict Eber, he also shall perish *for e.*
Deut. 4. 40. the earth which God giveth thee *for e.*
5. 29. it might be well with them *for e.* 12. 28.
13. 16. it shall be an heap *for e.* not built again
15. 17. take an awl, he shall be thy servant *for e.*

Deut. 18. 5. God hath chosen him and his sons *for e.*
23. 6. thou shalt not seek their peace *for e.*
28. 46. they shall be upon thee for a sign *for e.*
29. 29. those things revealed belong to us *for e.*
Josh. 4. 7. these stones shall be for a memorial *for e.*
24. that ye might fear the Lord your God *for e.*
8. 28. Joshua burnt Ai, and made it an heap *for e.*
14. 9. the land shall be thine inheritance *for e.*
1 *Sam.* 1. 22. appear before the Lord and abide *for e.*
2. 30. I said, thy house should walk before me *for e.*
32. there shall not be an old man in house *for e.*
35. he shall walk before mine Anointed *for e.*
3. 13. that I will judge his house *for e.* for iniquity
14. iniquity of Eli's house shall not be purged *f. e.*
20. 15. thou shalt not cut off thy kindness *for e.*
23. the Lord be between thee and me *for e.* 42.
27. 12. therefore he shall be my servant *for e.*
28. 2. I will make thee keeper of mine head *for e.*
2 *Sam.* 2. 26. Abner said, shall the sword devour *f. e.?*
3. 28. I and my kingd. are guiltless before L. *for e.*
7. 24. thou hast confirmed Israel to thee *for e.*
26. and let thy name be magnified *for e.*
29. that his house may continue *for e.* before thee
1 *Kings* 8. 13. settled place for thee to abide in *for e.*
9. 3. this house built, to put my name there *for e.*
10. 9. because the Lord loved Israel *for e.* therefore
11. 39. I will afflict David's seed, but not *for e.*
12. 7. they will be thy servants *for e.* 2 *Chr.* 10. 7.
2 *Kings* 5. 27. leprosy cleave to thee and seed *for e.*
1 *Chron.* 17. 22. didst thou make thine own *for e.*
23. 13. he and sons *for e.* to burn incense before L.
28. 9. if forsake him, he will cast thee off *for e.*
29. 18. O Lord God of Israel, keep this *for e.*
2 *Chron.* 7. 16. that my name may be there *for e.*
21. 7. he promised to give a light to his sons *for e.*
30. 8. his sanctuary which he hath sanctified *for e.*
33. 4. in Jerusalem shall my name be *for e.*
Neh. 13. 1. not come into congregation of God *for e.*
Job 4. 20. they perish *for e.* without any regarding it
14. 20. thou prevailest *for e.* ag. him, and he passeth
19. 24. graven with iron pen in the rock *for e.*
20. 7. yet he shall perish *for e.* like his own dung
23. 7. so should I be delivered *for e.* from my judge
36. 7. yea, he doth establish them *for e.*
Psal. 9. 7. but the Lord shall endure *for e.*
18. the expectation of poor shall not perish *for e.*
12. 7. O Lord, thou shalt preserve them *for e.*
13. 1. how long wilt thou forget me, O L. *for e.?*
19. 9. the fear of the Lord is clean, enduring *for e.*
21. 6. thou hast made him most blessed *for e.*
23. 6. I will dwell in the house of the Lord *for e.*
28. 9. feed them also, and lift them up *for e.*
29. 10. yea, the Lord sitteth king *for e.*
30. 12. I will give thanks to thee *for e.* 79. 13.
33. 11. the counsel of the Lord standeth *for e.*
37. 18. and their inheritance shall be *for e.*
28. and his saints are preserved *for e.*
29. the righteous shall dwell in the land *for e.*
41. 12. thou settest me before thy face *for e.*
44. 8. and we praise thy name *for e.* Selah
23. awake, O Lord, arise, cast us not off *for e.*
45. 2. therefore God hath blessed thee *for e.*
49. 8. for the redemption of their soul ceaseth *for e.*
11. thought is, that their houses continue *for e.*
52. 5. God shall likewise destroy thee *for e.*
9. I will praise thee *for e.* I will wait on thy name
61. 4. I will abide in thy tabernacle *for e.*
7. he shall abide before God *for e.* prepare mercy
8. I will sing praise unto thy name *for e.*
66. 7. he ruleth by his power *for e.*
68. 16. yea, the Lord will dwell in it *for e.*
72. 17. his name shall endure *for e.* be continued
19. and blessed be his glorious name *for e.*
73. 26. but God is my strength and portion *for e.*
74. 1. O God, why hast thou cast us off *for e.?*
10. shall the enemy blaspheme thy name *for e.?*
19. forget not the congregation of thy poor *for e.*
75. 9. I will declare *for e.* I will sing praises to G.
77. 7. will L. cast off *for e.?* favourable no more?
8. is mercy clean gone *for e.?* doth promise fail?
79. 5. how long, Lord, wilt thou be angry? *for e.?*
81. 15. but their time should have endured *for e.*
83. 17. let them be confounded and troubled *for e.*
85. 5. wilt thou be angry with us *for e.?*
89. 1. I will sing of the mercies of the Lord *for e.*
2. I have said, mercy shall be built up *for e.*
29. his seed also will I make to endure *for e.* 36.
46. how long wilt thou hide thyself? *for e.?*
92. 7. it is that they shall be destroyed *for e.*
93. 5. holiness becometh thine house, O L. *for e.*
103. 9. neither will he keep his anger *for e.*
105. 8. he hath remembered his covenant *for e.*
110. 4. thou art a priest *for e.* after the order of Melchizedek, *Heb.* 5. 6. | 6. 20. | 7. 17, 21.
111. 9. he hath commanded his covenant *for e.*
112. 6. surely he shall not be moved *for e.*
119. 89. *for e.* O Lord, thy word is settled in heaven
125. 2. from henceforth even *for e.* 131. 3. *Isa.* 9. 7.
132. 14. this is my rest *for e.* here will I dwell
146. 6. the Lord who keepeth truth *for e.*
10. the Lord shall reign *for e.* even thy God
Prov. 27. 24. for riches are not *for e.*
Eccl. 2. 16. no remembr. of wise more than fool *for e.*
3. 14. whatsoever God doth, it shall be *for e.*
9. 6. nor have they more a portion *for e.* in any thing
Isa. 26. 4. trust ye in Lord *for e.* for in L. Jehovah
32. 17. of righteousn. quietness, and assurance *for e.*
34. 10. the smoke thereof shall go up *for e.*
17. shall possess it *for e.* from generation to gener.
40. 8. but the word of our God shall stand *for e.*
47. 7. and thou saidst, I shall be a lady *for e.*
51. 6. but my salvation shall be *for e.* and righteous.
8. but my righteousness shall be *for e.* and salvat.
57. 16. will not contend *for e.* nor be always wroth
59. 21. and my words shall not depart *for e.*
60. 21. thy people shall inherit the land *for e.*
64. 9. be not wroth nor remember iniquity *for e.*
65. 18. be glad and rejoice *for e.* in what I create
Jer. 3. 5. will he reserve his anger *for e.?*
12. I am merciful, I will not keep anger *for e.*
17. 4. ye kindled a fire which shall burn *for e.*
25. Jerusalem and this city shall remain *for e.*

Jer. 31. 40. it shall not be plucked up any more *for e.*
32. 39. give one heart that they may fear me *for e.*
35. 6. Jonadab said, ye shall drink no wine *for e.*
19. Jonadab shall not want a man before me *for e.*
49. 33. Hazor be for dragons and a desolation *for e.*
50. 39. shall be no more inhabited *for e.* 51. 26, 62.
Lam. 3. 31. for the Lord will not cast off *for e.*
5. 19. thou, O L. remainest *for e.* thy throne
20. wherefore dost thou forget us *for e.?*
Ezek. 37. 25. they and their childr. shall dwell *for e.* and my servant David shall be their prince *for e.*
43. 7. I will dwell in the midst of Israel *for e.* 9.
Dan. 2. 44. but his kingdom shall stand *for e.*
4. 34. I praised and honoured him that liveth *for e.*
6. 26. G. of Daniel, he is living G. and stedfast *for e.*
7. 18. saints of most High shall possess kingd. *for e.*
12. 7. and sware by him that liveth *for e.*
Hos. 2. 19. I will betroth thee unto me *for e.* in right.
Joel 3. 20. but Jud. shall dwell *for e.* and Jerusalem
Amos 1. 11. Edom cast off pity and kept wrath *for e.*
Obad. 10. Edom, thou shalt be cut off *for e.*
Jonah 2. 6. earth with her bars was about me *for e.*
Mic. 2. 9. ye have taken away my glory *for e.*
4. 7. and the Lord shall reign over them *for e.*
7. 18. retaineth not anger *for e.* delights in mercy
Mal. 1. 4. against whom L. hath indignation *for e.*
Mat. 6. 13. for thine is the power and glory *for e.*
21. 19. no fruit grow on thee *for e.* *Mark* 11. 14.
Luke 1. 33. and he shall reign over Jacob *for e.*
55. as he spake to Abraham and his seed *for e.*
John 8. 35. servant abideth not in the house *for e.*
12. 34. we have heard that Christ abideth *for e.*
14. 16. the Comforter may abide with you *for e.*
Rom. 1. 25. more than Creator, who is blessed *for e.*
9. 5. Christ, who is over all, God blessed *for e.*
11. 36. to whom be glory *for e.* amen, 16. 27.
2 *Cor.* 9. 9. his righteousness remaineth *for e.*
Philem. 15. that thou shouldest receive him *for e.*
Heb. 10. 12. *for e.* sat down on the right hand of God
14. he perfected *for e.* them that are sanctified
13. 8. Jesus Christ, the same to-day and *for e.*
1 *Pet.* 1. 23. the word of God, which liveth *for e.*
25. but the word of the Lord endureth *for e.*
2 *Pet.* 2. 17. are clouds carried with a tempest, to whom mist of darkness is reserved *for e.* *Jude* 13.
2 *John* 2. for truth's sake which shall be with us *for e.*
See ESTABLISH, ESTABLISHED.

Live for EVER.

Gen. 3. 22. lest he eat of tree of life and *live for e.*
Deut. 32. 40. I lift up my hand and say, I *live for e.*
1 *Kings* 1. 31. said, let my lord king David *live for e.*
Neh. 2. 3. I said to the king, let the king *live for e.*
Ps. 22. 26. praise the L. your hearts shall *live for e.*
49. 9. that he should still *live for e.* not see
Dan. 2. 4. O king, *live for e.* 3. 9. | 5. 10. | 6. 6, 21.
Zech. 1. 5. and the prophets, do they *live for e.?*
John 6. 51. I am the living bread from heaven, if any man eat of this bread he shall *live for e.* 58.

For EVER *and* EVER.

Exod. 15. 18. the Lord shall reign *for e. and e.*
1 *Chron.* 16. 36. blessed be God *for e. and e.* people said amen, and praised Lord, 29. 10. *Dan.* 2. 20.
Neh. 9. 5. bless the Lord your God *for e. and e.*
Psal. 9. 5. thou hast put out their name *for e. and e.*
10. 16. the Lord is King *for e. and e.* the heathen
21. 4. thou gavest him length of days *for e. and e.*
45. 6. thy throne, O God, is *for e. and e.*
17. the people shall praise thee *for e. and e.*
48. 14. for this God is our God *for e. and e.*
52. 8. I trust in the mercy of God *for e. and e.*
111. 8. they stand fast *for e. and e.* are done in truth
119. 44. so shall I keep thy law *for e. and e.*
145. 1. and I will bless thy name *for e. and e.*
2. and I will praise thy name *for e. and e.* 21.
148. 6. he hath also stablished them *for e. and e.*
Isa. 30. 8. that it may be for time to come, *for e. and e.*
34. 10. none shall pass through it *for e. and e.*
Jer. 7. 7. dwell in the land that I gave *for e. and e.*
25. 5. L. given to you and your fathers *for e. and e.*
Dan. 7. 18. shall possess the kingdom *for e. and e.*
12. 3. they shall shine as the stars *for e. and e.*
Mic. 4. 5. will walk in the name of G. *for e. and e.*
Gal. 1. 5. of God, to whom be glory *for e. and e.*
Phil. 4. 20. 1 *Tim.* 1. 17. 2 *Tim.* 4. 18. *Heb.* 13. 21.
Heb. 1. 8. he saith, thy throne, O God, is *for e. and e.*
Rev. 4. 9. to him that sat on the throne, who liveth *for e. and e.* 10. | 5. 14. | 10. 6. | 15. 7.
5. 13. and honour be to the Lamb *for e. and e.*
7. 12. and power be unto our God *for e. and e.*
11. 15. and Christ shall reign *for e. and e.*
14. 11. the smoke ascendeth *for e. and e.* 19. 3.
20. 10. shall be torment. day and night *for e. and e.*
22. 5. and they shall reign *for e. and e.*

Statute for EVER.

Exod. 27. 21. it shall be a *statute for e.* 28. 43. | 30. 21. *Lev.* 6. 18. | 10. 9. | 17. 7. | 23. 14, 21, 31, 41. | 24. 3. *Num.* 18. 23.
29. 28. it shall be by a *statute for e.* *Lev.* 7. 34, 36. | 10. 15. | 16. 31. *Num.* 18. 11, 19
Lev. 6. 22. it is a *statute for e.* unto the Lord
Num. 19. 10. to the stranger for a *statute for e.*

EVERLASTING.

See *Signification* on ETERNAL.

Gen. 17. 8. land of Canaan for an *e.* possess. 48. 4.
21. 33. the *e.* God, *Isa.* 40. 28. *Rom.* 16. 26.
49. 26. to the utmost bound of the *e.* hills
Exod. 40. 15. an *e.* priesthood, *Num.* 25. 13.
Lev. 16. 34. be an *e.* statute || *Deut.* 33. 27. *e.* arms
Ps. 24. 7. be lift up, ye *e.* doors, 9. || 100. 5. mercy *e.*
112. 6. the righteous shall be in *e.* remembrance
119. 142. thy righteousness is an *e.* righteous. 144.
139. 24. search me, O God, and lead me in way *e.*
145. 13. thy kingdom is an *e.* kingdom, dominion thro' all generat. *Dan.* 4. 3. | 7. 27. 2 *Pet.* 1. 11.
Prov. 10. 25. but the righteous is an *e.* foundation
Isa. 9. 6. his name shall be called, the *e.* Father
26. 4. in the Lord JEHOVAH is *e.* strength
33. 14. who among us shall dwell with *e.* burnings?
35. 10. they shall come with *e.* joy, 51. 11. | 61. 7.
45. 17. with *e.* salvation || 54. 8. with *e.* kindness
55. 13. for an *e.* sign || 56. 5. an *e.* name, 63. 12.
60. 19. the Lord shall be unto thee an *e.* light, 20.

Jer. 10. 10. God is an *e.* King ‖ 20. 11. *e.* confusion
23. 40. I will bring an *e.* reproach upon you
31. 3. yea I have loved thee with an *e.* love
51. † 26. but thou shalt be *e.* desolations
Dan. 4. 34. whose dominion is an *e.* domin. 7. 14.
Hab. 3. 6. the *e.* mountains were scattered
Mat. 18. 8. to be cast into *e.* fire, 25, 41.
25. 46. these shall go away into *e.* punishment
Luke 16. 9. they may receive you into *e.* habitations
2 *Thess.* 1. 9. who shall be punish. with *e.* destruc.
2. 16. loved us, and hath given us *e.* consolation
1 *Tim.* 6. 16. to whom be honour and power *e.*
Jude 6. the angels he hath reserved in *e.* chains
Rev. 14. 6. having the *e.* gospel to preach to them
See COVENANT.

From EVERLASTING.

Ps. 41. 13. blessed be G. *from e.* to everlast. 106. 48.
90. 2. even *from e.* to everlasting thou art God
93. 2. thy throne is of old, thou art *from e.*
103. 17. but the mercy of the Ld. is *from e.* to ever.
Prov. 8. 23. I was set up *from e.* or ever the earth was
Isa. 63. 16. O Lord, thy name is *from e.*
Mic. 5. 2. whose goings forth have been *from e.*
Hab. 1. 12. art thou not *from e.* O Lord my God?

EVERLASTING *life.*

Dan. 12. 2. awake, some to *e. life*, some to ever. shame
Mat. 19. 29. and shall inherit *e. life*
Luke 18. 30. and in the world to come *e. life*
John 3. 16. whoso believeth should have *e. life*, 36.
4. 14. in him a well of water springing up to *e. life*
5. 24. he that heareth my words hath *e. life*
6. 27. labour for the meat which endureth to *e. life*
40. every one who seeth the Son may have *e. life*
47. he that believeth on me hath *e. life*
12. 50. I know that his commandment is *life e.*
Acts 13. 46. judge yourselves unworthy of *e. life*
Rom. 6. 22. being free from sin, ye have the end *e. life*
Gal. 6. 8. soweth to Spirit, shall of Spirit reap *life e.*
1 *Tim.* 1. 16. should hereafter believe on him to *life e.*

EVERMORE.

Deut. 28. 29. thou shalt be oppressed and spoiled *e.*
2 *Sam.* 22. 51. he sheweth mercy unto David *e.*
2 *Kings* 17. 37. ye shall observe to do for *e.*
1 *Chr.* 17. 14. his throne shall be established for *e.*
Psal. 16. 11. at right hand there are pleasures for *e.*
18. 50. sheweth mercy to David and his seed for *e.*
37. 27. depart from evil, do good, and dwell for *e.*
77. 8. is mercy gone? doth his promise fail for *e.?*
86. 12. I will praise and glorify thy name for *e.*
89. 28. my mercy will I keep for him for *e.*
52. blessed be the Lord for *e.* amen and amen
92. 8. but thou, Lord, art most high for *e.*
105. 4. seek the Lord, seek his face *e.*
106. 31. was counted to him for righteousn. for *e.*
113. 2. blessed be the name of the Lord for *e.*
115. 18. but we will bless the Lord for *e.*
121. 8. L. preserve thy going out and coming in *e.*
132. 12. their children shall sit upon throne for *e.*
133. 3. Lord commanded the blessing, life for *e.*
Ezek. 37. 26. I will make a covenant and will set
my sanctuary in the midst of them for *e.* 28.
John 6. 34. said to Jesus, Lord, *e.* give us this bread
2 *Cor.* 11. 31. the Father of our Lord blessed for *e.*
1 *Thess.* 5. 16. rejoice *e.* pray without ceasing
Heb. 7. † 25. he is able also to save them *e.*
28. maketh the Son, who is consecrated for *e.*
Rev. 1. 18. was dead, behold, I am alive for *e.*

EVERY.

Gen. 6. 5. *e.* imagination of his heart was evil
17. 10. *e.* man-child shall be circumcised
Lev. 19. 10. nor shalt gather *e.* grape of thy vineyard
Num. 5. 2. that they put out of the camp *e.* leper
1 *Sam.* 3. 18. Samuel told him *e.* whit, hid nothing
Psal. 119. 101. I have refrained from *e.* evil way
104. therefore I hate *e.* false way, 128.
Prov. 2. 9. then shalt thou understand *e.* good path
7. 12. now in streets, she lieth in wait at *e.* corner
14. 15. the simple believeth *e.* word, but prudent man
15. 3. the eyes of the Ld. are in *e.* place, beholding
20. 3. cease from strife, but *e.* fool will be meddling
30. 5. *e.* word of God is pure, he is a shield
Isa. 45. 23. *e.* knee shall bow, *e.* tongue shall swear
Jer. 51. 29. *e.* purpose of the Ld. shall be performed
Ezek. 12. 23. days at hand, and the effect of *e.* vision
Dan. 11. 36. and magnify himself above *e.* god
Zech. 12. 12. the land shall mourn, *e.* family apart
Mal. 1. 11. in *e.* place incense be offered to my name
Mat. 4. 4. but by *e.* word that proceedeth from God
19. 3. for a man to put away his wife for *e.* cause
Mark 1. 45. they came to him from *e.* quarter
Luke 4. 37. the fame of him went into *e.* place
6. 44. for *e.* tree is known by his own fruit
Acts 2. 43. and fear came upon *e.* soul, wonders done
15. 21. Moses hath in *e.* city them that preach him
Rom. 14. 11. *e.* knee shall bow, *e.* tongue shall confess
1 *Cor.* 4. 17. as I teach *e.* where in *e.* church
2 *Cor.* 10. 5. bringing into captivity *e.* thought
Eph. 1. 21. far above *e.* name named, *Phil.* 2. 9.
4. 16. *e.* joint supplieth, in the measure of *e.* part
Phil. 4. 21. salute *e.* saint in Christ Jesus
1 *Tim.* 4. 4. for *e.* creature of God is good if received
2 *Tim.* 2. 21. and prepared unto *e.* good work
Heb. 12. 1. let us lay aside *e.* weight, and the sin
Jam. 1. 17. *e.* good and perfect gift is from above
1 *Pet.* 2. 13. submit to *e.* ordinance of man for Lord
1 *John* 4. 1. beloved, believe not *e.* spirit, but try spi.
See BEAST, CITY, DAY, MAN, MORNING, WAY, SIDE, THING.

EVERY *one.*

Gen. 4. 14. that *e. one* that findeth me shall slay me
27. 29. cursed be *e. one* that curseth thee, blessed
Num. 16. 3. all congregation are holy, *e. one* of them
Deut. 4. 4. ye are alive *e. one* of you this day
1 *Kings* 22. 28. hearken, O people, *e. one* of you
2 *Kings* 18. 31. and then eat ye *e. one* of his fig tree
2 *Chron.* 30. 18. saying, the good Lord pardon *e. one*
Ezra 3. 5. of *e. one* that willingly offered an offering
9. 4. were assembled to me *e. one* that trembled
Job 40. 11. behold *e. one* that is proud, and abase him
12. look on *e. one* that is proud, and bring him low
Psal. 29. 9. in temple *e. one* doth speak of his glory
32. 6. for this shall *e. one* that is godly pray
Psal. 49. † 14. grave an habitation for *e. one* of them
63. 11. *e. one* that sweareth by him shall glory
68. 30. till *e. one* submit himself with silver
71. 18. and thy power to *e. one* that is to come
115. 8. so is *e. one* that trusteth in them, 135. 18.
119. 160. *e. one* of thy judgments endureth for ever
128. 1. blessed is *e. one* that fear the Lord
Eccl. 10. 3. he saith to *e. one* that he is a fool
Cant. 4. 2. whereof *e. one* bear twins, 6. 6.
Isa. 7. 22. honey shall *e. one* eat that is left in the land
9. 17. for *e. one* is an hypocrite and an evil doer
34. 15. vultures be gathered, *e. one* with her mate
43. 7. even *e. one* that is called by my name
55. 1. ho, *e. one* that thirsteth, come to the waters
Jer. 5. 6. *e. one* that goeth out shall be torn in pieces
8. *e. one* neighed after his neighbour's wife
6. 13. for *e. one* is given to covetousness
20. 7. I am in derision daily, *e. one* mocketh me
25. 5. turn ye now *e. one* from his evil way
Ezek. 7. 16. all of them mourning, *e. one* for iniquity
16. 25. hast opened thy feet to *e. one* that passed by
22. 6. behold *e. one* were in thee to shed blood
Dan. 12. 1. *e. one* that be found written in the book
Joel 2. 7. they shall march *e. one* on his ways
Zech. 5. 3. for *e. one* that stealeth shall be cut off
Mat. 7. 8. *e. one* that asketh, receiveth, *Luke* 11. 10.
Mark 7. 14. said to them, hearken to me, *e. one* of you
Luke 19. 26. to *e. one* which hath, shall be given
John 3. 8. so is *e. one* that is born of the Spirit
18. 37. *e. one* that is of the truth heareth my voice
Acts 2. 38. repent, and be baptized, *e. one* of you
17. 27. though he be not far from *e. one* of us
20. 31. I ceased not to warn *e. one* night and day
Rom. 14. 12. *e. one* shall give account of himself to G.
1 *Cor.* 7. 17. as the Lord hath called *e. one*, so walk
Gal. 3. 10. cursed is *e. one* that continueth not
2 *Tim.* 2. 19. *e. one* that nameth the name of Christ
1 *John* 4. 7. *e. one* that loveth is born of God
Rev. 6. 11. white robes were given to *e. one* of them

EVERY *where.*

1 *Chr.* 13. 2. send abroad to our brethren *e. where*
Mark 16. 20. they went forth and preached *e. where*
Luke 9. 6. preaching the gospel *e. where*, *Acts* 8. 4.
Acts 17. 30. commanding all men *e. where* to repent
28. 22. we know it is *e. where* spoken against
1 *Cor.* 4. 17. as I teach *e. where* in every church
Phil. 4. 12. *e. where*, and in all things instructed
1 *Tim.* 2. 8. I will therefore that men pray *e. where*

EVIDENCE.

Jer. 32. 10. I subscribed the *e.* and sealed it
11. so I took the *e.* ‖ 12. I gave the *e.* to Baruch
14. this *e.* both which is sealed, and this *e.* open
16. when I delivered the *e.* of the purchase
Heb. 11. 1. faith is the *e.* of things not seen

EVIDENCES.

Jer. 32. 14. thus saith the Lord, take these *e.*
44. men shall buy fields for money and subscribe *e.*

EVIDENT.

Job 6. 28. look upon me, for it is *e.* to you if I lie
Gal. 3. 11. that no man is justified by the law is *e.*
Phil. 1. 28. which is to them an *e.* token of perdition
Heb. 7. 14. it is *e.* our Lord sprang out of Judah
15. and it is yet far more *e.* for that after Melchis.

EVIDENTLY.

Acts 10. 3. Cornelius saw in a vision *e.* an angel
Gal. 3. 1. Jesus Christ hath been *e.* set forth crucified

EVIL.

Evil *is taken for sin and wickedness: thus it is said of the wicked kings of* Israel, *that* they did evil in the sight of the Lord, *they transgressed his law*, 1 Kings 16. 25, 30. *And in* Eccl. 9. 3. The heart of the sons of men is full of evil. *This is* criminal *or* moral evil. *It is likewise taken for afflictions or punishments which God inflicts upon a person or people.* Job 2. 10. Shall we receive good at the hand of God, and shall we not receive evil? *Isa.* 45. 7. I make peace and create evil. *Amos* 3. 6. Shall there be evil in a city, and the Lord hath not done it? *This is* the evil of punishment, *or* penal evil. *It is also taken for injuries or wrongs done by one man to another.* Prov. 17. 13. Whoso rewardeth evil for good, evil shall not depart from his house. *Mat.* 5. 39. But I say unto you that ye resist not evil. *It is put for dangers or calamities*, Prov. 22. 3. A prudent man foreseeth the evil, and hideth himself. *He sees public calamities approaching, and uses all lawful means to secure himself. It is taken both for corporal and spiritual evil, of sin and suffering.* Mat. 6. 13. Deliver us from evil.

It is said Mat. 5. 37. Let your communication be yea, yea; nay, nay; for whatsoever is more than these cometh of evil; *that is, Let your discourse be confirmed with a bare affirmation or denial only; for whatsoever is more than these proceedeth from an evil habit, or some such principle; and most commonly from the devil, that wicked one, who is evil in the highest degree; who commits evil without ceasing; and who practises all sorts and degrees of it by himself and his ministers.*

The evil of sin. *The internal malignity of sin, abstracted from its dreadful effects, renders it most worthy of our hatred; for it is in its own nature direct enmity against God, and obscures the glory of all his attributes: It is the violation of his majesty, who is the universal Sovereign of heaven and earth; a contrariety to his holiness, which shines forth in his law; a despising his goodness, the attractive to obedience; the contempt of his omniscience, which sees every sin when it is committed; the slighting of his terrible justice and power, as if the sinner could secure himself from his indignation; a denial of his truth, as if the threatenings were a vain terror to scare men from sin. Add to this the dreadful judgments and punishments which God inflicts upon sinners for sin, sometimes in this life, but especially the torments of hell, which are the just and full recompence of sin.*

Evil eye. *Prov* 23. 6. Eat not the bread of him that hath an evil eye; *that is, of the envious or covetous man; who secretly grudgeth thee the meat which he sets before thee. In the same sense this phrase is used,* Mat. 20. 15. Is thine eye evil because I am good? *Art thou envious, because I dispense my grace to others besides thyself?*

Evil day *or* days. *Prov.* 15. 15. All the days of the afflicted are evil; *that is, they are tedious and uncomfortable; he takes no content in any time or thing.* Eccl. 12. 1. When the evil days come not; *that is, the time of old age, which is burdensome and calamitous in itself; and far more grievous and more terrible when it is loaded with the sad remembrance of a man's youthful follies and lusts, and with the dreadful prospect of approaching death and judgment. And in* Amos 6. 3. Ye that put far away the evil day; *that is, ye that drive all thoughts of approaching death and judgment out of your heads; or else flatter yourselves as if it would never come, or at least not for a great while hence.*

Gen. 19. 19. lest some *e.* take me and I die
28. † 8. daughters of Canaan *e.* in eyes of Isaac
44. 5. ye have done *e.* in so doing
34. lest I see the *e.* that shall come on my father
50. 20. as for you, ye thought *e.* against me
Exod. 5. 23. since I came, he hath done *e.* to people
10. 10. look to it, for *e.* is before you
21. † 8. if she be *e.* in the eyes of her master
32. 14. the Lord repented of the *e.* he thought to do
to his people, 2 *Sam.* 24. 16. 1 *Chron.* 21. 15.
Num. 11. † 1. it was *e.* in the ears of the Lord
22. † 34. if it be *e.* in thine eyes, I will get back
Deut. 19. 20. commit no more such *e.* among you
29. 21. the L. shall separate him to *e.* out of tribes
30. 15. see, I have set before thee death and *e.*
31. 29. and *e.* will befall you in the latter days
Josh. 24. 15. if it seem *e.* to you to serve the Lord
Judg. 2. 15. the hand of the L. against them for *e.*
9. 57. the *e.* of the men of Shechem did God render
20. 34. but they knew not that *e.* was near them
1 *Sam.* 20. 7. be sure that *e.* is determined by him
9. if I knew certainly that *e.* were determined
24. 11. nor is *e.* nor transgression in mine hand
17. me good, whereas I have rewarded thee *e.*
25. 17. for *e.* is determined against our master
26. they that seek *e.* to my lord, be as Nabal
28. *e.* hath not been found in thee all thy days
26. 18. what have I done? what *e.* is in my hand?
29. 6. I have not found *e.* in thee since thy coming
2 *Sam.* 3. 39. the Lord shall reward the doer of *e.*
12. 11. behold I will raise up *e.* against thee
16. † 8. behold thee in thy *e.* thou bloody man
19. 7. will be worse than all the *e.* that befell thee
1 *Kings* 14. 9. but hast done *e.* above all before thee
16. 25. Omri wrought *e.* in the eyes of the Lord
22. 23. a lying spirit in thy prophets, and the Lord
hath spoken *e.* concerning thee, 2 *Chron.* 18. 22.
2 *Kings* 21. 2. I am bringing such *e.* on Jerusalem
22. 20. thine eyes shall not see all *e.* on this place
1 *Chron.* 21. † 7. it was *e.* in the eyes of the Lord
17. it is I that have sinned and done *e.* indeed
2 *Chron.* 20. 9. if when *e.* cometh on us, as the sword
Esth. 7. 7. he saw that there was *e.* determined
8. 6. for how can I endure to see *e.* to my people?
Job 1. 1. one that feared God and eschewed *e.* 8. | 2. 3.
5. 19. yea in seven there shall no *e.* touch thee
31. 29. or lift up myself when *e.* found him
42. 11. they comforted him over all the *e.* on him
Psal. 5. 4. neither shall *e.* dwell with thee
7. 4. if I have rewarded *e.* to him that was at peace
15. 3. nor doth *e.* to his neighbour, nor taketh up
21. 11. for they intended *e.* against thee
23. 4. I will fear no *e.* for thou art with me
34. 21. *e.* shall slay wicked, those hate righteous
36. 4. he deviseth mischief, he abhorreth not *e.*
40. 14. let them be put to shame that wish me *e.*
41. † 1. the Lord will deliver him in the day of *e.*
5. mine enemies speak *e.* of me ‖ † 7. devise *e.*
49. 5. wherefore should I fear in the days of *e.?*
50. 19. thou givest thy mouth to *e.* and thy tongue
54. 5. he shall reward *e.* unto mine enemies
56. 5. all their thoughts are against me for *e.*
90. 15. and the years wherein we have seen *e.*
91. 10. there shall no *e.* befall thee, *Jer.* 23. 17.
97. 10. ye that love the Lord, hate *e.*
109. 20. and of them that speak *e.* against my soul
140. 11. *e.* shall hunt violent man to overthrow him
Prov. 1. 16. for their feet run to *e.* *Isa.* 59. 7.
33. dwell safely, and shall be quiet from fear of *e.*
3. 29. devise not *e.* against thy neighbour
5. 14. I was almost in all *e.* in midst of congregation
11. 19. he that pursueth *e.* pursueth it to his death
12. 20. deceit in the heart of them that imagine *e.*
21. there shall no *e.* happen to the just
13. 21. *e.* pursueth sinners ‖ 14. 22. that devise *e.*
16. 4. yea, even the wicked for the day of *e.*
27. an ungodly man diggeth up *e.* fire in his lips
30. moving his lips he bringeth *e.* to pass
19. 23. he shall not be visited with *e.*
20. 8. a king scattereth away all *e.* with his eyes
22. say not thou, I will recompense *e.* wait on Lord
21. 10. the soul of the wicked desireth *e.*
22. 3. a prudent man foreseeth the *e.* 27. 12.
24. † 18. lest it be *e.* in the eyes of the Lord
30. 32. if thou hast thought *e.* lay thine hand
Eccl. 2. 21. this also is vanity, and a great *e.*
5. 13. there is a sore *e.* which I have seen, 16.
6. 1. an *e.* which I have seen under the sun, 10. 5.
9. 3. this is an *e.* among things that are done under
the sun, the heart of sons of men is full of *e.*
11. 2. thou knowest not what *e.* shall be on earth
Isa. 3. 9. for they have rewarded *e.* to themselves
13. 11. I will punish the world for their *e.*
33. 15. and shutteth his eyes from seeing *e.*
45. 7. I make peace and create *e.* I do these things
47. 11. therefore shall *e.* come upon thee
56. 2. and keepeth his hand from doing any *e.*
57. 1. that the righteous is taken away from the *e.*
Jer. 1. 14. out of the north an *e.* break forth, 6. 1.
2. 3. *e.* shall come upon them, saith the Lord
† 28. if they can save thee in the time of *e.*

Jer. 4. 4. lest my fury come forth like fire, because
of the e. of your doings, 23. 2. | 26. 3. | 44. 22.
5. 12. it is not he, neither shall e. come upon us
7. 30. children of Judah have done e. in my sight
11. † 12. shall not save them in the time of e.
† 14. I will not hear when they cry for their e.
15. when thou doest e. then thou rejoicest
17. hath pronounced e. against thee for e. of Israel
15. 11. will cause to entreat thee well in time of e.
17. 17. thou art my hope in the day of e.
18. bring on them the day of e. and destroy them
18. 8. if that nation turn from their e. I will repent
of the e. I thought to do, 26. 3, 13, 19. | 42. 10.
11. behold, I frame e. against you and devise
19. 15. I will bring all e. that I have pronounced
21. 10. I set my face against this city for e.
25. 32. e. shall go forth from nation to nation
28. 8. the prophets prophesied of war and of e.
29. 11. I think thoughts of peace, and not of e.
32. 30. the children of Judah have only done e.
32. because of all the e. of the children of Israel
35. 17. I will bring on Judah and Jerusalem all
the e. that I have pronounced against them, 36. 31.
38. 9. these men have done e. in all they have done
44. 11. I will set my face ag. you for e. and cut off
17. we had plenty, and were well, and saw no e.
27. I will watch over them for e. and not for good
29. my words shall stand against you for e.
48. 2. in Heshbon they have devised e. against it
51. 24. I will render to Babylon all e. done in Zion
60. wrote all the e. that should come on Babylon
Ezek. 7. 5. an e. an only e. behold it is come
14. 22. ye shall be comforted concerning the e.
Dan. 9. 14. the Lord hath watched upon the e.
Joel 2. 13. the Lord your God repenteth him of the e.
Amos 3. 6. shall there be e. in a city, L. not done it?
9. 10. who say, e. shall not overtake nor prevent us
Jonah 3. 10. and God repented of the e. he said, 4. 2.
Mic. 1. 12. but e. came down from Lord to Jerusalem
2. 1. woe to them that work e. upon their beds
3. behold, against this family do I devise an e.
3. 11. is not the Lord among us? no e. can come
Nah. 1. 11. that imagineth e. against the Lord
Hab. 1. 13. thou art of purer eyes than to behold e.
2. 9. he may be delivered from the power of e.
Zeph. 3. 15. thou shalt not see e. any more
Zech. 7. 10. let none of you imagine e. 8. 17.
Mal. 1. 8. ye offer the lame and sick, is it not e.?
2. 17. when ye say, every one that doeth e. is good
Mat. 5. 11. shall say all manner of e. against you
37. whatsoever is more than these, cometh of e.
39. but I say unto you, that ye resist not e.
6. 34. sufficient unto the day is the e. thereof
9. 4. wherefore think ye e. in your hearts?
27. 23. Pilate said to them, why, what e. hath he
done? Mark 15. 14. Luke 23. 22.
Mark 9. 39. that can lightly speak e. of me
Luke 6. 45. an evil man bringeth forth what is e.
John 3. 20. every one that doeth e. hateth the light
5. 29. they that have done e. to the resurrection of
18. 23. if I have spoken e. bear witness of the e.
Acts 9. 13. how much e. he hath done to thy saints
23. 9. a great cry, saying, we find no e. in this man
Rom. 2. 9. anguish on every soul of man that doeth e.
7. 19. but the e. which I would not, that I do
12. 9. abhor that which is e. cleave to what is good
17. recompense to no man e. for e. provide things
21. be not overcome of e. overcome e. with good
13. 4. a revenger to execute wrath on him doeth e.
14. 20. it is e. for that man who eateth with offence
16. 19. I would have you simple concerning e.
1 Cor. 13. 5. charity not provoked, thinketh no e.
1 Thess. 5. 15. see that none render e. for e. to any
22. abstain from all appearance of e.
1 Tim. 6. 10. the love of money is the root of all e.
Tit. 3. 2. put them in mind to speak e. of no man
Jam. 3. 8. the tongue is an unruly e. full of poison
1 Pet. 3. 9. not rendering e. for e. or railing, but bless.
3 John 11. he that doeth e. hath not seen God

Bring, Brought EVIL.

Josh. 23. 15. the Lord shall bring on you all e. things
2 Sam. 15. 14. lest he overtake and bring e. on us
17. 14. that the Lord might bring e. upon Absalom
1 Kings 14. 10. I will bring e. on the house of Jerob.
17. 20. he said, hast thou also brought e. on widow?
21. 21. behold, I will bring e. upon thee
29. not bring e. in his days, but in his son's days
2 Kings 22. 16. thus saith the Lord, behold, I will
bring e. upon this place, 2 Chron. 34. 24.
2 Chron. 34. 28. nor eyes see all the e. I will bring
Isa. 31. 2. I will bring e. and not call back his word
Jer. 4. 6. for I will bring e. from the north
6. 19. behold, I will bring e. upon this people
11. 11. behold, I will bring e. upon them
23. I will bring e. upon the men of Anathoth
19. 3. behold, I will bring e. on this place, 15.
23. 12. I will bring e. even year of their visitation
25. 29. for lo, I begin to bring e. on the city
35. 17. I will bring on Judah e. pronounced, 36. 31.
39. 16. I will bring my words on this city for e.
45. 5. I will bring e. upon all flesh, saith the Lord
See Did, Do.

EVIL, joined with *good*.

Gen. 2. 9. the tree of knowledge of good and e. 17.
3. 5. ye shall be as gods knowing good and e. 22.
44. 4. wherefore have ye rewarded e. for good?
Deut. 1. 39. had no knowledge between good and e.
1 Sam. 25. 21. he hath requited me e. for good
2 Sam. 19. 35. can I discern between good and e.?
1 Kings 22. 8. not prophesy g. concern. me, but e. 18.
2 Chron. 18. 7. never prophesieth good to me, but e.
17. he would not prophesy good to me, but e.
Job 2. 10. shall we receive good, and not receive e.?
30. 26. I looked for good, then e. came unto me
Psal. 35. 12. they rewarded me e. for good, 109. 5.
38. 20. that render e. for good are my adversaries
52. 3. thou lovest e. more than good, and lying
Prov. 15. 3. eyes of L. beholding the e. and the good
17. 13. whoso rewardeth e. for good, evil not depart
31. 12. she will do him good and not e. all her days
Isa. 5. 20. woe to them that call e. good, and good e.
7. 15. may know to refuse e. and choose good, 16.

Jer. 18. 20. shall e. be recompensed for good?
42. 6. whether it be good or e. we will obey Lord
Lam. 3. 38. of most High proceedeth not e. and g.
Amos 5. 14. seek good and not e. that ye may live
9. 4. I will set mine eyes on them for e. not for good
Mic. 3. 2. who hate the good and love the e.
Rom. 7. 21. when I would do good, e. present with me
9. 11. not born, neither having done good or e.
Heb. 5. 14. their senses exercised to discern g. and e.
3 John 11. follow not what is e. but what is good
See Great.

From EVIL.

Gen. 48. 16. the Angel who redeemed me from all e.
1 Sam. 25. 39. and hath kept his servant from e.
1 Chron. 4. 10. that thou wouldest keep me from e.
Job 28. 28. and to depart from e. is understanding
Psal. 34. 13. keep thy tongue from e. lips from guile
14. depart from e. do good, 37. 27. Prov. 3. 7.
121. 7. the Lord shall preserve thee from all e.
Prov. 4. 27. turn not, remove thy foot from e.
13. 19. it is abomination to fools to depart from e.
14. 16. a wise man feareth, and departeth from e.
16. 6. by the fear of the Lord men depart from e.
17. the high-way of upright is to depart from e.
Isa. 59. 15. that departeth f. e. makes hims. a prey
Jer. 9. 3. they proceed f. e. to evil, and know not me
23. 22. then they should have turned them from
their e. way, and from the e. of their doings
51. 64. Babylon not rise from e. I will bring on her
Mat. 6. 13. but deliver us from e. Luke 11. 4.
John 17. 15. but that thou shouldest keep them f. e.
2 Thess. 3. 3. shall stablish you, and keep you f. e.
1 Pet. 3. 10. let him refrain his tongue from e.

Put away EVIL.

Deut. 13. 5. put the e. away from the midst of thee
17. 7. so thou shalt put the e. away from among
you, 19. 19. | 21. 21. | 22. 21, 24. | 24. 7.
12 put e. away from Israel, 21. 22. Judg. 20. 13.
Eccl. 11. 10. and put away e. from thy flesh
Isa. 1. 16. wash ye, put away the e. of your doings

EVIL *in the sight of the Lord*.

Num. 32. 13. had done e. in sight of L. Judg. 3. 12.
Judg. 2. 11. Israel did e. in the sight of the Lord,
3. 7, 12. | 4. 1. | 6. 1. | 10. 6. | 13. 1. 1 Kings
11. 6. | 14. 22. | 15. 26, 34. | 16. 7, 30. | 22. 52.
2 Kings 8. 18, 27. | 13. 2, 11. | 14. 24. | 15. 9,
18, 24, 28. | 17. 2. | 21. 2, 20. 2 Chron. 22. 4. |
33. 2, 22. | 36. 5, 9, 12.
1 Sam. 15. 19. thou didst e. in the sight of the Lord
1 Kings 16. 19. in doing e. in the sight of the Lord
21. 20. sold to work e. in the sight of the Lord
2 Kings 3. 2. he wrought e. in the sight of the Lord
17. 17. sold themselves to do e. in the sight of L.
21. 16. to sin, in doing that which was e. in the
sight of the Lord, 23. 32, 37. | 24. 9, 19.
1 Chron. 2. 3. Er was e. in the sight of the Lord
2 Chr. 33. 6. he wrought much e. in the sight of L.

This EVIL.

Exod. 32. 12. and repent of this e. against thy people
1 Sam. 6. 9. then he hath done us this great e.
12. 19. we have added this e. to ask a king
2 Sam. 13. 16. this e. in sending me away is greater
1 Kings 9. 9. the Lord brought on them all this e.
2 Kings 6. 33. he said, behold, this e. is of the Lord
2 Chron. 7. 22. therefore he brought this e. on them
Neh. 13. 18. did not our God bring all this e. on us?
27. shall we hearken to you to do all this great e.?
Job 2. 11. when Job's three friends heard of this e.
Psal. 51. 4. I have done this e. in thy sight
Jer. 16. 10. the L. pronounced all this e. against us
32. 23. therefore thou hast caused all t. e. on them
42. like as I have brought all this e. on this people
40. 2. God hath pronounced this e. on this place
44. 7. why commit ye this great e. ag. your souls?
23. therefore this e. is happened unto you
Dan. 9. 13. it is written, all this e. is come upon us
Jonah 1. 7. know for whose cause this e. is on us, 8.

EVIL, *Adjective*.

Gen. 6. 5. thoughts of his heart were only e. 8. 21.
37. 20. some e. beast hath devoured him, 33.
Exod. 5. 19. Israel did see that they were in e. case
33. 4. people heard these e. tidings they mourned
Num. 14. 27. how long bear this e. congregation?
20. 5. to bring us in unto this e. place
Deut. 1. 35. not one of this e. generat. shall see land
6. † 22. the L. shewed signs, great and e. on Egypt
22. 14. and bring up an e. name upon her, 19.
28. 54. his eye shall be e. toward his brother
56. her eye shall be e. toward her husband
1 Sam. 2. 23. for I hear of your e. dealings
1 Kings 5. 4. there is neither advers. nor e. occurrent
Ezra 9. 13. after all that is come on us for e. deeds
Psal. 41. 8. an e. disease cleaveth fast unto him
64. 5. they encourage themselves in an e. matter
78. 49. trouble, by sending e. angels among them
112. 7. he shall not be afraid of e. tidings, heart fixed
140. 11. let not an e. speaker be established in earth
Prov. 6. 24. to keep thee from the e. woman
14. 19. the e. bow before the good, the wicked
Eccl. 5. 14. but those riches perish by e. travel
6. 2. this is vanity, and it is an e. disease
9. 12. as the fishes that are taken in an e. net
Isa. 7. 5. Ephraim have taken e. counsel against
thee
32. 7. the instruments also of the churl are e.
Jer. 8. 3. by them that remain of this e. family
12. 14. thus saith against all mine e. neighbours
13. 10. this e. people refuse to hear my words
23. 10. their course is e. their force not right
24. 3. e. figs, very e. they are so e. 8. | 29. 17.
49. 23. for they have heard e. tidings, faint-hearted
Ezek. 5. 16. I will send on them e. arrows of famine
17. so will I send on you famine and e. beasts
6. 11. alas, for all the e. abominations of Israel
34. 25. I will cause the e. beasts to cease from land
38. 10. and thou shalt think an e. thought
Hab. 2. 9. woe to him that coveteth an e. covetous.
Mat. 5. 45. he maketh his sun to rise on e. and good
7. 11. if ye then being e. Luke 11. 13.
18. a good tree cannot bring forth e. fruit
12. 34. how can ye being e. speak good things?
39. an e. generation seeketh a sign, Luke 11. 29.

Mat. 15. 19. for out of the heart proceed e. thoughts,
murders, adulteries, fornications, Mark 7. 21.
24. 48. if that e. servant shall say in his heart
Luke 6. 22. and shall cast out your name as e.
35. he is kind to the unthankful and to the e.
John 3. 19. loved darkness, for their deeds were e.
Acts 24. 20. if they have found any e. doing in me
1 Cor. 15. 33. e. communicat. corrupt good manners
Gal. 1. 4. that he might deliver us from this e. world
Eph. 4. 31. let e. speaking be put away from you
Phil. 3. 2. beware of dogs, beware of e. workers
Col. 3. 5. mortify therefore e. concupiscence
1 Tim. 6. 4. whereof cometh e. surmisings
Tit. 1. 12. the Cretians are e. beasts, slow bellies
Heb. 10. 22. your hearts sprinkled from e. conscience
Jam. 2. 4. and are become judges of e. thoughts
4. 16. ye rejoice in boastings, all such rejoicing is e.
1 Pet. 2. 1. laying aside all malice and e. speakings
Rev. 2. 2. how thou canst not bear them who are e.

EVIL *day* or *days*.

Gen. 47. 9. few and e. have the days of my life been
Prov. 15. 15. all the days of the afflicted are e.
Eccl. 12. 1. in youth, while the e. days come not
Amos 6. 3. ye that put far away the e. day
Eph. 5. 16. redeeming the time, because days are e.
6. 13. that ye may be able to withstand in the e. day
Day of EVIL; see Evil, *Substantive*.

EVIL *doer*, or *doers*.

Job 8. 20. neither will he help the e. doers
Psal. 26. 5. I hated the congregation of e. doers
37. 1. fret not thyself because of e. doers
9. e. doers shall be cut off, but those that wait on L.
94. 16. who will rise up for me against the e. doers?
119. 115. depart from me, ye e. doers, I will keep
Isa. 1. 4. ah, sinful nation, a seed of e. doers
9. 17. every one is an hypocrite, and an e. doer
14. 20. the seed of e. doers shall never be renowned
31. 2. but will arise against the house of e. doers
Jer. 20. 13. hath delivered soul of poor from e. doers
23. 14. they strengthen the hands of e. doers
2 Tim. 2. 9. wherein I suffer trouble as an e. doer
1 Pet. 2. 12. whereas they speak ag. you as e. doers
14. are sent by him for the punishment of e. doers
3. 16. whereas they speak evil of you as of e. doers
4. 15. let none of you suffer as a thief or an e. doer
See Doings, Eye.

EVIL *heart*.

Gen. 8. 21. imagina. of man's heart is e. from youth
Jer. 3. 17. nor walk after the imagination of e. heart
7. 24. walked in the imagination of their e. heart
11. 8. every one in imagination of their e. heart
16. 12. every one after imagination of his e. heart
18. 12. every one do the imagination of his e. heart
Heb. 3. 12. lest there be in any an e. heart of unbelief

EVIL *man* or *men*.

Job 35. 12. none answer because of pride of e. men
Psal. 10. 15. break thou the arm of the e. man
140. 1. deliver me, O Lord, from the e. man
Prov. 2. 12. to deliver thee from way of the e. man
4. 14. and go not in the way of e. men
12. 12. the wicked desireth the net of e. men
17. 11. an e. man seeketh only rebellion
24. 1. be not thou envious against e. men
19. fret not thyself because of e. men
20. for there shall be no reward to the e. man
28. 5. e. men understand not judgment
29. 6. in transgression of an e. man there is a snare
Mat. 12. 35. and an e. man out of the evil treasure
bringeth forth evil things, Luke 6. 45.
2 Tim. 3. 13. but e. men shall wax worse and worse
See Report.

EVIL *spirit* or *spirits*.

Judg. 9. 23. sent e. sp. between Abimelech and men
1 Sam. 16. 14. an e. sp. from the L. troubled him, 15.
16. when the e. spirit from God is upon thee
23. and the e. spirit departed from him
18. 10. the e. spirit from God came on Saul, 19. 9.
Luke 7. 21. that hour he cured many of e. spirits
8. 2. woman which had been healed of e. spirits
Acts 19. 12. and the e. spirits went out of them
13. to call over them which had e. spirits
15. the e. spirit said, Jesus I know, Paul I know
16. the man in whom the e. spirit was, leaped

EVIL *thing*.

Gen. 38. † 10. the thing he did was e. in eyes of Lord
2 Kings 4. † 41. there was no e. thing in the pot
Neh. 13. 17. what e. thing is this that ye do?
Psal. 141. 4. incline not my heart to any e. thing
Eccl. 8. 3. stand not in an e. thing, doth what pleases
5. keepeth commandment, shall feel no e. thing
12. 14. every secret thing, whether it be good or e.
Jer. 2. 19. know that it is an e. thing and bitter
Tit. 2. 8. having no e. thing to say of you

EVIL *things*.

Josh. 23. 15. the Lord shall bring on you all e. things
Prov. 15. 28. mouth of wicked poureth out e. things
Jer. 3. 5. thou hast done e. things as thou couldest
Mat. 12. 35. an evil man bringeth forth e. things
Mark 7. 23. all these e. things come from within
Luke 16. 25. and likewise Lazarus e. things
Rom. 1. 30. proud, boasters, inventors of e. things
1 Cor. 10. 6. we should not lust after e. things

EVIL *times*.

Psal. 37. 19. they shall not be ashamed in the e.
time
Eccl. 9. 12. so the sons of men are snared in an e. time
Amos 5. 13. prudent keep silence, for it is an e. time
Mic. 2. 3. nor shall go haughtily, for this time is e.

EVIL *way*.

1 Kings 13. 33. Jeroboam returned not from e. way
Psal. 119. 101. I refrained my feet from every e. way
Prov. 8. 13. the fear of the Lord is to hate the e. way
28. 10. who causeth righteous to go astray in e. way
Jer. 18. 11. return ye now every one from his e. way
25. 5. | 26. 3. | 35. 15. | 36. 3, 7.
23. 22. should have turned them from their e. way
Jonah 3. 8. let them turn every one from his e. way
10. and saw that they turned from their e. way

EVIL *ways*.

2 Kings 17. 13. turn from your e. ways, Ezek. 33. 11.
Ezek. 36. 31. then shall ye remember your own e. w.
Zech. 1. 4. turn ye now from your e. ways and doings

EVIL *work* or *works*.
Eccl. 4. 3. who hath not seen *e. work* that is done
8. 11. because sentence against an *e. work* is not
John 7. 7. I testify that the *works* thereof are *e.*
Rom. 13. 3. are not a terror to good *works* but *e.*
2 *Tim.* 4. 18. L. shall deliver me from every *e. work*
Jam. 3. 16. there is confusion, and every *e. work*
1 *John* 3. 12. because his own *works* were *e.*

EVIL, *Adverb.*
Exod. 5. 22. why hast thou so *e.* entreated people?
Deut. 26. 6. and the Egyptians *e.* entreated us
1 *Chron.* 7. 23. because it went *e.* with his house
Job 24. 21. he *e.* entreateth barren that beareth not
John 18. 23. if I have spoken *e.* bear witness
Acts 7. 6. they should entreat them *e.* 400 years
19. the same *e.* entreated our fathers
14. 2. their minds *e.* affected against the brethren
19. 9. but spake *e.* of that way before the multitude
23. 5. shall not speak *e.* of the ruler of thy people
Rom. 14. 16. let not your good be *e.* spoken of
1 *Cor.* 10. 30. why am I *e.* spoken of for that?
Jam. 4. 11. speak not *e.* one of another, brethren, he
that speaks *e.* of his brother, speaks *e.* of the law
1 *Pet.* 3. 16. that whereas they speak *e.* of you
17. better ye suffer for well-doing than for *e.* doing
4. 4. they think it strange, speaking *e.* of you
14. their part he is *e.* spoken of, but on your part
2 *Pet.* 2. 2. the way of truth shall be *e.* spoken of
10. are not afraid to speak *e.* of dignities, *Jude* 8.
12. these, as natural brute beasts, speak *e.* of the
things that they understand not, *Jude* 10.

EVILS.
Deut. 31. 17. many *e.* and troubles shall befall them,
they will say, are not these *e.* come upon us
18. for all the *e.* which they shall have wrought
21. when many *e.* and troubles are befallen them
Psal. 40. 12. innumerable *e.* have compassed me abt.
Jer. 2. 13. for my people have committed two *e.*
Ezek. 6. 9. shall lothe themselves for the *e.* commit.
20. 43. lothe yourselves in your sight for all your *e.*
Hos. 7. †1. the *e.* of Samaria were discovered
Luke 3. 19. for all the *e.* which Herod had done
Jam. 1. †13. God cannot be tempted with *e.*

EUNUCH
Comes from the Greek, Ευνουχος, *which signifies one who guards the bed; because generally in the courts of the eastern kings the care of the beds and apartments belonging to princes and princesses was committed to them; but chiefly of the princesses, who live in great confinement, remote from the sight and company of men. The* Hebrew *word* Saris, *signifies a real* eunuch, *or one deprived of his genitals: whether he be naturally born such, or made an* eunuch *by manual operation. But this word, as well as the* Greek Eunouchos, *is in scripture taken for an officer belonging to some prince attending at his court, and employed in the inner part of the palace, whether he be really an* eunuch *or not.* Potiphar, Pharaoh's *eunuch, and* Joseph's *master, had a wife,* Gen. 39. 1, 7. *and a child too, if* Asenath *was daughter to* Joseph's *master, as some think, though the generality of Commentators be of the contrary opinion.*

God forbad his people to make eunuchs, Deut. 23. 1. 'He that has that part wounded or cut off, which is intended for the preservation of the species, shall not enter into the congregation of the Lord. *Which words are differently explained. Some think that God here forbids* eunuchs *to marry with* Israelites: *others, that God forbids them to enter into his temple; others, that he excludes them from all offices of the magistracy; and others, that God debars them simply the possession of some outward privileges belonging to the* Israelites *and people of the Lord. They were looked upon in the commonwealth as dry and useless wood.* Isa. 56. 3. Behold I am a dry tree. *See* DRY.

There were eunuchs *in the courts of the kings of* Judah *and* Israel, *officers called* Sarism, *eunuchs.* Samuel, *describing to the people the manner of their king, tells them,* 1 Sam. 8. 15. He will take the tenth of your seed, and give to his *officers*, or eunuchs. *Some understand this properly, that he should against the command of God make some of his people* eunuchs. *But others think that these* eunuchs, *in all probability, were slaves taken from some foreign people: or if they were* Hebrews, *the name of* eunuchs, *which is given them, shews no more than their office and dignity. See also,* 1 Kings 22. 9. 2 Kings 9. 32. | 24. 12, 15. 1 Chron. 28. 1.

Our Saviour in Mat. 19. 12. *speaks of a sort of* eunuchs, *different from these mentioned persons,* who have made themselves eunuchs for the kingdom of heaven's sake; *that is, who, upon some religious motive, do abstain from marriage, and the use of all carnal pleasures; that they may be less encumbered with the cares of the world, and may devote themselves more closely to the service of God.*

Gen. 37. †36. to Potiphar an *e.* of Pharaoh's
2 *Kings* 8. †6. the king appointed an *e.* to restore
23. †11. the chamber of Nathan-melech the *e.*
25. †19. out of the city he took an *e. Jer.* 52. 25.
Isa. 56. 3. neither let the *e.* say, I am a dry tree
Acts 8. 27. an *e.* had come to Jerusalem to worship
34. *e.* said, of whom speaks the prophet this?
36. *e.* said, what doth hinder me to be baptized?
39. Spirit caught Philip, that *e.* saw him no more

EUNUCHS.
1 *Sam.* 8. †15. will give tenth of your seed to his *e.*
2 *Kings* 9. 32. there looked out two or three *e.*
20. 18. thy sons take away, and they shall be *e.* in
the palace of the king of Babylon, *Isa.* 39. 7.
24. †12. Jehoiachin went out, he and his *e.*
1 *Chron.* 28. †1. and David assembled the *e.*
2 *Chron.* 18. 8. Ahab called for one of his *e.*
Esth. 1. †12. Vashti refused to come by hand of his *e.*
4. †4. Esther's maids and *e.* came and told it her
Isa. 56. 4. saith the L. to the *e.* that keep my sabbath

Jer. 29. 2. after that the *e.* were departed from Jerus.
34. 19. *e.* which passed between the parts of the calf
38. 7. when Ebedmelech one of the *e.* heard
41. 16. the *e.* whom he had brought from Gibeon
Dan. 1. 3. the king spake to the master of his *e.*
7. to whom the prince of the *e.* gave names
8. Daniel requested of the prince of the *e.*
9. Daniel brought into favour with prince of *e.*
18. then the prince of the *e.* brought them in
Mat. 19. 12. some are *e.* who were so born, some are
made *e.* of men, some have made themselves *e.*

EUROCLYDON
Is *a wind which blows between the east and north. It is very dangerous, of the nature of a whirlwind, which falls on a sudden upon ships, makes them tack about, and sometimes causes them to founder, as* Pliny *observes.*
Acts 27. 14. there arose a tempestu. wind, called *e.*

EWE *or* EWES.
Gen. 21. 28. Abraham set seven *e.* lambs by thems.
29. he said, what mean these seven *e.* lambs?
31. 38. *e.* and she-goats have not cast their young
32. 14. two hundred *e.* and twenty rams for Esau
Lev. 14. 10. take one *e.* lamb of the first year
22. 28. whether cow or *e.* ye shall not kill it
2 *Sam.* 12. 3. poor man had nothing save one *e.* lamb
Psal. 78. 71. he took him from following the *e.*

EXACT.
Deut. 15. 2. shall not *e.* it of his neighbour or brother
3. of a foreigner thou mayest *e.* it again
Neh. 5. 7. you *e.* usury every one of his brother
10. I likewise might *e.* of them money and corn
11. restore hundredth part of money ye *e.* of them
Psal. 89. 22. the enemy shall not *e.* upon him
Isa. 58. 3. behold, in your fasts ye *e.* all your labours
Luke 3. 13. he said, *e.* no more than what is appointed

EXACTED.
2 *Kings* 15. 20. Menahem *e.* the money of Israel
23. 35. Jehoiakim *e.* the silver and the gold

EXACTETH.
Job 11. 6. G. *e.* of thee less than thine iniq. deserveth

EXACTION.
Neh. 10. 31. we would leave the *e.* of every debt

EXACTIONS.
Ezek. 45. 9. take away your *e.* from my people

EXACTOR.
Job 39. †7. nor regardeth he the crying of the *e.*

EXACTORS.
Isa. 60. 17. I will also make thine *e.* righteousness

EXALT.
Exod. 15. 2. he is my father's God, and I will *e.* him
1 *Sam.* 2. 10. he shall *e.* the horn of his anointed
Job 17. 4. therefore shalt thou not *e.* them
Psal. 34. 3. and let us *e.* his name together
37. 34. he shall *e.* thee to inherit the land
66. 7. let not the rebellious *e.* themselves
92. 10. but my horn shalt thou *e.* like the horn
99. 5. *e.* ye the Lord our God, and worship, 9.
107. 32. let them *e.* him in the congregation
118. 28. thou art my God, I will *e.* thee
140. 8. further not, lest the wicked *e.* themselves
Prov. 4. 8. *e.* her, and she shall promote thee
Isa. 13. 2. *e.* the voice unto them, shake the hand
14. 13. I will *e.* my throne above the stars of God
25. 1. O Lord, thou art my God, I will *e.* thee
Ezek. 21. 26. *e.* him that is low, abase the high
29. 15. nor shall it *e.* itself any more above nations
31. 14. to the end none of the trees *e.* themselves
Dan. 11. 14. robbers of thy people shall *e.* themselves
36. the king shall *e.* himself above every god
Hos. 11. 7. tho' they called, none at all would *e.* him
Obad. 4. though thou *e.* thyself as the eagle
Mat. 23. 12. whoso shall *e.* himself, shall be abased
2 *Cor.* 11. 20. if a man *e.* himself, if a man smite you
1 *Pet.* 5. 6. humble yoursel. that he may *e.* in due time

EXALTED.
Num. 24. 7. and his kingdom shall be *e.*
1 *Sam.* 2. 1. she said, mine horn is *e.* in the Lord
2 *Sam.* 5. 12. perceived that Lord had *e.* his kingdom
22. 47. the Lord liveth, and *e.* be the God of the
rock of my salvation, *Psal.* 18. 46.
1 *Kings* 1. 5. then Adonijah *e.* himself, saying
14. 7. I *e.* thee from among the people, 16. 2.
2 *Kings* 19. 22. against whom hast thou *e.* thy voice
and lift up thine eyes on high? *Isa.* 37. 23.
1 *Chr.* 29. 11. and thou art *e.* as head above all
Neh. 9. 5. which is *e.* above all blessing and praise
Job 5. 11. that those who mourn may be *e.* to safety
24. 24. they are *e.* for a little while, but are gone
36. 7. he doth establish them for ever, they are *e.*
Psal. 12. 8. wicked walk when the vilest men are *e.*
13. 2. how long shall my enemy be *e.* over me?
21. 13. be thou *e.* Lord, in thine own strength
46. 10. be still and know I am God, I will be *e.*
among the heathen, I will be *e.* in the earth
47. 9. shields of earth belong to G. he is greatly *e.*
57. 5. be thou *e.* O God, above the heavens, 11.
75. 10. but the horns of the righteous shall be *e.*
89. 16. in thy righteousness shall they be *e.*
17. and in thy favour our horn shall be *e.*
19. I have *e.* one chosen out of the people
24. and in my name shall his horn be *e.*
97. 9. thou, Lord, art *e.* far above all gods
108. 5. be thou *e.* O God, above the heavens
112. 9. his horn shall be *e.* with honour
118. 16. the right hand of the Lord is *e.*
140. †8. further not, let not the wicked be *e.*
Prov. 11. 11. by the blessing of the upright city is *e.*
Isa. 2. 2. the mountain of Lord's house shall be *e.*
above the hills, all nations flow to it, *Mic.* 4. 1.
11. the Lord shall be *e.* in that day, 17. | 5. 16.
12. 4. praise Ld. make mention that his name is *e.*
30. 18. will be *e.* that he may have mercy on you
33. 5. the Lord is *e.* ‖ 10. now will I be *e.*
40. 4. every valley shall be *e.* every mountain low
49. 11. and my high-ways shall be *e.*
52. 13. behold my servant shall be *e.* and extolled
Ezek. 17. 24. that I the Lord have *e.* the low tree
19. 11. and her stature was *e.* among branches, 31. 5.
Hos. 11. †7. together they *e.* not him
13. 1. Ephraim spake, he *e.* himself in Israel
6. they were filled, and their heart was *e.*

Mat. 11. 23. Capernaum *e.* to heaven, *Luke* 10. 15.
23. 12. *e.* himself be abased, that shall humble himself shall be *e.* *Luke* 14. 11. | 18. 14.
Luke 1. 52. and he hath *e.* them of low degree
Acts 2. 33. being by the right hand of God *e.*
5. 31. him hath God *e.* with his right hand
13. 17. the God of Israel *e.* the people in Egypt
2 *Cor.* 11. 7. abasing myself that you might be *e.*
12. 7. lest I should be *e.* above measure, 7.
Phil. 2. 9. wherefore God hath highly *e.* him
Jam. 1. 9. let the brother rejoice that he is *e.*

EXALTEST.
Exod. 9. 17. as yet *e.* thou thyself against my people

EXALTETH.
Job 36. 22. behold, God *e.* by his power
Psal. 113. †5. Lord our God, who *e.* hims. to dwell
148. 14. he also *e.* the horn of his people
Prov. 3. †35. wise inherit glory, but shame *e.* fools
14. 29. he that is hasty of spirit *e.* folly
34. righteousness *e.* a nation, but sin is a reproach
17. 19. he that *e.* his gate seeketh destruction
Luke 14. 11. he that *e.* hims. shall be abased, 18. 14.
2 *Cor.* 10. 5. casting down every thing that *e.* itself
2 *Thess.* 2. 4. who *e.* hims. above all that is called G.

EXAMINATION.
Acts 25. 26. that after *e.* had, I might have to write

EXAMINE,
When applied to God, denotes the particular strict notice he takes of his creatures. Psal. 26. 2. Examine me, O Lord, and prove me; try my reins and my heart. *As if the* Psalmist *had said, Because I may be mistaken, or be partial in my own cause, therefore I appeal to thee, and offer myself to thy trial concerning what my enemies charge me with.*

When applied to man, examination *is either private or public.* Private, *when a Christian tries himself by the word of God, and by what Christ has wrought by his spirit within him, whether he be a true believer in Jesus, and has any ground to hope for salvation through his blood and righteousness,* 2 Cor. 13. 5. Examine yourselves, whether ye be in the faith, prove your own selves. *And this duty is especially to be performed before persons partake of the Lord's supper.* 1 Cor. 11. 28. But let a man examine himself, and so let him eat of that bread, and drink of that cup. *Let him compare his heart and life by the word, to see whether he be duly qualified to partake of this ordinance, in regard of his knowledge, faith, repentance, love, and new obedience.*

Public examination *is, when rulers and governors, whether civil or ecclesiastical, bring such as are suspected of unsound principles, or detected of enormities, to a trial for the same. Thus it is said of the angel of the church of* Ephesus, *Rev.* 2. 2. Thou hast tried them which say they are apostles, and are not; and hast found them liars. *And our Saviour was examined by* Pilate, *though he was innocent, and the things laid to his charge were unjust,* Luke 23. 13, 14. *And the apostle* Paul *was ordered to be examined by scourging,* Acts 22. 24. *As to the manner of examining by scourging,* or putting one to the question. *See on* QUESTION.

Ezra 10. 16. sat down the first day to *e.* the matter
Psal. 26. 2. *e.* me, O Lord, prove me, try my reins
1 *Cor.* 9. 3. mine answer to them that *e.* me, is this
11. 28. let a man *e.* himself, and so let him eat of
2 *Cor.* 13. 5. *e.* yourselves, prove your own selves

EXAMINED.
Luke 23. 14. behold, I have *e.* him before you
Acts 4. 9. if we this day be *e.* of the good deed
12. 19. Herod *e.* keepers, and commanded to death
22. 24. brought, that he should be *e.* by scourging
29. they depart. from him, who should have *e.* him
28. 18. when they had *e.* me would have let me go

EXAMINING.
Acts 24. 8. by *e.* of whom thou mayest take knowl.

EXAMPLE
Is *taken either for a type, instance, or precedent, for our admonition, that we may be cautioned against the sins which others have committed, by the judgments which God inflicted on them,* 1 Cor. 10. 11. All these things happened unto them for ensamples. *Or example is taken for a pattern for our imitation, a model for us to copy after.* John 13. 15. I have given you an example, that ye should do as I have done to you. *And in* 1 Pet. 2. 21. Christ suffered for us, leaving us an example, that we should follow his steps. *This is one of the means by which our Redeemer restores his people to holiness, namely, by exhibiting a complete pattern of it in his life upon earth.*

That examples *have a peculiar power above the naked precept, to dispose us to the practice of holiness, may appear by considering,* (1) *That they most clearly express to us the nature of our duties in their subjects and sensible effects. General precepts form abstract ideas of virtue, but in examples, virtues are made visible in all their circumstances.* (2) *Precepts instruct us what things are our duty, but examples assure us that they are possible. When we see men like ourselves, who are united to frail flesh, and in the same condition with us, to command their passions, to overcome the greatest and most glittering temptations, we are encouraged in our spiritual warfare.* (3) Examples, *by a secret and lively incentive, urge us to imitation. We are touched in another manner by the visible practice of saints, which reproaches our defects, and obliges us to the same zeal, than by laws, though holy and good.*

The example of Christ *is most proper to form us to holiness, it being absolutely perfect, and accomodated to our present state. There is no example of a mere man, that is to be followed without limitation.* Be ye followers of me, as I am of Christ, *says the great apostle,* 1 Cor. 11. 1. *But the example of Christ is absolutely perfect. His conversation was a living law.* He was holy,

harmless, undefiled, and separate from sinners, *Heb.* 7. 26. *His example is also most accommodated to our present state. The divine nature is the supreme rule of moral perfection; for we are commanded to be holy, as God is holy. But such is the obscurity of our minds, and the weakness of our natures, that the pattern was too high and glorious to be expressed by us. And though we had not strength to ascend to him, yet he had goodness to descend to us; and in this present state, and in our nature, to set before us a pattern more fitted to our capacity: So that the divine attributes are sweetened in the Son of God incarnate; and being united with the graces proper for the human nature, are more perceptible to our minds, and more imitable by us.*
Mat. 1. 19. Joseph not willing to make her a public *e.*
John 13. 15. for I have given you an *e.* that ye do
Rom. 15. † 5. be like minded after the *e.* of Christ
1 *Tim.* 4. 12. but be thou an *e.* of the believers
Heb. 4. 11. lest any man fall after the same *e.*
8. 5. who serve unto the *e.* of heavenly things
Jam. 5. 10. take the prophets for an *e.* of suffering
1 *Pet.* 2. 21. Christ suffered for us, leaving us an *e.*
Jude 7. set forth for an *e.* suffering the vengeance

EXAMPLES.

1 *Cor.* 10. 6. now these things were our *e.* not to lust
See ENSAMPLE, S.

EXCEED.

Deut. 25. 3. forty stripes he may give, and not *e.*
lest if he should *e.* thy brother seem vile to thee
Mat. 5. 20. except your righteousness *e.* the scribes
2 *Cor.* 3. 9. ministration of righteousn. doth *e.* in glory

EXCEEDED.

1 *Sam.* 20. 41. and they wept, till David *e.*
1 *Kings* 10. 23. Solom. *e.* all kings of earth for riches
Job 36. 9. sheweth their transgressions that they *e.*

EXCEEDEST.

2 *Chron.* 9. 6. for thou *e.* the fame that I heard

EXCEEDETH.

1 *Kings* 10. 7. thy wisdom *e.* the fame which I heard

EXCEEDING.

Gen. 15. 1. I am thy shield, and thy *e.* great reward
17. 6. I will make thee *e.* fruitful, make nations
27. 34. and Esau cried with an *e.* bitter cry
Exod. 1. 7. the children of Israel waxed *e.* mighty
19. 16. and the voice of the trumpet *e.* loud
Num. 14. 7. the land we passed through is *e.* good
1 *Sam.* 2. 3. talk no more so *e.* proudly
2 *Sam.* 8. 8. king David took *e.* much brass
12. 2. the rich man had *e.* many flocks and herds
1 *Kings* 4. 29. God gave Solomon wisdom *e.* much
7. 47. left vessels unweighed, they were *e.* many
1 *Chr.* 20. 2. he brought *e.* much spoil out of the city
22. 5. and the house must be *e.* magnifical
2 *Chron.* 11. 12. and he made the cities *e.* strong
14. 14. for there was *e.* much spoil in them
16. 12. Asa diseased, until his disease waxed *e.* great
32. 27. Hezekiah had *e.* much riches and honour
Ps. 21. 6. thou hast made him *e.* glad with thy coun.
43. 4. then will I go unto God my *e.* joy
119. 96. but thy commandment is *e.* broad
Prov. 30. 24. there be four things which are *e.* wise
Eccl. 7. 24. that which is *e.* deep, who can find it out?
Jer. 48. 29. we heard the pride of Moab, he is *e.* proud
Ezek. 9. 9. the iniquity of Israel is *e.* great
16. 13. thou didst eat oil, and wast *e.* beautiful
23. 15. *e.* in dyed attire upon their heads
37. 10. stood up upon their feet an *e.* great army
47. 10. as the fish of the great sea, *e.* many
Dan. 3. 22. because the furnace was *e.* hot
6. 23. then was the king *e.* glad for him
7. 19. the fourth beast which was *e.* dreadful
8. 9. came forth a little horn, which waxed *e.* great
Jonah 3. 3. now Nineveh was an *e.* great city
4. 6. so Jonah was *e.* glad of the gourd
Mat. 2. 10. saw star, they rejoiced with *e.* great joy
16. Herod, when he was mocked, was *e.* wroth
4. 8. taketh him up into an *e.* high mountain
5. 12. rejoice and be *e.* glad, great is your reward
8. 28. met him two poss. with devils, *e.* fierce
17. 23. they shall kill him; they were *e.* sorry
26. 22. they were *e.* sorrowful, and began to say
38. my soul is *e.* sorrowful, *Mark* 14. 34.
Mark 6. 26. the king was *e.* sorry, yet for the oath
9. 3. his raiment became *e.* white as snow
Luke 23. 8. when Herod saw Jesus, he was *e.* glad
Acts 7. 20. Moses was born, and was *e.* fair
Rom. 7. 13. that sin might become *e.* sinful
2 *Cor.* 4. 17. worketh for us an *e.* weight of glory
7. 4. I am *e.* joyful in all our tribulation
9. 14. who long after you, for *e.* grace of God in you
Eph. 1. 19. what is the *e.* greatness of his power
2. 7. he might shew the *e.* riches of his grace
3. 20. to him that is able to do *e.* abundantly
1 *Tim.* 1. 14. the grace of our Lord was *e.* abundant
1 *Pet.* 4. 13. that ye may be glad also with *e.* joy
2 *Pet.* 1. 4. given to us *e.* great and precious promises
Jude 24. able to present you faultless with *e.* joy
Rev. 16. 21. for the plague thereof was *e.* great

EXCEEDINGLY.

Gen. 7. 19. the waters prevailed *e.* on the earth
13. 13. but the men of Sodom were sinners *e.*
16. 10. the angel said, I will multiply thy seed *e.*
17. 2. I will make my coven. and multiply thee *e.*
20. I will multiply Ishmael *e.* a great nation
27. 33. and Isaac trembled very *e.* and said
30. 43. and Jacob increased *e.* 47. 27.
1 *Sam.* 26. 21. I have played the fool and erred *e.*
2 *Sam.* 13. 15. then Amnon hated her *e.* and said
2 *Kings* 10. 4. the elders of Samaria were *e.* afraid
1 *Chr.* 29. 25. Ld. magnified Solom. *e.* 2 *Chr.* 1. 1.
2 *Chr.* 17. 12. Jehoshaphat waxed great *e.*
26. 8. Uzziah strengthened himself *e.*
Neh. 2. 10. they heard of it, it grieved them *e.*
Esth. 4. 4. the queen was *e.* grieved, and sent raiment
Job 3. 22. rejoice *e.* when they can find the grave
Psal. 68. 3. yea, let the righteous *e.* rejoice
106. 14. lusted *e.* in the wilderness, and tempted G.
119. 167. kept thy testimonies, I love them *e.*
123. 3. for we are *e.* filled with contempt, 4.
Isa. 24. 19. the earth is dissolved, earth is moved *e.*
Dan. 7. 7. and behold, a fourth beast strong *e.*
Jonah 1. 10. men were *e.* afraid, and said to him
16. then the men feared the Lord *e.* and offered
4. 1. but it displeased Jonah *e.* and he was angry
Mat. 19. 25. heard it, they were *e.* amazed, saying
Mark 4. 41. they feared *e.* and said one to another
15. 14. they cried out the more *e.* crucify him
Acts 16. 20. these men do *e.* trouble our city
26. 11. being *e.* mad against them, I persecuted
27. 18. and we being *e.* tossed with a tempest
2 *Cor.* 7. 13. yea, and *e.* the more joyed we for Titus
Gal. 1. 14. being more *e.* zealous of the traditions
1 *Thess.* 3. 10. night and day praying *e.* to see you
2 *Thess.* 1. 3. because that your faith groweth *e.*
Heb. 12. 21. Moses said, I *e.* fear and quake

EXCEL.

Gen. 49. 4. unstable as water, thou shalt not *e.*
1 *Chron.* 15. 21. with harps on the Sheminith to *e.*
Psal. 103. 20. ye his angels, that *e.* in strength
Isa. 10. 10. and whose graven images did *e.* them
1 *Cor.* 14. 12. seek that ye may *e.* to edifying

EXCELLED.

1 *Kings* 4. 30. Solomon's wisdom *e.* wisdom of Egypt

EXCELLEST.

Prov. 31. 29. done virtuously, but thou *e.* them all

EXCELLETH.

Eccl. 2. 13. wisdom *e.* folly, as far as light *e.* dark.
2 *Cor.* 3. 10. by reason of the glory that *e.*

EXCELLENCY.

Gen. 4. † 7. doest well, shalt thou not have the *e.*?
49. 3. the *e.* of dignity, and the *e.* of power
Exod. 15. 7. and in the greatness of thine *e.*
Deut. 33. 26. who rideth in his *e.* on the sky
29. shield of help, and who is the sword of thy *e.*
Job 4. 21. doth not their *e.* go away? they die
13. 11. shall not his *e.* make you afraid?
20. 6. though his *e.* mount up to the heavens
22. † 20. but their *e.* the fire consumeth
37. 4. he thundereth with the voice of his *e.*
40. 10. deck thyself now with majesty and *e.*
Psal. 47. 4. the *e.* of Jacob whom he loved
62. 4. they consult to cast him down from his *e.*
68. 34. his *e.* is over Israel, and his strength
Prov. 17. † 7. a lip of *e.* becometh not a fool
Eccl. 2. † 13. I saw that there is an *e.* in wisdom
7. 12. the *e.* of knowledge is, that wisdom gives life
Isa. 13. 19. Babylon the beauty of the Chaldees' *e.*
35. 2. *e.* of Carmel, Sharon; and the *e.* of our G.
60. 15. I will make thee an eternal *e.* a joy
Ezek. 16. † 56. Sodom not mentioned in day of *e.*
24. 21. my sanctuary, the *e.* of your strength
Amos 6. 8. saith the Lord, I abhor the *e.* of Jacob
8. 7. the Lord hath sworn by the *e.* of Jacob
Nah. 2. 2. for the Lord hath turned away the *e.* of
Jacob, as the *e.* of Israel, emptiers emptied them
Mal. 2. † 15. yet had he the *e.* of the Spirit
1 *Cor.* 2. 1. I came not to you with *e.* of speech
2 *Cor.* 4. 7. that the *e.* of the power may be of God
Phil. 3. 8. I count all things loss for the *e.* of Chr.

EXCELLENT.

Esth. 1. 4. Ahasuerus shewed his *e.* majesty
Job 37. 23. the Almighty is *e.* in power
Psal. 8. 1. how *e.* is thy name in all the earth! 9.
16. 3. and to the *e.* in whom is all my delight
36. 7. how *e.* is thy loving-kindness, O God!
76. 4. thou art more *e.* than the mountains of prey
141. 5. let him reprove me, it shall be an *e.* oil
148. 13. praise the Lord, his name alone is *e.*
150. 2. praise him according to his *e.* greatness
Prov. 8. 6. hear, for I will speak of *e.* things
12. 26. the righteous is more *e.* than his neighbour
17. 7. *e.* speech becometh not a fool
27. a man of understanding is of an *e.* spirit
22. 20. have I not written to thee *e.* things?
Cant. 5. 15. his countenance is *e.* as the cedars
Isa. 4. 2. and the fruit of the earth shall be *e.*
12. 5. sing to the Lord, he hath done *e.* things
22. † 17. Lord covered thee with an *e.* covering
28. 29. the Lord of hosts is *e.* in working
Ezek. 16. 7. and thou art come to *e.* ornaments
27. † 24. these were thy merchants in *e.* things
Dan. 2. 31. this image, whose brightness was *e.*
4. 36. an *e.* majesty was added unto me
5. 12. an *e.* spirit was found in Daniel, 6. 3.
14. I heard that *e.* wisdom is found in thee
Luke 1. 3. to write to thee, most *e.* Theophilus
Acts 23. 26. Claudius, to the *e.* governor Felix
Rom. 2. 18. and approvest things more *e.* *Phil.* 1. 10.
1 *Cor.* 12. 31. yet shew I unto you a more *e.* way
Heb. 1. 4. he obtained a more *e.* name than they
8. 6. but now hath he obtained a more *e.* ministry
11. 4. Abel offered to God a more *e.* sacrifice
2 *Pet.* 1. 17. there came a voice from the *e.* glory

EXCEPT.

Gen. 31. 42. *e.* the G. of my father had been with me
32. 26. I will not let thee go, *e.* thou bless me
42. 15. *e.* your youngest brother come, 43. 3, 5.
43. 10. *e.* we had lingered, we had now returned
47. 26. fifth part, *e.* the land of the priests only
Num. 16. 13. *e.* thou make thyself a prince over us
Deut. 32. 30. *e.* their Rock had sold them
Josh. 7. 12. *e.* you destroy accursed from among you
1 *Sam.* 25. 34. *e.* thou hadst hasted to meet me
2 *Sam.* 3. 9. *e.* as the Lord hath sworn to David
13. *e.* thou first bring Michal, Saul's daughter
5. 6. *e.* thou take away the blind and the lame
2 *Kings* 4. 24. slack not thy riding, *e.* I bid thee
Esth. 2. 14. *e.* the king delighted in her and called
4. 11. *e.* the king shall hold out the golden sceptre
Psal. 127. 1. *e.* the Lord build the house, *e.* the Lord
keep the city, the watchmen watch but in vain
Prov. 4. 16. sleep not, *e.* they have done mischief
Isa. 1. 9. *e.* the Lord had left a remnant, *Rom.* 9. 29.
Dan. 2. 11. none other can shew it, *e.* the gods
3. 28. nor worship any god, *e.* their own God
6. 5. *e.* we find it concerning the law of his God
Amos 3. 3. can two walk together, *e.* they be agreed?
Mat. 5. 20. *e.* your righteousness exceed that of
scribes
12. 29. *e.* he first bind the strong man, *Mark* 3. 27.
18. 3. I say to you, *e.* ye be converted, and become
19. 9. put away his wife, *e.* it be for fornication
Mat. 24. 22. and *e.* those days should be shortened
there should no flesh be saved, *Mark* 13. 20.
26. 42. if this cup may not pass, *e.* I drink it, thy will
Mark 7. 3. the Pharisees, *e.* they wash oft, eat not
Luke 9. 13. *e.* we go and buy meat for this people
13. 3. *e.* ye repent, ye shall all likewise perish, 5.
John 3. 2. can do these miracles, *e.* G. be with him
3. *e.* a man be born again, he cannot see the kingd.
5. *e.* a man be born of water and of the Spirit
27. can receive nothing, *e.* it be given from heaven
4. 48. *e.* ye see signs and wonders, ye will not bel.
6. 44. *e.* the Father who hath sent me draw him
53. *e.* ye eat the flesh of the Son of man
65. *e.* it were given unto him of my Father
12. 24. *e.* a corn of wheat fall into the ground
15. 4. ye cannot bear fruit, *e.* ye abide in me
19. 11. no power, *e.* it were given thee from above
20. 25. *e.* I shall see the prints of the nails
Acts 8. 1. they were all scattered, *e.* the apostles
31. how can I, *e.* some man should guide me?
15. 1. *e.* ye be circumcised, ye cannot be saved
24. 21. *e.* it be for this one voice, that I cried
26. 29. all were such as I am, *e.* these bonds
27. 31. Paul said, *e.* these abide in ship, ye cannot
Rom. 7. 7. I had not known lust, *e.* the law had said
10. 15. how shall they preach, *e.* they be sent
1 *Cor.* 7. 5. defraud not one anoth. *e.* it be with consent
14. 5. that speaketh with tongues, *e.* he interpret
6. *e.* I shall speak to you either by revelation
7. *e.* they give a distinction in the sounds
9. *e.* ye utter words easy to be understood
15. 36. that thou sowest is not quickened, *e.* it die
2 *Cor.* 12. 13. *e.* it be that I was not burdensome
13. 5. that Christ is in you, *e.* ye be reprobates?
2 *Thess.* 2. 3. *e.* there come a falling away first
2 *Tim.* 2. 5. he is not crowned, *e.* he strive lawfully
Rev. 2. 5. will remove thy candlestick, *e.* thou repent
22. into tribulation, *e.* they repent of their deeds

EXCEPTED.

1 *Cor.* 15. 27. he is *e.* who did put all things under him

EXCESS.

Mat. 23. 25. within are full of extortion and *e.*
Eph. 5. 18. be not drunk with wine, wherein is *e.*
1 *Pet.* 4. 3. when we walked in lusts, *e.* of wine
4. that ye run not with them to the same *e.*

EXCHANGE.

Gen. 47. 17. Joseph gave them bread in *e.* for horses
Lev. 27. 10. then it and the *e.* thereof shall be holy
Job 20. † 18. according to the substance of his *e.*
28. 17. and the *e.* of it shall not be for jewels
Mat. 16. 26. if gain world and lose his soul, what
shall a man give in *e.* for his soul? *Mark* 8. 37.

EXCHANGE.

Ezek. 48. 14. they shall not sell of it, nor *e.* first-fruits

EXCHANGERS.

Mat. 25. 27. oughtest to have put my money to *e.*

EXCLUDE.

Gal. 4. 17. they would *e.* you, that you might affect

EXCLUDED.

Rom. 3. 27. where is boasting then? it is *e.*

EXCOMMUNICATED.

Excommunication *is an ecclesiastical censure, whereby they who incur the guilt of any heinous sin, are separated from the communion of the church, and deprived of spiritual advantages; that they may be brought to repentance, and others, by their example, kept from the like enormities.* Mat. 18. 15, 16, 17. 1 Cor. 5. 5, 7. 2 Thess. 3. 14, 15.

There are generally three sorts of Excommunication, *distinguished among the* Jews. *The first is called* Niddui, *that is,* separation. *This is the lesser* Excommunication. *It lasted thirty days, and separated the excommunicated persons from the use of things holy. The second was called* Cherim, *that is* Anathema; *this was an aggravation of the first, and answers almost to our greater* excommunication. *It excluded a man from the synagogue, and deprived him of all civil commerce. The third sort of* Excommunication *is called* Scammatha, *and was of a higher nature than the greater* excommunication. *It was published, as they say, by sound of four hundred trumpets, and removed all hope of returning to the synagogue. Some affirm, that the penalty of death was annexed to it. But* Selden *maintains, that these three terms,* Niddui, Cherim, *and* Scammatha, *are oftentimes synonymous, and that the* Jews *never had, properly speaking, more than two sorts of* excommunication; *one greater the other less.* Selden *de synedriis veterum Hebræorum*, lib. 1. cap. 7. *and* 8.
John 9. † 34. dost thou teach us? and they *e.* him

EXCUSE.

Luke 14. 18. they with one consent began to make *e.*
John 15. † 22. now have they no *e.* for their sin
Rom. 1. 20. clearly seen, so that they are without *e.*

EXCUSE.

2 *Cor.* 12. 19. think you that we *e.* ourselves to you?

EXCUSED.

Luke 14. 18. I pray thee have me *e.* 19.

EXCUSING.

Rom. 2. 15. their thoughts accusing or else *e.* one an.

EXECRATION.

Jer. 42. 18. and ye shall be an *e.* and a curse
44. 12. and they shall be an *e.* and a reproach
Acts 23. † 12. bound themselves with an oath of *e.*

EXECUTE.

Exod. 12. 12. I will *e.* judgment on the gods of Egypt
Num. 5. 30. the priest shall *e.* upon her all this law
8. 11. that they may *e.* the service of the Lord
Deut. 10. 18. he doth *e.* the judgment of the widow
1 *Kings* 6. 12. if thou wilt *e.* my judgments
Psal. 119. 84. when wilt thou *e.* judgm. on them that
149. 7. to *e.* vengeance upon the heathen
9. to *e.* upon them the judgment written
Isa. 16. 3. take counsel, *e.* judgment, hide outcasts
Jer. 7. 5. *e.* judgm. between a man and his neighb.
21. 12. *e.* judgment in the morning, and deliver
22. 3. *e.* judgm. and righteousness, deliver spoiled
23. 5. branch shall *e.* judgm. and justice, 33. 15.
Ezek. 5. 8. I will *e.* judgments in thee, 10.

Ezek. 5. 15. when I shall *e.* judgments in thee in fury
11. 9. and I will *e.* judgments among you
16. 41. they shall *e.* judgments upon thee
25. 11. and I will *e.* judgments upon Moab
17. and I will *e.* great vengeance upon them
30. 14. I set fire in Zoan, and *e.* judgments in No
19. thus will I *e.* judgments in Egypt
45. 9. remove violence, *e.* judgment and justice
Hos. 11. 9. I will not *e.* the fierceness of mine anger
Mic. 5. 15. and I will *e.* vengeance in anger
7. 9. till he plead my cause, and *e.* judgm. for me
Zech. 7. 9. *e.* true judgment, and shew mercy
8. 16. *e.* the judgment of truth and peace
John 5. 27. hath given him authority to *e.* judgment
Rom. 13. 4. he is the minister of God to *e.* wrath
Jude 15. to *e.* judgment on all, and to convince

EXECUTED.

Num. 33. 4. on their gods the Lord *e.* judgments
Deut. 33. 21. he *e.* the justice of the Lord
2 *Sam.* 8. 15. David *e.* judgment, 1 *Chron.* 18. 14.
1 *Chron.* 6. 10. he it is that *e.* the priest's office
24. 2. Eleazar and Ithamar *e.* the priest's office
2 *Chron.* 24. 24. they *e.* judgment against Joash
Ezra 7. 26. let judgment be *e.* speedily on him
Ps. 106. 30. then stood up Phinehas, and *e.* judgment
Eccl. 8. 11. because sentence is not *e.* speedily
Jer. 23. 20. anger of L. shall not return till he have *e.*
Ezek. 11. 12. neither *e.* my judgments, 20. 24.
18. 8. hath *e.* true judgm. betw. man and man, 17.
23. 10. for they had *e.* judgment upon her
28. 22. when I shall have *e.* judgments, 26.
39. 21. heathen shall see my judgm. that I have *e.*
Luke 1. 8. while Zacharias *e.* the priest's office

EXECUTEDST.

1 *Sam.* 28. 18. nor *e.* his fierce wrath on Amalek

EXECUTEST.

Ps. 99. 4. thou *e.* judgm. and righteousness in Jacob

EXECUTETH.

Psal. 9. 16. Lord is known by the judgment he *e.*
103. 6. the Lord *e.* righteousness and judgment
146. 7. the Lord *e.* judgment for the oppressed
Isa. 46. 11. the man that *e.* my counsel from afar
Jer. 5. 1. if any *e.* judgment, I will pardon it
Joel 2. 11. for he is strong that *e.* his word

EXECUTING.

2 *Kings* 10. 30. thou hast done well in *e.* on Ahab
2 *Chron.* 11. 14. Jeroboam had cast them off from *e.*
22. 8. when Jehu was *e.* judgment on Ahab's house

EXECUTION.

Esth. 9. 1. his decree drew near to be put in *e.*

EXECUTIONER.

Mark 6. 27. the king sent an *e.* and commanded

EXECUTIONERS.

Gen. 37. † 36. sold him to Potiphar, chief of the *e.*
Jer. 39. † 9. Nebuzar-adan, chief of the *e.* 52. † 12.
Dan. 2. † 14. to Arioch the chief of the *e.*

EXEMPTED.

1 *Kings* 15. 22. Asa made proclamation, none was *e.*

EXERCISE.

1 *Tim.* 4. 8. bodily *e.* profiteth little, godliness profit.

EXERCISE.

Psal. 131. 1. nor do I *e.* myself in things too high
Jer. 9. 24. I am the Lord which *e.* loving-kindness
Mat. 20. 25. ye know that princes of the Gentiles *e.* dominion over them, and they that are great *e.* authority upon them, *Mark* 10. 42. *Luke* 22. 25.
Acts 24. 16. herein do I *e.* myself to have a conscience
1 *Tim.* 4. 7. and *e.* thyself rather unto godliness

EXERCISED.

Eccl. 1. 13. sore travail, to be *e.* therewith, 3. 10.
Ezek. 22. 29. the people of the land have *e.* robbery
Heb. 5. 14. senses *e.* to discern both good and evil
12. 11. fruit of right. to them which are *e.* thereby
2 *Pet.* 2. 14. an heart *e.* with covetous practices

EXERCISETH.

Rev. 13. 12. he *e.* all the power of the first beast

EXHORT.

Acts 2. 40. with many words did he testify and *e.*
27. 22. and now I *e.* you to be of good cheer
2 *Cor.* 9. 5. therefore I thought it necessary to *e.*
1 *Thess.* 4. 1. we beseech you, brethren, and *e.* you
† 18. wherefore *e.* one another with these words
5. † 11. wherefore *e.* yourselves together, edify
14. now we *e.* you, warn them that are unruly
2 *Thess.* 3. 12. such we command and *e.* by Christ
1 *Tim.* 2. 1. I *e.* that first of all, pray. be made for all
6. 2. these things teach and *e.*
2 *Tim.* 4. 2. *e.* with all long-suffering and doctrine
Tit. 1. 9. may be able to *e.* and convince gainsayers
2. 6. young men likewise *e.* to be sober-minded
9. *e.* servants to be obedient to their masters
15. speak, *e.* and rebuke with all authority
Heb. 3. 13. *e.* one another daily while it is called
1 *Pet.* 5. 1. the elders who are among you I *e.*
Jude 3. it was needful for me to write and *e.* you

EXHORTATION.

Luke 3. 18. many other things in his *e.* preached he
Acts 13. 15. if ye have any word of *e.* say on
15. † 31. when they read, they rejoiced for the *e.*
20. 2. and when Paul had given them much *e.*
Rom. 12. 8. he that exhorteth, let him wait on *e.*
1 *Cor.* 14. 3. speaketh unto men to *e.* and comfort
2 *Cor.* 8. 17. for indeed he accepted the *e.*
1 *Thess.* 2. 3. for our *e.* was not of deceit nor guile
1 *Tim.* 4. 13. till I come, give attendance to *e.*
Heb. 12. 5. ye have forgotten the *e.* which speaketh
13. 22. and I beseech you, suffer the word of *e.*

EXHORTED.

Acts 11. 23. Barnabas *e.* them to cleave to the Lord
15. 32. they *e.* the brethren with many words
1 *Thess.* 2. 11. as you know how we *e.* and comforted

EXHORTING.

Acts 14. 22. and *e.* them to continue in the faith
18. 27. brethren wrote *e.* disciples to receive him
Heb. 10. 25. but *e.* one another, and so much more
1 *Pet.* 5. 12. by Silvanus I have written briefly, *e.*

EXILE.

2 *Sam.* 15. 19. for thou art a stranger, and also an *e.*
Isa. 51. 14. the captive *e.* hasteneth to be loosed

EXORCISTS.

This word comes from the Greek Ἐξορκίζειν, Exorcisein, *which signifies to* adjure, *to* conjure, *to use the name of God, with a design to cast devils out of the bodies which they possess. When our Saviour sent out his disciples to preach the gospel, he gave them power over unclean spirits, to cast them out,* Mat. 10. 1. *And when the seventy returned, they told our Saviour,* Luke 10. 17. Lord, even the devils are subject to us, through thy name. *By this gift, they gained repute among the people, confirming them that they were sent of God.* St. Paul, *in* Acts 16. 18. *cast out a devil, in the name of* Christ; I command thee, in the name of Jesus Christ, to come out of her: and he came out the same hour. *This gift continued in the church, after the death of the apostles, as some say, for about two hundred years, and ceased by degrees.*
Those Jewish exorcists, *mentioned* Acts 19. 13. *were such as usurped and counterfeited this gift, though they had it not; but what they did was only by witchcraft, and compact with the devil.*
Josephus *relates strange stories concerning these exorcists. He says, that one* Eleazar, *a* Jew, *cured the possessed with the help of a ring, in which a root was set, said by some to have been discovered by* Solomon. *The smell of this root, put under the nose of the possessed person, made him fall on the ground; and the* exorcist *conjured the devil, forbidding him to return into that body;* Joseph. *Antiq.* lib. 8. cap. 2. Justin, Origen, *and* Tertullian, *speak of* Jews, *who boasted of a power to cast out devils, and, it is said, that sometimes in reality they did so, by calling upon the God of* Abraham.
Acts 19. 13. then certain of the vagabond Jews, *e.*

EXPANSION.

Gen. 1. † 6. let there be an *e.* in midst of the waters

EXPECTATION.

1 *Chron.* 29. † 15. days as a shadow, there is no *e.*
Job 6. † 8. O that God would grant me mine *e.*
Ps. 9. 18. the *e.* of the poor shall not perish for ever
62. 5. wait thou on God, for my *e.* is from him
Prov. 10. 28. the *e.* of the wicked shall perish, 11. 7.
11. 23. but the *e.* of the wicked is wrath
23. 18. thine *e.* shall not be cut off, 24. 14.
Isa. 20. 5. they shall be ashamed of their *e.*
6. the inhabitants shall say, behold, such is our *e.*
Jer. 29. † 11. I think to give you an end and *e.*
Zech. 9. 5. Ekron for her *e.* shall be ashamed
Luke 3. 15. and as the people were in *e.* John said
Acts 12. 11. Lord hath delivered me from *e.* of Jews
Rom. 8. 19. for the *e.* of the creature waiteth for
Phil. 1. 20. according to my earnest *e.* and hope

EXPECTED.

Job 32. † 4. Elihu had *e.* till Job had spoken
Jer. 29. 11. for I think to give you an *e.* end

EXPECTING.

Acts 3. 5. *e.* to receive something of them
Heb. 10. 13. *e.* till his enemies be made his footstool

EXPEDIENT.

John 11. 50. that it is *e.* for us that one man die
16. 7. I tell you, it is *e.* for you that I go away
18. 14. it was *e.* that one man die for the people
1 *Cor.* 6. 12. but all things are not *e.* 10. 23.
2 *Cor.* 8. 10. this is *e.* for you who have begun before
12. 1. it is not *e.* for me doubtless to glory

EXPEL.

Josh. 23. 5. God shall *e.* them from before you
Judg. 11. 7. did not ye hate me, *e.* me out of house?

EXPELLED.

Josh. 13. 13. Isr. *e.* not Geshurites, nor Maachathites
Judg. 1. 20. he *e.* thence the three sons of Anak
2 *Sam.* 14. 14. that his banished be not *e.* from him
Acts 13. 50. they *e.* them out of their coasts

EXPENCES.

Ezra 6. 4. let the *e.* be given out of the king's house
8. I decree that *e.* forthwith be given to these men

EXPERIENCE.

Gen. 30. 27. by *e.* that the Lord hath blessed me
Eccl. 1. 16. my heart had great *e.* of wisdom
Rom. 5. 4. and patience worketh *e.* and *e.* hope
Heb. 5. † 13. that useth milk hath no *e.* in the word

EXPERIMENT.

2 *Cor.* 9. 13. whiles by the *e.* of this ministration

EXPERT.

1 *Chron.* 12. 33. of Zebulun fifty thousand *e.* in war
35. of Danites 28,600 ‖ 36. of Asher, 40,000 *e.*
Cant. 3. 8. they all hold swords, being *e.* in war
Jer. 50. 9. their arrows shall be as of an *e.* man
Acts 26. 3. I know thee to be *e.* in all customs

EXPIATION.

Num. 35. † 33. and there can be no *e.* for the land

EXPIRED.

1 *Sam.* 18. 26. and the days were not *e.*
2 *Sam.* 11. 1. after the year was *e.* 1 *Chron.* 20. 1.
1 *Chron.* 17. 11. shall come to pass when days be *e.*
2 *Chron.* 36. 10. when year *e.* Nebuchadnezzar sent
Esth. 1. 5. when these days were *e.* the king made
Ezek. 43. 27. when these days are *e.* it shall be that
Acts 7. 30. and when forty years were *e.*
Rev. 20. 7. when 1000 years are *e.* Satan be loosed

EXPLOITS.

Dan. 11. 28. to his land he shall do *e.* and return
32. but the people shall be strong and do *e.*

EXPOSED.

Judg. 5. † 18. Zebulun and Naphtali a people *e.*

EXPOUND.

Lev. 24. † 12. put him in ward, to *e.* mind of God
Judg. 14. 14. they could not in three days *e.* riddle

EXPOUNDED.

Judg. 14. 19. garments to them who *e.* the riddle
Mark 4. 34. when they were alone, he *e.* all things
Luke 24. 27. he *e.* to them in all the scriptures
Acts 11. 4. but Peter *e.* it by order unto them
18. 26. Aquila and Priscilla *e.* to him way of God
28. 23. Paul *e.* and testified the kingdom of God

EXPRESS.

Heb. 1. 3. who being the *e.* image of his person

EXPRESS, ED.

Num. 1. 17. took men which are *e.* by their names
1 *Chr.* 12. 31. and of Manasseh 18,000, *e.* by name
16. 41. who were *e.* by name, to give thanks to L.
2 *Chron.* 28. 15. men *e.* took captives, clothed naked
2 *Chron.* 31. 19. men *e.* to give portions to the males
Ezra 8. 20. the Nethinims were *e.* by name
Job 6. † 3. therefore I want words to *e.* my grief

EXPRESSLY.

1 *Sam.* 20. 21. if I *e.* say to the lad, behold arrows
Ezek. 1. 3. the word came *e.* to Ezekiel the priest
1 *Tim.* 4. 1. now the Spirit speaketh *e.* some depart

EXPULSIONS.

Ezek. 45. † 9. take away your *e.* from my people

EXTEND.

Psal. 109. 12. let there be none to *e.* mercy to him
Isa. 66. 12. behold, I will *e.* peace to her like a river

EXTENDED.

Gen. 39. † 21. but the Lord *e.* kindness to Joseph
Ezra 7. 28. *e.* mercy to me ‖ 9. 9. *e.* mercy to us
Jer. 31. † 3. I have *e.* loving-kindness to thee

EXTENDETH.

Psal. 16. 2. my Lord, my goodness *e.* not to thee

EXTINCT.

Job 17. 1. my days are *e.* the graves are ready for me
Isa. 43. 17. they are *e.* they are quenched as tow

EXTINGUISH.

Ezek. 32. † 7. when I shall *e.* thee, I will cover heav

EXTINGUISHED.

Job 6. † 17. when it is hot, they are *e.* out of place

EXTOL.

Psal. 30. 1. I will *e.* thee, O Lord, hast lifted me up
68. 4. *e.* him that rideth upon the heavens
145. 1. I will *e.* thee, my God, O King, and bless
Dan. 4. 37. I Nebuchadnezzar *e.* King of heaven

EXTOLLED.

Psal. 66. 17. and he was *e.* with my tongue
Isa. 52. 13. behold, my servant shall be *e.*

EXTORTION.

Ezek. 22. 12. thou hast greedily gained by *e.*
Mat. 23. 25. but within they are full of *e.*

EXTORTIONER.

Psal. 109. 11. let the *e.* catch all that he hath
Isa. 16. 4. the *e.* is at an end, the spoiler ceaseth
1 *Cor.* 5. 11. if any man be a drunkard, an *e.*

EXTORTIONERS.

Luke 18. 11. that I am not as other men are, *e.*
1 *Cor.* 5. 10. yet not altogether with *e.* for then
6. 10. nor *e.* inherit the kingdom of God

EXTREME.

Deut. 28. 22. the L. shall smite thee with *e.* burning

EXTREMITY.

Job 35. 15. yet he knoweth it not in great *e.*

EYE.

The organ of sight, by which visible objects are discerned. Eye, *or* eyes, *in Scripture, are figuratively applied to God after the manner of man.* Prov. 15. 3. The eyes of the Lord are in every place; *that is, his infinite knowledge and providence. And as in men the eye is the organ which shews compassion or fury, vengeance or pardon, gentleness or severity; in these senses* eye *is referred to God;* Psal. 34. 15. The eyes of the Lord are upon the righteous: *He favours them, and heaps blessings on them.* 1 Kings 8. 29. That thine eyes may be opened toward this house night and day; *that is, that thou mayest behold it with an eye of favour and compassion. So likewise in* Jer. 24. 6. I will set mine eyes upon them for good. *On the contrary it is said,* Amos 9. 8. Behold, the eyes of the Lord are upon the sinful kingdom; *that is, in a way of severity and judgment. Also* Ezek. 5. 11. Neither shall mine eyes spare, neither will I have any pity.
Eye, *when referred to man, is not only taken for the organ of sight, but also for the understanding or judgment.* Deut. 16. 19. A gift doth blind the eyes of the wise: *It corrupteth and perverteth his mind, that as he will not, so oftentimes he cannot discern between right and wrong. So in* Acts 26. 18. I send thee to the Gentiles to open their eyes; *that is, To preach the gospel unto them whereby they may attain unto a spiritual understanding of their duty. Likewise in* Gen. 3. 7. The eyes of them both were opened. *Their consciences were touched with a sense of the heinousness of their sin, whereby they had defiled their souls: and of the greatness of the misery they had brought upon themselves and their posterity.*
The Hebrews *call colours,* eyes, *Num.* 11. 7. And the *eye,* or *colour* of the manna, was as the *eye,* or *colour* of bdellium. To set one's eyes upon any one *is to do him service, to favour him greatly;* or *barely to see him with friendship.* Gen. 44. 21. Thou saidst, bring Benjamin unto me, that I may set mine eyes upon him. *And* Nebuchadnezzar *recommends it to* Nebuzar-adan, *that he would set his eyes upon* Jeremiah, *and permit him to go where he pleased,* Jer. 39. † 12. ‖ 40. † 4. To find grace in one's eyes, *is to win his favour and friendship,* Ruth 2. 10. Job *says,* I was eyes to the blind, *Job* 29. 15. *that is, I instructed, directed, and assisted such as knew not how to manage their own affairs.*
To have the eyes towards, *or* upon one, *denotes that the person expects, or waits for something from him on whom the eyes are placed. Thus when* Adonijah, *without his father's knowledge, had usurped the kingdom,* Bathsheba *told king* David, 1 Kings 1. 20. The eyes of all *Israel* are upon thee, that thou shouldest tell them who shall sit upon the throne of my lord the king after him; *that is, The generality of the people are in suspense whether* Adonijah's *practices be with thy consent, or no, and wait for thy sentence concerning thy successor, which they will readily embrace. Also in* Psal. 25. 15. Mine eyes are ever towards the Lord; *that is, my expectation of help is only from him. And* Psal. 123. 2. As the eyes of servants look unto the hand of their masters; *either for the supply of their wants, which comes from their masters' hand: or, for help and defence against their oppressors.*
Solomon *says, that* the wise man's eyes are in his head, *Eccl.* 2. 14. *He knows where he goes, and what he has to do; he does not act ignorantly, rashly, or foolishly. He says likewise, that*

the eye is not satisfied with riches, *Eccl.* 4. 8. *The covetous mind, or desire, is insatiable.* Eye *is sometimes taken for something that is most delightful and dear to a person.* Mat. 5. 29. If thy right eye offend thee, pluck it out. *Gal.* 4. 15. You would have plucked out your own eyes, and have given them to me. *It is likewise taken for opinion, or conceit.* Prov. 3. 7. Be not wise in thine own eyes. *And for a diligent and careful inspection into affairs.* Prov. 20. 8. A king scattereth away all evil with his eyes. *Evil eye*; see on EVIL.

Gen. 45. † 20. let not your *e.* spare your stuff
Exod. 10. † 5. the locusts cover the *e.* of the earth
21. 24. *e.* for *e. Lev.* 24. 20. *Deut.* 19. 21. *Mat.* 5. 38.
26. if a man smite the *e.* of his servant, or the *e.*
Lev. 21. 20. or that hath a blemish in his *e.*
Num. 11. † 7. the *e.* of manna was as the *e.* of bdellium
Deut. 28. 54. his *e.* shall be evil toward his brother
56. her *e.* shall be evil towards her husband
32. 10. he kept him as the apple of his *e.*
34. 7. his *e.* was not dim, nor his force abated
Ezra 5. 5. the *e.* of their God was on the elders
Job 7. 8. *e.* that hath seen me, shall see me no more
10. 18. given up the ghost, and no *e.* had seen me
20. 9. the *e.* which saw him, shall see him no more
24. 15. the *e.* of the adulterer waiteth for twilight, saying, no *e.* shall see me, and disguiseth his face
28. 7. a path which the vulture's *e.* hath not seen
10. and his *e.* seeth every precious thing
29. 11. when the *e.* saw me, it gave witness to me
Psal. 33. 18. *e.* of the L. is on them that fear him
35. 19. neither let them wink with the *e.*
21. they said, aha, aha, our *e.* hath seen it
94. 9. he that formed the *e.* shall he not see?
Prov. 10. 10. that winketh with the *e.* causeth sorrow
20. 12. the seeing *e.* hearing ear, Lord hath made
22. 9. he that hath a bountiful *e.* shall be blessed
30. 17. the *e.* that mocketh at his father
Eccl. 1. 8. the *e.* is not satisfied with seeing
4. 8. neither is his *e.* satisfied with riches
Isa. 13. 18. their *e.* shall not spare children
52. 8. thy watchmen sing, for they shall see *e.* to *e.*
64. 4. neither hath the *e.* seen, 1 *Cor.* 2. 9.
Lam. 2. 4. and slew all that were pleasant to the *e.*
Ezek. 9. 5. let not your *e.* spare, neither have pity
16. 5. none *e.* pitied, to do any of these to thee
Mic. 4. 11. be defiled, and let our *e.* look on Zion
Mat. 6. 22. the light of the body is the *e. Luke* 11. 34.
7. 3. thou beholdest the mote in thy brother's *e.* and not the beam in thine own *e. Luke* 6. 41, 42.
18. 9. if thine *e.* offend thee, pluck it out
19. 24. easier for a camel to go through *e.* of a needle than a rich man, *Mark* 10. 25. *Luke* 18. 25.
1 *Cor.* 12. 16. because I am not the *e.* I am not of body
17. if the whole body were an *e.* ‖ 21. *e.* cannot say
15. 52. in twinkling of an *e.* at the last trump
Rev. 1. 7. he cometh, and every *e.* shall see him

Evil EYE.
Prov. 23. 6. the bread of him that hath an *evil e.*
28. 22. he that hasteth to be rich hath an *evil e.*
Mat. 6. 23. but if thine *e.* be *evil, Luke* 11. 34.
20. 15. is thine *e. evil* because I am good?
Mark 7. 22. out of the heart proceedeth an *evil e.*

Mine EYE.
1 *Sam.* 24. 10. bade kill thee, but *mine e.* spared thee
Job 7. 7. *mine e.* shall no more see good
13. 1. *mine e.* hath seen all this, mine ear heard
16. 20. but *mine e.* poureth out tears to God
17. 2. doth *mine e.* continue in their provocation?
7. *mine e.* also is dim by reason of sorrow
42. 5. heard of thee, but now *mine e.* seeth thee
Psal. 6. 7. *mine e.* is consumed with grief, 31. 9.
32. 8. instruct thee, I will guide thee with *mine e.*
54. 7. *mine e.* hath seen his desire on mine enemies
88. 9. *mine e.* mourneth by reason of affliction
92. 11. *mine e.* shall see my desire on mine enemies
Jer. 40. † 4. come to Babylon I will set *mine e.* on thee
Lam. 1. 16. *mine e. mine e.* runneth down, 3. 48.
3. 49. *mine e.* trickleth down and ceaseth not
51. *mine e.* affecteth my heart, because of daugh.
Ezek. 5. 11. neither shall *mine e.* spare, nor will I have any pity, 7. 4, 9. | 8. 18. | 9. 10.
20. 17. nevertheless *mine e.* spared them

Thine EYE.
Deut. 7. 16. *thine e.* shall not pity, nor shalt thou serve their gods, 13. 8. | 19. 13, 21. | 25. 12.
15. 9. and *thine e.* be evil against thy poor brother
Mat. 6. 22. if *thine e.* be single, *Luke* 11. 34.
7. 3. the beam that is in *thine* own *e. Luke* 6. 41.
18. 9. if *thine e.* offend thee pluck it out, *Mark* 9. 47.
See APPLE.

EYE-BROWS.
Lev. 14. 9. he shall shave all his hair off his *e.-brows*

EYE-LIDS.
Job 3. † 9. nor let it see the *e.* of the morning
16. 16. and on mine *e.* is the shadow of death
41. 18. his eyes are like the *e.* of the morning
Psal. 11. 4. his *e.* try the children of men
132. 4. sleep to mine eyes, or slumber to mine *e.*
Prov. 4. 25. let thine *e.* look straight before thee
6. 4. sleep to thine eyes, or slumber to thine *e.*
25. neither let her take thee with her *e.*
30. 13. how lofty their eyes, their *e.* are lifted up
Jer. 9. 18. that our *e.* may gush out with waters

Right EYE.
Zech. 11. 17. the sword shall be on his arm and on his *right e.* his *right e.* shall be utterly darkened
Mat. 5. 29. if thy *right e.* offend thee, pluck it out

EYE-SALVE.
Rev. 3. 18. anoint thine eyes with *e.-salve* to see

EYE-SERVICE.
Eph. 6. 6. not with *e.-service* as men-pleasers, but as the servants of Christ, *Col.* 3. 22.

EYE-SIGHT.
2 *Sam.* 22. 25. the Ld. hath recompensed me according to my cleanness in his *e.-sight, Psal.* 18. 24.

EYE-WITNESSES.
Luke 1. 2. who from beginning were *e.-witnesses*
2 *Pet.* 1. 16. but were *e.-witnesses* of his majesty

EYED.
1 *Sam.* 18. 9. and Saul *e.* David from that day

Tender-EYED
Gen. 29. 17. Leah was *tender-e.* Rachel beautiful

EYES.
Gen. 3. 6. was good for food and pleasant to the *e.*
7. and the *e.* of them both were opened
16. 4. her mistress was despised in her *e.*
5. she had conceived, I was despised in her *e.*
20. 16. behold, he is to thee a covering of the *e.*
21. 19. God opened Hagar's *e.* she saw a well
28. † 8. the daughters of Canaan evil in *e.* of Isaac
30. 41. Jacob laid the rods before the *e.* of the cattle
39. 7. his master's wife cast her *e.* on Joseph
41. 37. was good in the *e.* of Pharaoh, 45. † 16.
48. 10. now the *e.* of Israel were dim for age
Exod. 5. 21. to be abhorred in the *e.* of Pharaoh
21. † 8. if she be evil in the *e.* of her master
24. 17. glory of Lord was like fire in *e.* of Israel
Lev. 4. 13. if sin through ignorance, and the thing be hid from the *e.* of the assembly, *Num.* 15. † 24.
26. 16. the burning ague shall consume the *e.*
Num. 5. 13. be hid from the *e.* of her husband
10. 31. and thou mayest be to us instead of *e.*
16. 14. wilt thou put out the *e.* of these men?
20. 12. to sanctify me in the *e.* of Israel
22. 31. then the Lord opened the *e.* of Balaam
24. 3. the man whose *e.* are open hath said, 15.
Deut. 16. 19. a gift doth blind the *e.* of the wise
28. 65. the Lord shall give thee failing of *e.*
29. 4. the Lord hath not given you *e.* to see
Judg. 16. 28. that I may be avenged for my two *e.*
1 *Sam.* 8. † 6. the thing was evil in the *e.* of Samuel
16. † 7. man looketh on the *e.* the Lord on the heart
† 12. David was ruddy, and withal fair of *e.*
18. † 8. the saying was evil in the *e.* of Saul
29. † 6. thou art not good in the *e.* of the lords
† 7. that thou do not evil in the *e.* of the lords
2 *Sam.* 6. 20. who uncovered himself in *e.* of handm.
17. † 4. the saying was right in the *e.* of Absalom
24. 3. that the *e.* of my lord the king may see it
1 *Kings* 1. 20. the *e.* of all Israel are upon thee
2 *Kings* 6. 17. Lord opened the *e.* of the young man
20. Elisha said, Lord, open the *e.* of these men
9. † 30. Jezebel heard of it, put her *e.* in painting
25. 7. put out *e.* of Zedekiah, *Jer.* 39. 7. | 52. 11.
1 *Chron.* 13. 4. was right in the *e.* of all the people
2 *Chron.* 30. † 4. the thing was right in the *e.* of the king and all the congregation, *Esth.* 1. † 21.
Neh. 8. † 5. Ezra opened the book in *e.* of the people
Job 10. 4. hast thou *e.* of flesh? or seest as man seeth?
11. 20. but the *e.* of the wicked shall fail
17. 5. even the *e.* of his children shall fail
22. † 29. he shall save him that hath low *e.*
28. 21. seeing it is hid from the *e.* of all living
29. 15. I was *e.* to the blind, and feet to the lame
31. 16. or have caused the *e.* of the widow to fail
39. 29. seeketh prey, and her *e.* behold afar off
Psal. 15. 4. in whose *e.* a vile person is contemned
19. 8. commandment is pure, enlightening the *e.*
115. 5. *e.* have they, but they see not, 135. 16.
123. 2. as the *e.* of servants, the *e.* of a maiden
145. 15. the *e.* of all wait upon thee, thou givest
146. 8. the Lord openeth the *e.* of the blind
Prov. 1. † 17. in vain the net is spread in the *e.* of bird
6. † 17. haughty *e.* are abomination to the Lord
10. 26. as smoke to the *e.* so is the sluggard
15. 30. the light of the *e.* rejoiceth the heart
17. 8. a gift is as a precious stone in the *e.* of him
24. the *e.* of a fool are in the ends of the earth
23. 29. who hath wounds? who hath redness of *e.?*
27. 20. so the *e.* of man are never satisfied
Eccl. 2. 14. the wise man's *e.* are in his head
6. 9. better the sight of *e.* than wandering of desire
11. 7. It is pleasant for the *e.* to behold the sun
Cant. 1. 15. thou art fair, thou hast dove's *e.* 4. 1.
Isa. 3. 8. against Lord, to provoke the *e.* of his glory
16. the daughters of Zion walk with wanton *e.*
5. 15. the *e.* of the lofty shall be humbled
29. 18. the *e.* of the blind shall see out of obscurity
32. 3. the *e.* of them that see shall not be dim
35. 5. then the *e.* of the blind shall be opened
42. 7. to open the blind *e.* to bring out the prisoners
43. 8. bring forth the blind people that have *e.*
52. 10. Lord made bare his arm in *e.* of all nations
59. 10. like the blind we grope as if we had no *e.*
Jer. 4. † 30. thou rentest thine *e.* with painting
5. 21. which have *e.* and see not, *Ezek.* 12. 2.
Ezek. 1. 18. and their rings were full of *e.*
10. 12. the wheels were full of *e.* round about
23. 16. and as soon as she saw them with her *e.*
38. 23. I will be known in the *e.* of many nations
Dan. 7. 8. in this horn were *e.* like the *e.* of man
20. even of that horn that had *e.* and a mouth
Hab. 1. 13. thou art of purer *e.* than to behold evil
Zech. 3. 9. upon one stone shall be seven *e.*
8. 6. if it be marvellous in the *e.* of the remnant
9. 1. when the *e.* of man shall be towards the Lord
Mat. 18. 9. better to enter with one eye rather than having two *e.* to be cast into hell-fire, *Mark* 9. 47.
Mark 8. 18. having *e.* see ye not? and ears, hear not
Luke 4. 20. and the *e.* of all were fastened on him
10. 23. blessed are the *e.* which see the things
John 9. 6. he anointed the *e.* of the blind man
32. that any opened *e.* of one that was born blind?
10. 21. can a devil open the *e.* of the blind
11. 37. could not this man, which opened the *e.?*
Acts 9. 40. Dorcas opened her *e.* and sat up
Rom. 11. 8. hath given them *e.* they should not see
Gal. 3. 1. before whose *e.* Christ been set crucified
Eph. 1. 18. the *e.* of your understanding enlightened
Heb. 4. 13. but all things are naked and open to the *e.* of him with whom we have to do
2 *Pet.* 2. 14. having *e.* full of adultery, not cease sin
1 *John* 2. 16. the lust of the *e.* and pride of life
Rev. 4. 6. in the midst of throne four beasts full of *e.*
8. had each six wings, and were full of *e.* within
5. 6. a Lamb, as it had been slain, having seven *e.*

His EYES.
Gen. 27. 1. Isaac was old, and *his e.* were dim
49. 12. *his e.* shall be red with wine, teeth white
Num. 24. 4. into a trance, having *his e.* open, 16.
Deut. 24. 1. that if she find no favour in *his e.*
Judg. 16. 21. Philistines took him and put out *his e.*
1 *Sam.* 3. 2. Eli, *his e.* began to wax dim, 4. 15.
14. 27. he tasted, and *his e.* were enlightened
18. † 20. and the thing was right in *his e.*
2 *Sam.* 19. † 18. and to do the good in *his e.*
22. † 25. according to my cleanness before *his e.*
1 *Kings* 9. † 12. and they were not right in *his e.*
14. 4. Ahijah could not see, for *his e.* were set
2 *Kings* 4. 34. he lay on child and put *his e.* on *his e.*
35. the child sneezed seven times and opened *his e.*
6. 17. I pray thee, open *his e.* that he may see
25. 7. they slew the sons of Zedekiah before *his e.* and put out eyes of Zedekiah, *Jer.* 39. 6. | 52. 10.
1 *Chron.* 21. 23. let the king do what is good in *his e.*
Esth. 8. 5. if thing seem right, and I pleasing in *his e.*
Job 16. 9. mine enemy sharpeneth *his e.* on me
21. 20. *his e.* shall see his destruction, and drink
24. 23. he resteth, yet *his e.* are on their ways
27. 19. the rich man openeth *his e.* and he is not
34. 21. *his e.* are on the ways of man, and he seeth
36. 7. he withdraweth not *his e.* from the righteous
40. 24. he taketh it with *his e.* his nose pierceth
41. 18. *his e.* are like the eye-lids of the morning
Psal. 10. 8. *his e.* are privily set against the poor
11. 4. *his e.*-behold the children of men
36. 1. that there is no fear of God before *his e.*
66. 7. he ruleth by power, *his e.* behold the nations
Prov. 6. 13. he winketh with *his e.* he speaketh
16. 30. he shutteth *his e.* to devise froward things
20. 8. a king scattereth away all evil with *his e.*
21. 10. his neighbour findeth no favour in *his e.*
24. † 18. lest Lord see it, and it be evil in *his e.*
28. † 11. the rich man is wise in *his* own *e.*
27. he that hideth *his e.* shall have many a curse
Eccl. 8. 16. nor day nor night sleepeth with *his e.*
Cant. 5. 12. *his e.* are as the eyes of doves
8. 10. I was in *his e.* as one that found favour
Isa. 11. 3. he shall not judge after the sight of *his e.*
17. 7. *his e.* shall have respect to the holy One
33. 15. and shutteth *his e.* from seeing evil
59. † 15. evil in *his e.* that there was no judgment
Jer. 32. 4. and *his e.* shall behold *his e.*
Ezek. 12. 12. that he see not the ground with *his e.*
20. 7. cast ye away the abomination of *his e.*
Dan. 8. 5. had a notable horn between *his e.* 21.
10. 6. and *his e.* were as lamps of fire
Mark 8. 23. when he had spit on *his e.* and put hands
25. after that he put his hands again on *his e.*
John 9. 14. when Jesus made clay, and opened *his e.*
21. or who hath opened *his e.* we know not
Acts 3. 4. Peter fastening *his e.* upon him, said
9. 8. and when *his e.* were opened he saw no man
18. there fell from *his e.* as it had been scales
13. 9. then Saul set *his e.* on him, and said
1 *John* 2. 11. because darkness hath blinded *his e.*
Rev. 1. 14. *his e.* were as a flame of fire, 2. 18. | 19. 12.

Lift or *lifted up* EYES.
Gen. 13. 10. Lot *lifted up* his *e.* and beheld Jordan
14. *lift up* now thine *e.* and look, 31. 12. *Deut.* 3. 27. 2 *Kings* 19. 22. *Isa.* 49. 18. | 60. 4. *Jer.* 3. 2. *Ezek.* 8. 5. *Zech.* 5. 5.
18. 2. and Abraham *lift up* his *e.* 22. 4, 13.
24. 63. Isaac ‖ 64. Rebekah *lift up* her *e.*
31. 10. Jacob, 33. 1. ‖ 43. 29. Joseph *lift up* his *e.*
Exod. 14. 10. *lift up* their *e.* the Egyptians marched
Num. 24. 2. Balaam *lift up* his *e.* and saw Israel
Deut. 4. 19. lest thou *lift up* thine *e.* unto heaven
Josh. 5. 13. Joshua *lifted up* his *e.* and looked
Judg. 19. 17. the old man *lift up* his *e.* and saw a man
1 *Sam.* 6. 13. *lifted up* their *e.* and saw the ark
2 *Sam.* 13. 34. the watchman *lift up* his *e.* 18. 24.
1 *Chr.* 21. 16. David *lift up* his *e.* and saw the angel
Job 2. 12. they *lift up* their *e.* and knew him not
Psal. 121. 1. I will *lift up* mine *e.* to the hills
123. 1. to thee *lift I up* mine *e.* thou that dwellest
Isa. 37. 23. against whom hast thou *lifted up* thy *e.?*
51. 6. *lift up* your *e. Ezek.* 33. 25. *John* 4. 35.
Ezek. 18. 6. nor hath *lift up* his *e.* to idols, 15.
12. hath spoiled, hath *lift up* his *e.* to idols
23. 27. so that thou shalt not *lift up* thine *e.*
Dan. 4. 34. I Nebuchadnezzar *lift up* mine *e.*
8. 3. then I *lifted up* mine *e.* and saw, and behold, 10. 5. *Zech.* 1. 18. | 2. 1. | 5. 1, 5, 9. | 6. 1.
Mat. 17. 8. had *lift up* their *e.* they saw no man
Luke 6. 20. Jesus *l. up* his *e. John* 6. 5. | 11. 41. | 17. 1.
16. 23. in hell he *lift up* his *e.* being in torments
18. 13. would not *lift up* so much as his *e.* to heaven

EYES *of the Lord.*
Gen. 6. 8. Noah found grace in the *e. of the Lord*
38. † 10. the thing was evil in the *e. of the Lord*
Deut. 11. 12. the *e. of the Lord* are always on it
13. 18. to do what is right in the *e. of the Lord*
1 *Sam.* 26. 24. my life much set by in the *e. of the L.*
2 *Sam.* 11. † 27. but the thing that David did was evil in the *e. of the Lord*, 1 *Chron.* 21. † 7.
15. 25. if I find favour in the *e. of the Lord*
1 *Kings* 15. 5. because David did what was right in the *e. of the Lord*, 11. | 22. 43. 2 *Chron.* 14. 2.
2 *Chron.* 16. 9. the *e. of the Lord* run to and fro through the whole earth, *Zech.* 4. 10.
Psal. 34. 15. the *e. of the L.* are upon the righteous, and his ears are open to their cry, 1 *Pet.* 3. 12.
Prov. 5. 21. ways of man are before the *e. of the L.*
15. 3. the *e. of the Lord* are in every place
22. 12. the *e. of the Lord* preserve knowledge
Isa. 49. 5. yet shall I be glorious in the *e. of the Lord*
Amos 9. 8. the *e. of the L.* are on the sinful kingdom

Mine EYES.
Gen. 31. 40. and my sleep departed from *mine e.*
44. 21. bring him, that I may set *mine e.* upon him
Judg. 14. † 3. get her for me, she is right in *mine e.*
1 *Sam.* 12. 3. or received any bribe to blind *mine e.*
14. 29. see how *mine e.* have been enlightened
26. 24. thy life much set by this day in *mine e.*
1 *Kings* 1. 48. hath given one to sit, *mine e.* seeing it
9. 3. have hallowed this house, *mine e.* and mine heart shall be there perpetually, 2 *Chron.* 7. 16.
10. 7. until *mine e.* had seen it, 2 *Chron.* 9. 6.
11. 33. have not walked in my ways, to do that which is right in *mine e.* 14. 8. 2 *Kings* 10. 30.
2 *Chron.* 7. 15. now *mine e.* shall be open, ears attent
Job 3. 10. because it hid not sorrow from *mine e.*
4. 16. it stood still, an image was before *mine e.*

Job 19. 27. *mine e.* shall behold, and not another
31. 1. I made a covenant with *mine e.* why then
7. and mine heart walked after *mine e.*
*Ps.*13.3.lighten *mine e.* lest I sleep the sleep of death
25. 15. *mine e.* are ever toward the Lord
26. 3. for thy loving-kindness is before *mine e.*
38. 10. as for the light of *mine e.* it is gone from me
69. 3. *mine e.* fail, whilst I wait for my God
73. † 16. to know this, it was labour in *mine e.*
77. 4. thou holdest *mine e.* waking, I am troubled
101. 3. I will set no evil thing before *mine e.*
6. *mine e.* shall be on the faithful of the land
116. 8. thou hast delivered *mine e.* from tears
119. 18. open *mine e.* ‖ 37. turn away *mine e.*
82. *mine e.* fail for thy word, saying, comfort me
123. *mine e.* fail for thy salvation, and for the word
136. rivers of waters run down *mine e.*
148. *mine e.* prevent the night-watches
131. 1. mine heart is not haughty, nor *mine e.* lofty
132. 4. I will not give sleep to *mine e.* or slumber
141. 8. but *mine e.* are unto thee, O God, the Lord
Eccl. 2. 10. whatsoever *mine e.* desired, I kept not
Isa. 1. 15. I will hide *mine e.* from you
16. put away the evil doings from before *mine e.*
6. 5. *mine e.* have seen the King, the Lord of hosts
38. 14. *mine e.* fail with looking upward
65. 12. but did evil before *mine e.* 66. 4.
*16. and because they are hid from *mine e.*
Jer. 9. 1. O that *mine e.* were a fountain of tears
13. 17. *mine e.* shall weep sore, and run down
14. 17. shall say, let *mine e.* run down with tears
16. 17. *mine e.* are on their ways, they are not hid from me, nor is their iniquity hid from *mine e.*
24. 6. I will set *mine e.* upon them for good
Lam. 2. 11. *mine e.* do fail with tears, my bowels
Hos. 13. 14. repentance shall be hid from *mine e.*
Amos 9. 4. I will set *mine e.* on them for evil
Mic. 7. 10. *mine e.* shall behold her, be trodden down
Zech. 8. 6. should it also be marvellous in *mine e.*
9. 8. for now have I seen with *mine e.*
12. 4. I will open *mine e.* on the house of Judah
Luke 2. 30. for *mine e.* have seen thy salvation
John 9. 11. Jesus made clay, and anointed *mine e.* 15.
30. whence he is, yet he hath opened *mine e.*
Acts 11. 6. on the which when I had fastened *mine e.*

Our EYES.

Num. 11. 6. nothing but this manna before *our e.*
Deut. 6. 22. the Lord shewed signs before *our e.*
21. 7. not shed this blood, nor have *our e.* seen it
2 *Sam.* 20. † 6. lest Sheba deliver himself from *our e.*
2 *Chron.* 20. 12. but, O God, *our e.* are upon thee
Ezra 9. 8. that our God may lighten *our e.*
Psal. 118. 23. this is the Lord's doing, it is marvellous in *our e.* *Mat.* 21. 42. *Mark* 12. 11.
123. 2. so *our e.* wait upon the Lord our God
Jer. 9. 18. that *our e.* may run down with tears
Lam. 4. 17. *our e.* as yet failed for our vain help
5. 17. heart is faint, for these things *our e.* are dim
Joel 1. 16. is not the meat cut off before *our e.*
Mat. 20. 33. Lord, that *our e.* may be opened
1 *John* 1. 1. that which we have seen with *our e.*

Own EYES.

Num. 15. 39. that ye seek not after your *own e.*
Deut. 12. 8. ye shall not do, every man whatsoever is right in his *own e.* *Judg.* 17. 6. | 21. 25.
2 *Sam.* 4. † 10. was in his *own e.* a bringer of good
Neh. 6. 16. enemies much cast down in their *own e.*
Job 32. 1. because he was righteous in his *own e.*
Psal. 36. 2. he flattereth himself in his *own e.*
Prov. 3. 7. be not wise in thine *own e.* fear God
12. 15. the way of a fool is right in his *own e.*
16. 2. all the ways of man are clean in his *own e.*
21. 2. every way of man is right in his *own e.*
26. † 5. answer a fool, lest he be wise in his *own e.*
30. 12. a generation that are pure in their *own e.*
Isa. 5. 21. woe to them that are wise in their *own e.*
Gal. 4. 15. ye would have plucked out your *own e.*

Their EYES.

Gen. 42. 24. he took and bound Simeon before *their e.*
Exod. 8. 26. abomination of Egyptians before *their e.*
Lev. 20. 4. do any ways hide *their e.* from the man
Num. 20. 8. speak to the rock before *their e.*
27. 14. to sanctify me at the water before *their e.*
Josh. 22. † 30. it was good in *their e.* 2 *Sam.* 3. † 36.
2 *Kings* 6. 20. the Lord opened *their e.* and they saw
Ezra 3. 12. foundation was laid before *their e.*
Esth. 1. 17. they shall despise their husbands in *t. e.*
Job 21. 8. and their offspring before *their e.*
Psal. 17. 11. they have set *their e.* bowing down
69. 23. let *their e.* be darkened, that they see not
73. 7. *their e.* stand out with fatness, have more
Prov. 29. 13. the Lord lighteneth both *their e.*
30. 13. a generation, O how lofty are *their e.*
Eccl. 5. 11. saving the beholding them with *their e.*
Isa. 6. 10. make their ears heavy, shut *their e.* lest they see with *their e.* *Mat.* 13. 15. *Acts* 28. 27.
13. 16. children be dashed to pieces before *their e.*
44. 18. for he hath shut *their e.* they cannot see
Jer. 14. 6. *their e.* did fail, because there was no grass
Ezek. 6. 9. and with *their e.* which go a whoring
20. 8. not cast away the abominations of *their e.*
24. and *their e.* were after their father's idols
21. 6. and with bitterness sigh before *their e.*
22. 26. and have hid *their e.* from my sabbaths
24. 25. when I take from them the desire of *their e.*
36. 23. I shall be sanctified in you before *their e.*
37. 20. sticks shall be in thy hand before *their e.*
38. 16. sanctified in thee, O Gog, before *their e.*
Zech. 14. 12. and *their e.* shall consume away
Mat. 9. 29. then touched he *their e.* saying
30. *their e.* were opened, and Jesus charged them
13. 15. *their e.* they have closed, lest at any time
20. 34. Jesus touched *their e.* *their e.* received sight
26. 43. for *their e.* were heavy, *Mark* 14. 40.
Luke 24. 16. but *their e.* were holden, that they
31. *their e.* were opened, and they knew him
John 12. 40. he hath blinded *their e.* and hardened
Acts 26. 18. to open *their e.* and to turn them
Rom. 3. 18. there is no fear of God before *their e.*
11. 10. let *their e.* be darkened, that they see not
Rev. 7. 17. the Lamb shall feed them, and God shall wipe away all tears from *their e.* 21. 4.

Thine EYES.

Gen. 16. † 6. do to her that which is good in *thine e.*
20. † 15. Abimelech said, dwell as is good in *thine e.*
30. 27. if I have found favour in *thine e.* tarry
46. 4. Joseph shall put his hand on *thine e.*
47. 19. wherefore shall we die before *thine e.*?
Exod. 13. 9. for a memorial between *thine e.*
16. for frontlets between *thine e.* *Deut.* 6. 8.
Num. 22. † 34. if it be evil in *thine e.* I will go back
Deut. 3. 21. *thine e.* have seen all that the Lord
27. lift up *thine e.* behold it with *thine e.*
4. 9. forget the things which *thine e.* have seen
7. 19. the great temptations *thine e.* saw, 29. 3.
10. 21. terrible things which *thine e.* have seen
28. 31. thine ox shall be slain before *thine e.*
32. *thine e.* shall look, and fail with longing
34. thou shalt be mad for the sight of *thine e.* 67.
34. 4. I have caused thee to see it with *thine e.*
Judg. 10. † 15. Israel said, we have sinned, do to us whatsoever is good in *thine e.* 2 *Kings* 10. 5.
Ruth 2. 9. let *thine e.* be on the field they reap
10. she said, why have I found grace in *thine e.*?
1 *Sam.* 2. 33. shall be to consume *thine e.*
20. 3. knoweth that I have found grace in *thine e.*
29. and now if I have found favour in *thine e.*
24. 10. *thine e.* have seen how the Lord delivered
25. 8. let the young men find favour in *thine e.*
26. 21. my soul was precious in *thine e.* this day
27. 5. if I have found grace in *thine e.* give me
2 *Sam.* 10. † 3. the princes said to Hanun, in *thine e.* doth David honour thy father, 1 *Chron.* 19. † 3.
11. † 25. let not this thing be evil in *thine e.*
12. 11. I will take thy wives before *thine e.*
19. 27. do therefore what is good in *thine e.*
22. 28. *thine e.* are on the haughty to bring down
1 *Kings* 8. 29. that *thine e.* may be open toward this house night and day, 52. 2 *Chron.* 6. 20, 40.
20. 6. whatsoever is pleasant in *thine e.*
21. † 2. if it be good in *thine e.* I will give the worth
2 *Kings* 7. 2. behold, thou shalt see it with *thine e.*
19. 16. open, Lord, *thine e.* and see, *Isa.* 37. 17.
22. 20. and *thine e.* shall not see all the evil
1 *Chron.* 17. 17. this was a small thing in *thine e.*
2 *Chron.* 34. 28. nor shall *thine e.* see all the evil
Neh. 1. 6. let thine ear be attentive, and *thine e.* open
Job 7. 8. *thine e.* are upon me, and I am not
11. 4. my doctrine is pure, I am clean in *thine e.*
14. 3. dost thou open *thine e.* upon such an one?
15. 12. and what do *thine e.* wink at?
Psal. 5. † 5. the foolish shall not stand before *thine e.*
31. 22. I said, I am cut off from before *thine e.*
50. 21. and set them in order before *thine e.*
91. 8. only with *thine e.* shalt thou behold and see
139. 16. *thine e.* did see my substance unperfect
Prov. 3. 21. let them not depart from *thine e.* 4. 21.
4. 25. let *thine e.* look right on, and thine eyelids
6. 4. give not sleep to *thine e.* nor slumber to eyelids
20. 13. open *thine e.* and thou shalt be satisfied
23. 5. wilt thou set *thine e.* on that which is not?
26. give me thy heart, let *thine e.* observe my ways
33. *thine e.* shall behold strange women
25. 7. of the prince whom *thine e.* have seen
Eccl. 11. 9. O young man, walk in the sight of *thine e.*
Cant. 4. 9. hast ravished my heart with *thine e.*
6. 5. turn away *thine e.* from me, they overcome
7. 4. *thine e.* like the fish-pools in Heshbon
Isa. 30. 20. but *thine e.* shall see thy teachers
33. 17. *thine e.* shall see the king in his beauty
20. *thine e.* see Jerusalem a quiet habitation
Jer. 5. 3. O Lord, are not *thine e.* upon the truth?
20. 4. fall by the sword, *thine e.* shall behold it
22. 17. *thine e.* are not but for thy covetousness
31. 16. refrain weeping, and *thine e.* from tears
32. 19. *thine e.* are open on all the ways of men
34. 3. *thine e.* shall behold the king of Babylon
39. † 12. take Jeremiah, and set *thine e.* on him
42. 2. we are but few, as *thine e.* do behold us
Lam. 2. 18. let not the apple of *thine e.* cease
Ezek. 23. 40. for whom thou paintedst *thine e.*
24. 16. I take from thee the desire of *thine e.*
40. 4. son of man, behold with *thine e.* 44. 5.
Dan. 9. 18. open *thine e.* and behold our desolation
Luke 19. 42. but now they are hid from *thine e.*
John 9. 10. said to him, how were *thine e.* opened? 26.
17. sayest thou that he hath opened *thine e*?
Rev. 3. 18. and anoint *thine e.* with eye-salve

Your EYES.

Gen. 3. 5. in the day ye eat *your e.* shall be opened
19. 8. do ye to them as is good in *your e.*
34. 11. Shechem said, let me find grace in *your e.*
45. † 5. neither let there be anger in *your e.*
12. *your e.* and the eyes of my brother Benjamin
50. 4. if now I have found grace in *your e*
Num. 33. 55. those which ye let remain shall be pricks in *your e.* thorns in sides, *Josh.* 23. 13.
Deut. 1. 30. that he did before *your e.* 4. 34. | 29. 2.
4. 3. *your e.* have seen what the Lord did because of Baal-peor, 11. 7. *Josh.* 24. 7.
9. 17. I brake the two tables before *your e.*
11. 18. they may be as frontlets between *your e.*
14. 1. not make any baldness between *your e.*
1 *Sam.* 12. 16. what the Lord will do before *your e.*
2 *Chron.* 29. 8. and to hissing, as ye see with *your e.*
Isa. 29. 10. for the Lord hath closed *your e.*
40. 26. lift up *your e.* on high, *Jer.* 13. 20.
Jer. 7. 11. is this house a den of robbers in *your e.*
16. 9. cause to cease out of this place in *your e.*
29. 21. and he shall slay them before *your e.*
Ezek. 24. 21. the desire of *your e.* and what you pity
Zeph. 3. 20. when I turn your captivity before *your e.*
Hag. 2. 3. in *your e.* in comparison is nothing
Zech. 11. † 12. if good in *your e.* give me my price
Mal. 1. 5. *your e.* shall see, the L. will be magnified
Mat. 13. 16. but blessed are *your e.* for they see

Right EYES.

1 *Sam.* 11. 2. that I may thrust out all your *right e.*

F.

FABLES.

1 *Tim.* 1. 4. nor give heed to *f.* and genealogies
4. 7. but refuse profane and old wives' *f.*
2 *Tim.* 4. 4. and they shall be turned unto *f.*
Tit. 1. 14. not giving heed to Jewish *f.* and comm. of
2 *Pet.* 1. 16. have not followed cunningly devised *f.*

FACE,

Countenance, *or* visage, *is a part of the body well known: It is thereby that our inward motions are made known to others: Love, hatred, desire, dislike, joy, grief, confidence, despair, courage, cowardice, admiration, contempt, pride, modesty, cruelty, compassion, and the rest of the affections, are discovered by their proper aspects.* The countenance, *as one phrases it, is a crystal, wherein the thoughts and affections, otherwise invisible, appear; and is a natural sign, known to all. It is by the* face, *also, that one man is known and distinguished from another: And it is matter of admiration, that so few parts composing it, and in so small a compass, and always in the same situation, yet there is such a diversity of figures as of* faces *in the world. These innumerable different characters in the* faces *of men, is the counsel of a most wise Providence, for the universal benefit of the world: For human societies cannot be preserved without union and distinction: the one prevents division, the other confusion; and this distinction is caused by the variety of* countenances.

The Face *of a man is also taken for the man himself:* I had not thought to see thy *face*; *that is, thy person, says* Jacob *to his son* Joseph, *Gen.* 48. 11. Before one's face; *that is, in his sight or presence,* Num. 19. 3. To withstand a person to the face, *is to reprove him boldly.* Gal. 2. 11. The pride of *Israel* doth testify to his face, *Hos.* 5. 5. *It is so full and evident a witness against* Israel, *that no other testimony need be produced, to convince the most impudent and shameless among them.* To fall to the earth upon one's face, *was a posture of adoration.* Josh. 7. 6. *Joshua* fell to the earth upon his face, *in deep humiliation and fervent supplication.* To accept one's face, *is to shew one a favour and grant his request.* Gen. 19. † 21. Peradventure he will accept of my face; *he will be reconciled with me, and accept of my person.* To spit in one's face, *is a sign of the utmost contempt. The woman, whose husband died without children, if her husband's brother refused to marry her, spit in his face,* Deut. 25. 9.

Face *is likewise referred to God, and denotes sometimes his anger.* Psal. 34. 16. The face of the Lord is against them that do evil. *Rev.* 6. 16. Hide us from the face of him that sitteth on the throne. *At other times, it denotes his love and favour,* Psal. 31. 16. | 80. 7. Make thy face to shine upon thy servant. Cause thy face to shine and we shall be saved. *Dan.* 9. 17. Cause thy face to shine upon thy sanctuary which is desolate. *It is also taken for his omniscience,* 1 Sam. 26. 20. Let not my blood fall to the earth before the face of the Lord; *that is, if thou dost shed my blood, remember that God, the Judge of all the earth, seeth it, and will avenge it.*

The Lord promises Moses, *that his* face *shall go before the* Israelites, *Exod.* 33. 14. *My presence,* in Hebrew, *my face,* shall go with thee; *that is, I myself will go with thee. The Angel of my presence, namely, the* Messiah, *Isa.* 63. 9. *who is always in the bosom of the Father, and continually making intercession for his people: and likewise the pledge of my presence, shall go with thee, namely, the cloudy pillar.* Moses, *in the same chapter, begs of God* to shew him his glory. *God replies to him,* I will make all my goodness pass before thee, *or* all my glory; *thou shalt have a sudden transient view of it; and* I will proclaim my name, *which I will give thee as a signal of my presence, that thou mayest attend: but for* my face, thou canst not see it; for there shall no man see it and live: *Thou canst not see the majesty and glory attending that external shape I have now assumed; nor those manifestations of my glory which the saints are favoured with in another life; for such is the weakness of man in this life, that if I should display all the beams of my glory to him, it would certainly astonish, overwhelm, and destroy him. It was a certain persuasion, and very prevalent in the world, that no man could support the sight of God without expiring. See* Gen. 16. 13. | 32. 30. Exod. 20. 19. | 24. 11. Judg. 6. 22, 23. | 13. 22.

Nevertheless, it is said in Num. 12. 8. With *Moses* will I speak mouth to mouth, even apparently, and not in dark speeches. *And in* chap. 14. 14. The *Canaanites* have heard that thou art among this people, and that thou art seen face to face. *And in* Deut. 5. 4. *it is said, that* God talked with the *Israelites* face to face, out of the midst of the fire: *But in all these places,* face to face *is to be understood simply, as if he had said, that* God manifested himself *to the* Israelites, *that he made them hear his voice in a manner as distinct as if he had appeared to them face to face: That he spake to them personally and immediately, and not by an interpreter; and familiarly, so as not to overwhelm and confound them. The apostle, speaking of the difference between our knowledge here and in heaven, says,* Now we see through a glass darkly; but then face to face, 1 *Cor.* 13. 12. *that is, there is as much difference between our knowledge here and in heaven, as between looking through a perspective glass upon a thing a great way off, and covered with many obscurities; and looking immediately with the naked eye, upon the whole object nigh at hand.*

The bread of faces, *the* shew-bread, *which was always in the presence of God. See* BREAD.

Gen. 1. † 20. fowls may fly in *f.* of the firmament
3. 19. in the sweat of thy *f.* shalt thou eat bread
16. 8. I flee from the *f.* of my mistress Sarai
19. † 21. I have accepted thy *f.* concerning this
24. 47. and I put the ear-rings upon her *f.*
32. † 20. peradventure he will accept my *f.*
† 30. Jacob called the place, the *f.* of God

Gen. 35. 1. when thou fleddest from the f. of Esau, 7.
36. 6. Esau went from the f. of his brother Jacob
46. 28. he sent to Joseph to direct his f. to Goshen
48. 12. Joseph bowed with his f. to the earth
Exod. 2. 15. Moses fled from the f. of Pharaoh
14. 25. said, let us flee from the f. of Israel
25. † 37. may give light against the f. of it
34. 29. the skin of his f. shone, 30, 35.
33. till he had done speaking, he put a vail on his f.
Lev. 13. 41. that hath his hair fallen towards his f.
19. 32. thou shalt honour the f. of the old man
Num. 12. 14. if her father had but spit in her f.
19. 3. one shall slay the red heifer before his f.
Deut. 1. 17. ye shall not be afraid of the f. of man
7. 10. and repayeth them that hate him to their f.
† 23. the Lord shall deliver them before thy f. and shall destroy them, 9. 3. | 28. 7.
8. 20. the nations the Ld. destroyeth before your f.
25. 2. cause the wicked man be beaten before his f.
9. shall loose his shoe, and spit in his f. and say
28. 31. thine ass shall be taken before thy f.
† 50. a nation strong of f. which shall not regard
31. 5. the Lord shall give them up before your f.
Josh. 7. 10. wherefore liest thou upon thy f.?
Judg. 11. † 3. Jephthah fled from f. of his brethren
1 Sam. 5. 3. behold, Dagon was fallen on his f. 4.
17. † 24. they fled from Goliath's f. and were afraid
19. † 8. and the Philistines fled from his f.
24. 8. David stooped with his f. to the earth
25. 41. Abigail bowed on her f. and said
28. 14. Saul stooped with his f. to the ground
2 Sam. 2. 22. how should I hold up my f. to Joab?
7. † 9. I have cut off thine enemies from thy f.
14. 33. Absalom bowed on his f. to the ground
17. † 11. that thy f. or presence go to battle
24. 20. and Araunah went out and bowed himself before the king on his f. 1 Chron. 21. 21.
1 Kings 1. 23. Nathan bowed himself with his f.
31. Bath-sheba bowed with her f. to the earth
2. † 16. I ask one petition, turn not away my f.
8. 14. the king turned his f. about, 2 Chron. 6. 3.
10. † 24. all the earth sought the f. of Solomon
18. 42. Elijah put his f. between his knees
19. 13. that he wrapped his f. in his mantle
20. 38. prophet disguised himself with ashes on his f.
21. 4. Ahab turned away his f. and would not eat
2 Kings 4. 29. lay my staff upon the f. of the child
31. Gehazi laid his staff on the f. of the child
8. 15. Hazael spread it on his f. so that he died
9. 30. Jezebel painted her f. and tired her head
32. Jehu lift up his f. to the window, and said
13. 14. Joash wept over his f. and said, O my father
† 23. neither cast he them from his f. as yet
18. 24. how wilt thou turn away f. of one, Isa. 36. 9.
20. 2. Hezekiah turned his f. to the wall, Isa. 38. 2.
21. † 13. he wipeth and turneth it on the f. thereof
25. † 19. five men that saw king's f. Jer. 52. ‡ 25.
2 Chr. 6. 42. O Lord God, turn not away the f. of thine anointed, Psal. 132. 10.
30. 9. the Lord will not turn away his f. from you
32. † 2. when Hezekiah saw that his f. was to war
21. he returned with shame of f. to his own land
34. † 4. and strowed it upon the f. of the graves
35. 22. Josiah would not turn his f. from him
Ezra 9. 6. I blush to lift up my f. to thee, my God
7. to confusion of f. as it is this day, Dan. 9. 8.
Job 1. 11. and he will curse thee to thy f. 2. 5.
4. 15. then a spirit passed before my f.
6. † 28. for it is before your f. if I lie
11. 15. then shalt thou lift up thy f. without spot
† 19. yea, many shall entreat thy f.
16. 8. my leanness beareth witness to my f.
16. my f. is foul with weeping, on my eyelids
21. 31. who shall declare his way to his f.?
22. 26. and thou shalt lift up thy f. unto God
24. 15. no eye shall see me; and disguiseth his f.
26. 9. he holdeth back the f. of his throne
30. 10. and they spare not to spit in my f.
41. 13. who can discover the f. of his garment?
14. who can open the doors of his f.?
42. † 8. Job shall pray, for his f. will I accept
† 9. the Lord also accepted the f. of Job
Psal. 5. 8. make thy way straight before my f.
17. † 13. O Lord, prevent his f. cast him down
15. I will behold thy f. in righteousness
21. 12. make ready arrows against the f. of them
41. 12. thou settest me before thy f. for ever
45. † 12. even the rich shall entreat thy f.
68. † 1. let them that hate him flee from his f.
84. 9. and look upon the f. of thine anointed
89. 14. mercy and truth shall go before thy f.
23. I will beat down his foes before his f.
119. † 58. I entreated thy f. with my whole heart
Prov. 6. † 35. he will not accept the f. of a ransom
7. 13. and with an impudent f. said unto him
21. 29. a wicked man hardeneth his f.
Eccl. 8. 1. the boldness of his f. shall be changed
Isa. 5. † 21. woe to the prudent before their f.
16. 4. be a covert from the f. of the spoiler
21. † 15. for they fled from the f. of the sword
24. † 1. the Lord perverteth the f. of the earth
25. 7. he will destroy the f. of the covering
28. 25. when he hath made plain the f. thereof
29. 22. neither shall his f. now wax pale
49. 23. they shall bow down to thee with their f.
65. 3. that provoketh me continually to my f.
Jer. 1. † 13. f. thereof was from the f. of the north
2. 27. turned their back, and not the f. 32. 33.
4. 30. though thou rentest thy f. with painting
13. 26. therefore will I discover thy skirts upon thy f. that thy shame may appear, Nah. 3. 5.
18. 17. I will shew them the back, and not the f.
22. 25. from hand of them whose f. thou fearest
32. 31. I should remove it from before my f.
Lam. 3. 35. the right of man before f. of most High
Ezek. 1. 10. they four had the f. of a man, the f. of a lion, f. of an ox, the f. of an eagle
2. † 4. they are hard of f. and stiff-hearted
3. 8. I made thy f. strong against their faces
7. 22. my f. will I turn also from them
10. 14. f. of a man, f. of a lion, f. of an eagle, 41. 19.
14. 3. put stumbling-block before their f.

Ezek. 38. 18. that my fury shall come up in my f.
Dan. 8. 18. I was in a deep sleep on my f. 10. 9.
10. 6. his f. as the appearance of lightning
11. 18. he shall turn his f. unto the isles
Hos. 5. 5. the pride of Israel testifieth to his f. 7. 10.
7. 2. now their own doings, they are before my f.
Joel 2. 6. before their f. people be much pained
20. will drive him with his f. toward the east sea
Nah. 2. 1. that dasheth in pieces, come before thy f.
Zeph. 1. † 2. I will consume from the f. of the land
Mal. 1. † 9. now, I pray you, beseech the f. of God
Mat. 6. 17. anoint thine head, and wash thy f.
11. 10. behold, I send my messenger before thy f. to prepare thy way, Mark 1. 2. Luke 7. 27.
18. 10. their angels behold the f. of my Father
26. 67. then did they spit in his f. and buffeted
Luke 2. 31. thou hast prepared before f. of all people
9. 52. he sent messengers before his f. 10. 1.
53. his f. was as though he would go to Jerusalem
22. 64. they struck him on the f. and asked him
John 11. 44. his f. was bound about with a napkin
Acts 2. 25. I foresaw the Lord always before my f.
7. 45. God drave out before the f. of our fathers
1 Cor. 14. 25. so falling down on his f. will worship
2 Cor. 3. 7. could not stedfastly behold the f. of Moses
13. not as Moses, who put a vail over his f.
18. but we all with open f. beholding the glory
4. 6. the glory of God, in the f. of Jesus Christ
5. † 12. which glory in the f. and not in the heart
11. 20. ye suffer, if a man smite you on the f.
Gal. 1. 22. I was unknown by f. to the churches
2. 11. I withstood him to the f. because he was
Jam. 1. 23. beholding his natural f. in a glass
Rev. 4. 7. the third beast had a f. as a man
10. 1. and his f. was as it were the sun
12. 14. where nourished from the f. of the serpent
20. 11. from whose f. the earth and heaven fled
See Seek, Set, Shine, Sky, Waters, Wilderness, World.

FACE with cover, or covered.
Gen. 38. 15. an harlot, because she covered her f.
Exod. 10. 5. locusts shall cover the f. of the earth, 15.
Num. 22. 5. behold, they cover the f. of the earth
2 Sam. 19. 4. the king covered his f. and cried
Esth. 7. 8. word went out, they covered Haman's f.
Job 15. 27. he covereth his f. with his fatness
23. 17. nor hath he covered darkness from my f.
Psal. 44. 15. the shame of my f. hath covered me
69. 7. for thy sake shame hath covered my f.
Prov. 24. 31. nettles had covered the f. thereof
Isa. 6. 2. with twain he covered his f. and his feet
Ezek. 12. 6. thou shalt cover thy f. that thou see not
12. the prince shall cover his f. that he see not
Mark 14. 65. began to spit on him, and cover his f.

FACE of the country.
2 Sam. 18. 8. battle was scattered over f. of country

FACE of the deep.
Gen. 1. 2. darkness was upon the f. of the deep
Job 38. 30. and the f. of the deep is frozen
Prov. 8. 27. he set a compass on the f. of the depth

FACE of the earth.
Gen. 1. 29. every herb upon the f. of the earth
4. 14. thou hast driven me from the f. of the earth
6. 1. men began to multiply on the f. of the earth
7. 3. to keep seed alive on the f. of all the earth
4. I will destroy from off the f. of the earth, Deut. 6. 15. 1 Kings 13. 34. Amos 9. 8.
8. 9. the waters were on the f. of the whole earth
11. 4. lest we be scattered on the f. of the earth
41. 56. the famine was over all the f. of the earth
Exod. 32. 12. to consume them from f. of the earth
33. 16. from all people unto the f. of the earth
Num. 12. 3. meek above all men on f. of the earth
Deut. 7. 6. above all people on the f. of the earth
1 Sam. 20. 15. cut off every one from f. of the earth
2 Sam. 14. † 7. nor remainder on the f. of the earth
Psal. 104. 30. thou renewest the f. of the earth
Isa. 23. 17. with all kingdoms on the f. of the earth
Jer. 8. 2. be for dung on the f. of the earth, 16. 4.
28. 16. I will cast thee from the f. of the earth
Ezek. 38. 20. all men on the f. of the earth shake
Dan. 8. 5. an he-goat came on the f. of the earth
Amos 5. 8. poureth them on the f. of the earth, 9. 6.
Zech. 5. 3. curse that goeth over the f. of the earth
Luke 12. 56. ye can discern the f. of the earth
21. 35. that dwell on the f. of the whole earth
Acts 17. 26. to dwell on all the f. of the earth

FACE to FACE.
Gen. 32. 30. Peniel; for I have seen God f. to f.
Exod. 33. 11. and the Lord spake to Moses f. to f.
Num. 14. 14. that thou, Lord, art seen f. to f.
Deut. 5. 4. the Lord talked with you f. to f.
34. 10. like Moses, whom the Lord knew f. to f.
Judg. 6. 22. because I have seen an angel f. to f.
Prov. 27. 19. as in water f. answereth to f.
Ezek. 20. 35. there I will plead with you f. to f.
Acts 25. 16. before he have the accusers f. to f.
1 Cor. 13. 12. we see thro' a glass, but then f. to f.
2 John 12. I trust to come to you, and speak f. to f.
3 John 14. I trust to see thee and speak f. to f.

Fell on FACE or FACES.
Gen. 17. † 3. Abram fell on his f. and laughed, 17.
50. 1. Joseph fell on his father's f. and wept
18. his brethren fell down before his f.
Lev. 9. 24. when the people saw, they fell on their f.
Num. 14. 5. Moses and Aaron fell on f. 16. 22, 45.
16. 4. Moses || 22. 31. Balaam fell flat on his f.
Josh. 5. 14. Joshua fell on his f. to the earth, 7. 6.
Judg. 13. 20. Manoah and his wife fell on their f.
Ruth 2. 10. then she fell on her f. to the ground
1 Sam. 17. 49. Goliath || 20. 41. David fell on his f.
25. 23. Abigail || 2 Sam. 9. 6. Mephibosh. fell on f.
2 Sam. 14. 4. the woman of Tekoah fell on her f.
22. Joab || 18. 28. Ahimaaz fell on his f.
1 Kings 18. 7. Obadiah || 39. people fell on their f.
1 Chr. 21. 16. David and elders fell on their f.
Ezek. 1. 28. when I saw it I fell upon my f. 3. 23. | 9. 8. | 11. 13. | 43. 3. | 44. 4. Dan. 8. 17.
Dan. 2. 46. Nebuchadnezzar fell upon his f.
Mat. 17. 6. disciples || 26. 39. Jesus fell on his f.
Luke 5. 12. leper || 17. 16. Samaritan fell on his f.
Rev. 11. 16. the twenty-four elders fell on their f.

FACE of the field.
Lev. 14. † 7. living bird loose on the f. of the field
2 Kings 9. 37. Jezebel as dung on the f. of the field
Ezek. 29. † 5. thou shalt fall on the f. of the field
39. † 5. Gog shall fall on the f. of the field

FACE of the gate.
Ezek. 40. 15. from the f. of the gate of the entrance

FACE of the ground.
Gen. 2. 6. a mist watered the whole f. of the ground
7. 23. destroyed, that was on the f. of the ground
8. 8. were abated from off the f. of the ground
13. and behold, the f. of the ground was dry

Hide, hideth, or hid FACE.
Gen. 4. 14. and from thy f. shall I be hid
Exod. 3. 6. and Moses hid his f. for he was afraid
Deut. 31. 17. will hide my f. from them, 18. | 32. 20.
Job 13. 24. wherefore hidest thou thy f. and holdest me for thine enemy? Psal. 44. 24. | 88. 14.
34. 29. when he hideth his f. who can behold?
Psal. 10. 11. he hideth his f. he will never see it
13. 1. how long wilt thou hide thy f. from me?
22. 24. neither hath he hid his f. from him
27. 9. hide not thy f. 69. 17. | 102. 2. | 143. 7.
30. 7. hast made my mountain strong, thou didst hide thy f. and I was troubled, 104. 29.
51. 9. hide thy f. from my sins, and blot out all
Isa. 8. 17. hideth his f. from the house of Jacob
50. 6. I hid not my f. from shame and spitting
54. 8. in a little wrath I hid my f. from thee
59. 2. your sins have hid his f. from you
64. 7. thou hast hid thy f. from us and consumed
Jer. 16. 17. thy ways are not hid from my f.
33. 5. I have hid my f. from this city
Ezek. 39. 23. therefore hid I my f. from them, 24.
29. nor will I hide my f. any more from them
Mic. 3. 4. he will even hide his f. at that time
Rev. 6. 16. hide us from the f. of him that sitteth

FACE of the house.
Ezek. 41. 14. the breadth of the f. of the house

FACE of the Lord.
Gen. 19. 13. the cry great before the f. of the Lord
Exod. 32. † 11. Moses entreated the f. of the Lord
1 Sam. 26. 20. let not my blood fall before f. of Lord
1 Kings 13. 6. entreat now the f. of the Lord
Psal. 34. 16. the f. of the Lord is against them that do evil, to cut off from the earth, 1 Pet. 3. 12.
Jer. 26. † 19. Hezekiah besought the f. of the Lord
Lam. 2. 19. pour out thy heart before f. of the Lord
4. † 16. the f. of the Lord hath divided them
Luke 1. 76. thou shalt go before the f. of the Lord

FACE of the porch.
Ezek. 40. 15. to the f. of the porch were fifty cubits
41. 25. were thick planks on the f. of the porch

FACE with look, looked, see, saw, seen.
Gen. 32. 20. and afterward I will see his f.
33. 10. for therefore I have seen thy f. as though
43. 3. ye shall not see my f. except, 5. | 44. 23.
44. 26. for we may not see the man's f. except
46. 30. now let me die, since I have seen thy f.
48. 11. I had not thought to see thy f. and lo
Exod. 10. 28. Pharaoh said to him, see my f. no more
29. Moses said, I will see thy f. again no more
33. 20. and he said, thou canst not see my f.
23. see back parts, but my f. shall not be seen
34. 35. children of Israel saw the f. of Moses
2 Sam. 3. 13. not see my f. except thou bring Michal
14. 24. the king said, let him not see my f.
28. Absalom dwelt two years and saw not king's f.
32. now therefore let me see the king's f.
2 Kings 14. 8. sent messengers saying, come, let us look one another in the f. 2 Chron. 25. 17.
11. and they looked one another in the f.
Esth. 1. 14. the seven princes who saw the king's f.
Job 33. 26. and he shall see his f. with joy
Acts 6. 15. saw his f. as it had been f. of an angel
20. 25. I know that ye shall see my f. no more, 38.
Col. 2. 1. as many as have not seen my f. in the flesh
1 Thess. 2. 17. endeavoured to see your f. with desire
3. 10. praying, that we might see your f.
Rev. 22. 4. and they shall see his f. and his name

Seek FACE.
1 Chron. 16. 11. seek his f. continually, Psal. 105. 4.
2 Chron. 7. 14. if my people shall pray and seek my f.
Psal. 24. 6. a generation that seek thy f. O Jacob
27. 8. when thou saidst, seek ye my f. my heart said unto thee, thy f. Lord will I seek
Prov. 7. 15. I came diligently to seek thy f.
29. † 26. many seek the f. of a ruler
Hos. 5. 15. return to my place, till they seek my f.

Set FACE.
Gen. 31. 21. Jacob set his f. toward mount Gilead
Lev. 17. 10. I will set my f. against that soul, 20. 6.
20. 3. set my f. against that man, 5. Ezek. 14. 8.
26. 17. I will set my f. against you, Jer. 44. 11.
Num. 24. 1. Balaam set his f. toward wilderness
2 Kings 12. 17. Hazael set his f. to Jerusalem
1 Chron. 19. † 10. when Joab saw f. of battle was set
2 Chron. 20. † 3. Jehoshaphat set his f. to seek Lord
Isa. 50. 7. I have set my f. like a flint, not be ashamed
Jer. 21. 10. I have set my f. against this city
Ezek. 4. 3. set thy f. against it, it shall be besieged
7. thou shalt set thy f. towards the siege at Jerus.
6. 2. set thy f. towards the mountains of Israel
13. 17. set thy f. against the daughters of my peop
15. 7. and I will set my f. against them
20. 46. son of man, set thy f. toward the south
21. 2. son of man, set thy f. toward Jerusalem
16. go thee whithersoever thy f. is set
25. 2. son of man, set thy f. against the Ammonites
28. 21. f. against Zidon || 29. 2. f. against Pharaoh
35. 2. f. against mount Seir || 38. 2. f. against Gog
Dan. 9. 3. and I set my f. unto the Lord God
10. 15. I set my f. toward ground and became dumb
11. 17. he shall set his f. to enter with strength
Luke 9. 51. he stedfastly set his f. to go to Jerusal.

FACE shine.
Num. 6. 25. the Lord make his f. to shine upon thee
Psal. 31. 16. make thy f. to shine on thy servant, save me for thy mercies' sake, 119. 135.
67. 1. God bless us, and cause his f. to shine on us
80. 3. cause thy f. shine, we shall be saved, 7, 19.
104. 15. and oil to make his f. to shine

Eccl. 8. 1. a man's wisdom maketh his *f.* to *shine*
Dan. 9. 17. cause thy *f.* to *shine* on thy sanctuary
Mat. 17. 2. and his *f.* did *shine* as the sun

FACE *of the sky.*

Mat. 16. 3. O ye hypocrites, ye can discern the *f.*
of the sky, but can ye not the times? *Luke* 12. 56.

FACE *of the waters.*

Gen. 1. 2. Spirit of God moved on the *f. of the waters*
7. 18. the ark went upon the *f. of the waters*
Eccl. 11. † 1. cast thy bread on the *f. of the waters*
Hos. 10. † 7. her king cut off as foam on *f. of waters*

FACE *of the wilderness.*

Exod. 16. 14. on the *f. of the wilderness* lay manna

FACE *of the world.*

Job 37. 12. do what he commandeth on *f. of world*
Isa. 14. 21. nor fill the *f. of the world* with cities
27. 6. Israel shall fill the *f. of the world* with fruit

FACES.

Gen. 9. 23. their *f.* were backward, they saw not
30. 40. set *f.* of the flocks toward the ring-straked
40. † 7. wherefore are your *f.* evil to-day?
42. 6. they bowed with their *f.* to the earth
Exod. 19. 7. Moses laid before their *f.* all these words
20. 20. that his fear may be before your *f.*
25. 20. and their *f.* shall look one to another
37. 9. to the mercy-seat-ward were *f.* of cherubims
Deut. 1. † 17. shall not acknowledge *f.* in judgment
Judg. 18. 23. turned their *f.* and said, what aileth
2 *Sam.* 19. 5. thou hast shamed the *f.* of thy servants
1 *Kings* 2. 15. that all Israel set their *f.* on me
1 *Chron.* 12. 8. whose *f.* were like the *f.* of lions
2 *Chron.* 3. 13. and their *f.* were inward
29. 6. our fathers have turned away their *f.*
Neh. 8. 6. they worshipped with their *f.* to the ground
Job 9. 24. he covereth the *f.* of the judges
40. 13. hide in dust, and bind their *f.* in secret
Psal. 34. 5. and their *f.* were not ashamed
83. 16. fill their *f.* with shame, O Lord
Isa. 3. 15. and that ye grind the *f.* of the poor
13. 8. shall be amazed, their *f.* shall be as flames
25. 8. God will wipe away tears from off all *f.*
53. 3. and we hid as it were our *f.* from him
Jer. 1. 8. be not afraid of their *f.* I am with thee
17. be not dismay. at their *f.* lest I confound thee
5. 3. they have made their *f.* harder than a rock
7. 19. provoke to the confusion of their own *f.*
30. 6. and all *f.* are turned into paleness
42. 15. if ye set their *f.* to enter Egypt, 17. | 44. 12.
50. 5. the way to Zion, with their *f.* thitherward
51. 51. are confounded, shame hath covered our *f.*
Lam. 5. 12. the *f.* of the elders were not honoured
Ezek. 1. 6. and every one had four *f.* 10, 11, 15.
3. 8. I made thy face strong against their *f.*
7. 18. shame shall be on their *f.* and baldness
8. 16. twenty-five men, with their *f.* toward the east
14. 6. turn away your *f.* from all abominations
20. 47. and all *f.* shall be burnt therein
41. 18. and every cherub had two *f.*
Dan. 1. 10. for why should he see your *f.* worse
9. 7. but unto us confusion of *f.* as at this day
Joel 2. 6. be much pained, all *f.* shall gather blackn.
Nah. 2. 10. the *f.* of them all gather blackness
Hab. 1. 9. their *f.* shall sup up as the east-wind
Mal. 2. 3. behold, I will spread dung on your *f.*
† 9. but ye have accepted *f.* in the law
Mat. 6. 16. the hypocrites disfigure their *f.*
Luke 24. 5. as they were bowed down their *f.* to earth
Rev. 7. 11. fell before the throne on their *f.*
9. 7. the *f.* of the locusts were as the *f.* of men

See *Fell on* FACE, or FACES.

FACTIONS.

1 *Cor.* 3. † 3. for whereas there is among you *f.*

FADE.

Exod. 18. † 18. surely fading thou wilt *f.* away
2 *Sam.* 22. 46. strangers shall *f.* away, *Psal.* 18. 45.
Psal. 1. † 3. his leaf also shall not *f.* shall prosper
Isa. 64. 6. are all unclean, and we all *f.* as a leaf
Jer. 8. 13. I will consume them, and the leaf shall *f.*
Ezek. 47. 12. trees for meat, whose leaf shall not *f.*
Jam. 1. 11. so the rich man shall *f.* away in his ways

FADETH.

Job 14. † 18. surely the mountain falling *f.*
Isa. 1. 30. ye shall be as an oak, whose leaf *f.*
24. 4. the earth mourneth and *f.* the world *f.*
40. 7. the grass withereth, the flower *f.* 8.
1 *Pet.* 1. 4. to an inheritance that *f.* not away
5. 4. shall receive a crown of glory that *f.* not away

FADING.

Isa. 28. 1. whose glorious beauty is a *f.* flower
4. the glorious beauty shall be a *f.* flower

FAIL.

Josh. 3. 10. will without *f.* drive out Canaanites
Judg. 11. 30. if thou without *f.* deliver Ammon
1 *Sam.* 30. 8. pursue, thou shalt without *f.* recover all
Ezra 6. 9. let it be given day by day without *f.*

FAIL, *Verb.*

Gen. 47. 16. Jos. said, give your cattle, if money *f.*
Deut. 28. 32. thine eyes shall *f.* with longing for them
31. 6. Lord doth go with thee, he will not *f.* thee
nor forsake thee, 8. *Josh.* 1. 5. 1 *Chron.* 28. 20.
1 *Sam* 2. 16. let them not *f.* to burn fat presently
17. 32. David said, let no man's heart *f.* him
20. 5. I should not *f.* to sit with the king at meat
2 *Sam.* 3. 29. let there not *f.* from the house of Joab
1 *Kings* 2. 4. there shall not *f.* thee a man on the
throne of Israel, 8. 25. | 9. 5. 2 *Chron.* 6. 16.
17. 14. neither shall the cruse of oil *f.* 16.
Ezra 4. 22. take heed that ye *f.* not to do this
Esth. 6. 10. let nothing *f.* of all thou hast spoken
9. 27. not *f.* to keep these days of Purim, 28.
Job 11. 20. but the eyes of the wicked shall *f.*
14. 11. as waters *f.* from the sea, and flood drieth up
17. 5. even the eyes of his children shall *f.*
31. 16. or caused the eyes of the widow to *f.*
Psal. 12. 1. for the faithful *f.* from among men
69. 3. mine eyes *f.* while I wait for my God
77. 8. doth his promise *f.* for evermore?
89. 33. nor will I suffer my faithfulness to *f.*
119. 82. mine eyes *f.* for thy word, saying
123. mine eyes *f.* for thy salvation and for word
Prov. 22. 8. and the rod of his anger shall *f.*
Eccl. 12. † 3. the grinders *f.* because they grind little

Eccl. 12. 5. desire shall *f.* bec. man goeth to long home
Isa. 19. 3. the spirit of Egy. shall *f.* in midst thereof
5. waters shall *f.* || 21. 16. glory of Kedar *f.*
31. 3. and they all shall *f.* together
32. 6. he will cause the drink of the thirsty to *f.*
10. ye shall be troubled, for the vintage shall *f.*
34. 16. no one of these shall *f.* nor want her mate
38. 14. mine eyes *f.* with looking upward
42. 4. he shall not *f.* nor be discouraged
51. 14. hasteneth that his bread should not *f.*
57. 16. for the spirit should *f.* before me
58. 11. and like a spring whose waters *f.* not
Jer. 14. 6. their eyes did *f.* because there was no grass
15. 18. wilt thou be unto me as waters that *f.*?
48. 33. I caused wine to *f.* from presses, *Hos.* 9. 2.
Lam. 2. 11. mine eyes do *f.* with tears, my bowels
3. 22. not consumed, because his compassions *f.* not
Amos 8. 4. even to make the poor of the land to *f.*
Hab. 3. 17. although the labour of the olive shall *f.*
Luke 16. 9. that when ye *f.* they may receive you
17. earth to pass, than one tittle of the law to *f.*
22. 32. I have prayed that thy faith *f.* not
1 *Cor.* 13. 8. whether prophecies they shall *f.*
Heb. 1. 12. thou art the same, thy years shall not *f.*
11. 32. the time would *f.* me to tell of Gideon
12. 15. looking lest any man *f.* of the grace of God

FAILED.

Gen. 42. 28. their heart *f.* them, they were afraid
47. 15. and when money *f.* in the land of Egypt
Josh. 3. 16. the waters *f.* and were cut off
21. 45. there *f.* not any good thing which the Lord
promised to Israel, 23. 14. 1 *Kings* 8. 56.
Job 19. 14. my kinsfolk have *f.* and my friends
Psal. 142. 4. refuge *f.* me, no man cared for my soul
Cant. 5. 6. my soul *f.* when he spake, I sought him
Jer. 51. 30. their might *f.* they became as women
Lam. 4. 17. our eyes as yet *f.* for our vain help

FAILETH.

Gen. 47. 15. why should we die? for money *f.*
Lev. 25. † 35. if thy brother's hand *f.* relieve him
Job 21. 10. their bull gendereth and *f.* not
Psal. 31. 10. my strength *f.* me, 38. 10.
40. 12. therefore my heart *f.* me, 73. 26.
71. 9. forsake me not when my strength *f.*
109. 24. my knees are weak, my flesh *f.* of fatness
143. 7. hear me speedily, O Lord, my spirit *f.*
Eccl. 10. 3. when he walketh, his wisdom *f.* him
Isa. 15. 6. the grass *f.* there is no green thing
40. 26. for that he is strong in power, not one *f.*
41. 17. poor seek water, their tongue *f.* for thirst
44. 12. yea, he is hungry and his strength *f.*
59. 15. truth *f.* and he that departeth from evil
Ezek. 12. 22. days are prolonged and every vision *f.*
Zeph. 3. 5. bring his judgment to light, he *f.* not
Luke 12. 33. a treasure in the heavens that *f.* not
1 *Cor.* 13. 8. charity never *f.* but prophecies fail

FAILING.

Deut. 28. 65. the Lord shall give thee *f.* of eyes
Luke 21. 26. men's hearts *f.* them for fear

FAIN.

Job 27. 22. he would *f.* flee out of his hand
Luke 15. 16. would *f.* have filled his belly with husks

FAINT.

Gen. 25. 29. Esau came from field, and he was *f.* 30.
Deut. 25. 18. smote thee when thou wast *f.* and weary
Judg. 8. 4. passed over Jordan, *f.* yet pursuing them
5. give loaves of bread to the people, for they be *f.*
1 *Sam.* 14. 28. and the people were very *f.* 31.
30. 10. so *f.* that they could not go over, 21.
2 *Sam.* 16. 2. the wine, that such as be *f.* may drink
21. 15. David fought and waxed *f.*
Isa. 1. 5. the whole head is sick, the whole heart is *f.*
13. 7. therefore shall all hands be *f.* heart melt
29. 8. but he awaketh, and behold he is *f.*
40. 29. he giveth power to the *f.* and increaseth
44. 12. he drinketh no water, and is *f.*
Jer. 8. 18. I would comfort myself, my heart is *f.*
Lam. 1. 22. for my sighs are many, my heart is *f.*
5. 17. for this our heart is *f.* our eyes are dim
Zeph. 3. † 16. and to Zion, let not thine hands be *f.*

FAINT, *Verb.*

Deut. 20. 3. let not your hearts *f.* fear not
8. lest his brethren's heart *f.* as well as his heart
Josh. 2. 9. the inhabitants of land *f.* because of you
24. all the inhabitants of country *f.* because of us
Prov. 24. 10. if thou *f.* in the day of adversity
Isa. 40. 30. even the youths shall *f.* *Amos* 8. 13.
31. shall run and not be weary, walk and not *f.*
Jer. 51. 46. and lest your hearts *f.* and ye fear
Lam. 1. 13. he hath made me *f.* all the day
2. † 11. the sucklings *f.* || 19. young children *f.*
Ezek. 21. 7. every spirit shall *f.* knees shall be weak
15. their heart may *f.* and ruins be multiplied
Mat. 15. 32. not send them away fasting, lest they *f.*
Mark 8. 3. if I send them away fasting, they will *f.*
Luke 18. 1. that men ought always to pray, not to *f.*
2 *Cor.* 4. 1. as we have received mercy we *f.* not
16. for which cause we *f.* not, tho' outward man
Gal. 6. 9. in due season we shall reap, if we *f.* not
Eph. 3. 13. that ye *f.* not at my tribulations for you
2 *Thess.* 3. † 13. brethren, *f.* not in well-doing
Heb. 12. 3. lest ye be wearied, and *f.* in your minds
5. nor *f.* when thou art rebuked of him

FAINTED.

Gen. 45. 26. Jacob's heart *f.* for he believed not
47. 13. all the land of Canaan *f.* by reason of famine
Psal. 27. 13. I had *f.* unless I had believed to see
107. 5. hungry and thirsty, their soul *f.* in them
Isa. 51. 20. thy sons *f.* they lie at head of all streets
Jer. 45. 3. I *f.* in my sighing, I find no rest
Ezek. 31. 15. the trees of the field *f.* for him
Dan. 8. 27. I Daniel *f.* and was sick certain days
Jonah 2. 7. when my soul *f.* I remembered the Lord
4. 8. that he *f.* and wished in himself to die
Mat. 9. 36. with compassion on them, because they *f.*
Rev. 2. 3. thou hast laboured, and hast not *f.*

FAINTEST.

Job 4. 5. now it is come upon thee, and thou *f.*

FAINTETH.

Psal. 84. 2. my soul *f.* for the courts of the Lord
119. 81. my soul *f.* for thy salvation
Isa. 10. 18. they shall be as when a standard-bearer *f.*

Isa. 40. 28. the Creator of the ends of the earth *f.* not

FAINT-HEARTED.

Deut. 20. 8. who is fearful and *f.* let him return
Isa. 7. 4. fear not, nor be *f.* for the two tails
Jer. 49. 23. Hamath and Arpad are *f.*

FAINTNESS.

Lev. 26. 36. I will send a *f.* into their hearts

FAIR.

Gen. 6. 2. saw that the daughters of men were *f.*
12. 11. Sarah was *f.* 14. || 24. 16. Rebekah *f.* 26. 7.
1 *Sam.* 16. † 12. David was *f.* of eyes, 17. 42.
2 *Sam.* 13. 1. Tamar Absalom's sister was *f.* 14. 27.
1 *Kings* 1. 4. Abishag a *f.* damsel cherished David
Esth. 1. 11. Vashti the queen *f.* || 2. 7. Esther *f.*
2. 2. let *f.* young virgins be sought for the king
3. that they may gather the *f.* young virgins
Job 37. 22. *f.* weather cometh out of the north
42. 15. no women found so *f.* as Job's daughters
Prov. 7. 21. with *f.* speech she caused him to yield
11. 22. so is a *f.* woman without discretion
26. 25. when he speaketh *f.* believe him not
Cant. 1. 15. behold, thou art *f.* 16. | 4. 1, 7.
2. 10. rise up, my love, my *f.* one, come away, 13.
4. 10. how *f.* is thy love, my sister, my spouse!
6. 10. *f.* as the moon || 7. 6. how *f.* art thou, O love
Isa. 5. 9. many houses great and *f.* without inhabitant
54. 11. I will lay thy stones with *f.* colours
Jer. 4. 30. in vain shalt thou make thyself *f.*
11. 16. and olive-tree *f.* and of a goodly fruit
12. 6. though they speak *f.* words unto thee
46. 20. Egypt is like a very *f.* heifer, destruct. comes
Ezek. 16. 17. thou hast also taken thy *f.* jewels
39. and they shall take thy *f.* jewels, 23. 26.
31. 3. was a cedar in Lebanon with *f.* branches
7. thus was he *f.* in his greatness, in branches
9. I have made him *f.* by multitude of his branches
Dan. 4. 12. leaves thereof were *f.* fruit much, 21.
Hos. 10. 11. but I passed over upon her *f.* neck
Amos 8. 13. the *f.* virgins shall faint for thirst
Zech. 3. 5. let them set a *f.* mitre upon his head
Mat. 16. 2. it will be *f.* weather, for the sky is red
Acts 7. 20. Moses was born, and was exceeding *f.*
Rom. 16. 18. by *f.* speeches deceive the simple
Gal. 6. 12. a desire to make a *f.* shew in the flesh

FAIR *havens.*

Acts 27. 8. we came to a place called the *f. havens*

FAIRLY.

Mic. 1. † 11. pass ye away, thou that dwellest *f.*

FAIRER.

Judg. 15. 2. is not her younger sister *f.* than she?
Psal. 45. 2. thou art *f.* than the children of men
Dan. 1. 15. their countenances appeared *f.*

FAIREST.

Cant. 1. 8. O thou *f.* among women, 5. 9. | 6. 1.

FAIRS.

Ezek. 27. 12. they traded in thy *f.* 14, 16, 19, 22.
27. thy riches and thy *f.* shall fall into the seas

FAITH.

Faith *is a dependence on the veracity of another. Thus trust is called* faith, *because it relies upon the truth of a promise: And one is said to keep his faith inviolate, when he performs the promise that another relied on.* Faith, *in the propriety of expression, is an assent on account of the veracity of the speaker. Accordingly, divine faith is a firm assent of the mind to things upon the authority of divine revelation.* Faith *by divines is generally distinguished into four kinds, namely,* historical, temporary, the faith of miracles, *and* justifying *or* saving faith.

I. Historical faith *is a speculative knowledge of, and bare assent to, the truths revealed in the scripture: Of this kind of* faith *the apostle* James *speaks,* Jam. 2. 17, 24. Faith, if it have not works, is dead. Ye see how that by works a man is justified, and not by faith only; *that is, not by a mere profession of* faith, *or a bare assent to the truth, without good works, which proceed from* faith, *and shew it to be of the right kind. This kind of faith the devils themselves have.* Jam. 2. 19. Thou believest that there is one God; the devils also believe, and tremble. *They are fully persuaded that there is a God, and that* Christ *is the Son of God, and shall be their judge, as they acknowledge,* Mat. 8. 29.

II. Temporary faith, *together with the knowledge of, and assent to, revealed truths, has likewise in it, an approbation of, and joy in, receiving and hearing these truths; but this joy, arising from some worldly consideration, soon vanishes and comes to nothing: Of this kind of* faith *our Saviour speaks in the parable of the sower,* Mat. 13. 20. He that received the seed into stony places, receives it with joy; *he understands it, assents to it, he hears it gladly, considers, and approves of it; and it springs up in an outward profession and reformation:* Yet hath he not root in himself, but dureth for a while; *he has no sufficient or considerable root, because it wants the soil of a sincere heart, and true affections, firm and fixed resolutions, and habitual dispositions of grace: He has some good purposes and desires, but they are soon overpowered by unmortified corruption, and the force of temptation:* for when tribulation or persecution ariseth because of the word, by and by he is offended; *He stumbles, and falls off from all his former profession of religion.*

III. The faith of miracles *is a firm assent of the mind to some particular promise concerning any miraculous event, which, if performed by us, is called* an active miraculous faith; *of which our Saviour and the apostle* Paul *speak,* Mat. 17. 20. 1 Cor. 13. 2. *But if it be wrought upon us, it is called a* passive miraculous faith; *thus the lame man at* Lystra *had a firm persuasion that* Paul *and* Barnabas *were able to cure him,* Acts 14. 9.

IV. Justifying faith *is a saving grace wrought in the soul by the Spirit of God, whereby we receive* Christ *as he is revealed in the gospel, to be our Prophet, Priest, and King, trust in and rely upon him and his righteousness alone* for justification and salvation. This faith begets a sincere obedience in the life and conversation. The apostle to the Hebrews calls faith, the substance of things hoped for, the evidence of things not seen, Heb. 11. 1. It assures us of the reality and worth of eternal invisible things, and produces a satisfaction and assured confidence, that God will infallibly perform what he has promised, whereby the believer is as confident of them, as if they were before his eyes, and in his actual possession. The object of faith is the word of God in general, and especially the doctrines and promises that respect the salvation of men through Christ, which reason cannot discover by its own light, nor perfectly understand when revealed. The firm foundation of faith is the essential supreme perfections of God; his unerring knowledge, immutable truth, infinite goodness, and almighty power. Faith has a prevailing influence upon the will, it draws the affections, and renders the whole man obsequious to the gospel.

By this faith, we are said to be justified, Rom. 5. 1. We are justified by faith, not formally, as if it were our righteousness, or the meritorious cause of our justification before God; but instrumentally and relatively, as it apprehends and applies to us the righteousness and blood of Christ, which is the object of faith, and which only cleanseth us from all sin and renders us acceptable to God. It is called the faith through which we are saved, Eph. 2. 8. Faith is, as it were, a condition on our part, whereby we come to be partakers of the blessings of the new covenant. It is a faith which worketh by love, Gal. 5. 6. It is not an idle, unactive, and inoperative grace, but shows itself by producing in us love to God and our neighbour. It purifies the heart, Acts 15. 9. It is called the faith of God's elect, Tit. 1. 1. because it is bestowed only upon those. This grace increaseth from one degree to another, Rom. 1. 17. being in some strong and firm, Mat. 8. 10. in others weak and languishing, Mat. 14. 21. Lastly, this grace is the special gift of God, Eph. 2. 8. By grace ye are saved through faith; and that not of yourselves, it is the gift of God; that is, that you believe, is not by any ability of your own; and that you are saved, is not for any worth in yourselves. Likewise in Phil. 1. 29. Unto you it is given to believe on Christ.

Faith, in scripture, is taken for the truth and faithfulness of God, Rom. 3. 3. Shall their unbelief make the faith of God without effect? Shall their unbelief make the faithful promises of God, of sending the Messiah, and of redemption by him, not to be accomplished? It is also taken for a persuasion of the lawfulness of things indifferent, Rom. 14. 22, 23. Hast thou faith? have it to thyself before God. For whatsoever is not of faith is sin; that is, Hast thou a persuasion of the lawfulness of such and such meats, then keep it to thyself, without making an unseasonable discovery of it, to the offence of others: For whatever a man doeth with a wavering mind, without being persuaded that it is pleasing to God, and warranted by his word, he sinneth in the doing of it. Faith is also put for the doctrine of the gospel, which is the object of faith, Acts 24. 24. Felix heard Paul concerning the faith in Christ. Gal. 1. 23. He preacheth the faith which once he destroyed. And faith is taken for Christ, and his righteousness; that is, his active and passive obedience, which are apprehended by faith, and are the objects of it, in all those passages where we are said to be justified by faith. It is put for a belief and profession of the gospel, Rom. 1. 8. Your faith is spoken of throughout the whole world. And for fidelity in performing of promises, Deut. 32. 20. Children in whom is no faith; that is, They neither believe what I say, nor perform what themselves promise.

Deut. 32. 20. they are children in whom is no f.
Mat. 6. 30. O ye of little f. therefore take no thought, 8. 26. | 14. 31. | 16. 8. Luke 12. 28.
8. 10. found so great f. no not in Israel, Luke 7. 9.
17. 20. if ye have f. as a grain of mustard-seed
21. 21. if ye have f. ye shall not only do this
23. 23. and have omitted judgment, mercy, and f.
Mark 4. 40. he said to them, how is it ye have no f.?
11. 22. Jesus saith unto them, have f. in God
Luke 17. 5. the apostles said to the L. increase our f.
6. if ye had f. ye might say to this sycamine-tree
18. 8. when the Son of man cometh, shall he find f.?
Acts 3. 16. the f. which is by him, hath given him this perfect soundness in presence of you all
6. 5. and they chose Stephen, a man full of f. 8.
7. a great company of priests were obedient to the f.
11. 24. Barnabas was a good man, full of f.
13. 8. seeking to turn the deputy from the f.
14. 9. who perceiving that he had f. to be healed
22. and exhorting them to continue in the f.
27. how he had opened the door of f. to Gentiles
16. 5. the churches were established in the f.
17. † 31. whereof he hath offered f. to all men
20. 21. and f. toward our Lord Jesus Christ
24. 24. Felix heard Paul concerning the f.
Rom. 1. 5. we have received grace for obedience to f.
17. the righteousness of God revealed from f. to f.
3. 3. unbelief make the f. of God without effect
27. where boasting? It is excluded by law of f.
4. 5. his f. is counted for righteousness, 9.
11. circumcision a seal of the righteousness of f.
12. but also walk in steps of that f. of Abraham
13. but was through the righteousness of f.
14. if they of the law be heirs, f. is made void
16. it is of f. which is of the f. of Abraham
9. 30. even the righteousness, which is of f. 10. 6.
10. 8. that is the word of f. which we preach
17. f. cometh by hearing, hearing by word of God
12. 3. accord. as God hath dealt the measure of f.
6. prophesy according to the proportion of f.
14. 22. hast thou f.? have it to thyself before God
23. he eateth not of f. what is not of f. is sin
Rom. 16. 26. to all nations for the obedience of f.
1 Cor. 12. 9. to another f. by the same Spirit
13. 2. though I have all f. and have no charity
13. now abideth f. hope, charity, these three
2 Cor. 4. 13. we having the same Spirit of f.
Gal. 1. 23. now preached f. which once he destroyed
3. 2. by the works of law, or by the hearing of f. 5.
7. know ye, that they which are of f. 9.
12. law is not of f. but the man that doeth them
23. before f. came || 25. after that f. is come
5. 6. but f. which worketh by love
22. but the fruit of the Spirit is love, joy, f.
6. 10. unto them who are of the household of f.
Eph. 4. 5. one Lord, one f. one baptism
13. till we all come in the unity of the f.
6. 16. above all, taking the shield of f.
23. peace be to the brethren, with f. from God
Phil. 1. 25. for your furtherance and joy of f.
27. striving together for the f. of the gospel
1 Thess. 1. 3. remembering your work of f.
5. 8. putting on the breast plate of f. and love
2 Thess. 1. 4. we glory for your patience and f.
11. would fulfil the work of f. with power
3. 2. we may be delivered, for all men have not f.
1 Tim. 1. 5. f. unfeigned || 5. 8. he hath denied the f.
14. grace of our Lord exceeding abundant with f.
19. holding f. and a good conscience; which some put away concerning f. have made shipwreck
3. † 6. not one newly come to the f.
9. holding the mystery of f. in a pure conscience
4. 1. in latter times, some shall depart from the f.
6. nourished up in words of f. and good doctrine
5. 12. because they have cast off their first f.
6. 10. they have erred from the f. 21.
11. follow f. || 12. fight the good fight of f.
2 Tim. 1. 5. the unfeigned f. that is in thee
2. 18. and overthrow the f. of some
22. follow f. || 3. 8. reprobate concerning the f.
3. 10. but thou hast fully known my f. charity
4. 7. I have finished my course, I have kept the f.
Tit. 1. 1. according to the f. of God's elect
4. to Titus mine own son, after the common f.
Philem. 5. hearing of thy f. toward the Lord Jesus
Heb. 4. 2. word did not profit, not being mixed with f.
6. 1. not laying again the foundation of f.
10. 22. with a true heart in full assurance of f.
23. let us hold fast the profession of our f.
11. 1. f. is the substance of things hoped for
6. without f. it is impossible to please God
12. 2. Jesus, the author and finisher of our f.
13. 7. whose f. follow, considering the end
Jam. 2. 1. have not the f. with respect of persons
14. though a man say he hath f. can f. save him?
17. even so f. without works is dead, 20. 26.
18. a man may say, thou hast f. and I have works
22. seest thou how f. wrought with his works, and by works was f. made perfect
5. 15. and the prayer of f. shall save the sick
2 Pet. 1. 1. that have obtained like precious f.
1 John 5. 4. that overcometh the world, even our f.
Jude 3. ye should earnestly contend for the f.
20. building up yourselves on your most holy f.
Rev. 2. 13. thou holdest fast and hast not denied my f.
19. I know thy works, and f. and thy patience
13. 10. here is the patience and the f. of the saints
14. 12. here are they that keep the f. of Jesus

By FAITH.

Hab. 2. 4. but the just shall live by his f. Rom. 1. 17. Gal. 3. 11. Heb. 10. 38.
Acts 15. 9. purifying their hearts by f.
26. 18. who are sanctified by f. that is in me
Rom. 1. 12. may be comforted by the mutual f.
3. 22. the righteousness of God by f. of Jesus Chr.
28. a man is justified by f. 5. 1. Gal. 2. 16. | 3. 24.
30. which shall justify the circumcision by f.
5. 2. by whom we have access by f. to this grace
9. 32. because they sought it not by f.
11. 20. thou standest by f. 2 Cor. 1. 24.
2 Cor. 5. 7. for we walk by f. not by sight
Gal. 2. 20. I live by the f. of the Son of God
3. 22. that the promise by f. might be given
26. ye are the children of God by f. in Christ Jes.
5. 5. we wait for the hope of righteousness by f.
Eph. 3. 12. in whom we have access by f. of him
17. that Christ may dwell in your hearts by f.
Phil. 3. 9. the righteousness which is of God by f.
Heb. 4. † 2. because they were not united by f.
11. 4. by f. Abel || 5. by f. Enoch || 7. by f. Noah
8. by f. Abrah. 9, 17. || 20. by f. Isaac blessed Jac.
21. by f. Jacob || 22. by f. Joseph made mention
23. by f. Moses, 24, 27. || 31. by f. Rahab
29. by f. they passed through the Red sea
30. by f. the walls of Jericho fell down
Jam. 2. 24. you see then, how that by works a man is justified, not by f. only

In FAITH.

Rom. 4. 19. being not weak in f. he considered not
20. he staggered not, but was strong in f.
14. 1. him that is weak in the f. receive you
1 Cor. 16. 13. watch, stand fast in the f. be strong
2 Cor. 8. 7. as ye abound in f. and utterance
13. 5. examine yourselves whether ye be in the f.
Col. 1. 23. if ye continue in the f. grounded
2. 7. rooted in him, and stablished in the f.
1 Tim. 1. 2. unto Timothy my own son in the f.
4. rather than godly edifying which is in f.
2. 7. a teacher of the Gentiles in f. and verity
15. be saved, if they continue in f. and charity
3. 13. they purchase great boldness in the f.
4. 12. be thou an example of believers in f.
2 Tim. 1. 13. hold fast the form in f. and love
Tit. 1. 13. that they may be found in the f. 2. 2.
3. 15. greet them that love us in the f. grace be
Heb. 11. 13. these all died in f. not having received
Jam. 1. 6. but let them ask in f. not wavering
2. 5. God chosen the poor of this world, rich in f.
1 Pet. 5. 9. whom resist, stedfast in the f.

Their FAITH.

Mat. 9. 2. Jes. seeing their f. Mark 2. 5. Luke 5. 20.

Through FAITH.

Acts 3. 16. through f. in his name this man strong
Rom. 3. 25. a propitiation through f. in his blood
Rom. 3. 30. who shall justify uncircumcis. through f.
31. do we make void the law through f.? G. forbid
Gal. 3. 8. God would justify the heathen through f.
14. might receive the promise of the Spirit thro' f.
Eph. 2. 8. for by grace are ye saved through f.
Phil. 3. 9. but that righteousness which is thro' f.
Col. 2. 12. risen thro' the f. of the operation of God
2 Tim. 3. 15. make thee wise to salvation thro' f.
Heb. 6. 12. who through f. inherit the promises
11. 3. through f. we understand the worlds framed
11. through f. Sara received strength to conceive
28. thro' f. he kept the passover, and sprinkling
33. who thro' f. subdued kingdoms, wrought right.
39. having obtained a good report through f.
1 Pet. 1. 5. kept by power of G. thro' f. to salvation

Thy FAITH.

Mat. 9. 22. thy f. hath made thee whole, Mark 5. 34. | 10. 52. Luke 8. 48. | 17. 19.
15. 28. Jesus said, O woman, great is thy f.
Luke 7. 50. thy f. hath saved thee, go in peace, 18. 42.
22. 32. I prayed for thee, that thy f. fail not
Philem. 6. the communication of thy f. effectual
Jam. 2. 18. shew me thy f. without thy works

Your FAITH.

Mat. 9. 29. according to your f. be it unto you
Luke 8. 25. he said unto them, where is your f.?
Rom. 1. 8. your f. is spoken of through the world
1 Cor. 2. 5. your f. should not stand in wisdom of men
15. 14. and your f. is also vain, 17.
2 Cor. 1. 24. not have dominion over your f.
10. 15. having hope when your f. is increased
Eph. 1. 15. after I heard of your f. in the Lord
Phil. 2. 17. if I be offered on the service of your f.
Col. 1. 4. since we heard of your f. in Christ Jesus
2. 5. beholding the stedfastness of your f. in Christ
1 Thess. 1. 8. your f. to God-ward is spread abroad
3. 2. and to comfort you concerning your f.
5. I sent to know your f. lest the tempter
6. Timothy brought us good tidings of your f.
7. we were comforted over you by your f.
10. and might perfect what is lacking in your f.
2 Thess. 1. 3. that your f. groweth exceedingly
Jam. 1. 3. the trying of your f. worketh patience
1 Pet. 1. 7. the trial of your f. being more precious
9. receiving the end of your f. even salvation
21. that your f. and hope might be in God
2 Pet. 1. 5. add to your f. virtue, to virtue knowledge

FAITHFUL.

Num. 12. 7. Moses is f. in mine house, Heb. 3. 2, 5.
Deut. 7. 9. the f. God who keepeth covenant
1 Sam. 2. 35. I will raise me up a f. priest
3. † 20. Samuel was f. to be a prophet of the Lord
22. 14. Ahimelech said, who is so f. as David?
2 Sam. 20. 19. I am one of them that are f. in Israel
Neh. 7. 2. Hananiah was a f. man and feared God
9. 8. and foundest his heart f. before thee
13. 13. for they were counted f. to distribute
Job 12. † 20. he removeth the lip of the f.
Psal. 12. 1. for the f. fail from among men
31. 23. O love the Lord, for Lord preserveth the f.
89. 37. and as a f. witness in heaven
101. 6. mine eyes shall be on the f. of the land
119. 86. all thy commandments are f.
138. thy testimonies are righteous and very f.
Prov. 11. 13. a f. spirit concealeth the matter
13. 17. but a f. ambassador is health
14. 5. a f. witness will not lie, but a false utter lies
20. 6. but a f. man who can find?
25. 13. as snow in harvest, so is a f. messenger
27. 6. f. are the wounds of a friend, but the kisses
28. 20. a f. man shall abound with blessings
Isa. 1. 21. how is the f. city become an harlot!
26. afterwards thou shalt be called the f. city
8. 2. I took unto me f. witnesses to record
49. 7. kings shall see, because of the Lord that is f.
Jer. 42. 5. the Lord be a f. witness between us
Dan. 6. 4. could find none, forasmuch as he was f.
Hos. 11. 12. but Judah is f. with the saints
Mat. 24. 45. who then is a f. and wise servant?
25. 21. well done, thou good and f. servant
23. thou hast been f. in a few things, Luke 19. 17.
Luke 12. 42. who then is that f. and wise steward?
16. 10. he that is f. in the least is f. also in much
11. have not been f. in the unrighteous mammon
12. have not been f. in what is another man's
Acts 16. 15. if ye have judged me f. to the Lord
1 Cor. 1. 9. God is f. by whom ye were called, 10. 13.
4. 2. it is required in stewards, that a man be f.
17. I have sent you Timothy f. in the Lord
7. 25. that hath obtained mercy of the Lord to be f.
Gal. 3. 9. they are blessed with f. Abraham
Eph. 1. 1. to the saints and f. in Christ Jesus
6. 21. Tychicus a f. minister in the Lord
Col. 1. 2. to the saints and f. brethren in Christ
7. Epaphras, who is for you a f. minister, 4. 7.
4. 9. Onesimus, a f. brother, who is one of you
1 Thess. 5. 24. f. is he that calleth you, who will do it
2 Thess. 3. 3. the Lord is f. who shall stablish you
1 Tim. 1. 12. I thank Christ, that he counted me f.
15. this is a f. saying, 4. 9. Tit. 3. 8.
3. 11. their wives must be sober, and f. in all things
6. 2. rather do them service because they are f.
2 Tim. 2. 2. the same commit thou to f. men
11. it is a f. saying || 13. yet he abideth f.
Tit. 1. 6. if any be blameless, having f. children
9. holding fast the f. word, as he was taught
Heb. 2. 17. that he might be a f. high-priest
3. 2. who was f. to him that appointed him
10. 23. for he is f. that promised, 11, 11.
1 Pet. 4. 19. commit their souls, as unto a f. Creator
5. 12. I have written by Silvanus a f. brother
1 John 1. 9. if we confess, he is f. to forgive us
Rev. 1. 5. Christ who is the f. witness, 3. 14.
2. 10. be f. to death, I will give thee a crown of life
13. those days wherein Antipas was my f. martyr
17. 14. they that are with him, are called, and f.
19. 11. and he that sat upon him was called f.
21. 5. these words are true and f. 22. 6.

FAITHFULLY.

2 Kings 12. 15. for they dealt f. 22. 7.
2 Chron. 19. 9. thus do in the fear of the Lord f.
31. 12. and they brought in the offerings f.

2 Chron. 34. 12. and the men did the work f.
Prov. 29. 14. the king that f. judgeth the poor
Jer. 23. 28. hath my word, let him speak my word f.
3 John 5. thou doest f. whatsoever thou dost to bre- [thren

FAITHFULNESS.

1 Sam. 26. 23. the Lord render to every man his f.
Psal. 5. 9. for there is no f. in their mouth
36. 5. and thy f. reacheth unto the clouds
40. 10. I have declared thy f. and thy salvation
88. 11. or shall thy f. be declared in destruction?
89. 1. I will make known thy f. to all generations
2. thy f. shalt thou establish in the heavens
5. thy f. also in the congregation of the saints
8. who is like to thee, or to thy f. round about thee?
24. but my f. and my mercy shall be with him
33. nor will I suffer my f. to fail
92. 2. it is good to shew forth thy f. every night
119. 75. and that thou in f. hast afflicted me
† 86. all thy commandments are f.
90. thy f. is unto all generations
† 138. thy testimonies are righteous and very f.
143. 1. hear my prayer; in thy f. answer me
Isa. 11. 5. and f. shall be the girdle of his reins
25. 1. thy counsels of old are f. and truth
Lam. 3. 23. thy mercies are new, great is thy f.
Hos. 2. 20. I will betroth thee unto me in f.

FAITHLESS.

Mat. 17. 17. O f. generat. Mark 9. 19. Luke 9. 41.
John 20. 27. and be not f. but believing

FALL.

The fall of man. *Man's greatest excellency at first was a perfect conformity to the divine pattern.* God created man in his own image, in the image of God created he him, Gen. 1. 27. *This includes,*

I. *The similitude of God in the substance of the soul, as it is an intelligent, free, spiritual, and immortal being. This is assigned to be the reason of the law, that* whoso sheds man's blood, by man shall his blood be shed; for in the image of God made he man, *Gen.* 9. 6.

II. *A moral resemblance in its qualities and perfections. Man was conformed to God in holiness: this the apostle insinuates, when he sets forth the sanctification of corrupt man, by the expression of* renewing him in knowledge, righteousness, and holiness, after the image of the Creator, *Eph.* 4. 23, 24. *Col.* 3. 10. *The renovation of things, being a restoring of them to their primitive state; and is more or less perfect, by its proportion to, or distance from, the original. Man's understanding was enriched with knowledge, which was neither acquired by study, nor confined to that or the other particular creature, but reached through the whole compass of the creation. Besides, he had such a knowledge of the Deity as was sufficient for his duty and felicity. He discovered almighty power, admirable wisdom, and infinite goodness, from their effects in creating the world. The image of God was likewise resplendent in man's conscience, the seat of practical knowledge, and treasury of moral principles. The directive faculty was sincere and uncorrupt; it was clear from all prejudices, which might render it an incompetent judge of good and evil. There was also a divine impression on the will. Spiritual reason kept the throne, and the inferior faculties observed an easy and regular subordination to its dictates.*

III. *The image of God consisted, though in an inferior degree, in the happy state of man, which was the consequent and accession to his holiness: And herein he resembled that infinitely blessed Being, as he is perfectly exempt from all evils which might allay and lessen his felicity, and enjoys those pleasures which are worthy of his pure nature and glorious state. This happiness had relation to the two natures, which enter into man's composition.* (1) *The animal and sensitive, and this consisted both in the excellent disposition of his organs, and in the enjoyment of convenient objects. His body being formed immediately by God, was not liable to those defects which proceed from the weakness of second causes: no blemish or disease, which are the effects and footsteps of sin, were to be found in him: all his senses were quick and lively, able to perform with facility, vigour, and delight, their operations. Not only were his organs excellently disposed, but there were also convenient objects to entertain his sensitive faculties: he enjoyed nature in its original purity, crowned with the benediction of God, before it was blasted with the curse. The world was all harmony and beauty, becoming the goodness of the Creator; and not as it is since the fall, disordered and deformed in many parts, the effect of his justice. The earth was liberal to* Adam *of all its treasures; the heavens of their light and sweetest influences. And he was seated in* Eden, *a place of great beauty and delight. But* (2) *His chief happiness consisted in the exercise of his most noble faculties on their proper objects. The highest faculties in man are the understanding and will: and their happiness consists in union with God by knowledge and love. He saw the admirable beauty of the Creator through the transparent veil of the creatures: And from hence there arose in the soul a pleasure pure, solid, and satisfying.*

IV. *There was in man's dominion and power over the creatures a shining part of God's image. God gave him the solemn investiture of his dignity, when he brought the creatures to receive their names from him, which was a mark of their homage, and a token of his empire to command them by their names,* Psal. 8. 6, 7, 8. *Thus holy and blessed was* Adam *in his primitive state.*

Man only of all creatures on earth was in a state of moral dependence, and capable of a law. For, a law being the declaration of the Superior's will requiring obedience, and threatening punishment on the failure thereof, there must be a principle of reason and choice in that nature which is governed by it: both to discover the authority that enjoins it; to discern the matter of the law; and to determine itself, out of judgment and election, to obedience, as most excellent in itself, and advantageous to the performer. As therefore reason made man capable of a law, so it was impossible he should be exempt from a law; for as the notion of a God, that is, of the first and supreme Being, excludes all possibility of obligation to another, and of subjection to a law; so the quality of a creature includes the relation of dependence and natural subjection to the will of God.

The law of nature, to which man was subject upon his creation, contains those moral principles concerning good and evil, which have an essential equity in them, and are the measures of his duty to God, to himself, and to his fellow-creatures. This law was published by the voice of reason, and is holy, just, and good; and the obligation to it is eternal; it being the unchangeable will of God, grounded on the natural and invariable relations between God and man, and between man and the creatures. Besides the particular directions of the law of nature, this general principle was planted in the reasonable soul, to obey God in any instance wherein he did prescribe his pleasure. Accordingly, to declare his sovereign right in all things, and to make trial of man's obedience, God entered into covenant with man; he forbids him to eat of the tree of knowledge of good and evil, for in the day thou eatest thereof thou shalt surely die. *This established an inseparable connection between duty and felicity, disobedience and misery. In this threatening of death upon disobedience, the promise of life upon his obedience was implied, and easily suggested itself to the rational mind.*

Man was created perfectly holy, but in a natural, therefore mutable, state. He was invested with power to prevent his falling, yet under a possibility of it: he was complete in his own order, but receptive of sinful impressions. Being therefore set upon by the most subtle of those rebellious spirits, who had fallen from their obedience and glory, he was corrupted and seduced by him, and involved both himself and his posterity in sin and misery. As to the manner in which the devil seduced our first parents, see on DEVIL.

The honour and majesty of the whole law was violated in the breach of that symbolical precept: for in that grand apostasy many sins were included: as, 1. Infidelity *and* unbelief. *God had said,* Of the tree of knowledge of good and evil, thou shalt not eat of it; for in the day thou eatest thereof, thou shalt surely die. *This was the first step to ruin, as appears by the order of the temptation: it was first said by the devil,* Ye shall not die *to weaken their faith; then,* Ye shall be as gods, *to flatter their ambition. This infidelity is greatly aggravated, as it implies an accusation of God.* (1) *Of* envy; *as if he had denied them the perfections becoming the human nature, and they might ascend to an higher orb than that wherein they were placed, by eating the forbidden fruit.* (2) *Of* falsehood; *as if God had threatened to inflict a punishment upon man's disobedience which he had no design to do; and what heightens this is, that when he distrusted the fountain of truth, he gave credit to the father of lies; as appears by his compliance, the real evidence of his faith.*

II. *This sin included in it* prodigious pride. *He was scarcely out of the state of nothing, no sooner created but he aspired to be as God. Not content with his image, he affected an equality, to be like him in his inimitable attributes. He would rob God of his eternity, to live without end, to enjoy an immortality, not depending on God's will, but absolute, which is proper to God alone; of his sovereignty, to command without dependence; and of his wisdom, to know all things without reserve.*

III. Horrid ingratitude. *He was appointed heir apparent of all things; yet undervaluing his present portion, he entertains a project of improving his happiness. The excellent state newly conferred upon him, was a strong obligation to pay so small an acknowledgment to the Lord. The use of all the garden was allowed him, only a tree excepted. Now in the midst of such variety and plenty, to be inflamed with the intemperate appetite of the forbidden fruit, and to break a command so equal and easy, what was it but a despising the rich goodness of his great Benefactor?*

IV. A bloody cruelty to himself, and to all his posterity. *When God had made him a depository in a matter of infinite moment; that is, of his own happiness, and all mankind's, this should have been a powerful motive to have kept him vigilant: but giving a ready ear to the tempter, he betrayed his trust, and at once breaks both the tables of the law, and becomes the greatest sinner, being guilty of the highest impiety and cruelty.*

By voluntary disobedience our first parents fell from and lost their original rectitude and perfection of nature; which consisted in knowledge, holiness, and perfect happiness, Gen. 1. 26. Col. 3. 10. Eph. 4. 24.

By the fall of man all the powers of nature were depraved, polluted, and corrupted: [1] *The understanding was darkened,* Eph. 4. 18. [2] *The conscience defiled,* Heb. 10. 22. [3] *The will obstinate and rebellious,* Isa. 28. 14. Rom. 8. 7. [4] *The affections carnal and sensual,* Eph. 2. 3. [5] *All the thoughts uninterruptedly evil,* Gen. 6. 5. *and the whole mind, or heart, a nest of all manner of abominations,* Jer. 17. 9. Mat. 15. 19.

FALL, *Substantive.*

Prov. 16. 18. and an haughty spirit before a f.
29. 16. but the righteous shall see their f.
Jer. 49. 21. earth is moved at the noise of their f.
Ezek. 26. 15. the isles shake at the sound of their f.
18. the isles shall tremble in the day of thy f.
31. 16. the nations to shake at the sound of his f.
32. 10. every man for his life in the day of thy f.
Mat. 7. 27. the house fell, and great was the f. of it
Luke 2. 34. child is set for the f. and rising of many
Rom. 11. 11. but through their f. salvation is come unto the Gentiles
12. if the f. of them be the riches of the world

FALL, *Verb.*

Gen. 2. 21. God caused a deep sleep to f. upon Adam
43. 18. he may seek occasion against us, and f. on us
45. 24. he said, see that ye f. not out by the way
49. 17. so that his rider shall f. backward
Exod. 15. 16. fear and dread shall f. upon them
21. 33. if a man dig a pit, and an ox or ass f. therein
Lev. 11. 32. on whatsoever any of them doth f.
37. if their carcase f. on any sowing-seed, 38.
19. 29. lest land f. to whoredom and become wicked
26. 7. they shall f. before you by the sword, 8.
36. and they shall f. when none pursueth
37. and they shall f. one upon another
Num. 5. † 21. the Lord doth make thy thigh to f.
6. † 12. but the days that were before shall f.
11. 31. and let them f. by the camp round about
14. 29. your carcases shall f. in the wilderness, 32.
34. 2. this is the land that shall f. to you
Deut. 22. 8. if any man f. from thence
Judg. 8. 21. they said, rise thou, and f. upon us
15. 12. Samson said, swear ye will not f. upon me
18. and f. into the hand of the uncircumcised
Ruth 2. 16. let f. some handfuls of purpose for her
† 22. that they f. not on thee in another field
3. 18. until thou know how the matter will f.
1 Sam. 3. 19. let none of his words f. to the ground
14. 45. there shall not one hair of his head f. to the ground, 2 Sam. 14. 11. 1 Kings 1. 52. Acts 27. 34.
18. 25. Saul sought to make David f. by Philistines
22. 17. would not f. on the priests of the Lord
18. the king said, turn thou, and f. on the priests
26. 20. therefore let not my blood f. to the earth
2 Sam. 1. 15. go near and f. on him, 1 Kings 2. 29. 31.
24. 14. let us f. into the hand of God, let me not f. into the hand of man, 1 Chron. 21. 13.
1 Kings 22. 20. who shall persuade Ahab to go up and f. at Ramoth-gilead? 2 Chron. 18. 19.
2 Kings 7. 4. let us f. unto the host of the Syrians
10. 10. shall f. nothing of the word of the Lord
14. 10. why shouldst meddle, that thou shouldst f.?
1 Chron. 12. 19. he will f. to his master Saul
2 Chron. 21. 15. have sickness, till thy bowels f. out
25. 8. God shall make thee f. before the enemy
19. that thou shouldest f. and Judah with thee
Esth. 6. † 10. suffer not a whit to f. of all that
13. before whom thou hast begun to f. shall not prevail against him, but shalt surely f. before him
Job 6. † 27. yea, ye cause to f. upon the fatherless
12. † 3. I f. not lower than you
13. 11. and shall not his dread f. upon you
31. 22. let mine arm f. from my shoulder-blade
Psal. 5. 10. let them f. by their own counsels
9. 3. mine enemies shall f. and perish at thy presence
10. 10. that the poor may f. by his strong ones
35. 8. into that very destruction let him f.
37. 24. tho' he f. he shall not be utterly cast down
45. 5. arrows, whereby the people f. under thee
64. 8. make their tongue to f. on themselves
78. 28. and he let it f. in the midst of their camp
82. 7. but ye shall f. like one of the princes
91. 7. a thousand shall f. at thy side, and 10,000
106. † 27. make their seed f. among the nations
118. 13. thou hast thrust at me that I might f.
140. 10. let burning coals f. upon them
141. 10. let the wicked f. into their own nets
145. 14. the Lord upholdeth all that f.
Prov. 4. 16. unless they cause some to f.
10. 8. but a prating fool shall f. 10
11. 5. the wicked shall f. by his own wickedness
14. where no counsel is the people f.
28. he that trusteth in his riches shall f.
22. 14. he that is abhorred of the Ld. shall f. therein
24. 16. but the wicked shall f. into mischief
26. 27. whoso diggeth a pit shall f. therein, he who rolleth a stone it will return on him, Eccl. 10. 8.
28. 10. causeth to go astray shall f. into his own pit
14. but he that hardeneth his heart shall f.
18. but he that is perverse shall f. at once
Eccl. 4. 10. if they f. one will lift up his fellow
11. 3. if the tree f. toward the south or north
Isa. 8. 15. many among them shall stumble and f.
10. 4. and they shall f. under the slain
34. and Lebanon shall f. by a mighty one
22. 25. nail fastened in the sure place shall f.
24. 18. who fleeth from fear shall f. into the pit
20. the earth shall f. and not rise again
28. 13. that they might go and f. backward
30. 13. iniquity shall be as a breach ready to f.
25. in the day of slaughter, when the towers f.
40. 30. and the young men shall utterly f.
47. 11. therefore mischiefs shall f. upon thee
54. 15. whoso shall gather shall f. for thy sake
Jer. 3. 12. I will not cause mine anger to f. on you
6. 15. they shall f. among them that f. 8. 12.
21. the fathers and sons shall f. upon them
8. 4. saith the Lord, shall they f. and not arise?
9. 22. even the carcases of men shall f. as dung
15. 8. I have caused him to f. upon it suddenly
23. 12. they shall be driven on, and f. therein
19. a whirlwind f. on the head of wicked, 30. 23.
25. 27. drink ye, and be drunken, and spue, and f.
34. and ye shall f. like a pleasant vessel
37. 14. it is false, I f. not away to the Chaldeans
† 20. let my supplication f. before thee
42. † 2. let our supplication f. before thee
44. 12. they shall all f. in the land of Egypt
46. 6. they shall stumble and f. toward the north
16. he made many to f. yea one fell on another
48. 44. he that fleeth shall f. into the pit
49. 26. her young men f. in her streets, 50. 30.
50. 32. and the most proud shall stumble and f.
51. 4. the slain shall f. in land of Chaldeans, 47, 49.

Jer. 51. 44. yea, the wall of Babylon shall f.
49. as Babylon caused the slain of Israel to f.
Lam. 1. 14. he hath made my strength to f.
Ezek. 6. 7. the slain shall f. in the midst of you
13. 11. say unto them that it shall f. and ye, O great hailstones, shall f. and a stormy wind rent it
14. foundation shall be discovered, and it shall f.
24. 6. bring it out piece by piece, let no lot f. on it
27. 27. all thy company shall f. into the seas, 34.
29. 5. thou shalt f. upon the open fields, 39. 5.
30. 4. great pain, when the slain shall f. in Egypt
6. they also that uphold Egypt shall f.
22. I will cause the sword to f. out of his hand
32. 12. by swords will I cause thy multitude to f.
33. 12. not f. thereby in the day that he turneth
35. 8. and in all thy rivers shall they f.
36. † 14. nor cause to f. thy nations any more
38. 20. the steep places shall f. every wall shall f.
39. 3. arrows to f. ‖ 4. shalt f. on the mountains
44. 12. they caused Israel to f. into iniquity
45. † 1. when ye cause the land to f. by lot
47. 14. thus land shall f. to you for inheritance
Dan. 9. † 18. we cause not our supplications to f.
11. 14. also the robbers of thy people shall f.
19. but he shall stumble and f. and not be found
34. when they shall f. ‖ 35. some f. to try them
Hos. 4. 5. therefore shalt thou f. in the day, the prophet also shall f. with thee in the night
14. the people that doth not understand shall f.
5. 5. Israel and Ephraim shall f. Judah shall f.
10. 8. and they shall say to the hills, f. on us
14. 9. but the transgressors shall f. therein
Amos 3. 5. can a bird f. in a snare where no gin is?
14. the horns of the altar shall f. to the ground
8. 14. even they shall f. and never rise again
9. 9. yet shall not the least grain f. to the earth
Mic. 7. 8. rejoice not, O mine enemy, when I f.
Nah. 3. 12. they shall f. into the mouth of the eater
Mal. 2. † 8. ye have caused many to f. in the law
Mat. 10. 29. not one sparrow f. to ground without
12. 11. if it f. into a pit on the sabbath-day
15. 14. both shall f. into the ditch, Luke 6. 39.
27. eat crumbs which f. from masters' table
21. 44. whoso f. on this stone be broken, on whom it shall f. it will grind him to powder, Luke 20. 18.
24. 29. the sun shall be darkened, and the stars shall f. from heaven, Mark 13. 25.
Luke 10. 18. I beheld Satan as lightn. f. from heav.
23. 30. shall begin to say to the mountains f. on us
John 12. 24. except a corn f. into the ground and die
Acts 27. 17. fearing lest they should f. into quicks.
32. then the soldiers cut the ropes and let her f. off
34. shall not an hair f. from the head of any of you
Rom. 11. 11. have they stumbled that they should f.
14. 13. put an occasion to f. in his brother's way
1 Cor. 10. 12. him that standeth take heed lest he f.
1 Tim. 3. 6. he f. into the condemnation of the devil
7. have a good report, lest he f. into reproach
6. 9. they that will be rich f. into temptation
Heb. 4. 11. lest any f. after the same example
10. 31. it is fearful to f. into hands of living God
Jam. 1. 2. count it joy, when ye f. into temptation
5. 12. swear not, lest ye f. into condemnation
2 Pet. 1. 10. if ye do these things ye shall never f.
3. 17. beware lest ye f. from your stedfastness
Rev. 6. 16. said to the mountains and rocks, f. on us
9. 1. I saw a star f. from heaven unto the earth

FALL *away.*

Luke 8. 13. and in the time of temptation f. away
Heb. 6. 6. if they f. away to renew them again

FALL *down.*

Deut. 22. 4. see thy brother's ass f. down by the way
Josh. 6. 5. the wall of the city shall f. down flat
1 Sam. 21. 13. David let his spittle f. down
Psal. 72. 11. all kings shall f. down before him
Isa. 13. † 7. therefore shall all hands f. down
31. 3. and he that is holpen shall f. down
34. 4. their host shall f. down as the leaf falleth
44. 19. shall I f. down to the stock of a tree?
45. 14. the Sabeans shall f. down unto thee
46. 6. they f. down, yea, they worship
Ezek. 30. 25. and the arms of Pharaoh shall f. down
Dan. 3. 5. ye f. down and worship the image, 10.
15. if ye f. down and worship the image, well
11. 26. and many shall f. down slain
Mat. 4. 9. all these things will I give thee, if thou wilt f. down and worship me, Luke 4. 7.
Rev. 4. 10. the twenty-four elders f. down before him

FALL, *joined with sword.*

Exod. 5. 3. lest he f. on us with pestilence or sword
Num. 14. 3. brought us to this land to f. by sword
43. and ye shall f. by the sword
2 Kings 19. 7. Sennacherib f. by s. 2 Chr. 32. † 21.
Psal. 63. 10. they shall f. by the sword, Ezek. 6. 11.
Isa. 3. 25. thy men shall f. by the sword
13. 15. and every one shall f. by the sword
31. 8. then shall the Assyrian f. with the sword
37. 7. behold, I will cause him to f. by the sword in his own land, Jer. 19. 7.
Jer. 20. 4. Pashur's friends shall f. by the sword
39. 18. and thou shalt not f. by the sword
Ezek. 5. 12. a third part shall f. by the sword
6. 12. and he that is near shall f. by the sword
11. 10. ye shall f. by the sword, I will judge you
17. 21. his fugitives shall f. by the sword
23. 25. and thy remnant shall f. by the sword
24. 21. your sons and daughters shall f. by sword
25. 13. and they of Dedan shall f. by the sword
30. 5. the men in the league shall f. by the sword
6. from the tower of Syene, shall f. by the sword
17. the young men shall f. by the sword
22. I will cause the sword to f. out of his hand
33. 27. they in the wastes shall f. by the sword
Dan. 11. 33. they that understand shall f. by sword
Hos. 7. 16. their princes shall f. by the sword
13. 16. Samaria shall f. by the sword
Joel 2. 8. when they f. on the sword not be wounded
Amos 7. 17. thy sons and daughters f. by the sword
Luke 21. 24. they shall f. by the edge of the sword

FALLEN.

Gen. 4. 6. L. said to Cain, why is thy countenance f.?
Lev. 13. 41. that hath his hair f. off from his head
Lev. 25. 35. if thy brother be f. in decay with thee
Josh. 8. 24. all Ai were f. on the edge of the sword
Judg. 3. 25. behold, their lord was f. down dead
18. 1. their inheritance had not f. unto them
19. 27. behold, the woman was f. at the door
1 Sam. 5. 3. Dagon was f. ‖ 26. 12. a deep sleep f.
31. 8. they found Saul and his sons f. 1 Chr. 10. 8.
2 Sam. 1. 10. sure he could not live after he was f.
12. and they mourned, because they were f.
3. 38. there is a great man f. this day in Israel
17. † 9. when some of them be f. at the first
1 Kings 8. † 56. hath not f. one word of his promise
20. † 25. number an army like army that was f.
2 Kings 13. 14. now Elisha was f. sick of his sickness
25. † 11. the f. away did the captain carry away
2 Chron. 20. 24. were dead bodies f. to the earth
29. 9. for lo, our fathers have f. by the sword
Esth. 7. 8. Haman was f. on bed where Esther was
Psal. 20. 8. they are brought down and f.
36. 12. there are the workers of iniquity f.
Isa. 14. 12. how art thou f. from heaven, O Lucifer!
26. 18. nor have the inhabitants of the world f.
Ezek. 32. 22. all of them f. by the sword, 23, 24.
Hos. 14. 1. for thou hast f. by thine iniquity
Zech. 12. † 8. he that is f. at that day be as David
Luke 14. 5. which of you shall have ox f. into a pit?
Acts 8. 16. the Holy Ghost was f. on none of them
20. 9. Eutychus being f. into a deep sleep fell down
26. 14. when we were all f. I heard a voice
27. 29. fearing lest they should have f. on rocks
28. 6. looked when Paul should have f. down dead
Phil. 1. 12. f. out to the furtherance of the gospel
Rev. 2. 5. remember from whence thou art f.

Are FALLEN.

2 Sam. 1. 4. many of the people are f. and dead
19. how are the mighty f.! 25, 27.
22. 39. they are f. under my feet, Psal. 18. 38.
Psal. 16. 6. the lines are f. to me in pleasant places
55. 4. the terrors of death are f. upon me
57. 6. into the midst whereof they are f. themselves
69. 9. the reproaches of them are f. upon me
Isa. 9. 10. the bricks are f. down, but we will build
Jer. 38. 19. the Jews that are f. to the Chaldeans
46. 12. the mighty men, they are f. both together
50. 15. Babylon's foundations are f. walls down
Lam. 2. 21. my virgins are f. by the sword
Ezek. 31. 12. his branches are f. his boughs broken
32. 27. they shall not lie with the mighty that are f.
Hos. 7. 7. all their kings are f. none calleth to me
1 Cor. 15. 6. part remain, some are f. asleep, 18.
Gal. 5. 4. justified by the law, ye are f. from grace
Rev. 17. 10. are seven kings, five are f. and one is

Is FALLEN.

Lev. 13. 40. the man whose hair is f. off his head
Num. 32. 19. our lot is f. on this side Jordan
Josh. 2. 9. I know that your terror is f. upon us
Job 1. 16. the fire of God is f. from heaven
Psal. 7. 15. and is f. into the ditch which he made
Isa. 3. 8. Jerusalem is ruined, and Judah is f.
16. 9. the shouting for thy summer-fruits is f.
21. 9. Babylon is f. is f. Rev. 14. 8. | 18. 2.
59. 14. for truth is f. in the streets, equity cannot
Jer. 48. 32. the spoiler is f. on thy summer fruits
51. 8. Babylon is suddenly f. and destroyed
Lam. 5. 16. the crown is f. from our heads, woe to us
Ezek. 13. 12. lo, when the wall is f. shall it not be said
Amos 5. 2. the virgin of Isr. is f. shall no more rise
9. 11. I will raise up the tabernacle that is f.
Zech. 11. 2. howl, fir-tree, for the cedar is f.
Acts 15. 16. build tabernacle of David which is f.

FALLER.

Jer. 46. † 16. he multiplied the f. one fell on another

FALLEST.

Jer. 37. 13. saying, thou f. away to the Chaldeans

FALLETH.

Exod. 1. 10. when there f. out any war, they join
Lev. 11. 33. every vessel whereinto any of them f.
35. every thing whereupon their carcase f.
Num. 33. 54. inheritance shall be where his lot f.
2 Sam. 3. 29. not fail one that f. on the sword
34. as a man f. before wicked men, so fellest thou
17. 12. will light on him as dew f. on the ground
Job 4. 13. when deep sleep f. on men, 33. 15.
Prov. 13. 17. a wicked messenger f. into mischief
17. 20. a perverse tongue f. into mischief
24. 16. a just man f. seven times, riseth up again
17. rejoice not when thine enemy f.
Eccl. 4. 10. woe to him that is alone when he f.
9. 12. sons of men are snared when it f. on them
11. 3. where the tree f. there shall it be
Isa. 34. 4. as the leaf f. off from the vine
44. 15. maketh an image, and f. down thereto, 17.
Jer. 21. 9. he that f. to Chaldeans shall live
Dan. 3. 6. whoso f. not down, and worshippeth, 11.
Mat. 17. 15. for oft times he f. into the fire
Luke 11. 17. a house divided against a house f.
15. 12. give me the portion of goods that f. to me
Rom. 14. 4. to his own master he standeth or f.
Jam. 1. 11. the flower thereof f. 1 Pet. 1. 24.

FALLING.

Num. 24. 4. f. into a trance, but his eyes open, 16.
Deut. 19. † 16. to testify against him f. away
Job 4. 4. thy words have upholden him that was f.
14. 18. the mountain f. cometh to nought
Ps. 56. 13. wilt not deliver my feet from f. 116. 8.
Prov. 25. 26. a righteous man f. before the wicked
Isa. 34. 4. and as a f. fig from the fig-tree
Luke 8. 47. came trembling and f. down before him
22. 44. as it were great drops of blood f. down
Acts 1. 18. and Judas f. headlong, burst asunder
27. 41. and f. into a place where two seas met
1 Cor. 14. 25. and so f. down, he will worship God
2 Thess. 2. 3. except there come a f. away first
Jude 24. to him that is able to keep you from f.

FALLINGS.

Job 41. † 23. the f. of his flesh are joined together

FALLOW.

Jer. 4. 3. break up your f. ground, Hos. 10. 12.

See Deer.

FALSE.

Exod. 23. 1. thou shalt not raise a f. report
7. keep thee far from a f. matter
2 Kings 9. 12. and they said, it is f. tell us now
Job 36. 4. for truly my words shall not be f.
Psal. 119. 104. therefore I hate every f. way, 128.
120. 3. what shall be done to thee, thou f. tongue
Prov. 11. 1. a f. balance is an abomination to the L.
17. 4. a wicked doer giveth heed to f. lips
20. 23. and a f. balance is not good
25. 14. whoso boasteth of a f. gift, is like wind
Jer. 8. † 8. the f. pen of scribes worketh for falsehood
14. 14. they prophecy unto you a f. vision
23. 32. I am against them that prophesy f. dreams
37. 14. then said Jeremiah, it is f. I fall not away
Lam. 2. 14. but have seen for thee f. burdens
Ezek. 21. 23. it shall be to them as a f. divination
Zech. 8. 17. let none imagine evil, love no f. oath
10. 2. and the diviners have told f. dreams
Mal. 3. 5. I will be swift witness against f. swearers
Mat. 24. 24. for there shall arise f. Christs and f. prophets, and shall shew wonders, Mark 13. 22.
Luke 19. 8. have taken any thing by f. accusation
2 Cor. 11. 13. for such are f. apostles, deceitful
26. I have been in perils among f. brethren
Gal. 2. 4. because of f. brethren unawares brought in
2 Tim. 3. 3. without natural affection, f. accusers
Tit. 2. 3. aged women, that they be not f. accusers
2 Pet. 2. 1. there shall be f. teachers among you

See Prophet.

FALSE *prophets.*

Mat. 7. 15. beware of f. prophets in sheep's clothing
24. 11. and many f. prophets shall rise, 24.
Mark 13. 22. f. prophets shall rise, and shew signs
Luke 6. 26. so did their fathers to the f. prophets
2 Pet. 2. 1. there were f. prophets among the people
1 John 4. 1. f. prophets are gone out into the world

FALSE *witness.*

Exod. 20. 16. thou shalt not bear f. witness against thy neighbour, Deut. 5. 20. Mat. 19. 18.
Deut. 19. 16. if a f. witness rise up against any man
18. and behold, if the witness be a f. witness
Prov. 6. 19. a f. witness that speaketh lies
12. 17. a f. witness sheweth forth deceit, 14. 5.
19. 5. a f. witness shall not be unpunished, 9.
21. 28. a f. witness shall perish
25. 18. a man that beareth f. witness is a maul
Mat. 15. 19. for out of the heart proceed f. witness
26. 59. the elders sought f. witness against Jesus
Mark 14. 56. many bare f. witness against him, 57.

FALSE *witnesses.*

Psal. 27. 12. f. witnesses are risen up against me
35. 11. f. witnesses did rise, they laid to my charge
Mat. 26. 60. tho' many f. witnesses came, yet found they none, at the last came two f. witnesses
Acts 6. 13. and set up f. witnesses, who said
1 Cor. 15. 15. and we are found f. witnesses of God

FALSEHOOD.

2 Sam. 18. 13. should have wrought f. against my life
Job 21. 34. in your answers there remaineth f.
Psal. 7. 14. behold, he hath brought forth f.
119. 118. hast trodden them down, for deceit is f.
144. 8. their hand is a right hand of f. 11.
Prov. 20. † 17. bread of f. is sweet to a man
25. † 14. whoso boasteth himself in a gift of f.
Isa. 28. 15. and under f. have we hid ourselves
57. 4. are ye not a seed of f.? ‖ 59. 13. words of f.
Jer. 3. † 10. she hath turned to me but in f.
8. † 8. the false pen of scribes worketh for f.
10. 14. for his molten image is f. 51. 17.
13. 25. thou hast forgotten me, and trusted in f.
37. † 14. then said Jeremiah, it is a f.
Hos. 7. 1. for they commit f. and the thief cometh in
Mic. 2. 11. if a man walking in the spirit and f.

FALSELY.

Gen. 21. 23. swear to me that thou wilt not deal f.
Lev. 6. 3. have found what was lost, and sweareth f.
5. or all that about which he hath sworn f.
19. 11. neither deal f. nor lie one to another
12. and ye shall not swear by my name f.
Deut. 19. 18. if the witness have testified f.
Psal. 35. † 19. let not mine enemies f. rejoice
44. 17. nor have we dealt f. in thy covenant
Jer. 5. 2. tho' they say, the Lord liveth, they swear f.
31. the prophets prophesy f. unto you, 29. 9.
6. 13. prophet, priest, every one dealeth f. 8. 10.
7. 9. will ye steal, murder, and swear f.?
40. 16. for thou speakest f. of Ishmael
43. 2. thou speakest f. the Lord hath not sent thee
Hos. 10. 4. swearing f. in making a covenant
Mic. 2. † 11. if a man walk with the wind and lie f.
Zech. 5. 4. the curse enter his house that sweareth f.
Mat. 5. 11. say evil against you f. for my sake
Luke 3. 14. nor accuse any f. be content with wages
1 Tim. 6. 20. oppositions of science, f. so called
1 Pet. 3. 16. f. accuse your good conversa. in Christ

FALSIFYING.

Amos 8. 5. and f. the balances by deceit

FAME.

Gen. 45. 16. the f. was heard in Pharaoh's house
Num. 14. 15. nations that have heard the f. of thee
Josh. 6. 27. Joshua's f. was noised thro' the country
9. 9. we heard the f. of God, what he did in Egypt
1 Kings 4. 31. his f. was in all nations round about
10. 1. the queen heard f. of Solomon, 2 Chron. 9. 1.
7. thy wisdom exceedeth the f. 2 Chron. 9. 6.
1 Chron. 14. 17. the f. of David went to all lands
22. 5. and the house must be of f. and of glory
Esth. 9. 4. Mordecai's f. went through the provinces
Job 28. 22. we have heard the f. with our ears
Isa. 66. 19. to the isles that have not heard my f.
Jer. 3. † 9. thro' the f. of her whoredom she defiled
6. 24. we have heard the f. our hands wax feeble
Zeph. 3. 19. and I will get them f. in every land
Mat. 4. 24. the f. of Jesus went abroad, Mark 1. 28. Luke 4. 14, 37. | 5. 15
9. 26. the f. thereof went abroad into all that land
31. they, when departed, spread abroad his f.
14. 1. Herod the tetrarch heard of the f. of Jesus

FAMILIAR.

Job 19. 14. my f. friends have forgotten me
Psal. 41. 9. my f. friend hath lift up his heel ag. me

FAMILIAR *spirit.*

Lev. 20. 27. man or woman of a f. spirit put to dea

1 Sam. 28. 7. seek me a woman that hath a f. spirit to inquire of her; a f. spirit at Endor
8. divine to me by the f. spirit and bring him up
1 Chr. 10. 13. Saul inquired of one that had a f. sp.
2 Chron. 33. 6. Manasseh dealt with a f. spirit
Isa. 29. 4. thy voice as of one that hath a f. spirit

FAMILIAR spirits.

Lev. 19. 31. regard not them that have f. spirits
20. 6. against that soul that turneth after f. spirits
Deut. 18. 11. nor a consulter with f. spirits
1 Sam. 28. 3. Saul put away those that had f. spirits
9. how he hath cut off those that have f. spirits
2 Kings 21. 6. Manasseh dealt with f. spirits
23. 24. workers with f. spirits Josiah put away
Isa. 8. 19. when they say to you, seek f. spirits
19. 3. they shall seek to them that have f. spirits

FAMILIARS.

Jer. 20. 10. all my f. watched for my halting

FAMILY.

Lev. 20. 5. I will set my face against his f.
25. 10. ye shall return every man to his f. 41.
47. sell himself to the stock of the stranger's f.
49. his uncle or any of his f. may redeem him
Num. 3. 21. of Gershon was the f. of the Libnites
27. of Kohath was the f. of the Amramites
26. 5. the f. of the Hanochites, f. of the Palluites
FAMILY *mentioned often to the 59th verse.*
27. 4. why our father's name done away from f.?
11. give his inheritance to the next of his f.
36. 6. marry to f. of their father's tribe, 8, 12.
Deut. 29. 18. lest a f. turn away from Lord our God
Josh. 7. 14. the f. which the Lord taketh shall come
17. and he took the f. of the Zarhites
Judg. 1. 25. but they let go the man and all his f.
6. 15. behold, my f. is poor in Manasseh
9. 1. communed with the f. of his mother's father
13. 2. Manoah a man of the f. of the Danites
17. 7. a young man, a Levite of the f. of Judah
18. 2. the Danites sent of their f. five men to spy
19. or that thou be a priest to a f. in Israel
21. 24. Israel departed, every man to his f.
Ruth 2. 1. she had a kinsman of the f. of Elimelech
1 Sam. 9. 21. my f. the least of the tribe of Benjamin
10. 21. f. of Matri was taken, and Saul was taken
18. 18. what is my life, or my father's f. in Israel?
20. 6. a yearly sacrifice there for all the f. 29.
2 Sam. 14. 7. whole f. is risen against thine handmaid
16. 5. a man of the f. of Saul, his name Shimei
1 Chron. 4. 27. neither did all their f. multiply
6. 61. to the f. of Kohath were cities given, 70.
13. 14. the ark remained with the f. of Obed-edom
Esth. 9. 28. these days of Purim kept by every f.
Jer. 3. 14. I will take one of a city, and two of a f.
8. 3. death shall be chosen by residue of this evil f.
Amos 3. 1. against the f. I brought out of Egypt
Zech. 12. 12. every f. shall mourn apart, 13, 14.
14. 18. if the f. of Egypt go not up, and come not
Eph. 3. 15. whole f. in heaven and earth is named

FAMILIES.

Gen. 8. † 19. creepeth on the earth, after their f.
10. 5. the isles of Gentiles divided after their f.
18. were the f. of the Canaanites spread abroad
20. the sons of Ham after their f. ‖ 31. f. of Shem
12. 3. in thee all the f. of earth be blessed, 28. 14.
36. 40. the dukes of Esau according to their f.
47. 12. Joseph nourished his brethren with their f.
Exod. 6. 14. these be the f. of Reuben, the first-born of Israel, Num. 26. 7. Josh. 13. 15, 23.
15. these are the f. of Simeon, Num. 26. 12, 14. Josh. 19. 1, 8.
17. the f. of Gershon, Num. 3. 18, 21. | 4. 22, 24, 38, 40, 41. Josh. 21. 33.
19. these are the f. of Levi, 25. Num. 4. 46. | 26. 57, 58. Josh. 21. 27. 1 Chron. 6. 19.
12. 21. take you a lamb according to your f.
Lev. 25. 45. of the f. of strangers shall ye buy
Num. 1. 2. take the sum of Israel after their f.
3. 19. and the sons of Kohath by their f. 27. 29, 30. | 4. 37. Josh. 21. 4, 10.
20. the sons of Merari, by their f. 33, 35. | 4. 33, 42, 44, 45. Josh. 21. 34, 40. 1 Chron. 6. 63.
4. 18. cut not off the tribe of the f. of Kohathites
11. 10. Moses heard them weep through their f.
26. 15. the f. of Gad, 18. Josh. 13. 24, 28.
20. the f. of Judah, 22. Josh. 15. 1, 12, 20.
23. the sons of Issachar after their f. 25. Josh. 19. 17, 23. | 21. 6. 1 Chron. 6. 62. | 7. 5.
26. the f. of Zebulun, 27. Josh. 19. 10, 16.
28. the sons of Joseph after their f. 36. 1.
34. the f. of Manasseh, 36. 12. Josh. 13. 29. | 17. 2.
35. these are sons of Ephraim after their f. 37. Josh. 16. 5, 8. | 21. 5, 20. 1 Chron. 6. 66.
38. the sons of Benjamin after their f. 41. Josh. 18. 11, 20, 21. 1 Sam. 10. 21.
42. the sons of Dan after their f. Josh. 19. 40, 48.
44. sons of Asher after their f. Josh. 19. 24, 31.
48. sons of Naphtali after their f. 50. Josh. 19. 32.
27. 1. daughters of Zelophehad of Manasseh's f.
33. 54. divide your land by lot among your f.
36. 1. the chief fathers of the f. of Gilead
Josh. 6. † 23. brought out Rahab and all her f.
7. 14. tribe the Lord taketh come according to f.
13. 31. to half the children of Machir, by their f.
19. 40. the tribe of Dan according to their f. 48.
1 Sam. 9. 21. the least of all the f. of Benjamin
1 Chr. 2. 53. the f. of Kirjath-jearim, the Puhites
55. the f. of the scribes which dwelt at Jabez
4. 2. these are the f. of the Zorathites
21. the f. of them that wrought fine linen
38. these mentioned were princes in their f.
2 Chron. 35. 5. according to the divisions of the f. 12.
Neh. 4. 13. I set the people after their f.
Job 31. 34. did the contempt of f. terrify me?
Psal. 68. 6. God setteth the solitary in f.
107. 41. and maketh him f. like a flock
Jer. 1. 15. I will call all the f. of the north
2. 4. hear all the f. of the house of Israel
10. 25. fury on the f. that call not on thy name
15. † 3. and I will appoint over them four f.
25. 9. behold, I will take all the f. of the north
31. 1. I will be the God of all the f. of Israel

Jer. 33. 24. the two f. which the Lord hath chosen
Ezek. 20. 32. we will be as the f. of the countries
Amos 3. 2. you have I known of all f. of the earth
Nah. 3. 4. that selleth f. through her witchcrafts
Zech. 12. † 12. and the land shall mourn, f. f.
14. all the f. that remain, every family apart
14. 17. whoso will not come up of all the f.

FAMINE.

The scripture speaks of several famines *which have been in* Palestine, *and in the neighbouring countries: as that in the time of* Abraham, *and again in the time of* Isaac, *Gen.* 12. 10. | 26. 1. *But the most remarkable whereof we have any account, is that of seven years, which fell out in* Egypt, *while* Joseph *abode there,* Gen. 41. 27. *It is considerable for the continuance, extent, and greatness of it; and in this particular the more so, that* Egypt *is a country least subject to these calamities, by reason of its extreme fruitfulness.*

Famine *is sometimes a natural effect, as when the* Nile *does not overflow in* Egypt; *or the rains do not fall in* Judea, *at the customary times, that is, in spring or autumn; or when the caterpillars and locusts swarm in the country, and destroy the fruits of it. The prophets, in several places, take notice of these last causes of* famine, *Joel* 1. 3, 4, &c.

Famine *was also often the effect of God's anger against his people. For example: the Lord sent the prophet* Gad *to* David, *to tell him, that as a punishment of his vanity, whereby he had been induced to number his people, God gave him the option of seven years'* famine, *or of being for three months pursued by his enemies, or of seeing the plague raging for three days in his country,* 2 Sam. 24. 12, 13. *And in the reign of* Ahab, The Lord called for a famine, and it came upon the land seven years, 2 *Kings* 8. 1, 2. Amos *threatens the people of God with another sort of* famine, *want of heavenly bread, which was that* of hearing the word of God, *Amos* 8. 11. *The* Israelites *now despise a prophet's counsel, then they shall seek for it, but not have a prophet to give them counsel.*

Gen. 12. 10. for the f. was grievous in the land
26. 1. there was a f. in the land, besides the first f.
41. 27. seven empty ears shall be seven years of f.
30. and the f. shall consume the land
31. the plenty shall not be known by reason of f.
50. to Joseph were born two sons before the f.
56. the f. was over all the face of the earth
47. 13. the land fainted by reason of the f.
Ruth 1. 1. when the judges ruled there was a f.
2 Sam. 21. 1. there was a f. in the days of David
24. 13. shall seven years of f. come to thee in land?
1 Kings 8. 37. if there be in the land f. 2 Chr. 20. 9.
18. 2. there was a sore f. in Samaria, 2 Kings 6. 25.
2 Kings 7. 4. then the f. is in the city, we shall die
8. 1. the Lord hath called for a f. it shall come
25. 3. the f. prevailed in Jerusalem, no bread
2 Chr. 32. 11. Hezekiah persuadeth you to die by f.
Job 5. 20. in f. he shall redeem thee from death
22. at destruction and f. thou shalt laugh
30. 3. for want and f. they were solitary
Psal. 33. 19. and to keep them alive in f.
37. 19. in the days of f. they shall be satisfied
105. 16. moreover, he called for a f. on the land
Isa. 5. † 13. and their glory are men of f.
14. 30. and I will kill thy root with f.
51. 19. destruction, f. and sword, are come on thee
Jer. 5. 12. nor shall we see sword, nor f. 14. 13, 15.
14. 15. by sword and f. shall prophets be consumed
16. the people shall be cast out, because of the f.
18. then behold them that are sick with f.
15. 2. and such as are for the f. to the f.
18. 21. deliver up their children to the f.
21. 7. deliver from the f. to Nebuchadnezzar
24. 10. I will send the f. among them, 29. 17.
27. 8. that nation will I punish with the f.
29. 18. I will persecute with the sword and f.
32. 24. the city is given to Chaldeans because of f.
34. 17. I proclaim a liberty for you to the f.
42. 16. the f. shall follow close after you
52. 6. the f. was sore in the city, there was no bread
Lam. 5. 10. our skin was black, because of the f.
Ezek. 5. 12. a third part shall be consumed with f.
16. when I send on them the evil arrows of f.
17. so will I send on you f. 14. 13.
7. 15. f. within, f. and pestilence shall devour
12. 16. but I will leave a few men from the f.
36. 29. and I will lay no f. upon you
30. ye shall receive no more reproach of f.
Amos 8. 11. I will send a f. not of bread, but of word
Luke 4. 25. when great f. was thro' all the land
15. 14. there arose a mighty f. in that land
Rom. 8. 35. shall f. separate us from love of Christ?
Rev. 18. 8. her plagues come in one day, death, f.

By the FAMINE.

Jer. 11. 22. their sons and daught. shall die by the f.
14. 12. but I will consume them by the f. 15.
16. 4. they shall be consumed by f. 44. 12, 18, 27.
21. 9. he that abideth in the city shall die by the f.
27. 13. why will ye die by the f. and pestilence?
32. 36. be delivered to the king of Babylon by the f.
38. 2. remaineth in city shall die by f. Ezek. 6. 12.
42. 17. they shall die by the f. and pestilence
22. know certainly that ye shall die by the f.
44. 13. as I have punished Jerusalem by the f.
Ezek. 6. 11. they shall fall by the f. and pestilence

FAMINES.

Mat. 24. 7. there shall be f. pestilences, and earthquakes in divers places, Mark 13. 8. Luke 21. 11.

FAMISH *and* FAMISHED.

Gen. 41. 55. when all the land of Egypt was f.
Prov. 10. 3. the L. will not suffer the righteous to f.
Isa. 5. 13. and their honourable men are f.
Zeph. 2. 11. for he will f. all the gods of the earth

FAMOUS.

Num. 16. 2. princes f. in the congregation, 26. 9.
Ruth 4. 11. and be thou f. in Bethlehem
14. that his name may be f. in Israel
1 Chron. 5. 24. and these were f. men, 12. 30.
Psal. 74. 5. a man was f. as he had lifted up axes
136. 18. give thanks to him who slew f. kings
Ezek. 23. 10. and she became f. among women
32. 18. and the daughters of the f. nations

FAN, *Substantive.*

Isa. 30. 24. clean provender winnowed with the f.
Jer. 15. 7. I will fan them with a f. in the gates
Mat. 3. 12. whose f. is in his hand, Luke 3. 17.

FAN, *Verb.*

Isa. 41. 16. shalt f. them, wind shall carry them away
Jer. 4. 11. a dry wind not to f. nor to cleanse
15. 7. I will f. them with a fan in the gates
51. 2. I will send fanners that shall f. her

FAR.

Gen. 18. 25. that be f. from thee to slay righteous
Exod. 8. 28. only you shall not go very f. away
23. 7. keep thee f. from a false matter
Deut. 12. 21. if the place be too f. from thee, 14. 24.
29. 22. the stranger that shall come from a f. land
Josh. 3. 16. waters stood very f. from the city Adam
8. 4. go not very f. from the city, but be ready
9. 22. saying, we are f. from you, when ye dwell
Judg. 9. 17. my father adventured his life f.
18. 7. they were f. from the Zidonians, 28.
19. 11. they were by Jebus, day was f. spent
1 Sam. 20. 9. Jonathan said, f. be it from thee
1 Kings 8. 46. that they carry them away f. or near
2 Chr. 26. 15. and his name was spread f. abroad
Ezra 6. 6. now therefore be ye f. from thence
Neh. 4. 19. we are separated one f. from another
Esth. 9. 20. to all the Jews both nigh and f.
Job 5. 4. his children are f. from safety
11. 14. put iniquity f. away, 22. 23.
34. 10. f. be it from God to do wickedness
Psal. 10. 5. thy judgments are f. out of sight
22. 1. why art thou so f. from helping me?
73. 27. they that are f. from thee shall perish
97. 9. Lord, thou art exalted f. above all gods
103. 12. as f. as the east is from the west, so f. hath he removed our transgressions from us
109. 17. so let blessing be f. from him
119. 150. that follow mischief are f. from thy law
155. salvation is f. from the wicked
Prov. 4. 24. and perverse lips put f. from thee
5. 8. remove thy way f. from her, come not nigh her
15. 29. the Lord is f. from the wicked
19. 7. much more do his friends go f. from him
22. 5. doth keep his soul shall be f. from them
15. the rod of correction shall drive it f. from him
31. 10. for her price is f. above rubies
Eccl. 2. 13. as f. as light excelleth darkness
3. † 5. and a time to be f. from embracing
Isa. 6. 12. and the Lord have removed men f. away
19. 6. and they shall turn the rivers f. away
26. 15. thou hast removed the nations f.
46. 12. hear ye that are f. from righteousness
49. 19. that swallowed thee shall be f. away
54. 14. thou shalt be f. from oppression
59. 9. therefore is judgment f. from us
Jer. 12. 2. thou art f. from their reins
25. 26. all the kings of the north f. and near
27. 10. prophesy, to remove you f. from your land
48. 24. upon all the cities of Moab f. or near
47. thus f. is the judgment of Moab
51. 64. thus f. are the words of Jeremiah
Lam. 3. 17. thou hast removed my soul f. from peace
Ezek. 7. 20. therefore have I set it f. from them
11. 15. they have said, get ye f. from the Lord
Dan. 11. 2. the fourth king f. richer than they all
Joel 3. 6. that ye might remove them f. from border
Amos 6. 3. ye that put f. away the evil day
Mic. 7. 11. in that day shall decree be f. removed
Mat. 16. 22. Peter said, be it f. from thee, Lord
Mark 6. 35. and when the day was now f. spent
12. 34. thou art not f. from the kingdom of God
13. 34. Son of man is as a man taking a f. journey
Luke 7. 6. when he was not f. from the house
22. 51. Jesus said, suffer ye thus f. he healed him
24. 29. abide with us, for the day is f. spent
50. and he led them out as f. as to Bethany
John 21. 8. for they were not f. from land
Acts 11. 19. they travelled as f. as Phenice
22. that Barnabas should go as f. as Antioch
17. 27. though he be not f. from every one of us
22. 21. I will send thee f. hence to the Gentiles
28. 15. they came to meet us as f. as Appii forum
Rom. 13. 12. the night is f. spent, the day is at hand
2 Cor. 4. 17. worketh a f. more exc. weight of glory
10. 14. for we are come as f. as to you also
Eph. 1. 21. f. above all principality and power
4. 10. that ascended up f. above all heavens
Phil. 1. 23. to be with Christ, which is f. better
Heb. 7. 15. it is yet f. more evident, after Melchisedec
See COUNTRY, COUNTRIES.

FAR *from me.*

1 Sam. 2. 30. but now the Lord saith, be it f. from me, 22. 15. 2 Sam. 20. 20. | 23. 17.
Job 13. 21. withdraw thine hand f. from me
19. 13. he hath put my brethren f. from me
21. 16. the counsel of wicked is f. from me, 22. 18.
30. 10. they flee f. from me, and spare not to spit
Psal. 22. 11. O Lord, be not f. from me, for trouble is near, 19. | 35. 22. | 38. 21. | 71. 12.
27. 9. hide not thy face f. from me, leave me not
88. 8. thou hast put mine acquaintance f. from me
18. lover and friend hast thou put f. from me
Prov. 30. 8. remove f. from me vanity and lies
Eccl. 7. 23. I will be wise, but it was f. from me
Isa. 29. 13. but have removed their heart f. from me
Jer. 2. 5. they are gone f. from me, and become vain
Lam. 1. 16. because the comforter is f. from me
Ezek. 43. 9. the carcases of their kings f. from me
44. 10. the Levites that are gone f. from me
Mat. 15. 8. their heart is f. from me, Mark 7. 6.

From FAR.

Deut. 28. 49. a nation against thee from f. Jer. 5. 15.
Job 36. 3. I will fetch my knowledge from f.
Isa. 5. 26. he will lift up an ensign from f.
10. 3. desolation which shall come from f.
22. 3. they are bound which are fled from f.

Isa. 30. 27. the name of the Lord cometh *from f.*
43. 6. bring my sons *from f.* and daughters, 60. 9.
49. 1. listen, O isles, hearken, ye people, *from f.*
12. behold, these shall come *from f.*
60. 4. thy sons shall come *from f.* and daughters
Jer. 30. 10. for lo, I will save thee *from f.*
Ezek. 23. 40. that ye sent for men to come *from f.*
Hab. 1. 8. and their horsemen shall come *from f.*
Mark 8. 3. for divers of them came *from f.*
See Afar.

FAR *off.*

Gen. 44. 4. when they were gone, and not yet *f. off*
Num. 2. 2. they shall pitch *f. off* about the tabernacle
Deut. 13. 7. not consent to serve gods of people *f. off*
20. 15. thus do to all the cities very *f. off*
30. 11. neither is the commandment *f. off*
2 *Sam.* 15. 17. the king tarried in a place *f. off*
2 *Chron.* 6. 36. carry their captives to a land *f. off*
Psal. 55. 7. lo, then I would wander *f. off*
Prov. 27. 10. is better than a brother *f. off*
Eccl. 7. 24. that which is *f. off* who can find out?
Isa. 17. 13. they shall flee *f. off* and be chased
33. 13. hear, ye that are *f. off* what I have done
17. they shall behold the land that is *f. off*
46. 13. my righteousness shall not be *f. off*
57. 9. and thou didst send thy messengers *f. off*
19. peace to him that is *f. off* and him that is near
59. 11. we look for salvation, but it is *f. off*
Ezek. 6. 12. he that is *f. off* shall die of the pestilence
8. 6. that I should go *f. off* from my sanctuary
11. 16. although I have cast them *f. off*
12. 27. he prophesieth of times that are *f. off*
22. 5. those that be *f. off* from thee shall mock
Dan. 9. 7. confusion to Israel that are near and *f. off*
Joel 2. 20. I will remove *f. off* the northern army
3. 8. they shall sell them to the Sabeans *f. off*
Mic. 4. 7. make her that was cast *f. off* a nation
Zech. 6. 15. they *f. off* shall come and build in temple
Eph. 2. 13. ye who were *f. off* made nigh by Christ

FARTHER; *see* Further.

FARE.

1 *Sam.* 17. 18. and look how thy brethren *f.*

FARE.

Jonah 1. 3. so he paid the *f.* thereof, and went into it

FARED.

Luke 16. 19. the rich man *f.* sumptuously every day

FAREWELL.

Luke 9. 61. let me first go bid them *f.* at home
Acts 15. 29. if ye keep yourselves, ye do well, *f.*
18. 21. Paul bade them *f.* saying, I must keep
23. 30. to say what they had to say against him, *f.*
2 *Cor.* 13. 11. finally, brethren, *f.* be perfect

FARM.

Mat. 22. 5. they went their ways, one to his *f.*

FARTHING, S.

Mat. 5. 26. till thou hast paid the uttermost *f.*
10. 29. are not two sparrows sold for a *f.?*
Mark 12. 42. she threw in two mites which make a *f.*
Luke 12. 6. are not five sparrows sold for two *f.?*

FASHION.

Gen. 6. 15. this is the *f.* thou shalt make the ark of
Exod. 26. 30. the *f.* of the tabernacle as was shewed
37. 19. bowls made he after the *f.* of almonds
1 *Kings* 6. 38. according to all the *f.* of the house
2 *Kings* 16. 10. Ahaz sent the *f.* of the altar
Ezek. 43. 11. shew them the form and *f.* thereof
Hab. 2. † 18. the fashioner of his *f.* trusteth
Mark 2. 12. saying, we never saw it on this *f.*
Luke 9. 29. the *f.* of his countenance was altered
Acts 7. 44. make the tabernacle according to *f.* seen
1 *Cor.* 7. 31. for the *f.* of this world passeth away
Phil. 2. 8. being found in *f.* as a man, humbled hims.
Jam. 1. 11. and the grace of the *f.* of it perisheth

FASHION.

Job 31. 15. and did not one *f.* us in the womb?

FASHIONED.

Exod. 32. 4. Aaron *f.* the calf with a graving-tool
1 *Kings* 7. † 15. for he *f.* two pillars of brass
Job 10. 8. thine hands have *f.* me, *Psal.* 119. 73.
Psal. 139. 16. which in continuance were *f.*
Isa. 22. 11. neither had respect to him that *f.* it
Ezek. 16. 7. thy breasts are *f.* thine hair is grown
Phil. 3. 21. that it may be *f.* like his glorious body

FASHIONETH.

Psal. 33. 15. he *f.* their hearts alike, considers works
Isa. 44. 12. the smith *f.* it with the hammers
45. 9. clay say to him that *f.* it, what makest thou?

FASHIONING.

1 *Pet.* 1. 14. not *f.* yourselves to the former lusts

FASHIONS.

Ezek. 42. 11. their goings were according to their *f.*

FAST.

Ezra 5. 8. this work goeth *f.* on, and prospereth

FAST.

Gen. 20. 18. the Lord had *f.* closed up the wombs
Judg. 4. 21. Sisera was *f.* asleep and weary
15. 13. but we will bind thee *f.* and deliver thee
16. 11. he said, if they bind me *f.* with new ropes
Ruth 2. 8. Boaz said, abide here *f.* by my maidens
21. Boaz said to me, keep *f.* by my young men
Job 38. 38. when the clods cleave *f.* together
Psal. 65. 6. his strength setteth *f.* the mountains
33. 9. he commanded and it stood *f.*
Prov. 4. 13. take *f.* hold of instruction, keep her
Jer. 48. 16. the affliction of Moab hasteth *f.*
50. 33. all that took them captives held them *f.*
Jonah 1. 5. he lay in the ship, and was *f.* asleep
Acts 16. 24. who made their feet *f.* in the stocks
27. 41. the forepart stuck *f.* remained unmoveable

FAST.

Fasting *has, in all ages, and among all nations, been an exercise much in use in times of mourning, sorrow, and afflictions. The sense of it is in some sort inspired by nature, which, in these circumstances, denies itself nourishment, and takes off the edge of hunger. There is no example of fasting, properly so called, to be seen before* Moses; *yet it is presumable that the patriarchs fasted, since we see that there were very great mournings among them, and those too very particularly described, such as that of* Abraham *for* Sarah, Gen. 23. 2. *and that of* Jacob *for his son* Joseph, Gen. 37. 34.

Moses *enjoins no particular* fast *in his five books, excepting that upon the solemn day of expiation, which was generally and strictly observed,* Lev. 23. 27, 29. On the tenth day of this seventh month, ye shall afflict your souls; *that is, Ye shall humble yourselves deeply before God, both inwardly by godly sorrow, judging and loathing yourselves; and outwardly, by fasting and abstinence from all carnal comforts and delights. Since the time of* Moses, *examples of fasting have been very common among the* Jews. Joshua *and the elders of* Israel *remained prostrate before the ark from morning until evening without eating, after the* Israelites *were defeated by the men of* Ai, *Josh.* 7. 6. *The eleven tribes which had taken arms against that of* Benjamin, *seeing they could not hold out against the inhabitants of* Gibeah, *fell down before the ark upon their faces, and so continued till the evening without eating,* Judg. 20. 26. *The* Israelites, *perceiving themselves to be pressed by the* Philistines, *assembled before the Lord at* Mizpeh, *and fasted in his presence till the evening,* 1 Sam. 7. 6. *And* David *fasted while the first child he had by* Bathsheba, *the wife of* Uriah, *was sick,* 2 Sam. 12. 16.

Moses *fasted forty days on mount* Horeb, *Exod.* 34. 28. Elijah *passed as many days without eating any thing,* 1 Kings 19. 8. *And our Saviour fasted in the wilderness forty days and forty nights,* Mat. 4. 2. *These fasts were miraculous, and out of the common rules of nature.*

The very heathens themselves sometimes fasted; and the king of Nineveh, *terrified by* Jonah's *preaching, made an order, that not only men, but beasts also, should continue without eating or drinking; that both men and beasts should be covered with sackcloth, and each after their manner should cry unto the Lord,* Jonah 3. 6, 7, 8. *The* Jews, *in times of public calamity, made even the children at the breast fast,* Joel 2. 16.

It does not appear by our Saviour's own practice, or any commands that he gave to his disciples, that he instituted any particular fasts, or enjoined any to be kept out of pure devotion. But when the Pharisees *in the way of reproach told him, that his disciples did not fast so often as theirs, or* John the Baptist's, *he replied,* Can ye make the children of the bride-chamber fast, while the bridegroom is with them? but the days will come, when the bridegroom shall be taken away from them, and then shall they fast in those days, *Luke* 5. 33, 34, 35. *that is,* Fasting *is a duty fitted to a day of mourning and affliction: it is not yet a time of mourning to my disciples, while I am bodily present with them; yet the time shall come when I shall be taken from them, as to my bodily presence; and when they shall meet with many troubles and calamities, then it will be seasonable for them to perform this duty of* fasting. *Accordingly, the life of the apostles and first believers was a life of self-denial, of sufferings, austerities, and fasting, as appears from the life of the apostle* Paul, 2 Cor. 6. 4, 5. | 11. 27. Fasting *is likewise confirmed by our Saviour's discourse on the mount, though not as a stated, yet as an occasional, duty of Christians, in order to, and as an indication of, their humbling their souls for their sins, or under the afflicting hand of God,* Mat. 6. 16. *Where our Saviour requires that this duty be performed in sincerity, and not in hypocrisy; for the glory of God, not for ostentation and appearance unto men.*

2 *Sam.* 12. † 16. David fasted a *f.* and lay on earth
1 *Kings* 21. 9. proclaim a *f.* and set Naboth on high
12. they proclaimed a *f.* and set Naboth on high
2 *Chron.* 20. 3. Jehoshaphat proclaimed a *f.*
Ezra 8. 21. Ezra proclaimed a *f.* at the river Ahava
Isa. 58. 3. in the day of your *f.* you find pleasure
5. is it such *f.* I have chosen? wilt thou call this *f.?*
6. is not this the *f.* that I have chosen?
Jer. 36. 9. they proclaimed a *f.* before the Lord
Joel 1. 14. sanctify a *f.* call an assembly, 2. 15.
Jonah 3. 5. the people of Nineveh proclaimed a *f.*
Zech. 8. 19. the *f.* of the fourth month, of the fifth, seventh, and tenth months, be joy and gladness
Acts 27. 9. because the *f.* was now already past

FAST, *Verb.*

2 *Sam.* 12. 21. thou didst *f.* and weep for the child
23. but now he is dead, wherefore should I *f.?*
Esth. 4. 16. *f.* ye for me, I and my maidens will *f.*
Isa. 58. 4. ye *f.* for strife, ye shall not *f.* as ye do
Jer. 14. 12. when they *f.* I will not hear their cry
Zech. 7. 5. did ye at all *f.* unto me, even to me?
Mat. 6. 16. when ye *f.* be not as hypocrites of a sad countenance, that they may appear to men to *f.*
18. thou appear not to men to *f.* but to thy Father
9. 14. why do we *f.* disciples *f.* not? *Mark* 2. 18.
15. then shall they *f.* *Mark* 2. 20. *Luke* 5. 35
Mark 2. 18. the disciples of John used to *f.*
19. can children of the bride-chamber *f.* while bridegroom with them? they cannot *f.* *Luke* 5. 35.
Luke 5. 33. why do the disciples of John *f.* often?
18. 12. I *f.* twice in the week, I give tithes of all

FASTED.

Judg. 20. 26. the people *f.* that day until even
1 *Sam.* 7. 6. they drew water, and *f.* on that day
31. 13. buried them, and *f.* seven days, 1 *Chr.* 10. 12.
2 *Sam.* 1. 12. and they mourned and *f.* for Saul
12. 16. David *f.* ‖ 22. while the child was alive I *f.*
1 *Kings* 21. 27. Ahab *f.* ‖ *Ezra* 8. 23. so we *f.*
Neh. 1. 4. Nehemiah *f.* and prayed before God
Isa. 58. 3. why have we *f.* say they, and seest not?
Zech. 7. 5. when ye *f.* in the fifth and seventh month
Mat. 4. 2. Jesus *f.* forty days and forty nights
Acts 13. 2. as they ministered to the Lord and *f.*
3. when they had *f.* they laid their hands on them

FASTEST.

Mat. 6. 17. when thou *f.* anoint thy head, wash face

FASTING.

Neh. 9. 1. were assembled with *f.* and sackclothes
Esth. 4. 3. where the decree came, there was *f.*
Psal. 35. 13. I humbled my soul with *f.* and prayer
Psal. 69. 10. when I wept and chastened my soul with *f.*
109. 24. my knees are weak thro' *f.* my flesh fails
Jer. 36. 6. read the words of the Lord on the *f.* day
Dan. 6. 18. then the king passed the night *f.*
9. 3. Daniel set himself to seek by prayer and *f.*
Joel 2. 12. turn ye with *f.* weeping, and mourning
Mat. 15. 32. and I will not send them away *f.*
17. 21. this goeth not out but by *f.* *Mark* 9. 29.
Mark 8. 3. if I send them away *f.* they will faint
Acts 10. 30. four days ago I was *f.* till this hour
14. 23. had ordained elders, and had prayed with *f.*
27. 33. that is the fourteenth day ye continued *f.*
1 *Cor.* 7. 5. ye may give yourselves to *f.* and prayer

FASTINGS.

Esth. 9. 31. the matters of the *f.* and their cry
Luke 2. 37. Anna served God with *f.* and prayers
2 *Cor.* 6. 5. approving ourselves in stripes, in *f.*
11. 27. in *f.* often, in cold and nakedness

FASTEN.

Exod. 28. 14. shalt *f.* the chains to the ouches, 25.
39. 31. to *f.* the plate on high upon the mitre
Isa. 22. 23. I will *f.* him as a nail in a sure place
Jer. 10. 4. they *f.* it with nails and with hammers

FASTENED.

Exod. 10. † 19. and *f.* the locusts into the Red sea
39. 18. the ends of chains they *f.* in the two ouches
40. 18. Moses *f.* his sockets, set up the boards
Judg. 4. 21. Jael *f.* the nail into the ground
16. 14. Delilah *f.* it with a pin, and said to him
1 *Sam.* 31. 10. they *f.* Saul's body to the wall
2 *Sam.* 20. 8. with a sword *f.* upon his loins in sheath
1 *Kings* 6. 6. that the beams should not be *f.*
1 *Chron.* 10. 10. *f.* his head in the temple of Dagon
2 *Chron.* 9. 18. six steps were *f.* to the throne
Esth. 1. 6. hangings *f.* with cords of fine linen
Job 38. 6. whereupon are the foundations *f.*
Eccl. 12. 11. as nails *f.* by the masters of assemblies
Isa. 22. 25. the nail that is *f.* in the sure place
41. 7. *f.* it with nails that it should not be moved
Ezek. 40. 43. and within were hooks *f.* round about
Luke 4. 20. and the eyes of all were *f.* on him
Acts 11. 6. upon the which when I had *f.* mine eyes
28. 3. came a viper out of heat and *f.* on his hand

FASTENING.

Hab. 2. † 11. the *f.* of the timber shall answer it
Acts 3. 4. Peter *f.* his eyes upon him, said, look on us

FAT.

God forbade the Hebrews *to eat the fat of beasts,* Lev. 3. 16, 17. All the fat is the Lord's. It shall be a perpetual statute for your generations throughout all your dwellings, that ye eat neither fat nor blood. *Some interpreters take these words in all the rigour of the letter, and suppose the use of* fat *as well as* blood *to be entirely forbidden the* Jews. Josephus *says, that* Moses *forbids only the fat of oxen, goats, sheep, and their species, which agrees with the law in* Lev. 7. 23. Ye shall eat no manner of fat of ox, or of sheep, or of goat. *The modern* Jews *observe this custom; and with respect to the* fat *of every other sort of clean creature, they think it is allowed them, even that of beasts which have died of themselves: this is conformable to that other law,* Lev. 7. 24. And the fat of the beast that dieth of itself, and the fat of that which is torn with beasts, may be used in any other use.

But other interpreters maintain, that the law which seems to forbid generally the use of fat, is to be restrained to fat *separated from the flesh, such as that which covers the kidneys and intestines; and this only in the case of its being actually offered in sacrifice; which is confirmed by this passage in* Lev. 7. 25. Whosoever eateth of the fat of the beast, of which men offer an offering made by fire unto the Lord, even the soul that eateth it, shall be cut off from his people.

The word fat *in the* Hebrew *style signifies not only that of beasts, but every thing likewise which relates to it in other things, as in* Psal. 147. 14. He filleth thee with the finest of the wheat, *in Hebrew,* with the fat of wheat. *And in* Psal. 81. 16. He should have fed them with the fat of wheat. Fat *is also used sometimes for the source or cause of compassion or mercy. As the bowels are stirred at the recital of any great calamity; or at the view of some melancholy and afflicted object, it has been thought that sensibility resided principally in the bowels, which are commonly loaded with* fat. *The* Psalmist *upbraids the wicked with* being inclosed in their fat, *with having shut up their bowels against him, with being in no sort affected with compassion at the sight of his extreme grief.* Psal. 17. 10. Mine enemies compass me about, they are inclosed in their own fat. *And in* Psal. 119. 70. Their heart is as fat as grease. *They are stupid, and insensible, and past feeling; they are not affected either with the terrors or comforts of God.*

Fat *denotes abundance of spiritual blessings,* Jer. 31. 14. *I will satiate the souls* of the priests with fatness. *Psal.* 63. 5. My soul shall be satisfied as with marrow and fatness. *The fat of the earth implies the fruitfulness of it, Gen.* 27. 28. God give thee of the dew of heaven, and the fatness of the earth, and plenty of corn and wine.

Gen. 4. 4. Abel also brought of the *f.* of his flock
Exod. 23. 18. nor shall the *f.* of my sacrifice remain
29. 13. thou shalt take the *f.* that covereth the inwards, and the *f.* upon the kidneys, 22. *Lev.* 3. 3, 4, 9, 10, 14, 15. | 4. 8. | 7. 3, 4.
Lev. 1. 8. priests shall lay head and *f.* in order, 12.
3. 16. offering for a sweet savour, the *f.* is Lord's
4. 8. he shall take of the *f.* of the bullock, 31, 35.
26. burn his *f.* 6. 12. | 7. 3, 31. | 17. 6. *Num.* 18. 17.
7. 24. *f.* of the beast dieth of itself, or is torn to be used
30. the *f.* with the breast, it shall he bring
33. he that offereth *f.* shall have the right shoulder
8. 20. Moses burnt the head and the *f.* of the ram

Lev. 8. 26. he took one wafer and put them on the *f.*
9. 10. but the *f.* he burnt upon the altar, 20.
24. and fire from the Lord consumed the *f.*
16. 25. the *f.* of sin-offering shall burn on altar
Num. 18. † 12. the *f.* of the oil have I given thee
† 29. an heave offering to the Lord of all the *f.*
Deut. 32. 14. *f.* of lambs with *f.* of kidneys of wheat
Judg. 3. 22. and the *f.* closed upon the blade
† 29. they slew of Moab about 10,000 men all *f.*
1 *Sam.* 2. 15. before they burnt *f.* priest's serv. came
16. let them not fail to burn the *f.* presently
15. 22. to hearken is better than the *f.* of rams
2 *Sam.* 1. 22. from *f.* of the mighty, bow turned not
1 *Kings* 8. 64. altar was too little to receive the *f.*
2 *Chr.* 7. 7. offered the *f.* of peace-offerings, 29. 35.
35. 14. priests busied in offering the *f.* until night
Job 15. 27. he maketh collops of *f.* on his flanks
Psal. 17. 10. they are inclosed in their own *f.*
20. † 3. the Lord make *f.* thy burnt-sacrifice
23. † 5. thou makest *f.* my head with oil
73. † 4. but their strength is *f.* no bands in death
81. † 16. he should have fed them also with the *f.* of wheat, with honey out of rock, 147. † 14.
Isa. 1. 11. I am full of the *f.* of fed beasts
34. 6. made *f.* with the *f.* of the kidneys of rams
43. 24. nor hast filled me with *f.* of thy sacrifices
Ezek. 44. 7. when ye offer the *f.* and the blood
15. shall stand to offer to me the *f.* and the blood

Eat FAT.

Gen. 45. 18. and ye shall *eat* the *f.* of the land
Lev. 3. 17. a statute that ye *eat* no *f.* nor blood, 7. 23.
7. 25. whoso *eateth f.* of the beast shall be cut off
Deut. 32. 38. which did *eat* the *f.* of their sacrifices
Neh. 8. 10. go your way, *eat* the *f.* and drink sweet
Ezek. 34. 3. ye *eat f.* and clothe you with the wool
39. 19. ye shall *eat f.* till ye be full and drink blood
Zech. 11. 16. but he shall *eat* the flesh of the *f.*

FAT.

Gen. 41. 2. there came up seven kine *f.* fleshed
4. and they did eat up the seven *f.* kine, 20.
† 5. seven ears of corn came up *f.* and good
49. 20. out of Asher his bread shall be *f.*
Num. 13. 20. what the land is, whether *f.* or lean
Deut. 31. 20. waxen *f.* then they turn to other gods
32. 15. Jeshurun waxed *f.* and kicked, thou waxen *f.*
Judg. 3. 17. and Eglon was a very *f.* man
1 *Sam.* 2. 29. to make you *f.* with the offerings
28. 24. the woman had a *f.* calf in the house
1 *Kings* 1. 9. Adonijah slew sheep, *f.* cattle, 19. 25.
4. 23. his provision for one day was ten *f.* oxen
1 *Chron.* 4. 40. and they found *f.* pasture and good
Neh. 9. 25. they took a *f.* land and became *f.*
35. have not served thee in the large and *f.* land
Psal. 22. 29. that be *f.* on earth shall eat and worship
37. 20. the enemies of the Lord as the *f.* of lambs
92. 14. they shall be *f.* and flourishing
119. 70. their heart is *f.* as grease, I delight in law
Prov. 11. 25. the liberal soul shall be made *f.*
13. 4. the soul of the diligent shall be made *f.*
15. 30. a good report maketh the bones *f.*
28. 25. he that trusteth the Lord shall be made *f.*
Isa. 5. 17. waste places of *f.* ones shall strangers eat
6. 10. make the heart of this people *f.* ears heavy
10. 16. Lord shall send among his *f.* ones leanness
25. 6. make a feast of *f.* things full of marrow
28. 1. which are on the head of the *f.* valleys
4. the beauty which is on the head of the *f.* valley
30. 23. and bread shall be *f.* and plenteous
34. 6. the sword of the Lord is made *f.* with fatness
7. and their dust shall be made *f.* with fatness
58. 11. and the Lord shall make *f.* thy bones
Jer. 5. 28. they are waxen *f.* they shine
50. 11. ye are grown *f.* as the heifer at grass
Ezek. 34. 14. in a *f.* pasture shall they feed, in Israel
16. but I will destroy the *f.* and the strong
20. I will judge between the *f.* cattle and the lean
45. 15. one lamb out of the *f.* pastures of Israel
Amos 5. 22. nor will I regard the offering of *f.* beasts
Hab. 1. 16. because by them their portion is *f.*

FATHER.

This word, besides the common acceptation of it for an immediate father, is likewise taken in the scripture style for grand-father, great-grand-father, or the very author and first father of a family, how remote soever he may be from those who speak. For example, the Jews *in our Saviour's time, and their descendants of this present generation, call themselves sons of* Abraham, Isaac, *and* Jacob. *And* Nebuchadnezzar *is termed* Belshazzar's *father, though* Belshazzar *was his grand-son.*

By father *is likewise understood the inventor, the master of those who are of a certain profession,* Gen. 4. 20, 21, 22. *Jabal* was the father of such as dwell in tents, and such as have cattle. *Jubal* was the father of all such as handle the harp and organ. *The famous founder of* Tyre, Huram, *is called the* father *of the king of* Tyre, 2 *Chron.* 2. 13. *and even of* Solomon, 2 *Chron.* 4. 16. *because he was their principal workman, and the chief director of their undertakings. The principal, the eldest of the prophets, were considered as the masters and fathers of the rest, who were their disciples; for this reason the young prophets are called* the sons of the prophets, *and these style the eldest,* fathers. My father, my father, *said* Elisha *to* Elijah, the chariot of *Israel* and the horsemen thereof, 2 *Kings* 2. 12.

Father *is a term of respect which inferiors often give to their superiors, and servants to their masters;* My father, *said* Naaman's *servants to their master,* 2 Kings 5. 13. *The king of* Israel, *in like manner, called the prophet* Elisha *his* father, 2 *Kings* 6. 21. *My father,* shall I smite them? *And the same prophet being upon his death-bed,* Joash *came to see him, and said,* O my father, my father, the chariot of *Israel,* and the horsemen thereof, 2 *Kings* 13. 14.

A man is said to be a father, *to the poor and orphans when he takes care to supply their necessities, is affected with their miseries, and provides for their wants;* I was a father to the poor, *Job* 29. 16. *God declares himself to be a* Father *of the fatherless, and a Judge of the widow.* Psal. 68. 5.

God is frequently called heavenly Father, *and simply* Father. *He is truly and eminently the* Father, *Creator, Preserver, and Protector, of all creatures, and principally of those who call upon him, who know and serve him.* Is he not thy Father that bought thee? *Deut.* 32. 6. *Hath he not made thee, and established thee? And through* Christ, *who has merited adoption and filiation for his people, every believer has a right to call God* Father, *Rom.* 8. 15, 16.

Job *entitles God* the Father of rain, *Job* 38. 28. *He produces it, he makes it to fall. And in* chap. 17. 14. I have said to corruption, Thou art my father. *I acknowledge that I am sprung out of corruption, and shall return to the putrefaction of the grave; or, in the condition which I am reduced to, I look upon worms and putrefaction as my friends and relations.*

Joseph *says, that God had made him a* father to Pharaoh, *Gen.* 45. 8. *that he had given him very great authority in this prince's kingdom, and that* Pharaoh *looked upon him as his* father, *and had so much confidence in him, and consideration for his person, that he gave him the government of his house and of all his dominions.*

The devil is called the father *of the wicked;* Ye are of your father the *devil, says our* Saviour, *John* 8. 44. *Ye would imitate the desires of your father; he was a murderer from the beginning, he abode not in the truth.* He is a liar, and the *father* of it; *he is a falsifier, a deceiver, a seducer. He deceived* Eve *and* Adam; *he introduced sin and falsehood into the world: he inspires his followers with his spirit and sentiments; he keeps the school of fraud and deceit; his only business is to tempt and ensnare mankind.*

To be gathered unto their fathers; To sleep with their fathers; To go to their fathers; *are common expressions, to signify* death. *In these passages, the fathers signify those who lived before us, and whom we are going to meet again in another world.*

God is called the Father of spirits, *Heb.* 12. 9. *Our fathers are the fathers of our bodies only, but God is the Father of our spirits; he not only creates them, but he justifies them likewise, glorifies, and makes them happy. Our Saviour, in* Mat. 23. 9. *forbids us to give any man the name of* father, *because we have one only who is in heaven. Not that we should abandon or despise our earthly* fathers; *God requires us to honour them, and give them all necessary assistance; but when the interests of God are at stake, his glory, or our own salvation, if our fathers and mothers are an obstacle to them, we should say to them,* We know you not: *for what our parents have done for us, in comparison of what we owe to God, is so inconsiderable, that we may say, our fathers are nothing to us, and that God alone deserves the title of* our Father.

Gen. 4. 20. Jabal was *f.* of such as dwell in tents
21. Jubal was the *f.* of all such as handle harp
9. 18. went out of ark, and Ham is the *f.* of Canaan
17. 4. be the *f.* of many nations, 5. *Rom.* 4. 17, 18.
44. 19. have ye a *f.*? ‖ 20. and we said, we have a *f.*
45. 8. God made me a *f.* to Pharaoh, lord of house
Lev. 24. 10. whose *f.* was an Egyptian, he went out
Num. 11. 12. as a nursing *f.* beareth sucking child
30. 16. are statutes between *f.* and his daughter
Deut. 22. 15. *f.* shall bring forth tokens of virginity
29. the man shall give the damsel's *f.* fifty shekels
Judg. 9. 1. the family of the house of his mother's *f.*
17. 10. dwell with me, and be to me a *f.* and a priest
18. 19. go with us, and be to us a *f.* and a priest
19. 3. the *f.* of the damsel saw him, he rejoiced
4. damsel's *f.* retained him, he abode three days
1 *Sam.* 9. 3. and Kish was the *f.* of Saul, 14. 51.
1 *Chron.* 2. 51. Salma the *f.* of Bethlehem
55. of Hemath, the *f.* of the house of Rechab
4. 14. Joab the *f.* of the valley of Charashim
8. 29. at Gibeon dwelt the *f.* of Gibeon, 9. 35.
Esth. 2. 7. Esther had neither *f.* nor mother
Job 29. 16. I was a *f.* to the poor, and searched out
31. 18. he was brought up with me, as with a *f.*
38. 28. hath the rain a *f.*? or who begat the dew?
Ps. 68. 5. *f.* of fatherless, and judge of widows, is God
103. 13. as a *f.* pitieth his children, so Lord pities
Prov. 3. 12. the Lord correcteth, even as a *f.* the son
4. 1. hear, ye children, the instruction of a *f.*
10. 1. a wise son maketh a glad *f.* 15. 20.
17. 21. and the *f.* of a fool hath no joy
23. 24. the *f.* of the righteous shall rejoice
Isa. 9. 6. his name shall be called, the everlasting *F.*
22. 21. Eliakim shall be a *f.* to inhabitants of Jerus.
38. 19. the *f.* to child. shall make known thy truth
Jer. 31. 9. I will lead them, for I am a *f.* to Israel
Ezek. 18. 4. as the soul of the *f.* so of the son, is mine
19. doth not the son bear the iniquity of the *f.*?
20. the son shall not bear the iniquity of the *f.*
22. 7. in thee they set light by *f.* and mother
44. 25. for *f.* or mother they may defile themselves
Mic. 7. 6. for the son dishonoureth the *f.*
Mal. 1. 6. if I then be a *f.* where is mine honour?
2. 10. have we not all one *f.*? one God created us
Mat. 10. 21. *f.* deliver up the child, *Mark* 13. 12.
37. he that loveth *f.* or mother more than me
11. 25. Jesus said, I thank thee, O *F.* Lord of heav.
26. so *F.* it seemed good, *Luke* 10. 21. *John* 11. 41.
27. and no man knoweth the Son but the *F.*
15. 4. he that curseth *f.* let him die, *Mark* 7. 10.
19. 5. leave *f.* and mother, and cleave to his wife
29. every one that hath forsaken *f.* mother, or wife, for my name's sake, *Mark* 10. 29.
28. 19. baptizing them in the name of the *F.*
Mark 5. 40. he taketh *f.* of the damsel, *Luke* 8. 51.
9. 24. the *f.* of the child cried, Lord, I believe
Mark 13. 32. of that day knoweth no man, but the *F.*
14. 36. Abba, *F.* all things are possible to thee
15. 21. Simon, *f.* of Alexander, to bear his cross
Luke 10. 22. no man knows who the *F.* is but the Son
11. 11. if a son shall ask bread of any that is a *f.*
12. 53. the *f.* shall be divided against the son, and the son against the *f.* mother against daughter
15. 21. son said, *f.* I have sinned against heaven
22. the *f.* said, bring forth the best robe
16. 27. I pray thee, *f.* send to my father's house
22. 42. *F.* if thou be willing, remove this cup from
23. 34. *F.* forgive them, for they know not
46. *F.* into thy hands I commend my spirit
John 1. 14. the glory as of the only-begotten of the *F.*
18. the Son which is in the bosom of the *F.*
3. 35. the *F.* loveth the Son, and hath given, 5. 20.
4. 21. nor yet at Jerusalem worship the *F.*
23. shall worship the *F.* in spirit and in truth
53. the *f.* knew that it was at the same hour
5. 19. do nothing but what he seeth the *F.* do
21. for as the *F.* raiseth up the dead, so the Son
22. *F.* judgeth no man, but hath committed all
23. honour the Son, even as they honour the *F.* he that honours not the Son, honours not the *F.*
26. for as the *F.* hath life in himself, so hath given
30. I seek not mine own, but the will of the *F.*
36. for the works which the *F.* hath given me bear witness that the *F.* hath sent me
37. the *F.* which hath sent me, hath borne witness of me, 8. 16. | 12. 49. | 14. 24. 1 *John* 4. 14.
45. think not that I will accuse you to the *F.*
6. 27. for him hath God the *F.* sealed
37. all that the *F.* giveth me shall come to me
39. and this is the *F.'s* will, that I lose nothing
42. is not this Jesus, whose *f.* and mother we know?
44. no man can come, except the *F.* draw him
45. that hath learned of the *F.* cometh to me
46. not that any hath seen the *F.* he hath seen *F.*
57. as the *F.* hath sent me, and I live by the *F.*
8. 16. I am not alone, but I and the *F.* that sent me
18. the *F.* that sent me beareth witness of me
27. they understood not he spake to them of *F.*
29. *F.* hath not left me alone, I do those things
41. then said they, we have one *F.* even God
44. the devil is a liar, and the *f.* of it
10. 15. as the *F.* knoweth me, even so know I the *F.*
36. say ye of him whom the *F.* hath sanctified
38. believe that the *F.* is in me, and I in him
12. 27. what shall I say? *F.* save me from this hour
28. *F.* glorify thy name; then came there a voice
50. even as the *F.* said unto me, so I speak
13. 1. Jesus knew that he should depart unto the *F.*
3. knowing that the *F.* had given all things
14. 6. Jesus saith to him, I am the way, truth, and life, no man cometh to the *F.* but by me
8. Lord, shew us the *F.* and it sufficeth us
9. Philip, he that hath seen me, hath seen the *F.*
11. that I am in the *F.* and the *F.* in me, 17. 21.
13. that the *F.* may be glorified in the Son
16. and I will pray the *F.* for you, 16. 26.
26. but the Comforter whom the *F.* will send
31. I love the *F.* as the *F.* gave me commandment
15. 9. as the *F.* hath loved me, so have I loved you
16. that whatsoever ye shall ask of the *F.* in my name, he may give it you, 16. 23.
26. the Comforter whom I will send you from the *F.* the Spirit who proceedeth from the *F.*
16. 3. because they have not known the *F.* nor me
15. all things that the *F.* hath, are mine
16. ye shall see me, because I go to the *F.* 17.
25. but I shall shew you plainly of the *F.*
27. the *F.* loveth you, because ye have loved me
28. I came forth from the *F.* and go to the *F.*
32. I am not alone, because the *F.* is with me
17. 1. *F.* the hour is come, glorify thy Son
5. O *F.* glorify thou me with thine own self
11. Holy *F.* keep those whom thou hast given me
24. *F.* I will that they given me be where I am
25. O righteous *F.* the world hath not known thee
Acts 1. 4. but wait for the promise of the *F.*
7. the seasons, the *F.* hath put in his own power
2. 33. received of the *F.* the promise of the H. Ghost
Rom. 4. 11. he might be *f.* of all them that believe
12. and the *f.* of circumcision to them who are not
16. the faith of Abraham, who is the *f.* of us all
6. 4. as Christ was raised from the dead by the *F.*
8. 15. Spirit of adoption, whereby we cry, Abba, *F.*
11. 28. as to election, are beloved for *F's* sake
15. 6. may glorify God the *F.* of our Lord Jesus Christ, 2 *Cor.* 1. 3. | 11. 31. *Eph.* 1. 3. 1 *Pet.* 1. 3.
1 *Cor.* 8. 6. but to us there is but one God, the *F.*
15. 24. have delivered up the kingdom to God the *F.*
2 *Cor.* 1. 3. *F.* of mercies, the God of all comfort
6. 18. I will be a *F.* unto you, ye shall be my sons
Gal. 1. 1. Paul an apostle by Jes. C. and G. the *F.*
3. and peace from G. the *F.* 2 *Tim.* 1. 2. *Tit.* 1. 4.
4. according to the will of God and our *F.*
4. 2. until the time appointed of the *F.*
6. sent Spirit into your hearts, crying, Abba *F.*
Eph. 1. 17. the God of our L. Jesus the *F.* of glory
2. 18. by him have access by one Spirit to the *F.*
3. 14. for this cause I bow my knees unto the *F.*
4. 6. one God and *F.* of all, who is above all
5. 20. giving thanks to the *F.* *Col.* 1. 3, 12. | 3. 17.
6. 23. and love with faith from God the *F.* and Jes.
Phil. 2. 11. that Jesus is Lord to the glory of the *F.*
22. as a son with the *f.* he hath served with me
Col. 1. 19. it pleased *F.* that in him all fulness dwell
2. 2. the acknowledgment of the mystery of the *F.*
1 *Thess.* 1. 1. unto the church which is in God the *F.*
2. 11. we charged you, as a *f.* doth his children
1 *Tim.* 5. 1. rebuke not an elder, entreat him as a *f.*
Heb. 1. 5. will be to him a *F.* he shall be to me a Son
7. 3. Melchisedec without *f.* without mother
12. 7. what son is he whom the *F.* chasteneth not?
9. be in subjection to the *F.* of spirits, and live
Jam. 1. 17. every good gift cometh from *F.* of lights
27. pure and undefiled religion before God and *F.*
3. 9. therewith bless we God, even the *F.*
1 *Pet.* 1. 2. to the foreknowledge of God the *F.*
17. if ye call on the *F.* who judgeth man's work
2 *Pet.* 1. 17. he received from God the *F.* honour

1 John 1. 2. we shew eternal life, which was with *F.*
3. our fellowship is with the *F.* and his Son
2. 1. we have an Advocate with the *F.* Jesus Christ
13. I write to you, because ye have known the *F.*
15. if any love world, the love of *F.* is not in him
16. pride of life is not of the *F.* but of the world
22. he is antichrist that denieth the *F.* and Son
23. whoso denieth the Son, hath not the *F.* he that acknowledgeth the Son hath the *F.* also
24. ye shall continue in the Son and in the *F.*
3. 1. what manner of love *F.* hath bestowed on us
5. 7. three bear record, the *F.* Word, and Spirit
2 John 3. mercy and peace from God the *F.* and from the Lord Jesus Christ, the Son of the *F.*
4. as we received a commandment from the *F.*
9. he that abideth in Christ hath the *F.* and Son
Jude 1. to them that are sanctified by God the *F.*
See ABRAHAM.

Her FATHER.

Gen. 19. 33. the first-born went in and lay with *her f.*
29. 9. Rachel came with *h. f.'s* sheep, she kept them
12. he was *her f.'s* brother, she ran and told *her f.*
31. 19. Rachel had stolen images that were *her f.'s*
38. 11. Tamar went and dwelt in *her f.'s* house
Exod. 22. 17. if *her f.* utterly refuse to give her
Lev. 21. 9. she profaneth *her f.* she shall be burnt
22. 13. if she is returned to *her f.'s* house, as in her youth, she shall eat of *her f.'s* meat
Num. 12. 14. if *her f.* had but spit in her face
30. 3. if a woman vow a vow in *her f.'s* house
4. and *her f.* hear her, and shall hold his peace
5. if *her f.* disallow her in the day he heareth
16. being yet in her youth, in *her f.'s* house
36. 8. shall be wife to one of the tribe of *her f.*
Deut. 21. 13. and bewail *her f.* and mother a month
22. 21. bring to door of *her f.'s* house, because she wrought folly, to play the whore in *her f.'s* house
Josh. 6. 23. the spies brought out Rahab and *her f.*
25. he saved *her f.'s* household and all she had
15. 18. to ask of *her f.* a field, *Judg.* 1. 14.
Judg. 11. 39. in two months she returned to *her f.*
15. 1. but *her f.* would not suffer him to go in
6. the Philistines burnt her and *her f.* with fire
19. 3. she brought him into *her f.'s* house
Esth. 2. 7. when *her f.* and mother were dead

His FATHER.

Gen. 2. 24. therefore shall a man leave *his f.* and mother, and cleave to wife, *Mark* 10. 7. *Eph.* 5. 31.
9. 22. Ham saw the nakedness of *his f.* and told
11. 28. and Haran died before *his f.* Terah
27. 41. the blessing wherewith *his f.* blessed him
28. 7. Jacob obeyed *his f.* and mother, was gone
31. 53. Jacob sware by the fear of *his f.* Isaac
37. 1. in the land wherein *his f.* was a stranger
2. Joseph brought to *his f.* their evil report
10. he told the dream to *his f. his f.* rebuked him
11. brethren envied, but *his f.* observed the saying
22. he might rid him, to deliver him to *his f.*
44. 22. and we said, the lad cannot leave *his f.*
46. 1. he offered sacrifices to the God of *his f.*
29. and Joseph went up to meet Israel *his f.*
47. 12. Joseph nourished *his f.* and brethren
50. 10. he made a mourning for *his f.* seven days
Exod. 6. 20. and Amram took *his f.'s* sister to wife
21. 15. he that smiteth *his f.* shall be put to death
17. he that curseth *his f.* shall die, *Lev.* 20. 9.
Lev. 19. 3. shall fear every man his mother and *his f.*
20. 11. man that lieth with *his f.'s* wife, both die
17. if a man take *his f.'s* daughter, they shall die
21. 2. a son of Aaron may be defiled for *his f.*
11. the high-priest not defile himself for *his f.*
Num. 6. 7. a Nazarite not make unclean for *his f.*
27. 10. shall give inheritance to *his f.'s* brethren
11. if *his f.* have no brethren, to his kinsman
Deut. 21. 18. which will not obey *his f.* and mother
19. then shall *his f.* bring him to the elders
22. 30. a man shall not take *his f.'s* wife
27. 16. cursed be he that setteth light by *his f.*
22. cursed be he that lieth with daughter of *his f.*
33. 9. who said to *his f.* I have not seen him
Judg. 6. 27. Gideon feared *his f.'s* household
8. 32. Gideon was buried in the sepulchre of *his f.*
9. 56. God rendered the wickedness he did to *his f.*
14. 4. *his f.* knew not that it was of the Lord
1 Sam. 14. 1. but Jonathan told not *his f.*
27. heard not when *his f.* charged the people
19. 4. Jonathan spake good of David to *his f.*
20. 33. it was determined of *his f.* to slay David
34. because *his f.* had done him shame
2 Sam. 2. 32. Asahel buried in sepulchre of *his f.*
7. 14. I will be *his f.* and he shall be my son
10. 2. as *his f.* shewed kindness to me, *1 Chr.* 19. 2.
16. 22. Absalom went in to *his f.'s* concubines
17. 23. Ahithophel buried in the sepulchre of *his f.*
21. 14. Saul buried in the sepulchre of Kish *his f.*
1 Kings 7. 14. *his f.* was a man of Tyre, *2 Chr.* 2. 14.
51. which *his f.* had dedicated, 15. 15. *2 Chr.* 15. 18.
11. 4. not perfect, as the heart of David *his f.*
6. Solomon went not fully after the Lord, as did David *his f.* 15. 11. *2 Kings* 18. 3. *2 Chr.* 28. 1. | 29. 2.
33. not as did David *his f.* *2 Kings* 14. 3. | 16. 2.
15. 3. and he walked in all the sins of *his f.*
26. Nadab did evil and walked in the way of *his f.* 22. 43, 52. *2 Kings* 21. 21.
2 Kings 3. 2. Jehoram did evil, but not like *his f.*
9. 25. I and thou rode together after Ahab *his f.*
13. 25. the cities taken out of the hand of *his f.*
14. 5. Amaziah, the son of Joash, slew the servants who had slain the king *his f.* *2 Chron.* 25. 3.
21. him king instead of *his f.* 23. 30, 34.
1 Chr. 5. 1. Reub. defiled *his f.'s* bed, birth right given
17. 13. I will be *his f.* he shall be my son, 28. 6.
26. 10. not first-born, yet *his f.* made him the chief
2 Chron. 3. 1. the Lord appeared to David *his f.*
8. 14. according to the order of David *his f.*
17. 3. he walked in the first ways of *his f.* David
4. Jehoshaphat sought the Lord God of *his f.*
20. 32. he walked in the way of Asa *his f.*
22. 4. his counsellors after the death of *his f.*
34. 2. he walked in the ways of David *his f.* 3.
Psal. 72. † 17 as a son to continue *his f.'s* name

Prov. 13. 1. a wise son heareth the instruction of *his f.*
15. 5. a fool despiseth *his f.'s* instruction
17. 25. a foolish son is a grief to *his f.*
19. 13. a foolish son is the calamity of *his f.*
26. he that wasteth *his f.* is a son causeth shame
20. 20. whoso curseth *his f.* his lamp shall be put out
28. 7. a companion of riotous men shameth *his f.*
24. whoso robbeth *his f.* or mother, and saith
29. 3. whoso loveth wisdom, rejoiceth *his f.*
30. 17. the ravens pick out eye that mocketh *his f.*
Isa. 45. 10. woe to him that saith to *his f.* what begets
Ezek. 18. 14. beget a son that seeth all *his f.'s* sins
17. he shall not die for the iniquity of *his f.*
18. as for *his f.* because he cruelly oppressed
Dan. 5. 2. to bring the golden vessels *his f.* had taken
Amos 2. 7. a man and *his f.* go in to the same maid
Zech. 13. 3. *his f.* and mother shall thrust him thro'
Mal. 1. 6. a son honours *his f.* a servant his master
Mat. 10. 35. to set a man at variance against *his f.*
15. 5. whoso shall say to *his f.* it is a gift, *Mark* 7. 11.
6. and honour not *his f.* or mother, he shall be free
16. 27. the Son of man shall come in the glory of *his F.* with his angels, *Mark* 8. 38. *Luke* 9. 26.
21. 31. whether of them did the will of *his f.?*
Mark 9. 21. he asked *his f.* how long ago it is since
Luke 1. 32. Lord shall give him the throne of *his f.*
59. they called him after the name of *his f.*
62. they made signs unto *his f.* how to call him
67. *his f.* Zacharias was filled with the H. Ghost
9. 42. Jesus delivered him again to *his f.*
14. 26. if any man come to me, and hate not *his f.*
15. 12. and the younger of them said to *his f.*
20. arose and came to *his f. his f.* saw him, and ran
28. therefore came *his f.* and entreated him
John 5. 18. because he said, that God was *his f.*
Acts 16. 1. son of a Jewess, but *his f.* was a Greek
1 Cor. 5. 1. that one should have *his f.'s* wife
Heb. 7. 10. for he was yet in the loins of *his f.*
Rev. 1. 6. made us kings and priests to G. and *his F.*
14. 1. *his F.'s* name written in their foreheads
See HOUSE.

FATHER-*in-law.*

Gen. 38. 13. behold, thy *f. in law* goeth to Timnath
25. when brought forth, she went to her *f.-in-law*
Exod. 3. 1. the flock of Jethro his *f.-in-law*, 4. 18.
18. 1. Moses' *f.-in law*, 8, 14, 17. *Judg.* 1. 16. | 4. 11.
27. Moses let his *f.-in-law* depart, and he went
Num. 10. 29. Raguel the Midianite, Moses' *f.-in law*
Judg. 19. 4. his *f.-in-law* retained him, and he abode
7. when he rose to depart, his *f.-in-law* urged him
1 Sam. 4. 19. when she heard *f.-in law* was dead, 21.
John 18. 13. Annas was *f.-in-law* to Caiaphas

My FATHER.

Gen. 19. 34. behold, I lay yesternight with *my f.*
20. 12. she is daughter of *my f.* not of my mother
27. 12. *my f.* peradventure will feel me, I shall
34. Esau cried, bless me, even me also, O *my f.*
31. 5. the God of *my f.* 42. || 32. 9. *Exod.* 18. 4.
44. 24. when we came to thy servant *my f.* 27, 30.
32. for I became surety for the lad to *my f.*
45. 3. doth *my f.* yet live? || 9. haste to go up to *my f.*
13. tell *my f.* || 47. 1. *my f.* and brethren are come
48. 18. not so, *my f.* for this is the first-born
Deut. 26. 5. a Syrian ready to perish was *my f.*
Josh. 2. 13. ye will save alive *my f.* and mother
Judg. 9. 17. *my f.* fought for you, and delivered you
11. 36. *my f.* if thou hast opened thy mouth
14. 16. I have not told it *my f.* nor my mother
1 Sam. 9. 5. lest *my f.* leave caring for the asses
14. 29. Jonathan said, *my f.* troubled the land
18. 18. who am I, and what is *my f.'s* family?
19. 2. saying, Saul *my f.* seeketh to kill thee
3. and I will commune with *my f.* of thee
20. 2. *my f.* will do nothing, but he will shew it me
13. Lord be with thee, as he hath been with *my f.*
22. 3. let *my f.* and my mother be with you
23. 17. the hand of Saul *my f.* shall not find thee
2 Sam. 16. 3. restore me the kingdom of *my f.*
19. 37. that I may be buried by the grave of *my f.*
1 Kings 2. 26. thou barest the ark of the Lord before David *my f.* in all wherein *my f.* was afflicted
32. *my f.* David not knowing thereof
44. the wickedness that thou didst to David *my f.*
3. 6. thou hast shewed to David *my f.* great mercy
7. hast made thy servant king instead of *my f.*
5. 3. David *my f.* could not build an house
5. as the Lord spake to David *my f.* saying
8. 17. it was in the heart of David *my f.* to build
24. who hast kept with thy servant David *my f.*
26. let my word be verified to *my f.* *2 Chr.* 6. 16.
12. 10. thus thou shalt say, my little finger shall be thicker than *my f.'s* loins, *2 Chron.* 10. 10.
11. *my f.* lade you with a heavy yoke, *2 Chr.* 10. 11.
14. *my f.* chastised you with whips, *2 Chr.* 10. 14.
15. 19. league between *my f.* and thy *f.* *2 Chr.* 16. 3.
19. 20. let me, I pray thee, kiss *my f.* and mother
20. 34. the cities *my f.* took I will restore
2 Kings 2. 12. Elisha saw it, and he cried, *my f. my f.*
6. 21. *my f.* shall I smite them? shall I smite them?
13. 14. Elisha said, *my f. my f.* the chariot of Israel
1 Chr. 28. 4. Lord chose me before all the house of *my f.* and among the sons of *my f.* he liked me
2 Chr. 2. 3. as thou didst deal with *my f.* so deal
Neh. 2. 3. the place of *my f.'s* sepulchres lieth waste
5. send me to the city of *my f.'s* sepulchres
Job 17. 14. I said to corruption, thou art *my f.*
34. † 36. *my f.* let Job be tried to the end
Psal. 27. 10. when *my f.* and my mother forsake me
89. 26. he shall cry unto me, thou art *my F.* my G.
Prov. 4. 3. for I was *my f.'s* son, tender and beloved
Isa. 8. 4. the child have knowledge to cry, *my f.*
Jer. 2. 27. saying to a stock, thou art *my f.*
3. 4. wilt thou not cry unto me, *my F.?* 19.
20. 15. cursed be man who brought tidings to *my f.*
Dan. 5. 13. whom *my f.* brought out of Jewry
Mat. 7. 21. he that doeth the will of *my F.* 12. 50.
8. 21. suffer me to go and bury *my f.* *Luke* 9. 59.
10. 32. him will I confess before *my F.* in heaven
33. him will I also deny before *my F.* in heaven
11. 27. are delivered to me of *my F.* *Luke* 10. 22.
15. 13. plant *my* heavenly *F.* hath not planted
16. 17. but *my F.* who is in heaven revealed it

Mat. 18. 10. their angels behold the face of *my F.*
19. it shall be done of *my F.* who is in heaven
35. so shall *my* heavenly *F.* also do unto you
20. 23. for whom it is prepared of *my F.*
24. 36. that day knoweth no man but *my F.* only
25. 34. the King shall say, come ye blessed of *my F.*
26. 29. I drink it new with you in *my F.'s* kingdom
39 O *my F.* if it be possible, let this cup pass me
42. *my F.* if this cup may not pass, thy will be done
53. thinkest thou that I cannot pray to *my F.?*
Luke 2. 49. that I must be about *my F.'s* business
15. 17. how many hired serv. of *my f.* have bread?
18. I will arise, and go to *my f.* and will say, *f.*
16. 27. I pray thee, send him to *my f.'s* house
22. 29. as *my F.* hath appointed unto me
24. 49. I send the promise of *my F.* upon you
John 5. 17. *my F.* worketh hitherto, and I work
43. I am come in *my F.'s* name, ye receive me not
6. 32. but *my F.* giveth you the true bread
65. none come to me, except it be given of *my F.*
8. 19. Jesus said, ye neither know me, nor *my F.*
28. as *my F.* hath taught me, I speak these things
38. I speak that which I have seen with *my F.*
49. but I honour *my F.* and ye dishonour me
54. it is *my F.* that honoureth me, of whom ye say
10. 17. therefore doth *my F.* love me, because
18. this commandment have I received of *my F.*
25. works I do in *my F.'s* name bear witness of me
29. *my F.* who gave them me, is greater than all, none is able to pluck them out of *my F.'s* hand
30. I and *my F.* are one
32. many good works have I shewed from *my F.*
37. if I do not the works of *my F.* believe me not
12. 26. if any serve me, him will *my F.* honour
14. 7. if known me, should have known *my F.* also
12. greater works, because I go to *my F.* 16. 10.
20. at that day ye shall know that I am in *my F.*
21. he that loveth me, shall be loved of *my F.* 23.
28. I go to the Father, *my F.* is greater than I
15. 1. I am the vine, *my F.* is the husbandman
8. herein is *my F.* glorified, that ye bear fruit
10. even as I have kept *my F.'s* commandments
15. all that I heard of *my F.* I have made known
23. he that hateth me, hateth *my F.* also, 24.
18. 11. the cup *my F.* hath given, shall I not drink it?
20. 17. touch not, for I am not yet ascended to *my F.* say to them, I ascend to *my F.* and your Father
21. as *my F.* hath sent me, even so send I you
Rev. 2. 27. even as I received of *my F.*
3. 5. I will confess his name before *my F.* and angels

Our FATHER.

Gen. 19. 31. *our f.* is old || 32. make *our f.* drink wine
31. 1. Jacob hath taken away all that is *our f.* 16.
42. 13. the youngest is this day with *our. f.* 32.
43. 28. thy servant *our f.* is in good health
44. 31. bring *our f.* with sorrow to the grave
Num. 27. 3. *our f.* died in the wilderness, had no sons
4. why should the name of *our f.* be done away?
1 Chr. 29. 10. blessed be thou, L. God of Isr. *our F.*
Isa. 63. 16. doubtless, thou art *our F.* Abraham ignorant
64. 8. O Lord, thou art *our F.* we are the clay
Jer. 35. 6. *our f.* commanded us to drink no wine
8. we have obeyed the voice of *our f.* 10.
Mat. 6. 9. *our F.* which art in heaven, *Luke* 11. 2
Mark 11. 10. blessed be the kingdom of *our f.* David
Luke 1. 73. the oath which he sware to *our f.* Abrah.
3. 8. begin not to say, we have Abraham to *our f.*
John 4. 12. art thou greater than *our f.?* 8. 53.
Acts 7. 2. the God of glory appeared to *our f.*
Rom. 1. 7. grace to you, and peace from God *our F.* and the Lord Jesus Christ, *1 Cor.* 1. 3. *2 Cor.* 1. 2. *2 Thess.* 1. 2. *1 Tim.* 1. 2. *Philem.* 3.
9. 10. conceived by one, even by *our f.* Isaac
Gal. 1. 4. according to the will of God, and *our F.*
Eph. 1. 2. grace be to you, and peace from G. *our F.* and L. Jes. Ch. *Phil.* 1. 2. *Col.* 1. 2. *1 Thess.* 1. 1.
Phil. 4. 20. unto God *our F.* be glory for ever, amen
1 Thess. 1. 3. in the sight of God and *our F.*
3. 11. now God *our F.* direct our way unto you
13. may stablish you in holiness before G. *our F.*
2 Thess. 1. 1. Paul unto the church in God *our F.*
2. 16. now God, even *our F.* comfort your hearts

Their FATHER.

Gen. 9. 23. Shem and Japhet covered the nakedness of *their f.* and saw not the nakedness of *their f.*
19. 33. they made *their f.* drink wine that night
36. both Lot's daughters with child by *their f.*
37. 12. his brethren went to feed *their f.'s* flock
Exod. 2. 16. filled troughs to water *their f.'s* flock
40. 15. anoint them as thou didst anoint *their f.*
Num. 36. 6. to the tribe of *their f.* shall they marry
Josh. 19. 47. after Dan *their f.* *Judg.* 18. 29.
1 Sam. 2. 25. they hearkened not to voice of *their f.*
10. 12. one of the same place said, who is *their f.?*
1 Kings 13. 11. the prophet's sons told *their f.*
1 Chr. 7. 22. Ephraim *their f.* mourned many days
24. 2. Nadab and Abihu died before *their f.*
25. 3. under the hands of *their f.* Jeduthun, 6.
2 Chron. 21. 3. *their f.* gave them great gifts
Job 42. 15. *their f.* gave them inheritance
Prov. 30. 11. there is a generation that curseth *th. f.*
Jer. 16. 7. cup of consolation to drink for *their f.*
35. 14. Jonadab's sons obeyed *t. f.'s* command. 16
Ezek. 22. 10. they discovered *their f.'s* nakedness
Mat. 4. 21. in a ship with Zebedee *their f.*
22. they left ship and *their f.* and followed him
13. 43. righteous shall shine in kingdom of *their f*

Thy FATHER.

Gen. 12. 1. Lord said, get thee from *thy f.'s* house
27. 6. I heard *thy f.* speak to Esau thy brother
10. thou shalt bring it to *thy f.* that he eat
38. 11. Judah said, remain a widow at *thy f.'s* house
46. 3. I am the God of *thy f.* fear not to go down
49. 25. by the God of *thy f.* who shall help thee
26. the blessings of *thy f.* have prevailed above
50. 16. *thy f.* commanded before he died, saying
17. forgive the servants of the God of *thy f.*
Exod. 20. 12. honour *thy f.* and thy mother that thy days may be long, *Deut.* 5. 16. *Mat.* 15. 4. | 19. 19.
Num. 18. 2. thy brethren of the tribe of *thy f.* bring
Deut. 6. 3. as the God of *thy f.* promised thee

)eut. 32. 6. is not he thy f. that bought thee ?
7. ask thy f. and he will shew thee, thy elders
?uth 2. 11. how thou hast left thy f. and mother
Sam. 20. 1. and what is my sin before thy f.?
6. if thy f. at all miss me, then say, David asked
Sam. 6. 21. the Lord which chose me before thy f.
10. 3. thinkest thou that David doth honour thy f.
that he sent comforters to thee? 1 Chron. 19. 3.
16. 19. as I have served in thy f.'s presence
Kings 11. 12. I will not do it for David thy f.'s sake
12. 4. thy f. made yoke grievous, 10. 2 Chron. 10. 4.
15. 19. there is a league betw. my father and thy f.
20. 34. the cities which my father took from thy f.
Kings 3. 13. get thee to the prophets of thy f.
20. 5. thus saith the Lord, the God of David thy f.
2 Chron. 21. 12. Isa. 38. 5.
Chr. 28. 9. my son, know thou the God of thy f.
Chr. 7. 17. if thou wilt walk before me as thy f.
ob 15. 10. are aged men much elder than thy f.
Prov. 1. 8. hear the instruction of thy f. 23. 22.
5. 20. my son, keep thy f.'s commandment
23. 25. thy f. and mother shall be glad, she rejoice
27. 10. thine own and thy f.'s friend forsake not
sa. 43. 27. thy first f. hath sinned against me
58. 14. feed thee with the heritage of Jacob thy f.
er. 12. 6. house of t. f. dealt treacherously with thee
22. 15. did not thy f. eat, drink, and do judgment
Ezek. 16. 3. thy f. was an Amorite, mother an Hittite
Dan. 5. 11. in the days of thy f. the king, I say thy f.
18. God gave thy f. a kingdom and glory
Mat. 6. 4. thy F. which seeth in secret, 6, 18.
6. shut thy door, pray to thy F. who is in secret
Mark 7. 10. for Moses said, honour thy f. and mother, 10. 19. Luke 18. 20. Eph. 6. 2.
uke 2. 48. thy f. and I sought thee sorrowing
15. 27. and thy f. hath killed the fatted calf
ohn 8. 19. then said they unto him, where is thy f.?

Your FATHER.

Gen. 31. 6. with all my power I have served your f.
7. your f. hath deceived me, and changed my wages
43. 7. is your f. alive? have ye another brother?
44. 17. as for you, get you up in peace to your f.
45. 19. take you waggons, bring your f. and come
49. 2. sons of Jacob, hearken unto Israel your f.
er. 35. 18. because ye obeyed Jonadab your f.
Ezek. 16. 45. mother an Hittite, your f. an Amorite
Mat. 5. 16. may glorify your F. who is in heaven
45. may be the children of your F. in heaven
48. be ye perfect, as your F. in heaven is perfect
6. 1. otherwise ye have no reward of your F.
8. your F. knoweth what things ye have need of before ye ask them, 32. Luke 12. 30.
14. if ye forgive, your heavenly F. will forgive you
15. if ye forgive not, neither will your F. forgive your trespasses, Mark 11. 25, 26.
10. 29. not one sparrow shall fall without your F.
18. 14. it is not the will of your F. that one perish
23. 9. call no man your f. upon the earth, for one is your F. which is in heaven
Luke 6. 36. be ye merciful, as your F. also is merciful
12. 32. it is your F.'s pleasure to give you kingdom
John 8. 38. ye do what ye have seen with your f.
41. ye do the deeds of your f. then said they to him
42. Jes. said, if God were your F. ye would love me
44. ye are of your f. the devil, and the lusts of your f. ye will do, he was a murderer
20. 17. I ascend to my F. and your F. to my God

FATHERS.

Exod. 6. 14. these are the heads of their f.s' houses, 25. Josh. 14. 1. | 19. 51. | 21. 1. 1 Chr. 8. 10, 13, 28.
10. 6. neither thy father, nor thy f.s' father have seen
20. 5. visiting the iniquity of the f. upon the children, 34. 7. Num. 14. 18. Deut. 5. 9.
Deut. 24. 16. the f. shall not be put to death for the children, nor children for f. 2 Kings 14. 6.
ob 30. 1. whose f. I would have disdained to set
Prov. 19. 14. house and riches are inheritance of f.
sa. 49. 23. kings shall be thy nursing f. and queens
er. 6. 21. f. and sons shall fall on them, 13. 14.
7. 18. children gather wood, f. kindle the fire
31. 29. f. have eaten sour grapes, Ezek. 18. 2.
32. 18. recompensest iniquity of the f. on children
47. 3. the f. shall not look back to their children
Ezek. 5. 10. the f. shall eat the sons in midst of thee
Mal. 4. 6. he shall turn the heart of the f. to the children, and children to their f. Luke 1. 17.
ohn 7. 22. not because it is of Moses, but of the f.
Acts 7. 2. men, brethren, and f. hearken, 22. 1.
13. 32. the promise which was made unto the f.
22. 3. the perfect manner of the law of the f.
Rom. 9. 5. whose are the f. of whom Christ came
Cor. 4. 15. though instructors, yet have not many f.
Eph. 6. 4. f. provoke not your children, Col. 3. 21.
Heb. 1. 1. God who spake in times past to the f.
12. 9. we had f. of our flesh who corrected us
Pet. 3. 4. since the f. fell asleep, all things continue
John 2. 13. I write unto you f. ye have known, 14.

See BURIED, CHIEF.

His FATHERS.

Kings 15. 12. he removed the idols his f. made
Kings 12. 18. took the things his f. had dedicated
15. 9. he did what was evil as his f. had done
21. 22. he forsook Lord God of his f. 2 Chron. 21. 10.
23. 32. according to all his f. had done, 37. | 24. 9.
Chron. 21. 19. no burning like the burning of his f.
28. 25. Ahaz provoked the Lord God of his f.
30. 19. prepareth his heart to seek the God of his f.
33. 12. he humbled himself before God of his f.
Psal. 49. 19. he shall go to the generation of his f.
109. 14. let the iniquity of his f. be remembered
Dan. 11. 24. shall do what his f. have not done
37. neither shall he regard the God of his f.
38. and a god whom his f. knew not shall honour
Acts 13. 36. David was laid to his f. saw corruption

My FATHERS.

Gen. 47. 9. not attained to the years of my f.
30. I will lie with my f. carry me out of Egypt
48. 16. and the name of my f. be named on them
49. 29. bury me with my f. in the cave in field
Exod. 15. 2. he is my f. God, I will exalt him
Kings 19. 4. for I am no better than my f.
21. 3. give the inheritance of my f. to thee, 4.
2 Kings 19. 12. have gods of the nations delivered them my f. destroyed? 2 Chr. 32. 14. Isa. 37. 12.
2 Chr. 32. 13. know not what I and my f. have done
Psal. 39. 12. for I am a sojourner, as all my f. were
Dan. 2. 23. I thank and praise thee, O God of my f.
Acts 24. 14. so worship I the God of my f.
Gal. 1. 14. being zealous of the traditions of my f.

Our FATHERS.

Gen. 46. 34. till now both we and also our f. 47. 3.
Num. 20. 15. how our f. went down into Egypt
Deut. 5. 3. Lord made not this covenant with our f.
6. 23. land which he sware to our f. 26. 3, 15.
26. 7. cried to the God of our f. the Lord heard
Josh. 22. 28. the pattern of the altar our f. made
24. 17. brought our f. out of the land of Egypt
Judg. 6. 13. where be miracles which our f. told of?
1 Kings 8. 57. God be with us, as he was with our f.
58. his statutes, which he commanded our f.
2 Kings 22. 13. because our f. have not hearkened
1 Chron. 12. 17. the God of our f. look and rebuke it
29. 15. for we are sojourners, as were all our f.
18. O Lord God of our f. keep for ever in the thoughts of the heart of thy people, 2 Chr. 20. 6.
2 Chron. 6. 31. which thou gavest our f. Neh. 9. 36.
29. 6. for our f. have trespassed and done evil
9. for lo, our f. have fallen by the sword
34. 21. our f. have not kept the word of the Lord
Ezra 5. 12. but after our f. had provoked God
7. 27. blessed be the Lord God of our f.
9. 7. since the days of our f. in a great trespass
Neh. 9. 9. didst see the affliction of our f. in Egypt
16. our f. dealt proudly, and hardened their necks
Psal. 22. 4. our f. trusted in thee, they trusted
44. 1. our f. have told us what thou didst, 78. 3.
106. 6. we have sinned with our f. and committed
7. our f. understood not thy wonders in Egypt
Isa. 64. 11. house where our f. praised thee
Jer. 3. 24. shame hath devoured the labour of our f.
25. we and our f. have not obeyed the voice
16. 19. surely our f. have inherited lies, vanities
44. 17. as we have done, we and our f. our kings
Lam. 5. 7. our f. have sinned, and are not, have borne
Dan. 9. 8. confusion of face belongeth to our f.
16. for our sins and the iniquities of our f.
Mic. 7. 20. sworn to our f. from the days of old
Mal. 2. 10. by profaning the covenant of our f.
Mat. 23. 30. if we had been in the days of our f.
Luke 1. 55. as he spake to our f. to Abraham
72. to perform the mercy promised to our f.
John 4. 20. our f. worshipped in this mountain
6. 31. our f. did eat manna in the desert
Acts 3. 13. God of our f. hath glorified his Son Jesus
25. of the covenant which God made with our f.
5. 30. God of our f. raised up Jesus, whom ye slew
7. 11. came dearth, our f. found no sustenance
15. Jacob went down and died, he and our f.
19. and evil entreated our f. and cast out children
38. this is he which spake in Sinai and with our f.
39. to whom our f. would not obey, but thrust
44. our f. had the tabernacle of witness in wildern.
13. 17. God of this people of Israel chose our f.
15. 10. a yoke which our f. nor we were able to bear
26. 6. for the hope of the promise made to our f.
28. 25. well spake Holy Ghost by Esaias to our f.
1 Cor. 10. 1. all our f. were under the cloud

Slept with FATHERS.

1 Kings 2. 10. so David slept with his f. 11. 21.
43. Solomon slept with his f. 2 Chron. 9. 31.
14. 20. Jeroboam slept with his f. 2 Kings 14. 29.
31. Rehoboam slept with his f. 2 Chron. 12. 16.
15. 8. Abijam slept with his f. 2 Chron. 14. 1.
24. and Asa slept with his f. 2 Chron. 16. 13.
16. 6. so Baasha slept with f. ‖ 28. Omri slept with f.
22. 40. Ahab sl. w. f. ‖ 50. Jehoshaphat, 2 Chr. 21. 1.
2 Kings 8. 24. Joram slept with his f. ‖ 10. 35. Jehu
13. 9. Jehoahaz slept with his f. ‖ 13. Joash, 14. 16.
14. 22. after that the king slept with f. 2 Chr. 26. 2.
15. 7. Azariah slept with his f. ‖ 22. Menahem
38. Jotham slept with his f. 2 Chron. 27. 9.
16. 20. Ahaz slept with his f. 2 Chron. 28. 27.
20. 21. Hezekiah slept with his f. 2 Chron. 32. 33.
21. 18. Manasseh slept with his f. 2 Chron. 33. 20.
24. 6. Jehoiakim slept with his f.
2 Chron. 26. 23. Uzziah slept with his f.

Their FATHERS.

Exod. 4. 5. that the God of their f. hath appeared
6. 14. heads of their f. 25. Josh. 14. 1. | 19. 51. | 21. 1. 1 Chron. 5. 24. | 7. 2, 7. | 8. 6. | 9. 9, 13.
Lev. 26. 39. in iniquity of their f. shall pine away
40. if they confess the iniquity of their f.
Num. 11. 12. the land thou swarest to give to their f. 14. 23. Deut. 10. 11. | 31. 20. Josh. 1. 6. | 5. 6. | 21. 43, 44. Jer. 32. 22.
Deut. 29. 25. have forsaken the covenant of their f.
Josh. 4. 6. when your children ask their f. 21.
22. 14. each one a head of the house of their f.
Judg. 2. 10. that generation were gathered to their f.
12. they forsook the Lord God of their f.
17. they turned out of the way their f. walked in
19. they corrupted themselves more than their f.
20. my covenant which I commanded their f.
22. if they keep way of Lord, as their f. kept it
3. 4. wich he commanded their f. by Moses
1 Kings 8. 34. and bring them again to the land thou gavest to their f. 48. 2 Chron. 6. 25, 38.
9. 9. who brought forth their f. out of Egypt
14. 15. out of the land which he gave to their f. 2 Kings 21. 8. Jer. 16. 15. | 24. 10.
22. provoked above all that their f. had done
2 Kings 21. 15. since day their f. came out of Egypt
1 Chron. 4. 38. the house of their f. increased greatly
5. 25. transgressed against the God of their f.
29. 20. blessed the God of their f. and bowed down
2 Chr. 7. 22. forsook God of their f. 24. 24. | 28. 6.
11. 16. came to sacrifice to the God of their f.
13. 18. they relied on the Lord God of their f.
14. 4. commanded to seek God of their f. 15. 12.
19. 4. brought them back to the God of their f.
20. 33. not prepared their hearts to God of their f.
30. 7. which trespassed against the God of their f.
22. making confession to the God of their f.
34. 32. according to the covenant of God of their f.
2 Chr. 34. 33. from following Lord the God of their f.
36. 15. God of their f. sent by his messengers
Neh. 9. 2. confessed sins and iniquities of their f.
23. into the land thou promisedst to their f.
Job 8. 8. prepare thyself to the search of their f.
15. 18. which wise men have told from their f.
Psal. 78. 8. and might not be as their f. a stubborn
12. marvellous things did he in sight of their f.
57. they dealt unfaithfully like their f.
Prov. 17. 6. and the glory of children are their f.
Isa. 14. 21. slaughter for the iniquity of their f.
Jer. 7. 26. they did worse than their f.
9. 14. after Baalim, which their f. taught them
16. whom they nor their f. have known, 19. 4.
23. 27. as their f. have forgotten my name
31. 32. I will make a new covenant, not according to covenant I made with their f. 11. 10. Heb. 8. 9.
50. 7. have sinned against Lord, the hope of their f.
Ezek. 2. 3. they and their f. have transgressed
5. 10. the fathers shall eat sons, and sons eat their f.
20. 4. cause them to know abominations of their f.
24. their eyes were after their f. idols
Amos 2. 4. their lies, after which their f. walked
Mal. 4. 6. turn the heart of the children to their f.
Luke 6. 23. for in like manner did their f.
26. for so did their f. to the false prophets

Thy FATHERS.

Gen. 15. 15. thou shalt go to thy f. in peace
49. 8. thy f. children shall bow down before thee
Exod. 13. 5. into land which he sware to thy f. 11. Deut. 6. 10, 18. | 7. 12, 13. | 8. 18. | 9. 5. | 13. 17. | 19. 8. | 28. 11. | 29. 13. | 30. 20.
Deut. 1. 21. go up, possess it, as God of thy f. said
4. 31. nor forget the covenant of thy f. he sware
37. and because he loved thy f. 10. 15.
8. 3. humbled thee and fed thee with manna which thou knewest not, neither did thy f. know, 16.
10. 22. thy f. went into Egy. with seventy persons
12. 1. land which the God of thy f. giveth thee
13. 6. other gods thou nor thy f. known, 28. 64.
19. 8. give the land which he promised thy f. 27. 3.
28. 36. to a nation thou nor thy f. have known
30. 5. do thee good and multiply thee above thy f.
9. rejoice over thee, as he rejoiced over thy f.
31. 16. thou shalt sleep with thy f. 2 Sam. 7. 12.
1 Kings 13. 22. shall not come to sepulchre of thy f.
2 Kings 20. 17. what thy f. laid up be carried away
22. 20. I will gather thee to thy f. 2 Chr. 34. 28.
1 Chron. 17. 11. thou must go to be with thy f.
Ezra 4. 15. search the book of the records of thy f.
Psal. 45. 16. instead of thy f. shall be thy children
Prov. 22. 28. remove not the land-mark thy f. set
Jer. 34. 5. burned with the burnings of thy f.
Acts 7. 32. I am God of thy f. the G. of Abraham

Your FATHERS.

Gen. 48. 21. shall bring you to the land of your f.
Exod. 3. 13. the God of your f. hath sent me, Deut. 1. 11. | 4. 1. Josh. 18. 3. 2 Chron. 28. 9. | 29. 5.
Num. 32. 8. thus did your f. Neh. 13. 18.
14. behold ye are risen up in your f. stead
Deut. 1. 8. possess the land the Lord sware to your f. 35. | 7. 8. | 8. 1. | 11. 9, 21. Judg. 2. 1.
32. 17. sacrificed to gods whom your f. feared not
Josh. 24. 2. your f. dwelt on the other side the flood
6. I brought your f. out of Egypt, Egypt pursued
14. put away the gods which your f. served
15. whether the gods which your f. served
1 Sam. 12. 7. acts the Lord did to you and your f.
8. your f. cried, the Lord brought forth your f.
15. the hand of the Lord against you as ag. your f.
2 Kings 17. 13. the law which I commanded your f.
2 Chron. 13. 12. fight ye not ag. the God of your f.
30. 7. be not like your f. and brethren, 8. Zech. 1. 4.
33. 8. remove out of the land appointed for your f.
Ezra 8. 28. free-will offering to the God of your f.
10. 11. make confession to the God of your f.
Psal. 95. 9. when your f. tempted me, Heb. 3. 9.
Isa. 65. 7. your and the iniquities of your f. togeth.
Jer. 2. 5. what iniquity have your f. found in me?
3. 18. shall come to the land I have given to your f.
7. 7. dwell in the land I gave to your f. 14. | 23. 39. | 25. 5. | 35. 15. Ezek. 20. 42. | 36. 28. | 47. 14.
22. I spake not to your f. in the day I brought them
25. since the day your f. came forth out of Egypt
11. 4. which I commanded your f. 17. 22.
7. for I earnestly protested unto your f.
16. 11. because your f. have forsaken me
12. done worse than your f. ‖ 13. ye nor your f.
34. 13. I made a covenant with your f. in the day
14. but your f. hearkened not unto me
44. 3. whom they knew not, neither they nor your f.
9. have ye forgotten the wickedness of your f.?
10. in my statutes I set before you and your f.
21. the incense ye, your f. and kings, burn
Ezek. 20. 18. walk ye not in the statutes of your f.
27. in this your f. have blasphemed me
30. are ye polluted after the manner of your f.?
36. like as I pleaded with your f. so with you
37. 25 shall dwell in the land wherein your f. dwelt
Hos. 9. 10. I saw your f. as the first ripe of fig tree
Joel 1. 2. hath this been in the days of your f.?
Zech. 1. 2. the Lord hath been displeased with your f.
4. be not as your f. ‖ 5. your f. where are they?
6. did not my words take hold of your f.?
8. 14. when your f. provoked me to wrath
Mal. 3. 7. from days of your f. ye are gone away
Mat. 23. 32. fill ye up then the measure of your f.
Luke 11. 47. of prophets, and your f. killed them
48. ye witness that ye allow the deeds of your f.
John 6. 49. your f. did eat manna and are dead
58. not as your f. did eat manna and are dead
Acts 7. 51. ye resist Holy Ghost as your f. did, so ye
52. who of the proph. have not your f. persecuted?
1 Pet. 1. 18. received by tradition from your f.

FATHERLESS.

Exod. 22. 22. ye shall not afflict any f. child
24. your wives shall be widows, and children f.
Deut. 10. 18. he doth execute the judgment of the f. and widow, Psal. 82. 3. Isa. 1. 17.
Job 6. 27. ye overwhelm the f. and dig a pit
22. 9. the arms of the f. have been broken
24. 3. they drive away the ass of the f

Job 24. 9. they pluck the *f.* from the breast
29. 12. because I delivered the poor and the *f.*
31. 17. eaten alone, and *f.* hath not eaten thereof
21. if I have lifted up my hand against the *f.*
Psal. 10. 14. thou art the helper of the *f.*
18. to judge the *f.* and the oppressed
68. 5. a father of the *f.* a judge of the widows
109. 9. let his children be *f.* his wife a widow
12. nor let any favour his *f.* children
Prov. 23. 10. enter not into the fields of the *f.*
Isa. 1. 23. they judge not the *f.* *Jer.* 5. 28.
9. 17. the Lord shall not have mercy on their *f.*
10. 2. widows their prey, that they may rob the *f.*
Jer. 49. 11. leave thy *f.* children, I will preserve
*Lam.*5.3. we are orphans and *f.* our mothers widows
Ezek. 22. 7. in thee have they vexed the *f.* and widow
Hos. 14. 3. for in thee the *f.* findeth mercy
Mal. 3. 5. a witness against those that oppress the *f.*
Jam. 1. 27. pure religion is to visit the *f.* and widows

FATHERLESS, with *stranger.*

Deut. 14. 29. the *stranger*, and the *f.* and the widow shall come and eat, 24. 19, 20, 21. | 26. 12, 13.
16. 11. the *stranger* and *f.* rejoice with thee, 14.
24. 17. nor pervert judgment of *stranger* nor *f.*
27. 19. cursed that perverts judg. of *stranger* and *f.*
Psal. 94. 6. they slay the *stranger* and murder the *f.*
146. 9. the Lord preserveth the *strangers* and *f.*
Jer. 7. 6. if ye oppress not the *stranger*, the *f.* and the widow, 22. 3. *Zech.* 7. 10.

FATHOMS.

Acts 27. 28. they found it twenty *f.* again fifteen *f.*

FATLING.

*Isa.*11.6. the calf, the young lion, and the *f.* together

FATLINGS.

1 *Sam.* 15. 9. Saul spared Agag and the best of the *f.*
2 *Sam.* 6. 13. David sacrificed oxen and *f.*
Psal. 66. 15. I will offer to thee burnt sacrifices of *f.*
Ezek. 39. 18. all of them *f.* of Bashan
Mat. 22. 4. my oxen and my *f.* are killed, all ready

FATNESS.

Gen. 27. 28. God give thee of the *f.* of the earth
39. thy dwelling shall be the *f.* of the earth
Deut. 32. 15. thou art thick and covered with *f.*
Judg. 9. 9. the olive-tree said, should I leave my *f.*
Job 15. 27. because he covereth his face with his *f.*
36. 16. that set on thy table should be full of *f.*
Psal. 36. 8. shall be satisfied with the *f.* of thy house
63. 5. my soul be satisfied as with marrow and *f.*
65. 11. thou crownest year, all thy paths drop *f.*
73. 7. eyes stand out with *f.* have more than wish
109. 24. knees are weak, my flesh faileth of *f.*
Isa. 17. 4. once the *f.* of his flesh shall wax lean
34. 6. the sword of the Lord is made fat with *f.*
7. their dust shall be made fat with *f.*
55. 2. and let your soul delight itself in *f.*
Jer. 31. 14. I will satiate the soul of priests with *f.*
Rom. 11. 17. with them partakest of *f.* of the olive

FATS.

Joel 2. 24. the *f.* shall overflow with wine and oil
3. 13. for the press is full, the *f.* overflow

FATTED.

1 *Kings* 4. 23. ten oxen, beside harts, and *f.* fowl
Jer. 46. 21. her hired men are like *f.* bullocks

See CALF.

FATTER, *see* COUNTENANCES.

FATTEST.

Psal. 78. 31. the wrath of God slew the *f.* of them
Dan. 11. 24. shall enter on *f.* places of the province

FAULT, S.

Gen. 41. 9. butler said, I remember my *f.* this day
Exod. 5. 16. but the *f.* is in thine own people
Deut. 25. 2. cause to be beaten according to his *f.*
1 *Sam.* 29. 3. and I have found no *f.* in him
2 *Sam.* 3. 8. thou chargest me this day with a *f.*
Psal. 19. 12. cleanse thou me from secret *f.*
59. 4. they run and prepare without my *f.*
Dan. 6. 4. they could find no occasion or *f.* in him
Mat. 18. 15. if thy brother trespass, tell him his *f.*
Mark 7. 2. eat with unwashen hands, they found *f.*
Luke 23. 4. Pilate said, chief priests and people, I find no *f.* in this man, 14. *John* 18. 38. | 19. 4, 6.
Rom. 9. 19. thou wilt say, why doth he yet find *f.*?
1 *Cor.* 6. 7. now there is utterly a *f.* among you
Gal. 6. 1. if a man be overtaken in a *f.* restore him
Heb. 8. 8. for, finding *f.* with them, he saith, behold
9. † 14. who offered himself without *f.* to God
Jam. 5. 16. confess your *f.* one to another, pray one
1 *Pet.* 2. 20. if when ye be buffeted for your *f.*
Rev. 14. 5. are without *f.* before the throne of God

FAULTLESS.

Heb. 8. 7. if the first covenant had been *f.* then
Jude 24. him that is able to present you *f.* with joy

FAULTY.

Num. 35. † 31. no satisfaction for a murderer *f.* to die
2 *Sam.* 14. 13. the king doth speak as one which is *f.*
Hos. 10. 2. heart divided, now shall they be found *f.*

FAVOUR.

Gen. 39. 21. gave Joseph *f.* in the sight of the keeper
Exod. 3. 21. I will give this people *f.* in sight of the Egyptians, shall not go empty, 11. 3. | 12. 36.
Deut. 28. 50. which shall not shew *f.* to the young
33. 23. he said, O Naphtali, satisfied with *f.*
Josh. 11. 20. and that they might have no *f.*
1 *Sam.* 2. 26. Samuel was in *f.* with Lord and men
Job 10. 12. thou hast granted me life and *f.*
Psal. 5. 12. with *f.* wilt compass him as with a shield
30. 5. his *f.* is life, weeping may endure for a night
7. by thy *f.* thou hast made my mountain to stand
44. 3. because thou hadst a *f.* unto them
45. 12. even the rich shall entreat thy *f.*
89. 17. in thy *f.* our horn shall be exalted
106. 4. remember me with the *f.* thou bearest thine
112. 5. a good man sheweth *f.* and lendeth
119. 58. I entreated thy *f.* with my whole heart
Prov. 11. 27. he that seeketh good procureth *f.*
13. 15. good understanding giveth *f.*
14. 9. but among the righteous there is *f.*
35. the king's *f.* is toward a wise servant
16. 15. his *f.* is as a cloud of the latter rain
19. 6. many will entreat the *f.* of the prince
12. the king's *f.* is as dew upon the grass
21. 10. his neighbour findeth no *f.* in his eyes
Prov. 22. 1. loving *f.* rather to be chosen than silver
29. 26. many seek the ruler's *f.*
31. 30. *f.* is deceitful, and beauty is vain
Eccl. 9. 11. race not to swift, nor *f.* to men of skill
Isa. 26. 10. let *f.* be shewed to the wicked
27. 11. he who formed them will shew them no *f.*
60. 10. but in my *f.* have I had mercy on thee
Jer. 16. 13. a land, where I will not shew you *f.*
31. † 9. and with *f.* will I lead them
Dan. 1. 9. God had brought Daniel into *f.* and love
Luke 2. 52. Jesus increased in *f.* with God and men
Acts 2. 47. praising God, having *f.* with all people
7. 10. God gave Moses *f.* in sight of Pharaoh
25. 3. the high priest desired *f.* against him

Find, or *found*, FAVOUR.

Gen. 18. 3. if now I have *found f.* in thy sight, 30. 27. *Num.* 11. 15. 1 *Sam.* 20. 29. *Neh.* 2. 5. *Esth.* 5. 8. | 7. 3. | 8. 5.
Num. 11. 11. and wherefore have I not *found f.*?
Deut. 24. 1. it come to pass she *find* no *f.* in his eyes
Ruth 2. 13. let me *find f.* in thy sight, my lord
1 *Sam.* 16. 22. David hath *found f.* in my sight
25. 8. let the young men *find f.* in thy sight
2 *Sam.* 15. 25. if I shall *find f.* in eyes of the Lord
1 *Kings* 11. 19. Hadad *found f.* in sight of Pharaoh
Prov. 3. 4. so shalt thou *find f.* in the sight of God
28. 23. shall *find* more *f.* than he that flattereth
Cant. 8. 10. I was in his eyes as one that *found f.*
Luke 1. 30. fear not, for thou hast *found f.* with G.
Acts 7. 46. David *found f.* before God, and desired

Obtain, or *obtained*, FAVOUR.

Esth. 2. 15. now Esther *obtained f.* 17. | 5. 2.
Prov. 8. 35. whoso findeth me, shall *obtain f.* of Lord
12. 2. a good man *obtaineth f.* of the Lord
18. 22. whoso findeth a wife, *obtaineth f.* of Lord

FAVOUR.

1 *Sam.* 29. 6. nevertheless, the lords *f.* thee not
Psal. 35. 27. be glad, that *f.* my righteous cause
102. 13. the time, the set time to *f.* her is come
14. for thy servants *f.* the dust thereof
109. 12. nor let any to *f.* his fatherless children

FAVOURABLE.

Judg. 21. 22. be *f.* unto them for our sakes
Job 33. 26. shall pray, and God will be *f.* unto him
Psal. 77. 7. will the L. cast off, and be *f.* no more?
85. 1. Lord, thou hast been *f.* to thy land

FAVOURED.

Gen. 29. 17. Rachel was beautiful and well-*f.*
39. 6. Joseph was well-*f.* || 41. 2. kine well *f.* 18.
41. 3. out of the river ill *f.* kine, 4, 19, 21, 27.
Prov. 21. † 10. his neighbour is not *f.* in his eyes
Lam. 4. 16. Lord divided them, they *f.* not the elders
Dan. 1. 4. children well-*f.* and skilful in all wisdom
Nah. 3. 4. the whoredoms of the well-*f.* harlot
Luke 1. 28. hail, thou art highly *f.* Lord with thee

Evil-FAVOUREDNESS.

Deut. 17. 1. any bullock wherein is any *evil-f.*

FAVOUREST.

Psal. 41. 11. by this I know that thou *f.* me
86. † 2. preserve my soul, for I am one whom thou *f.*

FAVOURETH.

2 *Sam.* 20. 11. he that *f.* Joab, let him go after Joab

FEAR.

Fear *is a passion, implanted in nature, that causes a flight from an approaching evil, either real or imaginary.* The fear of God *is either* filial *or* servile. *The filial fear of God is a holy affection, or gracious habit wrought in the soul by God,* Jer. 32. 40. *whereby it is inclined and enabled to obey all God's commandments, even the most difficult,* Gen. 22. 12. Eccl. 12. 13. *and to hate and avoid evil,* Neh. 5. 15. Prov. 8. 13. | 16. 6. Slavish fear *is the consequence of guilt; it is a judicial impression from the sad thoughts of the provoked Majesty of heaven; it is an alarm within, that disturbs the rest of a sinner; thus* Felix *feared,* Acts 24. 25. *Though this fear be in wicked men, yet, through the mercy and grace of God, it often proves a preparative to faith,* Acts 2. 37. Rom. 8. 15.

Fear *is likewise used for the object of* fear. *Thus it is said,* the fear of *Isaac, to describe the God whom* Isaac *feared,* Gen. 31. 42. Except the fear of Isaac had been with me, surely thou hadst sent me away now empty. *And in* Prov. 1. 26. I will mock when your fear cometh; *that is, the calamity you feared. God says, that he will send* his fear *before his people; that is, a terror wrought by him, in order to terrify and destroy the inhabitants of* Canaan, *Exod.* 23. 27.

Fear *is put for the whole worship of God, in* Psal. 34. 11. I will teach you the fear of the Lord. *I will teach you the true and principal way of worshipping and serving God with his acceptation, and to your own salvation. It is likewise put for the law and word of God,* Psal. 19. 9. The fear of the Lord is clean, enduring for ever. *The law is so called, because it is the object, the cause, and the rule, of the grace of holy* fear.

Gen. 9. 2. the *f.* of you shall be on every beast
31. 42. except the *f.* of Isaac had been with me
53. Jacob sware by the *f.* of his father Isaac
Exod. 15. 16. *f.* and dread shall fall upon them
23. 27. I will send my *f.* before thee, and destroy
Deut. 2. 25. I will put the *f.* of thee on the nations
11. 25. the Lord shall lay the *f.* of you on the land
1 *Chron.* 14. 17. Lord brought *f.* of him on nations
Ezra 3. 3. *f.* was on them because of the people
Neh. 6. 14. think on them that put me in *f.* 19.
Esth. 8. 17. the *f.* of the Jews fell upon them, 9. 2.
9. 3. because the *f.* of Mordecai fell on them
Job 3. † 25. I feared a *f.* and it came upon me
4. 6. is not this thy *f.* thy confidence, thy hope?
14. *f.* came upon me and trembling
6. 14. he forsaketh the *f.* of the Almighty
9. 34. and let not his *f.* terrify me
15. 4. yea, thou castest off *f.* and restrainest prayer
21. 9. houses safe from *f.* nor rod of God on them
22. 10. snares round about, sudden *f.* troubleth thee
25. 2. dominion and *f.* are with him, makes peace
39. 22. he mocketh at *f.* and is not affrighted
Psal. 5. 7. in thy *f.* will I worship toward thy temple
Psal. 9. 20. put them in *f.* O Lord, that nations may
14. 5. there were they in great *f.* God is in generat.
31. 11. and I was a *f.* to mine acquaintance
13. *f.* was on every side, they took counsel ag. me
48. 6. *f.* took hold upon them there, and pain
53. 5. there were they in *f.* where no *f.* was
64. 1. preserve my life from *f.* of the enemy
90. 11. according to thy *f.* so is thy wrath
105. 38. for the *f.* of them fell upon them
119. 38. thy servant, who is devoted to thy *f.*
Prov. 1. 26. I will mock when your *f.* cometh
27. when your *f.* cometh as desolation and destruc.
33. and shall be quiet from *f.* of evil
3. 25. be not afraid of sudden *f.* nor desolation
10. 24. the *f.* of the wicked shall come upon him
20. 2. the *f.* of a king is as the roaring of a lion
29. 25. the *f.* of man bringeth a snare
Cant. 3. 8. hath his sword because of *f.* in the night
Isa. 7. 25. there shall not come the *f.* of briers
8. 12. neither fear ye their *f.* nor be afraid
13. the Lord, let him be your *f.* and your dread
14. 3. the Lord shall give thee rest from thy *f.*
21. 4. the night of pleasure be turned into *f.* to me
24. 17. *f.* and the pit, and the snare are upon thee
18. that fleeth from *f.* shall fall, *Jer.* 48. 44.
29. 13. their *f.* toward me is taught by men
63. 17. and hardened our heart from thy *f.*
Jer. 2. 19. an evil thing, that my *f.* is not in thee
6. 25. the sword and *f.* is on every side, 20. 10.
20. † 3. Lord hath called thy name *f.* round about
30. 5. we have heard a voice of *f.* not of peace
32. 40. but I will put my *f.* in their hearts
48. 43. *f.* and the pit shall be upon thee, O Moab
49. 5. behold, I will bring a *f.* upon thee, saith L.
24. *f.* hath seized on Damascus, anguish and sorr.
29. they shall cry to them, *f.* is on every side
Lam. 3. 47. *f.* and a snare is come upon us
Ezek. 21. † 15. *f.* of the sword against their gates
30. † 4. great *f.* shall be in Ethiopia
13. I will put a *f.* in the land of Egypt
Mal. 1. 6. if I be a master, where is my *f.*?
Luke 1. 12. when Zacharias saw him, *f.* fell upon him
65. *f.* came on all that dwelt round about them, 7. 16. *Acts* 2. 43. | 5. 5, 11. | 19. 17. *Rev.* 11. 11.
3. † 14. he said to the soldiers, put no man in *f.*
Rom. 13. 7. render to whom *f.* is due
1 *Cor.* 2. 3. I was with you in weakness and in *f.*
2 *Cor.* 7. 11. what *f.*! what vehement desire!
2 *Tim.* 1. 7. God hath not given us the spirit of *f.*
Col. 2. † 1. ye knew what great *f.* I have for you
Heb. 2. 15. and deliver them who thro' *f.* of death
12. 28. may serve God with reverence and godly *f.*
1 *Pet.* 1. 17. pass the time of your sojourn. here in *f.*
3. 15. give an answer with meekness and *f.*
1 *John* 4. 18. no *f.* in love, but love casteth out *f.*

For FEAR.

Deut. 28. 67. *for* the *f.* wherewith thou shalt fear
Josh. 22. 24. have not rather done it *for f.* of thing
Judg. 9. 21. dwelt *for f.* of Abimelech his brother
1 *Sam.* 21. 10. Dav. arose, fled that day *for f.* of Saul
23. 26. David made haste to get away *for f.* of Saul
Job 22. 4. will he reprove thee *for f.* of thee?
Isa. 31. † 8. they shall flee *for f.* of the sword
9. he shall pass over to his strong hold *for f.*
Jer. 35. 11. *for f.* of the army of the Chaldeans
37. 11. army broken up *for f.* of Pharaoh's army
41. 9. which Asa had made *for f.* of Baasha
46. 5. *for f.* was round about, saith the Lord
50. 16. *for f.* of the oppressing sword they return
Mal. 2. 5. *for f.* wherewith he feared me
Mat. 14. 26. the disciples cried out *for f.*
28. 4. *for f.* of him the keepers did shake
Luke 21. 26. men's hearts failing them *for f.*
John 7. 13. no man spake openly *for f.* of the Jews
19. 38. a disciple, but secretly *for f.* of the Jews
20. 19. disciples were assembled *for f.* of the Jews
Rev. 18. 10. afar off *for f.* of her torment, 15.

FEAR *of God.*

Gen. 20. 11. surely the *f. of God* is not in this place
2 *Sam.* 23. 3. must be just, ruling in the *f. of God*
2 *Chr.* 20. 29. the *f. of God* was on all kingdoms
Neh. 5. 9. ought ye not to walk in the *f. of God*?
15. but so did not I, because of the *f. of God*
Psal. 36. 1. there is no *f. of God* before his eyes
Rom. 3. 18. there is no *f. of God* before their eyes
2 *Cor.* 7. 1. perfecting holiness in the *f. of God*
Eph. 5. 21. submitting one to another in *f. of God*

FEAR *of the Lord.*

1 *Sam.* 11. 7. *f. of Lord* fell on people, 2 *Chr.* 17. 10.
2 *Chr.* 14. 14. the *f. of the Lord* came upon them
19. 7. let the *f. of the Lord* be upon you, take heed
9. thus shall ye do, in the *f. of the Lord*, faithfully
Job 28. 28. to man he said, the *f. of Lord* is wisdom
Psal. 19. 9. the *f. of Lord* is clean, enduring for ever
34. 11. children, I will teach you the *f. of the Lord*
111. 10. *f. of the Lord* is the beginning of wisdom
Prov. 1. 7. *f. of Ld.* beginning of knowledge, 9. 10.
29. and did not choose the *f. of the Lord*
2. 5. then shalt thou understand the *f. of the Lord*
8. 13. the *f. of the Lord* is to hate evil
10. 27. the *f. of the Lord* prolongeth days
14. 26. in the *f. of the Lord* is strong confidence
27. the *f. of the Lord* is a fountain of life
15. 16. better is a little with the *f. of the Lord*
33. the *f. of the Lord* is the instruction of wisdom
16. 6. by the *f. of the Lord* men depart from evil
19. 23. the *f. of the Lord* tendeth to life
22. 4. by the *f. of the Lord* are riches and honour
23. 17. be thou in the *f. of the Lord* all day long
Isa. 2. 10. hide thee in the dust for *f. of the Lord*
19. they shall go into caves for *f. of the Lord*
21. to go into clefts of rocks for *f. of the Lord*
11. 2. spirit of knowledge, and of the *f. of the Ld.*
3. of quick understanding in the *f. of the Lord*
33. 6. the *f. of the Lord* is his treasure
Acts 9. 31. walking in *f. of the Lord* and comfort

With FEAR.

Psal. 2. 11. serve the Lord *with f.* and rejoice
Jonah 1. † 10. then were the men *with* great *f.*
Mat. 28. 8. they departed *with f.* and great joy
Luke 5. 26. and they were all filled *with f.*
8. 37. the Gadarenes were taken *with* great *f.*

2 Cor. 7. 15. how *with f.* you received him
Eph. 6. 5. obedient to masters *with f.* and trembling
Phil. 2. 12. work out salvation *with f.* and trembling
Heb. 11. 7. Noah moved *with f.* prepared an ark
1 Pet. 2. 18. servants, be subject to masters *with f.*
3. 2. behold your chaste conversat. coupled *with f.*
Jude 23. and others save *with f.* pulling them out

Without FEAR.

Job 39. 16. her labour is in vain *without f.*
41. 33. there is not his like, who is made *without f.*
Luke 1. 74. that we might serve him *without f.*
1 Cor. 16. 10. that he may be with you *without f.*
Phil. 1. 14. are bold to speak the word *without f.*
Jude 12. they feast, feeding themselves *without f.*

FEARS.

Job 15. † 21. a sound of *f.* is in his ears
Psal. 34. 4. the Lord delivered me from all my *f.*
Eccl 12. 5. and when *f.* shall be in the way
Isa. 66. 4. and I will bring their *f.* upon them
2 Cor. 7. 5. without were fightings, within were *f.*

FEAR, *Verb.*

Lev. 19. 3. ye shall *f.* every man his mother and fath.
Num. 14. 9. neither *f.* ye the people of the land
Deut. 4. 10. hear, that they may learn to *f.* me
5. 29. O that they would *f.* me, keep my command.
28. 58. *f.* this glorious name, the Lord thy God
66. thou shalt *f.* day and night, have no assurance
67. for the fear of heart wherewith thou shalt *f.*
Judg. 7. 10. if thou *f.* to go down, go with Phurah
1 Kings 8. 40. that they may *f.* thee, *2 Chron.* 6. 31.
43. may know thy name to *f.* thee, *2 Chr.* 6. 33.
2 Kings 17. 38. neither shall ye *f.* other gods
39. but Lord your God ye shall *f.* and he deliver
1 Chron. 16. 30. *f.* before him all earth, *Psal.* 96. 9.
Neh. 1. 11. thy servants who desire to *f.* thy name
Job 31. 34. did I *f.* a great multitude?
Psal. 23. 4. I will *f.* no evil, for thou art with me
27. 1. the Lord is my salvation, whom shall I *f.*?
31. 19. thy goodness laid up for them that *f.* thee
40. 3. many shall see it, and *f.* and shall trust in L.
49. 5. wherefore should I *f.* in the days of evil?
52. 6. the righteous shall see and *f.* and laugh at him
60. 4. thou hast given a banner to them that *f.* thee
61. 5. the heritage of those that *f.* thy name
64. 9. all shall *f.* and declare the work of God
72. 5. they shall *f.* thee as long as the sun endureth
86. 11. unite my heart to *f.* thy name
102. 15. so the heathen shall *f.* thy name
119. 39. turn away my reproach which I *f.*
63. I am a companion of all them that *f.* thee
74. they that *f.* thee will be glad when they see me
79. let those that *f.* thee turn unto me
Eccl. 3. 14. God doeth it, men should *f.* before him
Isa. 8. 12. neither *f.* ye their fear, nor be afraid
19. 16. Egypt like to women, shall be afraid and *f.*
25. 3. the city of the terrible nations shall *f.* thee
44. 11. the workmen shall *f.* and be ashamed
59. 19. so shall they *f.* the name of the Lord
60. 5. thine heart shall *f.* and be enlarged
Jer. 10. 7. who would not *f.* thee, O King of nations?
23. 4. and they shall *f.* no more, nor be dismayed
32. 39. will give them one heart that may *f.* me
33. 9. they shall *f.* and tremble for all the goodness
51. 46. lest your heart faint, and ye *f.* for rumour
Dan. 1. 10. the prince said, I *f.* my lord the king
6. 26. that men *f.* before the God of Daniel
Hos. 10. 5. the inhabitants of Samaria shall *f.*
Mic. 7. 17. move as worms, and *f.* because of thee
Zeph. 3. 7. I said, surely thou wilt *f.* me
Hag. 1. 12. and the people did *f.* before the Lord
Zech. 9. 5. Ashkelon shall see it and *f.* Gaza also see
Mal. 4. 2. to you that *f.* my name shall sun of right.
Mat. 21. 26. if we shall say, of men, we *f.* the people
Luke 12. 5. I will forewarn you whom ye shall *f.*
Rom. 8. 15. not received spirit of bondage again to *f.*
11. 20. be not high-minded, but *f.*
2 Cor. 11. 3. I *f.* lest as the serpent beguiled Eve
12. 20. I *f.* lest I shall not find you such as I would
1 Tim. 5. 20. rebuke before all, that others may *f.*
Heb. 4. 1. let us *f.* lest promise being left us of entering
12. 21. Moses said, I exceedingly *f.* and quake
Rev. 2. 10. *f.* none of those things thou shalt suffer
11. 18. give reward to them that *f.* thy name

FEAR *God.*

Gen. 42. 18. he said, this do, and live, for I *f. God*
Exod. 18. 21. provide able men, such as *f. God*
Lev. 19. 14. but shalt *f.* thy *God*, I am the Lord, 32.
25. 17. but thou shalt *f.* thy *God*, 36, 43.
Job 1. 9. Satan said, doth Job *f. God* for nought?
Psal. 66. 16. come and hear, all ye that *f. God*
Eccl. 5. 7. in words are vanities, but *f.* thou *God*
8. 12. it shall be well with them that *f. God*
12. 13. *f. God*, and keep his commandments
Isa. 29. 23. and they shall *f.* the *God* of Israel
Luke 23. 40. rebuked him, saying, dost not *f. God?*
Acts 13. 16. and ye that *f. God* give audience
1 Pet. 2. 17. honour men, *f. God*, honour the king
Rev. 14. 7. saying, *f. God*, and give glory to him

Hear and FEAR.

Deut. 13. 11. all Israel shall *hear and f.* 21. 21.
17. 13. and all the people shall *hear and f.*
19. 20. those which remain shall *hear and f.*

FEAR *him.*

Gen. 32. 11. deliver me from Esau, for I *f. him*
Deut. 13. 4. ye shall walk after God, and *f. him*
2 Kings 17. 36. *him* shall ye *f. him* shall ye worship
Job 37. 24. men therefore *f. him*, he respecteth not
Psal. 22. 23. and *f. him* all ye the seed of Israel
25. I will pay my vows before them that *f. him*
25. 14. secret of the Lord is with them that *f. him*
33. 18. the eye of the Lord is on them that *f. him*
34. 7. angel encampeth about them that *f. him*
9. for there is no want to them that *f. him*
67. 7. all the ends of the earth shall *f. him*
85. 9. surely his salvation is nigh them that *f. him*
103. 11. great is his mercy to them that *f. him*
13. so the Lord pitieth them that *f. him*
17. the mercy of the Lord is on them that *f. him*
111. 5. he hath given meat to them that *f. him*
145. 19. he will fulfil the desire of them that *f. him*
147. 11. Lord taketh pleasure in them that *f. him*
Mat. 10. 28. *f. him* who is able to destroy, *Luke* 12. 5.

Luke 1. 50. his mercy is on them that *f. him*
Rev. 19. 5. praise God, ye that *f. him*, small and great

FEAR *the Lord.*

Deut. 6. 2. that thou mightest *f. the Lord* thy God
13. thou shalt *f. L.* thy God, 10. 20. *2 Kings* 17. 39.
24. to *f. the Lord* our God for our good always
10. 12. *f. the Lord*, walk in his ways, and love him
14. 23. learn to *f. the Lord*, 17. 19. | 31. 12, 13.
Josh 4. 24. that ye might *f. the Lord* your God
24. 14. now therefore *f. the Lord*, and serve him
1 Sam. 12. 14. if ye will *f. the Lord*, and serve him
24. only *f. the Lord*, and serve him in truth
1 Kings 18. 12. I thy servant *f. the L.* *2 Kings* 4. 1.
2 Kings 17. 28. taught them how they should *f. L.*
Psal. 15. 4. he honoureth them that *f. the L.*
22. 23. ye that *f. the Lord*, praise him
33. 8. let all the earth *f. the Lord*, and stand in awe
34. 9. O *f. the Lord*, ye his saints, there is no want
115. 11. ye that *f. the Lord*, trust in the Lord
13. he will bless them that *f. the Lord*
118. 4. that *f. the Lord*, say, his mercy endureth
135. 20. ye that *f. the Lord*, bless the Lord
Prov. 3. 7. *f. the Lord*, and depart from evil
24. 21. my son, *f.* thou *the Lord*, and the king
Jer. 5. 24. neither say they, let us *f. the Lord*
26. 19. did he not *f. the Lord*, and besought Lord?
Hos. 3. 5. afterward shall Israel *f. the Lord*
Jonah 1. 9. and I *f. the Lord*, the God of heaven

FEAR *not.*

Gen. 15. 1. *f. not*, Abram, I am thy shield and reward
21. 17. *f. not*, God hath heard the voice of the lad
26. 24. *f. not*, I am with thee, and will bless thee
35. 17. the midwife said to Rachel, *f. not*
43. 23. and he said, peace be to you, *f. not*
46. 3. he said, *f. not* to go down into Egypt
50. 19. Joseph said, *f. not*, for am I in place of God
21. *f. not*, I will nourish you and your little ones
Exod. 14. 13. *f. not*, stand and see salvation of Ld.
20. 20. Moses said, *f. not*, God is come to prove
Num. 14. 9. the Lord is with us, *f.* them *not*
21. 34. the Lord said to Moses, *f.* him *not*
Deut. 1. 21. go up and possess the land, *f. not*
3. 2. *f. not* Og, 22. || 20. 3. *f. not* your enemies
31. 6. *f. not* the Canaanites, *Josh.* 10. 8, 25.
8. the Lord will go before thee, he will not forsake thee, *f. not*, *Josh.* 8. 1. *1 Chron.* 28. 20.
Judg. 4. 18. turn in, my lord, turn in to me, *f. not*
6. 10. I said, *f. not* the gods of the Amorites
23. peace be to thee, *f. not*, thou shalt not die
Ruth 3. 11. and now, my daughter, *f. not*
1 Sam. 4. 20. women that stood by said to her, *f. not*
12. 20. and Samuel said to the people, *f. not*
22. 23. abide thou with me, *f. not*, he that seeketh
23. 17. Jonathan said unto David, *f. not*
2 Sam. 9. 7. David said to Mephibosheth, *f. not*
13. 28. he said to his servants, kill Amnon, *f. not*
1 Kings 17. 13. Elijah said to the widow, *f. not*
2 Kings 6. 16. *f. not* more with us than with them
17. 34. unto this day, they *f. not* the Lord
25. 24. *f. not* to serve Chaldees, *Jer.* 40. 9.
2 Chron. 20. 17. the Lord will be with you, *f. not*
Psal. 55. 19. no changes, therefore they *f. not* God
64. 4. suddenly do they shoot at him, and *f. not*
Isa. 7. 4. *f. not* the tails of smoking firebrands
35. 4. say to them that are of a fearful heart, *f. not*
41. 10. *f.* thou *not*, for I am with thee, 43. 5.
13. for I the Lord thy God will hold thy right hand, saying to thee, *f. not*, I will help thee
14. *f. not*, thou worm Jacob, and ye men of Isr.
43. 1. *f. not*, I have redeemed thee, thou art mine
44. 2. *f. not*, O Jacob my servant, and Jeshurun whom I have chosen, *Jer.* 30. 10. | 46. 27, 28.
8. *f.* ye *not*, nor be afraid, have not I told thee?
51. 7. hearken to me, *f. not* the reproach of men
54. 4. *f. not*, for thou shalt not be ashamed
Jer. 5. 22. *f.* ye *not* me, saith the Lord?
Lam. 3. 57. thou drewest near, thou saidst, *f. not*
Ezek. 3. 9. *f. not*, nor be dismayed at their looks
Dan. 10. 12. then said he to me, *f. not*, Daniel, 19.
Joel 2. 21. *f. not*, O land, be glad and rejoice
Zeph. 3. 16. it shall be said to Jerusalem, *f. not*
Hag. 2. 5. my Spirit remaineth among you, *f. not*
Zech. 8. 13. and ye shall be a blessing, *f. not*
15. again I will do well to Judah, *f.* ye *not*
Mal. 3. 5. a swift witness ag. them that *f. not* me
Mat. 1. 20. *f. not* to take to thee Mary thy wife
10. 26. *f.* them *not*, there is nothing covered
28. and *f. not* them which kill the body
31. *f. not*, ye are of more value, *Luke* 12. 7.
28. 5. the angel said to the women, *f. not*
Luke 1. 13. *f. not*, Zacharias, || 30. *f. not*, Mary
2. 10. to the shepherds, *f. not.* || 5. 10. Simon, *f. not*
8. 50. Jairus, *f. not* || 12. 32. *f. not*, little flock
18. 4. though I *f. not* God, nor regard man
John 12. 15. *f. not*, daughter of Sion, behold
Acts 27. 24. *f. not*, Paul, thou must be before Cesar
Rev. 1. 17. *f. not*, I am the first and the last

Not FEAR.

Exod. 9. 30. I know ye will *not* yet *f.* the Lord
2 Kings 17. 35. ye shall *not f.* other gods, 37.
Job 9. 35. then would I speak, and *not f.* him
11. 15. put iniquity far away, then thou shalt *not f.*
Psal. 27. 3. tho' an host encamp, my heart shall *not f.*
46. 2. we will *not f.* though the earth be removed
56. 4. I will *not f.* what flesh can do, 118. 6.
Isa. 54. 14. far from oppression, thou shalt *not f.*
Jer. 10. 7. who would *not f.* thee, O King of nations?
Amos 3. 8. the lion hath roared, who will *not f.*?
Luke 23. 40. the other said, dost *not* thou *f.* God?
Heb. 13. 6. I will *not f.* what man shall do to me
Rev. 15. 4. who shall *not f.* thee, O L. and glorify?

FEARED.

Gen. 19. 30. Lot *f.* to dwell in Zoar, dwelt in a cave
26. 7. Isaac *f.* to say of Rebekah, she is my wife
Exod. 2. 14. Moses *f.* and said, this thing is known
9. 20. he that *f.* the word of the Ld. made servants
Deut. 25. 18. Amalek smote thee, and *f.* not God
32. 17. to new gods whom your fathers *f.* not
27. were it not that I *f.* the wrath of the enemy
Josh. 4. 14. they *f.* Joshua as they did Moses
Judg. 6. 27. Gideon *f.* || 8. 20. Jether *f.* to slay them
1 Sam. 3. 15. Samuel *f.* to shew Eli the vision

1 Sam. 14. 26. honey dropped, for the peop. *f.* the oath
15. 24. because I *f.* the people, and obeyed them
2 Sam. 3. 11. Ish-bosheth not answer, he *f.* Abner
10. 19. the Syrians *f.* to help Ammon any more
12. 18. David's serv. *f.* to tell him child was dead
1 Kings 1. 50. Adonijah *f.* because of Solomon
3. 28. all Isr. heard the judgment, and *f.* the king
2 Kings 17. 7. *f.* other gods || 25. they *f.* not the L.
1 Chron. 16. 25. to be *f.* above all gods, *Psal.* 96. 4.
2 Chron. 20. 3. Jehoshaphat *f.* and proclaim. a fast
Job 32. † 6. Elihu said, I *f.* to shew mine opinion
Psal. 14. † 5. there they *f.* a great fear, 53. † 5.
76. 7. thou, even thou, art to be *f.* || 8. the earth *f.*
11. bring presents to him that ought to be *f.*
78. 53. he led them safely, so that they *f.* not
130. 4. there is forgiveness, that thou mayest be *f.*
Isa. 41. 5. the isles saw it and *f.* the ends of the earth
51. 13. and hast *f.* continually every day
57. 11. whom hast thou *f.* that thou hast lied
Jer. 3. 8. her treacherous sister Judah *f.* not
42. 16. the sword which ye *f.* shall overtake you
44. 10. they are not humbled, nor have they *f.*
Ezek. 11. 8. ye have *f.* the sword, I will bring it
Dan. 5. 19. all people and nations *f.* before him
Mal. 2. 5. for the fear wherewith he *f.* me
Mat. 14. 5. Herod *f.* the multitude, 21. 46.
Mark 4. 41. and they *f.* exceedingly, and said
6. 20. Herod *f.* John, knowing he was a just man
11. 18. the scribes and the chief priests *f.* Jesus
32. if we shall say of men, they *f.* the people 12, 12. *Luke* 20. 19. | 22. 2. *Acts* 5. 26.
Luke 9. 34. and they *f.* as they entered into the cloud
45. and they *f.* to ask him of that saying
18. 2. there was in a city a judge which *f.* not God
19. 21. I *f.* thee because thou art an austere man
John 9. 22. spake thus, because they *f.* the Jews
Acts 16. 38. the magistrates *f.* when they heard
Heb. 5. 7. Christ was heard in that he *f.*

FEARED *God.*

Exod. 1. 17. but the midwives *f. God*, saved children
21. because they *f. God*, he made them houses
Neh. 7. 2. he was faithful, and *f. God* above many
Job 1. 1. Job was one that *f. God*, and eschewed evil
Acts 10. 2. Cornelius was one *f. God* with his house

FEARED *greatly.*

Josh. 10. 2. the Canaanites *f. greatly*
1 Sam. 12. 18. all the people *greatly f.* the Lord
1 Kings 18. 3. now Obadiah *f.* the Lord *greatly*
Job 3. 25. the thing I *greatly f.* is come upon me
Psal. 89. 7. God is *greatly* to be *f.* in the assembly
Mat. 27. 54. centurion and they with him *f. greatly*

FEARED *the Lord.*

Exod. 14. 31. the people *f. the L.* and believed Moses
2 Kings 17. 32. so they *f. the Lord*, 33, 41.
Hos. 10. 3. no king, because we *f.* not *the Lord*
Jonah 1. 16. the men *f. the Lord* exceedingly
Mal. 3. 16. they that *f. L.* spake oft one to another, a book of remembrance for them that *f. the Lord*

FEAREST.

Gen. 22. 12. for now I know that thou *f.* God
Isa. 57. 11. of whom afraid or feared, have not I held my peace even of old, and thou *f.* me not?
Jer. 22. 25. give thee into hand of them thou *f.*

FEARETH.

1 Kings 1. 51. behold, Adonijah *f.* king Solomon
Job 1. 8. Job, one that *f.* G. and escheweth evil, 2. 3.
Psal. 25. 12. what man is he that *f.* the Lord?
112. 1. blessed is the man that *f.* the Lord
128. 1. blessed is every one that *f.* the Lord
4. thus shall the man be blessed that *f.* the Lord
Prov. 13. 13. that *f.* the commandment be rewarded
14. 2. he that walketh in his uprightness *f.* Lord
16. a wise man *f.* and departeth from evil
28. 14. happy is the man that *f.* always
31. 30. woman that *f.* the Lord shall be praised
Eccl. 7. 18. that *f.* God shall come forth of them all
8. 13. because the wicked *f.* not before God
9. 2. he that sweareth, as he that *f.* an oath
Isa. 50. 10. who is among you that *f.* the Lord
Acts 10. 22. Cornelius just, and one that *f.* God
35. he that *f.* him, is accepted with him
13. 26. and whosoever among you *f.* God
1 John 4. 18. he that *f.* is not perfect in love

FEARING.

Josh. 22. 25. our children cease from *f.* the Lord
Mark 5. 33. the woman *f.* and trembling came
Acts 23. 10. the chief captain *f.* lest Paul be pulled
27. 17. *f.* lest they fall into the quicksands, 29.
Gal. 2. 12. *f.* them which were of the circumcision
Col. 3. 22. but in singleness of heart *f.* God
Heb. 11. 27. forsook Egypt, not *f.* wrath of the king

FEARFUL.

Exod. 15. 11. O Lord, who is like thee, *f.* in praises
Deut. 20. 8. what man is *f.* let him return, *Judg.* 7. 3.
28. 58. mayest fear this *f.* name, the Lord thy God
Isa. 35. 4. say to them of a *f.* heart, be strong
Mat. 8. 26. why are ye *f.* O ye of little faith?
Mark 4. 40. he said to them, why are ye so *f.*?
Luke 21. 11. *f.* sights shall be in divers places
Heb. 10. 27. a certain *f.* looking for of judgment
31. *f.* to fall into the hands of the living God
Rev. 21. 8. the *f.* shall have their part in the lake

FEARFULNESS.

Psal. 55. 5. *f.* and trembling are come upon me
Isa. 21. 4. my heart panted, *f.* affrighted me
33. 14. *f.* hath surprised the hypocrites

FEARFULLY.

Psal. 139. 14. I am *f.* and wonderfully made

FEAST.

God out of his great wisdom appointed several festivals among the Jews for many reasons. 1. *To perpetuate the memory of those great events and wonders which he had wrought in favour of his people: the* Sabbath *brought to remembrance the creation of the world; the* Passover, *the departure out of Egypt; the* Pentecost, *the law given at Sinai,* &c. 2. *To keep them firm to their religion; with the view of ceremonies and the majesty of divine service.* 3. *To give them instruction; for in their religious assemblies the law of God was read and explained.* 4. *To renew the acquaintance, correspondence, and friendship of their tribes and families with one another, by coming from the several towns in the country, and meeting three times a year in the holy city.*

The Hebrews *had a great number of* feasts. *The first, and most ancient of all, was the* sabbath, *or the seventh day of the week, instituted to preserve the memory of the world's creation.* Gen. 2. 3. And God blessed the seventh day, and sanctified it, because in it he had rested from all his work. *Commentators are not agreed about the first institution of the sabbath: many are of opinion that the sabbath hath been observed among the righteous from the beginning of the world: that the ancients having preserved the memory of the creation, observed the sabbath also, in consequence of the natural law which obliged them thereto. Some are of opinion, that people did not begin to cease from work upon that day, till after the command which God gave the* Israelites *to that purpose, some time after their coming out of* Egypt, *when they were encamped at* Marah.

The Sabbatical Year, *which returned every seven years, and was entirely set apart for rest: and* Jubilee year, *which was at the end of seven times seven years, or of the forty-ninth year, were sorts of* feasts *too, and may be considered as consequences of the sabbath.*

The Passover *was celebrated on the fourteenth, or rather fifteenth, day of the first month in the ecclesiastical year, which was the seventh of the civil year. The feast began after noon on the fourteenth, and was celebrated properly on the fifteenth of* Nisan: *it lasted seven days. But the first and last days only of the octave were days of rest,* Exod. 12. 14, &c. See PASSOVER.

The feast of Pentecost *was celebrated on the fiftieth day after the* Passover, *in memory of the laws being given to* Moses *on mount* Sinai *fifty days, or seven weeks, after the departure out of* Egypt. See PENTECOST.

The feast of Trumpets *was celebrated at the beginning, or on the first day, of the civil year, upon which a trumpet was sounded, proclaiming the beginning of the year, which was in the month* Tisri, *answering to our* September. *This day was kept solemn, all servile business was forbid to be done upon it; and particular sacrifices were offered,* Lev. 23. 24, 25. *The Scripture does not acquaint us with the occasion of appointing this* feast. Theodoret *believes, it was in memory of the thunder and lightning upon mount* Sinai, *when God gave his law from hence. The Rabbins will have it, that it was in remembrance of the deliverance of* Isaac, *in whose stead a ram was sacrificed by* Abraham. *Others say, that as the seventh day of every week was a sabbath, and every seventh year was to be kept as a holy* sabbatical year, *so the seventh month was to be holy in some singular manner above the rest of the months, for the many sabbaths and solemn feasts that were to be observed in this more than any other month; such as the* feast of Expiation, *and of* Tabernacles.

The New Moons, *or first days of every month, were in some sort a consequence of the* feast of Trumpets. *And though these were not reckoned among the solemn feasts in* Lev. 23. *yet were celebrated as such, by the sound of trumpets,* Num. 10. 10. *by extraordinary sacrifices,* Num. 28. 11, 12, &c. *by abstaining from servile works,* Amos 8. 5. *and by attendance upon the ministry of God's word,* 2 Kings 4. 23. *Upon these days also some sort of entertainments were made,* 1 Sam. 20. 5, 18. *And God ordained it thus, that by giving him the first-fruits of every month they should acknowledge him as the Lord of all their time, and own his providence, by which all times and seasons are ordered.*

The feast of Expiation, *or* Atonement, *was kept upon the tenth day of the month* Tisri, *or* September. *The* Hebrews *call it* Kippur, *or* Chippur, *that is,* pardon, *or* expiation, *because it was instituted for the* expiation *of all the sins, irreverences, and pollutions of all the* Israelites, *from the high priest to the lowest of the people, committed by them throughout the whole year. Upon this day they fasted strictly, and offered several sacrifices. The high priest, after he had washed not only his hands and his feet, as usual in common sacrifices, but his whole body, dressed himself in plain linen, like the rest of the priests. He then neither wore his purple robe, nor the ephod, nor the breastplate, because he was going to expiate his own and the people's sins. He first of all offered a bullock and a ram for his own sins, and those of all the other priests. He put his hands upon the heads of these victims, and confessed his own sins, and the sins of his house: then he received from the princes of the people two goats for a sin-offering, and a ram for a burnt-offering, to be offered in the name of all the multitude,* Lev. 16. 2, 3, &c. *As to the ceremonies used with the goats,* see OFFERING.

The feast of Tents or Tabernacles. *See* TABERNACLE.

Besides these feasts mentioned by Moses, *we find the* feast of Lots, *or* Purim, *which was celebrated among the* Jews *of* Shushan, *on the fourteenth day of* Adar; *and among the other people of the* Persian *empire on the fifteenth of the same month, which answers to our* February, *Esth.* 9. 21. *The* Jews *observe the first of these days with fasting and crying, and other expressions of vehement grief and fear; and the latter with thanksgiving, and all demonstrations of joy and triumph. See* PURIM.

The feast of the Dedication of the Temple, *or rather of the restoration of the temple, which had been profaned by* Antiochus Epiphanes, *which is thought to be the* feast *mentioned in the gospel,* John 10. 22. *was celebrated in the winter.* Josephus *says, it was called* the feast of Lights; *probably this happiness befell them when they least expected it; and they looked upon it as a new light that had risen upon them,* Joseph. Antiq. lib. 12. cap. 11. *There is an account of this dedication in* 1 Maccab. 4. 52, 54, 55, &c. *where it is related, that* Judas Maccabeus *and his brethren having defeated the army of* Gorgias, *they went directly to the temple of* Jerusalem, *which they found forsaken and profaned, so that the courts were full of thick bushes and brambles, the doors were burnt, the altar profaned, and the buildings in ruins. After having shed abundance of tears on this occasion, they began to clean every thing, and employed the priests in demolishing the* altar *which had been polluted; and erected another of rough stone. They refitted the* holy place *and the* sanctuary, *and placed therein the* candlestick, *the* table of shew-bread, *and the* altar of perfumes. *They kindled the* lamps, *put the loaves upon the sacred table, set the incense on fire, offered sacrifices and burnt-offerings, and performed the dedication of the temple in eight days, with all the solemnity that circumstances would allow of. After which* Judas Maccabeus *made it a law, that the* feast *should be kept yearly for eight days, in memory of that mercy which God had shewed them. It is generally agreed that it was during this* feast *our Saviour was at* Jerusalem. *It was celebrated upon the twenty-fifth and following days of the month* Casleu, *which answers to our* November *and* December, *and it is therefore said,* that it was winter.

Love-feasts, *or* feasts of charity, *were used among the primitive Christians in the public meetings of the church, to shew their unity among themselves, to promote and maintain mutual charity, and for the relief of the poor among them, at the close whereof they administered the Lord's supper,* Jude 12. *But these feasts being abused, some think that the apostle* Paul *abolished them,* 1 Cor. 11. 21, 22, 34.

In the Christian church *we have no festival that appears clearly to have been instituted by* Christ Jesus, *or his apostles. Nevertheless, as some say, our Saviour seems to have instituted a* feast, *in a perpetual memory of his passion and death, when he instituted the sacrament of bread and wine as symbols of his body and blood, and pledges of spiritual blessings.* Christians *have always celebrated the memory of* Christ's *resurrection, and keep this feast on every first day of the week; which day was called the* Lord's day, *even so early as in* St. John's *time;* Rev. 1. 10. I was in the Spirit on the *Lord's day.*

Gen. 19. 3. Lot made a *f.* ‖ 21. 8. Abraham made a *f.*
26. 30. Isaac made a *f.* ‖ 29. 22. Laban made a *f.*
40. 20. Pharaoh made a *f.* to all his servants
Exod. 5. 1. that they may hold a *f.* unto me, 10. 9.
12. 14. you shall keep it a *f. Lev.* 23. 39, 41.
13. 6. the seventh day shall be a *f.* to the Lord
23. 14. three times thou shalt keep a *f.* in the year
16. the *f.* of harvest, the first-fruits of thy labours
32. 5. Aaron said, to-morrow is a *f.* to the Lord
Num. 28. 17. the fifteenth day of this month is the *f.*
29. 12. ye shall keep a *f.* to the Lord seven days
Deut. 16. 14. and thou shalt rejoice in thy *f.*
Judg. 14. 10. and Samson made there a *f.*
12. declare it within the seven days of the *f.*
17. and she wept before him while their *f.* lasted
1 *Sam.* 9. † 12. there is a *f.* to-day in the high place
20. † 6. there is a yearly *f.* for all the family
25. 36. Nabal held a *f.* in his house like a king
2 *Sam.* 3. 20. David made Abner and his men a *f.*
1 *Kings* 3. 15. Solomon made a *f.* to his serv. 8. 65.
8. 2. all the men of Israel assembled at the *f.*
12. 32. Jeroboam ordained a *f.* like to the *f.* that is in Judah, and he offered upon the altar
33. he ordained a *f.* to the children of Israel
2 *Chr.* 5. 3. the *f.* in the seventh month, *Neh.* 8. 14.
7. 8. Solomon kept the *f.* seven days, and all Israel with him, 9. | 30. 22. *Neh.* 8. 18. *Ezek.* 45. 25.
Esth. 1. 3. Ahasuerus made a *f.* 5. | 2. 18.
9. Vashti made a *f.* ‖ 8. 17. the Jews had a *f.*
Prov. 15. 15. a merry heart hath a continual *f.*
Eccl. 10. 19. *f.* is made for laughter, wine makes merry
Isa. 25. 6. the Lord shall make to all people a *f.*
Jer. 16. † 5. enter not the house of mourning *f.*
Ezek. 45. 23. seven days of the *f.* he shall prepare
Dan. 5. 1. Belshazzar the king made a great *f.*
Mat. 27. 15. at that *f.* the governor was wont to release to the people a prisoner, *Mark* 15. 6.
Luke 2. 42. they went up after the custom of the *f.*
5. 29. Levi made him a great *f.* in his house
14. 13. but when thou makest a *f.* call the poor
23. 17. he must release one unto them at the *f.*
John 2. 8. draw, and bear to the governor of the *f.*
9. when the ruler of the *f.* tasted the water
4. 45. the Galileans having seen all that he did at the *f.* at Jerusalem, for they also went to the *f.*
5. 1. after this there was a *f.* of the Jews
6. 4. the passover, a *f.* of the Jews, was nigh
7. 8. go ye up to this *f.* I go not up yet to this *f.*
10. then went he also up to the *f.* not openly
11. then the Jews sought him at the *f.* and said
14. now about the midst of the *f.* Jesus taught
37. in the last day, that great day of the *f.*
10. 22. it was at Jerusalem the *f.* of dedication
11. 56. what think ye, that he will not come to *f.*?
12. 12. next day much people that were come to *f.*
20. certain Greeks among them that came to *f.*
13. 29. buy what we have need of against the *f.*
Acts 18. 21. I must by all means keep this *f.*
1 *Cor.* 5. 8. let us keep the *f.* not with old leaven
10. 27. if any that believe not bid you to a *f.*

FEAST-*day, days.*

Hos. 2. 11. I will also cause her *f.-days* to cease
9. 5. what will ye do in *day* of the *f.* of the Lord?
Amos 5. 21. I hate, I despise your *f.-days*
Mat. 26. 5. they said, not on the *f.-day, Mark* 14. 2.
John 2. 23. in the *f.-day* many believed in his name

FEAST *of the passover.*

Exod. 34. 25. nor the sacrifice of *f. of passover* be left
Mat. 26. 2. after two days is *f. of passover, Mark* 14. 1.
Luke 2. 41. every year at *f. of pass.* his parents went
John 13. 1. before *f. of passover* Jesus knew his hour

Solemn FEAST.

Deut. 16. 15. seven days shalt thou keep a *solemn f.*
Psal. 81. 3. blow the trumpet on our *solemn f.*-day
Lam. 2. 7. made a noise as in the *solemn f.*-day

FEAST *of tabernacles.*

Lev. 23. 34. the fifteenth day shall be *f. of taber.*
Deut. 16. 13. thou shalt observe *f. of tab.* seven days
16. three times appear in *f. of tabernacles,* 31. 10. 2 *Chron.* 8. 13.
Ezra 3. 4. they kept *f. of tabernac.* as it is written
Zech. 14. 16. shall even go up to keep *f. of tabernac.*
18. heathen that come not to keep *f. of taber.* 19.
John 7. 2. now the Jews' *f. of tabernac.* was at hand

FEAST *of unleavened bread.*

Exod. 12. 17. ye shall obs. *f. of unl. br.* 23. 15. | 34. 18.
Lev. 23. 6. and on fifteenth day is *f. of unleav. br.*
Deut. 16. 16. appear in *f. of unl. br.* 2 *Chr.* 8. 13.
2 *Chr.* 30. 13. people assembled to keep *f. of unl. br.*
21. children of Isr. kept *f. of unl. br.* seven days
35. 17. *f. of un. b.* seven days, *Ezra* 6. 22. *Ezek.* 45. 21.
Mat. 26. 17. first day of *f. of unl. br.* disciples came
Mark 14. 1. after two days was *f. of un. br. Luke* 22. 1.

FEAST *of weeks.*

Exod. 34. 22. thou shalt obs. *f. of w. Deut.* 16. 10.
Deut. 16. 16. all thy males appear in the *f. of weeks*
2 *Chr.* 8. 13. Solomon offered burnt-offer. in *f. of w.*

FEAST, ED.

Job 1. 4. his sons went and *f.* in their houses
2 *Pet.* 2. 13. sporting, while they *f.* with you
Jude 12. these are spots, when they *f.* with you

FEASTING.

Esth. 9. 17. made it a day of *f.* and gladness, 18.
22. they should make them days of *f.* and joy
Job 1. 5. when the days of their *f.* were gone
Eccl. 7. 2. of mourning, than to go to the house of *f.*
Jer. 16. 8. thou shalt not go into the house of *f.*

FEASTS.

Lev. 23. 2. even these are my *f.* 4, 37, 44.
Psal. 35. 16. with hypocritical mockers in *f.*
Isa. 5. 12. the harp, pipe, and wine are in their *f.*
Jer. 51. 39. in their heat I will make their *f.*
Ezek. 45. 17. the princes part to give offerings in *f.*
46. 11. in *f.* the meat-offering shall be an ephah
Amos 8. 10. I will turn your *f.* into mourning
Zech. 8. 19. shall be joy, gladness, and cheerful *f.*
Mat. 23. 6. they love the uppermost rooms at *f.* and chief seats in synagog. *Mark* 12. 39. *Luke* 20. 46.
Jude 12. these are spots in your *f.* of charity

Appointed FEASTS.

Isa. 1. 14. your *app. f.* my soul hateth, a trouble

Set FEASTS.

Num. 29. 39. these things ye shall do in your *set f.*
1 *Chron.* 23. 31. to offer on the *set f. Ezra* 3. 5.
2 *Chron.* 31. 3. the king's portion for the *set f.*
Neh. 10. 33. we charged for offerings in the *set f.*

Solemn FEASTS.

Num. 15. 3. when you make offer. in your *sol. f.*
2 *Chr.* 2. 4. build an house for offering on *solemn f.*
8. 13. offering on *solemn f.* three times in a year
Lam. 1. 4. because none come to the *solemn f.*
2. 6. he hath caused the *solemn f.* to be forgotten
Ezek. 36. 38. as the flock of Jerusalem in *solemn f.*
46. 9. when people come before the Lord in *sol. f.*
Hos. 2. 11. I will cause to cease her *solemn f.*
12. 9. make thee dwell as in the days of *solemn f.*
Nah. 1. 15. O Judah, keep thy *sol. f.* perform vows
Mal. 2. 3. even the dung of your *solemn f.*

FEATHERED, *see* FOWL.

FEATHERS.

Lev. 1. 16. shall pluck away his crop with his *f.*
Job 39. 13. gavest thou the goodly wings to the peacock? or wings and *f.* to the ostrich?
Psal. 68. 13. and her *f.* covered with yellow gold
91. 4. shall cover thee with his *f.* under his wings
Ezek. 17. 3. an eagle long-winged, full of *f.* 7.
Dan. 4. 33. his hairs were grown like eagle's *f.*

FED.

Gen. 30. 36. Jacob *f.* the rest of Laban's flock
36. 24. as he *f.* the asses of Zibeon his father
41. 2. and the seven kine *f.* in a meadow, 18.
47. 17. he *f.* them with bread for their cattle
48. 15. the God who *f.* me all my life long
Exod. 16. 32. the bread wherewith I have *f.* you.
Deut. 8. 3. he *f.* thee with manna, thou knewest not
16. who *f.* thee in the wilderness with manna
2 *Sam.* 20. 3. put the concubines in ward, and *f.* them
1 *Kings* 18. 4. he *f.* them with bread and water, 13.
1 *Chron.* 27. 29. over the herds that *f.* in Sharon
Psal. 37. 3. trust in the Lord, verily thou shalt be *f.*
78. 72. so he *f.* them, according to his integrity
81. 16. he should have *f.* them with finest of wheat
Isa. 1. 11. I am full of the fat of *f.* beasts
Jer. 5. 7. when I had *f.* them to the full, they comm.
8. they were as *f.* horses in the morning
Ezek. 16. 19. and my honey wherewith I *f.* thee
34. 3. ye eat the fat, and kill them that are *f.*
8. the shepherds *f.* themselves, and *f.* not my flock
Dan. 4. 12. and all flesh was *f.* with it
5. 21. they *f.* Nebuchadnezzar with grass, like oxen
Zech. 11. 7. I took two staves, and I *f.* the flock
Mat. 25. 37. when saw we thee hungred, and *f.* thee?
Mark 5. 14. they that *f.* the swine fled, *Luke* 8. 34.
Luke 16. 21. desiring to be *f.* with crumbs that fell
1 *Cor.* 3. 2. I have *f.* you with milk, not with meat

FEE.

Dan. 2. † 6. ye shall receive of me, gifts and *f.*
5. † 17. give thy *f.* to another, yet I will read

FEEBLE.

Gen. 30. 42. when cattle were *f.* he put them not in
Deut. 25. 18. the Amalekites smote all that were *f.*
1 *Sam.* 2. 5. that hath many children, is waxen *f.*
2 *Sam.* 4. 1. Abner dead, Ish-bosheth's hands were *f.*
2 *Chron.* 28. 15. carried all the *f.* of them on asses
Neh. 4. 2. and he said, what do these *f.* Jews?
Job 4. 4. and thou hast strengthened the *f.* knees
Psal. 38. 8. I am *f.* and sore broken, I have roared
105. 37. was not one *f.* person amongst their tribes
Prov. 30. 26. the conies are but a *f.* folk, yet make
Isa. 16. 14. the remnant shall be very small and *f.*
35. 3. strengthen the weak hands, confirm *f.* knees

Jer. 6. 24. we have heard the fame, our hands wax *f.*
49. 24. Damascus is waxed *f.* and turneth to flee
50. 43. the king of Babylon's hands waxed *f.*
Ezek. 7. 17. all hands shall be *f.* 21. 7.
Zech. 12. 8. and he that is *f.* shall be as David
1 *Cor.* 12. 22. the members which seem to be more *f.*
1 *Thess.* 5. 14. brethren, comfort the *f.* minded
Heb. 12. 12. lift up the hands and the *f.* knees

FEEBLER.

Gen. 30. 42. so the *f.* were Laban's, stronger Jacob's

FEEBLENESS.

Jer. 47. 3. the fathers shall not look back for *f.*

FEED.

To feed *signifies to eat, to take meat or nourishment for the body, and this is common to man with the beasts.* Jude 12. Feeding themselves without fear. *Isa.* 27. 10. There shall the calf feed, and there shall he lie down. *It also signifies to furnish or supply others with food; thus* Joseph *fed the* Egyptians *for their cattle: that is, he gave them food and provision for one year, for which they gave him their cattle,* Gen. 47. 17. *And* Agar *prays that* God would feed him with food convenient for him; *that he would furnish him with food suitable to his necessities and occasions,* Prov. 30. 8.

But feeding, *generally in Scripture, is taken for the business and calling of a shepherd, and comprehends all the duties belonging to that office: not only that of feeding, or providing pasture for his flock, but also of guiding, observing, and defending them. In this sense,* feeding *is applied,*
I. *To* God, *and that* (1) *In respect of his church, which he rules, defends, directs, sustains, and nourishes, both inwardly, by the gifts and graces of his Spirit; and outwardly, by his power and providence,* Gen. 48. 15. The God which fed me all my life long unto this day. *And the* Psalmist, Feed them also, and lift them up for ever, *Psal.* 28. 9. *Hence God is called a* Shepherd, *Psal.* 23. 1. The Lord is my Shepherd: *he provides for me, he brings me out of the wrong way, and guides me in the right.* (2) *In respect of the ungodly, upon whom he executes his judgments.* Ezek. 34. 16. I will feed them with judgment. *And in* Hos. 4. 16. The Lord will feed them as a lamb in a large place; *he will make them to wander, like a lost lamb in a wilderness, and scatter them into* Assyria. (3) *In respect of the creatures which receive their supplies wholly from God.* Psal. 145. 15. The eyes of all wait upon thee, and thou givest them their meat in due season. *Mat.* 6. 26. The fowls of the air neither sow nor reap, yet your heavenly Father feedeth them.
II. *To* Christ. *Isa.* 40. 11. He shall feed his flock like a shepherd. *And our Saviour says of himself,* I am the good Shepherd, *John* 10. 11. Christ Jesus *performs all the offices of a tender and faithful Shepherd towards his people, carrying himself with great wisdom, and condescension, and compassion, to every one of them, according to their several capacities and infirmities: he feeds them by his word, Spirit, grace, fulness, redemption, ordinances, and providences.*
III. *To* man. *And then, besides the common acceptation of the word, for feeding cattle, it is taken,* (1) *For instructing and teaching others by wholesome doctrine; for ruling and censuring by ecclesiastical discipline,* John 21. 15, 16. Feed my lambs: Feed my sheep. *And in* Jer. 3. 15. I will give you pastors according to mine heart, which shall feed you with knowledge and understanding. (2) *For ruling and governing politically. Thus kings and magistrates are compared to shepherds,* 2 Sam. 5. 2. Thou shalt feed my people *Israel*, Psal. 78. 71. He brought *David* to feed Jacob his people.
IV. *To* the enemies of the church, *whom God sometimes makes use of for the chastisement of his people.* Jer. 6. 3. *The* Babylonian *princes, with their armies,* shall feed every one *in his place: they shall take up their quarters in the places assigned them, and make spoil of all they can find there.*
V. *To such as flatter themselves with vain hopes of help and assistance,* Hos. 12. 1. *Ephraim* feedeth on wind: *the ten tribes flatter themselves with hopes of help from the* Egyptians *and* Assyrians, *but they are supporting themselves with hopes as unfit to sustain them, as the wind is to feed the body and nourish it: they make new alliances and friendships, but all of them will prove lies to them at last, like the wind they feed upon.*
VI. *To* rulers, *both* political *and* ecclesiastical, *who contrive their own ease, advantage, honour, and ambitious projects; but feed not their flocks; take no care to support them, either with wholesome counsel, or necessary relief, as they ought to do, according to their respective offices.* Ezek. 34. 2, 3. Woe to the shepherds that do feed themselves: should not the shepherds feed the flocks? Ye kill them that are fed; but ye feed not the flock.

Gen. 37. 12. his brethren went to *f.* their father's flock
16. tell me, I pray, where they *f.* their flocks
46. 32. for their trade hath been to *f.* cattle
Exod. 22. 5. and shall *f.* in another man's field
34. 3. neither let flocks *f.* before that mount
2 *Sam.* 5. 2. thou shalt *f.* my people Israel
7. 7. whom I commanded to *f.* Israel, 1 *Chr.* 17. 6.
1 *Kings* 17. 4. have commanded the ravens to *f.* thee
Job 24. 2. they take away flocks and *f.* thereof
20. the worms shall *f.* sweetly on him
Psal. 28. 9. *f.* them, and lift them up for ever
49. 14. laid in the grave, death shall *f.* on them
78. 71. he brought David to *f.* Jacob his people
Prov. 10. 21. the lips of the righteous *f.* many
Cant. 4. 5. like two roes which *f.* among the lilies
6. 2. my beloved is gone to *f.* in the gardens
Isa. 5. 17. the lambs shall *f.* after their manner
11. 7. and the cow and the bear shall *f.*
14. 30. and the first-born of the poor shall *f.*
Isa. 27. 10. there shall the calf *f.* and shall lie down
30. 23. thy cattle shall *f.* in large pastures
40. 11. he shall *f.* his flock as a shepherd
49. 9. they shall *f.* in the ways and high places
61. 5. and strangers shall stand and *f.* your flocks
65. 25. the wolf and the lamb shall *f.* together
Jer. 2. † 16. the children of Noph *f.* on thy crown
3. 15. pastors who shall *f.* you with knowledge
6. 3. they shall *f.* every one in his place
23. 2. against the pastors that *f.* my people
4. I will set up shepherds which shall *f.* them
50. 19. Israel shall *f.* on Carmel and Bashan
Lam. 4. 5. they that *f.* delicately are desolate
Ezek. 34. 2. woe to the shepherds that do *f.* thems.
3. ye eat the fat, but ye *f.* not the flock
10. neither shall the shepherds *f.* themselves
23. even my servant David shall *f.* them
Dan. 11. 26. they that *f.* of his meat destroy him
Hos. 4. 16. now the Lord will *f.* them as a lamb
9. 2. the flour and the wine-press shall not *f.* them
Jonah 3. 7. let them not *f.* nor drink water
Mic. 5. 4. he shall *f.* in the strength of the Lord
Zeph. 2. 7. they shall *f.* thereupon, God shall visit
3. 13. they shall *f.* none shall make them afraid
Zech. 11. 9. then said I, I will not *f.* you
16. the shepherd shall not *f.* that standeth still
Mat. 2. † 6. out of thee a Governor that shall *f.*
Luke 15. 15. he sent him to his fields to *f.* swine
Acts 20. 28. take heed to *f.* the church of God
1 *Cor.* 9. † 13. they *f.* of the things of the temple
13. 3. though I give all my goods to *f.* the poor
Rev. 7. 17. for the Lamb shall *f.* them and lead them
12. 6. that they should *f.* her there 1260 days

FEED, *Imperatively.*

Gen. 25. 30. *f.* me with that same red pottage
29. 7. water ye the sheep, and go and *f.* them
1 *Kings* 22. 27. *f.* him with bread and water of affliction, until I come in peace, 2 *Chr.* 18. 26.
Prov. 30. 8. *f.* me with food convenient for me
Cant. 1. 8. *f.* thy kids beside the shepherds' tents
Mic. 7. 14. *f.* thy people with thy rod, the flock
Zech. 11. 4. saith Lord, *f.* the flock of the slaughter
John 21. 15. *f.* my lambs ‖ 16. *f.* my sheep, 17.
Rom. 12. 20. if thine enemy hunger, *f.* him
1 *Pet.* 5. 2. *f.* the flock of God which is among you

I will FEED.

Gen. 30. 31. *I will* again *f.* and keep thy flock
2 *Sam.* 19. 33. *I will f.* thee with me in Jerusalem
Isa. 49. 26. *I will f.* them that oppress thee
58. 14. *I will f.* thee with the heritage of Jacob
Jer. 9. 15. *I will f.* them with wormwood, 23. 15.
Ezek. 34. 13. *I will f.* them upon the mountains
14. *I will f.* them in a good pasture, on mountains
15. *I will f.* my flock, and cause them to lie down
16. *I will f.* the fat and the strong with judgment
Zech. 11. 7. *I will f.* the flock of slaughter, the poor

FEEDER.

Gen. 4. †2. Abel was *f.* of sheep, Cain tiller of ground

FEEDEST.

Psal. 80. 5. thou *f.* them with the bread of tears
Cant. 1. 7. tell me where thou *f.* thy flock

FEEDETH.

Prov. 15. 14. the mouth of fools *f.* on foolishness
28. † 7. he that *f.* gluttons, shameth his father
Cant. 2. 16. my beloved *f.* among the lilies, 6. 3.
Isa. 44. 20. he *f.* on ashes, a deceived heart turned him
Hos. 12. 1. Ephraim *f.* on wind followeth east-wind
Mat. 6. 26. yet your heavenly Father *f.* them
Luke 12. 24. the ravens sow not, yet God *f.* them
1 *Cor.* 9. 7. who *f.* a flock, and eateth not the milk

FEEDING.

Gen. 37. 2. Joseph was *f.* his flock with his brethren
Job 1. 14. the oxen were plowing, the asses *f.* by
Ezek. 34. 10. cause them to cease from *f.* the flock
Nah. 2. 11. where is the *f.* place of young lions?
Mat. 8. 30. an herd of swine *f.* *Mark* 5. 11. *Luke* 8. 32.
Luke 17. 7. which of you having a servant *f.* cattle
Jude 12. *f.* thems. without fear, clouds without water

FEEL.

Gen. 27. 12. my father peradventure will *f.* me
21. come near, that I may *f.* thee, my son
Judg. 16. 26. suffer me that I may *f.* the pillars
Job 20. 20. surely he shall not *f.* quietness
Psal. 58. 9. before your pots can *f.* the thorns
Eccl. 8. 5. whoso keepeth commandm. shall *f.* no evil
Acts 17. 27. seek the L. if haply they might *f.* after

FEELING.

Eph. 4. 19. who being past *f.* have given themselves
Heb. 4. 15. touched with the *f.* of our infirmities

FEET.

Gen. 29. † 1. then Jacob lift up his *f.* and came
49. 10. nor a lawgiver from between his *f.* till
33. Jacob gathered up *f.* in the bed, yielded ghost
Exod. 3. 5. put thy shoes from off thy *f.* *Acts* 7. 33.
11. † 8. get out, and the people that is at thy *f.*
12. 11. shall eat the passover with shoes on your *f.*
Lev. 11. 21. have legs above their *f.* ye may eat
Deut. 2. 28. only I will pass through on my *f.*
11. † 6. all the substance which was at their *f.*
28. 57. young one that cometh from between her *f.*
33. 3. and they sat down at thy *f.* every one
Josh. 3. 15. the *f.* of the priests were dipped in Jordan
9. 5. old shoes, and clouted upon their *f.*
10. 24. put your *f.* on the necks of these kings
14. 9. the land whereon thy *f.* have trodden
Judg. 1. † 7. having thumbs of hands and *f.* cut off
3. 24. surely he covereth his *f.* in his chamber
4. 15. so that Sisera fled away on his *f.* 17.
5. † 15. Barak was sent on his *f.* into the valley
27. at her *f.* bowed, at her *f.* he fell down dead
Ruth 3. 4. go in, uncover his *f.* and lay thee down
8. he turned, and behold a woman lay at his *f.*
1 *Sam.* 2. 9. he will keep the *f.* of his saints
14. 13. Jonathan climbed on his hands and *f.*
24. 3. and Saul went in to cover his *f.*
25. † 27. young men that walk at the *f.* of my lord
42. Abigail rode with five damsels at her *f.*
2 *Sam.* 2. † 18. Asahel was light of his *f.* as a roe
3. 34. hands not bound, nor thy *f.* put into fetters
4. 4. Jonathan's son was lame of his *f.* 9. 3, 13.
12. they cut off their hands and their *f.*
19. 24. Mephibosheth had not dressed his *f.*
2 *Sam.* 22. 34. maketh my *f.* like hinds' *f.* and setteth me upon high places, *Psal.* 18. 33. *Hab.* 3. 19
37. so that my *f.* did not slip, *Psal.* 18. 36.
1 *Kings* 2. 5. put the blood of war in shoes on his *f.*
14. 6. when Ahijah heard the sound of her *f.*
12. when thy *f.* enter the city, the child shall die
15. 23. Asa was diseased in his *f.* 2 *Chron.* 16. 12
2 *Kings* 3. † 9. no water for the cattle at their *f.*
4. 27. when she came, she caught him by the *f.*
6. 32. is not the sound of his master's *f.* behind him?
9. 35. but they found no more of her than the *f.*
13. 21. dead man revived, and stood upon his *f.*
18. † 27. that they may drink the water of their *f.*
21. 8. nor make the *f.* of Israel move any more
1 *Chron.* 28. 2. then David the king stood on his *f.*
Neh. 9. 21. clothes waxed not old, their *f.* swelled not
Job 12. 5. he that is ready to slip with his *f.*
13. 27. thou puttest my *f.* in the stocks, 33. 11. thou settest a print upon the heels of my *f.*
18. 8. for he is cast into a net by his own *f.*
11. terrors make afraid, and drive him to his *f.*
29. 15. I was eyes to the blind, *f.* was I to the lame
30. 12. the youth rise, they push away my *f.*
39. † 21. his *f.* dig in the valley, he rejoiceth
Psal. 22. 16. they pierced my hands and my *f.*
25. 15. for he shall pluck my *f.* out of the net
31. 8. thou hast set my *f.* in a large room
40. 2. he set my *f.* on rock, and established my goings
56. 13. wilt thou not deliver my *f.* from falling?
66. 9. and suffereth not our *f.* to be moved
73. 2. but as for me, my *f.* were almost gone
74. 3. lift up thy *f.* to the perpetual desolations
105. 18. whose *f.* they hurt with fetters
115. 7. *f.* have they, but they walk not, nor speak
116. 8. thou hast delivered my *f.* from falling
119. 59. I turned my *f.* unto thy testimonies
101. I refrained my *f.* from every evil way
105. thy word is a lamp to my *f.* a light to my path
122. 2. our *f.* shall stand within thy gates
Prov. 1. 16. their *f.* run to evil, 6. 18. *Isa.* 59. 7.
4. 26. ponder the path of thy *f.* ways be established
5. 5. her *f.* go down to death, steps take hold on hell
6. 13. the wicked man speaketh with his *f.*
28. can one go on coals, and his *f.* not be burnt?
7. 11. she is loud, her *f.* abide not in her house
19. 2. and he that hasteth with his *f.* sinneth
26. 6. cutteth off the *f.* and drinketh damage
29. 5. a flatterer spreadeth a net for his *f.*
Cant. 7. 1. how beautiful are thy *f.* with shoes!
Isa. 3. 16. and making a tinkling with their *f.*
18. Lord take away the ornaments about their *f.*
6. 2. with twain he covered his *f.* with twain did fly
7. 20. the Lord shall shave the hair of the *f.*
23. 7. her own *f.* shall carry her afar off to sojour.
26. 6. the *f.* of the poor shall tread it down
32. 20. that send forth the *f.* of the ox and ass
41. 3. by the way that he had not gone with his *f.*
49. 23. they shall lick up the dust of thy *f.*
52. 7. the *f.* of him that bringeth good tidings
60. 13. I will make the place of my *f.* glorious
Jer. 13. 16. before your *f.* stumble on the mountains
14. 10. loved to wander, have not refrained their *f.*
18. 22. they digged a pit, and hid snares for my *f.*
38. 22. thy *f.* are sunk in the mire, and are turned
Lam. 1. 13. he hath spread a net for my *f.*
Ezek. 1. 7. and their *f.* were straight *f.*
2. 1. he said to me, son of man, stand upon thy *f.*
2. and the Spirit set me upon my *f.* 3. 24.
16. 25. hast opened thy *f.* to every one that passed by
24. 17. and put on thy shoes upon thy *f.*
23. tires shall be on your heads, shoes on your *f.*
25. 6. because thou hast stamped with the *f.*
32. 2. thou troubledst the waters with thy *f.*
34. 18. but ye must foul the residue with your *f.*
19. what ye have trodden and fouled with your *f.*
37. 10. they lived, and stood up upon their *f.*
Dan. 2. 33. his *f.* part of iron, and part clay, 42.
34. a stone smote the image upon his *f.*
41. thou sawest the *f.* and toes part of clay
7. 7. and stamped the residue with the *f.* of it, 19.
10. 6. his *f.* like polished brass, *Rev.* 1. 15. | 2. 18.
Nah. 1. 3. and the clouds are the dust of his *f.*
15. the *f.* of him that bringeth good tidings
Zech. 14. 4. his *f.* shall stand upon mount of Olives
Mat. 10. 14. when ye depart out of that house or city, shake off the dust of your *f.* *Mark* 6. 11. *Luke* 9. 5.
15. 30. cast the lame and blind down at Jesus' *f.*
18. 8. rather than having two *f.* to be cast into fire
28. 9. they held him by the *f.* and worshipped him
Luke 1. 79. to guide our *f.* into the way of peace
7. 38. she kissed his *f.* and anointed them
45. this woman hath not ceased to kiss my *f.*
8. 35. they found a man sitting at the *f.* of Jesus
41. Jairus fell down at Jesus' *f.* and besought him
10. 39. Mary, who sat at Jesus' *f.* heard his word
15. 22. put a ring on his hand, and shoes on his *f.*
24. 39. behold my hands and my *f.* that it is I
40. he shewed them his hands and his *f.*
John 11. 2. and wiped his *f.* with her hair, 12. 3.
12. 3. and Mary anointed the *f.* of Jesus
20. 12. one angel at the head, the other at the *f.*
Acts 3. 7. and immediately his *f.* received strength
4. 35. laid them down at the apostles' *f.* 37. | 5. 2.
5. 9. the *f.* of them who have buried thy husband
7. 58. they laid their clothes at a young man's *f.*
13. 25. shoes of his *f.* I am not worthy to loose
51. they shook off the dust of their *f.* against them
14. 8. there sat at Lystra a man impotent in his *f.*
10. Paul said, stand upright on thy *f.* he leaped
16. 24. who made their *f.* fast in the stocks
21. 11. Agabus bound his own hands and *f.*
22. 3. yet brought up at the *f.* of Gamaliel
26. 16. but rise, and stand upon thy *f.*
Rom. 3. 15. their *f.* are swift to shed blood
10. 15. the *f.* of them that preach the gospel
1 *Cor.* 12. 21. nor head to the *f.* I have no need of you
Eph. 6. 15. your *f.* shod with the preparation of gospel
Heb. 12. 13. and make straight paths for your *f.*
Rev. 3. 9. make them come and worship before thy *f.*
10. 1. another mighty angel, his *f.* as pillars of fire
11. 11. the two witnesses stood upon their *f.*
13. 2. his *f.* were as *f.* of a bear, mouth of a lion

Rev. 22. 8. I fell down to worship before his f.
At his FEET.
Exod. 4. 25. Zipporah cast the foreskin at his f.
Judg. 4. 10. Barak went with ten thousand at his f.
Ruth 3. 14. she lay at his f. until the morning
1 Sam. 25. 24. Abigail fell at his f. and said
2 Kings 4. 37. the woman of Shunem fell at his f.
Esth. 8. 3. Esther fell down at his f. and besought him
Hab. 3. 5. and burning coals went forth at his f.
Mat. 18. 29. his fellow-servant fell down at his f.
Mark 5. 22. Jairus, when he saw him, fell at his f.
7. 25. Syrophenician woman came, and fell at his f.
Luke 7. 38. she stood at his f. behind him weeping
John 11. 32. Mary fell down at his f. saying
Acts 5. 10. Sapphira fell at his f. and yielded up ghost
10. 25. Cornelius met him, and fell down at his f.
Rev. 1. 17. when I saw him, I fell at his f. as dead
19. 10. and I fell at his f. to worship him
FEET joined with *sole* or *soles*.
Deut. 11. 24. soles of your f. tread shall be yours
Josh. 3. 13. as soon as soles of the priests' f. 4. 18.
1 Kings 5. 3. till L. put them under the soles of his f.
2 Kin. 19. 24. with s. of my f. have dried, Is. 37. 25.
Isa. 60. 14. shall bow down at the soles of thy f.
Ezek. 1. 7. the sole of their f. was like a calf's foot
43. 7. the place of soles of my f. no more defiled
Mal. 4. 3. wicked shall be ashes under s. of your f.
Under FEET.
Exod. 24. 10. under his f. as it were a sapphire stone
2 Sam. 22. 10. darkness was under his f. Psal. 18. 9.
39. yea, they are fallen under my f.
Psal. 8. 6. thou hast put all things under his f.
1 Cor. 15. 27. Eph. 1. 22.
47. 3. he shall subdue the nations under our f.
91. 13. the dragon shalt thou trample under f.
Isa. 14. 19. as a carcase trodden under f.
28. 3. drunkards of Ephraim shall be trod. under f.
Lam. 3. 34. to crush under his f. all prisoners
Mat. 7. 6. lest they trample them under their f.
Rom. 16. 20. God shall bruise Satan under your f.
1 Cor. 15. 25. till he hath put all enemies under his f.
Heb. 2. 8. for he put all in subjection under his f.
Rev. 12. 1. clothed with the sun, moon under her f.
FEET with *wash*, or *washed*.
Gen. 18. 4. let water be fetched, and wash your f.
19. 2. turn in, tarry all night, and wash your f.
24. 32. and Laban gave water to wash his f.
43. 24. gave them water, and they washed their f.
Exod. 30. 19. Aaron and his sons shall wash their hands and their f. thereat, 21. | 40. 31.
Judg. 19. 21. Levite and concubine washed their f.
1 Sam. 25. 41. to wash the f. of servants of my lord
2 Sam. 11. 8. Uriah, go to thy house, wash thy f.
Psal. 58. 10. shall wash his f. in blood of the wicked
Cant. 5. 3. have washed my f. how shall I defile them!
Luke 7. 38. she began to wash his f. with tears
44. but she hath washed my f. with tears
John 13. 5. he began to wash the disciples' f.
6. Peter saith to him, Lord, dost thou wash my f.?
8. Peter saith to him, thou shalt never wash my f.
10. needeth not save to wash his f. but is clean
12. so after he had washed their f. he said to them
14. if I your Ld. and Master have washed your f.
1 Tim. 5. 10. if she have washed the saints' f.
FEIGN.
2 Sam. 14. 2. I pray f. thyself to be a mourner
1 Kings 14. 5. she shall f. herself to be another wom.
Luke 20. 20. which should f. themselves just men
FEIGNED.
1 Sam. 21. 13. David f. himself mad in their hands
2 Sam. 22. † 45. strangers shall yield f. obedience unto me, Psal. 18. † 44.
Psal. 17. 1. to my prayer that goeth not out of f. lips
66. † 3. thine enemies shall yield f. obedience
81. † 15. the haters of the Lord yielded f. obedience
2 Pet. 2. 3. with f. words make merchandise of you
FEIGNEST.
1 Kings 14. 6. why f. thou thyself to be another?
Neh. 6. 8. but thou f. them out of thine own heart
FEIGNEDLY.
Jer. 3. 10. hath turned to me but f. saith the Lord
FELL.
Gen. 4. 5. Cain was wroth, and his countenance f.
14. 10. the kings of Sodom and Gomorrah f.
15. 12. a deep sleep f. on Abram, and lo, an horror
25. † 18. Ishmael f. in the presence of his brethren
33. 4. Esau ran, and f. on his brother's neck
44. 14. Joseph's brethren f. before him on ground
45. 14. Joseph f. on Benjamin's neck and wept
46. 29. Jacob f. on Joseph's neck and wept
Exod. 32. 28. there f. of the people 3000 men
Lev. 16. 9. the goat on which the Lord's lot f. 10.
Num. 11. 4. the mixt multitude f. a lusting
9. the dew f. on the camp, the manna f. upon it
14. 5. Moses and Aaron f. 16. 22, 45. | 20. 6.
Josh. 8. 25. that all that f. that day, were 12,000
11. 7. so Joshua came and f. upon them
22. 20. and wrath f. on all the congregation
Judg. 4. 16. Sisera's host f. on the edge of the sword
5. 27. Sisera f. || 8. 10. for there f. 120,000 men
7. 13. a cake of bread smote the tent that it f.
12. 6. there f. of Ephraimites at that time 42,000
16. 30. the house f. on the lords and on the people
20. 44. and there f. of Benjamin 18,000 men
1 Sam. 4. 10. there f. of Israel 30,000 footmen
18. Eli f. from his seat backward by the gate
11. 7. the fear of the Lord f. on the people
14. 13. the Philistines f. before Jonathan
19. † 24. Saul prophesied, and f. down that day
22. 18. Doeg turned, and f. upon the priests
25. 24. Abigail f. at David's feet, and said
28. 20. Saul f. straightway along on the earth
29. 3. I found no fault in him since he f. on me
30. 13. because three days agone I f. sick
31. 4. therefore Saul took a sword and f. upon it
5. his armour-bearer f. likewise, 1 Chr. 10. 4, 5.
2 Sam. 4. 4. Mephibosheth f. and became lame
11. 17. there f. some of the people of David
13. 2. Amnon f. sick for his sister Tamar
20. 8. Joab's sword f. out as he went forth
21. 9. they f. all seven together in days of harvest
22. they f. by the hand of David, 1 Chron. 20. 8.
1 Kings 2. 25. Benaiah f. on Adonijah that he died
32. who f. upon two men more righteous than he
34. Benaiah f. on Joab || 46. Benaiah f. on Shimei
12. † 19. so Israel f. from the house of David
14. 1. Abijah the son of Jeroboam f. sick
17. 17. the son of the woman f. sick, it was so sore
18. 38. fire of Lord f. and consumed the sacrifice
20. 30. a wall f. on 27,000 men that were left
2 Kings 1. 13. third captain f. on knees before Elijah
2. 13. he took mantle of Elijah that f. from him
4. 8. it f. on a day Elisha passed to Shunem, 11.
18. it f. on a day the child went to the reapers
37. Shunammite f. at his feet and bowed herself
6. 5. the axe-head f. into the water, and he cried
6. and the man of God said, where f. it?
7. 20. so it f. out to him, the people trode on him
25. 11. the fugitives that f. away to the king
1 Chr. 12. 19. there f. some of Manasseh to David
21. 14. and there f. of Israel 70,000 men
27. 24. because there f. wrath for it against Israel
2 Chron. 15. 9. for they f. to David out of Israel
17. 10. the fear of Ld. f. on all kingdoms of lands
20. 18. the inhabitants of Jerusalem f. before Ld.
21. 19. his bowels f. out by reason of sickness
25. 13. the soldiers of Israel f. on cities of Judah
Ezra 9. 5. I f. on my knees and spread my hands
Esth. 8. 17. for the fear of the Jews f. on them, 9. 2.
9. 3. because the fear of Mordecai f. upon them
Job 1. 15. the Sabeans f. on the asses, and took them
17. Chaldeans f. on camels, and carried them away
19. the house f. on young men, and they are dead
Psal. 27. 2. wicked came to eat up my flesh, they f.
78. 64. their priests f. by sword, widows not lament
105. 38. for the fear of Israel f. on Egypt
Jer. 39. 9. those that f. away, that f. to him, 52. 15.
46. 16. one f. upon another, and they said, arise
Lam. 1. 7. her people f. into the hand of the enemy
5. 13. and the children f. under the wood
Ezek. 8. 1. the hand of the Lord f. upon me, 11. 5.
39. 23. so f. they all by the sword
Dan. 4. 31. there f. a voice from heaven, saying
7. 20. other which came up, before whom three f.
10. 7. but a great quaking f. upon them
Jonah 1. 7. they cast lots, and the lot f. on Jonah
Mat. 7. 25. the house f. not || 27. it f. Luke 6. 49.
13. 4. seed f. by the way-side, Mark 4. 4. Luke 8. 5.
5. some f. upon stony places, Mark 4. 5. Luke 8. 6.
7. and some f. among thorns, Mark 4. 7. Luke 8. 7.
8. other f. into good ground, Mark 4. 8. Luke 8. 8.
Mark 5. 22. Jairus when he saw him, f. at his feet
7. 25. Syrophenician woman came, and f. at his feet
9. 20. he f. on the ground and wallowed foaming
14. 35. Jesus f. on the ground and prayed
Luke 1. 12. and fear f. upon Zacharias
8. 23. but as they sailed, Jesus f. asleep
10. 30. a certain man f. among thieves, 36.
13. 4. upon whom the tower in Siloam f.
15. 20. his father f. on his neck and kissed him
16. 21. crumbs which f. from the rich man's table
John 18. 6. went backward and f. to the ground
Acts 1. 25. from which Judas by transgression f.
26. gave forth lots, and the lot f. upon Matthias
7. 60. and when he had said this, he f. asleep
9. 4. Saul f. to the earth and heard a voice
18. there f. from his eyes as it had been scales
10. 10. Peter became hungry, and f. into a trance
44. the Holy Ghost f. on them all, 11. 15.
12. 7. the chains f. off from Peter's hands
13. 11. there f. on him a mist and a darkness
36. David f. on sleep and saw corruption
19. 17. and fear f. on all the Jews at Ephesus
20. 10. Paul went down, and f. on Eutychus
37. they all f. on Paul's neck, and kissed him
22. 7. I f. unto the ground, and heard a voice
Rom. 11. 22. on them which f. severity
15. 3. reproaches of them reproached thee f. on me
1 Cor. 10. 8. and f. in one day twenty-three thous.
Heb. 3. 17. whose carcases f. in the wilderness
2 Pet. 3. 4. since fathers f. asleep all things continue
Rev. 1. 17. when I saw him I f. at his feet as dead
6. 13. and the stars of heaven f. unto the earth
8. 10. and there f. a great star from heaven
11. 11. and great fear f. on them who saw them
13. the tenth part of the city f. by earthquake
16. 2. and there f. a noisome and grievous sore
19. the city was divided, and cities of nations f.
21. there f. on men, great hail out of heaven
19. 10. and I f. at his feet to worship him
See FACE, FACES.
FELL *down*.
Num. 22. 27. when the ass saw the angel, she f. d.
Deut. 9. 18. and I f. down before the Lord, 25.
Josh. 6. 20. the people shouted, the wall f. d. flat
Judg. 5. 27. where he bowed there he f. down dead
19. 26. the concubine f. down at door of the house
1 Sam. 17. 52. the Philistines f. down by the way
31. 1. men of Israel f. down in Gilboa, 1 Chr. 10. 1.
2 Sam. 2. 16. so they f. down together
23. Asahel f. down there, and died in the place
18. 28. Ahimaaz f. down || 19. 18. Shimei f. down
2 Kings 1. 2. and Ahaziah f. down through a lattice
1 Chr. 5. 22. there f. d. many slain, war was of G.
2 Chron. 13. 17. there f. d. of Israel 500,000 men
Esth. 8. 3. Esther f. down at Ahasuerus' feet
Job 1. 20. Job f. d. on the ground and worshipped
Psal. 107. 12. they f. down there was none to help
Dan. 3. 7. all nations f. d. and worshipped image
23. these three f. down bound in the furnace
Mat. 2. 11. wise men f. down and worshipped him
18. 26. the servant therefore f. down saying, 29.
Mark 3. 11. and unclean spirits f. down before him
5. 33. the woman with the issue of blood, f. down
Luke 5. 8. Simon Peter f. down at Jesus' knees
8. 28. man which had devils f. down before Jesus
41. Jairus f. down || 17. 16. the Samaritan f. d.
John 11. 32. Mary f. down at his feet, saying
Acts 5. 5. Ananias f. down || 10. Sapphira f. down
10. 25. Cornelius f. down || 16. 29. jailer f. down
19. 35. the image which f. down from Jupiter
20. 9. Eutychus f. down from the third loft
Heb. 11. 30. by faith the walls of Jericho f. down
Rev. 5. 8. elders f. d. before the Lamb. 14. | 19. 4.
Rev. 22. 8. John f. down to worship before the ange
FELL.
2 Kings 3. 19. and ye shall f. every good tree
FELLED.
2 Kings 3. 25. and they f. all the good trees
FELLER.
Isa. 14. 8. saying, no f. is come up against us
FELLEST.
2 Sam. 3. 34. as a man before wick. men, so f. thou
FELLING.
2 Kings 6. 5. as one was f. a beam, the axe-head fell
FELLOES.
1 Kings 7. 33. their f. and their spokes were molten
FELLOW.
Gen. 19. 9. they said, this one f. came in to sojourn
Exod. 2. 13. wherefore smitest thou thy f.?
18. † 16. and I judge between a man and his f.
Judg. 7. 13. there was a man told a dream to his f.
22. the Lord set every man's sword against his f. through all the host, 1 Sam. 14. 20.
1 Sam. 21. 15. that ye have brought this f. to play the madman; shall this f. come into my house?
25. 21. in vain have I kept all that this f. hath
29. 4. make this f. return, he may go to his place
2 Sam. 2. 16. caught every one his f. by the head
1 Kings 22. 27. put this f. in prison, 2 Chron. 18. 26.
2 Kings 9. 11. wherefore came this mad f. to thee?
Eccl. 4. 10. if they fall, one will lift up his f.
Isa. 34. 14. the satyr shall cry to his f.
Jonah 1. 7. they said every one to his f. cast lots
Zech. 11. † 9. eat every one the flesh of his f.
13. 7. awake, O sword, against my Shepherd, and against the man that is my f. saith Lord of hosts
Mat. 12. 24. this f. doth not cast out devils but by
26. 61. this f. said, I am able to destroy the temple
71. this f. was also with Jesus, Luke 22. 59.
Luke 23. 2. we found this f. perverting the nation
John 9. 29. as for this f. we know not whence he is
11. 16. Didymus said to his f. disciples, let us go
Acts 17. † 18. some said, what will this base f. say?
18. 13. this f. persuadeth men to worship God
22. 22. away with such a f. from the earth
24. 5. we have found this man a pestilent f.
FELLOW-*citizens*.
Eph. 2. 19. but f.-citizens with saints and household
FELLOW-*heirs*.
Eph. 3. 6. that the Gentiles should be f.-heirs
FELLOW-*helper*.
2 Cor. 8. 23. Titus my f.-helper concerning you
FELLOW-*helpers*.
3 John 8. that we might be f.-helpers to the truth
FELLOW-*labourer*.
1 Thess. 3. 2. we sent Timotheus our f.-labourer
Philem. 1. Paul to Philemon our f.-labourer
FELLOW-*labourers*.
Phil. 4. 3. Clement, with other my f.-labourers
Philem. 24. Marcus, Demas, Lucas, my f.-labourers
FELLOW-*prisoner*.
Col. 4. 10. Aristarchus my f.-prisoner saluteth you
Philem. 23. Epaphras my f.-prisoner in Christ
FELLOW-*prisoners*.
Rom. 16. 7. Andronicus and Junia my f.-prisoners
FELLOW-*servant*, or *servants*.
Mat. 18. 28. found one of his f.-serv. who owed him
29. his f.-servant fell down at his feet, saying
31. so when his f.-servants saw what was done
33. have had compassion on f.-servant as I on thee
24. 49. and shall begin to smite his f.-servants
Col. 1. 7. ye learned of Epaphras our f.-servant
4. 7. Tychicus, who is a f.-servant in the Lord
Rev. 6. 11. till their f.-servants should be fulfilled
19. 10. see thou do it not, I am thy f.-servant, 22. 9.
FELLOW-*soldier*.
Phil. 2. 25. to send Epaphroditus my f.-soldier
Philem. 2. Paul to Archippus our f.-soldier
FELLOW-*workers*.
Col. 4. 11. these only are my f.-workers to kingdom
FELLOWS.
Judg. 11. 37. bewail my virginity, I and my f.
18. 25. lest angry f. run on thee, and thou lose life
20. † 11. all Israel were gathered f. as one man
2 Sam. 6. 20. as one of the vain f. uncovereth himself
Psal. 45. 7. with oil of gladness above f. Heb. 1. 9.
Isa. 44. 11. behold all his f. shall be ashamed
Ezek. 37. 19. I will take the tribes of Israel his f.
Dan. 2. 13. they sought Daniel and his f. to be slain
18. that Daniel and his f. should not perish
7. 20. whose look was more stout than his f.
Zech. 3. 8. thou and thy f. that sit before thee
Mat. 11. 16. like to children calling to their f.
Acts 17. 5. Jews took lewd f. of the baser sort
FELLOWSHIP.
Lev. 6. 2. which was delivered him to keep, or in f.
Ps. 94. 20. shall the throne of iniq. have f. with thee?
Acts 2. 42. they contin. in apostles' doctrine and f.
1 Cor. 1. 9. ye were called to the f. of his Son
10. 20. not that ye should have f. with devils
2 Cor. 6. 14. what f. hath righteousness with unrighteousness? what communion light with darkn.?
8. 4. take on us the f. of ministering to the saints
Gal. 2. 9. they gave to me the right hand of f.
Eph. 3. 9. to make men see what is the f. of mystery
5. 11. have no f. with unfruitful works of darkness
Phil. 1. 5. for your f. in the gospel till now
2. 1. if there be any f. of the spirit, if bowels
3. 10. that I may know the f. of his sufferings
1 John 1. 3. that ye also may have f. with us, and truly our f. is with Father, and with Son J. C.
6. if we say that we have f. with him, and walk in
7. if we walk in light, we have f. one with another
FELT.
Gen. 27. 22. Jacob went near, and Isaac f. him
31. † 34. Laban f. all the tent, but found them not
Exod. 10. 21. over land, even darkness that may be f.
Prov. 23. 35. they have beaten me, and I f. it not
Mark 5. 29. she f. she was healed of that plague
Acts 28. 5. he shook off the beast and f. no harm
FEMALE.
Gen. 1. 27. male and f. created he them, 5. 2
6. 19. two of every sort, they shall be male and f.
7. 2. take to thee by sevens, the male and the f. 3.
9. there went in two and two, the male and the f.

Gen. 7. 16. they that went in, went in male and *f.*
Lev. 3. 1. if he offer it, whether it be male or *f.*
6. if his offering be of the flock, male or *f.*
4. 28. offering a *f.* without blemish, 32. | 5. 6.
12. 7. law for her that hath born a male or *f.*
27. 4. if it be a *f.* thy estimation shall be 30 shekels
5. thy estimation for the *f.* ten shekels, 7.
6. for the *f.* from a month old, three shekels
Num. 5. 3. both male and *f.* shall ye put out
Deut. 4. 16. graven image, the likeness of male or *f.*
7. 14. shall not be a male or *f.* barren among you
Mat. 19. 4. made them male and *f.* *Mark* 10. 6.
Gal. 3. 28. in Christ there is neither male nor *f.*

FENCE.

Ps. 62. 3. ye be as a bowing wall and a tottering *f.*

FENCED.

Job 10. 11. he hath *f.* me with bones and sinews
19. 8. he hath *f.* up my way that I cannot pass
Isa. 5. 2. my beloved hath a vineyard, and he *f.* it

FENCED.

Deut. 28. 52. till thy high and *f.* walls come down
2 *Sam.* 23. 7. man that shall touch them must be *f.*
2 *Kings* 3. 19. and ye shall smite every *f.* city
10. 2. there are with you a *f.* city and armour
17. 9. from the tower to the *f.* city, 18. 8.
19. † 24. I have dried up the rivers of *f.* places with the sole of my feet, *Isa.* 37. †25.
Isa. 2. 15. the day of the Lord on every *f.* wall
Jer. 15. 20. I will make thee a *f.* brazen wall
Ezek. 36. 35. the waste and ruined cities are become *f*
Hab. 2. † 1. I will set me upon the *f.* place

FENCED *cities.*

Num. 32. 17. our little ones shall dwell in *f. cities*
Deut. 3. 5. all these *cities* were *f.* with walls
9. 1. to possess *cities* great and *f.* up to heaven
Josh. 10. 20. the rest of them entered into *f.* cities
14. 12. and that the *cities* were great and *f.*
1 *Sam.* 6. 18. golden mice, according to number of *f. cities*
2 *Sam.* 20. 6. pursue, lest he get *f. cities* and escape
2 *Kings* 18. 13. Sennacherib came up against all the *f. cities* of Judah and took them, 2 *Chr.* 12. 4
19. 25. thou shouldest be to lay waste *f. cities*
2 *Chron.* 8. 5. Solomon built *f. cities* with walls
12. 4. Shishak took the *f. cities* of Judah
14. 6. Asa built *f. cities* in Judah, land had rest
17. 2. Jehoshaphat placed forces in the *f. cities*, 19.
19. 5. he set judges throughout all *f. cities* of Jud.
21. 3. Jehoshaphat gave them *f. cities* in Judah
33. 14. Manasseh put captains of war in *f. cities*
Jer. 5. 17. they shall impoverish thy *f. cities*
Dan. 11. 15. king of north shall take most *f. cities*
Hos. 8. 14. Judah hath multiplied *f. cities*
Zeph. 1. 16. day of alarm against *f. cities* and towers

FENS.

Job 40. 21. Behemoth lieth in covert of reed and *f*

FERRET.

Lev. 11. 30. the *f.* chameleon and lizard unclean

FERRY-*boat.*

2 *Sam.* 19. 18. there went a *f.-boat* for king's housh.

FERVENT.

Acts 18. 25. Apollos, being *f.* in spirit, taught
Rom. 12. 11. *f.* in spirit, serving the Lord
2 *Cor.* 7. 7. he told us your *f.* mind towards me
Jam. 5. 16. *f.* prayer of a righteous man avails much
1 *Pet.* 4. 8. above all things have *f.* charity
2 *Pet.* 3. 10. elements shall melt with *f.* heat, 12.

FERVENTLY.

Col. 4. 12. Epaphras labouring *f.* for you in prayers
1 *Pet.* 1. 22. see that ye love one another with a [pure heart *f.*

FETCH.

Gen. 18. 5. I will *f.* a morsel of bread and comfort
27. 9. go, *f.* me two kids of the goats, 13.
45. then I will send and *f.* thee from thence
Exod. 2. 5. when saw the ark, she sent maid to *f.* it
Num. 20. 10. must we *f.* water out of this rock?
Deut. 19. 12. the elders shall send and *f.* him
24. 10. thou shall not go to *f.* his pledge, 19.
30. 4. from whence will the Lord thy God *f.* thee
Judg. 11. 5. elders of Gilead went to *f.* Jephthah
20. 10. take men to *f.* victuals for the people
1 *Sam.* 4. 3. let us *f.* the ark of the covenant
6. 21. saying, come ye down, and *f.* it up to you
16. 11. Samuel said to Jesse, send *f.* Saul, 20. 31.
26. 22. let us come over and *f.* the spear
2 *Sam.* 5. 23. but *f.* a compass behind them
14. 13. the king doth not *f.* home his banished
20. to *f.* about this form of speech Joab done this
1 *Kings* 17. 10. *f.* me, I pray thee, a little water
11. as she was going to *f.* it, he called her
2 *Kings* 6. 13. go spy where he is, that I may *f.* him
2 *Chron.* 18. 8. *f.* quickly Micaiah the son of Imla
Neh. 8. 15. *f.* olive-branches, pine and myrtle
Job 36. 3. I will *f.* my knowledge from afar
Isa. 56. 12. come ye, say they, I will *f.* wine
Jer. 36. 21. the king sent Jehudi to *f.* the roll
Acts 16. 37. let them come themselves and *f.* us out

FETCHED.

Gen. 18. 4. let a little water, I pray you, be *f.*
7. Abraham *f.* a calf tender and good
27. 14. Jacob went and *f.* the kids to his mother
Judg. 18. 18. they *f.* the carved image, the ephod
1 *Sam.* 7. 1. men came and *f.* up the ark of the Lord
10. 23. and they ran, and *f.* Saul thence
2 *Sam.* 4. 6. as though they would have *f.* wheat
9. 5. king David sent and *f.* Mephibosheth
11. 27. David sent and *f.* Bath-sheba to his house
14. 2. Joab *f.* from Tekoah a wise woman
1 *Kings* 7. 13. king Solomon *f.* Hiram out of Tyre
9. 28. they *f.* from Ophir gold, 420 talents
2 *Kings* 3. 9. *f.* a compass of seven days' journey
11. 4. Jehoiada sent and *f.* rulers over hundreds
2 *Chron.* 1. 17. *f.* from Egypt a chariot and horse
12. 11. the guard came and *f.* the shields
Jer. 26. 23. and they *f.* forth Urijah out of Egypt
Acts 28. 13. and from thence we *f.* a compass

FETCHETH.

Deut. 19. 5. and his hand *f.* a stroke with the axe

FETTERS.

Judg. 16. 21. they bound Samson with *f.* of brass
2 *Sam.* 3. 34. thy hands were not bound, nor thy feet put into *f.*

2 *Kings* 25. 7. they put out the eyes of Zedekiah, and bound him with *f.* of brass, *Jer.* 39. † 7. | 52. † 11.
2 *Chron.* 33. 11. Manasseh was bound with *f.*
36. 6. Jehoiakim bound with *f.* to carry to Babylon
Psal. 105. 18. whose feet they hurt with *f.*
149. 8. to bind their nobles with *f.* of iron
Mark 5. 4. being often bound with *f.* *Luke* 8. 29.

FEVER.

Deut. 28. 22. the Lord shall smite thee with a *f.*
Mat. 8. 14. Jesus was come, he saw Peter's wife's mother sick of a *f.* *Mark* 1. 30. *Luke* 4. 38.
John 4. 52. yesterday at seventh hour the *f.* left him
Acts 28. 8. the father of Publius lay sick of a *f.*

FEW.

Gen. 24. 55. let the damsel abide with us a *f.* days
27. 44. tarry a *f.* days till thy brother's fury turn
34. 30. I being *f.* in number, they will slay me
47. 9. *f.* and evil have the days of my life been
Lev. 26. 22. I will make you *f.* *Deut.* 4. 27. | 28. 62.
Num. 9. 20. the cloud was a *f.* days on the tabern.
13. 18. see the people whether they be *f.* or many
26. 54. to *f.* shall give the less inheritance, 35. 8.
56. possession shall be divid. between many and *f.*
Deut. 26. 5. my father sojourned there with a *f.*
33. 6. let Reuben live, let not his men be *f.*
1 *Sam.* 14. 6. no restraint, to save by many or *f.*
17. 28. with whom hast thou left those *f.* sheep?
2 *Chron.* 29. 34. but the priests were too *f.*
Neh. 2. 12. I arose, I and some *f.* men with me
7. 4. the city large, but the people were *f.* therein
Job 10. 20. are not my days *f.*? cease then, let alone
14. 1. man is of *f.* days, and full of trouble
16. 22. when a *f.* years are come, then I shall go
32. † 6. I am *f.* of days, and ye are very old
Psal. 109. 8. let his days be *f.* and let another take
Eccl. 5. 2. God is in heaven, therefore let words be *f.*
9. 14. there was a little city, and *f.* men in it
12. 3. the grinders cease, because they are *f.*
Isa. 10. 19. the rest of the trees of forest shall be *f.*
24. 6. the inhabitants are burned, and *f.* men left
41. † 14. fear not Jacob, ye *f.* men of Israel
Ezek. 5. 3. thou shalt also take a *f.* in number
12. 16. I will leave a *f.* men from the sword
Dan. 11. 20. within *f.* days he shall be destroyed
Mat. 7. 14. strait is gate, and *f.* there be that find it
9. 37. but the labourers are *f.* *Luke* 10. 2.
15. 34. seven, and a *f.* little fishes, *Mark* 8. 7.
20. 16. many be called, but *f.* are chosen, 22. 14.
25. 21. thou hast been faithful in a *f.* things, 23.
Mark 6. 5. laid hands on a *f.* sick folk, healed them
Luke 12. 48. shall be beaten with *f.* stripes
13. 23. one said, Lord, are there *f.* that be saved?
Acts 24. 4. that thou wouldest hear us a *f.* words
Eph. 3. 3. the mystery as I wrote afore in *f.* words
Heb. 12. 10. for they verily for a *f.* days chastened us
13. 22. for I have written unto you in *f.* words
1 *Pet.* 3. 20. wherein *f.* that is, eight souls were saved
Rev. 2. 14. I have a *f.* things against thee, 20.
3. 4. thou hast a *f.* names even in Sardis

But a FEW.

Gen. 29. 20. they seemed to him *but a f.* days
Lev. 25. 52. if there remain *but f.* years to jubilee
Josh. 7. 3. the men of Ai are *but f.*
1 *Chron.* 16. 19. when ye were *but f.* *Psal.* 105. 12.
Jer. 42. 2. for we are left *but a f.* of many

Not a FEW.

2 *Kings* 4. 3. borrow empty vessels, borrow *not a f.*
Isa. 10. 7. to destroy, and cut off nations *not a f.*
Jer. 30. 19. multiply them, and they shall *not be f.*
Acts 17. 4. chief women *not a f.* || 12. of men *not a f.*

FEWER.

Num. 33. 54. to *f.* ye shall give the less inheritance
Job 30. † 1. but they that are of *f.* days than I

FEWEST.

Deut. 7. 7. for ye were the *f.* of all people

FEWNESS.

Lev. 25. 16. according to *f.* of years diminish pride

FIDELITY.

Tit. 2. 10. servants not purloining, shewing good *f.*

FIELD.

Gen. 23. 11. the *f.* give I thee, and the cave therein
20. the *f.* and cave were made sure to Abraham
27. 27. the smell of my son is as the smell of a *f.*
31. 4. Jacob called Rachel and Leah to the *f.*
49. 30. in the *f.* which Abraham bought, 50. 13.
Exod. 22. 5. if a man shall cause a *f.* to be eaten
6. so that the corn or *f.* be consumed therewith
Lev. 19. 19. shalt not sow thy *f.* with mingled seed
25. 3. six years shalt sow thy *f.* and prune vineyard
4. in the seventh year thou shalt not sow thy *f.*
27. 17. if he sanctify his *f.* from year of jubilee, 18.
20. if he will not redeem the *f.* or if he sold the *f*
Deut. 5. 21. nor shalt thou covet thy neighbour's *f*
Josh. 15. 18. to ask of her father a *f.* *Judg.* 1. 14.
Ruth 2. 8. go not to glean in another *f.* but abide
4. 5. Boaz said, what day thou buyest *f.* of Naomi
2 *Sam.* 2. † 16. place was called the *f.* of strong men
14. 30. Joab's *f.* is near mine, and he hath barley
31. why have thy servants set my *f.* on fire?
2 *Kings* 18. 17. they stood by upper pool, which is in the high-way of the fuller's *f.* *Isa.* 7. 3. | 36. 2.
Neh. 13. 10. the Levites fled every one to his *f.*
Psal. 96. 12. let the *f.* be joyful and all therein
Prov. 24. 30. I went by the *f.* of the slothful
27. 26. lambs for clothing, and goats the price of *f*
31. 16. she considereth a *f.* and buyeth it
Eccl. 5. 9. the king himself is served by the *f.*
Isa. 5. 8. woe to them that lay *f.* to *f.* till no place
16. 10. and joy is taken out of the plentiful *f.*
Jer. 12. 4. how long shall herbs of every *f.* wither?
26. 18. Zion shall be plowed like a *f.* *Mic.* 3. 12.
32. 7. buy thee my *f.* that is in Anathoth, 8. 25.
35. 9. neither have we vineyard, nor *f.* nor seed
48. 33. joy and gladness is taken from plentiful *f.*
Ezek. 17. † 8. was planted in a good *f.* by great waters
Joel 1. 10. the *f.* is wasted, the land mourneth
Mat. 13. 24. that soweth good seed in his *f.* 31.
38. the *f.* is the world, good seed childr. of kingd.
44. again the kingdom of heaven is like to treasure hid in a *f.* he selleth all, and buyeth that *f.*
27. 7. they bought with them the potter's *f.* 10.
8. the *f.* was called the *f.* of blood, *Acts* 1. 19.

Luke 17. 7. will say to him, when come from the *f.*
Acts 1. 18. this man purchased a *f.* with reward of

Fruitful FIELD.

2 *Kings* 19. † 23. I will enter his *f. f.* *Isa.* 37. † 24.
Isa. 10. 18. shall consume the glory of his *fruitful f.*
29. 17. Lebanon shall be turned into a *fruitful f.*
32. 15. till Spirit be poured out, and the wilderness be a *fruitful f.* and the *fruitful f.* be counted a forest
16. and righteousness in the *fruitful f.*
Ezek. 17. 5. he planted the seed in a *fruitful f.*

In the FIELD.

Gen. 4. 8. it came to pass when they were *in the f.*
24. 63. Isaac went out to meditate *in the f.*
29. 2. he looked, and behold a well *in the f.*
37. 15. behold, Joseph was wandering *in the f.*
Exod. 9. 19. send and gather all thou hast *in the f.*
25. the hail smote in Egypt all that was *in the f.*
16. 25. to-day ye shall not find it *in the f.*
Deut. 21. 1. if one be found slain, lying *in the f.*
22. 25. if a man find a betrothed damsel *in the f.*
28. 3. blessed shalt thou be in the city and *in the f.*
16. cursed shalt thou be in the city and *in the f.*
Judg. 13. 9. angel came to woman as she sat *in the f.*
1 *Sam.* 6. 18. which stone remaineth *in the f.* of Joshua
19. 3. I will stand beside my father *in the f.*
30. 11. and they found an Egyptian *in the f.*
2 *Sam.* 14. 6. two sons, and they two strove *in the f.*
1 *Kings* 11. 29. and they two were alone *in the f.*
14. 11. him that dieth of Jeroboam *in the f.*
21. 24. him that dieth of Ahab *in the f.* fowls eat
1 *Chron.* 19. 9. kings were by themselves *in t e f.*
27. 26. over them that did the work *in the f.*
Job 24. 6. they reap every one his corn *in the f.*
Psal. 78. 12. marvellous things *in the f.* of Zoan, 43.
Prov. 24. 27. make it fit for thyself *in the f.*
Jer. 14. 5. yea, the hind calved *in the f.*
17. 3. O my mountain *in the f.* I will give to spoil
41. 8. for we have treasures *in the f.* of wheat
Ezek. 7. 15. he that is *in the f.* shall die by the sword
26. 6. he shall slay thy daughters *in the f.* 8.
Mic. 4. 10. thou shalt dwell *in the f.* and go to Bab.
Zech. 10. 1. shall give to every one grass *in the f.*
Mal. 3. 11. nor shall your vine cast her fruit *in the f.*
Mat. 24. 18. neither let him who is *in the f.* return to take his clothes, *Mark* 13. 16. *Luke* 17. 31.
40. then shall two be *in the f.* *Luke* 17. 36.
Luke 2. 8. there were shepherds abiding *in the f.*
12. 28. clothe the grass which is to-day *in the f.*
15. 25. now his elder son was *in the f.* heard music

Into the FIELD.

Num. 22. 23. ass turned aside, and went *into the f.*
Judg. 9. 42. the people went out *into the f.*
1 *Sam.* 6. 14. the cart came *into the f.* of Joshua
20. 11. Jonathan said, come let us go *into the f.*
2 *Sam.* 11. 23. the men came out unto us *into the f.*
20. 12. removed Amasa out of the way *into the f.*
2 *Kings* 4. 39. one went *into f.* and gathered gourds
Cant. 7. 11. my beloved, let us go forth *into the f.*
Jer. 6. 25. go not forth *into f.* nor walk by the way
14. 18. if I go forth *into the f.* behold the slain

Of the FIELD.

Gen. 2. 5. God made every plant and herb *of the f.*
34. 7. and the sons of Jacob came out *of the f.*
47. 24. four parts your own, for seed *of the f.*
Lev. 26. 4. the trees *of the f.* yield fruit
27. 28. no devoted thing *of the f.* shall be sold
Deut. 20. 19. for the tree *of the f.* is man's life
Judg. 5. 4. when thou marchedst out *of the f.*
19. 16. came an old man from his work out *of the f.*
Ruth 2. 3. on a part *of the f.* belonging to Boaz
1 *Sam.* 11. 5. Saul came after the herd out *of the f.*
2 *Kings* 9. 25. cast him in portion *of the f.* of Naboth
37. carcase shall be as dung upon the face *of the f.*
Job 5. 23. shall be in league with the stones *of the f.*
Psal. 103. 15. as a flower *of the f.* he flourisheth
Cant. 2. 7. I charge you by the roes *of the f.* 3. 5.
Isa. 37. 27. the inhabitants were as grass *of the f.*
40. 6. all flesh is grass, and as the flower *of the f.*
43. 20. the beast *of the f.* shall honour me
55. 12. all the trees *of the f.* shall clap their hands
Jer. 4. 17. as keepers *of the f.* are they against her
18. 14. the snow of Lebanon from the rock *of the f.*
Lam. 4. 9. stricken for want of the fruits *of the f.*
Ezek. 16. 7. caused thee to multiply as bud *of the f.*
17. 24. all trees *of the f.* shall know that I Lord
34. 27. the tree *of the f.* shall yield her fruit
36. 30. I will multiply the increase *of the f.*
39. 10. so they shall take no wood out *of the f.*
Dan. 4. 15. in tender grass *of the f.* and wet with dew
Hos. 10. 4. as hemlock in the furrows *of the f.*
12. 11. their altars as heaps in furrows *of the f.*
Joel 1. 11. because the harvest *of the f.* is perished
12. even all the trees *of the f.* are withered
19. and the flame hath burnt all the trees *of the f.*
Mic. 1. 6. I will make Samaria as an heap *of the f.*
Mat. 6. 28. consider the lilies *of the f.* how they grow
30. wherefore, if God so clothe the grass *of the f.*
13. 36. declare the parable of the tares *of the f.*

See BEAST, BEASTS.

Open FIELD.

Lev. 14. 7. shall let living bird loose into the *open f.*
17. 5. bring sacrifices which they offer in the *open f.*
Jer. 9. 22. men's carcases as dung upon the *open f.*
Ezek. 16. 5. but thou wast cast out in the *open f.*
32. 4. I will cast thee forth upon the *open f.*
33. 27. him that is in the *open f.* I will give to beasts
39. 5. thou shalt fall upon the *open f.* saith Lord G.

FIELDS.

Exod. 8. 13. the frogs died out of the houses and *f.*
Lev. 25. 31. shall be counted as the *f.* of the country
27. 22. which is not of the *f.* of his possession
Num. 16. 14. thou hast not given us inheritance of *f*
20. 17. we will not pass thro' *f.* or vineyards, 21. 22
Deut. 11. 15. and I will send grass into thy *f.*
32. 13. that he might eat the increase of the *f.*
32. their vine is as the vine of the *f.* of Gomorrah
Josh. 21. 12. but the *f.* and villages gave they to Caleb
1 *Sam.* 8. 14. he will take your *f.* and vineyards
22. 7. will the son of Jesse give each of you *f.*?
25. 15. they were a wall to us when we were in *f.*
1 *Kings* 2. 26. get thee to Anathoth, to thine own *f.*

1 *Kings* 16. 4. him that dieth of Baasha in *f.* shall fowls eat
1 *Chron.* 16. 32. let the *f.* rejoice and all therein
27. 25. and over the store-houses in the *f.* in cities
2 *Chron.* 26. † 10. had vine-dressers in fruitful *f.*
Job 5. 10. and who sendeth waters upon the *f.*
Psal. 107. 37. and sow the *f.* and plant vineyards
132. 6. we found it in the *f.* of the wood
Prov. 8. 26. while as yet he had not made the *f.*
23. 10. and enter not into the *f.* of the fatherless
*Isa.*16.8. for *f.* of Heshbon languish and vine of Sib.
32. 12. they shall lament for teats, the pleasant *f.*
Jer. 6. 12. their *f.* shall be turned to others, 8. 10.
13. 27. I have seen thine abominations in the *f.*
32. 15. *f.* shall be possessed again in this land
43. *f.* bought ‖ 44. men shall buy *f.* for money
39. 10. Nebuzar-adan gave them *f.* at the same time
40. 7. the captains of forces which were in the *f.* 13.
Obad. 19. they shall possess the *f.* of Ephraim
Mic. 2. 2. they covet *f.* and take them by violence
4. turning away, he hath divided our *f.*
Hab. 3. 17. although the *f.* shall yield no meat
Mark 2. 23. he went through the corn-*f.* *Luke* 6. 1.
John 4. 35. lift up your eyes, and look on the *f.*
Jam. 5. 4. the labourers, which reaped down your *f.*

Open FIELDS.

Lev. 14.53. he shall let go the living bird into *open f.*
Num. 19. 16. one slain with a sword in the *open f.*
2 *Sam.* 11. 11. servants are encamped in the *open f.*
Ezek. 29. 5. thou shalt fall upon the *open f.*

FIERCE.

Gen. 49. 7. cursed be their anger, for it was *f.*
Deut. 28. 50. L. bring a nation of a *f.* countenance
Job 4. 10. the voice of *f.* lion and teeth are broken
10. 16. thou huntest me as a *f.* lion, thou shewest
28. 8. nor hath the *f.* lion passed by it
41. 10. none is so *f.* that dare stir him up
Isa. 19. 4. and a *f.* king shall rule over them, saith L.
33.19. thou shalt not see a *f.* people of deeper speech
Dan. 8. 23. a king of *f.* countenance shall stand up
*Hab.*1.8. horses are more *f.* than the evening wolves
Mat. 8. 28. two possessed with devils, exceeding *f.*
Luke 23. 5. and they were more *f.* saying, he stirreth
2 *Tim.* 3. 3. for men shall be incontinent, *f.* despisers
Jam. 3. 4. the ships which are driven of *f.* winds
See ANGER, WRATH.

FIERCENESS.

Job 39.24. he swalloweth the ground with *f.* and rage
Jer. 25. 38. land desolate for the *f.* of the oppressor
See ANGER, WRATH.

FIERCER.

2 *Sam.* 19. 43. words of Judah were *f.* than of Isr.

FIERY.

Num. 21. 6. the Ld. sent *f.* serpents among people
8. make thee a *f.* serpent, and set it upon a pole
Deut. 8. 15. wherein were *f.* serpents and scorpions
33. 2. from his right-hand went a *f.* law for them
Ps. 21. 9. shalt make them as a *f.* oven in thy anger
Isa. 14. 29. and his fruit shall be a *f.* flying serpent
Dan. 3. 6. into the midst of a *f.* furnace, 11, 15, 21.
17. if our G. is able to deliver us from *f.* furnace
23. three men fell down into midst of *f.* furnace
26. came near to the mouth of the *f.* furnace
7. 9. his throne was like the *f.* flame and his wheels
10. a *f.* stream issued and came forth from him
Nah. 2. † 3. the chariots shall be with *f.* torches
Eph. 6. 16. able to quench the *f.* darts of the wicked
Heb. 10. 27. a looking for of judgment, and *f.* indignation
1 *Pet.* 4. 12. think it not strange concerning *f.* trial

FIFTH.

Gen. 30. 17. Leah bare Jacob the *f.* son, Issachar
Josh. 19. 24. and the *f.* lot came out for Asher
2 *Sam.* 2. 23. Abner smote Asahel under the *f.* rib
3. 27. Abner under the *f.* rib ‖ 4. 6. Ish-bosheth
20. 10. Joab smote Amasa in the *f.* rib, he died
Neh. 6. 5. Sanballat sent the *f.* time to Nehemiah
Rev. 6. 9. when he had opened the *f.* seal I saw souls
9. 1. the *f.* angel sounded, and I saw a star fall
16. 10. *f.* angel poured out his vial on seat of beast
21. 20. the *f.* a sardonyx; the sixth, a sardius
See DAY, PART.

FIFTH *month.*

Num. 33. 38. Aaron died the first day of the *f. m.*
2 *Kings* 25. 8. *f. m.* came Nebuzar-adan, *Jer.* 52. 12.
1 *Chron.* 27. 8. the fifth captain for the *f. month*
Ezra 7. 8. Ezra came to Jerusalem in the *f. m.* 9.
Jer. 1. 3. carrying Jerusalem captive in the *f. m.*
28. 1. in the *f. month* Hananiah spake unto me
Ezek. 20. 1. in the *f. month* the elders sat before me
Zech. 7. 3. saying should I weep in the *f. month?*
5. when ye fasted and mourned in the *f. month*
8. 19. fast of fourth and of *f. m.* be joy and gladn.

FIFTH *year.*

Lev. 19. 25. in the *f. y.* ye shall eat the fruit thereof
1 *Kings* 14. 25. in the *f. year* of king Rehoboam, Shishak came up ag. Jerusalem, 2 *Chron.* 12. 2.
2 *Kings* 8. 16. in the *f. y.* of Joram, Jehoram began
Jer. 36. 9. in *f. y.* of Jehoiakim, proclaimed a fast
Ezek. 1. 2. was the *f. year* of Jehoiachin's captivity

FIFTEEN.

Gen. 7. 20. *f.* cubits upwards did the waters prevail
Exod. 27. 14. the hangings to be *f.* cubits, 15. | 38. 14.
Lev. 27. 7. then thy estimation shall be *f.* shekels
2 *Sam.* 9. 10. now Ziba had *f.* sons, and twenty serv.
19. 17. Ziba and his *f.* sons went over Jordan
1 *Kings* 7. 3. that lay on forty-five pillars, *f.* in a row
2 *Kings* 14. 17. Amaziah lived after Jehoash *f.* years
20. 6. I will add to thy days *f.* years, and deliver thee from Assyria, 2 *Chron.* 25. 25. *Isa.* 38. 5.
Ezek. 45. 12. *f.* shekels shall be your maneh
Hos. 3. 2. I bought her to me for *f.* pieces of silver
John 11. 18. Bethany was *f.* furlongs off Jerusalem
Acts 27. 28. they sounded, and found it *f.* fathoms
Gal. 1.18. I went to Jerus. I abode with Peter *f.* days

FIFTEENTH.

2 *Kings* 14. 23. in *f.* year of Amaziah, Jerobo. began
1 *Chr.* 24. 14. *f.* to Bilgah ‖ 25. 22. *f.* to Jerimoth
2 *Chr.* 15. 10. gathered to Jerusalem in the *f. year*
Luke 3. 1. in the *f.* year of the reign of Tiberius Cesar

FIFTEENTH *day.*

Exod. 16. 1. came to Sin, on *f. day* of second month
Lev. 23. 6. on the *f. day* of the same month is feast of unleavened bread to L. *Num.* 28. 17. | 33. 3.
34. the *f. day* of this seventh month shall be the feast of tabernacles to Ld. 39. *Num.* 29. 12.
1 *Kings* 12. 32. on the *f. d.* of the eighth month was Jeroboam's feast, he offered on the altar, 33.
Esth. 9. 18. on the *f. day* they rested yearly, 21.
Ezek. 32. 17. *f. day* of twelfth year came the word
45. 25. in *f. day* shall do like in feast of seven days

FIFTY.

Gen. 6. 15. the breadth of the ark shall be *f.* cubits
18. 24. not spare the place for *f.* righteous? 26.
Exod. 26. 5. *f.* loops shalt thou make, 10. | 36. 12. 17.
6. shalt make *f.* taches of gold, 11. | 36. 13, 18.
27. 12. shall be hangings of *f.* cubits, 38. 12.
30. 23. of cinnamon two hundred and *f.* shekels, of sweet calamus two hundred and *f.* shekels
Lev. 23. 16. after the 7th sabbath, number *f.* days
27. 3. of males thy estimation *f.* shekels of silver
16. an homer of barley-seed be valued at *f.* shek.
Num. 4. 3. from thirty years old and upward, even to *f.* years old, 23, 30, 35, 39.
8. 25. from the age of *f.* they shall serve no more
16. 2. two hundred and *f.* princes of the assembly
17. and bring two hundred and *f.* censers
26. 10. the fire devoured two hundred and *f.* men
31. 30. thou shalt take one portion of *f.* for Levites
47. Moses took one portion of *f.* of man and beast
Deut. 22. 29. shall give to damsel's father *f.* shekels
Josh. 7. 21. I took a wedge of gold of *f.* shekels
2 *Sam.* 15. 1. Absalom had *f.* men to run before him
1 *Kings* 1. 5. Adonijah had *f.* men to run before him
7. 2. the breadth of the house of the forest *f.* cubits
18. 4. hid them by *f.* in a cave, and fed them, 13.
2 *Kings* 1. 9. a captain of *f.* with his *f.* 11, 13.
10. then let fire consume thee and thy *f.* 12.
2. 7. *f.* men of sons of the prophets stood to view
17. they sent therefore *f.* men to seek Elijah
13. 7. he left to Jehoahaz but *f.* horsemen
15. 20. Menahem exacted of each *f.* shekels
25. but Pekah slew *f.* men of the Gileadites
2 *Chr.* 3. 9. the weight of nails was *f.* shekels of gold
Ezra 8. 6. Ebed son of Jonath. went up with *f.* males
Neh. 7. 70. the Tirshatha gave to treasure *f.* basins
Esth. 5. 14. let a gallows be made *f.* cubits high, 7. 9.
Isa. 3. 3. the Lord will take away the captain of *f.*
Ezek. 40. 15. to the face of the porch were *f.* cubits
21. the length *f.* cubits, 25, 29, 33, 36. | 42. 7.
42. 2. the breadth of the north door was *f.* cubits
Hag. 2. 16. when one came to draw out *f.* vessels
Luke 7. 41. the one owed 500 pence, the other *f.*
16. 6. he said, sit down quickly, and write *f.*
John 8. 57. thou art not yet *f.* years old, hast thou seen

FIFTY-*two.*

2 *Kings* 15. 2. Azariah reigned *f.-two* years
Ezra 2. 29. the children of Nebo *f.-two*, *Neh.* 7. 33.
Neh. 6. 15. the wall was finished in *f.-two* days

FIFTY-*six.*

Ezra 2. 22. the men of Netophah, *f.* and *six*

FIFTY *thousand.*

1 *Sam.* 6. 19. he smote of the people *f. thousand*
1 *Chr.* 5. 21. they took of their camels *f. thousand*
12. 33. of Zebulun *f. thousand* could keep rank
Acts 19. 19. price of books burnt *f. thousand* pieces [of silver

FIFTY-*three thousand.*

Num. 1. 43. of Naphtali numb. *f.-t. t.* 2. 30. | 26. 47.

FIFTY-*four thousand.*

Num. 1. 29. of Issachar *f.-four th.* four hundred, 2. 6.

FIFTY-*seven thousand.*

Num. 1. 31. of Zebulun *f.-seven th.* four hundred, 2. 8.

FIFTY-*nine thousand.*

Num. 1. 23. of Simeon numbered *f.-n. th.* three hund.

FIFTIES.

Exod. 18. 21. place such be rulers of *f.* 25. *Deut.* 1. 15.
1 *Sam.* 8. 12. the king appoint him captains over *f.*
2 *Kings* 1. 14. fire burnt up the two captains of *f.*
Mark 6. 40. and they sat down by *f.* *Luke* 9. 14.

FIFTIETH.

Lev. 25. 10. and ye shall hallow the *f.* year
11. a jubilee shall that *f.* year be to you, not sow
2 *Kings* 15. 23. in the *f.* year of Azariah king of Judah

FIG, S.

The fig-tree *and its fruit are well known: they were very common in* Palestine, *and there is mention often made of them in Scripture. Our first parents covered their nakedness with* fig-leaves, Gen. 3. 7. *gathered either from common fig-trees, or from some of another kind, the leaves whereof are much larger. This tree hath in it a milky or fat oily liquor; it is very fruitful.* M. Tournefort *says, that in the islands of the* Archipelago, *one of their fig-trees generally produces two hundred and four-score pound-weight of figs. It becomes barren, either through the defect of the above-mentioned liquor, which the husbandman cures by dung and sweet water; or through abundance thereof, which is remedied by causing the superfluous juice to extravasate. The prophet* Isaiah *gave orders to apply a lump of figs to* Hezekiah's *boil; and immediately after he was cured,* 2 Kings 20. 7. *Physicians agree that* figs *are employed with good success in bringing imposthumes to a ripeness, to healing ulcers, quinsies, and sore throats: and it is presumable that* Hezekiah *had some such disease, though the Scripture makes no particular mention of it.*

It is said in Mat. 21. 19. *that* Jesus *coming from* Bethany *early in the morning, and finding himself to be hungry, drew near to a* fig-tree, *with a design of gathering some* figs; *and seeing nothing but leaves upon it,* he cursed it, and immediately it withered to the root. *The generality both of the ancient and modern interpreters have looked upon this action of our Saviour's, as a figure of the rejection of the* Jews. *But a difficulty arises, from a passage which* St. Mark *adds to this history,* that this was not a time for figs, *Mark* 11. 13. *The earliest figs are in the months of* July *and* August, *and the latest in* September *and* October. *But what is related in the gospel came to pass four or five days before the passover, and consequently before the fifteenth day from the moon in* March. *This season therefore was not a time to expect* figs: *why then doth our Saviour curse this tree?*

To solve this difficulty, some interpreters have translated this passage, For this was not a year for figs; *they had failed this year. But this rather increases than lessens the difficulty; for why should our Saviour curse it for having no* figs, *when this was not a seasonable year for* figs, *when figs had failed this year? Others translate it thus,* For there where he was, it was a season for figs. *To support this version, both the pointing and the common accents of the text must be changed, and the Evangelist made to speak in too concise a manner, too different from the general style of* St. Mark.

But others say, that though this was not the time of figs, *as is evident from* St. Mark, *yet there might be some of the forward kind, and our Saviour might presume so, seeing the tree full of leaves. It is certain that there are forward* figs: Isaiah *compares the beauty of* Samaria *to these early* figs, *which people gathered, and ate as soon as they found them.* Isa. 28. 4. As the hasty fruit before the summer, which when he that looketh upon it, seeth it, while it is yet in his hand, he eateth it up. *And* Hosea *says, that the Lord* found *Israel* in the wilderness as the first ripe in the fig-tree at her first time, *Hos.* 9. 10. *And* Jeremiah *describes them as excellent figs.* Jer. 24. 2. One basket had very good figs, even like the figs that are first ripe. Pliny *acknowledges, that there is a sort of* fig-tree *always green, and always with fruit upon it; some ripe, or very far advanced, according to the season; the other in blossom, or buds,* Plin. *lib.* 13. cap. 8. *and lib.* 15. cap. 18. *In* Palestine, *where the winter is very mild, there might easily be forward* figs *in* March; *wherefore our Saviour might look for* figs *at this season upon a* fig-tree *that had leaves on; and his cursing the barren* fig-tree *upon this occasion, is an exact figure of the rejection of the* Jews. *The* fig-tree *had only leaves upon it; herein it resembled the* Jews, *who had only the appearances of piety and religion. The* fig-tree *may be said to be culpable for not bearing fruit at a time when, according to its kind, fruit might have been expected from it: so the* Jews *were criminal for not bringing forth the fruits of righteousness, when our Saviour appeared among them. He cursed the barren* fig-tree, *to show the malediction which was ready to fall upon the incredulous and impenitent* Jews.

To dwell under one's own vine, or fig-tree, *represents in Scripture a time of happiness and prosperity, safety, and security,* 1 Kings 4. 25.

Gen. 3. 7. they sewed *f.* leaves together for aprons
Num. 13. 23. they brought of the pomegranates and *f.*
20. 5. it is no place of seed, or of *f.* or vines
1 *Sam.* 25. 18. Abigail took 200 cakes of *f.*
30. 12. they gave the Egyptian a cake of *f.*
2 *Kings* 20. 7. he said, take a lump of *f.* *Isa.* 38. 21.
1 *Chron.* 12. 40. they that were nigh brought *f.*
Neh. 13. 15. on the sabbath some brought *f.*
Cant. 2. 13. the fig-tree putteth forth her green *f.*
Isa. 34. 4. as a falling *f.* from the fig-tree
Jer. 8. 13. there shall be no *f.* on the fig-tree
24. 1. two baskets of *f.* one had very good *f.* 2, 3.
8. as the evil *f.* that cannot be eaten, so evil
29. 17. I will make them like vile *f.* not to be eaten
Amos 7. † 14. but I was a gatherer of wild *f.*
Nah. 3. 12. shall be like fig-trees with first ripe *f.*
Mat. 7. 16. do men gather *f.* of thistles? *Luke* 6. 44.
Jam. 3. 12. can the fig-tree bear berries, or a vine *f.*?
Rev. 6. 13. as a fig-tree casteth her untimely *f.*

FIG-TREE.

Judg. 9. 10. the trees said to the *f.* come, reign, 11.
1 *Kings* 4. 25. dwelt safely under his *f.* *Mic.* 4. 4.
2 *Kings* 18. 31. eat every one of his *f.* *Isa.* 36. 16.
Prov. 27. 18. whoso keepeth *f.* shall eat the fruit
Hos. 9. 10. I saw fathers as first-ripe in the *f.* thereof
Joel 1. 7. he hath barked my *f.* and made it bare
12. the vine is dried, and the *f.* languisheth
2. 22. the *f.* and vine do yield their strength
Hab. 3. 17. although the *f.* shall not blossom
Hag. 2. 19. as yet the *f.* hath not brought forth
Zech. 3. 10. ye shall call every man under the *f.*
Mat. 21. 19. when he saw a *f.* in way, *Mark* 11. 13.
20. how soon is the *f.* withered? *Mark* 11. 20, 21.
24. 32. learn a parable of the *f.* *Mark* 13. 28.
Luke 13. 6. a man had a *f.* planted in his vineyard
7. behold, I come, seeking fruit on this *f.*
21. 29. behold the *f.* and all the trees
John 1. 48. when wast under the *f.* I saw thee, 50.

FIG-TREES.

Deut. 8. 8. a land of wheat, barley, vines, and *f.*
Psal. 105. 33. he smote their vines also and *f.*
Jer. 5. 17. they shall eat up thy vines and *f.*
Hos. 2. 12. I will destroy her vines and her *f.*
Amos 4. 9. when your gardens and *f.* increased
Nah. 3. 12. thy strong holds shall be like *f.*

FIGHT, *Substantive.*

1 *Sam.* 17. 20. as the host was going forth to the *f.*
1 *Tim.* 6. 12. fight the good *f.* of faith, lay hold on
2 *Tim.* 4. 7. I have fought a good *f.* I have finished
Heb. 10. 32. ye endured a great *f.* of afflictions
11. 34. were made strong, waxed valiant in *f.*

FIGHT, *Verb.*

Deut. 1. 41. then ye said, we will go up and *f.*
42. go not up, nor *f.* for I am not among you
2. 32. Sihon and his people came to *f.* at Jahaz
Judg. 11. 12. thou art come ag. me to *f.* in my land
1 *Sam.* 4. 9. quit yourselves like men, and *f.*
17. 10. give me a man that we may *f.* together
2 *Sam.* 11. 20. why went ye so nigh when ye did *f.*?
1 *Kings* 22. 31. *f.* not small nor great, 2 *Chr.* 18. 30.
2 *Chr.* 18. 31. compassed about Jehoshaphat to *f.*
20. 17. ye shall not need to *f.* in this battle
Psal. 144. 1. which teacheth my fingers to *f.*
Jer. 51. 30. the mighty men have forborn to *f.*

Zech. 10. 5. shall *f.* because the Lord is with them
14. 14. and Judah also shall *f.* at Jerusalem
John 18. 36. if kingdom, then would my servants *f.*
1 *Cor.* 9. 26. so *f.* I, not as one that beateth the air
1 *Tim.* 6. 12. *f.* the good fight of faith, lay hold on
Jam. 4. 2. ye kill, ye *f.* and war, yet ye have not
See BATTLES.

FIGHT *against.*

Exod. 1. 10. lest they join our enemies and *f. ag.* us
Deut. 20. 10. when come nigh to a city to *f. ag.* it
Josh. 10. 25. so do to enemies *against* whom ye *f.*
11. 5. they came and pitched to *f. against* Israel
19. 47. the Danites went up to *f. against* Leshem
Judg. 1. 1. who shall go up first to *f. against* them?
3. that we may *f. against* the Canaanites
10. 9. Ammon passed over Jordan to *f. ag.* Judah
11. 8. Jephthah to *f. against* Ammon, 9.
25. did he ever strive ag. Israel, or *f. ag.* them?
12. 3. why come ye this day to *f. against* me?
20. 20. Israel set themselves to *f. against* Benjamin
1 *Sam.* 15. 18. *f. against* Amalekites till consumed
23. 1. behold, the Philistines *f. against* Keilah
29. 8. that I may not *f. against* enemies of king
1 *Kings* 12. 21. Rehoboam assembled all Judah with Benjamin to *f. against* Israel, 2 *Chron.* 11. 1.
24. ye shall not *f. ag.* your brethren, 2 *Chr.* 11. 4.
20. 23. but let us *f. against* them in the plain, 25.
22. 32. they turned to *f. against* Jehoshaphat
2 *Kings* 3. 21. the kings were come to *f. ag.* them
19. 9. behold, he is come out to *f. against* thee
2 *Chron.* 13. 12. O Israel, *f.* ye not *ag.* the Lord
32. 2. Sennacherib purposed to *f. ag.* Jerusalem
35. 20. Necho came to *f. against* Carchemish
Neh. 4. 8. conspired to come and *f. ag.* Jerusalem
Psal. 35. 1. *f. against* them that *f. against* me
56. 2. they be many that *f. ag.* me, O most High
Isa. 19. 2. they shall *f.* every one *against* his brother
29. 7. all the nations that *f. against* Ariel
8. the nations that *f. against* mount Zion
Jer. 1. 19. shall *f. ag.* thee, but not prevail, 15. 20.
21. 4. wherewith ye *f. ag.* the king of Babylon
5. I myself will *f. against* you with strong arm
32. 24. behold, the city is given into the hand of Chaldeans that *f. against* it, 29. | 34. 22. | 37. 8.
37. 10. had smitten Chaldeans that *f. against* you
Zech. 14. 3. the Lord shall *f. against* those nations
Acts 5. 39. lest ye be found to *f. against* God
23. 9. if angel hath spoken, let us not *f. ag.* God
Rev. 2. 16. *f. ag.* them with the sword of my mouth

FIGHT *for.*

Exod. 14. 14. L. *f. for* you, *Deut.* 1. 30. | 3. 22. | 20. 4.
2 *Kings* 10. 3. and *f. for* your master's house
Neh 4. 14. *f. for* your brethren, sons, and wives
20. resort ye thither to us, our God shall *f. for* us
Isa. 31. 4. the Lord shall come to *f. for* mount Zion

FIGHT *with.*

Exod. 17. 9. choose men, go out *f. with* Amalek
Josh. 9. 2. Canaanites gathered to *f. with* Joshua
Judg. 8. 1. when wentest to *f. with* the Midianites
9. 38. go out now and *f. with* Abimelech
11. 6. that we may *f. with* the children of Ammon
1 *Sam.* 13. 5. Philist. gathered to *f. with* Israel, 28. 1.
17. 9. if he be able to *f. with* me, and to kill me
32. thy servant will go and *f. with* this Philistine
2 *Chron.* 35. 22. Josiah disguised hims. to *f. w.* him
Isa. 30. 32. in battles of shaking will he *f. with* it
Jer. 32. 5. though ye *f. with* Chaldeans, not prosper
33. 5. they came to *f. with* the Chaldeans
41. 12. they took men, and went to *f. w.* Ishmael
Dan. 10. 20. I will return to *f. with* prince of Persia
11. 11. the king of the south come and *f. with* him

FIGHTETH.

Exod. 14. 25. the L. *f.* for them against Egyptians
Josh. 23. 10. the Lord God, he it is that *f.* for you
1 *Sam.* 25. 28. my lord *f.* the battles of the Lord

FIGHTING.

Num. 22. † 11. peradventure I shall prevail in *f.*
1 *Sam.* 17. 19. Israel were *f.* with the Philistines
2 *Chron.* 26. 11. Uzziah had an host of *f.* men
Psal. 56. 1. be merciful, O God, he *f.* oppresseth me

FIGHTINGS.

2 *Cor.* 7. 5. without were *f.* within were fears
Jam. 4. 1. whence come wars and *f.* among you?

FIGURE.

Deut. 4. 16. lest ye make the similitude of any *f.*
Isa. 44. 13. he maketh it after the *f.* of a man
Rom. 5. 14. who is the *f.* of him that was to come
1 *Cor.* 4. 6. these I have in a *f.* transferred to myself
Heb. 9. 9. which was a *f.* of the time then present
11. 19. from whence also he received him in a *f.*
1 *Pet.* 3. 21. the like *f.* whereunto even baptism

FIGURES.

1 *Kings* 6. 29. he carved with carved *f.* of cherubims
Acts 7. 43. *f.* which ye made to worship them
1 *Cor.* 10. † 6. now these things were our *f.*
Heb. 9. 24. holy places, which are the *f.* of the true

FIGURED.

Lev. 26. † 1. neither shall ye set up any *f.* stone

FILE.

1 *Sam.* 13. 21. yet they had a *f.* for the mattocks

FILL, *Substantive.*

Lev. 25. 19. and ye shall eat your *f.* in safety
Deut. 23. 24. then thou mayest eat grapes thy *f*
Prov. 7. 18. come, let us take our *f.* of love

FILL, *Verb.*

Gen. 1. 22. multiply, and *f.* the waters in the seas
42. 25. Joseph commanded to *f.* their sacks, 44. 1.
Exod. 10. 6. the locusts shall *f.* thy houses
16. 32. Moses said, *f.* an homer of it to be kept
32. † 29. Moses said, *f.* your hands to-day to the L.
Lev. 16. † 32. the priest, he shall *f.* his hand
1 *Sam.* 16. 1. *f.* thine horn with oil, and go to Jesse
1 *Kings* 1. † 14. I will come in and *f.* up thy words
18. 33. *f.* four barrels with water, and pour it on
1 *Chr.* 29. † 5. who then is willing to *f.* his hand?
2 *Chron.* 13. † 9. whosoever cometh to *f.* his hand
Job 8. 21. till he *f.* thy mouth with laughing, and lips
15. 2. should a wise man *f.* his belly with east-wind?
20. 23. when he is about to *f.* his belly, God cast fury
23. 4. I would *f.* my mouth with arguments
38. 39. or *f.* the appetite of the young lions
41. 7. canst thou *f.* his skin with barbed irons?

Psal. 81. 10. open thy mouth wide, and I will *f.* it
83. 16. *f.* their faces with shame to seek thee, O L.
110. 6. he shall *f.* the places with the dead bodies
Prov. 1. 13. we shall *f.* our houses with spoil
8. 21. to inherit substance, I will *f.* their treasures
Isa. 8. 8. his wings shall *f.* the breadth of thy land
14. 21. nor *f.* the face of the world with cities
27. 6. Isr. shall *f.* the face of the world with fruit
56. 12. they say, we will *f.* ourselv. with strong drink
Jer. 13. 13. I will *f.* inhabitants with drunkenness
23. 24. do not I *f.* heaven and earth? saith the L.
33. 5. it is to *f.* them with the dead bodies of men
51. 14. surely I will *f.* thee with men as caterpillars
Ezek. 3. 3. son of man, *f.* thy bowels with this roll
7. 19. shall not satisfy their souls nor *f.* their bowels
9. 7. *f.* the courts with the slain, go ye forth
10. 2. go in, *f.* thine hand with coals of fire
24. 4. gather the pieces, *f.* it with the choice bones
30. 11. they shall *f.* the land with the slain
32. 4. I will *f.* the beasts of the whole earth with fire
5. I will *f.* the valleys with thy height
35. 8. I will *f.* his mountains with the slain
43. † 26. they shall purge altar, and *f.* their hands
Zeph. 1. 9. who *f.* their masters' houses with violence
Hag. 2. 7. I will *f.* this house with glory, saith Lord
Zech. 9. † 15. and they shall *f.* both the bowls
Mat. 9. 16. for that which is put in to *f.* it up
15. 33. whence have bread to *f.* such a multitude?
23. 32. *f.* ye up then the measure of your fathers
John 2. 7. *f.* the water-pots with water
Rom. 15. 13. G. of hope *f.* you with all joy and peace
Eph. 4. 10. he ascended, that he might *f.* all things
Col. 1. 24. *f.* up what is behind of sufferings of Christ
1 *Thess.* 2. 16. the Jews, to *f.* up their sins alway
Rev. 18. 6. the cup she hath filled, *f.* her double

FILLED.

Gen. 6. 13. the earth is *f.* with violence through men
21. 19. Hagar went and *f.* the bottle with water
24. 16. Rebekah *f.* her pitcher and came up
26. 15. the Philistines had *f.* the wells with earth
Exod. 1. 7. the children of Israel *f.* the land
2. 16. they *f.* the troughs to water their flock
28. 3. whom I have *f.* with wisdom, 35. 35.
31. 3. I have *f.* him with the Spirit of God, 35. 31.
40. 34. the glory of the Lord *f.* the tabernacle, 35.
Deut. 26. 12. they may eat within thy gates and be *f.*
31. 20. when they have eaten and *f.* themselves
Josh. 9. 13. these bottles we *f.* were new and are rent
1 *Kings* 8. 10. the cloud *f.* the house of the Lord
11. glory of L. *f.* the house, 2 *Chr.* 5. 14. | 7. 1, 2.
18. 35. and he *f.* the trench also with water
20. 27. but the Syrians *f.* the country
2 *Kings* 3. 25. they cast every man his stone and *f.* it
21. 16. Manasseh *f.* Jerusalem with blood, 24. 4.
23. 14. Josiah *f.* their places with the bones of men
Ezra 9. 11. which have *f.* it from one end to another
Job 3. 15. with princes who *f.* their houses with silver
16. 8. and thou hast *f.* me with wrinkles
22. 18. yet he *f.* their houses with good things
Psal. 38. 7. for my loins are *f.* with loathsome disease
71. 8. let my mouth be *f.* with thy praise and honour
72. 19. let the whole earth be *f.* with his glory
80. 9. didst cause it to take deep root, it *f.* the land
104. 28. thou openest thine hand, are *f.* with good
123. 3. for we are exceedingly *f.* with contempt
4. our soul is exceedingly *f.* with scorning
Prov. 5. 10. lest strangers be *f.* with thy wealth
25. 16. lest thou be *f.* with honey and vomit it
30. 16. the earth that is not *f.* with water
22. and for a fool when he is *f.* with meat
Eccl. 1. 8. nor is the ear *f.* with hearing
6. 3. and his soul be not *f.* with good
7. and yet the appetite is not *f.*
Cant. 5. 2. open to me, my head is *f.* with dew
Isa. 6. 1. high and lifted up, and his train *f.* the temp.
21. 3. therefore are my loins *f.* with pain
33. 5. the Lord hath *f.* Zion with judgment
34. 6. the sword of the Lord is *f.* with blood
43. 24. nor *f.* me with the fat of thy sacrifices
65. 20. nor an old man that hath not *f.* his days
Jer. 15. 17. for thou hast *f.* me with indignation
16. 18. they *f.* mine inheritance with carcases
19. 4. they have *f.* this place with blood of innocents
41. 9. Ishmael *f.* the pit with them that were slain
46. 12. and thy cry hath *f.* the land
51. 34. he hath *f.* his belly with my delicates
Lam. 3. 15. he hath *f.* me with bitterness
30. he is *f.* full with reproach
Ezek. 8. 17. they have *f.* the land with violence
10. 3. and the cloud *f.* the inner court
11. 6. ye have *f.* the streets with the slain
28. 16. they *f.* the midst of thee with violence
36. 38. waste cities shall be *f.* with flocks of men
43. 5. the glory of the Lord *f.* the house, 44. 4.
Dan. 2. 35. the stone cut out *f.* the whole earth
Nah. 2. 12. the lion *f.* his holes with prey
Hab. 2. 16. thou art *f.* with shame for glory
Hag. 1. 6. ye drink, but ye are not *f.* with drink
Zech. 9. 13. I have *f.* the bow with Ephraim
Mat. 27. 48. one of them ran, and *f.* a spunge with vinegar, *Mark* 15. 36. *John* 19. 29.
Mark 2. 21. new piece that *f.* it up taketh from old
7. 27. Jesus said, let the children first be *f.*
Luke 1. 53. he hath *f.* the hungry with good things
2. 40. Jesus waxed strong in spirit, *f.* with wisdom
5. 7. and they came and *f.* both the ships
14. 23. compel them to come, that my house be *f.*
15. 16. would fain have *f.* his belly with husks
John 2. 7. and they *f.* them up to the brim
6. 13. they *f.* twelve baskets with fragments
16. 6. I said these things, sorrow hath *f.* your heart
Acts 2. 2. as of a rushing mighty wind, *f.* the house
4. 8. then Peter, *f.* with the Holy Ghost, said
5. 3. why hath Satan *f.* thine heart to lie to H. Ghost?
28. ye have *f.* Jerusalem with your doctrine
9. 17. that thou mightest be *f.* with the Holy Ghost
13. 9. Paul, *f.* with the Holy Ghost, set his eyes
Rom. 1. 29. being *f.* with all unrighteousness
15. 14. that ye also are *f.* with all knowledge
24. if first I be somewhat *f.* with your company
2 *Cor.* 7. 4. I am *f.* with comfort, I am joyful
Eph. 3. 19. might be *f* with all the fulness of God

Eph. 5. 18. be not drunk with wine, but *f.* with Spirit
Phil. 1. 11. being *f.* with the fruits of righteousness
Col. 1. 9. might be *f.* with the knowledge of his will
2 *Tim.* 1. 4. that I may be *f.* with joy
Jam. 2. 16. depart in peace, be ye warmed and *f.*
Rev. 8. 5. angel *f.* the censer with the fire of the altar
15. 1. for in them is *f.* up the wrath of God
18. 6. in the cup which she hath *f.* fill to her double

Shall be FILLED.

Exod. 16. 12. in morning ye *shall be f.* with bread
Num. 14. 21. the earth *shall be f.* with glory of L.
2 *Kings* 3. 17. that valley *shall be f.* with water
Prov. 1. 31. they *shall be f.* with their own devices
3. 10. so *shall* thy barns *be f.* with plenty
12. 21. but the wicked *shall be f.* with mischief
14. 14. the backslider *shall be f.* with his own ways
18. 20. with the increase of his lips *shall* he *be f.*
20. 17. afterward his mouth *shall be f.* with gravel
24. 4. and by knowledge *shall* the chambers *be f.*
Jer. 13. 12. every bottle *shall be f.* with wine
Ezek. 23. 33. thou *shalt be f.* with drunkenness
39. 20. thus ye *shall be f.* at my table with horses
Hab. 2. 14. earth *shall be f.* with knowledge of Lord
Zech. 9. 15. and they *shall be f.* like bowls
Mat. 5. 6. blessed are they that hunger, they *shall be f.*
Luke 1. 15. John *shall be f.* with the Holy Ghost
3. 5. every valley *shall be f.* mountain brought low
6. 21. blessed ye that hunger now, ye *shall be f.*

Was FILLED.

Gen. 6. 11. and the earth *was f.* with violence
1 *Kings* 7. 14. and Hiram *was f.* with wisdom
2 *Kings* 3. 20. and the country *was f.* with water
2 *Chron.* 5. 13. then the house *was f.* with a cloud
16. 14. the bed which *was f.* with sweet odours
Psal. 126. 2. then our mouth *was f.* with laughter
Isa. 6. 4. and the house *was f.* with smoke
Jer. 51. 5. tho' their land *was f.* with sin ag. Holy
Ezek. 10. 4. and the house *was f.* with the cloud
Luke 1. 41. Elisabeth *was f.* with the Holy Ghost
67. Zacharias *was f.* with the Holy Ghost
John 12. 3. house *was f.* with the odour of ointment
Acts 19. 29. the whole city *was f.* with confusion
Rev. 15. 8. and the temple *was f.* with smoke

Were FILLED.

Hos. 13. 6. according to their pasture so were they *f.* they *were f.* and their heart was exalted
Luke 4. 28. when they heard, they *were f.* with wra.
5. 26. they glorified God, and *were f.* with fear
6. 11. they *were f.* with madness, and communed
8. 23. they *were f.* with water, and in jeopardy
John 6. 12. when they *were f.* he said, gather up
26. because ye did eat of the loaves, and *were f.*
Acts 2. 4. they *were* all *f.* with the Holy Ghost, 4. 31.
3. 10. they *were f.* with wonder and amazement
5. 17. rose up, and *were f.* with indignation
13. 45. the Jews *were f.* with envy, and spake
52. disciples *were f.* with joy and the Holy Ghost
Rev. 19. 21. all the fowls *were f.* with their flesh
See EAT.

FILLEDST.

Deut. 6. 11. and houses full, which thou *f.* not
Ezek. 27. 33. when wares went forth, *f.* many people

FILLEST.

Ps. 17. 14. whose belly thou *f.* with thy hid treasure

FILLETH.

Job 9. 18. but he *f.* me with bitterness
Psal. 84. 6. the rain also *f.* the pools
107. 9. he *f.* the hungry soul with goodness
129. 7. wherewith the mower *f.* not his hand
147. 14. he *f.* thee with the finest of the wheat
Eph. 1. 23. the fulness of him that *f.* all in all

FILLET.

Jer. 52. 21. a *f.* of twelve cubits did compass it

FILLETS.

Exod. 27. 10. the hooks of the pillars, and their *f.* shall be of silver, 11. | 38. 10, 11, 12, 17, 19.
36. 38. he overlaid their chapiters and *f.* with gold

FILLETED.

Exod. 27. 17. all shall be *f.* with silver, 38. 17.
38. 28. he overlaid their chapiters and *f.* them

FILLING.

Acts 14. 17. *f.* our hearts with food and gladness

FILTH.

Lev. 1. † 16. pluck away his crop with *f.* thereof
Isa. 4. 4. when the Lord washed away the *f.* of Zion
Nah. 3. 6. I will cast abominable *f.* upon thee
1 *Cor.* 4. 13. we are made as the *f.* of the world
1 *Pet.* 3. 21. not putting away the *f.* of the flesh

FILTHY.

Job 15. 16. how much more abomina. and *f.* is man?
Psal. 14. 3. they are altogether become *f.* 53. 3.
Isa. 64. 6. all our righteousnesses are as *f.* rags
Zeph. 3. 1. woe to her that is *f.* and polluted
Zech. 3. 3. Joshua was clothed with *f.* garments
4. take away the *f.* garments from him
Col. 3. 8. you also put off *f.* communicat. from mouth
1 *Tim.* 3. 3. no striker, not greedy of *f.* lucre, 8.
Tit. 1. 7. not soon angry, not given to *f.* lucre
11. teaching things for *f.* lucre's sake, 1 *Pet.* 5. 2.
2 *Pet.* 2. 7. Lot vexed with *f.* conversation of wicked
Jude 8. likewise these *f.* dreamers defile the flesh
Rev. 22. 11. he that is *f.* let him be *f.* still

FILTHINESS.

2 *Chron.* 29. 5. carry out the *f.* out of the holy place
Ezra 6. 21. had separated from the *f.* of the heathen
9. 11. unclean land with the *f.* of the people
Prov. 30. 12. and yet is not washed from their *f.*
Isa. 28. 8. for all tables are full of vomit and *f.*
Jer. 5. † 30. astonishment and *f.* is committed in land
23. † 14. I have seen *f.* in the prophets of Jerusalem
Lam. 1. 9. her *f.* is in her skirts, rememb. not her end
Ezek. 16. 36. because thy *f.* was poured out
22. 15. and I will consume thy *f.* out of thee
24. 11. that the *f.* of it may be molten in it
13. in thy *f.* is lewdness: because I have purged thee, and thou wast not purged, thou shalt not be purged from thy *f.*
36. 25. from all your *f.* will I cleanse you
2 *Cor.* 7. 1. let us cleanse ourselv. from all *f.* of flesh
Eph. 5. 4. nor let *f.* be once named among you
Jam. 1. 21. wherefore lay apart all *f.* receive the word
Rev. 17. 4. cup full of abominat. and *f.* of fornicat.

FINALLY.

2 *Cor.* 13. 11. *f.* my brethren, farewell, *Eph.* 6. 10. *Phil.* 3. 1. | 4. 8. 2 *Thess.* 3. 1. 1 *Pet.* 3. 8.

FIND

Signifies, [1] *To convert, or recover a thing that was lost,* Luke 15. 8, 9, 32. [2] *To invent, or discover,* 2 Chron. 2. 14. [3] *To know experimentally,* Rom. 4. 1. Rev. 2. 2. [4] *To obtain what we want and desire of God,* Mat. 7. 7. [5] *To come to,* Job 3. 22. [6] *To understand throughly,* Job 11. 7. [7] *To do, or perform,* Isa. 58. 13. [8] *To seek,* Job 33. 10. [9] *To happen upon without seeking,* Gen. 37. 15. [10] *To choose and appoint,* Acts 13. 22. [11] *To turn to, or light on,* Luke 4. 17. [12] *To observe,* Mat. 8. 10.

To find, *is used sometimes for* to attack, to surprise one's enemies, to discover their ambushes. *It is understood in this sense,* Judg. 1. 5. They found *Adoni-bezek* in Bezek. *They attacked him there. And,* 1 Sam. 31. 3. *according to the* Hebrew, *the archers belonging to the* Philistines found Saul, *they attacked him. In this sense some explain that passage in* Gen. 36. 24. This was that *Anah* that found the mules in the wilderness. *In the* Hebrew, he found the *Emims. These* Emims *are believed to be powerful people;* Deut. 2. 10, 11. The *Emims* dwelt therein in times past, a people great, and many, and tall, as the *Anakims, &c. who also were neighbours to the* Horites *here spoken of, as appears from* Gen. 14. 5, 6. Anah *therefore* found *a troop of these people: he surprised, attacked, and defeated them. Others render the* Hebrew *word* Jemim, *which is no where else used, by* waters; *that he found out some springs of water, which in those hot countries were rare and precious; or,* hot waters, *some hot and medicinal springs. Others again* mules, *as in our translation; that he found out the way of the generation of* mules, *by the copulation of an ass and a mare.*

Gen. 19. 11. they wearied themselves to *f.* the door
32. 19. you shall speak to Esau, when you *f.* him
Num. 32. 23. be sure your sin shall *f.* you out
35. 27. the revenger of blood *f.* him without city
Deut. 22. 25. a man *f.* a damsel and lie with her, 28.
Judg. 17. 8. to sojourn where he could *f.* a place, 9.
Ruth 1. 9. the L. grant ye may *f.* rest, each of you
1 *Sam.* 20. 21. saying, go, *f.* out the arrows, 36.
24. 19. if a man *f.* his enemy, will he let him go?
1 *Kings* 18. 5. peradv. we may *f.* grass to save horses
2 *Chron.* 2. 14. to *f.* out every device be put to him
32. 4. why should Assyria come and *f.* much water?
Job 23. 3. O that I knew where I might *f.* him
34. 11. cause every man to *f.* according to his ways
Psal. 10. 15. seek out his wickedn. till thou *f.* none
Prov. 2. 5. thou shalt *f.* the knowledge of God
4. 22. my words are life to those that *f.* them
8. 9. they are right to them that *f.* knowledge
12. I *f.* out knowledge of witty inventions
Eccl. 7. 14. a man should *f.* nothing for him
27. counting one by one, to *f.* out the account
12. 10. he sought to *f.* out acceptable words
Cant. 5. 8. if *f.* my beloved, tell him I am sick of love
Isa. 34. 14. the screech-owl shall *f.* a place of rest
58. 3. in the day of your fast you *f.* pleasure
Jer. 10. 18. will distress them, that they may *f.* it so
Lam. 1. 6. are become like harts that *f.* no pasture
2. 9. her prophets also *f.* no vision from God
Dan. 6. 4. the princes sought to *f.* occasion against Daniel, but could *f.* none occasion nor fault
5. shall not *f.* except we *f.* it concerning law of G.
Mat. 7. 14. strait is gate, and few there be that *f.* it
18. 13. and if so be that he *f.* it, he rejoiceth more
Mark 11. 13. if haply he might *f.* any thing thereon
13. 36. lest coming suddenly, he *f.* you sleeping
Luke 6. 7. that they might *f.* an accusation ag. him
12. 38. and *f.* them so, blessed are those servants
13. 7. he said I come seeking fruit and *f.* none
15. 4. and go after that which is lost, till he *f.* it
8. doth she not seek diligently till she *f.* it?
John 10. 9. he shall go in and out, and *f.* pasture
Acts 7. 46. desired to *f.* a tabernacle for G. of Jacob
17. 27. they might feel after him and *f.* him
23. 9. scribes, saying, we *f.* no evil in this man
Rom. 9. 19. thou wilt say, why doth he yet *f.* fault?
2 *Cor.* 9. 4. they come with me, and *f.* you unprepared
2 *Tim.* 1. 18. he may *f.* mercy of the L. in that day
See FAVOUR.

Can or *canst* FIND.

Gen. 41. 38. Phar. said, *can* we *f.* such a one as this is?
Exod. 5. 11. go, get you straw where you *can f.* it
Ezra 7. 16. all the silver and gold thou *canst f.*
Job 3. 22. and are glad when they *can f.* the grave
11. 7. *canst* thou by searching *f.* out God? *canst* thou *f.* out the Almighty unto perfection?
Prov. 20. 6. but a faithful man who *can f.*?
31. 10. who *can f.* a virt. woman price above rubies?
Eccl. 3. 11. no man *can f.* out the work God maketh
7. 24. that which is exceeding deep, who *can f.* it?
Jer. 5. 1. if ye *can f.* a man that seeketh truth

Cannot FIND.

Gen. 38. 22. he returned, and said, I *cannot f.* her
1 *Kings* 18. 12. if he *cannot f.* thee, he will slay me
Job 17. 10. I *cannot f.* one wise man among you
37. 23. touching Almighty, we *cannot f.* him out
Eccl. 8. 17. a man *cannot f.* out the work under sun

FIND *grace.*

Gen. 32. 5. I may *f. grace* in thy sight, *Exod.* 33. 13.
33. 8. these are to *f. grace* in the sight of my lord
15. let me *f. gr.* ‖ 34. 11. let me *f. gr.* in your eyes
47. 25. let us *f. grace* in the sight of my lord
Ruth 2. 2. in whose sight I shall *f. grace*
1 *Sam.* 1. 18. let thy handmaid *f. grace* in thy sight
2 *Sam.* 16. 4. that I may *f. grace* in thy sight, O king
Heb. 4. 16. that we may *f. gr.* to help in time of need

I FIND.

Gen. 18. 26. if *I f.* in Sodom fifty righteous in city
28. if *I f.* there forty-five ‖ 30. if *I f.* thirty there
Psal. 132. 5. till *I f.* out a place for the Lord
Eccl. 7. 26. and *I f.* more bitter than death the woman
Cant. 8. 1. when *I* should *f.* thee, I would kiss thee
Jer. 45. 3. I fainted in my sighing, and *I f.* no rest
Luke 23. 4. Pilate said to the chief priests, *I f.* no fault in this man, *John* 18. 38. | 19. 4, 6.
Rom. 7. 18. to perform that which is good *I f.* not
21. *I f.* then a law, that when I would do good

Not FIND, or FIND *not.*

Exod. 16. 25. to-day ye shall *not f.* it in the field
Lev. 12. † 8. if her hand *f. not* sufficiently
1 *Sam.* 23. 17. Saul my father shall *not f.* thee
2 *Sam.* 17. 20. had sought, and could *not f.* them
Prov. 1. 28. they shall seek me early, but they shall *not f.* me, *Hos.* 5. 6. *John* 7. 34, 36.
Eccl. 7. 28. which my soul seeketh, but I *f. not*
Cant. 5. 6. I sought him, but I could *not f.* him
Isa. 41. 12. seek them, but shalt *not f.* them, *Hos.* 2. 7.
Dan. 6. 5. we shall *not f.* any occasion against Dan.
Hos. 2. 6. make a wall that she shall *not f.* her paths
Amos. 8. 12. shall run to seek the word, and *not f.* it
Luke 5. 19. *not f.* what way they might bring him
19. 48. could *not f.* what they might do to Jesus
John 7. 35. whither go, that we shall *not f.* him
Rom. 7. 18. how to do that which is good, I *f. not*
2 *Cor.* 12. 20. I shall *not f.* you such as I would
Rev. 9. 6. shall men seek death, and shall *not f.* it

Shall, or *shalt* FIND.

Gen. 44. † 34. lest I see the evil that *shall f.* my father
Deut. 4. 29. if thence thou seek L. thou *shalt f.* him
28. 65. thou *shalt f.* no ease among these nations
Judg. 9. 33. then mayest do as thou *shalt f.* occasion
1 *Sam.* 9. 13. ye *shall f.* him before he go up to eat
10. 2. there *shall f.* two men by Rachel's sepulchre
† 7. thou shalt do as thy hand *shall f.*
2 *Kings* 7. † 9. if we tarry, we *shall f.* punishment
2 *Chr.* 20. 16. ye *shall f.* them at end of the brook
30. 9. your brethren and child. *shall f.* compassion
Ezra 4. 15. thou *shalt f.* in the book of records
Psal. 17. 3. thou hast tried me, and *shalt f.* nothing
21. 8. thy hand *shall f.* out all thine enemies
Prov. 1. 13. we *shall f.* all precious substance
8. 17. they that seek me early *shall f.* me, *Jer.* 29. 13.
16. 20. that handleth matter wisely, *shall f.* good
19. 8. he that keepeth understanding *shall f.* good
Eccl. 11. 1. for thou *shalt f.* it after many days
Jer. 2. 24. in her month they *shall f.* her
6. 16. ye *shall f.* rest to your souls, *Mat.* 11. 29.
Hos. 12. 8. in labours they *shall f.* none iniquity in me
Mat. 7. 7. seek and ye *shall f.* *Luke* 11. 9.
10. 39. he that loseth his life for my sake *shall f.* it
17. 27. thou *shalt f.* a piece of money, that take
21. 2. ye *shall f.* an ass tied, and a colt, *Mark* 11. 2.
22. 9. as many as ye *shall f.* bid to the marriage
24. 46. when cometh, *s. f.* so doing, *Luke* 12. 37, 43.
Luke 2. 12. ye *shall f.* babe wrapt in swaddl. clothes
18. 8. Son of man cometh, *shall* he *f.* faith on earth?
John 21. 6. cast the net on the right side, ye *shall f.*
Rev. 18. 14. and thou *shalt f.* them no more at all

FINDEST.

Gen. 31. 32. with whomsoever thou *f.* thy gods
Ezek. 3. 1. eat that thou *f.* eat this roll, and go speak

FINDETH.

Gen. 4. 14. every one that *f.* me shall slay me
Deut. 19. † 5. the head slippeth, and *f.* his neighbour
Job 33. 10. behold, he *f.* occasions against me
Psal. 119. 162. I rejoice at word, as one that *f.* spoil
Prov. 3. 13. happy is the man that *f.* wisdom
8. 35. whoso *f.* me, *f.* life, shall obtain favour of Ld.
14. 6. a scorner seeketh wisdom, and *f.* it not
17. 20. he that hath a froward heart, *f.* no good
18. 22. whoso *f.* a wife *f.* good thing, obtains favour
21. 10. his neighbour *f.* no favour in his eyes
21. he that followeth after mercy *f.* life and honour
Eccl. 9. 10. whatsoever thy hand *f.* to do, do it
Lam. 1. 3. she dwells among heathen, she *f.* no rest
Hos. 14. 3. for in thee the fatherless *f.* mercy
Mat. 7. 8. and he that seeketh *f.* *Luke* 11. 10.
10. 39. he that *f.* his life shall lose it
12. 43. walketh thro' dry places, seeking rest, *f.* none
44. *f.* it empty, swept, and garnished, *Luke* 11. 25.
26. 40. he *f.* his disciples asleep, *Mark* 14. 37.
John 1. 41. he first *f.* his own brother Simon
43. Jesus *f.* Philip ‖ 45. Philip *f.* Nathaneel
5. 14. afterward Jesus *f.* him in the temple

FINDING.

Gen. 4. 15. lest any *f.* Cain should kill him
Job 9. 10. who doeth things past *f.* out and wonders
Psal. 32. † 6. every one shall pray in a time of *f.*
Isa. 58. 13. *f.* thine own pleas. nor speaking words
Luke 11. 24. unclean spirit seeking rest and *f.* none
Acts 4. 21. *f.* nothing how they might punish them
19. 1. Paul came, and *f.* certain disciples, 21. 4.
21. 2. *f.* ship sailing over to Phenicia, went aboard
Rom. 11. 33. unsearchable, and his ways past *f.* out
Heb. 8. 8. for *f.* fault with them, he saith, behold

FINE.

Job 28. 1. there is a place for gold where they *f.* it

FINE.

Ezra 8. 27. and two vessels of *f.* copper, as gold
Job 28. † 15. *f.* gold shall not be given for wisdom
Isa. 19. 9. they that work in *f.* flax be confounded
Rev. 1. 15. his feet like unto *f.* brass, 2. 18.

FINE *flour.*

Lev. 2. 1. his offering shall be of *f. flour,* 24. 5.
4. cakes of *f. flour* mingled with oil, 5. 7. | 7. 12. 14. 10, 21. | 23. 13. *Num.* 6. 15. | 7. 13, 19, 25, 31, 37, 43, 49, 55, 61. | 8. 8.
5. 11. the tenth part of an ephah of *f. flour,* 6. 20.
1 *Kings* 4. 22. thirty measures of *f. flour* in one day
2 *Kings* 7. 1. measure *f. flour* sold for shekel, 16, 18.
1 *Chr.* 9. 29. were appointed to oversee *f. flour,* 23. 29.
Ezek. 16. 13. thou didst eat *f. flour,* honey, and oil
19. I gave thee *f. flour,* and oil, and honey
46. 14. an hin of oil to temper with the *f. flour*
Rev. 18. 13. none buyeth her merchandise of *f. flour*

FINE *gold.*

2 *Chr.* 3. 5. ceiling, which he overlaid with *f. gold*
8. the most holy he overlaid with *f. gold*
Job 28. † 15. *f. gold* shall not be given for wisdom
17. exchange of it shall not be for jewels of *f. gold*
31. 24. or said to *f. gold,* thou art my confidence
Psal. 19. 10. are more to be desired than much *f. gold*
119. 127. I love thy commandments above *f. gold*
Prov. 3. 14. and the gain of wisdom than *f. gold*
8. 19. my fruit is better than gold, than *f. gold*
Prov. 25. 12. as an ornament of *f. gold,* so is a reprover
Cant. 5. 11. his head is as most *f. gold* locks bushy
15. his legs are as pillars set on sockets of *f. gold*
Isa. 13. 12. will make a man more precious than *f. g.*
Lam. 4. 1. how is the most *f. gold* changed!
2. the precious sons of Zion comparable to *f. gold*
Dan. 2. 32. this image's head *f. gold,* breast of silver
10. 5. whose loins were girded with *f. gold* of Uphaz
Zech. 9. 3. Tyrus heaped *f. gold* as mire of the streets

FINE *linen.*

Gen. 41. 42. Pharaoh arrayed him in vest. of *f. linen*
Exod. 25. 4. this is the offering ye shall take, *f. linen*
26. 1. with ten curtains of *f.* twined *linen*
31. the vail of *f. linen,* 36. 35. 2 *Chron.* 3. 14.
36. thou shalt make an hanging of *f.* twined *linen,* 27. 9, 16, 18. | 36. 37. | 38. 9, 16, 18.
28. 5. take gold and *f. linen* to make garments
6. shall make the ephod of *f. linen,* 39. 2.
8. girdle *f. linen,* 39. 5, 29. ‖ 15. breast-plate, 39. 8.
39. thou shalt embroider the coat of *f. linen,* and thou shalt make the mitre of *f. linen*
35. 6. let him bring an offering of *f. linen*
23. every man with whom was found *f. linen*
25. the women brought of scarlet and *f. linen*
35. them hath he filled with wisdom to work all manner of work and *f. linen,* 38. 23. 2 *Chron.* 2. 14.
36. 8. that wrought curtains of *f. linen* and blue
39. 27. they made coats of *f. linen* for Aaron
28. made a mitre of *f. linen,* and bonnets of *f. linen*
1 *Chron.* 4. 21. families of them that wrought *f. linen*
15. 27. David was clothed with a robe of *f. linen*
Esth. 1. 6. were hangings fasten. with cords of *f. linen*
8. 15. Mordecai went with a garment of *f. linen*
Prov. 7. 16. I have decked my bed with *f. linen*
31. 24. she maketh *f. linen,* and selleth it
Isa. 3. 23. the Lord will take away the *f. linen*
Ezek. 16. 10. I girded thee about with *f. linen*
13. thy raiment was of *f. linen* and silk
27. 7. *f. linen* from Egypt was to be thy sail
16. Syria occupied in thy fairs with *f. linen*
Mark 15. 46. Joseph bought *f. linen* and wrapped
Luke 16. 19. rich man clothed in purple and *f. linen*
Rev. 18. 12. merchandise of *f. linen* depart. from thee
16. that city clothed in *f. linen* is come to nought
19. 8. to her was granted to be arrayed in *f. linen*
14. the armies in heaven were clothed in *f. linen*

FINE *meal.*

Gen. 18. 6. make ready three measures of *f. meal*

FINER.

Prov. 25. 4. there shall come forth a vessel for the *f*

FINEST.

Psal. 81. 16. have fed thee with the *f.* of the wheat
147. 14. he filleth thee with the *f.* of the wheat

FINING.

Prov. 17. 3. *f.* pot is for silv. furnace for gold, 27. 21.

FINGER.

The finger of God *signifies his power, his operation.* Pharaoh's *magicians discovered the* finger of God *in the miracles which* Moses *wrought,* Exod. 8. 19. *This legislator gave the law written with the finger of God to the* Hebrews, *Exod.* 31. 18. *It was written immediately by the power or Spirit of God, and not by any art of man. Our Saviour says, he cast out devils by the* finger, or Spirit, *of God, which he intimates was a sign that the kingdom of God was come; that God's spiritual government of his church was begun to be exercised among the* Jews *by the* Messiah, *Luke* 11. 20.

To put forth one's finger *is a bantering, insulting gesture.* Isa. 58. 9. If thou take away from the midst of thee the yoke, and the putting out of the finger. *If thou take away from the midst of thee the chain or yoke wherewith thou overwhelmest thy debtors, and forbear pointing at them, and using jeering and insulting gestures. Some take this for a menacing or threatening gesture.*

Exod. 8. 19. the magicians said, this is the *f.* of God
29. 12. put of the blood on the altar with thy *f.*
31. 18. tables written with the *f.* of God, *Deut.* 9. 10.
Lev. 4. 6. priest shall dip his *f.* in the blood and sprinkle it, 17, 25, 30, 34. | 8. 15. | 9. 9. | 16. 14, 19.
14. 16. the priest shall dip his right *f.* in the oil, and sprinkle of the oil with his *f.* seven times, 27.
Num. 19. 4. priest shall take of her blood with his *f.*
1 *Kings* 12. 10. my little *f.* thicker, 2 *Chron.* 10. 10.
Isa. 58. 9. if take away the putting forth of the *f.*
Luke 11. 20. if I with the *f.* of God cast out devils
16. 24. that he may dip the tip of his *f.* in water
John 8. 6. and with his *f.* wrote on the ground
20. 25. and put my *f.* into the print of the nails
27. reach hither thy *f.* and behold my hands

FINGERS.

2 *Sam.* 21. 20. on every hand six *f.* 1 *Chr.* 20. 6.
Psal. 8. 3. when consider thy heavens, work of thy *f.*
144. 1. the Lord, who teacheth my *f.* to fight
Prov. 6. 13. a wicked man teacheth with his *f.*
7. 3. bind them on thy *f.* write them on thy heart
Cant. 5. 5. and my *f.* with sweet-smelling myrrh
Isa. 2. 8. that which their own *f.* have made, 17. 8.
59. 3. hands defiled with blood, and *f.* with iniquity
Jer. 52. 21. the thickness of one pillar four *f.*
Dan. 5. 5. came forth *f.* of a man's hand, and wrote
Mat. 23. 4. they bind heavy burdens, but they will not move them with one of their *f.* *Luke* 11. 46.
Mark 7. 33. and he put his *f.* into his ears and he spit

FINISH.

To bring to pass, fulfil, perfect. Our blessed Lord said on the cross, It is finished, *John* 19. 30. *Our great Redeemer, by what he did and suffered, performed the will of God, and the whole work which the Father gave him to do; which was to obtain eternal redemption. He was the substance and end of all the types, and the legal dispensation. He completed and finished righteousness, removed the curse, and radically completed our salvation.*

Gen. 6. 16. and in a cubit shalt thou *f.* it above
Dan. 9. 24. to *f.* transgression, and make end of sin
Zech. 4. 9. Zerubbabel's hands shall also *f.* it

Mat. 10. † 23. ye shall not f. the cities of Israel
Luke 14. 28. whether he have sufficient to f.
29. after laid the foundation, and is not able to f. it
30. this man began to build, was not able to f.
John 4. 34. my meat is to do his will, and f. his work
5. 36. works which the Father hath given me to f.
Acts 20. 24. that I might f. my course with joy
Rom. 9. 28. for he will f. the work, and cut short
2 Cor. 8. 6. so he would also f. in you the same grace
Phil. 1. † 6. he that hath begun, will also f. it

FINISHED.

Gen. 2. 1. thus the heavens and the earth were f.
Exod. 39. 32. thus was all the work f. 40. 33.
Deut. 31. 24. an end of writing, till they were f.
Josh. 4. 10. the priest stood, till every thing was f.
Ruth 3. 18. the man not rest, till he have f. the thing
1 Kings 6. 9. Solomon built the house and f. it,
14, 22, 38. 2 Chron. 5. 1. | 7. 11.
7. 1. Solomon f. all his house, 9. 1, 25. 2 Chr. 8. 16.
22. so was the work of the pillars f.
1 Chr. 27. 24. Joab began to number, but he f. not
28. 20. Lord not fail thee, till thou hast f. the work
2 Chr. 24. 14. and when they had f. the repairing
29. 28. the singers sang, till burnt-offering was f.
31. 7. they f. the heaps in the seventh month
Ezra 4. † 12. the Jews have f. the walls
5. 16. hath it been in building, and yet it is not f.
6. 14. the elders of the Jews built and f. it, 15.
Neh. 6. 15. so the wall was f. in fifty-two days
Dan 5. 26. God hath numbered thy kingd. and f. it
12. 7. all these things shall be f.
Mat. 13. 53. when Jesus had f. these parables
19. 1. when Jesus had f. these sayings, 26. 1.
John 17. 4. I have f. the work thou gavest me to do
19. 30. he said, it is f. and he bowed his head
Acts 21. 7. when we had f. our course from Tyre
2 Tim. 4. 7. I have f. my course, I have kept the faith
Heb. 4. 3. the works were f. from the foundation
Jam. 1. 15. sin, when it is f. bringeth forth death
Rev. 10. 7. the mystery of God should be f.
11. 7. when witnesses shall have f. their testimony
20. 5. lived not, till the thousand years were f.

FINISHER.

Heb. 12. 2. looking to Jesus, author and f. of our faith

FINS.

Lev. 11. 9. whatever hath f. and scales eat, Deut. 14. 9.
10. that hath not f. shall be an abomination, 12.

FIRE

Is one of the four elements, which not only affords light and heat, but whereby likewise we try and purge metals. God hath often appeared in fire, *and encompassed with* fire; *as when he shewed himself in the burning bush, and descended on mount* Sinai *in the midst of flames, thunderings, and lightning,* Exod. 3. 2. | 19. 18. Fire *is a symbol of the holiness and justice of God:* The Lord thy God is a consuming fire, *Deut.* 4. 24. *He shewed himself to his prophets,* Isaiah, Ezekiel, *and St.* John *in the midst of* fire, *Isa.* 6. 4. *Ezek.* 1. 4. *Rev.* 1. 14. *The Psalmist describes the chariot of God as all in a flame,* Psal. 18. 12, 13, 14. *And it is said that God will appear in the midst of fire at his second coming,* 2 Thess. 1. 8. Daniel *says, that* a fiery stream issued and came forth from before him; *noting the speedy executing of his judgments for the terror of the wicked and comfort of the godly,* Dan. 7. 10. *The wrath of God is compared to* fire, *Psal.* 18. 8. *and the effects of his wrath, which are war, famine, and other scourges, are described under the same idea,* Psal. 66. 12. Jer. 48. 45.

Our Saviour is compared to fire. *Mal.* 3. 2. He is like a refiner's fire, and like fuller's soap. *He shall consume the wicked by his judgments, and purify those who are sincere by his doctrine. The Holy Ghost likewise is compared to* fire. *Mat.* 3. 11. He shall baptize you with the Holy Ghost and with fire. *To verify this prediction, Jesus sent the Holy Ghost who descended upon his disciples in the form of tongues, or like sparks of* fire, *Acts* 2. 3. *It is the work of the Holy Spirit to enlighten, purify, and sanctify the soul, and to inflame it with love to God, and zeal for his glory. The angels themselves, as the ministers of God, are compared to* a burning fire, *speedy and irresistible in the execution of his commands,* Psal. 104. 4. *The Lord, or his angel, led the* Israelites *in their journey through the wilderness, under the form of a pillar of* fire, *Exod.* 13. 21.

Fire *from heaven fell frequently on the victims sacrificed to the Lord, as a mark of his presence and approbation. It is thought that God in this manner expressed his acceptance of* Abel's *sacrifices,* Gen. 4. 4. *When the Lord made a covenant with* Abraham, *a fire, like that of a furnace, passed through the divided pieces of the sacrifices, and consumed them,* Gen. 15. 17. Fire *fell upon the sacrifices which* Moses *offered at the dedication of the tabernacle,* Lev. 9. 24. *And upon those of* Manoah, Samson's *father,* Judg. 13. 19, 20. *Upon* Solomon's *at the dedication of the temple,* 2 Chron. 7. 1. *And upon* Elijah's *at mount* Carmel, 1 *Kings* 18. 38.

The torments of hell are described by fire, *both in the Old and New Testament.* Moses *inveighing against the* Israelites, *who rebelled against the Lord, says to them;* A fire is kindled in mine anger, and shall burn unto the lowest hell, *Deut.* 32. 22. Isaiah *is still more express,* Who among us shall dwell with the devouring fire? who among us shall dwell with everlasting burnings? *Isa.* 33. 14. *And in* chap. 66. 24. Their worm shall not die, neither shall their fire be quenched. *Our Saviour makes use of the same similitude, to represent the punishment of the damned,* Mark 9. 44. *He likewise speaks frequently of the* eternal fire prepared for the devil, *his angels, and reprobates,* Mat. 25. 41. *The sting and remorse of conscience is the worm that will never die; and the wrath of God upon their souls and bodies, the* fire *that shall never go out. There are likewise who maintain that by worm is to be understood a common, living, and material, not an allegorical and figurative* worm; *and by* fire, *a real, elementary, and material* fire. *Among the maintainers of this opinion are* Austin, Cyprian, Chrysostom, Jerome, &c.

The word of God is compared to fire, *Jer.* 23. 29. Is not my word like as a fire? *It is full of life and efficacy; like a fire, it warms, melts, and heals my people, and is powerful to consume the dross, and burn up the chaff and stubble. And the apostle says, that every man's doctrine should be tried by fire, that is, by the light of the word, of what nature it is, whether it be true or false, sound and solid, or corrupt and frothy,* 1 Cor. 3. 13. Fire *is likewise taken for persecution, dissension, and division.* Luke 12. 49. I am come to send fire on the earth; *that is, Upon my coming and publishing the gospel, there will follow, through the devil's malice, and the corruption of men, much persecution to the professors thereof, and manifold divisions in the world, whereby men will be tried whether they be faithful or not. The church of God is compared to a* fire. *Obad.* 18. The house of *Jacob* shall be a *fire: The church shall subdue all her enemies. Carnal vain shifts of men's own devising, whereby they seek to support, relieve, and comfort themselves against the judgments denounced against them, are likewise compared to* fire, *Isa.* 50. 11. *As are also the lies, slanders, and other provoking speeches of ungodly men;* Prov. 16. 27. *And in* his lips there is a burning fire.

Gen. 15. † 17. a lamp of f. passed betw. those pieces
22. 6. Abraham took f. in his hand, and a knife
7. my father, behold the f. and the wood, but where
Exod. 3. 2. and behold, the bush burned with f.
9. 23. Lord sent hail and the f. along on ground
24. there was hail, and f. mingled with the hail
12. 8. shall eat the flesh in that night roast with f. 9.
19. 18. the Ld. descended upon mount Sinai in f.
22. 6. if f. break out, and catch in thorns
32. 24. then I cast gold into f. and came this calf
40. 38. and f. was on the tabernacle by night through all their journey, Num. 9. 16. Deut. 1. 33.
Lev. 1. 7. the sons of the priest shall put f. on the altar, and lay wood in order upon the f.
8. upon the wood that is in the f. 12, 17. | 3. 5.
2. 14. shalt offer green ears of corn dried by the f.
6. 9. the f. of the altar be burning in it, 10, 12, 13.
9. 24. there came a f. out from before the Lord
10. 1. the sons of Aaron put f. in their censers
2. there went out f. from Ld. and devoured them
16. 13. he shall put the incense upon the f.
18. 21. thou shalt not let any of thy seed pass thro' f. to Molech, Deut. 18. 10. 2 Kings 17. 17. | 23. 10.
Num. 6. 18. shall take the hair, and put it in the f.
11. 2. when Moses prayed the f. was quenched
16. 7. take ye censers, and put f. therein, 18.
37. that he take the censers, and scatter f. yonder
46. take a censer, and put f. therein from off altar
18. 9. be thine of most holy things reserved from f.
21. 28. for there is a f. gone out from Heshbon
31. 23. every thing that may abide f. go thro' the f.
Deut. 4. 11. and the mountain burnt with f. 9. 15.
36. and upon earth he shewed thee his great f.
5. 5. for ye were afraid by reason of the f.
18. 16. nor let me see this great f. any more
33. † 2. from his right hand went a f. of law for them
Josh. 7. 25. all Israel burned Achan with f.
Judg. 6. 21. and there rose up f. out of the rock
9. 15. let f. come out of bramble and devour cedars
16. 9. as a thread of tow when it toucheth the f.
1 Kings 18. 23. lay it on wood, put no f. under, 25.
24. the God that answereth by f. let him be God
38. then the f. of the Lord fell, 2 Chron. 7. 1, 3.
19. 12. after the earthquake a f. but the Lord was not in the f. after the f. a still small voice
2 Kings 1. 10. then let f. come down from heaven
12. and the f. of God came down from heaven
2. 11. there appeared a chariot and horses of f.
6. 17. the mountain was full of chariots of f.
16. 3. Ahaz made his son to pass through the f.
19. 18. and have cast their gods into the f.
21. 6. Manasseh made son pass thro' f. 2 Chr. 33. 6.
23. 10. no man might make his son pass thro' the f.
1 Chr. 21. 26. Lord answered him from heaven by f.
2 Chr. 35. 13. they roasted the passover with f.
Neh. 2. 3. the gates thereof are consumed with f. 13.
Job 1. 16. the f. of God is fallen from heaven
18. 5. and the spark of his f. shall not shine
28. 5. and under it is turned up as it were f.
41. 19. burning lamps, and sparks of f. leap out
Psal. 39. 3. while I was musing the f. burned
46. 9. he burneth the chariot in the f.
66. 12. we went through f. and through water
68. 2. as wax melteth before f. so let wicked perish
74. 7. they have cast f. into thy sanctuary
78. 14. all the night with a light of f. 105. 39.
83. 14. as the f. burneth the wood, and as the flame
97. 3. a f. goeth before him and burneth up enemies
105. 32. he gave hail and flaming f. in their land
118. 12. they are quenched as the f. of thorns
140. 10. let them be cast into the f. into deep pits
148. 8. f. and hail, stormy wind fulfilling his word
Prov. 6. 27. can a man take f. in his bosom
16. 27. and in his lips there is as a burning f.
26. 20. where no wood is, there the f. goeth out
21. as wood is to f. so is contentious man to kindle
30. 16. the grave and the f. saith not, it is enough
Isa. 9. 5. this shall be with burning and fuel of f.
18. for wickedness burneth as the f.
19. the people shall be as the fuel of the f.
10. 16. shall kindle a burning like burning of a f.
17. and the light of Israel shall be for a f.
30. 14. not be found a sherd to take f. from hearth
33. the pile thereof is f. and much wood
31. 9. saith the Lord, whose f. is in Zion
37. 19. kings of Assyria have cast their gods into f.
43. 2. when thou walkest through f. not be burnt
Isa. 44. 16. he burneth part thereof in the f. he warmeth himself, and saith, aha, I have seen the f.
47. 14. they shall be as stubble, the f. shall burn them
50. 11. walk in light of your f. and in the sparks
64. 2. as when the melting f. burneth, the f. causeth the waters to boil to make thy name known
65. 5. these are a f. that burneth all the day
66. 15. for behold, the Lord will come with f.
16. for by f. will the Lord plead with all flesh
24. worm not die, neither their f. be quenched
Jer. 4. 4. lest my fury come forth like f. and burn
5. 14. I will make my words in thy mouth f.
20. 9. his word was as a f. shut up in my bones
21. 12. lest my fury go out like f. and burn, that none
22. 7. shall cut down cast choice cedars in the f.
29. 22. whom the king of Babylon roasted in the f.
32. 35. high places, to cause their sons to pass thro' the f. to Molech, Ezek. 16. 21. | 20. 26, 31.
36. 22. and there was a f. on the hearth burning
23. Jehudi cut the roll, and cast it into the f.
48. 45. but a f. shall come forth out of Heshbon
51. 58. the folk shall labour in vain and in the f.
Lam. 2. 3. he burned against Jacob like a flaming f.
4. he bent his bow, he poured out his fury like f.
Ezek. 1. 4. I looked, behold, a f. infolding itself
13. the f. was bright, and out of the f. lightning
10. 6. saying, take f. from between the wheels
7. one cherub stretched forth his hand to the f.
21. 31. I will blow against thee in the f. 22. 21.
32. thou shalt be for fuel to f. no more remembered
22. 20. to blow f. upon it, to melt it, so gather you
24. 9. saith Lord, I will even make pile for f. great
12. her scum shall be in f. in filthiness is lewdness
28. 18. will bring forth a f. from the midst of thee
36. 5. in the f. of my jealousy have I spoken, 38. 19.
Dan. 3. 27. upon whose bodies the f. had no power, nor the smell of f. had passed on them
7. 9. his throne like flames, wheels like burning f.
10. 6. his face as lightning, his eyes as lamps of f.
Hos. 7. 6. in the morning it burneth as a flaming f.
Joel 2. 30. blood f. and pillars of smoke, Acts 2. 19.
Amos 5. 6. lest he break out like f. in house of Joseph
7. 4. behold, the Lord God called to contend by f.
Obad. 18. and the house of Jacob shall be a f.
Mic. 1. 4. shall be molten under him as wax before f.
Nah. 1. 6. fury poured out like f. rocks thrown down
Hab. 2. 13. the people shall labour in the very f.
Zech. 2. 5. will be unto her a wall of f. round about
3. 2. is not this a brand plucked out of the f.?
12. 6. like a hearth of f. and like torch of f. in sheaf
13. 9. I will bring the third part through the f.
Mal. 3. 2. he is like a refiner's f. and fuller's soap
Mat. 3. 10. every tree that bringeth not forth good fruit is cast into f. 7. 19. Luke 3. 9. John 15. 6.
11. baptize with Holy Ghost, and f. Luke 3. 16.
13. 42. and shall cast them into a furnace of f. 50.
17. 15. oft-times he falleth into the f. Mark 9. 22.
18. 8. rather than having two hands or two feet, to be cast into everlasting f. Mark 9. 43, 46.
25. 41. depart from me, ye cursed, into everlast. f.
Mark 9. 44. where the f. is not quenched, 45.
14. 54. and Peter warmed himself at the f.
Luke 9. 54. wilt thou that we command f. to come?
17. 29. the same day it rained f. and brimstone
22. 56. a maid beheld him as he sat by the f.
Acts 2. 3. appeared to them cloven tongues, like as f.
28. 3. when Paul had laid sticks on the f.
5. he shook off the beast into the f. felt no harm
1 Cor. 3. 13. it shall be revealed by f. and the f. shall try every man's work, of what sort it is
15. he himself shall be saved, yet so as by f.
2 Thess. 1. 8. in flaming f. taking vengeance on them
Heb. 1. 7. who maketh his ministers a flame of f.
11. 34. who thro' faith quenched the violence of f.
12. 18. are not come to mount that burned with f.
Jam. 3. 5. how great a matter a little f. kindleth!
6. and the tongue is a f. a world of iniquity
5. 3. and shall eat your flesh as it were f.
1 Pet. 1. 7. than of gold, tho' it be tried with f.
2 Pet 3. 7. reserved unto f. against day of judgment
12. the heavens being on f. shall be dissolved
Jude 7. suffering the vengeance of eternal f.
23. others save pulling them out of the f.
Rev. 3. 18. thee to buy of me gold tried in the f.
4. 5. seven lamps of f. burning before the throne
8. 5. the angel filled the censer with f. of the altar
7. there followed hail and f. mingled with blood
8. as it were a great mountain burning with f.
9. 17. and out of their mouths issued f. 11. 5.
18. the third part of men was killed by the f.
13. 13. he maketh f. come down from heaven
14. 18. another angel which had power over the f.
15. 2. I saw as it were a sea of glass mingled with f.
16. 8. power was given him to scorch men with f.
20. 9. and f. came down from God out of heaven
10. the devil was cast into lake of f. and brimstone
14. death and hell were cast into the lake of f.
15. whoso not written in book of life, cast into f.
21. 8. have part in the lake which burneth with f.
See BRIMSTONE, BURN, or BURNT, COALS, CONSUME, CONSUMING, DEVOUR, DEVOURED, DEVOURING, FLAME, HELL, MIDST.

Kindle, or *kindled* FIRE.

Exod. 22. 6. he that *kindled* the f. make restitution
35. 3. ye shall *kindle* no f. on the sabbath day
Deut. 32. 22. for a f. is *kindled* in my anger, and shall burn to lowest hell, Jer. 15. 14. | 17. 4.
2 Sam. 22. 13. before him were coals of f. *kindled*
Psal. 78. 21. so a f. was *kindled* against Jacob
106. 18. a f. was *kindled* in their company
Isa. 10. 16. he shall *kindle* a burning like a f.
50. 11. behold, all ye that *kindle* a f. that compass
Jer. 7. 18. children gathered wood, fathers *kindled* f
11. 16. he hath *kindled* f. on the green olive
17. 27. then will I *kindle* a f. in the gates thereof
21. 14. I will *kindle* a f. in the forest thereof
43. 12. I will *kindle* a f. in the houses of the gods
49. 27. I will *kindle* a f. in the wall of Damascus
50. 32. and I will *kindle* a f. in his cities
Lam. 4. 11. and the Lord hath *kindled* a f. in Zion
Ezek. 20. 47. I will *kindle* a f. in the forest
24. 10. heap on wood, *kindle* the f. consume the flesh

Amos 1. 14. I will *kindle* a *f.* in the wall of Rabbah
Mal. 1. 10. nor do ye *kindle f.* on my altar for nought
Luke 12. 49. to send *f.* and what if already *kindled?*
22. 55. when they had *kindled* a *f.* in the hall
Acts 28. 2. the barbarians *kindled* a *f.* and received us

Made, with FIRE.

Exod. 29. 18. an offering *made* by *f.* unto the Lord, 25, 41. *Lev.* 1. 9, 13, 17. | 2. 2, 9, 16. | 3. 3, 5, 9, 11, 14, 16. | 7. 5, 25. | 8. 21, 28. | 21. 6. | 22. 27. | 23. 8, 13, 18, 25, 27, 36, 37. | 24. 7. *Num.* 15. 3, 10, 13, 14. | 18. 17. | 28. 3.
Lev. 2. 3. the offerings of the Lord *made* by *f.* 10. | 4. 35. | 5. 12. | 6. 17, 18. | 7. 30, 35. | 10. 12, 15. | 21. 21. | 24. 9. *Deut.* 18. 1. 1 *Sam.* 2. 28.
10. 13. sacrifices *made* by *f.* *Num.* 28. 2. *Josh.* 13. 14.
Num. 15. 25. bring their sacrifice *made* by *f.* unto the Lord, 28. 6, 8, 13, 19, 24. | 29. 6, 13, 36.

Pillar of FIRE.

Exod. 14. 24. the Lord looked thro' the *pillar of f.*
Rev. 10. 1. face as the sun, and his feet as *pillars of f.*

See By NIGHT.

Send, or *sent* FIRE.

Lam. 1. 13. from above he *sent f.* into my bones
Ezek. 39. 6. and I will *send* a *f.* on Magog
Hos. 8. 14. but I will *send* a *f.* upon his cities
Amos 1. 4. I will *send* a *f.* into the house of Hazael
7. I will *send* a *f.* on the wall of Gaza
10. I will *send* a *f.* on wall of Tyrus || 12. on Teman
2. 2. I will *send* a *f.* on Moab || 5. *send f.* on Judah
Luke 12. 49. I am come to *send f.* on the earth

Set FIRE.

Deut. 32. 22. *set* on *f.* foundations of mountains
Josh. 8. 8. ye shall *set* the city of Ai on *f.*
19. and they hasted, and *set* the city on *f.*
Judg. 1. 8. now Judah had *set* Jerusalem on *f.*
9. 49. the people *set* the hold on *f.* upon them
15. 5. had *set* the brands on *f.* and burnt the corn
20. 48. they *set* on *f.* all the cities of Benjamin
2 *Sam.* 14. 30. servants *set* Joab's field on *f.*
31. why have thy servants *set* my field on *f.*?
2 *Kings* 8. 12. Hazael will *set* strong holds on *f.*
Psal. 57. 4. I lie among them that are *set* on *f.*
Prov. 29. † 8. scornful men *set* a city on *f.*
Isa. 27. 11. the women come and *set* them on *f.*
42. 25. he hath *set* him on *f.* round about
Jer. 6. 1. *set* up a sign of *f.* in Beth-haccerem
32. 29. the Chaldeans shall *set* on *f.* this city
Ezek. 30. 8. when I have *set* a *f.* in Egypt
14. I will *set f.* in Zoan || 16. *set f.* in Egypt
39. 9. *set* on *f.* and burn the weapons of Gog
Jam. 3. 6. the tongue is a fire, and *setteth* on *f.* the course of nature, and it is *set* on *f.* of hell

Strange FIRE.

Lev. 10. 1. Nadab and Abihu offered *strange f.*
Num. 3. 4. died when they offered *strange f.* 26. 61.

FIREBRAND, S.

Judg. 7. † 16. and he put *f.* within the pitchers
15. 4. Samson took *f.* and put a *f.* in the midst
Prov. 26. 18. as a mad man who casteth *f.*
Isa. 7. 4. for the two tails of these smoking *f.*
Amos 4. 11. ye were as a *f.* plucked out of burning

FIRE-PANS.

Exod. 27. 3. thou shalt make basons and *f.-pans*
38. 3. he made the *f.-pans* and all vessels of brass
2 *Kings* 25. 15. *f.-pans* carried he away, *Jer.* 52. 19.

FIRES.

Isa. 24. 15. wherefore glorify ye the Lord in the *f.*

FIRKINS.

John 2. 6. six water-pots containing two or three *f.*

FIRM.

Josh. 3. 17. the priests stood *f.* on dry ground
4. 3. the place where priests' feet stood *f.*
Job 41. 23. are *f.* in themselves, cannot be moved
24. his heart is as *f.* as a stone, yea, as hard
Psal. 73. 4. no bands in death, but their strength is *f.*
Dan. 6. 7. they consulted to make a *f.* decree
Heb. 3. 6. the rejoicing of the hope *f.* to the end

FIRMAMENT.

It is said, Gen. 1. 7. *that God made the* firmament *in the midst of the waters, in order to separate the inferior from the superior waters. The word there used is* rakiah, *which is translated* expansion, *something expanded; or* firmament, *something firm and solid. The verb* rakah, *from whence* rakiah *is derived, signifies to spread metal with the hammer, to make flat, to crush to pieces, to beat.* Moses *uses this word to describe the gold, which was beaten in order to cover the ark and the tables of the Holy with it,* Exod. 39. 3. Num. 16. 38, 39. Isaiah, *to denote the plates of gold wherewith the idols were covered,* Isa. 40. 19. *and the same prophet, and the* Psalmist, *to express the spreading forth of the earth, and its floating on the waters, for this was the conception which the* Hebrews *had of it,* Isa. 42. 5. Psal. 136. 6.

This intimates, that by the word firmament, rakiah, *the* Hebrews *understood the heavens, which, like a solid and immense arch (though it be soft and liquid) served as a bank and barrier between the upper and lower waters: and that the stars are set in this arch, like so many precious stones in gold and silver,* Gen. 1. 17. *When* firmament *is taken for the starry heaven, then by* upper waters *is meant, that sea or collection of water placed by God above all the visible heavens, and there reserved for ends known to himself. If by* firmament, *we understand the air, called the* expansion, *because it is extended far and wide; and the* firmament, *because it is fixed in its proper place, from whence it cannot be moved, unless by force; then by the superior waters are to be understood the waters in the clouds: and these may be said to be above the* firmament *or air, because they are above a considerable part of it.*

Gen. 1. 6. let there be a *f.* in midst of the waters
7. God made the *f.* waters under and above *f.*
8. and God called the *f.* Heaven
14. God said, let there be lights in the *f.* 15.
17. and God set them in the *f.* of heaven
Gen. 1. 20. and fowl that may fly above in the open *f.*
Psal. 19. 1. and the *f.* sheweth his handy work
150. 1. praise him in the *f.* of his power
Ezek. 1. 22. the likeness of the *f.* was as crystal
25. there was a voice from the *f.* over their heads
26. above the *f.* was the likeness of a throne
10. 1. in the *f.* that was above the cherubims
Dan. 12. 3. wise shall shine as the brightness of *f.*

FIR.

1 *Kings* 5. 8. I will do all concerning timber of *f.*
6. 15. he covered the floor with planks of *f.*
Cant. 1. 17. our beams are cedar, our rafters of *f.*

FIR-TREE.

1 *Kings* 6. 34. and the two doors were of *f.*
2 *Chron.* 3. 5. the greater house he ceiled with *f.*
Isa. 41. 19. I will set in the desert the *f.* and the pine
55. 13. instead of the thorn shall come up the *f.*
60. 13. the *f.* the pine-tree, and box together
Hos. 14. 8. I am like a green *f.* || *Zech.* 11. 2. howl, *f.*

FIR-TREES.

1 *Kings* 5. 10. so Hiram gave Solomon *f.* 9. 11.
2 *Kings* 19. 23. I will cut down tall *f.* *Isa.* 37. 24.
2 *Chron.* 2. 8. send me *f.* || *Isa.* 14. 8. the *f.* rejoice
Psal. 104. 17. as for the stork the *f.* are her house
Ezek. 27. 5. they made thy ship-boards of *f.* of Senir
31. 8. the *f.* were not like his boughs
Nah. 2. 3. and the *f.* shall be terribly shaken

FIR-WOOD.

2 *Sam.* 6. 5. Israel played on instruments made of *f.*

FIRST.

This *word signifies,* I. *That which is before another in respect of time; and then it is a word of order, and hath a reference to the second, third, fourth, &c.* Mat. 10. 2. The first is *Simon* called *Peter; that is, he was first called to be an apostle. And in* 1 Cor. 15. 47. The first man is of the earth, the second is from heaven. II. *That which is chief, or most excellent.* Rom. 3. 2. Chiefly, because unto them were committed the oracles of God. Chiefly, *in the original, is* first, *and shews the quality and excellence of the privilege here mentioned. So also in* Luke 15. 22. Bring forth the best, *in* Greek, the first robe. *A thing or person may be said to be* first, (1) *In number,* Gen. 8. 5, 13. (2) *In order,* Mat. 28. 1. (3) *By creation,* 1 Cor. 15. 47. (4) *By generation,* Deut. 21. 17. (5) *In dignity,* Dan. 6. 2. (6) *In time,* Heb. 9. 1.

FIRST-BORN. *This word is not always to be understood strictly according to the letter; it is sometimes taken for that which is first, most excellent, most distinguished in any thing. Thus it is said of* Christ, *Col.* 1. 15. *That* he is the *first-born of* every creature. *And in* Rev. 1. 5. *he is called,* The *first-begotten* of the dead; *that is, begotten of the Father before any creature was produced; and the first who rose from the dead by his own power.* The first-born of the poor, *Isa.* 14. 30. *signifies, the most miserable of all the poor; and in* Job 18. 13. The first-born of death; *that is, the most terrible of all deaths.*

The first-born *among the* Hebrews, *as well as among all other nations, enjoyed particular privileges: and as polygamy was in use with them, it was highly necessary to fix these rights.* Moses *regulates this particular in* Deut. 21. 15, 16, 17. *The privileges of the* first-born *consisted,* (1) *In a right to the priesthood, which, before the law, was fixed to the eldest of the family. This right continued in force only while brethren dwelt together in the same place and family; for as soon as they were separated, and made a family apart, every one became the priest and head of his own house.* (2) *The* first-born *had a double portion among his brethren. This is explained two ways: Some believe that half of the whole inheritance was given to the elder brother, and that the other half was shared in equal parts among the rest. But the* Rabbins *say, on the contrary, that the* first-born *for his share took twice as much as any one of his brothers. If a father left six sons, they made a division into seven equal parts; whereof the eldest had two, and each of the others one. If the eldest was dead, and had left children, his right devolved upon his children and his heirs.*

When God by the sword of the destroying angel had killed all the first-born *of the* Egyptians, *Exod.* 12. 29. *he ordained, that all the* first-born, *both of men and tame beasts for service, should be consecrated to him. The male children only were subject to this law. The children were offered in the temple, and their relations redeemed them, for the sum of five shekels,* Exod. 13. 12, 13. Num. 18. 16.

If it were a clean beast, as a calf, a lamb, or a kid, it was to be offered at the temple. It was not to be redeemed, but it was killed; the blood of it was sprinkled about the altar, the fat was burnt in the fire upon the altar, and the flesh was for the priest, Num. 18. 17, 18, 19. *If it were an unclean beast, and such as they were not allowed to eat, such as an horse, an ass, or a camel, it was either redeemed, or something else was given in exchange for it. The firstling of an ass was redeemed by giving a lamb; if it were not redeemed, it was to be killed,* Exod. 13. 13.

FIRST-FRUITS. *The presents were so called which the* Hebrews *made to God, consisting of part of the fruits of their harvest, to express their submission and dependence, and to acknowledge the sovereign dominion of God the author of all happiness. The day after the feast of the* Passover *they brought a sheaf into the temple, as the* first-fruits *of the barley-harvest. The sheaf was threshed in the court; and of the grain that came out they took a full homer; that is, about three pints. After it had been well winnowed, parched, and bruised, they sprinkled over it a log of oil; that is, near a pint. They added to it a handful of incense; and the priest that received this offering shook it before the Lord towards the four quarters of the world; he cast part of it upon the altar, and the rest was his own. After this, every one might begin their harvest,* Lev. 23. 10, 11, &c. *This was offered in the name of the whole nation, and by this the whole harvest was sanctified unto them.*

When the wheat harvest was over, that is, the day of Pentecost, they offered again first-fruits *of another kind in the name of all the nation, which consisted of two loaves of two tenth-deals: that is, of about three pints of flour each. The loaves were made of leavened dough.*

FIRST-FRUITS of the Spirit, see EARNEST.

Gen. 25. 25. the *f.* came out red all over
26. 1. there was a famine beside the *f.* famine
38. 28. the midwife said, this came out *f.*
Exod. 4. 8. if they will not hearken to the *f.* sign
23. 19. the *f.* of the first-fruits bring to the Lord
28. 17. the *f.* row shall be a sardius, 39. 10.
34. 1. two tables like to the *f.* 4. *Deut.* 10. 1, 3.
Lev. 5. 8. shall offer what is for the sin-offering *f.*
Num. 2. 9. camp of Judah, these shall *f.* set forth
10. 13. and they *f.* took their journey
13. 20. it was the time of the *f.* ripe grapes
15. 20. ye shall offer up a cake of the *f.* of your dough for an heave-offering, 21. *Ezek.* 44. 30.
18. 13. whatsoever is *f.* ripe shall be thine
24. 20. Amalek was the *f.* of the nations
Deut. 10. 10. according to the *f.* time, forty days
11. 14. I will give thee *f.* rain and latter rain
13. 9. thine hand shall be *f.* upon him
17. 7. the hands of witnesses shall be *f.* upon him
18. 4. the *f.* of the fleece of thy sheep give him
33. 21. he provided the *f.* part for himself
Josh. 21. 10. theirs was *f.* lot, 1 *Chr.* 24. 7. | 25. 9.
Judg. 1. 1. who shall go up *f.* to fight, 20. 18.
20. 39. Israel are smitten as in the *f.* battle
1 *Sam.* 14. 14. that *f.* slaughter was twenty men
35. the same was the *f.* altar Saul built to Lord
2 *Sam.* 3. 13. except thou *f.* bring Michal Saul's dau.
19. 20. I am come the *f.* this day to meet my lord
43. that advice should not be *f.* had in bringing
23. 19. he was their captain, howbeit he attained not unto the *f.* three, 23. 1 *Chron.* 11. 21, 25.
1 *Kings* 17. 13. but make thereof a little cake *f.*
18. 25. and dress it *f.* for ye are many
20. 17. the young men of the princes went out *f.*
1 *Chron.* 9. 2. now the *f.* inhabitants that dwelt
11. 6. whosoever smiteth the Jebusites *f.*
16. 7. that day David delivered *f.* this psalm
2 *Chron.* 3. 3. length by cubits after the *f.* measure
Ezra 3. 12. that had seen the glory of the *f.* house
Esth. 1. 14. which sat the *f.* in the kingdom
Job 15. 7. art thou the *f.* man that was born?
Prov. 18. 17. that is *f.* in his own cause seemeth just
Isa. 41. 27. the *f.* shall say to Zion, behold them
43. 27. thy *f.* father hath sinned against me
60. 9. the ships of Tarshish *f.* to bring thy sons
Jer. 4. 31. her that bringeth forth her *f.* child
16. 18. *f.* I will recompense their iniquity
24. 2. good figs, even like the figs that are *f.* ripe
36. 28. write the words that were in the *f.* roll
50. 17. *f.* the king of Assyria hath devoured him
Dan. 6. 2. Dan. was *f.* president, of an excellent sp.
7. 4. the *f.* beast was like a lion, *Rev.* 4. 7.
24. and another shall be diverse from the *f.*
8. 21. the great horn between his eyes is the *f.* king
10. † 13. but lo, Michael the *f.* came to help me
Hos. 2. 7. I will go and return to my *f.* husband
9. 10. the *f.* ripe in the fig tree at her *f.* time
Amos 6. 7. shall go captive with the *f.* that go capt.
Mic. 4. 8. to thee shall come the *f.* dominion
Nah. 3. 12. like fig-trees with the *f.* ripe figs
Hag. 2. 3. who is left that saw house in her *f.* glory?
Zech. 6. 2. in the *f.* chariot were red horses
12. 7. the Lord shall save the tents of Judah *f.*
Mat. 5. 24. *f.* be reconciled to thy brother, and come
6. 33. seek ye *f.* the kingdom of G. and righteousn.
7. 5. *f.* cast out the beam out of thine eye, *Luke* 6. 42.
8. 21. me *f.* to go and bury my father, *Luke* 9. 59.
12. 29. except he *f.* bind the strong man, *Mark* 3. 27.
45. latter state worse than the *f.* *Luke* 11. 26.
13. 30. gather ye together *f.* the tares, bind them
17. 10. that Elias must *f.* come, 11. *Mark* 9. 12.
27. and take up the fish that *f.* cometh up
20. 10. but when the *f.* came, they supposed
21. 28. he came to the *f.* and said, son, go work
31. who of the twain, they say unto him, the *f.*
36. he sent other servants more than the *f.*
22. 25. *f.* when married, *Mark* 12. 20. *Luke* 20. 29.
38. this is *f.* commandment, *Mark* 12. 28, 29, 30.
23. 26. Pharisee, cleanse *f.* that which is within
Mark 4. 28. *f.* the blade, then the ear, after that corn
7. 27. Jesus said to her, let the children *f.* be filled
9. 35. if any desire to be *f.* he shall be last
13. 10. and the gospel must *f.* be published
16. 9. he appeared *f.* to Mary Magdalene
Luke 1. 3. had perfect understanding from the *f.*
2. 2. was *f.* made when Cyrenius was governor
6. 1. on the second sabbath after the *f.* he went
10. 5. *f.* say, peace be to this house
11. 38. that he had not *f.* washed before dinner
14. 28. sitteth not down *f.* and counteth the cost
17. 25. but *f.* must he suffer many things
21. 9. for these things must *f.* come to pass
John 1. 41. he *f.* findeth his brother Simon
5. 4. whosoever *f.* stepped in, was made whole
8. 7. without sin, let him *f.* cast a stone at her
10. 40. into the place where John at *f.* baptized
18. 13. and led him away to Annas *f.*
19. 32. soldiers came, and brake the legs of the *f.*
20. 4. the disciple came *f.* to the sepulchre, 8.
Acts 3. 26. to you *f.* God sent him to bless you in
7. 12. Jacob sent out our fathers *f.*
11. 26. discip. were called Christians *f.* at Antioch
12. 10. they were past the *f.* and second ward
13. 24. when John had *f.* preached baptism
46. necessary it should *f.* have been spoken to you
16. † 12. Philippi the *f.* city of Macedonia
26. 20. but shewed *f.* unto them of Damascus
23. Christ should be *f.* that should rise from dead
27. 43. should cast themselves *f.* into the sea
Rom. 1. 8. *f.* I thank my God through Jesus Christ
2. 9. of the Jew *f.* and also of the Gentile, 10.

Rom. 11. 35. or who hath f. given to him?
15. 24. if f. I be somewhat filled with company
1 Cor. 12. 28. f. apostles, secondarily prophets
14. 30. let the f. hold his peace
15. 3. for I delivered f. of all that which I received
45. the f. man Adam was made a living soul
46. howbeit that was not f. which is spiritual
47. the f. man is of the earth, earthy
2 Cor. 8. 5. f. gave their own selves to the Lord
12. for if there be f. a willing mind, it is accepted
Eph. 1. 12. who f. trusted in Christ
4. 9. descended f. into the lower parts of the earth
6. 2. which is the f. commandment with promise
1 Thess. 4. 16. the dead in Christ shall rise f.
2 Thess. 2. 3. except there come a falling away f.
1 Tim. 1. 16. that in me f. Christ Jesus might shew
2. 13. for Adam was f. formed, then Eve
3. 10. let these also f. be proved, then let them use
5. 4. let them learn f. to shew piety at home
12. because they have cast off their f. faith
2 Tim. 1. 5. faith dwelt f. in thy grandmother Lois
2. 6. husbandman must be f. partaker of the fruits
4. 16. at my f. answer no man stood with me
Tit. 3. 10. after f. and second admonition, reject
Heb. 4. 6. to whom it was f. preached, entered not
5. 12. one teach you which be the f. principles
7. 2. f. being by interpretation, king of righteousn.
27. offer f. for his own sins, then for the people's
8. 7. the f. covenant, 13. | 9. 1, 15, 18.
9. 2. f. tabernacle, wherein was shew-bread, 6, 8.
10. 9. he taketh away the f. that he may establish
Jam. 3. 17. wisdom that is from above, is f. pure
1 Pet. 4. 17. if judgment f. begin at us, what end
2 Pet. 1. 20. knowing this f. that no prophecy, 3. 3.
1 John 4. 19. we love him, because he f. loved us
Jude 6. the angels who kept not their f. estate
Rev. 2. 4. because thou hast left thy f. love
5. repent, and do the f. works, else I will come
13. 12. he exerciseth all the power of the f. beast
20. 5. this is the f. resurrection
21. 1. the f. heaven and f. earth were passed away
19. the f. foundation was jasper, second sapphire

See DAY, LAST.

At the FIRST.

Gen. 13. 4. where Abram made the altar at the f.
28. 19. the city was called Luz at the f.
43. 18. because of the money returned at the f.
20. we came down indeed at the f. to buy food
Deut. 9. 18. I fell down before Lord as at the f. 25.
Josh. 8. 5. when they come against us at the f.
6. they will say, they flee before us as at the f.
Judg. 18. 29. name of the city was Laish at the f.
20. 32. are smitten down before us as at the f.
2 Sam. 17. 9. some of them be overthrown at the f.
1 Kings 20. 9. all thou didst send for to thy serv. at f.
1 Chron. 15. 13. because ye did it not at the f.
Neh. 7. 5. a register of them which came up at the f.
Isa. 1. 26. I will restore thy judges as at the f.
9. 1. when at the f. he lightly afflicted the land
Jer. 7. 12. my place where I set my name at the f.
33. 7. and I will build them as at the f.
11. return the captivity of the land, as at the f.
Dan. 8. 1. after that which appeared to me at the f.
John 12. 16. his disciples understood not at the f.
19. 39. which at the f. came to Jesus by night
Acts 15. 14. God at the f. did visit the Gentiles
26. 4. which was at the f. among mine own nation
Gal. 4. 13. I preached the gospel unto you, at the f.
Heb. 2. 3. which at the f. began to be spoken by Ld.

FIRST-BORN.

Gen. 19. 31. the f. said to the younger, 34.
33. the f. went in, and lay with her father
37. the f. bare a son, and called his name Moab
27. 19. and Jacob said, I am Esau, thy f. 32.
29. 26. not done to give the younger before the f.
43. 33. the f. according to his birth-right
48. 18. not so my father, for this is the f.
Exod. 4. 22. saith Lord, Israel is my son, even my f.
23. behold, I will slay thy son, even thy f.
11. 5. all the f. in the land of Egypt shall die
12. 12. and I will smite all the f. in the land
29. the Lord smote all the f. in Egypt, 13. 15.
13. 2. sanctify unto me all the f. it is mine
22. 29. the f. of thy sons shalt thou give to me
34. 20. f. of thy sons shalt redeem, Num. 18. 15.
Lev. 27. † 26. f. of beasts no man shall sanctify it
Num. 3. 12. instead of all the f. 41, 45. | 8. 17, 18.
13. because all the f. of Israel are mine, I hallowed to me all the f. of Israel
40. number all the f. of the males of Israel
42. Moses numbered all the f. of Israel
50. of the f. of Israel took he the money
33. 4. for the Egyptians buried all their f.
Deut. 21. 15. if the f. son be her's that was hated
17. beginning of strength, for the right of f. is his
25. 6. f. which she beareth, succeed in name
Josh. 6. 26. shall lay the foundation in his f.
1 Kings 16. 34. laid foundation in Abiram his f.
1 Chron. 5. 1. sons of Reuben the f. for he was the f.
26. 10. though he was not the f. yet his father
2 Chron. 21. 3. Jehoram, because he was the f.
Neh. 10. 36. to bring the f. to the house of God
Job 18. 13. the f. of death shall devour his strength
Psal. 78. 51. he smote all the f. in Egypt, the chief of their strength, 105. 36. | 135. 8. | 136. 10.
89. 27. will make him my f. higher than kings
Isa. 14. 30. and the f. of the poor shall feed
Jer. 31. 9. I am a father to Israel, Ephraim is my f.
Mic. 6. 7. shall I give my f. for my transgression?
Zech. 12. 10. as one in bitterness for his f.
Mat. 1. 25. Mary brought forth her f. son, Luke 2. 7.
Rom. 8. 29. might be the f. among many brethren
Col. 1. 15. who is the f. of every creature
18. who is the beginning, the f. from the dead
Heb. 11. 28. lest he that destroyed the f. touch them
12. 23. ye are come to the church of the f.

FIRST-FRUIT, or *fruits*.

Exod. 22. 29. not delay to offer the f. ripe fruits
23. 16. the f.-fruits of thy labour thou hast sown
19. first of f.-fruits of thy land, 34. 26. Deut. 26. 2.
34. 22. the feast of the f.-fruits of wheat harvest
Lev. 2. 12. oblation of the f.-fruits ye shall offer
Lev. 2. 14. the meat-offering of f.-fruits green ears
23. 10. bring a sheaf of the f.-fruits of harvest
17. they are the f.-fruits unto the Lord
20. wave them with the bread of the f.-fruits
Num. 18. 12. f.-fruits of oil, wine, wheat, I have given
28. 26. in the day of f.-fruits when ye offer to Lord
Deut. 18. 4. the f.-fruits of thy corn, wine, and oil
26. 10. I have brought the f.-fruits of the land
2 Kings 4. 42. and brought the man of God f.-fruits
2 Chron. 31. 5. brought in abundance the f.-fruits
Neh. 10. 35. bring f.-fruits of our ground, of trees
37. we should bring the f.-fruits of our dough
12. 44. appointed over chambers for f.-fruits, 13. 31.
Prov. 3. 9. honour the Lord with the f.-fruits
Jer. 2. 3. Israel was the f.-fruits of his increase
Ezek. 20. 40. there will I require the f.-fruits
44. 30. the first of all the f.-fruits of all things
48. 14. nor exchange the f.-fruits of the land
Amos 6. † 1. named the f.-fruits of the nations
Mic. 7. 1. my soul desired the f. ripe fruit
Rom. 8. 23. which have the f.-fruits of the Spirit
11. 16. if the f.-fruit be holy, the lump is holy
16. 5. who is the f.-fruits of Achaia, 1 Cor. 16. 15.
1 Cor. 15. 20. Christ f.-fruits of them that slept, 23.
Jam. 1. 18. a kind of f.-fruits of his creatures
Rev. 14. 4. being the f.-fruits unto God and Lamb

FIRST *month*.

Gen. 8. 13. in the f. month, the f. day of the month
Exod. 12. 2. shall be the f. month of the year to you
18. in f. month eat unleavened bread, Lev. 23. 5.
40. 2. first day of f. month set up tabernacle, 17.
Num. 9. 1. in the f. month keep the passover, 28. 16.
2 Chron. 35. 1. Ezra 6. 19. Ezek. 45. 21.
20. 1. came into the desert of Zin in the f. month
33. 3. departed from Rameses in the f. month
Josh. 4. 19. people came out of Jordan in f. month
1 Chron. 12. 15. these went over Jordan in f. month
27. 2. the captain that served the f. month, 3.
2 Chron. 29. 3. in the f. month opened the doors of the house of the Lord
17. they began on first day of f. month to sanctify and in the sixteenth day of f. month made an end
Ezra 7. 9. f. month began he to go from Babylon
8. 31. the f. month we departed from Ahava
10. 17. they made an end with them by f. month
Esth. 3. 7. in the f. month they cast Pur, on the thirteenth day of the f. month
Ezek. 45. 18. in the f. month take a young bullock
Joel 2. 23. cause former and latter rain in f. month

FIRST *year*.

Exod. 12. 5. your lambs shall be male of the f. year
29. 38. offer two lambs of the f. year day by day continually, Lev. 23. 19. Num. 28. 3, 9.
Lev. 9. 3. take a kid of the f. year without blemish
12. 6. he shall bring a lamb of the f. year, Num. 6. 12. | 7. 15, 21, 27, 33, 39, 45, 51, 57, 63, 69, 75, 81. Ezek. 46. 13.
14. 10. take an ewe-lamb of the f. year, Num. 6. 14.
23. 12. offer an he-lamb of the f. year, Num. 6. 14.
18. ye shall offer seven lambs of the f. year without blemish, Num. 28. 11, 19, 27. | 29. 2, 8, 36.
Num. 7. 17. for a peace-offering five lambs of the f. year, 23, 29, 35, 41, 47, 53, 59.
87. the lambs of the f. year twelve for burnt offer.
88. the lambs of the f. year sixty for a peace-offer.
15. 27. then he shall bring a she-goat of the f. year
29. 13. offer a burnt-offering, fourteen lambs of the f. year, 17, 20, 23, 26, 29, 32.
2 Chr. 29. 3. Hezekiah in the f. year of his reign
36. 22. in f. year of Cyrus, Ezra 1. 1. | 5. 13. | 6. 3.
Jer. 25. 1. that was the f. year of Nebuchadnezzar
52. 31. in the f. year of the reign of Evil-merodach
Dan. 1. 21. Daniel continued to the f. year of Cyrus
7. 1. in the f. year of Belshazzar Daniel dreamed
9. 1. in f. year of Darius I understood by books, 2.
11. 1. in the f. year of Darius I stood to confirm

FIRSTLING.

Exod. 13. 12. shalt set apart every f. that cometh of a beast, the males shall be the Lord's, 34. 19.
13. every f. of an ass thou shalt redeem, 34. 20.
Lev. 27. 26. the Lord's f. no man shall sanctify it
Num. 18. 15. the f. of unclean beasts shalt redeem
17. the f. of a cow, sheep, or goat, not redeem
Deut. 15. 19. all the f. males sanctify to the Lord
33. 17. Joseph's glory is like the f. of a bullock

FIRSTLINGS.

Gen. 4. 4. Abel brought of the f. of his flock
Num. 3. 41. instead of all the f. among the cattle
Deut. 12. 6. ye shall bring f. of your herds and flocks
17. thou mayest not eat within thy gates the f.
14. 23. eat the f. in the place the Lord shall choose
Neh. 10. 36. f. of our herds bring to the house of God

FISH.

Gen. 1. 26. let them have dominion over f. of sea, 28.
Exod. 7. 18. the f. in the river shall die, 21.
Num. 11. 5. we rememb. the f. we did eat in Egypt
22. shall all the f. of the sea be gathered together
Deut. 4. 18. nor likeness of any f. in the water
Neh. 13. 16. men of Tyre also, which brought f.
Psal. 8. 8. thou hast put the f. under his feet
105. 29. turned waters into blood, and slew their f.
Isa. 19. 10. all that make sluices and ponds for f.
50. 2. their f. stinketh because there is no water
Ezek. 29. 4. I will cause the f. to stick to thy scales
5. I will leave thee, and all the f. of thy rivers
47. 9. and there shall be a very great multitude of f.
10. their f. shall be as the f. of the great sea
Jonah 1. 17. the Ld. had prepared a great f. to swallow up Jonah, he was in belly of f. three days
2. 1. Jonah prayed to the Lord out of the f.'s belly
10. Lord spake to the f. and it vomited out Jonah
Mat. 7. 10. if he ask a f. will he give him a serpent?
17. 27. cast a hook, take up the f. that first cometh
Luke 24. 42. they gave him a piece of a broiled f.
John 21. 9. they saw f. laid thereon, and bread
10. bring of the f. which ye have now caught
13. Jesus taketh bread, and giveth them, and f.

FISH.

Jer. 16. 16. will send fishers, and they shall f. them

FISH-GATE.

2 Chr. 33. 14. Manasseh built to entering of f.-gate
Neh. 3. 3. the f.-gate did the sons of Hassenaah build
Neh. 12. 39. and I after them from above the f.-gate
Zeph. 1. 10. the noise of a cry from the f.-gate

FISH-HOOKS.

Amos 4. 2. I will take your posterity with f.-hooks

FISH-POOLS.

Cant. 7. 4. thine eyes like the f.-pools of Heshbon

FISH-SPEARS.

Job 41. 7. canst thou fill his head with f.-spears?

FISHERMEN.

Luke 5. 2. but the f. were gone out of them

FISHERS.

Isa. 19. 8. the f. also shall mourn and lament
Jer. 16. 16. behold, I will send for many f. saith Lord
Ezek. 47. 10. that the f. shall stand upon it
Mat. 4. 18. net into sea, for they were f. Mark 1. 16.
19. I will make you f. of men, Mark 1. 17.
John 21. 7. Peter girt f. coat to him, for he was naked

FISHES.

Gen. 9. 2. the fear of you shall be on all f. of the sea
48. † 16. let the lads grow as f. do increase
1 Kings 4. 33. he spake of creeping things and f.
Job 12. 8. the f. of the sea shall declare unto thee
Eccl. 9. 12. the f. that are taken in an evil net
Ezek. 38. 20. so that the f. of the sea shall shake
Hos. 4. 3. the f. of the sea shall be taken away
Hab. 1. 14. and makest men as the f. of the sea
Zeph. 1. 3. I will consume the f. of the sea
Mat. 14. 17. we have here but five loaves and two f. Mark 6. 38. Luke 9. 13. John 6. 9.
15. 34. seven loaves and a few little f. Mark 8. 7.
Luke 5. 6. they inclosed a great multitude of f.
9. for he was astonished at the draught of f.
John 21. 6. not able to draw it for multitude of f.
11. Simon Peter drew net to land full of great f.
1 Cor. 15. 39. one flesh of beasts, another of f.

FISHING.

John 21. 3. Simon Peter saith unto them, I go a f.

FISHY.

1 Sam. 5. † 4. the f. part of Dagon was left to him

FIST, S.

Exod. 21. 18. and one smite another with his f.
Prov. 30. 4. who hath gathered the wind in his f.?
Isa. 58. 4. and to smite with the f. of wickedness
Mark 7. † 3. they wash their hands with the f.

FIT.

Lev. 16. 21. send him away by the hand of a f. man
1 Chron. 7. 11. f. to go out to war and battle, 12. 8.
Job 34. 18. is it f. to say to a king, thou art wicked?
Prov. 24. 27. make it f. for thyself in the field
Ezek. 15. 5. the vine was made f. for no work
Luke 9. 62. looking back, is f. for kingdom of God
14. 35. it is not f. for the land nor dunghill
Acts 22. 22. it is not f. that he should live
Col. 3. 18. wives, submit as it is f. in the Lord

FITCHES.

Isa. 28. 25. doth he not cast abroad the f.?
27. the f. are not threshed, f. are beaten out
Ezek. 4. 9. take thou wheat, barley, millet, and f.

FITTED.

1 Kings 6. 35. with gold f. upon the carved work
Prov. 22. 18. they shall withal be f. in thy lips
Rom. 9. 22. the vessels of wrath f. to destruction
Heb. 10. † 5. but a body hast thou f. me

FITTETH.

Isa. 44. 13. the carpenter f. it with planes

FITLY.

Prov. 25. 11. a word f. spoken is like apples of gold
Cant. 5. 12. his eyes washed with milk, and f. set
Eph. 2. 21. in whom all building f. framed together
4. 16. from whom whole body f. joined together

FIVE.

Gen. 14. 9. battle in vale of Siddim, four kings with f.
18. 28. wilt thou destroy all for lack of f.?
43. 34. Benjamin's mess was f. times so much
45. 6. f. years in which no earing or harvest, 11.
22. to Benjamin he gave f. changes of raiment
47. 2. he presented f. of his brethren to Pharaoh
Exod. 13. † 18. but Israel went up f. in a rank
22. 1. the thief shall restore f. oxen for an ox
26. 3. other f. curtains coupled, 9. | 36. 10, 16.
26. make f. bars for the boards, 27. | 36. 31, 32.
37. f. pillars, 36. 38. || 36. 38. f. sockets of brass
27. 1. an altar f. cubits long, f. cubits broad
18. the height of the hangings f. cubits, 38. 18.
38. 1. f. cubits the breadth, and f. the length
Lev. 26. 8. f. of you shall chase an hundred
27. 5. if thy estimation be from f. years old
6. if it be from a month old to f. years old
Num. 3. 47. even take f. shekels apiece, 18. 16.
7. 17. for a sacrifice of peace-offerings, f. rams, f. goats, f. lambs, 23, 29, 35, 41, 47, 53.
31. 8. slew f. kings of Midian, Balaam son of Beor
Josh. 1. † 14. ye shall pass marshalled by f.
10. 5. f. kings of Amorites went against Gibeon
16. these f. kings fled and hid themselves
17. f. kings hid || 22. bring out the f. kings
23. they brought out these f. kings unto him
26. he slew them and hanged them on f. trees
13. 3. f. lords of the Philistines, Judg. 3. 3.
Judg. 7. † 11. he went to outside of ranks by f.
18. 2. the children of Dan sent f. men from coasts
1 Sam. 6. 4. f. golden emerods, f. golden mice
16. when the f. lords of the Philistines had seen it
17. 40. David chose him f. smooth stones
21. 3. give me f. loaves of bread in my hand
25. 18. she brought f. sheep, f. measures of corn
42. Abigail rode on an ass with f. damsels
2 Sam. 4. 4. Mephibosheth was f. years old when tidings came of Saul's and Jonathan's death
21. 8. but David took the f. sons of Michal
1 Kings 7. 39. f. bases on the right, f. on the left side
49. candlesticks of pure gold, f. on the right side, and f. on the left, 2 Chron. 4. 7.
2 Kings 6. 25. part of cab of dove's dung sold f. pieces
7. 13. let some take f. of the horses that remain
13. 19. thou shouldest have smitten f. or six times
25. 19. f. men that were in the king's presence
1 Chron. 2. 6. the sons of Zera, f. of them in all
11. 23. Benaiah slew an Egyptian f. cubits high
Isa. 17. 6. four or f. in the utmost fruitful branches
19. 18. f. cities in Egypt speak language of Canaan
30. 17. at the rebuke of f. shall ye flee

Mat. 14. 17. they said to him, we have here but *f.* loaves and two fishes, *Mark* 6. 38. *Luke* 9. 13.
16. 9. the *f.* loaves of the *f.* thousand, *Mark* 8. 19.
25. 2. *f.* of them were wise, and *f.* were foolish
15. and unto one he gave *f.* talents, 16.
Luke 12. 6. are not *f.* sparrows sold for two farthings
52. there shall be *f.* in one house divided
14. 19. another said, I have bought *f.* yoke of oxen
16. 28. send him to my father's, I have *f.* brethren
19. 18. Lord, thy pound hath gained *f.* pounds
19. be thou also over *f.* cities
John 4. 18. for thou hast had *f.* husbands
5. 2. there is a pool Bethesda having *f.* porches
6. 9. there is a lad which hath *f.* barley-loaves
13. with the fragments of the *f.* barley-loaves
1 *Cor.* 14. 19. I had rather speak *f.* words with unders.
2 *Cor.* 11. 24. *f.* times received I forty stripes
Rev. 17. 10. there are seven kings, *f.* are fallen

FIVE-SQUARE.

1 *Kings* 6. † 31. lintel and side-posts were *f.-square*

FIXED.

2 *Chron.* 12. † 14. Rehoboam *f.* not his heart
Psal. 57. 7. O God, my heart is *f.* I will sing, 108. 1.
112. 7. his heart is *f.* trusting in the Lord
Luke 16. 26. between us and you there is a gulf *f.*

FLAG, S.

Exod. 2. 3. she laid the ark in the *f.* by the river
5. and when she saw the ark among the *f.*
Job 8. 11. can the *f.* grow without water?
Isa. 19. 6. the reeds and *f.* shall wither

FLAGON.

2 *Sam.* 6. 19. to each a *f.* of wine, 1 *Chron.* 16. 3.

FLAGONS.

Cant. 2. 5. stay me with *f.* comfort me with apples
Isa. 22. 24. from cups, even to all the vessels of *f.*
Hos. 3. 1. who look to other gods, love *f.* of wine

FLAKES.

Job 41. 23. the *f.* of his flesh are joined together

FLAME.

Exod. 3. 2. angel appeared in a *f.* of fire, *Acts* 7. 30.
Num. 21. 28. a *f.* from the city of Sihon, *Jer.* 48. 45.
Judg. 13. 20. when *f.* went up, angel went in the *f.*
20. 38. that they should make a great *f.* to rise
40. the *f.* of the city ascended up to heaven
Job 15. 30. the *f.* shall dry up his branches
41. 21. and a *f.* goeth out of his mouth
Psal. 83. 14. as the *f.* setteth the mountains on fire
106. 18. the *f.* burnt up the wicked
Cant. 8. 6. coals of fire, which hath a vehement *f.*
Isa. 5. 24. and as the *f.* consumeth the chaff
10. 17. and his Holy One shall be for a *f.*
29. 6. shalt be visited with the *f.* of devouring fire
30. † 27. name of L. comes with grievousness of *f.*
30. the Lord shall shew his arm with the *f.*
43. 2. neither shall the *f.* kindle upon thee
47. 14. they shall not deliver themselves from *f.*
Ezek. 20. 47. the flaming *f.* shall not be quenched
Dan. 3. 22. *f.* slew those men that took up Shadrach
7. 9. his throne was like the fiery *f.* and his wheels
11. till his body was given to the burning *f.*
11. 33. yet they shall fall by the sword and by *f.*
Joel 1. 19. the *f.* hath burnt all the trees of the field
2. 3. a fire devours, and behind them a *f.* burneth
5. like the noise of a *f.* of fire that devoureth
Obad. 18. and the house of Joseph shall be a *f.*
Nah. 3. † 3. the horseman lifteth up the *f.* of sword
Luke 16. 24. for I am tormented in this *f.*
Heb. 1. 7. who maketh his ministers a *f.* of fire
Rev. 1. 14. eyes were as a *f.* of fire, 2. 18. | 19. 12.

FLAMES.

Psal. 29. 7. the voice of Lord divideth the *f.* of fire
Prov. 26. † 18. as a madman who casteth *f.* and death
Isa. 13. 8. shall be amazed, their faces shall be as *f.*
66. 15. Lord come to render rebuke with *f.* of fire

FLAMING.

Gen. 3. 24. he placed at garden of Eden a *f.* sword
Ezek. 20. 47. the *f.* flame shall not be quenched
Nah. 2. 3. the chariots shall be with *f.* torches
See FIRE.

FLANKS.

Lev. 3. 4. the fat that is on them, which is by the *f.* it shall he take away, 10. 15. | 4. 9. | 7. 4.
Job 15. 27. he maketh collops of fat on his *f.*

FLASH.

Ezek. 1. 14. as the appearance of a *f.* of lightning

FLAT.

Lev. 2. † 5. an offering baken on a *f.* plate, 7. † 9.
21. 18. he that hath a *f.* nose shall not approach
Num. 22. 31. Balaam bowed, and fell *f.* on his face
Josh. 6. 5. the wall of the city shall fall down *f.*
20. the people shouted, the wall fell down *f.*

FLATTER.

Psal. 5. 9. no faithfulness, they *f.* with their tongue
78. 36. they did *f.* him with their mouth, and lied

FLATTERETH.

Psal. 36. 2. for he *f.* himself in his own eyes
Prov. 2. 16. from stranger who *f.* with her words, 7. 5.
20. 19. meddle not with him that *f.* with his lips
28. 23. shall find more favour than he that *f.*
29. 5. a man that *f.* spreadeth a net for his feet

FLATTERING.

Job 32. 21. neither let me give *f.* titles to man
22. for I know not to give *f.* titles
Psal. 12. 2. with *f.* lips and double heart do speak
3. the Lord shall cut off all *f.* lips, and the tongue
Prov. 7. 21. with the *f.* of her lips she forced him
26. 28. and a *f.* mouth worketh ruin
Ezek. 12. 24. there shall be no more *f.* divination
1 *Thess.* 2. 5. neither used we at any time *f.* words

FLATTERY.

Job 17. 5. he that speaketh *f.* to his friends
Prov. 6. 24. to keep from the *f.* of a strange woman

FLATTERIES.

Dan. 11. 21. but he shall obtain the kingdom by *f.*
32. such as do wickedly shall he corrupt by *f.*
34. but many shall cleave to them with *f.*

FLAX.

Exod. 9. 31. *f.* and barley was smitten, *f.* was bolled
Josh. 2. 6. she hid them with the stalks of *f.*
Judg. 15. 14. cords became as *f.* that was burnt
Prov. 31. 13. she seeks wool and *f.* and worketh
Isa. 19. 9. they that work in fine *f.* confounded
Isa. 42. 3. smoking *f.* shall he not quench, *Mat.* 12. 20.
Ezek. 40. 3. a man with a line of *f.* in his hand
Hos. 2. 5. I will go after my lovers that give me *f.*
9. and I will recover my wool and my *f.*

FLAY.

Mic. 3. 3. *f.* their skins from off them, break bones

FLAYED.

2 *Chr.* 35. 11. sprinkled blood, the Levites *f.* them

FLEA.

1 *Sam.* 24. 14. is the king come after a *f.*? 26. 20.

FLED.

Gen. 14. 10. the kings of Sodom and Gomorrah *f.*
16. 6. Hagar *f.* || 31. 22. Jacob *f.* *Hos.* 12. 12.
Exod. 2. 15. Moses *f.* from Pharaoh, 4. 3. *Acts* 7. 29.
14. 5. it was told king of Egypt that the people *f.*
27. and the Egyptians *f.* against the sea
Num. 16. 34. Isr. round about *f.* at the cry of them
Deut. 34. † 7. nor was his natural force *f.*
Josh. 8. 15. Israel *f.* by the way of the wilderness
10. 16. these five kings *f.* and hid themselves
Judg. 1. 6. Adoni-bezek *f.* || 4. 15. Sisera *f.* away
7. 21. all the host ran and cried, and *f.* 22.
8. 12. Zalmunna *f.* || 9. 21. Jotham ran and *f.*
9. 51. to the tower *f.* all the men and women
11. 3. Jephthah *f.* || 20. 45. the Benjamites *f.* 47.
1 *Sam.* 4. 16. and I *f.* to-day out of the army
14. 22. when they heard that the Philistines *f.*
17. 24. the men of Israel *f.* from Goliath
19. 10. David *f.* and escaped, 12, 18. | 20. 1. | 21. 10.
22. 20. Abiathar escaped and *f.* after David, 23. 6.
30. 17. save four hundred which rode and *f.*
31. 1. Israel *f.* from the Philistines, 7. 2 *Sam.* 19. 8.
2 *Sam.* 4. 3. Beerothites *f.* to Gittaim and sojourned
4. and his nurse *f.* || 10. 14. the Syrians *f.* 18.
13. 29. Absalom and the king's sons *f.* 34. 37, 38.
18. 17. all Israel *f.* every one to his tent
1 *Kings* 2. 7. for so they came to me when I *f.*
28. Joab *f.* to the tabernacle, 29. || 11. 17. Hadad *f.*
11. 23. Rezon *f.* from his lord || 40. Jeroboam *f.*
20. 20. the Syrians *f.* 1 *Chr.* 19. 18. 2 *Kings* 7. 7.
2 *Kings* 8. 21. and the people *f.* to their tents
9. 10. the prophet opened door and *f.* || 23. Joram *f.*
25. 4. all the men of war *f.* by night, *Jer.* 52. 7.
1 *Chr.* 10. 1. the men of Isr. *f.* 11. 13. 2 *Chr.* 13. 16.
2 *Chron.* 14. 12. Lord smote Ethiopians and they *f.*
Neh. 13. 10. the Levites *f.* every one to his field
Esth. 6. † 1. king Ahasuerus's sleep *f.* away
Psal. 31. 11. they that did see me *f.* from me
114. 3. the sea saw it and *f.* Jordan was driven
Isa. 21. 14. they prevented with bread him that *f.*
22. 3. all thy rulers are *f.* together, they are bound
33. 3. at the noise of the tumult the people *f.*
Jer. 4. 25. all the birds of the heavens were *f.*
9. 10. the fowl and beast are *f.* they are gone
26. 21. Urijah heard and *f.* || 46. 5. Egyptians are *f.*
46. 21. also her hired men are *f.* away together
Jonah 4. 2. therefore I *f.* before to Tarshish
Zech. 14. 5. shall flee as ye *f.* before the earthquake
Mat. 8. 33. they that kept them *f.* and went away
26. 56. disciples forsook him and *f.* *Mark* 14. 50.
Mark 16. 8. they went out and *f.* from the sepulchre
Acts 16. 27. supposing the prisoners had been *f.*
Heb. 6. 18. *f.* for refuge to lay hold on the hope
Rev. 12. 6. the woman *f.* || 16. 20. every island *f.* away
20. 11. from whose face earth and heaven *f.* away

He FLED.

Gen. 31. 20. in that he told him not that *he f.*
21. so *he f.* || 35. 7. when *he f.* from his brother
39. 12. *he* left his garment and *f.* 13, 15, 18.
Josh. 20. 6. then the slayer shall come to his own house, to the city from whence *he f.* *Num.* 35. 25.
Judg. 9. 40. Abimelech chased Gaal, and *he f.*
1 *Sam.* 22. 17. because they knew when *he f.*
2 *Kings* 9. 27. Ahaziah fled, and *he f.* to Megiddo
14. 19. and *he f.* to Lachish, 2 *Chron.* 25. 27.
Jonah 1. 10. and *he f.* from the presence of the L.
Mark 14. 52. *he* left the linen cloth, and *f.* naked

Is FLED.

Num. 35. 32. take no satisfaction for him that is *f.*
1 *Sam.* 4. 17. Israel *is f.* before the Philistines
2 *Sam.* 19. 9. Dav. *is f.* out of the land for Absalom
Isa. 10. 29. Ramah is afraid, Gibeah of Saul *is f.*

They FLED.

Gen. 14. 10. *they* that remained *f.* to the mountains
Josh. 7. 4. *they f.* from before the men of Ai
10. 11. as *they f.* the Lord cast down great stones
1 *Sam.* 4. 10. Philistines fought, Israel was smitten, and *they f.* every man to his tent, 2 *Kings* 14. 12.
17. 51. when saw their champion was dead *they f.*
19. 8. David slew Philistines, and *they f.* from him
2 *Sam.* 10. 13. Joab drew nigh, *they f.* 1 *Chr.* 19. 14.
2 *Kings* 3. 24. smote Moabites, *they f.* before them
1 *Chron.* 10. 7. when all Israel saw that *they f.*
Psal. 104. 7. at thy rebuke *they f.* they hasted away
Isa. 21. 15. for *they f.* from the swords, and bent bow
Jer. 39. 4. then *they f.* and went forth of the city
Lam. 4. 15. when *they f.* away, and wandered
Dan. 10. 7. so that *they f.* to save themselves
Hos. 7. 13. woe unto them, for *they* have *f.* from me
Luke 8. 34. when they saw what was done, *they f.*
Acts 19. 16. so that *they f.* out of that house wounded

FLEDDEST.

Gen. 35. 1. when thou *f.* from the face of Esau
Psal. 114. 5. what ailed thee, O sea, that thou *f.*?

FLEECE.

Deut. 18. 4. the first of the *f.* of sheep give Levites
Judg. 6. 37. I will put a *f.* of wool in the floor
38. Gideon wringed the dew out of the *f.*
39. let it now be dry only upon the *f.*
Job 31. 20. if not warmed with the *f.* of my sheep

FLEE.

Gen. 16. 8. I *f.* from the face of my mistress Sarai
19. 20. behold this city is near to *f.* unto
27. 43. arise, *f.* to Laban my brother to Haran
Exod. 14. 25. let us *f.* from the face of Israel
21. 13. appoint a place whither he shall *f.*
Lev. 26. 17. ye shall *f.* when none pursueth, 36.
Num. 10. 35. that hate thee *f.* before thee, *Psal.* 68. 1.
24. 11. therefore now *f.* thou to thy place
35. 6. six cities, that the man slayer may *f.* thither, 11, 15. *Deut.* 4. 42. | 19. 3, 4, 5. *Josh.* 20. 3, 4, 9.
Deut. 28. 7. and *f.* before thee seven ways, 25.
Josh. 8. 5. as at first we will *f.* before them, 6.
20. had no power to *f.* this way or that way
Judg. 20. 32. let us *f.* and draw them from the city
2 *Sam.* 4. 4. as his nurse made haste to *f.* she fell
15. 14. *f.* else we shall not escape from Absalom
19. 3. as men steal away when they *f.* in battle
24. 13. wilt thou *f.* three months before enemies?
1 *Kings* 12. 18. Rehoboam made speed to get to his chariot, and *f.* to Jerusalem, 2 *Chron.* 10. 18.
2 *Kings* 9. 3. then open the door, and *f.* tarry not
Neh. 6. 11. I said, should such a man as I *f.*?
Job 20. 24. he shall *f.* from the iron weapon
27. 22. he would fain *f.* out of his hand
30. 10. they abhor me, they *f.* far from me
41. 28. the arrow cannot make him *f.*
Psal. 11. 1. how say ye, *f.* as bird to your mountain?
68. 12. kings of armies *f.* apace, she that tarried
139. 7. or whither shall I *f.* from thy presence?
143. 9. deliver me, O Lord, I *f.* to thee to hide me
Prov. 28. 1. the wicked *f.* when no man pursueth
17. he shall *f.* to the pit, let no man stay him
Isa. 10. 3. to whom will ye *f.* for help?
13. 14. and *f.* every one into his own land
15. 5. his fugitives shall *f.* unto Zoar
17. 13. they shall *f.* far off, and shall be chased
20. 6. such our expectation whither we *f.* for help
30. 16. but ye said no, for we will *f.* on horses
17. at the rebuke of five shall ye *f.*
48. 20. go from Babylon, *f.* ye from the Chaldeans
Jer. 4. 29. the city shall *f.* for the noise of horsemen
6. 1. gather yourselves to *f.* out of Jerusalem
25. 35. the shepherds shall have no way to *f.*
48. 6. *f.* save your lives, and be like the heath
9. give wings to Moab, that it may *f.* and get away
49. 8. Edom shall *f.* || 24. Damascus turned to *f.*
30. *f.* dwell deep, O ye inhabitants of Hazor
50. 16. they shall *f.* every one to his own land
28. voice of them that *f.* and escape from Babylon
51. 6. *f.* out of the midst of Babylon, *Zech.* 2. 6.
Amos 5. 19. as if a man did *f.* from a lion, and bear
Jonah 1. 3. Jonah rose up to *f.* to Tarshish
Nah. 3. 7. all they that look on, shall *f.* from thee
Mat. 2. 13. arise, take the young child and *f.*
3. 7. hath warned you *f.* from wrath? *Luke* 3. 7.
10. 23. when persecute you in city *f.* to another
24. 16. then let them which be in Judea *f.* to the mountains, *Mark* 13. 14. *Luke* 21. 21.
John 10. 5. a stranger will not follow, but *f.* from
Acts 27. 30. as the shipmen were about to *f.*
1 *Cor.* 6. 18. *f.* fornication || 10. 14. *f.* from idolatry
1 *Tim.* 6. 11. but thou, O man of God *f.* these things
2 *Tim.* 2. 22. *f.* also youthful lusts, follow faith
Jam. 4. 7. resist the devil, and he will *f.* from you
Rev. 9. 6. in those days death shall *f.* from them
12. 14. that the woman might *f.* into wilderness
See FLY.

FLEE *away.*

Gen. 31. 27. wherefore didst thou *f. away* secretly?
2 *Sam.* 18. 3. if we *f. away* they will not care for us
Job 9. 25. my days *f. away*, they see no good
20. 8. *f. away* as a dream, and shall not be found
Psal. 64. 8. all that see them, shall *f. away*
Cant. 2. 17. till day break, and shadows *f. away*, 4. 6.
Isa. 35. 10. sorrow and sighing shall *f. away*, 51. 11.
Jer. 46. 6. let not the swift *f. away*, nor escape
Amos 2. 16. he that is courageous shall *f. away*
7. 12. O thou seer, go *f. away* into the land of Judah
9. 1. he that fleeth of them, shall not *f. away*
Nah. 2. 8. Nineveh shall *f. away*, they shall cry
3. 17. as great grasshoppers in hedges they *f. away*

FLEEING.

Lev. 26. 36. they shall flee as *f.* from a sword
Deut. 4. 42. that *f.* to one of these cities he might live
Job 27. † 22. in *f.* he would flee out of his hand
30. 3. for want and famine *f.* to the wilderness

FLEETH.

Deut. 19. 11. smite him mortally, *f.* into one of cities
Job 14. 2. he *f.* as a shadow and continueth not
Isa. 24. 18. that he who *f.* from the noise of fear
Jer. 48. 19. ask him that *f.* and her that escapeth
44. he that *f.* from the fear, shall fall into the pit
Amos 9. 1. he that *f.* of them shall not flee away
John 10. 12. but he that is an hireling *f.* 13.

FLESH.

Flesh *is understood different ways, as,* (1) *For the flesh which is the matter of bodies, whether of men or animals,* Lev. 13. 10. Num. 11. 33. (2) *For living men, and even all animals in general,* Gen. 6. 13. The end of all flesh is come before me: *I am resolved to destroy every thing that hath life;* Gen. 7. 15, 16. They went in two and two of all flesh, *that is, animals of all species.* (3) Flesh *is taken for a relation, one of the same stock or kindred,* Gen. 37. 27. Let not our hand be upon him, for he is our flesh, *he is our brother. And in* 2 Sam. 19. 12, 13. Ye are my bones and my flesh. Art thou not of my bone, and of my flesh? (4) *For every man who is of the same nature with ourselves, and where we may contemplate our* own flesh: *In this latitude it is taken in* Isa. 58. 7. And that thou hide not thyself from thine own flesh; *from thy neighbour, from any one of thine own nature, to whom thou hast an opportunity of doing good.* (5) *For mankind, considered as impotent and feeble, unable to help either himself or others,* Jer. 17. 5. Cursed be the man that maketh *flesh* his arm; *that depends upon any human power for help.* (6) *For the quality of corruption, which is not sinful, but the effect of sin, to which our bodies are subject in this life.* 1 Cor. 15. 50. Flesh and blood cannot inherit the kingdom of God; *that is, our frail corruptible bodies cannot come to heaven: that which shall inherit heaven must be as incorrupt* flesh, *a body without corruption.* (7) *For the estate of this present life,* Phil. 1. 24. To abide in the flesh is more needful for you. (8) *For that which is according to the ordinary course of nature,* Gal. 4. 23. He who was of the bond-woman, was born after the flesh. Ishmael *was born after the manner of other men, by the mere and sole efficacy of na-*

ture, not by promise, as was Isaac, *when his mother was naturally past conception.* (9) Flesh *is taken for whatsoever in man is reputed most excellent and glorious without the grace of* Christ; *as nobility, wisdom, understanding or reason,* Mat. 16. 17. Flesh and blood hath not revealed it unto thee: *nothing of nature has done it. And in* John 1. 13. Born not of blood, nor of the will of the flesh: *that is, neither by their descent from such and such ancestors, nor by the power of their own free-will.* (10) *For all that in religion which is outward, and to be seen with the eye, as moral works, or ceremonies,* Rom. 4. 1. What hath *Abraham* found as pertaining to the flesh: *The word* flesh *in the following verse, is explained to be the works of* Abraham, *which did not justify him before God. Thus* Beza, Piscator, *and others, interpret the place. And in this sense* flesh *is taken,* Gal. 3. 3. Are ye now made perfect by the flesh? *that is, by works, and the carnal ceremonies of the law.* (11) *For the whole nature of man, as it cometh into the world corrupt, vile, and infected with sin,* Rom. 7. 5. | 8. 8. When we were in the flesh. They that are in the flesh; *that is, in a carnal, corrupt state; such cannot please God, namely, while they continue so, and till they be converted. Likewise in all other places where the word* flesh *is applied to men unregenerated, it signifies the whole corruption and depravity of our nature, raging and reigning both in the understanding and will: but in those places of Scripture, where* flesh *is attributed to persons that are converted, and is set in opposition to the Spirit, it signifies the remainder of natural corruption, even so much of that vicious quality of sin, as is still unmortified in regenerated persons. See* Rom. 7. 18, 25. Gal. 5. 17, 24.

To be one flesh, *denotes a most inseparable union, and an intimate communion, as if the two were but one person, or one body,* Gen. 2. 24. And they shall be one flesh. *This phrase is used by the apostle to show the union and communion that is between* Christ *and believers,* Eph. 5. 30, 31. Flesh *also signifies the human nature of* Christ, *Heb.* 10. 20. Through the vail, that is to say, his flesh. *It is called* flesh, *because it was subject to sinless weaknesses and infirmities, and whereby his divine nature was veiled and covered over; even as the ark of the covenant, the mercy-seat, and the most holy place, were by the vail.* The flesh of Christ *signifies whole* Christ, *both God and man in one person,* John 6. 55. My flesh is meat indeed, *that is, I myself, with all my benefits, being received and applied by faith.* A heart of flesh *denotes a tender, tractable temper and disposition of soul,* Ezek. 36. 26. Flesh *is also taken for the outward appearance,* John 8. 15. Ye judge after the flesh.

Gen. 2. 21. God closed up the *f.* instead thereof
24. shall cleave to his wife, and they shall be one *f.*
6. 3. shall not strive with man, for that he is *f.*
17. 11. ye shall circumcise the *f.* of your foreskin
14. whose *f.* is not circumcised shall be cut off
23. Abraham circumcised the *f.* of their foreskin
37. 27. for he is our brother and our *f.*
Exod. 4. 7. his hand was turned again as his other *f.*
28. † 42. make linen breeches to cover the *f.*
29. 14. burn the *f. Lev.* 9. 11. | 16. 27. *Num.* 19. 5.
30. 32. upon man's *f.* shall it not be poured
Lev. 6. 27. what shall touch *f.* thereof shall be holy
7. 19. as for *f.* all that are clean shall eat thereof
8. 31. boil the *f.* at the door of the tabernacle
13. 10. if there be quick raw *f.* 14, 15, 16, 24.
38. if in the skin of their *f.* have bright spots, 39.
15. 7. that toucheth the *f.* of him that hath an issue
19. if her issue in her *f.* be blood, she is put apart
21. 5. nor shall make any cuttings in their *f.*
Num. 11. 33. while the *f.* was between their teeth
12. 12. as dead, of whom the *f.* is half consumed
18. 18. and the *f.* of them shall be thine
Deut. 32. 42. and my sword shall devour *f.*
Judg. 6. 20. take the *f.* and the unleavened cakes
21. there rose up fire out of rock, and consumed *f.*
1 *Sam.* 2. 13. servant came, while *f.* was in seething
15. he said, give *f.* to roast for the priest
2 *Sam.* 6. 19. David dealt to each *f.* 1 *Chron.* 16. 3.
1 *Kings* 17. 6. the ravens brought him bread and *f.* in the morning, and bread and *f.* in the evening
19. 21. boiled their *f.* with the instruments of oxen
2 *Kings* 4. 34. and the *f.* of the child waxed warm
2 *Chr.* 32. 8. with him is an arm of *f.* with us is God
Neh. 5. 5. yet our *f.* is as the *f.* of our brethren
Job 10. 4. hast thou eyes of *f.*? or seest as man seeth?
11. thou hast clothed me with skin and *f.*
Psal. 56. 4. I will not fear what *f.* can do unto me
78. 20. can he provide *f.* for his people?
27. he rained *f.* also upon them as dust
39. for he remembered that they were but *f.*
79. 2. the *f.* of thy saints given to beasts of earth
Prov. 4. 22. my sayings are health to their *f.*
23. 20. be not among riotous eaters of *f.*
Isa. 10. † 18. consume the glory from soul to the *f.*
31. 3. and their horses are *f.* and not spirit
49. 26. I will feed them with their own *f.*
Jer. 11. 15. and the holy *f.* is passed from thee
12. 12. the spoilers are come, no *f.* shall have peace
17. 5. cursed be the man that maketh *f.* his arm
Ezek. 4. 14. nor came abominable *f.* into my mouth
10. † 12. their *f.* backs, wings, were full of eyes
11. 3. this city is the caldron, and we be the *f.*
7. your slain in midst of it, they are the *f.*
11. nor shall ye be the *f.* in the midst thereof
19. and I will give them a heart of *f.* 36. 26.
16. 26. great of *f.* and hast increased thy whoredoms
23. 20. paramours, whose *f.* is as *f.* of asses
24. 10. heap on wood, consume the *f.* spice it well
37. 6. and I will bring up *f.* upon you, 8.
Dan. 2. 11. the gods, whose dwelling is not with *f.*
7. 5. they said to it, arise, devour much *f.*
10. 3. neither came *f.* nor wine in my mouth
Hos. 8. 13. they sacrifice *f.* for sacrifices of offerings
Mic. 3. 2. who pluck the *f.* from off their bones

Zeph. 1. 17. their *f.* shall be poured out as dung
Hag. 2. 12. if one bear holy *f.* in skirt of his garment
Zech. 14. 12. their *f.* shall consume away
Mat. 16. 17. *f.* and blood hath not revealed it to thee
19. 5. shall cleave to his wife, and they twain shall be one *f.* 6. *Mark* 10. 8. 1 *Cor.* 6. 16. *Eph.* 5. 31.
24. 22. there should no *f.* be saved, *Mark* 13. 20.
26. 41. spirit willing, but *f.* is weak, *Mark* 14. 38.
Luke 24. 39. spirit hath not *f.* and bones, as ye see me
John 1. 14. the WORD was made *f.* and dwelt
6. 63. the Spirit quickeneth, the *f.* profiteth nothing
Acts 2. 30. the seed of Dav. according to *f. Rom.* 1. 3.
Rom. 3. 20. there shall no *f.* be justified in his sight
4. 1. that Abraham as pertaining to the *f.* found
7. 25. but with the *f.* I serve the law of sin
8. 3. in that the law was weak through the *f.* God sent his own Son in the likeness of sinful *f.*
9. 3. for my brethren and kinsmen according to *f.*
5. of whom as concerning the *f.* Christ came
13. 14. make not provision for the *f.* to fulfil
1 *Cor.* 1. 29. that no *f.* should glory in his presence
15. 39. there is one *f.* of men, another of beasts
50. *f.* and blood cannot inherit the kingd. of God
2 *Cor.* 1. 17. do I purpose according to the *f.*?
4. 11. that life of Jesus be made manifest in our *f.*
7. 5. our *f.* had no rest, but we were troubled
10. 2. as if we walked according to the *f.*
Gal. 1. 16. I conferred not with *f.* and blood
2. 16. by works of the law shall no *f.* be justified
3. 3. are ye now made perfect by the *f.*?
5. 13. use not liberty for an occasion to the *f.*
17. *f.* lusteth against the Spirit, Spirit against *f.*
24. they that are Christ's have crucified the *f.*
Eph. 2. 3. we all had our conversat. in lusts of our *f.*
6. 5. your masters according to the *f. Col.* 3. 22.
12. for we wrestle not against *f.* and blood
Heb. 2. 14. the children are partakers of *f.* and blood
12. 9. we had fathers of our *f.* who corrected us
Jude 7. and going after strange *f.* are an example
8. likewise these filthy dreamers defile the *f.*
23. hating even the garment spotted by the *f.*
Rev. 19. 18. may eat *f.* of captains, *f.* of mighty men
21. and all the fowls were filled with their *f.*

See EAT, EATETH.

After the FLESH.

John 8. 15. ye judge *after the f.* I judge no man
Rom. 8. 1. are in Christ, who walk not *after the f.* 4.
5. they that are *after the f.* mind things of the *f.*
12. not debtors to the flesh to live *after the f.*
13. for if ye live *after the f.* ye shall die
1 *Cor.* 1. 26. not many wise men *after the f.* are called
10. 18. behold Israel *after the f.*
2 *Cor.* 5. 16. we know no man *after the f.* though we have known Chr. *after f.* yet know him no more
10. 3. tho' walk in flesh, we do not war *after the f.*
11. 18. seeing that many glory *after the f.* I also
Gal. 4. 23. Ishmael was born *after the f.* 29.
2 *Pet.* 2. 10. chiefly them that walk *after the f.*

All FLESH.

Gen. 6. 12. for *all f.* had corrupted his way on earth
13. God said, the end of *all f.* is come before me
6. 19. of *all f.* two of every sort shalt thou bring into the ark to keep them alive, 7. 15.
7. 21. *all f.* died that moved upon the earth
8. 17. bring forth of *all f.* both of fowl and cattle
9. 11. nor shall *all f.* be cut off any more, 15.
16. covenant between me and *all f.* on earth, 17.
Lev. 17. 14. for the life of *all f.* is the blood
Num. 8. 7. let them shave *all* their *f.* and wash clothes
16. 22. the God of the spirits of *all f.* 27. 16.
18. 15. every thing that openeth the matrix of *all f.*
Deut. 5. 26. who of *all f.* heard the word of God
Job 12. † 10. in whose hand is breath of *all f.* of man
34. 15. *all f.* shall perish together, man turn to dust
Ps. 65. 2. thou hearest prayer, to thee shall *all f.* come
136. 25. who giveth food to *all f.* his mercy for ever
145. 21. let *all f.* bless his holy name for ever
Isa. 40. 5. and *all f.* shall see it together
6. *all f.* is grass, as flower of the field, 1 *Pet.* 1. 24.
49. 26. *all f.* shall know I am thy Sav. *Ezek.* 21. 5.
66. 16. for by fire will the Lord plead with *all f.*
23. *all f.* shall come to worship before me, saith L.
24. they shall be an abhorring to *all f.*
Jer. 25. 31. he will plead with *all f.* saith the Lord
32. 27. behold, I am the Lord the God of *all f.*
45. 5. for behold, I will bring evil on *all f.* saith L.
Ezek. 20. 48. *all f.* shall see that I have kindled it
21. 4. shall my sword go forth ag. *all f.* from south
Dan. 4. 12. fowls dwelt, and *all f.* was fed of it
Joel 2. 28. will pour out my Spirit on *all f. Acts* 2. 17.
Zech. 2. 13. be silent, O *all f.* before the Lord
Luke 3. 6. and *all f.* shall see the salvation of God
John 17. 2. thou hast given him power over *all f.*
1 *Cor.* 15. 39. *all f.* is not the same flesh, one of men

His FLESH.

Exod. 21. 28. and *his f.* shall not be eaten
29. 31. and seethe *his f.* in the holy place
Lev. 4. 11. burn all *his f.* with his head, 8. 17.
6. 10. he shall put linen breeches on *his f.* 16. 4.
13. 2. shall have a rising in the skin of *his f.*
3. priest look on the plague in the skin of *his f.*
4. if bright spot be white in the skin of *his f.*
11. it is an old leprosy in the skin of *his f.* 13.
14. 9. he shall wash his clothes, also wash *his f.* in water, 15. 16. | 16. 24, 28. *Num.* 19. 7.
15. 2. any man hath a running issue out of *his f.*
3. whether *his f.* run with his issue, or be stopped
17. 16. but if he wash them not, nor bathe *his f.*
22. 6. be unclean, unless he wash *his f.* with water
1 *Kings* 21. 27. Ahab put sackcloth on *his f.*
2 *Kings* 5. 14. *his f.* came again, and he was clean
6. 30. behold Joram had sackcloth on *his f.*
Job 2. 5. touch his bone and *his f.* he will curse thee
14. 22. but *his f.* upon him shall have pain
31. 31. if men said not, O that we had of *his f.*
33. 21. *his f.* is consumed away, it cannot be seen
25. *his f.* shall be fresher than a child's
41. 23. the flakes of *his f.* are joined togethe
Prov. 11. 17. he that is cruel troubleth *his f.*
Eccl. 4. 5. the fool foldeth his hands, and eateth *his f.*
Isa. 17. 4. the fatness of *his f.* shall wax lean
John 6. 52. can this man give us *his f.* to eat?

Acts 2. 31. neither *his f.* did see corruption
Gal. 6. 8. he that soweth to *his f.* shall reap corrup
Eph. 2. 15. having abolished in *his f.* the enmity
5. 29. no man ever yet hated *his* own *f.*
30. for we are members of his body, of *his f.*
Col. 1. 22. now hath reconciled in the body of *his f.*
Heb. 5. 7. who in days of *his f.* when offered prayers
10. 20. consecrated thro' vail, that is to say, *his f.*

In the FLESH, *or in* FLESH.

Gen. 17. 24. Abraham was circumcised *in the f.*
25. Ishmael circumcised *in the f.* of his foreskin
Ezek. 44. 7. brought in uncircumcised *in the f.*
9. uncircumcised *in the f.* not enter the sanctuary
Dan. 1. 15. counten. appeared fairer and fatter *in f.*
Rom. 2. 28. circumcision which is outward *in the f.*
7. 5. for when we were *in the f.* the motions of sin
8. 3. and for sin condemned sin *in the f.*
8. they that are *in the f.* cannot please God
9. but ye are not *in the f.* but in the Spirit
1 *Cor.* 7. 28. such shall have trouble *in the f.*
2 *Cor.* 10. 3. though we walk *in the f.* not war after *f.*
12. 7. there was given to me a thorn *in the f.*
Gal. 2. 20. life which I now live *in the f.* is by faith
6. 12. as desire to make a fair shew *in the f.*
Eph. 2. 11. in time past Gentiles *in the f.* called the circumcision *in the f.* made by hands
Phil. 1. 22. if I live *in the f.* this is the fruit of labour
24. to abide *in the f.* is more needful for you
3. 3. and have no confidence *in the f.*
4. though I might have confidence *in the f.*
Col. 2. 1. as many as have not seen my face *in the f.*
5. tho' I be absent *in the f.* I am with you in spirit
1 *Tim.* 3. 16. God was manifest *in the f.* justified
Philem. 16. how much more to thee, both *in the f.*
1 *Pet.* 3. 18. Christ being put to death *in the f.*
4. 1. Christ hath suffered for us *in the f.* for he that hath suffered *in the f.* hath ceased from sin
2. no longer live the rest of his time *in the f.*
6. might be judged according to men *in the f.*
1 *John* 4. 2. denieth that Christ is come *in the f.* 3.
2 *John* 7. confess not that Christ is come *in the f.*

My FLESH.

1 *Sam.* 25. 11. shall I then take my bread and *my f.*?
Job 4. 15. the hair of *my f.* stood up
6. 12. is my strength of stones? or is *my f.* brass?
7. 5. *my f.* is clothed with worms and dust
13. 14. wherefore do I take *my f.* in my teeth?
19. 20. my bone cleaveth to my skin, and *my f.*
22. why persecute, and not satisfied with *my f.*?
26. worms destroy body, yet in *my f.* shall I see G.
21. 6. and trembling taketh hold of *my f.*
Psal. 16. 9. *my f.* shall rest in hope, *Acts* 2. 26.
38. 3. there is no soundness in *my f.* 7.
63. 1. *my f.* longeth for thee in a dry thirsty land
73. 26. *my f.* faileth, but G. is my portion for ever
84. 2. my heart and *my f.* crieth out for God
102. † 5. by groaning my bones cleave to *my f.*
109. 24. my knees are weak, *my f.* faileth of fatness
119. 120. *my f.* trembleth for fear of thee
Eccl. 2. † 3. I sought to draw *my f.* with wine
Jer. 51. 35. the violence done to me, and to *my f.*
Lam. 3. 4. *my f.* and my skin hath he made old
John 6. 51. the bread that I will give, is *my f.*
54. whoso eateth *my f.* hath eternal life, 56.
55. *my f.* is meat indeed, my blood drink indeed
Rom. 7. 18. in *my f.* dwelleth no good thing
11. 14. if I may provoke them which are *my f.*
Gal. 4. 14. my temptation which was in *my f.*
Col. 1. 24. of the afflictions of Christ in *my f.*

See BONE.

Of the FLESH.

Exod. 12. 46. shalt not carry forth ought *of the f.*
29. 34. if ought *of the f.* remain unto morning
Deut. 28. 55. nor give *of the f.* of his children
Prov. 14. 30. a sound heart is the life *of the f.*
Eccl. 12. 12. much study is a weariness *of the f.*
John 1. 13. born, not of the will *of the f.* but of God
3. 6. that which is born *of the f.* is flesh
Rom. 8. 5. that after flesh do mind the things *of the f.*
† 6. for the minding *of the f.* is death
† 7. the minding *of the f.* is enmity against God
9. 8. that is, they which are the children *of the f.*
1 *Cor.* 5. 5. to Satan for the destruction *of the f.*
2 *Cor.* 7. 1. let us cleanse from all filthiness *of the f.*
Gal. 4. 13. through infirmity *of the f.* I preached
5. 16. ye shall not fulfil the lusts *of the f.*
19. now the works *of the f.* are manifest, adultery
6. 8. that soweth to *f.* shall *of the f.* reap corruption
Eph. 2. 3. walked in lusts *of the f.* desires *of the f.*
Col. 2. 11. putting off the body of sins *of the f.*
23. not in honour to the satisfying *of the f.*
Heb. 9. 13. sanctifieth to the purging *of the f.*
1 *Pet.* 3. 21. not the putting away the filth *of the f.*
2 *Pet.* 2. 18. they allure through the lusts *of the f.*
1 *John* 2. 16. the lust *of the f.* the lust of the eyes

Thy FLESH.

Gen. 40. 19. the birds shall eat *thy f.* from off thee
1 *Sam.* 17. 44. I will give *thy f.* unto fowls of the air
2 *Sam.* 5. 1. we are thy bone and *thy f.* 1 *Chr.* 11. 1.
2 *Kings* 5. 10. wash, and *thy f.* shall come again
Prov. 5. 11. mourn at last, when *thy f.* is consumed
Eccl. 5. 6. suffer not thy mouth to cause *thy f.* to sin
11. 10. therefore put away evil from *thy f.*
Isa. 58. 7. that thou hide not thyself from *thy* own *f.*
Ezek. 32. 5. I will lay *thy f.* on the mountains

Your FLESH.

Lev. 19. 28. ye shall not make cuttings in *your f.*
Judg. 8. 7. then I will tear *your f.* with the thorns
Ezek. 36. 26. I will take stony heart out of *your f.*
Rom. 6. 19. because of the infirmity of *your f.*
Gal. 6. 13. that they may glory in *your f.*
Col. 2. 13. being dead in uncircumcision of *your f.*
Jam. 5. 3. rust shall eat *your f.* as it were fire

FLESHED, *see* FAT, LEAN.

FLESH-HOOK.

1 *Sam.* 2. 13. the priest's servant came with a *f.-hook*
14. all that the *f.-hook* brought up, the priest took

FLESH-HOOKS.

Exod. 27. 3. shalt make his *f.-hooks* and his fire-pans
38. 3. he made all the vessels and the *f.-hooks*
Num. 4. 14. put upon the purple cloth the *f.-hooks*
1 *Chr.* 28. 17. David gave pure gold for the *f.-hooks*

2 *Chr.* 4. 16. he made also the pots and the *f.-hooks*

FLESHLY.

2 *Cor.* 1. 12. that in simplicity, not with *f.* wisdom
3. 3. not in stone, but in *f.* tables of the heart
Col. 2. 18. vainly puffed up by his *f.* mind
1 *Pet.* 2. 11. beloved, abstain from *f.* lusts that war

FLESH-POTS.

Exod. 16. 3. when we sat by the *f.-pots* and did eat

FLEW.

1 *Sam.* 14. 32. and the people *f.* upon the spoil
25. † 14. and our master *f.* upon them
Isa. 6. 6. then *f.* one of the seraphims unto me

FLIES.

Exod. 8. 21. I will send swarms of *f.* upon thee
31. he removed the swarms of *f.* from Pharaoh
Psal. 78. 45. he sent divers sorts of *f.* among them
105. 31. and there came divers sorts of *f.*
Eccl. 10. 1. dead *f.* cause the ointment to send f rth

FLIETH.

Deut. 4. 17. the likeness of any winged fowl that *f.*
14. 19. every creeping thing that *f.* is unclean
28. 49. shall bring a nation as swift as the eagle *f.*
Psal. 91. 5. nor for the arrow that *f.* by day
Nah. 3. 16. the cankerworm spoileth and *f.* away

FLIGHT.

Job 11. † 20. and *f.* shall perish from the wicked
Isa. 52. 12. shall not go out with haste nor go by *f.*
Jer. 46. † 5. their mighty ones are fled a *f.*
Dan. 9. † 21. Gabriel was caused to fly with *f.*
Amos 2. 14. the *f.* shall perish from the swift
Mat. 24. 20. pray *f.* be not in winter, *Mark* 13. 18.
Heb. 11. 34. turned to *f.* the armies of the aliens
See PUT.

FLINT.

Deut. 8. 15. brought water out of the rock of *f.*
Job 28. † 9. he putteth forth his hand on the *f.*
Psal. 114. 8. turning the *f.* into a fountain of waters
Isa. 5. 28. their horses shall be counted like *f.*
50. 7. therefore have I set my face like a *f.*
Ezek. 3. 9. harder than *f.* have I made thy forehead

FLINTY.

Deut. 32. 13. made him to suck oil out of the *f.* rock

FLIT.

Jer. 49. † 30. flee, *f.* greatly, O inhabitants of Hazor

FLOCK.

Gen. 4. 4. Abel brought of the firstlings of his *f.*
21. 28. Abraham set ewe-lambs of *f.* by themselves
27. 9. go now to the *f.* and fetch two good kids
29. 10. Jacob watered the *f.* of Laban
30. 31. I will again feed and keep thy *f.*
32. I will pass through all thy *f.* to-day
36. and Jacob fed the rest of Laban's *f.*
40. Jacob did separate all the brown in the *f.*
31. 4. Jacob called Rachel and Leah to his *f.*
38. the rams of thy *f.* have I not eaten
33. 13. if men overdrive them, the *f.* will die
37. 2. Joseph was feeding the *f.* with his brethren
12. his brethren went to feed their *f.* 13.
38. 17. I will send thee a kid from the *f.*
Exod. 2. 16. the troughs to water their father's *f.*
17. Moses helped, and watered their *f.* 19.
3. 1. Moses led the *f.* to the back-side of the desert
Lev. 1. 2. bring of your offering of the herd or *f.*
5. 6. he shall bring a female from the *f.*
18. he shall bring a ram without blemish out of the *f.* 6. 6. *Ezra* 10. 19. *Ezek.* 43. 23, 25.
27. 32. concerning the tithe of the herd or of the *f.*
Num. 15. 3. make a sweet savour of the herd or *f.*
Deut. 12. 21. then thou shalt kill of thy herd and *f.*
15. 14. thou shalt furnish him liberally out of thy *f.*
19. all the firstling males of thy *f.* shalt sanctify
16. 2. shalt sacrifice to the Lord thy God of the *f.*
1 *Sam.* 17. 34. a lion took a lamb out of the *f.*
2 *Sam.* 12. 4. he spared to take of his own *f.*
2 *Chron.* 35. 7. Josiah gave to the people of the *f.*
Job 30. 1. I disdained to set with the dogs of my *f.*
Cant. 1. 7. where thou makest thy *f.* to rest at noon
8. go thy way forth by the footsteps of the *f.*
4. 1. thy hair is as a *f.* of goats, 6. 5.
2. thy teeth are like a *f.* of sheep, 6. 6.
Isa. 40. 11. he shall feed his *f.* like a shepherd
63. 11. brought them with the shepherd of his *f.*
Jer. 13. 17. because the Lord's *f.* is carried captive
20. where is the *f.* was given thee, thy beautiful *f.*?
23. 2. ye have scattered my *f.* and driven them
3. I will gather the remnant of my *f.*
25. 34. cry and wallow, ye principal of the *f.*
35. nor the principal of the *f.* to escape
36. an howling of the principal of the *f.* be heard
31. 10. and keep him as a shepherd doth his *f.*
12. they shall sing for the young of the *f.*
49. 20. least of the *f.* shall draw them out, 50. 45.
51. 23. will break in pieces the shepherd and his *f.*
Ezek. 24. 5. take the choice of the *f.* burn the bones
34. 3. ye eat the fat, but ye feed not the *f.*
6. my *f.* was scattered on the face of the earth
8. surely because my *f.* became a prey, my *f.* meat
10. I will require my *f.* I will deliver my *f.*
12. as a shepherd seeketh out his *f.* in the day
15. I will feed my *f.* ‖ 17. as for you, O my *f.*
22. therefore will I save my *f.* no more a prey
31. ye my *f.* the *f.* of my pasture, are men
36. 38. as the holy *f.* as the *f.* of Jerusalem
45. 15. ye shall offer one lamb out of the *f.*
Amos 6. 4. and eat the lambs out of the *f.*
7. 15. the Lord took me as I followed the *f.*
Jonah 3. 7. let not herd nor *f.* taste any thing
Mic. 2. 12. as the *f.* in the midst of their fold
4. 8. thou, O tower of the *f.* the strong hold
7. 14. feed thy people, the *f.* of thine heritage
Hab. 3. 17. tho' the *f.* shall be cut off from the fold
Zech. 9. 16. save them as the *f.* of his people
10. 2. therefore they went their way as a *f.*
3. for the Lord of hosts hath visited his *f.*
11. 4. saith the Lord, will feed the *f.* of slaughter, 7.
7. the poor of the *f.* that waited on me, 11.
17. woe to the idol shepherd, that leaveth the *f.*
Mal. 1. 14. deceiver which hath in his *f.* a male
Mat. 26. 31. the sheep of the *f.* shall be scattered
Luke 2. 8. keeping watch over their *f.* by night
12. 32. fear not little *f.* it is your Father's pleasure
Acts 20. 28. take heed therefore to all the *f.*
29. grievous wolves shall enter, not sparing the *f.*
1 *Cor.* 9. 7. who feedeth a *f.* and eateth not of milk?
1 *Pet.* 5. 2. feed the *f.* of God which is among you
3. not as being lords, but being ensamples to the *f.*

Like a FLOCK.

Job 21. 11. send forth their little ones *like a f.*
Psal. 77. 20. thou leddest thy people *like a f.*
78. 52. he guided them in the wilderness *like a f.*
80. 1. thou that leadest Joseph *like a f.*
107. 41. and maketh him families *like a f.*
Ezek. 36. 37. I will increase them with men *like a f.*

FLOCKS.

Gen. 29. 2. and lo, three *f.* of sheep lying by the well, for out of that they watered the *f.*
3. and thither were all the *f.* gathered
8. we cannot, till all the *f.* be gathered together
30. 38. Jacob set the rods he pilled before the *f.*
39. and the *f.* conceived before the rods
40. Jacob set the faces of the *f.* towards the ring-straked, he put his own *f.* by themselves
32. 5. I have oxen, asses, *f.* and men-servants
7. he divided the *f.* and herds, and camels
37. 14. go, see whether it be well with the *f.*
16. tell me, I pray thee, where they feed their *f.*
47. 4. thy servants have no pasture for their *f.*
17. Joseph gave bread in exch. for horses and *f.*
Lev. 1. 10. if his offering be of the *f.* of the sheep
5. 15. bring a ram without blemish out of the *f.*
Num. 31. 9. Israel took spoil of all their *f.* and goods
30. thou shalt take one portion of the *f.*
32. 26. our wives, our *f.* and cattle, shall be there
Deut. 7. 13. he will also bless the *f.* of thy sheep
28. 4. blessed shall be the *f.* of thy sheep
18. cursed shall be the *f.* of thy sheep
51. who shall not leave the *f.* of thy sheep
Judg. 5. 16. to hear the bleatings of the *f.*
1 *Kings* 20. 27. pitched like two little *f.* of kids
1 *Chron.* 4. 39. they went to seek pasture for their *f.*
41. because there was pasture for their *f.*
27. 31. and over the *f.* was Jaziz the Hagarite
2 *Chron.* 17. 11. the Arabians brought him *f.*
Job 24. 2. violently take away *f.* and feed thereof
Psal. 8. † 7. *f.* and oxen all under his feet
65. 13. the pastures are clothed with *f.*
78. 48. he gave their *f.* to hot thunderbolts
Cant. 1. 7. turn aside by the *f.* of thy companions
Isa. 17. 2. cities of Aroer are forsaken, shall be for *f.*
32. 14. the palaces shall be a pasture of *f.*
60. 7. all the *f.* of Kedar shall be gathered together
61. 5. and strangers shall stand and feed your *f.*
65. 10. Sharon shall be a fold for *f.* valley of Achor
Jer. 6. 3. the shepherds with their *f.* shall come to her
10. 21. shall not prosper, all *f.* shall be scattered
31. 24. dwell in Judah they that go forth with *f.*
33. 12. shepherds causing their *f.* to lie down
13. the *f.* shall pass again under the rod
49. 29. their tents and *f.* shall they take away
50. 8. and be as the he-goats before the *f.*
Ezek. 25. 5. Ammonites a couching-place for *f.*
34. 2. should not the shepherds feed the *f.*?
36. 38. the waste cities shall be filled with *f.* of men
Joel 1. 18. the *f.* of sheep are made desolate
Mic. 1. † 11. inhabitant of country of *f.* came not forth
5. 8. as a young lion among the *f.* of sheep
Zeph. 2. 6. and the sea-coast shall be folds for *f.*
14. *f.* shall lie down in the midst of Nineveh

FLOCKS *with herds.*

Gen. 13. 5. Lot also had *f.* and *herds*, and tents
24. 35. the Lord hath given Abraham *f.* and *herds*
26. 14. Isaac had possession of *f.* and *herds*
32. 7. Jacob divided *f.* and *herds* into two bands
33. 13. the *f.* and *herds* with young are with me
45. 10. thou shalt be near me, thou, thy *f.* and *herds*
47. 1. my brethren, their *f.* and *herds* are come
50. 8. their *f.* and *herds* left they in land of Goshen
Exod. 10. 9. we will go with our *f.* and our *herds*
24. only let your *f.* and your *herds* be stayed
12. 32. also take your *f.* and *herds*, and be gone
34. 3. neither let *f.* nor *herds* feed before the mount
Num. 11. 22. shall the *f.* and *herds* be slain for them
Deut. 8. 13. when thy *herds* and thy *f.* multiply
12. 6. firstlings of *h.* and *f.* 17. | 14. 23. *Neh.* 10. 36.
1 *Sam.* 30. 20. David took all the *f.* and the *herds*
2 *Sam.* 12. 2. rich man had exceeding many *f.* and *h.*
2 *Chron.* 32. 29. provided possessions of *f.* and *herds*
Prov. 27. 23. know thy *f.* look well to thy *herds*
Jer. 3. 24. shame had devoured their *f.* and *herds*
5. 17. an ancient nation shall eat thy *f.* and *herds*
Hos. 5. 6. they shall go with *f.* and *herds* to seek Ld.

FLOOD.

Not *only that terrible inundation is in Scripture called* flood, *whereby God destroyed all mankind, and all the animals of the earth and air, which were not in the ark built by* Noah; *but likewise all sorts of inundations or extraordinary collections of waters. Thus the* Psalmist *speaking of the waters of the sea, or of a river, expresses it by the word* flood, *Psal.* 66. 6. They went through the flood on foot. *The same* Psalmist *sets forth extreme dangers under the notion of a* flood, *Psal.* 69. 15. Let not the water-flood overflow me. *And the violent assaults and sudden incursions of the devil and his instruments against the church are compared to a* flood, *Isa.* 59. 19. When the enemy shall come in like a flood. *By* floods *are also signified great plenty and abundance of spiritual and temporal blessings,* Isa. 44. 3. I will pour floods upon the dry ground.

Gen. 6. 17. I, even I, bring a *f.* of water on the earth
7. 6. when the *f.* of waters was upon the earth
7. Noah went in, because of the waters of the *f.*
10. after seven days the *f.* was on the earth
7. 17. the *f.* was forty days on the earth
9. 11. nor shall be any more a *f.* to destroy the earth
28. Noah lived after the *f.* 350 years
10. 1. to them were sons born after the *f.*
32. the nations were divided in the earth after *f.*
Josh. 24. 2. your fathers on either side of *f.* 3. 14, 15.
Job 14. 11. as the *f.* decayeth and drieth up
22. 16. whose foundation was overthrown with a *f.*
28. 4. the *f.* breaketh out from the inhabitant
Psal. 29. 10. the Lord sitteth upon the *f.* he is king
66. 6. they went thro' the *f.* on foot, we rejoiced
69. 15. let not the water-*f.* overflow me
74. 15. thou didst cleave the fountain and the *f.*
90. 5. thou carriest them away as with a *f.*
Isa. 28. 2. a strong one, which as a *f.* shall cast down
59. 19. the enemy shall come in like a *f.*
Jer. 46. 7. who is this that cometh up as a *f.*?
8. Egypt riseth up like a *f.* waters are moved
47. 2. behold, waters shall be an overflowing *f.*
Dan. 9. 26. the end thereof shall be with a *f.*
11. 22. with the arms of a *f.* shall they be overflown
Amos 8. 8. it shall rise up wholly as a *f.* 9. 5.
9. 5. and shall be drowned as by the *f.* of Egypt
Nah. 1. 8. with an overrunning *f.* make an end
Mat. 24. 38. in days before the *f.* they were eating
39. and knew not till the *f.* came, *Luke* 17. 27.
Luke 6. 48. when the *f.* arose the stream beat
2 *Pet.* 2. 5. bringing in the *f.* on world of ungodly
Rev. 12. 15. the dragon poured out water as a *f.*
16. the earth helped, and swallowed up the *f.*

FLOOD GATES.

Gen. 7. † 11. the *f.-gates* of heaven were opened

FLOODS.

Exod. 15. 8. the *f.* stood upright as an heap
2 *Sam.* 22. 5. *f.* of ungodly made me afraid, *Ps.* 18. 4.
Job 20. 17. he shall not see the rivers and the *f.*
28. 11. he bindeth the *f.* from overflowing
Psal. 24. 2. he hath established it upon the *f.*
32. 6. surely in the *f.* of great waters not come nigh
69. 2. into deep waters, where the *f.* overflow me
78. 44. and had turned their *f.* into blood
93. 3. the *f.* have lifted up, O Lord, *f.* have lifted up
98. 8. let the *f.* clap their hands, let hills be joyful
Cant. 8. 7. neither can the *f.* drown love
Isa. 44. 3. for I will pour *f.* upon the dry ground
Ezek. 31. 15. I restrained the *f.* thereof, waters stayed
Jonah 2. 3. the *f.* compassed me about, thy billows
Mat. 7. 25. the *f.* came, winds blew, and beat, 27.

FLOOR, *Verb.*

2 *Chron.* 34. 11. and for timber to *f.* the houses

FLOOR, *Substantive.*

Gen. 50. 10. they came to the threshing *f.* of Atad
11. when inhabitants saw mourning in *f.* of Atad
Num. 5. 17. the priests shall take dust that is in *f.*
15. 20. as ye do the heave-offering of threshing *f.*
18. 27. as tho' it were the corn of the threshing *f.*
30. be counted as the increase of the threshing *f.*
Deut. 15. 14. thou shalt furnish him out of thy *f.*
16. † 13. after thou hast gathered in thy *f.*
Judg. 6. 37. I will put a fleece of wool in the *f.*
Ruth 3. 2. he winnoweth in the threshing *f.*
2 *Sam.* 6. 6. came to Nachon's thresh. *f.* 1 *Chr.* 13. 9.
24. 18. rear an altar in the threshing *f.* of Araunah
21. David said, to buy the threshing *f.* of thee
1 *Kings* 6. 30. he overlaid the *f.* of house with gold
7. 7. with cedar from one side of the *f.* to the other
2 *Kings* 6. 27. out of the barn-*f.* or the wine-press?
1 *Chron.* 21. 28. L. had answered in the threshing *f.*
2 *Chron.* 3. 1. prepared in threshing *f.* of Ornan
18. † 9. they sat in a *f.* at the entering of the gate
Isa. 21. 10. O my threshing, and the corn of my *f.*
Jer. 51. 33. daughter of Bab. is like a threshing *f.*
Hos. 9. 1. thou hast loved a reward on every corn *f*
2. the *f.* and wine-press shall not feed them
13. 3. as the chaff that is driven out of the *f.*
Mic. 4. 12. shall gather them as sheaves into the *f*
Mat. 3. 12. he will throughly purge his *f.* *Luke* 3. 17.

FLOORS.

1 *Sam.* 23. 1. and they rob the threshing *f.*
Dan. 2. 35. like chaff of the summer threshing *f.*
Joel 2. 24. and the *f.* shall be full of wheat

FLOTES, or FLOATS.

1 *Kings* 5. 9. and I will convey them by sea in *f.* to the place thou shalt appoint me, 2 *Chr.* 2. 16.

FLOURISH.

Psal. 72. 7. in his days shall the righteous *f.*
16. they of the city shall *f.* like grass of the earth
92. 7. when all the workers of iniquity *f.*
12. the righteous shall *f.* like the palm-tree
13. they shall *f.* in the courts of our God
132. 18. but upon himself shall his crown *f.*
Prov. 11. 28. the righteous shall *f.* as a branch
14. 11. the tabernacle of the upright shall *f.*
Eccl. 12. 5. when the almond-tree shall *f.*
Cant. 7. 12. let us get up, let us see if the vine *f.*
Isa. 17. 11. in morning thou shalt make thy seed to *f.*
66. 14. your bones shall *f.* like an herb
Ezek. 17. 24. I the L. have made the dry tree to *f.*

FLOURISHED.

Cant. 6. 11. I went down to see whether the vine *f.*
Phil. 4. 10. your care of me hath *f.* again

FLOURISHETH.

Psal. 90. 6. in the morning it *f.* and groweth up
103. 15. as a flower of the field, so he *f.*

FLOURISHING.

Psal. 92. 14. in old age, they shall be fat and *f.*
Cant. 2. † 9. he looketh forth, *f.* through the lattice
Dan. 4. 4. I was at rest, and *f.* in my palace

FLOW.

Job 20. 28. his goods shall *f.* away in day of his wrath
Psal. 147. 18. he causeth the wind blow, and waters *f.*
Cant. 4. 16. that the spices thereof may *f.* out
Isa. 2. 2. and all nations shall *f.* unto it
48. 21. he caused waters to *f.* out of the rock
60. 5. then thou shalt see and *f.* together
64. 1. mountains might *f.* down at thy presence
Jer. 31. 12. shall *f.* to the goodness of the Lord
51. 44. nations shall not *f.* together any more to him
Joel 3. 18. in that day the hills shall *f.* with milk, and the rivers of Judah shall *f.* with waters
Mic. 4. 1. the people shall *f.* to the mountain of L.
John 7. 38. out of his belly shall *f.* living water

FLOWED.

Josh. 4. 18. Jordan *f.* over all his banks
Judg. 5. † 5. the mountains *f.* before the Lord
Isa. 64. 3. the mountains *f.* down at thy presence
Lam. 3. 54. the waters *f.* over mine head, then I said

FLOWETH.

Lev. 20. 24. a land that *f.* with milk and honey, *Num.* 13. 27. | 14. 8. | 16. 13, 14. *Deut.* 6. 3. | 11. 9. | 26. 15. | 27. 3. | 31. 20. *Josh.* 5. 6.

FLOWING.

Exod. 3. 8. to bring them to a land *f.* with milk and honey, 17. | 13. 5. | 33. 3. *Jer.* 11. 5. | 32. 22. *Ezek.* 20. 6, 15.
Prov. 18. 4. the well-spring of wisdom as a *f.* brook
Isa. 66. 12. the glory of the Gentiles like a *f.* stream
Jer. 18. 14. or shall the cold *f.* waters be forsaken?
49. 4. wherefore gloriest thou in thy *f.* valley?

FLOUR.

Exod. 29. 2. of wheaten *f.* shalt thou make them
Lev. 2. 2. he shall take his handful of the *f.* 6. 15.
Num. 28. 5. and a tenth part of an ephah of *f.* for a meat-offering, 20, 28. | 29. 3, 9, 14.
Judg. 6. 19. cakes of an ephah of *f.* 1 *Sam.* 1. 24.
1 *Sam* 28. 24. she took *f.* and kneaded it, 2 *Sam.* 13. 8.
2 *Sam.* 17. 28. brought *f.* parched corn, and beans
See DEAL, FINE.

FLOWER.

1 *Sam.* 2. 33. the increase shall die in *f.* of their age
1 *Cor.* 7. 36. if she pass *f.* of her age and need require

FLOWER.

Exod. 25. 33. with knop and *f.* in one branch, 37. 19.
Job 14. 2. he cometh forth as a *f.* and is cut down
15. 33. he shall cast off his *f.* as the olive
Psal. 103. 15. as a *f.* of field, so he flourisheth
Isa. 18. 5. and the sour grape is ripening in the *f.*
28. 1. whose glorious beauty is a fading *f.* 4.
40. 6. the goodliness thereof is as the *f.* of the field
7. *f.* fadeth, 8. *Neh.* 1. 4. *Jam.* 1. 10, 11. 1 *Pet.* 1. 24.

FLOWERS.

Exod. 25. 31. his *f.* shall be of the same, 37. 17.
37. 20. made like almonds, his knops and his *f.*
Num. 8. 4. to the *f.* thereof was beaten work
1 *Kings* 6. 18. cedar of the house within was carved with knops and open *f.* 29. 32, 35. | 7. 26, 49.
2 *Chr.* 4. 5. like the brim of a cup with *f.* of lilies
21. the *f.* lamps, and tongs made he of gold
Cant. 2. 12. the *f.* appear on earth, time of singing
5. 13. his cheeks are as a bed of spices, as sweet *f.*

FLOWERS.

Lev. 15. 24. if her *f.* be upon him, he shall be unclean
33. of her that is sick of her *f.* of him with issue

FLUTE, S.

1 *Kings* 1. † 40. all people piped with *f.* and rejoiced
Dan. 3. 5. when ye hear the sound of the *f.* 7. 10, 15.

FLUTTERETH.

Deut. 32. 11. as an eagle *f.* over her young

FLUX.

Acts 28. 8. the father of Publius lay sick of a *f.*

FLY.

Isa. 7. 18. the Lord shall hiss for the *f.* in Egypt

FLY, *Verb.*

Gen. 1. 20. and fowl that may *f.* above the earth
1 *Sam.* 15. 19. but didst *f.* on the spoil, and didst evil
2 *Sam.* 22. 11. he rode upon a cherub, and did *f.* and was seen on wings of the wind, *Psal.* 18. 10.
Job 5. 7. man born to trouble as sparks *f.* upward
39. 26. doth the hawk *f.* by thy wisdom?
Psal. 18. 10. he did *f.* upon the wings of the wind
55. 6. for then would I *f.* away, and be at rest
90. 10. for it is soon cut off, and we *f.* away
Prov. 23. 5. riches *f.* away as an eagle to heaven
Isa. 6. 2. each had six wings, and with twain he did *f.*
11. 14. but they shall *f.* upon shoulders of Philist.
60. 8. who are these that *f.* as a cloud, and as doves
Jer. 48. 40. behold, he shall *f.* as an eagle
Ezek. 13. 20. ye hunt the souls to make them *f.*
Dan. 9. 21. Gab. being caused to *f.* swiftly, touched
Hos. 9. 11. their glory shall *f.* away like a bird
Hab. 1. 8. they shall *f.* as the eagle that hasteth to eat
Rev. 14. 6. I saw another angel *f.* in midst of heaven
19. 17. to all the fowls that *f.* in the midst of heaven
See FLEE, FLIETH.

FLYING.

Lev. 11. 21. these may ye eat of every *f.* creeping [thing
23. but all other *f.* creeping things an abomination
Psal. 148. 10. all cattle and *f.* fowl, praise the Lord
Prov. 26. 2. as swallow by *f.* so the curse causeless
Isa. 14. 29. and his fruit shall be a fiery *f.* serpent
30. 6. from whence come viper and fiery *f.* serpent
31. 5. as birds *f.* so will the Lord defend Jerusalem
Zech. 5. 1. I looked, and behold, a *f.* roll, 2.
Rev. 4. 7. the fourth beast was like a *f.* eagle
8. 13. heard an angel *f.* thro' the midst of heaven

FOAL, S.

Gen. 32. 15. Jacob took ten bulls, twenty asses, ten *f.*
49. 11. binding his *f.* to the vine, and his ass's colt
Zech. 9. 9. upon a colt the *f.* of an ass, *Mat.* 21. 5.

FOAM.

Hos. 10. 7. the king of Samaria is cut off as *f.*

FOAMETH.

Mark 9. 18. *f.* and gnasheth with his teeth, *Luke* 9. 39.

FOAMING.

Mark 9. 20. he fell on the ground and wallowed, *f.*
Jude 13. raging waves of sea, *f.* out their own shame

FODDER.

Job 6. 5. or loweth the ox over his *f.*

FOES.

1 *Chron.* 21. 12. or to be destroyed before thy *f.*
Esth. 9. 16. the Jews slew of their *f.* 75,000
Psal. 27. 2. mine enemies and *f.* came upon me
30. 1. thou hast not made my *f.* to rejoice over me
89. 23. I will beat down his *f.* before his face
Mat. 10. 36. a man's *f.* shall be they of his household
Acts 2. 35. until I make thy *f.* thy footstool

FOLD.

Heb. 1. 12. as a vesture shalt thou *f.* them up

FOLD.

Isa. 13. 20. shall the shepherds make their *f.* there
65. 10. Sharon shall be *f.* for flocks, valley of Achor
Ezek. 34. 14. on the mountains shall their *f.* be
Mic. 2. 12. as the flock in the midst of their *f.*
Hab. 3. 17. the flock shall be cut off from the *f.*
Mat. 13. 8. brought forth fruit, some an hundred, some sixty, some thirty *f.* 23. *Mark* 4. 8, 20.
19. 29. hath forsaken houses, shall receive 100 *f.*
John 10. 16. and other sheep I have, which are not of this *f.* and there shall be one *f.* and one shepherd

FOLDS.

Num. 32. 24. build ye *f.* for your sheep, 36.
Psal. 50. 9. I will take no he-goats out of thy *f.*
Jer. 23. 3. I will bring them again to their *f.*

Zeph. 2. 6. the sea-coast shall be *f.* for flocks

FOLDEN.

Nah. 1. 10. while they be *f.* together as thorns

FOLDETH.

Eccl. 4. 5. the fool *f.* his hands together and eateth

FOLDING.

1 *Kings* 6. 34. the two leaves of one door were *f.*
Prov. 6. 10. a little *f.* of the hands to sleep, 24. 33.

FOLK.

Gen. 33. 15. let me now leave with thee some of the *f.*
Prov. 30. 26. the conies are but a feeble *f.* yet make
Jer. 51. 58. the *f.* shall labour in fire and be weary
Mark 6. 5. he laid his hands upon a few sick *f.*
John 5. 3. in these lay a multitude of impotent *f.*
Acts. 5. 16. a multitude round about, bringing sick *f.*

FOLLOW

Signifies, [1] *To come after one that goeth before, as servants come after their masters,* 1 Sam. 25. 27. Let it be given to the young men that follow my lord. [2] *To imitate, or do as another gives us an example,* Mat. 16. 24. Let him take up his cross, and follow me. 1 *Cor.* 11. 1. Be ye followers of me, even as I am of Christ. [3] *To believe and obey,* John 10. 27. My sheep hear my voice, and they follow me. *And in all passages where men are said to follow strange gods,* it signifies, *to put trust in them, to rely upon them, and yield them service.* 1 Kings 18. 21. If *Baal* be God, then follow him. *Judg.* 2. 12. They forsook the Lord, and followed other gods. [4] *To side, or take part with,* 2 Sam. 2. 10. 2 Kings 11. 16. [5] *To endeavour after, and pursue with great desire and diligence.* Phil. 3. 12. But I follow after, if that I may apprehend that for which I am apprehended of Christ Jesus. [6] *To die with one.* John 13. 36. Thou canst not follow me now, *that is, bear me company in my sufferings, and die with me.* To follow the Lamb, *Rev.* 14. 4. These are they that follow the Lamb: *that keep close to Christ in all his ordinances: are led by his word and Spirit, and depend upon the virtue and merit of his sacrifice alone for pardon and acceptance, and not on saints, or their own merits, as the followers of antichrist do.*

Gen. 24. 8. if the woman will not be willing to *f.* thee
44. 4. Joseph said, up, *f.* after the men
Exod. 11. 8. get thee out, and people that *f.* thee
14. 4. I will harden Pharaoh that he shall *f.* them
17. and the Egyptians shall *f.* them
21. 22. if hurt a woman, and yet no mischief *f.*
23. and if any mischief *f.* then life for life
23. 2. thou shalt not *f.* a multitude to do evil
Deut. 16. 20. what is altogether just shalt thou *f.*
18. 22. if the thing *f.* not, nor come to pass
Judg. 9. 3. their hearts inclined to *f.* Abimelech
1 *Sam.* 25. 27. it be given young men, who *f.* my lord
30. 21. so faint that they could not *f.* David
2 *Sam.* 17. 9. among the people that *f.* Absalom
1 *Kings* 19. 20. let me kiss father, then I will *f.* thee
Psal. 38. 20. because I *f.* the thing that good is
45. 14. the virgins her companions that *f.* her
94. 15. all the upright in heart shall *f.* it
119. 150. they draw nigh that *f.* after mischief
Isa. 5. 11. that they may *f.* strong drink
51. 1. hearken, ye that *f.* after righteousness
Jer. 17. 16. I hastened from being a pastor to *f.* thee
42. 16. the famine shall *f.* close after you
Ezek. 13. 3. the prophets that *f.* their own spirit
Hos. 2. 7. and she shall *f.* after her lovers
6. 3. we shall know, if we *f.* on to know the Lord
Mat. 8. 19. Master, I will *f.* thee, *Luke* 9. 57, 61.
Mark 16. 17. these signs *f.* them that believe
Luke 17. 23. go not after them, nor *f.* them
22. 49. when they about him saw what would *f.*
John 10. 5. and a stranger will they not *f.*
13. 37. Peter said, Lord, why cannot I *f.* thee now?
Acts 3. 24. all the prophets from Samuel, and that *f.*
Rom. 14. 19. let us *f.* things that make for peace
1 *Cor.* 14. 1. *f.* after charity, desire spiritual gifts
Phil. 3. 12. but I *f.* after, if that I may apprehend
1 *Thess.* 5. 15. but ever *f.* that which is good
2 *Thess.* 3. 7. for yoursel. know how ye ought to *f.* us
9. to make ourselves an ensample to you to *f.* us
1 *Tim.* 5. 24. and some men they *f.* after
6. 11. O man of God, *f.* righteousness, 2 *Tim.* 2. 22.
Heb. 12. 14. *f.* peace with all men, and holiness
13. 7. whose faith *f.* considering the end
1 *Pet.* 1. 11. when it testified the glory that should *f.*
2. 21. an example, that ye should *f.* his steps
2 *Pet.* 2. 2. many shall *f.* their pernicious ways
3 *John* 11. *f.* not that which is evil, but what is good
Rev. 14. 4. these are they that *f.* the Lamb
13. blessed are dead in Lord, that they may rest from their labours, and their works do *f.* them

FOLLOW *him.*

1 *Kings* 18. 21. if the Lord be God, *f. him*
Mark 5. 37. and he suffered no man to *f. him*
6. 1. he went out thence, and his disciples *f. him*
Luke 22. 10. *f. him* into the house, *Mark* 14. 13.
John 10. 4. he goeth before, and the sheep *f. him*

FOLLOW *me.*

Gen. 24. 5. the wom. will not be willing to *f. me,* 39.
Judg. 3. 28. Ehud said unto them, *f.* after *me*
8. 5. give bread, I pray, to the people that *f. me*
1 *Kings* 20. 10. for handfuls for the people that *f. me*
2 *Kings* 6. 19. *f. me,* I will bring you to man ye seek
Ps. 23. 6. goodness and mercy shall *f. me* all my life
Mat. 4. 19. Jesus saith, *f. me* and I will make you fishers of men, 8. 22. | 9. 9. *Mark* 2. 14. *Luke* 5. 27.
16. 24. let him deny himself and take up his cross and *f. me, Mark* 8. 34. | 10. 21. *Luke* 9. 23.
19. 21. sell that thou hast, *f. me, Luke* 18. 22.
Luke 9. 59. he said, *f. me, John* 1. 43. | 21. 22.
John 10. 27. my sheep hear my voice and *f. me*
12. 26. if any man will serve me, let him *f. me*
13. 36. thou canst not *f. me* now, but afterwards
Acts 12. 8. cast thy garment about thee, and *f. me*

FOLLOWED.

Gen. 24. 61. Rebekah and her damsels *f.* the man
32. 19. so commanded he all that *f.* the droves
Num. 32. 12. they have wholly *f.* the L. *Deut.* 1. 36.

Deut. 4. 3. for all the men that *f.* Baal-peor
11. † 6. swallowed the substance which *f.* them
Josh. 6. 8. and the ark of the covenant *f.* them
14. 8. but I wholly *f.* the Lord my God, 9. 14.
Judg. 2. 12. they forsook the Lord and *f.* other gods
9. 49. cut down his bough and *f.* Abimelech
1 *Sam.* 14. 22. they *f.* hard after the Philistines
17. 13. Jesse's three sons *f.* Saul to battle, 14.
31. 2. Philistines *f.* Saul, 2 *Sam.* 1. 6. 1 *Chr.* 10. 2.
2 *Sam.* 2. 10. but the house of Judah *f.* David
3. 31. and king David himself *f.* the bier
17. 23. Ahithophel saw his counsel was not *f.*
20. 2. Israel *f.* Sheba the son of Bichri
1 *Kings* 12. 20. there was none that *f.* house of David
16. 21. half of the people *f.* Tibni, half *f.* Omri, 22.
18. 18. have forsaken the Lord, thou hast *f.* Baalim
20. 19. came out, and the army which *f.* them
2 *Kings* 3. 9. was no water for the cattle that *f.* them
4. 30. Elisha arose and *f.* her
5. 21. so Gehazi *f.* after Naaman, is all well?
9. 27. Jehu *f.* after Ahaziah, and said, smite him
13. 2. Jehoahaz *f.* sins of Jeroboam son of Nebat
17. 15. and they *f.* vanity, and became vain
Psal. 68. 25. the players on instruments *f.* after
Ezek. 10. 11. whither the head looked, they *f.* it
Amos 7. 15. the Lord took me as I *f.* the flock
Mat. 27. 55. many women which *f.* Jes. from Galilee
Mark 10. 28. we left all and *f.* thee, *Luke* 18. 28.
32. were amazed, and as they *f.* they were afraid
Luke 22. 54. they took him, and Peter *f.* afar off
Acts 13. 43. religious proselytes *f.* Paul and Barnab.
16. 17. the same *f.* Paul and us, and cried
Rom. 9. 30. Gentiles who *f.* not after righteousness
31. who *f.* after the law of righteousness
1 *Cor.* 10. 4. they drank of that rock that *f.* them
1 *Tim.* 5. 10. if she have diligently *f.* every good work
2 *Pet.* 1. 16. we have not *f.* cunningly devised fables
Rev. 6. 8. his name was Death, and hell *f.* with him
8. 7. there *f.* hail and fire mingled with blood
14. 8. and there *f.* another angel, saying, Babylon is
9. and the third angel *f.* them, saying, if any man

FOLLOWED *him.*

Num. 16. 25. Moses rose up, the elders of Isr. *f. him*
Judg. 9. 4. hired vain and light persons who *f. him*
1 *Sam.* 13. 7. and all the people *f. him* trembling
2 *Sam.* 11. 8. there *f. him* a mess of meat from the k.
Mat. 4. 20. they left their nets and *f. him, Mark* 1. 18.
22. they immediately left the ship and *f. him*
25. and there *f. him* great multitudes of people, 8. 1. | 12. 15. | 19. 2. | 20. 29. *Mark* 2. 15. | 5. 24. *Luke* 23. 27. *John* 6. 2.
8. 23. when entered, his disciples *f. him, Luke* 22. 39.
9. 27. two blind men *f. him,* crying, and saying
26. 58. but Peter *f.* him afar off, *Mark* 14. 54.
Mark 14. 51. there *f. him* a certain young man
Luke 5. 11. they forsook all and *f. him,* 28.
7. 9. Jesus said to the people that *f. him,* not found
Acts 12. 9. Peter went out and *f. him* and wist not
Rev. 19. 14. the armies *f. him* on white horses

FOLLOWED *me.*

Num. 14. 24. my servant Caleb hath *f. me* fully
32. 11. because they have not wholly *f. me*
1 *Kings* 14. 8. David who *f. me* with all his heart
Neh. 4. 23. nor the men of the guard which *f. me*
Mat. 19. 28. ye that *f. me* in the regeneration

FOLLOWEDST.

Ruth 3. 10. thou *f.* not young men, poor or rich

FOLLOWER.

2 *Tim.* 3. † 10. hast been a diligent *f.* of my doctrine

FOLLOWERS.

1 *Cor.* 4. 16. have begotten you through the gospel I beseech you, be *f.* of me, 11. 1. *Phil.* 3. 17.
Eph. 5. 1. be ye *f.* of God as dear children
1 *Thess.* 1. 6. ye became *f.* of us and of the Lord
2. 14. for ye became *f.* of the churches of God
Heb. 6. 12. be *f.* of them who thro' faith inherit prom.
1 *Pet.* 3. 13. if ye be *f.* of that which is good

FOLLOWETH.

2 *Kings* 11. 15. him that *f.* her be killed, 2 *Chr.* 23. 14.
Ps. 63. 8. my soul *f.* hard after thee, hand upholds
Prov. 12. 11. but he that *f.* vain persons, 28. 19.
15. 9. he loveth him that *f.* righteousness, 21. 21.
Isa. 1. 23. every one loveth gifts and *f.* after rewards
Ezek. 16. 34. none *f.* thee to commit whoredoms
Hos. 12. 1. Ephraim feeds on wind, *f.* after east wind
Mat. 10. 38. he that taketh not up his cross and *f.* me
Mark 9. 38. because he *f.* not us, *Luke* 9. 49.
John 8. 12. he that *f.* me shall not walk in darkness

FOLLOWING.

Gen. 41. 31. plenty not known by reason of famine *f.*
Deut. 7. 4. they will turn away thy son from *f.* me
12. 30. take heed thou be not snared by *f.* them
Josh. 22. 16. from *f.* the Lord, 18. 23, 29. 1 *Sam.* 12. 20. 2 *Kings* 17. 21. 2 *Chr.* 25. 27. | 34. 33.
Judg. 2. 19. corrupted in *f.* other gods to serve them
Ruth 1. 16. or to return from *f.* after thee
1 *Sam.* 12. 14. if ye continue *f.* the Lord your God
14. 46. Saul went up from *f.* the Philistines
15. 11. Saul is turned back from *f.* me
24. 1. when Saul was returned from *f.* Philistines
2 *Sam.* 2. 19. Asahel turned not from *f.* Abner, 30.
26. bid the people return from *f.* their brethren
7. 8. I took thee from *f.* the sheep, to be ruler over my people, 1 *Chron.* 17. 7. *Psal.* 78. 71.
1 *Kings* 1. 7. and they *f.* Adonijah, helped him
9. 6. but if you shall at all turn from *f.* me
21. 26. Ahab did very abominably in *f.* idols
Psal. 48. 13. that ye may tell it to the generation *f.*
109. 13. in generat. *f.* let their name be blotted out
Mark 16. 20. and confirming the word with signs *f.*
Luke 13. 33. I must walk to-morrow, and the day *f.*
John 1. 38. then Jesus turned and saw them *f.*
43. the day *f.* || 6. 22. the day *f.* when the people saw
21. 20. Peter seeth the disciple whom Jesus loved *f.*
Acts 21. 1. we came the day *f.* unto Rhodes, 18.
23. 11. and the night *f.* the Lord stood by him
2 *Pet.* 2. 15. are gone astray, *f.* the way of Balaam

FOLLY.

Gen. 34. 7. because Shechem had wrought *f.* in Isr.
Deut. 22. 21. she wrought *f.* by playing the whore
Josh. 7. 15. because Achan wrought *f.* in Israel
Judg. 19. 23. nay, I pray you, do not this *f.*

Judg. 19. † 24. to this man do not the matter of this *f.*
20. 6. they have committed lewdness and *f.* in Isr.
10. according to the *f.* that they wrought in Isr.
1 *Sam.* 25. 25. Nabal is his name, and *f.* is with him
2 *Sam.* 13. 12. my brother, do not thou this *f.*
Job 1. † 22. in all this Job attributed not *f.* to God
4. 18. behold, his angels he charged with *f.*
24. 12. yet God layeth not *f.* to them
42. 8. lest I deal with you after your *f.*
Psal. 49. 13. this their way is their *f.* yet posterity
85. 8. but let them not turn again to *f.*
Prov. 5. 23. in the greatness of his *f.* he shall go astray
13. 16. but a fool layeth open his *f.*
14. 8. but the *f.* of fools is deceitful
18. the simple inherit *f.* but prudent are crowned
24. crown of wise is riches, foolishness of fools is *f.*
29. but he that is hasty of spirit exalteth *f.*
15. 21. *f.* is joy to him that is destitute of wisdom
16. 22. but the instruction of fools is *f.*
17. 12. let a bear meet a man rather than a fool in his *f.*
18. 13. before he heareth it, it is *f.* and shame to him
26. 4. answer not a fool accord. to his *f.* lest like him
5. ans. a fool accord. to his *f.* lest wise in conceit
11. as dog to vomit, so a fool returneth to his *f.*
Eccl. 1. 17. I gave my heart to know wisdom and *f.*
2. 3. I sought in my heart to lay hold on *f.*
12. turned to behold *f.* || 13. wisdom excelleth *f.*
7. 25. I applied to know the wickedness of *f.*
10. 1. so doth a little *f.* him that is in reputation
6. *f.* is set in great dignity, rich sit in low place
Isa. 9. 17. an evil doer, and every mouth speaketh *f.*
Jer. 23. 13. I have seen *f.* in the prophets of Samar.
Hos. 2. † 10. I will discov. her *f.* in sight of her lovers
2 *Cor.* 11. 1. ye could bear with me a little in my *f.*
2 *Tim.* 3. 9. their *f.* shall be made manifest to all men

FOOD.

Gen. 2. 9. every tree pleasant and that is good for *f.*
3. 6. the woman saw the tree was good for *f.*
6. 21. take thou to thee of all *f.* that is eaten
41. 35. let them gather all *f.* of those good years
42. 7. come to buy *f.* 10. | 43. 2, 4, 20, 22. | 44. 25.
33. take *f.* for the famine of your households
44. 1. he commanded to fill the sacks with *f.*
47. 24. for your *f.* and for *f.* for your little ones
Exod. 21. 10. her *f.* shall not be diminished
Lev. 3. 11. the *f.* of the offering made by fire, 16.
19. 23. shall have planted all manner of trees for *f.*
21. † 17. not approach to offer the *f.* of his God
22. 7. shall eat of holy things, because it is his *f.*
Deut. 10. 18. the stranger, in giving him *f.* and raim.
1 *Sam.* 14. 24. cursed that eateth *f.* till evening, 28.
2 *Sam.* 9. 10. that thy master's son may have *f.* to eat
1 *Kings* 5. 9. my desire, in giving *f.* for my househ.
11. Solom. gave Hiram wheat for *f.* to his househ.
Neh. 9. † 25. they possessed trees of *f.* in abundance
Job 23. 12. thy words more than my necessary *f.*
24. 5. wilderness yieldeth *f.* for them and children
38. 41. who provideth for the raven his *f.*?
40. 20. surely the mountains bring him forth *f.*
Psal. 78. 25. man did eat angels' *f.* he sent them meat
104. 14. he may bring forth *f.* out of the earth
136. 25. who giveth *f.* to all flesh, his mercy for ever
146. 7. the Lord who giveth *f.* to the hungry
147. 9. he giveth to the beast his *f.* to young ravens
Prov. 6. 8. the ant gathereth her *f.* in harvest
13. 23. much *f.* is in the tillage of the poor
27. 27. thou shalt have goats' milk enough for thy *f.*
28. 3. is like a sweeping rain which leaveth no *f.*
30. 8. feed me with *f.* convenient for me
31. 14. like ships, she bringeth her *f.* from afar
Ezek. 16. 27. I have diminished thine ordinary *f.*
48. 18. the increase thereof shall be for *f.* to them
Acts 14. 17. fruitful seasons, filling our hearts with *f.*
2 *Cor.* 9. 10. both minister bread for your *f.*
1 *Tim.* 6. 8. having *f.* and raiment, let us be content
Jam. 2. 15. if naked and destitute of daily *f.*

FOOL,

Folly, **Foolishness**, *are to be understood not only according to their natural and literal meaning, for one who is an idiot, or a very weak man, and for the discourses and notions of fools and madmen; but in the language of Scripture, especially in the book of* Proverbs, fool *is the usual character of* the sinner, *and* folly and foolishness *are put for* sin. *Psal.* 38. 5. My wounds stink, and are corrupt, because of my foolishness, *my sin. And* in Psal. 69. 5. O God, thou knowest my foolishness. Solomon *sets the* fool *in opposition to the* prudent man. *Prov.* 13. 16. Every prudent man dealeth with knowledge; but a fool layeth open his folly. *For as by* prudence *a man so governs himself, and regulates his actions, as to avoid impending evils, and to obtain that good which is suitable to his necessities: so it is the effect of* folly, *not to foresee evils to prevent them, and to neglect the season of obtaining what is good.*

In Prov. 13. 20. Solomon *opposes the* fool *to the* wise man. He that walketh with wise men, shall be wise; but a companion of fools shall be destroyed. *As it is with relation to the affairs of this life; the man of prudence and conduct in his affairs, who takes the best method of managing things to his own, his family's, and friend's, or any society's reputation, comfort, and advantage, and who minds his business more than his pleasure, is* the wise man; *and the inconsiderate, heedless, slothful man, who neglects the principal affairs of life, or goes into improper or unlikely methods of managing them to advantage, or who minds his pleasure more than his business, is* the fool *for this world; so it is with respect to another world: the truly* wise man *is he who proposes the things of God, and the everlasting interest of his immortal soul, as his highest end, and pursues them with the utmost care and diligence, in the way of God's appointment through* Jesus Christ *our only Saviour; and who seeks all things else with less solicitude and concern, and in subordination to these. And the* fool, *on the other hand, is he, who makes something in this world his highest end and aim, and spends his chief time and care, concern and labour, about it, to the neglect of the infinitely higher interests of God's glory and his own soul's everlasting happiness. So that the highest* folly *is justly charged upon every wilful impenitent sinner.*

Such also are called by the name of fools, *who, though they be godly, yet have much ignorance and unbelief remaining in them.* O fools, and slow of heart to believe, *says our Saviour to the disciples that were going to* Emmaus, *Luke* 24. 25. *And it is the character of all men, as they are born possessed of natural ignorance and corruption.* Tit. 3. 3. We ourselves were sometimes foolish. *The Apostle says,* 1 Cor. 4. 10. We are fools for Christ's sake: *that is, we are accounted so by the wise men of the world. And in* Rom. 1. 22. *he says,* Professing themselves to be wise, they became fools: *that is, While they pretended to, and boasted of, more than ordinary wisdom, their learned men being at first usually called* sophists, *or wise men, though afterwards* philosophers, *they entertained and vented many gross and absurd opinions and practices, and so shewed themselves to be real* fools. *The same apostle says, in* 1 Cor. 1. 18. The preaching of the cross is to them that perish foolishness. *The doctrine of* Christ *crucified, to purchase eternal salvation for believers, is by unbelievers, that judge only according to carnal reason and sense, accounted an absurd, ridiculous, impossible thing, and which none in their wits will believe, according to the principles of their philosophy. And in* 1 Cor. 2. 14. The things of God are foolishness to the natural man. *He counts them the most foolish things in the world; he looks upon them as either trifling and impertinent; or as containing means and ends disproportionate; or as undesirable in comparison of what may be set up in competition with them.*

1 *Sam.* 26. 21. behold I have played the *f.* and erred
Psal. 14. 1. the *f.* hath said in his heart, 53. 1.
49. 10. likewise the *f.* and brutish person perish
92. 6. neither doth a *f.* understand this
Prov. 10. 8. but a prating *f.* shall fall, 10.
23. it is a sport to a *f.* to do mischief
11. 29. the *f.* shall be servant to the wise of heart
12. 15. the way of a *f.* is right in his own eyes
16. a *f.* wrath is presently known, but prudent man
13. 16. wise man feareth, but *f.* layeth open his folly
14. 16. but the *f.* rageth and is confident
15. 5. a *f.* despiseth his father's instruction
17. 7. excellent speech becometh not a *f.*
10. a reproof more than a hundred stripes into a *f.*
12. let a bear meet a man rather than *f.* in his folly
16. why is a price in hand of a *f.* to get wisdom?
21. he that begetteth a *f.* doth it to his sorrow
28. a *f.* when he holdeth his peace is counted wise
18. 2. a *f.* hath no delight in understanding
6. *f.* lips enter into content. mouth calls for strokes
7. a *f.* mouth is his destruction, lips a snare
20. 3. but every *f.* will be meddling
26. 4. answer not a *f.* || 5. answer a *f.*
8. so is he that giveth honour to a *f.*
10. the great G. rewardeth the *f.* and transgressors
11. as a dog so a *f.* returneth to his folly
27. 3. but a *f.* wrath is heavier than them both
22. though thou shouldest bray a *f.* in a mortar
29. 11. a *f.* uttereth all his mind, but a wise man keeps
Eccl. 2. 14. but the *f.* walketh in darkness
15. as it happeneth to the *f.* so even to me
16. is no remembrance of wise man more than of *f.*
19. who knoweth whether he be wise or a *f.*?
4. 5. the *f.* foldeth his hands together, eats his flesh
5. 3. a *f.* voice is known by multitude of words
6. 8. for what hath the wise more than the *f.*?
10. 2. at right hand, but a *f.* heart is at his left hand
14. *f.* is full of words, man cannot tell what to be
Jer. 17. 11. and at his end he shall be a *f.*
Mat. 5. 22. whosoever shall say, thou *f.* be in danger
Luke 12. 20. *f.* this night thy soul shall be required
1 *Cor.* 3. 18. let him become a *f.* that he may be wise
15. 36. thou *f.* that thou sowest is not quickened
2 *Cor.* 11. 16. I say again, let no man think me a *f.*
12. 6. tho' I would desire to glory, shall not be a *f.*
11. I am become a *f.* in glorying, ye compelled me

As a FOOL.

2 *Sam.* 3. 33. David said, died Abner *as a f.* dieth?
Prov. 7. 22. *as a f.* to the correction of the stocks
Eccl. 2. 16. how dieth the wise man? *as the f.*
2 *Cor.* 11. 16. if otherwise, yet *as a f.* receive me
23. are they ministers? I speak *as a f.* I am more

For a FOOL.

Prov. 19. 10. delight is not seemly *for a f.*
24. 7. wisdom is too high *for a f.* opens not mouth
26. 1. so honour is not seemly *for a f.*
3. a bridle for the ass, and a rod *for the f.* back
30. 22. *for a f.* when he is filled with meat

Is a FOOL.

Prov. 10. 18. he that uttereth a slander *is a f.*
19. 1. than he that is perverse in his lips, and *is a f.*
28. 26. he that trusteth in his own heart *is a f.*
Eccl. 10. 3. when he that *is a f.* walketh, his wisdom faileth him, he saith to every one that he *is a f.*
Hos. 9. 7. the prophet *is a f.* the spiritual man is mad
1 *Tim.* 6. † 4. he *is a f.* and knoweth nothing

Of a FOOL.

Prov. 12. 15. the way *of a f.* is right in his own eyes
17. 21. and the father *of a f.* hath no joy
24. the eyes *of a f.* are in the ends of the earth
23. 9. speak not in the ears *of a f.* he will despise
26. 6. he that sendeth a message by the hand *of a f.*
12. there is more hope *of a f.* than of him, 29. 20.
Eccl. 7. 6. as crackling of thorns, so laughter *of the f.*
10. 12. but the lips *of a f.* will swallow up himself

FOOLS.

2 *Sam.* 13. 13. thou shalt be as one of the *f.* in Israel
Job 12. 17. and he maketh the judges *f.*
30. 8. they were children of *f.* children of base men
Psal. 75. 4. I said to the *f.* deal not foolishly
94. 8. and ye *f.* when will ye be wise?
107. 17. *f.* because of their transgress. are afflicted
Prov. 1. 7. but *f.* despise wisdom and instruction
Prov. 1. 22. how long, ye *f.* will ye hate knowledge?
32. and the prosperity of *f.* shall destroy them
3. 35. but shame shall be the promotion of *f.*
8. 5. and ye *f.* be ye of an understanding heart
10. 21. but *f.* die for want of wisdom
12. 23. but the heart of *f.* proclaimeth foolishness
13. 19. but it is abomination to *f.* to depart from evil
20. but a companion of *f.* shall be destroyed
14. 8. folly of *f.* is deceit || 9. *f.* make a mock at sin
24. crown of wise is riches, foolishness of *f.* is folly
33. what is in the midst of *f.* is made known
15. 2. the mouth of *f.* poureth out foolishness
14. the mouth of *f.* feedeth on foolishness
16. 22. but the instruction of *f.* is folly
19. 29. stripes are prepared for the back of *f.*
26. 7. so is a parable in the mouth of *f.* 9.
Eccl. 5. 1. more ready to hear, than give sacrifice of *f.*
4. he hath no pleasure in *f.* pay what hast vowed
7. 4. but the heart of *f.* is in the house of mirth
5. than for a man to hear the song of *f.*
9. be not hasty, for anger resteth in the bosom of *f.*
9. 17. more than cry of him that ruleth among *f.*
Isa. 19. 11. surely the princes of Zoan are *f.* 13.
35. 8. way-faring men, tho' *f.* shall not err therein
Mat. 23. 17. ye *f.* and blind, whether is greater, 19.
Luke 11. 40. ye *f.* did not he that made that without
24. 25. O *f.* and slow of heart to believe the prophets
Rom. 1. 22. professing to be wise, they became *f.*
1 *Cor.* 4. 10. we are *f.* for Christ's sake, ye wise in C.
2 *Cor.* 11. 19. for ye suffer *f.* gladly, seeing ye are wise
Eph. 5. 15. see then that ye walk not as *f.* but as wise

FOOLISH.

Deut. 32. 6. do ye thus requite the L. O *f.* people?
21. will provoke them with a *f.* nation, *Rom.* 10. 19.
Job 2. 10. thou speakest as one of *f.* women speaketh
5. 2. for wrath killeth the *f.* man, envy slays
3. I have seen the *f.* taking root, but I cursed
Psal. 5. 5. the *f.* shall not stand in thy sight
39. 8. make me not the reproach of the *f.*
73. 3. for I was envious at the *f.* when I saw prosp.
22. so *f.* was I and ignorant, I was as a beast
74. 18. the *f.* people have blasphemed thy name
22. remember how the *f.* man reproacheth thee daily
Prov. 9. 6. forsake the *f.* and live, go in way underst.
13. a *f.* woman is clamor. is simple, knows noth.
10. 1. but a *f.* son is the heaviness of his mother
14. but the mouth of the *f.* is near destruction
14. 1. but the *f.* plucketh it down with her hands
3. in the mouth of the *f.* is a rod of pride
7. go from the presence of a *f.* man
15. 7. but the heart of the *f.* doeth not so
20. but a *f.* man despiseth his mother
17. 25. a *f.* son is a grief to his father, and bitter.
19. 13. a *f.* son is the calamity of his father
21. 20. a *f.* man spendeth a treasure
29. 9. if a wise man contendeth with a *f.* man
Eccl. 4. 13. better is a wise child than a *f.* king
7. 17. be not overmuch wicked, neither be thou *f.*
10. 15. labour of the *f.* wearieth every one of them
Isa. 44. 25. he maketh their knowledge *f.*
Jer. 4. 22. for my people are *f.* they are sottish childr.
5. 4. I said, surely these are poor, they are *f.*
21. hear now this, O *f.* people, who see not
10. 8. but they are altogether brutish and *f.*
Lam. 2. 14. thy proph. have seen vain and *f.* things
Ezek. 13. 3. thus saith the Ld. woe to the *f.* prophets
Zech. 11. 15. take the instruments of a *f.* shepherd
Mat. 7. 26. shall be likened unto a *f.* man who built
25. 2. five of the virgins were wise, and five *f.*
Rom. 1. 21. and their *f.* heart was darkened
2. 20. an instructor of the *f.* a teacher of babes
1 *Cor.* 1. 20. hath not G. made *f.* wisd. of this world
Gal. 3. 1. O *f.* Galatians, who hath bewitched you?
3. are ye so *f.*? having begun in the spirit
Eph. 5. 4. neither filthiness, nor *f.* talking
1 *Tim.* 6. 9. they that will be rich fall into *f.* lusts
2 *Tim.* 2. 23. but *f.* questions avoid, *Tit.* 3. 9.
Tit. 3. 3. we ourselves were sometimes *f.* deceived
1 *Pet.* 2. 15. may put to silence the ignor. of *f.* men

FOOLISHLY.

Gen. 31. 28. thou hast now done *f.* in so doing, in my power to hurt you, 1 *Sam.* 13. 13. 2 *Chr.* 16. 9.
Num. 12. 11. the sin on us wherein we have done *f.*
2 *Sam.* 24. 10. I have done very *f.* 1 *Chron.* 21. 8.
Job 1. 22. in all this Job sinned not, nor charged G. *f.*
Psal. 75. 4. I said to the fools, deal not *f.*
Prov. 14. 17. he that is soon angry dealeth *f.*
30. 32. if thou hast done *f.* in lifting thyself
2 *Cor.* 11. 17. I speak it as it were *f.* in this boasting
21. I speak *f.* I am bold also, are they Hebrews?

FOOLISHNESS.

2 *Sam.* 15. 31. turn the counsel of Ahithophel into *f.*
Psal. 38. 5. my wounds stink because of my *f.*
69. 5. O God, thou knowest my *f.* sins are not hid
Prov. 12. 23. but the heart of fools proclaimeth *f.*
14. 24. but the *f.* of fools is folly
15. 2. but the mouth of fools poureth out *f.*
14. but the mouth of fools feedeth on *f.*
19. 3. the *f.* of man perverteth his way
22. 15. *f.* is bound in the heart of a child
24. 9. the thought of *f.* is sin, the scorner abominat.
27. 22. yet will not his *f.* depart from him
Eccl. 7. 25. to know the wicked. of *f.* and madness
10. 13. the beginning of the words of his mouth is *f.*
Mark 7. 22. thefts, pride, *f.* come from within
1 *Cor.* 1. 18. preaching of cross to them that perish *f.*
21. it pleased God by the *f.* of preaching to save
23. we preach Christ crucified, to the Greeks *f.*
25. because the *f.* of God is wiser than men
2. 14. the things of the Spirit of God are *f.* to him
3. 19. the wisdom of this world is *f.* with God

FOOT

Is a part of the body well known. In old times it was customary to wash the feet of strangers upon their coming off a journey, Gen. 18. 4. | 19. 2. | 24. 32. *because generally they were barefoot, or wore sandals only, which did not secure them from the dust or dirt.* St. Paul *enjoins inquiry to be made, whether the widows who were to be taken into the number of those who were to be maintained by the church,* had washed the feet of the saints; *whether they had been ready to do the meanest offices to the servants of God*, 1 Tim. 5. 10. Christ Jesus, *to give us an example of humility, washed the feet of his apostles; and thereby taught them to perform all the most humble services for one another*, John 13. 5.

Feet, *in the style of the sacred writers, often mean inclinations, affections, propensities, actions, motions*. Eccl. 5. 1. Keep thy foot when thou goest to the house of God. *Psal.* 36. 11. Let not the foot of pride come against me. *And in* Psal. 119. 59. I turned my feet unto thy testimonies. *Also in* Eph. 6. 15. And your feet shod with the preparation of the gospel of peace. To be at any one's feet, *is used for obeying, being in his service, following him*. Abigail *tells* David, *that the presents which she brought him, were* for the young men that walked at his feet; *for the soldiers who followed him*, 1 Sam. 25. † 27. Moses *says*, Deut. 33. 3. *that* the Lord loved his people, and they sat down at his feet: *like scholars, they heard him, they belonged to him, they were taught and instructed in his doctrine*. *St.* Paul *says, that he was brought up at the feet of* Gamaliel, *Acts* 22. 3. *And Mary* sat at our *Saviour's* feet, and heard his word, *Luke* 10. 39.

In Deut. 11. 10. *it is said, that the land of* Canaan *is not like the land of* Egypt, where thou sowedst thy seed, and wateredst it with thy foot; *that is, that* Palestine *is a country where the rains are not extremely rare, where the dews are plentiful, where there are many springs, rivulets, and brooks, without reckoning the river* Jordan, *which supply the earth with all the moisture that is necessary to its producing fruit; whereas* Egypt *is a country where there is no river but the* Nile, *where it never rains, and where the lands which are not within reach to be watered by the inundations of this river, continue parched and barren. To supply this want, ditches are dug, and water distributed throughout the several villages; the digging these ditches, and dispersing these waters, create a great deal of labour to the* feet.

But notwithstanding these precautions, there are many places which have no water; and in the course of the year, the places which are nearest to the Nile *require to be watered again in an artificial manner. It is done by the help of some machines, which* Philo *describes thus: It is a wheel which a man turns with the motion of his feet, by ascending successively the several steps which are within it. But as while he is thus continually turning, he cannot keep himself up, he holds a stay in his hands, which is not movable, and this supports him; so that in this work, the hands do the office of the feet, and the feet that of the hands: since the hands which should act, are at rest; and the feet which should be at rest, are in action, and give motion to the wheel. This is what is meant by* watering the earth with their feet.

It is said, in Jer. 2. 25. Withhold thy foot from being unshod, and thy throat from thirst. *Do not continue to prostitute yourselves, as you have hitherto done, to strange people. He speaks to the infidel and idolatrous* Jews. *So likewise* Ezek. 16. 25. Thou hast opened thy feet to every one that passed by. *It is a modest expression, for exposing one's nakedness, or going into the bed of lust.* Jacob *said to* Laban, *Gen.* 30. † 30. The Lord hath blessed thee at my foot; *that is, ever since I came to you; since my feet entered into thy house: or,* by my foot; *that is, by my ministry and labour, as the phrase is used,* Deut. 11. 10.

To be under any one's feet, to be a footstool to him, *is a figurative way of speaking, to signify the subjection of a subject to his sovereign, of a servant to his master,* Psal. 8. 6. | 18. 38. | 110. 1. Thou hast put all things under his feet. Mine enemies are fallen under my feet. Sit thou at my right hand, until I make thine enemies thy footstool. To lick the dust off one's feet, *Isa.* 49. 23. They shall bow down to thee with their face toward the earth, and lick up the dust of thy feet. *They shall highly reverence and honour thee, and shall most humbly and readily submit themselves unto thee. The expressions are borrowed from the practice of the eastern people in their prostrations and adorations, when they bowed so low as to touch and kiss the ground, whereby they did or might seem to lick up the very dust of the ground, which was about or under the feet of those whom they adored.*

Nakedness of feet *was a sign of mourning*: Forbear to cry, *says God to* Ezekiel, make no mourning for the dead, and put on thy shoes upon thy feet, *Ezek.* 24. 17. *It was also a mark of respect, reverence, and adoration,* Exod. 3. 5. Put off thy shoes from off thy feet, for the place where thou standest is holy ground. To wash one's foot with oil, or with butter, *signifies plenty of all sorts of good things,* Deut. 33. 24. Job 29. 6. To wash one's feet in the blood of sinners; *to take remarkable vengeance on them, to shed rivers of their blood,* Psal. 58. 10.

A wicked man speaketh with his feet, *says* Solomon, *Prov.* 6. 13. *He uses much gesture with his hands and feet while he is talking; he secretly signifies to his companions his intentions or desires of some evil towards another person, which he is afraid or ashamed to express openly. The ancient sages blamed those who used too much gesticulation, and spoke with all their members.* Ezekiel *reproaches the* Ammonites *with clapping their hands, and stamping with their feet in token of joy, upon seeing the desolation of* Jerusalem *and the temple,* Ezek. 25. 6. *And in* chap. 6. 11. *he makes the same motions the signs of grief, because of the ruin of his people.*

The prophet Isaiah *says,* Blessed are ye that sow beside all waters, that send forth thither the feet of the ox and the ass, *Isa.* 32. 20. *Happy are the people that sow their corn upon a well-watered soil, who with their oxen and asses plough a fat and fruitful land; or who feed there their oxen and their asses.* To send out their feet, *that is, to send them there, to feed them, to plough there with them. But this passage may be understood mystically, and seems to respect the times of the gospel: that is, Happy are the apostles and gospel-ministers, in comparison of those that lived before them, who shall find abundant success of their labours in the conversion of multitudes unto* Christ. *The same prophet says,* chap. 58. 13. If thou turn away thy foot from the sabbath, from doing thy pleasure on my holy day. *This is taken, either properly, if thou forbear walking, or taking any unnecessary journeys on the sabbath-day: or, metaphorically, that is, if thou keep thy mind and affections clear, and restrain thyself from whatever may profane it; feet being often put for affections, because the mind is moved by the affections, as the body is by the* feet.

Job *says, that* he was feet to the lame, and eyes to the blind, *Job* 29. 15. *He led, he directed, and instructed the one, and supported the other. And in* chap. 13. 27. *he says, that* God had put his feet in the stocks, and looked narrowly unto all his paths: *that he had encompassed him with his judgments, so that he had no way, or possibility to escape; he was like a bird taken by the foot in a snare.*

Gen. 41. 44. without thee no man shall lift up his *f.*
Exod. 12. 37. about six hundred thousand on *f.*
21. 24. thou shalt give *f.* for *f.* *Deut.* 19. 21.
30. 18. shalt make a laver of brass and his *f.* 28. | 31. 9. | 35. 16. | 38. 8. | 39. 39. | 40. 11. *Lev.* 8. 11.
Lev. 13. 12. if a leprosy cover from head to *f.*
Num. 22. 25. the ass crushed Balaam's *f.* agst. wall
Deut. 8. 4. nor did thy *f.* swell these forty years
11. 10. and wateredst it with thy *f.* as a garden
25. 9. she shall loose his shoe from off his *f.*
29. 5. thy shoe is not waxen old upon thy *f.*
32. 35. to me vengean. their *f.* shall slide in due time
33. 24. Moses said, let Asher dip his *f.* in oil
Josh. 1. 3. every place your *f.* shall tread upon
5. 15. loose thy shoe from off thy *f.* Joshua did so
Judg. 5. 15. Barak was sent on *f.* to the valley
1 *Sam.* 23. † 22. and see where his *f.* shall be
2 *Sam.* 2. 18. Asahel was as light of *f.* as a roe
21. 20. had on every *f.* six toes, 1 *Chron.* 20. 6.
2 *Kings* 9. 33. Jehu trod Jezebel under *f.*
2 *Chr.* 33. 8. nor any more removed the *f.* of Israel
Job 23. 11. my *f.* hath held his steps, his way I kept
28. 4. even the waters forgotten of the *f.*
31. 5. or if my *f.* hath hasted to deceit
39. 15. and forgetteth that the *f.* may crush them
Psal. 9. 15. in the net they hid is their *f.* taken
26. 12. my *f.* standeth in an even place
36. 11. let not the *f.* of pride come against me
38. 16. when my *f.* slippeth, magnify themselves
66. 6. they went through the flood on *f.*
68. 23. that thy *f.* may be dipped in blood
91. 12. his angels shall bear thee up, lest thou dash thy *f.* against a stone, *Mat.* 4. 6. *Luke* 4. 11.
94. 18. I said my *f.* slippeth, thy mercy held me up
121. 3. he will not suffer thy *f.* to be moved
Prov. 1. 15. refrain thy *f.* from their path
3. 23. shalt walk safely, and thy *f.* shall not stumble
26. the Lord shall keep thy *f.* from being taken
4. 27. turn not to right or left, remove thy *f.* from
25. 17. withdraw thy *f.* from thy neighbour's house
19. confidence in unfaith. men is like *f.* out of joint
Eccl. 5. 1. keep thy *f.* when goest into house of God
Isa. 14. 25. on my mountains tread him under *f.*
18. 7. a nation meted out and trodden under *f.*
20. 2. and put off thy shoe from off thy *f.*
26. 6. the *f.* shall tread it down, even of the poor
41. 2. who called the righteous man to his *f.*
58. 13. if thou turn away thy *f.* from my sabbath
Jer. 2. 25. withhold thy *f.* from being unshod
12. 10. they have trodden my portion under *f.*
Lam. 1. 15. Ld. hath trodden under *f.* mighty men
Ezek. 6. 11. stamp with thy *f.* and say, alas
16. † 6. when trodden under *f.* I said to thee, live
25. † 6. because thou hast stamped with the *f.*
29. 11. no *f.* of man, no *f.* of beast shall pass thro' it
32. 13. neither shall the *f.* of man trouble them
Dan. 8. 13. to give the host to be trodden under *f.*
Amos 2. 15. that is swift of *f.* shall not deliver himself
Mat. 5. 13. salt unsavoury, trodden under *f.* of men
14. 13. the people followed him on *f.* out of cities
18. 8. if thy *f.* offend thee, cut it off, *Mark* 9. 45.
22. 13. bind him hand and *f.* cast him into darkn.
Mark 6. 33. many ran a *f.* thither out of all cities
John 11. 44. was dead came forth bound hand and *f.*
Acts 7. 5. not so much as to set his *f.* on, yet promised
20. 13. so had appointed, minding himself to go a *f.*
1 *Cor.* 12. 15. if the *f.* say, because I am not the hand
Heb. 10. 29. hath trodden under *f.* the Son of God
Rev. 1. 13. Son of man clothed with a garm. to the *f.*
11. 2. the holy city shall they tread under *f.*

Sole of FOOT.

Gen. 8. 9. the dove found no rest for the *sole of* her *f.*
Deut. 28. 35. L. smite thee with a botch from *sole of f.*
56. not set *sole of* her *f.* on ground for delicateness
65. nor shall the *sole of* thy *f.* have rest [on
Josh. 1. 3. every place the *sole of* your *f.* shall tread
2 *Sam.* 14. 25. none like Absalom, from the *sole of f.*
Job 2. 7. Job smitten with boils from *sole of* the *f.*
Isa. 1. 6. from *sole of f.* to the head no soundness
Ezek. 1. 7. *sole of f.* was like the *sole of* a calf's *f.*

FOOT *breadth.*

Deut. 2. 5. will not give, no not so much as *f.-breadth*

Left FOOT.

Rev. 10. 2. and he set his *left f.* upon the earth

Right FOOT.

Rev. 10. 2. a little book, he set his *right f.* on the sea

See TOE.

FOOTED.

Lev. 11. 3. whatsoever is cloven-*f.* that ye shall eat
7. and the swine though he be cloven-*f.* is unclean
Lev. 21. 19. man that is broken-*f.* shall not approach
Acts 10. 12. all manner of four-*f.* beasts, 11. 6.
Rom. 1. 23. image made like birds and four-*f.* beasts

FOOTMEN.

Num. 11. 21. the people are six hundred thousand *f.*
1 *Sam.* 22. 17. Saul said to the *f.* slay priests of Ld.
Jer. 12. 5. if hast run with *f.* and they wearied thee

FOOTSTEPS.

Psal. 17. 5. hold up my goings that my *f.* slip not
77. 19. thy way is in the sea, thy *f.* are not known
89. 51. they reproached the *f.* of thine anointed
Cant. 1. 8. go thy way forth by the *f.* of the flock

FOOTSTOOL.

1 *Chron.* 28. 2. build an house for the *f.* of our God
2 *Chr.* 9. 18. were six steps to throne with *f.* of gold
Psal. 99. 5. worship at his *f.* for he is holy, 132. 7.
110. 1. sit thou at my right-hand till I make thine enemies thy *f.* *Mat.* 22. 44. *Mark* 12. 36. *Luke* 20. 43. *Acts* 2. 35. *Heb.* 1. 13.
Isa. 66. 1. heaven is my throne, and earth is my *f.* *Acts* 7. 49.
Lam. 2. 1. remembered not his *f.* in day of his anger
Mat. 5. 35. swear not by the earth, it is his *f.*
Heb. 10. 13. expecting till his enemies be made his *f.*
Jam. 2. 3. say to the poor, sit here under my *f.*

FOR.

Deut. 4. 7. so nigh in all things that we call on him *f.*
2 *Sam.* 11. 22. shewed David all Joab had sent him *f.*
Prov. 28. 21. *f.* piece of bread that man will transgress
Mat. 5. 45. *f.* maketh his sun to rise on evil and good
6. 7. they think to be heard *f.* their much speaking
25. 35. *f.* I was hungry, and ye gave me meat, 42.
John 1. 16. out of his fuln. we received grace *f.* grace
Rom. 13. 6. *f.* this cause ye pay tribute also
2 *Cor.* 5. 1. *f.* we know, if this house were dissolved
13. 8. *f.* we can do nothing against but *f.* the truth
2 *Pet.* 3. 12. looking *f.* the coming of the day of God

FORASMUCH.

Gen. 41. 39. *f.* as God hath shewed thee all this
Deut. 12. 12. *f.* as he hath no inheritance with you
Judg. 11. 36. *f.* as the Lord hath taken vengeance
1 *Sam.* 20. 42. *f.* as we have sworn both of us
2 *Sam.* 19. 30. *f.* as my lord is come again in peace
1 *Kings* 13. 21. *f.* as thou hast disobeyed the Lord
1 *Chron.* 5. 1. *f.* as Reuben defiled his father's bed
Isa. 29. 13. *f.* as this peo. draw near with their mouth
Jer. 10. 6. *f.* as there is none like to thee, O Lord
7. *f.* among all wise men of nations none like thee
Dan. 2. 40. *f.* as iron break. and subdu. all things
Luke 19. 9. *f.* as he also is the son of Abraham
Acts 11. 17. *f.* then as God gave them the like gift
17. 29. *f.* then as we are the offspring of God
24. 10. *f.* as I know that thou hast been a judge
1 *Cor.* 11. 7. *f.* as he is the image and glory of Go
14. 12. *f.* as ye are zealous of spiritual gifts
15. 58. *f.* as ye know your labour is not in vain
1 *Pet.* 1. 18. *f.* as ye know ye were not redeemed
4. 1. *f.* then as Christ hath suffered for us

FORBADE.

Deut. 2. 37. nor unto whatsoever the Lord *f.* us
Mat. 3. 14. but John *f.* him, saying, I have need
Mark 9. 38. we saw one casting out devils in thy name, we *f.* him, because he followeth not us, *Luke* 9. 49.
2 *Pet.* 2. 16. the ass *f.* the madness of the prophet

FORBARE.

1 *Sam.* 23. 13. Dav. escaped, and Saul *f.* to go forth
2 *Chron.* 25. 16. then the prophet *f.* and said, I know
Jer. 41. 8. so Ishmael *f.* and slew them not

FORBEARANCE.

Rom. 2. 4. or despisest thou the riches of his *f.*?
3. 25. for the remission of sins, through the *f.* of G.

FORBEAR.

Exod. 23. 5. if see his ass, and would *f.* to help him
Deut. 23. 22. if thou shalt *f.* to vow, it shall be no sin
1 *Sam.* 11. † 3. *f.* us seven days that we may send
1 *Kings* 22. 6. shall I go, or *f.*? 2 *Chron.* 18. 5, 14.
2 *Chron.* 25. 16. *f.* why shouldest thou be smitten?
35. 21. *f.* thee from meddling with God
Neh. 9. 30. yet many years didst thou *f.* them
Job 16. 6. and though I *f.* what am I eased?
Prov. 24. 11. thou *f.* to deliver them drawn to death
Jer. 40. 4. but if it seem ill to thee to come, *f.*
Ezek. 2. 5. whether they will hear or *f.* 7. | 3. 11.
3. 27. and he that forbeareth, let him *f.*
24. 17. *f.* to cry, make no mourning for the dead
Zech. 11. 12. I said, give me my price, if not, *f.*
1 *Cor.* 9. 6. have not we power to *f.* working?
2 *Cor.* 12. 6. *f.* lest any should think of me above what
1 *Thess.* 3. 1. wherefore when we could no longer *f.* 5.

FORBEARETH.

Num. 9. 13. that *f.* keep the passover shall be cut off
Ezek. 3. 27. and he that *f.* let him forbear

FORBEARING.

Prov. 25. 15. by long *f.* is a prince persuaded
Jer. 20. 9. I was weary with *f.* I could not stay
Eph. 4. 2. *f.* one another in love, *Col.* 3. 13.
6. 9. masters, do the same things, *f.* threatening
2 *Tim.* 2. † 24. the servant of the Lord must be *f.*

FORBID.

Num. 11. 28. Joshua said, my lord Moses, *f.* them
1 *Sam.* 24. 6. the Lord *f.* I should do this thing
26. 11. Lord *f.* I should stretch forth mine hand
1 *Kings* 21. 3. Naboth said to Ahab, the Ld. *f.* it me
1 *Chron.* 11. 19. my God *f.* it me, that I should do this
Mark 9. 39. but Jesus said, *f.* him not, *Luke* 9. 50.
10. 14. suffer little childr. *f.* them not, *Luke* 18. 16.
Luke 6. 29. taketh thy cloke, *f.* not to take coat also
Acts 10. 47. Peter answered, can any *f.* water, that these should not be baptized?
24. 23. should *f.* none of his acquaintance to come
1 *Cor.* 14. 39. and *f.* not to speak with tongues

God FORBID.

Gen. 44. 7. *God f.* 17. *Josh* 22. 29. | 24. 16. 1 *Sam.* 12. 23. | 14. 45. | 20. 2. *Job* 27. 5. *Luke* 20. 16. *Rom.* 3. 4, 6, 31. | 6. 2, 15. | 7. 7, 13. | 9. 14. | 11. 1, 11. 1 *Cor.* 6. 15. *Gal.* 2. 17. | 3. 21. | 6. 14.

FORBIDDEN.

Lev. 5. 17. if a soul commit any of these things *f.*
Deut. 4. 23. or the likeness of what the Lord hath *f.*
Acts 16. 6. and were *f.* to preach the word in Asia

FORBIDDETH.
3 John 10. and f. them that would receive brethren
FORBIDDING.
Luke 23. 2. and f. to give tribute to Cæsar, saying
Acts 28. 31. preaching kingd. of G. no man f. him
1 Thess. 2. 16. f. us to speak to the Gentiles
1 Tim. 4. 3. f. to marry, commanding to abstain
FORBORNE. [from
Jer. 51. 30. mighty men of Babylon have f. to fight
FORCE.
Gen. 31. 31. peradventure thou wouldest take by f.
Deut. 34. 7. eye not dim, nor was his natural f. abated
1 Sam. 2. 16. shalt give it, if not, I will take it by f.
Ezra 4. 23. they made them to cease by f. and power
Job 30. 18. by great f. of my disease, garm. changed
40. 16. and his f. is in the navel of his belly
Jer. 18. 21. pour out their blood by f. of the sword
23. 10. their course is evil, and their f. is not right
48. 45. they stood under the shadow, because of the f.
Ezek. 34. 4. with f. and cruelty have ye ruled them
35. 5. thou hast shed blood by the f. of the sword
Amos 2. 14. the strong shall not strengthen his f.
Mat. 11. 12. and the violent take it by f.
John 6. 15. when perceived they would take him by f.
Acts 23. 10. to take Paul by f. from among them
Heb. 9. 17. for a testament is of f. after men are dead
FORCE.
Deut. 22. 25. if the man f. her and lie with her
2 Sam. 13. 12. nay, my brother, do not f. me
Esth. 7. 8. will he f. the queen also before me in house
FORCED.
Judg. 1. 34. the Ammonites f. the children of Dan
20. 5. my concubine have they f. that she is dead
1 Sam. 13. 12. I f. myself therefore, and offered
2 Sam. 13. 14. Amnon f. Tamar and lay with her
22. hated Amnon, because he f. his sister Tamar
32. determined from the day that he f. his sister
Prov. 7. 21. with the flattering of her lips she f. him
FORCES.
2 Chr. 17. 2. Jehoshaphat placed f. in fenced cities
Job 36. 19. he will not esteem all the f. of strength
Isa. 60. 5. the f. of the Gentiles shall come to thee
11. men may bring to thee the f. of Gentiles
Jer. 40. 7. when the captains of the f. that were in the field, 13. | 41. 11, 13, 16. | 42. 1, 8. | 43. 4, 5.
Dan. 11. 10. and shall assemble a mult. of great f.
38. but in his estate shall he honour the God of f.
Obad. 11. that strangers carried away captive his f.
† 13. shouldest not have laid hands on their f.
FORCIBLE.
Job 6. 25. how f. right words, what arguing prove?
FORCING.
Deut. 20. 19. not destroy trees by f. axe against them
Prov. 30. 33. so the f. of wrath bringeth forth strife
FORD, S.
Gen. 32. 22. Jacob passed over the f. Jabbok
Josh. 2. 7. and the men pursued the spies to the f.
Judg. 3. 28. Israel went and took the f. of Jordan
Isa. 16. 2. the daughters of Moab at the f. of Arnon
FORECAST.
Dan. 11. 24. and he shall f. his devices, 25.
FOREFATHERS.
Jer. 11. 10. are turned to the iniquities of their f.
2 Tim. 1. 3. I thank God, whom I serve from my f.
FOREFRONT.
Exod. 26. 9. six curtains in the f. of the tabernacle
28. 37. a blue lace, on the f. of the mitre it shall be
Lev. 8. 9. upon his f. did he put the golden plate
1 Sam. 14. 5. f. of one rock was situate north-ward
2 Sam. 11. 15. set ye Uriah in the f. of the battle
2 Kings 16. 14. he brought the brazen altar from f.
2 Chron. 20. 27. Jehoshaphat in the f. of them
Ezek. 40. 19. from f. of lower gate to f. of inner court
47. 1. the f. of the house stood towards the east
FOREHEAD.
Gen. 24. † 22. the man took a jewel for the f.
Exod. 28. 38. the plate shall be on Aaron's f. always
Lev. 13. 41. he is f.-bald, yet is he clean
42. it is a leprosy sprung up in his bald f.
43. if the rising be reddish in his bald f.
† 55. whether it be in the head or f. thereof
1 Sam. 17. 49. David took a stone, slang it, and smote the Philistine in his f. the stone sunk in his f.
2 Chron. 26. 19. the leprosy rose up in Uzziah's f.
20. and behold he was leprous in his f.
Jer. 3. 3. and thou hadst a whore's f. not ashamed
Ezek. 3. † 7. Israel are stiff of f. and hard of heart
8. have made thy f. strong against their foreheads
9. as an adam. harder than flint have made thy f.
16. 12. I put a jewel upon thy f. and ear-rings in
Rev. 14. 9. and receive the mark of the beast in his f.
17. 5. and upon her f. was a name written, Mystery
FOREHEADS.
Ezek. 3. 8. made thy forehead strong against their f.
9. 4. set a mark on the f. of them that sigh and cry
Rev. 7. 3. have sealed the servants of God in their f.
9. 4. which have not the seal of God in their f.
13. 16. he causeth all to receive a mark in their f.
14. 1. having his Father's name written in their f.
20. 4. nor had received his mark upon their f.
22. 4. and his name shall be in their f.
FOREIGNER.
Exod. 12. 45. f. and hired servant shall not eat
Deut. 15. 3. of a f. thou mayest exact it again
FOREIGNERS.
Obad. 11. in the day that f. entered into his gates
Eph. 2. 19. ye are no more strangers and f.
FOREKNEW.
Rom. 11. 2. G. hath not cast away people which he f.
FOREKNOW.
Rom. 8. 29. whom he did f. he also did predestinate
FOREKNOWLEDGE.
Acts 2. 23. him being delivered by the f. of God
1 Pet. 1. 2. elect according to f. of God the Father
FOREMOST.
Gen. 32. 17. Jacob commanded the f. saying
33. 2. he put the handmaids and their children f.
2 Sam. 18. 27. the running of the f. is like Ahimaaz
FOREORDAINED.
Rom. 3. † 25. God hath f. to be a propitiation
1 Pet. 1. 20. who verily was f. before the world

FOREPART.
Exod. 28. 27. two rings towards f. of ephod, 39. 20.
1 Kings 6. 20. the oracle in the f. was twenty cubits
Ezek. 42. 7. the wall on the f. of the chambers
Acts 27. 41. the f. of ship stuck fast and remained
FORERUNNER.
Heb. 6. 20. whither the f. is for us entered, even Jesus
FORESAW.
Acts 2. 25. I f. the Lord always before my face
FORESEETH.
Prov. 22. 3. a prudent man f. the evil, 27. 12.
FORESEEING.
Gal. 3. 8. the scripture f. God would justify heathen
FORESEEN.
Heb. 11. † 40. God having f. some better thing for us
FORE-SHIP.
Acts 27. 30. they would have cast anchors out of f.
FORESKIN.
Gen. 17. 11. ye shall circumcise the flesh of your f.
14. whose flesh of his f. is not circumcised
23. and circumcised the flesh of their f. 24, 25.
Exod. 4. 25. then Zipporah cut off the f. of her son
Lev. 12. 3. the flesh of his f. shall be circumcised
Deut. 10. 16. circumcise therefore the f. of your heart
Hab. 2. 16. drink then, and let thy f. be uncovered
FORESKINS.
Josh. 5. 3. circumcised Israel at the hill of the f.
1 Sam. 18. 25. but an hundred f. of the Philistines
27. David brought their f. gave them to the king
2 Sam. 3. 14. which I espoused to me for an hund. f.
Jer. 4. 4. take away f. of your heart, ye men of Judah
FOREST.
1 Sam. 22. 5. David came into the f. of Hareth
1 Kings 7. 2. Solomon built the house of the f.
10. 17. put them in the house of the f. 2 Chron. 9. 16.
2 Kings 19. 23. into the f. of his Carmel, Isa. 37. 24.
Neh. 2. 8. a letter to Asaph, keeper of the king's f.
Psal. 50. 10. for every beast of the f. is mine
104. 20. wherein all beasts of the f. do creep forth
Isa. 9. 18. and shall kindle in the thickets of the f.
10. 18. and shall consume the glory of his f.
19. the rest of the trees of his f. shall be few
21. 13. in the f. of Arabia shall ye lodge
22. 8. thou didst look to the armour of the f.
29. 17. the field shall be esteemed as a f. 32. 15.
32. 19. when it shall hail, coming down on the f.
44. 14. taketh cypress from among trees of the f.
23. break forth into singing, ye mountains, O f.
56. 9. all ye beasts of the f. come to devour
Jer. 5. 6. wherefore a lion out of f. shall slay them
10. 3. for one cutteth a tree out of f. with the axe
12. 8. mine heritage is to me as a lion in the f.
21. 14. I will kindle a fire in the f. thereof
26. 18. become as high places of the f. Mic. 3. 12.
46. 23. they shall cut down her f. saith the Lord
Ezek. 15. 6. as the vine-tree among the trees of the f.
20. 46. prophesy against the f. of the south field
47. say unto the f. of the south, hear the word
Hos. 2. 12. I will make them a f. beasts shall eat them
Amos 3. 4. will lion roar in the f. when hath no prey?
Mic. 5. 8. as a lion among the beasts of the f.
Zech. 11. 2. the f. of the vintage is come down
FORESTS.
2 Chron. 27. 4. Jotham built castles in the f.
Psal. 29. 9. the voice of the Lord discovereth the f.
Isa. 10. 34. he shall cut down the thickets of the f.
Ezek. 39. 10. neither cut down any out of the f.
FORETELL.
2 Cor. 13. 2. I f. you as if I were present sec. time
FORETOLD.
Mark 13. 23. take heed, beh. I have f. you all things
Acts 3. 24. the proph. have likewise f. of these days
FOREWARN.
Luke 12. 5. but I will f. you whom ye shall fear
FOREWARNED.
1 Thess. 4. 6. as we also have f. you and testified
FORFEITED.
Ezra 10. 8. all his subst. should be f. he separated
FORGAT.
Gen. 40. 23. butler not remember Joseph, but f. him
Judg. 3. 7. the children of Israel f. the Lord
1 Sam. 12. 9. and when they f. the Lord their God
Psal. 78. 11. and they f. his works and his wonders
106. 13. soon f. his works || 21. f. G. their Saviour
Lam. 3. 17. removed far from peace, I f. prosperity
Hos. 2. 13. she went after her lov. and f. me, saith L.
FORGAVE.
Psal. 78. 38. he f. their iniquity, destroyed them not
Mat. 18. 27. he loosed him, and f. him the debt
32. O wicked servant, I f. thee all that debt
Luke 7. 42. had nothing to pay, he frankly f. them
43. I suppose that he to whom he f. most
2 Cor. 2. 10. for if I f. any thing to whom I f. it for your sakes f. I it in the person of Christ
Col. 3. 13. even as Christ f. you, so also do ye
FORGAVEST.
Ps. 32. 5. I will confess, thou f. the iniquity of my
99. 8. was G. that f. them, tho' tookest vengeance
FORGED.
Psal. 119. 69. the proud have f. a lie against me
FORGERS.
Job 13. 4. ye are f. of lies, are all physicians of no val.
FORGET
Signifies, [1] *To let things slip out of the memory,* Deut. 4. 9. Lest thou forget the things thine eyes have seen. [2] *To let God, his word, and benefits, slip out of mind: whereupon follow disobedience, neglect of God's worship, and wicked contempt of God, as a fruit and consequence of such forgetfulness.* Judg. 3. 7. The children of Israel did evil in the sight of the Lord, and forgat the Lord their God, and served Baalim and the groves. *Thus men forget God; the wicked wholly, the godly in part.* [3] *To cast off one, to cease to love, care, and provide for him,* Psal. 77. 9. Hath God forgotten to be gracious? *Thus God forgets the wicked: and the godly do sometimes think that they are thus forgotten, yet are not so. See also* Isa. 49. 15. Can a woman forget her sucking child? yea, they may forget, yet will I not forget thee. *She may cease to love her child, but I will not cease to love and provide for thee.* [4] *To omit to punish.* Amos 8. 7. Surely I will never forget any of their works; *I will not always defer to punish them, though it may seem I have forgotten.* [5] *Not to esteem, but to pass over a matter as unworthy our remembrance,* Phil. 3. 13. Forgetting those things which are behind: *not so much considering or regarding what I have already done, as what I have yet further to do.*

Joseph *called the name of his first-born,* Manasseh, *that is,* forgetting; *for God, said he,* hath made me forget all my toil, and all my father's house: *he has expelled all sorrowful remembrance of my slavery in* Egypt, *and of my sufferings from my brethren, by my present comfort and glory. In* Psal. 45. 10. *the* Psalmist *speaking to the church says,* Forget also thine own people, and thy father's house: *he alludes to the law of matrimony,* Gen. 2. 24. *Thou must forget and forsake all carnal relations, as far as they hinder from* Christ, *and likewise all those prejudices, false persuasions, corrupt inclinations, and evil practices, which are so natural to, and even part of, thyself,* Mat. 5. 29, 30. *And by these words he seems tacitly to foretell, that even the legal worship appointed by* Moses, *and delivered to them by their parents successively for many generations, should be relinquished by the believing* Jews, *and abolished by* Christ's *coming.*

Gen. 27. 45. till he f. that which thou hast done him
41. 51. for God hath made me f. all my toil
Deut. 4. 9. lest thou f. the things thine eyes have seen
23. lest ye f. the covenant of the Lord your God
31. the L. will not f. the covenant of thy fathers
6. 12. beware lest thou f. the Lord, 8. 11, 14, 19.
9. 7. f. not how thou provokedst the Lord thy God
25. 19. shalt blot out Amalek, thou shalt not f. it
1 Sam. 1. 11. if thou wilt not f. thine handmaid
2 Kings 17. 38. the covenant I made ye shall not f.
Job 8. 13. so are the paths of all that f. God
9. 27. if I say, I will f. my complaint
11. 16. because thou shalt f. thy misery
24. 20. womb shall f. him, worm shall feed on him
Psal. 9. 17. and all the nations that f. God
10. 12. arise, O Lord, f. not the humble
13. 1. how long wilt thou f. me, O Lord?
45. 10. f. also thine own people, and father's house
50. 22. now consider this, ye that f. God
59. 11. slay them not, lest my people f. scatter them
74. 19. f. not the congregation of thy poor for ever
23. f. not the voice of thine enemies
78. 7. that they might not f. the works of God
102. 4. heart smitten, so that I f. to eat my bread
103. 2. bless the Lord, and f. not all his benefits
119. 16. I will not f. thy word
83. yet do I not f. thy statutes, 109, 141.
93. I will never f. thy precepts, hast quickened me
153. deliver me, for I do not f. thy law
176. for I do not f. thy commandments
137. 5. if I f. thee, O Jerusalem, let my hand f.
Prov. 3. 1. my son, f. not my law, but let thy heart
4. 5. get wisdom, get understanding, f. it not
31. 5. lest they drink and f. the law, and pervert
7. let him drink and f. poverty, rememb. no more
Isa. 49. 15. can a woman f. her sucking child? yea, they may f. yet will I not f. thee
54. 4. for thou shalt f. the shame of thy youth
65. 11. ye are they that f. my holy mountain
Jer. 2. 32. can maid f. her ornaments, or bride attire?
23. 27. who think to cause my people to f. my name
39. behold, I, even I, will utterly f. you
Lam. 5. 20. wherefore dost thou f. us for ever?
Hos. 4. 6. forgotten the law, I will also f. thy childr.
Amos 8. 7. I will never f. any of their works
Heb. 6. 10. God is not unrighteous to f. your works
13. 16. to do good and communicate f. not
FORGETFUL.
Heb. 13. 2. be not f. to entertain strangers
Jam. 1. 25. he being not a f. hearer, but a doer
FORGETFULNESS.
Psal. 88. 12. and thy righteousness in the land of f.
FORGETTEST.
Psal. 44. 24. wherefore f. thou our affliction?
Isa. 51. 13. and f. the Lord thy Maker
FORGETTETH.
Job 39. 15. and f. that the foot may crush them
Psal. 9. 12. he f. not the cry of the humble
Prov. 2. 17. and f. the covenant of her God
Jam. 1. 24. he f. what manner of man he was
FORGETTING.
Gen. 41. † 51. Joseph called the first-born, f.
Phil. 3. 13. f. those things which are behind
FORGIVE.
Gen. 50. 17. f. I pray, the trespass of thy brethren, f. the trespass of serv. of God of thy father
Exod. 10. 17. f. I pray thee, my sin only this once
32. 32. yet now, if thou wilt f. their sin
Num. 30. 5. and the Lord shall f. her, 8, 12.
Josh. 24. 19. an holy God, he will not f. your sins
1 Sam. 25. 28. I pray, f. the trespass of thy handmaid
1 Kings 8. 30. when hearest f. 39. 2 Chron. 6. 21, 30
34. hear, and f. the sin of thy people Israel
36. f. the sin of thy servants, 2 Chron. 6. 25, 27, 39
50. f. thy people that have sinned against thee
2 Chron. 7. 14. then will I hear and f. their sin
Psal. 25. 18. look on my pain, and f. all my sins
86. 5. for thou, Lord, art good and ready to f.
Isa. 2. 9. the mean man boweth, therefore f. them
Jer. 18. 23. f. not their iniquity nor blot out their sin
31. 34. for I will f. their iniquity, not remember sin
36. 3. that I may f. their iniquity and their sin
Dan. 9. 19. O Lord hear, O Lord f. Lord hearken
Amos 7. 2. I said, O Lord God, f. I beseech thee
Mat. 6. 12. f. us, as we f. our debtors, Luke 11. 4.
14. if ye f. men their trespasses, your Father will f.
15. if ye f. not, nor will your Father f. your
9. 6. hath power to f. sin, Mark 2. 10. Luke 5. 24.
18. 21. how oft my brother sin, and I f. him?
35. if ye from your hearts f. not every one
Mark 2. 7. who can f. sins, but God only? Luke 5. 21.
11. 25. praying, f. that your Father may f. you

Mark 11. 26. but if ye do not f. Father will not f.
Luke 6. 37. f. and ye shall be forgiven
17. 3. and if thy brother repent, f. him, 4.
23. 34. Father, f. them, they know not what they do
2 Cor. 2. 7. ye ought rather to f. him and comfort him
10. to whom ye f. any thing, I f. also
12. 13. I was not burdensome, f. me this wrong
1 John 1. 9. he is faithful and just to f. us our sins

FORGIVEN.

Gen. 4. † 13. my iniquity is greater than may be f.
Lev. 4. 20. make atonement, and it shall be f. them, 26. 31, 35. | 5. 10, 13, 16, 18. | 6. 7. | 19. 22. Num. 15. 25, 26, 28. Deut. 21. 8.
Num. 14. 19. pardon, as thou hast f. from Egypt
Psa. 32. 1. blessed, whose transgress. is f. Rom. 4. 7.
85. 2. thou hast f. the iniquity of thy people
Isa. 33. 24. the people shall be f. their iniquity
Mat. 9. 2. son, be of good cheer, thy sins be f. thee, 5. Mark 2. 5, 9. Luke 5. 20, 23. | 7. 48.
12. 31. all sin and blasphemy shall be f. but ag. H. Gh. shall not be f. 32. Mark 3. 28. Luke 12. 10.
Mark 4. 12. and their sins should be f. them
Luke 6. 37. forgive, and ye shall be f.
7. 47. her many sins are f. but to whom little is f.
Acts 8. 22. the thought of thy heart may be f. thee
Eph. 4. 32. as God for Christ's sake hath f. you
Col. 2. 13. he quickened, having f. you all trespasses
Jam. 5. 15. if committed sins, they shall be f. him
1 John 2. 12. I write to you, because your sins are f.

FORGIVETH.

Ps. 103. 3. heals thy diseases, who f. all iniquities
Luke 7. 49. they began to say, who is this f. sins also

FORGIVENESS.

Ps. 130. 4. there is f. with thee that mayest be feared
Mark 3. 29. hath never f. but is in danger of hell
Acts 5. 31. him hath God exalted to give f. of sins
13. 38. thro' him is preached unto you f. of sins
26. 18. to God, that they may receive f. of sins
Eph. 1. 7. in whom we have f. of sins, Col. 1. 14.

FORGIVENESSES.

Dan. 9. 9. to Lord our God belong mercies and f.

FORGIVING.

Exod. 34. 7. f. iniquity, transgression, Num. 14. 18.
Eph. 4. 32. forbearing, f. one another, Col. 3. 13.

FORGOT.

Deut. 24. 19. and hast f. a sheaf in the field

FORGOTTEN.

Gen. 41. 30. and all the plenty shall be f.
Deut. 26. 13. not transgressed com. nor have I f. them
31. 21. it shall not be f. out of mouths of their seed
32. 18. thou hast f. God that formed thee
Job 19. 14. my familiar friends have f. me
28. 4. flood breaks out, even waters f. of the foot
Psal. 9. 18. for the needy shall not alway be f.
10. 11. he hath said in his heart, God hath f.
31. 12. I am f. as a dead man out of mind
42. 9. I will say, my rock, why hast thou f. me?
44. 17. all this is come on us, yet have we not f. thee
20. if we have f. name of our God, or stretched out
77. 9. hath G. f. to be gracious? hath he shut mercy
119. 61. but I have not f. thy law
139. because mine enemies have f. thy words
Eccl. 2. 16. in the days to come shall all be f.
8. 10. and the wicked were f. in the city
9. 5. for the memory of them is f.
Isa. 17. 10. thou hast f. the God of thy salvation
23. 15. that Tyre shall be f. seventy years
16. take an harp, thou harlot that hast been f.
44. 21. O Israel, thou shalt not be f. of me
49. 14. but Zion said, my Lord hath f. me
65. 16. because the former troubles are f.
Jer. 2. 32. my people have f. me, 13. 25. | 18. 15.
3. 21. they have f. the Lord their God
20. 11. their confusion shall never be f. 23. 40.
23. 27. to forget, as their fathers have f. my name
30. 14. all thy lovers have f. thee, they seek thee not
44. 9. have ye f. the wickedness of your fathers
50. 5. let us join in a covenant that shall not be f.
6. they turned away, have f. their resting-place
Lam. 2. 6. Lord caused the sabbath to be f. in Zion
Ezek. 22. 12. thou hast f. me, saith the Lord
23. 35. saith the Lord, because thou hast f. me
Hos. 4. 6. seeing thou hast f. the law of thy God
8. 14. for Israel hath f. Maker, and builds temples
13. 6. their heart exalted, therefore have f. me
Mat. 16. 5. they had f. to take bread, Mark 8. 14.
Luke 12. 6. and not one of them is f. before God
Heb. 12. 5. and ye have f. the exhortation that speaks
2 Pet. 1. 9. f. that he was purged from his old sins

FORKS.

1 Sam. 13. 21. yet they had a file for the f. and axes

FORM,

Is taken for the figure, shape, or likeness of a thing, Job 4. 16. It stood still, but I could not discern the form thereof. *Likewise for outward splendour, pomp, and dignity,* Isa. 53. 2. He hath no form nor comeliness; *no such outward splendour as the Jews expected in their Messiah. It is also taken for a draught or pattern,* 2 Tim. 1. 13. Hold fast the form of sound words, which thou hast heard of me. *Make thy discourses conform to the pattern of sound and true doctrine, wherein thou hast been instructed by me. The apostle* Paul, *advertising* Timothy *of what should come to pass in the latter times, says,* 2 Tim. 3. 5. That there should be men who had a form of godliness, but deny the power thereof: *they should have an outward appearance and shew of religion, pretend to a right way of worshipping God; to be the church, the only church of God; and yet not only be destitute of, but reject and refuse the inner part, which is lively, active, and powerful to make a thorough change.*

It is said, Mark 16. 12. *that after his resurrection,* Jesus appeared in another form to two of his disciples: another form *either in regard of his habit, or brightness of his countenance, or some such particular. And the apostle, speaking of* Christ, *says,* Phil. 2. 6. Who being in the form of God, thought it not robbery to be equal with God: *that is, Who being the essential image of the Father, and enjoying the divine essence and nature, with all its glory, knew that it was no usurpation in him, to account himself equal with the Father, and carry himself upon all occasions as such. So by the* form of God *is meant his essence and nature. It follows in verse* 7. But made himself of no reputation, and took upon him the form of a servant, and was made in the likeness of men. *Yet he emptied himself of that divine glory and majesty, by hiding it in the vail of his flesh; and took upon him the quality and condition of a mean person, not of a glorified saint, or of some great mortal; and was subject to all the frailties and infirmities of human nature, sin only excepted.*

Gen. 1. 2. the earth was without f. and void
Judg. 8. † 18. each according to the f. of a king
1 Sam. 28. 14. he said unto her, what f. is he of?
2 Sam. 14. 20. fetch about this f. of speech Joab done
Esth. 2. † 7. and the maid was fair of f.
Job 4. 16. but I could not discern the f. thereof
Isa. 52. 14. and his f. more than the sons of men
53. 2. he hath no f. nor comeliness
Jer. 4. 23. and, lo, it was without f. and void
Ezek. 10. 8. there appeared the f. of a man's hand
43. 11. shew them the f. of the house and fashion
Dan. 3. 19. and the f. of his visage was changed
25. the f. of the fourth is like the Son of God
Mark 16. 12. appeared in another f. to two of them
Rom. 2. 20. which hast f. of knowledge and of truth
6. 17. but ye have obeyed that f. of doctrine
Phil. 2. 6. who being in the f. of God, thought it no
7. but took upon him the f. of a servant
2 Tim. 1. 13. hold fast f. of sound words hast heard
3. 5. having f. of godliness, denying power thereof

FORM.

Isa. 45. 7. I f. the light and create darkness

FORMED.

Gen. 2. 7. the Lord God f. man of the dust
19. out of the ground God f. every beast of field
Deut. 32. 18. and hast forgotten God that f. thee
2 Kings 19. 25. that I have f. it, Isa. 37. 26.
Job 26. 5. dead things are f. from under the water
13. his hand hath f. the crooked serpent
33. 6. behold, I also am f. out of the clay
Psal. 90. 2. or ever thou hadst f. the earth
94. 9. he that f. the eye, shall he not see?
95. 5. the sea is his, and his hands f. the dry land
Prov. 26. 10. the great God that f. all things
Isa. 27. 11. he that f. them will shew them no favour
43. 1. thus saith he that f. thee, O Israel, fear not
7. I have f. him, yea, I have made him
10. before me there was no god f. nor after me
21. this peo. have I f. for myself, shall shew praise
44. 2. that made thee, and f. thee from the womb
10. who hath f. a god, or molten a graven image?
21. for thou art my servant, I have f. thee
24. thus saith he that f. thee from the womb
45. 18. God himself that f. the earth, he f. it
49. 5. Lord that f. me from womb to be his servant
54. 17. no weapon f. against thee shall prosper
Jer. 1. 5. before I f. thee in the belly, I knew thee
33. 2. the Lord that f. it to establish it
Amos 7. 1. and behold, he f. grasshoppers in beginn.
Rom. 9. 20. shall the thing f. say to him that f. it
Gal. 4. 19. I travail in birth, till Christ be f. in you
1 Tim. 2. 13. for Adam was first f. then Eve

FORMER.

Gen. 40. 13. shalt deliver the cup after the f. manner
Num. 21. 26. had fought against the f. king of Moab
Deut. 24. 4. her f. husband which sent her away
Ruth 4. 7. was the manner in f. time of redeeming
1 Sam. 17. 30. people answered after the f. manner
2 Kings 1. 14. the two captains of the f. fifties
17. 34. they do after the f. manner, 40.
Neh. 5. 15. the f. governors were chargeable
Job 8. 8. inquire, I pray thee, of the f. age
30. 3. the wilderness in f. time desolate and waste
Psal. 79. 8. O remember not against us f. iniquities
89. 49. where are thy f. loving-kindnesses?
Eccl. 1. 11. there is no remembrance of f. things
7. 10. that the f. days were better than these
Isa. 41. 22. let them shew the f. things, 43. 9.
42. 9. behold the f. things are come to pass
43. 18. remember ye not the f. things, nor consider
46. 9. remember the f. things of old, for I am God
48. 3. I have declared f. things from the beginning
61. 4. they shall raise up the f. desolations
65. 7. I will measure their f. work into their bosom
16. because the f. troubles are forgotten
17. the f. shall not be rememb. nor come to mind
Jer. 5. 24. the Lord our God that giveth the f. and latter rain in his season, Hos. 6. 3. Joel 2. 23.
10. 16. for he is the f. of all things, 51. 19.
34. 5. the f. kings which were before thee
36. 28. write in it all the f. words in the first roll
Ezek. 16. 55. thy daughter shall return to f. estate
Dan. 11. 13. set forth a multitude greater than the f.
29. but it shall not be as the f. or as the latter
Hag. 2. 9. the glory be greater than of the f. house
Zech. 1. 4. the f. prophets have cried, 7. 7, 12.
8. 11. I will not be to this people as in f. days
14. 8. waters go half of them toward the f. sea
Mal. 3. 4. shall be pleasant to the Lord as in f. years
Acts 1. 1. the f. treatise have I made, O Theophilus
Eph. 4. 22. put off concerning the f. conversation
1 Pet. 1. 14. not according to the f. lusts in ignorance
Rev. 21. 4. for the f. things are passed away

FORMETH.

Amos 4. 13. for, lo, he that f. the mountains
Zech. 12. 1. and f. the spirit of man within him

FORNICATION.

This word is taken (1) *For the sin of impurity committed between unmarried persons.* 1 Cor. 7. 2. To avoid fornication, let every man have his own wife, and let every woman have her own husband. (2) *For the sin of adultery, when one or both persons are married.* Mat. 5. 32. Whosoever putteth away his wife, saving for the cause of fornication, causeth her to commit adultery. (3) *For the sin of incest,* 1 Cor. 5. 1. Such fornication as is not so much as named among the Gentiles, &c. (4) *For the sin of idolatry, which is infidelity to, and forsaking of, the true God for false gods,* 2 Chron. 21. 11. Jehoram made high places in the mountains of Judah, and caused the inhabitants of Jerusalem to commit fornication. Rev. 19. 2. He hath judged the great whore, which did corrupt the earth with her fornication.

2 Chr. 21. 11. high places, caused Jerus. commit f.
Isa. 23. 17. Tyre shall commit f. with kingd. of world
Ezek. 16. 29. thou hast multiplied thy f. in Canaan
Mat. 5. 32. saving for the cause of f. 19. 9.
John 8. 41. then said they, we be not born of f.
Acts 15. 20. that they abstain from f. 29. | 21. 25.
Rom. 1. 29. being filled with all f. full of envy
1 Cor. 5. 1. that there is f. among you, and such f.
6. 13. the body is not for f. but for the Lord
18. flee f. ‖ 7. 2. nevertheless, to avoid f.
2 Cor. 12. 21. and have not repented of their f.
Gal. 5. 19. the works of the flesh, which are these, f.
Eph. 5. 3. f. let it not be once named among you
Col. 3. 5. mortify therefore f. uncleanness
1 Thess. 4. 3. will of G. that ye should abstain from f.
Jude 7. Sodom and cities giving themselv. over to f.
Rev. 2. 21. I gave her space to repent of her f.
9. 21. neither repented they of their f. nor thefts
14. 8. drink of the wine of the wrath of her f.
17. 2. have been made drunk with wine of her f.
4. a golden cup full of the filthiness of her f.
† 5. Babylon the great, mother of f. and abominations
18. 3. all nations drunk with wine of wrath of her f.
19. 2. which did corrupt the earth with her f.

FORNICATIONS.

Ezek. 16. 15. thou pouredst out thy f. on every one
Mat. 15. 19. out of heart proceed f. thefts, Mark 7. 21.
See COMMIT, COMMITTED.

FORNICATOR.

1 Cor. 5. 11. if any that is called a brother be a f.
Heb. 12. 16. lest there be any f. or profane person

FORNICATORS.

1 Cor. 5. 9. I wrote to you not to company with f.
10. yet not altogether with the f. of this world
6. 9. nor shall f. inherit the kingdom of God

FORSAKE.

Deut. 31. 16. this people will f. me and break coven.
17. in that day I will f. them and hide my face
Josh. 24. 16. God forbid we should f. the Lord
20. if ye f. the Lord and serve strange gods
Judg. 9. 11. should I f. my sweetness and my fruit?
2 Kings 21. 14. I will f. remnant of my inheritance
1 Chron. 28. 9. if thou f. him, will cast thee off for ever
2 Chron. 7. 19. if ye turn away, and f. my statutes
15. 2. but if ye f. him, he will f. you
Ezra 8. 22. his wrath is against them that f. him
Psal. 27. 10. when my father and mother f. me
37. 8. cease from anger and f. wrath, fret not
89. 30. if his children f. my law and walk not
94. 14. neither will he f. his inheritance
119. 53. horror taken hold, because wicked f. law
Prov. 3. 3. let not mercy and truth f. thee, bind them
9. 6. f. the foolish, and live, go in way of underst.
28. 4. they that f. the law, praise the wicked
Isa. 1. 28. they that f. the Lord shall be consumed
55. 7. let wicked f. his way, unright. his thoughts
65. 11. ye are they that f. L. forget my holy mount.
Jer. 17. 13. all that f. the Lord shall be ashamed
23. 33. I will even f. you, saith the Lord, 39.
51. 9. f. her, and let us go every one to his country
Lam. 5. 20. wherefore dost thou f. us so long time?
Dan. 11. 30. with them that f. the holy covenant
Jonah 2. 8. observe lying vanities, f. their own mercy
Acts 21. 21. thou teachest the Jews to f. Moses

FORSAKE *not*.

Deut. 12. 19. take heed that thou f. *not* the Levite
Job 20. 13. though he spare wickedness and f. it *not*
Psal. 38. 21. f. me *not*, O Lord my God, 71. 9, 18.
119. 8. I will keep thy statutes, O f. me *not* utterly
138. 8. f. *not* the works of thine own hands
Prov. 1. 8. and f. *not* the law of thy mother, 6. 20.
4. 2. I give you good doctrine, f. ye *not* my law
6. f. her *not* and she shall preserve thee
27. 10. thine own friend and father's friend f. *not*

***Not* FORSAKE.**

Deut. 4. 31. he will *not* f. thee, 31. 6, 8. 1 Chr. 28. 20.
14. 27. and the Levite, thou shalt *not* f. him
Josh. 1. 5. I will *not* fail nor f. thee, Heb. 13. 5.
1 Sam. 12. 22. L. will *not* f. his people, 1 Kings 6. 13.
1 Kings 8. 57. let him *not* leave us, nor f. us
Neh. 9. 31. thou didst *not* consume, nor f. them
10. 39. we will *not* f. the house of our God
Psal. 27. 9. *neither* f. me, O God of my salvation
Isa. 41. 17. I, the God of Israel, will *not* f. them
42. 16. these things will I do, and *not* f. them
Ezek. 20. 8. *nor* did they f. the idols of Egypt

FORSAKEN.

2 Chr. 21. 10. because he had f. the L. 24. 24. | 28. 6.
Neh. 13. 11. I said, why is the house of God f.?
Job 18. 4. shall the earth be f. for thee?
Psal. 37. 25. yet have I not seen the righteous f.
Isa. 7. 16. the land shall be f. of both her kings
17. 2. the cities of Aroer are f. shall be for flocks
9. shall be as a f. bough, and an uppermost branch
27. 10. and the habitation shall be f. and left
32. 14. because the palaces shall be f. city left
54. 6. the Lord hath called thee as a woman f.
62. 4. thou shalt no more be termed f.
Jer. 4. 29. every city shall be f. no man dwell therein
18. 14. shall cold waters from another place be f.?
Ezek. 36. 4. thus saith the Lord to the cities f.
Amos 5. 2. the virgin of Israel is f. on her land
Zeph. 2. 4. for Gaza shall be f. and Ashkelon desolate

***Have, hast, hath* FORSAKEN.**

Deut. 28. 20. thy doings, whereby thou *hast* f. me
29. 25. because they *have* f. the Lord, Judg. 10. 10.
Judg. 6. 13. but now the Lord *hath* f. us
10. 13. yet ye *have* f. me, and served other gods
1 Sam. 8. 8. the works wherewith they *have* f. me
12. 10. we have sinned, because we *have* f. the L.
1 Kings 11. 33. because that they *have* f. me
18. 18. ye *have* f. the commandments of the Lord
19. 10. for Israel *have* f. thy covenant, 14.

2 Kings 22. 17. because they have f. me and burnt
incense to gods, 2 Chr. 34. 25. Jer. 16. 11. | 19. 4.
2 Chron. 12. 5. ye have f. me, and I have left you
13. 11. we keep charge of the L. but ye have f. him
24. 20. because ye have f. the Lord, he hath f. you
29. 6. for fathers have done evil, and have f. him
Ezra 9. 10. for we have f. thy commandments
Job 20. 19. because he hath oppressed and f. the poor
Psal. 22. 1. my God, my God, why hast thou f.
me? Mat. 27. 46. Mark 15. 34.
71. 11. they take counsel, saying, God hath f. him
Isa. 1. 4. they have f. the L. and provoked Holy One
54. 7. for a small moment have I f. thee, Isa. 49. 14.
Jer. 1. 16. have f. me, burnt incense to other gods
2. 13. they have f. me the fountain of living waters
17. in that thou hast f. the Lord thy God, 19.
5. 7. how shall I pardon thee? thy child. have f. me
19. thou shalt answer, like as ye have f. me
9. 13. the Lord saith, because they have f. my law
19. are confounded, because ye have f. the land
12. 7. I have f. my house, I have left my heritage
15. 6. thou hast f. me, saith the Lord
17. 13. they have f. the fountain of living waters
22. 9. because they have f. the covenant of God
25. 38. he hath f. his covert as the lion
Ezek. 8. 12. the Lord hath f. the earth, 9. 9.
Mat. 19. 27. we have f. all and followed thee
29. every one that hath f. houses or brethren
2 Tim. 4. 10. Demas hath f. me, having loved world
2 Pet. 2. 15. which have f. the right way, gone astray

Not FORSAKEN.

2 Chron. 13. 10. but as for us, the Lord is our God,
we have not f. him, priests minister to the Lord
Ezra 9. 9. yet God hath not f. us in our bondage
Psal. 9. 10. thou hast not f. them that seek thee
Isa. 62. 12. shall be called, sought out, a city not f.
Jer. 51. 5. Isr. hath not been f. nor Judah of his God
2 Cor. 4. 9. we are persecuted, but not f. cast down

FORSAKETH.

Job 6. 14. but he f. the fear of the Almighty
Psal. 37. 28. for the Lord f. not his saints
40. † 12. more than my hairs, therefore heart f. me
Prov. 2. 17. from her who f. the guide of her youth
15. 10. correction grievous to him that f. the way
28. 13. whoso confesseth and f. shall have mercy
Luke 14. 33. whoso f. not all that he hath cannot

FORSAKING.

Isa. 6. 12. until there be a great f. in the land
Heb. 10. 25. not f. the assemb. of ourselves together

FORSOOK.

Deut. 32. 15. then he f. God that made him
Judg. 2. 12. and they f. the Lord God, 13. | 10. 6.
1 Sam. 31. 7. they f. their cities and fled, 1 Chr. 10. 7.
1 Kings 9. 9. because they f. the Lord their God
12. 8. but Rehoboam f. the counsel of old men, and
consulted with young men, 13. 2 Chr. 10. 8, 13.
2 Kings 21. 22. Amon f. the God of his fathers
2 Chron. 7. 22. they f. the God of their fathers
12. 1. Rehoboam f. law of the Lord and Israel
with him
Psal. 78. 60. he f. the tabernacle of Shiloh
119. 87. consumed me, but I f. not thy precepts
Isa. 58. 2. that f. not the ordinance of God
Jer. 14. 5. the hind calved in the field and f. it
Mat. 26. 56. disciples f. him and fled, Mark 14. 50.
Mark 1. 18. they f. their nets and followed him
Luke 5. 11. they f. all and followed him
2 Tim. 4. 16. none stood with me, all men f. me
Heb. 11. 27. by faith Moses f. Egypt, for he endured

FORSOOKEST.

Neh. 9. 17. art a God slow to anger, and f. them not
19. thou in thy mercies f. them not in wilderness

FORSWEAR.

Mat. 5. 33. thou shalt not f. thys. but perform oaths

FORT, S.

2 Sam. 5. 9. so David dwelt in the f. the city of Dav.
2 Kings 25. 1. they built f. ag. Jerus. Jer. 52. 4.
Isa. 25. 12. high f. of thy walls shall he bring down
29. 3. and I will raise f. against thee
32. 14. the f. and towers shall be for dens for ever
Ezek. 4. 2. and built a f. against it, 21. 22. | 26. 8.
17. 17. and building f. to cut off many persons
21. 22. was the divination for Jerus. to build a f.
26. 8. and he shall make a f. against thee
33. 27. and they that be in the f. shall die
Dan. 11. 19. shall turn toward the f. of his own land

FORTH.

Neh. 4. 16. from that time f. my servants wrought
13. 21. from that time f. came they no more
Psal. 113. 2. blessed be the name of the Lord, from
this time f. and for ever, 115. 18. | 121. 8.
Jer. 49. 5. ye shall be driven out every man right f.
Mat. 16. 21. from that time f. began Jesus to shew
22. 46. nor durst from that day f. ask him questions
John 11. 53. from that day f. they took counsel

FORTHWITH.

Ezra 6. 8. that f. expences be given to these men
Mat. 13. 5. f. sprung up, because no deepn. of earth
26. 49. he f. came to Jesus, and said, hail, Master
Mark 1. 29. and f. when come out of the synagogue
43. he straitly charged him, and f. sent him away
5. 13. and f. Jesus gave the unclean spirits leave
John 19. 34. and f. came thereout blood and water
Acts 9. 18. he received sight f. and arose, and was
baptized
12. 10. and f. the angel departed from him
21. 30. they drew Paul out, and f. doors were shut

FORTY.

Gen. 18. 29. he spake again, peradventure there shall
be f. found; he said, I will not do it for f. sake
Exod. 26. 19. thou shalt make f. sockets of silver
21. and their f. sockets of silver, 36. 24, 26.
Judg. 12. 14. Abdon had f. sons and thirty daugh.
2 Kings 8. 9. so Hazael went and took f. camels' burd.
Neh. 5. 15. the governors had taken f. shekels
Acts 23. 13. more than f. made this conspiracy, 21.

FORTY baths.

1 Kings 7. 38. made ten lavers, one contained f. baths

FORTY cubits.

1 Kings 6. 17. the house before it was f. cubits long
Ezek. 41. 2. he measured the length thereof f. cubits
46. 22. there were courts joined of f. cubits

See Days.

FORTY kine.

Gen. 32. 15. f. kine, ten bulls, a present to Esau

FORTY stripes.

Deut. 25. 3. f. str. he may give him, and not exceed
2 Cor. 11. 24. of the Jews I received f. str. save one

FORTY years.

Gen. 25. 20. Isaac was f. y. when he took Rebekah
26. 34. Esau f. years when he took to wife Judith
Exod. 16. 35. Israel did eat manna f. y. Neh. 9. 21.
Num. 14. 33. shall wander in wildern. f. y. 32. 13.
34. ye shall bear your iniquities f. years
Deut. 2. 7. he knoweth thy walking these f. years
8. 2. the way which God led thee f. years, 29. 5.
4. neither did thy foot swell these f. years
Josh. 5. 6. Israel walked f. years in the wilderness
14. 7. f. years old was I when Moses sent me
Judg. 3. 11. the land had rest f. years, 5. 31. | 8. 28.
13. 1. Israel into the hand of Philistines f. years
1 Sam. 4. 18. Eli had judged Israel f. years
2 Sam. 2. 10. Ish-bosheth f. y. old when he began
5. 4. David reigned f. years, 1 Kings 2. 11.
15. 7. after f. years Absalom said to the king
1 Kings 11. 42. time Solomon reigned was f. years
2 Kings 12. 1. Jehoash reigned f. years in Jerusalem
2 Chron. 24. 1. Joash reigned f. years in Jerusalem
Psal. 95. 10. f. y. was I grieved with this generation
Ezek. 29. 11. nor shall it be inhabited f. years
12. and her cities shall be desolate f. years
13. at the end of f. y. I will gather the Egyptians
Amos 2. 10. I led you f. years in the wilderness
5. 25. ye offered sacrifices f. years, Acts 7. 42.
Acts 4. 22. for the man healed was above f. y. old
7. 23. Moses was f. y. old, he visited his brethren
30. when f. y. expired, there appeared an angel
36. had shewed wonders in the wilderness f. y.
13. 18. the time of f. y. suffered he their manners
21. God gave them Saul by space of f. years
Heb. 3. 9. when your fathers saw my works f. years
17. but with whom was he grieved f. years?

FORTY-ONE years.

1 Kings 14. 21. Rehoboam was f.-one years old
when he began to reign, 2 Chron. 12. 13.
15. 10. Asa reigned f.-one years in Jerusalem
2 Kings. 14. 23. Joroboam reigned f.-one y. Samaria

FORTY-TWO.

Num. 35. 6. to cities of refuge add f.-two cities
2 Kings 2. 24. two bears tare f. and two children
10. 14. Jehu took them alive, even f. and two men
2 Chr. 22. 2. f.-two years old Ahaz. when he began
Ezra 2. 24. the children of Azmaveth f. and two
Neh. 7. 28. the men of Beth-azmaveth f. and two
Rev. 11. 2. holy city they tread f.-two months
13. 5. power was given him to continue f.-two months

FORTY-FOUR.

1 Chron. 5. 18. of Reuben and Gad, 44,760

FORTY-FIVE.

Gen. 18. 28. if I find f.-five, I will not destroy it
Josh. 14. 10. Lord kept me alive these f.-five years
1 Kings 7. 3. upon the beams that lay on f.-five pillars

FORTY-SIX.

John 2. 20. f.-six years was this temple in building

FORTY-EIGHT.

Num. 35. 7. cities of Levites f.-eight, Josh. 21. 41.

FORTY-NINE.

Lev. 25. 8. the space shall be to thee f.-nine years

FORTY thousand.

Num. 1. 33. those numbered of the tribe of Ephraim
were f. thousand five hundred, 2. 19. | 26. 18.
Josh. 4. 13. about f. thousand prepared for war
Judg. 5. 8. was a shield or spear seen among f. thous.
2 Sam. 10. 18. Dav. slew f. t. horsem. 1 Chr. 19. 18.
1 Kings 4. 26. Solo. had f. thousand stalls of horses
1 Chron. 12. 36. of Asher expert in war f. thousand

FORTY-ONE thousand.

Num. 1. 41. of Asher were f. and one thousand, 2. 28.

FORTY-TWO thousand.

Judg. 12. 6. there fell of Ephraimites f.-two thous.
Ezra 2. 64. whole congrega. was 42,360, Neh. 7. 66.

FORTY-THREE thousand.

Num. 26. 7. families of the Reubenites was 43,730

FORTY-FOUR thousand.

1 Chr. 5. 18. the children of Reuben were 44,760

An hundred FORTY-FOUR thousand.

See Hundred.

FORTY-FIVE thousand.

Num. 1. 25. that were numbered of Gad 45,650
26. 41. that were numbered of Benjamin 45,600
50. of Naphtali were numbered 45,400

FORTY-SIX thousand.

Num. 1. 21. of Reuben were 46,500, 2. 11.

FORTIETH.

Num. 33. 38. Aaron died there in the f. year after
Deut. 1. 3. in the f. year Moses spake to Israel
1 Chr. 26. 31. in the f. year of the reign of David
2 Chr. 16. 13. Asa died in one and f. year of his reign

FORTIFY.

Judg. 9. 31. and behold, they f. the city against thee
Neh. 4. 2. will these feeble Jews f. themselves?
Isa. 22. 10. houses have ye broken down to f. the wall
Jer. 51. 53. tho' she should f. height of her strength
Nah. 2. 1. watch the way, f. thy power mightily
3. 14. draw thee waters for siege, f. thy strong holds

FORTIFIED.

2 Chron. 11. 11. Rehoboam f. the strong holds
26. 9. Uzziah built towers and f. them
Neh. 3. 8. they f. Jerusalem to the broad wall
Mic. 7. 12. in that day he shall come from the f. cities

FORTRESS, ES.

2 Sam. 22. 2. the Lord is my rock and my f. Psal.
18. 2. | 31. 3. | 71. 3. | 91. 2. | 144. 2.
Prov. 12. † 12. wicked desireth the f. of evil men
Isa. 17. 3. the f. also shall cease from Ephraim
25. 12. the f. of the high fort shall he bring down
34. 13. nettles and brambles come up in the f.
Jer. 6. 27. I have set thee for a f. among my people
10. 17. gather thy wares, O inhabitant of the f.
16. 19. O Lord, my f. in the day of affliction
Dan. 11. 7. enter into the f. of the king of the north
10. shall he return and be stirred up even to his f.
† 39. thus shall he do in the f. of munitions
Hos. 10. 14. and all thy f. shall be spoiled
Amos 5. 9. that the spoiled shall come against the f.
Mic. 7. 12. in that day he shall come to thee from f.

FORWARD.

Num. 32. 19. we will not inherit on yonder side or f.
Jer. 7. 24. and they went backward and not f.
Ezek. 43. 27. it shall be upon the eighth day and so f.
Zech. 1. 15. and they helped f. the affliction
2 Cor. 8. 10. not only to do, but also to be f. year ago
17. but being more f. of his own accord he went
Gal. 2. 10. the same which I also was f. to do
3 John 6. whom if thou bring f. on their journey
See That Day, Go, Set, Went.

FORWARDNESS.

2 Cor. 8. 8. but by occasion of the f. of others
9. 2. for I know f. of your mind, for which I boast

FOUGHT.

Exod. 17. 8. then came Amalek and f. with Israel
10. so Joshua f. with Amalek, Moses went up
Num. 21. 1. then king Arad f. ag. Isr. and took some
23. Sihon came and f. against Israel, Judg. 11. 20.
26. Sihon f. against the former king of Moab
Josh. 10. 14. for the Lord f. for Israel, 42. | 23. 3.
29. Joshua and all Israel f. against Libnah
31. f. against Lachish || 34. Eglon || 36. Hebron
24. 8. the Amorites on the other side f. with you
11. and the men of Jericho f. against you
Judg. 1. 5. they found Adoni bezek and f. ag. him
8. Judah had f. against Jerusalem, and taken it
5. 19. the kings came, then f. the kings of Canaan
20. they f. from heaven, the stars in courses f.
9. 17. my father f. for you and delivered you
39. Gaal went out and f. with Abimelech
12. 4. all the men of Gilead f. with Ephraim
1 Sam. 4. 10. the Philistines f. 1 Chron. 10. 1.
14. 47. Saul f. against all his enemies on every side
15. † 5. Saul f. against Amalek in the valley
19. 8. so David f. with the Philistines, 23. 5.
2 Sam. 2. 28. people stood still, nor f. they any more
8. 10. he had f. against Hadadezer, 1 Chr. 18. 10.
10. 17. the Syrians f. against David, 1 Chr. 19. 17.
12. 29. David f. against Rabbah and took it
2 Kings 8. 29. Joram f. against Hazael, 9. 15.
12. 17. then Hazael went and f. against Gath
13. 12. Joash f. against Amaziah, 14. 15.
2 Chr. 20. 29. Lord f. against the enemies of Israel
Psal. 109. 3. they f. against me without a cause
Isa. 20. 1. Tartan f. against Ashdod and took it
63. 10. he was turned their enemy and f. ag. them
Jer. 34. 1. the people f. against Jerusalem, 7.
Zech. 14. 3. as when he f. in the day of battle
12. Lord will smite them that f. against Jerusalem
1 Cor. 15. 32. I have f. with beasts at Ephesus
2 Tim. 4. 7. I have f. a good fight, finished my course
Rev. 12. 7. Michael and his angels f. against dragon

FOUL.

Job 16. 16. my face is f. with weeping, on my eyelids
Mat. 16. 3. ye say, it will be f. weather to-day
Mark 9. 25. he rebuked the f. spirit, saying to him
Rev. 18. 2. Bab. the hold of every f. spirit and cage

FOUL.

Ezek. 34. 18. but ye must f. the residue with your feet

FOULED.

Ezek. 34. 19. they drink that ye have f. with your feet

FOULEDST.

Ezek. 32. 2. thou troubledst waters and f. their rivers

Fouls, see Fowls.

FOUND.

Gen. 2. 20. for Adam there was not f. an help meet
8. 9. the dove f. no rest for the sole of her foot
19. † 15. take thy two daughters which are f.
26. † 12. Isaac sowed, and f. an hundred fold
19. Isaac's servants digged and f. a well of water
32. Isaac's servants said to him, we have f. water
27. 20. how is it that thou hast f. it so quickly?
30. 14. Reuben went and f. mandrakes in the field
31. 33. Laban went into tents, but f. not images
37. what hast thou f. of all thy household stuff?
36. 24. Anah that f. the mules in the wilderness
37. 32. brought the coat, and said, this have we f.
38. 23. I sent this kid, and thou hast not f. her
44. 8. money which we f. in our sacks we brought
16. God hath f. out the iniquity of his servants
Exod. 15. 22. they went three days and f. no water
16. 27. they went to gather manna and f. none
18. † 8. Moses told all the travel that had f. them
Lev. 6. 3. or if he have f. that which was lost
† 5. restore it in the day of his being f. guilty
25. † 26. and it his hand hath f. sufficiency
Num. 15. 32. f. a man that gathered sticks on sabb.
33. they that f. him brought him to Moses
20. † 14. thou knowest the travel that hath f. us
31. † 50. we have brought what every man hath f.
Deut. 21. † 17. giving double portion of all f. with him
22. 3. with what thou hast f. shall do likewise
14. when I came to her I f. her not a maid, 17.
27. he f. her in the field, and the damsel cried
24. 1. because he hath f. some uncleanness in her
32. 10. he f. him in a desert land, he led him about
Josh. 2. 22. the pursuers sought, but f. them not
10. 17. five kings are f. hid in a cave at Makkedah
Judg. 1. 5. they f. Adoni-bezek and fought ag. him
14. 18. if not plowed with heifer, not f. out my riddle
15. 15. and he f. a new jaw-bone of an ass
21. 12. and they f. four hundred young virgins
1 Sam. 9. 4. passed thro' Shalisha, but they f. not asses
11. they f. young maidens going to draw water
20. as for thine asses they are f. 10. 2, 16.
12. 5. is witness ye have not f. ought in my hand
13. 19. now there was no smith f. in Israel
22. no sword nor spear f. in hand of the people
25. 28. and evil hath not been f. with thee
29. 3. I have f. no fault in him, since he fell to me
30. 11. and they f. an Egyptian in the field
31. 8. f. Saul and his three sons fallen in Gilboa
2 Sam. 7. 27. therefore thy servant f. in his heart to
pray this prayer to thee, 1 Chron. 17. 25.
1 Kings 7. 47. nor was the weight of the brass f. out
11. 29. the prophet Ahijah f. Jeroboam in the way
13. 28. he went and f. his carcase cast in the way
18. 10. he took an oath that they f. thee not
19. 19. Elijah departed thence and f. Elisha
20. 36. behold, a lion f. him and slew him

1 Kings 21. 20. hast thou f. me, O m. enemy? have f. thee
2 Kings 2. 17. they sought Elijah, but f. him not
9. † 21. they f. Jehu in the portion of Naboth
35. they f. no more of her than the skull
22. 8. I f. the book of the law in house of the Lord
25. 19. he took sixty men that were f. in the city
1 Chron. 4. 40. they f. fat pasture and good
29. 8. they with whom precious stones were f.
2 Chron. 19. 3. there are good things f. in thee
Ezra 2. 62. sought their register among those reckoned by genealogy, but they were not f. Neh. 7. 64.
8. 15. and I f. there none of the sons of Levi
Neh. 5. 8. then they f. nothing to answer
8. 14. they f. written in the law of Lord by Moses
Esth. 4. † 16. gather all the Jews f. in Shushan
Job 28. 13. nor is wisdom f. in the land of the living
31. † 25. if I rejoiced because my hand f. much
29. or lift up myself when evil f. mine enemy
32. 3. wrath kindled, because they had f. no answer
13. lest ye should say, we have f. out wisdom
33. 24. deliver from the pit, I have f. a ransom
42. 15. no women f. so fair as the daughters of Job
Psal. 69. 20. I looked for comforters, but f. none
76. 5. none of the men of might have f. their hands
84. 3. yea, sparrow hath f. an house, and swallow
89. 20. I have f. David my servant, I anointed him
107. 4. they wandered and f. no city to dwell in
116. † 3. I f. trouble and sorrow, pains of hell f. me
119. † 143. trouble and anguish have f. me
132. 6. we f. it in the fields of the wood
Prov. 7. 15. to seek thy face, and I have f. thee
24. 14. so shall wisdom be when thou hast f. it
25. 16. hast thou f. honey? eat so much as is sufficient
Eccl. 7. 27. behold, this have I f. saith the preacher
28. one man among a thousand have I f. but a woman among all those have I not f.
29. this only have I f. that God made man upright
Cant. 3. 1. I sought him, but I f. him not, 2.
3. the watchmen f. me, to whom I said, 5. 7.
4. but I f. him whom my soul loveth
Isa. 10. 10. as my hand hath f. kingdoms of idols
14. my hand hath f. the riches of the people
22. 3. all that are f. in thee are bound together
24. † 22. after many days shall they be f. wanting
57. 10. thou hast f. the life of thine hand
65. 1. I am f. of them that sought me not
Jer. 2. 5. what iniquity have your fathers f. in me?
34. in thy skirts is f. the blood of poor innocents
5. 26. for among my people are f. wicked men
14. 3. they came to the pits and f. no water
15. 16. thy words were f. and I did eat them
23. 11. in my house have I f. their wickedness
41. 8. ten men were f. that said, slay us not
50. 7. all that f. them have devoured them
Lam. 2. 16. this is the day, we have f. we have seen
Ezek. 22. 30. I sought for a man, but I f. none
Dan. 5. 12. an excellent spirit was f. in Daniel
27. thou art weighed, and art f. wanting
6. 4. nor was there any fault f. in Daniel
11. these men f. Daniel praying before his God
Hos. 9. 10. I f. Israel like grapes in the wilderness
12. 4. he f. him in Beth-el, and there spake with us
8. Ephraim said, I have f. me out substance
14. 8. I am like a tree, from me is thy fruit f.
Jonah 1. 3. he f. a ship for Tarshish, so he paid fare
Mic. 1. 13. the transgressions of Israel were f. in thee
Mat. 2. 8. when ye have f. him bring me word
8. 10. I have not f. so great faith in Israel, Luke 7. 9.
13. 44. which when a man hath f. he hideth it
46. when he had f. one pearl of great price
18. 28. and f. one of his fellow-servants who owed
20. 6. he went out and f. others standing idle
21. 19. f. nothing thereon, Mark 11. 13. Luke 13. 6.
22. 10. they gathered all as many as they f.
26. 43. he f. them asleep, Mark 14. 40. Luke 22. 45.
60. sought witnesses, yet f. they none, Mark 14. 55.
27. 32. they f. a man of Cyrene, Simon by name
Mark 1. 37. when they had f. him, they said to him
7. 2. some ate with defiled hands, they f. fault
30. when she was come, she f. the devil gone out
11. 4. they f. the colt tied by the door without
Luke 2. 16. they f. the babe lying in a manger
46. after three days they f. him in the temple
4. 17. he f. the place where it was written
7. 10. they returning f. the servant whole
8. 35. they f. man clothed and in his right mind
15. 5. when he hath f. the sheep, he layeth it
6. rejoice, for I have f. my sheep which was lost
9. when she hath f. the piece, she calleth friends
17. 18. are not any f. that returned to give glory
19. 32. they f. even as he had said to them, 22. 13.
23. 2. we f. this fellow perverting the nation
14. behold, I have f. no fault in this man
24. 2. and they f. the stone rolled away
3. they f. not the body of the Lord Jesus
23. when they f. not his body, they came, saying
33. and they f. the eleven gathered together
John 1. 41. and saith, we have f. the Messias, 45.
2. 14. Jesus f. in the temple those that sold oxen
Acts 5. 10. the young men came in, and f. her dead
22. when the officers f. them not in the prison
7. 11. and our fathers f. no sustenance
9. 2. that if he f. any of this way, whether men
10. 27. Peter f. many that were come together
12. 19. Herod sought for Peter, and f. him not
13. 6. they f. a certain sorcerer, a false prophet
22. I have f. David, a man after mine own heart
17. 23. I f. an altar with this inscription
24. 5. we have f. this man a pestilent fellow
20. if they have f. any evil doing in me
25. 25. I f. he hath done nothing worthy of death
28. 14. we came to Puteoli, where we f. brethren
Rom. 4. 1. what Abraham our father hath f.
7. 10. which was ordained to life, I f. to be to death
1 Cor. 15. 15. yea, we are f. false witnesses of God
2 Cor. 2. 13. because I f. not Titus my brother
Gal. 2. 17. we ourselves also are f. sinners
Phil. 2. 8. and being f. in fashion as a man
1 Tim. 3. 10. use the office, being f. blameless
2 Tim. 1. 17. Onesiphorus sought me and f. me
Heb. 12. 17. for he f. no place of repentance
1 Pet 1. 7. that your faith might be f. to praise

FOU

2 John 4. I f. of thy children walking in truth
Rev. 2. 2. thou hast tried them, and hast f. them liars
3. 2. I have not f. thy works perfect before God
12. 8. nor was their place f. any more in heaven
16. 20. and the mountains were not f.

Be FOUND.

Gen. 18. 29. peradventure there shall be forty f.
44. 9. with whomsoever of thy servants it be f.
Exod. 12. 19. seven days no leav. shall be f. in houses
21. 16. that stealeth a man, if he be f. in his hand
22. 2. if a thief be f. breaking up, 7.
4. if the theft be certainly f. in his hand
Deut. 22. 28. if a man lie with her, and they be f.
1 Sam. 10. 21. they sought him, he could not be f.
2 Sam. 17. 12. shall come on him where he shall be f.
1 Kings 1. 52. if wickedness be f. in him he shall die
1 Chron. 28. 9. if seek him, will be f. of thee, but if forsake him will cast off for ever, 2 Chron. 15. 2.
Job 20. 8. he shall fly away, and shall not be f.
28. 12. but where shall wisdom be f.?
Psal. 32. 6. shall pray in time when thou mayest be f.
36. 2. till his iniquity be f. to be hateful
37. 36. I sought him, but he could not be f.
Prov. 6. 31. if he be f. he shall restore seven-fold
16. 31. if it be f. in the way of righteousness
30. 6. lest he reprove thee and thou be f. a liar
10. lest he curse thee, and thou be f. guilty
Isa. 30. 14. there shall not be f. a sherd to take fire
35. 9. no lion, nor any beast shall be f. thereon
51. 3. joy and gladness shall be f. therein
55. 6. seek ye the Lord while he may be f.
Jer. 29. 14. I will be f. of you, saith the Lord
50. 20. sins of Judah be sought for, shall not be f.
Ezek. 26. 21. yet shalt thou never be f. again
Dan. 11. 19. he shall stumble and fall, and not be f.
12. 1. every one that shall be f. written in the book
Hos. 10. 2. now shall they be f. faulty
Zeph. 3. 13. nor a deceitful tongue be f. in mouth
Zech. 10. 10. and place shall not be f. for them
Acts 5. 39. lest ye be f. to fight against God
1 Cor. 4. 2. it is required that a steward be f. faithful
2 Cor. 5. 3. if clothed, we shall not be f. naked
11. 12. wherein glory, they may be f. even as we
12. 20. that I shall be f. such as ye would not
Phil. 3. 9. be f. in him, not having my own righteous.
2 Pet. 3. 14. that ye may be f. of him in peace
Rev. 18. 21. the city of Babylon be f. no more at all
22. no craftsman shall be f. any more in thee

See FAVOUR.

FOUND *grace.*

Gen. 6. 8. Noah f. grace in the eyes of the Lord
19. 19. thy servant hath f. grace in thy sight
33. 10. if I have f. g. in thy sight, 47. 29. | 50. 4.
39. 4. Joseph f. grace in his sight, he served him
Exod. 33. 12. thou hast also f. grace in my sight, 17.
13. if I have f. grace in thy sight, consider this nation thy people, 34. 9. Judg. 6. 17. 1 Sam. 27. 5.
16. how known that I and thy people have f. g.?
Num. 32. 5. if we have f. grace in thy sight
Ruth 2. 10. why have I f. grace in thine eyes?
1 Sam. 20. 3. thy father knoweth I have f. grace
2 Sam. 14. 22. thy servant knoweth I have f. grace
Jer. 31. 2. the people f. grace in the wilderness

Is FOUND.

Gen. 44. 10. he with whom it is f. be my servant, 16.
Deut. 20. 11. people that is f. shall be tributaries
1 Kings 14. 13. in him there is f. some good thing
2 Kings 22. 13. this book that is f. 2 Chron. 34. 21.
Ezra 4. 19. it is f. this city hath been rebellious
Job 19. 28. seeing the root of the matter is f.
Prov. 10. 13. in the lips of him wisdom is f.
Isa. 13. 15. every one that is f. shall be thrust thro'
37. † 4. lift up thy prayer for remnant that is f.
65. 8. as the new wine is f. in the cluster
Jer. 2. 26. as the thief is ashamed when he is f.
34. in thy skirts is f. the blood of innocents
11. 9. a conspiracy is f. among the men of Judah
Dan. 5. 12. excellent wisdom is f. in thee, 14.
Hos. 14. 8. I am like a tree, from me is thy fruit f.
Luke 15. 24. this my son was lost and is f. 32.
2 Cor. 7. 14. our boasting I made is f. a truth

Was FOUND.

Gen. 44. 12. the cup was f. in Benjamin's sack
47. 14. Joseph gathered the money that was f.
Exod. 35. 23. every man with whom was f. purple
24. every man with whom was f. shittim-wood
Judg. 20. † 48. smote with the sword all that was f.
1 Sam. 13. 22. with Saul and Jonathan there was f.
2 Kings 12. 10. high priest told the money that was f.
20. 13. shewed all that was f. in treasury, Isa. 39. 2.
22. 9. gathered the money that was f. 2 Chr. 34. 17.
23. 2. read book which was f. 2 Chron. 34. 30.
2 Chron. 15. 4. sought him, he was f. of them, 15.
21. 17. carried away the substance that was f.
Ezra 6. 2. there was f. at Achmetha a roll
Eccl. 9. 15. there was f. in it a poor wise man
Jer. 48. 27. was Isr. a derision? was he f. am. thieves?
Ezek. 28. 15. perfect till iniquity was f. in thee
Dan. 1. 19. among all none was f. like Daniel
2. 35. iron, clay broken, no place was f. for them
5. 11. like the wisdom of the gods was f. in him
6. 22. because before him innocency was f. in me
Mat. 1. 18. she was f. with child of the Holy Ghost
Luke 9. 36. when voice was past, Jesus was f. alone
Acts 8. 40. but Philip was f. at Azotus, he preached
Rom. 10. 20. I was f. of them that sought me not
1 Pet. 2. 22. neither was guile f. in his mouth
Rev. 5. 4. no man was f. worthy to open the book
14. 5. and in their mouth was f. no guile
18. 24. in her was f. the blood of the prophets
20. 11. and there was f. no place for them

Was not FOUND.

Mal. 2. 6. and iniquity was not f. in his lips
Heb. 11. 5. Enoch was not f. because God translated
Rev. 20. 15. whoso was not f. written in book of life

FOUNDATION

Is the ground-work, or lowest part, of a building, which supports the other parts; as the foundation of a house, of a castle, of a fort, tower, &c. Christ Jesus, *both in the Old and New Testament, is called a* Foundation, *Isa.* 28. 16. Behold, I lay in Zion for a foundation, a stone,

FOU

a tried stone, a precious corner-stone, a sure foundation. Christ *is the* foundation *on which the church is built; the* foundation *of all the hopes, and comfort, and happiness, of the people of God; the* foundation *of the covenant of grace made with the church, and of all the promises contained therein; he is a sure* foundation, *on whom his people may securely rest; one who will not fail them, nor deceive them; and he is the* corner-stone *that unites the several parts of the building together; he makes* Jews *and* Gentiles, *that once were implacable enemies, one church. So also in* 1 Cor. 3. 11. Other foundation can no man lay, than that is laid, which is *Jesus Christ. And the above-mentioned passage in* Isaiah *is cited by* St. Peter, *and applied to* Christ, 1 Pet. 2. 6.

God's decree of election is the firm immovable foundation *upon which the salvation of the elect depends.* 2 Tim. 2. 19. The foundation of God standeth sure, having this seal, The Lord knoweth them that are his. *See more of this passage on the word* SEAL. The foundation of the apostles and prophets, *is that foundation which they laid by their preaching and doctrine, namely,* Christ, *whom they held forth as the only mediator between God and man, the only Saviour and Head of the church.* Eph. 2. 20. Ye are built upon the foundation of the apostles and prophets: *Your faith is grounded upon the doctrine delivered by them.* Foundation *is likewise taken for the first principles of Christianity, taught in an easy and plain method, so as to make people of mean capacities to understand them; such as concerning the necessity and nature of repentance and faith; the nature, institution, signification, and use of the sacraments; concerning the last judgment, and the like; these the apostle calls the* foundation. *Heb.* 6. 1, 2. Not laying again the foundation of repentance, &c. *And in* Rom. 15. 20. *The apostle says,* So have I strived to preach the gospel, not where Christ was named, lest I should build upon another man's foundation. *I did not choose to preach the gospel, where the fundamentals, the first principles of religion, had been taught by another, lest I should seem to assume to myself the credit due to him. Heaven, which is the eternal inheritance of all believers, is described as a* city which hath foundations, *to denote that the state of the elect in heaven, and their glory there, is not subject to corruption, or the least alteration.* Heb. 11. 10. *Abraham* looked for a city which hath foundations, whose builder and maker is God.

Magistrates are also called foundations. *Psal.* 82. 5. All the foundations of the world are out of course: *all magistrates, rulers, and governors, that should settle and establish justice and order, have disturbed it by their irregular and disorderly proceedings.* Solomon *says,* Prov. 10. 25. The righteous is an everlasting foundation: *or,* hath an everlasting foundation: *His hope and happiness is built upon a sure foundation.*

Exod. 9. 18. as hath not been in Egypt since the f.
Josh. 6. 26. he shall lay the f. in his first-born
1 Kings 5. 17. they brought hewn stones to lay the f.
6. 37. in the fourth year was f. of house of L. laid
7. 9. were of costly stones even from the f. 10.
16. 34. he laid the f. of Jericho in his first-born
2 Chron. 8. 16. work was prepared to-day of the f.
31. 7. they began to lay the f. of the heaps
Ezra 3. 6. the f. of the temple was not yet laid
10. when the builders laid the f. of temple, 12.
5. 16. Sheshbazzar laid the f. of the house
7. † 9. on the first day was the f. of going up
Job 4. 19. how much less in them whose f. is in dust
22. 16. whose f. was overflown with a flood
Psal. 87. 1. his f. is in the holy mountains
102. 25. of old thou hast laid the f. of the earth
137. 7. rase it, rase it, even to the f. thereof
Prov. 10. 25. the righteous is an everlasting f.
Isa. 28. 16. I lay in Zion for a f. tried a stone
44. 28. saying to the temple, thy f. shall be laid
48. 13. my hand hath laid the f. of the earth
Ezek. 13. 14. the f. thereof shall be discovered
Hab. 3. 13. by discovering the f. to the neck
Hag. 2. 18. from the day that the f. was laid
Zech. 4. 9. Zerubbabel hath laid f. and shall finish
8. 9. prophets which were when the f. was laid
12. 1. the Lord, which layeth the f. of the earth
Luke 6. 48. digged deep, and laid the f. on a rock
49. like a man that without a f. built an house
14. 29. lest haply after he hath laid the f.
Rom. 15. 20. lest I should build on another man's f.
1 Cor. 3. 10. as a wise master-builder I laid the f.
11. for other f. can no man lay than is laid
12. if any man build on this f. gold, silver, wood
Eph. 2. 20. are built on the f. of the prophets
1 Tim. 6. 19. laying up in store for thems. a good f.
2 Tim. 2. 19. nevertheless f. of God standeth sure
Heb. 1. 10. thou, Lord, hast laid the f. of the earth
6. 1. not laying the f. of repentance and faith
Rev. 21. 19. the first f. jasper; second sapphire

FOUNDATION *of the world.*

Mat. 13. 35. kept secret from the f. of the world
25. 34. kingdom prepared from the f. of the world
Luke 11. 50. the blood shed from the f. of the world
John 17. 24. thou lovedst me before the f. of the world
Eph. 1. 4. chosen us in him before the f. of the world
Heb. 4. 3. works were finished from the f. of the world
9. 26. must have oft suffered since f. of the world
1 Pet. 1. 20. foreordained before the f. of the world
Rev. 13. 8. Lamb slain from the f. of the world
17. 8. names not written from the f. of the world

FOUNDATIONS.

Deut. 32. 22. and set on fire the f. of the mountains
2 Sam. 22. 8. the f. of heaven moved and shook
16. f. of the world were discovered, Ps. 18. 7, 15.
Ezra 4. 12. have set up the walls and joined the f.
6. 3. and let the f. thereof be strongly laid
Job 38. 4. where wast thou when I laid f. of earth?
6. whereupon are the f. thereof fastened
Psal. 11. 3. if f. be destroyed, what can righteous do?

Psal. 82. 5. all the *f.* of the earth are out of course
104. 5. who laid the *f.* of earth not to be removed
Prov. 8. 29. when he appointed the *f.* of the earth
Isa. 16. 7. for the *f.* of Kir-hareseth shall ye mourn
24. 18. and the *f.* of the earth do shake
40. 21. have ye not understood from *f.* of earth?
51. 13. the Lord that laid the *f.* of the earth
16. that I may lay the *f.* of the earth
54. 11. I will lay thy *f.* with sapphires
58. 12. thou shalt raise up *f.* of many generations
Jer. 31. 37. if the *f.* of the earth can be searched
50. 15. her *f.* are fallen, her walls are thrown down
51. 26. they shall not take of thee a stone for *f.*
Lam. 4. 11. and it hath devoured the *f.* thereof
Ezek. 30. 4. Egypt's *f.* shall be broken down
41. 8. the *f.* of the side chambers were a full reed
Mic. 1. 6. and I will discover the *f.* thereof
6. 2. hear, O mountains, and ye strong *f.* of earth
Acts 16. 26. the *f.* of the prison were shaken
Heb. 11. 10. for he looked for a city that hath *f.*
Rev. 21. 14. the walls of the city had twelve *f.*
19. the *f.* were garnished with precious stones

FOUNDED.

1 *Chron.* 9. † 22. these were porters whom David *f.*
2 *Chron.* 3. † 3. the things wherein Solomon was *f.*
Ezra 3. † 6. but the temple was not yet *f.*
Psal. 8. † 2. out of mouths of babes hast *f.* strength
24. 2. for he hath *f.* it upon the seas and the floods
78. † 69. like the earth which he hath *f.* for ever
89. 11. world and fulness thereof, thou hast *f.* them
104. † 5. he hath *f.* the earth upon her bases
8. to the place which thou hast *f.* for them
119. 152. thy testimonies, thou hast *f.* them for ever
Prov. 3. 19. the Lord by wisdom hath *f.* the earth
Isa. 14. 32. answer, that the Lord hath *f.* Zion
23. 13. this people was not till the Assyrian *f.* it
Amos 9. 6. and he hath *f.* his troop in the earth
Hab. 1. † 12. O God, thou hast *f.* them for correction
Mat. 7. 25. and it fell not, for it was *f.* on a rock
Luke 6. 48. could not shake it, it was *f.* on a rock

FOUNDER.

Judg. 17. 4. his mother gave them to the *f.*
Isa. 41. † 7. so the carpenter encouraged the *f.*
Jer. 6. 29. the bellows are burnt, *f.* melteth in vain
10. 9. the work of the hands of the *f.*
14. every *f.* confounded by graven image, 51. 17.

FOUNDEST.

Neh. 9. 8. and *f.* his heart faithful before thee

FOUNDING.

2 *Chron.* 24. † 27. concerning Joash *f.* the house

FOUNTAIN

Is properly the source or spring-head of waters. Metaphorically, God is called the fountain of living waters, *Jer.* 2. 13. *Springs or fountains are called* living, *when they never cease or intermit, but are always sending forth their waters: Such had God's care and kindness been over and to the* Jews, *of whom he complains,* That they had forsaken him, the fountain of living waters. *The blood of* Christ, *which washes believers from all uncleanness of sin, is called* a fountain. *Zech.* 13. 1. In that day there shall be a fountain opened to the house of *David*, and to the inhabitants of *Jerusalem*, for sin and uncleanness. *The legal washings were but shadows and types of this matchless healing and purging fountain, namely, the blood of* Christ, *which never failed to heal any that ever used it. All spiritual graces and refreshments communicated by the Spirit, are also compared to a* fountain. *Joel* 3. 18. A fountain shall come forth of the house of the Lord, and shall water the valley of *Shittim*. *As waters are of a cooling, refreshing, and fructifying nature, so these gifts and graces should make the most barren to become fruitful. And in* John 7. 38. He that believeth on me, out of his belly shall flow rivers of living water. *He shall be endued with the gifts and graces of the Spirit in a plentiful measure, which shall not only refresh himself, but shall break forth, and be communicated to others, also for their refreshing.*

Fountains *are taken for children, or posterity,* Prov. 5. 16. Let thy fountains be dispersed abroad: *May your posterity be numerous. In this passage* fountains *are put for* streams *or* rivers *flowing from them, by a metonymy of the cause for the effect. In the same sense it is used in* Deut. 33. 28. The fountain of *Jacob* shall be upon a land of corn and wine; *that is, the people that proceed from* Jacob. *The title of* fountains *may be the more fitly given to children, because as they are* rivers *in respect of their parents, so when they grow up, they also become fountains to their children. In* Prov. 5. 18. fountain *is put for a* wife. Let thy fountain be blessed. *Let thy wife be blessed with children: barrenness being esteemed a curse and reproach among the* Israelites; *or, let her be a blessing and comfort to thee, and not a curse and a snare, as a harlot will be: or, let her be made happy by the enjoyment of thy society, and cleaving to her alone.*

Solomon *says,* Prov. 13. 14. The law of the wise is a fountain of life, to depart from the snares of death; *that is, the doctrine, instruction, or counsel of a holy, pious man, is a means to preserve life, and to help men to depart from the snares of death. By* spring *and* fountain *in* Hos. 13. 15. *are meant a prosperous condition, and all blessings which seemed to be for a continuance;* His spring shall become dry, and his fountain shall be dried up. Fountain *is taken for the right ventricle of the heart, which is the spring of life, and of the vital spirits.* Eccl. 12. 6. Or the pitcher be broken at the fountain: *this may be said, when the veins do not return the blood to the heart, but suffer it to stand still, and cool within them, whence comes that coldness of the outward parts, which is a near forerunner of death.* Fountain of blood, *is the blood of a person incommoded with a loss of blood, whether natural or otherwise,* Lev. 20. 18. Mark 5. 29.

Gen. 16. 7. the angel of the Lord found Hagar by a *f.*
Lev. 11. 36. a *f.* wherein is water shall be clean
20. 18. he discovered her *f.* the *f.* of her blood
Deut. 33. 28. *f.* of Jacob shall be on a land of corn
1 *Sam.* 29. 1. the Israelites pitched by a *f.* in Jezreel
Psal. 36. 9. for with thee is the *f.* of life
68. 26. bless the Lord from the *f.* of Israel
74. 15. thou didst cleave the *f.* and the flood
114. 8. who turned the flint into a *f.* of water
Prov. 5. 18. let thy *f.* be blessed, rejoice with wife
13. 14. the law of the wise is a *f.* of life
14. 27. the fear of the Lord is a *f.* of life
25. 26. is as a troubled *f.* and corrupt spring
Eccl. 12. 6. or the pitcher be broken at the *f.*
Cant. 4. 12. a *f.* sealed ‖ 15. a *f.* of gardens
Jer. 2. 13. have forsaken *f.* of living waters, 17. 13.
6. 7. as a *f.* casteth out her waters, so she
9. 1. oh that mine eyes were a *f.* of tears
Joel 3. 18. a *f.* shall come forth of house of the Lord
Zech. 13. 1. in that day a *f.* shall be opened
Mark 5. 29. the *f.* of her blood was dried up
Jam. 3. 11. doth a *f.* send forth sweet waters?
12. no *f.* can yield salt water and fresh
Rev. 21. 6. I will give of the *f.* of life freely

FOUNTAINS.

Gen. 7. 11. the *f.* of the great deep were broken up
8. 2. the *f.* also of the deep were stopped
Deut. 8. 7. God bringeth thee into a land of *f.*
1 *Kings* 18. 5. go into the land, to all *f.* of water
2 *Chron.* 32. 3. he took counsel to stop waters of *f.*
4. there was much people, who stopt all the *f.*
Prov. 5. 16. let thy *f.* be dispersed abroad
8. 24. when there were no *f.* abounding with water
28. when he strengthened the *f.* of the deep
Isa. 41. 18. I will open *f.* in the midst of the valleys
Hos. 13. 15. and his *f.* shall be dried up
Rev. 7. 17. and he shall lead them to living *f.*
8. 10. the star fell upon the *f.* of waters
14. 7. worship him that made the *f.* of water
16. 4. the third angel poured his vial upon the *f.*

FOUR.

Gen. 2. 10. a river parted, and became *f.* heads
14. 9. *f.* kings joined battle with five
47. 24. and *f.* parts shall be your own for seed
Exod. 22. 1. he shall restore *f.* sheep for a sheep
25. 26. thou shalt make for it *f.* rings of gold
34. shall be *f.* bowls made like unto almonds
26. 2. the breadth of one curtain *f.* cubits, 8.
27. 16. their pillars *f.* their sockets *f.* 38. 19.
37. 20. and in the candlestick were *f.* bowls
38. 5. he cast *f.* rings for the *f.* ends of the grate
39. 10. *f.* rows of stones set in the breast-plate
Lev. 11. 20. all fowls that creep going on all *f.*
27. of beasts that go on all *f.* unclean, 42.
Num. 7. 7. two wagons, *f.* oxen to sons of Gershon
8. *f.* wagons, eight oxen to the sons of Merari
Deut. 22. 12. make thee fringes on the *f.* quarters
Judg. 11. 40. a custom to lament *f.* days in a year
2 *Sam.* 21. 22. these *f.* were born to the giant
1 *Kings* 18. 33. he said, fill *f.* barrels with water
2 *Kings* 7. 3. there were *f.* leprous men at the entry
Job 42. 16. saw his son's sons, even *f.* generations
Prov. 30. 15. yea, *f.* things say not, it is enough
18. yea, there be *f.* things which I know not
21. and for *f.* things which it cannot bear
24. there be *f.* things which are little on earth
29. yea, *f.* things are comely in going
Isa. 17. 6. *f.* or five in the utmost fruitful branches
Jer. 15. 3. I will appoint over them *f.* kinds
36. 23. when Jehudi had read three or *f.* leaves
Ezek. 1. 5. the likeness of *f.* living creatures
6. and every one had *f.* faces, 15. | 10. 14. and every one had *f.* wings, 10. 21.
16. and they *f.* had one likeness, 10. 10.
17. they went upon their *f.* sides, 10. 11.
14. 21. when I send my *f.* sore judgm. on Jerus.
37. 9. and say, come from the *f.* winds, O breath
40. 41. *f.* tables were on this side, *f.* on that
43. 15. the altar *f.* cubits, and upward *f.* horns
Dan. 1. 17. these *f.* children God gave knowledge
3. 25. lo, I see *f.* men loose, walking in the fire
7. 2. the *f.* winds of heaven strove on the sea
3. and *f.* great beasts came up from the sea
17. these *f.* beasts are *f.* kings who shall arise
8. 8. came *f.* notable horns towards the *f.* winds
22. whereas *f.* stood up, *f.* kingdoms shall stand
11. 4. his kingdom divided towards the *f.* winds
Amos 1. 3. and for *f.* I will not turn away the punishment thereof, 6, 9, 11, 13. | 2. 1, 4, 6.
Zech. 1. 18. I saw, and behold *f.* horns
20. and the Lord shewed me *f.* carpenters
6. 1. and behold, there came *f.* chariots out
Mat. 24. 31. he shall send his angels, and they shall gather his elect from the *f.* winds, *Mark* 13. 27.
Mark 2. 3. one sick of the palsy who was borne of *f.*
John 4. 35. are yet *f.* months, then cometh harvest
11. 17. Lazarus had lain in the grave *f.* days
19. 23. the soldiers made *f.* parts of his garment
Acts 10. 30. *f.* days ago I was fasting to this hour
21. 9. Philip had *f.* daughters, virgins, who proph.
23. we have *f.* men which have a vow on them
27. 29. they cast *f.* anchors out of the stern
Rev. 4. 6. round about the throne were *f.* beasts
8. the *f.* beasts had each of them six wings
5. 14. the *f.* beasts said, amen, and the elders fell
6. 6. I heard a voice in the midst of the *f.* beasts
7. 1. I saw *f.* angels, on *f.* corners, holding *f.* winds
9. 13. a voice from the *f.* horns of the golden altar
14. loose the *f.* ang. who are bound in Euphrates
14. 3. they sung a new song before the *f.* beasts
15. 7. one of the *f.* beasts gave seven vials
19. 4. the 24 elders and the *f.* beasts fell down
See CORNERS, DAYS.

FOUR *times.*

Neh. 6. 4. yet they sent to me *f. times* after this sort

FOURFOLD.

2 *Sam.* 12. 6. and he shall restore the lamb *f.*
Luke 19. 8. if I have taken any thing, I restore *f.*
See FOOTED, TWENTY, HUNDRED, THOUSAND.

FOUR-SQUARE.

Exod. 27. 1. altar shall be *f.-square*, height 3 cubits
28. 16. the breast-plate *f.-square*, being doubled
1 *Kings* 6. † 33. he made posts of olive-tree *f.-square*
Ezek. 40. 47. he measured the court *f.-square*
48. 20. ye shall offer the holy oblation *f.-square*
Rev. 21. 16. and the city lieth *f.-square*

FOURSCORE.

Exod. 7. 7. Moses was *f.* years old, and Aaron *f.* and three years old, when they spake to Pharaoh
Judg. 3. 30. and the land had rest *f.* years
2 *Sam.* 19. 32. Barzillai was *f.* years old, 35.
2 *Kings* 6. 25. an ass's head was sold for *f.* pieces
10. 24. Jehu appointed *f.* men without, and said
1 *Chron.* 15. 9. Eliel the chief, and his brethren *f.*
2 *Chron.* 26. 17. with him *f.* priests, valiant men
Ezra 8. 8. Zebadiah, and with him *f.* males
Psal. 90. 10. and if by strength they be *f.* years
Cant. 6. 8. are threescore queens, and *f.* concubines
Jer. 41. 5. there came from Samaria, *f.* men
Luke 2. 37. she was a widow about *f.* and four years
16. 7. he said to him, take thy bill, and write *f.*

FOURSCORE *and five.*

Josh. 14. 10. lo, I am this day *f. and five* years old
1 *Sam.* 22. 18. Doeg slew that day *f. and five* pers.

FOURSCORE *and six.*

Gen. 16. 16. Abra. was *f. and six* when Hagar bare

One hundred and FOURSCORE.

Gen. 35. 28. days of Isaac were *one hundred and f.*

Four hundred and FOURSCORE.

1 *Kings* 6. 1. in *four h. f.* years after come out of Eg.

FOURSCORE *thousand.*

1 *Kings* 5. 15. *f. thous.* hewers in mount, 2 *Chr.* 2. 18

FOURSCORE *and seven thousand.*

1 *Chr.* 7. 5. Issachar reckoned in all *f. and seven th.*

One hundred FOURSCORE *and five thousand.*

2 *Kings* 19. 35. angel smote in camp of Assyria *one h.*

FOURTEEN.

Gen. 31. 41. I served *f.* years for thy daughters
46. 22. who were born to Jacob, all the souls were *f.*
Num. 29. 13. ye shall offer for burnt-offering *f.* lambs of the first year, 17. 20, 23, 26, 29, 32.
Josh. 15. 36. the tribe of Judah had in the valley *f.* cities with their villages, 18. 28.
1 *Kings* 8. 65. Solomon and Isr. held a feast *f.* days
1 *Chr.* 25. 5. God gave to Heman *f.* sons, 3 daught.
2 *Chr.* 13. 21. Abijah waxed mighty, mar. *f.* wives
Ezek. 43. 17. the settle shall be *f.* cubits long
Mat. 1. 17. from Abraham to David *f.* from David to carrying to Babylon *f.* to Christ *f.* generations
2 *Cor.* 12. 2. I knew a man above *f.* years ago
Gal. 2. 1. then *f.* years after I went up to Jerusalem

FOURTEEN *thousand.*

Job 42. 12. Job had *f. th.* sheep, and 6,000 camels

FOURTEEN *thousand seven hundred.*

Num. 16. 49. that died in plague were *f. th. seven h.*

FOURTEENTH.

Gen. 14. 5. in the *f.* year came Chedorlaomer
2 *Kings* 18. 13. in the *f.* year of Hezekiah, *Isa.* 36. 1.
1 *Chron.* 24. 13. the *f.* lot came forth to Jeshebeab
25. 21. the *f.* lot came forth to Mattithiah
Ezek. 40. 1. in the *f.* year after the city was smitten
Acts 27. 27. but when the *f.* night was come
See DAY.

FOURTH.

Gen. 2. 14. and the *f.* river is Euphrates
15. 16. in *f.* generation they shall come hither
Exod. 20. 5. visiting iniquity of fathers to the *f.* generation, 34. 7. *Num.* 14. 18. *Deut.* 5. 9.
28. 20. and the *f.* row shall be a beryl, 39. 13.
Lev. 19. 24. in the *f.* year the fruit shall be holy
Josh. 19. 17. the *f.* lot came out to Issachar
2 *Sam.* 3. 4. David's *f.* son, Adonijah, 1 *Chron.* 3. 2.
2 *Kings* 10. 30. thy children of *f.* generation, 15. 12.
Ezek. 10. 14. the *f.* had the face of an eagle
Dan. 2. 40. the *f.* kingdom shall be strong as iron
3. 25. the form of the *f.* is like the Son of God
7. 7. behold, a *f.* beast dreadful and strong
19. then I would know the truth of the *f.* beast
23. the *f.* beast shall be the *f.* kingdom on earth
11. 2. the *f.* shall be far richer than they all
Zech. 6. 3. in the *f.* chariot were grisled horses
Mat. 14. 25. Jesus came in the *f.* watch of the night
Rev. 4. 7. the *f.* beast was like a flying eagle
6. 7. when he had opened the *f.* seal, I heard
8. 12. the *f.* angel sounded, the sun was smitten
16. 8. the *f.* angel poured out his vial on the sun
21. 19. the third, a chalcedony; the *f.* an emerald
See DAY, MONTH, PART.

FOURTH *year.*

1 *Kings* 6. 1. in the *f. year* of Solomon's reign over Israel he began to build, 37. 2 *Chron.* 3. 2.
22. 41. Jehoshaphat began to reign in *f. y.* of Ahab
2 *Kings* 18. 9. in the *f. year* of Hezekiah Shalmaneser came up against Samaria and besieged it
Jer. 25. 1. word came to Jerem. in *f. year* of Jehoiak.
28. 1. in the *f. year* of Zedekiah, Hananiah spake
36. 1. in the *f. year* of Jehoiakim this word came to Jeremiah from the Lord, 45. 1. | 46. 2
51. 59. commanded Seraiah in *f. year* of Zedekiah
Zech. 7. 1. in *f. year* of Darius word came to Zechar.

FOWL.

Gen. 1. 26. let them have dominion over the *f.* 28.
2. 19. out of the ground God formed every *f.* of air
7. 23. the *f.* of the heaven was destroyed
8. 17. bring forth of all flesh, of *f.* of cattle
9. 2. the fear of you shall be on every *f.* of the air
10. behold, I establish my covenant with the *f.*
Lev. 7. 26. eat no blood, whether of *f.* or beast
11. 46. this is the law of the beasts and *f.*
Deut. 4. 17. the likeness of any winged *f.* in the air
Job 28. 7. there is a path which no *f.* knoweth
Psal. 8. 8. to have dominion over the *f.* of the air
148. 10. beasts and flying *f.* praise the Lord
Jer. 9. 10. the *f.* of the heavens and beast are fled
Ezek. 17. 23. and under it shall dwell all *f.*
39. 17. son of man, speak to every feathered *f.*
44. 31. priest shall not eat any thing torn, *f.* or beast
Dan. 7. 6. had on the back of it four wings of a *f.*

FOWLS.

Gen. 7. 3. take of *f.* also of the air by sevens
15. 11. when the *f.* came down on the carcases
Lev. 1. 14. if the burnt-sacrifice to Lord be of *f.*
11. 13. these *f.* ye shall have in abomination
Deut. 14. 20. but of all clean *f.* ye may eat
28. 26. thy carcase shall be meat to all *f.* of the air

1 Sam. 17. 44. I will give thy flesh to the f. 46.
1 Kings 4. 33. Solomon spake of beasts and of f.
14. 11. that dieth in fields, f. eat, 16. 4. | 21. 24.
Neh. 5. 18. also f. were prepared for me, store of wine
Job 12. 7. ask the f. and they shall tell thee
Psal. 50. 11. I know all the f. of the mountains
78. 27. he rained f. like as the sand of the sea
Isa. 18. 6. they shall be left to the f. of the mountains, and the f. shall summer upon them
Dan. 4. 14. let the f. get from his branches
Mat. 6. 26. the f. they sow not, neither reap
13. 4. the f. devoured the seed, Mark 4. 4. Luke 8. 5.
Mark 4. 32. that f. may lodge under it, Luke 13. 19.
Luke 12. 24. how much more are ye better than f.
Acts 10. 12. a sheet wherein were f. 11. 6.
Rev. 19. 17. an angel cried to all the f. that fly
21. and all the f. were filled with their flesh

FOWLS *of the heaven.*

Job 28. † 21. kept close from the f. of the heaven
35. 11. who maketh us wiser than the f. of heaven
Psal. 79. 2. bodies of thy servants meat to f. of heav.
104. 12. by them the f. of hea. have their habitation
Jer. 7. 33. the carcases of this people shall be meat for the f. of the heaven, 16. 4. | 19. 7. | 34. 20.
15. 3. I will appoint the f. of the heaven to destroy
Ezek. 29. 5. given Pharaoh for meat to f. of heaven
31. 6. the f. of heaven made their nests in Assyria
13. on his ruin shall all the f. of heaven remain
32. 4. will cause all f. of heaven to remain on thee
38. 20. the f. of heaven shall shake at my presence
Dan. 2. 38. the f. of heaven given to Nebuchadnezz.
Hos. 2. 18. made a covenant for them with f. of h.
4. 3. every one shall languish with f. of heaven
7. 12. I will bring them down as the f. of heaven
Zeph. 1. 3. I will consume the f. of the heaven
Luke 13. 19. the f. of heaven lodged in the branches

FOWLER.

Psal. 91. 3. he shall deliver thee from snare of the f.
Prov. 6. 5. deliver as a bird from the hand of the f.
Hos. 9. 8. but the proph. is a snare of a f. in his ways

FOWLERS.

Psal. 124. 7. our soul is escaped out of the snare of f.
Jer. 5. † 26. my people pry, as f. lie in wait

FOX.

In Greek, Alopex, *in* Hebrew, Shual: *It is a creature very well known, and very remarkable, principally for its cunning. There is mention made of it in several places of the Scripture. Our Saviour calls* Herod *the tetrarch of* Galilee, fox, *signifying thereby his craft, and the refinements of his policy,* Luke 13. 32. *And to give an idea of his own extreme poverty, he says,* The foxes have holes, and the birds of the air have nests, but the Son of man hath not where to lay his head, *Luke* 9. 58. Ezekiel *compares the false prophets with* foxes, *Ezek.* 13. 4. Thy prophets are like the foxes in the deserts: *whether it was his design to heighten their cunning and hypocrisy in imitating the true prophets, and so covering themselves with sheep's clothing, though they were ravening wolves; or whether he intended to shew, that these false prophets, instead of supporting* Jerusalem, *endeavoured only to destroy it, by undermining its walls, and shaking its foundations, as* foxes *undermine the ground to make holes for themselves. In the same sense, seducers and false teachers are compared to* foxes. *Cant.* 2. 15. Take us the foxes that spoil the vines.

It is said, in Judg. 15. 4, 5. *that* Samson *took three hundred* foxes, *which he tied two and two together by the tails, and that having fastened a firebrand in the middle of the cord which bound them so together, he let them loose among the crops of standing corn belonging to the* Philistines, *and they burnt them. From the fields they went into the olive yards, and burnt them likewise. Some infidels are much scandalized at this history, and pretend it incredible that* Samson *could muster up so great a number of* foxes. *But to this it is replied, that foxes are very common in this country; which is proved from scripture, and the testimony of travellers.* Solomon *in his Song says, that* the little foxes spoiled the vines, *Cant.* 2. 15. Jeremiah *says, that* the foxes walk upon the mountain of Zion, which is desolate, *Lam.* 5. 18. *There are some provinces and cities in* Palestine *which take their name from* foxes, *doubtless by reason of the great number of these animals thereabouts. For example:* the land of Shual, *or the* fox, 1 *Sam.* 13. 17. Hazar-shual, *the fox's habitation, a city of* Judah, *or* Simeon, *Josh.* 15. 28. | 19. 3.

Belon *says, that in* Palestine, *particularly about* Cæsarea, *there is a kind of creature between a wolf and a fox, which so abounds there, that sometimes troops of two or three hundred of them are to be seen.* M. Morizon, *who has travelled in this country, says, that* foxes *swarm there, and that there are very great numbers of them in the hedges and ruins of buildings. Besides,* Samson *being so eminent a person, and the judge of* Israel, *might have employed abundance of people to catch this great number of* foxes, *and they might have provided them some time before for his purpose. Nor can it at all perplex any man's reason or faith, if it be allowed, that the God who made the world, and by his singular providence watched over* Israel, *and intended them deliverance at this time, could easily dispose things so that they might be taken.*

No animal was fitter for his design, especially when coupled together in this manner; for a fox *runs very swiftly, but uses a great many turnings and windings, not going straight on, but running sometimes on one side, sometimes on another, so that while one dragged one way, and another another way, they spread the fire over all the fields of the* Philistines, *and could not easily get into the woods, or holes in the rocks, where their fire brands had been extinguished, and* Samson's *stratagem rendered ineffectual.*

Many things are said concerning the craft and subtilty of foxes. *They lay their dung in the entrance of the badger's den, and by that means obtain it for their own use. They fright the wolves, who are their enemies, from their dens, by laying the herb sea onion at the mouth of them. They dig holes for themselves, but then they leave several outlets, that if the huntsman lays his snare at one, they may escape at the other. When sick, they eat the gum of pine trees, whereby they are not only cured, but their days lengthened. It is said, that when they are pursued by hunters, they make urine on their tails, and strike them upon the dog's faces. Some having been taken in a gin by the leg, have bit it off, and so escaped; others have feigned themselves dead, till they have been taken out, and then have run away. Being hungry, they feign themselves dead, on whom the fowls lighting for prey, they snatch and devour them. Many other things are storied of their cunning.*

Neh. 4. 3. a f. shall break down their stone wall
Luke 13. 32. go and tell that f. I cast out devils

FOXES.

Judg. 15. 4. Samson caught three hundred f.
Psal. 63. 10. they shall be a portion for f.
Cant. 2. 15. take the f. the little f. that spoil the vines
Lam. 5. 18. Zion is desolate, the f. walk upon it
Ezek. 13. 4. thy prophets are like f. in the deserts
Mat. 8. 20. f. have holes, the birds nests, Luke 9. 58.

FRAGMENTS.

Mat. 14. 20. they took up the f. twelve baskets full, Mark 6. 43. Luke 9. 17. John 6. 13.
Mark 8. 19. how many baskets full of f.? 20.
John 6. 12. gather up f. that remain, nothing be lost

FRAIL.

Psal. 39. 4. that I may know how f. I am

FRAME.

Psal. 103. 14. he knoweth our f. he remembereth
Jer. 7. † 18. to make cakes to the f. of heaven
44. † 17. to burn incense to the f. of heaven
Ezek. 40. 2. by which was as the f. of a city on south

FRAMES.

Jer. 18. † 3. behold, he wrought a work on the f.

FRAME, *Verb.*

Judg. 12. 6. for he could not f. to pronounce it right
Jer. 18. 11. behold, I f. evil against you and devise
Hos. 5. 4. they will not f. their doings to turn to God

FRAMED.

Isa. 29. 16. shall the thing f. say to him that f. it?
Eph. 2. 21. in whom all the building f. groweth to
Heb. 11. 3. the worlds were f. by the word of God

FRAMETH.

Psal. 50. 19. thy mouth to evil, thy tongue f. deceit
94. 20. throne of iniquity, f. mischief by a law

FRANKINCENSE.

Exod. 30. 34. take these spices with pure f.
Lev. 2. 1. put f. thereon, 15. | 5. 11. | 24. 7. Num. 5. 15.
2. he shall take the oil with all the f. thereof
16. the priest shall burn the oil with all f. 6. 15.
1 Chron. 9. 29. some were appointed to oversee the f.
Neh. 13. 5. where they laid the f. and vessels
9. thither brought I the vessels and the f.
Cant. 3. 6. who is this that comes perfumed with f.?
4. 6. till day break, I will get me to the hill of f.
14. calamus, cinnamon, with all trees of f.
Mat. 2. 11. they presented to him gifts, gold, f.
Rev. 18. 13. no man buyeth their f. wine and oil

FRANKLY.

Luke 7. 42. nothing to pay, he f. forgave them both

FRAUD.

Psal. 10. 7. his mouth is full of cursing and f.
Isa. 30. † 12. wherefore because ye trust in f.
Jam. 5. 4. hire by you, kept back by f. crieth

FRAY.

Deut. 28. 26. no man shall f. them away, Jer. 7. 33.
Zech. 1. 21. but these are come to f. them

FRECKLED.

Lev. 13. 39. it is a f. spot that groweth in the skin

FREE.

Exod. 21. 2. an Hebrew servant, in the seventh year he shall go out f. Deut. 15. 12. Jer. 34. 9, 14.
5. if the servant shall say, I will not go out f.
11. then shall she go out f. without money
26. he shall let him go f. for his eye's sake
27. he shall let him go f. for his tooth's sake
Lev. 19. 20. not be put to death because not f.
Num. 5. 19. be thou f. from this bitter water
28. if the woman be not defiled, she shall be f.
Deut. 15. 13. and when thou sendest him out f.
18. not seem hard when thou sendest him f.
24. 5. but he shall be f. at home one year
1 Sam. 17. 25. make his father's house f. in Israel
1 Kings 15. † 22. Asa made a proclam. none was f.
1 Chr. 9. 33. the singers, who remaining were f.
2 Chr. 26. † 21. Uzziah dwelt in a f. house
29. 31. and as many as were of f. heart offered
Job 3. 19. and the servant is f. from his master
39. 5. who hath sent out the wild ass f.?
Psal. 51. 12. and uphold me with thy f. Spirit
88. 5. f. among the dead, like slain in the grave
105. 20. the king loosed him, and let him go f.
Isa. 58. 6. and to let the oppressed go f.
Jer. 34. 9. each man should let his servant go f.
11. caused them whom they let go f. to return
Mat. 15. 6. and honour not his father, he shall be f.
17. 26. Jesus saith, then are the children f.
Mark 7. 11. if a man say, it is Corban, he shall be f.
John 8. 32. and the truth shall make you f.
33. how sayest thou, ye shall be made f.
36. if Son shall make you f. ye shall be f. indeed
Acts 22. 28. and Paul said, but I was f. born
Rom. 5. 15. not as the offence, so also is the f. gift
16. but the f. gift is of many offences to justificat.
18. even so the f. gift came upon all men to justif.
6. 18. being then made f. from sin, 22.
20. servants of sin ye were f. from righteousness
7. 3. if her husband be dead, she is f. from that law
8. 2. the Spirit of life made me f. from death
1 Cor. 7. 21. but if thou mayest be made f. use it
† 22. he that is called in the Lord is made f.
9. 1. am I not an apostle? am I not f.?
19. though I be f. from all men, yet a servant
12. 13. baptiz. by one Spirit whether bond or f.
Gal. 3. 28. there is neither bond nor f. Col. 3. 11.
4. 26. but Jerusalem which is above, is f.
31. not children of the bond-woman, but of the f.
5. 1. the liberty wherewith Christ hath made us f.
Eph. 6. 8. shall receive of Lord, whether bond or f.
2 Thess. 3. 1. pray that the word may have f. course
1 Pet. 2. 16. as f. and not using your liberty
Rev. 13. 16. causeth all, f. and bond, to rec. mark
19. 18. ye may eat the flesh of both bond and f.

FREED.

Josh. 9. 23. and there shall none of you be f.
Rom. 6. 7. for he that is dead is f. from sin

FREEDOM.

Lev. 19. 20. lieth with a woman, not f. given her
Ezek. 27. † 20. Dedan thy merchant in clothes of f.
Acts 22. 28. with a great sum obtained I this f.

FREELY.

Gen. 2. 16. of every tree thou mayest f. eat
Num. 11. 5. we remember the fish we did eat f.
1 Sam. 14. 30. if the people had eaten f. to-day
Ezra 2. 68. some of the chief fathers offered f.
7. 15. which the king hath offered f. to God
Psal. 54. 6. I will f. sacrifice to thee, O Lord
Hos. 14. 4. heal their backsliding, I will love them f.
Mat. 10. 8. f. ye have received, f. give
Acts 2. 29. men and brethren, let me f. speak
26. 26. the king knoweth, before whom I speak f.
Rom. 3. 24. being justified f. by his grace through the redemption that is in Christ Jesus
8. 32. will with him also f. give us all things
1 Cor. 2. 12. might know the things f. given us
2 Cor. 11. 7. have preached the gospel of God f.
Rev. 21. 6. I will give of the fountain of life f.
22. 17. and whosoever will let him take f.

FREEMAN.

1 Cor. 7. 22. he that is called, is the Lord's f.
Rev. 6. 15. every bondman and f. hid themselves

FREE *offerings.*

Exod. 36. 3. brought f. offerings every morning
Amos 4. 5. proclaim and publish the f. offerings

FREQUENT.

Prov. 27. † 6. but the kisses of an enemy are f.
2 Cor. 11. 23. in prisons more, f. in deaths oft

FREE-WILL.

Ezra 7. 13. of their f. will to go up to Jerusalem

FREE-WILL *offering.*

Lev. 22. 21. who offereth f.-w. off. it shall be perfect
23. a bullock thou mayest offer for a f.-will off.
Num. 15. 3. when ye will make sacrifice in f.-w. off.
Deut. 16. 10. keep feast, with a tribute of f.-will off.
23. 23. a f.-will offer. shalt thou keep and perform
Ezra 1. 4. help him with beasts besides f.-will offer.
3. 5. that willingly offered a f.-w. off. to the Lord
7. 16. all the silver thou canst find with f.-will off.
8. 28. the silver and gold are a f.-will off. to Lord

FREE-WILL *offerings.*

Lev. 22. 18. who will offer oblation for f.-will off.
23. 38. and beside all your f.-w. off. Num. 29. 39.
Deut. 12. 6. thither shall ye bring your f.-will off.
17. mayest not eat within thy gates thy f.-w. off.
2 Chron. 31. 14. Kore was over f.-will offer. of God
Psal. 119. 108. accept the f.-will offer. of my mouth

FREEWOMAN.

Gal. 4. 22. had two sons, by bond-maid, and by a f.
23. but he of the f. was by promise
30. shall not be heir with the son of the f.
31. we are not children of bond-woman, but of f.

FRESH.

Num. 11. 8. taste of manna was as the taste of f. oil
Job 29. 20. my glory was f. in me, my bow renewed
Psal. 92. 10. I shall be anointed with f. oil
Jam. 3. 12. no fountain can yield salt water and f.

FRESHER.

Job 33. 25. his flesh shall be f. than a child's

FRET.

Lev. 13. 55. shalt burn it in the fire, it is f. inward

FRET.

1 Sam. 1. 6. also provoked her to make her f.
Psal. 37. 1. f. not thyself, 7, 8. Prov. 24. 19.
Isa. 8. 21. when they be hungry, they shall f.

FRETTED.

Ezek. 16. 43. but thou hast f. me in these things

FRETTETH.

Prov. 19. 3. and his heart f. against the Lord

FRETTING.

Lev. 13. 51. the plague is a f. leprosy, 52. | 14. 44.

FRIED.

Lev. 7. 12. cakes mingled with oil of flour f.
1 Chr. 23. 29. Levites to wait about that which is f.

FRIEND

Is taken *for one whom we love and esteem above others, to whom we impart our minds more familiarly than to others; and that from a confidence of his integrity, and good will towards us; thus* Jonathan *and* David *were mutually friends.* Solomon *in his book of* Proverbs *gives the qualities of a true* friend. *Prov.* 17. 17. A friend loveth at all times; *not only in prosperity, but also in adversity.* Chap. 18. 24. There is a friend that sticketh closer than a brother; *he is more hearty in the performance of all friendly offices. He reproves and rebukes when he sees any thing amiss.* Prov. 27. 6. Faithful are the wounds of a friend; *his sharpest reproofs proceed from an upright, and truly loving and faithful soul. He is known by his good and faithful counsel, as well as by his seasonable rebukes.* Prov. 27. 9. Ointment and perfume rejoice the heart: so doth the sweetness of a man's friend by hearty counsel; *by such counsel as comes from his very heart and soul, and is the language of his most inward and serious thoughts. The company and conversation of a friend is refreshing and reviving to a person, who when alone is sad, and dull, and unactive.* Prov. 27. 17. Iron sharpeneth iron, so a man sharpeneth the countenance of his friend.

By friend *is meant also the favourite of a prince.* Hushai *was the* friend, *the favourite, of* David, 2 *Sam.* 15. 37. Zebud, *the son of* Nathan, *was* Solomon's *friend,* 1 Kings 4. 5. *And* Ahuzzath

was the particular friend of Abimelech *king of* Gerar, *Gen.* 26. 26.
The friend of God. *This title is principally given to* Abraham, *as in* 2 Chron. 20. 7. Art not thou our God, who gavest this land to the seed of *Abraham* thy friend for ever? *And in* Isa. 41. 8. But thou, *Israel*, art the seed of *Abraham* my friend. *The apostle* James *likewise makes mention of this*, Jam. 2. 23. And the scripture was fulfilled, which saith, *Abraham* believed God, and it was imputed to him for righteousness; and he was called the friend of God. *This title is given him not only because God frequently appeared to him, conversed familiarly with him, and revealed secrets to him*, Gen. 18. 17. Shall I hide from *Abraham* that thing which I do? *But also because he entered into a covenant of perpetual friendship, both with him and his seed*, Gen. 12. 2, 3. | 17. 2, 4, 7. *and especially because he renewed the covenant with him, upon the sacrificing of his son* Isaac, *and confirmed it by an oath, and thereby admitted him to a nearer degree of friendship and communion*, Gen. 22. 16, 17, &c. *And it is upon this trial of* Abraham's *obedience, namely, the offering up of his son, that the apostle* James *quotes the passage, where* Abraham *is called the friend of God*, Jam. 2. 21, 22, 23.
Our Saviour calls his apostles friends, *John* 15. 15. But I have called you friends; *he adds the reason of it*, for all things that I have heard of my Father, I have made known unto you. *As men used to communicate their counsels and their whole mind to their* friends, *especially in things which are of any concern, or may be of any advantage for them to know and understand; so I have revealed to you whatsoever is necessary for your instruction, office, comfort, and salvation. And this title is not peculiar to the apostles only, but is common with them to all true believers*, Cant. 5. 1. Eat, O friends.
The friend of the bridegroom, *is the bride-man; he who does the honours of the wedding, and leads his friend's spouse to the nuptial bed.* John *the* Baptist, *with respect to* Christ *and his church, was the friend of the Bridegroom; by his preaching he prepared the people of the* Jews *for* Christ, *John* 3. 29.
Friend *is a word of ordinary salutation, whether to* friend *or foe. He is called* friend *who had not on a wedding garment*, Mat. 22. 12. *And our Saviour calls* Judas *the traitor*, friend, *Mat.* 26. 50. *Some are of opinion that this title is given to the guest by an* irony *or* antiphrasis, *meaning the contrary to what the word importeth; or that he is called so, because he appeared to others to be* Christ's *friend, or was so in his own esteem and account, though falsely, being an hypocrite. However, this being spoken in the person of him who made the feast, it is generally taken for an usual compellation; and that* Christ, *following the like courteous custom of appellation, and friendly greeting, did so salute* Judas, *which yet left a sting behind it in his conscience, who knew himself to be the reverse of what he was called. The name of* friend *is likewise given to a neighbour.* Luke 11. 5. Which of you shall have a *friend*, and shall go unto him at midnight, and say, *friend*, lend me three loaves?
Gen. 38. 20. Judah sent the kid by the hand of his *f.*
Exod. 33. 11. God spake to Moses as a man to his *f.*
Deut. 13. 6. or if thy wife or *f.* entice thee secretly
Judg. 14. 20. to companion whom he used as his *f.*
2 *Sam.* 13. 3. Amnon had a *f.* his name was Jonadab
15. 37. Hushai, David's *f.* came into city, 16. 16.
16. 7. Absalom said to Hushai, is this thy kindness to thy *f.*? why wentest thou not with thy *f.*?
1 *Kings* 4. 5. Zabud was principal officer, king's *f.*
2 *Chr.* 20. 7. gavest to the seed of Abraham thy *f.*
Job 6. 14. to him afflicted pity be shewed from his *f.*
27. and ye dig a pit for your *f.*
16. † 21. O that one might plead for a man with God, as a man pleadeth for his *f.*!
Ps. 35. 14. as though he had been my *f.* or brother
41. 9. my familiar *f.* hath lifted up his heel ag. me
88. 18. lover and *f.* hast thou put far from me
Prov. 6. 1. my son, if thou be surety for thy *f.*
3. when in the hand of thy *f.* make sure thy *f.*
17. 17. *f.* loveth at all times, brother born for adver.
18. and becometh surety in the presence of his *f.*
18. 24. a *f.* that sticketh closer than a brother
19. 6. every man is a *f.* to him that giveth gifts
22. 11. for grace of his lips, the king shall be his *f.*
27. 6. faithful are the wounds of a *f.*
9. so doth sweetness of man's *f.* by hearty counsel
10. thine own *f.* and father's *f.* forsake not
14. he that blesseth his *f.* with a loud voice
17. a man sharpeneth the countenance of his *f.*
Cant. 5. 16. this is my beloved, this is my *f.* O daugh.
Isa. 41. 8. thou art the seed of Abraham my *f.*
Jer. 3. † 20. surely as a wife departeth from her *f.*
6. 21. the neighbour and his *f.* shall perish
19. 9. shall eat every one flesh of his *f.* in the siege
Hos. 3. 1. beloved of her *f.* yet an adulteress
Mic. 7. 5. trust ye not in a *f.* put not confidence
Mat. 11. 19. behold a *f.* of publicans, *Luke* 7. 34.
20. 13. he answered, *f.* I do thee no wrong
22. 12. he saith to him, *f.* how camest thou hither?
26. 50. Jesus said, *f.* wherefore art thou come?
Luke 11. 5. which of you shall have a *f.* and shall go at midnight and say, *f.* lend me three loaves
6. for a *f.* of mine in his journey is come to me
8. though he will not give him because he is his *f.*
14. 10. he that bade thee may say, *f.* go up higher
John 3. 29. the *f.* of the bridegroom rejoiceth
11. 11. he saith, our *f.* Lazarus sleepeth
19. 12. if thou let this man go, art not Cesar's *f.*
Acts 12. 20. and having made Blastus their *f.*
Jam. 2. 23. Abraham was called the *f.* of God
4. 4. will be a *f.* of the world, is the enemy of God

FRIENDLY.

Judg. 19. 3. the Levite went to speak *f.* to her
Ruth 2. 13. thou hast spoken *f.* to thine handmaid
Prov. 18. 24. that hath friends, must shew himself *f.*
Hos. 2. † 14. I will bring her, and speak *f.* to her

FRIENDS.

1 *Sam.* 30. 26. David sent of the spoil to his *f.*
2 *Sam.* 3. 8. which do shew kindness to Saul's *f.*
19. 6. thou lovest thine enemies, and hatest thy *f.*
1 *Kings* 16. 11. Zimri left him not one of his *f.*
Esth. 5. 10. Haman sent and called for his *f.*
14. then said his wife and all his *f.* to him
6. 13. Haman told his wife and *f.* every thing
Job 2. 11. when Job's three *f.* heard of this evil
16. 20. my *f.* scorn me, but mine eye poureth tears
17. 5. he that speaketh flattery to his *f.*
19. 14. my familiar *f.* have forgotten me
19. all my inward *f.* abhorred me
21. have pity on me, have pity on me, O ye *f.*
32. 3. Elihu's wrath was kindled against his *f.*
42. 7. Lord's wrath kindled against Eliphaz and *f.*
10. the Lord turned when he prayed for his *f.*
Psal. 38. 11. my *f.* stand aloof from my sore
Prov. 14. 20. the poor is hated, the rich hath many *f.*
16. 28. a whisperer separateth chief *f.*
17. 9. he that repeateth a matter, separateth *f.*
18. 24. that hath *f.* must shew himself friendly
19. 4. wealth maketh many *f.* but poor separated
7. how much more do his *f.* go far from him
Cant. 5. 1. eat, O *f.* drink, yea, drink abundantly
Jer. 20. 4. I will make thee a terror to thy *f.*
6. thou shalt be buried there, thou and all thy *f.*
38. 22. women shall say, thy *f.* have set thee on
Lam. 1. 2. all her *f.* have dealt treacherously
Zech. 13. 6. I was wounded in the house of my *f.*
Mark 3. 21. when his *f.* heard of it, they went out
5. 19. Jesus saith to him, go home to thy *f.*
Luke 7. 6. the centurion sent *f.* to him, saying
12. 4. my *f.* be not afraid of them that kill the body
14. 12. when thou makest a dinner, call not thy *f.*
15. 6. he calleth together his *f.* saying, rejoice
9. she calleth her *f.* and neighbours, saying
29. that I might make merry with my *f.*
16. 9. make to yourselves *f.* of the mammon
21. 16. ye shall be betrayed by parents and *f.*
23. 12. the same day Pilate and Herod were made *f.*
John 15. 13. that a man lay down his life for his *f.*
14. ye are my *f.* if ye do what I command you
15. not servants, but I have called you *f.*
Acts 10. 24. Cornelius called together his *f.*
19. 31. certain which were his *f.* sent to him
27. 3. Julius gave him liberty to go to his *f.*
Rom. 16. † 10. them which are of Aristobulus's *f.*
† 11. greet the *f.* of Narcissus in the Lord
3 *John* 14. our *f.* salute thee, greet the *f.* by name

FRIENDSHIP.

Prov. 22. 24. make no *f.* with an angry man
Jam. 4. 4. the *f.* of the world is enmity with God

FRINGE, S.

Num. 15. 38. bid them make *f.* put on *f.* a ribband
39. it shall be to you for a *f.* that ye may look
Deut. 22. 12. make thee *f.* on the four quarters

FROGS.

Exod. 8. 2. I will smite all thy borders with *f.*
7. the magicians brought up *f.* on the land
Psal. 78. 45. he sent *f.* which destroyed them
105. 30. and the land brought forth *f.*
Rev. 16. 13. I saw three unclean spirits like *f.*

To and FRO.

Gen. 8. 7. he sent a raven, which went *to and f.*
Exod. 29. † 24. shake *to and f.* a wave-offering
2 *Kings* 4. 35. Elisha walked in the house *to and f.*
Job 1. 7. Satan said, from going *to and f.* in earth, 2. 2.
7. 4. I am full of tossings *to and f.* to the dawning
13. 25. wilt thou break a leaf driven *to and f.*?
Psal. 107. 27. they reel *to and f.* and stagger
Prov. 21. 6. is a vanity tossed *to and f.* of them
Isa. 24. 20. earth shall reel *to and f.* like a drunkard
33. 4. as the running *to and f.* of locusts shall run
49. 21. a captive, and removing *to and f.*
Ezek. 27. 19. Dan also and Javan going *to and f.*
Zech. 1. 10. Lord sent to walk *to and f.* through earth
11. we have walked *to and f.* through the earth
6. 7. that they might walk *to and f.* through the earth, so they walked *to and f.* through the earth
Eph. 4. 14. be no more children tossed *to and f.*

See RUN.

FROM.

1 *Sam.* 6. 5. his hand *f.* off you, and *f.* off your land
Mat. 4. 25. then followed him multitudes *f.* Decapolis, *f.* Jerusalem, *f.* Judea, *f.* beyond Jordan

FRONT.

2 *Sam.* 10. 9. Joab saw *f.* of the battle against him
2 *Chron.* 3. 4. the porch in the *f.* of the house

FRONTIERS.

Ezek. 25. 9. from his cities which are on his *f.*

FRONTLETS.

These were square pieces of hard calf's skin, including four pieces of parchment, upon which the Jews *wrote four passages of the law, and bound them with strings on their foreheads. The four passages which they wrote are those: On the first piece of parchment*, Exod. 13. *from* verse 2. *to* 10. *On the second*, Exod. 13. *from* verse 11. *to* 16. *On the third*, Deut. 6. *from* verse 4. *to* 9. *And on the fourth*, Deut. 11. *from* verse 13. *to* 21. *Opinions are much divided whether the use of* frontlets, *and other phylacteries, was ordained by* Moses, *as an observance to which the* Jews *were obliged, and such as required a literal compliance, so that the* Hebrews *have at all times worn them; or have been obliged to wear them.*
They who believe the use of them to be rigorously binding, ground their persuasion on the text of Moses, *which speaks of it in a positive manner, as of other precepts of the law; he requires that the commandments of God* should be for a sign on their hands, and as *frontlets* between their eyes, *Deut.* 6. 8.
But the generality of interpreters on the contrary maintain, that the precepts of Moses *which mention these writings on the doors, the signs upon their hands, and* frontlets *between their eyes, should be taken in a figurative and allegorical sense; as meaning that they should be very careful to preserve the remembrance of God's law, and observe his commands; that they should always have them before them, and never forget them. It is certain that before the* Babylonish *captivity, not the least footsteps of them were to be seen in the history of the* Jews. *The prophets never inveighed against the omission or neglect of this practice; nor was there ever any question concerning them in the reformation of manners at any time proposed among the old* Hebrews.
Exod. 13. 16. it shall be for *f.* between thine eyes
Deut. 6. 8. shall be as *f.* between thine eyes, 11. 18.

FROST.

Gen. 31. 40. drought consumed by day, *f.* by night
Exod. 16. 14. round thing, as small as the hoar *f.*
Job 37. 10. by the breath of God *f.* is given
38. 29. the *f.* of heaven, who hath gendered it?
Psal. 78. 47. destroyeth their sycamore trees with *f.*
147. 16. he scattereth the hoar *f.* like ashes
Jer. 36. 30. Jehoiakim's body cast out to the *f.*

FROWARD.

Deut. 32. 20. for they are a very *f.* generation
2 *Sam.* 22. 27. with the pure thou wilt shew thyself pure, with the *f.* shew thyself *f.* *Psal.* 18. 26.
Job 5. 13. the counsel of the *f.* is carried headlong
Psal. 101. 4. a *f.* heart shall depart from me
Prov. 2. 12. from the man that speaketh *f.* things
15. ways are crooked, and they *f.* in their paths
3. 32. for the *f.* is abomination to the Lord
4. 24. put away from thee a *f.* mouth
6. 12. the wicked walketh with a *f.* mouth
8. 8. there is nothing *f.* or perverse in them
13. the evil way, and the *f.* mouth do I hate
10. 31. but the *f.* tongue shall be cut out
11. 20. of a *f.* heart, are abomination to the Lord
16. 28. a *f.* man soweth strife, whisperer separateth
30. he shutteth his eyes to devise *f.* things
17. 20. he that hath a *f.* heart, findeth no good
21. 8. the way of a man is *f.* and strange
22. 5. thorns and snares are in the way of the *f.*
1 *Pet.* 2. 18. servants be subject to masters, to the *f.*

FROWARDLY.

Isa. 57. 17. he went on *f.* in the way of his heart

FROWARDNESS.

Prov. 2. 14. who delight in the *f.* of the wicked
4. † 24. put away from thee *f.* of mouth
6. 14. *f.* is in his heart, he deviseth mischief
10. 32. the mouth of the wicked speaketh *f.*

FROWNED.

1 *Sam.* 3. † 13. his sons made vile, he *f.* not on them

FROZEN.

Job 38. 30. and the face of the deep is *f.*

FRUIT

Is the product of the earth, trees, plants, &c. Deut. 28. 4. Blessed shall be the *fruit* of thy ground and cattle. The *fruit* of the body *signifies children.* Deut. 28. 4. Blessed shall be the fruit of thy body. *Psal.* 132. 11. Of the *fruit* of thy body will I set upon thy throne. *By* fruit *is sometimes meant reward.* Prov. 1. 31. They shall eat of the *fruit* of their own way; *They shall receive the reward of their bad conduct, and punishments answerable to their sins.* The *fruit* of the lips *is the sacrifice of praise or thanksgiving*, Heb. 13. 15. The *fruit* of the righteous, *that is, the counsel, example, instruction, and reproof of the righteous*, is a tree of life; *is a means of much good, both temporal and eternal, and that not only to himself but to others also*, Prov. 11. 30. Solomon *says in* Prov. 12. 14. A man shall be satisfied with good by the *fruit* of his mouth; *that is, he shall receive abundant blessings from God as the reward of that good he has done by his pious and profitable discourses.* I will punish the *fruit* of the stout heart of the king of *Assyria.* Isa. 10. 12. *I will punish him for his insolent discourses against me.* Fruits meet for repentance, *are such holy lives and conversations as may manifest the reality and sincerity of repentance*, Mat. 3. 8.
The *fruits* of the Spirit *are those gracious habits which the Holy Spirit of God produces in those in whom he dwelleth and worketh, with those acts which flow from them as naturally as the tree produces its* fruit. *The apostle enumerates these* fruits *in* Gal. 5. 22, 23. But the *fruit* of the Spirit is love, *both to God, and our neighbours;* joy, *or a delight in God, arising from a sense of our interest in him;* peace *with God, quietude of conscience, and a peaceable disposition towards men, as opposed to strife, variance, emulation, &c.;* long-suffering, *patiently bearing and forgiving many provocations and injuries; this is opposed to a hastiness to revenge;* gentleness, *or an affableness, and easiness to be entreated, when any one has wronged us:* goodness, *kindness, friendliness, or readiness to do good to others;* faith, *or faithfulness, to speak nothing but the truth, and to perform all our engagements;* meekness, *forbearance of passion, rash anger, and hastiness of spirit;* and temperance, *or a curbing of all carnal desires, and a sparing use of all sensual delights.*
The apostle in Eph. 5. 9. *comprehends the fruits of the sanctifying Spirit in these three things*, (1) Goodness, *which is that quality or disposition which is contrary to malice and wickedness; or it may mean benignity and bounty.* (2) Righteousness, *which is opposed to injustice, whereby one becomes hurtful to another, through deceit, covetousness, oppression, and violence.* (3) Truth, *which is opposed to errors, lies, heresies, hypocrisy, both in common affairs, and also in matters of religion.*
The *fruits* of righteousness *are such good works and holy actions as spring from a gracious frame of heart.* Phil. 1. 11. Being filled with the *fruits* of righteousness. *Fruit is taken for a charitable contribution, which is the fruit or effect of faith and love.* Rom. 15. 28. When I have sealed unto them this *fruit*; *when I have safely delivered this contribution. When* fruit

is spoken of good men, then it is to be understood of the fruits *or works of holiness and righteousness: But when of evil men, then are meant the* fruits *of sin, immorality, and wickedness: This is our Saviour's doctrine,* Mat. 7. 16, 17, 18. First-fruits, *See* FIRST.

Uncircumcised *fruit, or impure, whereof there is mention in* Lev. 19. 23. *is the* fruit *for the three first years of a tree newly planted; it was reputed unclean, and no one was permitted to eat of it in all this time. In the fourth year it was offered to the Lord: after which it was common, and generally eaten. Various reasons are assigned for this precept, as,* (1) *Because the* first-fruits *were to be offered to God, who required the best; but in this time the* fruit *was not come to perfection.* (2) *It was serviceable to the trees themselves, which grew the better and faster, being early stript of those* fruits, *which otherwise would have derived to themselves, and drawn away much of the strength from the root and tree.* (3) *It tended to the advantage of men, both because the* fruit *was then waterish, indigestible, and unwholesome, and because hereby men were taught to bridle their appetites, a lesson of great use and absolute necessity in a godly life.*

Gen. 1. 29. I have given you every tree wherein is *f.*
4. 3. Cain brought of the *f.* of the ground
30. 2. hath withheld from thee the *f.* of the womb
Exod. 21. 22. so that her *f.* depart from her
Lev. 19. 23. ye shall count the *f.* uncircumcised
24. in the fourth year the *f.* shall be holy
23. + 40. take on first day the *f.* of goodly trees
25. 3. six years thou shalt gather in the *f.*
27. 30. the tithe of the *f.* is the Lord's, it is holy
Num. 13. 26. they shewed them the *f.* of the land
27. we came to the land, and this is the *f.* of it
Deut. 1. 25. they took of the *f.* in their hands
7. 13. he will also bless the *f.* of thy land
22. 9. lest *f.* of thy seed, *f.* of thy vineyard be defiled
26. 2. thou shalt take of the first of all the *f.*
28. 4. blessed shall be the *f.* of thy body and ground
11. make thee plenteous in *f.* of thy body, 30. 9.
18. cursed shall be the *f.* of thy body and of land
40. for thine olive shall cast his *f.*
42. all thy trees and *f.* shall the locust consume
Judg. 9. 11. should I forsake my sweetness and *f.?*
2 *Sam.* 16. 2. summer *f.* for the young men to eat
Ps. 21. 10. their *f.* shalt thou destroy from the earth
58. + 11. verily there is *f.* for the righteous
72. 16. the *f.* thereof shall shake like Lebanon
104. 13. the earth is satisfied with *f.* of thy works
105. 35. the locusts devoured the *f.* of their ground
127. 3. the *f.* of the womb is his reward
132. 11. of *f.* of thy body will I set on thy throne
Prov. 8. 19. my *f.* is better than fine gold
10. 16. the *f.* of the wicked tendeth to sin
11. 30. the *f.* of the righteous is a tree of life
12. 14. a man is satisfied by the *f.* of his mouth
18. 20. shall be satisfied with the *f.* of his mouth
31. 16. with the *f.* of her hand she planteth
31. give her of the *f.* of her hands
Cant. 2. 3. and his *f.* was sweet to my taste
8. 12. those that keep the *f.* thereof two hundred
Isa. 3. 10. they shall eat the *f.* of their doings
4. 2. the *f.* of the earth shall be excellent
10. 12. I will punish the *f.* of the stout heart
13. 18. they shall have no pity on the *f.* of the womb
14. 29. his *f.* shall be a fiery flying serpent
27. 6. and fill the face of the world with *f.*
9. this is all the *f.* to take away his sin
28. 4. as the hasty *f.* before the summer
57. 19. I create the *f.* of the lips, peace, peace
65. 21. shall plant vineyards, and eat *f.* of them
Jer. 6. 19. I will bring the *f.* of their thoughts
7. 20. my fury shall be on the *f.* of the ground
11. 16. a green olive-tree, fair, and of goodly *f.*
19. let us destroy the tree with the *f.* thereof
17. 10. according to *f.* of his doings, 21. 14. | 32. 19.
Ezek. 17. 9. cut off the *f.* thereof that it wither
19. 12. and the east-wind dried up her *f.*
14. fire is gone which hath devoured her *f.*
25. 4. they shall eat thy *f.* and drink thy milk
36. 30. I will multiply the *f.* of the tree
47. 12. nor shall the *f.* thereof be consumed
Dan. 4. 12. the leaves fair and the *f.* thereof much, 21.
14. he cried, and said thus, scatter his *f.*
Hos. 9. + 14. give them a womb that casteth the *f.*
10. 13. ye have eaten the *f.* of lies
14. 8. I like a green fir-tree, from me is thy *f.* found
Amos 2. 9. I destroyed his *f.* from above
6. 12. have turned *f.* of righteousness into hemlock
7. 14. I was an herdman, a gatherer of sycamore *f.*
8. 1. and behold a basket of summer *f.* 2.
Mic. 6. 7. shall I give *f.* of body for sin of my soul?
7. 13. the land desolate, for the *f.* of their doings
Hab. 3. 17. neither shall *f.* be in their vines
Hag. 1. 10. the earth is stayed from her *f.*
Zech. 8. 12. seed prosperous, the vine shall give her *f.*
Mal. 1. 12. the table is polluted, and the *f.* thereof
3. 11. nor shall your vine cast her *f.* before time
Mat. 12. 33. make tree good, and his *f.* good, tree corrupt, *f.* corrupt, for the tree is known by his *f.*
21. 19. he said, let no *f.* grow on thee for ever
34. when the time of the *f.* drew near he sent
26. 29. I will not drink of *f.* of the vine, till I drink it new in Father's kingdom, *Mark.* 14. 25.
Mark 12. 2. might receive the *f.* of the vineyard
Luke 1. 42. and blessed is the *f.* of thy womb
13. 6. he sought *f.* thereon, and found none
7. behold, I come seeking *f.* on this fig-tree
20. 10. that they should give him of the *f.*
John 4. 36. and gathereth *f.* to life eternal
Acts 2. 30. of the *f.* of his loins he would raise
Rom. 1. 13. that I might have some *f.* among you
6. 21. what *f.* had ye then in those things whereof
22. being free, ye have your *f.* unto holiness
15. 28. when I have sealed to them this *f.*
Gal. 5. 22. but the *f.* of the Spirit is love, joy, peace
Eph. 5. 9. the *f.* of the Spirit is in all goodness
Phil. 1. 22. if I live, this is the *f.* of my labour
Phil. 4. 17. I desire *f.* that may abound to your account
Heb. 13. 15. by him let us offer the *f.* of our lips
Jam. 3. 18. the *f.* of righteousness is sown in peace
5. 7. the husbandman waiteth for the precious *f.*
Jude 12. trees whose *f.* withereth, without *f.*
See EAT.

Bear, or *beareth* FRUIT.

2 *Kings* 19. 30. shall *bear f.* upward, *Isa.* 37. 31.
Ezek. 17. 8. in a good soil, that it might *bear f.*
23. in the height of Israel it shall *bear f.*
Hos. 9. 16. their root is dried up, they shall *bear* no *f.*
Joel 2. 22. be not afraid, the tree *beareth* her *f.*
Mat. 13. 23. in good ground, is he who *beareth f.*
Luke 8. 8. other fell on good ground, and *bare f.*
13. 9. if it *bear f.* well, if not, cut it down
John 15. 2. every branch in me that *beareth* not *f.* every branch that *beareth f.* he purgeth it
4. as the branch cannot *bear f.* of itself, except it
8. that ye *bear* much *f.* so shall ye be my disciples

Bring, bringeth, or *brought forth* FRUIT.

Lev. 25. 21. it shall *bring forth f.* for three years
Num. 13. 20. and *bring* of the *f.* of the land
Neh. 10. 35. to *bring* the *f.* of all trees, 37.
Psal. 1. 3. that bringeth *forth f.* in his season
92. 14. they shall still *bring forth f.* in old age
Cant. 8. 11. every one for the *f.* was to *bring* silver
Jer. 12. 2. the wicked grow, they *bring forth f.*
Ezek. 36. 11. they shall increase, and *bring forth f.*
47. 12. it shall *bring forth* new *f.* for meat
Hos. 10. 1. Israel *bringeth forth f.* to himself
Mat. 3. 10. *bring.* not *forth* good *f.* 7. 19. *Luke* 3. 9.
7. 17. every good tree *bringeth forth* good *f.*
18. a good tree cannot *bring forth* evil *f.*
13. 26. but when the blade *brought forth f.*
Mark 4. 20. such as hear the word and *bring forth f.*
28. for the earth *bringeth forth f.* of herself
Luke 8. 14. and *bring* no *f.* to perfection
15. they keep it and *bring forth f.* with patience
John 12. 24. if it die, it *bringeth forth* much *f.*
15. 2. purgeth it, that it may *bring forth* more *f.*
5. abideth in me, the same *bringeth forth* much *f.*
16. I ordained that you should *bring forth f.*
Rom. 7. 4. that we should *bring forth f.* to God
5. motions did work to *bring forth f.* unto death
Col. 1. 6. the gospel *bringeth forth f.* in you
Jam. 5. 18. Elijah prayed, the earth *brought forth f.*
See FIRST-FRUIT.

FRUIT-TREES.

Neh. 9. 25. and possessed *f.-trees* in abundance

Yield, yieldeth, yielding FRUIT.

Gen. 1. 11. and the fruit-tree *yielding f.* 12.
Lev. 25. 19. and the land shall *yield* her *f.*
26. 4. the trees of the field shall *yield* their *f.*
Deut. 11. 17. and that the land *yield* not her *f.*
Prov. 12. 12. the root of the righteous *yieldeth f.*
Jer. 17. 8. neither shall cease from *yielding f.*
Ezek. 34. 27. the tree of the field shall *yield* her *f.*
36. 8. and *yield* your *f.* to my people Israel
Mark 4. 7. the thorns choked it, it *yielded* no *f.*
8. other fell on good ground and did *yield f.*
Heb. 12. 11. *yieldeth* peaceable *f.* of righteousness
Rev. 22. 2. the tree *yielded* her *f.* every month

FRUITFUL.

Gen. 1. 22. God blessed them, saying, be *f.* and multiply, 28. | 8. 17. | 9. 7. | 35. 11.
17. 6. and I will make thee exceeding *f.*
20. I will make Ishmael *f.* || 48. 4. make Jacob *f.*
26. 22. God hath made room for us, we shall be *f.*
28. 3. God Almighty bless thee, and make thee *f.*
41. + 52. called him *f.* for God caused me to be *f.*
49. 22. Joseph is a *f.* bough, even a *f.* bough
Exod. 1. 7. and the children of Israel were *f.*
Lev. 26. 9. I will make you *f.* and multiply you
2 *Chr.* 26. + 10. Uzziah had husbandmen in *f.* fields
Psal. 107. 34. he turneth a *f.* land into barrenness
128. 3. thy wife shall be as a *f.* vine
148. 9. mountains and *f.* trees, praise the Lord
Isa. 5. 1. my beloved hath a vineyard in a *f.* hill
17. 6. four or five in the outmost *f.* branches thereof
32. 12. they shall lament for the *f.* vine
Jer. 4. 26. lo, the *f.* place was a wilderness
23. 3. and they shall be *f.* and increase
Ezek. 19. 10. she was *f.* and full of branches
Hos. 13. 15. though he be an east wind shall come
Acts 14. 17. and gave us rain and *f.* seasons
Col. 1. 10. being *f.* in every good work, and increasing
See FIELD.

FRUITS.

Gen. 43. 11. take of the best *f.* in the land in vessels
Exod. 22. 29. not delay to offer the first of thy ripe *f.*
23. 10. six years shalt gather in the *f.* thereof
Lev. 25. 15. according to the years of the *f.* 16.
22. till her *f.* come in, eat of the old store
26. 20. neither shall the trees yield their *f.*
Deut. 33. 14. for precious *f.* brought forth by the sun
2 *Sam.* 9. 10. thou and thy sons shall bring in *f.*
2 *Kings* 8. 6. restore to her all the *f.* of the field
19. 29. plant vineyards, and eat the *f.* thereof
Job 31. 39. if I have eaten the *f.* without money
Ps. 107. 37. sow fields, which may yield *f.* of increase
Eccl. 2. 5. I planted trees of all kind of *f.*
Cant. 4. 13. the plants are an orchard with pleasant *f.*
16. let my beloved eat his pleasant *f.*
6. 11. I went down to see the *f.* of the valley
7. 13. at our gates are all manner of pleasant *f.*
Isa. 33. 9. Bashan and Carmel shake off their *f.*
Lam. 4. 9. pine away for want of the *f.* of the earth
Mal. 3. 11. he shall not destroy the *f.* of your ground
Mat. 3. 8. bring *f.* meet for repentance, *Luke* 3. 8.
7. 16. ye shall know them by their *f.*
21. 34. that they might receive the *f.* of it
41. who shall render him the *f.* in their seasons
43. kingdom given to a nation bringing forth *f.*
Luke 12. 17. I have no room where to bestow my *f.*
18. and there will I bestow all my *f.*
2 *Cor.* 9. 10. increase the *f.* of your righteousness
Phil. 1. 11. filled with the *f.* of righteousness
2 *Tim.* 2. 6. the husbandman first partaker of the *f.*
Jam. 3. 17. wisdom from above is full of good *f.*
Rev. 18. 14. *f.* thy soul lusted after departed from
22. 2. the tree of life bare twelve manner of *f.*
See FIRST.

Summer FRUITS.

2 *Sam.* 16. 1. Ziba with an hundred of *summer f.*
Isa. 16. 9. thy *summer f.* and harvest are fallen
Jer. 40. 10. but gather ye wine and *summer f.*
12. Jews gathered wine and *summer f.* very much
48. 32. the spoiler is fallen on thy *summer f.*
Mic. 7. 1. as when they gathered the *summer f.*

FRUSTRATE.

Ezra 4. 5. and hired counsellors to *f.* their purpose
Psal. 33. + 10. Lord maketh *f.* counsel of heathen
Mark 7. + 9. full well ye *f.* the commandment of God
Gal. 2. 21. I do not *f.* the grace of God

FRUSTRATETH.

Isa. 44. 25. that *f.* the tokens of the liars

FRYING-PAN.

Lev. 2. 7. if oblation be a meat-offering in the *f.*
7. 9. all that is dressed in the *f.* shall be the priest's

FUEL.

Isa. 9. 5. this shall be with burning and *f.* of fire
19. the people shall be as the *f.* of the fire
Ezek. 15. 4. the vine-tree is cast into the fire for *f.* 6.
21. 32. thou shalt be for *f.* to the fire

FUGITIVE.

Gen. 4. 12. a *f.* and a vagabond shalt thou be
14. I shall be a *f.* and a vagabond in the earth

FUGITIVES.

Judg. 12. 4. ye Gileadites are *f.* of Ephraim
2 *Kings* 25. 11. and the *f.* that fell away to the king
Isa. 15. 5. shall cry for Moab, his *f.* shall flee to Zoar
Ezek. 17. 21. all his *f.* shall fall by the sword

FULFIL.

Gen. 29. 27. *f.* her week, and we will give thee this
Exod. 5. 13. *f.* your works, your daily task
23. 26. the number of thy days I will *f.*
1 *Kings* 2. 27. that he might *f.* the word of the Lord
1 *Chr.* 22. 13. if thou takest heed to *f.* statutes of L.
2 *Chron.* 36. 21. to *f.* threescore and ten years
Job 39. 2. canst thou number months that they *f.?*
Ps. 20. 4. the Lord grant thee to *f.* all thy counsel
5. the Lord *f.* all thy petitions
145. 19. he will *f.* the desire of them that fear him
Mat. 3. 15. it becometh us to *f.* all righteousness
5. 17. I am not come to destroy, but to *f.*
Acts 13. 22. found David, who shall *f.* all my will
Rom. 2. 27. uncircumcision, if it *f.* the law
13. 14. for the flesh, to *f.* the lusts thereof
Gal. 5. 16. ye shall not *f.* the lusts of the flesh
6. 2. bear burdens, and so *f.* the law of Christ
Eph. 4. + 10. ascended that he might *f.* all things
Phil. 2. 2. *f.* ye my joy, that ye be like-minded
Col. 1. 25. is given to me, to *f.* the word of God
4. 17. take heed thou *f.* the ministry, 2 *Tim.* 4. + 5.
2 *Thess.* 1. 11. *f.* all the good pleasure of his will
Jam. 2. 8. if ye *f.* the royal law, ye do well
Rev. 17. 17. for God put in their hearts to *f.* his will

FULFILLED.

Gen. 25. 24. when her days to be delivered were *f.*
29. 21. give me my wife, for my days are *f.*
50. 3. forty days were *f.* for so are *f.* the days
Exod. 5. 14. wherefore have ye not *f.* your task?
7. 25. seven days *f.* after Lord hath smitten river
Lev. 12. 4. till the days of purification be *f.* 6.
Num. 6. 13. when the days of his separation are *f.*
32. + 11. because they have not *f.* after me
Deut. 1. + 36. Caleb hath *f.* to go after me
1 *Sam.* 18. + 26. and the days were not *f.*
2 *Sam.* 7. 12. when days be *f.* and thou shalt sleep
14. 22. in that the king *f.* the request of servant
1 *Kings* 8. 15. and hath with his hand *f.* it
24. and hast *f.* it with thy hand, 2 *Chron.* 6. 15.
11. + 6. Solomon *f.* not after the Lord, as David
2 *Chr.* 6. 4. the Lord hath *f.* that which he spake
Ezra 1. 1. that the word of the Lord might be *f.*
Job 36. 17. thou hast *f.* the judgment of the wicked
Jer. 44. 25. ye and your wives have *f.* with your hand
Lam. 2. 17. he hath *f.* his word he had commanded
4. 18. our days are *f.* for our end is come
Ezek. 5. 2. when the days of the siege are *f.*
Dan. 4. 33. the same hour was the thing *f.*
10. 3. till three whole weeks were *f.*
Mat. 1. 22. that it might be *f.* 2. 15, 23. | 8. 17. | 12. 17. | 13. 35. | 21. 4. | 27. 35. *John* 12. 38. | 15. 25. | 17. 12. | 18. 9, 32. | 19. 24, 28, 36.
2. 17. then was *f.* that which was spoken, 27. 9.
5. 18. shall in no wise pass from the law till all be *f.*
13. 14. in them is *f.* the prophecy of Esaias
24. 34. shall not pass till all these things be *f.*
Mark 1. 15. the time is *f.* kingd. of God is at hand
13. 4. what sign when all these things shall be *f.?*
Luke 1. 20. my words which shall be *f.* in their season
2. 43. when they had *f.* the days, they returned
21. 22. that all things which are written may be *f.*
24. until the times of the Gentiles be *f.*
22. 16. not eat till it be *f.* in the kingdom of God
24. 44. all things must be *f.* spoken by Moses
John 3. 29. this my joy therefore is *f.*
17. 13. they might have my joy *f.* in themselves
Acts 3. 18. what God had shewed, he hath so *f.*
9. 23. after many days were *f.* Jews took counsel
12. 25. Paul and Barnabas *f.* their ministry
13. 25. and as John *f.* his course, he said
27. they have *f.* them in condemning him
29. when they had *f.* all that was written of him
33. God hath *f.* the same to us their children
14. 26. to grace of God for the work which they *f.*
Rom. 8. 4. the righteousness of law might be *f.* in us
13. 8. he that loveth another hath *f.* the law
2 *Cor.* 10. 6. when your obedience is *f.*
Gal. 5. 14. the law is *f.* in one word, even in this
Rev. 6. 11. till killing of their brethren should be *f.*
15. 8. till the seven plagues of seven angels were *f.*
17. 17. till the words of God shall be *f.*
20. 3. should deceive no more, till 1000 years be *f.*
See SCRIPTURE.

FULFILLING.

Psal. 148. 8. fire, hail, stormy wind *f.* his word
Rom. 13. 10. therefore love is the *f.* of the law
Eph. 2. 3. *f.* the desires of the flesh and of the mind

FULL.

Signifies, [1] *Satisfied with.* Isaiah 1. 11. I am full of the burnt offerings of rams. [2] *That which is perfect, complete, and which wants nothing.* 2 John 8. That we receive a full reward; *that whole portion of glory which God hath promised to diligent, persevering Christians.* [3] *Such as are proud, and puffed up with a high conceit of their own sufficiency and worth, so as they feel no need of* Christ. *Luke* 6. 25. Woe unto you that are full. [4] *One enabled both to conceive and bring forth.* 1 Sam. 2. 5. Full of years, *one who had lived long enough, as long as he desired,* Gen. 25. 8. Full of faith, and of the Holy Ghost, *that is, endued with a plentiful measure of faith, and of the gifts and graces of the Holy Spirit,* Acts 6. 5. The fulness of time, *is the time wherein the* Messiah *appeared, which was appointed by God, promised to the fathers, foretold by the prophets, expected by the* Jews *themselves, and earnestly longed for by all the faithful; the fulness of this time, is when that time was fully come.* Gal. 4. 4. When the fulness of the time was come, God sent his Son. The fulness of God, *is such a measure of perfection as God hath appointed to every one of the elect through* Christ. *Eph.* 3. 19. That ye might be filled with all the fulness of God; *that is, until you arrive at the highest degree of the knowledge and enjoyment of God, and immediate influence from him, and an entire conformity to him.*

The fulness of Christ, *is the infinite treasures of grace and mercy with which he was filled.* John 1. 16. Of his fulness have all we received. *And whereas men are said to be filled with the Holy Ghost, as* John *the* Baptist, *Luke* 1. 15. *and* Stephen, *Acts* 6. 5. *This differs from the fulness of* Christ *in these three respects,* (1) *Grace and the Spirit be in others by participation; as the moon hath her light from the sun, rivers their waters from the fountain, and the eye its sight from the soul; but in* Christ *they be originally, naturally, and of himself.* (2) *In Christ they be infinite and above measure,* John 3. 34. *But in the saints by measure, according to the gifts of God,* Eph. 4. 16. *The moon is full of light, but the sun is more full; rivers are full of waters, but the sea more full.* (3) *The saints cannot communicate their graces to others; whereas the gifts of the Spirit be in* Christ *as an head and fountain, to impart them to his members.* John 1. 16. We have received of his fulness. *It is said,* Col. 2. 9. That the fulness of the Godhead dwells in Christ bodily; *that is, The whole nature and attributes of God are in* Christ, *and that really, essentially, or substantially, and also personally, by nearest union, as the soul dwells in the body, so that the same person who is man, is God also.*

The church is called the fulness of Christ, *Eph.* 1. 23. *It is the church which makes him a complete and perfect Head, and without which he would account himself but empty and maimed, as it were; for though he has a natural and personal fulness, as God; yet as Mediator, he is not full and complete without his mystical body, (as a king is not complete without his subjects,) but receives an outward, relative, and mystical fulness from his members. And then the church does manifest and set forth his* fulness, *serving as an empty vessel for him to fill and to shew his fulness in; and this he does, by bringing every member to his full stature; by dispersing all variety of gifts and graces among them; and by bringing them all to heaven at last, so that not one shall be wanting.*

How much more their fulness! *Rom.* 11. 12. If the fall of them be the riches of the world, and the diminishing of them the riches of the Gentiles; how much more their fulness? *If the falling away of the* Jews, *from being God's people, through their rejecting the gospel, and the small number of believers among them, was the occasion of God's manifesting his abundant grace in the conversion of the* Gentiles, *and spreading the knowledge of* Christ *all the world over; how much more shall a general conversion of the* Jews, *towards the end of the world, confirm the faith of the believing* Gentiles, *and also be a means to convert those of them that do not yet believe, all over the world?*

Gen. 15. 16. the iniquity of the Amorites is not yet *f.*
25. 8. Abraham an old man, and *f.* of years
35. 29. Isaac being old and *f.* of days, died
41. 1. at the end of two *f.* years, Pharaoh dreamed
7. the thin ears devoured the seven *f.* ears, 22.
43. 21. every man's money in his sack *f.* weight
Exod. 8. 21. the houses shall be *f.* of swarms of flies
16. 33. and put an homer *f.* of manna therein
22. 3. for he should make *f.* restitution
Lev. 2. 14. shalt offer even corn beaten out of *f.* ears
16. 12. censer *f.* of coals, hands *f.* of incense
19. 29. and the land became *f.* of wickedness
25. 29. within a *f.* year may he redeem it
30. if not redeemed in a *f.* year, then the house
Num. 7. 13. both of them were *f.* of fine flour, 19, 25, 31, 37, 43, 49, 55, 61, 67, 73, 79.
14. one spoon of ten shekels *f.* of incense, 20, 26, 32, 38, 44, 50, 56, 62, 68, 74, 80, 86.
22. 18. if Balak give me house *f.* of silver, 24. 13.
Deut. 6. 11. and houses *f.* of all good things, when thou shalt have eaten and be *f.* 8. 10, 12.
11. 15. will send grass, that thou mayest eat and be *f.*
21. 13. she shall bewail her father a *f.* month
33. 23. Naphtali *f.* with the blessing of the Lord
34. 9. Joshua was *f.* of the Spirit of wisdom
Judg. 6. 38. wringed the dew, a bowl *f.* of water
16. 27. now the house was *f.* of men and women
Ruth 1. 21. I went out *f.* and the Lord hath brought
2. 12. and a *f.* reward be given thee of the Lord
1 *Sam.* 2. 5. they that were *f.* hired out themselves
18. 27. they gave them in *f.* tale to the king
27. 7. David dwelt in country of Philist. a *f.* year
2 *Sam.* 8. 2. and with one *f.* line to keep alive
1 *Kings* 17. † 15. she and her house did eat a *f.* year
2 *Kings* 3. 16. make this valley *f.* of ditches

2 *Kings* 4. 6. when vessels were *f.* she said to her son
6. 17. behold, the mountain was *f.* of horses
7. 15. and lo, all the way was *f.* of garments
10. 21. house of Baal was *f.* from one end to another
1 *Chron.* 21. 22. shall grant it me for the *f.* price
24. nay, but I will verily buy it for a *f.* price
23. 1. when David was old and *f.* of days, 29. 28.
Esth. 3. 5. then was Haman *f.* of wrath
5. 9. he was *f.* of indignation against Mordecai
Job 5. 26. thou shalt come to thy grave in a *f.* age
7. 4. I am *f.* of tossings to and fro to dawning of day
10. 15. I am *f.* of confusion, see mine affliction
11. 2. and should a man *f.* of talk be justified?
14. 1. man is of few days and *f.* of trouble
20. 11. his bones are *f.* of the sins of his youth
21. 23. one dieth in his *f.* strength, being at ease
24. his breasts are *f.* of milk, his bones moistened
32. 18. I am *f.* of matter, the Spirit constraineth me
36. 16. that on thy table should be *f.* of fatness
42. 17. so Job died, being old and *f.* of days
Psal. 17. 14. they are *f.* of children, and leave rest
69. 20. hath broken my heart, I am *f.* of heaviness
73. 10. waters of a *f.* cup are wrung out to them
74. 20. dark places are *f.* of habitations of cruelty
78. 25. man did eat angels' food, sent meat to the *f.*
104. 16. the trees of the Lord are *f.* of sap
127. 5. happy that hath his quiver *f.* of them
144. 13. that our garners may be *f.* affording store
Prov. 17. 1. than an house *f.* of sacrifices with strife
25. † 17. lest he be *f.* of thee, and hate thee
27. 7. the *f.* soul loatheth an honey-comb
20. hell and destruction are never *f.*
30. 9. lest I be *f.* and deny thee, and say, who is L.?
Eccl. 1. 7. run into the sea, yet the sea is not *f.*
8. all things are *f.* of labour, man cannot utter
4. 6. than both hands *f.* with travail and vexation
11. 3. if the clouds be *f.* of rain, they empty
Isa. 1. 11. I am *f.* of the burnt offerings of rams
15. I will not hear, your hands are *f.* of blood
21. the faithful city, it was *f.* of judgment
11. 9. the earth shall be *f.* of knowledge of the Ld.
13. 21. their houses shall be *f.* of doleful creatures
15. 9. the waters of Dimon shall be *f.* of blood
22. 2. *f.* of stirs ‖ 7. valleys shall be *f.* of chariots
25. 6. a feast of fat things, a feast *f.* of marrow
28. 8. for all tables are *f.* of vomit and filthiness
30. 27. his lips are *f.* of indignation, and his tongue
51. 20. they are *f.* of the fury of the Lord
Jer. 4. 12. a *f.* wind from those places shall come
5. 7. when I had fed them to the *f.* they committed
6. 11. therefore I am *f.* of the fury of the Lord
28. 3. within two *f.* years will I bring, 11.
35. 5. I set before the Rechabites pots *f.* of wine
Lam. 1. 1. how city sit solitary that was *f.* of peop.
3. 30. he is filled *f.* with reproach
Ezek. 1. 18. and their wings were *f.* of eyes
10. 4. court was *f.* of the brightness of Lord's glory
12. the wheels were *f.* of eyes round about
17. 3. a great eagle with wings *f.* of feathers
19. 10. she was fruitful and *f.* of branches
28. 12. the sum, *f.* of wisdom, and perfect in beauty
32. 6. and the rivers shall be *f.* of thee
37. 1. in midst of the valley which was *f.* of bones
39. 19. ye shall eat fat till ye be *f.* and drink blood
Dan. 3. 19. then was Nebuchadnezzar *f.* of fury
8. 23. when the transgressors are come to the *f.*
10. 2. in those days Daniel mourned three *f.* weeks
Joel 2. 24. the floors shall be *f.* of wheat
Mic. 3. 8. but truly I am *f.* of power by the Spirit
6. 12. the rich men thereof are *f.* of violence
Hab. 3. 3. and the earth was *f.* of his praise
Zech. 8. 5. the streets shall be *f.* of boys and girls
Mat. 6. 22. thy body shall be *f.* of light, *Luke* 11. 36.
13. 48. which when it was *f.* they drew to shore
14. 20. of fragments twelve baskets *f.* *Mark* 6. 43.
15. 37. they took up that was left seven baskets *f.*
23. 25. but within are *f.* of extortion and excess
27. but within are *f.* of dead men's bones
28. within ye are *f.* of hypocrisy and iniquity
Mark 7. 9. *f.* well ye reject commandment of God
15. 36. one ran and filled a spunge *f.* of vinegar
Luke 1. 57. now Elizab. *f.* time came to be deliver.
4. 1. Jesus being *f.* of the Holy Ghost, was led
5. 12. behold a man *f.* of leprosy, fell on his face
6. 25. woe unto you that are *f.* ye shall hunger
16. 20. Lazarus was laid at his gate *f.* of sores
John 1. 14. and dwelt among us, *f.* of grace and truth
7. 8. I go not up, for my time is not yet *f.* come
15. 11. and that your joy might be *f.* 16. 24.
19. 29. there was set a vessel *f.* of vinegar
Acts 2. 13. others said, these men are *f.* of new wine
28. shalt make me *f.* of joy with thy countenance
6. 3. look ye out men *f.* of the Holy Ghost
5. Stephen *f.* of faith and the H. Ghost, 8. | 7. 55.
7. 23. when Moses was *f.* forty years old
9. 36. Dorcas *f.* of good works and alms deeds
11. 24. Barnabas *f.* of the Holy Ghost and faith
13. 10. and said, O *f.* of all subtilty and mischief
19. 28. they were *f.* of wrath, and cried out
Rom. 1. 29. being *f.* of envy, murder, debate, deceit
15. 14. I am persuad. that ye also are *f.* of goodn.
1 *Cor.* 4. 8. now ye are *f.* now ye are rich
Phil. 2. 26. for he longed and was *f.* of heaviness
4. 12. I am instructed to be *f.* and to be hungry
18. but I have all, and abound, I am *f.*
2 *Tim.* 4. 5. make *f.* proof of thy ministry
Heb. 5. 14. but strong meat to them that are of *f.* age
Jam. 3. 8. tongue an unruly evil, *f.* of deadly poison
17. wisdom from above is pure, *f.* of mercy
1 *Pet.* 1. 8. ye rej. with joy unspeak. and *f.* of glory
2 *Pet.* 2. 14. eyes *f.* of adultery, not cease from sin
1 *John* 1. 4. we write to you, that your joy may be *f.*
2 *John* 8. but that we receive a *f.* reward
12. speak face to face, that our joy may be *f.*
Rev. 4. 6. there were four beasts *f.* of eyes, 8.
5. 8. having every one golden vials *f.* of odours
15. 7. seven golden vials *f.* of the wrath of God
16. 10. and his kingdom was *f.* of darkness
17. 3. I saw a woman *f.* of names of blasphemy
4. a golden cup *f.* of abominations and filthiness
21. 9. the seven vials *f.* of the seven last plagues

See ASSURANCE, COMPASSION.

Is FULL.

2 *Kings* 4. 4. thou shalt set aside that which *is f.*
Psal. 10. 7. his mouth *is f.* of cursing, *Rom.* 3. 14
26. 10. and their right hand *is f.* of bribes
29. 4. the voice of the Lord *is f.* of majesty
33. 5. the earth *is f.* of the goodness of the Lord
48. 10. thy right hand *is f.* of righteousness
65. 9. with the river of God, which *is f.* of water
75. 8. and the wine is red, it *is f.* of mixture
88. 3. my soul *is f.* of troubles, and my life
104. 24. O Lord, the earth *is f.* of thy riches
119. 64. the earth, O Lord, *is f.* of thy mercy
Eccl. 9. 3. the heart of the sons of men *is f.* of evil
10. 14. a fool *is f.* of words, man not tell what to be
Isa. 2. 7. their land *is f.* of silver, *is f.* of horses
8. their land also *is f.* of idols, they worship
6. 3. holy is Lord, the whole earth *is f.* of his glory
Jer. 5. 27. as a cage *is f.* of birds, houses full of deceit
6. 11. the aged, with him that *is f.* of days
23. 10. for the land *is f.* of adulterers
Ezek. 7. 23. land *is f.* of crimes, city *is f.* of violence
9. 9. land *is f.* of blood, city *is f.* of perverseness
Joel 3. 13. for the press *is f.* the fats overflow
Amos 2. 13. a cart is pressed, that *is f.* of sheaves
Nah. 3. 1. it *is* all *f.* of lies and robberies
Luke 11. 34. body *is f.* of light, *is f.* of darkness
39. but your inward part *is f.* of ravening

To the FULL.

Exod. 16. 3. when we sat and did eat bread *to the f.*
8. when L. shall give in the morn. bread *to the f.*
Lev. 26. 5. ye shall eat your bread *to the f.*

FULLER, S.

2 *Kings* 18. 17. they came and stood in the highway of the *f.* field, *Isa.* 7. 3. | 36. 2.
Mal. 3. 2. he is like a refiner's fire, and *f.* soap
Mark 9. 3. so as no *f.* on earth can white them

FULLY.

Num. 14. 24. but Caleb that followed me *f.*
Ruth 2. 11. Boaz said, it hath *f.* been shewed me
1 *Kings* 11. 6. Solomon went not *f.* after the Lord
Eccl. 8. 11. the heart of sons of men is *f.* set to do evil
Jer. 12. † 6. yea, they cried after thee *f.*
Nah. 1. 10. they shall be devoured as stubble, *f.* dry
Acts 2. 1. when the day of Pentecost was *f.* come
Rom. 4. 21. being *f.* persuaded, that what he promised
14. 5. let every man be *f.* persuad. in his own mind
15. 19. I have *f.* preached the gospel of Christ
Col. 1. † 25. made a minister *f.* to preach the word
2 *Tim.* 3. 10. thou hast *f.* known my doctrine
4. 17. that by me the preaching might be *f.* known
Rev. 14. 18. thrust in thy sickle, grapes are *f.* ripe

FULNESS.

Gen. 48. † 19. his seed become a *f.* of nations
Exod. 22. † 29. thou shalt not delay to offer thy *f.*
Num. 18. 27. reckoned as the *f.* of the wine press
Deut. 22. † 9. lest the *f.* of thy seed be defiled
33. 16. precious things of the earth, and *f.* thereof
1 *Sam.* 28. † 20. Saul fell with the *f.* of his stature
1 *Chron.* 16. 32. let the sea roar, and the *f.* thereof, *Psal.* 96. 11. | 98. 7.
Job 20. 22. in *f.* of sufficiency shall be in straits
Psal. 16. 11. in thy presence is *f.* of joy
24. 1. earth is the Lord's, and its *f.* 1 *Cor.* 10. 26, 28.
50. 12. the world is mine, and *f.* thereof, 89. 11.
Isa. 6. † 3. his glory is the *f.* of the whole earth
8. † 8. the *f.* of the breadth of thy land shall be the stretching out of his wings, O Immanuel
34. † 1. let the earth hear, and the *f.* thereof
42. † 10. ye that go down to sea, and the *f.* thereof
Jer. 8. † 16. have devoured the land and *f.* thereof
47. † 2. waters shall overflow the land and *f.* thereof
Ezek. 16. 49. iniquity of sister Sodom, *f.* of bread
12. † 19. land was desolate, and the *f.* 19. 7. | 30. † 12.
Amos 6. † 8. I will deliver up city, and the *f.* thereof
Mic. 1. † 2. hearken, O earth, and the *f.* thereof
John 1. 16. of his *f.* have we received grace for grace
Rom. 11. 12. how much more their *f.*?
25. till the *f.* of the Gentiles be come in
15. 29. I shall come in the *f.* of the gospel of Christ
Gal. 4. 4. when the *f.* of the time was come
Eph. 1. 10. that in the *f.* of times he might gather
23. the *f.* of him that filleth all in all
3. 19. that ye might be filled with all the *f.* of God
4. 13. we come to the stature of the *f.* of Christ
Col. 1. 19. pleased Father, in him should all *f.* dwell
2. 9. in him dwelleth the *f.* of the Godhead bodily

FUNDAMENT.

Judg. 3. † 22. not draw dagger, it came out at the *f.*

FURBISH.

Jer. 46. 4. *f.* the spears, put on the brigandines

FURBISHED.

Ezek. 21. 9. a sword is sharpened, and also *f.* 10.
11. given to be *f.* ‖ 28. sword *f.* to consume

FURY.

Gen. 27. 44. tarry, till thy brother's *f.* turn away
Lev. 26. 28. I will walk contrary to you in *f.*
Job 20. 23. God shall cast the *f.* of his wrath on him
Isa. 27. 4. *f.* is not in me, who would set briers
34. 2. and his *f.* is upon all their armies
51. 13. hast feared because of the *f.* of the oppressor; and where is the *f.* of the oppressor?
17. O Jerusalem, which hast drunk cup of his *f.*
20. as wild bull, they are full of the *f.* of the Lord
22. even the dregs of cup of my *f.* no more drink
59. 18. he will repay *f.* to his adversaries
63. 3. for I will trample them in my *f.*
5. my arm brought salvation, my *f.* it upheld me
6. and I will make them drunk in my *f.*
66. 15. Lord will come to render his anger with *f.*
Jer. 4. 4. lest my *f.* come forth like fire, and burn
6. 11. therefore I am full of the *f.* of the Lord
21. 5. I will fight against you in *f.* and wrath
12. lest my *f.* go out like fire, and burn
23. 19. a whirlwind is gone forth in *f.* 30. 23.
25. 15. take the wine-cup of this *f.* at my hand
32. 31. this city hath been a provocation of my *f.*
33. 5. whom I have slain in mine anger and *f.*
36. 7. great is the *f.* the Lord hath pronounced
Lam. 4. 11. the Lord hath accomplished his *f.*
Ezek. 5. 13. I will cause my *f.* to rest on them, they shall know when I have accomplished my *f*

Ezek. 5. 15. when I shall execute judgments in f.
6. 12. thus will I accomplish my f. on them
8. 18. therefore will I deal in f. my eye not spare
13. 13. I will rend with a stormy wind in my f.
16. 38. I will give thee blood in f. and jealousy
42. so will I make my f. towards thee to rest
19. 12. but she was plucked up in my f. cast down
20. 33. with f. poured out will I rule over you
21. 17. and I will cause my f. to rest
22. 20. so will I gather you in mine anger and f.
24. 8. that it might cause f. to come up to vengeance
13. not purged, till I have caused my f. to rest
25. 14. they shall do in Edom according to my f.
36. 6. I have spoken in my jealousy and in my f.
38. 18. that my f. shall come up in my face
Dan. 3. 13. Nebuchadnezzar in his f. commanded
19. then was Nebuchadnezzar full of f.
8. 6. and he ran unto him in the f. of his power
9. 16. let thy f. be turned away from thy city Jerus.
11. 44. he shall go forth with great f. to destroy
Mic. 5. 15. I will execute f. on the heathen
Nah. 1. † 2. the Lord revengeth, that hath f.
Zech. 8. 2. I was jealous for her with great f.
See POUR, POURED.

FURIOUS.

Prov. 22. 24. with a f. man thou shalt not go
29. 22. a f. man aboundeth in transgression
Ezek. 5. 15. execute judgment in f. rebukes, 25. 17.
Dan. 2. 12. Nebuchadnezzar the king was very f.
Nah. 1. 2. the Lord revengeth, and is f.

FURIOUSLY.

2 Kings 9. 20. like the driving of Jehu, he driveth f.
Ezek. 23. 25. and they shall deal f. with thee

FURLONGS.

Luke 24. 13. Emmaus was from Jerusalem sixty f.
John 6. 19. had rowed about five and twenty f.
11. 18. Bethany nigh Jerusalem about fifteen f.
Rev. 14. 20. blood came out by the space of 1600 f.
21. 16. he measured the city with reed, 12,000 f.

FURNACE

Signifies, [1] *A fire-place for melting gold and other metals*, Prov. 17. 3. | 27. 21. [2] *A place of cruel bondage and oppression; such was* Egypt *to the* Israelites, *who there met with much hardship, rigour, and severity, for to try and purge them*, Deut. 4. 20. Jer. 11. 4. [3] *Most sharp and grievous afflictions and judgments wherewith God tries his people*, Ezek. 22. 18, 20, 22. [4] *A place of temporal torment; such was* Nebuchadnezzar's *fiery* furnace, Dan. 3. 6, 11. [5] *Hell, the place of endless torment*, Mat. 13. 42.

Gen. 15. 17. a smoking f. and a burning lamp
19. 28. the smoke went up as the smoke of a f.
Exod. 9. 8. take you handfuls of ashes of the f.
10. and they took ashes of the f. and stood
19. 18. the smoke ascended as the smoke of a f.
Deut. 4. 20. the Lord hath taken you out of the f.
1 Kings 8. 51. from the midst of the f. Jer. 11. 4.
Psal. 12. 6. pure words, as silver tried in a f. of earth
Prov. 17. 3. fining pot for silver, f. for gold, 27. 21.
Isa. 31. 9. whose fire is in Zion, his f. in Jerusalem
48. 10. I have chosen thee in the f. of affliction
Ezek. 22. 18. Israel is dross in the midst of the f.
20. I will gather you as tin in the midst of the f.
22. as silver is melted in the midst of the f.
Dan. 3. 6. be cast into midst of a burning fiery f. 11.
Mat. 13. 42. and shall cast them into a f. of fire, 50.
Rev. 1. 15. his feet like brass, as if they burned in a f.
9. 2. arose a smoke, as the smoke of a great f.

FURNACES.

Neh. 3. 11. Hashub repaired the tower of the f.
12. 38. from the tower of the f. to the broad wall

FURNISH.

Deut. 15. 14. thou shalt f. him liberally out of flock
Psal. 78. 19. can God f. a table in the wilderness?
Isa. 65. 11. that f. the drink-offering to that number
Jer. 46. 19. f. thyself to go into captivity

FURNISHED.

1 Kings 9. 11. Hiram f. Solomon with cedar
Prov. 9. 2. she hath also f. her table
Mat. 22. 10. and the wedding was f. with guests
Mark 14. 15. will shew you a room f. Luke 22. 12.
2 Tim. 3. 17. thoroughly f. unto all good works

FURNITURE.

Gen. 31. 34. Rachel put them in the camels' f.
Exod. 31. 7. the tabernacle and his f. 39. 33.
8. table and his f. || 9. altar with all his f.
35. 14. the candlestick and his f. and his lamps
Nah. 2. 9. there is none end of all the pleasant f.

FURROW.

1 Sam. 14. † 14. slew twenty men within half a f.
Job 39. 10. canst thou bind the unicorn in the f.?

FURROWS.

Job 31. 38. or the f. thereof likewise complain
Psal. 65. 10. thou settlest the f. thereof
129. 3. the plowers plowed, they made long their f.
Ezek. 17. 7. might water it by f. of her plantation
10. it shall wither in the f. where it grew
Hos. 10. 4. judgment as hemlock in the f. of the field
10. when shall bind themselves in their two f.
12. 11. their altars as heaps in the f. of the fields

FURTHER.

Num. 22. 26. angel went f. and stood in narrow place
Deut. 20. 8. officers shall speak f. to the people
1 Sam. 10. 22. they inquired of the Lord f.
Job 38. 11. hitherto shalt thou come, but no f.
40. 5. yea, twice, but I will proceed no f.
Eccl. 8. 17. f. though a wise man think to know it
12. 12. f. by these, my son, be admonished
Mat. 26. 39. he went a little f. and fell on his face
65. saying, what f. need have we of witnesses? Mark 14. 63. Luke 22. 71.
Mark 1. 19. when he had gone a little f. thence
5. 35. why troublest thou the Master any f.?
Luke 24. 28. he made as tho' he would have gone f.
Acts 4. 17. that it spread no f. among the people
21. when had f. threatened them, they let them go
12. 3. Herod proceeded f. to take Peter also
21. 28. f. he brought Greeks also into the temple
24. 4. that I be not f. tedious unto thee
27. 28. they had gone a little f. they sounded
2 Tim. 3. 9. but they shall proceed no f.
Heb. 7. 11. what f. need another priest should rise

FURTHER, *Verb.*

Psal. 140. 8. O Lord, f. not his wicked device

FURTHERANCE.

Phil. 1. 12. the things which happened unto me have fallen out rather unto the f. of the gospel
25. shall abide with you for your f. and joy of faith

FURTHERED.

Ezra 8. 36. they f. the people and the house of God

FURTHERMORE.

Exod. 4. 6. Lord said f. to Moses, put thine hand
Ezek. 8. 6. Lord said f. to Ezekiel, son of man

G.

GADDEST.

Jer. 2. 36. why g. thou about to change thy way?

GAIN.

Judg. 5. 19. the kings of Canaan took no g. of money
Job 22. 3. is it g. to him to make thy way perfect?
Prov. 1. 19. so are the ways of every one greedy of g.
3. 14. the g. thereof is better than fine gold
15. 27. he that is greedy of g. troubleth his house
28. 8. that by usury and unjust g. increaseth
Isa. 33. 15. he that despiseth the g. of oppressions
56. 11. every one for his g. from his quarter
Ezek. 22. 13. have smitten hand at thy dishonest g.
27. her princes like as wolves to get dishonest g.
Dan. 11. 39. he shall divide the land for g.
Mic. 4. 13. I will consecrate their g. to the Lord
Hab. 2. † 9. woe to him that gaineth an evil g.
Acts 16. 16. which brought her masters much g.
19. 24. brought no small g. to the craftsmen
2 Cor. 12. 17. did I make a g. of you by any I sent?
18. did Titus make a g. of you?
Phil. 1. 21. for me to live is Christ, and to die is g.
3. 7. what things were g. to me, I counted loss
1 Tim. 6. 5. supposing that g. is godliness
6. but godliness with contentment is great g.
Jam. 4. 13. go to a city, there buy, sell, and get g.

GAIN, *Verb.*

Dan. 2. 8. I know that ye would g. the time
Mat. 16. 26. what profited if he should g. the whole world, and lose his soul? Mark 8. 36. Luke 9. 25.
1 Cor. 9. 19. servant to all, that I might g. the more
20. that I might g. the Jews || 22. g. the weak
21. that I might g. them that are without law

GAINED.

Job 27. 8. what hope hath hypocrite, tho' he hath g.?
Ezek. 22. 12. thou hast greedily g. by extortion
Mat. 18. 15. if he hear, thou hast g. thy brother
25. 17. that received two had also g. other two, 22.
20. I have g. besides them five talents more
Luke 19. 15. how much every man had g. by trading
16. Lord, thy pound hath g. ten pounds
18. Lord, thy pound hath g. five pounds
Acts 27. 21. and to have g. this harm and loss
2 John † 8. that ye lose not the things ye have g.

GAINS.

Acts 16. 19. saw that the hope of their g. was gone

GAINSAY.

Luke 21. 15. your adversaries shall not be able to g.

GAINSAYERS.

Tit. 1. 9. that ye might be able to convince the g.

GAINSAYING.

Acts 10. 29. therefore came I to you without g.
Rom. 10. 21. I stretched forth my hands to a g. peo.
Tit. 2. † 9. servants to please them, not g.
Jude 11. they have perished in the g. of Core

GALL

Is a bitter juice, one of the humours in the body of man and beast. It is put for any thing that is bitter and pernicious. Job 20. 14. Yet his meat in his bowels is turned, it is the gall of asps within him: *It will be very painful and destructive to him at last.* Psal. 69. 21. They gave me gall for my meat; *or poison, or bitter herbs.* St. Matthew *says, that they gave our Saviour* vinegar to drink mingled with gall, Mat. 27. 34. St. Mark *calls it* wine mingled with myrrh, Mark 15. 23. *It is generally thought that the* gall and myrrh *signify but one and the same thing, that is, something that was very bitter. It is said to have been an ordinary custom to give dying persons some intoxicating potion, to make them less sensible of their pain.* To give water of gall to drink, *denotes some very bitter affliction*, Jer. 8. 14. Their grapes are grapes of gall, Deut. 32. 32. *Their fruits, or actions, are displeasing to God, malicious and mischievous to others, and will at last be pernicious to themselves.* A root that beareth gall, Deut. 29. 18. *may denote some secret and subtle idolaters, who might secretly infect and poison others, by drawing them to idolatry; which will produce bitter fruits, how pleasant soever it may be for the present.* To be in the gall of bitterness, and bond of iniquity, *is to be in a state of great impiety, to be under the power of sin and corruption, of hypocrisy and ambition.* It is put for *great affliction*, Job 16. 13. *For wrong, injustice*, Amos 6. 12.

Deut. 29. 18. lest there should be a root that bear. g.
32. 32. their grapes are grapes of g. clusters bitter
Job 16. 13. he poureth out my g. on the ground
20. 14. his meat is the g. of asps within him
25. the glittering sword cometh out of his g.
Psal. 69. 21. they gave me also g. for my meat
Jer. 8. 14. God hath given us water of g. to drink
9. 15. I will give them water of g. 23. 15.
Lam. 3. 5. he hath compassed me with g. and travel
19. remembering the wormwood and the g.
Amos 6. 12. for ye have turned judgment into g.
Mat. 27. 34. they gave him vinegar mingled with g.
Acts 8. 23. I perceive thou art in the g. of bitterness

GALLANT.

Isa. 33. 21. no galley, nor shall g. ship pass thereby

GALLANTS.

Nah. 2. † 5. he shall recount his g. they shall stumble
Zech. 11. † 2. howl, because the g. are spoiled

GALLERY, IES.

Cant. 1. † 17. the beams are cedar, and our g. of fir
Cant. 7. 5. thy head like Carmel, king is held in the g.
Ezek. 41. 15. he measured the g. thereof on one side
42. 3. against the pavem. was g. against g. in stories

GALLEY.

Isa. 33. 21. wherein shall go no g. with oars

GALLOWS.

Esth. 6. 4. Haman spake to hang Mordecai on g.
7. 10. so they hanged Haman on the g. 8. 7.
9. 13. let Haman's ten sons be hanged on the g. 25.

GANGRENE.

2 Tim. 2. † 17. and their word will eat as doth a g.

GAP.

Ezek. 22. 30. a man that should stand in g. before me

GAPED.

Job 16. 10. they have g. upon me, Psal. 22. 13.

GAPETH.

Job 7. † 2. as a servant g. after the shadow

GAPS.

Ezek. 13. 5. ye have not gone up into the g. for Israel

GARDEN

Is *a plot of ground furnished with plants, flowers, &c.* Gen. 2. 15. *The church is resembled to a* garden, Cant. 4. 12. | 5. 1. *As a* garden *is taken out of the common waste ground to be appropriated to a more particular use, so the church of* Christ *is chosen from among the rest of the world to a particular use. In a* garden *nothing that is good comes up naturally of itself, but as it is planted and set; so nothing is good in the heart, but what is planted and set by the heavenly Husbandman. In a* garden *nothing uses to be planted, but what is useful and delightful; so there is no grace in the heart of a christian but what is useful and necessary. In a* garden *there are variety of flowers and spices; so in a christian there is somewhat of every grace. As men delight much in their* gardens, *to walk there and take their pleasure, and take care to fence, weed, water, and plant them; so* Christ's *care and delight is for his church. As* gardens *use to have fountains and streams running through them, as* Paradise *had four streams which ran through it; so the church is* Christ's *Paradise, and his Spirit is a spring in the midst of it, to refresh the souls of believers. A* garden *stands always in need of weeding and dressing; so in the hearts of christians,* Christ *hath always somewhat to do, they would else soon be overgrown and turn wild. The prophet* Isaiah *upbraids the Jews with the abominations and acts of idolatry which they committed in their* gardens. Ye shall be confounded for the gardens which ye have chosen, Isa. 1. 29. *These gardens were either consecrated to idols, or were such as the heathens worshipped idols in; there they sacrificed,* Isa 65. 3. *after which they thought that they were well purified, when they had washed themselves in the water,* Isa. 66. 17.

Gen. 2. 15. God took the man and put him in the g.
3. 23. Lord sent him forth from the g. of Eden
13. 10. the plain of Jordan was as the g. of the Ld.
Deut. 11. 10. and waterest it as a g. of herbs
1 Kings 21. 2. that I may have it for a g. of herbs
Job 8. 16. his branch shooteth forth in his g.
Cant. 4. 12. a g. inclosed is my sister, my spouse
16. blow upon my g. let him come into his g.
5. 1. I am come into my g. my sister, my spouse
6. 2. my beloved is gone down into his g. 11.
Isa. 1. 8. the daughter of Zion is as a lodge in a g.
30. ye shall be as a g. which hath no water
51. 3. he will make her desert like the g. of God
58. 11. and thou shalt be like a watered g.
61. 11. as the g. causeth things sown to spring
Jer. 31. 12. their souls shall be as a watered g.
Lam. 2. 6. taken away his tabernac. as it were of a g.
Ezek. 28. 13. thou hast been in Eden the g. of God
31. 8. cedars in g. of God could not hide him
9. all the trees in the g. of God envied him
36. 35. desolate land is become like the g. of Eden
Joel 2. 3. land is as the g. of Eden before them
Luke 13. 19. which a man took and cast into his g.
John 18. 1. over the brook Cedron, where was a g.
26. did not I see thee in the g. with him?
19. 41. there was a g. and in the g. a sepulchre

GARDENS.

Num. 24. 6. thy tents as g. by the river side
Eccl. 2. 5. I made me g. and orchards, and planted
Cant. 4. 15. a fountain of g. a well of waters
6. 2. to feed in the g. and to gather lilies
8. 13. thou that dwellest in the g. cause me to hear
Isa. 1. 29. and ye shall be confounded for the g.
65. 3. a people that sacrificeth in g. burns incense
66. 17. they that purify themselves in the g.
Jer. 29. 5. plant g. and eat the fruit of them, 28.
Amos 4. 9. I sent blasting, when your g. increased
9. 14. they shall also make g. and eat fruit of them

GARDENER.

John 20. 15. she supposing he had been the g.

GARRISON, S.

1 Sam. 10. 5. to hill where is g. of the Philistines
13. 3. Jonathan smote the g. of the Philistines
14. 1. let us go over to the Philistines' g. 6.
15. the g. and the spoilers, they also trembled
2 Sam. 8. 6. David put g. in Syria, 1 Chron. 18. 6.
14. David put g. in Edom, 1 Chron. 18. 13.
23. 14. g. of Philist. in Beth-lehem, 1 Chron. 11. 16.
2 Chr. 17. 2. Jehoshap. set g. in Judah and Ephraim
Ezek. 26. 11. thy strong g. shall go down to ground
2 Cor. 11. 32. the governor kept the city with a g.

GARLANDS.

Acts 14. 13. the priest of Jupiter brought oxen and g.

GARLICK.

Num. 11. 5. we remember the g. we did eat in Egypt

GARMENT

Is *that wherewith one is clothed.* Mat. 27. 35. They parted my garments. *By the* wedding-garment *is meant* Christ *with his perfect righteousness imputed, which as a garment doth hide the spiritual nakedness, and decks and adorns the soul with spiritual beauty.* Mat. 22. 11. *Some by* wedding-garment *understand the grace of sanctification, or a holy life, answerable to one's profession; in which sense* garment *is taken in* Rev. 3. 4. Thou hast a few

names in Sardis which have not defiled their garments; *who are of unblameable lives.* He was clothed with a garment down to his foot, Rev. 1. 13. *Some are of opinion that this denoted the purity and innocency of that priesthood, which* Christ *did exercise for his church: Others, that it denoted the dignity and majesty of* Christ, *as King of his church: it being usual for kings to wear long robes in token of majesty.* Garments rolled or dyed in blood, Isa. 9. 5. | 63. 2. *are garments sprinkled and stained with the blood of the slain, such as warriors wear, which have overcome their enemies in battle.*
Gen. 9. 23. Shem and Japhet took a g. and laid it
25. 25. the first came out red, like a hairy g.
39. 12. she caught Joseph by his g. he left his g.
15. he left his g. with me and fled out, 18.
39. 16. she laid up his g. till her lord came home
Lev. 6. 27. sprinkled of the blood thereof on any g.
13. 47. g. wherein is the plague of leprosy, 49.
51. if plague be spread in the g. in warp or woof
59. the law of the plague of leprosy in a g. 14. 55.
15. 17. every g. whereon is the seed of copulation
19. 19. nor g. mingled come on thee, Deut. 22. 11.
Deut. 22. 5. a man shall not put on a woman's g.
Josh. 7. 21. when I saw a goodly Babylonish g.
24. Joshua took Achan, the silver, and the g.
Judg. 8. 25. they spread a g. and cast ear-rings
2 Sam. 13. 18. Tamar had a g. of divers colours on her
19. she rent her g. and went on crying
1 Kings 11. 29. Jeroboam clad himself with a new g.
2 Kings 4. †42. brought him ears of corn in his g.
9. 13. took every man his g. and put under him
Ezra 9. 3. when I heard this I rent my g. and mantle
5. having rent my g. and mantle I fell on knees
Esth. 8. 15. Mordecai went with a g. of purple
Job 13. 28. consumeth, as a g. that is moth-eaten
30. 18. by force of my disease is my g. changed
38. 9. when I made the cloud the g. thereof
14. it is turned as clay to the seal, they stand as a g.
41. 13. who can discover the face of his g.?
Psal. 69. 11. I made sackcloth also my g.
73. 6. pride compasseth, violence cover. them as g.
102. 26. they shall perish, yea, all of them shall wax old like a g. Isa. 50. 9. | 51. 6. Heb. 1. 11.
104. 2. thou coverest thyself with light, as with a g.
6. thou coveredst it with the deep as with a g.
109. 18. he clothed himself with cursing as a g.
19. let it be to him as the g. which covereth him
Prov. 20. 16. take his g. that is surety, 27. 13.
25. 20. as he that taketh away a g. in cold weather
30. 4. who hath bound the waters in a g.?
Isa. 51. 8. the moth shall eat them up like a g.
61. 3. to give g. of praise for the spirit of heaviness
Jer. 43. 12. as a shepherd putteth on his g.
Ezek. 18. 7. hath covered the naked with a g. 16.
Dan. 7. 9. whose g. was white as snow
Mic. 2. 8. ye pull off the robe with the g. from them
Hag. 2. 12. if one bear holy flesh in the skirt of his g.
Zech. 13. 4. neither shall wear a rough g. to deceive
Mal. 2. 16. for one covereth violence with his g.
Mat. 9. 16. new cloth to old g. Mark 2. 21. Luke 5. 36.
20. behold, a woman diseased touched the hem of his g. 21. | 14. 36. Mark 5. 27. Luke 8. 44.
22. 11. I saw a man who had not on a wedding g. 12.
Mark 13. 16. not turn back again to take up his g.
16. 5. a young man clothed with a long white g.
Luke 22. 36. let him sell his g. and buy one
Acts 12. 8. cast thy g. about thee and follow me
Jude 23. hating even the g. spotted by the flesh
Rev. 1. 13. Son of man clothed with a g. down to foot

GARMENTS.

Gen. 35. 2. and be clean, and change your g.
38. 14. Tamar put her widow's g. off from her
49. 11. washed his g. in wine, his clothes in grapes
Exod. 28. 3. may make Aaron's g. to consecrate him
29. 21. sprinkled the blood on Aaron's g. Lev. 8. 30.
31. 10. I have given them wisdom to make g.
Lev. 6. 11. put off his g. put on other g. 16. 23, 24.
Num. 15. 38. make fringes in the borders of their g.
20. 26. strip Aaron of his g. put them on Eleazar
28. Moses stript Aaron of g. put them on Eleazar
Josh. 9. 5. Gibeonites brought old g. mouldy bread
Judg. 14. 12. I will give you thirty change of g.
17. †10. I will give thee ten shekels and order of g.
1 Sam. 18. 4. Jonathan gave David his g.
2 Sam. 10. 4. cut off their g. in the middle, 1 Chr. 19. 4.
13. 31. David tare his g. and lay on the earth
2 Kings 5. 26. is it a time to receive money and g.?
7. 15. all the way was full of g. and vessels
22. †14. Huldah, wife of Shallum, keeper of g.
25. 29. he changed Jehoiakim's g. Jer. 52. 33.
Ezra 2. 69. they gave one hundred priests' g.
Neh. 7. 70. the Tirshatha gave 530 priests' g.
72. the people gave sixty-seven priests' g.
Job 37. 17. how thy g. are warm, when he quieteth
Psal. 22. 18. they part my g. among them, cast lots
45. 8. all thy g. smell of myrrh, aloes, and cassia
133. 2. ointment that went down to skirts of his g.
Prov. 31. †21. her household clothed with double g.
Eccl. 9. 8. let thy g. be always white, and thy head
Cant. 4. 11. smell of thy g. is like smell of Lebanon
Isa. 9. 5. every battle is with g. rolled in blood
52. 1. put on thy beautiful g. O Jerusalem
59. 6. their webs shall not become g.
17. he put on the g. of vengeance for clothing
61. 10. he hath clothed me with the g. of salvation
63. 1. that cometh with dyed g. from Bozrah?
3. their blood shall be sprinkled upon my g.
Jer. 36. 24. yet they were not afraid, nor rent g.
Lam. 4. 14. so that men could not touch their g.
Ezek. 16. 18. tookest thy broid. g. and coveredst them
42. 14. there shall lay their g. they ministered in
44. 19. they shall not sanctify people with their g.
Dan. 3. 21. were bound in their coats and other g.
Joel 2. 13. rend your heart, and not your g.
Zech. 3. 3. Joshua was clothed with filthy g.
4. saying, take away the filthy g. from him
Mat. 21. 8. spread their g. in the way, Mark 11. 8.
23. 5. they enlarge the borders of their g.
27. 35. they parted his g. casting lots, Mark 15. 24.
Mark 10. 50. Bartimeus casting away his g. arose
Mark 11. 7. they cast their g. on the colt, Luke 19. 35.
Luke 24. 4. two men stood by them in shining g.
John 13. 4. he laid aside his g. and took a towel
Acts 9. 39. shewing coats and g. which Dorcas made
Jam. 5. 2. and your g. are moth-eaten
Rev. 3. 4. few names which have not defiled their g.
16. 15. blessed that watcheth and keepeth his g.

Holy GARMENTS.

Exod. 28. 2. thou shalt make *holy* g. for Aaron, 4.
31. 10. I have put wisdom to make *holy* g.
Lev. 16. 4. these are *holy* g. he shall wash, 32.
Ezek. 42. 14. lay their *holy* g. wherein they minister

GARNER.

Mat. 3. 12. gather his wheat into the g. Luke 3. 17.

GARNERS.

Psal. 144. 13. our g. may be full, affording store
Joel 1. 17. the g. are laid desolate, barns broken down

GARNISH, ED.

2 Chron. 3. 6. he g. the house with precious stones
Job 26. 13. by his Spirit he hath g. the heavens
Mat. 12. 44. findeth it swept and g. Luke 11. 25.
23. 29. you g. the sepulchres of the righteous
Rev. 21. 19. the foundations of the wall are g.

GAT.

Exod. 24. 18. Moses g. him up into the mount
Num. 16. 27. they g. up from tabernacle of Korah
Judg. 9. 51. and g. them up to the top of the tower
2 Sam. 8. 13. and David g. him a name
1 Kings 1. 1. they covered him, but he g. no heat
Psal. 116. 3. the pains of hell g. hold on me
Eccl. 2. 8. I g. men-singers, and women-singers
Lam. 5. 9. we g. our bread with the peril of our lives

GATE

Is *the entrance into a house or city.* Judg. 16. 3. Samson took the doors of the gate of the city. *The word gate is often used in scripture to denote the place of public assemblies, where justice was administered. One particular form of these judgments is to be seen in that, which was given at the gate of* Beth-lehem, *between* Boaz *and another person, a relation of* Naomi's *upon the subject of* Ruth's *marriage, who was a* Moabitess, Ruth 4. 1. *And in* Abraham's *purchase of a field to bury* Sarah, Gen. 23. 10, 18. Jerom *says, that as the* Jews *were for the most part employed in labouring in the field, it was wisely provided, that assemblies should be held at the city gates, and justice administered there in a summary manner, that those laborious men, who were busy at their work, might lose no time, and that the country people who had affairs upon their hands in the town, might not be obliged to enter and spend time there.*

The word gate is likewise sometimes put to signify power or dominion. God *promises* Abraham, *that his posterity* should possess the gates of their enemies, *their towns, their fortresses,* Gen. 22. 17. *They should conquer them, they should have dominion over them.* The gates of hell shall not prevail against the church, Mat. 16. 18. *that is, neither the power nor policy of the devil and his instruments. For the gates of cities were the places both of jurisdiction or judicature, and of fortification and chief strength in war,* Judg. 5. 8. Psal. 147. 13. The gates of brass, *are the strongest helps and defences.* Psal. 107. 16. He hath broken the gates of brass; *he restored them to liberty, in spite of all impediments and oppositions.* The strait gate *signifies regeneration and conversion, and true holiness in heart and life, which prepares the soul for heaven.* Mat. 7. 13. Enter ye in at the strait gate.

The gates of death *are the brink, or mouth of the grave.* Psal. 9. 13. Thou that liftest me up from the gates of death, *that preservedst me when I was, as it were, dropping into the grave. And king* Hezekiah, *having received a message of death, represents in his hymn the condition he had been in when he was sick, and expresses himself thus:* I said, I shall go to the gates of the grave; *I perceive I must die, without any hopes of prevention,* Isa. 38. 10. *The* Hebrews *looked upon death or the grave, as a place, whither people came from all parts of the world, there to enter upon another life.* The gates of righteousness, Psal. 118. 19. *are those of the Lord's tabernacle, where the righteous, the saints, the priests of the Lord, the true* Israelites, *paid their vows and praises to the Lord; where none were to enter but purified* Israelites, *a nation of righteous men.* The gates or everlasting doors *mentioned in* Psal. 24. 7, 9. *are either the gates of the temple, which by faith and the spirit of prophecy* David *beheld as already built; these gates he bids lift up their heads, to receive the glorious King* Jehovah, *who dwelt in the temple, and between the cherubim: or the passage may admit of a mystical sense; for as the temple was a type of* Christ, *and of his church, and of heaven itself; so this place may also contain a representation, either of* Christ's *entrance into his church, or into the hearts of his faithful people, who are here commanded to set open their hearts and souls for his reception: or, it may represent his ascension into heaven, where the saints or angels are poetically introduced as preparing the way, and opening the heavenly gates to receive their Lord and King, returning to his royal habitation with triumph and glory.*

Gen. 22. 17. thy seed possess the g. of enemies, 24. 60.
28. 17. Jacob said, this is the g. of heaven
Exod. 32. 27. go in and out from g. to g. thro' camp
Deut. 21. 19. his father shall bring him to the g.
22. 24. bring them both out to the g. of the city
25. 7. let his brother's wife go up to the g.
Josh. 2. 7. they were gone out, they shut the g.
Judg. 16. 3. Samson took the doors of the g.
Ruth 4. 1. then went Boaz to the g. and sat down
10. the name of the dead be not cut off from the g.
1 Sam. 4. 18. Eli fell backward by the side of the g.
2 Sam. 15. 2. Absalom stood beside the way of the g.
18. 33. the king went up to the chamber over the g.
2 Sam. 23. 15. water of Beth-leh. by g. 16. 1 Chr. 11. 18.
1 Kings 17. 10. when Elijah came to the g. of the city
2 Kings 7. 17. a lord to have the charge of the g.
1 Chron. 26. 13. and they cast lots for every g.
2 Chron. 8. 14. he appointed the porters at every g.
Neh. 13. 19. I commanded the g. should be shut
Esth. 4. 2. Mordecai came before the king's g. 6. 12.
Job 29. 7. when I went out to the g. and prepared
Psal. 118. 20. this g. of the Lord, the righteous enter
Cant. 7. 4. thine eyes like the fish-pools by the g.
Isa. 14. 31. howl, O g. cry, O city, shall come smoke
24. 12. the g. is smitten with destruction
28. 6. to them that turn the battle to the g.
Jer. 36. 10. Baruch read at the entry of new g.
Lam. 5. 14. the elders have ceased from the g.
Ezek. 8. 3. brought me to the door of the inner g.
11. 1. at the door of the g. twenty-five men
43. 4. the glory of the Lord came by way of the g.
44. 2. this g. shall be shut, none shall enter
3. prince shall enter by the way of the g. 46. 2, 8.
45. 19. put the blood on the posts of the g.
46. 1. the g. of the inner court shall be shut
2. but the g. shall not be shut till evening
12. one shall open him the g. one shall shut the g.
48. 31. one g. of Reuben, one g. of Judah, of Levi
Obad. 13. not entered into the g. of my people
Mic. 1. 9. he is come into the g. of my people to Jer.
12. evil came down from Lord to the g. of Jerus.
2. 13. they have passed through the g.
Mat. 7. 13. enter in at the strait g. wide is the g. and broad is the way, 14. Luke 13. 24.
Luke 7. 12. when he came nigh the g. of the city
16. 20. a beggar Lazarus laid at his g. full of sores
Acts 10. 17. men from Cornelius stood before the g.
12. 10. they came to the iron g. which opened
14. Rhoda opened not the g. for gladness
Heb. 13. 12. Jesus also suffered without the g.
Rev. 21. 21. every several g. was of one pearl
See Entering, Entereth.

GATE.

Prov. 17. 19. that exalteth his g. seeketh destruction

At the GATE.

Gen. 23. 10. of all that went in *at the* g. of city, 18.
2 Kings 9. 31. as Jehu entered in *at the* g. she said
11. 6. a third part shall be *at the* g. of Sur, and a third *at the* g. behind the guard, 2 Chr. 23. 5.
23. 8. which were on a man's left hand *at the* g.
2 Chr. 24. 8. set a chest *at the* g. of the house of Lord
Esth. 5. 13. I see Mordecai sitting *at the* king's g.
Isa. 22. 7. horsemen set themselves in array *at the* g.
Acts 3. 2. they laid daily *at the* g. of the temple
10. who sat for alms *at* beautiful g. of the temple
See Fish-gate.

High GATE.

2 Chron. 23. 20. they came through the *high* g.
27. 3. Jotham built the *high* g. of the house
Jer. 20. 2. put Jeremiah in the stocks in the *high* g.
See Horse-gate.

In the GATE.

Gen. 19. 1. and Lot sat *in the* g. of Sodom
Exod. 32. 26. Moses stood *in the* g. of the camp
Deut. 22. 15. bring tokens of virginity to elders *in* g.
Judg. 16. 2. they laid wait for Samson *in the* g.
Ruth 4. 11. people *in the* g. said, we are witnesses
1 Sam. 9. 18. Saul drew near to Samuel *in the* g.
2 Sam. 3. 27. Joab took Abner aside *in the* g.
19. 8. king sat *in the* g. they told all the people
2 Kings 7. 1. two measures for a shekel *in the* g. 18.
20. the people trod on him *in the* g. and he died
Esth. 2. 19. Mordecai sat *in the* king's g. 21.
5. 9. when Haman saw him *in the* king's g.
Job 5. 4. his children are crushed *in the* g.
31. 21. when I saw my help *in the* g.
Psal. 69. 12. they that sit *in the* g. speak against me
127. 5. but they shall speak with the enemies *in* g.
Prov. 22. 22. nor oppress the afflicted *in the* g.
24. 7. he openeth not his mouth *in the* g.
Isa. 29. 21. lay a snare for him that reproveth *in* g.
Jer. 7. 2. stand *in the* g. of the Lord's house
17. 19. stand *in the* g. of the children of the people
37. 13. when he was *in the* g. of Benjamin
38. 7. the king then sitting *in the* g. of Benjamin
39. 3. all the princes of Babylon sat *in the* g.
Dan. 2. 49. but Daniel sat *in the* g. of the king
Amos 5. 10. they hate him that rebuketh *in the* g.
12. they turn aside the poor *in the* g.
15. hate evil, and establish judgment *in the* g.

Old GATE.

Neh. 3. 6. the *old* g. repaired Jehoiada son of Paseah
12. 39. the priests went above the *old* g. and fish-gate

Prison-GATE.

Neh. 12. 39. and they stood still in the *prison*-g.

Sheep-GATE.

Neh. 12. 39. they went even unto the *sheep*-g.
John 5. †2. by the *sheep*-g. there is a pool

Valley-GATE.

2 Chron. 26. 9. Uzziah built towers at the *valley*-g.
Neh. 2. 13. and I went out by the g. of the *valley*
15. and I entered by the g. of the *valley*
3. 13. the *valley* g. repaired Hanun

Water-GATE.

Neh. 3. 26. Nethinims dwelt over against *water*-g.
8. 1. gathered into the street before the *water*-g.
3. he read in the law before the *water*-g.
16. made booths in the street of the *water*-g.
12. 37. priests went even to the *water*-g. eastward

GATES.

Deut. 12. 12. rejoice, ye and Levite, within your g.
Josh. 6. 26. in his youngest son set up g. 1 Kings 16. 34.
Judg. 5. 8. chose new gods, then was war in the g.
5. 11. the people of the Lord shall go to the g.
2 Chron. 31. 2. Hezekiah appointed to praise in the g.
Neh. 1. 3. the g. are burnt with fire, 2. 3, 13, 17.
7. 3. let not the g. of Jerusalem be opened
12. 30. the priests and Levites purified the g.
13. 19. some of my servants set I at the g.
22. I commanded the Levites to keep the g.
Psal. 9. 14. may shew forth thy praise in the g.
24. 7. lift up your heads, O ye g. and be ye lift up, 9.
87. 2. the Lord loveth the g. of Zion, more than
100. 4. enter into his g. with thanksgiving
107. 16. for he hath broken the g. of brass

Psal. 118. 19. open to me the g. of righteousness
Prov. 1. 21. wisdom crieth in the openings of g. 8. 3.
8. 34. that heareth me, watching daily at my g.
14. 19. the wicked at the g. of the righteous
31. 23. her husband is known in the g.
31. let her own works praise her in the g.
Cant. 7. 13. at our g. are all manner of pleasant fruits
Isa. 3. 26. and her g. shall lament and mourn
13. 2. they may go into the g. of the nobles
26. 2. open ye the g. that the righteous may enter
38. 10. I shall go to the g. of the grave
45. 1. to open before him the two-leaved g.
2. I will break in pieces the g. of brass
62. 10. go thro' go thro' the g. prepare the way
Jer. 7. 2. hear, ye that enter in at the g. 17. 20. | 22. 2.
14. 2. Judah mourneth, and the g. languish
15. 7. I will fan them with a fan in g. of the land
17. 19. go and stand in all the g. of Jerusalem
21. bear no burden on the sabbath by the g. 24.
25. then shall there enter into the g. 22. 4.
27. I will kindle a fire in the g. of Jerusalem
22. 19. shall be drawn and cast forth beyond the g.
Lam. 1. 4. Zion's g. are desolate, her priests sigh
2. 9. her g. are sunk into the ground, bars broken
4. 12. the adversary should have entered the g.
Ezek. 21. 15. I have set point of sword against their g.
22. to appoint battering rams against the g.
26. 2. she is broken that was the g. of the people
48. 32. at the east side three g. one of Joseph
Obad. 11. in the day that foreigners entered his g.
Nah. 2. 6. the g. of the rivers shall be opened
3. 13. the g. of thy land shall be set wide open
Zech. 8. 16. exec. judg. of truth and peace in your g.
Mat. 16. 18. the g. of hell shall not prevail against it
Acts 9. 24. and they watched the g. to kill Paul
14. 13. Jupiter's priests brought oxen to the g.
Rev. 21. 12. the city had twelve g. at g. twelve angels
13. on the east three g. on the north three g.
21. the twelve g. were twelve pearls
25. the g. of it shall not be shut at all by day
See Bars, Death.

Thy GATES.

Exod. 20. 10. thy stranger within thy g. Deut. 5. 14.
Deut. 6. 9. thou shalt write them on thy g. 11. 20.
12. 15. thou mayest eat flesh in thy g. 21.
17. thou mayest not eat within thy g. the tithe
18. thou must eat, thou and Levite in thy g.
14. 21. give it to the stranger that is in thy g.
27. Levite within thy g. thou shalt not forsake
28. thou shalt lay up the tithe within thy g.
29. the widow within thy g. shall come and eat
15. 7. if there be a poor man within any of thy g.
22. thou shalt eat the firstling within thy g.
16. 5. not sacrifice the passover within thy g.
11. shalt rejoice, and Levite in thy g. 14. | 26. 12.
18. judges and officers shalt thou make in all thy g.
17. 5. bring forth that man or woman to thy g.
18. 6. if a Levite come from any of thy g.
23. 16. servant escaped dwell in one of thy g.
24. 14. thou shalt not oppress within thy g.
28. 52. he shall besiege thee in all thy g.
55. thine enemies shall distress thee in all thy g.
31. 12. gather the people within thy g. to hear
Psal. 122. 2. our feet shall stand within thy g. O Jer.
Isa. 54. 12. I will make thy g. of carbuncles
60. 11. therefore thy g. shall be open continually
18. call thy walls salvation, and thy g. praise
Ezek. 26. 10. when he shall enter thy g. as men

GATHER.

Gen. 31. 46. he said, g. stones, and they took stones
41. 35. let them g. all the food of those years
Exod. 5. 7. let them go and g. straw || 12. g. stubble
9. 19. g. thy cattle || 16. 4. shall g. a certain rate
16. 5. g. twice as much || 26. six days g. it
23. 10. six years sow thy land and g. Lev. 25. 3.
Lev. 19. 9. shalt not g. the gleanings, 23. 22.
10. thou shalt not g. every grape of thy vineyard
25. 5. nor g. grapes of the vine undressed, 11.
20. we shall not sow, nor g. in our increase
Num. 10. 4. if with one trumpet, then princes g.
11. 16. g. seventy men of the elders of Israel
19. 9. a man that is clean shall g. the ashes
Deut. 11. 14. I will give rain that thou mayest g.
13. 16. thou shalt g. all the spoil of it into street
28. 30. plant a vineyard and not g. grapes, 39.
38. carry much seed out, and g. but little in
30. 3. he will g. thee from all nations, Ezek. 36. 24.
Josh. 2. † 18. shalt g. thy father and mother home
2 Kings 4. 39. one went into the field to g. herbs
22. 20. I will g. thee to thy fathers, 2 Chr. 34. 28.
1 Chron. 13. 2. send to brethren and Levites to g.
2 Chron. 24. 5. g. money to repair house of the Ld.
Neh. 1. 9. yet will I g. them from thence
12. 44. some appointed to g. for the priests
Job 24. 6. they g. the vintage of the wicked
34. 14. if he g. to himself his spirit and his breath
39. 12. will he bring seed, and g. it into thy barn?
Psal. 26. 9. g. not my soul with sinners, nor life
27. † 10. when Father and mother forsake, L. will g.
39. 6. and knoweth not who shall g. them
104. 28. that thou givest them they g.
106. 47. save us, and g. us from among the heathen
Prov. 28. 8. shall g. for him that will pity the poor
Eccl. 2. 26. to sinner travel to g. and heap up
Cant. 6. 2. my beloved is gone down to g. lilies
Isa. 34. 15. there the owl g. under her shadow
40. 11. he shall g. the lambs with his arms
43. 5. fear not, I will g. thee from the west
52. † 12. the God of Israel will g. you up, 58. † 8.
54. 7. but with great mercies will I g. thee
56. 8. yet will I g. others to him, besides those
62. 10. cast up the high-way, g. out the stones
66. 18. I will g. all nations and tongues
Jer. 6. 1. g. to flee || 7. 18. the children g. wood
9. 22. none shall g. them || 10. 17. g. up thy wares
23. 3. I will g. the remnant of my flock
29. 14. I will g. you from all the nations
31. 8. I will g. them from the coasts of the earth,
32. 37. Ezek. 20. 34, 41. | 34. 13.
10. he that scattered Israel will g. him
40. 10. g. ye wine, and summer-fruits, and oil
47. † 6. O sword, g. thyself into thy scabbard

Jer. 49. 5. and none shall g. up him that wandereth
Ezek. 11. 17. I will even g. you from the people
16. 37. I will g. all thy lovers against thee
22. 19. I will g. you into the midst of Jerusalem
20. as they g. silver, so will I g. you in fury, 21.
24. 4. g. the pieces || 29. 13. I will g. the Egyptians
37. 21. I will g. them on every side, 39. 17.
Hos. 8. 10. though hired among the nations, I will g.
9. 6. Egypt shall g. them up, Memphis bury them
Joel 1. 14. g. the elders and the inhabitants of land
2. 6. people much pained, all faces shall g. blackn.
16. g. the people, g. the children that suck
3. 2. I will g. all nations, and bring them down
Mic. 2. 12. I will surely g. the remnant of Israel
4. 6. I will g. her that was driven out, Zeph. 3. 19.
12. he shall g. them as sheaves into the floor
5. 1. g. thyself in troops, O daughter of troops
Nah. 2. 10. the faces of them all g. blackness
Hab. 1. 9. they shall g. the captivity as the sand
15. they catch them, and g. them in their drag
Zeph. 3. 8. for my determination is to g. the nations
18. I will g. them that are sorrowful for assembly
20. bring you even in the time that I g. you
Zech. 10. 8. I will hiss for them and g. them
10. and I will g. them out of Assyria
14. 2. I will g. all nations against Jerusalem
Mat. 3. 12. g. his wheat into his garner, Luke 3. 17.
6. 26. they sow not, nor do they g. into barns
7. 16. do men g. grapes of thorns? Luke 6. 44.
13. 28. wilt thou that we go and g. them up?
29. he said, nay, lest while ye g. up the tares
30. burn tares, but g. the wheat into my barn
41. shall g. out of his kingd. all things that offend
25. 26. and that I g. where I have not strawed
Luke 13. 34. as a hen doth g. her brood under wings
John 6. 12. g. up the fragments that remain
15. 6. men g. them and cast them into the fire
Rev. 14. 18. g. the clusters of the vine of the earth
16. 14. g. them to the battle of that day of God

GATHER together.

Gen. 34. 30. I being few they shall g. tog. ag. me
49. 1. g. yourselves together, ye sons of Jacob, 2.
Exod. 3. 16. go g. the elders of Israel together
Lev. 8. 3. g. congregation of Israel tog. Num. 8. 9.
Num. 20. 8. and g. thou the assembly together
21. 16. g. the people together, Deut. 4. 10. | 31. 12.
2 Sam. 12. 28. g. the rest together and encamp
1 Chron. 16. 35. save us, O God, and g. us together
22. 2. David commanded to g. tog. the strangers
Neh. 7. 5. God put in my heart to g. together nobles
Esth. 2. 3. may g. together all the fair virgins
4. 16. g. together the Jews present in Shushan
Job 11. 10. if he g. together, who can hinder him?
Psal. 50. 5. g. my saints together unto me
56. 6. they g. themselves tog. to mark my steps
94. 21. they g. together against the righteous
104. 22. the sun ariseth, they g. themselves tog.
Eccl. 3. 5. there is a time to g. stones together
Isa. 11. 12. he shall g. tog. the dispersed of Judah
49. 18. these g. together and come to me, 60. 4.
54. 15. they shall surely g. together, but not by me
Jer. 4. 5. blow the trumpet, cry, g. together
49. 14. g. ye together and come against Edom
Dan. 3. 2. the king sent to g. together the princes
Joel 3. 11. g. yourselves together round about
Zeph. 2. 1. g. tog. yea, g. tog. O nation not desired
Mat. 13. 30. g. together first the tares, and bind
24. 31. they shall g. together his elect, Mark 13. 27.
John 11. 52. he should g. together in one, Eph. 1. 10.
Rev. 19. 17. g. tog. to the supper of the great God
20. 8. to g. Gog and Magog together to battle

GATHERED.

Gen. 25. 8. Abraham died and was g. to his people
17. Ishmael was g. || 35. 29. Isaac was g. to people
49. 29. Jacob was g. to his people, 33.
Exod. 16. 17. and they g. some more, some less
18. he that g. much, he that g. little, 2 Cor. 8. 15.
21. they g. it every morning, every man according
23. 16. when thou hast g. in thy labours out of field
Lev. 23. 39. when ye have g. in the fruits of the land
Num. 11. 32. the people g. quails || 15. 32. g. sticks
16. 19. Korah g. congregation against Moses, 42.
20. 24. Aaron shall be g. to his people, 26.
27. 13. Moses g. to his people, 31. 2. Deut. 32. 50.
Judg. 1. 7. kings g. their meat under my table
2. 10. that generation was g. to their fathers
6. 34. and Abiezer was g. after him
11. 3. there were g. vain men to Jephthah
1 Sam. 5. 8. they g. all the lords of the Philistines
22. 2. every one that was in distress g. to David
2 Sam. 14. 14. as water spilt which cannot be g. up
2 Kings 3. 21. they g. all able to put on armour
22. 20. Josiah be g. to grave in peace, 2 Chr. 34. 28.
Neh. 5. 16. all my servants were g. to the work
Job 27. 19. rich man lie down, but shall not be g.
Psal. 59. 3. the mighty are g. against me
107. 3. and he g. them out of the lands
Prov. 27. 25. and herbs of the mountains are g.
30. 4. who hath g. the wind in his fists?
Eccl. 2. 8. I g. me also silver and gold and treasure
Cant. 5. 1. I have g. my myrrh with my spice
Isa. 5. 2. he fenced it, and g. out the stones
10. 14. as one gathereth eggs, have I g. the earth
27. 12. ye shall be g. one by one, O Israel
34. 15. vultures be g. || 16. his Spirit g. them
49. 5. tho' Israel be not g. yet shall I be glorious
56. 8. I will gather others, besides those that are g.
62. 9. but they that have g. it shall eat it
Jer. 3. 17. and all nations shall be g. unto it
8. 2. they shall not be g. nor buried, 25. 33.
26. 9. all people g. against Jeremiah in house of L.
40. 15. all the Jews g. to thee should be scattered
Ezek. 28. 25. when I shall have g. the house of Israel
29. 5. thou shalt not be brought together nor g.
38. 13. hast thou g. thy company to take a prey?
39. 27. have g. them out of their enemies' lands
28. but I have g. them to their own land
Hos. 10. 10. the people shall be g. against them
Mic. 7. 1. I am as when they g. the summer-fruits
Mat. 13. 40. as tares are g. and burnt in the fire
47. a net cast into the sea, and g. of every kind
25. 32. before him shall be g. all nations

Mat. 27. 27. and g. to him the whole band of soldiers
John 11. 47. then g. chief priests a council, and said
Acts 17. 5. g. a company, set the city on an uproar
28. 3. when Paul had g. a bundle of sticks
Rev. 14. 19. the angel g. the vine of the earth

GATHERED together.

Exod. 8. 14. they g. them together upon heaps
Num. 10. 7. when the congregation is to be g. together
11. 22. shall all the fish of the sea be g. together?
Judg. 20. 1. the congregation was g. together as one man, 11. Ezra 3. 1. Neh. 8. 1.
2 Chron. 20. 4. Judah g. together to ask help of Ld.
Job 16. 10. they g. themselves together against me
30. 7. under the nettles were they g. together
Psal. 35. 15. the abjects g. themselves together ag. me
47. 9. the princes of the people are g. together
102. 22. when people are g. together to serve the L.
140. 2. continually are they g. together for war
Prov. 30. † 27. locusts go forth all g. together
Hos. 1. 11. then shall children of Judah be g. together
Mic. 4. 11. many nations are g. together ag. thee
Zech. 12. 3. tho' all people be g. together against it
Mat. 18. 20. where two or three are g. together
23. 37. how often would I have g. thy children together, as a hen her chickens, Luke 13. 34.
24. 28. there will eagles be g. together, Luke 17. 37.
Mark 1. 33. all the city was g. together at the door
Luke 15. 13. the younger son g. all together
24. 33. they found the eleven g. together
Acts 4. 26. rulers were g. together against the Ld.
12. 12. where many were g. together praying
14. 27. when they had g. the church together
1 Cor. 5. 4. when ye are g. together and my spirit
Rev. 16. 16. g. t. into a place called Armageddon
19. 19. beast and his army g. together to make war

GATHERER, S.

Jer. 6. 9. turn back thy hand as a grape g. into baskets
49. 9. if grape g. come to thee, Obad. 5.
Amos 7. 14. but I was a g. of sycamore-fruit

GATHEREST.

Deut 24. 21. when thou g. the grapes of vineyard

GATHERETH.

Num. 19. 10. that g. the ashes shall wash his clothes
Judg. 19. † 18. there is no man that g. me to house
Psal. 33. 7. he g. the waters of the sea together
41. 6. his heart g. iniquity to itself
147. 2. he g. the outcasts of Israel, Isa. 56. 8.
Prov. 6. 8. the ant g. her food in the harvest
10. 5. he that g. in summer is a wise son
13. 11. but he that g. by labour shall increase
Isa. 10. 14. as one g. eggs that are left
17. 5. it shall be as when the harvest-man g.
Jer. 17. † 11. as the partridge g. young which she hath not brought forth, so he that gets riches
Nah. 3. 18. thy people is scattered, and no man g.
Hab. 2. 5. but g. to him all nations, and heapeth
Mat. 12. 30. he that g. not scattereth, Luke 11. 23.
23. 37. as a hen g. her chickens under her wings
John 4. 36. he that reapeth g. fruit to life eternal

GATHERING.

Gen. 49. 10. to him shall the g. of the people be
Exod. 7. † 19. stretch thy hand on all g. of waters
Lev. 11. † 36. a g. together of waters shall be clean
Num. 15. 33. they that found him g. sticks
1 Kings 17. 10. the widow woman was there g. sticks
2 Chron. 20. 25. they were three days in g. spoils
Isa. 24. † 22. be gathered with the g. of prisoners
32. 10. the vintage shall fail, the g. shall not come
33. 4. your spoil like the g. of the caterpillar
Ezek. 22. † 20. according to the g. of silver, brass
Mat. 25. 24. and g. where thou hast not strawed
Acts 16. 10. assuredly g. the Lord hath called us
2 Thess. 2. 1. and by our g. together unto him

GATHERINGS.

1 Chron. 26. † 15. to Obed-edom the house of g.
Mic. 7. † 1. I am as the g. of summer-fruits
1 Cor. 16. 2. that there be no g. when I come

GAVE.

Gen. 2. 20. Adam g. names to all cattle and to fowl
3. 12. the woman g. me of the tree, and I did eat
14. 20. and he g. him tithes of all, Heb. 7. 2, 4.
25. 5. and Abraham g. all that he had to Isaac
28. 4. the land which God g. to Abraham, 35. 12.
Exod. 11. 3. the Lord g. the people favour, 12. 36.
14. 20. the cloud g. light by night to these
Num. 11. 25. Ld. took of the Spirit, and g. to seventy
Deut. 22. 16. I g. my daughter to this man to wife
Josh. 19. 50. they g. him the city which he asked
21. 43. the Lord g. to Israel all the land
44. the Lord g. them rest, 2 Chron. 15. 15. | 20. 30.
Judg. 6. 9. I drave them out, and g. you their land
Ruth 4. 13. the Lord g. her conception, and she bare
1 Sam. 10. 9. God g. to Saul another heart
2 Sam. 12. 8. and I g. thee thy master's house
1 Kings 4. 29. the Lord g. Solomon wisdom, 5. 12.
2 Kings 13. 5. and the Lord g. Israel a saviour
1 Chron. 25. 5. God g. to Heman fourteen sons
2 Chron. 32. 24. and God g. Hezekiah a sign
Neh. 8. 8. read in book of the law, and g. the sense
Job 1. 21. Lord g. and the Lord hath taken away
42. 10. God g. Job twice as much as he had before
Psal. 18. 13. and the Highest g. his voice
68. 11. the Ld. g. the word, great was the company
69. 21. they g. me also gall, they g. me vinegar
78. 29. for he g. them their own desire, 106. 15.
Eccl. 12. 7. the spirit shall return to God that g. it
Isa. 42. 24. who g. Jacob for a spoil, and Israel
43. 3. I g. Egypt for thy ransom, Seba for thee
50. 6. I g. my back to the smiters, and my cheeks
Jer. 1. † 5. I g. thee a prophet to the nations
Ezek. 16. 19. my meat also which I g. thee
20. 11. I g. them my statutes, and shewed them
12. moreover also, I g. them my sabbaths
25. I g. them also statutes that were not good
Dan. 1. 17. God g. these four children knowledge
6. 10. Daniel prayed and g. thanks before God
Hos. 2. 8. for she did not know that I g. her corn
13. 11. I g. thee a king in mine anger
Amos 2. 12. ye g. the Nazarites wine to drink
Mal. 2. 5. I g. my covenant to Levi of life
Mat. 10. 1. Jesus g. them power against unclean spirits to cast them out, Mark 6. 7. Luke 9. 1

Mat. 14. 19. he brake and *g.* the loaves to his disciples, 15. 36. | 26. 16. *Mark* 6. 41. | 8. 6. | 14. 22. *Luke* 9. 16. | 22. 19.
21. 23. who *g.* thee author.? *Mark* 11. 28. *Luke* 20. 2.
25. 35. ye *g.* me meat, ye *g.* me drink, took me in
42. ye *g.* me no meat, and ye *g.* me no drink
Luke 15. 16. with husks, and no man *g.* unto him
John 1. 12. to them *g.* he power to become sons of G.
3. 16. God so loved world that he *g.* his only Son
6. 31. he *g.* them bread from heaven to eat
10. 29. my Fath. who *g.* them me is greater than all
14. 31. as the Father *g.* me commandment, so I do
Acts 2. 4. to speak as the Spirit *g.* them utterance
7. 5. and he *g.* them no inheritance in it
10. God *g.* Joseph favour and wisdom before Pha.
10. 2. Cornelius *g.* much alms to the people
11. 17. as God *g.* them the like gift as he did to us
12. 23. smote him, because he *g.* not God the glory
13. 21. afterward God *g.* them Saul forty years
14. 17. he did good, and *g.* us rain from heaven
15. 24. to whom we *g.* no such commandment
26. 10. when put to death, I *g.* my voice ag. them
Rom. 2. 28. God *g.* them over to a reprobate mind
1 *Cor.* 3. 5. even as the Lord *g.* to every man
6. Apollos watered, but God *g.* the increase
2 *Cor.* 8. 5. but first *g.* their own selves to the Lord
Gal. 1. 4. who *g.* himself for our sins, *Tit.* 2. 14.
2. 20. who loved me, and *g.* himself for me
3. 18. but God *g.* it to Abraham by promise
Eph. 1. 22. and *g.* him to be head over all things
4. 8. he led captivity captive and *g.* gifts to men
11. and he *g.* some apostles; some prophets
5. 25. Christ loved the church, and *g.* himself for it
1 *Thess.* 4. 2. ye know what commandment we *g.* you
1 *Tim.* 2. 6. who *g.* himself a ransom for all
Heb. 12. 9. who corrected us, we *g.* them reverence
Jam. 5. 18. he prayed, and the heavens *g.* rain
1 *John* 3. 23. love one another, as he *g.* us command.
5. 10. he believeth not the record God *g.* of his Son
Rev. 1. 1. the revelation of Jes. Christ which God *g.*
2. 21. I *g.* her space to repent of her fornication
13. 2. the dragon *g.* him his power and his seat, 4.

GAVE *up*.

Gen. 25. 8. Abraham *g. up* the ghost and died
17. Ishmael || 35. 29. and Isaac *g. up* ghost and died
2 *Sam.* 24. 9. Joab *g. up* the sum of the number
2 *Chr.* 30. 7. who *g.* them *up* to desolation, as ye see
Psal. 78. 48. he *g. up* their cattle also to the hail
81. 12. I *g.* them *up* to their own hearts' lust
Lam. 1. 19. my elders *g. up* the ghost in the city
Mark 15. 37. Jesus cried with a loud voice, and *g. up* the ghost, 39. *Luke* 23. 46. *John* 19. 30.
Acts 5. 5. Ananias *g. up* the ghost || 12. 23. Herod
7. 42. God *g.* them *up* to worship the host of heaven
Rom. 1. 24. God also *g.* them *up* to uncleanness
26. for this cause God *g.* them *up* to vile affections
Rev. 20. 13. the sea *g. up* the dead that were in it

GAVEST.

Gen. 3. 12. the woman whom thou *g.* to be with me
1 *Kings* 8. 34. the land which thou *g.* to their fathers, 40, 48. 2 *Chron.* 6. 25, 31, 38. *Neh.* 9. 35.
Neh. 9. 7. thou *g.* him the name of Abraham
13. thou *g.* them right judgments, true laws
15. *g.* them bread from heaven for their hunger
20. thou *g.* also thy good Spirit, *g.* water for thirst
22. thou *g.* them kingdoms and nations
27. thou *g.* them saviours who saved them
Job 39. 13. *g.* thou the goodly wings to the peacocks?
Psal. 21. 4. he asked life of thee; thou *g.* it him
74. 14. thou *g.* him to be meat to the people
Luke 7. 44. thou *g.* me no water for my feet
45. thou *g.* me no kiss, but this woman not ceased
15. 29. yet thou never *g.* me a kid, to make merry
John 17. 4. I have finished work thou *g.* me to do
6. manifested to the men whom thou *g.* me out of the world, thine they were, and thou *g.* them me
8. I have given them the words which thou *g.* me
12. those that thou *g.* me I have kept, none lost
22. the glory which thou *g.* me, I have given
18. 9. of them whom thou *g.* me have I lost none

GAY.

Jam. 2. 3. respect to him that weareth *g.* clothing

GAZE.

Exod. 19. 21. lest they break thro' to the Lord to *g.*

GAZING.

Nah. 3. 6. and I will set thee as a *g.* stock
Acts 1. 11. why stand ye *g.* up into heaven?
Heb. 10. 33. partly whilst ye were made a *g.* stock

GENDER.

Lev. 19. 19. shalt not let cattle *g.* with diverse kinds
2 *Tim.* 2. 23. knowing that they do *g.* strifes

GENDERED, ETH.

Job 21. 10. their bull *g.* and faileth not
38. 29. the hoary frost of heaven, who hath *g.* it?
Gal. 4. 24. from mount Sinai, which *g.* to bondage

GENEALOGY

Comes from the Greek *word* Genealogia, *which signifies a list of our ancestors, a description of the stock, lineage, or pedigree of any person or family. The common* Hebrew *expression for it is* Sepher toledoth, Liber generationis. *The* Hebrews *were very careful in preserving their* genealogies; *and perhaps there never was any nation more circumspect in this point than that of the* Jews. *At this day we find* genealogies *in their sacred writings, carried on for above three thousand five hundred years; and in the Evangelists we have the* genealogy *of* Jesus Christ *deduced for four thousand years, from* Adam *to* Joseph *or* Mary, *Luke* 3. 23, &c. *The* Jews *were very exact in their* genealogies, *partly from their own choice and interest, that they might preserve the distinctions of the several tribes and families, which was necessary both to make out their claims or titles to offices or inheritances which might belong to them by death, or otherwise; and to govern themselves thereby in the matter of marriages, and some other things, wherein the practice of some laws required the knowledge of these things. It is observed in* Ezra 2. 62. *that such priests as were not able to produce an exact* genealogy *of their families, were not permitted to exercise their functions: This their exactness was likewise ordered by the special providence of God, that so it might be certainly known of what tribe and family the* Messiah *was born.*

Josephus *says, that they had in his nation an uninterrupted succession of priests for two thousand years. He adds, that the priests were particularly careful to preserve their* genealogies, *and that not only in* Judea, *but also in* Babylon *and* Egypt: *and wherever they were, they never married below themselves, and had exact genealogical tables prepared from those authentic monuments which were kept at* Jerusalem, *and to which they had recourse upon occasion: that in all their wars, persecutions, and public calamities, they always were particularly diligent in securing those monuments, and to renew them from time to time.*

Notwithstanding, since the war which the Romans *carried on against the* Jews, *about thirty years after the death of our Saviour, and since their entire dispersion in the reign of* Adrian, *the* Jews *have lost their ancient* genealogies; *and perhaps there is not one of those who say they are of the sacerdotal race, that is able to produce any authentic proofs of his* genealogy. Jerom *says, that the* Jews *are so versed in the reading of their books, and know so perfectly the* genealogies, *which are there set forth, that they can repeat all the names from* Abraham *to* Zerubbabel, *as easily as they can pronounce their own.* St. Paul *seems to condemn the affectation of knowing old* genealogies: *he looks upon them to be useless and vain, as in reality they are, when they serve only for ostentation, and not for edification: This study was of great use before the* Messiah *came, that it might be known distinctly of what tribe and family he was born; but he being come, this study is vain, though still the* Jews *are addicted to it.*

The genealogies *set down by* Ezra *and* Nehemiah, *in some particulars vary: The reason whereof is assigned by* Dr. Prideaux *in these terms.* "*For the true settling of these* genealogies," *says he,* "*search was made by* Nehemiah *for the old registers, and having among them found the register of the* genealogies *of those who came up at first from* Babylon *with* Zerubbabel *and* Joshua; *he settled this matter according to it, adding such as afterwards came up, and expunging others, whose families were extinguished: and this hath caused the difference that is between the accounts which we have of these* genealogies *in* Ezra *and* Nehemiah. *For in the second chapter of* Ezra, *we have the old register made by* Zerubbabel; *and in the seventh of* Nehemiah, *from the sixth verse, we have a copy of it as settled by* Nehemiah, *with the alterations that are now mentioned.*" Prideaux's Connection, Part I. Book VI.

1 *Chron.* 5. 1. and the *g.* is not to be reckoned after the birth-right
Ezra 2. 62. these sought their *g.* *Neh.* 7. 64.
8. 1. this is the *g.* of them that went up with me
Neh. 7. 5. I found a register of the *g.* which came up

GENEALOGIES.

1 *Chron.* 9. 1. so all Israel were reckoned by *g.*
2 *Chr.* 12. 15. the book of Shemaiah concerning *g.*
31. 19. to give portions to all reckoned by *g.*
1 *Tim.* 1. 4. give no heed to fables and endless *g.*
Tit. 3. 9. avoid foolish questions, *g.* and contentions

GENERAL.

1 *Chron.* 27. 34. the *g.* of the king's army was Joab
Heb. 12. 23. to *g.* assembly and church of first-born

GENERALLY.

2 *Sam.* 17. 11. I counsel that Israel be *g.* gathered
Jer. 48. 38. be lamentation *g.* on house-tops of Moab

GENERATION.

This word is used for the history and genealogy of any man. For example: This is the book of the generations of *Adam*, Gen. 5. 1. *This is the history of* Adam's *creation, and that of his posterity.* These are the generations of the heavens and of the earth, *Gen.* 2. 4. *This is a recital of the creation of heaven and earth. And in* Mat. 1. 1. The book of the generation of *Jesus Christ*, the Son of *David*. *This is the genealogy of* Jesus Christ, *and the history of his life, death, and resurrection. It is likewise taken for persons or people who live in some one age.* Heb. 3. 10. I was grieved with that generation; *with those men that came out of* Egypt, *and rebelled against me in the wilderness.* Mat. 24. 34. This generation shall not pass, till all these things be fulfilled. *All who are at present living, shall not be dead, when this shall come to pass. There are some at this day living, who shall be witnesses of the evils which I have foretold shall befall the* Jews. The men of this generation, *the men who are now alive, Luke* 11. 31. O faithless and perverse generation! *Luke* 9. 41. *And,* save yourselves from this untoward generation, *from these perverse men.* Acts 2. 40. To generation and generation, *denotes future ages,* Psal. 33. † 11. Who shall declare his generation? *Isa.* 53. 8. *Who can declare or number the* Messiah's *spiritual seed, the number of those who shall believe in him, and be converted to him by the preaching of the gospel?* Generation *is also taken for men of like quality and disposition, though neither of one place nor age.* Psal. 14. 5. God is in the generation of the righteous.

The ancients sometimes computed by generations, *and the Scripture follows frequently this method,* Gen. 15. 16. | 50. 23. In the fourth generation thy descendants shall come hither again. *Joseph* saw *Ephraim's* children of the third generation. *A bastard shall not enter into the congregation* even to his tenth generation, *Deut.* 23. 2. *By some of the ancients a generation was fixed at an hundred years, by others at an hundred and ten, by others at thirty-three, thirty, five-and-twenty, and even at twenty years. So that there was nothing uniform and settled in this matter. Only it is remarked, that the continuance of generations is so much longer, as it comes nearer to the more ancient times.*

Gen. 7. 1. thee have I seen righteous in this *g.*
Exod. 1. 6. Joseph died, and all that *g.*
17. 16. will have war with Amalek from *g.* to *g.*
Num. 32. 13. till that *g.* was consumed, *Deut.* 2. 14.
Deut. 1. 35. not one of this evil *g.* shall see that land
23. 2. a bastard shall not enter even to his tenth *g.*
3. an Ammonite to tenth *g.* shall not enter
8. Edomite and Egypt. in the third *g.* shall enter
29. 22. so that the *g.* to come shall rise up and say
32. 5. they are a perverse and crooked *g.* 20.
† 7. consider the years of *g.* and *g.*
Judg. 2. 10. all that *g.* were gathered to their fathers, and there arose another *g.* after them
Esth. 9. 28. these days shall be rememb. in every *g.*
Psal. 10. † 6. I shall not be moved to *g.* and *g.*
12. 7. thou shalt keep them, O Lord, thou shalt preserve them from this *g.* for ever
14. 5. for God is in the *g.* of the righteous
22. 30. it shall be accounted to the Lord for a *g.*
24. 6. this is the *g.* of them that seek him
48. 13. that ye may tell it to the *g.* following
49. 19. he shall go to the *g.* of his fathers
71. 18. till I have shewed thy strength to this *g.*
73. 15. I should offend ag. the *g.* of thy children
77. † 8. doth his promise fail to *g.* and *g.*?
78. 4. shewing to the *g.* to come the praises of Ld.
6. that the *g.* to come might know them
8. might not be a stubborn and rebellious *g.*
95. 10 forty years grieved with this *g.* *Heb.* 3. 10.
102. 18. this shall be written for the *g.* to come
109. 13. in *g.* following let their name be blotted out
112. 2. the *g.* of the upright shall be blessed
145. 4. one *g.* shall praise thy works to another
Prov. 27. 24. doth the crown endure to every *g.*?
30. 11. there is a *g.* that curseth their father
12. there is a *g.* that are pure in their own eyes
13. a *g.* lofty || 14. a *g.* whose teeth are swords
Eccl. 1. 4. one *g.* passeth away, another *g.* cometh
Isa. 13. 20. not dwelt in from *g.* to *g.* *Jer.* 50. 39.
34. 10. from *g.* to *g.* it shall lie waste
17. from *g.* to *g.* they shall dwell therein
51. 8. but my salvation shall be from *g.* to *g.*
53. 8. who shall declare his *g.*? *Acts* 8. 33.
Jer. 2. 31. O *g.* see ye the word of the Lord
7. 29. the Lord hath rejected the *g.* of his wrath
Lam. 5. 19. thy throne, O L. remains from *g.* to *g.*
Dan. 4. 3. and his dominion is from *g.* to *g.* 34.
Joel 1. 3. and let their children tell another *g.*
3. 20. Jerusalem shall dwell from *g.* to *g.*
Mat. 1. 1. the book of the *g.* of Jesus Christ
3. 7. O *g.* of vipers, 12. 34 | 23. 33. *Luke* 3. 7.
11. 16. whereto shall I liken this *g.* *Luke* 7. 31.
12. 39. an evil and adulterous *g.* seeketh after a sign, 16. 4. *Mark* 8. 12. *Luke* 11. 29
41. shall rise in judgment with this *g.* *Luke* 11. 32.
42. queen of the south rise up with *g.* *Luke* 11. 31.
45. even so shall it be also to this wicked *g.*
17. 17. O perverse *g.* *Mark* 9. 19. *Luke* 9. 41.
23. 36. all these things shall come on this *g.*
24. 34. this *g.* sh ll not pass, *Mark* 13. 30. *Luke* 21. 32.
Mark 8. 38. shall be ashamed of me in this sinful *g.*
Luke 1. 50. his mercy is on them from *g.* to *g.*
11. 30. so shall the Son of man be to this *g.*
50. the blood of the prophets required of this *g.* 51.
16. 8. children of this world in their *g.* are wiser
17. 25. the Son of man must be rejected of this *g.*
Acts 2. 40. save you from this untoward *g.*
13. 36. David, after he had served his own *g.*
1 *Pet.* 2. 9. ye are a chosen *g.* a royal priesthood
See FOURTH.

GENERATIONS.

Gen. 2. 4. these are the *g.* of the heavens and earth
5. 1. the *g.* of Adam || 6. 9. the *g.* of Noah, 10. 1.
6. 9. Noah was a just man, and perfect in his *g.*
9. 12. of the covenant I make for perpetual *g.*
11. 10. these are the *g.* of Shem || 27. *g.* of Terah
17. 7. covenant between me and thy seed in their *g.*
9. thou and thy seed after thee in their *g.*
12. every man-child in your *g.* must be circumcised
25. 12. these are the *g.* of Ishmael, 13. 1 *Chr.* 1. 29.
19. these are the *g.* of Isaac || 36. 1. the *g.* of Esau, 9.
37. 2. these are the *g.* of Jacob, Joseph 17 years old
Exod. 3. 15. and this is my memorial unto all *g.*
6. 16. the sons of Levi according to their *g.* 19.
12. 14. a feast to the Lord throughout your *g.*
17. ye shall observe this day in your *g.*
42. a night to be much observed by Isr. in their *g.*
16. 32. fill an homer to be kept for your *g.* 33.
27. 21. it shall be a statute for ever to their *g.* 30. 21. *Lev.* 3. 17. | 6. 18. | 7. 36. | 10. 9. | 17. 7. | 23, 14, 21, 31, 41.
29. 42. a contin. burnt-offering throughout your *g.*
30. 8. burn incense || 31. oil throughout your *g.*
31. 13. my sabbaths a sign throughout your *g.* 16.
40. 15. an everlasting priesthood through their *g.*
Lev. 21. 17. of thy seed in their *g.* that hath blemish
23. 43. your *g.* may know that I made Israel dwell
24. 3. a statute for ever in *g.* *Num.* 10. 8. | 18. 23.
Deut. 7. 9. Lord keepeth covenant to a thousand *g.*
32. 7. consider the years of many *g.*
Josh. 22. 27. a witness between you and our *g.*
28. when they should say to our *g.* in time to come
Judg. 3. 2. the *g.* of Israel might teach them war
Ruth 4. 18. now these are the *g.* of Pharez
1 *Chron.* 16. 15. of his covenant, the word which he commanded to a thousand *g.* *Psal.* 105. 8.
Job 42. 16. Job saw his sons' sons, even four *g.*
Psal. 33. 11. the thoughts of his heart to all *g.*
45. 17. make thy name to be remembered in all *g.*
49. 11. their dwelling-places continue to all *g.*
61. 6. thou wilt prolong the king's years as many *g.*
72. 5. they shall fear thee throughout all *g.*
79. 13. we will shew forth thy praise to all *g.*
85. 5. wilt thou draw out thine anger to all *g.*?
89. 1. I will make known thy faithfulness to all *g.*
4. and I will build up thy throne to all *g.*

Psal. 90. 1. thou hast been our dwelling-place in all g.
100. 5. and his truth endureth to all g.
102. 12. and thy remembrance unto all g.
24. thy years are throughout all g.
106. 31. was counted to him for righteous. to all g.
119. 90. thy faithfulness is unto all g.
135. 13. and thy memorial throughout all g.
145. 13. and thy dominion throughout all g.
146. 10. thy God, O Zion, shall reign to all g.
Isa. 41. 4. calling the g. from the beginning
51. 9. awake, O arm of the Ld. as in the g. of old
58. 12. shalt raise up the foundations of many g.
60. 15. I will make thee a joy of many g.
61. 4. they shall repair the desolations of many g.
Joel 2. 2. even to the years of many g.
Mat. 1. 17. the g. from Abraham to David are 14 g.
Luke 1. 48. behold, all g. shall call me blessed
Col. 1. 26. mystery hath been hid from ages and g.

GENTILE.

The Hebrews *call the* Gentiles *by the general name of Goiim, which signifies the nations that have not received the faith, or law of God. All who are not* Jews, *and circumcised, are comprised under the word* Goiim. *Before* Christ, *the door to life and justification was opened to the world by the belief only and profession of the* Jewish *religion. Those who were converted, and embraced* Judaism, *they called Proselytes. Since the preaching of the gospel, the true religion is not confined to any one nation and country, only, as heretofore. God, who had promised by his prophets to call the* Gentiles *to the faith, with a superabundance of grace, has executed this promise: So that the* christian *church is composed of scarcely any other beside* Gentile *converts; and the* Jews, *who were too proud of their particular privileges, for the most part have been abandoned to their reprobated sense of things, and have disowned* Jesus Christ *their* Messiah *and Redeemer, for whom, for so many ages, they wished so impatiently.*

The apostle Paul *generally comprehends the* Gentiles *under the name of* Greeks, *Rom.* 1. 16. Jew *and* Greek *signify* Jew *and* Gentile. *See also* Rom. 2. 9, 10. | 3. 9. | 10. 12. 1 Cor. 1. 22, 24. Gal. 3. 28. *And* St. Luke, *in the* Acts, *expressed himself in the same manner,* Acts 11. 20. | 18. 4. St. Paul *is commonly called the* Apostle of the Gentiles, *or the* Greeks, 1 *Tim.* 2. 7. *because he was principally sent to idolatrous people, to preach* Christ *to them; whereas* St. Peter, *and the other apostles, preached more generally to the* Jews; *for which reason they are called the apostles of the* circumcision. *Gal.* 2. 7. The gospel of the uncircumcision was committed unto me, as the gospel of the circumcision was unto *Peter.*

The old prophets declared in a very particular manner the calling of the Gentiles. Jacob *foretold, that when* Shiloh, *or the* Messiah *should come,* to him should the gathering of the people be; *that is, the* Gentiles *should yield obedience to* Christ, *and acknowledge him for their Lord and Saviour. And how sincerely and heartily the ancient and godly* Jews *desired the conversion of the* Gentiles, *may appear from the prayer which* Solomon *addresses to God after the dedication of the temple which he had built.* 1 Kings 8. 41, 42, 43. *When the stranger shall come and pray towards this house, hear thou in heaven,* that all people of the earth may know thy name, to fear thee as thy people *Israel. The* Psalmist *says, that the Lord shall give the* Gentiles *to the* Messiah *for an inheritance.* Psal. 2. 8. *That* the kings of *Tarshish* and of the isles *shall* bring presents; the kings of *Sheba* and *Seba* shall offer gifts; yea, all kings shall fall down before him, *Psal.* 72. 10, 11. *And in* Psal. 87. 4. I will make mention of *Egypt* and *Babylon*, to them that know me: behold, *Philistia* and *Tyre*, with *Ethiopia:* this man was born there. Isaiah *abounds with prophecies of the like nature; see* Isa. 2. 2, 3, 4. | 11. 10. | 42. 1, 6.

In the New Testament we see the Gentiles *came sometimes to* Jerusalem *to worship God there. Some of these arriving there a little before the death of our Saviour, addressed themselves to* Philip, *desiring him to shew them* Jesus, *John* 12. 20, &c. Philip *told* Andrew, *and both of them informed* Jesus; *who answered them,* The hour is come, that the Son of man should be glorified; *that is, Do the* Gentiles *seek me? why, the time approaches wherein I shall be glorified by their conversion, and owning of me; but I must die first, like a grain of corn, and from thence will spring up a plentiful crop among the* Gentiles. *Queen* Candace's *eunuch, who came to* Jerusalem, *was likewise a* Gentile, *as several affirm,* Acts 8. 27.

Mark 7. † 26. the woman was a g. a Syrophenician
Rom. 2. 9. of the Jew first, and also of the g. 10.

GENTILES.

Gen. 10. 5. by these the isles of the g. were divided
Judg. 4. 2. Sisera dwelt in Harosheth of the g.
Isa. 11. 10. a root of Jesse, to it shall the g. seek
42. 1. he shall bring judgment to the g. Mat. 12. 18.
6. for a light to g. 49. 6. Luke 2. 32. Acts 13. 47.
49. 22. behold, I will lift up mine hand to the g.
54. 3. and thy seed shall inherit the g.
60. 3. and the g. shall come to thy light
5. the forces of the g. shall come to thee, 11.
16. thou shalt also suck the milk of the g.
61. 6. ye shall eat the riches of the g.
9. and their seed shall be known among the g.
62. 2. and the g. shall see thy righteousness
66. 12. the glory of the g. like a flowing stream
19. they shall declare my glory among the g.
Jer. 4. 7. the destroyer of the g. is on his way
14. 22. can any of the vanities of the g. cause rain?
16. 19. the g. shall come to thee from ends of earth
46. 1. the word came to Jeremiah against the g.
Lam. 2. 9. her king and princes are among the g.
Ezek. 4. 13. eat their defiled bread among the g.
Hos. 8. 8. now shall they be among the g.
Joel 3. 9. proclaim ye this among the g. prepare war
Mic. 5. 8. the remnant of Jacob shall be among the g.
Zech. 1. 21. are come to cast out the horns of g.
Mal. 1. 11. my name shall be great among the g.
Mat. 4. 15. beyond Jordan, Galilee of the g.
6. 32. for after all these things do the g. seek
10. 5. saying, go not into the way of the g.
18. for a testimony against them and the g.
12. 21. and in his name shall the g. trust
20. 19. deliv. him to the g. Mark 10. 33. Luke 18. 32.
25. princes of the g. exercise domin. Luke 22. 25.
Luke 21. 24. Jerusalem shall be trodden down of the g. till the times of the g. be fulfilled
John 7. 35. to the dispersed among g. and teach g.
Acts 4. 27. Pilate with g. were gathered together
7. 45. with Jesus into the possession of the g.
9. 15. to bear my name before the g. and kings
10. 45. on the g. also was poured out the gift
11. 1. heard that the g. received the word of God
18. hath God to the g. granted repentance to life?
13. 42. g. besought these words might be preached
46. Paul and Barnabas said, lo, we turn to the g.
48. when the g. heard this, they were glad
14. 2. the unbelieving Jews stirred up the g.
5. there was an assault made both of Jews and g.
27. he had opened the door of faith to the g.
15. 3. declaring the conversion of the g. great joy
7. that the g. by my mouth should hear the word
12. what wonders God had wrought among the g.
14. Simeon declared how God at first did visit g.
17. and all the g. on whom my name is called
19. we trouble not them, which from among the g.
23. send greeting to the brethren of the g.
18. 6. from henceforth I will go to the g.
21. 11. shall deliver Paul into the hands of the g.
19. God wrought among the g. by his ministry
21. teachest the Jews among g. to forsake Moses
25. as touching the g. which believe, have written
22. 21. for I will send thee far hence to the g.
26. 17. delivering thee from the people and the g.
20. shewing to the g. that they should repent
23. that Christ should shew light to the g.
28. 28. the salvation of God is sent to the g.
Rom. 1. 13. have some fruit, as among other g.
2. 14. for when the g. which have not the law
24. the name of God is blasphemed among the g.
3. 9. we have proved both Jews and g. under sin
29. is he not also of the g.? yes, of the g. also
9. 24. not of Jews only, but also of the g.
30. g. which followed not after righteousness
11. 11. salvation is come to the g. to provoke them
12. the diminishing of them the riches of the g.
13. I speak to you g. as the apostle of the g.
25. till the fulness of the g. be come in
15. 9. that the g. might glorify God for his mercy; for this cause I will confess to thee among the g.
10. he saith, rejoice, ye g. with his people
11. praise Lord, all ye g. and laud him, all people
12. to reign over the g. in him shall the g. trust
16. that I should be the minister of Jesus Christ to the g. that the offering up of the g.
18. to make the g. obedient by word and deed
27. for if the g. have been made partakers of
16. 4. not only I, but all the churches of the g.
1 Cor. 5. 1. is not so much as named among the g.
10. 20. the things which the g. sacrifice to devils
32. give none offence, neither to Jews nor g.
12. 2. ye know ye were g. carried away to idols
13. into one body, whether we be Jews or g.
Gal. 2. 2. that gospel which I preach among the g.
8. the same was mighty in me towards the g.
12. for before some came, he did eat with the g.
14. livest after manner of g. why compellest g.?
15. we who are Jews, and not sinners of the g.
3. 14. blessing of Abraham might come on the g.
Eph. 2. 11. ye being in time past g. in the flesh
3. 1. I Paul the prisoner of Jesus Christ for you g.
6. that g. should be fellow heirs of the same body
8. preach among the g. the unsearchable riches
4. 17. that ye henceforth walk not as other g.
Col. 1. 27. the glory of this mystery among the g.
1 Thess. 2. 16. forbidding us to speak to the g.
4. 5. not in the lust of concupiscence, as the g.
1 Tim. 2. 7. I am ordained a teacher of the g.
3. 16. preached to the g. believed on in the world
2 Tim. 1. 11. am appoint. an apostle and teacher of g.
4. 17. and that all the g. might hear
1 Pet. 2. 12. your conversation honest among the g.
4. 3. to have wrought the will of the g.
3 John 7. they went forth, taking nothing of the g.
Rev. 11. 2. for the court is given to the g.

GENTLE.

1 Thess. 2. 7. we were g. among you, even as a nurse
2 Tim. 2. 24. the servant of the Lord must be g.
Tit. 3. 2. but g. shewing all meekness to all men
Jam. 3. 17. the wisdom from above is pure and g.
1 Pet. 2. 18. be subject not only to the good and g.

GENTLENESS.

2 Sam. 22. 36. thy g. hath made me great, Ps. 18. 35.
2 Cor. 10. 1. I beseech you by the g. of Christ
Gal. 5. 22. the fruit of the Spirit is g. goodness

GENTLY.

2 Sam. 18. 5. deal g. with the young man Absalom
Isa. 40. 11. he will g. lead those with young

GET.

Gen. 34. 4. saying, g. me this damsel to wife
Exod. 1. 10. and so g. them up out of the land
14. 17. and I will g. me honour upon Pharaoh
Lev. 14. 21. if he be poor and cannot g. so much
22. two pigeons, such as he is able to g. 30, 31.
32. the law of him whose hand is not able to g.
Num. 6. 21. besides that that his hand shall g.
22. 34. now therefore I will g. me back again
Deut. 8. 18. it is he giveth thee power to g. wealth
28. 43. the strangers shall g. up above thee
Judg. 14. 2. therefore g. her for me to wife, 3.
1 Sam. 20. 29. let me g. away and see my brethren
23. 26. David made haste to g. away for fear
2 Sam. 20. 6. lest Sheba g. fenced cities and escape
1 Kings 1. 2. that my lord the king may g. heat
12. 18. king Rehoboam made speed to g. up to his chariot to flee to Jerusalem, 2 Chron. 10. 18.
2 Kings 7. 12. shall catch them alive, and g. the city
Psal. 119. 104. thro' thy precepts I g. understanding
Prov. 4. 5. g. wisdom, g. understanding, 7.
6. 33. a wound and dishonour shall he g.
16. 16. much better it is to g. wisdom than gold, and to g. understanding rather to be chosen than silver
17. 16. a price in the hand of a fool to g. wisdom
22. 25. lest thou learn his ways and g. a snare
Eccl. 3. 6. there is a time to g. and a time to lose
Cant. 4. 6. I will g. me to the mountains of myrrh
7. 12. let us g. up early to the vineyards and see if
Jer. 5. 5. I will g. me to great men, and will speak
19. 1. and g. a potter's earthen bottle
46. 4. harness the horses, and g. up, ye horsemen
48. 9. give wings to Moab, that it may g. away
Lam. 3. 7. he hath hedged me about, I cannot g. out
Ezek. 22. 27. to destroy souls, to g. dishonest gain
Dan. 4. 14. let the beasts g. away from under it
Zeph. 3. 19. I will g. them praise from every land
Mat. 10. † 9. g. neither gold nor silver in your purses
14. 22. constr. them to g. into ship, Mark 6. 45.
Luke 9. 12. that they may lodge and g. victuals
Acts 27. 43. cast themselves into sea, and g. to land
2 Cor. 2. 11. lest Satan should g. the advantage of us
Jam. 4. 13. continue there, buy, sell, and g. gain

GET thee.

Gen. 12. 1. g. thee out of thy country, Acts 7. 3.
22. 2. he said, g. thee into the land of Moriah
31. 13. g. thee out from this land, and return
Exod. 7. 15. g. thee to Pharaoh in the morning
10. 28. g. thee from me, take heed to thyself
11. 8. g. thee out, and all the people that follow thee
19. 24. Lord said to Moses, away, g. thee down and thou shalt come up, 32. 7. Deut. 9. 12.
Num. 27. 12. g. thee to mount Abarim, Deut. 32. 49.
Deut. 3. 27. g. thee up to the top of Pisgah
17. 8. g. thee up to the place the Lord shall choose
Josh. 7. 10. g. thee up, wherefore liest thou thus?
17. 15. then g. thee up to the wood country
Judg. 7. 9. arise, g. thee down unto the host
Ruth 3. 3. wash thyself, g. thee down to the floor
4. † 11. g. thee riches in Ephratah, and be famous
1 Sam. 22. 5. depart, g. thee into the land of Judah
1 Kings 1. 13. go, g. thee in to king David, and say
2. 26. g. thee to Anathoth to thine own fields
14. 2. g. thee to Shiloh, behold there is Ahijah
12. arise therefore, g. thee to thine own house
17. 3. g. thee hence ‖ 9. g. thee to Zarephath
18. 41. Elijah said, g. thee up, eat and drink
44. g. thee down, that the rain stop thee not
2 Kings 3. 13. g. thee to the prophets of thy father
Neh. 9. 10. so didst thou g. thee a name as this day
Isa. 22. 15. g. thee to this treasurer, to Shebnah
30. 22. thou shalt say unto it, g. thee hence
40. 9. O Zion, g. thee up into the high mountain
47. 5. sit thou silent, and g. thee into darkness
Jer. 13. 1. g. thee a linen girdle, put it on thy loins
Ezek. 3. 4. son of man, g. thee to the house of Israel
11. and go, g. thee to them of the captivity
Mat. 4. 10. Jesus saith to him, g. thee hence, Satan
16. 23. he turned, and said to Peter, g. thee behind me, Satan, Mark 8. 33. Luke 4. 8.
Luke 13. 31. g. thee out, for Herod will kill thee
Acts 10. 20. arise, g. thee down, go with them
22. 18. g. thee quickly out of Jerusalem, will not

GET ye.

Gen. 19. 14. Lot said, up, g. ye out of this place
Isa. 30. 11. g. ye out of the way, turn aside from path
Jer. 49. 31. arise, g. ye up to the wealthy nation
Ezek. 11. 15. have said, g. ye far from the Lord
Joel 3. 13. come, g. ye down, for the press is full
Zech. 6. 7. he said, g. ye hence, walk to and fro

GET you.

Gen. 34. 10. dwell and trade, g. you possessions there.
42. 2. g. you down thither and buy for us thence
44. 17. rise up, g. you up in peace unto your father
Exod. 5. 4. the king said, g. you to your burdens
11. go you, g. you straw where you can find it
12. 31. rise up, g. you forth from among my people
Num. 14. 25. turn you, g. you into the wilderness
16. 24. g. you up from about tabernacle of Korah
22. 13. Balaam said, g. you into your land
Deut. 5. 30. g. you into your tents again, Josh. 22. 4.
Josh. 2. 16. g. y. to the mountain, lest pursuers meet
Judg. 19. 9. to-morrow g. you early on your way
1 Sam. 9. 13. g. you up, for ye shall find him
15. 6. g. you down from among the Amalekites
25. 5. g. you up to Carmel, and go to Nabal
Jer. 49. 30. flee g. you far off, dwell deep, ye of Hazor

GETTETH.

2 Sam. 5. 8. whosoever g. up to the gutter, be chief
Prov. 3. 13. happy is the man that g. understanding
9. 7. he that reproveth a scorner g. to himself shame, he that rebuketh a wicked man g. a blot
15. 32. he that heareth reproof g. understanding
18. 15. the heart of the prudent g. knowledge
19. 8. he that g. wisdom loveth his own soul
Jer. 17. 11. so he that g. riches, and not by right
48. 44. he that g. out of the pit shall be taken

GETTING.

Gen. 31. 18. Jacob carried away the cattle of his g.
Prov. 4. 7. with all thy g. get understanding
21. 6. the g. of treasures by a lying tongue is vanity

GHOST.

Gen. 49. 33. Jacob yielded up the g. was gathered
Job 10. 18. O that I had given up the g. no eye seen
11. 20. their hope shall be as the giving up of g.
14. 10. yea, man giveth up the g. and where is he?
Jer. 15. 9. hath born seven, she hath given up the g.
Mat. 27. 50. Jesus cried, and yielded up the g.
Acts 5. 10. Sapphira fell down and yielded up the g.
See GAVE, GIVE, HOLY.

GIANT.

In Greek, Gigas, *in* Hebrew, Nephel, *or* Nephilim, *which may signify* a monster, *or* a terrible man, *who beats and bears down other men. The Scripture speaks of* Giants *who lived before the flood; they are called* Nephilim, mighty men which were of old, men of renown, *Gen.* 6. 4. Aquila, *instead of* Gigantes, *translates this word* Nephilim, Ἐπιπίπτοντες, men who attack, *who fall with impetuosity upon their enemies; a translation, says one, which renders very well the whole force of the* Hebrew *term.*

Symmachus translates it Βιαιοι, violent men, cruel, whose only rule of their actions is violence, and force of arms.

The Scripture calls them sometimes Rephaims. For example: Chedorlaomer and his allies beat the Rephaims or giants at Ashteroth Karnaim, Gen. 14. 5. The Emims, ancient inhabitants of the land of Moab, were of a gigantic stature, they were of the number of the Rephaims or giants, Deut. 2. 10, 11. The Rephaims and the Perizzites are joined together as old inhabitants of the land of Canaan, Gen. 15. 20. Job says, that the ancient Rephaims mourn or groan under the waters, Job 26. 5. These giants of the old world, who once carried themselves insolently towards God and men, but were quickly subdued by the divine power, and drowned with a deluge, do now mourn or groan from under the waters where they were buried, or in their subterranean and infernal habitations. But this passage is otherwise explained by some. Solomon in Prov. 2. 18. says, that the paths of a debauched woman lead to the Rephaims, that is, to hell, where the rebellious giants are; and that he who deviates from the ways of wisdom, shall go and dwell in the assembly of the giants in hell, Prov. 21. 16.

The Anakims, or the sons of Anak, were the most famous giants of Palestine. They dwelt at Hebron, and thereabouts. Their stature was so much above what was common, that the Israelites, who were sent to view the promised land, told the people at their return, that they had seen giants of the race of Anak in this country, who were of so monstrous a size, that the Israelites, in comparison, were but grasshoppers to them, Num. 13. 33.

The Septuagint sometimes translate the Hebrew word Gibbor, giant, though literally it signifies no more than a strong man, a man of valour and bravery, a warrior. For example: they say that Nimrod was a giant before the Lord, Gen. 10. 8, 9. That the sun rises like a giant to run its course, Psal. 19. 5. That the Lord will destroy the giant and the warlike man, Isa. 3. 2. That he will call his giants in his wrath, to take vengeance of his enemies, Isa. 13. 3. That he will destroy the power of Egypt by the sword of his giants; that is, of his warriors, Ezek. 32. 12, 21, 27.

As to the existence of giants, several writers, both ancient and modern, have imagined, that the giants spoken of in Scripture were indeed men of an extraordinary stature, but not so much above what was common as they have fancied, who describe giants as three or four times larger than men are at present. They were, say they, men famous for the violences which they committed, and for their crimes rather than for their strength, or the greatness of their stature.

It is very probable, that the first men were all of a strength and stature much superior to those of mankind at present, since they lived a much longer time; long life being commonly the effect of a strong and vigorous constitution. And that formerly there were men of a stature much above that of common men cannot be denied, at least not without contradicting the holy Scriptures. The Israelites who traversed the Holy Land, told their brethren, that they had seen giants in this country of Anak's race, who were so unmeasureably large, that other men were but grasshoppers in comparison to them, Num. 13. 33. Moses speaks of Og the king of Bashan's bed, which was nine cubits long, and four wide; that is, fifteen feet four inches and a half long, Deut. 3. 11. Goliath was six cubits and a span in height, that is to say, ten feet seven inches, 1 Sam. 17. 4. These sorts of giants were still common in Joshua's and David's times, when the life of men was already so much shortened, and as may be presumed, the size and strength of human bodies were very much diminished. Besides the giants, mentioned in Scripture, several historians make mention of giants; as Herodotus, Diodorus Siculus, Pliny, Homer, Plutarch, &c.

2 Sam. 21. 16. was of sons of the g. 18. 1 Chr. 20. 4.
1 Chron. 20. 6. the son of the g. ‖ 8. born to the g.
Job 16. 14. he runneth upon me like a g.

GIANTS.

Gen. 6. 4. there were g. in the earth in those days
Num. 13. 33. there we saw the g. the sons of Anak
Deut. 2. 11. Emims were counted g. as the Anakims
3. 11. for only Og of Bashan remained of the remnant of g. Josh. 12. 4. | 13. 12.
13. Bashan which was called the land of g.
Josh. 15. 8. the lot of Judah went up at valley of g.
17. 15. then get thee up to the land of the g.
18. 16. Benjamin came to the valley of the g.

GIER-EAGLE.

Lev. 11. 18. these in abomination, the g. Deut. 14. 17.

GIFT

Signifies, [1] A present, Esth. 2. 18. Mat. 2. 11. [2] A reward, Dan. 5. 17. [3] A recompence for the reparation of an injury or wrong done to a person, or something given in testimony of respect and kindness, Gen. 34. 12. [4] A bribe, or something given to a judge by one who has a cause depending in order to bring the judge to side with him; which is forbidden by the law, Deut. 16. 19. because such gifts corrupt and bias the mind, that as the judge will not, so oft times he cannot, discern between right and wrong. [5] An oblation, or free-will offering, Mat. 5. 23.

Christ Jesus is called the gift of God, John 4. 10. He is the greatest gift that God ever gave to the world. The Holy Ghost and his miraculous gifts are also called the gift of God. Acts 8. 20. Thou hast thought that the gift of God may be purchased with money. Every good thing which men receive is the gift of God. Jam. 1. 17. Every good gift is from above. The gift of righteousness signifies those benefits which Christ by his righteousness or obedience has purchased for us, Rom. 5. 17. By unspeakable gift, in 2 Cor. 9. 15. some understand Christ; others understand the gospel, by which the hearts of men are subdued, effectually disposed, and inclined to obey the will of God: Others think it is to be understood of that habit of brotherly love, which from the Spirit of Christ, by the gospel, was wrought in the hearts of these Corinthians.

Gen. 34. 12. ask me never so much dowry and g.
Exod. 23. 8. take no g. a g. blindeth, Deut. 16. 19.
Num. 8. 19. I have given the Levites as a g. 18. 6.
18. 7. I have given your office as a service of g.
11. this is thine, the heave-offering of their g.
Deut. 16. † 17. every man according to g. of his hand
2 Sam. 19. 42. or hath he given us any g.?
Psal. 45. 12. daughter of Tyre shall be there with g.
Prov. 17. 8. a g. is as a precious stone in the eyes
23. a wicked man taketh a g. out of the bosom
18. 16. a man's g. maketh room for him
21. 14. a g. in secret pacifieth anger
25. 14. whoso boasteth himself of a false g.
Eccl. 3. 13. enjoy good, it is the g. of God, 5. 19.
7. 7. and a g. destroyeth the heart
Ezek. 46. † 5. meat-offering the g. of his hand
16. if a prince give a g. to any of his sons
17. if he give a g. to one of his servants
Mat. 5. 23. if thou bring thy g. to the altar
24. leave there thy g. before the altar and go
8. 4. and offer the g. that Moses commanded
15. 5. but ye say, it is a g. by whatsoever thou mightest be profited by me, Mark 7. 11.
23. 18. whoso sweareth by the g. is guilty, 19.
John 4. 10. he said, if thou knewest the g. of God
Acts 2. 38. ye shall receive the g. of the Holy Gh.
8. 20. thought the g. of God may be purchased
10. 45. on the Gentiles also was poured out the g.
11. 17. God gave them the like g. as he did to us
Rom. 1. 11. I may impart to you some spiritual g.
5. 15. not as the offence, so also is free g. the grace of God and the g. by grace abounded to many
16. so is the g. the free g. is of many offences
17. they which receive the g. of righteousness
18. the free g. came on all men to justification
6. 23. the g. of God is eternal life thro' Jesus Christ
1 Cor. 1. 7. so that ye come behind in no g. waiting
7. 7. every man hath his proper g. of God
13. 2. tho' I have the g. of prophecy and understand
16. † 3. I will send them to bring your g. to Jerusal.
2 Cor. 1. 11. that for the g. bestowed upon us
8. 4. praying us that we would receive the g.
† 19. was chosen to travel with us with this g.
9. 15. thanks be to God for his unspeakable g.
Eph. 2. 8. faith is not of yourselves, it is the g. of God
3. 7. I was made a minister, according to the g.
4. 7. according to the measure of the g. of Christ
Phil. 4. 17. not because I desire a g. but fruit
1 Tim. 4. 14. neglect not the g. that is in thee
2 Tim. 1. 6. stir up the g. that is in thee by putting
Heb. 6. 4. and have tasted of the heavenly g.
Jam. 1. 17. every good g. and perfect g. is from above
1 Pet. 4. 10. as every man hath received the g.

GIFTS.

Gen. 25. 6. Abraham gave g. to sons of concubines
Exod. 28. 38. which Israel shall hallow in their g.
Lev. 23. 38. these are your feasts, besides your g.
Num. 18. 29. out of all your g. offer the best
2 Sam. 8. 2. the Moabites and Syrians became David's servants, and brought g. 6. 1 Chron. 18. 2.
2 Chron. 19. 7. with the Lord is no taking of g.
21. 3. Jehoshaphat gave great g. of silver and gold
26. 8. the Ammonites gave g. to Uzziah
32. 23. and many brought g. unto the Lord
Esth. 2. 18. Ahasuerus made a feast and gave g.
9. 22. make them days of sending g. to the poor
Psal. 16. † 4. that give g. to another god
68. 18. thou hast received g. for men, for rebellious
72. 10. the kings of Sheba and Seba shall offer g.
Prov. 6. 35. not content, though thou givest many g.
15. 27. but he that hateth g. shall live
19. 6. every man is friend to him that giveth g.
29. 4. he that receiveth g. overthroweth judgment
Isa. 1. 23. every one loveth g. followeth after rewards
Ezek. 16. 33. they give g. to whores, g. to lovers
20. 26. and I polluted them in their own g.
31. when ye offer your g. ye pollute yourselves
39. pollute my holy name no more with your g.
22. 12. in thee have they taken g. to shed blood
Dan. 2. 6. if ye shew the dream, ye shall receive g.
48. the king gave Daniel many great g.
5. 17. then Daniel said, let thy g. be to thyself
Mat. 2. 11. they presented to him g. gold, myrrh
7. 11. if ye know how to give good g. Luke 11. 13.
Luke 21. 1. the rich casting their g. into the treasury
5. temple was adorned with goodly stones and g.
Rom. 11. 29. the g. of God are without repentance
12. 6. having g. differing according to the grace
1 Cor. 12. 1. now concerning spiritual g. brethren
4. there are diversities of g. but the same Spirit
9. to another the g. of healing, 28, 30.
31. but covet earnestly the best g.
14. 1. follow after charity and desire spiritual g.
12. forasmuch as ye are zealous of spiritual g.
Eph. 4. 8. he led captivity captive, and gave g. to men
Heb. 2. 4. God also bearing them witness with g.
5. 1. that he may offer g. and sacrifices for sins
8. 3. every high-priest is ordained to offer g.
4. seeing that there are priests that offer g.
9. 9. which were offered, both g. and sacrifices
11. 4. God testifying of Abel's g. dead yet speaketh
Rev. 11. 10. they that dwell on earth shall send g.

GILDED.

Rev. 17. † 4. and the woman was g. with gold

GIN.

Job 40. † 24. will any bore his nose with a g.?
Isa. 8. 14. be for a g. to the inhabitants of Jerusalem
Amos 3. 5. can a bird fall in a snare where no g. is?

GIRD.

Gen. 3. † 7. made themselves things to g. about
Exod. 29. 5. g. him with the curious girdle, 9.
Judg. 3. 16. Ehud did g. his dagger under raiment
1 Sam. 25. 13. g. ye on every man his sword
2 Kings 3. † 21. that were able to g. themselves
Psal. 45. 3. g. thy sword on thy thigh, O most
Isa. 8. 9. g. yourselves, and ye shall be broken
Ezek. 44. 18. not g. with what causeth sweat
Joel 1. 13. g. yourselves, and lament, ye priests
Luke 12. 37. shall g. himself, and make them sit down
17. 8. g. thyself, and serve me, till I have eaten
John 21. 18. when old, another shall g. thee
Acts 12. 8. g. thyself and bind on thy sandals
See Loins, Sackcloth.

GIRDED.

Lev. 8. 7. he g. him with the girdle and clothed him
Deut. 1. 41. when ye g. on every man his weapons
Judg. 18. 11. six hundred men g. with weapons
1 Sam. 2. 18. Samuel g. with a linen ephod
2 Sam. 6. 14. David danced, and was g. with an ephod
20. 8. and Joab's garment was g. unto him
22. 40. thou hast g. me with strength, Psal. 18. 39.
1 Kings 20. 32. they g. sackcloth on their loins
Psal. 30. 11. thou hast g. me with gladness
65. 6. setteth fast mountains, being g. with power
† 12. little hills are g. with joy on every side
93. 1. strength wherewith he hath g. himself
109. 19. and for a girdle wherewith he is g.
Isa. 45. 5. I g. thee, tho' thou hast not known me
Lam. 2. 10. the elders of Zion g. with sackcloth
Ezek. 16. 10. I g. thee about with fine linen
23. 15. images of the Chaldeans g. with girdles
Joel 1. 8. lament like a virgin g. with sackcloth
John 13. 4. he took a towel and g. himself
5. to wipe with the towel wherewith he was g.
Rev. 15. 6. seven angels, breasts g. with golden girdle
See Loins, Sword.

GIRDEDST.

John 21. 18. when thou wast young thou g. thyself

GIRDETH.

1 Kings 20. 11. let not him that g. on his harness
Job 12. 18. and he g. their loins with a girdle
Psal. 18. 32. it is God that g. me with strength
Prov. 31. 17. she g. her loins with strength

GIRDING.

Isa. 3. 24. instead of a stomacher, a g. of sackcloth
22. 12. the Lord did call to g. with sackcloth

GIRDLE.

The Hebrews generally wore no girdle in the house, nor even abroad, unless when they were at work, or upon a journey. At these times they tucked themselves up, and girt their clothes about them, as the eastern people still at this day wear them. This appears from many passages of the Old and New Testament. Elijah girded up his loins, and ran before Ahab, 1 Kings 18. 46. And Elisha ordered his servant Gehazi to gird up his loins, and to go and lay his staff on the face of the Shunammite's child, 2 Kings 4. 29. Our Saviour putting himself in a proper condition to wash the feet of his disciples, girt himself about with a towel, John 13. 4. The soldiers likewise had their belts generally girt about them, to which the Psalmist alludes, Psal. 18. 39. Thou hast girded me with strength unto the battle.

Belts or girdles were often made of very precious stuff. The virtuous woman made rich girdles, and sold them to the merchants, Prov. 31. 24. These girdles were used in common both by men and women. Our Lord appeared to St. John in a girdle of gold, Rev. 1. 13. noting the excellency of his ministration as priest. And in Rev. 15. 6. the seven angels, who came out of the temple, were clothed with linen, and girt about with golden girdles. On the contrary, the prophets, and persons who made particular professions of humility and contempt of the world, wore girdles of leather. The prophet Elijah had one of this sort, 2 Kings 1. 8. as well as John the Baptist, Mat. 3. 4. In times of mourning they used girdles of sackcloth, as marks of humiliation and sorrow. God threatens the daughters of Zion, who had offended him with the excess of their ornaments, to reduce them to the wearing of sackcloth, Isa. 3. 24. And in chap. 22. 12. the Lord threatens Jerusalem with bringing her into captivity, with cutting off her hair, the instrument of her pride, and obliging her to gird herself about with sackcloth.

The military girdle, or belt, did not come over the shoulder, as among the old Greeks, but was worn upon the loins; whence the following expressions have their original. Every man had his sword girded by his side, or upon his loins, Neh. 4. 18. Girded with girdles upon their loins, Ezek. 23. 15. These belts were generally rich, and sometimes given as rewards to soldiers. Joab tells him who had seen Absalom hanging on a tree, that if he had smitten him to the ground, he would have given him ten shekels of silver and a girdle, 2 Sam. 18. 11. Jonathan the son of Saul made David a present of his girdle, 1 Sam. 18. 4. Job, exalting the power of God, says, That he looseth the bond of kings, and girdeth their loins with a girdle; he deposeth them from their thrones, and reduceth them to a mean and servile condition, Job 12. 18.

The priest's girdle or sash was of several colours, of gold, of blue, and purple, and scarlet, and fine twined linen, Exod. 28. 4, 8. Josephus says, that the priests wore it upon their breasts, under their arms; that a kind of flower-work was there represented, with threads of purple, scarlet, and hyacinth; that it went twice round the body, was tied before, and the ends hung down to the feet, to render the priests more venerable. When they were in the act of sacrificing, they threw this girdle over the left shoulder, that they might perform their office with the greater freedom.

The girdle was used formerly for a purse, as appears from Mat. 10. 9. where our Saviour forbids his apostles to carry money in their purses, or girdles. These girdles were large and hollow, much like the cast skin of a serpent, or an eel.

Our Saviour says, Luke 12. 35. Let your loins be girded about; that is, be always prepared *for any service that God requires of you, and diligent about it: be like servants who are girded, and ready to obey their master's commands, or like soldiers who wait for orders from their commanders. The Apostle* Paul, *describing the Christian's armour, makes* truth *the* girdle *of the loins.* Eph. 6. 14. Having your loins girt about with truth; *that is, Let your minds and spirits be strengthened and established with soundness of judgment and sincerity of heart, and in stedfastly endeavouring to have a conscience void of offence towards God and men. See* LOINS.

Exod. 28. 4. these garments they shall make a g.
8. the curious g. of the ephod which is upon it, 27, 28. | 29. 5. | 39. 5, 20. Lev. 8. 7.
39. thou shalt make the g. of needle-work
39. 29. they made a g. of fine twined linen
1 Sam. 18. 4. Jonathan gave David his bow and g.
2 Sam. 18. 11. and I would have given thee a g.
1 Kings 2. 5. he put the blood of war on his g.
2 Kings 1. 8. Elijah was girt with a g. of leather
3. † 21. that could gird themselves with a g.
Job 12. 18. he girdeth the loins of kings with a g.
† 21. he looseth the g. of the strong
Psal. 109. 19. for a g. wherewith he is girded
Isa. 3. 24. instead of a g. there shall be a rent
5. 27. nor shall the g. of their loins be loosed
11. 5. and righteousness shall be the g. of his loins, and faithfulness the g. of his reins
22. 21. I will strengthen Eliakim with thy g.
23. † 10. O daught. of Tarshish, thy no more g.
Jer. 13. 1. go, get thee a linen g. put it on thy loins
10. this people shall be as this g. good for nothing
Mat. 3. 4. John had a leathern g. Mark 1. 6.
Acts 21. 11. took Paul's g. man that owneth this g.
Rev. 1. 13. girt about the paps with a golden g.

GIRDLES.

Exod. 28. 40. thou shalt make for Aaron's sons g.
29. 9. and thou shalt gird Aaron and sons with g.
Lev. 8. 13. Moses did gird Aaron's sons with g.
Prov. 31. 24. she delivereth g. to the merchant
Ezek. 23. 15. the images of Chaldeans girded with g.
Dan. 5. † 6. that the g. of his loins were loosed
Rev. 15. 6. seven angels girded with golden g.

GIRL, S.

Joel 3. 3. they have sold a g. for wine to drink
Zech. 8. 5. streets of city shall be full of boys and g.

GIRT.

1 Sam. 2. 4. they that stumbled are g. with strength
2 Kings 1. 8. he was g. with a girdle of leather
John 21. 7. Simon Peter g. his fisher's coat to him
Eph. 6. 14. stand, having your loins g. with truth
Rev. 1. 13. g. about the paps with a golden girdle

GITTITH.

This is the title prefixed to Psalms 8, 81, *and* 84. *The conjectures of interpreters are various concerning this word. Some think it signifies a sort of musical instrument, or tune to which they were set; others, that the hymns of this kind were invented in the city of* Gath; *others, that* Gittith *signifies* wine-presses, *and that the* Psalms *with this title were sung after the vintage; others that* winepresses *were meant by it, it should be* Gitteth; *and that* Gittith *signifies* a woman of Gath; *and that these* Psalms *were given to the class of young women, or songstresses of* Gath, *to be sung by them. Dr.* Hammond *thinks that the* Psalms *with this title were all set to the same tune, and made on* Goliath *the* Gittite.

GIVE.

Gen. 15. 2. what wilt g. me, seeing I go childless?
23. 11. the field I g. thee, and the cave therein
28. 22. of all thou shalt g. me, I will g. the tenth
29. 19. better I g. her thee, than g. her to another
34. 16. then will we g. our daughters to you
Exod. 10. 25. thou must g. us also sacrifices
22. 17. if her father utterly refuse to g. her to him
30. on the eighth day thou shalt g. it me
30. 12. then they shall g. every man a ransom
13. this they shall g. every one half a shekel
Num. 3. 9. thou shalt g. the Levites unto Aaron
11. 4. they said, who shall g. us flesh to eat? 18.
22. 18. if Balak would g. me his house full, 24. 13.
25. 12. I g. to Phinehas my covenant of peace
26. 54. to many g. thou the more inheritance, to few thou shalt g. the less inheritance, 33. 54.
35. 2. ye shall g. to Levites suburbs for the cities
Deut. 15. 10. thou shalt g. him thine heart, 14.
16. 17. every man g. as he is able, Ezek. 46. 5, 11.
24. 15. at his day thou shalt g. him his hire
25. 3. forty stripes he may g. him, and not exceed
Josh. 20. 4. that fleeth, they shall g. him a place
Judg. 7. 2. to g. the Midianites into their hands
8. 25. they answered, we will willingly g. them
1 Sam. 2. 16. nay, but thou shalt g. it me now
32. in all the wealth which God shall g. Israel
17. 25. the king will g. him his daughter
22. 7. will the son of Jesse g. every one fields?
25. 11. shall I then g. it to men whom I know not
2 Sam. 23. 15. oh that one would g. me drink of the water of the well of Beth lehem, 1 Chr. 11. 17.
24. 23. all these did Araunah g. 1 Chron. 21. 23.
1 Kings 13. 8. if thou wilt g. me half thine house
2 Chron. 30. † 8. but g. the hand unto the Lord
12. the hand of God was to g. them one heart
Ezra 9. 8. and to g. us a nail in his holy place
9. to g. us a reviving, to g. us a wall in Judah
Job 2. 4. all that a man hath will he g. for his life
14. † 4. who will g. a clean thing out of unclean?
Psal. 2. 8. ask of me, and I shall g. thee the heathen
14. † 7. who will g. salvation out of Zion. 53. † 6.
37. 4. he shall g. thee the desires of thine heart
49. 7. none can g. to God a ransom for him
51. 16. thou desirest not sacrifice, else would I g. it
68. † 33. lo, he doth g. out his mighty voice
78. 20. can he g. bread also? can he provide flesh?
91. 11. he shall g. his angels charge, Mat. 4. 6.
109. 4. but I g. myself unto prayer
120. † 3. what shall the deceitful tongue g. thee?
Prov. 29. 15. the rod and reproof g. wisdom
17. he shall g. thee rest, shall g. delight to thy soul
Eccl. 2. 26. that he may g. to him that is good
Cant. 8. 7. if a man would g. substance of his house
Isa. 30. 23. then he shall g. the rain of thy seed
55. 10. that it may g. seed to the sower, and bread
61. 3. to g. unto them beauty for ashes
Jer. 3. 19. how shall I g. thee a pleasant land!
6. 10. to whom shall I speak and g. warning?
9. † 1. who will g. my head waters, my eyes tears?
17. 10. to g. man according to his ways, 32. 19.
29. 11. I think to g. you an expected end
Ezek. 2. 8. open thy mouth, eat that I g. thee
3. 3. fill thy bowels with this roll that I g. thee
16. 36. by blood of thy childr. which didst g. them
20. 28. when I had brought them to land, I lifted up mine hand to g. it to them, 42. | 47. 14.
33. 15. if wicked g. again that he had robbed
46. 16. if the prince g. a gift to his sons, 17.
Dan. 9. 22. I am come forth to g. thee skill
Mic. 6. 7. shall I g. my first-b. for my transgression?
Zech. 8. 12. the vine shall g. her fruit, the ground shall g. increase, and the heavens g. their dew
Mat. 7. 9. if he ask bread, will he g. him a stone?
10. if he ask fish, will he g. a serpent? Luke 11. 11.
11. how to g. gifts to your children, so your Father to g. them that ask him, Luke 11. 13.
10. 42. whoso shall g. to drink a cup of cold water
14. 7. he promised to g. her what she would ask
16. 26. g. in exchange for his soul? Mark 8. 37.
19. 7. why comm. to g. a writing of divorcement?
20. 23. sit on hand is not mine to g. Mark 10. 40.
26. 15. what will ye g. me, and I will deliver him
Mark 6. 25. I will that thou g. me the head of John
12. 9. and he will g. the vineyard unto others
Luke 4. 6. and to whomsoever I will, I g. it
6. 38. good measure shall men g. into your bosom
11. 8. he will g. him as many as he needeth
16. 12. who shall g. you that which is your own?
John 4. 14. whoso drinketh the water I shall g. him
6. 27. meat which the Son of man shall g. you
52. how can this man g. us his flesh to eat?
10. 28. and I g. to them eternal life, never perish
11. 22. what thou wilt ask, God will g. it thee
13. 29. that he should g. something to the poor
14. 16. he shall g. you another Comforter to abide
27. peace I leave with you, my peace I g. to you not as world giveth g. I to you, be not troubled
15. 16. whatsoever ye shall ask, he may g. it
16. 23. whatsoever ye ask he will g. it you
17. 2. that he should g. eternal life to as many
Acts 3. 6. such as I have g. I thee, rise and walk
6. 4. but we will g. ourselves to prayer
7. 5. he promised he would g. it for a possession
20. 35. it is more blessed to g. than to receive
Rom. 8. 32. with him also freely g. us all things
1 Cor. 7. 5. that ye may g. yourselves to fasting
Eph. 1. 17. God may g. you the spirit of wisdom
4. 28. that he may have to g. to him that needeth
2 Tim. 4. 8. which the righteous Judge shall g. me
Heb. 2. 1. we ought to g. the more earnest heed
1 John 5. 16. g. life for them that sin not to death
Rev. 13. 15. he had power to g. life to the image
† 16. to g. a mark in their right hand or foreheads
16. 19. to g. her the cup of the wine of his wrath
22. 12. to g. every man according to his work
See ACCOUNT, GLORY, SWARE.

GIVE, *Imperatively.*

Gen. 14. 21. g. me the persons, and take the goods
27. 28. therefore God g. thee of dew of heaven
29. 21. g. me my wife || 30. 1. g. children else I die
30. 26. g. me my wives and my children
Num. 6. 26. and the Lord g. thee peace
Josh. 2. 12. swear to me, and g. me a true token
14. 12. now therefore g. me this mountain
15. 19. g. me a blessing, g. springs, Judg. 1. 15.
1 Sam. 8. 6. when they said, g. us a king to judge us
17. 10. g. me a man that we may fight together
21. 9. David said, none like that, g. it me
1 Kings 3. 9. g. thy servant an understanding heart
26. O my lord, g. her the living child, 27.
8. 39. g. every man according to his ways
17. 19. he said, g. me thy son, and he took him
2 Kings 6. 29. I said, g. thy son, that we may eat him
10. 15. if it be, g. me thine hand, and he gave it
14. 9. saying, g. thy daughter to my son to wife
1 Chr. 16. 28. g. to Lord, ye kindreds of the people, glory and strength, 29. Psal. 29. 1, 2. | 96. 7, 8.
22. 12. the Lord g. thee wisdom and understanding
2 Chron. 1. 10. g. me now wisdom and knowledge
Neh. 4. 4. and g. them for a prey in land of captivity
Job 32. 21. nor let me g. flattering titles to man
Psal. 28. 4. g. them according to their deeds
60. 11. g. us help from trouble, 108. 12.
86. 16. O turn, g. thy strength to thy servant
119. 34. g. me understanding, 73, 125, 144, 169.
Prov. 9. 9. instruct. to a wise man he will be wiser
23. 26. my son, g. me thine heart, observe my
25. 21. if enemy hunger, g. him bread, Rom. 12. 20.
30. 8. g. me neither poverty nor riches, feed me
15. horse-leech hath two daughters, crying, g. g.
Eccl. 11. 2. g. a portion to seven, also to eight
Isa. 49. 20. g. place to me, that I may dwell
62. 7. g. him no rest till he establish Jerusalem
Jer. 18. 19. g. heed to me, O Lord, and hearken
35. 2. bring them, and g. them wine to drink
Lam. 2. 18. let tears run down, g. thyself no rest
3. 65. g. them sorrow of heart, thy curse to them
Ezek. 3. 17. and g. them warning from me
Dan. 5. 17. and g. thy rewards to another
Hos. 4. 18. her rulers with shame do love, g. ye
9. 14. g. them, O Lord, what wilt thou g.?
13. 10. thou saidst, g. me a king and princes
14. † 2. take away all iniquity, and g. good
Zech. 11. 12. g. me my price, if not forbear
Mat. 5. 42. g. to him that asketh thee
6. 11. g. us this day our daily bread, Luke 11. 3.
9. 24. g. place || 10. 8. freely ye received, freely g.
14. 16. g. ye them to eat, Mark 6. 37. Luke 9. 13.
17. 27. that take, and g. to them for me and thee
19. 21. go sell, and g. to the poor, Mark 10. 21.
20. 8. call the labourers, and g. them their hire
25. 8. g. us of your oil, for our lamps are gone out
Luke 6. 38. g. and it shall be given unto you
11. 41. g. alms of such things as ye have, 12. 33.
14. 9. he that bade thee say, g. this man place
15. 12. the younger said, g. me the portion of goods
John 4. 7. Jesus saith to her, g. me to drink, 10.
6. 34. they said, Lord, evermore g. us this bread
9. 24. g. God the praise, this man is a sinner
Acts 8. 19. Simon said, g. me also this power
Rom. 12. 19. avenge not, but rather g. place to wrath
1 Cor. 10. 32. g. none offence, neither to the Jews
2 Cor. 9. 7. so let him g. not grudgingly or of necessity
Col. 4. 1. g. to your servants that which is just
1 Tim. 4. 13. g. attendance to reading, to doctrine
15. meditate, g. thyself wholly to them
Rev. 10. 9. g. me the little book, he said, take it
18. 7. so much torment and sorrow g. her
See CHARGE, EAR, GLORY, LIGHT.

I will GIVE.

Gen. 17. 8. *I will* g. to thee and thy seed the land wherein thou art a stranger, 48. 4. Deut. 34. 4.
16. *I will* g. thee a son also of her, and bless her
28. 22. *I will* surely g. the tenth to thee
34. 11. what ye shall say to me *I will* g. 12.
Exod. 3. 21. and *I will* g. this people favour
33. 14. my presence with thee, and *I will* g. thee rest
Lev. 26. 4. *I will* g. you rain in season, Deut. 11. 14.
6. *I will* g. peace in the land, ye shall lie down
1 Sam. 1. 11. *I will* g. him to the Lord all his life
18. 21. *I will* g. her, that she may be a snare to him
2 Sam. 12. 11. *I will* g. thy wives to thy neighbour
1 Kings 11. 13. not rend all, but *I will* g. one tribe
31. behold, *I will* g. ten tribes to thee
13. 7. come home, and *I will* g. thee a reward
21. 2. *I will* g. thee for it a better vineyard
7. *I will* g. thee the vineyard of Naboth
1 Chr. 22. 9. *I will* g. him rest, *I will* g. peace to Isr.
2 Chr. 1. 12. *I will* g. thee riches, wealth, honour
Psal. 30. 12. O Lord, *I will* g. thanks to thee
57. 7. *I will* sing and g. praise, 108. 1.
Prov. 3. 28. to-morrow *I will* g. when thou hast it
Isa. 3. 4. *I will* g. them children to be princes
41. 27. shall say to Zion, behold, and *I will* g. to Jerusalem one that bringeth good tidings
42. 6. *I will* g. thee for covenant of the people, 49. 8.
45. 3. *I will* g. thee the treasures of darkness
49. 6. *I will* g. thee for a light to the Gentiles
56. 5. *I will* g. them an everlasting name
Jer. 3. 15. *I will* g. pastors according to my heart
9. 15. *I will* g. them waters of gall to drink
14. 13. *I will* g. you assured peace in this land
15. † 4. *I will* g. them for a removing into kingdoms
17. 3. *I will* g. thy substance to the spoil
24. 7. *I will* g. them an heart to know me
32. 39. *I will* g. them one heart, Ezek. 11. 19.
34. 18. *I will* g. the men that have transgressed
Ezek. 7. 21. *I will* g. it into the hand of strangers
11. 17. and *I will* g. you the land of Israel
16. 38. *I will* g. thee blood in fury, and jealousy
39. *I will* also g. thee into their hand
61. *I will* g. them to thee for daughters
21. 27. he come whose right it is, *I will* g. it him
23. 46. *I will* g. them to be removed and spoiled
29. 19. *I will* g. land of Egypt to Nebuchadnezzar
21. *I will* g. thee the opening of the mouth
36. 26. and *I will* g. you an heart of flesh
Hos. 2. 15. *I will* g. her vineyards from thence
Mat. 11. 28. come unto me, and *I will* g. you rest
16. 19. *I will* g. unto thee the keys of the kingdom
20. 4. and whatsoever is right, *I will* g. you
14. *I will* g. to this last even as unto thee
Mark 6. 22. ask what thou wilt, *I will* g. it thee
Luke 21. 15. for *I will* g. you a mouth and wisdom
John 6. 51. I am living bread, the bread *I will* g. is my flesh, which *I will* g. for the life of the world
Acts 13. 34. *I will* g. you the sure mercies of David
Heb. 8. † 10. *I will* g. my laws into their mind
Rev. 2. 10. be faithful, *I will* g. thee a crown of life
17. *I will* g. him a white stone and a new name
23. *I will* g. to every one according to your works
28. and *I will* g. him the morning star
11. 3. and *I will* g. power to my two witnesses
21. 6. *I will* g. to him that is athirst water of life

Will I GIVE.

Gen. 12. 7. to thy seed *will I* g. this land, 13. 15. | 24. 7. | 28. 13. | 35. 12. Exod. 32. 13. | 33. 1.
Deut. 1. 36. save Caleb, to him *will I* g. the land
39. they shall go in thither, to them *will I* g. it
Josh. 15. 16. to him *will I* g. Achsah, Judg. 1. 12.
1 Sam. 9. 8. that *will I* g. to the man of God to tell
18. 17. my daughter Merab, her *will I* g. thee
1 Chr. 16. 18. to thee *will I* g. land, Psal. 105. 11.
Psal. 18. 49. therefore *will I* g. thanks to thee
Cant. 7. 12. there *will I* g. thee my loves
Isa. 43. 4. therefore *will I* g. men for thee
56. 5. to them *will I* g. in mine house a place
Jer. 24. 8. so *will I* g. Zedekiah king of Judah
45. 5. thy life *will I* g. to thee for a prey
Ezek. 15. 6. so *will I* g. inhabitants of Jerusalem
36. 26. new heart also *will I* g. you, and new spirit
Hag. 2. 9. and in this place *will I* g. peace
Mat. 4. 9. devil said, all these things *will I* g. thee
Luke 4. 6. all this power *will I* g. thee, and glory
Rev. 2. 7. to him that overcometh *will I* g. 17, 26.

Lord GIVE.

Exod. 12. 25. when ye come to the land which *L.* will g. you, Lev. 14. 34. | 23. 10. | 25. 2. Num. 15. 2.
16. 8. when the *Lord* shall g. you flesh to eat
Num. 11. 18. therefore the *Lord* will g. you flesh
14. 8. if the *Lord* delight in us, he will g. it us
22. 13. the *Lord* refuseth to g. me leave to go
34. 13. the *Lord* commanded to g. the nine tribes
36. 2. the *Lord* commanded to g. the land by lot
Deut. 1. 25. it is a good land the *Lord* doth g.
28. 65. the *Lord* shall g. thee a trembling heart
Josh. 9. 24. the *Lord* commanded Moses to g. the land
17. 4. the *Lord* commanded to g. us inheritance
21. 2. the *Lord* commanded to g. us cities
Ruth 4. 12. which the *L.* shall g. thee of this woman
1 Kings 15. 4. the *Lord* his God did g. him a lamp
2 Chron. 25. 9. the *Lord* is able to g. thee much
Psal. 29. 11. the *Lord* will g. strength to his people
84. 11. the *Lord* will g. grace and glory
85. 12. the *Lord* shall g. that which is good
Isa. 7. 14. the *Lord* himself shall g. you a sign

Isa. 14. 3. the *Lord* shall *g.* thee rest from sorrow
30. 20. though the *Lord g.* you bread of adversity
Zech. 10. 1. the *Lord* shall *g.* them showers of rain
Luke 1. 32. *Lord* shall *g.* him the throne of his Father
2 *Tim.* 1. 16. *Lord g.* mercy to house of Onesiphorus

Not GIVE, or GIVE *not.*

Gen. 30. 31. Jacob said, thou shalt *not g.* me anything
Exod. 5. 10. I will *not g.* you straw, go, get straw
30. 15. the rich shall *not g.* more, poor *not g.* less
Lev. 25. 37. thou shalt *not g.* thy money on usury
Deut. 2. 5. I will *not g.* you of their land, 9, 19.
7. 3. thy daughter thou shalt *not g.* to his son
28. 55. he will *not g.* of the flesh of his children
Judg. 21. 1. shall *not* any of us *g.* his daught. to Benj.
7. we have sworn we will *not g.* them wives
1 *Sam.* 30. 22. we will *not g.* them ought of the spoil
1 *Kings* 21. 4. I will *not g.* inheritance of my fathers
Ezra 4. † 13. then will they *not g.* toll, tribute
9. 12. *g. not* your daughters, *Neh.* 10. 30. | 13. 25.
Psal. 132. 4. I will *not g.* sleep to mine eyes
Prov. 6. 4. *g. not* sleep to thine eyes, nor slumber
31. 3. *g. not* thy strength unto women
Eccl. 7. † 21. *g. not* thy heart unto all words
Isa. 13. 10. constellations shall *not g.* their light
42. 8. my glory will I *not g.* to another, 48. 11.
62. 8. I will *no* more *g.* thy corn to enemies
Jer. 18. 18. let us *not g.* heed to any of his words
26. 24. *not g.* Jeremiah into the hand of the people
Ezek. 32. 7. I will cover sun with a cloud, the moon shall *not g.* her light, *Mat.* 24. 29. *Mark* 13. 24.
Dan. 11. 21. to whom *not g.* honour of kingdom
Hos. 5. † 4. *not g.* their doings to turn to the Lord
Joel 2. 17. *g. not* thine heritage to reproach
Mat. 7. 6. *g. not* that which is holy to the dogs
Mark 12. 15. shall we *g.* or shall we *not g.?*
Eph. 4. 27. *neither g.* place to the devil
Jam. 2. 16. and *g. not* those things they need

GIVE *thanks.*

2 *Sam.* 22. 50. I will *g. thanks* to thee, *Psal.* 18. 49.
1 *Chron.* 16. 8. *g. thanks* to the Lord, call upon his name, *Psal.* 105. 1. | 106. 1. | 107. 1. | 118. 1, 29. | 136. 1, 3.
35. save us, O God of our salvation, that we may *g. thanks* to thy holy name, *Psal.* 106. 47.
41. who were expressed by name, to *g. thanks*
25. 3. sons of Jeduthun with a harp to *g. thanks*
2 *Chr.* 31. 2. Hezekiah appointed Levites to *g. th.*
Psal. 6. 5. in the grave who shall *g.* thee *thanks*
30. 4. sing to Lord, ye saints of his, and *g. thanks* at the remembrance of his holiness, 97. 12.
12. O Lord, I will *g. thanks* to thee for ever
35. 18. I will *g. thanks* in the great congregation
42. † 5. I shall *g. thanks* for help of countenance
75. 1. to thee, O God, do we *g. thanks,* do *g. thanks*
79. 13. so we thy people will *g.* thee *thanks*
92. 1. it is a good thing to *g. thanks* to the Lord
106. 47. save us to *g. thanks* to thy holy name
119. 62. at midnight I will rise to *g. thanks*
122. 4. whither the tribes go up to *g. thanks*
136. 2. O *g. thanks* unto the God of gods
26. O *g. thanks* unto the God of heaven
140. 13. righteous shall *g. thanks* to thy name
Rom. 16. 4. to whom not only I *g. thanks*
1 *Cor.* 10. 30. for that for which I *g. thanks*
Eph. 1. 16. I cease not to *g. thanks* for you
Col. 1. 3. we *g. thanks* to God and the Father
1 *Thess.* 1. 2. we *g. thanks* to God always for you
5. 18. in every thing *g. thanks,* this is the will of God
2 *Thess.* 2. 13. we are bound to *g. thanks* for you
Rev. 11. 17. we *g.* thee *thanks,* Lord God Almighty

GIVE *up.*

Deut. 23. 14. Lord walketh to *g. up* thine enem. 31. 5.
1 *Kings* 14. 16. he shall *g.* Isr. *up,* because of sins
Job 3. 11. why did not I *g. up* the ghost?
13. 19. if I hold my tongue, I shall *g. up* the ghost
Isa. 43. 6. I will say to north, *g. up,* and to south
Hos. 11. 8. how shall I *g.* thee *up,* Ephraim?
Mic. 5. 3. therefore will he *g.* them *up*
6. 14. that which thou deliverest will I *g. up*

GIVEN.

Gen. 21. 7. Sarah should have *g.* children suck
Lev. 20. 3. because he hath *g.* his seed to Molech
Num. 18. 6. they are *g.* as a gift for the Lord
Deut. 12. 15. according to the blessing *g.* 16. 17.
Ruth 2. 12. a full reward be *g.* thee of the Lord
1 *Sam.* 2. † 32. wealth which God would have *g.* Isr.
2 *Sam.* 4. 10. who thought I would have *g.* a reward
12. 8. I would have *g.* thee such and such things
18. 11. I would have *g.* thee ten shekels of silver
19. 42. or hath the king *g.* us any gift?
1 *Kings* 13. 5. the sign which the man of G. had *g.*
1 *Chr.* 29. 14. and of thine own have we *g.* thee
Ezra 6. 9. let it be *g.* them day by day without fail
Esth. 3. 11. the silver is *g.* to thee, the people also
7. 3. let my life be *g.* me at my petition and people
Job 3. 20. why is light *g.* to him that is in misery?
23. why is light *g.* to a man whose way is hid?
15. 19. to whom alone the earth was *g.*
Psal. 79. 2. dead bodies of thy servts. *g.* to be meat
112. 9. he hath *g.* to the poor, 2 *Cor.* 9. 9.
115. 16. the earth hath he *g.* to the children of men
Prov. 19. 17. that which he hath *g.* will he pay him
Eccl. 8. 8. nor wickedn. deliver those that are *g.* to it
12. 11. which are *g.* from one shepherd
Isa. 9. 6. for to us a Child is born, to us a Son is *g.*
47. 8. therefore hear, thou that art *g.* to pleasures
Jer. 6. 13. every one is *g.* to covetousness, 8. 10.
44. 20. he said to all who had *g.* him that answer
Lam. 5. 6. we have *g.* the hand to the Egyptians
Ezek. 11. 15. unto us is this land *g.* 33. 24.
35. 12. they are desolate, they are *g.* to consume
Dan. 2. 38. beasts, fowls hath he *g.* into thine hand
7. 4. like a lion, and a man's heart was *g.* to it
† 12. yet a prolonging in life was *g.* them
11. 6. she shall be *g.* up, and they that brought her
Mat. 13. 11. it is *g.* to you to know the mysteries of the kingdom, *Mark* 4. 11. *Luke* 8. 10.
19. 11. all cannot receive, save they to whom it is *g.*
21. 43. be *g.* to a nation bringing forth fruits
22. 30. are *g.* in marriage, *Mark* 12. 25. *Luke* 20. 35.
26. 9. sold for much and *g.* to the poor, *Mark* 14. 5.
28. 18. all power is *g.* to me in heaven and earth

Mark 4. 24. unto you that hear more shall be *g.*
Luke 12. 48. to whom much *g.* of him much required
John 3. 27. can receive nothing, except it be *g.*
5. 26. he hath *g.* to the Son to have life in himself
6. 39. of all he hath *g.* me, I should lose nothing
65. no man can come to me, except it were *g.* him
19. 11. except it were *g.* thee from above
Acts 4. 12. there is none other name *g.* among men
24. 26. he hoped that money should be *g.* him
Rom. 5. 5. by the Holy Ghost which is *g.* to us
11. 35. or who hath first *g.* to him, and recompensed
15. 15. because of the grace that is *g.* me of God
1 *Cor.* 2. 12. might know things freely *g.* us of God
2 *Cor.* 1. 11. that thanks may be *g.* by many
Gal. 3. 21. been a law *g.* which could have *g.* life
Eph. 3. 2. dispensation, which is *g.* me to you-ward
8. to me who am the least is this grace *g.*
4. 19. who have *g.* themselves over to lasciviousness
5. 2. Christ hath loved us, and *g.* himself for us
Phil. 1. 29. to you it is *g.* in behalf of Christ
2. 9. and hath *g.* him a name above every name
Heb. 4. 8. for if Jes. had *g.* them rest, then not spoken
1 *John* 3. 24. by the Spirit which he hath *g.* us
4. 13. because he hath *g.* us of his Spirit
Rev. 6. 11. white robes were *g.* to every one of them
13. 5. power was *g.* him to continue 42 months
7. it was *g.* to him to make war with the saints

God or Lord hath, had GIVEN.

Gen. 24. 35. the *L. hath g.* Abrah. flocks and herds
30. 6. and Rachel said, *God hath g.* me a son
18. and Leah said, *God hath g.* me mine hire
31. 9. thus *God hath g.* me your father's cattle
33. 5. the children which *G. hath* graciously *g.* me
43. 23. *God hath g.* you treasure in your sacks
48. 9. the children *God hath g.* me in this place
Exod. 16. 15. the bread which the *Lord hath g.* you
29. for that the *Lord hath g.* you the sabbath
Num. 32. 7. from going over to the land which the *Lord hath g.* them, 9. *Deut.* 3. 18. | 28. 52. *Josh.* 2. 9, 14. | 23. 13, 15. *Jer.* 25. 5.
Josh. 6. 16. shout, for the *Lord hath g.* you the city
18. 3. to possess land which the *Lord hath g.* you
1 *Sam.* 1. 27. *Lord hath g.* me my petition I asked
15. 28. *L. hath g.* it to a neighbour of thine, 28. 17.
30. 23. not to do so with what the *Lord hath g.*
2 *Chr.* 36. 23. kingdoms *hath God g.* me, *Ezra* 1. 2.
Eccl. 5. 19. every man to whom *G. hath g.* riches.
Isa. 8. 18. I and the children *L. hath g. Heb.* 2. 13.
23. 11. the *Lord hath g.* a commandment against
50. 4. the *L. hath g.* me the tongue of the learned
Jer. 11. 18. the *Lord hath g.* me knowledge of it
47. 7. seeing the *Lord hath g.* it a charge
John 6. 23. after that the *Lord had g.* thanks
Acts 5. 32. whom *G. hath g.* to them that obey him
27. 24. *God hath g.* thee all that sail with thee
Rom. 11. 8. *God hath g.* them the spirit of slumber
2 *Cor.* 10. 8. the *L. hath g.* us for edification, 13. 10.
1 *Thess.* 4. 8. but G. who *hath g.* us his Holy Spirit
1 *John* 5. 11. this is the record *God hath g.* to us

See REST.

I have, or *have I* GIVEN.

Gen. 27. 37. brethren *have I g.* him for servants
1 *Kings* 3. 13. *I have g.* thee that thou hast not asked
Isa. 43. 28. therefore *I have g.* Jacob to the curse
55. 4. *I have g.* him for a witness to the people
Jer. 8. 13. things *I have g.* shall pass from them
27. 5. *I have g.* it to whom it seemed meet to me
Ezek. 4. 15. *I have g.* thee cow's dung for man's dung
29. 20. *I have g.* him the land of Egypt for labour
Amos 4. 6. *I* also *have g.* you cleanness of teeth
9. 15. no more be pulled out of land *I have g.* them
John 13. 15. *I have g.* you an example, that ye do
17. 8. *I have g.* them the words thou gavest me, 14.
22. the glory thou gavest me, *I have g.* them
1 *Cor.* 16. 1. as *I have g.* order to the churches

Not GIVEN.

Gen. 38. 14. and she was *not g.* unto him to wife
Deut. 26. 14. I have *not g.* ought thereof for the dead
29. 4. yet Lord hath *not g.* you an heart to perceive
1 *Chr.* 22. 18. hath he *not g.* you rest on every side?
Neh. 13. 10. the portion of Levites had *not* been *g.*
Job 22. 7. thou hast *not g.* water to the weary
Psal. 78. 63. their maidens were *not g.* to marriage
118. 18. but he hath *not g.* me over to death
124. 6. who hath *not g.* us as a prey to their teeth
Isa. 37. 10. Jerus. *not* be *g.* into the hand of Assyria
Jer. 39. 17. thou shalt *not* be *g.* into hand of the men
Ezek. 3. 20. because thou hast *not g.* him warning
18. 8. he that hath *not g.* forth upon usury
Mat. 13. 11. it is given to you, to them it is *not g.*
John 7. 39. for the Holy Ghost was *not* yet *g.*
1 *Tim.* 3. 3. bishop *not g.* to wine, no striker, *Tit.* 1. 7.
8. deacons *not g.* to much wine, not greedy
2 *Tim.* 1. 7. God hath *not g.* us the spirit of fear
Tit. 2. 3. aged women likewise *not g.* to much wine

Shall be GIVEN.

Num. 26. 54. to every one *shall* inheritance *be g.*
Deut. 28. 31. thy sheep *shall be g.* to thine enemies
32. thy sons *shall be g.* to another people
Ezra 4. 21. till another commandment *shall be g.*
Esth. 5. 3. it *shall be g.* to half of the kingdom
Psal. 72. 15. to him *shall be g.* of gold of Sheba
120. 3. what *shall be g.* to thee, thou false tongue?
Isa. 3. 11. the reward of his hands *shall be g.* him
33. 16. bread *shall be g.* him, waters shall be sure
35. 2. the glory of Lebanon *shall be g.* to it
Jer. 21. 10. this city *shall be g.* into the hand of king of Babylon, and he shall burn it, 38. 3, 18.
Ezek. 47. 11. the marishes, they *shall be g.* to salt
Dan. 7. 25. the saints *shall be g.* into his hand
27. the kingdom *shall be g.* to the saints
Mat. 7. 7. ask, and it *shall be g.* you, *Luke* 11. 9.
10. 19. it *shall be g.* you in same hour, *Mark* 13. 11.
12. 39. no sign *shall be g. Mark* 8. 12. *Luke* 11. 29.
13. 12. for whosoever hath, to him *shall be g.* and more abundance, 25. 29. *Mark* 4. 25. *Luke* 8. 18.
20. 23. it *shall be g.* them for whom it is prepared
21. 43. the kingdom of God *shall be g.* to a nation
Luke 6. 38. give, and it *shall be g.* you, good measure
Philem. 22. that thro' your prayers I *shall be g.* you
Jam. 1. 5. let him ask of God, and it *shall be g.* him

Thou hast, or *hast thou* GIVEN.

Gen. 15. 3. Abram said, to me *thou hast g.* no seed
Deut. 26. 15. bless the land which *thou hast g.* us
Josh. 15. 19. *thou hast g.* me south land, *Judg.* 1. 15.
17. 14. why *hast thou g.* me but one lot to inherit?
Judg. 15. 18. *thou hast g.* this great deliverance
1 *Sam.* 22. 13. *thou hast g.* him bread and a sword
2 *Sam.* 12. 14. by this deed *thou hast g.* occasion
22. 36. *thou hast* also *g.* me the shield of thy salvation, and gentleness made me great, *Psal.* 18. 35.
41. *thou hast g.* me the necks of enemies, *Ps.* 18. 40.
1 *Kings* 3. 6. *thou hast g.* him a son to sit on throne
8. 36. rain on thy land *thou hast g.* 2 *Chron.* 6. 27.
9. 13. what cities are these *thou hast g.* me?
2 *Chr.* 20. 11. cast us out of possession *thou hast g.*
Ezra 9. 13. *thou hast g.* us such deliverance as this
Psal. 21. 2. *thou hast g.* him his heart's desire
44. 11. *thou hast g.* us like sheep for meat
60. 4. *thou hast g.* a banner to them that fear thee
61. 5. *thou hast g.* me the heritage of those that fear
71. 3. *thou hast g.* commandment to save me
John 17. 2. as *thou hast g.* him power over all flesh
7. that all things *thou hast g.* me, are of thee
9. I pray not but for them which *thou hast g.* me
11. keep through thy name those *thou hast g.* me
Rev. 16. 6. *thou hast g.* them blood to drink

GIVER.

Isa. 24. 2. as with the taker of usury, so with the *g.*
2 *Cor.* 9. 7. not grudgingly, God loveth a cheerful *g.*

GIVEST.

Deut. 15. 9. thou *g.* him nought, and he cry to Ld.
10. thy heart not be grieved when thou *g.* him
Job 35. 7. if thou be righteous, what *g.* thou him?
Psal. 50. 19. thou *g.* thy mouth to evil, thy tongue
80. 5. thou *g.* them tears to drink in great measure
104. 28. that thou *g.* them, they gather
145. 15. thou *g.* them their meat in due season
Prov. 2. † 3. if thou *g.* thy voice, for understanding
6. 35. nor rest content, though thou *g.* many gifts
Ezek. 3. 18. thou *g.* not warning, to save his life
16. 33. but thou *g.* thy gifts to all thy lovers
34. in that thou *g.* a reward, and none is given
1 *Cor.* 14. 17. for thou verily *g.* thanks well

GIVETH.

Exod. 16. 29. he *g.* you on sixth day bread of two
20. 12. thy days may be long in the land which L thy God *g.* thee, *Deut.* 4. 40. | 5. 16. | 25. 15.
25. 2. every man that *g.* it willingly with his heart
Lev. 27. 9. all that any man *g.* of such shall be holy
Deut. 2. 29. into the land which the Lord our God *g.* thee, 4. 1, 21. | 11. 17, 31. | 12. 1, 10. | 15. 4, 7. | 16. 20. | 17. 14. | 18. 9. | 19. 1, 2, 10, 14. | 21. 1, 23. | 24. 4. | 26. 1, 2. | 27. 2, 3. | 28. 8. *Josh.* 1. 11, 15.
8. 18. it is he that *g.* thee power to get wealth
9. 6. God *g.* not this land for thy righteousness
12. 10. when he *g.* you rest from enemies, 25. 19.
13. 1. if a prophet *g.* thee a sign or a wonder
16. 5. in thy gates which Lord *g.* thee, 18. | 17. 2.
2 *Sam.* 22. † 48. it is God *g.* avengement for me, and bringeth down people under me, *Psal.* 18. † 47.
1 *Kings* 17. † 14. till the day the Ld. *g.* rain on earth
Job 5. 10. who *g.* rain upon the earth and field
33. 13. he *g.* no account of any of his ways
34. 29. when he *g.* quietness ‖ 35. 10. who *g.* songs
36. 6. but *g.* right to the poor ‖ 31. he *g.* meat
Psal. 18. 50. great deliverance *g.* he to his king
37. 21. but the righteous sheweth mercy and *g.*
68. 35. the God of Israel is he that *g.* strength
119. 130. the entrance of thy words *g.* light
127. 2. for so he *g.* his beloved sleep
136. 25. who *g.* food to all flesh, 146. 7. | 147. 9.
144. 10. *g.* salvation to kings ‖ 147. 16. he *g.* snow
Prov. 2. 6. the Lord *g.* wisdom out of his mouth
3. 34. he *g.* grace to the lowly, *Jam.* 4. 6. 1 *Pet.* 5. 5.
13. 15. good understanding *g.* favour
21. 26. the righteous *g.* and spareth not, 22. 9.
28. 27. he that *g.* to the poor shall not lack
Eccl. 2. 26. God *g.* to a man that is good, wisdom and knowledge, but to sinner he *g.* travel
6. 2. yet God *g.* him not power to eat thereof
Isa. 40. 29. he *g.* power to the faint ‖ 42. 5. *g.* breath
Jer. 5. 24. *g.* rain ‖ 31. 35. *g.* the sun for a light
22. 13. woe to him that *g.* him not for his work
Lam. 3. 30. he *g.* his cheek to him that smiteth him
Dan. 2. 21. he *g.* wisdom to the wise, and knowledge
4. 17. and *g.* it to whomsoever he will, 25, 32.
Hos. 10. † 1. a vine emptying the fruit which it *g.*
Hab. 2. 15. woe to him that *g.* his neighbour drink
Mat. 5. 15. it *g.* light to all that are in the house
John 3. 34. God *g.* not the Spirit by measure to him
6. 32. but my Father *g.* you the true bread
33. who cometh down and *g.* life to the world
37. all that the Father *g.* me shall come to me
10. 11. the good shepherd *g.* his life for the sheep
14. 27. not as the world *g.* give I unto you
Acts 17. 25. he *g.* to all life, breath, and all things
Rom. 12. 8. he that *g.* let him do it with simplicity
14. 6. he eateth to the Lord, for he *g.* God thanks
1 *Cor.* 3. 7. but God that *g.* the increase
7. 38. he that *g.* her in marriage doth well
15. 38. God *g.* it a body as it hath pleased him
57. but thanks be to God who *g.* us the victory
2 *Cor.* 3. 6. the letter killeth, but the Spirit *g.* life
1 *Tim.* 6. 17. who *g.* us richly all things to enjoy
Jam. 1. 5. ask of God, that *g.* to all men liberally
4. 6. *g.* more grace, God *g.* grace to the humble
1 *Pet.* 4. 11. let him do it as of the ability that God *g.*
Rev. 22. 5. for the Lord God *g.* them light

GIVING.

Deut. 10. 18. he loveth the stranger in *g.* him food
21. 17. by *g.* him a double portion of all he hath
Ruth 1. 6. Lord visited his people in *g.* them bread
1 *Kings* 5. 9. shalt accomplish my desire, in *g.* food
2 *Chr.* 6. 23. by *g.* him according to righteousness
Job 11. 20. their hope be as the *g.* up of the ghost
Mat. 24. 38. were marrying and *g.* in marriage
Acts 8. 9. *g.* out that himself was some great one
15. 8. *g.* them the Holy Ghost, as he did to us
Rom. 4. 20. was strong in faith, *g.* glory to God
9. 4. the *g.* of the law, and the service of God

1 Cor. 14. 7. things g. sound || 16. at thy g. of thanks
2 Cor. 6. 3. g. no offence in any thing, ministry not
Phil. 4. 15. concerning g. and receiving, but ye only
1 Tim. 4. 1. g. heed to seducing spirits and doctrines
1 Pet. 3. 7. g. honour to the wife as to weaker vessel
2 Pet. 1. 5. g. all diligence, add to faith virtue
Jude 7. g. themselves over to fornication

See THANKS.

GLAD.

Exod. 4. 14. when he seeth thee, he will be g. in heart
Judg. 18. 20. and the priest's heart was g.
1 Sam. 11. 9. and the men of Jabesh were g.
1 Kings 8. 66. Israel went to tents g. 2 Chron. 7. 10.
Esth. 5. 9. Haman g. || 8. 15. the city Shushan was g.
Job 3. 22. and are g. when they can find the grave
22. 19. righteous see it and are g. Psal. 64. 10.
Psal. 16. 9. therefore my heart is g. glory rejoiceth
21. 6. thou hast made him g. with thy countenance
34. 2. the humble shall hear and be g. 69. 32.
35. 27. them be g. that favour my righteous cause
45. 8. whereby they have made thee g.
46. 4. the streams shall make g. the city of God
67. 4. let the nations be g. and sing for joy
90. 15. make us g. || 92. 4. thou L. hast made me g.
97. 1. let the isles be g. || 8. Zion heard, and was g.
104. 15. wine that maketh g. the heart of man
34. I will be g. in the Lord || 105. 38. Egypt was g.
107. 30. then are they g. because they be quiet
119. 74. they that fear thee will be g. when
122. 1. I was g. when they said to me, let us go
126. 3. done great things for us, whereof we are g.
Prov. 10. 1. a wise son maketh a g. father, 15. 20.
12. 25. but a good word maketh it g.
17. 5. that is g. at calamities, not be unpunished
23. 25. thy father and thy mother shall be g.
24. 17. let not thy heart be g. when he stumbleth
27. 11. my son, be wise, and make my heart g.
Eccl. 10. † 19. and wine maketh g. the life
Isa. 35. 1. the wilderness shall be g. for them
39. 2. Hezekiah was g. of them, and shewed them
Jer. 20. 15. a child is born, making him very g.
50. 11. because ye were g. O ye destroyers
Lam. 1. 21. they are g. that thou hast done it
Dan. 6. 23. then was the king exceeding g.
Hos. 7. 3. they make the king g. with their wickedn.
Jonah 4. 6. Jonah was g. because of the gourd
Zech. 10. 7. their children shall see it and be g.
Mark 14. 11. were g. and promised money, Luke 22. 5
Luke 1. 19. I am sent to shew thee these g. tidings
8. 1. shewing the g. tidings of the kingdom
15. 32. was meet we should make merry and be g.
John 8. 56. Abraham saw my day and was g.
11. 15. I am g. for your sakes that I was not there
Acts 11. 23. when had seen the grace of G. he was g.
13. 48. the Gentiles heard this, they were g.
Rom. 16. 19. I am g. therefore on your behalf
1 Cor. 16. 17. I am g. of the coming of Stephanas
2 Cor. 2. 2. who is he then that maketh me g.?
13. 9. we are g. when we are weak, and ye strong
1 Pet. 4. 13. his glory revealed, ye may be g. also

GLAD joined with *rejoice*.

1 Chron. 16. 31. let the heavens be g. and let the earth *rejoice*, the Lord reigneth, Psal. 96. 11.
Psal. 9. 2. I will be g. and *rejoice* in thee
14. 7. Jacob shall *rejoice*, Israel shall be g. 53. 6.
31. 7. I will be g. and *rejoice* in thy mercy
32. 11. be g. and *rejoice*, ye righteous, 68. 3.
40. 16. that seek thee, be g. and *rejoice*, 70. 4.
48. 11. let Zion *rejoice*, daughters of Judah be g.
90. 14. that we may be g. and *rejoice* all our days
118. 24. this is the day, we will *rej.* and be g. in it
Cant. 1. 4. we will be g. and *rejoice* in thee
Isa. 25. 9. we will *rejoice* and be g. in his salvation
65. 18. but be you g. and *rejoice* for ever
66. 10. *rej.* ye with Jerusalem, and be g. with her
Lam. 4. 21. *rejoice* and be g. O daughter of Edom
Joel 2. 21. fear not, O land, be g. and *rejoice*
23. be g. ye children of Zion, and *rejoice* in Lord
Hab. 1. 15. therefore they *rejoice* and are g.
Zeph. 3. 14. be g. and *rej.* O daughter of Jerusalem
Mat. 5. 12. *rejoice* and be g. great is your reward
Acts 2. 26. my heart did *rejoice*, my tongue was g.
Rev. 19. 7. be g. and *rejoice* the marriage is come

GLADLY.

Mark 6. 20. Herod feared John, and heard him g.
12. 37. the common people heard Christ g.
Acts 2. 41. that g. received the word were baptized
21. 17. when come, the brethren received us g.
2 Cor. 11. 19. ye suffer fools g. seeing ye are wise
12. 9. most g. therefore will I rather glory
15. I will very g. spend and be spent for you

GLADNESS.

Num. 10. 10. in the day of your g. ye shall blow
Deut. 28. 47. servedst not the Lord with g. of heart
2 Sam. 6. 12. David brought up the ark with g.
1 Chron. 16. 27. strength and g. are in his place
29. 22. and did eat and drink that day with great g.
2 Chron. 29. 30. and they sang praises with g.
30. 21. Israel kept feast of unleavened bread with g.
23. and they kept other seven days with g.
Neh. 8. 17. and there was very great g.
12. 27. Levites, to keep the dedication with g.
Esth. 8. 16. the Jews had light, and g. and joy, 17.
9. 17. they made it a day of feasting and g. 18. 19.
Psal. 4. 7. thou hast put g. in my heart more than
30. 11. and thou hast girded me with g.
43. † 4. I will go to God the g. of my joy
45. 7. hath anointed thee with oil of g. Heb. 1. 9.
15. with g. and rejoicing shall they be brought
51. 8. make me to hear joy and g. that the bones
97. 11. and g. is sown for the upright in heart
100. 2. serve the Lord with g. come with singing
105. 43. he brought forth his chosen with g.
106. 5. that I may rejoice in the g. of thy nation
Prov. 10. 28. the hope of the righteous shall be g.
Cant. 3. 11. and in the day of the g. of his heart
Isa. 16. 10. joy and g. is taken away out of the field
22. 13. and, behold, joy and g. slaying oxen
30. 29. ye shall have a song and g. of heart
35. 10. they shall obtain joy and g. 51. 11.
51. 3. joy and g. shall be found therein
Jer. 7. 34. cease voice of mirth and g. 16. 9. | 25. 10.
31. 7. sing with g. for Jacob, shout among nations
33. 11. there shall be heard a voice of joy and g.
48. 33. joy and g. taken from the plentiful field
Joel 1. 16. joy and g. from the house of our God
Zech. 8. 19. shall be to house of Judah joy and g.
Mark 4. 16. who immediately receive it with g.
Luke 1. 14. shalt have joy and g. and many rejoice
Acts 2. 46. did eat their meat with g. of heart
12. 14. she opened not the gate for g. but ran
14. 17. filling our hearts with food and g.
Phil. 2. 29. receive him in the Lord with all g.

GLASS.

1 Cor. 13. 12. for now we see through a g. darkly
2 Cor. 3. 18. with open face, beholding as in a g.
Jam. 1. 23. a man beholding his natural face in a g.
Rev. 4. 6. there was a sea of g. like unto crystal
15. 2. and I saw a sea of g. mingled with fire
21. 18. the city was pure gold, like clear g. 21.

GLASSES.

Isa. 3. 23. the Lord will take away the g. and vails

See LOOKING.

GLEAN.

Lev. 19. 10. thou shalt not g. vineyard, Deut. 24. 21.
Ruth 2. 2. let me now go to the field and g. ears
Jer. 6. 9. they shall thoroughly g. the remnant

GLEANED.

Judg. 1. † 7. kings g. their meat under my table
20. 45. and they g. of them in the high-ways
Ruth 2. 3. she came and g. after the reapers

GLEANING, S.

Lev. 19. 9. not gather the g. of harvest, 23. 22.
Judg. 8. 2. is not the g. of the grapes of Ephraim?
Isa. 17. 6. yet g. grapes shall be left in it as shaking
24. 13. as the g. grapes when vintage is done
Jer. 49. 9. would they not leave some g.? Obad. † 5.
Mic. 7. 1. I am as the grape g. of the vintage

GLEDE.

Deut. 14. 13. ye shall not eat the g. kite, vulture

GLISTERING.

1 Chron. 29. 2. now I have prepared g. stones
Job 20. 25. the g. sword cometh out of his gall
Luke 9. 29. and his raiment was white and g.

GLITTER, ING.

Deut. 32. 41. if I whet my g. sword I will render
Job 39. 23. the g. spear rattleth against him
Ezek. 21. 10. it is furbished that it may g.
28. it is furbished to consume, because of the g.
Nah. 3. 3. the horseman lifteth up the g. spear
Hab. 3. 11. they went at the shining of thy g. spear

GLOOMINESS.

Joel 2. 2. a day of darkness and g. Zeph. 1. 15.

GLORIFY.

To glorify, *signifies to make glorious*, Rom. 8. 30. Whom he justified, them he also glorified. *Thus God glorifies the elect, by adorning them with gifts and graces in this world, and by bringing them to the full possession of glory and blessedness in the other world. When man is said to glorify God, it is not to be understood as if he could add any thing to God's essential glory: but we may be said to glorify God, when we acknowledge him to be glorious, and ascribe to him the glory of every excellency whether of nature or grace, and confess that he is worthy to receive honour, glory, might, and majesty,* Rev. 4. 11. *When we confess that all the glory, gifts, and dignity which we have above other men, are given us of God,* 1 Chron. 29. 11, 12. *When we are willing to abase ourselves in the acknowledgment of our own vileness, that God may be magnified in any of his attributes or ordinances by it,* Jer. 13. 16. Mal. 2. 2. *When we believe God's promises, and wait for the performance of them, though we see no means likely for their accomplishment,* Rom. 4. 20. *When we publicly acknowledge true religion, or any special truth of God, when it is generally opposed,* Luke 23. 47. *When we suffer for God,* 1 Pet. 4. 16. *When on the sabbath we devote ourselves only to the service of God,* Isa. 58. 13. *When we give thanks to God for benefits, or deliverances,* Psal. 113. 4. Luke 17. 18. *When we love, praise, admire, and esteem* Christ *above all,* John 1. 14. | 11. 4.

God the Father is glorified in Christ *the Mediator by his obedience unto death, and thereby consummating the work of man's redemption, which tends so much to the advancement of the justice, wisdom, mercy, and holiness of God: but* Christ *the Son is glorified of the Father, as touching his human nature, by sustaining it against the gates of hell in his agony and passion on the cross; by manifestly owning him to be his Son; by enabling him to triumph over his and his people's enemies, in his resurrection, ascension, and exaltation to his Father's right hand.* John 17. 1. Father, glorify thy Son, that thy Son also may glorify thee.

Psal. 22. 23. all ye the seed of Jacob g. him and fear
50. 15. I will deliver thee, and thou shalt g. me
86. 9. all nations shall come and g. thy name
12. and I will g. thy name for evermore
Isa. 24. 15. wherefore g. ye the Lord in the fires
25. 3. therefore shall the strong people g. thee
60. 7. and I will g. the house of my glory
Jer. 30. 19. I will multiply, I will also g. them
Mat. 5. 16. g. your Father which is in heaven
John 12. 28. Father, g. thy name; I will g. it
13. 32. God shall also g. him in himself
16. 14. he shall g. me; for he shall receive of mine
17. 1. g. thy Son, that thy Son also may g. thee
5. now, O Father, g. me with thine own self
21. 19. signifying by what death he should g. God
Rom. 15. 6. ye may with one mind and mouth g. God
9. that the Gentiles might g. God for his mercy
1 Cor. 6. 20. g. G. in body and spirit which are God's
2 Cor. 9. 13. g. God for your professed subjection
1 Pet. 2. 12. may g. God in the day of visitation
4. 16. but let him g. God on this behalf
Rev. 15. 4. who shall not fear thee, and g. thy name?

GLORIFIED.

Lev. 10. 3. before all the people I will be g.
Isa. 26. 15. thou hast increased nation, thou art g.
44. 23. for the Lord hath g. himself in Israel
49. 3. art my servant, O Isr. in whom I will be g.
55. 5. the Holy One of Isr. he hath g. thee. 60. 9.
60. 21. the work of my hands, that I may be g.
61. 3. the planting of the Lord that he might be g
66. 5. your brethren said, let the Lord be g.
Ezek. 28. 22. I will be g. in the midst of thee
39. 13. be a renown in the day that I shall be g.
Dan. 5. 23. and the God in whose hand thy breath is, and whose are all thy ways, hast thou not g.
Hag. 1. 8. I will take pleasure in it, and be g.
Mat. 9. 8. marvelled, and g. G. Mark 2. 12. Luke 5. 26.
15. 31. and they g. the God of Israel
Luke 4. 15. he taught in synagogues, being g. of all
7. 16. there came fear on all, and they g. God
13. 13. and she was made straight, and g. God
17. 15. the leper g. God || 23. 47. the centurion g. G.
John 7. 39. H. Ghost not given, because Jesus not g.
11. 4. that the Son of God might be g. thereby
12. 16. but when Jes. was g. then remembered they
23. the hour is come the Son of man should be g.
28. I have both g. it, and will glorify it again
13. 31. now is the Son of man g. God is g. in him
32. if God be g. in him, God shall glorify him
14. 13. that the Father may be g. in the Son
15. 8. herein is my Father g. that ye bear fruit
17. 4. I have g. thee on earth, I have finished
10. and thine are mine, and I am g. in them
Acts 3. 13. the God of our fathers hath g. his Son
4. 21. for all men g. God for what was done
11. 18. they held their peace, and g. God, saying
13. 48. Gentiles heard this, they g. word of Lord
21. 20. they of Jerusalem g. the Lord, and said
Rom. 1. 21. they knew God, they g. him not as God
8. 17. if we suffer with him, that we may be also g.
30. and whom he justified, them he also g.
Gal. 1. 24. and they g. God in me
2 Thess. 1. 10. when he shall come to be g. in saints
12. that the name of Jesus may be g. in you
3. 1. that the word of the Lord may be g.
Heb. 5. 5. so Christ g. not himself to be high-priest
1 Pet. 4. 11. God in all things may be g. thro' Jesus
14. is evil spoken of, but on your part he is g.
Rev. 18. 7. how much she hath g. herself

GLORIFIETH, ING.

Psal. 50. 23. whoso offereth praise g. me
Luke 2. 20. the shepherds returned, g. God
5. 25. he departed to his own house, g. God
18. 43. the blind man followed him, g. God

GLORY

Is *taken for worldly splendour and magnificence, which make kings glorious before men,* Mat. 6. 29. *Solomon* in all his glory, *in all his lustre, and in his richest ornaments, was not so beautiful as a lily. Thus riches, authority, sumptuous buildings and garments, which men are ready to praise, and which make their possessors glorious before men, are called in Scripture* glory. *Psal.* 49. 16. When the glory of his house is increased. *By* glory *is meant the tongue, which is that peculiar excellency, wherein chiefly, except reason, man surpasses all other creatures.* Psal. 16. 9. My heart is glad, and my glory rejoiceth: *My tongue breaks out into holy boastings and praises. So in* Psal. 108. 1. I will sing and give praise, even with my glory. The glory of the king of *Assyria, is his splendid princes, brave captains, valiant commanders, and powerful armies, which would make a gallant shew, and wherein he would glory, and boast exceedingly.* Isa. 8. 7. The Lord bringeth upon them the king of *Assyria*, and all his glory. Glory *is put for the ark of the covenant, which was a glorious type and assurance of God's presence, and the great safeguard and ornament of* Israel, *which they could glory in above all other nations.* 1 Sam. 4. 21. The glory is departed from *Israel.* Rom. 9. 4. To whom pertaineth the glory.

Glory *is put for the church, which God makes glorious, not only in his own eyes, but even in the eyes of the world.* Isa. 4. 5. Upon all the glory shall be a defence; *upon all holy assemblies of sincere Christians. It is put for grace,* 2 Cor. 3. 18. We are changed into the same image, from glory to glory; *growing from one degree of glorious grace to another, till it come to its perfection in eternal glory. The apostle calls man* the image and glory of God, *and for this reason* he ought not to cover his head; *that is, Since God would have the male sex to be a kind of representation of his glory, majesty, and power, a man ought not, by hiding his face, wherein these things are most conspicuous, to conceal the glory of God shining in him.* David *calls God his* glory, Psal. 3. 3. Thou art my glory; *thou art the Author of that royal dignity to which I am advanced: or, thou art the matter of my glorying, thou hast formerly given, and wilt further give, me occasion of glorying or boasting of thy power and favour to me.* Glory *is taken for the unspeakable blessedness, joy, and felicity of the saints in heaven.* Psal. 73. 24. Thou shalt guide me with thy counsel, and afterwards receive me to glory. *God promises to be to his church* a wall of fire round about, and the glory in the midst, *Zech.* 2. 5. *that he would protect his church, and that his presence and power should make her glorious. It is put for the presence of God,* Psal. 63. 2.

When the Israelites *forsook God in the wilderness,* they changed their glory into the similitude of an ox that eateth grass, *Psal.* 106. 20. They changed their glory; *that is, their God, who was indeed their glory, into the golden image of an ox or calf.* Joshua *speaking to* Achan *says,* Give glory to God, *Josh.* 7. 19. *Confess the truth, and ascribe unto God the glory of his omniscience in knowing thy sin, and of his justice in punishing thee according to thy desert. When God thought fit to call his servant* Moses *to himself, he directed him to go up to mount* Abarim, *and die there*, Num. 27. 12, &c. Moses *hereupon desired of God that he would provide a man who should be set over the multitude. The Lord therefore commanded him to take* Joshua, *the son of* Nun, *saying*, He is a man who is filled with the Spirit, lay thine hand upon him, and give him a charge in the presence *of the multitude, and put some of thine honour, in* Hebrew, *of thy glory or splendour, upon him. The question is, what glory this was, which* Moses *communicated to* Joshua. Onkelos, *and some of the* Rabbins, *are of opinion, that* Moses *imparted to him some of that lustre which appeared upon his countenance, after the conversation which he had been admitted to with God.* Moses, *they say, shined like the sun, and* Joshua *like the moon: this was a weak and borrowed brightness. But it is to be understood of that authority, and empire, whereof he stood in need for the government of the people.* Moses *laid his hands on him, and by this ceremony appointed him for his successor in the conduct of the* Israelites: *He gave him his orders and instructions, that he might acquit himself with honour in this employment.*

The glory of God. Moses *earnestly begged of God to shew him his glory.* Exod. 33. 18. I beseech thee, shew me thy glory; *that is, the highest manifestation of thy divine glory that I am capable of; or that glorious shape, which, together with an human voice, thou hast now assumed.* The heavens declare the glory of God, *Psal.* 19. 1. *The visible heavens afford matter and occasion, in respect of their vast extent, glorious furniture, and powerful influences, to acknowledge and admire the glorious being, infinite power, wisdom, and goodness of God.* The glory of the Lord hath filled the house of the Lord; *that is, the cloud, which was an usual token of God's glorious presence*, 1 Kings 8. 11. Christ *says to* Martha, *John* 11. 40. If thou wouldest believe, thou shouldest see the glory of God; *that is, an admirable instance of the divine power, in raising thy dead brother. The miracles which our Saviour wrought, manifested his glory, or his divine power*, John 2. 11. The glory of the Lord shall be revealed, *Isa.* 40. 5. *that is, the glorious power and goodness of God shall be manifested in the deliverance of the* Jews *from* Babylon, *but more especially in the redemption of all nations by our Lord* Jesus Christ. Whether ye eat or drink, or whatsoever ye do, do all to the glory of God, 1 *Cor.* 10. 31. *that is, let the glory and honour of God be habitually and really the chief end of all your actions.*

Gen. 31. 1. of our fathers hath he gotten all this *g.*
Exod. 28. 2. make garments for Aaron for *g.* 40.
1 *Sam.* 2. 8. to make them inherit the throne of *g.*
4. 21. the *g.* is departed from Israel, 22.
† 21. where is the *g.?* there is no *g.*
1 *Chr.* 22. 5. house for Lord must be of *g.* and fame
29. 11. thine is greatness, power, and *g. Mat.* 6. 13.
Esth. 5. 11. Haman told of the *g.* of his riches
Job 39. 20. the *g.* of his nostrils is terrible
40. 10. and array thyself with *g.* and beauty
Psal. 24. 7. and the King of *g.* shall come in, 9.
10. who is this King of *g.?* the Lord is King
29. 3. the God of *g.* thundereth, Lord on waters
49. 16. when the *g.* of his house is increased
73. 24. thou shalt afterward receive me to *g.*
79. 9. help us, O God, for the *g.* of thy name
85. 9. that *g.* may dwell in our land
89. 17. for thou art the *g.* of their strength
106. 20. they changed their *g.* into similitude
145. 11. speak of the *g.* of thy kingdom
149. 5. let the saints be joyful in *g.*
Prov. 3. 35. the wise shall inherit *g.*
17. 6. the *g.* of children are their fathers
20. 29. the *g.* of young men is their strength
25. † 6. set not out thy *g.* in presence of the king
27. so for men to search their own *g.* is not *g.*
28. 12. when the righteous men rejoice there is *g.*
Isa. 2. 10. hide thee for the *g.* of his majesty, 19. 21.
4. † 2. branch of the Lord shall be beauty and *g.*
5. for upon all the *g.* shall be a defence
5. † 13. and their *g.* are men of famine
14. their *g.* and pomp shall descend unto it
10. 3. and where will ye leave your *g.?*
12. I will punish the *g.* of his high looks
18. and shall consume the *g.* of his forest
11. † 10. a root of Jesse, his rest shall be *g.*
13. 19. Babylon the *g.* of kingd. shall be as Sodom
14. 18. all of them lie in *g.* each in his house
16. 14. the *g.* of Moab shall be contemned
17. 3. they shall be as the *g.* of the children of Isr.
4. that the *g.* of Jacob shall be made thin
20. 5. they shall be ashamed of Egypt their *g.*
21. 16. and all the *g.* of Kedar shall fail
22. 24. shall hang on him *g.* of his Father's house
23. 9. hath purposed to stain the pride of all *g.*
24. 16. we heard songs, even *g.* to the righteous
† 23. there shall be *g.* before his ancients
35. 2. the *g.* of Lebanon shall be given to it
61. 6. in their *g.* ye shall boast yourselves
66. 11. be delighted with the abundance of her *g.*
12. the *g.* of the Gentiles as a flowing stream
Jer. 2. 11. but my people have changed their *g.*
13. 11. that they might be to me for a *g.*
18. shall come down, even the crown of your *g.*
Ezek. 20. 6. which is the *g.* of all lands, 15.
24. 25. when I take from them the joy of their *g.*
25. 9. I will open the *g.* of the country
26. 20. I shall set *g.* in the land of the living
31. 18. to whom art thou thus like in *g.?*
Dan. 2. 37. God hath given thee power and *g.* 7. 14.
4. 36. the *g.* of my kingdom returned to me
11. 39. shall acknowledge, and increase with *g.*
Hos. 4. 7. I will change their *g.* into shame
9. 11. as for Ephraim, their *g.* shall fly away
10. 5. the priests that rejoiced for the *g.* thereof
Mic. 1. 15. he shall come to Adullam the *g.* of Isr.
Nah. 2. 9. there is none end of the store and *g.*
Hab. 2. 16. thou art filled with shame for *g.*
Hag. 2. 3. who saw this house in her first *g.?*
7. I will fill this house with *g.* saith the Lord
Hag. 2. 9. *g.* of this latter house greater than of form.
Zech. 2. 5. I will be the *g.* in the midst of her
8. after the *g.* hath he sent me to the nations
6. 13. he shall build temple, he shall bear the *g.*
11. 3. their *g.* is spoiled, a voice of roaring of lions
12. 7. *g.* of the house of David, *g.* of Jerusalem
Mat. 4. 8. kingdoms of the world, and *g.* of them
6. 2. sound trumpet, that they may have *g.* of men
16. 27. shall come in the *g.* of his Father, *Mark* 8. 38.
24. 30. they shall see the Son of Man coming with power and great *g. Mark* 13. 26. *Luke* 21. 27.
Luke 2. 14. saying, *g.* to God in the highest, 19. 38.
32. light to Gentiles, and the *g.* of thy people Isr.
4. 6. all this power will I give thee, and the *g.*
9. 31. who appeared in *g.* and spake of his decease
John 17. 5. with the *g.* which I had with thee
22. the *g.* thou gavest me, I have given them
Acts 7. 2. the God of *g.* appeared to our father
12. 23. because he gave not God the *g.*
22. 11. when I could not see for the *g.* of light
Rom. 4. 20. was strong in faith, giving *g.* to God
6. 4. raised from the dead by the *g.* of the Father
8. 18. are not worthy to be compared with the *g.*
9. 4. to whom pertaineth the *g.* and covenants
23. which he had afore prepared unto *g.*
11. 36. of him are all things, to whom be *g.* for ever, *Gal.* 1. 5. 2 *Tim.* 4. 18. *Heb.* 13. 21. 1 *Pet.* 5. 11.
16. 27. to God only wise be *g.* 1 *Tim.* 1. 17.
1 *Cor.* 2. 7. which God hath ordained to our *g.*
8. they would not have crucified the Lord of *g.*
11. 7. but the woman is the *g.* of the man
15. if a woman have long hair, it is a *g.* to her
15. 40. *g.* of celestial is one, the *g.* of the terrestrial
41. one *g.* of the sun, another *g.* of the moon
43. it is sown in dishonour, it is raised in *g.*
2 *Cor.* 3. 7. for the *g.* of his countenance, which *g.*
9. if the ministration of condemnation be *g.* the ministration of righteousness doth exceed in *g.*
10. had no *g.* by reason of the *g.* that excelleth
18. but we all are changed from *g.* to *g.*
4. 17. worketh for us an eternal weight of *g.*
8. 19. administered to us to the *g.* of the same Ld.
23. they are messengers, and the *g.* of Christ
Eph. 1. 6. to the praise of the *g.* of his grace
17. the Father of *g.* may give you the Spirit
18. ye may know what is the riches of the *g.*
3. 13. my tribulations for you, which is your *g.*
21. to him be *g.* in the church by Christ Jesus
Phil. 1. 11. fruits, which are by Christ to *g.* of God
3. 19. and whose *g.* is in their shame
4. 19. according to his riches in *g.* by Christ
20. now to God and our Father be *g.* for ever
Col. 1. 27. what is the riches of the *g.* of this mystery, which is Christ in you the hope of *g.*
3. 4. then shall ye appear with him in *g.*
1 *Thess.* 2. 6. nor of men sought we *g.* nor of you
12. who hath called you to his kingdom and *g.*
20. for ye are our *g.* and joy
2 *Thess.* 1. 9. punished from the *g.* of his power
2. 14. to the obtaining of the *g.* of our Lord
1 *Tim.* 3. 16. seen of angels, received up into *g.*
2 *Tim.* 2. 10. salvation in Christ, with eternal *g.*
Heb. 2. 10. in bringing many sons to *g.* to make
3. 3. this man was counted worthy of more *g.*
9. 5. over it the cherubims of *g.* shadowing
Jam. 2. 1. the faith of our Lord Jesus, the Lord of *g.*
1 *Pet.* 1. 8. rejoice with joy unspeakable, full of *g.*
11. it testified the *g.* that should follow
21. that God raised him up, and gave him *g.*
24. and all the *g.* of man, as the flower of grass
2. 20. for what *g.* is it, if when ye be buffeted?
4. 14. the Spirit of *g.* and of God resteth on you
5. 1. a partaker of the *g.* that shall be revealed
10. hath called us to eternal *g.* by Christ Jesus
2 *Pet.* 1. 3. that hath called us to *g.* and virtue
17. came such a voice to him from excellent *g.*
3. 18. to him be *g.* both now and ever, *Rev.* 1. 6.
Jude 25. to the only wise God our Saviour be *g.*
Rev. 4. 11. thou art worthy to receive *g.* 5. 12.
7. 12. blessing and *g.* and wisdom be to our God
11. 13. remnant were affrighted, and gave *g.* to God
See CROWN, HONOUR, VAIN.

Give GLORY.

Josh. 7. 19. my son, *give g.* to the God of Israel
1 *Sam.* 6. 5. ye shall *give g.* to the God of Israel
1 *Chron.* 16. 28. *give* to the Lord *g. give* to Lord *g.* and strength, 29. *Psal.* 29. 1, 2. | 96. 7, 8. *Jer.* 13. 16.
Psal. 84. 11. the Lord will *give* grace and *g.*
115. 1. not to us, but to thy name *give* the *g.*
Isa. 42. 12. let them *give g.* unto the Lord
Mal. 2. 2. if ye will not lay it to heart to *give g.*
Luke 17. 18. that returned to *give g.* to God
Rev. 4. 9. when those beasts *give g.* and honour
14. 7. fear God, and *give g.* to him, worship him
16. 9. were scorched, and repented not to *give g.*

GLORY *of God.*

Psal. 19. 1. the heavens declare the *g. of God*
Prov. 25. 2. it is the *g. of God* to conceal a thing
Ezek. 8. 4. the *g. of* the *God* of Israel was there
9. 3. the *g. of God* was gone up from the cherub
10. 19. the *g. of God* was over them above, 11. 22.
43. 2. the *g. of God* came from the way of the east
John 11. 4. this sickness is for the *g. of God*
40. if believe, thou shouldest see the *g. of God*
Acts 7. 55. Stephen looked up and saw the *g. of God*
Rom. 3. 23. all sinned and come short of the *g. of God*
5. 2. we rejoice in hope of the *g. of God*
15. 7. as Christ also received us to the *g. of God*
1 *Cor.* 10. 31. ye eat or drink, do all to the *g. of G.*
11. 7. for a man is the image and *g. of God*
2 *Cor.* 1. 20. promises in him yea and amen, to *g. of G.*
4. 6. the light of the knowledge of the *g. of God*
15. thanksgiving of many redound to *g. of God*
Phil. 1. 11. which are by Christ to the *g. of God*
2. 11. confess that Jesus is Lord to the *g. of God*
Rev. 15. 8. temple filled with smoke from *g. of God*
21. 11. the holy Jerusalem, having the *g. of God*
23. no need of the sun, *g. of God* did lighten it

His GLORY.

Deut. 5. 24. the Lord our G. hath shewed us *his g.*
33. 17. *his g.* like the firstling of a bullock
1 *Chr.* 16. 24. declare *his g.* among heath. *Ps.* 96. 3.
Psal. 21. 5. *his g.* is great in thy salvation
29. 9. in his temple doth every one speak of *his g.*
49. 17. *his g.* shall not descend after him
72. 19. let the whole earth be filled with *his g.*
78. 61. delivered *his g.* into the enemies' hand
89. 44. thou hast made *his g.* to cease
97. 6. and all the people see *his g.*
102. 16. when L. build Zion, shall appear in *his g.*
113. 4. and *his g.* above the heavens, 148. 13.
Prov. 19. 11. it is *his g.* to pass over transgression
Isa. 3. 8. to provoke the eyes of *his g.*
6. 3. one cried, the whole earth is full of *his g.*
8. 7. the king of Assyria and *his g.* shall come up
10. 16. under *his g.* he shall kindle a burning
59. 19. shall fear *his g.* from rising of the sun
60. 2. and *his g.* shall be seen upon thee
Jer. 22. 18. not lament, saying, ah lord, or ah *his g.*
Ezek. 43. 2. and the earth shined with *his g.*
Dan. 5. 20. and they took *his g.* from him
Hab. 3. 3. God came, *his g.* covered the heavens
Mat. 6. 29. Solomon in all *his g. Luke* 12. 27.
19. 28. Son of man shall sit in *his g. Luke* 9. 26
Luke 9. 32. when they were awake, they saw *his g.*
24. 26. to have suffered, and to enter into *his g.*
John 1. 14. we beheld *his g.* the glory as of the only
2. 11. thus did Jesus, and manifested forth *his g.*
7. 18. but he that seeketh *his g.* that sent him
12. 41. these things said Esaias, when he saw *his g.*
Rom. 3. 7. hath abounded through my lie unto *his g.*
9. 23. might make known the riches of *his g.*
Eph. 1. 12. should be to the praise of *his g.* 14.
3. 16. grant you according to the riches of *his g.*
Heb. 1. 3. who being the brightness of *his g.*
1 *Pet.* 4. 13. that when *his g.* shall be revealed
Jude 24. present you before the presence of *his g.*
Rev. 18. 1. the earth was lightened with *his g.*

My GLORY.

Gen. 45. 13. tell my father of all *my g.* in Egypt
Exod. 29. 43. tabernacle shall be sanctified by *my g.*
33. 22. while *my g.* passeth by, I will put thee
Num. 14. 22. those men which have seen *my g.*
Job 19. 9. he hath stript me of *my g.* and taken
29. 20. *my g.* was fresh in me, my bow renewed
Psal. 3. 3. thou art *my g.* and lifter up of my head
4. 2. how long will ye turn *my g.* into shame?
16. 9. *my g.* rejoiceth || 30. 12. *my g.* may sing
57. 8. awake up *my g.* || 62. 7. in God is *my g.*
108. 1. I will sing and give praise with *my g.*
Isa. 42. 8. *my g.* will I not give to another, 48. 11.
43. 7. for I have created him for *my g.*
46. 13. I will place salvation for Israel, *my g.*
60. 7. I will glorify the house of *my g.*
66. 18. and they shall come and see *my g.*
19. have not seen *my g.* they shall declare *my g.*
Ezek. 39. 21. I will set *my g.* among the heathen
Mic. 2. 9. from children have ye taken away *my g.*
John 8. 50. and I seek not *mine* own *g.* one seeks
17. 24. be with me, that they may behold *my g.*

GLORY *of the Lord.*

Exod. 16. 7. in morning ye shall see *g. of the Lord*
10. the *g. of the Lord* appeared in the cloud, *Lev.* 9. 23. *Num.* 14. 10. | 16. 19, 42. | 20. 6.
24. 16. the *g. of the Lord* abode on mount Sinai
17. the *g. of the Lord* was like devouring fire
40. 34. the *g. of the Lord* filled the tabernacle, 35.
Lev. 9. 6. the *g. of the Lord* shall appear unto you
Num. 14. 21. earth shall be filled with *g. of the Lord*
1 *Kings* 8. 11. the *g. of the Lord* filled the house, 2 *Chr.* 5. 14. | 7. 1, 2, 3. *Ezek.* 43. 5. | 44. 4.
Ps. 104. 31. the *g. of the Lord* shall endure for ever
138. 5. for great is the *g. of the Lord*
Isa. 35. 2. they shall see the *g. of the Lord*
40. 5. and the *g. of the Lord* shall be revealed
58. 8. the *g. of the Lord* shall be thy rereward
60. 1. and the *g. of the Lord* is risen upon thee
Ezek. 1. 28. appearance of the likeness of *g. of Lord*
3. 12. blessed be the *g. of the Lord* from his place
23. and behold, the *g. of the Lord* stood there
10. 4. the *g. of the Lord* went up from the cherub
18. *g. of the Lord* departed from the threshold
11. 23. the *g. of the Lord* went up from the city
43. 4. the *g. of the Lord* came into the house
Hab. 2. 14. filled with knowledge of *g. of the Lord*
Luke 2. 9. *g. of the Lord* shone round about them
2 *Cor.* 3. 18. beholding as in a glass *g. of the Lord*

Thy GLORY.

Exod. 33. 18. he said, I beseech thee shew me *thy g.*
Psal. 8. 1. who hast set *thy g.* above the heavens
45. 3. gird thy sword on thy thigh with *thy g.*
57. 5. let *thy g.* be above all the earth, 11. | 108. 5.
63. 2. to see thy power and *thy g.* as I have seen
90. 16. let *thy g.* appear unto their children
102. 15. and all the kings of the earth *thy g.*
Isa. 22. 18. the chariots of *thy g.* shall be the shame
60. 19. thy God *thy g.* || 62. 2. kings shall see *thy g.*
63. 15. behold from the habitation of *thy g.*
Jer. 14. 21. do not disgrace the throne of *thy g.*
48. 18. come down from *thy g.* and sit in thirst
Hab. 2. 16. and shameful spewing shall be on *thy g.*
Mark 10. 37. the other on thy left hand in *thy g.*

GLORIOUS.

Exod. 15. 6. thy right hand, O Lord, is become *g.*
11. who is like thee, O Lord, *g.* in holiness
Deut. 28. 58. that thou mayest fear this *g.* name
2 *Sam.* 6. 20. how *g.* was the king of Israel to day
1 *Chron.* 29. 13. we thank and praise thy *g.* name
Neh. 9. 5. blessed be thy *g.* name which is exalted
Psal. 29. † 2. worship Ld. in *g.* sanctuary, 96. † 9.
45. 13. the king's daughter is all *g.* within
66. 2. sing forth his honour, make his praise *g.*
72. 19. and blessed be his *g.* name for ever
76. 4. thou art more *g.* than the mountains of prey
87. 3. *g.* things are spoken of thee, O city of God
111. 3. his work is honourable and *g.*
145. 5. I will speak of the *g.* honour of thy majesty
12. to make known the *g.* majesty of his kingdom
Isa. 4. 2. the branch of the Lord shall be *g.*
11. 10. be a root of Jesse, and his rest shall be *g.*
22. 23. he shall be for a *g.* throne to his F. house
28. 1. whose *g.* beauty is a fading flower
4. the *g.* beauty which is on head of the fat valley
30. 30. the Lord shall cause his *g.* voice to be heard

Isa. 33. 21. *g.* Lord will be to us a place of streams
49. 5. yet shall I be *g.* in the eyes of the Lord
60. 13. I will make the place of my feet *g.*
63. 1. who is this that is *g.* in his apparel?
12. that led them by Moses with his *g.* arm
14. didst lead people to make thyself a *g.* name
Jer. 17. 12. a *g.* high throne from the beginning
Ezek. 27. 25. made very *g.* in the midst of the seas
Dan. 11. 16. and he shall stand in the *g.* land
41. he shall enter also into the *g.* land
45. between the seas in the *g.* holy mountain
Luke 13. 17. people rejoiced for the *g.* things done
Rom. 8. 21. into the *g.* liberty of the children of G.
2 *Cor.* 3. 7. if ministration engraven in stones was *g.*
3. 8. the ministration of the Spirit be rather *g.*
4. 4. lest light of *g.* gospel should shine unto them
Eph. 5. 27. he might present it to himself a *g.* church
Phil. 3. 21. that it may be fashioned like to his *g.* body
Col. 1. 11. strengthened according to his *g.* power
1 *Tim.* 1. 11. according to the *g.* gospel of blessed G.
Tit. 2. 13. looking for the *g.* appearing of the great G.

GLORIOUSLY.

Exod. 15. 1. sing to the Lord, he hath triumphed *g.*
Isa. 24. 23. the Ld. shall reign before his ancients *g.*

GLORY, *Verb.*

Exod. 8. 9. *g.* over me, when shall I entreat for thee
2 *Kings* 14. 10. *g.* of this, and tarry at home
1 *Chr.* 16. 10. *g.* ye in his holy name, *Psal.* 105. 3.
35. we may give thanks, and *g.* in thy praise
Psal. 63. 11. every one that sweareth by him shall *g.*
64. 10. and all the upright in heart shall *g.*
106. 5. that I may *g.* with thine inheritance
Isa. 41. 16. and shalt *g.* in the holy One of Israel
45. 25. in the Lord shall all the seed of Israel *g.*
Jer. 4. 2. bless in him, and in him shall they *g.*
9. 23. let not the wise, mighty, the rich man *g.*
24. let him *g.* in this, that he knoweth me
Rom. 4. 2. he hath whereof to *g.* but not before God
5. 3. not only so, but we *g.* in tribulations also
15. 17. I have therefore whereof I may *g.* thro' Jesus
1 *Cor.* 1. 29. that no flesh should *g.* in his presence
31. he that glorieth *g.* in the Lord, 2 *Cor.* 10. 17.
3. 21. therefore let no man *g.* in men, all are yours
4. 7. why dost thou *g.* as if thou hadst not received
9. 16. though I preach, I have nothing to *g.* of
2 *Cor.* 5. 12. give occasion to *g.* on our behalf; to answer them who *g.* in appearance, not in heart
11. 12. wherein they *g.* they may be found as we
18. seeing many *g.* after the flesh, I will *g.* also
30. if I must needs *g.* I will *g.* of my infirmities
12. 1. it is not expedient for me doubtless to *g.*
5. of such an one will I *g.* of myself I will not *g.*
6. for though I would desire to *g.* I shall not be a f.
9. therefore I will rather *g.* in mine infirmities
Gal. 6. 13. you circumcised, that they may *g.* in flesh
14. G. forbid I should *g.* save in the cross of Jesus
2 *Thess.* 1. 4. that we ourselves *g.* in you in churches
Jam. 1. † 9. let the brother of low degree *g.*
3. 14. if ye have envying in your hearts, *g.* not

GLORIEST.

Jer. 49. 4. wherefore *g.* thou in the valleys?

GLORIETH.

Jer. 9. 24. let him that *g.* 1 *Cor.* 1. 31. 2 *Cor.* 10. 17.
Jam. 2. † 13. and mercy *g.* against judgment

GLORYING.

1 *Cor.* 5. 6. your *g.* is not good, a little leaven
9. 15. than that any man should make my *g.* void
2 *Cor.* 7. 4. great is my boldness, great my *g.* of you
12. 11. I am become a fool in *g.* ye compelled me
1 *Thess.* 2. † 19. what is our crown of *g.*? are not ye

GLUTTON, S.

Deut. 21. 20. this our son, is a *g.* and a drunkard
Prov. 23. 21. drunkard and *g.* shall come to poverty
28. † 7. he that feedeth *g.* shameth his father

GLUTTONOUS.

Mat. 11. 19. they said, behold a man *g.* *Luke* 7. 34.

GNASH.

Ps. 112. 10. he shall *g.* with his teeth, and melt away
Lam. 2. 16. all thine enemies hiss and *g.* the teeth

GNASHED.

Psal. 35. 16. they *g.* upon me with their teeth
Acts 7. 54. and they *g.* on him with their teeth

GNASHETH.

Job 16. 9. he *g.* on me with his teeth, *Psal.* 37. 12.
Mark 9. 18. he foameth and *g.* with his teeth

GNASHING.

Mat. 8. 12. there shall be weeping and *g.* of teeth, 13. 42, 50. | 22. 13. | 24. 51. | 25. 30. *Luke* 13. 28.

GNAT.

Mat. 23. 24. who strain at a *g.* and swallow a camel

GNAW.

Zeph. 3. 3. her judges *g.* not the bones till the morrow

GNAWED.

Rev. 16. 10. and they *g.* their tongues for pain

GO.

To go down, and go up; We go up to *Jerusalem*, Mat. 20. 18. He goes down to *Jericho*, Luke 10. 30. *Abraham* went up out of *Egypt*, Gen. 13. 1. *Jacob* went down into *Egypt*, Gen. 46. 3. Go up to *Ai*, Josh. 7. 3. He went down to *Cesarea*, Acts 12. 19. *By all which nothing more is meant, than that they went to* Jerusalem, *into* Egypt, *to* Jericho, Ai, *and* Cesarea; *but the situation of the place they were going to, is described by the words* going up *and* going down.

To go down into hell, *or* scheol; *to go down to the grave, the place where the dead are.* Psal. 55. 15. Let them go down quick into hell; *Let them go down alive into the grave; cut them off by a sudden and violent death, like* Korah, Dathan, *and* Abiram. The dead praise not the Lord, neither any that go down into silence; *into the* grave, *Psal.* 115. 17. All they that go down to the dust, shall bow before him, *Psal.* 22. 29. *Such as are poor, and in great misery and distress, shall own, submit unto, and adore* Christ *as their supreme Lord.* They who go down into the sea, *are the merchants or mariners who make voyages upon the sea,* Psal. 107. 23. Jonah *says that* he went down to the very bottoms of the mountains; *that is, to the bottom of the sea, where the mountains have their basis and foundation,* Jonah 2. 6. *See on* HELL.

To go in and out, *signifies all the actions of life.* Psal. 121. 8. The Lord shall preserve thy going out and thy coming in: *He shall guard and assist thee in all thy expeditions, affairs, and actions, either at home or abroad. And in* 2 Sam. 3. 25. *Abner* came to know thy going out and thy coming in; *to search out thy counsels and secret designs.* To go in and out, *denotes also freedom and security,* John 10. 9. He shall go in and out, and find pasture: *He shall have much spiritual freedom and security of mind.* To go into a woman's chamber, *to enter her apartment, was allowable only for her husband,* Judg. 15. 1. To go in unto her, *that is, to use the marriage bed, or the particular rights which the husband claims over his wife's person,* Gen. 29. 23. | 30. 3.

Gen. 3. 14. on thy belly shalt thou *go*, and eat dust
16. 8. whence camest thou? whither wilt thou *go*?
24. 42. if now thou do prosper my way which I *go*
55. abide a few days, after that Rebekah shall *go*
56. send me away, that I may *go* to my master
58. wilt thou *go* with this man? she said, I will *go*
26. 16. and Abimelech said to Isaac, *go* from us
28. 20. if God will keep me in this way that I *go*
30. 25. send me away that I may *go* to my place
32. 26. let me *go*, for the day breaketh; and Jacob said, I will not let thee *go*, except thou bless
37. 30. the child is not, and I, whither shall I *go*?
43. 8. send lad with me, and we will arise, and *go*
Exod. 3. 19. king of Egypt will not let you *go*, 4. 21.
20. and after that he will let you *go*, 11. 1.
21. that when ye *go*, ye shall not *go* empty
4. 23. let my son *go*; if thou refuse to let him *go*, I will slay thy first-born, 8. 2, 21. | 9. 2. | 10. 4.
26. so he let him *go*, then she said, a bloody husb.
5. 1. thus saith the Lord God of Israel, let my people *go*, 7. 16. | 8. 1, 20. | 9. 1, 13 | 10. 3.
2. I know not the Lord, nor will I let Israel *go*
8. 8. and I will let thy people *go*, 28. | 9. 28.
32. Pharaoh hardened his heart, neither would he let the people *go*, 7. 14. | 9. 35. | 10. 26, 27.
10. 7. let the men *go* || 8. who are they that shall *go*?
9. we will *go* with our young and with our old
13. 21. light to *go* by day and night, *Neh.* 9. 12. 19.
14. 5. that we have let Israel *go* from serving us
† 25. chariot-wheels, and made them *go* heavily
17. 5. Lord said to Moses, *go* on before the people
23. 23. mine Angel shall *go* before thee, 32. 34.
32. 23. make us gods to *go* before us, *Acts* 7. 40.
33. 14. he said, my presence shall *go* with thee
34. 9. if I have found grace in sight, *go* amongst us
Num. 10. 32. and it shall be, if thou *go* with us
20. 17. we will *go* by the king's high-way, 19.
22. 13. the Lord refuseth to give me leave to *go*
20. if men call thee, rise up, and *go* with them, 35.
24. 14. and now behold, I *go* unto my people
31. 23. shall make it *go* through the fire and water
32. 6. shall your brethr. *go* to war, and ye sit here?
17. but we will *go* ready armed before Israel
Deut. 1. 33. to shew you by what way ye should *go*
4. 5. in land whither ye *go*, 26. | 11. 8, 11. | 30. 18.
40. that it may *go* well with thee, 5. 16. | 19. 13.
11. 28. a curse, if ye *go* after other gods, 28. 14.
20. 5. let him *go* and return to his house, 6, 7, 8.
21. 14. then thou shalt let her *go* whither she will
22. 7. thou shalt in anywise let the dam *go*
24. 2. she may *go* and be another man's wife
31. 6. thy God, he it is that doth *go* with thee
7. for thou must *go* with this people to the land
8. the Lord, he it is that doth *go* before thee
16. the land whither they *go* to be amongst them
21. I know their imagination they *go* about
Josh. 1. 16. whither thou sendest us we will *go*
3. 4. ye may know the way by which ye must *go*
Judg. 1. 25. but they let *go* the man and his family
4. 8. if thou wilt *go* with me, then I will *go*
6. 14. the Lord said to him, *go* in this thy might
7. 4. of whom I say, this shall *go*, the same shall *go*
11. 8. we turn to thee, that thou mayest *go* with us
16. 17. if I be shaven, then my strength will *go*
18. 5. whether our way we *go* shall be prosperous?
6. before the Lord is your way wherein ye *go*
9. be not slothful to *go* to possess the land
10. when ye *go* || 19. hold thy peace, *go* with us
19. 25. when day began to spring, they let her *go*
Ruth 1. 11. turn again, why will ye *go* with me?
18. she saw she was stedfastly minded to *go*
2. 2. let me *go* to the field and glean, *go* my daugh.
1 *Sam.* 5. 11. let it *go* again to its own place
6. 6. did they not let people *go*? and they departed
8. take the ark, send it away, that it may *go*
9. 6. let us go thither, he can shew us our way
7. if we *go* what shall we bring the man?
19. *go* up before me, to-morrow I will let thee *go*
10. 9. when he turned his back to *go* from Samuel
12. 21. for then should ye *go* after vain things
16. 2. how can I *go*? if Saul hear it he will kill me
17. 33. thou art not able to *go* against this Philistine
18. 2. Saul would let him *go* no more home
19. 17. he said, let me *go*, why should I kill thee?
20. 5. but let me *go*, that I may hide myself in field
23. 13. David and his men went whither could *go*
26. 19. driven me out, saying, *go* serve other gods
28. 7. a woman, that I may *go* and inquire of her
2 *Sam.* 12. 23. I shall *go* to him, he shall not return
13. 13. whither shall I cause my shame to *go*?
15. 7. Absalom said, let me *go* and pay my vow
20. seeing I *go* whither I may, return thou
17. 11. that thou *go* to battle in thy person
19. 36. thy servant will *go* a little way over
20. 11. that is for David, let him *go* after Joab
1 *Kings* 2. 2. I *go* the way of all the earth, be strong
11. 21. let me depart, that I may *go* to my country
22. nothing, howbeit, let me *go* in any wise
12. 27. shall kill me, and *go* to Rehoboam
13. 17. nor turn to *go* by the way thou camest
20. 42. because thou hast let *go* a man appointed
22. 4. wilt thou *go* with me to battle? 2 *Chr.* 18. 3.
2 *Kings* 3. 7. wilt thou go with me against Moab?
4. 23. wherefore wilt thou *go* to him to-day?
6. 22. set bread and water, that they may *go* and eat
10. 24. he that letteth him *go* his life be for him

2 *Kings* 18. 21. it will *go* into hand pierce it, *Isa.* 36. 6.
2 *Chr.* 14. 11. in thy name we *go* ag. this multitude
25. 7. let not the army of Israel *go* with thee
8. if thou wilt *go*, do it, be strong for battle
Job 6. 18. they *go* to nothing and perish
10. 21. before I *go* whence shall not return, 16. 22.
20. 26. it shall *go* ill with him that is left in tabern.
21. 29. have ye not asked them that *go* by the way?
27. 6. my righteousness I will not let *go*
Psal. 32. 8. and teach thee in the way thou shalt *go*
39. 13. before I *go* hence, and be no more
42. 9. I will say to God, why *go* I mourning, 43. 2.
49. 19. he shall *go* to the generation of his fathers
84. 7. they *go* from strength to strength, till appear
85. 13. righteousness shall *go* before him
89. 14. mercy and truth shall *go* before thy face
107. 7. that they might *go* to a city of habitation
132. 7. we will *go* into his tabernacles, will worship
139. 7. whither shall I *go* from thy presence?
Prov. 2. 19. none that *go* unto her return again
3. 28. *go* and come again, to-morrow I will give
6. 28. can one *go* on hot coals, and not be burnt?
9. 15. to call passengers who *go* right on their way
14. 7. *go* from the presence of a foolish man
15. 12. neither will the scorner *go* to the wise
19. 7. much more do his friends *go* far from him
22. 6. train up a child in the way he should *go*
23. 30. they that *go* to seek mixt wine
30. 29. there be three things which *go* well
Eccl. 1. † 7. rivers come, thither they return to *go*
3. 20. all *go* unto one place, all are of the dust
5. 15. naked shall he return to *go* as he came, 16.
6. 6. hath seen no good, do not all *go* to one place?
7. 2. it is better to *go* to the house of mourning
9. 3. and after that, they *go* to the dead
10. 15. because he knoweth not how to *go* to city
12. 5. and the mourners *go* about the streets
Cant. 3. 4. I held him, I would not let him *go*
Isa. 3. 16. walking and mincing as they *go*
6. 8. whom shall I send, and who will *go* for us?
9. he said, *go* and tell this people, *Acts* 28. 26.
27. 4. I will *go* through them, I would burn them
28. 13. that they might *go* and fall backward
45. 13. he shall let *go* my captives, not for price
48. 17. leadeth thee by the way thou shouldest *go*
58. 8. thy righteousness shall *go* before thee
62. 10. *go* thro', *go* thro' the gates, prepare the way
Jer. 1. 7. thou shalt *go* to all that I send thee
9. 2. I might leave my people, and *go* from them
12. † 2. they have taken root, they *go* on
29. 12. ye shall *go* and pray to me, I will hearken
31. 22. how long wilt thou *go* about, O daughter
34. 3. thou shalt *go* to Babylon, *Mic.* 4. 10.
40. 4. whither it seemeth good to *go*, there *go*, 5.
5. he gave him reward, and let him *go*
15. saying, let me *go*, and I will slay Ishmael
42. 22. ye shall die, in place whither ye desire to *go*
46. 22. the voice thereof shall *go* like a serpent
48. † 2. O Madmen, the sword shall *go* after thee
50. 4. they shall *go* and seek the Lord their God
33. held them fast, they refused to let them *go*
Ezek. 1. 12. whither the Spirit was to *go*, 20.
8. 6. that I should *go* far from my sanctuary
9. 4. *go* through the midst of the city, 5.
14. 17. or if I say, sword, *go* through the land
20. 29. what is the high place whereto ye *go*?
21. 16. *go* thee one way or other, either on right
Hos. 5. 6. they shall *go* with flocks to seek the Lord
7. 11. they call to Egypt, they *go* to Assyria
12. when they shall *go* will spread my net on them
11. 3. I taught Ephraim also to *go*, they knew not
Mic. 5. 8. who, if he *go* through, both treadeth down
Zech. 6. 7. the bay went forth, and sought to *go*
8. these *go* towards north, have quieted my spirit
8. 21. inhabitants of one city shall *go* to another
23. we will *go* with you, for we have heard
9. 14. and shall *go* with whirlwinds of the south
Mat. 2. 22. Joseph was afraid to *go* thither
5. 41. compel thee to *go* a mile, *go* twain, *Luke* 7. 8.
8. 9. and I say to this man, *go*, and he goeth
32. he said to them, *go*, they went into the herd
9. 13. but *go* ye and learn what that meaneth
10. 6. *go* rather to the lost sheep of house of Israel
21. 30. he answered, I *go*, sir, and went not
25. 9. but *go* rather to them that sell, and buy
26. 36. sit ye here, while I *go* and pray yonder
28. 10. *go*, tell my brethren that they *go* to Galilee
19. *go* ye therefore and teach all nations
Mark 6. 38. *go* and see || 11. 6. and they let them *go*
Luke 1. 17. shall *go* before him in the power of Elias
9. 51. he stedfastly set his face to *go* to Jerusalem
60. but *go* thou and preach the kingdom of God
10. 37. then said Jesus, *go*, and do likewise
14. 18. I bought ground and must needs *go* and see
22. 33. I am ready to *go* with thee to prison
68. you will not answer me, nor let me *go*
23. 22. I will chastise him, and let him *go*
John 6. 68. Peter said, Lord, to whom shall we *go*?
7. 33. and then I *go* unto him that sent me
8. 14. but I know whence I came and whither I *go*
21. I *go* my way, whither I *go* ye cannot come
11. 44. Jesus saith, loose him, and let him *go*
13. 36. whither I *go* thou canst not follow now
14. 2. I *go* to prepare a place for you
4. whither I *go* ye know, the way ye know
12. because I *go* unto my Father, 16. 10.
28. because I said, I *go* to the Father, 16. 17, 28.
19. 12. the Jews cried, if thou let this man *go*
21. 3. I *go* a fishing, they say, we also *go* with thee
Acts 1. 25. that he might *go* to his own place
3. 13. when he was determined to let him *go*
4. 21. when had threatened them, they let them *go*
23. being let *go* they went to their company
5. 40. that they should not speak, and let them *go*
11. 22. that Barnabas should *go* as far as Antioch
16. 7. they essayed to *go* into Bithynia, but Spirit
35. magistrates sent, saying, let those men *go*
17. 9. had taken security of Jason, they let them *go*
20. 22. I *go* bound in the Spirit to Jerusalem
25. 12. hast appealed to Cesar, to Cesar shalt thou *go*
28. 18. had examined me, would have let me *go*
Rom. 15. 25. but now I *go* to Jerusalem to minister

1 Cor. 6. 1. dare you go to law before the unjust?
10. 27. if any bid you and ye be disposed to go
16. 4. if it be meet that I go also, they shall go
2 Cor. 9. 5. exhort the brethren that they go before
Phil. 2. 23. as I shall see how it will go with me
Jam. 4. 13. we will go into such a city and buy
See Free.
GO aside.
Num. 5. 12. if any man's wife go aside and commit
Deut. 28. 14. thou shalt not go aside from words
Jer. 15. 5. who shall go aside to ask how thou dost
Acts 4. 15. when they commanded them to go aside
GO astray.
Deut. 22. 1. thou shalt not see brother's ox go astray
Psal. 58. 3. they go astray as soon as they be born
Prov. 5. 23. in greatness of his folly he shall go astray
7. 25. decline not to her ways, go not astray into path
28. 10. whoso causeth the righteous to go astray
Jer. 50. 6. their shepherds caused them to go astray
Ezek. 14. 11. house of Israel may go no more astray
GO away.
Exod. 8. 28. only you shall not go very far away
Deut. 15. 13. thou shalt not let him go away empty
16. if he say, I will not go away from thee
1 Sam. 15. 27. as Samuel turned about to go away
24. 19. find his enemy, will he let him go away?
Job 4. 21. doth not their excellency go away?
15. 30. by breath of his mouth shall he go away
Jer. 51. 50. ye that escaped the sword, go away
Hos. 5. 14. I, even I, will tear and go away
Mat. 8. 31. suffer us to go away into the swine
25. 46. these go away into everlasting punishment
John 6. 67. then said Jesus will ye also go away?
14. 28. ye have heard how I said, I go away, 16. 7.
GO his way.
Judg. 19. 27. her lord rose up and went to go his w.
GO their way.
John 18. 8. if ye seek me, let these go their way
GO thy way.
Gen. 12. 19. behold thy wife, take her, go thy way
1 Sam. 20. 22. go thy way, the Lord hath sent thee
2 Kings 4. 29. he said, take my staff, and go thy w.
Eccl. 9. 7. go thy way, eat thy bread with joy
Cant. 1. 8. go thy way forth by footsteps of the flock
Dan. 12. 9. go thy way, for the words are closed up
13. go thy way till the end be, for thou shalt rest
Mat. 5. 24. go thy way, be reconciled to thy brother
8. 4. go thy way, shew thyself to the priest
20. 14. take that thine is, and go thy way
Mark 7. 29. he said, for this saying, go thy way
10. 21. go thy way, sell whatsoever thou hast
52. go thy w. faith made thee whole, Luke 17. 19.
John 4. 50. Jesus saith, go thy way, thy son liveth
Acts 9. 15. go thy way, for he is a chosen vessel
24. 25. Felix answered, go thy way for this time
GO your way.
Gen. 19. 2. ye shall rise up and go on your ways
Josh. 2. 16. afterward go your way, Judg. 19. 5.
Ruth 1. 12. turn again my daughters, go your way
Neh. 8. 10. go your w. eat the fat, drink the sweet
Mat. 27. 65. go your w. make it as sure as you can
Mark 11. 2. go your way into village over against
16. 7. go your way, tell his disciples that he goeth
Luke 7. 22. go your w. tell John what things ye heard
10. 3. go your ways, I send you as lambs am. wolves
10. they receive you not, go your ways to streets
Rev. 16. 1. go your ways, pour out the vials of wrath
GO back.
Exod. 14. 21. the Lord caused the sea to go back
Josh. 23. 12. else if ye do in any wise go back
Judg. 11. 35. I opened my mouth, I cannot go back
1 Kings 19. 20. go b. again, what have I done to thee?
2 Kings 20. 9. shall the shadow go b. ten degrees?
Psal. 80. 18. so will not we go back from thee
Jer. 40. 5. go back to Gedaliah, son of Ahikam
Ezek. 24. 14. I will not go back, nor will I spare
GO down.
Gen. 11. 7. let us go d. and confound their language
18. 21. I will go down now, and see whether
26. 2. the Lord said, go not down into Egypt
43. 5. if thou wilt not send him, we will not go d.
44. 26. we cannot go down, then will we go down
46. 3. fear not, Jacob, to go down into Egypt
Exod. 19. 21. Lord said, go down, charge the people
Num. 16. 30. and they go down quick into the pit
Deut. 24. 15. nor shall the sun go down on his hire
Josh. 10. 13. sun hasted not to go down about a day
Judg. 7. 10. if thou fear to go down, go with Phurah
1 Sam. 10. 8. thou shalt go down before me to Gilgal
14. 36. let us go down after Philistines by night
23. 4. go down to Keilah, I will deliver Philistines
26. 6. who will go down with me to Saul?
29. 4. let him not go down with us to battle
2 Sam. 11. 8. David said, go down to thy house
10. why didst thou not go down to thine house?
15. 20. should I this day make thee go up and down
1 Kings 21. 18. go down to meet Ahab king of Israel
2 Kings 1. 15. go down with him, be not afraid
20. 10. for the shadow to go down ten degrees
2 Chron. 20. 16. to-morrow go down against him
Job 21. 13. in a moment go down to the grave
Psal. 22. 29. all that go down to the dust shall bow
28. 1. I become like them that go down to the pit
55. 15. and let them go down quick into hell
107. 23. they that go down to the sea in ships
115. 17. neither any that go down into silence
143. 7. lest I be like them that go down to the pit
Prov. 5. 5. her feet go down to death, her steps take
Isa. 14. 19. thou art cast out, as those that go down
30. 2. woe to them that walk to go d. to Egypt, 31. 1.
38. 18. they that go down into pit cannot hope
60. 20. sun shall not go down nor moon withdraw
Jer. 50. 27. let them go down to the slaughter
Ezek. 24. † 16. neither shall thy tears go down
26. 11. and thy strong garrisons shall go down
20. when I shall set thee with them that go down
to the pit, 31. 14. | 32. 18, 24, 25, 29, 30.
47. 8. these waters go down into the desert
Amos 6. 2. then go down to Gath of the Philistines
8. 9. I will cause the sun to go down at noon
Mic. 3. 6. the sun shall go down over the prophets
Mark 13. 15. let him that is on house-top not go down

Acts 25. 5. which are able to go down with me
Eph. 4. 26. let not the sun go down on your wrath
GO forth.
Gen. 8. 16. go forth of the ark, thou and thy wife
42. 15. not go forth hence, except brother come
Lev. 14. 3. the priest shall go forth of the camp
Num. 1. 3. all able to go forth to war, 2 Chr. 25. 5.
Deut. 23. 12. thou shalt have a place to go forth
1 Sam. 23. 13. and he forbare to go forth
2 Sam. 11. 1. at time when kings go forth to battle
18. 2. I will surely go forth with you myself
19. 7. if thou go not forth, there will not tarry
1 Kings 2. 36. and go not forth thence any whither
22. 22. he said, I will go forth: go forth and do so
2 Kings 9. 15. if it be your minds, let none go forth
19. 31. out of Jerusalem shall go forth a remnant
they that escape out of mount Zion, Isa. 37. 32.
Job 24. 5. as wild asses go they forth to their work
Psal. 78. 52. he made his own people to go forth
108. 11. wilt not thou go forth with our hosts?
Prov. 25. 8. go not forth hastily to strive, lest thou
30. 27. have no king, yet go they forth by bands
Cant. 3. 11. go forth, O ye daughters of Zion
7. 11. come, let us go forth into the villages
Isa. 2. 3. out of Zion shall go forth the law, Mic. 4. 2.
42. 13. the Lord shall go forth as a mighty man
48. 20. go forth of Babylon, flee ye, Jer. 50. 8.
49. 9. that thou mayest say to prisoners, go forth
17. they that made thee waste shall go forth
62. 1. till the righteousness thereof go forth
Jer. 6. 25. go not forth into the field, nor walk
11. † 11. they shall not be able to go forth
14. 18. if I go forth into the field, then the slain
15. 1. let them go forth || 2. whither shall we go f.?
25. 32. evil shall go forth from nation to nation
31. 4. O Israel, thou shalt go forth in the dances
39. the measuring-line shall yet go forth
38. 17. if thou wilt go forth to the king of Babylon
18. but if thou wilt not go forth to the princes, 21.
43. 12. he shall go forth from thence in peace
Ezek. 12. 4. go forth as they that go forth into capt.
12. prince go forth || 21. 4. my sword shall go forth
30. 9. in that day messengers shall go forth
46. 8. and he shall go forth by the way thereof
9. but he shall go forth over against it
Dan. 11. 44. he shall go forth with great fury
Joel 2. 16. let the bridegr. go forth of his chamber
Hab. 1. 4. and judgment doth never go forth
Zech. 6. 5. these are the four spirits which go forth
6. black horses go forth into the north country
14. 3. then shall the Lord go forth and fight
Mal. 4. 2. ye shall go forth and grow up as calves
Mat. 24. 26. behold, he is in the desert, go not forth
Acts 16. 3. him would Paul have to go forth
Heb. 13. 13. let us go forth to him without the camp
Rev. 16. 14. the spirits of devils which go forth
GO forward.
Exod. 14. 15. speak to Israel that they go forward
Num. 2. 24. they shall go forward in the third rank
2 Kings 20. 9. shall shadow go forward ten degrees?
Job 23. 8. behold, I go forward, but he is not there
GO in, or into, or not GO in.
Gen. 11. 31. from Ur, to go into land of Canaan, 12. 5.
Exod. 30. 20. when go into tabernacle, shall wash
32. 27. go in and out from gate to gate thro' camp
Lev. 10. 9. do not drink wine, when ye go into tabern.
14. 36. empty the house, before the priest go in
21. 11. neither shall he go in to any dead body
23. only he shall not go in to the vail or near altar
Num. 4. 19. Aaron and his sons shall go in and ap.
20. but they shall not go in to see when holy things
8. 15. and after that shall the Levites go in
27. 17. which may go out, and go in before them
32. 9. that they should not go into the land
Deut. 1. 37. thou also shalt not go in thither, 4. 21.
38. but Joshua son of Nun he shall go in thither
4. 1. that ye may live, and go in and possess, 8. 1.
6. 18. that thou mayest go in and possess, 10. 11.
11. 8. that ye may be strong, and go in and possess
24. 10. not go into his house to fetch his pledge
Judg. 19. 15. they turned aside to go in and lodge
Ruth 3. 4. thou shalt go in, and uncover his feet
2 Sam. 11. 11. shall I then go into mine house to eat?
1 Kings 13. 8. I will not go in, nor eat with thee
16. I may not return, nor go in with thee
17. 12. may go in, and dress it for me and my son
2 Kings 9. 2. look out Jehu, and go in, make him arise
10. 25. go in and slay them, let none come forth
2 Chron. 18. 24. thou shalt go into an inner chamber
23. 6. they that minister of the Levites shall go in
Neh. 6. 11. who is there as I am would go into the
temple to save his life? I will not go in
Esth. 2. 15. when Esther's turn was come to go in
4. 8. and to charge her that she should go in
16. and so will I go in unto the king, if I perish
5. 14. then go thou in merrily unto the king
Job 34. † 23. he should go into judgment with God
Psal. 26. 4. nor will I go in with dissemblers
118. 19. open the gates, I will go in to them
119. 35. make me go in path of thy commandment
132. 7. we will go into his tabernacle and worship
Prov. 27. 10. nor go into thy brother's house
Isa. 2. 19. they shall go into the holes of the rocks
Jer. 4. 5. and let us go into the defenced cities
36. 5. I cannot go into the house of the Lord
42. 14. no, but we will go into the land of Egypt
19. the Lord hath said, go ye not into Egypt
Ezek. 7. † 17. all knees shall go into water, 21. † 7.
46. 10. the prince when they go in shall go in
Nah. 3. 14. go into clay, and tread the mortar
Zech. 6. 10. go into house of Josiah son of Zephaniah
Mat. 2. 20. take the young child, and go into Isr.
7. 13. and many there be that go in thereat
20. 4. go into the vineyard, and they went, 7.
21. 2. go into village over-against you, Luke 19. 30.
31. harlots go into kingdom of God before you
22. 9. go into the high-ways, as many as ye find, bid
23. 13. ye neither go in, nor suffer others to go in
26. 18. go into the city, to such a man, Mark 14. 13.
Mark 6. 36. that they may go into the country
8. 26. nor go into the town, nor tell it to any
16. 15. go into all the world, preach the gospel

Luke 8. 51. he suffered no man to go in, save Peter
15. 28. and he was angry, and would not go in
John 10. 9. he shall go in and out, and find pasture
Acts 1. 11. shall so come, as ye see him go into heaven
Rev. 17. 8. the beast was, is not, shall go into perdition
See Captivity.
GO in.
Gen. 16. 2. Sarai said, I pray thee, go in unto my maid
19. 34. make him drink wine, and go thou in
30. 3. behold my maid Bilhah, go in unto her
38. 8. go in unto thy brother's wife, and marry her
Deut. 21. 13. after that thou shalt go in unto her
22. 13. if take a wife, and go in unto her, hate her
25. 5. her husband's brother shall go in unto her
Josh. 23. 12. make marriages, and go in unto them
Judg. 15. 1. I will go in to my wife into the chamber
2 Sam. 16. 21. go in unto thy father's concubines
1 Kings 11. 2. ye shall not go in to them, nor they
Ezek. 23. 44. went to her as they go in to a woman
Amos 2. 7. a man and his father go in to same maid
GO in peace.
Gen. 15. 15. thou shalt go to thy fathers in peace
Exod. 4. 18. Jethro said to Moses, go in peace
18. 23. this people shall go to their place in peace
Judg. 18. 6. the priest said to Danites, go in peace
1 Sam. 1. 17. Eli said to Hannah, go in peace
20. 42. Jonathan said to David, go in peace
25. 35. David said to Abigail, go up in peace
29. 7. Achish said to David, go in peace
2 Sam. 15. 9. the king said to Absalom, go in peace
1 Kings 2. 6. let not his hoary head go down in peace
2 Kings 5. 19. Elisha said to Naaman, go in peace
Isa. 57. † 2. he shall go in peace, they shall rest
Mark 5. 34. go in peace, and be whole of thy plague
Luke 7. 50. faith hath saved thee, go in peace, 8. 48.
Acts 15. 33. they were let go in peace from brethren
Let us GO.
Gen. 37. 17. I heard them say, let us go to Dothan
Exod. 3. 18. now let us go three days' journey, 5. 3.
5. 8. therefore they say, let us go sacrifice, 17.
13. 15. when Pharaoh would hardly let us go
Deut. 13. 2. let us go after other gods, 6. 13.
1 Sam. 9. 9. thus he spake, let us go to the seer, 10.
11. 14. let us go to Gilgal, and renew the kingdom
14. 1. let us go over to the Philistines' garrison, 6.
2 Kings 6. 2. let us go to Jordan, take thence a beam
Psal. 122. 1. let us go into the house of the Lord
Isa. 2. 3. let us go up to the mountain of the Lord
Jer. 4. 5. let us go into the defenced cities
6. 5. let us go by night, and destroy her palaces
35. 11. let us go to Jerusalem for fear of Chaldeans
46. 16. arise, let us go again to our own people
51. 9. let us go, every one to his own country
Zech. 8. 21. let us go to pray before the Lord
Mark 1. 38. he said, let us go into the next towns
14. 42. rise up, let us go, he that betrayeth is at hand
Luke 2. 15. let us go to Bethlehem, see this thing
John 11. 7. then saith he, let us go to Judea again
15. let us go to him || 16. let us go that we may die
14. 31. even so I do; arise, let us go hence
Acts 15. 36. let us go again, and visit our brethren
Heb. 6. 1. let us go on to perfection, not laying again
I will GO.
Gen. 13. 9. I will go to the right, I will go to the left
24. 58. wilt thou go with this man? I will go
33. 12. let us go, I will go before thee, Isa. 45. 2.
45. 28. my son is alive, I will go see him before I die
Num. 20. 19. I will only go through on my feet
23. 3. stand by thy burnt-offering, and I will go
Deut. 2. 27. I will go along by the high-way
Judg. 1. 3. I will go likewise with thee into thy lot
4. 8. if thou wilt go with me, then will I go
9. and she said, I will surely go with thee
16. 20. I will go out as at other times before
Ruth 1. 16. Ruth said, whither thou goest, I will go
2 Kings 6. 3. go with servant, he answered, I will go
2 Chron. 18. 29. he said, I will go to the battle
Psal. 43. 4. then will I go to the altar of God
66. 13. I will go into thy house with burnt-offering
71. 16. I will go in the strength of the Lord God
118. 19. open the gates of righteousness, I will go in
Jer. 2. 25. I loved strangers, after them I will go
Ezek. 38. 11. I will go to them that are at rest
Hos. 2. 5. for she said, I will go after my lovers
7. I will go and return to my first husband
5. 15. I will go to my place, till they seek my face
Mic. 1. 8. I will wail, I will go stript and naked
Zech. 8. 21. go to seek the Lord; I will go also
Mat. 26. 32. I will go before into Galilee, Mark 14. 28.
Luke 15. 18. I will arise and go to my father
Acts 18. 6. henceforth I will go to the Gentiles
GO near.
Deut. 5. 27. go near, and hear all the Lord says
2 Sam. 1. 15. David said, go near, and fall on him
Job 31. 37. as a prince would I go near unto him
Acts 8. 29. go near, join thyself to this chariot
GO not, or not GO.
Exod. 33. 15. if thy presence go not with me
Num. 10. 30. Hobab said, I will not go, but depart
20. 20. and he said, thou shalt not go through
22. 12. God said to Balaam, shalt not go with them
18. I cannot go beyond the word of Lord, 24. 13.
Deut. 3. 27. thou shalt not go over this Jordan
6. 14. ye shall n. go after other gods, 1 Kings 11. 10.
15. 16. if he say, I will not go away from thee
24. 19. thou shalt not go again to fetch it
32. 52. but thou shalt not go thither to the land
Josh. 8. 4. go not far from the city, but be ready
Judg. 4. 8. if thou wilt not go with me, I will not go
7. 4. I say, this shall not go, the same shall not go
20. 8. we will not any of us go to his tent
Ruth 3. 17. go not empty to thy mother-in law
1 Sam. 17. 39. David said, I cannot go with these
29. 8. that I may not go fight ag. enemies of the king
2 Sam. 13. 25. let not all go, howbeit he would not go
2 Kings 2. 18. he said, did I not say to you, go not?
1 Chron. 21. 30. but David could not go before it
2 Chron. 25. 13. soldiers that should not go to battle
Prov. 4. 13. take hold of instruction, let her not go
14. and go not into the way of evil men
22. 24. with a furious man thou shalt not go
Isa. 52. 12. for ye shall not go out with haste

Jer. 10. 5. they must be borne, because they cannot go
16. 8. thou shalt not go into the house of feasting
25. 6. go not after other gods to serve them, 35. 15.
27. 18. that the vessels left go not to Babylon
43. 2. go not into Egypt to sojourn there, 42. 19.
49. 12. thou shalt not go unpunished, but drink of it
Lam. 4. 18. hunt steps, that we cannot go in our str.
Ezek. 42. 14. when the priests enter, shall not go out
Mat. 10. 5. go not into the way of the Gentiles
Luke 10. 7. go not from house to house
17. 23. see here or there, go not after them, 21. 8.

GO over.

Deut. 3. 25. I pray thee let me go over and see land
28. Joshua shall go over before the people, 31. 3.
4. 14. land whither ye go over, 26. | 31. 13. | 32. 47.
22. I must not go over Jordan, ye shall go over
24. 20. thou shalt not go over the boughs again
30. 13. who shall go over sea for us and bring it?
31. 3. the Lord thy God will go over before thee
34. 4. but thou shalt not go over thither
Josh. 1. 2. therefore arise, go over this Jordan
Judg. 12. 5. the Ephraimites said, let me go over
1 Sam. 14. 1. come, let us go over to the Philistines, 6.
30. 10. so faint, they could not go over the brook
2 Sam. 16. 9. let me go over and take off his head
19. 37. thy servant Chimham, let him go over
Isa. 8. 7. he shall come and go over all his banks
11. 15. he shall make men go over dry-shod
51. 23. which said, bow down, that we may go over
54. 9. the waters of Noah should no more go over
Jer. 41. 10. Ishmael depart. to go over to Ammonites
Luke 8. 22. let us go over to the other side

GO out.

Gen. 9. 10. from all that go out of the ark
24. 11. the time that women go out to draw water
45. 1. he cried, cause every man to go out from me
Exod. 6. 11. that he let children of Israel go out
8. 29. behold, I go out from thee, I will entreat
11. 8. after that I will go out, and he went out
10. he would not let the children of Israel go out
12. 22. none of you shall g. o. at the door of house
16. 4. people shall g. o. and gather a rate every day
29. let no man go out of his place on seventh day
21. 2. in the seventh year he shall go out free
3. if he came in by himself, shall go out by himself;
if married, his wife shall go out with him
4. her master's, and he shall go out by himself
5. if the servant say, I will not go out free
7. a maid-servant not go out as men-servants do
11. then shall she go out free without money
Lev. 6. 13. the fire on the altar shall never go out
8. 33. shall not go out of tabernacle in seven days
10. 7. ye shall not go out at the door, lest ye die
14. 38. then the priest shall go out of the house
15. 16. if any man's seed of copulation go out
16. 18. he shall go out to the altar before the Lord
21. 12. nor shall he go out of the sanctuary
25. 28. and in the jubilee it shall go out, 31, 33.
30. it shall not go out in jubil. || 54. he shall go out
Deut. 24. 5. taken a wife, he shall not go out to war
28. 25. thou shalt go out one way, flee seven ways
Josh. 2. 19. who shall go out, his blood be on his
Judg. 9. 38. go out, I pray now, and fight with them
16. 20. he said, I will go out as at other times
20. 28. shall I yet again g. o. to battle ag. Benjamin
Ruth 2. 22. it is good thou go out with his maidens
1 Sam. 19. 3. I will go out and stand beside my father
20. 11. come, let us go out into the field
28. 1. Achish said, thou shalt go out with me
2 Sam. 5. 24. then the Lord shall go out before thee
21. 17. thou shalt go no more out with us to battle
1 Kings 15. 17. that he might not suffer any to go
out, or come in to Asa, 2 Chron. 16. 1.
20. 31. put ropes on heads, and go out to the king
1 Chron. 20. 1. at the time kings go out to battle
2 Chron. 18. 21. go out and be a lying spirit, go out
20. 17. fear not, to-morrow go out against them
26. 18. go out of sanctuary, for thou hast trespassed
20. yea, himself hasted also to go out
Job 15. 13. lettest such words go out of thy mouth
Psal. 60. 10. which didst not go out with our armies
109. † 7. when he is judged, let him go out guilty
Prov. 22. 10. cast out the scorner, contention go out
Eccl. 8. 3. be not hasty to go out of his sight
Isa. 52. 11. depart ye, go ye out from thence
12. ye shall not go out with haste or by flight
55. 12. ye shall go out with joy, and be led forth
Jer. 21. 12. lest my fury go out like fire and burn
51. 45. my people, go ye out of the midst of her
Ezek. 15. 7. they shall go out from one fire
44. 3. the prince shall go out the same way
46. 9. entereth by north, shall go out by south-gate
Amos 4. 3. and ye shall go out at the breaches
Zech. 14. 8. that living waters go out from Jerusalem
Mat. 25. 6. bridegroom cometh, go ye out to meet him
Luke 9. 5. when ye go out of the city shake off dust
14. 21. go out quickly into the streets and lanes
23. go out into the highways and hedges
1 Cor. 5. 10. then must ye needs go out of the world
Heb. 11. 8. Abraham, when he was called to go out
Rev. 3. 12. he that overcometh, shall go no more out
20. 8. and shall go out to deceive the nations

GO to.

Gen. 11. 3. go to, let us make brick, and burn them
4. go to, let us build || 7. go to, let us confound
Eccl. 2. 1. go to now, I will prove thee with mirth
Isa. 5. 5. go to, I will tell you what I will do
Jam. 4. 13. go to now, ye that say, to-day, or to-mor.
5. 1. go to now, ye rich men, weep and howl

GO up.

Gen. 35. 1. arise, go up to Bethel, dwell there, 3.
44. 33. and let the lad go up with his brethren
34. how shall I go up to my father? 45. 9.
50. 6. Pharaoh said, go up and bury thy father
Exod. 8. 3. frogs shall go up and come into thy house
19. 12. take heed ye go not up into the mount
20. 26. nor shalt thou go up by steps to my altar
24. 2. neither shall the people go up with him
32. 30. ye have sinned a great sin, I will go up
33. 1. depart and go up, thou and the people
3. for I will not go up in the midst of thee
34. 24. not desire thy land, when thou shalt go up
Lev. 19. 16. shalt not go up and down as a tale-bearer
Num. 13. 30. let us go up at once and possess it
31. we be not able to go up against this people
14. 40. lo, we be here, and will go up, Deut. 1. 41.
42. go not up || 44. but they presumed to go up
Deut. 25. 7. let his brother's wife go up to the gate
30. 12. who shall go up for us to heaven, and bring
Josh. 7. 3. let not all go up, let 3000 men go up
22. 33. did not intend to go up ag. them in battle
Judg. 1. 1. who shall go up for us to fight them?
2. the Lord said, Judah shall go up, 20. 18.
2. 1. an angel said, I made you go up out of Egypt
9. † 9. should I go up and down for other trees?
11. 37. that I may go up and down on the mountains
18. 9. arise, that we may go up against them
20. 9. we will go up by lot against Gibeah
18. which of us shall go up first to battle?
23. shall I go up again? || 28. go up against him
1 Sam. 1. 22. I will not go up till the child be weaned
6. 9. if it go up by the way of his own coast
20. and to whom shall he go up from us?
9. 13. ye shall find him before he go up to eat
14. Samuel came to go up to the high place, 19.
14. 9. if they say, tarry, we will not go up
10. if they say, come up unto us, we will go up
2 Sam. 2. 1. David said, shall I go up to any of the
cities of Judah? the Lord said, go up to Hebron
5. 19. shall I go up against the Philistines?
15. 20. should I make thee go up and down with us?
19. 34. how long have I to live, that I should go up
24. 18. go up, rear an altar in floor, 1 Chr. 21. 18.
1 Kings 12. 24. ye shall not go up, 2 Chron. 11. 4.
27. if this people go up to do sacrifice at Jerusal.
28. it is too much for you to go up to Jerusalem
18. 43. go up, look towards the sea, and he went
22. 6. go up, for the Lord shall deliver it into the
hand of the king, 12. 2 Chron. 18. 11, 14.
20. may go up and fall at Ramoth, 2 Chr. 18. 19.
2 Kings 1. 3. go up, meet the messengers of the king
2. 23. go up thou bald-head, go up thou bald-head
3. 7. wilt thou go up with me against Moab?
8. and he said, which way shall we go up
12. 17. Hazael set his face to go up to Jerusalem
18. 25. Lord said, go up against the land, Isa. 36. 10.
20. 5. on third day thou shalt go up to the house
8. what the sign that I shall go up? Isa. 38. 22.
22. 4. go up to Hilkiah high-priest to sum silver
1 Chr. 14. 10. shall I go up || 14. go not up after them
2 Chron. 18. 5. shall we go up to Ramoth-gilead?
36. 23. God be with him, let him go up, Ezra 1. 3.
Ezra 7. 9. he began to go up from Babylon
13. all which are minded to go up go with me
Neh. 4. 3. if a fox go up he shall even break down
Psal. 104. 8. they go up by the mountains;
132. 3. surely I will not go up into my bed
Cant. 6. 6. as a flock of sheep that go up from washing
7. 8. I said, I will go up to the palm-tree
Isa. 2. 3. let us go up to mountain of Lord, Mic. 4. 2.
7. 6. let us go up against Judah and vex it
15. 5. with weeping shall they go it up
21. 2. go up, O Elam, || 34. 10. the smoke shall go up
35. 9. nor any ravenous beast shall go up there
36. 10. go up against this land, and destroy it
Jer. 5. 10. go ye up upon her walls and destroy
6. 4. arise, and let us go up at noon, woe unto us
21. 2. that Nebuchadnezzar may go up from us
22. 20. go up to Lebanon, and cry, lift up thy voice
31. 6. let us go up to Zion, to the Lord our God
46. 8. he saith, I will go up and cover the earth
11. go up into Gilead, and take balm, O virgin
48. 5. continual weeping shall go up
49. 28. go up to Kedar, and spoil men of the east
50. 21. go up against the land of Merathaim
Ezek. 38. 11. I will go up to land of unwalled villages
40. 26. there were seven steps to go up to it
Hos. 4. 15. neither go up to Beth-aven, nor swear
Hag. 1. 8. go up to the mountain, and bring wood
Zech. 14. 16. go up from year to year to worship
Mat. 20. 18. we go up to Jerusalem, Son of man
shall be betrayed, Mark 10. 33. Luke 18. 31.
Luke 14. 10. he may say to thee, friend, go up higher
John 7. 8. go ye up to this feast, I go not up yet
Acts 15. 2. go up to Jerusalem about this question
21. 4. that Paul should not go up to Jerusalem
12. we besought him not to go up to Jerusalem
25. 9. wilt thou go up to Jerusalem and be judged?

GO a whoring.

Exod. 34. 15. lest they go a whoring after their gods
16. and thy sons go a whoring after their gods
Lev. 20. 5. I will cut off all that go a whor. after him
6. I will cut off such as go a whor. after wizards
Num. 15. 39. ways, after which ye use to go a whor.
Deut. 31. 16. this people will go a whor. after gods
2 Chron. 21. 13. Jehoram made Judah go a whoring
Psal. 73. 27. destroyed all that go a whor. from thee
Ezek. 6. 9. eyes which go a whoring after idols

GOEST.

Gen. 28. 15. will keep thee in places whither thou g.
32. 17. whose art thou? whither g. thou? Judg. 19.
17. Zech. 2. 2. John 13. 36. | 16. 5.
Exod. 33. 16. is it not in that thou g. with us?
34. 12. no coven. with inhabitants whither thou g.
Num. 14. 14. and thou g. before them by day-time
Deut. 7. 1. when Lord God shall bring thee into the
land whither thou g. to possess it, 11. 29.
11. 10. the land whither thou g. is not as Egypt
12. 29. God shall cut off nations whither thou g.
20. 1. when thou g. to battle and seest, 21. 10.
23. 20. God may bless thee in all that thou settest
thine hand to, whither thou g. Josh. 1. 7.
28. 6. blessed shalt thou be when thou g. out
19. cursed shalt thou be when thou g. out
21. make pestilence cleave to thee whither thou g.
63. shall be plucked off the land whither thou g.
32. 50. and die in the mount whither thou g.
Josh. 1. 9. the Lord is with thee whither thou g.
Judg. 14. 3. that thou g. to take a wife of Philist.
Ruth 1. 16. for whither thou g. I will go
2 Sam. 15. 19. wherefore g. thou also with us?
1 Kings 2. 37. on the day thou g. over the brook, 42.
Psal. 44. 9. but thou g. not forth with our armies
Prov. 4. 12. when thou g. steps shall not be straitened
Prov. 6. 22. when thou g. it shall lead thee
Eccl. 5. 1. keep thy foot when thou g. to house of G
9. 10. nor wisdom in the grave whither thou g.
Jer. 45. 5. I will give for a prey whither thou g.
Mat. 8. 19. I will follow thee whither g. Luke 9. 57.
Luke 12. 58. when thou g. with thine adversary
John 11. 8. sought to stone thee, g. thither again?
14. 5. Lord, we know not whither thou g.

GOETH.

Exod. 7. 15. lo, he g. out unto the water
22. 26. shall deliver it by that the sun g. down
28. 29. Aaron shall bear them when he g. in
30. they shall be on Aaron's heart when he g. in
35. his sound shall be heard when he g. in
Lev. 11. 21. these ye may eat that g. on all four
14. 46. he that g. into the house shall be unclean
15. 32. law of him whose seed g. from him, 22. 4.
16. 17. none in the tabernacle when he g. in
22. 3. who g. to holy things having uncleanness
27. 21. the field, when it g. out in jubilee, be holy
Num. 5. 29. this is the law, when a wife g. aside
Deut. 1. 30. the Lord which g. before shall fight
9. 3. thy God is he that g. over before you
19. 5. as when a man g. into wood with his neighb.
20. 4. the Lord your God is he that g. with you
23. 9. when the host g. forth against thy enemies
24. 13. deliver the pledge when the sun g. down
Judg. 5. 31. be as the sun when he g. forth in might
1 Sam. 22. 14. as David who g. at thy bidding
30. 24. as his part is that g. down to the battle
2 Kings 5. 18. my master g. to house of Rimmon
11. 8. be with the king as he g. out, 2 Chron. 23. 7.
Ezra 5. 8. this work g. fast on and prospereth
Job 7. 9. that g. down to grave come up no more
9. 11. lo, he g. by me, and I see him not
16. † 6. and though I forbear, what g. from me
34. 8. when g. in company with workers of iniquity
37. 2. hear the sound that g. out of his mouth
39. 21. he g. on to meet the armed men
Psal. 17. 1. prayer that g. not out of feigned lips
41. 6. when he g. abroad, he telleth it
68. 21. such a one as g. on in his trespasses
88. 16. thy fierce wrath g. over me
97. 3. a fire g. before him, and burneth up enemies
104. 23. man g. forth to his work until evening
126. 6. he that g. forth and weepeth, bearing
146. 4. his breath g. forth; he returneth to earth
Prov. 6. 29. so he that g. in to his neighbour's wife
7. 22. g. after her, as an ox g. to the slaughter
11. 10. when it g. well with righteous, city rejoices
16. 18. pride g. before destruction, a haughty spirit
20. 19. that g. about as a tale-bearer reveals secrets
26. 9. as a thorn g. up into the hand of a drunkard
20. where no wood is, there the fire g. out
31. 18. her candle g. not out by night
Eccl. 1. 5. the sun g. down and hasteth to his place
3. 21. spirit of man g. up, spirit of beast g. down
12. 5. because man g. to his long home
Cant. 7. 9. that g. down sweetly, causing the lips
Isa. 28. 19. from the time it g. forth, it shall take
30. 29. when one g. with a pipe to come to mount
55. 11. so shall my word be that g. forth of mouth
59. 8. whoso g. therein shall not know peace
63. 14. as a beast g. down into the valley
Jer. 5. 6. every one that g. out thence shall be torn
6. 4. woe unto us, for the day g. away
21. 9. that g. out to Chaldeans shall live, 38. 2.
22. 10. but weep sore for him that g. away
30. 23. whirlwind of the Lord g. forth with fury
44. 17. we will do what g. out of our own mouth
49. 17. every one that g. by it be astonished, 50. 13.
Ezek. 7. 14. they have blown, but none g. to battle
33. 31. their heart g. after their covetousness
44. 27. in the day that he g. into the sanctuary
Hos. 6. 4. your goodn. is as the early dew, it g. away
5. thy judgments are as light that g. forth
Zech. 5. 3. this is the curse that g. forth
6. he said, this is an ephah that g. forth
Mat. 8. 9. I say to this man, go, and he g. Luke 7. 8.
12. 45. then g. he and taketh, Luke 11. 26.
13. 44. for joy thereof g. and selleth all he hath
15. 11. not that which g. into mouth defileth a man
17. 21. this kind g. not out but by prayer
26. 24. the Son of man g. as it is written of him,
Mark 14. 21. Luke 22. 22.
28. 7. he g. before you into Galilee, Mark 16. 7.
John 3. 8. but canst not tell whither it g.
7. 20. thou hast a devil; who g. about to kill thee?
10. 4. he g. before them, the sheep follow him
11. 31. she g. unto the grave to weep there
12. 35. knoweth not whither he g. 1 John 2. 11.
1 Cor. 6. 6. but brother g. to law with brother
9. 7. who g. a warfare any time at his own charges
Jam. 1. 24. he beholdeth himself and g. his way
Rev. 14. 4. that follow the Lamb whithersoever he g.
17. 11. and is of the seven, and g. into perdition
19. 15. and out of his mouth g. a sharp sword

GOING.

Gen. 15. 12. sun g. down, a deep sleep fell on Abram
25. † 32. Esau said, behold, I am g. to die
Exod. 17. 12. his hands steady, to g. down of the sun
23. 4. if thou meet thine enemy's ox g. astray
Num. 34. 4. g. forth of border from south to Kadesh
Deut. 16. 6. sacrifice the passover at g. down of sun
33. 18. he said, rejoice, Zebulun, in thy g. out
Josh. 7. 5. and smote them in the g. down
10. 11. as they were in the g. down to Beth horon
27. at the g. down of the sun carcases taken down
23. 14. I am g. the way of all the earth
Judg. 8. † 30. Gideon had 70 sons g. out of his thigh
19. 18. I am now g. to the house of the Lord
28. up, let us be g. but none answered
1 Sam. 10. 3. meet thee three men g. up to God
2 Sam. 2. 19. in g. turned not from following Abner
5. 24. hearest a sound of g. in trees, 1 Chr. 14. 15.
1 Kings 17. 11. as she was g. to fetch it, he called
22. 36. went a proclamation at g. down of the sun
2 Kings 2. 23. g. by the way, children mocked him
9. 27. they smote Ahaziah at the g. up to Gur
1 Chron. 11. † 9. David went in g. and increasing
2 Chron. 18. 34. at time of sun g. down, he died
Ezra 7. † 9. foundation of the g. from Babylon

Job 1. 7. from *g.* to and fro in the earth, 2. 2.
33. 24. deliver him from *g.* down to the pit
28. he will deliver his soul from *g.* into the pit
Psal. 19. 6. his *g.* forth is from the end of heaven
50. 1. the mighty God calleth the earth, from rising of sun to *g.* down, 113. 3. *Mal.* 1. 11.
104. 19. the sun knoweth his *g.* down
Prov. 7. 27. *g.* down to the chambers of death
14. 15. but the prudent man looketh well to his *g.*
30. 29. three go well, yea, four are comely in *g.*
Isa. 13. 10. the sun shall be darkened in his *g.* forth
Jer. 48. 5. in the *g.* up to Luhith, continual weeping shall go up; in the *g.* down of Horonaim
50. 4. *g.* and weeping they shall seek the Lord
Ezek. 40. 31. the *g.* up had eight steps, 34, 37.
44. 5. with every *g.* forth of the sanctuary
46. 12. after his *g.* forth, one shut the gate
Dan. 6. 14. and laboured till *g.* down of the sun
9. 25. from the *g.* forth of the commandment
Hos. 6. 3. his *g.* forth is prepared as the morning
Zech. 8. † 7. from the country of *g.* down of the sun
† 21. *g.* speedily to entreat the face of the Lord
Mat. 25. † 8. give oil, for our lamps are *g.* out
26. 46. rise, let us be *g.* behold, he is at hand
Luke 14. 31. what king *g.* to war with another
John 8. 59. *g.* through midst of them, so passed by
Acts 20. 5. these *g.* before, tarried at Troas
Rom. 10. 3. *g.* about to establish their righteousness
1 *Tim.* 5. 24. some men's sins *g.* before to judgment
Heb. 7. 18. is a disannulling of command *g.* before
Jude 7. *g.* after strange flesh are set forth an examp.
See COMING.

GOINGS.

Num. 33. 2. and Moses wrote their *g.* out
34. 5. the *g.* out of their borders, 8, 9, 12. *Josh.* 15. 4, 7, 11. | 16. 3, 8. | 18. 12, 14.
Job 34. 21. his eyes are on man, he seeth all his *g.*
Psal. 17. 5. hold up my *g.* in thy paths that footsteps
37. † 31. none of his *g.* shall slide
40. 2. he set my feet on a rock, established my *g.*
44. † 18. nor have our *g.* declined from thy way
68. 24. they have seen thy *g.* even the *g.* of G.
140. 4. who have purposed to overthrow my *g.*
Prov. 5. 21. before Lord, and he pondereth all his *g.*
20. 24. man's *g.* are of the Lord, how can a man
Isa. 59. 8. there is no judgment in their *g.*
Ezek. 42. 11. their *g.* out were according to fashion
43. 11. shew them *g.* out thereof and comings in
Mic. 5. 2. whose *g.* forth have been from of old

GOAD, S.

Judg. 3. 31. Shamgar slew 600 men with an ox *g.*
1 *Sam.* 13. 21. they had a file to sharpen the *g.*
Eccl. 12. 11. the words of the wise are as *g.* and nails

GOAT.

Gen. 15. 9. take a heifer, a she-*g.* of three years
Exod. 22. † 1. if a man steal an ox or a *g.*
Lev. 3. 12. if his offering be a *g.* then shall offer it
4. 24. he shall lay his hand on the head of the *g.*
7. 23. he shall eat no fat of ox, sheep, or of *g.*
9. 15. he took the *g.* which was the sin-offering
10. 16. Moses sought the *g.* of the sin-offering
16. 9. Aaron shall bring the *g.* on which the lot fell
22. he shall let go the *g.* in the wilderness
17. 3. whosoever killeth a *g.* in the camp
22. 27. when a *g.* is brought forth seven days
Num. 15. 27. if sin thro' ignorance shall bring a *g.*
18. 17. the firstling of a *g.* thou shalt not redeem
28. 22. one *g.* for a sin-offering, to make an atonement for you, 29. 22, 28, 31, 34, 38.
Deut. 14. 4. ye shall eat the ox, sheep, and the *g.*
17. † 1. not sacrifice a *g.* wherein is blemish
Judg. 6. † 4. the Midianites left no ox, or *g.* or ass
Ezek. 43. 25. seven days prepare every day a *g.*
Dan. 8. 5. the *g.* had a notable horn between his eyes
21. the rough *g.* is the king of Grecia

He-GOAT.

Prov. 30. 31. four are comely in going, an *he-g.*
Jer. 51. 40. bring them down like rams with *he-g.*
Dan. 8. 5. behold, an *he-g.* came from the west
8. therefore the *he-g.* waxed very great

Live GOAT.

Lev. 16. 20. bring *live g.* || 21. lay both hands on *l.-g.*

Scape-GOAT.

See Signification on OFFERING.
Lev. 16. 8. and the other lot for the *scape-g.*
10. to let him go for a *scape-g.* into the wilderness
26. he that let go *scape-g.* shall wash his clothes

Wild GOAT.

Deut. 14. 5. ye shall eat the *wild g.* and wild ox

GOATS.

Gen. 4. † 4. Abel brought the firstling of the *g.*
27. 9. fetch me from thence two kids of the *g.*
16. she put the skins of the *g.* on his hands
30. 32. all the spotted and speckled among the *g.*
33. is not speckled among *g.* || 35. he removed *g.*
31. 38. thy she-*g.* have not cast their young
32. 14. two hundred she-*g.* and twenty he-*g.*
37. 31. Joseph's brethren killed a kid of the *g.*
38. † 17. I will send thee a kid from the *g.*
Exod. 12. 5. ye shall take it out from the sheep or *g.*
Lev. 1. 10. if his offering be of the sheep or *g.*
4. 23. if his sin come to his knowledge, he shall bring his offering, a kid of the *g.* 28. | 5. 6.
9. 3. take a kid of the *g.* for a sin offering
16. 5. two kids of the *g.* || 7. two *g.* present them
22. 19. ye shall offer a male of the sheep or *g.*
† 21. a free-will offering in beeves or *g.*
23. 19. then ye shall sacrifice one kid of the *g.* for a sin offering, *Num.* 7. 16. | 15. 24.
Num. 7. 17. five rams, five he-*g.* five lambs, 23, 29, 35, 41, 47, 53, 59, 65, 71, 77, 83.
87. the kids of the *g.* for a sin offering, twelve
88. the he-*g.* sixty, the lambs of first year sixty
31. † 30. thou shalt take one portion of the *g.*
Deut. 32. 14. rams and he-*g.* of the breed of Bashan
Judg. 6. † 19. Gideon made ready a kid of the *g.*
1 *Sam.* 25. 2. Nabal had a thousand *g.* was shearing
2 *Chron.* 17. 11. the Arabians brought 7,700 he-*g.*
29. 21. they brought seven he-*g.* for a sin offering
Ezra 6. 17. offered at the dedication twelve he-*g.*
8. 35. children out of captivity offered 12 he-*g.*
Psal. 50. 9. I will take no he-*g.* out of thy fold
50. 13. or will I drink the blood of *g.?*
66. 15. I will offer to thee bullocks with *g.*
Prov. 27. 26. the *g.* are the price of thy field
27. thou shalt have *g.* milk enough for food
Cant. 4. 1. thy hair is as a flock of *g.* 6. 5.
Isa. 1. 11. I delight not in the blood of he-*g.*
14. † 9. it stirreth up for thee all great *g.*
34. 6. sword of the Lord fat with the blood of *g.*
Jer. 50. 8. and be as the he-*g.* before the flocks
Ezek. 27. 21. Arabia occupied with thee in *g.*
34. 17. I judge between the rams and he-*g.*
39. 18. ye shall drink the blood of lambs and *g.*
43. 22. on the second day offer a kid of the *g.*
45. 23. a kid of the *g.* daily for a sin offering
Mic. 5. † 8. as a young lion among the flocks of *g.*
Zech. 10. 3. my anger was kindled, I punished the *g.*
Mat. 25. 32. a shepherd divideth the sheep from the *g.*
33. he shall set the *g.* on his left hand
Heb. 9. 12. nor entered by blood of *g.* and calves
13. if the blood of bulls and *g.* sanctifieth
19. he took the blood of *g.* and sprinkled the book
10. 4. is not possible the blood of *g.* take away sins

GOATS-HAIR.

Exod. 25. 4. this is the offering ye shall take, *g.-hair*
26. 7. thou shalt make curtains of *g.-hair*
35. 6. who is willing, let him bring *g.-hair*
23. every man with whom was found *g.-hair*
26. and all the women spun *g.-hair*
36. 14. she made curtains of *g.-hair* for the tent
Num. 31. 20. purify all work of *g.-hair* and wood
1 *Sam.* 19. 13. put a pillow of *g.-hair* for bolster, 16.

GOAT-SKINS.

Heb. 11. 37. wandering in sheep-skins and *g.-skins*

Wild GOATS.

1 *Sam.* 24. 2. to seek David on rocks of the *wild g.*
Job 39. 1. knowest thou when the *wild g.* bring forth?
Psal. 104. 18. high hills are a refuge for the *wild g.*

GOBLET.

Cant. 7. 2. thy navel is like a round *g.*

GOD, referred to *man.*

Exod. 4. 16. thou shalt be to Aaron instead of *g.*
7. 1. I have made thee a *g.* to Pharaoh

GOD, for *idol.*

Deut. 32. 21. moved me with that which is not *g.*
Judg. 6. 31. if he be a *g.* let him plead for himself
8. 33. they made Baal-berith their *g.*
9. 27. they went into the house of their *g.* and eat
11. 24. possess that which Chemosh thy *g.* giveth
16. 23. the Philistines' *g.* was Dagon, 24.
1 *Sam.* 5. 7. his hand is sore on us, and our *g.*
1 *Kings* 11. 33. Israel worshipped the *g.* of Moabites
18. 27. he is a *g.* either talking, or pursuing
2 *Kings* 1. 2. Baal-zebub the *g.* of Ekron, 3, 6, 16.
19. 37. worshipping in the house of Nisroch his *g.* smote with sword, 2 *Chr.* 32. 21. *Isa.* 37. 38.
Psal. 16. 4. sorrows multiplied, hasten after other *g.*
Isa. 44. 10. who hath formed a *g.* or molten image?
15. he maketh a *g.* and worshippeth it, 17.
45. 20. and that pray to a *g.* that cannot save
46. 6. he maketh it a *g.* they fall down, they worship
Dan. 1. 2. he carried the vessels into house of his *g.*
4. 8. Belteshazzar according to the name of my *g.*
11. 36. and magnify himself above every *g.*
Amos 5. 26. the star of your *g.* ye made, *Acts* 7. 43.
8. 14. that swear, and say, thy *g.* O Dan, liveth
Jonah 1. 5. the mariners cried, every man to his *g.*
Mic. 4. 5. all people will walk in the name of his *g.*
Hab. 1. 11. imputing this his power to his *g.*
Acts 12. 22. it is the voice of a *g.* not of a man

Any GOD.

Exod. 22. 20. that sacrifice to *any g.* save the Lord
2 *Sam.* 7. 22. nor is there *any G.* beside, 1 *Chr.* 17. 20.
Dan. 3. 28. that they might not worsh. *any g.* except
6. 7. who shall ask a petition of *any g.* or man, 12.
11. 37. neither shall he regard *any g.*

Other GOD.

Exod. 34. 14. thou shalt worship no *other g.*
Dan. 3. 29. because there is no *other g.* can deliver
1 *Cor.* 8. 4. there is none *other g.* but one.

Strange GOD.

Deut. 32. 12. there was no *strange g.* with them
Psal. 44. 20. stretched out our hands to a *strange g.*
81. 9. no *strange g.* be in thee, nor worsh. *strange g.*
Isa. 43. 12. when there was no *strange g.* among them
Dan. 11. 39. thus shall he do with a *strange g.*

GOD.

This is one of the names which we give to that eternal, infinite, and incomprehensible Being, the Creator of all things, who preserves and governs every thing by his almighty power and wisdom, and is the only object of our worship. The Hebrews give to God *generally the name of* JEHOVAH, *he who exists of himself, and gives being and existence to others: this is a name ineffable and mysterious, which denotes the eternity, immutability, and independence of God, and the infallible certainty of his word and promises. The import of this name is opened and predicated of* Christ, *in* Rev. 1. 4, 8. *The* Hebrews *had such a veneration for this holy name, that they never pronounced it, but instead of it made use of that of* Adonai, *which signifies properly* My Lords, *in the plural number: and of* Elohi, Eloi, *or* Elohim. *They likewise called him* El *which signifies* Strong; *or* Shaddai, *whereby may be meant one who is self-sufficient: or, according to another pronunciation, the Destroyer, the powerful One; or* Elion, *the most High, or* El-sabaoth, *the God of Hosts; or* Ja, *God.*

This name JEHOVAH, *in the* Hebrew, *consists of four letters, as for the most part it doth in all languages. Thus among the* Persians *the name is* Eopy; *among the* Arabians, Alla; *among the* Assyrians, Adad; *among the* Ægyptians, Θωυθ, *or* Θευθ; *with the* Grecians, Θεος; *the* Latins, Deus; *the* French, Dieu; *the* Spaniards, Dios; *the* Italians, Idio; *and with the* Germans, Gott. *Hereof some give this reason, that the number of four is a perfect number, and so hereby the perfection of God is noted. Others say, that God is he who created all things, consisting of four elements.*

God declared to Moses, *that he was not known by the name* JEHOVAH *to* Abraham, Isaac, *and* Jacob; *and yet God is called by the name* Jehovah, *in* Gen. 15. 7. | 26. 24. *This is not to be understood of the name, but of the thing signified by that name. For that denotes all his perfections, and, among others, the constancy and immutability of his nature and will, and the infallible certainty of his word and promises. And, though this was believed by* Abraham, Isaac, *and* Jacob; *yet God had not given any actual being to his promises for their deliverance, by the accomplishment of them: for they only saw the promises afar off. This expression may likewise be understood comparatively; they knew this but darkly and imperfectly, which was now to be made known more clearly and fully.*

GOD *is taken,* I. Properly; *and that either* essentially, *for the whole Trinity,* Isa. 40. 28. John 4. 24. *Or,* personally, (1) *For the Father,* Eph. 1. 3. (2) *The Son,* John 1. 1. (3) *For the Holy Ghost,* Acts 5. 3, 4. II. Improperly, (1) *For an idol, or false and imaginary god,* Exod. 22. 20. Judg. 11. 24. (2) *For princes, magistrates, and judges,* Exod. 22. 28. Psal. 82. 1, 6. (3) *For the ark of God. Thus, when the ark came into the camp of the* Israelites, *the* Philistines *said, God is come into their camp; this name they give to the ark, as they used to do to the images of their false gods,* 1 Sam. 4. 7. *The Lord tells* Moses, *Exod.* 7. 1. See, I have made thee a god to *Pharaoh: Thou shalt represent my person, and act like God, by requiring his obedience to thy commands, and by punishing his disobedience with such punishments as none but God can inflict; to which end, thou shalt have my omnipotent assistance. Satan is called* the god of this world, 2 *Cor.* 4. 4. *because he rules over the greatest part of the world, and they are his servants and slaves. St.* Paul, *in* Phil. 3. 19. *speaks of some* that make their belly their god; *that is, who mind nothing but the satisfaction of their fleshly appetites.* God forbid, *is a strong form of denial, with a lothing of what is objected,* Rom. 3. 31. | 9. 14. *In the original it is,* Let it not be.

Gen. 16. 13. called name of Lord, thou *G.* seest me
17. 7. to be a *G.* to thee and thy seed after thee
31. 13. I am the *G.* of Beth-el, where thou vowedst
42. 28. what is this that *G.* hath done to us?
45. 8. it was not you that sent me hither, but *G.*
48. 21. behold, I die, but *G.* shall be with you
Exod. 6. 7. I will take you to me, and be to you a *G.*
18. 19. give thee counsel, and *G.* shall be with thee
Num. 23. 23. said of Jacob, what hath *G.* wrought?
24. 23. alas, who shall live when *G.* doth this?
Deut. 4. 7. what nation which hath *G.* so nigh?
29. 13. that he may be to thee a *G.* as he said
1 *Sam.* 3. 17. *G.* do so and more also, 14. 44. | 25. 22. 2 *Sam.* 3. 9, 35. | 19. 13. 1 *Kings* 2. 23. 2 *Kings* 6. 31.
17. 46. all may know that there is a *G.* in Israel
22. 3. till I know what *G.* will do for me
2 *Sam.* 22. 32. who is *G.* save the Ld.? *Ps.* 18. 31.
1 *Kings* 18. 21. if the Lord be *G.* follow him
39. the Lord, he is the *G.* the Lord, he is the *G.*
2 *Kings* 19. 15. thou art the *G.* even thou alone
2 *Chr.* 20. 6. O Lord *G.* art not thou *G.* in heaven?
Ezra 1. 3. his *G.* be with him, he is the *G.*
Neh. 9. 17. art a *G.* ready to pardon, slow to anger
Job 22. 13. sayest, how doth *G.* know? *Psal.* 73. 11.
Ps. 5. 4. art not a *G.* that hast pleasure in wickedn.
52. 7. the man that made not *G.* his strength
86. 10. thou art great, thou art *G.* alone, *Isa.* 37. 16.
Isa. 12. 2. behold, *G.* is my salvation, I will trust
44. 8. is there a *G.* besides me? yea, there is no *G.*
45. 22. look unto me, I am *G.* there is none else
46. 9. I am *G.* there is none else, none like me
Jer. 31. 33. I will be their *G.* they my people, 32. 38.
Ezek. 28. 2. hast said, I am a god, I sit in seat of *G.*
9. but thou shalt be a man, and no *g.*
Hos. 8. 6. workman made it, therefore it is not *G.*
11. 9. for I am *G.* and not man, the holy One
Mic. 7. 18. who is a *G.* like to thee, that pardons
Mat. 1. 23. name Immanuel, which is *G.* with us
6. 24. ye cannot serve *G.* and mammon, *Luke* 16. 13.
19. 17. there is none good but one, that is *G.* *Mark* 10. 18. *Luke* 18. 19.
Mark 12. 32. there is one *G.* and none other but he
John 1. 1. the Word was with *G.* and Word was *G.*
3. 2. can do miracles, except *G.* be with him
8. 41. they said, we have one Father, even *G.*
42. for I proceeded forth, and came from *G.*
17. 3. they might know thee, the only true *G.*
Acts 2. 22. by wonders, which *G.* did by him
5. 29. we ought to obey *G.* rather than men
7. 9. patriarchs sold Joseph, but *G.* was with him
10. 34. I perceive *G.* is no respecter of persons
Rom. 3. 4. let *G.* be true, and every man a liar
8. 31. if *G.* be for us, who can be against us?
15. 5. now the *G.* of patience and consolation
1 *Cor.* 8. 6. to us there is but one *G.* the Father
15. 28. that *G.* may be all in all
2 *Cor.* 1. 21. he which hath anointed us, is *G.*
4. 4. the *g.* of this world hath blinded minds
13. 11. *G.* of love and peace shall be with you
2 *Thess.* 2. 4. above all called *G.* so that he as *G.*
1 *Tim.* 3. 16. *G.* was manifest in the flesh
Tit. 1. 16. they profess that they know *G.*
Heb. 3. 4. but he that built all things is *G.*
4. 10. ceased from his works, as *G.* did from his
8. 10. I will be to them a *G.* they to me a people
1 *John.* 1. 5. *G.* is light, in him is no darkness at all
4. 12. no man hath seen *G.* at any time
Rev. 21. 3. and *G.* himself shall be with them
4. *G.* shall wipe away all tears
7. I will be his *G.* and he shall be my son

Against GOD.

Gen. 39. 9. how do this wickedness, and sin *ag. G.?*
Num. 21. 5. the people spake *ag. G.* *Psal.* 78. 19.
1 *Chron.* 5. 25. and they transgressed *against G.*
2 *Chron.* 32. 19. spake *against* the *G.* of Jerusalem

Job 15. 13. thou turnest thy spirit *against* G.
25. for he stretcheth out his hand *against* G.
34. 37. he multiplieth his words *against* G.
Dan. 3. 29. which speak amiss *ag.* G. of Shadrach
11. 36. speak marvellous things *ag.* G. of gods
Hos. 13. 16. she hath rebelled *against* her G.
Acts 5. 39. lest ye be found to fight *against* G.
6. 11. he hath spoken blasphemous words *ag.* G.
23. 9. let us not fight *against* G.
Rom. 8. 7. the carnal mind is enmity *against* G.
9. 20. who art thou that repliest *against* G.?
Rev. 13. 6. opened his mouth in blasphemy *ag.* G.
See ALMIGHTY.

Before GOD.

Gen. 6. 11. the earth was corrupt *before* G.
Exod. 18. 12. eat bread with Moses' father *before* G.
Josh. 24. 1. they presented themselves *before* G.
Judg. 21. 2. the people abode till even *before* G.
1 Chron. 13. 8. David and all Isr. played *before* G.
10. and there Uzza died *before* G.
16. 1. they offered burnt-sacrifices *before* G.
2 Chr. 33. 12. Manasseh humbled himself *before* G.
34. 27. Josiah's heart was humbled *before* G.
Ezra 7. 19. deliver *before* the G. of Jerusalem
Job 15. 4. yea, thou restrainest prayer *before* G.
Psal. 42. 2. when shall I appear *before* G.?
56. 13. may walk *before* G. in light of living
61. 7. he shall abide *before* G. for ever
68. 3. let the righteous rejoice *before* G.
84. 7. every one in Zion appeareth *before* G.
Eccl. 2. 26. give to him that is good *before* G.
5. 2. heart hasty to utter any thing *before* G.
8. 13. because he feareth not *before* G.
Dan. 2. † 18. would desire mercies from *before* G.
6. 10. gave thanks *before* his G. as aforetime
11. found him making supplication *before* G.
26. that men tremble *before* the G. of Daniel
Luke 1. 6. they were both righteous *before* G.
12. 6. not one of them is forgotten *before* G.
24. 19. a prophet mighty in deed and word *bef.* G.
Acts 7. 46. who found favour *before* G.
10. 4. thine arms are come for a memorial *before* G.
33. we are all here present *before* G. to hear
23. 1. I lived in all good conscience *before* G.
Rom. 2. 13. not hearers of law are just *before* G.
3. 19. the world may become guilty *before* G.
4. 2. hath whereof to glory, but not *before* G.
14. 22. hast thou faith? have it to thyself *before* G.
2 Cor. 12. 19. we speak *before* G. in Christ
Gal. 1. 20. behold, *before* G. I lie not
1 Thess. 3. 13. he may establish your hearts *bef.* G.
1 Tim. 5. 4. that is good and acceptable *before* G.
21. I charge thee *before* G. 2 Tim. 4. 1.
Jam. 1. 27. pure religion and undefiled *before* G.
Rev. 3. 2. not found thy works perfect *before* G.
9. 13. a voice from the horns of the altar *before* G.
12. 10. which accused them *bef.* G. day and night
16. 19. Babylon came in remembrance *before* G.
20. 12. I saw dead, small and great, stand *bef.* G.
See CALLED, CHOSEN, COMMANDED.

Eternal GOD.

Deut. 33. 27. the *eternal* G. is thy refuge

Everlasting GOD.

Gen. 21. 33. Abraham called on name of *ever.* G.
Isa. 40. 28. the *ever.* G. fainteth not, nor is weary
Rom. 16. 26. according to commandment of *ever.* G.
See FATHER, FEAR, FORBID, GAVE, GLORIFY.

High GOD.

Gen. 14. 18. was priest of the most *high* G. Heb. 7. 1.
19. blessed be Abraham of the most *high* G.
20. blessed be the most *high* G. which delivered
22. I have lift up my hand to the most *high* G.
Psal. 57. 2. I will cry unto G. most *high*, unto G.
78. 35. G. was their rock, the *high* G. their Redeem.
56. they tempted and provoked the most *high* G.
Dan. 3. 26. servants of most *high* G. come forth
4. 2. shew the wonders the *high* G. hath wrought
5. 18. *high* G. gave Nebuchadnezzar a kingdom
21. till he knew that the most *high* G. ruled
Mic. 6. 6. and bow myself before the most *high* G.
Mark 5. 7. thou Son of the most *high* G. Luke 8. 28.
Acts 16. 17. these men are servants of most *high* G.

Holy GOD.

Josh. 24. 19. he is an *holy* G. he is a jealous God
1 Sam. 6. 20. who is able to stand before this *holy* G.?
Psal. 99. 9. for the Lord our G. is *holy*
Isa. 5. 16. G. that is *holy* shall be sanctified in right.

GOD *of heaven.*

2 Chron. 36. 23. all kingdoms of the earth hath the Lord G. *of heaven* given me, Ezra 1. 2.
Ezra 5. 11. we are the servants of the G. *of heaven*
12. our fathers have provoked the G. *of heaven*
6. 9. for burnt-offerings of the G. *of heaven*, 10.
7. 12. a scribe of the law of the G. *of heaven*, 21.
23. whatever is commanded by the G. *of heaven*
Neh. 1. 4. I fasted and prayed before the G. *of h.*
2. 4. so I prayed to the G. *of heaven*, and said
Psal. 136. 26. O give thanks to the G. *of heaven*
Dan. 2. 18. they would desire mercies of G. *of h.*
19. then Daniel blessed the G. *of heaven*
44. the G. *of heaven* shall set up a kingdom
Jonah 1. 9. I fear the Lord, the G. *of heaven*
Rev. 11. 13. the remnant gave glory to G. *of hea.*
16. 11. and they blasphemed the G. *of heaven*

GOD *of hosts.*

Psal. 80. 7. turn us again, O G. *of hosts*, 19.
14. return, we beseech thee, O G. *of hosts*
Amos 5. 27. saith Lord, whose name is the G. *of hosts*
See LORD God.

GOD *is.*

Gen. 21. 22. G. *is* with thee in all that thou doest
31. 50. see, G. *is* witness betwixt me and thee
Exod. 20. 20. fear not, for G. *is* come to prove you
Num. 23. 19. G. *is* not a man, that he should lie
Deut. 3. 24. what G. *is* there in heaven who can do?
33. 27. the eternal G. *is* thy refuge, and underneath
Josh. 24. 19. our holy G. *is* a jealous God, Nah. 1. 2.
1 Sam. 4. 7. G. *is* come into the camp, woe unto us
10. 7. for G. *is* come with thee, 1 Chron. 17. 2.
28. 15. G. *is* departed from me, he answereth not
2 Sam. 22. 33. G. *is* my strength and power
1 Chron. 14. 15. G. *is* gone forth before thee to smite
2 Chr. 13. 12. G. himself *is* with us for our captain
Job 33. 12. I answer thee, G. *is* greater than man
36. 5. behold, G. *is* mighty and despiseth not any
26. behold, G. *is* great, and we know him not
Psal. 7. 11. G. *is* angry with the wicked every day
10. 4. G. *is* not in all his thoughts, not seek after G.
14. 5. for G. *is* in the generation of the righteous
33. 12. blessed nation, whose G. *is* Lord, 144. 15.
46. 1. G. *is* our refuge and strength, 62. 8.
5. G. *is* in the midst of her, she shall not be moved
47. 5. G. *is* gone up with a shout || 7. for G. *is* King
48. 3. G. *is* known in her palaces for a refuge
50. 6. for G. *is* judge himself, Selah, 75. 7.
54. 4. behold, G. *is* my helper, Lord is with them
56. 9. turn back; this I know, for G. *is* for me
59. 9. I will wait, for G. *is* my defence, 17.
62. 7. in G. *is* my salvation and glory, Isa. 12. 2.
68. 5. a father of the fatherless *is* G. in his habitation
73. 1. truly G. *is* good to Israel, even to such as are
26. G. *is* strength of my heart, and portion for ever
74. 12. G. *is* my King of old, working salvation
89. 7. G. *is* greatly to be feared in the assembly
116. 5. gracious is the Lord, our G. *is* merciful
118. 27. G. *is* the Lord that hath shewed us light
Eccl. 5. 2. for G. *is* in heaven, and thou on earth
Isa. 5. 16. G. that *is* holy shall be sanctified in right.
8. 10. for G. *is* with us || 45. 14. surely G. *is* in thee
Zech. 8. 23. we have heard that G. *is* with you
Mat. 3. 9. G. *is* able of these stones to raise, Luke 3. 8.
22. 32. G. *is* not God of the dead, but of the living
John 3. 33. hath set to his seal that G. *is* true
4. 24. G. *is* a Spirit || 13. 31. G. *is* glorified in him
Acts 10. 34. G. *is* no respecter of persons
Rom. 1. 9. for G. *is* my witness, whom I serve
11. 23. for G. *is* able to graff them in again
14. 4. for G. *is* able to make him stand
1 Cor. 1. 9. G. *is* faithful, by whom ye were called
10. 13. G. *is* faithful who will not suffer you
14. 25. and report that G. *is* in you of a truth
33. G. *is* not author of confusion, but of peace
2 Cor. 1. 18. as G. *is* true, our word was not yea, nay
9. 8. G. *is* able to make all grace abound to you
Gal. 3. 20. but G. *is* one || 6. 7. G. *is* not mocked
Eph. 2. 4. but G. who *is* rich in mercy quickened us
Phil. 1. 8. G. *is* my record, how greatly I long after
3. 19. for many walk, whose *g. is* their belly
1 Thess. 2. 5. nor cloke of covetousness, G. *is* witness
Heb. 6. 10. G. *is* not unright. to forget your work
11. 16. G. *is* not ashamed to be called their God
12. 29. for our G. *is* a consuming fire
13. 16. for with such sacrifices G. *is* well pleased
1 John 1. 5. G. *is* light || 4. 8. for G. *is* love, 16.
3. 20. G. *is* greater than our heart, knows all things

GOD *of Israel.*

Exod. 24. 10. they went up, and saw the G. *of Isr.*
Num. 16. 9. the G. *of Israel* hath separated you
Josh. 7. 19. to give glory to the G. *of Isr.* 1 Sam. 6. 5.
13. 33. the G. *of Israel* was their inheritance
22. 16. what trespass ye committed ag. G. *of Israel*
24. what have ye to do with the G. *of Israel*?
24. 23. incline your heart to the G. *of Israel*
Judg. 11. 23. G. *of Israel* dispossessed the Amorites
Ruth 2. 12. a full reward be given thee of G. *of Isr.*
1 Sam. 1. 17. the G. *of Israel* grant thy petition
5. 11. send away the ark of the G. *of Israel*
1 Kin. 8. 23. L. G. *of Isr.* no G. like thee, 2 Chr. 6. 14.
14. 13. some good thing toward the G. *of Israel*
1 Chron. 4. 10. Jabez called on the G. *of Israel*
17. 24. the Lord of hosts is the G. *of Israel*
2 Chron. 15. 13. who would not seek the G. *of Isr.*?
Ezra 7. 15. have freely offered to the G. *of Israel*
9. 4. trembled at the words of the G. *of Israel*
Ps. 41. 13. blessed be the L. G. *of Isr.* from everlast. to everlasting, 72. 18. | 106. 48. Luke 1. 68.
Isa. 41. 17. I the G. *of Israel* will not forsake them
45. 3. I which call thee by name, am G. *of Israel*
48. 2. they stay themselves on the G. *of Israel*
Ezek. 8. 4. the glory of the G. *of Israel* was there
Mat. 15. 31. the multitude glorified the G. *of Israel*

Living GOD.

Deut. 5. 26. that heard the voice of the *living* G.
Josh. 3. 10. hereby know the *living* G. is among you
1 Sam. 17. 26. should defy the armies of *living* G. 36.
2 Kings 19. 4. whom the king of Assyria hath sent to reproach the *living* G. 16. Isa. 37. 4, 17.
Psal. 42. 2. my soul thirsteth for God, the *living* G.
84. 2. my heart and flesh crieth out for *living* G.
Jer. 10. 10. he is the *living* G. an everlasting King
23. 36. have perverted the words of the *living* G.
Dan. 6. 26. he is the *living* G. and stedfast for ever
Hos. 1. 10. shall be said, ye are sons of the *living* G.
Mat. 16. 16. art Christ, Son of *living* G. John 6. 69.
26. 63. I adjure thee by the *living* G. tell us
Acts 14. 15. turn from these vanities to the *living* G.
Rom. 9. 26. they shall be called children of *living* G.
2 Cor. 3. 3. but with the Spirit of the *living* G.
6. 16. for ye are the temple of the *living* G.
1 Thess. 1. 9. from idols to serve *living* and true G.
1 Tim. 3. 15. which is the church of the *living* G.
4. 10. because we trust in the *living* G. 6. 17.
Heb. 3. 12. an evil heart in departing from *living* G.
9. 14. purge your conscience to serve the *living* G.
10. 31. it is fearful to fall into hands of *living* G.
12. 22. ye are come to Zion, the city of *living* G.
Rev. 7. 2. angel having the seal of the *living* G.

Lord GOD, *Lord his* GOD, *Lord my, Lord our, their, your* GOD. See these in the divisions of the word LORD.

Merciful GOD.

Exod. 34. 6. the Lord, the Lord G. *merciful*, gracious
Deut. 4. 31. the Lord thy God is a *merciful* G.
2 Chr. 30. 9. Lord your G. is *merciful* if ye turn
Neh. 9. 31. thou art a gracious and *merciful* G.
Psal. 116. 5. gracious is the Lord, our G. is *merciful*
Jonah 4. 2. I knew that thou art a G. *merciful*

Mighty GOD.

Gen. 49. 24. bow abode by hands of *mighty* G. of Jac.
Deut. 7. 21. Lord is among you, a *mighty* G. 10. 17.
Neh. 9. 32. now therefore our God, the *mighty* G.
Job 36. 5. behold, G. is *mighty*, and despiseth not any
Psal. 50. 1. the *mighty* G. the Lord hath spoken
132. 2. how he vowed to the *mighty* G. of Jacob
Psal. 132. 5. till I find an habitation *m.* G. of Jacob
Isa. 9. 6. his name shall be called the *mighty* G.
10. 21. the remnant shall return to the *mighty* G.
Jer. 32. 18. *mighty* G. the Lord of hosts is his name
Hab. 1. 12. O *mighty* G. thou hast stablished them

My GOD.

Gen. 28. 21. Jacob said, then shall the Ld. be *my* G.
Exod. 15. 2. he is *my* G. *my* father's G. I will exalt
Ruth 1. 16. thy people be my people, thy God *my* G.
2 Sam. 22. 7. I cried to *my* G. he heard, Psal. 18. 6.
22. and have not departed from *my* G. Psal. 18. 21.
30. by *my* G. I have leaped over a wall, Ps. 18. 29.
1 Chr. 28. 20. for God, even *my* G. will be with thee
2 Chr. 18. 13. what *my* G. saith, that will I speak
Neh. 5. 19. think upon me, *my* G. for good, 13. 31.
13. 14. remember me, *my* G. concerning this, 22.
Psal. 22. 1. *my* G. *my* G. why hast thou forsaken me? why so far from helping me? Mat. 27. 46.
10. thou art *my* G. from my mother's belly
31. 14. I trusted in thee, I said, thou art *my* G.
38. 21. O *my* G. be not far from me, 71. 12.
89. 26. he shall cry, thou art my Father, *my* G.
104. 33. I will sing praises to *my* G. 146. 2.
118. 28. thou art *my* G. and I will praise thee
145. 1. I will extol thee, *my* G. O King, and bless
Prov. 30. 9. and take the name of *my* G. in vain
Isa. 7. 13. but will ye weary *my* G. also?
40. 27. my judgment is passed over from *my* G.
44. 17. he saith, deliver me, for thou art *my* G.
61. 10. my soul shall be joyful in *my* G.
Dan. 6. 22. *my* G. hath sent his angel, hath shut lions'
Hos. 2. 23. they shall say, thou art *my* G. Zech. 13. 9.
8. 2. Israel shall cry to me, *my* G. we know thee
9. 17. *my* G. will cast them away, not hearken
Mic. 7. 7. I will wait, for *my* G. will hear me
John 20. 17. and say, I ascend to *my* G. and your G.
28. Thomas answered and said, my L. and *my* G.
Rom. 1. 8. I thank *my* G. through Jesus Christ, for you all, 1 Cor. 1. 4. | 14. 18. Phil. 1. 3. Philem. 4.
2 Cor. 12. 21. lest when I come, *my* G. will humble
Phil. 4. 19. *my* G. shall supply all your need
Rev. 3. 12. I will write on him the name of *my* G.
See LORD *my God.*

No GOD.

Deut. 32. 39. I, even I am he, there is *no* G. with me
1 Kings 8. 23. there is *no* G. like thee, 2 Chr. 6. 14.
2 Kings 1. 16. is it because there is *no* G. in Israel?
5. 15. now I know there is *no* G. in all the earth
2 Chron. 32. 15. *no* G. of any nation able to deliver
Psal. 14. 1. the fool hath said, there is *no* G. 53. 1.
Isa. 43. 10. before me there was *no* G. formed
44. 6. besides me there is *no* G. 8. | 45. 5, 14, 21.
Ezek. 28. 9. but thou shalt be a man, and *no* G.
Hos. 13. 4. and thou shalt know *no* G. but me

O GOD.

Num. 12. 13. heal her now, *O* G. I beseech thee
Judg. 16. 28. strengthen me, only this once, *O* G.
Psal. 4. 1. hear me, *O* G. of my righteousness
25. 22. redeem Israel, *O* G. out of all his troubles
51. 14. deliver me from blood-guiltiness, *O* G.
56. 12. thy vows are upon me, *O* G. I will render
Isa. 64. 4. nor hath the eye seen, *O* G. besides thee
Heb. 10. 7. I said, lo, I come to do thy will, *O* G. 9.

Of GOD.

Exod. 9. † 28. entreat there be no more voices *of* G.
1 Sam. 14. † 15. so it was a trembling *of* G.
2 Chr. 10. 15. hearkened not, for the cause was *of* G.
25. 20. Amaziah would not hear, for it came *of* G.
Psal. 7. 10. my defence is *of* G. who saveth upright
Isa. 29. † 1. woe to the lion *of* G. add year to year
53. 4. we did esteem him smitten *of* G. and afflicted
Mat. 16. 23. savourest not things *of* G. Mark 8. 33.
John 1. 13. born not of the will of man, but *of* G.
6. 46. he which is *of* G. hath seen the Father
7. 17. shall know of doctrine whether it be *of* G.
8. 47. he that is *of* G. heareth: ye are not *of* G.
9. 16. this man is not *of* G. || 33. if he were not *of* G.
12. 43. loved the praise of men more than *of* G.
Acts 5. 39. if it be *of* G. ye cannot overthrow it
Rom. 2. 29. whose praise is not of men, but *of* G.
9. 16. but *of* G. that sheweth mercy
13. 1. no power but *of* G. powers ordained *of* G.
1 Cor. 1. 30. who *of* G. is made unto us wisdom
6. 19. which ye have *of* G. ye are not your own
11. 12. but all things are *of* G. 2 Cor. 5. 18.
2 Cor. 2. 17. but as *of* G. in the sight *of* G. speak we
3. 5. we are not sufficient, our sufficiency is *of* G.
Phil. 1. 28. but to you of salvation, and that *of* G.
3. 9. the righteousness which is *of* G. by faith
Heb. 5. 4. he that was called *of* G. as was Aaron
1 John 3. 10. doeth not righteousness, is not *of* G.
4. 1. beloved, try the spirits whether they are *of* G.
3. confesseth not that Christ is come, is not *of* G.
6. we are *of* G. || 5. 19. we know that we are *of* G.
3 John 11. follow good, he that doeth good is *of* G.
See ANGEL, ARK, BORN, CHILDREN, CHOSEN, CHURCH, COUNSEL, FEAR, GLORY, GRACE, HAND, HOUSE, KINGDOM, KNOWLEDGE, LOVE, MAN, PEOPLE, POWER, SERVANT, SIGHT, SON, SONS, SPIRIT, WILL, WORDS, WORK, WORKS, WORLD, WRATH.

Our GOD.

Exod. 5. 8. they cry, let us go and sacrifice to *our* G.
Deut. 31. 17. because *our* G. is not amongst us
32. 3. ascribe ye greatness unto *our* G.
Josh. 24. 18. we will serve the Lord, he is *our* G.
Judg. 10. 10. because we have forsaken *our* G.
1 Sam. 2. 2. neither is there any rock like *our* G.
2 Sam. 10. 12. and let us play the men for *our* people, and for the cities of *our* G. 1 Chron. 19. 13.
22. 32. who is a rock, save *our* G.? Psal. 18. 31.
1 Chr. 29. 13. now therefore, *our* G. we thank thee
2 Chron. 2. 5. for great is *our* G. above all gods
14. 11. O Lord, thou art *our* G. let not man prevail
20. 7. art not thou *our* G. who didst drive out
Ezra 9. 10. now, O *our* G. what shall we say after?
Neh. 4. 4. hear, O *our* G. || 20. *our* G. shall fight for us
6. 16. that this work was wrought of *our* G.
9. 32. now therefore *our* G. the great, mighty God
13. 2. *our* G. turned the curse into a blessing
Ps. 40. 3. hath put a new song, even praise to *our* G.
48. 14. this God is *our* G. for ever and ever

Psal. 50. 3. our G. shall come and not keep silence
67. 6. and God, even our own G. shall bless us
68. 20. he that is our G. is the God of salvation
77. 13. who is so great a God as our G.?
95. 7. he is our G. || 115. 3. our G. is in the heavens
116. 5. gracious is the Lord, our G. is merciful
Isa. 25. 9. lo, this is our G. we have waited for him
55. 7. to our G. for he will abundantly pardon
59. 13. and departing away from our G.
61. 2. to proclaim the day of vengeance of our G.
Dan. 3. 17. our G. whom we serve is able to deliver
Zech. 9. 7. he that remaineth shall be for our G.
1 Cor. 6. 11. ye are sanctified by the Spirit of our G.
Heb. 12. 29. for our G. is a consuming fire
Rev. 5. 10. hast made us to our G. kings and priests
7. 10. salvation to our G. who sitteth on the throne
12. blessing, and honour, and power be to our G.
See Peace, Said, Saith, Serve, Sent, Speak, Speed, Spoken.

Their GOD.

Gen. 17. 8. I will be their G. Exod. 29. 45. Jer. 24. 7. | 31. 33. | 32. 38. Ezek. 11. 20. | 34. 24. | 37. 23, 27. Zech. 8. 8. 2 Cor. 6. 16. Rev. 21. 3.
Lev. 21. 6. they shall be holy to their G. for offerings of the Lord, and bread of their G. they do offer
26. 45. that I might be their G. Ezek. 14. 11.
2 Sam. 7. 24. thou art become their G. 1 Chr. 17. 22.
Ezra 5. 5. the eye of their G. was on the elders
Psal. 79. 10. where is their G.? 115. 2. Joel 2. 17.
Isa. 8. 19. should not a people seek to their G.?
21. shall fret, and curse their king, and their G.
58. 2. and forsook not the ordinance of their G.
Jer. 5. 4. they know not the judgment of their G. 5.
Dan. 11. 32. but the people that know their G.
Hos. 4. 12. have gone a whor. from under their G.
5. 4. not frame their doings to turn to their G.
Zech. 12. 5. my strength in the Lord of hosts their G.
Heb. 11. 16. he is not ashamed to be called their G.
See Lord their God.

Thy GOD.

Lev. 19. 14. thou shalt fear thy G. 25. 17, 36, 43.
Deut. 10. 21. he is thy praise, and he is thy G.
26. 17. hast avouched this day the Ld. to be thy G.
Ruth 1. 16. thy people my people, thy G. my God
2 Kings 19. 10. let not thy G. deceive thee, Isa. 37. 10.
1 Chr. 12. 18. peace to thee, for thy G. helpeth thee
2 Chr. 9. 8. beca se thy G. loved Isr. made thee king
Ezra 7. 14. according to law of thy G. in thy hand
25. after the wisdom of thy G. laws of thy G.
Neh. 9. 18. this is thy G. that brought thee up
Ps. 42. 3. continually say to me, where is thy G.? 10.
45. 7. God, thy G. hath anointed thee, Heb. 1. 9.
50. 7. hear, O Israel, I am God, even thy G.
68. 28. thy G. hath commanded thy strength
147. 12. praise the Lord, praise thy G. O Zion
Isa. 41. 10. be not dismayed, for I am thy G.
51. 20. they are full of the rebuke of thy G.
52. 7. that saith to Zion, thy G. reigneth
60. 19. Lord shall be a light, and thy G. thy glory
62. 5. so shall thy G. rejoice over thee
Dan. 6. 16. thy G. whom thou servest will deliver
20. is thy G. whom thou servest continually able?
10. 12. and to chasten thyself before thy G.
Hos. 4. 6. thou hast forgotten the law of thy G.
9. 1. thou hast gone a whoring from thy G.
12. 6. turn thou to thy G. and wait on thy G.
Amos 4. 12. prepare to meet thy G. O Israel
Jonah 1. 6. O sleeper, arise, call upon thy G.
Mic. 6. 8. and to walk humbly with thy G.
See Lord thy God.

To, or unto GOD.

Gen. 40. 8. do not interpretations belong to G.?
Exod. 2. 23. they cried, and their cry came up to G.
Lev. 21. 7. for he is holy unto his G.
Deut. 32. 17. sac. to devils not to G. 1 Cor. 10. 20.
33. 26. there is none like to the G. of Jeshurun
Judg. 13. 5. shall be a Nazarite unto G. 7. | 16. 17.
1 Sam. 10. 3. shall meet the three men going up to G.
1 Chron. 26. 32. for every matter pertaining to G.
Job 22. 2. can a man be profitable to G.?
34. 31. surely it is meet to be said unto G. I have
Psal. 62. 11. I have heard, power belongeth to G.
68. 20. to G. the Lord belong the issues from death
31. Ethiopia shall stretch her hands to G.
73. 28. it is good for me to draw near to G.
77. 1. I cried to G. even to G. with my voice
Eccl. 12. 7. and the spirit shall return unto G.
Isa. 58. 2. they take delight in approaching to G.
Lam. 3. 41. let us lift up our heart with hands to G.
Mat. 22. 21. render unto G. the things which are God's, Mark 12. 17. Luke 20. 25.
John 13. 3. that he was come from God, went to G.
Acts 4. 19. to hearken to you more than unto G.
5. 4. thou hast not lied unto men, but unto G.
26. 18. to turn them from power of Satan unto G.
20. turn to G. and do works meet for repentance
Rom. 6. 10. he liveth unto G. || 11. but alive unto G.
13. yield yourselves unto G. as alive from dead
7. 4. that we should bring forth fruit unto G.
12. 1. present your bodies a living sacrifice unto G.
14. 12. every one give account of himself to G.
1 Cor. 14. 2. speaketh not unto men but unto G.
15. 24. he shall have delivered up kingdom to G.
Phil. 4. 20. now unto G. and our Father be glory
Heb. 7. 25. he is able to save them that come unto G.
11. 6. he that cometh to G. must believe that he is
12. 23. but ye are come to G. the Judge of all
Jam. 4. 7. submit yourselves therefore to G.
1 Pet. 3. 18. Christ once suffered, might bring us to G.
4. 6. but live according to G. in the Spirit
Rev. 5. 9. thou hast redeemed us to G. by thy blood
12. 5. her child was caught up unto G. to his throne
14. 4. being the first-fruits unto G. and the Lamb
See True.

With GOD.

Gen. 5. 22. Enoch walked with G. and was not, 24.
6. 9. Noah walked || 32. 28. Jacob hath power w. G.
Exod. 19. 17. Moses brought people to meet with G.
1 Sam. 14. 45. he hath wrought with G. this day
2 Sam. 23. 5. although my house be not so with G.
2 Chron. 35. 21. forbear from meddling with G.
Job 9. 2. how should man be just with G.?
Job 13. 3. and I desire to reason with G.
16. 21. O that one might plead for a man with G.
25. 4. how then can a man be justified with G.?
27. 13. this the portion of a wicked man with G.
34. 9. that he should delight himself with G.
23. that he should enter into judgment with G.
37. 22. with G. is terrible majesty
Psal. 78. 8. whose spirit is not stedfast with G.
Hos. 11. 12. but Judah yet ruleth with G.
12. 3. Jacob by his strength had power with G.
Mat. 19. 26. with men this is impossible, but with G. all things possible, Mark 10. 27. Luke 1. 37. | 18. 27.
Luke 1. 30. for thou hast found favour with G.
2. 52. Jesus increased in favour with G. and man
John 1. 1. the Word was with G. the Word was God
5. 18. making himself equal with G. Phil. 2. 6.
Rom. 2. 11. there is no respect of persons with G.
5. 1. being justified by faith, we have peace with G.
9. 14. is there unrighteousn. with G.? God forbid
1 Cor. 3. 9. we are labourers together with G.
19. the wisdom of this world is foolishness with G.
7. 24. let every man therein abide with G.
2 Thess. 1. 6. a righteous thing with G. to recompense
Jam. 4. 4. the friendship of world is enmity with G.
1 Pet. 2. 20. take patiently, this is acceptable with G.
Would GOD, see Would.

Your GOD.

Gen. 43. 23. your G. hath given you treasure in sacks
Exod. 8. 25. go ye, sacrifice to your G. in the land
Lev. 11. 45. Lord that bringeth you out of Egypt to be your G. 22. 33. | 25. 38. Num. 15. 41.
26. 12. I will be your G. and ye shall be my people, Jer. 7. 23. | 11. 4. | 30. 22. Ezek. 36. 28.
Num. 10. 10. be to you a memorial before your G.
15. 40. do my commandments, be holy to your G.
Josh. 24. 27. stone be witness, lest ye deny your G.
1 Sam. 10. 19. ye have this day rejected your G.
2 Chron. 32. 14. that your G. should deliver you
15. how much less shall your G. deliver you?
Ezra 4. 2. let us build, for we seek your G. as ye do
Isa. 35. 4. your G. will come with vengeance
40. 1. comfort ye my people, saith your G.
9. say to the cities of Judah, behold your G.
59. 2. iniquities separated between you and your G.
Ezek. 34. 31. I am your G. saith the Lord God
Dan. 2. 47. of a truth it is, your G. is a God of gods
Hos. 1. 9. ye are not my people, I will not be your G.
John 8. 54. of whom ye say that he is your G.
20. 17. I ascend to my God and your G.
See Lord your God.

GODDESS.

1 Kings 11. 5. Solom. went after the g. of Zidonians
33. they have worshipped Ashtoreth, the g.
Acts 19. 27. the temple of great g. Diana be despised
35. Ephesians are worshippers of the g. Diana
37. nor yet blasphemers of your g.

GODHEAD.

Acts 17. 29. nor think that the g. is like to gold
Rom. 1. 20. even his eternal power and g.
Col. 2. 9. in him dwelleth the fulness of the g. bodily

GODLY.

Psal. 4. 3. the Lord hath set apart him that is g.
12. 1. help, Lord, for the g. man ceaseth
32. 6. for this shall every one that is g. pray
Mic. 7. †2. the g. man is perished out of the earth
Mal. 2. 15. that he might seek a g. seed
2 Cor. 1. 12. in g. sincerity had our conversation
7. 9. we were made sorry after a g. manner, 11.
10. for g. sorrow worketh repentance
11. 2. I am jealous over you with g. jealousy
2 Tim. 3. 12. all that will live g. in Christ, suffer
Tit. 2. 12. that ye should live g. in this world
Heb. 12. 28. let us serve God with rever. and g. fear
2 Pet. 2. 9. the Lord knoweth how to deliver the g.
3 John 6. if thou bring forward after a g. sort

GODLINESS.

Isa. 57. †1. and men of g. are taken away
1 Tim. 2. 2. that we may lead a quiet life in all g.
10. which becometh women professing g.
3. 16. great is the mystery of g. God in the flesh
4. 7. and exercise thyself rather unto g.
8. but g. is profitable unto all things
6. 3. to the doctrine which is according to g.
5. corrupt men, supposing that gain is g.
6. but g. with contentment is great gain
11. follow after righteousness, g. faith, love
2 Tim. 3. 5. having a form of g. but denying power
Tit. 1. 1. acknowledging the truth which is after g.
2 Pet. 1. 3. all things that pertain to life and g.
6. add to patience g. to g. brotherly kindness, 7.
3. 11. what manner of persons ought to be in all g.

GOD-WARD.

Exod. 18. 19. God with thee, be thou for people to G.
2 Cor. 3. 4. such trust have we through Christ to G.
1 Thess. 1. 8. your faith to G. is spread abroad

GODS.

Gen. 3. 5. ye shall be as g. knowing good and evil
31. 30. yet wherefore hast thou stolen my g.?
Exod. 12. 12. against all g. of Egypt I will execute
20. 23. shalt not make with me g. of silver or gold
22. 28. thou shalt not revile the g. nor curse ruler
23. 24. thou shalt not bow down to their g.
32. shalt make no covenant with them nor their g.
32. 1. up, make us g. to go before us, 23. Acts 7. 40.
4. these be thy g. O Israel, which brought, 8.
31. Moses said, they have made them g. of gold
34. 15. lest they go a whoring after their g.
Num. 25. 2. called people to the sacrifices of their g.
33. 4. upon the Egyptians' g. also the Lord executed judgment, Jer. 43. 12, 13. | 46. 25.
Deut. 7. 25. the images of their g. shall ye burn
10. 17. Lord your God is God of g. Lord of lords
12. 3. ye shall hew down the images of their g.
30. that thou enquire not after their g.
31. have done every abomination to their g. burnt their sons and daughters in the fire to their g.
13. 7. entice thee to the g. of people round about
20. 18. not to do as they have done to their g.
29. †17. and ye have seen their dungy g.
32. 37. and ye shall say, where are their g.?
Josh. 22. 22. the Lord God of g. knoweth
Josh. 23. 7. nor make mention of the name of their g.
Judg. 5. 8. they chose new g. then was war in gates
6. 10. I said, fear not the g. of the Amorites
10. 14. go and cry to the g. which ye have chosen
17. 5. the man Micah had an house of g.
18. 24. ye have taken away my g. which I made
Ruth 1. 15. thy sister-in-law is gone back to her g.
1 Sam. 4. 8. these are the g. that smote Egyptians
6. 5. will lighten his hand from off you and your g
17. 43. the Philistine cursed David by his g.
28. 13. she said, I saw g. ascending out of the earth
2 Sam. 7. 23. thou redeemest from Egypt and their g.
1 Kings 11. 2. they will turn your heart after their g.
8. Solomon burnt incense and sacrificed to their g
12. 28. it is too much to go up, behold thy g.
18. 24. and call ye on the name of your g. 25.
19. 2. let the g. do so to me and more also, 20. 10.
20. 23. their g. are g. of the hills, therefore
2 Kings 17. 29. every nation made g. of their own
33. they feared the Lord, and served their own g.
18. 33. hath any of the g. delivered his land? 19. 12. 2 Chron. 32. 13, 14. Isa. 36. 18. | 37. 12.
34. where are the g. of Hamath? Isa. 36. 19.
19. 18. have cast their g. into fire, they were no g.
1 Chron. 5. 25. went a whoring after g. of the land
10. 10. put Saul's armour in the house of their g.
14. 12. they left their g. David burnt them
2 Chron. 13. 8. golden calves Jeroboam made for g.
9. the same may be a priest to them that are no g.
25. 14. Amaziah brought g. of Seir to be his g.
28. 23. Ahaz sacrificed to the g. of Damascus
32. 17. the g. of the nations have not delivered
Ezra 1. 7. Nebuch. put vessels in the house of his g.
Psal. 82. 1. God standeth, he judgeth among the g.
6. I have said, ye are g. John 10. 34.
136. 2. O give thanks unto the God of g.
138. 1. before the g. will I sing praise unto thee
Isa. 21. 9. Babylon is fallen, and her g. broken
41. 23. that we may know that ye are g.
42. 17. that say to molten images, ye are our g.
Jer. 2. 11. hath a nation changed her g. are no g.?
28. where are thy g. thou hast made? according to the number of thy cities are thy g. 11. 13.
5. 7. children have sworn by them that are no g.
10. 11. the g. that have not made the heavens
11. 12. cry to the g. to whom they offer incense
16. 20. shall a man make g. and they are no g.?
48. 35. to cease him that burneth incense to his g.
Dan. 2. 11. no other can shew it, except the g.
47. of a truth it is, that your God is a God of g.
4. 8. in whom is the spirit of the holy g.
9. I know spirit of holy g. is in thee, 18. | 5. 14.
5. 4. they praised the g. of gold and silver, 23.
11. and wisdom like the wisdom of the g.
11. 8. carry captives into Egypt g. with princes
36. shall speak marvellous things against G. of g.
Hos. 14. 3. neither will we say more, ye are our g
Nah. 1. 14. out of the house of thy g. I will cut off
John 10. 35. if he called them g. to whom the word
Acts 14. 11. the g. are come down to us like men
17. †23. I beheld your g. that you worship
19. 26. they be no g. which are made with hands
1 Cor. 8. 5. be that are called g. there be g. many
Gal. 4. 8. did service to them which by nature no g.
See Serve.

All GODS.

Exod. 18. 11. I know the Lord is greater than all g.
1 Chr. 16. 25. to be feared above all g. Psal. 96. 4.
26. all g. of the people are idols, Psal. 96. 5.
2 Chr. 2. 5. great is God above all g. Psal. 135. 5.
Psal. 95. 3. the Lord is a great King above all g.
97. 7. worship him, all ye g. || 9. exalted above all g.
Zeph. 2. 11. he will famish all the g. of the earth

Among the GODS.

Exod. 15. 11. among the g. who is like thee, O Lord?
2 Kings 18. 35. who among the g. could deliver their country? 2 Chron. 32. 14. Isa. 36. 20.
Psal. 86. 8. among the g. there is none like thee

Molten GODS.

Exod. 34. 17. shalt make no molten g. Lev. 19. 4.

Other GODS.

Exod. 20. 3. shalt have no o. g. before me, Deut. 5. 7.
23. 13. make no mention of names of other g.
Deut. 6. 14. ye shall not go after other g. 11. 28. | 28. 14. 1 Kings 11. 10. Jer. 25. 6. | 35. 15.
7. 4. they will turn thy son to serve other g.
8. 19. if thou walk after other g. and serve them
13. 2. let us go after other g. and serve them, 6, 13.
17. 3. hath gone and served other g. 29. 26. Josh. 23. 16. Judg. 10. 13. 1 Sam. 8. 8. Jer. 11. 10.
18. 20. prophet that shall speak in name of other g.
30. 17. but shalt be drawn away, and worship other g. and serve them, Jer. 22. 9.
31. 18. in that day they turned to other g.
20. then will they turn to other g. and provoke me
Judg. 2. 12. forsook the Lord, and followed other g.
17. went a whoring after other g. bowed to them
19. in following other g. to serve them, and to bow
1 Sam. 26. 19. driven me out, saying, go serve other g.
1 Kings 9. 9. have taken hold upon other g. 2 Chr. 7. 22.
11. 4. his wives turned his heart after other g.
14. 9. for thou hast gone and made thee other g.
2 Kings 5. 17. I will not offer sacrifice to other g.
17. 7. Israel had sinned, and had feared other g.
35. ye shall not fear other g. nor bow to them, nor serve them, nor sacrifice to them, 37, 38.
22. 17. have forsaken me, and burnt incense to other g. 2 Chron. 34. 25. Jer. 1. 16. | 19. 4.
2 Chron. 28. 25. Ahaz burnt incense to other g.
Jer. 7. 6. nor walk after other g. to your hurt
9. walk after other g. whom ye know not, 13. 10.
16. 11. have forsaken me, and walked after other g.
44. 5. hearkened not to burn no incense to other g.
8. burning incense to other g. in land of Egypt, 15.
Hos. 3. 1. look to other g. and love flagons of wine
See Serve.

Strange GODS.

Gen. 35. 2. put away the strange g. 1 Sam. 7. 3.
4. they gave Jacob the strange g. Josh. 24. 23.
Deut. 32. 16. provoked him to jealousy with str. g
Josh. 24. 20. if ye forsake Lord, and serve strange g.

Judg. 10. 16. they put away their strange g.
2 Chr. 14. 3. Asa took away the altar of strange g.
33. 15. Josiah took away the strange g. and idol
Jer. 5. 19. as ye served strange g. so serve strangers
Acts 17. 18. seemeth to be a setter forth of strange g.

GOLD.

Gen. 2. 11. whole land of Havilah, where there is g.
12. the g. of that land is good, there is bdellium
41. 42. he put a chain of g. on Joseph's neck
Exod. 20. 23. nor shall ye make you gods of g.
25. 12. thou shalt cast four rings of g. for the ark,
26. | 26. 29. | 28. 23, 26, 27. | 37. 3, 13.
13. shalt make staves of shittim wood, overlay
them with g. 28. | 26. 29, 37. | 30. 5. | 37. 4, 15, 28.
18. thou shalt make two cherubims of g. 37. 7.
26. 6. thou shalt make fifty taches of g. 36. 13.
32. their hooks shall be of g. 37. | 36. 38.
28. 6. ephod g. || 8. girdle g. || 15. breast-plate g.
11. to be set in ouches of g. 13. | 39. 6, 13, 16.
24. chains of g. || 33. thou shalt make bells of g.
32. 24. who hath any g. let him break it off
31. oh, this people have made them gods of g.
35. 22. they brought jewels of g. an offering of g.
36. 34. he overlaid the boards with g. bars with g.
38. he overlaid their chapiters and fillets with g.
38. 24. all the g. that was occupied in the work
39. 3. they did beat the g. into thin plates
40. 5. thou shalt set the altar of g. before the ark
Num. 7. 14. one spoon of ten shekels of g. 20.
84. at dedication of the altar twelve spoons of g.
86. all the g. of the spoons was 120 shekels
31. 50. the captains' oblation, jewels of g. chains
Josh. 7. 21. Achan took a wedge of g. of 50 shekels
24. Joshua took Achan and the wedge of g.
Judg. 8. 26. the ear-rings 1700 shekels of g.
1 Sam. 6. 8. and put the jewels of g. in a coffer
11. they laid coffer and the mice of g. on the cart
15. Levites took the coffer with the jewels of g.
2 Sam. 8. 7. David took shields of g. 1 Chr. 18. 7.
1 Kings 6. 22. house, altar, he overlaid with g.
28. he overlaid cherubims with g. 2 Chron. 3. 10.
7. 48. Solomon made the altar and table of g.
49. lamps and tongs of g. || 50. hinges of g.
9. 11. Hiram king of Tyre furnished Solomon with
g. and cedar trees, 10. 11. 2 Chron. 9. 10.
10. 2. queen of Sheba came with g. 2 Chron. 9. 1.
14. the weight of g. come in one year, 2 Chr. 9. 13.
16. Solomon made 200 targets of beaten g.
17. he made three hundred shields of g.
18. he overlaid the throne with the best g.
12. 28. Jeroboam made two calves of g.
22. 48. Jehoshaphat made ships to go for g.
2 Kings 18. 16. Hezekiah cut off g. from the doors
1 Chron. 28. 14. David gave of g. by weight for g.
2 Chron. 3. 6. and the g. was g. of Parvaim
4. 7. ten candlesticks of g. || 8. basins of g.
22. snuffers, censers, and spoons of pure g.
9. 18. steps to the throne, with a footstool of g.
12. 9. Shishak carried away the shields of g.
Ezra 8. 27. basins of g. copper precious as g.
Neh. 7. 70. Tirshatha gave thousand drachms of g.
71. chief of the fathers gave g. || 72. people gave g.
Job 22. 24. lay up g. as dust, the g. of Ophir
† 25. yea, the Almighty shall be thy g.
23. 10. when tried, I shall come forth like g.
28. 6. as for the earth, it hath the dust of g.
15. wisdom cannot be gotten for g. nor silver
16. it cannot be valued with the g. of Ophir
17. the g. and the crystal cannot equal it
31. 24. if I made g. my hope, or said to fine g.
36. 19. will he esteem thy riches? no not g.
37. † 22. g. cometh out of the north
42. 11. every one gave Job an ear ring of g.
Psal. 19. 10. more to be desired are they than g.
45. 9. did stand the queen in g. of Ophir
72. 15. to him shall be given of the g. of Sheba
Prov. 11. 22. as a jewel of g. in a swine's snout
16. 16. much better it is to get wisdom than g.
20. 15. there is g. and a multitude of rubies
Cant. 1. 10. thy neck is comely with chains of g.
5. 14. his hands are as g. rings set with beryl
Isa. 14. † 4. how hath the exactness of g. ceased
30. 22. ye shall defile ornament of thy images of g.
40. 19. the goldsmith spreadeth it over with g.
60. 17. for brass I will bring g. for iron bring silver
Jer. 4. 30. thou deckest thee with ornaments of g.
Lam. 4. 1. how is the g. become dim! fine g. changed!
Ezek. 27. 22. merchants of Sheba occupied with g.
Dan. 2. 38. art head of g. || 3. 1. Neb. made image of g.
5. 23. and thou hast praised the gods of g.
29. they put a chain of g. about Daniel's neck
Zech. 4. 2. and behold a candlestick all of g.
13. 9. and I will try them as g. is tried
Mat. 2. 11. they presented to him g. and myrrh
23. 16. whoso shall swear by the g. of the temple
17. for whether is greater, the g. or the temple?
1 Tim. 2. 9. not adorned with g. or pearls, 1 Pet. 3. 3.
Heb. 9. 4. the ark overlaid round about with g.
Jam. 2. 2. if there come a man with a g. ring
1 Pet. 1. 7. the trial of faith more precious than g.
Rev. 3. 18. I counsel thee to buy of me g. tried
4. 4. the elders had on their heads crowns of g.
9. 7. the locusts had on their heads crowns of g.
17. 4. the woman was decked with g. and pearls
18. 16. that great city that was decked with g.
See Beaten, Crown, Fine.

Pure GOLD.

Exod. 25. 11. thou shalt overlay the ark with pure g.
within and without, 24. | 30. 3. | 37. 2, 11, 26.
17. thou shalt make a mercy seat of pure g. 37. 6.
29. dishes, spoons and covers of p. g. 37. 16, 23.
31. make a candlest. of p. g. 37. 17. 1 Kings 7. 49.
38. snuff dishes p. g. 1 Kings 7. 50. 2 Chr. 4. 22.
28. 14. two chains of pure g. at ends, 22. | 39. 15.
36. thou shalt make a plate of pure g. 39. 30.
1 Kings 6. 20. the oracle he overlaid with pure g.
10. 21. vessels of Lebanon of pure g. 2 Chr. 9. 20.
1 Chron. 28. 17. pure g. for flesh-hooks, bowls, cups
2 Chron. 3. 4. overlaid the porch within with pure g.
9. 17. he overlaid the throne with pure g.
Job 28. 19. wisdom not to be valued with pure g.
Psal. 21. 3. settest a crown of pure g. on his head

Rev. 21. 18. city was pure g. || 21. street of pure g.

GOLD with silver.

Gen. 13. 2. Abram was rich in silver and g. 24. 35.
44. 8. steal out of my lord's house silver or g.
Exod. 3. 22. jewels of silver and g. 11. 2. | 12. 35.
25. 3. this is the offering, take silver and g.
31. 4. to work in g. silver, and brass, 35. 32.
Num. 22. 18. his house full of silver and g. 24. 13.
31. 22. only g. and silver that may abide the fire
Deut. 7. 25. shalt not desire silver and g. on idols
8. 13. when thy silver and g. is multiplied
17. 17. nor shall he greatly multiply silver and g.
29. 17. ye have seen their idols, silver and g.
Josh. 6. 19. silver and g. are consecrated to Ld. 24.
22. 8. return to your tents with silver and g.
2 Sam. 8. 11. silv. and g. Dav. dedicated, 1 Kings 7. 51.
21. 4. we will have no silver or g. of Saul
1 Kings 15. 15. Asa brought into house of Ld. silver
and g. he had dedicated, 2 Chron. 15. 18.
18. Asa took all the silver and g. 2 Chron. 16. 2.
19. I have sent a present of silv. and g. 2 Chr. 16. 3.
20. 3. silv. and g. is mine || 5. deliver silv. and g.
2 Kings 7. 8. carried thence silver and g. raiment
14. 14. Jehoash took the silv. and g. 2 Chr. 25. 24.
16. 8. Ahaz took silv. and g. found in Ld.'s house
20. 13. Hezek. shewed them silv. and g. Isa. 39. 2.
23. 35. Jehoiak. gave silv. and g. exacted silv. and g.
25. 15. things of g. in g. of silv. in silv. Jer. 52. 19.
1 Chr. 29. 3. of my own proper good, of g. and silv.
2 Chr. 1. 15. the king made silver and g. plenteous
Ezra 1. 4. men of his place help with silver and g.
2. 69. gave silv. and g. || 7. 15. to carry silv. and g.
8. 25. they weighed them the silver and g. 33.
Esth. 1. 6. beds were of g. and silver on a pavement
Job 28. 1. there is a vein for silver, a place for g.
Psal. 68. 13. covered with silv. her feathers with g.
105. 37. he brought them out with silver and g.
115. 4. their idols are silver and g. 135. 15.
119. 72. thy law is better than g. and silver
Prov. 8. 10. not silv. receive knowl. rather than g.
17. 3. fining-pot for silver, furnace for g. 27. 21.
22. 1. loving favour rather than silver or g.
25. 11. like apples of g. in pictures of silver
Eccl. 2. 8. I gathered me also silver and g.
Cant. 1. 11. make borders of g. with studs of silv.
3. 10. he made the pillars of silver, bottom of g.
Isa. 2. 7. the land also is full of silver and g.
20. a man shall cast his idols of silv. and g. 31. 7.
13. 17. which shall not regard silver or g.
46. 6. they lavish g. out of the bag, and weigh silv.
60. 9. to bring their silver and g. with them
Jer. 10. 4. they deck it with silver and g.
Ezek. 7. 19. they shall cast away their silver and g.
silver and g. not able to deliver them, Zeph. 1. 18.
16. 13. thus wast thou decked with g. and silver
Dan. 2. 35. then was silv. and g. broken to pieces, 45.
5. 4. they praised the gods of silver and g. 23.
11. 38. a god shall he honour with g. and silver
43. have power over treasures of g. and silver
Hos. 2. 8. did not know I multiplied her silv. and g.
8. 4. of their silver and g. have they made idols
Joel 3. 5. because ye have taken my silver and g.
Nah. 2. 9. take the spoil of silver and spoil of g.
Hab. 2. 19. behold, it is laid over with silv. and g.
Hag. 2. 8. the silver is mine, and the g. is mine
Zech. 6. 11. then take silver and g. and make crowns
Mal. 3. 3. he shall purge them as g. and silver
Mat. 10. 9. provide neither g. nor silver, nor brass
Acts 3. 6. Peter said, silv. and g. have I none
17. 29. nor think Godhead is like to silver and g.
20. 33. I have coveted no man's silver or g.
1 Cor. 3. 12. if any build on this foundation g. silver
2 Tim. 2. 20. in a great house vessels of silv. and g.
Jam. 5. 3. your g. and silver cankered, rust of them
1 Pet. 1. 18. we were not redeemed with silv. and g.
Rev. 9. 20. repented not of idols of silver and g.

Talent and talents of GOLD.

Exod. 25. 39. of a talent of pure g. shall he make it
37. 24. of a talent of pure g. made he it
2 Sam. 12. 30. weight of crown a t. of g. 1 Chr. 20. 2.
1 Kings 9. 14. Hiram sent Solomon 120 talents of g.
28. they sent from Ophir 420 talents of g.
10. 10. she gave Solomon 120 t. of g. 2 Chr. 9. 9.
14. in one year came to Solomon 666 talents of g.
2 Kings 23. 33. put the land to a t. of g. 2 Chr. 36. 3.
1 Chron. 22. 14. David prepared 100,000 talents of g.
29. 4. prepared of my proper good 3000 talents of g.
7. the chief of the fathers gave 5000 talents of g.
2 Chron. 8. 18. took from Ophir 450 talents of g.
Ezra 8. 26. I weighed of g. vessels 100 talents

Vessels of GOLD.

2 Sam. 8. 10. Toi sent to Dav. vessels of g. 1 Chr. 18. 10.
1 Kings 10. 21. Solomon's drinking vessels were of
g. 2 Chron. 9. 20.
25. every man brought present, v. of g. 2 Chr. 9. 24.
2 Kings 12. 13. not made for house of Lord v. of g.
24. 13. Nebuchadnezzar cut in pieces vessels of g.
2 Chr. 24. 14. of rest of money made they v. of g.
Ezra 1. 11. all the vessels of g. and silver 5400
5. 14. the vessels of g. Cyrus delivered to one
8. 26. I weighed of vessels of g. 100 talents
Esth. 1. 7. they gave them drink in vessels of g.
Dan. 11. 8. shall also carry into Egypt vessels of g.
2 Tim. 2. 20. not only vessels of g. but of wood

GOLDEN.

Exod. 25. 25. a g. crown to the border round about
28. 34. a g. bell || 30. 4. two g. rings, 39. 20.
32. 2. Aaron said, break off the g. ear-rings
Lev. 8. 9. upon forefront he put the g. plate
Num. 7. 26. one g. spoon of ten shek. full of incense
Judg. 8. 24. had g. ear-rings, because Ishmaelites
26. the weight of g. ear rings he requested
1 Sam. 6. 4. five g. emerods, five g. mice, 17, 18.
2 Kings 10. 29. Jehu departed not from the g. calves
1 Chron. 28. 17. for the g. basins he gave gold
2 Chron. 13. 8. there are with you g. calves
Ezra 6. 5. and also let the g. vessels be restored
Esth. 4. 11. king shall hold out a g. sceptre, 5. 2. | 8. 4.
Eccl. 12. 6. or the g. bowl be broken, or pitcher
Isa. 13. 12. man more prec. than g. wedge of Ophir
14. 4. how hath the oppressor, the g. city ceased
Jer. 51. 7. Babylon hath been g. cup in Lord's hand

Dan. 3. 5. fall down and worship the g. image, 12.
5. 2. Belshazzar commanded to bring the g. vessels
3. they brought the g. vessels taken out of temple
Zech. 4. 12. through the g. pipes, empty the g. oil
Heb. 9. 4. had the g. censer and ark where was g. pot
Rev. 1. 12. being turned, I saw seven g. candlesticks
13. one girt about the paps with a g. girdle
20. the mystery of the seven g. candlesticks
2. 1. who walketh in the midst of the g. candlesticks
5. 8. g. vials, 15. 7. || 8. 3. having a g. censer
14. 14. on his head a g. crown || 17. 4. a g. cup full
21. 15. had a g. reed to measure the city and gates
See Altar.

GOLDSMITH, S.

Neh. 3. 8. Uzziel of the g. repaired next to him
31. the g. son || 32. g. and merchants repaired
Isa. 40. 19. the g. spreadeth it over with gold
41. 7. so the carpenter encouraged the g.
46. 6. they hire a g. and he maketh it a god

GONE.

Gen. 24. † 1. Abraham was old, and g. into days
31. 30. and now though thou wouldest needs be g.
34. 17. take our daughter, and we will be g.
42. 33. take food for your households, and be g.
Exod. 12. 32. take your flocks and herds, and be g.
Deut. 32. 36. when he seeth their power is g.
1 Sam. 14. 3. the people knew not Jonathan was g.
17. number now, and see who is g. from us
15. 20. I have g. the way which the Lord sent me
20. 41. as soon as the lad was g. David arose
2 Sam. 3. 7. wherefore g. in to my father's concubine
24. he is quite g. || 13. 15. Amnon said, arise, be g.
1 Kings 2. 41. that Shimei had g. from Jerusalem
13. 24. when he was g. a lion met him by the way
14. 10. as a man takes away dung till it be all g.
18. 12. as soon as I am g. Spirit shall carry thee
20. 40. as I was busy here and there, he was g.
22. 13. the messenger that was g. to call Micaiah
1 Chron. 17. 5. but have g. from tent to tent
Job 7. 4. when shall I rise, and the night be g.?
19. 10. he hath destroyed me, and I am g.
24. 24. they are exalted for a while, but are g.
28. 4. they are dried up and g. away from men
Psal. 38. 10. as for light of mine eyes, it also is g.
42. 4. I had g. with the multitude to house of God
73. 2. but as for me, my feet were almost g.
77. 8. is his mercy clean g. for ever?
103. 16. the wind passeth over it, and it is g.
109. 23. I am g. like the shadow that declineth
Prov. 7. 19. the good man is g. a long journey
20. 14. when he is g. his way, then he boasteth
Eccl. 8. 10. who had come and g. from place of holy
Cant. 2. 11. winter is past, the rain is over and g.
5. 6. but my beloved had withdrawn, and was g.
6. 1. whither is thy beloved g. O thou fairest?
Isa. 5. 13. therefore my people are g. into captivity
24. 11. all joy darkened, the mirth of the land g.
41. 3. by the way he had not g. with his feet
Jer. 2. 5. what iniquity in me, that they are g.
23. how canst thou say, I have not g. after Baalim?
5. 23. but this people are revolted and g.
9. 10. beasts are g. || 15. 6. thou art g. backward
44. 14. none that are g. into Egypt shall escape
28. all the remnant that are g. shall know
50. 6. they have g. from mountain to hill
Lam. 1. 3. Judah is g. || 5. Zion's children are g.
6. g. without strength || 18. my virgins are g.
Ezek. 37. 21. take Israel from heathen whither g.
Dan. 2. 5. the king said, the thing is g. from me, 8.
Hos. 4. † 18. their drink is g. they committed
9. 6. for lo, they are g. because of destruction
Amos 8. 5. when will new moon be g. that we may
Luke 2. 15. angels were g. from them into heaven
24. 28. he made as if he would have g. further
John 4. 8. for his disciples were g. to buy meat
12. 19. behold, the world is g. after him
Acts 16. 19. their masters saw hope of gains was g.
20. 25. among whom I have g. preaching the
kingdom of God.
1 Pet. 3. 22. who is g. into heaven on right hand
Jude 11. they have g. in the way of Cain

GONE about.

1 Sam. 15. 12. Saul is g. about and passed to Gilgal
Job 1. 5. when days of their feastings were g. about
Isa. 15. 8. for the city is g. about the borders of Moab
Acts 24. 6. hath g. about to profane the temple

GONE aside.

Num. 5. 19. if thou hast not g. aside to uncleanness
20. if hast g. aside to anoth. instead of husband
Psal. 14. 3. they are all g. aside, they are filthy
Acts 26. 31. when they were g. aside, they talked

GONE astray.

Psal. 119. 176. I have g. astray like a lost sheep
Isa. 53. 6. all we like sheep have g. astray
Mat. 18. 12. if a man have 100 sheep, one of them be
g. astray, he seeketh that which is g. astray
2 Pet. 2. 15. forsaken the right way, and are g. astray

GONE away.

2 Sam. 3. 22. but Abner was g. away in peace, 23.
23. 9. and the men of Israel were g. away
Job 28. 4. even the waters are g. away from men
Isa. 1. 4. they are g. away backward
Ezek. 44. 10. Levites which are g. away from me
Mal. 3. 7. ye are g. away from mine ordinances
John 6. 22. but his disciples were g. away alone

GONE back.

Ruth 1. 15. behold, thy sister-in-law is g. back
Job 23. 12. nor have I g. back from commandment
Psal. 53. 3. every one is g. back, none doeth good
Jer. 40. 5. while he was not yet g. b. he said, go back

GONE down.

1 Sam. 15. 12. Saul is passed, and g. down to Gilgal
1 Kings 1. 25. Adonijah is g. down, and slain oxen
21. 18. Ahab g. down to possess Naboth's vineyard
2 Kings 20. 11. by which the shadow had g. down
in the dial of Ahaz, Isa. 38. 8.
Cant. 6. 2. my beloved is g. down into his garden
Jer. 15. 9. her sun is g. down while it was yet day
48. 15. his young men are g. down to slaughter
Ezek. 31. 12. all people g. down from his shadow
32. 21. the strong are g. down slain by the sword
24. there is Elam || 27. Tubal || 30. Zidon g. down

Jonah 1. 5. Jonah was *g. down* to sides of the ship

GONE *forth.*

Gen. 19. † 23. sun *g. forth* when Lot entered Zoar
Exod. 19. 1. in third month when Isr. was *g. forth*
2 Kings 6. 15. when servant of Elisha was *g. forth*
1 Chron. 14. 15. God is *g. forth* before thee to smite
Isa. 51. 5. my salvation is *g. forth*, and my arms
Jer. 4. 7. he is *g. forth* to make thy land desolate
10. 20. my children are *g. forth* of me, and are not
23. 15. is profaneness *g. forth* into all the land
19. a whirlwind of the Lord is *g. forth* in fury
29. 16. brethren that are not *g. forth* into captivity
Ezek. 7. 10. day is come, the morning is *g. forth*
36. 20. these are people of the L. and are *g. forth*
Dan. 2. 14. *g. forth* to slay wise men of Babylon
10. 20. when I am *g. forth*, prince of Grecia come
Mark 10. 17. when he was *g. forth* one came running

GONE *out.*

Exod. 9. 29. as soon as I am *g. out* I will spread hands
Num. 16. 46. there is wrath *g. out* from the Lord
Deut. 13. 13. certain men *g.* out, and withdrawn
23. 23. that which is *g. out* of thy lips, shalt keep
Judg. 4. 14. is not the Lord *g. out* before thee?
Ruth 1. 13. hand of the Lord is *g. out* against me
1 Sam. 9. † 7. bread is *g. out* of our vessels
25. 37. when the wine was *g. out* of Nabal
2 Kings 5. 2. the Syrians had *g. out* by companies
7. 12. we be hungry, therefore they are *g. out*
20. 4. afore Isaiah was *g. out* into the court
Psal. 19. 4. their line is *g. out* through all the earth
89. 34. alter the thing that is *g. out* of my lips
Isa. 45. 23. the word is *g. out* of my mouth
Ezek. 24. 6. pot, whose scum is not *g. out* of it
Mat. 12. 43. when unclean spir. is *g. out*, Luke 11. 24.
25. 8. give us of your oil, our lamps are *g. out*
Mark 5. 30. that virtue had *g. out* of him, Luke 8. 46.
7. 29. devil is *g. out* of daughter, 30. Luke 11. 14.
John 13. 31. when he was *g. out*, Jesus said
Rom. 3. 12. they are all *g. out* of way, unprofitable
1 John 4. 1. many false prophets are *g. out* into world

GONE *over.*

2 Sam. 17. 20. they be *g. over* the brook of water
Psal. 38. 4. mine iniquities are *g. over* my head
42. 7. all thy waves and billows are *g. over* me
124. 4. then the stream had *g. over* our soul
5. the proud waters had *g. over* our soul
Isa. 10. 29. they are *g. over* the passage, and taken up
16. 8. they are *g. over* the sea, Jer. 48. 32.
Mat. 10. 23. shall not have *g. over* the cities of Isr.

GONE *up.*

Gen. 49. 9. from the prey, my son, thou art *g. up*
2 Kings 1. 4. not come off bed on which *g. up*, 6, 16.
Psal. 47. 5. God is *g. up* with a shout, sing praises
Isa. 15. 2. he is *g. up* to Bajith and to Dibon
57. 8. discovered to another than me, and art *g. up*
Jer. 3. 6. she is *g. up* on every high mountain
14. 2. and the cry of Jerusalem is *g. up*
34. 21. the king of Babylon's army, which are *g. up*
48. 15. Moab is spoiled, and *g. up* out of her cities
Ezek. 9. 3. the glory of the God of Israel was *g. up*
13. 5. ye have not *g. up* into the gaps
Hos. 8. 9. for they are *g. up* to Assyria, a wild ass
John 7. 10. but when his brethren were *g. up*
Acts 18. 22. when he had *g. up* and salut. the church

GONE *a whoring.*

Lev. 17. 7. after whom they have *g. a whoring*
Ezek. 23. 30. because thou hast *g. a whoring*
Hos. 4. 12. *g. a whoring* from under their God
9. 1. for thou hast *g. a whoring* from thy God

GOOD

Is taken, (1) *For that sort of happiness which all men desire, as being pleasant and agreeable to them.* Psal. 4. 6. Who will shew us any good? (2) *For that which is virtuous, morally honest, and just.* Psal. 34. 14. Depart from evil and do good. (3) *For that which is beautiful and agreeable; for something perfect in its kind. God beheld every thing he had created, and it* was very good, Gen. 1. 31. *Every creature had the goodness, beauty, and perfection which it required. And in* 2 Chron. 18. 7. This man never prophesieth good unto me, *nothing agreeable.* (4) *For that which is pleasing and acceptable to God.* Psal. 14. 1. There is none that doeth good. (5) *That which is expedient or convenient.* Gen. 2. 18. It is not good that the man should be alone: *It is not convenient either for my purpose of the increase of mankind, or for man's personal comfort. Also in* 1 Cor. 7. 1. It is good for a man not to touch a woman. *It were more convenient for a man not to marry.* (6) *It signifies seasonable and commendable.* Mat. 26. 10. The woman hath wrought a good work on me. (7) *Cheerful and festival.* 1 Sam. 25. 8. We come in a good day; *in a time of feasting and rejoicing.* (8) *Lawful to be used.* 1 Tim. 4. 4. Every creature of God is good. (9) *Christian liberty.* Rom. 14. 16. Let not your good be evil spoken of: *Use not your Christian liberty unduly, whereby it should come to be reproached, as if it were only profane licentiousness, and matter of contention.* (10) *Kind, merciful, bountiful.* Rom. 5. 7. For a good man some would even dare to die. (11) *Useful and valuable,* Deut. 6. 11. (12) *Pleasant and agreeable,* Psal. 133. 1. (13) *Sweet.* Prov. 24. 13. Eat honey, because it is good. (14) *Pious and religious,* Acts 11. 24. The good of the land *denotes all sorts of temporal blessings,* Isa. 1. 19. The good hand of God, *that is, the favour and kind providence of God,* Neh. 2. 8.

GOOD, *Substantive.*

Gen. 32. 12. thou saidst, I will surely do thee *g.*
45. 18. I will give you the *g.* of the land of Egypt
20. for the *g.* of the land of Egypt is yours
50. 20. God meant it unto *g.* to bring to pass
Num. 10. 29. Lord hath spoken *g.* concerning Israel
Deut. 23. † 6. thou shalt not seek their peace nor *g.*
Josh. 24. 20. consume you, after he hath done you *g.*
1 Sam. 20. 12. behold, if there be *g.* toward David
24. 17. for thou hast rewarded me *g.* for evil
19. wherefore the Lord rewarded thee *g.*
1 Sam. 25. 30. according to all the *g.* he hath spoken
2 Sam. 14. 32. it had been *g.* for me to been there
16. 12. Lord will requite *g.* for his cursing this day
1 Kings 22. 13. words of the prophets declare *g.* to the king with one mouth, 2 Chron. 18. 12.
1 Chr. 29. 3. I have prepared of mine own proper *g.*
2 Chron. 24. 16. because he had done *g.* in Israel
Ezra 9. 12. be strong, and eat the *g.* of the land
Esth. 7. 9. who had spoken *g.* for the king
Job 2. 10. shall we receive *g.* at the hand of God?
5. 27. hear it, and know thou it for thy *g.*
7. 7. mine eye shall no more see *g.*
9. 25. my days flee away, they see no *g.*
15. 3. or with speeches wherewith he can do no *g.*
21. 16. lo, their *g.* is not in their hand
22. 21. be at peace, thereby *g.* shall come to thee
24. 21. and he doeth not *g.* to the widow
Psal. 4. 6. many say, who will shew us any *g.?*
14. 1. none doeth *g.* not one, 3. | 53. 1, 3. Rom. 3. 12.
34. 12. and loveth many days, that he may see *g.*
39. 2. I was dumb, I held my peace, even from *g.*
104. 28. thou openest hand, they are filled with *g.*
106. 5. that I may see the *g.* of thy chosen
122. 9. because of house of Lord I will seek thy *g.*
128. 5. shalt see the *g.* of Jerusalem all thy life
Prov. 3. 27. withhold not *g.* from them to whom due
11. 17. the merciful man doth *g.* to his own soul
27. he that diligently seeketh *g.* procureth
12. 14. a man satisfied with *g.* by fruit of his mouth
13. 2. a man shall eat *g.* by the fruit of his mouth
21. but to the righteous *g.* shall be repaid
14. 22. mercy and truth be to them that devise *g.*
16. 20. handleth a matter wisely, shall find *g.*
17. 20. he that hath a froward heart, findeth no *g.*
22. a merry heart doeth *g.* like a medicine
19. 8. he that keepeth understanding shall find *g.*
Eccl. 2. 24. make his soul enjoy *g.* 3. 13. | 5. 18.
3. 12. I know that there is no *g.* in them
4. 8. whom do I labour, and bereave my soul of *g.?*
5. 11. and what *g.* is there to the owners thereof?
6. 3. his soul be not filled with *g.* and no burial
6. yet hath he seen no *g.* all go to one place
7. 20. not a man just, that doeth *g.* and sinneth not
9. 18. but one sinner destroyeth much *g.*
Isa. 1. 19. if willing, ye shall eat the *g.* of the land
52. 7. that bringeth good tidings of *g.* of salvation
Jer. 8. 15. we looked for peace, no *g.* came, 14. 19.
17. 6. he shall not see when *g.* cometh
18. 10. if it do evil, I will repent of the *g.*
20. I stood before thee to speak *g.* for them
29. 32. neither shall he behold the *g.* I will do
32. 42. I will bring all the *g.* I have promised
33. 9. which shall hear all the *g.* that I do them
Lam. 3. † 17. my soul far from peace, I forgat *g.*
Ezek. 16. 50. I took them away as I saw *g.*
Hos. 14. † 2. take away all iniquity, and give *g.*
Zech. 1. † 17. my cities through *g.* shall be spread
11. 12. I said, if ye think *g.* give me my price
Mat. 26. 24. been *g.* for that man had not been born
Mark 10. † 42. think *g.* to rule over the Gentiles
John 5. 29. that have done *g.* to the resurrection
Acts 10. 38. who went about doing *g.* and healing
14. 17. in that he did *g.* and gave us rain
Rom. 2. 10. honour to every man that worketh *g.*
1 Thess. 3. 1. we thought it *g.* to be left at Athens
1 John 3. 17. who hath this world's *g.* and shutteth up

For GOOD.

Deut. 6. 24. to fear the Lord *for* our *g.* always
10. 13. which I command thee this day *for* thy *g.*
28. † 11. Ld. shall make thee plenteous *for g.* 30. 9.
30. 9. the Lord will again rejoice over thee *for g.*
Ezra 8. 22. hand of our God on all of them *for g.*
Neh. 5. 19. think upon me, O my God, *for g.* 13. 31.
Job 5. 27. hear it, and know thou it *for* thy *g.*
Psal. 86. 17. shew me a token *for g.* they may see
119. 122. be surety for thy servant *for g.*
Jer. 14. 11. pray not for this people *for* their *g.*
24. 5. whom I sent out of this place *for* their *g.*
6. for I will set mine eyes on them *for g.*
32. 39. may fear me for ever, *for* the *g.* of them
Mic. 1. 12. Maroth waited carefully *for g.*
Rom. 8. 28. we know all things work together *for g.*
13. 4. he is the minister of God to thee *for g.*
15. 2. let every one please his neighbour *for g.*

See BAD, EVIL.

GOOD, *Adjective.*

Gen. 21. 16. Hagar sat her down a *g.* way off
24. 12. I pray thee, send me *g.* speed this day
† 16. Rebekah was *g.* of countenance, a virgin
26. 29. as we have done to thee nothing but *g.*
27. 46. Rebekah said, what *g.* shall my life do me?
41. 5. *g.* ears || 26. *g.* kine || 35. *g.* years
43. 28. thy servant our father is in *g.* health
46. 29. Joseph wept on his father's neck a *g.* while
Deut. 33. 16. for *g.*-will of him that dwelt in bush
1 Sam. 2. 24. my sons, it is no *g.* report that I hear
12. 23. I will teach you the *g.* and right way
25. 15. men were very *g.* to us, we were not hurt
29. 9. I know that thou art *g.* in my sight
2 Sam. 15. 3. see thy matters are *g.* and right
19. 18. and to do what the king thought *g.*
1 Kings 8. 36. that thou teach them the *g.* way
56. hath not failed one word of his *g.* promise
12. 7. and speak *g.* words to them, 2 Chron. 10. 7.
2 Kings 20. 19. *g.* is the word of the Lord, Isa. 39. 8.
2 Chron. 19. 11. the Lord shall be with the *g.*
30. 18. saying, the *g.* Lord pardon every one
Ezra 7. 9. the *g.* hand of his God on him, Neh. 2. 8.
8. 18. and by the *g.* hand of our God upon us
Neh. 9. 13. thou gavest them true laws, *g.* statutes
20. thou gavest thy *g.* Spirit to instruct them
Job 10. 3. is it *g.* that thou shouldest oppress?
13. 9. is it *g.* that he should search you out?
22. † 2. doth his *g.* success depend thereon?
39. 4. their young ones are in *g.* liking
Psal. 25. 8. *g.* and upright is the Lord, therefore
37. 23. steps of a *g.* man are ordered by the Lord
45. 1. my heart is inditing a *g.* matter
86. 5. thou, Lord, art *g.* ready to forgive, 119. 68.
112. 5. a *g.* man sheweth favour, and lendeth
119. 39. turn reproach, thy judgments are *g.*
66. teach me *g.* judgment and knowledge
Prov. 2. 9. thou shalt understand every *g.* path
20. that thou mayest walk in the way of *g.* men
12. 25. but a *g.* word maketh the heart glad
14. 19. the evil bow before the *g.* and the wicked
15. 23. and a word in due season, how *g.* is it!
30. and a *g.* report maketh the bones fat
20. 18. and with *g.* advice make war
22. 1. a *g.* name rather to be chosen than riches
Eccl. 4. 9. they have a *g.* reward for their labour
5. 11. what *g.* is there to the owners thereof?
9. 2. there is one event to the *g.* and to the clean
11. 6. or whether they both shall be alike *g.*
Jer. 6. 16. where is the *g.* way, and walk therein
24. 2. *g.* figs || 3. very *g.* || 5. like *g.* figs, so will I
29. 10. I will perform my *g.* word toward you
Ezek. 17. 8. planted in a *g.* soil by great waters
24. 4. gather every *g.* piece, thigh, and shoulder
Dan. 4. 2. I thought it *g.* to shew the signs
Zech. 1. 13. Lord answered the angel with *g.* words
Mal. 2. 13. receiveth it with *g.*-will at your hand
Mat. 7. 11. know how to give *g.* gifts, Luke 11. 13.
17. every *g.* tree bringeth forth *g.* fruit, 18.
9. 22. daughter, be of *g.* comfort, Luke 8. 48.
13. 8. fell in *g.* gr. 23. Mark 4. 8, 20. Luke 8. 8, 15.
24. *g.* seed || 19. 16. *g.* Master, what *g.* thing
19. 17. why callest thou me *g.?* none *g.* but one
20. 15. is thine eye evil because I am *g.?*
25. 21. well done, thou *g.* and faithful servant
Luke 2. 14. peace on earth, *g.*-will towards men
6. 38. *g.* measure, pressed down, shaken together
10. 42. and Mary hath chosen that *g.* part
12. 32. it is your Father's *g.* pleasure to give you
John 2. 10. but thou hast kept the *g.* wine until now
10. 11. I am the *g.* Shepherd, the *g.* Shepherd giveth
Acts 15. 7. ye know how that a *g.* while ago
Rom. 7. 12. commandment is holy, and just, and *g.*
12. 2. what is that *g.* and perfect will of God
1 Cor. 15. 33. evil communications corrupt *g.* mann.
1 Thess. 3. 6. that ye have *g.* remembrance of us
2 Tim. 3. 3. despisers of those that are *g.*
Tit. 1. 8. a bishop must be a lover of *g.* men
Heb. 6. 5. that have tasted the *g.* word of God
Jam. 1. 17. every *g.* gift || 2. 3. sit in a *g.* place
1 Pet. 2. 18. be subject not only to the *g.* and gentle
3. 10. he that will love life, and see *g.* days

See BAD, CHEER, CONSCIENCE, COURAGE, DO, DAY, OLD *age.*

As GOOD.

Heb. 11. 12. sprang of one, and him *as g.* as dead

GOOD *heed.*

Deut. 2. 4. take ye *g. heed*, 4. 15. Josh. 23. 11.
Eccl. 12. 9. preacher gave *g. heed*, and sought out

Is GOOD.

Gen. 2. 12. and the gold of that land *is g.*
16. † 6. do as *is g.* in thine eyes, 19. 8. | 20. † 15.
Deut. 1. 14. the thing which thou hast spoken *is g.*
6. 18. do that which *is g.* in the sight of the Lord
23. † 16. he shall dwell where it *is g.* for him
Judg. 9. † 2. speak whether it *is g.* for you
1 Sam. 29. 6. coming in with me in the host *is g.*
1 Kings 2. 38. and Shimei said, the saying *is g.*
42. the word that I have heard *is g.* 18. † 24.
22. 13. and speak that which *is g.*
2 Kings 20. 3. I have done that which *is g.* Isa. 38. 3.
1 Chron. 16. 34. the Lord *is g.* 2 Chr. 5. 13. | 7. 3.
Ezra 3. 11. Psal. 100. 5. | 106. 1. | 107. 1. | 118. 1, 29. | 135. 3. | 136. 1. | 145. 9. Jer. 33. 11. Lam. 3. 25. Nah. 1. 7.
19. 18. the Lord do that which *is g.* in his sight
Job 34. 4. know among ourselves what *is g.*
Psal. 34. 8. O taste and see that the Lord *is g.*
69. 16. hear me, for thy loving-kindness is *g.*
73. 1. truly God *is g.* to Israel, to such as are
85. 12. the Lord shall give that which *is g.*
109. 21. because thy mercy *is g.* deliver me
143. 10. thy Spirit *is g.* lead me into the land
Prov. 11. 23. the desire of the righteous *is* only *g.*
25. 25. so *is g.* news from a far country
31. 18. she perceiveth her merchandise *is g.*
Eccl. 2. 26. God giveth to a man that *is g.* in his sight, may give to him that *is g.* before God
6. 12. who knoweth what *is g.* for man in life?
7. 11. wisdom *is g.* with an inheritance
† 26. that *is g.* before God shall escape
9. 2. as *is* the *g.* so is the sinner
Isa. 55. 2. eat ye that which *is g.* let your soul
Jer. 13. 10. this girdle which *is g.* for nothing
Hos. 4. 13. because the shadow thereof *is g.*
Mic. 6. 8. he hath shewed thee, O man, what *is g.*
Mal. 2. 17. ye say, every one that doeth evil *is g.*
Mark 9. 50. salt *is g.* but if the salt, Luke 14. 34.
Luke 6. 45. bringeth forth that which *is g.*
18. 19. none *is g.* save one, that is God
Rom. 7. 13. was then that which *is g.* made death
18. but how to perform that *is g.* I find not
12. 9. abhor evil, cleave to that which *is g.*
16. 19. I would have you wise to that which *is g.*
1 Cor. 7. 26. that this *is g.* for the present
Eph. 4. 29. no communication but that *is g.*
1 Thess. 5. 15. follow that which *is g.* 3 John 11.
21. prove all things, hold fast that which *is g.*
1 Tim. 1. 8. but we know that the law *is g.*
2. 3. this *is g.* and acceptable in the sight of God
4. 4. for every creature of God *is g.*
5. 4. for that *is g.* and acceptable before God
1 Pet. 3. 13. if ye be followers of that which *is g.*

It is GOOD.

Psal. 52. 9. I will wait on thy name, for *it is g.* 54. 6.
73. 28. *it is g.* for me to draw near to God
92. 1. *it is a g.* thing to give thanks unto the Lord
119. 71. *it is g.* for me that I have been afflicted
147. 1. *it is g.* to sing praises unto our God
Prov. 24. 13. my son, eat thou honey, because *it is g.*
Eccl. 5. 18. *it is g.* and comely for one to eat and dr.
7. 18. *it is g.* that thou shouldest take hold
Isa. 41. † 7. saying of the soder, *it is g.*
Lam. 3. 26. *it is g.* that a man should both hope
27. *it is g.* that a man bear the yoke in his youth
Mat. 5. 13. *it is g.* for nothing but to be cast out
17. 4. *it is g.* for us to be here, Mark 9. 5. Luke 9. 33.
Rom. 7. 16. I consent unto the law, that *it is g.*
14. 21. *it is g.* neither to eat flesh nor drink wine

1 Cor. 7. 1. it is g. for a man not to touch a woman, 8.
26. I say, it is g. for a man so to be
Gal. 4. 18. it is g. to be zealously affected always

GOOD land.

Exod. 3. 8. come to bring them to g. land, Deut. 8. 7.
Num. 14. 7. the land we searched is a g. land
Deut. 1. 25. it is a g. land which the Lord doth give
35. none of that generation see that g. land
3. 25. I pray, let me go over, and see the g. land
4. 21. Lord sware I should not go unto that g. land
22. ye shall go over and possess that g. land
6. 18. thou mayest go in and possess the g. land
8. 7. the Lord thy God bringeth thee into a g. land
10. shalt bless the Lord thy God for the g. land
9. 6. giveth not this g. land for thy righteousness
11. 17. lest ye perish from off g. land Lord giveth
Josh. 23. 13. until ye perish from this g. land, 15.
16. ye shall perish quickly from off the g. land
Judg. 18. 9. we have seen the land, and it is very g.
1 Kings 14. 15. shall root Israel out of this g. land
2 Kings 3. 19. mar every g. piece of land, 25.
1 Chron. 28. 8. that ye may possess this g. land

GOOD with make. { Affirmative. Negative.

Exod. 21. 34. the owner of pit shall make it g. 22. 14.
22. 11. the owner shall not make it g. 13. 15.
Lev. 24. 18. he that killeth a beast shall make it g.
Num. 23. 19. hath spoken, shall he not make it g.?
Jer. 18. 11. and make your ways and doings g.

GOOD man.

2 Sam. 18. 27. the king said, Ahimaaz is a g. man
Psal. 37. 23. steps of a g. man are ordered by the L.
112. 5. a g. man sheweth favour and lendeth
Prov. 7. 19. the g. man is not at home, he is gone
12. 2. a g. man obtaineth favour of the Lord
13. 22. a g. man leaveth an inheritance to
14. 14. a g. man is satisfied from himself, 12. 14.
Mic. 7. 2. the g. man is perished out of the earth
Mat. 12. 35. g. man out of good treasure, Luke 6. 45.
20. 11. they murmured against the g. man
24. 43. if the g. man of the house had known in what watch the thief would come, Luke 12. 39.
Luke 23. 50. Joseph was a g. man, and a just
John 7. 12. some said, he is a g. man, others said, nay
Acts 11. 24. Barnabas was a g. man, full of Holy G.
Rom. 5. 7. for a g. man some would even dare to die

Not GOOD.

Gen. 2. 18. it is not g. that man should be alone
1 Sam. 29. †6. thou art not g. in the eyes of the lords
2 Sam. 17. 7. the counsel is not g. at this time
Psal. 36. 4. setteth himself in a way that is not g.
Prov. 16. 29. leadeth him into way that is not g.
17. 26. also to punish the just is not g.
18. 5. is not g. to accept the person of the wicked
19. 2. that the soul be without knowledge is not g.
20. 23. and a false balance is not g.
24. 23. not g. to have respect of persons, 28. 21.
25. 27. it is not g. to eat much honey
Isa. 65. 2. which walketh in a way that is not g.
Ezek. 18. 18. and did that which is not g. among
20. 25. I gave them statutes that were not g.
36. 31. remember your doings that were not g.
Mat. 19. 10. if the case be so, it is not g. to marry
Acts 15. 38. Paul thought not g. to take him with
1 Cor. 5. 6. your glorying is not g. know ye not

Seem, seemed, seemeth GOOD.

Josh. 9. 25. as it seemeth g. to thee to do unto us, do, Judg. 10. 15. 1 Sam. 14. 36, 40. Ezra 7. 18. Esth. 3. 11. Jer. 26. 14. | 40. 4.
Judg. 19. 24. do to them what seemeth g. unto you
1 Sam. 1. 23. do what seemeth g. 3. 18. | 11. 10. | 24. 4.
2 Sam. 3. 19. Abner spake all seemed g. to Israel
10. 12. the Lord do that seemeth him g. 15. 26.
19. 37. do to Chimham what shall seem g. 38.
24. 22. take and offer up what seemeth g. unto him
1 Kings 21. 2. if it seem g. to thee, Jer. 40. 4.
1 Chron. 13. 2. if it seem g. to you, let us send
Ezra 5. 17. if it seem g. to the king, Esth. 5. 4.
Jer. 18. 4. as seemed g. to the potter to make it
Mat. 11. 26. so it seemed g. in sight, Luke 10. 21.
Luke 1. 3. it seemed g. to me, having perfect unders.
Acts 15. 25. it seemed g. unto us, being assembled
28. it seemed g. to the Holy Ghost and to us

GOOD with thing.

Exod. 18. 17. the thing that thou doest is not g.
Deut. 26. 11. thou shalt rejoice in every g. thing
Josh. 21. 45. there failed not aught of any g. thing
1 Sam. 26. 16. this thing is not g. thou hast done
1 Kings 14. 13. in him there is found some g. thing
2 Kings 8. 9. Hazael took of every g. thing of Damas.
Psal. 34. 10. that seek Lord not want any g. thing
38. 20. because I follow the thing that g. is
84. 11. no g. thing will he withhold from them
92. 1. it is a g. thing to give thanks unto the Lord
Prov. 18. 22. whoso findeth a wife, findeth a g. thing
Jer. 33. 14. I will perform g. thing I have promised
Hos. 8. 3. Israel hath cast off the thing that is g.
Mat. 19. 16. what g. thing shall I do to inherit life?
John 1. 46. can any g. thing come out of Nazareth?
Rom. 7. 18. that is in my flesh, dwelleth no g. thing
Gal. 4. 18. good to be zealously affected in a g. thing
Eph. 4. 28. working with his hands thing which is g.
6. 8. knowing that what g. thing any man doeth
2 Tim. 1. 14. that g. thing committed unto thee, keep
Philem. 6. by acknowledging every g. thing in you
Heb. 13. 9. it is a g. thing the heart be established

GOOD things.

Deut. 6. 11. to give thee houses full of all g. things
Josh. 23. 14. not one failed of all the g. things
15. that as all g. things are come upon you
2 Kings 25. †28. he spake g. t. with him, Jer. 52. †32.
2 Chron. 12. 12. in Judah there were g. things
19. 3. in Jehoshaphat there are g. things found
Job 22. 18. yet he filled their houses with g. things
Ps. 103. 5. who satisfieth thy mouth with g. things
Prov. 28. 10. the upright shall have g. things
Jer. 5. 25. your sins have withholden g. things
12. †6. believe not, though they speak g. things
Mat. 7. 11. give g. things to them that ask him?
12. 34. how can ye being evil speak g. things?
35. a good man bringeth forth g. things
Luke 1. 53. he hath filled the hungry with g. things
16. 25. in thy life-time receivedst thy g. things
Rom. 10. 15. and bring glad tidings of g. things
Gal. 6. 6. communicate unto him in all g. things
Tit. 2. 3. the aged women be teachers of g. things
3. 8. these things are g. and profitable unto men
Heb. 9. 11. Christ being an high-priest of g. things
10. 1. the law having a shadow of g. things to come

GOOD tidings.

2 Sam. 4. 10. thinking to have brought g. tidings
18. 27. a good man, and cometh with g. tidings
1 Kings 1. 42. a valiant man, and bringest g. tidings
2 Kings 7. 9. this day is a day of g. tidings
Isa. 40. 9. O Zion, that bringest g. tidings
41. 27. I will give Jerusalem one that bringeth g. t.
52. 7. the feet of him that bringeth g. tidings
61. 1. he hath anointed me to preach g. tidings
Nah. 1. 15. behold feet of him who bringeth g. tid.
Luke 2. 10. I bring you g. tidings of great joy
1 Thess. 3. 6. brought us g. tidings of your faith

Was GOOD.

Gen. 1. 4. God saw that it was g. 10, 12, 18, 21, 25.
31. God saw every thing, behold it was very g.
3. 6. the woman saw that the tree was g. for food
40. 16. the baker saw the interpretation was g.
41. 37. thing was g. in eyes of Pharaoh, 45. †16.
49. 15. Issachar saw that rest was . and the land
Josh. 22. †30. it was g. in the eyes of Phinehas
1 Sam. 15. 9. Saul and people spared all that was g.
2 Chron. 14. 2. Asa did that which was g. and right
31. 20. Hezekiah wrought that which was g.
Neh. 2. 18. the hand of my God which was g.
Eccl. 2. 3. till I might see what was that g. for sons

GOOD understanding.

1 Sam. 25. 3. Abigail was a woman of g. understand.
Psal. 111. 10. g. und. have all that do his command.
Prov. 3. 4. so shalt thou find favour and g. underst.
13. 15. g. understanding giveth favour

GOOD work.

Neh. 2. 18. strengthen their hands for this g. work
Mat. 26. 10. she hath wrought a g. work, Mark 14. 6.
John 10. 33. for a g. work we stone thee not
2 Cor. 9. 8. that ye may abound to every g. work
Phil. 1. 6. that he which hath begun a g. work
Col. 1. 10. being fruitful in every g. work
2 Thess. 2. 17. stablish you in every g. word and work
1 Tim. 3. 1. office of a bishop, desireth a g. work
5. 10. if she diligently followed every g. work
2 Tim. 2. 21. and prepared unto every g. work
Tit. 1. 16. and unto every g. work reprobate
3. 1. put them in mind to be ready to every g. work
Heb. 13. 21. God make you perfect in every g. work

GOOD works.

1 Sam. 19. 4. his works to thee have been very g.
Mat. 5. 16. that they may see your g. works
John 10. 32. many g. works have I shewed you
Acts 9. 36. Dorcas full of g. works and alms-deeds
Rom. 13. 3. for rulers are not a terror to g. works
Eph. 2. 10. created in Christ Jesus unto g. works
1 Tim. 2. 10. that women be adorned with g. works
5. 10. a widow well reported of for g. works
25. the g. works of some are manifest before-hand
6. 18. charge the rich, that they be rich in g. works
2 Tim. 3. 17. thoroughly furnished to all g. works
Tit. 2. 7. shewing thyself a pattern in g. works
14. a peculiar people, zealous of g. works
3. 8. they be careful to maintain g. works, 14.
Heb. 10. 24. to provoke unto love and g. works
1 Pet. 2. 12. they may by your g. works glorify God

GOODLY.

Gen. 27. 15. Rebekah took g. raiment of her son
39. 6. Joseph was a g. person, and well-favoured
49. 21. Naphtali a hind let loose, giveth g. words
Exod. 2. 2. when she saw he was a g. child
39. 28. they made g. bonnets of fine linen
Lev. 23. 40. on the first day boughs of the g. trees
Num. 24. 5. how g. are thy tents, O Jacob!
31. 10. they burnt all their g. castles with fire
Deut. 3. 25. let me see that g. mount. and Lebanon
6. 10. great and g. cities which thou buildest not
8. 12. lest when thou hast built g. houses
Josh. 7. 21. I saw a g. Babylonish garment
1 Sam. 9. 2. Saul, a choice young man, and a g.
16. 12. David was ruddy and g. to look to
2 Sam. 23. 21. Benaiah slew an Egyptian, a g. man
1 Kings 1. 6. Adonijah also was a very g. man
2 Chron. 36. 10. brought to Babylon the g. vessels
19. burnt palaces, and destroyed the g. vessels
Job 39. 13. gavest thou g. wings to the peacocks?
Psal. 16. 6. yea, I have a g. heritage
80. 10. the boughs were like the g. cedars
Jer. 3. 19. how shall I give thee a g. heritage!
11. 16. a green olive-tree, fair, and of g. fruit
Ezek. 17. 8. was planted, that it might be a g. vine
23. it shall bear fruit, and be a g. cedar
Dan. 11. †16. he shall stand in the g. land, †41.
†45. he shall plant in the g. holy mountain
Hos. 10. 1. they have made g. images
Joel 3. 5. carried into your temples my g. things
Zech. 10. 3. hath made them as his g. horse in battle
11. 13. a g. price that I was prized at of them
Mat. 13. 45. a merchant-man seeking g. pearls
Luke 21. 5. how it was adorned with g. stones
Jam. 2. 2. if there come a man in g. apparel
Rev. 18. 14. all things dainty and g. are departed

GOODLIER.

1 Sam. 9. 2. not in Israel a g. person than Saul

GOODLIEST.

1 Sam. 8. 16. he will take your g. young men
1 Kings 20. 3. thy children, even the g. are mine

GOODLINESS.

Isa. 40. 6. the g. thereof as the flower of the field

GOODNESS.

Exod. 18. 9. Jethro rejoiced for all g. Lord had done
33. 19. I will make all my g. pass before thee
34. 6. the Lord God abundant in g. and truth
Num. 10. 32. that what g. the Lord shall do to us
2 Sam. 7. 28. thou promisedst this g. 1 Chron. 17. 26.
1 Kings 8. 66. joyful for g. L. had done, 2 Chr. 7. 10.
10. †7. thou hast added wisdom and g. to the fame
2 Chron. 6. 41. let thy saints rejoice in g.
32. 32. Hezekiah his g. || 35. 26. Josiah and his g.
Neh. 9. 25. and delighted themselves in thy g.
9. 35. they have not served thee in thy great g
Psal. 16. 2. my g. extendeth not to thee
21. 3. for thou preventest him with blessings of g.
23. 6. surely g. and mercy shall follow me
25. 7. remember thou me, for thy g. sake, O Lord
†13. his soul shall lodge in g. seed inherit earth
27. 13. I had believed to see the g. of the Lord
31. 19. O how great is thy g. thou hast laid up
33. 5. the earth is full of the g. of the Lord
52. 1. the g. of God endureth continually
65. 4. we shall be satisfied with the g. of thy house
11. thou crownest the year with thy g.
68. 10. thou hast prepared of thy g. for the poor
107. 8. praise the Lord for his g. 15. 21, 31.
9. and filleth the hungry soul with g.
144. 2. my g. and my fortress, my high tower
145. 7. they shall utter the memory of thy g.
Prov. 20. 6. most men will proclaim every one his g.
Isa. 63. 7. the great g. toward the house of Israel
Jer. 2. 7. I brought you to eat the g. thereof
31. 12. they shall flow together to the g. of the Ld.
14. people shall be satisfied with my g. saith Ld.
33. 9. they shall fear and tremble for all the g.
Hos. 3. 5. they shall fear the Lord and his g.
6. 4. your g. is as a morning cloud and early dew
10. 1. according to g. of his land they made images
Zech. 9. 17. for how great is his g. and his beauty!
Rom. 2. 4. or despisest thou the riches of his g. not knowing the g. of God leadeth thee to repentance
11. 22. behold, therefore, the g. and severity of God, toward thee g. if thou continue in his g.
15. 14. I am persuaded that you are full of g.
Gal. 5. 22. the fruit of the Spirit is g. Eph. 5. 9.
2 Thess. 1. 11. fulfil all the good pleasure of his g.

GOODS.

Gen. 14. 16. Abram brought back all the g. and Lot
21. give me the persons, and take the g. to thyself
24. 10. the g. of his master were in his hand
31. 18. Jacob carried away all his g. 46. 6.
Exod. 22. 8. not put hand to his neighbour's g. 11.
Num. 16. 32. the earth swallowed them and their g.
31. 9. Israel took the spoil of Midian and their g.
35. 3. the suburbs shall be for Levites' cattle and g.
Deut. 28. 11. Lord shall make thee plenteous in g.
2 Chr. 21. 14. the Lord will smite thy wives, thy g.
Ezra 1. 4. let the men of his place help him with g.
6. all about them strengthened their hands with g.
6. 8. that of king's g. expenses be given to these men
7. 26. to banishment or to confiscation of g.
Neh. 9. 25. they possessed houses full of all g.
Job 20. 10. and his hands shall restore their g.
21. therefore shall no man look for his g.
28. his g. shall flow away in the day of his wrath
Eccl. 5. 11. when g. increase, they are increased
Ezek. 38. 12. which have gotten cattle and g.
13. art thou come to take away cattle and g.?
Zeph. 1. 13. their g. shall become a booty
Mat. 12. 29. how enter a strong man's house, and spoil his g. except he bind strong man, Mark 3. 27.
24. 47. he shall make him ruler over all his g.
25. 14. who called and delivered to them his g.
Luke 6. 30. of him that taketh away thy g. ask not
11. 21. keepeth his palace, his g. are in peace
12. 18. there will I bestow all my fruits and my g.
19. thou hast much g. laid up for many years
15. 12. give me the portion of g. that falleth to me
16. 1. was accused to him that he wasted his g.
19. 8. the half of my g. I give to the poor
Acts 2. 45. sold their g. and parted them to all men
1 Cor. 13. 3. tho' I bestow all my g. to feed the poor
Heb. 10. 34. ye took joyfully the spoiling of your g.
Rev. 3. 17. I am rich, and increased with g.

GOPHER wood.

Gen. 6. 14. make thee an ark of g. wood, rooms

GORE, ED.

Exod. 21. 28. if an ox g. man or woman that they
31. whether he have g. a son or a daughter

GORGEOUS.

Luke 23. 11. Herod arrayed Jesus in a g. robe

GORGEOUSLY.

Ezek. 23. 12. she doted on Assyrians clothed most g.
Luke 7. 25. that are g. apparelled in king's courts

GOSPEL.

The Gospel *is a revelation of the grace of God to fallen man through a Mediator.* Or, *it is a wise, a holy, and gracious constitution of God, for the recovery of fallen, sinful, and miserable man, from that deplorable state into which sin had brought him, by sending his own Son* Jesus Christ *into the flesh, to obey his law which man had broken, to make a proper atonement for sin by his death, and thus to procure pardon, and the favour of God, and eternal happiness for all that believe and repent, and receive the gospel-salvation; together with a promise of the Holy Spirit to work this faith and repentance in their hearts, to renew their sinful natures unto holiness, to form them on earth fit for this happiness, and to bring them to the full possession of it in heaven.*

Hence it is called the gospel of God, *as it came originally from the Father,* Rom. 1. 1. *It is called* the gospel of the grace of God, *Acts* 20. 24. *because it proceeds from, and manifests his favour, and is the means whereby his grace is bestowed. It is called* the gospel of Christ, *Rom.* 1. 16. *as he is the immediate Author, and the subject matter of it. In the same passage it is said* to be the power of God unto salvation: *it is the means which, by the influence of the Spirit of God, is made effectual to salvation. It is called* the gospel of salvation, *Eph.* 1. 13. *It brings the good news that salvation is to be had; it offers this salvation; it shews the way how it is attained; it works grace to fit for, and bring men to salvation.*

This gospel *the Spirit of God preached to* Abraham *under the Old Testament.* Gal. 3. 8, The Scripture foreseeing that God would justify the heathen through faith, preached before the gospel unto *Abraham*, saying, In thee shall all nations be blessed. *The glad tidings of justification and salvation by faith in* Christ, *were preached to* Abraham, *and were contained in*

that promise made to him, which is the sum of the covenant, In thy seed shall all nations be blessed, Gen. 22. 18.
The word gospel, in the original, Ευαγγελιον, signifies good news, or glad tidings. And surely when a sinner, who is exposed to the wrath of God, is sensible of his guilt and danger, it must needs be glad tidings to him to hear of a way of salvation, and an all-sufficient Saviour.
Gospel is taken for an historical narration of what Christ did and spake, of his life, miracles, death, resurrection, and doctrine; as the Gospel according to Matthew, Mark, &c. The beginning of the gospel of Christ, Mark 1. 1. Sometimes it is taken for the preaching and publication of the gospel, and administration of affairs that concern it. Rom. 1. 9. Whom I serve with my spirit in the gospel of his Son. It is put for the doctrines of free grace, Rom. 11. 28.
Mark 1. 1. the beginning of the g. of Jesus Christ
15. Jesus came, saying, repent and believe the g.
8. 35. whoso shall lose his life for my sake and g.
10. 29. that hath left house for my sake and g.
13. 10. the g. must be published among all nations
Acts 15. 7. that the Gentiles by my mouth hear g.
20. 24. to testify the g. of the grace of God
Rom. 1. 1. an apostle, separated to the g. of God
9. whom I serve with my spirit in g. of his Son
16. for I am not ashamed of the g. of Christ
2. 16. shall judge secrets of men according to my g.
10. 16. but they have not all obeyed the g.
11. 28. as concerning the g. they are enemies
15. 16. to the Gentiles, ministering the g. of God
29. in the fulness of the blessing of the g. of Christ
16. 25. of power to stablish you according to g.
1 Cor. 4. 15. in Jesus I have begotten you thro' the g.
9. 12. lest we should hinder the g. of Christ
17. a dispensation of the g. is committed to me
18. when I preach g. I may make the g. of Christ without charge; that I abuse not my power in g.
23. this I do for the g. sake to be partaker thereof
2 Cor. 4. 3. if our g. be hid, it is hid to them are lost
4. lest light of glorious g. of Christ should shine
8. 18. sent the brother, whose praise is in the g.
9. 13. for your professed subjection to g. of Christ
11. 4. if ye receive another Spirit or g. Gal. 1. 6.
Gal. 1. 7. and would pervert the g. of Christ
2. 2. I communicated to them the g. I preach
5. that the truth of the g. might continue
7. when saw the g. of uncircum. committed to me
14. not uprightly according to the truth of the g.
Eph. 1. 13. the word of truth the g. of your salvation
3. 6. be partakers of his promise in Christ by the g.
6. 15. shod with the preparation of the g. of peace
19. to make known the mystery of the g.
Phil. 1. 5. for your fellowship in the g. till now
7. in the defence and confirmation of the g. 17.
12. have fallen out to the furtherance of the g.
27. only let your conversation be as becometh the g. striving together for the faith of the g.
2. 22. he hath served with me in the g.
4. 3. help women who laboured with me in the g.
15. know also that in the beginning of the g.
Col. 1. 5. ye heard before in word of truth of the g.
23. be not moved away from the hope of the g.
1 Thess. 1. 5. g. came not in word but in power
2. 2. we were bold to speak the g. of God to you
4. were allowed of God to be put in trust with g.
8. were willing to have imparted not the g. only
3. 2. Timothy our fellow-labourer in the g.
2 Thess. 1. 8. on them that obey not the g. 1 Pet. 4. 17.
2. 14. whereunto he called you by our g.
1 Tim. 1. 11. according to the g. of the blessed God
2 Tim. 1. 8. be partaker of the afflictions of the g.
10. brought immortality to light through the g.
2. 8. Jesus Christ was raised according to my g.
Philem. 13. have ministered to me in bonds of the g.
GOSPEL joined with preach, preached, preaching.
Mat. 4. 23. Jesus went preaching g. 9. 35. Mark 1. 14.
11. 5. the poor have the g. preached, Luke 7. 22.
24. 14. this g. shall be preached, 26. 13. Mark 14. 9.
Mark 16. 15. go, preach the g. to every creature
Luke 4. 18. he hath anointed me to preach the g.
9. 6. they departed, preaching the g. and healing
20. 1. that as he taught, and preached the g.
Acts 8. 25. and preached the g. to the Samaritans
14. 7. and there they preached the g.
21. when they had preached the g. to that city
16. 10. that the Lord had called us to preach the g.
Rom. 1. 15. I am ready to preach the g. at Rome
10. 15. how beautiful feet of them that preach g.
15. 19. I have fully preached the g. of Christ
20. so have I strived to preach the g. not where
1 Cor. 1. 17. sent me not to baptize, but to preach g.
9. 14. that preach the g. should live of the gospel
16. though I preach the g. have nothing to glory of, for necessity on me, woe to me if I preach not g.
18. that when I preach the g. I may make gospel
15. 1. I declare to you the g. which I preached
2 Cor. 2. 12. when I came to Troas to preach the g.
10. 14. come as far as to you in preaching the g.
11. 7. because I preached to you freely the g.
Gal. 1. 8. though we or an angel preach any other g. 9.
11. the g. preached of me is not after man
3. 8. preached before the g. to Abraham, saying
4. 13. through infirmity of flesh I preached the g.
1 Thess. 2. 9. we preached to you the g. of God
Heb. 4. 2. to us was the g. preached as well as to them
1 Pet. 1. 12. by them that preached the g. to you
25. this is the word which by g. is preached to you
4. 6. for this cause was the g. preached to the dead
Rev. 14. 6. having everlasting g. to preach to them

GOT.

Gen. 39. 12. Joseph fled from her and g. him out, 15.
Psal. 44. 3. they g. not the land by their own sword
Eccl. 2. 7. I g. me servants and maidens
Jer. 13. 2. I g. a girdle according to word of Lord
4. take the girdle that thou hast g. and arise

GOTTEN.

Gen. 4. 1. she said, I have g. a man from the Lord
31. 1. what was our father's hath he g. all this
Exod. 14. 18. when I have g. me honour on Pharaoh
Lev. 6. 4. or the thing he hath deceitfully g.
Num. 31. 50. what every man hath g. of jewels
Deut. 8. 17. might of my hand hath g. this wealth
2 Sam. 17. 13. moreover if he be g. into a city
Job 28. 15. wisdom cannot be g. for gold
31. 25. if I rejoiced because my hand had g. much
Psal. 98. 1. his holy arm hath g. him the victory
Prov. 13. 11. wealth g. by vanity shall be diminished
20. 21. an inheritance may be g. hastily at begin.
31. † 29. many daughters have g. riches
Eccl. 1. 16. have g. more wisdom than all before me
Isa. 15. 7. the abundance g. they shall carry away
Jer. 48. 36. because riches he hath g. are perished
Ezek. 28. 4. with thy wisdom thou hast g. riches
Dan. 9. 15. thou hast g. thee renown as at this day
Mat. 11. † 12. the kingdom of heaven is g. by force
Rev. 15. 2. I saw them that had g. the victory

GOVERN.

1 Kings 21. 7. dost thou now g. the kingdom of Isr.?
Job 34. 17. shall even he that hateth right g.?
Psal. 67. 4. for thou shalt g. the nations upon earth

GOVERNMENT, S.

Isa. 9. 6. and the g. shall be upon his shoulder
7. of the increase of his g. there shall be no end
22. 21. I will commit thy g. into his hand
1 Cor. 12. 28. helps, g. diversities of tongues
2 Pet. 2. 10. but chiefly them that despise g.

GOVERNOR.

Gen. 42. 6. Joseph was g. over the land, 45. 26.
1 Kings 18. 3. Obadiah was g. over Ahab's house
1 Chr. 29. 22. they anointed Solomon to be chief g.
Ezra 5. 14. Cyrus delivered the vessels to the g.
Neh. 5. 14. I have not eaten the bread of the g.
18. for all this I required not the bread of the g.
10. † 1. those that sealed were, Nehemiah the g.
Psal. 22. 28. he is the g. among the nations
Jer. 30. 21. their g. shall proceed from midst of them
40. 5. he said, go back also to Gedaliah the g.
41. 2. then Ishmael smote Gedaliah the g. 18.
Hag. 1. 14. the Lord stirred up Zerubbabel the g.
2. 2. speak to Zerubbabel the g. and to Joshua, 21.
Zech. 9. 7. and he shall be as a g. in Judah
Mal. 1. 8. offer it now to thy g. will he accept person
Mat. 2. 6. out of thee shall come a g. to rule Israel
27. 2. they delivered him to Pontius Pilate the g.
28. 14. and if this come to the g.'s ears
John 2. 8. draw out, and bear to the g. of the feast
Acts 24. 1. who informed the g. against Paul
2 Cor. 11. 32. the g. under Aretas the king kept city
Jam. 3. 4. the ships turned whither the g. listeth

GOVERNORS.

Judg. 5. 9. my heart is towards the g. of Israel
14. out of Machir came down g.
Ezra 8. 36. delivered the king's commissions to g.
Neh. 2. 7. let letters be given me to g. beyond river
5. 15. but the former g. were chargeable to people
Isa. 19. † 13. they have seduced the g. of Egypt
Dan. 2. 48. the king made Daniel chief of the g.
Zech. 12. 5. the g. of Judah shall say in their heart
6. I will make the g. of Judah like a hearth
Mat. 10. 18. ye shall be brought before g. and kings
Gal. 4. 2. but the heir is under tutors and g. till
1 Pet. 2. 14. submit yourselves to g. as sent by him

GOURD.

In Hebrew, Kikajon. This word is found in Jonah 4. 6. where the Septuagint translate it Κολοκυνθη. Jerom uses Hedera, Ivy; as also does Aquila. Jerom acknowledges, that the word Ivy does not answer the signification of the Hebrew Kikajon; but as he could not find any Latin words proper to express it, he chose rather to set down Hedera, than to leave Kikajon, which might be taken for a monstrous animal in the Indies, or mountains of Bœotia. His account of Kikajon is this: It is a shrub which grows in the sandy places of Palestine; and increases so suddenly, that within few days it comes to a considerable height. The leaves of it are large, and like those almost of the vine. It is supported by its trunk without being upheld by any thing else, and furnishes a very agreeable shade under the thickness of its leaves.
Modern interpreters almost all agree that the Hebrew Kikajon signifies the Palma Christi, or Ricinus, in Egyptian called Kiki, and in Greek, Selicyprion. It is a plant like a lily, the leaves whereof are smooth, scattered here and there, and spotted with black spots. Dioscorides says, that there is a sort of it which grows large like a tree, and as high as a fig-tree. The leaves of it are like those of the plum-tree; though broader, smoother, and blacker. The branches and trunk of it are hollow like a reed. Some think, that Jonah speaks of this last species.
Wild gourd, in Hebrew, Pekaah. This is a plant which produces leaves and branches much like garden cucumbers, which creep upon the earth, and are divided into several branches. Its fruit is of the size and figure of an orange. It is of a light, white substance, if you pare off the rind; and so bitter to the taste, that it has been called the gall of the earth. Mention is made of this plant in 2 Kings 4. 39.
Jonah 4. 6. God prepared a g. Jonah glad of the g.
7. a worm smote the g. that it withered
10. thou hast had pity on the g. for which hast not

GOURDS.

1 Kings 6. † 18. cedar of the house carved with g.

Wild GOURDS.

2 Kings 4. 39. one gathered wild g. his lap full

GRACE

Is taken (1) For the free and eternal love and favour of God, which is the spring and source of all the benefits which we receive from him. Rom. 11. 6. And if by grace, then it is no more of works. 2 Tim. 1. 9. Who hath saved us, and called us with an holy calling, according to his own purpose and grace. This free and unmerited love of God is the original mover in our salvation, and hath no cause above it to excite or draw it forth, but merely arises from his own will. It was this mercy or love of God that found out redemption for mankind: God so loved the world, that he gave his only-begotten Son to die for us, John 3. 16. And what could his love give more than the life of his Son? (2) Grace is taken for the free imputation of Christ's righteousness, by the merit whereof true believers become righteous in the sight of God. Rom. 5. 20. Where sin abounded grace did much more abound. (3) For the work of the Spirit, renewing the soul after the image of God, and continually guiding and strengthening the believer to obey his will, to resist and mortify sin, and to overcome it. Rom. 6. 14. Ye are not under the law, but under grace. 2 Cor. 12. 9. My grace is sufficient for thee. (4) For that excellent and blessed state of reconciliation, friendship, and favour with God, which God graciously bestows upon his people. Rom. 5. 2. By whom also we have access by faith, into this grace wherein we stand. (5) For the free love, favour, and bounty of Christ. 2 Cor. 8. 9. Ye know the grace of our Lord Jesus Christ. (6) For the doctrine of the gospel, which proceeds from the grace of God, and wherein his grace is offered and bestowed upon all penitent believers. 1 Pet. 5. 12. This is the true grace of God wherein ye stand; the true and only doctrine of the gospel. (7) For a liberal and charitable disposition, wrought in the heart by the grace of God. 2 Cor. 8. 7. As ye abound in every thing, see that ye abound in this grace also. (8) For spiritual instruction and edification. Eph. 4. 29. That your communication may minister grace to the hearers; that it may be a means of some spiritual advantage to them. (9) Grace is taken for the office of apostleship, which was given of grace, together with ability and other qualifications necessary for the faithful discharge of that office. Rom. 15. 15. I have written the more boldly to you, because of the grace that is given me of God. Eph. 3. 8. To me, who am less than the least of all saints, is this grace given, that I should preach, &c. (10) For the free and undeserved love and favour of God, and a lively sense thereof in the soul; this the apostle wishes to be continued with and increased in the Romans, Rom. 1. 7. (11) For the love and fear of God dwelling in the heart; or, for the assistance of divine grace. 2 Cor. 1. 12. By the grace of God, we have had our conversation in the world. (12) For faith, patience, and other graces that enable to bear, and support under sufferings, 2 Pet. 3. 18. Phil. 1. 7. Ye all are partakers of my grace. (13) For eternal life, or final salvation, which God will graciously bestow upon his people, at the appearing of Christ, at the day of judgment. 1 Pet. 1. 13. The grace that is to be brought to you at the revelation of Jesus Christ. (14) For something acceptable, beautiful, and graceful. Prov. 4. 9. She shall give to thine head an ornament of grace; a beautiful ornament. (15) For favour or friendship with men. Joseph found grace in the sight of Potiphar, Gen. 39. 4. See SAVE.
Ezra 9. 8. for a little space g. hath been shewed
Esth. 2. 17. Esther obtained g. in his sight
Psal. 45. 2. g. is poured into lips, G. hath anointed
84. 11. the Lord is a sun, he will give g. and glory
Prov. 1. 9. they shall be an ornament of g. to head
3. 22. so shall they be life and g. to thy neck
34. but he giveth g. to the lowly, Jam. 4. 6.
4. 9. shall give to thine head an ornament of g.
22. 11. for the g. of his lips the king be his friend
Eccl. 10. † 12. words of a wise man's mouth are g.
Zech. 4. 7. with shoutings, crying, g. unto it
12. 10. I will pour the Spirit of g. and supplications
John 1. 14. begotten of Father, full of g. and truth
16. of his fulness we have all received, g. for g.
17. but g. and truth came by Jesus Christ
Acts 4. 33. and great g. was on them all
14. 3. which gave testimony to the word of his g.
18. 27. helped them which had believed through g.
20. 32. I commend you to the word of his g.
Rom. 1. 5. by whom we received g. and apostleship
7. g. and peace to you from God our Father, 1 Cor. 1. 3. 2 Cor. 1. 2. Gal. 1. 3. Eph. 1. 2. Phil. 1. 2. Col. 1. 2. 1 Thess. 1. 1. 2 Thess. 1. 2. Philem. 3.
3. 24. being justified freely by his g. through redem.
4. 4. the reward is not reckoned of g. but of debt
16. it is of faith, that it might be by g.
5. 2. we have access into this g. wherein we stand
17. much more they who receive abundance of g.
20. where sin abounded g. did much more abound
21. even so might g. reign through righteousness
6. 1. shall we continue in sin, that g. may abound?
14. under g. || 15. shall we sin, because under g.?
11. 5. a remnant according to the election of g.
6. and if by g. then it is no more of works
12. 3. for I say, through the g. given unto me
6. gifts differing according to the g. given to us
15. 15. because of the g. given to me of God
1 Cor. 10. 30. for if I by g. be a partaker, why
15. 10. his g. bestowed upon me was not in vain
2 Cor. 1. † 15. that ye might have a second g.
4. 15. abundant g. might redound to glory of God
8. 6. so he would also finish in you the same g. also
7. see that ye abound in this g. also
19. who was chosen to travel with us with this g.
9. 8. and God is able to make all g. abound to you
12. 9. he said, my g. is sufficient for thee
Gal. 1. 6. removed from him who called you to g.
15. when it pleased God, who called me by his g.
2. 9. when James perceived the g. given to me
5. 4. justified by the law, ye are fallen from g.
Eph. 1. 6. to the praise of the glory of his g.
7. forgiveness, according to the riches of his g.
2. 5. by g. ye are saved through faith, 8.
7. he might shew the exceeding riches of his g.
3. 8. to me the least of all saints is this g. given
4. 7. but unto every one of us is given g.
29. that it may minister g. to the hearers
6. 24. g. be with all that love our Lord Jesus
Phil. 1. 7. ye all are partakers of my g.

Col. 3. 16. singing with g. in your hearts to the Lord
4. 6. let speech be alway with g. seasoned with salt
18. g. be with you, 2 Tim. 4. 22. Tit. 3. 15. Heb. 13. 25.
2 Thess. 2. 16. hath given us good hope through g.
1 Tim. 1. 2. g. mercy, and peace from G. our Father and our L. J. Chr. 2 Tim. 1. 2. Tit. 1. 4. 2 John 3.
14. the g. of our Lord was exceeding abundant
6. 21. g. be with thee. Amen
2 Tim. 1. 9. who called us according to his g.
2. 1. be strong in the g. that is in Christ Jesus
Tit. 3. 7. being justified by his g. we should be heirs
Heb. 4. 16. let us come boldly to the throne of g.
10. 29. and hath done despite to the Spirit of g.
12. 28. let us have g. to serve God acceptably
13. 9. it is good the heart be established with g.
Jam. 1. 11. the g. of the fashion of it perisheth
4. 6. he giveth more g. giveth g. to the humble
1 Pet. 1. 2. g. and peace be multiplied, 2 Pet. 1. 2.
10. who prophesied of the g. to come to you
13. hope for the g. || 3. 7. as being heirs of g.
5. 5. God resisteth the proud, giveth g. to humble
10. the God of g. who hath called us to glory
2 Pet. 3. 18. grow in g. and knowledge of Jes. Chr.
Jude 4. turning the g. of God into lasciviousness
Rev. 1. 4. g. and peace from him which is and was
See FIND, or FOUND.

GRACE of God.

Luke 2. 40. and the g. of God was upon him
Acts 11. 23. when he had seen g. of God, was glad
13. 43. persuaded them to continue in the g. of G.
14. 26. had been recommended to g. of G. 15. 40.
20. 24. to testify the gospel of the g. of God
Rom. 5. 15. much more the g. of God hath abounded
1 Cor. 1. 4. the g. of God given you by Jesus Christ
3. 10. according to g. of God which is given to me
15. 10. by the g. of God I am what I am, yet not I, but the g. of God which was with me
2 Cor. 1. 12. by the g. of God we had our conversation
6. 1. that ye receive not the g. of God in vain
8. 1. of the g. of God bestowed on the churches
9. 14. for the exceeding g. of God in you
Gal. 2. 21. I do not frustrate the g. of God
Eph. 3. 2. if have heard of dispensation of g. of God
7. according to the gift of the g. of God given me
Col. 1. 6. since the day ye knew the g. of God
2 Thess. 1. 12. and ye in him, according to g. of God
Tit. 2. 11. the g. of God that bringeth salvation
Heb. 2. 9. that he by g. of God should taste death
12. 15. looking lest any man fail of the g. of God
1 Pet. 4. 10. good stewards of the manifold g. of God
5. 12. testifying that this is the true g. of God

GRACE of our Lord Jesus.

Acts 15. 11. through g. of L. J. we shall be saved as
Rom. 16. 20. the g. of our Lord Jesus Christ be with you, 24. 1 Cor. 16. 23. Phil. 4. 23. 1 Thess. 5. 28. 2 Thess. 3. 18.
2 Cor. 8. 9. for ye know the g. of our Lord J. Christ
13. 14. the g. of our L. J. Christ, love of God, and communion of Holy Ghost, be with you all
Gal. 6. 18. g. of L. J. Chr. be with spirit, Philem. 25.
Rev. 22. 21. g. of L. J. Christ be with you all. Amen

GRACIOUS.

Gen. 43. 29. and he said, God be g. to thee my son
Exod. 22. 27. when he crieth, I will hear, for I am g.
33. 19. I will be g. to whom I will be g.
34. 6. the Lord, the Lord God, g. 2 Chron. 30. 9. Psal. 103. 8. | 116. 5. | 145. 8. Joel 2. 13.
Num. 6. 25. the Lord make his face shine, and be g.
2 Sam. 12. 22. who can tell whether God will be g.
2 Kings 5. † 1. now Naaman was g. with his master
13. 23. and the Lord was g. unto them
Neh. 9. 17. a God ready to pardon, g. merciful, 31.
Job 33. 24. then he is g. to him, and saith, deliver
Psal. 4. † 1. be g. unto me, and hear my prayer
77. 9. hath God forgotten to be g.?
86. 15. but thou, O Lord, art G. g. 111. 4. | 112. 4.
Prov. 11. 16. a g. woman retaineth honour
26. † 25. when he maketh voice g. believe him not
Eccl. 10. 12. the words of a wise man's mouth are g.
Isa. 30. 18. the Lord will wait that he may be g.
19. he will be very g. to thee || 33. 2. be g. to us
Jer. 22. 23. how g. when pangs come upon thee
Amos 5. 15. may be the Lord will be g. to remnant
Jonah 4. 2. for I knew that thou art a g. God
Mal. 1. 9. beseech God that he will be g. to us
Luke 4. 22. wondered at g. words which proceeded
1 Pet. 2. 3. if ye have tasted that the Lord is g.

GRACIOUSLY.

Gen. 33. 5. the children which G. hath g. given me
11. because God hath dealt g. with me
Psal. 119. 29. and grant me thy law g.
Hos. 14. 2. take away all iniquity, and receive us g.
Luke 1. † 28. hail, thou that art g. accepted

GRAFT, ED.

Rom. 11. 17. thou being a wild olive-tree wert g. in
19. branches were broken that I might be g. in
23. they shall be g in, for God is able to g. them
24. were cut out and g. much more these be g.

GRAIN, S.

Joel 1. † 17. the g. are rotten under the clods
Amos 9. 9. yet shall not the least g. fall on the earth
Mat. 13. 31. the kingdom of heaven is like a g. of mustard-seed, Mark 4. 31. Luke 13. 19.
17. 20. if ye have faith as a g. of mustard seed, ye shall say unto this mountain, remove, Luke 17. 6.
1 Cor. 15. 37. bare g. wheat, or some other g.

GRANDFATHER.

Dan. 5. † 11. in days of thy g. in him whom thy g.
† 13. that Daniel whom g. brought out of Jewry

GRANDMOTHER.

1 Kings 15. † 10. his g.'s name was Maachah
2 Tim. 1. 5. faith which dwelt first in thy g. Lois

GRANT.

Ezra 3. 7. according to the g. they had of Cyrus

GRANT.

Lev. 25. 24. ye shall g. a redemption for the land
Ruth 1. 9. the Lord g. you that you may find rest
1 Sam. 1. 17. the God of Israel g. thee thy petition
1 Chron. 21. 22. g. me the place of this threshing-floor; thou shalt g. it me for the full
2 Chron. 12. 7. but I will g. them some deliverance
Neh. 1. 11. and g. him mercy in sight of this man
Esth. 5. 8. if it please the king to g. my petition
Job 6. 8. that God would g. the thing I long for
Psal. 20. 4. g. thee according to thine own heart
85. 7. shew us thy mercy, O Lord, g. us salvation
119. 29. and g. me thy law graciously
140. 8. g. not O Lord, the desires of the wicked
Mat. 20. 21. g. my two sons may sit, Mark 10. 37.
Luke 1. 74. g. to us, that we being delivered
Acts 4. 29. g. that with boldness we may speak
Rom. 15. 5. now God g. you to be like-minded
Eph. 3. 16. g. you to be strengthened with might
2 Tim. 1. 18. the Lord g. that he may find mercy
Rev. 3. 21. will I g. to sit with me in my throne

GRANTED.

1 Chron. 4. 10. God g. him that which he requested
2 Chron. 1. 12. wisdom and knowledge is g. thee
Ezra 7. 6. and the king g. him all his requests
Neh. 2. 8. the king g. according to good hand of G.
Esth. 5. 6. what thy petition, shall be g. 7. 2. | 9. 12.
9. 13. let it be g. to the Jews in Shushan
Job 10. 12. thou hast g. me life and favour
Prov. 10. 24. the desire of the righteous shall be g.
Acts 3. 14. and desired a murderer to be g. you
11. 18. then hath God also to the Gentiles g. repentance unto life
14. 3. who g. signs to be done by their hands
Rev. 19. 8. to her was g. she should be arrayed in

GRAPE.

There was abundance of fine vineyards, and excellent grapes *in* Palestine. *How large this fruit was in that country, we may judge by the bunch of* grapes *which was cut in the valley of* Eshcol, *and was brought upon a staff between two men to the camp of* Israel *at* Kadeshbarnea, Num. 13. 23, 24. *Travellers relate, that there was some to be seen there of a prodigious size.* Strabo *and* Pliny *affirm the same. Some affirm, that in the valley of* Eshcol *there were bunches of grapes to be found still of ten and twelve pounds.*

Moses *in the law commanded, that when the* Israelites *gathered their* grapes, *they should not be careful to pick up those which fell, nor be so exact as to leave none upon the vines. What fell, and was left behind, he ordered should be for the poor,* Lev. 19. 10. Deut. 24. 20, 21. *People who were passing that way were permitted to go into another man's vineyard, and eat what grapes they would; but they were not allowed to carry any away with them,* Deut. 23. 24.

Some learned men are of opinion, that the prohibition delivered by Moses *against gleaning grapes after the vintage, may signify a second vintage after the first, which was never so good or so plentiful as the former; for this, they say, was over in the hot countries about the end of* August, *and the other in* September. *God requires therefore that this second vintage should be left to the poor, as well as the grapes of the first which had escaped the observation of the gatherers.*

It is frequent in Scripture to describe an almost total destruction, by the similitude of a vine stripped in such a manner that there was not a bunch of grapes left for those who came a gleaning. Isa. 24. 13. Thus it shall be in the midst of the land, there shall be as the gleaning grapes when the vintage is done. *And* Jer. 6. 9. They shall thoroughly glean the remnant of *Israel* as a vine. *See* Jer. 49. 9. Obad. 5.

The blood of grapes, *Gen.* 49. 11. *signifies wine.* He washed his clothes in the blood of grapes. *His habitation shall be in a country where there are vineyards. And* Deut. 32. 14. Thou didst drink the pure blood of the grape; *pure, unmixed wine.* The fathers have eaten a sour grape, and the children's teeth are set on edge, *Jer.* 31. 29. *Ezek.* 18. 2. *This is a proverbial way of speaking in the sacred text; meaning, that the fathers have sinned, and the children have borne the punishment of their crimes. It was a complaint made by the* Jews *to God, who punished those sins in them, whereof they pretended they were not guilty. But the Lord said, he would cause this proverb to cease in* Israel, *and that for the future every one should suffer the punishment of his own iniquity.*

Lev. 19. 10. nor gather every g. of thy vineyard
Deut. 32. 14. thou didst drink the blood of the g.
Job 15. 33. he shall shake off his unripe g. as vine
Cant. 2. 13. vines with tender g. give a good smell
7. 12. let us see whether the tender g. appear
Isa. 18. 5. the sour g. is ripening in the flower
Jer. 31. 29. the fathers have eaten a sour g.
30. every man that eateth the sour g.
Mic. 7. 1. I am as the g.-gleanings of the vintage

GRAPE-gatherer.

Jer. 6. 9. turn back thy hand as a g.-gatherer
49. 9. if g.-g. come, would they not leave? Obad. 5.

GRAPES.

Gen. 40. 10. the clusters thereof brought forth ripe g.
49. 11. he washed his clothes in the blood of g.
Lev. 25. 5. nor gather the g. of thy vine undressed
11. in jubilee, nor gather the g. of thy vine
Num. 6. 3. nor shall he eat moist g. or dried
13. 20. the time was the time of the first ripe g.
23. they cut down a branch with one cluster of g.
Deut. 23. 24. then thou mayest eat g. thy fill
24. 21. when thou gatherest the g. of thy vineyard
28. 30. shalt plant a vineyard, not gather the g. 39.
32. 32. their g. are g. of gall, their clusters bitter
Judg. 8. 2. is not the gleaning of the g. of Ephraim
9. 27. they trode the g. and cursed Abimelech
Neh. 13. 15. bringing in wine and g. on the sabbath
Cant. 2. 15. for our vines have tender g.
7. 7. and thy breasts are like to clusters of g.
Isa. 5. 2. he looked it should bring forth g.
4. should bring forth g. brought it forth wild g.?
17. 6. yet gleaning g. shall be left in it
24. 13. as the gleaning g. when vintage is done
Jer. 8. 13. there shall be no g. on the vine
25. 30. shall give a shout, as they that tread the g.
49. 9. would not leave some gleaning g. Obad. 5.
Ezek. 18. 2. the fathers have eaten sour g.
Hos. 3. † 1. look to gods, and love flagons of g.
9. 10. I found Israel like g. in the wilderness
Amos 9. 13. treader of g. shall overtake the sower
Mat. 7. 16. do men gather g. of thorns, figs of thistles?
Luke 6. 44. nor of a bramble-bush gather they g.
Rev. 14. 18. thrust in sickle, her g. are fully ripe

GRASS.

Gen. 1. 11. God said, let the earth bring forth g.
12. and the earth brought forth g. and herb
Num. 22. 4. as the ox licketh up the g. of the field
Deut. 11. 15. I will send g. in thy fields for thy cattle
29. 23. it is not sown, nor any g. groweth therein
32. 2. my speech shall distil as showers upon the g.
2 Sam. 23. 4. as the g. springing out of the earth
1 Kings 18. 5. peradventure find g. to save horses
2 Kings 19. 26. they were as the g. of the field, as green herb, as g. on the house-tops, Isa. 37. 27.
Job 5. 25. thine offspring is the g. of the earth
6. 5. doth the wild ass bray when he hath g.?
40. 15. behold, behemoth eateth g. as an ox
Psal. 23. † 2. to lie down in pastures of tender g.
37. 2. for they shall soon be cut down like the g.
72. 6. he shall come down like rain upon mown g.
16. they of the city shall flourish like g. of earth
90. 5. in the morn. they are like g. which groweth
92. 7. when the wicked spring as the g. and flourish
102. 4. my heart is smitten, and withered like g.
11. my days like a shadow, am withered like g.
103. 15. as for man, his days are as g. as a flower
104. 14. he causeth g. to grow for cattle
106. 20. in the similitude of an ox that eateth g.
129. 6. let them be as the g. upon the house tops
147. 8. who maketh g. to grow upon the mountains
Prov. 19. 12. the king's favour is as dew upon the g.
27. 25. hay appeareth, the tender g. sheweth itself
Isa. 15. 6. the g. faileth, there is no green thing
35. 7. in the habitation of dragons shall be g.
40. 6. the voice said, cry, all flesh is g. 1 Pet. 1. 24
7. the g. withereth, surely the people is g. 8
44. 4. they shall spring up as among the g.
51. 12. the son of man which shall be made as g.
Jer. 14. 5. hind forsook it, because there was no g. 6.
50. 11. ye are grown fat as the heifer at g.
Dan. 4. 15. leave the stump in the tender g. 23.
25. shall make thee eat g. as oxen, 32, 33. | 5. 21.
Amos 7. 2. they had made an end of eating g. of land
Mic. 5. 7. as showers upon the g. that tarrieth not
Zech. 10. 1. Lord shall give every one g. in the field
Mat. 6. 30. if God so clothe the g. Luke 12. 28.
14. 19. the multitude to sit down on g. Mark 6. 39.
John 6. 10. now there was much g. in the place
Jam. 1. 10. as the flower of the g. he shall pass away
11. sun is no sooner risen, but it withereth the g.
Rev. 8. 7. and all green g. was burnt up
9. 4. that they should not hurt the g. of the earth

GRASSHOPPER, S.

Lev. 11. 22. these ye may eat, the g. after his kind
Num. 13. 33. and we were in our own sight as g.
Judg. 6. 5. they came as g. for multitude, 7. 12.
Job 39. 20. canst thou make him afraid as a g.?
Eccl. 12. 5. and the g. shall be a burden, desire fail
Isa. 40. 22. the inhabitants thereof are as g.
Jer. 46. 23. because they are more than the g.
Amos 7. 1. behold, he formed g. in the beginning
Nah. 3. 17. thy captains are as the great g.

GRATE, See BRASEN.

GRAVE, Substantive.

Gen. 35. 20. Jacob set up a pillar upon her g. that is the pillar of Rachel's g. unto this day
37. 35. I will go down to g. to my son, mourning
42. 38. bring grey hairs with sorrow to g. 44. 31.
50. 5. bury me in my g. which I have digged
Num. 19. 16. whosoever toucheth a g. is unclean
18. sprinkle it on him that touched one dead or g.
1 Sam. 2. 6. the Lord bringeth down to the g.
2 Sam. 3. 32. the king and people wept at Abner's g.
19. 37. and be buried by the g. of my father
1 Kings 2. 6. let not his head go to the g. in peace
9. his head bring down to the g. with blood
13. 30. and he laid his carcase in his own g.
14. 13. he only of Jeroboam shall come to the g.
2 Kings 22. 20. thou gathered to thy g. 2 Chr. 34. 28.
Job 3. 22. who are glad when they can find the g.
5. 26. thou shalt come to thy g. in a full age
7. 9. so he that goeth to g. shall come up no more
10. 19. I should have been carried from womb to g.
14. 13. O that thou wouldest hide me in the g.
17. 13. if I wait, the g. is my house
21. 13. and in a moment they go down to the g.
32. yet shall he be brought to the g. and in tomb
24. 19. so doth the g. those that have sinned
30. 24. he will not stretch out his hand to the g.
33. 22. yea, his soul draweth near to the g.
Psal. 6. 5. in the g. who shall give thee thanks?
30. 3. thou hast brought up my soul from the g.
31. 17. let the wicked be silent in the g.
49. 14. like sheep laid in the g. consume in the g.
15. redeem my soul from the power of the g.
55. † 15. let them go down quick into the g.
86. † 13. thou hast delivered my soul from the g.
88. 3. and my life draweth nigh to the g.
5. free among the dead, like slain that lie in the g.
11. thy loving-kindness be declared in the g.
89. 48. shall he deliver his soul from hand of g.?
141. 7. our bones are scattered at the g.'s mouth
Prov. 1. 12. let us swallow them alive as the g.
30. 16. g. and barren womb, say not, it is enough
Eccl. 9. 10. no wisdom in the g. whither thou goest
Cant. 8. 6. love is strong, jealousy is cruel as the g.
Isa. 14. † 9. the g. is moved for thee to meet thee
11. thy pomp is brought down to the g.
19. thou art cast out of thy g. like a branch
38. 10. I said, I shall go to the gates of the g.
18. the g. cannot praise thee, death cannot
53. 9. he made his g. with the wicked, and with rich
Jer. 20. 17. that my mother might have been my g.
Ezek. 31. 15. the day when he went down to the g.
32. 23. and her company is round about her g.
Hos. 13. 14. I will ransom them from the power of g.
I will redeem from death, O g. I will be destruction
Jonah 2. † 2. out of the belly of the g. cried I
Nah. 1. 14. I will make thy g. for thou art vile

John 11. 17. he found he had lain in the g. four days
31. saying, she goeth to the g. to weep there
38. Jesus again groaning, cometh to the g.
12. 17. when he called Lazarus out of his g.
1 Cor. 15. 55. O g. where is thy victory?
Rev. 20. † 13. death and g. delivered up the dead

GRAVE-clothes.

John 11. 44. Lazarus came forth bound with g.-cl.

GRAVE, Adjective.

1 Tim. 3. 8. deacons must be g. ‖ 11. wives must be g.
Tit. 2. 2. that aged men be sober, g. temperate

GRAVE.

Exod. 28. 9. thou shalt g. on the onyx-stones names
36. shalt make a plate of pure gold, and g. on it
Chron. 2. 7. send me a man that can skill to g.
14. I have sent a cunning man to g. any graving

GRAVED.

1 Kings 7. 36. on the borders he g. cherubims
2 Chron. 3. 7. and he g. cherubims on the walls

GRAVEL.

Prov. 20. 17. but his mouth shall be filled with g.
Isa. 48. 19. offspring of thy bowels like g. thereof
Lam. 3. 16. hath broken my teeth with g. stones

GRAVEN, Verb.

Isa. 49. 16. I have g. thee on the palms of my hands
Hab. 2. 18. that the maker thereof hath g. it

GRAVEN.

Exod. 32. 16. was the writing of God g. on tables
39. 6. g. as signets are g. with the names of Israel
Job 19. 24. that they were g. with an iron pen
Jer. 17. 1. it is g. upon the table of their heart
Acts 17. 29. that the Godhead is like gold g. by art

GRAVEN image.

Exod. 20. 4. thou shalt not make unto thee any g. image, Lev. 26. 1. Deut. 5. 8.
Deut. 4. 16. lest ye corrupt and make a g. image, 25.
27. 15. cursed the man that maketh any g. image
Judg. 17. 3. the silver for my son to make a g. image
4. gave them to the founder, who made a g. image
18. 14. there is in these houses a g. image
17. the g. image ‖ 30. Dan set up the g. image, 31.
2 Kings 21. 7. Manasseh set g. image in house of G.
Isa. 40. 19. the workman melteth a g. image
20. he seeketh a workman to prepare a g. image
44. 9. they that make a g. image are vanity
10. who hath molten a g. image not profitable
17. with the residue thereof he maketh his g. im.
45. 20. that set up the wood of their g. image
48. 5. and my g. image hath commanded them
Jer. 10. 14. founder confounded by g. image, 51. 17.
Nah. 1. 14. I will cut off the g. and molten image
Hab. 2. 18. what profiteth the g. image?

GRAVEN images.

Deut. 7. 5. ye shall burn their g. images with fire, 25.
12. 3. ye shall hew down the g. im. of their gods
Judg. 3. † 19. Ehud turned by the g. images at Gilgal
2 Kings 17. 41. feared the Lord and served g. im.
2 Chron. 33. 19. set up g. im. before he was humbled
34. 7. when he had beaten the g. images to powder
Psal. 78. 58. moved him to jealousy with g. images
97. 7. confounded be all they that serve g. images
Isa. 10. 10. whose g. im. did excel them of Jerusal.
21. 9. Babylon is fallen, and all the g. images
30. 22. shall defile the covering of thy g. images
42. 8. neither will I give my praise to g. images
17. shall be greatly ashamed that trust in g. im.
Jer. 8. 19. provoked me to anger with their g. im.
50. 38. it is the land of g. images, they are mad
51. 47. I will do judgment on the g. images, 52.
Hos. 11. 2. they burnt incense to g. images
Mic. 1. 7. all the g. images shall be beaten to pieces
5. 13. thy g. images also will I cut off

GRAVES.

Exod. 14. 11. because there were no g. in Egypt
Num. 11. † 34. he called the place the g. of lusts
2 Kings 23. 6. cast the powder on the g. of the peo.
2 Chron. 34. 4. strowed it on the g. of them that
Job 17. 1. days extinct, the g. are ready for me
21. † 32. yet shall he be brought to the g.
Isa. 65. 4. which remain among the g. and lodge
Jer. 8. 1. shall bring the priest's bones out of their g.
26. 23. and cast his dead body into g. of the people
Ezek. 32. 22. his g. are about him, 23. 25, 26.
37. 12. I will open your g. and cause you to come up out of your g.
13. when I have opened your g. brought out of g.
39. 11. I will give Gog a place of g. in Israel
Mat. 27. 52. the g. were opened, many saints arose
53. and many bodies of the saints came out of g.
Luke 11. 44. for ye are as g. which appear not
John 5. 28. all that are in the g. shall hear his voice
Rev. 11. 9. not suffer their bodies to be put in g.

GRAVETH.

Isa. 22. 16. as he that g. an habitation in a rock

GRAVING.

Exod. 32. 4. he fashioned golden calf with a g. tool

GRAVING.

2 Chr. 2. 14. skilful to grave any manner of g. † 7.
Zech. 3. 9. I will engrave g. thereof, saith the Lord

GRAVINGS.

1 Kings 7. 31. upon the mouth of the laver were g.

GRAVITY.

1 Tim. 3. 4. having children in subjection with all g.
Tit. 2. 7. in doctrine shewing g. sincerity

GRAY, see HAIRS and HEAD.

GRAY-headed.

1 Sam. 12. 2. I am old and g.-h. my sons are with you
Job 15. 10. with us are the g.-headed and aged
Psal. 71. 18. when I am old and g.-h. forsake me not

GREASE.

Psal. 119. 70. their heart is as fat as g. but I delight

GREAT.

This word is put for rich, powerful, celebrated, magnificent, illustrious, ancient. Naaman *was a great man with the king his master; he was in great consideration with him,* 2 Kings 5. 1. I will make of thee a great nation, *Gen.* 12. 2. *I will make thee head or father of a numerous and powerful people.* Moses was very great in the land of Egypt, Exod. 11. 3. *The whole country looked upon him as an extraordinary man, and as one sent from God.* The Great Sea, *Num.* 34. 6. *in the way of eminence, is the* Mediterranean, *greater beyond comparison than the* Dead sea, *and the sea of* Gennesareth, *which are but lakes. The king of* Assyria *is called the* great king, *the* Euphrates, *the great river, the city of* Nineveh, *the great city; because the king of* Assyria *was the most powerful king in the east; the* Euphrates *the greatest river in* Syria; *and* Nineveh *the greatest city in the dominions of the king of* Assyria, *and of all the countries round about.*

Gen. 12. 2. I will bless thee, and make thy name g.
24. 35. Abraham my master is become g.
30. 8. with g. wrestlings have I wrestled with sister
39. 9. how can I do this g. wickedness and sin!
45. 7. to save your lives by a g. deliverance
48. 19. I know it, my son, he also shall be g.
Deut. 3. 5. beside unwalled towns a g. many
10. 17. the Lord your God is a g. God, 2 Chr. 2. 5.
11. 7. your eyes have seen the g. acts of the Lord
18. 16. neither let me see this g. fire any more
29. 24. what meaneth the heat of this g. anger?
Josh. 7. 9. what wilt thou do unto thy g. name?
14. 12. thou heardest the cities were g. and fenced
22. 10. built there a g. altar by Jordan to see to
24. 17. for he did those g. signs in our sight
Judg. 5. 15. divisions of Reuben g. thoughts of heart
1 Sam. 12. 17. may perceive your wickedness is g.
22. † 15. I knew nothing of all this, little or g.
2 Sam. 5. 10. Dav. went on, and grew g. L. with him
7. 9. I have made thee a g. name, I was with thee
22. thou art g. O Lord God, none is like thee
12. 14. given g. occasion to enemies to blaspheme
22. 36. thy gentleness hath made me g. Ps. 18. 35.
1 Kings 8. 42. shall hear of thy g. name, 2 Chr. 6. 32.
19. 7. because the journey is too g. for thee
2 Kings 4. 8. passed to Shunem, where was g. woman
22. 13. g. is the wrath of the Lord that is kindled
1 Chron. 16. 25. g. is the Lord, and greatly to be praised, Psal. 48. 1. | 96. 4. | 135. 5. | 145. 3.
21. 13. into Lord's hand, for very g. are his mercies
29. 12. and in thine hand it is to make g.
2 Chron. 2. 5. the house I build is g. for g. is our G.
9. the house I am to build shall be wonderful g.
17. 12. Jehoshaphat waxed g. exceedingly
28. 13. our trespass is g. ‖ 34. 21. g. wrath poured
Neh. 4. 14. remember the L. who is g. and terrible
9. 32. now therefore our God, the g. the mighty God
Esth. 1. 20. published thro' all his empire, for it is g.
Job 5. 25. thou shalt know that thy seed shall be g.
22. 5. is not thy wickedness g. iniquities infinite?
30. 18. by g. force of my disease garment changed
35. 15. yet he knoweth it not in g. extremity
36. 18. a g. ransom ‖ 26. God is g. we know him not
38. 21. or because the number of thy days is g.
39. 11. wilt thou trust him, because strength is g.?
Psal. 12. † 3. cut off tongue that speaks g. things
14. 5. there were they in g. fear, 53. 5.
19. 11. and in keeping of them there is g. reward
21. 5. his glory is g. in thy salvation, honour
25. 11. O Lord, pardon mine iniquity, for it is g.
31. 19. O how g. is thy goodness thou hast laid up
86. 10. thou art g. and doest wondrous things
92. 5. how g. are thy works ‖ 103. † 8. g. of mercy
139. 17. O God, how g. is the sum of them!
Eccl. 9. 13. this wisdom seemed g. unto me
Isa. 5. 9. houses even g. and fair without inhabitant
9. 2. sat in darkness, have seen g. light, Mat. 4. 16.
12. 6. g. is the Holy One of Israel in midst of thee
19. 20. he shall send them a Saviour and a g. one
53. 12. I will divide him a portion with the g.
54. 13. and g. shall be the peace of thy children
Jer. 5. 27. therefore they are become g. and rich
10. 6. thou art g. and thy name is g. in might
20. 17. and her womb to be always g. with me
32. 18. the g. the mighty God is his name
19. g. in counsel, and mighty in work
44. 26. behold, I have sworn by my g. name
Lam. 3. 23. they are new, g. is thy faithfulness
Ezek. 16. 7. thou hast increased and waxed g.
17. 3. a g. eagle with g. wings, long-winged, 7.
24. 9. I will even make the pile for fire g.
29. 18. to serve a g. service against Tyrus
31. 4. the waters made him g. the deep set him up
36. 23. and I will sanctify my g. name
Dan. 4. 3. how g. his signs, how mighty his wonders!
8. 4. I saw the ram pushing, and he became g.
Joel 3. 13. get you down, for their wickedness is g.
Amos 6. 2. and from thence go to Hamath the g.
Mic. 5. 4. now shall he be g. unto ends of the earth
Zech. 9. 17. how g. his goodness, how g. his beauty!
Mal. 1. 11. my name shall be g. among Gentiles, 11.
Mat. 5. 12. rejoice and be exceeding glad, for g. is your reward in heaven, Luke 6. 23, 35.
19. shall be called g. in the kingdom of heaven
6. 23. if light be darkness, how g. is that darkness!
13. 46. one pearl of g. price ‖ 15. 28. g. is thy faith
19. 22. for he had g. possessions, Mark 10. 42.
20. 25. they that are g. exercise authority
26. whosoever will be g. among you, Mark 10. 43.
22. 36. Master, which is the g. commandment?
38. this is the first and g. commandment
Luke 1. 15. he shall be g. in sight of the Lord
9. 48. that is least among you, the same shall be g.
10. 2. the harvest truly is g. but the labourers few
16. 26. between us and you there is a g. gulf
Acts 8. 9. giving out that he was some g. one
19. 28. g. is Diana of the Ephesians! 34.
2 Cor. 7. 4. g. is my boldness, g. is my glorying
Col. 4. 13. that he hath a g. zeal for you and them
1 Tim. 3. 16. g. is mystery of godliness, G. manifest
2 Tim. 2. 20. in g. house not only vessels of gold
Tit. 2. 13. the glorious appearing of the g. God
Heb. 7. 4. now consider how g. this man was
Jam. 3. 5. how g. a matter a little fire kindleth
Rev. 15. 1. and I saw another sign in heaven, g.
16. 19. g. Babylon came in remembrance before G.
17. 5. Babylon the g. the mother of harlots, 18. 2.
19. 17. gather together unto the supper of the g. G.

See CITY, COMPANY, CONGREGATION, CRY, DAY, DESTRUCTION.

GREAT evil.

1 Sam. 6. 9. then he hath done us this g. evil
Neh. 13. 27. hearken unto you to do all this g. evil
Eccl. 2. 21. this also is vanity, and a g. evil
Jer. 16. 10. wherefore Lord pronounced this g. evil
26. 19. thus might we procure g. evil ag. our souls
32. 42. I have brought this g. evil upon this people
44. 7. why commit this g. evil against your souls?
Dan. 9. 12. confirmed, by bringing upon us a g. evil

See EXCEEDING, JOY.

GREAT king or kings.

2 Kings 18. 19. thus saith the g. k. 28. Isa. 36. 4, 13.
Ezra 5. 11. which a g. king of Israel builded
Psal. 47. 2. the Lord is a g. King over all the earth
48. 2. is mount Zion, the city of the g. King
95. 3. the Lord is a g. King above all gods
136. 17. give thanks to him that smote g. kings
Eccl. 9. 14. and there came a g. king against it
Jer. 25. 14. g. kings shall serve themselves, 27. 7.
Mal. 1. 14. for I am a g. King, saith the Lord
Mat. 5. 35. Jerusalem is the city of the g. King

GREAT men.

2 Sam. 7. 9. like name of g. m. in earth, 1 Chr. 17. 8.
2 Kings 10. 6. Ahab's sons were with g. men of city
11. Jehu slew all Ahab's g. men and kinsfolks
Neh. 11. 14. Zabdiel overseer, son of one of g. men
Job 32. 9. g. men are not always wise, nor the aged
Prov. 18. 16. a gift bringeth him before g. men
25. 6. and stand not in the place of g. men
Jer. 5. 5. I will get me unto the g. men and speak
52. 13. all the houses of the g. men burnt he
Ezek. 21. 14. it is the sword of the g. men slain
Jonah 3. † 7. with the consent of his g. men
Nah. 3. 10. all her g. men were bound in chains
Rev. 6. 15. g. men hid themselves in dens and rocks
18. 23. thy merchants were the g. men of the earth

GREAT multitude, multitudes.

Num. 32. 1. Reuben, Gad had a g. multitude of cattle
1 Kings 20. 13. hast thou seen all this g. multitude?
28. I will deliver this g. multitude into thine hand
2 Chr. 13. 8. ye be a g. mult. ye have golden calves
20. 2. there cometh a g. multitude against thee
15. not dismayed by reason of this g. multitude
28. 5. carried a g. multitude captives to Damascus
Job 31. 34. did I fear a g. multitude or did contempt
Isa. 16. 14. all that g. multitude shall be contemned
Jer. 44. 15. women that stood by, even a g. mult.
Ezek. 47. 9. there shall be a very g. multitude of fish
Dan. 11. 11. king of south shall set forth a g. mult.
Mat. 4. 25. g. multitudes followed him, 8. 1. | 12. 15. | 19. 2. | 20. 29. Mark 3. 7. John 6. 2.
8. 18. when Jesus saw g. mult. 14. 14. Mark 9. 14.
15. 30. g. mults. came, having lame, blind, dumb
33. whence so much bread as to fill so g. a mult.
21. 8. a g. multitude spread their garments in way
26. 47. with Judas a g. m. with swords, Mark 14. 43.
Luke 5. 6. they inclosed a g. multitude of fishes
15. a g. m. came together to hear and be healed
John 5. 3. in these lay a g. mult. of impotent folk
Acts 14. 1. a g. mult. of Jews and Greeks believed
17. 4. and of the devout Greeks a g. multitude
Rev. 7. 9. a g. mult. which no man could number
19. 6. I heard as it were the voice of a g. multit.

GREAT nation and nations.

Gen. 12. 2. I will make of thee a g. nation, and will bless thee, 18. 18. | 46. 3. Exod. 32. 10.
17. 20. I will make Ishmael a g. nation, 21. 18.
Deut. 4. 6. surely this g. nation is a wise people
26. 5. he became there a nation g. and mighty
Josh. 23. 9. hath driven out before you g. nations
Psal. 135. 10. who smote g. nations, and slew kings
Jer. 6. 22. a g. nation shall be raised from the sides
50. 9. I will raise against Bab. an assembly of g. n.
41. people shall come from the north, a g. nation
Ezek. 31. 6. under his shadow dwelt all g. nations

GREAT people.

Deut. 2. 10. the Emims dwelt therein, a people g.
21. Zamzummims, a people g. many and tall
9. 2. a people g. and tall, children of Anakims
Josh. 17. 14. why but one lot, seeing I am a g. people
15. if thou be a g. people ‖ 17. thou art a g. people
1 Kings 3. 8. a g. people that cannot be numbered
9. who is able to judge this g. people? 2 Chr. 1. 10.
5. 7. given David a wise son over this g. people
Isa. 13. 4. the noise in mountains like as of g. people
Joel 2. 2. a g. people hath not been ever the like

GREAT power.

Exod. 32. 11. thy people thou hast brought out of Egypt with g. power, 2 Kings 17. 36. Neh. 1. 10.
Num. 14. 17. let the power of my lord be g.
Josh. 17. 17. thou art a great people and hast g. p.
Job 23. 6. will he plead against me with g. power?
Psal. 147. 5. great is our Lord, and of g. power
Jer. 27. 5. I have made the earth, the man and the beast on the ground, by my g. power, 32. 17.
Ezek. 17. 9. it shall wither even without g. power
Nah. 1. 3. the Lord is slow to anger, g. in power
Mark 13. 26. coming in the clouds with g. power
Acts 4. 33. with g. power gave the apostles witness
8. 10. saying, this man is the g. power of God
Rev. 11. 17. thou hast taken to thee thy g. power
18. 1. angel come from heaven, having g. power

GREAT sea.

Num. 34. 6. ye shall have the g. sea for a border
Josh. 1. 4. from the wilderness unto the g. sea
9. 1. when the kings in the coasts of g. sea heard
15. 12. the west border was to the g. sea and coast
47. inheritance of Judah, to the g. sea and border
23. 4. with all nations I have cut off to the g. sea
Ezek. 47. 10. as fish of the g. sea, exceeding many
15. border of land toward north from the g. sea
Dan. 7. 2. the four winds strove upon the g. sea

See SIN.

GREAT slaughter.

Josh. 10. 10. slew them with a g. s. at Gibeon
20. made an end of slaying them with g. s.
Judg. 11. 33. Jephthah smote Ammon. with g. s.
15. 8. Samson smote the Philistines with g. s.
1 Sam. 4. 10. Philistines smote Isr. with g. s. 17.
6. 19. Lord had smitten the people with a g. s.
19. 8. David slew Philistines with a g. s. 23. 5.
2 Sam. 18. 7. a g. slaughter that day of 20,000 men
1 Kings 20. 21. king of Israel slew Assyr. with g. s.
2 Chron. 13. 17. Abijah slew Israel with a g. s.

2 Chr. 28. 5. king of Israel smote Ahaz with a *g. s.*
Isa. 30. 25. in day of *g. s.* when the towers fall
34. 6. Lord hath a *g. slaughter* in land of Idumea

So GREAT.

Exod. 32. 21. thou hast brought *so g.* a sin upon them
Deut. 4. 7. what nation *so g.* hath God so nigh? 8.
1 Kings 3. 9. who able to judge *so g.* people? *2 Ch.* 1. 10.
Psal. 77. 13. who is *so g.* a God as our God?
103. 11. *so g.* is his mercy to them that fear him
Mat. 8. 10. not found *so g.* faith in Israel, *Luke* 7. 9.
15. 33. so much bread as to fill *so g.* a multitude
2 Cor. 1. 10. who delivered us from *so g.* a death
Heb. 2. 3. how escape, if we neglect *so g.* salvation?
12. 1. are compassed with *so g.* a cloud of witnesses
Jam. 3. 4. ships tho' *so g.* yet turned with an helm
Rev. 16. 18. so mighty an earthquake and *so g.*
18. 17. in one hour *so g.* riches come to nought

Small and GREAT.

Gen. 19. 11. smote men with blindness *small and g.*
Deut. 1. 17. but ye shall hear *small* as well as *g.*
25. 13. shalt not have divers weights, a *g. and sm.*
14. shalt not have divers measures, a *g. and sm.*
1 Sam. 5. 9. smote the men *sm. and g.* with emerods
20. 2. my father will do nothing *g.* or *small*
30. 2. they slew not any either *g.* or *small*
19. there was nothing lacking neither *sm.* nor *g.*
1 Kings 22. 31. fight not with *sm.* nor *g.* *2 Chr.* 18. 30.
2 Kings 23. 2. *sm. and g.* went to house, *2 Chr.* 34. 30.
25. 26. all the people *small and g.* came to Egypt
1 Chron. 26. 13. they cast lots as well the *small* as *g.*
2 Chron. 15. 13. be put to death, whether *sm.* or *g.*
31. 15. to give to brethren by courses, *g. and sm.*
36. 18. gave into his hand vessels, *g. and small*
Esth. 1. 5. Ahasuerus made a feast unto *g. and sm.*
20. shall give to husbands honour *g. and small*
Job 3. 19. *small and g.* are there, servant is free
37. 6. he saith to the *small* rain, and to *g.* rain
Psal. 104. 25. are things creeping, *small and g.*
115. 13. bless them that fear the Lord, *small and g.*
Eccl. 2. 7. I had possessions of *g. and small* cattle
Jer. 16. 6. *g. and small* shall die in this land
Amos 8. 5. making the ephah *small*, the shekel *g.*
Acts 26. 22. I continue witnessing to *small and g.*
Rev. 11. 18. reward to them that fear him, *sm. and g.*
13. 16. he caused *small and g.* to receive a mark
19. 5. praise our God, ye that fear him, *small and g.*
18. that ye may eat flesh of all men, *small and g.*
20. 12. I saw the dead, *sm. and g.* stand before God

GREAT *stone* and *stones.*

Gen. 29. 2. a *g. stone* was upon the well's mouth
Deut. 27. 2. that set up *g. stones* and plaster them
Josh. 10. 11. Lord cast down *g. stones* from heaven
18. roll *g. stones* upon the mouth of the cave
24. 26. Joshua took a *g. stone*, and set it up there
1 Sam. 6. 14. the cart came where there was a *g. stone*
15. and the Levites put them on the *g. stone*
18. to the *g. stone* of Abel, whereon they set ark
14. 33. ye have transgressed, roll a *g. stone* unto me
2 Sam. 20. 8. when they were at *g. stone* in Gibeon
1 Kings 5. 17. they brought *g. stones* to lay foundat.
7. 10. the foundation was of *g. stones*, *Ezra* 5. 8.
2 Chron. 26. 15. he made engines to shoot *g. stones*
Ezra 6. 4. three rows of *g. stones* and a row of timber
Jer. 43. 9. take *g. stones* and hide them in clay
Mat. 27. 60. he rolled a *g. stone* to door of sepulchre

GREAT *thing* and *things.*

Deut. 4. 32. whether any such thing as this *g. thing* is
10. 21. he is thy God that hath done *g. things*
1 Sam. 12. 16. stand and see this *g. thing* Lord will do
24. consider how *g. things* he hath done for you
26. 25. thou shalt both do *g. things* and prevail
2 Sam. 7. 21. for word's sake hast thou done *g. things*
23. and to do for you *g. things* and terrible
2 Kings 5. 13. if prophet had bid thee do some *g. t.*
8. 4. tell me all the *g. things* Elisha hath done
13. is he a dog, that he should do this *g. thing?*
1 Chron. 17. 19. in making known these *g. things*
Job 5. 9. to God who doeth *g. things*, 9. 10. | 37. 5.
Psal. 71. 19. who hast done *g. things*, who is like thee
106. 21. they forgat God who had done *g. things*
126. 2. the Lord hath done *g. things* for them, 3.
Jer. 33. 3. I will shew thee *g.* and mighty *things*
45. 5. and seekest thou *g. things* for thyself?
Dan. 7. 8. a mouth speaking *g. th.* 20. *Rev.* 13. 5.
Hos. 8. 12. I have written the *g. things* of my law
Joel 2. 20. because he hath done *g. things*
21. fear not, O land, the Lord will do *g. things*
Mark 3. 8. when they heard what *g. things* he did
5. 19. tell how *g. things* Lord hath done, *Luke* 8. 39.
Luke 1. 49. he that is mighty hath done *g. things*
8. 39. he published how *g. things* Jesus had done
Acts 9. 16. I will shew how *g. things* he must suffer
1 Cor. 9. 11. is it a *g. thing* if we reap carnal things?
2 Cor. 11. 15. no *g. th.* if his ministers be transform.
Jam. 3. 5. tongue a little member boasteth *g. things*

Very GREAT.

Gen. 26. 13. Isaac grew till he became *very g.*
Exod. 11. 3. the man Moses was *very g.* in the land
Num. 11. 33. Ld. smote people with a *very g.* plague
13. 28. and the cities are walled and *very g.*
22. 17. I will promote thee unto *very g.* honour
1 Sam. 2. 17. the sin of the young men was *very g.*
4. 10. and there was a *very g.* slaughter
14. 15. *very g.* trembling || 20. *very g.* discomfiture
25. 2. Nabal was a *very g.* man, he had 3000 sheep
2 Sam. 18. 17. they laid a *very g.* heap on Absalom
19. 32. for Barzillai was a *very g.* man
1 Kings 10. 2. qu. of Sheba came with a *very g.* train
1 Chron. 21. 13. for *very g.* are his mercies
2 Chron. 16. 14. they made a *very g.* burning for Asa
24. 24. Ld. delivered a *very g.* host into their hand
30. 13. assembled a *very g.* congregation, *Ezra* 10. 1.
33. 14. Manass. raised up the wall a *very g.* height
Neh. 8. 17. and there was a *very g.* gladness
Job 1. 3. Job a *very g.* household, greatest in the east
2. 13. for they saw that his grief was *very g.*
Psal. 104. 1. O Lord my God, thou art *very g.*
Ezek. 47. 9. there shall be a *very g.* multitude of fish
Dan. 8. 8. therefore the he-goat waxed *very g.*
11. 25. king of south stirred up with a *very g.* army
Joel 2. 11. for his camp is *very g.* he is strong
Zech. 14. 4. and there shall be a *very g.* valley

Mat. 21. 8. a *very g.* multitude spread their garments
Mark 8. 1. the multitude *very g.* having nothing
16. 4. the stone was rolled away, for it was *very g.*

Was GREAT.

Gen. 6. 5. God saw the wickedness of man *was g.*
13. 6. their substance *was g.* so that they could not
1 Kings 3. 4. to Gibeon, that *was* the *g.* high place
2 Kings 3. 27. there *was g.* indignation against Isr.
Esth. 4. 3. where the decree came *was g.* mourning
9. 4. Mordecai *was g.* in the king's house, 10. 3.
Job 31. 25. if I rejoiced because my wealth *was g.*
Eccl. 2. 9. I *was g.* and increas. more than all before
Lam. 1. 1. she that *was g.* among the nations
Dan. 4. 10. the tree's height *was g.* and it grew
Mat. 7. 27. it fell, and *g. was* the fall of it, *Luke* 6. 49.

GREAT *waters.*

2 Sam. 22. † 17. drew me out of *g. w.* *Psal.* 18. † 16.
Psal. 29. † 3. the voice of Lord is upon *g. waters*
32. 6. in floods of *g. waters* shall not come nigh
77. 19. thy way is in the sea, thy path in *g. waters*
107. 23. they that do business in *g. waters*
144. 7. send from above, deliver me out of *g. waters*
Isa. 23. 3. and by *g. waters* the seed of Sihor
Jer. 41. 12. found Ishmael by *g. waters* of Gibeon
51. 55. when her waves do roar like *g. waters*
Ezek. 1. 24. the noise of their wings like *g. waters*
17. 5. he placed of the seed by *g. waters*, set it
8. it was planted in a good soil by *g. waters*
26. 19. when *g. waters* shall cover thee
27. 26. thy rowers brought thee into *g. waters*
31. 7. he was fair, for his root was by *g. waters*
15. I restrained floods, the *g. waters* were stayed
32. 13. I will destroy all the beasts beside *g. waters*
Hab. 3. 15. didst walk through the heap of *g. waters*

GREAT *while.*

2 Sam. 7. 19. but thou hast spoken also of thy servant's house for a *g. while* to come, *1 Chron.* 17. 17.
Mark 1. 35. rising up a *g. while* before day, he went
Luke 10. 13. had *g. while* ago repented in sackcloth
Acts 28. 6. after the barbarians looked a *g. while*

GREAT *work* and *works.*

Exod. 14. 31. Israel saw that *g. work* the Lord did
Judg. 2. 7. who had seen all the *g. works* of the Lord
1 Chron. 29. 1. my son is young, and the *work* is *g.*
Neh. 4. 19. the *work* is *g.* and we are separated
6. 3. I am doing a *g. work*, I cannot come down
Psal. 111. 2. the *works* of the Lord are *g.* *Rev.* 15. 3.
Eccl. 2. 4. I made *g. works*, I builded me houses

GREATER.

Gen. 1. 16. God made the *g.* light to rule the day
4. 13. my punishment is *g.* than I can bear
39. 9. there is none *g.* in this house than I
41. 40. only in the throne will I be *g.* than thou
48. 19. his younger brother shall be *g.* than he
Exod. 18. 11. I know the Lord is *g.* than all gods
Num. 14. 12. make of thee *g.* nation, *Deut.* 9. 14.
Deut. 1. 28. the people is *g.* and taller than we
4. 38. drive nations *g.* than thou, 7. 1. | 9. 1. | 11. 23.
Josh. 10. 2. because Gibeon was *g.* than Ai
1 Sam. 14. 30. had there been a much *g.* slaughter
2 Sam. 13. 15. the hatred was *g.* than the love
16. this evil is *g.* than the other thou didst me
1 Kings 1. 37. make his throne *g.* than David, 47.
1 Chron. 11. 9. David waxed *g.* and *g.* Ld. was with
2 Chron. 3. 5. the *g.* house he ceiled with fir-tree
Esth. 9. 4. for this man Mordecai waxed *g.* and *g.*
Job 33. 12. I will answer, that God is *g.* than man
Lam. 4. 6. is *g.* than the punishment of Sodom
Ezek. 8. 6. thou shalt see *g.* abominations, 13, 15.
Dan. 11. 13. shall set forth a multitude *g.* than former
Amos 6. 2. or their border *g.* than your border
Hag. 2. 9. the glory of latter house *g.* than former
Mat. 11. 11. not risen up a *g.* than John the Baptist, least in kingdom of heaven *g.* than he, *Luke* 7. 28.
12. 6. in this place is one *g.* than the temple
41. behold, a *g.* than Jonas is here, *Luke* 11. 32.
42. behold, a *g.* than Solomon is here, *Luke* 11. 31.
23. 14. receiving *g.* damn. *Mark* 12. 40. *Luke* 20. 47.
17. for whether is *g.* the gold, or the temple?
19. for whether is *g.* the gift or the altar?
Mark 4. 32. sown, it becometh *g.* than all herbs
12. 31. there is no other command. *g.* than these
Luke 12. 18. I will pull down my barns, and build *g.*
22. 27. whether is *g.* he that sitteth or that serveth?
John 1. 50. thou shalt see *g.* things, 5. 20. | 14. 12.
4. 12. art thou *g.* than our father Jacob?
5. 36. I have a *g.* witness than that of John
8. 53. art thou *g.* than our father Abraham?
10. 29. my Father is *g.* than all, 14. 28.
13. 16. the servant is not *g.* than his lord, 15. 20.
15. 13. *g.* love hath no man than this to lay down
19. 11. he that delivered me to thee hath the *g.* sin
Acts 15. 28. to lay upon you no *g.* burden than these
Rom. 9. † 12. it was said, the *g.* shall serve the lesser
1 Cor. 14. 5. for *g.* is he that prophesieth, than he
15. 6. of whom the *g.* part remain unto this present
Heb. 6. 13. because he could swear by no *g.* he swore
16. for men verily swear by the *g.* and an oath
9. 11. by a *g.* and more perfect tabernacle
11. 26. esteeming the reproach of Christ *g.* riches
Jam. 3. 1. knowing we shall receive *g.* condemnation
2 Pet. 2. 11. whereas angels which are *g.* in power
1 John 3. 20. God is *g.* than our heart, and knoweth
4. 4. *g.* is he that is in you, than he in the world
5. 9. witness of God is *g.* this is the witness of God
3 John 4. I have no *g.* joy than to hear that children

GREATEST.

1 Chr. 12. 14. least was over 100, *g.* over a thousand
29. hitherto the *g.* part had kept the ward of Saul
Job 1. 3. this man was the *g.* of all in the east
Jer. 6. 13. from least to *g.* given to covetousn. 8. 10.
31. 34. all know me, from least to the *g.* *Heb.* 8. 11.
42. 1. all people from the least to the *g.* came near
8. Jeremiah called the people from least to the *g.*
44. 12. they shall die, from the least to the *g.*
Jonah 3. 5. put on sackcloth, from the *g.* to the least
Mat. 13. 32. when grown, it is the *g.* among herbs
18. 1. who is the *g.* in the kingdom of heaven
4. humble himself as this little child, same is *g.*
23. 11. but he that is *g.* shall be your servant
Mark 9. 34. disputed who should be *g.* *Luke* 9. 46.
Luke 22. 24. there was a strife who should be *g.*

Luke 22. 26. but he that is *g.* let him be as the younger
Acts 8. 10. all gave heed from the least to the *g.*
1 Cor. 13. 13. but the *g.* of these is charity

GREATLY.

Gen. 3. 16. he said, I will *g.* multiply thy sorrow
19. 3. Lot pressed upon them *g.* and they turned in
24. 35. the Lord hath blessed my master *g.*
27. † 33. Isaac trembled with a trembling *g.*
32. 7. then Jacob was *g.* afraid and distressed
Exod. 19. 18. and the whole mount quaked *g.*
Num. 11. 10. the anger of the Lord was kindled *g.*
14. 39. Moses told, and the people mourned *g.*
Deut. 15. 4. the Lord shall *g.* bless thee in the land
17. 17. nor shall he *g.* multiply silver and gold
Judg. 2. 15. Lord ag. them, they were *g.* distressed
6. 6. Israel was *g.* impoverished by Midian
1 Sam. 11. 6. Saul's anger was kindled *g.*
15. Saul and all the men of Israel rejoiced *g.*
12. 18. the people *g.* feared the Lord and Samuel
16. 21. he loved him *g.* became his armour-bearer
17. 11. when heard Philistine they were *g.* afraid
28. 5. Saul saw the Philist. his heart trembled *g.*
30. 6. David was *g.* distressed, for the people spake
2 Sam. 10. 5. the men were *g.* ashamed, *1 Chr.* 19. 5.
12. 5. David's anger was *g.* kindled ag. the man
13. † 15. Amnon hated her with great hatred *g.*
† 36. the king wept with a great weeping *g.*
14. † 25. was not a beautiful man in Isr. to praise *g.*
24. 10. David said, I have sinned *g.* *1 Chr.* 21. 8.
1 Kings 2. 12. Solomon's kingdom was established *g.*
5. 7. Hiram heard Solomon's words, he rejoiced *g.*
18. 3. now Obadiah feared the Lord *g.*
1 Chr. 4. 38. the house of their fathers increased *g.*
16. 25. great is the Lord, *g.* to be praised, to be feared above all gods, *Ps.* 48. 1. | 96. 4. | 145. 3.
2 Chr. 25. 10. their anger was *g.* kindled ag. Judah
33. 12. Manasseh humbled himself *g.* before God
Ezra 10. † 13. we have *g.* offended in this thing
Job 8. 7. yet thy latter end should *g.* increase
Psal. 21. 1. in thy salvation how *g.* shall he rejoice
28. 7. therefore my heart *g.* rejoiceth, I will praise
38. 6. I am bowed down *g.* go mourning all the day
45. 11. so shall the king *g.* desire thy beauty
47. 9. shields of earth belong to God, he is *g.* exalted
62. 2. he is my defence, I shall not be *g.* moved
65. 9. thou *g.* enrichest it with the river of God
71. 23. my lips shall *g.* rejoice when I sing unto thee
78. 59. he was wroth, and *g.* abhorred Israel
105. 24. he increased his people *g.* 107. 38.
109. 30. I will *g.* praise the Lord with my mouth
112. 1. blessed that delighteth *g.* in his command.
116. 10. I was *g.* afflicted, I said in my haste
119. 51. the proud have had me *g.* in derision
Prov. 23. 24. the father of righteous shall *g.* rejoice
Isa. 42. 17. shall be *g.* ashamed that trust in images
61. 10. I will *g.* rejoice in the Lord, soul be joyful
Jer. 3. 1. shall not that land be *g.* polluted?
4. 10. surely thou hast *g.* deceived this people
9. 19. we are *g.* confounded, have forsaken the land
20. 11. persecutors shall be *g.* ashamed not prosper
Ezek. 20. 13. and my sabbaths they *g.* polluted
25. 12. because that Edom hath *g.* offended
Dan. 5. 9. then was king Belshazzar *g.* troubled
9. 23. for thou art *g.* beloved, 10. 11, 19.
Obad. 2. I made thee small, thou art *g.* despised
Jonah 4. † 4. art thou *g.* angry? || † 9. I am *g.* angry
Zeph. 1. 14. the great day of the Lord hasteth *g.*
Zech. 9. 9. rejoice *g.* O daughter of Zion, shout
Mat. 27. 14. insomuch that governor marvelled *g.*
Mark 5. 23. Jairus besought him *g.* saying, my daug
38. he seeth them that wept and wailed *g.*
9. 15. when they beheld, they were amazed *g.*
12. 27. the God of the living, ye therefore do *g.* err
John 3. 29. rejoiceth *g.* because of bridegroom's voice
Acts 3. 11. all the people ran to porch, *g.* wondering
6. 7. number of disciples multiplied in Jerusalem *g.*
1 Cor. 16. 12. I *g.* desired Apollos to come unto you
Phil. 1. 8. how *g.* I long after you all in Jesus Christ
4. 10. I rejoiced in the Lord *g.* that at last your care
1 Thess. 3. 6. desiring *g.* to see us, as we to see you
2 Tim. 1. 4. *g.* desiring to see thee, that I may be filled
4. 15. for he hath *g.* withstood our words
1 Pet. 1. 6. ye *g.* rejoice tho' now ye are in heaviness
2 John 4. I rejoiced *g.* that I found children walking
3 John 3. I rejoiced *g.* when the brethren testified
See FEARED.

GREATNESS.

Exod. 15. 7. in *g.* of thy excellency overthrow them
16. by *g.* of thine arm they shall be still as a stone
Num. 14. 19. pardon according to *g.* of thy mercies
Deut. 3. 24. thou hast begun to shew thy serv. thy *g.*
5. 24. the Lord hath shewed us his glory and *g.*
9. 26. which thou hast redeemed through thy *g.*
11. 2. not with children who have not seen his *g.*
32. 3. ascribe ye *g.* unto our God, he is the rock
1 Chr. 17. 19. to thy own hurt hast done all this *g.*
21. to make thee a name of *g.* and terribleness
29. 11. thine, O Lord, is the *g.* power and glory
2 Chr. 9. 6. one half of *g.* of thy wisdom not shewed
24. 27. and the *g.* of the burdens laid upon him
Neh. 13. 22. spare me according to *g.* of thy mercy
Esth. 10. 2. the declaration of the *g.* of Mordecai
Psal. 66. 3. by *g.* of thy power enemies submit to
71. 21. thou shalt increase my *g.* and comfort me
79. 11. according to the *g.* of thy power, preserve
145. 3. his *g.* is unsearchable || 6. I declare thy *g.*
150. 2. praise him according to his excellent *g.*
Prov. 5. 23. in the *g.* of his folly he shall go astray
Isa. 40. 26. he calleth by name, by *g.* of his might
57. 10. thou art wearied in the *g.* of thy way
63. 1. travelling in the *g.* of his strength
Jer. 13. 22. for *g.* of iniquity thy skirts discovered
Ezek. 31. 2. whom art thou like in thy *g.?*
7. thus was he fair in his *g.* in his branches
Dan. 4. 22. thy *g.* is grown and reacheth to heaven
7. 27. the *g.* of the kingdom shall be given to saints
Eph. 1. 19. what is the exceeding *g.* of his power

GREAVES.

1 Sam. 17. 6. Goliath had *g.* of brass upon his legs

GREEDY.

Psal. 17. 12. like as a lion that is *g.* of his prey
Prov. 1. 19. so is every one that is *g.* of gain

Prov. 15. 27. he that is g. of gain troubleth his house
Isa. 56. 11. they are g. dogs, can never have enough
1 Tim. 3. 3. not g. of filthy lucre, but patient, 8.

GREEDILY.

Prov. 21. 26. he coveteth g. all the day long
Ezek. 22. 12. thou hast g. gained of thy neighbours
Jude 11. they ran g. after the error of Balaam

GREEDINESS.

Eph. 4. 19. given over to work all unclean. with g.

GREEK.

Luke 23. 38. superscription written in G. John 19. 20.
Acts 21. 37. chief captain said, canst thou speak G.
Rev. 9. 11. but in G. tongue hath his name Apollyon

GREEN. [meat

Gen. 1. 30. to beast I have given every g. herb for
9. 3. as the g. herb have I given you all things
30. 37. Jacob took rods of g. poplar and hazel
Exod. 10. 15. there remained not any g. thing in trees
Lev. 2. 14. offer for thy first-fruits g. ears of corn
23. 14. eat no g. ears, till ye have brought an offer.
Judg. 16. 7. if they bind me with seven g. withs
8. then they brought to her seven g. withs
2 Kings 19. 26. inhabit. were as g. herbs, Isa. 37. 27.
Esth. 1. 6. where were white, g. and blue hangings
Job 8. 16. he is g. before the sun, branch shooteth
15. 32. and his branch shall not be g.
39. 8. the wild ass searcheth after every g. thing
Psal. 23. 2. he maketh me lie down in g. pastures
37. 2. and they shall wither as the g. herb
35. I have seen wicked spread. like a g. bay-tree
92. † 14. in old age they shall be fat and g.
Cant. 1. 16. thou art fair, also our bed is g.
2. 13. the fig-tree putteth forth her g. figs
Isa. 15. 6. the grass faileth, there is no g. thing
Jer. 11. 16. the Lord called thy name, a g. olive
17. 8. as tree spreadeth her roots, leaf shall be g.
Hos. 14. 8. I am like a g. fir-tree, from me thy
Amos 7. † 1. he formed g. worms in the beginning
Mark 6. 39. sit down by companies on the g. grass
Rev. 8. 7. hail and fire, and all g. grass was burnt up
9. 4. were commanded not to hurt any g. thing

GREEN tree.

Deut. 12. 2. nations served gods under every g. tree
1 Kings 14. 23. images und. every g. t. 2 Kings 17. 10.
2 Kings 16. 4. Asa sacr. und. every g. t. 2 Chr. 28. 4.
Ps. 52. 8. I am like a g. olive-tree in house of God
Isa. 57. 5. inflaming yourselves under every g. tree
Jer. 2. 20. when under every g. tree thou wanderest
3. 6. under every g. tree, there played the harlot
13. hast scattered thy ways under every g. tree
Ezek. 6. 13. thy slain shall be under every g. tree
17. 24. know that I have dried up the g. tree
20. 47. it shall devour every g. tree and dry tree
Luke 23. 31. if they do these things in a g. tree

GREEN trees.

Jer. 17. 2. whilst children remember groves by g. tr.

GREENISH.

Lev. 13. 49. if the plague be g. in the garment
14. 37. if plague be with hollow strakes g. or red

GREENNESS.

Job 8. 12. whilst it is yet in his g. and not cut

GREET.

1 Sam. 25. 5. go to Nabal and g. him in my name
Rom. 16. 3. g. Priscilla and Aquila helpers in C. J.
5. g. church ‖ 6. g. Mary who bestowed labour
8. g. Amplias ‖ 11. g. the household of Narcissus
1 Cor. 16. 20. all the brethren g. you, Phil. 4. 21.
20. g. ye one another, 2 Cor. 13. 12. 1 Pet. 5. 14.
Col. 4. 14. Luke the physician and Demas g. you
1 Thess. 5. 26. g. the brethren with an holy kiss
Tit. 3. 15. g. them that love us in the faith
2 John 13. the children of thy elect sister g. thee
3 John 14. peace be to thee, g. the friends by name

GREETETH.

2 Tim. 4. 21. Eubulus g. thee, Pudens, and Linus

GREETING, S.

Mat. 23. 7. g. in markets, Luke 11. 43. | 20. 46.
Acts 15. 23. apostles, elders, and brethren, send g.
23. 26. Claudius Lysias to Felix sendeth g.
Jam. 1. 1. to the twelve tribes scattered abroad, g.

GREW.

Gen. 2. 5. the Lord made every herb before it g.
19. 25. he overthrew that which g. upon the ground
21. 8. Isaac g. 26. 13. ‖ 21. 20. Ishmael g.
25. 27. boys g. ‖ 47. 27. Israel g. and multiplied
Exod. 1. 12. the more they afflicted, more they g.
2. 10. Moses g. ‖ Judges 11. 2. his wife's sons g. up
Judg. 13. 24. Samson g. and the Lord blessed him
1 Sam. 2. 21. the child Samuel g. before the Lord, 26
2 Sam. 5. 10. and David went on and g. great
12. 3. it g. up together with him, did eat of his meat
Ezek. 17. 6. it g. and became a spreading vine
Dan. 4. 11. the tree g. and was strong, it reached
Jonah 1. † 11. the sea g. more and more tempestuous
Mark 4. 7. and the thorns g. up and choked it
5. 26. was nothing bettered, but rather g. worse
Luke 1. 80. child g. and waxed strong in spirit, 2. 40.
13. 19. and it g. and waxed a great tree
Acts 7. 17. the people g. and multiplied in Egypt
12. 24. but the word of God g. and multiplied
19. 20. so mightily g. the word of God and prevailed

GREY-hound.

Prov. 30. 31. four comely in going, a g.-hound

GRIEF, S.

Gen. 26. 35. which were a g. unto Isaac and Rebekah
1 Sam. 1. 16. out of the abundance of g. have I spoken
25. 31. this shall be no g. to thee, or offence of heart
2 Chron. 6. 29. when every one shall know his own g.
Job 2. 13. they saw that his g. was very great
6. 2. oh that my g. were thoroughly weighed
† 3. therefore I want words to express my g.
16. 5. the moving of my lips should assuage your g.
6. though I speak, my g. is not assuaged
Psal. 6. 7. my eye is consumed because of g. 31. 9.
31. 10. my life is spent with g. my years with sigh.
69. 26. they talk to g. of those thou hast wounded
139. † 24. see if there be any way of g. in me
147. † 3. he healeth and bindeth up their g.
Prov. 17. 25. a foolish son is a g. to his father
Eccl. 1. 18. for in much wisdom is much g.
2. 23. for all his days are sorrows, and his travail g.
Isa. 1. † 13. it is g. even the solemn meeting
Isa. 17. 11. the harvest shall be a heap in day of g.
53. 3. a man of sorrows, and acquainted with g.
4. he hath borne our g. and carried our sorrows
10. it pleased Ld. to bruise him, he put him to g.
Jer. 6. 7. before me continually is g. and wounds
10. 19. I said, truly this is a g. and I must bear it
45. 3. for the Lord hath added g. to my sorrow
Lam. 3. 32. tho' he cause g. he will have compassion
Ezek. 32. † 9. I will provoke many people to g.
Jonah 4. 6. a gourd, a shadow to deliver him from g.
2 Cor. 2. 5. if any caused g. he hath not grieved me
Heb. 13. 17. may do it with joy and not with g.
1 Pet. 2. 19. for conscience toward God endure g.

GRIEVANCE.

Hab. 1. 3. why dost thou cause me to behold g.?
† 13. thou art of purer eyes than to look on g.

GRIEVE.

1 Sam. 2. 33. the man shall be to g. thine heart
2 Kings 3. † 19. he shall g. every good piece of land
1 Chr. 4. 10. keep from evil, that it may not g. me
Psal. 78. 40. how oft did they g. him in the desert?
Lam. 3. 33. doth not willingly g. the children of men
Eph. 4. 30. g. not the Holy Spirit of God, whereby

GRIEVED.

Gen. 6. 6. and it repented the Lord that he had made man on the earth, and it g. him at his heart
34. 7. Jacob's sons heard and were g. and wroth
45. 5. now be not g. that ye sold me hither
49. 23. the archers have sorely g. him, and shot
Exod. 1. 12. and they were g. because of Israel
Deut. 15. 10. shall not be g. when thou givest unto him
Judg. 10. 16. his soul was g. for the misery of Israel
1 Sam. 1. 8. why weepest thou? why is thy heart g.?
15. 11. it g. Samuel, and he cried unto the Lord
20. 3. let not Jonathan know this lest he be g.
34. Jonathan arose, for he was g. for David
30. 6. because the soul of all the people was g.
2 Sam. 19. 2. heard how the king was g. for his son
Neh. 2. 10. it g. them exceedingly, that there was
13. 8. it g. me sore, and I cast forth all the stuff
Esth. 4. 4. then was the queen exceedingly g.
Job 4. 2. if we assay to commune, wilt thou be g.?
30. 25. was not my soul g. for the poor?
Psal. 73. 21. thus my heart was g. I was pricked
95. 10. forty years was I g. with this generation
112. 10. the wicked shall see it, and be g.
119. 158. I beheld the transgressors and was g.
139. 21. am not I g. with those that rise up ag. thee
Isa. 54. 6. the L. called thee as a woman g. in spirit
57. 10. therefore thou wast not g.
Jer. 5. 3. thou hast stricken them, they have not g.
Dan. 7. 15. I Dan. was g. in spirit in midst of body
11. 30. therefore he shall be g. and return
Amos 6. 6. they are not g. for the affliction of Joseph
Mark 3. 5. being g. for the hardness of their hearts
10. 22. he went away g. for he had great possessions
John 21. 17. Peter was g. because he said third time
Acts 4. 2. being g. that they taught the people
9. † 38. that he would not be g. to come to them
16. 18. Paul being g. said to the spirit, come out
Rom. 14. 15. if thy brother be g. with thy meat
2 Cor. 2. 4. I wrote not that ye should be g.
5. caused grief, he hath not g. me, but in part
Heb. 3. 10. wherefore I was g. with that generation
17. but with whom was he g. forty years?

GRIEVETH.

Ruth 1. 13. for it g. me much for your sakes
Prov. 26. 15. it g. him to bring it again to his mouth

GRIEVING.

Ezek. 28. 24. shall be no more a g. thorn unto Israel

GRIEVOUS.

Gen. 12. 10. for the famine was g. in the land
18. 20. Lord said, because their sin is very g.
21. 11. the thing was very g. in Abraham's sight
12. God said, let it not be g. in thy sight
41. 31. for the famine shall be very g.
50. 11. this is a g. mourning to the Egyptians
Exod. 8. 24. there came a g. swarm of flies
9. 3. a g. murrain ‖ 18. to rain a very g. hail, 24.
10. 14. locusts were very g. before were no such
1 Kings 2. 8. Shimei, who cursed me with a g. curse
12. 4. make the g. service lighter, 2 Chron. 10. 4.
Psal. 10. 5. his ways always g. judgment out of sight
31. 18. which speak g. things against the righteous
Prov. 15. 1. but g. words stir up anger
10. correction is g. unto him that forsaketh the way
Eccl. 2. 17. work wrought under the sun is g. to me
Isa. 15. 4. his life shall be g. unto him
21. 2. a g. vision is declared unto me
Jer. 6. 28. they are all g. revolters, walking with
10. 19. woe is me for my hurt, my wound is g.
14. 17. virgin of my people broken with a g. blow
16. 4. they shall die of g. deaths, not be buried
23. 19. a g. whirlwind shall fall on the wicked
30. 12. bruise incurable, thy wound is g. Nah. 3. 19.
Mat. 23. 4. bind heavy burdens and g. Luke 11. 46.
Acts 20. 29. shall g. wolves enter in among you
25. 7. Jews laid many g. complaints against Paul
Phil. 3. 1. to me indeed is not g. but for you safe
Heb. 12. 11. no chastening seems joyous, but g.
1 John 5. 3. and his commandments are not g.
Rev. 16. 2. a g. sore on men that had mark of beast

GRIEVOUSLY.

Isa. 9. 1. and afterward did more g. afflict her
Jer. 23. 19. it shall fall g. on the head of the wicked
Lam. 1. 8. Jerusal. hath g. sinned, therefore removed
20. my heart is turned, for I have g. rebelled
Ezek. 14. 13. when land sinneth by trespassing g.
Mic. 1. † 9. she is g. sick of her wounds
Mat. 8. 6. g. tormented ‖ 15. 22. daughter g. vexed

GRIEVOUSNESS.

Isa. 10. 1. that write g. which they have prescribed
21. 15. for they fled from the g. of war

GRIND.

Judg. 16. 21. Samson did g. in the prison-house
Job 31. 10. then let my wife g. unto another
Eccl. 12. † 3. the grinders cease because they g. little
Isa. 3. 15. what mean ye to g. the faces of the poor?
47. 2. take millstones and g. meal, uncover locks
Lam. 5. 13. they took the young men to g.
Mat. 21. 44. it will g. him to powder, Luke 20. 18.

GRINDERS.

Job 29. † 17. I brake the g. of the wicked
Eccl. 12. 3. the g. cease, because they are few

GRINDING.

Eccl. 12. 4. when the sound of the g. is low
Mat. 24. 41. two women g. at the mill, Luke 17. 35

GRIN.

Job 18. 9. the g. shall take him by the heel

GRINS.

Psal. 140. 5. they spread a net, they set g. for me
141. 9. keep me from the g. of the workers of iniq.
See GIN.

GRISLED.

Gen. 31. 10. the rams were speckled and g. 12.
Zech. 6. 3. in the fourth chariot were g. horses
6. the g. go forth toward the south country

GROAN.

Job 24. 12. men g. from out of the city
Jer. 51. 52. thro' all her land the wounded shall g.
Ezek. 30. 24. Pharaoh shall g. before him
Joel 1. 18. how do the beasts g. herds have no pasture
Rom. 8. 23. we ourselves g. within ourselves
2 Cor. 5. 2. in this we g. desiring to be clothed upon
4. we in this tabernacle do g. being burdened

GROANED.

John 11. 33. he g. in spirit, and was troubled

GROANETH.

Rom. 8. 22. we know that the whole creation g.

GROANING, S.

Exod. 2. 24. God heard their g. and remembered
6. 5. I have heard the g. of Israel, Acts 7. 34.
Judg. 2. 18. it repented the Lord because of their g.
Job 23. 2. my stroke is heavier than my g.
Psal. 6. 6. I am weary with g. all the night
38. 9. and my g. is not hid from thee
102. 5. by reason of my g. bones cleave to my skin
20. to hear the g. of the prisoner, to loose those
Ezek. 30. 24. with the g. of a deadly-wounded man
Rom. 8. 26. for us with g. that cannot be uttered

GROANING.

John 11. 38. Jesus g. in himself, cometh to the grave

GROPE, ETH.

Deut. 28. 29. thou shalt g. at noon as the blind g.
Job 5. 14. they g. in noon-day as in the night
12. 25. they g. in the dark without light
Isa. 59. 10. we g. for the wall like the blind, we g.

GROSS.

Isa. 60. 2. and g. darkness shall cover the people
Jer. 13. 16. while look for light, make it g. darkness
Mat. 13. 15. people's heart is waxed g. Acts 28. 27.

GROVE.

Gen. 21. 33. Abraham planted a g. in Beer-sheba
Deut. 16. 21. thou shalt not plant a g. near the altar
Judg. 6. 25. and cut down the g. that is by it
28. the g. was cut down that was by it
1 Sam. 22. † 6. Saul abode under a g. in a high place
1 Kings 15. 13. because she had made an idol in a g. 2 Chron. 15. 16.
16. 33. Ahab made a g. and did more to provoke G.
2 Kings 13. 6. there remained the g. in Samaria
17. 16. Israel made a g. and served Baal
21. 3. Manasseh reared up altars, and made a g.
23. 4. to bring out the vessels made for the g.
6. he brought out the g. from house of the Lord
15. Josiah burnt the high place and the g.

GROVES.

Exod. 34. 13. ye shall cut down their g. Deut. 7. 5.
Deut. 12. 3. ye shall burn their g. with fire
Judg. 3. 7. forgat Lord, and served g. 2 Chr. 24. 18.
1 Kings 14. 15. shall root up Israel out of this good land, because they have made their g.
23. built them g. on every high hill, 2 Kings 17. 10.
18. 19. the prophets of the g. four hundred
2 Kings 18. 4. Hezek. cut down g. and brake serp.
23. 14. Josiah cut down the g. 2 Chron. 34. 3, 4.
2 Chr. 14. 3. Asa brake images, and cut down the g.
17. 6. Jehoshaphat took away the g. out of Judah
19. 3. in that thou hast taken away the g.
31. 1. all Israel that were present cut down the g.
33. 3. Manasseh made g. ‖ 19. where he set up g.
34. 3. Josiah began to purge Judah from the g.
7. when he had broken down the altars and the g.
Isa. 17. 8. neither shall he respect the g. or images
27. 9. the g. and the images shall not stand up
Jer. 17. 2. whilst children remember altars and g.
Mic. 5. 14. I will pluck up thy g. out of midst of thee

GROUND.

Exod. 32. 20. he g. the calf to powder, Deut. 9. 21.
Num. 11. 8. the people g. the manna in mills

GROUND corn.

2 Sam. 17. 19. spread g. corn on the well's mouth

GROUND.

Gen. 2. 5. and there was not a man to till the g.
7. the Lord God formed man of the dust of the g.
19. out of the g. the Lord formed every beast
3. 17. he said, cursed is the g. for thy sake
4. 2. Abel a keeper of sheep, but Cain a tiller of g.
10. thy brother's blood crieth to me from the g.
5. 29. because of the g. the Lord hath cursed
8. 21. I will not again curse the g. any more
18. 2. Abram bowed himself toward the g.
19. 1. Lot bowed himself with his face toward g.
Exod. 3. 5. where thou standest is holy g. Acts 7. 33.
8. 21. g. whereon they are shall be full of flies
Num. 16. 31. the g. clave asunder under them
Deut. 28. 4. blessed shall be the fruit of thy g. 11.
Judg. 4. 21. Jael fastened the nail into the g.
1 Sam. 8. 12. he will set them to ear his g. and reap
26. 7. his spear stuck in the g. at his bolster
2 Sam. 23. 11. where was a piece of g. full of lentiles
12. he stood in the midst of the g. and defended it
2 Kings 2. 19. but the water is naught, and g. barren
9. 26. now take him and cast him into the plat of g.
1 Chr. 11. 13. where was a parcel of g. full of barley
2 Chr. 4. 17. the king did cast them in the clay g.
Neh. 10. 35. and to bring the first-fruits of our g.
37. and bring the tithes of our g. to the Levites
Job 5. 6. nor doth trouble spring out of the g.
14. 8. and though the stock thereof die in the g.
18. 10. the snare is laid for him in the g.
38. 27. to satisfy the desolate and waste g.
39. 24. he swallows the g. with fierceness and rage

Psal. 105. 35. locusts devoured the fruit of their *g.*
107. 33. he turneth the water springs into dry *g.*
35. and he turneth dry *g.* into water springs
Isa. 28. 24. doth he open and break clods of his *g.?*
29. 4. and thou shalt speak out of the *g.*
30. 23. seed that thou shalt sow the *g.* withal
24. oxen and young asses that ear the *g.* shall eat
35. 7. and the parched *g.* shall become a pool
51. 23. and thou hast laid thy body as the *g.*
Jer. 4. 3. break up your fallow *g.* *Hos.* 10. 12.
7. 20. my fury shall be poured on the fruit of the *g.*
14. 4. because the *g.* is chapt, there was no rain
Lam. 2. 2. her gates are sunk into the *g.*
Ezek. 12. 6. cover thy face, thou see not the *g.* 12.
41. 16. ceiled from the *g.* up to the windows
Dan. 8. 5. an he-goat came, and touched not the *g.*
18. Daniel's face was towards the *g.* 10. 9, 15.
Hos. 2. 18. make covenant with them for things of *g.*
Zech. 8. 12. and the *g.* shall give her increase
Mal. 3. 11. he shall not destroy the fruits of your *g.*
Mat. 13. 8. but other fell into good *g.* *Luke* 8. 8.
23. he that received seed into good *g.* *Luke* 8. 15.
Mark 4. 26. as if a man should cast seed into the *g.*
Luke 12. 16. the *g.* of a certain rich man brought forth
13. 7. cut it down, why cumbereth it the *g.?*
14. 18. the first said, I have bought a piece of *g.*
19. 44. they shall lay thee even with the *g.*
John 4. 5. near the parcel of *g.* Jacob gave Joseph
12. 24. except a corn of wheat fall into the *g.*
See DRY, FACE.

On or *upon the* GROUND.

Gen. 38. 9. he spilled it *on the g.* lest he should give
44. 14. Joseph's brethren fell before him *on the g.*
Exod. 4. 3. cast the rod *on the g.* he cast it *on the g.*
9. 23. thunder, and the fire ran along *upon the g.*
14. 16. Israel shall go *on* dry *g.* through the sea, 22.
16. 14. as small as the hoar frost *on the g.*
Deut. 15. 23. pour the blood *upon the g.* as water
22. 6. if a bird's nest chance to be *on the g.*
28. 56. woman that would not set her foot *upon g.*
Judg. 6. 39. and *upon* all *the g.* let there be dew
40. and there was dew *upon* all *the g.*
1 *Sam.* 14. 25. and there was honey *upon the g.*
32. the people slew oxen and calves *on the g.*
20. 31. as long as the son of Jesse liveth *on the g.*
2 *Sam.* 14. 14. for we are as water spilt *on the g.*
17. 12. shall light on him as dew falleth *on the g.*
2 *Kings* 13. 18. he said, smite *upon the g.* he smote
Job 1. 20. Job fell *upon the g.* and worshipped
2. 13. they sat down with him *upon the g.* seven days
16. 13. he poureth out my gall *upon the g.*
Isa. 3. 26. she being desolate shall sit *on the g.*
47. 1. O daughter of Babylon, sit *on the g.*
Jer. 25. 33. they shall be dung *upon the g.*
27. 5. I have made man and beast *upon the g.*
Lam. 2. 10. the elders of daught. of Zion sit *on the g.*
21. young and old lie *on the g.* in the streets
Ezek. 24. 7. she poured it not *upon the g.* to cover it
26. 16. then all the princes shall sit *upon the g.*
Mat. 15. 35. the multitude to sit *on the g.* *Mark* 8. 6.
Mark 4. 5. some fell *on* stony *g.* it had not earth, 16.
8. and other fell *on* good *g.* 20. *Luke* 8. 8, 15.
9. 20. he fell *on the g.* and wallowed foaming
14. 35. he went forward, and fell *on g.* and prayed
John 8. 6. he wrote *on the g.* 8. ‖ 9. 6. he spat *on the g.*

To or *unto the* GROUND.

Gen. 3. 19. till thou return *unto the g.* for out of it
33. 3. Jacob bowed himself *to the g.* seven times
Judg. 13. 20. Manoah and his wife fell *to the g.*
20. 21. Benjamin destroyed *to the g.* 22,000 men
25. and destroyed *to the g.* of Israel 18,000 men
Ruth 2. 10. Ruth bowed and fell *to the g.*
1 *Sam.* 3. 19. let none of his words fall *to the g.*
5. 4. Dagon was fallen on his face *to the g.*
14. 45. shall not one hair of his head fall *to the g.*
20. 41. David arose and fell on his face *to the g.*
25. 23. Abigail bowed *to the g.* before David
28. 14. Saul stooped with his face *to the g.*
2 *Sam.* 2. 22. wherefore should I smite thee *to the g.?*
8. 2. he smote Moab, casting him down *to the g.*
14. 4. woman of Tekoah fell on her face *to the g.*
22. Joab fell *to the g.* ‖ 33. Absalom bowed *to the g.*
18. 11. why didst not thou smite him *to the g.?*
20. 10. Joab shed out Amasa's bowels *to the g.*
1 *Kings* 1. 23. Nathan bowed *to the g.* before the king
2 *Kings* 2. 15. sons of the prophets bowed *to the g.*
4. 37. woman of Shunam bowed herself *to the g.*
1 *Chron.* 21. 21. Ornan bowed *to the g.* to David
2 *Chron.* 7. 3. all Israel bowed with their faces *to g.*
20. 18. Jehoshaphat bowed with his face *to the g.*
Neh. 8. 6. worshipped Lord with their faces *to the g.*
Psal. 74. 7. the dwelling-place of thy name *to the g.*
89. 39. profaned his crown, by casting it *to the g.*
44. thou hast cast his throne down *to the g.*
143. 3. he hath smitten my life down *to the g.*
147. 6. he casteth the wicked down *to the g.*
Isa. 14. 12. how art thou cut down *to the g.!*
21. 9. Babylon's images he hath broken *to the g.*
25. 12. lay low, bring *to the g.* even to the dust
26. 5. the lofty city he layeth even *to the g.*
Jer. 14. 2. her gates languish, are black *to the g.*
Lam. 2. 2. hath brought strong holds of Judah *to g.*
10. virgins of Jerusal. hang their heads *to the g.*
Ezek. 13. 14. I will bring down the wall *to the g.*
19. 12. thy mother was cast down *to the g.*
26. 11. thy strong garrison shall go down *to the g.*
28. 17. I will cast thee *to the g.* I will lay thee
Dan. 8. 7. he cast the ram down *to the g.* and stamped
10. it cast down some of hosts and stars *to the g.*
12. and cast down the truth *to the g.*
Amos 3. 14. the horns of the altar shall fall *to the g.*
Obad. 3. saith, who shall bring me down *to the g.?*
Mat. 10. 29. one of them shall not fall *to the g.*
Luke 22. 44. as drops of blood falling *to the g.*
John 18. 6. they went backward, and fell *to the g.*
Acts 22. 7. I fell *to the g.* and heard a voice

GROUND.

1 *Tim.* 3. 15. which is the pillar and *g.* of truth
Heb. 11. † 1. faith is *g.* of things hoped for

GROUNDED.

Isa. 30. 32. in every place where *g.* staff shall pass
Eph. 3. 17. that ye being rooted and *g.* in love

Col. 1. 23. if ye continue in the faith, *g.* and settled

GROW.

Gen. 2. 9. the Lord God made every tree to *g.*
48. 16. and let them *g.* into a multitude
Num. 6. 5. and shall let the locks of his hair *g.*
Deut. 21. † 12. she shall suffer her nails to *g.*
Judg. 16. 22. the hair of his head began to *g.*
2 *Sam.* 23. 5. all my desire, tho' he make it not to *g.*
2 *Kings* 19. 29. eat such things as *g.* of themselves
Ezra 4. 22. why should damage *g.* to hurt of kings?
Job 8. 11. can the rush *g.* up without mire?
19. and out of the earth shall others *g.*
14. 19. thou washest away things that *g.* out of dust
31. 40. let thistles *g.* instead of wheat, and cockle
39. 4. they *g.* up with corn, they go forth
Psal. 92. 12. he shall *g.* like a cedar in Lebanon
104. 14. he causeth grass to *g.* for the cattle, 147. 8.
Eccl. 11. 5. nor how the bones *g.* in the womb
Isa. 11. 1. and a branch shall *g.* out of his roots
17. 11. in the day shalt thou make thy plant *g.*
53. 2. he shall *g.* up before him as a tender plant
Jer. 12. 2. they *g.* yea they bring forth fruit
33. 15. the branch of righteousness to *g.* to David
Ezek. 44. 20. nor suffer their locks to *g.* long
47. 12. by the river shall *g.* all trees for meat
Hos. 14. 5. he shall *g.* as the lily, cast forth his roots
7. they shall revive as the corn, and *g.* as the vine
Jonah 4. 10. nor madest it *g.* which came up in night
Zech. 6. 12. whose name is the BRANCH, he shall *g.*
9. † 17. corn shall make the young men *g.*
Mal. 4. 2. ye shall *g.* up as calves of the stall
Mat. 6. 28. consider the lilies how they *g.* *Luke* 12. 27.
13. 30. let both *g.* together till the harvest
21. 19. let no fruit *g.* on thee henceforward
Mark 4. 27. seed should *g.* up, he knoweth not how
Acts 5. 24. they doubted whereunto this would *g.*
Eph. 4. 15. may *g.* up into him in all things
1 *Pet.* 2. 2. desiring the milk of word, that ye may *g.*
2 *Pet.* 3. 18. *g.* in grace and in knowledge of Lord

GROWN.

Gen. 38. 11. till Shelah be *g.* ‖ 14. Shelah was *g.*
Exod. 2. 11. that when Moses was *g.* he went out
9. 32. were not smitten, for they were not *g.* up
Deut. 32. 15. thou art *g.* thick, covered with fatness
Ruth 1. 13. would ye tarry for them till they were *g.*
2 *Sam.* 10. 5. tarry till your beards be *g.* 1 *Chr.* 19. 5.
1 *Kings* 12. 8. consulted with young men *g.* 10.
2 *Kings* 4. 18. when the child was *g.* up, it fell sick
19. 26. as corn blasted before it be *g.* *Isa.* 37. 27.
Ezra 9. 6. our trespass is *g.* up to the heavens
Psal. 144. 12. that our sons may be as plants *g.* up
Prov. 24. 31. and lo, it was all *g.* over with thorns
Jer. 50. 11. because ye are *g.* fat as the heifer
Ezek. 16. 7. thy breasts are fashioned, thy hair is *g.*
Dan. 4. 22. thou art *g.* strong, thy greatness is *g.*
33. till his hairs were *g.* like eagle's feathers
Mat. 13. 32. when it is *g.* it is greatest among herbs

GROWETH.

Exod. 10. 5. the locusts shall eat every tree that *g.*
Lev. 13. 39. a freckled spot that *g.* in the skin
25. 5. which *g.* of its own accord, not reap, 11.
Deut. 29. 23. nor any grass *g.* therein, like Sodom
Judg. 19. 9. behold, the day *g.* to an end, lodge here
Job 38. 38. when the dust *g.* into hardness and clods
Psal. 37. † 35. the wicked spreadeth as tree that *g.*
90. 5. in the morning like grass which *g.* up, 6.
129. 6. as the grass, which withereth afore it *g.* up
Isa. 37. 30. ye shall eat this year such as *g.* of itself
Mark 4. 32. when it is sown it *g.* up and becometh
Eph. 2. 21. *g.* unto an holy temple in the Lord
2 *Thess.* 1. 3. because your faith *g.* exceedingly

GROWTH.

Amos 7. 1. shooting up of latter *g.* lo, it was latter *g.*

GRUDGE.

Lev. 19. 18. nor bear any *g.* against thy people
Mark 6. † 19. Herodias had a *g.* against John

GRUDGE.

Psal. 59. 15. let them *g.* if they be not satisfied
Jam. 5. 9. *g.* not one against another, brethren

GRUDGING.

1 *Pet.* 4. 9. use hospitality one to another without *g.*

GRUDGINGLY.

2 *Cor.* 9. 7. let him give, not *g.* or of necessity

GUARD.

Gen. 37. 36. Joseph sold to a captain of the *g.* 39. 1.
41. 12. an Hebrew, servant to a captain of the *g.*
1 *Sam.* 22. † 17. king said to the *g.* slay the priests
2 *Sam.* 23. 23. Dav. set him over his *g.* 1 *Chr.* 11. 25.
1 *Kings* 14. 27. shields to captain of *g.* 2 *Chr.* 12. 10.
28. *g.* bare them and brought them, 2 *Chron.* 12. 11.
2 *Kings* 11. 6. a third part at the gate behind the *g.*
25. 8. captain of *g.* came to Jerusalem, *Jer.* 52. 12.
10. captain of *g.* brake down walls, *Jer.* 52. 14.
11. the rest of people captain of *g.* carried away
12. the capt. of the *g.* left of the poor of the land
Neh. 4. 22. that in the night they may be a *g.* to us
23. nor I nor men of the *g.* put off our clothes
Jer. 39. 11. charge to captain of *g.* concerning Jere.
40. 1. when the captain of the *g.* had let him go
5. the captain of the *g.* gave him victuals
52. 30. the captain of the *g.* took captive 4600
Ezek. 38. 7. be thou prepared, and be a *g.* to them
Dan. 2. 14. Daniel answered the captain of the *g.*
Mark 6. † 27. king sent one of his *g.* and commanded
Acts 28. 16. delivered the prisoners to captain of *g.*

GUARD *chamber.*

1 *Kings* 14. 28. guard bare them to *g. ch.* 2 *Chr.* 12. 11.

GUEST.

Luke 19. 7. he was gone to be *g.* with a sinner

GUEST *chamber.*

Mark 14. 14. where is the *g. chamber?* *Luke* 22. 11.

GUESTS.

1 *Kings* 1. 41. Adonijah and all *g.* with him heard it
49. all *g.* with Adonijah were afraid and rose up
Prov. 9. 18. that her *g.* are in the depths of hell
Zeph. 1. 7. for the Lord hath prepared and bid *g.*
Mat. 22. 10. and the wedding was furnished with *g.*
11. when the king came in to see the *g.* he saw

GUIDE, S.

Psal. 48. 14. he will be our *g.* even unto death
55. 13. it was thou, a man, my *g.* my acquaintance
Prov. 2. 17. who forsaketh the *g.* of her youth

Prov. 6. 7. which having no *g.* overseer, or ruler
Jer. 3. 4. my father, thou art the *g.* of my youth
Mic. 7. 5. trust not friend, put ye not confidence in *g.*
Mat. 23. 16. woe to you, ye blind *g.* 24.
Acts 1. 16. who was *g.* to them that took Jesus
Rom. 2. 19. art confident that thou art *g.* of the blind
Heb. 13. † 7. remember them that are *g.* over you

GUIDE.

Job 38. 32. canst thou *g.* Arcturus with his sons?
Psal. 25. 9. the meek will he *g.* in judgment
31. 3. for thy name's sake lead me and *g.* me
32. 8. I will teach and *g.* thee with mine eye
73. 24. thou shalt *g.* me with thy counsel
112. 5. he will *g.* his affairs with discretion
Prov. 11. 3. the integrity of the upright shall *g.* them
23. 19. be wise, and *g.* thine heart in the way
Isa. 49. 10. by springs of water shall he *g.* them
51. 18. there is none to *g.* her among all the sons
58. 11. the Lord shall *g.* thee continually
Luke 1. 79. to *g.* our feet into the way of peace
John 16. 13. he will *g.* you into all truth
Acts 8. 31. how can I, except some man *g.* me?
1 *Thess.* 3. ‖ 11. now G. himself *g.* our way to you
1 *Tim.* 5. 14. younger women bear children, *g.* house
Heb. 13. † 17. obey them that *g.* you, and submit

GUIDED, ING.

Gen. 48. 14. Israel *g.* his hands wittingly
Exod. 15. 13. thou hast *g.* them in thy strength
2 *Chron.* 32. 22. the Lord *g.* them on every side
Job 31. 18. I have *g.* her from my mother's womb
Psal. 78. 52. *g.* them in the wilderness like a flock
72. hast *g.* them by the skilfulness of his hands

GUILE.

Exod. 21. 14. if a man slay with *g.* let him die
Psal. 32. 2. and in whose spirit there is no *g.*
34. 13. keep lips from speaking *g.* 1 *Pet.* 3. 10.
55. 11. deceit and *g.* depart not from her streets
John 1. 47. an Israelite indeed, in whom is no *g.*
2 *Cor.* 12. 16. being crafty, I caught you with *g.*
1 *Thess.* 2. 3. for our exhortation was not in *g.*
1 *Pet.* 2. 1. laying aside all malice and *g.* and envies
22. who did no sin, nor was *g.* found in his mouth
Rev. 14. 5. and in their mouth was found no *g.*

GUILT.

Deut. 19. 13. put away *g.* of innocent blood, 21. 9.

GUILTY.

Gen. 42. 21. we are verily *g.* concerning our brother
Exod. 34. 7. will by no means clear *g.* *Num.* 14. 18.
Lev. 4. 13. which should not be done, are *g.* 22, 27.
5. 2. if hid from him, he shall be unclean and *g.*
3. when he knoweth of it, he shall be *g.* 4.
5. when he shall be *g.* he shall confess his sin
17. tho' he wist it not, yet is he *g.* and shall bear
6. 4. because he sinned and is *g.* he shall restore
Num. 35. 27. tho' he kill the slayer shall not be *g.*
31. take no satisfaction for a murderer *g.* of death
Judg. 21. 22. ye did not give, that you should be *g.*
Ezra 10. 19. being *g.* offered a ram of the flock
Ps. 5. † 10. to make them *g.* let them fall from coun.
34. † 21. they that hate the righteous shall be *g.*
109. † 7. when he shall be judged, let him go out *g.*
Prov. 30. 10. lest he curse, and thou be found *g.*
Ezek. 22. 4. art become *g.* in blood thou hast shed
Hos. 5. † 15. I will return to the place till they be *g.*
Zech. 11. 5. slay them, and hold themselves not *g.*
Mat. 23. 18. swear by the *g.* on it, he is *g.*
26. 66. they said, he is *g.* of death, *Mark* 14. 64.
Rom. 3. 19. all the world may become *g.* before G.
1 *Cor.* 11. 27. shall be *g.* of the body and blood of L.
Jam. 2. 10. shall offend in one point, he is *g.* of all

GUILTINESS.

Gen. 26. 10. thou shouldest have brought *g.* on us
Ezra 9. † 6. our *g.* is grown up to the heavens
Psal. 51. 14. deliver me from blood-*g.* O God
69. † 5. and my *g.* is not hid from thee

GUILTLESS.

Exod. 20. 7. Lord will not hold him *g.* *Deut.* 5. 11.
Num. 5. 31. then shall the man be *g.* from iniquity
32. 22. afterward shall return and be *g.* before Lord
Josh. 2. 19. his blood be on him, and we will be *g.*
1 *Sam.* 26. 9. hand agst. Lord's anointed and be *g.*
2 *Sam.* 3. 28. I and my kingdom are *g.* of blood
14. 9. women said, the king and his throne be *g.*
1 *Kings* 2. 9. hold him not *g.* for thou art a wise man
Mat. 12. 7. ye would not have condemned the *g.*

GULF.

Luke 16. 26. between us and you is a great *g.* fixed

GUSH, ED.

1 *Kings* 18. 28. till the blood *g.* out upon them
Psal. 78. 20. he smote the rock, the waters *g.* out
105. 41. he opened the rock, the waters *g.* out
Isa. 48. 21. he clave the rock, and the waters *g.* out
Jer. 9. 18. and our eye-lids *g.* out with waters
Acts 1. 18. he burst asunder, and his bowels *g.* out

GUTTER, S.

Gen. 30. 38. Jacob set rods in the *g.* before the cattle
41. laid rods before the eyes of the cattle in the *g.*
2 *Sam.* 5. 8. who getteth up to the *g.* and smiteth

H.

HA.

Job 39. 25. he saith among the trumpets, *ha, ha.*

HABERGEON.

Exod. 28. 32. as it were the hole of an *h.* 39. 23.
Job 41. 26. the spear, the dart, the *h.* cannot hold

HABERGEONS.

2 *Chron.* 26. 14. *h.* and bows Uzziah prepared
Neh. 4. 16. half of my servants held bows and *h.*

HABITABLE.

Prov. 8. 31. rejoicing in the *h.* part of his earth

HABITATION.

Exod. 15. 2. he is my God, I will prepare him an *h.*
Lev. 13. 46. without the camp shall his *h.* be
Deut. 12. 5. even to his *h.* shall ye seek and come
1 *Sam.* 2. 29. why kick at offerg. commanded in *h.?*
32. and thou shalt see an enemy in my *h.*
2 *Sam.* 15. 25. he will shew me both it and his *h.*
2 *Chron.* 6. 2. I have built an house of *h.* for thee
29. 6. and have turned from the *h.* of the Lord
30. † 27. prayer came up to the *h.* of his holiness

Ezra 7. 15. to God of Israel whose h. is in Jerusa.
Job 5. 3. foolish taking root, but suddenly I cursed h.
24. thou shalt visit thy h. and shalt not sin
8. 6. make the h. of thy righteousness prosperous
18. 15. brimstone shall be scattered upon his h.
Psal. 26. 8. I have loved the h. of thy house
33. 14. from the place of his h. he looketh
49. † 14. the grave an h. for every one of them
69. 25. let their h. be desolate, none dwell in tents
71. 3. be thou my strong h. whereunto I may resort
89. 14. and judgment the h. of thy throne, 97. 2.
91. 9. thou hast made the most High thy h.
104. 12. the fowls of the heaven have their h.
107. 7. that they might go to a city of h. 36.
132. 5. find an h. for the mighty God of Jacob
13. for the Lord hath desired it for his h.
Prov. 3. 33. but he blesseth the h. of the just
Isa. 22. 16. and that graveth an h. for himself
27. 10. and the h. shall be forsaken and left
32. 18. my people shall dwell in a peaceable h.
33. 20. thine eyes shall see Jerusalem a quiet h.
34. 13. it shall be an h. of dragons, and a court
35. 7. in the h. of dragons shall be grass with reeds
63. 15. and behold from the h. of thy holiness
Jer. 9. 6. thine h. is in the midst of deceit
10. 25. and they have made his h. desolate
25. 30. the Lord shall mightily roar on his h.
31. 23. the Lord bless thee, O h. of justice, 50. 7.
33. 12. the cities thereof be an h. of shepherds
41. 17. and they dwelt in the h. of Chimham
49. 19. he shall come against h. of strong, 50. 44.
50. 19. I will bring Israel again to his h.
45. surely he shall make their h. desolate
Ezek. 16. † 3. thy h. is of the land of Canaan
29. 14. I will cause Egypt to return to their h.
Amos 6. † 3. and cause the h. of violence to come near
Obad. 3. whose h. is high, that saith in his heart
Hab. 3. 11. the sun and moon stood still in their h.
Acts 1. 20. it is written, let his h. be desolate
17. 26. hath determined the bounds of their h.
Eph. 2. 22. for an h. of God through the Spirit
Jude 6. the angels which left their own h.
Rev. 18. 2. Babylon is become the h. of devils

Holy HABITATION.

Exod. 15. 13. thou hast guided them to thy *holy* h.
Deut. 26. 15. look down from thy *holy* h. from heav.
Psal. 68. 5. a Judge of widows is God in his *holy* h.
Jer. 25. 30. Lord shall utter his voice from *holy* h.
Zech. 2. 13. for he is raised up out of his *holy* h.

HABITATIONS.

Gen. 49. 5. instruments of cruelty are in their h.
Exod. 12. 20. in all your h. shall ye eat unleav. bread
35. 3. shall kindle no fire thro' your h. on sabbath
Num. 15. 2. when ye be come into the h. I give you
Psal. 74. 20. dark places of earth full of h. of cruelty
78. 28. he let it fall round about their h.
Isa. 54. 2. let them stretch forth curtains of thy h.
Jer. 9. 10. for the h. of the wilderness a lamentation
21. 13. which say, who shall enter into our h.?
25. 37. and the peaceable h. are cut down
49. 20. surely he shall make their h. desolate
Lam. 2. 2. Lord hath swallowed up the h. of Jacob
Ezek. 6. 14. in all their h. make the land desolate
Hos. 10. † 10. I shall bind them in their two h.
Joel 1. † 19. fire hath devoured h. of the wilderness
Amos 1. 2. the h. of the shepherds shall mourn
Luke 16. 9. they may receive you into everlasting h.

HAD.

Gen. 21. 2. his servants that ruled over all that he h.
39. 6. he knew not ought he h. save bread he eat
Exod. 16. 18. he that gathered much h. nothing
Deut. 10. 15. the Lord h. a delight in thy fathers
Josh. 6. 25. Joshua saved Rahab and all that she h.
7. 24. Joshua took Achan and all that he h.
2 Sam. 6. 22. of them shall I be h. in honour
12. 6. because he did this thing, and h. no pity
23. 8. the names of mighty men whom David h.
2 Kings 9. 31. she said, h. Zimri peace who slew mast.
1 Chr. 13. 14. Lord blessed his house and all he h.
28. 2. as for me, I h. in my heart to build an
12. and the pattern of all that he h. by the Spirit
Job 3. 26. I was not in safety, neither h. I rest
31. 31. if men said not, oh that we h. of his flesh!
42. 10. the Lord gave him twice as much as he h.
Psal. 55. 6. I said, O that I h. wings like a dove
84. 10. I h. rather be a door-keeper in house of God
89. 7. to be h. in reverence of all them about him
119. 51. the proud have h. me greatly in derision
Eccl. 4. 1. as were oppressed, they h. no comforter
Isa. 38. 17. behold, for peace I h. great bitterness
59. 10. we grope as if we h. no eyes, we stumble
60. 10. in my favour have I h. mercy on thee
Jer. 4. 23. I beheld the heavens, and they h. no light
44. 17. for then h. we plenty of victuals, were well
Lam. 1. 7. her pleasant things she h. in days of old
9. she came down wonderfully, h. no comforter
Ezek. 29. 18. yet h. he no wages for the service
36. 21. but I h. pity for mine holy name
Hos. 12. 3. by his strength Jacob h. power with God
4. yea, he h. power over the angel and prevailed
Zech. 1. 12. against which thou hast h. indignation
Mal. 2. 15. yet h. he the residue of the Spirit
Mat. 13. 46. he sold all that he h. and bought it
22. 28. whose wife of seven, for they all h. her?
Mark 12. 44. she of her want did cast in all she h.
John 4. 18. for thou hast h. five husbands
5. 4. was made whole of whatsoever disease he h.
12. 6. Judas h. the bag, and bare what was in it
15. 22. if I h. not come they h. not h. sin
17. 5. the glory I h. with thee before the world was
Acts 2. 44. all that believed h. all things common
18. 18. having shorn his head, for he h. a vow
25. 26. that after examination h. I might write
Rom. 4. 11. a seal he h. yet being uncircumcised, 12.
6. 21. what fruit h. ye in things whereof ashamed
1 Cor. 7. 29. that have wives be as tho' they h. none
2 Cor. 1. 9. but we h. the sentence of death in us
1 Thess. 1. 9. what manner of entering in h. to you
Heb. 7. 6. and blessed him that h. the promises
1 John 2. 7. old command. which ye h. from begin.
2 John 5. that which we h. from the beginning
See ALL, COMPASSION.

HADST.

Gen. 30. 30. for it was little thou h. before I came
Psal. 44. 3. because thou h. a favour to them
Jer. 3. 3. and thou h. a whore's forehead
Heb. 10. 8. and offering for sin thou h. no pleasure

HAFT.

Judg. 3. 22. and the h. also went in after the blade

HAIL.

Exod. 9. 18. I will cause it to rain a very grievous h.
23. the Lord sent thunder and h. the fire ran along
26. where children of Israel were, was there no h.
29. nor shall there be any more h. || 33. h. ceased
10. 5. that which remaineth from the h. 12, 15.
Job 38. 22. or hast thou seen the treasures of the h.?
Psal. 78. 47. he destroyed their vines with h.
48. he gave up their cattle also to the h.
105. 32. he gave them h. for rain, and flaming fire
148. 8. fire, h. snow, and vapour, fulfilling his word
Isa. 28. 2. which as a tempest of h. shall cast down
17. the h. shall sweep away the refuge of lies
Hag. 2. 17. I smote you with h. in all the labours
Rev. 8. 7. there followed h. and fire mingled blood
11. 19. temple was opened, and there was great h.
16. 21. there fell on men a great h. out of heaven

HAIL.

Isa. 32. 19. my people shall dwell when it shall h.

HAIL.

Mat. 26. 49. Judas said, h. master, and kissed him
27. 29. h. king of the Jews, Mark 15. 18. John 19. 3.
Luke 1. 28. the angel came to Mary, and said, h.

HAILSTONES.

Josh. 10. 11. there were more which died with h.
Psal. 18. 12. clouds passed, h. and coals of fire, 13.
Isa. 30. 30. the Lord shall shew indignation with h.
Ezek. 13. 11. and ye, O great h. shall fall, and a wind
13. there shall be great h. in my fury to consume it
38. 22. I will rain great h. fire, and brimstone

HAIR.

Lev. 13. 3. when the h. in the plague is turned white
30. if in plague a yellow h. || 31. no black h. in it
37. there is black h. grown || 14. 8. shave off h. 9.
Num. 6. 19. after the h. of his separation is shaven
Judg. 20. 16. every one could sling stones at h. brea.
2 Sam. 14. 11. not one h. of thy son fall to the earth
26. because the h. was heavy on him, he polled it
1 Kings 1. 52. there shall not an h. of him fall to earth
Neh. 13. 25. I plucked off their h. and made them
Job 4. 15. then a spirit passed, h. of my flesh stood up
Cant. 4. 1. thy h. is as a flock of goats, 6. 5.
Isa. 3. 24. and instead of well set h. baldness
7. 20. the Lord shall shave the head, and h. of feet
50. 6. my cheeks to them that plucked off h.
Jer. 7. 29. cut off thy h. O Jerusalem, cast away
Ezek. 5. 1. and divide the h. || 16. 7. thy h. is grown
Zech. 13. † 4. nor shall they wear a garment of h.
Mat. 3. 4. John had raiment of camel's h. Mark 1. 6.
5. 36. thou canst not make one h. white or black
John 11. 2. and wiped his feet with her h. 12. 3.
1 Cor. 11. 14. if a man have long h. it is a shame
15. if a woman have long h. it is a glory to her
1 Tim. 2. 9. not with broidered h. or gold, or pearls
1 Pet. 3. 3. not of plaiting the h. and wearing gold
Rev. 6. 12. the sun became black as sackcloth of h.
9. 8. and they had h. as the h. of women
See GOATS, HEAD.

HAIRS.

Gen. 42. 38. ye shall bring down my h. 44. 29, 31.
Lev. 13. 21. if there be no white h. therein
Deut. 32. 25. the suckling also with man of gray h.
Ruth 4. † 15. he shall be a nourisher of thy gray h.
Psal. 40. 12. are more than the h. of my head, 69. 4.
71. † 18. now to gray h. O God, forsake me not
Isa. 46. 4. and even to hoar h. will I carry you
Dan. 4. 33. till h. were grown like eagle's feathers
Hos. 7. 9. gray h. are here and there upon him
Mat. 10. 30. the h. of our head numbered, Luke 12. 7.
Luke 7. 38. did wipe them with h. of her head, 44.
Rev. 1. 14. his head and h. were white like wool

HAIRY.

Gen. 25. 25. the first red, all over like an h. garment
27. 11. Esau is an h. man || 23. his hands were h.
2 Kings 1. 8. Elijah was an h. man, and girt with
Psal. 68. 21. the h. scalp of such a one as goeth on

HALE.

Luke 12. 58. lest the adversary h. thee to the judge

HALING.

Acts 8. 3. Saul h. men and women, committed them

HALF.

Exod. 24. 6. Moses took h. the blood, h. he sprinkled
30. 23. take thou of sweet cinnamon h. so much
Lev. 6. 20. h. of it in the morning, and h. at night
Num. 12. 12. of whom the flesh is h. consumed
31. 29. take it of their h. and give it to Eleazar
Josh. 8. 33. h. of them over against mount Ebal
1 Sam. 14. 14. within as it were an h. acre of land
2 Sam. 10. 4. Hanun shaved off one h. of their beards
18. 3. nor if h. of us die, will they care for us
19. 40. h. the people of Israel conducted David
1 Kings 3. 25. give h. of the child to one, h. to other
10. 7. and behold, the h. was not told, 2 Chr. 9. 6.
13. 8. if thou wilt give me h. thine house, I will not
16. 21. h. of the people followed Tibni, h. Omri
Neh. 3. 9. the ruler of the h. part of Jerusalem, 12.
16. h. part of Bethzur || 17. h. of Keilah, 18.
13. 24. children spake h. in the speech of Ashdod
Esth. 5. 3. to the h. of the kingdom, 7. 2. Mark 6. 23.
Psal. 55. 23. bloody men shall not live h. their days
Ezek. 16. 51. nor hath Samaria committed h. thy sins
Dan. 12. 7. be for time, times, and an h. Rev. 12. 14.
Hos. 3. 2. I bought her for h. an homer of barley
Zech. 14. 2. h. of the city shall go into captivity
4. h. of mount toward the south || 8. h. toward sea
Luke 10. 30. and departed, leaving him h. dead
19. 8. behold, the h. of my goods I give to the poor
Rev. 8. 1. was silence about space of h. an hour
11. 9. shall see dead bodies three days and an h. 11.
See SHEKEL, HIN, TRIBE.

HALL.

Mat. 27. 27. the soldiers took Jesus into common h.
Mark 15. 16. the soldiers led him away to the h.
Luke 22. 55. had kindled a fire in the midst of the h.
See JUDGMENT.

HALLOW.

Exod. 28. 38. which the children of Israel shall h.
29. 1. h. them to minister to me in priest's office
Lev. 22. 2. in those things which they h. to me, 3.
32. I will be hallowed, I am the Lord who h. you
25. 10. shall h. the fiftieth year, proclaim liberty
Num. 6. 11. and he shall h. his head that same day
1 Kings 8. 64. same day did king h. court, 2 Chr. 7. 7.
Jer. 17. 22. but h. ye the sabbath-day, 24. 27.
Ezek. 20. 20. and h. my sabbaths, they shall be a sign
44. 24. they shall keep laws and h. my sabbaths

HALLOWED.

Exod. 20. 11. Ld. blessed the sabbath-day and h. it
29. 21. Aaron shall be h. and his garments
Lev. 12. 4. she shall touch no h. thing, nor come
19. 8. because he hath profaned the h. thing of L.
22. 32. I will be h. among the children of Israel
Num. 3. 13. I h. unto me all the first-born in Israel
5. 10. and every man's h. things shall be his
16. 37. take up the censers, for they are h. 38.
18. 8. of all the h. things I have given unto thee
29. even the h. part thereof out of it
Deut. 26. 13. I have brought away the h. things
1 Sam. 21. 4. is no common, but there is h. bread
6. so Ahimelech the priest gave him h. bread
1 Kings 9. 3. I have h. this house thou hast built, 7.
2 Kings 12. 18. Jehoash took all the h. things
2 Chron. 36. 14. polluted the house of L. he had h.
Mat. 6. 9. h. be thy name, Luke 11. 2.

HALT.

Mat. 18. 8. is better to enter into life h. Mark 9. 45.
Luke 14. 21. bring in hither the h. and the blind
John 5. 3. of h. waiting for the moving of the water

HALT.

To halt, *to be lame on both sides. With this* Elijah *reproaches the* Israelites *of the ten tribes,* 1 Kings 18. 21. How long halt ye between two opinions? *They did not adore God with a pure and unmixed worship, but were for reconciling the worship of God with that of idols. God says,* I will assemble her that halteth, and her that is driven out, Mic. 4. 6. *That is, I will restore my people of the* Jews, *though now in a weak, banished, afflicted condition, to their former privileges, and plant them in their own country; I will determine such of them to return, who seem unresolved whether to go or not. The Psalmist says, that his enemies rejoiced to see him halt,* Psal. 35. 15. But in mine adversity, *Heb.* halting, they rejoiced. *When I was in great danger of falling into trouble; when I had any sickness, or ill success in my affairs. And in* Jer. 20. 10. All my familiars watched for my halting: *They lay in wait to take me tripping in any thing, if they could, that they might give mine adversaries any advantage against me.*

1 Kings 18. 21. how long h. ye between two opinions?
Psal. 38. 17. am ready to h. my sorrow is before me

HALTED.

Gen. 32. 31. as Jacob passed, he h. upon his thigh
Mic. 4. 7. I will make her that h. a remnant

HALTETH.

Mic. 4. 6. in that day I will assemble her that h.
Zeph. 3. 19. behold at that time I will save her that h.

HALTING.

Jer. 20. 10. all my familiars watched for my h.

HAMMER.

Judg. 4. 21. then Jael took an h. in her hand
5. 26. with h. she smote Sisera, smote off his head
1 Kings 6. 7. was neither h. nor axe heard in house
Isa. 41. 7. and he that smootheth with the h.
Jer. 23. 29. like a h. that breaketh rock in pieces
50. 23. how is the h. of whole earth cut asunder
Nah. 2. † 1. the h. is come up before thy face

HAMMERS.

Psal. 74. 6. break down the carved work with h.
Isa. 44. 12. the smith fashioneth it with h.
Jer. 10. 4. they fasten it with nails and with h.

HAND

Is a part of the body well known. By hand, *is sometimes understood the vengeance of God exercised upon any one;* 1 Sam. 5. 6, 7. The hand of the Lord was heavy upon them of *Ashdod, after they had taken the ark, and had been told that it should continue to oppress them, till they should send it back with presents.*

To pour water on any one's hands, *signifies to serve him. Thus* Elisha *is said to have poured water on* Elijah's *hands, thereby meaning that he was his servant,* 2 Kings 3. 11.

To wash one's hands, *denoted that the person was innocent of manslaughter, when the murderer was not known,* Deut. 21. 6, 7. Pilate *washed his hands,* Mat. 27. 24. *to denote his being innocent of what was required of him, when he proceeded to condemn* Jesus, *in whom he found nothing to deserve such a sentence. Some think that* Pilate, *living among the* Jews, *had learned this rite from them; but others are of opinion, that it was a ceremony used in protestations of innocency among other people as well as the* Jews.

To kiss one's hand, *is an act of adoration,* Job 31. 27. If I beheld the sun when it shined, and my mouth hath kissed my hand.

To fill one's hand, *signifies to put one in possession of the priesthood, to enter him in the enjoyment of the sacerdotal dignity; because in this ceremony the parts of the victim which were to be offered were put into the new priest's hand.* Exod. 28. 41. Thou shalt consecrate them; *in Hebrew,* fill their hand. *See also* Judg. 17. 5, 12. 1 Kings 13. 33.

To lean upon any one's hand, *is a mark of familiarity and superiority. The king of Israel had one of his confidents upon whom he leaned,* 2 Kings 7. 2, 17. *And in like manner the king of* Syria *leaned on* Naaman, *when he went up to the temple of his god* Rimmon, *2 Kings* 5. 18.

To lift up one's hand, *is a way of taking an oath in use with all nations,* Gen. 14. 22. I have lifted up mine hands unto the Lord. *It was likewise a posture used in praying for a blessing upon the people.* Lev. 9. 22. *Aaron* lifted up his hands towards the people, and blessed them. To lift up the hand against one, *is to rebel against him.* 2 Sam. 20. 21. *Sheba* hath lifted up his hand against king *David.*

To give one's hand, *signifies to grant peace, to swear friendship, to promise all security, to make alliance.* 2 Kings 10. 15. *Jehu* said to *Jehonadab,* Is thine heart right, as my heart is with thy heart? If it be, give me thine hand; and he gave him his hand. *The* Jews *say, they were obliged* to give the hand *to the* Egyptians *and* Assyrians, *that they might procure bread: that is, to surrender to them, to make an alliance with them, that they might be enabled to subsist, that in their extreme necessity they might preserve their lives. Others think that by this phrase is meant, that the* Jews *were glad to labour with their hands, and work for them, in order to procure the necessaries of life,* Lam. 5. 6.

Right hand. *The* right hand *denotes power, strength. The scripture generally imputes to God's* right hand *all the effects of his omnipotence.* Exod. 15. 6. Thy right hand, O Lord, is become glorious in power; thy right hand, O Lord, hath dashed in pieces the enemy. *See* Psal. 17. 7. | 20. 6. | 44. 3.

To sit down on the right hand of God. *The Son of God is often represented as sitting at the* right hand *of his heavenly Father.* Psal. 110. 1. The Lord said to my Lord, sit thou at my right hand. *Thou hast done thy work upon earth, now take possession of that sovereign kingdom and glory; which by right belongeth to thee; do thou rule with authority and honour, as thou art Mediator.*

The right hand *commonly denotes the south, as the left hand denotes the north. For the* Hebrews *speak of the quarters of the world in respect of themselves, having their faces turned towards the east, their backs to the west, their* right hands *to the south, and their left to the north. Thus* Kedem, *which signifies* before, *stands also for the east; and* Achor, *which signifies* behind, *marks out the west;* Jamin, *the* right hand, *is the south; and* Shemol, *the* left hand, *is the north. For example:* Doth not David hide himself with us in strong holds in the woods, in the hill of Hachilah, which is on the south of Jeshimon? Heb. *on the* right hand *of* Jeshimon. *See* EAST.

The accuser was commonly at the right hand *of the accused.* Psal. 109. 6. Let Satan stand at his right hand. *And in* Zech. 3. 1. *Satan was at the* right hand *of the high priest* Joshua *to accuse him.*

Often, in a contrary sense, to be at one's right hand *signifies to defend, to protect, to support him.* Psal. 16. 8. | 109. 31. I have set the Lord always before me; because he is at my right hand I shall not be moved. For he shall stand at the right hand of the poor, to save him from those that condemn his soul.

To turn from the law of God, neither to the *right hand,* nor to the left, *is a frequent Scripture expression,* Josh. 1. 7. | 23. 6. 2 Kings 22. 2. *The meaning is, that we must not depart from it at all, neither by attempting to go beyond it, and doing more than it requires, nor by doing less. But we must observe it closely, constantly, and invariably, as a traveller, who does not go out of his way, either to the right or to the left.*

Our Saviour, in Mat. 6. 3. *to shew with what privacy we should do good works, says,* That our left hand should not know what our right hand does. *Above all things we should avoid vanity and ostentation in all the good we undertake to do, and should not think that thereby we merit any thing.*

To stretch or spread out the hands, *is sometimes a gesture that denotes mercy.* Isa. 65. 2. I have spread out my hands all the day unto a rebellious people; *I have invited them by my prophets, and used all means to allure them to myself. So in* Prov. 1. 24. I have called, and ye have refused; I have stretched out my hand, and no man regarded. I would not put forth my hand against the Lord's anointed, *I would not kill him,* 1 Sam. 24. 10. To put forth one's hand upon any thing, *to take, to steal it.* Exod. 22. 8, 11. He shall swear that he hath not put his hands to his neighbour's goods.

Hand *is likewise frequently taken for the power and impression of the Holy Spirit felt by some prophet.* 1 Kings 18. 46. The hand of the Lord was on Elijah. *See* 2 Kings 3. 15. Ezek. 1. 3. | 3. 14. *It is said in several places, that God gave his law, or sent his orders,* by the hand of Moses, *or some other prophet; that he spake to his people* by the hand of prophets, &c. *that is, by their means, by their mouth.*

Laying on hands, *or* imposition of hands, *is understood in different ways both in the Old and New Testament.* (1) *It is often taken for ordination and consecration of priests and ministers, as well among the* Jews *as* Christians, *Num.* 8. 10. *Acts* 6. 6. | 13. 3. 1 *Tim.* 4. 14. (2) *It is sometimes also made use of to signify the establishment of judges and magistrates, on whom it was usual to lay hands, when they were intrusted with these employments: Thus when* Moses *constituted* Joshua *his successor, God appointed him to* lay his hands upon him, *Num.* 27. 18. Jacob *laid his hands upon* Ephraim *and* Manasseh, *when he gave them his last blessing,* Gen. 48. 14.

The high priest stretched out his hands to the people, as often as he recited the solemn form of blessing, Lev. 9. 22. *The* Israelites *who presented sin-offerings at the tabernacle, confessed their sins, while they laid their hands upon them,* Lev. 1. 4. *This testified that the person acknowledged himself worthy of death, that he laid his sins upon the sacrifice, that he trusted in* Christ *for the expiation of his sins, and that he devoted himself to God. Witnesses laid their hands upon the head of the accused person, as it were to signify that they charged upon him the guilt of his blood, and freed themselves from it,* Deut. 13. 9. | 17. 7. *Our Saviour laid his hands upon the children that were presented to him, and blessed them,* Mark 10. 16. *And the Holy Ghost was conferred on those who were baptized, by the laying on of the apostle's hands,* Acts 8. 17. | 19. 6.

Hand when referred, I. *To God, signifies,* [1] *His eternal purposes, and executive power,* Acts 4. 28. 30. [2] *His providential bounty and goodness,* Psal. 104. 28. [3] *His mighty power to preserve and defend,* John 10. 28, 29. [4] *His frowns and corrections,* Judg. 2. 15. Psal. 32. 4. | 38. 2. [5] *His sovereign dispose,* Psal. 31. 15. [6] *His help,* Neh. 2. 8. Psal. 74. 11. [7] *His favour,* Luke 1. 66. [8.] *His Spirit,* 1 Kings 18. 46. Ezek. 1. 3. | 37. 1. [9] *His providence,* 1 Chron. 29. 16. Job 2. 10.

Referred, II. *To men, signifieth,* [1] *An instrument,* Exod. 4. 13. Hag. 1. † 1. [2] *Power,* Prov. 3. 27. [3] *His help,* 2 Kings 15. 19. [4] *Possession,* 1 Kings 11. 31. [5] *Advice,* 2 Sam. 14. 19. [6] *Tyranny,* Exod. 18. 9. [7] *Work,* Acts 20. 34.

Gen. 9. 2. into your *h.* are they delivered
39. 6. he left all that he had in Joseph's *h.*
44. 17. but the man in whose *h.* the cup is found
Exod. 6. 1. with a strong *h.* shall he drive them out
13. 3. by strength of *h.* Lord brought out
14. 8. Israel went out with an high *h. Num.* 33. 3.
16. stretch out thine *h.* over the sea
† 31. Israel saw that great *h.* Lord did on Egypt
17. † 16. the *h.* upon the throne of the Lord
19. 13. there shall not a *h.* touch it, but he shall
21. 24. *h.* for *h.* foot for foot, *Deut.* 19. 21.
28. † 41. anoint them, and fill their *h.* 29. † 9.
34. 29. two tables of the testimony in Moses' *h.*
38. 15. on this *h.* and that *h.* were hangings
Lev. 12. † 8. if her *h.* find not sufficiency, then
25. 28. remain in the *h.* of him that bought it
Num. 15. † 30. soul that doeth ought with an high *h.*
35. † 17. if he smite him with the stone of the *h.*
Deut. 13. 9. afterwards the *h.* of all the people
25. 12. thou shalt cut off her *h.* pity her not
32. † 36. repent, when he seeth their *h.* is gone
Josh. 2. 19. his blood on our head if any *h.* on him
Judg. 1. 35. the *h.* of the house of Joseph prevailed
4. 9. the Lord shall sell Sisera into *h.* of a woman
15. 18. now fall into the *h.* of the uncircumcised
17. † 5. Micah filled the *h.* of one of his sons
20. 48. Isr. smote all that came to *h.* of Benjamin
1 *Sam.* 12. 3. of whose *h.* have I received any bribe?
13. 22. nor spear found in the *h.* of any of Israel
17. 50. there was no sword in the *h.* of David
20. 19. didst hide thyself when the business was in *h.*
22. 17. because their *h.* also is with David
2 *Sam.* 13. 5. that I may see, and eat it at her *h.* 6.
14. 19. is not the *h.* of Joab with thee in all this?
21. 20. had on every *h.* six fingers, 1 *Chron.* 20. 6.
24. 14. let me not fall into *h.* of men, 1 *Chr.* 21. 13.
1 *Kings* 2. 46. kingdom established in *h.* of Solomon
13. 6. and the king's *h.* was restored again
18. 44. there ariseth a cloud like a man's *h.*
22. 6. they said, go up, for the Lord shall deliver it into the king's *h.* 12, 15. 2 *Chron.* 28. 5.
2 *Kings* 7. 2. lord on whose *h.* the king leaned, 17.
13. 5. went out from under the *h.* of the Syrians
19. † 26. inhabitants were short of *h. Isa.* 37. † 27.
1 *Chr.* 29. † 24. sons of Dav. gave *h.* under Solom.
2 *Chron.* 12. 5. hath Lord left you in *h.* of Shishak
Ezra 7. 9. according to good *h.* of his God on him
9. 2. the *h.* of princes have been chief in trespass
Job 9. 24. earth is given into the *h.* of the wicked
12. 6. into whose *h.* God bringeth abundantly
10. in whose *h.* is the soul of every living thing
20. 22. every *h.* of the wicked shall come on him
21. 16. lo, their good is not in their *h.*
34. 20. the mighty shall be taken away without *h.*
37. 7. he sealeth up the *h.* of every man
Psal. 31. 8. thou hast not shut me into *h.* of enemy
36. 11. let not the *h.* of the wicked remove me
71. 4. deliv. me out of *h.* of wicked, 82. 4. | 97. 10.
123. 2. as eyes of servants look to the *h.* of masters
127. 4. as arrows are in the *h.* of a mighty man
149. 6. let a two-edged sword be in their *h.*
Prov. 6. 3. when thou art come into *h.* of thy friend
10. 4. he becometh poor that dealeth with a slack *h.* but the *h.* of the diligent maketh rich
11. 21. tho' *h.* join *h.* wicked not unpunished, 16. 5.
12. 24. the *h.* of the diligent shall bear rule
17. 16. why a price in *h.* of a fool to get wisdom?
26. 9. as a thorn goeth up into the *h.* of a drunkard
Eccl. 4. † 1. on the *h.* of their oppressors was power
Isa. 10. 5. the staff in their *h.* is my indignation
13. 2. shake the *h.* that they may go into the gates
14. 26. and this is the *h.* that is stretched out
19. 4. I will give over into the *h.* of a cruel lord
28. 2. Ld. shall cast down to the earth with the *h.*
Jer. 12. 7. have given dearly belov. into *h.* of ene.
18. 4. vessel was marred in the *h.* of the potter
6. as clay in the potter's *h.* so are ye in mine
21. 5. with an outstretched *h.* I will fight ag. you
26. 24. the *h.* of Ahikam was with Jeremiah, not to give him into *h.* of people to put him to death
50. 15. shout agst. her round, she hath given her *h.*
Lam. 5. 6. we have given the *h.* to the Egyptians
12. princes are hanged up by their *h.*
Ezek. 2. 9. an *h.* was sent me, and lo, a roll
8. 3. and he put forth the form of an *h.* 10. 8.
16. 49. nor did she strengthen the *h.* of the needy
21. † 14. prophesy, and smite *h.* to *h.* together
24. I say, ye shall be taken with the *h.*
28. 9. be no god in the *h.* of him that slayeth thee
34. 10. behold, I will require my flock at their *h.*
37. 19. take the stick which is in the *h.* of Ephraim
40. 5. and in the man's *h.* a measuring reed
Dan. 5. 5. there came forth the fingers of a man's *h.*
23. God, in whose *h.* thy breath is, hast not glorif.
8. 25. but he shall be broken without *h.*
10. 10. behold, an *h.* touched me, which set me

Joel 3. 8. sell sons and daughters into *h.* of Judah
Mic. 2. 1. because it is in the power of their *h.*
Zech. 4. 10. shall see plummet in *h.* of Zerubbabel
Mat. 8. 15. he touched her *h.* ‖ 22. 13. bind him *h.*
Mark 3. 1. a man who had a withered *h.* 3. *Luke* 6. 8
14. 41. the Son of man is betrayed into *h.* of sinners
Luke 1. 1. as many have taken in *h.* to set forth
74. being delivered out of the *h.* of our enemies
22. 21. the *h.* of him that betrayeth me is with me
John 10. 39. but he escaped out of their *h.*
11. 44. that was dead came forth, bound *h.* and foot
Acts 12. 17. Peter beckoning to them with the *h.*
1 *Cor.* 12. 15. because I am not the *h.* I am not body
21. eye cannot say to the *h.* I have no need of thee
Gal. 3. 19. ordained by angels in the *h.* of a mediator
Rev. 10. 8. take little book open in *h.* of the angel
17. 4. the woman, having a golden cup in her *h.*
19. 2. hath avenged the blood of servants at her *h.*

At HAND, or *at the* HAND.

Gen. 9. 5. *at the h.* of every beast I will require it, *at the h.* of man, *at the h.* of man's brother
27. 41. the days of mourning for my father are *at h.*
33. 19. field Jacob bought *at h.* of child. of Hamor
Deut. 15. 9. saying, the year of release is *at h.*
32. 35. for the day of their calamity is *at h.*
1 *Sam.* 9. 8. I have here *at h.* fourth part of a shekel
20. 16. let Lord require it *at h.* of David's enemies
2 *Kings* 9. 7. may avenge blood *at the h.* of Jezebel
Neh. 11. 24. Pethahiah was *at the* king's *h.* in all
Isa. 13. 6. day of Lord is *at h. Joel* 1. 15. *Zeph.* 1. 7
Jer. 23. 23. am I a God *at h.* and not a God afar off?
Ezek. 12. 23. the days are *at h.* and effect of vision
33. 6. but his blood will I require *at* watchman's *h.*
36. 8. and yield fruit, for they are *at h.* to come
Joel 2. 1. the day of the Lord cometh, it is nigh *at h.*
Mat. 3. 2. kingdom of heaven is *at h.* 4. 17. | 10. 7.
26. 18. my time is *at h.* ‖ 45. the hour is *at h.*
46. he is *at h.* that doth betray me, *Mark* 14. 42.
Mark 1. 15. kingdom of God is *at h. Luke* 21. 31.
Luke 21. 30. that summer is now nigh *at h.*
John 2. 13. and the Jews' passover was *at h.* 11. 55.
7. 2. now the Jews' feast of tabernacles was *at h.*
19. 42. for the sepulchre was nigh *at h.*
Rom. 13. 12. the night is far spent, the day is *at h.*
Phil. 4. 5. let moderation be known, the Lord is *at h.*
2 *Thess.* 2. 2. as that the day of Christ is *at h.*
2 *Tim.* 4. 6. the time of my departure is *at h.*
1 *Pet.* 4. 7. the end of all things is *at h.* be ye sober
Rev. 1. 3. for the time is *at h.* 22. 10.

By the HAND.

Exod. 4. 13. send *by h.* of him whom thou wilt send
38. 21. sum of tabernacle counted *by h.* of Ithamar
Lev. 8. 36. which Lord commanded *by h.* of Moses, 10. 11. | 26. 46. *Num.* 4. 37, 45, 49. | 9. 23. | 10. 13. | 15. 23. | 16. 40. | 27. 23. | 36. 13. *Josh.* 14. 2. | 20. 2. | 21. 2, 8. | 22. 9. *Judg.* 3. 4. 1 *Kings* 8. 53, 56. 2 *Chron.* 33. 8. | 35. 6. *Neh.* 9. 14. *Psal.* 77. 20.
16. 21. send him away *by the h.* of a fit man
Josh. 20. 9. not die *by the h.* of the avenger of blood
Judg. 16. 26. Samson said to lad that held *by the h.*
1 *Sam.* 18. 25. make Dav. fall *by the h.* of Philistines
27. 1. I shall one day perish *by h.* of Saul
2 *Sam.* 3. 18. *by the h.* of my servant David I will save
10. 2. David sent to comfort him *by h.* of servants
11. 14. David wrote a letter, sent it *by h.* of Uriah
12. 25. he sent *by the h.* of Nathan the prophet
21. 22. they fell *by the h.* of David, 1 *Chr.* 20. 8.
1 *Kings* 2. 25. Solomon sent *by the h.* of Benaiah
14. 18. which he spake *by the h.* of his serv. Ahijah
16. 7. also *by the h.* of Jehu came word of the Lord
2 *Kings* 14. 25. which he spake *by the h.* of Jonah
27. he saved them *by the h.* of Jeroboam
2 *Chr.* 10. 15. word which he spake *by h.* of Ahijah
12. 7. not pour out wrath *by the h.* of Shishak
Ezra 1. 8. bring out vessels *by the h.* of Mithredath
8. 33. the vessels weighed *by the h.* of Meremoth
Job 8. † 20. nor will he take ungodly *by the h.*
Prov. 26. 6. that sendeth a message *by h.* of a fool
Isa. 51. 18. nor any that taketh her *by the h.*
Jer. 27. 3. send yokes *by the h.* of the messengers
31. 32. in the day I took them *by the h. Heb.* 8. 9.
Ezek. 25. 14. my vengeance on Edom *by h.* of Israel
30. 12. I will lay the land waste *by h.* of strangers
Hos. 12. † 10. used similitudes *by the h.* of prophets
Mat. 9. 25. he went in and took her *by the h. Mark* 1. 31. | 5. 41. *Luke* 8. 54.
Mark 8. 23. he took the blind man *by h.* and led him
9. 27. Jesus took him that was possessed *by the h.*
Acts 7. 35. send to be a deliverer *by h.* of the angel
9. 8. he saw no man, but they led him *by the h.*
13. 11. he went seeking some to lead him *by the h.*
Col. 4. 18. the salutation *by the h.* of me, Paul

See CHALDEANS, ENEMY.

HAND joined with *enemies.*

1 *Sam.* 4. 3. the ark of the covenant may save us out of the *h.* of our *enemies,* 12. 10. 2 *Sam.* 3. 18.
12. 11. deliv. you out of *h.* of *e.* 2 *Kings* 17. 39.
2 *Sam.* 18. † 19. Lord judged him from *h.* of *enemies*
19. 9. the king saved us out of the *h.* of our *enemies*
2 *Kings* 21. 14. I will deliver them into the *h.* of their *enemies,* 2 *Chron.* 25. 20. *Neh.* 9. 27.
Neh. 9. 28. leftest thou them in *h.* of their *enemies*
Ps. 31. 15. deliver me from the *h.* of mine *enemies*
Jer. 20. 5. I will give this city into the *h.* of their *enemies,* 21. 7. | 34. 20, 21. *Ezek.* 39. 23.
44. 30. I will give Pharaoh into *h.* of his *enemies*
Mic. 4. 10. redeem thee from the *h.* of thy *enemies*
Luke 1. 74. delivered out of the *h.* of our *enemies*

From the HAND.

Gen. 32. 11. deliver me *from h.* of my brother Esau
Deut. 7. 8. L. redeemed you *from the h.* of Pharaoh
Judg. 8. 22. thou hast delivered us *from h.* of Midian
1 *Sam.* 25. 39. pleaded my reproach *from h.* of Nabal
Job 5. 15. he saveth the poor *from the h.* of mighty
6. 23. or redeem me *from the h.* of the mighty
Ps. 22. † 20. deliver my darling *from h.* of the dog
49. † 15. God will redeem my soul *from h.* of grave
89. 48. deliver his soul *from the h.* of the grave
106. 10. he saved them *from the h.* of him that hated them, and redeemed them *from h.* of the enemy

Ps. 144. 7. deliver me from h. of strange children, 11.
Prov. 6. 5. deliver thyself as a roe from h. of hunter
Jer. 20. 13. he hath delivered poor from h. of evil
31. 11. from h. of him that was stronger than he
Dan. 6. † 27. delivered Daniel from h. of the lions
Hos. 13. † 14. I will ransom them from h. of the grave
Luke 1. 71. be saved from the h. of all that hate us

HAND *of God*.

1 Sam. 5. 11. h. of God was heavy on them of Ashdod
2 Chr. 30. 12. h. of God was to give them one heart
Ezra 7. 9. according to the good h. of God, Neh. 2. 8.
8. 18. by good h. of God upon us, they brought us
22. h. of God is upon all them for good that seek
31. the h. of God is upon us, and he delivered us
Neh. 2. 18. then I told them of the h. of God on me
Job 2. 10. shall we receive good at the h. of God?
19. 21. have pity on me, h. of God hath touched me
27. 11. I will teach you by the h. of God
Eccl. 2. 24. this I saw that it was from the h. of God
9. 1. the wise and their works are in the h. of God
Isa. 62. 3. shalt be a royal diadem in h. of thy God
Mark 16. 19. into heaven, and sat on right h. of God,
Rom. 8. 34. Col. 3. 1. Heb. 10. 12. 1 Pet. 3. 22.
Acts 2. 33. being by the right h. of God exalted
7. 55. saw Jesus standing on the right h. of God, 56.
1 Pet. 5. 6. humble yourselves under the h. of God

His HAND.

Gen. 3. 22. lest he put forth his h. and take tree of life
16. 12. his h. will be against every man, and every man's hand against him
19. 16. while he lingered, men laid hold on his h.
24. 10. all the goods of his master were in his h.
32. 13. Jacob took of that which came to his h.
39. 3. Lord made all that he did prosper in his h.
41. 42. Pharaoh took the ring off his h. and put it
Exod. 4. 4. he put forth his h. it became a rod in his h.
6. when he took it out, his h. was leprous as snow
20. Moses took the rod of God in his h.
8. 6. Aaron stretched out his h. over the waters, 17.
10. 22. Moses stretched forth his h. toward heaven
17. 11. when Moses held up his h. let down his h.
21. 13. but God delivered him into his h.
16. if found in his h. || 20. he die under his h.
22. 4. if the theft be certainly found in his h. alive
8. to see whether he hath put his h. to goods, 11.
24. 11. on the nobles of Israel he laid not his h.
32. 15. two tables of testimony were in his h. 34. 4.
Lev. 1. 4. he shall put his h. on head of burnt-offering
5. † 7. if his h. cannot reach to sufficiency of a lamb
16. † 32. the priest whom he shall fill his h.
Num. 5. 18. priest shall have in his h. bitter water
6. 21. besides that that his h. shall get
21. 26. and had taken all his land out of his h.
22. 23. his sword drawn in his h. 31. 1 Chr. 21. 16.
25. 7. Phinehas took a javelin in his h. and went
Deut. 19. 5. his h. fetcheth a stroke with the axe
Josh. 5. 13. a man with his sword drawn in his h.
8. 26. Joshua drew not his h. back till destroyed
20. 5. shall not deliver the slayer up into his h.
Judg. 6. 21. put forth the end of the staff in his h.
7. 14. into his h. hath God delivered Midian
1 Sam. 6. 3. known why his h. is not remov. from you
9. that it is not his h. that smote us, but chance
14. 26. but no man put his h. to his mouth
27. but Jonathan put his h. to his mouth
16. 16. that he shall play with his h. thou be well
23. took an harp and played with his h. 18. 10.
17. 40. David took his staff and his sling in his h.
57. with the head of the Philistine in his h.
19. 5. he put his life in his h. and slew the Philistine
23. 16. and Jonathan strengthened his h. in God
2 Sam. 6. 6. Uzzah put his h. to ark, 1 Chr. 13. 10.
1 Kings 8. 15. and hath with his h. fulfilled it
11. 34. nor take the whole kingdom out of his h.
13. 4. his h. which he put forth against him dried up
2 Kings 5. 11. call on Ld. and strike his h. over place
10. 15. he gave him his h. took him up in chariot
11. 8. ye shall compass the king every man with his weapons in his h. 11. 2 Chron. 23. 7.
14. 5. the kingdom was confirmed in his h.
15. 19. his h. might be with him to confirm kingdom
18. 21. on which if a man lean will go into his h.
19. 19. I beseech thee, save us out of his h.
1 Chr. 28. 19. made me understand by his h. on me
29. † 5. who is willing to fill his h. this day?
2 Chron. 26. 19. Uzziah had a censer in his h.
36. 17. he gave them all into his h.
Neh. 6. 5. sent his servant with open letter in his h.
Job 6. 9. he would let loose his h. and cut me off
15. 23. the day of darkness is ready at his h.
25. for he stretcheth out his h. against God
26. 13. his h. hath formed the crooked serpent
27. 22. he would fain flee out of his h.
28. 9. he putteth forth his h. upon the rock
Psal. 37. 24. the Lord upholdeth him with his h.
33. the Lord will not leave him in his h.
78. 42. they remembered not his h. nor the day
89. 25. I will set his h. also in the sea, and right hand
95. 4. in his h. are the deep places of the earth
7. sheep of his h. to-day if ye will hear his voice
106. 26. therefore he lifted up his h. against them
129. 7. wherewith the mower filleth not his h.
Prov. 7. † 20. hath taken a bag of money in his h.
19. 24. a slothful man hideth his h. 26. 15.
Eccl. 5. 14. begets a son, and nothing is in his h.
15. nothing which he may carry away in his h.
Cant. 5. 4. my beloved put in his h. by hole of door
Isa. 5. 25. his anger not turned away, but his h. is stretched out still, 9. 12, 17, 21. | 10. 4. | 14. 27.
10. 32. he shall shake his h. against mount Zion
11. 11. Lord shall set his h. again the second time
15. and he shall shake his h. over the river
22. 21. I will commit thy government into his h.
28. 4. while it is yet in his h. he eateth it up
31. 3. when the Lord shall stretch out his h.
37. 20. therefore, O Lord, save us from his h.
40. 12. who measured waters in hollow of his h.
44. 5. another shall subscribe with his h. to Lord
49. 2. in the shadow of his h. hath he hid me
53. 10. the pleasure of Lord shall prosper in his h.
56. 2. and keepeth his h. from doing any evil
Jer. 27. 8. till I have consumed them by his h.
Lam. 1. 14. yoke of my transgression bound by h. h.
2. 8. he hath not withdrawn his h. from destroying
3. 3. he turneth his h. against me all the day
Ezek. 8. 11. even every man with his censer in his h.
9. 1. every man with his destroying weapon in h. h.
17. 18. despiseth oath, when lo, he had given his h.
30. 22. I will cause the sword to fall out of his h.
24. and I will put my sword in his h.
46. 7. for lambs according as his h. shall attain unto
Dan. 4. 35. none can stay h. h. or say, what doest thou
8. 4. neither any that could deliver out of his h. 7.
25. he shall cause craft to prosper in his h.
11. 11. but the multitude shall be given into his h.
41. but these shall escape out of h. h. even Edom
Hos. 7. 5. he stretched out his h. with scorners
12. 7. the balances of deceit are in his h.
Hab. 3. 4. he had horns coming out of his h.
Zeph. 2. 15. passeth her shall hiss and wag his h.
Zech. 8. 4. every man with staff in his h. for very age
14. 13. his h. rise up ag. the hand of his neighbour
Mat. 3. 12. whose fan is in his h. Luke 3. 17.
26. 23. he that dippeth his h. with me in the dish
Mark 3. 5. and his h. was restored whole, Luke 6. 10.
7. 32. they beseech him to put his h. upon him
Luke 9. 62. no man having put his h. to the plough
15. 22. put a ring on his h. and shoes on his feet
John 3. 35. and hath given all things into his h.
18. 22. an officer struck him with the palm of his h.
Acts 7. 25. how God by his h. would deliver them
28. 3. a viper fastened on his h. || 4. hang on his h.
Rev. 6. 5. he that sat had a pair of balances in his h.
10. 2. and he had in his h. a little book open
14. 9. receive his mark in his forehead, or in his h.
14. having golden crown, and in h. h. sharp sickle
20. 1. an angel came with a great chain in his h.

HAND *of the Lord*, or *Lord's* HAND.

Exod. 9. 3. the h. of the Lord is upon thy cattle
16. 3. would to God we had died by h. of the Lord
Num. 11. 23. said to Moses, is Lord's h. waxed short?
Deut. 2. 15. h. of the L. was against them to destroy
Josh. 4. 24. all people know that h. of Lord is mighty
22. 31. ye have delivered Israel out of h. of the L.
Judg. 2. 15. the h. of the Lord was ag. them for evil
Ruth 1. 13. the h. of the Lord is gone out against me
1 Sam. 5. 6. h. of L. was heavy on them of Ashdod
9. h. of L. was against the city with destruction
7. 13. the h. of the Lord was against the Philistines
12. 15. then shall the h. of the Lord be against you
2 Sam. 24. 14. let us fall into h. of L. 1 Chr. 21. 13.
1 Kings 18. 46. the h. of the Lord was on Elijah
2 Kings 3. 15. that the h. of L. came upon Elisha
Ezra 7. 6. king granted according to h. of L. on him
Job 12. 9. h. of Lord hath wrought this, Isa. 40. 20.
Psal. 75. 8. in the h. of the Lord there is a cup
Prov. 21. 1. king's heart is in the h. of the Lord
Isa. 19. 16. because of the shaking of the h. of Lord
25. 10. in this mountain shall the h. of the L. rest
40. 2. she hath received of the Lord's h. double
51. 17. hast drunk at h. of Lord the cup of his fury
59. 1. Lord's h. is not shortened, that it cannot save
62. 3. thou shalt be a crown of glory in h. of Lord
66. 14. h. of Lord shall be known toward servants
Jer. 25. 17. then took I the cup at the Lord's h.
51. 7. Babylon hath been a golden cup in Lord's h.
Ezek. 1. 3. the h. of the Lord was there upon him
3. 14. the h. of the L. was upon me, 22. | 8. 1. | 37. 1.
33. 22. the h. of the Lord was on me in the evening
40. 1. the self-same day the h. of Lord was with him
Luke 1. 66. and the h. of the Lord was with him
Acts 11. 21. the h. of the Lord was with them
13. 11. behold, the h. of the Lord is upon thee

See LAY, or LAID.

Left HAND.

Gen. 13. 9. if thou wilt take left h. I will go to right
14. 15. Hobah which is on left h. of Damascus
24. 49. that I may turn to the right h. or to the left
48. 13. Joseph took Ephraim in his right hand toward Israel's left h. and Manasseh in his left h.
14. Israel laid his left h. upon Manasseh's head
Exod. 14. 22. waters a wall on the right h. and left
Lev. 14. 15. pour the oil into his own left h. 27.
Num. 20. 17. we will not turn to the right h. nor to the left, Deut. 2. 27. | 5. 32. | 17. 11, 20. | 28. 14.
22. 26. no way to turn either to right h. or left
Josh. 1. 7. turn not from it to right h. or to left, that thou mayest prosper, 23. 6. 1 Sam. 6. 12. Prov. 4. 27.
Judg. 3. 21. Ehud put forth left h. and took dagger
7. 20. the companies held lamps in their left h.
16. 29. Samson took hold of other pillar with left h.
2 Sam. 2. 19. he turned not to left h. from following
14. 19. none can turn to the right h. or to the left
16. 6. all the mighty men were on right h. and left
1 Kings 22. 19. host of heaven on his left h. 2 Chr. 18. 18.
2 Kings 22. 2. Josiah turned not to the right h. or left
23. 8. which were on a man's left h. at the gate
1 Chr. 6. 44. the sons of Merari stood on the left h.
12. 2. they could use both right h. and left in hurl.
2 Chr. 3. 17. he called name of that on left h. Boaz
4. 6. and he put five on the left h. to wash in them
7. five candlesticks on the right, five on the left h.
Neh. 8. 4. Ezra on pulpit, on his left h. stood Pedaiah
Job 23. 9. on left h. he doth work, not behold him
Prov. 3. 16. and in her left h. riches and honour
Eccl. 10. 2. but a fool's heart is at his left h.
Cant. 2. 6. left h. is under my head, right embraces
8. 3. his left h. under my head, right embrace me
Isa. 9. 20. he shall eat on left h. and not be satisfied
30. 21. ears hear a word, when ye turn to the left h.
54. 3. thou shalt break forth on the right h. and left
Ezek. 16. 46. her daughters dwell at thy left h.
21. 16. go thee either on the right h. or on the left
39. 3. I will smite thy bow out of thy left h.
Dan. 12. 7. when he held up his left h. to heaven
Jonah 4. 11. cannot discern between right h. and left
Zech. 12. 6. shall dev. all people on right h. and left
Mat. 6. 3. let not left h. know what thy right doeth
20. 21. one on right h. other on left, Mark 10. 37.
23. to sit on right h. and left not mine, Mark 10. 40.
25. 33. he shall set sheep on his right h. goats on left
41. he shall say to them on left h. depart from me
Mat. 27. 38. were two thieves, one crucified on right h. other on the left, Mark 15. 27. Luke 23. 33
Acts 21. 3. we left Cyprus on the left h. and sailed
2 Cor. 6. 7. armour of righteousn. on right h. and left

See LIFT hand or hands.

Mighty HAND.

Exod. 3. 19. will not let you go, no not with mighty h.
32. 11. people thou broughtest forth with mighty h.
Deut. 3. 24. hast began to shew servant thy mighty h.
4. 34. assayed to take him a nation by a mighty h.
5. 15. God brought thee out of Egypt by a mighty h. 6. 21. | 7. 8, 19. | 9. 26. | 11. 2. | 26. 8. | 34. 12.
2 Chr. 6. 32. stranger that is come for thy mighty h.
Ezek. 20. 33. with a mighty h. will I rule over you
34. and I will bring you out with a mighty h.
Dan. 9. 15. brought you out of Egypt with mighty h.
1 Pet. 5. 6. humble yourselves under mighty h. of G.

Mine and *my* HAND.

Gen. 14. 22. I have lifted up mine h. unto the Lord
21. 30. seven ewe-lambs shalt thou take of my h.
31. 29. it is in the power of my h. to do you hurt
39. I bear loss, of my h. didst thou require it
33. 10. I pray thee, receive my present at my h.
42. 37. deliver him into my h. I will bring him thee
43. 9. I'll be surety, of my h. shalt thou require him
Exod. 7. 17. I'll smite with the rod that is in mine h.
15. 9. my h. shall destroy them || 17. 9. rod in mine h.
33. 22. I will cover thee with my h. while I pass
23. I will take away mine h. and thou shalt see
Num. 21. 2. if thou wilt deliver this people into my h.
22. 29. I would there were a sword in mine h.
Deut. 8. 17. might of my h. hath gotten me this wealth
10. 3. went up, having the two tables in mine h.
32. 39. nor any that can deliver out of my h. Isa. 43. 13.
40. I lift up my h. to heav. and say, I live for ever
41. and if mine h. take hold on judgment
Judg. 6. 36. if thou wilt save Israel by my h. 37.
7. 2. lest vaunt, saying, mine own h. hath saved me
8. 7. when Lord hath delivered Zeba into mine h.
9. 29. would to God this people were under my h.
12. 3. and the Lord delivered them into my h.
17. 3. dedicated the silver to the Lord from my h.
1 Sam. 12. 5. that ye have not found ought in my h.
17. 46. Lord will deliver thee this day into mine h.
18. 17. Saul said, let not mine h. be upon him
21. 4. there is no common bread under mine h.
23. 7. God hath delivered him into mine h.
24. 6. to stretch mine h. against Lord's anointed
11. see skirt in mine h. no transgression in m. h.
12. but mine h. shall not be upon thee, 13.
26. 18. what have I done? what evil is in mine h.?
23. Lord delivered thee into my h. to-day, 24. 10.
28. 21. I have put my life in my h. and hearkened
2 Sam. 3. 12. my h. shall be with thee to bring Israel
5. 19. wilt thou deliver the Philistines into mine h.? I will doubtless deliver, 1 Chron. 14. 10
18. 12. yet not put forth mine h. against Absalom
1 Kings 13. 6. that my h. may be restored me again
2 Kings 5. 18. he leaneth on my h. in house of Rimm.
18. 34. have they delivered Samaria out of my h.?
35. have delivered their country out of my h. that the L. should deliver Jerusalem out of mine h.
1 Chr. 22. 18. given inhabitants of land into my h.
2 Chr. 32. 15. shall G. deliver you out of my h.? 17.
Job 13. 14. wherefore do I put my life in mine h.?
29. 20. and my bow was renewed in my h.
31. 25. rejoiced because mine h. had gotten much
27. or my mouth hath kissed my h.
33. 7. neither shall my h. be heavy upon thee
Psal. 77. † 2. my h. ran in the night, and ceased not
81. 14. and turned my h. against their enemies
89. 21. with whom my h. shall be established
119. 109. my soul is continually in my h.
Prov. 1. 24. I have stretched out my h. none regarded
Isa. 1. 25. I will turn my h. upon me and purge dross
10. 10. as my h. hath found the kingdoms of idols
13. by the strength of my h. I have done it
14. my h. hath found as a nest the riches of people
36. 19. have they delivered Samaria out of my h.?
20. that L. should deliver Jerusalem out of my h.
48. 13. mine h. also hath laid foundation of earth
50. 2. is my h. shortened || 11. this ye have of my h.
51. 16. have covered thee in the shadow of mine h.
66. 2. all those hath mine h. made, Acts 7. 50.
Jer. 6. 12. I will stretch out my h. 15. 6. | 51. 25.
16. 21. will cause them to know mine h. and might
18. 6. so are ye in mine h. O house of Israel
25. 15. take the wine-cup of this fury at my h.
Ezek. 6. 14. so will I stretch out my h. upon them
12. 7. in the even I digged thro' the wall with my h.
13. 9. mine h. shall be upon prophets that see vanity
20. 5. I lifted up mine h. saying, I am the Lord your God, 6. 23, 28, 42. | 36. 7. | 44. 12. | 47. 14.
22. I withdrew my h. and wrought for name's sake
22. 13. I have smitten mine h. at thy dishonest gain
37. 19. one stick, and they shall be one in mine h.
Hos. 2. 10. none shall deliver her out of mine h.
Amos 1. 8. I will turn mine h. against Ekron
9. 2. tho' into hell, thence shall mine h. take them
Zech. 2. 9. behold, I will shake mine h. on them
13. 7. I will turn mine h. upon the little ones
John 10. 28. nor shall any pluck them out of my h.
29. none is able to pluck them out of my Father's h.
20. 25. except I shall thrust my h. into his side
1 Cor. 16. 21. the salutation of me Paul with mine own h. the grace of Lord J. C. 2 Thess. 3. 17.
Gal. 6. 11. I have written with my h. Philem. 19.

Our HAND.

Gen. 37. 27. let not our h. be on him, he is our brother
43. 21. and we have brought it again in our h.
Num. 31. † 49. taken sum of men of war under our h.
Deut. 32. 27. lest adversaries should say, our h. is high
Judg. 16. 23. our god hath delivered Sams. into our h.
1 Sam. 14. 10. L. hath deliv. them into our h. 30. 23.
Jer. 11. 21. prophesy not, that thou die not by our h.
2 Cor. 10. 16. to boast in things made ready to our h.

Out of HAND, or *out of the* HAND.

Gen. 48. 22. which I took out of the h. of Amorite
Exod. 2. 19. Egyptian delivered us out of h. of shep.
3. 8. to deliver them out of h. of Egyptians, 14. 30.
Num. 5. 25. take jealousy-offering out of woman's h.

Num. 11. 15. if thus, kill me, I pray thee, out of h.
35. 25. deliver him out of h. of the aveng. of blood
Josh. 9. 26. deliver them out of the h. of Israel
Judg. 2. 16. judges which delivered them out of the h.
6. 9. I delivered you out of the h. of Egyptians
13. 5. deliver Israel out of the h. of the Philistines
1 Sam. 4. 8. who shall deliv. us out of h. of these gods?
17. 37. L. will deliver me out of h. of this Philistine
2 Sam. 12. 7. I delivered thee out of h. of Saul, 22. 1.
23. 21. plucked the spear out of the Egyptian's h.
1 Kings 11. 12. will rend king. out of h. of Solom. 31.
22. 3. we take it not out of h. of the king of Syria
2 Kings 13. 25. took again out of h. of Ben-hadad
20. 6. out of h. of the king of Assyria, Isa. 38. 6.
Psal. 71. 4. deliver me out of the h. of the wicked
82. 4. rid them out of the h. of the wicked
97. 10. he delivereth them out of h. of the wicked
Jer. 15. 21. I will deliver thee out of h. of the wicked
21. 12. him spoiled out of h. of the oppressor, 22. 3.
32. 4. not escape out of h. of Chaldeans, 38. 18, 23.
Lam. 5. 8. none doth deliver us out of their h.
Zech. 11. 6. out of their h. I will not deliver them
John 10. 39. to take him, but he escaped out of their h.
Acts 12. 11. deliver me out of the h. of Herod
Rev. 8. 4. ascended before G. out of angel's h. 10. 10.

Right HAND.

Gen. 35. † 18. Jacob called him son of the right h.
48. 14. put his right h. on Ephraim's head, 18.
Exod. 15. 6. thy right h. O Lord, is become glorious
29. 20. put the blood on the thumb of their right h. Lev. 8. 23, 24. | 14. 14, 17, 25, 28.
Deut. 33. 2. from his right h. went a fiery law
Judg. 5. 26. her right h. to the workman's hammer
2 Sam. 20. 9. Joab took Amasa with right h. to kiss
1 Kings 2. 19. Bath-sheba sat on Solomon's right h.
2 Kings 23. 13. on right h. of the mount of corruption
Job 23. 9. he hideth himself on the right h.
30. 12. upon my right h. rise the youth, they push
40. 14. that thine own right h. can save thee
Psal. 16. 8. he is at my right h. I shall not be moved
11. at thy right h. are pleasures for evermore
17. 7. savest by thy right h. them that trust in thee
18. 35. and thy right h. hath holden me up
20. 6. with the saving strength of his right h.
21. 8. thy right h. shall find out those that hate thee
26. 10. and their right h. is full of bribes
44. 3. but thy right h. and thy arm saved them
45. 4. thy right h. shall teach thee terrible things
9. on thy right h. did stand queen in gold of Ophir
48. 10. thy right h. is full of righteousness;
60. 5. save with thy right h. and hear me
63. 8. my soul followeth, thy right h. upholdeth me
73. 23. thou hast holden me by my right h.
74. 11. why withdrawest thou thy right h.?
77. 10. I will remember the years of the right h.
78. 54. to mountain which his right h. purchased
80. 15. the vineyard which thy right h. planted
17. let thy hand be upon the man of thy right h.
89. 13. strong is thy hand, high is thy right h.
25. I will also set his right h. in the rivers
42. thou hast set up the right h. of his adversaries
91. 7. ten thousand shall fall at thy right h.
98. 1. his right h. hath gotten him the victory
108. 6. save with thy right h. and answer me
109. 6. and let Satan stand at his right h.
31. for he shall stand at the right h. of the poor
110. 1. sit thou at my right h. till I make enemies thy footstool, Luke 20. 42. Acts 2. 34. Heb. 1. 13.
5. the Lord at thy right h. shall strike thro' kings
118. 15. the right h. of the Lord doeth valiantly
16. right h. of the Lord is exalted, doeth valiantly
121. 5. the Lord is thy shade upon thy right h.
137. 5. if I forget, let my right h. forget her cunning
138. 7. and thy right h. shall save me
139. 10. even there thy right h. shall hold me
142. 4. looked on my right h. none would know me
144. 8. their right h. is a right h. of falsehood, 11.
Prov. 3. 16. length of days is in her right h.
27. 16. the ointment of his right h. bewrayeth
Eccl. 10. 2. a wise man's heart is at his right h.
Cant. 2. 6. and his right h. doth embrace me
8. 3. and his right h. should embrace me
Isa. 41. 10. I will uphold thee with right h. of right.
13. I the Lord thy God will hold thy right h.
44. 20. nor say, is there not a lie in my right h.
45. 1. to Cyrus whose right h. I have holden
48. 13. my right h. hath spanned the heavens
62. 8. the Lord hath sworn by his right h.
63. 12. that led them by the right h. of Moses
Jer. 22. 24. tho' Coniah were the signet on my right h.
Lam. 2. 3. hath drawn back his right h. from enemy
4. he stood with his right h. as an adversary
Ezek. 21. 22. at right h. divination for Jerusalem
Hab. 2. 16. cup of Lord's right h. shall be turned to
Zech. 3. 1. Satan standing at his right h. to resist him
Mat. 5. 30. if thy right h. offend thee, cut it off
6. 3. let not thy left know what thy right h. doeth
Mark 14. 62. ye shall see Son of man sitting on the r. h. of power, coming in clouds, Luke 22. 69.
16. 19. received to heaven, sat on right h. of God, Heb. 1. 3. | 8. 1. | 10. 12. | 12. 2. 1 Pet. 3. 22.
Luke 6. 6. was a man whose right h. was withered
Acts 2. 25. he is on my right h. I shall not be moved
33. being by the right h. of God exalted, 5. 31.
3. 7. he took him by the right h. and lift him up
7. 55. saw Jesus standing on right h. of God, 56.
Rom. 8. 34. who is even at the right h. of God
Eph. 1. 20. set him at his right h. in heavenly places
Col. 3. 1. where Christ sitteth on the right h. of God
Rev. 1. 16. he had in his r. h. seven stars, 20. | 2. 1.
17. laid right h. upon me, saying, fear not
5. 1. I saw in his right h. a book written within, 7.
13. 16. to receive mark in their right h. or foreheads
See Left HAND.

Right HANDS.

Gal. 2. 9. gave to me and Barnab. right h. of fellow.

To stretch forth or out HAND.

Gen. 22. 10. Abraham stretched forth his h. to slay
Exod. 3. 20. I will stretch out my h. on Eg. 7. 5. | 9. 15.
14. 16. stretch out thy h. over the sea, 26. 7, 19.
21. Moses stretched out his h. over the sea, 27.
1 Sam. 26. 9. who can st. f. h. aga. Lord's anointed
2 Sam. 1. 14. how wast not afraid to stretch f. thy h.
Psal. 138. 7. will stretch forth thine h. aga. enemies
Prov. 31. 20. she stretcheth out her h. to the poor
Ezek. 14. 9. I will stretch out my h. on that prophet
13. then will I stretch out mine h. upon the land
25. 7. I will str. out mine h. upon the Ammonites
13. I will also stretch out mine h. upon Edom
16. I will stretch out mine h. on the Philistines
35. 3. I will stretch out mine h. against mount Seir
Dan. 11. 42. shall stretch f. his h. on the countries
Zeph. 1. 4. on Judah || 2. 13. against Assyria
See STRONG.

Thine or thy HAND.

Gen. 4. 11. to receive thy brother's blood from thy h.
16. 6. thy maid is in thy h. do to her as it pleaseth
22. 12. and he said, lay not thine h. upon the lad
24. 2. put, I pray, thy h. under my thigh, 47. 29.
49. 8. thy h. shall be in the neck of thy enemies
Exod. 4. 2. what is that in thine h.? he said, a rod
17. thou shalt take this rod in t. h. 7. 15. | 17. 5.
8. 5. stretch forth thine h. over the rivers, 9. 22. | 10. 12, 21. Mat. 12. 13. Mark 3. 5.
13. 9. it shall be for a sign on t. h. 16. Deut. 6. 8.
23. 1. put not thine h. with wicked to be witness
Num. 21. 34. for I have delivered Og into thy h.
Deut. 2. 7. L. thy God hath blessed thee in works of thy h. 14. 29. | 15. 10. | 23. 20. | 28. 8, 12, 20.
24. behold, I have given into thy h. Sihon
3. 2. I will deliver Og and his people into thy h.
13. 9. thy h. shall be first on him, to put him to death
17. shall cleave nought of cursed thing to thine h.
14. 25. thou shalt bind up the money in thine h.
15. 7. nor shut thine h. from thy poor brother
8. thou shalt open thine h. wide to thy brother
23. 25. thou mayest pluck the ears with thine h.
28. 32. there shall be no might in thine h.
30. 9. make thee plenteous in every work of t. h.
33. 3. he loved the people, all his saints are in thy h.
Josh. 6. 2. I have given into thine h. Jericho
8. 18. for I will give Ai into thine h.
9. 25. now behold, we are in thine h. to do to us
10. 6. slack not thy h. from thy servants, save us
8. I have delivered kings of Canaan into thy h.
Judg. 4. 7. I will deliver Sisera into thine h.
7. 7. I will deliver the Midianites into thine h.
8. 15. are hands of Zeba and Zalmunna in thine h.
18. 19. hold thy peace, lay thine h. on thy mouth
20. 28. I will deliver Benjamin into thine h.
1 Sam. 14. 19. Saul said to the priest, withdraw thy h.
21. 3. what is under thine h.? give me five loaves
23. 4. I will deliv. Philistines into t. h. 2 Sam. 5. 19.
2 Sam. 13. 10. bring meat, that I may eat of thine h.
24. 16. it is enough, stay thine h. 1 Chron. 21. 15.
17. let thine h. I pray, be ag. me, 1 Chron. 21. 17.
1 Kings 8. 24. hast fulfilled it with t. h. 2 Chr. 6. 15.
17. 11. she said, bring me a morsel of bread in t. h.
20. 13. I will deliver Syrians into thine h. 28.
42. because thou hast let go out of thy h. a man
2 Kings 4. 29. and take my staff in thine h.
8. 8. the king said, take a present in thine h.
9. 1. Elisha said, take this box of oil in thine h.
10. 15. give me thine h. and he gave him his hand
13. 16. and he said, put thine h. upon the bow
1 Chron. 4. 10. and that thine h. might be with me
29. 12. in thine h. power; and to make great
16. all this store for house cometh of thine h.
2 Chron. 20. 6. in t. h. is there not power and might?
Ezra 7. 14. the law of thy God which is in thine h.
25. after wisdom of God, that is in thine h.
Job 1. 11. but put forth thine h. and touch, 2. 5.
12. only upon himself put not forth thine h.
2. 6. behold, he is in thine h. but save his life
10. 7. there is none that can deliver out of thine h.
11. 14. if iniquity be in thine h. put it far away
13. 21. withdraw t. h. far from me, let not thy dread
35. 7. or what receiveth he of thine h.?
Psal. 10. 12. arise, O Lord, O God, lift up thine h.
14. beholdest spite to requite it with thy h.
17. 14. from men which are thy h. O Lord
21. 8. thine h. shall find out all thine enemies
31. 5. into thine h. I commit my spirit
15. my times are in thy h. deliv. me from enemies
32. 4. for day and night thy h. was heavy upon me
38. 2. thy h. presseth me || 39. 10. by blow of thine h.
74. 11. why withdrawest thou thy h.? pluck it out
80. 17. let thy h. be upon the man of thy right h.
88. 5. and they are cut off from thy h.
104. 28. thou openest thy h. filled with good, 145. 16.
109. 27. that they may know that this is thy h.
119. 173. let thy h. help me || 139. 5. laid t. h. on me
139. 10. even there shall thy h. lead me
144. 7. send thine h. from above, rid me, deliver me
Prov. 3. 27. when it is in power of thine h. to do it
6. 1. if thou hast stricken thy h. with a stranger
30. 32. if thought evil, lay thy h. upon thy mouth
Eccl. 7. 18. yea also from this withdraw not thine h.
9. 10. whatsoever thy h. findeth to do, do it
11. 6. in the evening withhold not thine h.
Isa. 3. 6. and let this ruin be under thy h.
26. 11. when thy h. is lifted up, they will not see
42. 6. I the Lord will hold thine h. and keep thee
47. 6. I have given my inheritance into thine h.
51. 22. I have taken out of thy h. cup of trembling
57. 10. thou hast found the life of thine h.
64. 8. art our Father, we are the work of thy h.
Jer. 6. 9. turn back thine h. as a grape-gatherer
15. 17. I sat alone because of thy h. thou hast filled
25. 28. if they refuse to take the cup at thine h.
36. 14. take in thy h. the roll, wherein thou hast read
40. 4. free from chains which were upon thine h.
Ezek. 3. 18. his blood will I require at t. h. 20. | 33. 8.
6. 11. smite with thine h. and stamp with thy foot
10. 2. and fill thine h. with coals of fire
23. 31. therefore I will give her cup into thine h.
29. 7. when they took hold of thee by thy h.
37. 17. go in and they shall become one in thine h.
38. 12. to turn thine h. upon the desolate places
Dan. 2. 38. the fowls hath he given into thine h.
3. 17. our God will deliver us out of thine h.
Mic. 5. 9. th. h. shall be lift up on thine adversaries
12. I will cut off witchcrafts out of thine h.
Mat. 18. 8. if thy h. or foot offend thee, Mark 9. 43.
John 20. 27. reach thy h. and thrust it into my side
Acts 4. 28. to do whatever t. h. and counsel determ.
30. by stretching forth thine h. to heal

Your HAND.

Gen. 9. 2. into your h. are they delivered
43. 12. and take double money in your h.
Exod. 12. 11. with shoes on your feet, staff in your h.
23. 31. the inhabitants of the land into your h.
Deut. 12. 7. ye shall rejoice in all ye put your h. to
Josh. 8. 7. God will deliver it into your h. 20.
10. 19. the Lord hath delivered them into your h.
24. 8. I gave the Amorites into your h. 11.
Judg. 3. 28. Moabites || 7. 15. Midianites into your h.
2 Sam. 4. 11. shall I not require his blood of your h.?
2 Chr. 18. 14. they shall be delivered into your h.
28. 9. God hath delivered them into your h.
Isa. 1. 12. who hath required this at your h.?
Jer. 26. 14. I am in y. h. do with me as seemeth good
38. 5. Zedekiah said, behold, he is in your h.
44. 25. ye have spoken and fulfilled with your h.
Ezek. 13. 21. and they shall be no more in your h.
23. I will deliver my people out of your h.
Mal. 1. 10. nor will I accept an offering at your h.
13. should I accept this of your h.? saith the Lord
2. 13. or receiveth it with good-will at your h.

HANDED, see LEFT, WEAK.

HAND-BREADTH.

Exod. 25. 25. a border of an h. round about, 37. 12.
1 Kings 7. 26. a molten sea a h. thick, 2 Chron. 4. 5.
Psal. 39. 5. thou hast made my days as an h.
Ezek. 40. 5. a reed of six cubits long, and an h.
43. 13. the cubit is a cubit and an h.

HAND-broad.

Ezek. 40. 43. within were hooks an h.-broad fastened

HANDFUL.

Lev. 2. 2. the priest shall take thereout an h. of flour, 5. 12. | 6. 15. | 9. 17. Num. 5. 26.
1 Kings 17. 12. an h. of meal in a barrel, oil in a cruse
Ps. 72. 16. there shall be an h. of corn in the earth
Eccl. 4. 6. better is h. with quietness, than both hands
Jer. 9. 22. and as the h. after the harvest-man

HANDFULS.

Gen. 41. 47. and the earth brought forth by h.
Exod. 9. 8. take to you h. of ashes of the furnace
Ruth 2. 16. let fall also some h. of purpose for her
1 Kings 20. 10. if dust of Samaria shall suffice for h.
Ezek. 13. 19. will ye pollute me for h. of barley?

HANDY.

Psal. 19. 1. and the firmament sheweth his h. work

HANDKERCHIEFS.

Acts 19. 12. from his body were brought to the sick h.

HANDLE.

Gen. 4. 21. Jubal was father of such as h. the harp
Judg. 5. 14. they that h. the pen of the writer
1 Chr. 12. 8. men that could h. spear, 2 Chr. 25. 5.
Psal. 115. 7. they have hands, but they h. not
Jer. 2. 8. and they that h. the law knew me not
46. 9. and the Libyans that h. the shield
Ezek. 27. 29. all that h. the oar, and all the pilots
Luke 24. 39. h. me and see || Col. 2. 21. taste not, h. not

HANDLED.

Ezek. 21. 11. to be furbished, that it may be h.
Mark 12. 4. and they sent him away shamefully h.
1 John 1. 1. our hands have h. of the word of life

HANDLETH.

Prov. 16. 20. he that h. matter wisely, shall find good
Jer. 50. 16. cut off him that h. sickle in time of harvest
Amos 2. 15. nor shall he stand that h. the bow

HANDLING.

Ezek. 38. 4. great company, all of them h. swords
2 Cor. 4. 2. not h. the word of God deceitfully

HANDLES.

Cant. 5. 5. hands dropped with myrrh on h. of lock

HANDMAID.

Gen. 16. 1. Sarai had an h. whose name was Hagar
29. 24. Laban gave Zilpah to be Leah's h. 35. 26.
29. La. gave Bilhah to be Rachel's h. 30. 4. | 35. 25.
Exod. 23. 12. that son of thy h. may be refreshed
Judg. 19. 19. there is bread and wine for me and thy h.
Ruth 2. 13. for that thou hast spoken friendly to thy h.
3. 9. and she answered, I am Ruth thine h.
1 Sam. 1. 11. if wilt look on the affliction of thine h.
16. count not thine h. for a daughter of Belial
18. Hannah said, let thy h. find grace in thy sight
25. 24. let thy h. speak || 31. remember thy h.
41. let thy h. be a servant to wash feet of servants
2 Sam. 14. 6. thy h. had two sons, they two strove
20. 17. she said to him, hear the words of thy h.
1 Kings 1. 13. didst not thou, my lord, swear to thy h.?
17. thou swarest by the Lord thy God to thy h.
3. 20. she took my son while thine h. slept
2 Kings 4. 2. thy h. hath not any thing, save pot of oil
16. nay, thou man of God, do not lie to thine h.
Psal. 86. 16. turn to me, and save the son of thy h.
116. 16. I am thy servant, and the son of thy h.
Prov. 30. 23. and an h. that is heir to her mistress
Jer. 34. 16. ye caused every man his h. to return
Luke 1. 38. behold the h. of the Lord, be it to me

HANDMAIDEN.

Luke 1. 48. he hath regarded the low estate of his h.

HANDMAIDS.

Gen. 33. 1. Jacob divided the children to the two h.
2. he put the h. and their children foremost
Ruth 2. 13. though I be not like to one of thy h.
2 Sam. 6. 20. who uncovered himself in eyes of the h.
Jer. 34. 11. they caused the h. to return for h.
Joel 2. 29. on the h. will I pour my spirit, Acts 2. 18.

HANDS.

Gen. 16. 9. return and submit thyself under her h.
27. 22. the voice is Jacob's, the h. are the h. of Esau
49. 24. h. were made strong by h. of mighty God
Exod. 17. 12. but Moses' h. were heavy, took a stone
26. † 17. two h. shall be in one board set in order
29. 24. and thou shalt put all in the h. of Aaron
32. † 29. Moses said, fill your h. to-day to the Lord
Lev. 8. 27. put all on Aaron's h. and on his son's h.
Num. 5. 18. put the offering of memorial in her h.
6. 19. and shall put them on the h. of the Nazarite
Deut. 4. 28. there ye shall serve gods, the work of men's h. 27. 15. 2 Kings 19. 18. 2 Chr. 32. 19.
9. 15. the tables of the covenant were in my two h.
17. I cast them out of my two h. and brake them

Deut. 17. 7. the *h.* of witnesses shall be first on him
31. 29. to provoke him through the work of your *h.*
Judg. 2. 14. he delivered them into *h.* of the spoilers
6. 13. into *h.* of Midianites ‖ 10. 7. into *h.* of Philist.
8. 6. are *h.* of Zeba and Zalmunna in thy hand? 15.
34. delivered them out of *h.* of enem. 1 *Sam.* 14. 48.
18. 10. for God hath given Laish into your *h.*
19. 27. and her *h.* were upon the threshold
1 *Sam.* 30. 15. nor deliver me into *h.* of my master
2 *Sam.* 2. 7. let your *h.* be strong, *Zech.* 8. 9, 13.
16. 21. then the *h.* of all with thee shall be strong
21. 9. delivered them into the *h.* of the Gibeonites
23. 6. because they cannot be taken with *h.*
1 *Kings* 10. † 19. there were *h.* on seat, 2 *Chr.* 9. † 18.
14. 27. into the *h.* of the guard, 2 *Chron.* 12. 10.
2 *Kings* 3. 11. who poured water on the *h.* of Elijah
9. 35. they found the skull and the palms of her *h.*
10. 24. the men whom I brought into your *h.*
1 *Chron.* 25. 2. sons of Asaph under the *h.* of Asaph
3. under the *h.* of Jeduthun ‖ 6. *h.* of their father
2 *Chron.* 15. 7. be strong, let not your *h.* be weak
23. † 18. was ordained by the *h.* of David, 29. † 27.
Ezra 4. 4. weakened the *h.* of the people of Judah
Job 4. 3. thou hast strengthened the weak *h.*
5. † 20. redeem in war from the *h.* of the sword
16. 11. God hath turned me into the *h.* of the wicked
17. 3. who is he that will strike *h.* with me?
9. that hath clean *h.* shall be stronger and stronger
Psal. 24. 4. who shall ascend? he that hath clean *h.*
26. 10. in whose *h.* is mischief ‖ 47. 1. clap your *h.*
58. 2. ye weigh the violence of your *h.* in the earth
63. † 10. make him run out by the *h.* of the sword
68. 31. Ethiopia shall stretch out her *h.* unto God
115. 4. idols, the work of men's *h.* 135. 15. *Is.* 37. 19.
7. they have *h.* but handle not, feet, but walk not
134. 2. lift up your *h.* in the sanctuary, and bless L.
140. 4. keep me, O Lord, from the *h.* of the wicked
Prov. 6. 10. a little folding of the *h.* to sleep, 24. 33.
17. Ld. doth hate the *h.* that shed innocent blood
12. 14. the recompence of man's *h.* be rendered him
14. 1. the foolish plucketh it down with her *h.*
17. 18. a man striketh *h.* and becometh surety
22. 26. be not thou one of them that strike *h.*
30. 28. spider taketh hold with her *h.* is in palaces
31. 13. and she worketh willingly with her *h.*
19. she layeth her *h.* to the spindle, her *h.* hold
20. yea, she reacheth forth her *h.* to the needy
31. give her of the fruit of her *h.* and let her works
Eccl. 4. 6. than both *h.* full with travel and vexation
7. 26. her *h.* are as bands ‖ 10. 18. the idleness of *h.*
Cant. 7. 1. the work of the *h.* of a cunning workman
Isa. 1. 15. when ye spread forth your *h.* I will hide
my eyes from you; your *h.* are full of blood
2. 8. they worship the work of their own *h.*
13. 7. therefore shall all *h.* be faint, and heart melt
31. 7. idols which your own *h.* have made to you
33. † 21. the Lord will be a place broad of *h.*
35. 3. strengthen ye the weak *h.* and confirm knees
45. 9. or shall thy work say, he hath no *h.*
59. 3. *h.* are defiled with blood, fingers with iniquity
Jer. 4. 31. that spreadeth her *h.* saying, woe is me
10. 3. a tree, the work of the *h.* of the workman
9. and of the *h.* of the founder, blue and purple
19. 7. cause them to fall by *h.* that seek their lives
21. 4. will turn back weapons that are in your *h.*
23. 14. they strengthen also the *h.* of evil doers,
that none return from wickedness, *Ezek.* 13. 22.
25. 6. provoke me not with the works of your *h.* 7.
33. 13. shall pass under *h.* of him that telleth them
38. 4. he weakeneth *h.* of men of war, *h.* of people
48. 37. upon all the *h.* shall be cuttings
Lam. 1. 17. Zion spreadeth her *h.* none to comfort
4. 2. how esteemed as the work of *h.* of the potter!
6. that was overthrown, and no *h.* stayed on her
10. *h.* of pitiful women have sodden their children
Ezek. 7. 17. all *h.* shall be feeble, 21. 7.
35. † 5. hast shed blood of Israel by *h.* of the sword
Dan. 2. 34. till a stone was cut out without *h.* 45.
Mic. 7. 3. that they may do evil with both *h.* earnestly
Nah. 3. 19. all shall clap the *h.* over thee
Hag. 2. 17. in all labour of your *h.* I smote you
Zech. 4. 9. the *h.* of Zerubbabel laid the foundation
Mat. 15. 20. to eat with unwashen *h.* *Mark* 7. 2, 5.
17. 22. the Son of man shall be betrayed into the
h. of men, 26. 45. *Mark* 9. 31. *Luke* 9. 44.
18. 8. having two *h.* to be cast into fire, *Mark* 9. 43.
Mark 14. 58. temple made with *h.* another without *h.*
Luke 22. 53. ye stretched forth no *h.* against me
24. 7. must be delivered into the *h.* of sinful men
Acts 2. 23. by wicked *h.* have crucified and slain
5. 12. by *h.* of the apostles were wonders wrought
48. dwelleth not in temples made with *h.* 17. 24.
8. 18. that through laying on of the apostles' *h.*
11. 30. sent to elders by the *h.* of Barnabas and Saul
17. 25. neither is worshipped with men's *h.*
19. 26. that they be no gods which are made with *h.*
20. 34. that these *h.* have ministered to my necessit.
28. 17. shall deliver him into the *h.* of the Gentiles
2 *Cor.* 5. 1. we have an house not made with *h.*
Eph. 2. 11. the circumcision in flesh made by *h.*
Col. 2. 11. with the circumcision made without *h.*
1 *Thess.* 4. 11. that ye study to work with your own *h.*
1 *Tim.* 2. 8. men pray every where lifting up holy *h.*
4. 14. by laying on of *h.* of the presbytery, *Heb.* 6. 2.
Heb. 9. 11. by a greater tabernacle not with *h.*
24. Christ not entered into holy place made with *h.*
10. 31. fearful to fall into the *h.* of the living God
12. 12. wherefore lift up the *h.* which hang down
Jam. 4. 8. cleanse your *h.* ye sinners, purify your
See CLAP.

His HANDS.

Gen. 27. 23. *his h.* were hairy ‖ 48. 14. guiding *his h.*
Exod. 17. 12. and Aaron and Hur stayed up *his h.*
32. 19. and Moses cast the tables out of *his h.*
Lev. 7. 30. *his* own *h.* shall bring the offering
15. 11. and hath not rinsed *his h.* in water
16. 12. *his h.* full of sweet incense beaten small
21. Aaron shall lay both *his h.* on head of live g.
Num. 24. 10. and Balak smote *his h.* together
Deut. 33. 7. let *his h.* be sufficient for him
11. bless, Lord, and accept the work of *his h.*
34. 9. for Moses had laid *his h.* upon Joshua
Judg. 9. 16. done according to the deserving of *his h.*
† 24. who strengthened *his h.* to kill his brethren
1 *Sam.* 5. 4. both the palms of *his h.* were cut off
14. 13. Jonathan climbed up on *his h.* and his feet
23. 16. Jonathan went and strengthened *his h.* in G.
2 *Sam.* 4. 1. when Saul's son heard, *his h.* were feeble
1 *Kings* 8. 22. Solomon stood and spread forth *his h.*
toward heaven, 38. 54. 2 *Chron.* 6. 12, 13, 29.
16. 7. in provoking him with the work of *his h.*
2 *Kings* 4. 34. he went up and put *his h.* upon *his h.*
5. 20. hath spared Naaman in not receiving at *his h.*
13. 16. Elisha put *his h.* upon the king's hands
2 *Chron.* 6. 4. who hath with *his h.* fulfilled that
Neh. 4. 17. with one of *his h.* wrought in the work
Job 1. 10. thou hast blessed the work of *his h.*
5. 18. he woundeth, and *his h.* make whole
20. 10. and *his h.* shall restore their goods
34. 19. for they all are the works of *his h.*
37. for he clappeth *his h.* amongst us
Psal. 9. 16. the wick. is snared in the work of *his h.*
28. 5. they regard not the operation of *his h.*
78. 72. he guided them by the skilfulness of *his h.*
81. 6. *his h.* were delivered from the pots
95. 5. the sea is his, and *his h.* formed dry land
111. 7. the works of *his h.* are verity and judgment
Prov. 21. 25. for *his h.* refuse to labour
Eccl. 4. 5. the fool foldeth *his h.* together
Cant. 5. 14. *his h.* are as gold rings set with beryl
Isa. 3. 11. the reward of *his h.* shall be given him
5. 12. nor consider the operation of *his h.*
17. 8. he shall not look to altars, the work of *his h.*
25. 11. L. shall spread forth *his h.* in midst of them,
as he that swimmeth spreadeth *his h.* to swim
33. 15. that shaketh *his h.* from holding bribes
Jer. 30. 6. why see every man with *his h.* on his loins?
50. 43. king heard the report, *his h.* waxed feeble
Hab. 3. 10. the deep lifted up *his h.* on high
Zech. 4. 9. *his h.* shall also finish the house
Mat. 19. 13. should put *his h.* on them, *Mark* 10. 16.
27. 24. he washed *his h.* before the multitude
Mark 6. 2. such mighty works are wrought by *his h.*
8. 23. when he had put *his h.* on his eyes, 25.
Luke 24. 40. shewed them *his h.* and feet, *John* 20. 20.
50. and he lifted up *his h.* and blessed them
John 13. 3. the Fath. had given all things into *his h.*
20. 25. except I see in *his h.* the print of the nails
Acts 9. 17. putting *his h.* on him, said, brother Saul
12. 1. Herod stretch. forth *his h.* to vex the church
7. and his chains fell off from *his h.*
2 *Cor.* 11. 33. was let down by a wall, and escap. *his h.*
Eph. 4. 28. working with *his h.* thing that is good
See LAY, LAID.

Mine HANDS, *my* HANDS.

Gen. 20. 5. in innocency of *my h.* have I done this
31. 42. God hath seen the labour of *my h.*
Exod. 9. 29. I will spread abroad *my h.* *Ezra* 9. 5.
Judg. 12. 3. I put my life in *my h.* and passed over
2 *Sam.* 22. 21. accord. to clean. of my *h.* *Ps.* 18. 20, 24.
35. he teacheth *my h.* to war, *Ps.* 18. 34. ‖ 144. 1.
1 *Chr.* 12. 17. seeing there is no wrong in *mine h.*
Neh. 6. 9. now, therefore, O God, strengthen *my h.*
Job 9. 30. and if I make *my h.* never so clean
16. 17. not for any injustice in *mine h.*
31. 7. and if any blot hath cleaved to *mine h.*
Psal. 7. 3. O Lord, if there be iniquity in *my h.*
22. 16. they pierced *my h.* and my feet
26. 6. I will wash *m. h.* in innocency, so will I com.
28. 2. when I lift up *my h.* toward thy holy oracle
63. 4. I will lift up *my h.* in thy name
73. 13. in vain I have washed *my h.* in innocency
88. 9. I have stretched out *my h.* unto thee
119. 48. *my h.* will I lift to thy commandments
141. 2. lifting up of *my h.* as the evening sacrifice
143. 6. I stretch forth *my h.* to thee, my soul
Eccl. 2. 11. on all the works that *my h.* had wrought
Cant. 5. 5. I rose, and *my h.* dropped with myrrh
Isa. 19. 25. blessed be Assyria the work of *my h.*
29. 23. when he seeth the work of *mine h.* in thee
45. 11. ask me concerning the work of *my h.*
12. even *my h.* have stretched out the heavens
49. 16. I have graven thee on the palms of *my h.*
60. 21. thy people also the work of *my h.*
65. 2. I have spread out *my h.* all day to rebellious
Ezek. 21. 17. I will also smite *mine h.* together
Dan. 3. 15. who is God to deliver you out of *my h?*
10. 10. an hand which set me on the palms of *my h.*
Luke 24. 39. behold *my h.* and my feet, *John* 20. 27.
John 13. 9. not feet only, but also *my h.* and head
Rom. 10. 21. all day I have stretched forth *my h.*
2 *Tim.* 1. 6. the gift in thee by putting on of *my h.*

Our HANDS.

Gen. 5. 29. shall comfort us concerning toil of *our h.*
43. 22. other money have we brought in *our h.*
Deut. 3. 3. G. deliver. into *our h.* Og king of Bashan
21. 7. shall say, *our h.* have not shed this blood
Josh. 2. 24. L. hath delivered into *our h.* all the land
Judg. 13. 23. not received a meat-offering at *our h.*
16. 24. our G. hath delivered into *our h.* our enemy
1 *Sam.* 17. 47. and he will give you into *our h.*
Psal. 44. 20. or stretched out *our h.* to a strange god
90. 17. establish thou the work of *our h.* upon us
Jer. 6. 24. we have heard the fame, *our h.* wax feeble
Lam. 3. 41. let us lift up our heart with *our h.* to G.
Hos. 14. 3. nor say to work of *our h.* ye are our gods
Acts 24. 7. Lysias took him away out of *our h.*
1 *Cor.* 4. 12. and labour working with *our* own *h.*
1 *John* 1. 1. *our h.* have handled the word of life

Their HANDS.

Gen. 37. 21. he delivered him out of *their h.* 22.
Exod. 29. 10. shall put *their h.* on head of the bullock
15. shall put *their h.* on the head of the ram, 19.
25. thou shalt receive them of *their h.* *Lev.* 8. 28.
Num. 8. 10. Israel shall put *their h.* on the Levites
12. the Levites shall lay *their h.* on the bullock
Deut. 1. 25. they brought of fruit of land in *their h.*
21. 6. the elders shall wash *their h.* over the heifer
Judg. 7. 2. too many to give Midianites into *their h.*
12. 2. ye delivered me not out of *their h.*
2 *Sam.* 4. 12. and they cut off *their h.* and their feet
2 *Kin.* 11. 12. they clapped *their h.* said, G. save king
22. 17. that they might provoke me to anger with
all the works of *their h.* 2 *Chron.* 34. 25.
Ezra 1. 6. strengthened *their h.* with vessels of silver
5. 8. work goeth fast on and prospereth in *their h.*
6. 22. to strengthen *their h.* in the work of the house
10. 19. they gave *their h.* that they would put away
Neh. 2. 18. so they strengthened *their h.* for the work
6. 9. *their h.* shall be weakened from the work
9. 24. gavest them into *their h.* with their kings
Job 5. 12. *their h.* cannot perform their enterprise
30. 2. whereto might strength of *their h.* profit me?
Psal. 28. 4. give them after the work of *their h.*
76. 5. the men of might have not found *their h.*
91. 12. the angels shall bear thee up in *their h.*
125. 3. lest righteous put forth *their h.* to iniquity
Isa. 25. 11. pride, together with the spoils of *their h.*
59. 6. and the act of violence is in *their h.*
65. 22. mine elect shall enjoy the work of *their h.*
Jer. 1. 16. worshipped the works of *their* own *h.*
5. † 31. the priests take into *their h.* by their means
25. 14. accord. to the works of *their h.* *Lam.* 3. 64.
32. 30. provoked to anger with works of *their h.*
Lam. 1. 14. the Lord hath delivered me into *their h.*
2. † 20. women eat children swaddled with *their h.*
Ezek. 10. 12. *their h.* and wings full of eyes round
23. 37. committed adultery, blood is in *their h.* 45.
43. † 26. they shall purge altar and fill *their h.*
Jonah 3. 8. turn from the violence that is in *their h.*
Hag. 2. 14. so is every work of *their h.* unclean
Mat. 4. 6. with *th. h.* they sh. bear thee up, *Luke* 4. 11.
15. 2. they wash not *their h.* when they eat bread
26. 67. smote with palms of *their h.* *Mark* 14. 65.
Mark 7. 3. Jews, except they wash *their h.* eat not
Luke 6. 1. and did eat, rubbing them in *their h.*
John 19. 3. and they smote him with *their h.*
Acts 7. 41. they rejoiced in the works of *their h.*
14. 3. granted signs and wonders to be done by *th. h.*
Rev. 7. 9. with white robes, and palms in *their h.*
9. 20. yet repented not of the works of *their h.*
20. 4. nor had received his mark in *their h.*

Thine or *thy* HANDS.

Exod. 15. 17. in sanctuary which *thy h.* have estab.
Deut. 16. 15. the Lord shall bless thee in all works
of *thine h.* therefore shalt surely rejoice, 24. 19.
Judg. 7. 11. afterward shall *thine h.* be strengthened
2 *Sam.* 3. 34. *thy h.* were not bound, nor feet in fetters
Job 10. 3. is it good to despise the work of *thine h.?*
8. *thine h.* have made and fashioned me together
14. 15. thou wilt have desire to the work of *thine h.*
22. 30. and it is delivered by pureness of *thine h.*
Psal. 8. 6. to have dominion over the works of *thy h.*
92. 4. I will triumph in the works of *thy h.*
102. 25. and the heavens are the work of *thy h.*
119. 73. *thy h.* have made me and fashioned me
128. 2. for thou shalt eat the labour of *thine h.*
138. 8. forsake not the works of *thine* own *h.*
143. 5. I meditate, I muse on the work of *thy h.*
144. † 7. send *thine h.* from above, rid me, deliv. me
Eccl. 5. 6. why should G. destroy the work of *th. h.*
Jer. 2. 37. thou shalt go forth, and *th. h.* on thy head
Lam. 2. 19. lift up *thy h.* for the life of thy children
Ezek. 21. 14. prophesy and smite *thine h.* together
22. 14. can *thine h.* be strong in the day that I deal?
Mic. 5. 13. shalt no more worship the work of *th. h.*
Zeph. 3. 16. and to Zion, let not *thine h.* be slack
Zech. 13. 6. what are these wounds in *thine h.?*
Luke 23. 46. Father, into *thy h.* I commend my spirit
John 21. 18. thou shalt stretch forth *thy h.*
Heb. 1. 10. the heavens are the works of *thine h.*
2. 7. thou didst set him over the works of *thy h.*

HAND-*staves.*

Ezek. 39. 9. and shall burn the *h.-staves* and spears

HAND-*weapon.*

Num. 35. 18. or if he smite him with a *h.-weapon*

HAND-*writing.*

Col. 2. 14. blotting out the *h.-writing* of ordinances

HANG.

Gen. 40. 19. Pharaoh shall *h.* thee on a tree
Num. 25. 4. *h.* them before the Lord against the sun
Deut. 21. 22. and if thou *h.* him on a tree, his body
28. 66. and thy life shall *h.* in doubt before thee
2 *Sam.* 21. 6. and we will *h.* them up unto the Lord
Esth. 6. 4. to speak to the king to *h.* Mordecai
7. 9. then the king said, *h.* him thereon
Cant. 4. 4. whereon there *h.* a thousand bucklers
Isa. 22. 24. they shall *h.* upon him all the glory
Lam. 2. 10. the virgins of Jerusalem *h.* their heads
Ezek. 15. 3. will men take pin to *h.* any vessel
thereon?
Mat. 22. 40. on these two *h.* all the law and prophets
Acts 28. 4. saw the venomous beast *h.* on his hand
Heb. 12. 12. lift up hands *h.* down and feeble knees

HANGED.

Gen. 40. 22. but he *h.* the chief baker, 41. 13.
Deut. 21. 23. for he that is *h.* is accursed of God
Josh. 8. 29. and the king of Ai he *h.* on a tree
10. 26. the five kings *h.* he on five trees
2 *Sam.* 4. 12. Rechab and Baanah *h.* over the pool
17. 23. Ahithophel *h.* himself ‖ 18. 10. Absalom *h.*
21. 9. the seven sons of Saul *h.* they in the hill
Ezra 6. 11. and being set up, let him be *h.* thereon
Esth. 2. 23. the two chamberlains were *h.* on a tree
7. 10. they *h.* Haman ‖ 9. 14. they *h.* his ten sons
Psal. 137. 2. we *h.* our harps on the willows
Lam. 5. 12. princes are *h.* up by their hands
Ezek. 27. 10. they *h.* the shield and helmet in thee
11. they *h.* their shields upon thy walls round about
Mat. 18. 6. it were better for him that a millstone
were *h.* about his neck, *Mark* 9. 42. *Luke* 17. 2.
27. 5. Judas departed, and went and *h.* himself
Luke 19. † 48. all the people *h.* on him to hear him
23. 39. one of the thieves who were *h.* railed on him
Acts 5. 30. whom ye slew and *h.* on a tree, 10. 39.

HANGETH.

Job 26. 7. and he *h.* the earth upon nothing
Gal. 3. 13. cursed is every one that *h.* on a tree

HANGING.

Josh. 10. 26. they were *h.* on trees till the evening

HANGING.

Exod. 26. 36. thou shalt make an *h.* for door of tent
37. thou shalt make for the *h.* five pillars
27. 16. *h.* for court gate, 38. 18. ‖ 39. 40. ‖ 40. 8, 33.
35. 15. the *h.* for the door at the entering in of
the tabernacle, 36. 37. ‖ 39. 38. ‖ 40. 5, 28.

HANGINGS.

Exod. 27. 9. *h.* of an hundred cubits, 11 | 38. 9, 11.
12. there shall be *h.* of fifty cubits, 38. 12.
14. the *h.* on either side of gate, 15. | 38. 14, 15.
35. 17. the *h.* of court, his pillars and their sockets, 38. 9, 16, 18. | 39. 40. *Num.* 3. 36. | 4. 26.
2 *Kings* 23. 7. where women wove *h.* for the grove
Esth. 1. 6. blue *h.* fastened with cords of lin. and purp.

HAP.

Ruth 2. 3. and her *h.* was to light on Boaz' field

HAPLY.

1 *Sam.* 14. 30. if *h.* the people had eaten freely
Mark 11. 13. if *h.* he might find any fruit thereon
Luke 14. 29. lest *h.* after he had laid the foundation
Acts 5. 39. lest *h.* ye be found to fight against God
17. 27. if *h.* they might feel after him and find him
2 *Cor.* 9. 4. lest *h.* if they of Macedonia come with me

HAPPEN.

1 *Sam.* 28. 10. no punishment *h.* to thee for this thing
Prov. 12. 21. there shall no evil *h.* to the just
Isa. 41. 22. and let them shew us what shall *h.*
Mark 10. 32. began to tell what thing should *h.* to him

HAPPENED.

Ruth 2. † 3. her hap *h.* to light on Boaz' field
1 *Sam.* 6. 9. it was a chance that *h.* to us
2 *Sam.* 1. 6. as I *h.* by chance upon mount Gilboa
20. 1. and there *h.* to be there a man of Belial
Esth. 4. 7. Mordecai told him of all that had *h.*
Jer. 44. 23. therefore this evil is *h.* to you at this day
Luke 24. 14. they talked of all things that had *h.*
Acts 3. 10. were filled with wonder at that which *h.*
Rom. 11. 25. that blindness in part is *h.* to Israel
1 *Cor.* 10. 11. now all things *h.* to them for ensamples
Phil. 1. 12. the things which *h.* to me have fallen
1 *Pet.* 4. 12. as though some strange thing *h.* to you
2 *Pet.* 2. 22. it is *h.* to them according to the proverb

HAPPENETH.

Eccl. 2. 14. I perceived that one event *h.* them all
15. I said, as it *h.* to the fool, so it *h.* even to me
8. 14. there be just men, wicked men to whom it *h.*
9. 11. but time and chance *h.* to them all

HAPPY.

Gen. 30. 13. *h.* am I, for daughters will call me bless.
† 13. and Leah called his name Asher, *h.*
Deut. 33. 29. *h.* art thou, O Isr. who is like to thee?
1 *Kings* 10. 8. *h.* thy men, *h.* thy servants, 2 *Chr.* 9. 7.
Job 5. 17. *h.* is the man whom God correcteth
Psal. 127. 5. *h.* man who hath quiver full of them
128. 2. *h.* shalt thou be, it shall be well with thee
137. 8. *h.* shall he be that rewardeth thee, 9.
144. 15. *h.* is that people that is in such a case, yea *h.* is that people whose God is the Lord
146. 5. *h.* is he that hath God of Jacob for his help
Prov. 3. 13. *h.* is the man that findeth wisdom
18. and *h.* is every one that retaineth her
14. 21. *h.* is he that hath mercy on the poor
16. 20. and whoso trusteth in the Lord, *h.* is he
28. 14. *h.* is the man that feareth alway
29. 18. but he that keepeth the law, *h.* is he
Jer. 12. 1. why are they *h.* that deal treacherously?
Mal. 3. 15. and now we call the proud *h.*
John 13. 17. if ye know these things, *h.* if do them
Acts 26. 2. I think myself *h.* king Agrippa
Rom. 14. 22. *h.* is he that condemneth not himself
Jam. 5. 11. behold, we count them *h.* who endure
1 *Pet.* 3. 14. if ye suffer for righteousness' sake, *h.* ye
4. 14. if reproached for name of Christ, *h.* are ye

HAPPIER.

1 *Cor.* 7. 40. but she is *h.* if she so abide, after my

HARD

Is *taken for difficult, sad, or sorrowful, cruel, austere, &c.* Pharaoh *overwhelmed the Israelites* with hard bondage, *with cruel and insupportable slavery,* Exod. 1. 14. The sons of *Zeruiah* are too hard for me; *they are too powerful, they treat me with insolence, with unseasonable cruelty,* 2 Sam. 3. 39. *Joseph* spake hard things with his brethren; *he spake roughly, or harshly to them,* Gen. 42. † 7. The hard, *or difficult* causes they brought to *Moses,* Exod. 18. 26. Thou art not sent unto a people of an hard language, *of an unintelligible language: that is, they will need no interpreter to understand thee, neither wilt thou, to understand them.* Hannah *said to* Eli, I am a woman of a sorrowful spirit, *Heb.* hard of spirit. I know thee that thou art an hard man, *a severe, auste e, rigorous, and churlish man.* Mat. 25. 24. Solomon *says,* that the way of transgressors is hard, *or* rough, *it is offensive and hateful to God and men, as rough ways are to a traveller. Or, he is fierce, intractable, and incorrigible in his sinful course,* Prov. 13. 15.

When God is said to harden the heart, *it is not to be understood as if God did properly and positively make men's hearts hard, but only privately, either by denying to them, or withdrawing from them that grace, which alone can make the hearts of men soft, flexible, and pliable to the divine will; as the sun hardens the clay by drawing out of it that moisture which made it soft; or by exposing them to those temptations of the world, or the devil, which meeting with a corrupt heart, are apt to harden it.*

Gen. 18. 14. is any thing too *h.* for the Lord?
35. 16. Rachel travailed, and had *h.* labour, 17.
42. † 7. Joseph spake *h.* things with them, † 30.
Exod. 1. 14. they made their lives bitter with *h.* bond.
18. 26. the *h.* causes they brought unto Moses
Deut. 1. 17. cause that is too *h.* you bring it to me
15. 18. it shall not seem *h.* to thee when thou send.
17. 8. if there arise matter too *h.* for thee in judg.
26. 6. Egyptians afflicted and laid on *h.* bondage
Judg. 4. † 24. the hand of Israel was *h.* against Jabin
1 *Sam.* 1. † 15. no, my lord, I am a woman *h.* of spirit
2. † 3. let not *h.* come out of your mouth
2 *Sam.* 3. 39. the sons of Zeruiah be too *h.* for me
13. 2. Amnon thought it *h.* to do any thing to her
1 *Kings* 10. 1. to prove with *h.* questions, 2 *Chr.* 9. 1.
14. † 6. for I am sent to thee with *h.* tidings
2 *Kings* 2. 10. he said, thou hast asked a *h.* thing
Job 30. † 25. did not I weep for him was *h.* of day?

Job 41. 24. as *h.* as a piece of the nether millstone
Psal. 31. † 18. let the lying lips, which speak a *h.* thing
60. 3. thou hast shewed thy people *h.* things
88. 7. thy wrath lieth *h.* on me, thou hast afflicted
94. 4. how long shall the wicked speak *h.* things!
Prov. 13. 15. but the way of transgressors is *h.*
Isa. 14. 3. Lord shall give thee rest from *h.* bondage
21. † 2. a *h.* vision is declared unto me
Jer. 32. 17. and there is nothing too *h.* for thee
27. I am Ld. is there any thing too *h.* for me?
Ezek. 2. † 4. for they are children *h.* of face
3. 5. thou art not sent to a people of *h.* language, 6.
Dan. 5. 12. and shewing *h.* sentences, were found
Mat. 25. 24. Lord, I knew that thou art an *h.* man
Mark 10. 24. how *h.* for them trust in riches to enter
John 6. 60. this is an *h.* saying, who can hear it?
Acts 9. 5. it is *h.* for thee to kick ag. pricks, 26. 14.
Heb. 5. 11. many things to say, and *h.* to be uttered
2 *Pet.* 3. 16. in which are things *h.* to be understood
Jude 15. to convince all ungodly of their *h.* speeches

HARD.

Lev. 3. 9. the rump shall take off *h.* by the back-bone
Judg. 9. 52. Abimelech went *h.* to the door of tower
20. 45. Israel pursued *h.* after Benjamin to Gideon
1 *Sam.* 14. 22. followed *h.* after Philistines in battle
31. 2. the Philistines followed *h.* upon Saul, and upon his sons, 2 *Sam.* 1. 6. 1 *Chr.* 10. 2.
1 *Kings* 21. 1. Naboth had a vineyard *h.* by the pal.
1 *Chr.* 19. 4. cut off garments *h.* by their buttocks
Psal. 63. 8 my soul followeth *h.* after thee
Jonah 1. 13. the men rowed *h.* to bring it to the land
Acts 18. 7. whose house joined *h.* to the synagogue

HARDEN.

Exod. 4. 21. I will *h.* Pharaoh's heart, 7. 3. | 14. 4.
14. 17. I will *h.* the hearts of the Egyptians
Deut. 15. 7. shalt not *h.* thy heart, nor shut thy hand
Josh. 11. 20. it was of the Lord to *h.* their hearts
1 *Sam.* 6. 6. wherefore then do ye *h.* your hearts?
2 *Chr.* 30. † 8. *h.* not your necks as your fathers
Job 6. 10. yea, I would *h.* myself in sorrow
Psal. 95. 8. *h.* not your hearts, *Heb.* 3. 8, 15. | 4. 7.

HARDENED.

Exod. 7. 13. Lord *h.* Pharaoh's heart, he hearkened not to them, 9. 12. | 10. 1, 20, 27. | 11. 10. | 14. 8.
14. Pharaoh's heart is *h.* ‖ 22. was *h.* 8. 19. | 9. 7, 35.
8. 15. he *h.* his heart and hearkened not, 32. | 9. 34.
Deut. 2. 30. the Lord thy G. *h.* his spirit and heart
1 *Sam.* 6. 6. as Egyptians and Phar. *h.* their hearts
2 *Kings* 17. 14. they *h.* their necks like to their fath.
2 *Chr.* 36. 13. Zedekiah *h.* heart from turning to L.
Neh. 9. 16. they and our fathers *h.* their necks, 17, 29.
Job 9. 4. who hath *h.* himself ag. him and prospered
39. 16. she is *h.* against her young ones, as not hers
Isa. 63. 17. why hast thou *h.* our heart from thy fear?
Jer. 7. 26. they hearkened not, but *h.* their neck
19. 15. have *h.* their necks not to hear my words
Dan. 5. 20. but when his mind was *h.* in pride
Mark 6. 52. they consider. not, for their heart was *h.*
8. 17. perceive ye not? have ye your heart yet *h.?*
John 12. 40. he hath blind. their eyes, *h.* their heart
Acts 19. 9. but when divers were *h.* and believed not
Rom. 11. † 7. election obtained it, and rest were *h.*
Heb. 3. 13. lest any of you be *h.* thro' deceitfulness

HARDENETH.

Prov. 21. 29. a wicked man *h.* his face, but he directs
28. 14. he that *h.* his heart shall fall into mischief
29. 1. he that being often reproved *h.* his neck
Rom. 9. 18. mercy on whom he will, whom he will *h.*

HARD-*hearted.*

Ezek. 3. 7. all the house of Israel are *h.-hearted*

HARDER.

Prov. 18. 19. brother offended *h.* to be won than city
Jer. 5. 3. they have made their faces *h.* than a rock
Ezek. 3. 9. *h.* than flint have I made thy forehead

HARDLY.

Gen. 16. 6. when Sarai dealt *h.* with her she fled
Exod. 13. 15. and when Pharaoh would *h.* let us go
Isa. 8. 21. shall pass thro' it *h.* bestead and hungry
Mat. 19. 23. I say that rich man shall *h.* enter into the kingdom of God, *Mark* 10. 23. *Luke* 18. 24.
Luke 9. 39. a spir. taketh him, *h.* depart. from him
Acts 27. 8. *h.* passing it, we came to the fair havens

HARDNESS.

Job 38. 38. when dust groweth into *h.* clods cleave
Psal. 81. † 12. I gave them up to the *h.* of their hearts
Mat. 19. 8. because of *h.* of your hearts, *Mark* 10. 5.
Mark 3. 5. he being grieved for the *h.* of their hearts
16. 14. he upbraided them with their *h.* of heart
Rom. 2. 5. but after thy *h.* and impenitent heart
11. † 25. not ignorant that *h.* in part happen. to Isr.
2 *Tim.* 2. 3. endure *h.* as a good soldier of Jes. Chr.

HARE.

Lev. 11. 6. the *h.* is unclean to you, *Deut.* 14. 7.

HARLOT

Is *taken for whore or prostitute,* Prov. 29. 3. *Also for one who forsakes the true God and his pure worship, to follow idols and false gods.* Isa. 1. 21. How is the faithful city become an harlot! *that is, like an harlot, leaving God her husband, to cleave to false gods. By* harlots *may also be understood the most infamous and scandalous sinners,* Mat. 21. 31. Publicans and harlots go into the kingdom of heaven before you.

Rahab *who received into her house and concealed the spies sent by* Joshua *to view the city of* Jericho, *is called an* harlot. *The* Hebrew *text,* Josh. 2. 1. *calls her* Zona, *which* St. Jerom *and many others understand of a woman of an ill life. The* Septuagint *render it by* πορνη, *as also the apostle* Paul *in* Heb. 11. 31. *And* James, *Jam.* 2. 25. *Some think that she was only an hostess or inn-keeper; and that this is the true signification of the original word. Had she been a woman of ill fame, say they, would* Salmon, *a prince of the tribe of* Judah, *and one of our Saviour's ancestors, have taken her to wife, or could he have done it by the law? Besides, the spies of* Joshua *would hardly have gone to lodge with a prostitute, a common harlot, they who were charged with so nice and dangerous a commission.*

Gen. 34. 31. should deal with our sister as with *h.?*
38. 15. Judah saw her, he thought her to be an *h.*
24. Tamar thy daughter-in-law hath played *h.*
Lev. 21. 14. the high-priest shall not take an *h.*
Josh. 2. 1. spies came into an *h.'s* house named Rahab
6. 17. only Rahab the *h.* shall live, and all with her
Judg. 11. 1. now Jephthah was the son of an *h.*
16. 1. Samson saw there an *h.* and went in unto her
Prov. 7. 10. a woman met him with attire of an *h.*
Isa. 1. 21. how is the faithful city become an *h.!*
23. 15. after seventy years shall Tyre sing as an *h.*
16. take an harp, thou *h.* that hast been forgotten
Jer. 2. 20. when thou wanderest, playing the *h.*
3. 1. thou hast played the *h.* with many lovers
6. under every gr. tree, and there hath played *h.*
8. Judah feared not, but went and played *h.* also
Ezek. 16. 15. playedst the *h.* because of thy renown
16. playedst *h.* thereon ‖ 28. played *h.* with them
31. hast not been as an *h.* ‖ 35. O *h.* hear the word
41. I will cause thee to cease from playing the *h.*
23. 5. Aholah played the *h.* when she was mine
19. the days wherein she had played the *h.*
44. as they go in unto a woman that playeth the *h.*
Hos. 2. 5. for their mother hath played the *h.*
3. 3. I said unto her, thou shalt not play the *h.*
4. 15. tho' Israel play the *h.* let not Judah offend
Joel 3. 3. they have given a boy for a *h.*
Amos 7. 17. thy wife shall be an *h.* in the city
Mic. 1. 7. they shall return to the hire of an *h.*
Nah. 3. 4. the whoredoms of the well-favoured *h.*
1 *Cor.* 6. 15. shall I make them the members of an *h.?*
16. that he who is joined to an *h.* is one body
Heb. 11. 31. by faith the *h.* Rahab perished not
Jam. 2. 25. was not Rahab the *h.* justified by works?

HARLOTS.

1 *Kings* 3. 16. there came two women *h.* to the king
Prov. 29. 3. that keepeth company with *h.* spendeth
Jer. 5. 7. they assemble by troops in *h.* houses
Hos. 4. 14. separated with whores, sacrifice with *h.*
Mat. 21. 31. publicans and *h.* go into kingdom of G.
32. but the publicans and the *h.* believed him
Luke 15. 30. who hath devoured thy living with *h.*
Rev. 17. 5. mystery, Babylon the great, mother of *h*

HARM.

Gen. 31. 52. shalt not pass over this pillar to me for *h.*
Lev. 5. 16. shall make amends for *h.* he hath done
Num. 35. 23. was not his enemy, nor sought his *h.*
1 *Sam.* 26. 21. return, I will no more do thee *h.*
2 *Sam.* 20. 6. now shall Sheba do more *h.* than Absal.
2 *Kings* 4. 41. and there was no *h.* in the pot
1 *Chr.* 16. 22. do my prophets no *h.* *Psal.* 105. 15.
Prov. 3. 30. strive not, if he have done thee no *h.*
Jer. 39. 12. look well to him, and do him no *h.*
Acts 16. 28. do thyself no *h.* ‖ 27. 21. gained this *h.*
28. 5. he felt no *h.* ‖ 6. saw no *h.* ‖ 21. spake any *h.*

HARM.

1 *Pet.* 3. 13. who will *h.* you, if followers of good?

HARMLESS.

Mat. 10. 16. be wise as serpents, and *h.* as doves
Rom. 16. † 19. would have you *h.* concerning evil
Phil. 2. 15. that ye may be *h.* the sons of God
Heb. 7. 26. is holy, *h.* undefil. separate from sinners

HARNESS, *Substantive.*

1 *Kings* 20. 11. let not him girdeth on *h.* boast hims.
22. 34. between joints of his *h.* 2 *Chron.* 18. 33.
2 *Chr.* 9. 24. they brought every man *h.* and spices

HARNESS, *Verb.*

Jer. 46. 4. *h.* the horses, and get up, ye horsemen

HARNESSED.

Exod. 13. 18. Israel went up *h.* out of land of Egypt

HARP.

Gen. 4. 21. Jubal was father of them that handle *h.*
31. 27. might have sent thee away with tabr. and *h.*
1 *Sam.* 10. 5. meet a company of prophets with a *h.*
16. 16. a man who is a cunning player on an *h.*
23. David took an *h.* and played with his hand
1 *Chr.* 25. 3. six prophesied with a *h.* to give thanks
Job 21. 12. they take the timbrel and *h.* and rejoice
30. 31. my *h.* also is turned to mourning, and organ
Psal. 33. 2. praise the Lord with the *h.* 150. 3.
43. 4. yea, on the *h.* will I praise thee, O my God
49. 4. I will open my dark saying upon the *h.*
57. 8. awake psaltery and *h.* I will awake, 108. 2.
71. 22. sing with *h.* 92. 3. | 98. 5. | 147. 7. | 149. 3.
81. 2. bring hither the pleasant *h.* with the psaltery
Isa. 5. 12. the *h.* and the viol are in their feasts
16. 11. my bowels shall sound like an *h.* for Moab
23. 16. take an *h.* ‖ 24. 8. the joy of the *h.* ceaseth
Dan. 3. 5. at sound of the *h.* fall down, 7, 10, 15.
1 *Cor.* 14. 7. whether pipe or *h.* except they give

HARPS.

2 *Sam.* 6. 5. David and all Isr. played on *h.* and corn.
1 *Kings* 10. 12. the king made of the almug-trees *h*
Psal. 137. 2. we hanged our *h.* upon the willows
Isa. 30. 32. it shall be with tabrets and *h.*
Ezek. 26. 13. the sound of thy *h.* shall be no more
Rev. 5. 8. having every one of them *h.* and vials
14. 2. harping with their *h.* ‖ 15. 2. the *h.* of God
See CYMBAL.

HARPED.

1 *Cor.* 14. 7. how shall be known what is piped or *h.*

HARPERS.

Rev. 14. 2. I heard the voice of *h.* harping with harps
18. 22. the voice of *h.* shall be heard no more at all

HARROW.

Job 39. 10. or will he *h.* the valleys after thee?

HARROWS.

2 *Sam.* 12. 31. he put them under saws and *h.* of iron
1 *Chr.* 20. 3. and cut them with saws and *h.* of iron

HART.

Deut. 12. 15. may eat flesh as of the *h.* 14. 5. | 15. 22.
Psal. 42. 1. as the *h.* panteth after the water-brooks
Isa. 35. 6. then shall the lame man leap as an *h.*
See YOUNG.

HARTS.

1 *Kings* 4. 23. ten fat oxen, besides *h.* and roe-bucks
Lam. 1. 6. her princes become like *h.* without pasture

HARVEST

Is *the time of reaping corn and other fruits of the earth,* Gen. 8. 22. *It is taken for a seasonable and proper time for business.* Prov. 10. 5. He that sleepeth in harvest, is a son that causeth

shame. *He that neglecteth and misimproveth the proper seasons and opportunities of doing good to himself and to others, causeth shame both to himself for his folly, and the poverty and misery which follows thereupon; and also to his parents, to whose negligent or evil education such things are often, and sometimes justly imputed.*
Harvest *is put for a people whose sins are ripe for judgment.* Joel 3. 13. Put ye in the sickle, for the harvest is ripe: *Cut down these sinners that are ripe for judgment.* The time of *Babylon's* harvest shall come: *the time when she shall be cut down*, Jer. 51. 33. *Our Saviour, in the parable of the sower, calls the end of the world, or the day of judgment, the harvest*, Mat. 13. 39. *Then God will separate the tares from the wheat, the wicked from the godly. In* Mat. 9. 36, 37. Christ, *seeing multitudes coming to hear him, said to his disciples*, The harvest truly is plenteous; *many are willing to receive instruction. This was spoken at the feast of Tabernacles, which was in* harvest.
Gen. 8. 22. while earth remaineth *h.* shall not cease
30. 14. Reuben went in days of wheat-*h.*
45. 6. in five years shall neither be earing nor *h.*
Exod. 23. 16. thou shalt keep the feast of *h.* 34. 22.
34. 21. in earing-time and in *h.* thou shalt rest
Lev. 19. 9. when ye reap *h.* 23. 10, 22. *Deut.* 24. 19.
25. 5. what grows of its own accord of *h.* not reap
Ruth 1. 22. came to Beth-lehem in begin. of barley-*h.*
2. 21. tarry with my maidens till end of *h.* 23.
1 *Sam.* 6. 13. men of Beth-shemesh reaping their *h.*
8. 12. and he will set them to reap his *h.*
12. 17. is it not wheat-*h.* to-day, I will call to Ld.
2 *Sam.* 21. 9. were put to death in *h.* in barley-*h.*
10. spread it for her from beginning of barley-*h.*
Job 5. 5. whose *h.* the hungry eateth up and taketh it
Prov. 6. 8. the ant gathereth her food in the *h.*
10. 5. he that sleepeth in *h.* causeth shame
26. 1. as rain in *h.* so honour is not seemly for a fool
Isa. 9. 3. they joy before thee according to joy in *h.*
16. 9. for the shouting for thy *h.* is fallen
17. 11. but the *h.* shall be a heap in the day of grief
18. 4. and like a cloud of dew in the heat of *h.*
5. for afore the *h.* when the bud is perfect
23. 3. the *h.* of the river is her revenue
Jer. 5. 17. they shall eat up thine *h.* and thy bread
24. he reserveth to us the appointed weeks of *h.*
8. 20. the *h.* is past, summer is ended, we not saved
Hos. 6. 11. O Judah, he hath set an *h.* for thee
Joel 1. 11. because the *h.* of the field is perished
3. 13. put in the sickle, for the *h.* is ripe, come
Amos 4. 7. when there were yet three months to *h.*
Mat. 9. 37. the *h.* is plenteous, the labourers are few
38. pray ye the Lord of the *h.* to send, *Luke* 10. 2.
13. 30. let both grow together until *h.* in time of *h.*
39. the *h.* is end of the world, reapers the angels
Mark 4. 29. put in the sickle because *h.* is come
Luke 10. 2. he said unto them, the *h.* truly is great
John 4. 35. then cometh *h.* the fields are white to *h.*
Rev. 14. 15. time is come, for the *h.* of earth is ripe

HARVEST-*man.*

Isa. 17. 5. it shall be as when the *h.* gathereth corn
Jer. 9. 22. carcases shall fall as the handful after *h.*

HARVEST-*time.*

Josh. 3. 15. Jordan overfloweth all the *time* of *h.*
Judg. 15. 1. in *time* of wheat *h.* Samson visited wife
2 *Sam.* 23. 13. three chiefs came to David in *h.-time*
Prov. 25. 13. as the cold of snow in the *time* of *h.*
Jer. 50. 16. cut off him handleth sickle in *h.-time*
51. 33. a little while the *time* of her *h.* shall come
Mat. 13. 30. in the *time* of *h.* I will say to the reapers

HAST.

Gen. 19. 12. the men said to Lot, *h.* thou here any besides? whatsoever thou *h.* in city bring out
27. 38. Esau said, *h.* thou but one blessing, father?
32. 28. as a prince *h.* thou power with G. and men
33. 9. Esau said, keep that thou *h.* to thyself
45. 10. come thou, thy flock, and all that thou *h.*
Exod. 9. 19. send and gather all that thou *h.* in field
13. 12. every firstling thou *h.* shall be the Lord's
Deut. 8. 13. silver, gold, and all thou *h.* is multiplied
Judg. 18. 3. what makest thou? what *h.* thou here?
1 *Sam.* 25. 6. peace be to thee and all that thou *h.*
2 *Sam.* 15. 35. *h.* thou not here with thee Zadok?
2 *Kings* 4. 2. Elisha said, tell me, what *h.* in house
Job 10. 4. *h.* thou eyes of flesh, or seest as man?
40. 9. *h.* thou an arm like God? or canst thunder?
Prov. 3. 28. say not, go, when thou *h.* it by thee
Isa. 22. 16. what *h.* thou here? whom *h.* thou here?
Mat. 19. 21. sell all thou *h.* *Mark* 10. 21. *Luke* 18. 22.
25. 25. lo, there thou *h.* that is thine
John 4. 11. from whence then *h.* thou living water?
18. and he whom thou now *h.* is not thine husband
6. 68. to whom go? thou *h.* words of eternal life
7. 20. the people said, thou *h.* a devil, 8. 48, 52.
13. 8. if I wash thee not, thou *h.* no part with me
Acts 8. 21. thou *h.* neither part nor lot in this matter
Rom. 2. 20. thou who *h.* the form of knowledge
14. 22. *h.* thou faith? have it to thyself before God
1 *Cor.* 4. 7. what *h.* thou that thou didst not receive?
Jam. 2. 18. a man may say, thou *h.* faith and I works
Rev. 2. 3. thou *h.* patience, and for my name's sake
6. but this thou *h.* ‖ 3. 1. thou *h.* a name to live, 4.
8. thou *h.* a little strength ‖ 11. hold what thou *h.*

HASTE, *Substantive.*

Exod. 10. 16. Pharaoh called for Moses and Aaron *h.*
12. 11. ye shall eat it in *h.* with your loins girded
33. might send them out of land in *h.* *Deut.* 16. 3.
1 *Sam.* 21. 8. because the king's business required *h.*
2 *Kings* 7. 15. the Syrians had cast away in their *h.*
Ezra 4. 23. they went up in *h.* to Jerusalem
Psal. 31. 22. I said in my *h.* I am cut off from thee
116. 11. I said in my *h.* all men are liars
Isa. 52. 12. ye shall not go out with *h.* nor by flight
Dan. 2. 25. Arioch brought Dan. before king in *h.*
3. 24. the king rose up in *h.* and spake, and said
6. 19. the king went in *h.* unto the den of lions
Mark 6. 25. she came in straightway with *h.* to king
Luke 1. 39. Mary went into the hill-country with *h.*
2. 16. the shepherds came with *h.* and found Mary

HASTE.

Gen. 19. 22. *h.* thee, escape thither, for I cannot do
Gen. 45. 9. *h.* ye and go up to my father, say, 13.
1 *Sam.* 20. 38. Jonathan cried, make speed *h.* stay not
23. 27. *h.* thee, for Philistines have invaded the land
Psal. 22. 19. O my strength, *h.* thee to help me

See MAKE *haste.*

HASTED.

Gen. 18. 7. give it to young man, and he *h.* to dress it
24. 18. she said, drink, my lord, and she *h.* 20.
Exod. 5. 13. and the task-masters *h.* them, saying
Josh. 4. 10. the people *h.* and passed over Jordan
8. 14. and when the king of Ai saw it, they *h.*
19. the ambush *h.* and set the city on fire
10. 13. the sun *h.* not to go down a whole day
Judg. 20. 37. liers in wait *h.* and rushed on Gibeah
1 *Sam.* 17. 48. David *h.* ‖ 25. 23. Abigail *h.* 42.
25. 34. except thou hadst *h.* and come to meet
28. 24. the witch at En-dor *h.* and killed the calf
2 *Sam.* 19. 16. Shimei, who was of Bahurim, *h.*
1 *Kings* 20. 41. the prophet *h.* and took ashes away
2 *Kings* 9. 13. they *h.* and put garments under Jehu
2 *Chron.* 26. 20. yea, himself *h.* also to go out
Esth. 6. 12. Haman *h.* to his house mourning
14. they *h.* to bring Haman unto the banquet
Job 31. 5. or if my foot hath *h.* to deceit
Psal. 48. 5. they were troubled and *h.* away, 104. 7.
Acts 20. 16. Paul *h.* to be at Jerusalem at Pentecost

HASTEN.

1 *Kings* 22. 9. *h.* hither Micaiah the son of Imlah
2 *Chron.* 24. 5. and see that ye *h.* the matter
Psal. 16. 4. sorrows multiplied *h.* after another god
55. 8. I would *h.* my escape from the windy storm
Eccl. 2. 25. or who else can *h.* hereunto more than I?
Isa. 5. 19. let him *h.* his work that we may see it
60. 22. I the Lord will *h.* it in his time
Jer. 1. 12. I will *h.* my word to perform it

HASTENED, ETH.

Gen. 18. 6. Abraham *h.* into the tent unto Sarah
19. 15. angels *h.* Lot, saying, arise, take thy wife
2 *Chron.* 24. 5. howbeit the Levites *h.* it not
Esth. 3. 15. posts went out, being *h.* by king, 8. 14.
Isa. 51. 14. the captive exile *h.* to be loosed
Jer. 17. 16. I have not *h.* from being a pastor

HASTETH.

Job 9. 26. as the eagle that *h.* to the prey
40. 23. behold, he drinketh up a river, and *h.* not
Prov. 7. 23. as a bird *h.* to snare, and knoweth not
19. 2. and he that *h.* with his feet sinneth
28. 22. he that *h.* to be rich, hath an evil eye
Eccl. 1. 5. the sun *h.* to the place where he arose
Jer. 48. 16. the affliction of Moab *h.* fast
Hab. 1. 8. they shall fly as the eagle that *h.* to eat
Zeph. 1. 14. the great day of the Lord *h.* greatly

HASTILY.

Gen. 41. 14. they brought Joseph *h.* out of dungeon
Judg. 2. 23. left nations without driving them out *h.*
9. 54. Abimelech called *h.* unto his armour-bearer
1 *Sam.* 4. 14. and the man came in *h.* and told Eli
1 *Kings* 20. 33. the men did *h.* catch it, and they said
Prov. 20. 21. an inheritance may be gotten *h.*
25. 8. go not forth *h.* to strive, lest thou know not
John 11. 31. when Jews saw Mary that she rose *h.*

HASTING.

Isa. 16. 5. seeking judgment, and *h.* righteousness
2 *Pet.* 3. 12. and *h.* unto the coming of day of the L.

HASTY.

Prov. 14. 29. but he that is *h.* of spirit exalteth folly
21. 5. but of every one that is *h.* only to want
29. 20. seest thou a man that is *h.* in his words
Eccl. 5. 2. let not thy heart be *h.* to utter before G.
7. 9. be not *h.* in thy spirit to be angry
8. 3. be not too *h.* to go out of his sight
Isa. 28. 4. as the *h.* fruit before the summer
32. †4. the heart of the *h.* shall understand
35. †4. say to them that are of *h.* heart, be strong
Dan. 2. 15. why is the decree so *h.* from the king?
Hab. 1. 6. the Chaldeans, that bitter and *h.* nation

HATCH.

Isa. 34. 15. owl shall *h.* and gather under her shad.
59. 5. they *h.* cockatrice-eggs, weave spiders' web

HATCHETH.

Jer. 17. 11. as partridge sitteth on eggs and *h.* not

HATE.

To hate, *is not always to be understood rigorously. It frequently signifies no more than a lesser degree of love.* Deut. 21. 15. If a man have two wives, one beloved, and another hated; *that is, less beloved. Thus our Saviour says, that he who would follow him*, must hate father and mother; *that is, should love them less than* Christ, *less than his own salvation; he ought not to prefer them to God.* Solomon *says*, that he that spareth his rod, hateth his son, *Prov.* 13. 24. *Fathers often spare their children out of an excessive love to them; but this is not a proper instance of affection, to forbear correcting them; their fond affection is as pernicious to their children, as other men's hatred could be; they keep back from them what would do them good. There is a malicious hatred of the persons of men, not of their sins; thus* Ahab *hated the Lord's prophet* Micaiah, 1 *Kings* 22. 8. *And wicked men do thus hate the righteous.* Psal. 34. 21. They that hate the righteous shall be desolate. *There is also an hatred of the sins of men, not of their persons; thus the righteous hate even the garment spotted with corruption*, Jude 23. What I hate, that do I, *Rom.* 7. 15. *The godly hate sin, because it is a breach of God's law.*
Gen. 24. 60. let seed possess gate of those that *h.*
50. 15. they said, Joseph will peradventure *h.* us
Lev. 19. 17. thou shalt not *h.* thy brother in heart
26. 17. they that *h.* you shall reign over you
Num. 10. 35. let them that *h.* thee flee before thee
Deut. 7. 10. and repayeth them that *h.* him to face
15. he will lay them upon them that *h.* thee, 30. 7.
19. 11. if any man *h.* his neighbour and lie in wait
22. 13. if take a wife, and go in unto her and *h.* her
24. 3. if the latter husband *h.* her and write a bill
33. 11. smite through the loins of them that *h.* him
2 *Chr.* 19. 2. and love them that *h.* the Lord?
Job 8. 22. that *h.* thee shall be clothed with shame
Psal. 21. 8. thy hand shall find those that *h.* thee
34. 21. they that *h.* the righteous shall be desolate
Psal. 44. 10. they which *h.* us spoil for thems.
68. 1. let them also that *h.* him flee before him
83. 2. they that *h.* thee have lifted up the head
89. 23. and I will plague them that *h.* him
97. 10. ye that love the Lord *h.* evil
105. 25. he turned their heart to *h.* his people
129. 5. let them be turned back that *h.* Zion
Prov. 1. 22. how long, fools, will ye *h.* knowledge
6. 16. these six doth the Lord *h.* a proud look
8. 13. fear of the Lord is to *h.* evil; pride do I *h.*
9. 8. reprove not a scorner, lest he *h.* thee
19. 7. all the brethren of the poor do *h.* him
25. 17. lest he be weary of thee, and so *h.* thee
29. 10. the blood-thirsty *h.* the upright
Eccl. 3. 8. a time to love and a time to *h.*
Ezek. 16. 27. delivered unto will of them that *h.* thee
Dan. 4. 19. the dream be to them that *h.* thee
Amos 5. 10. they *h.* him that rebuketh in the gate
15. *h.* the evil, and love the good, establish judgm.
Mic. 3. 2. who *h.* the good, and love evil, who pluck
Mat. 5. 43. been said, love thy neighbour, *h.* enemy
44. do good to them that *h.* you, *Luke* 6. 27.
6. 24. either he will *h.* the one, *Luke* 16. 13.
24. 10. and shall betray and shall *h.* one another
Luke 1. 71. saved from the hand of all that *h.* us
6. 22. blessed are ye when men shall *h.* you
14. 26. and *h.* not his father, and mother, and wife
John 7. 7. the world cannot *h.* you, but me it hateth
15. 18. marvel not if the world *h.* you, 1 *John* 3. 13.
Rev. 17. 16. the ten horns, these shall *h.* the whore

I HATE.

1 *Kings* 22. 8. there is one man, *I h.* him, 2 *Chr.* 18. 7.
Psal. 101. 3. *I h.* the work of them that turn aside
119. 104. therefore *I h.* every false way, 128.
113. *I h.* vain thoughts ‖ 163. *I h.* and abhor lying
139. 21. do not *I h.* them, O Lord, that hate thee?
22. yea, *I h.* them with perfect hatred
Prov. 8. 13. the evil way and froward mouth do *I h.*
Isa. 61. 8. *I h.* robbery for burnt-offering
Jer. 44. 4. do not this abominable thing that *I h.*
Amos 5. 21. *I h.* I despise your feast-days
6. 8. *I h.* his palaces, therefore will I deliver city
Zech. 8. 17. for all these are things that *I h.* saith L.
Rom. 7. 15. but what *I h.* that do I
Rev. 2. 6. the deeds of the Nicolaitanes *I h.* 15.

HATE *me.*

Gen. 26. 27. why come ye to me, seeing ye *h. me?*
Exod. 20. 5. visiting iniquity to the third and fourth generation of them that *h. me*, *Deut.* 5. 9.
Deut. 32. 41. and I will reward them that *h. me*
Judg. 11. 7. do not ye *h. me?* ‖ 14. 16. thou dost *h. me*
2 *Sam.* 22. 41. destroy them that *h. me*, *Ps.* 18. 40.
Psal. 9. 13. trouble which I suffer of them that *h. me*
25. 19. and they *h. me* with cruel hatred
35. 19. let them wink that *h. me* without a cause
38. 19. they that *h. me* wrongfully are many, 69. 4.
41. 7. all that *h. me* whisper together against me
55. 3. they cast iniquity upon me, in wrath *h. me*
69. 14. let me be delivered from them that *h. me*
86. 17. that they which *h. me* may see it
118. 7. I shall see my desire upon them that *h. me*
Prov. 8. 36. all they that *h. me* love death

HATED.

Gen. 27. 41. Esau *h.* Jacob, because of the blessing
29. 31. the L. saw Leah was *h.* ‖ 33. that I was *h.*
37. 4. his brethren *h.* Joseph yet the more, 5, 8.
49. 23. the archers shot at him and *h.* him
Deut. 1. 27. and said, because the Lord *h.* us, 9. 28.
4. 42. *h.* him not in times past, 19. 4, 6. *Josh.* 20. 5.
21. 15. another *h.* ‖ 16. before the son of the *h.*
17. shall acknowledge the son of *h.* for first-born
Judg. 15. 2. I thought that thou hadst utterly *h.* her
2 *Sam.* 5. 8. the lame and blind that are *h.* of David's
13. 15. Amnon *h.* Tamar ‖ 22. Absalom *h.* Amnon
22. 18. he delivered me from my strong enemy, and from them that *h.* me, *Psal.* 18. 17.
Esth. 9. 1. the Jews had rule over them that *h.* them
5. did what they would unto those that *h.* them
Job 31. 29. at the destruction of him that *h.* me
Psal. 26. 5. I have *h.* the congregation of evil doers
31. 6. I have *h.* them that regard lying vanities
44. 7. thou hast put them to shame that *h.* us
55. 12. neither was it he that *h.* me, that did magnify
106. 10. he saved them from him that *h.* them
41. and they that *h.* them ruled over them
Prov. 1. 29. they *h.* knowledge, and did not choose
5. 12. and say, how have I *h.* instruction
14. 17. and a man of wicked devices is *h.*
20. the poor is *h.* even of his own neighbour
Eccl. 2. 17. therefore I *h.* life ‖ 18. I *h.* labour
Isa. 60. 15. whereas thou hast been forsaken and *h.*
66. 5. brethren that *h.* you said, Lord be glorified
Jer. 12. 8. therefore have I *h.* mine heritage
Ezek. 16. 37. I will gather all them that thou hast *h.*
35. 6. sith thou hast not *h.* blood, blood pursue
Hos. 9. 15. for there I *h.* them for wickedn. of doings
Mal. 1. 3. I loved Jacob, and *h.* Esau, *Rom.* 9. 13.
Mat. 10. 22. ye shall be *h.* *Mark* 13. 13. *Luke* 21. 17.
24. 9. ye shall be *h.* of all nations for my name
Luke 19. 14. his citizens *h.* him, and sent a message
John 15. 18. ye know that it *h.* me before it *h.* you
24. have both seen and *h.* both me and my Father
25. written in their law, they *h.* me without a cause
17. 14. world hath *h.* them, because not of world
Eph. 5. 29. no man ever yet *h.* his own flesh
Heb. 1. 9. thou hast loved righteousn. and *h.* iniquity

HATEFUL.

Psal. 36. 2. until his iniquity be found to be *h.*
Tit. 3. 3. we were *h.* and hating one another
Rev. 18. 2. a cage of every unclean and *h.* bird

HATEFULLY.

Ezek. 23. 29. and they shall deal with thee *h.*

HATERS.

Psal. 81. 15. the *h.* of Lord should have submitted
Rom. 1. 30. backbiters, *h.* of God, despiteful

HATEST.

2 *Sam.* 19. 6. lovest thine enemies, and *h.* thy friends
Psal. 5. 5. thou *h.* all workers of iniquity
45. 7. thou lovest righteousness, and *h.* wickedness
50. 17. thou *h.* instruction, and castest my words
Ezek. 23. 28. deliver thee into hand whom thou *h.*
Rev. 2. 6. thou *h.* the deeds of the Nicolaitanes

HATETH.

Exod. 23. 5. if see the ass of him that h. thee lying
Deut. 7. 10. Lord not be slack to him that h. him
12. 31. every abomination he h. have they done
16. 22. nor set up any image which the Lord h.
22. 16. I gave my daughter unto this man, he h. her
Job 16. 9. he teareth me in his wrath, who h. me
34. 17. shall even he that h. right, govern?
Psal. 11. 5. him that loveth violence, his soul h.
120. 6. my soul long dwelt with him that h. peace
Prov. 11. 15. and he that h. suretyship is sure
12. 1. but he that h. reproof is brutish
13. 5. a righteous man h. lying, but a wicked man
24. he that spareth his rod h. his son
15. 10. and he that h. reproof shall die
27. but he that h. gifts shall live
26. 24. he that h. dissembleth with his lips
28. a lying tongue h. those that are afflicted
28. 16. he that h. covetousness shall prolong days
29. 24. whoso is partner with a thief h. his own soul
Isa. 1. 14. and your appointed feasts my soul h.
Mal. 2. 16. the Lord saith, that he h. putting away
John 3. 20. every one that doeth evil h. the light
7. 7. but me the world h. because I testify of it
12. 25. he that h. his life in this world shall keep it
15. 19. ye are not of world, therefore world h. you
23. he that h. me h. my Father also
1 John 2. 9. he that h. his brother is in darkness, 11.
3. 15. whosoever h. his brother is a murderer
4. 20. if say, I love God, and h. his brother, is a liar

HATING.

Exod. 18. 21. provide men of truth, h. covetousness
Tit. 3. 3. in times past hateful, and h. one another
Jude 23. h. even the garment spotted by the flesh

HATH.

Gen. 24. 36. and unto him h. he giv. all that he h.
Lev. 22. 5. whatsoever uncleanness he h.
27. 28. no devoted thing of all he h. shall be sold
Num. 23. 22. he h. the strength of an unicorn, 24. 8.
27. 4. why name done away because he h. no son
Deut. 21. 16. his sons to inherit that which he h.
17. the first-born a double portion of all he h.
Josh. 6. 22. bring out thence woman and all she h.
7. 15. he shall be burnt with fire, he and all he h.
1 Sam. 15. 22. h. Lord as great delight in offerings?
2 Kings 4. 2. thine handmaid h. not any thing in hou.
14. verily she h. no child, her husband is old
Job 1. 10. hedge about all he h. ‖ 11. touch all he h.
12. behold, all that he h. is in thy power
2. 4. all that a man h. will he give for his life
5. 16. so the poor h. hope ‖ 38. 28. h. rain a father?
Psal. 37. 16. a little that a righteous man h. is better
109. 11. let the extortioner catch all that he h.
127. 5. happy is the man h. his quiver full of them
146. 5. happy he that h. God of Jacob for his help
Prov. 12. 9. he that is despised and h. a servant is bet.
13. 4. the sluggard desireth, and h. nothing
7. there is that maketh himself rich, yet h. nothing
16. 22. understanding is life unto him who h. it
17. 8. a precious stone in eyes of him that h. it
19. 23. and he that h. it shall abide satisfied
23. 29. who h. woe? who h. sorrow? who h. wounds?
Eccl. 4. 8. yea, he h. neither child nor brother
10. for he h. not another to help him up
6. 8. for what h. the wise more than the fool?
8. 8. neither h. he power in the day of death
Cant. 8. 8. we have a little sister, and she h. no breasts
Isa. 29. 8. behold he is faint, and his soul h. appetite
45. 9. he h. no hands ‖ 50. 10. and h. no light
53. 2. he h. no form nor comeliness, when see him
55. 1. he that h. no money, come ye, buy and eat
Jer. 23. 28. prophet that h. a dream, let him tell, and
he that h. my word, let him speak my word
49. 1. h. Israel no sons? h. he no heir? why then
Mal. 1. 14. cursed be deceiver which h. in flock a male
Mat. 8. 20. h. not where to lay head, Luke 9. 58.
11. 15. he that h. ears to hear, let him hear, 13. 9,
43. Mark 4. 9. Luke 8. 8. | 14. 35. Rev. 2. 7.
18. nor eating, nor drinking, they say he h. a devil
13. 12. whosoever h. to him shall be given, and more
abundance; who h. not, from him shall be taken
that he h. 25. 29. Mark 4. 25. Luke 8. 18. | 19. 26.
44. selleth all that he h. and buyeth that field
56. whence h. this man these things? Mark 6. 2.
Mark 3. 22. he h. Beelzebub, and casteth out devils
30. because they said, he h. an unclean spirit
Luke 7. 33. and ye say, he h. a devil, John 10. 20.
12. 44. he will make him ruler over all that he h.
14. 33. that forsaketh not all that he h. cannot be
20. 24. whose superscription h. it? they said Cesar's
22. 36. he that h. a purse, he that h. no sword
24. 39. a spirit h. not flesh and bones, as ye see me
John 3. 29. he that h. the bride, is the bridegroom
36. believeth h. everlasting life, 5. 24. | 6. 47, 54.
5. 26. as the Father h. life in himself, so h. given
12. 48. h. one judgeth him, the word I have spoken
14. 21. he that h. my commandm. and keepeth them
30. the prince of this world h. nothing in me
15. 13. greater love h. no man than this, that a man
16. 15. all things that the Father h. are mine
19. 11. delivered thee unto me, h. the greater sin
Rom. 3. 1. what advantage then h. the Jew?
4. 2. if justified by works, he h. whereof to glory
9. 21. h. not the potter power over the clay?
1 Cor. 7. 4. the wife h. not power of her own body
7. but every man h. his proper gift of God
14. 26. every one of you h. a psalm, h. a doctrine
2 Cor. 6. 14. what fellowship h. righteousness with
unright.? what communion h. light with darkn.?
15. what concord h. Christ? ‖ 16. h. temple of G.
8. 12. it is accepted according to that a man h.
Gal. 4. 27. for the desolate h. more children than she
Eph. 5. 5. nor idolater h. any inheritance in kingdom
Phil. 3. 4. if any thinketh he h. whereof may trust
Heb. 3. 3. the builder h. more honour than the house
7. 24. this man h. an unchangeable priesthood
10. 35. confidence, which h. recompense of reward
Jam. 2. 14. though a man say he h. faith, not works
1 John 2. 23. who denieth Son, same h. not Father
3. 3. every man that h. this hope in him purifieth
15. ye know that no murderer h. eternal life
17. whoso h. this world's good, and seeth brother

1 John 4. 16. we have bel. the love that God h. to us
18. there is no fear in love, because fear h. torm.
5. 10. he that believeth on Son of G. h. the witness
12. he that h. the Son h. life, h. not Son h. not life
2 John 9. whoso abideth not in doctrine of Christ h.
not God, that abideth h. both the Father and Son
Rev. 3. 7. that h. key of David opens, no man shuts
12. 6. wildern. where she h. a place prepared of G.
12. because he knoweth that he h. but a short time
17. 7. beast which h. the seven heads and ten horns
9. and here is the mind which h. wisdom
20. 6. on such the second death h. no power

HATRED.

Gen. 26. †21. they digged another well, called it h.
Num. 35. 20. if he thrust him of h. or hurl at him
2 Sam. 13. 15. h. wherewith he hated her greater
Psal. 25. 19. and they hate me with cruel h.
109. 3. they compassed me about with h.
5. they have rewarded me h. for my love
139. 22. I hate them with perfect h. I count them
Prov. 10. 12. h. stirs up strifes, love covers all sins
18. he that hideth h. with lying lips, is a fool
15. 17. better than a stalled ox, and h. therewith
26. 26. whose h. is covered by deceit, his wickedn.
Eccl. 9. 1. no man knoweth either love or h.
6. their love, their h. and envy is now perished
Ezek. 25. 15. vengeance to destroy it for the old h.
35. 5. because thou hast had a perpetual h.
11. I will do according to envy hast used out of h.
Hos. 9. 7. for multitude of iniquity, and for great h.
8. but the prophet is h. in the house of his God
Gal. 5. 20. witchcraft, h. the works of the flesh

HATS.

Dan. 3. 21. men were bound in their hosen and h.

HAUGHTY.

2 Sam. 22. 28. thine eyes are upon h. to bring down
Psal. 131. 1. Lord, my heart is not h. nor eyes lofty
Prov. 6. †17. the Lord hateth h. eyes, a lying tongue
16. 18. and a h. spirit goeth before a fall
18. 12. before destruction the heart of man is h.
21. 24. proud and h. scorner is his name
Isa. 3. 16. because the daughters of Zion are h.
10. 33. high hewn down, and h. shall be humbled
24. 4. the h. people of the earth do languish
Ezek. 16. 50. were h. before me, I took them away
Zeph. 3. 11. no more be h. because of holy mountain

HAUGHTILY.

Mic. 2. 3. neither shall ye go h. this time, is evil

HAUGHTINESS.

Prov. 21. †4. the h. of eyes and a proud heart is sin
Isa. 2. 11. h. of men shall be bowed down, L. exalted
17. and the h. of men shall be made low
13. 11. and I will lay low the h. of the terrible
16. 6. we heard of the h. of Moab, Jer. 48. 29.

HAUNT.

1 Sam. 23. 22. go and see his place where his h. is

HAUNT.

1 Sam. 30. 31. where David and men were wont to h.
Ezek. 26. 17. cause their terror to be on all that h. it

HAVE.

Gen. 11. 6. the Lord said, they h. all one language
43. 7. h. ye another brother? ‖ 44. 19. h. ye a father?
46. 32. and they have brought all that they h.
Exod. 20. 3. thou shalt h. no other gods, Deut. 5. 7.
Lev. 7. 7. priest that maketh atonement shall h. it, 8.
10. every meat-offering the sons of Aaron shall h.
19. 36. a just ephah and a just hin shall ye h.
22. 13. priest's daughter h. no child, Num. 27. 8, 9.
Num. 11. 13. whence should I h. flesh to give unto all
22. 38. h. I now any power at all to say any thing?
25. 13. covenant of peace he and his seed shall h. it
35. 8. from them that h. many, them that h. few
Deut. 5. 26. who hath heard voice of God, as we h.?
Josh. 2. 13. ye will save alive father and all they h.
17. 18. though they h. iron chariots and be strong
22. 24. what h. you to do with Lord God of Israel?
Judg. 14. 15. h. ye called us to take that we h.?
18. 24. ye h. taken my gods, and what h. I more?
Ruth 1. 12. turn again, for I am too old to h. an husband, if I should h. an husband also to night
1 Sam. 8. 19. but we will h. a king over us
9. 7. there is not a present to bring; what h. we?
15. 3. go and utterly destroy all that they h.
18. 8. what can he h. more but the kingdom?
21. 15. h. I need of madmen, that ye h. brought?
2 Sam. 13. 9. Amnon said, h. out all men from me
15. 36. they h. there with them their two sons
16. 10. what h. I to do with you, ye sons of Zeruiah?
18. 18. I h. no son to keep my name in remembrance
19. 28. what right h. I yet to cry any more to king?
34. Barzillai said unto king, how long h. I to live?
43. Israel said, we h. ten parts in the king
1 Kings 8. 28. h. thou respect unto prayer of thy serv.
12. 16. saying, what portion h. we in David
17. 12. I h. not a cake, but an handful of meal
20. 4. my lord, O king, I am thine, and all I h.
21. 2. that I may h. it for a garden of herbs
22. 17. Israel scattered as sheep that h. no shepherd
2 Kings 11. 15. h. her forth without, 2 Chr. 23. 14.
20. 9. Isaiah said, this sign shalt thou h. of the L.
2 Chron. 1. 12. nor shall any after thee h. the like
16. 9. from henceforth thou shalt h. wars
35. 21. what h. I to do with thee, king of Judah?
23. he said, h. me away, for I am sore wounded
Neh. 5. 5. other men h. our lands and vineyards
Job 3. 9. let it look for light but h. none
6. 8. O that I might h. my request, that God would
10. then should I yet h. comfort, yea, I would
21. 15. what profit should we h. if pray unto him?
30. 13. they mar my path, they h. no helper
35. 3. what profit shall I h. if be cleansed from sin?
Psal. 2. 4. the Lord shall h. them in derision
14. 4. h. workers of iniquity no knowledge? 53. 4.
16. 6. in pleasant places, I h. a goodly heritage
35. 25. let them not say, ah, so would we h. it
73. 25. whom h. I in heaven but thee? none upon
104. 33. I will sing to my God while I h. my being
111. 10. a good understanding h. all they that do
115. 5. they h. mouths; eyes h. they, but see not
6. they h. ears; noses h. they, 7. | 135. 16, 17.
119. 42. so shall I h. wherewith to answer him
165. great peace h. they which love thy law

Psal. 146. 2. sing pr. unto my G. while I h. any being
149. 9. this honour h. all his saints, praise Lord
Prov. 1. 14. cast in thy lot, let us all h. one purse
20. 4. the slug. shall beg in harvest, and h. nothing
29. 21. shall h. him become his son at the length
30. 2. and I h. not the understanding of a man
3. nor h. I the knowledge of the Holy
Eccl. 3. 19. yea, they h. all one breath, so that a man
7. 12. that wisdom giveth life to them that h. it
9. 5. neither h. they any more a reward
6. neither h. they any more portion for ever
Cant. 8. 8. we h. a little sister and she hath no breasts
12. thou, O Solomon, must h. a thousand
Isa. 5. 13. are gone, because they h. no knowledge
23. 12. pass over, there also shalt thou h. no rest
26. 1. we h. a strong city, salvation will G. appoint
30. 29. ye shall h. a song as in the night when a holy
43. 8. bring the blind that h. eyes, death that h. ears
45. 21. h. not I the Lord? there is no G. beside me
24. say, in the L. h. I righteousness and strength
49. 20. the children which thou shalt h. shall say
50. 2. is my hand shortened? h. I no power to deliv.?
11. this h. of my hand, ye shall lie down in sorrow
52. 5. therefore what h. I here, saith the Lord
56. 11. are greedy dogs, which can never h. enough
61. 7. for your shame you shall h. double
Jer. 5. 21. which h. eyes and see not, which h. ears
31. my people love to h. it so, what will ye do in
12. 12. sword of L. devour, no flesh shall h. peace
16. 2. neither shalt h. sons nor daugh. in this place
23. 17. the Lord hath said, ye shall h. peace, 29. 7.
35. 7. ye shall not plant vineyard, nor h. any
36. 30. he shall h. none to sit upon throne of David
38. 2. he shall h. his life for a prey, and shall live
44. 14. to the which they h. a desire to return
49. 9. they will destroy till they h. enough
31. the nation which h. neither gates nor bars
Lam. 3. 21. this I recall to my mind, theref. h. I hope
Ezek. 5. 11. neither will I h. pity, 7. 4. | 8. 18. | 9. 10.
9. 5. let not your eye spare, neither h. ye pity
18. 23. h. I any pleasure that the wicked die?
32. I h. no pleasure in the death of him, 33. 11.
21. 25. when iniquity shall h. an end, 29.
Dan. 2. 30. for any wisdom that I h. more than any
3. 25. I see four men loose, and they h. no hurt
5. 7. shall h. a chain of gold about his neck, 16.
6. 2. and the king should h. no damage
Hos. 10. 3. for now they shall say we h. no king
Mic. 3. 6. night shall be unto you, ye shall not h. vis.
Zeph. 2. 10. this shall they h. for their pride
Hag. 1. 6. ye eat, but ye h. not enough; ye drink
Mal. 2. 10. h. we not all one father? hath not God
Mat. 3. 9. we h. Abraham to our father, Luke 3. 8.
5. 40. take thy coat, let him h. thy cloak also
46. if love them who love you what reward h. ye?
6. 2. verily I say, they h. their reward, 5, 16.
8. 20. the foxes h. holes, birds h. nests, Luke 9. 58.
29. what h. we to do with thee, Jesus, thou Son of
God? Mark 1. 24. Luke 4. 34.
13. 12. and he shall h. more abundance, 25. 29.
14. 4. it is not lawful for thee to h. her, Mark 6. 18.
15. 33. whence should we h. so much bread in wild.
34. how many loaves h. ye? Mark 6. 38. | 8. 5.
17. 20. if h. faith as a grain of mustard, 21. 21.
19. 16. what shall I do, that I may h. eternal life?
27. followed thee, what shall we h. therefore?
26. 11. ye h. the poor always with you, but me ye
h. not always, Mark 14. 7. John 12. 8.
65. what further need h. we of witnesses?
27. 19. h. nothing to do with that just man
43. let him deliver him now, if he will h. him
Mark 2. 17. the whole h. no need of the physician
19. as long as they h. the bridegroom with them
4. 23. if any man h. ears to hear, 7. 16. Rev. 13. 9.
40. why are ye so fearful, how is it ye h. no faith?
8. 16. saying, it is because we h. no bread
9. 50. h. salt in yourselves, h. peace one with anoth.
10. 21. thou shalt h. treasure in heaven, Luke 18. 22.
11. 23. but shall believe, shall h. whatsoev. he saith
24. believe ye receive them, and ye shall h. them
Luke 6. 32. who love you, what thank h. ye? 33, 34.
8. 18. from him be taken what he seemeth to h.
11. 5. which of you shall h. a friend, and shall go
41. but rather give alms of such things as ye h.
12. 4. and after that h. no more that they can do
24. which neither h. store-house nor barn
33. sell that ye h. and give alms, provide bags
14. 18. must go and see it, I pray h. me excused, 19.
15. 31. thou art ever with me, all that I h. is thine
19. 14. we will not h. this man to reign over us
22. 31. Satan hath desired to h. you, that he may
24. 17. what communications ye h. one to another?
39. spirit hath not flesh and bones, as ye see me h.
41. he said, h. ye here any meat? John 21. 5.
John 2. 3. the mother of Jesus said, they h. no wine
4. woman, what h. I to do with thee?
3. 15. should not perish, but h. everlast. life, 16.
4. 17. the woman answered and said, I h. no husb.
5. 26. he hath given the Son to h. life in himself
38. and ye h. not his word abiding in you
42. I know that ye h. not the love of God in you
6. 40. believeth on him may h. everlasting life
53. except ye eat his flesh, ye h. no life in you
8. 6. tempting, that they might h. to accuse him
12. he that followeth me, shall h. the light of life
41. h. one father, even God ‖ 49. I h. not a devil
9. 41. if ye were blind, ye should h. no sin
10. 10. I am come that they might h. life and more
16. other sheep I h. which are not of this fold
12. 35. walk while ye h. light, lest darkness, 36.
16. 33. that in me ye might h. peace, in the world
ye shall h. tribulation, I h. overcome the world
18. 39. but ye h. a custom that I should release one
19. 7. we h. a law ‖ 15. we h. no king but Cesar
20. 31. that believing ye might h. life thro' Jesus
Acts 3. 6. silver and gold h. I none, but such as I h.
9. 6. he said, Lord, what wilt thou h. me to do?
17. 28. in him we live, move, and h. our being
19. 25. know that by this craft we h. our wealth
21. 23. we h. four men which h. a vow
Rom. 2. 14. when the Gentiles, which h. not the law
6. 22. ye h. your fruit unto holiness, the end life

Rom. 8. 9. now if any man *h.* not Spirit of Christ
9. 9. this time I will come, and Sara shall *h.* a son
12. 4. and all members *h.* not the same office
14. 22. hast thou faith? *h.* to thyself before God
15. 17. I *h.* whereof I may glory through Christ
1 *Cor.* 2. 16. but we *h.* the mind of Christ
4. 11. are naked, and *h.* no certain dwelling-place
15. though instructors, yet *h.* ye not many fathers
5. 1. that one should *h.* his father's wife
6. 19. Holy Gh. which is in you, which ye *h.* of G.
7. 2. to avoid fornication, let every man *h.* his own wife, let every woman *h.* her own husband
28. yet such shall *h.* trouble in the flesh
29. they that *h.* wives be as tho' they had none
32. I would *h.* you without carefulness
40. I think also that I *h.* the Spirit of God
8. 1. we know, that we all *h.* knowledge
9. 4. *h.* we not power to eat and drink? 5, 6.
11. 14. if a man *h.* long hair, it is a shame to him
15. if a woman *h.* long hair, it is a glory to her
16. we *h.* no such custom, nor the churches of G.
22. what, *h.* ye not houses to eat and drink in?
12. 21. eye not say to hand, I *h.* no need of thee
30. *h.* all the gifts of healing? do all interpret?
13. 1. *h.* not charity, I am become sounding brass
2. though I *h.* all faith and *h.* not charity, 3.
15. 31. by your rejoicing which I *h.* Christ Jesus
34. for some *h.* not the knowledge of God
2 *Cor.* 3. 4. such trust *h.* we thro' Christ to God-ward
4. 1. seeing we *h.* this ministry, we faint not
8. 11. a performance out of that which ye *h.*
Eph. 4. 28. he may *h.* to give to him that needeth
5. 11. *h.* no fellowship with the unfruitful works
Phil. 1. 7. I *h.* you in my heart ‖ 4. 18. but I *h.* all
Col. 1. 4. and love which ye *h.* to all the saints
2. 1. ye knew what great conflict I *h.* for you
3. 13. if any man *h.* a quarrel against any
4. 1. knowing that ye also *h.* a Master in heaven
1 *Thess.* 2. 14. ye suffered, as they *h.* of the Jews
2 *Thess.* 3. 2. pray for us, for all men *h.* not faith
9. not because we *h.* not power, but to make
1 *Tim.* 2. 4. who will *h.* all men to be saved
Heb. 4. 13. the eyes of him with whom we *h.* to do
14. seeing then that we *h.* a great high-priest
5. 14. by reason of use *h.* their senses exercised
6. 19. which hope we *h.* as an anchor of the soul
8. 1. we *h.* such an High-Priest, set on right-hand
3. that this man *h.* somewhat also to offer
10. 34. that ye *h.* in heaven a better substance
13. 5. be content with such things as ye *h.*
10. we *h.* an altar whereof they *h.* no right to eat
14. here *h.* we no continuing city, we seek one
Jam. 1. 4. but let patience *h.* her perfect work
2. 1. *h.* not faith of Christ with respect of persons
14. and *h.* not works, can faith save him?
17. even so faith, if it *h.* not works, is dead
18. a man may say, thou hast faith, and I *h.* works
3. 14. if ye *h.* bitter envy, and strife in your hearts
4. 2. ye lust and *h.* not, ye desire to *h.* ye fight and war, yet ye *h.* not, because ye ask not
1 *Pet.* 4. 8. above all things *h.* fervent charity
2 *Pet.* 1. 19. we *h.* a more sure word of prophecy
2. 14. an heart they *h.* exercised with covetousness
1 *John* 1. 8. if we say, we *h.* no sin, deceive ourselv.
2. 1. we *h.* an Advocate with the Father, Jesus
20. but ye *h.* an unction from the Holy One
4. 21. and this commandment *h.* we from him
5. 13. that ye may know that ye *h.* eternal life
14. this is the confidence that we *h.* in him
15. know we *h.* the petitions we desired of him
3 *John* 4. I *h.* no greater joy than to hear that my
9. Diotrephes, who loveth to *h.* the pre-eminence
Rev. 1. 18. I *h.* the keys of hell and of death
2. 4. yet I *h.* somewhat against thee, 14, 20.
10. and ye shall *h.* tribulation ten days
24. to you, and to as many as *h.* not this doctrine
25. but what ye *h.* already, hold fast till I come
9. 4. which *h.* not the seal of God in their foreh.
12. 17. and *h.* the testimony of Jesus Christ
14. 11. they *h.* no rest day nor night who worship
17. 13. these *h.* one mind, and give their power
19. 10. of brethren that *h.* the testimony of Jesus
21. 8. liars shall *h.* their part in the lake that burns
22. 14. that they may *h.* right to the tree of life

See COMPASSION, DOMINION.

HAVING.

Lev. 7. 20. *h.* his uncleanness upon him, 22. 3.
20. 18. *h.* her sickness ‖ 22. 22. *h.* a wen or scurvy
Num. 24. 4. into a trance, but *h.* his eyes open, 16.
Ruth 1. 13. would ye stay for them from *h.* husbands
1 *Chron.* 21. 16. *h.* a drawn sword in his hand
2 *Chron.* 11. 12. *h.* Judah and Benjamin on his side
Esth. 6. 12. mourning, and *h.* his head covered
Prov. 6. 7. which *h.* no guide, overseer, or ruler
Ezek. 38. 11. and *h.* neither bars nor gates
Mic. 1. 11. pass ye away, *h.* thy shame naked
Zech. 9. 9. thy king cometh to thee, *h.* salvation
Mat. 7. 29. he taught as one *h.* authority
8. 9. under authority, *h.* soldiers under me, *Luke* 7. 8.
9. 36. were as sheep *h.* no shepherd, *Mark* 6. 34.
18. 8. rather than *h.* two hands or two feet
9. rather than *h.* two eyes to be cast, *Mark* 9. 43.
22. 12. how camest, not *h.* a wedding-garment?
24. if a man die, *h.* no children, *Luke* 20. 28.
25. and *h.* no issue, left his wife to his brother
26. 7. woman *h.* an alabaster box, *Mark* 14. 3.
Mark 8. 1. and *h.* nothing to eat, Jesus called
18. *h.* eyes, see ye not? *h.* ears, hear ye not?
11. 13. a fig tree *h.* leaves ‖ 12. 6. *h.* one son
Luke 8. 43. woman *h.* an issue of blood twelve years
15. 4. what man of you *h.* an hundred sheep?
8. either what woman *h.* ten pieces of silver?
17. 7. but which of you *h.* a servant ploughing
John 7. 15. how knows he letters, *h.* never learned?
18. 10. then Simeon Peter *h.* a sword drew it
Acts 4. 37. *h.* land, sold it, and brought the money
22. 12. *h.* a good report of the Jews who dwelt
24. 22. *h.* more perfect knowledge of that way
Rom. 2. 14. *h.* not the law, are a law to themselves
12. 6. *h.* then gifts differing accord. to grace given
1 *Cor.* 6. 1. *h.* a matter against another, go to law
7. 37. he that standeth stedfast *h.* no necessity
2 *Cor.* 4. 13. we *h.* the same spirit of faith, as written
6. 10. as *h.* nothing, and yet possessing all things
7. 1. *h.* therefore these promises, beloved, cleanse
9. 8. ye always *h.* all sufficiency in all things
10. 6. *h.* in a readiness to revenge all disobedience
15. but *h.* hope, when your faith is increased
Eph. 2. 12. *h.* no hope ‖ 5. 27. not *h.* spot or wrinkle
6. 14. *h.* your loins girt about with truth
Phil. 1. 23. *h.* a desire to depart, and be with Christ
25. *h.* this confidence ‖ 30. *h.* the same conflict
2. 2. *h.* same love ‖ 3. 9. not *h.* my own righteousn.
Col. 1. 20. *h.* made peace thro' the blood of his cross
2. 19. *h.* nourishment ministered, and knit together
1 *Tim.* 3. 4. *h.* his chil. in subjection with all gravity
4. 8. *h.* the promise of the life that now is
5. 12. *h.* damnation, because they have cast off
6. 8. and *h.* food and raiment, let us be content
2 *Tim.* 2. 19. *h.* this seal, the Lord knoweth his
3. 5. *h.* a form of godliness, but denying the power
4. 3. they shall heap teachers, *h.* itching ears
Tit. 1. 6. *h.* faithful children, not accused of riot
1 *Pet.* 2. 12. *h.* conversation honest among Gentiles
3. 16. *h.* a good conscience, they may be ashamed
2 *Pet.* 2. 14. *h.* eyes full of adult. that cannot cease
Jude 19. these be sensual, *h.* not the Spirit
Rev. 5. 6. *h.* seven horns ‖ 8. *h.* every one harps
7. 2. I saw an angel, *h.* the seal of the living God
8. 3. *h.* a golden censer ‖ 9. 17. *h.* breast-plates
12. 3. *h.* seven heads ‖ 12. *h.* great wrath
14. 6. *h.* the everlasting gospel to preach to them
15. 2. *h.* the harps of God ‖ 17. 4. *h.* a golden cup
18. 1. *h.* great power ‖ 20. 1. *h.* the key of the pit
21. 11. the holy Jerusalem, *h.* the glory of God

HAVEN.

Gen. 49. 13. Zebul. shall dwell at the *h.* an *h.* of ships
Psal. 107. 30. he bringeth them to their desired *h.*
Acts 27. 12. *h.* not commodious, an *h.* of Crete

Fair HAVENS.

Acts 27. 8. came to a place which is called the *f. h.*

HAVOCK.

Acts 8. 3. as for Saul, he made *h.* of the church

HAWK.

Lev. 11. 16. *h.* had in abomination, *Deut.* 14. 15.
Job 39. 26. doth the *h.* fly by thy wisdom?

HAY.

Prov. 27. 25. the *h.* appeareth and tender grass
Isa. 15. 6. the *h.* is withered away, the grass faileth
1 *Cor.* 3. 12. who buildeth on this foundation, *h.*

HAZEL.

Gen. 30. 37. Jacob took him rods of *h.* and chesnut

HE.

Gen. 3. 16. and *he* shall rule over thee
6. 3. not always strive with man, for *he* is flesh
44. 10. *he* with whom it is found shall be my servant
48. 19. younger brother shall be greater than *he*
49. 8. art *he* whom thy brethren shall praise
Exod. 4. 16. *he* shall be thy spokesman to the people, and *he* shall be to thee instead of a mouth
9. 34. and hardened his heart, *he* and his servants
35. 34. *he* hath put in his heart that he may teach both *he* and Aholiab of the tribe of Dan
Lev. 7. 33. *he* among the sons of Aaron that offereth
25. 54. shall go out in jubilee, *he* and his children
Num. 24. 9. and cursed is *he* that curseth thee
Deut. 3. 1. came, *he* and all his people to battle
8. 18. it is *he* that giveth power to get wealth
27. 16. cursed be *he*. *So to the end of the chapter*
31. 6. *he* that doth go with thee, *he* will not fail, 8.
32. 6. is not *he* thy Father that hath bought thee?
39. I, even I am *he*, and there is no God with me, *Isa.* 41. 4. | 43. 10, 13. | 46. 4. | 48. 12.
Josh. 23. 3. L. your G. is *he* that fought for you, 10.
Judg. 10. 18. what man is *he* that will begin to fight?
1 *Sam.* 4. 16. I am *he* that came out of the army
9. 2. there was not a goodlier person than *he*
16. 12. this is *he* ‖ 25. 25. as his name is so is *he*
1 *Kings* 2. 32. who fell on two men better than *he*
17. 15. she and *he* and her house did eat many days
18. 17. art thou *he* that troubleth Israel?
2 *Kings* 18. 22. is not that *he* whose places, *Isa.* 36. 7.
2 *Chron.* 29. 3. *he* in first year of reign opened doors
Job 9. 24. if not, where, and who is *he*?
13. 19. who is *he* that will plead with me?
14. 10. man dieth, and where is *he*? 20. 7. *Isa.* 63. 11.
Psal. 22. 9. thou art *he* that took me out of the womb
60. 12. *he* it is shall tread down enemies, 108. 13.
68. 20. *he* that is our God is the God of salvation
100. 3. *he* is God, it is *he* that hath made us
144. 10. it is *he* that giveth salvation to kings
Prov. 16. 20. that trusteth in L. happy is *he*, 29. 18.
Eccl. 5. 8. *he* that is higher than the highest regard.
6. 3. I say that an untimely birth is better than *he*
Isa. 40. 22. it is *he* sitteth on the circle of the earth
51. 12. I, even I, am *he* that comforteth you, 52. 6. *John* 18. 5, 6, 8. *Rev.* 1. 18. | 2. 23.
Jer. 5. 12. have belied the Lord, and said, it is not *he*
14. 22. art not thou *he*, O Lord our God
38. 5. the king is not *he* that can do any thing
48. 26. and *he* also shall be in derision
Ezek. 38. 17. art thou *he* of whom I have spoken?
Hab. 1. 13. the man that is more righteous than *he*
Mat. 2. 2. where is *he* that is born king of the Jews?
3. 3. this is *he* that was spoken of by the prophet
11. 3. art thou *he* that should come? *Luke* 7. 19, 20.
12. 30. *he* that is not with me is against me, and *he* that gathereth not with me, *Luke* 11. 23.
22. 42. what think ye of Christ? whose son is *he*?
24. 26. *he* is in the desert, *he* is in the secret chamb.
26. 48. the same is *he*, hold him fast, *Mark* 14. 44.
Mark 12. 32. and there is none other but *he*
Luke 10. 22. *he* to whom the Son will reveal him
11. 7. and *he* from within shall answer and say
20. 2. who is *he* that gave thee this authority?
22. 27. *he* that sitteth at meat, or *he* that serveth
24. 6. they said, *he* is not here, but is risen
21. we trusted *he* should have redeemed Israel
John 1. 15. this was *he* of whom I spake, 30.
4. 26. Jesus saith, I that speak to thee, am *he*
7. 11. where is *he*? ‖ 25. is not this *he* they seek to k.?
8. 24. if ye believe not that I am *he*, ye shall die
28. then shall ye know that I am *he*
9. 8. they said, is not this *he* that sat and begged?
John 9. 9. some said, this is *he*, but *he* said, I am *he*
36. who is *he*, Ld. ‖ 37. *he* that talketh with thee
13. 19. I tell you that ye may believe that I am *he*
Acts 3. 10. they knew it was *he* who sat for alms
7. 38. this is *he* that was in the church in wildern.
9. 21. is not this *he* that destroyed them who called
10. 21. Peter said, I am *he* whom ye seek
42. *he* that was ordained of God to be the judge
13. 25. whom think ye that I am? I am not *he*
Rom. 2. 28. *he* is not a Jew that is one outwardly
29. but *he* is a Jew that is one inwardly
14. 18. *he* that in these things serveth Christ
1 *Cor.* 10. 22. are we stronger than *he*?
2 *Cor.* 10. 7. of himself think this again, that as *he* is Christ's, even so are we Christ's
1 *Thess.* 5. 24. faithful is *he* that calleth you, will do it
2 *Thess.* 2. 7. *he* who letteth, will let till *he* be taken
Heb. 12. 7. what son is *he* the father chasteneth not?
10. but *he* for our profit, that we might be partak.
1 *Pet.* 1. 15. as *he* which hath called you is holy
1 *John* 1. 7. if we walk in light, as *he* is in the light
2. 28. when he shall appear, we may have confidence
3. 7. is righteous, even as *he* is righteous
24. dwelleth in him, and *he* in him, 4. 15.
4. 4. greater is *he* that is in you, than *he* in world
17. because as *he* is so are we in this world
5. 12. *he* that hath the Son, hath life; and *he* that hath not the Son of God, hath not life
3 *John* 11. follow not evil, *he* that doeth good is of God; *he* that doeth evil hath not seen God
Rev. 20. 6. holy is *he* that hath part in first resurrec.
22. 11. *he* that is unjust, *he* that is filthy

See BLESSED, DID, SAITH.

HEAD.

The head *is the uppermost and chief part of the body. It is sometimes taken for the whole man.* Prov. 10. 6. Blessings are upon the head of the just, *that is, upon their persons. And God says of the wicked,* I will recompense their way upon their head, *Ezek.* 9. 10. *It is taken also for the life.* Dan. 1. 10. Ye shall make me endanger my head to the king. *It also signifies a chief or capital city.* Isa. 7. 8. The head of *Syria* is *Damascus. It denotes a chief or principal member in any society.* Isa. 9. 14, 15. The Lord will cut off from *Israel* head and tail. The ancient and honourable, he is the head. *It is said,* Gen. 3. 15. The seed of the woman shall bruise the serpent's head; *that is,* Christ Jesus, *the blessed seed of the woman, shall overthrow the power, policy, and works of the devil.*

Head *is taken for one that hath rule and pre-eminence over others. Thus God is the* head *of Christ, as Mediator; from him he derives all his dignity and authority:* Christ *is the only spiritual* head *of his church, both in respect of eminence and influence; he communicates life, motion, and strength to every believer: also the husband is the* head *of his wife, because by God's ordinance he is to rule over her,* Gen. 3. 16. *Also in regard of pre-eminence of sex,* 1 Pet. 3. 7. *and excellency of knowledge,* 1 Cor. 14. 35. *The apostle mentions this subordination of persons in* 1 Cor. 11. 3. But I would have you know, that the head of every man is *Christ:* and the head of the woman is the man; and the head of *Christ* is God.

The river in Paradise was divided into four heads, *into four springs, four branches,* Gen. 2. 10. The stone which the builders rejected, was made the head of the corner, *Psal.* 118. 22. *it was the first in the angle, whether it were disposed at the top of that angle to adorn and crown it, or at the bottom to support it. This in the New Testament is applied to* Christ, *who is the strength and beauty of the church, to unite the several parts thereof, namely, both* Jews *and* Gentiles, *together.* Thou hast caused men to ride over our heads, *Psal.* 66. 12. *Thou hast given us masters who use us like slaves, yea, like beasts to carry their burdens.* The Lord shall make thee the head, and not the tail, *Deut.* 28. 13. *Thou shalt be always master, and never in subjection.*

Head *is taken sometimes for poison, because the* Hebrew *word* Rosch, *which signifies* head, *signifies likewise poison.* Job 20. 16. He shall suck the poison, or head of asps. *In times of mourning, they covered their heads, they cut and plucked off their hair;* I will bring baldness upon every head, *says the prophet, speaking of calamitous times,* Amos 8. 10. *On the contrary, in prosperity they anointed their heads with sweet oils.* Eccl. 9. 8. Let thy head lack no ointment. To shake the head at one, *is a gesture of contempt and insult.* Psal. 22. 7. They shoot out the lip, they shake the head.

Gen. 3. 15. it shall bruise thy *h.* thou bruise his heel
40. 13. yet Pharaoh shall lift up thy *h.* 19.
49. 26. blessings shall be on the *h.* of Joseph, and on the top of the *h.* of him, *Deut.* 33. 16.
Exod. 29. 10. Aaron and his sons shall put their hands upon *h.* of the bullock, *Lev.* 4. 4. | 8. 14.
15. put hands on *h.* of the ram, 19. *Lev.* 8. 18, 22.
Lev. 1. 4. shall put hand on the *h.* of burnt-offering
3. 2. shall lay his hand on the *h.* of his offering
4. 29. lay his hand on the *h.* of sin-offering, 33.
13. 44. he is leprous, his plague is in his *h.*
45. his clothes shall be rent, and his *h.* bare
21. 5. they shall not make baldness on their *h.*
10. shall not uncover his *h.* nor rend his clothes
Num. 5. 18. the priest shall uncover the woman's *h.*
6. 5. there shall no razor come on the Nazarite's *h.*
7. the consecration of his God is on his *h.*
9. then he shall shave his *h.* 18. *Deut.* 21. 12.
11. and he shall hallow his *h.* that same day
Josh. 2. 19. his blood be on his *h.* blood on our *h.*
Judg. 5. 26. she smote off Sisera's *h.* when she had
13. 5. shall bear a son, no razor shall come on his *h.*
1 *Sam.* 17. 57. Goliath's *h.* ‖ 31. 9. cut off Saul's *h.*
25. 39. the wickedness of Nabal on his own *h.*
28. 2. I will make thee keeper of my *h.* for ever
2 *Sam.* 1. 2. a man came, and earth upon his *h.* 15. 32.
16. thy blood be upon thy *h.* 1 *Kings* 2. 37.
3. 8. Abner was wroth, and said, am I a dog's *h.*?

2 Sam. 3. 29. let it rest on h. of Joab, on his house
16. 9. let me go over, and take off his h.
2 Kings 2. 3. take thy master from thy h. to day, 5.
4. 19. and he said unto his father, my h. my h.
6. 31. if the h. of Elisha shall stand on him
32. son of a murderer sent to take away my h.
19. 21. the virgin despised thee, the daughter of Jerusalem hath shaken her h. at thee, Isa. 37. 22.
25. 27. did lift up the h. of Jehoiachin, Jer. 52. 31.
2 Chron. 6. 23. by recompensing his way on his h.
Ezra 9. 6. our iniquities are increased over our h.
Neh. 4. 4. and turn their reproach on their own h.
Esth. 9. 25. his device should return on his own h.
Job 1. 20. Job arose, shaved his h. and fell down
10. 15. if righteous, yet will I not lift up my h.
16. 4. and I could shake my h. at you
Psal. 3. 3. my glory and the lifter up of mine h.
7. 16. his mischief shall return on his own h.
22. 7. they shoot out the lip, they shake the h.
23. 5. thou anointest my h. with oil, cup runneth
27. 6. now shall my h. be lifted up above enemies
38. 4. mine iniquities are gone over mine h.
44. 14. a shaking of the h. among the people
60. 7. Ephraim is the strength of my h. 108. 8.
68. 21. God shall wound the h. of his enemies
83. 2. they that hate thee have lift up the h.
110. 7. therefore shall he lift up the h.
140. 9. as for the h. of those that compass me
141. 5. be an oil, which shall not break my h.
Prov. 10. 6. blessings are on the h. of the just
11. 26. blessing on the h. of him which selleth corn
25. 22. shalt heap coals of fire on his h. Rom. 12. 20.
Eccl. 2. 14. the wise man's eyes are in his h.
Cant. 2. 6. his left hand is under my h. 8. 3.
5. 2. my h. is filled with dew, my locks with drops
11. his h. as most fine gold || 7. 5. thy h. as Carmel
Isa. 1. 5. the whole h. is sick and the heart faint
51. 11. everlasting joy shall be on their h.
58. 5. is it to bow down his h. as a bulrush?
59. 17. he put on an helmet of salvation on his h.
Jer. 2. 37. go forth, and thine hands on thy h.
9. 1. O that my h. were waters, mine eyes tears
23. 19. fall grievously on the h. of wicked, 30. 23.
Ezek. 9. 10. recompense their way on their h.
29. 18. every h. was made bald, shoulder peeled
Dan. 2. 38. O king, thou art this h. of gold
Joel 3. 4. return your recompense on your h. 7.
Amos 2. 7. that pant after dust on the h. of the poor
8. 10. and I will bring baldness on every h.
9. 1. he said, cut them in the h. all of them
Zech. 1. 21. so that no man did lift up his h.
6. 11. then set the crowns on the h. of Joshua
Mat. 5. 36. neither shalt thou swear by thy h.
27. 30. and they smote him on the h. Mark 15. 19.
Mark 6. 24. she said, the h. of John the Baptist
Luke 7. 46. my h. with oil thou didst not anoint
John 13. 9. not feet only, but also my hands and h.
1 Cor. 11. 4. his h. covered, dishonoureth his h.
10. the woman ought to have power on her h.
12. 21. the h. to the feet, I have no need of you
Eph. 1. 22. put all things under his feet, and gave him as h. to the church, 4. 15. Col. 1. 18.
Col. 2. 19. not holding the h. from which the body
Rev. 19. 12. eyes flame of fire, and his h. many crowns
See Beard, Bald, Bow, Bowed, Cover, Covered, Crown.

Axe-HEAD.

Deut. 19. 5. and the axe-h. slippeth from the helve
2 Kings 6. 5. axe-h. fell into the water, and he cried

Bed's-HEAD.

Gen. 47. 31. Israel bowed himself on the bed's-h.

Spear's-HEAD.

1 Sam. 17. 7. s.-h. weighed 600 shekels, 2 Sam. 21. 16.

HEAD-*stone*.

Psal. 118. 22. is become the h.-stone of the corner
Zech. 4. 7. bring forth the h.-stone with shoutings

HEAD *of the corner*.

Mat. 21. 42. is become the h. of the corner, Mark 12. 10. Luke 20. 17. Acts 4. 11. 1 Pet. 2. 7.

HEAD, for *Ruler, Governor*.

Num. 17. 3. one rod shall be for the h. of the house
25. 15. he was h. over a people of a chief house
Deut. 28. 13. Lord will make thee the h. not the tail
44. he shall be the h. and thou shalt be the tail
Josh. 22. 14. each one an h. of house of their fathers
Judg. 10. 18. he shall be h. over all Gilead, 11. 8.
11. 9. shall I be your h.? || 11. the people made him h.
1 Sam. 15. 17. wast thou not made the h. of Israel?
2 Sam. 22. 44. thou hast kept me to be h. Psal. 18. 43.
1 Chron. 11. † 6. who smiteth Jebusites, shall be h.
29. 11. and thou art exalted as h. above all
Isa. 7. 8. h. of Damascus is Rezin, h. of Samaria, 9.
9. 14. Lord will cut off from Israel h. and tail
15. the ancient and honourable, he is the h.
19. 15. nor work which h. or tail, or rush, may do
Jer. 22. 6. thou art Gilead to me, h. of Lebanon
Hos. 1. 11. they shall appoint themselves one h.
Hab. 3. 13. woundest the h. out of house of wicked
14. thou didst strike through the h. of his villages
1 Cor. 11. 3. that the h. of every man is Christ, the h. of the woman is the man, the h. of Christ is God
Eph. 5. 23. the husband is the h. of the wife, even as Christ is h. of the church, and Saviour of body
Col. 2. 10. who is the h. of all principality and power

HEAD, for *Top, Chief*.

Psal. 137. † 6. prefer Jerusalem before h. of my joy
Isa. 28. 1. which are on the h. of fat valleys, 4.
51. 20. they lie at the h. of all the streets
Ezek. 16. 25. built high places at h. of the way
21. 19. choose it at the h. of the way to the city
21. king of Babylon stood at the h. of two ways

HEAD, with *hair* or *hairs*.

Lev. 13. 40. the man whose hair is fallen off his h. 41.
14. 9. the leper shall shave all his hair off his h.
Num. 6. 5. let the locks of the hair of his h. grow
18. and shalt take the hair of h. of his separation
Judg. 16. 22. the hair of his h. began to grow again
1 Sam. 14. 45. not an hair of his h. shall fall to ground
2 Sam. 14. 26. weighed hair of his h. at 200 shekels
Ezra 9. 3. I plucked off the hair of my h. and beard
Psal. 40. 12. they are more than hairs of my h. 69. 4.
Cant. 7. 5. and the hair of thine h. like purple
Dan. 3. 27. nor was an hair of their h. singed
7. 9. the hair of his h. like the pure wool
Mat. 10. 30. hairs of your h. are numbered, Luke 12. 7.
Luke 7. 38. did wipe them with hairs of her h. 44.
21. 18. there shall not an hair of your h. perish
Acts 27. 34. not an hair fall from the h. of any
Rev. 1. 14. his h. and his hairs were white like wool

Hoary HEAD.

Lev. 19. 32. thou shalt rise before the hoary h.

HEADBANDS.

Isa. 3. 20. Lord will take away the h. and tablets

HEADY.

2 Tim. 3 4. for men shall be h. high-minded

HEADLONG.

Job 5. 13. the counsel of the froward is carried h.
Luke 4. 29. that they might cast him down h.
Acts 1. 18. and falling h. he burst asunder in midst

HEADS.

Gen. 43. 28. they bowed down their h. Exod. 4. 31.
Lev. 10. 6. uncover not your h. lest ye die
Josh. 7. 6. and put dust upon their h. Job 2. 12.
Judg. 8. 28. so that they lifted up their h. no more
9. 57. all the evil did God render upon their h.
1 Sam. 29. 4. should it not be with the h. of these
1 Kings 20. 31. let us, I pray, put ropes on our h.
32. put ropes on their h. and came to the king
2 Kings 10. 6. take ye the h. of your master's sons
8. they have brought the h. of the king's sons
1 Chron. 12. † 19. he will fall to Saul on our h.
Psal. 24. 7. lift up your h. O ye gates, and be lift, 9.
66. 12. thou hast caused men to ride over our h.
74. 13. thou brakest the h. of the dragons in waters
14. thou brakest the h. of leviathan in pieces
109. 25. they looked on me, they shaked their h.
Isa. 15. 2. on all their h. shall be baldness
35. 10. to Zion songs, and everlasting joy on their h.
Jer. 14. 3. they were ashamed and covered their h.
4. plowmen were ashamed, they covered their h.
Ezek. 7. 18. and baldness shall be on all their h.
11. 21. I will recompense their way on their h. 22. 31.
32. 27. they laid their swords under their h.
44. 18. shall have linen bonnets on their h.
20. nor shall they shave, they shall poll their h.
Mat. 27. 39. reviled, wagging their h. Mark 15. 29.
Luke 21. 28. then look up, and lift up your h.
Acts 18. 6. he said, your blood be upon your own h.
Rev. 9. 7. and on their h. were as it were crowns
19. their tails were like to serpents, and had h.
13. 1. I saw a beast having seven h. and on his h.
3. I saw one of his h. as it were wounded to death
17. 9. the seven h. are seven mountains, on which
18. 19. they cast dust on their h. and cried, alas!

HEADS, for *Governors*.

Exod. 18. 25. and made them h. over the people
Num. 1. 16. they were h. of thousands in Israel
25. 4. take all the h. of the people and hang them
Josh. 22. 21. Reuben and Gad answered the h.
23. 2. Joshua called for their h. and for their judges
1 Chron. 12. 32. the h. of Israel were two hundred
2 Chron. 5. 2. Solomon assembled all the h. to bring
28. 12. certain of the h. of Ephraim stood up
Psal. 110. 6. shall wound the h. over many countries
Isa. 29. † 10. the prophets and h. hath he covered
Mic. 3. 1. hear, O h. of Jacob, and princes of Isr. 9.
11. h. thereof judge for reward, and priests teach
See Fathers.

HEAL.

Num. 12. 13. h. her now, O God, I beseech thee
Deut. 32. 39. I kill and make alive, I wound, I h.
2 Kings 20. 5. I will h. thee, and add to thy days
8. what shall be the sign that the L. will h. me?
2 Chr. 7. 14. I will forgive their sin, and will h. land
Psal. 6. 2. O Lord, h. me, for my bones are vexed
41. 4. h. my soul, for I have sinned against thee
60. 2. h. the breaches thereof, for it shaketh
Eccl. 3. 3. a time to kill, and a time to h.
Isa. 19. 22. shall smite and h. it, and he shall h. them
57. 18. I have seen his ways, and will h. him, 19.
Jer. 3. 22. return, and I will h. your backslidings
17. 14. h. me, O Lord, and I shall be healed
30. 17. I will h. thee of thy wounds, saith the L.
Lam. 2. 13. for thy breach is great, who can h. thee?
Hos. 5. 13. yet could he not h. you, nor cure you
6. 1. let us return, he hath torn, and will h. us
14. 4. I will h. their backslidings, I will love freely
Zech. 11. 16. he shall not h. that that is broken
Mat. 8. 7. Jesus saith, I will come and h. him
10. 1. to h. all manner of sickness, Mark 3. 15.
8. h. the sick, cleanse the lepers, Luke 9. 2. || 10. 9.
12. 10. is it lawful to h. on sabbath-day? Luke 14. 3.
13. 15. I should h. them, John 12. 40. Acts 28. 27.
Mark 3. 2. whether he would h. on sabbath, Luke 6. 7.
Luke 4. 18. he hath sent me to h. the broken-hearted
23. ye will surely say, physician, h. thyself
5. 17. the power of the Lord was present to h. them
7. 3. beseeching that he would come and h. his serv.
John 4. 47. that he would come down and h. his son
Acts 4. 30. by stretching forth thine hand to h.

HEALED.

Gen. 20. 17. God h. Abimelech and his wife
Exod. 21. 19. he shall cause him to be thoroughly h.
Lev. 13. 18. the bile is h. || 37. the scall is h.
14. 3. and if the plague of leprosy be h. 48.
Deut. 28. 27. with itch, whereof thou canst not be h.
1 Sam. 6. 3. return an offering, then he shall be h.
2 Kings 2. 21. have h. the waters || 22. waters were h.
8. 29. king Joram went to be h. in Jezreel
9. 15. Joram was returned to be h. 2 Chron. 22. 6.
2 Chron. 30. 20. the L. hearkened and h. the people
Psal. 30. 2. I cried to thee, and thou hast h. me
107. 20. he sent his word, and h. them
Isa. 6. 10. lest they see, and convert, and be h.
53. 5. he was bruised, and with his stripes we are h.
Jer. 6. 14. they have h. the hurt slightly, 8. 11.
15. 18. my wound incurable, which refuseth to be h.
17. 14. heal me, O Lord, and I shall be h.
51. 8. howl for her, take balm, if so be she may be h.
9. we would have h. Babylon, but she is not h.
Ezek. 30. 21. and lo, it shall not be bound up to be h.
34. 4. neither have ye h. that which was sick
47. 8. brought forth into sea, the waters shall be h. 9.
11. and the marishes thereof shall not be h.
Hos. 7. 1. when I would have h. Isr. then iniquity
11. 3. but they knew not that I h. them
Mat. 4. 24. those that had the palsy, and he h. them
8. 8. speak, and my servant shall be h. Luke 7. 7.
12. 15. multitudes followed him, he h. them, 14. 14
Mark 5. 23. that she may be h. and she shall live
Luke 8. 43. had spent all, nor could be h. of any
13. 14. therefore come and be h. and not on sabbath
17. 15. when he saw that he was h. turned back
22. 51. and he touched his ear, and h. him
John 5. 13. he that was h. wist not who it was
Acts 4. 14. and beholding the man who was h.
5. 16. and they were h. every one
14. 9. and perceiving that he had faith to be h.
28. 8. Paul prayed, and h. the father of Publius
Heb. 12. 13. be out of the way, but let it rather be h.
Jam. 5. 16. pray one for another, that ye may be h.
1 Pet. 2. 24. by whose stripes ye were h.
Rev. 13. 3. and his deadly wound was h. 12.

HEALER.

Isa. 3. 7. shall swear, saying, I will not be an h.

HEALETH.

Exod. 15. 26. for I am the Lord that h. thee
Psal. 103. 3. bless the Lord who h. all thy diseases
147. 3. he h. the broken in heart, and bindeth up
Isa. 30. 26. and he h. the stroke of their wound

HEALING, *Substantive*.

2 Chron. 24. † 13. and the h. went up upon the work
36. † 16, wrath of Lord arose, till there was no h.
Prov. 15. † 4. the h. of a tongue is a tree of life
Jer. 14. 19. there is no h. for us, the time of h.
Dan. 4. † 27. if it may be an h. of thy error
Nah. 3. 19. there is no h. of thy bruise, wound grievous
Mal. 4. 2. shall Sun of right. arise with h. in his wings
Luke 9. 11. and he healed them that had need of h.
Acts 4. 22. on whom this miracle of h. was shewed
1 Cor. 12. 9. is given to another the gift of h. 28.
30. have all the gifts of h.? do all interpret?
Rev. 22. 2. leaves of the tree were for h. of nations

HEALING.

Jer. 30. 13. none to plead, thou hast no h. medicines
Mat. 4. 23. went about h. all manner of sickness
Luke 9. 6. preaching the gospel, and h. every where
Acts 10. 38. h. all that were oppressed of the devil

HEALTH.

Gen. 43. 28. our father is in good h. he is yet alive
2 Sam. 20. 9. Joab said, art thou in h. my brother?
Psal. 38. † 3. neither is there any h. in my bones
42. 11. who is the h. of my countenance, 43. 5.
67. 2. thy saving h. may be known among all nations
Prov. 3. 8. it shall be h. to thy navel and marrow
4. 22. for they are h. to all their flesh
12. 18. but the tongue of the wise is h.
13. 17. but a faithful ambassador is h.
16. 24. sweet to the soul, and h. to the bones
Isa. 58. 8. thy h. shall spring forth speedily
Jer. 8. 15. looked for a time of h. behold trouble
22. why is not the h. of my people recovered!
30. 17. for I will restore h. unto thee, and heal thee
33. 6. behold, I will bring it h. and cure
Acts 27. 34. take some meat, for this is for your h.
3 John 2. mayest be in h. as thy soul prospereth

HEAP, *Substantive*.

Gen. 31. 46. they made a h. and did eat on the h.
52. this h. be witness, and this pillar be witness
Exod. 15. 8. waters gathered, the floods stood upright as an h. Josh. 3. 13, 16. Psal. 33. 7. | 78. 13.
Deut. 13. 16. shall be an h. for ever, not built again
Josh. 7. 26. they raised over him a great h. of stones
8. 28. Joshua burnt Ai, and made it an h. for ever
29. raise on the king of Ai a great h. of stones
11. † 13. the cities that stood still on their h.
Judg. 15. † 16. with the jaw-bone of an ass, an h.
Ruth 3. 7. to lie down at the end of the h. of corn
2 Sam. 18. 17. they laid very great h. on Absalom
Job 21. † 32. yet shall he watch in the h.
30. † 24. he will not stretch out his hand to the h.
Prov. 26. † 8. that putteth a precious stone in an h.
Cant. 7. 2. thy belly is like an h. of wheat set about
Isa. 17. 1. Damascus shall be a ruinous h.
11. harvest shall be an h. in the day of grief
25. 2. for thou hast made of a city an h.
Jer. 30. 18. the city shall be builded on her own h.
49. 2. and Rabbah shall be a desolate h.
Mic. 1. 6. will make Samaria as an h. of the field
Hab. 3. 15. didst walk through the h. of great waters
Hag. 2. 16. when one came to an h. of 20 measures

HEAP.

Deut. 32. 23. I will h. mischiefs upon them
Job 16. 4. I could h. up words against you
27. 16. though he h. up silver as the dust
36. 13. but the hypocrites in heart h. up wrath
Prov. 25. 22. thou shalt h. coals of fire, Rom. 12. 20.
Eccl. 2. 26. to sinner he giveth to gather and to h. up
Ezek. 24. 10. h. on wood, kindle the fire, consume
Hab. 1. 10. for they shall h. dust and take it
2 Tim. 4. 3. h. to themselves teachers, having itching

HEAPED.

Zech. 9. 3. Tyrus h. up silver as the dust, and fine gold
Jam. 5. 3. ye have h. treasure together for last days

HEAPETH.

Psal. 39. 6. he h. up riches, and knoweth not who
Hab. 2. 5. and he h. unto him all people

HEAPS.

Exod. 8. 14. they gathered them together on h.
Judg. 15. 16. with the jaw-bone of an ass, h. on h.
2 Kings 10. 8. lay ye them in two h. at entering in
19. 25. to lay waste fenced cities into ruinous h.
2 Chr. 31. 6. they brought tithe, and laid them by h.
7. in the third month they began to lay the h.
8. when the princes came and saw the h.
Neh. 4. 2. will they revive the stones out of the h.
Job 15. 28. in houses which are ready to become h.
Psal. 79. 1. they have laid Jerusalem on h.
Jer. 9. 11. and I will make Jerusalem h. 26. 18.
31. 21. set thee up way-marks, make thee high h.
50. 26. cast Babylon up as h. and destroy her utterly
51. 37. and Babylon shall become h.
Hos. 12. 11. their altars are as h. in the furrows
Mic. 3. 12. and Jerusalem shall become h.

HEAR

Signifies, (1) *To receive a voice or sound by the ear*

2 Sam. 15. 10. (2) *To grant or answer our prayer.* Psal. 116. 1. I love the Lord because he hath heard my voice. *It is often used in this sense, in the* Psalms *and elsewhere. And God is said* not to hear, *when he does not grant one's desires.* John 9. 31. We know that God heareth not sinners. (3) *To listen to God's word only with the outward sense of the ear.* Mat. 13. 19. When any one heareth the word of the kingdom, and understandeth it not. *Thus all wicked men who are within the church do hear the word; they hear the sound of the words, but then they have not so much as a notional knowledge of these things, or else regard them not, never consider, or lay them to heart.* (4) *To yield a willing assent in our minds to the word of God, with a firm purpose to obey it.* John 8. 47. He that is of God, heareth God's word; *he believes and obeys it. So in* John 10. 27. My sheep hear my voice, and follow me. *It is used often in this sense.* Deut. 1. 43. I spake unto you, and ye would not hear; *ye would not obey me.* 1 Sam. 24. 9. Wherefore hearest thou men's words? *Why believest thou what mine enemies say against me? So in* Mat. 17. 5. This is my beloved Son, hear him; *believe and obey him.* (5) *To learn,* John 8. 26, 40. I speak to the world those things which I have heard of him; *those things which he hath taught me, which he hath communicated to me.* (6) *To approve of, and embrace.* 1 John 4. 5. They speak of the world, and the world heareth them; *these seducers and false teachers preach such doctrines as may gratify and comply with the corrupt affections of worldly men; and they greedily hearken to, approve and embrace such doctrines.* (7) *To judge and determine.* 2 Sam. 15. 3. Thy matters are good and right, but there is no man deputed of the king to hear thee; *to determine thy cause with justice and equity.*

Gen. 21. 6. so that all that *h.* will laugh with me
23. 6. *h.* us, my lord, thou art a mighty prince
Exod. 19. 9. that the people may *h.* when I speak
32. 18. but the noise of them that sing do I *h.*
Num. 16. 8. *h.* I pray you, ye sons of Levi
23. 18. rise up, Balak, and *h.* hearken unto me
30. 4. and her father *h.* her vow and her bond
Deut. 1. 16. *h.* the causes between your brethren
4. 10. and I will make them *h.* my words
5. 1. *h.* Israel the statutes and judgments, 6. 3. | 9. 1. | 20. 3. *Isa.* 48. 1. *Mark* 12. 29.
27. and *h.* all that the Lord our God doth say
12. 28. *h.* all these words which I command thee
13. 12. if thou shalt *h.* say in one of thy cities
30. 12. bring it, that we may *h.* it and do it, 13.
31. 12. that they may *h.* and fear Ld. 13. *Jer.* 6. 10.
Josh. 3. 9. *h.* the words of the Lord your God
6. 5. when ye *h.* the sound of the trumpet, the people shall shout, *Neh.* 4. 20. *Dan.* 3. 5, 15.
Judg. 5. 3. *h.* O ye kings, give ear, O ye princes
16. why abodest, to *h.* the bleatings of the flocks?
14. 13. put forth thy riddle, that we may *h.* it
1 *Sam.* 2. 23. for I *h.* of your evil dealings by all
24. nay, my sons, it is no good report that I *h.*
15. 14. and the lowing of the oxen which I *h.*
16. 2. how can I go? if Saul *h.* it, he will kill me
25. 24. *h.* the words of thy handmaid, 2 *Sam.* 20. 17.
26. 19. let my lord the king *h.* words of his servant
2 *Sam.* 14. †17. so is my lord the king to *h.* good
15. 3. there is no man deputed of the king to *h.* thee
10. as soon as ye *h.* the sound of the trumpet
35. that what thing soever thou shalt *h.*
36. ye shall send to me every thing that ye *h.*
17. 5. and let us *h.* likewise what Hushai saith
20. 16. a wise woman cried out of the city, *h. h.*
22. 45. soon as they *h.* shall be obedient, *Ps.* 18. 44.
1 *Kings* 3. †11. asked understanding to *h.* judgment
4. 34. to *h.* the wisdom of Solomon, 10. 8, 24. 2 *Chron.* 9. 7, 23. *Mat.* 12. 42. *Luke* 11. 31.
8. 30. then *h.* thou in heaven and forgive, 32, 34, 36, 39, 43, 45, 49. 2 *Chron.* 6. 21.
18. 26. they called on Baal, saying, O Baal, *h.* us
2 *Kings* 7. 6. made the host to *h.* a noise of chariots
18. 28. *h.* the word of the great king, *Isa.* 36. 13.
19. 16. *h.* the words of Sennacherib, *Isa.* 37. 17.
1 *Chr.* 14. 15. when thou shalt *h.* a sound of going
Neh. 1. 6. that thou mayest *h.* the prayer of servant
4. 4. *h.* O our G. for we are despised, turn reproach
8. 2. and all that could *h.* with understanding
Job 5. 27. *h.* it, and know thou it for thy good
13. 17. *h.* diligently my speech with ears, 21. 2.
27. 9. will God *h.* his cry? || 34. 2. *h.* my words
42. 4. *h.* I beseech thee, and I will speak
Psal. 4. 1. have mercy upon me, *h.* my prayer, O God, 39. 12. | 54. 2. | 84. 8. | 102. 1. | 143. 1.
20. 1. the Lord *h.* thee in the day of trouble
9. save, Lord, let the king *h.* us when we call
27. 7. *h.* O Lord, when I cry with my voice
30. 10. *h.* O Lord, and have mercy upon me
49. 1. *h.* this, all ye people, give ear, all inhabitants
50. 7. *h.* O my people, and I will speak, 81. 8.
51. 8. make me to *h.* joy and gladness, that the bones
59. 7. swords in lips, for who, say they, doth *h.*?
61. 1. *h.* my cry, O God, attend to my prayer
66. 16. come, and *h.* all ye that fear God
102. 20. *h.* groaning of the prisoner, to loose those
138. 4. when they *h.* the words of thy mouth
143. 8. cause me to *h.* thy loving-kindness in morn.
Prov. 1. 8. my son, *h.* the instruction of thy father
4. 1. *h.* ye children, the instruction of a father
10. *h.* O my son, and receive my sayings, 19. 20.
8. 6. *h.* for I will speak of excellent things
33. *h.* instruction, and be wise, refuse it not
19. 27. cease to *h.* instruction that causeth to err
22. 17. bow thine ear, *h.* the words of the wise
23. 19. *h.* thou, my son, be wise, and guide thy heart
Eccl. 5. 1. and be more ready to *h.* than to give
7. 5. it is better to *h.* the rebuke of the wise
12. 13. let us *h.* the conclusion of the matter
Cant. 8. 13. hearken to thy voice, cause me to *h.* it
Isa. 1. 2. *h.* O heavens, and give ear, O earth
6. 9. *h.* ye indeed, but understand not, *Mark* 4. 12.
18. 3. and when he bloweth a trumpet, *h.* ye
33. 13. *h.* ye that are afar off what I have done

Isa. 34. 1. let the earth *h.* and all that is therein
42. 18. *h.* ye deaf || 23. who will *h.* for time to come
43. 9. or let them *h.* and say, it is truth
48. 14. all ye, assemble yourselves and *h.*
16. *h.* ye this, I have not spoken in secret
55. 3. *h.* and your soul shall live, *John* 5. 25.
Jer. 4. 21. shall I *h.* the sound of the trumpet?
6. 18. therefore *h.* ye nations || 19. *h.* O earth
11. 2. *h.* ye the words of this covenant, 6.
10. forefathers who refused to *h.* 13. 10.
13. 15. *h.* ye, give ear, for the Lord hath spoken
18. 2. then I will cause thee to *h.* my words
23. 22. and had caused my people to *h.* my words
38. 25. if the princes *h.* that I have talked
49. 20. therefore *h.* the counsel of the Ld. 50. 45.
Lam. 1. 18. *h.* I pray you, all people, and behold
Ezek. 2. 8. *h.* what I say || 3. 17. *h.* at my mouth 33. 7.
3. 27. he that heareth, let him *h.* he that forbears
13. 19. by your lying to my people, that *h.* your lies
33. 30. *h.* what is the word that cometh forth
31. they *h.* thy words, but will not do them, 32.
Dan. 9. 17. O God, *h.* the prayer of thy servant
19. O Lord, *h.* O Lord, forgive, hearken, and do
Hos. 5. 1. *h.* ye this, O priests, and hearken, give ear
Joel 1. 2. *h.* this, ye old men, and give ear, all inhabit.
Amos 3. 1. *h.* this wd. L. hath spoken, 4. 1. | 5. 1. | 8. 4.
Mic. 1. 2. *h.* all ye people, hearken, O earth
3. 1. I said, *h.* I pray you, O heads of Jacob, 9.
6. 2. *h.* ye, O mountains || 9. *h.* ye the rod and him
Nah. 3. 19. all that *h.* the bruit of thee shall clap
Zech. 7. 12. lest they should *h.* the law and words
Mat. 11. 4. shew John the things which ye *h.* and
5. lame walk, and deaf *h.* *Mark* 7. 37. *Luke* 7. 22.
13. 17. to *h.* those things that ye *h.* *Luke* 10. 24.
15. 10. he said to the multitude *h.* and understand
17. 5. this is my beloved Son, *h.* him, *Mark* 9. 7.
18. 17. he neglect to *h.* them, to *h.* the church
Mark 4. 18. are such as *h.* the word, 20. *Luke* 8. 12, 13.
24. take heed what ye *h.* you that *h.* more given
Luke 5. 1. pressed on him to *h.* the word of God
15. multitudes came together to *h.* and be healed
6. 17. which came to *h.* him, and to be healed
27. I say to you which *h.* love your enemies
8. 18. take heed therefore how ye *h.* whoever hath
21. are these which *h.* the word and do it, 11. 28.
9. 9. but who is this of whom I *h.* such things?
15. 1. then drew near publicans and sinn. to *h.* him
16. 2. he said, how is it that I *h.* this of thee?
29. they have Moses and proph. let them *h.* them
18. 6. Lord said, *h.* what the unjust judge saith
19. 48. the people were very attentive to *h.* him
21. 38. came to him in the temple for to *h.* him
John 5. 30. as I *h.* I judge || 6. 60. who can *h.* it?
7. 51. doth our law judge a man before it *h.* him
9. 27. wherefore would ye *h.* it again
10. 3. the sheep *h.* his voice, and he calleth by name
12. 47. if any man *h.* my words, and believe not
14. 24. and the word which ye *h.* is not mine
Acts 2. 8. how *h.* we every man in our own tongue
33. hath shed forth this, which ye now see and *h.*
10. 22. to send for thee, and to *h.* words of thee
33. to *h.* all things that are commanded thee
13. 7. and desired to *h.* the word of God
44. the whole city came together to *h.* the word
15. 7. Gentiles by my mouth should *h.* the word
17. 21. either to tell or to *h.* some new thing
19. 26. ye *h.* Paul hath turned away much people
22. 1. *h.* ye my defence which I make now to you
24. 4. that thou wouldest *h.* us of thy clemency
25. 22. Agrippa said, I would *h.* the man myself
28. 22. but we desire to *h.* what thou thinkest
1 *Cor.* 11. 18. I *h.* there be divisions among you
Phil. 1. 27. or else be absent, I may *h.* of your affairs
2 *Thess.* 3. 11. we *h.* that some walk disorderly
1 *Tim.* 4. 16. shalt save thyself and them that *h.* thee
2 *Tim.* 4. 17. and that all the Gentiles might *h.*
Jam. 1. 19. let every one be swift to *h.* slow to speak
1 *John* 5. 15. we know that he *h.* us, what we ask
3 *John* 4. than to *h.* my children walk in truth
Rev. 1. 3. blessed that *h.* words of this prophecy
9. 20. which neither can see, nor *h.* nor walk
See Ear, Ears, Voice.

HEAR *me.*

Exod. 6. 12. how then shall Pharaoh *h. me?*
1 *Kings* 18. 37. *h. me,* O Lord *h. me,* that this people
1 *Chron.* 28. 2. *h. me,* my brethren, and my people
2 *Chron.* 13. 4. *h. me,* thou Jeroboam, and all Israel
15. 2. *h. me,* Asa || 20. 20. and he said, *h. me,* O Judah
29. 5. *h. me,* ye Levites, sanctify now yourselves
Job 15. 17. I will shew thee, *h. me,* I will declare
31. 35. O that one would *h. me,* my desire is
Psal. 4. 1. *h. me* when I call, O G. of my righteousn.
13. 3. consider, and *h. me,* O Lord my God
17. 6. I called upon thee, for thou wilt *h. me*
38. 16. for I said, *h. me,* lest they should rejoice
55. 2. attend unto me, and *h. me,* I mourn
60. 5. save with thy right-hand, and *h. me*
69. 13. O God, in the multitude of thy mercy *h. me*
17. for I am in trouble, *h. me* speedily, 143. 7.
Mic. 7. 7. I will wait for God, my God will *h. me*
Acts 26. 3. wherefore I beseech thee to *h. me*
29. but also all that *h. me,* were such as I am
1 *Cor.* 14. 21. yet for all that will they not *h. me*

HEAR *not,* or *not* HEAR.

Deut. 28. †49. whose tongue thou shalt *not h.*
30. 17. so thou wilt *not h.* but worship other gods
1 *Sam.* 8. 18. the Lord will *not h.* you in that day
Job 30. 20. I cry unto thee, and thou dost *not h.* me
35. 13. surely God will *not h.* vanity, nor regard it
Psal. 66. 18. if I regard iniquity, Lord will *not h.* me
94. 9. he that planted the ear, shall he *not h.*?
Isa. 1. 15. when make many prayers, I will *not h.* *Jer.* 7. 16. | 11. 14. | 14. 12. *Ezek.* 8. 18. *Amos* 5. 23.
30. 9. children that will *not h.* the law of the Lord
59. 1. neither his ear heavy that it *cannot h.*
2. he will *not h.* || 65. 12. when I spake ye did *not h.*
66. 4. when I spake, they did *not h.* *Zech.* 1. 4.
Jer. 5. 21. have ears and *h. not, Ezek.* 12. 2. *Mark* 8. 18.
13. 17. but if ye will *not h.* 22. 5. *Mal.* 2. 2.
17. 23. that they might *not h.* 19. 15. *Zech.* 7. 11.
22. 21. I spake, but thou saidst, I will *not h.*

Dan. 5. 23. thou hast praised the gods of silver, which see *not,* nor *h.* nor know, *Rev.* 9. 20.
Mic. 3. 4. shall cry to Lord, but he will *not h.* them
Hab. 1. 2. how long shall I cry, and thou wilt *not h.*
Mat. 10. 14. not receive you, *nor h.* your words
18. 16. if he will *not h.* thee, then take one or two
Luke 16. 31. if they *h. not* Moses and the prophets
John 8. 43. even because ye *cannot h.* my word
47. ye therefore *h.* them *not,* because not of God
9. 27. he answered, I told you, and ye did *not h.*
10. 8. are robbers, but the sheep did *not h.* them
Acts 3. 23. every soul which will *not h.* be destroy.
1 *Cor.* 14. 21. yet for all that will they *not h.* me
Gal. 4. 21. ye under the law, do ye *not h.* the law

Would not HEAR.

Gen. 42. 21. when he besought us, we *would not h.*
22. do not sin against the child, ye *would not h.*
Exod. 7. 16. behold, hitherto, thou *wouldest not h.*
Deut. 1. 43. Israel *would not h.* 3. 26. 2 *Kings* 17. 14.
2 *Kings* 14. 11. Amaziah *would not h.* 2 *Chr.* 25. 20.
18. 12. Israel *would not h.* *Neh.* 9. 29. *Zech.* 7. 13.
Isa. 28. 12. this is the refreshing, yet they *would not h.*
Jer. 13. 11. might be for praise, they *w. n. h.* 29. 19.
36. 25. he *would not h.* || *Zech.* 7. 13. *I would not h.*

HEAR *now,* or *now* HEAR.

Num. 12. 6. and he said, *h. now* my words, 20. 10.
1 *Sam.* 22. 7. then Saul said, *h. now,* ye Benjamites
12. *h. now,* thou son of Ahitub, he answered
Job 13. 6. *h. now* my reasoning, and hearken
Prov. 5. 7. *h.* me *now,* therefore, O ye children
Isa. 7. 13. and he said, *h.* ye *now,* O house of David
44. 1. yet *now h.* O Jacob my servant, and Israel
47. 8. *h. now,* thou that art given to pleasures
51. 21. therefore, *h. now* this, thou afflicted
Jer. 5. 21. therefore, *h. now* this, O foolish people
28. 15. *h. now* Hananiah || *Zech.* 3. 8. *h. now,* O Josh.
37. 20. *h. now,* I pray thee, O my lord the king
Mic. 6. 1. *h.* ye *now* what the Lord saith, arise
Acts 2. 33. shed forth this which ye *now* see and *h.*
Phil. 1. 30. which ye saw in me, and *now h.* to be in

Shall HEAR.

Exod. 15. 14. the people *shall h.* and be afraid, *Deut.* 13. 11. | 17. 13. | 19. 20. | 21. 21.
Num. 14. 13. Moses said, then the Egypt. *shall h.* it
Deut. 1. 17. ye *shall h.* small as well as great
2. 25. who *shall h.* report of thee, and shall tremble
4. 6. which *shall h.* all these statutes and say
Josh. 7. 9. the inhabitants of the land *shall h.* of it
Judg. 7. 11. and thou *shalt h.* what they say
2 *Sam.* 16. 21. Israel *shall h.* that thou art abhorred
1 *Kings* 8. 42. for they *shall h.* of thy great name
2 *Kings* 19. 7. and he *shall h.* a rumour, *Isa.* 37. 7.
Job 22. 27. shalt make prayer to him, he *shall h.*
Psal. 34. 2. the humble *shall h.* thereof, and be glad
55. 17. I will pray and cry, and he *shall h.* my voice
19. God *shall h.* and afflict them, even he that
92. 11. mine ears *shall h.* desire of the wicked
141. 6. they *shall h.* my words, for they are sweet
Isa. 29. 18. in that day *shall* the deaf *h.* the words
30. 19. when he *shall h.* it he will answer thee
21. thine ears *shall h.* a word behind thee
Jer. 33. 9. which *shall h.* all the good that I do
Hos. 2. 21. and the heaven *shall h.* the earth
22. the earth *shall h.* the corn and the wine
Mat. 13. 14. by hearing, ye *shall h.* *Acts* 28. 26.
18. 15. if he *shall h.* thee thou hast gained thy
24. 6. ye *shall h.* of wars, *Mark* 13. 7. *Luke* 21. 9.
John 5. 25. the dead *shall h.* voice of the Son of God
16. 13. whatsoever he *shall h.* that shall he speak
Acts 3. 22. him *shall* ye *h.* in all things, 7. 37.
25. 22. to-morrow, said he, thou *shalt h.* him
Rom. 10. 14. how *shall* they *h.* without a preacher

Will HEAR.

Exod. 20. 19. speak with us, we *will h.* *Deut.* 5. 27.
22. 23. if they cry, I *will* surely *h.* their cry, 27.
Num. 9. 8. I *will h.* what the Lord will command
2 *Sam.* 14. 16. king *will h.* to deliver his handmaid
2 *Kings* 19. 4. it may be thy God *will h.* the words
2 *Chr.* 7. 14. then *will* I *h.* from heaven, *Ps.* 20. 6.
20. 9. then thou *wilt h.* and help, *Psal.* 38. 15.
Psal. 4. 3. the Lord *will h.* || 17. 6. thou *wilt h.* me
85. 8. I *will h.* what God the Lord will speak
145. 19. he also *will h.* their cry, and save them
Prov. 1. 5. wise man *will h.* and increase learning
Isa. 41. 17. the Lord *will h.* them, and not forsake
65. 24. while they are yet speaking, I *will h.*
Jer. 36. 3. it may be the house of Judah *will h.*
Ezek. 2. 5. whether they *will h.* or forbear, 7. | 3. 11.
Hos. 2. 21. I *will h.* the heavens, they the earth
Mic. 7. 7. I will wait for God, my God *will h.* me
Zech. 10. 6. I am their God and *will h.* them, 13. 9.
Acts 17. 32. we *will h.* thee again of this matter
21. 22. for they *will h.* that thou art come
23. 35. I *will h.* thee, when thy accusers are come
28. 28. salvation is sent to the Gentiles, they *will h.*

HEAR *the word of the Lord.*

1 *Kings* 22. 19. *h.* therefore *the word of the Lord,* 2 *Chr.* 18. 18. *Jer.* 29. 20. | 42. 15. *Amos* 7. 16.
2 *Kings* 7. 1. then Elisha said *h. the word of the Lord, Jer.* 17. 20. | 21. 11.
20. 16. Isaiah said to Hezekiah, *h. word of Lord,* all in thy house be carried to Babylon, *Isa.* 39. 5.
Isa. 1. 10. *h. word of the Lord,* ye rulers of Sodom
28. 14. *h. the word of the Lord,* ye scornful men
66. 5. *h. word of Lord,* ye that tremble at his word
Jer. 2. 4. *h. word of Lord,* O house of Jacob, 10. 1.
7. 2. *h. the word of the Lord,* all ye of Judah
9. 20. yet *h. the word of the Lord,* O ye women
19. 3. *h. word of Lord,* O kings of Judah, 22. 2.
22. 29. O earth, earth, *h. the word of the Lord*
31. 10. *h. the word of the Lord,* O ye nations
34. 4. yet *h. word of Lord,* O Zedekiah king of Jud.
44. 24. *h. the word of the Lord,* all Judah, 26.
Ezek. 6. 3. ye mountains of Israel, *h. the word of the Lord,* I will bring a sword on you, 36. 1, 4.
13. 2. say to prophets *h.* ye *the word of the Lord*
16. 35. wherefore, O harlot, *h. the word of the Lord*
20. 47. forest of the south, *h. the word of the Lord*
25. 3. say to Ammonites, *h. the word of the Lord*
34. 7. ye shepherds, *h. the word of the Lord,* 9.
37. 4. say, O ye dry bones, *h. the word of the Lord*
Hos. 4. 1. *h. word of the Lord,* ye children of Israel

Amos 7. 16. Amaziah, *h.* thou *the word of the Lord*

HEARD.

Gen. 16. 11. because the Lord hath *h.* thy affliction
21. 26. neither yet *h.* I of it, but to-day
29. 33. because the Lord hath *h.* that I was hated
45. 2. Joseph wept aloud, and the Egyptians *h.*
Exod. 2. 24. God *h.* their groaning, and remembered
16. 9. for he hath *h.* your murmurings
23. 13. neither let it be *h.* out of thy mouth
28. 35. his sound shall be *h.* when he goeth in and
33. 4. when the people *h.* these evil tidings
Lev. 24. 14. let all that *h.* him lay their hands
Num. 11. 1. the people complained, the Lord *h.* it
12. 2. Miriam spake against Moses, the Lord *h.* it
14. 14. they have *h.* thou art among this people
15. the nations which have *h.* the fame of thee
30. 7. held his peace at her in the day he *h.* it, 14.
Josh. 9. 16. they *h.* that they were their neighbours
1 *Sam.* 7. 9. Samuel cried, and the Lord *h.* him
23. 11. will Saul come, as thy servant hath *h.*?
1 *Kings* 1. 11. hast not *h.* that Adonijah doth reign
6. 7. nor was any tool of iron *h.* in the house
10. 7. the half not told me, thy wisdom and prosperity exceedeth the fame which I *h.* 2 *Chr.* 9. 6.
2 *Kings* 19. 25. hast thou not *h.* long ago, *Isa.* 37. 26.
2 *Chr.* 5. 13. make one sound to be *h.* in praising
33. 13. he was entreated and *h.* his supplications
Ezra 3. 13. people shouted, the noise was *h.* afar
Neh. 12. 43. the joy of Jerusalem *h.* even afar off
Job 15. 8. hast thou *h.* the secret of God?
19. 7. I cry out of wrong, but I am not *h.*
26. 14. but how little a portion is *h.* of him
29. 11. when the ear *h.* me, then it blessed me
Psal. 6. 9. the Lord hath *h.* my supplication
10. 17. thou hast *h.* the desire of the humble
22. 21. save me, for thou hast *h.* me from the horns
24. but when he cried he *h.* 34. 6. | 40. 1. | 120. 1.
34. 4. I sought the Lord, and he *h.* me, and deliv.
38. 13. but I as a deaf man *h.* not, I was dumb
61. 5. thou, O G. hast *h.* my vows, thou hast given
66. 19. verily God hath *h.* me, he hath attended
76. 8. cause judgment to be *h.* from heaven
78. 21. therefore the Lord *h.* this and was wroth
59. when God *h.* this, was wroth, and abhorred
81. 5. where I *h.* a language that I understood not
97. 8. Zion *h.* and was glad, and Judah rejoiced
106. 44. he regarded their affliction, when he *h.*
118. 21. for thou hast *h.* me, and art my salvation
132. 6. lo, we *h.* of it at Ephratah, we found it
Prov. 21. 13. he shall cry himself, but not be *h.*
Isa. 10. 30. cause it to be *h.* unto Laish, O Anathoth
40. 21. have ye not *h.*? hath it not been told you?
28. hast thou not *h.* everlasting God fainteth not?
48. 6. thou hast *h.* see all this, will not ye declare?
52. 15. which they had not *h.* shall they consider
60. 18. violence shall no more be *h.* in thy land
64. 4. men have not *h.* what he hath prepared
65. 19. the voice of weeping shall be no more *h.*
66. 8. who hath *h.* such a thing, who hath seen?
19. to the isles afar off, that have not *h.* my fame
Jer. 4. 19. because thou hast *h.* sound of trumpet
6. 7. she casteth out wickedness, spoil is *h.* in her
7. 13. I spake unto you, rising early, but ye *h.* not
8. 6. I hearkened and *h.* but they spake not aright
18. 13. ask the heathen, who hath *h.* such things
22. let cry be *h.* from houses when shalt bring
25. 36. an howling of the flock shall be *h.*
26. 11. for he hath prophesied as ye have *h.*
34. 10. *h.* every one should let his man-servant go
35. 17. I have spoken, but they have not *h.*
46. 12. the nations have *h.* of thy shame
50. 46. and the cry is *h.* among the nations
51. 46 a rumour that shall be *h.* in the land
Lam. 1 21. they have *h.* that I sigh, there is none
3. 61. thou hast *h.* their reproach, O Lord
Ezek. 19. 4. the nations *h.* of him, he was taken
26. 13. the sound of thy harps shall be no more *h.*
33. 5. he *h.* the sound of the trumpet, and took
Dan. 12. 8. and I *h.* but I understood not
Hos. 7. 12. chastise them, as their congrega. hath *h.*
Jonah 2. 2. I cried unto the Lord, and he *h.* me
Mic. 5. 15. in fury, such as they have not *h.*
Hab. 3. 16. when I *h.* my belly trembled
Mal. 3. 16. and the Lord hearkened and *h.* it
Mat. 5. 21. ye have *h.* it was said, 27, 33, 38, 43.
6. 7. they shall be *h.* for their much speaking
13. 17. ye hear, and have not *h.* them, *Luke* 10. 24.
15. 12. were offended after they *h.* this saying
22. 7. when the king *h.* thereof, he was wroth
26. 65. ye have *h.* his blasphemy, *Mark* 14. 64.
Mark 4. 15. but when they have *h.* Satan cometh
14. 11. and when they *h.* it they were glad
Luke 1. 13. fear not, thy prayer is *h.* *Acts* 10. 31.
12. 3. what ye have spoken, shall be *h.* in the light
20. 16. when they *h.* it, they said, God forbid
John 3. 32. what he hath *h.* that he testifieth
6. 45. every man that hath *h.* of the Father
8. 6. wrote on the ground, as tho' he *h.* them not
9. 32. since the world began was it not *h.*
11. 41. Father, I thank thee that thou hast *h.* me
18. 21. ask them which *h.* me, what I have said
21. 7. when Simon Peter *h.* that it was the Lord
Acts 1. 4. wait for the promise ye have *h.* of me
2. 37. when they *h.* this, they were pricked in heart
4. 4. many of them which *h.* the word believed
5. 5. fear came on all them that *h.* these things
13. 48. when the Gentiles *h.* this they were glad
14. 9. the same *h.* Paul speak, who beholding
16. 14. a woman which worshipped God, *h.* us
25. sang praises to God, and the prisoners *h.* them
19. 5. when they *h.* this, they were baptized
22. 15. shalt witness of what thou hast seen and *h.*
24. 24. *h.* him concerning the faith in Christ
Rom. 10. 14. in him of whom they have not *h.*
18. but I say, have they not *h.*? yes, verily
15. 21. they that have not *h.* shall understand
1 *Cor.* 2. 9. eye hath not seen, nor ear *h.* neither
Gal. 1. 13. for ye have *h.* of my conversation
Eph. 1. 13. after that ye *h.* the word of truth
15. after I *h.* of your faith in the Lord Jesus
4. 21. if so be ye have *h.* him and been taught
Phil. 2. 26. that ye had *h.* that he had been sick

Phil. 4. 9. those things ye have *h.* and seen in me, do
Col. 1. 4. since we *h.* of your faith in Christ
6. since day ye *h.* of it, and knew the grace of G.
9. since day we *h.* it, do not cease to pray for you
2 *Tim.* 2. 2. things thou hast *h.* of me, commit to
Heb. 2. 3. was confirmed to us by them that *h.* him
3. 16. for some when they had *h.* did provoke
4. 2. not being mixed with faith in them that *h.*
5. 7. offer. up prayers, and was *h.* in that he feared
Jam. 5. 11. ye have *h.* of the patience of Job
1 *John* 2. 18. ye *h.* that antichrist shall come, 4. 3.
24. have *h.* from the beginning, 3. 11. 2 *John* 6.
Rev. 3. 3. remember therefore how thou hast *h.*
5. 13. and all that are in them *h.* I, saying
7. 4. I *h.* the number of them which were sealed
9. 16. and I *h.* the number of the horsemen
16. 5. and I *h.* the angel of the waters say
18. 22. the voice of trumpeters shall be *h.* no more
23. the voice of bride shall be *h.* no more in thee
22. 8. I saw these things, and *h.* them, when I *h.*

I have HEARD.

Gen. 17. 20. and as for Ishmael *I have h.* thee
41. 15. I have dreamed a dream, *I have h.* say of thee thou canst interp. dreams, *Dan.* 5. 14, 16.
42. 2. *I have h.* that there is corn in Egypt
Exod. 3. 7. *I have h.* their cry || 6. 5. *I h.* *h.* groaning
16. 12. *I have h.* the murmuring, *Num.* 14. 27.
Deut. 5. 28. *I have h.* the voice of your words
1 *Sam.* 25. 7. now *I have h.* that thou hast shearers
1 *Kings* 2. 42. the word that I *have h.* is good
9. 3. *I have h.* thy prayer thou hast made before me, 2 *Kings* 20. 5. 2 *Chron.* 7. 12. *Isa.* 38. 5.
2 *Kings* 19. 20. that which thou hast prayed *I. h. h.*
22. 19. I also *have h.* thee, saith L. 2 *Chr.* 34. 27.
Job 16. 2. *I have h.* many such things, miserable com.
20. 3. *I have h.* the check of my reproach
42. 5. *I have h.* of thee by the hearing of the ear
Psal. 31. 13. for *I have h.* the slander of many
62. 11. twice *I have h.* this, power belongeth to G.
Isa. 21. 10. that which *I have h.* of Lord of hosts
28. 22. *I have h.* from the Lord a consumption
49. 8. in an acceptable time *have I h.* 2 *Cor.* 6. 2.
Jer. 23. 25. *I have h.* what the prophets said
31. 18. *I have h.* Ephraim bemoaning himself thus
42. 4. *I have h.* you, behold, I will pray unto the L.
49. 14. *I have h.* a rumour from the Lord
Ezek. 35. 12. know *I have h.* all thy blasphemies
Hos. 14. 8. *I have h.* him and observed him
Hab. 3. 2. O L. *I have h.* thy speech, and was afraid
Zeph. 2. 8. *I have h.* the reproach of Moab
John 8. 26. I speak those things *I have h.* of him
40. told you the truth, which *I have h.* of God
15. 15. all things that *I have h.* of my Father
Acts 7. 34. *I have h.* their groaning, and am come
9. 13. Lord *I have h.* by many of this man, how

HEARD, joined with *voice*.

Gen. 3. 8. they *h. voice* of the L. walking in garden
10. I *h.* thy *voice*, and was afraid, because naked
21. 17. God *h.* the *voice* of the lad, the angel called
30. 6. God hath *h.* my *voice*, and given me a son
39. 15. when he *h.* that I lifted up my *voice*
Num. 7. 89. then he *h.* the *voice* of one speaking
20. 16. we cried, he *h.* our *voice*, and sent an angel
Deut. 1. 34. the Lord *h.* the *voice* of your words
4. 12. saw no similitude, only he *h.* a *voice*
33. hear *v.* of God as thou hast *h.* and live, 5. 26.
5. 23. ye *h.* the *voice* out of the midst of darkness
24. we have *h.* his *voice* out of the midst of the fire
28. and the Lord *h.* the *voice* of your words
26. 7. we cried, the Lord *h.* our *voice*, and looked
Judg. 18. 25. let not thy *voice* be *h.* among us
1 *Sam.* 1. 13. her lips moved, her *voice* was not *h.*
1 *Kings* 17. 22. the Lord *h.* the *voice* of Elijah
2 *Chron.* 30. 27. their *voice* was *h.* prayer came up
Job 4. 16. there was silence, I *h.* a *voice*, saying
33. 8. I have *h.* the *voice* of thy words, saying
37. 4. he will not stay them when his *voice* is *h.*
Psal. 3. 4. I cried to the L. with my *voice*, he *h.* me
6. 8. the Lord hath *h.* the *voice* of my weeping
18. 6. I called, he *h.* my *voice* out of his temple
19. 3. there is no speech where their *voice* is not *h.*
28. 6. because he hath *h.* the *voice* of my supplica.
66. 8. and make the *voice* of his praise to be *h.*
116. 1. I love the Lord, because he hath *h.* my *voice*
Cant. 2. 12. the *voice* of the turtle is *h.* in our land
Isa. 6. 8. also I *h.* the *voice* of the Lord, saying
15. 4. their *voice* shall be *h.* even unto Jahaz
30. 30. Lord shall cause his glorious *voice* to be *h.*
42. 2. nor cause his *voice* to be *h.* in the street
58. 4. not fast, to make your *voice* be *h.* on high
65. 19. *voice* of weeping shall no more be *h.* in her
Jer. 3. 21. a *voice* was *h.* upon the high places
4. 31. I have *h.* a *voice* as of a woman in travail
9. 19. for a *voice* of wailing is *h.* out of Zion
30. 5. we have *h.* a *voice* of trembling, of fear
31. 15. a *voice* was *h.* in Ramah, *Mat.* 2. 18.
Lam. 3. 56. thou hast *h.* my *voice*, hide not thine ear
Ezek. 1. 28. and I *h.* a *voice* of one that spake
3. 12. I *h.* behind me a *voice* of great rushing
19. 9. that his *voice* should no more be *h.*
27. 30. and shall cause their *voice* to be *h.* ag. thee
Dan. 8. 16. I *h.* a man's *voice* between the banks
10. 9. yet *h.* I the *voice* of his words, when I *h.*
Nah. 2. 13. *voice* of thy messengers no more be *h.*
John 5. 37. ye have neither *h.* his *voice* at any time
Acts 9. 4. *h.* a *voice*, saying, Saul, Saul, 22. 7. | 26. 14.
11. 7. I *h.* a *voice* saying to me, arise, slay and eat
22. 9. they *h.* not the *voice* of him that spake
Heb. 12. 19. which *voice* they that *h.* entreated
2 *Pet.* 1. 18. the *voice* which came from heaven we *h.*
Rev. 1. 10. I *h.* a great *voice*, 16. 1. | 19. 1. | 21. 3.
4. 1. the first *voice* I *h.* was as it were of a trumpet
5. 11. I beheld, and *h.* the *voice* of many angels
6. 6. I *h.* a *voice* in the midst of the four beasts
7. I *h.* a *voice* of the fourth beast say, come and see
9. 13. I *h.* a *voice* from the four horns of the altar
10. 4. I *h.* a *voice* from heaven, 8. | 14. 2, 13. | 18. 4.
12. 10. and I *h.* a loud *voice*, saying in heaven
14. 2. I *h.* the *voice* of harpers harping with harps
19. 6. I *h.* as it were the *voice* of a great multitude

We have HEARD.

Josh. 2. 10. *we have h.* how the Lord dried Red sea
Josh. 2. 11. soon as *we had h.* these things hearts melt
9. 9. *we have h.* the fame of him, and all he did
2 *Sam.* 7. 22. there is none like thee according to all *we have h.* with our ears, 1 *Chr.* 17. 20.
1 *Kings* 20. 31. *we have h.* kings of Isr. are merciful
Job 28. 22. *we have h.* the fame thereof, *Jer.* 6. 24.
Psal. 44. 1. *we have h.* with our ears, our fathers told
48. 8. as *we have h.* so have we seen in city of Lord
78. 3. dark sayings which *we have h.* and known
Isa. 16. 6. *we have h.* of pride of Moab, *Jer.* 48. 29.
24. 16. *we have h.* songs, glory to the righteous
Jer. 30. 5. *we have h.* a voice of trembling, of fear
51. 51. confounded, because *we have h.* reproach
Obad. 1. *we have h.* a rumour from the Lord
Zech. 8. 23. for *we have h.* that God is with you
Mark 14. 58. *we have h.* him say, I will destroy
Luke 4. 23. whatever *we have h.* done in Capernaum
22. 71. *we* ourselves *have h.* of his own mouth
John 4. 42. we believe, *we have h.* him ourselves
12. 34. *we have h.* out of the law that Christ abideth
Acts 4. 20. we cannot but speak things *we have h.*
6. 11. *we have h.* him speak blasphemous words
14. *we have h.* him say, this Jesus shall destroy
15. 24. *we have h.* that certain have troubled you
19. 2. *we have* not *h.* whether there be any Holy Gh.
Heb. 2. 1. to give heed to things which *we have h.*
1 *John* 1. 1. that which *we have h.* and seen, 3.
5. this is the message which *we have h.* of him

HEARD, joined with *word* or *words*.

Gen. 24. 30. and when he *h.* the *words* of Rebekah
52. when Abraham's servant *h.* their *words*
27. 34. and when Esau *h.* the *words* of his father
31. 1. Jacob *h.* the *words* of Laban's sons, saying
39. 19. when his master *h.* the *words* of his wife
Num. 24. 4. he hath said, which *h. words* of God, 16.
Josh. 22. 30. when heads of Isr. *h. words* of Reuben
24. 27. for it hath *h.* all the *words* of the Lord
Judg. 9. 30. when Zebul *h.* the *words* of Gaal
1 *Sam.* 8. 21. Samuel *h.* all the *words* of the people
17. 11. Saul and Israel *h.* Goliath's *words*
23. accord. to the same *words*, and David *h.* them
31. when the *words* were *h.* which David spake
1 *Kings* 2. 42. the *word* that I have *h.* is good
5. 7. when Hiram *h.* Solomon's *words* he rejoiced
21. 27. when Ahab *h.* those *words*, rent his clothes
2 *Kings* 6. 30. when the king *h. words* of the woman
19. 6. be not afraid of *words* thou hast *h.* *Isa.* 37. 6.
22. 11. when the king had *h.* the *words* of book of law, he rent his clothes, 18. 2 *Chr.* 34. 19.
2 *Chron.* 15. 8. Asa *h.* these *words*, he took courage
Neh. 1. 4. *h.* these *words*, I sat down and wept
5. 6. and I was angry when I *h.* these *words*
8. 9. the people wept, when they *h. words* of the law
Job 33. 8. I have *h.* the voice of thy *words*, saying
Eccl. 9. 16. the poor man's *words* are not *h.*
17. the *words* of wise men are *h.* in quiet
Isa. 37. 4. will reprove the *words* which God hath *h.*
Jer. 23. 18. hath perceived, marked, and *h.* his *word*
25. 8. therefore because ye have not *h.* my *words*
26. 12. against this city all the *words* ye have *h.*
21. when the king and all the princes *h.* his *words*
36. 13. declared unto them all the *words* he had *h.*
24. they were not afraid that *h.* these *words*
38. 1. Pashur *h.* the *words* Jeremiah had spoken
Dan. 6. 14. when Darius *h.* these *words* was displeased
10. 12. thy *words* were *h.* I am come for thy words
Mat. 22. 22. when they *h.* these *words* they marvelled
Mark 5. 36. as soon as Jesus *h.* the *word* spoken
Luke 10. 39. Mary sat at Jesus' feet, and *h.* his *word*
Acts 10. 44. Holy Ghost fell on them who *h. word*
2 *Cor.* 12. 4. caught up, and *h.* unspeakable *words*
Eph. 1. 13. after that ye *h.* the *word* of truth
Col. 1. 5. whereof ye *h.* in the *word* of the gospel
1 *Thess.* 2. 13. received the *word* which ye *h.* of us
2 *Tim.* 1. 13. hold fast form of sound *w.* hast *h.* of me
Heb. 12. 19. they that *h.* entreateth that the *word*
1 *John* 2. 7. the *word* ye have *h.* from the beginning

HEARDEST.

Deut. 4. 36. and thou *h.* his words out of the fire
Josh. 14. 12. for thou *h.* in that day how Anakims
2 *Kings* 22. 19. when thou *h.* what I spake against this place, hast rent thy clothes, 2 *Chr.* 34. 27.
Neh. 9. 9. and thou *h.* their cry by the Red sea
27. they cried, thou *h.* them from heaven, 28.
Psal. 31. 22. thou *h.* the voice of my supplications
119. 26. I have declared my ways, and thou *h.* me
Isa. 48. 7. before the day when thou *h.* them not
8. yea, thou *h.* not, yea, thou knewest not
Jonah 2. 2. out of belly of hell I cried, thou *h.*

HEARER.

Jam. 1. 23. if any be a *h.* of the word, and not a doer
25. he being not a forgetful *h.* but doer of work

HEARERS.

Rom. 2. 13. not the *h.* of the law are justified
Eph. 4. 29. that it may minister grace unto the *h.*
2 *Tim.* 2. 14. but to the subverting of the *h.*
Jam. 1. 22. be doers of the word, and not *h.* only

HEAREST.

Ruth 2. 8. Boaz to Ruth, *h.* thou not, my daughter?
1 *Sam.* 24. 9. wherefore *h.* thou men's words?
2 *Sam.* 5. 24. when *h.* sound in the mulberry-trees
1 *Kings* 8. 30. when thou *h.* forgive, 2 *Chron.* 6. 21.
Psal. 22. 2. I cry in the day-time, but thou *h.* not
65. 2. thou that *h.* prayer, unto thee all flesh come
Mat. 21. 16. said unto him, *h.* thou what these say?
27. 13. *h.* thou not how many things they witness
John 3. 8. wind bloweth, and thou *h.* the sound
11. 42. and I knew that thou *h.* me always

HEARETH.

Exod. 16. 7. for that he *h.* your murmurings, 8.
Num. 30. 5. if father disallow her in day that he *h.*
Deut. 29. 19. when he *h.* the words of this curse
1 *Sam.* 3. 9. speak, Lord, for thy servant *h.* 10.
11. I will do a thing at which ears of every one that *h.* shall tingle, 2 *Kings* 21. 12. *Jer.* 19. 3.
2 *Sam.* 17. 9. whosoever *h.* it will say, there is a slaugh.
Job 34. 28. and he *h.* the cry of the afflicted
Psal. 34. 17. the righteous cry, and the Lord *h.*
38. 14. thus I was as a man that *h.* not
69. 33. Ld. *h.* poor, and despiseth not his prisoners
Prov. 8. 34. blessed is the man that *h.* me, watching
13. 1. a wise son *h.* his father's instruction

Prov. 13. 8. ransom his riches, but poor h. not rebuke
15. 29. but he h. the prayer of the righteous
31. the ear that h. the reproof of life, 32.
18. 13. he that answereth a matter before he h. it
21. 28. but the man that h. speaketh constantly
25. 10. lest he that h. it put thee to shame
29. 24. he h. cursing, and bewrayeth it not
Isa. 41. 26. yea, there is none that h. your words
42. 20. opening the ears, but he h. not
Ezek. 3. 27. thou shalt say, he that h. let him hear
33. 4. whosoever h. the sound of the trumpet
Mat. 7. 24. whoso h. these sayings, 26. Luke 6. 47, 49.
13. 19. when any one h. the word of the kingdom
20. the same is he that h. the word, 22, 23.
Luke 10. 16. he that h. you h. me, and that despiseth
John 3. 29. who standeth and h. him rejoiceth greatly
5. 24. he that h. my word, and believeth on him
8. 47. he that is of God h. God's words
9. 31. God h. not sinners, but if any man be a worshipper of God, and doeth his will, him he h.
18. 37. every one that is of the truth, h. my voice
2 Cor. 12. 6. think of me above that he h. of me
1 John 4. 5. are of the world, and the world h. them
6. we are of God, he that knoweth God h. us
5. 14. if we ask according to his will, he h. us
Rev. 22. 17. and let him that h. say, come
18. for I testify to every man that h. the words

HEARING.

Gen. 29. † 13. when Laban heard the h. of Jacob
† 33. she called his name Simeon, that is, h.
Deut. 31. 11. shalt read this law to Israel in their h.
2 Sam. 18. 12. for in our h. the king charged thee
2 Kings 4. 31. but there was neither voice nor h.
Neh. 8. † 2. the law before all that understood in h.
Job 33. 8. surely thou hast spoken in my h.
37. † 2. hear in h. the noise of his voice and sound
42. 5. I have heard of thee by the h. of the ear
Psal. 18. † 44. at the h. of the ear they will obey
Isa. 6. † 9. hear ye in h. but understand not
11. 3. nor reprove after the h. of his ears
21. 3. I was bowed down at the h. of it
28. † 9. whom shall he make to understand the h.?
33. 15. he that stoppeth his ears from h. of blood
53. † 1. who hath believed our h.? Rom. 10. † 16.
Ezek. 9. 5. to others he said in my h. go after him
10. 13. it was cried unto them in my h. O wheel
16. † 56. thy sister Sodom was not for h. in the day
Amos 8. 11. a famine of h. the word of the Lord
Hab. 3. † 2. O Ld. I have heard thy h. I was afraid
Acts 25. 21. to be reserved to the h. of Augustus
23. Agrippa was entered into the place of h.
Rom. 10. 17. faith cometh by h. and h. by word of G.
1 Cor. 12. 17. where were the h.? if whole were h.
Gal. 3. 2. the works of law, or by the h. of faith, 5.
Heb. 5. 11. many things hard, seeing ye are dull of h.

HEARING.

1 Kings 3. † 9. give thy servant an h. heart to judge
Prov. 20. 12. the h. ear, the Lord hath made
28. 9. that turneth away the ear from h. the law
Eccl. 1. 8. nor is the ear filled with h.
Ezek. 33. † 4. he that h. heareth the sound of trumpet
Mat. 13. 13. and h. they hear not, nor understand
14. by h. ye shall hear, and shall not understand
15. their ears dull of h. Acts 28. 27. Heb. 5. 11.
Mark 6. 2. many h. him were astonished, saying
Luke 2. 46. both h. them and asking them questions
Acts 5. 5. Ananias h. these words fell down
8. 6. h. and seeing the miracles which he did
9. 7. the men stood, h. a voice, but seeing no man
18. 8. many of the Corinthians h. believed
Philem. 5. h. of thy love and faith toward Ld. Jesus
2 Pet. 2. 8. Lot in seeing and h. vexed his righteous

HEARKEN.

Exod. 6. 30. behold, how shall Pharaoh h. to me?
Deut. 7. 12. if ye h. to these judgments, and keep them
11. 13. if ye will h. diligently to my commands
15. 5. if thou carefully h. to voice of Ld. Jer. 17. 24.
18. 15. a prophet like to me, to him ye shall h.
28. 13. if thou h. to commandments, 1 Kings 11. 38.
Josh. 1. 17. as to Moses, so will we h. unto thee
1 Sam. 15. 22. and to h. than the fat of rams
30. 24. for who will h. to you in this matter?
1 Kings 8. 28. have thou respect to h. to cry and prayer
29. mayest h. to the prayer, 52. 2 Chron. 6. 19, 20.
Neh. 13. 27. shall we h. then to you to do all this?
Psal. 81. 8. O Israel, if thou wilt h. unto me
Prov. 29. 12. if a ruler h. to lies, servants are wicked
Isa. 32. 3. and the ears of them that hear shall h.
42. 23. who will h. and hear for the time to come
Jer. 26. 3. if so be they will h. and turn from evil?
5. to h. to the prophets whom I sent unto you
29. 12. ye shall pray to me, and I will h. unto you
35. 13. will ye not receive instruction to h. to words
Zech. 7. 11. but they refused to h. stopped their ears
Acts 4. 19. to h. unto you more than unto God
12. 13. as Peter knocked, a damsel came to h.

HEARKEN, *Imperatively.*

Gen. 4. 23. ye wives of Lamech, h. to my speech
23. 15. my lord, h. to me || 49. 2. h. to Isr. your father
Num. 23. 18. rise up, h. unto me, thou son of Zippor
Deut. 4. 1. h. O Israel, to the statutes I teach you
27. 9. take heed, and h. O Israel, this day thou art
Judg. 9. 7. he cried, h. to me, ye men of Shechem
1 Kings 8. 30. h. to the supplications, 2 Chr. 6. 21.
22. 28. he said, h. O people, every one of you
2 Chron. 18. 27. and he said, h. all ye people
20. 15. h. ye, all Judah, and ye inhabitants of Jeru.
Job 13. 6. and h. to the pleadings of my lips
32. 10. h. to me, 33. 31. || 33. 1. h. to all my words
34. 10. h. unto me, ye men of understanding
34. let a wise man h. || 37. 14. h. to this, O Job
Psal. 34. 11. h. I will teach you || 45. 10. h. O daught.
Prov. 7. 24. h. to me, therefore, O children, 8. 32.
Isa. 28. 23. hear my voice, h. and hear my speech
34. 1. come near, ye nations, h. ye people, 49. 1.
46. 3. h. to me, O house of Jacob, 48. 12. Hos. 5. 1.
12. h. to me, stout-hearted, are far from righteous.
51. 1. h. to me, ye that follow after righteousness
4. h. unto me, my people, give ear, O my nation
7. h. to me, ye that know righteousness
55. 2. h. diligently unto me, eat that which is good
Jer. 6. 17. saying, h. to the sound of the trumpet
Dan. 9. 19. O Lord, h. and do; defer not, O my God
Mic. 1. 2. h. O earth, and all that therein is
Mark 7. 14. he said, h. to me, every one of you
Acts 2. 14. ye men of Judah, h. to my words
7. 2. he said, men, brethren, and fathers, h.
15. 13. saying, men and brethren, h. to me
Jam. 2. 5. h. my beloved brethren, hath not God
See VOICE.

HEARKEN *not*, or *not* HEARKEN.

Gen. 34. 17. if ye will not h. to be circumcised
Exod. 7. 4. Pharaoh shall not h. to you, 22. | 11. 9.
Lev. 26. 14. but if ye will not h. to me, 18, 21, 27.
Deut. 13. 3. thou shalt not h. to that dreamer
8. not h. unto him, nor shall thine eye pity him
17. 12. the man that will not h. to the priest
18. 19. that whosoever will not h. to my words
21. 18. when chastened, he will not h. to them
23. 5. Lord would not h. to Balaam, Josh. 24. 10.
Josh. 1. 18. and will not h. to thy words in all
Judg. 2. 17. yet they would not h. to their judges
11. 17. the king of Edom would not h. thereto
19. 25. the men of Gibeah would not h. to him
20. 13. the children of Benjamin would not h.
1 Kings 20. 8. elders said, h. not to him, nor consent
2 Kings 17. 40. did not h. but did after their manner
18. 31. h. not to Hezekiah, Isa. 36. 16.
2 Chr. 10. 16. king Rehoboam would not h. to them
33. 10. and the Lord spake, but they would not h.
Job 33. 33. if not h. hold thy peace, I shall teach thee
Psal. 58. 5. who will not h. to the voice of charmers
81. 11. but my people would not h. to my voice
Jer. 6. 10. their ear is uncircumcised, they cannot h.
17. but they said, we will not h. 44. 16.
7. 27. thou shalt speak, they will not h. unto thee
11. 11. tho' they cry to me, I will not h. to them
16. 12. after evil heart, that they may not h. to me
17. 27. if ye will not h. to me, 26. 4. Ezek. 20. 39.
23. 16. h. not to prophets, 27. 9, 14, 16, 17. | 29. 8.
38. 15. if I give counsel, wilt thou not h. to me?
Ezek. 3. 7. not h. to thee, for they will not h. to me
20. 8. they rebelled, and would not h. unto me
Hos. 9. 17. because they did not h. to him, Zech. 1. 4.

HEARKENED.

Gen. 23. 16. Abraham h. to Ephron, and weighed
30. 17. God h. to Leah || 22. God h. to Rachel
34. 24. to Hamor h. all that went out of the gate
39. 10. that Joseph h. not to her, to lie by her
Exod. 6. 9. but they h. not to Moses, 16. 20.
12. the children of Israel have not h. to me
7. 13. Pharaoh h. not to them, 8. 15, 19. | 9. 12.
Deut. 9. 19. Lord h. to me at that time, 10. 10.
18. 14. these nations h. to observers of times
34. 9. Israel h. to Joshua as to Moses, Josh. 1. 17.
Judg. 11. 28. king of Ammonites h. not to Jephthah
1 Sam. 28. 21. the woman of Endor h. to Saul's words
1 Kings 12. 15. king h. not to people, 16. 2 Chr. 10. 15.
24. they h. therefore to the word of the Lord
15. 20. Ben-hadad h. to king Asa, 2 Chron. 16. 4.
2 Kings 13. 4. and the Lord h. to Jehoahaz
16. 9. the king of Assyria h. to Asa
20. 13. Hezekiah h. to the messengers from Babylon
21. 9. Judah h. not to the law, Manasseh seduced
22. 13. our fathers h. not to the words of the book
2 Chr. 24. 17. then Joash h. to the princes of Judah
25. 16. Amaziah h. not to the prophet's counsel
30. 20. Lord h. to Hezekiah, and healed the people
35. 22. Josiah h. not to Pharaoh-necho
Neh. 9. 16. our fathers dealt proudly, and h. not to thy commandments, 29, 34. Jer. 34. 14.
Esth. 3. 4. now when Mordecai h. not to them
Psal. 81. 13. O that my people had h. to me
Isa. 21. 7. and he h. diligently with much heed
48. 18. O that thou hadst h. to my commandments
Jer. 6. 19. they have not h. to my word, 7. 24, 26. | 25. 3, 4, 7. | 26. 5. | 29. 19. | 32. 33. | 34. 17. | 35. 14, 15, 16. | 36. 31. | 44. 5.
37. 14. Irijah, h. not to Jeremiah, so he took him
Ezek. 3. 6. had I sent, they would have h. to thee
Dan. 9. 6. neither have we h. to thy servants
Mal. 3. 16. the Lord h. and heard it, Jer. 8. 6.
Acts 27. 21. Paul said, sirs, ye should have h. to me
See VOICE.

HEARKENEDST.

Deut. 28. 45. because thou h. not to voice of the L.

HEARKENETH.

Prov. 1. 33. but whoso h. to me shall dwell safely
12. 15. but he that h. to counsel is wise

HEARKENING.

Psal. 103. 20. ye angels h. to the voice of his word

HEART.

The Hebrews *look upon the* heart *as the source of wit, understanding, love, courage, grief, and pleasure. Hence are derived many ways of speaking.* An honest and good heart; *that is, a heart studious of holiness, being prepared by the Spirit of God, to entertain the word with due affections, dispositions, and resolutions.* Luke 8. 15. *We read of* a broken heart, a clean heart, an evil heart, a hardened heart, a liberal heart, *a heart that does an act of kindness, freely, voluntarily, with generosity.* To incline the heart to God; *to beseech him to* change our stony hearts into hearts of flesh; to love with all one's heart, &c. To turn the heart of the fathers to the children, and the heart of the children to their fathers, Mal. 4. 6. *that is, to cause them to be perfectly reconciled, and that they should be of the same mind.* Let no man's heart fail; *let no man be discouraged,* 1 Sam. 17. 32.

To want heart, *sometimes denotes to want understanding and prudence.* Hos. 7. 11. Ephraim is like a silly dove, without heart; they call to Egypt, they go to Assyria. *They have no judgment or understanding of the right way, to free themselves from their troubles, which is seen in their seeking to* Egypt *and* Assyria. O fools and slow of heart, *ignorant men without insight and understanding,* Luke 24. 25. This people's heart is waxed gross, lest they should understand with their heart, Mat. 13. 15. *Their heart is stupified, so as to be destitute of understanding; they resist the light, and reject all impressions of truth.* The prophets prophesy out of their own hearts, Ezek. 13. 2. *They prophesy according to their own inclinations and affections, and what their own imaginations suggest to them, without any warrant from God.* To lay any thing to heart, to set one's heart on any thing; *that is, to remember it, to apply oneself to it, to have it at heart.* No man layeth it to heart, *no one concerns himself about it,* Jer. 12. 11.

The heart *dilates with joy, contracts with sadness, breaks with sorrow, grows fat, and hardens in prosperity; it resists truth; God opens it, prepares and turns it as he pleases.* To steal one's heart *is an expression in* Gen. 31. † 20. Jacob stole away the heart of Laban; *that is, he went away without his knowledge and consent.* The heart melts, *under discouragement;* the heart forsakes one, *under terror;* the heart is desolate, *in amazement;* the heart is fluctuating, *in doubt.* To speak to one's heart, *to comfort him, to say pleasing and affecting things to him.*

By the heart *likewise the middle of any thing is meant:* Tyre is in the heart of the seas, *in the midst of the seas,* Ezek. 27. 4. We will not fear, though the mountains be carried into the heart, *or midst of the sea,* Psal. 46. 2. As Jonas was three days and three nights in the whale's belly; so shall the Son of man be three days and three nights in the heart of the earth, *in the grave,* Mat. 12. 40.

Gen. 31 † 20. Jacob stole away the h. of Laban
34. † 3. Shechem spake to the h. of Dinah
45. 26. Jacob's h. fainted, for he believed them not
Exod. 23. 9. for ye know the h. of a stranger
28. 30. they shall be on Aaron's h. when he goeth in
35. 5. whoso is of a willing h. let him bring it
35. them hath he filled with wisdom of h.
Lev. 26. 16. shall consume eyes, cause sorrow of h.
Num. 32. 7. wherefore discourage ye the h. of Israel?
9. they discouraged the h. of the children of Isr.
Deut. 5. 29. O that there were such an h. in them
28. 28. Lord shall smite with astonishment of h.
47. thou servedst not the Lord with gladness of h.
65. the Lord shall give thee there a trembling h.
29. 4. the Lord hath not given you a h. to perceive
Josh. 14. 8. they made the h. of the people melt
Judg. 5. 15. for divisions there were great thoughts of h.
16. for divisions there were great searchings of h.
18. 20. the priest's h. was glad, he took the ephod
1 Sam. 1. 13. now Hannah, she spake in her h.
4. † 20. she answered not, nor set her h. to it
10. 9. it was so that God gave him another h.
16. 7. but the Lord looketh on the h.
17. 32. Dav. said, let no man's h. fail because of him
24. 5. David's h. smote him, because he cut off
25. 31. shall be no grief, nor offence of h. to my ld.
36. and Nabal's h. was merry within him
2 Sam. 6. 16. she despised him in h. 1 Chron. 15. 29.
13. 28. when Amnon's h. is merry with wine
14. 1. that the king's h. was toward Absalom
18. 14. Joab thrust darts through the h. of Absal.
19. † 7. go forth and speak to h. of thy servants
14. he bowed the h. of all the men of Judah
1 Kings 3. 9. give thy servant an understanding h.
12. I have given thee an understanding h.
4. 29. G. gave Solomon wisdom and largeness of h.
8. 17. it was in the h. of David, 2 Chron. 6. 7.
66. people went to tents glad of h. 2 Chron. 7. 10.
10. 2. communed of all was in her h. 2 Chron. 9. 1
11. 4. perfect, as was the h. of David his father
12. 27. then shall the h. of this people turn
2 Kings 6. 11. the h. of king of Assyria was troubled
12. 4. that cometh into any man's h. 2 Chr. 29. 31.
1 Chron. 12. 33. they were not of double h.
† 33. they were without a h. and a h.
16. 10. let the h. of them rejoice, Psal. 105. 3.
29. 17. I know thou triest the h. 18. Jer. 11. 20.
2 Chr. 7. 11. and all that came into Solomon's h.
30. † 22. Hezekiah spake to the h. of the Levites
Ezra 6. 22. turned the h. of the king of Assyria
7. 27. put such a thing as this in the king's h.
Neh. 2. 2. this is nothing else but sorrow of h.
Esth. 1. 10. when the h. of the king was merry
5. 9. Haman went forth that day with a glad h.
Job 9. 4. he is wise in h. and mighty in strength
12. † 3. but I have an h. as well as you
24. he taketh away the h. of the chief of people
29. 13. I caused the widow's h. to sing for joy
34. † 10. therefore hearken to me, ye men of h.
† 34. let men of h. tell me, let a wise man hear
36. 13. but the hypocrites in h. heap up wrath
37. 24. he respecteth not any that are wise of h.
38. 36. who hath given understanding to the h.
Psal. 12. 2. and with a double h. do they speak
19. 8. the statutes of Lord are right, rejoicing the h.
34. 18. the Ld. is nigh them that are of a broken h.
44. 21. for he knoweth the secrets of the h.
45. 5. thine arrows are sharp in the h. of enemies
58. 2. in h. ye work wickedness || 64. 6. the h. is deep
73. 7. they have more than h. could wish
101. 4. a froward h. shall depart from me
5. an high look, and a proud h. will not I suffer
104. 15. wine, that maketh glad the h. of man; bread, which strengtheneth man's h.
Prov. 6. 18. an h. that deviseth wicked imaginations
† 32. whoso committeth adultery, lacketh h.
7. 10. behold, there met him a woman subtle of h.
8. 5. and ye fools, be ye of an understanding h.
10. 8. the wise in h. will receive commandments
20. the h. of the wicked is little worth
11. 20. they of a froward h. are abomination to Ld.
29. the fool shall be servant to the wise of h.
12. 8. but he that is of perverse h. shall be despised
20. deceit is in the h. of them who imagine evil
25. heaviness in the h. of man maketh it stoop
13. 12. hope deferred maketh the h. sick
14. 10. the h. knoweth his own bitterness
13. even in laughter the h. is sorrowful
14. backslider in h. be filled with his own ways
30. a sound h. is the life of the flesh, but envy the
33. wisdom resteth in h. of him that hath underst.
15. 7. but the h. of the foolish doeth not so
13. a merry h. maketh a cheerful countenance; but by sorrow of the h. the spirit is broken

Prov. 15. 14. h. of him that hath underst. seeketh kn.
15. he that is of a merry h. hath a continual feast
28. the h. of the righteous studieth to answer
30. the light of the eyes rejoiceth the h.
† 32. he that heareth reproof possesseth an h.
16. 1. the preparations of h. in man from the Lord
5. every one proud in h. is an abomination to Ld.
9. a man's h. deviseth his way, but Lord directs
23. the h. of the wise teacheth his mouth
17. 16. a price in hand, seeing he hath no h. to it
20. he that hath a froward h. findeth no good
22. a merry h. doeth good like a medicine
18. 12. before destruction the h. of man is haughty
15. the h. of the prudent getteth knowledge
19. 21. there are many devices in a man's h.
20. 5. counsel in the h. of man is like deep water
21. 1. the king's h. is in the hand of the Lord
4. an high look, and a proud h. is sin
22. 11. that loveth pureness of h. the king his friend
15. foolishness is bound in the h. of a child
24. 12. doth not he that pondereth the h. consider it?
25. 3. and the h. of kings is unsearchable
20. so is he that singeth songs to an heavy h.
26. 23. a wicked h. is like a potsherd covered with
27. 9. ointment and perfume rejoice the h.
19. so the h. of man answereth to man
28. 25. he that is of a proud h. stirreth up strife
31. 11. the h. of her husband doth safely trust in her
Eccl. 7. 3. by sadness of countenance the h. is better
4. the h. of the wise is in the house of mourning,
but the h. of fools is in the house of mirth
7. oppression makes mad, a gift destroyeth the h.
8. 5. wise man's h. discerneth both time and judgm.
11. the h. of men is fully set in them to do evil
9. 3. also the h. of the sons of men is full of evil
7. eat thy bread, and drink thy wine with merry h.
10. 2. a wise man's h. is at right hand, fool's h. at left
Isa. 6. 10. make their h. fat, Mat. 13. 15. Acts 28. 27.
9. 9. that say in the pride and stoutness of h.
10. 12. will punish the fruit of the stout h. of king
13. 7. all hands faint, every man's h. shall melt
30. 29. ye shall have gladness of h. as when one
32. 4. the h. of the rash shall understand knowledge
35. 4. say to them that are of fearful h. be strong
40. † 2. speak ye to the h. of Jerusalem
42. 25. it burned him, yet he laid it not to h.
44. 20. a deceived h. hath turned him aside
57. 1. and no man layeth it to h. Jer. 12. 11.
15. and to revive the h. of the contrite ones
59. 13. uttering from the h. words of falsehood
65. 14. behold, my servants shall sing for joy of h.
but ye shall cry for sorrow of h. and howl
† 17. the former heavens not come upon the h.
Jer. 2. † 24. that snuffeth wind at the desire of her h.
3. † 16. neither shall it come upon the h.
4. 9. the h. of the king and princes shall perish
5. 23. but this people hath a rebellious h.
9. 26. the house of Israel are uncircumcised in h.
11. 20. O Lord, that triest the reins and the h.
17. 9. the h. is deceitful above all things
10. I the Lord search the h. I try the reins
20. 12. O Lord, that seest the reins and h.
23. 26. how long shall this be in the h. of prophets?
24. 7. and I will give them a h. to know me
48. 41. be as the h. of a woman in her pangs, 49. 22.
Lam. 3. 65. give them sorrow of h. thy curse to them
Ezek. 6. 9. I am broken with their whorish h.
11. 19. I will take the stony h. out of their flesh
13. 22. with lies ye made h. of the righteous sad
18. 31. and make you a new h. and a new spirit
21. 7. every h. shall melt, all hands shall be feeble
25. 6. rejoiced in h. with all thy despite ag. Israel
15. have taken vengeance with a despiteful h.
27. 31. shall weep for thee with bitterness of h.
36. 26. and I will give you a h. of flesh
44. 7. strangers uncircumcised in h. 9. Acts 7. 51.
Dan. 4. 16. let a beast's h. be given unto him
7. 4. and a man's h. was given to it
Hos. 2. † 14. I will allure her, and speak to her h.
4. 11. whoredom and wine take away the h.
7. 11. Ephraim is like a silly dove without h.
Nah. 2. 10. the h. melteth, and the knees smite
Zeph. 2. 15. this the city that said in her h. I am
Mal. 2. 2. if ye will not lay it to h. to give glory, I
will send a curse, because ye do not lay it to h.
4. 6. shall turn the h. of fathers, and h. of children
Mat. 11. 29. come to me, I am meek and lowly in h.
12. 34. out of the abundance of the h. Luke 6. 45.
35. out of the treasure of the h. Luke 6. 45.
15. 18. come forth from the h. and defile the man
19. out of the h. proceed evil thoughts, Mark 7. 21.
Mark 16. 14. he upbraided them with hardness of h.
Luke 2. 19. Mary kept and pondered them in her h.
51. but his mother kept these sayings in her h.
8. 15. which in a good h. having heard the word
24. 25. O fools, slow of h. to believe the prophets
John 13. 2. the devil having put into the h. of Judas
Acts 2. 46. did eat their meat with singleness of h.
5. 33. heard that, they were cut to the h. 7. 54.
11. 23. with purpose of h. they would cleave to Ld.
Rom. 2. 5. after thy impenitent h. treasurest up
29. circumcision is that of the h. in the Spirit
6. 17. ye have obeyed from the h. that doctrine
10. 10. with the h. man believeth to righteousness
1 Cor. 2. 9. neither have entered into the h. of man
7. 37. hath so decreed in his h. that he will keep
2 Cor. 2. 4. out of much anguish of h. I wrote you
3. 3. not in stone, but written in fleshly tables of h.
5. 12. which glory in appearance, and not in h.
8. 16. the same earnest care into the h. of Titus
Eph. 6. 6. doing the will of God from the h.
Col. 3. 22. but in singleness of h. fearing God
1 Thess. 2. 17. taken from you in presence, not in h.
Heb. 4. 12. is a discerner of the intents of the h.
10. 22. let us draw near with a true h. in assurance
13. 9. it is good that the h. be established with grace
1 Pet. 3. 4. let it be the hidden man of the h.
2 Pet. 2. 14. an h. exercised with covetous practices
Rev. 18. 7. for she saith in her h. I sit a queen

HEART.

Exod. 15. 8. depths were congealed in h. of the sea
Deut. 4. † 11. mountain burnt to the h. of heaven
Ps. 46. † 2. though mountains be carried into h. of
Prov. 23. † 34. as he that lieth down in h. of sea
30. † 19. the way of a ship in the h. of the sea
Isa. 19. 1. h. of Egypt shall melt in the midst of it
Mat. 12. 40. so shall Son of man be in h. of earth

HEART with all.

Deut. 11. 13. to serve him with all your h. and with
all your soul, Josh. 22. 5. 1 Sam. 12. 20, 24.
13. 3. love the Ld. with all your h. and soul, 30. 6.
Mat. 22. 37. Mark 12. 30, 33. Luke 10. 27.
26. 16. thou shalt keep and do them with all thy h.
30. 2. return to the L. with all thine h. 10. Joel 2. 12.
Judg. 16. 17. that Samson told her all his h. 18.
1 Kings 2. 4. walk before me with all their h. 8. 23.
8. 48. and so return to thee with all their h. and
all their soul, 2 Kings 23. 25. 2 Chron. 6. 38.
14. 8. David, who followed me with all his h.
2 Kings 10. 31. Jehu took no heed to walk with all h.
23. 3. made a covenant to walk before the L. with
all their h. and all their soul, 2 Chron. 34. 31.
2 Chr. 15. 12. seek God of fathers with all their h.
15. for they had sworn with all their h.
22. 9. Jehoshaphat sought the Lord with all his h.
31. 21. he did it with all his h. and prospered
Psal. 86. 12. I will praise thee, O L. with all my h.
Prov. 3. 5. trust in the L. with all thy h. lean not
Jer. 29. 13. when ye search for me with all your h.
Ezek. 36. 5. with the joy of all their h. to cast it out
Zeph. 3. 14. be glad with all the h. O Jerusalem
Acts 8. 37. if thou believest with all thy h. mayest
See APPLY, BROKEN, CLEAN, EVIL, HARDEN, HARDENED.

His HEART.

Gen. 6. 5. every imagination of his h. was only evil
6. it repented the Lord and grieved him at his h.
8. 21. L. said in his h. || 17. 17. Abraham in his h.
27. 41. Esau said in his h. the days of mourning
Exod. 4. 14. when seeth thee, he will be glad in his h.
7. 23. neither did he set his h. to this also
25. 2. every man that giveth willingly with his h.
28. 29. in the breast-plate of judgment upon his h.
35. 34. he hath put in his h. that he may teach
Deut. 2. 30. the Lord hath made his h. obstinate
17. 17. multiply wives, that his h. turn not away
20. his h. be not lifted up above his brethren
19. 6. lest the avenger pursue, while his h. is hot
20. 8. lest his brethren's heart faint as well as his h.
24. 15. for he is poor, and setteth his h. upon it
29. 19. that he bless himself in his h. saying
Ruth 3. 7. his h. was merry, he went to lie down
1 Sam. 4. 13. his h. trembled for the ark of God
21. 12. David laid up these words in his h.
25. † 25. let not my lord lay it to his h.
37. it came to pass that his h. died within him
27. 1. David said in his h. || 28. 5. his h. trembled
2 Sam. 7. 27. thy servant hath found in his h. to
pray this prayer unto thee, 1 Chron. 17. 25.
13. 33. let not my lord take the thing to his h.
1 Kin. 10. 24. which G. had put in his h. 2 Chr. 9. 23.
11. 3. and his wives turned away his h. 4. 9.
12. 26. Jeroboam said in his h. the kingdom return
2 Kings 9. 24. the arrow went out at his h. and sunk
2 Chron. 12. 14. because he prepared not his h. to
17. 6. his h. was lifted up in the ways of the Lord
26. 16. his h. was lifted up to his destruction
30. 19. that prepareth his h. to seek God, Lord G.
32. 25. for his h. was lifted up, therefore was wrath
26. he humbled himself for the pride of his h.
31. that he might know all that was in his h.
Ezra 7. 10. Ezra prepared his h. to seek law of L.
Neh. 9. 8. and foundest his h. faithful before thee
Esth. 6. 6. Haman thought in his h. to whom the kg.
7. 5. where is he that durst presume in his h. to do
Job 34. 14. if he set his h. upon man, if he gather
41. 24. his h. is as firm as a stone, yea as hard
Psal. 10. 3. the wicked boasteth of his h. desire
6. he hath said in his h. 11. 13. | 14. 1. | 53. 1.
15. 2. that speaketh truth in his h. shall dwell
21. 2. thou hast given him his h. desire, hast not
33. 11. the thoughts of his h. to all generations
37. 31. law of his God is in his h. none of his steps
41. 6. his h. gathereth iniquity to itself
55. 21. words were smooth, but war was in his h.
78. 72. he fed them according to integrity of his h.
112. 7. his h. is fixed, trusting in the Lord
8. his h. is established, he shall not be afraid
Prov. 6. 14. frowardness is in his h. deviseth mischf.
18. 2. but that his h. may discover itself
19. 3. and his h. fretteth against the Lord
23. 7. for as he thinketh in his h. so is he; eat and
drink, saith he, but his h. is not with thee
28. 14. but he that hardeneth his h. shall fall
Eccl. 2. 23. yea his h. taketh not rest in the night
5. 20. God answereth him in the joy of his h.
Cant. 3. 11. in the day of the gladness of his h.
Isa. 7. 2. his h. was moved, and the h. of his people
10. 7. he meaneth not so, neither doth his h. think
so, but it is in his h. to destroy and cut off nations
32. 6. his h. will work iniquity, to practise hypocrisy
44. 19. none considereth in his h. neither is there
57. 17. he went on frowardly in the way of his h.
Jer. 9. 8. but in h. he layeth his wait
23. 20. he have performed the thoughts of his h.
30. 21. that engaged his h. to approach unto me
24. until he have performed the intents of his h.
48. 29. we have heard the haughtiness of his h.
Ezek 14. 4. that setteth up his idols in his h. 7.
31. 10. his h. lifted up in his height, Dan. 5. 20.
Dan. 1. 8. Daniel purposed in his h. that he would
4. 16. let his h. be changed from man's, 5. 21.
6. 14. the king set his h. on Daniel to deliver him
8. 25. and he shall magnify himself in his h.
11. 12. his h. shall be lifted up, shall cast down
28. his h. shall be against the holy covenant
Obad. 3. that saith in his h. who shall bring me down?
Mat. 5. 28. hath committed adultery with her in h. h.
13. 19. and catcheth away that was sown in his h.
24. 48. if evil servant shall say in his h. Luke 12. 45.
Mark 7. 19. because it entereth not into his h.
11. 23. and shall not doubt in his h. but believe
Luke 6. 45. good man out of good treasure of his h. an
evil man out of the evil treasure of his h.
Acts 7. 23. it came into his h. to visit his brethren
1 Cor. 7. 37. he that standeth stedfast in his h.
14. 25. thus are the secrets of his h. made manifest
2 Cor. 9. 7. as he purposeth in his h. so let him give

Mine or my HEART.

Gen. 20. 5. in the integrity of my h. have I done this
24. 45. done speaking in mine h. Rebekah came
Deut. 29. 19. tho' I walk in the imagination of m. h.
Josh. 14. 7. I brought him word as it was in mine h.
Judg. 5. 9. my h. is toward the governors of Israel
1 Sam. 2. 1. she said, my h. rejoiceth in the Lord
35. shall do according to that which is in mine h.
1 Kings 9. 3. to put my name, and my eyes and mine
h. shall be there perpetually, 2 Chron. 7. 16.
2 Kings 5. 26. went not mine h. with thee, when
10. 15. is thine h. right, as my h. is with thy h.?
30. hast done according to all that was in mine h.
1 Chr. 12. 17. if to help, mine h. shall be knit unto
28. 2. I had in mine h. to build an house of rest
2 Chr. 29. 10. it is in mine h. to make a covenant
Neh. 2. 12. what God had put in my h. to do, 7. 5.
5. † 7. then my h. consulted in me, I rebuked
Job 17. 11. the thoughts of my h. are broken off
23. 16. God maketh my h. soft, and the Almighty
27. 6. my h. shall not reproach me so long as I live
31. 7. and mine h. walked after mine eyes
9. if mine h. have been deceived by a woman
27. and my h. hath been secretly enticed
33. 3. my words shall be of the uprightness of my h.
37. 1. at this also my h. trembleth, and is moved
Ps. 4. 7. thou hast put gladness in my h. more than
13. 2. how long take counsel, sorrow in my h. daily
5. but I trusted, my h. shall rejoice in thy salvat.
16. 9. my h. is glad || 17. 3. thou hast proved mine h.
19. 14. let the meditation of my h. be acceptable
22. 14. m. h. is like wax || 26. 2. try my reins and m. h.
25. 17. the troubles of my h. are enlarged, O bring
27. 3. my h. shall not fear though war should rise
8. my h. said to thee, thy face, Lord, will I seek
28. 7. my h. trusted in him, my h. greatly rejoiceth
36. 1. the transgression of the wicked saith in my h.
38. 8. by reason of the disquietness of my h.
10. my h. panteth, my strength faileth, Isa. 21. 4.
39. 3. my h. was hot within me, while musing
40. 8. yea, thy law is within my h.
10. I have not hid thy righteousness within my h.
12. not able to look up, therefore my h. faileth me
45. 1. my h. is inditing a good matter, I speak
49. 3. the meditation of my h. be of understanding
55. 4. my h. is sore pained within me, terrors of death
57. 7. my h. is fixed, O God, my h. is fixed, 108. 1.
61. 2. I will cry, when my h. is overwhelmed
66. 18. if I regard iniquity in my h. L. will not hear
69. 20. reproach hath broken my h. I am full
73. 13. verily I have cleansed my h. in vain
21. my h. was grieved, I was pricked in my reins
26. my h. faileth, but God is the strength of my h.
84. 2. my h. and flesh crieth out for the living God
86. 11. unite my h. to fear thy name
102. 4. my h. is smitten and withered like grass
109. 22. and my h. is wounded within me
119. 11. thy word have I hid in my h. not to sin
32. I will run, when thou shalt enlarge my h.
36. incline my h. to thy testimonies, not to covet.
80. let my h. be sound in thy statutes
111. thy testimonies are the rejoicing of my h.
112. I have inclined mine h. to perform thy stat.
131. 1. Lord, my h. is not haughty, nor eyes lofty
139. 23. search me, and know my h. try me
141. 4. incline not my h. to any evil thing
143. 4. my h. within me is desolate
Prov. 5. 12. how hath my h. despised reproof
20. 9. who can say, I have made my h. clean?
23. 15. if thine heart be wise, my h. shall rejoice
Eccl. 1. 13. I gave my h. to seek and search out
16. my h. had great experience of wisdom
17. I gave my h. to know wisdom and madness
2. 1. I said in mine h. I will prove thee, 15. | 3.
17, 18.
3. I sought in mine h. to give myself to wine, yet
acquainting mine h. with wisdom, to lay hold
on folly
10. I withheld not my h. from any joy
20. to cause my h. to despair of all the labour
7. 25. I applied mine h. to know and search, 8. 9, 16.
9. 1. for all this I considered in my h.
Cant. 4. 9. thou hast ravished my h. my sister, 9.
5. 2. I sleep, but my h. waketh, it is the voice
Isa. 15. 5. my h. shall cry out for Moab
63. 4. for the day of vengeance is in mine h.
Jer. 3. 15. I will give you pastors according to m. h.
4. 19. I am pained at my h. my h. maketh a noise
7. 31. I commanded not, neither came it into my h.
8. 18. when I comfort myself, my h. is faint in me
12. 3. hast seen me, and tried mine h. toward thee
15. 16. thy word the joy and rejoicing of mine h.
20. 9. his word was in mine h. as a burning fire
23. 9. mine h. is broken || 48. 31. my h. shall mourn
48. 36. therefore mine h. shall sound for Moab
Lam. 1. 20. behold, mine h. is turned within me
22. my sighs are many, and my h. is faint
3. 51. mine eye affecteth mine h. because of all
Dan. 7. 28. but I kept the matter in my h.
Hos. 11. 8. mine h. is turned within me, my repent.
Acts 2. 26. therefore did my h. rejoice, tongue glad
21. 13. what mean ye to weep, and break mine h.?
Rom. 9. 2. I have continual sorrow in my h.
10. 1. my h. desire to God for Isr. is, they be saved
Phil. 1. 7. because I have you in my h. inasmuch
See APPLIED.

One HEART.

2 Chr. 30. 12. hand of God was to give them one h.
Jer. 32. 39. I will give them one h. Ezek. 11. 19.
Acts 4. 32. multitude that believed were of one h.

Own HEART.

Num. 15. 39. that ye seek not after your own h.
1 Sam. 13. 14. sought man after his o. h. Acts 13. 22.
2 Sam. 7. 21. for thy word's sake, according to thine
own h. hast thou done these things, 1 Chron. 17. 19.
1 Kings 8. 38. know every man plague of his own h.
12. 33. which he had devised of his own h.
Neh. 6. 8. thou feignest them out of thine own h.

Psal. 4. 4. commune with your *own h.* on your bed
20. 4. grant thee according to thine *own h.*
37. 15. their sword shall enter into their *own h.*
77. 6. I commune with my *own h.* and my spirit
Prov. 28. 26. he that trusteth in his *own h.* is a fool
Eccl. 1. 16. I communed with mine *own h.* saying
7. 22. thy *own h.* knows thou hast cursed others
Jer. 9. 14. after imagination of their *own h.* 23. 17.
23. 16. they speak a vision of their *own h.*
26. prophesy the deceit of their *o. h.* *Ezek.* 13. 17.
Ezek. 14. 5. may take house of Israel in their *own h.*
Jam. 1. 26. but deceiveth his *own h.* this man's

Our HEART.

Deut. 1. 28. our brethren have discouraged *our h.*
Psal. 33. 21. for *our h.* shall rejoice in him
44. 18. *our h.* is not turned back, neither our
Lam. 3. 41. let us lift up *our h.* with our hands
5. 15. the joy of *our h.* is ceased ‖ 17. *our h.* is faint
Luke 24. 32. did not *our h.* burn within us, while he
2 *Cor.* 6. 11. our mouth is open, *our h.* is enlarged
1 *John* 3. 20. if *our h.* condemn us, God is greater
21. if *our h.* condemn us not, we have confidence

Perfect HEART.

1 *Kings* 8. 61. let your *h.* be *perfect* with the Lord
11. 4. his *h.* was not *perfect* with the Lord, 15. 3.
15. 14. nevertheless Asa's *h.* was *perfect* with the
Lord all his days, 2 *Chron.* 15. 17.
2 *Kings* 20. 3. Hezekiah said, remember how I have
walked before thee with a *perfect h.* *Isa.* 38. 3.
1 *Chr.* 12. 38. came with *perf. h.* to make D. king
28. 9. Solomon, my son, serve God with a *per. h.*
29. 9. because with *perf. h.* they offered willingly
19. and give unto Solomon my son a *perfect h.*
2 *Chr.* 16. 9. in behalf of them whose *h.* is *perfect*
19. 9. thus shall ye do in fear of Ld. with *perf. h.*
25. 2. Amaziah did right, but not with a *perfect h.*
Psal. 101. 2. I will walk in my house with *perf. h.*

Pure HEART.

Psal. 24. 4. who shall ascend? that hath a *pure h.*
Mat. 5. 8. blessed are *pure* in *h.* they shall see God
1 *Tim.* 1. 5. end of command. is charity out of *p. h.*
2 *Tim.* 2. 22. that call on the Lord out of a *pure h.*
1 *Pet.* 1. 22. love one another with a *p. h.* fervently

Their HEART.

Gen 42. 28. *their h.* failed them, they were afraid
Josh. 5. 1. the kings of Amorites heard *t. h.* melted
2 *Sam.* 18. † 3. if we flee, they will not set *t. h.* on us
1 *Kings* 8. † 47. if they bring back to *t. h.* 2 *Chr.* 6. † 37.
18. 37. thou hast turned *their h.* back again
1 *Chron.* 29. 18. and prepare *their h.* unto thee
Job 8. 10. shall they not utter words out of *t. h.?*
17. 4. thou hast hid *their h.* from understanding
Psal. 10. 17. Lord, thou wilt prepare *their h.*
78. 8. a generation that set not *their h.* aright
18. they tempted God in *their h.* by asking meat
37. *their h.* was not right with him, nor were
95. 10. it is a people that do err in *their h.*
105. 25. he turned *their h.* to hate his people
107. 12. therefore he brought down *their h.*
119. 70. *t. h.* is as fat as grease, I delight in thy law
140. 2. which imagine mischiefs in *t. h.* with labour
Prov. 24. 2. for *their h.* studieth destruction
Eccl. 3. 11. also he hath set the world in *their h.*
9. 3. madness is in *their h.* while they live
Isa. 6. 10. lest they hear with their ears and understand with *their h.* *Mat.* 13. 15. *Acts* 28. 27.
29. 13. *t. h.* is far from me, *Mat.* 15. 8. *Mark* 7. 6.
Jer. 5. 24. neither say they in *t. h.* let us fear the Ld.
13. 10. which walk in the imagination of *their h.*
14. 14. the prophets prophesy the deceit of *their h.*
17. 1. sin of Judah is graven on the table of *their h.*
Lam. 2. 18. *their h.* cried to the L. O wall of Zion
Ezek. 14. 3. these have set up their idols in *their h.*
20. 16. for *their h.* went after their idols
21. 15. that *their h.* may faint, ruins be multiplied
33. 31. but *their h.* goeth after their covetousness
Hos. 4. 8. they set *their h.* on their iniquity
7. 6. they have made ready *their h.* like an oven
14. they have not cried unto me with *their h.*
10. 2. *their h.* is divided ‖ 13. 6. *their h.* was exalt.
13. 8. I will rend the caul of *their h.* and devour
Zeph. 1. 12. I will punish the men that say in *t. h.*
Zech. 10. 7. *their h.* shall rejoice in the Lord
12. 5. the governors of Judah shall say in *their h.*
Mark 6. 52. for *their h.* was hardened, *Rom.* 1. 21.
Luke 9. 47. Jesus perceiving the thought of *their h.*
John 12. 40. he hath hardened *their h.* that they
should not see nor understand with *their h.*
Acts 2. 37. were pricked in *their h.* and said to Peter
2 *Cor.* 3. 15. when Moses is read, vail is on *their h.*
Eph. 4. 18. because of the blindness of *their h.*

Thine, thy HEART.

Gen. 20. 6. thou didst this in the integrity of *thy h.*
Exod. 9. 14. I will send all my plagues upon *thine h.*
Lev. 19. 17. thou shalt not hate thy brother in *t. h.*
Deut. 4. 9. lest they depart from *thy h.* all thy life
29. shalt find, if thou seek him with all *thy h.*
4. 39. know and consider it in *thine h.* 8. 5.
6. 5. thou shalt love the Lord with all *thine h.*
7. 17. if thou shalt say in *thine h.* these nations
are more than I, 8. 17. | 18. 21. *Jer.* 13. 22.
8. 2. led thee, to know what was in *thine h.*
14. then *thine h.* be lifted up, and thou forget L.
9. 4. speak not thou in *thine h.* after that the Lord
5. not for uprightness of *thine h.* dost thou go to
10. 12. to serve the Lord thy God with all *thy h.*
15. 9. there be not a thought in *thy* wicked *h.*
10. *thine h.* shall not be grieved when thou givest
28. 67. for the fear of *thine h.* wherewith shalt fear
30. 6. circumcise *thine h.* and the *h.* of thy seed
14. but the word is very nigh to thee in *thy h.*
17. if *thine h.* turn, so that thou wilt not hear
Judg. 16. 15. when *thine h.* is not with me
19. 6. and let *thine h.* be merry, 9. 1 *Kings* 21. 7.
8. the damsel's father said, comfort *thine h.*
1 *Sam.* 1. 8. why weepest thou? why is *thy h.* griev.?
2. 33. the man of thine shall be to grieve *thine h.*
9. 19. I will tell thee all that is in *thine h.*
14. 7. do all that is in *thine h.* 2 *Sam.* 7. 3. 1 *Chron.*
17. 2. behold, I am with thee, according to *thy h.*
17. 28. I know thy pride and naughtiness of *thy h.*
2 *Sam.* 3. 21. reign over all that *thine h.* desireth
2 *Sam.* 13. † 20. he is thy brother, set not *th. h.* on this
1 *Kings* 2. 44. knowest wickedness *thine h.* is privy
8. 18. in *thine h.* to build, 2 *Chron.* 1. 11. | 6. 8.
2 *Kings* 10. 15. Jehu said, is *thine h.* right as my *h.*
is with *thy h.* Jehonadab answered, it is
14. 10. *thine h.* hath lifted thee up, 2 *Chr.* 25. 19.
22. 19. because *thine h.* was tender, 2 *Chr.* 34. 27.
2 *Chron.* 19. 3. hast prepared *thine h.* to seek God
Job 1. † 8. hast thou set *thy h.* on my servant Job?
7. 17. and that thou shouldest set *thine h.* upon him
10. 13. and these things hast thou hid in *thine h.*
11. 13. if thou prepare *thine h.* and stretch out
15. 12. why doth *thine h.* carry thee away
22. 22. receive, and lay up his words in *thine h.*
Psal. 27. 14. and he shall strengthen *thine h.*
37. 4. and he shall give thee the desires of *thine h.*
Prov. 2. 2. and apply *thine h.* to understanding
10. when wisdom entereth into *thine h.*
3. 1. my son, let *thine h.* keep my commandments
3. write them upon the table of *thine h.* 7. 3.
4. 4. he said, let *thine h.* retain my words, 21.
23. keep *thy h.* with all diligence, for out of it
6. 21. bind them continually upon *thine h.*
25. lust not after her beauty in *thine h.*
7. 25. let not *thine h.* decline to her ways
23. 15. my son, if *thine h.* be wise, my *h.* rejoice
17. let not *thine h.* envy sinners, but be in fear
19. hear, my son, and guide *thine h.* in the way
26. my son, give me *thine h.* let thy eyes observe
33. and *thine h.* shall utter perverse things
24. 17. let not *thine h.* be glad when he stumbleth
27. † 23. and set *thy h.* to thy herds
Eccl. 5. 2. not *thine h.* be hasty to utter any thing
7. † 21. also give not *thine h.* unto all words
11. 9. let *thy h.* cheer thee; walk in ways of *thy h.*
10. therefore remove sorrow from *thy h.*
Isa. 14. 13. thou hast said in *thine h.* I will ascend
33. 18. *thine h.* shall meditate terror, where is
47. 7. thou didst not lay these things to *thy h.* 57. 11.
8. that sayest in *thine h.* I am, and none else, 10.
49. 21. then shalt thou say in *thine h.* who hath
Jer. 4. 14. O Jerus. wash *thine h.* from wickedness
18. it is bitter, because it reacheth unto *thine h.*
22. 17. *thine h.* are not but for thy covetousness
31. 21. set *thine h.* toward the high-way, turn
49. 16. the pride of *thine h.* deceived thee, *Obad.* 3.
Lam. 2. 19. pour out *thine h.* like water before Ld.
Ezek. 3. 10. receive in *thine h.* hear with thine ears
16. 30. how weak is *thine h.* saith the Lord God
22. 14. can *thine h.* endure in days I deal with thee
28. 2. because *thine h.* is lifted up for thy riches, 5.
6. thou hast set *thine h.* as the heart of God
17. *thine h.* was lifted up because of thy beauty
40. 4. set *thine h.* upon all that I shall shew thee
Dan. 2. 30. mightest know the thoughts of *thy h.*
5. 22. and thou hast not humbled *thine h.*
10. 12. thou didst set *thine h.* to understand
Acts 5. 3. why hath Satan filled *thine h.* to lie
4. why hast thou conceived this in *thine h.?*
8. 21. for *thy h.* is not right in the sight of God
Acts 8. 22. thought of *thine h.* may be forgiven thee
Rom. 10. 6. say not in *thine h.* who shall ascend
9. and shalt believe in *thine h.* that God raised

Upright in HEART.

2 *Chr.* 29. 34. Levites were more *upright in h.*
Psal. 7. 10. which saveth the *upright in h.*
11. 2. that they may shoot at the *upright in h.*
32. 11. shout for joy, ye that are *upright in h.*
36. 10. continue thy righteousness to *upright in h.*
64. 10. and all the *upright in h.* shall glory
94. 15. and all the *upright in h.* shall follow it
97. 11. gladness is sown for the *upright in h.*

Uprightness of HEART.

1 *Kings* 3. 6. he walketh in *uprightness of h.* 9. 4.
Psal. 119. 7. I will praise thee with *uprightness of h.*

Whole HEART.

Psal. 9. 1. I will praise thee, O Lord, with my *whole*
h. will shew forth thy works, 111. 1. | 138. 1.
119. 2. blessed that seek him with the *whole h.*
10. with my *whole h.* have I sought thee
34. yea, I shall observe it with my *whole h.*
58. I entreated thy favour with my *whole h.*
69. I will keep thy precepts with my *whole h.*
145. I cried with my *whole h.* hear me, O Lord
Isa. 1. 5. the whole head is sick, the *whole h.* is faint
Jer. 3. 10. not turned with *whole h.* but feignedly
24. 7. they shall return unto me with their *w. h.*
32. 41. I will plant them in land with my *whole h.*

Whose HEART.

Exod. 35. 21. *whose h.* stirred him up, 29. | 36. 2.
26. all the women *whose h.* stirred them up
Deut. 29. 18. *whose h.* turneth away this day from Ld
2 *Sam.* 17. 10. *whose h.* is as the heart of a lion
1 *Kings* 8. 39. *whose h.* thou knowest, 2 *Chr.* 6. 30.
2 *Chron.* 16. 9. in behalf of them *whose h.* is perfect
Psal. 84. 5. in *whose h.* are the ways of them
Eccl. 7. 26. the woman *whose h.* is snares and nets
Isa. 51. 7. hearken ye people, in *whose h.* is my law
Jer. 17. 5. *whose h.* departeth from the Lord
Ezek. 11. 21. *whose h.* walketh after detestable things
Acts 16. 14. *whose h.* the Lord opened, she attended

Your HEART.

Deut. 10. 16. circumcise foreskin of *your h.* *Jer.* 4. 4.
11. 16. take heed that *your h.* be not deceived
18. ye shall lay up these my words in *your h.*
1 *Kings* 11. 2. surely they will turn away *your h.*
1 *Chr.* 22. 19. set *your h.* and soul to seek the Lord
Psal. 22. 26. meek shall eat, *your h.* shall live for ever
31. 24. he shall strengthen *your h.* ye that hope
62. 8. ye people, pour out *your h.* before him
10. if riches increase, set not *your h.* upon them
69. 32. and *your h.* shall live that seek God
Isa. 66. 14. when ye see this, *your h.* shall rejoice
Jer. 51. 46. and lest *your h.* faint, and ye fear
Joel 2. 13. and rend *your h.* and not your garments
Zech. 7. 10. let none of you imagine evil in *your h.*
Mat. 6. 21. there will *your h.* be also, *Luke* 12. 34.
Mark 8. 17. have ye *your h.* yet hardened?
10. 5. for the hardness of *your h.* he wrote
John 14. 1. let not *your h.* be troubled, 27.
16. 6. because I said this, sorrow hath filled *your h.*
22. I will see you, and *your h.* shall rejoice
Eph. 6. 5. in singleness of *your h.* as unto Christ

HEARTED.

Exod. 35. 22. they came, as many as were willing-*h.*
Psal. 76. 5. the stout-*h.* are spoiled, they slept
Isa. 24. 7. new wine mourns, all the merry-*h.* do sigh
61. 1. he hath sent me to bind up the broken-*h.*
Ezek. 3. 7. all the house of Israel are hard-*h.*

Faint-HEARTED.

Deut. 20. 8. what man is there that is *faint-h.?*

Tender-HEARTED.

2 *Chron.* 13. 7. Rehoboam was young and *tender-h.*
Eph. 4. 32. and be kind one to another, *tender-h.*

Wise-HEARTED.

Exod. 28. 3. thou shalt speak unto all that are *w.-h.*
31. 6. and in the hearts of all that are *wise-h.*
35. 10. and every *wise-h.* among you shall come
25. all the women that were *wise-h.* did spin
36. 1. then wrought every *wise-h.* man, 2, 8.

HEARTH.

Gen. 18. 6. knead it, and make cakes upon the *h.*
Psal. 102. 3. and my bones are burnt as an *h.*
Isa. 30. 14. not a sherd to take fire from the *h.*
Jer. 36. 22. a fire on the *h.* burning before him
23. cast the roll into fire that was on the *h.*
Zech. 12. 6. make governm. of Judah like *h.* of fire

HEARTILY.

Luke 22. † 15. I have *h.* desired to eat this passover
Col. 3. 23. what ye do, do it *h.* as to the Lord, not to

HEARTS.

Josh. 7. 5. wherefore the *h.* of the people melted
1 *Sam.* 10. 26. band of men, whose *h.* G. had touched
2 *Sam.* 15. 6. so Absalom stole the *h.* of Israel
13. the *h.* of the men of Israel are after Absalom
1 *Kings* 8. 39. thou only knowest the *h.* 2 *Chr.* 6. 30.
1 *Chron.* 28. 9. for the Lord searcheth all *h.*
Ps. 7. 9. the righteous God trieth the *h.* *Prov.* 17. 3
Prov. 15. 11. how much more then the *h.* of men
21. 2. but the Lord pondereth the *h.*
31. 6. give wine to those that be of heavy *h.*
Jer. 48. 41. mighty men's *h.* of Moab like a woman
Ezek. 32. 9. I will also vex the *h.* of many people
Dan. 11. 27. both these k.'s *h.* shall be to do mischief
Luke 1. 17. turn the *h.* of the fathers to the children
2. 35. that the thoughts of *h.* may be revealed
21. 26. signs in the sun, men's *h.* failing them
Acts 1. 24. which knowest the *h.* of all men, 15. 8.
Rom. 8. 27. he that searcheth the *h.* knoweth the
16. 18. by fair speeches deceive the *h.* of the simple
1 *Cor.* 4. 5. make manifest the counsels of the *h.*
Rev. 2. 23. I am he that searcheth the reins and *h.*

Our HEARTS.

Josh. 2. 11. as soon as we heard, *our h.* did melt
1 *Kings* 8. 58. that he may incline *our h.* to him
Acts 14. 17. filling *our h.* with food and gladness
Rom. 5. 5. the love of God is shed abroad in *our h.*
2 *Cor.* 1. 22. given the earnest of the Spirit in *our h.*
3. 2. ye are our epistle written in *our h.*
4. 6. God hath shined in *our h.* to give the light
7. 3. that you are in *our h.* to die and live with you
1 *Thess.* 2. 4. but pleasing God, who trieth *our h.*
Heb. 10. 22. *our h.* sprinkled from an evil conscience
1 *John* 3. 19. and shall assure *our h.* before him

Their HEARTS.

Lev. 26. 36. I will send a faintness into *their h.*
41. if then *their* uncircumcised *h.* be humbled
Judg. 9. 3. *their h.* inclined to follow Abimelech
16. 25. when *their h.* were merry, they said
19. 22. as they were making *their h.* merry
2 *Chron.* 6. 14. walk before thee with all *their h.*
11. 16. such as set *their h.* to seek the Lord God
20. 33. the people had not prepared *their h.* to God
Job 1. 5. it may be my sons have cursed G. in *their h.*
Psal. 28. 3. speak peace, but mischief is in *their h.*
33. 15. he fashioneth *their h.* alike, he considers
35. 25. let them not say in *their h.* ah, so would we
74. 8. they said in *their h.* let us destroy them
81. 12. I gave them up to *their* own *h.* lust
125. 4. and to them that are upright in *their h.*
Isa. 44. 18. hath shut *t. h.* they cannot understand
Jer. 31. 33. and write my law in *their h.* *Heb.* 8. 10.
32. 40. but I will put my fear in *t. h.* not to depart
Ezek. 13. 2. that prophesy out of *their* own *h.*
Hos. 7. 2. and they consider not in *their h.*
Zech. 7. 12. yea, they made *their h.* as an adamant
Mark 2. 6. sitting there, and reasoning in *their h.*
3. 5. being grieved for the hardness of *their h.*
4. 15. taketh away word sown in *t. h.* *Luke* 8. 12.
Luke 1. 51. scattered proud in imaginations of *t. h.*
66. all that heard laid them up in *their h.*
3. 15. all men mused in *t. h.* of John, whether Ch.
Acts 7. 39. in *their h.* turned back again to Egypt
Rom. 1. 24. through the lust of *their h.* to dishonour
2. 15. shew the work of the law written in *their h.*
Col. 2. 2. that *their h.* might be comforted, being knit
Heb. 3. 10. said, they do always err in *their h.*
Rev. 17. 17. God hath put in *their h.* to fulfil his will

Your HEARTS.

Gen. 18. 5. comfort ye *your h.* after that pass on
Deut. 20. 3. O Israel, let not *your h.* faint, fear not
32. 46. set *your h.* to all the words which I testify
Josh. 23. 14. and ye know in all *your h.* and souls
24. 23. incline *your h.* to the Lord God of Israel
1 *Sam.* 6. 6. wherefore then do ye harden *your h.?*
7. 3. if ye return to the Lord with all *your h.* and
prepare *your h.* to the Lord to serve him only
Jer. 42. 20. ye dissembled in *your h.* when ye sent
Zech. 8. 17. let none of you imagine evil in *your h.*
Mat. 9. 4. Jesus said, wheref. think ye evil in *y. h.?*
18. 35. if ye from *your h.* forgive not every one
19. 8. because of the hardness of *y. h.* suffered you
Mark 2. 8. why reason ye these things in *your h.?*
Luke 5. 22. Jesus said, what reason ye in *your h.?*
16. 15. ye justify yourselves, God knoweth *your h.*
21. 14. settle it in *your h.* not to meditate before
34. lest at any time *your h.* be overcharged
24. 38. and why do thoughts arise in *your h.?*
Gal. 4. 6. God sent the Spirit of his Son into *your h.*
Eph. 3. 17. that Christ may dwell in *your h.* by faith
5. 19. making melody in *y. h.* to the Lord, *Col.* 3. 16.
6. 22. I sent that he might comfort *your h.*
Phil. 4. 7. shall keep *your h.* and minds through
Christ Jesus

Col. 3. 15. let the peace of God rule in your h.
4. 8. might know your estate and comfort your h.
1 Thess. 3. 13. he may establish your h. unblameable
2 Thess. 2. 17. comfort your h. and stablish you
3. 5. the Lord direct your h. into the love of God
Jam. 3. 14. if ye have strife in your h. glory not
4. 8. and purify your h. ye double-minded
5. 5. have been wanton, ye have nourished your h.
8. be ye also patient, stablish your h. the coming
1 Pet. 3. 15. sanctify the Lord God in your h.
2 Pet. 1. 19. till day dawn, and day-star arise in y. h.

HEARTY.

Prov. 27. 9. so the sweetness of a friend by h. couns.

HEAT.

Gen. 8. 22. cold, h. summer, winter, shall not cease
18. 1. sat in the tent-door in the h. of the day
Exod. 11. † 8. and he went out in the h. of anger
Deut. 29. 24. what meaneth the h. of this great anger?
32. 24. they shall be devoured with burning h.
1 Sam. 11. 11. slew the Ammonites till h. of the day
2 Sam. 4. 5. and they came about the h. of the day
1 Kings 1. 1. but he gat no h. || 2. my lord may get h.
Job 6. † 17. ice and snow vanish in the h. thereof
24. 19. drought and h. consume the snow waters
30. 30. my skin black, my bones are burnt with h.
Psal. 19. 6. there is nothing hid from the h. thereof
Eccl. 4. 11. if two lie together, then they have h.
Isa. 4. 6. a shadow in the day-time from h. 25. 4.
18. 4. I will take my rest, like a clear h. on herbs, and like a cloud of dew in the h. of harvest
25. 5. as the h. in a dry place, even the h.
49. 10. neither shall the h. nor sun smite them
Jer. 17. 8. and shall not see when h. cometh
36. 30. dead body shall be cast out in the day to h.
51. 39. in their h. I will make their feasts
Ezek. 3. 14. and I went in the h. of my spirit
Hos. 7. † 5. have made him sick with h. through wine
Mat. 20. 12. have borne the burden and h. of the day
Luke 12. 55. when south-wind blow, there will be h.
Acts 28. 3. there came a viper out of the h.
Jam. 1. 11. the sun no sooner risen with a burning h.
2 Pet. 3. 10. the elements shall melt with fervent h.

HEAT.

Dan. 3. 19. h. the furnace more than wont to be heated

HEATED.

Dan. 3. 19. the furnace more than wont to be h.
Hos. 7. 4. are adulterers, as an oven h. by the baker

HEATH.

Jer. 17. 6. he shall be like the h. in the desert
48. 6. flee, and be like the h. in the wilderness

HEATHEN.

Lev. 25. 44. bond-men shall be of the h. round you
26. 45. whom I brought forth in sight of the h.
2 Sam. 22. 44. kept me to be head of h. Psal. 18. 43.
2 Kings 16. 3. walked according to the abominations of the h. 17. 15. | 21. 2. 2 Chr. 28. 3. | 36. 14.
17. 8. Israel walked in the statutes of the h.
11. as did the h. whom the Lord carried away
1 Chron. 16. 35. save us, and deliver us from the h.
2 Chron. 20. 6. thou rulest over all kingdoms of h.
33. 2. but did like to the abominations of the h.
9. Manasseh made Judah to do worse than the h.
Ezra 6. 21. as had separated from filthiness of the h.
Neh. 5. 8. we redeemed the Jews who were sold to h.
9. because of the reproach of the h. our enemies
6. 16. all the h. that were about us saw these things
Psal. 2. 1. why do the h. rage? Acts 4. 25.
8. I shall give thee the h. for thy inheritance
9. 5. thou hast rebuked the h. thou hast destroyed
15. the h. are sunk in the pit that they made
9. 19. arise, let the h. be judged in thy sight
10. 16. the h. are perished out of his land
33. 10. the Lord brings the counsel of h. to nought
44. 2. we heard how thou didst drive out the h.
46. 6. the h. raged, the kingdoms were moved
47. 8. God reigneth over the h. God sitteth on
59. 5. thou, therefore, awake to visit all the h.
8. thou shalt have all the h. in derision
78. 55. he cast out the h. also before them, 80. 8.
79. 1. the h. are come into thine inheritance
6. pour out thy wrath upon the h. Jer. 10. 25.
10. wherefore should the h. say, where is their God? let him be known among the h. 115. 2.
94. 10. he that chastiseth the h. shall not he correct?
98. 2. he hath openly shewed in the sight of the h.
102. 15. the h. shall fear the name of the Lord
105. 44. and gave them the lands of the h.
106. 41. and he gave them into the hand of the h.
111. 6. he may give them the heritage of the h.
135. 15. the idols of the h. are silver and gold
149. 7. to execute vengeance upon the h.
Isa. 16. 8. the lords of the h. have broken down
Jer. 10. 2. learn not way of the h. be not dismayed at signs of heaven, for the h. dismayed at them
49. 14. an ambassador is sent to the h. saying
Lam. 1. 10. seen that the h. entered into her sanctuary
Ezek. 7. 24. I will bring the worst of the h.
11. 12. but have done after the manners of h.
20. 9. should not be polluted before the h. 14. 22.
32. that ye say, we will be as the h.
41. I will be sanctified before the h. 28. 25.
22. 4. I have made thee a reproach to the h.
16. take thine inheritance in sight of the h.
23. 30. thou hast gone a whoring after the h.
25. 7. I will deliver thee for a spoil to the h.
8. behold, the house of Judah is like to all the h.
30. 3. day is near, it shall be time of the h.
31. 11. into the hand of the mighty one of the h.
17. that dwelt under his shadow in midst of the h.
34. 28. they shall no more be a prey to the h.
29. neither bear the shame of the h. any more
36. 3. might be a possession to the residue of the h.
4. which became a derision to the residue of the h.
6. because ye have borne the shame of the h.
20. when they entered unto the h. whither
23. h. know I am L. 36. | 37. 28. | 38. 16. | 39. 7.
39. 21. and all the h. shall see my judgment
Joel 2. 17. that the h. should rule over them
3. 11. and come, all ye h. and gather yourselves
12. let the h. be wakened, and come up to valley of Jehoshaphat, there will I sit to judge all the h.
Amos 9. 12. they may possess remnant of all the h.
Obad. 15. the day of the Lord is near on all the h.
16. so shall all the h. drink continually
Mic. 5. 15. I will execute fury upon the h.
Hab. 3. 12. thou didst thresh the h. in anger
Zeph. 2. 11. all the isles of the h. shall worship him
Hag. 2. 22. I will destroy the strength of the h.
Zech. 1. 15. I am sore displeased with the h.
9. 10. and he shall speak peace to the h.
14. 14. the wealth of all the h. shall be gathered
18. the plague wherewith Lord will smite the h.
Mat. 6. 7. use not vain repetitions as the h. do
18. 17. let him be to thee as an h. man and publican
2 Cor. 11. 26. in perils by the h. in perils in the sea
Gal. 2. 9. that we should go unto the h.
3. 8. that God would justify the h. through faith

Among the HEATHEN.

Lev. 26. 33. I will scatter you among the h. and land be desolate, Jer. 9. 16. Ezek. 20. 23. | 22. 15.
38. and ye shall perish among the h. and the land
Deut. 4. 27. ye shall be left few in number among h.
2 Sam. 22. 50. I will give thanks to thee, O Lord, among h. and sing praises to thy name, Ps. 18. 49.
1 Chron. 16. 24. declare his glory among h. Ps. 96. 3.
Neh. 5. 17. that came to us from among the h.
6. 6. it is reported among the h. Gashmu saith it
Psal. 44. 11. thou hast scattered us among the h.
14. thou makest us a by-word among the h.
46. 10. I am God, I will be exalted among the h.
79. 10. let him be known among the h. in sight
96. 10. say among the h. that the Lord reigneth
106. 35. but they were mingled among the h.
47. save us, O Lord, and gather us from among h.
110. 6. he shall judge among the h. he shall fill
126. 2. said among the h. L. hath done great things
Jer. 18. 13. ask among the h. who heard such things
49. 15. I will make thee small among the h.
Lam. 1. 3. she dwelleth among the h. she findeth
4. 15. said among the h. they shall no more sojourn
20. under his shadow we shall live among the h.
Ezek. 11. 16. tho' I have cast them far off among the h.
12. 16. may declare their abominations among t. h.
16. 14. thy renown went forth among the h.
36. 19. and I did scatter them among the h.
21. which Israel profaned among the h. 22, 23.
24. I will take you from among the h. 37. 21.
30. no more reproach of famine among the h.
39. 21. and I will set my glory among the h.
28. caused them to be led into captivity among h.
Joel 2. 19. no more make you a reproach among t. h.
Obad. 1. an ambassador is sent among the h.
2. behold, I have made thee small among the h.
Hab. 1. 5. behold ye among the h. regard, wonder
Zech. 8. 13. that as ye were a curse among the h.
Mal. 1. 11. my name shall be great among the h.
14. and my name is dreadful among the h.
Gal. 1. 16. that I might preach him among the h.

HEAVE.

Num. 15. 20. as ye do heave-offering, so shall ye h. it

HEAVED.

Exod. 29. 27. is h. of the ram of consecration
Num. 18. 30. when ye have h. the best thereof, 32.

See OFFERING, SHOULDER.

HEAVEN.

Heaven and earth, *in* Gen. 1. 1. *are used for the substance and common matter of all sensible creatures.* Heaven *is often taken for the air:* The fowls of heaven, *are the birds which fly in the air,* Job 35. 11. The dew of heaven, the clouds of heaven, the winds of heaven; *in all which passages,* heaven *is put for the air.*

The stars are placed in heaven, *or* in the firmament, *Gen.* 1. 17. *They are called* the host or army of heaven, *Deut.* 17. 3. *God, like a powerful monarch, calleth them by their names, and giveth them his orders. The God of the* Hebrews *is named, not only by the* Jews, *but also by the heathens and strange people,* the God of Heaven, *Ezra* 1. 2. | 5. 11. | 6. 9, 10. | 7. 12. *Jonah* 1. 9. *because the* Jews *adored nothing sensible, and said, their God was in heaven; that there he had his throne, and exercised his sovereign dominion over all creatures.*

The heaven of heavens *is the highest heaven, as the* song of songs *is the most excellent song,* the God of gods, the Lord of lords; *the greatest of the gods, the most powerful of lords. From these passages it appears, that the* Hebrews *acknowledged three* heavens: (1) *The aerial heaven, where the birds fly, the winds blow, and the showers are formed.* (2) *The heaven, or firmament, wherein the stars are disposed.* (3) *The heaven of heavens, or the third heaven, which is the place of God's residence, the dwelling of angels and the blessed. This is the true palace of God, entirely separated from the impurities and imperfections, the alterations and changes, of the lower world; where he reigns in eternal peace. It is the temple of the divine Majesty, where his excellent glory is revealed in the most conspicuous manner.* It is the habitation of his holiness, the place where his honour dwells. *It is the sacred mansion of light, and joy, and glory.*

Heaven, *or* heavens, *is put for God, who dwelleth and reigneth there.* Dan. 4. 26. After thou shalt have known that the heavens do rule. *So in* Luke 15. 21. I have sinned against heaven. *Also for the angels in heaven.* Job 15. 15. The heavens are not clean in his sight; *the angels that dwell in heaven are not pure simply, perfectly, and comparatively to God. It is put also for the visible church.* Rev. 12. 7, 9. There was war in heaven. Heaven *by an hyperbole is put for a great height.* Deut. 1. 28. Their cities are walled up to heaven. *It is taken for great glory and royal majesty,* Isa. 14. 12. How art thou fallen from heaven, O Lucifer, son of the morning! *speaking of the overthrow of the king of* Babylon *by the* Medes *and* Persians.

The enjoyment of the divine presence in heaven, is the supreme and everlasting felicity of the saints; whatsoever is requisite to their complete blessedness is enjoyed there; there is an exemption from all evils; sin and all the penal consequences are abolished; the body is revived to a glorious life, and the soul lives in communion with God and Christ. The understanding there shall be clearly enlightened with the knowledge of God. Here the revelation of God, in his works and word, is according to our capacities, but in heaven it is most glorious, and our faculties are raised and refined to receive it. The communion also of the angels and saints in heaven affords the purest pleasure. And the fulness of joy in heaven is everlasting, without defect, and without end.

Gen. 1. 1. in the beginning God created h. and earth
8. and God called the firmament h.
14. let there be lights in the firmament of h. 15.
20. fowl that may fly in the open firmament of h.
7. 11. and the windows of h. were opened
8. 2. and the windows of h. were stopped
14. 19. most high God, possessor of h. and earth, 22.
19. 24. Lord rained fire from the Lord out of h.
21. 17. the angel of God called to Hagar out of h.
22. 11. the angel called to Abraham out of h. 15.
27. 28. God give thee of the dew of h. 39.
28. 17. and he said, this is the gate of h.
49. 25. shall bless thee with blessings of h. above
Exod. 20. 11. six days Ld. made h. and earth, 31. 17.
24. 10. as it were the body of h. in his clearness
Lev. 26. 19. I will make your h. as iron, earth brass
Deut. 4. 11. the mountain burned to the midst of h.
26. I call h. and earth to witness, 30. 19. | 31. 28.
32. ask from the one side of h. to the other
36. out of h. he made thee hear his voice
10. 14. behold, the h. and h. of heavens, Ps. 115. 16.
11. 11. and drinketh water of the rain of h.
17. he shut up h. 1 Kings 8. 35. 2 Chr. 6. 26. | 7. 13.
21. be multiplied as the days of h. on the earth
28. 12. open the h. to give thee rain in his season
23. the h. that is over thy head shall be brass
30. 4. scatter thee to the utmost part of h. Neh. 1. 9.
33. 13. for the precious things of h. for the dew
26. God of Jeshurun rideth upon the h. in thy help
1 Sam. 2. 10. out of h. shall he thunder on them
2 Sam. 18. 9. he was taken up between h. and earth
21. 10. till water dropped on them out of h.
22. 8. the foundations of h. moved and shook
1 Kings 8. 27. behold, the h. and the h. of heavens cannot contain thee, 2 Chron. 2. 6. | 6. 18.
35. when h. is shut up, and there is no rain
18. 45. mean while the h. was black with clouds
2 Kings 19. 15. thou art God of all kingdoms, thou hast made h. and earth, 2 Chr. 2. 12. Neh. 9. 6.
1 Chron. 21. 16. angel stood between h. and earth
Job 11. 8. it is as high as h. what canst thou do
20. 27. the h. shall reveal his iniquity, earth rise up
22. 12. is not God in height of h.? behold height
14. and he walketh in the circuit of h.
26. 11. the pillars of h. tremble at his reproof
38. 29. the hoary frost of h. who hath gendered it?
33. knowest thou the ordinances of h.?
37. or who can stay the bottles of h.?
Psal. 19. 6. his going forth is from the end of h.
20. 6. he will hear him from his holy h.
69. 34. let h. and earth praise him, the seas
78. 23. and though he opened the doors of h.
24. and had given them of the corn of h.
89. 29. his throne to endure as the days of h.
103. 11. for as the h. is high above the earth
105. 40. he satisfied them with the bread of h.
115. 15. the Lord who made h. and earth, 121. 2. | 124. 8. | 134. 3. | 146. 6. Isa. 37. 16. Jer. 32. 17. Acts 4. 24. | 14. 15. Rev. 14. 7.
147. 8. who covereth h. with clouds, who prepares
148. 13. his glory is above the earth and h.
Prov. 25. 3. the h. for height, the earth for depth
Isa. 13. 5. they come from far, from the end of h.
40. 12. who hath meted out h. with a span?
66. 1. h. my throne, earth my footstool, Acts 7. 49.
Jer. 7. 18. to make cakes to the queen of h.
10. 2. and be not dismayed at the signs of h.
23. 24. do not I fill h. and earth? saith the Lord
31. 37. if h. above can be measured
33. 25. if I have not appointed ordinances of h.
44. 17. to burn incense to queen of h. 18, 19, 25.
49. 36. four winds from the four quarters of h.
51. 15. hath stretched out the h. by his understand.
48. the h. and earth shall sing for Babylon
Lam. 4. 19. our enemies swifter than the eagles of h.
Ezek. 8. 3. the Spirit lifted me between earth and h.
32. 7. I will cover the h. and make the stars dark
8. the lights of h. will I make dark over thee
Dan. 4. 15. be wet with dew of h. 23. 25, 33. | 5. 21.
35. doeth according to his will in the army of h.
37. now I extol and honour the King of h.
5. 23. hast lifted up thyself against the Lord of h.
7. 2. the four winds of h. strove upon the sea
13. one like Son of man, came with clouds of h.
8. 8. four horns toward the four winds of h.
11. 4. his kingdom divided toward four winds of h.
Amos 9. 6. he that buildeth his stories in the h.
Hag. 1. 10. the h. over you is stayed from dew
Zech. 2. 6. I have spread you as the four winds of h.
5. 9. lifted the ephah between the earth and h.
Mal. 3. 10. if I will not open the windows of h.
Mat. 5. 18. till h. and earth pass, one jot not pass
34. nor swear by h. it is God's throne, Jam. 5. 12.
11. 25. I thank thee, Father, Lord of h. Luke 10. 21.
23. 22. he that shall swear by h. sweareth by God
24. 30. then shall appear the sign of the Son of man coming in the clouds of h. 26. 64. Mark 14. 62.
31. gather elect from one end of h. to the other
35. h. earth shall pass away, Mark 13. 31. Luke 21. 33.
36. no, not the angels of h. but my Father only
Mark 13. 27. gather his elect from utmost part of h.
Luke 3. 21. and Jesus praying, the h. was opened
4. 25. when the h. was shut up three years
15. 18. father, I have sinned against h. 21.
16. 17. it is easier for h. and earth to pass
21. 26. for the powers of h. shall be shaken
John 1. 51. hereafter ye shall see h. open, and angels

Acts 3. 21. whom the h. must receive until the times
10. 11. I saw h. opened, and a vessel, Rev. 19. 11.
17. 24. seeing that he is Lord of h. and earth
Jam. 5. 18. he prayed again, and the h. gave rain
Rev. 3. 12. cometh down out of h. from my God
6. 14. h. departed as a scroll when it is rolled
8. 13. an angel flying through the midst of h. 14. 6.
10. 6. who created h. and the things therein
11. 6. these have power to shut h. that it rain not
16. 17. came a great voice out of the temple of h.
21. there fell on men a great hail out of h.
18. 20. rejoice over her, thou h.
19. 17. to all the fowls that fly in the midst of h.
20. 9. and fire came down from God out of h.
11. earth and h. fled away, and there was no place
21. 1. I saw a new h. and earth, the first h. passed
10. holy Jerusalem descending out of h. from God
See Fowl, Fowls.

From HEAVEN.

Gen. 8. 2. and the rain from h. was restrained
Exod. 16. 4. I will rain bread from h. for you
20. 22. I have talked with you from h. Neh. 9. 13.
Deut. 26. 15. look down from h. Isa. 63. 15. Lam. 3. 50.
28. 24. as dust from h. shall it come down on thee
Josh. 10. 11. Lord cast great stones from h. on them
Judg. 5. 20. they fought from h. the stars fought
2 Sam. 22. 14. Lord thundered from h. and uttered
2 Kings 1. 10. then let fire come down from h. and
there came down fire from h. 12. 14.
1 Chron. 21. 26. he answered him from h. by fire
2 Chron. 6. 21. hear thou from h. 23, 27, 30.
7. 1. the fire came down from h. and consumed
14. then will I hear from h. and will forgive
Neh. 9. 15. gavest them bread from h. for hunger
27. they cried, thou heardest them from h. 28.
Job 1. 16. the fire of God is fallen from h.
Psal. 14. 2. the Lord looked down from h. 53. 2.
33. 13. the Lord looketh from h. and beholdeth
57. 3. shall send from h. and save me from reproach
76. 8. didst cause judgment to be heard from h.
80. 14. O God, look down from h. and behold
85. 11. righteousness shall look down from h.
102. 19. from h. did the Lord behold the earth
Isa. 14. 12. how art thou fallen from h. O Lucifer!
55. 10. as snow falleth from h. and returneth not
Lam. 2. 1. Lord cast down from h. beauty of Israel
Dan. 4. 13. behold, a watcher came down from h.
23. the king saw an holy one coming down from h.
31. fell a voice from h. saying, kingd. is departed
from thee, Mat. 3. 17. Luke 3. 22. John 12. 28.
Mat. 16. 1. he would shew them a sign from h.
21. 25. the baptism of John, whence was it? from
h. or of men? Mark 11. 30. Luke 20. 4.
28. 2. there was a great earthquake, for the angel
descended from h. Rev. 10. 1. | 18. 1. | 20. 1.
Mark 8. 11. seeking of him a sign f. h. Luke 11. 16.
Luke 9. 54. we command fire to come down from h.
10. 18. I beheld Satan as lightning fall from h.
17. 29. it rained fire and brimstone f. h. on Sodom
21. 11. and great signs shall there be from h.
22. 43. appeared an angel f. h. strengthening him
John 1. 32. I saw the Spirit descending from h.
3. 13. but he that came down from h. 6. 33.
27. receive nothing, except it be given him from h.
31. he that cometh from h. is above all
6. 31. he gave them bread from h. to eat
32. Moses gave you not that bread from h.
38. I came from h. not to do mine own will, 42.
41. bread which came down from h. 50, 51, 58.
Acts 2. 2. suddenly there came a sound from h.
9. 3. a light f. h. shined about him, 22. 6. | 26. 13.
11. 5. as it had been a great sheet let down from h.
9. but the voice answered me again from h.
14. 17. in that he did good, and gave us rain f. h.
Rom. 1. 18. the wrath of God is revealed from h.
1 Cor. 15. 47. the second man is the Lord from h.
2 Cor. 5. 2. clothed on with our house that is from h.
Gal. 1. 8. an angel from h. preach any other gospel
1 Thess. 1. 10. and to wait for his Son from h.
4. 16. the Lord himself shall descend from h.
2 Thess. 1. 7. the Lord Jesus shall be revealed f. h.
Heb. 12. 25. if turn from him that speaketh from h.
1 Pet. 1. 12. by them that have preached the gospel
to you with the Holy Ghost sent down from h.
Rev. 8. 10. and there fell a great star from h.
9. 1. and I saw a star fall from h. to the earth
10. 4. I heard a voice f. h. seal up those things, and
write them not, 8. | 11. 12. | 14. 2, 13. | 18. 4.
13. 13. that he maketh fire come down from h.
See God of heaven.

Host, or hosts of HEAVEN.

Deut. 4. 19. seest the h. of h. shouldest worship him
17. 3. hath gone and worshipped the host of h.
1 Kings 22. 19. I saw the Lord sitting on the throne,
and the host of h. standing by him, 2 Chr. 18. 18.
2 Kings 17. 16. Israel worshipped the host of h.
21. 3. Manasseh worshipped host of h. 2 Chr. 33. 3.
5. he built altars for the host of h. 2 Chron. 33. 5.
23. 4. Josiah brought out vessels made for h. of h.
5. put down them that burnt incense to h. of h.
Neh. 9. 6. thou hast made the h. of heavens with
their host, and the host of h. worshippeth thee
Isa. 34. 4. all the host of h. shall be dissolved
Jer. 8. 2. they shall spread them before the h. of h.
19. 13. they burnt incense to all the host of h.
33. 22. as the host of h. cannot be numbered
Dan. 8. 10. it waxed great, even to the host of h.
Zeph. 1. 5. I will cut off them that worship h. of h.
Acts 7. 42. gave them up to worship the host of h.

In HEAVEN.

Exod. 20. 4. nor likeness of any thing in h. Deut. 5. 8.
Deut. 3. 24. what god in h. can do like thy works?
4. 39. that the Lord he is G. in h. above and earth
30. 12. it is not in h. that thou shouldest say, who
Josh. 2. 11. for Lord your G. he is God in h. above
1 Kings 8. 23. is no God like thee in h. 2 Chr. 6. 14.
30. hear thou in h. 32, 34, 36, 39, 43, 45, 49.
2 Kings 7. 2. if the Lord make windows in h. 19.
1 Chron. 29. 11. all that is in h. and earth is thine
2 Chr. 20. 6. O Lord God, art not thou God in h.?
Job 16. 19. also now behold, my witness is in h.
Psal. 11. 4. the Lord's throne is in h. his eyes behold
Ps. 73. 25. whom have I in h. but thee, none on earth
77. 18. the voice of thy thunder was in the h.
78. 26. he caused an east wind to blow in the h.
89. 6. who in h. can be compared to the Lord?
37. shall be established as a faithful witness in h.
113. 6. humbleth himself to behold things in h.
119. 89. for ever, Lord, thy word is settled in h.
135. 6. that did he in h. and earth, in the seas
Eccl. 5. 2. for God is in h. and thou upon earth
Isa. 34. 5. for my sword shall be bathed in h. behold
Jer. 8. 7. yea, the stork in h. knoweth her times
Dan. 2. 28. there is a God in h. that revealeth secrets
6. 27. worketh signs and wonders in h. and earth
Amos 9. 6. he that buildeth his stories in the h.
Mat. 5. 12. rejoice, for great is your reward in h.
16. and glorify your Father who is in h.
45. the children of your Father who is in h.
48. be perfect, as your Father in h. is perfect
6. 9. pray ye, our Father which art in h. Luke 11. 2.
10. will be done on earth, as it is in h. Luke 11. 2.
20. but lay up for yourselves treasures in h.
7. 11. shall your Father in h. give good things
21. that doth the will of my Father in h. 12. 50.
10. 32. him will I confess before my Father in h.
33. him will I deny before my Father in h.
16. 17. but my Father which is in h. revealed it
19. shall be bound in h. be loosed in h. 18. 18.
18. 10. despise not these little ones, in h. angels do
always behold the face of my Father in h.
19. shall be done for them of my Father in h.
19. 21. thou shalt have treasure in h. Luke 18. 22.
22. 30. are as the angels of God in h. Mark 12. 25.
23. 9. for one is your Father who is in h.
24. 30. shall appear the sign of the Son of man in h.
28. 18. all power is given to me in h. and in earth
Mark 11. 26. nor will your Father in h. forgive you
13. 25. the powers that are in h. shall be shaken
32. no, not the angels which are in h. nor the Son
Luke 6. 23. for behold, your reward is great in h.
10. 20. because your names are written in h.
15. 7. joy shall be in h. over one sinner that repent.
19. 38. peace in h. and glory in the highest
John 3. 13. even the Son of man who is in h.
Acts 2. 19. I will shew wonders in h. above and signs
1 Cor. 8. 5. and called gods, whether in h. or in earth
Eph. 1. 10. he might gather in one, things in h.
3. 15. of whom the whole family in h. is named
6. 9. knowing that your master is in h. Col. 4. 1.
Phil. 2. 10. every knee should bow, of things in h.
3. 20. our conversation is in h. from whence we look
Col. 1. 5. for the hope which is laid up for you in h.
16. by him were all things created that are in h.
20. by him to reconcile all things in h. and earth
Heb. 10. 34. that ye have in h. a better substance
12. 23. the first-born which are written in h.
1 Pet. 1. 4. to an inheritance reserved in h. for you
1 John 5. 7. there are three that bear record in h.
Rev. 4. 1. and behold, a door was opened in h.
2. a throne was set in h. and one sat on the throne
5. 3. no man in h. or earth was able to open book
13. every creature in h. saying, blessing, honour
8. 1. was silence in h. || 11. 15. great voices in h.
11. 19. the temple of God was opened in h.
12. 1. there appeared a great wonder in h. 3.
7. there was war in h. Michael and his angels
8. nor was their place found any more in h.
10. I heard a loud voice saying in h. 19. 1.
13. 6. to blaspheme them that dwell in h.
14. 17. angel came out of the temple which is in h.
15. 1. I saw another sign in h. great and marvell.
5. the tabernacle of testimony in h. was opened
19. 14. the armies that were in h. followed him

Into HEAVEN.

2 Kings 2. 1. the Lord would take up Elijah into h.
11. Elijah went up by a whirlwind into h.
Psal. 139. 8. if I ascend into h. thou art there
Prov. 30. 4. who hath ascended into h.? Rom. 10. 6.
Isa. 14. 13. thou hast said, I will ascend into h.
Mark 16. 19. the Lord was received up into h.
Luke 2. 15. as the angels were gone away into h.
24. 51. he was parted from them, carried up into h.
Acts 1. 11. gazing up into h. taken from you into h.
Jesus shall come as ye have seen him go into h.
7. 55. Stephen looked up stedfastly into h. and saw
10. 16. the vessel was received up into h. 11. 10.
Heb. 9. 24. but into h. itself, to appear for us
1 Pet. 3. 22. who is gone into h. on right hand of God
See Kingdom.

HEAVEN joined with stars.

Gen. 1. 17. God set stars in the firmament of h.
22. 17. I will multiply thy seed as stars of h. 26. 4.
Exod. 32. 13. 1 Chron. 27. 23. Neh. 9. 23.
Deut. 1. 10. you are this day as stars of h. 10. 22.
28. 62. whereas ye were as stars of h. for multitude
Isa. 13. 10. the stars of h. shall not give light
Ezek. 32. 7. I will cover h. and make stars dark
Nah. 3. 16. multiplied merchants as stars of h.
Mat. 24. 29. the stars shall fall from h. Mark 13. 25.
Rev. 6. 13. and the stars of h. fell on the earth
12. 4. his tail drew the third part of stars of h.

To HEAVEN, or unto HEAVEN.

Gen. 11. 4. a tower whose top may reach unto h.
28. 12. a ladder, and the top of it reached to h.
Deut. 1. 28. the cities great and walled up to h. 9. 1.
4. 19. and lest thou lift up thine eyes unto h.
30. 12. who shall go up for us to h. and bring it to us
32. 40. for I lift up my hand to h. and say, I live
Josh. 8. 20. the smoke of the city ascended up to h.
Judg. 20. 40. the flame of the city ascended up to h.
1 Sam. 5. 12. and the cry of the city went up to h.
1 Kings 8. 54. with his hands spread up to h.
2 Chron. 28. 9. in a rage that reacheth up unto h.
30. 27. their prayer came up even unto h.
32. 20. the prophet Isaiah prayed and cried to h.
Psal. 107. 26. they mount up to h. they go down
Jer. 51. 9. for her judgment reacheth unto h.
Dan. 4. 11. the tree whose height reached to h. 20.
12. 7. when he held up his left hand unto h.
Amos 9. 2. though they climb up to h. thence will I
Mat. 11. 23. Capernaum, which art exalted to h.
14. 19. and looking up to h. Mark 6. 41. Luke 9. 16.
Mark 7. 34. looking up to h. he sighed, and saith
Luke 18. 13. not lift up so much as his eyes unto h.
John 3. 13. and no man hath ascended up to h.
17. 1. Jesus lift up his eyes to h. and said, Father
2 Cor. 12. 2. such an one caught up to third h.
Rev. 10. 5. the angel lifted up his hand to h.
11. 12. and they ascended up to h. in a cloud
18. 5. for her sins have reached unto h.

Toward HEAVEN.

Gen. 15. 5. look now toward h. and tell the stars
Exod. 9. 8. let Moses sprinkle it toward the h.
10. and Moses sprinkled it up toward h.
22. stretch forth thine hand toward h. 10. 21.
23. Moses stretched forth his rod toward h.
10. 22. Moses stretched forth his hand toward h.
Judg. 13. 20. when the flame went up toward h.
1 Kings 8. 22. Solomon stood before altar of Lord,
and spread forth his hands toward h. 2 Chr. 6. 13.
Job 2. 12. sprinkled dust on their heads toward h.
Prov. 23. 5. they fly away as an eagle toward h.
Acts 1. 10. while they looked stedfastly toward h

Under HEAVEN.

Gen. 1. 9. let the waters under h. be gathered
6. 17. a flood to destroy all flesh from under h.
7. 19. the high hills under the whole h. were cover.
Exod. 17. 14. I will utterly put out the remem
brance of Amalek from under h. Deut. 25. 19.
Deut. 2. 25. the fear of thee on nations under h.
4. 19. God hath divided to all nations under h.
7. 24. shalt destroy their name from under h. 9. 14.
29. 20. Lord shall blot out his name from under h.
2 Kings 14. 27. blot out name of Isr. from under h.
Job 28. 24. for God seeth under the whole h.
37. 3. he directeth it under the whole h.
41. 11. whatsoever is under the whole h. is mine
Eccl. 1. 13. to search out all things done under h.
2. 3. what was that good they should do under h.
3. 1. a time to every purpose under the h.
Luke 17. 24. that lighteneth out of one part under h.
Acts 2. 5. devout men of every nation under h.
4. 12. none other name under h. given among men
Col. 1. 23. gospel preached to every creature und. h.

HEAVENLY.

Mat. 6. 14. your h. Father will forgive you
26. yet your h. Father feedeth them
32. your h. Father knoweth that ye have need
15. 13. every plant my h. Father hath not planted
18. 35. so shall my h. Father do also to you
Luke 2. 13. a multitude of the h. host praising God
11. 13. your h. Father shall give the Spirit to them
John 3. 12. how believe, if I tell you of h. things
Acts 26. 19. I was not disobedient to the h. vision
1 Cor. 15. 48. as is the h. such are they that are h.
49. we shall also bear the image of the h.
Eph. 1. 3. with spiritual blessings in h. places in Chr.
1. 20. set him at his right hand in h. places, 2. 6.
3. 10. that now unto the powers in h. places
2 Tim. 4. 18. Ld. will preserve me to his h. kingdom
Heb. 3. 1. brethren, partakers of the h. calling
6. 4. once enlightened, and have tasted of the h. gift
8. 5. who serve to example and shadow of h. things
9. 23. but h. things with better sacrifices than these
11. 16. an h. country || 12. 22. the h. Jerusalem

HEAVENS.

Gen. 2. 1. thus the h. and the earth were finished
4. these are the generations of the h. and the earth
in the day that the Ld. made the h. and earth
Deut. 32. 1. give ear, O h. I will speak, Isa. 1. 2.
33. 28. also his h. shall drop down dew
Judg. 5. 4. the earth trembled, the h. dropped
2 Sam. 22. 10. he bowed the h. and came, Ps. 18. 9.
1 Kings 8. 27. the heaven of h. cannot contain thee
1 Chr. 16. 26. the gods are idols, but the Lord made
the h. Neh. 9. 6. Psal. 96. 5. | 102. 25. | 136. 5.
31. let the h. be glad, let the earth rejoice
2 Chron. 6. 25. then hear from the h. 33, 35, 39.
Ezra 9. 6. our trespass is grown up to the h.
Job 9. 8. which alone spreadeth out the h.
14. 12. man riseth not till the h. be no more
15. 15. yea, the h. are not clean in his sight
20. 6. though his excellency mount up to the h.
26. 13. by his Spirit he hath garnished the h.
35. 5. look to the h. and see, and behold the clouds
Psal. 8. 1. thou hast set thy glory above the h. 113. 4.
3. when I consider thy h. the work of thy fingers
19. 1. the h. declare the glory of God, and firmam.
33. 6. by the word of the Lord were the h. made
50. 4. shall call to the h. from above, and to earth
6. the h. shall declare his righteousn. G. is judge
57. 5. be thou exalted, O God, above h. 11. | 108. 5.
10. for thy mercy is great unto the h. 108. 4.
68. 4. extol him that rideth upon the h. 33.
8. the h. also dropped at the presence of God
73. 9. they set their mouth against the h.
89. 5. the h. shall praise thy wonders, O Lord
11. the h. are thine, the earth also is thine
96. 11. let the h. rejoice, earth be glad, Rev. 12. 12.
97. 6. h. declare his righteousness, people his glory
104. 2. who stretchest out the h. Isa. 40. 22.
108. 4. for thy mercy is great above the h.
115. 16. the heaven, even the h. are the Lord's
144. 5. bow thy h. O Lord, and come down, touch
148. 1. praise ye the Lord from the h. praise him
4. praise him ye h. of h. and waters above the h.
Prov. 3. 19. by understanding he established the h.
8. 27. when he prepared the h. I was there
Isa. 13. 13. will shake the h. and earth, Hag. 2. 6, 21.
34. 4. the h. shall be rolled together as a scroll
42. 5. thus saith he that created the h. 45. 18.
44. 23. sing, O ye h. for the Lord hath done it
24. saith the Lord, that stretcheth forth the h.
45. 12. | 51. 13. Jer. 10. 12. Zech. 12. 1.
45. 8. drop down ye h. from above, let the skies pour
48. 13. my right hand hath spanned the h.
49. 13. sing, O h. and be joyful, O earth
50. 3. I clothe h. with blackness, I make sackcloth
51. 6. lift up your eyes to the h. and look, the h.
shall vanish away like smoke, and earth wax old
16. that I may plant the h. and lay foundations
55. 9. for as the h. are higher than the earth
64. 1. that thou wouldest rend the h. and come down
65. 17. behold, I create new h. and a new earth
66. 22. for as the new h. which I will make

Jer. 2. 12. be astonished, O ye *h.* and be afraid
4. 23. I beheld the *h.* and they had no light
25. all the birds of the *h.* were fled, 9. 10.
28. for this shall the earth mourn, *h.* above black
10. 11. the gods that have not made the *h.* and the earth shall perish, and from under these *h.*
14. 22. or can the *h.* give showers? art not thou he
Lam. 3. 66. destroy them from under the *h.* of [the Lord
Ezek. 1. 1. that the *h.* were opened, *Mat.* 3. 16.
Dan. 4. 26. shalt have known that the *h.* do rule
Hos. 2. 21. I will hear the *h.* they shall hear the earth
Joel 2. 10. the *h.* shall tremble, sun and moon be dark
3. 16. and the *h.* and the earth shall shake
Hab. 3. 3. God came, his glory covered the *h.*
Zech. 6. 5. these are the four spirits of the *h.*
8. 12. and the *h.* shall give their dew
Mat. 24. 29. the powers of the *h.* shall be shaken
Mark 1. 10. and coming up, he saw the *h.* opened
Acts 2. 34. for David is not ascended into the *h.*
7. 56. behold, I see the *h.* opened, and Son of man
Heb. 1. 10. the *h.* are the work of thine hands
4. 14. we have an High-Priest that is passed into *h.*
7. 26. an High-Priest made higher than the *h.*
2 *Pet.* 3. 5. by the word of God the *h.* were of old
7. but the *h.* which are now, are kept in store
10. the *h.* shall pass away with a great noise
12. wherein the *h.* being on fire shall be dissolved

In the HEAVENS.

Psal. 2. 4. he that sitteth *in the h.* shall laugh
18. 13. the Lord also thundered *in the h.*
36. 5. thy mercy, O Lord, is *in the h.* thy faithfuln.
89. 2. thy faithfulness shalt thou establish *in the h.*
103. 19. the Lord hath prepared his throne *in the h.*
115. 3. God is *in the h.* he hath done what pleased
123. 1. I lift my eyes, O thou that dwellest *in the h.*
Isa. 5. 30. the light is darkened *in the h.* thereof
Jer. 10. 13. a multitude of waters *in the h.* 51. 16.
Lam. 3. 41. let us lift up our hearts to God *in the h.*
Joel 2. 30. I will shew wonders *in the h.*
Luke 12. 33. a treasure *in the h.* which faileth not
2 *Cor.* 5. 1. house not made with hands, eternal *in h.*
Heb. 8. 1. of the throne of the Majesty *in the h.*
9. 23. necessary that the patterns of things *in the h.*

HEAVY.

Gen. 41. † 31. for the famine shall be very *h.*
48. † 10. now the eyes of Israel were *h.* for age
Exod. 5. † 9. let the work be *h.* upon the men
17. 12. Moses' hands were *h.* they took a stone
18. 18. for this thing is too *h.* for thee, thou art not able to perform it thyself alone
Num. 11. 14. not able, because it is too *h.* for me
Judg. 1. † 35. the hand of the house of Joseph was *h.*
1 *Sam.* 4. 18. for Eli was an old man and *h.*
5. 6. hand of the L. was *h.* on them of Ashdod, 11.
2 *Sam.* 14. 26. because the hair was *h.* on him
1 *Kings* 12. 4. thy father's *h.* yoke lighter, we will serve thee, 10, 11, 14. 2 *Chr.* 10. 4, 10, 11, 14.
14. 6. for I am sent to thee with *h.* tidings
20. 43. king Ahab went to his house *h.* 21. 4.
2 *Kings* 6. † 14. the king sent to Dothan an *h.* host
18. † 17. Sennacherib sent to Hezekiah an *h.* host
Neh. 5. 18. because the bondage was *h.* on people
Job 33. 7. neither shall my hand be *h.* upon thee
Psal. 32. 4. day and night thy hand was *h.* on me
38. 4. as an *h.* burden they are too *h.* for me
Prov. 25. 20. he that singeth songs to an *h.* heart
27. 3. stone is *h.* and sand weighty, but fool's wrath
31. 6. give wine to those that be of *h.* hearts
Isa. 6. 10. make their ears *h.* shut their eyes
24. 20. the transgression thereof shall be *h.* upon it
30. 27. with his anger, and the burden thereof is *h.*
46. 1. your carriages were *h.* loaden, are a burden
58. 6. is not this the fast, to undo the *h.* burdens?
59. 1. neither his ear *h.* that it cannot hear
Lam. 3. 7. hedged me about, hath made my chain *h.*
Mat. 11. 28. come to me, all ye that are *h.* laden
23. 4. for they bind *h.* burdens, and grievous to be
26. 37. he began to be sorrowful, and very *h.*
43. for their eyes were very *h.* *Mark* 14. 33, 40.
Luke 9. 32. that were with him, were *h.* with sleep

HEAVIER.

Job 6. 3. now it would be *h.* than the sand of the sea
23. 2. my stroke is *h.* than my groaning
Prov. 27. 3. a fool's wrath is *h.* than them both

HEAVILY.

Exod. 14. 25. take off wheels, so that drave them *h.*
Psal. 35. 14. I bowed down *h.* as one that mourneth
Isa. 47. 6. on the ancient hast thou *h.* laid thy yoke

HEAVINESS.

Ezra 9. 5. at the evening sacrifice I rose from my *h.*
Job 9. 27. if I say, I will leave off my *h.* and comfort
Psal. 69. 20. broken my heart, and I am full of *h.*
119. 28. my soul melteth for *h.* strengthen thou me
Prov. 10. 1. a foolish son is the *h.* of his mother
12. 25. *h.* in the heart of man maketh it stoop
14. 13. and the end of that mirth is *h.*
Isa. 1. † 4. ah sinful nation, a people of *h.* with iniq.
29. 2. and there shall be *h.* and sorrow
30. † 27. with his anger, and the burd. thereof is *h.*
61. 3. to give the garment of praise for spirit of *h.*
Rom. 9. 2. that I have great *h.* and continual sorrow
2 *Cor.* 2. 1. I would not come again to you in *h.*
Phil. 2. 26. Epaphroditus my brother was full of *h.*
Jam. 4. 9. let your joy be turned into *h.*
1 *Pet.* 1. 6. tho' now for a season, if need, ye are in *h.*

HEDGE.

Job 1. 10. hast thou not made an *h.* about him?
Prov. 15. 19. the way of slothful is an *h.* of thorns
Eccl. 10. 8. whoso breaketh a *h.* a serpent shall bite
Isa. 5. 5. I will take away the *h.* thereof
Lam. 2. † 6. he hath violently taken away his *h.*
Ezek. 13. 5. nor made up the *h.* for the house of Israel
22. 30. I sought a man that should make up the *h.*
Mic. 7. 4. the most upright sharper than a thorn *h.*
Mark 12. 1. he set a *h.* about it, digged for wine-fat

HEDGE.

Hos. 2. 6. behold, I will *h.* up thy way with thorns

HEDGED.

Job 3. 23. whose way is hid, whom God hath *h.* in
10. † 11. thou hast *h.* me with bones and sinews
Lam. 3. 7. he hath *h.* me about, I cannot get out

Ezek. 13. † 5. ye have not *h.* up the hedge for Israel
Mat. 21. 33. planted a vineyard, and *h.* it round about

HEDGES.

1 *Chr.* 4. 23. those that dwelt amongst plants and *h.*
Psal. 80. 12. hast thou broken down her *h.*? 89. 40.
Jer. 49. 3. lament and run to and fro by the *h.*
Nah. 3. 17. as grasshoppers which camp in the *h.*
Luke 14. 23. go out into the high-ways and *h.*

HEED.

2 *Sam.* 20. 10. but Amasa took no *h.* to the sword
2 *Kings* 10. 31. Jehu took no *h.* to walk in the law
Psal. 119. 9. by taking *h.* according to thy word
Prov. 17. 4. a wicked doer giveth *h.* to false lips
Eccl. 12. 9. the preacher gave good *h.* and sought out
Isa. 21. 7. he hearkened diligently with much *h.*
Jer. 18. 18. let us not give *h.* to any of his words
19. give *h.* to me, O Lord, and hearken to voice
Acts 3. 5. he gave *h.* unto them, expecting to receive
8. 6. the people of Samaria gave *h.* to Philip
10. they gave *h.* to Simon from least to greatest
1 *Tim.* 1. 4. neither give *h.* to fables, *Tit.* 1. 14.
4. 1. some giving *h.* to seducing spirits and doctrines
Heb. 2. 1. we ought to give the more earnest *h.*

See TAKE.

HEEL, S.

Gen. 3. 15. it bruise thy head, thou shalt bruise his *h.*
25. 26. his hand took hold on Esau's *h.* *Hos.* 12. 3.
49. 17. Dan be an adder that biteth the horse *h.*
Job 13. 27. thou settest a print on the *h.* of my feet
18. 9. the gin shall take him by the *h.* robber
Ps. 41. 9. hath lift up his *h.* against me, *John* 13. 18.
49. 5. when iniquity of my *h.* compass me about
Jer. 13. 22. for thine iniquity are thy *h.* made bare

HEIFER.

Gen. 15. 9. take me an *h.* of three years old, and goat
Num. 19. 2. bring a red *h.* ‖ 5. burn the *h.* in his sight
9. gather up the ashes of the *h.* and lay them up
Deut. 21. 3. the elders of that city shall take an *h.*
4. shall strike off *h.* neck ‖ 6. wash hands over the *h.*
Judg. 14. 18. if ye had not plowed with my *h.*
1 *Sam.* 16. 2. the Lord said, take an *h.* with thee
Isa. 15. 5. cry out for Moab as an *h.* of three years old
Jer. 46. 20. Egypt is like a fair *h.* destruction comes
48. 34. uttered their voice as an *h.* of three years
50. 11. because ye are grown fat as an *h.* at grass
Hos. 4. 16. for Israel slideth back, as a backsliding *h.*
10. 11. and Ephraim is as an *h.* that is taught
Heb. 9. 13. the ashes of an *h.* sprinkling the unclean

HEIGHT.

Gen. 6. 15. the *h.* of the ark shall be thirty cubits
Exod. 25. 10. shalt make an ark of shittim-wood, a cubit and a half shall be *h.* of it, 23. | 37. 1, 10.
27. 1. *h.* of the altar shall be three cubits, 38. 1.
18. *h.* of the court shall be five cubits, 38. 18.
30. 2. *h.* of altar of incense two cubits, 37. 25.
1 *Sam.* 16. 7. look not on the *h.* of his stature
17. 4. Goliath's *h.* was six cubits and a span
1 *Kings* 6. 2. the *h.* of house of God was thirty cubits
20. the oracle twenty cubits in the *h.* thereof
26. the *h.* of the one cherub was ten cubits
7. 2. the *h.* of the house of Lebanon thirty cubits
16. the *h.* of the one chapiter was five cubits
23. the *h.* of the molten sea was five cubits
27. the *h.* of one base was three cubits
2 *Kings* 19. 23. with multitudes of chariots I am come up to the *h.* of the mountains, *Isa.* 37. 24.
25. 17. the *h.* of one pillar was eighteen cubits
2 *Chr.* 33. 14. and raised it up a very great *h.*
Ezra 6. 3. the *h.* of God's house sixty cubits
Job 22. 12. is not God in the *h.* of heaven? and behold the *h.* of the stars, how high they are
Psal. 102. 19. Lord looked from *h.* of his sanctuary
Prov. 25. 3. the heaven for *h.* the earth for depth
Isa. 7. 11. ask it in the depth, or in the *h.* above
Jer. 31. 12. they shall come and sing in the *h.* of Zion
49. 16. O thou that holdest the *h.* of the hill
51. 53. tho' she should fortify the *h.* of her strength
Ezek. 17. 23. in mountain of the *h.* of Israel, 20. 40.
19. 11. she appeared in her *h.* with her branches
31. 5. therefore his *h.* was exalted above all the trees
10. because thou hast lifted up thyself in *h.*
14. that none of the trees exalt themselves for *h.*
32. 5. I will fill the valleys with thy *h.*
Dan. 3. 1. image of gold whose *h.* was sixty cubits
4. 10. I saw and beheld a tree whose *h.* was great
11. and the *h.* thereof reached unto heaven, 20.
Amos 2. 9. whose *h.* was like the *h.* of cedars
Rom. 8. 39. nor *h.* nor depth shall be able to separate
Eph. 3. 18. what is the *h.* of the love of Christ?
Rev. 21. 16. the breadth and *h.* of the city are equal

HEIGHTS.

Job 9. † 8. which treadeth upon the *h.* of the sea
11. † 8. it is the *h.* of heaven, what canst thou do?
Psal. 95. † 4. the *h.* of the hills are his also
148. 1. praise the Lord, praise him in the *h.*
Eccl. 10. † 6. folly is set in great *h.* rich sit low
Isa. 14. 14. I will ascend above the *h.* of the clouds
33. † 16. he shall dwell on *h.* his place of defence

HEINOUS.

Job 31. 11. for this is an *h.* crime, yea, an iniquity

HEIR, S.

Gen. 15. 3. and lo, one born in my house is mine *h.*
4. word came, saying, this shall not be thine *h.*
21. 10. Ishmael shall not be *h.* with my son Isaac
Judg. 18. † 7. there was no *h.* of restraint in the land
2 *Sam.* 14. 7. and we will destroy the *h.* also
Prov. 30. 23. an handmaid that is *h.* to her mistress
Jer. 49. 1. hath Israel no sons? hath he no *h.*?
2. Israel shall be *h.* unto them that were his *h.*
Mic. 1. 15. yet will I bring an *h.* unto thee, O inhab.
Mat. 21. 38. this is the *h.* *Mark* 12. 7. *Luke* 20. 14.
Rom. 4. 13. that he should be *h.* of the world
14. for if they which are of the law be *h.*
8. 17. if children, then *h.* *h.* of God, and joint *h.* with Christ; if we suffer to be glorified
Gal. 3. 29. ye are *h.* according to the promise
4. 1. I say, that the *h.* as long as he is a child
7. if a son, then an *h.* of God through Christ
30. the son of the bond-woman shall not be *h.*
Eph. 3. 6. that the Gentiles should be fellow-*h.*
Tit. 3. 7. *h.* according to the hope of eternal life
Heb. 1. 2. whom he appointed *h.* of all things

Heb. 1. 14. for them who shall be *h.* of salvation
6. 17. God willing to shew unto the *h.* of promise
11. 7. became *h.* of the righteousness by faith
9. and Jacob *h.* with him of the same promise
Jam. 2. 5. *h.* of the kingdom he hath promised
1 *Pet.* 3. 7. as *h.* together of the grace of life

HELD.

Gen. 48. 17. Joseph *h.* up his father's hand
Exod. 17. 11. when Moses *h.* up hand, Isr. prevailed
36. 12. the loops *h.* one curtain to another
Judg. 7. 20. and *h.* the lamps in their left-hands
16. 26. Samson said unto lad that *h.* him by the hand
Ruth 3. 15. when she *h.* it, he measured six measures
1 *Sam.* 25. 36. Nabal *h.* a feast in his house
2 *Sam.* 18. 16. for Joab *h.* back the people
1 *Kings* 8. 65. at that time Solomon *h.* a feast
1 *Chron.* 11. † 10. these *h.* strongly with David
2 *Chron.* 4. 5. the sea *h.* three thousand baths
Neh. 4. 16. the other half of them *h.* both spears, 21.
17. and with the other hand he *h.* a weapon
Esth. 5. 2. the king *h.* out the golden sceptre
7. 4. if we had been sold, I had *h.* my tongue
Job 23. 11. my foot *h.* his steps, his way have I kept
Psal. 32. 9. whose mouth must be *h.* in with bit
94. 18. my foot slippeth, thy mercy, O L. *h.* me up
Prov. 16. † 5. not be *h.* innocent, 17. † 5. | 19. † 5.
Cant. 3. 4. I *h.* him, and would not let him go
7. 5. hair like purple, the king is *h.* in the galleries
Jer. 50. 33. that took them captives, *h.* them fast
Dan. 12. 7. when he *h.* up his right-hand and sware
Mat. 12. 14. *h.* a counsel against him, *Mark* 15. 1
Luke 22. 63. the men that *h.* Jesus mocked him
Acts 3. 11. the same man that was healed, *h.* Peter
14. 4. part *h.* with the Jews, part with the apostles
Rom. 7. 6. that being dead wherein we were *h.*
Rev. 6. 9. were slain for the testimony which they *h.*

HELD *peace.*

Gen. 24. 21. the man wondering at her, *h.* his *peace*
34. 5. Jacob *h.* his *peace* until they were come
Lev. 10. 3. I will be glorified, and Aaron *h.* his *peace*
Num. 30. 7. her husband *h.* his *peace* at her, 11. 14.
1 *Sam.* 10. 27. they despised Saul, he *h.* his *peace*
2 *Kings* 18. 36. but people *h.* their *peace*, would not
Neh. 5. 8. they *h.* their *peace*, and found nothing
Job 29. 10. nobles *h.* their *peace*, their tongue cleaved
Psal. 39. 2. I was dumb, I *h.* my *peace* from good
Isa. 36. 21. they *h.* their *peace*, *Mark* 3. 4. | 9. 34.
57. 11. have not I *h.* my *peace*, even of old?
Mat. 26. 63. but Jesus *h.* his *peace*
Luke 14. 4. they *h.* their *peace*, 20. 26. *Acts* 11. 18.
Acts 15. 13. they *h.* their *peace*, James answered

HELL,

In Hebrew, Scheol. *This word most commonly signifies the grave, or the place or state of the dead.* Jacob *says*, Gen. 37. 35. I will go down into the grave unto my son, mourning. *I will die with grief, I will never leave mourning till I die. So in* Gen. 42. 38. If mischief befall Benjamin, then shall ye bring down my grey hairs with sorrow to the grave. *You will make me, who am worn away already, to die with grief. The conspirators,* Korah, Dathan, and Abiram, *were swallowed up in the earth,* and descended quick into the grave; *they were buried alive,* Num. 16. 30, 31. Thou wilt not leave my soul in hell; *thou wilt not suffer my body to putrefy in the grave,* Psal. 16. 10. *which is prophetically spoken of the* Messiah. *And in* Psal. 55. 15. Let death seize upon them, and let them go down quick into hell, *into the grave.* Jonah *says,* that he cried to the Lord out of the belly of hell; *that is, out of the belly of a fish, wherein he was shut up as in the grave,* Jonah 2. 2. *This word* Scheol *is sometimes put for hell, the place where the wicked or the damned are tormented; as in* Job 11. 8. *The secrets of God's providence* are high as heaven, and deeper than hell. *And in* Prov. 15. 11. Hell and destruction are before the Lord; *the place and state of the damned are known to God.* The wicked shall be turned into hell, *Psal.* 9. 17.

As the happiness of heaven is expressed in Scripture under the idea of a feast or wedding, at which there is a great deal of light, joy, and pleasure; so hell, in the New Testament, is set forth by such representations as may powerfully instruct and terrify even the most carnal man. Nothing is more intolerably painful than suffering the violence of fire enraged with brimstone; and hell *is described by a lake of fire and brimstone,* Rev. 19. 20. | 21. 8. *It is represented as a dismally dark place, where there is nothing but grief, sadness, vexation, rage, despair, and gnashing of teeth, like one excluded or shut out, during the obscurity of the night, and severity of the cold,* Mat. 8. 12. *The wicked* in hell *not only undergo the punishment of sense, but also that of loss, which is a separation from God, a privation of his sight, and of the beatific vision. Add to these the eternity of their misery, which above all other considerations makes it intolerable:* Their worm dieth not, and their fire is not quenched, *Mark* 9. 48.

By the gates of hell, *Mat.* 16. 18. *is meant the power and policy of the devil and his instruments.* The sorrows of hell, the pains of hell; *that is, deadly or killing pains, such agonies and horrors as dying persons used to feel within themselves, or such sorrows as bring to the brink of the grave.* Psal. 18. 5. | 116. 3.

Deut. 32. 22. a fire shall burn unto the lowest *h.*
2 *Sam.* 22. 6. sorrows of *h.* compassed me, *Ps.* 18. 5.
Job 11. 8. deeper than *h.* what canst thou know?
26. 6. *h.* is naked before him, and destruction
Psal. 9. 17. the wicked shall be turned into *h.*
16. 10. thou wilt not leave my soul in *h.* *Acts* 2. 27.
49. † 15. redeem my soul from power of *h.* 86. 13.
55. 15. and let them go down quick into *h.*
116. 3. and the pains of *h.* gat hold upon me
139. 8. if I make my bed in *h.* thou art there
Prov. 5. 5. her feet to death, her steps take hold on *h.*
7. 27. her house is the way to *h.* going down

Prov. 9. 18. that her guests are in the depths of *h.*
15. 11. *h.* and destruction are before the Lord
24. that he may depart from *h.* beneath
23. 14. and shalt deliver his soul from *h.*
27. 20. *h.* and destruction are never full
Isa. 5. 14. therefore *h.* hath enlarged herself
14. 9. *h.* from beneath is moved for thee to meet
15. yet thou shalt be brought down to *h.*
28. 15. and with *h.* are we at agreement
18. your agreement with *h.* shall not stand
57. 9. and didst debase thyself even unto *h.*
Ezek. 31. 16. when I cast him down to *h.* with them
17. they also went down unto *h.* with him
32. 21. shall speak to him out of the midst of *h.*
27. which are going down to *h.* with weapons
Amos 9. 2. tho' they dig into *h.* thence my hand take
Jonah 2. 2. out of the belly of *h.* cried I, thou heardest
Hab. 2. 5. who enlargeth his desire as *h.* is as death
Mat. 5. 22. say, fool, shall be in danger of *h.* fire
29. thy whole body should be cast into *h.* 30.
10. 28. to destroy soul and body in *h.* *Luke* 12. 5.
11. 23. Capernaum brought down to *h.* *Luke* 10. 15.
16. 18. the gates of *h.* shall not prevail against it
18. 9. having two eyes, to be cast into *h.* *Mark* 9. 47.
23. 15. make him twofold more the child of *h.*
33. how can ye escape the damnation of *h.?*
Luke 16. 23. in *h.* he lifted up his eyes, in torments
Acts 2. 31. that his soul was not left in *h.*
1 *Cor.* 15. † 55. O *h.* where is thy victory?
Jam. 3. 6. the tongue is set on fire of *h.*
2 *Pet.* 2. 4. if God spared not, cast angels down to *h.*
Rev. 1. 18. and I have the keys of *h.* and of death
6. 8. name was Death, and *h.* followed with him
20. 13. death and *h.* delivered up the dead in them
14. death and *h.* were cast into the lake of fire

HELM.

Jam. 3. 4. they are turned about with a small *h.*

HELMET.

1 *Sam.* 17. 5. he had a *h.* of brass upon his head, 38.
Isa. 59. 17. and an *h.* of salvation upon his head
Ezek. 23. 24. shall set against the shield and *h.*
27. 10. they hanged the shield and *h.* in thee
38. 5. all of them with shield and *h.*
Eph. 6. 17. take *h.* of salvation, and sword of Spirit
1 *Thess.* 5. 8. and for an *h.* the hope of salvation

HELMETS.

2 *Chron.* 26. 14. Uzziah prepared spears and *h.*
Jer. 46. 4. get up and stand forth with your *h.*

HELP, *Substantive.*

Gen. 2. 18. I will make him an *h.* meet for him
20. there was not found an *h.* meet for him
Exod. 18. 4. God of my father, said he, was my *h.*
Deut. 33. 7. be thou an *h.* to him from his enemies
26. who rideth upon the heavens in thy *h.*
29. O people, saved by the L. the shield of thy *h.*
Judg. 5. 23. they came not to the *h.* of the Lord
1 *Sam.* 11. 9. by time sun be hot, ye shall have *h.*
2 *Chron.* 20. 4. Judah gathered to ask *h.* of the Lord
Job 6. 13. is not my *h.* in me? is wisdom driven?
31. 21. lift my hand, when I saw my *h.* in the gate
Psal. 3. 2. say of my soul, there is no *h.* for him
20. 2. the Lord send thee *h.* from the sanctuary
27. 9. thou hast been my *h.* leave me not, O God
33. 20. our soul waits for L. he is our *h.* and shield
35. 2. take hold of shield, stand up for mine *h.* 44. 26.
40. 17. thou art my *h.* and my deliverer, 70. 5.
42. 5. praise him for the *h.* of his countenance
46. 1. God is a very present *h.* in time of trouble
60. 11. give us *h.* for vain is the *h.* of man, 108. 12.
63. 7. because thou hast been my *h.* therefore
71. 12. O my God, make haste for my *h.*
89. 19. I have laid *h.* upon one that is mighty
94. 17. unless the Lord had been my *h.* my soul
115. 9. he is their *h.* and their shield, 10. 11.
121. 1. to the hills, from whence cometh my *h.*
2. my *h.* cometh from Lord which made heaven
124. 8. our *h.* is in name of the Lord, who made
146. 3. trust not in man, in whom there is no *h.*
5. happy that hath the God of Jacob for his *h.*
Isa. 10. 3. to whom will ye flee for *h.?* and where
20. 6. whither we flee for *h.* to be deliver. from king
30. 5. nor be an *h.* nor profit, but shame and reproach
31. 1. woe to them that go down to Egypt for *h.*
2. against the *h.* of them that work iniquity
Lam. 4. 17. our eyes as yet failed for our vain *h.*
Dan. 11. 34. they shall be holpen with a little *h.*
Hos. 13. 9. hast destroyed thys. but in me is thine *h.*
Acts 26. 22. having obtained *h.* of God, I continue

HELP, *Verb.*

Gen. 49. 25. by the G. of thy father, who shall *h.* thee
Exod. 23. 5. lying under his burden, wouldest forbear to *h.* him, thou shalt surely *h.* him, *Deut.* 22. 4.
Deut. 32. 38. let them rise and *h.* you, and be your
Josh. 1. 14. pass before your brethren, and *h.* them
10. 4. come unto me, and *h.* me, that we may smite
6. come up to us quickly, and save us, and *h.* us
33. Horam king of Gezer came up to *h.* Lachish
2 *Sam.* 10. 11. then *h.* me, will *h.* thee, 1 *Chron.* 19. 12.
19. Syrians feared to *h.* Ammon, 1 *Chron.* 19. 19.
14. 4. woman said, *h.* O king, 2 *Kings* 6. 26.
1 *Chron.* 12. 17. if ye be come unto me to *h.* me
22. day by day there came to David to *h.* him
18. 5. Syrians of Damascus came to *h.* Hadarezer
22. 17. David commanded to *h.* Solomon his son
2 *Chron.* 14. 11. it is nothing with thee to *h.* his. us, O Ld. our G. we rest on thee, and in thy name go
19. 2. shouldest thou *h.* the ungodly, and love them
20. 9. if we cry, then thou wilt hear and *h.*
25. 8. for God hath power to *h.* and to cast down
26. 13. made war with mighty power to *h.* the king
28. 16. send unto the kings of Assyria to *h.* him
23. the gods of Syria *h.* them, that they may *h.* me
29. 34. their brethren the Levites did *h.* them
32. 3. his princes and his mighty men did *h.* him
8. but with us is the Lord our God, to *h.* us
Ezra 1. 4. let the men of his place *h.* him with silver
8. 22. I was ashamed to require horsemen to *h.*
Job 8. 20. neither will he *h.* the evil-doers
29. 12. I delivered him that had none to *h.* him
Psal. 12. 1. *h.* Lord || 22. 11. for there is none to *h.*
22. 19. haste thee to *h.* me, 38. 22. | 40. 13. | 70. 1.
37. 40. Lord shall *h.* them || 46. 5. God shall *h.* her

Ps. 59. 4. awake to *h.* me || 79. 9. *h.* us, O G. of salv.
107. 12. they fell there was none to *h.* *Isa.* 63. 5.
109. 26. *h.* me, O Lord my God, O save me
118. 7. Lord taketh my part with them that *h.* me
119. 86. *h.* thou me || 173. let thine hand *h.* me
175. let my soul live, and let thy judgments *h.* me
Eccl. 4. 10. for he hath not another to *h.* him up
Isa. 30. 7. for the Egyptians shall *h.* in vain
41. 10. fear not, I will *h.* thee, 13, 14. | 44. 2.
50. 7. for the Lord God will *h.* me, 9.
Jer. 37. 7. Pharaoh's army, which is come to *h.* you
Lam. 1. 7. her people fell, and none did *h.* her
Ezek. 12. 14. I will scatter all about him to *h.* him
32. 21. speak out of hell with them that *h.* him
Dan. 10. 13. lo, one of the princes came to *h.* me
11. 45. shall come to his end, and none shall *h.* him
Mat. 15. 25. she worshipped him, saying, L. *h.* me
Mark 9. 22. have compassion on us, and *h.* us
24. Lord, I believe, *h.* thou mine unbelief
Luke 5. 7. they beckon. that they should come and *h.*
10. 40. bid her therefore that she *h.* me
Acts 16. 9. come over into Macedonia, and *h.* us
21. 28. the Jews crying out, men of Israel *h.*
Phil. 4. 3. *h.* those women which laboured with me
Heb. 4. 16. we may find grace to *h.* in time of need

HELPED.

Exod. 2. 17. but Moses stood up and *h.* them
1 *Sam.* 7. 12. Ebenezer, hitherto hath the Ld. *h.* us
1 *Kings* 1. 7. and they following Adonijah, *h.* him
20. 16. the thirty and two kings that *h.* him
1 *Chron.* 5. 20. and they were *h.* against them
12. 19. but they *h.* them not, for the lords sent
21. they *h.* David against the band of the rovers
15. 26. when God *h.* the Levites that bare the ark
2 *Chr.* 18. 31. the Lord *h.* Jehoshaphat, and moved
20. 23. every one *h.* to destroy another
26. 7. God *h.* him against the Philistines
15. for he was marvellously *h.* till he was strong
28. 21. but the king of Assyria *h.* him not
Ezra 10. 15. and Shabbethai the Levite *h.* them
Esth. 9. 3. the officers of the king *h.* the Jews
Job 26. 2. how hast thou *h.* him that is without power
Ps. 28. 7. and I am *h.* || 118. 13. but the Ld. *h.* me
116. 6. I was brought low, and he *h.* me
Isa. 41. 6. they *h.* every one his neighbour
49. 8. in a day of salvation have I *h.* thee
Zech. 1. 15. and they *h.* forward the affliction
Acts 18. 27. who, when he was come, *h.* them much
Rev. 12. 16. the earth *h.* the woman, and opened

HELPER.

2 *Kings* 14. 26. nor was there any *h.* for Israel
Job 30. 13. they mar my path, they have no *h.*
Psal. 10. 14. thou art the *h.* of the fatherless
22. † 11. be not far from me, for there is not a *h.*
30. 10. Lord, be thou my *h.* || 54. 4. God is my *h.*
72. 12. he shall deliver him that hath no *h.*
Jer. 47. 4. cut off from Tyrus and Zidon every *h.*
Rom. 16. 9. salute Urbane, our *h.* in Christ
Heb. 13. 6. the L. is my *h.* I will not fear what man

HELPERS.

1 *Chr.* 12. 1. among the mighty men, *h.* of the war
18. peace be to thee, and peace be to thine *h.*
Job 9. 13. the proud *h.* do stoop under him
Ezek. 30. 8. when all her *h.* shall be destroyed
Nah. 3. 9. Put and Lubim were thy *h.*
Rom. 16. 3. Priscilla and Aquila my *h.* in Christ
2 *Cor.* 1. 24. but are *h.* of your joy; by faith ye stand
3 *John* 8. that we might be fellow-*h.* to the truth

HELPS.

Acts 27. 17. they used *h.* undergirding the ship
1 *Cor.* 12. 28. gifts of healings, *h.* governments

HELPETH.

1 *Chr.* 12. 18. peace unto thee, for thy God *h.* thee
Isa. 31. 3. both he that *h.* shall fall, and he that is holpen
Rom. 8. 26. the Spirit also *h.* our infirmities
1 *Cor.* 16. 16. ye submit to every one that *h.* with us

HELPING.

Ezra 5. 2. where the prophets of God *h.* them
Psal. 22. 1. why art thou so far from *h.* me?
2 *Cor.* 1. 11. ye also *h.* together by prayer for us

HELVE.

Deut. 19. 5. and the head slippeth from the *h.*

HEMLOCK.

Hos. 10. 4. thus judgment springeth up as *h.* in field
Amos 6. 12. ye turned fruit of righteousness into *h.*

HEM, S.

Exod. 28. 33. upon the *h.* of it thou shalt make pomegranates of blue and purple, 34. | 39. 24, 25, 26.
Mat. 9. 20. woman touched *h.* of his garment, 14. 36.

HEN.

Mat. 23. 37. as a *h.* gathereth chickens, *Luke* 13. 34.

HENCE.

Gen. 37. 17. the man said, they are departed *h.*
42. 15. by the life of Phar. ye shall not go forth *h.*
50. 25. carry up my bones from *h.* *Exod.* 13. 19.
Exod. 11. 1. he will let you go *h.* thrust you out *h.*
33. 1. depart and go up *h.* thou and the people
15. if thy presence not with me, carry us not up *h.*
Deut. 9. 12. arise, get thee down quickly from *h.*
Josh. 4. 3. take *h.* out of Jordan twelve stones
Judg. 6. 18. depart not *h.* I pray thee, until I come
Ruth 2. 8. neither go *h.* but abide fast by my maidens
1 *Kings* 17. 3. get thee *h.* *Isa.* 30. 22. *Mat.* 4. 10.
Ps. 39. 13. O spare, before I go *h.* and be no more
Jer. 38. 10. saying, take from *h.* thirty men with thee
Zech. 6. 7. he said, get you *h.* walk to and fro
Mat. 17. 20. shall say, remove *h.* to yonder place
Luke 4. 9. if Son of God, cast thyself down from *h.*
13. 31. get thee out, and depart *h.* *John* 7. 3.
16. 26. they which would pass from *h.* to you cannot
John 2. 16. take things *h.* make not my Father's
14. 31. arise, let us go *h.* || 18. 36. my kingd. not *h.*
20. 15. sir, if thou have borne him *h.* tell me where
Acts 1. 5. baptized with Holy G. not many days *h.*
22. 21. I will send thee far *h.* unto the Gentiles
Jam. 4. 1. come they not *h.* even of your lusts?

HENCEFORTH.

Gen. 4. 12. the ground not *h.* yield thee her strength
Num. 18. 22. neither must Israel *h.* come nigh taber.
Deut. 17. 16. ye shall *h.* return no more that way
19. 20. shall *h.* commit no more any such evil
Judg. 2. 21. I will not *h.* drive out any before them

2 *Kings* 5. 17. thy serv. will *h.* not offer to other gods
2 *Chron.* 16. 9. from *h.* thou shalt have wars
Psal. 125. 2. so is Lord about his people from *h.*
131. 3. Israel hope in the Lord from *h.* and for ever
Isa. 9. 7. to establish it with justice from *h.* for ever
52. 1. *h.* there shall no more come the unclean
59. 21. out of mouth of thy seed's seed *h.* and for ever
Ezek. 36. 12. thou shalt no more *h.* bereave them
Mic. 4. 7. the Lord shall reign in mount Zion from *h.*
Mat. 23. 39. ye shall not see me *h.* till ye say
26. 29. I will not drink *h.* of this fruit of vine
Luke 1. 48. *h.* all generations shall call me blessed
5. 10. fear not, from *h.* thou shalt catch men
12. 52. *h.* there shall be five in one house
John 14. 7. *h.* ye know him, and have seen him
15. 15. *h.* I call you not servants, but friends
Acts 4. 17. they speak *h.* to no man in this name
18. 6. I am clean, *h.* I will go unto the Gentiles
Rom. 6. 6. that *h.* we should not serve sin
2 *Cor.* 5. 15. should not *h.* live unto themselves, but to
16. *h.* know we no man, *h.* know we him no more
Gal. 6. 17. from *h.* let no man trouble me, for I bear
Eph. 4. 14. we *h.* be no more childr. tossed to and fro
17. that ye *h.* walk not as other Gentiles walk
2 *Tim.* 4. 8. *h.* there is laid up for me a crown of right.
Heb. 10. 13. *h.* expecting till enemies be made
Rev. 14. 13. blessed are they who die in Lord, from *h.*

HENCEFORWARD.

Num. 15. 23. and *h.* among your generations
Mat. 21. 19. let no fruit grow on thee *h.* for ever

HERALD.

Dan. 3. 4. an *h.* cried aloud, to you it is commanded

HERB.

Gen. 1. 11. bring forth the *h.* yielding seed, 12.
29. I have given you every *h.* bearing seed
2. 5. made every *h.* || 3. 18. thou shalt eat the *h.*
9. 3. even as the *h.* I have given you all things
Exod. 9. 22. the hail smote every *h.* of the field, 25.
10. 12. the locusts eat every *h.* of the land, 15.
Deut. 32. 2. as the small rain upon the tender *h.*
2 *Kings* 19. 26. were as the green *h.* *Isa.* 37. 27.
Job 8. 12. flag withereth before any other *h.*
38. 27. to cause the bud of the tender *h.* to spring
Psal. 37. 2. for they shall wither as the green *h.*
104. 14. he causeth *h.* to grow for service of man
Isa. 66. 14. your bones shall flourish like an *h.*

HERBS.

Exod. 12. 8. and with bitter *h.* eat it, *Num.* 9. 11.
Deut. 11. 10. and wateredst it as a garden of *h.*
1 *Kings* 21. 2. that I may have it for a garden of *h.*
2 *Kings* 4. 39. one went into the field to gather *h.*
Psal. 105. 35. and did eat up all the *h.* in their land
Prov. 15. 17. better is a dinner of *h.* where love is
27. 25. and *h.* of the mountains are gathered
Isa. 18. 4. I will consider like a clear heat upon *h.*
26. 19. for thy dew is as the dew of *h.* and earth
42. 15. I will dry up all their *h.* make rivers islands
Jer. 12. 4. how long the *h.* of every field wither?
Mat. 13. 32. is greatest among all *h.* *Mark* 4. 32.
Luke 11. 42. for ye tithe all manner of *h.*
Rom. 14. 2. another who is weak eateth *h.*
Heb. 6. 7. and bringeth forth *h.* meet for them

HERD, S.

Gen. 18. 7. Abraham ran to the *h.* and fetched a calf
32. 7. Jacob divided his *h.* into two bands
47. 18. my lord also hath our *h.* of cattle
Exod. 10. 9. with our flocks and *h.* will we go
Lev. 1. 2. ye shall bring your offering of the *h.*
3. 1. if ye offer it of *h.* male or female, *Num.* 15. 3.
27. 32. concerning the tithe of the *h.* or flock
Deut. 12. 21. thou shalt kill of thy *h.* and flock
15. 19. the firstling males that come of thy *h.*
1 *Sam.* 11. 5. Saul came after the *h.* out of the field
2 *Sam.* 12. 4. he spared to take of his *h.* to dress
1 *Chr.* 27. 29. over the *h.* in Sharon, *h.* in valleys
Isa. 65. 10. Achor a place for the *h.* to lie down in
Jer. 31. 12. shall flow together for young of the *h.*
Joel 1. 18. the *h.* of cattle are perplexed, no pasture
Jonah 3. 7. let not the *h.* nor flock taste any thing
Hab. 3. 17. and there shall be no *h.* in the stalls
Mat. 8. 30. *h.* of swine feed. *Mark* 5. 11. *Luke* 8. 32.
32. whole *h.* ran violently, *Mark* 5. 13. *Luke* 8. 33.
See FLOCKS.

HERDMAN.

Amos 7. 14. I was no prophet, but I was an *h.*

HERDMEN.

Gen. 13. 7. a strife between the *h.* of Abram and Lot
8. let there be no strife between my *h.* and thy *h.*
26. 20. the *h.* of Gerar did strive with Isaac's *h.*
1 *Sam.* 21. 7. Doeg chiefest of *h.* belonged to Saul
Amos 1. 1. who was among the *h.* of Tekoa

HERE.

Gen. 19. 12. the men said, hast thou *h.* any besides?
15. arise, take thy two daughters which are *h.*
21. 23. now therefore swear unto me *h.* by God
22. 1. *h.* I am, 7. 11. | 27. 1, 18. | 31. 11. | 37. 13. | 46. 2. *Exod.* 3. 4. 1 *Sam.* 3. 4, 5, 6, 8, 16. 2 *Sam.* 1. 7. | 15. 26. *Isa.* 6. 8.
5. abide ye *h.* with the ass, I and lad will go yond.
24. 13. behold, I stand *h.* by the well of water
31. 37. set it *h.* before my brethren that they may
40. 15. and *h.* also have I done nothing to put me
42. 33. leave one of your brethren *h.* with me
47. 23. lo, *h.* is seed for you, ye shall sow the land
Exod. 24. 14. tarry ye *h.* for us, till we come to you
Num. 14. 40. saying, lo, we be *h.* and will go up
22. 8. lodge *h.* this night, I will bring you word, 19.
23. 1. build *h.* seven altars, prepare *h.* oxen, 29.
32. 6. shall your breth. go to war, and you sit *h.?*
16. we will build sheep-folds *h.* for our cattle
Deut. 5. 3. even us, who are all of us *h.* alive this day
12. 8. after all the things we do *h.* this day
29. 15. with him that standeth *h.* that is not *h.*
Josh. 18. 6. that I may cast lots for you *h.* 8.
Judg. 4. 20. is there any man *h.?* thou shalt say, no
18. 3. and what hast thou *h.?* || 19. 9. lodge *h.*
19. 24. behold, *h.* is my daughter, a maiden
20. 7. give *h.* your advice and counsel
Ruth 2. 8. but abide *h.* fast by my maidens
4. 1. unto whom he said, turn aside, sit down *h.* 2.
1 *Sam.* 1. 26. I am the woman that stood by thee *h.*
9. 11. they went up the hill and said, is the seer *h.?*

1 *Sam.* 12. 3. behold, *h.* I am, 22. 12. *Isa.* 58. 9.
14. 34. slay them *h.* and eat, and sin not against L.
16. 11. Samuel said to Jesse, are *h.* all thy children
21. 8. is there not *h.* under thine hand a spear?
9. it is *h.* wrapped in a cloth, none save that *h.*
23. 3. behold, we be afraid *h.* in Judah; how much
29. 3. the princes said, what do these Hebrews *h.?*
2 *Sam.* 11. 12. tarry *h.* to-day ‖ 18. 30. turn aside *h.*
20. 4. be thou *h.* present ‖ 24. 22. *h.* be oxen
1 *Kings* 2. 30. and he said, nay, but I will die *h.*
18. 8. tell thy lord, behold, Elijah is *h.* 11. 14.
19. 9. he said, what doest thou *h.* Elijah? 13.
20. 40. as thy servant was busy *h.* and there
22. 7. is there not *h.* a prophet of L. 2 *Kings* 3. 11.
2 *Kings* 2. 2. Elijah said, tarry *h.* I pray thee, 6.
3. 11. *h.* is Elisha ‖ 7. 3. why sit we *h.* until we die?
7. 4. the lepers said, if we sit still *h.* we die also
10. 23. look there be *h.* none of the servants of Lord
1 *Chr.* 29. 17. with joy thy people present *h.* to offer
Job 38. 11. *h.* shall thy proud waves be stayed
35. that lightnings may say unto thee, *h.* we are
Psal. 132. 14. this is my rest, *h.* will I dwell
Isa. 21. 9. behold, *h.* cometh a chariot of men
22. 16. what hast thou *h.?* whom hast thou *h.?*
28. 10. *h.* a little, and there a little, 13.
52. 5. now therefore, what have I *h.?* saith Lord
Ezek. 8. 6. the house of Israel committeth *h.* 17.
Hos. 7. 9. gray hairs are *h.* and there upon him
Mat. 12. 41. a greater than Jonas is *h.* *Luke* 11. 32.
42. a greater than Solomon is *h.* *Luke* 11. 31.
14. 8. give me *h.* John Baptist's head in a charger
17. we have *h.* but five loaves, and two fishes
16. 28. there be some standing *h.* *Luke* 9. 27.
17. 4. Lord, it is good for us to be *h.* let us make *h.*
24. 2. shall not be left *h.* one stone upon another
23. if any say to you, lo, *h.* is Chr. *Mark* 13. 21.
26. 36. sit ye *h.* while I go and pray, *Mark* 14. 32.
38. tarry ye *h.* and watch with me
28. 6. he is not *h.* he is risen, *Mark* 16. 6. *Luke* 24. 6.
Mark 6. 3. and are not his sisters *h.* with us?
13. 1. Master, see what stones and buildings are *h.*
Luke 4. 23. what heard done, do *h.* in thy country
9. 12. for we are *h.* in a desert place
17. 21. neither shall they say, lo *h.* or lo there
23. say to you, see *h.* or see there, go not after th.
19. 20. behold, *h.* is thy pound which I have kept
22. 38. *h.* are two swords, he said, it is enough
24. 41. he said unto them, have ye *h.* any meat?
John 6. 9. there is a lad *h.* which hath five loaves
11. 21. Lord, if thou hadst been *h.* my brother, 32.
Acts 8. 36. *h.* is water ‖ 9. 10. behold, I am *h.* Lord
9. 14. and *h.* he hath authority from the priests
10. 33. are we all *h.* present before God, to hear
16. 28. do thyself no harm, for we are all *h.*
24. 19. who ought to have been *h.* before thee
25. 24. and all men which are *h.* present with us
Col. 4. 9. make known unto you all things done *h.*
Heb. 7. 8. and *h.* men that die receive tithes
13. 14. for *h.* have we no continuing city, seek one
Jam. 2. 3. sit *h.* in a good place, or sit *h.* under
1 *Pet.* 1. 17. pass time of your sojourning *h.* in fear
Rev. 13. 10. *h.* is the patience of the saints, 14. 12.
18. *h.* is wisdom; let him that hath understanding
14. 12. *h.* are they that kept the commandments
17. 9. and *h.* is the mind which hath wisdom
See STAND.

HEREAFTER.

Isa. 41. 23. shew the things that are to come *h.*
Ezek. 20. 39. *h.* also, if ye will not hearken unto me
Dan. 2. 29. what should come to pass *h.* 45.
Mat. 26. 64. *h.* shall ye see the Son of man sitting
Mark 11. 14. no man eat fruit of thee *h.* for ever
Luke 22. 69. *h.* shall Son of man sit on right hand
John 1. 51. I say, *h.* ye shall see heaven opened
13. 7. thou knowest not now, thou shalt know *h.*
14. 30. *h.* I will not talk much with you
1 *Tim.* 1. 16. pattern to them which *h.* believe on him
Rev. 1. 19. write the things which shall be *h.*
4. 1. I will shew thee things which must be *h.*
9. 12. and behold, there come two woes more *h.*

HEREBY.

Gen. 42. 15. *h.* ye shall be proved, by life of Pharaoh
33. *h.* shall I know that ye are true men
Num. 16. 28. *h.* know that the Lord hath sent me
Josh. 3. 10. *h.* know that the living God is among
1 *Cor.* 4. 4. I know nothing, yet am I not *h.* justified
1 *John* 2. 3. *h.* we do know that we know him
5. keepeth word, *h.* know we that we are in him
3. 16. *h.* perceive we the love of God, because
19. and *h.* we know that we are of the truth
24. and *h.* we know that he abideth in us
4. 2. *h.* know ye the Spirit of God, every spirit
6. *h.* know we the Spirit of truth and of error
13. *h.* know we that we dwell in him, and he in us

HEREIN.

Gen. 34. 22. only *h.* will the men consent unto us
2 *Chr.* 16. 9. *h.* thou hast done foolishly, therefore
John 4. 37. *h.* is that saying true, one soweth
9. 30. *h.* is a marvellous thing, that ye know not
15. 8. *h.* is my Father glorified, that ye bear fruit
Acts 24. 16. *h.* do I exercise myself to have conscien.
2 *Cor.* 8. 10. *h.* I give my advice, for this expedient
1 *John* 4. 10. *h.* is love ‖ 17. *h.* is love made perfect

HERESY.

This word comes from the Greek, Hæresis, *and signifies in general*, a sect, *or* choice. *It is sometimes taken in a good sense, as in* Acts 26. 5. After the most straitest sect, *or* heresy, of our religion, I lived a Pharisee. *St.* Paul *commends the sect, opinion, and way of the* Pharisees, *as being more learned and strict, and as coming nearer to the truth in many things, than the other sect, of the* Sadducees. *But most commonly it is taken in a bad sense, for some fundamental error in matters of religion, adhered to with obstinacy. St.* Paul *enumerates* heresies *among the works of the flesh*, Gal. 5. 20. *And St.* Peter *says*, There shall be false teachers among you, who privily shall bring in damnable heresies, even denying the Lord that bought them, 2 *Pet.* 2. 1. *St.* Paul *says in* 1 Cor. 11. 19. There must be also heresies among you, that they which are approved may be made manifest among you. *It is not simply and absolutely necessary that there should be such schisms and divisions in the church, but God has decreed to permit Satan to shew his malice, and men to discover the lusts and corruptions of their nature, by causing such divisions, that the sincerity of his people may be tried and known by their stedfastness to the truth, and opposition to these corruptions. Christianity was called* a sect, *or* heresy, *by* Tertullus *and the profane* Jews, *Acts* 24. 5, 14. We have found this man a pestilent fellow, and ringleader of the sect of the *Nazarenes.* This I confess, *says* St. Paul, that after the way which they call heresy, so worship I the God of my fathers.

As to the Sects, *or* Heresies *among the* Jews, *See* SECT.

From the very beginning of the Christian *church there were very dangerous and pernicious heresies; for the most essential doctrines of religion were attacked, such as the divinity of* Christ, *his quality of* Messiah, *the reality and truth of his incarnation, the resurrection of the dead, the liberty of Christians, and their freedom from the legal ceremonies, and other points of this nature. The most ancient of these founders of* heresy, *is* Simon *the magician, who desired to buy the gift of God with money, and afterwards set himself up for the* Messiah, *and God Almighty the Creator*, Acts 8. 9, 10. *The false apostles, against whom* St. Paul *so often speaks in his epistles, had a mind that the faithful should receive circumcision, and subject themselves to all the legal observances*, Gal. 5. 11. | 6. 12.

The Nicolaitanes *allowed of a community of women, and without any scruple committed the most ignominious actions, and followed the superstitions of heathenism. It is said, they went over to the* sect *of the* Cainists, *who acknowledged a power superior to that of the Creator.* St. John *speaks of the* Nicolaitanes, *as a sect of heretics then subsisting, and producing great disorders in the churches of* Asia, *Rev.* 2. 6, 15. *At the same time there were false* Christs, *and false prophets*, 1 John 2. 18, 22. 2 John 7. St. Paul *speaks of* Hymeneus *and* Philetus, *who departed from the truth, saying, that the resurrection is already past*, 2 Tim. 2. 17, 18. *He foretold that in the last times there would be some who should forsake the faith, and give themselves up to the spirit of error, and the doctrines of devils*, 1 Tim. 4. 1. St. Peter *and* Jude *foretell the same thing*, 2 Pet. 2. 1. Jude 18. *And herein they only copy what* Jesus Christ *himself had said in the gospel*, Mat. 7. 15. | 24. 24. Beware of false prophets, which come to you in sheep's clothing, but inwardly they are ravening wolves. For there shall arise false Christs, and false prophets, and shall shew great signs and wonders; insomuch that, if it were possible, they shall deceive the very elect.
Acts 24. 14. after the way which they call *h.*

HERESIES.

1 *Cor.* 11. 19. there must be also *h.* among you
Gal. 5. 20. the works of the flesh, wrath, strife, *h.*
2 *Pet.* 2. 1. who privily bring in damnable *h.*

HERETIC.

Tit. 3. 10. an *h.* after the second admonition, reject

HERETOFORE.

Exod. 4. 10. I am not eloquent, neither *h.* nor since
5. 7. no more give straw to make brick as *h.*
Josh. 3. 4. for ye have not passed this way *h.*
Ruth 2. 11. to a people which thou knewest not *h.*
1 *Sam.* 4. 7. there hath not been such a thing *h.*
2 *Cor.* 13. 2. I write to them which *h.* have sinned

HEREUNTO.

Eccl. 2. 25. or who else can hasten *h.* more than I?
1 *Pet.* 2. 21. for even *h.* were ye called, because

HEREWITH.

Ezek. 16. 29. and yet thou wast not satisfied *h.*
Mal. 3. 10. that there may be meat in mine house,
and prove me now *h.* saith the Lord of hosts

HERITAGE.

Exod. 6. 8. the land, I will give it you for an *h.*
Job 20. 29. and the *h.* appointed by God for him
27. 13. the *h.* of oppressors which they shall receive
Ps. 16. 6. in pleasant places, yea, I have a goodly *h.*
61. 5. give me the *h.* of those that fear thy name
94. 5. they break thy people, they afflict thy *h.*
111. 6. he may give them the *h.* of the heathen
119. 111. thy testimonies have I taken as an *h.*
127. 3. lo, children are an *h.* of the Lord
135. 12. and gave their land for an *h.* 136. 21, 22.
Isa. 54. 17. this is the *h.* of the servants of the Lord
58. 14. I will feed thee with the *h.* of Jacob
Jer. 2. 7. and ye made mine *h.* an abomination
3. 19. how shall I give thee a goodly *h.?*
12. 7. I have left mine *h.* ‖ 8. mine *h.* is as a lion
9. mine *h.* is unto me as a speckled bird, the birds
15. I will bring them again every man to his *h.*
17. 4. thou shalt discontinue from thine *h.* I give
50. 11. O destroyers of mine *h.* because grown fat
Joel 2. 17. and give not thine *h.* to reproach
3. 2. I will plead with them for my *h.* Israel
Mic. 2. 2. so they oppress a man and his *h.*
7. 14. feed the flock of thine *h.* with thy rod
18. that passeth by the transgression of his *h.*
Mal. 1. 3. I laid Esau's mountains and *h.* waste
1 *Pet.* 5. 3. neither as being lords over God's *h.*

HERITAGES.

Isa. 49. 8. to cause to inherit the desolate *h.*

HERODIANS.

See Signification on SECT.
Mat. 22. 16. they sent unto him their disciples, with
H. saying, we know thou art true, *Mark* 12. 13.
Mark 3. 6. the Pharisees took counsel with the *H.*

HERON.

Lev. 11. 19. the stork, the *h.* unclean, *Deut.* 14. 18.

HERSELF, *See* SELF.

HER'S.

Job 39. 16. ostrich is hardened as tho' they were not *h.*

HEW.

Exod. 34. 1. *h.* thee two tables of stone, *Deut.* 10. 1.
Deut. 12. 3. ye shall *h.* down the graven images
19. 5. when a man goeth with neighbour to *h.* wood
1 *Kings* 5. 6. that they *h.* me cedar-trees out of Leb.
18. Solomon's and Hiram's builders did *h.* them
1 *Chr.* 22. 2. David set masons to *h.* stones
2 *Chr.* 2. 2. Solomon told 80,000 to *h.* in mountains
Jer. 6. 6. *h.* ye down trees and cast a mount
Dan. 4. 14. he cried aloud, *h.* down the tree, 23.

HEWED.

Exod. 34. 4. he *h.* two tables like the first, *Deut.* 10. 3.
1 *Sam.* 11. 7. Saul *h.* oxen in pieces, and sent them
15. 33. and Samuel *h.* Agag in pieces in Gilgal
1 *Kings* 5. 17. *h.* stones to lay foundation of house
6. 36. with three rows of *h.* stones, 7. 12.
7. 9. according to the measures of *h.* stones, 11.
2 *Kings* 12. 12. buy *h.* stone to repair the breaches
Isa. 22. 16. thou hast *h.* thee out a sepulchre
Jer. 2. 13. my people have *h.* them out cisterns
Hos. 6. 5. therefore have I *h.* them by the prophets

HEWER.

Deut. 29. 11. from *h.* of wood, unto drawer of water

HEWERS.

Josh. 9. 21. let them be *h.* of wood and drawers, 23.
27. Joshua made them that day *h.* of wood
1 *Kings* 5. 15. and 80,000 *h.* in mountains, 2 *Chr.* 2. 18.
2 *Kings* 12. 12. laid out money to masons and *h.*
1 *Chron.* 22. 15. are *h.* with thee in abundance
2 *Chr.* 2. 10. I will give to thy servants the *h.*
Jer. 46. 22. shall come against Egypt as *h.* of wood

HEWETH.

Isa. 10. 15. shall the axe boast against him that *h.?*
22. 16. as he that *h.* him out a sepulchre on high
44. 14. he *h.* him down cedars, and taketh cypress

HEWN.

Prov. 9. 1. she hath *h.* out her seven pillars
Isa. 10. 33. the high ones of stature shall be *h.* down
33. 9. Leban. is ashamed, and *h.* down, Sharon like
51. 1. look unto the rock whence ye are *h.*
Mat. 3. 10. *h.* down and cast into fire, 7. 19. *Luke* 3. 9.
27. 60. and laid it in a sepulchre which he had *h.*
out in the rock, *Mark* 15. 46. *Luke* 23. 53.
See STONE.

HID.

Gen. 3. 8. and Adam and his wife *h.* themselves
10. afraid because I was naked, and I *h.* myself
35. 4. Jacob *h.* them under the oak by Shechem
Exod. 2. 2. goodly child, she *h.* Moses three months
12. Moses slew the Egyptian, and *h.* him in sand
3. 6. Moses *h.* his face, for he was afraid to look
Josh. 2. 4. Rahab *h.* the spies with stalks of flax, 6.
6. 17. because she *h.* the messengers we sent, 25.
7. 21. and behold they are *h.* in the earth
10. 16. the five kings *h.* themselves in a cave
Judg. 9. 5. yet Jotham was left, for he *h.* himself
1 *Sam.* 3. 18. Samuel told Eli and *h.* noth. from him
10. 22. Saul *h.* himself ‖ 20. 24. David *h.* himself
1 *Kings* 18. 4. Obadiah *h.* the prophets, 13.
2 *Kings* 4. 27. and the Lord hath *h.* it from me
6. 29. I said, give thy son, she hath *h.* her son
7. 8. lepers went and *h.* it, carried thence, and *h.* it
11. 2. they *h.* him and his nurse, 2 *Chron.* 22. 11.
1 *Chron.* 21. 20. Ornan and four sons *h.* themselves
Job 3. 10. nor *h.* sorrow from mine eyes
10. 13. these things hast thou *h.* in thine heart
17. 4. thou hast *h.* their heart from understanding
23. † 12. I have *h.* the words of his mouth
29. 8. the young men saw me and *h.* themselves
Psal. 9. 15. in net which they *h.* their own foot taken
22. 24. neither hath he *h.* his face from him
35. 7. without cause they *h.* for me their net
8. let his net that he hath *h.* catch himself
55. 12. then I would have *h.* myself from him
119. 11. thy word have I *h.* in mine heart
140. 5. the proud have *h.* a snare for me, and cords
Isa. 28. 15. under falsehood have we *h.* ourselves
49. 2. in shadow of his hand, in quiver he *h.* me
50. 6. I *h.* not my face from shame and spitting
53. 3. and we *h.* as it were our faces from him
54. 8. in a little wrath I *h.* my face from thee
57. 17. I *h.* me and was wroth, and he went
59. 2. and your sins have *h.* his face from you
64. 7. for thou hast *h.* thy face from us
65. 16. because they are *h.* from mine eyes
Jer. 13. 5. so I went and *h.* it by Euphrates
7. I took girdle from the place where I had *h.* it
18. 22. for they have *h.* snares for my feet
33. 5. I have *h.* my face from this city
36. 26. to take them, but the Lord *h.* them
43. 10. will set his throne on these stones I have *h.*
Ezek. 22. 26. have *h.* their eyes from my sabbaths
39. 23. therefore *h.* I my face from them, 24.
Mat. 11. 25. thou hast *h.* from the wise, *Luke* 10. 21.
13. 33. *h.* in three measures of meal, *Luke* 13. 21.
25. 18. but he went and *h.* his lord's money
25. I went and *h.* thy talent in the earth
Luke 1. 24. Elizabeth *h.* herself five months
John 8. 59. but Jesus *h.* himself, and went out
Rev. 6. 15. bond-man and free-man *h.* themselves

HID.

Deut. 33. 19. they shall suck of treasures *h.* in sand
Josh. 7. 22. and behold, it was *h.* in his tent
10. 17. the five kings are found *h.* in a cave
2 *Sam.* 17. 9. behold, he is *h.* now in some pit
18. 13. no matter *h.* from king, 1 *Kings* 10. 3.
2 *Chron.* 9. 2.
2 *Kings* 11. 3. he was *h.* in house of G. 2 *Chr.* 22. 12.
2 *Chron.* 22. 9. Ahaziah was *h.* in Samaria
Job 3. 21. and dig for it more than for *h.* treasures
23. why is light given to a man whose way is *h.?*
6. 16. stream of brooks, wherein the snow is *h.*
28. 11. the thing that is *h.* bringeth he forth
21. seeing it is *h.* from the eyes of all living
29. † 10. the voice of the nobles was *h.*
38. 30. the waters are *h.* as with a stone
Ps. 17. 14. whose belly thou fillest with *h.* treasure
19. 6. nothing is *h.* from the heat thereof
Prov. 2. 4. and searchest for her as for *h.* treasures
Isa. 40. 27. why sayest, my way is *h.* from the Ld.
42. 22. and they are *h.* in prison-houses
Jer. 16. 17. nor their iniquity *h.* from mine eyes

Jer. 32. † 17. and there is nothing *h.* from thee
Hos. 13. 12. sin of Ephraim bound up, his sin is *h.*
Mat. 10. 26. there is nothing *h.* that shall not be known, *Mark* 4. 22. *Luke* 8. 17. | 12. 2.
Luke 9. 45. this saying was *h.* from them, 18. 34.
19. 42. but now they are *h.* from thine eyes
Eph. 3. 9. from the beginning hath been *h.* in God
Col. 1. 26. mystery which hath been *h.* from ages
2. 3. in whom are *h.* all the treasures of wisdom
3. 3. and your life is *h.* with Christ in God
Heb. 11. 23. by faith Moses was *h.* three months

Be HID.

Gen. 4. 14. hast driven me, from thy face shall I *be h.*
Lev. 4. 13. thing *be h.* from the assembly, 5. 3, 4.
Num. 5. 13. and it *be h.* from the eyes of her husb.
Job 5. 21. shall *be h.* from the scourge of the tongue
20. 26. darkness shall *be h.* in his secret places
Isa. 29. 14. the understanding of prudent men *be h.*
Hos. 13. 14. repentance shall *be h.* from mine eyes
Amos 9. 3. and though they *be h.* from my sight
Nah. 3. 11. thou shalt be drunken, thou shalt *be h.*
Zeph. 2. 3. it may be ye shall *be h.* in the day
2 *Cor.* 4. 3. if our gospel *be h.* it is hid to the lost

Not be HID.

Mat. 5. 14. a city that is set on an hill can*not be h.*
Mark 7. 24. entered an house, but he could *not be h.*
1 *Tim.* 5. 25. they that are otherwise can*not be h.*

Not HID.

Job 15. 18. told from their fathers, and *not h.* it
Psal. 32. 5. and mine iniquity have I *not h.*
38. 9. and my groaning is *not h.* from thee
40. 10. I have *not h.* thy righteousness within
69. 5. and my sins are *not h.* from thee
139. 15. my substance was *not h.* when I was made
Jer. 16. 17. my eyes upon their ways, they are *not h.* from my face, neither is iniq. hid from my eyes
Hos. 5. 3. I know Ephraim, Israel is *not h.* from me
Luke 8. 47. woman saw that she was *not h.* she came

HIDDEN.

Exod. 9. † 32. for the wheat and the rye were *h.*
Lev. 5. 2. if it be *h.* from him, he shall be unclean
Deut. 30. 11. it is not *h.* from thee, nor is it afar off
Job 3. 16. as an *h.* untimely birth, I had not been
15. 20. the number of years is *h.* to the oppressor
18. † 10. the snare is *h.* for him in the ground
24. 1. seeing times are not *h.* from thee
Psal. 51. 6. in *h.* part shalt make me know wisdom
Prov. 28. 12. when the wicked rise, a man is *h.*
Isa. 45. 3. I will give thee *h.* riches of secret places
48. 6. I have shewed thee new things, *h.* things
Jer. 33. † 3. and I will shew thee *h.* things
Obad. 6. how are his *h.* things sought up!
Zech. 11. † 16. shepherd not visit those who be *h.*
Acts 26. 26. none of these things are *h.* from him
1 *Cor.* 2. 7. even the *h.* wisdom which God ordained
4. 5. will bring to light the *h.* things of darkness
2 *Cor.* 4. 2. have renounced *h.* things of dishonesty
1 *Pet.* 3. 4. but let it be the *h.* man of the heart
Rev. 2. 17. I will give to eat of the *h.* manna

HIDDEN *ones.*

Psal. 83. 3. they consulted against thy *h. ones*

HIDE, *Substantive.*

Lev. 8. 17. his *h.* and flesh he burnt with fire, 9. 11.

HIDE

Signifies, [1] *To conceal, or keep any thing from the sight and knowledge of others.* 1 Sam. 20. 2. Why should my father hide this thing from me? *Gen.* 18. 17. Shall I hide from Abraham that thing which I do? *I will not, I cannot hide it; it is against the laws of friendship to conceal my secrets from him.* [2] *Not to confess one's sins, or to excuse and extenuate them.* Psal. 32. 5. I acknowledged my sin unto thee, and mine iniquity have I not hid. *And in* Prov. 28. 13. He that covereth his sins shall not prosper. *That does not confess them to God, and men too, when occasion requires it: that being convinced, or admonished of his sins, either justifieth, or denieth, or excuseth them.* [3] *To cover sin by free pardon and forgiveness.* Psal. 51. 9. Hide thy face from my sins; *look not upon them with an eye of revenge, but forget and forgive them.* [4] *To protect and keep safe.* Psal. 27. 5. In the time of trouble he shall hide me in his pavilion. *The saints are called* the hidden ones. *Psal.* 83. 3. They have consulted against thy hidden ones; *against thy people, whom thou hidest as a precious treasure, and protectest from the rage of their enemies.* [5] *To put oneself under the protection of the Almighty by faith, prayer, and repentance.* Prov. 22. 3. The prudent man foreseeth the evil, and hideth himself. *Thus the godly hide themselves under the wings of God's promises.*

The Psalmist *says,* I have not hid thy righteousness within my heart, *Psal.* 40. 10. *that is, I have not smothered, or shut it up there, but spread it abroad for thy glory, and the good of the world. Our first parents hid themselves from the presence of God, after they had eaten the forbidden fruit, being filled with shame and conscience of their guilt, and dread of judgment,* Gen. 3. 8. The Psalmist *prays,* That God would not hide himself from his supplication, *Psal.* 55. 1. *that is, that he would not turn away his face and ear, as one resolved not to hear nor help; but that he would be pleased to hear him, to look favourably upon him. It is spoken after the manner of men, who show their aversion and estrangement, by hiding their face, by turning from any one. In* Psal. 119. 19. David *prays to God,* not to hide his commandments from him; *to discover to him the sense and meaning of them.*

Gen. 18. 17. shall I *h.* from Abraham what I do?
47. 18. we will not *h.* it from my lord, how that
Exod. 2. 3. and when she could not longer *h.* him
Lev. 20. 4. any ways *h.* their eyes from the man
Deut. 22. 1. go astray, and *h.* thyself from them, 4.
3. with all lost things, thou mayest not *h.* thyself
Josh. 2. 16. and *h.* yourselves there three days
7. 19. tell what thou hast done, *h.* it not from me
Judg. 6. 11. to *h.* the wheat from the Midianites
1 *Sam.* 3. 17. *h.* it not from me, if thou *h.* 2 *Sam.* 14. 18.
19. 2. abide in a secret place, and *h.* thyself
20. 2. why should my father *h.* this thing from me?
5. let me go, that I may *h.* myself in the field
19. come to the place where thou didst *h.* thyself
1 *Kings* 17. 3. and *h.* thyself by the brook Cherith
22. 25. into an inner chamber to *h.* 2 *Chr.* 18. 24.
Job 13. 20. then will I not *h.* myself from thee
14. 13. O that thou wouldest *h.* me in the grave
20. 12. though he *h.* it under his tongue
33. 17. from his purpose, and *h.* pride from man
40. 13. *h.* them in the dust together, and bind
Psal. 17. 8. *h.* me under the shadow of thy wings
27. 5. time of trouble he shall *h.* me in his pavilion, in secret of his tabernacle shall he *h.* me
30. 7. thou didst *h.* thy face and I was troubled
31. 20. thou shalt *h.* them in secret of thy presence
55. 1. and *h.* not thyself from my supplication
64. 2. *h.* me from the secret counsel of the wicked
78. 4. we will not *h.* them from their children
89. 46. how long, O Lord, wilt thou *h.* thyself?
119. 19. *h.* not thy commandments from me
143. 9. deliver me, O Lord, I flee to thee to *h.* me
Prov. 2. 1. and *h.* my commandments with thee
Isa. 1. 15. I will *h.* my eyes from you, I will not hear
2. 10. and *h.* thee in the dust, for fear of the Lord
3. 9. they *h.* not their sin || 16. 3. *h.* the outcasts
26. 20. *h.* thyself as it were for a little moment
29. 15. woe to them that seek deep to *h.* their couns.
58. 7. that thou *h.* not thyself from thine own flesh
Jer. 13. 4. and *h.* it there in a hole of the rock
6. girdle which I commanded thee to *h.* there
36. 19. go, *h.* thee, thou, and Jeremiah, and let
38. 14. I will ask thee a thing, *h.* nothing from me
25. *h.* it not from us || 43. 9. *h.* them in the clay
Lam. 3. 56. *h.* not thine ear at my breathing, my cry
Ezek. 28. 3. there is no secret they can *h.* from thee
31. 8. cedars in garden of God could not *h.* him
39. 29. neither will I *h.* my face any more from th.
Jam. 5. 20. and shall *h.* a multitude of sins
Rev. 6. 16. *h.* us from the face of him that sitteth

See FACE.

HIDE *himself.*

1 *Sam.* 23. 19. doth not David *h. himself?* 26. 1.
Jer. 23. 24. can any *h. himself* in secret places?
49. 10. and he shall not be able to *h. himself*
John 12. 36. and Jesus did *h. himself* from them

HIDE *themselves.*

Deut. 7. 20. till they that *h. themselves* be destroyed
1 *Sam.* 13. 6. the people did *h. themselves* in caves
2 *Kings* 7. 12. Syrians gone to *h. themselves* in field
Job 24. 4. the poor of the earth *h. themselves*
34. 22. where workers of iniquity may *h. themselves*
Psal. 56. 6. they *h. themselves,* they mark my steps
Prov. 28. 28. when the wicked rise, men *h. themselves*
Dan. 10. 7. so that they fled to *h. themselves*
Amos 9. 3. tho' they *h. themselves* in top of Carmel

HIDEST.

Job 13. 24. why *h.* thy face? *Psal.* 44. 24. | 88. 14.
Psal. 10. 1. why *h.* thou thyself in times of trouble?
104. 29. thou *h.* thy face, they are troubled
Isa. 45. 15. verily thou art a God that *h.* thyself

HIDETH.

1 *Sam.* 23. 23. find the lurking places where he *h.*
Job 23. 9. he *h.* himself on the right hand, that
34. 29. when he *h.* his face, who can behold him?
42. 3. who is he that *h.* counsel without knowledge
Psal. 10. 11. he *h.* his face, he will never see it
139. 12. yea, the darkness *h.* not from thee
Prov. 10. 18. he that *h.* hatred with lying lips
19. 24. the slothful *h.* his hand in his bosom, 26. 15.
22. 3. a prudent man foreseeth and *h.* himself, 27. 12.
27. 16. whosoever *h.* her, *h.* the wind
28. 27. he that *h.* his eyes shall have many a curse
Isa. 8. 17. that *h.* his face from the house of Jacob
Mat. 13. 44. which when a man hath found, he *h.*

HIDING.

Job 31. 33. by *h.* mine iniquity in my bosom
Psal. 32. 7. thou art my *h.* place, 119. 114.
Isa. 28. 17. the waters shall overflow the *h.* place
32. 2. a man shall be as an *h.* place from the wind
Hab. 3. 4. and there was the *h.* of his power

HIGH.

High places, *in* Hebrew, Bamoth. *They are often spoken of in Scripture, and the prophets upbraid the* Israelites *for nothing with so much zeal as for worshipping upon the* high places. *The destroying of these* high places *is a commendation given but to few princes in the scripture; and many of them, though otherwise zealous for the observance of the law, had not the courage to ruin these eminences, and prevent the people from sacrificing upon them. While the temple was not built, there was nothing in* high places *expressly contrary to the law, provided God only was adored there, and that no incense or victims were offered to idols. Under the Judges they seem to have been tolerated; and* Samuel *offered sacrifices in several places besides the tabernacle, where the ark was not present. Even in* David's *time, they sacrificed to the Lord at* Shiloh, Jerusalem, *and* Gibeon. *But after that the temple was built, and a place prepared for the fixed settlement of the ark, it was no more allowed of to sacrifice out of* Jerusalem. Solomon, *in the beginning of his reign, went to* Gibeon *to sacrifice there,* 1 Kings 3. 4. *But from that time we see no lawful sacrifices offered out of the temple.*

Dr. Prideaux *thinks it probable that the* Proseuchæ, *which he says were open courts, built like those in which the people prayed at the tabernacle, and at the temple, and in one of which our Saviour is said to have continued all night in prayer to* God, Luke 6. 12. *were the same which in the Old Testament are called* high places. *And he says, that he is confirmed in this opinion, in that the* Proseuchæ *had groves in or about them, in the same manner as the* high places *had.* Connect. Part i. Book 6.

Gen. 29. 7. and he said, lo, it is yet *h.* day
Exod. 14. 8. Israel went out with *h.* hand, *Num.* 33. 3.
Num. 11. 31. brought quails as it were two cubits *h.*
Deut. 3. 5. the cities were fenced with *h.* walls
12. 2. served their gods on the *h.* mountains
26. 19. and to make thee *h.* above all nations
28. 43. the stranger shall get up above thee very *h.*
52. till thy *h.* and fenced walls come down
32. 27. lest they should say, our hand is *h.*
1 *Kings* 9. 8. at this house which is *h.* every one hiss
1 *Chr.* 17. 17. to the estate of a man of *h.* degree
2 *Chr.* 7. 21. this house is *h.* shall be an astonishment
Esth. 5. 14. a gallows be made of fifty cubits *h.* 7. 9.
Job 11. 8. it is as *h.* as heaven, what canst thou do?
21. 22. seeing he judgeth those that are *h.*
22. 12. and behold the stars, how *h.* they are
38. 15. and the *h.* arm shall be broken
41. 34. he beholdeth all *h.* things, he is a king
Psal. 18. 27. but thou wilt bring down *h.* looks
49. 2. give ear, both low and *h.* rich and poor
62. 9. and men of *h.* degree are a lie
71. 19. thy righteousness also, O God, is very *h.*
78. 69. he built his sanctuary like *h.* palaces
89. 13. strong is thy hand, *h.* is thy right hand
97. 9. thou, Lord, art *h.* above earth, 99. 2. | 113. 4.
101. 5. him that hath an *h.* look and proud heart
103. 11. for as the heaven is *h.* above the earth
131. 1. nor do I exercise in things too *h.* for me
138. 6. though the Lord be *h.* yet hath he respect
139. 6. such knowledge, it is *h.* cannot attain to it
149. 6. let the *h.* praises of God be in their mouth
150. 5. praise him on *h.* sounding cymbals
Prov. 18. 11. and as an *h.* wall in his own conceit
21. 4. an *h.* look and a proud heart, is sin
24. 7. wisdom is too *h.* for a fool, he openeth not
Eccl. 12. 5. when shall be afraid of that which is *h.*
Isa. 2. 13. day of the Lord on all cedars that are *h.*
14. and upon all the *h.* mountains and hills
6. 1. the Lord sitting on a throne *h.* and lifted up
10. 12. I will punish the glory of his *h.* looks
33. the *h.* ones of stature shall be hewn down
24. 21. punish the host of the *h.* ones that are on *h.*
25. 12. the fortress of *h.* fort shall he bring down
30. 13. as a breach swelling out in an *h.* wall
52. 13. behold my servant shall be very *h.*
57. 15. for thus saith the *h.* and lofty One
Jer. 17. 12. a glorious *h.* throne from the beginning
31. 21. set up way-marks, make thee *h.* heaps
49. 16. though thou make thy nest *h.* as the eagle
51. 58. her *h.* gates shall be burnt with fire
Ezek. 1. 18. as for their rings they were so *h.*
17. 24. that I have brought down the *h.* tree
21. 26. exalt the low, and abase him that is *h.*
31. 3. behold the Assyrian was of *h.* stature
34. 14. I will feed them on the *h.* mountains
Dan. 8. 3. the two horns were *h.* one was higher
Obad. 3. whose habitation is *h.* that saith in his heart
Zeph. 1. 16. a day of alarm against the *h.* towers
John 19. 31. for that sabbath day was an *h.* day
Acts 13. 17. with an *h.* arm brought he them out
Rom. 12. 16. mind not *h.* things || 13. 11. it is *h.* time
2 *Cor.* 10. 5. casting down every *h.* thing that exalts
Phil. 3. 14. for the prize of the *h.* calling of God
Rev. 21. 12. holy Jerusalem had a wall great and *h.*

See GATE, GOD, HILL, HILLS.

Most HIGH.

Num. 24. 16. and knew the knowledge of the *most H.*
Deut. 32. 8. when the *most H.* divided to the nations
2 *Sam.* 22. 14. when the *most H.* uttered his voice
Psal. 7. 17. I will praise the Lord, and sing praise to the name of the Lord *most H.* 9. 2. | 92. 1.
21. 7. thro' mercy of the *most H.* shall not be moved
46. 4. holy place of the tabernacle of the *most H.*
47. 2. the Lord *most H.* is terrible, a great king
50. 14. offer to God, and pay thy vows to the *most H.*
56. 2. that fight against me, O thou *most H.*
57. 2. I will cry unto God *most H.* unto God that
73. 11. and is there knowledge in the *most H.?*
77. 10. the years of the right hand of the *most H.*
78. 17. by provoking the *most H.* in wilderness, 56.
82. 6. all of you are the children of the *most H.*
83. 18. that thou art *most H.* over all the earth
91. 1. dwelleth in the secret place of the *most H.*
9. thou hast made the *most H.* thy habitation
92. 8. but thou, Lord, art *most H.* for evermore
107. 11. contemned the counsel of the *most H.*
Isa. 14. 14. I will ascend, I will be like the *most H.*
Lam. 3. 35. turn aside before the face of the *most H.*
38. out of mouth of *most H.* proceedeth not evil
Dan. 4. 17. that the *most H.* ruleth in the kingdom
24. and this is the decree of the *most H.*
25. that the *most H.* rules in kingdom of men, 32.
34. and I blessed the *most H.* and I praised him
7. 18. the saints of *most H.* shall take the kingdom
22. judgment was given to the saints of *most H.*
25. shall speak great words against the *most H.*
27. to the people of the saints of the *most H.*
Hos. 7. 16. they return, but not to the *most H.*
11. 7. though they called them to the *most H.*
Acts 7. 48. the *most H.* dwelleth not in temples made

See MOUNTAIN.

On HIGH.

Exod. 25. 20. cherubims stretch wings *on h.* 37. 9.
39. 31. they tied a lace of blue, to fasten it *on h.*
Deut. 28. 1. thy God will set thee *on h.* above
2 *Sam.* 22. 49. thou also hast lifted me up *on h.*
23. 1. and the man who was raised up *on h.* said
1 *Kings* 21. 9. set Naboth *on h.* among the people, 12.
2 *Kings* 19. 22. against whom hast thou lifted up thine eyes *on h.?* against Holy One of Israel? *Isa.* 37. 23.
1 *Chron.* 14. 2. for his kingdom was lifted up *on h.*
2 *Chr.* 20. 19. stood up to praise God of Israel *on h.*
Job 5. 11. to set up *on h.* those that be low
16. 19. witness is in heaven, and my record is *on h.*
31. 2. what inheritance of the Almighty from *on h.*
39. 18. what time she lifteth up herself *on h.*
27. the eagle mount up and make her nest *on h.?*
Psal. 7. 7. for their sakes therefore return *on h.*
68. 18. thou hast ascended *on h.* thou hast led
69. 29. let thy salvation, O God, set me up *on h.*
75. 5. lift not up your horn *on h.* speak not with
91. 14. I will set him *on h.* because he hath known
93. 4. the Lord *on h.* is mightier than the noise
107. 41. setteth he the poor *on h.* from affliction

Psal.113. 5. who is like to our God, who dwell. on h.?
Isa. 22. 16. that heweth him out a sepulchre on h.?
24. 18. for the windows from on h. are open
21 punish the host of high ones that are on h.
26. 5. he bringeth down them that dwell on h.
32. 15. till the Spirit be poured on us from on h.
33. 5. he dwelleth on h. ‖ 16. he shall dwell on h.
40. 26. lift up your eyes on h. and behold
58. 4. to make your voice to be heard on h.
Jer. 25. 30. the Lord shall roar from on h.
Ezek. 31. 4. the deep set him up on h. with her rivers
Hab. 2. 9. that he may set his nest on h. to be deliver.
3. 10. the deep lifted up his hands on h.
Luke 1. 78. the day-spring from on h. hath visited us
24. 49. till ye be endued with power from on h.
Eph. 4. 8. when he ascended up on h. he led captivity
Heb. 1. 3. on the right hand of the Majesty on h.
See Place, Places, Priest, Tower.

HIGH-way, or ways.

Lev. 26. 22. and your h.-ways shall be desolate
Num. 20. 17. by king's h.-way, 19. | 21. 22. Deut. 2. 27.
Judg. 5. 6. in days of Jael h.-ways were unoccupied
20. 31. they began to kill the people in the h.-ways
32. let us flee, and draw them unto the h.-ways
45. gleaned of them in the h.-ways 5000 men
1 Sam. 6. 12. the kine went along the h.-way lowing
2 Sam. 20. 12. Amasa wallowed in blood in h.-way
2 Kings 18. 17. h.-w. of fuller's field, Isa. 7. 3. | 36. 2.
Prov. 16. 17. h.-w. of upright to depart from evil
Isa. 11. 16. an h.-way for the remnant of his people
19. 23. shall be a h.-way out of Egypt to Assyria
33. 8. h.-ways lie waste, way-faring man ceaseth
35. 8. and an h.-way shall be there, and a way
40. 3. make in the desert a h.-way for our God
49. 11. and my h.-ways shall be exalted
62. 10. cast up, cast up the h.-way, gather stones
Jer. 31. 21. set thine heart toward the h.-way
Amos 5. 16. they shall say in all the h.-ways, alas
Mat. 22. 9. go therefore into the h.-ways, Luke 14. 23.
Mark 10. 46. Bartimeus sat by the h. way begging

HIGHER.

Num. 24. 7. and his king shall be h. than Agag
1 Sam. 9. 2. Saul was h. than any of the people
2 Kings 15. 35. Jotham built h. gate of the house
Neh. 4. 13. on the h. places, I even set the people
Job 35. 5. behold the clouds, which are h. than thou
Psal. 61. 2. lead me to the rock that is h. than I
89. 27. I will make him h. than kings of the earth
Eccl. 5. 8. he regardeth, and there be h. than they
Isa. 55. 9. as the heavens are h. than earth, so my ways h. than your ways, thoughts than yours
Jer. 36. 10. then read Baruch in the h. court
Ezek. 9. 2. six men came from the way of the h. gate
42. 5. for the galleries were h. than these
43. 13. and this shall be the h. place of the altar
Dan. 8. 3. one horn h. than the other, h. came last
Luke 14. 10. he may say to thee, friend, go up h.
Rom. 13. 1. let every soul be subject to the h. powers
Heb. 7. 26. an High Priest made h. than the heavens

HIGHEST.

2 Chr. 32. † 33. buried Hezekiah in h. of sepulchres
Psal. 18. 13. Lord thundered, the H. gave his voice
87. 5. and the H. himself shall establish her
Prov. 8. 26. nor the h. part of the dust of the world
9. 3. she crieth upon the h. places of the city
Eccl. 5. 8. he that is higher than the h. regardeth
Ezek. 17. 3. and took the h. branch of the cedar
22. I will take of the h. branch of the cedar
41. 7. so increased from lowest chamber to the h.
Mat. 21. 9. saying, Hosanna in the h. Mark 11. 10.
Luke 1. 32. and shall be called the Son of the H.
35. the power of the H. shall overshadow thee
76. thou shalt be called the prophet of the H.
2. 14. glory to God in the h. on earth peace, 19. 38.
6. 35. and ye shall be the children of the H.
14. 8. when bidden sit not down in the h. room
20. 46. and love the h. seats in the synagogues

HIGHLY.

Luke 1. 28. the angel said, thou art h. favoured
16. 15. that which is h. esteemed amongst men
Acts 12. 20. Herod was h. displeased with Tyre
Rom. 12. 3. not to think of himself more h. than
Phil. 2. 9. wherefore God also hath h. exalted him
1 Thess. 5. 13. and to esteem them very h. in love

HIGH-MINDED.

Rom. 11. 20. be not h. but fear, 1 Tim. 6. 17.
2 Tim. 3. 4. traitors, heady, h. lovers of pleasure

HIGHNESS.

Job 31. 23. by reason of his h. I could not endure
Isa. 13. 3. even them that rejoice in my h.

HILL.

Exod. 24. 4. Moses built an altar under the h.
Num. 14. 45. the Canaanites which dwelt in that h.
Deut. 1. 41. ye were ready to go up into the h. 43.
Josh. 5. 3. circumcised Israel at the h. of fore-skins
17. 16. they said, the h. is not enough for us
24. 30. Joshua buried on the h. Gaash, Judg. 2. 9.
33. Eleazar was buried in a h. that pertained
Judg. 7. 1. the Midianites were by the h. of Moreh
1 Sam. 7. 1. ark into the house of Abinadab in the h.
9. 11. as Saul and his servants went up the h.
10. 5. after that thou shalt come to h. of God, 10.
23. 19. David hid in the h. of Hachilah, 26. 1.
25. 20. Abigail came down by the covert of the h.
2 Sam. 2. 24. when they were come to h. of Ammah
13. 34. much people came by the h. behind him
16. 13. Shimei went along on the h. side, cursing
21. 9. they hanged them in the h. before the Lord
1 Kings 11. 7. Solomon built in the h. for Chemosh
16. 24. Omri bought the h. Samaria, built on h.
2 Kings 4. 27. she came to the man of God to the h.
Ps. 24. 3. who shall ascend into the h. of the Lord
42. 6. I will remember thee from the h. Mizar
68. 15. the h. of God is as the h. of Bashan
16. this is the h. which God desireth to dwell in
Cant. 4. 6. I will get me to the h. of frankincense
Isa. 5. 1. hath a vineyard in a very fruitful h.
10. 32. shall shake his hand against h. of Jerusalem
30. 17. till ye be left as an ensign on an h.
31. 4. Lord of hosts shall fight for the h. thereof
40. 4. every mountain and h. shall be made low
Jer 16. 16. they shall hunt them from every h.

Jer. 31. 39. the measuring line upon the h. Gareb
49. 16. thou that holdest the height of the h.
50. 6. they have gone from mountain to h.
Ezek. 34. 26. will make places about my h. a blessing
Mat. 5. 14. a city that is set on an h. cannot be hid
Luke 3. 5. and every h. shall be brought low
4. 29. and they led him to the brow of the h.
9. 37. when they were come down from the h.
Acts 17. 22. then Paul stood in the midst of Mar's h.

HILL-country.

Josh. 13. 6. inhabitants of h.-country will I drive out
21. 11. gave to the sons of Aaron, Arba in h.-coun.
Luke 1. 39. and Mary went into the h. country
65. were noised thro' all the h.-country of Judea

High HILL, S.

Gen. 7. 19. all high h. under heaven were covered
1 Kings 14. 23. groves on every high h. 2 Kings 17. 10.
Psal. 68. 15. is a high h. as the hill of Bashan
16. why leap ye, ye high. h.? this is hill G. desires
104. 18. high h. are a refuge for the wild goats
Isa. 30. 25. and on every high h. rivers of waters
Jer. 2. 20. when on every high h. thou wanderest, 23.
17. 2. whilst children remember groves on high h.
Ezek. 6. 13. slain men among idols on every high h.
20. 28. then they saw every high h. and thick trees
34. 6. my sheep wandered on every high h.

Holy HILL.

Psal. 2. 6. I have set my king on my holy h. of Zion
3. 4. I cried to Lord, he heard me out of his holy h.
15. 1. Lord, who shall dwell in thy holy h.?
43. 3. let them lead me, bring me to thy holy h.
99. 9. worship at his holy h. the Lord is holy

HILL, with top.

Exod. 17. 9. to-morrow I will stand on top of the h.
10. Moses, Aaron, and Hur, went to top of the h.
Num. 14. 44. they presumed to go up to the h. top
Judg. 16. 3. Samson carried them to the top of an h.
1 Sam. 26. 13. David stood on the top of an h.
2 Sam. 2. 25. and Abner stood on the top of an h.
16. 1. David was a little past the top of the h.
2 Kings 1. 9. Elijah sat on the top of an h.

HILLS.

Gen. 49. 26. to the utmost bound of the everlasting h.
Num. 23. 9. and from the h. I behold him
Deut. 8. 7. that spring out of the valleys and h.
9. out of whose h. thou mayest dig brass
11. 11. it is a land of h. and valleys, and drinketh
33. 15. for the precious things of the lasting h.
Josh. 10. 40. Joshua smote all the country of the h.
11. 16. so Joshua took all that land, the h.
1 Kings 20. 23. their gods are the gods of the h. 28.
22. 17. I saw all Israel scattered on the h.
2 Kings 16. 4. burnt incense on the h. 2 Chron. 28. 4.
Job 15. 7. or wast thou made before the h.?
Psal. 18. 7. the foundations also of the h. moved
50. 10. the cattle on a thousand h. are mine
65. 12. the little h. rejoice on every side
72. 3. and the little h. by righteousness
80. 10. the h. were covered with the shadow of it
95. 4. the strength of the h. is his also
97. 5. the h. melted like wax at the presence of L.
98. 8. let the h. be joyful together
104. 10. he sendeth springs, which run among the h.
13. he watereth the h. from his chambers
32. he toucheth the h. and they smoke
114. 4. and the little h. skipped like lambs, 6.
121. 1. I will lift up mine eyes to the h. whence
148. 9. mountains and all h. praise the Lord
Prov. 8. 25. before the h. was I brought forth
Cant. 2. 8. he cometh skipping upon the h.
Isa. 2. 2. and shall be exalted above the h.
14. the day of the Lord shall be on all the h.
5. 25. the h. did tremble, their carcases were torn
7. 25. on all h. shall not come the fear of briers
40. 12. who hath weighed the h. in a balance?
41. 15. and thou shalt make the h. as chaff
42. 15. I will make waste mountains and h.
54. 10. mountains shall depart, the h. be removed
55. 12. the h. shall break forth into singing
65. 7. which have blasphemed me upon the h.
Jer. 3. 23. in vain is salvation hoped for from the h.
4. 24. I beheld, and lo, the h. moved lightly
13. 27. I have seen thy abominations on the h.
Ezek. 6. 3. thus saith the Lord to the h. 36. 4.
35. 8. with his slain men in thy h. and valleys
36. 6. and say to the h. to the rivers, and valleys
Hos. 4. 13. they burn incense on the h. under oaks
10. 8. and they shall say to the h. fall on us
Joel 3. 18. and the h. shall flow with milk
Amos 9. 13. drop wine, and all the h. shall melt
Mic. 4. 1. and it shall be exalted above the h.
6. 1. arise, and let the h. hear thy voice
Nah. 1. 5. the h. melt, and the earth is burnt
Hab. 3. 6. the perpetual h. did bow, his ways
Zeph. 1. 10. and a great crashing from the h.
Luke 23. 30. they shall begin to say to the h. cover us

HIM.

Gen. 41. 13. me he restored, and h. he hanged
Exod. 32. 33. whoso. hath sinned, h. I will blot out
Num. 14. 24. Caleb, h. will I bring into the land
16. 5. to come near, even h. whom he hath chosen
Deut. 10. 20. h. shalt thou serve, and to h. cleave
18. 5. the Lord hath chosen h. and his sons for ever
1 Sam. 10. 24. see ye h. whom the Ld. hath chosen
1 Kings 14. 11. h. that dieth in city, 16. 4. | 21. 24.
21. 21. h. that pisseth against the wall, 2 Kings 9. 8.
2 Kings 11. 2. and they hid h. even h. and his nurse
15. and h. that followed her, kill with the sword
17. 36. h. shall ye fear, h. shall ye worship
Neh. 13. 26. h. did outlandish women cause to sin
Esth. 8. 7. h. they have hanged on the gallows
Job 15. 31. let not h. that is deceived trust in vanity
29. 12. I delivered h. that had none to help h.
36. 22. behold, who teacheth like h.?
40. 9. or canst thou thunder with a voice like h.?
42. 8. Job shall pray for you, for h. will I accept
Psal. 4. 3. the Lord hath set apart h. that is godly
25. 12. h. shall he teach in the way he shall choose
45. 11. worship h. ‖ 72. 12. h. who hath no helper
101. 5. h. will I cut off, h. that hath an high look
Prov. 6. 19. h. that soweth discord among brethren
24. 24. h. shall the people curse, nations shall abhor

Eccl. 10. 1. a little folly h. that is in reputation
Jer. 48. 35. h. that offereth in the high places
Ezek. 35. 7. and cut off from it h. that passeth out
Amos 1. 5. and h. that holdeth the sceptre
Mal. 2. 12. will cut off h. that offereth an offering
Mat. 4. 10. h. only shalt thou serve, Luke 4. 8.
10. 32. whosoever shall confess me before men, h. will I confess also bef. my Father, Luke 12. 8.
33. h. will I deny before my Father in heaven
40. receiveth h. that sent me, Mark 9. 37.
17. 5. this is my Son, hear ye h. Acts 3. 22. | 7. 37.
18. 15. go tell h. between thee and h. alone
24. 18. nor let h. in the field return, Mark 13. 16.
27. 32. h. they compelled to bear his cross
Mark 13. 14. let h. that readeth understand
15. let h. that is on the house-top not go down
Luke 23. 25. h. that for sedition and murder was
24. 24. as the women had said, but h. they saw not
John 5. 38. whom he hath sent, h. ye believe not
43. come in his own name, h. ye will receive
6. 27. for h. hath God the Father sealed
37. h. that cometh unto me, I will in no wise cast out
9. 31. h. he heareth ‖ 12. 26. h. will my Father hon.
13. 32. God shall also glorify h. in himself
Acts 2. 23. h. being delivered ‖ 5. 31. h. God exalted
10. 40. h. God raised up the third day, and shewed
16. 3. h. would Paul have to go forth with h.
17. 23. whom ye worship h. declare I unto you
Rom. 14. 1. h. that is weak in the faith receive
3. let not h. that eateth, despise h. that eateth not
1 Cor. 3. 17. any defile temple, h. shall God destroy
10. 12. let h. that thinketh he standeth take heed
2 Cor. 5. 21. for he hath made h. to be sin for us
Gal. 6. 6. let h. that is taught in the word
Eph. 4. 28. let h. that stole steal no more
Phil. 2. 23. h. therefore I hope to send presently
29. receive h. therefore in the Ld. with gladness
2 Thess. 2. 9. h. whose coming is after the working
Heb. 2. 14. might destroy h. that had power of death
11. 12. sprang there of one and h. as good as dead

Above HIM.

Dan. 11. 5. shall be strong above h. and have domin.

About HIM.

1 Sam. 22. 6. his servants were standing about h. 7.
17. king said to the footmen that stood about h.
1 Kings 5. 3. not build for wars which were about h.
2 Chron. 18. 31. they compassed about h. to fight
Job 1. 10. hast not thou made an hedge about h.
Psal. 76. 11. let all round about h. bring presents
89. 7. and to be had in reverence of all about h.
Jer. 48. 17. all ye that are about h. bemoan him
39. Moab shall be a dismaying to all about h.
50. 32. and it shall devour all round about h.
Lam. 1. 17. his adversaries shall be round about h.
Ezek. 12. 14. scatter all that are about h. to help him
32. 22. his graves are round about h. 25. 26.
Mat. 8. 18. when Jesus saw great multitudes about h.
Mark 3. 32. the multitude sat about h. and said
John 10. 24. then came the Jews round about h.
Rev. 4. 8. four beasts had each six wings about h.

After HIM.

Gen. 17. 19. with him and with his seed after h.
18. 19. he will command his household after h.
Exod. 28. 43. it shall be a statute for his seed after h.
29. 29. the holy garments shall be his son's after h.
Lev. 20. 5. will cut off all that go a whoring after h.
Num. 32. 15. for if ye turn away from after h.
Josh. 20. 5. if the avenger of blood pursue after h.
Judg. 1. 6. Adoni-bezek fled, they pursued after h.
3. 28. they went after h. and took the fords
6. 34. and Abiezer was gathered after h. 35.
1 Sam. 14. 13. and his armour-bearer after h.
17. 35. I went out after h. and smote him
26. 3. and David saw that Saul came after h.
2 Sam. 1. 6. the horsemen followed hard after h.
15. 17. king went forth and all the people after h.
23. 10. the people returned after h. only to spoil
1 Kings 1. 20. on the throne of my lord after h. 27
15. 4. to set up his son after h. and establish Jer.
2 Kings 5. 20. I will run after h. and take somewha
9. 27. Jehu followed after h. and said, smite
14. 19. sent after h. to Lachish, 2 Chron. 25. 27.
18. 5. so that after h. was none like him, 23. 25.
1 Chron. 27. 7. Joab, and Zebadiah his son after h.
2 Chron. 26. 17. Azariah the priest went in after h.
Neh. 3. 16. after h. repaired. So to the 31st verse
Job 18. 20. they that come after h. shall be astonied
21. 21. what pleasure hath he in his house after h.
33. and every man shall draw after h.
41. 32. he maketh a path to shine after h.
Psal. 49. 17. his glory shall not descend after h.
Prov. 20. 7. his children are blessed after h.
Eccl. 3. 22. bring to see what shall be after h. 6. 12
7. 14. that man should find nothing after h.
10. 14. what shall be after h. who can tell him?
Ezek. 9. 5. go ye after h. thro' the city, and smite
Luke 19. 14. and sent a message after h. saying
John 12. 19. behold, the world is gone after h.
Acts 5. 37. and drew away much people after h.
7. 5. he would give it to him, and to his seed after h.
17. 27. seek Lord, if haply they might feel after h.
19. 4. believe on him which should come after h.

Against HIM.

Gen. 16. 12. and every man's hand against h.
32. 25. he saw that he prevailed not against h.
37. 18. they conspired against h. 1 Kings 15. 27. | 16. 9. 2 Kings 14. 19. | 15. 10, 25. | 21. 23.
Exod. 16. 8. Lord heareth your murmurings which ye murmur against h. Num. 14. 36. | 16. 11.
Num. 22. 22. stood for an adversary against h.
Deut. 19. 11. but if any man rise up against h.
16. if a false witness rise to testify against h.
33. 11. smite through the loins that rise against h.
Josh. 5. 13. there stood a man over against h.
Judg. 14. 5. behold a young lion roared against h.
15. 14. the Philistines shouted against h.
20. 23. and the Lord said, go up against h.
2 Sam. 10. 9. the front of the battle was against h.
1 Kings 13. 4. hand he put forth against h. dried up
21. 10. sons of Belial to bear witness against h.
2 Kings 23. 29. and king Josiah went up against h.
24. 2. Lord sent against h. bands of Chaldees

2 Chron. 32. 17. to rail and to speak against h.
Esth. 6. 13. thou shalt not prevail against h.
Job 2. 3. although thou movedst me against h.
8. 4. if thy children have sinned against h.
9. 4. who hardened himself ag. h. and prospered?
14. 20. thou prevailest for ever against h.
33. 13. why dost thou strive against h.?
35. 6. if thou sinnest, what doest thou against h.?
Psal. 78. 17. and they sinned yet more against h.
Prov. 17. 11. a cruel messenger shall be sent agst. h.
Eccl. 4. 12. and if one prevail against h. two withst.
Isa. 10. 15. shall the axe boast agst. h. that heweth?
or the saw magnify itself ag. h. that shaketh it?
31. 4. when shepherds are called forth against h.
45. 24. all that are incensed against h. be ashamed
59. 19. Spirit of L. shall lift up a standard agst. h.
Jer. 20. 10. be enticed and we shall prevail agst. h.
31. 20. for since I spake agst. h. I remember him
51. 3. against h. that bendeth, let the archer bend
Ezek. 29. 2. and prophesy agst. h. and Egypt, 38. 2.
38. 21. and I will call for a sword against 38.
22. I will plead ag. h. with pestilence and blood
Dan. 9. 11. because we have sinned against h.
11. 16. but he that cometh agst. h. shall do accord.
Mic. 3. 5. they even prepare war against h.
7. 9. I will bear, because I have sinned against h.
Hab. 2. 6. shall not these take up a parable ag. h.?
Mat. 12. 14. and held a counsel against h. Mark 3. 6.
Luke 14. 31. to meet him that cometh against h.
Acts 22. 24. wherefore they cried so against h.
23. 30. to say before thee what they had against h.
25. 3. the high-priest desired favour against h.
15. Jews desiring to have judgment against h:
Jude 9. durst not bring against h. a railing accusat.
15. which ungodly sinners have spoken against h.
Rev. 19. 19. make war against h. that sat on the horse

At HIM.

Gen. 49. 23. the archers shot at h. and hated him
1 Sam. 20. 33. Saul cast a javelin at h. to smite him
2 Sam. 16. 13. Shimei threw stones at h. and cast dust
Job 27. 23. men shall clap their hands at h.
Psal. 12. 5. in safety from him that puffeth at h.
37. 13. the Lord shall laugh at h. for he seeth
52. 6. the righteous also shall see and laugh at h.
64. 4. suddenly do they shoot at h. and fear not
Isa. 52. 15. the kings shall shut their mouths at h.
Dan. 11. 40. the king of the south shall push at h.
Nah. 1. 5. the mountains quake at h. and hills melt
Mark 6. 3. and they were offended at h.
12. 4. at h. they cast stones, and wound. him in head
17. and they marvelled at h.
Luke 7. 9. he marvelled at h. and turned about
8. 19. they could not come at h. for the press
John 6. 41. the Jews then murmured at h.
8. 59. then took they up stones to cast at h.

Before HIM.

Gen. 24. 33. there was set meat before h. to eat
32. 3. Jacob sent messengers before h. to Esau
21. so went the present over before h.
41. 43. and they cried before h. bow the knee
43. 33. they sat before h. || 44. 14. fell before h.
Exod. 34. 6. and the Lord passed by before h.
Num. 11. 20. and have wept before h. saying
Josh. 6. 5. ascend up every man straight before h.
22. 27. might do the service of the Lord before h.
Judg. 9. 40. Abimelech chased, he fled before h.
14. 16. Samson's wife wept before h. and said, 17.
1 Sam. 16. 6. surely the Lord's anointed is before h.
21. and David came to Saul and stood before h.
17. 7. and one bearing a shield went before h.
2 Sam. 10. 13. they fled before h. 1 Chron. 19. 14.
11. 13. Uriah did eat and drink before h.
12. 20. when he required, they set bread before h.
15. 1. and fifty men to run before h. 1 Kings 1. 5.
22. 24. I was also upright before h. Psal. 18. 23.
1 Kings 3. 16. then came two harlots, stood before h.
16. 25. Omri did worse than all before h. 30, 33.
21. 10. and set two men, sons of Belial, before h.
2 Kings 2. 15. they bowed to the ground before h.
4. 12. the Shunammite when called, stood before h.
38. the sons of the prophets were sitting before h.
6. 32. and the king sent a man from before h.
10. 4. kings stood not before h. how shall we stand
17. 2. not as kings of Israel that were before h.
18. 5. nor any that were before h. were like him
21. 11. that the Amorites did, which were before h.
23. 25. like to Josiah there was no king before h.
25. 29. did eat bread continually before h. Jer. 52. 33.
1 Chr. 16. 29. bring an offering, and come before h.
30. fear before h. Psal. 96. 9. Eccl. 3. 14. | 8. 12.
29. 25. not any before h. like Solomon for majesty
2 Chron. 2. 4. to burn before h. sweet incense, 6.
14. 5. and the kingdom was quiet before h.
29. 11. the Lord hath chosen you to stand before h.
Neh. 2. 1. it came to pass that wine was before h.
Esth. 4. 8. to make request before h. for her people
6. 9. proclaim before h. 11. || 13. fall before h.
Job 13. 15. but I will maintain my ways before h.
16. an hypocrite shall not come before h.
21. 33. as there are innumerable before h.
23. 4. I would order my cause before h. and fill
26. 6. hell is naked before h. and destruction
35. 14. judgment is before h. therefore trust in him
41. 22. and sorrow is turned into joy before h.
Psal. 18. 6. my cry came before h. even to his ears
12. at the brightness that was before h.
22. 29. all that go to the dust shall bow before h.
50. 3. God shall come, a fire shall devour before h.
62. 8. ye people, pour out your heart before h.
68. 1. let them that hate him flee before h.
4. sing unto God, sing and rejoice before h.
72. 9. they that dwell in wildern. shall bow before h.
11. kings shall fall before h. nations shall serve h.
85. 13. righteousness shall go before h. and set us
96. 6. honour and majesty are before h. strength
9. worship the Lord, fear before h. all the earth
97. 3. a fire goeth before h. and burneth enemies
106. 23. had not Moses his chosen stood before h.
142. 2. I showed before h. my trouble
Prov. 8. 30. his delight, rejoicing always before h.
17. 24. wisdom is before h. that hath understanding
Isa. 40. 10. reward with him, work before h. 62. 11.
Isa. 40. 17. all nations before h. are as nothing
41. 2. gave nations before h. and made him rule
45. 1. I have holden to subdue nations before h.
Jer. 42. 9. to present your supplications before h.
Ezek. 28. 9. wilt thou say before h. that slayeth thee
30. 24. shall groan before h. with groanings
Dan. 7. 10. ten thousand times 10,000 stood before h.
8. 4. so that no beasts might stand before h.
7. there was no power in the ram to stand before h.
11. 16. to his own will, none shall stand before h.
22. they shall be overflown from before h.
Mic. 6. 6. shall I come before h. with burnt offerings
Hab. 2. 20. let all the earth keep silence before h.
3. 5. before h. went the pestilence and burning coals
Mal. 3. 16. a book of remembrance written before h.
Mat. 25. 32. before h. be gathered all nations
27. 29. they bowed the knee before h. and mocked
Mark 3. 11. fell down before h. and cried, 5. 33.
Luke 1. 17. he shall go before h. in the spirit of Elias
75. in holiness and righteousness before h.
5. 18. they sought means to lay him before h.
11. 6. a friend is come, I have nothing to set bef. h.
John 3. 28. I said, that I am sent before h.
Acts 23. 33. they presented Paul also before h.
Rom. 4. 17. before h. whom he believed, even God
Eph. 1. 4. holy and without blame before h. in love
Heb. 12. 2. who for the joy that was set before h.
1 John 2. 28. not be ashamed before h. at his coming
3. 19. and shall assure our hearts before h.
Rev. 13. 12. all the power of the first beast before h.
19. 20. false prophet that wrought miracles before h.

Behind HIM.

Gen. 18. 10. Sarah heard in the tent-door behind h.
2 Sam. 2. 23. that the spear came out behind h.
2 Kings 6. 32. is not sound of his master's feet beh. h.?
Joel 2. 14. and repent, and leave a blessing behind h.
Zech. 1. 8. beh. h. were red horses speckled and white
Mat. 9. 20. a woman diseased with an issue of blood
came beh. h. and touched the hem, Luke 8. 44.
Mark 12. 19. brother die, and leave his wife beh. h.
Luke 7. 38. stood at his feet behind h. weeping

Beside HIM.

Deut. 4. 35. the Lord is God, there is none beside h.
2 Sam. 15. 18. his servants passed on beside h.
Neh. 8. 4. beside h. stood Mattithiah and Shema

Between HIM.

Lev. 26. 46. laws the L. made between h. and Isrl.
Mal. 3. 18. shall discern between h. that serveth God

Beyond HIM.

1 Sam. 20. 36. Jonathan shot an arrow beyond h.

By HIM.

Deut. 2. 30. but Sihon would not let us pass by h.
33. 12. the beloved of L. shall dwell in safety by h.
Judg. 3. 15. by h. children of Israel sent a present
19. all that stood by h. went out from him
1 Sam. 2. 3. and by h. actions are weighed
20. 7. then be sure that evil is determined by h.
1 Kings 22. 19. the host of heaven standing by h.
2 Kings 3. 11. we may inquire of the L. by h. 8. 8.
5. 1. by h. the Lord had given deliverance to Syria
1 Chr. 11. 11. three hundred slain by h. at one time
Neh. 2. 6. king said to me, the queen also sitting by h.
4. 3. now Tobia the Ammonite was by h.
Psal. 63. 11. every one that sweareth by h. glory
Isa. 27. 7. the slaughter of them that are slain by h.
Dan. 8. 11. by h. daily sacrifice was taken away
12. 7. sware by h. that liveth for ever, Rev. 10. 6.
Nah. 1. 6. and the rocks are thrown down by h.
Mat. 23. 21. sweareth by h. who dwelleth therein
22. sweareth by h. that sitteth thereon
Luke 3. 19. Herod being reproved by h. shut up John
9. 7. Herod heard of all that was done by h.
13. 17. the glorious things that were done by h.
John 1. 3. all things were made by h. without him
10. the world was made by h. and knew him not
Acts 2. 22. by miracles and wonders God did by h.
3. 16. the faith which is by h. hath given, 4. 10.
13. 39. by h. all that believe justif. from all things
23. 11. the night following the Lord stood by h.
1 Cor. 1. 5. in every thing ye are enriched by h.
8. 6. by whom are all things, and we by h.
Eph. 4. 21. heard him, and have been taught by h.
Col. 1. 16. for by h. were all things created in heaven
17. he is before all things, by h. all things consist
20. by h. to reconcile all things to himself by h.
3. 17. giving thanks to God the Father by h.
2 Tim. 2. 26. who are taken captive by h. at his will
Heb. 7. 25. to save them that come to God by h.
13. 15. by h. let us offer the sacrifice of praise
1 Pet. 1. 21. who by h. do believe in G. that raised
2. 14. are sent by h. for punishment of evil-doers

Concerning HIM.

Judg. 21. 5. made an oath conc. h. that came not up
2 Kings 19. 21. word L. hath spoken con. h. Is. 37. 22.
Esth. 3. 2. the king had so commanded concerning h.
Dan. 5. 29. and made a proclamation concerning h.
John 7. 12. murmuring among people concern. h. 32.
9. 18. the Jews did not believe concerning h.
Acts 2. 25. for David speaketh concerning h.
23. 15. ye would inquire something concerning h.
1 Cor. 5. 3. concerning h. that hath so done this
See Fear.

For HIM.

Gen. 2. 18. I will make him an help meet for h. 20.
37. 35. thus Joseph's father wept for h.
43. 9. I will be surety for h. of my hand require
Exod. 22. 2. no blood shed f. h. || 3. blood shed for h.
Lev. 1. 4. and it shall be accepted for h. to make
atonement for h. 4. 26, 31. | 5. 13. | 14. 18, 19,
20, 31. | 15. 15. | 19. 22. Num. 5. 8. | 6. 11. |
15. 28.
Num. 27. 21. the priest, who shall ask counsel for h.
35. 32. ye shall take no satisfaction for h. that is fled
Deut. 19. 11. lie in wait for h. and rise up against him
33. 7. let his hands be sufficient for h. be help to him
Judg. 6. 31. he that will plead for h. let him die
1 Sam. 2. 25. if a man sin, who shall entreat for h.?
15. 2. how he laid wait for h. in the way, when
17. 31. they rehearsed them, and Saul sent for h.
22. 10. and he inquired of the Lord for h. 15.
27. 4. and he sought no more again for h.
2 Sam. 9. 10. thy servants shall till the land for h.
1 Kings 2. 22. ask for h. the kingdom, even for h.
13. 23. saddled for h. the ass, to wit, for the proph.
14. 13. all Israel shall mourn for h. and bury him
2 Chr. 16. 14. they made very great burning for h.
21. 19. and his people made no burning for h.
Esth. 5. 4. to the banquet that I have prepared for h.
9. when Haman saw that he moved not for h.
6. 3. the servants said, there is nothing done for h.
4. to hang on the gallows he had prepared for h.
Job 13. 7. and will you talk deceitfully for h.?
30. 25. did not I weep for h. that was in trouble?
Psal. 3. 2. who say, there is no help for h. in God
37. 7. rest in the Lord, and wait patiently for h.
49. 7. nor give to God a ransom for h.
72. 15. prayer also shall be made for h. continually
Prov. 9. 4. as for h. that wanteth understanding, 16.
28. 8. he shall gather it for h. that will pity the poor
Cant. 5. 4. and my bowels were moved for h.
Isa. 8. 17. I will wait upon the Lord and look for h.
25. 9. we have waited for h. he will save us, 9.
29. 21. that lay a snare for h. that reproveth in gate
30. 18. blessed are all they that wait for h.
40. 10. Lord will come, his arm shall rule for h.
64. 4. what he hath prepared for h. that waiteth for h.
Jer. 22. 18. they shall not lament for h. 18.
31. 20. therefore my bowels are troubled for h.
Lam. 3. 25. Lord is good to them that wait for h.
Ezek. 17. 17. nor shall Pharaoh make for h. in war
31. 15. I covered the deep for h. I caused Lebanon
to mourn for h. trees of the field fainted for h.
45. 20. so shalt thou do for h. that is simple
Dan. 11. 17. not on his side, nor shall she be for h.
Amos 3. 5. fall in a snare where no gin is for h.
Zeph. 1. 6. have not sought Ld. nor inquired for h.
Zech. 12. 10. shall mourn for h. be in bitterness for h.
Mat. 12. 4. which was not lawful for h. to eat
18. 6. it were better for h. that a millstone were
hanged about his neck, Mark 9. 42. Luke 17. 2.
24. 50. when he looketh not for h. Luke 12. 46.
Mark 5. 20. how great things Jesus had done for h.
Luke 2. 27. brought in the child Jesus, to do for h.
after the custom of the law
8. 40. for they were all waiting for h.
9. 52. and they went to make ready for h.
Acts 12. 5. but prayer was made unto God for h.
1 Cor. 16. 11. for I look for h. with the brethren
Col. 1. 16. all things were created by him and for h.
Heb. 9. 28. to them that look for h. shall he appear

From HIM.

Gen. 35. 13. and God went up from h. in the place
Lev. 5. 3. it be hid from h. when he knoweth of it
Judg. 3. 19. all that stood by him, went out from h.
16. 19. to shave locks, his strength went from h.
1 Sam. 3. 18. and Samuel hid nothing from h.
2 Sam. 11. 15. retire from h. || 13. 9. went out fr. h.
1 Kings 20. 33. whether any thing would come fr. h.
2 Kings 25. 5. all his army were scattered from h.
2 Chron. 12. 12. the wrath of the L. turned from h.
Job 14. 6. turn from h. that he may rest, till he shall
Psal. 22. 24. nor hath he hid his face from h.
35. 10. the poor from h. that spoileth him
55. 12. then I would have hid myself from h.
62. 1. waiteth on God, fr. h. cometh my salvation
Isa. 5. 23. the righteousness of the righteous fr. h.
53. 3. and we hid as it were our faces from h.
Jer. 3. 1. she go from h. and become another man's
Dan. 5. 24. then was part of the hand sent from h.
Amos 5. 11. ye take from h. burdens of wheat
Jonah 3. 6. he arose, and laid his robe from h.
Mat. 5. 42. from h. that would borrow of thee
13. 12. fr. h. shall be taken, Mark 4. 25. Luke 8. 18.
25. 29. fr. h. hath not shall be taken, Luke 19. 26.
Mark 14. 35. prayed, that the hour might pass fr. h.
Luke 11. 22. he taketh from h. all his armour
John 7. 29. I am fr. h. || 10. 5. but will flee from h.
Gal. 1. 6. are so soon removed fr. h. that called you
Heb. 12. 25. if we turn away from h. that speaketh
1 John 3. 17. shutteth up bowels of compassion fr. h.
4. 21. and this commandment have we from h.
Rev. 1. 4. and peace from h. which is, which was
See Depart, Departed.

In HIM.

Gen. 18. 18. all nations of earth shall be blessed in h.
Exod. 23. 21. beware of him, for my name is in h.
Judg. 9. 26. men of Shechem put confidence in h.
1 Sam. 28. 20. and there was no strength in h.
29. 3. I have found no fault in h. John 19. 4, 6.
2 Sam. 22. 3. in h. will I trust, Psal. 91. 2.
31. he is a buckler to all that trust in h. Isa. 36. 6.
1 Kings 1. 52. if wickedness be in h. he shall die
3. 28. they saw that the wisdom of God was in h.
14. 13. because in h. there is found some good thing
17. 17. sickness, that there was no breath left in h.
1 Chron. 5. 20. because they put their trust in h.
Job 13. 15. though he slay me, yet will I trust in h.
35. 14. judgment is before him, trust thou in h.
Psal. 2. 12. blessed are they that put their trust in h.
18. 30. a buckler to all those that trust in h.
28. 7. my heart trusted in h. and I am helped
33. 21. our heart shall rejoice in h. 66. 6. | 149. 2.
34. 8. blessed is the man that trusteth in h.
22. none of them that trust in h. shall be desolate
37. 5. trust in h. || 40. because they trust in h.
62. 8. trust in h. at all times, ye people, pour out
64. 10. the righteous shall be glad and trust in h.
72. 17. men shall be blessed in h. all nations call
92. 15. is no unrighteousness in h. John 7. 18.
Prov. 14. 7. perceivest not in h. lips of knowledge
30. 5. he is a shield to them that put their trust in h.
Eccl. 4. 16. that come after shall not rejoice in h.
Jer. 4. 2. the nations shall bless themselves in h.
46. 25. Pharaoh and all them that trust in h.
48. 11. therefore his taste remained in h.
Lam. 3. 24. my portion, therefore will I hope in h.
Dan. 3. 28. delivered his servants who trusted in h.
6. 4. nor was any error or fault found in h.
Obad. 7. there is none understanding in h.
Nah. 1. 7. he knoweth them that trust in h.
Hab. 2. 4. behold, his soul is not upright in h.
Mat. 13. 57. and they were offended in h.
14. 2. mighty works do shew themselves in h.
Luke 23. 22. I have found no cause of death in h.

John 1. 4. in h. was life, the life was light of men
3. 15. whosoever believeth in h. 16. Acts 10. 43.
4. 14. shall be in h. a well of water springing up
6. 56. dwelleth in me and I in h. 10. 38. | 15. 5.
7. 5. neither did his brethren believe in h.
8. 44. because there is no truth in h.
9. 3. made manifest in h. || 11. 10. no light in h.
13. 31. God is glorified in h. || 32. if glorified in h.
Acts 17. 28. in h. we live, move, and have our being
Rom. 10. 14. how shall they believe in h. of whom
15. 12. in h. shall the Gentiles trust
1 Cor. 2. 11. save the spirit of man which is in h.
8. 6. of whom are all things, we in h. 1 John 5. 20.
2 Cor. 1. 19. was not yea, nay, but in h. was yea. 20.
5. 21. might be made the righteousn. of God in h.
13. 4. for we are weak in h. but shall live with him
Eph. 1. 4. chosen us in h. || 10. gather even in h.
Phil. 3. 9. that I may win Christ, and be found in h.
Col. 1. 19. that in h. should all fulness dwell, 2. 9.
2. 6. so walk ye in h. || 7. rooted and built up in h.
9. in h. dwelleth the fulness of the Godhead bodily
10. ye are complete in h. who is the head of all
Heb. 2. 13. and again, I will put my trust in h.
10. 38. my soul shall have no pleasure in h.
1 John 2. 4. is a liar, and the truth is not in h.
5. whoso keepeth his word, in h. verily is love of
God perfected, hereby know we that we are in h.
6. he that saith he abideth in h. ought to walk
8. which thing is true in h. and in you
10. and there is none occasion of stumbling in h.
15. the love of the Father is not in h. 3. 17.
27. as it hath taught you, ye shall abide in h. 28.
3. 3. and every man that hath this hope in h.
5. in h. is no sin || 6. who abideth in h. sinneth not
9. for his seed remaineth in h. he cannot sin
15. no murderer hath eternal life abiding in h.
24. dwelleth in h. and he in h. 4. 13, 15, 16.
5. 14. this is the confidence that we have in h.

Into HIM.

1 Kings 17. 21. let this child's soul come into h.
22. the soul of the child came into h. again
Luke 8. 30. because many devils were entered into h.
John 13. 27. after the sop, Satan entered into h.
Eph. 4. 15. may grow up into h. in all things

Of HIM.

Gen. 25. 21. and the Lord was entreated of h.
Exod. 23. 21. beware of h. and obey his voice
32. 1. we wot not what is become of h. 23.
Lev. 15. 7. that toucheth flesh of h. hath the issue, 33.
25. 36. take thou no usury of h. nor increase
Num. 35. 33. but by the blood of h. that shed it
Deut. 18. 19. not hearken, I will require it of h.
22. thou shalt not be afraid of h. 2 Kings 1. 15.
1 Sam. 17. 32. let no man's heart fail because of h.
2 Kings 5. 20. I will run and take somewhat of h.
10. 24. his life shall be for the life of h.
1 Chr. 5. 2. of h. came the chief ruler, but birth-right
2 Chr. 28. 23. they were the ruin of h. and Israel
33. 13. prayed, and he was entreated of h. 19.
Ezra 8. 21. to seek of h. a right way for us
Job 7. 8. eye of h. hath seen me shall see me no more
12. 5. despised in the thought of h. that is at ease
18. 21. this is the place of h. that knoweth not God
23. 15. when I consider, I am afraid of h.
Ps. 37. 7. fret not thyself because of h. who prospers
Prov. 16. 26. for his mouth craveth it of h.
23. 24. begetteth a wise child, shall have joy of h.
26. 12. is more hope of a fool than of h. 29. 20.
27. 13. take a pledge of h. for a strange woman
Isa. 29. 16. shall the work say of h. that made it
52. 7. the feet of h. bringeth good tidings, Nah. 1. 15.
Jer. 20. 9. I said, I will not make mention of h.
42. 11. be not afraid of h. saith the Lord
Ezek. 14. 10. as the punishment of h. that seeketh
17. 13. king of Babylon hath taken an oath of h.
18. 32. no pleasure in the death of h. that dieth
19. 4. the nations also heard of h. he was taken
28. 9. in the hand of h. that slayeth thee
Zech. 8. 23. take hold of skirt of h. that is a Jew
9. 8. I will encamp because of h. that returneth
Mat. 26. 24. as it is written of h. Mark 9. 13. | 14. 21.
27. 19. I suffered in a dream, because of h.
Mark 8. 30. that they should tell no man of h.
38. of h. shall Son of man be ashamed, Luke 9. 26.
Luke 6. 30. of h. that taketh thy goods, ask not again
12. 48. much given, of h. shall much be required
John 10. 36. say ye of h. whom Father sanctified
Rom. 3. 26. the justifier of h. that believeth in Jesus
9. 11. not of works but of h. that calleth
16. it is not of h. that willeth, but of God
11. 36. for of h. and through him are all things
1 Cor. 1. 30. but of h. are ye in Christ, who of God
1 Pet. 2. 9. shew forth praises of h. who called you
2 Pet. 3. 14. that ye may be found of h. in peace
1 John 1. 5. is the message which we have heard of h.
2. 27. the anointing which ye have received of h.
29. he that doeth righteousness is born of h.
Rev. 1. 7. all kindr. of earth shall wail because of h.

On, or upon HIM.

Exod. 21. 30. shall give whatsoever is laid upon h.
Lev. 7. 20. eateth, having his uncleanness upon h.
15. 24. if her flowers be upon h. he is unclean
19. 17. thou shalt rebuke, and not suffer sin upon h.
20. 9. he cursed father, his blood shall be upon h.
21. 12. crown of anointing oil of his God is upon h.
Num. 11. 25. took of the spirit that was upon h.
15. 31. shall be cut off, his iniquity shall be upon h.
35. 23. seeing him not, cast it upon h. that he die
Deut. 13. 9. thine hand shall be first upon h.
17. 7. the hands of witnesses shall be first upon h.
29. 20. all curses written in this book lie upon h.
Josh. 2. 19. be on our head, if any hand be upon h.
Judg. 3. 10. the Spirit of the Lord came upon h. 14. 6,
19. | 15. 14. Num. 24. 2. 1 Sam. 10. 10. | 19. 23.
1 Sam. 18. 17. the hand of the Philistines be upon h.
2 Sam. 17. 2. I will come upon h. while he is weary
1 Kings 8. 31. an oath be laid upon h. 2 Chr. 6. 22.
13. 4. put forth his hand, saying, lay hold on h.
2 Kings 4. 21. she shut the door upon h. and went out
6. 31. if the head of Elisha stand on h. this day
7. 17. the people trode upon h. in the gate, 20.
2 Chron. 32. 25. therefore there was wrath upon h.

Ezra 7. 6. the hand of the Lord his God upon h. 9.
Job 7. 17. that thou shouldest set thy heart upon h.
15. 21. in prosperity the destroyer shall come u. h.
20. 22. the hand of the wicked shall come upon h.
23. and shall rain it upon h. while he is eating
25. the sword cometh, terrors are upon h.
27. 9. will God hear, when trouble cometh upon h.?
Psal. 116. 2. I will call upon h. as long as I live
145. 18. Ld. is nigh to all that call upon h. in truth
Isa. 44. 3. I will pour water upon h. that is thirsty
53. 5. the chastisement of our peace was upon h.
55. 6. seek the Lord, call ye upon h. while he is near
7. return to Lord, and he will have mercy upon h.
Jer. 31. 20. I will surely have mercy upon h.
Ezek. 12. 13. my net also will I spread upon h.
18. 20. the righteousness of the righteous shall be
upon h. wickedness of the wicked shall be upon h.
Hos. 7. 9. yea, gray hairs are here and there upon h.
12. 14. therefore he shall leave his blood upon h.
Mat. 12. 18. and I will put my Spirit upon h.
27. 30. and they spit upon h. and smote him
Luke 23. 26. and on h. they laid the cross
John 1. 32. it abode upon h. || 33. remaining on h.
3. 18. he that believeth on h. is not condemned, 5.
24. | 6. 40. Rom. 9. 33. 1 Pet. 2. 6.
19. 37. they shall look on h. whom they pierced
Acts 13. 9. then Saul set his eyes on h. and said
Phil. 1. 29. not only to believe on h. but to suffer
2. 27. but God had mercy on h. and not on h. only
Heb. 2. 16. he took not on h. the nature of angels
Rev. 6. 2. and he that sat on h. 5, 8. | 19. 11.
20. 3. shut him up, and he set a seal upon h.

Over HIM.

Gen. 4. 7. be his desire, thou shalt rule over h.
Lev. 16. 21. and confess over h. all the iniquities
25. 43. thou shalt not rule over h. with rigour, 53.
2 Sam. 3. 34. all the people wept again over h.
1 Kings 13. 30. they mourned over h. saying, alas
16. 18. burnt the king's house over h. with fire
Psal. 109. 6. set thou a wicked man over h. let Satan
Ezek. 19. 8. the nations spread their net over h.
Dan. 4. 16. and let seven times pass over h. 23.
Acts 8. 2. devout men made lamentation over h.
Rom. 6. 9. death hath no more dominion over h.
Jam. 5. 14. is any sick? let them pray over h.

Through HIM.

John 1. 7. that all men through h. might believe
3. 17. that the world through h. might be saved
Rom. 5. 9. we shall be saved from wrath, thro' h.
8. 37. more than conquerors thro' h. that loved us
11. 36. of him, thro' h. and to him, are all things
Eph. 2. 18. through h. we have access to the Father
1 John 4. 9. sent his Son that we might live t. h.

To, or unto HIM.

Gen. 4. 26. to Seth, to h. also there was born a son
12. 7. an altar to the Lord, who appeared unto h.
17. 17. shall a child be born unto h. that is old?
21. 2. at set time of which God had spoken to h.
24. 36. unto h. hath he given all that he hath
49. 10. unto h. shall the gathering of the people be
Exod. 4. 16. thou shalt be to h. instead of God
22. 25. thou shalt not be to h. as an usurer
28. 43. it shall be a statute for ever unto h. 30. 21.
Deut. 1. 36. and to h. will I give the land
18. 15. raise up a prophet, unto h. ye shall hearken
Judg. 15. 10. to do to h. as he hath done to us
1 Sam. 28. 17. the Lord hath done to h. as he spake
2 Sam. 3. 9. hath sworn to David, even so I do to h.
2 Kings 4. 23. wherefore wilt thou go to h. to-day?
7. 20. so it fell out unto h. for the people trode
2 Chron. 13. 5. even to h. and his sons by covenant
34. 26. as for the king, so shall ye say unto h.
Job 6. 14. to h. that is afflicted, pity should be shewed
35. 6. if thou sinnest, what doest thou unto h.?
Psal. 68. 33. to h. that rideth on the heavens
72. 15. to h. shall be given of the gold of Sheba
136. 7. to h. that made great lights, for his mercy
17. to h. that smote great kings, for his mercy
Eccl. 9. 2. all things come alike to all, one event to
h. that sacrificeth, and to h. that sacrificeth not
Isa. 9. 13. people turneth not to h. that smiteth
31. 6. turn to h. from whom Israel have revolted
40. 17. they are counted to h. less than nothing
18. or what likeness will ye compare unto h.?
45. 24. even to h. shall men come, and all that are
49. 7. thus saith the L. to h. whom man despiseth
57. 19. peace to h. that is afar off, and to h. near
66. 2. I will look, even to h. that is poor and contrite
Mat. 7. 8. to h. that knocketh, it shall be opened
Luke 6. 29. to h. that smiteth thee on one cheek
8. 18. whosoever hath, to h. shall be given
12. 10. to h. that blasphemeth against Holy Ghost
20. 38. the God of the living, for all live unto h.
John 7. 33. then I go unto h. that sent me, 16. 5.
10. 3. to h. the porter openeth, the sheep hear
Acts 5. 40. to h. they agreed, and called apostles
8. 11. to h. they had regard, because he had bewitch.
10. 43. to h. give all the prophets witness, that thro'
Rom. 4. 4. now to h. that worketh, is the reward
5. to h. that worketh not, but believeth on him
7. 4. even to h. who is raised from the dead
11. 36. and to h. are all things, to whom be glory
14. 14. to h. that esteemeth, to h. it is unclean
16. 25. now to h. that is of power to stablish you
1 Cor. 14. 11. I be to h. who speaketh a barbarian
Gal. 3. 6. it was accounted to h. for righteousness
Eph. 3. 21. unto h. be glory in the church by Christ
Heb. 1. 5. I will be to h. a Father, he to me a son
5. 7. to h. that was able to save him from death
Jam. 2. 23. it was imputed unto h. for righteousness
4. 17. to h. that knoweth to do good, to h. it is sin
Rev. 1. 5. unto h. that loved us, and washed us
2. 7. to h. that overcometh will I give, 17. | 3. 21.
26. to h. will I give power over the nations
21. 6. I will give unto h. that is athirst, of fountain

Toward HIM.

Gen. 31. 2. behold, it was not toward h. as before
Judg. 8. 3. their anger was abated toward h.
2 Chr. 16. 9. of them whose heart is perfect toward h.
Job 11. 13. and stretch out thine hands toward h.
Lam. 2. 19. lift up thy hands toward h. for thy child.
Ezek. 17. 6. whose branches turned toward h.
2 Cor. 2. 8. ye would confirm your love toward h.

Under HIM.

Exod. 17. 12. they took a stone and put it under h.
2 Sam. 18. 9. the mule that was under h. went away
Job 9. 13. the proud helpers do stoop under h.
Isa. 58. 5. to spread sackcloth and ashes under h.
Ezek. 17. 6. the roots thereof were under h.
1 Cor. 15. 27. all things put under h. 28. Heb. 2. 8.

With HIM.

Gen. 39. 3. his master saw that the Lord was with h
Exod. 31. 6. I have given with h. Aholiab, 38. 23
Num. 12. 8. with h. will I speak mouth to mouth, even
apparently, not in dark speeches, Jer. 32. 4.
23. 21. the Lord his God is with h. and the shout
Deut. 29. 15. with h. that standeth here with us, also
with h. that is not here with us this day
32. 12. and there was no strange god with h.
1 Sam. 3. 19. and the Lord was with h. 18. 12, 14.
16. 18. the Lord is with h. || 25. 25. folly is with h.
2 Sam. 5. 10. Lord of hosts was with h. 1 Chr. 11. 9.
16. 18. his will I be, and with h. will I abide
1 Kings 8. 65. Solomon held a feast, and all Israel
with h. from Hamath to Egypt, 2 Chr. 7. 8.
2 Kings 3. 12. said, the word of the Lord is with h.
15. 19. gave silver, that his hand might be with h.
18. 7. the Lord was with h. and he prospered,
1 Chron. 9. 20. 2 Chron. 1. 1. | 15. 9.
2 Chron. 15. 2. Lord is with you, while ye be with h.
26. 17. with h. fourscore priests of the Lord
32. 7. for there be more with us than with h.
8. with h. is an arm of flesh, with us the Lord
36. 23. the Lord his God be with h. Ezra 1. 3.
Ezra 8. 3. with h. 150 males || 4. with h. 200 males
6. with h. 50 males || Job 12. 13. with h. is wisdom, 16.
Job 18. 6. and his candle shall be put out with h.
22. 21. acquaint thyself with h. and be at peace
Psal. 89. 24. and my mercy shall be with h.
91. 15. I will be with h. in trouble, I will deliver him
130. 7. and with h. is plenteous redemption
Prov. 8. 30. then was I as one brought up with h.
Eccl. 8. 15. that shall abide with h. of his labour
Isa. 3. 10. say to the righteous, it shall be well with h.
11. woe unto the wicked, it shall be ill with h.
40. 10. behold, his reward is with h. 62. 11.
57. 15. with h. also that is of a contrite spirit
Jer. 22. 15. and then it was well with h. 16.
Ezek. 31. 11. the mighty one, he shall deal with h.
Mal. 2. 5. my covenant was with h. of life
Mat. 5. 25. agree whiles thou art in the way with h.
Mark 3. 14. ordained 12, that they should be with h.
5. 18. prayed that he might be with h. Luke 8. 38.
Luke 1. 66. and the hand of the Lord was with h.
22. 56. a maid said, this man was also with h.
John 3. 2. do these miracles, except God be with h.
14. 23. we will come and make our abode with h.
Acts 7. 9. sold Joseph, but God was with h. 10. 38.
10. 35. he that feareth him is accepted with h.
21. 36. multitude followed, crying, away with h.
Rom. 6. 4. we are buried with h. by baptism, Col. 2. 12.
8. live with h. 2 Cor. 13. 4. 1 Thess. 5. 10. 2 Tim. 2. 11.
8. 32. how shall he not with h. give us all things
1 Thess. 4. 14. sleep in Jesus, will God bring with h.
2 Tim. 2. 12. we also shall reign with h. Rev. 20. 6.
Heb. 11. 9. the heirs with h. of the same promise
2 Pet. 1. 18. when we were with h. in the holy mount
Rev. 3. 20. and I will sup with h. and he with me
14. 1. with h. 144,000 having his Father's name
17. 14. they that are with h. are called chosen

Within HIM.

Job 14. 22. and his soul within h. mourn
20. 14. his meat is the gall of asps within h.
Prov. 26. 24. and layeth up deceit within h.
Isa. 63. 11. is he that put his Holy Spirit within h.
Zech. 12. 1. and formeth the spirit of man within h.

Without HIM.

John 1. 3. and without h. was not any thing made

See HYMN.

HIMSELF.

Gen. 43. 32. they set on for him by h. and for them
Exod. 21. 3. if he came in by h. he shall go out by h.
Lev. 9. 8. sin-offering which was for h. 16. 6, 11.
16. 11. shall make an atonement for h. 17, 24.
Num. 16. 9. separated you to bring you near to h.
31. 53. men of war had taken spoil, every man for h.
Deut. 7. 6. Lord hath chosen thee to be a people to
h. 14. 2. | 28. 9. | 29. 13. 2 Sam. 7. 23.
33. 21. and he provided the first part for h.
Josh. 22. 23. let the Lord h. require it
Judg. 3. 19. he h. turned again from the quarries
1 Sam. 30. 6. but David encouraged h. in the Lord
1 Kings 19. 4. but Elijah h. went a day's journey,
and he requested for h. that he might die
2 Chron. 13. 12. God h. is with us for our captain
26. 20. thrust him out, yea, h. hasted also to go out
Ezra 10. 8. h. separated from the congregation
Job 1. 12. only on h. put not forth thine hand
22. 2. he that is wise may be profitable to h.
27. 10. will he delight h. in the Almighty?
32. 2. because he justified h. rather than God
34. 9. that he should delight h. with God
41. 25. when he raiseth h. the mighty are afraid
Psal. 4. 3. hath set apart him that is godly for h.
10. 14. the poor committeth h. unto thee
35. 8. let his net that he hath hid catch h.
36. 4. he setteth h. in a way that is not good
50. 6. for God is judge h. Selah
87. 5. and the Highest h. shall establish her
132. 18. but on h. shall his crown flourish
135. 4. for the Lord hath chosen Jacob to h.
Prov. 5. 22. his own iniquities shall take wicked h.
11. 25. he that watereth shall be watered also h.
13. 7. that maketh h. rich, that maketh h. poor
14. 14. and a good man shall be satisfied from h.
16. 4. the Lord hath made all things for h.
26. he that laboureth, laboureth for h.
21. 13. he also shall cry h. but shall not be heard
22. 3. foreseeth the evil, and hideth h. 27. 12.
29. 15. but a child left to h. bringeth to shame
Cant. 5. 6. but my beloved had withdrawn h.
Isa. 7. 14. the Lord h. shall give you a sign
38. 15. he hath spoken, and h. hath done it
44. 5. another shall call h. by the name of Jacob

Isa. 59. 15. departeth from evil, maketh *h.* a prey
63. 12. to make *h.* an everlasting name
Jer. 10. 23. I know that the way of man is not in *h.*
29. 26. man that is mad, and maketh *h.* a prophet
51. 14. the Lord hath sworn by *h. Amos* 6. 8.
Ezek. 45. 22. on that day shall prince prepare for *h.*
Dan. 9. 26. Messiah shall be cut off, but not for *h.*
Hos. 5. 6. he hath withdrawn *h.* from them
10. 1. Israel an empty vine, bringeth forth fruit to *h.*
Amos 2. 14. nor shall the mighty deliver *h.*
15. he that is swift of foot shall not deliver *h.*
Mat. 6. 4. *h.* shall reward thee openly
8. 17. *h.* took our infirmities, bare our sicknesses
13. 21. yet hath he not root in *h.* but dureth a while
27. 42. saved others, *h.* he cannot save, *Mark* 15. 31.
Mark 3. 21. for they said, he is beside *h.*
8. 34. let him deny *h.* and take his cross, *Luke* 9. 23.
12. 33. to love his neighbour as *h.* is more than
Luke 10. 1. sent them, whither he *h.* would come
11. 26. he taketh seven spirits more wicked than *h.*
12. 47. who knew his lord's will, and prepared not *h.*
15. 17. and when he came to *h.* he said, how many
19. 12. a nobleman went to receive for *h.* a kingdom
23. 2. saying, that he *h.* is Christ, a king
51. who also *h.* waited for the kingdom of God
24. 27. he expounded the things concerning *h.*
36. Jesus *h.* stood in the midst of them, and saith
John 4. 2. tho' Jesus *h.* baptized not, but his disciples
5. 18. God was his Father, making *h.* equal with G.
19. verily I say, the Son can do nothing of *h.*
26. for as the Father hath life in *h.* so the Son
6. 6. for he *h.* knew what he would do
61. when Jesus knew in *h.* that his disciples
7. 4. and he *h.* seeketh to be known openly
18. he that speaketh of *h.* seeketh his own glory
9. 21. he is of age, ask him, he shall speak for *h.*
11. 51. this spake he not of *h.* but being high-priest
13. 32. God shall glorify him in *h.* and glorify him
16. 13. he shall not speak of *h.* but whatsoever
27. the Father *h.* loveth you, because ye loved me
19. 12. whoso maketh *h.* a king, speaketh ag. Cæsar
21. 1. Jesus shewed *h.* again to the disciples, 14.
Acts 5. 13. of the rest durst no man join *h.* to them
36. rose up Theudas, boasting *h.* to be somebody
8. 9. giving out that *h.* was some great one
34. of whom speaketh the prophet this? of *h.*
10. 17. now while Peter doubted in *h.* what this
12. 11. and when Peter was come to *h.* he said
14. 17. he left not *h.* without witness, in that
25. 8. while he answered for *h.* 26. 1.
26. 24. as he spake for *h.* Festus said with loud voice
28. 16. but Paul was suffered to dwell by *h.*
Rom. 12. 3. not to think of *h.* more highly than he
14. 7. none of us liveth to *h.* no man dieth to *h.*
15. 3. for even Christ pleased not *h.* but as is written
1 *Cor.* 2. 15. yet he *h.* is judged of no man
3. 15. but he *h.* shall be saved, yet so as by fire
11. 28. but let a man examine *h.* so let him eat
15. 28. then shall the Son *h.* be subject to him
2 *Cor.* 5. 18. who hath reconciled us to *h.* by Jesus, 19.
10. 7. if any man trust to *h.* let him of *h.* think
11. 20. for ye suffer if a man exalt *h.* if a man smite
Gal. 1. 4. who gave *h.* for our sins, that he might
2. 20. gave *h.* for me || 6. 3. think *h.* to be something
6. 4. then shall he have rejoicing in *h.* alone
Eph. 2. 15. to make in *h.* of twain one new man
20. Jesus *h.* being the chief corner stone
5. 2. hath given *h.* for us || 25. gave *h.* for it
27. he might present it to *h.* a glorious church
28. loveth *h.* || 33. so love his wife, even as *h.*
Col. 1. 20. and by him to reconcile all things to *h.*
2. + 15. triumphing over them in *h.*
2 *Thess.* 2. 4. sitteth, shewing *h.* that he is God
1 *Tim.* 2. 6. who gave *h.* a ransom for all
Tit. 2. 14. who gave *h.* for us, to purify to *h.*
3. 11. he sinneth, being condemned of *h.*
Heb. 1. 3. when he had by *h.* purged our sins
2. 14. he also *h.* likewise took part of the same
18. in that he *h.* hath suffered, being tempted
5. 2. for that he *h.* also is compassed with infirmity
3. as for the people, so also for *h.* to offer for sins
4. no man taketh this honour to *h.* but he that
5. Christ glorified not *h.* to be made an high-priest
6. 13. he sware by *h.* || 7. 27. when he offered up *h.*
9. 26. appeared to put away sin by sacrifice of *h.*
1 *Pet.* 2. 23. but committed *h.* to him that judgeth
1 *John* 2. 6. ought *h.* to walk, even as he walked
3. 3. hath this hope, purifieth *h.* even as he is pure
5. 10. he that believeth hath the witness in *h.*
3 *John* 10. nor doth he *h.* receive the brethren
Rev. 19. 12. had a name that no man knew but *h.*
21. 3. God *h.* shall be with them, and be their God
See Bowed, Hide.

HIN

Was a liquid measure of the Hebrews; *it was the sixth part of a* Bath, *and held one gallon and two pints.*
Exod. 29. 40. with the fourth part of an *h.* of oil
30. 24. take also unto thee of oil-olive an *h.*
Lev. 19. 36. a just ephah and *h.* shall ye have
23. 13. the drink offering shall be of wine, the fourth part of an *h.* of oil, *Num.* 15. 4. | 28. 14.
Num. 15. 5. the fourth part of an *h.* of wine
6. the third part of an *h.* of oil || 9. half an *h.*
Ezek. 4. 11. shalt drink sixth part of an *h.* of water
45. 24. an *h.* of oil for an ephah, 46. 5, 7, 11.
46. 14. third part of an *h.* of oil to temper with

HIND, S.

Gen. 49. 21. Naphtali is a *h.* let loose, he giveth
2 *Sam.* 22. 34. he maketh my feet like *h.* feet, and setteth me on high places, *Ps.* 18. 33. *Hab.* 3. 19.
Job 39. 1. or canst thou mark when the *h.* do calve?
Ps. 29. 9. the voice of Lord maketh the *h.* to calve
Prov. 5. 19. let her be as the loving *h.* and roe
Cant. 2. 7. I charge you by the *h.* of the field, 3. 5.
Jer. 14. 5. the *h.* calved in the field, and forsook it

HINDER.

Gen. 24. 56. *h.* me not, seeing the L. hath prospered
Num. 22. 16. let nothing *h.* thee from coming to me
Neh. 4. 8. to come and fight, and *h.* the building
Job 9. 12. behold, he taketh away, who can *h.* him?
11. 10. if he cut off, and shut up, who can *h.* him?
Acts 8. 36. what doth *h.* me to be baptized?
1 *Cor.* 9. 12. lest we should *h.* the gospel of Christ
Gal. 5. 7. who did *h.* you, that should not obey truth?

HINDERED.

Ezra 6. 8. expences be given, that they be not *h.*
Luke 11. 52. and them that were entering in, ye *h.*
Rom. 15. 22. have been much *h.* from coming to you
1 *Thess.* 2. 18. we would have come, but Satan *h.*
1 *Pet.* 3. 7. as heirs of life, that your prayers be not *h.*

HINDERETH.

Isa. 14. 6. he that ruled is persecuted, and none *h.*

HINDER *end.*

2 *Sam.* 2. 23. Abner smote him with *h. end* of spear

HINDERMOST, *or* HINDMOST.

Gen. 33. 2. and he put Rachel and Joseph *h.*
Num. 2. 31. they shall go *h.* with their standards
Deut. 25. 18. he met thee, and smote the *h.* of thee
Josh. 10. 19. pursue, and smite the *h.* of them
Jer. 50. 12. the *h.* of the nations shall be a wildern.

HINDER *part.*

Joel 2. 20. and his *h. part* toward the utmost sea
Mark 4. 38. Jesus was in the *h. part* of the ship
Acts 27. 41. the *h. part* was broken with waves

HINDER *parts.*

1 *Kings* 7. 25. their *h. parts* were inward, 2 *Chr.* 4. 4.
Psal. 78. 66. he smote his enemies in the *h. parts*

HINDER *sea.*

Zech. 14. 8. and half of them toward the *h. sea*

HINGES.

1 *Kings* 7. 50. and the *h.* of gold for doors of house
Prov. 26. 14. as the door turneth upon his *h.*

HIP.

Judg. 15. 8. he smote them *h.* and thigh with slaugh.

HIRE, *Substantive.*

Gen. 30. 18. given me my *h.* + called his name an *h.*
32. among the goats, and of such shall be my *h.*
33. when it shall come for my *h.* before thy face
31. 8. if he said, the ring-straked shall be thy *h.*
Exod. 22. 15. if an hired thing, it came for his *h.*
Deut. 23. 18. thou shalt not bring the *h.* of a whore
24. 15. at his day thou shalt give him his *h.*
1 *Kings* 5. 6. to thee will I give *h.* for thy servants
Isa. 23. 17. she shall turn to her *h.* and commit
18. and her *h.* shall be holiness to the Lord
Ezek. 16. 31. not as an harlot in that thou scornest *h.*
41. and thou also shalt give no *h.* any more
29. + 20. I have given him Egypt for his *h.*
Mic. 1. 7. for she gathered it of the *h.* of an harlot, and they shall return to the *h.* of an harlot
3. 11. and the priests thereof teach for *h.*
Zech. 8. 10. there was no *h.* for man, any *h.* for beast
Mat. 20. 8. give them their *h.* beginning from last
Luke 10. 7. for the labourer is worthy of his *h.*
Jam. 5. 4. behold, the *h.* of the labourers is kept back

HIRE.

Isa. 46. 6. they *h.* a goldsmith, and he maketh it a god
Mat. 20. 1. went out to *h.* labourers into his vineyard

HIRED.

Gen. 30. 16. I have *h.* thee with my son's mandrakes
Exod. 22. 15. if it be an *h.* thing it came for his hire
Lev. 19. 13. the wages of him that is *h.* not abide
Deut. 23. 4. they *h.* against thee Balaam, *Neh.* 13. 2.
Judg. 9. 4. wherewith Abimelech *h.* vain persons
18. 4. Micah hath *h.* me, and I am his priest
1 *Sam.* 2. 5. that were full, have *h.* out themselves
2 *Sam.* 10. 6. Ammon *h.* the Syrians, 1 *Chr.* 19. 7.
2 *Kings* 7. 6. the king of Israel hath *h.* against us
2 *Chron.* 24. 12. *h.* masons and carpenters to repair
25. 6. Amaziah *h.* 100,000 mighty men of valour
Ezra 4. 5. *h.* counsellors against them to frustrate
Neh. 6. 12. Tobiah and Sanballat had *h.* him, 13.
Isa. 7. 20. shall Lord shave with a razor that is *h.*
Jer. 46. 21. her *h.* men are like fatted bullocks
Hos. 8. 9. are gone up, Ephraim hath *h.* lovers
10. yea, though they have *h.* among the nations
Mat. 20. 7. they say, because no man hath *h.* us
9. when they came that were *h.* ab. eleventh hour
Acts 28. 30. Paul dwelt two years in his own *h.* hou.

HIRED *servant.*

Exod. 12. 45. an *h. serv.* not eat thereof, *Lev.* 22. 10.
Lev. 25. 6. the sabbath shall be meat for thy *h. serv.*
40. but as an *h. servant* he shall be with thee
50. according to the time of an *h. serv.* shall it be
53. as a yearly *h. servant* shall he be with him
Deut. 15. 18. hath been worth a double *h. servant*
24. 14. thou shalt not oppress an *h. servant*

HIRED *servants.*

Mark 1. 20. left Zebedee in the ship with *h. serv.*
Luke 15. 17. how many *h. serv.* have bread enough
19. make me as one of thy *h. servants*

HIRELING.

It is commanded in the law, that the hireling *should be paid as soon as his work is over.* Lev. 19. 13. The wages of him that is hired shall not abide with thee all night until the morning; *because his urgent necessities require it for present subsistence.* An hireling's day or year, *is a kind of proverb, signifying a full year, without abating any thing of it.* Are not his days like the days of an hireling? Job 7. 1. *The days of man are like those of an* hireling; *as nothing is deducted from them, so nothing is added to them. And in* Job 14. 6. Till he shall accomplish as an hireling his day; *to the time of his death, which he waits for as the* hireling *for the end of the day. See* Isa. 16. 14. | 21. 16. *In* John 10. 12, 13. *the* hireling *is set in opposition to the true shepherd; the first neglects the sheep, and aims only at his own advantage; the second loves and guides them carefully. The* hirelings *whom the Father of the family, that is, God, sends into his vineyard, are the prophets and apostles,* Jews *and* Christians; *the second succeeded the first, and all receive their reward when their work is done,* Mat. 20. 1—16.
Job 7. 1. are not his days like the days of an *h.*?
2. as an *h.* looketh for the reward of his work
14. 6. till he shall accomplish as an *h.* his day
Isa. 16. 14. in three years as the years of an *h.* 21. 16.
Mal. 3. 5. witness against those that oppress the *h.*
John 10. 12. he that is an *h.* and not the shepherd
13. the *h.* fleeth, because he is an *h.* and careth not

HIREST.

Ezek. 16. 33. thou *h.* them, that they may come

HIRES.

Mic. 1. 7. all the *h.* thereof shall be burnt with fire

HIS.

Gen. 38. 9. Onan knew the seed should not be *h.*
Exod. 21. 34. and the dead beast shall be *h.*
22. 9. which another challengeth to be *h.*
Lev. 27. 15. add the fifth part, and it shall be *h.*
Num. 5. 10. a man's hallowed things shall be *h.*
16. 5. to morrow the Lord will shew who are *h.*
23. 10. righteous, and let my last end be like *h.*
Deut. 21. 17. the right of the first-born is *h.*
2 *Sam.* 16. 18. *h.* will I be, with him will I abide
1 *Kings* 2. 15. for it was *h.* from the Lord
2 *Kings* 15. 25. a captain of *h.* conspired ag. him
Esth. 4. 11. is one law of *h.* to put him to death
Job 12. 16. the deceived and the deceiver are *h.*
18. 15. in his tabernacle, because it is none of *h.*
Psal. 30. 4. sing unto the Lord, all ye saints of *h.*
95. 4. the strength of the hills is *h.* also
103. 21. ye ministers of *h.* that do his pleasure
Cant. 2. 16. my beloved is mine, and I am *h.*
Ezek. 16. 15. on every one that passeth by, *h.* it was
46. 17. then it shall be *h.* to the year of liberty
Dan. 2. 20. blessed be G. wisdom and might are *h.*
Obad. 14. to cut off those of *h.* that did escape, nor shouldest have deliver. up those of *h.* that remain
Hab. 2. 6. woe to him increaseth that which is not *h.*
John 7. 16. doctrine is not mine, but *h.* that sent me
Acts 16. 33. was baptized, he and all *h.* straightway
Rom. 8. 9. if any have not the Spirit, he is none of *h.*
2 *Tim.* 2. 19. the Lord knoweth them that are *h.*
Heb. 4. 10. hath ceased from works, as G. did from *h.*

HISS.

To hiss, *is a kind of insult and contempt.* 1 Kings 9. 8. All they, *who shall see the destruction of this temple,* shall be astonished, and shall hiss, and say, why hath the Lord done thus unto this land, and to this house? *And* Job, *speaking of the wicked under calamities, says, that* they shall clap their hands at him, and shall hiss him out of his place, *Job* 27. 23. *And in* Jer. 19. 8. I will make this city desolate and an hissing; every one that passeth thereby shall be astonished, and hiss, because of all the plagues thereof? *I will make this city the subject of ridicule and scorn.*
To hiss, *to call any one with* hissing, *is a mark of power and authority. The Lord says, that in his anger he will* hiss, *and call the enemy against* Jerusalem. *Isa.* 5. 26. He will hiss unto them from the end of the earth. *He will bring them with an hiss from the very extremities of the earth. And in* Isa. 7. 18. The Lord shall hiss for the fly, *and shall bring it to him,* that is in the uttermost part of the rivers of *Egypt,* and for the bee that is in the land of *Assyria. The fly and the bee, which God will bring thus with a* hiss, *are the kings of* Egypt and Assyria: *they shall come with their troops into the territories of* Israel, *and shall disperse themselves over the whole country.* Theodoret, *writing upon* Isaiah, *remarks, that in* Syria, *and* Palestine, *they who looked after bees drew them out of their hives, carried them into the fields, and brought them back again with the sound of a flute and the noise of* hissing. Zechariah, *speaking of the return from the* Babylonish *captivity, says, that the* Lord will gather them, as it were with an hiss, and bring them back into their country, *Zech.* 10. 8. *Which shows the ease and authority with which he will perform this great work.*
1 *Kings* 9. 8. and at this house every one shall *h.*
Job 27. 23. men shall *h.* him out of his place
Isa. 5. 26. he will *h.* to them from end of the earth
7. 18. the Lord shall *h.* for the fly in Egypt
Jer. 19. 8. passeth thereby shall *h.* 49. 17. | 50. 13.
Lam. 2. 15. they *h.* at the daughter of Jerusalem
16. thy enemies *h.* and gnash the teeth against thee
Ezek. 27. 36. the merchants shall *h.* at thee
Zeph. 2. 15. every one that passeth by her shall *h.*
Zech. 10. 8. I will *h.* for them and gather them

HISSING.

2 *Chron.* 29. 8. and he hath delivered them to *h.*
Jer. 18. 16. to make their land a perpetual *h.*
19. 8. I will make this city desolate and an *h.*
25. 9. and I will make them an *h.* 18. | 29. 18.
51. 37. Babylon shall be an *h.* without inhabitant
Mic. 6. 16. should make inhabitants thereof an *h.*

HIT.

1 *Sam.* 31. 3. and the archers *h.* him, 1 *Chron.* 10. 3.

HITHER.

Gen. 45. 5. now be not angry that ye sold me *h.*
8. it was not you that sent me *h.* but God
13. ye shall haste and bring down my father *h.*
Exod. 3. 5. draw not nigh *h.* put off thy shoes
Josh. 2. 2. behold, there came men in *h.* to night
18. 6. ye shall bring the description *h.* to me
Judg. 18. 3. they said to him, who brought thee *h.*?
19. 12. we will not turn aside *h.* into the city
1 *Sam.* 13. 9. bring *h.* a burnt-offering to me
14. 18. and Saul said, bring *h.* the ark of God
34. bring me *h.* every man his ox and his sheep
36. the priest said, let us draw near *h.* unto God
15. 32. bring *h.* Agag || 17. 28. why camest thou *h.*
23. 9. said to Abiathar, bring *h.* the ephod, 30. 7.
2 *Sam.* 1. 10. I have brought them *h.* unto my lord
1 *Kings* 22. 9. hasten *h.* Micaiah the son of Imlah
2 *Kings* 2. 8. Jordan divided *h.* and thither, 14.
2 *Chron.* 28. 13. ye shall not bring in captives *h.*
Ezra 4. 2. king of Assur, which brought us up *h.*
Psal. 73. 10. therefore his people return *h.*
81. 2. take a psalm, and bring *h.* the timbrel
Prov. 9. 4. whoso is simple, let him turn in *h.* 16.
Isa. 57. 3. draw near *h.* ye sons of the sorceress
Mat. 14. 18. he said, bring them *h.* to me
17. 17. Jesus said, bring him *h.* to me, *Luke* 9. 41.
22. 12. friend, how camest thou in *h.* not having
Luke 14. 21. bring in *h.* the poor and the maimed
15. 23. bring *h.* the fatted calf and kill it
19. 27. bring *h.* and slay them before me
30. shall find a colt tied, loose him, bring him *h.*

John 6. 2 they said, Rabbi, when camest thou *h.?*
20. 27. reach *h.* thy finger, reach *h.* thy hand
Acts 9. 21. that came *h.* for that intent, that he
10. 32. call *h.* Simon, whose surname is Peter
19. 37. ye have brought *h.* these men, which are
See COME.

HITHERTO.

Exod. 7. 16. behold, *h.* thou wouldest not hear
Num. 14. † 19. as thou hast forgiven this people *h.*
Josh. 17. 14. as the Lord hath blessed me *h.*
Judg. 16. 13. *h.* thou hast mocked me, and told lies
1 *Sam.* 1. 16. for out of my grief have I spoken *h.*
7. 12. and saying, *h.* hath the Lord helped us
2 *Sam.* 7. 18. thou hast brought me *h.* 1 *Chr.* 17. 16.
15. 34. as I have been thy father's servant *h.*
1 *Chron.* 9. 18. who *h.* waited in the king's gate
12. 29. *h.* the greatest part kept the ward
Job 38. 11. *h.* shalt thou come, but no further
Psal. 71. 17. *h.* have I declared thy wondrous works
Isa. 18. 2. a people terrible from their beginning *h.* 7.
John 5. 17. my Father worketh *h.* and I work
16. 24. *h.* have ye asked nothing in my name
Rom. 1. 13. I purposed to come, but was let *h.*
1 *Cor.* 3. 2. for *h.* ye were not able to bear it

HO.

Ruth 4. 1. to whom he said, *ho* such a one, sit down
Isa. 55. 1. *ho* every one that thirsteth, come ye
Zech. 2. 6. *ho, ho,* come forth, flee from the land

HOAR, HOARY, *See* FROST, HAIRS, HEAD.

HOARY.

Job 41. 32. one would think the deep to be *h.*

HOISED.

Acts 27. 40. they *h.* up the main-sail to the wind

HOLD, *Substantive.*

Judg. 9. 46. they entered into a *h.* of the god Berith
49. they put them to the *h.* and set the *h.* on fire
1 *Sam.* 22. 4. Dav. in *h.* 24. 22. 2 *Sam.* 5. 17. | 23. 14.
5. abide not in the *h.* depart and get thee into land
1 *Chr.* 12. 16. there came of Judah to *h.* to David
Acts 4. 3. and put them in *h.* unto the next day
Rev. 18. 2. is become the *h.* of every foul spirit
See STRONG.

HOLD.

Gen. 21. 18. lift up the lad, *h.* him in thine hand
Exod. 5. 1. that they may *h.* a feast to me in wildern.
9. 2. refuse to let them go, and wilt *h.* them still?
10. 9. for we must *h.* a feast unto the Lord
20. 7. Lord will not *h.* him guiltless, *Deut.* 5. 11.
Deut. 22. † 25. if the man take strong *h.* of her
Ruth 3. 15. he said, bring the vail, and *h.* it
2 *Sam.* 2. 22. how should I *h.* up my face to Joab
6. 6. Uzzah put forth his hand to ark of God, and took *h.* of it, oxen shook it, 1 *Chron.* 13. 9.
1 *Kings* 2. 9. now therefore *h.* him not guiltless
Esth. 4. 11. the king shall *h.* out the golden sceptre
Job 6. 24. teach me, and I will *h.* my tongue
9. 28. I know that thou wilt not *h.* me innocent
13. 19. if I *h.* my tongue, I shall give up the ghost
17. 9. the righteous also shall *h.* on his way
41. 26. the spear, dart, the habergeon cannot *h.*
Psal. 17. 5. *h.* up my goings in thy paths
119. 53. horror hath taken *h.* upon me, because
117. *h.* thou me up, and I shall be safe
139. 10. and thy right hand shall *h.* me
Prov. 31. 19. and her hands *h.* the distaff
Cant. 3. 8. they all *h.* swords, being expert in war
Isa. 41. 13. I the Lord will *h.* thy right hand
42. 6. and I will *h.* thine hand, and keep thee
Jer. 2. 13. hewed broken cisterns, can *h.* no water
8. 21. astonishment hath taken *h.* on me
50. 42. they shall *h.* the bow and the lance
43. anguish took *h.* of him, and pangs as of wom.
Ezek. 30. 21. to make it strong to *h.* the sword
41. 6. that they might have *h.* they had not *h.*
Amos 6. 10. then shall he say, *h.* thy tongue
Zech. 11. 5. slay them, and *h.* themselves not guilty
Mat. 6. 24. else he will *h.* to the one, *Luke* 16. 13.
21. 26. for all *h.* John as a prophet
Mark 7. 4. other things they have received to *h.*
8. ye *h.* the tradition of men, as washing of pots
Rom. 1. 18. who *h.* the truth in unrighteousness
Phil. 2. 29. receive him, and *h.* such in reputation
2 *Thess.* 2. 15. *h.* the traditions ye have been taught
Heb. 3. 14. if we *h.* the beginning of our confidence
Rev. 2. 14. hast them that *h.* the doctrine of Balaam
15. hast them that *h.* doctrine of the Nicolaitanes
See CAUGHT.

HOLD *fast.*

Job 8. 15. he shall *h.* it *fast,* but it shall not endure
27. 6. my righteousness I *h. fast,* I will not let it go
Jer. 8. 5. they *h. fast* deceit, they refuse to return
1 *Thess.* 5. 21. prove all things, *h. fast* that is good
2 *Tim.* 1. 13. *h. fast* the form of sound words which
Heb. 3. 6. if we *h. fast* the confid. and the rejoicing
4. 14. let us *h. fast* our profession, 10. 23.
Rev. 2. 25. that ye have already *h. fast* till I come
3. 3. *h. fast* and repent || 11. *h. fast* which thou hast

HOLD *peace.*

Exod. 14. 14. Lord shall fight, ye shall *h.* your *peace*
Num. 30. 4. if her father *h.* his *peace* at her
14. if her husband altogether *h.* his *peace* at her
Judg. 18. 19. *h.* thy *peace,* lay hand on thy mouth
2 *Sam.* 13. 20. *h.* thy *peace,* my sister, he is brother
2 *Kings* 2. 3. he said, I know it, *h.* you your *peace,* 5.
7. 9. a day of good tidings, and we *h.* our *peace*
Neh. 8. 11. saying, *h.* your *peace,* the day is holy
Job 11. 3. should thy lies make men *h.* their *peace?*
13. 5. that ye would altogether *h.* your *peace*
13. *h.* your *peace,* let me alone that I may speak
33. 31. mark well, *h.* thy *peace* and I will speak
33. *h.* thy *peace,* and I will teach thee wisdom
Psal. 83. 1. O G. *h.* not thy *p.* be not still, 109. 1.
Isa. 62. 1. for Zion's sake will I not *h.* my *peace*
6. which shall never *h.* their *peace* day nor night
64. 12. wilt thou *h.* thy *peace* and afflict us sore?
Jer. 4. 19. I am pained at heart, I cannot *h.* my *p.*
Zeph. 1. 7. *h.* thy *peace* at the presence of the Lord
Mat. 20. 31. multitude rebuked them, because they should *h.* their *peace, Mark* 10. 48. *Luke* 18. 39.
Mark 1. 25. *h.* thy *p.* come out of him, *Luke* 4. 35.
Luke 19. 40. if they should *h.* their *peace* the stones
Acts 12. 17. beckoning to them to *h.* their *peace*
Acts 18. 9. be not afraid, but speak, and *h.* not thy *p.*
1 *Cor.* 14. 30. to another, let the first *h.* his *peace*
See TAKE.

HOLDEN.

2 *Kings* 23. 22. there was not *h.* such a passover, 23.
Job 36. 8. if they be *h.* in cords of affliction
Psal. 18. 35. and thy right hand hath *h.* me up
71. 6. by thee have I been *h.* up from the womb
73. 23. thou hast *h.* me up by my right hand
Prov. 5. 22. and shall be *h.* with the cords of his sins
Isa. 42. 14. I have long *h.* my peace and been still
45. 1. whose right hand I have *h.* to subdue nations
Luke 24. 16. eyes were *h.* they should not know him
Acts 2. 24. it was not possible he should be *h.* of it
Rom. 14. 4. yea, he shall be *h.* up, for God is able

HOLDEST.

Esth. 4. 14. if thou altogether *h.* thy peace this time
Job 13. 24. wherefore *h.* thou me for thine enemy?
Psal. 77. 4. thou *h.* my eyes waking, I am troubled
Jer. 49. 16. O thou that *h.* the height of the hill
Hab. 1. 13. *h.* thy tong. when the wicked devoureth
Rev. 2. 13. thou *h.* fast my name, hast not denied

HOLDETH.

Job 2. 3. and still he *h.* fast his integrity
26. 9. he *h.* back the face of his throne, and spread.
Psal. 66. 9. bless God who *h.* our soul in life
Prov. 11. 12. a man of understanding *h.* his peace
17. 28. a fool when he *h.* his peace is counted wise
Dan. 10. 21. and none *h.* with me but Michael
Amos 1. 5. I will cut off him that *h.* the sceptre, 8.
Rev. 2. 1. that *h.* the seven stars in his right hand

HOLDING.

Isa. 33. 15. that shaketh his hands from *h.* of bribes
Jer. 6. 11. I am weary with *h.* in, I will pour fury
Mark 7. 3. eat not, *h.* the tradition of the elders
Phil. 2. 16. *h.* forth the word of life, that I may
Col. 2. 19. not *h.* the head, from which the body
1 *Tim.* 1. 19. *h.* faith and a good conscience
3. 9. *h.* the mystery of faith in a pure conscience
Tit. 1. 9. *h.* fast faithful word, as hath been taught
Rev. 7. 1. I saw four angels *h.* the four winds

HOLDS.

Jer. 51. 30. they have remained in their *h.*
Ezek. 19. 9. and they brought him into *h.*
See STRONG.

HOLE.

Exod. 28. 32. there shall be an *h.* in the top of it
2 *Kings* 12. 9. Jehoiada bored a *h.* in the lid of it
Cant. 5. 4. put in his hand by the *h.* of the door
Isa. 11. 8. suck. child shall play on the *h.* of the asp
51. 1. look to *h.* or the pit whence ye are digged
Jer. 13. 4. and hide it there in a *h.* of the rock
Ezek. 8. 7. when I looked, behold a *h.* in the wall
Jam. 3. † 11. a fountain send at same *h.* sweet water

HOLES.

Gen. 40. † 16. I had baskets full of *h.* on my head
1 *Sam.* 14. 11. the Hebrews come forth out of the *h.*
Isa. 2. 19. they shall go into *h.* of the rocks, 7. 19.
42. 22. they are all of them snared in *h.* are hid
Jer. 16. 16. hunt them out of the *h.* of the rocks
48. 28. maketh her nest in sides of the *h.* mouth
Mic. 7. 17. they shall not move out of their *h.*
Nah. 2. 12. the lion filled his *h.* with prey, and dens
Hag. 1. 6. earneth wages to put it in a bag with *h.*
Zech. 14. 12. their eyes shall consume in their *h.*
Mat. 8. 20. Jesus saith, the foxes have *h. Luke* 9. 58.

HOLIER.

Isa. 65. 5. come not near, for I am *h.* than thou

HOLIEST.

Heb. 9. 3. the tabernacle which is called the *h.*
8. the way into the *h.* was not yet made manifest
10. 19. to enter into the *h.* by the blood of Jesus

HOLILY.

1 *Thess.* 2. 10. ye are witnesses how *h.* we behaved

HOLINESS.

Exod. 15. 11. who is like thee, glorious in *h.?*
28. 36. *h.* to the L. 35. † 2. | 39. 30. *Zech.* 14. 20, 21.
1 *Chr.* 16. 29. come before the Lord, worship the Lord in the beauty of *h. Psal.* 29. 2. | 96. 9.
2 *Chr.* 8. † 11. Solom. said, because the places are *h.*
20. 21. singers, that should praise the beauty of *h.*
31. 18. in office they sanctified themselves in *h.*
Psal. 30. 4. at the remembrance of his *h.* 97. 12.
47. 8. God sitteth upon the throne of his *h.*
48. 1. greatly to be praised in the mountain of his *h.*
60. 6. God hath spoken in his *h.* 108. 7.
89. 35. once have I sworn by my *h.* I will not lie
93. 5. *h.* becometh thine house, O Lord, for ever
110. 3. thy peopl shall be willing, in beauties of *h.*
Isa. 23. 18. and her hire shall be *h.* to the Lord
35. 8. and it shall be called the way of *h.*
62. 9. they shall drink it in the courts of my *h.*
63. 15. behold from habitation of thy *h.* and glory
18. the people of thy *h.* have possessed it
Jer. 2. 3. Israel was *h.* to the L. and the first fruits
23. 9. and because of the words of his *h.*
31. 23. the Lord bless thee, O mountain of *h.*
Amos 4. 2. the Lord God hath sworn by his *h.*
Obad. 17. but upon mount Zion there shall be *h.*
Mal. 2. 11. Judah hath profaned the *h.* of the Lord
Luke 1. 75. might serve him in *h.* and righteousness
Acts 3. 12. as though by our *h.* made this man walk
Rom. 1. 4. with power, according to the Spirit of *h.*
6. 19. yield members servants to right. unto *h.*
22. ye have your fruit unto *h.* and the end life
2 *Cor.* 7. 1. perfecting *h.* in the fear of God
Eph. 4. 24. new man created in righteousn. and *h.*
1 *Thess.* 3. 13. stablish your hearts unblameab. in *h.*
4. 7. hath not called us to uncleanness, but to *h.*
1 *Tim.* 2. 15. if they continue in faith and *h.*
Tit. 2. 3. that they be in behaviour as becometh *h.*
Heb. 12. 10. that we might be partakers of his *h.*
14. follow peace with men, and *h.* without which

HOLLOW.

Gen. 32. 25. he touched the *h.* of his thigh, 32.
Exod. 27. 8. shalt make the altar *h.* with bds. 38. 7.
Lev. 14. 37. if the plague be in walls with *h.* strakes
Judg. 15. 19. God clave an *h.* place in the jaw
Isa. 40. 12. who measured waters in *h.* of his hand
Jer. 52. 21. concerning the pillar, it was *h.*

HOLPEN.

Psal. 83. 8. they have *h.* the children of Lot
Psal. 86. 17. because thou, Lord, hast *h.* me
Isa. 31. 3. and he that is *h.* shall fall down
Dan. 11. 34. they shall be *h.* with a little help
Luke 1. 54. hath *h.* his servant Isr. in remembrance

HOLY.

Holiness. *True holiness consists in a conformity to the nature and will of God, whereby a saint is distinguished from the unrenewed world, and is not actuated by their principles and precepts, nor governed by their maxims and customs. There are different degrees of holiness in the Saints, but sincerity is inseparable from the being of it. All gold, as one observes, is not refined to the same degree and height of purity; but true gold, though in the lowest degree of fineness, will endure the furnace and the touchstone, and by that trial is discerned from counterfeit metal. The Holy Spirit, in renewing a man, infuses an universal habit of holiness, that is, comprehensive of all the variety of graces to be exercised in the life of a Christian.* Gal. 5. 22, 23. The fruit of the Spirit is love, joy, peace, long-suffering, gentleness, goodness, faith, meekness, temperance. *See* SANCTIFY.

Holy *is applied,* I. *To God the Father, Son, and Spirit, who is infinitely holy above all creatures, and is called by way of emphasis,* THE HOLY ONE. *All the holiness and perfection that creatures do or shall enjoy and possess to eternity, is derived from the immeasurable abyss of God's holiness, for he is the fountain of all holiness and purity.* II. *To his saints who are holy,* [1] *By separation and choice,* 1 Pet. 2. 9. [2] *By the imputation of Christ's holiness or righteousness to them,* Ezek. 16. 14. 2 Cor. 5. 21. [3] *By partaking of a holy principle of grace, whereby the soul is renewed in holiness by degrees, till it attains a perfection of it,* Heb. 12. 23. III. *To angels,* Mat. 25. 31. IV. *To persons and things dedicated to God,* Exod. 30. 35. | 31. 14. Lev. 16. 4.

The prophets call the Lord, The Holy One of Israel, *as if the name of* Holy *were synonymous with that of God.* They provoked the Holy One of Israel to anger, *Isa.* 1. 4. They shall stay upon the Lord, the Holy One of *Israel,* Isa. 10. 20. *And in* Isa. 29. 19. The poor among men shall rejoice in the Holy One of *Israel. The* Messiah *in like manner is called the* Holy One. *Psal.* 16. 10. Thou wilt not suffer thine Holy One to see corruption. *And in* Luke 4. 34. I know thee who thou art, the Holy One of God. *So in* Luke 1. 35. That holy thing which shall be born of thee, shall be called the Son of God. Christ *is called simply the* Holy One, *Acts* 3. 14. Holy *is likewise the common epithet given to the third person of the glorious Trinity,* Holy Ghost.

The Israelites *are often called holy in scripture, because they were the Lord's, who sanctified them; they professed the true religion, were called to holiness, which they were to endeavour to acquire, and which many in reality did attain to under the old law.* Exod. 19. 6. Ye shall be an holy nation. *See* Exod. 22. 31. Lev. 11. 44, 45. Num. 16. 3.

Christians *are still more particularly declared* holy. *They having received the earnests of the Holy Spirit in a more plentiful and perfect manner than were enjoyed under the law. In the* Acts, *and in* St. Paul's *Epistles, Christians are generally described under the name of* Saints. *Acts* 9. 13, 32, 41. Lord, I have heard by many of this man, how much evil he hath done to thy saints. *St.* Peter *came down to the* saints *which dwelt in* Lydda; *he raised* Tabitha *from the dead, and presented her to the* saints. *St.* Paul *directs his Epistle to the* Romans *thus,* To the beloved of God, called to be *saints,* Rom. 1. 7.

Holy place *is put for the* holy of holies, *or the most holy place.* Exod. 28. 29. *Aaron* shall bear the names of the children of *Israel* in the breast-plate of judgment upon his heart, when he goeth in unto the holy place. *Sometimes it is put for the court of the priests.* Lev. 10. 18. Behold, the blood of it was not brought in within the holy place; ye should indeed have eaten it in the holy place; *the court of the priests is called holy, compared with the court of the people; as in* Ezek. 42. 14. The priests shall not go out of the holy place into the outer court. *It is also taken for the whole temple.* Acts 6. 13. This man ceaseth not to speak blasphemous words against this holy place and the law. *And sometimes for heaven itself.* Isa. 57. 15. I dwell in the high and holy place; *so in* Heb. 9. 12. Neither by the blood of goats and calves, but by his own blood he entered in once into the *holy place.*

Exod. 3. 5. place whereon thou standest is *h.* ground
16. 23. to-morrow is the rest of the *h.* sabbath
19. 6. ye shall be to me a *h.* nation, 1 *Pet.* 2. 9.
20. 8. remember the sabbath day to keep it *h.*
28. 38. Israel shall hallow in all their *h.* gifts
29. 6. and put the *h.* crown upon the mitre
33. because they are *h.* || 34. because it is *h.*
30. 25. make it an oil of *h.* ointment compound
32. it is *h.* and it shall be *h.* unto you
35. perfume tempered together, pure and *h.*
31. 14. keep the sabbath, for it is *h.* unto you, 15.
Lev. 8. 9. and he put upon Aaron the *h.* crown
10. 10. ye may put difference between *h.* and unholy
16. 4. he shall put on the *h.* linen coat
33. he shall make atonement for the *h.* sanctuary
19. 2. for I the Lord your God am *h.* 21. 8.
20. 7. be ye *h.* || 21. 7. for he is *h.* unto his God
27. 14. a man sanctify his house to be *h.* to the L.
30. the tithe of the land is *h.* unto the Lord
Num. 5. 17. and the priest shall take *h.* water
15. 40. that ye may remember, and be *h.* to your G
16. 3. seeing all the congregation are *h.* every one
5. the Lord will shew who are his, and who is *h.*
18. 17. thou shalt not redeem them, they are *h.*
31. 6. sent Phinehas with the *h.* instruments

1 *Sam.* 2. 2. for there is none *h.* as the Lord
21. 5. and the vessels of the young men are *h.*
1 *Kings* 8. 4. they brought up the ark and the tabernacle, and all the *h.* vessels, 2 *Chron.* 5. 5.
2 *Kings* 4. 9. I perceive this is an *h.* man of God
1 *Chr.* 22. 19. bring the *h.* vessels into house of God
29. 3. above all that I have prepared for the *h.* house
2 *Chron.* 23. 6. they shall go in, for they are *h.*
35. 3. said to the Levites which were *h.* to the Ld. put the *h.* ark into the house Solomon built
13. but the other *h.* offerings sod they in pots
Ezra 8. 28. ye are *h.* to the Lord, vessels are *h.* also
9. 2. the *h.* seed mingled themselves with people
Neh. 9. 14. madest known unto them thy *h.* sabbath
Psal. 20. 6. he will hear him from his *h.* heaven
22. 3. thou art *h.* O thou that inhabitest praises
28. 2. when I lift my hands towards thy *h.* oracle
86. 2. preserve my soul, for I am *h.* O God, save
98. 1. his *h.* arm hath gotten him the victory
99. 5. worship at his footstool, for he is *h.*
9. exalt the Lord, and worship at his *h.* hill
105. 42. for he remembered his *h.* promise
145. 17. the Lord is *h.* in all his works
Prov. 9. 10. the knowledge of the *h.* is understanding
20. 25. to man, who devoureth that which is *h.*
30. 3. nor have I the knowledge of the *h.*
Isa. 4. 3. remaineth in Jerusalem shall be called *h.*
6. 3. one cried *h. h. h.* is the Lord of hosts
13. the *h.* seed shall be the substance thereof
27. 13. shall worship in the *h.* mountain at Jerusalem
30. 29. a song, as when a *h.* solemnity is kept
52. 10. the Lord hath made bare his *h.* arm
58. 13. call sabbath, the *h.* of the Lord, honourable
64. 10. thy *h.* cities are a wilderness, Zion a wilder.
11. our *h.* and beautiful house is burnt up
Jer. 11. 15. and the *h.* flesh is passed from thee
Ezek. 22. 26. put no difference between *h.* and profane
36. 38. I will increase them as the *h.* flock
42. 13. they be *h.* chambers where priests eat
14. there lay their garments, for they are *h.*
44. 19. and lay them in the *h.* chambers
23. shall teach difference between *h.* and profane
45. 1. shall offer an *h.* portion of the land, 4.
6. against the oblation of *h.* portion, 7. | 48. 18.
46. 19. into the *h.* chambers of the priests
48. 10. for the priests shall be this *h.* oblation
14. not sell first-fruits, for it is *h.* unto the Lord
20. shall offer the *h.* oblation four-square, 21.
Dan. 4. 8. but Daniel came in before me, in whom is the spirit of the *h.* gods, 9, 18. | 5. 11.
11. 28. his heart shall be against the *h.* covenant
30. indignation against the *h.* covenant, intelligence with them that forsake the *h.* covenant
Hag. 2. 12. if one bear *h.* flesh, and with his skirt touch bread, or pottage, or wine, or oil, shall it be *h.*?
Zech. 2. 12. Lord shall inherit Judah in the *h.* land
13. Lord is raised up out of his *h.* habitation
Mat. 7. 6. give not that which is *h.* unto the dogs
25. 31. shall come and all the *h.* angels with him
Mark 6. 20. knowing that he was a just man and *h.*
8. 38. cometh in glory with *h.* angels, *Luke* 9. 26.
Luke 1. 70. by the mouth of *h.* prophets, *Acts* 3. 21.
72. and to remember his *h.* covenant
2. 23. every male shall be called *h.* to the Lord
John 17. 11. *h.* Fath. keep those thou hast given me
Acts 4. 27. against thy *h.* child Jesus, whom thou
30. wonders may be done by name of thy *h.* child
7. 33. the place where thou standest is *h.* ground
10. 22. was warned from God by an *h.* angel
Rom. 1. 2. which he had promised in the *h.* scriptures
7. 12. the commandment is *h.* just, and good
11. 16. if the first-fruit be *h.* it the root be *h.*
12. 1. that ye present your bodies a *h.* sacrifice to G.
16. 16. salute one another with an *h.* kiss, 1 *Cor.* 16. 20. 2 *Cor.* 13. 12. 1 *Thess.* 5. 26. 1 *Pet.* 5. 14.
1 *Cor.* 3. 17. the temple of God is *h.* which temple
7. 14. but now are they *h.* || 34. that she may be *h.*
Eph. 1. 4. we should be *h.* and without blame, 5. 27.
Col. 1. 22. to present you *h.* and unblameable
3. 12. put on, as the elect of God, *h.* and beloved
1 *Thess.* 5. 27. this epistle be read to all the *h.* brethren
1 *Tim.* 2. 8. lifting up *h.* hands without wrath
2 *Tim.* 1. 9. who hath called us with an *h.* calling
3. 15. thou hast known *h.* scriptures able to make
Tit. 1. 8. a bishop must be sober, *h.* temperate
Heb. 3. 1. *h.* brethr. partakers of heavenly calling
7. 26. such an high-priest became us, who is *h.*
1 *Pet.* 1. 15. so be ye *h.* in all conversation, 16.
2. 5. an *h.* priesthood to offer up spiritual sacrifices
3. 5. the *h.* women also who trusted in God
2 *Pet.* 1. 18. when we were with him in *h.* mount
21. but *h.* men spake as moved by Holy Ghost
2. 21. than to turn from the *h.* commandment
3. 2. the words spoken before by the *h.* prophets
11. what persons to be in all *h.* conversation
Rev. 3. 7. write these things, saith he that is *h.*
4. 8. saying, *h. h. h.* Ld. God Almighty, which was
6. 10. cried, saying, how long, O Lord, *h.* and true
14. 10. be tormented in presence of the *h.* angels
15. 4. who shall not fear thee? for thou art *h.*
18. 20. rejoice over her, ye *h.* apostles and prophets
20. 6. *h.* is he that hath part in the first resurrection
21. 10. and he shewed me the *h.* Jerusalem
22. 6. Lord God of the *h.* prophets sent his angel
11. and he that is *h.* let him be *h.* still
See Convocation.

HOLY *day.*

Exod. 35. 2. the seventh shall be an *h. day*
Neh. 8. 9. this *day* is *h.* unto the Lord, 10, 11.
10. 31. not buy it of them on sabbath or *h. day*
Psal. 42. 4. with a multitude that kept *h. day*
Isa. 58. 13. from doing thy pleasure on my *h. day*
Col. 2. 16. let no man judge you in respect of an *h. d.*
See Garments.

HOLY *Ghost.*

Mat. 1. 18. she was found with child of the *H. Ghost*
20. what is conceived in her is of the *H. Ghost*
3. 11. shall baptize you with *H. Ghost* and with fire, *Mark* 1. 8. *Luke* 3. 16. *John* 1. 33. *Acts* 1. 5.
12. 31. blasphemy against the *H. Ghost* shall not be forgiven unto men, *Mark* 3. 29. *Luke* 12. 10.
32. whosoever speaketh against the *H. Ghost*
Mat. 28. 19. baptize in name of Father, Son, and *H. G.*
Mark 12. 36. David said by the *H. Ghost*, *Acts* 1. 16.
13. 11. it is not ye that speak, but the *H. Ghost*
Luke 1. 15. John shall be filled with the *H. Ghost*
35. the *H. Ghost* shall come upon thee
41. and Elisabeth was filled with the *H. Ghost*
67. his father Zacharias was filled with *H. Ghost*
2. 25. name was Simeon, and *H. Ghost* was upon him
26. and it was revealed unto him by the *H. Ghost*
3. 22. the *H. Ghost* descended in a bodily shape
4. 1. Jesus being full of the *H. Ghost* returned
12. 12. *H. Ghost* shall teach you in the same hour
John 7. 39. for the *H. Ghost* was not yet given
14. 26. but the Comforter, who is the *H. Ghost*
20. 22. he saith, receive ye the *H. G. Acts* 2. 38.
Acts 1. 2. after that he through the *H. G.* had given
8. after that the *H. Ghost* is come upon you
2. 4. they were all filled with the *H. Ghost*, 4. 31.
33. having received the promise of the *H. Ghost*
4. 8. Peter, filled with the *H. G.* said unto them
5. 3. Satan filled thy heart to lie to the *H. Ghost*
32. we are his witnesses, so is also the *H. Ghost*
6. 3. look out men full of the *H. G.* and wisdom
5. they chose Stephen, a man full of the *H. G.*
7. 51. ye stiff-necked, ye always resist the *H. G.*
55. he being full of *H. G.* looked up to heaven
8. 15. prayed that they might receive the *H. G.*
17. hands on them, and they received the *H. G.*
18. when Simon saw that the *H. G.* was given
19. on whom I lay hands, he may receive *H. G.*
9. 17. thou mightest be filled with the *H. Ghost*
31. walking in the comfort of the *H. Ghost*
10. 38. how God anointed Jesus with the *H. G.*
44. *H. G.* fell on all which heard the word
45. on Gentiles was poured the gift of the *H. G.*
47. which have received the *H. G.* as well as we
11. 15. *H. G.* fell on them as on us at beginning
16. but ye shall be baptized with the *H. Ghost*
24. Barnabas, full of the *H. Ghost* and faith
13. 2. the *H. G.* said, separate Barnabas and Saul
4. being sent forth by the *H. Ghost*, departed
9. Paul, filled with the *H. G.* set his eyes on him
52. the disciples were filled with the *H. Ghost*
15. 8. giving them the *H. Ghost* as he did unto us
28. it seemed good to the *H. Ghost*, and to us
16. 6. were forbidden of the *H. G.* to preach in Asia
19. 2. have ye received the *H. Ghost*? we have not heard whether there be any *H. Ghost*
6. laid hands on them, the *H. G.* came on them
20. 23. save that the *H. G.* witnesseth in every city
28. over which *H. G.* hath made you overseers
21. 11. thus saith the *H. Ghost*, so shall the Jews
28. 25. well spake the *H. G.* by Esaias the prophet
Rom. 5. 5. love of God shed in hearts by the *H. G.*
9. 1. conscience bearing me witness in the *H. Gh.*
14. 17. the kingdom of God is joy in the *H. Ghost*
15. 13. abound in hope through power of the *H. G.*
16. acceptable, being sanctified by the *H. Ghost*
1 *Cor.* 2. 13. but in words which the *H. G.* teacheth
6. 19. your body is the temple of the *H. Ghost*
12. 3. say that Jesus is Lord, but by the *H. Ghost*
2 *Cor.* 6. 6. by kindness, by the *H. Ghost*, by love
13. 14. the communion of the *H. G.* be with you
1 *Thess.* 1. 5. for our gospel came in the *H. Ghost*
6. received the word with joy of the *H. Ghost*
2 *Tim.* 1. 14. that good thing keep by the *H. Ghost*
Tit. 3. 5. he saved us by the renewing of the *H. G.*
Heb. 2. 4. bearing witness with gifts of the *H. Ghost*
3. 7. as the *H. Ghost* saith, to-day if ye will hear
6. 4. and were made partakers of the *H. Ghost*
9. 8. the *H. Ghost* this signifying, that the way
10. 15. whereof the *H. Ghost* is a witness to us
1 *Pet.* 1. 12. with the *H. G.* sent down from heaven
2 *Pet.* 1. 21. spake as they were moved by the *H. G.*
1 *John* 5. 7. the Father, the Word, and the *H. Gh.*
Jude 20. but ye, beloved, praying in the *H. Ghost*
See God, Habitation, Hill.

Most HOLY.

Exod. 26. 33. between the holy place and the *most h.*
34. on ark of the testimony in the *most h.* place
29. 37. and it shall be an altar *most h.* 40. 10.
30. 10. it is *most h.* || 29. that they may be *most h.*
36. the perfume shall be to you *most h.*
Lev. 2. 3. the remnant of the meat offering shall be Aaron's, it is *most h.* 10. | 6. 17. | 10. 12.
6. 25. the sin offering is *most h.* 29. | 10. 17.
7. 1. the trespass offering is *most h.* 6. | 14. 13.
21. 22. eat bread of God, both of *most h.* and holy
24. 9. the cakes of fine flour are *most h.* to him
27. 28. every devoted thing is *most h.* to the Lord
Num. 4. 4. this shall be service about *most h.* things
19. thus do, when they approach the *most h.* things
18. 9. the offering they render to me shall be *m. h.*
10. in the *most h.* place shalt thou eat it
1 *Kings* 6. 16. he built them for the *most h.* place
7. 50. Solomon made vessels for the *most h.* place
8. 6. brought the ark unto *m. h.* place, 2 *Chr.* 5. 7.
1 *Chron.* 6. 49. Aaron and sons for work of *most h.*
23. 13. Aaron separated to sanctify *most h.* things
2 *Chron.* 3. 8. Solomon made the *most h.* house
10. in the *most h.* house he made two cherubims
4. 22. the inner doors thereof for the *most h.* place
31. 14. and Kore to distribute the *most h.* things
Ezra 2. 63. not eat of the *most h.* things, *Neh.* 7. 65.
Ezek. 43. 12. the whole limit shall be *most h.*
44. 13. shall not come near in the *most h.* place
45. 3. in it shall be the sanctuary and *most h.* place
48. 12. this oblation shall be a thing *most h.*
Dan. 9. 24. seventy weeks to anoint the *most h.*
Hos. 11. † 12. Judah is faithful with the *most h.*
Jude 20. building yourselves on your *most h.* faith

HOLY *mountain.*

Psal. 87. 1. his foundation is in the *h. mountains*
Isa. 11. 9. nor destroy in my *h. mountain*, 65. 25.
56. 7. even them will I bring to my *h. mountain*
57. 13. and he shall inherit my *h. mountain*
65. 11. ye are they that forget my *h. mountain*
66. 20. on mules and swift beasts to my *h. mount.*
Ezek. 20. 40. in my *h. mountain* they shall serve me
28. 14. thou wast upon the *h. mountain* of God
Dan. 9. 16. let thy anger be turned from thy *h. m.*
20. presenting supplication for the *h. mountain*
Dan. 11. 45. plant tabernacles in glorious *h. mount.*
Joel 2. 1. sound an alarm in my *h. mountain*
3. 17. I am the Lord, dwelling in Zion my *h. moun.*
Obad. 16. for as ye have drunk on my *h. mountain*
Zeph. 3. 11. no more haughty, because of *h. mount.*
Zech. 8. 3. mountain of the Lord called the *h. mount.*

HOLY *name.*

Lev. 20. 3. seed to Molech, to profane my *h. name*
22. 2. and that they profane not my *h. name*
32. neither shall ye profane my *h. name*
1 *Chron.* 16. 10. glory ye in his *h. name*, *Ps.* 105. 3.
35. we give thanks to thy *h. name*, *Psal.* 106. 47.
29. 16. to build thee an house for thy *h. name*
Psal. 33. 21. because we trusted in his *h. name*
99. 3. praise thy terrible *name*, for it is *h.*
103. 1. bless the Lord, bless his *h. name*, 145. 21.
111. 9. *h.* and reverend is his *name*, *Luke* 1. 49.
Isa. 57. 15. saith the lofty One, whose *name* is *h.*
Ezek. 20. 39. but pollute you my *h. name* no more
36. 20. they profaned my *h. name* when they said
21. but I had pity for mine *h. name*
22. not for your sakes, but for my *h. name's* sake
39. 7. I will make my *h. name* known in Isr. I will not let them pollute my *h. name* any more
25. and I will be jealous for my *h. name*
43. 7. my *h. name* shall Israel no more defile
8. they have defiled my *h. n.* by their abominat.
Amos 2. 7. go in to same maid, to profane my *h. n.*

HOLY *One.*

Deut. 33. 8. Thummim and Urim be with thy *h. O.*
Job 6. 10. not concealed the words of the *h. One*
Ps. 16. 10. not leave my soul in hell, nor suffer thine *h. One* to see corruption, *Acts* 2. 27. | 13. 35.
89. 19. then thou spakest in vision to thy *h. One*
Isa. 10. 17. and his *h. One* shall be for a flame
29. 23. they shall sanctify the *h. One* of Jacob
40. 25. to whom shall I be equal? saith the *h. One*
43. 15. I am the Lord your *h. One*, the Creator
49. 7. thus saith the Redeemer of Isr. his *h. One*
Dan. 4. 13. an *h. One* came down from heaven, 23.
Hos. 11. 9. for I am the *h. One* in the midst of thee
Hab. 1. 12. art thou not from everlast. O L. my *h. O.*
3. 3. the *h. One* came from mount Paran
Mark 1. 24. man with unclean spir. said, I know thee who thou art, the *h. One* of God, *Luke* 4. 34.
Acts 3. 14. but ye denied the *h. One* and the Just
1 *John* 2. 20. ye have an unction from the *h. One*

HOLY *One of Israel.*

2 *Kings* 19. 22. thou hast exalted thy voice, and lifted thy eyes against the *h. One of Isr. Isa.* 37. 23.
Psal. 71. 22. to thee will I sing, O thou *h. One of Isr.*
78. 41. yea, they limited the *h. One of Israel*
89. 18. and the *h. One of Israel* is our king
Isa. 1. 4. they have provoked the *h. One of Israel*
5. 19. let counsel of the *h. One of Israel* draw nigh
24. and despised the word of the *h. one of Israel*
10. 20. shall stay on the Lord, the *h. One of Israel*
12. 6. great is the *h. One of Israel* in midst of thee
17. 7. his eyes shall have respect to *h. One of Isr.*
29. 19. the poor shall rejoice in the *h. One of Isr.*
30. 11. cause the *h. One of Israel* to cease from us
12. thus saith the *h. One of Israel*, 15.
31. 1. they look not unto the *h. One of Israel*
41. 14. saith thy Redeemer, the *h. One of Israel*
16. and thou shalt glory in the *h. One of Israel*
20. and the *h. One of Israel* hath created it
43. 3. I am the Ld. the *h. One of Isr.* thy Saviour
14. thus saith your Redeemer, the *h. One of Isr.*
45. 11. the Ld. the *h. One of Israel*, and his Maker
47. 4. Lord of hosts is his name, the *h. One of Isr.*
48. 17. saith thy Redeemer, the *h. One of Isr.* 51. 5.
49. 7. the Redeemer *of Israel*, and his *h. One*
55. 5. nations run unto thee, for the *h. One of Isr.*
60. 9. bring their gold to the *h. One of Israel*
14. shall call thee, the Zion of the *h. One of Isr.*
Jer. 50. 29. Babylon proud ag. the *h. One of Isr.*
51. 5. land filled with sin against the *h. One of Isr.*
Ezek. 39. 7. that I am the Lord, the *h. One in Isr.*

HOLY *ones.*

Dan. 4. 17. the demand by the word of the *h. ones*

HOLY *oil.*

Exod. 30. 25. it shall be an *h.* anointing *oil*, 31.
37. 29. and he made the *h.* anointing *oil*
Num. 35. 25. the high-priest was anointed with *h. oil*
Psal. 89. 20. with my *h. oil* have I anointed him

HOLY *people.*

Deut. 7. 6. thou art an *h. peo.* to the Lord, 14. 2, 21.
26. 19. that thou mayest be an *h. people* to the Ld.
28. 9. L. shall establish thee an *h. people* to himself
Isa. 62. 12. they shall call them, the *h. people*
Dan. 8. 24. he shall prosper, and destroy the *h. peo.*
12. 7. to scatter the power of the *h. people*

HOLY *place.*

Exod. 28. 29. when he goeth in unto the *h. place*, 35.
43. come near to minister in the *h. place*, 29. 30.
29. 31. thou shalt seeth his flesh in the *h. place*
31. 11. may make sweet incense for the *h. place*
35. 19. to do service in the *h. place*, 39. 1, 41.
38. 24. the gold in all the work of the *h. place*
Lev. 6. 16. with unleavened bread it shall be eaten in the *h. place*, 26. | 7. 6. | 10. 13. | 24. 9.
27. thou shalt wash that in the *h. place*
30. brought to reconcile withal in the *h. place*
10. 17. have ye not eaten sin offering in the *h. place*?
18. blood was not brought in within the *h. place*
14. 13. shall slay the burnt offering in the *h. place*
16. 2. that he come not at all times into the *h. place*
3. thus shall Aaron come into the *h. place*
16. he shall make an atonement for the *h. place*
17. goeth to make atonement in the *h. place*, 27.
20. hath made an end of reconciling the *h. place*
23. he put on when he went into the *h. place*
24. shall wash his flesh with water in the *h. place*
Josh. 5. 15. the *place* whereon thou standest is *h.*
1 *Kings* 8. 8. the staves were seen out in the *h. place*
10. priests come out of the *h. place*, 2 *Chr.* 5. 11.
1 *Chron.* 23. 32. keep the charge of the *h. place*
2 *Chron.* 29. 5. carry filthiness out of the *h. place*
7. nor offered burnt offerings in the *h. place*
30. 27. prayer came up to his *h.* dwelling-*place*
35. 5. stand in the *h. place* according to divisions
Ezra 9. 8. and to give us a nail in his *h. place*

Psal. 24. 3. and who shall stand in his *h. place?*
46. 4. the streams whereof make glad the *h. place*
68. 17. among them as in Sinai, in the *h. place*
Eccl. 8. 10. who had gone from the *place* of the *h.*
Isa. 57. 15. I dwell in the high and *h. place*
Ezek. 41. 4. he said to me, this is the most *h. place*
42. 13. the *place* is *h.* ‖ 14. not go out of the *h. place*
45. 4. it shall be an *h. place* for the sanctuary
Mat. 24. 15. ye see the abomination stand in *h. place*
Acts 6. 13. blasphemous words against this *h. place*
21. 28. this man hath polluted this *h. place*
Heb. 9. 12. Christ entered in once into the *h. place*
25. the high priest entered every year into *h. place*

HOLY *places.*

2 *Chron.* 8. 11. because the *places* are *h.* whereunto
Psal. 68. 35. thou art terrible out of thy *h. places*
Ezek. 7. 24. and their *h. places* shall be defiled
21. 2. and drop thy word toward the *h. placos*
Heb. 9. 24. Christ is not entered into *h. places* made

Shall be HOLY.

Exod. 22. 31. and ye *shall be h.* men unto me
29. 37. whatsoever toucheth the altar *shall be h.*
30. 29. whatsoever toucheth them *s. be h. Lev.* 6. 18.
32. it is holy, and it *shall be h.* unto you, 37.
40. 9. shalt anoint the tabernacle, and it *shall be h.*
Lev. 6. 27. shall touch the flesh thereof *shall be h.*
11. 44. ye *s. be h.* for I am holy, 45. | 19. 2. | 20. 26.
19. 24. fruit thereof *shall be h.* to praise the Lord
21. 6. priests *shall be h.* unto their God
23. 20. they *shall be h.* to the Lord for the priest
25. 12. it is the jubilee, it *shall be h.* unto you
27. 9. that any man giveth to the Lord *shall be h.*
10. then the exchange thereof *shall be h.* 33.
21. in the jubilee it *shall be h.* to the Lord
32. the tenth *shall be h.* unto the Lord
Num. 6. 5. the Nazarite *shall be h.* unto the Lord
16. 7. the man whom Lord doth choose he *shall be h.*
18. 10. every male shall eat it, it *shall be h.* unto thee
Deut. 23. 14. therefore *shall* thy camp *be h.*
Jer. 31. 40. the gate towards the east *shall be h.*
Ezek. 45. 1. the holy portion *shall be h.* with borders
Joel 3. 17. I dwell in Zion, then *shall* Jerusalem *be h.*

HOLY *Spirit.*

Psal. 51. 11. and take not thy *h. Spirit* from me
Isa. 63. 10. they rebelled and vexed his *h. Spirit*
11. where is he that put his *h. Spirit* within him?
Luke 11. 13. your heavenly Father give the *h. Spirit*
Eph. 1. 13. sealed with that *h. Spirit* of promise
4. 30. grieve not the *h. Spirit* of God, whereby
1 *Thess.* 4. 8. who hath given unto us his *h. Spirit*

HOLY *temple.*

Psal. 5. 7. I will worship toward thy *h. temple*, 138. 2.
11. 4. the Lord is in his *h. temple*, his eyes behold
65. 4. be satisfied with the goodness of thy *h. tem.*
79. 1. thy *h. temple* have they defiled, they laid
Jonah 2. 4. I will look again toward thy *h. temple*
7. my prayer came in unto thee, to thy *h. temple*
Mic. 1. 2. the Lord from his *h. temple* be witness
Hab. 2. 20. but the Lord is in his *h. temple*
Eph. 2. 21. groweth to an *h. temple* in the Lord

HOLY *thing.*

Lev. 22. 10. no stranger shall eat of the *h. thing*
14. if a man eat of the *h. thing* unwittingly
27. 23. thy estimation as an *h. thing* to the Lord
Num. 4. 15. but they shall not touch any *h. thing*
Ezek. 48. 12. oblation be to them a *thing* most *h.*
Luke 1. 35. therefore that *h. thing* born of thee

HOLY *things.*

Exod. 28. 38. Aaron may bear the iniquity of *h. t.*
Lev. 5. 15. sin thro' ignorance in the *h. things* of L.
22. 2. separate themselves from the *h. things* of Isr.
3. whosoever he be that goeth unto the *h. things*
4. not eat of the *h. things* till he be clean, 6, 12.
7. be clean, and shall afterward eat of the *h. th.*
15. they shall not profane the *h. things* of Israel
16. to bear iniquity, when they eat *h. things*
Num. 4. 20. not go in to see, when *h. t.* are covered
5. 9. every offering of *h. things* shall be his, 18. 19.
18. 32. neither shall ye pollute the *h. things*
Deut. 12. 26. thy *h. things* take and go to the place
1 *Chron.* 23. 28. their office was in purifying *h. th.*
2 *Chron.* 31. 6. they brought in the tithe of *h. things*
Neh. 10. 33. we made ordinances for the *h. things*
12. 47. they sanctified the *h. things* to the Levites
Ezek. 20. 40. there will I require your *h. things*
22. 8. thou hast despised mine *h. things*
26. her priests have profaned my *h. things*
44. 8. ye have not kept the charge of my *h. things*
13. shall not come near to any of my *h. things*
1 *Cor.* 9. 13. they who minister about *h. things*
Heb. 8. † 2. an high priest, a minister of *h. things*

HOME.

Gen. 39. 16. laid up garment till her lord came *h.*
43. 16. bring these men *h.* slay and make ready
Exod. 9. 19. man and beast not brought *h.* shall die
Deut. 21. 12. then thou shalt bring her *h.* to thy hou.
24. 5. but he shall be free at *h.* one year
Josh. 2. 18. bring all thy father's household *h.* to thee
Judg. 11. 9. if ye bring me *h.* again to fight
19. 9. get on your way, that thou mayest go *h.*
Ruth 1. 21. the Lord hath brought me *h.* empty
1 *Sam.* 2. 20. and they went unto their own *h.*
6. 7. and bring their calves *h.* from them
10. and the men shut up their calves at *h.*
10. 26. and Saul also went *h.* to Gibeah, 24. 22.
18. 2. let him go no more *h.* to his father's house
2 *Sam.* 13. 7. then David sent *h.* to Tamar, saying
14. 13. the king doth not fetch *h.* his banished
17. 23. Ahithophel gat him *h.* to his house
1 *Kings* 5. 14. a month in Lebanon, two months at *h.*
13. 7. come *h.* with me and refresh thyself, 15.
2 *Kings* 14. 10. and tarry at *h.* 2 *Chron.* 25. 19.
1 *Chron.* 13. 12. bring the ark of God *h.* to me
13. so David brought not the ark *h.* to himself
2 *Chron.* 25. 10. Amaziah separated the army of Ephr. to go *h.* they returned *h.* in great anger
Esth. 5. 10. when Haman came *h.* called his friends
Job 39. 12. believe that he will bring *h.* thy seed
Psal. 68. 12. she that tarried at *h.* divided the spoil
Prov. 7. 19. the good man is not at *h.* he is gone
20. and he will come *h.* at the day appointed
Eccl. 12. 5. because man goeth to his long *h.*
Jer. 6. † 2. likened Zion to a woman dwelling at *h.*
39. 14. that Gedaliah should carry him *h.*
Lam. 1. 20. abroad the sword, at *h.* there is as death
Hab. 2. 5. he is a proud man, neither keepeth at *h.*
Hag. 1. 9. when ye brought it *h.* I did blow upon it
Mat. 8. 6. my servant lieth at *h.* sick of the palsy
Mark 5. 19. go *h.* to thy friends and tell them
Luke 9. 61. let first bid them farewell which are at *h.*
15. 6. when he cometh *h.* he calleth his friends
John 16. † 32. scattered, every man to his own *h.*
19. 27. that disciple took her to his own *h.*
20. 10. the disciples went away to their own *h.*
Acts 2. † 46. contin. in temple breaking bread at *h.*
21. 6. we took ship, and they returned *h.* again
1 *Cor.* 11. 34. if any man hunger let him eat at *h.*
14. 35. let them ask their husbands at *h.*
2 *Cor.* 5. 6. that whilst we are at *h.* in the body
1 *Tim.* 5. 4. let them learn to shew piety at *h.*
Tit. 2. 5. to be discreet, chaste, keepers at *h.*

HOME-*born.*

Exod. 12. 49. one law shall be to him that is *h.-born*
Lev. 18. 9. thy sister whether *born* at *h.* or abroad
Jer. 2. 14. is Israel a servant? is he a *h.-born* slave?

HOMER

Was a measure of capacity in use among the Hebrews, *containing six pints very nearly. It was the tenth part of the* Ephah, *and was the measure of manna which God appointed for every* Israelite, *Exod.* 16. 16, 36. *See* EPHAH.

Lev. 27. 16. an *h.* of barley-seed at fifty shekels
Isa. 5. 10. the seed of an *h.* shall yield an ephah
Ezek. 45. 11. the measure shall be after the *h.*
13. the sixth part of an ephah of an *h.* of wheat
14. tenth part of a bath, for ten baths are an *h.*
Hos. 3. 2. I bought her for an *h.* and half an *h.*

HONEST.

Luke 8. 15. which in an *h.* and good heart, having
Acts 6. 3. look out among you seven men of *h.* report
Rom. 12. 17. provide things *h.* in sight of all men
2 *Cor.* 8. 21. provid. *h.* things in sight of L. and men
13. 7. but that ye should do that which is *h.*
Phil. 4. 8. whatsoever things are *h.* just, pure, lovely
Tit. 3. † 14. let ours learn to profess *h.* trades
1 *Pet.* 2. 12. having our conversation *h.* am. Gentiles

HONESTLY.

Rom. 13. 13. let us walk *h.* as in the day, not in riot.
1 *Thess.* 4. 12. may walk *h.* toward them without
Heb. 13. 18. conscience, in all things willing to live *h.*

HONESTY.

1 *Tim.* 2. 2. may lead peaceable life in godli. and *h.*

HONOUR,

Or to honour, *in scripture style, is taken not only for the inward or outward respect which people have and pay to persons who are superior to them; and to whom they owe particular marks of deference and distinction: but likewise for real services which are due to them.* Exod. 20. 12, Honour thy father and thy mother. *This precept requires, not only that we should shew our parents respect and deference, but likewise that we should assist and relieve them, and perform such services for them as they may stand in need of; as this precept is explained by our Saviour;* Mat. 15. 4, 5, 6. Honour *is likewise taken in the same sense in* 1 Tim. 5. 3, 17. Honour widows that are widows indeed. *Not only respect, but also relieve them.* Let elders that rule well be counted worthy of double honour. *Let them have a liberal maintenance.* Honour *is taken for a recompense or reward,* Num. 24. 11. I thought to promote thee unto great honour, but lo, the Lord hath kept thee back from honour; *that is, hath deprived thee of the reward I designed for thee. By* honour *is also understood that adoration which is due to God only.* Psal. 29. 2. Give unto the Lord the honour due unto his name. *So in* Mal. 1. 6. If then I be a father, where is mine honour? *And in* 1 Tim. 1. 17. Unto the only wise God be honour and glory. *It is put for an honourable function, or office, such as was that of the holy priesthood under the law,* Heb. 5. 4. No man taketh this honour, *this honourable office,* unto himself, but he that is called of God, as was *Aaron. And for those great blessings and enjoyments which are bestowed on the saints in heaven.* Rom. 2. 10, Glory, honour, and peace to every man that worketh good.

Gen. 49. 6. to their assembly, my *h.* be not united
Exod. 8. † 9. Moses said, have this *h.* over me
14. 17. and I will get me *h.* upon Pharaoh
18. when I have gotten me *h.* upon Pharaoh
Num. 22. 17. I will promote thee unto great *h.* 37.
24. 11. the Lord hath kept thee back from *h.*
27. 20. thou shalt put some of thine *h.* upon him
Deut. 26. 19. make thee high above all nations in *h.*
Judg. 4. 9. the journey shall not be for thine *h.*
13. 17. thy sayings come to pass, we may do thee *h.*
2 *Sam.* 6. 22. of them shall I be had in *h.*
1 *Kings* 3. 13. I have also given thee riches and *h.*
1 *Chr.* 16. 27. glory and *h.* are in his presence
17. 18. what can Dav. say more for *h.* of thy serv.
29. 12. both riches and *h.* come of thee
28. David died in old age, full of riches and *h.*
2 *Chr.* 1. 11. thou hast not asked riches or *h.*
12. I will give thee riches, and wealth, and *h.*
17. 5. Jehoshaphat had *h.* in abundance, 18. 1.
26. 18. nor shall it be for thy *h.* from the Lord
32. 27. Hezekiah had much riches and *h.*
33. the inhabitants of Jerusalem did him *h.*
Esth. 1. 4. to shew the *h.* of his excellent majesty
20. all wives shall give to their husbands *h.*
6. 3. what *h.* hath been done Mordecai for this?
† 6. the man in whose *h.* the king delighteth
8. 16. the Jews had light and gladness, joy and *h.*
Job 14. 21. his sons come to *h.* he knoweth it not
Psal. 7. 5. let the enemy lay mine *h.* in the dust
8. 5. thou hast crowned him with *h. Heb.* 2. 7, 9.
21. 5. *h.* and majesty hast thou laid upon him
26. 8. I loved the place where thine *h.* dwelleth
29. † 2. give unto the Lord the *h.* of his name
49. 12. nevertheless man being in *h.* abideth not
20. man that is in *h.* and understandeth not
Psal. 66. 2. sing forth the *h.* of his name, make his
71. 8. let my mouth be filled with thy *h.* all the day
96. 6. *h.* and majesty are before him, strength
104. 1. thou art clothed with *h.* and majesty
112. 9. his horn shall be exalted with *h.*
145. 5. I will speak of the *h.* of thy majesty
149. 9. this *h.* have all his saints, praise the Lord
Prov. 3. 16. and in her left hand are riches and *h.*
4. 8. exalt her, and she shall bring thee to *h.*
5. 9. lest thou give thine *h.* to others, thy years
8. 18. riches and *h.* are with me, durable riches
11. 16. a gracious woman retaineth *h.*
14. 28. in the multitude of people is the king's *h.*
15. 33. and before *h.* is humility, 18. 12.
20. 3. it is an *h.* for a man to cease from strife
21. 21. he that followeth mercy, findeth *h.*
22. 4. by the fear of the Lord are riches and *h.*
25. 2. the *h.* of kings is to search out a matter
26. 1. so *h.* is not seemly for a fool
8. so is he that giveth *h.* to a fool
29. 23. *h.* shall uphold the humble in spirit
31. 25. strength and *h.* are her clothing
Eccl. 6. 2. a man to whom God hath given *h.*
10. 1. so folly him that is in reputation for *h.*
Jer. 33. 9. be to me an *h.* before all nations of earth
Dan. 2. 6. ye shall receive rewards and great *h.*
4. 30. that I have built for the *h.* of my majesty
36. mine *h.* and brightness returned unto me
5. 18. O king, God gave thy father glory and *h.*
11. 21. they shall not give the *h.* of the kingdom
Mal. 1. 6. if then I be a father, where is mine *h.?*
Mat. 13. 57. Jesus said, a prophet is not without *h.* save in his own country, *Mark* 6. 4. *John* 4. 44.
John 5. 41. I receive not *h.* from men
44. who receive *h.* one of another, and seek not *h.*
8. 54. if I honour myself, my *h.* is nothing
Rom. 2. 7. in well doing seek for glory and *h.*
10. but *h.* to every man that worketh good
9. 21. of the same lump to make one vessel to *h.*
12. 10. kindly affectioned, in *h.* preferring one ano.
13. 7. render therefore *h.* to whom *h.* is due
1 *Cor.* 12. 23. we bestow more abundant *h.* 24.
2 *Cor.* 6. 8. by *h.* and dishonour, by evil report
Col. 2. 23. not in any *h.* to the satisfying of the flesh
1 *Thess.* 4. 4. know how to possess his vessel in *h.*
1 *Tim.* 1. 17. to the only wise God be *h.* and glory
5. 17. let elders be counted worthy of double *h.*
6. 1. count their own masters worthy of all *h.*
16. to whom be *h.* and power everlasting
2 *Tim.* 2. 20. vessels, some to *h.* some to dishon. 21.
Heb. 3. 3. who builded, hath more *h.* than the house
5. 4. no man taketh this *h.* to himself, but he called
1 *Pet.* 1. 7. might be found to praise, *h.* and glory
2. † 7. unto you that believe he is an *h.*
3. 7. giving *h.* to the wife as to the weaker vessel
2 *Pet.* 1. 17. he received from God the Father *h.*
Rev. 4. 9. when those beasts give glory and *h.*
11. thou art worthy to receive glory and *h.* 5. 12.
5. 13. *h.* power, and might be to him, 7. 12. | 19. 1.
19. 7. let us be glad, rejoice, and give *h.* to him
21. 24. kings bring their glory and *h.* to it, 26.

HONOURS.

Acts 28. 10. who also honoured us with many *h.*

HONOUR, *Verb.*

Exod. 20. 12. *h.* thy father and thy moth. *Deut.* 5. 16. *Mat.* 15. 4. | 19. 19. *Mark* 7. 10. | 10. 19. *Luke* 18. 20. *Eph.* 6. 2.
Lev. 19. 15. shalt not *h.* the person of the mighty
32. thou shalt *h.* the face of the old man
Judg. 9. 9. wherewith by me they *h.* God and man
1 *Sam.* 2. 30. Ld. saith, for them that *h.* me I will *h.*
15. 30. yet *h.* me now, I pray thee, before elders
2 *Sam.* 10. 3. thinkest thou that David doth *h.* thy father, that he sent to thee, 1 *Chron.* 19. 3.
Esth. 6. 6. whom the king delighteth to *h.* 7, 9, 11.
Psal. 91. 15. I will deliver him and *h.* him
Prov. 3. 9. *h.* the L. with thy substance and first-fru.
Isa. 29. 13. this people with their lips do *h.* me
43. 20. the beast of the field shall *h.* me
58. 13. and shalt *h.* him, not doing thine own ways
Dan. 4. 37. I extol and *h.* the King of heaven
11. 38. in his estate shall he *h.* the God of forces, a god whom his fathers knew not, shall he *h.*
Mat. 15. 6. and *h.* not his father or his mother
John 5. 23. that all men should *h.* Son as they *h.* Fa.
8. 49. but I *h.* my Father, and ye dishonour me
54. if I *h.* myself, my *h.* is nothing
12. 26. if any serve me, him will my Father *h.*
1 *Tim.* 5. 3. *h.* widows that are widows indeed
1 *Pet.* 2. 17. *h.* all men, fear God, *h.* the king

HONOURABLE.

Gen. 34. 19. Shechem was more *h.* than all house
Num. 22. 15. Balak sent princes more *h.* than they
1 *Sam.* 9. 6. there is in the city a man of God, and he is an *h.* man, all he saith cometh to pass
22. 14. faithful as David, who is *h.* in thy house
2 *Sam.* 23. 19. was he not most *h.* of three? therefore he was their captain, 1 *Chron.* 11. 21.
23. was more *h.* than the thirty, but attained not
2 *Kings* 5. 1. now Naaman was *h.* with his master
1 *Chron.* 4. 9. Jabez was more *h.* than his brethren
11. 25. behold, was *h.* among thirty, attained not
Job 22. 8. had the earth, and the *h.* man dwelt in it
Psal. 45. 9. kings' daughters among thy *h.* women
111. 3. his work is *h.* and glorious
Isa. 3. 3. the Lord doth take away the *h.* man
5. the base shall behave proudly against the *h.*
5. 13. and their *h.* men are famished
9. 15. the ancient and *h.* he is the head
23. 8. whose traffickers are the *h.* of the earth
9. bring into contempt all the *h.* of the earth
42. 21. he will magnify the law, and make it *h.*
43. 4. thou hast been *h.* ‖ 58. 13. holy of the L. *h.*
Nah. 3. 10. and they cast lots for her *h.* men
Mark 15. 43. Joseph of Arimathea an *h.* counsellor
Luke 14. 8. lest a more *h.* man be bidden of him
Acts 13. 50. the Jews stirred up the *h.* women
17. 12. also of *h.* women not a few believed
1 *Cor.* 4. 10. we are weak, but ye are strong, ye are *h.*
12. 23. those members which we think less *h.*
Heb. 13. 4. marriage is *h.* and the bed undefiled

HONOURED.
Exod. 14. 4. I will be *h.* on Pharaoh and his host
Prov. 13. 18. he that regardeth reproof shall be *h.*
27. 18. he that waiteth on his master shall be *h.*
Isa. 43. 23. nor hast thou *h.* me with thy sacrifices
Lam. 1. 8. all that *h.* her, despise her, they have seen
5. 12. the faces of the elders were not *h.*
Dan. 4. 34. I praised and *h.* him that liveth for ever
Acts 28. 10. who also *h.* us with many honours
1 *Cor.* 12. 26. or one member be *h.* all rejoice with it

HONOUREST.
1 *Sam.* 2. 29. and *h.* thy sons above me, to make fat

HONOURETH.
Psal. 15. 4. but he *h.* them that fear the Lord
Prov. 12. 9. is better than he that *h.* himself
14. 31. but he that *h.* him hath mercy on the poor
Mal. 1. 6. a son *h.* his father, where is my honour?
Mat. 15. 8. and *h.* me with their lips, *Mark* 7. 6.
John 5. 23. he that *h.* not the Son, *h.* not the Father
8. 54. it is my Father that *h.* me, of whom ye say

HONEY.
Bees are some of the smallest creatures that fly, and the produce of them is the sweetest thing in the world. The scripture, describing a troop of enemies pursuing with obstinacy and warmth, makes use of the similitude of bees. *Deut.* 1. 44. The *Amorites* chased you as bees. *And in* Psal. 118. 12. They compassed me about like bees. *As to* honey, *God did not permit any to be offered to him upon his altar.* Lev. 2. 11. Ye shall burn no leaven, nor any honey, in any offering of the Lord made by fire. *There are many reasons given for the expediency of this law; such as, that* honey *does not agree well with other things, which are offered in the way of sacrifice, that it makes bread sour, and is not good with roast meat; or because bees are insects which are judged to be unclean,* Lev. 11. 23. *Or because* honey *is the symbol of carnal pleasures; or, lastly, to keep at a distance from the customs of the heathens, who were used to offer* honey *in their sacrifices.*

But at the same time that God forbids any honey *to be offered to him in sacrifice, he commands the first-fruits of it to be presented to him,* Lev. 2. 12. As for the oblation of the first-fruits, ye shall offer them unto the Lord; *but these first-fruits and offerings were designed for the support and sustenance of the priests, and were not offered upon the altar. The* Rabbins, *by the word* honey *in the above-cited place, understand not only the* honey *of bees, but likewise the* honey *of dates, or the fruit of the palm-tree, or the dates themselves, from which* honey *is extracted.*

The expressions of scripture which import so frequently that Palestine *was a land* flowing with milk and honey, *are a good proof that* honey *was formerly very common in that country.* Moses *says, that the Lord made his people* to suck honey out of the rock, and oil out of the flinty rock, *Deut.* 32. 13. Honey *ran upon the ground in the forest, where* Jonathan *dipped the end of his staff in this liquor, and conveyed it to his mouth,* 1 Sam. 14. 25, 26, 27. John *the* Baptist *fed upon wild* honey, *which was to be found in the rocks up and down the country, or in hollow trees,* Mat. 3. 4. *Children were fed with milk, cream, and* honey. Isa. 7. 15. Butter and honey shall he eat, that he may know to refuse the evil, and choose the good. *This was the sweetest and most delicious thing which was then known before the invention and preparation of sugar, and therefore things that are sweet, pleasant, and agreeable, are in scripture compared to it. As the word of God,* Psal. 119. 103. *Wisdom,* Prov. 24. 13, 14. *God complains of* Jerusalem *for offering that bread, oil, and* honey *to idols, which he had given to the inhabitants thereof for their nourishment,* Ezek. 16. 13, 19. *And* Solomon *observes, that too great a quantity of* honey *is hurtful to the stomach, and creates a loathing,* Prov. 25. 16.

Gen. 43. 11. carry a little *h.* spices, myrrh, nuts
Exod. 16. 31. taste of it was like wafers made with *h.*
Lev. 2. 11. ye shall burn no leaven, nor any *h.*
Deut. 8. 8. a land of oil-olive and *h.* 2 *Kings* 18. 32.
32. 13. he made him to suck *h.* out of the rock
Judg. 14. 8. there was *h.* in carcase of the lion, 9.
18. what sweeter than *h.*? what stronger than lion?
1 *Sam.* 14. 25. and there was *h.* upon the ground
26. *h.* dropped ‖ 29. I tasted a little *h.* 43.
2 *Sam.* 17. 29. brought *h.* and butter to David
1 *Kings* 14. 3. take a cruse of *h.* and go to him
2 *Chron.* 31. 5. Israel brought the first-fruits of *h.*
Job 20. 17. he shall not see the brooks of *h.* and but.
Psal. 19. 10. judgment sweeter than *h.* 119. 103.
81. 16. with *h.* out of the rock have satisfied thee
Prov. 24. 13. my son, eat *h.* because it is good, 25. 16.
25. 27. it is not good to eat much *h.*
Cant. 4. 11. *h.* and milk are under thy tongue
5. 1. I have eaten my honey-comb with my *h.*
Isa. 7. 15. but. and *h.* shall he eat, that he may know
22. for butter and *h.* shall every one eat that is left
Jer. 41. 8. we have treasures of *h.* in the field
Ezek. 3. 3. it was in my mouth as *h.* for sweetness
16. 13. thou didst eat fine flour, *h.* and oil, 19.
27. 17. Judah traded in *h.* and balm with Tyrus
Mat. 3. 4. John the Baptist's raiment of camel's hair, and his meat was locusts and wild *h.* *Mark* 1. 6.
Rev. 10. 9. but it shall be in thy mouth sweet as *h.*
10. and it was in my mouth sweet as *h.*

See FLOWETH, FLOWING.

HONEY-*comb.*
1 *Sam.* 14. 27. put forth rod and dipt it in a *h.-comb*
Psal. 19. 10. sweeter also than honey and *h.-comb*
Prov. 5. 3. the lips of a strange woman drop as *h.-c.*
16. 24. pleasant words are as an *h.-comb*, sweet
24. 13. eat the *h.-comb* which is sweet to thy taste
27. 7. the full soul loatheth an *h.-comb*
Cant. 4. 11. thy lips, O my spouse, drop as an *h.-comb*
5. 1. I have eaten my *h.-comb* with my honey
Luke 24. 42. they gave him a piece of an *h.-comb*

HOODS.
Isa. 3. 23. I will take away the *h.* and the vails

HOOF.
Exod. 10. 26. there shall not an *h.* be left behind
Lev. 11. 3. whatever parteth *h.* and is cloven-footed
4. of them that divide the *h.* but divideth not *h.*
5. but divideth not the *h.* 6. *Deut.* 14. 7.
7. the swine, tho' he divide the *h.* *Deut.* 14. 8.

HOOFS.
Judg. 5. 22. then were the horse *h.* broken
Psal. 69. 31. please Lord better than an ox with *h.*
Isa. 5. 28. their horses' *h.* shall be counted like flint
Jer. 47. 3. at the noise of the stamping of the *h.*
Ezek. 26. 11. with *h.* of horses shall tread thy streets
32. 13. nor shall the *h.* of beasts trouble them
Mic. 4. 13. I will make thy *h.* brass, and shall beat

HOOK.
2 *Kings* 19. 28. I will put my *h.* in thy nose, *Isa.* 37. 29.
Job 41. 1. canst thou draw leviathan with an *h.*? 2.
Mat. 17. 27. go, and cast an *h.* and take up a fish

HOOKS.
Exod. 26. 32. their *h.* shall be of gold, 37. | 36. 36.
27. 10. the *h.* of the pillars shall be of silver, and their fillets of silver, 11, 17. | 38. 10, 11, 12, 17, 19.
Isa. 2. 4. their spears into pruning *h.* *Mic.* 4. 3.
18. 5. he shall cut off the sprigs with pruning *h.*
Ezek. 29. 4. but I will put *h.* in thy jaws, 38. 4.
40. 43. and within were *h.* an hand broad
Joel 3. 10. beat your pruning *h.* into spears
Amos 4. 2. that he will take you away with *h.*

HOPE.
Christian hope *is a firm expectation of all promised good things, so far as they may be for God's glory and our good, but especially of eternal salvation and happiness in heaven, where we shall be conformed to the Son of God; which hope is founded on the grace, blood, righteousness, and intercession of* Christ, *and the earnest of the Holy Spirit in our hearts, and the unchangeable truth and almighty power of God, which always second his word.*

This hope *is distinguished from worldly hopes,* (1) *By the excellency of the object, which is an eternal state of glory and joy; whereas worldly hopes are terminated on empty vanishing things, gilded over with the thin appearance of good.* (2) *By the stability of its foundation, namely, God's unchangeable truth, and almighty power.* God cannot lie, *and consequently neither deceive our faith, nor disappoint our hopes; and he can do all things, which the apostle makes the ground of his confidence.* 2 Tim. 1. 12. I know whom I have believed, and I am persuaded that he is able to keep that which I have committed to him against that day. *But worldly hopes are always uncertain: There is so much of impotence or deceit in all the means used to obtain human desires, that the success is doubtful.* (3) *Divine hope is distinguished from carnal presumption, by its inseparable effect, it has a cleansing efficacy.* 1 John 3. 3. Every man that hath this hope in him purifieth himself, even as he is pure. *He endeavours to shun all sin, and to be perfecting holiness. He purifies himself by the assistance of the Holy Spirit, from whom the spiritual life, and all the operations of it, do proceed. But vain and groundless hopes are inspirations of wind, loose and ineffective.*

The hope of Israel, *is the* Messiah, *the* Lord Jesus Christ. *Acts* 28. 20. For the hope of Israel I am bound with this chain. Christ *is so called in respect of the fathers, who looked for his promised coming. Some by this understand the belief of the resurrection.* Christ *is called* our hope; *that is, the only foundation we have to build our hope of heaven, or any good thing, upon,* 1 Tim. 1. 1. Hope *is taken for that eternal salvation, which is the object or end of our hope.* Tit. 2. 13. Looking for that blessed hope. *The Lord is called* the hope of his people, *Jer.* 14. 8. *He is that God in whom alone they hope for help; and their hope shall not be confounded: On the contrary,* the hope of the ungodly shall perish, *Prov.* 10. 28. | 11. 7. *their hope shall be without effect: or they shall live and die without hope.* Hope deferred maketh the heart sick: *delays in obtaining that good, which a man passionately desires and hopes for, make the heart sad and sorrowful; but when any one possesses what he desires, his soul is comforted and revived,* Prov. 13. 12. My flesh shall rest in hope, *Psal.* 16. 9. *My body shall quietly and sweetly rest in the grave, in confident assurance of its resurrection to a blessed and immortal life. Abraham* against hope believed in hope, *when being advanced in years, God promised him a son,* Rom. 4. 18. *He confidently believed God's promise that he should have a son, against all grounds of hope, when it was most unlikely in a way of nature and reason.* The prisoners of hope, *Zech.* 9. 12. *are the* Israelites, *who were captives in* Babylon, *but were in hopes of deliverance. Or,* ye prisoners of hope, *ye who, though captives to sin and Satan, yet have good grounds to hope for deliverance:* turn ye to the strong hold, *repent, believe, and apply to the* Lord Jesus Christ, *your only help and refuge.*

Ruth 1. 12. if I should say, I have *h.* if I should have
Ezra 10. 2. there is *h.* in Israel concerning this
Job 4. 6. is not this thy fear, confidence, thy *h.*?
5. 16. poor hath *h.* and iniquity stoppeth her mouth
7. 6. my days are spent without *h.*
8. 13. and the hypocrite's *h.* shall perish, 14.
11. 18. thou shalt be secure, because there is *h.*
20. their *h.* shall be as the giving up of the ghost
14. 7. for there is *h.* of a tree if it be cut down
19. and thou destroyest the *h.* of man
27. 8. what is *h.* of hypocrite tho' he hath gained?
41. 9. behold, the *h.* of him is in vain
Psal. 78. 7. that they might set their *h.* in God
146. 5. happy is he whose *h.* is in the Lord his God
Prov. 10. 28. the *h.* of the righteous shall be gladness
11. 7. and the *h.* of unjust men perisheth
13. 12. *h.* deferred maketh the heart sick
14. 32. but the righteous hath *h.* in his death
19. 18. chasten thy son while there is *h.*
26. 12. is more *h.* of a fool than of him, 29. 20.
Eccl. 9. 4. to him who is joined to living, there is *h.*
Isa. 57. 10. there is no *h.* *Jer.* 2. 25. | 18. 12.
Jer. 14. 8. O thou *h.* of Israel, the Saviour, 17. 13.
17. 7. blessed is the man whose *h.* the Lord is
31. 17. there is *h.* in the end, saith the Lord
50. 7. even the Lord, the *h.* of their fathers
Lam. 3. 21. this I recall to my mind, theref. have I *h.*
29. his mouth in the dust, if so be there may be *h.*
Ezek. 19. 5. when she saw that her *h.* was lost
37. 11. behold, they say, our bones dried, our *h.* lost
Hos. 2. 15. the valley of Achor for a door of *h.*
Joel 3. 16. the Lord will be the *h.* of his people
Zech. 9. 12. turn to the strong hold ye prisoners of *h.*
Acts 16. 19. when saw the *h.* of their gains was gone
23. 6. of the *h.* and resurrection of the dead
24. 15. I have *h.* toward G. which they also allow
26. 6. now I am judged for the *h.* of the promise
7. for which *h.* sake, I am accused of the Jews
27. 20. all *h.* that we should be saved was gone
28. 20. for *h.* of Israel I am bound with this chain
Rom. 5. 4. patience, experience; experience, *h.*
5. *h.* maketh not ashamed, because love of God
8. 24. for we are saved by *h.* but *h.* seen is not *h.*
15. 4. that we through patience might have *h.*
13. that ye may abound in *h.* thro' the H. Ghost
1 *Cor.* 9. 10. that he should be partaker of his *h.*
13. 13. now abideth faith, *h.* charity, these three
15. 19. if in this life only we have *h.* in Christ
2 *Cor.* 1. 7. and our *h.* of you is stedfast, knowing
3. 12. seeing that we have such *h.* we use plainness
10. 15. having *h.* when your faith is increased
Gal. 5. 5. for we thro' the Spirit wait for *h.* of right.
Eph. 1. 18. may know what is the *h.* of his calling
2. 12. having no *h.* and without God in the world
4. 4. one Spirit, even as ye are called in one *h.*
Col. 1. 5. for the *h.* laid up for you in heaven
23. be not moved away from the *h.* of the gospel
27. which is Christ in you, the *h.* of glory
1 *Thess.* 1. 3. your patience of *h.* in our Lord Jesus
2. 19. for what is our *h.* or joy? are not even ye
4. 13. ye sorrow not, even as others who have no *h.*
5. 8. and for an helmet the *h.* of salvation
2 *Thess.* 2. 16. who hath given us good *h.* thro' grace
1 *Tim.* 1. 1. of our Lord Jesus, who is our *h.*
Tit. 2. 13. looking for that blessed *h.* and appearing
3. 7. made heirs according to the *h.* of eternal life
Heb. 3. 6. rejoicing of the *h.* firm to the end
6. 11. to the full assurance of *h.* unto the end
18. who have fled to lay hold on *h.* set before us
19. which *h.* we have as an anchor of the soul
7. 19. but the bringing in of a better *h.* did
1 *Pet.* 1. 3. who hath begotten us again to a lively *h.*
21. that your faith and *h.* might be in God
3. 15. that asketh a reason of the *h.* that is in you
1 *John* 3. 3. every man that hath this *h.* in him

In HOPE.
Psal. 16. 9. my flesh shall rest *in h.* *Acts* 2. 26.
Rom. 4. 18. who against hope believed *in h.*
5. 2. and rejoice *in h.* of the glory of God
8. 20. of him who hath subjected the same *in h.*
12. 12. rejoicing *in h.* patient in tribulation
15. 13. that ye may abound *in h.* thro' Holy Ghost
1 *Cor.* 9. 10. that ploweth *in h.* that thresheth *in h.*
Tit. 1. 2. *in h.* of eternal life which God promised

My HOPE.
Job 17. 15. and where is now *my h.*? as for *my h.*
19. 10. and *my h.* hath he removed like a tree
31. 24. if I have made gold *my h.* or have said
Psal. 39. 7. Lord, what wait I for? *my h.* is in thee
71. 5. for thou art *my h.* O Lord God, *Jer.* 17. 17.
119. 116. and let me not be ashamed of *my h.*
Lam. 3. 18. and *my h.* is perished from the Lord
Phil. 1. 20. accord. to *my h.* that in nothing I shall

HOPE, *Verb.*
Job 6. 11. what is my strength, that I should *h.*?
Psal. 22. 9. thou didst make me *h.* when I was upon
31. 24. be of courage, all ye that *h.* in the Lord
33. 18. upon them that *h.* in his mercy, 147. 11.
22. thy mercy be on us, according as we *h.* in thee
38. 15. for in thee, O Lord, do I *h.* thou wilt hear
42. 5. why cast down? *h.* thou in God, 11. | 43. 5.
71. 14. but I will *h.* continually, and praise thee
119. 49. word on which thou hast caused me to *h.*
81. my soul faint. I *h.* in thy word, 114. | 130. 5.
130. 7. let Israel *h.* in the Lord, 131. 3.
Isa. 38. 18. they in the pit cannot *h.* for thy truth
Lam. 3. 24. my portion, therefore will I *h.* in him
26. it is good that a man should both *h.* and wait
Ezek. 13. 6. and they have made others to *h.*
Luke 6. 34. if lend to them of whom ye *h.* to receive
Acts 26. 7. to which promise our tribes *h.* to come
Rom. 8. 24. what a man seeth, why doth he *h.* for?
25. if we *h.* for that we see not, then do we wait
Phil. 2. 23. him I *h.* to send presently, soon as I see
1 *Pet.* 1. 13. wherefore be sober, and *h.* to the end

HOPED.
Esth. 9. 1. the enemies of the Jews *h.* to have power
Job 6. 20. they were confounded because they had *h.*
Psal. 119. 43. for I have *h.* in thy judgments
74. because I have *h.* in thy word, 147.
166. Lord, I have *h.* for thy salvation
Jer. 3. 23. in vain is salvation *h.* for from the hills
Luke 23. 8. he *h.* to have seen some miracle done
Acts 24. 26. he *h.* money should have been given
2 *Cor.* 8. 5. and this they did, not as we *h.*
Heb. 11. 1. faith is the substance of things *h.* for

HOPETH.
1 *Cor.* 13. 7. charity *h.* all things, endureth all things

HOPING.
Luke 6. 35. do good, and lend, *h.* for nothing again
1 *Tim.* 3. 14. I write, *h.* to come unto thee shortly

HORN.
The principal defence and greatest strength of horned beasts consist in their horns; *and the scripture mentions the* horn *as the symbol of strength.* Moses *compares* Joseph *to a young bullock, and says, that* his horns are like the horns of unicorns; *that is, his strength and power shall be very great,* Deut. 33. 17. *And in* Psal. 132. 17. I will make the horn of *David* to bud; *I will make his power and glory*

to flourish and increase. I will cut off the horns of the wicked, *Psal.* 75. 10. *So in* Jer. 48. 25. The horn of *Moab is* cut off. *In* Psal. 44. 5, *a victory over enemies is expressed by these words,* Through thee we will push down our enemies: *in* Hebrew, we will smite with the horn, *we will subdue, destroy, and disperse them, as a bull disperses every thing that comes before him with his* horns.

Horn *signifies likewise glory, honour, brightness, and rays.* 1 Sam. 2. 1, Mine horn is exalted in the Lord; *my glory is advanced and manifested; God hath loaded me with honour.* Job *says,* I have defiled my horn in the dust: *I have parted with all my glory and dignity, and been contented to lie in the dust,* Job 16. 15. *The* Psalmist *says,* I said to the wicked, lift not up the horn; *Do not carry yourselves either arrogantly, boasting of your own strength, or scornfully and maliciously towards me,* Psal. 75. 4. *In* Hab. 3. 4, *it is said,* God came from *Paran,* and his brightness was as the light, and he had horns coming out of his hand, *or, beams and rays of light, that is, glorious manifestations of his power in these his acts. Or, according to others, having his hands armed with flaming darts, and fiery arrows.*

Kingdoms and great powers are often described by the word horns. *It is thus* Daniel *represents the power of the* Persians, *of the* Greeks, *of* Syria *and* Egypt. *He represents* Darius *and* Alexander *like a goat and a ram running violently at each other with their* horns, *Dan.* 8. 3, 5, 6. *The* Hebrews, *by the word* horn, *sometimes understood an eminence, an angle, a corner.* Isa. 5. 1. My well-beloved hath a vineyard in a very fruitful hill, *Heb.* in the horn of the son of oil: *my beloved has a vineyard situated on an eminence, or on the corner of a rich and fertile mountain. The* horns *of the altar of burnt offerings were eminences or spires at the four corners of it, which were not only for ornament, but also for use, either to keep things put upon them from falling, or that beasts to be offered might be bound to them, as the* Psalmist *seems to insinuate,* Psal. 118. 27. *As the ancients frequently made use of* horns *to hold liquors, the vessels wherein oil was put, and perfumes, are called often* horns, *whether they really were of* horn, *or of any other matter.* Fill thine horn with oil, *says the Lord to* Samuel, and go anoint *David* king, 1 *Sam.* 16. 1.

Exod. 21. 29. if ox were wont to push with his *h.*
1 *Sam.* 2. 1. Hannah said, mine *h.* is exalted in the Lord
10. and he shall exalt the *h.* of his anointed
16. 1. fill thine *h.* with oil, go, I will send thee
13. Samuel took the *h.* of oil, and anointed him
2 *Sam.* 22. 3. the *h.* of my salvation, *Psal.* 18. 2.
1 *Kings* 1. 39. Zadok the priest took an *h.* of oil
1 *Chr.* 25. 5. in the words of God, to lift up the *h.*
Job 16. 15. I have defiled my *h.* in the dust
Psal. 75. 4. to the wicked, lift not up the *h.* 5.
89. 17. and in thy favour our *h.* shall be exalted
24. and in my name shall his *h.* be exalted
92. 10. my *h.* shalt thou exalt like *h.* of an unicorn
112. 9. his *h.* shall be exalted with honour
132. 17. I will make the *h.* of David to bud
148. 14. he also exalteth the *h.* of his people
Jer. 48. 25. the *h.* of Moab is cut off, and his arm
Lam. 2. 3. he hath cut off all the *h.* of Israel
17. he hath set up the *h.* of thine adversaries
Ezek. 29. 21. I will cause the *h.* of Israel to bud
Dan. 7. 8. among them a little *h.* in this *h.* 20.
11. of the great words which the *h.* spake
21. the same *h.* made war with the saints
8. 5. the goat had a notable *h.* between his eyes
8. 8. when he was strong great *h.* was broken
9. out of one of them came forth a little *h.*
21. the great *h.* that is between his eyes
Mic. 4. 13. for I will make thy *h.* iron, and hoofs brass
Zech. 1. 21. which lift up their *h.* over the land
Luke 1. 69. hath raised up an *h.* of salvation for us

HORNS.

Gen. 22. 13. a ram caught in a thicket by his *h.*
Exod. 27. 2. make the *h.* of it on the four corners, his *h.* shall be of the same, 30. 2. | 37. 25. | 38. 2.
29. 12. and put of the blood on the *h.* of the altar, *Lev.* 4. 7, 18, 25, 30, 34. | 8. 15. | 9. 9. | 16. 18.
30. 3. with pure gold shalt overlay the *h.* 37. 26.
10. make an atonement on *h.* of it once a year
Deut. 33. 17. his *h.* are like the *h.* of unicorns
1 *Kings* 2. 28. Joab caught hold on the *h.* of the altar
22. 11. Zedekiah made *h.* of iron, 2 *Chron.* 18. 10.
Psal. 22. 21. hast heard me from the *h.* of unicorns
69. 31. than a bullock that hath *h.* and hoofs
75. 10. all the *h.* of the wicked will I cut off, but the *h.* of the righteous shall be exalted
118. 27. bind the sacrifice to the *h.* of the altar
Ezek. 27. 15. they brought for a present *h.* of ivory
34. 21. ye pushed all the diseased with your *h.*
43. 15. from the altar and upwards shall be four *h.*
Dan. 7. 7. behold a fourth beast had ten *h.* 20.
8. I considered the *h.* three *h.* were plucked up
24. the ten *h.* are ten kings that shall arise
8. 3. the ram had two *h.* the two *h.* were high
6. the he-goat came to the ram which had two *h.*
7. and he smote the ram, and brake his two *h.*
20. two *h.* are the kings of Media and Persia
Amos 6. 13. have we not taken *h.* by our strength?
Hab. 3. 4. he had *h.* coming out of his hand
Zech. 1. 18. then I saw, and behold, four *h.*
19. these the *h.* which have scattered Judah, 21.
21. are come to cast out the *h.* of the Gentiles
Rev. 5. 6. in midst stood a Lamb having seven *h.*
12. 3. a red dragon, having seven heads and ten *h.*
13. 1. a beast having ten *h.* and on his *h.* ten crowns
11. another beast had two *h.* like a lamb
17. 3. a scarlet-coloured beast having ten *h.*
7. the beast which hath the seven heads and ten *h.*
12. the ten *h.* thou sawest are ten kings, 16.
See RAMS.

HORNET.

Hornets *are a sort of strong flies which the Lord used as instruments to plague the enemies of his people. They are of themselves very troublesome and mischievous; but those the Lord made use of were, it is thought, like the flies wherewith he plagued* Egypt, *of an extraordinary bigness and perniciousness. It is said, they live as the wasps, that they have a king or captain, and pestilent stings as bees, and that if twenty-seven of them sting man or beast, it is certain death to either. Nor is it strange that such creatures did drive out the* Canaanites *from their habitations; for many heathen writers give instances of some people driven from their seats by frogs, others by mice, others by bees and wasps; of which see* Herodotus, Diodorus, Pliny, Ælian, Justin, *&c. And it is said, that* "*a christian city, being besieged by* Sapores, *king* "*of* Persia, *was delivered by* hornets; *for the* "*elephants and beasts being stung by them, waxed* "*unruly, and so the whole army fled.*"

Deut. 7. 20. the Lord will send the *h.* among them
Josh. 24. 12. I sent the *h.* before you, which drave

HORNETS.

Exod. 23. 28. I will send *h.* before thee, which drive

HORRIBLE.

Psal. 11. 6. on the wicked he shall rain a *h.* tempest
40. 2. he brought me up also out of a *h.* pit
Jer. 5. 30. a *h.* thing is committed in the land
18. 13. the virgin of Israel hath done a *h.* thing
23. 14. I have seen in the prophets a *h.* thing
Hos. 6. 10. I have seen a *h.* thing in house of Israel

HORRIBLY.

Jer. 2. 12. be *h.* afraid, O ye heavens, at this, saith L.
Ezek. 32. 10. their kings shall be *h.* afraid for thee

HORROR.

Gen. 15. 12. a *h.* of great darkness fell on Abram
Job 18. †20. they that went before laid hold on *h.*
Psal. 55. 5. and *h.* hath overwhelmed me
119. 53. *h.* hath taken hold on me, because
Ezek. 7. 18. *h.* shall cover them, and shame on all faces

HORSE

Is *a very common beast, and very well known in these countries; but very rare among the* Hebrews *till* Solomon's *time. Before him we find no horsemen mentioned in the armies of* Israel. *God forbids the kings of his people* to keep many horses, *Deut.* 17. 16. *Hereby God would prevent oppression and tyranny, and the imposition of unnecessary burdens and taxes upon his people; as also carnal confidence in the kings, which by this means would be promoted. As in* Psal. 20. 7. Some trust in chariots, and some in horses. *By this God would likewise prevent their having commerce with* Egypt, *which was famous for horses.* David *having won a great battle against* Hadadezer *king of* Zobah, *took seventeen hundred horses, and lamed all belonging to the chariots of war, reserving only an hundred chariots,* 2 Sam. 8. 4. *The Judges and Princes of* Israel *used generally to ride on mules, or asses.*

Solomon *is the first king of* Judah *who had a great number of horses, and he kept them rather for pomp than for war. He had forty thousand stalls of horses for his chariots, and twelve thousand horsemen distributed in his fortified places,* 1 Kings 4. 26. *He had his horses from* Egypt, 1 Kings 10. 28. *although the Lord had forbidden the king of the* Hebrews *to multiply horses, and that in order to prevent the* Israelites *having commerce with the* Egyptians, *lest they should be infected with their idolatry, and their other wickednesses,* Deut. 17. 16.

HORSES consecrated to the Sun. *In* 2 Kings 23. 11. *it is said, that* Josiah *took away the* horses *which the kings of* Judah, *his predecessors, had given to the sun. It is known, that the sun was worshipped over all the east, and that the horse, the swiftest of tame beasts, was consecrated to this deity, who was represented as riding in a chariot drawn by the most beautiful and swiftest horses in the world, and performing every day his journey from east to west, in order to communicate his light to mankind.*

Some are of opinion, that these horses were sacrificed to the sun: Others, that every morning they were put to the chariots dedicated to the sun, whereof there is mention made in the same passage, and that the king, or some of his officers, got up and rode to meet the sun in its rising, as far as from the eastern gate of the temple to the suburbs of Jerusalem. Xenophon *testifies that both these were the customs of the* Persians *and* Armenians: *He describes a solemn sacrifice of horses, which was made with ceremony to the sun: they were all of the finest, and were led with a white chariot, crowned, and consecrated to the same god. Lastly, others are of opinion, that these horses were of wood, stone, or metal, erected in the temple in honour of the sun.*

Gen. 49. 17. an adder in path that biteth the *h.* heels
Exod. 15. 21. the *h.* and rider hath he thrown into sea
Judg. 5. 22. then were *h.* hoofs broken by prancing
1 *Kings* 10. 29. a *h.* for 150 shekels, 2 *Chron.* 1. 17.
20. 20. Benhadad king escaped on *h.* with horsemen
25. number an army like the army lost, *h.* for *h.*
Esth. 6. 8. let the *h.* the king rideth on be brought
9. let this *h.* be delivered to one of the princes
10. take the apparel and *h.* as thou hast said
11. then took Haman the apparel and the *h.*
Job 39. 18. she scorneth the *h.* and his rider
19. hast thou given *h.* strength? hast thou clothed
Psal. 32. 9. be ye not as the *h.* or as the mule
33. 17. an *h.* is a vain thing for safety
76. 6. the chariot and *h.* are cast into a dead sleep
147. 10. he delighteth not in the strength of the *h.*
Prov. 21. 31. the *h.* is prepared against day of battle
26. 3. a whip for the *h.* a rod for the fool's back
Isa. 43. 17. which bringeth forth the chariot and *h.*
63. 13. that led them thro' the deep, as a *h.*
Jer. 8. 6. as the *h.* rusheth into the battle
Jer. 51. 21. with thee will I break in pieces *h.*
Amos 2. 15. nor shall he that rideth *h.* deliver hims.
Zech. 1. 8. and behold, a man riding upon a red *h.*
9. 10. and I will cut off the *h.* from Jerusalem
10. 3. hath made them as his goodly *h.* in battle
12. 4. I will smite every *h.* with blindness
14. 15. so shall be the plague of the *h.* of the mule
Rev. 6. 2. and I saw and behold white *h.* 19. 11.
4. a red *h.* ‖ 5. a black *h.* ‖ 8. behold, a pale *h.*
14. 20. and blood came even to the *h.* bridles
19. 19. to make war against him that sat on the *h.*
21. slain with the sword of him that sat on the *h.*

HORSEBACK.

2 *Kings* 9. 18. there went one on *h.* to meet Jehu
19. then he sent out a second on *h.* which came
Esth. 6. 9. and bring him on *h.* through the city
11. Haman brought him on *h.* through the city
8. 10. and Mordecai sent letters by posts on *h.*

HORSE-GATE.

2 *Chr.* 23. 15. when she was come to entering of *h.-g.*
Neh. 3. 28. from above the *h.-g.* repaired the priests
Jer. 31. 40. the fields to the corner of the *h.-gate*

HORSES.

Gen. 47. 17. Joseph gave bread in exchange for *h.*
Exod. 9. 3. the hand of the Lord is upon the *h.*
Deut. 17. 16. but he shall not multiply *h.* to himself, to the end that he should multiply *h.*
1 *Kings* 4. 28. barley also and straw for the *h.*
10. 25. they brought *h.* and mules, 2 *Chron.* 9. 24.
28. Sol. had *h.* out of Egypt, 2 *Chr.* 1. 16, 17. | 9. 28.
18. 5. may find grass to save the *h.* and mules alive
22. 4. and my *h.* are as thy *h.* 2 *Kings* 3. 7.
2 *Kings* 2. 11. there appeared *h.* of fire, and parted
5. 9. Naaman came with his *h.* and his chariot
7. 7. they left their *h.* and fled for their life
10. but *h.* tied ‖ 13. some take five of the *h.*
9. 33. Jezebel's blood was sprinkled on the *h.*
14. 20. brought Amaziah on *h.* 2 *Chron.* 25. 28.
18. 23. I will deliver thee 2000 *h.* *Isa.* 36. 8.
23. 11 Josiah took away the *h.* given to the sun
Ezra 2. 66. their *h.* were 736, *Neh.* 7. 68.
Eccl. 10. 7. I have seen servants on *h.* and princes
Isa. 2. 7. their land is also full of *h.* and chariots
5. 28. their *h.* hoofs shall be counted like flint
30. 16. but ye said, no, for we will flee upon *h.*
31. 1. and stay on *h.* and trust in chariots
3. and their *h.* are flesh, and not spirit
Jer. 4. 13. his *h.* are swifter than eagles
5. 8. they were as fed *h.* in the morning
6. 23. they ride on *h.* set in array as men for war
8. 16. the snorting of his *h.* was heard from Dan
12. 5. then how canst thou contend with *h.*?
46. 4. harness the *h.* and get up, ye horsemen
47. 3. noise of the stamping of the hoofs of his *h.*
50. 42. and they shall ride upon *h.* put in array
51. 27. cause the *h.* to come up as caterpillars
Ezek. 17. 15. that they might give him *h.* and people
23. 6. young men, horsemen riding on *h.* 12.
20. and whose issue is like the issue of *h.*
23. renowned, all of them riding on *h.* 38. 15.
26. 10. because of the abundance of his *h.*
27. 14. Togarmah traded in thy fairs with *h.*
38. 4. I will bring thee forth, and all thy army, *h.*
Hos. 1. 7. I will not save them by battle nor *h.*
14. 3. Ashur shall not save, we will not ride on *h.*
Joel 2. 4. as the appearance of *h.* and horsemen
Amos 4. 10. and I have taken away your *h.*
6. 12. shall *h.* run upon the rock? will one plow?
Mic. 5. 10. that I will cut off thy *h.* out of thee
Hab. 1. 8. their *h.* also are swifter than the leopards
3. 8. that thou didst ride on thy *h.* and chariots
15. thou didst walk through the sea with thy *h.*
Hag. 2. 22. I will overthrow the *h.* and riders
Zech. 1. 8. and behind him there were red *h.*
6. 2. in first chariot red *h.* in the second black *h.*
3. in third white *h.* in fourth chariot bay *h.*
6. the black *h.* go forth into the north country
10. 5. the riders on *h.* shall be confounded
14. 20. on bells of *h.* HOLINESS TO THE LORD
Jam. 3. 3. behold, we put bits in the *h.* mouths
Rev. 9. 7. the locusts were like *h.* prepared to battle
17. I saw the *h.* the heads of *h.* as heads of lions
18. 13. no man buyeth the merchandise of *h.*
19. 14. the armies followed him upon white *h.*
18. that ye may eat the flesh of kings and *h.*
See CHARIOTS.

HORSELEECH.

Prov. 30. 15. the *h.* hath two daughters, crying, give

HORSEMAN.

2 *Kings* 9. 17. Joram said, take an *h.* send to meet
Nah. 3. 3. *h.* lifteth up the bright sword and spear

HORSEMEN.

Gen. 50. 9. there went with Joseph chariots and *h.*
Exod. 14. 9. the *h.* of Pharaoh pursued after them
17. I will get me honour on Pharaoh and his *h.*
15. 19. Pharaoh and *h.* went into sea, *Josh.* 24. 6.
1 *Sam.* 8. 11. he will take your sons to be his *h.*
13. 5. the Philist. gathered 6000 *h.* against Israel
2 *Sam.* 1. 6. lo, the *h.* followed hard after him
8. 4. and David took from Hadadezer 700 *h.*
10. 18. David slew 40,000 *h.* smote Shobach
1 *Kings* 1. 5. Adonijah prepared chariots and *h.*
4. 26. Solomon had 12,000 *h.* 10. 26.
9. 19. Solomon had cities of store for his chariots, and cities for his *h.* 22. 2 *Chr.* 8. 6, 9.
20. 20. Ben-hadad escaped on an horse with his *h.*
2 *Kings* 2. 12. the chariot of Isr. and the *h.* thereof
13. 7. nor did he leave to Jehoahaz but fifty *h.*
14. Joash said, O my father, the *h.* of Israel
18. 24. put thy trust in Egypt for chariots and *h.*
2 *Chron.* 12. 3. Shishak came up with 60,000 *h.*
16. 8. the Ethiopians a huge host with many *h.*
Ezra 8. 22. was ashamed to ask soldiers but *h.* to help
Neh. 2. 9. now king had sent captains and *h.* with me
Isa. 21. 7. he saw a chariot with a couple of *h.* 9.
22. 7. the *h.* shall set themselves in array at the gate
28. 28. because he will not bruise it with his *h.*
31. 1. and trust in *h.* because they are very strong
36. 9. how wilt thou put thy trust on Egypt for *h.*
Jer. 4. 29. whole city shall flee for the noise of the *h.*
46. 4. get up, ye *h.* and stand with your helmets
Ezek. 23. 6. all of them *h.* riding on horses, 12.

Ezek. 26. 7. bring Nebuchadnezzar against Tyrus with *h.*
10. thy walls shall shake at the noise of the *h.*
27. 14. they of Togarmah traded in fairs with *h.*
38. 4. Gog I will bring thee forth, horses and *h.*
Dan. 11. 40. the king of the north shall come with *h.*
Hos. 1. 7. I will not save them by horses, nor by *h.*
Joel 2. 4. appearance of horses, as *h.* so shall they run
Hab. 1. 8. their *h.* shall spread themselves, and their *h.* shall come from far, shall fly as the eagle
Acts 23. 23. make ready *h.* threescore and ten
32. on morrow they left the *h.* to go with him
Rev. 9. 16. the number of the army of *h.* were

HOSANNA

Is an Hebrew *word, which signifies,* Save I beseech you. *It is a form of acclamation, of blessing, or wishing one well. Thus at our Saviour's entrance into* Jerusalem, *when the people cried,* Hosanna to the Son of *David; their meaning was,* Lord preserve this Son of *David;* this king: *heap favours and blessings on him. The word is found in* Mat. 21. 9, 15. Mark 11. 9, 10. John 12. 13.

HOSEN.

Dan. 3. 21. these men were bound in their *h.* and hats

HOSPITALITY

Signifies *love to strangers, expressed in entertaining and using them kindly,* Rom. 12. 13. *It has always been very much in esteem among civilized people. The Scripture furnishes us with several examples of* hospitality *exercised by the patriarchs.* Abraham *received three angels, and earnestly invited them, and served them himself; while* Sarah *his wife took care to make ready provisions for his guests,* Gen. 18. 2, 3, &c. Lot *waited at the city-gate to receive such guests as might come thither,* Gen. 19. 1, 2, &c. *St.* Paul *makes use of* Abraham's *and* Lot's *example to encourage the faithful, and persuade them to the exercise of hospitality, saying, that they who have practised it, have had the honour of receiving angels under the form of men,* Heb. 13. 2.

The apostles Peter *and* Paul, *who abounded with the spirit of their Master, with great care recommended* hospitality *to the faithful.* 1 Pet. 4. 9. Use hospitality one to another without grudging. *And St.* Paul *recommends this duty, particularly to such as are overseers in the church of God,* 1 Tim. 3. 2. *Our Saviour tells his apostles,* Mat. 10. 40, 42. He that receiveth you receiveth me: And whosoever shall give to drink unto one of these little ones, a cup of cold water only, he shall in no wise lose his reward. *And in* Mat. 25. 41, 43, 45. *at the day of judgment he will say to the wicked,* Depart from me, ye cursed, into everlasting fire; I was a stranger, and ye took me not in. In as much as ye did it not to one of the least of these, ye did it not to me.

The primitive Christians made one principal part of their duty to consist in the exercise of hospitality; *and they were so exact in the discharge of it that the very heathens admired them for it. They were hospitable to all strangers, but chiefly to those that were of the same faith and communion. Believers scarce ever went without letters of communion, which testified the purity of their faith; this was sufficient to procure them reception in all those places where the name of* Jesus Christ *was known.*

Rom. 12. 13. distributing, given to *h.* 1 *Tim.* 3. 2.
Tit. 1. 8. but a lover of *h.* a lover of good men
1 *Pet.* 4. 9. use *h.* one to another without grudging

HOST.

Luke 10. 35. he took two pence, and gave them to *h.*
Rom. 16. 23. Gaius mine *h.* and of church saluteth you

HOST.

Gen. 2. 1. the earth was finished, and all *h.* of them
21. 22. Phichol the chief captain of his *h.* 32.
32. 2. Jacob saw them, he said, this is God's *h.*
Exod. 14. 4. I will be honoured on all his *h.* 17.
24. Lord looked to *h.* of Egyptians thro' pillar of fire and of cloud, and troubled the *h.* of Egypt.
28. the waters covered all the *h.* of Pharaoh
16. 13. in morning the dew lay round about the *h.*
Num. 2. 4. and his *h.* and those that were numbered of them, 6, 8, 11, 13, 15, 19, 21, 23.
4. 3. all that entered into the *h.* to do the work
10. 14. over the *h.* of Judah ‖ 15. the *h.* of Issachar
16. over *h.* of Zebulun ‖ 18. Reuben ‖ 19. Simeon
31. 14. Moses was wroth with the officers of the *h.*
48. the officers of the *h.* came near to Moses
Deut. 2. 14. the men of war were wasted from the *h.*
15. to destroy them from among *h.* till consumed
23. 9. when the *h.* goeth forth against enemies
Josh. 1. 11. pass thro' the *h.* and command the peo.
3. 2. after three days the officers went thro' the *h.*
5. 14. as captain of the *h.* of the Lord am I come
18. 9. and came again to Joshua to the *h.* at Shiloh
Judg. 4. 2. the captain of whose *h.* was Sisera
16. and all the *h.* of Sisera fell on the sword
7. 8. the *h.* of Midian was beneath in the valley
9. God said, arise, get thee down unto the *h.* 10.
13. a cake of bread tumbled into the *h.* of Midian
21. and all the *h.* ran, and cried, and fled
8. 11. Gideon went up and smote the *h.* the *h.* sec.
12. Gideon pursued and discomfited all the *h.*
1 *Sam.* 11. 11. Saul came into the *h.* in the morning
14. 15. there was trembling in the *h.* in the field
19. the noise of the *h.* went on and increased
50. the captain of Saul's *h.* was Abner son of Ner
17. 20. Dav. came as the *h.* was going forth to fight
28. 5. when Saul saw the *h.* of the Philistines
19. Ld. shall deliver the *h.* of Isr. to Philistines
29. 6. thy going and coming in with me in *h.* is good
2 *Sam.* 5. 24. L. shall smite the *h.* of the Philistines
8. 9. when Toi king of Hamath heard that David had smitten all the *h.* of Hadadezer, 1 *Chr.* 18. 9.
10. 18. Syrians fled, Dav. smote Shobach the captain of their *h.* who died there, 1 *Chron.* 19. 18.
17. 25. Absalom made Amasa captain of the *h.*
19. 13. if thou be not captain of *h.* in room of Joab
20. 23. Joab was over all the *h.* 1 *Chron.* 18. 15.
23. 16. these three brake thro' the *h.* 1 *Chr.* 11. 18
1 *Kings* 2. 32. Abner the son of Ner capt. of the *h.* of Isr. and Amasa captain of the *h.* of Judah
35. the king put Benaiah over the *h.* 4. 4.
16. 16. Israel made Omri captain of the *h.* king
20. 1. Benhadad gathered all his *h.* together
22. 34. turn thy hand and carry me out of the *h.*
2 *Kings* 3. 9. there was no water for the *h.* and cattle
4. 13. wouldest be spoken for to the capt. of the *h.?*
6. 14. therefore sent he horses and great *h.* to Dothan
24. Benhadad gathered his *h.* and went up
7. 4. come and let us fall unto the *h.* of the Syrians
6. Lord made the *h.* to hear the noise of a great *h.*
9. 5. behold the captains of the *h.* were sitting
18. 17. Sennacherib sent a great *h.* against Jerus.
25. 1. Nebuchadnezzar came and his *h.* against Jerusalem
19. the principal scribe of the *h.* *Jer.* 52. 25.
1 *Chron.* 9. 19. their fathers over the *h.* of the Lord
12. 22. till it was a great *h.* like the *h.* of God
27. 3. was the chief of all the captains of the *h.*
2 *Chron.* 14. 9. against them Zerah came with an *h.*
16. 7. not relied, therefore the *h.* of Syria escaped
8. were not the Ethiopians and Lubims a huge *h.?*
18. 33. turn thy hand and carry me out of the *h.*
24. 24. the Ld. delivered a great *h.* into their hand
26. 11. Uzziah had an *h.* of fighting men for war
28. 9. Oded went out before the *h.* and said, behold
Ps. 27. 3. though an *h.* should encamp against me
33. 6. all *h.* of them made by breath of thy mouth
16. no king is saved by the multitude of an *h.*
136. 15. but overthrew Pharaoh and *h.* in Red sea
Isa. 13. 4. Lord of hosts mustereth the *h.* of battle
24. 21. Lord shall punish the *h.* of the high ones
40. 26. that bringeth out their *h.* by number
45. 12. and all their *h.* have I commanded
Jer. 51. 3. spare not, destroy ye utterly all her *h.*
Ezek. 1. 24. the voice of speech, as the noise of an *h.*
Dan. 8. 10. and it cast down some of the *h.*
11. he magnified himself to the prince of the *h.*
12. an *h.* was given him against the daily sacrifice
13. to give the *h.* to be trodden under foot
Obad. 20. the captivity of this *h.* shall possess that
Luke 2. 13. multitude of the heavenly *h.* praising G.
See HEAVEN.

HOSTAGES.

2 *Kings* 14. 14. Jehoash took all the gold and silver and *h.* and returned to Samaria, 2 *Chr.* 25. 24.

HOSTS.

Gen. 32. † 2. he called the name of that place, two *h.*
Exod. 12. 41. the *h.* of Lord went out of Egypt
Josh. 10. 5. the kings of Canaan and all their *h.* 11. 4.
Judg. 8. 10. Zeba and Zalmunna with their *h.*
1 *Kings* 15. 20. Benhadad sent the captains of the *h.*
Psal. 103. 21. bless ye the Lord, all ye his *h.*
108. 11. wilt not thou, O God, go forth with *h.?*
148. 2. praise ye him, all his angels, all his *h.*
Jer. 3. 19. a goodly heritage of the *h.* of nations
See GOD, LORD.

HOT.

Exod. 16. 21. when the sun waxed *h.* it melted
Lev. 13. 24. any flesh, wherein there is a *h.* burning
Deut. 9. 19. I was afraid of anger and *h.* displeasure
19. 6. lest the avenger pursue, while his heart is *h.*
Josh. 9. 12. this our bread we took *h.* for provision
Judg. 2. 14. anger of Lord was *h.* against Israel, and he delivered to the spoilers, 20. ‖ 3. 8. ‖ 10. 7.
6. 39. Gideon said, let not thine anger be *h.* ag. me
9. † 30. when Zabul heard Gaal, his anger was *h.*
1 *Sam.* 11. 9. by the sun be *h.* ye shall have help
21. 6. put *h.* bread in day when it was taken away
1 *Kings* 3. † 26. for her bowels were *h.* upon her son
Neh. 7. 3. let not gates be opened till the sun be *h.*
Job 6. 17. when it is *h.* they are consumed
Psal. 6. 1. neither chasten in thy *h.* displeasure, 38. 1.
39. 3. my heart was *h.* within me, while musing
78. 48. he gave their flocks to *h.* thunderbolts
85. † 3. hast turned thine anger from waxing *h.*
Prov. 6. 28. can one go upon *h.* coals and not be burnt?
Ezek. 24. 11. that the brass of it may be *h.* and burn
Dan. 3. 22. because the furnace was exceeding *h.*
Hos. 7. 7. they are all *h.* as an oven, and devoured
1 *Tim.* 4. 2. their conscience seared with a *h.* iron
Rev. 3. 15. I know thy works, that thou art neither cold nor *h.* I would thou wert cold or *h.* 16.
See WAX, *Verb.*

HOTLY.

Gen. 31. 36. that thou hast so *h.* pursued after me

HOTTEST.

2 *Sam.* 11. 15. set Uriah in forefront of the *h.* battle

HOUGH.

Josh. 11. 6. the Lord said, thou shalt *h.* their horses

HOUGHED.

Josh. 11. 9. *h.* their horses, burnt chariots with fire
2 *Sam.* 8. 4. and David *h.* all the chariot horses

HOUR.

The ancient Hebrews *did not divide the day by* hours: *The day was divided into four parts, morning, high day or noon, the first evening, and the last evening; and the night was divided into three parts, night, mid-night, and the morning-watch. But afterwards, when the* Jews *came to be under the* Romans, *they followed them in dividing the night into four parts, which they called* watches, *because they relieved their centinels every three hours. Thus in* Mat. 14. 25. *it is said, that* in the fourth watch of the night, Jesus went to his disciples, walking on the sea; *that is, about three* hours *before the rising of the sun.*

In the books of the New Testament we see clearly the day divided into twelve equal hours, *after the manner of the* Greeks *and* Romans, Mat. 20. 1, 2, 3, &c. John 11. 9. *These* hours *were equal to each other, but unequal with respect to the different seasons. The twelve* hours *of the longest days in summer were much longer than those of the shortest days in winter. The first* hour *was that which followed the rising of the sun, and was answerable to our six o'clock in the morning in the equinox; and to other times in proportion to the length or shortness of the days. The third* hour *was answerable to nine o'clock of the morning in the equinox; the sixth at all times to noon, and so on.*

Dan. 4. 19. then Daniel was astonied for one *h.*
Mat. 9. 22. woman was made whole from that *h.*
15. 28. her daughter made whole from that very *h.*
17. 18. the child was cured from that very *h.*
20. 3. he went out about the third *h.* and saw
5. about the sixth and ninth *h.* ‖ 6. the eleventh *h.*
12. saying, these last have wrought but one *h.*
24. 36. that *h.* knoweth no man, 42. *Mark* 13. 32.
44. such an *h.* as ye think not, 50. *Luke* 12. 40, 46
25. 13. for ye know neither the day nor the *h.*
26. 40. could ye not watch one *h.?* *Mark* 14. 37.
45. the *h.* is at hand, the Son of man is betrayed
27. 45. from the sixth *h.* was darkness over the land to the ninth *h.* *Mark* 15. 33. *Luke* 23. 44.
46. about the ninth *h.* Jesus cried, *Mark* 15. 34.
Mark 13. 11. whatsoever shall be given you in that *h.*
14. 35. that if possible the *h.* might pass from him
15. 25. it was the third *h.* and they crucified him
Luke 10. 21. in that *h.* Jes. rejoiced in spirit and said
12. 39. had known what *h.* the thief would come
22. 14. and when the *h.* was come, he sat down
53. but this is your *h.* and the power of darkness
59. about the space of one *h.* after another affirmed
John 1. 39. abode that day, for it was about tenth *h.*
2. 4. Jesus saith, woman, mine *h.* is not yet come
4. 6. Jesus sat, it was about the sixth *h.* 19. 14.
21. woman, believe me, the *h.* cometh, 23
52. then inquired he the *h.* when he began to amend, yesterday at seventh *h.* the fever left him
5. 25. the *h.* is coming, and now is, 28. ‖ 16. 32.
7. 30. because his *h.* was not yet come, 8. 20.
12. 23. the *h.* is come, Son should be glorified, 17. 1.
27. my soul is troubled, Father, save me from this *h.* for this cause came I to this *h.*
13. 1. when Jesus knew that his *h.* was come
16. 21. woman hath sorrow, because her *h.* is come
19. 27. from that *h.* that disciple took her home
Acts 2. 15. not drunken, seeing it is third *h.* of day
3. 1. at the *h.* of prayer being the ninth *h.*
10. 3. he saw about the ninth *h.* an angel coming
9. Peter went up to pray about the sixth *h.*
30. four days ago I was fasting until this *h.*
23. 23. make ready at the third *h.* of the night
1 *Cor.* 4. 11. to this present *h.* both hunger and thirst
8. 7. some with conscience of the idol unto this *h.*
15. 30. and why stand we in jeopardy every *h.?*
Gal. 2. 5. to whom we gave place, no not for an *h.*
Rev. 3. 3. not know what *h.* I will come upon thee
10. I will keep thee from the *h.* of temptation
8. 1. there was silence about the space of half an *h.*
9. 15. which were prepared for an *h.* and a day
14. 7. fear God, for the *h.* of his judgment is come
17. 12. but receive power as kings one *h.* with beast
18. 10. for in one *h.* is thy judgment come
17. in one *h.* so great riches is come to nought
19. that great city in one *h.* is she made desolate

Same HOUR.

Dan. 3. 6. the *same h.* be cast into the furnace, 15.
4. 33. the *same h.* was the thing fulfilled on Nebuc.
5. 5. in the *same h.* came forth fingers, and wrote
Mat. 8. 13. his servant was healed the *same h.*
10. 19. it shall be given you the *same h.* *Luke* 12. 12.
26. 55. in the *same h.* said Jesus to the multitude
Luke 7. 21. that *same h.* cured many of their plagues
20. 19. scribes *same h.* sought to lay hands on him
24. 33. they rose up the *same h.* returned to Jerusal.
John 4. 53. the father knew that it was at the *same h.*
Acts 16. 18. and he came out the *same h.*
33. he took them *same h.* of the night and washed
22. 13. and the *same h.* I looked up upon him
Rev. 11. 13. the *same h.* was there a great earthquake

HOURS.

John 11. 9. are there not twelve *h.* in the day?
Acts 5. 7. wife came in about space of three *h.* after
19. 34. all cried about two *h.* great is Diana of Eph.

HOUSE

Signifies, (1) *A place to dwell in,* Gen. 19. 3. (2) *The household, or persons dwelling in the house.* Acts 10. 2. *Cornelius* feared God with all his house, *with all his family. So in* Heb. 11. 7. *Noah* prepared an ark to the saving of his house. *And in many other places.* (3) *Kindred, stock, or lineage,* 2 Sam. 7. 18. What is my house, that thou hast brought me hitherto? *And* Luke 1. 27. *Gabriel* was sent to a virgin espoused to *Joseph,* of the house of *David, of the lineage or family of* David. (4) *Wealth, riches, or estates.* Mat. 23. 14. Ye devour widows' houses; *ye consume their estates.* (5) *The grave, or a sepulchre.* Job 30. 23. I know that thou wilt bring me to the house appointed for all living. *And* Isa. 14. 18. Every one in his own house. (6) *One's family affairs and concerns.* 2 Kings 20. 1. Set thine house in order. (7) *This frail, corruptible, mortal body, wherein the soul lodges for a time.* 2 Cor. 5. 1. If our earthly house of this tabernacle were dissolved; *if our bodily frame of nature were taken to pieces by death.* (8) *The church among the* Jews. *Heb.* 3. 2. Moses was faithful in all his house. *He ordered all things in the* Jewish *church according to the command of God.*

Our Saviour, in John 14. 2. *calls heaven* his Father's house, *in which there are many mansions, wherein saints and blessed spirits shall dwell with God for ever in immortal glory. The church of God is called* his house. 1 *Tim.* 3. 15. That thou mayest know how to behave thyself in the house of God, which is the church of the living God; *a people in and among whom he dwelleth. And in* Heb. 3. 6. But Christ as a Son over his own house, whose house are we. *Believers are set apart from profane uses, and dedicated to the service of God; among whom he manifests his gracious presence by his Spirit. The tabernacle is also called* the house of God, *Judg.* 18. 31. *as also the temple,* 2 Chron. 5. 14. *Persons are said to* join house to house, *when they watch all opportunities to dispossess others by any means whatsoever, and to engross all to them*

selves. Isa. 5. 8. Woe unto them that join house to house. Egypt was the house of bondage; here the people of Israel were in great bondage and slavery, Deut. 5. 6.
Gen. 19. 4. men of Sodom compassed the h. round
24. 27. Ld. led me to the h. of my master's brethren
31. I have prepared the h. and room for camels
28. 2. go to the h. of Bethuel, thy mother's father
39. 5. Lord blessed the Egyptian's h. for Joseph's sake
45. 2. the Egyptians and the h. of Pharaoh heard
Exod. 8. 3. frogs shall come into the h. of thy servants
12. 3. a lamb according to the h. of their fathers
30. was not an h. where there was not one dead
46. thou shalt not carry of the flesh out of the h.
13. 3. remember day ye came out from Egypt, out of the h. of bondage, 14. Deut. 5. 6. | 6. 12.
20. 17. shalt not covet neighbour's h. Deut. 5. 21.
Lev. 14. 36. priest shall command they empty the h.
14. 38. priest shall go out of the h. and shut up
45. he shall break down the h. and mortar of h.
46. he that goeth into the h. shall be unclean
49. he shall take to cleanse the h. two birds
25. 30. h. sold in walled city, not go out in jubilee
Num. 30. 10. and if she vowed in her husband's h.
Deut. 7. 8. redeemed you out of the h. of bondmen
8. 14. which brought you out of the land of Egypt, from the h. of bondage, 13. 5, 10 Josh. 24. 17. Judg. 6. 8. Jer. 34. 13. Mic. 6. 4.
25. 10. the h. of him that hath his shoe loosed
Josh. 2. 15. for her h. was upon the town wall
Judg. 8. 35. neither shewed kind. to h. of Jerubbaal
9. 6. all the h. of Millo made Abimelech king
20. let fire come from h. of Millo, and devour
10. 9. Ammon fought against the h. of Ephraim
16. 26. that I may feel pillars whereon h. standeth
27. the h. was full of men || 30. h. fell on the lords
17. 5. Micah had an h. of gods, made an ephod
18. 13. and they came unto the h. of Micah
19. 18. there is no man that receiveth me to h.
22. the sons of Belial beset the h. round, 20. 5.
1 Sam. 3. 14. therefore I have sworn unto h. of Eli
5. 2. they brought the ark into the h. of Dagon
7. 1. and brought the ark into the h. of Abinadab
9. 18. tell me, I pray thee, where the seer's h. is
25. 3. Nabal was churlish, and of the h. of Caleb
28. the Ld. will certainly make my lord a sure h.
2 Sam. 3. 1. long war betw. h. of Saul and h. of David
8. do shew kindness to the h. of Saul thy father
29. let there not fail from the h. of Joab one
4. 5. came to h. of Ishbosheth, who lay on bed at
5. 8. the lame and blind shall not come into the h.
6. 11. the Ld. blessed the h. of Obed-edom, David brought the ark from his h. 12. 1 Chron. 13. 14.
7. 6. I have not dwelt in any h. 1 Chron. 17. 5.
11. Lord telleth thee, he will make thee an h.
29. to bless the h. of thy servant, 1 Chron. 17. 27.
9. 1. is there any that is left of the h. of Saul?
12. 8. and I gave thee thy master's h. and wives
13. 7. go now to thy brother Amnon's h. and dress
16. 5. came a man of the family of the h. of Saul
1 Kings 2. 24. who made me an h. as he promised
27. which he spake concerning the h. of Eli
6. 22. and the whole h. he overlaid with gold
9. 25. he burnt incense, so Solomon finished the h.
11. 18. they came to Pharaoh, who gave him an h.
12. 31. Jeroboam made an h. of his high places
14. 10. I will bring an evil on the h. of Jerob. 14.
15. 29. Baasha smote all the h. of Jeroboam
16. 11. Zimri slew all the h. of Baasha, he left none
17. 15. she, and he, and her h. did eat many days
21. 22. I will make thy h. like the h. of Jeroboam
2 Kings 8. 3. to cry to the king for her h. and land
18. as did the h. of Ahab, 27. 2 Chron. 21. 6. | 22. 4.
9. 8. for the whole h. of Ahab shall perish
10. 3. look out the best, fight for your master's h.
21. h. of Baal was full from one end to another
27. and they made the h. of Baal a draught h.
12. 12. for all that was laid out for h. to repair it
20. 13. Hezekiah shewed them h. of his precious things, all the h. of his armour, Isa. 39. 2.
23. 27. h. of which I said, my name shall be there
25. 9. every great man's h. he burnt with fire
1 Chr. 2. 54. sons of Salma; Ataroth the h. of Joab
26. 15. and to his sons, the h. of Asuppim
2 Chr. 7. 1. glory of L. filled the h. Ezek. 43. 4, 5.
12. chosen this place to myself for h. of sacrifice
22. 9. so the h. of Ahaziah had no power to keep
35. 21. but against the h. wherewith I have war
Ezra 5. 8. that we went to the h. of the great God
6. 3. let the h. be builded, the place where offered
Neh. 2. 8. and for the h. which I shall enter into
Esth. 2. 3. gather all the virgins to the h. of women
8. 1. king did give the h. of Haman to Esther, 7.
Job 1. 13. drinking wine in eldest brother's h. 18.
19. a wind came and smote the corners of the h.
20. 19. hath taken away a h. which he builded not
21. 28. for ye say, where is the h. of the prince?
30. 23. and to the h. appointed for all living
38. 20. thou shouldest know paths to the h. thereof
39. 6. whose h. I have made the wilderness
Ps. 31. 2. my rock be for a h. of defence to save me
84. 3. yea, the sparrow hath found an h.
104. 17. as for the stork, fir-trees are her h.
Prov. 2. 18. her h. inclineth to death, paths to dead
7. 8. the young man went the way to her h.
11. loud and stubborn, her feet abide not in her h.
27. her h. is the way to hell, going to death
9. 1. wisdom hath builded her h. hath hewn pillars
12. 7. but the h. of the righteous shall stand
14. 11. the h. of the wicked shall be overthrown
15. 25. the Lord will destroy the h. of the proud
17. 1. than an h. full of sacrifices with strife
19. 14. h. and riches are the inheritance of fathers
21. 9. is better to dwell in corner of h. top, 25. 24.
12. righteous wisely considereth the h. of wicked
24. 3. thro' wisdom is an h. built and established
25. 17. withdraw thy foot from thy neighbour's h.
27. 10. nor go into brother's h. in day of calamity
Eccl. 7. 2. to go to h. of mourning, than h. of feasting
10. 18. thro' idlen. of hands the h. droppeth thro'
12. 3. when the keepers of the h. shall tremble

Cant. 1. 17. the beams of our h. are cedar, and raft.
2. 4. brought me to the banqueting h. his banner
3. 4. till I had brought him into my mother's h.
8. 2. I would bring thee into my mother's h.
Isa. 5. 8. woe to them that join h. to h. field to field
6. 4. and the h. was filled with smoke
14. 17. that opened not the h. of his prisoners
23. 1. so that there is no h. || 24. 10. every h. shut
31. 2. he will arise against the h. of evil doers
60. 7. and I will glorify the h. of my glory
64. 11. our holy and beautiful h. is burned up
Jer. 16. 5. enter not into the h. of mourning
8. thou shalt not go into h. of feasting with them
21. 11. touching the h. of the king of Judah, 22. 1.
35. 2. go to the h. of the Rechabites and speak
37. 20. not to return to h. of Jonathan, 38. 26.
Ezek. 2. 5. for they are a rebellious h. yet shall know a prophet been among them, 3. 9, 26, 27. | 12. 3.
8. be not thou rebellious like that rebellious h.
9. 7. he said to them, defile the h. go ye forth
12. 2. thou dwellest in the midst of a rebellious h.
25. in your days, O rebellious h. will I say
17. 12. say now to the rebellious h. know ye not
24. 3. and utter a parable to the rebellious h.
43. 11. if ashamed, shew them the form of the h.
12. this is the law of h. on the top of mountain
45. 20. so shall ye reconcile the h.
Dan. 1. 2. which he carried to the h. of his god
Hos. 1. 4. avenge blood of Jezreel on the h. of Jehu
Amos 1. 4. I will send a fire into the h. of Hazael
5. that holdeth the sceptre from the h. of Eden
3. 15. I will smite the winter h. with summer h.
5. 19. or went into h. and leaned his hand on wall
6. 11. he will smite the great h. and the little h.
7. 9. I will rise against h. of Jeroboam with sword
16. drop not thy word against the h. of Isaac
Obad. 18. the h. of Esau shall be for stubble
Mic. 3. 12. Jerus. become heaps, and the mountain of the h. shall be as high places of the forest
4. 2. let us go up to the h. of the God of Jacob
6. 16. all the works of the h. of Ahab are kept
Nah. 1. 14. out of the h. of thy gods will I cut off
Zech. 5. 4. it shall enter into the h. of the thief, into the h. of him that sweareth falsely by my name
12. 12. the family of the h. of Nathan apart
Mat. 7. 25. and beat upon that h. 27. Luke 6. 48.
10. 12. and when ye come into an h. salute it
13. if h. be worthy, let your peace come, Luke 10. 5.
12. 25. every h. divided against itself, Mark 3. 25.
29. how enter into a strong man's h. Mark 3. 27.
20. 11. murmured against the good man of the h.
23. 38. your h. is left to you desolate, Luke 13. 35.
24. 43. if the good man of the h. had known in what watch the thief would come, Luke 12. 39.
Mark 3. 25. a h. divided agst. itself, that h. cannot
10. 29. that hath left h. or brethren for my sake
14. 14. Master saith, where is the guest-chamber? say ye to the good man of the h. Luke 22. 11.
Luke 10. 7. in that h. remain, go not from h. to h.
38. named Martha, received him into her h.
15. 8. doth not light candle and sweep h. and seek
John 12. 3. h. was filled with the odour of ointment
Acts 2. 2. a sound from heaven filled all the h.
46. breaking bread from h. to h. did eat their
5. 42. in every h. ceased not to teach and preach J.
10. 6. Simon a tanner, whose h. is by the sea-side
11. 12. and we entered into the man's h.
12. 12. he came to the h. of Mary, mother of John
17. 5. but the Jews assaulted the h. of Jason
18. 7. whose h. joined hard to the synagogue
19. 16. they fled out of that h. naked and wounded
20. 20. I taught you publicly, and from h. to h.
21. 8. entered into the h. of Philip the evangelist
Rom. 16. 5. greet the church in their h. 1 Cor. 16. 19.
1 Cor. 1. 11. by them which are of the h. of Chloe
16. 15. ye know the h. of Stephanas the first-fruits
2 Cor. 5. 1. if earthly h. be dissolved, we have an h.
2. desiring to be clothed upon with h. from heaven
1 Tim. 5. 13. wandering about from h. to h. and tattlers
14. that the younger women guide the h.
2 Tim. 1. 16. Lord give mercy to h. of Onesiphorus
2. 20. in a great h. there are vessels of gold and [silver
Heb. 3. 3. he who built the h. more honour than h.
4. for every h. is built by some man, he that built
6. whose h. are we, if we hold fast the confidence
2 John 10. receive him not into your h. nor bid him
See AARON, BORN, BUILD or BUILT, CHIEF, DAVID, DOOR, DWELL.

HOUSE joined with father.

Gen. 12. 1. Lord said, get thee from thy father's h.
20. 13. when God caused to wander from father's h.
24. 7. God, which took me from my father's h.
38. thou shalt go to my f.'s h. and take a wife
40. shalt take a wife for my son of my father's h.
31. 14. is there any portion for us in our father's h.?
38. 11. remain a widow at thy father's h. till Shelah be grown, Tamar went and dwelt in her father's h.
41. 51. God hath made me forget my father's h.
46. 31. my brethren and father's h. are come to me
50. 22. Joseph dwelt in Egypt, he and his f.'s h.
Exod. 12. 3. a lamb, according to h. of their fathers
Lev. 22. 13. if she is returned to her father's h.
Num. 1. 2. take sum of Israel by h. of their fathers, with number of their names, 18, 20, 22, 24.
4. there shall be a man of every tribe, every one head of the h. of his fathers, 44. Josh. 22. 14.
45. that were numbered by the h. of their fathers
2. 2. every man pitch with ensign of their f.'s h.
3. 15. number of the children of Levi after the h. of their fathers, by their families 20. | 4. 46.
4. 38. Gershon || 42. Merari after h. of their fathers
17. 2. according to h. of their f.'s twelve rods, 3.
18. 1. thou and f.'s h. bear iniquity of sanctuary
30. 3. woman vow a vow, being in her father's h. 16.
34. 14. Reuben, Gad, according to the h. of their f.
Deut. 22. 21. to play the whore in her father's h.
Josh. 2. 12. ye will shew kindness to my father's h.
Judg. 6. 15. and I am the least in my father's h.
9. 18. and ye are risen up against my father's h.
11. 2. thou shalt not inherit in our father's h.

Judg. 14. 15. lest we burn thee and thy f.'s h. with fire
16. 31. all the h. of his father came and buried him
19. 2. his concubine went to his father's h.
3. and she brought him into her father's h.
1 Sam. 2. 27. did I plainly appear to h. of thy father
30. I said the h. of thy f. should walk before me
9. 20. is it not on thee, and on all thy father's h.?
17. 25. king will make his father's h. free in Israel
18. 2. let him go no more home to his father's h.
22. 11. the king sent to call all his father's h.
16. thou and all thy father's h. shall die
24. 21. wilt not destroy my name out of father's h.
2 Sam. 3. 29. let it rest on Joab and all his f.'s h.
14. 9. the iniquity be on me, and on my father's h.
19. 28. all of my father's h. were but dead men
24. 17. let thy hand, I pray thee, be against me and against my father's h. 1 Chron. 21. 17.
1 Kings 2. 31. take innocent blood from me and f. h.
18. 18. thou and father's h. have troubled Israel
1 Chron. 2. 55. Hemath father of the h. of Rechab
4. 38. the h. of their fathers increased greatly
5. 15. Ahi son of Abdiel, son of Guni, chief of the house of their father's h. 24. | 7. 2, 7, 9, 40.
7. 4. with them after the h. of fathers were bands
9. 9. chief in the h. of their fathers, 13. 12. 30.
12. 28. of Zadok, his fath.'s h. twenty-two captains
28. 4. God chose me before the h. of my father
2 Chron. 21. 13. slain thy brethren of thy father's h.
Ezra 2. 59. could not shew their father's h. Neh. 1. 6.
10. 16. chief of the h. of their father examined
Neh. 1. 6. both I and my father's h. have sinned
Esth. 4. 14. thou and thy father's h. shall be destroy.
Psal. 45. 10. forget thy people and thy father's h.
Isa. 3. 6. take hold of his brother of h. of his father
7. 17. bring on thy f.'s h. days that have not come
22. 23. shall be for glorious throne to his father's h.
24. hang on him all the glory of his father's h.
Jer. 12. 6. the h. of thy father dealt treacherously
Luke 16. 27. I pray thee, send him to my father's h.
John 2. 16. make not my Father's h. an house of merchandise
14. 2. in my Father's h. are many mansions
Acts 7. 20. Moses was nourished in his father's h.

HOUSE of God.

Gen. 28. 17. this is none other but the h. of God
22. and this stone which I set shall be God's h.
Josh. 9. 23. from being drawers of water for h. of G.
Judg. 18. 31. all the time h. of God was in Shiloh
20. 18. Israel arose and went up to the h. of God
26. all the people came unto the h. of God, 21. 2.
31. high-way of which one goeth up to h. of God
1 Chr. 9. 11. Azariah ruler of h. of G. Neh. 11. 11.
24. 5. the governors of h. of G. were sons of Eleazar
2 Chr. 5. 14. glory of the Lord filled the h. of God
22. 12. he was with them hid in h. of G. six years
24. 13. and they set the h. of God in his state
33. 7. Manasseh set a carved image in the h. of God
36. 19. they burnt the h. of God and brake the wall
Ezra 5. 8. we went to the h. of the great God
15. let the h. of God be builded in his place, 6. 7.
7. 20. what more shall be needful for the h. of God?
23. let it be done for the h. of the God of heaven
Neh. 6. 10. let us meet in h. of God in the temple
13. 11. then I said, why is the h. of God forsaken?
Psal. 42. 4. I went with them to the h. of God, 55. 14.
52. 8. I am like a green olive-tree in the h. of God
84. 10. I had rather be door-keeper in h. of God
Eccl. 5. 1. keep thy foot when thou goest to h. of G.
Isa. 2. 3. come, let us go up to the h. of G. Mic. 4. 2.
Hos. 9. 8. the prophet is hated in the h. of God
Joel 1. 13. drink-offering withholden from h. of God
16. joy and gladness cut off from the h. of God
Zech. 7. 2. when they had sent to h. of G. men to pray
Mat 12. 4. how he entered into the h. of God, and did eat the shew-bread, Mark 2. 26. Luke 6. 4.
1 Tim. 3. 15. how to behave thyself in the h. of God
Heb. 10. 21. having an High-Priest over the h. of G.
1 Pet. 4. 17. judgment must begin at the h. of G.

His HOUSE.

Gen. 12. 17. the Lord plagued Pharaoh and his h.
17. 27. all the men of his h. were circumcised
39. 4. and he made him overseer over his h. 5.
45. 8. hath made me lord of all his h. Acts 7. 10.
Lev. 16. 6. and make an atonement for his h. 11.
27. 14. and when a man shall sanctify his h.
15. if he that sanctified it will redeem his h.
Num. 22. 18. if Balak would give me his h. full of silver and gold, I cannot go beyond word of L. 24. 13.
Deut. 20. 5. let him go and return to his h. 6, 7, 8.
24. 1. then let him send her out of his h.
10. thou shalt not go into his h. to fetch his pledge
Judg. 8. 27. which thing became a snare to his h.
9. 16. if dealt well with Jerubbaal and his h. 19.
1 Sam. 3. 12. which I have spoken concerning his h.
13. I told, that I will judge his h. for ever
7. 17. his return was to Ramah, for there was his h.
25. 1. Israel buried Samuel in his h. at Ramah
2 Sam. 6. 19. the people departed every one to his h.
21. which chose me before thy father and his h.
7. 1. it came to pass, when the king sat in his h.
25. hast spoken concerning his h. 1 Chron. 17. 23.
11. 9. but Uriah went not down to his h. 10, 13.
27. David fetched her to his h. became his wife
19. 11. why last to bring the king back to his h.?
21. 1. it is for Saul and his bloody h. because he slew
4. have no silver nor gold of Saul, nor of his h.
1 Kings 2. 33. on his h. there shall be peace from Lord
7. 1. Solomon was building, and finished all his h.
12. 24. return every man to his h. for thing is from me, 22. 17. 1 Chr. 16. 43. 2 Chr. 11. 4. | 18. 16.
13. 19. did eat bread in his h. and drank water
16. 7. came the sword against Baasha and his h.
20. 43. king of Israel went to his h. heavy, 21. 4.
2 Kings 6. 32. Elisha sat in his h. and elders with him
20. 13. nothing in his h. Hezekiah shewed not
1 Chron. 7. 23. because it went evil with his h.
10. 6. Saul, his sons, and all his h. died together
13. 14. the ark remained in his h. three months
2 Chr. 24. 16. had done good toward God and his h.
Ezra 6. 11. let his h. be made a dunghill for this
Neh. 3. 28. every one repaired over-against his h.
5. 13. so God shake out every man from his h.

Neh. 7. 3. and every one to be over-against his h.
Job 1. 10. hast not thou made an hedge about his h.?
7. 10. he shall return no more to his h.
8. 15. he shall lean on his h. it shall not stand
20. 28. the increase of his h. shall depart
21. 21. for what pleasure hath he in his h. after him?
27. 18. he buildeth his h. as a moth, as a booth
Psal. 49. 16. when the glory of his h. is increased
105. 21. he made him Lord of his h. and ruler
112. 3. wealth and riches shall be in his h.
Prov. 6. 31. give the substance of his h. Cant. 8. 7.
17. 13. evil shall not depart from his h.
Jer. 23. 34. I will even punish that man and his h.
Mic. 2. 2. so they oppress a man and his h.
Hab. 2. 9. coveteth an evil covetousness to his h.
Zech. 5. 4. it shall remain in the midst of his h.
Mat. 12. 29. then he will spoil his h. Mark 3. 27.
24. 17. to take any thing out of his h. Mark 13. 15.
43. not have suffered his h. to be broken up
Luke 8. 41. besought that he would come into his h.
18. 14. this man went down to his h. justified
John 4. 53. and himself believed and his whole h.
Acts 10. 2. one that feared God, with all his h.
22. was warned to send for thee into his h.
11. 13. shewed how he had seen an angel in his h.
16. 32. they spake to him and to all in his h.
34. when the jailer brought them into his h. he rejoiced, believing in God with all his h. 18. 8.
Col. 4. 15. salute the church which is in his h.
Heb. 3. 2. Moses was faithful in all his h. 5.
11. 7. Noah prepared an ark for the saving of his h.

HOUSE of Jacob.

Gen. 46. 27. all the souls of h. of Jacob were seventy
Exod. 19. 3. thus shalt thou say to the h. of Jacob
Psal. 114. 1. h. of J. from people of strange language
Isa. 2. 5. O h. of Jacob, let us walk in light of Lord
6. thou hast forsaken thy people, the h. of Jacob
8. 17. Lord that hideth his face from h. of Jacob
10. 20. such as are escaped of the h. of Jacob
14. 1. and they shall cleave to the h. of Jacob
29. 22. thus saith the Lord concerning h. of Jacob
46. 3. hearken unto me, O h. of Jacob and Israel
48. 1. hear ye this, O h. of Jacob, which are called
58. 1. spare not, shew the h. of Jacob their sins
Jer. 2. 4. hear the word of the Lord, O h. of Jacob
5. 20. declare this in the h. of Jacob, publish it
Ezek. 20. 5. I lifted up my hand to the h. of Jacob
Amos 3. 13. hear ye, and testify in the h. of Jacob
9. 8. I will not utterly destroy the h. of Jacob
Obad. 17. the h. of Jacob shall possess possessions
18. h. of Jacob shall be a fire
Mic. 2. 7. O thou that art named the h. of Jacob
3. 9. hear this, I pray, ye heads of the h. of Jacob
Luke 1. 33. he shall reign over the h. of Jacob

HOUSE of Joseph.

Gen. 43. 17. he brought the men into Joseph's h.
Josh. 18. 5. the h. of Joseph shall abide in their coast
Judg. 1. 22. the h. of Joseph went up against Bethel
23. the h. of Joseph sent to descry Bethel
35. yet the hand of the h. of Joseph prevailed
2 Sam. 19. 20. am come first of all the h. of Joseph
1 Kings 11. 28. ruler over the charge of h. of Joseph
Amos 5. 6. lest he break out like fire in h. of Joseph
Obad. 18. and the h. of Joseph shall be a flame
Zech. 10. 6. and I will save the h. of Joseph

HOUSE of Israel.

Lev. 10. 6. let h. of Israel bewail the burning
17. 3. what man soever there be of the h. of Israel that killeth an ox or lamb, 8. 10. | 22. 18.
Num. 20. 29. all the h. of Israel mourned for Aaron
1 Sam. 7. 2. the h. of Israel lamented after the Lord
2 Sam. 1. 12. they mourned for the h. of Israel
6. 5. all the h. of Israel played before the Lord
15. David and the h. of Israel brought up the ark
12. 8. I gave thee the h. of Israel and Judah
16. 3. to-day shall h. of Israel restore the kingdom
1 Kings 20. 31. kings of h. of Isr. are merciful kings
Psal. 98. 3. remembered his truth toward h. of Israel
115. 12. he will bless us, he will bless h. of Israel
135. 19. bless ye the Lord, O h. of Isr. bless Lord
Isa. 5. 7. the vineyard of the Lord is the h. of Israel
14. 2. the h. of Israel shall possess them in the land
46. 3. the remnant of the h. of Israel, hearken to me
63. 7. the great goodness toward the h. of Israel
Jer. 2. 4. hear, all the families of the h. of Israel
26. as a thief, so is the h. of Israel ashamed
3. 18. the house of Judah shall walk with h. of Isr.
20. you dealt treacherously, O h. of Israel, 5. 11.
9. 26. all the h. of Isr. are uncircumcised in heart
11. 10. the h. of Israel have broken my covenant
17. pronounced evil for evil, of the h. of Israel
13. 11. caused to cleave to me the whole h. of Isr.
23. 8. the Lord liveth, who led the h. of Israel
31. 27. I will sow the h. of Israel with seed of man
31. I will make new covenant with h. of Israel, 33.
33. 14. perform that I promised to the h. of Israel
48. 13. as the h. of Israel was ashamed of Beth-el
Ezek. 3. 1. eat this roll, and go, speak to h. of Israel, 17. 2. | 20. 27, 30. | 24. 21. | 33. 10. | 36. 22.
4. go, get thee unto the h. of Israel, and speak
5. but thou art sent to the h. of Israel
7. the h. of Isr. will not hearken to me, for all the h. of Israel are impudent and hard-hearted
17. I made thee a watchman to h. of Israel, 33. 7.
4. 3. this shall be a sign to the h. of Israel
4. and lay the iniquity of the h. of Israel upon it
5. thou shalt bear the iniquity of the h. of Israel
5. 4. a fire shall come forth into the h. of Israel
6. 11. the evil abominations of the h. of Israel, 8. 6.
8. 10. all the idols of the h. of Israel are pourtrayed
11. seventy men of the ancients of h. of Israel, 12.
9. 9. the iniquity of the h. of Israel is exceeding great
11. 5. thus have ye said, O h. of Israel, for I know
15. and all the h. of Israel wholly are they
12. 9. hath not the h. of Israel said, 27. | 18. 29.
24. nor any more divination within the h. of Israel
13. 5. nor made up the hedge for the h. of Israel
9. written in the writing of the h. of Israel
14. 4. every one of h. of I. that setteth up idols, 7.
11. that the h. of Israel may go no more astray
18. 6. nor lift his eyes to the idols of h. of Isr. 15.

Ezek. 18. 25. hear, O h. of Isr. is not my way equal?
30. therefore I will judge you, O h. of Israel
31. for why will ye die, O h. of Israel? 33. 11.
20. 13. but the h. of Israel rebelled against me
39. as for you, O h. of Isr. go ye, serve ye every one his idols, if ye will not hearken to me
40. there shall all the h. of Israel serve me
44. according to your corrupt doings, O h. of Isr.
22. 18. the h. of Israel is to me become dross
28. 24. no more a pricking briar to the h. of Israel
25. when I shall have gathered the h. of Israel
29. 6. have been a staff of a reed to the h. of Israel
16. shall be no more the confidence of h. of Israel
21. I will cause the horn of the h. of Israel to bud
34. 30. that they, even the h. of Isr. are my people
36. 10. and I will multiply all the h. of Israel
17. when the h. of Israel dwelt in their own land
21. my holy name which the h. of Israel profaned
22. I do not this for your sakes, O h. of Israel
32. be ashamed for your ways, O h. of Israel
37. I will for this be inquired of by the h. of Isr.
37. 11. these bones are the whole h. of Israel
16. write on it, for the h. of Israel his companions
39. 12. seven months shall h. of Israel be burying
22. the h. of Israel shall know that I am the Lord
23. that the h. of Israel went into captivity
25. I will have mercy on the whole h. of Israel
29. I have poured out my Spirit on the h. of Isr.
40. 4. declare all that thou seest to the h. of Israel
43. 10. son of man, shew the house to h. of Israel
44. 6. say to the rebellious, even to the h. of Israel
12. and caused the h. of Isr. to fall into iniquity
22. shall take maidens of the seed of the h. of Isr.
45. 6. possession shall be for the whole h. of Israel
8. the rest of the land shall they give to h. of Isr.
17. to make reconciliation for the h. of Israel
Hos. 1. 4. cause to cease the kingdom of h. of Isr.
6. I will no more have mercy on the h. of Israel
5. 1. and hearken, ye h. of Israel, and give ear
6. 10. have seen an horrible thing in h. of Israel
11. 12. h. of Isr. compasseth me about with deceit
Amos 5. 3. the city shall leave ten to the h. of Isr.
4. saith the Lord to the h. of Israel, seek ye me
25. have ye offered sacrifices 40 years, O h. of Is.?
6. 1. chief of nations, to whom the h. of Isr. came
14. I will raise against you a nation, O h. of Isr.
7. 10. hath conspired against thee in the h. of Isr.
9. 9. I will sift the h. of Israel among all nations
Mic. 1. 5. for the sins of the h. of Israel is all this
3. 1. hear, ye princes of the h. of Israel, 9.
Zech. 8. 13. that as ye were a curse, O h. of Isr.
Mat. 10. 6. go to lost sheep of the h. of Israel, 15. 24.
Acts 2. 36. let all the h. of Israel know assuredly
7. 42. O h. of Israel, have ye offered to me beasts?
Heb. 8. 8. make a new covenant with h. of Isr. 10.

HOUSE of Judah.

2 Sam. 2. 4. the men of Judah came and anointed David king over h. of Judah, 7, 11. 1 Chr. 28. 4.
12. 8. I gave thee the h. of Judah and of Israel
1 Kings 12. 21. he assembled all the h. of Judah
23. speak to all the h. of Judah and Benjamin
2 Kings 19. 30. the remnant that is escaped of the h. of Judah shall take root, and bear fruit, Isa. 37. 31.
2 Chr. 19. 11. Zebadiah the ruler of the h. of Judah
Neh. 4. 16. the rulers were behind the h. of Judah
Isa. 22. 21. he shall be a father to the h. of Judah
Jer. 3. 18. h. of Judah shall walk with house of Isr.
5. 11. the h. of Judah hath dealt treacherously
11. 10. the h. of Judah hath broken my covenant
17. for evil of the h. of Judah that they have done
12. 14. I will pluck h. of Judah from among them
13. 11. I caused to cleave to me the h. of Judah
31. 27. I will sow the h. of Judah with seed of man
31. I will make a new covenant with h. of Judah
33. 14. perform that good I promised to h. of Judah
36. 3. it may be h. of Judah will hear all the evil
Ezek. 4. 6. bear the iniquity of h. of Judah forty days
8. 17. is it a light thing to the h. of Judah?
9. 9. the iniquity of the h. of Judah is great
25. 3. Ammonites said, aha, against the h. of Jud.
8. the h. of Judah is like to all the heathen
12. Edom hath dealt against the h. of Judah
Hos. 1. 7. but I will have mercy upon the h. of Jud.
5. 12. I will be to the h. of Judah as rottenness
14. I will be as a young lion to the h. of Judah
Zeph. 2. 7. coast shall be for remnant of h. of Judah
Zech. 8. 13. as ye were a curse, O h. of Judah
15. I have thought to do well to the h. of Judah
19. the fast shall be to h. of Judah joy and gladness
10. 3. for the Lord hath visited the h. of Judah
6. and I will strengthen the h. of Judah
12. 4. I will open mine eyes unto the h. of Judah
Heb. 8. 8. I will make new covenant with h. of Judah

King's HOUSE.

2 Sam. 11. 2. David walked on roof of the king's h.
8. and Uriah departed out of the king's h.
15. 35. what thou shalt hear out of the king's h.
1 Kings 9. 1. when Solomon had finished the king's h.
14. 26. he took away the treasure of the king's h. 15. 18. 2 Kings 16. 8. 2 Chr. 12. 9. | 25. 24.
16. 18. Zimri burnt the king's h. over him with fire
2 Kings 7. 11. they told it to the king's h. within
25. 9. he burnt the king's h. Jer. 39. 8. | 52. 13.
2 Chr. 23. 5. a third part shall be at the king's h.
26. 21. Jotham his son was over the king's h.
28. 21. took away a portion out of the h. of the king
Ezra 6. 4. let expences be given out of the king's h.
Esth. 2. 9. gave her seven maidens out of king's h.
4. 13. think not thou shalt escape in the king's h.
9. 4. for Mordecai was great in the king's h.
Hos. 5. 1. and give ye ear, O h. of the k.

HOUSE of Levi.

Exod. 2. 1. and there went a man of the h. of Levi
Num. 17. 8. rod of Aaron for h. of Levi was budded
Psal. 135. 20. bless the Lord, O h. of Levi
Zech. 12. 13. the family of the h. of Levi apart

In the HOUSE.

Gen. 27. 15. she took raiment of Esau that were in h.
34. 29. they spoiled even all that was in the h.
39. 5. the blessing of the Lord was on all in the h.
8. my master wotteth not what is with me in the h.
45. 16. the fame thereof was heard in Pharaoh's h.

Exod. 12. 46. in one h. shall the passover be eaten
Lev. 14. 34. I put the plague of leprosy in a h. 35.
43. if plague come again and break out in the h.
44. behold, if the plague be spread in the h.
47. he that lieth, that eateth in the h. shall wash
48. behold, the plague hath not spread in the h.
Josh. 2. 19. whoso with thee in the h. his blood on us
6. 17. Rahab live, all that are with her in the h.
Judg. 17. 4. and they were in the h. of Micah, 12.
Ruth 1. 9. may find rest, each in h. of her husband
2. 7. until now, that she tarried a little in the h.
1 Sam. 28. 24. the woman had a fat calf in the h.
31. 9. sent to publish it in the h. of their idols
10. they put his armour in the h. of Ashtaroth
1 Kings 3. 17. I and this woman dwell in one h. and I was delivered of a child with her in the h.
6. 7. there was not any tool of iron heard in the h.
14. 13. is found some good in the h. of Jeroboam
16. 9. drinking himself drunk in the h. of Arza
2 Kings 4. 2. tell me what hast thou in the h.? thine handmaid hath not any thing in the h.
35. he returned, and walked in the h. to and fro
5. 18. leaneth on my hand, bow in h. of Rimmon
24. he took them, and bestowed them in the h.
19. 37. worshipping in h. of Nisroch, Isa. 37. 38.
21. 7. Manasseh set a graven image in the h.
2 Chr. 36. 17. slew young men in the h. of sanctua.
Ezra 1. 7. and had put them in the h. of his gods
6. 1. search was made in the h. of the rolls where
Esth. 7. 8. will he force the queen also in the h.?
9. behold, the gallows standeth in h. of Haman
Psal. 68. † 6. God setteth the solitary in a h.
119. 54. been my songs in the h. of my pilgrimage
Prov. 3. 33. curse of Lord is in the h. of the wicked
5. 10. thy labours be in the h. of a stranger
7. 11. she is loud, her feet abide not in her h.
15. 6. in the h. of the righteous is much treasure
Eccl. 7. 4. the heart of the wise is in h. of mourning; but the heart of fools is in the h. of mirth
Isa. 44. 13. maketh idol that it may remain in the h.
Jer. 7. 30. set their abominations in the h. 32. 34.
34. 15. ye made a covenant before me in the h.
37. 15. put him in the h. of Jonathan the scribe
Amos 6. 9. if there remain ten men in one h.
Mic. 1. 10. in the h. of Aphrah roll thyself in dust
6. 10. treasures of wickedness in the h. of wicked
Zech. 13. 6. I was wounded in the h. of my friends
Mat. 5. 15. giveth light unto all that are in the h.
Mark 2. 1. and it was noised that he was in the h.
9. 33. being in the h. he asked them what was it
10. 10. in the h. his disciples asked of the matter
14. 3. being in Bethany, in the h. of Simon the leper
Luke 8. 27. nor abode in any h. but in the tombs
John 8. 35. the servant abideth not in the h.
11. 20. Martha met him, Mary sat still in the h.
Acts 9. 11. inquire in the h. of Judas for one Saul
10. 32. Peter is lodged in the h. of Simon a tanner

HOUSE, joined with Lord.

Exod. 23. 19. the first-fruits thou shalt bring into the h. of the Lord, 34. 26. Neh. 10. 35.
Deut. 23. 18. not bring price of a dog into h. of Ld.
Josh. 6. 24. put into the treasury of h. of the Lord
Judg. 19. 18. I am now going to the h. of the Lord
1 Sam. 1. 7. when she went up to the h. of the Lord
24. Hannah brought him unto the h. of the Lord, 2 Kings 12. 4, 9, 13. | 22. 4. 2 Chron. 31. 14.
2 Sam. 12. 20. then David came into h. of the Ld.
1 Kings 3. 1. made an end of building the h. of L.
6. 37. was the foundation of the h. of the Lord laid, 2 Chron. 8. 16. Ezra 3. 11. Zech. 8. 9.
7. 40. the work he made for the h. of the Lord, 45, 51. 2 Chron. 4. 16. | 5. 1. | 24. 14.
8. 10. that the cloud filled the h. of the Lord, 11. 2 Chron. 5. 13. | 7. 2. Ezek. 44. 4.
63. so Israel dedicated the h. of the Lord
10. 5. he went up unto the h. of Lord, 2 Chr. 9. 4.
2 Kings 11. 3. he was hid in the h. of Lord six years
4. he took an oath of them in the h. of the Lord
15. let her not be slain in h. of L. 2 Chr. 23. 14.
18. appointed officers over h. of L. 2 Chr. 23. 18.
19. they brought from the h. of the Lord, 23. 6.
12. 10. found in h. of the L. 14. 14. | 16. 8. | 18. 15.
11. had the oversight of the h. of the Lord
16. trespass-money was not brought into h. of L.
16. 18. the king's entry, turned he from h. of Ld.
2 Kings 20. 5. third day shalt go up unto h. of Lord
8. what sign Lord will heal me, and that I shall go up to the h. of the L. Isa. 38. 22.
23. 2. read words of the covenant which were found in the h. of the Lord, 24. 2 Chron. 34. 17, 30.
7. houses of Sodomites that were by h. of the L.
11. the horses at entering in of the h. of the L.
25. 9. and he burnt the h. of the Lord, Jer. 52. 13.
1 Chr. 6. 31. service of song in the h. of the Lord
22. 1. then David said, this is the h. of the L.
11. now, my son, build the h. of the Lord thy G.
14. have prepared for the h. of the Lord
23. 4. to set forward the work of the h. of the L.
26. 12. porters, to minister in the h. of the L.
2 Chron. 8. 16. so the h. of the Lord was perfected
26. 21. for he was cut off from h. of L. Joel 1. 9.
29. 5. ye Levites, sanctify the h. of the L.
15. they came to cleanse the h. of the Lord
33. 15. Manasseh took the idol out of h. of Lord
34. 15. I found the book of the law in h. of Lord
36. 14. the priests polluted the h. of the Lord
Ezra 7. 27. to beautify h. of the Lord in Jerusalem
Psal. 23. 6. I will dwell in the h. of the Lord for ever
27. 4. that I may dwell in the h. of Lord all my life
92. 13. those that be planted in the h. of the Lord
116. 19. I will pay my vows in courts of Lord's h.
118. 26. we have blessed you out of the h. of Lord
122. 1. when they said, let us go into h. of the L.
9. because of the h. of Lord I will seek thy good
134. 1. ye that stand in the h. of the Lord, 135. 2.
Isa. 2. 2. mountain of the Lord's h. be established in the top of the mountains, Mic. 4. 1.
37. 14. Hezekiah went up unto the h. of the Lord
Jer. 17. 26. sacrifices of praise to the h. of the Lord
20. 1. Pashur was governor in the h. of the Lord
2. the high gate, which was by h. of the Lord

Jer. 26. 2. which come to worship in the Lord's h.
7. speaking these words in the h. of the Lord
28. 1. Hananiah spake to me in the h. of the Lord
5. the people that stood in the h. of the Lord
29. 26. ye should be officers in the h. of the Lord
35. 2. bring the Rechabites into the h. of the Lord
36. 5. I am shut up, I cannot go into h. of Lord
6. read in the Lord's h. upon the fasting-day
38. 14. the third entry that is in the h. of the Lord
41. 5. to bring them to the h. of the Lord
51. 51. are come into the sanctuaries of Lord's h.
Lam. 2. 7. they have made a noise in the h. of the Lord
Hag. 1. 2. the time that the Lord's h. should be built
See COURT, DOOR, GATE, TREASURES, VESSELS.

Mine, or *my* HOUSE.

Gen. 15. 2. the steward of my h. is this Eliezer
3. and lo, one born in my h. is mine heir
34. 30. and I shall be destroyed, I and my h.
41. 40. thou shalt be over my h. and according to
Num. 12. 7. Moses not so, who is faith. in all mine h.
Deut. 26. 13. the hallowed things out of mine h.
Josh. 24. 15. as for me and my h. we will serve Lord
Judg. 11. 31. cometh forth of the doors of my h.
19. 23. seeing this man come into m. h. do not thus
1 Sam. 20. 15. not cut off thy kindness from my h.
21. 15. shall this fellow come into my h.?
2 Sam. 7. 18. who am I, and what is my h. that thou hast brought me hitherto? 1 Chron. 17. 16.
11. 11. shall I then go into mine h. to eat and drink?
23. 5. tho' my h. be not so with God, yet he hath
1 Kings 21. 2. give it me, because it is near to my h.
2 Kings 20. 15. all things that are in mine h. have they seen, nothing have I not shewn them, Isa. 39. 4.
1 Chron. 17. 14. I will settle him in mine h. for ever
Job 17. 13. if I wait, the grave is mine h. I have made
Psal. 101. 2. I will walk in my h. with a perfect heart
132. 3. I will not come into the tabernacle of my h.
Prov. 7. 6. at the window of my h. I looked through
Isa. 3. 7. in my h. is neither bread nor clothing
56. 5. unto them will I give in mine h. a name
7. I will make them joyful in my h. of prayer, mine h. shall be called an h. of prayer for all people, Mat. 21. 13. Mark 11. 17. Luke 19. 46.
Jer. 11. 15. what hath my beloved to do in mine h.?
12. 7. I have forsaken mine h. I left mine heritage
23. 11. in my h. have I found their wickedness
Ezek. 8. 1. as I sat in mine h. and elders before me
23. 39. thus have they done in midst of mine h.
44. 7. in my sanctuary to pollute it, even my h.
Dan. 4. 4. I Nebuchadnezzar was at rest in mine h.
Hos. 9. 15. I will drive them out of mine h.
Hag. 1. 9. why? because of mine h. that is waste
Zech. 3. 7. then thou shalt also judge my h. and keep
9. 8. I will encamp about mine h. for the army
Mal. 3. 10. that there may be meat in mine h.
Mat. 12. 44. I will return into my h. Luke 11. 24.
Luke 9. 61. let me bid them farewell at my h.
14. 23. compel them, that my h. may be filled
Acts 10. 30. at the ninth hour I prayed in my h.
16. 15. saying, come into my h. and abide there

Own HOUSE.

Gen. 14. 14. armed his servants born in his own h.
30. 30. when shall I provide for mine own h. also
Deut. 22. 2. thou shalt bring it unto thine own h.
Josh. 20. 6. shall return and come unto his own h.
Judg. 8. 29. Jerubbaal went and dwelt in his own h.
2 Sam. 4. 11. slain a righteous person in his own h.
12. 11. raise evil against thee out of thy own h.
14. 24. let him turn to his own h. and not see my face, so Absalom returned to his own h.
19. 30. the king is come again in peace to his own h.
1 Kings 2. 34. Joab buried in his own h. in wildern.
3. 1. he had made an end of building his own h.
7. 1. Solomon was building his own h. 13 years
9. 15. Solomon raised a levy to build his own h.
12. 16. see to thine own h. David, 2 Chron. 10. 16.
14. 12. arise therefore, get thee into thine own h.
2 Kings 21. 18. Manasseh slept with his fathers, was buried in the garden of his own h. 2 Chron. 33. 20.
23. slew the king in his own h. 2 Chron. 33. 24.
2 Chr. 7. 11. came in his heart to make in his own h.
8. 1. at the end of twenty years, wherein Solomon had built the house of the Lord and his own h.
Esth. 1. 22. every man should bear rule in his own h.
Prov. 11. 29. he that troubleth his own h. shall
15. 27. that is greedy of gain troubleth his own h.
Isa. 14. 18. lie in glory, every one in his own h.
Mic. 7. 6. a man's enemies are the men of his own h.
Hag. 1. 9. and ye run every man unto his own h.
Mat. 13. 57. Jesus said to them, a prophet is not without honour, save in his own h. Mark 6. 4.
Luke 1. 23. he departed to his own h. 5. 25.
56. and Mary returned to her own h.
5. 29. Levi made him a great feast in his own h.
8. 39. return to thy o. h. and shew how great things
John 7. 53. and every man went unto his own h.
Acts 28. 30. Paul dwelt two years in his own h.
1 Tim. 3. 4. a bishop, one that ruleth well his own h.
5. for if a man know not how to rule his own h.
5. 8. and especially for those of his own h.
Heb. 3. 6. but Christ as a Son over his own h.

This HOUSE.

Gen. 39. 9. there is none greater in this h. than I.
40. 14. think on me, and bring me out of this h.
1 Kings 6. 12. concerning this h. thou art building
8. 27. how much less this h. that I have builded
29. eyes be opened toward this h. 2 Chron. 6. 20.
31. before thine altar in this h. 2 Chron. 6. 22.
33. shall confess thy name, pray and make supplication to thee in this h. 42. 2 Chr. 6. 24, 32.
38. and spread forth his hands towards this h.
9. 3. I have hallowed this h. 2 Chron. 7. 16, 20.
8. at this h. every one shall hiss, 2 Chron. 7. 21.
2 Kings 21. 7. t. h. which I have chosen, 2 Chr. 33. 7.
2 Chron. 20. 9. if when evil cometh upon us we stand before this h. for thy name is in this h.
Ezra 3. 12. the foundation of this h. was laid before
5. 12. Nebuchadnezzar who destroyed this h.
6. 15. this h. was finished on third day of Adar

Jer. 7. 10. and come and stand before me in this h.
11. is this h. become a den of robbers in your eyes
14. therefore will I do to this h. as to Shiloh
22. 4. then shall there enter in by the gates of t. h.
5. that this h. shall become a desolation
26. 6. then will I make this h. like Shiloh
9. saying, this h. shall be like Shiloh
12. the Lord sent me to prophesy against this h.
Hag. 1. 4. to dwell in houses, and this h. lie waste?
2. 3. who is left that saw this h. in her first glory?
7. I will fill this h. with glory, saith the Lord
9. the glory of this latter h. greater than former
Zech. 4. 9. Zerubb. laid the foundation of this h.
Luke 10. 5. ye enter, first say, peace be to this h.
19. 9. Jesus said, this day is salv. come to this h.

Thine, or *thy* HOUSE.

Gen. 7. 1. come thou and all thy h. into the ark
31. 41. thus have I been twenty years in thy h.
Exod. 8. 3. frogs shall go up and come into thine h.
Num. 18. 11. every one that is clean in thy h. 13.
Deut. 6. 7. talk when thou sittest in thine h. 11. 19.
9. shalt write them on the posts of thy h. 11. 20.
7. 26. nor shalt bring an abomination into thine h.
15. 16. because he loveth thee and thine h.
21. 12. then thou shalt bring her home to thine h.
13. shall remain in thine h. and bewail her father
22. 8. that thou bring not blood upon thine h.
25. 14. shalt not have in thine h. divers measures
26. 11. good thing God given to thee and thine h.
Josh. 2. 3. bring men which are entered into thine h.
19. whosoever shall go out of the doors of thy h.
Judg. 12. 1. we will burn thine h. on thee with fire
19. 22 bring forth the man that came into thine h.
Ruth 4. 11. make woman that is come into thine h.
12. and let thy h. be like the house of Pharez
1 Sam. 2. 30. that thy h. should walk before me
31. there shall not be an old man in thine h.
33. the incr. of thine h. shall die in flower of age
36. every one in thine h. shall crouch to him
22. 14. as David, who is honourable in thine h.
25. 6. peace be to thine h. and to all thou hast
35. David said to her, go up in peace to thine h.
2 Sam. 7. 16. thine h. shall be established for ever
11. 8. go down to thy h. and wash thy feet
10. why then didst not thou go down to thine h.?
12. 10. the sword shall never depart from thine h.
14. 8. the king said, go to thine h. 1 Kings 1. 53.
1 Kings 13. 8. if thou wilt give me half thine h.
18. bring him back with thee into thine h.
16. 3. make thy h. like the h. of Jeroboam, 21. 22.
20. 6. my servants, they shall search thine h.
2 Kings 20. 1. set thine h. in order, Isa. 38. 1.
15. what have they seen in thine h.? Isa. 39. 4.
17. all in thine h. shall be carried, Isa. 39. 6.
Ps. 5. 7. I will come to t. h. in multit. of thy mercy
26. 8. I have loved the habitation of thy h.
36. 8. they shall be satisfied with fatness of thy h.
50. 9. I will take no bullock out of thy h.
65. 4. we shall be satisfied with goodness of thy h.
66. 13. I will go into thy h. with burnt offerings
69. 9. zeal of thine h. hath eaten me up, John 2. 17.
93. 5. holiness becometh thine h. O Lord, for ever
128. 3. wife shall be as a fruitful vine by sides of thine h.
Isa. 58. 7. bring the poor that are cast out to thy h.
Jer. 38. 17. go forth, thou shalt live, and thine h.
Ezek. 3. 24. Spirit said, shut thyself within thine h.
44. 30. may cause the blessing to rest in thine h.
Hab. 2. 10. thou hast consulted shame to thy h.
Mat. 9. 6. arise, go to t. h. Mark 2. 11. Luke 5. 24.
26. 18. I will keep the passover at thy h.
Luke 7. 44. I entered t. h. thou gavest me no water
19. 5. come down, for to-day I must abide at thy h.
Acts 11. 14. thou and all thy h. shall be saved, 16. 31.
Philem. 2. to the church in thy h. grace to you
See TOPS.

HOUSES.

Gen. 42. 19. go, carry corn for the famine of your h.
Exod. 1. 21. midwives feared God, he made them h.
6. 14. these be the heads of their fathers' h.
8. 9. to destroy the frogs from thee and thy h. 11.
13. and the frogs died out of the h. and the fields
21. I will send swarms of flies into thy h. 24.
9. 20. he made his servants and cattle flee into the h.
10. 6. the locusts shall fill thy h. and the h. of all thy servants, and the h. of all the Egyptians
12. 7. strike it on the upper door-posts of the h.
13. blood be for a token upon the h. where you are
15. ye shall put away leaven out of your h.
19. there shall be no leaven found in your h.
23. not suffer the destroyer to come in to your h.
27. who passed over and delivered our h. in Egypt
Lev. 25. 31. the h. of villages be counted as the fields
32. the h. of the cities of their possession, 33.
Num. 4. 22. sum of Gershon thro' h. their fathers, 40.
16. 32. the earth swallowed them up and their h.
17. 6. for each prince, according to their fathers' h.
32. 18. we will not return unto our h. till Israel
Deut. 6. 11. to give thee h. full of all good things
8. 12. when hast built goodly h. and dwelt therein
19. 1. dwellest in their cities and h. Neh. 9. 25.
Josh. 9. 12. we took hot provision out of our h.
Judg. 18. 14. do ye know that there is in these h.?
22. the men that were in the h. near to Micah's
1 Kings 13. 32. he cried against the h. of high places
20. 6. they shall search the h. of thy servants
2 Kings 17. 29. put them in the h. of the high places
32. which sacrificed in the h. of the high places
23. 7. he brake down the h. of the Sodomites
19. the h. of the high places Josiah took away
25. 9. he burnt all the h. of Jerusalem, Jer. 52. 13.
1 Chron. 15. 1. David make h. in the city of David
28. 11. David gave to Solom. the pattern of the h.
29. 4. to overlay the walls of the h. withal
2 Chron. 34. 11. to buy timber to floor the h.
35. 4. and prepare yourselves by h. of your fathers
Neh. 4. 14. fight for your wives and your h.
5. 3. some said, we have mortgaged our lands and h.
11. restore to them their vineyards and h.
7. 4. but the people are few, and h. not builded
10. 34. we cast lots after the h. of our fathers
Job 1. 4. his sons went and feasted in their h.

Job 3. 15. with princes, who filled their h. with silver
4. 19. much less in them that dwell in h. of clay
15. 28. he dwelleth in h. which no man inhabiteth
21. 9. their h. are safe from fear, nor is the rod of G.
22. 18. yet he filled their h. with good things
24. 16. in the dark they dig through h. which they
Psal. 49. 11. that their h. shall continue for ever
83. 12. let us take the h. of God in possession
Prov. 1. 13. we shall fill our h. with spoil
30. 26. yet make they their h. in the rocks
Eccl. 2. 4. I builded me h. I planted me vineyards
Isa. 3. 14. the spoil of the poor is in your h.
5. 9. of a truth, many h. shall be desolate, 6. 11.
8. 14. for a rock of offence to both the h. of Israel
13. 16. their h. be spoiled, their wives ravished
21. their h. shall be full of doleful creatures
22. the wild beasts shall cry in their desolate h.
15. 3. on the tops of their h. every one shall howl
22. 10. ye have numbered the h. of Jerusalem, and the h. have ye broken down to fortify the wall
32. 13. yea, upon all the h. of joy in the joyous city
65. 21. they shall build h. and inhabit them
Jer. 5. 7. and assembled by troops in the harlot's h.
27. as cage is full of birds, are their h. full of dec.
6. 12. and their h. shall be turned unto others
18. 22. let a cry be heard from their h.
19. 13. the h. of Jerusalem and the h. of the kings of Judah shall be defiled as the place of Tophet
29. 5. build ye h. and dwell in them, 28.
32. 15. h. and fields shall be possessed in this land
29. h. on whose roofs they offered incense to Baal
33. 4. concerning h. of this city, and h. of kings
39. 8. they burnt the h. of the people with fire
43. 12. I will kindle a fire in h. of gods of Egypt, 13.
Lam. 5. 2. our h. are turned to aliens, we are orphans
Ezek. 7. 24. the heathen shall possess their h.
11. 3. which say, it is not near, let us build h.
16. 41. they shall burn thine h. with fire, 23. 47.
26. 12. and they shall destroy thy pleasant h.
28. 26. they shall build h. and plant vineyards
33. 30. talking against thee in the doors of the h.
45. 4. the holy portion shall be a place for their h.
Dan. 2. 5. and your h. shall be made a dunghill
3. 29. and their h. shall be made a dunghill
Hos. 11. 11. I will place them in their h. saith Lord
Joel 2. 9. they shall climb up upon the h. shall enter
Amos 3. 15. will smite winter and summer-house, h. of ivory shall perish, great h. shall have an end
Mic. 1. 14. the h. of Achzib shall be a lie to kings
2. 2. and they covet h. and take them away
9. the women ye cast out from their pleasant h.
Zeph. 1. 9. which fill their master's h. with violence
13. their h. shall become a desolation, they shall build h. but not inhabit them, plant vineyards
2. 7. in the h. of Ashkelon shall they lie down
Hag. 1. 4. is time for you to dwell in yo. ceiled h.?
Zech. 14. 2. h. shall be rifled, and the wom. ravished
Mat. 11. 8. they that wear soft cloth. are in kings' h.
19. 29. every one that hath forsaken h. or wife
23. 14. dev. widows' h. Mark 12. 40. Luke 20. 47.
Mark 8. 3. if send them away fasting to their own h.
Luke 16. 4. that they may receive me into their h.
Acts 4. 34. as many as were possessors of h. sold
1 Cor. 11. 22. have ye not h. to eat and drink in?
1 Tim. 3. 12. deacons ruling their own h. well
2 Tim. 3. 6. of this sort are they which creep into h.
Tit. 1. 11. who subvert whole h. teaching things

HOUSEHOLD, *or* HOUSEHOLDS.

Gen. 18. 19. he will command his h. after him
35. 2. Jacob said to his h. put away strange gods
42. 33. take food for the famine of your h. be gone
45. 11. lest thou and thy h. come to poverty
18. take your father and your h. and come to me
47. 12. Joseph nourished his father's h. with bread
24. four parts shall be for food for your h.
Exod. 1. 1. every man and his h. came with Jacob
12. 4. if the h. be too little for the lamb
Lev. 16. 17. till he have made an atonem. for his h.
Num. 18. 31. ye shall eat it in every place, and your h.
Deut. 6. 22. the Lord shewed wonders upon all his h.
11. 6. the earth swallowed them and their h.
14. 26. thou shalt rejoice, thou and thy h.
15. 20. thou shalt eat it before L. thou and thy h.
Josh. 2. 18. bring all thy father's h. home to thee
6. 25. saved Rahab, her father's h. and all she had
7. 14. and the family shall come by h.
18. and he brought his h. man by man
Judg. 6. 27. so it was, bec. he feared his father's h.
18. 25. thou lose thy life, with the lives of thy h.
1 Sam. 25. 17. evil is determined against his h.
27. 3. every man with his h. 2 Sam. 2. 3.
2 Sam. 6. 11. the Lord blessed him and all his h.
20. then David returned to bless his h.
15. 16. and the king went forth and all his h.
16. 2. the asses be for the king's h. to ride on
17. 23. put his h. in order and hanged himself
19. 18. a ferry-boat to carry over the king's h.
41. why have Judah brought the king and his h.
1 Kings 4. 6. and Ahishai was over the h.
7. which provided victuals for the king and his h.
5. 9. shall do my desire, in giving food for my h.
11. Solomon gave Hiram wheat for food to his h.
11. 20. and Genubath was in Pharaoh's h.
2 Kings 7. 9. that we may go and tell the king's h.
8. 1. go and thine h. to sojourn where thou canst
18. 18. there came out to them Eliakim son of Hilkiah who was over the h. 19. 2. Isa. 36. 22. | 37. 2.
1 Chr. 24. 6. one principal h. being taken for Eleaz.
Job 1. 3. three thousand camels and a great h.
Prov. 27. 27. have goats' milk for food of thy h.
31. 15. she riseth and giveth meat to her h.
21. she is not afraid of the snow for her h. for all her h. are clothed with scarlet
27. she looketh well to the ways of her h.
Mat. 10. 25. much more shall they call them of his h.
36. a man's foes shall be they of his own h.
24. 45. hath made ruler over his h. Luke 12. 42.
Acts 16. 15. when she was baptized and her h.
Rom. 16. 10. salute them which are of Aristobulus' h.
11. greet them that be of the h. of Narcissus
1 Cor. 1. 16. I baptized also the h. of Stephanas
Gal. 6. 10. to them who are of the h. of faith

Eph. 2. 19. no more strangers, but of the h. of God
Phil. 4. 22. chiefly they that are of Cesar's h.
2 Tim. 4. 19. salute the h. of Onesiphorus
HOUSEHOLDER.
Mat. 13. 27. so the servants of the h. came and said
52. is like unto a man that is an h. 20. 1.
21. 33. there was a certain h. planted a vineyard
HOUSEHOLD-servants.
Acts 10. 7. Cornelius called two of his h.-servants
HOUSEHOLD-stuff.
Gen. 31. 37. what hast thou found of all thy h.-stuff?
Neh. 13. 8. I cast out all the h.-stuff of Tobiah
HOW.
Gen. 26. 9. and h. saidst thou, she is my sister?
27. 20. h. is it thou hast found it so quickly?
28. 17. Jacob said, h. dreadful is this place
39. 9. h. then can I do this great wickedness
44. 8. h. then should we steal out of thy lord's h.
16. what shall we speak? h. shall we clear ourselv.
34. h. shall I go to my father, lad not with me?
Exod. 2. 18. h. is it that ye are come so soon to-day
6. 12. h. then shall Pharaoh hear me of uncircum.
30. and h. shall Pharaoh hearken unto me?
18. 8. Moses told h. the Lord delivered them
19. 4. ye have seen h. I bare you, Deut. 1. 31.
Num. 10. 31. h. we are to encamp in the wilderness
23. 8. h. shall I curse G. not cursed? h. shall I defy?
24. 5. h. goodly are thy tents, O Jacob, and tabern.
Deut. 1. 12. h. can I myself bear your cumbrance?
7. 17. if thou shalt say, h. can I dispossess them?
11. 6. h. the earth opened her mouth and swallowed
12. 30. h. did these nations serve their gods?
25. 18. h. he met thee by the way and smote thee
29. 16. ye know h. we have dwelt in Egypt, and
h. we came through nations which ye passed by
32. 30. h. should one chase a thousand, and two put
Josh. 9. 7. h. shall we make a league with you?
Judg. 13. 12. h. shall we order the child, h. do to him?
16. 15. she said, h. canst thou say, I love thee?
20. 3. they said, tell us, h. was this wickedness
21. 7. h. do for wives for them that remain? 16.
Ruth 3. 18. till thou know h. the matter will fall
1 Sam. 10. 27. said, h. shall this man save us?
14. 29. see h. mine eyes have been enlightened
16. 2. h. can I go? if Saul hear he will kill me
2 Sam. 1. 4. h. went the matter, I pray thee, tell me
5. h. knowest thou that Saul and Jonath. be dead?
19. h. are the mighty fallen! 25, 27.
11. 7. h. Joab did, h. the people did, and h. the war
12. 18. h. then will he vex himself, if we tell him
1 Kings 3. 7. I know not h. to go out or come in
12. 6. h. do you advise, that I may answer people
14. 19. h. Jeroboam warred, and h. he reigned
18. 13. h. I hid an hundred men of Lord's prophets
20. 7. and see h. the man seeketh mischief
2 Kings 5. 7. h. he seeketh a quarrel against me
10. 4. two kings stood not, h. then shall we stand?
17. 28. taught them h. they should fear the Lord
18. 24. h. then wilt thou turn away? Isa. 36. 9.
19. 25. heard long ago, h. I have done it, Isa. 37. 26.
20. 3. h. I have walked before thee, Isa. 38. 3.
2 Chron. 20. 11. behold, I say, h. they reward us
33. 19. his prayer, and h. God was entreated of him
Neh. 2. 17. ye see h. Jerusal. lieth waste, gates burnt
Esth. 2. 11. Mordecai walked, to know h. Esther did
8. 6. h. can I endure to see evil that shall come
Job 9. 2. but h. should a man be just with God?
22. 13. and thou sayest, h. doth God know?
26. 2. h. hast thou helped him that is without power!
h. savest thou arm that hath no strength!
14. but h. little a portion is heard of him!
Psal. 11. 1. h. say ye to my soul, flee as a bird
44. 2. h. thou didst drive out heathen, h. afflict
66. 3. say to God, h. terrible art thou in thy works
73. 11. h. doth G. know? || 89. 47. h. short my time
84. 1. h. amiable are thy tabernacles, O Lord
104. 24. O Lord, h. manifold are thy works
119. 97. O h. love I thy law, it is my meditation
103. h. sweet are thy words unto my taste
159. consider h. I love thy precepts, quicken me
132. 2. h. he sware unto the Lord and vowed
139. 17. h. precious are thy thoughts unto me!
Prov. 15. 23. a word in due season, h. good is it!
30. 13. there is a generation, O h. lofty their eyes
Eccl. 10. 15. he knoweth not h. to go to the city
11. 5. knowest not h. the bones grow in the womb
Cant. 4. 10. h. fair is thy love, my sister, spouse, 7. 6.
5. 3. I have put off my coat, h. shall I put it on?
7. 1. h. beautiful are thy feet with shoes, O daugh.
Isa. 14. 12. h. art thou fallen from heaven, O Lucifer
20. 6. shall say in that day, and h. shall we escape?
48. 11. for h. should my name be polluted?
50. 4. I should know h. to speak a word in season
52. 7. h. beautiful are the feet of him, Rom. 10. 15.
Jer. 2. 23. h. canst thou say, I am not polluted?
3. 19. I said, h. shall I put thee among the children?
5. 7. h. shall I pardon || 8. 8. h. do ye say? 48. 14.
9. 19. h. are we spoiled? || 15. 5. to ask h. thou doest?
47. 7. h. can it be quiet, seeing the Lord hath given
50. 23. h. is the hammer of the whole earth cut?
Lam. 1. 1. h. doth the city sit solitary as a widow?
Ezek. 16. 30. h. weak is thy heart, saith the Lord
33. 10. if we pine away in sins, h. should we live?
Hos. 11. 8. h. shall I give thee up, Ephraim? h.
deliver thee? h. make thee as Admah and Zeboim?
Joel 1. 18. h. do the beasts groan? herds of cattle
Obad. 5. if thieves came to thee, h. art thou cut off
Zeph. 2. 15. h. is she become desolat. place for beasts
Hag. 2. 3. h. do you see it now? is it not as nothing?
Zech. 9. 17. h. great is his goodness and his beauty!
Mat. 6. 23. if light be darkn. h. great is that darkn.
7. 4. h. wilt thou say to thy brother, let me pull
11. if ye know h. to give good gifts, Luke 11. 13.
10. 19. take no thought h. or what ye shall speak
12. 14. h. they might destr. him, Mark 3. 6. | 11. 18.
26. h. shall his kingdom stand? Luke 11. 18.
34. h. can ye, being evil, speak good things?
16. 11. h. is it that ye do not underst. that I spake
18. 12. h. think ye? if a man have an hundr. sheep
21. 20. h. soon is the fig-tree withered away
22. 12. h. camest thou in hither not having a garm.
45. if call him Ld. h. is he his son? Luke 20. 44.

Mat. 23. 33. h. can ye escape the damnation of hell?
26. 54. h. then shall the scriptures be fulfilled?
Mark 2. 16. h. is it that he eateth with sinners?
26. h. he went into the house of God, Luke 6. 4.
4. 27. the seed should grow up, he knoweth not h.
40. he said, h. is it that ye have no faith?
10. 23. h. hardly shall they that have riches enter?
14. 1. sought h. they might take him by craft
11. sought h. he might betray him, Luke 22. 4.
Luke 1. 34. h. shall this be, seeing I know not a man
2. 49. h. is it that ye sought me? wist ye not that I
8. 18. take heed h. ye hear || 10. 26. h. readest thou
12. 50. and h. am I straitened till it be accomplis.
56. h. is it that ye do not discern this time?
16. 2. he said, h. is it that I hear this of thee?
24. 6. remember h. he spake unto you in Galilee?
35. h. he was known of them in breaking bread
John 3. 4. h. can a man be born when he is old?
9. h. can these things be? || 5. 44. h. can ye believe
5. 47. if not his writing, h. believe my words?
6. 52. h. can this man give us his flesh to eat?
7. 15. saying, h. knoweth this man letters?
9. 10. h. were thy eyes opened? || 26. h. opened eyes?
11. 36. h. loved him || 14. 5. h. can we know the way?
14. 22. h. is it thou wilt manifest thyself to us?
Acts 4. 21. finding noth. h. they might punish them
5. 9. h. is it that ye have agreed together to tempt?
7. 25. h. God by his hand would deliver them
8. 31. h. can I, except some man should guide me?
9. 27. told, h. he had seen the Lord in the way
10. 38. h. G. anointed Jesus of Naz. with Holy G.
11. 13. shewed h. he had seen an angel in his house
14. 27. h. he had opened the door of faith
15. 36. let us go again, and see h. they do
20. 20. h. kept back nothing that was profitable
35. h. so labouring, ye ought to support the weak
Rom. 3. 6. for then h. shall God judge the world?
6. 2. h. we that are dead to sin live longer therein?
7. 18. h. to perform what is good, I find not
8. 32. h. shall he not with him freely give all things?
10. 14. h. shall they call? h. shall believe? h. hear?
11. 2. h. he maketh intercession to G. against Isr.
33. h. unsearchable his judgments, and ways past
1 Cor. 3. 10. take heed h. he buildeth thereupon
7. 32. unmarried careth h. he may please the Lord
33. that is mar. careth h. he may please his wife
34. she careth h. she may please her husband
14. 7. h. shall it be known what is piped or harped?
9. h. shall it be known what is spoken?
15. 12. h. say some that there is no resurrection?
35. some man will say, h. are the dead raised up?
2 Cor. 7. 15. h. with fear and trembling received him
8. 2. h. that in a great trial of affliction their joy
13. 5. know ye not h. that Jesus Christ is in you?
Gal. 4. 9. h. turn ye again to the weak elements?
6. 11. ye see h. large a letter I have written to you
Eph. 6. 21. but that ye also may know h. I do
Phil. 2. 23. so soon as I shall see h. it will go with me
4. 12. I know h. to be abased, and know h. to abound
Col. 4. 6. that ye may know h. ye ought to answer
1 Thess. 1. 9. and h. ye turned to G. from idols to
2. 10. h. holily we behaved ourselves among you
11. h. we exhorted you || 4. 1. h. ye ought to walk
4. 4. should know h. to possess his vessel in honour
2 Thess. 3. 7. for you know h. ye ought to follow us
1 Tim. 3. 5. for if a man know not h. to rule his own
house, h. shall he take care of the church of God?
15. mayest know h. thou oughtest to behave
Heb. 2. 3. h. shall we escape if we neglect so great sa.
7. 4. now consider h. great this man was, to whom
Jam. 2. 24. ye see h. that by works a man is justified
3. 5. behold h. great a matter a little fire kindleth
2 Pet. 2. 9. the Lord knoweth h. to deliver the godly
1 John 3. 17. h. dwelleth the love of God in him?
4. 20. h. can he love God whom he hath not seen?
Jude 5. h. that the Lord having saved the people
Rev. 2. 2. h. thou canst not bear them who are evil
3. 3. remember h. thou hast received and heard
See Do.
HOW long.
Exod. 10. 3. h. long wilt refuse to humble thyself?
7. h. long shall this man be a snare unto us?
16. 28. h. long refuse to keep my commandments?
Num. 14. 11. h. long will this people provoke me?
h. long will it be ere they believe me?
27. h. long shall I bear with this evil congregation
Josh. 18. 3. h. long are ye slack to go to possess land?
1 Sam. 1. 14. Eli said, h. long wilt thou be drunken?
16. 1. h. l. wilt thou mourn for Saul, seeing I have
2 Sam. 19. 34. Barzillai said, h. long have I to live?
1 Kings 18. 21. h. long halt ye between two opinions?
Neh. 2. 6. king said, for h. l. shall thy journey be?
Job 7. 19. h. long wilt thou not depart from me?
8. 2. h. long wilt thou speak? h. long shall words
of thy mouth be like a strong wind?
18. 2. h. long will it be ere you make end of words?
19. 2. h. long will ye vex my soul and break me?
Psal. 4. 2. h. l. will ye turn my glory into shame?
h. l. will ye love vanity, and seek after leasing
6. 3. my soul is vexed; but thou, O Lord, h. long?
13. 1. h. long wilt thou forget me, O Ld. for ever?
2. h. long shall I take counsel in my soul? h. long
shall my enemy be exalted over me?
35. 17. Ld. h. l. wilt thou look on? rescue my soul
62. 3. h. long will ye imagine mischief against man?
74. 9. nor is there any among us that knoweth h. l.
10. O God, h. l. shall the adversary reproach?
79. 5. h. long wilt thou be angry for ever? 80. 4.
82. 2. h. l. wilt judge unjustly and accept persons?
89. 46. h. l. Lord, wilt thou hide thyself? for ever?
90. 13. return, O Lord, h. long? let it repent thee
94. 3. render a reward to the proud, Lord, h. long
shall the wicked, h. long shall wicked triumph?
4. h. long shall they utter and speak hard things?
Prov. 1. 22. h. long simple ones, will love simplicity
6. 9. h. l. wilt thou sleep, O sluggard? when arise
Isa. 6. 11. then said I, Lord, h. long? he answered
Jer. 4. 14. h. l. shall vain thoughts lodge in thee?
21. h. long shall I see standard, and hear trump.?
12. 4. h. long shall land mourn and herbs wither?
23. 26. h. l. shall this be in the heart of prophets?
47. 5. baldness on Gaza, h. long wilt cut thyself?

Jer. 47. 6. O sword of the L., h. long ere thou be quiet
Dan. 8. 13. h. long shall be vision of daily sacrifice?
12. 6. h. long shall it be to end of these wonders?
Hos. 8. 5. h. long will it be ere they attain innocency?
Hab. 1. 2. h. long shall I cry, and thou wilt not hear?
2. 6. woe to him increaseth what not his, h. long?
Zech. 1. 12. h. long wilt thou not have mercy on Jer.
Mat. 17. 17. h. l. shall I be with you, h. l. suffer
you, bring him me, Mark 9. 19. Luke 9. 41.
Mark 9. 21. h. long is it ago since this came to him?
John 10. 24. h. long dost thou make us to doubt?
Rev. 6. 10. h. long, O L. holy and true, dost thou not
HOW many.
Job 13. 23. h. many are mine iniquities and sins?
Psal. 119. 84. h. many are the days of thy servants?
Mat. 15. 34. h. m. loaves have ye? Mark 6. 38. | 8. 5.
16. 9. h. m. baskets ye took up? Mark 8. 19, 20.
Mark 15. 4. h. many things they witness against thee
Luke 15. 17. h. m. hired servts. of my father's have
2 Tim. 1. 18. in h. many things he ministered to me
HOW many times.
1 Kings 22. 16. h. m. times shall I adjure thee, thou
tell nothing but what is true? 2 Chron. 18. 15.
HOW much.
2 Kings 5. 13. h. much rather when he saith, wash
Ezra 7. 22. and salt without prescribing h. much
Prov. 16. 16. h. much better is it to get wisd. than gold
Cant. 4. 10. h. much better is thy love than wine
Mat. 12. 12. h. much is a man better than a sheep
Luke 16. 5. h. much owest thou to my lord? 7.
19. 15. h. much every man hath gained by trading
Acts 9. 13. h. much evil he hath done thy saints at Jer.
Heb. 8. 6. by h. much he is Mediator of better coven.
10. 29. of h. much sorer punishment, suppose ye
Rev. 18. 7. h. much she hath glorified herself
HOW much less.
1 Kings 8. 27. heaven cannot contain thee, h. much
less this house which I have built, 2 Chr. 6. 18.
2 Chron. 32. 15. h. much less shall your God deliver
Job 4. 19. h. much less in them dwell in houses of clay
9. 14. h. much less shall I answer him, choose words
25. 6. h. much less is man that is worm and son of man
34. 19. h. much less to him that accepteth not persons
Ezek. 15. 5. h. much less shall it be meet for work
HOW much more.
Deut. 31. 27. and h. much more after my death?
1 Sam. 14. 30. h. much more if people had eaten freely
23. 3. h. much more then if we come to Keilah
2 Sam. 4. 11. h. m. more when wicked men have slain
16. 11. h. much more now may this Benjamite do it?
Job 15. 16. h. much m. abominable and filthy is man?
Prov. 15. 11. h. much more then the hearts of men?
19. 7. h. m. more do his friends go far from him?
21. 27. h. much more when with a wicked mind
Ezek. 14. 21. h. m. more when send sore judgments?
Mat. 7. 11. h. m. more shall your heavenly Father
give good things to them that ask? Luke 11. 13.
10. 25. h. m. more shall call them of his household?
Luke 12. 24. h. m. m. are ye better than the fowls?
28. h. m. more will clothe you, O ye of little faith?
Rom. 11. 12. h. much more their fulness?
24. h. m. more these which be natural branches?
1 Cor. 6. 3. h. much more things that pertain to life?
Philem. 16. a brother to me, h. m. more to thee?
HOW oft, often.
Job 21. 17. h. oft is the candle of the wicked put out?
h. oft cometh their destruction upon them?
Psal. 78. 40. h. oft did they provoke him in wildern.
Mat. 18. 21. h. oft shall my brother sin against me?
23. 37. O Jerusalem, h. often would I have gathered
thy children as a hen her chickens, Luke 13. 34.
HOWBEIT.
Judg. 4. 17. h. Sisera fled on his feet to tent of Jael
11. 28. h. the king of Ammonites hearkened not
16. 22. h. the hair of his head began to grow again
18. 29. h. the name of the city was Laish at first
21. 18. h. we may not give them wives of our daugh.
Ruth 3. 12. h. there is a kinsman nearer than I
1 Sam. 8. 9. h. yet protest solemnly unto them
2 Sam. 2. 23. h. Asahel refused to turn aside
12. 14. h. because by this deed hast given occasion
13. 14. h. he would not hearken unto her voice
25. h. he would not go, but blessed him
23. 19. h. he attained not first three, 1 Chr. 11. 21.
1 Kings 2. 15. h. the kingdom is turned about
10. 7. h. I believed not the words, 2 Chron. 9. 6.
11. 13. h. I will not rend all the kingdom, 34.
22. I have lacked nothing, h. let me go in any wise
2 Kings 3. 25. h. slingers went about it and smote it
8. 10. h. Lord shewed me, that he shall surely die
10. 29. h. from sins of Jeroboam Jehu turned not
12. 13. h. there were not made for house bowls
14. 4. h. high places were not taken away, as yet
people did sacrifice, 15. 35. 2 Chr. 20. 33.
17. 29. h. every nation made gods of their own
40. h. they did not hearken, but did after their
22. 7. h. there was no reckoning made with them
1 Chr. 28. 4. h. the Lord God of Israel chose me
2 Chr. 18. 34. h. the king of Isr. stayed himself up
24. 5. h. the Levites hastened it not
27. 2. h. he entered not into the temple of the Lord
32. 31. h. in the business of ambassadors, G. left him
Neh. 9. 33. h. thou art just in all brought on us
13. 2. h. our God turned the curse into a blessing
Job 30. 24. h. he will not stretch out his hand
Isa. 10. 7. h. he meaneth not so, nor thinketh so
Jer. 44. 4. h. I sent to you all my servants, prophets
Mat. 17. 21. h. this kind goeth not out but by prayer
Mark 5. 19. h. Jesus suffered him not, but saith to him
7. 7. h. in vain do they worship me, teaching
John 6. 23. h. there came boats from Tiberias
7. 13. h. no man spake openly of him for fear
27. h. we know this man whence he is
11. 13. if he sleep, do well, h. Jesus spake of his
16. 13. h. when he the Spirit of truth is come
Acts 4. 4. h. many who heard the word believed
7. 48. h. the Most High dwelleth not in temples
14. 20. h. he rose up and came into the city
17. 34. h. certain men clave to him and believed
27. 26. h. we must be cast upon a certain island
28. 6. h. they looked when he should have swollen
1 Cor. 2. 6. h. we speak wisdom among the perfect

1 Cor. 8. 7. h. there is not in every man that knowl.
14. 2. h. in the Spirit he speaketh mysteries
20. h. in malice be children, in understanding, men
15. 46. h. that was not first which is spiritual
2 Cor. 11. 21. h. wherein soever any is bold, I am also
Gal. 4. 8. h. when ye knew not God ye did service
1 Tim. 1. 16. h. for this cause I obtained mercy
Heb. 3. 16. h. not all that came out of Egypt by Mos.

HOWL.

Isa. 13. 6. h. ye, for the day of the Lord is at hand
14. 31. h. O gate ‖ 15. 2. Moab shall h. 3. | 16. 7.
23. 1. h. ye ships of Tarshish, for it is laid waste
6. pass over to Tarshish, h. ye inhabitants of isle
52. 5. make them to h. ‖ 65. 14. h. for vexation
Jer. 4. 8. lament and h. 48. 20. ‖ 25. 34. h. ye shep
47. 2. and all the inhabitants of the land shall h.
48. 31. I will h. for Moab ‖ 39. they shall h.
49. 3. h. O Heshbon ‖ 51. 8. h. for Babylon
Ezek. 21. 12. cry and h. son of man, for it shall be
30. 2. prophesy and say, h. ye, woe worth the day
Joel 1. 5. h. ye drinkers ‖ 11. h. ye vine-dressers
13. lament and h. ye ministers of the altar
Mic. 1. 8. therefore I will wail and h. will go stripped
Zeph. 1. 11. h. ye inhabitants of Maktesh
Zech. 11. 2. h. fir-tree, h. O ye oaks of Bashan
Jam. 5. 1. go to, now, ye rich men, weep and h.

HOWLED.

Hos. 7. 14. not cried to me, when they h. on their beds

HOWLING.

Isa. 15. 8. h. thereof is gone to Eglaim and Beer-elim
Jer. 25. 36. an h. of principal of the flock be heard
Zeph. 1. 10. there shall be an h. from the second gate
Zech. 11. 3. there is a voice of the h. of the shepherds

HOWLING.

Deut. 32. 10. he found him in the waste h. wilderness

HOWLINGS.

Amos 8. 3. songs of the temple shall be h. in that day

HUGE.

2 Chron. 16. 8. the Ethiopians and Lubims a h. host

HUMBLE.

Humility *is a most excellent grace of the spirit, evidences the subject of it to be a child of God, and is accompanied with contentment, peace, and submission to the will of God. The sense of the weakness of our understanding, which is the effect of* humility, *is a temper of soul that prepares it for faith: partly, as it puts us on a serious consideration of those things which are revealed to us in the word; partly, as it stops all curious inquiries into those things which are unsearchable; and principally, as it graciously entitles to the promise, God* giveth grace to the humble, 1 Pet. 5. 5. *This our Saviour makes a necessary qualification in all those who shall enter into his kingdom.* Mat. 18. 3. Except ye be converted, and become as little children, ye shall not enter into the kingdom of heaven. *And since pride arises out of ignorance, the gospel, to cause in us a lowly sense of our unworthiness, discovers the sinfulness, nakedness, and misery of the human nature, divested of its primitive righteousness. We have the example of our Saviour, in whom there is an union of all divine and human perfections, debasing himself to the form of a servant, to instruct us to be meek and lowly.* Mat. 11. 29. Learn of me, for I am meek and lowly. Humility *is put for an humble, dejected, and low estate.* Luke 1. 48. He hath regarded the low estate of his handmaiden; *in* Greek, ταπεινωσιν, *the* humility.

To humble *signifies to afflict, to prove, to try,* Deut. 8. 2. God led thee in the wilderness to humble thee. To humble a woman, *is to lie with her, to rob her of her honour.* Deut. 21. 14. Thou shalt not make merchandise of her, because thou hast humbled her. *And in* Ezek. 22. 10. In thee have they humbled her that was set apart for pollution: *they came near a woman at a certain particular time when the law forbids it.*

Job 22. 29. and he shall save the h. person
Psal. 9. 12. he forgetteth not the cry of the h.
10. 12. arise, O Lord, O God, forget not the h.
17. Lord, thou hast heard the desire of the h.
34. 2. the h. shall hear thereof and be glad
69. 32. the h. shall see this and be glad
Prov. 16. 19. better be of a h. spirit with the lowly
29. 23. but honour shall uphold the h. in spirit
Isa. 57. 15. with him also that is of a contrite and h. spirit, to revive spirit of h. and heart of contrite
Jam. 4. 6. but giveth grace to the h. 1 Pet. 5. 5.

HUMBLE.

Exod. 10. 3. how long wilt thou refuse to h. thyself?
Deut. 8. 2. to h. thee and to prove thee, 16.
Judg. 19. 24. h. ye them, and do with them as seem.
2 Chr. 7. 14. my people shall h. themsel. and pray
34. 27. because thou didst h. thyself before God
Prov. 6. 3. go, h. thyself, and make sure thy friend
Jer. 13. 18. say to the king, h. yourselves, sit down
Mat. 18. 4. whosoever shall h. himself, 23. 12.
2 Cor. 12. 21. my God will h. me among you
Jam. 4. 10. h. yourselves in the sight of the Lord
1 Pet. 5. 6. h. yourselves under mighty hand of God

HUMBLED.

Lev. 26. 41. if their uncircumcised hearts be h.
Deut. 8. 3. he h. thee and suffered thee to hunger
21. 14. not sell her, because thou hast h. her, 22. 29.
22. 24. because he hath h. his neighbour's wife
2 Kings 22. 19. because hast h. thyself before the Ld.
2 Chr. 12. 6. the princes and the king h. themselves
7. when the Lord saw that they h. themselves
12. when he h. himself, wrath turned from him
30. 11. divers of Asher and Zebulun h. themselves
32. 26. Hezekiah h. hims. for the pride of his heart
33. 12. Manasseh h. himself greatly before God
19. he set up graven images before he was h.
23. Amon h. not himself before the Lord, as Manasseh his father h. himself, trespassed more
36. 12. Zedekiah h. not himself before Jeremiah
Psal. 35. 13. as for me, I h. my soul with fasting
Isa. 2. 11. the lofty looks of man shall be h.
5. 15. mighty man shall be h. eyes of the lofty be h.
10. 33. high hewn down, and the haughty shall be h.

Jer. 44. 10. they are not h. even to this day
Lam. 3. 20. my soul hath in remembrance and is h.
Ezek. 22. 10. in thee have they h. her set apart
11. and another in thee hath h. his sister
Dan. 5. 22. thou his son hast not h. thine heart
Phil. 2. 8. he h. himself and became obedient to death

HUMBLEDST.

2 Chron. 34. 27. because thou h. thyself before me

HUMBLETH.

1 Kings 21. 29. how Ahab h. because he h. himself
Psal. 10. 10. he croucheth and h. himself, that poor
113. 6. who h. himself to behold things in heaven
Isa. 2. 9. mean man boweth, the great man h. himself
Luke 14. 11. he that h. hims. shall be exalted, 18. 14.

HUMBLENESS.

Col. 3. 12. put on kindness, h. of mind, meekness

HUMBLY.

2 Sam. 16. 4. I h. beseech thee that I may find grace
Mic. 6. 8. to love mercy, and to walk h. with thy G.

HUMILIATION.

Acts 8. 33. in his h. his judgment was taken away

HUMILITY.

Prov. 15. 33. and before honour is h. 18. 12.
22. 4. by h. are riches, and honour, and life
Acts 20. 19. serving the Lord with all h. of mind
Col. 2. 18. let no man beguile you in a voluntary h.
23. have a shew of wisdom in will-worship and h.
1 Pet. 5. 5. be subject one to another, clothed with h.

HUNDRED-FOLD. *See* FOLD.

HUNDRED.

Gen. 11. 10. Shem was an h. years old and begat
17. 17. shall a child be born to him that is a h. years old, and shall Sarah bear? 21. 5. Rom. 4. 19.
33. 19. Jacob bought for an h. pieces, Josh. 24. 32.
Exod. 27. 9. hangings h. cubits long, 11. | 38. 9, 11.
18. the length of the court shall be an h. cubits
38. 27. an h. sockets were cast of the h. talents
Lev. 26. 8. five shall chase a h. and a h. put to flight
Deut. 22. 19. shall amerce him in h. shekels of silv.
Judg. 7. 19. so Gideon and the h. men with him came
20. 10. we will take ten of an h. an h. of a 1000
35. Israel destroyed of Benjm. 25,000 and an h.
1 Sam. 18. 25. but an h. foreskins, 2 Sam. 3. 14.
25. 18. an h. clusters of raisins, 2 Sam. 16. 1.
2 Sam. 8. 4. reserved for an h. chariots, 1 Chr. 18. 4.
1 Kings 4. 23. Solom. provision for one day h. sheep
7. 2. length of the house of the forest an h. cubits
18. 4. Obadiah took an h. proph. and hid them, 13.
2 Kings 4. 43. what should I set this bef. an h. men?
23. 33. Pharaoh-necho put Jehoahaz in bands, and put land to a tribute of an h. talents, 2 Chron. 36. 3.
1 Chron. 12. 14. one of the least was over an h.
25. children of Simeon seven thousand and one h.
21. 3. Lord make his people an h. times so many
2 Chron. 3. 16. Solomon made an h. pomegranates
4. 8. and he made an h. basins of gold
25. 6. he hired also men for an h. talents of silver
9. what shall we do for the h. talents I have given
27. 5. Ammon gave Jotham an h. talents of silver
29. 32. the congregation brought an h. rams
Ezra 2. 69. they gave one h. priests' garments
6. 17. and offered at the dedication an h. bullocks
7. 22. let it be done to an h. talents of silver, an h. measures of wheat and wine, and an h. baths of oil
8. 26. silver vessels an h. talents of gold, an h. talts.
Neh. 5. 11. restore to them the h. part of the money
Prov. 17. 10. more than an h. stripes into a fool
Eccl. 6. 3. if a man beget an h. childr. and live years
8. 12. tho' sinner do evil h. times, days be prolong.
Isa. 65. 20. for the child shall die an h. years old, but the sinner being an h. years old shall be accursed
Ezek. 40. 19. he measured an h. cubits eastward
23. he measured from gate to gate an h. cubits, 27.
47. the court an h. cubits long, an h. cubits broad
41. 13. so he measured the house an h. cubits long
14. of the separate place toward east, an h. cubits
15. the galleries on one side and other, an h. cubits
42. 8. and lo, before the temple were an h. cubits
Amos 5. 3. city that went out by a 1000, shall leave an h. that which went forth by an h. shall leave ten.
Mat. 18. 12. if a man have an h. sheep, Luke 15. 4.
28. went and found one who owed him an h. pence
Luke 16. 6. and he said, an h. measures of oil
7. how much owest thou? an h. meas. of wheat
John 19. 39. mixt. of myrrh and aloes an h. weight

One HUNDRED *and five.*

Gen. 5. 6. Seth lived *one h. and five years,* beg. Enos

One HUNDRED *and ten.*

Gen. 50. 22. Joseph lived *one h. and ten* years, 26.
Josh. 24. 29. Josh. died an h. *ten* years old, Judg. 2. 8.
Ezra 8. 12. with Johanan an h. *and ten* males

One HUNDRED *and twelve.*

1 Chr. 15. 10. of the sons of Uzziel an h. *and twelve*
Ezra 2. 18. the children of Jorah, an h. *and twelve*
Neh. 7. 24. the children of Hariph, an h. *and twelve*

One HUNDRED *and nineteen.*

Gen. 11. 25. Nahor lived after beg. Terah h. *nineteen*

One HUNDRED *and twenty.*

Gen. 6. 3. yet his days shall be h. *and twenty* years
Num. 7. 86. gold of spoons was an h. *and twenty* [shekels
Deut. 31. 2. I am an h. *and twenty* years old this day
34. 7. Moses an h. *and twenty* years old when he died
1 Kings 10. 10. she gave king an h. *and twenty* talents of gold, spices, and precious stones, 2 Chron. 9. 9.
1 Chron. 15. 5. Uriel and brethren an h. *and twenty*
2 Chron. 3. 4. height of porch an h. *and twenty* cubits
5. 12. with them an h. *and twenty* priests, sounding
Dan. 6. 1. to set over kingdom an h. *and tw.* princes
Acts 1. 15. number of names were about an h. *and t.*

One HUNDRED *twenty-two.*

Ezra 2. 27. men of Michmash, h. *tw.-two,* Neh. 7. 31.

One HUNDRED *twenty-three.*

Num. 33. 39. Aaron h. *tw.-three* years when he died
Ezra 2. 21. the children of Beth-lehem went up out of captivity an h. *twenty and three,* Neh. 7. 32.

One HUNDRED *twenty-seven.*

Gen. 23. 1. Sarah was an h. *tw.-seven* years, and died
Esth. 1. 1. this is Ahasuerus who reigned over an h. and *twenty-seven* provinces, 8. 9. | 9. 30.

One HUNDRED *twenty-eight.*

Ezra 2. 23. men of Anathoth h. *tw.-eight,* Neh. 7. 27.
41. the children of Asaph an h. *twenty-eight*
Neh. 11. 14. their brethren an h. and *twenty-eight*

One HUNDRED *thirty.*

Gen. 5. 3. Adam lived h. *thirty years,* and begat son
47. 9. years of my pilgrimage are an h. and *thirty*
Num. 7. 13. weight thereof was a h. *t.* shekels, 19, 25.
85. each charger weighing an h. *thirty* shekels
1 Chr. 15. 7. Joel and brethren an h. and *thirty*
2 Chr. 24. 15. Jehoiada was an h. *t.* years old

One HUNDRED *thirty-three.*

Exod. 6. 18. years of life of Kohath an h. *thirty-three*

One HUNDRED *thirty-seven.*

Gen. 25. 17. life of Ishmael an h. and *t.-seven* years
Exod. 6. 16. the years of Levi were h. and *thirty-seven*
20. the years of Amram were an h. *thirty-seven*

One HUNDRED *thirty-eight.*

Neh. 7. 45. the children of Shobai of Ater. h. *th.-eight*

One HUNDRED *thirty-nine.*

Ezra 2. 42. children of Shobai in all an h. *thirty-nine*

One HUNDRED *forty.*

Job 42. 16. after this lived Job an h. *forty* years

One HUNDRED *forty-four.*

Rev. 21. 17. measured the wall an h. *f.-f.* cubits

One HUNDRED *forty-seven.*

Gen. 47. 28. whole age of Jacob an h. *forty-seven* y.

One HUNDRED *forty-eight.*

Neh. 7. 44. singers, the children of Asaph h. *f.-eight*

One HUNDRED *fifty.*

Gen. 7. 24. waters prevailed an h. *fifty* days, 8. 3.
1 Kings 10. 29. a chariot went out of Egypt, and an horse for an h. and *fifty* shekels, 2 Chr. 1. 17.
1 Chr. 8. 40. Ulam's sons and sons' sons an h. *fifty*
Ezra 8. 3. were reckoned of males, an h. and *f.*
Neh. 5. 17. there were at my table an h. *f.* Jews

One HUNDRED *fifty-three.*

John 21. 11. drew the net full of fishes an h. *f.-t.*

One HUNDRED *fifty-six.*

Ezra 2. 30. the children of Magbish, an h. *f.-six*

One HUNDRED *sixty.*

Ezra 8. 10. Shelomith, and with him h. *sixty* males

One HUNDRED *sixty-two.*

Gen. 5. 18. Jared lived h. *s.-two* years, begat Enoch

One HUNDRED *seventy-two.*

Neh. 11. 19. the porters and brethren h. *seventy-two*

One HUNDRED *seventy-five.*

Gen. 25. 7. Abraham's life was an h. *seventy-five*

One HUNDRED *eighty.*

Gen. 35. 28. the days of Isaac an h. and *eighty* years
Esth. 1. 4. Ahasuerus feast for an h. and *eighty* days

One HUNDRED *eighty-two.*

Gen. 5. 28. Lamech lived h. *eig.-two* and begat Noah

One HUNDRED *eighty-seven.*

Gen. 5. 25. Methuselah lived h. *eig.-seven* begat Lam.

One HUNDRED *eighty-eight.*

Neh. 7. 26. the men of Beth-lehem an h. *eighty-eight*

HUNDRED *thousand.*

Num. 2. 9. all numbered in Judah were an h. *thous.*
16. numbered in the camp of Reuben an h. *thous.*
1 Kings 20. 29. slew of the Syrians h. *thous.* footmen
2 Kings 3. 4. Mesha king of Moab rendered to king of Israel an h. *thous.* lambs, an h. *thous.* rams
1 Chr. 5. 21. took from Hagarites an h. *thous.* men
21. 5. of Israel a thousand thousand and h. *thous.*
22. 14. for house of Lord h. *thous.* talents of gold
29. 7. and gave an h. *thousand* talents of iron
2 Chr. 25. 6. he hired an h. *thousand* men of valour

HUNDRED *eight thousand and an* HUNDRED.

Num. 2. 24. numbered of camp of Ephraim, 108,100

An HUNDRED *twenty thousand.*

Judg. 8. 10. there fell of the Midianites 120,000
1 Kings 8. 63. Solomon offered a sacrifice of an h. and *twenty thousand* sheep, 2 Chron. 7. 5.
1 Chr. 12. 37. of Reuben, Gad, and Manasseh, 120,000
2 Chr. 28. 6. Pekah slew in Judah in one day 120,000
Jonah 4. 11. in Nineveh were about 120,000 persons

An HUNDRED *forty-four thousand.*

Rev. 7. 4. were sealed 144,000 of all the tribes of Isr.
14. 1. with him 144,000, having his Father's name
3. no man could learn that song but the 144,000

An HUNDRED *fifty thousand.*

2 Chron. 2. 17. strangers that were in the land of Israel were found an h. *fifty thousand*

An HUNDRED *eighty thousand.*

1 Kings 12. 21. with Benjamin 180,000, 2 Chr. 11. 1.
2 Chr. 17. 18. with Jehozabad were 180,000, for war

An HUNDRED *eighty-five thousand.*

2 Kings 19. 35. that night the angel of the Lord smote of the Assyrians, 185,000, Isa. 37. 36.

Two HUNDRED.

Gen. 11. 23. Serug lived aft. begat Nahor *two h.* years
32. 14. *two h.* she-goats, and *two h.* ewes for Esau
Josh. 7. 21. Achan saw *two h.* shekels of silver
Judg. 17. 4. his mother took *two h.* shekels of silver
1 Sam. 18. 27. David slew of the Philist. *two h.* men
25. 13. *two h.* abode by the stuff, 30. 10, 21.
18. Abigail took *two h.* loaves, *two h.* cakes of figs
2 Sam. 14. 26. Absalom weighed hair *two h.* shekels
15. 11. with Absalom went *two h.* men out of Jerus.
16. 1. Ziba brought David *two h.* loaves of bread
1 Kings 7. 20. the pomegranates were *two h.* in rows
10. 16. Solomon made *two h.* targets, 2 Chr. 9. 15.
2 Chron. 29. 32. for burnt offerings *two h.* lambs
Ezra 2. 65. were among them *two h.* singing men
6. 17. and offered at the dedication *two h.* rams
Cant. 8. 12. those that keep the fruit thereof *two h.*
Ezek. 45. 15. ye shall offer one lamb out of *two h.*
John 6. 7. *two h.* pennyworth is not sufficient
Acts 23. 23. he called, saying, make ready *two h.* soldiers to go to Cesarea, and spearmen *two h.*

Two HUNDRED *five.*

Gen. 11. 32. the days of Terah were *two h. five* years

Two HUNDRED *seven.*

Gen. 11. 21. Reu lived *two h. seven* years and begat

Two HUNDRED *nine.*

Gen. 11. 19. Peleg lived *two h. nine* years and begat

Two HUNDRED *twelve.*
1 *Chron.* 9. 22. porters in the gates were *two h. twelve*
Two HUNDRED *eighteen.*
Ezra 8. 9. with Obadiah *two h. eighteen* males
Two HUNDRED *twenty.*
Ezra 8. 20. for service of Levites *two h. tw.* Nethin.
Two HUNDRED *twenty-three.*
Ezra 2. 28. men of Beth-el and Ai *two h. tw.-three*
Two HUNDRED *thirty-two.*
1 *Kings* 20. 15. of princes of provinces *two h. th.-two*
Two HUNDRED *forty-two.*
Neh. 11. 13. chief of the fathers *two h. forty two*
Two HUNDRED *forty-five.*
Ezra 2. 66. their mules *two h.* and *forty five*
Neh. 7. 67. had *two h.* 45 singing men and women
68. their mules *two h.* and *forty-five*
Two HUNDRED *fifty.*
Exod. 30. 23. take thou to thee of cinnamon *two h.* and *fifty,* of calamus *two h.* and *fifty* shekels
Num. 16. 2. *two h.* and *fifty* princes of the assembly
17. and bring ye before L. *two h.* and *fifty* censers
35. a fire consumed the *two h.* and *fifty* men
2 *Chron.* 8. 10. *two h.* and *fifty* that bare rule
Ezek. 48. 17. suburbs toward north *two h. fifty*
Two HUNDRED *seventy-six.*
Acts 27. 37. in all the ship *two h. seventy-six* souls
Two HUNDRED *eighty-four.*
Neh. 11. 18. Levites in the holy city *two h. eighty-f.*
Two HUNDRED *eighty-eight.*
1 *Chr.* 25. 7. all cunning in songs *two h. eighty-eight*
Two HUNDRED *fifty thousand.*
1 *Chr.* 5. 21. took away of sheep *two h. fifty thous.*
Three HUNDRED.
Gen. 5. 22. Enoch walked with God *three h.* years and begat sons and daughters
6. 15. the length of the ark shall be *three h.* cubits
45. 22. he gave Benjamin *three h.* pieces of silver
Judg. 7. 6. the number that lapped were *three h.* men
8. and he retained those *three h.* men
8. 4. the *three h.* men that were with him were faint
11. 26. Israel by the coast of Arnon *three h.* years
15. 4. Samson went and caught *three h.* foxes
2 *Sam.* 21. 16. whose spear weighed *three h.* shekels
23. 18. Abishai Joab's brother lifted up his spear against *three h.* and slew them, 1 *Chr.* 11. 11, 20.
1 *Kings* 10. 17. he made *three h.* shields of beat. gold
11. 3. Solomon had *three h.* concubines
2 *Kings* 18. 14. appointed to Hezek. *three h.* talents
2 *Chr.* 9. 16. *th. h.* shekels of gold went to one shield
14. 9. Zera came against Asa with *th. h.* chariots
35. 8. gave to priests for passover-offer. *th. h.* oxen
Ezra 8. 5. with Shechaniah *three h.* males
Esth. 9. 15. the Jews slew *three h.* men at Shushan
John 12. 5. this ointment sold for *three h.* pence
Three HUNDRED *eighteen.*
Gen. 14. 14. Abram went with *th. h. eight.* servants
Three HUNDRED *twenty.*
Ezra 2. 32. the children of Harim *th. h.* and *twenty*
Neh. 7. 35. the children of Harim *th. h.* and *twenty*
Three HUNDRED *twenty-three.*
Ezra 2. 17. the children of Bezai 323, *Neh.* 7. 23.
Three HUNDRED *twenty-eight.*
Neh. 7. 22. childr. of Hashum *three h. twenty-eight*
Three HUNDRED *forty-five.*
Ezra 2. 34. children of Jericho 345, *Neh.* 7. 36.
Three HUNDRED *fifty.*
Gen. 9. 28. Noah lived after flood *th. h. fifty* years
Three HUNDRED *sixty.*
2 *Sam.* 2. 31. so that of Israel *th. h. sixty* men died
Three HUNDRED *sixty-five.*
Gen. 5. 23. Enoch's days were *th. h. sixty five* years
Three HUNDRED *seventy-two.*
Ezra 2. 4. the childr. of Shephatiah 372, *Neh.* 7. 9.
Three HUNDRED *ninety.*
Ezek. 4. 5. according to number of days, *th. h. n.* 9.
Three HUNDRED *thousand.*
Num. 31. 36. of them that went out to war 300,000
1 *Sam.* 11. 8. Israel were 300,000, 2 *Chron.* 14. 8.
2 *Chron.* 17. 14. with Adnah mighty men 300,000
25. 5. found Judah and Benjamin to be 300,000
Three HUNDRED *thousand seven thousand five* HUNDRED.
2 *Chron.* 26. 13. Uzziah had an army of 307,500
Three HUNDRED *and thirty thousand seven thousand five* HUNDRED.
Num. 31. 43. now the half that pertained unto the congregation was 337,500 sheep
Four HUNDRED.
Gen. 15. 13. afflict them *four h.* years, *Acts* 7. 6.
23. 15. land is worth *four h.* shekels of silver, 16.
32. 6. Esau cometh to thee with *four h.* men, 33. 1.
Judg. 21. 12. found *four h.* virgins of Jabesh-gilead
1 *Sam.* 22. 2. were with Dav. *four h.* 25. 13. | 30. 10.
30. 17. save *four h.* young men on camels that fled
1 *Kings* 7. 42. *four h.* pomegranates for net-works
18. 19. and the prophets of the groves *four h.*
22. 6. Ahab gathered of the prophets about *four h.* and said, shall I go ag. Ramoth! 2 *Chr.* 18. 5.
2 *Kings* 14. 13. Jehoash came and brake down the wall of Jeru. *four h.* cubits, 2 *Chr.* 25. 23.
Ezra 6. 17. offered at dedication of house *f. h.* lambs
Acts 5. 36. to whom about *four h.* joined themselves
Four HUNDRED *and three.*
Gen. 11. 13. Arphaxad lived *f. h. th.* years, and begat
15. Salah lived after he begat Eber 403 years
Four HUNDRED *and ten.*
Ezra 1. 10. silver basins of a second sort *four h. ten*
Four HUNDRED *and twenty.*
1 *Kings* 9. 28. they fetched from thence gold, 420 tal.
Four HUNDRED *thirty.*
Gen. 11. 17. Eber lived 430 years and begat sons
Exod. 12. 40. sojourning in Egypt 430 years, 41.
Gal. 3. 17. the law which was 430 years after cannot
Four HUNDRED *thirty-five.*
Ezra 2. 67. their camels were 435, *Neh.* 7. 69.
Four HUNDRED *and fifty.*
1 *Kings* 18. 19. gather the prophets of Baal 450, 22.
Acts 13. 20. gave judges about *four h. fifty* years
Four HUNDRED *fifty-four.*
Ezra 2. 15. the children of Adin *four h. fifty-four*
Four HUNDRED *sixty-eight.*
Neh. 11. 6. all the sons of Perez were 468 men

Four HUNDRED *eighty.*
1 *Kings* 6. 1. in 480 years Solomon began to build
Four HUNDRED *thousand.*
Judg. 20. 2. Israel besides Benjamin 400,000, 17.
2 *Chr.* 13. 3. set the battle in array with 400,000 men
Four HUNDRED *seventy thousand.*
1 *Chr.* 21. 5. Judah was 470,000 that drew the sword
Five HUNDRED.
Gen. 5. 32. Noah was *five h.* years old and begat Shem
11. 11. Shem lived after *five h.* years and begat
Exod. 30. 23. take of pure myrrh *five h.* shekels
24. of cassia *fi. h.* shekels after shekel of sanctuary
Num. 31. 28. levy one soul of *five h.* for the Lord
2 *Chron.* 35. 9. for passover-offerings *five h.* oxen
Esth. 9. 6. Jews slew at Shushan *five h.* men, 12.
Job 1. 3. *five h.* yoke of oxen, *five h.* she-asses
Ezek. 42. 16. he measur. *five h.* reeds, 17, 18, 19, 20.
45. 2. of this there shall be for the sanctuary *five h.* in length, with *five h.* in breadth, square round
Luke 7. 41. the one owed *fi. h.* pence, the other fifty
1 *Cor.* 15. 6. was seen of above *five h.* brethr. at once
Five HUNDRED *and thirty.*
Neh. 7. 70. gave *five h. and thirty* priests' garments
Five HUNDRED *and fifty.*
1 *Kings* 9. 23. *five h. and fifty* bare rule over people
Five HUNDRED *thousand.*
2 *Sam.* 24. 9. the men of Judah were 500,000 men
2 *Chr.* 13. 17. there were slain of Israel 500,000 men
Six HUNDRED.
Gen. 7. 6. Noah *six h.* years old when flood came, 11.
Exod. 14. 7. Phar. took *six h.* chariots to pursue Isr.
Judg. 3. 31. Shamgar slew with an ox goad *six h.*
18. 11. Danites sent out of Eshtaol *six h.* 16, 17.
20. 47. *six h.* Benjamites fled to rock Rimmon
1 *Sam.* 13. 15. Saul numbered the people *six h.* 14. 2.
17. 7. Goliath's spear head weighed *six h.* shekels
23. 13. Dav. and his men about *six h.* 27. 2. | 30. 9.
2 *Sam.* 15. 18. all the Gittites were *six h.* men
1 *Kings* 10. 16. Solomon made targets, *six h.* shekels of gold went to one target, 2 *Chron.* 9. 15.
29. a chariot went for *six h.* shekels, 2 *Chr.* 1. 17.
1 *Chron.* 21. 25. David gave Ornan *six h.* shekels
2 *Chr.* 3. 8. overlaid house with gold to *six h.* talents
29. 33. the consecrated things were *six h.* oxen
Six HUNDRED *twenty-one.*
Ezra 2. 26. child. of Ramah *six h. tw. one, Neh.* 7. 30.
Six HUNDRED *twenty-three.*
Ezra 2. 11. the children of Bebai, *six h. twenty-three*
Six HUNDRED *twenty-eight.*
Neh. 7. 16. the children of Bebai, *six h. twenty-eight*
Six HUNDRED *forty-two.*
Ezra 2. 10. the children of Bani, *six h. forty-two*
Neh. 7. 62. the children of Nekoda, *six h. forty-two*
Six HUNDRED *forty-eight.*
Neh. 7. 15. the children of Binnui, *six h. forty-eight*
Six HUNDRED *and fifty.*
Ezra 8. 26. weighed to their hand *six h. fifty talents*
Six HUNDRED *fifty-two.*
Ezra 2. 60. the children of Nekoda, *six h. fifty-two*
Neh. 7. 10. the children of Arah, *six h.* and *fifty-two*
Six HUNDRED *sixty-six.*
1 *Kings* 10. 14. gold to Sol. in year *six h. sixty-six* tal.
Ezra 2. 13. children of Adonikam, *six h. sixty-six*
Rev. 13. 18. and his number is *six h.* and *sixty-six*
Six HUNDRED *sixty-seven.*
Neh. 7. 18. children of Adonikam, *six h. sixty-seven*
Six HUNDRED *seventy-five.*
Num. 31. 37. Lord's trib. of sheep was *six h. sev. five*
Six HUNDRED *ninety.*
1 *Chron.* 9. 6. Jeuel and brethren were *six h. ninety*
Six HUNDRED *thousand.*
Exod. 12. 37. Israel journeyed about 600,000 on foot
38. 26. a bekah for every man for 600,000 men
Num. 1. 46. all that were numbered were 600,000
11. 21. Moses said, the people are 600,000 footmen
Six HUNDRED *seventy-five thousand.*
Num. 31. 32. the rest of the prey was 675,000 sheep
Seven HUNDRED.
Judg. 20. 15. of Gibeah were *sev. h.* chosen men, 16.
2 *Sam.* 8. 4. David took from him *sev. h.* horsemen
10. 18. Dav. slew men of *sev. h.* chariots of Syrians
1 *Kings* 11. 3. Solom. had *seven h.* wives, princesses
2 *Kings* 3. 26. the king of Moab took *seven h.* men
2 *Chr.* 15. 11. they offered to the Lord *seven h.* oxen
Seven HUNDRED *twenty one.*
Neh. 7. 37. children of Lod, Hadid, Ono, 721.
Seven HUNDRED *twenty-five.*
Ezra 2. 33. children of Lod, Hadid, Ono, 725
Seven HUNDRED *thirty-six.*
Ezra 2. 66. their horses were 736, *Neh.* 7. 68.
Seven HUNDRED *forty-three.*
Ezra 2. 25. the children of Kirjath-arim, 743
Seven HUNDRED *forty-five.*
Jer. 52. 30. took away captive of the Jews 745
Seven HUNDRED *sixty.*
Ezra 2. 9. the children of Zaccai 760, *Neh.* 7. 14.
Seven HUNDRED *seventy-five.*
Ezra 2. 5. the children of Arah, *seven h. seventy-five*
Seven HUNDRED *seventy-seven.*
Gen. 5. 31. all the days of Lamech were 777 years
Seven HUNDRED *eighty-two.*
Gen. 5. 26. Methusal. lived 782 years, begat Lamech
Eight HUNDRED.
Gen. 5. 4. Adam after he begat Seth lived 800 years
19. Jared after he begat Enoch lived 800 years
2 *Sam.* 23. 8. he lifted up his spear against 800
Eight HUNDRED *seven.*
Gen. 5. 7. Seth lived after he begat Enos 807 years
Eight HUNDRED *fifteen.*
Gen. 5. 10. Enos after he begat Cainan 815 years
Eight HUNDRED *twenty-two.*
Neh. 11. 12. their brethren that did work were 822
Eight HUNDRED *thirty.*
Gen. 5. 16. Mahalaleel after he begat Jared 830 yrs.
Eight HUNDRED *thirty-two.*
Jer. 52. 29. Nebuchadnezzar carried captive 832
Eight HUNDRED *forty.*
Gen. 5. 13. Cainan after he begat Mahalaleel 840
Eight HUNDRED *forty-five.*
Neh. 7. 13. the children of Zattu were 845
Eight HUNDRED *ninety-five.*
Gen 5. 17. all the days of Mahalaleel were 895 yrs.

Nine HUNDRED.
Judg. 4. 3. Jabin had *nine h.* chariots of iron, 13.
Nine HUNDRED *five.*
Gen. 5. 11. all the days of Enos were 905 years
Nine HUNDRED *ten.*
Gen. 5. 14. all the days of Cainan 910 years
Nine HUNDRED *twelve.*
Gen. 5. 8. all the days of Seth were 912 years
Nine HUNDRED *twenty-eight.*
Neh. 11. 8. and after him Gabbai, Sallai, 928
Nine HUNDRED *thirty.*
Gen. 5. 5. all days that Adam lived were 930 years
Nine HUNDRED *forty-five.*
Ezra 2. 8. the children of Zattu 945
Nine HUNDRED *fifty.*
Gen. 9. 29. all the days of Noah were 950 years
Nine HUNDRED *fifty-six.*
1 *Chron.* 9. 9. brethren according to generations 956
Nine HUNDRED *sixty-two.*
Gen. 5. 20. all the days of Jared were 962 years
Nine HUNDRED *sixty-nine.*
Gen. 5. 27. the days of Mathuselah were 969 years
Nine HUNDRED *seventy-three.*
Ezra 2. 36. the children of Jedaiah 973, *Neh.* 7. 39.
HUNDREDS.
Exod. 18. 21. be rulers of *h.* and tens, 25. *Deut.* 1. 15.
Num. 31. 14. Moses was wroth with captains over *h.*
54. Moses took the gold of the captains of *h.*
1 *Sam.* 22. 7. will son of Jesse make you captains of *h.*
29. 2. the lords of the Philistines passed on by *h.*
2 *Sam.* 18. 1. David set captains of *h.* over them
4. the king stood, all the people came out by *h.*
2 *Kings* 11. 4. Jehoiada sent and set the rulers over *h.*
10. to captains over *h.* did the priest give spears and shields that were in the temp. 2 *Chr.* 23. 9.
1 *Chr.* 13. 1. David consulted with the captains of *h.*
26. 26. which the captains over *h.* had dedicated
28. 1. David assembled the captains over the *h.*
29. 6. then the captains of *h.* offered willingly
2 *Chr.* 23. 1. Jehoiada took captains of *h.* into cov.
25. 5. Amaziah made them captains over *h.*
Mark 6. 40. they sat down in ranks by *h.* and fifties
HUNGER, *Substantive.*
Exod. 16. 3. to kill this whole assembly with *h.*
Deut. 28. 48. thou shalt serve thine enemies in *h.*
32. 24. they shall be burnt with *h.* and devoured
Neh. 9. 15. thou gavest bread from heav. for their *h.*
Psal. 34. 10. the young lions do lack and suffer *h.*
Prov. 19. 15. and an idle soul shall suffer *h.*
Jer. 38. 9. he is like to die for *h.* where he is
42. 14. we shall see no war, nor have *h.* of bread
Lam. 2. 19. that faint for *h.* in the top of every street
4. 9. are better than they that be slain with *h.*
Ezek. 34. 29. they shall be no more consum. with *h.*
Luke 15. 17. have bread enough, and I perish with *h.*
2 *Cor.* 11. 27. I have been in *h.* and thirst, in fastings
Rev. 6. 8. and power was given them to kill with *h.*
HUNGER, *Verb.*
Deut. 8. 3. he suffered thee to *h.* and fed with manna
Isa. 49. 10. they shall not *h.* nor thirst, nor sun smite
Mat. 5. 6. blessed are they that *h. Luke* 6. 21.
Luke 6. 25. woe to you who are full, for ye shall *h.*
John 6. 35. he that cometh to me shall never *h.*
Rom. 12. 20. therefore if thine enemy *h.* feed him
1 *Cor.* 4. 11. we both *h.* and thirst, and are naked
11. 34. and if any man *h.* let him eat at home
Rev. 7. 16. they shall *h.* no more, neither thirst
HUNGER-*bitten.*
Job 18. 12. his strength shall be *h.-bit.* destruction
HUNGERED.
Mat. 4. 2. he was afterwards an *h. Luke* 4. 2.
12. 1. his discip. were an *h.* and began to pluck ears
3. what David did when he was an *h. Mark* 2. 25.
21. 18. now as he returned into the city he *h.*
25. 35. for I was an *h.* and ye gave me meat
37. L. when saw we thee an *h.* and fed thee? 44.
42. for I was an *h.* and ye gave me no meat
Luke 6. 3. what David did when himself was an *h*
HUNGRY.
1 *Sam.* 2. 5. and they that were *h.* ceased
2 *Sam.* 17. 29. the people is *h.* weary, and thirsty
2 *Kings* 7. 12. they know that we be *h.* therefore
Job 5. 5. whose harvest the *h.* eateth up and taketh it
22. 7. thou hast withholden bread from the *h.*
24. 10. they take away the sheaf from the *h.*
Psal. 50. 12. if I were *h.* I would not tell thee
107. 5. *h.* and thirsty, their soul fainted in them
9. for he filleth the *h.* soul with goodness
36. and there he maketh the *h.* to dwell
146. 7. hope is in Lord who giveth food to the *h.*
Prov. 6. 30. if he steal to satisfy his soul when he is *h.*
25. 21. if thine enemy be *h.* give him bread to eat
27. 7. to the *h.* soul every bitter thing is sweet
Isa. 8. 21. they shall pass thro' it, hardly bestead and *h.* when they shall be *h.* they shall fret themselves
9. 20. he shall snatch on the right hand, and be *h.*
29. 8. it shall even be as when a *h.* man dreameth
32. 6. to make empty the soul of the *h.*
44. 12. yea, he is *h.* and his strength faileth
58. 7. is it not to deal thy bread to the *h.?*
10. and if thou draw out thy soul to the *h.*
65. 13. my servants shall eat, but ye shall be *h.*
Ezek. 18. 7. hath given his bread to the *h.* 16.
Mark 11. 12. when were come from Bethany he was *h.*
Luke 1. 53. he hath filled the *h.* with good things
Acts 10. 10. Peter became very *h.* would have eaten
1 *Cor.* 11. 21. one is *h.* and another is drunken
Phil. 4. 12. I know how to be full and to be *h.*
HUNT.
Hunting *has been called a kind of an apprenticeship to war, and an imitation of it.* Nimrod was a mighty hunter before the Lord, *Gen.* 10. 9. *Some think he did good with his* hunting, *served his country by ridding it of the wild beasts which did infest it, and so insinuated himself into the affections of his neighbours, and got to be their prince. Others think, under pretence of* hunting, *he gathered men under his command, and by their help established a tyrannical and absolute power over men: He was a* mighty hunter; *that is, he was*

a violent invader of his neighbours' rights and properties, and a persecutor of innocent men; carrying all before him, and endeavouring to make all his own by force and violence.
The prophets sometimes express war under the name of hunting. *Jer.* 16. 16. I will send for many hunters, and they shall hunt them from every mountain, and from every hill, and out of the holes of the rocks. *He speaks of the* Chaldeans *or* Persians, *who took the* Jews, *and held them under their dominion. Some are of opinion, that the* hunters *mentioned by* Jeremiah *are the* Persians, *who set the* Hebrews *at liberty, and, in a more elevated sense, the Apostles, who were as hunters, that endeavoured to take men with their preaching.* Micah *complains that every one lays ambuscades for his neighbour, and that one brother hunts after another to destroy him.* Mic. 7. 2. They all lie in wait for blood, they hunt every man his brother with a net. Ezekiel *inveighs against the false prophetesses, who place cushions under the elbows of sinners, thereby promising them ease and security, while really they were spreading a net as hunters do, to catch the prey and devour it,* Ezek. 13. 18. 20
Gen. 27. † 3. now therefore go *h.* me some venison
5. Esau went to field to *h.* venison, and
1 *Sam.* 26. 20. as when one doth *h.* a partridge
Job 38. 39. wilt thou *h.* the prey for the lion?
Ps. 140. 11. evil shall *h.* violent man to overth. him
Prov. 6. 26. the adulteress will *h.* for the precious life
Jer. 16. 16. they shall *h.* them from every mountain
Lam. 4. 18. they *h.* our steps that we cannot go
Ezek. 13. 18. will ye *h.* the souls of my people?
20. pillows wherewith ye there *h.* the souls
Mic. 7. 2. they *h.* every man his brother with a net

HUNTED.

Gen. 27. † 33. where is he that hath *h.* venison?
Ezek. 13. 21. shall be no more in your hand to be *h.*

HUNTER, S.

Gen. 10. 9. he was a mighty *h.* before the Ld. wherefore it is said, even as Nimrod the mighty *h.*
25. 27. Esau was a cunning *h.* a man of the field
Prov. 6. 5. deliver as a roe from the hand of the *h.*
Jer. 16. 16. and after will I send for many *h.*

HUNTEST.

1 *Sam.* 24. 11. yet thou *h.* my soul to take it
Job 10. 16. thou *h.* me as a fierce lion, again shewest

HUNTETH.

Lev. 17. 13. which *h.* and catcheth any beast

HUNTING.

Gen. 27. 30. that Esau his brother came in from *h.*
Prov. 12. 27. roasteth not that which he took in *h.*

HURL.

Num. 35. 20. if *h.* at him by lying in wait that he die

HURLETH.

Job 27. 21. and as a storm *h.* him out of his place

HURLING.

1 *Chr.* 12. 2. could use right hand and left in *h.* stones

HURT, *Substantive.*

Gen. 4. 23. for I have slain a young man to my *h.*
26. 29. make a covenant, that thou wilt do us no *h.*
31. 29. it is in the power of my hand to do you *h.*
Josh. 24. 20. if forsake, then will he turn and do you *h.*
1 *Sam.* 20. 21. there is peace to thee, and no *h.*
24. 9. saying, behold, David seeketh thy *h.*
2 *Sam.* 18. 32. that rise to do *h.* be as that young man
2 *Kings* 14. 10. for why shouldest thou meddle to thy *h.* that thou shouldest fall? 2 *Chron.* 25. 19.
Ezra 4. 22. why damage grow to the *h.* of kings?
Esth. 9. 2. to lay hands on such as sought their *h.*
Psal. 15. 4. that sweareth to his *h.* and changeth not
35. 4. brought to confusion that devise my *h.* 70. 2.
26. let them be ashamed that rejoice at my *h.*
38. 12. seek my *h.* speak mischievous things ag. me
41. 7. against me do they devise my *h.*
71. 13. be covered with reproach that seek my *h.*
24. they are brought to shame that seek my *h.*
Eccl. 5. 13. riches kept for the owners to their *h.*
8. 9. one man ruleth over another to his own *h.*
Jer. 6. 14. have healed *h.* of my people slightly, 8. 11.
7. 6. neither walk after other gods to your *h.*
8. 21. for the *h.* of my people am I h. I am black
10. 19. woe is me for my *h.* my wound is grievous
24. 9. will deliver them to be removed for their *h.*
25. 6. provoke me not, and I will do you no *h.*
7. that ye might provoke me to your own *h.*
38. 4. seeketh not welfare of this people, but the *h.*
Dan. 3. 25. they have no *h.* ‖ 6. 22. I have done no *h.*
6. 23. and no manner of *h.* was found upon him
Acts 27. 10. that this voyage will be with *h.* I perceive

HURT, *participle.*

Exod. 22. 10. if a beast be *h.* no man seeing it
14. if it be *h.* and die the owner thereof not with it
1 *Sam.* 25. 15. the men were good and we were not *h.*
Eccl. 10. 9. whoso removeth stones shall be *h.* therew.
Jer. 8. 21. for the h. of my people am I *h.* I am black
Rev. 2. 11. overcomes, shall not be *h.* of second death

HURT, *Verb.*

Gen. 31. 7. but God suffered him not to *h.* me
Exod. 21. 22. if men strive and *h.* woman with child
35. if one man's ox *h.* another's that die, shall sell
Num. 16. 15. neither have I *h.* one of them
1 *Sam.* 25. 7. thy shepherds with us, we *h.* them not
Job 35. 8. thy wickedness may *h.* a man as thou art
Psal. 105. 18. whose feet *h.* with fetters, laid in iron
Isa. 11. 9. they shall not *h.* nor destroy in all my holy mountain, earth full of knowledge of Lord, 65. 25.
27. 3. lest any *h.* it, I will keep it night and day
Dan. 6. 22. that the lions have not *h.* me
Mark 16. 18. any deadly thing, it shall not *h.* them
Luke 4. 35. the devil came out of him, and *h.* him not
10. 19. and nothing shall by any means *h.* you
Acts 18. 10. no man shall set on thee to *h.* thee
Rev. 6. 6. see thou *h.* not the oil and the wine
7. 2. to whom it was given to *h.* earth and sea
3. saying, *h.* not the earth, neither the sea
9. 4. they should not *h.* the grass of the earth
10. and their power was to *h.* men five months
19. and had heads, and with them they do *h.*
11. 5. if any *h.* them, fire proceedeth out of mouth

HURTFUL.

Ezra 4. 15. shalt find that this city is *h.* to kings
Ps. 144. 10. who delivereth David from the *h.* sword
1 *Tim.* 6. 9. they that will be rich fall into *h.* lusts

HURTING.

1 *Sam.* 25. 34. Lord who hath kept me from *h.* thee

HUSBAND.

Gen. 20. † 3. dead man, for she is married to a *h.*
Exod. 4. 25. surely a bloody *h.* art thou to me, 26.
21. 22. as the woman's *h.* will lay upon him
Lev. 19. 20. that is betrothed to a *h.* *Deut.* 22. 23.
21. 3. his sister who had hath no *h.* *Ezek.* 44. 25.
Num. 30. 6. if she had at all an *h.* when she vowed
Deut. 22. 22. lying with a woman married to a *h.*
24. 3. and if the latter *h.* hate her or die
4. her former *h.* may not take her again to wife
25. 5. and perform the duty of a *h.* brother to her
28. 56. her eye shall be evil toward *h.* of her bosom
Judg. 20. 4. the *h.* of the woman slain, answered
Ruth 1. 3. Elimelech, Naomi's *h.* died, she was left
12. I am too old to have an *h.* if I should have a *h.*
Jer. 6. 11. the *h.* with the wife shall be taken
31. 32. although I was a *h.* to them, saith the Lord
Joel 1. 8. girded with sackcloth for *h.* of her youth
Mat. 1. 16. and Jacob begat Joseph the *h.* of Mary
Luke 2. 36. she had lived with a *h.* seven years
John 4. 17. I have no *h.* hast well said, I have no *h.*
Rom. 7. 2. if *h.* be dead, she is loosed from her *h.* 3.
1 *Cor.* 7. 3. let the *h.* render to the wife due benevolence, and likewise also the wife to the *h.*
4. also the *h.* hath not power of his own body
11. and let not the *h.* put away his wife
13. the woman who hath a *h.* that believeth not
14. unbelieving *h.* is sanctified by the wife, and unbelieving wife is sanctified by the *h.*
2 *Cor.* 11. 2. for I have espoused you to one *h.*
Gal. 4. 27. more children than she who hath a *h.*
Eph. 5. 23. the *h.* is head of wife, as Christ of church
1 *Tim.* 3. 2. bishop be blameless, *h.* of one wife, *Tit.* [1. 6.

Her HUSBAND.

Gen. 3. 6. Eve did eat of the fruit, and gave to *her h.*
16. 3. Sarai Abram's wife gave Hagar to *h. h.* Abr.
Lev. 21. 7. not take a woman put away from *her h.*
Num. 5. 13. if it be hid from the eyes of *her h.*
27. if she have done trespass against *her h.*
29. when one goeth aside to another instead of *h. h.*
30. 7. and *h. h.* heard it, and held his peace, 11, 14.
8. if *her h.* disallow her on the day he heard it
10. and if she vowed in *her h.* house or bound
12. if *her h.* hath utterly made them void on day
13. *her h.* may establish it, or may make it void
Deut. 21. 13. thou shalt go in unto her, and be *her h.*
25. 5. *her h.* brother shall go in unto her, and take
11. the wife draweth near to deliver *her h.*
Judg. 13. 6. then the woman came and told *her h.*
9. but Manoah *her h.* was not with her
10. the woman made haste, and shewed *her h.*
19. 3. *her h.* arose and went after her, to speak
Ruth 1. 5. Naomi left of her two sons and *her h.*
9. find rest each of you in the house of *her h.*
2. 1. Naomi had kinsman of *her h.* a man of wealth
1 *Sam.* 1. 8. then said Elkanah *her h.* to her, 23.
22. she said unto *her h.* I will not go up till child
2. 19. when she came up with *her h.* to offer sacrifice
4. 19. she heard that her father and *her h.* were dead
21. because of *her h.* ‖ 25. 19. she told not *her h.*
2 *Sam.* 3. 15. Ish-bosheth sent and took her from *h. h.*
16. *her h.* went with her along weeping behind her
11. 26. when the wife of Uriah heard that *her h.* was dead, she mourned for *her h.*
2 *Kings* 4. 9. she said to *her h.* behold, now I perceive
14. verily she hath no child, and *her h.* is old
22. she called unto *her h.* and said, send me one
Prov. 12. 4. a virtuous wife is a crown to *her h.*
31. 11. the heart of *her h.* doth safely trust in her
23. *her h.* is known in the gates among the elders
28. *her h.* also riseth up, and he praiseth her
Jer. 3. 20. surely as a wife departeth from *her h.*
Ezek. 16. 32. who taketh strangers instead of *her h.*
45. that loatheth *her h.* and her children, thou art
Hos. 2. 2. she is not my wife, neither am I *her h.*
Mat. 1. 19. now Joseph *her h.* being a just man
Mark 10. 12. if a woman shall put away *her h.*
Luke 16. 18. whoso marrieth her put away from *h. h.*
Acts 5. 10. and carrying her forth, buried her by *her h.*
Rom. 7. 2. is bound by law to *h. h.* so long as he liveth
3. if *her h.* be dead, she is free from that law
1 *Cor.* 7. 2. and let every woman have *her* own *h.*
10. let not the wife depart from *her h.*
11. let her remain unmar. or be reconciled to *her h.*
34. is married, careth how she may please *her h.*
39. is bound by the law as long as *her h.* liveth
Eph. 5. 33. and the wife see that she reverence *her h.*
Rev. 21. 2. prepared as a bride adorned for *her h.*

My HUSBAND.

Gen. 29. 32. now therefore *my h.* will love me
34. now this time will *my h.* be joined to me
30. 15. is it small matter that thou hast taken *my h.*?
18. because I have given my maiden to *my h.*
20. Leah said, now will *my h.* dwell with me
Deut. 25. 7. *my h.* brother refuseth to raise a name
2 *Sam.* 14. 5. am a widow, *my h.* is dead, 2 *Kings* 4. 1.
7. shall not leave to *my h.* a name on the earth
Hos. 2. 7. shall say, will go and return to *my* first *h.*
† 16. in that day thou shalt call me *my h.*

Thy HUSBAND.

Gen. 3. 16. thy desire shall be to *thy h.* he shall rule
Num. 5. 19. with another instead of *thy h.* 20.
Judg. 14. 15. they said to Samson's wife, entice *thy h.*
Ruth 2. 11. done to thy mother since death of *thy h.*
2 *Kings* 4. 26. and say to her, is it well with *thy h*?
Isa. 54. 5. thy Maker is *thy h.* the Lord is his name
John 4. 16. go call *thy h.* ‖ 18. he is not *thy h.*
Acts 5. 9. the feet of them that have buried *thy h.*
1 *Cor.* 7. 16. knowest whether thou shalt save *thy h.*

HUSBANDMAN.

Gen. 9. 20. Noah began to be an *h.* and plant. viney.
Jer. 51. 23. with thee will I break in pieces the *h.*
Amos 5. 16. alas! they shall call the *h.* to mourning
Zech. 13. 5. he shall say, I am no prophet, I am a *h.*
John 15. 1. I am the true vine, my Father is the *h.*
2 *Tim.* 2. 6. the *h.* that laboureth must be first partak.
Jam. 5. 7. *h.* waiteth for the precious fruit of earth

HUSBANDMEN.

2 *Kings* 25. 12. he left of the poor to be *h.* *Jer.* 52. 16.
2 *Chron.* 26. 10. Uzziah had *h.* also in Carmel
Jer. 31. 24. and there shall dwell in Judah itself *h.*
Joel 1. 11. be ashamed, O ye *h.* howl, O vine-dress.
Mat. 21. 33. he let it out to *h.* *Mark* 12. 2. *Luke* 20. 9.
34. sent his servants to *h.* *Mark* 12. 2. *Luke* 20. 10.
38. when *h.* saw the son, *Mark* 12. 7. *Luke* 20. 14.
40. when he cometh, what will he do to those *h.*?
41. he will let out his vineyard to other *h.*
Mark 12. 2. he might receive from the *h.* of the fruit
9. he will come and destroy the *h.* and give viney.

HUSBANDRY.

2 *Chr.* 26. 10. Uzziah had husbandmen, for loved *h.*
Job 1. † 3. Job had a very great *h.*
1 *Cor.* 3. 9. ye are God's *h.* ye are God's building

HUSBANDS.

Ruth 1. 11. are there more sons, they may be your *h.*?
13. would ye stay for them from having *h.*?
Esth. 1. 17. so they shall despise their *h.* in their eyes
20. the wives shall give to their *h.* honour
Jer. 29. 6. and give your daughters to *h.*
Ezek. 16. 45. which loathed their *h.* and their child.
John 4. 18. thou hast had five *h.* he not thy husband
1 *Cor.* 14. 35. let them ask their *h.* at home
Eph. 5. 22. wives, submit yourselves to your *h.* 24.
25. *h.* love your wives, even as Christ also loved the church, and gave himself for it, *Col.* 3. 19.
Col. 3. 18. wives, submit yourselves to your own *h.*
1 *Tim.* 3. 12. let the deacons be the *h.* of one wife
Tit. 2. 4. teach young women to love their *h.*
5. to be chaste, obedient to their own *h.*
1 *Pet.* 3. 1. ye wives, be in subjection to your own *h.*
7. ye *h.* dwell with them according to knowledge

HUSK, S.

Num. 6. 4. from the kernels even to the *h.*
2 *Kings* 4. 42. brought full ears of corn in *h.* thereof
Luke 15. 16. would fain have filled his belly with *h.*

HYMN, S.

Mat. 26. 30. when they had sung an *h.* *Mark* 14. 26.
Eph. 5. 19. speaking to yourselves in psalms and *h.*
Col. 3. 16. admonishing one another in psalms and *h.*

HYPOCRISY

Comes from the Greek, ὑποκρισις: *It is a counterfeiting religion and virtue; an affectation of the name, joined with a disaffection to the thing; or,* the having a form of godliness with denying the power of it. *Thus he is a* hypocrite *who feigns to be what he is not, who puts on a false person, like the actors in tragedies and comedies. Our Saviour frequently accused the* Pharisees *of* hypocrisy, *Mat.* 23. 13, 14, *&c. Their character is drawn out in that chapter; as,* (1) *They say and do not,* verse 3. *their practice was not agreeable to their doctrine, and therefore their example was not to be imitated; for they imposed many strict injunctions, over and above what the law required, and severely exacted obedience thereto from others, but did not observe the least part thereof themselves,* verse 4. (2) *What good things they did, were only for ostentation, to be seen of men,* verse 5. (3) *They ambitiously affected titles, vain applause, and the precedency at entertainments,* verse 6–12. (4) *They hid their crying sins under the colourable appearance of virtues, and pretended to holiness, that they might sin with less suspicion and more security,* verse 14. *These our Saviour compares to* whited sepulchres, *that within contain sordid dust and rottenness,* verses 27, 28. (5) *They were exact in light matters, they tithed mint and cummin, but neglected substantial duties: They were zealous in the outward parts of religious worship, and neglected righteousness and mercy, thinking to compensate their defects in the duties of one table, by strictly observing the duties of the other,* verses 23, 24. (6) *They studied rather an external purity, than the inward purity of the heart,* verse 25. (7) *These hypocritical* Scribes *and* Pharisees *pretended a great deal of respect to the ancient prophets, and to disallow what their fathers did to them, and yet were as ready to practise the like themselves to Christ and his apostles,* verses 29, 30, 31. (8) Hypocrites *pray to God only in the time of sickness and danger, when by their afflictions they are driven to it, but shew no love to prayer or delight in God in time of prosperity,* Job 27. 8, 9, 10. (9) *They judged and censured others severely for smaller faults, being in the mean time themselves guilty of greater crimes,* Mat. 7. 5. (10) *They were more for outward ceremonies and human traditions than for the true and spiritual worship of God,* Mat. 12. 1, 2, 7. ‖ 15. 2, 7, 8, 9. (11) *In worldly affairs they were quick-sighted, not so in spiritual and heavenly things,* Mark 3. 4. (12) Hypocrites *in public calamities are fearful,* Isa. 33. 14.
This sin of hypocrisy *is difficultly cured, in that it is not easily discovered by men, and does not expose to shame, but is subservient to many carnal ends Men cannot dive into the hearts of others, and cannot discern between the paint of* hypocrisy *and the life of holiness.* Hypocrisy *also turns the means of salvation into poison; for the frequent exercise of religious duties, which is the means to sanctify others, confirms and hardens* hypocrites.
The effectual means to cure it, is a stedfast belief of the pure and all-seeing eye of God; who sees sin wherever it is, and will bring it into judgment. A hypocrite *may hide his sin from the eyes of others, and sometimes from his own conscience, but can never impose upon God. The stedfast belief of this truth will cause frequent and solemn thoughts of God, as our Inspector and Judge: Our Saviour makes use of it as an argument against* hypocrisy. *Luke* 12. 1, 2, 3. Beware ye of the leaven of the Pharisees, which is hypocrisy. For there is nothing covered that shall not be revealed; neither hid that shall not be known, &c.

Isa. 32. 6. his heart will work iniquity, to practise *h.*
Mat. 23. 28. within ye are full of *h.* and iniquity
Mark 12. 15. he knowing their *h.* said unto them
Luke 12. 1. beware of leaven of Pharisees, which is *h.*
1 *Tim.* 4. 2. speaking lies in *h.* their conscience seared
Jam. 3. 17. wisdom from above is pure and without *h.*

HYPOCRISIES.

1 *Pet.* 2. 1. wherefore laying aside all malice and *h.*

HYPOCRITE.

Job 8. 13. and the *h.* hope shall perish
13. 16. for an *h.* shall not come before him
17. 8. the innocent shall stir up himself against *h.*
20. 5. and the joy of the *h.* is but for a moment
27. 8. what is the hope of the *h.* tho' he hath gained
34. 30. that the *h.* reign not, lest the people be snared
Prov. 11. 9. an *h.* with his mouth destroy. neighbour
Isa. 9. 17. for every one is an *h.* and an evil doer
Mat. 7. 5. thou *h.* first cast out the beam out of eye
Luke 6. 42. thou *h.* cast beam out of thy own eye
13. 15. thou *h.* doth not each one loose his ox?

HYPOCRITES.

Job 15. 34. the congregation of *h.* shall be desolate
36. 13. but the *h.* in heart heap up wrath
Isa. 33. 14. fearfulness hath surprised the *h.*
Mat. 6. 2. do not sound a trumpet, as the *h.* do
5. when thou prayest, thou shalt not be as *h.* are
16. moreover, when ye fast, be not as the *h.*
15. 7. ye *h.* well did Esaias prophesy, *Mark* 7. 6.
16. 3. O ye *h.* ye can discern the face of sky, but can ye not discern the signs of times? *Luke* 12. 56.
22. 18. but Jesus said, why tempt ye me, ye *h.?*
23. 13. woe unto you, scribes and Pharisees, *h.* ye shut up kingd. against men, 14, 15, 23, 25, 27, 29.
24. 51. shall appoint him his portion with the *h.*
Luke 11. 44. woe unto you, scribes and Pharisees, *h.*

HYPOCRITICAL.

Ps. 35. 16. with *h.* mockers in feasts, they gnashed
Isa. 10. 6. I will send him against an *h.* nation

HYSSOP

Is an herb very generally known, and in Hebrew *called* Esob. *It was commonly made use of in purification instead of a sprinkler: Thus God commanded the* Hebrews, *when they came out of* Egypt, *to take a bunch of* hyssop, *to dip it in the blood of the Paschal lamb, and sprinkle the lintel and two side-posts with it,* Exod. 12. 22. *Sometimes they added a little wool to it, of a scarlet colour. So in the purification of lepers, they dipped a bunch composed of* hyssop, *the branches of cedar, and red wool, in water, mingled with the blood of a bird, and with it sprinkled the leper,* Lev. 14. 4, &c.

David *alludes to these ceremonial purifications.* Psal. 51. 7. Purge me with hyssop, and I shall be clean: *that is, As lepers and other unclean persons are by thy appointment purified by the use of* hyssop *and other things, so do thou cleanse me, a most leprous and polluted creature, by thy grace, and by the virtue of the blood of* Christ, *which is represented and signified by those ceremonial usages.*

Hyssop *is a shrub, which shoots out abundance of suckers from one root only: it is as hard as any large wood, and grows about a foot and a half high. At particular distances on both sides of its stock it pushes out longish leaves, which are hard, odoriferous, warm, and a little bitter to the taste. The blossom of it appears at the top of the stem, of an azure colour, and like an ear of corn. There are two sorts of it, the garden, and mountain* hyssop. *It is very probable that* hyssop *grows to a very great height in* Judea, *since it is said in the gospel, that the soldiers having filled a spunge with vinegar, they put it upon a stick of* hyssop, *and presented it to our Saviour's mouth, who was then upon the cross,* John 19. 29.

Exod. 12. 22. ye shall take a bunch of *h.* and dip it
Lev. 14. 4. take cedar-wood, scarlet, and *h.* 6, 49, 51.
52. shall cleanse the house with the *h.* and scarlet
Num. 19. 6. shall cast *h.* into the midst of the burning
18. a clean person shall take *h.* and dip it in water
1 *Kings* 4. 33. from the cedar-tree even unto the *h.*
Psal. 51. 7. purge me with *h.* and I shall be clean
John 19. 29. they filled a spunge, and put it on *h.*
Heb. 9. 19. he took blood with *h.* and sprinkled people

I.

I *is* referred (I) *To God,* to set forth, [1] *The dignity of his person,* Psal. 81. 10. Isa. 45. 5, 6. [2] *His great power and might,* Gen. 17. 1. [3] *His eternal and unchangeable being in himself,* Exod. 3. 14. [4] *The certainty of his promises and threatenings,* Exod. 6. 2. Num. 14. 35. (II) *To the Son of God.* [1] *Before his manifestation in the flesh,* Cant. 2. 1. [2] *When manifested,* Mark 14. 62. Luke 24. 39. (III) *To the Holy Ghost,* Acts 10. 20. (IV) *To the church,* Cant. 2. 16. | 6. 3. (V) *To the good angels,* Luke 1. 19. | 2. 10. Rev. 22. 9. (VI) *To evil angels,* 1 Kings 22. 21, 22. (VII) *To men and women,* denoting, [1] *Their pride,* Isa. 47. 8, 10. [2] *The certainty of what is spoken,* Gal. 5. 2. Philem. 19. [3] *The readiness of the speaker to perform his duty, or what is enjoined him,* Mic. 3. 8. Mat. 21. 30. (VIII) *To the creatures,* Num. 22. 30. Judg. 9. 9, 11, 13.

Gen. 6. 17. behold *I,* even *I,* do bring a flood on earth
9. 9. *I,* behold *I,* establish my covenant with you
34. 30. *I* shall be destroyed, *I* and my house
37. 10. shall *I,* thy moth. and brethr. come to bow?
30. the child is not, and *I,* whither shall *I* go?
39. 9. there is none greater in this house than *I*
Exod. 3. 11. who am *I,* that *I* should go to Pharaoh?
9. 27. L. is righteous, *I* and my people are wicked
14. 17. and *I,* behold *I,* will harden the hearts
18. 6. *I* thy father-in-law Jethro am come to thee
31. 6. *I,* behold *I,* have given with him Aholiab
Lev. 26. 28. *I,* even *I,* will chastise you for your sins
Num. 3. 12. *I,* behold *I,* have taken the Lev. 18. 6.
Deut. 7. 17. nations more than *I,* how can *I* dispose.
Deut. 32. 39. *I,* even *I,* am he, there is no G. with me
Josh. 14. 7. forty years old was *I* when Moses sent me
Judg. 5. 3. *I,* even *I,* will sing to the Lord God of Isr.
7. till *I* Deborah arose, that *I* arose mother in Isr.
7. 18. when *I* blow, *I* and all that are with me
11. 37. may bewail my virginity, *I* and my fellows
12. 2. *I* and my people were at strife with Ammon
20. 4. *I* came to Gibeah, *I* and my concubine
1 *Sam.* 24. 17. he said, thou art more righteous than *I*
2 *Sam.* 3. 28. *I* and my kingd. are guiltless before L.
13. 13. *I,* whither shall *I* cause my shame to go?
1 *Kings* 1. 21. *I* and son Solom. be counted offenders
18. 22. *I,* even *I,* only remain a prophet, 19. 10, 14.
1 *Chr.* 29. 14. who am *I,* what my peop. 2 *Chr.* 2. 6.
2 *Chr.* 32. 13. what *I* and fathers have done to peo.
Ezra 7. 21. *I,* even I Artaxerxes, make a decree
Neh. 5. 15. but so did not *I,* because of fear of G.
Esth. 4. 16. *I* also and my maidens will fast likewise
Job 1. 15. *I* only am escaped to tell thee, 16, 17, 19.
15. 6. thy own mouth condemneth thee, and not *I*
34. 33. whether thou refuse or choose, and not *I*
Ps. 61. 2. lead me to the rock that is higher than *I*
142. 6. persecutors, for they are stronger than *I*
Eccl. 2. 25. who can hasten hereunto more than *I?*
Cant. 2. 1. *I* am the rose of Sharon, and lily of vall.
6. 3. *I* am my beloved's, 7. 10. || 8. 10. *I* am a wall
Isa. 8. 18. *I* and child. L. hath given me, *Heb.* 2. 13.
41. 4. *I* the Lord the first, I am he, 43. 11, 25.
10. *I* am with thee, for *I* am thy God, 43. 5.
44. 6. *I* am the first, *I* am the last, 48. 12. *Rev.* 1. 17.
7. who as *I* shall call, and shall declare it?
45. 12. *I,* even my hands have stretched out heav.
46. 4. even to your old age *I* am he, *I* have made
9. *I* am God, and there is none else, *I* am God
48. 15. *I,* even *I* have spoken, *I* have called him
16. from time that it was, there am *I,* *Mat.* 18. 20.
49. 5. yet shall *I* be glorious in the eyes of the L.
51. 12. *I,* even *I* am he, 52. 6. || 52. 6. behold, it is I
65. 5. stand by thyself, for *I* am holier than thou
Jer. 20. 7. *I* was deceived, thou art stronger than *I*
23. 39. behold *I,* even *I,* will utterly forget you
Ezek. 5. 8. behold *I,* even *I,* am against thee
6. 3. behold *I,* even *I,* will bring a sword upon you
34. 11. beh. *I,* even *I,* will search sheep and seek
20. *I,* even *I,* will judge between fat catt. and lean
44. 28. I am their inherit. I am their possession
Dan. 8. 15. when *I,* even *I* Dan. had seen the vision
Hos. 5. 14. *I,* even *I,* will tear, *I* will take away
Hag. 1. 13. Haggai spoke, *I* am with you, saith Lord
Zech. 1. 15. for *I* was but little displeased, they help
Mal. 1. 13. should *I* accept of your hands? saith Ld.
Mat. 3. 11. after me is mightier than *I,* *Mark* 1. 7.
14. 27. it is *I,* be not afraid, *Mark* 6. 50. *John* 6. 20.
16. 13. whom do men say that *I* the Son of man am?
18. 20. two or three, there am *I* in midst of them
24. 5. many shall come in name, saying, *I* am Chr.
26. 22. every one began to say, Lord, is it *I?*
Mark 14. 29. tho' all shall be offended, yet will not *I*
Luke 2. 48. thy father and *I* sought thee sorrowing
11. 19. if *I* by Beelzeb. cast out devils, by whom do
20. if *I* with the finger of God cast out devils
21. 8. shall come in my name, saying, *I* am Christ
22. 27. but *I* am among you as he that serveth
24. 39. that it is *I* myself, handle me and see
John 1. 20. he confessed, *I* am not the Christ, 3. 28.
33. *I* knew him not || 4. 26. *I* that speak am he
8. 16. *I* am not alone, but *I* and Fath. that sent me
23. *I* am from above, *I* am not of this world
28. shall know that *I* am he, *I* do nothing of myself
58. Jesus said, verily, before Abraham was, *I* am
10. 30. *I* and my Father are one
38. the Father in me, and *I* in him, 17. 21. | 15. 5.
12. 32. and *I,* if *I* be lifted up, will draw all men to
13. 14. if *I* then your Ld. and Master have washed
14. 20. *I* in my Fath. || 15. 4. abide in me, *I* in you
28. *I* go to Fath. for my Father is greater than *I*
17. 23. *I* in them, 26. || 25. but *I* have known thee
18. 35. Pilate answered, am *I* a Jew?
Acts 11. 17. what was *I,* that *I* could withstand God?
22. 28. *I* obtained this freedom; *I* was free born
Rom. 7. 17. it is no more *I,* but sin dwell. in me, 20.
1 *Cor.* 1. 12. *I* am of Paul, *I* of Apollos, *I* of Chr. 3. 4.
2. 1. and *I* brethren when *I* came to you declaring
3. 1. and *I,* brethr. could not speak to you as to sp.
7. 7. *I* would that all men were even as *I* myself
8. if they abide even as *I* || 10. yet not *I,* but Lord
9. 6. or *I* only and Barnabas, have not we power
26. *I* therefore so run, so fight *I,* not as one that
11. 1. be ye followers of me, even as *I* am of Christ
15. 10. by the grace of G. *I* am what *I* am, yet not *I*
11. whether it were *I* or they, so we preached
16. 10. for he worketh the work of Christ, even as *I*
2 *Cor.* 11. 22. are they Hebrews? so am *I*
23. *I* am more || 29. who is offended, *I* burn not?
Gal. 2. 19. *I* thro' the law am dead to the law, that *I*
20. *I* live, yet not *I,* but Christ liveth in me
4. 12. brethren be as *I* am, for *I* am as ye are
5. 11. *I,* brethren, if *I* yet preach circumcision
6. 14. that *I* should glory in cross, and *I* to world
Eph. 1. 15. *I* also, after *I* heard of your faith in Jesus
4. 1. *I* therefore, prisoner of the Lord, beseech you
1 *Pet.* 1. 16. it is written, be ye holy, for *I* am holy
2 *John* 1. whom *I* love in the truth, and not *I* only
Rev. 1. 8. *I* am Alpha and Omega, begin. and end
3. 19. as many as *I* love, *I* rebuke and chasten
21. as *I* also overcame || 21. 2. *I* John saw, 22. 8.
22. 9. see thou do it not, *I* am thy fellow servant
16. *I* Jesus have sent my angel to testify these things, *I* am the root and offspring of David

JACINTH.

Rev. 9. 17. having breast-plates of fire, *j.* and brimst.
21. 20. the eleventh foundation of the city was a *j.*

JAILER.

Acts 16. 23. charging the *j.* to keep them safely

JANGLING.

1 *Tim.* 1. 6. having swerved, turned aside to vain *j.*

JASPER.

Exod. 28. 20. the fourth row an onyx and a *j.* 39. 13.
Ezek. 28. 13. topaz, the diamond and *j.* thy covering
Rev. 4. 3. he that sat, was to look upon like a *j.*
21. 11. her light was like to a *j.* stone, clear as
18. building of the wall of city was of *j.*
Rev. 21. 19. with prec. stones, the first found. was *j*

JAVELIN.

Num. 25. 7. and Phinehas took a *j.* in his hand
1 *Sam.* 18. 10. there was a *j.* in Saul's hand, 19. 9.
11. Saul cast the *j.* for he said, I will smite Dav.
19. 10. he smote the *j.* into the wall, David fled

JAW.

Judg. 15. 19. but God clave an hollow place in the *j.*
Job 41. 2. canst thou bore his *j.* thro' with a thorn?

JAW-BONE.

Judg. 15. 15. Samson found a new *j.-bone* of an ass
15. 16. with the *j.-bone* of an ass have I slain
17. he cast away the *j.-bone* out of his hand

JAWS.

Job 29. 17. and I brake the *j.* of the wicked
Psal. 22. 15. and my tongue cleaveth to my *j.*
Isa. 30. 28. there shall be a bridle in *j.* of the people
Hos. 11. 4. as they that take off the yoke on their *j*

JAW-TEETH.

Prov. 30. 14. and their *j.-teeth* as knives to devour

ICE, *See* YCE.

IDLE

Signifies [1] *One who is slothful or lazy,* Exod. 5. 8, 17. [2] *One that would work, but is not employed or hired,* Mat. 20. 3, 6. [3] *Unprofitable, not tending to edification,* Mat. 12. 36.

Exod. 5. 8. for they be *i.* therefore they cry
17. but he said, ye are *i.* ye are *i.* ye say, let us go
Prov. 19. 15. and an *i.* soul shall suffer hunger
Mat. 12. 36. that every *i.* word men shall speak
20. 3. he saw others standing *i.* in market-place, 6.
Luke 24. 11. and their words seemed as *i.* tales
1 *Tim.* 5. 13. withal they learn to be *i.* and not only *i.*

IDLENESS.

Prov. 31. 27. she eateth not the bread of *i.*
Eccl. 10. 18. through *i.* the house droppeth through
Ezek. 16. 49. and abundance of *i.* was in her

IDOLATER.

1 *Cor.* 5. 11. if any called a brother be an *i.* not to eat
Eph. 5. 5. who is an *i.* hath any inheritance in kingd.

IDOLATERS.

1 *Cor.* 5. 10. yet not altogeth. with the covetous or *i.*
6. 9. *i.* shall not inherit the kingdom of God
10. 7. neither be ye *i.* as were some of them
Rev. 21. 8. but *i.* shall have their part in the lake
22. 15. without are murderers and *i.* and all liars

IDOLATRY

Signifies, [1] *The superstitious worship which is given to idols or false gods,* Acts 17. 16. 1 Cor. 10. 7. [2] *The making of any image or likeness of God or any creature for a religious end,* Deut. 5. 8. Gal. 5. 20. [3] *All human inventions thrust into the worship of God,* Deut. 12. 32. [4] *The setting of the heart inordinately upon any creature,* Phil. 3. 19. [5] *An inordinate love to, and distrustful care for, the things of the world,* Col. 3. 5.

1 *Sam.* 15. 23. stubbornness is as iniquity and *i.*
Acts 17. 16. when he saw the city wholly given to *i.*
1 *Cor.* 10. 14. my dearly beloved, flee from *i.*
Gal. 5. 20. the works of the flesh are *i.* witchcraft
Col. 3. 5. mortify covetousness, which is *i.*

IDOLATRIES.

1 *Pet.* 4. 3. when he walked in abominable *i.*

IDOLATROUS.

2 *Kings* 23. 5. Josiah put down the *i.* priests

IDOL.

Zech. 11. 17. woe to the *i.* shepherd that leaveth flock

IDOL

Signifies, [1] *An image or statue representing some false deity,* 2 Cor. 6. 16. [2] *Any thing too much and sinfully indulged,* 1 John 5. 21. [3] *Devils,* Isa. 19. 3. 1 Cor. 10. 21.

1 *Kings* 15. 13. she made an *i.* in grove, 2 *Chr.* 15. 16.
2 *Chron.* 33. 7. he set the *i.* in the house of God
15. he took the *i.* out of the house of the Lord
Isa. 48. 5. lest thou shouldst say, my *i.* hath done
66. 3. he that burneth incense as if he blessed an *i.*
Jer. 22. 28. is this man Coniah a despised broken *i.*
Acts 7. 41. made a calf and offered sacrifice to the *i.*
1 *Cor.* 8. 4. we know an *i.* is nothing in world, 10. 19.
7. some with conscience of the *i.* to this hour eat it

IDOLS.

Lev. 19. 4. turn ye not unto *i.* || 26. 1. shall make no *i.*
26. 30. will cast your carcases on carcases of your *i.*
Deut. 29. 17. ye have seen their *i.* wood and stone
1 *Sam.* 31. 9. to publish it in the house of their *i.*
1 *Kings* 15. 12. Asa removed the *i.* his father made
21. 26. Ahab did very abominable in following *i.*
2 *Kings* 17. 12. for they served *i.* 2 *Chron.* 24. 18.
21. 11. Manasseh hath made Judah to sin with his *i.*
21. Amon served the *i.* that his father served
23. 24. the *i.* that were spied in the land of Judah
1 *Chron.* 10. 9. to carry tidings to their *i.* and people
16. 26. for all the gods of the people are *i.*
2 *Chr.* 15. 8. Asa put away abominable *i.* out of Jud.
34. 7. Josiah cut down all the *i.* in the land of Isr.
Psal. 96. 5. for all the gods of the nations are *i.*
97. 7. confounded, they that boast themselves of *i.*
106. 36. they serv. their *i.* that were snare to them
38. whom they sacrificed to the *i.* of Canaan
115. 4. their *i.* are silver and gold, 135. 15.
Isa. 2. 8. their land is full of *i.* worship work of ha.
18. and the *i.* he shall utterly abolish
20. shall cast away his *i.* of silver and gold, 31. 7.
10. 10. as my hand hath found kingdoms of the *i.*
11. to Samaria and her *i.* so do to Jerus. and her *i.*
19. 1. *i.* of Egypt shall be moved at his presence
3. they shall seek to the *i.* and to the charmers
45. 16. the makers of *i.* shall go to confusion
46. 1. their *i.* were on the beasts and on the cattle
57. 5. inflaming yourselves with *i.* under green tree
Jer. 50. 2. her *i.* are confounded, her images broken
38. land of images, and they are mad upon their *i.*
Ezek. 6. 4. cast your slain men before your *i.* 5, 13.
6. alt. laid waste, your *i.* may be broken and cease
9. with their eyes which go a whoring after their *i.*
13. where they did offer sweet savour to all th. *i.*
8. 10. I saw all the *i.* of Israel pourtrayed on wall
14. 3. these men set up their *i.* in their heart, 4. 7.
5. they are estranged from me through their *i.*
6. repent, and turn yourselves from your *i.*

Ezek. 16. 36. and with all the *i.* of thy abominations
18. 6. nor hath lift up his eyes to the *i.* of Israel, 15.
12. oppressed the poor, hath lift up his eyes to *i.*
20. 7. defile not yourselves with the *i.* of Egypt, 18.
8. nor did they forsake the *i.* of Egypt, I will pour
16. polluted my sabb. for their heart went after *i.*
24. polluted sabb. their eyes went after father's *i.*
31. ye pollute yourselves with all your *i.* even unto this day, 22. 4. | 23. 7, 30, 37.
39. but pollute ye my holy name no more with *i.*
22. 3. the city maketh *i.* against herself to defile
23. 39. when they had slain their children to their *i.*
49. and ye shall bear the sins of your *i.* I am L.
30. 13. I will destroy *i.* and will cause their images
33. 25. and ye lift up your eyes towards your *i.*
36. 18. for their *i.* wherewith they polluted it
25. from all your *i.* will I cleanse you, 37. 23.
44. 10. which went astray from me after their *i.*
12. because they minister. to them before their *i.*
Hos. 4. 17. Ephraim is joined to *i.* let him alone
8. 4. of their silv. and gold have they made them *i.*
13. 2. have made *i.* according to their understand.
14. 8. what have I to do any more with *i.*
Mic. 1. 7. and all the *i.* thereof will I lay desolate
Hab. 2. 18. maker trusteth therein to make dumb *i.*
Zeph. 1. † 3. I will consume *i.* with the wicked
Zech. 10. 2. for the *i.* have spoken vanity, and divin.
13. 2. I will cut off names of the *i.* out of the land
Acts 15. 20. they abstain from pollutions of *i.*
29. abstain from meats offered to *i.* 21. 25.
17. † 16. when he saw the city full of *i.*
Rom. 2. 22. thou that abhorrest *i.* dost thou commit
1 *Cor.* 8. 1. as touching things offered to *i.* 4, 10. | 10. 19, 28. *Rev.* 2. 14. 20.
12. 2. were Gentiles carried away to these dumb *i.*
2 *Cor.* 6. 16. what agreement temple of God with *i.*?
1 *Thess.* 1. 9. how ye turned to God from *i.*
1 *John* 5. 21. children keep yourselves from *i.*
Rev. 9. 20. not worship devils and *i.* of gold and sil.

JEALOUS.

Exod. 20. 5. for I the Lord thy God am a *j.* God, 34. 14. *Deut.* 4. 24. | 5. 9. | 6. 15. *Josh.* 24. 19.
Num. 5. 14. and he be *j.* of his wife, 14, † 30.
1 *Kings* 19. 10. I have been *j.* for the L. of hosts, 14.
Ezek. 39. 25. and will be *j.* for my holy name
Joel 2. 18. then will the Lord be *j.* for his land
Nah. 1. 2. God is *j.* and the Lord revengeth
Zech. 1. 14. I am *j.* for Jerus. || 8. 2. was *j.* for Zion
2 *Cor.* 11. 2. for I am *j.* over you with godly jealousy

JEALOUSY

Signifies, [1] *Suspicion between married persons of their fidelity one to another,* Num. 5. 14. [2] *An earnest desire and concern for the welfare of others, joined with some degree of fear of them,* 2 Cor. 11. 2. [3] *The hot displeasure and indignation of God,* Psal. 79. 5. 1 Cor. 10. 22.
Num. 5. 14. the spirit of *j.* come upon him, 14, † 30.
15. for it is an offering of *j.* and of memorial, 18.
25. then priest shall take *j.* offering from woman
25. 11. that I consumed not Israel in my *j.*
Deut. 29. 20. his *j.* shall smoke against that man
32. 16. they provoked him to *j.* 1 *Kings* 14. 22.
21. have moved me to *j.* I will move them to *j.*
Psal. 78. 58. they moved him to *j.* with images
79. 5. how long, Lord, shall thy *j.* burn like fire?
Prov. 6. 34. for *j.* is the rage of man, he will not spare
27. † 4. but who is able to stand before *j.*?
Cant. 8. 6. *j.* is cruel as the grave, the coals thereof are
Isa. 42. 13. he shall stir up *j.* like a man of war
Ezek. 8. 3. where was the seat of the image of *j.*?
5. behold at gate of altar this image of *j.* in entry
16. 38. and I will give thee blood in fury and *j.*
42. my *j.* shall depart from thee and will be quiet
23. 25. I will set my *j.* against thee, they shall deal
36. 5. in the fire of *j.* have I spoken, 6. | 38. 19.
Zeph. 1. 18. whose land devoured by fire of his *j.* 3. 8.
Zech. 1. 14. I am jealous for Zion with great *j.* 8. 2.
Rom. 10. 19. Moses saith, will provoke you to *j.*
11. 11. salvation to Gentiles, to provoke them to *j.*
1 *Cor.* 10. 22. do we provoke the Lord to *j.*?
2 *Cor.* 11. 2. for I am jealous over you with godly *j.*

JEALOUSIES.

Num. 5. 29. this is law of *j.* when a wife goeth aside

JEOPARDED.

Judg. 5. 18. were people that *j.* their lives unto death

JEOPARDY.

2 *Sam.* 23. 17. went in *j.* of their lives, 1 *Chr.* 11. 19.
1 *Chr.* 12. 19. he will fall to Saul, to *j.* of our heads
Luke 8. 23. ship was filled with water, they were in *j.*
1 *Cor.* 15. 30. and why stand we in *j.* every hour?

JESTING.

Eph. 5. 4. nor filthiness, nor *j.* not convenient

JEWEL

Signifies, [1] *A precious and costly ornament,* Gen. 24. 53. [2] *God's children,* Mal. 3. 17.
Prov. 11. 22. as a *j.* of gold in a swine's snout
20. 15. but the lips of knowledge are a precious *j.*
Ezek. 16. 12. I put a *j.* on thy forehead, and ear-rings

JEWELS.

Gen. 24. 53. the servant brought forth *j.* of silver
Exod. 3. 22. shall borrow *j.* of gold, 11. 2. | 12. 35.
35. 22. they brought all *j.* of gold, *Num.* 31. 50.
Num. 31. 51. took the gold, even all wrought *j.*
1 *Sam.* 6. 8. and put the *j.* of gold in a coffer, 15.
2 *Chron.* 20. 25. they found riches and precious *j.*
32. 27. made treasuries for all manner pleasant *j.*
Job 28. 17. the exchange of it shall not be for *j.* of
Cant. 1. 10. thy cheeks are comely with rows of *j.*
7. 1. the joints of thy thighs are like *j.*
Isa. 61. 10. as a bride adorneth herself with her *j.*
Ezek. 16. 17. hast taken thy *j.* of my gold and silver
39. and they shall take thy fair *j.* 23. 26.
Hos. 2. 13. she decked herself with ear-rings and *j.*
Mal. 3. 17. they shall be mine, when I make up my *j.*

IF

Signifies, [1] *Surely,* Num. 14. † 23. [2] *Whether or no,* Gen. 8. 8. [3] *When,* Judg. 21. 21. John 12. 32. It denotes, (1) *A condition,* Deut. 28. 15. Luke 9. 23. (2) *A supposition,* Rom. 4. 2. 1 Pet. 3. 17. (3) *A reason of a matter,* Eph. 4. 21.
Gen. 25. 22. she said, *if* it be so, why am I thus?
Gen. 31. 8. *if* he said thus || 34. 15. *if* ye be as we be
43. 11. *if* it must be so now, take of the best fruits
Josh. 14. 12. *if* so be the Lord will be with me
1 *Sam.* 14. 9. *if* they say to us, tarry till we come
20. 7. *if* he say thus, it is well, 2 *Sam.* 15. 26.
2 *Kings* 7. 4. *if* we say, *if* we sit here; *if* they kill us
10. 6. *if* ye be mine, *if* ye will hearken to my voice
Job 9. 29. *if* I be wicked, 10. 15. || 24. 25. *if* it be not so
Psal. 7. 3. *if* I have done this, *if* there be iniquity
Jer. 27. 18. *if* they be prophets, *if* the word of Lord
51. 8. take balm for her pain, *if* so be may be heal.
Dan. 3. 17. *if* it be so, our God is able to deliver us
4. 27. *if* it may be a lengthening of thy tranquillity
Hos. 8. 7. *if* so be it yield, strangers shall swall. it up
Mat. 4. 3. *if* thou be the Son of God, command that these stones be made bread, 27. 40. *Luke* 4. 3.
14. 28. *if* it be thou, bid me come to thee on water
27. 43. let him deliver him, *if* he will have him
Mark 1. 40. *if* thou wilt, thou canst make me clean
11. 32. *if* we shall say, of men, they feared people
Luke 23. 35. *if* he be Christ, 39. *John* 10. 24.
John 1. 25. *if* thou be not Elias, nor that prophet
15. 18. *if* the world hate you, 1 *John* 3. 13.
19. 12. Jews cried out, *if* thou let this man go
Acts 5. 39. *if* it be of God ye cannot overthrow it
1 *Cor.* 15. 19. *if* in this life only we have hope in Chr.
Gal. 4. 7. *if* a son, then an heir of God thro' Christ
Phil. 2. 1. *if* any consolation, *if* any comfort of love
Heb. 3. † 11. *if* they shall enter into rest, 4. 3, 5.
1 *John* 2. 19. *if* they had been of us, they would

IF *not.*

Gen. 18. 21. *if not* I will know || 24. 49. *if n.* tell me
Exod. 32. 32. *if not,* blot me, I pray, out of thy book
Judg. 9. 15. *if n.* let fire come out of the bramble, 20.
1 *Sam.* 2. 16. and *if not,* I will take it by force
6. 9. *if not,* then we shall know it is not his hand
2 *Sam.* 13. 26. *if not,* I pray thee, let Amnon go
17. 6. shall we do after his say.? *if not* speak thou
2 *Kings* 2. 10. but *if not,* it shall not be so
Job 9. 24. *if not,* where, and who is he?
33. 33. *if not,* hearken unto me, hold thy peace.
Dan. 3. 18. but *if not,* be it known to thee, O king
Zech. 11. 12. give me my price; *if not,* forbear
Luke 10. 6. but *if not,* it shall turn to you again
13. 9. *if not,* after that thou shalt cut it down

See WERE.

IF *now.*

Gen. 18. 3. *if now* I have found favour in thy sight
24. 42. O God, *if now* thou do prosper my way
49. *if now* you will deal kindly with me
33. 10. Jacob said, *if now* I have found grace in thy sight, 47. 29. *Exod.* 34. 9. *Judg.* 6. 17.
1 *Cor.* 4. 7. *if n.* thou didst receive it, why dost glory?

IGNOMINY.

Prov. 18. 3. cometh contempt, and with *i.* reproach

IGNORANCE

Signifies, [1] *Want of the true knowledge of God and of heavenly things,* Eph. 4. 18. [2] *Unbelief, which follows ignorance,* 1 Pet. 1. 14. [3] *Error, imprudence, or surprise,* Lev. 4. 2, 13. [4] *Idolatry,* Acts 17. 30.
Lev. 4. 2. if a soul shall sin thro' *i.* against any commandment, 5. 15. *Num.* 15. 24, 27, 28, 29.
13. the whole congregation of Israel sin thro' *i.*
22. when a ruler hath done somewhat through *i.*
27. if any of the common people sin through *i.*
Num. 15. 25. it shall be forgiven them, for it is *i.*
Acts 3. 17. I wot that thro' *i.* ye did it, as your rulers
17. 30. and the times of this *i.* God winked at
Eph. 4. 18. being alienated thro' the *i.* that is in them
1 *Pet.* 1. 14. according to the former lusts in your *i.*
2. 15. that ye may put to silence *i.* of foolish men

IGNORANT

Signifies, [1] *One that wants understanding,* Isa. 56. 10. [2] *One that is not in a capacity to know one's condition, or deliver from troubles,* Isa. 63. 16. [3] *Without the knowledge of the true God,* Acts 17. 23. [4] *One sinning unwittingly, not knowing that the Christian religion was the true religion,* 1 Tim. 1. 13. [5] *One that has not been trained up in schools of polite learning, nor attained his knowledge by the ordinary way of learning it from men,* Acts 4. 13. [6] *One not rightly conceiving or apprehending,* Rom. 10. 3. [7] *One that sinneth for want of the knowledge of his duty, and through inconsideration,* Heb. 5. 2.
Psal. 73. 22. so foolish was I and *i.* I was as a beast
Isa. 56. 10. they are all *i.* they are all dumb dogs
63. 16. thou art our father, tho' Abraham be *i.* of us
Acts 4. 13. and perceived that they were *i.* men
Rom. 1. 13. now I would not have you *i.* brethren, 1 *Cor.* 10. 1. | 12. 1. 2 *Cor.* 1. 8. 1 *Thess.* 4. 13.
10. 3. they being *i.* of God's righteous. going about
11. 25. that ye should be *i.* of this mystery
1 *Cor.* 14. 38. if any man be *i.* let him be *i.*
2 *Cor.* 2. 11. for we are not *i.* of Satan's devices
Heb. 5. 2. who can have compassion on the *i.*
2 *Pet.* 3. 5. for this they willingly are *i.* of
8. but, beloved, be not *i.* of this one thing

IGNORANTLY.

Num. 15. 28. priests atone for the soul that sinneth *i.*
Deut. 19. 4. the case, whoso killeth his neighbour *i.*
Acts 17. 23. whom therefore ye *i.* worship I declare
1 *Tim.* 1. 13. had mercy, because I did it *i.* in unbel.

ISLAND.

Job 22. 30. he shall deliver the *i.* of the innocent
Isa. 34. 14. shall meet with the wild beasts of the *i.*
Acts 27. 16. and running under a certain *i.* Clauda
26. howbeit, we must be cast on a certain *i.*
28. 1. they knew that the *i.* was called Melita
7. were possessions of the chief man of the *i.*
9. others who had diseases in the *i.* were healed
Rev. 6. 14. every *i.* was moved out of its place
16. 20. every *i.* fled away, mountains not found

ISLANDS.

Isa. 11. 11. to receive his people from the *i.* of the sea
13. 22. wild beasts of the *i.* shall cry in their houses
41. 1. keep silence before me, O *i.* and let people
42. 12. and declare the Lord's praise in the *i.*
15. I will make the rivers *i.* and dry up the pools
59. 18. to the *i.* he will repay recompence
Jer. 50. 39. wild beasts of the *i.* shall dwell there

ISLE.

Isa. 20. 6. the inhabitants of the *i.* say in that day
23. 2. be still, ye inhabitants of the *i.*
6. pass over to Tarshish, howl, inhabitants of *i.*
Acts 13. 6. they had gone through the *i.* to Paphos
28. 11. in a ship which had wintered in the *i.*
Rev. 1. 9. I John was in the *i.* that is called Patmos

ISLES.

Gen. 10. 5. by these were the *i.* of the Gentiles divided
Esth. 10. 1. Ahasuerus laid a tribute on the *i.*
Psal. 72. 10. the kings of the *i.* shall bring presents
97. 1. let the multitude of the *i.* be glad thereof
Isa. 24. 15. glorify ye the Lord in the *i.* of the sea
40. 15. he taketh up the *i.* as a very little thing
41. 5. the *i.* saw it and feared, the ends of the earth
42. 4. and the *i.* shall wait for his law
10. the *i.* and the inhabit. thereof sing his praise
49. 1. listen, O *i.* unto me, and hearken ye people
51. 5. the *i.* shall wait upon me and trust, 60. 9.
66. 19. the *i.* afar off that have not heard my fame
Jer. 2. 10. for pass over the *i.* of Chittim, and see
25. 22. the kings of the *i.* shall drink after them
31. 10. hear and declare it in the *i.* afar off
Ezek. 26. 15. shall not *i.* shake at sound of thy fall?
26. 18. the *i.* tremble, the *i.* shall be troubled
27. 3. who art a merchant of the people for many *i.*
6. benches of ivory, brought out of *i.* of Chittim
7. blue and purple from the *i.* of Elisha
15. many *i.* were the merchandise of thy hand
35. inhabitants of the *i.* shall be astonished at thee
39. 6. among them that dwell carelessly in the *i.*
Dan. 11. 18. after this he shall turn his face to the *i.*
Zeph. 2. 11. all the *i.* of heathen shall worship him

ILL.

Gen. 41. 3. kine came up *i.*-favoured, 4, 19, 20, 21.
43. 6. why dealt ye so *i.* with me as to tell the man?
Deut. 15. 21. hath any *i.* blemish thou shalt not offer
Job 20. 26. it shall go *i.* with him that is left
Psal. 106. 32. it went *i.* with Moses for their sakes
Isa. 3. 11. woe to the wicked, it shall be *i.* with him
Jer. 40. 4. if it seem *i.* to thee to come with me
Joel 2. 20. his stink and his *i.* savour shall come up
Mic. 3. 4. they behaved themselves *i.* in their doings
Rom. 13. 10. love worketh no *i.* to his neighbour

ILL *favouredness.*

Deut. 17. 1 not sacrifice goat wherein *i.-favouredness*

ILLUMINATED.

Heb. 10. 32. after ye were *i.* ye endured a great fight

IMAGE

Signifies, [1] *A representation or likeness of a person or thing,* 1 Sam. 19. 13. Mat. 22. 20. [2] *Any shape or picture representing God, or any creature, made for the sake of divine worship,* Exod. 20. 4. [3] *Our resemblance of God in righteousness and holiness,* Gen. 1. 26. [4] *Our likeness to God in respect of dominion and power,* 1 Cor. 11. 7. [5] *An essential, substantial, real, and adequate resemblance of the person of another,* Col. 1. 15. Heb. 1. 3. It is taken, [1] *Essentially, as Christ is the image of his Father,* Heb. 1. 3. [2] *Accidentally, or respecting qualities, spiritual and heavenly,* Gen. 1. 26, 27. [3] *Existentially, for the substance of the things whereof they be images,* 1 Cor. 15. 49. Heb. 10. 1. [4] *Mystically,* Rev. 13. 14, 15. | 14. 9, 11. [5] *Representatively,* 1 Cor. 11. 7. [6] *Civilly,* Mat. 22. 20. [7] *Imaginarily, as in apparitions,* Job 4. 16. [8] *Figuratively, for the transitory felicity and glory of the wicked,* Psal. 73. 20. [9] *Idolatrously,* 2 Kings 17. 10, 16.
Gen. 1. 26. let us make man in our *i.* 27. | 9. 6.
5. 3. Adam begat a son in his own *i.* after his *i.*
Lev. 26. 1. nor rear up a standing *i.* *Deut.* 16. 22.
1 *Sam.* 19. 13. Michal took an *i.* and laid it in bed
16. behold there was an *i.* in the bed with pillow
2 *Kings* 3. 2. for Jehoram put away the *i.* of Baal
10. 27. they brake down the *i.* and house of Baal
2 *Chr.* 33. 7. Manasseh set carved *i.* in the house of G.
Job 4. 16. an *i.* was before mine eyes was silence
Psal. 39. † 6. surely every man walketh in an *i.*
73. 20. when thou awakest, shalt despise their *i.*
Ezek. 8. 3. there was the seat of the *i.* of jealousy, 5.
Dan. 2. 31. behold, a great *i.* stood before thee
35. stone that smote *i.* became a great mountain
3. 1. Nebuchadnezzar the king made an *i.* of gold
5. fall down and worship the golden *i.* 10, 15.
Hos. 3. 4. Isr. shall abide many days without an *i.*
Mat. 22. 20. whose is this *i.*? *Mark* 12. 16. *Luke* 20. 24.
Acts 19. 35. of the *i.* which fell down from Jupiter
Rom. 1. 23. and changed the glory of G. into an *i.*
8. 29. to be conformed to the *i.* of his Son
11. 4. who have not bowed the knee to *i.* of Baal
1 *Cor.* 11. 7. forasmuch as he is the *i.* and glory of G.
15. 49. and as we have borne the *i.* of the earthy
2 *Cor.* 3. 18. and changed into the same *i.* from glory
4. 4. of Christ, who is the *i.* of God, *Col.* 1. 15.
Col. 3. 10. after the *i.* of him that created him
Heb. 1. 3. by his Son, the express *i.* of his person
10. 1. a shadow, not the very *i.* of the things
Rev. 13. 14. that they should make an *i.* to the beast
15. had power to give life unto the *i.* of the beast
14. 9. if any man worship the beast and his *i.*
11. they have no rest, who worsh. beast and his *i.*
15. 2. that have gotten victory over beast and his *i.*
16. 2. grievous sore fell on them that worshipped his *i.*
19. 20. he deceived them that worshipped his *i.*
20. 4. who had not worshipped the beast nor his *i.*

See GRAVEN.

IMAGE-*work.*

2 *Chron.* 3. 10. he made two cherubims of *i.-work*

Molten IMAGE.

Deut. 9. 12. they have made them a *molten i.*
Judg. 17. 3. the silver for my son to make a *molten i.*
Psal. 106. 19. made a calf and worshipped *molten i.*
Jer. 10. 14. for his *molten i.* is falsehood, 51. 17.
Hab. 2. 18. what profiteth the graven and *molten i.*

IMAGES.

Gen. 31. 19. Rachel had stolen her father's *i.* 34.
35. Laban searched but found not the *i.*
Exod. 23. 24. thou shalt overthrow and quite break down their *i.* 34. 13. *Deut.* 7. 5. *Num.* 33. 52.
Lev. 26. 30. I will cut down your *i.* and cast carcases

1 Sam.6.5. ye shall make i. of your emerods and mice
11. they laid the i. of their emerods on the cart
2 Sam.5.21. there they left their i. David burnt them
1 Kings 14. 9. hast made molten i. to provoke me
23. they also built them high places, i. and groves
2 Kings 10. 26. they brought i. out of house of Baal
11. 18. i. brake they in pieces, 18. 4. | 23. 14.
17. 10. set up i. || 16. they made them molten i.
23. 24. Josiah put away i. that were spied in land
2 Chron. 14. 3. and Asa broke down the i. 5.
23. 17. Jehoiada brake i. || 31. 1. Hezekiah brake i.
28. 2. Ahaz made also molten i. for Baalim
33. 22. for Amon sacrificed to all the carved i.
34. 3. Josiah cut down the carved and molten i. 4.
Isa. 17. 8. he shall not look to groves or i.
27. 9. the groves and i. shall not stand up
30. 22. ye shall defile the ornaments of molten i.
41. 29. their molten i. are wind and confusion
Jer. 43. 13. he shall break the i. of Beth-shemesh
50. 2. idols confounded, her i. are broken in pieces
Ezek.6.4. altars desolate, and your i. shall be broken
6. idols broken, and that your i. may be cut down
7. 20. but they made the i. of their abominations
16. 17. taken gold, and madest to thyself i. of men
21. 21. the king of Babylon consulted with i.
23. 14. the i. of the Chaldeans pourtrayed
30. 13. I will cause their i. to cease out of Noph
Hos. 10. 1. increas. altars, they have made goodly i.
2. shall break down their altars, spoil their i.
13. 2. they have made their molten i. of silver
Amos 5. 26. ye have borne the tabernacle of your i.
Mic. 5. 13. thy graven and standing i. will I cut off

IMAGERY.
Ezek. 8. 12. every man in the chamber of his i.

IMAGINE.
Job 6. 26. do ye i. to reprove words and speeches?
21. 27. the devices ye wrongfully i. against me
Psal. 2. 1. why do the people i. a vain thing?
38. 12. they seek my hurt and i. deceits all day long
62. 3. how long will ye i. mischief against me?
140. 2. which i. misch. in their heart, are for war
Prov. 12. 20. deceit is in the heart of them that i. evil
Hos. 7. 15. yet do they i. mischief against me
Nah. 1. 9. what do ye i. against the Lord?
Zech. 7. 10. let none i. evil against neighbour, 8. 17.
Acts 4. 25. why do the people i. vain things?

IMAGINATION
Signifies, [1] The first ideas, purposes, and motions of the soul, Gen. 6. 5. [2] Stubbornness, Deut. 29. † 19. Jer. 27. † 17. [3] Corrupt reasonings, 2 Cor. 10. † 5.
Gen. 6. 5. every i. of his heart was evil continually
8. 21. the i. of man's heart is evil from his youth
Deut. 29. 19. though I walk in the i. of mine heart
31. 21. for I know their i. 1 Chron. 28. 9.
1 Chron. 29. 18. keep this for ever in the i. of heart
Jer. 23. 17. say to every one walketh aft. i. of his h.
Luke 1. 51. scattered the proud in i. of their hearts

IMAGINATIONS.
1 Chr. 28. 9. L. understands all the i. of thoughts
Psal. 81. † 12. I gave them up to the hardness of i.
Prov. 6. 18. an heart that deviseth wicked i.
Lam. 3. 60. thou hast seen all their i. against me
61. thou hast heard all their i. against me
Rom. 1. 21. but became vain in their i. heart darken.
2 Cor. 10. 5. casting down i. that exalt. against God
See Heart.

IMAGINED.
Gen. 11. 6. nothing restrained, which they have i.
Ps. 10. 2. let them be taken in devices they have i.
21. 11. intended evils, they i. mischievous device

IMAGINETH.
Nah. 1. 11. there is one that i. evil against the Lord

IMMEDIATELY.
Mat. 4. 22. they i. left the ship and followed him
8. 3. i. his leprosy was cleans. Mark 1.42. Luke 5.13.
20. 34. i. received sight, Mark 10. 52. Luke 18. 43.
26. 74. i. the cock crew, Luke 22. 60. John 18. 27.
Mark 1. 12. i. the Spirit driveth him into wilderness
31. he lifted her up, and i. the fever left her
4. 15. Satan cometh i. and taketh away the word
17. when affliction ariseth, i. they are offended
Luke 1. 64. Zacharias, his mouth was opened i.
6. 49. i. it fell || 8. 44. i. her issue of blood staunched
13. 13. i. she was made straight and glorified God
19. 11. that the kingdom of God should i. appear
John 5. 9. and i. the man was made whole
Acts 9. 34. Eneas arose i. || 10. 33. I sent i. to thee
12. 23. i. the angel of the Lord smote him
16. 26. and i. all the doors were opened
Gal. 1. 16. i. I conferred not with flesh and blood
Rev. 4. 2. and i. I was in the Spirit, and behold

IMMORTAL
Signifies, [1] One who is simply and every way incorruptible, without possibility of perishing or dying, 1 Tim. 1. 17. [2] That which being once dead shall rise again, never to die more, 1 Cor. 15. 53. [3] The consummate glory and eternal blessedness of the saints in heaven, Rom. 2. 7.
1 Tim. 1. 17. now to the King eternal, i. invisible

IMMORTALITY.
Rom. 2. 7. to them who seek for i. eternal life
1 Cor. 15. 53. and this mortal must put on i.
54. when this mortal shall have put on i.
1 Tim. 6. 16. who only hath i. dwelling in the light
2 Tim. 1. 10. who brought i. to light thro' the gospel

IMMUTABLE.
Heb. 6. 18. that by two i. things, in which it was

IMMUTABILITY.
Heb. 6. 17. the i. of his counsel, confirmed it by an oath

IMPART.
Luke 3.11. two coats, let him i. to him that hath none
Rom. 1. 11. that I may i. to you some spiritual gift

IMPARTED.
Job 39. 17. nor hath he i. to her understanding
1 Thess.2.8. we were willing to have i. our own souls

IMPEDIMENT.
Mark 7. 32. they bring one that had i. in his speech

IMPENITENT.
Rom.2.5. thou, after thy i. heart, treasurest up wrath

IMPERIOUS.
Ezek. 16. 30. the work of an i. whorish woman

IMPLACABLE.
Rom. 1. 31. without natural affection, i. unmerciful

IMPLEAD.
Acts 19. 38. the law is open, let them i. one another

IMPORTUNITY.
Luke 11. 8. because of his i. he will rise and give him

IMPOSE.
Ezra 7. 24. it shall not be lawful to i. toll upon them

IMPOSED.
Heb. 9. 10. stood only in carnal ordinances i. on them

IMPOSSIBLE.
Mat. 17. 20. and nothing shall be i. unto you
19. 26. with men is i. Mark 10. 27. Luke 18. 27.
Luke 1. 37. for with God nothing shall be i. 18. 27.
17. 1. he said, it is i. but that offences will come
Heb. 6. 4. it is i. for those who were once enlightened
18. in which it was i. for God to lie, we might have
11. 6. but without faith it is i. to please God

IMPOTENT.
John 5. 3. in these lay a great multitude of i. folk
Acts 4. 9. of the good deed done to the i. man
14. 8. there sat a man at Lystra i. in his feet

IMPOVERISH.
Jer. 5. 17. they shall i. thy fenced cities thou trust.

IMPOVERISHED.
Judg. 6. 6. Isr. was greatly i. because of Midianites
Psal. 106. † 43. they were i. for their iniquity
Isa. 40. 20. he that is so i. chooseth a tree will not rot
Mal. 1. 4. whereas Edom saith, we are i. but will ret.

IMPRISONED.
Acts 22. 19. they know that I i. and beat them

IMPRISONMENT.
Ezra 7. 26. whether it be to death, banishment, or i.
Heb. 11. 36. others had trial of mockings, bonds, i.

IMPRISONMENTS.
2 Cor. 6. 5. approving ourselves in stripes, in i.

IMPUDENT.
Prov. 7. 13. and with an i. face she said to him
Ezek. 2. 4. for they are i. children, and stiff-hearted
3. 7. the house of Israel are i. and hard-hearted

IMPUTE
Signifies, [1] Freely to account or ascribe to a person that which he himself hath not, or did not, Rom. 4. 22. [2] To lay to one's charge, 2 Sam. 19. 19. [3] To be held guilty, Lev. 17. 4. [4] To suspect, 1 Sam. 22. 15.
1 Sam. 22. 15. let not king i. any thing to his servant
2 Sam. 19. 19. let not my Lord i. iniquity to me
Rom. 4. 8. blessed, to whom the Lord will not i. sin

IMPUTED.
Lev. 7. 18. nor shall it be i. to him that offereth it
17. 4. blood shall be i. to that man, he shed blood
Rom. 4. 11. that righteousn. might be i. to them also
22. therefore it was i. to him for righteousness, 23. Jam. 2. 23. Gal. 3. † 6.
24. for us also, to whom it shall be i. if we believe
5. 13. but sin is not i. when there is no law

IMPUTETH.
Psal. 32. 2. blessed to whom the L. i. not iniquity
Rom. 4. 6. to whom G. i. righteousn. without works

IMPUTING.
Hab. 1. 11. he shall pass over, i. his power to his god
2 Cor. 5. 19. G. in Chr. not i. their trespasses to them

IN
Signifies, [1] By or through, John 17. 10. Gal. 3. 8. [2] Out of, Exod. 31. 4. [3] With, or together with, Mat. 16. 27. [4] As, Mat. 10. 41. [5] From, Col. 3. 16. [6] Before, John 1. 1. [7] Upon, John 14. 1. [8] After, Mark 13. 24. compared with Mat. 24. 29.
Gen. 7. 16. Noah in the ark, and the L. shut him in
John 14. 10. that I am in the Father, 11, 20.
See Him, We, Thee, Them, Us, You.

INASMUCH.
Deut. 19. 6. i. as he hated him not in time past
Ruth 3. 10. i. as thou followedst not young men
Mat. 25. 40. i. as have done it to one of least of these
45. i. as ye did it not to one of the least of these

INCENSE
Signifies, [1] A rich perfume used in sacrifices, Exod. 37. 29. [2] The merits of Christ's death, Rev. 8. 3.
Exod. 30. 8. shall burn a perpetual i. before the L.
9. ye shall offer no strange i. thereon, nor sacrifice
37. 29. he made the pure i. of sweet spices
40. 5. shalt set the altar of gold for i. before the ark
Lev. 10. 1. each took his censer, and put i. thereon
16. 13. he shall put i. on the fire before the Lord
Num. 7. 14. one spoon of ten shekels full of i. 86.
16. 7. put i. in them before the L. to morrow, 17.
35. a fire consumed the 250 men that offered i.
46. Moses said to Aaron, put on i. and go quickly
47. he put on i. and made an atonem. for people
Deut. 33. 10. they shall put i. bef. thee, and sacrifi.
2 Chron. 30. 14. the altars of i. took they away
34. 25. forsaken me, and burned i. to other gods
Psal. 66. 15. I will offer to thee the i. of rams
141. 2. let my prayer be set forth before thee as i.
Isa. 1. 13. no oblations, i. is an abomination to me
43. 23. I have not wearied thee with i.
60. 6. shall bring gold and i. and shew forth praises
65. 3. sacrificeth and burneth i. on altars of brick
66. 3. he that burneth i. as if he blessed an idol
Jer. 6. 20. why cometh there to me i. from Sheba?
11. 12. and cry to the gods to whom they offer i.
17. to provoke me to anger, in offering i. to Baal
41. 5. offerings and i. in their hand to bring them
48. 35. and him that burneth i. to his gods
Ezek. 8. 11. and a thick cloud of i. went up
16. 18. thou hast set mine oil and i. before them
23. 41. whereupon thou hast set mine i. and oil
Mal. 1. 11. in every place i. shall be offered to my
Luke 1. 10. people were praying without at time of i.
Rev. 5. † 8. having harps, and golden vials full of i.
8. 3. there was given to him much i. to offer
4. the smoke of thy i. ascended up before God
See Altar, Burn, Burnt.

Sweet INCENSE.
Exod. 25. 6. spices for sweet i. 35. 8, 28. Num. 4. 16.
31. 11. to make oil and sweet i. for the holy place
Exod. 39. 38. they brought the oil and sweet i. to Moses
Lev. 16. 12. Aaron took a censer, hands full of sw. i.

INCENSED.
Isa. 41. 11. all they that were i. ag. thee be ashamed
45. 24. all that are i. against him shall be ashamed

INCHANTER.
Deut. 18. 10. there shall not be found an i. or a witch

INCHANTERS.
Jer. 27. 9. therefore hearken not to dreamers nor i.

INCHANTMENTS.
Exod. 7. 11. magicians did so with i. 22. | 8. 7, 18.
Lev. 19. 26. nor shall ye use i. nor observe times
Num. 23. 23. there is no i. against Jacob, nor divinat.
24. 1. Balaam went not to seek for i. but set his face
2 Kings 17. 17. Isr. used divinat. and i. and did evil
21. 6. Manasseh used i. 2 Chron. 33. 6.
Eccl. 10. 11. surely the serpent will bite without i.
Isa. 47. 9. and for the great abundance of thine i.
12. stand now with thine i. and thy sorceries

INCLINE.
Josh. 24. 23. i. your heart to the Lord God of Israel
1 Kings 8. 58. that he may i. our hea. to keep his law
Psal. 78. 1. i. your ears to the words of my mouth
119. 36. i. my heart unto thy testimoni. not to cov.
141. 4. i. not my heart to any evil thing
See Ear.

INCLINED.
Judg. 9. 3. and their hearts i. to follow Abimelech
Ps. 40. 1. L. i. unto me, and heard my cry, 116. 2.
119. 112. I have i. mine heart to perform thy stat.
Prov. 5. 13. nor i. mine ear to them who instruct. me
Jer. 7. 24. nor i. ear, 26. | 11. 8. | 17. 23. | 34. 14.
25. 4. but ye have not i. your ear, 35. 15. | 44. 5.

INCLINETH.
Prov. 2. 18. her house i. to death, and paths to dead

INCLOSE.
Cant. 8. 9. if she be a door, we will i. her with cedar

INCLOSED.
Exod. 39. 6. onyx-stone i. in ouches of gold, 13.
Judg. 20. 43. Israel i. the Benjamites round about
Ps. 17. 10. they are i. in their own fat, speak proudly
22. 16. the assembly of the wicked have i. me
Cant. 4. 12. a garden i. is my sister, my spouse
Lam. 3. 9. he hath i. my ways with hewn stone
Luke 5. 6. they i. great multit. of fishes, net brake

INCLOSINGS.
Exod. 28. 20. stones shall be set in gold in i. 39. 13.

INCONTINENCY.
1 Cor. 7. 5. that Satan tempt you not for your i.

INCONTINENT.
2 Tim. 3. 3. without natural affection, i. fierce

INCORRUPTIBLE.
Rom. 1. 23. and changed the glory of the i. God
1 Cor. 9. 25. we do it to obtain an i. crown
15. 52. and the dead shall be raised i. we changed
1 Pet. 1. 4. begotten us to an inheritance i. undefiled
23. being born of i. seed, by the word of God

INCORRUPTION.
1 Cor. 15. 42. it is sown in corrupt. it is raised in i.
50. neither doth corruption inherit i.
53. for this corruptible must put on i.
54. so when this corruptible shall have put on i.

INCREASE
Signifies, [1] The profit which cometh of the earth and of cattle, Deut. 7. 13. | 32. 13. Prov. 14. 4. [2] To grow, advance, or improve, Col. 1. 10. 1 Thess. 3. 12. [3] To be of more esteem and authority, John 3. 30. [4] To swell up, Gen. 7. 17. [5] To recruit, or reinforce, Judg. 9. 29. [6] To multiply, 1 Chron. 27. 23. [7] To aggravate or make greater, Ezra 10. 10. [8] To strengthen and enlarge, Luke 17. 5. [9] To make profitable and fruitful, 1 Cor. 3. 6, 7.

INCREASE, Substantive.
Lev. 19. 25. that it may yield you the i. thereof
25. 7. for thy cattle shall all the i. thereof be meat
36. take thou no usury of him or i. but fear God
37. not money for usury, lend him victuals for i.
26. 4. the land shall yield her i. and trees of field
20. your land shall not yield her i. or trees of field
Num. 18. 30. as the i. of the threshing floor
32. 14. risen up in father's stead an i. of sinful men
Deut. 7. 13. I will also bless the i. of thy kine, 28. 4.
14. 22. thou shalt truly tithe all the i. of thy seed
28. shall bring forth all tithe of the i. same year
16. 15. the Lord thy G. shall bless thee in all thy i.
28. 18. cursed shall be the i. of thy kine, 51.
1 Sam. 2. 33. i. of thy house shall die in flower of age
Neh. 9. 37. it yieldeth much i. to the kings over us
Job 20. 28. the i. of his house shall depart, and goods
31. 12. it is a fire would root out all mine i.
Psal. 67. 6. earth shall yield her i. and God bless us
78. 46. he gave also their i. to the caterpillar
85. 12. what is good, and our land shall yield her i.
Prov. 14. 4. but much i. is by the strength of the ox
18. 20. and with the i. of his lips he shall be filled
Eccl. 5. 10. shall not be satisfied with i. this is vanity
Isa. 9. 7. of the i. of his government shall be no end
Jer. 2. 3. first-fruits of his i. was holiness to the Lord
Ezek. 18. 8. not usury, nor hath taken any i. 17.
13. he hath given on usury, and taken i. 22. 12.
34. 27. tree yield fruit, and earth shall yield her i.
Zech. 8. 12. and the ground shall give her i.
1 Cor. 3. 6. I have planted, but God gave the i. 7.
Eph. 4. 16. maketh i. of the body to edifying in love
Col. 2. 19. all the body increaseth with the i. of God

INCREASE, Verb.
Lev. 25. 16. by years thou shalt i. the price thereof
Deut. 6. 3. hear, O Israel, that ye may i. mightily
7. 22. not at once, lest beasts of the field i. on thee
Judg. 9. 29. he said, i. thy army, and come out
1 Chr. 27. 23. he would i. Israel like to the stars
Ezra 10. 10. taken strange wives to i. trespass of Isr.
Job 8. 7. tho' small, yet thy lat. end should greatly i.
Psal. 44. 12. dost not i. thy wealth by their price
62. 10. if riches i. set not your heart upon them
71. 21. thou shalt i. my greatness, and comfort
73. 12. who prosper in the world, they i. in riches
115. 14. the Lord shall i. you more and more
Prov. 1. 5. a wise man will i. learning, 9. 9.
22. 16. he that oppresseth the poor to i. his riches
28. 28. but when they perish, the righteous i.

Eccl. 5. 11. goods *i.* they are increased that eat them
6. 11. there be many things that *i.* vanity
Isa. 29. 19. the meek shall *i.* their joy in the Lord
57. 9. and didst *i.* thy perfumes and didst send
Ezek. 5. 16. I will *i.* the famine on you and break
36. 29. I will *i.* it, and lay no famine on you
37. I will *i.* them with men like a flock
Dan. 11. 39. whom he shall *i.* with glory
Hos. 4. 10. they commit whoredom, and shall not *i.*
Zech. 10. 8. they shall *i.* as they have increased
Luke 17. 5. the apostles said, Lord, *i.* our faith
John 3. 30. he must *i.* but I must decrease
2 *Cor.* 9. 10. and *i.* the fruits of your righteousness
1 *Thess.* 3. 12. the Lord make you to *i.* in love
4. 10. we beseech you, that ye *i.* more and more
2 *Tim.* 2. 16. they will *i.* to more ungodliness

INCREASED.
Gen. 7. 17. the waters *i.* and bare up the ark, 18.
30. 30. it was little thou hadst, and it is now *i.*
43. Jacob *i.* ‖ *Exod.* 1. 7. Israel *i.* abundantly
Exod. 23. 30. till thou be *i.* and inherit the land
1 *Sam.* 14. 19. the noise in the host went on and *i.*
2 *Sam.* 15. 12. the people *i.* with Absalom
1 *Kings* 22. 35. the battle *i.* that day, 2 *Chr.* 18. 34.
1 *Chron.* 4. 38. the house of their fathers *i.* greatly
Ezra 9. 6. for our iniquities are *i.* over our head
Psal. 3. 1. how are they *i.* that trouble me
4. 7. in the time that their corn and wine *i.*
49. 16. when the glory of his house is *i.*
105. 24. and he *i.* his people greatly
Prov. 9. 11. the years of thy life shall be *i.*
Eccl. 2. 9. I *i.* more than all before me
5. 11. goods increase, they are *i.* that eat them
Isa. 9. 3. multiplied the nation, and not *i.* the joy
26. 15. thou hast *i.* the nation, O Lord
Jer. 5. 6. and their backslidings are *i.*
15. 8. their widows are *i.* above the sand of the seas
29. 6. take wives, that ye may be *i.* there
30. 14. wounded thee, because thy sins were *i.* 15.
Lam. 2. 5. hath *i.* in daughter of Judah mourning
Ezek. 16. 26. and hast *i.* thy whoredoms, 23. 14.
28. 5. by thy great wisdom hast thou *i.* thy riches
Dan. 12. 4. many run, and knowledge shall be *i.*
Hos. 4. 7. as they were *i.* so they sinned against me
10. 1. according to the fruit, he hath *i.* the altars
Zech. 10. 8. they shall increase, as they have *i.*
Mark 4. 8. other did yield fruit, that sprang up and *i.*
Luke 2. 52. Jesus *i.* in wisdom and stature
Acts 6. 7. and the word of God *i.* and the number
9. 22. but Saul *i.* the more in strength
16. 5. the churches *i.* in number daily
2 *Cor.* 10. 15. but having hope when your faith is *i.*
Rev. 3. 17. sayest, I am rich, and *i.* with goods

INCREASEST.
Job 10. 17. and *i.* thine indignation upon me

INCREASETH.
Job 10. 16. my affliction *i.* ‖ 12. 23. he *i.* nations
Psal. 74. 23. the tumult of those *i.* continually
Prov. 11. 24. there is that scattereth, and yet *i.*
23. 28. she *i.* the transgressors among men
24. 5. a man of knowledge *i.* strength
28. 8. he that by unjust gain *i.* his substance
29. 16. when wicked are multiplied, transgression *i.*
Eccl. 1. 18. he that *i.* knowledge, *i.* sorrow
Isa. 40. 29. to them that have no might, he *i.* strength
Hos. 12. 1. he daily *i.* lies and desolation
Hab. 2. 6. woe to him that *i.* that which is not his
Col. 2. 19. the body *i.* with the increase of God

INCREASING.
Col. 1. 10. and *i.* in the knowledge of God

INCREDIBLE.
Acts 26. 8. why thought *i.* God should raise dead?

INCURABLE.
2 *Chr.* 21. 18. Lord smote him with an *i.* disease
Job 34. 6. my wound is *i.* without transgression
Jer. 15. 18. why is my wound *i.* which refuseth
30. 12. thy bruise is *i.* ‖ 15. thy sorrow is *i.*
Mic. 1. 9. for her wound is *i.* it is come to Judah

INDEBTED.
Luke 11. 4. we forgive every one that is *i.* to us

INDEED.
Gen. 17. 19. Sarah thy wife shall bear a son *i.*
20. 12. yet *i.* she is my sister, she is daughter
37. 8. shalt thou *i.* reign over us, shalt thou *i.*?
10. shall I, thy mother, and brethren *i.* come
40. 15. for *i.* I was stolen away out of the land
Exod. 19. 5. if you will obey my voice *i.* 23. 22.
Lev. 10. 18. ye should *i.* have eaten it in holy place
Num. 12. 2. hath the Ld. *i.* spoken only by Moses?
21. 2. if thou wilt *i.* deliver this people
22. 37. am I not able *i.* to promote thee to honour?
Deut. 2. 15. *i.* the hand of the L. was against them
21. 16. son of the hated, which is *i.* the first-born
Josh. 7. 20. *i.* I have sinned against the Lord
1 *Sam.* 1. 11. if thou wilt *i.* look on the affliction
1 *Kings* 8. 27. God *i.* dwell on earth, 2 *Chr.* 6. 18.
2 *Kings* 14. 10. thou hast *i.* smitten Edom
1 *Chron.* 4. 10. O that thou wouldest bless me *i.*
21. 17. it is I that have sinned and done evil *i.*
Job 19. 4. and be it *i.* that I have erred
Psal. 58. 1. do ye *i.* speak righteousness, O congre.
Isa. 6. 9. hear ye *i.* see ye *i.* but perceive not
Jer. 22. 4. for if ye do this thing *i.* then kings
Mat. 3. 11. I *i.* baptize, *Mark* 1. 8. *Luke* 3. 16.
Mark 11. 32. men counted that he was a prophet *i.*
Luke 23. 41. we *i.* justly ‖ 24. 34. Lord is risen *i.*
John 1. 47. behold an Israelite *i.* in whom no guile
4. 42. that this is *i.* the Christ, the Saviour
6. 55. my flesh is meat *i.* my blood is drink *i.*
7. 26. do the rulers know *i.* that this is very Christ?
8. 31. if ye continue, then are ye my disciples *i.*
36. if the Son make you free, ye shall be free *i.*
Acts 4. 16. for that *i.* a notable miracle been done
Rom. 8. 7. not subject to the law, neither *i.* can be
14. 20. all things *i.* are pure, but it is evil for that
2 *Cor.* 11. 1. you could bear, and *i.* bear with me
Phil. 1. 15. some *i.* preach Christ, even of envy
3. 1. to write to you to me *i.* is not grievous
Col. 2. 23. which things *i.* have a shew of wisdom
1 *Thess.* 4. 10. *i.* ye do it towards all the brethren
1 *Tim.* 5. 3. honour widows that are widows *i.*
5. she that is a widow *i.* and desolate, 16.

1 *Pet.* 2. 4. disallowed *i.* of men, but chosen of God
See ENDEAVOUR.

INDIGNATION
Signifies, [1] *Wrath, anger*, Neh. 4. 1. Esth. 5. 9. [2] *Envy*, Acts 5. 17. [3] *The judgments of God, or the dreadful effects of his anger*, Isa. 26. 20. [4] *Messages of wrath*, Jer. 15. 17. [5] *A holy displeasure against one's self for sin, accompanied with a fear of falling into temptations, so as to be overcome by them*, 2 Cor. 7. 11.
2 *Kings* 3. 27. there was great *i.* against Israel
Neh. 4. 1. Sanballat took great *i.* mocked the Jews
Esth. 5. 9. Haman was full of *i.* against Mordecai
Job 5. † 2. and *i.* slayeth the silly one
10. 17. and there increasest thine *i.* upon me
Psal. 69. 24. pour out thy *i.* on them, and let none
78. 49. he cast on them wrath, *i.* and trouble
102. 10. because of thine *i.* and thy wrath
Isa. 10. 5. and the staff in their hand is mine *i.*
25. for yet a little while, and the *i.* shall cease
13. 5. Lord, and weapons, of his *i.* *Jer.* 50. 25.
26. 20. hide thyself till the *i.* be overpast
30. 27. his lips are full of *i.* his tongue as fire
30. with the *i.* of his anger, and with the flame
34. 2. for the *i.* of the Lord is on all nations
66. 14. *i.* shall be known towards his enemies
Jer. 10. 10. nations shall not be able to abide his *i.*
15. 17. for thou hast filled me with *i.*
Lam. 2. 6. hath despised in *i.* of his anger the king
Ezek. 21. 31. I will pour out mine *i.* upon thee
22. 24. the land not rained on in the day of his *i.*
31. therefore I poured out mine *i.* on them
Dan. 11. 30. and have *i.* against the holy covenant
Mic. 7. 9. I will bear the *i.* of the Lord
Nah. 1. 6. who can stand before his *i.*?
Hab. 3. 12. thou didst march through the land in *i.*
Zech. 1. 12. thou hast had *i.* these seventy years
Mal. 1. 4. people against whom the Lord hath *i.*
Mat. 20. 24. they were moved with *i.* against two
26. 8. they had *i.* saying, to what purpose is this
Luke 13. 14. ruler of synagogue answered with *i.*
Acts 5. 17. and they were filled with *i.*
Rom. 2. 8. but obey unrighteousness, *i.* wrath
2 *Cor.* 7. 11. yea what *i.*? yea what fear!
Heb. 10. 27. a fearful looking for of fiery *i.*
Rev. 14. 10. poured out into the cup of his *i.*

INDITING.
Psal. 45. 1. my heart is *i.* a good matter

INDUSTRIOUS.
1 *Kings* 11. 28. seeing the young man that he was *i.*

INEXCUSABLE.
Rom. 2. 1. therefore thou art *i.* O man, that judgest

INFALLIBLE.
Acts 1. 3. he shewed himself by many *i.* proofs

INFAMY.
Prov. 25. 10. and thine *i.* turn not away
Ezek. 36. 3. and ye are an *i.* of the people

INFAMOUS.
Ezek. 22. 5. they shall mock thee which art *i.*

INFANT.
1 *Sam.* 15. 3. slay man, woman, *i.* and suckling
Isa. 65. 20. shall be no more thence an *i.* of days

INFANTS.
Job 3. 16. or as *i.* which never saw light
Hos. 13. 16. their *i.* shall be dashed in pieces
Luke 18. 15. and they brought also *i.* to him

INFERIOR.
Job 12. 3. understanding I am not *i.* to you, 13. 2.
Dan. 2. 39. shall arise another kingdom *i.* to thee
2 *Cor.* 12. 13. what were ye *i.* to other churches
Heb. 2. † 7. madest him little *i.* to the angels

INFIDEL.
2 *Cor.* 6. 15. hath he that believeth with an *i.*?
1 *Tim.* 5. 8. denied faith, and is worse than an *i.*

INFINITE.
Job 22. 5. and are not thine iniquities *i.*?
Psal. 147. 5. great is Lord, his understanding is *i.*
Nah. 2. † 9. take the spoil of their *i.* store
3. 9. and Egypt were her strength, and it was *i.*

INFIRMITY
Signifies, [1] *Sickness, or feebleness of body*, 1 Tim. 5. 23. [2] *Afflictions, reproaches, and persecutions*, 2 Cor. 12. 10. [3] *Spiritual weakness, and defects in grace*, Rom. 6. 19. | 8. 26. [4] *Failings and mistakes, either through ignorance or weakness*, Rom. 15. 1.
Lev. 12. 2. the days of separation for her *i.*
Psal. 77. 10. I said, this is mine *i.* but I will
Prov. 18. 14. the spirit of a man will sustain his *i.*
Luke 13. 11. a woman which had a spirit of *i.*
12. woman, thou art loosed from thine *i.*
John 5. 5. which had an *i.* thirty-eight years
Rom. 6. 19. because of the *i.* of your flesh
Gal. 4. 13. ye know how through *i.* I preached
Heb. 5. 2. for he himself also is compassed with *i.*
7. 28. the law maketh high-priests which have *i.*

INFIRMITIES.
Mat. 8. 17. himself took our *i.* and bare our
Luke 5. 15. came to be healed by him of their *i.*
7. 21. in that hour he cured many of their *i.* 8. 2.
Rom. 8. 26. the Spirit also helpeth our *i.*
15. 1. strong ought to bear the *i.* of the weak
2 *Cor.* 11. 30. of the things which concern mine *i.*
12. 5. of myself I glory not, but in mine *i.* 9.
10. therefore I take pleasure in mine *i.*
1 *Tim.* 5. 23. use a little wine for thine often *i.*
Heb. 4. 15. be touched with the feeling of our *i.*

INFLAME.
Isa. 5. 11. woe to those continue till wine *i.* them

INFLAMING.
Isa. 57. 5. *i.* yourselves with idols under every tree

INFLAMMATION.
Lev. 13. 28. for it is an *i.* of the burning
Deut. 28. 22. the Lord shall smite thee with an *i.*

INFLICTED.
2 *Cor.* 2. 6. punishment which was *i.* of many

INFLUENCES.
Job 38. 31. canst thou bind the *i.* of Pleiades?

INFOLDING.
Ezek. 1. 4. a fire *i.* itself, and a brightness

INFORM.
Deut. 17. 10. according to all that they *i.* thee

INFORMED.
Dan. 9. 22. *i.* me, and talked with me, and said
Acts 21. 21. are *i.* of thee that thou teachest, 24.
24. 1. *i.* the governor against Paul, 25. 2, 15.

INGATHERING.
Exod. 23. 16. feast of the *i.* in the end of the year

INGRAFTED.
Jam. 1. 21. and receive with meekness the *i.* word

INHABIT.
Num. 35. 34. defile not the land which ye shall *i.*
Prov. 10. 30. the wicked shall not *i.* the earth
Isa. 42. 11. the villages that Kedar doth *i.*
65. 21. they shall build houses and *i.* them
22. they shall not build, and another *i.*
Jer. 17. 6. but shall *i.* the parched places
48. 18. thou daughter, that dost *i.* Dibon
Ezek. 33. 24. they that *i.* those wastes of Israel
Amos 9. 14. shall build the waste cities and *i.* them
Zeph. 1. 13. shall build houses, but not *i.* them

INHABITANT.
Isa. 5. 9. many houses great and fair without *i.*
6. 11. till the cities be wasted without *i.*
9. 9. Ephraim and the *i.* of Samaria shall know
12. 6. cry out and shout, thou *i.* of Zion
20. 6. the *i.* of this isle shall say in that day
24. 17. the pit and snare are on thee, O *i.* of earth
33. 24. the *i.* shall not say, I am sick
Jer. 2. 15. his cities are burned without *i.*
4. 7. thy cities shall be laid waste without an *i.*
9. 11. | 26. 9. | 33. 10. | 34. 22.
10. 17. gather thy wares, O *i.* of the fortress
21. 13. *i.* of the valley ‖ 22. 23. *i.* of Lebanon
44. 22. your land is a curse without an *i.*
46. 19. waste and desolate, without *i.* 51. 29, 37.
48. 19. O *i.* of Aroer ‖ 43. O *i.* of Moab
51. 35. be upon Babylon, shall the *i.* of Zion say
Amos 1. 5. I will cut off the *i.* from plain of Aven
8. and I will cut off the *i.* from Ashdod
Mic. 1. 11. pass away *i.* of Saphir, *i.* of Zaanan
12. the *i.* of Maroth waited carefully for good
13. O thou *i.* of Lachish, bind the chariot
15. will bring an heir to thee, O *i.* of Mareshah
Zeph. 2. 5. I will destroy, that there shall be no *i.*
3. 6. their cities destroyed, so that there is none *i.*

INHABITANTS.
Gen. 19. 25. he overthrew all the *i.* of the cities
Exod. 15. 14. shall take hold of the *i.* of Palestina
15. all the *i.* of Canaan shall melt away
Lev. 18. 25. the land itself vomiteth out her *i.*
25. 10. shall proclaim liberty to all the *i.* thereof
Num. 13. 32. is a land that eateth up the *i.* thereof
Deut. 13. 13. have withdrawn the *i.* of their city
15. thou shalt surely smite the *i.* of that city
Josh. 2. 24. even the *i.* of the country do faint
11. 19. that made peace, save the *i.* of Gibeon
17. 12. could not drive out the *i.* *Judg.* 1. 19, 27.
Judg. 2. 2. make no league with the *i.* of this land
5. 7. the *i.* of the villages ceased till I arose
23. curse ye bitterly the *i.* thereof
10. 18. be head over all the *i.* of Gilead, 11. 8.
21. 9. were none of the *i.* of Jabesh-gilead there
10. go and smite the *i.* of Jabesh gilead
Ruth 4. 4. saying, buy it before the *i.* and elders
1 *Kings* 17. 1. Elijah who was of the *i.* of Gilead
2 *Kings* 19. 26. their *i.* were of small power
1 *Chron.* 9. 2. first *i.* that dwelt in their possessions
2 *Chron.* 20. 23. stood against the *i.* of mount Seir
Job 26. 5. are formed from under the *i.* thereof
Psal. 33. 8. all the *i.* of world stand in awe of him
14. he looketh on all the *i.* of the earth
49. 1. hear this, give ear, all ye *i.* of the world
75. 3. the earth and all the *i.* thereof are dissolved
Isa. 10. 13. put down the *i.* like a valiant man
18. 3. all ye *i.* of the world, see ye, when he
23. 2. be still, ye *i.* of the isle, thou whom, 6.
24. 1. and scattereth abroad the *i.* thereof
5. the earth is defiled under the *i.* thereof
6. therefore the *i.* of the earth are burned
26. 9. the *i.* of the world will learn righteousness
18. nor have the *i.* of the world fallen
38. 11. behold man no more with the *i.* of the world
40. 22. the *i.* thereof are as grasshoppers
42. 10. isles and *i.* sing to the Lord a new song
11. let the *i.* of the rock sing, let them shout
49. 19. land too narrow by reason of the *i.*
Jer. 13. 13. I will fill the *i.* with drunkenness
19. 12. thus will I do to the *i.* thereof
21. 6. I will smite the *i.* of this city, man and beast
23. 14. as Sodom, and the *i.* thereof as Gomorrah
25. 29. for a sword upon the *i.* thereof, 50. 35.
26. 15. ye shall bring innocent blood on the *i.*
49. 8. turn back, dwell deep, O *i.* of Dedan, 30.
50. 34. the Lord will disquiet the *i.* of Babylon
51. 35. and my blood upon the *i.* of Chaldea
Lam. 4. 12. *i.* of the world would not have believed
Ezek. 29. 6. *i.* of Egypt shall know I am the Lord
Dan. 4. 35. *i.* of the earth are reputed as nothing
Mic. 6. 12. the *i.* thereof have spoken lies
16. that I should make the *i.* thereof an hissing
Zech. 8. 20. there shall come the *i.* of many cities
21. the *i.* of one city shall go to another
Rev. 17. 2. the *i.* of the earth have been made drunk
See JERUSALEM.

INHABITANTS *of the land.*
Gen. 34. 30. to make me to stink among the *i. of l.*
Exod. 23. 31. I will deliv. the *i. of l.* into your hand
34. 12. lest thou make a coven. with *i. of land*, 15.
Num. 32. 17. dwell in cities because of the *i. of land*
33. 52. shall drive out the *i. of l.* 55. 2 *Chr.* 20. 7.
Josh. 2. 9. all the *i. of the land* faint because of you
7. 9. all the *i. of land* shall hear of it and environ
9. 24. to destroy all the *i. of the land* from bef. you
1 *Sam.* 27. 8. these nations were of old the *i. of land*
1 *Chr.* 22. 18. he hath given *i. of l.* into my hand
Jer. 1. 14. an evil shall break forth on all the *i. of l.*
10. 18. behold, I will fling out the *i. of l.* at once
47. 2. men shall cry, and all the *i. of l.* shall howl
Hos. 4. 1. Lord hath a controversy with the *i. of l.*
Joel 2. 1. let all the *i. of the l.* tremble for the day
Zech. 11. 6. for I will no more pity the *i. of the l.*

INHABITED.
Exod. 16. 35. eat manna, till they came to a land *i.*

Lev. 16.22. goat bear their iniquities to a land not *i.*
2 *Sam.* 24. † 6. came to the nether land newly *i.*
Isa. 13. 20. it shall never be *i.* nor dwelt in
44. 26. thou shalt be *i.* || 45. 18. formed it to be *i.*
54. 3. and make the desolate cities to be *i.*
Jer. 6. 8. lest I make thee a land not *i.*
17. 6. shall inhabit in a salt land and not *i.*
22. 6. I will make thee cities which are not *i.*
46. 26. afterward it shall be *i.* as in the days of old
50. 13. it shall not be *i.* || 39. no more *i.* for ever
Ezek. 12. 20. the cities that are *i.* shall be laid waste
26. 20. when I shall set thee, that thou be not *i.*
29. 11. nor shall it be *i.* forty years
36. 10. the cities shall be *i.* and the wastes builded
38. 12. upon the desolate places that are now *i.*
Zech. 2. 4. Jerusalem be *i.* as towns without walls
9. 5. from Gaza, and Ashkelon shall not be *i.*
12. 6. Jerusalem shall be *i.* again in her place
14. 10. it shall be lifted up, and *i.* in her place
11. no destruction, but Jerus. shall be safely *i.*

INHABITERS.

Rev. 8. 13. saying, woe, woe, woe, to *i.* of the earth
12. 12. woe to the *i.* of the earth and of the sea

INHABITEST.

Psal. 22. 3. O, thou that *i.* the praises of Israel

INHABITETH.

Job 15. 28. he dwelleth in houses which no man *i.*
Isa. 57. 15. thus saith the lofty One that *i.* eternity

INHABITING.

Psal. 74. 14. be meat to the people *i.* the wilderness

INHERIT

Signifies, [1] *To possess by right of inheritance or succession,* Deut. 21. 16. [2] *To subdue by grace, and gain to the church of Christ,* Psal. 82. 8. Isa. 54. 3. [3] *To come into,* Luke 18. 18. 1 Cor. 6. 9. [4] *To be led away with,* Jer. 16. 19.

Gen. 15. 8. whereby shall I know that I shall *i.* it?
Exod. 32. 13. and they shall *i.* it for ever
Num. 18. 24. I have given it to the Levites to *i.*
26. 55. accord. to the names of tribes they shall *i.*
32. 19. we will not *i.* on yonder side Jordan
Deut. 1. 38. for he shall cause Israel to *i.* it
12. 10. which the Lord God giveth you to *i.*
21. 16. he maketh his sons to *i.* what he hath
Judg. 11. 2. thou shalt not *i.* in our father's house
1 *Sam.* 2. 8. to make them *i.* the throne of glory
Psal. 25. 13. and his seed shall *i.* the earth
37. 9. that wait on the Lord shall *i.* the earth
11. but the meek shall *i.* the earth, *Mat.* 5. 5.
22. such as be blessed of him shall *i.* the earth
69. 36. the seed also of his servants shall *i.* it
82. 8. arise, O God, for thou shalt *i.* all nations
Prov. 3. 35. the wise shall *i.* glory, but shame
8. 21. cause those who love me to *i.* substance
11. 29. troubleth his own house, shall *i.* the wind
14. 18. the simple *i.* folly, but the prudent
Isa. 49. 8. to cause to *i.* the desolate heritages
54. 3. and thy seed shall *i.* the Gentiles
65. 9. and mine elect shall *i.* it, and my servants
Jer. 12. 14. I have caused my people Israel to *i.*
49. 1. why then doth their king *i.* Gad?
Ezek. 7. † 24. they shall *i.* their holy places
47. 14. ye shall *i.* it, one as well as another
Zech. 2. 12. the Lord shall *i.* Judah his portion
Mat. 19. 29. and shall *i.* everlasting life
25. 34. come *i.* the kingdom prepared for you
Mark 10. 17. *i.* eternal life, *Luke* 10. 25. | 18. 18.
1 *Cor.* 6. 9. unrighteous not *i.* the kingdom of God
10. neither shall extortioners *i.* *Gal.* 5. 21.
15. 50. flesh and blood cannot *i.* the kingdom of God, nor doth corruption *i.* incorruption
Heb. 6. 12. who through faith *i.* the promises
1 *Pet.* 3. 9. are called, that ye should *i.* a blessing
Rev. 21. 7. he that overcometh shall *i.* all things

INHERIT *land.*

Gen. 15. 7. to give thee this *land* to *i.* it
28. 4. that thou mayest *i.* *land* wherein a stranger
Lev. 20. 24. I have said, ye shall *i.* their *land*
Num. 34. 13. this is the *land* ye shall *i.* by lot
Deut. 2. 31. possess, that thou mayest *i.* his *land*
16. 20. *i.* the *land* the Lord giveth thee, 19. 3.
Psal. 37. 29. the righteous shall *i.* the *land*
34. and he shall exalt thee to *i.* the *land*
Isa. 60. 21. they shall *i.* the *land* for ever
Ezek. 47. 13. border, whereby ye shall *i.* the *land*

INHERITANCE

Signifies, [1] *An estate, whether come by succession, or donation,* Num. 26. 54. Prov. 13. 22. [2] *Those whom God chooseth as his peculiar people,* Psal. 28. 9. | 94. 14. [3] *The land of Canaan,* Psal. 79. 1. [4] *The nations that should become the subjects of Christ's kingdom, and be governed and saved by him,* Psal. 2. 8. [5] *The kingdom of heaven,* 1 Pet. 1. 4. [6] *Hereditary,* Deut. 4. 20. [7] *Possession,* Num. 34. 2.

Gen. 31. 14. is there any portion or *i.* for us?
48. 6. after the name of their brethren in their *i.*
Exod. 15. 17. plant them in mountain of thine *i.*
Lev. 25. 46. for ever take them as an *i.* for ever
Num. 16. 14. or given us *i.* of fields or vineyards
18. 20. have no *i.* for I am thy part and thine *i.*
27. 8. shall cause his *i.* to pass to his daughters
9. *i.* to brethren || 10. *i.* to father's brethren
32. 19. our *i.* is fallen on this side, 32. | 34. 15.
34. 18. take one prince, to divide the land by *i.*
36. 3. and shall be put to the *i.* of the tribe, 4.
9. nor *i.* remove from one tribe to another
Deut. 4. 20. a people of *i.* as ye are this day
9. 26. destroy not thine *i.* || 29. they are thy *i.*
32. 9. Jacob is the lot of his *i.*
Josh. 13. 14. sacrifices of Lord their *i.* 18. 7.
33. the Lord God of Israel was their *i.*
14. 2. by lot was their *i.* *Psal.* 78. 55.
14. Hebron therefore became the *i.* of Caleb
17. 6. daughters of Manasseh had *i.* among sons
24. 28. every man to his *i.* *Judg.* 2. 6. | 21. 24.
Judg. 21. 17. must be an *i.* for them that escaped
Ruth 4. 6. cannot redeem *i.* lest mar mine own *i.*
1 *Sam.* 10. 1. hath anointed thee captain over his *i.*
26. 19. from abiding in the *i.* of the Lord
2 *Sam.* 20. 1. nor *i.* in son of Jesse, 1 *Kings* 12. 16.
2 *Sam.* 21. 3. that ye may bless the *i.* of the Lord
1 *Kings* 8. 51. they be thy people and thy *i.* 53.
21. 3. give the *i.* of my fathers to thee, 4.
2 *Kings* 21. 14. will forsake the remnant of mine *i.*
1 *Chron.* 16. 18. land of Canaan, the lot of your *i.*
Neh. 11. 20. in all cities, every one in his *i.*
Job 31. 2. what *i.* of the Almighty from on high?
Psal. 16. 5. the Lord is the portion of mine *i.*
28. 9. bless thine *i.* || 33. 12. chosen for his *i.*
37. 18. and their *i.* shall be for ever
47. 4. he shall choose our *i.* for us
68. 9. whereby thou didst confirm thine *i.*
74. 2. the rod of thine *i.* thou hast redeemed
78. 62. and was wroth with his *i.*
71. he brought him to feed Israel his *i.*
79. 1. O God, the heathen are come into thine *i.*
94. 14. not cast off, neither will he forsake his *i.*
105. 11. the land of Canaan, the lot of your *i.*
106. 5. that I may glory with thine *i.*
40. insomuch, that he abhorred his own *i.*
Prov. 13. 22. a good man leaveth an *i.* to children
17. 2. shall have part of the *i.* among the brethren
19. 14. house and riches are the *i.* of fathers
20. 21. an *i.* may be gotten hastily at the beginning
Eccl. 7. 11. wisdom is good with an *i.*
Isa. 19. 25. blessed be Israel mine *i.*
47. 6. I have polluted mine *i.* and given them
63. 17. for thy servants' sake, the tribes of thine *i.*
Jer. 10. 16. Israel is the rod of his *i.* 51. 19.
32. 8. for right of *i.* is thine, redemption is thine
Lam. 5. 2. our *i.* is turned to strangers, our houses
Ezek. 36. 12. shall possess thee, thou shalt be their *i.*
44. 28. it shall be unto them for an *i.* I am their *i.*
46. 16. the *i.* thereof shall be his son's, 17.
18. shall not take of the people's *i.* by oppression
47. 22. they shall have *i.* with you among tribes, 23.
Mat. 21. 38. kill him, and let us seize on his *i.*
Mark 12. 7. and the *i.* shall be ours, *Luke* 20. 14.
Luke 12. 13. speak, that he divide the *i.* with me
Acts 20. 32. to give you an *i.* among all sanctified
26. 18. and *i.* among them sanctified by faith in me
Gal. 3. 18. if the *i.* be of the law, it is no more
Eph. 1. 11. in whom also we have obtained an *i.*
14. which is the earnest of our *i.* till redemption
18. the riches of the glory of his *i.* in the saints
5. 5. hath any *i.* in the kingdom of Christ and God
Col. 1. 12. to be partakers of the *i.* of the saints
3. 24. and ye shall receive the reward of the *i.*
Heb. 1. 4. as he hath by *i.* obtained a name
9. 15. might receive the promise of eternal *i.*
1 *Pet.* 1. 4. begotten us to an *i.* incorruptible

For INHERITANCE.

Exod. 34. 9. pardon our sin, and take us *for* thine *i.*
Num. 18. 21. all the tenth in Israel *for* an *i.* 26.
26. 53. the land shall be divided *for* an *i.* 33. 54. | 34. 2. | 36. 2. *Deut.* 4. 21, 30. | 15. 4. | 19. 10. *Josh.* 13. 6, 7, 32. | 14. 1. | 19. 49, 51. *Ezek.* 45. 1. | 47. 22. | 48. 29.
Deut. 20. 16. the Lord doth give thee *for* an *i.* 21. 23. | 24. 4. | 25. 19. | 26. 1. *Josh.* 11. 23. | 13. 6. | 14. 13. 1 *Kings* 8. 36. 2 *Chron.* 6. 27. *Jer.* 3. 18.
1 *Chr.* 28. 8. leave it *for* an *i.* *for* children, *Ezra* 9. 12.
Psal. 2. 8. I shall give thee the heathen *for* thy *i.*
Ezek. 33. 24. the land is given us *for* an *i.*
44. 28. it shall be to them *for* an *i.* I am their
47. 14. this land shall fall unto you *for* an *i.*
Heb. 11. 8. which he should after receive *for* an *i.*

No or none INHERITANCE.

Num. 18. 20. thou shalt have no *i.* 23, 24. | 26. 62. *Deut.* 10. 9. | 14. 27, 29. | 18. 1, 2. *Josh.* 13. 14, 33. | 14. 3.
2 *Chron.* 10. 16. we have *no i.* in the son of Jesse
Acts 7. 5. and he gave him *none i.* in it

INHERITANCES.

Josh. 19. 51. these are the *i.* Joshua divided by lot

INHERITED.

Num. 32. 18. we will not return till Israel have *i.*
Josh. 14. 1. children of Israel *i.* the land of Canaan
Psal. 105. 44. they *i.* the labour of the people
Jer. 16. 19. surely our fathers have *i.* lies
Ezek. 33. 24. Abraham was one, and he *i.* the land
Heb. 12. 17. when he would have *i.* the blessing

INHERITETH.

Num. 35. 8. according to his inheriting which he *i.*

INHERITOR.

Isa. 65. 9. out of Judah an *i.* of my mountains

See ENJOY, ENJOIN.

INIQUITY

Signifies, [1] *Sin and wickedness in general,* Mat. 7. 23. [2] *Original corruption,* Psal. 51. 5. [3] *Punishment for sin,* Gen. 19. 15. Lev. 5. 1.

Gen. 15. 16. the *i.* of the Amorites is not yet full
19. 15. lest thou be consumed in the *i.* of the city
44. 16. God hath found out the *i.* of thy servants
Exod. 20. 5. visiting the *i.* of the fathers upon the children, 34. 7. *Num.* 14. 18. *Deut.* 5. 9.
34. 7. forgiving *i.* and transgression, *Num.* 14. 18.
9. go amongst us, and pardon our *i.* and our sin
Lev. 18. 25. therefore I do visit the *i.* thereof
Num. 5. 15. an offering bringing *i.* to remembrance
31. then shall the man be guiltless from *i.*
14. 19. pardon, I pray thee, the eye of this people
23. 21. he hath not beheld *i.* in Jacob, nor seen
Deut. 19. 15. nor rise up against a man for any *i.*
32. 4. he is a God of truth and without *i.* just
Josh. 22. 17. is the *i.* of Peor too little for us?
1 *Sam.* 3. 13. judge for the *i.* which he knoweth
14. the *i.* of Eli's house shall not be purged
15. 23. and stubbornness is as *i.* and idolatry
20. 8. if there be in me *i.* slay me thyself
25. 24. upon me let this *i.* be, 2 *Sam.* 14. 9
2 *Sam.* 14. 32. if there be *i.* in me, let him kill me
19. 19. let not my Lord impute *i.* to me
24. 10. to take away *i.* of thy servant, 1 *Chron.* 21. 8.
2 *Chr.* 19. 7. for there is no *i.* with Lord our God
Job 4. 8. they that plow *i.* reap the same
5. 16. the poor hath hope, and *i.* stoppeth her mouth
6. 29. return, I pray you, let it not be *i.* return
30. is there *i.* in my tongue? cannot my taste
11. 6. God exacteth less than thine *i.* deserveth
Job 11. 14. if *i.* be in thy hand, put it far away
15. 5. for thy mouth uttereth thine *i.*
16. filthy is man which drinketh *i.* like water
22. 23. thou shalt put away *i.* far from thy tabern.
31. 11. it is an *i.* to be punished by judges, 28.
33. 9. I am innocent, nor is there *i.* in me
34. 32. if I have done *i.* I will do no more
36. 10. he commandeth that they return from *i.*
21. take heed, regard not *i.* for this hast chosen
23. or who can say, thou hast wrought *i.*?
Psal. 7. 3. O Lord, if there be *i.* in my hands
14. behold, he travaileth with *i.* and conceived
10. † 7. under his tongue is mischief and *i.*
32. 2. blessed to whom the Lord imputeth not *i.*
5. and thou forgavest the *i.* of my sin
36. 3. the words of his mouth are *i.* and deceit
39. 11. when thou dost correct man for *i.*
41. 6. his heart gathereth *i.* to itself
49. 5. when the *i.* of my heels shall compass me
51. 5. behold I was shapen in *i.* and in sin mother
53. 1. they are corrupt, and have done abominable *i.*
55. 3. they cast *i.* upon me, and in wrath hate me
56. 7. shall they escape by *i.*? cast down, O God
66. 18. if I regard *i.* in my heart, Lord not hear me
85. 2. thou hast forgiven the *i.* of thy people
94. 20. throne of *i.* have fellowship with thee
107. 42. and all *i.* shall stop her mouth
109. 14. let the *i.* of his fathers be remembered
119. 3. they also do no *i.* they walk in his ways
133. let not any *i.* have dominion over me
125. 3. lest they put forth their hands to *i.*
Prov. 16. 6. by mercy and truth *i.* is purged
19. 28. the mouth of the wicked devoureth *i.*
22. 8. he that soweth *i.* shall reap vanity
Eccl. 3. 16. place of righteousness that *i.* was there
Isa. 1. 4. a people laden with *i.* a seed of evil doers
13. it is *i.* even the solemn meeting
5. 18. woe to them that draw *i.* with cords
6. 7. thine *i.* is taken away, and thy sin purged
14. 21. prepare for the *i.* of their fathers
22. 14. this *i.* shall not be purged from you
27. 9. by this shall the *i.* of Jacob be purged
29. 20. and all that watch for *i.* are cut off
30. 13. this *i.* shall be to you as a breach
40. 2. cry unto her, her *i.* is pardoned
53. 6. the Lord hath laid on him the *i.* of us all
57. 17. for the *i.* of his covetousness was I wroth
59. 3. for your fingers are defiled with *i.*
4. bring forth *i.* || 6. their works are works of *i.*
7. their thoughts are thoughts of *i.* wasting
64. 9. be not wroth, nor remember *i.* for ever
Jer. 2. 5. what *i.* have your fathers found in me
22. thine *i.* is marked before me, saith the Lord
3. 13. only acknowledge thine *i.* that thou hast
13. 22. for the greatness of thine *i.* are thy skirts
14. 20. we acknowledge the *i.* of our fathers
16. 10. what is our *i.* || 17. *i.* hid from mine eyes
30. 14. for multitude of thine *i.* 15. *Hos.* 9. 7.
32. 18. recompensest *i.* of fathers into the bosom
50. 20. the *i.* of Israel be sought for, and none
51. 6. flee out of Babylon, be not cut off in her *i.*
Lam. 2. 14. they have not discovered thine *i.*
4. 6. for the punishment of the *i.* of my people
22. the punishment of thine *i.* is accomplished, he will visit thine *i.* O daughter of Edom
Ezek. 4. 4. lay *i.* of the house of Israel upon it
7. 13. nor strengthen himself in the *i.* of his life
9. 9. the *i.* of the house of Israel is great
16. 49. this was the *i.* of thy sister Sodom
18. 8. that hath withdrawn his hand from *i.*
17. he shall not die for the *i.* of his father
30. repent, so *i.* shall not be your ruin
21. 23. he will call to remembrance your *i.* 24.
25. when *i.* shall have an end, 29. | 35. 5.
28. 15. wast perfect, till *i.* was found in thee
18. defiled thy sanctuaries by *i.* of thy traffic
44. 12. caused the house of Israel to fall into *i.*
Dan. 9. 24. to make reconciliation for *i.*
Hos. 7. 1. the *i.* of Ephraim was discovered
10. 9. against children of *i.* || 13. ye reaped *i.*
12. 8. find no *i.* in me || 11. is there *i.* in Gilead?
13. 12. the *i.* of Ephraim is bound up, his sin hid
14. 1. return, for thou hast fallen by thine *i.*
2. take away all *i.* and receive us graciously
Mic. 2. 1. woe to them that devise *i.* on their beds
3. 10. they build up Jerusalem with *i.*
7. 18. who is a God like to thee, that pardoneth *i.*?
Hab. 1. 3. why dost thou shew me *i.* and cause me
13. of purer eyes, and thou canst not look on *i.*
2. 12. woe to him that establisheth a city by *i.*
Zeph. 3. 5. the just Lord, he will not do *i.*
13. the remnant of Israel shall not do *i.*
Zech. 3. 4. I have caused thine *i.* to pass from thee
9. I will remove the *i.* of that land in one day
Mal. 2. 6. and *i.* was not found in his lips, he walked in peace, and did turn many away from *i.*
Mat. 13. 41. they shall gather them which do *i.*
23. 28. within ye are full of hypocrisy and *i.*
24. 12. because *i.* shall abound, love shall wax cold
Acts 1. 18. purchased a field with the reward of *i.*
8. 23. for I perceive thou art in the bond of *i.*
Rom. 6. 19. your members servants to *i.* unto *i.*
1 *Cor.* 13. 6. rejoiceth not in *i.* but in the truth
2 *Thess.* 2. 7. the mystery of *i.* doth already work
2 *Tim.* 2. 19. that nameth Christ, depart from *i.*
Tit. 2. 14. that he might redeem us from all *i.*
Heb. 1. 9. and thou hast hated *i.* therefore God
Jam. 3. 6. the tongue is a fire, a world of *i.*

See BEAR, COMMIT, COMMITTED.

His INIQUITY.

Num. 15. 31. *his i.* shall be upon him
Josh. 22. 20. that man perished not alone in *his i.*
Job 20. 27. the heavens shall reveal *his i.*
21. 19. God layeth up *his i.* for his children
Psal. 36. 2. until *his i.* be found to be hateful
Jer. 31. 30. die for *h. i.* *Ezek.* 3. 18, 19. | 7. 16. | 18. 26.
Ezek. 14. 7. the stumbling block of *his i.* 14.
18. 18. even he shall die in *his i.* 33. 8, 9.
33. 6. he is taken away in *his i.* but his blood
2 *Pet.* 2. 16. Balaam was rebuked for *his i.*

Mine INIQUITY.

Gen. 4. † 13. *mine i.* is greater than may be forgiven

1 Sam. 20. 1. what is mine i. and what is my sin?
2 Sam. 22. 24. I kept thyself from mine i. Ps. 18. 23.
Job 7. 21. why dost thou not take away mine i.?
10. 6. that thou inquirest after mine i.
14. thou wilt not acquit me from mine i.
14. 17. sealed in a bag, thou sewest up mine i.
31. 33. if I covered, by hiding mine i. in my bosom
Psal. 25. 11. O Lord, pardon mine i. for it is great
31. 10. my strength faileth because of mine i.
32. 5. and mine i. have I not hid, I said
38. 18. for I will declare mine i. I will be sorry for
51. 2. wash me throughly from mine i. cleanse

Their INIQUITY.

Lev. 26. 39. left of you, shall pine away in their i.
40. if they confess their i. and the iniquity of fath.
41. accept of the punishment of their i. 43.
Neh. 4. 5. and cover not their i. let not their sin be
Psal. 69. 27. add iniquity unto their i. and let them
78. 38. he forgave their i. ‖ 89. 32. I will visit their i.
94. 23. he shall bring upon them their i.
106. 43. they were brought low for their i.
Isa. 13. 11. I will punish the wicked for their i.
26. 21. to punish the inhabitants of earth for th. i.
33. 24. the people shall be forgiven their i.
Jer. 14. 10. he will now remember their i.
16. 18. and first, he will recompense their i.
18. 23. forgive not their i. nor blot out their sin
25. 12. that I will punish that nation for their i.
31. 34. all know me, for I will forgive their i.
33. 8. I will cleanse them from all their i.
36. 3. that I may forgive their i. and sin
31. I will punish his servants for their i.
Ezek. 4. 5. I have laid on thee the years of their i.
17. they may consume away for their i.
7. 19. the stumbling block of their i. 14. 3.
14. 10. they shall bear the punishment of their i.
29. 16. which bringeth their i. to remembrance
39. 23. Israel went into captivity for their i.
Hos. 4. 8. and they set their heart on their i.
5. 5. shall Israel and Ephraim fall in their i.
9. 9. he will remember their i. he will visit sins

Work INIQUITY.

Psal. 141. 4. to practise works with men that work i.
Isa. 31. 2. against the help of them that work i.
32. 6. his heart will work i. to practise hypocrisy
Hos. 6. 8. Gilead is a city of them that work i.
Mat. 7. 23. depart from me, ye that work i.

Workers of INIQUITY.

Job 31. 3. a strange punishment to the workers of i.
34. 8. which goeth in company with the work. of i.
22. where the workers of i. may hide themselves
Ps. 5. 5. foolish shall not stand, thou hatest all w. of i.
6. 8. depart from me all ye work. of i. Luke 13. 27.
14. 4. have all the work. of i. no knowledge? 53. 4.
28. 3. draw me not away with the workers of i.
36. 12. there are the w. of i. fallen, they are cast down
37. 1. nor be thou envious against the workers of i.
59. 2. deliver me from the work. of i. and save me
64. 2. from the insurrection of the workers of i.
92. 7. and when all the workers of i. do flourish
9. all the workers of i. shall be scattered
94. 4. and all the workers of i. boast themselves
16. or who will stand up for me against the w. of i.
125. 5. lead them forth with the workers of i.
141. 9. keep me from the gins of the workers of i.
Prov. 10. 29. destruction shall be to w. of i. 21. 15.

INIQUITIES.

Lev. 16. 21. confess over the goat all the i.
26. 39. in the i. of their fathers shall they pine
Ezra 9. 6. our i. are increased over our head
7. for our i. have we, our kings, been delivered
13. thou hast punished us less than our i. deserve
Neh. 9. 2. Israel confessed the i. of their fathers
Job 13. 23. how many are mine i. and sins
26. thou makest me to possess the i. of my youth
22. 5. thy wickedness great, and thine i. infinite
Psal. 38. 4. and mine i. are gone over my head
40. 12. mine i. have taken hold on me
51. 9. hide thy face from my sins, and blot out all i.
64. 6. they search out i. ‖ 65. 3. i. prevail against
79. 8. remember not against us former i.
90. 8. hast set our i. before thee, our secret sins
103. 3. bless the Lord, who forgiveth all thine i.
10. nor rewarded us according to our i.
130. 3. if thou, L. shouldest mark i. who stand?
8. and he shall redeem Israel from all his i.
Prov. 5. 22. his own i. shall take the wicked himself
Isa. 43. 24. thou hast wearied me with thine i.
53. 5. but he was bruised for our i.
59. 12. and as for our i. we know them
64. 6. our i. like the wind have taken us away
7. thou hast consumed us because of our i.
Jer. 11. 10. turned back to i. of their forefathers
14. 7. O Lord, though our i. testify against us
Lam. 4. 13. for i. of her priests that shed blood
Ezek. 28. 18. by the multitude of thine i. defiled
Dan. 4. 27. break off thine i. by shewing mercy
9. 13. that we might turn from our i. and underst.
16. for our sins, and for the i. of our fathers
Mic. 7. 19. he will turn, he will subdue our i.
Acts 3. 26. to bless in turning every one from his i.
Rom. 4. 7. blessed are they whose i. are forgiven
Rev. 18. 5. for God hath remembered her i.

Their INIQUITIES.

Lev. 16. 22. the goat shall bear on him all their i.
Psal. 107. 17. fools because of their i. are afflicted
Isa. 53. 11. justify many, for he shall bear their i.
Jer. 33. 8. and I will pardon all their i. whereby
Lam. 5. 7. our fathers sinned, we have borne their i.
Ezek. 32. 27. but their i. shall be on their bones
43. 10. that they may be ashamed of their i.
Heb. 8. 12. their i. will I remember no more, 10. 17.

Your INIQUITIES.

Num. 14. 34. forty years shall ye bear your i.
Isa. 50. 1. for your i. have you sold yourselves
59. 2. your i. separated between you and your God
65. 7. your i. I will recompense, and iniq. of fathers
Jer. 5. 25. your i. have turned away these things
Ezek. 24. 23. ye shall pine away for your i.
36. 31. and shall loathe yourselves for your i.
33. I shall have cleansed you from all your i.
Amos 3. 2. therefore I will punish you for all your i.

INJURED.

Gal. 4. 12. I am as ye are, ye have not i. me at all

INJURIOUS.

1 Tim. 1. 13. who was before a persecutor and i.

INJUSTICE.

Job 16. 17. not for i. in my hands, my prayer pure

INK.

Jer. 36. 18. I wrote them with i. in the book
2 Cor. 3. 3. written not with i. but the Spirit
2 John 12. I would not write with i. 3 John 13.

INK-HORN.

Ezek. 9. 2. with a writer's i. by his side, 3, 11.

INN.

Gen. 42. 27. to give his ass provender in the i.
43. 21. when we came to the i. we opened our sacks
Exod. 4. 24. by the way in the i. the Lord met him
Luke 2. 7. there was no room for them in the i.
10. 34. brought him to an i. and took care of him

INNER.

1 Kings 6. 27. he set the cherubims in the i. house
1 Chron. 28. 11. gave patterns of the i. parlours
Esth. 4. 11. shall come to the king into the i. court
5. 1. Esther stood in the i. court of the house
Ezek. 10. 3. and the cloud filled the i. court
42. 15. he made an end of measuring the i. house
46. 1. the gate of the i. court shall be shut six days
Acts 16. 24. who thrust them into the i. prison
Eph. 3. 16. strengthened with might in the i. man
See CHAMBER.

INNERMOST.

Prov. 18. 8. into the i. parts of the belly, 26. 22.

INNOCENCY.

Gen. 20. 5. in the i. of my hands have I done this
Psal. 26. 6. I will wash my hands in i. so compass
73. 13. in vain I have washed my hands in i.
Dan. 6. 22. before him i. was found in me
Hos. 8. 5. how long will it be ere they attain to i.?

INNOCENT.

Exod. 23. 7. the i. and the righteous slay thou not
Deut. 27. 25. that taketh reward to slay the i.
1 Sam. 14. †41. Saul said to the Lord, shew the i.
Job 4. 7. remember, whoever perished being i.?
9. 23. he will laugh at the trial of the i.
28. but I know that thou wilt not hold me i.
17. 8. the i. shall stir up against the hypocrite
22. 19. and the i. laugh them to scorn
30. he shall deliver the island of the i.
27. 17. and the i. shall divide the silver
33. 9. hast said, I am i. nor is iniquity in me
Psal. 10. 8. in secret places doth he murder the i.
15. 5. nor taketh reward against the i.
19. 13. I shall be i. from the great transgression
Prov. 1. 11. if they say, let us lurk privily for the i.
6. 29. whosoever toucheth her shall not be i.
28. 20. maketh haste to be rich shall not be i.
Jer. 2. 35. yet thou sayest, because I am i.
Mat. 27. 24. I am i. of the blood of this person
See BLOOD.

INNOCENTS.

Jer. 2. 34. is found the blood of the poor i.
19. 4. have filled this place with the blood of i.

INNUMERABLE.

Job 21. 33. after him, as there are i. before him
Psal. 40. 12. i. evils have compassed me about
104. 25. sea, wherein are things creeping i.
Jer. 46. 23. more than grasshoppers, and are i.
Luke 12. 1. an i. multitude gathered together
Heb. 11. 12. as the sand which is by the sea-shore i.
12. 22. ye are come to an i. company of angels

INORDINATE.

Ezek. 23. 11. she was the more corrupt in her i. love
Col. 3. 5. mortify fornication, i. affection

INQUISITION.

Deut. 19. 18. the judges shall make diligent i.
Esth. 2. 23. when i. was made of the matter
Psal. 9. 12. when he maketh i. for blood

INSCRIPTION.

Acts 17. 23. I found an altar with this i.

INSIDE.

1 Kings 6. 15. covered the walls on i. with wood

INSPIRATION.

Job 32. 8. i. of Almighty giveth understanding
2 Tim. 3. 16. all scripture is given by i. of God

INSTANT

Signifies, [1] *A short moment of time,* Isa. 29. 5.
[2] *To be very eager, or pressing,* Luke 23. 23.
[3] *To set about any thing with care and diligence,* Acts 26. 7.
Isa. 29. 5. yea, it shall be at an i. suddenly
30. 13. whose breaking cometh suddenly at an i.
Jer. 18. 7. at what i. I speak concerning, 9.
Luke 2. 38. she coming in that i. gave thanks
23. 23. and they were i. with loud voices
Acts 12. †5. i. prayer was made of the church
Rom. 12. 12. patient, continuing i. in prayer
2 Tim. 4. 2. preach the word, be i. in season, out of

INSTANTLY.

Luke 7. 4. they besought him i. saying
Acts 26. 7. our twelve tribes i. serving God

INSTRUCT

Signifies, *To train up, or teach,* Psal. 32. 8. We are instructed by, [1] *God,* Deut. 4. 36. Isa. 28. 26. [2] *Christ is a prophet, who teaches inwardly, and spiritually,* Acts 3. 22. [3] *The Spirit,* Neh. 9. 20. [4] *The church,* Cant. 8. 2. [5] *Ministers,* Dan. 11. 33. 2 Tim. 2. 25. [6] *The law,* Rom. 2. 18. [7] *The scriptures,* 2 Tim. 3. 16. [8] *Corrections,* Jer. 31. 19. [9] *The godly,* Job 4. 3. Acts 18. 25. [10] *The wicked,* Prov. 24. 32.
Deut. 4. 36. made thee hear, that he might i. thee
Neh. 9. 20. thou gavest thy good Spirit to i. them
Job 40. 2. shall he that contendeth i. him?
Psal. 16. 7. my reins also i. me in night seasons
32. 8. I will i. thee and teach thee in the way
Cant. 8. 2. in my mother's house, who will i. me
Isa. 28. 26. his God doth i. him to discretion
Dan. 11. 33. they that understand shall i. many
1 Cor. 2. 16. the mind of Lord, that he may i. him

INSTRUCTED.

Gen. 14. †14. Abraham armed his i. servants
Deut. 32. 10. the Lord led him about, he i. him
2 Kings 12. 2. wherein Jehoiada the priest i. him
1 Chron. 15. 22. Chenaniah i. about the song
25. 7. that were i. in the songs of the Lord
2 Chron. 3. 3. Solomon was i. for the building
Job 4. 3. behold thou hast i. many, and hast
Psal. 2. 10. be i. ye judges of the earth
Prov. 5. 13. inclined mine ear to them that i. me
21. 11. the wise is i. he receiveth knowledge
Isa 8. 11. the Lord spake thus to me and i. me
40. 14. who i. him, and taught him the path
Jer. 6. 8. be i. O Jerusalem, lest my soul depart
31. 19. after that I was i. I smote on my thigh
Mat. 13. 52. every scribe who is i. to the kingdom
14. 8. and she, being before i. of her mother
Luke 1. 4. of things wherein thou hast been i.
Acts 18. 25. this man was i. in the way of the Ld.
Rom. 2. 18. knowest his will, being i. out of law
Phil. 4. 12. every where, and in all things, I am i.

INSTRUCTING.

2 Tim. 2. 25. i. those that oppose themselves

INSTRUCTOR.

Gen. 4. 22. Tubal-Cain, an i. of every artificer
Rom. 2. 20. an i. of the foolish, a teacher of babes

INSTRUCTORS.

1 Cor. 4. 15. though ye have 10,000 i. in Christ, yet

INSTRUCTION.

Job 33. 16. he openeth the ears, and sealeth i.
Psal. 50. 17. seeing thou hatest i. and casteth my
Prov. 1. 2. to know wisdom and i. to perceive
3. to receive the i. of wisdom, justice, and judgm.
7. but fools despise wisdom and i. 15. 5.
8. my son, hear the i. of thy father, 4. 1.
4. 13. take fast hold of i. let her not go, keep her
5. 12. how have I hated i. and my heart despised
23. he shall die without i. and shall go astray
6. 23. and reproofs of i. are the way of life
8. 10. receive my i. ‖ 33. hear i. and be wise
9. 9. give i. to a wise man and he will be wiser
10. 17. he is in the way of life that keepeth i.
12. 1. whoso loveth i. loveth knowledge
13. 1. a wise son heareth his father's i.
18. shame shall be to him that refuseth i.
15. 32. he that refuseth i. despiseth his own soul
33. the fear of the Lord is the i. of wisdom
16. 22. but the i. of fools is folly
19. 20. hear counsel, and receive i. that thou
27. cease to hear the i. that causeth to err
23. 12. apply thy heart to i. and thine ears
23. buy the truth, also i. and understanding
24. 32. I looked upon it and received i.
Jer. 17. 23. they might not hear, nor receive i.
32. 33. they have not hearkened to receive i.
35. 13. will ye not receive i. to hearken to my
Ezek. 5. 15. it shall be a reproach, a taunt, an i.
Zeph. 3. 7. I said, surely thou wilt receive i.
2 Tim. 3. 16. all scripture is profitable for i.

INSTRUMENT.

Num. 35. 16. if he smite him with an i. of iron
Ps. 33. 2. sing to him with an i. of ten strings, 92. 3.
71. †22. I will praise with the i. of psaltery
144. 9. I will sing a new song, O God, on an i.
Isa. 28. 27. fitches not threshed with a threshing i.
41. 15. I will make thee a new sharp threshing i.
54. 16. that bringeth forth an i. for his work
Ezek. 33. 32. song of one that can play on an i.

INSTRUMENTS.

Gen. 49. 5. i. of cruelty are in their habitations
Exod. 25. 9. the pattern of all the i. thereof
Num. 3. 8. shall keep all the i. of the tabernacle
4. 12. they shall take all the i. of ministry
7. 1. sanctified all the i. ‖ 31. 6. with the holy i.
1 Sam. 8. 12. to make i. of war, and i. of chariots
18. 6. to meet king Saul with i. of music
1 Kings 19. 21. boiled their flesh with i. of oxen
1 Chron. 9. 29. to oversee all the i. of the sanctuary
16. 42. make a sound with musical i. of God
2 Chron. 30. 21. singing with loud i. to the Lord
Neh. 12. 36. Hanani with the musical i. of David
Psal. 7. 13. hath prepared for him the i. of death
68. 25. the players on i. followed after
87. 7. as the players on i. shall be there
150. 4. praise him with stringed i. and organs
Eccl. 2. 8. as musical i. and that of all sorts
Isa. 22. †24. hang on him all the i. of viols
32. 7. the i. also of the churl are evil
38. 20. we will sing my songs to the stringed i.
Jer. 46. †19. make thee i. of captivity
Ezek. 12. †3. prepare thee i. for removing
16. †39. shall take i. of thy ornament, 23. †26.
Dan. 6. 18. nor i. of music brought before him
Amos 1. 3. threshed Gilead with threshing i. of iron
6. 5. and invent to themselves i. of music
Hab. 3. 19. to the chief singer on my stringed i.
Zech. 11. 15. take thee i. of a foolish shepherd
Rom. 6. 13. nor yield members i. of unrighteousness
members as i. of righteousness to God

INSURRECTION.

Ezra 4. 19. this city hath made i. against kings
Psal. 64. 2. from the i. of the workers of iniquity
Mark 15. 7. lay bound with them that had made i.
who had committed murder in the i.
Acts 18. 12. the Jews made i. with one accord

INTANGLE

Signifies, *To perplex.* This may be, [1] *Corporeally,* Exod. 14. 3. [2] *Verbally,* Mat. 22. 15. [3] *Ceremonially,* Gal. 5. 1. [4] *Worldly,* 2 Tim. 2. 4. [5] *Spiritually, to return to, and continue in, sin,* 2 Pet. 2. 20.
Mat. 22. 15. how they might i. him in his talk

INTANGLED.

Exod. 14. 3. Pharaoh will say, they are i. in the land
Gal. 5. 1. be not i. again with the yoke of bondage
2 Pet. 2. 20. they are again i. therein and overcome

INTANGLETH.

2 Tim. 2. 4. i. himself with the affairs of this life

INTEGRITY.

Gen. 20. 5. in i. of my heart I have done this
6. I know thou didst this in the i. of thy heart
1 Kings 9. 4. as David thy father walked in i.
Job 2. 3. and still he holdeth fast his i.
9. his wife said, dost thou still retain thine i.?
27. 5. I will not remove my i. from me

Job 31. 6. be weighed, that God may know my *i.*
Psal. 7. 8. according to my *i.* that is in me
25. 21. let *i.* and uprightness preserve me
26. 1. I walked in my *i.* || 11. I will walk in *i.*
41. 12. as for me, thou upholdest me in my *i.*
78. 72. he fed them according to *i.* of his heart
Prov. 11. 3. the *i.* of the upright shall guide them
19. 1. better is the poor that walketh in his *i.*
20. 7. just man walketh in his *i.* children blessed

INTELLIGENCE.

Dan. 11. 30. *i.* with them that forsake covenant

INTEND.

Josh. 22. 33. did not *i.* to go up against them
2 Chron. 28. 13. ye *i.* to add more to our sins
Acts 5. 28. ye *i.* to bring this man's blood on us
35. what ye *i.* to do as touching these men

INTENDED.

Psal. 21. 11. for they *i.* evil against thee

INTENDEST.

Exod. 2. 14. *i.* thou to kill me, as the Egyptian

INTENDING.

Luke 14. 28. which of you *i.* to build a tower
Acts 12. 4. *i.* after Easter to bring him forth
† 20. Herod *i.* war with them of Tyre and Sidon
20. 13. sailed to Assos, there *i.* to take in Paul

INTENT.

2 Sam. 17. 14. to the *i.* the Lord might bring evil
2 Kings 10. 19. to *i.* he might destroy worshippers
2 Chron. 16. 1. to the *i.* he might let none go out
Ezek. 40. 4. to the *i.* that I might shew them
Dan. 4. 17. to the *i.* that the living may know
John 11. 15. not there to the *i.* ye may believe
13. 28. for what *i.* he spake this unto him
Acts 9. 21. and came hither for that *i.*
10. 29. I ask for what *i.* ye have sent for me.
1 Cor. 10. 6. to the *i.* we should not lust after
Eph. 3. 10. to the *i.* that now to the principalities

INTENTS.

Jer. 30. 24. till he have performed *i.* of his heart
Heb. 4. 12. is a discerner of the *i.* of the heart

INTERCESSION

Signifies, *A pleading or entreating in behalf of another*, Jerem. 7. 16. It is spoken, (I) *Of the intercession of Christ*, Isa. 53. 12. Heb. 7. 25. Which he performs, [1] *By appearing for us before the Father*, Heb. 9. 24. [2] *By presenting the merit of his sacrifice once offered*, Heb. 10. 12, 14. [3] *By declaring his will, that such and such blessings may be bestowed on the elect*, Heb. 10. 10. [4] *By the Father's consenting and agreeing to this will of his Son*, John 11. 42. (II) *Of the Holy Ghost in God's children*, Rom. 8. 26. (III) *Of men interceding*, [1] *For temporal blessings*, Jer. 7. 16. [2] *For spiritual blessings*, 1 Tim. 2. 1. (IV) *Of Elias*, *who complained against the ten tribes, who were generally become idolaters*, Rom. 11. 2.

Isa. 53. 12. and made *i.* for the transgressors
Jer. 7. 16. neither lift up cry, nor make *i.* to me
27. 18. let them now make *i.* to the Lord
36. 25. Elnathan and Gemariah had made *i.*
Rom. 8. 26. but the Spirit maketh *i.* for us, 27, 34.
11. 2. how he maketh *i.* to God against Israel
Heb. 7. 25. he ever liveth to make *i.* for them

INTERCESSIONS.

1 Tim. 2. 1. that prayers and *i.* be made for all men

INTERCESSOR.

Isa. 59. 16. he wondered that there was no *i.*

INTERMEDDLE.

Prov. 14. 10. a stranger doth not *i.* with his joy

INTERMEDDLETH.

Prov. 18. 1. seeketh and *i.* with all wisdom

INTERMISSION.

Lam. 3. 49. mine eye ceaseth not without any *i.*

INTERPRET.

Gen. 41. 8. none that could *i.* them to Pharaoh
12. to each according to his dream he did *i.*
1 Cor. 12. 30. do all *i.*? || 14. 5. except he *i.*
14. 13. pray that he may *i.* || 27. let one *i.*

INTERPRETATION

Signifies, [1] *A translation, or turning from one language into another*, 1 Cor. 12. 10. [2] *The gift of expounding visions and dreams*, Gen. 40. 8. [3] *Exposition, or shewing the sense and import of any thing*, 2 Pet. 1. 20.

Gen. 40. 5. each according to *i.* of dream, 41. 11.
12. this is the *i.* of it, 18. *Dan.* 4. 24. | 5. 26.
16. when the baker saw that the *i.* was good
Judg. 7. 15. when Gideon heard the *i.* thereof
Prov. 1. 6. to understand a proverb and the *i.*
Dan. 2. 4. and we shall shew the *i.* 7, 36.
45. the dream is certain, and the *i.* thereof sure
4. 19. and the *i.* thereof be to thy enemies
5. 12. he will shew the *i.* || 15. not shew the *i.*
7. 16. and made me to know the *i.* of the things
John 1. 42. Cephas, which is by *i.* a stone
9. 7. in the pool of Siloam, which is by *i.* sent
Acts 9. 36. named Tabitha, by *i.* is called Dorcas
13. 8. Elymas the sorcerer, so is his name by *i.*
1 Cor. 12. 10. to another the *i.* of tongues
14. 26. every one of you hath an *i.*
Heb. 7. 2. being by *i.* king of righteousness
2 Pet. 1. 20. no prophecy is of any private *i.*

INTERPRETATIONS.

Gen. 40. 8. Joseph said, do not *i.* belong to God?
Dan. 5. 16. I have heard that thou canst make *i.*

INTERPRETED.

Gen. 40. 22. as Joseph had *i.* to them, 41. 13.
Ezra 4. 7. written and *i.* in the Syrian tongue
Mat. 1. 23. which being *i.* is, God with us
Mark 5. 41. which is, being *i.* damsel, arise
15. 22. which is, being *i.* the place of a skull
34. *i.* my God, my God, why hast forsaken me
John 1. 38. being *i.* master || 41. *i.* the Christ
Acts 4. 36. is, being *i.* the son of consolation

INTERPRETER, S.

Gen. 40. 8. we dreamed, and there is no *i.* of it
42. 23. for Joseph spake to them by an *i.*
2 Chron. 32. † 31. howbeit in the business of *i.*
Job 33. 23. there be an *i.* one among a thousand
Isa. 43. † 27. and thy *i.* have transgressed
1 Cor. 14. 28. but if there be no *i.* let him keep

INTERPRETING.

Dan. 5. 12. *i.* of dreams was found in Daniel

INTREAT

Signifies, [1] *To supplicate or pray to*, Exod. 8. 8. Judg. 13. 8. [2] *To intercede, or speak in one's behalf*, Gen. 23. 8. 1 Sam. 2. 25. [3] *To entertain, or use kindly*, Gen. 12. 16. [4] *To urge, or press earnestly*, Ruth 1. 16. [5] *To hear, grant, or accept of*, Gen. 25. 21. [6] *To seek*, Prov. 19. 6. [7] *To give good words*, 1 Cor. 4. 13.

Gen. 23. 8. *i.* for me to Ephron the son of Zoar
Exod. 8. 8. then Pharaoh called for Moses, and said, *i.* the Lord, 28. | 9. 28. | 10. 17.
9. when shall I *i.* for thee || 29. I will *i.* Lord
Ruth 1. 16. Ruth said, *i.* me not to leave thee
1 Sam. 2. 25. if a man sin, who shall *i.* for him?
1 Kings 13. 6. *i.* the face of the Lord thy God
Job 11. † 19. yea, many shall *i.* thy face
Psal. 45. 12. among the people, shall *i.* thy favour
Prov. 19. 6. many will *i.* the favour of the prince
Jer. 15. 11. I will cause the enemy to *i.* thee well
Acts 7. 6. and should *i.* them evil 400 years
1 Cor. 4. 13. being defamed, we *i.* we are made
Phil. 4. 3. I *i.* thee also, true yoke-fellow
1 Tim. 5. 1. rebuke not, but *i.* him as a father

INTREATED.

Gen. 12. 16. he *i.* Abraham well for her sake
25. 21. Isaac *i.* for his wife, Lord was *i.* of him
Exod. 5. 22. why hast thou so evil *i.* this people?
8. 30. Moses went out and *i.* the Lord, 10. 18.
Deut. 26. 6. and the Egyptians evil *i.* us
Judg. 13. 8. then Manoah *i.* the Lord, and said
2 Sam. 21. 14. after that God was *i.* for the land
24. 25. Lord was *i.* for the land, the plague [stayed
1 Chron. 5. 20. they cried and he was *i.* of them
2 Chron. 33. 13. Manasseh prayed, and God was *i.*
Ezra 8. 23. we besought God, and he was *i.* of us
Job 19. 16. I called, I *i.* him with my mouth
17. tho' I *i.* for the children's sake of my body
Psal. 119. 58. I *i.* thy favour with my whole heart
Isa. 19. 22. he shall be *i.* of them and heal them
Mat. 22. 6. and *i.* them spitefully, *Luke* 18. 32.
Luke 15. 28. then came his father out, and *i.* him
20. 11. *i.* him shamefully, and sent him away
Acts 7. 19. the same evil *i.* our fathers
27. 3. and Julius courteously *i.* Paul
1 Thess. 2. 2. after that we were shamefully *i.*
Heb. 12. 19. *i.* the word should not be spoken
Jam. 3. 17. wisdom from above is easy to be *i.*

INTREATETH.

Job 24. 21. he evil *i.* the barren that beareth not

INTREATIES.

Prov. 18. 23. the poor useth *i.* but the rich
2 Cor. 8. 4. praying us with much *i.* that we receive

INTRUDING.

Col. 2. 18. *i.* into those things he hath not seen

INVADE.

2 Chr. 20. 10. whom thou wouldest not let Israel *i.*
Hab. 3. 16. he will *i.* them with his troops

INVADED.

1 Sam. 23. 27. the Philistines have *i.* the land
27. 8. David and his men *i.* the Geshurites
30. 1. the Amalekites *i.* the south, and Ziklag
2 Kings 13. 20. a band of Moabites *i.* the land
2 Chron. 28. 18. the Philistines had *i.* the cities

INVASION.

1 Sam. 30. 14. we made an *i.* on the south

INVENT.

Amos 6. 5. *i.* instruments of music, like David

INVENTED.

2 Chron. 26. 15. made engines *i.* by cunning men

INVENTIONS

Signify, [1] *Contrivances*, Prov. 8. 12. [2] *Sinful practices*, Psal. 99. 8. [3] *Idolatrous acts*, Psal. 106. 29, 39. [4] *New ways of making oneself more wise and happy than God has made him*, Eccl. 7. 29.

Psal. 99. 8. thou tookest vengeance of their *i.*
106. 29. provoked him to anger with their *i.*
39. and went a whoring with their own *i.*
Prov. 8. 12. and find out knowledge of witty *i.*
Eccl. 7. 29. but they have sought out many *i.*

INVENTORS.

Rom. 1. 30. *i.* of evil things, disobedient to parents

INVISIBLE.

Rom. 1. 20. the *i.* things of him are clearly seen
Col. 1. 15. who is the image of the *i.* God
16. that are in heaven and earth, visible and *i.*
1 Tim. 1. 17. now to the King immortal, *i.*
Heb. 11. 27. he endured, as seeing him who is *i.*

INVITED.

1 Sam. 9. 24. since I said, I have *i.* the people
2 Sam. 13. 23. Absalom *i.* all the king's sons
Esth. 5. 12. to-morrow am I *i.* to her with the king

INWARD.

Gen. 41. † 21. when they had come to the *i.* parts
Lev. 13. 55. shalt burn it in the fire, it is fret *i.*
1 Kings 7. 25. and all their hinder parts were *i.*
17. † 21. this child's soul come into his *i.* parts
2 Chron. 3. 13. they stood and their faces were *i.*
Job 19. 19. all my *i.* friends abhorred me
38. 36. who hath put wisdom in the *i.* parts
Psal. 5. 9. their *i.* part is very wickedness
49. 11. their *i.* thought is, that their houses
51. 6. behold, thou desirest truth in the *i.* parts
62. † 4. but they curse in their *i.* parts
64. 6. *i.* thought of every one of them is deep
Prov. 20. 27. searching all the *i.* parts of the belly
30. so do stripes the *i.* parts of the belly
Isa. 16. 11. my *i.* parts sound for Kir-haresh
Jer. 31. 33. I will put my law in their *i.* parts
Mark 6. † 19. Herodias had an *i.* grudge against him
Luke 11. 39. your *i.* part is full of ravening
Rom. 7. 22. I delight in the law of God after *i.* man
2 Cor. 4. 16. yet the *i.* man is renewed day by day
7. 15. his *i.* affection is more abundant to you

INWARDLY.

Psal. 62. 4. they bless with their mouth, but curse *i.*
Mat. 7. 15. but *i.* they are ravening wolves
Rom. 2. 29. but he is a Jew who is one *i.*

INWARDS.

Exod. 29. 13. the fat that covereth the *i.* 22. *Lev.* 3. 3, 9, 14. | 4. 8. | 7. 3. | 9. 19.
17. thou shalt wash the *i.* *Lev.* 1. 9, 13. | 9. 14.
Lev. 4. 11. his *i.* and dung burn in a clean place
8. 16. the fat on the *i.* Moses burnt on the altar
21. and he washed the *i.* and the legs with water

JOIN

Signifies, [1] *To knit, or unite together*, Job 41. 17. [2] *To make leagues and alliances*, Dan. 11. 6. [3] *To go close to*, Acts 8. 29. [4] *To be numbered, or reckoned with*, Job 3. 6. It is spoken, (I) *Materially, of things*, Isa. 5. 8. (II) *Personally, as* [1] *In marriage*, Eph. 5. 31. [2] *In affinity*, 2 Chron. 18. 1. [3] *In aiding or assisting*, Exod. 1. 10. [4] *In battle, army against army*, 1 Sam. 4. 2. 1 Kings 20. 29. (III) *Mentally*, 1 Cor. 1. 10. [4] *Carnally*, 1 Cor. 6. 16. [V] *Idolatrously*, Hos. 4. 17. [6] *Spiritually*, Jer. 50. 5. 1 Cor. 6. 17.

Exod. 1. 10. lest they *j.* to our enemies, and fight
2 Chron. 20. 35. did Jehoshaphat *j.* with Ahaziah
Ezra 9. 14. and *j.* in affinity with the people
Prov. 11. 21. hand *j.* in hand, the wicked, 16. 5.
Isa. 5. 8. woe to them that *j.* house to house
9. 11. the Lord shall *j.* his enemies together
56. 6. sons of stranger that *j.* themselves to Lord
Jer. 50. 5. come, let us *j.* ourselves to the Lord
Ezek. 37. 17. *j.* them one to another into one stick
Dan. 11. 6. they shall *j.* in the end of years
Acts 5. 13. of the rest durst no man *j.* himself
8. 29. go near and *j.* thyself to this chariot
9. 26. Saul assayed to *j.* himself to the disciples

JOINED.

Gen. 14. 3. all these kings were *j.* together in vale
8. they *j.* battle with them in the vale of Siddim
29. 34. this time will my husband be *j.* to me
Num. 18. 2. thy brethren of Levi be *j.* to thee, 4.
1 Sam. 4. 2. when they *j.* battle, Israel was smitten
1 Kings 20. 29. in the seventh day the battle was *j.*
2 Chron. 18. 1. Jehoshaphat *j.* affinity with Ahab
20. 36. he *j.* with Ahaziah to make ships, 37.
Ezra 4. 12. set up walls, and *j.* the foundations
Neh. 4. 6. all the wall was *j.* together unto half
Esth. 9. 27. all that *j.* should keep Purim
Job 3. 6. let it not be *j.* to the days of the year
41. 17. Leviathan's scales are *j.* one to another
23. the flakes of his flesh are *j.* together
Psal. 83. 8. Assur also is *j.* with them
Eccl. 9. 4. to him that is *j.* to all the living is hope
Isa. 13. 15. every one *j.* to them shall fall by sword
14. 1. and the strangers shall be *j.* with them
20. thou shalt not be *j.* with them in burial
56. 3. nor him that hath *j.* to the Lord speak
Ezek. 1. 9. their wings were *j.* one to another
46. 22. there were courts *j.* of forty cubits long
Hos. 4. 17. Ephraim is *j.* to idols, let him alone
Zech. 2. 11. many nations shall be *j* to the Lord
Mat. 19. 6. what God hath *j.* together, *Mark* 10. 9.
Luke 15. 15. he went and *j.* himself to a citizen
Acts 5. 36. about four hundred *j.* themselves
18. 7. whose house *j.* hard to the synagogue
1 Cor. 1. 10. that ye be perfectly *j.* in the same mind
6. 16. he which is *j.* to an harlot is one body
17. he that is *j.* to the Lord is one spirit
Eph. 4. 16. the whole body fitly *j.* together
5. 31. and shall be *j.* to his wife, and they two

See BAAL-PEOR.

JOINING, S.

1 Chron. 22. 3. David prepared iron for the *j.*
2 Chron. 3. 12. *j.* to the wing of the other cherub

JOINT.

Gen. 32. 25. hollow of Jacob's thigh was out of *j.*
Psal. 22. 14. and all my bones are out of *j.*
Prov. 25. 19. confidence is like a foot out of *j.*
Eph. 4. 16. by that which every *j.* supplieth

JOINTS.

1 Kings 22. 34. smote the king of Israel between the *j.* of the harness, 2. *Chron.* 18. 33.
Cant. 7. 1. the *j.* of thy thighs are like jewels
Dan. 5. 6. that the *j.* of his loins were loosed
Col. 2. 19. all the body by *j.* knit together
Heb. 4. 12. to dividing asunder of *j.* and marrow

JOINT-*heirs.*

Rom. 8. 17. heirs of God, and *j.-heirs* with Christ

JOT.

Mat. 5. 18. one *j.* or tittle shall in no wise pass

JOURNEY.

Gen. 24. 21. the Lord had made his *j.* prosperous
29. 1. Jacob went on his *j.* and came to the east
31. 23. Laban pursued after him seven days' *j.*
33. 12. let us take our *j.* || 46. 1. Israel took his *j.*
Exod. 13. 20. they took their *j.* from Succoth
16. 1. Israelites took their *j.* from Elim
Num. 9. 10. be in a *j.* yet shall keep the passover
13. is not in a *j.* and forbeareth to keep passover
10. 13. they first took their *j.* according to the
Deut. 1. 2. there are eleven days' *j.* from Horeb
10. 11. arise, take thy *j.* before the people
Josh. 9. 11. take victuals with you for your *j.*
13. become old, by reason of the very long *j.*
Judg. 4. 9. the *j.* thou takest is not for thy honour
1 Sam. 15. 18. and the Lord sent thee on a *j.*
2 Sam. 11. 10. camest thou not from thy *j.*?
1 Kings 18. 27. or he is in a *j.* || 19. 7. the *j.* is great
2 Kings 3. 9. fetched a compass of seven days' *j.*
Neh. 2. 6. for how long shall thy *j.* be?
Prov. 7. 19. the good man is gone a long *j.*
Mat. 10. 10. nor scrip for your *j.* nor two coats
Mark 6. 8. take nothing for their *j.* *Luke* 9. 3.
Luke 11. 6. a friend of mine in his *j.* is come to me
15. 13. the younger took his *j.* into a far country
John 4. 6. Jesus wearied with his *j.* sat thus
Rom. 1. 10. I might have a prosperous *j.* to come
15. 24. for I trust to see you in my *j.*
1 Cor. 16. 6. that ye may bring me on my *j.*
Tit. 3. 13. bring Zenas and Apollos on their *j.*
3 John 6. whom if thou bring forward on their *j.*

Days' JOURNEY.

Num. 11. 31. the quails fall a *day's j.* on this side
1 Kings 19. 4. himself went a *day's j.* into wildern
Jonah 3. 4. began to enter city a *day's j.* and cried
Luke 2. 44. went a *day's j.* among their acquaint.

Acts 1. 12. is from Jerusalem a sabbath *ay's j.*
See three DAYS.

JOURNEYED.

Gen. 11. 2. that as they *j.* they found a plain
12. 9. Abram *j.* going on toward the south, 20. 1.
13. 11. Lot *j.* east ‖ 33. 17. Jacob *j.* to Succoth
35. 5. Israel *j.* toward Bethel, and the terror
16. *j.* from Bethel ‖ 21. *j.* to the tower of Edar
Exod. 40. † 36. when cloud was taken up, Israel *j.*
37. cloud not taken up, they *j.* not, *Num.* 9. 21.
Num. 9. 17. after that the children of Israel *j.* 18.
19. kept the charge of the Lord, and *j.* not
20. at the commandment of the Lord they *j.* 23.
12. 15. *j.* not till Miriam was brought in again
Judg. 17. 8. came to the house of Micah as he *j.*
Acts 9. 3. as Saul *j.* he came near to Damascus
7. the men which *j.* with him stood, 26. 13.

JOURNEYING.

Gen. 12. † 9. Abram in going and *j.* toward
Num. 10. 2. make trumpets for *j.* of the camps
29. we are *j.* to the place of which Lord said
Luke 13. 22. and as he was *j.* towards Jerusalem
2 *Cor.* 11. 26. in *j.* often, in perils of waters

JOURNEYINGS.

Num. 10. 28. thus were the *j.* of Israel's armies

JOURNEYS.

Gen. 13. 3. Abram went on his *j.* from the south
Exod. 17. 1. *j.* according to the commandment
40. 36. taken up, they went on in *j.* *Num.* 10. 12.
38. the cloud was on tabernacle thro' all their *j.*
Num. 10. 6. they shall blow an alarm for their *j.*
33. 1. these are the *j.* of Israel with armies, 2.

JOY

Signifies, [1] *An agreeable and sweet affection of the soul, arising from some present or hoped-for good,* 1 Chron. 12. 40. [2] *The delight and satisfaction of the reasonable soul in its union with God in Christ, as the greatest and highest good, with an actual rejoicing in what is for his honour and glory,* Gal. 5. 22. [3] *That joyful and glorious state, unto which Christ himself should attain after his sufferings, and which he will communicate to all who believe in him,* Heb. 12. 2. [4] *That free, gracious, and liberal reward, which God will bestow on the righteous in the kingdom of heaven,* Mat. 25. 21, 23. [5] *The matter or cause of joy,* 1 Thess. 2. 20. [6] *Songs of thanksgiving and praise,* Psal. 42. 4. It is, (1) *Natural,* Prov. 23. 24. Eccl. 2. 10. (2) *Worldly,* Job 29. 13. Isa. 9. 3. (3) *Hypocritical,* Job 20. 5. Mat. 13. 20. (4) *Ungodly,* Prov. 15. 21. Hos. 9. 1. (5) *Mixed, worldly, and spiritual,* 1 Chron. 12. 40. Luke 10. 17. (6) *Heavenly,* Mat. 25. 21, 23. Luke 15. 7, 10. (7) *Spiritual,* Psal. 51. 12. Rom. 14. 17.

JOY, *Substantive.*

1 *Sam.* 18. 6. came out to meet king Saul with *j.*
1 *Chron.* 12. 40. for there was *j.* in Israel
15. 16. singers, by lifting up the voice with *j.*
25. went to bring the ark of the covenant with *j.*
29. 17. now have I seen with *j.* the people offer
2 *Chron.* 20. 27. to go again to Jerusalem with *j.*
Ezra 3. 13. not discern noise of the shout of *j.*
6. 16. dedication of the house of God with *j.*
22. and kept the feast seven days with *j.*
Neh. 8. 10. the *j.* of the Lord is your strength
12. 43. the *j.* of Jerusalem was heard afar off
† 44. for the *j.* of Judah and Levites which
Esth. 8. 16. the Jews had light, *j.* and honour
9. 22. turned to them from sorrow to *j.* they should make them days of feasting and *j.*
Job 8. 19. behold, this is the *j.* of his way
† 21. till he fill thy lips with shouting for *j.*
20. 5. the *j.* of the hypocrite is but for a moment
29. 13. I caused the widow's heart to sing for *j.*
33. 26. and he will see his face with *j.*
41. 22. and sorrow is turned into *j.* before him
Psal. 16. 11. in thy presence is fulness of *j.*
27. 6. offer in his tabernacles sacrifices of *j.*
30. 5. but *j.* cometh in the morning
42. 4. I went with the voice of *j.* and praise
43. 4. then will I go to God my exceeding *j.*
48. 2. the *j.* of the whole earth is mount Zion
51. 12. restore to me the *j.* of thy salvation
65. † 12. the little hills are girded with *j.*
67. 4. let the nations be glad and sing for *j.*
105. 43. he brought forth his people with *j.*
126. 5. they that sow in tears shall reap in *j.*
137. 6. if prefer not Jerusalem above my chief *j.*
Prov. 12. 20. but to the counsellors of peace is *j.*
14. 10. a stranger not intermeddle with his *j.*
15. 21. folly is *j.* to him destitute of wisdom
23. a man hath *j.* by the answer of his mouth
17. 21. and the father of a fool hath no *j.*
21. 15. it is *j.* to the just to do judgment
23. 24. who begetteth a wise child shall have *j.*
Eccl. 2. 10. I withheld not my heart from *j.*
26. God giveth him wisdom, knowledge, and *j.*
5. 20. God answered him in the *j.* of his heart
9. 7. go thy way, eat thy bread with *j.*
Isa. 9. 3. not increased the *j.* according to the *j.*
17. Lord shall have no *j.* in their young men
12. 3. with *j.* shall ye draw water out of wells
16. 10. *j.* is taken out of the plentiful field
24. 8. *j.* of the harp ceaseth ‖ 11. *j.* is darkened
29. 19. the meek shall increase their *j.* in Lord
32. 13. on all houses of *j.* ‖ 14. a *j.* of wild asses
35. 2. and rejoice even with *j.* and singing
10. with everlasting *j.* on their heads, 51. 11.
52. 9. break forth into *j.* ‖ 55. 12. go out with *j.*
60. 15. I will make thee a *j.* of many generations
61. 3. to give them the oil of *j.* for mourning
7. everlasting *j.* shall be unto them
65. 14. my servants shall sing for *j.* of heart
18. for behold, I create her people a *j.*
66. 5. but he shall appear to your *j.*
10. rejoice for *j.* with her, all ye that mourn
Jer. 15. 16. the word was to me the *j.* of my heart
31. 13. I will turn their mourning into *j.*
33. 9. it shall be to me a name of *j.* a praise
11. again there shall be heard the voice of *j.*
48. 27. since thou spakest, thou skippedst for *j.*

Jer. 48. 33. *j.* is taken from the plentiful field
49. 25. the city of praise, the city of my *j.*
Lam. 2. 15. the city, the *j.* of the whole earth
5. 15. the *j.* of our heart is ceased, our dance
Ezek. 24. 25. take from them the *j.* of their glory
36. 5. appointed, with the *j.* of all their heart
Hos. 9. 1. rejoice not, O Israel, for *j.* as other people
Joel 1. 12. because *j.* is withered away from men
Zeph. 3. 17. he will rejoice over thee with *j.*
Mat. 13. 20. anon with *j.* receiveth it, *Luke* 8. 13.
44. for *j.* thereof goeth and selleth all he hath
25. 21. enter thou into the *j.* of thy Lord, 23.
Luke 1. 44. the babe leaped in my womb for *j.*
6. 23. rejoice ye in that day, and leap for *j.*
10. 17. the seventy returned again with *j.*
15. 7. *j.* shall be in heaven over one sinner that
10. there is *j.* in the presence of the angels
24. 41. while they yet believed not for *j.*
John 3. 29. this my *j.* therefore is fulfilled
15. 11. I have spoken to you, that my *j.* might remain in you, and that your *j.* might be full
16. 20. your sorrow shall be turned into *j.*
21. for *j.* that a man is born into the world
22. and your *j.* no man taketh from you
24. ye shall receive, that your *j.* may be full
17. 13. might have my *j.* fulfilled in themselves
Acts 2. 28. make me full of *j.* with thy countenance
13. 52. disciples filled with *j.* and the Holy Ghost
20. 24. that I might finish my course with *j.*
Rom. 14. 17. kingdom of God is *j.* in the H. Ghost
15. 13. God fill you with all *j.* in believing
32. may come to you with *j.* by the will of God
2 *Cor.* 1. 24. but we are helpers of your *j.*
2. 3. that my *j.* is the *j.* of you all
7. 13. the more joyed we for the *j.* of Titus
8. 2. the abundance of their *j.* abounded to riches
Gal. 5. 22. the fruit of the Spirit is love, *j.* peace
Phil. 1. 4. in prayer, making request with *j.*
25. abide for your furtherance and *j.* of faith
2. 2. fulfil ye my *j.* ‖ 4. 1. my *j.* and crown
1 *Thess.* 1. 6. received the word with *j.* of Holy G.
2. 19. what is our hope or *j.* ‖ 20. ye are our *j.*
3. 9. for the *j.* wherewith we joy before God
2 *Tim.* 1. 4. that I may be filled with *j.*
Philem. 20. let me have *j.* of thee in the Lord
Heb. 12. 2. who for the *j.* that was set before him
13. 17. they may do it with *j.* and not with grief
Jam. 1. 2. count it *j.* when ye fall into temptation
4. 9. and your *j.* be turned into heaviness
1 *Pet.* 1. 8. ye rejoice with *j.* unspeakable
4. 13. ye may be glad also with exceeding *j.*
1 *John* 1. 4. that your *j.* may be full, 2 *John* 12.
3 *John* 4. I have no greater *j.* than to hear that my
Jude 24. to present you faultless with exceeding *j.*
See GLADNESS.

Great JOY.

1 *Kings* 1. 40. the people rejoiced with *great j.*
1 *Chr.* 29. 9. David the king rejoiced with *great j.*
2 *Chr.* 30. 26. so there was *great j.* in Jerusalem
Neh. 12. 43. G. had made them rejoice with *great j.*
Mat. 2. 10. saw the star, they rejoiced with *great j.*
28. 8. went from sepulchre with fear and *great j.*
Luke 2. 10. I bring you good tidings of *great j.*
24. 52. they returned to Jerusalem with *great j.*
Acts 8. 8. and there was *great j.* in that city
15. 3. they caused *great j.* to all the brethren
Philem. 7. for we have *great j.* in thy love

Shout, or *shouted for* JOY.

Ezra 3. 12. and many *shouted* aloud *for j.*
Job 38. 7. and all the sons of God *shouted for j.*
Psal. 5. 11. let those that put their trust in thee rejoice; let them ever *shout for j.* 35. 27.
32. 11. *shout for j.* all ye that are upright in heart
65. 13. the valleys *shout for j.* they also sing
132. 9. and let thy saints *shout for j.* 16.

JOY, *Verb.*

Psal. 21. 1. the king shall *j.* in thy strength
Isa. 9. 3. they *j.* before thee according to the joy
65. 19. I will rejoice and *j.* in my people
Hab. 3. 18. I will *j.* in the God of my salvation
Zeph. 3. 17. he will *j.* over thee with singing
Rom. 5. 11. but we also *j.* in G. thro' our Lord Jesus
Phil. 2. 17. yea, I *j.* and rejoice with you all
18. for the same cause also do ye *j.* and rejoice
1 *Thess.* 3. 9. for all the joy wherewith we *j.* for you

JOYED.

2 *Cor.* 7. 13. the more *j.* we for the joy of Titus

JOYFUL.

1 *Kings* 8. 66. they went to their tents *j.* and glad
Ezra 6. 22. for the Lord hath made them *j.*
Esth. 5. 9. then Haman went forth that day *j.*
Job 3. 7. let no *j.* voice come therein
Ps. 5. 11. let them that love thy name be *j.* in thee
35. 9. and my soul shall be *j.* in the Lord
63. 5. my mouth shall praise thee with *j.* lips
66. 1. make a *j.* noise to God, all ye lands
81. 1. make a *j.* noise to the God of Jacob
89. 15. blessed is the people that know the *j.* sound
95. 1. make a *j.* noise to the rock of our salvation
2. a *j.* noise to him with psalms, 98. 4. | 100. 1.
98. 6. make a *j.* noise before the Lord the king
8. let the hills be *j.* together before the Lord
113. 9. the barren to be a *j.* mother of children
149. 2. let the children of Zion be *j.* in their king
5. let the saints be *j.* in glory; let them sing
Eccl. 7. 14. in the day of prosperity be *j.* but in
Isa. 49. 13. sing, O heavens, and be *j.* O earth
56. 7. I will make them *j.* in my house of prayer
61. 10. my soul shall be *j.* in my God
2 *Cor.* 7. 4. I am exceeding *j.* in all our tribulation

JOYFULLY.

Eccl. 9. 9. live *j.* with the wife whom thou lovest
Luke 19. 6. Zaccheus came down and received him *j.*
Heb. 10. 34. ye took *j.* the spoiling of your goods

JOYFULNESS.

Deut. 28. 47. because servedst not the Lord with *j.*
Col. 1. 11. strengthened to long-suffering with *j.*

JOYING.

Col. 2. 5. absent, yet am I with you in the spirit, *j.*

JOYOUS.

Isa. 22. 2. thou art full of stirs, a *j.* city
23. 7. is this your *j.* city, whose antiquity is

Isa. 32. 13. on all the houses of joy in the *j.* city
Heb. 12. 11. no chastening seemeth to be *j.*

IRON

Signifies, [1] *The metal so called,* Deut. 3. 11. [2] *An axe,* Isa. 10. 34. [3] *Insensible hardness,* 1 Tim. 4. 2. [4] *Hard, dry, and barren, like iron,* Deut. 28. 23. [5] *Unbendable,* Isa. 48. 4. [6] *Mighty and irresistible power,* Psal. 2. 9. [7] *Fetters, or chains,* Psal. 107. 10. [8] It denotes *strength,* Dan. 2. 33, 41.

IRON, *Substantive.*

Num. 35. 16. smite him with an instrument of *i.*
Deut. 3. 11. Og's bedstead was a bedstead of *i.*
4. 20. Lord brought you out of the *i.* furnace, out of Egypt, 1 *Kings* 8. 51. *Jer.* 11. 4.
8. 9. a land whose stones are *i.* and out of hills
28. 23. the earth that is under thee shall be *i.*
48. put a yoke of *i.* on thy neck, *Jer.* 28. 14.
Josh. 8. 31. altar of stones, over which no man lift *i.*
17. 16. Canaanites have chariots of *i.* *Judg.* 1. 19.
Judg. 4. 3. had nine hundred chariots of *i.* 13.
1 *Sam.* 17. 7. his spear weighed 600 shekels of *i.*
2 *Sam.* 12. 31. under harrows of *i.* 1 *Chron.* 20. 3.
23. 7. but the man must be fenced with *i.*
1 *Kings* 6. 7. nor any tool of *i.* heard in the house
22. 11. Zedekiah made him horns of *i.* 2 *Chr.* 18.10.
2 *Kings* 6. 6. and the *i.* did swim
1 *Chron.* 22. 3. David prepared *i.* in abundance
29. 2. I prepared *i.* for the things of *i.* 7.
Job 28. 2. *i.* is taken out of the earth, and brass
40. 18. behemoth's bones are like bars of *i.*
41. 27. he esteemeth *i.* as straw, brass as wood
Psal. 2. 9. thou shalt break them with a rod of *i.*
105. 18. whose feet they hurt, he was laid in *i.*
107. 10. being bound in *i.* ‖ 16. cut bars of *i.*
149. 8. to bind their nobles with fetters of *i.*
Prov. 27. 17. *i.* sharpeneth *i.* so a man his friend
Eccl. 10. 10. if the *i.* be blunt, and he do not whet
Isa. 10. 34. cut down thickets of the forest with *i.*
45. 2. I will cut asunder the bars of *i.*
60. 17. for *i.* I will bring silver, for stones *i.*
Jer. 15. 12. shall *i.* break the northern *i.* and steel?
17. 1. the sin of Judah is written with a pen of *i.*
28. 13. thou shalt make for them yokes of *i.*
Ezek. 4. 3. take an *i.* pan, and set it for a wall of *i.*
27. 12. Tarshish was thy merchant with *i.*
19. Dan and Javan occupied with bright *i.*
Dan. 2. 33. his legs of *i.* feet part *i.* 34, 41, 42.
35. then was the *i.* and clay broken in pieces
40. the fourth kingdom shall be strong as *i.*
7. 19. the fourth beast, whose teeth were of *i.*
Amos 1. 3. thresh Gilead with instruments of *i.*
Mic. 4. 13. for I will make thy horn *i.* and hoofs
1 *Tim.* 4. 2. their conscience seared with a hot *i.*
Rev. 2. 27. rule them with a rod of *i.* 12. 5. | 19. 15.
9. 9. and they had as it were breast-plates of *i.*
See BRASS.

IRON.

Deut. 27. 5. shalt not lift up any *i.* tool on them
Josh. 17. 18. tho' they have *i.* chariots, and be strong
Job 19. 24. that they were graven with an *i.* pen
20. 24. he shall flee from the *i.* weapon
Isa. 48. 4. thy neck is an *i.* sinew, thy brow brass
Jer. 1. 18. I have made thee this day an *i.* pillar
Ezek. 4. 3. take thou unto thee an *i.* pan
Dan. 7. 7. it had great *i.* teeth, it devoured
Acts 12. 10. they came to the *i.* gate that leads

IRONS.

Job 41. 7. canst thou fill his skin with barbed *i.?*

IS

Signifies, [1] *The existence of a person, or thing,* 1 Cor. 8. 4. Heb. 11. 6. [2] *Represents,* Exod. 12. 11. Mat. 26. 26, 28. [3] *Leads or brings unto,* Rom. 6. 23. | 7. 7. [4] *Ought to be, or let it be,* Heb. 13. 4. [5] *Causeth, deserveth,* Rom. 8. 6.

Job 11. 6. that they are double to that which *is*
Luke 10. 22. who the son *is,* and who the Father *is*
John 1. 47. an Israelite indeed, in whom *is* no guile
3. 6. born of flesh *is* flesh, of the Spirit *is* spirit
13. but the Son of man which *is* in heaven
29. he that hath the bride *is* the bridegroom
4. 23. but the hour cometh, and now *is*
7. 27. no man knoweth whence he *is*
8. 47. he that *is* of God ‖ 18. 37. that *is* of the truth
9. 29. we know not from whence he *is,* 30.
Acts 4. 24. made the sea, and all that in them *is*
17. 19. what new doctrine whereof thou speakest *is*
Eph. 5. 17. understanding what the will of Lord *is*
2 *Thess.* 2. 4. above all that *is* called God, or that *is* worshipped, shewing himself that he *is* God
1 *Tim.* 4. 8. having promise of life that now *is*
Heb. 11. 6. must believe he *is,* and *is* a rewarder
1 *John* 3. 2. for we shall see him as he *is*
3. as he *is* pure ‖ 4. sin *is* the transgression of law
Rev. 1. 4. which *is,* was, and *is* to come, 8. | 4. 8.
17. 8. behold the beast that was, *is* not, yet *is*
10. and one *is* and the other *is* not yet come
See BETTER, CHRIST, CLEAN, DEAD, EPHRAIM, FOOL, GOOD, RIGHT.

IS *it.*

Gen. 19. 20. this city near, *is it* not a little one?
32. 29. wherefore *is it* thou askest after my name
42. 14. that *is it* that I spake to you, ye are spies
49. 28. this *is it* that their fathers spake to them
Exod. 2. 18. how *is it* that you are come so soon
20. why *is it* that ye have left the man?
5. 22. Moses said, why *is it* that thou hast sent
32. 18. neither *is it* the voice of them that cry
33. 16. *is it* not in that thou goest with us?
Deut. 3. 11. *is it* not in Rabbath of Ammon?
30. 11. nor *is it* far off ‖ 13. nor *is it* beyond the sea
Judg. 14. 15. to take that we have, *is it* not so?
1 *Sam.* 9. 20. *is it* not on thee, and on father's house?
10. 1. *is it* not because the Lord hath anointed
12. 17. *is it* not wheat-harvest to-day? I will call
2 *Kings* 1. 3. *is it* not because no God in Isr. 6, 16.
4. 26. *is it* well with thee, *is it* well with husband
9. 17. and let him say, *is it* peace, 18, 19, 22.
20. 19. *is it* not good, if peace be in my days
1 *Chr.* 21. 17. *is it* not I that commanded the people
Job 10. 3. *is it* good, 13. 9. ‖ 15. 23. saying, where *is it*

Job 22. 3. is it any pleasure to the Almighty that
Prov. 15. 23. a word in due season, how good is it!
Isa. 7. 13. is it a small thing for you to weary men
29. 17. is it not yet a very little while, and Lebanon
36. 7. is it not he whose high places and altars
58. 5. is it such a fast that I have chosen?
7. is it not to deal thy bread to the hungry?
Jer. 10. 5. neither also is it in them to do good
Lam. 1. 12. is it nothing to you, all ye that pass by?
Dan. 3. 14. is it true, O Shadrach, Meshach?
Amos 2. 11. is it not even thus, O children of Israel?
Mic. 1. 5. transgression of Jacob, is it not Samaria?
3. 1. is it not for you to know judgment?
Hab. 2. 13. is it not of the Lord of hosts that people
Hag. 2. 3. is it not in your eyes as nothing?
Zech. 5. 6. what is it? Mat. 26. 62. Mark 14. 60.
Acts 10. 4. | 21. 22. 2 Cor. 12. 13. Eph. 4. 9.
Mal. 1. 8. is it not e il || 3. 14. what profit is it
Mat. 12. 10. is it lawful to heal on, Luke 14. 3.
16. 11. how is it ye do not understand, Mark 8. 21.
19. 3. is it lawful to put away his wife, Mark 10. 2.
20. 15. is it not lawful for me to do what I will
22. 17. is it lawful to give tribute to Cesar, or not?
Mark 12. 14. Luke 20. 22.
26. 22. began to say, Lord, is it I? 25. Mark 14. 19.
62. what is it which these witness, Mark 14. 60.
Mark 2. 9. whether is it easier to say, thy sins
16. how is it that he eateth with publicans
3. 4. is it lawful to do good on sabbath, Luke 6. 9.
4. 40. he said, how is it that you have no faith?
9. 21. how long is it ago since this came to him?
10. 24. hard is it for them that trust in riches
11. 17. saying to them, is it not written, John 10. 34.
Luke 2. 49. he said to them, how is it ye sought me
12. 56. how is it that ye do not discern this time?
16. 2. how is it that I hear this of thee?
22. 64. prophesy, who is it that smote thee?
John 4. 9. how is it thou being a Jew askest of me?
14. 22. how is it that thou wilt manifest thyself?
Acts 5. 9. how is it that ye have agreed together
22. 25. is it lawful for you to scourge a Roman
1 Cor. 6. 5. is it so, that there is not a wise man
9. 11. is it a great matter if we reap your carnal
10. 16. is it not the communion of blood of Christ
12. 15. is it therefore not of the body, 16.
14. 26. how is it every one of you hath a psalm
1 Pet. 2. 20. what glory is it if when ye be buffeted
1 John 4. 3. even now already is it in the world

It IS.

Gen. 31. 29. it is in the power of my hand to do hurt
41. 16. and Joseph answered, it is not in me
Num. 13. 18. go up and see the land what it is
Deut. 31. 8. he it is that doth go before thee
1 Sam. 3. 18. it is the Lord, let him do what seems
2 Sam. 13. 35. so it is, Job 5. 27. Luke 12. 54.
21. 1. it is for Saul and for his bloody house
2 Kings 10. 15. is thine heart right as my heart? it is
1 Chr. 6. 10. he it is that executeth the priest's office
21. 17. even I it is that have sinned, and done evil
2 Chron. 5. 9. and there it is unto this day
Job 26. 3. how hast thou declared the thing as it is
Ps. 39. 4. to know the measure of my days what it is
Jer. 30. 7. it is even the time of Jacob's trouble
Lam. 3. 22. it is of Lord's mercies not consumed
Ezek. 21. 27. till he come whose right it is
Mat. 6. 10. will be done on earth, as it is in heaven
14. 27. of good cheer, it is I, be not afraid, John 6. 20.
16. 7. it is because we have no bread, Mark 8. 16.
John 1. 27. he it is who coming after me is preferred
1. 22. not because it is of Moses, but the fathers
13. 26. he it is to whom I shall give a sop
14. 21. hath commandments, he it is that loveth
Acts 12. 15. then said they, it is his angel
1 Cor. 3. 13. try every man's work, of what sort it is
11. 14. that if a man have long hair it is a shame
15. if a woman have long hair it is a glory to her
2 Cor. 5. 13. it is to God, or if we be sober it is for
Gal. 4. 29. but as then, even so it is now
Col. 1. 6. is come to you, as it is in all the world
2 Thess. 3. 1. be glorified, even as it is with you

See BEHOLD, BETTER, GOOD, WRITTEN.

IS not.

Gen. 37. 30. the child is not || 42. 13. and one is not, 32.
42. 36. and Jacob said, Joseph is not, Simeon is not
44. 5. is not this it in which my lord drinketh?
Exod. 4. 14. is not Aaron the Levite thy brother?
14. 12. is not this the word that we did tell thee?
Num. 12. 7. my servant Moses is not so, who is
16. 40. is not of seed of Aaron, come near to offer
23. 19. God is not a man that he should lie
Deut. 11. 10. the land is not as the land of Egypt
29. 15. also with him that is not here this day
31. 17. because our God is not amongst us
32. 6. is not he thy Father that bought thee?
31. for their rock is not as our rock
34. is not this laid up in store with me?
Judg. 4. 14. is not the Lord gone out before thee?
19. 12. a city that is not of the children of Israel
1 Sam. 15. 29. he is not a man that he should repent
20. 37. he cried, is not the arrow beyond thee?
21. 11. is not this David king of the land? 29. 3, 5.
2 Sam. 11. 3. is not this Bathsheba wife of Uriah?
14. 19. is not the hand of Joab with thee in this
20. 21. and Joab said, the matter is not so
23. 17. is not this the blood of the men that went
1 Kings 8. 41. stranger that is not of Isr. 2 Chr. 6. 32.
2 Kings 6. 19. this is not the way, nor this the city
32. is not the sound of his master's feet behind
1 Chron. 22. 18. is not the Lord your God with you
2 Chron. 25. 7. for the Lord is not with Israel
Esth. 4. 16. which is not according to the law
Job 4. 6. is not this thy fear, thy confidence
6. 13. is not my help in me || 9. 32. he is not a man as
21. 16. lo, their good is not in their hand
22. 5. is not thy wickedness great and infinite?
12. is not God in the height of heaven?
23. 8. behold, I go forward, but he is not there
27. 19. the rich man openeth his eyes, and he is not
Prov. 7. 19. for the good man is not at home, he is
23. 5. wilt thou set thy eyes on that which is not
7. eat, saith he, but his heart is not with thee
Eccl. 9. 11. I saw the race is not to the swift
Isa. 10. 9. is not Calno, is not Hamath, is not Samar.
17. 14. and behold, before the morning he is not
55. 2. spend money for that which is not bread
Jer. 5. 13. and the word is not in the prophets
8. 19. is not the Lord in Zion, is not her King in her
10. 16. the portion of Jacob is not like them, 51. 19.
23. I know that the way of man is not in himself
23. 29. is not my word like as a fire, saith the Lord
38. 5. the king is not he that can do any thing
49. 10. and Esau is not || 51. 9. but she is not healed
Ezek. 18. 25. ye say the way of the Lord is not equal,
is not my way equal? 29. | 33. 17, 20.
Dan. 2. 11. the gods, whose dwelling is not with flesh
30. as for me, this secret is not revealed to me
4. 30. is not this great Babylon, that I have built
Hos. 2. 2. for she is not my wife, nor I her husband
Mic. 2. 10. arise, depart, for this is not your rest
3. 11. yet will they say, is not the Lord among us
Hab. 2. 4. his soul which is lifted up is not upright
Zech. 3. 2. is not this a brand plucked out of the fire?
Mat. 13. 55. is not this the carpenter's son, is not his
20. 23 on my left, is not mine to give, Mark 10. 40.
22. 32. God is not the God of the dead, but of the
living, Mark 12. 27. Luke 20. 38.
24. 6. come to pass, but the end is not yet, Luke 21. 9.
28. 6. he is not here for he is risen, Luke 24. 6.
Luke 6. 40. the disciple is not above his master
22. 27. is not he that sitteth at meat greater
John 3. 18. he that believeth is not condemned
5. 31. my witness is not true || 9. 16. this man is not
11. 4. Jesus said, this sickness is not unto death
14. 24. the word which you hear is not mine, 7. 16.
18. 36. my kingdom is not of this world
Rom. 2. 28. he is not a Jew that is one outwardly
29. whose praise is not of men but of God
3. 29. is not he also of the Gentiles, yes, of Gentiles
8. 24. but hope that is seen is not hope
14. 17. the kingdom of God is not meat and drink
23. for whatsoever is not of faith is sin
1 Cor. 4. 20. for the kingdom of God is not in word
6. 13. now the body is not for fornication
7. 15. a brother or sister is not under bondage
11. 8. for the man is not of the woman, but the
20. this is not to eat the Lord's supper
12. 14. for the body is not one member, but many
13. 4. charity envieth not, is not puffed up
15. 39. all flesh is not the same flesh, but there is
58. that your labour is not in vain in the Lord
Gal. 1. 7. which is not another, but some trouble you
11. the gospel preached by me is not after man
3. 12. law is not of faith || 20. is not a mediator of one
6. 7. be not deceived, God is not mocked
Phil. 3. 1. to write the same to me is not grievous
Heb. 6. 10. for God is not unrighteous, to forget
2 Pet. 3. 9. the Lord is not slack concerning his
1 John 1. 8. the truth is n. in us, 2. 4. || 1. 10. word is n.
2. 15. the love of the Father is not in him
16. is not of the Father, but is of the world
3. 10. doth not righteousness, is not of God, 4. 3, 6.
5. 16. if brother sin a sin which is not unto death
Rev. 17. 8. beast thou sawest, was, and is not, 11.

It IS not.

Gen. 2. 18. it is not good, Prov. 18. 5. | 25. 27. | 28.
21. Hos. 8. 6. Mat. 19. 10.
31. 5. that it is not towards me as before
41. 16. it is not in me, God shall give an answer
Exod. 8. 26. and Moses said, it is not meet so to do
Deut. 32. 47. for it is not a vain thing for you
1 Sam. 6. 9. shall know it is not his hand that smote
20. 2. Jonathan said, God forbid, it is not so
Ezra 5. 16. been in building, yet it is not finished
Job 9. 35. I would speak, but it is not so with me
28. 14. it is not in me, the sea saith, it is not with me
35. 15. but now because it is not so, he hath visited
Prov. 31. 4. it is not for kings, O Lemuel, to drink
Jer. 5. 12. it is not he || 10. 23. it is not in man to direct
Ezek. 11. 3. which say, it is not near, let us build
Mat. 10. 20. for it is not ye that speak, but the Spirit
13. 11. to you it is given, but to them it is not given
14. 4. it is not law. to have her, 27. 6. Mark 6. 18.
15. 26. it is not meet to take children's, Mark 7. 27.
18. 14. even so it is not the will of your Father
Acts 1. 7. it is not for you to know the times
6. 2. it is not reason that we should leave the word
22. 22. for it is not fit that he should live
25. 16. it is not the manner of the Romans
Rom. 9. 16. so then it is not of him that willeth
2 Cor. 12. 1. it is not expedient for me to glory

IS there.

Gen. 31. 14. is there yet any portion or inheritance
Deut. 3. 24. what God is there in heaven or earth
4. 7. what nation is there so great, who hath God, 8.
5. 26. who is there of all flesh that hath heard
20. 5. what man is there that hath built, 7, 8.
32. 28. nor is there any understanding in them
Judg. 4. 20. is there any man || 14. 3. is there never a
21. 5. who is there among all the tribes of Israel, 8.
1 Sam. 2. 2. neither is there any rock like our God
17. 29. and David said, is there not a cause?
2 Sam. 7. 22. nor is t. any God besides thee, Isa. 44. 8.
9. 1. is there any that is left of Saul's house, 3.
1 Kings 22. 7. is there not here a prophet of the Lord
besides? 2 Kings 3. 11. 2 Chron. 18. 6.
2 Chr. 20. 6. in thy hand is t. not power and might?
36. 23. who is t. among you his people? Ezra 1. 3.
Neh. 6. 11. and who is there being as I am would go
Job 6. 30. is there iniquity in my tongue, 33. 9.
15. 11. is there any secret thing with thee?
Psal. 30. 9. what profit is t. in my blood when I go
Prov. 17. 16. is there a price in the hand of a fool
Eccl. 1. 10. is there any thing whereof it may be said
5. 11. what good is there to the owners thereof
Isa. 2. 7. nor is there any end of their treasures, nor
is there any end of their chariots
44. 19. nor is there knowledge to say, I have burnt
20. nor say, is there not a lie in my right hand?
Jer. 8. 22. is t. no balm in Gilead, is t. no physician
32. 27. I am Lord, is t. any thing too hard for me
37. 17. asked him, is there any word from the Lord
Hos. 12. 11. is there iniquity in Gilead, surely vanity
Amos 6. 10. is t. yet any with thee, ye shall say, no
Mat. 7. 9. what man is there of you, whom if his son
Acts 4. 12. nor is there salvation in any other, for no
Rom. 3. 1. what profit is there of circumcision?
9. 14. is there unrighteousness with God?

There IS.

Lev. 14. 35. there is as it were a plague in the house
Num. 11. 6. there is nothing at all besides manna
Deut. 32. 39. I am he, and there is no god with me
Judg. 19. 19. yet there is both straw and provender
21. 19. there is a feast of the Lord in Shiloh
1 Sam. 14. 6. for there is no restraint to the Lord
17. 46. may know that there is a God in Israel
20. 3. there is but a step between me and death
21. then come thou, for there is peace to thee
1 Kings 5. 4. there is neither adversary nor evil
8. 23. t. is no God like thee in heaven, 2 Chr. 6. 14.
46. there is no man that sinneth not, 2 Chr. 6. 36.
14. 2. behold there is Ahijah the prophet who told
1 Kings 22. 8. t. is yet one man, Micaiah son of Imlah
2 Kings 5. 8. he shall know t. is a prophet in Israel
Ezra 10. 2. yet there is hope in Israel, Job 11. 18.
Esth. 3. 8. there is a certain people scattered
Job 19. 29. that ye may know there is a judgment
22. 29. then thou shalt say, there is lifting up
32. 8. but there is a spirit in man, the inspiration
Psal. 14. 1. the fool hath said, there is no G. 53. 1.
19. 11. in keeping them there is great reward
34. 9. there is no want to them that fear him
46. 4. there is a river whose streams make glad
58. 11. verily there is a reward for the righteous
68. 27. there is little Benjamin with their ruler
146. 3. put not trust in man, in whom t. is no help
Prov. 11. 24. there is that scattereth, yet increaseth
13. 7. there is that maketh himself rich, yet hath
14. 9. but among the righteous there is favour
12. t. is a way that seemeth right to a man, 16. 25.
23. in all labour th. is profit || 23. 18. th. is an end
30. 11. there is a generation that curseth, 12, 13, 14.
Eccl. 3. 1. to every thing th. is a season, and a time
7. 15. there is a just man, there is a wicked man
8. 4. where the word of a king is, there is power
16. there is that neither day nor night seeth sleep
9. 2. there is one event || 4. for to him there is hope
Isa. 43. 11. and besides me there is no Saviour
44. 6. and beside me there is no God, 8. | 45. 5.
47. 1. t. is no throne, O daughter of the Chaldeans
48. 22. t. is no peace to wicked, 57. 21. Jer. 6. 14.
50. 2. because t. is no water || 53. 2. t. is no beauty
57. 10. saidst not, t. is no hope, Jer. 2. 25. | 18. 12.
Jer. 31. 17. t. is hope in thy end || 37. 17. he said, t. is
Ezek. 22. 25. there is a conspiracy of her prophets
32. 24. th. is Elam || 29. there is Edom, her kings
34. 5. were scattered, because there is no shepherd
Dan. 2. 28. there is a God that revealeth secrets
5. 11. there is a man in thy kingdom in whom is
Hos. 4. 1. because there is no truth nor mercy
Nah. 3. 19. t. is no healing of thy bruise, thy wound
Mat. 22. 23. the Sadducees, who say, there is no
resurrection, Mark 12. 18. 1 Cor. 15. 12.
Mark 10. 18. there is none good but one, that is God
Luke 14. 22. and yet t. is room || 15. 10. t. is joy in
John 8. 44. because there is no truth in him
11. 10. he stumbleth, because t. is no light in him
1 Cor. 3. 3. there is among you envying and strife
5. 1. it is reported there is fornication among you
8. 6. but to us there is but one God, the Father
15. 44. t. is a natural body, t. is a spiritual body
Gal. 5. 23. temperance, against such there is no law
Col. 3. 25. and there is no respect of persons
1 John 4. 18. there is no fear in love, but perfect love
5. 16. there is a sin unto death, I do not say he shall
17. and there is a sin not unto death

See NONE, ONE.

There IS not.

Gen. 47. 18. there is not ought left in sight of my lord
2 Sam. 13. 30. slain the king's sons, th. is not one left
1 Kings 5. 6. th. is n. among us that can skill to hew
2 Kings 1. 3. not because there is not a God in
Israel, 6.
19. 3. to birth, and th. is not strength to bring forth
Job 41. 33. upon earth there is not his like
Eccl. 4. 8. there is one alone, and there is not second
Cant. 6. 6. and there is not one barren among them
Luke 7. 28. there is not a greater prophet than John
1 Cor. 6. 5. that there is not a wise man amongst you
8. 7. there is not in every man that knowledge

ISLAND, &c. See after IGNORANTLY.

ISSUE

Signifies, [1] *A passage, way, or outlet*, Psal. 68. 20.
[2] *Children or posterity*, Gen. 48. 6. [3] *A flux or running*, Lev. 12. 7. [4] *Seed*, Ezek. 23. 20.
[5] *To spring or proceed from*, 2 Kings 20. 18.
[6] *To flow*, Ezek. 47. 8. [7] *To come forth hastily and violently*, Josh. 8. 22.

ISSUE, *Substantive*.

Gen. 48. 6. thy i. which thou begettest after them
Lev. 12. 7. the i. of her blood, 15. 25. Mat. 9. 20.
Mark 5. 25. Luke 8. 43, 44.
15. 2. running i. 3. | 22. 4. || 15. 8. hath the i. 28.
2 Sam. 3. 29. from the house of Joab, one hath an i.
Isa. 22. 24. shall hang on him the offspring and i.
Ezek. 23. 20. whose i. is like the i. of horses
Mat. 22. 25. having no i. left his wife

ISSUE.

2 Kings 20. 18. thy sons that i. from thee, Isa. 39. 7.
Ezek. 47. 8. these waters i. toward the east country

ISSUED.

Josh. 8. 22. other i. out of the city against them
Job 38. 8. break forth as if it i. out of the womb
Ezek. 47. 1. waters i. from under the threshold
12. because their waters i. out of the sanctuary
Dan. 7. 10. a fiery stream i. and came forth
Rev. 9. 17. and out of their mouths i. fire, 18.

ISSUES.

Psal. 68. 20. to God belong the i. from death
Prov. 4. 23. keep heart, for out of it are the i. of life

IT.

Prov. 4. 23. keep heart, for out of it are issues of life
Isa. 6. 13. in it shall be a tenth, and it shall return
7. 7. thus saith the Lord, it shall not stand
11. 10. to it shall the Gentiles seek, and his rest
30. 21. a word, saying, this is the way, walk in it
51. 9. art thou not it that hath cut Rahab?

Isa. 51. 10. art thou not *it* which hath dried the sea?
See BETTER, GOOD, WRITTEN, SELF.

ITCH.

Deut. 28. 27. the Lord will smite thee with the *i.*

ITCHING.

2 *Tim.* 4. 3. shall they heap teachers having *i.* ears

JUDGE

Signifies, [1] *To try and determine a cause,* Exod. 18. 13. 1 Cor. 6. 2. [2] *Rightly to understand and discern,* 1 Cor. 2. 15. [3] *To censure rashly,* Mat. 7. 1. 1 Cor. 4. 3. [4] *To proceed against,* Acts 24. 6. [5] *To esteem or reckon,* Acts 16. 15. [6] *To rule and govern,* Psal. 67. 4. Heb. 10. 30. [7] *To punish,* Ezek. 7. 3, 8. Heb. 13. 4. It is spoken, (I) *Of God,* Gen. 18. 25. Heb. 12. 23. (II) *Of Christ,* Acts 10. 42. (III) *Of men called gods,* Psal. 82. 1, 6. [1] *Ordinary,* Deut. 1. 16. [2] *Extraordinary,* Judg. 2. 18, 19.

JUDGE, *Substantive.*

Gen. 18. 25. shall not the *J.* of all the earth do right
19. 9. this one fellow came, and will needs be a *j.*
Exod. 2. 14. made thee a *j.* over us, *Acts* 7. 27, 35.
Deut. 17. 9. come to the *j.* that shall be in those days
12. the man that will not hearken to the *j.*
25. 2. that the *j.* shall cause him to lie down
Judg. 2. 18. then the Lord was with the *j.*
19. the *j.* was dead, they corrupted themselves
11. 27. the Lord the *J.* be *j.* this day between
1 *Sam.* 2. 25. if a man sin, the *j.* shall judge him
2 *Sam.* 15. 4. Absalom said, O that I were made *j.*
Job 9. 15. I would make supplication to my *j.*
23. 7. I should be delivered for ever from my *j.*
31. 28. an iniquity to be punished by the *j.*
Psal. 7. † 11. God is a righteous *j.* and is angry
50. 6. heavens declare, for God is *j.* himself, selah
68. 5. a *j.* of the widows ‖ 75. 7. God is the *j.*
94. 2. lift up thyself, thou *J.* of the earth, render
Isa. 3. 2. doth take away from Jerusalem the *j.*
Amos 2. 3. I will cut off the *j.* from the midst thereof
Mic. 5. 1. they shall smite the *j.* of Israel with a rod
7. 3. prince asketh, and the *j.* asketh for a reward
Mat. 5. 25. the adversary deliver thee to the *j.* the *j.* deliver thee to the officer, *Luke* 12. 58.
Luke 12. 14. man, who made me a *j.* over you?
18. 2. saying, there was in a city, a *j.* feared not G.
6. the Lord said, hear what the unjust *j.* saith
Acts 10. 42. of God to be the *j.* of quick and dead
18. 15. for I will be no *j.* of such matters
24. 10. hast been of many years a *j.* of this nation
2 *Tim.* 4. 8. the Lord the righteous *j.* shall give me
Heb. 12. 23. ye are come to God the *J.* of all
Jam. 4. 11. thou art not a doer of the law, but a *j.*
5. 9. behold, the *J.* standeth before the door

JUDGE, *Verb, applied to* GOD *and* CHRIST.

Gen. 16. 5. *j.* between me and thee, 1 *Sam.* 24. 12, 15.
31. 53. the God of their father *j.* betwixt us
Exod. 5. 21. they said, the Lord look on you and *j.*
Deut. 32. 36. for the Lord shall *j.* his people, *Psal.* 50. 4. | 135. 14. *Heb.* 10. 30.
1 *Sam.* 2. 10. the Lord shall *j.* the ends of the earth
24. † 15. the Lord *j.* me out of thy hand
1 *Kings* 8. 32. hear and *j.* thy servants, 2 *Chr.* 6. 23.
1 *Chr.* 16. 33. cometh to *j.* the earth, *Ps.* 96. 13. | 98. 9.
2 *Chron.* 20. 12. O our God, wilt thou not *j.* them?
Job 22. 13. sayest, can he *j.* through the dark cloud?
Psal. 7. 8. the Lord shall *j.* the people righteously, 9. 8. | 50. 4. | 96. 10.
10. 18. *j.* the fatherless and poor, 82. † 3. *Isa.* 11. 4.
26. 1. *j.* me, O Lord, 7. 8. | 35. 24. | 43. 1. | 54. 1. *Lam.* 3. 59.
82. 8. arise, O God, *j.* the earth: thou shalt inherit
96. 13. he shall *j.* the world with righteousness, 98. 9. *Acts* 17. 31.
110. 6. he shall *j.* among the heathen
Eccl. 3. 17. God shall *j.* the righteous and wicked
Isa. 2. 4. and he shall *j.* among the nations
3. 13. the Lord standeth to *j.* the people
11. 3. he shall not *j.* after the sight of his eyes
51. 5. and mine arm shall *j.* the people
Ezek. 7. 3. and will *j.* thee according to thy ways
34. 17. behold I *j.* between cattle and cattle
Joel 3. 12. there will I sit to *j.* the heathen
Mic. 4. 3. he shall *j.* among many people
John 5. 30. as I hear I *j.* my judgment is just
8. 15. I *j.* no man ‖ 16. and yet if I *j.*
26. I have many things to say and to *j.* of you
12. 47. I *j.* him not, I came not to *j.* the world
Rom. 2. 16. when God shall *j.* the secrets of men
3. 6. for then how shall God *j.* the world?
2 *Tim.* 4. 1. who shall *j.* quick and dead, 1 *Pet.* 4. 5.
Heb. 13. 4. whoremongers and adulterers G. will *j.*
Rev. 6. 10. dost thou not *j.* and avenge our blood
19. 11. in righteousness he doth *j.* and make war
See further, I *will* JUDGE.

JUDGE, *applied to* MAN, *or other things.*

Gen. 31. 37. that they may *j.* betwixt us both
49. 16. Dan shall *j.* his people as one of the tribes
Exod. 18. 13. that Moses sat to *j.* the people
16. they come, I *j.* between one and another
22. but every small matter they shall *j.*
Lev. 19. 15. in righteousness shalt thou *j.* thy neighbour, *Deut.* 1. 16. | 16. 18.
Num. 35. 24. the congregation *j.* between the slayer
Deut. 25. 1. come, that the judges may *j.* them
1 *Sam.* 2. 25. if a man sin, the judge shall *j.* him
8. 5. thou art old, make us a king to *j.* us, 6. 20.
1 *Kings* 3. 9. give an understanding heart to *j.* who is able to *j.* this great people? 2 *Chron.* 1. 10.
7. 7. a porch for the throne where he might *j.*
2 *Chron.* 1. 11. that thou mayest *j.* my people
19. 6. for ye *j.* not for man, but for the Lord
Ezra 7. 25. set judges which may *j.* all the people
Psal. 58. 1. do ye *j.* uprightly, O ye sons of men?
72. 2. he shall *j.* thy people with righteousness
4. he shall *j.* the poor of the people, *Prov.* 31. 9.
82. 2. how long will ye *j.* unjustly, and accept
Isa. 1. 17. *j.* the fatherless, plead for the widow
23. they *j.* not the fatherless, *Jer.* 5. 28.
5. 3. *j.* I pray you betwixt me and my vineyard
Jer. 21. † 12. *j.* judgment, *Zech.* 7. † 9. | 8. † 16.
Ezek. 20. 4. wilt thou *j.* them, son of man? 22. 2.
23. 24. and they shall *j.* thee, 45. | 24. 14.
36. son of man, wilt *j.* Aholah and Aholibah?
44. 24. they shall *j.* it according to my judgments
Obad. 21. saviours come to *j.* the mount of Esau
Mic. 3. 11. the heads thereof *j.* for reward
Zech. 3. 7. then thou shalt also *j.* my house
Mat. 7. 1. *j.* not that ye be not judged
2. for with what judgment ye *j.* *Luke* 6. 37.
Luke 12. 57. yea, and why *j.* ye not what is right?
John 7. 24. *j.* not according to the appearance, but *j.* righteous judgment
51. doth our law *j.* any man before it hear
8. 15. ye *j.* after flesh ‖ 12. 48. same shall *j.* him
18. 31. take and *j.* him according to your law
Acts 4. 19. *j.* ye ‖ 13. 46. *j.* yourselves unworthy
23. 3. for sittest thou to *j.* me after the law?
Rom. 2. 27. uncircumcision if it fulfil the law, *j.* thee
14. † 1. not to *j.* his doubtful thoughts
3. *j.* him that eateth ‖ 10. why *j.* thy brother
13. let us not *j.* one another, but *j.* this rather
1 *Cor.* 4. 3. I *j.* not myself, ‖ 5. *j.* not, before time
5. 12. what have I to do to *j.* them that are without, do ye not *j.* them that are within?
6. 2. do ye not know the saints shall *j.* the world?
3. know ye not that we shall *j.* angels?
4. set them to *j.* who are least esteemed in church
5. shall be able to *j.* between his brethren
10. 15. *j.* ye what I say, ‖ 11. 13. *j.* in yourselves
31. for if we would *j.* ourselves, we should
14. 29. let the prophets speak, and the other *j.*
2 *Cor.* 5. 14. because we thus *j.* that if one died
Col. 2. 16. let no man therefore *j.* you in meat
Jam. 4. 11. but if thou *j.* the law, thou art not

I *will* JUDGE.

1 *Sam.* 3. 13. I told that *I will j.* his house for ever
Psal. 75. 2. when shall receive, *I will j.* uprightly
Ezek. 7. 3. —*j.* according to thy ways, 8. 27. ‖ 33. 20.
11. 10. *I will j.* you in the border of Israel, 11.
16. 38. *I will j.* thee as women that break wedlock
18. 30. therefore *I will j.* you, O house of Israel
21. 30. *I will j.* thee in the place where thou wast
34. 20. I, even *I, will j.* between fat cattle, 22.

Will I JUDGE.

Gen. 15. 14. the nation they shall serve —*j.* *Acts* 7. 7.
Luke 19. 22. out of thine own mouth *will I j.* thee

JUDGED.

Gen. 30. 6. God hath *j.* me and heard my voice
Exod. 18. 26. *j.* the people, small matter they *j.*
Judg. 3. 10. Othniel *j.* ‖ 4. 4. Deborah *j.* Israel
10. 2. Tola *j.* ‖ 3. Jair *j.* ‖ 12. 7. Jephthah *j.*
12. 8. Ibzan *j.* ‖ 11. Elon *j.* ‖ 14. Abdon *j.* Israel
15. 20. Samson *j.* Israel twenty years, 16. 31.
Ruth 1. † 1. when judges *j.* there was a famine
1 *Sam.* 4. 18. Eli *j.* ‖ 7. 6. Samuel *j.* Israel, 15, 16, 17.
2 *Sam.* 18. † 19. the Lord *j.* him from his enemies
1 *Kings* 3. 28. heard the judgment the king had *j.*
2 *Kings* 23. 22. from the days of the judges that *j.*
Psal. 9. 19. let the heathen be *j.* in thy sight
37. 33. not condemn him when he is *j.*
109. 7. when he shall be *j.* let him be condemned
Jer. 22. 16. he *j.* the cause of the poor and needy
Ezek. 16. 38. as women that shed blood are *j.*
52. thou also who hast *j.* thy sisters, bear shame
28. 23. and the wounded shall be *j.* in her
35. 11. make myself known, when I have *j.* thee
36. 19. according to their doings I *j.* them
Dan. 9. 12. and against our judges that *j.* us
Mat. 7. 1. that ye be not *j.* ‖ 2. shall be *j.* *Luke* 6. 37.
Luke 7. 43. he said to him, thou hast rightly *j.*
John 16. 11. the prince of this world is *j.*
Acts 16. 15. if ye have *j.* me to be faithful
24. 6. we would have *j.* according to our law
25. 9. there be *j.* of these things before me, 20.
10. Paul said, I stand, where I ought to be *j.*
26. 6. and am *j.* for the hope of the promise
Rom. 2. 12. shall be *j.* by the law, *Jam.* 2. 12.
3. 4. thou mightest overcome when thou art *j.*
7. why yet am I also *j.* as a sinner?
1 *Cor.* 2. 15. yet he himself is *j.* of no man
4. 3. a small thing that I should be *j.* of you
5. 3. I have *j.* already, as though I were present
6. 2. and if the world shall be *j.* by you
10. 29. for why is my liberty *j.* of another man's
11. 31. if we would judge we should not be *j.*
32. when we are *j.* we are chastened of the Lord
14. 24. he is convinced of all, he is *j.* of all
Heb. 11. 11. because she *j.* him faithful who had
1 *Pet.* 4. 6. they might be *j.* according to men
Rev. 11. 18. time of the dead, that they should be *j.*
16. 5. art righteous because thou hast *j.* thus
19. 2. righteous, for he hath *j.* the great whore
20. 12. the dead were *j.* out of those things
13. were *j.* every man according to his works

JUDGES.

Exod. 21. 6. his master shall bring him to the *j.*
22. and he shall pay as the *j.* determine
22. 8. then the master shall be brought to the *j.*
9. the cause of both shall come before the *j.*
† 28. thou shalt not revile the *j.*
Num. 25. 5. Moses said to the *j.* slay each his men
Deut. 1. 16. I charged your *j.* at that time, saying
16. 18. *j.* shalt thou make in all thy gates
19. 17. both the men shall stand before priests and *j.*
18. the *j.* shall make diligent inquisition
21. 2. thy elders and thy *j.* shall come forth
25. 1. they come that the *j.* may judge them
32. 31. even our enemies themselves being *j.*
Josh. 8. 33. their *j.* stood on this side the ark
23. 2. Joshua called for their heads and *j.* 24. 1.
Judg. 2. 16. the Lord raised up *j.* who delivered, 18.
17. they would not hearken to their *j.*
Ruth 1. 1. when the *j.* ruled a famine was
1 *Sam.* 8. 1. he made his sons *j.* over Israel, 2.
2 *Sam.* 7. 11. I commanded *j.* to be over my people
2 *Kings* 23. 22. from the days of the *j.* that judged
1 *Chr.* 17. 6. spake I a word to any of the *j.* 10.
23. 4. and six thousand were officers and *j.*
26. 29. Chenaniah and his sons were for *j.*
2 *Chron.* 1. 2. then Solomon spake to the *j.*
19. 5. he set *j.* in the land ‖ 6. said to the *j.*
Ezra 7. 25. set *j.* which may judge the people
10. 14. and with them the *j.* of every city
Job 9. 24. he covereth the face of the *j.* thereof
12. 17. and he maketh the *j.* fools
31. 11. it is an iniquity to be punished by the *j.*
Psal. 2. 10. be instructed ye *j.* of the earth
109. † 31. to save him from the *j.* of his soul
141. 6. when *j.* are overthrown in stony places
148. 11. princes, and all *j.* of the earth
Prov. 8. 16. by me princes rule, and all *j.* of earth
Isa. 1. 26. I will restore thy *j.* as at the first
40. 23. he maketh the *j.* of the earth as vanity
Dan. 3. 2. Nebuchadnezzar sent to gather the *j.* 3.
9. 12. his words against our *j.* that judged us
Hos. 7. 7. and they have devoured their *j.*
13. 10. where are thy *j.* of whom thou saidst
Zeph. 3. 3. her *j.* are evening wolves, they gnaw
Mat. 12. 27. they shall be your *j.* *Luke* 11. 19.
Acts 13. 20. and after that he gave to them *j.*
Jam. 2. 4. and are become *j.* of evil thoughts

JUDGEST.

Psal. 51. 4. thou mightest be clear when thou *j.*
Jer. 11. 20. Lord of hosts, that *j.* righteously
Rom. 2. 1. O man, whosoever thou art that *j.*
3. O man, that *j.* them which do such things
14. 4. who art thou that *j.* another man's servant?
Jam. 4. 12. who art thou that *j.* another

JUDGETH.

Job 21. 22. seeing he *j.* those that were high
36. 31. for by them *j.* he the people
Psal. 7. 11. God *j.* the righteous, is angry with
58. 11. verily he is a God that *j.* in the earth
82. 1. in congregation of mighty, he *j.* among gods
Prov. 29. 14. the king that faithfully *j.* the poor
John 5. 22. for the Father *j.* no man, but hath
8. 50. there is one that *j.* ‖ 12. 48. one that *j.* him
1 *Cor.* 2. 15. he that is spiritual *j.* all things
4. 4. but he that *j.* me is the Lord
5. 13. but them that are without, God *j.*
Jam. 4. 11. he that *j.* his brother, *j.* the law
1 *Pet.* 1. 17. who without respect of persons *j.*
2. 23. but committed himself to him that *j.*
Rev. 18. 8. for strong is the Lord that *j.* her

JUDGING.

Gen. 30. † 6. Rachel called his name, *j.*
2 *Kings* 15. 5. *j.* the people of the land, 2 *Chr.* 26. 21.
Psal. 9. 4. thou sattest in the throne *j.* right
Isa. 16. 5. he shall sit *j.* and seeking judgment
Mat. 19. 28. *j.* the twelve tribes, *Luke* 22. 30.

JUDGMENT

Signifies, [1] *The sentence, or decision of a judge,* 1 Kings 3. 28. [2] *The spirit of wisdom and prudence, enabling to know and discern right from wrong, and good from evil,* Psal. 72. 1. [3] *Those remarkable punishments, which God inflicts upon people for their sins and transgressions,* Prov. 19. 29. Ezek. 30. 14. [4] *The spiritual government of the world, which is committed by God the Father to Christ the Mediator, and which he manages with a perfect rectitude and equity,* John 5. 22. | 9. 39. [5] *Those afflictions and chastisements which God brings upon his children for their trial and instruction,* 1 Pet. 4. 17. [6] *God's merciful moderation in chastising his people,* Jer. 10. 24. [7] *The solemn action and trial at the great and last day,* Eccl. 12. 14. Jude 6. [8] *The righteous statutes and commandments of God,* Psal. 119. 7, 20. [9] *The punishment inflicted on Christ for our sins,* Isa. 53. 8. [10] *The doctrine of the gospel, or God's word,* Mat. 12. 18. Psal. 119. 7, 20. [11] *Justice and equity,* Isa. 1. 17. Luke 11. 42. [12] *The deliverance and vindication of mankind from the power and tyranny of the devil,* John 12. 31. [13] *God's decrees and purposes concerning nations or persons,* Rom. 11. 33. [14] *The sentence of damnation upon the wicked, and of absolution in favour of the godly,* Jude 15. [15] *Courts of judgment,* Mat. 5. 21. [16] *Differences and controversies to be decided,* 1 Cor. 6. 4. [17] *Sentiment, or opinion,* 1 Cor. 1. 10. [18] *Advice,* 1 Cor. 7. 25. [19] *The gospel, or kingdom of grace,* Mat. 12. 20.

Gen. 30. † 21. Leah called her name *j.*
Exod. 12. 12. against the gods I will execute *j.*
21. 31. according to this *j.* be it done to him
23. 2. to decline after many, to wrest *j.* 6.
28. 15. thou shalt make the breast-plate of *j.*
29. Aaron bear names in breast-plate of *j.* 30.
Num. 27. 11. to Israel a statute of *j.* 35. 29.
21. after the *j.* of Urim before the Lord
Deut. 1. 17. not afraid of man, for the *j.* is God's
10. 18. he doth execute the *j.* of the fatherless
16. 18. they shall judge the people with just *j.*
19. not wrest *j.* ‖ 17. 11. according to the *j.*
17. 9. they shall shew thee the sentence of *j.*
24. 17. thou shalt not pervert the *j.* of the stranger
25. 1. be a controversy, and they come unto *j.*
27. 19. cursed be he that perverteth *j.* of stranger
32. 4. for all his ways are *j.*; a God of truth
41. if my hand take hold on *j.* I will render
Josh. 20. 6. stand before the congregation for *j.*
Judg. 4. 5. Israel came up to Deborah for *j.*
1 *Sam.* 8. 3. his sons took bribes and perverted *j.*
2 *Sam.* 8. 15. David executed *j.* 1 *Chron.* 18. 14.
15. 2. when any man came to the king for *j.* 6.
1 *Kings* 3. 11. hast asked understanding to discern *j.*
28. all Israel heard of the *j.* the king judged
7. 7. the porch of *j.* ‖ 20. 40. so shall thy *j.* be
2 *Kings* 25. 6. took the king and gave *j.* upon him
2 *Chron.* 19. 8. chief of fathers for *j.* of the Lord
20. 9. when evil cometh on us as the sword, *j.*
22. 8. when Jehu was executing *j.* on Ahab
24. 24. so they executed *j.* against Joash
Ezra 7. 26. let *j.* be executed speedily on him
Esth. 1. 13. towards all that knew law and *j.*
Job 8. 3. doth God pervert *j.* or pervert justice?
9. 19. if I speak of *j.* ‖ 19. 7. but there is no *j.*
19. 29. that ye may know there is a *j.*
32. 9. neither do the aged understand *j.*
34. 4. let us choose to us *j.* know what is good
12. neither will the Almighty pervert *j.*
35. 14. yet *j.* is before him, trust in him
36. 17. thou hast fulfilled the *j.* of the wicked, *j.* and justice take hold on thee

Psal. 7. 6. awake for me to the j. thou hast comm.
9. 7. he hath prepared his throne for j.
8. shall minister j. to the people in righteousness
16. the Lord is known by the j. he executeth
33. 5. he loveth righteousness and j. 37. 28.
37. 6. he shall bring forth thy j. as the noon-day
30. and his tongue talketh of j.
72. 2. and he shall judge thy poor with j.
76. 8. thou didst cause j. to be heard from heaven
9. when God arose to j. to save the meek of the earth
89. 14. justice and j. are the habitation, 97. 2.
94. 15. but j. shall return to righteousness
99. 4. the king's strength also loveth j. thou executest j. and righteousness in Jacob
101. 1. I will sing of mercy and j. to thee, O Lord
103. 6. Lord executeth j. for the oppressed, 146. 7.
106. 3. blessed are they that keep j.
30. then Phinehas stood up and executed j.
111. 7. the works of his hands are verity and j.
112. † 5. he will guide his affairs with j.
119. 66. teach me good j. and knowledge
121. I have done j. and justice: leave me not
149. O Lord, quicken me according to thy j.
122. 5. for there are set thrones of j.
149. 9. to execute upon them the j. written
Prov. 1. 3. to receive the instruction of wisdom and j.
2. 8. he keepeth the paths of j. and preserveth
9. then shalt thou understand j. and equity
8. 20. I lead in the midst of the paths of j.
13. 23. there is that is destroyed for want of j.
17. 23. taketh a gift to pervert the ways of j.
19. 28. an ungodly witness scorneth j.
20. 8. a king that sitteth in the throne of j.
28. 5. evil men understand not j. but they that seek
29. 4. the king by j. establisheth the land
26. every man's j. cometh from the Lord
31. 5. nor pervert the j. of any of the afflicted
Eccl. 3. 16. I saw under the sun the place of j.
5. 8. if thou seest violent perverting of j. and justice
8. 5. and a wise man discerneth both time and j.
6. because to every purpose there is time and j.
Isa. 1. 17. seek j. ‖ 21. it was full of j.
27. Zion shall be redeemed with j.
4. 4. shall have purged Jerusalem by the spirit of j.
5. 7. and looked for j. ‖ 16. 5. seeking j.
9. 7. and to establish it with j. and with justice
10. 2. to turn aside the needy from j.
16. 3. execute j. Jer. 21. 12. | 22. 3. Ezek. 18. 8. | 45. 9. Zech. 7. 9. | 8. 16.
28. 6. for a spirit of j. | 17. I will lay j. to the line
30. 18. will have mercy, for the Lord is a God of j.
32. 16. then j. shall dwell in the wilderness
33. 5. Lord hath filled Zion with j. and righteousn.
34. 5. and upon the people of my curse to j.
40. 14. and who taught him in the path of j.?
41. 1. let us come near together to j.
42. 1. he shall bring forth j. to the Gentiles
3. he shall bring forth j. unto truth
4. he shall not fail, till he have set j. in the earth
53. 8. he was taken from prison and from j.
56. 1. keep ye j. and do justice, Hos. 12. 6.
59. 8. and there is no j. in their goings
9. therefore is j. far from us, neither doth justice
11. we look for j. but there is none
14. j. is turned away backward, and justice
15. it displeased him that there was no j.
61. 8. I the Lord love j. I hate robbery
Jer. 5. 1. if there be any that executeth j.
4. they know not the j. of their God, 8. 7.
5. they have known the j. of their God
7. 5. if ye thoroughly execute j. between a man
9. 24. which exercise j. and righteousness in earth
10. 24. correct me, but with j. not in thine anger
21. 12. execute j. in the morning, and deliver him
23. 5. branch shall execute j. in the earth, 33. 15.
26. † 11. the j. of death is for this man
39. 5. to Riblah, where he gave j. upon him, 52. 9.
48. 21. and j. is come upon the plain country
47. thus far is the j. of Moab
49. 12. they whose j. was not to drink of the cup
51. 9. forsake her, for her j. reacheth unto heaven
Ezek. 23. 10. for they had executed j. on her
24. I will set j. before them, they shall judge
Dan. 4. 37. king of heaven, all whose ways are j.
7. 10. j. was set ‖ 26. but the j. shall sit
22. j. was given to the saints of the most High
Hos. 5. 1. give ye ear, for j. is toward you
10. 4. thus j. springeth up as hemlock in the field
Amos 5. 7. ye who turn j. into wormwood
15. love the good, and establish j. in the gate
24. but let j. run down as waters and righteousn.
6. 12. for ye have turned j. into gall
Mic. 3. 1. is it not to know j. ‖ 8. I am full of j.
9. that abhor j. ‖ 7. 9. and execute j. for me
Hab. 1. 4. law is slacked, j. doth never go forth
7. their j. shall proceed of themselves
12. O Lord, thou hast ordained them for j.
Zeph. 2. 3. all ye which have wrought his j.
3. 5. every morning doth he bring j. to light
Mal. 2. 17. yet ye say, where is the God of j.?
Mat. 5. 21. shall be in danger of the j. 22.
7. 2. with what j. ye judge, ye shall be judged
12. 18. he shall shew j. to the Gentiles
20. till he send forth j. unto victory
23. 23. and have omitted j. mercy, and faith
Luke 11. 42. and pass over j. and the love of God
John 5. 22. but hath committed all j. to the Son
27. hath given him authority to execute j. also
7. 24. not to appearance, but judge righteous j.
9. 39. for j. I am come into this world
12. 31. now is the j. of this world, now shall
16. 8. he will reprove the world of j. 11.
Acts 8. 33. in his humiliation his j. was taken away
24. 25. as he reasoned of j. Felix trembled
25. 15. the Jews desiring to have j. against him
† 21. Paul appealed to the j. of Augustus
Rom. 1. † 28. G. gave them over to a mind void of j.
32. who knowing the j. of God, that they which
2. 2. are sure that the j. of G. is according to truth
3. thinkest that thou shalt escape the j. of God?

Rom. 2. 5. and revelation of the righteous j. of God
3. † 19. world may be subject to the j. of God
5. 16. for the j. was by one to condemnation
18. j. came on all men to condemnation
1 Cor. 1. 10. but be joined together in the same j.
4. 3. that I should be judged of man's j.
11. † 29. eateth and drinketh j. to himself
† 34. that ye come not together to j.
2 Thess. 1. 5. token of the righteous j. of God
1 Tim. 5. 24. some sins are open, going before to j.
2 Tim. 3. † 8. men of no j. concerning the faith
Tit. 1. † 16. to every good work void of j.
Heb. 6. 2. and of eternal j. ‖ 9. 27. after this the j.
10. 27. but a certain fearful looking for of j.
Jam. 2. 13. he shall have j. without mercy that shewed no mercy, and mercy rejoiceth against j.
3. † 1. knowing we shall receive greater j.
1 Pet. 4. 17. that j. must begin at the house of God
2 Pet. 2. 3. whose j. lingereth not ‖ 4. reserved to j.
Jude 6. to j. of the great day ‖ 15. to execute j.
Rev. 14. 7. fear God, for the hour of his j. is come
17. 1. will shew thee the j. of the great whore
18. 10. alas, alas, for in one hour is thy j. come
20. 4. they sat on them, and j. was given to them

See BEAR, DAY.

Do JUDGMENT.

Gen. 18. 19. to do justice and j. 1 Kings 10. 9. Prov. 21. 3. Jer. 22. 15.
1 Kings 3. 28. wisdom of God was in him to do j.
2 Chron. 9. 8. set over them to do justice and j.
Prov. 21. 7. because they refuse to do j.
15. it is joy to the just to do j. but destruction
Jer. 51. 47. I will do j. on the graven images
52. I will do j. on her graven images
Ezek. 18. † 5. if a man do j. and justice, 33. † 14.

JUDGMENT-hall.

John 18. 28. then they led Jesus to the hall of j. they themselves went not into the j.-hall
33. then Pilate entered into the j.-hall again
19. 9. went into the j.-hall, and saith to Jesus
Acts 23. 35. to be kept in Herod's j.-hall.

In JUDGMENT.

Lev. 19. 15. do no unrighteousness in j. 35.
Num. 35. 12. stand before the congregation in j.
Deut. 1. 17. ye shall not respect persons in j.
17. 8. if there arise a matter too hard for thee in j.
Judg. 5. 10. ye that sit in j. and walk by the way
2 Chron. 19. 6. for the Lord, who is with you in j.
Job 9. 32. and we should come together in j.
37. 23. he is excellent in power and in j.
Psal. 1. 5. the ungodly shall not stand in j.
25. 9. the meek will he guide in j. and teach
Prov. 16. 10. his mouth transgresseth not in j.
18. 5. not good to overthrow the righteous in j.
24. 23. not good to have respect of persons in j.
Isa. 5. 16. but the Lord of hosts shall be exalted in j.
28. 6. him that sitteth in j. ‖ 7. they stumble in j.
32. 1. behold princes shall rule in j.
† 7. when he speaketh against the poor in j.
54. 17. every tongue that shall rise against thee in j.
Jer. 4. 2. the Lord liveth in righteousness and in j.
49. † 19. who will convent me in j.?
Ezek. 44. 24. in controversy they stand in j.
Hos. 2. 19. I will betroth thee to me in j.
5. 11. Ephraim is oppressed and broken in j.
Mal. 3. 5. and I will come near to you in j.
Mat. 12. 41. the men of Nineveh shall rise in j.
42. queen of south shall rise in j. Luke 11. 31, 32.
Phil. 1. 9. I pray, that your love may abound in j.

Into JUDGMENT.

Job 14. 3. and bringest me into j. with thee
22. 4. will he reprove, will he enter with thee into j.
34. 23. that he should enter into j. with God
Psal. 143. 2. enter not into j. with thy servant
Eccl. 11. 9. for these God will bring thee into j.
12. 14. God shall bring every work into j.
Isa. 3. 14. Lord will enter into j. with ancients

My JUDGMENT.

Job 27. 2. who hath taken away my j. 34. 5.
29. 14. my j. was as a robe and a diadem
40. 8. wilt thou also disannul my j.? wilt thou
Psal. 9. † 4. for thou hast made my j.
35. 23. stir up thyself, and awake to my j.
Isa. 40. 27. my j. is passed over from my God
49. 4. yet surely my j. is with the Lord
51. 4. I will make my j. to rest for a light of people
Ezek. 39. 21. all the heathen shall see my j.
John 5. 30. and my j. is just ‖ 8. 16. my j. is true
1 Cor. 7. 25. yet I give my j. ‖ 40. happier in my j.

JUDGMENT-seat.

Mat. 27. 19. he was set down on j.-s. John 19. 13.
Acts 18. 12. the Jews brought him to the j.-seat
16. and he drave them from the j.-seat
17. the Greeks beat Sosthenes before the j.-seat
25. 10. I stand at Cesar's j.-seat ‖ 17. I sat on j.-seat
Rom. 14. 10. stand before j.-s. of Christ, 2 Cor. 5. 10.
Jam. 2. 6. rich men draw you before the j.-seats

JUDGMENTS.

Exod. 6. 6. I will redeem you with great j. 7. 4.
21. 1. these are the j. thou shalt set before them
24. 3. and Moses told the people all the j.
Num. 33. 4. on their gods the Lord executed j.
35. 24. shall judge according to these j.
36. 13. these are the j. which the Lord commanded
Deut. 7. 12. if ye hearken to these j. and keep them
33. 10. they shall teach Jacob thy j. and law
21. he executed the j. of the Lord with Israel
2 Sam. 22. 23. his j. were before me, Psal. 18. 22.
1 Chron. 16. 12. remem. j. of his mouth, Ps. 105. 5.
14. his j. are in all the earth, Psal. 105. 7.
Neh. 9. 29. but sinned against thy j.
Psal. 10. 5. thy j. are far above out of sight
19. 9. the j. of the Lord are true and righteous
36. 6. thy j. are a great deep; O L. thou preservest
48. 11. let Judah be glad because of thy j.
72. 1. give the king thy j. O God, and righteousn.
97. 8. Judah rejoiced, because of thy j. O Lord
119. 7. when I have learned thy righteous j.
13. with my lips I declared all the j. of thy mouth
20. for the longing that it hath unto thy j.
30. thy j. have I laid before me
39. turn away my reproach, for thy j. are good

Psal. 119. 43. I hoped in thy j. ‖ 52. I rememb. thy j.
62. give thanks, because of thy righteous j. 164.
75. I know, O Lord, that thy j. are right
102. I have not departed from thy j.
106. I have sworn that I will keep thy righteous j.
108. teach me thy j. ‖ 120. I am afraid of thy j.
137. righteous art thou, and upright are thy j.
156. O Lord, quicken me according to thy j.
160. every one of thy righteous j. endureth
175. let my soul live, and let thy j. help me
147. 20. his j. they have not known them
Prov. 19. 29. j. are prepared for scorners, stripes
Isa. 26. 8. in the way of thy j. we waited for thee
9. for when thy j. are in the earth, inhabitants
Jer. 4. † 12. nor will I utter j. against them
12. 1. yet let me talk with thee of thy j.
Ezek. 5. 7. nor done according to the j. of the nations
8. execute j. in the midst of thee, 10. 15. | 11. 9.
7. † 27. with their j. will I judge them
16. 41. execute j. on thee in sight of women
23. 24. they shall judge thee according to their j.
25. 11. and I will execute j. on Moab
28. 26. executed j. on all those that despise them
30. 14. I will execute j. in No
19. thus will I execute j. in Egypt
34. 16. I will destroy, I will feed them with j.
Dan. 9. 5. we sinned by departing from thy j.
Hos. 6. 5. thy j. are as the light that goeth forth
Zeph. 3. 15. the Lord hath taken away thy j.
Rom. 11. 33. how unsearchable are his j. and ways
1 Cor. 6. 4. if ye have j. of things of this life
Rev. 15. 4. for thy j. are made manifest
16. 7. true and righteous are thy j. 19. 2.

My JUDGMENTS.

Lev. 18. 4. ye shall do my j. I am the Lord
5. ye shall therefore keep my j. 25. 18.
26. 15. if your soul abhor my j. so that ye do not
43. because, even because they despised my j.
1 Chron. 28. 7. if ye be constant to do my j.
Psal. 89. 30. if his children walk not in my j.
Jer. 1. 16. I will utter my j. against them
Ezek. 5. 6. she changed my j. into wickedness
5. 7. neither have kept my j. nor done
14. 21. when I send my four sore j. on Jerusalem
36. 27. and ye shall keep my j. and do them
44. 24. they shall judge it according to my j.

Statutes and JUDGMENTS.

Lev. 18. 5. keep my statutes and my j. 26. | 20. 22. Deut. 7. 11. | 11. 1. | 26. 16, 17. | 30. 16. 1 Kings 2. 3. | 8. 58. | 9. 4. | 11. 33.
19. 37. ye shall observe all my statutes and j. Deut. 11. 32. | 12. 1. 2 Chron. 7. 17.
26. 46. these are the st. and j. L. made, Deut. 4. 45.
Deut. 4. 1. hearken to st. and j. which I teach, 5. 1.
5. I taught you st. and j. ‖ 8. hath st. and j. so right
14. commanded to teach st. and j. 6. 1. Ezra 7. 10.
5. 31. I will speak the stat. and j. thou shalt teach
6. 20. thy son asketh thee, what mean the st. and j.
8. 11. forget L. in not keep. his st. and j. Neh. 1. 7.
1 Kings 6. 12. walk in my stat. and execute my j.
1 Chron. 22. 13. if thou takest heed to fulfil st. and j.
2 Chr. 19. 10. what cause shall come betw. st. and j.
Neh. 9. 13. and thou gavest them right stat. and j.
10. 29. entered into a curse, to do all his st. and j.
Psal. 147. 19. he sheweth his stat. and j. to Israel
Ezek. 5. 6. for they refused my j. and my statutes
11. 12. for ye have not walked in my statutes, nor executed my j. 20. 13, 16, 21.
18. 9. walked in my st. and j. 17. | 20. 19. | 37. 24.
20. 11. give them my statutes, and shewed my j.
18. not in stat. of fathers, nor observe their j.
25. gave them stat. not good, and j. whereby
Mal. 4. 4. remember ye law of Mos. with st. and j.

JUICE.

Cant. 8. 2. to drink wine of the j. of my pomegranate

JUMPING.

Neh. 3. 2. the noise of horses and the j. chariots

JUNIPER.

1 Kings 19. 4. Elijah came and sat under a j. tree, 5.
Job 30. 4. who cut up j. roots for their meat
Psal. 120. 4. arrows of the mighty with coals of j.

IVORY.

1 Kings 10. 18. king made a throne of i. 2 Chr. 9. 17.
22. bringing gold, silver, and i. 2 Chron. 9. 21.
22. 39. and the i. house which Ahab made
Psal. 45. 8. out of the i. places, whereby they made
Cant. 5. 14. his belly is as bright i. overlaid with
7. 4. thy neck is as a tower of i. thine eyes
Ezek. 27. 6. the Ashurites made thy benches of i.
15. they brought thee for a present horns of i.
Amos 3. 15. and the houses of i. shall perish
6. 4. that lie upon beds of i. and stretch themselves
Rev. 18. 12. for no man buyeth vessels of i.

JURISDICTION.

1 Kings 8. † 37. besiege in the land of their j.
Luke 23. 7. as he knew that he belonged to Herod's j.

JUST

Signifies, [1] *One who is upright and sincere in his actions and dealings with others*, Luke 23. 50. [2] *The great Creator, who is essentially just and righteous, and the fountain of justice*, Deut. 32. 4. [3] *One who is exceeding faithful, keeping his word and promise*, 1 John 1. 9. [4] *One who in his life and death answered the perfect justice of the law of God*, 1 Pet. 3. 18. [5] *One who is righteous by the imputation of Christ's righteousness*, Rom. 1. 17. [6] *One who is not truly convinced of his own sinfulness, and is only righteous in his own opinion*, Luke 18. 9. [7] *One that is good-natured, mild, and indulgent*, Mat. 1. 19. [8] *One of a charitable, liberal disposition*, Psal. 37. 26.

Gen. 6. 9. Noah was a j. man, and perfect, and walked
Lev. 19. 36. j. balances, j. weights, a j. ephah, and a j. hin shall ye have, Deut. 25. 15. Ezek. 45. 10.
Deut. 16. 18. they shall judge peo. with j. judgments
20. that is altogether j. shalt thou follow
32. 4. a God without iniquity, j. and right is he
2 Sam. 23. 3. he that ruleth over men must be j.
Neh. 9. 33. thou art j. in all that is brought on us
Job 4. 17. shall mortal man be more j. than God?

Job 9. 2. but how should man be j. with God?
12. 4. the j. upright man is laughed to scorn
27. 17. he may prepare it, but the j. shall put it on
33. 12. behold, in this thou art not j.
Psal. 7. 9. let wickedness end, but establish the j.
37. 12. the wicked plotteth against the j.
Prov. 3. 33. but he blesseth the habitation of the j.
4. 18. the path of the j. is as the shining light
9. 9. teach a j. man, and he will increase in learning
10. 6. blessings are upon the head of the j.
7. the memory of the j. is blessed
20. the tongue of the j. is as choice silver
31. the mouth of the j. bringeth forth wisdom
11. 1. but a j. weight is his delight
9. but through knowledge shall the j. be delivered
12. 13. but the j. shall come out of trouble
21. there shall no evil happen to the j.
13. 22. the wealth of the sinner is laid up for the j.
16. 11. a j. weight and balance are the Lord's
17. 15. he that condemneth the j. is abomination
26. also to punish the j. is not good
18. 17. he that is first in his own cause seemeth j.
20. 7. the j. man walketh in his integrity
21. 15. it is a joy to the j. to do judgment
24. 16. a j. man falleth seven times and riseth again
29. 10. hate the upright, but the j. seek his soul
27. an unjust man is an abomination to the j.
Eccl. 7. 15. there is a j. man that perisheth in his
20. not a j. man upon earth that sinneth not
8. 14. there be j. men to whom it happeneth
Isa. 26. 7. the way of the j. is uprightness, thou most upright dost weigh the path of the j.
29. 21. turn aside the j. for a thing of nought
45. 21. I the Lord, a j. God, and a Saviour
49. † 24. or the captivity of the j. delivered
Lam. 4. 13. that have shed the blood of the j. in her
Ezek. 18. 5. but if a man be j. and do that is right
9. he is j. he shall surely live, saith the Lord God
Hos. 14. 9. ways of Lord right, j. shall walk in them
Amos 5. 12. they afflict the j. they take a bribe
Hab. 2. 4. but the j. shall live by faith, Rom. 1. 17. Gal. 3. 11. Heb. 10. 38.
Zeph. 3. 5. the j. Lord is in the midst thereof
Zech. 9. 9. he is j. and having salvation, lowly
Mat. 1. 19. Joseph her husband, being a j. man
5. 45. and sendeth rain on the j. and on unjust
13. 49. and sever the wicked from among the j.
27. 19. have nothing to do with that j. man
24. I am innocent of the blood of this j. person
Mark 6. 20. knowing that he was a j. man and holy
Luke 1. 17. the disobedient to the wisdom of the j.
2. 25. Simeon was j. and devout, waiting for
14. 14. be recompensed at the resurrection of the j.
15. 7. more than over ninety and nine j. persons
20. 20. spies which should feign themselves j.
23. 50. Joseph of Arimathea was a good man and j.
John 5. 30. as I hear I judge, and my judgment is j.
Acts 10. 22. Cornelius the centurion, a j. man
24. 15. shall be resurrection both of j. and unjust
Rom. 2. 13. for not the hearers of the law are j.
3. 8. whose damnation is j. || 26. he might be j.
7. 12. and the commandment holy, j. and good
Phil. 4. 8. finally, whatsoever things are j. pure
Col. 4. 1. give servants that which is j. and equal
Tit. 1. 8. a bishop must be j. holy, temperate
Heb. 2. 2. received a j. recompence of reward
12. 23. and to the spirits of j. men made perfect
Jam. 5. 6. ye have condemned and killed the j.
1 Pet. 3. 18. Christ suffered, the j. for the unjust
2 Pet. 2. 7. delivered j. Lot, vexed with conversation
1 John 1. 9. if we confess, he is j. to forgive us our sins
Rev. 15. 3. j. and true are thy ways, thou King

Most JUST.

Job 34. 17. wilt thou condemn him that is most j.?

JUST One.

Acts 3. 14. ye denied the Holy One and the J. One
7. 52. shewed before of the coming of the J. One
22. 14. shouldest know his will, and see that J. One

JUSTICE

Is, (I) *That essential perfection in God, whereby he is infinitely righteous and just, both in his nature, and in all his proceedings with his creatures*, Psal. 89. 14. (II) *That political virtue which renders to every man his due, and is*, [1] *Distributive, which concerns princes, magistrates, &c.* Job 29. 14. [2] *Commutative, which concerns all persons in their dealings one with another*, Gen. 18. 19.

Gen. 18. 19. keep way of L. to do j. and judgment
Deut. 16. † 20. what is j. shalt thou follow
33. 21. he executeth the j. of Lord and judgments
2 Sam. 8. 15. David executed j. 1 Chron. 18. 14.
15. 4. O that I were made judge, I would do j.
Job 8. 3. or doth the Almighty pervert j.?
31. † 6. let him weigh me in the balance of j.
36. 17. judgment and j. take hold on thee
37. 23. is excellent in plenty of j. will not afflict
Psal. 82. 3. do j. to the afflicted and needy
89. 14. j. and judgment are habitation of thy throne
119. 121. I have done judgment and j. leave me not
Prov. 1. 3. to receive the instruction of j. and equity
8. 15. by me kings reign, and princes decree j.
Eccl. 5. 8. if thou seest the perverting of j.
Isa. 9. 7. to establish his throne with j. and judgm.
56. 1. keep ye judgment, and do j. for my salvation
58. 2. they ask of me the ordinances of j.
59. 4. none calleth for j. || 9. nor doth j. overtake us
14. j. standeth afar off, truth is fallen in the str.
Jer. 23. 5. shall execute judgment and j. in the earth
31. 23. Lord bless thee, O habitation of j.
50. 7. sinned against the Lord, the habitation of j.
Ezek. 45. 9. O princes, execute judgment and j.
See Do JUDGMENT, before.

JUSTIFICATION

Signifies, *A gracious act of God, whereby he pardons and accepts of sinners on the account of Christ's righteousness imputed to them, and received by faith*, Rom. 5. 16, 18. *Our justification was*, [1] *Confirmed and ratified by the resurrection of Christ*, Rom. 4. 25. [2] *And it is manifested by the good works of believers*, Jam. 2. 21, 24, 25. See SANCTIFY.

Rom. 4. 25. Christ was raised again for our j.
5. 16. but the free gift is of many offences to j.
18. the free gift came on all men to j. of life

JUSTIFY

Signifies, [1] *To absolve or declare one innocent*, Prov. 17. 15. [2] *To absolve and acquit a sinner from the guilt and punishment of sin, through the imputation of Christ's righteousness*, Rom. 3. 28. | 5. 9. [3] *To declare another to be less guilty than ourselves*, Ezek. 16. 51. [4] *To acknowledge a thing or person to be just*, Mat. 11. 19. Luke 7. 35. [5] *To prove and manifest one's self to be in a justified state*, Jam. 2. 21. It is fourfold, [1] *Falsely and vaingloriously*, Luke 10. 29. | 16. 15. [2] *Politically*, Deut. 25. 1. Isa. 5. 23. [3] *Legally*, Rom. 3. 20. Gal. 2. 16. [4] *Evangelically*, Rom. 5. 1. This is said to be, [1] *By Christ*, Gal. 2. 16. [2] *By grace freely*, Rom. 3. 24. Tit. 3. 7. [3] *By faith*, Gal. 3. 8. [4] *By his blood*, Rom. 5. 9. [5] *By his knowledge*, Isa. 53. 11.

Exod. 23. 7. for I will not j. the wicked
Deut. 25. 1. then they shall j. the righteous
Job 9. 20. if I j. myself, my own mouth shall cond.
27. 5. God forbid that I should j. you
33. 32. answer me, speak, for I desire to j. thee
Isa. 5. 23. which j. the wicked for reward
53. 11. by knowl. shall my righteous serv. j. many
Luke 10. 29. he, willing to j. himself, said to Jesus
16. 15. ye are they which j. yourselves before men
Rom. 3. 30. one God shall j. circumcision by faith
Gal. 3. 8. foreseeing that God would j. the heathen

JUSTIFIED.

Job 11. 2. should a man full of talk be j.?
13. 18. behold now, I know that I shall be j.
25. 4. how then can man be j. with G. or be clean?
32. 2. because he j. himself rather than God
Psal. 51. 4. thou mightest be j. when thou speakest
143. 2. in thy sight shall no man living be j.
Isa. 43. 9. they may be j. || 26. thou mayest be j.
45. 25. in the Lord shall all the seed of Israel be j.
Jer. 3. 11. the backsliding Israel hath j. herself
Ezek. 16. 51. j. thy sisters in all abominations, 52.
Dan. 8. † 14. then shall the sanctuary be j.
Mat. 11. 19. wisdom is j. of her children, Luke 7. 35.
12. 37. for by thy words thou shalt be j.
Luke 7. 29. all the people and publicans j. God
18. 14. this man went down j. rather than the other
Acts 13. 39. all that believe are j. from all things from which ye could not be j. by the law
Rom. 2. 13. but the doers of the law shall be j.
3. 4. that thou mightest be j. in thy sayings
20. there shall no flesh be j. in his sight
24. being j. freely by his grace, Tit. 3. 7.
28. a man is j. by faith, 5. 1. Gal. 2. 16. | 3. 24.
4. 2. if Abraham were j. by works, he hath
5. 1. being j. by faith we have peace with God
9. being now j. by his blood, we shall be saved
8. 30. and whom he j. them he also glorified
1 Cor. 4. 4. I know nothing, yet am I not hereby j.
6. 11. ye are j. in the name of the Lord Jesus
Gal. 2. 16. a man is not j. by the works of law, 3. 11.
5. 4. whosoever of you is j. by law, ye are fallen
1 Tim. 3. 16. G. manifest in the flesh, j. in the Spirit
Jam. 2. 21. was not Abraham our father j. by works?
24. ye see how that by works a man is j.
25. was not Rahab the harlot j. by works?

JUSTIFIER.

Rom. 3. 26. the j. of him who believeth in Jesus

JUSTIFIETH.

Prov. 17. 15. he that j. the wicked is abomination
Isa. 50. 8. he is near that j. who will contend with me
Rom. 4. 5. but believeth on him that j. the ungodly
8. 33. to the charge of God's elect? it is God that j.

JUSTIFYING.

1 Kings 8. 32. and j. the righteous, 2 Chron. 6. 23.

JUSTLE.

Nah. 2. 4. the chariots shall j. one against another

JUSTLY.

Mic. 6. 8. what doth the Lord require but to do j.?
Luke 23. 41. we indeed j. for we receive the reward
1 Thess. 2. 10. how holily and j. we behaved

K.

KAB.

2 Kings 6. 25. a k. of doves' dung sold for five pieces

KEEP

Signifies, [1] *To retain or hold fast*, 2 Tim. 1. 14. [2] *To remember*, Luke 2. 51. [3] *To defend and protect*, Psal. 127. 1. [4] *To observe and practise*, Psal. 119. 4. Acts 16. 4. [5] *To save or deliver*, John 17. 15. [6] *To celebrate*, Mat. 26. 18. [7] *To perform fully and perfectly*, Mat. 19. 17.

Gen. 2. 15. Lord put him in the garden of Eden to k. it
18. 19. and they shall k. the way of the Lord
28. 15. and behold I am with thee to k. thee, 20.
30. 31. I will again feed and k. thy flock
33. 9. my brother, k. that thou hast to thyself
41. 35. and let them k. food in the cities
Exod. 6. 5. whom the Egyptians k. in bondage
12. 6. shall k. it till the fourteenth day of month
14. ye shall k. it a feast to the Lord through your generations, 23. 15. | 34. 18. Lev. 23. 41.
25. that ye shall k. this service, 13. 5.
47. and the congregation of Israel shall k. it
13. 10. thou shalt k. this ordinance in his season
20. 8. remember the sabbath day to k. it holy, 31. 13, 14, 16. Deut. 5. 12, 15.
22. 7. if a man deliver money or stuff to k. 10.
23. 7. k. thee far from a false matter
14. three times shalt thou k. a feast to me
20. I send an angel to k. thee in the way
Lev. 6. 2. and lie in that delivered him to k. 4.
18. 4. ye shall k. my ordinances, I am the Lord, 30. | 22. 9. Ezek. 11. 20.
19. 3. shall k. my sabbaths, 30. | 26. 2. Isa. 56. 4.
23. 39. shall k. a feast seven days, 2 Chr. 30. 13.
Lev. 25. 18. ye shall k. my judgments and do them
Num. 6. 24. the Lord bless thee and k. thee
9. 3. in the fourteenth day at even ye shall k. it
11. day of second month at even they shall k. it
18. 7. thou and thy sons shall k. your priests' office
29. 12. ye shall k. a feast to the Lord seven days
36. 7. shall k. himself to the inheritance of tribe, 9.
Deut. 4. 6. k. therefore and do them, 5. 1.
7. 8. because the Ld. loved you, would k. the oath
12. if ye k. them, the Lord shall k. the covenant
16. 10. thou shalt k. the feast of weeks to the Lord
15. shalt k. a solemn feast to the Lord thy God
17. 19. may learn to k. all the words of this law
23. 9. then k. thee from every wicked thing
23. that which is gone out of thy lips thou shalt k.
29. 9. k. therefore the words of this covenant
Josh. 6. 18. k. yourselves from the accursed thing
10. 18. and set men by the cave for to k. them
23. 6. to k. all that is written in the law of Moses
Judg. 2. 22. whether they will k. the way of Lord
Ruth 2. 21. thou shalt k. fast by my young men
1 Sam. 2. 9. he will k. the feet of his saints
7. 1. Eleazar his son, to k. the ark of the Lord
2 Sam. 15. 16. the king left ten women which were concubines to k. the house, 16. 21. | 20. 3.
18. 18. I have no son to k. my name in remembr.
1 Kings 8. 25. k. with thy servant Dav. 2 Chr. 6. 16.
20. 39. brought a man to me and said, k. this
1 Chr. 4. 10. that thou wouldest k. me from evil
12. 33. fifty thousand, which could k. rank, 38.
22. 12. that thou mayest k. the law of the Lord
29. 18. k. this for ever in the imagination of heart
2 Chron. 22. 9. had no power to k. still the kingdom
28. 10. ye purpose to k. under the children of Judah
30. 3. for they could not k. it at that time
23. assembly took counsel to k. other seven days
Ezra 8. 29. watch and k. them till ye weigh them
Neh. 12. 27. to k. the dedication with gladness
13. 22. that the Levites should k. the gates
Esth. 3. 8. nor k. they the king's laws
9. 27. that they would k. those two days of Purim
Job 14. 13. O that thou wouldest k. me secret till
20. 13. though he k. it still within his mouth
Psal. 12. 7. thou shalt k. them, O Lord, 31. 20.
17. 8. k. me as the apple of the eye, hide me
19. 13. k. back also from presumptuous sins
25. 20. O k. my soul, and deliver me, I trust
34. 13. k. thy tongue from evil, and thy lips
37. 34. and k. his way || 39. 1. I will k. my mouth
89. 28. my mercy will I k. for him for ever
91. 11. his angels charge, to k. thee in all thy ways
103. 9. nor chide, nor will he k. his anger for ever
105. 45. they might observe and k. his laws
106. 3. blessed are they that k. judgment
113. 9. he maketh the barren woman to k. house
119. 2. blessed are they that k. his testimonies
4. thou hast commanded us to k. thy precepts
17. that I may live and k. thy word, 101.
33. teach me, and I shall k. it to the end
34. give understanding, I shall k. thy law, 44.
57. O Lord, I have said, that I would k. thy words
63. I am a companion of them that k. thy precepts
69. I will k. thy precepts with my heart, 134.
88. I will k. the testimony of thy mouth
100. I understand, because I k. thy precepts
106. I will k. thy righteous judgments
129. wonderful, therefore doth my soul k. them
136. down my eyes, because they k. not thy law
146. save me, and I shall k. thy testimonies
127. 1. except the Lord k. the city the watchman
140. 4. k. me from the hands of the wicked
141. 3. O Lord, k. the door of my lips
9. k. me from the snares they have laid for me
Prov. 2. 11. understanding shall k. thee
20. thou mayest k. the paths of the righteous
3. 21. my son, k. sound wisdom and discretion
26. Lord shall k. thy foot from being taken
4. 6. love wisdom, and she shall k. thee
13. k. instruction, let her not go, for she is thy life
21. k. my sayings in the midst of thy heart
23. k. thy heart with all diligence, for out of it
5. 2. and that thy lips may k. knowledge
6. 22. when thou sleepest it shall k. thee
24. to k. thee from the evil woman
7. 1. my son, k. my words, and lay up my command.
5. they may k. thee from the strange woman
8. 32. for blessed are they that k. my ways
22. 5. he that doth k. his soul shall be far from them
18. it is pleasant if thou k. them within thee
24. † 19. k. not company with the wicked
28. 4. such as k. the law contend with them
Eccl. 3. 6. there is a time to k. and to cast away
5. 1. k. thy foot when thou goest to the house
Cant. 8. 12. that k. the fruit thereof, two hundred
Isa. 26. 3. thou wilt k. him in perfect peace
27. 3. I the Lord do k. it, I will k. it night and day
42. 6. I the Lord have called thee, I will k. thee
43. 6. k. not back || 56. 1. k. ye judgment
Jer. 3. 5. will he k. his anger to the end?
12. and I will not k. anger for ever
31. 10. and k. him as a shepherd doth his flock
42. 4. I will k. nothing back from you
Ezek. 20. 19. k. my judgments and do them, 36. 27.
43. 11. that they may k. the whole form thereof
Hos. 12. 6. k. mercy and judgment, wait on God
Mic. 6. † 16. he doth much k. statutes of Omri
7. 5. the k. the doors of thy mouth from her that
Nah. 1. 15. k. thy feasts || 2. 1. k. the munition
Zech. 3. 7. then thou shalt also k. my courts
13. 5. man taught me to k. cattle from my youth
14. 16. and to k. the feast of tabernacles, 18, 19.
Mal. 2. 7. for the priests' lips should k. knowledge
Mark 7. 9. that ye may k. your own tradition
Luke 4. 10. he shall give his angels charge to k. thee
8. 15. they who having heard the word k. it
11. 28. blessed are they that hear the word and k. it
19. 43. thy enemies shall k. thee in on every side
John 8. 51. if k. my saying shall never see death, 52.
55. but I know him, and k. his saying
12. 25. he that hateth his life in this world shall k. it
14. 23. if a man love me he will k. my words
15. 20. if kept my saying, they will k. yours also

John 17. 11. k. thro' thy name || 15. k. from evil
Acts 5. 3. and to k. back part of the price of land
10. 28. for a man that is a Jew to k. company
12. 4. and delivered him to soldiers to k. him
15. 5. to command them to k. the law of Moses
24. ye must be circumcised, and k. the law
29. from which if ye k. yourselves, ye do well
16. 4. they delivered them the decrees for to k.
23. charging the jailer to k. them safely
18. 21. I must by all means k. this feast in Jerus.
21. 25. k. themselves from things offered to idols
24. 23. he commanded a centurion to k. Paul
Rom. 2. 25. circumcision profiteth, if thou k. the law
26. if uncircumcision k. the righteousness of law
1 Cor. 5. 8. let us k. the feast || 11. not k. company
7. 37. decreed that he will k. his virgin, doeth well
9. 27. I k. under my body and bring it into subj.
11. 2. that ye k. the ordinances, as I delivered them
15. 2. if ye k. in memory what I preached to you
2 Cor. 11. 9. kept myself, and so will I k. myself
Gal. 6. 13. neither do circumcised k. the law
Eph. 4. 3. endeavouring to k. the unity of the Spirit
Phil. 4. 7. the peace of God shall k. your hearts
2 Thess. 3. 3. who shall establish and k. you from evil
1 Tim. 5. 22. nor partaker of sins, k. thyself pure
6. 20. k. that which is committed to thy trust
2 Tim. 1. 12. able to k. that I committed to him
14. good thing committed to thee k. by Holy G.
Jam. 1. 27. and to k. himself unspotted from world
2. 10. for whosoever shall k. the whole law
1 John 5. 21. children, k. yourselves from idols
Jude 21. k. yourselves in the love of God, looking
24. to him that is able to k. you from falling
Rev. 1. 3. blessed are they that hear and k. those th.
3. 10. I will k. thee from the hour of temptation
22. 9. of them who k. the sayings of this book

KEEP *alive.*

Gen. 6. 19. bring into the ark to k. them *alive*, 20.
7. 3. to k. seed *alive* on the face of all the earth
Num. 31. 18. women, children k. *alive* for yourselves
2 Sam. 8. 2. he measured with one full line to k. *alive*
Psal. 22. 29. and none can k. *alive* his own soul
33. 19. to deliver and k. them *alive* in famine
41. 2. the Lord will preserve him and k. him *alive*

KEEP *charge.*

Lev. 8. 35. and k. the *charge* of the L. 1 Kings 2. 3.
Num. 1. 53. Levites k. *charge* of the tabernacle of testimony, 18. 4. | 31. 30. 1 Chron. 23. 32.
3. 7. they shall k. his c. 8. 26. | 18. 3. Deut. 11. 1.
8. they shall k. the *charge* of the children of Israel
32. k. c. of the sanctuary, 18. 5. 1 Chron. 23. 32.
Ezek. 44. 16. to minister to me, and k. my *charge*
Zech. 3. 7. if thou wilt k. my *charge* then shalt judge

KEEP *commandments.*

Exod. 16. 28. how long refuse ye to k. my *command.*
20. 6. shewing mercy to them that k. my *commandments*, Deut. 5. 10. | 7. 9. Dan. 9. 4.
Lev. 22. 31. therefore shall ye k. my *commandments* and do them, Deut. 4. 40. | 6. 17. | 7. 11.
26. 3. if ye k. my *commandments*, Deut. 11. 22. | 19. 9. | 28. 9. | 30. 10. 1 Kings 3. 14.
Deut. 4. 2. that ye may k. the c. of the Lord
5. 29. O that they would fear me and k. my c.
8. 2. know whether thou wouldest k. his *command.*
6. thou shalt k. the *command.* 11. 1, 8. | 13. 4, 18.
10. 13. doth Lord require him to k. c. 27. 1. | 30. 16.
26. 17. thou hast avouched the Lord to k. his c.
18. Lord avouched thee, that thou shouldest k. c.
28. 45. because thou hearkenedst not to k. his c.
Josh. 22. 5. take heed to k. c. to cleave to him
1 Kings 2. 3. keep the charge of the Lord to k. his c.
6. 12. k. my c. 2 Kings 17. 13. Prov. 4. 4. | 7. 2.
8. 58. that he may incline our hearts to k. his c.
61. let your heart be perfect to k. his *command.*
9. 6. if ye will not k. my c. I will cut off Israel
11. 38. if thou wilt k. my c. Neh. 1. 9. John 15. 10.
2 Kings 23. 3. made a covenant to k. c. 2 Chr. 34. 31.
1 Chr. 28. 8. k. and seek for all the c. of the Lord
29. 19. give to Solomon a perfect heart to k. thy c.
Psal. 78. 7. not forget the works of God, but k. his c.
119. 60. I made haste and delayed not to k. thy c.
115. depart ye evil doers, for I will k. c. of my G.
Prov. 3. 1. forget not my law, let thy heart k. my c.
6. 20. my son, k. thy father's c. forsake not the law
Eccl. 8. 2. I counsel thee to k. the king's *command.*
12. 13. fear God and k. his c. this is the whole duty
Mat. 19. 17. if thou wilt enter into life, k. the c.
John 14. 15. if ye love me, k. my *commandments*
1 Tim. 6. 14. that thou k. this c. without spot
1 John 2. 3. we know that we know him if we k. his c.
3. 22. what we ask we receive, because we k. his c.
5. 2. when we love God and k. his *command.*
3. this is the love of God, that we k. his *com.*
Rev. 12. 17. make war with her seed which k. c.
14. 12. here are they which k. the c. of God

See COVENANT.

KEEP *passover.*

Exod. 12. 48. when a stranger will k. p. to Lord, let his males be circumcised, then let him k. p.
Num. 9. 2. let the children of Israel k. *passover* in its season, 4. Deut. 16. 1. 2 Kings 23. 21.
6. could not k. the *pass.* || 10. yet he shall k. *pass.*
12. all the ordinances of *passover* they shall k. it
13. and forbeareth to k. the *pass.* that soul cut off
14. if a stranger will k. the *passover* to the Lord
2 Chr. 30. 1. come to k. the p. to the God of Israel
2. taken counsel, to k. *pass.* in the second month
35. 16. all the service was prepared to k. *passover*
18. nor did all the kings of Israel k. such a *pass.*
Mat. 26. 18. say to him, I will k. *pass.* at thy house

KEEP *silence.*

Judg. 3. 19. who said, k. *silence*, and all went out
Ps. 35. 22. k. not *silence*, 83. 1. || 50. 3. come and not k. *silence*
Eccl. 3. 7. a time to k. *silence* and a time to speak
Isa. 41. 1. k. s. before me, O islands, and let people
62. 6. k. not s. || 65. 6. behold, I will not k. s.
Lam. 2. 10. the elders of daughter of Zion k. *silence*
Amos 5. 13. the prudent shall k. *silence* in that time
Hab. 2. 20. Lord in his temple, let the earth k. *silence*
1 Cor. 14. 28. let him k. *silence* in the church
34. let your women k. *silence* in the churches

KEEP *statutes.*

Exod. 15. 26. if thou wilt k. all his *statutes*, Deut. 30. 10. 1 Kings 9. 4. | 11. 38.
Lev. 18. 5. you shall k. my *statutes* and judgments, 26. | 19. 19. | 20. 8, 22. Ezek. 44. 24.
Deut. 4. 40. thou shalt k. therefore his *sta.* 26. 16.
6. 2. that thou mightest fear Lord to k. his *statutes*
26. 17. thou hast avouched the Lord to k. his *stat.*
28. 45. thou hearkenedst not to k. his *statutes*
1 Kings 11. 33. not walked in my ways to k. my *stat.*
Ps. 119. 5. that my ways were directed to k. thy *st.*
8. I will k. thy *stat.* forsake me not utterly, 145.
Ezek. 18. 21. if the wicked will turn and k. my *stat.*

KEEPER.

Gen. 4. 2. Abel was a k. of sheep || 9. my brother's k.
39. 21. Lord gave Joseph favour in sight of the k.
22. the k. of the prison committed to Joseph
23. the k. of the prison looked not to any thing
1 Sam. 17. 20. David left the sheep with a k.
22. David left his carriage in the hand of the k.
28. 2. I will make the k. of mine head for ever
2 Kings 22. 14. k. of the wardrobe, 2 Chr. 34. 22.
Neh. 2. 8. Asaph the k. of the king's forest
3. 29. after him Shemaiah k. of the east gate
Esth. 2. 3. custody of Hege k. of women, 8, 15.
Job 27. 18. and as a booth that the k. maketh
Psal. 121. 5. Lord is thy k. the Lord is thy shade
Cant. 1. 6. they made me the k. of the vineyards
Jer. 35. 4. Maaseiah the son of Shallum k. of the door
Acts 16. 27. and the k. of the prison awaking
36. the k. of the prison told this saying to Paul
19. † 35. the city of the Ephesians is a temple k.

KEEPERS.

2 Kings 11. 5. a third part shall be k. of the watch
1 Chron. 9. 19. k. of the gates of the tabernacle
Eccl. 12. 3. when the k. of the house tremble
Cant. 5. 7. the k. took away my vail from me
8. 11. Solomon let out the vineyard to k.
Jer. 4. 17. as k. of the field are they against her
Ezek. 40. 45. k. of charge of house, 46. | 44. 8, 14.
Mat. 28. 4. for fear of him the k. did shake
Acts 5. 23. the k. standing before the doors
12. 6. k. kept the prison || 19. Herod examined the k.
Tit. 2. 5. to be discreet, chaste, k. at home, good

See DOOR.

KEEPEST.

1 Kings 8. 23. who k. covenant and mercy with thy servants, 2 Chron. 6. 14. Neh. 9. 32.
Acts 21. 24. thou walkest orderly and k. the law

KEEPETH.

Exod. 21. 18. and he died not, but k. his bed
Deut. 7. 9. faithful G. which k. covenant, Neh. 1. 5.
1 Sam. 16. 11. and behold he k. the sheep
Job 33. 18. he k. back his soul from the pit
Psal. 34. 20. he k. all his bones, none is broken
121. 3. he that k. thee will not slumber, 4.
146. 6. Lord God, which k. truth for ever
Prov. 2. 8. he k. the paths of judgment
10. 17. he is in the way of life that k. instruction
13. 3. he that k. his mouth k. his life, 21. 23.
6. righteousness k. him upright in the way
16. 17. that k. his way preserveth his soul, 19. 16.
19. 8. he that k. understanding shall find good
24. 12. that k. thy soul, doth not he know
27. 18. whoso k. the fig-tree shall eat fruit
28. 7. whoso k. the law is a wise son, but he
29. 3. that k. company with harlots, spendeth
11. but a wise man k. it in till afterwards
18. but he that k. the law, happy is he
Eccl. 8. 5. k. the commandments shall feel no evil
Isa. 26. 2. that nation which k. truth may enter in
56. 2. that k. the sabbath from polluting it, and k. his hand from doing any evil, 6.
Jer. 48. 10. cursed be he that k. back his sword
Lam. 3. 28. he sitteth alone and k. silence
Hab. 2. 5. he is a proud man, neither k. at home
Luke 11. 21. when a strong man armed k. his palace
John 7. 19. and yet none of you k. the law
9. 16. is not of God, because he k. not the sabbath
14. 21. that hath my commandments and k. them
24. he that loveth me not, k. not my sayings
1 John 2. 4. that saith, I know him, and k. not
5. whoso k. his word, in him is love, 3. 24.
5. 18. he that is begotten of God k. himself
Rev. 2. 26. he that overcometh and k. my works
16. 15. blessed is he that k. his garments, lest he
22. 7. blessed is he that k. the sayings of this book

KEEPING.

Exod. 34. 7. the Lord God k. mercy for thousands
Num. 3. 28. k. the charge of the sanctuary, 38
Deut. 8. 11. forget not God, in not k. his commands
1 Sam. 25. 16. while we were with them k. sheep
1 Chron. 12. † 36. of Asher k. rank, forty thousand
Neh. 12. 25. were porters k. the ward at the gates
Psal. 19. 11. and in k. of them is great reward
Prov. 4. † 23. keep thy heart above all k. out of it
Ezek. 17. 14. by k. of his covenant it might stand
Dan. 9. 4. O Lord the great God, k. covenant
Luke 2. 8. there were shepherds k. watch by night
1 Cor. 7. 19. but k. the commandments of God
Heb. 4. † 9. there remaineth a k. of a sabbath
1 Pet. 4. 19. commit the k. of their souls to him

KEPT.

Gen. 26. 5. Abraham k. my charge and my laws
29. 9. Rachel came with sheep, for she k. them
39. 9. neither hath he k. back any thing from me
42. 16. send one, and ye shall be k. in prison
Exod. 3. 1. now Moses k. the flock of Jethro
16. 23. lay up for you, to be k. till the morning
32. pot of manna to be k. for generations, 33, 34.
21. 29. if the owner hath not k. him in, 36.
Num. 5. 13. and it be k. close, and she be defiled
9. 5. they k. the passover || 7. why are we k. back
19. then Israel k. the charge of the Lord, 23.
17. 10. bring Aaron's rod to be k. for a token
19. 9. water of separation k. for the congregation
24. 11. Lord hath k. thee back from honour
31. 47. which k. the charge of the tabernacle
Deut. 32. 10. he k. them as the apple of his eye
33. 9. they observed thy word, k. thy covenant
Josh. 5. 10. Israel k. the passover in Gilgal
14. 10. the Lord hath k. me alive these 45 years

Josh. 22. 2. you have k. all that Moses commanded
3. have k. the charge of commandment of Lord
Ruth 2. 23. so she k. fast by the maidens of Boaz
1 Sam. 9. 24. to this time it hath been k. for thee
13. 13. hast not k. the commandment of Lord, 14.
17. 34. David said, thy servant k. his father's sheep
21. 4. have k. themselves at least from women
25. 21. David said, surely in vain have I k. all that
33. blessed be thou who hast k. me this day
34. the Lord God hath k. me from evil, 39.
26. 15. why hast thou not k. thy lord the king?
16. because ye have not k. your master, the Lord's
2 Sam. 13. 34. the young man that k. the watch
22. 22. I have k. the ways of the Lord, Ps. 18. 21.
24. I have k. myself from iniquity, Psal. 18. 23.
44. thou hast k. me to be head of the heathen
1 Kings 2. 43. why hast thou not k. the oath of L.
3. 6. thou hast k. for him this great kindness
8. 24. who hast k. with thy servant David my father that thou promisedst him, 2 Chron. 6. 15.
11. 10. Solomon k. not that the Lord commanded
11. and thou hast not k. my covenant and statutes
34. because David k. my commandments, 14. 8.
13. 21. man of God from Judah not k. commandm.
20. † 7. I k. not back silver and gold from him
2 Kings 17. 19. Judah k. not the commandments
18. 6. Hezekiah k. the commandments of the Lord
1 Chron. 10. 13. the word of the Lord Saul k. not
12. 1. while David k. himself close because of Saul
2 Chron. 7. 8. Solomon k. the feast seven days
9. for they k. the dedication of the altar seven days
30. 21. k. feast of unleavened bread, Ezra 6. 22.
23. and they k. other seven days with gladness
34. 21. because our fathers have not k. the word
35. 1. Josiah and Israel k. the passover, 17, 19.
18. there was no passover like to that k. in Israel
Ezra 3. 4. they k. also the feast of tabernacles
6. 16. k. the dedication of this house with joy
19. the children of the captivity k. the passover
Neh. 1. 7. we have not k. the commandments
8. 18. and they k. the feast seven days
9. 34. nor our priests nor our fathers k. thy law
Esth. 9. 28. that these days of Purim should be k.
Job 23. 11. his ways have I k. and not declined
28. 21. and k. close from the fowls of the air
Ps. 17. 4. I have k. me from paths of the destroyer
30. 3. hast k. me alive || 42. 4. that k. holy day
78. 10. they k. not the covenant of God
56. they tempted God, and k. not his testimonies
99. 7. they k. his testimonies and the ordinance
119. 22. for I have k. thy testimonies, 167.
55. I have k. thy law || 56. I k. thy precepts, 168
67. now have I k. thy word || 158. k. not thy word
Eccl. 2. 10. what my eyes desired I k. not from them
5. 13. riches k. for the owners thereof to their hurt
Cant. 1. 6. but my own vineyard have I not k.
Isa. 30. 29. a song as when a holy solemnity is k.
Jer. 16. 11. not k. my laws || 35. 18. k. his precepts
Ezek. 5. 7. nor have k. my judgments, 20. 21.
18. 9. hath k. my judgments || 19. k. my statutes
44. 8. ye have not k. the charge of my holy things
15. that k. the charge of my sanctuary, 48. 11.
Dan. 5. 19. whom he would, he k. alive, he set up
7. 28. but I k. the matter in my heart
Hos. 12. 12. Israel served for a wife, and k. sheep
Amos 1. 11. and Edom k. his wrath for ever
2. 4. Judah hath not k. his commandments
Mic. 6. 16. for the statutes of Omri are k.
Mal. 2. 9. according as ye have not k. my ways, 3. 7.
3. 14. what profit that we have k. his ordinance
Mat. 8. 33. and they that k. the swine fled, and told
13. 35. will utter things which have been k. secret
14. 6. but when Herod's birth-day was k.
19. 20. these have I k. from my youth, Luke 18. 21.
Mark 4. 22. nor was any thing k. secret, but that it
9. 10. and they k. that saying, Luke 9. 36.
Luke 2. 19. Mary k. these things in her heart, 51.
8. 29. and he was k. bound with chains, in fetters
19. 20. thy pound, which I have k. in a napkin
John 2. 10. but thou hast k. the good wine till now
12. 7. against day of my burying hath she k. this
15. 10. as I have k. my father's commandments
20. if they have k. my saying, they will keep yours
17. 6. thine they were, and have k. thy word
12. k. in thy name, those thou gavest me I have k.
18. 16. and spake to her that k. the door
17. then saith the damsel that k. the door to Peter
Acts 5. 2. sold, and k. back part of the price
7. 53. who received the law, and have not k. it
9. 33. Eneas had k. his bed eight years, was sick
12. 5. Peter was k. in prison || 6. k. the prison
20. 20. I k. back nothing profitable to you
22. 20. and k. the raiment of them that slew him
23. 35. and he commanded him to be k. 25. 21.
25. 4. Festus answered that Paul should be k.
27. 43. the centurion k. them from their purpose
28. 16. Paul dwelt with a soldier that k. him
Rom. 16. 25. mystery k. secret since the world began
2 Cor. 11. 9. I k. myself from being burdensome
32. the governor k. the city with a garrison
Gal. 3. 23. before faith came, we were k. under law
2 Tim. 4. 7. have finished my course, I k. the faith
Heb. 11. 28. through faith Moses k. the passover
Jam. 5. 4. the hire that is k. back by fraud, crieth
1 Pet. 1. 5. who are k. by the power of G. thro' faith
2 Pet. 3. 7. which by the same word are k. in store
Jude 6. the angels which k. not their first estate
Rev. 3. 8. hast k. my word, and not denied my name
10. because thou hast k. the word of my patience

KEPT *silence.*

Job 29. 21. men gave ear, and k. *sil.* at my counsel
31. 34. did I fear a great multitude, that I k. *sil.*
Psal. 32. 3. when I k. *silence*, my bones waxed old
50. 21. these things hast thou done, and I k. *silence*
Acts 15. 12. then all the multitude k. *silence*
22. 2. that he spake Hebrew, they k. the more *sil.*

KERCHIEFS.

Ezek. 13. 18. make k. on head of every stature to hunt
21. your k. also will I tear, and deliver my people

KERNELS.

Num. 6. 4. eat nothing from the k. even to the husk

KETTLE.
1 Sam. 2. 14. priest's servant struck into the k. or pot

KEY
Signifies, [1] *An instrument to open a lock*, Judg. 3. 25. [2] *The gift and ability to interpret the scripture, whereby an entrance is made to the knowledge thereof*, Luke 11. 52. [3] *The whole administration of the Gospel with reference both to the publication of its doctrine, and the dispensing the ordinances of it*, Mat. 16. 19. It is an emblem of *government and power*, Isa. 22. 22.
Judg. 3. 25. therefore they took a k. and opened
Isa. 22. 22. the k. of house of David lay on Eliakim
Luke 11. 52. ye have taken away the k. of knowledge
Rev. 3. 7. saith he that hath the k. of David
9. 1. to him was given the k. of bottomless pit, 20. 1.

KEYS.
Mat. 16. 19. I will give the k. of kingdom of heaven
Rev. 1. 18. and have the k. of hell and of death

KICK.
1 Sam. 2. 29. wherefore k. ye at my sacrifice ?
Acts 9. 5. it is hard to k. against the pricks, 26. 14.

KICKED.
Deut. 32. 15. but Jeshurun waxed fat and k.

KID.
Gen. 37. 31. Joseph's brethren killed a k. of the goats
38. 17. I will send thee a k. from the flock
Exod. 23. 19. thou shalt not see the k. in his mother's milk, 34. 26. Deut. 14. 21.
Lev. 4. 23. he shall bring his offering, a k. of the goats, 28. | 9. 3. Ezek. 43. 22. | 45. 23.
5. 6. bring a lamb or a k. for a sin offering
23. 19. then ye shall sacrifice one k. of the goats, Num. 7. 16, 22, 28. | 15. 24. | 28. 15, 30. | 29. 5, 11, 16, 19, 25. Ezek. 45. † 15.
Num. 15. 11. thus shall it be done for a lamb or a k.
Judg. 6. 19. Gideon went and made ready a k.
13. 19. so Manoah took a k. with a meat-offering
14. 6. Samson rent lion as a k. nothing in his hand
15. 1. Samson visited his wife with a k. and said
1 Sam. 16. 20. Jesse took an ass laden, and a k.
Isa. 11. 6. the leopard shall lie down with the k.
Luke 15. 29. and yet thou never gavest me a k.

KIDS.
Gen. 27. 9. fetch me from thence two k. of goats
16. she put the skins of the k. on his hands
Lev. 16. 5. he shall take two k. of the goats
Num. 7. 87. the k. of the goats for sin offering twelve
1 Sam. 10. 3. one carrying three k. another bread
1 Kings 20. 27. pitched like two little flocks of k.
2 Chron. 35. 7. Josiah gave lambs and k. for offerings
Cant. 1. 8. feed thy k. beside the shepherds' tents

KIDNEYS
Signify, [1] *Those natural parts of the body in man or beast*, Lev. 3. 4. [2] *The kernels of wheat*, Deut. 32. 14. [3] *The innermost affections and desires*, Psal. 16. 7.
Exod. 29. 13. thou shalt take the two k. and burn 22. Lev. 3. 4, 10, 15. | 4. 9. | 7. 4. | 8. 16, 25.
Lev. 9. 10. but fat and k. burn on the altar, 19.
Deut. 32. 14. rams, with the fat of k. of wheat
Isa. 34. 6. the sword of Lord, with fat of k. of rams

KILL
Is spoken. (I) *Of* God, *who has many ways to deprive of life*, Lam. 2. 21. (II) *Of* man. [1] *Lawfully, when a malefactor is put to death by the sentence of a magistrate*, Deut. 13. 9. [2] *Unlawfully*, 2 Sam. 13. 28. 1 Kings 21. 19. (III) *Of* wrath, *which kills men, either as it preys upon their spirits, and wasteth them inwardly; or, as it prompts them to such rash, furious, and wicked actions, as may procure their death; or, as it provoketh God to cut them off*, Job 5. 2. (IV) *Of the* desire of the slothful, *which exposeth him to extreme want, and so to death: or puts him upon such wicked courses to supply his wants, as bring him to an untimely death*, Prov. 21. 25. (V) *Of the* letter, that is, *the law which is said to kill, because it accuseth, condemneth, and denounceth the wrath of God against men, for not doing their duty, but gives no strength for the doing of it*, 2 Cor. 3. 6.
Gen. 4. 15. lest any finding Cain, should k. him
12. 12. they will k. me, but will save thee alive
26. 7. lest the men of the place should k. me
27. 42. doth comfort himself, purposing to k. thee
37. 21. Reuben heard and said, let us not k. him
43. † 16. bring these men home, k. a killing
Exod. 1. 16. if it be a son, then ye shall k. him
2. 14. intendest thou to k. me? Acts 7. 28.
4. 24. the Lord met him, and sought to k. him
12. 6. the congregation of Israel shall k. it, 21.
16. 3. to k. this whole assembly with hunger
17. 3. to k. us and our children with thirst
20. 13. thou shalt not k. Deut. 5. 17. Mat. 5. 21. Rom. 13. 9.
22. 1. if a man steal an ox or sheep, and k. it
24. and I will k. you with the sword
29. 11. k. bullock before the Lord, Lev. 1. 5. | 4. 4.
20. then shalt k. the ram, and take of his blood
Lev. 1. 11. shall k. it on the side of the altar, 16. 15.
3. 2. and k. it at the door of the tabernacle
8. he shall k. it before the tabernacle, 13.
4. 24. he shall k. it in the place where they k.
33. where they k. the burnt-offering, 7. 2.
14. 13. where he shall k. the sin offering, 16. 11.
25. he shall k. the lamb of the trespass offering
50. and he shall k. one of the birds
20. 4. giveth his seed to Molech, and k. him not
16. thou shalt k. the woman and the beast
22. 28. whether cow or ewe, ye shall not k. it
Num. 11. 15. if thou deal thus with me, k. me
14. 15. if thou k. all this people as one man
16. 13. hast brought us to k. us in the wilderness
22. 29. were a sword, for now would I k. thee
31. 17. now k. every male among the little ones, k. every woman that hath known man
35. 27. and the revenger of blood k. the slayer
Deut. 4. 42. who should k. his neighbour unawares
12. 15. thou mayest k. and eat flesh in thy gates

Deut. 12. 21. then thou shalt k. of thy herd and flock
13. 9. but thou shalt surely k. him, thine hand
16. † 5. not k. the passover within thy gates
32. 39. I k. and I make alive, I wound and I heal
Judg. 9. † 24. which strengthened his hands to k.
13. 23. if the Lord were pleased to k. us, would not
15. 13. saying, surely we will not k. thee
16. 2. morning, when it is day, we shall k. him
20. 31. they began to k. as at other times, 39.
1 Sam. 16. 2. if Saul hear it, he will k. me
17. 9. if he be able to k. me, then we will serve
19. 1. to all his servants, that they should k. David
2. saying, Saul my father seeketh to k. thee
17. why should I k. thee || 24. 10. bade me k. thee
30. 15. swear thou wilt neither k. me, nor deliver
2 Sam. 13. 28. I say, smite Amnon, then k. him
14. 7. that we may k. him, for life of his brother
32. if any iniquity be in me, let him k. me
21. 4. nor for us shalt thou k. any man in Israel
1 Kings 11. 40. Solomon sought to k. Jeroboam
12. 27. and they shall k. me, and go again to Rehob.
2 Kings 5. 7. am I a God, to k. and make alive?
7. 4. and if they k. us, we shall but die
11. 15. him that followeth her k. with the sword
2 Chron. 35. 6. k. the passover, sanctify yourselves
Esth. 3. 13. letters were sent by posts to k. all Jews
7. † 4. are sold, that they should destroy and k.
Eccl. 3. 3. a time to k. and a time to heal
Isa. 14. 30. and I will k. thy root with famine
29. 1. add ye year to year, let them k. sacrifices
Ezek. 34. 3. ye k. them that are fed, but feed not
Mat. 5. 21. who shall k. shall be in danger of judgm.
10. 28. fear not them which k. the body, Luke 12. 4.
17. 23. and they shall k. him, Mark 9. 31. | 10. 34.
21. 38. this is the heir, come let us k. him, Mark 12. 7. Luke 20. 14.
23. 34. and some of them ye shall k. and crucify
24. 9. then shall they deliv. you up, and shall k. you
26. 4. they might take Jesus by subtilty and k. him
Mark 3. 4. is it lawful to save life, or to k.?
10. 19. do not k. Luke 18. 20. Jam. 2. 11.
Luke 13. 31. depart hence, for Herod will k. thee
15. 23. and bring hither the fatted calf and k. it
22. 2. the priests and scribes sought how to k. him
John 5. 18. Jews sought the more to k. him, 7. 1.
7. 19. keepeth the law, why go ye about to k. me?
20. thou hast a devil, who goeth about to k. thee?
25. is not this he whom they seek to k.?
8. 22. will he k. himself? || 37. ye seek to k. me, 40.
10. 10. the thief cometh not but to steal and k.
Acts 9. 23. the Jews took counsel to k. Paul, 26. 21.
24. watched the gates day and night to k. him
10. 13. came a voice to him, rise, Peter, k. and eat
21. 31. as they went about to k. him, tidings
23. 15. we, ere he come near, are ready to k. him
25. 3. laying wait in the way to k. him
27. 42. the soldiers' counsel was to k. the prisoners
Jam. 2. 11. if thou commit no adultery, yet if thou k.
4. 2. ye k. and desire to have, and cannot obtain
Rev. 2. 23. and I will k. her children with death
6. 4. and that they should k. one another
8. power was given them to k. with the sword
9. 5. it was given that they should not k. them
11. 7. the beast shall overcome them and k. them

KILLED.
Gen. 31. † 54. then Jacob k. beasts on the mount
37. 31. they took Joseph's coat, and k. a kid
Exod. 21. 29. the beast hath k. a man or woman
Lev. 4. 15. the bullock shall be k. before the Lord
6. 25. in the place where the burnt offering is k. shall the sin offering be k. before the Lord
8. 19. the ram he k. || 14. 5. one of the birds be k.
14. 6. shall dip them in the blood of the bird k.
Num. 16. 41. ye have k. the people of the Lord
31. 19. whosoever hath k. any person, purify
1 Sam. 24. 11. the skirt of thy robe, and k. thee not
25. 11. take my flesh I have k. for my shearers
28. 24. the woman hasted and k. the calf
2 Sam. 12. 9. thou hast k. Uriah with the sword
21. 17. Abishai smote the Philistine and k. him
1 Kings 16. 7. like Jeroboam, and because he k. him
10. Zimri went and smote Ela, and k. him
21. 19. hast thou k. and also taken possession?
2 Kings 15. 25. Pekah k. Pekahiah, and reigned
1 Chron. 19. 18. David k. Shophach the captain
2 Chron. 18. 2. Ahab k. sheep and oxen in abundance
25. 3. he slew those that had k. the king his father
29. 22. so they k. the bullocks, rams, lambs
24. the priests k. them and made reconciliation
30. 15. k. the passover, 35. 1, 11. Ezra 6. 20.
Psal. 44. 22. for thy sake are we k. all the day long
Prov. 9. 2. hath k. her beasts, mingled her wine
Lam. 2. 21. thou hast k. and not pitied
Mat. 16. 21. k. and raised again, Mark 8. 31. | 9. 31.
21. 35. beat one, and k. another, Mark 12. 5.
22. 4. my oxen and my fatlings are k. all things
23. 31. are children of them that k. the prophets
Mark 6. 19. and Herodias would have k. him
12. 8. k. him and cast him out of the vineyard
14. 12. the first day, when they k. the passover
Luke 11. 47. and your fathers k. them, 48.
12. 5. after he hath k. hath power to cast into hell
15. 27. thy father hath k. the fatted calf, 30.
22. 7. the day when the passover must be k.
Acts 3. 15. k. the Prince of life || 12. 2. he k. James
16. 27. he drew his sword, and would have k. himself
23. 12. not eat nor drink till they had k. Paul
27. taken of the Jews, and should have been k.
Rom. 8. 36. for thy sake we are k. all the day long
11. 3. Lord, they have k. thy prophets, and digged
2 Cor. 6. 9. as dying we live, as chastened and not k.
1 Thess. 2. 15. who k. the Lord Jesus and prophets
Jam. 5. 6. ye have condemned and k. the just
Rev. 6. 11. brethren who should be k. as they were
9. 18. by these three was the third part of men k.
20. the rest which were not k. by these plagues
11. 5. if any hurt him he must in this manner be k.
13. 10. killeth with sword, must be k. with sword
15. not worship image of the beast, should be k.

KILLEDST.
Exod. 2. 14. to kill me, as thou k. the Egyptian
1 Sam. 24. 18. forasmuch as thou k. me not

KILLEST.
Mat. 23. 37. that k. the prophets, Luke 13. 34.

KILLETH.
Lev. 17. 3. who k. an ox, goat in the camp, or k. out
24. 17. he that k. any man shall surely be put to death, 21. Num. 35. 30.
18. he that k. a beast, shall make it good, 21.
Num. 35. 11. the slayer may flee, who k. any person unawares, 15. Deut. 19. 4. Josh. 20. 3, 9.
1 Sam. 2. 6. the Lord k. and maketh alive
17. 25. man who k. him, king will enrich, 26, 27.
Job 5. 2. for wrath k. the foolish man
24. 14. the murderer k. the poor and needy
Prov. 21. 25. the desire of the slothful k. him
Isa. 66. 3. he that k. an ox, as if he slew a man
John 16. 2. who k. you, think he doeth God service
2 Cor. 3. 6. for the letter k. the Spirit giveth life
Rev. 13. 10. he that k. with sword must be killed

KILLING.
Gen. 43. † 16. bring these men home, kill a k.
Judg. 9. 24. which aided him in k. his brethren
2 Chr. 30. 17. the Levites had charge of k. passover
Psal. 42. † 10. as with a k. mine enemies reproach
Prov. 9. † 2. wisdom hath killed her k.
Isa. 22. 13. slaying oxen, and k. sheep, eating flesh
Hos. 4. 2. by swearing, lying, k. and stealing
Mark 12. 5. sent others, beating some, and k. some

KIN.
Lev. 18. 6. none shall approach to any near of k.
20. 19. for he uncovereth his near k.
21. 2. for his k. that is near, he may be defiled
25. 25. if any of his k. come to redeem it, 49.
Ruth 2. 20. Naomi said, the man is near of k. to us
2 Sam. 19. 42. the king is near of k. to us
Mark 6. 4. a prophet is not, but among his own k.

KIND, *Substantive.*
Gen. 1. 11. fruit-tree yielding fruit after his k. 12.
12. herb yielding seed after his k. and the tree
21. the waters brought forth abundantly after their k. and every winged fowl after his k.
24. earth, and beast of earth after their k.
25. God made the beast of the earth after his k.
6. 20. of fowls after their k. and of cattle after their k. every creeping thing after his k.
7. 14. beast, cattle, and fowl, after their k.
Lev. 11. 14. in abomination, vulture, kite, raven, hawk after his k. 15, 16, 19. Deut. 14. 14.
29. the weasel, mouse, and tortoise after his k.
19. 19. not let thy cattle gender with a diverse k.
1 Chron. 28. 14. for all instruments of every k.
Neh. 13. 20. sellers of all k. of ware, lodged
Eccl. 2. 5. I planted trees of all k. of fruits
Ezek. 27. 12. the multitude of all k. of riches
Mat. 13. 47. like a net, and gathered of every k.
17. 21. k. goeth not out but by prayer, Mark 9. 29.
1 Cor. 15. 39. there is one k. of flesh of men
Jam. 1. 18. that we should be a k. of first-fruits
3. 7. for every k. of beasts and birds is tamed

KIND.
2 Chron. 10. 7. saying, if thou be k. to this people
Luke 6. 35. God is k. to the unthankful and evil
1 Cor. 13. 4. charity suffereth long and is k.
Eph. 4. 32. be k. one to another, tender-hearted

KINDS.
Gen. 8. 19. whatsoever creepeth after their k.
2 Chron. 16. 14. filled with divers k. of spices
Jer. 15. 3. I will appoint over them four k.
Ezek. 47. 10. their fish shall be according to their k.
Dan. 3. 5. dulcimer, and all k. of music, 7, 10, 15.
1 Cor. 12. 10. to another divers k. of tongues
14. 10. there are, it may be, so many k. of voices

KINDLE.
Prov. 26. 21. a contentious man to k. strife
Isa. 9. 18. it shall k. in the thickets of the forest
10. 16. k. a burning like the burning of fire
30. 33. the breath of the Lord doth k. it
43. 2. nor shall the flame k. upon thee
Jer. 33. 18. never want a man to k. meat-offerings
Obad. 18. fire and flame shall k. in them

KINDLED.
Gen. 39. 19. Potiphar's wrath was k.
Lev. 10. 6. bewail the burning the Lord hath k.
Num. 11. 33. the wrath of the Lord was k. Deut. 11. 17. 2 Kings 22. 13, 17. Psal. 106. 40.
2 Sam. 22. 9. coals were k. by it, Psal. 18. 8.
Job 19. 11. he hath also k. his wrath against me
32. 2. then was k. the wrath of Elihu, against Job was his wrath k. because he justified himself
3. against his three friends was his wrath k. 5.
42. 7. my wrath is k. against thee, and friends
Psal. 2. 12. when his wrath is k. but a little
124. 3. when their wrath is k. against us
Isa. 50. 11. walk in the sparks that ye have k.
Jer. 44. 6. my wrath was k. in the cities of Judah
Ezek. 20. 48. shall see, that I the Lord have k. it
Hos. 11. 8. my repentings are k. together
Luke 12. 49. what will I, if it be already k.
See Anger, Fire.

KINDLETH.
Job 41. 21. his breath k. coals, a flame goeth
Isa. 44. 15. yea, he k. it, and baketh bread
Jam. 3. 5. how great a matter a little fire k.

KINDLY.
Gen. 24. 49. if you will deal k. with me, 47. 29.
34. 3. Shechem spake k. to the damsel
50. 21. Joseph spake k. to his brethren
Josh. 2. 14. that we will deal k. and truly with thee
Ruth 1. 8. the Lord deal k. with you, as ye dealt
1 Sam. 20. 8. thou shalt deal k. with thy servant
2 Kings 25. 28. spake k. to Jehoiachin, Jer. 52. 32.
Rom. 12. 10. be k. affectioned one to another

KINDNESS.
Gen. 20. 13. this is thy k. thou shalt shew to me
21. 23. according to the k. I have done to thee
24. 12. O Lord, shew k. to my master Abraham
14. know that thou hast shewed k. to my master
39. † 21. the Lord extended k. to Joseph
40. 14. think on me, and shew k. I pray thee
Josh. 2. 12. swear, since I have shewed you k. that ye will also shew k. to my father's house
Judg. 8. 35. nor shewed k. to the house of Jerubbaal
Ruth 2. 20. not left off his k. to living and dead

Ruth 3. 10. thou hast showed more k. in latter end
1 Sam. 15. 6. ye shewed k. to Israel when they came
20. 14. thou shalt shew me the k. of the Lord
15. thou shalt not cut off thy k. from my house
2 Sam. 2. 5. ye have shewed this k. unto your lord
6. now Lord shew k. to you, I also will requite you this k. because ye have done this thing
3. 8. against Judah shew k. to the house of Saul
9. 1. that I may shew him k. for Jonathan's sake
3. any, that I may shew the k. of God to him
7. I will surely shew thee k. for Jonathan's sake
10. 2. I will shew k. to Hanun son of Nahash, as his father shewed k. to me, 1 Chron. 19. 2.
16. 17. Absalom said, is this thy k. to thy friend?
1 Kings 2. 7. but shew k. to the sons of Barzillai
3. 6. thou hast kept for David this great k.
2 Chr. 24. 22. Joash remembered not k. of Jehoiada
Neh. 9. 17. but thou art a God gracious, of great k.
Esth. 2. 9. and the maiden obtained k. of him
† 17. she obtained k. more than all the virgins
Psal. 31. 21. he hath shewed me his marvellous k.
117. 2. for his merciful k. is great toward us
119. 76. let thy merciful k. be for my comfort
141. 5. let the righteous smite me, it shall be a k.
Prov. 19. 22. the desire of a man is his k. and a poor
31. 26. and in her tongue is the law of k.
Isa. 54. 8. with everlasting k. will I have mercy on
10. but my k. shall not depart from thee
57. † 1. men of k. taken away, none considering
Jer. 2. 2. I remember thee, the k. of thy youth
Hos. 6. † 4. your k. as a morning cloud and early dew
Joel 2. 13. for he is gracious, of great k. Jonah 4. 2.
Acts 28. 2. the barbarous peop. shewed us no little k.
2 Cor. 6. 6. by pureness, by long-suffering, by k.
Eph. 2. 7. in his k. toward us through Christ Jesus
Col. 3. 12. put on k. humbleness of mind, meekness
1 Tim. 5. † 4. let them learn to shew k. at home
Tit. 3. 4. after the k. of God our Saviour appeared
2 Pet. 1. 7. to godliness brotherly k. to k. charity

Loving-KINDNESS.

Psal. 17. 7. shew thy marvellous loving-k. 92. 2.
26. 3. thy l.-k. is before mine eyes, I have walked
36. 7. how excellent is thy loving-k. O God!
10. O continue thy loving-k. to them that know
40. 10. I have not concealed thy lov.-k. and truth
11. let thy loving-k. continually preserve me
42. 8. yet the Lord will command his loving-k.
48. 9. we have thought of thy loving-k. O God
51. 1. have mercy on me according to thy loving-k.
63. 3. because thy loving-k. is better than life
69. 16. hear me, O Lord, for thy loving-k. is good
88. 11. shall thy lov.-k. be declared in the grave?
89. 33. my lov.-k. will I not utterly take from him
92. 2. to shew forth thy loving-k. in the morning
103. 4. who crowneth thee with lov.-k. and mercies
107. 43. they shall understand lov.-k. of the Lord
119. 88. quicken me after thy loving-k. 159.
149. hear my voice according to thy loving-k.
138. 2. I will praise thy name for thy loving-k.
143. 8. cause me to hear thy loving-k. in the morn.
Jer. 9. 24. I am the Lord which exercise loving-k.
16. 5. I have taken away my peace, even loving-k.
31. 3. therefore with loving-k. have I drawn thee
32. 18. thou shewest loving-k. unto thousands
Hos. 2. 19. I will betroth thee to me in loving-k.

Loving-KINDNESSES.

Psal. 25. 6. remember Ld. thy mercies and loving-k.
89. 49. Lord, where are thy former loving-k.?
Isa. 63. 7. I will mention the loving-k. of the Lord, according to the multitude of his loving-k.

KINDRED.

Gen. 12. 1. God said, get thee from thy k. Acts 7. 3.
24. 4. go to k. and take a wife to my son, 38. 40.
7. Lord who took me from my k. shall send
41. when thou comest to my k. if they give not
31. 3. the Lord said, return to thy k. 13. | 32. 9.
43. 7. the man asked us straitly of our k.
Num. 10. 30. I will depart to my own land and k.
Josh. 6. 23. and they brought out all her k.
Ruth 2. 3. Boaz was of the k. of Elimelech, 3. 2.
1 Chron. 12. 29. of Benjamin the k. of Saul 3000
Esth. 2. 10. Esther shewed not her people or k. 20.
8. 6. how endure to see the destruction of my k.
Job 32. 2. the wrath of Elihu, of the k. of Ram.
Ezek. 11. 15. men of thy k. said, get far from the L.
Luke 1. 61. none of thy k. called by this name
Acts 4. 6. as were of the k. of the high priest
7. 13. Joseph's k. was made known to Pharaoh
14. called his father Jacob to him and all his k.
19. the same dealt subtilly with our k.
1 Tim. 5. † 8. provide not for those of his own k.
Rev. 5. 9. redeemed us out of every k. and tongue
14. 6. the everlasting gospel to preach to every k.

KINDREDS.

1 Chr. 16. 28. give to the Lord, ye k. Psal. 96. 7.
Ps. 22. 27. all k. of nations shall worship bef. thee
Acts 3. 25. shall all the k. of the earth be blessed
Rev. 1. 7. and all k. of the earth shall wail because
7. 9. a great multitude of all k. stood before throne
11. 9. of k. shall see their dead bodies three days
13. 7. and power was given him over all k.

KINE

Is taken, [1] Properly, for cows, Deut. 7. 13. [2] Figuratively, for the proud, wealthy, and potent rulers of Israel, Amos 4. 1.

Gen. 32. 15. forty k. ten bulls, a present to Esau
41. 2. there came up seven well-favoured k. 18.
3. seven other k. came out of the river, 4, 19, 20.
26. the seven good k. are seven years
27. the seven thin ill favoured k. are seven years
Deut. 7. 13. he will bless the increase of thy k.
28. 4. blessed shall be the increase of thy k.
18. cursed shall be the increase of thy k.
51. which shall not leave the increase of thy k.
32. 14. butter of k. milk of sheep, fat of lambs
1 Sam. 6. 7. take two milch k. and tie the k.
10. took two k. || 12. the k. took the straight way
14. they clave the wood of cart, and offered the k.
2 Sam. 17. 29. butter, and cheese of k. for David
Amos 4. 1. hear this word, ye k. of Bashan

KING

Signifies, A sovereign prince, or chief ruler in a kingdom, Prov. 8. 15. It is applied, [1] To God, the supreme Ruler and Governor of the world, Psal. 44. 4. [2] To Christ, the King and Head of his church, Psal. 2. 6. | 45. 1. [3] To all real christians who are heirs of the kingdom of glory, and are enabled to war against, and at last to conquer, sin, Satan, and all their spiritual enemies, Rev. 1. 6. [4] To the devil, Rev. 9. 11.

Gen. 14. 18. Melchizedeck k. of Salem, Heb. 7. 1.
36. 31. kings that reigned in Edom, before there reigned any k. over Israel, 1 Chron. 1. 43.
Exod. 1. 8. there arose up a new k. over Egypt
Num. 23. 21. the shout of a k. is among them
24. 7. and his k. shall be higher than Agag
Deut. 17. 14. shalt say, I will set a k. over me
15. thou shalt in any wise set him k. over thee
28. 36. Ld. shall bring thee and thy k. to a nation
33. 5. and he was k. in Jeshurun when the heads
Judg. 8. 18. each resembled the children of a k.
9. 8. the trees went to anoint a k. over them
17. 6. in those days no k. in Israel, but every man did right in his own eyes, 18. 1. | 19. 1. | 21. 25.
1 Sam. 2. 10. Lord shall give strength to his k.
8. 5. go make us a k. to judge us like the nations
6. give us a k. || 9. shew the manner of the k. 11.
18. ye shall cry out on that day because of your k.
19. we will have a k. || 22. and make them a k.
20. that our k. may judge us, and go before us
10. 19. ye said unto him, nay, but set a k. over us
24. the people shouted, and said, God save the k. 2 Sam. 16. 16. 2 Kings 11. 12. 2 Chr. 23. 11.
12. 1. behold, I have made a k. over you
2. and now behold, the k. walketh before you
12. ye said unto me, nay, but a k. shall reign over us, when the Lord your God was your k.
13. behold the k. whom ye have chosen
17. that your wickedness is great in asking a k.
19. have added to our sins this evil, to ask us a k.
25. ye shall be consumed, both you and your k.
15. 1. the Lord sent me to anoint thee to be k.
23. he hath rejected thee from being k. 26.
16. 1. I have provided me a k. among his sons
19. 4. let not the k. sin against his servant David
20. 5. I should not fail to sit with the k. at meat
22. 15. let not the k. impute any thing to his serv.
24. 20. I know that thou shalt surely be k.
25. 36. Nabal held a feast like the feast of a k.
29. 8. against the enemies of my lord the k.
2 Sam. 2. 9. he made Ish-bosheth k. over Gilead
3. 36. what the k. did, pleased all the people
37. that it was not of the k. to slay Abner
5. 12. the Lord had established him k. over Israel
11. 8. there followed him a mess of meat from k.
12. 7. thus saith Lord, I anointed thee k. over Isr.
13. 13. therefore I pray thee, speak to the k.
14. 9. and the k. and his throne be guiltless
17. as an angel of G. so is my Lord the k. 19. 27.
15. 2. that had a controversy, came to the k.
3. there is none deputed of the k. to hear thee
19. abide with the k. for thou art a stranger
21. in what place my lord the k. shall be
16. 9. why should this dead dog curse the k.?
17. 2. people shall flee, I will smite the k. only
18. 13. there is no matter hid from the k.
19. 9. the k. saved us out of the hand of our enemies
11. the speech of all Israel is come to the k.
19. that the k. should take it to his heart
22. I know that I am this day k. over Israel
28. what right have I to cry any more to the k.?
42. because the k. is near of kin to us
43. and said, we have ten parts in the k.
22. 51. he is the tower of salvation for his k.
24. 23. these did Araunah as a k. give to the k.
1 Kings 1. 5. then Adonijah said, I will be k.
35. for Solomon shall be k. in my stead
2. 18. well, I will speak for thee to the k.
38. as the k. hath said, so will thy servant do
3. 7. hast made thy servant k. instead of David
22. thus the women spake before the k.
28. Israel heard the judgment the k. judged
8. 62. the k. and all Israel offered sacrifice
10. 3. there was not any thing hid from the k.
11. 26. Jeroboam lifted up his hand against the k.
37. thou shalt reign and shalt be k. over Israel
14. 2. Ahijah, who told me I should be k.
14. the Lord shall raise him up a k. over Israel
16. 16. Zimri conspired and hath slain the k.
21. 10. thou didst blaspheme God and the k.
22. 13. prophets declare good to the k. 2 Chr. 18. 12.
47. there was then no k. in Edom, a deputy was k.
2 Kings 1. 11. O man of God, k. said, come down, 9.
4. 13. wouldest thou be spoken for to the k.?
7. 2. then a lord on whose hand the k. leaned
8. 3. she went to cry to the k. for her house
13. the Lord hath shewed that thou shalt be k.
20. Edom revolted, made a k. over themselves
10. 5. sent, saying, we will not make any k.
11. 8. and be with the k. as he goeth out and cometh
17. Jehoiada made a covenant between the Lord and the k. between the k. also and the people
14. 5. had slain the k. his father, 2 Chron. 25. 3.
22. 9. brought the k. word, 20. 2 Chron. 34. 16, 28.
10. Shaphan read it before the k. 2 Chron. 34. 18.
25. 6. they took the k. and brought him, Jer. 52. 9.
1 Chron. 4. 23. they dwelt with the k. for his work
24. 6. Shemaiah wrote them before the k.
29. 20. bowed and worshipped the Lord and the k.
2 Chron. 2. 11. he hath made thee k. over them, 9. 8.
10. 15. so the k. hearkened not to the people
11. 22. for he thought to make him k.
24. 21. they stoned him at the command of the k.
25. 16. art thou made of the k. counsel? forbear
Ezra 4. 12. be it known to the k. that, 13. | 5. 8.
6. 10. and pray for the life of k. and sons
7. 26. who will not do the law of the k.
27. which hath put in the k. heart to beautify
8. 22. to require of the k. a band of soldiers
Neh. 1. 11. for I was the k. cup-bearer
2. 19. what do ye? will ye rebel against the k.?
6. 6. mayest be their k. according to these words
7. to preach, saying, there is a k. in Judah
Neh. 13. 26. yet among many nations was there no k. like him, God made him k. over all Israel
Esth. 4. 16. so will I go in unto the k. if I perish
6. 6. whom the k. delighteth to honour, 7.
7. 8. as the word went out of the k. mouth
9. for Mordecai, who had spoken good for the k.
Job 15. 24. shall prevail, as a k. ready to the battle
18. 14. it shall bring him to the k. of terrors
29. 25. I sat chief, and dwelt as a k. in the army
34. 18. is it fit to say to the k. thou art wicked?
41. 34. he is a k. over all the children of pride
Psal. 2. 6. I set my k. upon my holy hill of Zion
5. 2. hearken to my cry, my k. and my God, 84. 3.
10. 16. the Lord is k. for ever and ever, 29. 10.
18. 50. great deliverance giveth he to his k.
20. 9. let the k. hear us when we call
21. 1. the k. shall joy in thy strength, O Lord
7. for the k. trusteth in the L. and not be moved
24. 7. and the k. of glory shall come in, 9.
8. who is k. of glory? the Lord strong and mighty
10. the Lord of hosts he is the k. of glory
33. 16. no k. saved by the multitude of an host
44. 4. art my k. O God, command deliverances
45. 1. of the things I have made touching the k.
11. so shall the k. greatly desire thy beauty
14. she shall be brought to the k. in raiment
47. 6. sing praises to our k. || 7. God is the k.
61. 6. thou wilt prolong the k. life and years
63. 11. but the k. shall rejoice in God, every one
68. 24. they have seen the goings of my God, my k.
72. 1. give the k. thy judgments, O God
74. 12. God is my k. of old, working salvation
89. 18. the holy One of Israel is our k.
98. 6. make a joyful noise before the Lord the k.
99. 4. the k. strength also loveth judgment
105. 20. the k. sent and loosed him, let him go free
149. 2. let the children of Zion be joyful in their k.
Prov. 14. 28. in multitude of people is the k. honour
35. the k. favour is toward a wise servant
20. 28. mercy and truth preserve the k.
22. 11. for grace of his lips, the k. shall be his friend
24. 21. my son, fear thou the Lord and the k.
25. 5. take away the wicked from before the k.
30. 27. the locusts have no k. yet go they forth
31. and a k. against whom there is no rising up
Eccl. 2. 12. what can the man do that cometh after k.
5. 9. the k. himself is served by the field
8. 4. where the word of a k. is, there is power
10. 16. woe to thee, O land, when thy k. is a child
17. blessed when thy k. is the son of nobles
20. curse not the k. no, not in thy thought
Cant. 1. 4. the k. brought me into his chamber
12. while the k. sitteth at his table, my spikenard
3. 11. behold k. Solomon with the crown
7. 5. the k. is held in the galleries
Isa. 6. 5. mine eyes have seen the k. the L. of hosts
7. 6. let us set a k. in the midst of it, son of Tabeal
8. 21. curse their k. and their God, and look up
19. 4. and a fierce k. shall rule over them
23. 15. according to the days of one k.
30. 33. for Tophet, yea, for the k. it is prepared
32. 1. behold, a k. shall reign in righteousness
33. 17. thine eyes shall see the k. in his beauty
22. the Lord is our k. he will save us
41. 21. bring your reasons, saith the k. of Jacob
43. 15. I am the Creator of Israel your k.
57. 9. and thou wentest to the k. with ointment
Jer. 4. 9. that the heart of the k. shall perish
8. 19. is not the L. in Zion? is not her k. in her?
10. 10. the Lord is the true God, an everlasting k.
13. 18. say to the k. and queen, humble yourselves
23. 5. a k. shall reign and prosper and execute
29. 16. thus saith the Lord, of the k. that sitteth
38. 5. for the k. is not he that can do any thing
25. declare what hast said to the k. the k. to thee
46. 18. as I live, saith the k. whose name is the Lord of hosts, 48. 15. | 51. 57.
49. 1. why doth their k. inherit Gad and dwell in
38. I will destroy from thence the k. and princes
Lam. 2. 6. the Lord hath despised the k. and priest
Ezek. 7. 27. the k. shall mourn, and the prince
17. 12. hath taken the k. and princes thereof
13. hath taken of the k. seed and made a covenant
16. where the k. dwelleth that made him k.
26. 7. I will bring a k. of kings from the north
37. 22. and one k. shall be k. to them all, 24.
Dan. 2. 10. there is no k. asked such things at any
11. there is none that can shew it before the k.
24. bring me in before the k. and I will shew the k.
3. 13. they brought these men before the k.
4. 24. decree which is come upon my lord the k.
31. while the word was in the k. mouth
37. I praise, extol, and honour the k. of heaven
5. 5. the k. saw the part of the hand that wrote
6. 6. the princes assembled together to the k.
8. 23. a k. of fierce countenance shall stand up
11. 3. and a mighty k. shall stand up to rule
36. the k. shall do according to his will
Hos. 3. 4. Israel shall abide many days without a k.
5. Israel shall seek the Lord, and David their k.
5. 13. then Ephraim sent to k. Jareb, 10. 6.
7. 3. they make the k. glad with their wickedness
5. in the day of our k. princes made him sick
10. 3. we have no k. what then should a k. do?
7. her k. is cut off, as the foam upon the water
11. 5. but the Assyrian shall be his k. because
13. 10. I will be thy k. give me a k. and princes
11. I gave thee a k. in mine anger and took him
Amos 1. 15. and their k. shall go into captivity
7. 13. for it is the k. chapel, the k. court
Mic. 2. 13. and their k. shall pass before them
4. 9. why dost thou cry? is there no k. in thee?
Zech. 9. 5. the k. shall perish from Gaza
9. behold thy k. cometh to thee, Mat. 21. 5.
11. 6. will deliver every one into the hand of his k.
14. 9. the Lord shall be k. over all the earth
16. every one shall even go up to worship the k. 17.
Mat. 18. 23. kingdom likened to a certain k. 22. 2.
22. 11. when the k. came in to see the guests
Mark 6. 25. she came with haste to the k. and asked
Luke 14. 31. what k. goeth to war against another k.
19. 38. blessed be the k. that cometh in name of L.

Luke 23. 2. saying, that he himself is Christ, a *k.*
John 6. 15. to make him a *k.* ‖ 12. 15. thy *k.* cometh
18. 37. Pilate said to him, art thou a *k.* then?
19. 12. whosoever maketh himself a *k.* speaketh ag.
14. Pilate saith to the Jews, behold your *k.*
15. shall I crucify your *k.*? have no *k.* but Cesar
Acts 7. 18. till another *k.* arose, who knew not Joseph
13. 21. afterward they desired a *k.* and God gave
17. 7. saying, that there is another *k.* one Jesus
26. 26. for the *k.* knoweth of these things
1 *Tim.* 1. 17. now to the *k.* eternal, immortal
6. 15. who is the *k.* of kings, and Lord of lords
Heb. 11. 23. not afraid of the *k.* commandment
27. Moses not fearing the wrath of the *k.*
1 *Pet.* 2. 13. whether to the *k.* as supreme, or govern.
17. honour all men, fear God, honour the *k.*
Rev. 9. 11. they had a *k.* over them, the angel
15. 3. just are thy ways, thou *K.* of saints
17. 14. he is Lord of lords, *K.* of kings, 19. 16.

KING *of the Amorites*, *See* SIHON.

KING *of Assyria.*

2 *Kings* 15. 19. Pul the *k. of Assy.* came agst. land
20. Menahem exacted money to give *k. of Assy.*
16. 18. turned he from house of Lord to *k. of Assy.*
17. 6. in ninth year of Hoshea *k. of A.* took Samaria
18. 11. *k. of Assy.* did carry away Israel to Assy.
19. speak, thus saith great king the *k. of Assyria*
33. delivered his land out of hand of *k. of Assyria*
19. 32. saith L. concerning *k. of Assyria*, *Isa.* 37. 33.
Ezra 6. 22. turned the heart of *k. of Assy.* to them
Isa. 7. 17. Lord shall bring upon thee the *k. of Assy.*
20. shall shave by *k. of Assyria* the head and hair
Jer. 50. 17. first the *k. of Assyria* hath devoured him
18. I will punish Baby. as I punished *k. of Ass.*
Nah. 3. 18. thy shepherds slumber, O *k. of A.* thy nob.
See BASHAN, BABYLON, DAVID.

KING *of Egypt.*

Exod. 1. 17. midwives did not as *k. of Egypt* comm.
3. 19. I am sure the *k. of Egypt* will not let you go
6. 13. the L. gave them a charge to the *k. of Egypt*
2 *Kings* 24. 7. the *k. of E.* came not again any more,
had taken all that pertained to the *k. of Egypt*
2 *Chr.* 12. 2. *k. of Eg.* came up against Jerusalem
36. 3. the *k. of Egypt* put him down at Jerusalem
4. the *k. of Egypt* made Eliakim his brother king
Isa. 36. 6. so is the *k. of Egypt* to all that trust in him
See PHARAOH.
See GREAT, HOUSE, JEWS.

KING *of Israel.*

1 *Sam.* 24. 14. after whom is the *k. of Isr.* come out
26. 20. for the *k. of Isr.* is come out to seek a flea
2 *Sam.* 6. 20. how glorious was the *k. of Israel* to-day
1 *Kings* 20. 31. let us, I pray thee, go out to *k. of Isr.*
22. 31. fight not, save only with the *k. of Israel*
32. they said, surely it is *k. of Israel*, 2 *Chr.* 18. 31.
2 *Kings* 6. 11. shew me which of us is for *k. of Israel*
16. 7. save me out of the hand of *k. of Israel*
2 *Chr.* 18. 30. fight ye not, save only with *k. of Israel*
32. captains perceived that it was not *k. of Israel*
35. 3. son of David *k. of Isr.* did build, *Ezra* 5. 11.
Neh. 13. 26. did not Solomon *k. of Isr.* sin by these
Isa. 44. 6. thus saith the Lord, the *k. of Israel*
Hos. 10. 15. in a morning shall the *k. of Is.* be cut off
Zeph. 3. 15. the *k. of Israel* is in the midst of thee
Mat. 27. 42. if he be *k.* let him descend, *Mark* 15. 32.
John 1. 49. thou art *k. of Is.* ‖ 12. 13. blessed is *k. of I.*

KING *of Judah.*

2 *Kings* 8. 16. Jehoshaphat being then *k. of Judah*
22. 18. but to *k. of Judah* which sent you to inquire
2 *Chron.* 34. 26. and as for *k. of Judah* who sent you
35. 21. what have I to do with thee, thou *k. of Jud.*
Jer. 34. 4. hear the word of the Ld. O *k. of Judah*
37. 7. thus shall ye say to *k. of Judah* who sent you

KING *of Moab.*

Num. 23. 7. Balak *k. of Moab* brought me from Aram
Josh. 24. 9. the *k. of Moab* warred against Israel
Judg. 3. 14. Israel served Eglon the *k. of M.* 18 years
11. 17. Israel in like manner sent to the *k. of Moab*
25. art thou any thing better than Balak *k. of M.*?
1 *Sam.* 12. 9. sold them into the hand of *k. of Moab*
22. 4. David brought father and mother to *k. of M.*
2 *Kings* 3. 4. and Mesha *k. of M.* was a sheep-master
5. the *k. of Moab* rebelled against Israel, 7.
26. when the *k. of M.* saw the battle was too sore
Jer. 27. 3. send bonds and yokes to the *k. of Moab*

O KING.

1 *Sam.* 17. 55. Abner said, *O k.* I cannot tell
23. 20. now, therefore, *O k.* come down
26. 17. my lord, *O k.* 2 *Sam.* 14. 9, 22. | 16. 4.
| 19. 26. 1 *Kings* 1. 13, 20, 24. | 20. 4.
2 *Kings* 6. 12, 26. | 8. 5.
2 *Sam.* 14. 4. the woman of Tekoah said, help, *O k.*
15. 34. if thou say, I will be thy servant, *O k.*
2 *Chron.* 25. 7. *O k.* let not the army of Israel go
Psal. 145. 1. I will extol thee, my God, *O k.*
Jer. 10. 7. who would not fear thee, *O k.* of nations?
Dan. 2. 4. *O k.* live for ever, 3. 9. | 5. 10. | 6. 21.
29. as for thee, *O k.* ‖ 31. thou, *O k.* sawest an image
37. thou, *O k.* art a king of kings, for God hath
3. 10. thou, *O k.* hast made a decree, that every man
17. he will deliver us out of thy hand, *O k.*
18. be it known to thee, *O k.* ‖ 24. true, *O k.*
4. 22. it is thou, *O k.* ‖ 27. *O k.* let my counsel be
31. saying, *O k.* Nebuchadnez. to thee it is spoken
5. 18. *O* thou *k.* the most high God gave thy father
6. 7. shall ask a petition save of thee, *O k.*
8. now, *O k.* establish the decree, and sign it
13. regardeth not thee, *O k.* ‖ 15. know, *O k.*
22. also before thee, *O k.* have I done no hurt
Acts 26. 13. at mid-day, *O k.* I saw in the way a light
19. whereupon, *O k.* I was not disobedient

KING *of Persia.*

Ezra 4. 3. as Cyrus, *k. of Persia* hath commanded us
5. even till the reign of Darius *k. of Persia*
7. Bishlam wrote unto Artaxerxes *k. of Per.* 6. 14.
9. 9. extended mercy to us in sight of the *k. of Per.*
See CYRUS.

KING *of Syria.*

1 *Kings* 20. 20. Benhadad *k. of S.* escaped on a horse
22. the *k. of Syria* will come up against thee
2 *Kings* 5. 1. Naaman captain of host of *k. Syria*
8. 7. *k. of S.* was sick ‖ 9. *k. of S.* hath sent me to thee
13. 4. because the *k. of Syria* oppressed them
7. for the *k. of Syria* had destroyed them
16. 7. save me out of the hand of the *k. of Syria*
2 *Chr.* 16. 7. because thou hast relied on *k. of Syria*,
the host of the *k. of S.* is escaped out of thy hand
See BENHADAD, HAZAEL, REZIN.

KING *of Tyre.*

2 *Sam.* 5. 11. Hiram *k. of Tyre* sent messengers to
David, and they built him an house, 1 *Chr.* 14. 1.
1 *Kings* 5. 1. the *k. of Tyre* sent servants to Solomon
9. 11. Hiram the *k. of Tyre* had furnished Solomon
2 *Chr.* 2. 3. Solomon sent to Huram the *k. of Tyre*
11. Huram the *k. of Tyre* answered in writing

KINGS.

Gen. 17. 6. *k.* shall come out of thee, 16. | 35. 11.
36. 31. these are the *k.* that reigned in Edom
Num. 31. 8. and they slew the *k.* of Midian
Deut. 3. 21. the Lord hath done to these two *k.*
7. 24. he shall deliver their *k.* into thy hand
Josh. 10. 5. five *k.* of Amorites gathered together
16. these five *k.* fled ‖ 22. bring out those five *k.*
24. come near, put your feet on necks of these *k.*
40. so Joshua smote all their *k.* 11. 17.
12. 24. all these *k.* thirty and one
Judg. 1. 7. seventy *k.* having their thumbs cut off
5. 3. hear, O ye *k.* ‖ 19. the *k.* came and fought
2 *Sam.* 11. 1. the time when *k.* go forth to battle
1 *Kings* 3. 13. there shall not be any among the *k.*
like thee, 10. 23. 2 *Chron.* 1. 12. | 9. 22.
4. 24. Solomon over all the *k.* on this side the river
20. 1. Benhadad and thirty-two *k.* with him
2 *Kings* 3. 10. hath called these three *k.* together
23. this is blood, the *k.* are surely slain
7. 6. hath hired against us the *k.* of the Hittites
10. 4. behold, two *k.* stood not before him
1 *Chr.* 16. 21. he reproved *k.* for them, *Ps.* 105. 14.
2 *Chr.* 9. 23. all *k.* sought the presence of Solomon
21. 20. but not in the sepulchres of the *k.* 24. 25.
26. 23. in field of the burial which belonged to *k.*
Ezra 4. 13. shalt endamage the revenue of the *k.*
15. this city hath been hurtful to *k.* and provinces
19. this city hath made insurrection against *k.*
20. there have been mighty *k.* over Jerusalem
6. 12. God destroy *k.* that shall alter this house
7. 12. Artaxerxes king of *k.* to Ezra the priest
9. 7. our *k.* and priests have been deliver. *Neh.* 9. 24.
Neh. 9. 32. trouble seem little to us and our *k.*
34. nor have our *k.* or princes kept thy law
Job 3. 14. had I been at rest with *k.* and counsellors
12. 18. he looseth the bond of *k.* and girdeth
36. 7. but with *k.* are they on the throne
Psal. 2. 2. *k.* of the earth set themselves, *Acts* 4. 26.
10. be wise, therefore, O ye *k.* be instructed
45. 9. *k.* daughters among thy honourable women
48. 4. lo, the *k.* were assembled, they passed by
68. 12. *k.* of armies did flee apace, she that tarried
14. when the Almighty scattered *k.* in it
29. shall *k.* bring presents to thee
72. 11. yea, all *k.* shall fall down before him
76. 12. he is terrible to the *k.* of the earth
89. 27. make him higher than the *k.* of the earth
102. 15. the *k.* of the earth shall fear thy glory
110. 5. he shall strike thro' *k.* in the day of wrath
119. 46. I will speak of thy testimonies before *k.*
135. 10. smote great nations, and slew mighty *k.*
136. 17. to him which smote great *k.* 18.
138. 4. all *k.* of the earth shall praise thee, 148. 11.
144. 10. it is he that giveth salvation to *k.*
149. 8. to bind their *k.* with chains, their nobles
Prov. 8. 15. by me *k.* reign, and princes decree justice
16. 12. an abomination for *k.* to commit wickedness
13. righteous lips are the delight of *k.*
22. 29. the diligent in business shall stand before *k.*
25. 2. it is the honour of *k.* to search a matter
3. and the heart of *k.* is unsearchable
30. 28. and the spider is in *k.* palaces
31. 3. nor thy ways to that which destroyeth *k.*
4. it is not for *k.* O Lemuel, to drink wine
Eccl. 2. 8. gold and the peculiar treasure of *k.*
Isa. 7. 16. the land shall be forsaken of both her *k.*
10. 8. are not my princes altogether *k.*?
14. 9. it hath raised all the *k.* of the nations
18. all the *k.* of the nations lie in glory
19. 11. how say ye, I am the son of ancient *k.*
24. 21. L. shall punish the *k.* of the earth on earth
41. 2. who raised up and made him ruler over *k.*
45. 1. I will loose the loins of *k.* to open gates
49. 7. *k.* shall see and arise, princes shall worship
23. *k.* shall be thy nursing fathers and queens
52. 15. the *k.* shall shut their mouths at him
60. 3. and *k.* to the brightness of thy rising
10. and their *k.* shall minister to thee
11. thy gates open, that their *k.* may be brought
16. thou shalt also suck the breast of *k.*
62. 2. and all *k.* shall see thy glory
Jer. 2. 26. they, their *k.* and princes ashamed
13. 13. even *k.* that sit upon David's throne
17. 25. shall enter into the gates of this city, *k.*
22. 4. *k.* sitting upon the throne of David
25. 18. I made Judah and *k.* drink of the cup
22. *k.* of Tyrus ‖ 24. all the *k.* of Arabia
25. the *k.* of Zimri ‖ 26. all the *k.* of the north
32. 32. to provoke me to anger, they, their *k.*
34. 5. and with the burnings of former *k.* bef. thee
44. 17. as we, our *k.* and princes to burn incense
21. your *k.* and princes burnt incense in Judah
46. 25. I will punish their *k.* and their gods
49. 3. for their *k.* shall go into captivity, and priests
50. 41. many *k.* shall be raised up from the earth
51. 11. Lord raised up the spirit of *k.* of the Medes
Lam. 4. 12. *k.* of the earth would not have believed
Ezek. 27. 35. their *k.* shall be sore afraid, 32. 10.
28. 17. I will lay thee before *k.* to behold thee
32. 29. there is Edom, her *k.* and all her princes
43. 7. their *k.* shall no more defile my holy name
Dan. 2. 21. he removeth *k.* and setteth up *k.*
44. in the days of these *k.* shall G. set up a kingd.
47. of a truth it is, that your God is a Lord of *k.*
7. 17. the four great beasts are four *k.* shall arise
24. the ten horns are ten *k.* shall subdue three *k.*
9. 6. which spake in thy name to our *k.* our princes
8. to our *k.* and princes belongs confusion of face
Dan. 10. 13. I remained there with the *k.* of Persia
11. 2. stand up three *k.* ‖ 27. both these *k.* hearts
Hos. 7. 7. are hot as an oven, all their *k.* are fallen
8. 4. they have set up *k.* but not by me
Hab. 1. 10. they shall scoff at *k.* and princes
Mat. 10. 18. ye shall be brought before governors
and *k.* for my sake, *Mark* 13. 9. *Luke* 21. 12.
11. 8. they that wear soft clothing are in *k.* houses
17. 25. of whom do the *k.* of the earth take custom?
Luke 10. 24. prophets and *k.* have desired to see
22. 25. *k.* of Gentiles exercise lordship over them
Acts 9. 15. a chosen vessel to bear my name before *k.*
1 *Cor.* 4. 8. ye have reigned as *k.* without us
1 *Tim.* 2. 2. that prayers be made for *k.* and for all
6. 15. King of *k.* Lord of lords, *Rev.* 17. 14. | 19. 16.
Heb. 7. 1. Abraham returned from slaughter of the *k.*
Rev. 1. 5. Jes. Christ the prince of the *k.* of the earth
6. hath made us *k.* and priests unto God, 5. 10.
6. 15. the *k.* of the earth hid themselves in the dens
10. 11. thou must prophesy again before *k.*
16. 12. the way of the *k.* of east might be prepared
14. spirits which go forth to the *k.* of the earth
17. 2. with whom *k.* of earth committed fornication
10. there are seven *k.* five are fallen, and one is
12. are ten *k.* which receive power as *k.* with beasts
18. that great city which reigneth over *k.* of earth
18. 3. *k.* of the earth have committed fornication
9. *k.* of earth who shall bewail her and lament
19. 18. that ye may eat the flesh of *k.* and captains
19. *k.* of the earth gathered to make war against
21. 24. the *k.* of the earth do bring their glory

KINGS *of the Amorites.* [24. 12.

Deut. 4. 47. two *k. of A.* 31. 4. *Josh.* 2. 10. | 9. 10. |
Josh. 5. 1. came to pass, when all *k. of Am.* heard
10. 5. therefore five *k. of Am.* gathered together, 6.
See BOOK, GREAT.

KINGS *of Israel.*

1 *Kings* 14. 19. written in the book of the Chronicles
of the *k. of Israel*, 15. 31. | 16. 5, 14, 20, 27.
| 22. 39. 2 *Kings* 1. 18. | 10. 34. | 13. 8, 12.
| 14. 15, 28. | 15. 11, 15, 21, 26, 31.
16. 33. Ahab provoked L. more than all *k. of Isr.*
20. 31. we heard that *k. of Isr.* are merciful kings
2 *Kings* 8. 18. Jehoram walked in way of *k. of Isr.*
13. 13. Joash was buried with the *k. of Isr.* 14. 16.
14. 29. Jeroboam slept with his fathers *k. of Israel*
16. 3. Ahaz walked in the way of the *k. of Israel*
17. 2. Hoshea did evil, but not as the *k. of Israel*
8. Israel walked in the statutes of the *k. of Israel*
23. 19. Josiah took away houses the *k. of Isr.* made
22. not such a passover in the days of the *k. of Isr.*
1 *Chr.* 9. 1. were written in the book of *k. of Israel*
and Judah, 2 *Chron.* 16. 11. | 25. 26. | 27. 7. | 28.
26. | 32. 32. | 33. 18.
2 *Chron.* 20. 34. in book of Jehu who is mentioned
in the book of the *k. of Isr.* 35. 27. | 36. 8.
28. 27. Ahaz was not brought into sep. of *k. of Isr.*
Mic. 1. 14. houses of Achzib shall be a lie to *k. of Is.*

KINGS *of Judah.*

1 *Sam.* 27. 6. Ziklag pertained to the *k. of Judah*
1 *Kings* 14. 29. acts of Rehoboam in the book of the
Chronicles of the *k. of Judah*, 15. 7, 23. | 22. 45.
2 *Kings* 8. 23. | 15. 6, 36. | 16. 19. | 20. 20. | 21.
17, 25. | 23. 28. | 24. 5.
2 *Kings* 12. 18. hallowed things the *k. of Judah* had
dedicated, 19. written in the book of the Chronicles of the *k. of Judah*, 14. 18. 2 *Chron.* 25. 26.
| 28. 26. | 32. 32. | 35. 27. | 36. 8.
18. 5. there was none like him of all the *k. of Judah*
23. 5. Josiah put down priests *k. of Judah* ordained
11. took horses *k. of Judah* had given to the sun
12. beat down altars which *k. of Judah* had made
22. not such a passover in all days of *k. of Judah*
2 *Chr.* 34. 11. to floor houses *k. of Judah* destroyed
Isa. 1. 1. the vision of Isaiah in days of the *k. of Jud.*
Jer. 1. 18. I have made an iron pillar against *k. of J.*
8. 1. they shall bring out bones of the *k. of Judah*
17. 19. stand in gate, whereby *k. of Judah* come in
20. hear the word of the Lord, ye *k. of Jud.* 19. 3.
19. 4. burnt incense to gods *k. of J.* have not known
13. the houses of the *k. of Judah* shall be defiled
20. 5. treasures of *k. of Judah* will I give to enem.
33. 4. concerning houses of *k. of Judah* thrown down
44. 9. have ye forgotten wickedness of *k. of Judah*?
Hos. 1. 1. the word of the Lord that came to Hosea
in the days of the *k. of Judah*, *Mic.* 1. 1.
See KINGS *of Israel.*

KINGDOM

Signifies, [1] *One or more countries subject to a king*, Deut. 3. 4. [2] *Sovereignty, or universal dominion*, 1 Chr. 29. 11. Psal. 22. 28. | 103. 19. [3] *Heaven*, Mat. 26. 29. 2 Tim. 4. 18. [4] *A right to be king*, 1 Sam. 20. 31. [5] *Government, or supreme administration*, 1 Sam. 18. 8. There is, (I) *The kingdom of God*, [1] *Of his power*, Psal. 145. 12, 13. Dan. 4. 3. [2] *Of his grace*, Mat. 4. 23. | 6. 10, 33. [3] *Of his glory*, Luke 22. 16. 1 Cor. 6. 9. (II) *Of Christ*, Mat. 16. 28. Col. 1. 13. (III) *Of heaven*, signifying, [1] *The state of the church under the gospel, or the kingdom of the Messiah, wherein great spiritual blessings and privileges were to be bestowed*, Mat. 3. 2. [2] *The visible church, which is heavenly, and prepares for the kingdom of glory*, Mat. 5. 19, 20. | 13. 47. [3] *The state of the church or gospel in the world, or of grace in the soul, which should increase, notwithstanding its small appearance at first*, Mat. 13. 31. *Or, for grace in the heart*, Luke 17. 21. [4] *The place of eternal happiness and glory*, Mat. 5. 10. (IV) *Of priests*, Exod. 19. 6. 1 Pet. 2. 9. (V) *Of men*, Dan. 5. 21.

Exod. 19. 6. and ye shall be to me a *k.* of priests
Num. 32. 33. Moses gave to Gad, Reuben, and Manasseh, the *k.* of Sihon and the *k.* of Og, *Deut* 3. 13. *Josh.* 13. 12, 21, 27, 30.
Deut. 3. 4. took the *k.* of Og in Bashan sixty cities
1 *Sam.* 10. 16. of the matter of *k.* he told him not
25. then Samuel told the manner of the *k.*
11. 14. renew the *k.* there ‖ 14. 47. Saul took *k.*
15. 28. Lord hath rent the *k.* of Israel, 28. 17.
18. 8. and what can he have more but the *k.*?
2 *Sam.* 3. 10. to translate the *k.* from house of Saul

2 *Sam.* 16. 3. Israel shall restore me *k.* of my father
8. hath delivered the *k.* into hand of Absalom
1 *Kings* 2. 15. thou knowest that the *k.* was mine
22. ask for him the *k.* for he is my elder brother
10. 20. not the like made in any *k.* 2 *Chron.* 9. 19.
11. 11. I will surely rend the *k.* from thee, 31. 35.
13. I will not rend away all the *k.* 34.
12. 21. to bring *k.* again to Rehoboam, 2 *Chr.* 11. 1.
26. now shall *k.* return again to house of David
14. 8. I rent the *k.* away from the house of David
18. 10. no *k.* where my lord hath not sent to seek
21. 7. dost thou now govern the *k.* of Israel?
2 *Kings* 14. 5. as soon as the *k.* was confirmed
15. 19. with him, to confirm the *k.* in his hand
1 *Chr.* 10. 14. and turned the *k.* to David, 12. 23.
16. 20. from one *k.* to another people, *Ps.* 105. 13.
29. 11. all in heaven and earth is thine, thine is the *k.* O Lord, *Psal.* 22. 28. *Mat.* 6. 13.
2 *Chr.* 13. 8. think to withstand the *k.* of the Lord
14. 5. and the *k.* was quiet before him
21. 3. the *k.* gave he to Jehoram the first-born
4. Jehoram was risen up to the *k.* of his father
22. 9. Ahaziah had no power to keep still the *k.*
29. 21. for a sin-offering for the *k.* and Judah
32. 15. for no god of any nation or *k.* was able
Neh. 9. 35. for they have not served thee in their *k.*
Esth. 1. 14. seven princes which sat first in the *k.*
4. 14. thou art come to the *k.* for such a time
5. 3. it shall be given to the half of the *k.* 6. | 7. 2.
Isa. 19. 2. they shall fight, *k.* against *k.* *Mat.* 24. 7. *Mark* 13. 8. *Luke* 21. 10.
34. 12. they shall call the nobles thereof to the *k.*
60. 12. the *k.* that will not serve thee, *Jer.* 27. 8.
Jer. 18. 7. I speak concerning a *k.* to destroy it
9. concerning a *k.* to build and to plant it
Lam. 2. 2. he hath polluted the *k.* and the princes
Ezek. 16. 13. and thou didst prosper into a *k.*
17. 14. that the *k.* might be base, and not lift itself
29. 14. and they shall be there a base *k.*
Dan. 2. 37. the God of heaven hath given thee a *k.*
44. in their days shall God of heaven set up a *k.*
4. 17. the Most High ruleth in the *k.* of men, 25. 32.
31. O king, the *k.* is departed from thee
6. 4. no fault against Daniel concerning the *k.*
7. 18. the saints shall take the *k.* and possess the *k.*
22. the time came that the saints possessed the *k.*
27. the Most High, whose *k.* is an everlasting *k.*
11. 21. they shall not give the honour of the *k.*
Hos. 1. 4. and will cause to cease the *k.* of Israel
Amos 9. 8. the eyes of the L. are upon the sinful *k.*
Obad. 21. and the *k.* shall be the Lord's
Mic. 4. 8. *k.* shall come to the daughter of Jerusal.
Mat. 4. 23. the gospel of the *k.* 9. 35. | 24. 14.
8. 12. the children of the *k.* shall be cast out
12. 25. every *k.* divided against itself is brought to desolation, *Mark* 3. 24. *Luke* 11. 17.
13. 38. the good seed are the children of the *k.*
43. shall shine as the sun in the *k.* of their father
25. 34. inherit the *k.* prepared for you from the
26. 29. till I drink it new in my Father's *k.*
Mark 11. 10. blessed be the *k.* of our father David
Luke 12. 32. Father's good pleasure to give you *k.*
19. 12. a nobleman went to receive for himself a *k*
15. he was returned, having received the *k.*
22. 29. I appoint unto you a *k.* as my Father
Acts 1. 6. wilt thou restore again the *k.* to Israel
1 *Cor.* 15. 24. when he shall have delivered up the *k.*
Col. 1. 13. hath translated us into the *k.* of his Son
Heb. 12. 28. wherefore we receiving a *k.* that cannot
Jam. 2. 5. heirs of the *k.* which he hath promised
2 *Pet.* 1. 11. an entrance ministered into everlast. *k.*
Rev. 1. 9. companion in the *k.* and patience of Jesus
17. 12. ten kings, which have received no *k.* as yet
17. to agree, and give their *k.* to the beast

See ESTABLISH, ESTABLISHED, THRONE.

KINGDOM *of God.*

Mat. 6. 33. but seek ye first the *k.* of G. *Luke* 12. 31.
12. 28. *k.* of G. is come unto, *Luke* 10. 9, 11. | 11. 20.
19. 24. through eye of needle, than for a rich man to enter into *k.* of G. *Mark* 10. 23. *Luke* 18. 24.
21. 31. the harlots go into the *k.* of G. before you
43. the *k.* of God shall be taken from you
Mark 1. 14. preaching *k.* of God, *Acts* 8. 12. | 20. 25. | 28. 31.
15. the *k.* of God is at hand, repent and believe
4. 11. to know the mystery of *k.* of G. *Luke* 8. 10.
26. and he said, so is the *k.* of G. as if a man cast
30. whereunto shall liken *k.* of G.? *Luke* 13. 18. 20.
9. 1. till they have seen *k.* of G. come with power
47. better to enter into the *k.* of G. with one eye
10. 14. children, for of such is *k.* of G. *Luke* 18. 16.
15. whoso shall not receive *k.* of G. *Luke* 18. 17.
24. how hard is it for them that trust in riches to enter into the *k.* of God, 25. *Luke* 18. 25.
12. 34. he said, thou art not far from the *k.* of God
14. 25. till that day I drink it new in the *k.* of G.
15. 43. which waited for the *k.* of G. *Luke* 23. 51.
Luke 4. 43. I must preach the *k.* of G. to other cities
6. 20. blessed be ye poor, for yours is the *k.* of G.
7. 28. that is least in the *k.* of G. is greater than he
8. 1. preaching and shewing glad tidings of *k.* of G.
9. 2. and he sent them to preach the *k.* of God, 60.
11. received them, and spake to them of *k.* of G.
27. shall not taste of death, till they see *k.* of G.
62. and looking back, is fit for the *k.* of God
13. 28. ye shall see all the prophets in the *k.* of God
29. and they shall sit down in the *k.* of God
14. 15. blessed is he that shall eat bread in *k.* of G.
16. 16. since that time the *k.* of God is preached
17. 20. was demanded when *k.* of G. should come
20. the *k.* of God cometh not with observation
21. for behold, the *k.* of God is within you
18. 29. left wife or children for the *k.* of G. sake
19. 11. they thought that *k.* of G. should appear
21. 31. know ye that the *k.* of G. is nigh at hand
22. 16. nor eat till it be fulfilled in the *k.* of God
18. I will not drink until the *k.* of G. shall come
John 3. 3. except man be born again, cannot see *k.*
5. born of water, he cannot enter into the *k.* of G.
Acts 1. 3. things pertaining to *k.* of G. 8. 12. | 19. 8.
14. 22. thro' much tribulation enter into *k.* of God
28. 23. to whom he expounded, and testif. *k.* of G.

Rom. 14. 17. for the *k.* of G. is not meat and drink
1 *Cor.* 4. 20. the *k.* of G. is not in word, but in power
6. 9. the unrighteous shall not inherit the *k.* of G.
10. nor extortioners inherit *k.* of G. *Gal.* 5. 21. *Eph.* 5. 5.
15. 50. flesh and blood cannot inherit the *k.* of G.
Col. 4. 11. my fellow-workers unto the *k.* of God
2 *Thess.* 1. 5. may be counted worthy of the *k.* of G.
Rev. 12. 10. now is come the *k.* of our God

KINGDOM *of heaven.*

Mat. 3. 2. repent, for *k.* of h. is at hand, 4. 17. | 10. 7.
5. 3. blessed are poor in spirit, theirs is *k.* of h. 10.
19. shall be called least in *k.* of h. great in *k.* of h.
20. shall in no case enter into *k.* of heaven, 18. 3.
7. 21. not that saith, Lord, shall enter *k.* of h.
8. 11. shall sit down with Abraham in *k.* of h.
11. 11. he that is least in *k.* of h. is greater than he
12. *k.* of h. suffer. violence, violent take it by force
13. 11. to know the mysteries of the *k.* of heaven
24. the *k.* of h. is like, 31. 33, 44, 45, 47, 52. | 18. 23. | 20. 1. | 22. 2. | 25. 1, 14.
16. 19. I will give to thee the keys of *k.* of heaven
18. 1. who is the greatest in the *k.* of heaven, 4.
23. 13. for ye shut up the *k.* of h. against men

His KINGDOM.

Gen. 10. 10. and the beginning of *his k.* was Babel
Num. 24. 7. and *his k.* shall be exalted
Deut. 17. 18. he sitteth on the throne of *his k.*
20. that he may prolong his days in *his k.*
2 *Sam.* 5. 12. perceived that he had exalted *his k.*
1 *Chron.* 11. 10. strengthened with him in *his k.*
14. 2. for *his k.* was lift up on high for Israel
2 *Chr.* 1. 1. Solomon was strengthened in *his k.*
2. 1. determined to build a house for *his k.* 12.
33. 13. brought him again to Jerusalem into *his k.*
Psal. 103. 19. and *his k.* ruleth over all
145. 12. and the glorious majesty of *his k.*
Eccl. 4. 14. whereas he that is born in *his k.*
Isa. 9. 7. upon *his k.* to order and establish it
Dan. 4. 3. the high God, *his k.* is an everlasting k.
34. *his k.* from generation to gener. 6. 26. | 7. 14.
11. 4. *his k.* shall be broken and plucked up
9. the king of the south shall come into *his k.*
Mat. 12. 26. how shall *his k.* stand? *Luke* 11. 18.
13. 41. they shall gather out of *his k.* all things
16. 28. they see the Son of man coming in *his k.*
Luke 1. 33. and of *his k.* there shall be no end
1 *Thess.* 2. 12. who hath called you to *h. k.* and glory
2 *Tim.* 4. 1. who shall judge at his appearing and *h. k.*
Rev. 16. 10. and *his k.* was full of darkness

My KINGDOM.

Gen. 20. 9. hast brought on me and *my k.* a great sin
2 *Sam.* 3. 28. I and *my k.* are guiltless before the L.
1 *Chron.* 17. 14. I will settle him in *my k.* for ever
Dan. 4. 36. and for the glory of *my k.* in *my k.*
6. 26. in every dominion of *my k.* men tremble
Mark 6. 23. I will give it, to the half of *my k.*
Luke 22. 30. may eat and drink at my table in *my k.*
John 18. 36. Jesus said, *my k.* is not of this world, if *my k.* were, but now *my k.* is not from hence

Thy KINGDOM.

1 *Sam.* 13. 14. but now *thy k.* shall not continue
Ps. 45. 6. sceptre of *t. k.* a right sceptre, *Heb.* 1. 8.
145. 11. they shall speak of the glory of *thy k.*
13. *thy k.* is an everl. kingd. thy domin. endureth
Dan. 4. 26. *thy k.* shall be sure to thee, after that
5. 11. there is a man in *thy k.* || 26. G. numb. *thy k.*
28. *thy k.* is divided to the Medes and Persians
Mat. 6. 10. *thy k.* come, thy will be done, *Luke* 11. 2.
20. 21. and the other on the left in *thy k.*
Luke 23. 42. rememb. me when thou comest to *thy k.*

KINGDOMS.

Deut. 3. 21. so shall the L. do to all the *k.* whither
28. 25. be removed into all the *k.* of the earth
Josh. 11. 10. Hazor was the head of all those *k.*
1 *Sam.* 10. 18. I delivered you out of hand of all *k.*
1 *Kings* 4. 21. Solomon reigned over all *k.* from river
2 *Kings* 19. 15. the God of all the *k.* of the earth
19. that all the *k.* may know, *Isa.* 37. 20.
1 *Chron.* 29. 30. times that went over all the *k.*
2 *Chron.* 12. 8. they may know the service of the *k.*
17. 10. the fear of the Lord fell on the *k.* 20. 29.
20. 6. thou rulest over all the *k.* of the heathen
36. 23. all *k.* hath the Lord given me, *Ezra* 1. 2.
Neh. 9. 22. thou gavest them *k.* and nations
Psal. 46. 6. the heathen raged, the *k.* were moved
68. 32. sing unto God, ye *k.* of the earth
79. 6. thy wrath on the *k.* that have not called
102. 22. the *k.* are gathered to serve the Lord
135. 11. who smote all the *k.* of Canaan
Isa. 10. 10. as my hand hath found the *k.* of idols
13. 4. the noise of the *k.* of nations gathered
19. Babylon the glory of *k.* as Sodom, 47. 5.
14. 16. is this the man that did shake *k.*?
23. 11. he shook the *k.* || 37. 16. God of all *k.*
Jer. 1. 10. and over the *k.* I have set thee
10. 7. and in all their *k.* none like thee
15. 4. to be removed into all *k.* 24. 9. | 34. 17.
25. 26. all the *k.* of the world shall drink
28. 8. the prophets prophesied against great *k.*
29. 18. I will make them a terror to all *k.*
34. 1. all the *k.* fought against Jerusalem
49. 28. concerning Kedar and the *k.* of Hazor
51. 20. and with thee will I destroy *k.*
27. call together against her the *k.* of Ararat
Ezek. 29. 15. it shall be the basest of the *k.*
37. 22. nor shall they be divided into two *k.*
Dan. 2. 44. and it shall consume all these *k.*
7. 23. which shall be diverse from all *k.*
8. 22. four *k.* shall stand up out of the nation
Amos 6. 2. go to Gath; be they better than these *k.*?
Nah. 3. 5. and I will shew the *k.* thy shame
Zeph. 3. 8. that I may assemble the *k.* to pour on
Hag. 2. 22. I will overthrow the throne of *k.* and I will destroy the strength of the *k.* of the heathen
Mat. 4. 8. shewed him all the *k.* of world, *Luke* 4. 5.
Heb. 11. 33. who through faith subdued *k.* wrought
Rev. 11. 15. *k.* of this world become *k.* of the Lord

KINGLY.

Dan. 5. 20. he was deposed from his *k.* throne

KINSFOLK.

Job 19. 14. my *k.* have failed and forgotten me

Luke 2. 44. sought Jesus among their *k.* and acquaint.

KINSFOLKS.

1 *Kings* 16. 11. Zimri left none of Baasha's *k.*
2 *Kings* 10. 11. Jehu slew Ahab's *k.* and priests
Luke 21. 16. ye shall be betrayed by *k.* and friends

KINSMAN.

Num. 5. 8. if the man have no *k.* to recompense
27. 11. ye shall give his inheritance to his *k.*
Deut. 25. † 5. her husband's next *k.* shall go in
† 7. if a man like not to take his next *k.* wife
Ruth 2. 1. Naomi had a *k.* his name was Boaz
3. 9. thou art a near *k.* || 12. a *k.* nearer than I
13. if he will perform to thee the part of a *k.* well; if not, I will do the part of a *k.* to thee
4. 1. behold the *k.* of whom Boaz spake, came by
6. the *k.* said, I cannot redeem it for myself
8. the *k.* said unto Boaz, buy it for thee
14. hath not left thee this day without a *k.*
John 18. 26. being his *k.* whose ear Peter cut off
Rom. 16. 11. salute Herodion my *k.* greet them

KINSMEN.

Ruth 2. 20. the man is near of kin, one of our next *k.*
1 *Chron.* 15. † 5. Uriel and his *k.* two hundred twenty
Psal. 38. 11. my lovers and *k.* stood afar off
Mark 3. † 21. when *k.* heard, they went to lay hold
Luke 14. 12. call not friends, brethren, nor *k.*
Acts 10. 24. Cornelius had called together his *k.*
Rom. 9. 3. accursed, for my *k.* according to the flesh
16. 7. salute my *k.* || 21. thy *k.* salute you

KINSWOMAN.

Lev. 18. 12. father's sister, she is my father's near *k.*
13. mother's sister, she is thy mother's near *k.*
Prov. 7. 4. and call understanding thy *k.*

KINSWOMEN.

Lev. 18. 17. not uncover, for they are her near *k.*

KISS.

They are signs, [1] *Of reverence and subjection to a superior,* 1 Sam. 10. 1. 1 Kings 19. 18. [2] *Of spiritual submission and adoration to Christ,* Psal. 2. 12. [3] *Of love and affection,* Gen. 27. 26, 27. 1 Sam. 20. 41. [4] *Of idolatrous reverence and adoration,* Hos. 13. 2. They are, [1] *Traitorous, such as Joab's to Amasa, when he kissed him and slew him, and Judas's to Christ, when he kissed him and betrayed him,* 2 Sam. 20. 9. Mat. 26. 49. [2] *Hypocritical,* 2 Sam. 15. 5. [3] *Idolatrous,* 1 Kings 19. 18. [4] *Carnal and whorish,* Prov. 7. 13. [5] *Spiritual, those sensible, familiar, and frequent discoveries of Christ's love communicated to his church by his word and Spirit.* Cant. 1. 2. | 8. 1. [6] *Holy, proceeding from, and a pledge of, christian and holy love.* Rom. 16. 16. 1 Cor. 16. 20.

KISS, ES.

Prov. 27. 6. but the *k.* of an enemy are deceitful
Cant. 1. 2. let him *k.* me with the *k.* of his mouth
Luke 7. 45. thou gavest me no *k.* but this woman
22. 48. betrayest thou the Son of man with a *k.*?
Rom. 16. 16. salute one another with an holy *k.*
1 *Cor.* 16. 20. greet with an holy *k.* 2 *Cor.* 13. 12.
1 *Thess.* 5. 26. greet the brethren with an holy *k.*
1 *Pet.* 5. 14. greet ye one another with a *k.* of charity

KISS.

Gen. 27. 26. come near now and *k.* me, my son
31. 28. not suffered me to *k.* my sons and daughters
41. † 40. at thy word shall all my people *k.*
2 *Sam.* 20. 9. Joab took Amasa by the beard to *k.*
1 *Kings* 19. 20. let me *k.* my father and mother
Psal. 2. 12. *k.* the Son, lest he be angry and ye perish
Prov. 24. 26. every man shall *k.* his lips that gives
Cant. 1. 2. let him *k.* me with the kisses of his mouth
8. 1. I would *k.* thee, yet I should not be despised
Hos. 13. 2. let men that sacrifice *k.* the calves
Mat. 26. 48. give a sign, saying, whomsoever I *k.* the same is he, hold him fast, *Mark* 14. 44.
Luke 7. 45. this woman hath not ceased to *k.* my feet
22. 47. Judas drew near to Jesus to *k.* him

KISSED.

Gen. 27. 27. and Jacob came near and *k.* him
29. 11. and Jacob *k.* Rachel and wept
13. Laban *k.* Jacob || 33. 4. Esau *k.* Jacob
31. 55. and Laban *k.* his sons and his daughters
45. 15. moreover Joseph *k.* all his brethren
48. 10. Jacob *k.* and embraced Joseph's sons
50. 1. Joseph fell on his father's face and *k.* him
Exod. 4. 27. Aaron met Moses in mount and *k.* him
18. 7. Moses met his father-in-law and *k.* him
Ruth 1. 9. Naomi *k.* her daughters-in-law, they wept
14. and Orpah *k.* her mother-in-law, but Ruth
1 *Sam.* 10. 1. Samuel poured oil and *k.* Saul
20. 41. Jonathan and David *k.* one another
2 *Sam.* 14. 33. he bowed, and the king *k.* Absalom
15. 5. Absalom *k.* any man that came nigh to him
19. 39. the king *k.* Barzillai, and blessed him
1 *Kings* 19. 18. every mouth which hath not *k.* him
Job 31. 27. or my mouth hath *k.* my hand
Psal. 85. 10. righteousness and peace *k.* each other
Prov. 7. 13. so she caught him and *k.* him
Ezek. 3. † 13. wings of creatures *k.* one another
Mat. 26. 49. hail Master, and *k.* him, *Mark* 14. 45.
Luke 7. 38. Mary *k.* his feet and anointed them
15. 20. his father fell on his neck and *k.* him
Acts 20. 37. they fell on Paul's neck and *k.* him

KITE.

Lev. 11. 14. the *k.* after his kind uncl. *Deut.* 14. 13.

KNEAD.

Gen. 18. 6. *k.* it, and make cakes on the hearth
Jer. 7. 18. and the women *k.* their dough

KNEADED.

1 *Sam.* 28. 24. woman at Endor took flour and *k.* it
2 *Sam.* 13. 8. Tamar took flour *k.* and made cakes
Hos. 7. 4. the baker *k.* the dough till it be leavened

KNEADING.

Exod. 8. 3. frogs shall come into thy *k.*-troughs
12. 34. their *k.*-troughs being bound up in clothes

KNEE

Signifies, [1] *That part of the body which joins the leg and thigh together,* Judg. 7. 5. [2] *The body,* Psal. 109. 24. [3] *Persons,* Job 4. 4. Heb. 12. 12. To bow the KNEE signifies, [1] *To worship,* 1 Kings 19. 18. Rom. 11. 4. [2] *To pray,* Eph. 3. 14. [3] *To be in subjection,* Phil. 2. 10.

Gen. 41. 43. they cried before him, bow the k.
Isa. 45. 23. that unto me every k. shall bow, every tongue shall swear, Rom. 14. 11. Phil. 2. 10.
Mat. 27. 29. bowed the k. before him
Rom. 11. 4. who have not bowed the k. to Baal

KNEES.

Gen. 30. 3. my maid Bilhah shall bear on my k.
48. 12. Joseph brought them out from betw. his k.
50. 23. children were brought up on Joseph's k.
Deut. 28. 35. the Lord shall smite thee in the k.
Judg. 7. 5. that boweth down on his k. to drink, 6.
16. 19. and she made Samson sleep on her k.
1 Kings 8. 54. Solom. arose from kneeling on his k.
18. 42. Elijah put his face between his k.
19. 18. all the k. which have not bowed to Baal
2 Kings 1. 13. third capt. fell on his k. before Elijah
4. 20. he sat on his mother's k. till noon, and died
2 Chron. 6. 13. Solomon kneeled down on his k.
Ezra 9. 5. I fell on my k. and spread my hands
Job 3. 12. why did the k. prevent me, or breasts
4. 4. and thou hast strengthened the feeble k.
Ps. 109. 24. my k. are weak thro' fasting, my flesh
Isa. 35. 3. weak hands, and confirm the feeble k.
66. 12. ye shall suck and be dandled on her k.
Ezek. 7. 17. all k. shall be weak as water, 21. 7.
47. 4. he measured, the waters were to the k.
Dan. 5. 6. his k. smote one against another
6. 10. kneeled on k. three times a day, and prayed
10. 10. behold an hand set me upon my k.
Nah. 2. 10. she is empty, and the k. smite together
Mark 15. 19. bowing their k. worshipped him
Luke 5. 8. Simon Peter fell down at Jesus' k.
Eph. 3. 14. for this cause I bow my k. to the Father
Heb. 12. 12. lift up hands that hang down, feeble k.

KNEEL.

Gen. 24. 11. he made his camels k. down by a well
Psal. 95. 6. let us k. before the Lord our Maker

KNEELED.

2 Chron. 6. 13. Solomon k. down on his knees
Dan. 6. 10. Dan. k. three times a day on his knees
Luke 22. 41. and Jesus k. down and prayed
Acts 7. 60. Stephen k. and cried with a loud voice
9. 40. Pet. k. and prayed ‖ 20. 36. Paul k. and prayed
21. 5. and we k. down on the shore, and prayed

KNEELING.

1 Kings 8. 54. Solomon rose up from k. on his knees
Mat. 17. 14. a man k. to him, saying, Mark 10. 17.
Mark 1. 40. there came a leper k. down to him

KNEW.

Gen. 4. 1. Adam k. Eve his wife, she conceived, 25.
17. Cain k. wife ‖ 38. 26. Judah k. her no more
Judg. 11. 39. Jephthah's daughter k. no man
19. 25. they k. her and abused her all the night
1 Sam. 1. 19. Elkanah k. Hannah his wife
1 Kings 1. 4. she was fair, but the king k. her not
Mat. 1. 25. Joseph k. her not, till she brought forth

KNEW.

Gen. 3. 7. Adam and Eve k. that they were naked
9. 24. Noah k. what his younger son had done
37. 33. Jacob k. it, and said, it is my son's coat
38. 9. Onan k. the seed should not be his
42. 7. Joseph saw and k. his brethren, 8.
Num. 24. 16. and k. the knowledge of the Most High
Deut. 9. 24. been rebellious from the day I k. you
34. 10. a prophet whom the Lord k. face to face
Judg. 3. 2. such as before k. nothing thereof
13. 21. Manoah k. that he was an angel of God
18. 3. they k. the voice of the young man
1 Sam. 3. 20. all Israel k. Samuel was a prophet
18. 28. Saul k. that the Lord was with David
20. 9. for if I k. then would I not tell thee
33. Jonathan k. that it was determined by Saul
39. only David and Jonathan k. the matter
22. 15. for the servant k. nothing of all this
17. slay the priests, because they k. when he fled
22. David said to Abiathar, I k. it that day
23. 9. David k. that Saul secretly practised against
26. 17. Saul k. David's voice, and said, is this thy
2 Sam. 11. 16. where he k. that valiant men were
1 Kings 18. 7. Obadiah k. Elijah, and fell on his face
2 Chr. 33. 13. then Manasseh k. the Lord was God
Esth. 1. 13. manner to all that k. law and judgment
Job 23. 3. O that I k. where I might find him!
Isa. 48. 4. because I k. that thou art obstinate
7. lest thou shouldest say, behold I k. them
8. I k. that thou wouldest deal very treacherously
Jer. 1. 5. before I formed thee, I k. thee
32. 8. then I k. this was the word of the Lord
41. 4. he had slain Gedaliah, and no man k. it
44. 15. men which k. their wives had burnt incense
Ezek. 10. 20. I k. that they were the cherubims
19. 7. and he k. their desolate palaces, laid waste
Dan. 5. 21. till he k. that the Most High ruled
6. 10. when Daniel k. the writing was signed
Jonah 4. 2. I k. that thou art a gracious God
Zech. 11. 11. k. that it was the word of the Lord
Mat. 7. 23. I will profess I never k. you
12. 15. when Jesus k. he withdrew himself
25. Jesus k. their thoughts, Luke 6. 8.
25. 24. I k. thee, that thou art an hard man
27. 18. he k. that for envy they had delivered
Mark 1. 34. not to speak because they k. him
6. 54. out of the ship, straightway they k. him
12. 12. k. he had spoken the parable against them
Luke 4. 41. the devils, for they k. that he was Christ
12. 47. that servant which k. his lord's will
18. 34. nor k. they the things that were spoken
24. 31. their eyes were opened, and they k. him
John 2. 9. but the servants k. whence it was
24. not commit himself, because he k. all men
25. any testify, for he k. what was in man
4. 53. the father k. it was at the same hour
5. 6. Jesus k. he had been long in that case
6. 6. for he himself k. what he would do
61. Jesus k. that his disciples murmured
64. Jesus k. from the beginning who believed not
11. 42. I k. that thou hearest me always
57. that if any man k. where he were, to shew it
13. 1. when Jesus k. that his hour was come
11. for he k. who should betray him
28. no man at the table k. for what intent
16. 19. Jesus k. that they were desirous to ask

John 18. 2. Judas which betrayed him k. the place
Acts 3. 10. k. that it was he that sat for alms
9. 30. which when the brethren k. they brought
12. 14. when Rhoda k. Peter's voice she opened
16. 3. they k. all that his father was a Greek
19. 34. but when they k. that he was a Jew
22. 29. afraid after he k. that he was a Roman
26. 5. which k. me from the beginning, a Pharisee
28. 1. then they k. the island was called Melita
Rom. 1. 21. because that when they k. God
1 Cor. 2. 8. which none of the princes of this world k.
2 Cor. 5. 21. he made him to be sin, who k. no sin
12. 2. I k. a man in Christ above 14 years ago, 3.
Col. 1. 6. in you since ye k. the grace of God in truth
2. 1. I would you k. what great conflict I have
Jude 5. put in remembrance, tho' ye once k. this
Rev. 19. 12. he had a name written that no man k.

KNEW not.

Gen. 28. 16. Lord is in this place, and I k. it not
31. 32. Jacob k. not that Rachel had stolen them
38. 16. Judah k. not she was his daughter-in-law
39. 6. he k. not aught he had ‖ 42. 8. but they k. n. him
Exod. 1. 8. there arose a new king which k. n. Joseph
Num. 22. 34. I k. not that thou stoodest in the way
Deut. 8. 16. with manna which thy fathers k. not
29. 26. served gods which thy fathers k. not, 32. 17.
Judg. 2. 10. a generation which k. not the Lord
13. 16. Manoah k. not that he was an angel
14. 4. his father k. not that it was of the Lord
20. 34. Benjamin k. not that evil was near
1 Sam. 2. 12. now the sons of Eli k. not the Lord
14. 3. the people k. not that Jonathan was gone
20. 39. the lad k. not any thing, only Jonathan
2 Sam. 3. 26. sent after Abner, but David k. it not
11. 20. k. ye not they would shoot from the wall?
15. 11. they went in simplicity, and k. not any thing
18. 29. I saw a tumult, but I k. not what it was
22. 44. a people which I k. not shall serve me
2 Kings 4. 39. gathered gourds for they k. them not
Neh. 2. 16. the rulers k. not whither I went
Job 2. 12. Job's friends k. him not, and wept
29. 16. the cause which I k. not I searched out
42. 3. things which I k. not too wonderful for me
Psal. 35. 11. they laid to my charge things I k. not
15. abjects gathered against me, and I k. it not
73. † 22. so foolish was I, and k. not, I was a beast
Prov. 23. † 35. they have beaten me, and I k. it not
24. 12. if thou sayest, behold, we k. it not
Isa. 42. 16. I will bring the blind by a way they k. not
25. it hath set him on fire, yet he k. not
55. 5. and nations that k. not thee, shall run to thee
Jer. 2. 8. and they that handle the law k. me not
11. 19. I k. not that they had devised devices
44. 3. went to serve other gods whom they k. not
Dan. 11. 38. honour a god whom his fathers k. not
Hos. 8. 4. they have made princes and I k. it not
11. 3. but they k. not that I healed them
Zech. 7. 14. among nations whom they k. not
Mat. 17. 12. Elias is come, and they k. him not
24. 39. k. not till the flood came and took them
Luke 2. 43. Joseph and his mother k. not of it
12. 48. that k. not and did commit things worthy
John 1. 10. the world k. him not ‖ 31. I k. him not, 33.
2. 9. when the governor k. not whence it was
20. 9. for as yet they k. not the scriptures that he
14. and k. not that it was Jesus, 21. 4.
Acts 13. 27. for they, because they k. him not
19. 32. the more part k. not wherefore they came
27. 39. when it was day, they k. not the land
1 Cor. 1. 21. the world by wisdom k. not God, it pleased
Gal. 4. 8. howbeit, then when ye k. not God, ye did
1 John 3. 1. world knoweth us not, because k. him not

KNEWEST.

Deut. 8. 3. he fed thee with manna, which thou k. not
Ruth 2. 11. art come to a people which thou k. not
Neh. 9. 10. thou k. that they dealt proudly against
Psal. 142. 3. then thou k. my path in the way
Isa. 48. 8. thou heardest not, yea, thou k. not
Dan. 5. 22. not humbled thy heart, thou k. all this
Mat. 25. 26. thou k. I reaped where, Luke 19. 22.
Luke 19. 44. thou k. not the time of thy visitation
John 4. 10. if thou k. the gift of God, and who it is

KNIFE.

Gen. 22. 6. Abraham took the k. in his hand, 10.
Exod. 4. † 25. then Zipporah took a sharp k.
Judg. 19. 29. took a k. and laid hold on his concub.
Prov. 23. 2. and put a k. to thy throat, if given to
Ezek. 5. 1. son of man, take thee a sharp k.
2. take a third part, and smite about it with a k.

KNIVES.

Josh. 5. 2. make thee sharp k. and circumcise
3. Joshua made him sharp k. and circumcised
1 Kings 18. 28. cut themsel. with k. and lancets
Ezra 1. 9. nine and twenty k. Cyrus brought
Prov. 30. 14. their jaw-teeth as k. to devour the poor
Ezek. 21. † 21. the king of Babylon made bright k.

KNIT.

Judg. 20. 11. Israel were k. together as one man
1 Sam. 18. 1. the soul of Jonathan was k. to David
1 Chr. 12. 17. if come, my heart shall be k. to you
Acts 10. 11. I saw a sheet k. at the four corners
Col. 2. 2. their hearts being k. together in love
19. body k. togeth. increaseth with increase of G.

KNOCK

Signifies, [1] *To beat, hit, or strike upon*, Acts 12. 13, 16. [2] *To pray with fervency, constancy, and importunity*, Mat. 7. 8. Luke 11. 10. [3] *Christ calling and inviting us by his word, providence, and Spirit, to admit him into our hearts, and receive him by faith and love*, Cant. 5. 2. Rev. 3. 20.

Mat. 7. 7. k. and it shall be opened, Luke 11. 9.
Luke 13. 25. ye begin to k. at the door, saying, open
Rev. 3. 20. behold, I stand at the door and k. if any

KNOCKED.

Acts 12. 13. and as Peter k. at the door of the gate

KNOCKETH.

Cant. 5. 2. it is voice of my belov. that k. open to me
Mat. 7. 8. to him that k. shall be opened, Luke 11. 10.
Luke 12. 36. when he cometh and k. they may open

KNOCKING.

Acts 12. 16. Peter contin. k. and when they saw him

KNOP, S.

Exod. 25. 31. his k. and his flowers, 34. 36. ‖ 37. 17.
33. with a k. and flower in one branch, 37. 19.
36. and k. branches of the same, 37. 17, 20, 22.
1 Kings 6. 18. cedar carved with k. and open flowers
7. 24. were k. compassing it, k. cast into two rows
Amos 9. † 1. he said, smite the k. of the door
Zeph. 2. † 14. the bittern shall lodge in k. of it

KNOW

Signifies, [1] *To understand or perceive*, Ruth 3. 11. [2] *To approve of, love, and delight in*, Psal. 1. 6. [3] *To cherish and take care of*, John 10. 27. [4] *To have the experience of*, Gen. 3. 5. ‖ 22. 12. [5] *To possess, or have it in one's power*, Psal. 50. 11. [6] *Lawfully to use the marriage-bed*, Gen. 4. 1, 17. [7] *To consider and ponder seriously*, Psal. 90. 11. [8] *To believe upon undoubted testimony*, John 4. 22. ‖ 11. 24. [9] *To have a bare speculative knowledge*, Luke 12. 47. [10] *To commit the sin against nature*, Gen. 19. 5. Judg. 19. 22. [11] *To be fully persuaded*, Judg. 6. 37. ‖ 18. 5. [12] *To have a vain and groundless assurance*, Judg. 17. 13. [13] *To discern and find out*, Mat. 7. 16. [14] *To teach and excite men to know thoroughly and practically*, Prov. 1. 2. [15] *To hear or be informed of*, Acts 22. 24. [16] *To acknowledge persons with due respect, so as to perform our duty to them*, 1 Thess. 5. 12. [17] *To choose*, Amos 3. 2. [18] *To commit, or have*, 2 Cor. 5. 21. [19] *To take particular notice of*, Gen. 39. 6.

Gen. 3. 5. God doth k. your eyes shall be opened
22. man is become as one of us, to k. good and evil
15. 13. said to Abram, k. thy seed shall be a stranger
18. 21. I will go down and see, and if not, I will k.
20. 7. if thou restore her not, k. thou shalt die
Exod. 18. 16. I make them k. the statutes of God
33. 12. hast not let me k. whom thou wilt send
Num. 14. 31. they shall k. the land ye have despised
Deut. 4. 39. k. this day and consider it, 11. 2.
8. 2. to prove thee and k. what was in thy heart
3. nor did thy father k. he might make thee k.
13. 3. proveth you, to k. whether ye love the Lord
Josh. 4. 22. then ye shall let your children k.
22. 22. the Lord knoweth, and Israel he shall k.
Judg. 3. 4. to k. whether they would hearken to
Ruth 3. 11. city of my people doth k. thou art
14. she rose up before one could k. another
18. sit still, my daughter, till thou k. how matter
1 Sam. 17. 47. and all this assembly shall k. the Lord
20. 3. he saith, let not Jonathan k. this, lest grieved
21. 2. let no man k. any thing of the business
24. 11. k. and see that there is no evil in me
25. 17. therefore k. and consider what thou
28. 1. Achish said to David, k. assuredly that
2. surely thou shalt k. what thy servant can do
2 Sam. 3. 25. to k. thy going out, to k. all thou doest
7. 21. done these things to make thy servant k. them
14. 20. to k. all things that are in the earth
19. 20. thy servant doth k. that I have sinned
1 Kings 8. 38. k. every man the plague, 2 Chr. 6. 29.
2 Kings 5. 8. he shall k. that there is a prophet in Isr.
7. 12. they k. that we be hungry, therefore
10. 10. k. now that there shall fall nothing of word
1 Chr. 12. 32. Issachar, to k. what Isr. ought to do
28. 9. my son, k. thou the God of thy father
2 Chr. 13. 5. ought ye not to k. that the Lord gave
Ezra 4. 15. k. that this city is a rebellious city
7. 25. all such as k. the laws of thy God and teach
Esth. 2. 11. Mordecai walked to k. how Esther did
4. 5. to k. what it was, and why it was
11. people k. whosoever shall come to the king
Job 5. 24. thou shalt k. thy tabernacle in peace
25. thou shalt k. that thy seed shall be great
27. hear it, and k. thou it for thy good
7. 10. nor shall his place k. him any more
8. 9. we are but of yesterday, and k. nothing
11. 6. k. therefore that God exacteth less than thine
8. it is deeper than hell, what canst thou k.?
13. 23. make me to k. my transgression and sin
19. 6. k. now that God hath overthrown me
21. 19. God rewardeth him, and he shall k. it
22. 13. and thou sayest, how doth God k.
24. 1. do they that k. him not see his days?
17. if one k. them, they are in terrors of shadow
34. 4. let us k. among ourselves what is good
37. 15. dost thou k. when God disposed them
16. dost thou k. the balancings of the clouds
38. 12. and caused the day-spring to k. his place
20. that thou shouldest k. the paths to the house
Psal. 4. 3. but k. the Lord hath set apart the godly
9. 10. they that k. thy name put their trust in thee
36. 10. continue thy loving-kindness to them k. thee
39. 4. Lord, make me to k. mine end, and measure
46. 10. be still, and k. that I am God, I will be
51. 6. in hidden part thou shalt make me to k.
59. 13. and let them k. that God ruleth in Jacob
73. 11. how doth God k. ‖ 16. I thought to k. this
87. 4. I will mention Babylon to them that k. me
89. 15. blessed are they that k. the joyful sound
103. 16. the place thereof shall k. it no more
139. 23. k. my heart, try me, and k. my thoughts
142. 4. there was no man that would k. me
143. 8. cause me k. the way wherein I should walk
Prov. 1. 2. to k. wisdom and instruction, to perceive
4. 1. hear, and attend to k. understanding
10. 32. the lips of righteous k. what is acceptable
27. 23. be thou diligent to k. the state of thy flocks
Eccl. 1. 17. and I gave my heart to k. wisdom
7. 25. I applied my heart to k. wisdom and folly
8. 16. when I applied my heart to k. wisdom and see
17. tho' a wise man think to k. it yet not able
9. 5. the living k. they shall die, but the dead
11. 9. but k. that God will bring thee to judgment
Isa. 7. 16. for before the child shall k. to refuse evil
9. 9. and all the people shall k. even Ephraim
19. 21. the Egyptians shall k. the Lord in that day
41. 20. that they may see and k. and consider
22. that we may k. the latter end of them
49. 26. all flesh shall k. that I am thy Saviour
50. 4. should k. how to speak in season to weary
52. 6. therefore my people shall k. my name

Isa. 58. 2. they seek me, and delight to k. my ways
60. 16. thou shalt k. that I the Lord am thy Saviour
Jer. 2. 19. k. and see that it is an evil thing to forsake
23. see thy way in valley, k. what thou hast done
6. 18. k. O congregation, what is among them
9. 6. thro' deceit they refuse to k. me, saith Lord
15. 15. k. that for thy sake I have suffered rebuke
16. 21. I will cause them to k. my hand and my might, and they shall k. that my name is the L.
17. 9. the heart is deceitful, who can k. it?
22. 16. was not this to k. me? saith the Lord
24. 7. I will give them an heart to k. me
31. 34. k. the L. for they shall all k. me, Heb. 8. 11.
36. 19. go, hide thee, let no man k. where ye be
38. 24. he said, let no man k. of these words
40. 15. slay Ishmael and no man shall k. it
44. 28. Judah shall k. whose words shall stand
Ezek. 2. 5. k. that there hath been a prophet, 33. 33.
5. 13. shall k. I the Lord hath spoken in my zeal
16. 2. Jerus. to k. her abomination, 20. 4. | 22. †2.
20. † 11. and made them to k. my judgments
25. 14. and they shall k. my vengeance, saith Lord
28. 19. all that k. thee shall be astonished at thee
34. 30. thus shall they k. that I am with them
37. 28. and the heathen shall k. 39. 23.
Dan. 2. 21. givest knowl. to them who k. understand.
4. 25. till thou k. that the Most High ruleth, 32.
7. 16. and made me k. the interpretation
19. I would k. the truth of the fourth beast
8. 19. I will make thee k. what shall be
9. 25. k. therefore and understand, that from
11. 32. people that k. their God shall be strong
Hos. 2. 20. thou shalt k. the Lord || 9. 7. shall k. it
13. 4. and thou shalt k. no God but me
14. 9. who is prudent, and he shall k. them
Mic. 3. 1. is it not for you to k. judgment?
Zech. 2. 11. thou shalt k. that the Lord sent me, 4. 9.
Mal. 2. 4. and ye shall k. that I have sent this
Mat. 6. 3. let not thy left hand k. what thy right doeth
7. 11. if ye k. how to give good gifts, Luke 11. 13.
9. 30. see no man k. it, Mark 5. 43. | 7. 24. | 9. 30.
13. 11. it is given to you to k. Mark 4. 11. Luke 8. 10.
24. 33. k. desolat. is near, Mark 13. 29. Luke 21. 20.
43. but k. this, if the goodman, Luke 12. 39.
John 4. 42. we k. that this is indeed the Christ
7. 17. if any do his will, he shall k. of the doctrine
26. do the rulers k. indeed || 51. k. what he doeth
10. 4. the sheep follow him, for they k. his voice
14. I k. my sheep || 13. 7. thou shalt k. hereafter
13. 35. by this shall all men k. ye are my disciples
18. 21. ask them, behold, they k. what I said
Acts 1. 7. it is not for you to k. the times or seasons.
2. 36. let all the house of Isr. k. assuredly that God
22. 14. shouldest k. his will and see that Just One
19. they k. I imprisoned them that believed on thee
26. 4. my manner of life from my youth k. all Jews
Rom. 7. 1. I speak to them that k. the law
10. 19. but I say, did not Israel k.? first Moses
1 Cor. 2. 14. neither can he k. them, because they are
8. 2. he knoweth nothing as he ought to k.
11. 3. but I would have you k. that the head is Chr.
Eph. 3. 19. and to k. the love of Christ, which passeth
1 Thess. 3. 5. for this cause I sent to k. your faith
4. 4. every one should k. how to possess his vessel in
5. 12. to k. them who labour among you, and are
1 Tim. 4. 3. of them which believe and k. the truth
2 Tim. 3. 1. this k. also that in the last days perilous
Tit. 1. 16. they profess that they k. God, but in works
Jam. 2. 20. but wilt thou k. O vain man, that
5. 20. let him k. he which converteth a sinner
Jude 10. but what they k. naturally, as brute beasts
Rev. 2. 23. all the churches shall k. that I am he who
3. 9. I will make them to k. that I have loved thee
See CERTAIN, CERTAINLY, CERTAINTY.

I KNOW.

Gen. 12. 11. now I k. that thou art a fair woman
15. 8. whereby shall I k. that I shall inherit it?
18. 19. I k. that he will command his children
20. 6. I k. thou didst this in integrity of thy heart
22. 12. for now I k. that thou fearest God
24. 14. thereby shall I k. that thou hast shewed
48. 19. his father said, I k. it, my son, I k. it
Exod. 3. 7. the Lord said, I k. their sorrows
4. 14. Aaron thy brother I. k. he can speak well
9. 30. I k. that ye will not yet fear the Lord God
18. 11. I k. the Lord is greater than all gods
33. 12. yet thou hast said, I k. thee by name, 17.
Deut. 31. 21. I k. their imagination even now
27. for I k. thy rebellion and thy stiff neck
29. I k. that after my death ye will utterly corrupt
Josh. 2. 9. I k. the Lord hath given you the land
Judg. 6. 37. then shall I k. that thou wilt save
17. 13. now k. I that the Lord will do me good
1 Sam. 17. 28. I k. thy pride and naughtiness of heart
20. 30. do not I k. thou hast chosen son of Jesse?
22. 3. till I k. what God will do for me
24. 20. I k. well that thou shalt surely be king
29. 9. I k. that thou art good in my sight, as angel
2 Kings 2. 3. yea I k. it, hold you your peace, 5.
5. 15. I k. that there is no God in earth, but in Israel
8. 12. I k. the evil that thou wilt do to Israel
19. 27. I k. thy abode and going out, Isa. 37. 28.
1 Chron. 29. 17. I. k. that thou triest the heart
2 Chron. 25. 16. I k. that God hath determined
Job 9. 2. I k. it is so of a truth, but how should
28. I k. thou wilt not hold me innocent
10. 13. things hast hid, I k. that this is with thee
13. 2. what ye know, the same do I k. also, not infer.
18. behold, I k. that I shall be justified
19. 25. I k. that my Redeemer liveth and shall stand
21. 27. I k. your thoughts and devices ye imagine
30. 23. for I k. that thou wilt bring me to death
42. 2. I k. that thou canst do every thing
Psal. 20. 6. I k. that the Lord saveth his anointed
41. 11. by this I k. that thou favourest me
50. 11. I k. all the fowls of the mountains
56. 9. this I. k. for God is for me
119. 75. I k. O Lord, that thy judgments are right
135. 5. for I k. the Lord is great and above all gods
140. 12. I k. the Lord will maintain the cause
Eccl. 3. 12. I k. that there is no good in them
14. I k. that whatsoever God doeth, it shall be for
Eccl. 8. 12. I k. it shall be well with them that fear G.
Isa. 47. 8. nor shall I k. the loss of children
50. 7. and I k. that I shall not be ashamed
66. 18. I k. their works and their thoughts
Jer. 10. 23. I k. the way of man is not in himself
11. 18. Lord hath given me knowledge, and I k. it
29. 11. for I k. the thoughts that I think
23. I k. and am a witness, saith the Lord
48. 30. I k. his wrath, saith the Lord, it shall
Ezek. 11. 5. I k. things that come into your mind
Dan. 2. 9. therefore tell me the dream, and I shall k.
Hos. 5. 3. I k. Ephraim, and Israel is not hid
13. 5. I did k. thee in the wilderness
Amos 5. 12. I k. your manifold transgressions
Jonah 1. 12. I k. that for my sake this tempest is
Mat. 28. 5. fear not ye, I k. that ye seek Jesus
Mark 1. 24. I k. thee who thou art, Luke 4. 34.
Luke 1. 18. whereby shall I k. this, for I am old
John 4. 25. I k. that Messias cometh, called Christ
5. 42. but I k. you || 8. 14. I k. whence I came
8. 37. I k. that ye are Abraham's seed
55. but I k. him || 9. 25. one thing I k.
10. 15. as Father knoweth me, so I k. the Father
27. and I k. my sheep, and they follow me
11. 22. I k. that what thou wilt ask of God
24. Martha said, I k. that he shall rise again
12. 50. I k. his commandment is life everlasting
13. 18. I speak not of all, I k. whom I have chosen
Acts 12. 11. now I k. of a surety that the Lord sent
19. 15. Jesus I k. and Paul I k. but who are ye?
20. 25. I k. that ye shall see my face no more
29. I k. this, that after my departing, wolves
24. 22. I will k. the uttermost of your matter
26. 3. because I k. thee to be expert in customs
27. king Agrippa, I k. that thou believest
Rom. 7. 18. I k. that in me dwelleth no good thing
1 Cor. 4. 4. for I k. nothing by myself, yet am I not
13. 12. now I k. in part, then shall I k. as I am kno.
2 Cor. 9. 2. I k. the forwardness of your mind
Phil. 1. 19. I k. this shall turn to my salvation
25. I k. that I shall abide with you all, and contin.
2. 19. be of good comfort, when I k. your estate
4. 12. I k. how to be abased, I k. how to abound
2 Tim. 1. 12. for I k. whom I have believed
1 John 2. 4. he that saith, I k. him, and keepeth
Rev. 2. 2. I k. thy works, 9. 13, 19. | 3. 1, 8, 15.
2. 9. I k. the blasphemy of them, who say

KNOW not, or not KNOW.

Gen. 4. 9. Lord said, where is Abel? he said, I k. not
27. 2. I am old, I k. not the day of my death
Exod. 5. 2. I k. not the Lord, nor will I let Israel go
10. 26. we k. not with what we must serve the Lord
Deut. 22. 2. or if thou k. him not, then bring it
1 Sam. 3. 7. now Samuel did not yet k. the Lord
25. 11. take my bread, give to men whom I k. not?
1 Kings 3. 7. I k. not how to go out or come in
18. 12. the Spirit shall carry thee whither I k. not
2 Kings 17. 26. they k. not the manner of G. of land
Ezra 7. 25. and teach ye them that k. them not
Neh. 4. 11. they shall not k. nor see, till we come
Job 9. 21. though perfect, yet would I not k. my soul
15. 9. what knowest thou that we k. not?
21. 29. and do ye not k. their tokens?
24. 13. they k. not the ways thereof, nor abide in
16. they dig in the dark, they k. not the light
32. 22. for I k. not to give flattering titles
36. 26. God is great, and we k. him not
Psal. 71. 15. for I k. not the numbers thereof
82. 5. they k. not, neither will they understand
94. 10. he that teacheth man, shall not he k.?
101. 4. I will not k. a wicked person
Prov. 4. 19. they k. not at what they stumble
5. 6. ways are moveable, that thou canst not k. them
24. 12. doth not he k. it, and shall not he render
25. 8. lest thou k. not what to do in the end
29. 7. but the wicked regardeth not to k. it
30. 18. yea, there are four things which I k. not
Eccl. 9. 5. but the dead k. not any thing
Cant. 1. 8. if thou k. not, O fairest among women
Isa. 1. 3. but Israel doth not k. nor consider
43. 19. shall ye not k. it? || 44. 8. I k. not any
47. 11. thou shalt not k. from whence it ariseth
48. 6. even hidden things, and thou didst not k. them
59. 8. way of peace they k. not, shall not k. peace
Jer. 5. 4. for they k. not the way of the Lord
7. 9. will ye walk after other gods, whom ye k. not?
8. 7. but my people k. not the judgments of the Lord
9. 3. and they k. not me, saith the Lord
10. 25. thy fury on the heathen that k. thee not
14. 18. go about into a land that they k. not, 22. 28.
Ezek. 38. 14. dwelleth safely, shalt thou not k. it?
Hos. 2. 8. she did not k. that I gave her corn, wine
Amos 3. 10. for they k. not to do right, saith the L.
Mic. 4. 12. they k. not the thoughts of the Lord
Mat. 25. 12. verily I say unto you, I k. you not
26. 70. Peter said, I k. not what thou sayest
Mat. 26. 72. then began he to curse and swear, saying, I k. not the man, 74. Mark 14. 68, 71.
Mark 10. 38. Jesus said, ye k. not what ye ask
12. 24. ye err, because ye k. not the scriptures
Luke 1. 34. how shall this be, seeing I k. not a man
13. 25. he shall say, I k. not whence you are, 27.
22. 57. denied him, saying, woman, I k. him not
60. Peter said, man, I k. not what thou sayest
23. 34. forgive them, they k. not what they do
24. 16. eyes holden, that they should not k. him
John 1. 26. standeth one among you whom ye k. not
8. 55. if I should say, I k. him not, I should lie
9. 12. the blind man said, I k. not, 25.
21. or who hath opened his eyes, we k. not
29. for this fellow, we k. not from whence he is
10. 5. for they k. not the voice of strangers
14. 5. Lord, we k. not whither thou goest
15. 21. because they k. not him that sent me
20. 2. we k. n. || 13. I k. not where they have laid him
Acts 21. 34. and when he could not k. the certainty
Rom. 8. 26. for we k. not what we should pray for
1 Cor. 1. 16. I k. not whether I baptized any other
2. 2. I determined not to k. any thing among you
14. 11. if I k. not the meaning of the voice
1 Thess. 4. 5. as the Gentiles which k. not God
2 Thess. 1. 8. vengeance on them that k. not God
1 Tim. 3. 5. if a man k. not how to rule his house
Jude 10. these speak evil of things they k. not
Rev. 3. 3. thou shalt not k. what hour I will come
See, Ye KNOW.

KNOW that I am the Lord.

Exod. 6, 7. ye shall k. that I am the Lord, 16. 12.
1 Kings 20. 28. Ezek. 6. 7, 13. | 7. 4, 9. | 11. 10,
12. | 12. 20. | 13. 9, 14, 21, 23. | 14. 8. | 15. 7.
| 20. 38, 42, 44. | 23. 49. | 24. 24. | 25. 5. | 35. 9.
| 36. 11. | 37. 6, 13. Joel 3. 17.
7. 5. and the Egyptians shall k. t. I am L. 14. 4, 18
17. thou shalt k. I am L. 1 Kings 20. 13. Isa. 49.
23. Ezek. 16. 62. | 22. 16. | 25. 7. | 35. 4, 12.
8. 22. to end that thou mayest k. that I am the Lord
10. 2. that ye may k. t. I am L. 31. 13. Ezek. 20. 20.
29. 46. they shall k. that I am the Lord, Ezek. 6. 10.
14. | 7. 27. | 12. 15, 16. | 24. 27. | 25. 11, 17. | 26.
6. | 28. 22, 23, 24, 26. | 29. 9, 16, 21. | 30. 8, 19,
25, 26. | 32. 15. | 33. 29. | 34. 27. | 35. 15. | 36. 38.
| 38. 23. | 39. 6, 28.
Deut. 29. 6. that ye might k. that I am the Lord
Jer. 24. 7. I will give them an heart to k. I am Ld.
Ezek. 20. 12. my sabbat. that they might k. I am L. 26.
36. 23. and the heathen shall k. I am the L. 39. 7.
39. 22. the house of Israel shall k. that I am the L.

May, mayest, or might KNOW.

Exod. 8. 10. thou mayest k. there is none like G. 9. 14.
9. 29. that thou mayest k. that the earth is the Lord's
11. 7. ye may k. the Lord doth put a difference
33. 5. that I may k. what to do to thee
13. shew me thy way, that I may k. thee
Lev. 23. 43. that your generations may k. that
Num. 22. 19. that I may k. what the Lord will say
Deut. 4. 35. that thou mightest k. that the L. he is G.
Josh. 3. 4. ye may k. the way by which ye should go
7. they may k. that as I was with Moses, so I will
4. 24. all people might k. the hand of the Lord
Judg. 3. 2. that Israel might k. to teach them war
18. 5. we may k. whether our way be prosperous
Ruth 4. 4. if not, then tell me, that I may k.
1 Sam. 17. 46. that all the earth may k. there is a G. in Israel, 1 Kings 8. 43, 60. 2 Kings 19. 19.
2 Sam. 24. 2. that I may k. the number of the peop.
1 Kings 18. 37. this people may k. that thou art God
2 Chron. 6. 33. that all people may k. thy name, and may k. that this house is called by thy name
12. 8. his servants, that they may k. my service
Job 19. 29. that ye may k. there is a judgment
31. 6. be weighed, that God may k. my integrity
37. 7. that all men may k. his work
Psal 9. 20. nations may k. themselves to be but men
39. 4. measure of days, that may k. how frail I am
78. 6. that the generation to come might k. them
83. 18. that men may k. that thou art the Most High
109. 27. that they may k. that this is thy hand
119. 125. that I may k. thy testimonies
Isa. 5. 19. let counsel draw nigh that we may k. it
7. 15. that he may k. to refuse the evil
37. 20. that all may k. that thou art the Lord
41. 23. that we may k. ye are gods, yea, do good
26. who hath declared, that we may k. and before
43. 10. ye may k. and believe me, and understand
45. 3. that thou mayest k. that I am the G. of Isr.
6. that they may k. from the rising of the sun
Jer. 6. 27. that thou mayest k. and try their way
44. 29. that ye may k. that my words shall stand
Ezek. 21. 5. all flesh may k. I have drawn my sword
38. 16. against the land, that heathen may k. me
Dan. 2. 30. mightest k. the thoughts of thy heart
4. 17. to the intent that the living may k.
Jonah 1. 7. come, let us cast lots, that we may k.
Mic. 6. 5. ye may k. the righteousness of the Lord
Mat. 9. 6. but that ye may k. that the Son of man hath power to forgive, Mark 2. 10. Luke 5. 24.
John 10. 38. ye may k. and believe the Fath. is in me
14. 31. that the world may k. I love Fath. 17. 23.
17. 3. that they might k. thee the only true God
19. 4. that ye may k. that I find no fault in him
Acts 17. 19. may we k. what this new doctrine is?
21. 24. all may k. that those things are nothing
1 Cor. 2. 12. we might k. the things given us of God
2 Cor. 2. 4. that ye might k. the love I have to you
9. that I might k. the proof of you, whether ye be
Eph. 1. 18. that ye may k. the hope of his calling
6. 22. whom I sent, that ye might k. our affairs
Phil. 3. 10. that I may k. him, and the power of his
Col. 4. 6. that ye may k. how to answer every man
8. whom I sent, that he might k. your estate
1 Tim. 3. 15. thou may k. how thou oughtest to beh.
1 John 5. 13. that ye may k. ye have eternal life
20. given us, that we may k. him that is true

We KNOW, or KNOW we.

Gen. 29. 5. know ye Laban? they said, we k. him
Deut. 18. 21. if thou say, how shall we k. the word
1 Sam. 6. 9. then shall we k. it is not his hand
2 Chr. 20. 12. we have no might, nor k. we what to do
Job 36. 26. behold, God is great, and we k. him not
Isa. 59. 12. as for our iniquities, we k. them
Hos. 6. 3. then shall we k. if we follow on to know
8. 2. Israel shall cry to me, my God, we k. thee
Mat. 22. 16. we k. thou art true, and teachest the way of God, Mark 12. 14. Luke 20. 21.
John 3. 2. we k. thou art a teacher come from God
11. verily I say to thee, we speak that we do k.
4. 22. we k. what we worship; for salvation is of
6. 42. Jesus, whose father and mother we k.?
7. 27. howbeit, we k. whence this man is
8. 52. now we k. that thou hast a devil
9. 20. we k. that this is our son who was blind
24. said to him, we k. that this man is a sinner
29. we k. that God spake to Moses, as for this
31. now we k. that God heareth not sinners
14. 5. Thomas saith to him, Ld. we k. not whither thou goest, and how can we k. the way?
21. 24. and we k. that his testimony is true
Acts 17. 20. we would k. what these things mean
28. 22. we k. it is every where spoken against
Rom. 3. 19. we k. that what things the law saith
7. 14. for we k. that the law is spiritual, but I am
8. 22. we k. the whole creation groaneth and travail.
28. we k. that all things work together for good
1 Cor. 8. 1. we k. that we all have knowledge

1 Cor. 8. 4. *we k.* that an idol is nothing in the world
13. 9. for *we k.* in part, and prophesy in part
2 Cor. 5. 1. for *we k.* that if our earthly house
16. *k. we* no man after the flesh, *k. we* him no more
1 Tim. 1. 8. but *we k.* that the law is good
Heb. 10. 30. for *we k.* him that hath said, vengeance
1 John 2. 3. hereby *we k.* that *we k.* him, if we keep
5. hereby *k. we* that we are in him
18. whereby *we k.* that it is the last time
3. 2. but *we k.* that when he shall appear
14. *we k.* that we have passed from death to life
19. hereby *we k.* that we are of the truth
24. hereby *we k.* that he abideth in us
4. 6. hereby *k. we* the spirit of truth and error
13. hereby *k. we* that we dwell in him
5. 2. by this *we k.* we love the children of God
15. and if *we k.* that he heareth us, *we k.* that we have the petitions that we desired of him
18. *we k.* whosoever is born of God, sinneth not
19. *we k.* that we are of God, and the world lieth
20. and *we k.* that the Son of God is come, an understanding, that *we* may *k.* him that is true

Ye KNOW, or KNOW *ye*.

Gen. 29. 5. he said, *k. ye* Laban the son of Nahor?
31. 6. *ye k.* that with all my power I served your
44. 27. *ye k.* that my wife bare me two sons
Exod. 16. 6. at even *ye* shall *k.* the Lord brought
23. 9. *ye k.* the heart of a stranger, seeing ye were
Num. 14. 34. *ye* shall *k.* my breach of promise
16. 28. *ye* shall *k.* that the Lord hath sent me
Josh. 3. 10. *ye* shall *k.* the living God is among you
23. 14. and *ye k.* in all your hearts and souls
Judg. 18. 14. *ye k.* there is in these houses an ephod
1 Kings 22. 3. *k. ye* that Ramoth in Gilead is ours?
2 Kings 9. 11. *ye k.* the man and his communication
Job 13. 2. what *ye k.* the same do I know
Psal. 100. 3. *k. ye* that the Lord he is God, he made
Isa. 51. 7. hearken, *ye* that *k.* righteousness
Jer. 26. 15. *k. ye* for certain, if ye put me to death
48. 17. all *ye* that *k.* his name, say, how is
Ezek. 14. 23. *ye* shall *k.* that I have not done
17. 21. *ye* shall *k.* I the Lord have spoken, 37. 14.
Joel 2. 27. *ye* shall *k.* that I am in midst of Israel
Zech. 2. 9. *ye* shall *k.* the Lord hath sent me, 6. 15.
Mat. 7. 16. *ye* shall *k.* them by their fruits, 20.
20. 25. *ye k.* princes of the Gentiles, Mark 10. 42.
24. 32. *ye k.* summer nigh, Mark 13. 28. Luke 21. 30.
25. 13. watch, for *ye k.* neither day nor hour
Mark 4. 13. he said to them, *k. ye* not this parable?
Luke 21. 31. *k. ye* that the kingdom of God is nigh
John 7. 28. *ye* both *k.* me, and know whence I am
8. 28. *ye* shall *k.* I am he ‖ 32. *ye* shall *k.* the truth
11. 49. *k. ye* nothing ‖ 13. 12. *k. ye* what I have [done
13. 17. if *ye k.* these things, happy are ye if do them
14. 4. whither I go *ye k.* and the way *ye k.*
7. from henceforth *ye k.* him, and have seen, 17.
20. *ye* shall *k.* I am in my Father, and you in me
15. 18. *ye k.* that it hated me before it hated you
Acts 2. 22. man approved, as *ye* yourselves also *k.*
10. 28. *ye k.* how that it is unlawful for a Jew
15. 7. brethren, *ye k.* how that a good while ago
19. 25. *ye k.* that by this craft we have our wealth
20. 18. *ye k.* from the first day that I came
1 Cor. 12. 2. *ye k.* that ye were Gentiles, carried
15. 58. *ye k.* your labour is not in vain in the Lord
16. 15. brethren, *ye k.* the house of Stephanas
2 Cor. 8. 9. *ye k.* the grace of our Lord Jesus Christ
13. 6. I trust *ye* shall *k.* we are not reprobates
Gal. 3. 7. *k. ye* that they which are of faith
4. 13. *ye k.* how through infirmities I preached
Eph. 5. 5. for this *ye k.* that no whoremonger
Phil. 2. 22. *ye k.* the proof of him, that as a son
1 Thess. 1. 5. as *ye k.* what manner of men we were
2. 2. and were shamefully entreated, as *ye k.*
5. nor used we flattering words, as *ye k.*
11. *ye k.* how we exhorted and comforted
3. 4. even as it came to pass, and *ye k.*
4. 2. *ye k.* what commandments we gave by Lord
2 Thess. 2. 6. and now *ye k.* what withholdeth
Heb. 12. 17. *ye k.* when he would have inherited
13. 23. *k. ye* that our brother Timothy is set at
1 Pet. 1. 18. *ye k.* that ye were not redeemed with
2 Pet. 1. 12. put you in remembrance, tho' *ye k.* them
3. 17. seeing *ye k.* these things before, beware
1 John 2. 20. *ye k.* all things ‖ 21. because *ye k.* it
29. if *ye k.* he is righteous, *ye k.* that every one
3. 5. *ye k.* he was manifested to take away our sins
15. *ye k.* no murderer hath eternal life in him
4. 2. hereby *k. ye* the Spirit of God, every spirit
3 John 12. and *ye k.* that our record is true

Ye KNOW *not*, or KNOW *ye not*.

2 Sam. 3. 38. *k. ye not* that there is a prince fallen
2 Chr. 32. 13. *k. ye not* what I and my fathers have
Job 21. 29. have not asked, do *ye not k.* their tokens
Ezek. 17. 12. *k. ye not* what these things mean?
Mat. 20. 22. Jesus said, *ye k. not* what ye ask
24. 42. *ye k. not* what hour your Lord doth come
Mark 4. 13. he said to them, *k. ye not* this parable?
12. 24. ye err, because *ye k. not* the scriptures
13. 33. watch, for *ye k. not* when the time is, 35.
Luke 9. 55. *ye k. not* what manner of spirit ye be of
John 1. 26. standeth one among you, whom *ye k. not*
4. 22. ye worship *ye k. not* what ‖ 32. meat *ye k. not* of
7. 28. he that sent me is true, whom *ye k. not*
8. 19. *ye* neither *k.* me nor my Father
9. 30. that *ye k. not* from whence he is, and yet
Rom. 6. 3. *k. ye not* that so many as were baptized
16. *k. ye not* that to whom ye yield servants
7. 1. *k. ye not*, brethren, for I speak to them that
1 Cor. 3. 16. *k. ye not* ye are temple of G. 6. 15, 19.
5. 6. *k. ye not* that a little leaven leaveneth the lump
6. 2. do *ye not k.* the saints shall judge the world?
3. *k. ye not* that we shall judge angels?
9. *k. ye not*, the unrighteous shall not inherit
16. *k. ye not*, that he which is joined to an harlot
9. 13. do *ye not k.* that they which minister
24. *k. ye not*, that they which run in a race, run all
2 Cor. 13. 5. *k. ye not* yourselves, that Jesus is in you
Jam. 4. 4. *k. ye not* that the friendship of the world
14. *ye k. not* what shall be on the morrow
1 John 2. 21. not written, because *ye k. not* the truth

KNOWEST.

Gen. 30. 26. thou *k.* my service that I have done
29. thou *k.* how I have served thee, and thy cattle
47. 6. and if thou *k.* any man of activity among
Exod. 10. 7. *k.* thou not that Egypt is destroyed
32. 22. thou *k.* the people are set on mischief
Num. 10. 31. for thou *k.* how we are to encamp
20. 14. thou *k.* the travel that hath befallen
Deut. 7. 15. the diseases of Egypt, which thou *k.*
9. 2. the children of the Anakims, whom thou *k.*
28. 33. a nation thou *k.* not, shall eat up
Josh. 14. 6. thou *k.* the thing that the Lord said
Judg. 15. 11. *k.* thou not the Philistines are rulers
1 Sam. 28. 9. woman said, thou *k.* what Saul hath done
2 Sam. 1. 5. how *k.* thou that Saul and Jonath. be dead
2. 26. *k.* thou not that it will be bitterness in end?
3. 25. thou *k.* Abner the son of Ner, that he came
7. 20. thou, Lord, *k.* thy servant, 1 Chron. 17. 18.
17. 8. for, said Hushai, thou *k.* thy father
1 Kings 1. 18. my lord the king, thou *k.* it not
2. 5. thou *k.* also what Joab did to me
9. thou *k.* what thou oughtest to do to him
15. thou *k.* that the kingdom was mine
44. thou *k.* all the wickedness thou didst to David
8. 39. whose heart thou *k.* thou only *k.* 2 Chr. 6. 30.
2 Kings 2. 3. *k.* thou the Ld. will take thy master, 5.
4. 1. thou *k.* that thy servant did fear the Lord
Job 10. 7. thou *k.* that I am not wicked
15. 9. what *k.* thou that we know not?
20. 4. *k.* thou not this of old, since man was
34. 33. therefore speak what thou *k.*
38. 5. who hath laid measures of earth, if thou *k.*?
18. breadth of the earth, declare, if thou *k.* it all
21. *k.* thou it, because thou wast then born?
33. *k.* thou the ordinances of heaven?
39. 1. *k.* thou when the wild goats bring forth, 2.
Psal. 40. 9. not refrained, O Ld. thou *k.* Jer. 15. 15.
69. 5. O God, thou *k.* my foolishness
139. 2. thou *k.* my down-sitting and up-rising
4. lo, O Lord, thou *k.* it altogether
Prov. 27. 1. thou *k.* not what a day may bring forth
Eccl. 11. 2. thou *k.* not what evil shall be
5. as thou *k.* not what is the way of the Spirit, even so thou *k.* not the works of God
6. for thou *k.* not whether shall prosper
Isa. 55. 5. thou shalt call a nation that thou *k.* not
Jer. 5. 15. a nation whose language thou *k.* not
12. 3. but thou, O Lord, *k.* me, thou hast seen me
15. 14. into a land which thou *k.* not, 17. 4.
17. 16. nor have I desired the woeful day, thou *k.*
18. 23. thou *k.* all their counsel to slay me
33. 3. I will shew thee things which thou *k.* not
Ezek. 37. 3. and I answered, O Lord God, thou *k.*
Dan. 10. 20. said, *k.* thou wherefore I come to thee
Zech. 4. 5. angel said, *k.* thou not what these be, 13.
Mat. 15. 12. *k.* thou that the Pharisees were offended
Mark 10. 19. thou *k.* commandments, Luke 18. 20.
Luke 22. 34. shall thrice deny that thou *k.* me
John 1. 48. Nathanael said, whence *k.* thou me?
3. 10. art thou a master, and *k.* not these things?
13. 7. Jesus said, what I do, thou *k.* not now
16. 30. we are sure thou *k.* all things, 21. 17.
19. 10. *k.* thou not I have power to crucify
21. 15. yea, Lord, thou *k.* that I love thee, 16.
Acts 1. 24. thou which *k.* the hearts of all men
25. 10. I have done no wrong, as thou very well *k.*
Rom. 2. 18. *k.* his will, and approvest the things
1 Cor. 7. 16. what *k.* thou, O wife, *k.* thou, O man?
2 Tim. 1. 15. thou *k.* that all they in Asia be turned
18. how he ministered to me, thou *k.* very well
Rev. 3. 17. and *k.* not that thou art wretched, blind
7. 14. and I said unto him, sir, thou *k.*

KNOWETH.

Gen. 33. 13. my lord *k.* the children are tender
Lev. 5. 3. when he *k.* of it, he shall be guilty, 4.
Deut. 2. 7. he *k.* thy walking thro' this wilderness
34. 6. no man *k.* of Moses' sepulchre to this day
Josh. 22. 22. the Lord God of gods, he *k.* and Israel
1 Sam. 3. 13. Eli's house for the iniquity which he *k.*
20. 3. thy father certainly *k.* that I found grace
23. 17. and that also Saul my father *k.*
2 Sam. 14. 22. thy servant *k.* that I found grace
17. 10. all Israel *k.* thy father is a mighty man
Job 11. 11. he *k.* vain men, he seeth wickedness
15. 23. he *k.* the day of darkness is ready at his hand
23. 10. but he *k.* the way that I take
28. 7. there is a path which no fowl *k.*
23. God understandeth and *k.* the place thereof
34. 25. therefore he *k.* their works and overturneth
Psal. 1. 6. the Lord *k.* the way of the righteous
37. 18. the Lord *k.* the days of the upright
44. 21. for he *k.* the secrets of the heart
74. 9. nor is there any among us that *k.* how long
94. 11. Lord *k.* the thoughts of man are vanity
103. 14. he *k.* our frame, remembereth we are dust
104. 19. moon for seasons, the sun *k.* his going down
138. 6. but the proud he *k.* afar off
139. 14. thy works, and that my soul *k.* right well
Prov. 9. 13. foolish woman is simple and *k.* nothing
14. 10. the heart *k.* his own bitterness, and stranger
Eccl. 6. 8. the poor, that *k.* to walk before the living
7. 22. thine own heart *k.* thou hast cursed others
9. 1. no man *k.* either love or hatred by all that
Isa. 1. 3. the ox *k.* his owner, the ass his master's crib
Jer. 8. 7. the stork *k.* her appointed times, and turtle
9. 24. glory, that he understandeth and *k.* me
Dan. 2. 22. he *k.* what is in the darkness, and light
Nah. 1. 7. Lord is good, he *k.* them that trust in him
Zeph. 3. 5. he faileth not, but the unjust *k.* no shame
Mat. 6. 8. your Father *k.* what things ye need
32. *k.* ye have need of all these things, Luke 12. 30.
11. 27. no man *k.* the Son but the Father, nor any *k.* the Father save the Son, Luke 10. 22.
24. 36. of that day *k.* no man, Mark 13. 32.
Luke 16. 15. ye justify, but God *k.* your hearts
John 7. 15. saying, how *k.* this man letters?
27. when Christ cometh, no man *k.* whence he is
10. 15. as the Father *k.* me ‖ 14. 17. nor *k.* him
19. 35. he saw it, and he *k.* that he saith true
Acts 15. 8. God which *k.* the hearts bare witness
26. 26. for the king *k.* of these things before whom
Rom. 8. 27. he *k.* what is the mind of the Spirit

1 Cor. 2. 11. for what man *k.* the things of a man, even so the things of God *k.* no man but Spirit
8. 2. if any man think he *k.* any thing, he *k.* nothing
2 Cor. 11. 11. because I love you not? God *k.*
31. God *k.* I lie not ‖ 12. 2. I cannot tell, God *k.* 3.
2 Tim. 2. 19. the Lord *k.* them that are his
Jam. 4. 17. to him that *k.* to do good, and doeth not
2 Pet. 2. 9. the Lord *k.* how to deliver the godly
1 John 3. 20. and *k.* all things ‖ 4. 6. he that *k.* God
4. 7. he that loveth is born of God, and *k.* God
Rev. 2. 17. a new name written, which no man *k.*
12. 12. because he *k.* that he hath but a short time

Who KNOWETH, or KNOWETH *not*.

1 Kings 1. 11. doth reign, and Dav. our Ld. *k.* it *not*
Esth. 4. 14. *who k.* whether thou art come to kingd.
Job 12. 3. yea, *who k. not* such things as these?
9. *who k. not* in all these, that the hand of Lord
14. 21. his sons come to honour, he *k.* it *not*
18. 21. this is the place of him that *k. not* God
28. 13. man *k. not* the price thereof, nor is it found
35. 15. he hath visited in anger, yet he *k.* it *not*
Ps. 39. 6. riches, and *k. not* who shall gather them
90. 11. *who k.* the power of thine anger?
92. 6. a brutish man *k. not*, nor a fool understand this
Prov. 7. 23. and *k. not* that it is for his life
9. 18. but he *k. not* that the dead are there
24. 22. and *who k.* the ruin of them both?
Eccl. 2. 19. *who k.* whether he be wise or a fool
3. 21. *who k.* the spirit of man that goeth upward
6. 12. for *who k.* what is good for man in life
8. 1. *who k.* the interpretation of a thing?
7. for he *k. not* that which shall be
9. 12. for man also *k. not* his time, as the fishes
10. 15. because he *k. not* how to go to the city
Isa. 29. 15. and they say, who seeth us, *who k.* us?
Hos. 7. 9. gray hairs here and there, yet he *k. not*
Joel 2. 14. *who k.* if he will return and repent
Mark 4. 27. and seed should grow up, he *k. not* how
John 7. 49. but this people, *who k. not* the law
12. 35. walketh in darkness, *k. not* whither he goeth
15. 15. the servant *k. not* what his lord doeth
Acts 19. 35. what man that *k. not* that Ephesians
1 John 2. 11. walketh in darkness, *k. not* whither go
3. 1. therefore the world *k.* us *not*, it knew him not
4. 8. he that loveth not, *k. not* God, for God is love

KNOWING.

Gen. 3. 5. ye shall be as gods, *k.* good and evil
43. † 7. *k.* could we know he would say, bring
1 Kings 2. 32. slew them, my father David not *k.*
2 Chron. 2. † 12. to David a wise son, *k.* prudence
Mat. 9. 4. Jesus *k.* their thoughts, Luke 11. 17.
22. 29. ye err, not *k.* the scriptures nor power of G.
Mark 5. 30. Jesus immediately *k.* in himself virtue
33. but the woman *k.* what was done in her
6. 20. feared John, *k.* that he was a just man
12. 15. but he *k.* their hypocrisy, said to them
Luke 8. 53. they laughed, *k.* that she was dead
9. 33. and one for Elias, not *k.* what he said
John 13. 3. Jesus *k.* the Father had given all things
18. 4. Jesus *k.* all things that should come upon him
19. 28. Jesus *k.* that all things were accomplished
21. 12. none durst ask him, *k.* that it was the Lord
Acts 2. 30. *k.* that God had sworn with an oath
5. 7. his wife not *k.* what was done, came in
18. 25. he taught, *k.* only the baptism of John
20. 22. not *k.* the things that shall befall me there
Rom. 1. 32. who *k.* the judgment of God that they
2. 4. not *k.* that the goodness of God leadeth thee
5. 3. *k.* that tribulation worketh patience
6. 6. *k.* this, that our old man is crucified with him
9. *k.* Chr. being raised from dead, dieth no more
13. 11. *k.* the time, now it is high time to awake
2 Cor. 1. 7. *k.* that as ye are partakers of sufferings
4. 14. *k.* that he which raised the Lord Jesus
5. 6. *k.* that whilst we are at home in the body
11. *k.* the terror of the Lord, we persuade men
Gal. 2. 16. *k.* that a man is not justified by the law
Eph. 6. 8. *k.* that whatsoever good any man doeth
9. *k.* that your master is in heaven, Col. 4. 1.
Phil. 1. 17. *k.* that I am set for defence of gospel
Col. 3. 24. *k.* that of the L. ye shall receive reward
1 Thess. 1. 4. *k.* beloved, your election of God
1 Tim. 1. 9. *k.* this, that the law is made for lawless
6. 4. is proud, *k.* nothing, but doting about questions
2 Tim. 2. 23. questions, *k.* that they do gender strifes
3. 14. *k.* of whom thou hast learned them
Tit. 3. 11. *k.* that he that is such, is subverted
Philem. 21. *k.* that thou wilt do more than I say
Heb. 10. 34. *k.* ye have in heaven a better substance
11. 8. he went out, not *k.* whither he went
Jam. 1. 3. *k.* this, that the trying of your faith
3. 1. *k.* we shall receive greater condemnation
1 Pet. 3. 9. blessing, *k.* that ye are thereunto called
5. 9. *k.* the same afflictions are accomplished in
2 Pet. 1. 14. *k.* that shortly I must put off this tabern.
20. *k.* this, that no prophecy of scripture is of
3. 3. *k.* that there shall come scoffers in last days

KNOWLEDGE

Signifies, [1] *The essential and infinite understanding of God, by which he knows every thing in the most perfect manner,* 1 Sam. 2. 3. [2] *A bare understanding of divine truths, without faith in Christ, and love to our Christian brethren,* 1 Cor. 8. 1. [3] *A right understanding and conception of spiritual things,* 2 Cor. 6. 6. [4] *That knowledge of God's will, and of the way of salvation which is in Christ in its highest perfection, and which by him is revealed to his people, and imprinted on their minds and hearts by his Spirit, so as to produce faith, love, and obedience,* Isa. 53. 11. [5] *Christian prudence and holy experience in the ways of God,* 2 Cor. 8. 7. 2 Pet. 1. 5. 6. [6] *That imperfect knowledge of divine things which we have in this world,* 1 Cor. 13. 8. [7] *The gift of interpreting dreams,* Dan. 5. 12. It is [1] Natural, *that knowledge which men have by the light of nature,* Rom. 1. 21, 28. Jude 10. [2] Artificial, *such as is bestowed on men for devising curious and excellent pieces of workmanship,* Exod. 35. 31. [3] Legal, *namely, that knowledge of our guilt and danger which were taught by the law,* Rom. 3. 20. | 7. 7. [4] Evangelical, *such is that*

knowledge of Christ, and of salvation through him, which the gospel acquaints us with, 2 Cor. 2. 14.
Gen. 2. 9. and the tree of *k.* of good and evil, 17.
Exod. 31. 3. I have filled Bezaleel in *k.* 35. 31.
Lev. 4. 23. or if his sin come to his *k.* 28.
Num. 24. 16. and knew the *k.* of the most High
Ruth 2. 10. that thou shouldest take *k.* of me
19. blessed be he that did take *k.* of thee
1 *Sam.* 2. 3. for the Lord is a God of *k.*
23. 23. see, take *k.* of all the lurking places
1 *Kings* 9. 27. shipmen that had *k.* of sea, 2 *Chr.* 8. 18.
2 *Chron.* 1. 10. give me *k.* that I may go out
11. but hast asked *k.* || 12. *k.* is granted thee
Neh. 10. 28. every one having *k.* separated
Job 15. 2. should a wise man utter vain *k.?*
21. 14. for we desire not the *k.* of thy ways
22. shall any teach God *k.* seeing he judgeth
33. 3. and my lips shall utter *k.* clearly
34. 2. give ear unto me, ye that have *k.*
36. 3. I will fetch my *k.* from afar, and will ascribe
4. he that is perfect in *k.* is with thee, 37. 16.
Psal. 19. 2. and night unto night sheweth *k.*
73. 11. and is there *k.* in the Most High?
94. 10. he that teacheth man *k.* shall not he know?
119. 66. teach me good judgment and *k.*
139. 6. such *k.* is too wonderful for me
144. 3. what is man that thou takest *k.* of him?
Prov. 1. 4. to give the young man *k.* and discretion
7. the fear of the Lord is the beginning of *k.*
22. fools hate *k.* || 2. 3. if thou criest after *k.*
29. for that they hated *k.* and did not choose
2. 6. out of his mouth cometh *k.* and understanding
10. and when *k.* is pleasant to thy soul
3. 20. by his *k.* the depths are broken up
5. 2. and that thy lips may keep *k.*
8. 9. they are right to them that find *k.*
10. *k.* rather than gold || 12. and find out *k.*
9. 10. and the *k.* of the Holy is understanding
10. 14. wise men lay up *k.* but the foolish
11. 9. but through *k.* shall the just be delivered
12. 1. whoso loveth instruction loveth *k.*
23. a prudent man concealeth *k.* but fools
13. 16. every prudent man dealeth with *k.*
14. 6. *k.* is easy to him that understandeth
7. thou perceivest not in him the lips of *k.*
18. but the prudent are crowned with *k.*
15. 2. the tongue of the wise useth *k.* aright
7. the lips of the wise disperse *k.*
14. the heart that hath understanding seeketh *k.*
17. 27. he that hath *k.* spareth his words
18. 15. the heart of the prudent getteth *k.* and the ear of the wise seeketh *k.*
19. 25. reprove, and he will understand *k.*
27. cease, my son, to err from the words of *k.*
20. 15. the lips of *k.* are a precious jewel
21. 11. when the wise is instructed, he receiveth *k.*
22. 12. the eyes of the Lord preserve *k.*
17. and apply thine heart unto my *k.*
20. written excellent things in counsels and *k.*
23. 12. and apply thine ears to the words of *k.*
24. 4. by *k.* shall the chambers be filled with riches
5. yea, a man of *k.* increaseth strength
14. so shall the *k.* of wisdom be to thy soul
28. 2. by a man of *k.* the state shall be prolonged
30. 3. nor learned wisdom, nor have the *k.* of Holy
Eccl. 1. 16. yea, my heart had experience of *k.*
18. he that increaseth *k.* increaseth sorrow
2. 21. for there is a man whose labour is in *k.*
26. God giveth to a man wisdom, *k.* and joy
7. 12. but the excellency of *k.* is that wisdom giveth
9. 10. nor *k.* in the grave, whither thou goest
12. 9. the preacher still taught the people *k.*
Isa. 8. 4. for before the child shall have *k.* to cry
11. 2. the spirit of *k.* and of the fear of the Lord
28. 9. whom shall he teach *k.?* them that are wean.
32. 4. the heart of the rash shall understand *k.*
33. 6. wisdom and *k.* shall be stability of thy times
40. 14. who taught him *k.* || 44. 19. nor is there *k.*
44. 25. and maketh their *k.* foolish
47. 10. thy wisdom and thy *k.* hath perverted thee
53. 11. by his *k.* my righteous servant justify many
Jer. 3. 15. pastors, which shall feed you with *k.*
10. 14. every man is brutish in his *k.* every founder
11. 18. the Lord hath given me *k.* of it
51. 17. every man is brutish by his *k.* every founder
Dan. 1. 4. children well favoured and cunning in *k.*
17. God gave them *k.* || 2. 21. he giveth *k.* to them
5. 12. excellent spirit and *k.* were found in Daniel
12. 4. many run to and fro, and *k.* shall be increased
Hos. 4. 6. my people are destroyed for lack of *k.* because thou hast rejected *k.* I will reject thee
Hab. 2. 14. the earth filled with the *k.* of the Lord
Mal. 2. 7. for the priest's lips should keep *k.*
Mat. 14. 35. the men of that place had *k.* of him
Luke 1. 77. to give *k.* of salvat. by remission of sins
11. 52. ye have taken away the key of *k.*
Acts 4. 13. they marvelled and took *k.* of them
24. 22. having more perfect *k.* of that way
Rom. 1. 28. did not like to retain God in their *k.*
2. 20. which hast the form of *k.* and of truth
3. 20. no flesh justified, for by law is the *k.* of sin
10. 2. they have a zeal, but not according to *k.*
15. 14. that ye also are filled with all *k.* able to
1 *Cor.* 1. 5. are enriched in all utterance and all *k.*
8. 1. we know that we all have *k.* *k.* puffeth up
7. howbeit there is not in every man that *k.*
10. if any man see thee which hast *k.* sit at meat
11. through thy *k.* shall thy weak brother perish
12. 8. to another the word of *k.* by the same Spirit
13. 2. though understand all mysteries and all *k.*
8. whether there be *k.* it shall vanish away
14. 6. except I speak to you by revelation or *k.*
2 *Cor.* 2. 14. maketh manifest the savour of his *k.*
4. 6. to give the light of the *k.* of the glory of God
6. 6. by pureness, by *k.* by long-suffering, by kind.
8. 7. as ye abound in faith, utterance, and *k.*
11. 6. though I be rude in speech, yet not in *k.*
Eph. 1. 17. may give you wisdom in the *k.* of him
3. 4. when ye read, ye may understand my *k.*
19. the love of Christ which passeth *k.*
4. 13. till we come in the unity of the *k.* of the Son
Phil. 1. 9. that your love may abound more in *k.*
3. 8. I count all things but loss for the *k.* of Christ
Col. 1. 9. that ye might be filled with the *k.* of his will
2. 3. in whom are hid the treasures of wisd. and *k.*
3. 10. put on the new man which is renewed in *k.*
1 *Tim.* 2. 4. all men to come to the *k.* of the truth
2 *Tim.* 3. 7. never able to come to the *k.* of the truth
Heb. 10. 26. if we sin after we have received the *k.*
Jam. 3. 13. who is a wise man, and endued with *k.?*
1 *Pet.* 3. 7. husbands dwell with them according to *k.*
2 *Pet.* 1. 3. thro' the *k.* of him that hath called us
5. add to virtue *k.* and to *k.* temperance
8. nor unfruitful in the *k.* of our Lord Jes. Christ
3. 18. grow in grace and in the *k.* of our Lord Jesus

KNOWLEDGE *of God.*

Prov. 2. 5. then shalt thou find the *k. of God*
Hos. 4. 1. there is no truth, nor *k. of God* in the land
6. 6. desired the *k. of God* more than burnt-offerings
Rom. 11. 33. the riches both of wisdom, and *k. of G.*
1 *Cor.* 15. 34. for some have not the *k. of God*
2 *Cor.* 10. 5. high thing exalteth itself against *k. of G.*
Col. 1. 10. and increasing in the *k. of God*
2 *Pet.* 1. 2. peace be multiplied, thro' the *k. of God*

KNOWLEDGE *of the Lord.*

2 *Chron.* 30. 22. that taught the good *k. of the Lord*
Isa. 11. 9. the earth shall be full of the *k. of the Lord*
2 *Pet.* 2. 20. escaped pollutions thro' the *k. of the L.*

No KNOWLEDGE.

Deut. 1. 39. your childr. which in that day had *no k.*
Psal. 14. 4. have the workers of iniquity *no k.* 53. 4.
Isa. 5. 13. gone into captiv. because they have *no k.*
45. 20. they have *no k.* that set up their images
58. 3. we afflicted our soul, and thou takest *no k.*
Jer. 4. 22. but to do good, they have *no k.*

Without KNOWLEDGE.

Num. 15. 24. committed *without k.* of the congregat.
Job 34. 35. Job hath spoken *without k.* and wisdom
35. 16. he multiplieth words *without k.*
36. 12. shall perish by sword, and die *without k.*
38. 2. darkeneth counsel by words *without k.* 42. 3.
Prov. 19. 2. it is not good that the soul be *without k.*

KNOWN.

Gen. 24. 16. was a virgin, nor had any man *k.* her
Exod. 2. 14. Moses said, surely this thing is *k.*
21. 36. if it be *k.* that the ox hath used to push
33. 16. for wherein shall it be *k.* here that I and
Lev. 4. 14. when the sin they have sinned is *k.*
5. 1. is a witness whether he hath seen or *k.* of it
Num. 31. 17. kill every woman that hath *k.* man
Deut. 1. 13. take wise men, and *k.* among tribes, 15.
21. 1. and it be not *k.* who hath slain him
Josh. 24. 31. and which had *k.* the works of the Ld.
1 *Sam.* 6. 3. and it shall be *k.* to you why his hand
1 *Kings* 18. 36. let it be *k.* that thou art God in Isr.
Ezra 4. 12. be it *k.* to the king, 13. | 5. 8.
Neh. 4. 15. when enemies heard that it was *k.* to us
Esth. 2. 22. the thing was *k.* to Mordecai who told it
Psal. 9. 16. the Lord is *k.* by the judgment which
31. 7. thou hast *k.* my soul in adversities
48. 3. God is *k.* in her palaces for a refuge
67. 2. that thy way may be *k.* on earth, thy health
69. 19. thou hast *k.* my reproach and my shame
76. 1. in Judah is God *k.* his name is great in Isr.
77. 19. thy way in the sea, thy footsteps are not *k.*
78. 3. sayings of old, which we have heard and *k.*
79. 10. let him be *k.* among the heath. in our sight
88. 12. shall thy wonders be *k.* in the dark?
91. 14. set him on high, because he hath *k.* my name
119. 79. those that have *k.* thy testimonies
152. I have *k.* of old thou hast found. them for ever
139. 1. O Lord, thou hast searched me, and *k.* me
Prov. 10. 9. but he that pervert. his ways shall be *k.*
12. 16. a fool's wrath is presently *k.* but a prudent
20. 11. a child is *k.* by his doings whether his work
31. 23. her husband is *k.* in the gates, when he sitt.
Eccl. 5. 3. a fool's voice is *k.* by multitude of words
6. 10. and it is *k.* that it is man, nor may contend
Isa. 12. 5. excellent things, this is *k.* in all the earth
19. 21. and the Lord shall be *k.* to Egypt
61. 9. their seed shall be *k.* among the Gentiles
66. 14. hand of the Lord shall be *k.* to his servants
Jer. 5. 5. for they have *k.* the way of the Lord
28. 9. then shall prophet be *k.* the Lord sent him
Ezek. 36. 32. saith the Lord God, be it *k.* to you, *Acts* 4. 10. | 13. 38. | 28. 28.
38. 23. I will be *k.* in the eyes of many nations
Dan. 3. 18. but if not, be it *k.* to thee, O king
4. 26. after thou shalt have *k.* the heavens rule
Amos 3. 2. you only have I *k.* of all families of earth
Zech. 14. 7. a day which shall be *k.* to the Lord
Mat. 12. 7. but if ye had *k.* what this meant
33. the tree is *k.* by his fruit, *Luke* 6. 44.
24. 43. if the good man of house had *k. Luke* 12. 39.
Luke 7. 39. if he were a prophet, he would have *k.*
19. 42. saying, if thou hadst *k.* in this thy day
24. 35. how he was *k.* of them in breaking of bread
John 7. 4. he himself seeketh to be *k.* openly
8. 19. nor know me nor my Father, if ye had *k.* me ye should have *k.* my Father also, 14. 7.
10. 14. I know my sheep, and am *k.* of mine
17. 7. now they have *k.* || 8. and have *k.* surely
25. I have *k.* thee, these have *k.* that thou sent me
18. 15. that disciple which was *k.* to high-priest, 16.
Acts 1. 19. and it was *k.* to all dwellers at Jerus.
2. 14. be this *k.* unto you, and hearken to my words
9. 24. but their laying await was *k.* of Saul
42. it was *k.* throughout all Joppa many believed
15. 18. *k.* unto God are all his works from beginn.
19. 17. this was *k.* to all the Jews and Greeks
22. 30. he would have *k.* the certainty, 23. 28.
Rom. 1. 19. because that which may be *k.* of God
11. 34. who hath *k.* the mind of Lord, 1 *Cor.* 2. 16.
1 *Cor.* 2. 8. for had they *k.* it || 8. 3. same is *k.* of him
13. 12. then shall I know, even as I also am *k.*
14. 7. how shall it be *k.* what is piped or harped
9. how shall it be *k.* what is spoken?
2 *Cor.* 3. 2. are our epistle *k.* and read of all men
5. 16. though we have *k.* Christ after the flesh
6. 9. as unknown and yet well *k.* as dying and
Gal. 4. 9. after ye have *k.* God or are *k.* of God
Eph. 3. 10. might be *k.* by church the wisd. of God
Phil. 4. 5. let your moderation be *k.* to all men
2 *Tim.* 3. 10. thou hast fully *k.* my doctrine
15. from a child thou hast *k.* the holy scriptures
4. 17. that by me the preaching might be fully *k.*
1 *John* 2. 13. I write, because ye have *k.* him, 14.
4. 16. we have *k.* and believed the love God hath
2 *John* 1. 1. and all them that have *k.* the truth

Made or *madest* KNOWN.

Gen. 45. 1. while Joseph *made* himself *k.* to brethren
Neh. 9. 14. and *madest k.* to them thy holy sabbath
Psal. 98. 2. the Lord hath *made k.* his salvation
103. 7. he *made k.* his ways to Moses, his acts
Prov. 14. 33. that which is in the midst of fools is *m. k.*
22. 19. I have *made k.* to thee this day, even to thee
Ezek. 20. 5. and *made* myself *k.* to them, 9.
Dan. 2. 15. then Arioch *made* the thing *k.* to Daniel
17. Daniel *made* the thing *k.* to Hananiah
23. hast *ma. k.* to me, *ma. k.* to us the king's matter
† 28. a God in heaven hath *made k.* to the king
45. the great God hath *made k.* to the king
Hos. 5. 9. have I *made k.* that which shall surely be
Luke 2. 15. which the Lord hath *made k.* to us
17. had seen it, they *made k.* abroad the saying
John 15. 15. all that I heard, I have *made k.* to you
Acts 2. 28. thou hast *made k.* to me the ways of life
7. 13. at the second time Joseph was *made k.* to his breth. and Joseph's kindred *made k.* to Pharaoh
Rom. 16. 26. *m. k.* to all nations for obedience of f.
Eph. 1. 9. having *m. k.* to us the mystery of his will
3. 3. how by revelation he *m. k.* to me the mystery
Phil. 4. 6. let your requests be *made k.* to God
2 *Pet.* 1. 16. when we *ma. k.* the coming of our Ld.

Make KNOWN.

Num. 12. 6. I will *make* myself *k.* to him in a vision
1 *Sam.* 28. 15. thou mayest *m. k.* to me what I shall do
1 *Chr.* 16. 8. *m. k.* his deeds among people, *Ps.* 105. 1.
17. 19. in *making k.* all these great things
Psal. 78. 5. that they should *make* them *k.*
89. 1. with my mouth will I *make k.* thy faithfuln.
106. 8. that he might *make k.* his mighty power
145. 12. to *make k.* to sons of men his mighty acts
Prov. 1. 23. I will *make k.* my words to you
Isa. 38. 19. the father to children shall *m. k.* thy truth
64. 2. to *make* thy name *k.* to thy adversaries
Ezek. 35. 11. I will *make* myself *k.* among them
39. 7. so will I *make* my holy name *k.* in Israel
Dan. 2. 25. found a man that will *make k.* to the king
26. art thou able to *make k.* to me the dream?
28. but the Lord *maketh k.* to the king, 29.
30. shall *make k.* the interpretation, 5. 15, 16, 17.
Hab. 3. 2. O Lord, in the midst of the years *make k.*
Rom. 9. 22. God willing to *make* his power *k.*
23. that he might *make k.* the riches of his glory
Eph. 6. 19. to *make k.* the mystery of the gospel
21. Tychicus shall *make k.* to you all things
Col. 1. 27. to whom G. will *m. k.* what is the riches
4. 9. they shall *make k.* to you all things done here

Not KNOWN.

Gen. 19. 8. I have two daughters which have *not k.* man, *Num.* 31. 18, 35. *Judg.* 21. 12.
41. 21. it could *not* be *k.* they had eaten them
31. and the plenty shall *not* be *k.* in the land
Exod. 6. 3. by my name JEHOVAH was I *not k.*
Deut. 11. 2. with children which have *not k.* 31. 13.
28. to go after gods which ye have *not k.* 13. 6, 13.
28. 36. neither thou *nor* thy fathers have *k.* 64.
Judg. 3. 1. as many as had *not k.* the wars of Canaan
16. 9. brake the withs, so his strength was *not k.*
Ruth 3. 3. but make *not* thyself *k.* to the man
14. let it *not* be *k.* that a woman came in
2 *Sam.* 17. 19. spread corn, and the thing was *not k.*
1 *Kings* 14. 2. be *not k.* to be the wife of Jeroboam
Ps. 18. 43. people whom I have *not k.* shall serve me
77. 19. way is in the sea, and thy footsteps are *not k.*
79. 6. pour wrath on heathen that have *not k.* thee
95. 10. and they have *not k.* my ways, *Heb.* 3. 10.
147. 20. thy judgments, they have *not k.* them
Eccl. 6. 5. he hath not seen the sun, *nor k.* any thing
Isa. 40. 21. have ye *not k.?* || 28. hast thou *not k.?*
42. 16. lead them in paths that they have *not k.*
44. 18. they have *not k.* nor understood, he hath shut
45. 4. I surnamed thee, tho' thou hast *not k.* me, 5.
Jer. 4. 22. my people is foolish, they have *not k.* me
Ezek. 32. 9. into countries which thou hast *not k.*
Dan. 2. 5. if ye will *not* make *k.* the dream, 9.
4. 7. they did *not* make *k.* to me interpretation, 5. 8.
Hos. 5. 4. and they have *not k.* the Lord
Nah. 3. 17. their place is *not k.* where they are
Mat. 10. 26. fear them not, for there is nothing hid that shall *not* be *k. Luke* 8. 17. | 12. 2.
12. 16. they should *not* make him *k. Mark* 3. 12.
Luke 24. 18. a stranger, and hast *not k.* these things
John 8. 55. yet ye have *not k.* him, but I know him
14. 9. so long time, and yet hast thou *n. k.* me, Philip
16. 3. because they have *not k.* the Father nor me
17. 25. O righteous Fath. the world hath *n. k.* thee
Rom. 3. 17. the way of peace have they *not k.*
7. 7. I had *not k.* sin but by the law, I had *n. k.* lust
Eph. 3. 5. which in other ages was *not* made *k.*
2 *Pet.* 2. 21. been better *not k.* way of righteousness
1 *John* 3. 6. the sinner hath not seen *nor k.* him
Rev. 2. 24. which have *not k.* the depths of Satan

L.

LABOUR

Signifies, [1] *Diligent care and pains,* Prov. 14. 23. Eccl. 1. 3. [2] *The increase and fruit of labour,* Exod. 23. 16. Eccl. 2. 10. [3] *The pangs of a woman in child-birth,* Gen. 35. 16, 17. [4] *The work done or performed by labour,* Eccl. 2. 11. [5] *All evils both of sin and misery, particularly those of persecution,* Rev. 14. 13. [6] *To endeavour earnestly,* Isa. 22. 4. Heb. 4. 11. [7] *To journey or travel,* Josh. 7. 3. [8] *To perform christian offices,* Rom. 16. 6. [9] *Diligently and carefully to discharge pastoral duties,* 1 Tim. 5. 17.

LABOUR, *Substantive.*

Gen. 31. 42. God hath seen the *l.* of my hands
35. 16. Rachel travailed and had hard *l.* 17.
Deut. 26. 7. the Lord heard, and looked on our *l.*
Neh. 5. 13. so God shake out every man from his *l.*

Job 5. † 7. yet man is born to l. as sparks fly upward
39. 11. or wilt thou leave thy l. to him
16. her l. is in vain without fear
Psal. 73. † 16. to know, it was l. in mine eyes
78. 46. he gave their l. to the locust
90. 10. yet is their strength l. and sorrow, soon cut
104. 23. man goeth to his l. till the evening
105. 44. they inherited the l. of the people
107. 12. he brought down their heart with l.
109. 11. let the stranger spoil his l.
128. 2. thou shalt eat the l. of thy hands
Prov. 10. 16. the l. of the righteous tendeth to life
13. 11. he that gathereth by l. shall increase
14. 23. in all l. there is profit, but the talk of lips
Eccl. 1. 3. what profit hath a man of all his l.
8. all things are full of l. man cannot utter it
2. 10. rejoiced in all my l. my portion of all my l.
18. yea, I hated all my l. which I had taken
19. yet shall he have rule over all my l.
20. to cause my heart to despair of the l. I took
21. for there is a man whose l. is in wisdom
22. what hath man of all his l. under the sun?
24. make his soul enjoy good in l. 3. 13. | 5. 18.
4. 8. yet there is no end of all his l. nor eye satisfied
9. because they have a good reward for their l.
5. 15. nothing of his l. which he may carry away
19. to rejoice in his l. this is the gift of God
6. 7. all the l. of man is for his mouth, and yet
8. 15. for that shall abide with him of his l.
9. 9. that is thy portion in thy l. under the sun
10. 15. the l. of the foolish wearieth every one
Isa. 45. 14. the l. of Egypt shall come over to thee
55. 2. why spend your l. for that which satisfi. not?
Jer. 3. 24. shame devoured the l. of our fathers
20. 18. wherefore came I out of the womb to see l.
Ezek. 23. 29. they shall take away all thy l.
29. 20. I have given him the land of Egypt for his l.
Hab. 3. 17. though the l. of the olive should fail
Hag. 1. 11. a drought on all the l. of the hands
John 4. 38. to reap that whereon ye bestowed no l.
Rom. 16. 6. greet Mary, who bestowed much l. on us
1 Cor. 3. 8. every man shall receive accord. to his l.
15. 58. you know that your l. is not in vain
Gal. 4. 11. I am afraid of you, lest I bestowed l. in vain
Phil. 1. 22. if I live in the flesh, this is fruit of my l.
2. 25. Epaphroditus, my companion in l. brother
1 Thess. 1. 3. remembering your l. of love, and patience
2. 9. for ye remember, brethren, our l. and travail
3. 5. tempter have tempted you, and our l. be in vain
2 Thess. 3. 8. but wrought with l. and travail night
Heb. 6. 10. not unrighteous to forget your l. of love
Rev. 2. 2. I know thy works, and l. and patience

LABOUR, Verb.

Exod. 5. 9. more work, that they may l. therein
20. 9. six days shalt thou l. Deut. 5. 13.
Josh. 7. 3. make not all the people to l. thither
24. 13. given you a land, for which he did not l.
Neh. 4. 22. may be a guard to us, and l. on the day
Job 9. 29. if I be wicked, why then l. I in vain?
Psal. 127. 1. except the Lord build they l. in vain
144. 14. that our oxen may be strong to l.
Prov. 21. 25. the slothful, his hands refuse to l.
23. 4. l. not to be rich, cease from thy own wisdom
Eccl. 4. 8. nor saith he, for whom do I l.?
8. 17. because tho' a man l. to seek it out, not find it
Isa. 22. 4. I will weep bitterly, l. not to comfort me
65. 23. they shall not l. in vain, nor bring forth
Jer. 51. 58. and the people shall l. in vain
Lam. 5. 5. under persecution we l. and have no rest
Mic. 4. 10. be in pain, and l. to bring forth, O Zion
Hab. 2. 13. that the people should l. in the fire
Mat. 11. 28. come to me all ye that l. and are laden
John 6. 27. l. not for the meat that perisheth
Rom. 16. 12. and Tryphosa, who l. in the Lord
1 Cor. 4. 12. and l. working with our own hands
2 Cor. 5. 9 wherefore we l. to be accepted of him
Eph. 4. 28. but rather l. working with his hands
Col. 1. 29. whereunto I also l. striving according to
1 Thess. 5. 12. to know them which l. among you
1 Tim. 4. 10. therefore we both l. and suffer reproach
5. 17. especially they that l. in word and doctrine
Heb. 4. 11. let us l. therefore to enter into that rest

LABOURED.

Neh. 4. 21. so we l. in the work, and held the spears
Job 20. 18. that which he l. for, shall he restore
Eccl. 2. 11. I looked on the labour I had l. to do
19. have rule over all my labour wherein I have l.
21. yet to a man that hath not l. therein
22. of the vexation of his heart wherein he hath l.
5. 16. what profit hath he that hath l. for the wind?
Isa. 47. 12. with thy sorceries wherein thou hast l.
15. shall they be to thee with whom thou hast l.
49. 4. I said, I have l. in vain, spent my strength
62. 8. stranger not drink, for which thou hast l.
Dan. 6. 14. then the king l. to deliver Daniel
Jonah 4. 10. the gourd for which thou hast not l.
John 4. 38. other men l. and ye are entered into their
Rom. 16. 12. salute Persis, who l. much in the Lord
1 Cor. 15. 10. but I l. more abundantly than they all
Phil. 2. 16. that I have not run nor l. in vain
4. 3. help those that l. with me in the gospel
Rev. 2. 3. hast borne, and for my name's sake l.

LABOURER.

Luke 10. 7. for the l. is worthy of his hire
1 Tim. 5. 18. the l. is worthy of his reward

LABOURERS.

Mat. 9. 37. harvest plenteous, but l. few, Luke 10. 2.
38. pray the Lord that he will send l. Luke 10. 2.
20. 1. went out early to hire l. into his vineyard
2. when he had agreed with the l. || 8. call the l.
1 Cor. 3. 9. for we are l. together with God
Jam. 5. 4. behold the hire of the l. that reaped

LABOURETH.

Prov. 16. 26. he that l. l. for himself
Eccl. 3. 9. what profit in that wherein he l.?
1 Cor. 16. 16. submit to every one that helpeth and l.
2 Tim. 2. 6. the husbandman that l. must be first

LABOURING.

Eccl. 5. 12. the sleep of a l. man is sweet
Acts 20. 35. so l. ye ought to support the weak
Col. 4. 12. always l. for you in prayer, that ye
1 Thess. 2. 9. l. night and day we preached to you

LABOURS.

Exod. 23. 16. the first-fruits of thy l. when thou hast gathered in thy l. out of the field
Deut. 28. 33. and all thy l. shall a nation eat up
Prov. 5. 10. and thy l. be in the house of a stranger
Isa. 58. 3. in day of your fast you exact all your l.
Jer. 20. 5. I will deliver all their l. to their enemies
Hos. 12. 8. in my l. shall they find no iniquity in me
Hag. 2. 17. I smote you in all the l. of your hands
John 4. 38. and ye are entered into their l.
2 Cor. 6. 5. in tumults, in l. in watchings, in fastings
10. 15. not boasting of other men's l.
11. 23. in l. more abund. in stripes above measure
Rev. 14. 13. that they may rest from their l.

LACE.

Exod. 28. 28. shall bind the breast-plate with l. of blue
37. and thou shalt put it on a blue l.
39. 31. and they tied to it a l. of blue to fasten it

LACK, Substantive.

Gen. 18. 28. wilt thou destroy all for l. of five?
Exod. 16. 18. that gathered little had no l. 2 Cor. 8. 15.
Job 4. 11. the old lion perisheth for l. of prey
38. 41. when his young ones wander for l. of meat
Hos. 4. 6. my peo. are destroyed for l. of knowledge
Phil. 2. 30. his life to supply your l. of service
1 Thess. 4. 12. and that ye may have l. of nothing

LACK, Verb.

Gen. 18. 28. if there shall l. five of the fifty
Deut. 8. 9. thou shalt not l. any thing in it
Psal. 34. 10. the young lions do l. and suffer hunger
Prov. 28. 27. that giveth to the poor shall not l.
Eccl. 9. 8. and let thy head l. no ointment
Mat. 19. 20. these things have I kept, what l. I yet?
Jam. 1. 5. if any of you l. wisdom, let him ask of God

LACKED.

Deut. 2. 7. Ld. been with thee, thou hast l. nothing
2 Sam. 2. 30. there l. of David's serv. nineteen men
1 Kings 4. 27. officers provided victual, they l. noth.
11. 22. but what hast thou l. with me?
Neh. 9. 21. thou didst sustain them, they l. nothing
Luke 8. 6. it withered away, because it l. moisture
22. 35. I sent you without purse, l. ye any thing?
Acts 4. 34. nor was there any among them that l.
1 Cor. 12. 24. given more honour to that part which l.
Phil. 4. 10. ye were careful, but l. opportunity

LACKEST.

Mark 10. 21. but one thing thou l. Luke 18. 22.

LACKETH.

Num. 31. 49. and there l. not one man of us
2 Sam. 3. 29. let there not fail one that l. bread
Prov. 6. 32. committeth adultery, l. understanding
12. 9. than he that honoureth himself, and l. bread
2 Pet. 1. 9. but he that l. these things is blind

LACKING.

Lev. 2. 13. nor shalt thou suffer salt to be l.
22. 23. not offer a lamb that hath any thing l.
Judg. 21. 3. that there should be one tribe l. in Israel
1 Sam. 30. 19. and there was nothing l. to them
Jer. 23. 4. they shall fear no more, nor shall be l.
1 Cor. 16. 17. for that which was l. they supplied
2 Cor. 11. 9. what was l. to me the brethren supplied
1 Thess. 3. 10. might perfect what is l. in your faith

LAD, S,

Signifies, *A boy, or one young in years*, Gen. 21. 12, 17. It is applied, [1] *To one who was seventeen years old*, Gen. 37. 2. [2] *To a married man*, Gen. 43. 8. compared with 46. 21. [3] *To a servant*, 1 Sam. 20. 36.

Gen. 21. 12. let it not be grievous because of the l.
17. and God heard the voice of the l.
18. arise, lift up the l. || 19. she gave the l. drink
20. God was with the l. and he grew and dwelt
22. 5. I and the l. will go yonder and worship
12. he said, lay not thine hand upon the l.
37. 2. the l. was with the sons of Bilhah
43. 8. send the l. with me, and we will arise and go
44. 22. we said, the l. cannot leave his father
30. my father, and the l. be not with us, 31, 34. his life is bound up in the l. life
32. thy servant became surety for the l.
33. abide instead of the l. let the l. go up
48. 16. the Angel who redeemed me, bless the l.
Judg. 16. 26. Samson said to the l. that held him
1 Sam. 20. 21. and behold I will send a l. saying, go
36. Jonathan said to the l. run, as the l. ran
37. Jonathan cried after the l. make speed, 38.
39. but the l. knew not any thing, only David
40. Jonathan gave his artillery to his l.
2 Sam. 17. 18. a l. saw them and told Absalom
John 6. 9. there is a l. here hath five barley loaves

LADDER.

Gen. 28. 12. Jacob dreamed, and behold a l. set up

LADE

Signifies, [1] *To lay on a burden*, Neh. 4. 17. | 13. 15. [2] *To oppress*, 1 Kings 12. 11. [3] *To impose the performance of unnecessary traditions, or strict injunctions, over and above what the law requires*, Luke 11. 46. [4] *To be burdened not with the sense, but with the guilt and bondage, of sin*, Isa. 1. 4. [5] *To be sensible of and mourn under the burden of sin*, Mat. 11. 28.

That ladeth himself with thick clay, Hab. 2. 6. *that burdens and defiles himself with amassed treasures, gotten by extortion and oppression.*

Gen. 45. 17. l. your beasts and go to land of Canaan
Lev. 22. † 16. l. themselves with the iniquity
1 Kings 12. 11. my father did l. you with a yoke
Luke 11. 46. for ye l. men with grievous burdens

LADED.

Gen. 42. 26. they l. their asses with the corn, 44. 13.
Neh. 4. 17. those that l. wrought in the work
Acts 28. 10. they l. us with such things as necessary

LADEN.

Gen. 45. 23. sent ten asses l. with good things of Egypt
1 Sam. 16. 20. Jesse took an ass l. with bread
Isa. 1. 4. a people l. with iniquity, seed of evil doers
Mat. 11. 28. come, all ye that labour and are heavy l.
2 Tim. 3. 6. silly women, l. with sins, led away with

LADETH.

Hab. 2. 6. woe to him that l. himself with thick clay

LADING.

Neh. 13. 15. I saw some on the sabbath l. asses

LADING.

Acts 27. 10. much damage not only of l. and ship

LADY.

Isa. 47. 5. shall no more be called a l. of kingdoms
7. and thou saidst, I shall be a l. for ever
2 John 1. the elder to the elect l. and her children
5. now I beseech, thee, l. that we love one another

LADIES.

Judg. 5. 29. wise l. answered her, yea, she returned
Esth. 1. 18. likewise shall l. of Persia and Media say

LAID, *see after* LAY.

LAKE

Signifies, [1] *A large place full of water encompassed with land*, Luke 5. 1, 2. [2] *Hell*, Rev. 19. 20. | 20. 10.

Luke 5. 1. Jesus stood by the l. of Gennesaret
2. and saw two ships standing by the l.
8. 22. let us go over to the other side of the l.
23. there came down a storm of wind on the l.
33. herd ran violently down a steep place into l.
Rev. 19. 20. these both were cast into a l. of fire
20. 10. devil was cast into l. of fire and brimstone
14. death and hell were cast into the l. of fire
15. was not found in the book of life, cast into l.
21. 8. murderers have their part in the l. burneth

LAMB

Signifies, *A sheep under a year old, of a meek, gentle, and tractable nature, which is useful for food and clothing, and under the law was used for sacrifice, particularly in the passover*, Gen. 21. 28. Exod. 12. 3, 5. Prov. 27. 26. To which are compared, [1] *Christ Jesus, who was typified by the lamb in the passover, and became a sacrifice for sin*, John 1. 29. Rev. 5. 6, 8. [2] *All true christians, who are humble, meek, and tractable*, Isa. 11. 6. John 21. 15. [3] *An innocent, inoffensive, and harmless teacher, who had done nothing to merit the cruelty and barbarity of his enemies, and was as ignorant of their inhuman devices against him, as a lamb is of the design of such as lead it to the slaughter*, Jer. 11. 19. [4] *A man's wife*, 2 Sam. 12. 3, 4. [5] *Antichrist, who by his pardons and indulgences presumptuously assumes the power and prerogative of Christ Jesus the Lamb of God*, Rev. 13. 11.

Gen. 22. 7. but where is the l. for a burnt-offering?
8. my son, God will provide himself a l.
Exod. 12. 3. they shall take to them every man a l. 21.
5. your l. shall be without blemish, a male
13. 13. an ass shalt thou redeem with a l. 34. 20.
29. 39. one l. thou shalt offer in the morning, and the other l. shalt offer at evening, 41. Num. 28. 4.
40. with a l. a tenth deal of flour mingled, Num. 28. 21, 29. | 29. 4, 10, 15.
Lev. 3. 7. if he offer a l. 4. 32. | 5. 6. | 22. 23. | 23. 12.
4. 35. he shall take away the fat, as the fat of a l.
5. 7. if he be not able to bring a l. 12. 8.
9. 3. take a l. of the first year without blemish, 14. 10. Num. 6. 12. | 7. 15, 21.
14. 12. the priest shall take the l. and offer him
13. slay the l. 25. || 24. l. of trespass-offering
17. 3. that killeth an ox, or a l. or goat in the camp
23. 12. shall offer a l. without blemish
Num. 6. 14. he shall offer one he-l. of first year for a burnt-offering, ewe-l. of first year for a sin-offer.
15. 5. shalt prepare with the sacrifice for one l.
11. thus done for one l. 28. 7, 13, 14. Ezek. 46. 15.
1 Sam. 7. 9. Samuel offered a sucking l. to the Lord
17. 34. there came a lion and bear and took a l.
2 Sam. 12. 4. took the poor man's l. and dressed it
6. and he shall restore the l. four-fold
Isa. 11. 6. the wolf also shall dwell with the l.
16. 1. send ye the l. to the ruler of the land
53. 7. was brought as l. to the slaughter, Jer. 11. 19.
65. 25. the wolf and the l. shall feed together
66. 3. that sacrificeth a l. as if he cut off dog's neck
Ezek. 45. 15. one l. out of flock for a peace-offering
46. 13. a l. of the first year thou shalt prepare
Hos. 4. 16. Ld. will feed them as l. in a large place
John 1. 29. behold l. of God that takes away sin, 36.
Acts 8. 32. like a l. dumb before the shearer
1 Pet. 1. 19. as of a l. without blemish and spot
Rev. 5. 6. in the midst of the elders stood a l. slain
8. the four beasts fell down before the l.
12. saying, worthy is the l. that was slain
13. honour, glory, and power, be to the l. for ever
6. 1. I saw when the l. opened one of the seals
16. and hide us from the wrath of the l. that sits
7. 9. a great multitude stood before l. clothed
10. saying, salvation to our God and to the l.
14. and made them white in the blood of the l.
17. for the l. shall feed and lead them to fountains
12. 11. they overcame him by the blood of the l.
13. 8. the l. slain from the foundation of the world
11. he had two horns like a l. and spake as dragon
14. 1. I looked, and lo, a l. stood on the mount Sion
4. these are they that follow the l. whithersoever
10. tormented in the presence of angels and the l.
15. 3. they sing the song of Moses and song of the l.
17. 14. war with the l. and the l. shall overcome
19. 7. for the marriage of the l. is come, and his wife
9. that are called to the marriage-supper of the l.
21. 9. I will shew thee the bride, the l. wife
14. the names of the twelve apostles of the l.
22. God Almighty and the l. are the temple of it
23. God did lighten it, and the l. is light thereof
27. but they who are written in the l. book of life
22. 1. proceeding out of throne of God and of l. 3.

LAMBS.

Gen. 30. 40. and Jacob did separate the l.
33. † 19. Jacob bought it for 100 l. Josh. 24. † 32.
Num. 7. 87. rams twelve, l. of the first year twelve
88. sixty l. || 29. 13. fourteen l. 17, 20, 23.
29. 18. drink-offerings for the bullocks, l. and rams
Deut. 32. 14. milk of sheep, with fat of l. and rams
1 Sam. 15. 9. but Saul spared the best of the l.
2 Kings 3. 4. Moab rendered to Israel 100,000 l.
1 Chron. 29. 21. they offered to the L. a thousand l.
2 Chron. 29. 22. priests killed l. and sprinkled blood
32. the number of burnt-offerings two hundred l.
35. 7. Josiah gave to the people l. and kids
Ezra 7. 17. that thou mayest buy speedily l.

Psal. 37. 20. the wicked shall be as the fat of l.
114. 4. mountains skipped, little hills skipped like l.
6. ye little hills that skipped like l.
Prov. 27. 26. l. are for thy clothing, and goats
Isa. 1. 11. I delight not in the blood of l. or goats
5. 17. then shall the l. feed after their manner
34. 6. the sword of the Lord filled with blood of l.
40. 11. he shall gather the l. with his arm, carry
Jer. 51. 40. I will bring them like l. to slaughter
Ezek. 27. 21. Arabia occupied with thee in l.
39. 18. ye shall drink the blood of l. and rams
46. 4. in the sabbath six l. ‖ 6. in new moons six l.
5. and meat-offering for the l. as able to give, 7.
Amos 6. 4. and eat the l. out of the flock, and calves
Luke 10. 3. I send you forth as l. among wolves
John 21. 15. Jesus saith to Peter, feed my l.

Five LAMBS.

Num. 7. 17. five l. of the first year, 23, 29, 35, 41, 47.

Seven LAMBS.

Gen. 21. 28. Abraham set seven ewe-l. by themselves
29. what mean these seven ewe-l. set by themselves
30. these seven ewe-l. thou shalt take of my hand
Lev. 23. 18. ye shall offer with the bread seven l.
Num. 28. 11. ye shall offer seven l. of the first year without spot, 19. 27. | 29. 2, 8, 36.
21. a tenth deal throughout seven l. 29. | 29. 4, 10.
2 Chr. 29. 21. they brought seven l. for a sin-offer.

Two LAMBS.

Exod. 29. 38. two l. of the first year offer, Num. 28. 3.
Lev. 14. 10. on the eighth day he shall take two l.
23. 19. then ye shall sacrifice two l. of the first year
Num. 28. 9. and on the sabbath two l. of the first year

LAME

Signifies, *One that is maimed or enfeebled in his limbs*, Prov. 26. 7. And is taken, (I.) Corporally, *and that either by accident or birth*, 2 Sam. 4. 4. Acts 3. 2. (II.) Figuratively, [1] *For idols*, 2 Sam. 5. 6. [2] *The weakest or meanest*, Isa. 33. 23. (III.) Spiritually, *for such as are halting in their minds between two opinions*, Heb. 12. 13.

Lev. 21. 18. a blind or l. man shall not approach
Deut. 15. 21. if it be l. thou shalt not sacrifice it
2 Sam. 4. 4. Jonath. had a son l. of his feet, 9. 3, 13.
5. 6. except thou take away the blind and the l.
8. whosoever smiteth the l. and the blind
19. 26. that I may ride, because thy servant is l.
Job 29. 15. I was eyes to the blind, feet to the l.
Prov. 26. 7. the legs of the l. are not equal, so is
Isa. 33. 23. then is prey divided, the l. take the prey
35. 6. then shall the l. man leap as an hart
Jer. 31. 8. bring with them the blind and the l.
Mal. 1. 8. if ye offer the l. for sacrifice, is it not evil?
13. and ye brought that which was torn and l.
Mat. 11. 5. the l. walk, 15. 31. | 21. 14. Luke 7. 22.
Luke 14. 13. call the poor, the l. and the blind
Acts 3. 2. a certain man, l. from womb, was carried
11. and as the l. man held Peter and John
8. 7. many with palsies and that were l. were healed
Heb. 12. 13. lest the l. be turned out of the way

LAMENT.

Judg. 11. 40. the daughters of Israel went yearly to l.
Isa. 3. 26. and her gates shall l. and mourn
19. 8. the fishers also shall mourn and l.
32. 12. they shall l. for the teats and pleasant fields
Jer. 4. 8. for this l. and howl, for the anger of Lord
16. 5. neither go to l. nor bemoan them, 6.
22. 18. they shall not l. for him, saying, ah, Lord
34. 5. they will l. thee, saying, ah, Lord
49. 3. ye daughters of Rabbah, l. and run
Lam. 2. 8. he made the rampart and the wall to l.
Ezek. 27. 32. they shall l. over Tyrus, saying, what
32. 16. the daughters of the nations shall l. her
Joel 1. 8. l. like a virgin girded with sackcloth
13. gird yourselves, and l. ye priests, howl
Mic. 2. 4. l. with a doleful lamentation and song
John 16. 20. verily I say, ye shall weep and l.
Rev. 18. 9. the kings of the earth shall l. Babylon

LAMENTED.

1 Sam. 6. 19. people l. because the Lord had smitten
7. 2. all the house of Israel l. after the Lord
25. 1. all the Israelites l. Samuel, 28. 3.
2 Sam. 1. 17. David l. over Saul and Jonathan
3. 33. the king l. over Abner and said
2 Chron. 35. 25. and Jeremiah l. for Josiah
Jer. 16. 4. they shall die and not be l. 25. 33.
Mat. 11. 17. we mourned to you, but ye have not l.
Luke 23. 27. and a great company of people l. Jesus

LAMENTABLE.

Dan. 6. 20. the king cried with a l. voice to David

LAMENTATION

Signifies, [1] *Mourning, bemoaning, and bewailing*, Jer. 31. 15. [2] *Songs of lamentation*, 2 Chron. 35. 25. [3] *Such dreadful judgments as would cause most bitter lamentation*, Ezek. 2. 10. [4] *The title of a book, the subject whereof is lamentation*, 2 Chron. 35. 25.

Gen. 50. 10. there they mourned with a sore l.
2 Sam. 1. 17. and David lamented with this l.
Psal. 78. 64. and their widows made no l.
Jer. 6. 26. wallow thyself in ashes, make bitter l.
7. 29. and take up a l. on the high places
9. 10. for the habitations of wilderness a l.
20. and teach every one her neighbour l.
31. 15. in Ramah l. and weeping, Mat. 2. 18.
48. 38. there shall be l. generally on the tops
Lam. 2. 5. Lord hath increased mourning and l.
Ezek. 19. 1. take thou up a l. for the princes
14. this is a l. and shall be for a l.
26. 17. they shall take up a l. for Tyrus, 27. 2, 32.
28. 12. take up a l. upon the king of Tyrus
32. 2. son of man take up a l. for Pharaoh, 16.
Amos 5. 1. a l. against you, O house of Israel
16. shall call such as are skilful of l. to wailing
8. 10. and I will turn all your songs into l.
Mic. 2. 4. and lament with a doleful l.
Acts 8. 2. and made great l. over Stephen

LAMENTATIONS.

2 Chron. 35. 25. the singers spake of Josiah in their l. and behold, they are written in the l.
Ezek. 2. 10. there was written therein l. mourning

LAMP

Signifies, [1] *A light made with oil in a proper vessel*, 1 Sam. 3. 3. [2] *A sincere profession of religion, flowing from an inward principle of holiness*, Mat. 25. 4. [3] *A form of godliness, without saving faith and true repentance*, Mat. 25. 3. [4] *A son, or successor, who preserves one name and memory from being extinguished and forgotten*, 1 Kings 15. 4. Psal. 132. 17. [5] *Outward prosperity*, Prov. 13. 9. | 20. 20. It is spoken, [1] Of God, *who enlightens, directs, and comforts his people*, 2 Sam. 22. 29. [2] Of his word, *which affords direction and comfort in all doubts, difficulties, and distresses*, Psal. 119. 105.

Gen. 15. 17. a burning l. that passed between pieces
Exod. 27. 20. to cause the l. to burn always
1 Sam. 3. 3. ere l. went out, Samuel was laid to sleep
2 Sam. 21. † 17. that thou quench not the l. of Israel
22. 29. thou art my l. O Lord, Lord will lighten
1 Kings 11. † 36. David my servant may have a l.
15. 4. for David's sake God gave him a l. in Jerus.
Job 12. 5. is as a l. despised in the thought of him
18. † 6. wicked man's l. put out, 21. † 17.
29. † 3. when his l. shined on my head
Psal. 18. † 28. for thou wilt light my l.
119. 105. thy word is a l. to my feet, and a light
132. 17. I have ordained a l. for mine anointed
Prov. 6. 23. for commandment is a l. the law is light
13. 9. the l. of the wicked shall be put out
20. 20. who curseth his father, his l. shall be put out
† 27. the spirit of man is the l. of the Lord
Isa. 62. 1. salvation thereof as a l. that burneth
Rev. 8. 10. a great star burning as it were a l.

LAMPS.

Exod. 25. 37. they shall light the l. thereof, 40. 4.
30. 7. when he dresseth the l. burn incense on it
8. when Aaron lighteth the l. at even, burn incense
35. 14. and his l. with the oil for the light
39. 37. and they brought the l. to Moses
40. 25. he lighted the l. before the L. Num. 8. 2, 3.
Lev. 24. 2. l. to burn continually, 2 Chron. 13. 11.
4. order the l. ‖ Num. 4. 9. and cover his l.
Judg. 7. 16. he put l. within the pitchers
20. and held the l. in their left hand, and trumpets
1 Kings 7. 49. he made l. of gold, 2 Chr. 4. 20, 21.
Job 41. 19. out of his mouth go burning l. and sparks
Ezek. 1. 13. was like the appearance of l.
Dan. 10. 6. body like beryl, and his eyes as l. of fire
Mat. 25. 1. ten virgins which took their l. 3. 4.
7. those virgins arose, and trimmed their l.
8. give us of your oil, for our l. are gone out

Seven LAMPS.

Exod. 25. 37. thou shalt make the seven l. thereof
37. 23. he made his seven l. of pure gold
Num. 8. 2. the seven l. shall give light over against
Zech. 4. 2. and behold a candlestick and seven l.
Rev. 4. 5. there were seven l. of fire burning before

LANCE.

Jer. 50. 42. they that hold the l. are cruel, will not

LANCETS.

1 Kings 18. 28. cut themselves with l. till blood

LAND

Signifies [1] *The whole continent of the earth, as distinguished from sea*, Mat. 23. 15. [2] *One particular country*, Mat. 9. 26. [3] *Arable ground*, Gen. 26. 12. [4] *The inhabitants of a country*, Isa. 37. 11. [5] *A certain possession*, 2 Sam. 19. 29. Acts 4. 37.

Gen. 2. 12. and the gold of that l. is good
10. 11. out of that l. went forth Ashur
12. 1. get thee into a l. I will shew thee, Acts 7. 3.
13. 6. and the l. was not able to bear them
9. is not the whole l. before thee, separate
17. 8. I will give thee and seed the l. 28. 13. | 35. 12.
20. 15. behold, my l. is before thee, dwell where
24. 37. of the Canaanite, in whose l. I dwell
26. 12. Isaac sowed in that l. and received in year
47. 20. bought the l. so the l. became Pharaoh's
22. only the l. of the priests bought he not
Exod. 8. 24. the l. was corrupted by the flies
10. 15. so that the l. was darkened, and they eat
20. 12. that thy days may be long upon the l.
Lev. 16. 22. goat bear iniquities into l. not inhabited
18. 25. and the l. is defiled, therefore, 27.
28. that the l. spue not you out also, 20. 22.
25. 2. then shall the l. keep a sabbath, 26. 34.
23. the l. shall not be sold, for the l. is mine
26. 4. the l. shall yield her increase, 25. 19.
38. the l. of your enemies shall eat you up
42. and I will remember the l.
43. the l. also shall be left of them, and enjoy
Num. 13. 18. see the l. what it is, and the people
32. the l. is a l. that eateth up the inhabitants
14. 23. surely they shall not see the l. I sware to
24. my servant Caleb will I bring to the l.
15. 2. when ye be come into the l. of your habitation, 18. Deut. 17. 14. | 18. 9. | 26. 1.
21. 34. delivered into thy hand his l. Deut. 3. 2.
32. 4. the country the Lord smote is a l. for cattle
35. 33. for blood defileth the l. and the l. cannot
Deut. 1. 36. to him will I give the l. he hath
2. 20. that was accounted a l. of giants, 3. 13.
8. 8. a l. of wheat, and barley, and vines
9. l. wherein eat bread, l. whose stones are iron
9. 28. was not able to bring them into the l.
10. 7. to Jotbath, a l. of rivers of waters
11. 12. a l. which the Lord thy God careth for
29. 23. the whole l. thereof is brimstone and salt
28. cast them into another l. as at this day
32. 10. he found him in a desert l. and in wilderness
43. he will be merciful to his l. and people
33. 13. he said, blessed of the Lord be his l.
34. 1. and the Lord shewed him all the l.
Josh. 2. 1. sent two men, saying, go view the l.
9. the Lord hath given you the l. 21. 43.
11. 16. Joshua took all that l. the hills, 23.
14. 15. and the l. had rest from war
24. 13. given you a l. for which ye did not labour
Judg. 3. 11. the l. had rest forty years, 5. 31.
30. and the l. had rest fourscore years
11. 12. thou art come to fight against me in my l.
18. 10. when ye go ye shall come to a large l.
30. till the day of the captivity of the l.
1 Sam. 14. 29. my father hath troubled the l.
1 Sam. 21. 11. is not this David the king of the l.?
2 Sam. 3. 12. Abner sent, saying, whose is the l.?
9. 7. I will restore thee all the l. of Saul
21. 14. God was entreated for the l. 24. 25.
1 Kings 9. 13. and he called them the l. of Cabul
11. 18. appointed him victuals and gave him l.
2 Kings 8. 3. went to cry to the king for her l.
6. since the day that she left the l. even till now
17. 26. the manner of the God of the l. 27.
18. 32. take you to l. of corn and wine, Isa. 36. 17
33. any god delivered his l. Isa. 36. 18.
21. 8. move any more out of the l. 2 Chr. 33. 8.
24. 7. the king of Egypt came no more out of his l
25. 12. left of the poor of the l. Jer. 52. 16.
1 Chron. 4. 40. and the l. was wide, and quiet
7. 21. men of Gath, who were born in that l.
2 Chron. 7. 20. I will pluck them up out of my l.
14. 7. make walls, while the l. is yet before us
34. 8. when he had purged the l. and the house
Ezra 9. 12. that ye may eat the good of l. Isa. 1. 19.
Neh. 5. 16. work of wall, nor bought we any l.
9. 36. for the l. behold we are servants in it
Job 31. 38. if my l. cry against me, or furrows
37. 13. whether for correction, or his l. or mercy
39. 6. and the barren l. his dwellings
Psal. 10. 16. the heathen are perished out of his l.
42. 6. remember thee from the l. of Jordan
44. 3. for they got not the l. in possession
52. 5. and root thee out of the l. of the living
80. 9. to take deep root, and it filled the l.
101. 6. mine eyes shall be on the faithful of the l.
8. I will destroy all the wicked of the l.
105. 16. he called for a famine on the l.
30. the l. brought forth frogs in abundance
106. 24. yea, they despised the pleasant l.
38. and the l. was polluted with blood
107. 34. he turneth the fruitful l. into barrenness
143. 6. my soul thirsts after thee as a thirsty l.
10. lead me into the l. of uprightness
Prov. 12. 11. that tilleth his l. shall be satisfied, 28. 19.
28. 2. for the transgression of a l. many princes
Eccl. 10. 16. woe to thee, O l. when thy king is a child
17. blessed art thou, O l. when thy king is son
Isa. 5. 30. if one look unto the l. behold sorrow
7. 16. the l. that thou abhorrest shall be forsaken
24. because all l. shall become briers and thorns
9. 1. l. of Zebulun, l. of Naphtali, Mat. 4. 15.
19. through the wrath of the Lord is l. darkened
13. 5. they come to destroy the whole l.
14. 25. I will break the Assyrian in my l.
18. 1. woe to the l. shadowing with wings!
2. whose l. the rivers have spoiled, 7.
19. 24. shall be a blessing in the midst of the l.
21. 1. cometh from the desert, from a terrible l.
23. 1. from the l. of Chittim it is revealed
24. 3. the l. shall be utterly emptied and spoiled
11. joy is darkened, the mirth of the l. is gone
30. 6. into the l. of trouble and anguish
32. 2. as the shadow of a great rock in a weary l.
13. on the l. of my people shall come thorns
33. 17. and behold the l. that is very far off
34. 9. the l. thereof shall become burning pitch
35. 7. and the thirsty l. springs of water
49. 12. and lo, these from the l. of Sinim
19. the l. of thy destruction be too narrow
53. 8. he was cut off out of the l. of the living
Jer. 1. 18. an iron pillar against the whole l.
2. 2. wentest after me, in a l. that was not sown
6. led us through a l. of deserts, a l. of drought
7. when he entered, ye defiled my l. 3. 9.
15. the young lions made his l. waste
3. 19. how shall I give thee a pleasant l.?
4. 20. the whole l. is spoiled, suddenly are
5. 19. serve strangers in a l. that is not yours
6. 8. lest I make thee a l. not inhabited
8. 16. the whole l. trembled at the sound
9. 12. for what the l. perisheth and is burnt
19. because we have forsaken the l.
11. 19. let us cut him off from the l. of the living
12. 4. how long shall the l. mourn, herbs wither?
12. from one end of the l. even to the other
15. I will bring again every man to his l.
16. 15. brought Israel from l. of the north, 31. 16.
18. because they have defiled my l. they filled
17. 6. inhabit wilderness in a salt l. not inhabited
22. 27. to the l. whereunto they desire to return
23. 15. is profaneness gone forth into the l.
25. 13. I will bring on that l. all my words
27. 7. till the very time of his l. come
40. 4. behold, all the l. is before thee
46. 12. thy shame, and thy cry hath filled the l.
50. 18. I will punish the king of Babylon and his l.
38. for it is the l. of graven images, they are mad
51. 43. a dry l. a l. wherein no man dwelleth
47. her whole l. shall be confounded
Ezek. 7. 23. for the l. is full of bloody crimes
8. 17. they have filled the l. with violence
9. 9. and the l. is full of blood, and the city
14. 13. when the l. sinneth against me
17. bring a sword on l. ‖ 19. a pestilence into l.
17. 5. he took also of the seed of the l. and planted
13. he hath taken the mighty of the l.
21. 19. both shall come forth out of one l.
22. 24. thou art the l. is not cleansed nor rained on
30. should stand in the gap before me for the l.
32. 4. then will I leave thee upon the l. I will cast
33. 2. when I bring the sword upon a l.
3. if when he seeth the sword come upon the l.
24. the l. is given us for inheritance
36. 5. have appointed my l. into their possession
13. thou l. devourest up men, and hast bereaved
38. 9. thou shalt be like a cloud to cover the l. 16.
11. I will go up to the l. of unwalled villages
16. and I will bring thee against my l.
39. 12. that they may cleanse the l.
16. thus shall they cleanse the l.
47. 15. and this shall be the border of the l.
Dan. 11. 16. he shall stand in the glorious l. 41.
Hos. 4. 3. therefore shall the l. mourn and languish
Joel 1. 6. for a nation is come up upon my l. strong
2. 3. the l. is as the garden of Eden before them
18. then will the lord be jealous for his l.

Joel 2.21. fear not, O *l.* be glad || 3. 2. and parted my *l.*
Amos 5. 2. she is forsaken upon her *l.* there is none
7. 10. the *l.* is not able to bear all his words
8. 4. even to make the poor of the *l.* to fail
8. shall not the *l.* tremble for this?
9. 5. the Lord God of hosts is he that toucheth the *l.*
Zeph. 1. 2. I consume all things from off the *l.*
18. whole *l.* shall be devoured by fire of jealousy
3. 19. I will get them praise and fame in every *l.*
Zech. 2. 6. ho, ho, flee from the *l.* of the north
3. 9. I will remove the iniquity of that *l.* in one
9. 16. of a crown lifted up, as an ensign upon his *l.*
12. 12. the *l.* shall mourn, every family apart
13. 2. and the unclean spirit to pass out of the *l.*
8. in all the *l.* two parts therein shall be cut off
14. 10. all the *l.* shall be turned as a plain
Mal. 3. 12. for ye shall be a delightsome *l.*
Mat. 9. 26. fame hereof went abroad into all that *l.*
10. 15. more tolerable for the *l.* of Sodom, 11. 24.
23. 15. ye compass sea and *l.* to make one proselyte
27. 45. was darkness over all the *l.* *Mark* 15. 33.
Mark 6. 47. ship was in the sea, and he alone on the *l.*
Luke 14. 35. neither fit for the *l.* nor dunghill
15. 14. there arose a great famine in that *l.*
John 6. 21. immediately the ship was at the *l.*
21. 11. Peter drew the net to *l.* full of great fishes
Acts 4. 37. having *l.* sold it, and brought the money
5. 8. tell me whether ye sold the *l.* for so much
27. 39. when it was day, they knew not the *l.*
43. cast themselves into the sea, and get to *l.*
44. that they escaped all safe to *l.*
See Benjamin, Chaldeans, Canaan, Darkness, Desolate, Divide, Divided.

Dry LAND.

Gen. 1. 9. let *dry l.* appear || 10. called *dry l.* earth
7. 22. of all that was in the *dry l.* died
Exod. 4. 9. take and pour water on the *dry l.* and the waters shall become blood on the *dry l.*
14. 21. and the Lord made the sea *dry l.*
29. Israel walked on *dry l.* || 15. 19. *Neh.* 9. 11.
Josh. 4. 18. the priests' feet were lifted up on *dry l.*
22. Israel came over this Jordan on *dry l.*
Psal. 63. 1. my flesh longeth for thee in a *dry l.*
66. 6. he turned the sea into *dry l.*
68. 6. but the rebellious dwell in a *dry l.*
95. 5. sea is his, and his hands formed the *dry l.*
Isa. 41. 18. I will make *dry l.* springs of water
Jer. 50. 12. hindermost of nations shall be a *dry l.*
51. 43. her cities are a *dry l.* and wilderness
Hos. 2. 3. lest I set her as a *dry l.* and slay her
Jonah 1. 9. I fear God, who made the sea and *dry l.*
2. 10. the fish vomited out Jonah on the *dry l.*
Hag. 2. 6. and I will shake the sea and *dry l.*
Heb. 11. 29. they passed the Red sea as by *dry l.*
See Dwell, Egypt, Good.

In the LAND.

Gen. 13. 7. and the Canaanite dwelt then *in the l.*
26. 22. and we shall be fruitful *in the l.*
41. 31. the plenty shall not be known *in the l.*
42. 34. I shall know, and ye shall traffick *in the l.*
47. 4. for to sojourn *in the l.* are we come
Exod. 8. 25. go ye, sacrifice to your God *in the l.*
9. 5. to-morrow the Lord shall do this thing *in the l.*
14. 3. he will say, they are entangled *in the l.*
Lev. 26. 6. and I will give peace *in the l.* and ye
Deut. 4. 14. that ye may do them *in t. l.* whither ye go
5. 16. that it may go well with thee *in the l.*
11. 9. that you may prolong days *in t. l.* 21. | 25. 15.
25. 19. God hath given thee rest *in the l.*
28. 8. he shall bless thee *in the l.* 11. | 30. 16.
31. 13. fear the Lord as long as ye live *in the l.*
Judg. 18. 7. and there was no magistrate *in the l.*
1 *Sam.* 23. 23. and if he be *in the l.* I will search
2 *Sam.* 15. 4. O that I were made judge *in the l.*
1 *Kings* 8. 37. if there be famine *in the l.* 2 *Chr.* 6. 28.
2 *Chr.* 6. 31. fear thee so long as they live *in the l.*
19. 5. and Jehoshaphat set judges *in the l.*
32. 31. inquire of the wonder that was done *in the l.*
Job 28. 13. nor is it found *in the l.* of the living
Psal. 27. 13. goodness of the L. *in the l.* of the living
35. 20. they devise deceitful matter *in the l.*
74. 8. they burnt the synagogues of God *in the l.*
116. 9. I will walk before the Lord *in the l.* of [the living
142. 5. thou art my portion *in the l.* of the living
Isa. 7. 22. for honey shall every one eat *in the l.*
26. 10. *in the l.* of uprightness he will deal unjustly
38. 11. I shall not see the L. *in the l.* of the living
Ezek. 20. 40. shall all of them *in the l.* serve me
26. 20. I shall set glory *in the l.* of the living
32. 23. caused terror *in the l.* of the living, 24. 32.
37. 22. I will make them one nation *in the l.*
45. 8. *in the l.* shall be his possession in Israel
Hos. 4. 1. because there is no truth *in the l.*
Zech. 11. 16. I will raise up a Shepherd *in the l.*
Luke 21. 23. there shall be great distress *in the l.*
Heb. 11. 9. by faith he sojourned *in the l.* of promise
See Inhabitants, Inherit, Israel, Judah.

Our LAND.

Gen. 47. 19. buy us and *o. l.* for bread, and we and *o. l.*
Psal. 85. 12. and *our l.* shall yield her increase
Cant. 2. 12. the voice of the turtle is heard in *our l.*
Mic. 5. 5. the Assyrian shall come into *our l.*
6. he shall deliver us when he cometh into *our l.*

Own LAND.

Exod. 18. 27. Jethro went into his *own l.* *Num.* 10. 30.
1 *Kings* 10. 6. a true report I heard in my *l.* 2 *Chr.* 9. 5.
2 *Kings* 17. 23. Israel carried out of their *own l.*
18. 32. take you to a land like your *own l.* *Isa.* 36. 17.
19. 7. and he shall return to his *own l.*
2 *Chr.* 32. 21. he returned with shame to his *own l.*
Isa. 13. 14. and flee every one to his *own l.*
14. 1. choose Israel, and set them in their *own l.*
37. 7. and fall by the sword in his *own l.*
Jer. 23. 8. they shall dwell in their *own l.* 27. 11.
37. 7. return to Egypt, into their *own l.* 42. 12.
50. 16. they shall flee every one to his *own l.*
Ezek. 34. 13. I will bring them into their *own l.* 36. 24. | 37. 14, 21. | 39. 28.
36. 17. when Israel dwelt in their *own l.*
Amos 7. 11. Israel led captive out of their *own l.*
See People, Possess, Possession, Strange.

Their LAND, S.

Gen. 47. 22. wherefore the priests sold not *their l.*
Lev. 20. 24. but I said, ye shall inherit *their l.*
Num. 18. 20. Aaron had no inheritance in *their l.*
Deut. 2. 5. for I will not give you of *their l.* 9.
4. 38. bring thee, and give thee *their l.* *Judg.* 6. 9.
29. 8. we took *their l.* and gave it, *Josh.* 10. 42.
28. and the Lord rooted them out of *their l.*
1 *Kings* 8. 48. return and pray to thee toward *their l.*
2 *Chron.* 7. 14. forgive their sin and heal *their l.*
Psal. 105. 32. he gave them flaming fire in *their l.*
135. 12. and gave *their l.* for an heritage, 136. 21.
Isa. 2. 7. *their l.* is full of silver and horses
8. *their l.* also is full of idols, they worship
34. 7. *their l.* shall be soaked with blood
Jer. 12. 14. behold, I will pluck them out of *their l.*
16. 15. I will bring them again into *their l.*
51. 5. not forsaken, tho' *their l.* was filled with sin
Ezek. 34. 27. and they shall be safe in *their l.*
39. 26. when they dwelt safely in *their l.* and
Amos 9. 15. and I will plant them on *their l.*

This LAND.

Gen. 12. 7. the Lord said, unto thy seed I will give *this l.* 15. 18. | 24. 7. | 48. 4. *Exod.* 32. 13.
28. 15. I will bring thee again into *this l.*
31. 13. get thee out from *this l.* and return to land
50. 24. and God will bring you out of *this l.*
Num. 14. 3. why hath the Lord brought us unto *this l.*
8. then he will bring us into *this l.* and give it
32. 5. let *this l.* be given to thy servants
22. *this l.* shall be your possession before the Ld.
34. 2. *this l.* shall fall to you, 13. *Josh.* 13. 2.
Deut. 4. 22. but I must die in *this l.* and not go over
26. 9. and he hath given us *this l.* *Josh.* 1. 13.
29. 24. wherefore hath the Lord done thus to *this l.*? 27. 1 *Kings* 9. 8. 2 *Chron.* 7. 21.
Judg. 2. 2. no league with the inhabitants of *this l.*
2 *Kings* 18. 25. Ld. said, go up ag. *this l.* *Isa.* 36. 10.
2 *Chron.* 30. 9. they shall come again into *this l.*
Jer. 14. 15. say, the sword shall not be in *this l.*
16. 3. their fathers that begat them in *this l.*
6. both great and small shall die in *this l.*
13. therefore I will cast you out of *this l.*
22. 12. and he shall see *this l.* no more
24. 6. and I will bring them again to *this l.*
25. 9. and I will bring them against *this l.*
11. and *this* whole *l.* shall be a desolation
26. 20. a man who prophesied against *this l.*
32. 15. houses shall be possessed again in *this l.*
41. and I will plant them in *this l.* assuredly
36. 29. the king of Babylon shall destroy *this l.*
37. 19. shall not come against you, nor *this l.*
42. 10. if ye will abide in *this l.* I will build you
13. if ye say, we will not dwell in *this l.*
45. 4. I will pluck up even *this* whole *l.*
Ezek. 11. 15. to us is *this l.* given in possession
47. 14. *this l.* shall fall unto you for inheritance
48. 29. *this* is the *l.* which ye shall divide
Acts 7. 4. he removed him into *this l.* wherein

Thy LAND.

Exod. 23. 10. six years thou shalt sow *thy l.*
26. nothing shall cast their young in *thy l.*
33. they shall not dwell in *thy l.* lest they
34. 24. nor shall any man desire *thy l.*
Num. 21. 22. Israel said, let me pass through *thy l.* *Deut.* 2. 27. *Judg.* 11. 17, 19.
Deut. 7. 13. he will bless the fruit of *thy l.*
21. 23. bury him, that *thy l.* be not defiled
28. 12. to give the rain to *thy l.* in his season
18. cursed shall be the fruit of *thy l.* 42.
2 *Sam.* 7. 23. and to do great things for *thy l.*
24. 13. shall famine come to thee in *thy l.*?
Psal. 85. 1. thou hast been favourable to *thy l.*
Isa. 8. 8. his wings shall fill the breadth of *thy l.*
14. 20. because thou hast destroyed *thy l.*
23. 10. pass through *thy l.* as a river, O Tarshish
60. 18. violence shall no more be heard in *thy l.*
62. 4. nor shall *thy l.* be termed desolate; the Lord delighteth in thee, and *thy l.* shall be married
Ezek. 32. 8. and I will set darkness upon *thy l.*
Amos 7. 17. and *thy l.* shall be divided by line
Mic. 5. 11. I will cut off the cities of *thy l.*
Nah. 3. 13. the gates of *thy l.* shall be set wide open

Your LAND.

Gen. 47. 23. I have bought you and *your l.* this day
Lev. 19. 9. when ye reap the harvest of *your l.* 23. 22.
25. 45. children, which they begat in *your l.*
26. 5. ye shall eat, and dwell in *your l.* safely
6. nor shall the sword go through *your l.*
20. for *your l.* shall not yield her increase
Num. 10. 9. if you go to war in *your l.* then blow
22. 13. get into *your l.* || 34. 12. this shall be *your l.*
Deut. 11. 14. give you the rain of *your l.* in season
1 *Sam.* 6. 5. he will lighten his hand from off *your l.*
Jer. 5. 19. and have served strange gods in *your l.*
27. 10. prophesy, to remove you far from *your l.*
44. 22. therefore is *your l.* a desolation and astonish.

LANDED.

Acts 18. 22. when we had *l.* at Cesarea
21. 3. and sailed into Syria, and *l.* at Tyre

LANDING.

Acts 28. 12. *l.* at Syracuse we tarried three days

LAND-*mark.*

Deut. 19. 14. thou shalt not remove thy neighbour's *l.-mark*, *Prov.* 22. 28. | 23. 10.
27. 17. cursed that removeth neighbour's *l.-mark*

LAND-*marks.*

Job 24. 2. some remove the *l.-marks*, and take away

LANDS.

Gen. 41. 54. and the dearth was in all *l.* 57.
47. 18. not ought left but our bodies and *l.*
22. wherefore they sold not their *l.*
Judg. 11. 13. restore those *l.* again peaceably
2 *Kings* 19. 11. thou hast heard what the kings of Assyria have done to all *l.* *Isa.* 37. 11.
1 *Chron.* 14. 17. the fame of David went into all *l.*
2 *Chron.* 13. 9. priests after the manner of other *l.*
17. 10. fear fell on all the *l.* round about
32. 17. as the gods of other *l.* have not delivered
Ezra 9. 1. have not separated from the people of *l.*
2. have mingled with the people of those *l.* 11.
Neh. 5. 3. some said, we have mortgaged our *l.* 4.
Neh. 5. 5. for other men have our *l.* and vineyards
11. restore I pray you, this day their *l.*
10. 28. that had separated from the people of the *l.*
Psal. 49. 11. they call their *l.* after their own names
66. 1. make a joyful noise all ye *l.* 100. 1.
105. 44. and gave them the *l.* of the heathen
106. 27. lifted his hand, to scatter them in the *l.*
107. 3. gathered them out of the *l.* from east
Jer. 16. 15. that brought up Israel from *l.* whither
27. 6. have given all these *l.* to Nebuchadnezzar
Ezek. 20. 6. into a land which is the glory of all *l.* 15.
39. 27. gathered them out of their enemies' *l.*
Mat. 19. 29. hath forsaken houses, *l.* *Mark* 10. 29.
Mark 10. 30. shall receive an hundred fold, *l.*
Acts 4. 34. as many as were possessors of *l.* sold

LANES.

Luke 14. 21. go out quickly into the *l.* of the city

LANGUAGE

Signifies, [1] *A set of words which a particular nation or people make use of to express their thoughts*, 2 Kings 18. 26. [2] *The Hebrew tongue*, Gen. 11. 1, 6.

Shall speak the language of Canaan, *Isa.* 19. 18. *Shall make profession of the true religion, and become members of the gospel church.*

I will turn to the people a pure language, *Zeph.* 3. 9. *I will renew them by my Spirit and give them a pure way of worshipping me in prayer and praises, as the fruit and issue of a purified heart.*

Gen. 11. 1. the whole earth was of one *l.* and speech
6. the people is one, and they have all one *l.*
7. go down, and there confound their *l.* 9.
2 *Kings* 18. 26. speak in the Syrian *l.* *Isa.* 36. 11.
28. Rab-shakeh cried in the Jews' *l.* *Isa.* 36. 13.
Neh. 13. 24. their children could not speak in the Jews' *l.* but according to the *l.* of each people
Esth. 1. 22. to every people after their *l.* 3. 12. | 8. 9.
Psal. 19. 3. no *l.* where their voice is not heard
81. 5. where I heard a *l.* that I understood not
114. 1. house of Jacob from a people of strange *l.*
Isa. 19. 18. five cities speak the *l.* of Canaan
Jer. 5. 15. a nation, whose *l.* thou knowest not
Ezek. 3. 5. not sent to a people of hard *l.* 6.
Dan. 3. 29. I decree, every *l.* that speaketh amiss
Zeph. 3. 9. I will turn to the people a pure *l.*
Acts 2. 6. every man heard them speak in his own *l.*

LANGUAGES.

Dan. 3. 4. to you, O people, nations, and *l.*
7. all *l.* fell down and worshipped the image
4. 1. Nebuchadnezzar to all *l.* || 6. 25. Darius to all *l.*
5. 19. all *l.* trembled and feared before him
7. 14. all people, nations, and *l.* should serve him
Zech. 8. 23. ten men out of all *l.* shall take hold

LANGUISH.

Isa. 16. 8. for the fields of Heshbon *l.* and vine
19. 8. and they that spread nets on waters shall *l.*
24. 4. the haughty people of the earth do *l.*
Jer. 14. 2. gates of Judah *l.* and are black to ground
Hos. 4. 3. every one that dwelleth therein shall *l.*

LANGUISHED.

Lam. 2. 8. rampart and wall to lament, *l.* together

LANGUISHETH.

Isa. 24. 4. the world *l.* and fadeth away
7. the vine *l.* || 33. 9. the earth mourneth and *l.*
Jer. 15. 9. she that hath born seven *l.* given up ghost
Joel 1. 10. the oil *l.* || 12. the fig-tree *l.*
Nah. 1. 4. Bashan *l.* and Carmel, the flower *l.*

LANGUISHING.

Psal. 41. 3. Lord will strengthen him on the bed of *l.*

LANTERNS.

John 18. 3. Judas cometh with *l.* and torches

LAP.

2 *Kings* 4. 39. and gathered wild gourds, his *l.* full
Neh. 5. 13. I shook my *l.* and said, so God shake
Prov. 16. 33. the lot is cast into the *l.* but disposing

LAPPED.

Judg. 7. 6. the number that *l.* were three hundred
7. the Lord said, by them that *l.* I will save you

LAPPETH.

Judg. 7. 5. every one that *l.* of the water as a dog

LAPWING. *See* Bat.

LARGE.

Gen. 34. 21. the land, behold it is *l.* enough for them
Exod. 3. 8. to bring them into a good and *l.* land
Judg. 18. 10. when ye go, ye shall come into a *l.* land
2 *Sam.* 22. 20. he brought me into *l.* place, *Ps.* 18. 19.
Neh. 4. 19. I said to people, the work is great and *l.*
7. 4. the city was *l.* and great, but the people few
9. 35. have not served thee in the *l.* and fat land
Psal. 31. 8. thou hast set my feet in a *l.* room
118. 5. Lord answered me, and set me in a *l.* place
119. † 45. I will walk at *l.* for I seek thy precepts
Isa. 22. 18. he will toss thee into a *l.* country
30. 23. in that day shall thy cattle feed in *l.* pastures
33. Tophet is ordained, he made it deep and *l.*
Jer. 22. 14. that saith, I will build *l.* chambers
Ezek. 23. 32. drink of thy sister's cup deep and *l.*
Hos. 4. 16. Ld. will feed them as a lamb in a *l.* place
Mat. 28. 12. they gave *l.* money to the soldiers
Mark 14. 15. will shew a *l.* upper room, *Luke* 22. 12.
Gal. 6. 11. ye see how *l.* a letter I have written
Rev. 21. 16. the length is as *l.* as the breadth

LARGENESS.

1 *Kings* 4. 29. God gave Solomon *l.* of heart

LASCIVIOUSNESS.

Mark 7. 22. out of the heart of men proceed *l.*
2 *Cor.* 12. 21. and have not repented of the *l.*
Gal. 5. 19. the works of the flesh are manifest, *l.*
Eph. 4. 19. who have given themselves over to *l.*
1 *Pet.* 4. 3. when we walked in *l.* lusts, excess
Jude 4. turning the grace of our God into *l.*

LAST.

Gen. 49. 19. but Gad shall overcome at the *l.*
Num. 23. 10. and let my *l.* end be like his
2 *Sam.* 19. 11. why are ye *l.* to bring the king? 12.
23. 1. now these be the *l.* words of David
1 *Chron.* 23. 27. for by the *l.* words of David
29. 29. now the acts of David the king, first and *l.*
2 *Chron.* 9. 29. the acts of Solomon first and *l.*
12. 15. of Rehoboam first and *l.* || 16. 11. of Asa
20. 34. the acts of Jehoshaphat first and *l.*

2 *Chron.* 25. 26. the acts of Amaziah first and *l.*
26. 22. of Uzziah first and *l.* || 28. 26. of Ahaz
35. 27. Josiah's deeds first and *l.* are written
Ezra 8. 13. and of the *l.* sons of Adonikam
Neh. 8. 18. from the first day to the *l.* he read
Prov. 5. 11. and thou mourn at the *l.* when thy
23. 32. at the *l.* it biteth like a serpent, and stingeth
Isa. 41. 4. I the Lord, the first, and with the *l.* 41. 6.
| 48. 12. *Rev.* 1. 11, 17 | 2. 8. | 22. 13.
Jer. 12. 4. they said, he shall not see our *l.* end
50. 17. at *l.* Nebuchadnezzar hath broken his bones
Lam. 1. 9. she remembereth not her *l.* end
Dan. 4. 8. at the *l.* Daniel came in before me
8. 3. but one was higher, and the higher came up *l.*
19. make thee know what shall be in the *l.* end
Amos 9. 1. I will slay the *l.* of them with sword
Mat. 12. 45. *l.* state of that man is worse, *Luke* 11. 26.
19. 30. many that are first shall be *l.* and the *l.*
first, 20. 16. *Mark* 10. 31. *Luke* 13. 30.
20. 8. beginning from the *l.* to the first
12. these *l.* have wrought but one hour
14. I will give to this *l.* even as unto thee
21. 37. *l.* of all he sent his son, saying, *Mark* 12. 6.
22. 27. and *l.* of all the woman died also, in resurrection whose wife? *Mark* 12. 22. *Luke* 20. 32.
26. 60. at the *l.* came two false witnesses
27. 64. the *l.* error shall be worse than the first
Mark 9. 35. if desire to be first, the same shall be *l.*
Luke 12. 59. till thou hast paid the *l.* mite
John 8. 9. beginning at the eldest, even to the *l.*
1 *Cor.* 4. 9. God hath set forth us the apostles *l.*
15. 8. and *l.* of all he was seen of me also
26. the *l.* enemy is death || 45. the *l.* Adam
52. all be changed in a moment, at the *l.* trump
Phil. 4. 10. at *l.* your care of me flourished again
Rev. 2. 19. the *l.* works to be more than the first
15. 1. seven angels, having the seven *l.* plagues
21. 9. seven vials full of the seven *l.* plagues

LAST *day, days,*

Signifies, [1] *The eighth and great day of the feast of tabernacles, wherein there used to be the greatest assemblies,* John 7. 37. [2] *The day of judgment,* John 11. 24. | 12. 48. [3] *From the time of Christ's first coming to his second,* Acts 2. 17. Heb. 1. 2.

Gen. 49. 1. which shall befall you in the *l. days*
Isa. 2. 2. come to pass in *l. days, Mic.* 4. 1. *Acts* 2. 17.
John 6. 39. should raise it up at the *l. day,* 40, 44, 54.
7. 37. in the *l. day,* the great day of the feast
11. 24. I know that he shall rise again at the *l. day*
12. 48. the same shall judge him in the *l. day*
2 *Tim.* 3. 1. in *l. days* perilous times shall come
Heb. 1. 2. hath spoken in these *l. days* by his Son
Jam. 5. 3. ye have heaped treasure for the *l. days*
2 *Pet.* 3. 3. there shall come in the *l. days* scoffers

LAST *time, times.*

1 *Pet.* 1. 5. ready to be revealed in the *l. time*
20. but was manifest in these *l. times* for you
1 *John* 2. 18. little children, it is the *l. time,* are many antichrists, whereby we know that it is the *l. time*
Jude 18. told there should be mockers in the *l. time*

LASTED.

Judg. 14. 17. and she wept while the feast *l.*

LASTING.

Deut. 33. 15. for the precious things of the *l.* hills

LATCHET.

Isa. 5. 27. nor the *l.* of their shoes be broken
Mark 1. 7. the *l.* of whose shoes, *Luke* 3. 16.

LATE.

Psal. 127. 2. it is in vain for you to sit up *l.*
Mic. 2. 8. of *l.* my people is risen up as an enemy
John 11. 8. the Jews of *l.* sought to stone thee

LATELY.

Acts 18. 2. found Aquila a Jew *l.* come from Italy

LATIN.

Luke 23. 38. written in Hebrew and *l. John* 19. 20.

LATTER.

Exod. 4. 8. they will believe the voice of the *l.* sign
Deut. 11. 14. will give you the first rain, and *l.* rain
24. 3. and if her *l.* husband hate her or die
Job 19. 25. my Redeemer shall stand at the *l.* day
29. 23. they opened their mouth, as for the *l.* rain
Prov. 16. 15. his favour is as a cloud of the *l.* rain
19. 20. that thou mayest be wise in the *l.* end
Jer. 3. 3. and there hath been no *l.* rain
5. 24. both the former and *l.* rain in his season
Ezek. 38. 8. in the *l.* years thou shalt come
Dan. 8. 23. in the *l.* time of their kingdom
11. 29. but it shall not be as the former or the *l.*
Hos. 6. 3. he shall come as the *l.* and former rain
Joel 2. 23. and the *l.* rain in the first month
Amos 7. 1. in the beginning of the *l.* growth
Hag. 2. 9. the glory of the *l.* house shall be greater
Zech. 10. 1. ask ye rain in the time of the *l.* rain
1 *Tim.* 4. 1. that in the *l.* times some shall depart

See DAYS, END.

LATTICE.

Judg. 5. 28. Sisera's mother cried though the *l.*
2 *Kings* 1. 2. Ahaziah fell down through the *l.*
Cant. 2. 9. shewing himself through the *l.*

LAUD.

Rom. 15. 11. praise the Ld. and *l.* him, all ye people

LAVER.

Exod. 30. 18. thou shalt also make a *l.* of brass
28. the *l.* and his foot, 31. 9. | 35. 16. | 39. 39.
38. 8. he made the *l.* of brass, and the foot brass
40. 7. thou shalt set the *l.* || 30. and he set the *l.*
11. and thou shalt anoint the *l.* and his foot
Lev. 8. 11. he anointed both the *l.* and his foot
1 *Kings* 7. 30. under the *l.* were undersetters molten
38. every *l.* was forty baths, and every *l.* was
2 *Kings* 16. 17. and king Ahaz removed the *l.*

LAVERS.

1 *Kings* 7. 38. then made he ten *l.* of brass
40. and Hiram made the *l.* and the shovels
43. and the ten *l.* on the bases, 2 *Chron.* 4. 6, 14.

LAUGH

Signifies, [1] *To rejoice greatly in a blessing promised, or already conferred,* Gen. 17. 17. | 21. 6. [2] *To distrust, or doubt of, the fulfilment of a promise,* Gen. 18. 12. [3] *To receive comfort and joy,* Luke 6. 21. [4] *To be merry in a sinful manner,* Luke 6. 25. [5] *To carry oneself familiarly and pleasantly towards another,* Job 29. 24.

At destruction and famine thou shalt laugh, *Job* 5. 22. *Thou shalt rejoice, that by God's watchful and gracious providence thou hast been secured from them, when others are destroyed thereby.*

Gen. 18. 13. wherefore did Sarah *l.* saying
15. and he said, nay, but thou didst *l.*
21. 6. God hath made me to *l.* all will *l.* with me
Job 5. 22. at destruction and famine thou shalt *l.*
9. 23. he will *l.* at the trial of the innocent
22. 19. and the innocent *l.* them to scorn
Psal. 2. 4. he that sitteth in the heavens shall *l.*
22. 7. all they that see me *l.* me to scorn
37. 13. the Lord shall *l.* at him, for he seeth
52. 6. the righteous also shall *l.* at him
59. 8. but thou, O Lord, shalt *l.* at them
80. 6. and our enemies *l.* among themselves
Prov. 1. 26. I also will *l.* at your calamity
29. 9. whether he rage or *l.* there is no rest
Eccl. 3. 4. a time to weep, and a time to *l.*
Luke 6. 21. blessed are ye that weep, ye shall *l.*
25. woe unto you that *l.* now, ye shall weep

LAUGHED.

Gen. 17. 17. Abraham *l.* || 18. 12. Sarah *l.* in herself
18. 15. then Sarah denied, saying, I *l.* not
2 *Kings* 19. 21. daughter of Zion hath *l. Isa.* 37. 22.
2 *Chron.* 30. 10. they *l.* them to scorn, and mocked
Neh. 2. 19. they *l.* us to scorn, and despised us
Job 12. 4. the just and upright man is *l.* to scorn
29. 24. if I *l.* on them, they believed not
Ezek. 23. 32. thou shalt be *l.* to scorn, and had
Mat. 9. 24. they *l.* to scorn, *Mark* 5. 40. *Luke* 8. 53.

LAUGHETH.

Job 41. 29. he *l.* at the shaking of a spear

LAUGHING.

Job 8. 21. till he fill thy mouth with *l.* and thy lips

LAUGHTER.

Psal. 126. 2. then was our mouth filled with *l.*
Prov. 14. 13. even in *l.* the heart is sorrowful
Eccl. 2. 2. I said of *l.* it is mad, and of mirth
7. 3. sorrow is better than *l.* || 6. so is *l.* of the fool
Jam. 4. 9. let your *l.* be turned to mourning

LAVISH.

Isa. 46. 6. they *l.* gold out of the bag, and weigh

LAUNCH.

Luke 5. 4. he said to Simon, *l.* out into the deep

LAUNCHED.

Luke 8. 22. let us go over, and they *l.* forth
Acts 21. 1. that after we had *l.* 27. 2, 4.

LAW

Signifies, [1] *A rule directing and obliging a rational creature in moral and religious actions,* Prov. 28. 4. [2] *That which often hath the force of governing and over-ruling our actions in our present imperfect state,* Rom. 7. 23, 25. [3] *The whole doctrine of the word delivered by God to his church,* Psal. 1. 2. | 19. 7. [4] *The decalogue, or ten moral precepts,* Rom. 2. 25. | 7. 7. [5] *The second table of the law,* Rom. 13. 8. [6] *The precepts of God, moral, ceremonial, and judicial,* John 1. 17. [7] *The principles of reason, or the law of nature written in man's heart,* Rom. 2. 14. [8] *The old testament,* John 10. 34. | 15. 25. 1 Cor. 14. 21. [9] *The doctrine of the gospel, which no less obliges men to the belief and practice of it, than the law did,* Isa. 2. 3. | 42. 4. Rom. 3. 27. [10] *The works commanded by the law,* Gal. 3. 11. [11] *A strict and precise observation of the law,* Phil. 3. 5. [12] *The covenant that God made with the Jews, with all the constitution of worship thereto belonging,* Heb. 10. 1.

Gen. 47. 26. Joseph made it a *l.* over the land
Exod. 12. 49. one *l.* to him that is home-born and to the stranger, *Lev.* 24. 22. *Num.* 15. 16, 29.
24. 12. I will give thee a *l.* and commandment
Deut. 17. 11. according to the sentence of the *l.*
33. 2. from his right hand went a fiery *l.* for them
4. Moses commanded us a *l.* even the inheritance
Josh. 1. 7. mayest obs. to do according to all the *l.*
8. 32. wrote on the stones a copy of the *l.* of Mos.
34. afterward he read all the words of the *l.*
22. 5. take heed to the *l.* 2 *Kings* 17. 13, 37. | 21. 8.
2 *Kings* 17. 34. nor do after the *l.* and commandment
23. 24. that he might perform the words of the *l.*
25. according to all the *l.* of Moses
1 *Chron.* 16. 17. hath confirmed to Jacob for a *l.*
22. 12. that thou mayest keep the *l.* of God
2 *Chron.* 14. 4. commanded Judah to do the *l.*
19. 10. between *l.* and commandment, statutes
30. 16. stood in their place according to *l.* of Moses
31. 21. Hezekiah did in every work, and in the *l.*
33. 8. take heed to do according to the whole *l.*
34. 19. when Josiah heard the words of the *l.*
Ezra 7. 6. he was a ready scribe in the *l.* 12. 21.
14. to inquire according to the *l.* of thy God
26. will not do the *l.* of God and *l.* of the king
10. 3. and let it be done according to the *l.*
Neh. 8. 2. and Ezra the priest brought the *l.* before
7. Levites caused the people to understand the *l.*
9. people wept when they heard the words of *l.*
13. were gathered together to understand the *l.*
10. 28. had separated themselves to *l.* of God
29. entered into an oath to walk in God's *l.*
12. 44. to gather into them the portions of the *l.*
13. 3. when they had heard the *l.* they separated
Esth. 1. 8. the drinking was according to the *l.*
15. what do to the queen Vashti according to the *l.*
4. 11. there is one *l.* of his to put him to death
16. I will go in, which is not according to the *l.*
Job 22. 22. receive the *l.* from his mouth, lay up
Psal. 1. 2. in his *l.* he meditates day and night
37. 31. the *l.* of his God is in his heart
78. 5. for he appointed a *l.* in Israel, which he
10. and they refused to walk in his *l.*
81. 4. this was a *l.* of the God of Jacob
94. 20. which frameth mischief by a *l.*
105. 10. and confirmed the same to Jacob for a *l.*
119. 72. the *l.* of thy mouth is better than gold
Prov. 1. 8. forsake not the *l.* of thy mother, 6. 20.
6. 23. commandment is a lamp, and the *l.* is light
Prov. 13. 14. the *l.* of the wise is a fountain of life
28. 4. they that forsake the *l.* praise the wicked, but such as keep the *l.* contend with them
7. whoso keepeth the *l.* is a wise son
9. he that turns away his ear from hearing the *l.*
29. 18. but he that keepeth the *l.* happy is he
31. 5. lest they drink and forget the *l.*
26. and in her tongue is the *l.* of kindness
Isa. 1. 10. and give ear to the *l.* of our God
2. 3. out of Zion shall go forth the *l. Mic.* 4. 2.
8. 16. seal the *l.* || 20. to the *l.* and the testimony
42. 4. and the isles shall wait for his *l.*
21. the Lord will magnify the *l.* and make it
24. neither were they obedient to his *l.*
51. 4. for a *l.* shall proceed from me
Jer. 2. 8. they that handle the *l.* knew me not
18. 18. the *l.* shall not perish from the priest
32. 11. evidence was sealed accord. to *l.* and custom
44. 23. ye have not obeyed, nor walked in his *l.*
Lam. 2. 9. the *l.* is no more, prophets find no vision
Ezek. 7. 26. the *l.* shall perish from the priests
Dan. 6. 5. except concerning the *l.* of his God
12. true according to the *l.* of the Medes, 15.
Hos. 4. 6. thou hast forgotten the *l.* of thy God
Hab. 1. 4. therefore the *l.* is slacked, and judgment
Zeph. 3. 4. her priests have done violence to the *l.*
Hag. 2. 11. ask now the priests concerning the *l.*
Zech. 7. 12. lest they should hear the *l.* and words
Mal. 2. 6. the *l.* of truth was in his mouth
7. and they should seek the *l.* at his mouth
8. ye have caused many to stumble at the *l.*
9. not kept my ways, but have been partial in the *l.*
4. 4. remember the *l.* of Moses my servant
Mat. 5. 17. think not I am come to destroy the *l.*
18. one tittle shall in no wise pass from the *l.*
40. and if any man will sue thee at the *l.*
11. 13. the *l.* prophesied till John, *Luke* 16. 16.
12. 5. have ye not read in the *l.* how that on
22. 36. which is the great commandment in *l.*
40. on these two commandments hang all the *l.*
23. 23. have omitted the weightier matters of the *l.*
Luke 2. 27. to do for him after the custom of the *l.*
5. 17. there were doctors of the *l.* sitting by
16. 17. than for one tittle of the *l.* to fail
John 1. 17. for the *l.* was given by Moses, but grace
45. him of whom Moses in the *l.* did write
7. 19. did not Moses give you the *l.* and yet none of you keepeth the *l.* why go ye to kill me?
23. that the *l.* of Moses should not be broken
49. people who knoweth not the *l.* are cursed
51. doth our *l.* judge any man before it hear him?
8. 5. now Moses in the *l.* commanded us
10. 34. is it not written in your *l.* ye are gods?
12. 34. we have heard out of the *l.* that Christ
15. 25. might be fulfilled what is written in their *l.*
18. 31. and judge him according to your *l.*
19. 7. we have a *l.* and by our *l.* he ought to die
Acts 5. 34. then stood up Gamaliel, a doctor of the *l.*
6. 13. to speak blasphemous words against the *l.*
7. 53. who have received the *l.* by angels
13. 15. after reading of the *l.* and prophets
39. ye could not be justified by the *l.* of Moses
15. 5. to command them to keep the *l.* of Moses
24. ye must be circumcised and keep the *l.*
18. 13. men to worship God contrary to the *l.*
15. but if it be a question of your *l.* look ye to it
19. 38. the *l.* is open || 21. 20. zealous of the *l.*
21. 24. but that thou thyself keepest the *l.*
28. this is the man that teacheth against the *l.*
22. 3. taught according to the manner of the *l.*
12. Ananias a devout man according to the *l.*
23. 3. for sittest thou to judge me after the *l.* and commandest me to be smitten contrary to the *l.*
24. 6. and would have judged according to our *l.*
25. 8. nor against the *l.* of the Jews, nor temple
28. 23. persuading them out of the *l.* and prophets
Rom. 2. 12. sinned in the *l.* shall be judged by the *l.*
13. not the hearers of the *l.* are just before God
14. when the Gentiles which have not the *l.* do by nature things contained in the *l.* these having not the *l.* are a *l.* unto themselves
15. which shew the work of the *l.* written in
17. thou art called a Jew, and restest in the *l.*
18. knowest, being instructed out of the *l.*
20. which hast the form of the truth in the *l.*
23. thou that makest thy boast of the *l.* through breaking the *l.* dishonourest thou God?
25. circumcision verily profiteth if thou keep the *l.* but if thou be a breaker of the *l.*
26. therefore if keep the righteousness of the *l.*
27. uncircumcision, if it fulfil the *l.* judge thee who by circumcision dost transgress the *l.*
3. 19. we know what things soever the *l.* saith
20. by the deeds of *l.* no flesh be justified, for by the *l.* is the knowledge of sin, 28. *Gal.* 2. 16.
21. the righteousness of G. is witnessed by the *l.*
27. by what *l.* excluded? by the *l.* of faith
31. do we make void the *l.*? we establish the *l.*
4. 13. for the promise was not through the *l.*
14. for if they which are of the *l.* be heirs
15. the *l.* worketh wrath, for where no *l.* is
16. be sure, not to that only which is of the *l.*
5. 13. for until the *l.* sin was in the world, but sin is not imputed where there is no *l.*
20. the *l.* entered, that the offence might abound
7. 1. I speak to them which know the *l.* the *l.* hath dominion over a man as long as he liveth
2. the woman is bound by the *l.* to her husband; if he be dead, she is loosed from the *l.* 3.
4. ye also are become dead to the *l.* by Christ
5. the motions of sins which were by the *l.*
6. but now we are delivered from the *l.*
7. is the *l.* sin? I had not known sin but by *l.* nor lust, except *l.* had said, thou shalt not covet
8. for without the *l.* sin was dead
12. the *l.* is holy, and commandment holy, just
14. the *l.* is spiritual || 16. the *l.* is good, 1 *Tim.* 1. 8.
21. I find then a *l.* || 22. I delight in the *l.* of God
23. I see another *l.* warring against the *l.* of my mind, bringing me into captivity to *l.* of sin
25. with mind I serve *l.* of God, flesh, *l.* of sin
8. 2. the *l.* of life made me free from the *l.* of sin

Rom. 8. 3. for what the *l.* could not do, in that weak
4. the righteousness of the *l.* might be fulfilled
7. the carnal mind is not subject to the *l.* of God
9. 4. to whom pertaineth the giving of the *l.*
31. Israel followed after the *l.* of righteousness
32. because they sought it by the works of the *l.*
10. 4. Christ is the end of the *l.* for righteousness
5. describes the righteousness which is of the *l.*
13. 8. he that loveth another, hath fulfilled the *l.*
10. therefore love is the fulfilling of the *l.*
1 *Cor.* 6.1. dare any of you go to *l.* before the unjust?
6. but brother goeth to *l.* with brother
7. because ye go to *l.* one with another
7. 39. wife is bound by the *l.* as long as her husband
9. 8. or saith not the *l.* the same also?
14. 34. to be under obedience, as also saith the *l.*
15. 56. of death is sin, and strength of sin is the *l.*
Gal. 2. 16. man is not justified by the works of the *l.*
19. I thro' the *l.* am dead to the *l.* that I might live
21. for if righteousness come by the *l.* then
3. 2. received ye the Spirit by the works of the *l.*?
5. miracles, doeth he it by the works of the *l.*?
10. as many as are of the works of the *l.*
11. that no man is justified by the *l.* is evident
12. and the *l.* is not of faith, but the man
13. Christ hath redeemed us from the curse of *l.*
17. the covenant in Christ, the *l.* cannot disannul
18. if the inheritance be of the *l.* not of promise
19. wherefore then serveth the *l.*? it was added
21. is the *l.* then against the promises? if a *l.* had been given, righteousness had been by the *l.*
24. the *l.* was our schoolmaster to bring us to Chr.
4. 21. tell me, do ye not hear the *l.*?
5. 3. that he is a debtor to do the whole *l.*
4. for whosoever of you are justified by the *l.*
14. all the *l.* is fulfilled in one word, even in this
23. temperance, against such there is no *l.*
6. 2. bear ye, and so fulfil the *l.* of Christ
13. nor themselves keep the *l.* but desire to have
Eph. 2. 15. having abolished in his flesh the *l.*
Phil. 3. 5. as touching the *l.* a Pharisee
6. touching the righteousness in the *l.* blameless
9. not having mine own righteousness, of the *l.*
1 *Tim.* 1. 7. desiring to be teachers of the *l.*
9. the *l.* is not made for a righteous man
Tit. 3. 9. but avoid contentions about the *l.*
Heb. 7. 5. to take tithes of people according to the *l.*
11. for under it the people received the *l.*
12. there is made of necessity a change of the *l.*
16. not after the *l.* of a carnal commandment
19. for the *l.* made nothing perfect, but bringing
28. the *l.* maketh men high-priests, but the word of the oath which was since the *l.* maketh Son
8. 4. there are priests offer gifts according to the *l.*
9. 19. when Moses had spoken according to the *l.*
22. all things are by the *l.* purged with blood
10. 1. the *l.* having a shadow of good things
28. he that despised Moses' *l.* died without mercy
Jam. 1. 25. whoso looketh into perfect *l.* of liberty
2. 8. if ye fulfil the royal *l.* ye do well
9. and are convinced of the *l.* as transgressors
10. for whosoever shall keep the whole *l.*
11. if thou kill, thou art a transgressor of the *l.*
12. they that shall be judged by the *l.* of liberty
4. 11. that speaketh evil of the *l.* and judgeth the *l.*
1 *John* 3. 4. whosoever committeth sin transgresseth also the *l.* for sin is the transgression of the *l.*

See BOOK.

LAW *of the Lord.*

Exod. 13. 9. that *the Lord's l.* may be in thy mouth
2 *Kings* 10. 31. Jehu took no heed to walk in *l. of L.*
2 *Chron.* 12. 1. Rehoboam forsook *l. of L.* and Isr.
31. 4. that they might be encouraged in the *l. of L.*
35. 26. Josiah's goodness according to *l. of L.*
Ezra 7. 10. prepared his heart to seek the *l. of Lord*
Psal. 1. 2. his delight is in the *l. of the Lord*, and in his law
19. 7. the *l. of the L.* is perfect, converting the soul
119. 1. blessed are they who walk in the *l. of the L.*
Isa. 5. 24. because they have cast away the *l. of L.*
30. 9. children that will not hear the *l. of the Lord*
Jer. 8. 8. how do ye say, the *l. of the Lord* is with us
Amos 2. 4. because they have despised the *l. of the L.*
Luke 2. 39. had performed according to the *l. of L.*

My LAW.

Exod. 16. 4. whether they will walk in *my l.* or no
2 *Chron.* 6. 16. so that thy children walk in *my l.*
Psal. 78. 1. give ear, O my people, to *my l.* incline
89. 30. if his children forsake *my l.* and walk
Prov. 3. 1. my son, forget not *my l.* but keep
4. 2. forsake not *my l.* ‖ 7. 2. keep *my l.* as the apple
Isa. 51. 7. the people in whose heart is *my l.*
Jer. 6. 19. they have not hearkened unto *my l.*
9. 13. because they have forsaken *my l.*
16. 11. have forsaken me, and have not kept *my l.*
26. 4. if ye will not hearken to walk in *my l.*
31. 33. I will put *my l.* in their inward parts
44. 10. nor have they feared nor walked in *my l.*
Ezek. 22. 26. her priests have violated *my l.*
Hos. 8. 1. because they trespassed against *my l.*
12. have written to him the great things of *my l.*

This LAW.

Lev. 14. 2. *this* shall be the *l.* of leper in cleansing
Num. 5. 30. the priest shall execute on her *this l.*
19. 2. *this* is the ordinance of the *l.* 31. 21.
Deut. 1. 5. began Moses to declare *this l.* saying
4. 8. all *this l.* which I set before you this day
17. 18. he shall write him a copy of *this l.* in a book
19. he may learn to keep all the words of *this l.*
27. 3. shall write on them the words of *this l.* 8.
26. cursed that confirmeth not the words of *this l.*
28. 58. if thou wilt not observe the words of *this l.*
29. 29. that we may do all the words of *this l.* 31. 12.
31. 9. Moses wrote *this l.* ‖ 11. thou shalt read *this l.*
24. of writing the words of *this l.* in a book
32. 46. your children to do the words of *this l.*

This is the LAW.

Lev. 6. 9. *this is the l.* of the burnt offering, 7. 37.
14. *this is the l.* of meat offering ‖ 25. of sin offering
7. 1. *this is the l.* of the trespass offering, it is holy
11. 46. *this is the l.* of the beasts and of the fowl
12. 7. *t. is the l.* of her that hath born male and fem.
13. 59. *this is the l.* of plague of lepr. 14. 32, 57.
14. 54. *this is the l.* for all manner of plag. of scall
15. 32. *this is the l.* of him that hath an issue
Num. 5. 29. *this is the l.* of jealousies, when a wife
6. 13. *this is the l.* of the Nazarite, when days, 21.
19. 14. *this is the l.* when a man dieth in a tent
Deut. 4. 44. *this is the l.* which Moses set before Israel
Ezek. 43. 12. *this is the l.* of the house, on top of mount.
Mat. 7. 12. do to them, for *this is the l.* and prophets

Thy LAW.

Deut. 33. 10. they shall teach Israel *thy l.*
Neh. 9. 26. they cast *thy l.* behind their backs
29. that thou mightest bring them again to *thy l.*
34. nor our kings, nor our princes kept *thy l.*
Psal. 40. 8. yea, *thy l.* is within my heart
94. 12. chastenest, and teachest him out of *thy l.*
119. 18. behold wondrous things out of *thy l.*
29. the way of lying, and grant me *thy l.* graciously
34. give me understanding, and I shall keep *thy l.*
44. so shall I keep *thy l.* continually for ever
51. yet have I not declined from *thy l.*
53. because of the wicked that forsake *thy l.*
55. I remembered thy name, and kept *thy l.*
61. have robbed me, but I have not forgotten *thy l.*
70. their heart is fat, but I delight in *thy l.*
77. I may live, for *thy l.* is my delight, 92, 174.
85. the proud digged pits; which are not after *t. l.*
97. O how I love *t. l.* ‖ 109. yet do I not forget *t. l.*
113. but *t. l.* do I love, 163. ‖ 126. made void *t. l.*
136. waters run down, because they keep not *t. l.*
142. and *thy l.* is the truth ‖ 150. are far from *thy l.*
165. great peace have they who love *thy l.*
Jer. 32. 23. they obeyed not, nor walked in *thy l.*
Dan. 9. 11. all Israel have transgressed *thy l.*

Under the LAW.

Rom. 3. 19. it saith to them that are *under the l.*
6. 14. for ye are not *under the l.* but under grace
15. shall we sin because we are not *under the l.*?
1 *Cor.* 9. 20. to them that are *under the l.* as *under the l.* that I might gain them that are *under the l.*
21. not without law to God, but *under l.* to Christ
Gal. 3. 23. we were kept *under the l.* ‖ 4. 4. made *u. l.*
4. 5. sent his Son to redeem them that were *under l.*
21. tell me, ye that desire to be *under the l.*
Gal. 5. 18. if ye be led by Spirit, are not *under the l.*

Without LAW.

2 *Chron.* 15. 3. a long season, Israel hath been *w. l.*
Rom. 2. 12. as many as sinned *without l.* perish *w. l.*
3. 21. the righteousness of God *w. l.* is manifested
7. 8. for *w. l.* sin was dead ‖ 9. I was alive *w. l.* once
1 *Cor.* 9. 21. that are *w. l.* as *w. l.* being not *w. l.* to G.

Written in the LAW.

1 *Kings* 2. 3. as it is *written in the l.* of Moses, 2 *Chron.* 23. 18. | 25. 4. | 31. 3. *Ezra* 3. 2. *Neh.* 10. 34, 36. *Dan.* 9. 13. *Luke* 2. 23.
1 *Chron.* 16. 40. do according to all *w. l.* 2 *Chr.* 35. 26.
Neh. 8. 14. and they found *writ. in the l.* that Israel
Dan. 9. 11. and the oath that is *writ. in l.* of Moses
Luke 10. 26. what is *writ. in the l.* how readest thou?
24. 44. all must be fulfilled, which were *writ. in l.*
Acts 24. 14. believing all things that are *writ. in l.*
1 *Cor.* 9. 9. it is *w. l.* ‖ 14. 21. *in the l.* it is *written*

LAWS.

Gen. 26. 5. Abraham kept my statutes and my *l.*
Exod. 16. 28. how long refuse ye to keep my *l.*?
18. 16. I do make them know the *l.* of God
20. thou shalt teach them ordinances and *l.*
Lev. 26. 46. these are the *l.* which the Lord made
Ezra 7. 25. all such as know the *l.* of thy God
Neh. 9. 13. camest down, thou gavest them true *l.*
14. and commandedst them statutes and *l.*
Esth. 1. 19. to be written among the *l.* of the Persians
3. 8. a certain people, their *l.* are diverse from all people, neither keep they the king's *l.*
Psal. 105. 45. that they might keep his *l.*
Isa. 24. 5. because they have transgressed the *l.*
Ezek. 43. 11. shew them all the *l.* thereof
44. 5. hear all the *l.* ‖ 24. they shall keep my *l.*
Dan. 7. 25. and think to change times and *l.*
9. 10. nor have we obeyed to walk in his *l.*
Heb. 8. 10. I will put my *l.* into their mind
10. 16. I will put my *l.* into their hearts

LAWFUL.

Ezra 7. 24. shall not be *l.* to impose toll on them
Isa. 49. 24. shall the *l.* captive be delivered?
Ezek. 18. 5. do that which is *l.* 21. 27. | 33. 14, 19.
19. the son hath done that which is *l.* 33. 16.
Mat. 12. 2. do what is not *l.* *Mark* 2. 24. *Luke* 6. 2.
4. was not *l.* for him to eat, *Mark* 2. 26. *Luke* 6. 4.
10. they asked him, is it *l.* to heal on the sabbath days? 12. *Mark* 3. 4. *Luke* 6. 9. | 14. 3.
14. 4. it is not *l.* for thee to have her, *Mark* 6. 18.
19. 3. is it *l.* for man to put away wife? *Mark* 10. 2.
22. 17. tell us, is it *l.* to give tribute to Cesar or not? *Mark* 12. 14. *Luke* 20. 22.
27. 6. it is not *l.* to put them in the treasury
John 5. 10. it is not *l.* for thee to carry thy bed
18. 31. it is not *l.* for us to put any man to death
Acts 16. 21. teach customs which are not *l.* to receive
19. 39. it shall be determined in a *l.* assembly
22. 25. is it *l.* for you to scourge a Roman?
1 *Cor.* 6. 12. all things are *l.* to me, *l.* for me, 10. 23.
2 *Cor.* 12. 4. which is not *l.* for a man to utter

LAWFULLY.

1 *Tim.* 1. 8. the law is good, if a man use it *l.*
2 *Tim.* 2. 5. yet is not crowned, except he strive *l.*

LAWGIVER.

Gen. 49. 10. nor a *l.* from between his feet
Num. 21. 18. digged the well by direction of the *l.*
Deut. 33. 21. in a portion of the *l.* was he seated
Psal. 60. 7. Gilead is mine, Judah is my *l.* 108. 8.
Isa. 33. 22. the Lord is our *l.* and our king
Jam. 4. 12. there is one *l.* who is able to save

LAWLESS.

1 *Tim.* 1. 9. the law is for the *l.* and disobedient

LAWYER.

Mat. 22. 35. one that was a *l.* asked him, *Luke* 10. 25.
Tit. 3. 13. bring Zenas the *l.* and Apollos

LAWYERS.

Luke 7. 30. the *l.* rejected the counsel of God
11. 45. then answered one of the *l.* and said
46. woe unto you, *l.* 52. ‖ 14. 3. Jesus spake to *l.*

LAY, *as with a woman.*

Gen. 19. 33. the first-born *l.* with her father, 34, 35.
30. 16. and Jacob *l.* with Leah that night
34. 2. Shechem *l.* with Dinah and defiled her
35. 22. Reuben went and *l.* with Bilhah
Deut. 22. 22. man that *l.* with woman, both shall die
25. the man only that *l.* with her shall die
29. the man that *l.* with her give fifty shekels
1 *Sam.* 2. 22. Eli heard they *l.* with the women
2 *Sam.* 11. 4. she came, and he *l.* with her, 12. 24.
13. 14. Amnon forced Tamar and *l.* with her
Ezek. 23. 8. for in her youth they *l.* with her

LAY.

Exod. 5. 8. the tale of bricks ye shall *l.* upon them
16. 13. the dew *l.* round about the host, 14.
21. 22. as woman's husband will *l.* upon him
22. 25. neither shalt thou *l.* upon him usury
Lev. 1. 7. and *l.* the wood in order on the fire
8. the priests shall *l.* the parts in order, 12.
2. 15. thou shalt *l.* the frankincense thereon
6. 12. and *l.* the burnt-offering in order upon it
Num. 12. 11. alas, my Lord, *l.* not the sin upon us
Deut. 7. 15. but will *l.* them on them that hate thee
11. 25. shall *l.* the fear of you upon all the land
21. 8. *l.* not innocent blood to thy people Israel
Josh. 2. † 1. they came to Rahab's house, and *l.* there
8. 2. *l.* thee an ambush for the city behind it
Judg. 16. 3. Samson *l.* till midnight, and arose
Ruth 3. 8. and behold, a woman *l.* at his feet
1 *Sam.* 3. 15. and Samuel *l.* till the morning
11. 2. and *l.* it for a reproach on all Israel
25. † 25. let not my lord *l.* it to his heart
26. 5. Saul *l.* in the trench, people about him, 7.
2 *Sam.* 4. 5. Ish-bosheth, who *l.* on a bed at noon
12. 3. ewe lamb eat of his meat, and *l.* in his bosom
16. David *l.* all night on the earth, 13. 31.
1 *Kings* 13. 31. *l.* my bones beside his bones
18. 23. *l.* it on wood and put no fire under
19. 5. and as he *l.* and slept under a juniper tree
21. 27. Ahab fasted and *l.* in sackcloth
2 *Kings* 4. 34. he went up and *l.* upon the child
10. 8. *l.* ye them in two heaps at the gate
2 *Chr.* 36. 21. long as she *l.* desolate, she kept sabb.
Esth. 4. 3. many *l.* in sackcloth and ashes
Job 29. 19. the dew *l.* all night upon my branch
34. 23. he will not *l.* on man more than right
Psal. 7. 5. let him *l.* mine honour in the dust
38. 12. they that seek my life, *l.* snares for me
84. 3. found a nest, where she may *l.* her young
Eccl. 7. 2. and the living will *l.* it to heart
Isa. 5. 8. woe to them that *l.* field to field
10. † 6. give them charge to *l.* them a treading
13. 9. to *l.* the land desolate, *Ezek.* 33. 28.
11. I will *l.* low the haughtiness of the terrible
22. 22. key of house of David *l.* on his shoulder
25. 12. and the fortress shall he *l.* low
28. 16. behold, I will *l.* in Zion a tried stone
17. judgment will I *l.* to the line, and righteousn.
29. 21. that *l.* a snare for him that reproveth
30. 32. the staff which the Lord shall *l.* on him
34. 15. there shall the great owl *l.* and hatch
38. 21. a lump of figs, and *l.* it for a plaister
47. 7. so thou didst not *l.* these things to thy heart
54. 11. I will *l.* thy stones with fair colours
Jer. 6. 21. I will *l.* stumbling-block, *Ezek.* 3. 20.
Ezek. 4. 1. take thee a tile, and *l.* it before thee
2. *l.* siege against it, 3. ‖ 8. *l.* bands on thee
4. *l.* the iniquity of the house of Israel upon it
25. 14. I will *l.* my vengeance on Edom, 17.
28. 17. I will *l.* thee before kings to behold thee
32. 5. I will *l.* thy flesh on the mountains, and fill
36. 29. and I will *l.* no famine upon you
34. the land shall be tilled, whereas it *l.* desolate
37. 6. I will *l.* sinews upon you and bring flesh
42. 13. there *l.* the most holy things, 14. | 44. 19.
Jonah 1. 14. O Lord, *l.* not on us innocent blood
Mic. 1. 7. the idols thereof will I *l.* desolate
Mal. 2. 2. if ye will not *l.* it to heart, I will send a curse upon you; because ye do not *l.* it to heart
Mat. 8. 20. hath not where to *l.* his head, *Luke* 9. 58.
23. 4. bind, and *l.* them on men's shoulders
28. 6. come, see the place where the Lord *l.*
Mark 2. 4. the bed wherein the sick of the palsy *l.*
Luke 19. 44. and shall *l.* thee even with the ground
John 5. 3. in these *l.* impotent folk, blind, halt
11. 38. it was a cave, and a stone *l.* upon it
Acts 7. 60. Lord, *l.* not this sin to their charge
15. 28. to *l.* on you no greater burden than these
27. 20. and no small tempest *l.* on us, all hope
Rom. 8. 33. *l.* any thing to the charge of God's elect
9. 33. behold, I *l.* in Zion a stumbling-stone
1 *Cor.* 16. 2. let every one *l.* by him in store
Heb. 12. 1. let us *l.* aside every weight, and the sin
Jam. 1. 21. wherefore *l.* apart all filthiness
1 *Pet.* 2. 6. I *l.* in Zion a chief corner-stone

See FOUNDATION.

LAY *down.*

Gen. 19. 4. before they *l. d.* men of Sodom compass.
33. and Lot perceived not when she *l. down*, 35.
28. 11. Jacob *l. down* in that place to sleep
Num. 24. 9. couched, he *l. d.* as a lion, as a young
Judg. 5. 27. he *l. down* at her feet, he bowed, he fell
Ruth 3. 4. uncover his feet, and *l.* thee *down*
1 *Sam.* 3. 5. lie down, and Samuel went and *l. d.* 9.
19. 24. Saul *l. down* naked all that day and night
2 *Sam.* 13. 5. Jonadab said, *l.* thee *down* on thy bed
6. so Amnon *l. down* and made himself sick
1 *Kings* 14. † 20. Jeroboam *l. down* with his fathers
Job 17. 3. *l. down* now, put me in surety with thee
Psal. 4. 8. I will *l.* me *down* in peace and sleep
104. 22. young lions *l.* them *down* in their dens
Ezek. 19. 2. thy mother *l. down* among lions
Amos 2. 8. they *l.* themselves *down* on clothes
Mat. 9. † 36. because they were tired and *l. down*
John 10. 15. and I *l. down* my life for my sheep, 17
18. I *l.* it *d.* of myself, I have power to *l.* it *d.*
13. 37. I will *l. down* my life for thy sake, 38.
15. 13. that a man *l. down* his life for his friends
1 *John* 3. 16. we ought to *l. d.* our lives for the breth

LAY *hand.*

Gen. 22. 12. he said, *l.* not thy *hand* on the lad
37. 22. shed no blood, *l.* no *hand* upon Joseph

Exod. 7. 4. that I may *l.* my *hand* upon Egypt
Lev. 3. 2. *l.* his *hand* on the head of his offering, 8.
13. *l.* his *hand* on the head of the goat, 4. 24.
4. 4. he shall *l.* his *hand* on the bullock's head, 15.
29. he shall *l.* his *hand* on the sin offering, 33.
Num. 27. 18. the Lord said, *l.* thy *hand* on Joshua
Judg. 18. 19. *l.* thy *hand* upon thy mouth, and go
Esth. 2. 21. and sought to *l.* *hand* on the king
9. 2. to *l.* *hand* on such as sought their hurt
Job 9. 33. any days-man to *l.* his *hand* on us both
21. 5. mark me, and *l.* your *hand* upon your mouth
40. 4. shall I answ. I will *l.* my *hand* on my mouth
41. 8. *l.* thy *hand* upon him, remember the battle
Prov. 30. 32. if thou thought evil, *l.* *hand* on mouth
Isa. 11. 14. they shall *l.* their *hand* on Edom
Mic. 7. 16. they shall *l.* their *hand* on their mouth
Mat. 9. 18. come, and *l.* thy *hand* on her
LAY *hands.*
Lev. 16. 21. Aaron shall *l.* both his *hands* on the goat
24. 14. all that heard him *l.* their *hands* on head
Num. 8. 12. the Levites *l.* their *h.* on the bullocks
Neh. 13. 21. if ye do so again, I will *l.* *hands* on you
Esth. 3. 6. he thought scorn to *l.* *h.* on Mordec. alone
Mat. 21. 46. they sought to *l.* *h.* on him, *Luke* 20. 19.
Mark 5. 23. come and *l.* thy *hands* on her
16. 18. *l.* *hands* on the sick, and they shall recover
Luke 21. 12. they shall *l.* *hands* on you, and persec.
Acts 8. 19. on whomsoever I *l.* *h.* he may receive
1 *Tim.* 5. 22. *l.* *hands* suddenly on no man, nor be
LAY *hold.*
Deut. 21. 19. then shall his father *l.* *hold* on him
22. 28. and *l.* *hold* on her, and lie with her
2 *Sam.* 2. 21. *l.* thee *hold* on one of the young men
1 *Kings* 13. 4. put forth his hand, saying, *l.* *h.* on him
Prov. 3. 18. a tree of life to them that *l.* *hold* on her
Eccl. 2. 3. and I sought to *l.* *h.* on folly, till I might
Isa. 5. 29. they shall roar, and *l.* *hold* on the prey
Jer. 6. 23. they shall *l.* *hold* on bow and spear
Zech. 14. 13. every one shall *l.* *h.* on his neighbour
Mat. 12. 11. will he not *l.* *h.* on it, and lift it out?
Mark 3. 21. his friends went out to *l.* *hold* on him
12. 12. they sought to *l.* *hold* on him, but feared
1 *Tim.* 6. 12. *l.* *hold* on eternal life, whereunto, 19.
Heb. 6. 18. to *l.* *hold* on the hope set before us
LAY *up.*
Gen. 41. 35. *l.* *up* corn under the hand of Pharaoh
Exod. 16. 23. *l.* *up* manna for you till the morning
33. *l.* *up* a pot of manna to be kept for generations
Num. 17. 4. shall *l.* them *up* in the tabernacle
19. 9. *l.* them *up* without the camp in a clean place
Deut. 11. 18. *l.* *up* these my words in your heart
14. 28. and shall *l.* it *up* within thy gates
Job 22. 22. and *l.* *up* his words in thy heart
24. then shalt *l.* *up* gold as dust and stones
Prov. 7. 1. *l.* *up* my commandments with thee
10. 14. wise men *l.* *up* knowledge, but the foolish
Mat. 6. 19. *l.* not *up* for you treasures on earth
20. *l.* *up* for yourselves treasures in heaven
2 *Cor.* 12. 14. children not to *l.* *up* for the parents
LAY *wait.*
Ezra 8. 31. delivered us from such as *l.* in *wait*
Psal. 71. 10. that *l.* *wait* for my soul take counsel
Prov. 1. 11. let us *l.* *wait* for blood, let us lurk
18. and they *l.* *wait* for their own blood, and lurk
24. 15. *l.* not *wait* against the righteous
Jer. 5. 26. they *l.* *wait* as he that setteth snares
LAY *waste.*
2 *Kings* 19. 25. that shouldest be to *l.* *w.* *Isa.* 37. 26.
Isa. 5. 6. I will *l.* it *waste*, it shall not be pruned
Ezek. 35. 4. I will *l.* thy cities *waste*, thou shalt
LAID.
Gen. 9. 23. and *l.* it on both their shoulders
22. 6. Abraham took wood, and *l.* it on Isaac
30. 41. Jacob *l.* the rods before the cattle
38. 19. she went away, and *l.* by her veil from her
48. 14. right hand, and *l.* it on Ephraim's head
Exod. 2. 3. she *l.* it in the flags by the river
5. 9. let more work be *l.* on the men
21. 30. he shall give whatsoever is *l.* on him
Deut. 26. 6. the Egyptians *l.* on us hard bondage
Josh. 2. 6. with stalks of flax she had *l.* in order
7. 23. they took and *l.* them out before the Lord
Judg. 9. 24. their blood be *l.* on Abimelech
Ruth 4. 16. took the child, and *l.* it in her bosom
2 *Sam.* 18. 17. *l.* a great heap of stones on Absalom
1 *Kings* 3. 20. she arose and took my son, and *l.* it in
her bosom, and *l.* her dead child in my bosom
8. 31. an oath be *l.* on him to cause, 2 *Chron.* 6. 22.
13. 29. the prophet *l.* the carcase on the ass
30. he *l.* his carcase in his own grave
17. 19. he carried him up, and *l.* him on his own bed
2 *Kings* 4. 21. she went, and *l.* him on the bed
9. 25. the Lord *l.* this burden on him
20. 7. and they took and *l.* it on the boil
2 *Chron.* 24. 9. Moses *l.* on Israel in the wilderness
Neh. 13. 5. where they *l.* the meat offerings
Job 6. 2. and my calamity *l.* in the balances
18. 10. the snare is *l.* for him in the ground
38. 6. or who *l.* the corner-stone thereof
Psal. 21. 5. honour and majesty hast *l.* on him
31. 4. pull me out of the net they have *l.* for me
49. 14. like sheep they are *l.* in the grave
62. 9. to be *l.* in the balance, they are vanity
79. 1. they have *l.* Jerusalem on heaps
88. 6. thou hast *l.* me in the lowest pit
89. 19. I have *l.* help upon one that is mighty
105. 18. feet hurt with fetters, he was *l.* in iron
119. 30. thy judgments have I *l.* before me
110. the wicked have *l.* a snare for me, 141. 9.
139. 5. thou hast *l.* thine hand upon me
142. 3. they have privily *l.* a snare for me
Isa. 6. 7. and he *l.* it upon my mouth, and said
42. 25. it burned him, yet *l.* it not to heart, 57. 11.
47. 6. thou hast very heavily *l.* thy yoke
53. 6. the Lord *l.* on him the iniquity of us all
Jer. 50. 24. I have *l.* a snare for thee, O Babylon
Ezek. 32. 19. be thou *l.* with the uncircumcised
33. 29. when I have *l.* the land most desolate
35. 12. hast spoken, saying, they are *l.* desolate
Hos. 11. 4. I drew them, and I *l.* meat unto them
Joel 1. 17. the garners are *l.* desolate, the barns
Amos 2. 8. on clothes *l.* to pledge by every altar
Obad. 7. they have *l.* a wound under thee
Jonah 3. 6. he arose and *l.* his robe from him
Mic. 5. 1. now gather, he hath *l.* siege against us
Hab. 2. 19. it is *l.* over with gold and silver
Hag. 2. 15. from before a stone was *l.* on a stone
Zech. 3. 9. behold the stone that I have *l.*
7. 14. for they *l.* the pleasant land desolate
Mat. 3. 10. now the axe is *l.* to the root, *Luke* 3. 9.
27. 60. he *l.* it in his own new tomb, and rolled
Mark 7. 30. and her daughter *l.* on the bed
15. 47. and Mary beheld where he was *l.*
16. 6. behold the place where they *l.* him
Luke 2. 7. her first-born and *l.* him in a manger
16. 20. Lazarus was *l.* at his gate full of sores
23. 53. wherein never man before was *l.* *John* 19. 41.
John 11. 34. and said, where have ye *l.* him?
13. 4. *l.* aside his garments and took a towel
19. 42. there *l.* they Jesus therefore, because
20. 2. we know not where they have *l.* him, 13.
Acts 3. 2. whom they *l.* at the gate of the temple
4. 37. and *l.* the money at the apostles' feet, 5. 2.
5. 15. *l.* them on beds and couches, that at least
9. 37. when washed, they *l.* her in an upper chamb.
13. 36. David was *l.* to his fathers, and saw corrupt.
23. 29. nothing *l.* to his charge worthy of death
25. 7. *l.* many complaints they could not prove
16. concerning the crime *l.* against him
1 *Cor.* 9. 16. necessity is *l.* upon me, woe to me
2 *Tim.* 4. 16. I pray it be not *l.* to their charge
See FOUNDATION.
LAID *down.*
Josh. 2. 8. before they were *l.* *down*, she came up
4. 8. carried them, and *l.* them *down* there
Ruth 3. 7. Ruth uncovered his feet and *l.* her *down*
1 *Sam.* 3. 2. Eli was *l.* *down* || 3. Sam. *l.* *down* to sleep
2 *Sam.* 13. 8. Amnon was *l.* *down*, and she took flour
1 *Kings* 19. 5. Elijah did eat, and *l.* him *down* again
21. 4. Ahab came and *l.* him *down* on his bed
Psal. 3. 5. I *l.* me *down* and slept, I awaked
Isa. 14. 8. since thou art *l.* *d.* no feller is come up
Luke 19. 22. taking up that I *l.* not *d.* and reaping
Acts 4. 35. and *l.* them *down* at the apostles' feet
7. 58. the witnesses *l.* *d.* their clothes at a young
Rom. 16. 4. who for my life *l.* *down* their necks
1 *John* 3. 16. because he *l.* *down* his life for us
LAID *hand.*
Exod. 24. 11. and on the nobles he *l.* not his *hand*
2 *Sam.* 13. 19. Tamar *l.* her *h.* on her head, crying
Esth. 8. 7. because he *l.* his *hand* on the Jews
9. 10. but they *l.* not their *h.* on the spoil, 15, 16.
Job 29. 9. the princes *l.* their *hand* on their mouth
Psal. 139. 5. thou hast *l.* thine *hand* upon me
Ezek. 39. 21. my *hand* that I have *l.* on them
Rev. 1. 17. he *l.* his right *hand* upon me, saying
LAID *hands.*
Lev. 8. 14. Aaron and his sons *l.* their *h.* on, 18. 22.
Num. 27. 23. Moses *l.* his *h.* on Joshua, *Deut.* 34. 9.
2 *Kings* 11. 16. and they *l.* *hands* on her, 2 *Chr.* 23. 15.
2 *Chr.* 29. 23. they *l.* their *hands* on the he-goats
Obad. 13. nor have *l.* *hands* on their substance
Mat. 18. 28. he *l.* *hands* and took him by the throat
19. 15. and he *l.* his *hands* on them, and departed
26. 50. they came and *l.* *h.* on Jesus, *Mark* 14. 46.
Mark 6. 5. save that he *l.* *hands* on a few sick folk
Luke 4. 40. he *l.* his *hands* on every one of them
13. 13. he *l.* his *hands* on her, she was made straight
John 7. 30. but no man *l.* *hands* on him, 44. | 8. 20.
Acts 4. 3. and they *l.* *hands* on the apostles, 5. 18.
6. 6. had prayed, they *l.* *hands* on the deacons
8. 17. then *l.* they their *hands* on them, and they
13. 3. they *l.* their *hands* on Paul and Barnabas
19. 6. and when Paul had *l.* his *hands* on them
21. 27. stirred up the people, and *l.* *hands* on Paul
28. 8. Paul *l.* *hands* on Publius' father, and healed
LAID *hold.*
Gen. 19. 16. the men *l.* *h.* on Lot's hand and his wife's
Judg. 19. 29. took a knife, and *l.* *hold* on his concubine
1 *Sam.* 15. 27. Saul *l.* *h.* on Samuel's skirt, and it rent
2 *Chron.* 7. 22. *l.* *hold* on other gods and worshipped
Job 18. † 20. they that went before *l.* *hold* on horror
Mat. 14. 3. Herod had *l.* *hold* on John, *Mark* 6. 17.
26. 55. *l.* no *h.* on me || 57. *l.* *h.* on Jes. *Mark* 14. 51.
Luke 23. 26. they *l.* *hold* on one Simon a Cyrenian
Rev. 20. 2. he *l.* *hold* on the dragon, and bound him
LAID *up.*
Gen. 39. 16. and she *l.* *up* his garment by her
41. 48. Joseph *l.* *up* food in the cities
Exod. 16. 24. they *l.* it *up* till the morning, as Moses
34. Aaron *l.* *up* the pot of manna to be kept
Num. 17. 7. Moses *l.* *up* the rods before the Lord
Deut. 32. 34. is not this *l.* *up* in store with me?
1 *Sam.* 10. 25. Samuel *l.* it *up* before the Lord
21. 12. David *l.* *up* these words in his heart
2 *Kings* 20. 17. which thy fathers *l.* *up* in store
Ezra 6. 1. where treasures were *l.* *up* in Babylon
Job 23 † 12. I have *l.* *up* the words of his mouth
Psal. 31. 19. thou hast *l.* *up* for them that fear thee
Prov. 13. 22. wealth of sinners is *l.* *up* for the just
Cant. 7. 13. fruits which I have *l.* *up* for thee
Isa. 10. 28. at Michmash he *l.* *up* his carriages
15. 7. that *l.* *up* shall they carry away to the brook
23. 18. her hire shall not be treasured or *l.* *up*
39. 6. which fathers *l.* *up* be carried to Babylon
Jer. 36. 20. they *l.* *up* the roll in the chamber
Luke 1. 66. all *l.* them *up* in their hearts, saying
12. 19. soul, thou hast much goods *l.* *up* for years
19. 20. thy pound I have kept *l.* *up* in a napkin
Col. 1. 5. for the hope which is *l.* *up* for you
2 *Tim.* 4. 8. is *l.* *up* for me a crown of righteousness
LAID *wait.*
Judg. 9. 34. and they *l.* *wait* against Shechem
16. 2. they *l.* *wait* all night for Samson in the gate
1 *Sam.* 15. 2. Amalek *l.* *wait* for him in the way
5. and Saul came and *l.* *wait* in the valley
Job 31. 9. or if I have *l.* *wait* at my neighbour's door
Lam. 4. 19. they *l.* *wait* for us in the wilderness
Acts 20. 3. when the Jews *l.* *wait* for him, 23. 30.
LAID *waste.*
Psal. 79. 7. for they *l.* *waste* his dwelling-place
Isa. 15. 1. Ar and Kir *l.* *waste* || 23. 1. Tyre, it is *l.* *waste*
23. 14. howl, ye ships, your strength is *l.* *waste*
37. 18. the kings of Assyria *l.* *waste* all the nations
Isa. 64. 11. and all pleasant things are *l.* *waste*
Jer. 4. 7. thy cities shall be *l.* *waste* without an inhabitant, *Ezek.* 6. 6. | 12. 20. | 19. 7. | 29. 12.
27. 17. wherefore should this city be *l.* *waste*?
Ezek. 26. 2. I shall be replenished now she is *l.* *waste*
Joel 1. 7. *l.* my vine *waste*, and barked my fig-tree
Amos 7. 9. the sanctuaries of Isr. shall be *l.* *waste*
Nah. 3. 7. all shall flee and say, Nineveh is *l.* *waste*
Mal. 1. 3. I *l.* his heritage *waste* for dragons
LAIDEST.
Psal. 66. 11. thou *l.* affliction on our loins
Luke 19. 21. thou takest up that thou *l.* not down
LAIN.
John 20. 12. where the body of Jesus had *l.*
LAYEST.
Num. 11. 11. thou *l.* the burden of this people on me
1 *Sam.* 28. 9. wherefore *l.* thou a snare for my life?
LAYETH.
Job 21. 19. God *l.* up his iniquity for his children
24. 12. soul crieth out, yet God *l.* not folly to them
41. 26. the sword of him that *l.* at him cannot hold
Psal. 33. 7. he *l.* up the depth in store-houses
104. 3. he *l.* the beams of his chambers in waters
Prov. 2. 7. he *l.* up wisdom for the righteous
13. 16. deals with knowledge, but a fool *l.* open folly
26. 24. dissembleth, and *l.* up deceit with him
31. 19. she *l.* her hands to the spindle, her hands
Isa. 26. 5. the lofty city he *l.* low to the ground
56. 2. blessed is the man that *l.* hold on it
57. 1. righteous perisheth, and no man *l.* it to heart
Jer. 9. 8. in heart he *l.* wait || 12. 11. *l.* it to heart
Zech. 12. 1. Lord *l.* the foundation of the earth
Luke 12. 21. so is he that *l.* up treasure for himself
15. 5. found, he *l.* it on his shoulders rejoicing
LAYING.
Num. 35. 20. or hurl at him by *l.* wait, that he die
22. have cast on him any thing without *l.* wait
Psal. 64. 5. they commune of *l.* snares privily
Mark 7. 8. for *l.* aside the commandment of God
Luke 11. 54. *l.* wait for him, and seeking to catch
Acts 8. 18. that through *l.* on of the apostles' hands
9. 24. but their *l.* wait was known of Saul
23. 16. Paul's kinsmen heard of their *l.* in wait
25. 3. send for him, *l.* wait in the way to kill him
1 *Tim.* 4. 14. with *l.* on of the hands of the presbytery
6. 19. *l.* up in store a good foundation for time to
Heb. 6. 1. not *l.* again the foundation of repentance
2. of doctrine of baptisms, and of *l.* on of hands
1 *Pet.* 2. 1. *l.* aside all malice, guile, and hypocrisies
LEAD.
Exod. 15. 10. they sank as *l.* in the mighty waters
Num. 31. 22. and the *l.* that may abide the fire
Job 19. 24. that they were graven with iron and *l.*
Jer. 6. 29. the *l.* is consumed of the fire
Ezek. 22. 18. they are *l.* in the midst of the furnace
20. as they gather *l.* so will I gather you in anger
27. 12. with iron, tin, and *l.* Tarshish traded in fairs
Zech. 5. 7. behold, there was lifted up a talent of *l.*
8. he cast the weight of *l.* on the mouth thereof
LEAD
Signifies, [1] *To guide or conduct*, Psal. 31. 3. | 139. 10. [2] *To live*, 1 Tim. 2. 2. [3] *To govern or direct*, Rom. 8. 14. [4] *To seduce*, 2 Tim. 3. 6. [5] *To walk*, Prov. 8. † 20.
Gen. 33. 14. I will *l.* on softly as the cattle
Exod. 13. 21. a pillar of cloud to *l.* them the way
32. 34. now go, *l.* the people to the place
Num. 27. 17. which may *l.* them out and bring
Deut. 4. 27. whither the Lord shall *l.* you, 28. 37.
20. 9. they shall make captains to *l.* the people
32. 12. so the Lord alone did *l.* him, there was
Judg. 5. 12. arise, Barak, *l.* thy captivity captive
1 *Sam.* 30. 22. they may *l.* them away and depart
2 *Chron.* 30. 9. find compassion before them that *l.*
Neh. 9. 19. the pillar of cloud to *l.* them in the way
Psal. 5. 8. *l.* me, O Lord, in thy righteousness
25. 5. *l.* me in thy truth || 27. 11. *l.* in a plain path
31. 3. for thy name's sake *l.* me and guide me
43. 3. send thy light and truth, let them *l.* me
60. 9. who will *l.* me into Edom? 108. 10.
61. 2. *l.* me to the rock that is higher than I
125. 5. *l.* them forth with the workers of iniquity
139. 10. even there shall thine hand *l.* me
24. and *l.* me in the way everlasting
143. 10. *l.* me into the land of uprightness
Prov. 6. 22. when thou goest, it shall *l.* thee
8. 20. I *l.* in the way of righteousness
Cant. 8. 2. I would *l.* thee to my mother's house
Isa. 3. 12. they that *l.* thee cause thee to err
11. 6. and a little child shall *l.* them
20. 4. the king of Assyria *l.* Egyptians prisoners
40. 11. he shall gently *l.* those that are with young
42. 16. I will *l.* them in paths not known
49. 10. that hath mercy on them, shall *l.* them
57. 18. I will *l.* him, and restore comforts
63. 14. so didst thou *l.* thy people to make
Jer. 31. 9. with supplications will I *l.* them
32. 5. and he shall *l.* Zedekiah to Babylon
Nah. 2. 7. her maids *l.* her, as with voice of doves
Mat. 6. 13. *l.* us not into temptation, *Luke* 11. 4.
15. 14. if the blind *l.* the blind, *Luke* 6. 39.
Mark 13. 11. when they shall *l.* you and deliver up
14. 44. take him and *l.* him away safely
Luke 13. 15. loose his ox and *l.* him to watering
Acts 13. 11. he went about seeking some to *l.* him
1 *Cor.* 9. 5. have we not power to *l.* about a sister?
1 *Tim.* 2. 2. we may *l.* a quiet life in godliness
2 *Tim.* 3. 6. *l.* captive silly women laden with sins
Heb. 8. 9. to *l.* them out of the land of Egypt
Rev. 7. 17. the Lamb shall feed and *l.* them
LEADER.
1 *Chr.* 12. 27. Jehoiada was *l.* of the Aaronites
13. 1. David consulted with captains and every *l.*
Isa. 55. 4. I have given him a *l.* to the people
LEADERS.
2 *Chron.* 32. 21. Lord sent an angel which cut off *l.*
Isa. 9. 16. the *l.* of this people cause them to err
14. † 9. it stirreth up all the *l.* of the earth
Ezek. 4. † 2. set chief *l.* against it round about
Mat. 15. 14. they be blind *l.* of the blind
LEADEST.
Psal. 80. 1. thou that *l.* Joseph like a flock

LEADETH.
1 *Sam.* 13. 17. turned to the way that *l.* to Ophrah
Job 12. 17. he *l.* counsellors away spoiled
19. he *l.* princes away spoiled, and overthroweth
† 23. he enlargeth the nations and *l.* in
Psal. 23. 2. he *l.* me beside the still waters
3. he *l.* me in the paths of righteousness
Prov. 16. 29. *l.* him into the way that is not good
Isa. 48. 17. I am the Lord thy God which *l.* thee
Mat. 7. 13. wide is the way that *l.* to destruction
14. narrow is the way that *l.* to life, few find it
Mark 9. 2. Jesus *l.* them into an high mountain
John 10. 3. he calleth his sheep and *l.* them
Acts 12. 10. the iron gate that *l.* into the city
Rom. 2. 4. the goodness of God *l.* to repentance
Rev. 13. 10. he that *l.* shall go into captivity

LEAF.
Signifies, [1] *The product or clothing of trees and plants,* Gen. 8. 11. [2] *An evidence of grace,* Psal. 1. 3. [3] *A form of godliness, or a bare profession of Christianity, without the fruit of righteousness,* Mat. 21. 19. [4] *The least cause of fear,* Lev. 26. 36.
The leaves were for the healing of the nations, *Rev.* 22. 2. *Grace from* Christ, the tree of life, *heals his people whom he chooses out of all nations, and gives them perfect freedom from all spiritual diseases.*
Gen. 8. 11. and lo, in her mouth was an olive *l.*
Lev. 26. 36. sound of a shaken *l.* shall chase them
Job 13. 25. wilt thou break a *l.* driven to and fro?
Psal. 1. 3. his *l.* also shall not wither, shall prosper
Isa. 1. 30. shall be as an oak, whose *l.* fadeth
34. 4. their host fall as a *l.* ‖ 64. 6. we fade as a *l.*
Jer. 8. 13. there shall be no grapes, the *l.* shall fade
17. 8. but her *l.* shall be green, and not be careful
Ezek. 47. 12. *l.* shall not fade, the *l.* for medicine

LEAVES.
Gen. 3. 7. they sewed fig *l.* and made aprons
Isa. 6. 13. as an oak, when they cast their *l.*
Jer. 36. 23. when Jehudi read three or four *l.*
Ezek. 17. 9. it shall wither in all the *l.* of her spring
Dan. 4. 12. *l.* thereof fair, 21. ‖ 14. shake off his *l.*
Mat. 21. 19. nothing thereon but *l.* *Mark* 11. 13.
24. 32. his branch putteth forth *l.* *Mark* 13. 28.
Rev. 22. 2. the *l.* were for the healing of the nations

LEAVES for *doors.*
1 *Kings* 6. † 32. the *l.* of the doors were of olive trees
34. the two *l.* of the one door were folding
Ezek. 41. 24. doors had two *l.* apiece, two *l.* for one

LEAGUE.
Josh. 9. 6. make therefore a *l.* with us, 11.
15. Joshua made a *l.* with the Gibeonites, 16.
Judg. 2. 2. make no *l.* with the inhabitants of land
1 *Sam.* 22. 8. my son hath made a *l.* with David
2 *Sam.* 5. 3. king David made a *l.* with them
1 *Kings* 5. 12. Hiram and Solomon made a *l.*
15. 19. there is a *l.* between me and thee
2 *Chron.* 16. 3. go break thy *l.* with Baasha king of
Job 5. 23. shalt be in *l.* with the stones of the field
Ezek. 30. 5. men of the land that is in *l.* shall fall
Dan. 11. 23. after the *l.* he shall work deceitfully

LEAN.
Gen. 41. 3. kine came out of the river *l.*-fleshed, 19.
4. the *l.*-fleshed eat up the seven fat kine, 20.
Num. 13. 20. what the land is, whether fat or *l.*
2 *Sam.* 13. 4. why art thou being the king's son *l.*
Isa. 17. 4. the fatness of his flesh shall wax *l.*
Ezek. 34. 20. I will judge between fat cattle and *l.*
Zeph. 2. † 11. Lord make *l.* the gods of the earth

LEANNESS.
Job 16. 8. my *l.* rising up in me, beareth witness
Ps. 106. 15. gave request, but sent *l.* into their soul
Isa. 10. 16. Lord shall send among his fat ones *l.*
24. 16. but I said, my *l.* my *l.* woe unto me
Mic. 6. † 10. the measure of *l.* is abominable

LEAN.
Signifies, [1] *To incline or rest against,* Judg. 16. 26. [2] *To trust or depend upon,* 2 Kings 18. 21. [3] *Spiritually by faith and love to cleave to and rely upon,* Cant. 8. 5.
Judg. 16. 26. that I may *l.* on the pillars
2 *Kings* 18. 21. on which if a man *l.* *Isa.* 36. 6.
Job 8. 15. shall *l.* on his house, but it shall not stand
Prov. 3. 5. *l.* not to thine own understanding
Mic. 3. 11. yet will they *l.* on the Lord, and say

LEANED.
Judg. 16. † 29. the middle pillars on which he *l.*
2 *Sam.* 1. 6. behold, Saul *l.* upon his spear
2 *Kings* 7. 2. then a lord, on whose hand the king *l.*
2 *Chron.* 32. † 8. people *l.* on the words of Hezekiah
Ezek. 29. 7. when they *l.* on thee, thou brakest
Amos 5. 19. *l.* his hand on wall, a serpent bit him
John 21. 20. who also *l.* on his breast at supper

LEANETH.
Num. 21. † 15. brooks *l.* on the border of Moab
2 *Sam.* 3. 29. not fail one that *l.* on a staff
2 *Kings* 5. 18. *l.* on my hand in the house of Rimm.

LEANING.
Cant. 8. 5. that cometh up *l.* on her beloved
John 13. 23. now there was *l.* on Jesus' bosom
Heb. 11. 21. Jacob worshipped, *l.* on top of his staff

LEAP
Signifies, [1] *To skip, or jump to and fro,* Acts 3. 8. ‖ 14. 10. [2] *To come violently and suddenly upon,* Acts 19. 16. [3] *To rejoice and be glad,* Isa. 35. 6.
Gen. 31. 12. all the rams which *l.* on the cattle
Lev. 11. 21. have legs to *l.* withal upon the earth
Deut. 33. 22. and of Dan, he shall *l.* from Bashan
Job 41. 19. burning lamps, and sparks of fire *l.* out
Psal. 68. 16. why *l.* ye, ye high hills, this is the hill
Isa. 35. 6. then shall the lame man *l.* as an hart
Joel 2. 5. like the noise of chariots shall they *l.*
Zeph. 1. 9. shall punish those that *l.* on the threshold
Luke 6. 23. rejoice ye in that day, and *l.* for joy

LEAPED.
Gen. 31. 10. the rams which *l.* upon the cattle
2 *Sam.* 22. 30. by my God, I *l.* over a wall, *Ps.* 18. 29.
1 *Kings* 18. 26. they *l.* upon the altar which was
Luke 1. 41. the babe *l.* in her womb for joy, 44.
Acts 14. 10. stand upright, and he *l.* and walked
19. 16. he in whom evil spirit was, *l.* on them

LEAPING.
2 *Sam.* 6. 16. Michal saw David *l.* and dancing
Cant. 2. 8. behold he cometh *l.* on the mountains
Acts 3. 8. and he *l.* up, stood and walked, entered

LEARN
Signifies, [1] *To receive instruction,* 1 Cor. 14. 31. 1 Tim. 2. 11. [2] *To imitate,* Mat. 11. 29. [3] *To take heed,* 1 Tim. 1. 20. [4] *To know, or hear one's opinion, or sentiment concerning any thing,* Gal. 3. 2. [5] *To practise,* Psal. 106. 35.
No man could learn that song, *Rev.* 14. 3. *None of the antichristian party could join in this pure gospel-worship; they could not learn to ascribe power, riches, wisdom, honour, glory, and blessing to Jesus Christ alone; but gave Christ's honour and glory to the Virgin Mary, angels, saints, &c.*
Deut. 4. 10. that they may *l.* to fear me, 14. 23.
5. 1. that ye may *l.* them, and keep and do them
17. 19. he shall read therein, that he may *l.* to fear
18. 9. thou shalt not *l.* to do after the abominations
31. 12. they may hear, and *l.* and fear the Lord
13. that their children may *l.* to fear the Lord
Psal. 119. 71. that I might *l.* thy statutes, 73.
Prov. 22. 25. lest thou *l.* his ways and get a snare
Isa. 1. 17. *l.* to do well, seek judgment, relieve
2. 4. neither shall they *l.* war any more, *Mic.* 4. 3.
26. 9. the inhabitants of world shall *l.* righteousness
10. yet will not the wicked *l.* righteousness
29. 24. they that murmured shall *l.* doctrine
Jer. 10. 2. *l.* not the way of the heathen
12. 16. if they will diligently *l.* ways of my people
Mat. 9. 13. but go and *l.* what that meaneth
11. 29. *l.* of me, for I am meek and lowly
24. 32. *l.* a parable of the fig-tree. *Mark* 13. 28.
1 *Cor.* 4. 6. that ye might *l.* in us not to think
14. 31. may all prophesy one by one, that all may *l.*
35. if they will *l.* any thing, let them ask
Gal. 3. 2. this would I *l.* of you, received ye Spirit
1 *Tim.* 1. 20. that they may *l.* not to blaspheme
2. 11. let the woman *l.* in silence with all subjection
5. 4. let them *l.* first to shew piety at home
13. and withal they *l.* to be idle, wandering about
Tit. 3. 14. let ours *l.* to maintain good works
Rev. 14. 3. no man could *l.* that song but 144,000

LEARNED.
Gen. 30. 27. tarry, for I have *l.* by experience
Ps. 106. 35. among the heathen, and *l.* their works
119. 7. when I shall have *l.* thy righteous judgments
Prov. 30. 3. I neither *l.* wisdom, nor have knowledge
Isa. 29. 11. which men deliver to one that is *l.*
12. to him that is not *l.* he saith, I am not *l.*
50. 4. the Lord God hath given me the tongue of the *l.* he wakeneth mine ear to hear as the *l.*
Ezek. 19. 3. it *l.* to catch the prey, it devoured, 6.
John 6. 45. every man that hath *l.* of the Father
7. 15. knoweth this man letters, having never *l.*
Acts 7. 22. Moses was *l.* in all the wisdom of Egypt
Rom. 16. 17. contrary to the doctrine ye have *l.*
Eph. 4. 20. but ye have not so *l.* Christ
Phil. 4. 9. those things ye have *l.* and heard, do
11. I have *l.* in every state to be content
Col. 1. 7. as ye *l.* of Epaphras our fellow-servant
2 *Tim.* 3. 14. but continue thou in the things thou hast *l.* knowing of whom thou hast *l.* them
Heb. 5. 8. though he were a son, yet *l.* he obedience

LEARNING.
Prov. 1. 5. a wise man will hear and increase *l.*
9. 9. teach a just man, and he will increase in *l.*
16. 21. the sweetness of the lips increaseth *l.*
23. the heart of the wise addeth *l.* to his lips
Dan. 1. 4. whom they might teach *l.* of the Chaldeans
17. God gave them skill in all *l.* and wisdom
Acts 26. 24. Festus said, much *l.* doth make thee mad
Rom. 15. 4. for things were written for our *l.*
2 *Tim.* 3. 7. ever *l.* and never able to come to truth

LEASING.
Psal. 4. 2. how long will ye seek after *l.*?
5. 6. thou shalt destroy them that speak *l.*

LEAST
Signifies, [1] *The smallest quantity,* Num. 11. 32. [2] *Most humble and lowly,* Luke 9. 48. [3] *The meanest person, or one of the least judgment, skill, and experience,* Judg. 6. 15.
Called least in the kingdom of heaven, *Mat.* 5. 19. *Shall be of little or no value and esteem in the church of God, and without true repentance, shall never come into the kingdom of glory.*
Gen. 32. 10. not worthy of the *l.* of the mercies
Num. 11. 32. that gathered *l.* gathered ten homers
Judg. 6. 15. I am the *l.* in my father's house
1 *Sam.* 9. 21. my family, the *l.* of all families
2 *Kings* 18. 24. one captain of *l.* of master's servants
Jer. 49. 20. *l.* of flock shall draw them, 50. 45.
Amos 9. 9. not the *l.* grain fall upon the earth
Mat. 2. 6. art not the *l.* among the princes of Judah
5. 19. shall break one of these *l.* commandments, shall be called *l.* in the kingdom of heaven
11. 11. John Baptist, he that is *l.* in the kingdom of heaven, is greater than he, *Luke* 7. 28.
13. 32. which indeed is the *l.* of all seeds
25. 40. as ye have done it to the *l.* of these, 45.
Luke 9. 48. he that is *l.* among you, the same shall
12. 26. if ye be not able to do that which is *l.*
16. 10. he that is faithful in the *l.* unjust in *l.*
1 *Cor.* 6. 4. set them to judge who are *l.* esteemed
15. 9. for I am the *l.* of the apostles, not meet
Eph. 3. 8. who am less than the *l.* of all saints

See GREATEST.

At the LEAST.
Gen. 24. 55. damsel abide with us, *at the l.* ten days
Judg. 3. 2. *at the l.* such as before knew nothing
1 *Sam.* 21. 4. if kept themselves *at l.* from women
Luke 19. 42. hadst known *at l.* in this thy day
Acts 5. 15. that *at the l.* the shadow of Peter passing

LEATHER.
2 *Kings* 1. 8. an hairy man, girt with a girdle of *l.*

LEATHERN.
Mat. 3. 4. John had a *l.* girdle about his loins

LEAVE
Signifies, [1] *Licence or permission,* Num. 22. 13. Mark 5. 13. [2] *To depart from,* John 16. 28. [3] *To bid farewell to,* Acts 18. 18. [4] *Not to dwell or live with,* Mat. 19. 5. [5] *To lay down,* Mat. 5. 24.

LEAVE, *Substantive.*
Num. 22. 13. for the Lord refuseth to give me *l.* to
1 *Sam.* 20. 6. David earnestly asked *l.* of me, 28.
Neh. 13. 6. after certain days obtain. I *l.* of the king
Mark 5. 13. and forthwith Jesus gave them *l.*
John 19. 38. Pilate gave him *l.* to take away body
Acts 18. 18. Paul took his *l.* of the brethren
21. 6. when we had taken our *l.* one of another
2 *Cor.* 2. 13. taking my *l.* I went to Macedonia

LEAVE.
Gen. 2. 24. shall a man *l.* father and mot. and cleave to his wife, *Mat.* 19. 5. *Mark* 10. 7. *Eph.* 5. 31.
33. 15. let me *l.* with thee some of the folk
42. 33. *l.* one of your brethren here with me
44. 22. the lad cannot *l.* his father, if he *l.* him
Exod. 16. 19. let no man *l.* manna till the morning
23. † 5. cease to *l.* thy business, thou shalt *l.* it
11. what they *l.* the beasts of the field shall eat
Lev. 7. 15. not *l.* any of the peace offering, 22. 30.
16. 23. shall put off garments and *l.* them there
19. 10. thou shalt *l.* them for the poor, 23. 22.
Num. 9. 12. *l.* none of the passover till morning
10. 31. and he said, *l.* us not, I pray thee
32. 15. will yet again *l.* them in the wilderness
Deut. 28. 51. shall not *l.* thee either corn, wine, or oil
54. the remnant of children which he shall *l.*
Josh. 4. 3. and *l.* them in the lodging place
Judg. 9. 9. the olive said, should I *l.* my fatness
13. vine said, should I *l.* my wine, which cheereth
Ruth 1. 16. Ruth said, entreat me not to *l.* thee
1 *Sam.* 9. 5. lest my father *l.* caring for the asses
14. 36. Saul said, let us not *l.* a man of them
25. 22. if I *l.* of all that pertain to him
2 *Sam.* 14. 7. shall not *l.* to my husband a name
1 *Kings* 8. 57. let him not *l.* us nor forsake us
2 *Kings* 4. 43. they shall eat and shall *l.* thereof
13. 7. nor did he *l.* of the people but fifty horsemen
1 *Chron.* 28. 8. may possess this good land, and *l.* it
Ezra 9. 8. grace from L. to *l.* us a remnant to escape
12. *l.* it for an inheritance to your children for ever
Neh. 4. † 2. the Jews, will they *l.* to themselves
5. 10. I pray you let us *l.* off this usury
6. 3. why should the work cease whilst I *l.* it?
10. 31. that we would *l.* the seventh year
Job 39. 11. or wilt thou *l.* thy labour to him?
Ps. 16. 10. thou wilt not *l.* my soul in hell, *Acts* 2. 27.
17. 14. they *l.* their substance to their babes
27. 9. thou hast been my help, *l.* me not, 119. 121.
49. 10. they die and *l.* their wealth to others
141. 8. O God, my trust, *l.* not my soul destitute
Prov. 2. 13. who *l.* the paths of uprightness
17. 14. *l.* off contention, before it be meddled with
Eccl. 2. 18. because I should *l.* it to the man after me
21. yet shall he *l.* it for his portion
10. 4. if ruler rise up against thee, *l.* not thy place
Isa. 10. 3. and where will ye *l.* your glory?
65. 15. and ye shall *l.* your name for a curse
Jer. 9. 2. I might *l.* my people, and go from them
14. 9. O Lord, we are called by thy name, *l.* us not
17. 11. riches, he shall *l.* them in midst of his days
18. 14. will a man *l.* the snow of Lebanon
44. 7. child and suckling, to *l.* you none to remain
48. 28. *l.* the cities, and dwell in the rock
49. 9. would they not *l.* some gleaning-grapes?
11. *l.* thy fatherless children, I will preserve them
Ezek. 16. 39. and *l.* thee naked and bare, 23. 29.
39. 2. will turn thee, and *l.* but a sixth part of thee
Dan. 4. 15. *l.* the stump of his root, 23, 26.
Hos. 12. 14. therefore shall he *l.* his blood upon him
Joel 2. 14. will return, and *l.* a blessing behind him
Amos 5. 3. shall *l.* an hundred, shall *l.* ten to Israel
7. ye, who *l.* off righteousness in the earth
Obad. 5. grape gatherers, would they not *l.* grapes?
Mal. 4. 1. that it shall *l.* them neither root nor branch
Mat. 5. 24. *l.* there thy gift before the altar
18. 12. doth he not *l.* the ninety and nine, *Luke* 15. 4.
23. 23. to have done, and not to *l.* other undone
Mark 12. 19. and *l.* his wife, and *l.* no children
Luke 19. 44. they shall not *l.* in thee one stone
John 14. 27. my peace I *l.* with you, peace I give
16. 28. I *l.* the world and go to the Father
32. ye shall *l.* me alone, yet I am not alone, becau.
Acts 6. 2. it is not reason we should *l.* the word
1 *Cor.* 7. 13. to dwell with him, let her not *l.* him
Heb. 13. 5. I will never *l.* thee nor forsake thee
Rev. 11. 2. the court *l.* out, and measure it not

I will, or *will* I LEAVE.
1 *Kings* 19. † 18. yet *I will l.* seven thousand in Isr.
Job 9. 27. if I say, *I will l.* off my heaviness
10. 1. *I will l.* my complaint on myself, I will speak
Ezek. 6. 8. yet *I w. l.* a rem. ‖ 12. 16. but *I w. l.* a few
22. 20. and *I will l.* you there and melt you
29. 5. *I will l.* thee thrown into the wilderness
32. 4. then *I will l.* thee upon the land and cast
Zeph. 3. 12. *I will l.* in midst of thee a poor people

I will not LEAVE.
Gen. 28. 15. *I will not l.* thee until I have done that
2 *Kings* 2. 2. as the L. liveth, *I w. not l.* thee, 4. 30.
4. he said, as thy soul liveth, *I will not l.* thee, 6.
Ps. 37. 33. L. *I w. n. l.* him in his hand, nor condemn
Jer. 30. 11. *I w. n. l.* thee together unpunished, 46. 28.
John 14. 18. *I w. n. l.* you comfortless, I will come

LEAVED.
Isa. 45. 1. to open before him the two *l.* gates

LEAVETH.
Job 39. 14. the ostrich *l.* her eggs in the earth
Prov. 13. 22. a good man *l.* an inheritance to his
28. 3. is like a sweeping rain which *l.* no food
Zech. 11. 17. woe to the idol shepherd, that *l.* the flock
Mat. 4. 11. then the devil *l.* him, and behold
John 10. 12. the hireling *l.* the sheep and fleeth

LEAVEN
Signifies, *A piece of dough salted and soured, to ferment and relish a mass of dough for bread,* Hos. 7. 4. 1 Cor. 5. 6. To which are compared, [1] *The doctrine of the gospel, which was to be successful in converting many sinners,* Mat. 13. 33. [2] *The erroneous doctrines, and vicious*

practices of the Pharisees and Sadducees; the corrupt glosses of the law, the doctrine of traditions, invented and promoted by the former, and that poisonous doctrine of the mortality of the soul, strenuously maintained by the latter; which, like leaven, are not only of a sour, but also of a contagious and infectious nature, and suited to men of atheistical hearts and lives, Mat. 16. 6, 12. [3] *Notorious scandalous sinners, who infect and cast a blot upon a church,* 1 Cor. 5. 6.
Exod. 12. 15. ye shall put away *l.* seven days, 19.
13. 7. neither shall be *l.* seen in all thy quarters
34. 25. not offer the blood of my sacrifice with *l.*
Lev. 2. 11. no meat offering shall be made with *l.*
6. 17. it shall not be baken with *l.* I have given
10. 12. take and eat the meat-offering without *l.*
23. 17. be of fine flour, they shall be baken with *l.*
Amos 4. 5. offer a sacrifice of thanksgiving with *l.*
Mat. 13. 33. kingdom of heaven is like *l. Luke* 13. 21.
16. 6. Jesus said, beware of the *l.* of the Pharisees, and of the Sadducees, 11. *Mark* 8. 15. *Luke* 12. 1.
12. bade them not beware of the *l.* of bread
1 *Cor.* 5. 6. little *l.* leaveneth the whole lump, *Gal.* 5. 9.
7. purge out therefore the old *l.* that ye may be
8. let us keep the feast, not with old *l.* or of malice

LEAVENED.

Exod. 12. 15. for whosoever eateth *l.* bread, 19.
20. ye shall eat nothing *l.* in all your habitations
34. people took their dough before it was *l.* 39.
13. 3. there shall no *l.* bread be eaten, 7.
Hos. 7. 4. after he hath kneaded the dough till it be *l.*
Mat. 13. 33. till the whole was *l. Luke* 13. 21.
See Bread.

LEAVENETH.

1 *Cor.* 5. 6. a little leaven *l.* the whole lump, *Gal.* 5. 9.

LEAVING.

Mat. 4. 13. Jesus *l.* Nazareth, dwelt in Capernaum
Luke 10. 30. thieves departed, *l.* him half dead
Rom. 1. 27. men *l.* the natural use of the woman
Heb. 6. 1. *l.* the principles of the doctrine of Christ
1 *Pet.* 2. 21. Christ suffered for us, *l.* us an example

LED.

Gen. 14. † 14. he *l.* forth his trained servants
24. 27. I being in the way, the Lord *l.* me
48. blessed the Lord, who had *l.* me in right way
47. † 17. he *l.* them with bread for that year
Exod. 3. 1. Moses *l.* the flock to back side of desert
13. 17. God *l.* them not thro' the land of Philistines
18. but God *l.* them about thro' the wilderness
15. 13. thou in mercy hast *l.* forth the people
Deut. 8. 2. the way which the L. *l.* thee forty years
15. who *l.* thee through that great wilderness
29. 5. I have *l.* you forty years in the wilderness
32. 10. he *l.* him about, he instructed him
Josh. 24. 3. I *l.* him through all the land of Canaan
1 *Kings* 8. 48. enemies, which *l.* them away captive
2 *Kings* 6. 19. but Elisha *l.* them to Samaria
1 *Chr.* 20. 1. Joab *l.* forth the power of the army
2 *Chron.* 25. 11. and Amaziah *l.* forth his people
Psal. 78. 14. in the day he *l.* them with a cloud
53. he *l.* them on safely, so that they feared not
106. 9. so he *l.* them thro' the depths as thro' a wilderness, 136. 16. *Isa.* 63. 13.
107. 7. he *l.* them forth by the right way
Prov. 4. 11. I have *l.* thee in right paths
Isa. 9. 16. they that are *l.* of them are destroyed
48. 21. they thirsted not when they *l.* them thro'
55. 12. for ye shall be *l.* forth with peace
63. 12. that *l.* them by the right hand of Moses
Jer. 2. 6. where is the Ld. that *l.* us thro' wilderness
17. hath forsaken God, when he *l.* thee by the way
22. 12. shall die in the place whither they have *l.* him
23. 8. the Lord liveth which *l.* the house of Israel
Lam. 3. 2. he hath *l.* me into darkness, not light
Ezek. 17. 12. and *l.* them with him to Babylon
39. 28. who caused them to be *l.* into captivity
47. 2. *l.* me about to the outer gate eastward
Amos 2. 10. also I *l.* you 40 years thro' the wildern.
7. 11. Israel shall surely be *l.* captive out of land
Nah. 2. 7. and Huzzah shall be *l.* away captive
Mat. 4. 1. then was Jesus *l.* of the Spirit, *Luke* 4. 1.
26. 57. they *l.* him to Caiaphas the high-priest, *Mark* 14. 53. *Luke* 22. 54. *John* 18. 13.
27. 2. they *l.* him to Pont. Pilate the governor, 31. *Mark* 15. 16, 20. *Luke* 22. 54. *John* 18. 13.
Mark 8. 23. he took the blind man and *l.* him out
Luke 4. 29. they *l.* Jesus to the brow of the hill
21. 24. they shall be *l.* away captive into all nations
22. 66. and *l.* him into their council, saying
23. 1. the whole multitude *l.* him to Pilate
32. two other malefactors were *l.* with him
24. 50. he *l.* them out as far as Bethany
John 18. 28. they *l.* Jesus unto the hall of judgment
Acts 8. 32. he was *l.* as a sheep to the slaughter
9. 8. they *l.* Saul by the hand to Damascus, 22. 11.
21. 37. as Paul was to be *l.* into the castle
Rom. 8. 14. as many as are *l.* by the Spirit of God
1 *Cor.* 12. 2. carried away to idols, even as ye were *l.*
Gal. 5. 18. but if ye be *l.* by the Spirit, ye are
2 *Tim.* 3. 6. silly women, *l.* away with divers lusts
2 *Pet.* 3. 17. beware, lest ye also being *l.* away with the error of the wicked, fall from stedfastness

LEDDEST.

2 *Sam.* 5. 2. wast he that *l.* out Israel, 1 *Chr.* 11. 2.
Neh. 9. 12. *l.* them in the day by a cloudy pillar
Psal. 77. 20. thou *l.* thy people like a flock
Acts 21. 38. and *l.* into the wilderness four thousand men that were murderers

LEDGES.

1 *Kings* 7. 28. the borders were between the *l.*
35. the *l.* and borders thereof were of the same
36. on the plates of the *l.* he graved cherubims

LEEKS.

Num. 11. 5. we remember the *l.* and the onions

LEES.

Isa. 25. 6. a feast of wine on the *l.* well refined
Jer. 48. 11. and Moab hath settled on his *l.*
Zeph. 1. 12. I will punish men settled on their *l.*

LEFT.

Gen. 18. 33. he had *l.* communing with Abraham
24. 27. who hath not *l.* destitute my master
29. 35. his name Judah, and *l.* bearing, 30. 9.
Gen. 32. 8. then the other company which is *l.*
39. 6. he *l.* all that he had in Joseph's hand
12. he *l.* his garment in her hand, 13, 15, 18.
41. 49. Joseph gathered corn till he *l.* numbering
44. 12. at the eldest, and *l.* at the youngest
47. 18. not enough *l.* but our bodies and lands
50. 8. their little ones *l.* they in Goshen
Exod. 2. 20. why is it that ye have *l.* the man?
9. 21. *l.* his servants and his cattle in the field
10. 12. eat every herb, all that the hail *l.* 15.
26. there shall not an hoof be *l.* behind
16. 20. but some of them *l.* of it till morning
34. 25. nor sacrifice of passover be *l.* till morning
Lev. 2. 10. that which is *l.* of the meat offering
10. 12. and to Ithamar, his sons that were *l.*
26. 39. they that are *l.* of you shall pine away
43. the land also shall be *l.* of them and enjoy
Num. 26. 65. there was not *l.* a man of them, *Josh.* 8. 17. *Judg.* 4. 16. *Hos.* 9. 12.
Deut. 2. 34. we utterly destroyed, we *l.* none to remain, *Josh.* 10. 33, 37, 39, 40. | 11. 8, 11, 14.
4. 27. ye shall be *l.* few in number among the heathen, 28. 62. *Isa.* 24. 6. *Jer.* 42. 2.
7. 20. till they that are *l.* be destroyed
28. 55. he hath nothing *l.* him in the siege
32. 36. power gone, and there is none shut up or *l.*
Josh. 6. 23. and *l.* them without the camp of Israel
8. 17. they *l.* the city open, and pursued Israel
11. 15. he *l.* nothing undone of all commanded
22. there was none of the Anakims *l.* in the land
22. 3. ye have not *l.* your brethren to this day
Judg. 2. 21. of nations which Joshua *l.* when he died
23. therefore the Lord *l.* those nations, 3. 1.
6. 4. *l.* no sustenance for Israel, neither sheep
9. 5. yet Jotham the youngest son was *l.*
Ruth 1. 3. and she was *l.* and her two sons, 5.
18. was minded to go, then she *l.* speaking to her
2. 11. how thou hast *l.* thy father and mother
14. Ruth did eat and was sufficed, and *l.*
4. 14. Lord not *l.* thee this day without kinsman
1 *Sam.* 2. 36. every one that is *l.* in thy house
5. 4. only the stump of Dagon was *l.* to him
9. 24. that which is *l.* set it before thee and eat
10. 2. thy father hath *l.* the care of the asses
11. 11. so that two of them were not *l.* together
17. 20. David rose up and *l.* the sheep with a keeper
22. David *l.* his carriage in the hand of a keeper
25. 34. not been *l.* any that pisseth against the wall
27. 9. David *l.* neither man nor woman alive
2 *Sam.* 5. 21. and there they *l.* their images
9. 1. is there yet any *l.* of the house of Saul?
13. 30. the king's sons, there is not one of them *l.*
14. 7. so they shall quench my coal which is *l.*
15. 16. the king *l.* ten concubines, 16. 21.
17. 12. there shall not be *l.* so much as one
1 *Kings* 9. 21. their children that were *l.* 2 *Chr.* 8. 8.
14. 10. cut off him that is shut up and *l.* 2 *Kings* 9. 8.
15. 29. he *l.* not Jeroboam any that breathed
16. 11. he *l.* Baasha not one that pisseth against
17. 17. sickness that there was no breath *l.* in him
19. 3. and *l.* his servant there || 10. I only am *l.*
18. yet I have *l.* me 7000 || 20. he *l.* oxen and ran
2 *Kings* 4. 44. and they did eat and *l.* thereof
7. 7. they arose and *l.* tents || 13. all that are *l.*
8. 6. since the day she *l.* the land even until now
10. 11. Jehu slew all, till he *l.* him none remaining
21. so that there was not a man *l.* that came not
14. 26. for there was not any *l.* nor any helper
17. 16. they *l.* the commandments of the Lord
19. 4. this prayer for remnant that are *l. Isa.* 37. 4.
20. 17. nothing shall be *l.* saith the Lord
25. 12. *l.* of poor of the land, *Jer.* 39. 10. | 52. 16.
1 *Chron.* 13. 2. send to our brethren that are *l.*
2 *Chron.* 11. 14. for the Levites *l.* their suburbs
12. 5. I have also *l.* you in the hand of Shishak
21. 17. so that there was never a son *l.* him
24. 18. and they *l.* the house of the Lord God
25. for they *l.* Joash in great diseases
31. 10. we had enough to eat, and have *l.* plenty
32. 31. God *l.* him to try him, that he might know
34. 21. go, inquire for them that are *l.* in Israel
Neh. 1. 2. I asked concerning the Jews which had *l.*
3. the remnant that are *l.* are in great affliction
6. 1. the wall that there was no breach *l.* therein
Job 20. 21. there shall none of his meat be *l.*
26. it shall go ill with him that is *l.* in his tabern.
Psal. 106. 11. there was not one of them *l.*
Prov. 29. 15. a child *l.* to himself bringeth to shame
Isa. 1. 8. Zion is *l.* as a cottage in a vineyard
9. except Lord had *l.* us a remnant, *Rom.* 9. 29.
4. 3. he that is *l.* in Zion shall be called holy
7. 22. butter and honey shall every one eat that is *l.*
10. 14. as one gathereth eggs that are *l.*
11. 16. a high-way for the remnant that shall be *l.*
17. 6. yet gleaning-grapes shall be *l.* in it
24. 12. in the city is *l.* desolation, and the gate
30. 17. till ye be *l.* as a beacon on a mountain
39. 6. nothing shall be *l.* saith the Lord
Jer. 12. 7. I *l.* my heritage || 31. 2. *l.* of the sword
49. 25. how is the city of praise not *l.* the city of joy
50. 26. destroy her, let nothing of her be *l.*
Ezek. 14. 22. behold, therein shall be *l.* a remnant
23. 8. nor *l.* her whoredoms brought from Egypt
31. 12. strangers have cut him off and have *l.* him
Dan. 2. 44. the kingd. shall not be *l.* to other people
Joel 1. 4. what the palmer-worm *l.* the locust hath *l.*
Hag. 2. 3. who is *l.* that saw this house in her glory?
Zech. 13. 8. the third part shall be *l.* therein
Mat. 4. 20. *l.* their nets || 22. they *l.* their ships
8. 15. he touched her, and fever *l.* her, *Mark* 1. 31.
15. 37. took up of the meat that was *l. Mark* 8. 8.
22. 25. he *l.* his wife to his brother, *Mark* 12. 20.
23. 38. your house is *l.* unto you desolate
24. 2. there shall not be *l.* one stone upon another, *Mark* 13. 2. *Luke* 21. 6.
40. one taken, other *l.* 41. *Luke* 17. 34, 35, 36.
26. 44. Jesus *l.* them, and prayed the third time
Mark 10. 28. we have *l.* all and followed thee
29. no man that hath *l.* house, *Luke* 18. 28, 29.
12. 22. and the seven had her, and *l.* no seed
Luke 5. 28. he *l.* all, rose up, and followed him
10. 40. that my sister hath *l.* me to serve alone
John 4. 28. the woman then *l.* her water-pot
52. at the seventh hour the fever *l.* him
Acts 2. 31. of Christ, that his soul was not *l.* in hell
14. 17. he *l.* not himself without witness
21. 32. when saw captain, they *l.* beating of Paul
24. 27. and Felix *l.* Paul bound, 25. 14.
1 *Thess.* 3. 1. we thought good to be *l.* at Athens alone
2 *Tim.* 4. 13. the cloak that I *l.* at Troas bring
20. Trophimus have I *l.* sick at Miletum
Tit. 1. 5. for this cause *l.* I thee at Crete
Heb. 2. 8. he *l.* nothing that is not put under
4. 1. let us fear, lest a promise being *l.* of entering
Jude 6. the angels which *l.* their own habitation
Rev. 2. 4. because thou hast *l.* thy first love
See Alone.

LEFT *off.*

Gen. 11. 8. and they *l. off* to build the city
17. 22. *l. off* talking with him, and God went up
Ruth 2. 20. who hath not *l. off* his kindness
1 *Kings* 15. 21. Baasha *l. off* building, 2 *Chr.* 16. 5.
Job 32. 15. answered no more, they *l. off* speaking
Psal. 36. 3. he hath *l. off* to be wise and to do good
Jer. 38. 27. so they *l. off* speaking with him
44. 18. since we *l. off* to burn incense to the queen
Hos. 4. 10. because they have *l. off* to take heed

LEFT *corner.*

2 *Kings* 11. 11. guard stood to the *l. c.* about king
See HAND.

LEFT-HANDED.

Judg. 3. 15. raised Ehud a Benjamite, a man *l.-han.*
20. 16. were seven hundred chosen men *l.-handed*

LEFT *pillar.*

1 *Kings* 7. 21. he set up the *l. pil.* and called it Boaz

LEFT *side.*

1 *Kings* 7. 39. five bases on the *l. side* of the house
49. five candlesticks on the *l. side* before
2 *Chr.* 23. 10. with his weapon from right to *l. side*
Ezek. 1. 10. they had the face of an ox on the *l. side*
4. 4. lie also on thy *l. side*, and lay the iniquity
Zech. 4. 3. other olive tree upon *l. side* thereof, 11.

LEG

Signifies, [1] Properly, *the limbs or parts of an animal, which are the instruments of local motion, and the supporters of the body,* Exod. 12. 9. 1 Sam. 17. 6. [2] Figuratively, *strength,* Psal. 147. 10.

His legs are as pillars of marble, Cant. 5. 15. *The dispensations of his providence are wisely and skilfully contrived: or, it may denote, the firmness and stability of Christ's kingdom, in spite of all opposition.*

Isa. 47. 2. make bare the *l.* uncover the thigh

LEGS.

Exod. 12. 9. but roast with fire his head and *l.*
29. 17. wash the inwards and his *l. Lev.* 9. 14.
Lev. 4. 11. the skin, his head, and his *l.* burn
8. 21. he washed the inwards and *l.* in water
11. 21. which have *l.* above their feet, these eat
Deut. 28. 35. he shall smite thee in the knees and *l.*
1 *Sam.* 17. 6. he had greaves of brass upon his *l.*
Ps. 147. 10. he taketh no pleasure in the *l.* of a man
Prov. 26. 7. the *l.* of the lame are not equal
Cant. 5. 15. his *l.* are as pillars of marble
Isa. 3. 20. the Ld. will take away the ornaments of *l*
Dan. 2. 33. his *l.* of iron, his feet part of iron
Amos 3. 12. out of the mouth of the lion two *l.*
John 19. 31. they besought their *l.* might be broken
32. the soldiers came and brake the *l.* of the first
33. and saw he was dead, they brake not his *l.*

LEISURE.

Mark 6. 31. and they had no *l.* so much as to eat

LEND.

Exod. 22. 25. if thou *l.* money to any, thou shalt
Lev. 25. 37. not *l.* him thy victuals for increase
Deut. 15. 6. and thou shalt *l.* to many nations
8. thou shalt surely *l.* him sufficient for his need
23. 19. thou shalt not *l.* upon usury to thy brother
20. to a stranger thou mayest *l.* upon usury
24. 10. when thou dost *l.* thy brother any thing
11. the man to whom thou dost *l.* shall bring
28. 12. thou shalt *l.* to many nations, and not borrow
44. he shall *l.* to thee, thou shalt not *l.* to him
Luke 6. 34. if ye *l.* them of whom ye hope to receive, sinners also *l.* sinners, to receive as much again
35. but love ye your enemies, do good and *l.*
11. 5. and say to him, friend, *l.* me three loaves

LENDER.

Prov. 22. 7. the borrower is servant to the *l.*
Isa. 24. 2. as with the *l.* so with the borrower

LENDETH.

Deut. 15. 2. every creditor that *l.* aught to neighbour
Psal. 37. 26. he is ever merciful, and *l.* seed blessed
112. 5. a good man sheweth favour and *l.* will guide
Prov. 19. 17. he that hath pity on the poor, *l.* to L.
22. † 7. the borrower is servant to the man that *l.*

LENGTH.

Gen. 13. 17. arise, walk thro' the land in the *l.* of it
Deut. 30. 20. he is thy life, and the *l.* of thy days
Job 12. 12. and in *l.* of days, understanding
Psal. 21. 4. even *l.* of days for ever and ever
23. † 6. dwell in the house of Lord to *l.* of days
91. † 16. with *l.* of days will I satisfy
Prov. 3. 2. for *l.* of days shall they add to thee
16. *l.* of days is in her right hand, riches
Zech. 2. 2. and to see what is the *l.* thereof
5. 2. the *l.* of the roll is twenty cubits
Eph. 3. 18. be able to comprehend *l.* of love of Christ
Rev. 21. 16. and the *l.* as large as the breadth

At LENGTH.

Ps. 36. † 10. O draw out *at l.* thy loving-kindness!
Prov. 29. 21. shall have him become his son *at l.*
Rom. 1. 10. if now *at l.* I may have a journey

LENGTHEN.

1 *Kings* 3. 14. walk as David, then will I *l.* thy days
Isa. 54. 2. *l.* thy cords, and strengthen thy stakes

LENGTHENED.

Deut. 25. 15. that thy days may be *l.* in the land

LENGTHENING.

Dan. 4. 27. if it may be a *l.* of thy tranquillity

LENT.

Exod. 12. 36. they *l.* to them such as they required
Deut. 23. 19. usury of any thing that is *l.* on usury

1 *Sam.* 1. 28. I *l.* him to the Lord, he shall be *l.*
2. 20. for the loan which is *l.* to the Lord
Jer. 15. 10. I have not *l.* on usury nor have men *l.* me

LENTILES.

Gen. 25. 34. when Jacob gave Esau pottage of *l.*
2 *Sam.* 23. 11. there was a piece of ground full of *l.*
See BEANS.

LEOPARD

Is *a wild beast, called by some a* libbard ; *it is full of spots, also exceeding swift, subtle, and fierce, enraged against men, and of such a sweet savour that it allures other beasts to it ; by which means they are caught and devoured,* Hos. 13. 7. Hab. 1. 8. To which are compared, [1] *Antichrist, with his followers and adherents,* Rev. 13. 2. [2] *Men of a fierce untractable disposition,* Isa. 11. 6.

Can the leopard change his spots? &c. *Jer.* 13. 23. *It is as much labour in vain to endeavour to reclaim these Jews, who by their continual customary sinning have inured themselves to wicked practices, as to use means to take out the natural spots of a leopard.*

Isa. 11. 6. the *l.* shall lie down with the kid
Jer. 5. 6. a *l.* shall watch over their cities
13. 23. or can the *l.* change his spots?
Dan. 7. 6. I beheld, and lo, another like a *l.*
Hos. 13. 7. therefore I will be to them as a *l.*
Rev. 13. 2. and the beast was like to a *l.*

LEOPARDS.

Cant. 4. 8. look from the mountains of the *l.*
Hab. 1. 8. their horses are swifter than *l.*

LEPER.

Lev. 13. 45. and the *l.* in whom the plague is
14. 2. this shall be the law of the *l.* in the day
3. behold, if the leprosy be healed in the *l.*
22. 4. what man of the seed of Aaron is a *l.*
Num. 5. 2. they put out of the camp every *l.*
2 *Sam.* 3. 29. from the house of Joab, one that is a *l.*
2 *Kings* 5. 1. Naaman was a *l.* ‖ 11. recover the *l.*
27. went from his presence a *l.* as white as snow
15. 5. Azariah was a *l.* to the day of his death
2 *Chron.* 26. 21. and Uzziah the king was a *l.*
23. they buried him, for they said, he is a *l.*
Mat. 8. 2. and behold, there came a *l.* *Mark* 1. 40.
26. 6. in the house of Simon the *l.* *Mark* 14. 3.

LEPERS.

2 *Kings* 7. 8. when the *l.* came to the uttermost part
Mat. 10. 8. heal the sick, cleanse *l.* raise the dead
11. 5. the lame walk, the *l.* are cleansed, *Luke* 7. 22.
Luke 4. 27. many *l.* were in Israel in time of Eliseus
17. 12. there met him ten men that were *l.*

LEPROSY.

Lev. 13. 2. and it be in the skin like the plague of *l.*
3. it is a plague of *l.* 8, 11, 15, 25, 27, 30, 42, 49.
9. when the plague of *l.* is in a man, then he shall
12. if a *l.* break out ‖ 13. if the *l.* covered his flesh
43. as the *l.* appeareth in the skin of the flesh
47. the garment that the plague of *l.* is in
59. this is the law of the plag. of *l.* 14. 54, 55, 57.
14. 3. if the plague of *l.* be healed in the leper
7. shall sprinkle him that is to be cleansed from *l.*
32. the law of him in whom is the plague of *l.*
Deut. 24. 8. take heed in the plague of *l.* to observe
2 *Kings* 5. 3. for he would recover him of his *l.* 7.
6. that thou mayest recover him of his *l.*
27. the *l.* of Naaman shall cleave unto thee
2 *Chron.* 26. 19. the *l.* rose up in his forehead
Mat. 8. 3. his *l.* was cleansed, *Mark* 1. 42. *Luke* 5. 13.
Luke 5. 12. behold, a man full of *l.* besought him
See FRETTING.

LEPROUS.

Exod. 4. 6. behold, his hand was *l.* as snow
Lev. 13. 44. he is a *l.* man, he is unclean
Num. 12. 10. Miriam became *l.* behold she was *l.*
2 *Kings* 7. 3. there were four *l.* men at the gate
2 *Chron.* 26. 20. and Uzziah was *l.* in his forehead

LESS

Signifies, [1] *A smaller quantity,* Exod. 16. 17. [2] *Not in proportion to,* Ezra 9. 13. [3] *An inferior,* Heb. 7. 7.

Gen. 32. † 10. I am *l.* than least of all the mercies
Exod. 16. 17. and gathered some more, some *l.*
30. 15. the poor shall not give *l.* than half a shekel
Num. 22. 18. go beyond the word of the Ld. to do *l.*
26. 54. to few thou shalt give *l.* inheritance, 33. 54.
1 *Sam.* 22. 15. thy servant knew nothing *l.* or more
25. 36. Abigail told him nothing *l.* or more
Ezra 9. 13. punished us *l.* than our iniquities deserve
Job 11. 6. God exacteth *l.* than iniquity deserveth
Prov. 17. 7. much *l.* do lying lips a prince
19. 10. much *l.* for a servant to rule over princes
Isa. 40. 17. all nations are counted *l.* than nothing
Mark 4. 31. when it is sown is *l.* than all seeds
15. 40. Mary the mother of James the *l.*
1 *Cor.* 8. † 8. nor if we eat not, have we the *l.*
12. 23. those members we think *l.* honourable
2 *Cor.* 12. 15. the more I love, the *l.* I am loved
Eph. 3. 8. who am *l.* than the least of all saints
Phil. 2. 28. and that I may be the *l.* sorrowful
Heb. 7. 7. the *l.* is blessed of better without contrad.

LESSER.

Gen. 1. 16. made the *l.* light to rule the night
Isa. 7. 25. and for the treading of *l.* cattle
Ezek. 16. † 46. thy sister *l.* than thou is Sodom
43. 14. from the *l.* settle to the greater settle

LEST.

Gen. 3. 3. neither shall ye touch it, *l.* ye die, *Lev.* 10. 6, 7, 9. *Num.* 18. 32.
11. 4. *l.* we be scattered abroad on the earth
14. 23. *l.* thou say, I have made Abram rich
19. 15. *l.* thou be consumed in the iniquity of city
19. *l.* I die, 26. 9. ‖ 32. 11. *l.* he come and smite me
38. 11. *l.* he die, as his breth. did, *Deut.* 20. 5, 6, 7.
23. let her take it to her, *l.* we be ashamed
45. 11. *l.* thou and thy household come to poverty
Exod. 5. 3. go. *l.* he fall on us with pestilence
13. 17. *l.* peradventure the people repent in war
19. 21. *l.* they break through to the Lord to gaze
22. sanctify, *l.* the Lord break forth upon them
20. 19. let not God speak with us, *l.* we die
33. 3. I will not go, *l.* I consume thee in the way

Num. 4. 20. shall not go in to see, *l.* they die, 18. 22.
Deut. 11. 17. *l.* ye perish quickly from off the land
24. 15. *l.* he cry against thee to Lord, and it be sin
25. 3. *l.* if he should exceed and beat him above these
Josh. 9. 20. let them live, *l.* wrath be upon us
24. 27. shall be a witness, *l.* ye deny your God
Judg. 7. 2. *l.* Israel vaunt themselves against me
1 *Sam.* 20. 3. let him not know, *l.* he be grieved
2 *Sam.* 12. 28. *l.* I take the city, and it be called
Job 36. 18. *l.* he take thee away with his stroke
42. 8. *l.* I deal with you after your folly
Ps. 2. 12. kiss the Son *l.* he be angry, and ye perish
13. 3. lighten mine eyes, *l.* I sleep the sleep of death
50. 22. consider this, *l.* I tear you in pieces
91. 12. *l.* thou dash thy foot, *Mat.* 4. 6. *Luke* 4. 11.
106. 23. Moses stood, *l.* he should destroy them
140. 8. grant not, *l.* they exalt themselves
143. 7. *l.* I be like them that go down into the pit
Prov. 9. 8. reprove not a scorner, *l.* he hate thee
20. 13. love not sleep, *l.* thou come to poverty
22. 25. *l.* thou learn his ways, and get a snare
24. 18. *l.* the Lord see it, and it displease him
25. 8. *l.* thou know not what to do in the end
10. *l.* he that heareth it, put thee to shame
17. *l.* he be weary of thee, and so hate thee
26. 4. answer not a fool, *l.* thou also be like unto him
30. 6. add not to his words, *l.* he reprove thee
9. *l.* I be full and deny thee, or *l.* I be poor
Isa. 6. 10. *l.* they see with their eyes, *Acts* 28. 27.
27. 3. *l.* any hurt it, I will keep it night and day
28. 22. not mockers, *l.* your bands be made strong
48. 5. *l.* thou shouldest say, my idol hath done, 7.
Jer. 1. 17. be not dismayed, *l.* I confound thee
4. 4. *l.* my fury come forth like fire, 21. 12.
6. 8. be instructed, *l.* my soul depart from thee
37. 20. cause me not to return, *l.* I die there
Hos. 2. 3. *l.* I strip her naked, and set her as in day
Amos 5. 6. seek the Lord, *l.* he break out like fire
Zech. 7. 12. as an adamant, *l.* they should hear the l.
Mal. 4. 6. *l.* I come and smite the earth with a curse
Mat. 17. 27. *l.* we should offend, go to the sea
25. 9. *l.* there be not enough for us and you
Mark 13. 5. take heed, *l.* any man deceive you
36. *l.* coming suddenly, he find you sleeping
14. 38. watch and pray, *l.* ye enter into temptation
Luke 8. 12. *l.* they should believe and be saved
21. 34. *l.* your hearts overcharged with surfeiting
John 5. 14. sin no more, *l.* a worse thing come to thee
18. 28. they went out *l.* they should be defiled
Acts 5. 39. *l.* ye be found to fight against God
13. 40. beware therefore, *l.* that come upon you
Rom. 11. 21. take heed, *l.* he spare not thee, 44.
1 *Cor.* 9. 12. *l.* we hinder the gospel of Christ
10. 12. let him that standeth take heed *l.* he fall
2 *Cor.* 2. 11. *l.* Satan should get advantage of us
12. 7. *l.* I should be exalted above measure
Gal. 2. 2. *l.* by any means I should run in vain
6. 1. considering thyself, *l.* thou also be tempted
Eph. 2. 9. not of works, *l.* any man should boast
Col. 2. 4. *l.* any man beguile you with enticing words
3. 21. provoke not children, *l.* they be discouraged
1 *Tim.* 3. 6. *l.* being lifted up with pride he fall into
Heb. 2. 1. *l.* at any time we should let them slip
3. 12. *l.* there be in any an evil heart of unbelief
13. *l.* any of you be hardened through sin
4. 11. *l.* any man fall after the same example
12. 3. *l.* ye be weary and faint in your minds
13. *l.* what is lame be turned out of the way
15. *l.* any man fail of the grace of God
Jam. 5. 9. grudge not, *l.* ye be condemned
12. swear not, *l.* ye fall into condemnation
2 *Pet.* 3. 17. beware, *l.* ye also being led away
Rev. 16. 15. keepeth his garments, *l.* he walk naked

LET.

Gen. 49. 21. Naphtali is a hind *l.* loose, goodly words
Exod. 3. 19. king of Egy. will not *l.* you go, 4. 21. | 7. 14. | 8. 32. | 9. 7, 17, 35. | 10. 20, 27. | 11. 10.
20. my wonders, and after that he will *l.* you go
5. 1. *l.* my peo. go, 7. 16. | 8. 1, 20. | 9. 1, 13. | 10. 3.
4. why do ye *l.* the people from their works?
8. 28. Phar. said, I will *l.* you go, 9. 28. | 13. 17.
14. 5. why have we *l.* Israel go from serving
18. 27. and Moses *l.* his father-in-law depart
21. 8. then shall he *l.* her be redeemed
26. he shall *l.* him go free for his eye, 27.
23. 11. seventh year thou shalt *l.* it rest and lie still
33. 12. hast not *l.* me know whom thou wilt send
Lev. 14. 7. and shall *l.* the living bird loose
18. 21. not *l.* seed pass through the fire to Molech
19. 19. not *l.* cattle gender with a diverse kind
Deut. 15. 12. thou shalt *l.* him go free from thee
13. thou shalt not *l.* him go away empty
Josh. 10. 28. and all therein, he *l.* none remain, 30.
24. 28. so Joshua *l.* the people depart every man
Judg. 1. 25. they *l.* the man go and his family
1 *Sam.* 18. 2. Saul would *l.* him go no more home
2 *Sam.* 11. 12. to-morrow I will *l.* thee depart
13. 6. I pray thee, *l.* Tamar my sister come
1 *Kings* 18. 40. Elijah said, *l.* none of them escape
2 *Chron.* 20. 10. thou wouldest not *l.* Israel invade
Esth. 5. 12. queen did *l.* no man come in but myself
Job 6. 9. even that he would *l.* loose his hand
27. 6. my righteousness I will not *l.* it go
Psal. 69. 6. *l.* not those that wait on thee be ashamed, *l.* not those that seek thee be confounded
109. 6. and *l.* Satan stand at his right hand
119. 10. *l.* me not wander from thy commandments
Cant. 3. 4. I held him, and would not *l.* him go
8. 11. he *l.* out the vineyard to keepers
Isa. 43. 13. I will work, and who shall *l.* it?
Jer. 27. 11. those will I *l.* remain in the land
Ezek. 39. 7. I will not *l.* them pollute my name
Mat. 21. 33. a householder planted a vineyard and *l.* it out to husbandmen, *Mark* 12. 1. *Luke* 20. 9.
Luke 22. 68. ye will not answer me nor *l.* me go
John 19. 12. the Jews cried, if thou *l.* this man go
Acts 27. 15. ship could not bear up, we *l.* her drive
Rom. 1. 13. to come to you, but was *l.* hitherto
2 *Thess.* 2. 7. only he who now letteth, will *l.*
Heb. 2. 1. lest at any time we should *l.* them slip
See ALONE.

LET *down.*

Gen 24. 14. *l. down* thy pitcher, I pray thee, 18, 46.
Exod. 17. 11. when he *l. d.* his hands, Amalek prevail.
Josh. 2. 15. then Rahab *l.* them *down* by a cord, 18.
1 *Sam.* 19. 12. Michal *l.* David *d.* through a window
2 *Kings* 13. 21. and when the man was *l. down*
Jer. 38. 6. they *l. down* Jeremiah with cords
Ezek. 1. 24. they stood they *l. down* their wings, 25.
Mark 2. 4. they *l. down* the bed wherein, *Luke* 5. 19.
Luke 5. 4. and *l. down* your nets for a draught
5. at thy word I will *l. down* the net
Acts 9. 25. and *l.* him *d.* in a basket, 2 *Cor.* 11. 33.
10. 11. *l. d.* to the earth ‖ 27. 30. had *l. d.* the boat

LETTED.

Num. 22. † 16. be not thou *l.* from coming.

LETTER

Signifies, [1] *An epistle sent by one person to another,* 2 Sam. 11. 14. [2] *A proclamation,* Esth. 3. 13. [3] *Learning, or the knowledge of the mysterious sense and meaning of the law of God,* John 7. 15. [4] *The outward ceremony of circumcision, without the inward grace signified thereby,* Rom. 2. 29. [5] *The legal dispensation, which consisted chiefly in a multitude of carnal ordinances, and where they had the letter of the command, without strength to obey,* Rom. 7. 6. 2 Cor. 3. 6.

2 *Sam.* 11. 14. David wrote a *l.* to Joab and sent
2 *Kings* 5. 5. I will send a *l.* to the king of Israel
6. now when this *l.* is come to thee, behold
10. 2. now as soon as this *l.* cometh to thee
19. 14. Hezekiah received the *l.* *Isa.* 37. 14.
Ezra 4. 7. the *l.* was written in the Syrian tongue
8. Rehum wrote a *l.* against Jerusalem
7. 11. now this is the copy of the *l.* 5. 6, 7.
Neh. 2. 8. a *l.* to Asaph the keeper of the forest
6. 5. sent to me with an open *l.* in his hand
Esth. 9. 29. wrote to confirm this *l.* of Purim
Jer. 29. 1. the words of the *l.* that Jeremiah sent
29. Zephaniah priest read this *l.* in the ears of Jer.
Acts 23. 25. Claudius wrote a *l.* to Felix in this
34. when the governor had read the *l.* he asked
Rom. 2. 27. who by the *l.* dost transgress the law
29. circumcision of the heart, not in the *l.*
7. 6. we should serve, not in the oldness of the *l.*
2 *Cor.* 3. 6. ministers not of the *l.* but of the Spirit
7. 8. tho' I made you sorry with *l.* I do not repent
Gal. 6. 11. ye see how large a *l.* I have written
2 *Thess.* 2. 2. be not soon shaken by word or by *l.*
Heb. 13. 22. I have written a *l.* to you in few words

LETTERS.

1 *Kings* 21. 8. Jezebel wrote *l.* in Ahab's name, 9.
2 *Kings* 10. 1. Jehu wrote *l.* and sent to Samaria
20. 12. king of Babylon sent *l.* to Hezekiah
2 *Chron.* 30. 1. Hezekiah wrote *l.* also to Ephraim
6. so the posts went with the *l.* from the king
32. 17. Sennacherib wrote *l.* to rail on God of Isr.
Neh. 2. 7. let *l.* be given me to the governors
6. 17. sent *l.* to Tobiah, and *l.* came to them
19. and Tobiah sent *l.* to put me in fear
Esth. 1. 22. Ahasuerus sent *l.* to the provinces
3. 13. the *l.* were sent by posts to provinces, 8. 10.
8. 5. to reverse *l.* devised by Haman to destroy Jews
9. 20. Mordecai sent *l.* to all the Jews, 30.
Jer. 29. 25. because thou hast sent *l.* in thy name
Luke 23. 38. was written in *l.* of Hebrew, this is
John 7. 15. how knoweth this man *l.* having never
Acts 9. 2. and desired of him *l.* to Damascus
15. 23. the apostles wrote *l.* after this manner
22. 5. from whom also I received *l.* to the brethren
28. 21. we neither received *l.* out of Judea
1 *Cor.* 16. 3. whom ye shall approve by your *l.*
2 *Cor.* 3. 1. nor need we *l.* of commendation
10. 9. may not seem as if I would terrify you by *l.*
10. for his *l.* are weighty and powerful, but his
11. such as we are in word, by *l.* when absent

LETTEST.

Job 15. 13. *l.* such words go out of thy mouth
41. 1. or his tongue with a cord thou *l.* down?
Luke 2. 29. Lord, now *l.* thou thy servant depart

LETTETH.

2 *Kings* 10. 24. he that *l.* him go, his life be for his
Prov. 17. 14. strife is as when one *l.* out water
2 *Thess.* 2. 7. only he that now *l.* will let until taken

LETTING.

Exod. 8. 29. deal deceitfully in not *l.* the people go

LEVIATHAN.

Job 3. † 8. who are ready to raise up a *l.*
41. 1. canst thou draw out *l.* with an hook?
Psal. 74. 14. thou breakest the heads of *l.* in pieces
104. 26. there is that *l.* thou hast made to play
Isa. 27. 1. shall punish *l.* even *l.* that crooked serpent

LEVITE.

Exod. 4. 14. is not Aaron the *l.* thy brother?
Deut. 12. 12. rejoice ye before the Lord your God, and the *l.* 18. | 16. 11, 14. | 26. 11, 13.
14. 29. and the *l.* shall come and eat, 26. 12.
18. 6. if a *l.* come from any of thy gates
Judg. 17. 7. a young man a *l.* 9. ‖ 10. so the *l.* went in
11. the *l.* was content to dwell with the man
12. Micah consecrated the *l.* ‖ 13. a *l.* to my priest
18. 3. they knew the voice of the young man the *l.*
19. 1. there was a certain *l.* sojourning on mount
20. 4. the *l.* said, I came into Gibeah of Benjamin
2 *Chr.* 20. 14. on Jahaziel the *l.* came the Spirit
31. 12. Cononiah the *l.* over the dedicated things
14. Kore the *l.* over the free-will offerings
Ezra 10. 15. Shabbethai the *l.* helped them
Luke 10. 32. likewise a *l.* came and looked on
Acts 4. 36. Barnabas a *l.* having land, sold it

LEVITES.

Exod. 6. 25. these heads of the fathers of the *l.*
38. 21. it was counted for the service of the *l.*
Lev. 25. 32. cities of *l.* may *l.* redeem at any time
33. the cities of the *l.* are their possession
Num. 1. 47. but the *l.* were not numbered, 2. 33.
50. shalt appoint the *l.* over the tabernacle
51. the *l.* shall take it down ‖ 53. the *l.* shall pitch
3. 9. and thou shalt give the *l.* unto Aaron
12. I have taken the *l.* the *l.* shall be mine
39. all that were numbered of the *l.* 4. 46.
41. and thou shalt take the *l.* for me, 45. | 8. 14.

Num. 7. 5. and thou shalt give waggons unto the l.
8. 6. take the l. from Israel and cleanse them
9. bring the l. before the tabernacle, 10.
11. Aaron shall offer the l. before the Lord
15. then after that shall the l. go in, 22.
24. this is it that belongeth unto the l.
26. thus shalt thou do to the l. touching their
18. 6. I have taken the l. to do service, 23.
24. the tithes I have given to the l. to inherit
35. 2. that they give to the l. cities round, 8.
Deut. 18. 7. minister, as his brethren the l. do
Josh. 14. 3. to the l. he gave none inheritance
21. 3. Israel gave these cities to the l. 8.
41. all the cities of the l. were forty-eight
1 Sam. 6. 15. the l. took down the ark of the Lord
2 Sam. 15. 24. Zadok and the l. were with him
1 Chron. 15. 15. the children of the l. bare the ark
26. when God helped the l. that bare the ark
24. 6. one of the l. wrote them before the king
2 Chron. 5. 12. the l. which were singers stood, 7. 6.
11. 14. the l. left their suburbs and possession
13. 9. have ye not cast out the sons of Aaron and l.
19. 11. also the l. shall be officers before you
23. 6. the l. shall compass the king round about, 7.
24. 5. howbeit, the l. hastened it not
29. 5. hear me, ye l. sanctify now yourselves
30. 22. Hezekiah spake comfortably to the l.
34. 13. of the l. there were scribes and officers
35. 3. Josiah said to the l. which taught Israel
9. the chief of the l. gave to the l. 500 oxen
14. therefore the l. prepared for themselves, 15.
Ezra 6. 18. they set the l. in their courses
Neh. 3. 17. after him repaired the l. Rehum
8. 7. the l. caused the people to understand the law
11. the l. stilled the people, saying, hold your peace
11. 22. the overseer of the l. was Uzzi
12. 27. at the dedication they sought the l.
13. 10. the portions of the l. had not been given
them, for the l. were fled every one to his field
29. they have defiled the priesthood of the l.
Jer. 33. 22. I will multiply the l. that minister
Ezek. 44. 10. the l. that are gone shall bear iniquity
48. 11. went not astray when the l. went astray

Priests and LEVITES.

Deut. 17. 9. thou shalt come to p. and l. and judge
24. 8. to do all that the priests and l. shall teach
Josh. 3. 3. when ye see the p. and l. bearing the ark
1 Kings 8. 4. p. and l. brought up the ark of the Ld.
2 Chron. 23. 4. p. and l. shall be porters of the doors
29. 34. p. and l. were more upright in heart than
30. 15. priests and l. were ashamed, and sanctified
21. l. and the priests praised the Lord day by day
27. then the priests and l. blessed the people
31. 9. Hezekiah questioned with the priests and l.
35. 8. his princes gave willingly to the priests and l.
Ezra 2. 70. so priests and l. dwelt in their cities
6. 20. for the priests and l. were purified together
7. 7. there went up of the priests and l. and singers
9. 1. the p. and l. have not separated themselves
10. 5. Ezra arose and made the p. and l. to swear
Neh. 9. 38. our princes, l. and priests, seal to it
10. 34. we cast lots among priests and l. and people
12. 30. the p. and l. purified themselves and the wall
44. Judah rejoiced for the p. and l. that waited
Isa. 66. 21. I will take of them for priests and l.
Jer. 33. 18. priests and l. not want a man to offer
21. and with the l. the priests my ministers
Ezek. 44. 15. but the p. and l. that kept the charge
John 1. 19. when the Jews sent p. and l. to ask him

LEVITICAL.

Heb. 7. 11. if perfection were by the l. priesthood

LEVY, Substantive.

1 Kings 5. 13. Solomon raised a l. of 300,000 men
14. and Adoniram was over the l.
9. 15. this is the reason of the l. Solomon raised

LEVY, Verb.

Num. 31. 28. and l. a tribute to the Lord
1 Kings 9. 21. upon those did Solomon l. a tribute

LEWD.

Ezek. 16. 27. which are ashamed of thy l. way
23. 44. so went they in, as unto the l. woman
Acts 17. 5. Jews took l. fellows of the baser sort

LEWDLY.

Ezek. 22. 11. another hath l. defiled his daughter

LEWDNESS.

Judg. 20. 6. they have committed l. in Israel
Jer. 11. 15. she hath wrought l. with many
13. 27. I have seen the l. of thy whoredom
Ezek. 16. 43. and thou shalt not commit this l.
58. thou hast borne thy l. and abominations
22. 9. in the midst of thee they commit l.
† 11. by l. hath defiled his daughter-in-law
23. 21. calledst to remembrance the l. of thy youth
27. thus will I make thy l. to cease, 48.
29. shall be discovered, both thy l. and whoredom
35. therefore bear thou also thy l. and whoredom
49. and they shall recompense your l. on you
24. 13. in thy filthiness is l. because I purged thee
Hos. 2. 10. and now will I discover her l. in sight
6. 9. priests murder in way, they commit l.
Acts 18. 14. if it were a matter of wrong or l.

LIAR, see LYAR.

LIBERAL.

Prov. 11. 25. the l. soul shall be made fat
Isa. 32. 5. the vile person shall not be called l.
8. the l. deviseth l. things, and by l. things
2 Cor. 9. 13. they glorify G. for your l. distribution

LIBERALITY.

1 Cor. 16. 3. to bring your l. to Jerusalem
2 Cor. 8. 2. abounded to the riches of their l.

LIBERALLY.

Deut. 15. 14. thou shalt furnish him l. out of
Jam. 1. 5. ask of God, who giveth to all men l.

LIBERTINES.

Acts 6. 9. which is called the synagogue of the l.

LIBERTY

Signifies, [1] *A power which a person has to do or forbear any particular action,* 1 Cor. 7. 39. [2] *Freedom from any servitude or bondage,* Lev. 25. 10. Heb. 13. 23. [3] *Freedom from the curse of the moral law, and from the servitude of the ceremonial law.* Gal. 5. 1. [4] *Full and perfect deliverance from all miseries whatsoever,* Rom. 8. 21. [5] *A power or freedom in using things indifferent,* 1 Cor. 8. 9. | 10. 29. [6] *Freedom from the veil of ignorance and spiritual blindness, the yoke of the law, and the slavery of sin,* 2 Cor. 3. 17.

Lev. 25. 10. ye shall proclaim l. through all the land
Psal. 119. 45. and I will walk at l. for I seek
Isa. 61. 1. he sent me to proclaim l. to the captives
Jer. 34. 8. made a covenant to proclaim l. to them
15. done right in my sight, in proclaiming l.
16. his servant whom he had set at l. to return
17. ye have not hearkened to me in proclaiming l.
I proclaim a l. for you to famine, to sword
Ezek. 46. 17. it shall be his to the year of l.
Luke 4. 18. to set at l. them that are bruised
Acts 24. 23. to keep Paul, and let him have l.
26. 32. this man might have been set at l.
27. 3. and gave him l. to go to his friends
Rom. 8. 21. from bondage into the glorious l.
1 Cor. 7. 39. she is at l. to marry whom she will
8. 9. take heed lest this l. of yours become
10. 29. for why is my l. judged of another
2 Cor. 3. 17. where the Spirit of the Lord is, there is l.
Gal. 2. 4. who came in privily, to spy out our l.
5. 1. stand fast in the l. wherewith Christ made
13. ye have been called to l. use not your l.
Heb. † 19. having l. to enter the holiest
13. 23. that our brother Timothy is set at l.
Jam. 1. 25. whoso looketh into the law of l.
2. 12. that shall be judged by the law of l.
1 Pet. 2. 16. as free, and not using l. for a cloak
2 Pet. 2. 19. while they promise them l. they

LICE.

Exod. 8. 16. the dust became l. through all Egypt
17. smote dust, it became l. in man and beast
18. magicians did so with their enchantments to
bring forth l. so there were l. upon man and beast
Psal. 105. 31. there came l. in all their coasts

LICENCE.

Acts 21. 40. and when he had given Paul l.
25. 16. till the accused have l. to answer for himself

LICK.

Num. 22. 4. now shall this company l. up all around
1 Kings 21. 19. shall dogs l. thy blood, even thine
Psal. 72. 9. and his enemies shall l. the dust
Isa. 49. 23. and shall l. up the dust of thy feet
Mic. 7. 17. they shall l. the dust like a serpent

LICKED.

1 Kings 18. 38. fire l. up the water in the trench
21. 19. where dogs l. the blood of Naboth
22. 38. and the dogs l. up his blood and washed
Luke 16. 21. the dogs came and l. his sores

LICKETH.

Num. 22. 4. shall lick up all, as the ox l. up grass

LID.

2 Kings 12. 9. and bored a hole in the l. of it

LIE.

Gen. 19. 32. drink wine, and we will l. with him
34. and go thou in, and l. with him
30. 15. therefore he shall l. with thee to-night
39. 7. she said, come l. with me, 12. 2 Sam. 13. 11.
14. he came in unto me to l. with me
Exod. 22. 16. if a man l. with a maid not betrothed
Lev. 15. 18. woman with whom man shall l. with seed
24. if any man l. with her at all, he is unclean
18. 20. not l. carnally with thy neighbour's wife
22. shalt not l. with mankind || 23. nor l. with beast
20. 12. and if a man l. with his daughter-in-law
13. if l. with mankind || 15. if l. with a beast
18. if a man l. with a woman having her sickness
20. if a man l. with his uncle's wife, he hath
Num. 5. 13. if a man l. with her, and it be hid from
Deut. 22. 23. and a man find her, and l. with her
25. if the man force her, and l. with her
28. if find a damsel not betrothed, and l. with her
28. 30. betroth a wife, and another l. with her
2 Sam. 11. 11. shall I then go to l. with my wife?
Cant. 1. 13. he shall l. all night betwixt my breasts

LIE.

Gen. 47. 30. I will l. with my fathers, not in Egypt
Exod. 23. 11. thou shalt let the ground l. still
Deut. 29. 20. all the curses in this book shall l. on him
Josh. 8. 9. and they went to l. in ambush, 12.
Judg. 19. 20. let all thy wants l. on me, only lodge
Ruth 3. 4. thou shalt mark the place where he shall l.
1 Kings 1. 2. and let her l. in thy bosom, that king
Psal. 57. 4. I l. among them that are set on fire
88. 5. like the slain that l. in the grave
Eccl. 4. 11. if two l. together they have heat
Isa. 13. 21. wild beasts of the desert shall l. there
14. 18. all the kings of the nations l. in glory
51. 20. thy sons l. at the head of all the streets
Lam. 2. 21. the young and old l. on the ground
Ezek. 4. 4. l. thou also upon thy left side and lay
6. l. again on thy right side || 9. shalt l. 390 days
31. 18. shalt l. in the midst of the uncircumcised
32. 21. they l. uncircumcised, slain by sword, 30.
27. and they shall not l. with the mighty
28. l. with the slain || 29. l. with uncircumcised
34. 14. there shall they l. in a good fold
Joel 1. 13. come, l. all night in sackcloth
Amos 6. 4. that l. on beds of ivory, and stretch
John 5. 6. when Jesus saw him l. he saith to him
20. 6. Simon Peter seeth the linen clothes l.

LIE down.

Lev. 18. 23. before a beast, to l. down thereto, 20. 16.
26. 6. ye shall l. down and none shall make you afraid
Num. 23. 24. Israel shall not l. down till he eat prey
Deut. 25. 2. judge cause him to l. down and beaten
31. † 16. thou shalt l. down with thy fathers
Ruth 3. 7. Boaz went to l. down at the end of heap
13. tarry this night, l. down until the morning
1 Sam. 3. 5. Eli said, I called not, l. down again, 6, 9.
2 Sam. 11. 13. at even he went to l. down on his bed
Job 7. 4. when I l. down I say, when shall I arise
11. 19. thou shalt l. d. and none make thee afraid
20. 11. which shall l. down with him in the dust
21. 26. they shall l. down alike in the dust
27. 19. the rich man shall l. d. but not be gathered
Psal. 23. 2. he maketh me l. down in green pastures
Prov. 3. 24. thou shalt l. down and thy sleep be sweet
Isa. 11. 6. the leopard shall l. down with the kid
7. their young ones shall l. down together
14. 30. and the needy shall l. down in safety
17. 2. they shall be for flocks which shall l. down
27. 10. there shall the calf feed and l. down
43. 17. the army and the power shall l. d. together
50. 11. this ye have, ye shall l. down in sorrow
65. 10. shall be a place for the herds to l. down in
Jer. 3. 25. we l. down in our shame and confusion
33. 12. shepherds causing their flocks to l. down
50. † 6. have forgotten their place to l. down in
Ezek. 34. 15. and I will cause them to l. down
Hos. 2. 18. I will make them to l. down safely
Zeph. 2. 7. they shall l. down in the evening
14. flocks shall l. down || 15. for beasts to l. down in
3. 13. the remnant of Israel shall feed and l. down

LIE in wait.

Exod. 21. 13. if a man l. not in wait, but God deliver
Deut. 19. 11. if a man hate his neighbour, and l. in w.
Josh. 8. 4. ye shall l. in wait against the city
Judg. 9. 32. up by night, and l. in wait in the field
21. 20. saying, go and l. in wait in the vineyards
1 Sam. 22. 8. hast stirred up my servant to l. in w. 13.
Job 38. 40. and abide in the covert to l. in wait
Psal. 59. 3. for lo, they l. in wait for my soul
Prov. 12. 6. the words of the wicked are to l. in wait
Hos. 7. 6. heart like an oven, whiles they l. in wait
Mic. 7. 2. they all l. in wait for blood, they hunt
Acts 23. 21. there l. in w. for him more than 40 men
Eph. 4. 14. whereby they l. in wait to deceive me

LIE waste.

Isa. 33. 8. the high-ways l. waste || 34. 10. it shall l. w.
Hag. 1. 4. to dwell in houses, and this house l. waste

LIEN, or LAIN.

Gen. 26. 10. one might have l. with thy wife
Num. 5. 19. if no man have l. with thee, be free
20. but if some man have l. with thee beside thy
Judg. 21. 11. destroy every woman that hath l.
Job 3. 13. for now should I have l. still
Psal. 68. 13. though ye have l. among the pots, yet
Jer. 3. 2. see where thou hast not been l. with
John 11. 17. he had l. in the grave four days

LIERS in wait.

Josh. 8. 14. he wist not that there were l. in wait
Judg. 9. 25. the men of Shechem set l. in w. for him
16. 12. there were l. in wait abiding in the chamber
20. 29. Israel set l. in wait round about Gibeah
33. the l. in w. came forth || 37. l. hasted and rush.
36. they trusted to the l. in wait which they set
Jer. 51. † 12. prepare l. in wait against Babylon

LIEST.

Gen. 28. 13. the land whereon thou l. I will give
Deut. 6. 7. when thou l. down and risest up, 11. 19.
Josh. 7. 10. up, wherefore l. thou on thy face?
Prov. 3. 24. when thou l. down shalt not be afraid

LIETH.

Gen. 4. 7. if thou doest not well, sin l. at the door
49. 25. bless blessings of the deep that l. under
Lev. 14. 47. he that l. in the house shall wash
15. 4. every bed whereon he l. is unclean
20. every thing that she l. on is unclean, 26.
24. all the bed whereon he l. shall be unclean, 33.
26. 34. sabbaths, as long as it l. desolate, 35.
43. the land enjoy sabbaths, while she l. desolate
Judg. 16. 5. see wherein his great strength l.
6. tell me wherein thy great strength l. 15.
Job 40. 21. he l. under the shady trees, in covert
Psal. 41. 8. now that he l. he shall rise no more
88. 7. thy wrath l. hard on me, thou hast afflicted
Mat. 8. 6. my servant l. at home sick of the palsy
Mark 5. 23. my daughter l. at the point of death
Rom. 12. 18. as much as l. in you, live peaceably
1 John 5. 19. the whole world l. in wickedness

LIETH down.

Ruth 3. 4. it shall be when he l. down, mark the place
Job 14. 12. so man l. down, and riseth not till heavens
Prov. 23. 34. as he that l. down in the midst of the sea

LIETH in wait.

Psal. 10. 9. he l. in w. secretly as a lion, l. in w. to
Prov. 7. 12. and she l. in wait at every corner
23. 28. she also l. in wait as for a prey

LIETH waste.

Neh. 2. 3. the place of my father's sepulchres l. w.
17. then said I, you see how Jerusalem l. waste

LIETH, as with a woman.

Exod. 22. 19. whoso l. with beast surely put to death
Lev. 19. 20. whoso l. carnally with a bond-maid
20. 11. the man that l. with his father's wife
13. lie with mankind as he l. with a woman
Deut. 27. 20. cursed be he that l. with father's wife
21. l. with beast || 22. sister || 23. mother-in-law
Mic. 7. 5. thy mouth from her that l. in thy bosom

LIEUTENANTS.

Ezra 8. 36. they deliver. the king's commissions to l.
Esth. 3. 12. Haman had commanded the king's l.
8. 9. Mordecai had commanded to the l.
9. 3. all the rulers and l. helped the Jews

LIFE

Signifies, [1] *That space of time which passes between the birth and death of any person,* Psal. 17. 14. Prov. 3. 2. [2] *A power to move, and do the actions of life,* Job 3. 20. Eccl. 2. 17. [3] *A spiritual, supernatural, and heavenly life, whereby we live to God, and enjoy peace with him, which also is the way to eternal life,* Rom. 8. 6. Col. 3. 3. [4] *That eternal happiness, glory, and blessedness, which the saints enjoy in heaven,* Rom. 5. 17. [5] *That quickening and strengthening power of the Spirit of Christ, which supports believers under afflictions and sufferings, so that they are not overwhelmed and conquered by them,* 2 Cor. 4. 10. [6] *Christ's resurrection and intercession,* Rom. 5. 10. [7] *The appetite, or stomach,* Job 33. 20. [8] *The nourishment, or support of life,* Deut. 20. 19. [9] *Blessings pertaining to this life,* 1 Tim. 4. 8. [10] *This world,* Luke 8. 14. [11] *Conversation,* Acts 26. 4. It is spoken, [1] Of Christ, *who is the fountain of natural, spiritual, and eternal life, who has promised eternal life to his people, purchased and prepared it for them: and who prepares them for it, and will actually bestow it upon them,* John

1. 4. | 11. 25. Col. 3. 4. [2] Of the doctrine of the gospel, *which points out the way to eternal life*, John 6. 63. [3] Of the blood, *which, with the spirits contained in it, is the seat and support of life*, Gen. 9. 4.
Gen. 1. 20. the moving creature that hath *l.*
30 and to every thing wherein there is *l.*
2. 7. God breathed into his nostrils the breath of *l.*
9. the tree of *l.* in the midst of the garden, 3. 22.
3. 24. cherubims to keep the way of the tree of *l.*
6. 17. to destroy all wherein is the breath of *l.* 7. 22.
9. 4. flesh with the *l.* shall ye not eat, *Lev.* 17. 14.
5. of every man will I require the *l.* of man
18. 10. I will return according to the time of *l.* 14.
23. 1. these were the years of the *l.* of Sarah
25. 7. the years of Abraham's *l.* ‖ 17. Ishmael's *l.*
42. 15. by the *l.* of Pharaoh, ye shall not go, 16.
45. 5. God did send me before to preserve *l.*
47. 9. not attained to the years of *l.* of my fathers
Exod. 6. 16. the years of the *l.* of Levi were 137.
18. years of the *l.* of Kohath ‖ 20. *l.* of Amram
21. 23. shalt give *l.* for *l.* *Lev.* 24. † 18. *Deut.* 19. 21.
Lev. 17. 11. for the *l.* of the flesh is in the blood
18. 18. besides the other in her *l.* time
24. † 17. he that smiteth *l.* of man, *Deut.* 19. † 6, 11.
Deut. 12. 23. blood is the *l.* not eat *l.* with flesh
20. 19. for the tree of the field is man's *l.*
24. 6. for he taketh a man's *l.* to pledge
30. 15. I have set before thee *l.* 19. *Jer.* 21. 8.
32. 47. it is not a vain thing, because it is your *l.*
Josh. 2. 14. the men answered, our *l.* for yours
1 *Sam.* 25. 29. shall be bound up in the bundle of *l.*
2 *Sam.* 14. 7. for the *l.* of his brother whom he slew
† 14. because God hath not taken away his *l.*
15. 21. whether in death or *l.* there will I be
1 *Kings* 3. 11. hast not asked for thyself long *l.* nor asked the *l.* of thine enemies, 2 *Chr.* 1. 11.
2 *Kings* 4. 16. time of *l.* thou shalt embrace a son, 17.
7. 7. left the camp as it was, and fled for their *l.*
Ezra 6. 10. they may pray for the *l.* of the king
Esth. 8. 11. granted the Jews to stand for their *l.*
Job 3. 20. why is *l.* given to the bitter in soul?
10. 12. thou hast granted me *l.* and favour
12. † 10. in whose hand is the *l.* of every thing
24. 22. he riseth up, and no man is sure of *l.*
31. 39. or the owners thereof to lose their *l.*
33. 4. the breath of the Almighty hath given me *l.*
36. 6. he preserveth not the *l.* of the wicked
14. and their *l.* is among the unclean
38. † 39. wilt thou fill the *l.* of the young lions?
Psal. 16. 11. thou wilt shew me the path of *l.*
21. 4. he asked *l.* of thee, thou gavest him
30. 5. in his favour is *l.* weeping may endure
34. 12. what man is he that desireth *l.*?
36. 9. for with thee is the fountain of *l.*
61. 6. thou wilt prolong the king's *l.*
63. 3. thy loving-kindness is better than *l.*
66. 9. bless God, who holdeth our soul in *l.*
78. 50. but gave their *l.* over to the pestilence
91. 16. with long *l.* will I satisfy him
133. 3. the blessing, even *l.* for evermore
Prov. 1. 19. which taketh away the *l.* of the owners
2. 19. nor take they hold of the paths of *l.*
3. 2. long *l.* and peace shall they add to thee
18. she is a tree of *l.* to them that lay hold on her
22. so shall they be *l.* to thy soul
4. 22. for they are *l.* to those that find them
23. keep thy heart, for out of it are the issues of *l.*
5. 6. lest thou shouldest ponder the path of *l.*
6. 23. reproofs of instruction are the way of *l.*
26. adulteress will hunt for the precious *l.*
8. 35. whoso findeth me findeth *l.* and shall obtain
10. 11. the mouth of the righteous is a well of *l.*
17. is in the way of *l.* that keepeth instruction
11. 30. the fruit of the righteous is a tree of *l.*
12. 10. righteous regardeth the *l.* of his beast
28. in the way of righteousness is *l.* and no death
13. 8. the ransom of a man's *l.* are his riches
12. when desire cometh, it is a tree of *l.*
14. the law of the wise is a fountain of *l.*
14. 27. the fear of the Lord is a fountain of *l.*
30. a sound heart is the *l.* of the flesh, but envy
15. 4. a wholesome tongue is a tree of *l.*
24. the way of *l.* is above to the wise
31. heareth reproof of *l.* abideth among the wise
16. 15. in the light of the king's countenance is *l.*
22. understanding is a well-spring of *l.* to him
18. 21. death and *l.* are in the power of the tongue
21. 21. he that followeth mercy, findeth *l.*
22. 4. by humility are riches, honour, and *l.*
27. † 27. goats'-milk for *l.* for thy maidens
31. 12. she will do him good all the days of her *l.*
Eccl. 2. 3. good they should do all the days of their *l.*
17. therefore I hated *l.* ‖ 7. 12. wisdom giveth *l.*
9. † 9. enjoy *l.* with the wife whom thou lovest
Isa. 38. 16. in all these thin s is the *l.* of my spirit
20. we will sing songs all the days of our *l.*
57. 10. thou hast found the *l.* of thy hand
Jer. 8. 3. and death shall be chosen rather than *l.*
21. 7. hands of them that seek their *l.* 34. 20, 21.
8. I set before you the way of *l.* and of death
49. 37. I will cause Elam to be dismayed before their enemies, before them that seek their *l.*
Lam. 2. 19. lift up thy hands for the *l.* of thy childr.
Ezek. 1. † 20. spirit of *l.* in wheels, † 21. | 10. † 17.
7. † 13. though their *l.* was yet among the living
13. 22. should not return by promising him *l.*
33. 15. if the wicked walk in the statutes of *l.*
Dan. 7. † 12. a prolonging in *l.* was given them
Jonah 1. 14. let us not perish for this man's *l.*
Mal. 2. 5. my covenant was with him of *l.*
Mat. 2. 20. are dead which sought the child's *l.*
3. † 8. bring fruit meet for amendment of *l.*
6. 25. take no thought for your *l.* *Luke* 12. 22.
18. 8. to enter into *l.* halt or maimed, *Mark* 9. 43.
9. better to enter into *l.* with one eye, *Mark* 9. 45.
19. 17. if wilt enter into *l.* keep the commandments
Mark 3. 4. is it lawful to save *l.* or to kill, *Luke* 6. 9.
Luke 1. 75. in holiness all the days of our *l.*
12. 15. for a man's *l.* consisteth not in abundance
23. the *l.* more than meat, the body than raiment
John 1. 4. in him was *l.* and the *l.* was light of men

John 3. 36. that believeth not the Son, shall not see *l.*
5. 26. for as the Father hath *l.* in himself, so hath he given to the Son to have *l.* in himself
29. have done good, to the resurrection of *l.*
40. will not come to me that might have *l.* 10. 10.
6. 33. giveth *l.* unto world ‖ 35. I am bread of *l.* 48.
51. which I will give for the *l.* of the world
53. and drink his blood, ye have no *l.* in you
63. the words that I speak to you, they are *l.*
8. 12. not in darkness, but shall have the light of *l.*
11. 25. I am the resurrection and the *l.* 14. 6.
20. 31. believing ye might have *l.* through his name
Acts 2. 28. hast made known to me the ways of *l.*
3. 15. and killed the Prince of *l.* whom God raised
17. 25. seeing he giveth to all *l.* and breath
26. 4. the manner of *l.* from my youth, Jews know
27. 22. there shall be no loss of any man's *l.*
Rom. 5. 17. shall reign in *l.* by one, Jesus Christ
18. came on all men to justification of *l.*
6. 4. even so we should walk in newness of *l.*
8. 2. the law of the Spirit of *l.* in Christ Jesus
6. to be spiritually minded is *l.* and peace
10. the Spirit is *l.* because of righteousness
38. I am persuaded that neither death nor *l.*
11. 15. the receiving them be, but *l.* from the dead
1 *Cor.* 3. 22. the world, or *l.* or death, all are yours
14. 7. even things without *l.* giving sound
2 *Cor.* 1. 8. insomuch that we despaired even of *l.*
2. 16. to the other the savour of *l.* unto *l.*
3. 6. the letter killeth, but the Spirit giveth *l.*
4. 10. that the *l.* of Jesus might be manifested
12. death worketh in us, but *l.* in you
5. 4. that mortality might be swallowed up of *l.*
Gal. 2. 20. the *l.* which I now live in the flesh
3. 21. a law given which could have given *l.*
Eph. 4. 18. being alienated from the *l.* of God
Phil. 1. 20. whether it be by *l.* or by death
2. 16. holding forth word of *l.* that I may rejoice
Col. 3. 3. and your *l.* is hid with Christ in God
4. when Christ who is our *l.* shall appear
1 *Tim.* 2. 2. we may lead a peaceable *l.* in all godlin.
4. 8. having the promise of the *l.* that now is
2 *Tim.* 1. 1. according to the promise of *l.* in Christ
10. and hath brought *l.* to light by the gospel
3. 10. thou hast fully known my manner of *l.*
Heb. 2. 15. were all their *l.*-time subject to bondage
7. 3. neither beginning of days, nor end of *l.*
16. who is made after the power of an endless *l.*
Jam. 1. 12. he shall receive the crown of *l.*
4. 14. for what is your *l.*? it is even a vapour
1 *Pet.* 3. 7. as being heirs together of the grace of *l.*
10. for he that will love *l.* and see good days
4. 3. for the time past of our *l.* may suffice us
2 *Pet.* 1. 3. hath given us all things pertaining to *l.*
1 *John* 1. 1. our hands have handled the word of *l.*
2. for the *l.* was manifested, and we have seen it
2. 16. the pride of *l.* is not of the Fath. but of world
5. 12. he that hath the Son hath *l.* and he that hath not the Son of God hath not *l.*
16. he shall give him *l.* for them that sin not
Rev. 2. 7. to him will I give to eat of the tree of *l.*
10. be faithful, and I will give thee a crown of *l.*
8. 9. third part of the creatures that had *l.* died
11. 11. the Spirit of *l.* from God entered into them
13. 15. he had power to give *l.* to the beast
21. 6. I will give to thirsty of the water of *l.* freely
22. 1. he shewed me a pure river of water of *l.*
2. the tree of *l.* bare twelve manner of fruits
14. that they may have right to the tree of *l.*
17. let him take the water of *l.* freely

See Book, Eternal, Everlasting.

His LIFE.

Gen. 44. 30. seeing *his l.* is bound up in the lad's life
Exod. 21. 30. he shall give for the ransom of *his l.*
Deut. 17. 19. shall read therein all the days of *his l.*
Josh. 4. 14. they feared him all the days of *his l.*
Judg. 9. 17. for my father adventured *his l.* far
16. 30. more than they which he slew in *his l.*
1 *Sam.* 19. 5. he did put *his l.* in his hand, and slew
23. 15. saw that Saul was come out to seek *his l.*
2 *Sam.* 18. 18. Absalom in *his l.*-time had taken
1 *Kings* 2. 23. if not spoken this word against *his l.*
19. 3. when he saw that, he arose and went for *his l.*
† 4. Elijah sat down, and requested for *his l.*
20. 39. then shall thy life be for *his l.* 42.
2 *Kings* 10. 24. *his l.* shall be for the life of him
Neh. 6. 11. would go into the temple to save *his l.*
Esth. 7. 7. Haman stood to make request for *his l.*
Job 2. 4. all that a man hath will he give for *his l.*
6. behold, he is in thy hand, but save *his l.*
33. 18. and *his l.* from perishing by the sword
20. *his l.* abhorreth bread ‖ 22. *his l.* to destroyers
28. he will deliver, and *his l.* shall see the light
Psal. 49. † 18. though in *his l.* he blessed his soul
Prov. 7. 23. and knoweth not that it is for *his l.*
13. 3. he that keepeth his mouth, keepeth *his l.*
Eccl. 3. 12. for a man to rejoice and do good in *his l.*
7. 15. there is a wicked man that prolongeth *his l.*
8. 15. shall abide of his labours all the days of *his l.*
Isa. 15. 4. Moab, *his l.* shall be grievous to him
Jer. 21. 9. *his l.* shall be to him for a prey, 38. 2.
44. 30. into the hand of them that seek *his l.*
Ezek. 3. 18. nor speakest to warn, to save *his l.*
7. 13. nor strengthen himself in iniquity of *his l.*
32. 10. shall tremble, every man for *his l.*
Amos 2. † 14. nor shall the mighty deliver *his l.*
Mat. 10. 39. he that findeth *his l.* shall lose it; he that loseth *his l.* shall find it, 16. 25. *Mark* 8. 35. *Luke* 9. 24. | 17. 33. *John* 12. 25.
20. 28. to give *h. l.* a ransom for many, *Mark* 10. 45.
Luke 14. 26. yea, and hate not *his* own *l.* also
John 10. 11. good Shepherd giveth *his l.* for sheep
15. 13. that a man lay down *his l.* for his friends
Acts 8. 33. for *his l.* is taken from the earth
20. 10. trouble not yourselves, *his l.* is in him
Rom. 5. 10. much more we shall be saved by *his l.*
Phil. 2. 30. not regarding *his l.* to supply your lack
1 *John* 3. 16. love of G. because he laid down *his l.*

See Days.

My LIFE.

Gen. 19. 19. mercy thou hast shewed in saving *my l.*
27. 46. I am weary of *my l.* what good shall *my l.* do

Gen. 32. 30. *my l.* is preserved ‖ 48. 15. fed me all *my l*
Num. 23. † 10. let *my l.* die the death of righteous
Judg. 12. 3. I put *my l.* in my hands, and passed over
1 *Sam.* 18. 18. what is *my l.* or my father's family
20. 1. what is my sin, that he seeketh *my l.*?
22. 23. he that seeketh *my l.* seeketh thy life
26. 24. so that *my l.* be much set by in the eyes
28. 9. wherefore layest thou a snare for *my l.*?
21. I put *my l.* in my hand, and hearkened to
2 *Sam.* 1. 9. because *my l.* is yet whole in me
16. 11. behold, my son of my bowels seeketh *my l.*
18. 13. have wrought falsehood against *my l.*
19. † 34. how many days are the years of *my l.*
1 *Kings* 19. 4. it is enough, now, take away *my l.*
10. they seek *my l.* to take it away, 14. *Rom.* 11. 3.
2 *Kings* 1. 13. let *my l.* be precious in thy sight, 14.
Esth. 7. 3. let *my l.* be given me at my petition
Job 6. 11. my end that I should prolong *my l.*
7. 7. O remember that *my l.* is but wind
15. my soul chooseth death rather than *my l.*
9. 21. tho' I were perfect, yet I would despise *my l.*
10. 1. my soul is weary of *my l.* I will leave
13. 14. wherefore do I put *my l.* in my hand?
Psal. 7. 5. let him tread down *my l.* on the earth
23. 6. mercy shall follow me all the days of *my l.*
26. 9. gather not *my l.* with bloody men
27. 1. the Lord is the strength of *my l.* of whom
4. dwell in the house of the Lord all days of *my l.*
31. 10. *my l.* is spent with grief and sighing
13. they devised to take away *my l.*
38. 12. that seek after *my l.* lay snares for me
42. 8. and my prayer to the God of *my l.*
64. 1. preserve *my l.* from fear of the enemy
88. 3. and *my l.* draweth nigh to the grave
143. 3. he hath smitten *my l.* to the ground
Isa. 38. 12. I have cut off like a weaver *my l.*
Lam. 3. 53. they cut off *my l.* in the dungeon
58. O Lord, thou hast redeemed *my l.*
Jonah 2. 6. hast brought up *my l.* from corruption
4. 3. O Lord, take, I beseech thee, *my l.* from me
John 10. 15. and I lay down *my l.* for the sheep
17. my Fath. loveth me, because I lay down *my l.*
13. 37. Lord, I will lay down *my l.* for thy sake
Acts 20. 24. nor count I *my l.* dear to myself

This LIFE.

Psal. 17. 14. men which have their portion in *this l.*
Eccl. 6. 12. knoweth what is good for a man in *this l*
9. 9. that is thy portion in *this l.* and in labour
Luke 8. 14. are choked with the cares of *this l.*
21. 34. hearts overcharged with the cares of *this l.*
Acts 5. 20. go, speak all the words of *this l.*
1 *Cor.* 6. 3. much more things that pertain to *this l.*
4. have judgment of things pertaining to *this l.*
15. 19. if in *this l.* only we have hope in Christ
2 *Tim.* 2. 4. entangleth himself with affairs of *this l.*
1 *John* 5. 11. eternal life, and *this l.* is in his Son

Thy LIFE.

Gen. 19. 17. escape for *thy l.* look not behind thee
47. † 8. how many are the days of the years of *thy l.*
Exod. 4. 19. the men are dead which sought *thy l.*
Deut. 28. 66. and *thy l.* shall hang in doubt before thee, and thou shalt have no assurance of *thy l.*
Judg. 18. 25. they run on thee, and thou lose *thy l.*
Ruth 4. 15. he shall be to thee a restorer of *thy l.*
1 *Sam.* 19. 11. if thou save not *thy l.* to-night
22. 23. he that seeketh my life seeketh *thy l.*
26. 24. as *t. l.* was much set by this day, so my life
2 *Sam.* 4. 8. the head of thine enemy that sought *thy l.*
19. 5. thy servants which this day saved *thy l.*
1 *Kings* 1. 12. come that thou mayest save *thy l.*
19. 2. if I make not *thy l.* as the life of one of them
20. 31. go out, peradventure he will save *thy l.*
39. if he be missing *thy l.* be for his life, 42.
Psal. 103. 4. who redeemeth *thy l.* from destruction
Prov. 4. 10. and the years of *t. l.* shall be many, 9. 11.
13. let her not go, keep her, for she is *thy l.*
9. 11. and the years of *thy l.* shall be increased
Isa. 43. 4. therefore will I give people for *thy l.*
Jer. 4. 30. thy lovers, they will seek *thy l.*
11. 21. of the men that seek *thy l.* 22. 25. | 38. 16.
39. 18. *thy l.* shall be for a prey to thee, 45. 5.
Luke 16. 25. thou in *thy l.* receivedst good things
John 13. 38. wilt thou lay down *thy l.* for my sake?

To LIFE.

2 *Kings* 8. 1. whose son he had restored *to l.* 5.
Prov. 10. 16. the labour of the righteous tendeth *to l.*
11. 19. as righteousness tendeth *to l.* so that pursueth
19. 23. the fear of the Lord tendeth *to l.*
Mat. 7. 14. narrow is the way that leadeth *to l.*
John 5. 24. but is passed from death *to l.* 1 *John* 3. 14.
Acts 11. 18. G. to Gentiles granted repentance *to l.*
Rom. 7. 10. the commandment ordained to *l.*
Heb. 11. 35. women received their dead raised *to l.*

LIFT

Signifies, [1] *To raise or heave up*, Gen. 37. 28. [2] *To put to death, or crucify*, John 8. 28. | 12. 32. To Lift up the eyes, signifies, [1] *To direct and make known our desires to God by prayer, with hope and expectation of a gracious answer*, Psal. 121. 1. | 123. 1. [2] *To behold, contemplate, and consider with wonder and admiration*, Isaiah 40. 26. To Lift up the head, signifies, [1] *To restore a person to his former dignity*, Gen. 40. 13. [2] *To recover former strength and courage, so as to oppress others*, Judg. 8. 28. [3] *To rejoice and be glad*, Luke 21. 28. [4] *To be advanced above others, and obtain a complete victory over them*, Psal. 27. 6. To Lift up the hand, signifies, [1] *To swear, or by oath to confirm a thing*, Gen. 14. 22. [2] *To bless*, Lev. 9. 22. *It was an usual posture in* blessing, *which denoted both the place whence the* blessing *was expected, and an earnest desire for obtaining it.* [3] *To pray*, Psal. 28. 2. [4] *To rise in rebellion*, 2 Sam. 18. 28. | 20. 21. [5] *To oppress, threaten, injure, or wrong any manner of way*, Job 31. 21. [6] *To shake off sloth, and heartily to engage in our duty*, Heb. 12. 12.

Thou shalt lift up thy face unto God, *Job* 22. 26. *Thou shalt look up to him by meditation and prayer, not with horror and grief, but with cheerfulness, confidence, and comfort.*

Be ye lift up, ye everlasting doors, *Psal.* 24. 7. *All ye true members of the church, raise up your hearts and souls, which are of an everlasting and immortal nature, from all earthly things, and set them open for the reception of Christ the King of glory.*

Hath lift up his heel against me, *Psal.* 41. 9. *Hath behaved himself insolently, contemptuously, and injuriously towards me. It is a phrase taken from an unruly horse, who kicks at him that owns and feeds him.*

Lift not up the horn, *Psal.* 75. 4. *Carry not yourselves arrogantly, scornfully, or maliciously toward me or any of God's people.*

Lift up thy feet, *Psal.* 74. 3. *Come speedily to our help, and for our deliverance.*

To lift up oneself in height, *that is, to grow proud, insolent, and oppressive,* Ezek. 31. 10.

Gen. 7. 17. the ark was *l.* up above the earth
21. 18. *l.* up the lad, and hold him in thine hand
29. † 1. then Jacob *l.* up his feet and came
37. 28. they *l.* up Joseph out of the pit
40. 13. Pharaoh shall *l.* up thine head, 19.
Exod. 7. 20. *l.* up the rod and smote waters, 14. 16.
20. 25. if thou *l.* up a tool on it thou hast polluted
Num. 6. 26. Lord *l.* up his countenance upon thee
16. 3. wherefore then *l.* ye up yourselves?
23. 24. and *l.* up himself as a young lion
Deut. 22. 4. shalt help him to *l.* them up again
27. 5. not *l.* up an iron tool on them, *Josh.* 8. 31.
Josh. 4. 18. the soles of the priests' feet were *l.* up
Ruth 3. † 4. *l.* up the clothes that are on his feet
2 *Sam.* 23. 8. he *l.* up his spear against 800
18. he *l.* up his spear against 300, 1 *Chr.* 11. 11.
2 *Kings* 9. 32. he *l.* up his face to the window
19. 4. *l.* up thy prayer for the remnant, *Isa.* 37. 4.
25. 27. *l.* up the head of Jehoiachin king of Judah
1 *Chron* 25. 5. all these were to *l.* up the horn
Ezra 1. † 4. let the men of the place *l.* him up
9. 6. I blush to *l.* up my face to thee, my God
Job 5. † 7. the sons of burning coal *l.* up to fly
10. 15. if righteous, yet will I not *l.* up my head
11. 15. then shalt thou *l.* up thy face, 22. 26.
Psal. 4. 6. *l.* up the light of thy countenance on us
7. 6. arise, O Lord, in thine anger, *l.* up thyself
24. 7. *l.* up your heads, O ye gates, be *l.* ye doors, 9.
25. 1. to thee, O Lord, I *l.* my soul, 86. 4. | 143. 8.
28. 2. hear my voice when I *l.* up my hands
9. feed them also, and *l.* them up for ever
41. 9. hath *l.* up his heel against me, *John* 13. 18.
74. 3. *l.* up thy feet to the perpetual desolations
75. 4. and to the wicked, *l.* not up the horn, 5.
93. 3. the floods have *l.* up their waves
94. 2. *l.* up thyself, thou judge of the earth
110. 7. therefore shall he *l.* up the head
Eccl. 4. 10. if they fall, the one will *l.* up his fellow
Isa. 2. 4. nation shall not *l.* up sword against nation, neither shall they learn war any more, *Mic.* 4. 3.
5. 26. he will *l.* up an ensign to the nations
10. 15. as if staff should *l.* up itself as if no wood
24. smite, and shall *l.* up his staff against thee
26. so shall *l.* it up after the manner of Egypt
13. 2. *l.* ye up a banner upon the high mountain
33. 10. now will I rise, now will I *l.* up myself
59. 19. the Lord shall *l.* up a standard against him
62. 10. *l.* up a standard for the people, *Jer.* 50. † 2.
Jer. 7. 16. nor *l.* up cry nor prayer for them, 11. 14.
51. 14. they shall *l.* up a shout against thee
Lam. 3. 41. let us *l.* up our heart with our hands
Ezek. 8. 3. Spirit *l.* me up between the earth, 11. 1.
17. 14. that it might not *l.* itself up, but stand
26. 8. and shall *l.* up the buckler against thee
Zech. 1. 21. so that no man did *l.* up his head, which *l.* up their horn over land of Judah to scatter it
Mat. 12. 11. will he not *l.* it out on the sabbath?
Mark 1. 31. took her by the hand, and *l.* her up
Luke 13. 11. and could in no wise *l.* up herself
21. 28. *l.* up your heads, your redemption draweth
Jam. 4. 10. humble yourselves, and he shall *l.* up

See EYES.

LIFT *hand* or *hands.*

Gen. 14. 22. I have *l.* up mine *hand* to the Lord
41. 44. without thee shall no man *l.* up his *hand*
Deut. 32. 40. I *l.* up my *h.* and say I live for ever
Psal. 10. 12. *l.* up thine *hand*, forget not the humble
28. 2. when I *l.* up my *hands* toward thine oracle
63. 4. I will *l.* up my *hands* in thy name
119. 48. my *h.* will I *l.* up to thy commandments
134. 2. *l.* up your *hands* in the sanctuary and bless
Isa. 49. 22. I will *l.* up mine *hand* to the Gentiles
Lam. 2. 19. *l.* up thy *hands* towards him for the life
Heb. 12. 12. wherefore *l.* up the *h.* that hang down

LIFT *voice.*

Gen. 21. 16. and Hagar *l.* up her *voice* and wept
Job 38. 34. canst thou *l.* up thy *voice* to the clouds
Isa. 10. 30. *l* up thy *voice*, O daughter of Gallim
24. 14. they shall *l.* up their *voice*, shall sing
40. 9. *l.* up thy *voice* with strength, lift it up
42. 2. he shall not cry nor *l.* up his *voice*
11. let the wilderness and cities *l.* up their *voice*
52. 8. thy watchmen shall *l.* up the *voice*
58. 1. cry, spare not, *l.* up thy *voice* like a trumpet
Jer. 22. 20. cry, and *l.* up thy *voice* in Bashan
Ezek. 21. 22. to *l.* up the *voice* with shouting

LIFTED.

Gen 13. 10. Lot *l.* up his eyes and beheld Jordan
18. 2. Abraham *l.* up his eyes and looked, 22. 13.
27. 38. Esau *l.* up voice ‖ 39. 18. as I *l.* up my voice
29. 11. and Jacob *l.* up his voice and wept
31. 10. Jacob *l.* up his eyes saw in a dream, 33. 1.
40. 20. Pharaoh *l.* up the head of the butler
Lev. 9. 22. Aaron *l.* up his hand towards the people
Num. 14. 1. the congregation *l.* up their voice
20. 11. Moses *l.* up his hand and smote the rock
Deut. 8. 14. then thy heart be *l.* up and thou forget
17. 20. that his heart be not *l.* above his brethren
Judg. 2. 4. when the angel of Lord spake, the people *l.* up their voice and wept, 21. 2. 1 *Sam.* 11. 4.
8. 28. so they *l.* up their heads no more
9. 7. Jotham *l.* up his voice and cried, hearken to me
Ruth 1. 9. Orpah and Ruth *l.* up voice and wept, 14
1 *Sam.* 24. 16. and Saul *l.* up his voice and wept
1 *Sam.* 30. 4. David and people *l.* up voice, 2 *Sam.* 3. 32.
2 *Sam.* 13. 36. king's sons came and *l.* up their voice
20. 21. Sheba hath *l.* up his hand against king
22. 49. thou also hast *l.* me up on high
1 *Kings* 11. 26. Jeroboam *l.* up hand against king, 27.
2 *Kings* 14. 10. and thine heart hath *l.* thee up
1 *Chron.* 14. 2. his kingdom was *l.* up on high
2 *Chr.* 5. 13. as trumpeters and singers *l.* up voice
17. 6. his heart was *l.* up in the ways of the Lord
26. 16. heart was *l.* up to destruction, 32. 25.
Job 2. 12. they *l.* up their voice and wept
6. † 2. my calamity *l.* up in the balances
31. 21. if I have *l.* up my hand against the fatherless
29. or *l.* up myself when evil found him
Psal. 24. 4. who hath not *l.* up his soul unto vanity
27. 6. now shall my head be *l.* up above
30. 1. extol thee, for thou hast *l.* me up, 102. 10.
74. 5. as he *l.* up axes upon the thick trees
83. 2. they that hate thee have *l.* up the head
93. 3. the floods have *l.* up their voice, O Lord
106. 26. therefore he *l.* up his hand against them
Prov. 26. † 7. the legs of the lame are *l.* up
30. 13. lofty eyes, and their eyelids are *l.* up
Isa. 2. 12. day of the Lord on every one that is *l.* up
13. on cedars that are *l.* ‖ 14. mountains *l.* up
6. 1. the Lord sitting on a throne high and *l.* up
26. 11. when thy hand is *l.* up they will not see
30. † 25. there shall be on every *l.* up hill rivers
37. 23. against whom hast thou *l.* up thine eyes?
Jer. 51. 9. her judgment is *l.* up to the skies
Ezek. 1. 19. creatures were *l.* up from the earth
20. the wheels were *l.* up, 21. | 10. 17.
3. 14. so the Spirit *l.* me up and took me away
10. 16. cherubims *l.* up their wings, 19. | 11. 22.
20. 5. and *l.* up my hand to the seed of Jacob, 6.
15. yet *l.* up mine hand in the wilderness, 23.
28. when I brought into the land for the which I *l.* up mine hand to give it to them, 42. | 47. 14.
28. 2. because thine heart is *l.* up, 5, 17. | 31. 10.
36. 7. thus saith the Lord, I have *l.* up mine hand
44. 12. have I *l.* up my hand against them
Dan. 5. 20. when his heart was *l.* up and hardened
23. but hast *l.* up thyself against the Lord
7. 4. the first beast was *l.* up from the earth
8. 3. then I *l.* up mine eyes and saw, 10. 5.
Mic. 5. 9. thine hand shall be *l.* up on adversaries
Hab. 2. 4. his soul which is *l.* up is not upright
3. 10. the deep *l.* up his hands on high
Zech. 5. 7. behold, there was *l.* up a talent of lead
9. and they *l.* up the ephah between the earth
9. 16. shall be as the stones of a crown, *l.* up
14. 10. the land shall be *l.* up and inhabited
Mal. 2. † 9. as ye have *l.* up the face against my law
Mark 9. 27. but Jesus *l.* him up, and he arose
Luke 6. 20. he *l.* up his eyes on his disciples
11. 27. a certain woman *l.* up her voice and said
17. 13. ten lepers *l.* up their voices and said
24. 50. and he *l.* up his hands and blessed them
John 3. 14. and as Moses *l.* up the serpent in the wilderness, even so must the Son of man be *l.* up
8. 28. when ye have *l.* up the Son of man
12. 32. I, if I be *l.* up, will draw all men to me
34. sayest thou, Son of man must be *l.* up
Acts 2. 14. Peter *l.* up his voice and said to them
4. 24. *l.* up their voice to God with one accord
14. 11. *l.* up their voices in the speech of Lycaonia
22. 22. and then *l.* up their voices and said, away
1 *Tim.* 3. 6. lest being *l.* up with pride he fall
Rev. 10. 5. the angel *l.* up his hand to heaven

LIFTER.

Psal. 3. 3. my glory, and the *l.* up of mine head

LIFTEST.

Job 30. 22. thou *l.* me up to the wind, thou causest
Psal. 9. 13. that *l.* me up from the gates of death
18. 48. *l.* above those that rise up against me
Prov. 2. 3. and *l.* up thy voice for understanding

LIFTETH.

Deut. 24. † 15. he is poor, and *l.* his soul to it
1 *Sam.* 2. 7. the Lord bringeth low, and *l.* up, 8.
2 *Chron.* 25. 19. thine heart *l.* thee up to boast
Job 39. 18. what time the ostrich *l.* up herself
Psal. 107. 25. wind which *l.* up the waves thereof
113. 7. he *l.* the needy out of the dunghill
147. 6. the Lord *l.* up the meek, he casteth wicked
Isa. 18. 3. see ye when he *l.* up an ensign on mount
Jer. 51. 3. that *l.* himself up in his brigandine
Nah. 3. 3. the horseman *l.* up the bright sword

LIFTING.

Judg. 15. † 17. called the place, *l.* up of the jaw-bone
1 *Chron.* 11. 20. Abishai chief, for *l.* up his spear
15. 16. sounding, by *l.* up the voice with joy
2 *Chron.* 32. † 26. humbled for *l.* up of his heart
Neh. 8. 6. answered, amen, with *l.* up their hands
Job 22. 29. then thou shalt say, there is *l.* up
Psal. 141. 2. *l.* up of my hands as the evening sacrifice
Prov. 30. 32. hast done foolishly in *l.* up thyself
Isa. 9. 18. they shall mount up like the *l.* up of smoke
33. 3. at *l.* up of thyself nations are scattered
1 *Tim.* 2. 8. men pray every where, *l.* up holy hands

LIGHT.

Gen. 44. 3. as soon as the morning was *l.* the men
Judg. 19. 26. fell at door of the house till it was *l.*
1 *Sam.* 14. 36. and spoil them till the morning *l.*
Psal. 139. 11. even the night shall be *l.* about me
Mic. 2. 1. when morning is *l.* they practise it
Zech. 14. 7. that at evening time it shall be *l.*

LIGHT.

Num. 21. 5. our soul loatheth this *l.* bread
Mat. 11. 30. my yoke is easy, and my burden is *l.*
2 *Cor.* 4. 17. our *l.* affliction worketh for us a far

LIGHT.

Judg. 9. 4. Abimelech hired vain and *l.* persons
Zeph. 3. 4. her prophets are *l.* and treacherous

LIGHT.

2 *Sam.* 2. 18. Asahel was *l.* of foot as a wild roe

LIGHT.

Deut. 27. 16. cursed that setteth *l.* by his father
Ezek. 22. 7. in thee they set *l.* by father and mother
Mat. 22. 5. but made *l.* of it, and went their ways

LIGHT *thing.*

1 *Sam.* 18. 23. seemeth it a *l. thing* to be the king's son
1 *Kings* 16. 31. as if it had been a *l. thing* for him
2 *Kings* 3. 18. is but a *l. thing* in the sight of the L.
20. 10. it is a *l. thing* for the shadow to go down
Isa. 49. 6. a *l. thing* that thou shouldest be my servant
Ezek. 8. 17. is it a *l. thing* they commit abominations

LIGHT

Signifies, [1] *The sensation which arises from beholding any bright object,* Exod. 10. 23. | 14. 20. [2] *The sun and moon, which are the springs of light,* Gen. 1. 16. [3] *A son or successor, who keeps one's name and memory from being extinguished,* 1 Kings 11. 36. 2 Chron. 21. 7. [4] *A window,* 1 Kings 7. 4, 5. [5] *Joy, comfort, and felicity,* Esth. 8. 16. Psal. 97. 11. [6] *The appearance of the day,* Job 24. 14. [7] *True saving knowledge,* Isa. 8. 20. [8] *Happiness and prosperity,* Isa. 58. 8. [9] *Support, comfort, and deliverance,* Mic. 7. 8. [10] *The gospel, which is the means of spiritual comfort,* Mat. 4. 16. [11] *The understanding or judgment,* Mat. 6. 23. It is spoken, [1] Of God, *who is a Being of infinite wisdom, truth, holiness, purity, &c.* 1 John 1. 5. [2] Of Jesus Christ, *who is the fountain and author of all knowledge, both natural and spiritual,* Luke 2. 32. John 1. 9. [3] Of the word of God, *which conducts and guides christians in this world, and points out the way to eternal happiness,* Psal. 119. 105. 2 Pet. 1. 19. [4] Of John the Baptist, *who was eminent for his knowledge and zeal,* John 5. 35. [5] Of the apostles, or ministers of the gospel, *who assist others, and direct them to Christ and salvation,* Mat. 5. 14. [6] Of true christians, *who are enlightened by the Spirit of God, and brought to the saving knowledge of God and Christ,* Luke 16. 8. Eph. 5. 8. [7] Of good kings, *both for their splendour, and the counsel and comfort that their people have from them,* 2 Sam. 21. 17.

The light of my countenance they cast not down, *Job* 29. 24. *They were very careful not to abuse my smiles, and to give me no occasion to change my countenance or carriage towards them.*

Let your light so shine before men, &c. *Mat.* 5. 16. *Let your gifts and graces be so apparent to others in your doctrines and lives, that they may be brought to own, and believe in, the true God, and look on you as his true and faithful servants.*

Gen. 1. 3. God said, let there be *l.* and there was *l.*
4. God saw the *l.* ‖ 5. God called the *l.* day
16. the greater *l.* the lesser *l.* to rule the night
Exod. 10. 23. Israel had *l.* in their dwellings
14. 20. but the pillar gave *l.* by night to these
25. 6. this is the offering, oil for the *l.* 27. 20. | 35. 8, 14, 28. | 39. 37. *Lev.* 24. 2.
Num. 4. 16. to Eleazar pertaineth oil for the *l.*
1 *Sam.* 29. 10. and as soon as ye have *l.* depart
2 *Sam.* 21. 17. that thou quench not the *l.* of Israel
23. 4. he shall be as the *l.* of the morning
1 *Kings* 7. 4. *l.* was against *l.* in three ranks, 5.
11. 36. that David my servant may have a *l.*
Neh. 8. † 3. Ezra read from the *l.* till mid-day
9. 19. nor pillar of fire by night to shew them *l.*
Esth. 8. 16. the Jews had *l.* joy and gladness
Job 3. 4. neither let the *l.* shine upon it
9. let it look for *l.* but have none
16. I had been as infants which never saw *l.*
20. wherefore is *l.* given to him in misery, 23.
4. † 18. nor in his angels in whom he put *l.*
10. 22. without order, where the *l.* is as darkness
12. 22. bringeth out to *l.* the shadow of death
25. they grope in the dark without *l.*
18. 5. the *l.* of the wicked shall be put out
6. the *l.* shall be dark in his tabernacle
22. 28. and the *l.* shall shine on thy ways
24. 13. they are of those that rebel against the *l.*
14. the murderer rising with the *l.* killeth
16. marked in the day-time, they know not the *l.*
25. 3. and upon whom doth not his *l.* arise?
28. 11. the thing that is hid bringeth he to *l.*
31. † 26. if I beheld the *l.* when it shined
33. 28. will deliver, and his life shall see the *l.*
30. to be enlightened with the *l.* of the living
36. 30. behold he spreadeth his *l.* upon it
32. with clouds he covereth *l.* and commandeth
37. † 3. he directeth his *l.* to the ends of the earth
† 11. he scattereth the cloud of his *l.*
15. and caused the *l.* of his cloud to shine
21. men see not the bright *l.* in the clouds
38. 15. from the wicked their *l.* is withholden
19. where is the way where *l.* dwelleth?
24. by what way is the *l.* parted? which scattereth
41. 18. by his neesings a *l.* doth shine, and his eyes
Psal. 4. 6. lift up the *l.* of thy countenance on us
27. 1. the Lord is my *l.* and my salvation
37. 6. he shall bring forth thy righteousness as *l.*
38. 10. *l.* of mine eyes is gone, it is gone from me
49. 19. he shall go, they shall never see *l.*
74. 16. thou hast prepared the *l.* and the sun
78. 14. and all the night with a *l.* of fire
97. 11. *l.* is sown for the righteous, and gladness
104. 2. who coverest thyself with *l.* as with garment
118. 27. God is the Lord, who hath shewed us *l.*
119. 105. thy word is a lamp, and a *l.* to my paths
130. the entrance of thy words giveth *l.*
139. 12. darkness and *l.* are both alike to thee
148. 3. praise him, sun, and all ye stars of *l.*
Prov. 4. 18. the path of the just is as the shining *l.*
6. 23. for the commandment is a lamp, the law is *l.*
13. 9. *l.* of righteous rejoiceth, but lamp of wicked
15. 30. the *l.* of the eyes rejoiceth the heart
21. † 4. a proud heart and *l.* of the wicked is sin
Eccl. 11. 7. truly the *l.* is sweet and pleasant
12. 2. while the sun or the *l.* be not darkened
Isa. 5. 20. put darkness for *l.* and *l.* for darkness
30. and the *l.* is darkened in the heavens thereof
8. 20. it is because there is no *l.* in them
9. 2. have seen a great *l.* on them hath *l.* shined
10. 17. the *l.* of Israel shall be for a fire
13. 10. the sun darkened, the moon shall not cause her *l.* to shine, *Mat.* 24. 29. *Mark* 13. 24.
30. 26. the *l.* of the moon shall be as the *l.* of th sun, the *l.* of the sun as the *l.* of seven day

Isa. 51. 4. my judgment to rest for a *l.* to people
59. 9. we wait for *l.* but behold obscurity
60. 19. the Lord shall be to thee an everlasting *l.*
Jer. 4. 23. I beheld the heavens, and they had no *l.*
25. 10. I will take from them the *l.* of the candle
31. 35. the Lord giveth the sun for a *l.* by day, and
ordinances of the moon and stars for *l.* by night
Ezek. 32. † 8. the *l.* of the *l.* I will make dark
Dan. 2. 22. and the *l.* dwelleth with him
5. 11. *l.* and understanding found in Daniel, 14.
Hos. 6. 5. thy judgments as *l.* that goeth forth
Mic. 7. 9. the Lord will bring me forth to the *l.*
Hab. 3. 4. and his brightness was as the *l.*
11. at the *l.* of thine arrows they went
Zeph. 3. 5. every morning bring judgment to *l.*
Zech. 14. 6. in that day the *l.* shall not be clear
Mat. 4. 16. to them that sat in death, *l.* is sprung up
5. 14. ye are the *l.* of the world ‖ 15. it giveth *l.*
16. let your *l.* so shine before men, that they see
6. 22. the *l.* of body is the eye, if eye single, thy
whole body shall be full of *l.* *Luke* 11. 34, 36.
17. 2. and his raiment was white as the *l.*
Luke 2. 32. a *l.* to lighten the Gentiles, and the glory
8. 16. they which enter in may see the *l.* 11. 33.
16. 8. of this world are wiser than the children of *l.*
John 1. 4. in him was life, and life was the *l.* of men
7. the same came to bear witness of that *l.* 8.
9. that was the true *l.* which lighteth every man
3. 19. condemnation, that *l.* is come into the world
20. every one that doeth evil hateth the *l.*
21. but he that doeth truth cometh to the *l.*
5. 35. he was a burning and a shining *l.* and ye
were willing to rejoice for a season in his *l.*
8. 12. Jesus saying, I am the *l.* of the world, 9. 5.
he that followeth me shall have the *l.* of life
11. 9. he stumbleth not, because he seeth the *l.*
10. he stumbleth, because there is no *l.* in him
12. 35. yet a little while is the *l.* with you
36. while ye have the *l.* believe in the *l.* that ye
46. I am come a *l.* into the world, that whosoever
Acts 9. 3. there shined about him a *l.* from heaven
12. 7. a *l.* shined in the prison, and he smote
13. 47. I have set thee to be a *l.* to the Gentiles
16. 29. then he called for a *l.* and sprang in
22. 6. there shone a great *l.* round about me
9. they that were with me saw indeed the *l.*
11. when I could not see for the glory of that *l.*
26. 13. at mid-day, O king, I saw in the way a *l.*
23. should shew *l.* to the people and Gentiles
Rom. 2. 19. a *l.* of them which are in darkness
13. 12. and let us put on the armour of *l.*
1 *Cor.* 4. 5. who will bring to *l.* hidden things
2 *Cor.* 4. 4. lest the *l.* of the gospel should shine
6. who commanded *l.* to shine out of darkness
11. 14. Satan is transformed into an angel of *l.*
Eph. 5. 8. but now are ye *l.* walk as children of *l.*
13. all things that are reproved are made manifest
by the *l.* whatsoever doth make manifest is *l.*
Col. 1. 12. meet for inheritance of the saints in *l.*
1 *Thess.* 5. 5. ye are all children of the *l.* and day
1 *Tim.* 6. 16. dwelling in *l.* no man can approach
2 *Tim.* 1. 10. who brought life and immortality to *l.*
1 *Pet.* 2. 9. who called you into his marvellous *l.*
2 *Pet.* 1. 19. take heed, as to a *l.* shining in dark place
1 *John* 1. 5. God is *l.* and in him is no darkness
Rev. 18. 23. the *l.* of a candle shall shine no more
21. 11. her *l.* was like a stone most precious
23. glory lighten it, and the Lamb is the *l.* thereof
22. 5. they need not *l.* of the sun, the Lord giveth *l.*
See COUNTENANCE, DARKNESS.

Give LIGHT.

Gen. 1. 15. and let them be to *give l.* on the earth
17. and God set the stars to *give l.* on the earth
Exod. 13. 21. in a pillar of fire to *give* them *l.*
25. 37. the lamps may *g. l.* over against it, *Num.* 8. 2.
2 *Kings* 8. 19. he promised to *g.* him a *l.* 2 *Chr.* 21. 7.
Neh. 9. 12. to *g.* them *l.* in the way they should go
Psal. 105. 39. and fire to *give l.* in the night
Isa. 13. 10. the stars of heaven shall not *give* their *l.*
42. 6. I will *g.* thee for a *l.* to the Gentiles, 49. 6.
60. 19. nor shall the moon *g. l.* to thee, *Ezek.* 32. 7.
Mat. 5. 15. it *g. l.* to all in the house, *Luke* 11. 36.
2 *Cor.* 4. 6. to *give* the *l.* of the knowledge of God
Eph. 5. 14. awake, and Christ shall *give* thee *l.*

In the LIGHT.

Psal. 56. 13. that I may walk *in the l.* of the living
Isa. 2. 5. come, let us walk *in the l.* of the Lord
50. 11. walk *in the l.* of your fire, and in the sparks
John 12. 36. while ye have the light, believe *in the l.*
1 *John* 1. 7. but if we walk *in the l.* as he is *in the l.*
2. 9. he that saith he is *in l.* and hateth his brother
10. that loveth his brother, abideth *in the l.*
Rev. 21. 24. nations that are saved shall walk *in l.*

Thy LIGHT.

Psal. 36. 9. and in *thy l.* shall we see light
43. 3. O send out *thy l.* and thy truth, let them lead
Isa. 58. 8. then shall *thy l.* break forth as morning
10. then shall *thy l.* rise in obscurity, and thy dark.
60. 1. arise, shine, for *thy l.* is come, the glory
3. the Gentiles shall come to *thy l.* and kings
19. the sun shall be no more *thy l.* by day
20. for the Lord shall be *thy* everlasting *l.*

LIGHT, ED.

Exod. 25. 37. and they shall *l.* the lamps, 40. 4.
40. 25. he *l.* the lamps before the Lord, *Num.* 8. 3.
Psal. 18. 28. for thou wilt *l.* my candle, L. enlighten
Mat. 5. 15. nor do men *l.* a candle, and put it under
Luke 8. 16. no man, when he hath *l.* a candle, 11. 33.
15. 8. doth not *l.* a candle, and sweep the house
Rev. 7. 16. nor shall the sun *l.* on them, nor heat

LIGHT.

Ruth 2. 3. her hap was to *l.* on a part of Boaz' field

LIGHT.

2 *Sam.* 17. 12. and we will *l.* on him as the dew

LIGHTED.

Gen. 24. 64. when she saw Isaac, she *l.* off the camel
Josh. 15. 18. and she *l.* off her ass, *Judg.* 1. 14.
Judg. 4. 15. Sisera *l.* off his chariot and fled
1 *Sam.* 25. 23. Abigail hasted and *l.* off the ass
2 *Kings* 5. 21. Naaman *l.* down from the chariot

LIGHTED.

Gen. 28. 11. Jacob *l.* on a certain place, and tarried
2 *Kings* 10. 15. Jehu *l.* on Jehonadab son of Rechab

LIGHTED.

Isa. 9. 8. sent a word to Jacob and it *l.* on Israel

LIGHTEN.

2 *Sam.* 22. 29. the Lord will *l.* my darkness
Ezra 9. 8. that our God may *l.* our eyes and give
Psal. 13. 3. *l.* mine eyes, lest I sleep the sleep
Luke 2. 32. a light to *l.* the Gentiles and the glory
Rev. 21. 23. had no sun, the glory of God did *l.* it

LIGHTEN.

1 *Sam.* 6. 5. peradventure he will *l.* his hand
Jonah 1. 5. cast wares into the sea, to *l.* it of them

LIGHTER.

1 *Kings* 12. 4. make thou yoke *l.* 9. 10. 2 *Chr.* 10. 10.
Psal. 62. 9. they are altogether *l.* than vanity
Isa. 49. † 6. art thou *l.* than to be my servant
Ezek. 8. † 17. any thing *l.* than to commit abominat.

LIGHTEST.

Num. 8. 2. say to him, when thou *l.* the lamps

LIGHTETH.

Exod. 30. 8. and when Aaron *l.* the lamps at even
John 1. 9. that was the true light which *l.* every man

LIGHTETH.

Deut. 19. 5. axe-head slippeth and *l.* on his neighb.

LIGHTING.

Isa. 30. 30. Lord shall shew the *l.* down of his arm
Mat. 3. 16. descending like a dove, and *l.* on him

LIGHTLY.

Gen. 26. 10. one might *l.* have lien with thy wife
Isa. 9. 1. when at first he *l.* afflicted the land
Jer. 4. 24. I beheld, and all the hills moved *l.*
Mark 9. 39. do a miracle, can *l.* speak evil of me
See ESTEEMED.

LIGHTENED.

Psal. 34. 5. they looked to him and were *l.* and faces
77. 18. the lightnings *l.* the world, earth trembled
Rev. 18. 1. the earth was *l.* with his glory
See ENLIGHTENED.

LIGHTENED.

Acts 27. 18. being tossed, next day they *l.* ship, 38.

LIGHTNESS.

Jer. 3. 9. thro' *l.* of her whoredoms she defiled land
23. 32. tell them cause my people to err by their *l.*
2 *Cor.* 1. 17. when I was thus minded, did I use *l.*?

LIGHTENETH.

Prov. 29. 13. the Lord *l.* both their eyes
Luke 17. 24. for as lightning that *l.* out of one part

LIGHTNING.

2 *Sam.* 22. 15. he sent *l.* and discomfited them
Job 28. 26. when he made a way for the *l.* of thunder
37. 3. he directeth his *l.* to the ends of the earth
38. 25. who divided a way for the *l.* of thunder
Psal. 144. 6. cast forth *l.* and scatter them
Ezek. 1. 13. and out of the fire went forth *l.*
14. living creatures ran as the appearance of *l.*
Dan. 10. 6. and his face as the appearance of *l.*
Nah. 3. † 3. horsemen lifted up *l.* of the spear
Zech. 9. 14. his arrow shall go forth as the *l.*
Mat. 24. 27. as *l.* cometh out of the east, *Luke* 17. 24.
28. 3. his countenance was as *l.* his raiment white
Luke 10. 18. I beheld Satan as *l.* fall from heaven

LIGHTNINGS.

Exod. 19. 16. thunders, *l.* and thick cloud on mount
20. 18. all the people saw the *l.* and noise of trump.
Job 38. 35. canst thou send *l.* that they may go?
Psal. 18. 14. he shot out *l.* and discomfited them
77. 18. *l.* lighted the world, earth trembled, 97. 4.
78. † 48. he gave their cattle to hail and flocks to *l.*
135. 7. he maketh *l.* for the rain, he bringeth wind
Jer. 10. 13. he maketh *l.* with rain, 51. 16.
Nah. 2. 4. the chariots shall run like the *l.*
Zech. 10. † 1. so the Lord shall make *l.*
Rev. 4. 5. out of the throne proceeded *l.* thunderings
8. 5. there were voices, thunderings, and *l.* 11. 19.
16. 18. there were *l.* and a great earthquake

LIGHTS.

Gen. 1. 14. let there be *l.* in the firmament of heaven
15. and let them be for *l.* in the firmament
16. God made two great *l.* greater to rule the day
1 *Kings* 6. 4. he made windows of narrow *l.*
Psal. 136. 7. to him that made great *l.* for his mercy
Ezek. 32. 8. all the bright *l.* will I make dark
Luke 12. 35. let your loins be girded, your *l.* burn.
Acts 20. 8. there were many *l.* in the upper chamber
Phil. 2. 15. among whom ye shine as *l.* in the world
Jam. 1. 17. cometh down from the Father of *l.*

LIGN-ALOES.

Num. 24. 6. as trees of *l.* which the Ld. hath planted

LIGURE.

Exod. 28. 19. the third row a *l.* an agate, 39. 12.

LIKE.

Gen. 13. 10. Sodom was *l.* the land of Egypt
Exod. 15. 11. who is *l.* unto thee? *Deut.* 33. 29.
1 *Kings* 8. 23. 2 *Chr.* 6. 14. *Psal.* 35. 10. | 71. 19.
16. 31. manna was *l.* coriander-seed, white
24. 17. the glory of the Lord was *l.* devouring fire
30. 32. nor shall ye make any ointment *l.* it
33. whosoever compoundeth any *l.* it, 38.
34. of each shall there be a *l.* weight
34. 1. hew two tables *l.* to the first, 4. *Deut.* 10. 1, 3.
Num. 23. 10. and let my last end be *l.* his
Deut. 4. 32. or any thing that hath been heard *l.* it
7. 26. lest thou be a cursed thing *l.* it
17. 14. set king over me *l.* all nations, 1 *Sam.* 8. 5, 20.
18. 8. they shall have *l.* portions to eat
15. prophet of thy brethren *l.* me, *Acts* 3. 22. | 7. 37.
18. I will raise a prophet from brethren *l.* to thee
29. 23. *l.* the overthrow of Sodom and Gomorrah
34. 10. there arose not a prophet *l.* to Moses
Josh. 10. 14. no day *l.* that before or after it
Judg. 13. 6. his countenance *l.* an angel of God
16. 12. he brake them from his arms *l.* a thread
17. I shall become weak and *l.* any other man
Ruth 2. 13. tho' I be not *l.* to one of thy handmaidens
4. 11. Lord make the woman *l.* Rachel and *l.* Leah
12. let thy house be *l.* the house of Pharez
1 *Sam.* 2. 2. nor is there any rock *l.* our God
4. 9. be strong, quit yourselves *l.* men, 1 *Cor.* 16. 13.
17. 7. the staff of his spear was *l.* a weaver's beam
25. 36. Nabal held a feast *l.* the feast of a king
26. 15. a valiant man, and who is *l.* to thee in Isr.
2 *Sam.* 7. 9. *l.* to the name of the great men
2 *Sam.* 7. 23. one nation in earth is *l.* thy people Isr.
22. 34. he maketh my feet *l.* hinds' feet
1 *Kings* 3. 12. none *l.* thee bef. not arise *l.* thee, 13.
10. 20. there was not the *l.* made in any kingdom
12. 32. Jeroboam ordained a feast *l.* that in Judah
16. 3. *l.* the house of Jerob. 7. | 21. 22. 2 *Kings* 9. 9.
18. 44. there ariseth a little cloud *l.* a man's hand
20. 25. number thee an army *l.* the army thou lost
27. pitched before them *l.* two little flocks of kids
22. 13. word *l.* word of one of those, 2 *Chr.* 18. 12.
2 *Kings* 3. 2. but not *l.* his father and *l.* his mother
5. 14. his flesh came again *l.* flesh of a little child
9. 9. and *l.* the house of Baasha son of Ahijah
13. 7. had made them *l.* dust by threshing
14. 3. yet not *l.* David his fath. 16. 2. 2 *Chr.* 28. 1.
17. 15. the L. charged they should not do *l.* them
18. 32. take you to a land *l.* your own, *Isa.* 36. 17.
23. 25. *l.* to him was there no king, *Neh.* 13. 26.
1 *Chron.* 12. 22. a great host *l.* the host of God
27. 23. would increase Israel *l.* the stars of heaven
2 *Chr.* 1. 9. over a people, *l.* the dust of the earth
21. 19. no burning for him *l.* burning of fathers
30. 7. be not ye *l.* your fathers and your brethren
33. 2. *l.* to the abominations of the heathen
35. 18. there was no passover *l.* to that in Israel
Job 5. 26. to grave *l.* as a shock of corn cometh in
10. 10. hast thou not curdled me *l.* cheese?
11. 12. though man be born *l.* a wild ass's colt
12. 25. he maketh them to stagger *l.* a drunken man
13. 12. your remembrances are *l.* to ashes
14. 2. he cometh forth *l.* a flower and is cut down
15. 16. filthy is man, who drinketh iniquity *l.* water
16. 14. he runneth upon me *l.* a giant
20. 7. he shall perish for ever *l.* his own dung
21. 11. they send their little ones *l.* a flock
34. 7. what man is *l.* Job, who drinketh scorning
36. 22. God exalteth by power, who teacheth *l.* him?
38. 3. gird up now thy loins *l.* a man, 40. 7.
40. 9. hast thou an arm *l.* God, or canst thunder
41. 33. on earth there is not his *l.* who is made
42. 8. ye have not spoken right *l.* my servant Job
Ps. 1. 3. he shall be *l.* a tree planted by the rivers
4. ungodly are not so, but are *l.* the chaff
7. 2. lest he tear my soul *l.* a lion, rending it
17. 12. *l.* as a lion that is greedy of his prey
22. 14. I am poured out *l.* water, my heart *l.* wax
28. 1. I become *l.* them that go down to the pit
31. 12. I am forgotten, I am *l.* a broken vessel
36. 6. thy righteousness is *l.* the great mountains
37. 2. they shall be soon cut down *l.* grass
35. and spreading himself *l.* a green bay-tree
39. 11. thou makest his beauty to consume *l.* moth
44. 11. thou hast given us *l.* sheep for meat
49. 12. man is *l.* the beasts that perish, 20.
52. 2. thy tongue is *l.* a sharp razor working
8. but I am *l.* a green olive-tree in the house of G.
55. 6. O that I had wings *l.* a dove, I would fly
58. 4. *l.* the poison of a serpent, *l.* the deaf adder
59. 6. they make a noise *l.* a dog, they go, 14.
64. 3. who whet their tongue *l.* a sword
72. 6. he shall come down *l.* rain on the grass
73. 5. nor are they plagued *l.* other men
77. 20. thou leddest thy people *l.* a flock, 78. 52.
78. 57. they dealt unfaithfully *l.* their fathers
79. 3. their blood have shed *l.* water round Jerus.
80. 10. the boughs thereof *l.* the goodly cedars
82. 7. but shall die *l.* men, and fall *l.* one of princes
83. 13. O my God, make them *l.* a wheel
89. 8. a strong Lord *l.* to thee, 113. 5. *Mic.* 7. 18.
92. 12. the righteous shall flourish *l.* the palm-
tree, he shall grow *l.* a cedar in Lebanon
102. 4. my heart is smitten, withered *l.* grass, 11.
6. I am *l.* a pelican, *l.* an owl of the desert
26. all of them shall wax old *l.* a garment
103. 13. *l.* as a father pitieth his children, so Lord
104. 2. who stretchest out the heavens *l.* a curtain
105. 41. they ran in the dry places *l.* a river
107. 27. they reel and stagger *l.* a drunken man
109. 18. *l.* water, *l.* oil let it come into his bones
115. 8. they that make them are *l.* to them, 135. 18.
126. 1. captivity of Zion, we were *l.* them dream
143. 7. lest I be *l.* them that go down to the pit
144. 4. man is *l.* to vanity, his days as a shadow
147. 16. he giveth snow *l.* wool, hoar frost *l.* ashes
Prov. 18. 19. their contentions *l.* the bars of a castle
20. 5. counsel in the heart of man is *l.* deep water
23. 32. it biteth *l.* a serpent, stingeth *l.* an adder
25. 19. in an unfaithful man is *l.* a broken tooth
28. *l.* a city broken down, and without walls
26. 4. answer not a fool, lest thou be *l.* to him
Cant. 2. 9. my beloved is *l.* a roe or young hart
17. turn, my beloved, and be thou *l.* a roe, 8. 14.
3. 6. who is this that cometh *l.* pillars of smoke?
4. 2. thy teeth are *l.* a flock of sheep even shorn
3. thy lips *l.* scarlet, temples *l.* a pomegranate
4. thy neck is *l.* the tower of David for armoury
5. thy two breasts are *l.* two young roes, 7. 3.
5. 13. his lips *l.* lilies dropping sweet myrrh
6. 12. my soul made me *l.* chariots of Ammi-nadib
7. 1. the joints of thy thighs are *l.* jewels
2. thy navel is *l.* a goblet, thy belly is *l.* wheat
4. eyes ‖ 5. head, hair ‖ 7. stature *l.* a palm-tree
8. and the smell of thy nose *l.* apples
Isa. 1. 9. should have been *l.* Gomorrah, *Rom.* 9. 29.
18. tho' your sins be red *l.* crimson, shall be as wool
10. 13. put down the inhabitants *l.* a valiant man
11. 7. and the lion shall eat straw *l.* the ox
16. and shall be an highway, *l.* as it was to Israel
14. 10. they shall say, art thou become *l.* to us?
14. I will ascend, I will be *l.* the Most High?
19. thou art cast out *l.* an abominable branch
16. 11. my bowels shall sound *l.* an harp for Moab
19. 16. in that day shall Egypt be *l.* unto women
20. 3. *l.* as my servant Isaiah hath walked naked
22. 18. will toss thee *l.* a ball into a large country
26. 17. *l.* a woman with child that draweth near
30. 33. breath of the Lord *l.* a stream of brimstone
33. 9. Sharon is *l.* a wilderness, Bashan and Carmel
38. 12. I have cut off *l.* a weaver my life
14. *l.* a crane or swallow so did I chatter
42. 14. now will I cry *l.* a travailing woman
46. 5. to whom will ye compare me that we may be *l.*

Isa. 57. 20. the wicked are l. the troubled sea
58. 1. spare not, lift up thy voice l. a trumpet
11. be l. a watered garden, and l. a spring
59. 10. we grope for the wall l. the blind
11. we roar all l. bears, and mourn sore l. doves
19. when the enemy shall come in l. a flood
63. 2. l. him that treadeth in the wine-fat
64. 6. our iniquities l. wind have taken us away
66. 12. I will extend peace to her l. a river
Jer. 4. 4. lest my fury come forth l. fire, 21. 12.
5. 19. l. as ye have forsaken me, and served gods
10. 16. the portion of Jacob is not l. them
11. 19. I was l. a lamb brought to the slaughter
17. 6. for he shall be l. the heath in the desert
23. 29. is not my word l. fire, and l. a hammer?
26. 6. then will I make this house l. Shiloh, 9.
18. saying, Zion shall be plowed l. a field
29. 22. make thee l. Zedekiah and l. Ahab
36. 32. were added besides to them many l. words
38. 9. he is l. to die with hunger where he is
46. 20. Egypt is l. a very fair heifer, but destruct.
48. 6. flee, be l. the heath in the wilderness
28. be l. dove || 49. 19. shall come l. a lion, 50. 44.
49. 19. who is l. me, who will appoint?
51. 19. the portion of Jacob is not l. them
Ezek. 5. 9. whereto I will not do any more the l.
12. 11. l. as I have done, so shall it be done them
18. 10. and doth the l. to any of these things
25. 8. the house of Judah is l. to all the heathen
31. 2. whom art thou l. in thy greatness, 18.
8. not any tree was l. to him in his beauty
45. 25. in the seventh month shall he do the l.
Dan. 3. 25. the form of the fourth is l. the Son of G.
5. 21. his heart was made l. the beasts, l. oxen
7. 13. one l. the Son of man came with clouds
Hos. 4. 9. and there shall be l. people, l. priest
5. 10. the princes l. them that remove the bound
6. 7. but they l. men have transgressed the coven.
14. 8. I am l. a green fir-tree, from me is fruit
Joel 2. 2. there hath not been ever the l. nor shall be
Amos 5. 6. lest he break out l. fire in Joseph
6. 5. and invent instruments of music l. David
Zech. 1. 6. l. as the Lord of hosts thought to do
12. 6. make the governors of Judah l. a hearth
Mat. 3. 16. the Spirit descending l. a dove, and lighting on him, Mark 1. 10. Luke 3. 22. John 1. 32.
6. 8. be not ye therefore l. unto them
29. was not arrayed l. one of these, Luke 12. 27.
11. 16. l. childr. sitting in the market, Luke 7. 32.
12. 13. it was restored whole l. as the other
13. 31. the kingdom of heaven is l. to a grain of mustard seed, Mark 4. 31. Luke 13. 19.
33. kingdom of heaven is l. leaven, Luke 13. 21.
44. is l. to a treasure || 45. is l. to a merchant
47. is l. to a net || 52. is l. an householder, 20. 1.
22. 2. the kingdom of heaven is l. to a certain king
39. and the second is l. to it, Mark 12. 31.
23. 27. for ye are l. to whited sepulchres
28. 3. his countenance was l. lightning, and raiment
Luke 6. 47. I will shew you to whom he is l.
7. 31. and to what are they l.? || 32. are l. childr.
13. 18. he said, to what is the kingdom of God l.?
John 7. 46. answered, never man spake l. this man
8. 55. I shall be a liar l. unto you, but I know
9. 9. some, this is he, others said, he is l. him
Acts 8. 32. l. a lamb dumb before his shearer
11. 17. forasmuch as God gave them the l. gift
14. 15. we also are men of l. passions with you
17. 29. not to think the Godhead is l. gold or silver
19. 25. with the workmen of l. occupation
Rom. 1. 23. an image made l. to corruptible man
6. 4. l. as Christ was raised up from the dead
Phil. 3. 21. fashioned l. unto his glorious body
1 Thess. 2. 14. suffered l. things of your countrymen
Heb. 2. 17. it behoved him to be made l. his brethren
4. 15. was in all points tempted l. as we are
7. 3. but made l. to the Son of God, abideth a priest
Jam. 1. 6. that wavereth is l. a wave of the sea
23. he is l. a man beholding his natural face
5. 17. Elias was a man subject to l. passions
1 Pet. 3. 21. l. figure whereunto baptism save us
2 Pet. 1. 1. have obtained l. precious faith with us
1 John 3. 2. he shall appear, we shall be l. him
Rev. 1. 13. one l. the Son of man, clothed, 14. 14.
13. 4. worshipped, saying, who is l. to the beast?
11. he had two horns l. a lamb, and he spake as
16. 13. I saw three unclean spirits l. frogs come
18. 18. saying, what city is l. to this great city?

LIKE *manner*.

Exod. 7. 11. did in l. man. with their enchantments
23. 11. in l. man. thou shalt deal with thy vineyard
Deut. 22. 3. in l. manner shalt thou do with his ass
Judg. 11. 17. in l. manner they sent to king of Moab
1 Sam. 19. 24. he prophesied before Samuel in l. ma.
Neh. 6. 5. Sanballat sent in l. manner the fifth time
Isa. 51. 6. that dwell there shall die in l. manner
Mark 13. 29. ye, in l. man. when ye see these things
Luke 6. 23. in l. man. did their fathers to prophets
20. 31. third took her, in l. man. the seventh also
Acts 1. 11. shall so come in l. man. as ye have seen
1 Tim. 2. 9. in l. m. that women adorn themselves
Jude 7. in l. man. giving themselves to fornication

LIKE-MINDED.

Rom. 15. 5. the God of patience grant you to be l. m.
Phil. 2. 2. that ye be l. m. || 20. I have no man l. m.

***None* LIKE.**

Exod. 8. 10. there is none l. the Lord our G. 9. 14. Deut. 33. 26. 2 Sam. 7. 22. 1 Chron. 17. 20.
9. 24. none l. the hail || 11. 6. none l. cry of Egypt
1 Sam. 10. 24. none l. Saul among all the people
21. 9. David said, there is none l. that, give it me
1 Kings 3. 12. there was n. l. Sol. || 21. 25. n. l. Ahab
2 Kings 18. 5. so that after there was n. l. Hezekiah
Job 1. 8. that there is none l. him in the earth, 2. 3.
Ps. 86. 8. among the gods n. l. to thee, Jer. 10. 6, 7.
Isa. 46. 9. for I am God, and there is none l. me
Jer. 30. 7. alas, that day is great, so that none l. it
Dan. 1. 19. among all was found none l. Daniel

***Such* LIKE.**

Ezek. 18. 14. considereth, and doeth not such l.
Mark 7. 8. many other such l. things ye do, 13.
Gal. 5. 21. envyings, drunkenness, and such l.

LIKE.

Deut. 25. 7. if the man l. not to take her, 8.
Rom. 1. 28. even as they did not l. to retain God

LIKED.

1 Chr. 28. 4. among the sons of my father he l. me

LIKEN.

Isa. 40. 18. to whom then will ye l. God? 25. | 46. 5.
Lam. 2. 13. what thing shall I l. to thee?
Mat. 7. 24. and doeth them, I will l. him to a man
11. 16. whereto l. this generation, Luke 7. 31.
Mark 4. 30. whereunto l. the kingdom, Luke 13. 20.

LIKENED.

Ps. 89. 6. who among the sons can be l. to Lord?
Jer. 6. 2. I have l. the daughter of Zion to a comely
Mat. 7. 26. shall be l. to a foolish man who built
13. 24. kingdom of heaven is l. 18. 23. | 25. 1.

LIKENESS

Signifies, [1] *The external visible form or representation of a thing*, Ezek. 1. 5. [2] *An image representing a person or thing*, Deut. 4. 12, 15. Isa. 40. 18. [3] *A true and real resemblance between one person and another*, Gen. 5. 3.

Gen. 1. 26. let us make man after our l. 5. 1.
5. 3. Adam begat a son in his own l.
Exod. 20. 4. not make the l. of any thing
Deut. 4. 16. lest ye make a graven image, the l. of male or female, 17, 18, 23, 25. | 5. 8.
Psal. 17. † 12. l. of him is as a lion that desireth
17. 15. I shall be satisfied, when awake with thy l.
Isa. 13. † 4. l. of great people gathered together
40. 18. or what l. will ye compare to him?
Ezek. 1. 5. came the l. of four living creatures
10. as for the l. of their faces, 10. 22.
13. l. of lamps || 16. they four had one l. 10. 10.
22. the l. of the firmament was as crystal
26. l. of a throne, 10. 1. | 8. 2. lo, a l. as of fire
28. this was the l. of the glory of the Lord
10. 21. and the l. of the hands of a man
19. † 10. thy mother is like a vine in thy l.
Acts 14. 11. gods are come down in the l. of men
Rom. 6. 5. if we have been planted in the l. of his death, we shall be also in the l. of his resurrection
8. 3. God sending his Son in the l. of sinful flesh
Phil. 2. 7. and was made in the l. of men

LIKETH.

Deut. 23. 16. he shall dwell where it l. him best
Esth. 8. 8. write ye also for the Jews as it l. you
Amos 4. 5. for this l. you, O children of Israel

LIKING.

Job 39. 4. their young ones are in good l. grow up

LIKING.

Dan. 1. 10. why should he see your faces worse l.

LIKEWISE.

Exod. 22. 30. l. shalt thou do with thine oxen
Deut. 12. 30. serve their gods, even so will I do l.
15. 17. to thy maid-servant thou shalt do l.
22. 3. to thy brother's lost goods shalt thou do l.
Judg. 7. 17. he said to them, look on me, and do l.
1 Sam. 19. 21. sent messengers, and they prophesied l.
31. 5. fell l. on his sword, and died with him
2 Sam. 17. 5. and let us hear l. what he saith
1 Kings 11. 8. and l. did he for all his strange wives
1 Chron. 19. 15. l. fled before Abishai his brother
23. 30. to praise every morning and l. at even
Neh. 5. 10. I l. might exact of them money
Esth. 4. 16. I also and my maidens will fast l.
Psal. 49. 10. l. the fool and brutish person perish
52. 5. God shall l. destroy thee for ever
Eccl. 7. 22. knowest thou thys. l. hast cursed others
Nah. 1. 12. though they be quiet and l. many, yet
Mat. 17. 12. l. shall also Son of man suffer of them
18. 35. so l. shall my heavenly Father do to you
20. 5. he went about the sixth hour, and did l.
10. they l. received every man a penny
21. 30. he came to the second and said l.
36. other servants, and they did unto them l.
22. 26. l. the second and third died, Mark 12. 21.
24. 33. so l. when ye see these things, Luke 21. 31.
25. 17. l. he that had received two talents
26. 35. l. also said all his disciples, Mark 14. 31.
27. 41. l. the chief priests mocked, Mark 15. 31.
Luke 2. 38. and she gave thanks l. to the Lord
3. 11. let him do l. || 6. 31. do ye also to them l.
10. 37. go and do l. || 13. 3. ye shall l. perish, 5.
14. 33. l. who forsaketh not all that he hath
15. 7. l. joy shall be in heaven over one, 10.
16. 25. l. Lazarus received evil things, but now
17. 10. so l. when ye shall have done all things
22. 20. l. also the cup after supper, saying
John 5. 19. what he doeth, these also doeth the Son l.
Acts 3. 24. prophets have l. foretold of these days
Rom. 1. 27. l. the men leaving the natural use
6. 11. l. reckon yourselves to be dead to sin
8. 26. l. the Spirit helpeth our infirmities
1 Cor. 7. 3. and l. also the wife to the husband
Gal. 2. 13. other Jews dissembled l. with him
1 Tim. 5. 25. l. the good works of some are manifest
Tit. 2. 6. young men l. exhort to be sober-minded
Heb. 2. 14. he also himself l. took part of the same
1 Pet. 4. 1. arm yourselves l. with the same mind
Jude 8. l. these filthy dreamers defile the flesh
Rev. 8. 12. the day shone not, and the night l.

LIKE *wise*.

Mat. 21. 24. I in l. wise will tell by what authority

LILY

Signifies, *The beautiful, fragrant, and medicinal flower so called*, Mat. 6. 28. To which are compared, [1] *Christ, who is refreshing and beautiful to true believers*, Cant. 2. 1. [2] *His church and people*, Cant. 2. 2, 16.

Cant. 2. 1. I am the rose of Sharon, and l. of valleys
2. as the l. among thorns, so is my love among
Hos. 14. 5. Israel shall grow as the l. and cast forth

LILIES.

1 Kings 7. 26. wrought with flowers of l. 2 Chr. 4. 5.
Cant. 2. 16. my beloved feedeth among the l. 6. 3.
4. 5. like two young roes which feed among the l.
5. 13. his lips like l. dropping sweet myrrh
7. 2. thy belly is like wheat set about with l.
Mat. 6. 28. consid. the l. how they grow, Luke 12. 27.

LILY *work*.

1 Kings 7. 19. the chapiters were of l. w. in the porch
1 Kin. 7. 22. and on the top of the pillars was l. work

LIME.

Isa. 33. 12. the people shall be as the burnings of l.
Amos 2. 1. he burned bones of king of Edom to l.

LIMIT.

Ezek. 43. 12. the l. thereof shall be most holy

LIMITED.

Psal. 78. 41. they l. the Holy One of Israel

LIMITETH.

Heb. 4. 7. again, he l. a certain day, saying, to-day

LINE

Signifies, [1] *A cord or instrument to measure any thing by*, 1 Kings 7. 15, 23. [2] *Direction or instruction given us by any thing*, Psalm 19. 4. [3] *A portion measured by line*, Psalm 16. 6. [4] *The doctrine of the word briefly and plainly delivered*, Isa. 28. 10, 13. [5] *Judgment and destruction laid along upon some place or person as it were by line*, 2 Kings 21. 13. [6] *A building or edifice made by line*, Zech. 1. 16.

Josh. 2. 18. bind this l. of scarlet thread in window
21. she bound the scarlet l. in the window
2 Sam. 8. 2. he measured Moab with a l. with one l.
1 Kings 7. 15. and a l. of twelve cubits did compass
23. a l. of thirty cubits did compass, 2 Chr. 4. 2.
2 Kings 21. 13. stretch over Jerusalem l. of Samaria
Job 38. 5. or who hath stretched the l. on the earth?
Psal. 19. 4. their l. is gone through all the earth
78. 55. he divided them an inheritance by l.
Isa. 18. † 2. a nation of l. l. and treading under foot
28. 10. for l. must be upon l. l. upon l. 13.
17. judgment also will I lay to the l. and right.
34. 11. shall stretch out on it the l. of confusion
17. his hand hath divided it to them by l.
44. 13. he marketh it out with a l. he fitteth it
Jer. 31. 39. the measuring l. shall yet go forth
Lam. 2. 8. the Lord hath stretched out a l.
Ezek. 40. 3. a man that had the l. of flax in his hand
47. 3. the man that had the l. went eastward
Amos 7. 17. thy land shall be divided by l. and die
Zech. 1. 16. a l. shall be stretched on Jerusalem
2. 1. a man with a measuring l. in his hand
2 Cor. 10. 16. not to boast in another man's l.

LINEAGE.

Luke 2. 4. because he was of the l. of David

LINES.

2 Sam. 8. 2. with two l. measured he to put to death
Psal. 16. 6. the l. are fallen in pleasant places

LINGERED.

Gen. 19. 16. while Lot l. the men laid hold on hand
43. 10. except we had l. surely we had returned

LINGERETH.

2 Pet. 2. 3. whose judgment of a long time l. not

LINEN.

Exod. 28. 42. thou shalt make them l. breeches
Lev. 6. 10. put on l. garment and l. breeches 16. 4.
13. 47. whether woollen or l. garment, 48, 52, 59.
16. 23. Aaron shall put off the l. garments
32. l. clothes and l. garments, Ezek. 44. 17, 18.
1 Sam. 2. 18. Samuel ministered with a l. ephod
22. 18. slew 85 persons that did wear a l. ephod
2 Sam. 6. 14. David was girded with a l. ephod
1 Kings 10. 28. Solomon had l. yarn brought, the merchants received the l. yarn, 2 Chron. 1. 16.
Jer. 13. 1. get thee a l. girdle, put it on thy loins
Mat. 27. 59. wrapped it in a l. cloth, John 19. 40.
Mark 14. 51. a l. cloth cast about his naked body
52. and he left the l. cloth and fled naked
Luke 24. 12. Peter beheld the l. clothes, John 20. 6.
John 20. 5. John saw the l. clothes, yet went not in

LINEN.

Lev. 19. 19. nor shall a garment mingled of l. and woollen come upon thee, Deut. 22. 11.
1 Chron. 15. 27. David had on him an ephod of l.
Mark 15. 46. wrapped him in the l. Luke 23. 53.
Rev. 15. 6. seven angels clothed in pure and white l.

See FINE.

LINTEL.

Exod. 12. 22. and strike the l. and two side-posts
23. when he seeth blood on the l. he will pass
1 Kings 6. 31. the l. and side-posts were a fifth part
Amos 9. 1. smite the l. that the posts may shake

LINTELS.

Zeph. 2. 14. bittern shall lodge in the upper l. of it

LION

Is taken, properly, *for the most courageous and generous of all wild beasts, an emblem of strength and valour*, Job 38. 39. Prov. 28. 1. To which are compared, [1] *Christ Jesus, the great, mighty, and invincible lion of the tribe of Judah, who conquers and leads captive his own and his people's enemies*, Rev. 5. 5. [2] *The tribe of Judah and its kings, who were valiant, courageous, and terrible to their enemies, and made a prey of them*, Gen. 49. 9. [3] *The devil, who, like a fierce and hungry lion, seeks all opportunities and advantages to insnare and destroy mankind*, 1 Pet. 5. 8. [4] *Tyrants and violent oppressors*, 2 Tim. 4. 17. [5] *Enemies and evils of every kind*, Psal. 91. 13. [6] *Some pretended difficulties and hinderances to divert one from his duty*, Prov. 22. 13.

Gen. 49. 9. Judah couched as a l. who shall rouse
Num. 24. 9. Israel lay down as a l. as a great l.
Deut. 33. 20. Gad dwelleth as a l. and teareth
Judg. 14. 8. he turned to see the carcase of l. there was a swarm of bees and honey in carcase of l.
18. the men said, what is stronger than a l.?
1 Sam. 17. 34. there came a l. and took a lamb
2 Sam. 17. 10. whose heart is as the heart of a l.
23. 20. slew a l. in the midst of a pit, 1 Chr. 11. 22.
1 Kings 13. 24. when gone, a l. met him by the way and slew him, the l. also stood by the carcase
25. men saw the l. standing by the carcase, 28.
26. the Lord hath delivered him to the l.
20. 36. as soon as thou art departed from me, a l. shall slay thee; a l. found him and slew him
Job 4. 10. the roaring of the l. voice of the fierce l
10. 16. thou huntest me as a fierce l.
28. 8. nor the fierce l. passed by it
38. 39. wilt thou hunt the prey for the l.?
Psal. 7. 2. lest he tear my soul like a l. rending

Psal. 10. 9. he lieth in wait secretly as a *l.*
17. 12. like a *l.* that is greedy of his prey
22. 13. they gaped on me as a roaring *l.*
91. 13. thou shalt tread on the *l.* and adder
Prov. 19. 12. the king's wrath is as the roaring of a *l.*
20. 2. the fear of a king is as the roaring of a *l.*
22. 13. the slothful saith, there is a *l.* in the way
26. 13. there is a *l.* in the way, a *l.* in the street
28. 1. but the righteous are bold as a *l.*
30. 30. a *l.* which is strongest among beasts
Eccl. 9. 4. a living dog is better than a dead *l.*
Isa. 5. 29. their roaring shall be like a *l.* shall roar
11. 7. the *l.* shall eat straw like the ox, 65. 25.
21. 8. he cried, a *l.* my lord, I stand on watch
29. † 1. woe to the *l.* of God, city where Dav. dwelt
35. 9. no *l.* shall be there, nor ravenous beast
38. 13. as a *l.* so will he break all my bones
Jer. 2. 30. hath devoured your prophets like a *l.*
4. 7. the *l.* is come up from his thicket
5. 6. a *l.* out of the forest shall slay them
12. 8. my heritage is to me as a *l.* in the forest
25. 38. he hath forsaken his covert as the *l.*
49. 19. behold, he shall come up like a *l.* 50. 44.
Lam. 3. 10. he was to me as a *l.* in secret places
Ezek. 1. 10. and the face of a *l.* on the right side
10. 14. and the third was the face of a *l.*
22. 25. a conspiracy of prophets like a roaring *l.*
Dan. 7. 4. the first was like a *l.* and had wings
Hos. 5. 14. for I will be to Ephraim as a *l.*
11. 10. he shall roar like a *l.* when he shall roar
13. 7. I will be to them as a *l.* ‖ 8. I will devour as a *l.*
Joel 1. 6. teeth of a *l.* cheek-teeth of a great *l.*
Amos 3. 4. will a *l.* roar when he hath no prey?
8. the *l.* hath roared, who will not fear?
12. as shepherd taketh out of the mouth of the *l.*
Mic. 5. 8. the remnant of Jacob shall be as a *l.*
Nah. 2. 12. *l.* did tear in pieces enough for his whelps
2 *Tim.* 4. 17. I was delivered out of mouth of the *l.*
1 *Pet.* 5. 8. the devil as a roaring *l.* walketh about
Rev. 4. 7. and the first beast was like a *l.*
5. 5. the *l.* of the tribe of Judah hath prevailed
10. 3. cried with a loud voice, as when a *l.* roareth
13. 2. and his mouth as the mouth of a *l.*

See BEAR.

LION-LIKE.

2 *Sam.* 23. 20. slew two *l.-l.* men of Moab, 1 *Chr.* 11. 22.

Old LION.

Gen. 49. 9. as an *old l.* who shall rouse him up?
Job 4. 11. the *old l.* perisheth for lack of prey
Isa. 30. 6. from whence come the young and *old l.*?
Nah. 2. 11. where the lion, even the *old l.* walked

Young LION.

Num. 23. 24. and shall lift up himself as a *young l.*
Judg. 14. 5. behold, a *young l.* roared against him
Psal. 17. 12. as it were a *young l.* lurking in secret
91. 13. the *young l.* shalt thou trample under feet
Isa. 11. 6. the calf and *young l.* lie down together
31. 4. like as the *young l.* roaring on his prey
Ezek. 19. 3. it became a *y. l.* and learned to catch, 6.
5. then she took another, and made him a *young l.*
32. 2. thou art like a *young l.* of the nations
41. 19. face of a *young l.* was towards the palm tree
Hos. 5. 14. I will be as a *y. l.* to the house of Judah
Amos 3. 4. will a *young l.* cry out of his den, if taken?
Mic. 5. 8. as a *young l.* among the flocks of sheep

LIONESS.

Ezek. 19. 2. and say, what is thy mother? a *l.*

LIONESSES.

Nah. 2. 12. the lion strangled for his *l.* and filled

LIONS.

2 *Sam.* 1. 23. Saul and Jonathan stronger than *l.*
1 *Kings* 7. 29. on the borders were *l.* beneath the *l.*
36. he graved cherubims, *l.* and palm-trees
10. 19. two *l.* stood beside the stays, 2 *Chr.* 9. 18.
20. twelve *l.* stood on the one side, 2 *Chr.* 9. 19.
2 *Kings* 17. 25. the Lord sent *l.* among them
26. therefore he hath sent *l.* among them
1 *Chron.* 12. 8. whose faces were like faces of *l.*
Psal. 22. 21. save me from the *l.* mouth for thou
35. 17. Lord, rescue my darling from the *l.*
57. 4. my soul is among *l.* I lie even among them
Cant. 4. 8. look from top of Amana, from the *l.* dens
Isa. 15. 9. *l.* upon him that escapeth of Moab
Jer. 50. 17. the *l.* have driven Israel away
51. 38. they shall roar together like *l.*
Ezek. 19. 2. a lioness, she lay down among *l.*
6. he went up and down among the *l.*
Dan. 6. 24. and the *l.* had the mastery of them
27. who delivered Daniel from the power of the *l.*
Nah. 2. 11. where is the dwelling of the *l.*?
Zeph. 3. 3. her princes within are roaring *l.*
Heb. 11. 33. through faith stopped the mouths of *l.*
Rev. 9. 8. their teeth were as the teeth of *l.*
17. the heads of the horses were as the heads of *l.*

See DEN.

LION'S *whelp, whelps.*

Gen. 49. 9. Judah is *l. whelp,* from the prey, my son
Deut. 33. 22. Dan is a *l. whelp,* he shall leap from
Job 4. 11. the stout *l. whelps* are scattered abroad
28. 8. the *l. whelps* have not trodden it, nor fierce
Jer. 51. 38. shall roar, they shall yell as *l. whelps*

Young LIONS.

Job 4. 10. the teeth of the *young l.* are broken
38. 39. wilt thou fill the appetite of the *young l.*?
Psal. 34. 10. the *young l.* do lack and suffer hunger
58. 6. break out the great teeth of the *young l.*
104. 21. the *young l.* roar after their prey
Isa. 5. 29. they shall roar like *young l.* and lay hold
Jer. 2. 15. the *young l.* roared upon him and yelled
Ezek. 19. 2. she nourished her whelps among *y. l.*
38. 13. with all the *young l.* shall say to thee
Nah. 2. 11. where is the feeding-place of the *young l.*?
13. and the sword shall devour thy *young l.*
Zech. 11. 3. there is a voice of the roaring of *young l.*

LIP

Signifies, [1] *The upper and nether part of the mouth,* Lev. 13. 45. [2] *Words, or impatient and unbecoming expressions,* Job 2. 10. [3] *Language or speech,* Gen. 11. † 1. [4] *The mouth, together with an ability and liberty to speak to God's honour, and sing to his praise,* Psal. 51. 15. [5] *The tongue,* Prov. 10. 19. Isa. 28. 11. [6] *Outward devotion, and profession of religion,* Isa. 29. 13.

Gen. 11. † 1. the whole earth was of one *l.*
Lev. 13. 45. he shall put a covering on his *l.*
Judg. 7. † 22. host fled to the *l.* of Abel-meholah
1 *Kings* 9. † 26. in Ezion-geber on *l.* of the Red sea
2 *Kings* 2. † 13. Elisha stood by the *l.* of Jordan
Psal. 22. 7. they shoot out the *l.* they shake the head
Prov. 12. 19. the *l.* of truth shall be established
Ezek. 36. † 3. made to come on the *l.* of the tongue
Mic. 3. † 7. they shall cover the upper *l.*

LIPS.

Exod. 6. 12. who am of uncircumcised *l.* 30.
Num. 30. 6. or uttered ought out of her *l.* 8, 12.
1 *Sam.* 1. 13. spake in her heart, only her *l.* moved
2 *Kings* 18. † 20. they are but words of *l.* *Isa.* 36. † 5.
Psal. 12. 2. with flattering *l.* do they speak
3. the Lord shall cut off all flattering *l.*
4. our *l.* are our own, who is lord over us?
17. 1. my prayer that goeth not out of feigned *l.*
31. 18. let the lying *l.* be put to silence, which speak
59. 7. behold, swords are in their *l.* who doth hear?
12. for the words of their *l.* let them be taken
63. 5. my mouth shall praise thee with joyful *l.*
120. 2. deliver my soul, O Lord, from lying *l.*
140. 3. adders' poison is under their *l.*
9. let the mischief of their own *l.* cover them
Prov. 4. 24. and perverse *l.* put far from thee
5. 3. *l.* of a strange woman drop as an honey comb
7. 21. with flattering of her *l.* she forced him
10. 13. in the *l.* of him that hath understanding
18. he that hideth hatred with lying *l.* is a fool
21. the *l.* of the righteous feed many, but fools
32. the *l.* of righteous know what is acceptable
12. 22. lying *l.* are an abomination to the Lord
14. 3. but the *l.* of the wise shall preserve them
7. when perceivest not in him the *l.* of knowledge
23. the talk of the *l.* tendeth only to penury
15. 7. the *l.* of the wise disperse knowledge
16. 10. a divine sentence is in the *l.* of the king
13. righteous *l.* are the delight of kings
21. the sweetness of the *l.* increaseth learning
17. 4. a wicked doer giveth heed to false *l.*
7. much less do lying *l.* become a prince
18. 6. a fool's *l.* enter into contention
20. 15. the *l.* of knowledge are a precious jewel
24. 2. and their *l.* talk of mischief
26. 23. burning *l.* are like a potsherd covered
Eccl. 10. 12. the *l.* of a fool will swallow himself
Cant. 7. 9. causing the *l.* of those asleep to speak
Isa. 6. 5. woe is me, I am undone, a man of unclean
l. I dwell in the midst of a people of unclean *l.*
28. 11. for with stammering *l.* will he speak
29. 13. this people with their *l.* do honour me
57. 19. I create the fruit of the *l.* peace to him
59. 3. your *l.* have spoken lies, your tongue
Lam. 3. 62. the *l.* of those that rose against me
Ezek. 24. 22. ye shall not cover your *l.* nor eat
36. 3. ye are taken up in the *l.* of talkers
Hos. 14. 2. so will we render the calves of our *l.*
Mic. 3. 7. they shall cover their *l.* no answer of God
Mal. 2. 7. the priest's *l.* should keep knowledge
Mat. 15. 8. honoureth me with their *l.* *Mark* 7. 6.
Rom. 3. 13. the poison of asps is under their *l.*
1 *Cor.* 14. 21. with other *l.* will I speak to this
Heb. 13. 15. the fruit of our *l.* giving thanks

His LIPS.

Lev. 5. 4. pronouncing with *his l.* to do evil
Job 2. 10. in all this did not Job sin with *his l.*
11. 5. O that God would open *his l.* against thee
23. 12. nor gone back from commandment of *his l.*
Psal. 21. 2. not withholden the request of *his l.*
106. 33. so that he spake unadvisedly with *his l.*
Prov. 10. 19. he that refraineth *his l.* is wise
12. 13. wicked is snared by transgression of *his l.*
13. 3. openeth wide *his l.* shall have destruction
16. 23. the heart of the wise addeth learning to *his l.*
27. and in *his l.* there is as a burning fire
30. moving *his l.* he bringeth evil to pass
17. 28. shutteth *his l.* is a man of understanding
18. 7. and *his l.* are the snare of his soul
20. with the increase of *his l.* shall he be filled
19. 1. than he that is perverse in *his l.* and is a fool
20. 19. with him that flattereth with *his l.*
22. 11. for grace of *his l.* the king will be his friend
24. 26. shall kiss *his l.* that gives a right answer
26. 24. he that hateth dissembleth with *his l.*
Cant. 5. 13. *his l.* like lilies dropping myrrh
Isa. 11. 4. with breath of *his l.* shall he slay wicked
30. 27. *his l.* are full of indignation, and his tongue
Mal. 2. 6. and iniquity was not found in *his l.*
1 *Pet.* 3. 10. and *his l.* that they speak no guile

My LIPS.

Job 13. 6. hear now, hearken to the pleading of *my l.*
16. 5. moving of *my l.* should assuage your grief
27. 4. *my l.* shall not speak wickedness
32. 20. I will speak, I will open *my l.* and answer
33. 3. and *my l.* shall utter knowledge clearly
Psal. 16. 4. nor take up their names into *my l.*
40. 9. lo, I have not refrained *my l.* O Lord
51. 15. open thou *my l.* ‖ 63. 3. *my l.* shall praise thee
66. 14. I will pay vows, which *my l.* have uttered
71. 23. *my l.* shall greatly rejoice when I sing
89. 34. nor alter the thing that is gone out of *my l.*
119. 13. with *my l.* have I declared thy judgments
171. *my l.* shall utter thy praise, when hast taught
141. 3. O Lord, keep the door of *my l.*
Prov. 8. 6. the opening of *my l.* shall be right things
7. wickedness is an abomination to *my l.*
Jer. 17. 16. that which came out of *my l.* was right
Dan. 10. 16. one like the sons of men touched *my l.*
Hab. 3. 16. I heard, *my l.* quivered at the voice

Thy LIPS.

Deut. 23. 23. that which is gone out of *thy l.* perform
2 *Kings* 19. 28. I will put my bridle in *thy l.* *Isa.* 37. 29.
Job 8. 21. till he fill *thy l.* with rejoicing
15. 6. yea, *thy* own *l.* testify against thee
Ps. 17. 4. by the word of *thy l.* I have kept me from
34. 13. keep *thy l.* from speaking guile
45. 2. grace is poured into *thy l.* therefore G. blessed
Prov. 5. 2. and that *thy l.* may keep knowledge
22. 18. they shall withal be fitted in *thy l.*
Prov. 23. 16. rejoice when *thy l.* speak right things
24. 28. deceive not with *thy l.* say not, I will do so
27. 2. let another praise thee, and not *thy* own *l.*
Cant. 4. 3. *thy l.* are like a thread of scarlet
11. *thy l.* O my spouse, drop as the honey-comb
Isa. 6. 7. and said, lo, this hath touched *thy l.*
Ezek. 24. 17. cover not *thy l.* and eat not bread

LIQUOR.

Num. 6. 3. nor shall he drink any *l.* of grapes
Cant. 7. 2. a round goblet, which wanteth not *l.*

LIQUORS.

Exod. 22. 29. nor delay to offer the first of thy *l.*

LISTED.

Mat. 17. 12. done to him whatsoever *l.* *Mark* 9. 13.

LISTEN.

Isa. 49. 1. *l.* O isles, unto me, and hearken from far

LISTETH.

John 3. 8. the wind bloweth where it *l.* thou hearest
Jam. 3. 4. the ships, whithersoever the governor *l.*

LITTERS.

Isa. 66. 20. shall bring your breth. in chariots and *l.*

LITTLE

Signifies, [1] *A small quantity,* Exod. 16. 18. 1 Sam. 14. 29. [2] *Few in number,* Exod. 12. 4. Luke 12. 32. [3] *Light, or of small account,* Josh. 22. 17. [4] *Modest, humble, and submissive,* 1 Sam. 9. 21. | 15. 17. [5] *A short way or time,* 2 Sam. 16. 1. Job 10. 20. [6] *Weak,* Luke 12. 28. [7] *Young,* Gen. 45. 19. Esth. 3. 13. [8] *Low,* Luke 19. 3.

Gen. 18. 4. let a *l.* water, I pray you, be fetched
24. 17. let me drink a *l.* water of thy pitcher
30. 30. it was but *l.* thou hadst before I came
35. 16. there was but a *l.* way to Ephrath, 48. 7.
43. 2. buy us a *l.* food, 44. 25. ‖ 11. *l.* balm, *l.* honey
Exod. 12. 4. if the household be too *l.* for the lamb
16. 18. he that gathered *l.* had no lack, 2 *Cor.* 8. 15.
23. 30. by *l.* and *l.* I will drive them out, *Deut.* 7. 22.
Deut. 28. 38. carry much out, and gather but *l.* in
Josh. 19. 47. coast of Dan went out too *l.* for them
22. 17. is the iniquity of Peor too *l.* for us?
Judg. 4. 19. give me *l.* water to drink, 1 *Kings* 17. 10
Ruth 2. 7. that she tarried a *l.* in the house
1 *Sam.* 2. 19. his mother made him a *l.* coat
14. 29. because I tasted a *l.* of this honey, 43.
15. 17. when thou wast *l.* in thine own sight
22. † 15. knew nothing of all this, *l.* or great
2 *Sam.* 12. 3. had nothing, save one *l.* ewe-lamb
8. if that had been too *l.* I would have given such
19. 36. thy servant will go a *l.* way over Jordan
1 *Kings* 8. 64. because the brasen altar was too *l.*
12. 10. my *l.* finger thicker than, 2 *Chron.* 10. 10.
17. 12. and a *l.* oil in a cruse ‖ 13. make a *l.* cake
18. 44. there ariseth a *l.* cloud like a man's hand
20. 27. Israel pitched like two *l.* flocks of kids
2 *Kings* 5. 2. had brought away captive a *l.* maid
10. 18. Ahab served Baal a *l.* but Jehu much
Ezra 9. 8. for a *l.* space, give us a *l.* reviving
Neh. 9. 32. let not all the trouble seem *l.*
Job 4. 12. and my ear received a *l.* thereof
10. 20. cease then, that I may take comfort a *l.*
26. 14. but how *l.* a portion is heard of him!
36. 2. suffer me a *l.* and I will shew thee
Psal. 2. 12. when his wrath is kindled but a *l.*
8. 5. made him a *l.* lower than the angels, *Heb.* 2. 7.
37. 16. a *l.* that a righteous man hath is better
42. † 6. I will remember thee from the *l.* hill
65. 12. the *l.* hills rejoice on every side
68. 27. there is *l.* Benjamin, with their ruler
72. 3. and the *l.* hills by righteousness
114. 4. and the *l.* hills skipped like lambs, 6.
Prov. 6. 10. a *l.* sleep, *l.* slumber, a *l.* folding, 24. 33.
10. 20. the heart of the wicked is *l.* worth
15. 16. better is a *l.* with the fear of the Lord
16. 8. better is a *l.* with righteousness, than great
30. 24. four things that are *l.* on the earth
Eccl. 5. 12. is sweet, whether he eat *l.* or much
9. 14. there was a *l.* city, and few men in it
10. 1. so a *l.* folly him that is in reputation
12. † 3. the grinders fail because they grind *l.*
Cant. 2. 15. take us the foxes, the *l.* foxes
3. 4. was but a *l.* that I passed from them
8. 8. we have a *l.* sister, and she hath no breasts
Isa. 26. 20. hide thyself for a *l.* moment till indigna
28. 10. line upon line, here a *l.* and there a *l.* 13.
40. 15. he taketh up the isles as a very *l.* thing
54. 8. in a *l.* wrath I hid my face from thee
Jer. 30. † 18. city shall be built on her own *l.* hill
Ezek. 11. 16. I will be to them a *l.* sanctuary
16. 47. but as if that were a very *l.* thing
31. 4. and sent out her *l.* rivers to the trees
Dan. 7. 8. there came up another *l.* horn, 8. 9.
11. 34. they shall be holpen with a *l.* help
Hos. 8. 10. they shall sorrow a *l.* for the burden
Amos 6. 11. he will smite the *l.* house with clefts
Mic. 5. 2. though *l.* among the thousands of Judah
Hag. 1. 6. ye have sown much, and bring in *l.*
9. ye looked for much, and lo, it came to *l.*
Zech. 1. 15. for I was but a *l.* displeased
Mat. 6. 30. shall he not much more clothe you, O ye of *l.* faith? 8. 26. | 16. 8. *Luke* 12. 28.
14. 31. O thou of *l.* faith, why didst thou doubt
15. 34. they said, seven, and a few *l.* fishes
26. 39. he went a *l.* further, *Mark* 1. 19. | 14. 35.
Mark 5. 23. my *l.* daughter lieth at point of death
Luke 7. 47. to whom *l.* is forgiven, the same loveth *l.*
12. 32. fear not, *l.* flock ‖ 19. 3. he was *l.* of stature
19. 17. thou hast been faithful in a very *l.*
John 6. 7. that every one of them may take a *l.*
Acts 5. 34. to put the apostles forth a *l.* space
20. 12. young man alive, and were not a *l.* comforted
28. 2. the barbarians shewed us no *l.* kindness
1 *Cor.* 5. 6. a *l.* leaven leaveneth the lump, *Gal.* 5. 9.
2 *Cor.* 11. 1. could bear with me a *l.* in my folly
16. receive me, that I may boast myself a *l.*
Eph. 3. † 3. as I wrote a *l.* before in few words
1 *Tim.* 4. 8. bodily exercise profiteth *l.* but godliness
5. 23. use a *l.* wine for thy stomach's sake
Heb. 2. 9. who was made a *l.* lower than the angels
Jam. 3. 5. tongue is a *l.* member, a *l.* fire kindleth
4. 14. life, a vapour that appeareth for a *l.* time
2 *Pet.* 2. † 18. those who were for a *l.* escaped

Rev. 3. 8. thou hast a l. strength, and hast kept
6. 11. rest a l. season || 20. 3. be loosed a l. season
See Book, Chambers, Child, Children.

LITTLE one, or ones.

Gen. 19. 20. Lot said, it is a l. one, is it not a l. one?
34. 29. all their l. ones took they captive
43. 8. we may live, both we, and thou, and our l. o.
44. 20. we have a l. one, and his brother is dead
45. 19. take waggons out of Egypt for your l. ones
46. 5. carried their l. o. || 47. 24. food for your l. o.
47. † 12. with bread according to their l. ones
50. 8. only their l. ones left they in Goshen
21. fear not, I will nourish you and your l. ones
Exod. 10. 10. I will let you go and your l. ones, 24.
Num. 14. 31. but your l. ones, them will I bring
31. 9. took women of Midian captives and l. ones
17. therefore kill every male among the l. ones
32. 16. we will build cities for our l. ones
17. our l. ones shall dwell in the fenced cities, 26.
Deut. 2. 34. we destroyed men, women, and l. ones
20. 14. but the women and l. ones take to thyself
Josh. 8. 35. Joshua read before the women and l. ones
Judg. 18. 21. so they put the l. ones before them
2 Sam. 15. 22. Ittai passed over and all the l. ones
2 Chr. 20. 13. Judah stood before Lord and l. ones
31. 18. and to the genealogy of all their l. ones
Ezra 8. 21. to seek a right way for our l. ones
Esth. 8. 11. to cause to perish l. ones and women
Job 21. 11. they send forth their l. ones like a flock
Psal. 137. 9. that dasheth thy l. ones ag. the stones
Isa. 60. 22. a l. one shall become a thousand
Jer. 14. 3. their nobles sent their l. ones to the pit
48. 4. her l. ones have caused a cry to be heard
Zech. 13. 7. and I will turn my hand on the l. ones
Mat. 10. 42. give to drink to one of these l. ones
18. 6. who should offend one of these l. o. Mark 9. 42.
10. take heed that ye despise not one of these l. o.
14. that one of these l. ones should perish
Luke 17. 2. than that he offend one of these l. ones

LITTLE while.

2 Chr. 12. † 7. therefore I will grant them a l. while
Job 24. 24. they are exalted for a l. w. but are gone
Psal. 37. 10. yet a l. w. and the wicked shall not be
Isa. 10. 25. yet a l. w. and the indignation shall cease
29. 17. is it not yet a very l. while, and Lebanon
63. 18. thy people have possessed it but a l. while
Jer. 51. 33. yet a l. w. and her harvest shall come
Hos. 1. 4. yet a l. while and I will avenge the blood
Hag. 2. 6. a l. while and I will shake the heavens
Luke 22. 58. and after a l. while another saw him
John 7. 33. yet a l. w. and I am with you, 13. 33.
12. 35. yet a l. while is the light with you, walk
14. 19. a l. while, and the world seeth me no more
16. 16. again a l. while, and ye shall see me, 17, 19.
I go to Father a l. while and ye shall not see me
18. a l. while; we cannot tell what he saith
Heb. 2. † 7. thou madest him a l. w. inferior to angels
10. 37. for yet a l. while, and he that shall come

LIVE.

Exod. 21. 35. then they shall sell the l. ox
Isa. 6. 6. a seraphim, having a l. coal in his hand
See Goat.

LIVE

Signifies, [1] *To move and do the actions of life,* Gen. 45. 3. [2] *To be in health, or to be recovered from sickness,* John 4. 50. [3] *To preserve alive,* Gen. 42. 2. [4] *To have a maintenance for this life,* 1 Cor. 9. 13. [5] *Faithfully to serve God, to have a share in his favour and gracious covenant,* Gen. 17. 18. [6] *To enjoy communion with God,* Psal. 69. 32. [7] *To enjoy eternal life in heaven,* John 14. 19. [8] *To be greatly comforted,* Psal. 22. 26. It is taken, (1) *Naturally,* Gen. 9. 3. John 4. 50. (2) *Morally,* Acts 23. 1. | 26. 5. (3) *Spiritually, to live a life of faith in Christ, to the glory of God's free grace,* Gal. 2. 19, 20. 2 Tim. 3. 12. (4) *Wickedly,* 2 Pet. 2. 6. (5) *Eternally,* John 6. 51, 58. Rom. 6. 8.

To live after the flesh, Rom. 8. 13. *To lead such a course of life as is agreeable to corrupt nature; to bestow all our time and pains in the service of the flesh, and so make provision only for a present life.*

Man shall not live by bread alone, but by every word, &c. Mat. 4. 4. *Though men live ordinarily by usual and common food, yet God's power is not restrained; he can uphold the life of man when that is wanting, as he supported the Israelites with manna; yea, by his power and will only, without any means at all, if he so pleases: and therefore men ought not absolutely to rest upon the means, and without warrant run to an extraordinary course for supply, but trust in God, and leave him to provide as he pleases.*

Gen. 3. 22. lest he take of tree of life, and l. for ever
12. 13. and my soul shall l. because of thee
17. 18. O that Ishmael might l. before thee!
19. 20. O let me escape, and my soul shall l.
20. 7. he shall pray for thee, and thou shalt l.
27. 40. by sword shalt thou l. and serve thy brethr.
31. 32. and findest thy goods, let him not l.
42. 18. Joseph said, this do, and l. for I fear God
45. 3. I am Joseph, doth my father yet l.?
Exod. 1. 16. if it be a daughter, then she shall l.
33. 20. for there shall no man see me and l.
Lev. 18. 5. which if a man do, he shall l. in them, I am the Lord, Neh. 9. 29. Ezek. 20. 11, 13, 21.
Num. 21. 8. when he looketh upon serpent, shall l.
24. 23. alas, who shall l. when God doeth this?
Deut. 4. 10. may fear me all the days they shall l.
33. did ever people hear, as thou hast, and l.?
8. 3. but by every word of the Lord doth man l.
12. 1. all the days that ye l. on the earth
19. 5. he shall flee to one of these cities and l.
31. 13. learn to fear L. as long as ye l. 1 Kings 8. 40.
33. 6. let Reuben l. and not die, men not be few
Josh. 6. 17. only Rahab harlot shall l. and her house
9. 15. Josh. made a league with them to let them l.
20. we will let them l. lest wrath be on us, 21.
1 Sam. 10. † 24. said, let the king l. 2 Sam. 16. † 16.
1 Kings 1. † 25. 2 Kings 11. † 12. 2 Chron. 23. † 11.
1 Sam. 20. 14. not only while I l. shew me kindness of Lord
2 Kings 4. 7. l. thou and thy children of the rest
7. 4. if they save us alive, we shall l.
2 Chron. 6. 31. walk in thy ways so long as they l.
Job 7. † 8. thine eyes are on me, I can l. no longer
14. 14. if a man die, shall he l. again? all days
21. 7. wherefore do the wicked l. become old?
Ps. 22. 26. praise Lord, your heart shall l. for ever
49. 9. that he should still l. and not see corruption
63. 4. thus will I bless thee while I l. lift up hands
69. 32. your hearts shall l. that seek God
72. 15. he shall l. || 118. 17. I shall not die, but l.
119. 144. give me understanding, and I shall l.
175. let my soul l. and it shall praise thee
146. 2. while I l. will I praise the Lord
Prov. 4. 4. keep my commandments, and l. 7. 2.
9. 6. forsake foolish and l. go in way of understand.
15. 27. but he that hateth gifts shall l.
Eccl. 6. 3. if a man l. many years, 6. | 11. 8.
9. 3. madness is in their heart while they l.
9. l. joyfully with the wife whom thou lovest
Isa. 26. 19. thy dead men shall l. together with my
38. 16. O Ld. by these things men l. make me to l.
55. 3. come to me, hear, and your soul shall l.
Jer. 21. 9. to Chaldeans shall l. 27. 12, 17. | 38. 2, 17.
38. 20. obey, I pray thee, and thy soul shall l.
Lam. 4. 20. we said, under his shadow we shall l.
Ezek. 3. 21. he shall surely l. 18. 9, 17. | 33. 13, 15, 16.
16. 6. I said, when thou wast in thy blood, l.
18. 19. kept my statutes shall l. 21, 22. | 20. 11, 25.
24. shall he l. || 32. turn yourselves and l. 33. 11.
33. 10. if our sins be on us, how should we then l.?
19. do that which is lawful and right, he shall l.
37. 3. he said, son of man, can these bones l.?
5. cause breath to enter you, and ye shall l. 6, 14.
47. 9. every thing which liveth and moveth shall l. every thing shall l. whither the river cometh
Hos. 6. 2. he will revive us, we shall l. in his sight
Amos 5. 4. saith the Lord, seek me, and ye shall l. 6.
Jonah 4. 3. it is better for me to die than to l. 8.
Hab. 2. 4. the just shall l. by his faith, Rom. 1. 17.
Zech. 10. 9. they shall l. with their children and turn
Mat. 4. 4. man shall not l. by bread alone, Luke 4. 4.
9. 18. lay hand on her, and she shall l. Mark 5. 23.
Luke 7. 25. they which l. delicately are in courts
10. 28. he said to him, this do, and thou shalt l.
20. 38. he is not a God of dead, for all l. unto him
John 5. 25. dead hear voice of the Son of God, and l.
6. 57. as living Father sent me, and I l. by Father, so he that eateth me, even he shall l. by me
11. 25. believeth, tho' he were dead, yet shall he l.
14. 19. because I l. ye shall l. also
Acts 17. 28. for in him we l. and move, and have
22. 22. for it is not fit that he should l.
Rom. 6. 2. that are dead to sin, l. any longer therein
8. we believe that we shall also l. with him
8. 12. we are debtors, not to l. after the flesh
13. if ye l. after the flesh, ye shall die, if ye thro' the Spirit mortify deeds of the body, ye shall l.
10. 5. doeth these things shall l. by them, Gal. 3. 12.
12. 18. if possible, l. peaceably with all men
14. 8. for whether we l. we l. to the Lord; whether we l. therefore, or die, we are the Lord's
1 Cor. 9. 13. they l. of the things of the temple
14. they who preach gospel should l. of gospel
2 Cor. 4. 11. for we which l. are delivered to death
6. 9. as dying, and behold, we l. as chastened
7. 3. ye are in our hearts to die and l. with you
13. 4. we shall l. with him by the power of God
11. brethren, be of one mind, l. in peace
Gal. 2. 14. why compellest the Gentiles to l. as Jews
19. dead to the law, that I might l. unto God
20. I l. yet not I, but Christ liveth in me, the life I now l. in flesh, I l. by faith of Son of God
3. 11. the just shall l. by faith, Heb. 10. 38.
5. 25. if we l. in the Spirit, let us walk in the Spirit
Phil. 1. 21. for me to l. is Christ, and to die is gain
22. if I l. in the flesh, this is the fruit of my labour
1 Thess. 3. 8. for now we l. if ye stand fast in Lord
5. 10. died, that we should l. together with him
2 Tim. 2. 11. if dead, we shall also l. with him
3. 12. all that will l. godly shall suffer persecution
Tit. 2. 12. teaching us that we should l. soberly
Heb. 12. 9. be in subjection to Father of spirits and l.
13. 18. in all things willing to l. honestly
Jam. 4. 15. if the Lord will we shall l. and do this
1 Pet. 2. 24. that we should l. to righteousness
4. 2. that he should no longer l. in the flesh
6. but l. according to God in the Spirit
2 Pet. 2. 6. an ensample to those that l. ungodly
18. those that escaped from them who l. in error
1 John 4. 9. sent his Son, that we might l. thro' him
Rev. 13. 14. beast which had the wound and did l.
See For Ever.

As I LIVE.

Num. 14. 21. as truly as I l. earth shall be filled, 28.
Job 27. 6. so long as I l. Psal. 104. 33. | 116. 2.
Isa. 49. 18. as I l. saith the Lord, Jer. 22. 24. Ezek. 5. 11. | 14. 16, 18, 20. | 16. 48. | 17. 16, 19. | 18. 3. | 20. 3, 33. | 33. 11, 27. | 34. 8. | 35. 6, 11. Zeph. 2. 9. Rom. 14. 11.
Jer. 46. 18. as I l. saith the king, surely as Tabor

May, might, or mayest LIVE.

Gen. 42. 2. that we m. l. and not die, 43. 8. | 47. 19.
Lev. 25. 35. relieve him that he may l. with thee
36. take no usury, that thy brother may l.
Num. 4. 19. but thus do to them that they may l.
Deut. 4. 1. do to them, ye m. l. 5. 33. | 8. 1. | 30. 6, 16.
42. that fleeing to one of these cities he might l.
16. 20. what is just follow, that thou mayest l.
30. 19. choose life, that thou and thy seed may l.
2 Sam. 12. 22. gracious to me, that the child may l.
2 Kings 18. 32. to a land of bread, that you may l.
Esth. 4. 11. hold out the sceptre, that he may l.
Psal. 119. 17. deal bountifully, that I may l.
77. let thy mercies come to me, that I may l.
116. uphold me according to thy word, that I m. l.
Jer. 35. 7. dwell in tents, that ye may l. many days
Ezek. 37. 9. breathe on these slain, that they may l.
Amos 5. 14. seek good, and not evil, that ye may l.
Eph. 6. 3. and thou mayest l. long on the earth

Not LIVE.

Exod. 19. 13. that touch the mountain shall not l.
22. 18. thou shalt not suffer a witch to l.
Deut. 8. 3. man doth not l. by bread only, but by the word of the Lord, Mat. 4. 4. Luke 4. 4.
2 Sam. 1. 10. for I was sure that he could not l.
2 Kings 10. 19. whosoever is wanting he shall not l.
20. 1. set house in order, thou shalt not l. Isa. 38. 1.
Job 7. 16. I loath it, I would not l. always
Psal. 55. 23. the wicked shall not l. half their days
Isa. 26. 14. they are dead, they shall not l.
Ezek. 13. 19. to save the souls that should not l.
18. 13. shall he then live? he shall not l.
Zech. 13. 3. shall say to him, thou shalt not l.
Luke 12. † 29. l. not in careful suspense
Acts 7. 19. cast out children, that they might not l.
25. 24. crying, that he ought not to l. any longer
28. 4. yet vengeance suffereth not to l.
2 Cor. 5. 15. they should not l. to themselves, but him

LIVED.

Gen. 25. 6. from Isaac his son, while he yet l.
47. 28. Jacob l. in the land of Egypt 17 years
Num. 14. 38. but Joshua and Caleb l. still
21. 9. when he beheld the serpent of brass he l.
Deut. 5. 26. that heard the voice of God and l.
2 Sam. 19. 6. if Absalom had l. and we had died
1 Kings 12. 6. the old men that stood before Solomon his father while he yet l. 2 Chron. 10. 6.
2 Kings 14. 17. Amaziah l. after the death of Jehoash fifteen years, 2 Chron. 25. 25.
Psal. 49. 18. while he l. he blessed his soul
Ezek. 37. 10. breath came into them, and they l.
Luke 2. 36. she had l. with a husband seven years
Acts 23. 1. I have l. in all good conscience before G.
26. 5. after the sect of our religion I l. a Pharisee
Col. 3. 7. ye walked sometime, when ye l. in them
Jam. 5. 5. ye have l. in pleasure on the earth
Rev. 18. 7. how much she hath l. deliciously, 9.
20. 4. they l. with Christ || 5. the rest l. not again

LIVELY.

Exod. 1. 19. because the Hebrew women are l.
Psal. 38. 19. but my enemies are l. and are strong
Acts 7. 38. who received the l. oracles to give to us
1 Pet. 1. 3. who hath begotten us again to a l. hope
2. 5. ye, as l. stones, are built up a spiritual house

LIVER.

Exod. 29. 13. the caul above the l. 22. Lev. 3. 4, 10, 15. | 4. 9. | 7. 4. | 8. 16, 25. | 9. 10, 19.
Prov. 7. 23. till a dart strike through his l.
Lam. 2. 11. my l. is poured upon the earth
Ezek. 21. 21. he consulted, he looked in the l.
See Caul.

LIVES.

Gen. 9. 5. surely your blood of your l. will I require
45. 7. to save your l. by a great deliverance
47. 25. thou hast saved our l. let us find grace
Exod. 1. 14. they made their l. bitter with bondage
Josh. 2. 13. and deliver our l. from death
9. 24. therefore we were sore afraid of our l.
Judg. 5. 18. were a people that jeoparded their l.
18. 25. thou lose thy life with l. of thy household
2 Sam. 1. 23. Saul and Jonathan lovely in their l.
19. 5. who saved l. of thy sons, wives, and concu.
23. 17. that went in jeopardy of their l. 1 Chr. 11. 19.
Esth. 9. 16. other Jews gathered and stood for their l.
Prov. 1. 18. they lurk privily for their own l.
Jer. 19. 7. fall by them which seek their l. 46. 26.
9. they that seek their l. shall straiten them
48. 6. flee, save your l. be like the heath in wildern.
Lam. 5. 9. we gat our bread with the peril of our l.
Dan. 7. 12. their l. were prolonged for a season
Luke 9. 56. Son of man is not come to destroy men's l.
Acts 15. 26. men that have hazarded their l. for our
27. 10. this voyage will be with damage of our l.
1 John 3. 16. to lay down our l. for the brethren
Rev. 12. 11. they loved not their l. to the death

LIVEST.

Deut. 12. 19. forsake not the Levite as long as thou l.
Gal. 2. 14. if thou being a Jew l. after the manner
Rev. 3. 1. hast a name that thou l. and art dead

LIVETH.

Gen. 9. 3. every thing that l. shall be meat for you
16. † 14. the well of him that l. and seeth me
Deut. 5. 24. that God doth talk with man, and he l.
1 Sam. 1. 28. have lent him to the L. as long as he l.
20. 31. for as long as son of Jesse l. on the ground
25. 6. thus shall say to him that l. in prosperity
2 Sam. 2. 27. as God l. unless thou hadst spoken
15. 21. as my lord the king l. surely in what place
22. 47. the Lord l. blessed be my rock, Ps. 18. 46.
1 Kings 3. 23. one saith, this is my son that l.
17. 23. and Elijah said, see thy son l.
Job 19. 25. for I know that my Redeemer l.
27. 2. as G. l. who hath taken away my judgment
Psal. 89. 48. what man that l. and shall not see death?
Jer. 4. 2. thou shalt swear, the Lord l. in truth
5. 2. tho' they say, the Lord l. they swear falsely
12. 16. to swear by my name, the Lord l. 15. | 23. 7, 8.
16. 14. no more be said, the Lord l. 15. | 23. 7, 8.
44. 26. in the land of Egypt, saying, the Lord l.
Ezek. 47. 9. every thing that l. and moveth shall live
Hos. 4. 15. nor go ye up, nor swear, the Lord l.
Amos 8. 14. they that swear, and say, thy God, O Dan, l. and the manner of Beer-sheba l.
John 4. 50. Jesus said, go thy way, thy son l. 51, 53.
11. 26. whosoever l. and believeth in me never die
Rom. 6. 10. but in that he l. he l. to God
7. 1. law hath dominion over man as long as he l. 2.
3. so if while her husband l. she be married
14. 7. for none of us l. or dieth to himself
1 Cor. 7. 39. the wife is bound as long as her husb. l.
2 Cor. 13. 4. yet he l. by the power of God
Gal. 2. 20. I live, yet not I, but Christ l. in me
1 Tim. 5. 6. that l. in pleasure is dead while she l.
Heb. 7. 8. of whom it is witnessed that he l.
25. seeing he ever l. to make intercession for them
9. 17. testament is of no strength while testator l.
Rev. 1. 18. I am he that l. and was dead, behold
See For Ever.

As the Lord LIVETH.

Judg. 8. 19. as the L. l. if ye have saved them alive
Ruth 3. 13. I will do the part of kinsman, as the L. l.

1 *Sam.* 14. 39. for *as the L. l.* tho' it be in Jonathan
45. *as the Lord l.* 19. 6. | 20. 21. | 25. 26. | 26. 10,
16. | 28. 10. | 29. 6. 2 *Sam.* 4. 9. | 12. 5. | 14. 11.
1 *Kings* 1. 29.
20. 3. *as the Lord l.* there is but a step between me
25. 34. *as the Lord* God of Israel *l.* who kept me
2 *Sam.* 15. 21. *as the L. l.* and as my lord the king *l.*
1 *Kings* 2. 24. *as the Lord l.* 2 *Kings* 5. 20. 2 *Chron.*
18. 13. *Jer.* 38. 16.
17. 1. *as the Lord* God of Israel *l.* 18. 15.
12. *as the Lord* thy God *l.* 18. 10.
2 *Kings* 2. 2. *as L. l.* and thy soul liveth, 4. 6. | 4. 30.
3. 14. *as L.* of hosts *l.* before whom I stand, 5. 16.

As thy soul LIVETH.

1 *Sam.* 1. 26. *as s. l.* I am woman who stood praying
17. 55. Abner said, *as thy s. l.* O king, I cannot tell
20. 3. *as s. l.* there is but one step betw. me and death
25. 26. *as thy soul l.* seeing L. hath withholden thee
2 *Sam.* 11. 11. *as thy soul l.* I will not do this thing
14. 19. *as soul l.* none can turn to right or left hand
2 *Kings* 2. 2. *as s. l.* I will not leave thee, so they went

LIVING

Signifies, [1] *One who is alive, or enjoys life,* 1 Kings 3. 22. [2] *Never dry, but always springing and running,* Cant. 4. 15. [3] *Christ risen from the dead,* Luke 24. 5. [4] *The godly, departed this life,* Mat. 22. 32. [5] *Spiritual,* Rom. 12. 1. [6] *That which procureth and bringeth to life spiritual and eternal,* Heb. 10. 20. 1 Pet. 2. 4. [7] *A person's wealth, goods, or estate,* Luke 15. 12.

Man became a living soul, *Gen.* 2. 7. *His lifeless body was endued with a soul, whereby he became a living rational creature.*

Living water, *John* 4. 10. | 7. 38. *The Spirit of God and his grace, which will never fail, but endure to eternal life.*

Gen. 1. 28. have dominion over every *l.* thing
2. 7. man bec. a *l.* soul || 3. 20. Eve, mother of all *l.*
6. 19. and of every *l.* thing of all flesh, two
7. 4. and every *l.* substance I will destroy
23. and every *l.* substance was destroyed
8. 1. God remembered Noah and every *l.* thing
21. I will not smite any more every thing *l.*
26. † 19. and found there a well of *l.* water
Lev. 11. 10. of any *l.* thing which is in the water
13. † 10. if there be a quickening of *l.* flesh
14. 6. as for the *l.* bird he shall take it, 7. 53.
20. 25. not make abominable by any *l.* thing
Num. 16. 48. he stood between the dead and the *l.*
19. † 17. for unclean *l.* water shall be given
Ruth 2. 20. hath not left off his kindness to the *l.*
2 *Sam.* 20. 3. they were shut up *l.* in widowhood
1 *Kings* 3. 22. the *l.* is my son, the dead thy son, 23.
25. divide the *l.* child in two, and give half to one
26. whose the *l.* child was, give her the *l.* child
27. then the king said, give her the *l.* child
Job 12. 10. in whose hand is soul of every *l.* thing
28. 13. nor is it found in the land of the *l.*
21. seeing it is hid from the eyes of all *l.*
30. 23. and to the house appointed for all *l.*
33. 30. to be enlightened with light of *l.*
Ps. 27. 13. to see goodness of the Lord in land of *l.*
38. † 19. for mine enemies being *l.* are strong
52. 5. and root thee out of the land of the *l.*
56. 13. that I may walk in the light of the *l.*
58. 9. shall take them away both *l.* and in wrath
69. 28. let them be blotted out of the book of the *l.*
116. 9. walk before the Lord in the land of the *l.*
142. 5. thou art my portion in the land of the *l.*
143. 2. in thy sight shall no man *l.* be justified
145. 16. thou satisfiest the desire of every *l.* thing
Eccl. 4. 2. dead, more than the *l.* which are alive
15. I considered all the *l.* under the sun
6. 8. poor, that knoweth to walk before the *l.*
7. 2. end of all men, and the *l.* will lay it to heart
9. 4. that is joined to all the *l.* a *l.* dog is better
5. for the *l.* know that they shall die, but dead
Cant. 4. 15. a well of *l.* water, streams from Lebanon
Isa. 4. 3. that is written among the *l.* in Jerusalem
8. 19. seek to their God for the *l.* to the dead
19. † 10. be broken that make ponds of *l.* things
38. 11. not see the Lord in the land of the *l.*
19. the *l.* the *l.* he shall praise thee, as I do
53. 8. he was cut off out of the land of the *l.*
57. † 10. thou hast found the *l.* of thy hand
Jer. 2. 13. forsaken fountain of *l.* waters, 17. 13.
11. 19. let us cut him off from the land of the *l.*
Lam. 3. 39. wherefore doth a *l.* man complain?
Ezek. 7. † 13. though his life be yet among the *l.*
26. 20. I shall set glory in the land of the *l.*
32. 23. all of them slain, which caused terror in
the land of the *l.* 24, 25, 26, 27, 32.
Dan. 2. 30. any wisdom that I have more than any *l.*
4. 17. to the intent that the *l.* may know
Zech. 14. 8. *l.* waters shall go out from Jerusalem
Mat. 22. 32. God is not the God of the dead, but
of the *l.* *Mark* 12. 27. *Luke* 20. 38.
Mark 12. 44. she cast in all she had, even all her *l.*
Luke 8. 43. woman had spent all her *l.* on physicians
15. 12. and he divided unto them his *l.*
13. there wasted his substance with riotous *l.* 30.
24. 5. why seek ye the *l.* among the dead?
John 4. 10. he would have given thee *l.* water?
11. from whence hast thou that *l.* water?
6. 51. I am the *l.* bread which came down from
57. as the *l.* Father hath sent me, and I live
7. 38. out of his belly shall flow rivers of *l.* water
Rom. 12. 1. that ye present your bodies a *l.* sacrifice
14. 9. that he might be Lord both of dead and *l.*
1 *Cor.* 15. 45. the first man Adam was made a *l.* soul
Col. 2. 20. *l.* in the world, are ye subject to ordinan.
Tit. 3. 3. *l.* in malice, envy, and hating one another
Heb. 10. 20. boldness to enter by a new and *l.* way
1 *Pet.* 2. 4. to whom coming as to a *l.* stone, chosen
Rev. 7. 17. the Lamb shall lead them to *l.* fountains
16. 3. and every *l.* soul died in the sea

See BIRD, CREATURE, GOD.

LIZARD.

Lev. 11. 30. the *l.* snail, and mole unclean to you

LO

Denotes, [1] *Matter of attention and consideration,* Isa. 25. 9. Luke 13. 16. [2] *Readiness,* Psal. 40. 7. [3] *Certainty and affirmation,* Ezek. 30. 9. [4] *Demonstration of a thing present,* Gen. 29. 7.

Gen. 18. 10. *l.* Sarah thy wife shall have a son
29. 7. *l.* it is yet high day, water ye the sheep
50. 5. *l.* I die || *Exod.* 19. 9. *l.* I come in a cloud
Num. 14. 40. *l.* we be here, and will go up to place
24. 11. *l.* the Lord hath kept thee from honour
1 *Sam.* 14. 43. I did but taste honey, and *l.* I must die
2 *Sam.* 24. 17. *l.* I have sinned and done wickedly
Job 9. 19. if I speak of strength, *l.* he is strong
Psal. 37. 36. he passed away, and *l.* he was not
40. 7. *l.* I come || 132. 6. *l.* we heard it at Ephratah
52. 7. *l.* the man that made not God his strength
73. 27. *l.* they that are far from thee shall perish
92. 9. *l.* thine enemies, for *l.* thine enemies perish
Eccl. 7. 29. *l.* this only have I found, that God made
Cant. 2. 11. *l.* the winter is past, the rain is over
Isa. 25. 9. *l.* this is our God, we have waited for him
Jer. 4. 23. the earth, and *l.* it was without form
25. I beheld, and *l.* there was no man, birds fled
8. 8. *l.* certainly in vain made he it, pen in vain
25. 29. for *l.* I begin to bring evil on the city
Ezek. 17. 18. when *l.* he had given him his hand
30. 9. for *l.* it cometh || 33. 33. *l.* it will come
Hos. 9. 6. for *l.* they are gone, because of destruction
Amos 4. 2. that *l.* the days shall come upon you
Hag. 1. 9. ye looked for much, and *l.* it came to little
Mat. 3. 16. and *l.* the heavens were opened
24. 23. *l.* here is Christ, or there, believe it not
28. 7. *l.* I have told you || 20. *l.* I am with you
Luke 13. 16. Satan bound, *l.* these eighteen years
23. 15. *l.* nothing worthy of death is done to him
Acts 13. 46. unworthy, *l.* we turn to the Gentiles
Heb. 10. 7. *l.* I come to do thy will, O God, 9.

LOADEN.

Psal. 144. † 14. that our oxen may be *l.* with flesh
Isa. 46. 1. on the cattle your carriages were heavy *l.*

LOADETH.

Psal. 68. 19. Lord, who daily *l.* us with benefits

LOAF.

Exod. 29. 23. one *l.* of bread, one cake of oiled bread
1 *Chr.* 16. 3. David dealt to every one a *l.* of bread
Mark 8. 14. neither had they more than one *l.*

LOAN.

1 *Sam.* 2. 20. for the *l.* which is lent to the Lord

LOATH, *see* LOTHE.

LOAVES.

1 *Sam.* 17. 17. take ten *l.* and run to the camp
25. 18. Abigail made haste and took 200 *l.*
1 *Kings* 14. 3. take with thee ten *l.* and cracknels
2 *Kings* 4. 42. a man brought the man of God 20 *l.*
Mat. 14. 17. they say, we have here but five *l.*
19. and he took the five *l.* *Mark* 6. 38. *Luke* 9. 13.
15. 34. said, how many *l.* have ye? *Mark* 6. 38. | 8. 5.
36. he took the seven *l.* and the fishes, *Mark* 8. 6.
16. 9. nor remember the five *l.* of the 5000
10. nor the seven *l.* of the 4000, and how many
Mark 6. 44. they that did eat of the *l.* were 5000
52. they considered not the miracle of the *l.*
Luke 11. 5. say to him, friend, lend me three *l.*
John 6. 9. a lad here who hath five barley *l.*
11. Jesus took the *l.* and distributed to the disciples
13. with the fragments of the five barley *l.*
26. because ye did eat of the *l.* and were filled

See BREAD.

Wave LOAVES.

Lev. 23. 17. shall bring two *w. l.* of two tenth deals

LOCK.

Cant. 5. 5. dropping myrrh on the handles of the *l.*

LOCK.

Ezek. 8. 3. and he took me by a *l.* of my head

LOCKS.

Num. 6. 5. let the *l.* of the hair of his head grow
Judg. 16. 13. if thou weavest the seven *l.* of my head
19. she caused him to shave off the seven *l.*
Neh. 3. 3. set up doors, and *l.* thereof, 6, 13, 14, 15.
Cant. 4. 1. thou hast doves' eyes within thy *l.*
3. like a piece of pomegranate within thy *l.*
5. 2. my *l.* are filled with the drops of the night
11. his *l.* are bushy, and black as a raven
6. 7. a pomegranate are thy temples within thy *l.*
Isa. 47. 2. uncover thy *l.* make bare the leg
Ezek. 44. 20. nor suffer their *l.* to grow long

See BARS.

LOCKED.

Judg. 3. 23. Ehud shut the doors and *l.* them
24. behold, the doors of the parlour were *l.*

LOCUST

Signifies, [1] *A certain vile insect. Their nature is to be many together, therefore vast multitudes are resembled by them,* Nah. 3. 15. *In* Arabia, *and other countries that are infested by them, they come in vast numbers upon their corn when ripe, and what they do not eat they infect with their touch and the moisture coming from them; and afterwards dying in great numbers, they poison the air, and cause a pestilence. God plagued the Egyptians, by sending swarms of them into their land,* Exod. 10. 14. [2] *Either a large sort of grasshoppers, or a kind of green herb,* Lev. 11. 22. Mat. 3. 4. [3] *Authors, or teachers of false doctrine, who infect others by distilling their poisonous doctrines into them,* Rev. 9. 3

Exod. 10. 19. there remained not one *l.* in all Egypt
Lev. 11. 22. *l.* after his kind, and bald *l.* ye may eat
Deut. 28. 42. all thy trees shall the *l.* consume
1 *Kings* 8. 37. if there be in the land *l.* 2 *Chr.* 6. 28.
Psal. 78. 46. he gave also their labour to the *l.*
109. 23. I am tossed up and down as the *l.*
Joel 1. 4. hath the *l.* eaten, and that which *l.* left
2. 25. I will restore the years that the *l.* hath eaten

LOCUSTS.

Exod. 10. 4. behold, to-morrow I will bring *l.*
12. stretch out thy hand over Egypt for the *l.*
13. in the morning the east wind brought the *l.*
14. no such *l.* || 19. the west wind took away the *l.*
Deut. 28. 38. for the *l.* shall consume it
2 *Chron.* 7. 13. if I command the *l.* to devour
Psal. 105. 34. he spake, and *l.* came, and caterpillars
Prov. 30. 27. the *l.* have no king, ye go by bands
Isa. 33. 4. as the running to and fro of *l.* shall he run
Nah. 3. 15. make thyself many as the *l.*
17. thy crowned are as the *l.* and thy captains
Mat. 3. 4. his meat was *l.* and wild honey, *Mark* 1. 6.
Rev. 9. 3. there came out of the smoke *l.* on the earth
7. shapes of *l.* were like to horses for battle

LODGE.

Isa. 1. 8. the daughter of Zion is left as a *l.* in garden

LODGE.

Gen. 24. 23. is there room in the house for us to *l.* in?
25. we have provender enough, and room to *l.* in
Num. 22. 8. he said to them, *l.* here this night
Josh. 4. 3. in the place where ye shall *l.* this night
Judg. 19. 9. *l.* here, that thy heart may be merry
13. to *l.* in Gibeah or in Ramah, 15. | 20. 4.
20. the old man said, only *l.* not in the street
Ruth 1. 16. where thou lodgest I will *l*
2 *Sam.* 17. 8. thy father will not *l.* with the people
16. *l.* not this night in the plains of the wilderness
Neh. 4. 22. let every one *l.* within Jerusalem
13. 21. I said, why *l.* ye about the wall?
Job 17. † 2. doth not my eye *l.* in their provocation?
24. 7. they cause the naked to *l.* without clothing
31. 32. the stranger did not *l.* in the street
Psal. 25. † 13. his soul shall *l.* in goodness
91. † 1. shall *l.* under the shadow of the Almighty
Cant. 7. 11. come, my beloved, let us *l.* in the villages
Isa. 21. 13. in the forest in Arabia shall ye *l.*
65. 4. and *l.* in monuments, and eat swine's flesh
Jer. 4. 14. how long shall vain thoughts *l.* in thee?
Zeph. 2. 14. the beasts shall *l.* in the upper lintels
Mat. 13. 32. so that birds of the air come and *l.* in
the branches thereof, *Mark* 4. 32.
Acts 21. 16. brought Mnason with whom we should *l.*

LODGED.

Gen. 32. 13. Jacob *l.* there that same night
21. and himself *l.* that night in the company
Josh. 2. 1. the spies came into an harlot's house, and *l.*
3. 1. to Jordan, he and all Israel, and *l.* there
4. 8. carried them over to the place where they *l.*
6. 11. they came into the camp, and *l.* in the camp
8. 9. but Joshua *l.* that night among the people
Judg. 18. 2. came to house of Micah, they *l.* there
19. 4. so they did eat and drink, and *l.* there
7. urged him, therefore he *l.* there again
1 *Kings* 19. 9. came into a cave, and *l.* there
1 *Chr.* 9. 27. they *l.* round about the house of God
Neh. 13. 20. the merchants *l.* without Jerusalem
Isa. 1. 21. righteousness *l.* in it, but now murderers
Mat. 21. 17. he went to Bethany and *l.* there
Acts 10. 18. asked whether Simon were *l.* there
23. then called he them in, and *l.* them
28. 7. Publius *l.* us three days courteously
1 *Tim.* 5. 10. if she have *l.* strangers, if she washed

LODGEST.

Ruth 1. 16. Ruth said, where thou *l.* I will lodge

LODGETH.

Acts 10. 6. he *l.* with one Simon a tanner

LODGING.

Josh. 4. 3. twelve stones, and leave them in the *l.*
Judg. 19. 15. no man took them to his house to *l.*
Isa. 10. 29. they have taken up their *l.* at Geba
Jer. 9. 2. that I had in the wilderness a *l.* place
Acts 28. 23. there came many to him into his *l.*
Philem. 22. but withal prepare me also a *l.*

LODGINGS.

2 *Kings* 19. 23. I will enter into the *l.* of his borders

LOFT.

1 *Kings* 17. 19. he took him and carried him into a *l.*
Acts 20. 9. Eutychus fell down from the third *l.*

LOFTY.

Psal. 131. 1. heart is not haughty, nor mine eyes *l.*
Prov. 30. 13. a generation, O how *l.* are their eyes!
Isa. 2. 11. the *l.* looks of man shall be humbled, 5. 15.
12. the day of the Lord be on every one that is *l.*
26. 5. the *l.* city he layeth low to the ground
57. 7. on a *l.* mountain hast thou set thy bed
15. thus saith the high and *l.* One, that inhabiteth

LOFTILY.

Psal. 73. 8. they are corrupt, they speak *l.*

LOFTINESS.

Isa. 2. 17. the *l.* of man shall be bowed down
Jer. 48. 29. we heard the pride of Moab, his *l.*

LOG.

Lev. 14. 10. the priest shall take a *l.* of oil, 12, 24.
15. shall take some of the *l.* of oil, and pour it
21. if he be poor, then he shall take a *l.* of oil

LOINS

Signify, [1] *The lower parts of the back, or the waist,* Exod. 28. 42. [2] *The whole man,* Job 31. 20. Psal. 66. 11.

Gird up the loins of your mind, 1 *Pet.* 1. 13. *Let your minds be intent upon, ready, and prepared for your spiritual work, restrained from all those thoughts, cares, affections, and lusts, which may entangle, detain, and hinder them, or make them unfit for it. It is an allusion to the custom of the* Oriental *nations, who wearing long loose garments were wont to gird them about their loins, that they might not hinder them in their travelling or working,* 1 Kings 18. 46. 2 Kings 4. 29. *It may also have a special respect to the like rite used at the passover when the Israelites were just ready to enter upon their journey and march out of Egypt,* Exod. 12. 11.

Gen. 35. 11. and kings shall come out of thy *l.*
37. 34. and Jacob put sackcloth upon his *l.*
46. 26. the souls which came out of his *l.* *Exod.* 1. 5.
Exod. 12. 11. ye shall eat it, with your *l.* girded
28. 42. breeches reach from the *l.* unto the thighs
Deut. 33. 11. smite through the *l.* of them that rise
2 *Sam.* 20. 8. a girdle with a sword fastened on his *l.*
1 *Kings* 2. 5. put the blood in the girdle about his *l.*
8. 19. son shall come forth of thy *l.* 2 *Chron.* 6. 9.
12. 10 thicker than my father's *l.* 2 *Chr.* 10. 10.
18. 46. Elijah girded up his *l.* and ran before Ahab
20. 31. let us, I pray, put sackcloth on our *l.*
32. so they girded sackcloth on their *l.* and ropes
2 *Kings* 1. 8. was an hairy man, and girt with girdle
of leather about his *l.* *Mat.* 3. 4. *Mark* 1. 6.
4. 29. gird up thy *l.* 9. 1. *Job* 38. 3. | 40. 7. *Jer.* 1. 17.

Neh. 4. † 18. had each his sword girded on his *l.*
Job 12. 18. he girdeth the *l.* of kings with a girdle
31. 20. if his *l.* have not blessed me
40. 16. lo, now his strength is in his *l.*
Psal. 38. 7. my *l.* are filled with a loathsome disease
66. 11. thou laidest affliction upon our *l.*
69. 23. and make their *l.* continually to shake
Prov. 30. † 31. a horse girt in the *l.* and a king
31. 17. she girdeth her *l.* with strength
Isa. 5. 27. neither shall the girdle of their *l.* be loosed
11. 5. righteousness shall be the girdle of his *l.*
20. 2. loose the sackcloth from off thy *l.* put off
21. 3. therefore are my *l.* filled with pain
32. 11. make bare, gird sackcloth upon your *l.*
45. 1. I will loose the *l.* of kings to open before
Jer. 13. 1. get a linen girdle and put it upon thy *l.*
11. as the girdle cleaveth to the *l.* of a man
30. 6. see every man with his hands on his *l.*
48. 37. and upon the *l.* shall be sackcloth
Ezek. 1. 27. from the appearance of his *l.* upward
8. 2. from his *l.* downward, fire; from his *l.* upward
9. † 2. with a writer's inkhorn on his *l.*
21. 6. sigh with the breaking of thy *l.* and bitterness
23. 15. girded with girdles upon their *l.*
29. 7. thou madest all their *l.* to be at a stand
44. 18. they shall have linen breeches on their *l.*
47. 4. he measured, the waters were to the *l.*
Dan. 5. 6. so the joints of his *l.* were loosed
10. 5. whose *l.* were girded with fine gold of Uphaz
Amos 8. 10. I will bring sackcloth on your *l.*
Nah. 2. 1. make thy *l.* strong ‖ 10. pain is in all *l.*
Luke 12. 35. let your *l.* be girded about, and lights
Acts 2. 30. that of his *l.* he would raise up Christ
Eph. 6. 14. having your *l.* girt about with truth
Heb. 7. 5. tho' they came out of the *l.* of Abraham
10. for he was yet in the *l.* of his father
1 *Pet.* 1. 13. wherefore gird up the *l.* of your mind

LONG

Signifies, [1] *Of great extent in length*, Ezek. 31. 5. [2] *To love greatly*, Gen. 34. 8. [3] *To thirst*, 2 Sam. 23. 15. [4] *To desire very earnestly*, Job 3. 21. Thus do, [1] *Such as are greatly afflicted for death*, Job 3. 21. [2] *The father after the son*, 2 Sam. 13. 39. [3] *The absent for his native place*, Gen. 31. 30. [4] *The godly after God's word*, Psal. 119. 40, 131, 174. [5] *The faithful teacher after his flock*, Phil. 2. 26. [6] *Saints after saints*, Rom. 1. 11. Phil. 1. 8.

Gen. 48. 15. G. who fed me all my life *l.* to this day
Exod. 19. 13. when the trumpet soundeth *l.* 19.
20. 12. that thy days may be *l.* on the land
Num. 9. 19. when the cloud tarried *l.* on tabernacle
Deut. 1. 6. ye dwelt *l.* enough in this mount, 2. 3.
4. 25. and shalt have remained *l.* in the land
14. 24. and if the way be too *l.* for thee
19. 6. and overtake him, because the way is *l.*
28. 59. make great plagues and of *l.* continuance
Josh. 6. 5. when they make a *l.* blast with the horn
9. 13. are old, by reason of the very *l.* journey
24. 7. ye dwelt in the wilderness a *l.* season
2 *Sam.* 3. 1. there was *l.* war between house of Saul
1 *Kings* 3. 11. and hast not asked *l.* life, 2 *Chr.* 1. 11.
2 *Chr.* 15. 3. for a *l.* season Israel was without God
Ps. 91. 16. with *l.* life will I satisfy him
95. 10. forty years *l.* was I grieved with this genera.
120. 6. my soul *l.* dwelt with him that hateth peace
129. 3. the plowers made *l.* their furrows
143. 3. to dwell, as those that have been *l.* dead
Prov. 3. 2. and *l.* life shall they add to thee
7. 19. the good man is gone a *l.* journey
23. 30. they that tarry *l.* at the wine, that go
25. 15. by *l.* forbearing is a prince persuaded
Eccl. 12. 5. because man goeth to his *l.* home
Isa. 65. 22. my elect shall *l.* enjoy work of their hands
Jer. 29. 28. this captivity is *l.* build ye houses
Lam. 2. 20. shall women eat their children of span *l.*?
Ezek. 17. 3. a great eagle *l.* winged, full of feathers
31. 5. his branches became *l.* because of waters
44. 20. nor shave, nor suffer their locks to grow *l.*
Dan. 10. 1. but the time appointed was *l.*
Hos. 13. 13. not stay *l.* in the place of breaking forth
Mat. 11. 21. repented *l.* ago in sackcloth and ashes
23. 14. ye devour widows' houses, and for pretence make *l.* prayers, *Mark* 12. 40. *Luke* 20. 47.
Mark 12. 38. who go in *l.* clothing, *Luke* 20. 46.
16. 5. sitting clothed in a *l.* white garment
Luke 18. 7. avenge, though he bear *l.* with them
23. 8. for he was desirous to see him of a *l.* season
Acts 20. 9. as Paul was *l.* preaching, he sunk with
27. 14. not *l.* after there arose a tempest Euroclydon
21. but after *l.* abstinence Paul stood in midst of
1 *Cor.* 11. 14. if a man have *l.* hair, it is a shame
15. if a woman have *l.* hair, it is a glory to her
Eph. 6. 3. that thou mayest live *l.* on the earth
1 *Tim.* 3. 15. if I tarry *l.* that thou mayest know
Jam. 5. 7. the husbandman hath *l.* patience for it

See Ago.

As LONG *as.*

Lev. 18. 19. *as l. as* she is put apart for uncleanness
26. 34. enjoy sabbaths, *as l. as* it lieth desolate, 35.
Num. 9. 18. *as l. as* the cloud abode, they rested
Deut. 12. 19. forsake not the Levite *as l. as* thou liv.
31. 13. fear the Lord *as l. as* you live in the land
1 *Sam.* 1. 28. lent to the Lord, *as l. as* he liveth
20. 31. *as l. as* son of Jesse liveth on the ground
25. 15. any thing *as l. as* we were conversant
2 *Chr.* 26. 5. *as l. as* he sought the L. he prospered
36. 21. *as l. as* she lay desolate she kept sabbath
Psal. 72. 5. fear thee *as l. as* sun and moon endure
17. his name shall be continued *as l. as* the sun
104. 33. I will sing to the Lord *as l. as* I live
116. 2. I will call upon him *as l. as* I live
Ezek. 42. 11. *as l. as* they, and as broad as they
Mat. 9. 15. *as l. as* bridegr. is with them, *Mark* 2. 19.
John 9. 5. *as l. as* I am in the world, I am the light
Rom. 7. 1. dominion over a man *as l. as* he liveth
1 *Cor.* 7. 39. wife is bound *as l. as* her husband liveth
Gal. 4. 1. the heir, *as l. as* he is a child, differeth not
1 *Pet.* 3. 6. whose daughters ye are *as l. as* ye do well
2 *Pet.* 1. 13. *as l. as* I am in this tabernacle

See Cubits, Day, Hour.

So LONG.

Judg. 5. 28. why is his chariot *so l.* in coming?
1 *Sam.* 29. 8. what found in thy servant, *so l.* as I have
2 *Kings* 9. 22. *so l.* as the whoredoms of thy mother
2 *Chron.* 6. 31. they may fear thee *so l.* as they live
Esth. 5. 13. *so l.* as I see Mordecai sitting at the gate
Job 27. 6. shall not reproach me *so l.* as I live
Psal. 72. 7. peace *so l.* as the moon endureth
Luke 1. 21. and marvelled that he tarried *so l.*
Rom. 7. 2. bound to her husband *so l.* as he liveth
Heb. 4. 7. to-day, after *so l.* a time, as it is said

LONG *time.*

Gen. 26. 8. when he had been there a *l. time*
Num. 20. 15. and we have dwelt in Egypt a *l. time*
Deut. 20. 19. when thou shalt besiege a city a *l. time*
Josh. 11. 18. Joshua made war a *l. time* with kings
23. 1. a *l. time* after that Joshua waxed old
1 *Sam.* 7. 2. while the ark abode the *time* was *l.*
2 *Sam.* 14. 2. as a woman that had *l. time* mourned
2 *Chron.* 30. 5. for they had not done it of a *l. time*
Isa. 42. 14. I have *l. time* holden my peace, been still
Lam. 5. 20. forget us, and forsake us so *l. time*
Mat. 25. 19. after a *l. time* the lord of those servants cometh and reckoneth with them, *Luke* 20. 9.
Luke 8. 27. a certain man which had devils *l. time*
20. 9. a man went into a far country for a *l. time*
John 5. 6. knew that he had been a *l. time* in that case
14. 9. have I been so *l. time* with you, and yet
Acts 8. 11. because of *l. time* he had bewitched them
14. 3. *l. time* abode they with the disciples, 28.
2 *Pet.* 2. 3. whose judgment of a *l. time* lingereth not

LONG *while.*

Acts 20. 11. he talked a *l. while* till break of day

LONG.

Job 3. 21. which *l.* for death, but it cometh not
6. 8. O that God would grant me thing that I *l.* for!
Rom. 1. 11. for I *l.* to see you, that I may impart
2 *Cor.* 9. 14. and by their prayer which *l.* after you
Phil. 1. 8. how greatly I *l.* after you all in bowels

LONGED.

2 *Sam.* 13. 39. David *l.* to go forth unto Absalom
23. 15. David *l.* and said, O that one, 1 *Chr.* 11. 17.
Psal. 119. 40. behold, I have *l.* after thy precepts
131. for I *l.* for thy commandments
174. I have *l.* for thy salvation, O Lord
Phil. 2. 26. for he *l.* after you all ‖ 4. 1. and *l.* for

LONGEDST.

Gen. 31. 30. thou sore *l.* after thy father's house

LONGER.

Exod. 2. 3. when she could no *l.* hide him
9. 28. I will let you go, and ye shall stay no *l.*
Judg. 2. 14. could not any *l.* stand before enemies
2 *Sam.* 20. 5. he tarried *l.* than the set time
2 *Kings* 6. 33. should I wait for the Lord any *l.*?
Job 7. †8. thine eyes are on me, I can live no *l.*
11. 9. the measure thereof is *l.* than the earth
Jer. 44. 22. so that the Lord could no *l.* bear
Luke 16. 2. for thou mayest be no *l.* steward
Acts 18. 20. when they desired him to tarry *l.*
25. 24. crying, that he ought not to live any *l.*
Rom. 6. 2. that are dead to sin, live any *l.* therein
Gal. 3. 25. we are no *l.* under a school-master
1 *Thess.* 3. 1. when we could no *l.* forbear, 5.
1 *Tim.* 5. 23. drink no *l.* water, but use a little wine
1 *Pet.* 4. 2. that he no *l.* live the rest of his time
Rev. 10. 6. that there should be time no *l.*

LONGETH.

Gen. 34. 8. my son Shechem *l.* for your daughter
Deut. 12. 20. because thy soul *l.* to eat flesh
Psal. 63. 1. my flesh *l.* for thee in a dry land
84. 2. my soul *l.* for the courts of the Lord

LONGING.

Deut. 28. 32. thine eyes shall fail with *l.* for them
Psal. 107. 9. for he satisfieth the *l.* soul
119. 20. my soul breaketh for the *l.* that it hath

LONG-*suffering.*

Exod. 34. 6. Lord God merciful and gracious, *l.-suffering*, *Num.* 14. 18. *Psal.* 86. 15. 2 *Pet.* 3. 9.
Jer. 15. 15. O Lord take me not away in thy *l. suff.*
Rom. 2. 4. or despisest thou riches of his *l.-suffer.*
9. 22. endured with much *l.-suffer.* vessels of wrath
2 *Cor.* 6. 6. by knowledge, by *l. suffer.* by kindness
Gal. 5. 22. fruit of the Spirit is love, *l.-suffering*
Eph. 4. 2. with *l.-suffering*, forbearing one another
Col. 1. 11. strengthened to all *l.-suff.* with joyfulness
3. 12. put on, as elect of God, meekness, *l.-suffer.*
1 *Tim.* 1. 16. that in me Christ might shew all *l.-s.*
2 *Tim.* 3. 10. thou hast fully known my faith, *l.-suff.*
4. 2. rebuke, exhort with all *l.-suffer.* and doctrine
1 *Pet.* 3. 20. when *l.-suffering* of God waited in days
2 *Pet.* 3. 15. the *l.-suffering* of our Lord is salvation

LOOK, S.

Psal. 18. 27. but thou wilt bring down high *l.*
101. 5. that hath a high *l.* I will not suffer
Prov. 6. 17. the Lord hateth a proud *l.* a lying
21. 4. a high *l.* and proud heart is sin
Isa. 2. 11. the lofty *l.* of man shall be humbled
10. 12. I will punish the glory of his high *l.*
Ezek. 2. 6. nor be dismayed at their *l.* 3. 9.
Dan. 7. 20. whose *l.* was more stout than his fellows

LOOK

Signifies, [1] *To behold or see*, Deut. 28. 32. [2] *To consider or take particular notice of*, Lev. 13. 5. [3] *To expect or wait for*, Jer. 13. 16. Mat. 11. 3. [4] *To believe and trust in*, Isa. 45. 22.

Gen. 13. 14. *l.* from the place where thou art
15. 5. *l.* towards heaven, and tell the stars
19. 17. escape for thy life, *l.* not behind thee
40. 7. wherefore *l.* ye so sadly to-day?
41. 33. now let Pharaoh *l.* out a man discreet
42. 1. Jacob said, why *l.* ye one upon another?
Exod. 10. 10. *l.* to it; for evil is before you
25. 20. and their faces shall *l.* one to another
40. *l.* that thou make them after their pattern
Lev. 13. 39. then the priest shall *l.* if the spots
53. if the priest shall *l.* and behold, 56.
14. 3. then the priest shall *l.* if the plague, 39, 44.
Deut. 9. 27. *l.* not to the stubbornness of this people
28. 32. thine eyes shall *l.* and fail with longing
1 *Sam.* 16. 12. David was ruddy, and goodly to *l.* to
17. 18. *l.* how brethren fare, and take pledge

1 *Kings* 18. 43. go up now, *l.* toward the sea
2 *Kings* 3. 14. I would not *l.* toward thee, nor see
6. 32. *l.* when messenger cometh, shut the door
9. 2. *l.* out there, Jehu, and go in, make him rise
10. 3. *l.* even out best and meetest of master's sons
23. *l.* there be none of the servants of the Lord
14. 8. come, let us *l.* one another in the face
1 *Chron.* 12. 17. the God of our fathers *l.* thereon
Job 3. 9. let it *l.* for light, but have none
5. † 1. to which of the saints wilt thou *l.*?
20. 21. therefore shall no man *l.* for his goods
21. † 5. *l.* unto me and be astonished, lay your hand
35. 5. *l.* to heavens and see, and behold the clouds
Ps. 5. 3. I will direct my prayer to thee, and *l.* up
40. 12. iniquities so that I am not able to *l.* up
123. 2. as the eyes of servants *l.* to their masters
Prov. 4. 25. let thine eyes *l.* right on, and eye-lids
27. 23. to know thy flocks, and *l.* well to thy herds
Eccl. 12. 3. that *l.* out at the windows be darkened
Cant. 4. 8. *l.* from top of Amana, Shenir, Hermon
Isa. 5. 30. if one *l.* unto the land, behold darkness
8. 17. I will wait on the Lord, I will *l.* for him
21. shall curse their king and God, and *l.* upward
22. they shall *l.* unto earth, and behold trouble
17. 7. at that day shall a man *l.* to his Maker
8. he shall not *l.* to the altars, work of his hands
22. 4. *l.* away from me, I will weep bitterly
8. thou didst *l.* in that day to the armour
31. 1. they *l.* not to the Holy One of Israel
42. 18. hear, ye deaf, *l.* ye blind, that ye may see
45. 22. *l.* unto me, and be saved, all ends of earth
51. 1. *l.* to the rock whence ye are hewn
2. *l.* to Abraham your father, and to Sarah
56. 11. they all *l.* to their own way for gain
59. 11. we *l.* for judgment, but there is none
66. 2. but to this man will I *l.* that is poor
Jer. 13. 16. and while ye *l.* for light, he turn it
39. 12. take and *l.* well to him, do him no harm
40. 4. come with me, and I will *l.* well to thee
46. 5. their mighty ones are fled, and *l.* not back
47. 3. the fathers shall not *l.* back to their children
Ezek. 23. 15. all of them princes to *l.* us to Babylon
29. 16. iniquity to remembrance when they *l.*
Hos. 3. 1. who *l.* to other gods, and love wine
Jonah 2. 4. I will *l.* again towards thy holy temple
Mic. 7. 7. therefore will I *l.* to the Lord, will wait
Nah. 2. 8. stand, stand, but none shall *l.* back
Mat. 11. 3. or do we *l.* for another? *Luke* 7. 19, 20.
Mark 8. 25. put hands on eyes, and made him *l.* up
Luke 21. 28. when these things begin, then *l.* up
John 7. 52. search and *l.* for out of Galilee no prophet
Acts 6. 3. *l.* ye out seven men of honest report
18. 15. if it be a question of words, *l.* ye to it
1 *Cor.* 16. 11. *l.* for him with the brethren
2 *Cor.* 3. 13. Israel could not stedfastly *l.* to the end
4. 18. while we *l.* at things which are seen
Phil. 3. 20. from whence we *l.* for the Saviour
Heb. 9. 28. to them that *l.* for him shall he appear
1 *Pet.* 1. 12. which the angels desire to *l.* into
2 *Pet.* 3. 13. nevertheless we *l.* for new heavens
14. seeing ye *l.* for such things, be diligent that
2 *John* 8. *l.* to yourselves, that we lose not
Rev. 5. 3. and no man was able to *l.* thereon
4. found worthy to read the book, nor *l.* thereon

LOOK *down.*

Deut. 26. 15. *l. down* from thy holy habitation
Psal. 80. 14. *l. down*, behold, and visit this vine
85. 11. righteousness shall *l. down* from heaven
Isa. 63. 15. *l. down* from heaven, and behold from
Lam. 3. 50. till L. *l. down*, and behold from heaven

LOOK *on*, or *upon.*

Gen. 9. 16. bow shall be in cloud, and I will *l. upon* it
12. 11. I know thou art a fair woman to *l. upon*
24. 16. Rebekah was very fair to *l. upon*, 26. 7.
Exod. 3. 6. Moses was afraid to *l. upon* God
5. 21. the Lord *l. upon* you, and judge, because
39. 43. and Moses did *l. upon* all the work
Lev. 13. 3. the priest shall *l. on* the plague in the skin of the flesh, 21, 25, 26, 31, 32, 34, 43, 50.
3. the priest shall *l. on* him, 5, 6, 27, 36.
14. 48. the priest shall *l. upon* it, and behold
Num. 15. 39. for a fringe, that ye may *l. upon* it
Judg. 7. 17. Gideon said, *l. on* me, and do likewise
1 *Sam.* 1. 11. if thou wilt indeed *l. on* the affliction
16. 7. *l.* not *on* his countenance or stature
2 *Sam.* 9. 8. shouldest *l. upon* such a dead dog as I am
11. 2. the woman was very beautiful to *l. upon*
16. 12. it may be the Lord will *l. on* my affliction
2 *Chr.* 24. 22. he said, Lord, *l. upon* it, and require it
Esth. 1. 11. Vashti the queen was fair to *l. on*
Job 6. 28. now, therefore, be content, *l. upon* me
40. 12. *l. on* every one that is proud, and bring low
Psal. 22. 17. my bones stare and *l. upon* me
25. 18. *l. upon* mine affliction and my pain, forgive
35. 17. Lord, how long wilt thou *l. on*? rescue
84. 9. and *l. upon* the face of thine Anointed
119. 132. *l.* thou *upon* me, and be merciful to me
142. † 4. *l. on* the right hand, and see
Prov. 4. 25. let thine eyes *l.* right *on*, and eye-lids
23. 31. *l.* not thou *upon* the wine when it is red
Cant. 1. 6. *l.* not *upon* me because I am black
6. 13. return, return, that we may *l. upon* thee
Isa. 14. 16. that see thee, shall narrowly *l. upon* thee
33. 20. *l. upon* Zion ‖ 51. 6. *l. upon* the earth beneath
66. 24. go forth and *l. upon* the carcases of the men
Mic. 4. 11. be defiled, and let our eye *l. upon* Zion
Nah. 3. 7. that *l. upon* thee, shall flee from thee
Hab. 1. 13. of purer eyes than to *l. upon* iniquity
2. 15. that thou mayest *l. upon* their nakedness
Zech. 12. 10. shall *l. upon* me whom they pierced
Luke 9. 38. master, I beseech thee, *l. upon* my son
John 4. 35. lift up your eyes, and *l. upon* the fields
19. 37. they shall *l. upon* him whom they pierced
Acts 3. 4. Peter and John said, *l. on* us, 12.
2 *Cor.* 10. 7. *l. upon* things after outward appearance
Phil. 2. 4. *l.* not every man *on* his own things
Rev. 4. 3. he that sat was to *l. upon* like a jasper

LOOKED.

Gen. 6. 12. God *l.* on the earth, and it was corrupt
18. 16. the men rose up, and *l.* toward Sodom
19. 26. his wife *l.* back ‖ 26. 8. *l.* out at a window
29. 32. the Lord hath *l.* upon my affliction

Gen. 39. 23. keeper of the prison l. not to any thing
40. 6. Joseph l. on them, behold they were sad
Exod. 2. 11. Moses went and l. on their burdens
12. he l. this way and that way, and saw no man
25. and God l. upon the children of Israel
4. 31. Lord had l. on their affliction, Deut. 26. 7.
14. 24. the Lord l. on the host of the Egyptians
16. 10. that they l. toward the wilderness
33. 8. the people l. after Moses till he was gone
Num. 12. 10. Aaron l. on Miriam, she was leprous
16. 42. that they l. towards the tabernacle
24. 20. he l. on Amalek, he took up his parable
21. l. on the Kenites, and took up his parable
Josh. 8. 20. when the men of Ai l. behind them
Judg. 5. 28. the mother of Sisera l. out at a window
6. 14. the Lord l. upon him, and said, go in might
13. 19. and Manoah and his wife l. on, 20.
20. 40. the Benjamites l. behind them, and behold
1 Sam. 6. 19. because they had l. into the ark
9. 16. I have l. on my people, because cry came to
14. 16. the watchmen of Saul l. and behold
16. 6. when they were come, he l. on Eliab
17. 42. the Philistine l. about, and saw David
24. 8. Saul l. behind him, David stood, 2 Sam. 1. 7.
2 Sam. 2. 20. Abner l. behind him and said
6. 16. Michal l. through a window, and saw David
22. 42. they l. but there was none to save
1 Kings 18. 43. Elijah's servant went up and l.
2 Kings 2. 24. Elisha turned back and l. on them
6. 30. the people l. and behold he had sackcloth
9. 30. Jezebel painted, and l. out at a window
14. 11. l. one another in the face at Beth-shemesh
2 Chron. 13. 14. when Judah l. back, the battle
26. 20. l. on him, and behold he was leprous
Esth. 2. 15. favour in the sight of all who l. on her
Job 6. 19. the troops of Tema l. Sheba waited
Psal. 14. 2. the Lord l. to see if any did understand
34. 5. they l. to him, and were lightened
53. 2. God l. down on the children of men
102. 19. he hath l. down from his sanctuary
109. 25. when they l. they shaked their heads
Cant. 1. 6. because the sun hath l. on me
Isa. 5. 2. he l. that it should bring forth grapes
7. he l. for judgment, but behold oppression
22. 11. but ye have not l. to the maker thereof
64. 3. didst terrible things which we l. not for
Jer. 8. 15. we l. for peace, no good came, 14. 19.
Lam. 2. 16. certainly this is the day that we l. for
Ezek. 10. 11. whither the head l. they followed
16. + 4. wast not washed when I l. upon thee, 8.
21. 21. he consulted with images, he l. in the liver
Dan. 1. 13. let our countenances be l. on before thee
Obad. 12. not have l. on the day of thy brother
13. thou shouldest not have l. on their affliction
Hag. 1. 9. ye l. for much, and lo it came to little
Mark 3. 5. when he l. round about, 5. 32. | 10. 23.
6. 41. he l. up to heaven, and blessed and brake
8. 24. he l. and said, I see men as trees walking
16. 4. when they l. they saw the stone rolled
Luke 1. 25. l. on me, to take away my reproach
2. 38. spake to all that l. for redemption in Jerusa.
10. 32. likewise a Levite came and l. on him
22. 61. the Lord turned, and l. upon Peter
John 13. 22. then the disciples l. one on another
Acts 1. 10. while they l. stedfastly toward heaven
28. 6. after they had l. a great while and saw no
Heb. 11. 10. for he l. for a city which hath foundat.
1 John 1. 1. that which we have l. upon, declare we

LOOKED, with eyes.

Gen. 33. 1. Jacob lifted up his eyes and l. Esau came
37. 25. they lifted up their eyes and l. and behold
Dan. 10. 5. then I lifted up mine eyes l. and behold
Zech. 2. 1. Zechariah lifted his eyes and l. 5. 9. | 6. 1.

I LOOKED.

Gen. 16. 13. have I also here l. after him that seeth
Deut. 9. 16. I l. and behold ye had sinned
Job 30. 26. when I l. for good, then evil came
Psal. 69. 20. and I l. for some to take pity, but
142. 4. I l. on my right hand, and beheld
Prov. 7. 6. at the window, I l. through my casement
24. 32. I l. upon it, and received instruction
Eccl. 2. 11. I l. on all the works that my hands
Isa. 5. 4. I l. it should bring forth grapes, it brought
63. 5. and I l. and there was none to help, I wond.
Ezek. 1. 4. I l. and behold, 2. 9. | 8. 7. | 10. 1, 9. | 44. 4.
Dan. 12. 5. then I Daniel l. and behold there stood
Zech. 4. 2. I have l. and behold a candlestick
Acts 22. 13. and the same hour I l. up upon him
Rev. 4. 1. I l. and behold, 6. 8. | 14. 1, 14. | 15. 5.

LOOKEST.

Job 13. 27. thou l. narrowly to all my paths
Hab. 1. 13. why l. on them that deal treacherously?

LOOKETH.

Lev. 13. 12. if leprosy cover wheresoever priest l.
Num. 21. 8. when he l. on the serpent, he shall live
20. Pisgah, which l. toward Jeshimon, 23. 28.
1 Sam. 16. 7. man l. on the outward appearance
Job 7. 2. as an hireling l. for the reward of work
28. 24. for he l. to the ends of the earth
33. 27. he l. on men, and if any say, I have sinned
Psal. 33. 13. the Lord l. from heaven, he beholdeth
14. he l. on all the inhabitants of the world
104. 32. he l. on the earth, and it trembleth
Prov. 14. 15. the prudent l. well to his goings
31. 27. she l. well to the ways of her household
Cant. 2. 9. behold, he l. forth at the window
6. 10. who is she that l. forth as the morning?
7. 4. as the tower which l. toward Damascus
Isa. 28. 4. when he that l. upon it seeth it
Ezek. 8. 3. the door that l. toward the north
11. 1. the gate which l. eastward, 40. 6, 22. | 43. 1.
| 44. 1. | 46. 1, 12. | 47. 2.
40. 20. gate of the court that l. toward the north
Mat. 5. 28. whosoever l. on a woman to lust after
24. 50. lord come when l. not for him, Luke 12. 46.
Jam. 1. 25. whoso l. into the perfect law of liberty

LOOKING.

1 Kings 7. 25. three oxen l. toward the north
1 Chr. 15. 29. Michal l. out at a window, saw Dav.
2 Chron. 4. 4. three oxen l. toward the south
Isa. 38. 14. mine eyes fail with l. upward
Mat. 14. 19. l. up to heaven, he blessed, Luke 9. 16.
Mark 7. 34. and l. up to heaven, he sighed
15. 40. there were also women l. on afar off
Luke 6. 10. l. round about upon them all, he said
9. 62. and l. back, is fit for the kingdom of God
21. 26. men's hearts failing them for l. after
John 1. 36. John l. on Jes. saith, behold the Lamb
20. 5. l. in, saw linen clothes lying, yet went not in
Acts 6. 15. l. stedfastly on him, saw his face as it
23. 21. are they ready, l. for a promise from thee
Tit. 2. 13. l. for that blessed hope and appearing
Heb. 10. 27. but a certain fearful l. for of judgment
12. 2. l. unto Jesus the author and finisher of faith
15. l. diligently, lest any fail of the grace of God
2 Pet. 3. 12. l. for the coming of the day of God
Jude 21. l. for the mercy of our Lord Jesus Christ

LOOKING-GLASS.

Job 37. 18. spread out the sky as a molten l.-glass

LOOKING-GLASSES.

Exod. 38. 8. made laver and foot of l.-glass. of wom.

LOOPS.

Exod. 26. 4. thou shalt make l. of blue, 5.
5. l. shalt thou make, 10. || 11. put taches in the l.
36. 11. made l. of blue || 12. fifty l. made he, 17.

LOOSE.

Gen. 49. 21. Naphtali is a hind let l. giveth goodly
Lev. 14. 7. let the living bird l. into the open field
Job 6. 9. that he would let l. his hand and cut me off
30. 11. they have let l. the bridle before me
Isa. 14. + 17. did not let prisoners l. homeward
Dan. 3. 25. lo I see four men l. walking in the fire

LOOSE, Verb,

Signifies, [1] To unbind, John 11. 44. [2] To open, Rev. 5. 2, [3] To put off, Josh. 5. 15. [4] To remit and absolve, Mat. 16. 19. [5] To set at liberty, Psal. 105. 20. [6] To set sail, Acts 13. 13. | 27. 21.

Deut. 25. 9. and l. his shoe from off his foot
Josh. 5. 15. l. thy shoe from off thy foot, for
Job 38. 31. canst thou l. the bands of Orion
Psal. 102. 20. to l. those that are appointed to death
Isa. 20. 2. go and l. the sackcloth from thy loins
45. 1. I will l. the loins of kings, to open gates
52. 2. O Jerusalem, l. thyself from the bands
58. 6. to l. the bands of wickedness, to undo burd.
Jer. 40. 4. and now behold I l. thee this day
Mat. 16. 19. whatsoever ye l. on earth, 18. 18.
21. 2. ye shall find an ass tied and colt, l. and bring them to me, Mark 11. 2, 4. Luke 19. 30.
Luke 19. 31. if any man ask, why do ye l. him? 33.
John 11. 44. Jesus said, l. him, and let him go
Acts 13. 25. shoes of his feet I am not worthy to l.
24. 26. money have been given, that he might l.
Rev. 5. 2. who is worthy to l. the seals thereof
5. hath prevailed to l. the seven seals thereof?
9. 14. l. the four angels bound in Euphrates

LOOSED.

Exod. 28. 28. that the breast-plate be not l. 39. 21.
Deut. 25. 10. the house of him that hath his shoe l.
Judg. 15. 14. his bands l. from off his hands
Job 30. 11. because he l. my cord and afflicted me
39. 5. who hath l. the bands of the wild ass?
Psal. 105. 20. the king sent and l. him, let him go
116. 16. I am thy servant, thou hast l. my bands
Eccl. 12. 6. or ever the silver cord be l. or bowl
Isa. 5. 27. nor shall the girdle of their loins be l.
33. 23. thy tacklings are l. they could not spread
51. 14. captive exile hasteneth that he may be l.
Jer. 6. + 8. lest my soul be l. from thee
Ezek. 23. + 17. and her mind was l. from them
Dan. 5. 6. so that the joints of his loins were l.
Mat. 16. 19. be l. on earth, l. in heaven, 18. 18.
18. 27. was moved with compassion, and l. him
Mark 7. 35. the string of his tongue was l. Luke 1. 64.
Luke 13. 12. woman, thou art l. from thy infirmity
16. ought not this daughter to be l. on sabbath?
Acts 2. 24. raised up, having l. the pains of death
13. 13. when Paul and company l. from Paphos
16. 26. and every one's bands were l.
22. 30. on the morrow he l. him from his bands
27. 21. have hearkened, and not have l. from Crete
40. l. the rudder-bands, and hoised up the sail
Rom. 7. 2. if the husband be dead, she is l. from
1 Cor. 7. 27. art thou l. from wife? seek not a wife
Rev. 9. 15. the four angels were l. which were
20. 3. after that he must be l. a little season, 7.

LOOSETH.

2 Sam. 22. + 33. God my strength, and he l. my way
Job 12. 18. he l. the bond of kings, and girdeth
+ 21. he l. the girdle of the strong
Ps. 146. 7. food to hungry, the L. l. the prisoners

LOOSING.

Mark 11. 5. said to them, what do you l. the colt?
Luke 19. 33. as they were l. the colt, the owners
Acts 16. 11. therefore l. from Troas, we came
27. 13. l. thence, they sailed close by Crete

LOP.

Isa. 10. 33. behold the Lord shall l. the bough

LORD

Is, (I) A word of authority, signifying a ruler or governor; and is applied, to the three Divine Persons, [1] To the Father, Gen. 2. 4. [2] To the Son, Psal. 110. 1. Col. 3. 24. [3] To the Holy Spirit, 2 Thess. 3. 5. Because they support and uphold the kingdom of nature, grace, and glory, Deut. 33. 27. Heb. 1. 3. [4] To kings, Gen. 40. 1. 2 Sam. 19. 19, 20. [5] To princes and nobles, Gen. 42. 10, 30. Dan. 4. 36. [6] To tyrants, Isa. 26. 13. 1 Pet. 5. 3. (II) A word of reverence and respect, and is applied, [1] To an husband, Gen. 18. 12. [2] To a master, John 15. 15. [3] To prophets, 1 Kings 18. 7. 2 Kings 2. 19. [4] To persons of worth and merit, Gen. 24. 18.

Gen. 18. 14. is any thing too hard for the L.?
24. 40. the L. before whom I walk will send
26. 28. we saw certainly the L. was with thee
28. 21. I come again, then shall the L. be my God
39. 2. and the L. was with Joseph, 21, 23.
Exod. 5. 2. who is the L. that I should obey him?
8. 24. and the L. did so, and there came flies
9. 29. the earth is the L. Psal. 24. 1. 1 Cor. 10. 26.
10. 10. the L. be so with you, as I will let you go
13. 8. because of that which the L. did to me
Exod. 13. 12. every firstl. of beast the male shall be L.
30. 37. it shall be unto thee holy for the L.
32. 26. who is on the L. side, let him come to me
34. 14. for L. whose name is jealous, is a jealous G.
Lev. 3. 16. food of the offering, all the fat is the L.
16. 8. Aaron shall cast one lot for the L. 25. 4. | 27. 2.
Num. 14. 14. they heard that thou, L. art among this people, that thou, L. art seen face to face
43. therefore the L. will not be with you
18. 6. to you they are given as a gift for the L.
22. 19. that I may know what the L. will say
23. 26. all that the L. speaketh that must I do
24. 11. the L. hath kept thee back from honour
31. 50. we have brought an oblation for the L.
32. 12. they have followed the L. Deut. 1. 36.
Deut. 3. 21. so shall the L. do to all kingdoms
4. 35. know that the L. he is G. 39. 1 Kings 18. 39.
5. 5. I stood between the L. and you at that time
10. 14. behold the heaven of heavens is the L.
17. and L. of lords a great G. a mighty, a terrible
29. 2. ye have seen all that the L. did in Egypt
4. yet the L. hath not given you an heart to
24. wherefore hath the L. done thus to this land?
1 Kings 9. 8. 2 Chron. 7. 21.
31. 4. L. shall do to them as he did to Sihon
32. 6. do ye thus requite the L. O foolish people
30. to flight, except the L. had shut them up
33. 29. happy art thou, O people, saved by the L.
Josh. 2. 12. swear unto me by the L. 1 Sam. 24. 21.
3. 11. even the L. of all the earth passeth over, 13.
10. 25. thus shall the L. do to all your enemies
14. 12. if so be the L. will be with me, then
Judg. 1. 19. the L. was with Judah, and he drave
22. and the L. was with the house of Joseph
2. 10. arose a generation which knew not the L.
4. 14. is not the L. gone out before thee?
6. 13. if the L. be with us, why is this befallen us
11. 31. cometh to meet me shall surely be the L.
17. 13. now know I that the L. will do me good
Ruth 1. 17. L. do so to me and more, 1 Sam. 20. 13.
2. 4. the L. be with you, 2 Chr. 20. 17. 2 Thess. 3. 16.
1 Sam. 2. 2. there is none holy as the L. for there is
8. for the pillars of the earth are the L.
3. 18. it is the L. let him do what seems, John 21. 7.
19. Samuel grew, and the L. was with him, 18. 12, 14. 2 Kings 18. 7. 1 Chron. 9. 20.
12. 16. this great thing which the L. will do
17. 37. the L. be with thee, 20. 13. 1 Chr. 22. 11, 16.
20. 23. the L. be between thee and me, 42.
2 Sam. 7. 24. L. art become their G. 1 Chr. 17. 22.
10. 12. L. do what seemeth him good, 1 Chr. 19. 13.
1 Kings 18. 21. if the L. be God, follow him, if Baal
2 Kings 6. 27. if the L. do not help, whence shall I
33. what shall I wait for the L. any longer?
10. 16. come with me and see my zeal for the L.
18. 25. am I now come without the L. Isa. 36. 10.
1 Chr. 16. 25. for great is the L. Psal. 48. 1. | 145. 3.
17. 26. and now, L. thou art G. and hast promised
21. 24. not take that which is thine for the L.
2 Chr. 19. 6. ye judge not for man, but for the L.
11. and the L. shall be with the good
33. 13. Manasseh knew that the L. was God
Neh. 9. 6. even that thou art L. alone, Isa. 37. 20.
Psal. 4. 3. know the L. hath set apart the godly
33. 12. blessed is the nation, whose God is the L.
35. 10. my bones say, L. who is like unto thee?
45. 11. for he is thy L. worship thou him
66. 18. if I regard iniquity, the L. will not hear me
86. 5. for thou L. art good, ready to forgive
92. 8. thou L. art most high for ever, 97. 9.
100. 3. know ye that the L. he is God, he made us
109. 21. do thou for me, O God the L. 140. 7.
27. they may know that thou L. hast done it
116. 5. gracious is the L. and righteous
118. 23. this is the L. doing || 27. God is the L.
124. 1. if it had not been the L. who was on, 2.
130. 3. if thou L. shouldest mark iniquity, who stand
132. 5. till I find out a place for the L.
Prov. 24. 18. lest the L. see it, and it displease him
30. 9. lest I deny thee, and say, who is the L.?
Isa. 10. 20. but shall stay upon the L. the holy one
19. 21. and the L. shall be known to Egypt
33. 21. the L. will be to us a place of broad rivers
42. 24. did not the L. he against whom we sinned?
44. 23. sing, O heavens, for the L. hath done it
52. 12. the L. will go bef. you, your rereward
Jer. 2. 6. where is the L. that brought us, 8.
5. 10. her battlements, for they are not the L.
8. 19. is not the L. in Zion? is not her King in her?
16. 21. they shall know that my name is the L.
21. 2. if so be that the L. will deal with us
23. 6. called, the L. our Righteousness, 33. 16.
31. 34. saying, know the L. Heb. 8. 11.
50. 7. even the L. the hope of their fathers
51. 50. remember the L. afar off, let Jerusalem
Lam. 3. 31. for the L. will not cast off for ever
50. till the L. look down, and behold from heaven
Ezek. 35. 10. possess it, whereas the L. was there
Dan. 2. 47. truth it is, your God is a L. of kings
9. 17. cause thy face to shine for the L. sake
Hos. 2. 20. betroth thee, and thou shalt know the L.
5. 4. and they have not known the L.
11. 10. they shall walk after the L. he shall roar
12. 14. his reproach shall his L. return to him
Joel 2. 21. fear not, for the L. will do great things
Amos 3. 6. be evil in the city, and L. hath not done
5. 14. and so the L. shall be with you
Obad. 21. and the kingdom shall be the L.
Mic. 2. 13. and the L. on the head of them
3. 11. lean on the L. and say, is not the L. among
4. 7. the L. shall reign over them in mount Zion
6. 8. and what doth the L. require of thee?
Zeph. 1. 5. that swear by the L. and by Malcham
Zech. 9. 1. when eyes of man shall be toward the L.
14. the L. shall be seen over them
14. 3. then shall the L. go forth and fight against
9. in that day shall there be one L. his name one
Mat. 7. 21. not every one that saith, L. L. shall enter into the kingdom, 22. 22, 44. Luke 13. 25.
8. 2. L. if thou wilt, thou canst make, Luke 5. 12.
25. L. save us || 9. 28. they said, yea, L. 13. 51.
14. 30. L. save me || 15. 25. saying, L. help me

Mat. 15. 27. she said, truth *L.* ‖ 25. 11. *L. L.* open to
21. 3. *L.* hath need of, *Mark* 11. 3. *Luke* 19. 31, 34.
22. 43. he saith to him, how then doth David call
him *L.?* 45. *Mark* 12. 37. *Luke* 20. 44.
24. 42. ye know not what hour your *L.* will come
46. whom his *L.* shall find so doing, *Luke* 12. 43.
50. the *L.* of that servant shall come, *Luke* 12. 46.
25. 21. enter thou into the joy of thy *L.*
37. *L.* when saw we thee an hungered? 44.
26. 22. *L.* is it I? ‖ 28. 6. the place where the *L.* lay
Mark 2. 28. Son of man is *L.* of sabbath, *Luke* 6. 5.
5. 19. how great things the *L.* hath done for thee
9. 24. *L.* I believe, help thou, *John* 9. 38. | 11. 27.
10. 51. *L.* that I may receive my sight, *Mat.* 20. 33.
16. 20. preached, the *L.* working with them
Luke 1. 17. to make ready a people for the *L.*
25. thus *L.* dealt with me, to take my reproach
2. 11. born a Saviour, which is Christ the *L.*
6. 46. why call ye me *L. L.* and do not what I say?
9. 57. a man said to him, *L.* I will follow thee, 61.
11. 1. *L.* teach us to pray, as John taught his discip.
13. 8. *L.* let it alone this year, till I dig about it
14. 21. that servant shewed his *L.* these things
17. 5. apostles said unto the *L.* increase our faith
37. where *L.?* ‖ 23. 42. *L.* remember me when thou
24. 34. saying, the *L.* is risen indeed, and appeared
John 6. 68. *L.* to whom shall we go, thou hast life
8. 11. no man *L.* ‖ 9. 36. who is the *L.* that I might
11. 34. they said to him, *L.* come and see
13. 13. ye call me Master and *L.* and say well
25. *L.* who is it? ‖ 20. 25. we have seen the *L.*
20. 2. they have taken the *L.* out of the sepulchre
21. 12. none durst ask him, knowing it was the *L.*
21. Peter saith, *L.* what shall this man do?
Acts 2. 36. whom ye crucified, both *L.* and Christ
4. 24. *L.* thou art *G.* ‖ 29. now *L.* behold threatenings
9. 5. and he said, who art thou *L.?* 26. 15.
10. 4. and said, what is it, *L.* ‖ 14. not so, *L.* 11. 8.
10. 36. peace by Jesus Christ, he is *L.* of all
22. 10. and I said, what shall I do, *L.?*
Rom. 9. 28. because a short work will the *L.* make
10. 12. for the same *L.* over all is rich unto all
14. 9. that he might be *L.* of the dead and living
1 *Cor.* 2. 8. not have crucified the *L.* of glory
3. 5. even as the *L.* gave to every man
4. 4. but he that judgeth me is the *L.*
19. I will come to you, if the *L.* will, *Jam.* 4. 15.
6. 13. but for the *L.* ‖ 7. 10. yet not I, but the *L.*
12. 5. differences of administrations, but the same *L.*
15. 47. second man is the *L.* from heaven
2 *Cor.* 5. 8. and to be present with the *L.*
11. 17. I speak it not after the *L.* but as it were
Eph. 4. 5. one *L.* ‖ 5. 29. even as the *L.* the church
Phil. 2. 11. tongue confess that Jesus Christ is *L.*
4. 5. moderation be known, the *L.* is at hand
1 *Thess.* 4. 17. so shall we ever be with the *L.*
1 *Tim.* 6. 15. the King of kings, and *L.* of lords
2 *Tim.* 2. 22. with them that call on the *L.*
3. 11. out of them all the *L.* delivered me
4. 8. which the *L.* shall give me at that day
17. notwithstanding the *L.* stood with me
Heb. 2. 3. which at first began to be spoken by the *L.*
8. 11. saying, know the *L.* for all shall know
Jam. 5. 15. and the *L.* shall raise the sick up
2 *Pet.* 3. 8. one day is with the *L.* as a thousand
Jude 9. Michael said, the *L.* rebuke thee
Rev. 11. 8. where also our *L.* was crucified
15. are become the kingdoms of our *L.* and his C.
17. 14. overcome, for he is *L.* of lords, 19. 16.

Against the LORD.

Exod. 10. 16. I have sinned *against the L.* your God,
Josh. 7. 20. 2 *Sam.* 12. 13.
16. 7. that he heareth your murmurings *ag. the L.* 8.
Lev. 5. 19. have trespassed *ag. t. L. Num.* 5. 6. | 31. 16.
6. 2. if a soul commit trespass *against the L.*
Num. 14. 9. only rebel not *against the L. Josh.* 22. 19.
16. 11. are gathered together *against the L.* 27. 3.
Psal. 2. 2. *Acts* 4. 26.
21. 7. we have sinned, for we have spoken *ag. the L.*
26. 9. company of Korah, when they strove *ag. t. L.*
32. 23. ye have sinned *ag. the L. Jer.* 40. 3. | 44. 23.
Deut. 1. 41. have sinn. *ag the L.* 1 *Sam.* 7. 6. *Jer.* 8. 14.
9. 7. ye have been rebellious *ag. the L.* 24. | 31. 27.
13. †5. because he hath spoken revolt *against the L.*
Josh. 22. 16. that ye might rebel this day *ag. the L.*
18. it will be, seeing ye rebel this day *ag. the L.*
22. or if in transgression *ag. the L.* save us not
29. God forbid we should rebel *against the L.*
31. have not committed this trespass *ag. the L.*
1 *Sam.* 2. 25. if a man sin *ag. t. L.* who shall entreat
12. 23. sin *against the L.* in ceasing to pray for you
14. 33. behold, the people sin *against the L.* in that
34. slay them here and eat, and sin not *ag. the L.*
2 *Kings* 17. 7. Israel had sinned *ag. the L.* their God
9. did secretly things not right *against the L.* God
1 *Chr.* 10. 13. transgression he committed *ag. the L.*
2 *Chr.* 12. 2. because they had transgressed *ag. the L.*
19. 10. warn them that they trespass not *ag. the L.*
28. 13. whereas we have offended already *ag. the L.*
19. Ahaz transgressed sore *against the L.*
22. in distress did he trespass yet more *ag. the L.*
Psal. 2. 2. rulers take counsel *ag. the L.* and Anoint.
Prov. 19. 3. and his heart fretteth *against the L.*
21. 30. there is no wisdom nor counsel *ag. the L.*
Isa. 3. 8. because their doings are *against the L.*
32. 6. will work iniquity to utter error *ag. the L.*
59. 13. in transgressing and lying *against the L.*
Jer. 28. 16. hast taught rebellion *ag. the L.* 29. 32.
48. 26. for he magnified himself *against the L.* 42.
50. 7. because they have sinned *against the L.*
14. against Babyl. she hath sinned *ag. the L.* 29.
24. because thou hast striven *ag. the L. Zeph.* 1. 17.
Dan. 5. 23. but hast lifted up thyself *against the L.*
Hos. 5. 7. they have dealt treacherously *ag. the L.*
Nah. 1. 9. what do ye imagine *ag. the L.* he will make
11. there is one that imagineth evil *against the L.*
See LIVETH, ANOINTED, APPEARED.

Before the LORD.

Gen. 10. 9. Nimrod was a mighty hunter *bef. the L.*
13. 10. well watered, *bef. the L.* destroyed Sodom
13. men of Sod. were sinners *b. the L.* exceedingly
18. 22. but Abraham stood yet *b. the L.* and said
Gen. 27. 7. that I may eat and bless thee *b. the L.*
Exod. 16. 9. say to congregation, come near *b. the L.*
33. lay it up *b. the L.* to be kept, 1 *Sam.* 10. 25.
23. 17. three times in the year all thy males appear
before the L. 34. 24. *Deut.* 16. 16. 1 *Sam.* 1. 22.
27. 21. Aaron shall order the lamps *b. the L.* 40. 25.
28. 12. Aaron shall bear their names *bef. the L.*
29. for a memorial *b. the L.* 30. 16. *Num.* 31. 54.
Lev. 4. 6. sprinkle seven times *b. the L.* 17. | 14. 16, 27.
9. 24. there came a fire out from *before the L.*
10. 2. went out fire, and they died *b. the L. Num.* 3. 4.
Num. 5. 16. bring her near, set her *b. the L.* 18, 30.
10. 9. ye shall be remembered *b. the L.* your God
18. 19. it is a covenant of salt for ever *b. the L.*
25. 4. and hang them up *b. the L.* against the sun
27. 5. Moses brought their cause *before the L.*
Deut. 9. 18. and I fell down *before the L.* forty days
12. 18. but thou must eat them *before the L.* thy God
18. 7. his brethren which stand there *before the L.*
19. 17. the controversy is, shall stand *before the L.*
Josh. 6. 26. cursed be the man *b. the L.* that buildeth
Judg. 11. 11. uttered his words *bef. the L.* in Mizpeh
18. 6. *before the L.* is your way wherein ye go
20. 26. all the people sat there *b. the L.* 2 *Sam.* 7. 18.
1 *Sam.* 2. 17. sin of the men was very great *b. the L.*
12. 3. here I am, witness against me *before the L.*
7. that I may reason with you *before the L.*
21. 7. was there that day detained *b. the L.*
26. 19. but if they be men, cursed be they *b. the L.*
2 *Sam.* 6. 21. it was *b. the L.* which chose me before
21. 9. and they hanged them in the hill *b. the L.*
2 *Kings* 19. 14. Hezekiah spread it *b. the L. Isa.* 37. 14.
1 *Chron.* 22. 18. and the land is subdued *b. the L.*
29. 22. and did eat and drink *b. the L.* with gladness
Psal. 96. 13. *b. the L.* for he cometh to judge, 98. 9.
109. 15. let them be *before the L.* continually
116. 9. I will walk *bef. the L.* in the land of living
Prov. 15. 11. hell and destruction are *before the L.*
Isa. 23. 18. shall be for them that dwell *bef. the L.*
Jer. 36. 7. present their supplications *before the L.*
Ezek. 44. 3. shall sit in it to eat bread *before the L.*
Dan. 9. 13. yet made we not our prayer *bef. the L.*
Mic. 6. 6. wherewith shall I come *b. the L.* and bow
Zech. 2. 13. be silent, O all flesh, *bef. the L.* for he
7. 2. and their men to pray *bef. the L.* 8. 21, 22.
Mal. 3. 14. we have walked mournfully *b. the L.*
2 *Tim.* 2. 14. charging them *b. the L.* that they strive
2 *Pet.* 2. 11. bring no railing accusation *bef. the L.*
See BLESS, BLESSED, CALLED, CAST *Out*,
CHOSEN, CHOOSE, COMMANDED, FEAR,
FEARED, REJOICE.

From the LORD.

Gen. 4. 1. I have gotten a man *f. L.* ‖ 19. 24. fire *f. L.*
24. 50. Laban said, the thing proceedeth *f. the L.*
Num. 11. 31. and there went forth a wind *f. the L.*
16. 35. there came out a fire *f. the L.* and consumed
46. there is wrath gone out *f. the L.* the plague
1 *Sam.* 16. 14. evil spirit *f. the L.* troubled him, 19. 9.
26. 12. a deep sleep *f. the L.* was fallen on them
1 *Kings* 2. 15. it was his *f. L.* ‖ 33. shall be peace *f. L.*
Psal. 24. 5. he shall receive the blessing *fr. the L.*
109. 20. reward of mine adversaries *from the L.*
121. 2. my help cometh *f. the L.* who made heaven
Prov. 16. 1. and the answer of the tongue is *f. the L.*
19. 14. and a prudent wife is *from the L.*
29. 26. but every man's judgment cometh *f. the L.*
Isa. 29. 15. seek to hide their counsel *from the L.*
40. 27. why sayest thou, my way is hid *f. the L.*
Jer. 7. 1. the word that came to Jeremiah *f. the L.*
11. 1. | 18. 1. | 21. 1. | 26. 1. | 27. 1. | 30. 1. |
32. 1. | 34. 1, 8, 12. | 35. 1. | 36. 1. | 40. 1.
17. 5. cursed whose heart departeth *from the L.*
37. 17. the king asked, is there any word *f. the L.*
49. 14. I have heard a rumour *f. the L.* an ambas.
Lam. 2. 9. her prophets find no vision *from the L.*
3. 18. my strength and hope is perished *f. the L.*
Ezek. 11. 15. Jerusalem said, get ye far *fr. the L.*
33. 30. hear what is the word that cometh *fr. the L.*
Hos. 1. 2. committed whoredom, departing *f. the L.*
Obad. 1. we have heard a rumour *f. the L.* arise
Mic. 1. 12. but evil came down *f. the L.* to the gate
5. 7. remnant of Jacob shall be as a dew *f. the L.*
Zeph. 1. 6. and them that are turned back *f. the L.*
Zech. 14. 13. tumult *f. the L.* shall be among them
Luke 1. 45. things which were told her *from the L.*
2 *Cor.* 5. 6. in the body we are absent *from the L.*
See GIVE, GIVEN.

LORD *God.*

Gen. 9. 26. he said, blessed be the *L. God* of Shem
15. 2. Abram said, *L. God* what wilt thou give me
8. *L. God*, whereby shall I know I shall inherit
24. 27. blessed be the *L. G.* of my master Abraham
28. 13. I am the *L. God* of Abraham thy father
Exod. 32. 27. the *L. God* of Israel, *Josh.* 9. 18, 19.
| 10. 40, 42. | 13. 14, 33. | 14. 14.
34. 6. the Lord, the *L. God* merciful and gracious
Josh. 7. 7. Joshua said, alas, O *L. God*, wherefore
22. 22. the *L. God* of gods, the *L. God* of gods
24. what have ye to do with the *L. God* of Israel?
24. 2. the *L. God* of Israel, *Judg.* 4. 6. | 5. 3, 5.
| 11. 21, 23. | 21. 3. *Ruth* 2. 12. 1 *Sam.* 2. 30.
| 14. 41. | 20. 12. | 23. 10. | 25. 32, 34. 1 *Kings*
1. 30. 1 *Chron.* 23. 25. | 24. 19.
Judg. 6. 22. Gideon said, alas, O *L. God*, because
16. 28. O *L. God*, remember me only this once
1 *Sam.* 6. 20. who is able to stand bef. this holy *L. G.?*
2 *Sam.* 5. 10. and the *L. God* of hosts was with him
7. 18. who am I, O *L. God*, and what is my house?
19. and is this the manner of man, O *L. God?*
20. for thou, *L. God*, knowest thy servant
22. wherefore thou art great, O *L. G.*, none like
1 *Kings* 1. 36. the *L. G.* of my lord the king say so
48. the king said, blessed be the *L. God* of Israel
8. 15. 1 *Chron.* 16. 36. | 29. 10.
14. 13. found some good thing toward the *L. God*
17. 1. Elijah said, as the *L. God* of Israel liveth
18. 37. may know thou art *L. G.* ‖ 2 *Kings* 19. 19.
2 *Kings* 2. 14. and said, where is *L. God* of Elijah?
1 *Chr.* 17. 17. state of a man of high degree, O *L. G.*
2 *Chr.* 13. 12. fight ye not against *L. God* of fathers
24. 18. they left the house of the *L. God* of fathers
26. 18. nor shall it be for thy honour from *L. God*
2 *Chr.* 32. 16 his servants spake more against *L. G.*
Neh. 9. 7. thou art the *L. God*, didst choose Abram
Psal. 31. 5. hast redeemed me, O *L. God* of truth
41. 13. blessed be *L. God* of Isr. from everlasting
to everlasting, 72. 18. | 106. 48. *Luke* 1. 68.
68. 18. that the *L. God* might dwell among them
71. 5. thou art my hope, O *L. G.* thou art my trust
84. 11. for *L. G.* is a sun and shield, will give grace
85. 8. I will hear what the *L. God* will speak
Isa. 28. 22. for I have heard from the *L. G.* of hosts
50. 7. for the *L. God* will help me, therefore, 9.
65. 15. for *L. G.* shall slay thee, and call servants
Jer. 44. 26. not named, saying, the *L. God* liveth
Ezek. 5. 11. as I live, saith the *L. God*, 14. 16.
13. 9. know I am the *L. God*, 23. 49. | 24. 24.
16. 19. and thus it was, saith the *L. God*
23. woe, woe unto thee, saith the *L. God*
18. 30. according to his ways, saith the *L. God*
21. 7. be brought to pass, saith the *L. God*
13. it shall be no more, saith the *L. God*
22. 12. and hast forgotten me, saith the *L. God*
29. 20. because they wrought for me, saith *L. G.*
34. 31. and I am your God, saith the *L. God*
36. 23. know that I am the Lord, saith the *L. God*
32. not for your sakes do I this, saith the *L. God*
37. 3. and I answered, O *L. God*, thou knowest
39. 5. for I have spoken it, saith the *L. God*, 23.
34. | 26. 14. | 28. 10.
8. it is come, and it is done, saith the *L. God*
43. 27. I will accept you saith the *L. God*
Dan. 9. 3. I set my face unto the *L. God*, to seek
Hos. 12. 5. even *L. God* of hosts is his memorial
Amos 1. 8. a remn. of Phil. shall perish, saith *L. G*
3. 7. *L. God* will do nothing, but he revealeth
8. the *L. G.* hath spoken, who can but prophesy?
4. 5. for this liketh you, saith the *L. God*
9. 5. *L. God* of hosts is he that toucheth the land
Mic. 1. 2. let the *L. God* be witness against you
Hab. 3. 19. the *L. God* is my strength, he will make
1 *Pet.* 3. 15. sanctify the *L. God* in your hearts
Rev. 4. 8. holy, holy, *L. G.* Almighty, 11. 17 | 16. 7.
15. 3. marvellous are thy works, *L. G.* Almighty
18. 8. for strong is the *L. God* who judgeth her
19. 6. for the *L. God* omnipotent reigneth
21. 22. the *L. God* and the Lamb are the temple
22. 5. for the *L. God* giveth them light
See AH, FATHERS.

LORD *his God.*

Exod. 32. 11. Moses besought the *L. his G.* and said
Lev. 4. 22. the commandments of the *L. his God*
Num. 23. 21. the *L. his God* is with him, the shout
Deut. 17. 19. that he may learn to fear the *L. his G.*
18. 7. he shall minister in name of the *L. his G.*
1 *Sam.* 30. 6. David encouraged hims. in *L. his God*
1 *Kings* 5. 3. an house unto the name of *L. his G.*
11. 4. heart was not perfect with *L. his G.* 15. 3.
15. 4. did the *L. his G.* give him a lamp in Jerusal.
2 *Kings* 16. 2. not right in the sight of the *L. his G.*
2 *Chr.* 1. 1. the *L. h. G.* was with him, and magnified
14. 2. good and right in the eyes of the *L. his God*
11. Asa cried unto the *L. his God*, and said
15. 9. when they saw that *L. his G.* was with him
26. 16. Uzziah transgressed against the *L. his G.*
27. 6. Jotham prepared his ways before *L. his G.*
28. 5. *L. his G.* delivered Ahaz into hands of Syria
31. 20. Hezekiah wrought right before *L. his God*
33. 12. Manasseh in affliction besought *L. his God*
34. 8. Josiah sent to repair the house of *L. his God*
36. 5. Jehoiakim did evil in sight of *L. his G.* 12.
23. the *L. his G.* be with him, and let him go up
Ezra 7. 6. accord. to hand of the *L. his G.* upon him
Ps. 146. 5. happy he whose hope is in the *L. his G.*
Jonah 2. 1. then Jonah prayed to the *L. his G.* out
Mic. 5. 4. feed in majesty of the name of *L. his G.*

LORD *my God.*

Num. 22. 18. not go beyond the word of *L. my G.*
Deut. 4. 5. even as the *L. my* God commanded me
18. 16. not hear again the voice of the *L. my God*
26. 14. have hearkened to the voice of *L. my God*
Josh. 14. 8. but I wholly followed the *L. my God*
2 *Sam.* 24. 24. I offer burnt offerings to the *L. my G.*
1 *Kings* 3. 7. O *L. my G.* 8. 28. | 17. 20, 21. 1 *Chron.*
21. 17. 2 *Chron.* 6. 19. *Psal.* 7. 1, 3. | 13. 3.
| 30. 2, 12. | 35. 24. | 38. 15. | 40. 5. | 86. 12.
| 109. 26. *Jonah* 2. 6. *Hab.* 1. 12.
5. 4. the *L. my G.* hath given me rest on every side
5. I purpose to build an house unto the name of
the *L. my God*, 1 *Chron.* 22. 7. 2 *Chron.* 2. 4.
Ezra 7. 28. as the hand of the *L. my G.* was upon me
9. 5. and I spread out my hands to the *L. my God*
Ps. 18. 28. the *L. my God* will enlighten my darkn.
Jer. 31. 18. turn thou me, for thou art *L. my God*
Dan. 9. 4. I prayed unto the *L. my God*, and said
20. while I was present. my supplic. bef. *L. m. G.*
Zech. 11. 4. thus saith the *L. my God*, feed the flock
14. 5. and the *L. my G.* shall come, and all saints

LORD *our God.*

Exod. 3. 18. sacrifice to *L. G.* 5. 3. | 8. 27. | 10. 25.
8. 10. there is none like to *L. our God*, *Ps.* 113. 5.
10. 26. thereof must we take to serve the *L. our G.*
Deut. 1. 6. the *L. our God* spake unto us in Horeb
19. we went through all that wilderness, as the
L. our God commanded us, 41. | 6. 20.
20. which *L. our G.* doth give unto us, 25. | 2. 29.
2. 33. *L. our God* delivered him before us, 36. | 3. 3.
37. nor unto whatsoever *L. our God* forbade us
4. 7. so nigh to them as *L. our G.* is in all things
5. 2. *L. our G.* made a covenant with us in Horeb
24. the *L. our God* hath shewed us his glory
25. if we hear the voice of *L. our God* any more
27. go and hear all that the *L. our G.* shall say
6. 4. O Israel, *L. our God* is one Lord, *Mark* 12. 29
24. to fear *L. our G.* ‖ 25. to do before *L. our G*
29. 15. that standeth this day before the *L. our G*
29. the secret things belong to the *L. our God*
Josh. 18. 6. cast lots for you before the *L. our God*
22. 19. an altar, beside the altar of *L. our God*, 29.
24. 17. *L. our God*, he it is that brought us up out of
24. the people said, the *L. our God* will we serve
Judg. 11. 24. whomsoever *L. our G.* shall drive out
1 *Sam.* 7. 8. cease not to cry to the *L. our G.* for us
1 *Kings* 8. 57. *L. our G.* be with us, as with fathers

1 Kings 8. 59. let these my words be nigh L. our G.
2 Kings 18. 22. but if ye say, we trust in L. our God
19. 19. O L. our God, save thou us out of his hand
1 Chron. 13. 2. and that it be of L. our G. let us send
15. 13. the L. our G. made a breach on us, for that
16. 14. he is L. our G. his judgments, Psal. 105. 7.
29. 16. O L. our God, 2 Chron. 14. 11. Psal. 99. 8. | 106. 47. Isa. 26. 13. | 37. 20. Jer. 14. 22. Dan. 9. 15.
2 Chron. 13. 11. we keep the charge of the L. our G.
14. 7. because we have sought the L. our God
19. 7. there is no iniquity with the L. our God
32. 8. but with us is the L. our God to help us
11. L. our God shall deliver us out of the hand
Ezra 9. 8. grace hath been shewed from the L. our G.
Psal. 20. 7. will rememb. the name of the L. our G.
90. 17. let the beauty of the L. our God be on us
94. 23. yea, the L. our God shall cut them off
99. 5. exalt ye the L. our G. and worship at his, 9.
9. for the L. G. is holy || 105. 7. for he is the L. G.
122. 9. because of the house of the L. our G.
123. 2. so our eyes wait on the L. our God
Jer. 3. 22. we come to thee, for thou art the L. our G.
23. in the L. our God is the salvation of Israel
25. we have sinned against the L. our God, we and fathers, and have not obeyed voice of L. our G.
5. 19. wherefore doth the L. our God these things?
24. let us now fear the L. our God that giveth rain
8. 14. for the L. our God hath put us to silence
16. 10. sin we have committed ag. the L. our God
26. 16. hath spoken to us in the name of L. our G.
31. 6. arise, and let us go up to Zion, to the L. our G.
37. 3. saying, pray now to L. our G. for us, 42. 20.
42. 6. we will obey the voice of the L. our God
43. 2. the L. our G. hath not sent thee to say, go not
50. 28. to declare the vengeance of the L. our G.
51. 10. let us declare in Zion the work of L. our G.
Dan. 9. 9. to the L. our G. belong mercies, tho' we
10. nor have we obeyed the voice of the L. our G.
14. for the L. our G. is righteous in all his works
Mic. 4. 5. we will walk in the name of the L. our G.
7. 17. they shall be afraid of the L. our God
Acts 2. 39. as many as the L. our God shall call
Rev. 19. 1. glory, honour, and power to the L. our G.

LORD their God.

Exod. 10. 7. serve L. t. G. 2 Chr. 34. 33. Jer. 30. 9.
29. 46. they shall know that I am the L. their God, Ezek. 28. 26. | 34. 30. | 39. 22, 28.
Lev. 26. 44. break covenant, I am L. t. G. Zech. 10. 6.
Judg. 3. 7. forgat L. t. G. 8. 34. 1 Sam. 12. 9. Jer. 3. 21.
1 Kings 9. 9. because they forsook L. t. G. Jer. 22. 9.
2 Kings 17. 7. Israel had sinned against the L. t. G.
9. that were not right against the L. their God
14. fathers, that did not believe in the L. their G.
16. they left all the commandments of the L. t. G.
19. Judah kept not commandments of the L. t. G.
18. 12. obeyed not voice of the L. t. G. Jer. 7. 28.
2 Chron. 31. 6. were consecrated to the L. their God
33. 17. did sacrifice unto the L. their God only
Jer. 43. 1. spake all the words of the L. their God for which the L. their God had sent him to them
50. 4. they shall go and seek the L. t. G. Hos. 3. 5.
Hos. 1. 7. and I will save them by the L. their God
7. 10. and they do not return to the L. their God
Hag. 1. 12. people obeyed the voice of the L. their G.
Zech. 9. 16. the L. t. G. shall save them in that day
Luke 1. 16. and many shall he turn to the L. their G.

LORD thy God.

Exod. 20. 2. I am the L. thy God, Psal. 81. 10. Isa. 51. 15. Hos. 12. 9. | 13. 4.
5. for I the L. thy G. am a jealous God, Deut. 5. 9.
Deut. 2. 7. the L. thy God hath been with thee
4. 24. the L. t. G. is a consuming fire, a jealous G.
31. for the L. thy God is a merciful God
7. 9. know therefore that the L. thy God, he is God
21. for the L. thy God is among you, 23. 14.
8. 5. as a man his son, so the L. t. G. chasteneth thee
12. 31. thou shalt not do so to the L. thy God
20. 1. for the L. thy God is with thee who brought
26. 5. and thou shalt say before the L. thy God, 13.
28. 58. mayest fear this fearful name, the L. thy G.
Josh. 1. 9. be strong, for the L. thy God is with thee
17. only the L. thy G. be with thee as with Moses
2 Sam. 14. 17. therefore the L. t. G. will be with thee
24. 23. Araunah said, the L. thy God accept thee
1 Kings 13. 6. entreat now the face of the L. thy G.
17. 12. as the L. t. G. liv. I have not a cake, 18. 10.
Isa. 43. 3. I am the L. t. G. the holy One of Israel
55. 5. shall run to thee, because of the L. thy God
Jer. 42. 2. pray for us to the L. thy G. even for this
3. that the L. t. G. may shew us the way wherein
Mic. 7. 10. which said to me, where is the L. thy G.?
Zeph. 3. 17. the L. thy G. in midst of thee is mighty
Mat. 4. 7. thou shalt not tempt the L. t. G. Luke 4. 12.

LORD your God.

Lev. 19. 2. ye shall be holy, for I L. y. G. am holy
Deut. 1. 10. L. y. G. hath multiplied you as stars
30. the L. your God he shall fight for you, 3. 22.
6. 16. ye shall not tempt the L. y. G. as in Massah
10. 17. the L. y. G. is God of gods, Lord of lords
20. 4. the L. your God is he that goeth with you
Josh. 2. 11. the L. your God is God in heaven above
23. 3. the L. y. G. is he that hath fought for you, 10.
1 Sam. 12. 12. when the L. your God was your king
2 Kings 17. 39. but the L. your God ye shall fear
1 Chr. 22. 18. is not the L. your God with you?
2 Chron. 20. 20. believe in the L. your G. so shall ye
Jer. 42. 20. ye dissembled, when ye sent me to L. G.
Joel 3. 17. so shall ye know that I am the L. your G.
Acts 3. 22. a prophet shall the L. your G. raise, 7. 37.
See, I am the LORD your God.

LORD of hosts.

1 Sam. 1. 11. O L. of hosts, Psal. 59. 5. | 84. 1, 3, 12. 2 Sam. 7. 27. Jer. 11. 20. | 20. 12.
2 Sam. 6. 2. called by the name of the L. of hosts
7. 26. saying, the L. of hosts is God over Israel
1 Kin. 18. 15. Elijah said, as L. h. liveth, 2 Kin. 3. 14.
2 Kings 19. 31. the zeal of the L. of hosts shall do this, Isa. 9. 7. | 37. 32.
1 Chr. 11. 9. greater, for the L. of h. was with him
17. 24. the L. of h. God of Israel, even a G. to Isr.
Ps. 24. 10. the L. of hosts he is the King of glory

Ps. 46. 7. the L. of h. is with us, 11. || 48. 8. in city L. h.
Isa. 1. 24. therefore saith the Lord, the L. of hosts
2. 12. the day of the L. of hosts shall be on the proud
6. 3. and one said, holy, holy, holy is the L. of hosts
5. mine eyes have seen the King, the L. of hosts
8. 13. sanctify the L. of hosts himself, let him be
14. 27. for the L. of hosts hath purposed it, 23. 9.
19. 18. five cities shall swear to the L. of hosts
47. 4. L. of hosts is his name, 48. 2. | 51. 15. | 54. 5. Jer. 10. 16. | 31. 35. | 32. 18. | 50. 34. | 51. 19.
Jer. 46. 18. king, whose name is the L. of h. 48. 15.
25. L. of hosts saith, I will punish the multitude
Hab. 2. 13. is it not of the L. of hosts that the people
Hag. 2. 4. work, for I am with you, saith L. of hosts
Zech. 1. 6. like as the L. of hosts thought to do to us
2. 9. shall know that the L. of h. sent me, 11. | 4. 9.
7. 12. came a great wrath from the L. of hosts
13. they cried, I would not hear, saith the L. of h.
8. 21. let us go to pray, and to seek the L. of hosts
22. many people shall come to seek the L. of hosts
14. 16. go up to worship the King, L. of hosts, 17.
21. every pot shall be holiness unto the L. of h.
Mal. 1. 14. for I am a great King, saith L. of h.
See, Saith the LORD.

I the LORD.

Lev. 19. 2. for I t. L. your G. am holy, 20. 26. | 21. 8.
21. 15. for I t. L. do sanctify him, 23. | 22. 9, 16.
Num. 14. 35. I L. have said it, I will do it, Ezek. 21. 17.
Isa. 27. 3. I t. L. do keep it, I will water it every
41. 4. I the L. the first, and with the last I am he
17. when the needy seek, I t. L. will hear them
42. 6. I the L. have called thee in righteousness
45. 3. that I the L. which call thee by thy name
7. I t. L. do all these things || 8. I t. L. created it
19. I the L. speak righteousness, I declare things
21. have not I the L. and there is no God else
60. 16. shalt know that I the L. am thy Saviour
22. I the L. will hasten it in his time
61. 8. for I the L. love judgment, I hate robbery
Jer. 17. 10. I t. L. search the heart, and try reins
Ezek. 5. 13. I t. L. have spoken it, 15, 17. | 17. 21. | 21. 32. | 22. 14. | 24. 14. | 26. 14. | 30. 12.
14. 4. I the L. will answer him that cometh, 7.
9. I the L. have deceived that prophet
17. 24. I L. have brought down, I L. have done it
20. 48. all shall see that I the L. have kindled it
21. 5. that I the L. have drawn forth my sword
34. 24. I t. L. will be their G. David their prince
30. know that I the L. their God am with them
36. 36. that I the L. do build, I the L. will do it
37. 14. know that I the L. have performed it
28. shall know that I the L. do sanctify Israel

I am the LORD.

Gen. 15. 7. I am the L. that brought thee out of Ur
Exod. 6. 2. I am the L. 6, 8, 29. | 12. 12. Lev. 18. 5, 6, 21. Num. 3. 13. Isa. 43. 11, 15.
20. 2. I L. thy G. who brought thee out of Egypt
Lev. 22. 32. I L. which hallow you, that brought
Isa. 42. 8. I L. that is my name || 44. 5. shall say, I L.
Jer. 9. 24. glory, that he knoweth that I am the L.
32. 27. behold, I am the L. the God of all flesh
Mal. 3. 6. for I am the L. I change not, therefore
See KNOW.

I am the LORD your God.

Exod. 6. 7. ye shall know that I am L. y. G. 16. 12.
Lev. 11. 44. I am the L. your God, 18. 30. | 19. 3. | 20. 7. | 23. 22. Judg. 6. 10. Ezek. 20. 5, 7, 19, 20. Joel 2. 27.

LORD Jesus, see JESUS.

In the LORD.

Gen. 15. 6. he believed in the L. and he counted it
Josh. 22. 25. Reuben, Gad, ye have no part in L. 27.
1 Sam. 2. 1. my heart rejoiceth in L. is exalted in L.
Psal. 4. 5. offer sacrifice, and put your trust in t. L.
11. 1. in the L. put I my trust, 26. 1. | 31. 6. | 73. 28.
31. 24. all ye that hope in L. || 32. 11. be glad in L.
34. 2. my soul shall make her boast in the L.
35. 9. my soul shall be joyful in the L.
37. 4. delight also thyself in the L. Isa. 58. 14.
7. rest in t. L. || 56. 10. in t. L. will I praise his w.
64. 10. the righteous shall be glad in the L. 104. 34.
Prov. 3. 5. trust in the L. with all thine heart
29. 25. putteth his trust in the L. shall be safe
Isa. 26. 4. in the L. Jehovah is everlasting strength
29. 19. the meek shall increase their joy in the L.
45. 17. but Israel shall be saved in the L.
24. in the L. have I righteousness and strength
25. in the L. shall all the seed of Israel be justified
Jer. 3. 23. in the L. is the salvation of Israel
Zeph. 3. 2. she trusted not in the L. drew not near
Zech. 12. 5. Jerusalem shall be my strength in the L.
Acts 9. 42. it was known, and many believed in t. L.
14. 3. they abode, speaking boldly in the L.
Ro. 16. 2. ye receive her in L. || 8. great Amplias in L.
12. salute Persis, who laboured much in the L.
13. salute Rufus, chosen in the L. and his mother
22. I Tertius who wrote this salute you in the L.
1 Cor. 1. 31. glorieth, let him glory in L. 2 Cor. 10. 17.
4. 17. and faithful in the L. || 7. 22. called in the L.
7. 39. be married to whom she will, only in the L.
9. 1. am I not an apostle, are not ye my work in L.
2. the seal of my apostleship are ye in the L.
11. 11. nor the woman without the man in the L.
15. 58. that your labour is not in vain in the L.
Eph. 2. 21. groweth to an holy temple in the L.
4. 17. and testify in L. || 5. 8. now are ye light in L.
6. 1. children obey your parents in the L. for this
10. finally, my brethren, be strong in the L.
21. Tychicus a faithful minister in the L.
Phil. 1. 14. brethren in the L. waxing confident
2. 24. I trust in the L. I shall come to you shortly
29. receive him therefore in the L. with gladness
4. 1. my brethren, stand fast in the L. 1 Thess. 3. 8.
2. that they be of the same mind in the L.
10. but I rejoiced in the L. greatly, that at last
Col. 3. 18. submit to your own husbands in the L.
4. 7. Tychicus who is a fellow-servant in the L.
17. ministry which thou hast received in the L.
1 Thess. 5. 12. know them which are over you in L.
2 Thess. 3. 4. we have confidence in the L. touching
Philem. 16. to thee, both in the flesh and in the L.
20. joy of thee in t. L. refresh my bowels in the L.
Rev. 14. 13 blessed are the dead which die in the L.
See REJOICE, TRUST.

LORD is.

Gen. 28. 16. surely the L. is in this place
Exod. 9. 27. the L. is righteous, I wicked, 2 Chr. 12. 6.
15. 2. the L. is my strength and song, he is my G.
3. the L. is a man of war, the L. is his name
18. 11. I know that L. is greater than all gods
Num. 14. 9. the L. is with us, fear them not
18. the L. is long-suffering, of great, Nah. 1. 3.
42. go not up, for the L. is not among you
16. 3. are holy every one, and the L. is among them
Deut. 10. 9. the L. is his inheritance, according
18. 2. the L. is their inheritance, as he said
Josh. 22. 34. shall be a witness, that L. is God
Judg. 6. 12. and said, the L. is with thee, Luke 1. 28.
1 Sam. 2. 3. for the L. is a God of knowledge
16. 18. the L. is with David, 2 Sam. 7. 3.
28. 16. seeing the L. is departed from thee
2 Sam. 22. 2. he said, the L. is my rock, Ps. 18. 2.
1 Kings 8. 60. people may know that the L. is God
20. 28. Syrians said, the L. is the God of the hills
2 Chron. 13. 10. but as for us, the L. is our God
15. 2. the L. is with you while ye be with him
Psal. 9. 16. the L. is known by the judgment which he
10. 16. the L. is king for ever and ever
11. 4. the L. is in his holy temple, his eyes behold
14. 6. counsel of poor, because the L. is his refuge
16. 5. the L. is the portion of mine inheritance
23. 1. the L. is my shepherd, I shall not want
27. 1. the L. is my light and my salvation, the L. is the strength of my life, of whom be afraid
28. 7. the L. is my strength and shield, 118. 14.
8. L. is their strength, and he is saving strength
34. 8. O taste and see that the L. is good, blessed is
47. 2. for the L. most high is terrible, a great king
89. 18. the L. is our defence and Holy One our king
92. 15. to shew that L. is upright, he is my rock
93. 1. the L. is clothed with strength, wherewith
94. 22. but the L. is my defence and my rock
95. 3. the L. is a great God, 96. 4. | 99. 2. | 135. 5.
100. 5. the L. is good, 31. 8. | 135. 3. | 145. 9. Jer. 33. 11. Lam. 3. 25. Nah. 1. 7.
103. 8. L. is merciful and gracious, 111. 4. | 145. 8.
113. 4. the L. is high || 118. 6. the L. is on my side
121. 5. the L. is thy keeper, the L. is thy shade
125. 2. so the L. is round about his people
129. 4. L. is right. 145. 17. Lam. 1. 18. Dan. 9. 14.
145. 18. the L. is nigh to all them that call on him
Prov. 15. 29. the L. is far from the wicked
22. 2. the L. is the maker of them all
Isa. 30. 18. for the L. is a God of judgment
33. 5. the L. is exalted || 22. L. is our judge, our
42. 21. L. is well pleased for his righteousness
Jer. 10. 10. the L. is the true God, the living God
17. 7. whose hope the L. is || 20. 11. the L. is with me
Lam. 3. 24. the L. is my portion, saith my soul
Ezek. 48. 35. the name of the city, the L. is there
Amos 5. 8. maketh the stars, the L. is his name, 9. 6.
Hab. 2. 20. but the L. is in his holy temple
Zeph. 3. 5. the just L. is in the midst thereof, 15.
Zech. 10. 5. they shall fight because L. is with them
13. 9. and they shall say, the L. is my God
Luke 24. 34. the L. is risen indeed, and appeared
2 Cor. 3. 17. now the L. is that Spirit, and where
Phil. 4. 5. moderation be known, the L. is at hand
1 Thess. 4. 6. the L. is the avenger of all such
2 Thess. 3. 3. but the L. is faithful, who shall keep
Heb. 13. 6. the L. is my helper, I will not fear
Jam. 5. 11. L. is very pitiful, and of tender mercy
1 Pet. 2. 3. if ye have tasted that the L. is gracious
2 Pet. 3. 9. the L. is not slack concerning his promise
See MADE.

My LORD.

Gen. 19. 18. Lot said unto him, oh, not so, my L.
Exod. 4. 10. Moses said, O my L. I am not eloquent
13. O my L. send by hand of whom thou wilt send
Num. 14. 17. now let the power of my L. be great
Josh. 5. 14. he said, what saith my L. to his servant?
Judg. 6. 13. O my L. if the L. be with us, why is this
15. O my L. wherewith shall I save Israel?
13. 8. O my L. let the man of G. come again to us
Psal. 16. 2. thou hast said to the L. thou art my L.
35. 23. stir up thyself, my God, my L. John 20. 28.
110. 1. the L. said to my L. Mat. 22. 44. Mark 12. 36. Luke 20. 42. Acts 2. 34.
Isa. 21. 8. my L. I stand on the watch-tower
49. 14. but Zion saith, my L. hath forgotten me
Dan. 10. 16. O my L. by the vision my sorrows
17. can the servant of my L. talk with this my L.?
19. and I said, let my L. speak, for thou hast
12. 8. O my L. what shall be end of these things?
Zech. 1. 9. then said I, O my L. what are these? 4. 4. | 6. 4. || 4. 5. no, my L. 13.
Luke 1. 43. that the mother of my L. should come
John 20. 13. because they have taken away my L.
Phil. 3. 8. the knowledge of Christ Jesus my L.

O LORD.

Gen. 49. 18. I have waited for thy salvation, O L.
Exod 15. 11. who is like to thee, O L. among gods?
Num. 10. 36. return, O L. unto Israel, Psal. 6. 4.
Deut. 26. 10. which thou, O L. hast given me
Josh. 7. 8. O L. what shall I say, Israel turneth
Judg 5. 31. so let all thy enemies perish, O L.
2 Sam. 15. 31. O L. turn counsel of Ahithophel
22. 29. thou art my lamp, O L. and Lord will
23. 17. be it far from me, O L. that I should
1 Chron. 17. 20. O L. there is none like thee
29. 11. thine, O L. is the greatness, thine, O L.
2 Chr. 14. 11. help us, O. L. our G. O L. thou art
Psal. 3. 7. arise, O L. save me || 5. 8. lead me, O L.
6. 2. O L. heal me || 3. but thou, O L. how long?
7. 6. arise, O L. 9. 19. | 10. 12. | 17. 13.
8. judge me, O L. accord. to my righteous. 26. 1.
8. 1. O L. our L. 9. || 9. 1. I will praise thee, O L.
9. 13. have mercy upon me, O L. consider my trouble, 31. 9. | 86. 3. | 123. 3.
18. 1. I will love thee, O L. my strength, 19. 14.
22. 19. be not thou far from me, O L. 35. 22.
27. 7. hear, O L. 30. 10. | 39. 12. | 69. 16. | 86. 6. | 102. 1. | 119. 145. | 140. 6.
31. 14. I trusted in thee, O L. I said

Psal. 86. 8. among the gods none like to thee, O L.
11. teach me thy way, O L. I walk, 25. 4. | 27. 11.
115. 1. not unto us, O L. not unto us, but to thy name
119. 151. thou art near, O L. thy commands truth
143. 1. hear my prayer O L. 7. Isa. 37. 17. Dan. 9. 19.
Isa. 25. 1. O L. thou art my God, I will exalt thee
63. 16. thou, O L. art our Fath. our Redeem. 64. 8.
Jer. 10. 6. O L. thou art great || 11. 5. so be it, O L.
12. 3. but thou, O L. knowest me, thou hast seen
14. 9. yet thou, O L. art in the midst of us
17. 13. O L. the hope of Israel, all that forsake
14. heal me, O L. and I shall be healed, save me
Lam. 1. 11. see, O L. and consider I am vile, 2. 20.
5. 19. thou, O L. remainest for ever, thy throne
21. turn us unto thee, O L. we shall be turned
Jonah 1. 14. we beseech thee, O L. we beseech thee
Hab. 1. 12. O L. thou hast ordained them for judgm.
3. 2. O L. revive thy work in midst of the years
Mat. 15. 22. O L. thou Son of David, 20. 30, 31.
Luke 5. 8. depart, for I am a sinful man, O L.
Rev. 4. 11. thou art worthy, O L. to receive glory
6. 10. saying, how long, O L. holy and true
15. 4. who shall not fear thee, O L. and glorify
16. 5. O L. which art, and wast, and shalt be
See LORD God.

Of the LORD.

Josh. 11. 20. for it was of the L. to harden hearts
1 Sam. 1. 20. because I have asked him of the L.
8. 21. he rehearsed them in the ears of the L.
23. 21. Saul said, blessed be ye of L. 2 Sam. 2. 5.
2 Sam. 12. 25. his name Jedidiah because of the L.
1 Kings 15. 29. according to the saying of the L.
2 Kings 6. 33. he said, behold this evil is of the L.
8. 8. meet the man of G. and enquire of L. by him
10. 17. according to the saying of the L. to Elijah
2 Chr. 18. 7. one man, by whom we may enquire - L.
34. 21. go, enquire of the L. for me, and for Israel
Psal. 91. 2. I will say of the L. he is my refuge
Prov. 16. 33. but the disposing thereof is of the L.
20. 24. man's goings are - L. || 21. 31. safety is of L.
Isa. 49. 7. worship because of the L. that is faithful
51. 9. O arm of the L. awake as in ancient days
Jer. 21. 2. enquire, I pray thee, of the L. for us
Lam. 3. 22. it is - L. mercies we are not consumed
Jonah 2. 9. pay that I vowed, salvation is of the L.
Acts 21. 14. ceased, saying, the will of L. be done
1 Cor. 11. 23. I have received of the L. that which
2 Cor. 2. 12. and a door was opened to me of the L.
Eph. 6. 8. the same shall he receive of the L.
Col. 3. 24. knowing that of the L. ye receive reward
2 Tim. 1. 18. grant that he may find mercy of the L.
Jam. 1. 7. that he shall receive any thing of the L.
5. 11. and ye have seen the end of the L.
2 Pet. 3. 15. long-suffering of the L. is salvation
See ANGEL.

Anger of the LORD.

Exod. 4. 14. anger of the L. was kindled ag. Moses
Num. 11. 10. anger of the L. was kindled against
Israel, 25. 3. Josh. 7. 1. Judg. 2. 14, 20. | 3. 8.
| 10. 7. 2 Sam. 24. 1. 2 Kings 13. 3. Isa. 5. 25.
Num. 12. 9. - L. kindled against Aaron and Miriam
25. 4. that the fierce an. of L. may be turned away
32. 14. to augment yet the an. of the L. toward Isr.
Deut. 6. 15. lest the an. of the L. be kindled ag. thee
7. 4. so will anger of the L. be kindled against you
29. 20. then the an. of the L. shall smoke ag. that man
27. anger of the L. was kindled against this land
Josh. 23. 16. the anger of the L. be kindled ag. you
2 Sam. 6. 7. - L. kindled against Uzzah, 1 Chr. 13. 10.
2 Kings 24. 20. thro' - L. it came to pass, Jer. 52. 3.
2 Chr. 25. 15. a. of the L. kindled against Amaziah
Jer. 4. 8. fierce a. of L. is not turned back from us
12. 13. ashamed because of the fierce a. of the L.
23. 20. anger of the L. shall not return till, 30. 24.
51. 45. deliver every man his soul from a. of the L.
Lam. 2. 22. so that in day of L. anger none escaped
4. 16. the anger of the L. hath divided them
Zeph. 2. 2. before the fierce a. of L. come upon you
3. it may be ye shall be hid in the day of the
anger of the L.
See COMMANDMENT, CONGREGATION, COUNSEL, DAY, EYES, FACE, FEAR, FEAST, GLORY, HAND, HOUSE, KNOWLEDGE, LAW.

Mouth of the LORD.

Deut. 8. 3. word that proceedeth out of mouth of L.
Josh. 9. 14. and asked not counsel at the mouth of L.
1 Kings 13. 21. thou hast disobeyed the mouth of L.
Isa. 1. 20. for the mouth of L. hath spoken it, 40. 5.
| 58. 14. Jer. 9. 12. Mic. 4. 4.
62. 2. by a new name, which the - L. shall name
Jer. 23. 16. and they speak not out of mouth of t. L.

Name of the LORD.

Gen. 12. 8. Abraham called on the name of the L.
16. 13. she called the name of L. that spake to her
26. 25. Isaac called on n. of L. and pitched there
Exod. 20. 7. shalt not take - L. in vain, Deut. 5. 11.
33. 19. I will proclaim n. of the L. before thee
34. 5. and the Lord proclaimed n. of the L.
Lev. 24. 11. woman's son blasphemed the - L. 16.
Deut. 18. 5. to stand to minister in n. of the L. 7.
22. when a prophet speaketh in the n. of the L.
21. 5. them hath God chosen to bless in n. of the L.
28. 10. see that thou art called by the n. of the L.
32. 3. because I will publish name of the L. ascribe
Josh. 9. 9. thy servants are come beca. of n. of the L.
1 Sam. 17. 45. I come to thee in n. of the L. of hosts
20. 42. we have sworn both of us in name of the L.
2 Sam. 6. 2. whose name is called by the n. of the L.
18. blessed the people in the n. of L. 1 Chr. 16. 2.
1 Kings 3. 2. no house built to the name of the
Lord, 5. 3, 5. | 8. 17, 20. 1 Chron. 22. 7, 19.
2 Chron. 2. 1, 4. | 6. 10.
10. 1. queen of Sheba heard concerning name of L.
18. 32. Elijah built an altar in the name of the L
22. 16. that which is true in n. L. 2 Chron. 18. 15.
2 Kings 2. 24. and Elisha cursed them in n. of the L.
1 Chr. 21. 19. which he spake in n. L. 2. Chr. 33. 18.
Job 1. 21. blessed be the n. of the L. Psal. 113. 2.
Psal. 7. 17. I will sing praises to n. of the L. most high
20. 7. but we will remember n. of the L. our God
102. 15. so the heathen shall fear the n. of the L.
21. to declare n. of the L. in Zion, and his praise
Ps. 113. 1. praise the - L. 135. 1. | 148. 5, 13. Joel 2. 26.
3. from rising of sun the L. name is to be praised
116. 4. then called I on n. of L. O Lord, deliver
118. 10. but in the - L. will I destroy them, 11, 12.
26. blessed be he that cometh in the n. of the L.
122. 4. to give thanks unto the name of the L.
124. 8. our help is in n. of the L. who made heaven
129. 8. they which go by say, we bless you in - L.
Prov. 18. 10. the - L. is a strong tower, the righteous
Isa. 18. 7. to the place of the na. of the L. of hosts
24. 15. glorify the name of the L. in the isles of sea
30. 27. the na. of L. cometh from far, burning with
48. 1. which swear by na. of L. and make mention
50. 10. let him trust in n. of the L. and stay on God
56. 6. and to love the na. of L. to be his servants
59. 19. so shall they fear the name of L. from west
60. 9. to bring their silver and gold to name of t. L.
Jer. 3. 17. all nations gathered to name of the Lord
11. 21. saying, prophesy not in the name of the L.
26. 9. why hast thou prophesied in the name of L.
16. he hath spoken to us in the name of L. 44. 16.
20. Urijah that prophesied in the name of the L.
Amos 6. 10. we may not make mention of n. of t. L.
Mic. 4. 5. we will walk in n. of L. for ever and ever
5. 4. ye shall feed in the majesty of the n. of the L.
Zeph. 3. 12. and they shall trust in name of the L.
Zech. 13. 3. thou speakest lies in the name of the L.
Mat. 21. 9. blessed is he that cometh in the name of
the L. 23. 39. Mark 11. 9, 10. Luke 13. 35. |
19. 38. John 12. 13.
Acts 9. 29. and he spake boldly in n. of the L. Jesus
10. 48. commanded them to be baptized in n. of L.
19. 13. to call over them the n. of L. Jesus, saying
17. and the n. of the L. Jesus was magnified
21. 13. for I am ready to die for the n. of L. Jesus
22. 16. wash away thy sins, calling on the n. of L.
2 Thess. 1. 12. that the n. of L. Jes. may be glorified
3. 6. we command you in the n. of L. Jesus Christ
Jam. 5. 10. prophets, who have spoken in n. of L.
14. anointing him with oil in the name of the L.
See CALL, OFFERINGS.

Prophet and prophets of the LORD.

1 Sam. 3. 20. Samuel established to be a p. of the L.
1 Kings 18. 4. when Jezebel cut off the p. of the L.
13. Jezebel slew the - L. || 22. I only remain a - L.
22. 7. is there not here a proph. of the L. to inquire
of him? 2 Kings 3. 11. 2 Chron. 18. 6.
2 Chr. 28. 9. a - L. was there, whose name was Oded
See SABAOTH, SABBATH.

Servant, servants of the LORD.

Deut. 34. 5. Moses the s. of t. L. died there in Moab
Josh. 1. 1. after the death of Moses the s. of the L.
13. which Moses the servant of the L. commanded,
8. 31, 33. | 11. 12. | 22. 2, 5. 2 Kings 18. 12.
15. which Moses the servant of the L. gave you,
12. 6. | 13. 8. | 18. 7. | 22. 4.
12. 6. them did Moses the servant of the L. smite
14. 7. when Moses the s. of L. sent me from Kadesh
24. 29. Joshua son of Nun the - L. died, Judg. 2. 8.
2 Kings 9. 7. avenge the blood of all the servts. of L.
10. 23. see there be here none of the servants of L.
2 Chr. 1. 3. tabernacle Moses the s. of the L. made
24. 6. according to commandment of Moses the - L.
Psal. 113. 1. praise the Ld. praise, O ye - L. 135. 1.
134. 1. behold, bless ye the Lord, O all ye ser. of L.
Isa. 42. 19. who is blind or deaf as the L. servant
54. 17. this is the heritage of the servants of the L.
2 Tim. 2. 24. and the serv. of the L. must not strive

Sight of the LORD.

Gen. 38. 7. Er was wicked in s. of L. and he slew him
Lev. 10. 19. should have been accepted in sight of L.
Deut. 6. 18. do that which is good in s. of L. 12. 28.
12. 25. do what is right in sight of the L. 21. 9.
2 Kings 12. 2. | 14. 3. | 15. 3, 34. | 18. 3. | 22. 2.
2 Chron. 20. 32. | 24. 2. | 25. 2. | 26. 4. | 27. 2. |
29. 2. | 34. 2.
1 Sam. 12. 17. wickedness is great ye have done in
the sight of L. 1 Kings 21. 25. 2 Kings 21. 6.
2 Kings 3. 18. this is but a light thing in sight of L.
16. 2. did not what was right in - L. 2 Chron. 28. 1.
Psal. 116. 15. precious in - L. is death of his saints
Mal. 2. 17. ye say, he that doth evil, is good in - L.
Luke 1. 15. for he shall be great in the sight of L.
2 Cor. 8. 21. not only in the s. of the L. but of men
Jam. 4. 10. humble yourselves in the sight of the L.
See EVIL.

Spirit of the LORD.

Judg. 3. 10. S. of L. came on Othniel, and he judged
6. 34. S. of L. came on Gideon || 11. 29. on Jephtha
13. 25. - L. began to move Sams. 14. 6, 19. | 15. 14.
1 Sam. 10. 6. - L. will come on Saul || 16. 13. on Dav.
16. 14. but the Spirit of the L. departed from Saul
2 Sam. 23. 2. - L. spake by me, his word was in
1 Kings 18. 12. Spirit of the L. shall carry thee
whither I know not
22. 24. which way went the Sp. of the L. from me
to speak unto thee? 2 Chron. 18. 23.
2 Kings 2. 16. lest the S. of the L. hath taken him up
2 Chr. 20. 14. on Jahaziel came S. of L. in midst
Isa. 11. 2. - L. shall rest upon him, Spirit of wisd.
40. 7. - L. bloweth upon it || 13. hath directed - L.
59. 19. the Spirit of the L. shall lift up a standard
61. 1. - L. is upon me, because the Ld. Luke 4. 18.
63. 14. Spir. of L. caused him to rest, so didst thou
Ezek. 11. 5. - L. fell upon me || 37. 1. carried in - L.
Mic. 2. 7. O house of Jac. is the S. of L. straitened
3. 8. but truly I am full of power by the S. of the L.
Acts 5. 9. how is it ye have agreed to tempt S. of L.
8. 39. when come up, the - L. caught away Philip
2 Cor. 3. 17. where the S. of t. L. is, there is liberty
18. from glory to glory, even as by the Spi. of L.

Temple of the LORD.

1 Sam. 1. 9. Eli sat on a seat by a post of the t. of L.
3. 3. and ere the lamp of God went out in the - L.
2 Kings 11. 13. she came to the people into t. of L.
18. 16. Hezekiah cut gold off from doors of t. of L.
23. 4. bring out of the - L. vessels made for Baal
24. 13. all vessels Solomon had made in the t. of L.
2 Chr. 26. 16. Uzziah went in t. of L. to burn inc.
27. 2. Jotham entered not into the temple of the L.
29. 16. took away uncleanness found in t. of the L.
Ezra 3. 6. foundation of the t. of L. was not yet laid
Ezra 3. 10. laid foundation of t. of the L. Hag. 2. 18.
Jer. 7. 4. saying, the t. of L. the t. of L. are these
24. 1. basket of figs were set before the t. of the L.
Ezek. 8. 16. at the door of the t. of L. were 25 men
with their backs toward - L. and faces to east
Hag. 2. 15. consider before a stone was laid in - L.
Zech. 6. 12. and he shall build the t. of the L. 13, 15.
14. crown shall be for a memorial in temple of L.
Luke 1. 9. when Zacharias went into the t. of L.

Voice of the LORD.

Deut. 30. 8. and obey voice of L. Jer. 26. 13. | 38. 20.
Josh. 5. 6. because they obeyed not the v. of L. 1 Sam.
28. 18. 1 Kings 20. 36. Jer. 3. 25. | 7. 28. | 42.
13, 21. | 43. 4, 7. | 44. 23. Dan. 9. 10.
1 Sam. 15. 19. wherefore didst thou not obey v. of L.
20. Saul said, yea, I have obeyed the v. of the L.
22. and sacrifices, as in obeying the voice of the L.
Psal. 29. 3. the voice of the L. is upon the waters
4. the v. of the L. is powerful, full of majesty, 5.
7. the voice of the L. divideth the flames of fire
8. the v. of L. shaketh the wilderness of Kadesh
9. the voice of the L. maketh the hinds to calve
106. 25. they hearkened not to the voice of the L.
Isa. 6. 8. I heard the v. of the L. saying, who will go
30. 31. thro' v. of the L. shall Assyrians be beaten
66. 6. a voice of the L. that rendereth recompence
Jer. 42. 6. we will obey the v. of the L. our God that
it may be well with us when we obey the v. of L.
Mic. 6. 9. the L. voice crieth unto the city
Hag. 1. 12. remnant of the people obeyed v. of the L.
Zech. 6. 15. if ye will diligently obey the v. of the L.
Acts 7. 31. the v. of the L. came to Moses, saying

Way of the LORD.

Gen. 18. 19. command his household to keep w. of L.
Judg. 2. 22. whether they will keep the w. of the L.
2 Kings 21. 22. Amon walked not in the w. of the L.
Psal. 119. 1. bless. are they who walk in w. of the L.
Prov. 10. 29. the w. of the L. is strength to the upright
Isa. 40. 3. prepare ye the w. of the L. make
straight, Mat. 3. 3. Mark 1. 3. Luke 3. 4.
Jer. 5. 4. are foolish, they know not way of the L.
5. great men, for they have known way of the L.
Ezek. 18. 25. the w. L. is not equal, 29. | 33. 17, 20.
John 1. 23. one crying, make straight way of the L.
Acts 18. 25. Apollos was instructed in way of the L.

Ways of the LORD.

2 Sam. 22. 22. for I have kept the w. of L. Ps. 18. 21.
2 Chr. 17. 6. Jehoshaphat was lifted up in w. of L.
Psal. 138. 5. yea, they shall sing in the w. of the L.
Hos. 14. 9. for the w. of the L. are right, and the just
Acts 13. 10. cease to pervert the right w. of the L.

Word of the LORD.

Exod. 9. 20. he that feared the w. of the L. amongst
21. and he that regarded not the w of the L. left
Num. 3. 16. according to the word of the L. 51.
| 4. 45. | 36. 5. Deut. 34. 5. Josh. 8. 27. | 19.
50. | 22. 9. 1 Kings 12. 24. | 13. 26. | 14. 18. |
16. 12, 34. | 17. 5, 16. | 22. 38. 2 Kings 1. 17.
| 4. 44. | 7. 16. | 9. 26. | 14. 25.
15. 31. because he hath despised the word of the L.
22. 18. I cannot go beyond the word of L. my God
Deut. 5. 5. at that time to shew you the word of L.
1 Sam. 3. 1. the w. of L. was precious in those days
7. nor was word of the L. yet revealed to Samuel
15. 23. because thou hast rejected the w. of L. 26.
2 Sam. 22. 31. the word of L. is tried, Psal. 18. 30.
1 Kings 2. 27. might fulfil w. of t. L. 2 Chr. 36. 21.
12. 24. they hearkened therefore to the word of the
L. and returned, 2 Chron. 11. 4. Jer. 37. 2.
13. 1. came a man of God by w. of L. to Beth-el
2. he cried against the altar in the word of the L.
5. the sign the man of God had given by w. of L.
9. so it was charged me by w. of L. saying
18. angel spake by w. of L. saying, bring him back
26. the man who was disobedient unto the w. of L.
32. for the saying he cried by the word of the L.
14. 18. they buried him according to the w. of L.
17. 24. and that w. of the L. in my mouth is truth
20. 35. prophet said in w. of L. smite me, I pray
22. 5. enquire, I pray thee, at w. of L. 2 Chr. 18. 4.
2 Kings 3. 12. Jehoshaphat said, w. of L. is with him
9. 36. this is w. of L. || 15. 12. this was the w. of L.
10. 10. fall to the earth nothing of the word of L.
20. 19. Hezek. said, good is the w. of L. Isa. 39. 8.
23. 16. according to the word of the L. 24. 2.
1 Chron. 11. 3, 10. | 12. 23. | 15. 15. Jer. 13. 2.
| 32. 8. Jonah 3. 3.
1 Chron. 10. 13. committed even against w. of the L.
2 Chr. 30. 12. to do commandm. of king by w. of L.
34. 21. our fathers have not kept the w. of the L.
36. 22. that w. of L. might be accomp. Ezra 1. 1.
Psal. 33. 4. for the w. of L. is right, and his works
6. by w. of L. were heavens made, and all host
105. 19. till his word came, the w. of L. tried him
Isa. 2. 3. and the w. of L. from Jerus. Mic. 4. 2.
28. 13. the w. of L. was to them precept on precept
Jer. 2. 31. O generation, see ye the word of the L.
6. 10. the w. of the L. is to them a reproach, 20. 8.
8. 9. lo, they have rejected the word of L. and what
17. 15. behold, they say to me, where is the w. of L.
25. 3. to this day the w. of L. hath come unto me
27. 18. if the w. of L. be with them, let them make
32. 8. then I knew that this was the word of the L.
Hos. 1. 2. the w. of L. that came to Hosea son of
Amos 8. 12. they shall wander to seek the w. of L.
Zeph. 2. 5. the w. of the L. is against you, O Canaan
Zech. 4. 6. this is w. of the L. to Zerubbabel, saying
9. 1. the burden of the word of the L. in the land of
Hadrach and Damascus, 12. 1. Mal. 1. 1.
11. 11. poor of the flock knew that it was w. of L.
Luke 22. 61. Peter remembered w. of L. Acts 11. 16.
Acts 8. 25. they had testified, and had preached the
word of the L. 13. 49. | 15. 35, 36. | 16. 32.
13. 48. and glorified the word of the L.
19. 10. heard the word of the L. Jesus
1 Thess. 1. 8. for from you sounded out the w. of L.
4. 15. for this we say to you by the word of the L.
2 Thess. 3. 1. that the w. of L. may have free course
1 Pet. 1. 25. but the word of L. endureth for ever

Words of the LORD.

Exod. 24. 3. Moses told peo. all w. of L. Num. 11. 24.
4. and Moses wrote all the w. of L. and rose up

Josh. 24. 27. this stone heard all the words of the L.
1 Sam. 8. 10. Samuel told the people words of the L.
15. 1. hearken thou to the voice of the w. of the L.
2 Chr. 29. 15. came by w. of L. to cleanse the house
Psal. 12. 6. words of the L. are pure words, as silver
Jer. 36. 4. Baruch wrote all w. of L. from mouth of
6. read in the roll thou hast written w. of L. 8.
11. had heard out of the book all the w. of the L.
Amos 8. 11. but a famine of hearing the w. of the L.
See CAME, HEAR.

Work of the LORD.

Exod. 34. 10. all the people shall see the w. of the L.
Isa. 5. 12. they regard not the w. of L. nor consider
Jer. 48. 10. cursed that doeth the w. of L. deceitfully
50. 25. this is the w. of L. || 51. 10. declare the w. of L.
1 Cor. 15. 58. always abounding in the w. of the L.
16. 10. for he worketh the w. of the L. as I also do

Works of the LORD.

Josh. 24. 31. which had known all the w. of the L.
Judg. 2. 7. which had seen all the great w. of the L.
Psal. 28. 5. because they regard not the w. of the L.
46. 8. come, behold the w. of the L. what desolations
77. 11. I will remember the w. of L. thy wonders
107. 24. these see the w. of the L. and his wonders
111. 2. the w. of L. are great || 118. 17. declare w. of L.

Wrath of the LORD.

Num. 11. 33. ere it was chewed w. of L. was kindl.
Deut. 11. 17. then the L. w. be kindled against you
2 Kings 22. 13. for great is the w. of L. 2 Chr. 34. 21.
2 Chron. 12. 12. the w. of L. turned from him, that
29. 8. the w. of L. was upon Judah and Jerusalem
32. 26. so that the w. of the L. came not upon them
36. 16. until w. of the L. arose against his people
Psal. 106. 40. therefore was wrath of the L. kindled
Isa. 9. 19. thro' the w. of the L. is the land darkened
13. 13. the earth shall remove in the w. of the L.
Jer. 50. 13. because of w. of the L. not be inhabited
Ezek. 7. 19. their silver and gold shall not be able to deliver them in day of w. of the L. Zeph. 1. 18.
See PRAISE.

LORD said.

Gen. 8. 21. the L. said in his heart, I will not curse
Exod. 7. 13. he hearkened not as the L. said, 22. | 8. 15, 19. Deut. 9. 3. Judg. 2. 15. | 6. 27.
16. 23. this is that which the L. said, to-morrow
24. 3. Moses told them all the words the L. said
7. all that the L. said we will do, Num. 32. 31.
Num. 10. 29. journeying to place of which L. said
16. 40. as the L. said to him by the hand of Moses
26. 65. the L. had said, they shall surely die
Deut. 31. 3. as the L. hath s. Josh. 14. 12. Joel 2. 32.
Josh. 11. 23. according to all the L. said to Moses
14. 6. thou knowest the thing that the L. said
1 Sam. 3. 17. what is the thing that L. said to thee
15. 16. tell thee what the L. said to me this night
24. 4. behold, the day of which the L. said to thee
2 Sam. 16. 10. bec. the L. said to him, curse David
1 Kings 8. 12. L. said he would dwell, 2 Chr. 6. 1.
11. 2. nations, concerning which L. said to Israel
2 Kings 14. 27. L. said not that he would blot out
17. 12. whereof the L. had said, ye shall not do
21. 4. of which L. said in Jerusal. 7. 2 Chr. 33. 4.
24. 13. Solomon had made in temple as the L. said
Psal. 2. 7. the L. hath said unto me, thou art my Son
110. 1. the L. said unto my Lord, Mat. 22. 44. Mark 12. 36. Luke 20. 42. Acts 2. 34.
Isa. 7. 3. then said the L. 8. 3. Ezek. 44. 2. Hos. 3. 1. Jonah 4. 10. Luke 20. 13.
18. 4. for so L. said unto me, I will take my rest
21. 16. thus hath L. said unto me, Jer. 4. 27. | 6. 6.
29. 13. wherefore L. said, forasmuch as this people
Ezek. 21. 17. cause my fury rest, I the L. have said
Mat. 25. 21. his L. said unto him, well done, 23.
Acts 9. 10. to him said the L. in a vision, Ananias
11. 16. I remembered the word of L. how he said

Saith the LORD.

Exod. 4. 22. thus saith the L. 5. 1. | 7. 17. 1 Sam. 2. 27. 2 Sam. 12. 11. | 24. 12.
Num. 24. 13. what the L. saith, that will I speak
Josh. 7. 13. thus saith the L. God of Israel, 24. 2. Judg. 6. 8. 2 Sam. 12. 7.
1 Sam. 2. 30. but now the L. saith, be it far from me
15. 2. thus saith the L. of hosts, 2 Sam. 7. 8. 1 Chron. 17. 7. Jer. 6. 9. | 7. 3, 21.
1 Kings 22. 14. what the L. saith, that will I speak
Isa. 22. 14. iniquity shall not be purged, saith the L. God of hosts, Jer. 5. 14. | 35. 17. | 49. 5. | 50. 31.
33. 10. now will I rise s. t. L. now will I, Ps. 12. 5.
49. 5. now s. the L. that formed me from the womb
54. 10. be removed, s. t. L. that hath mercy on thee
Jer. 1. 8. for I am with thee, saith the L. 19. | 30. 11.
2. 19. and that my fear is not in thee, saith the L.
3. 1. played the harlot, yet return unto me, s. the L.
4. 1. if thou wilt return, s. the L. return unto me
5. 22. fear ye not me, s. L. || 7. 11. I have seen it, s. L.
9. 3. from evil to evil, they know not me, s. the L.
22. 16. was not this to know me? saith the L.
23. 23. am I a G. at hand, s. the L. and not afar off?
24. can any hide, that I shall not see him, s. the L.
33. what burden? I will even forsake you, s. the L.
27. 15. for I have not sent him, s. the L. yet they
29. 9. they prophesy, I have not sent them, s. the L.
Ezek. 13. 6. L. s. and the Lord hath not sent them, 7.
8. I am against you, s. L. || 16. 19. thus it was, s. L.
21. 13. even the rod, it shall be no more, s. the L. G.
34. 31. ye my flock are men, and I am your G. s. L.
39. 8. behold, it is come, and it is done, s. the L. G.
43. 27. and I will accept you, saith the L. God
Amos 2. 11. is it not even thus, O Isr.? saith the L.
4. 5. this liketh you, s. t. L. || 7. 3. shall not be, s. L.
9. 12. are called by my name, s. the L. that doeth this
Mic. 6. 1. hear ye now what the L. saith, arise thou
Nah. 2. 13. behold, I am against thee, s. the L. 3. 5.
Zeph. 3. 8. therefore wait ye upon me, saith the L.
Hag. 1. 9. why? s. L. of hosts || 13. I am with you, s. L.
Zech. 2. 5. for I, s. the L. will be to her a wall of fire
4. 6. not by might or power, but by my Spirit, s. t. L.
Mal. 1. 2. I have loved you, saith the L. yet ye say
13. should I accept this of your hand, saith the L.
14. for I am a great king, saith the L. of hosts
3. 5. that oppress, and fear not me, s. t. L. of hosts
10. and prove me now herewith, s. the L. of hosts
Mal. 3. 17. and they shall be mine, s. the L. of hosts
4. 3. in the day that I shall do this, s. t. L. of hosts
Acts 15. 17. saith the L. who doeth all these things
Rom. 12. 19. vengeance is mine, I will repay s. t. L.
1 Cor. 14. 21. they will not hear me for all this, s. the L.
2 Cor. 6. 17. come out and be ye separate, s. the L.
Heb. 8. 9. and I regarded them not, saith the L.
10. 30. who hath said, I will recompense, s. the L.
Rev. 1. 8. I am the Beginning and Ending, s. the L.
See LIVE, SAVED.

LORD joined with seek.

Deut. 4. 29. if from thence thou shalt seek the L.
1 Chron. 16. 10. heart rejoice, that seek L. Ps. 105. 3.
11. seek the L. and his strength, Psal. 105. 4.
22. 19. set your heart to seek the L. 2 Chron. 11. 16.
2 Chron. 12. 14. prepared not his heart to seek the L.
14. 4. and commanded Judah to seek the L. God
15. 12. they entered into a covenant to seek the L.
13. that whosoever would not seek the L. God
20. 3. Jehoshaphat set himself to seek the L.
4. out of the cities of Judah they came to seek L.
Ezra 6. 21. were come to seek the L. God of Israel
Psal. 22. 26. they shall praise the L. that seek him
34. 10. they that seek the L. shall not want any good
Prov. 28. 5. they that seek L. understand all things
Isa. 9. 13. neither do they seek L. 31. 1. Hos. 7. 10.
51. 1. hearken to me, ye that seek the L. look to
55. 6. seek ye the L. while he may be found
Jer. 50. 4. they shall go and seek the L. their God
Hos. 3. 5. shall return and seek the L. their God
5. 6. they shall go with their herds to seek the L.
10. 12. for it is time to seek the L. till he come
Amos 5. 6. seek the L. and ye shall live, lest he break
Zeph. 2. 3. seek ye the L. all ye meek of the earth
Zech. 8. 21. saying, let us go to seek the L. of hosts
22. many people shall come to seek the L.
Mal. 3. 1. the L. whom ye seek shall suddenly come
Acts 15. 17. that the residue of men might seek the L.
17. 27. that they should seek the L. if haply might

LORD joined with sent.

Gen. 3. 23. the L. sent him forth from the garden
19. 13. we will destroy, the L. sent us to destroy it
Exod. 4. 28. told all the words of L. who had sent him
7. 16. the L. God of the Hebrews sent me to thee
9. 23. and L. sent thunder and hail on Egypt
Num. 16. 28. ye shall know that the L. hath sent me
29. if die common death, then L. hath not sent
20. 16. and when we cried, the L. sent an angel
21. 6. the L. sent fiery serpents among the people
Deut. 9. 23. when L. sent you from Kadesh-barnea
34. 11. in all wonders which the L. sent him to do
Judg. 6. 8. that the L. sent a prophet unto Israel
1 Sam. 12. 8. then the L. sent Moses and Aaron
11. and the L. s. Jerubbaal || 18. the L. s. thunder
15. 1. the L. sent me to anoint thee king over Israel
18. the L. sent thee on a journey, and said, go
20. I have gone the way which the L. sent me
20. 22. go thy way, the L. hath sent thee away
2 Sam. 12. 1. the L. s. Nathan to David, and he came
24. 15. L. sent pestilence on Israel, 1 Chr. 21. 14.
2 Kings 2. 2. tarry, for the L. hath sent me to Beth-el
4. L. hath sent me to Jericho || 6. L. s. me to Jordan
17. 25. therefore the L. sent lions among them
24. 2. the L. sent against him bands of the Chaldees
2 Chron. 32. 21. the L. sent an angel, who cut off
Isa. 9. 8. the L. sent a word into Jacob, and it lighted
Jer. 19. 14. whither the L. sent him to prophesy
25. 4. and the L. hath sent to you all his servants
17. nations to drink to whom the L. had sent me
26. 12. L. sent me to prophesy agst. this house, 15.
28. 9. be known that the L. hath truly sent him
15. hear Hananiah, the L. hath not sent thee
Ezek. 13. 6. Lord saith, and the L. hath not s. them
Jonah 1. 4. the L. sent out a great wind into the sea
Hag. 1. 12. obeyed, as the L. their God had sent him
Zech. 1. 10. whom the L. hath sent to walk to and fro
2. 9. know L. of hosts hath s. me, 11. | 4. 9. | 6. 15.
7. 12. lest hear the words which the L. hath sent
Acts 9. 17. Saul, the L. Jesus hath sent me, that thou
12. 11. now know I that the L. hath sent his angel

Serve the LORD.

Exod. 10. 7. men go, that they may s. the L. their G.
8. Phar. said, go s. the L. your G. 11. 24. | 12. 31.
26. for thereof must we take to serve the L. our God, we know not with what we must s. the L.
23. 25. ye shall serve the L. your God, ye shall bless
Deut. 10. 12. to s. the L. thy God with all thy heart
Josh. 24. 14. therefore fear and serve the L.
15. if it seem evil unto you to s. the L. choose you
18. therefore will we s. the L. he is our God, 21. 24.
19. Joshua said, ye cannot s. the L. for he is holy
22. that ye have chosen you the L. to serve him
1 Sam. 12. 20. but serve the L. with all your heart
2 Sam. 15. 8. will bring me again, then I will s. t. L.
2 Chron. 30. 8. but yield, and s. t. L. your G. 35. 3.
33. 16. and commanded Judah to s. the L. 34. 33.
Ps. 2. 11. s. t. L. with fear, and rejoice with trembl.
100. 2. serve the L. with gladness and come be- [fore his presence
102. 22. and the kingdoms gathered to serve the L.
Col. 3. 24. receive reward, for ye serve the L. Christ
See SHEWED, SMITE.

LORD spake.

Gen. 16. 13. called the name of L. that spake to her
Lev. 10. 3. this is it that the L. spake, saying, I will
Num. 3. 1. in the day the L. spake with Moses, 9. 1.
5. 4. as the L. spake unto Moses, so did Israel
21. 16. that is the well whereof L. spake to Moses
Deut. 4. 12. L. spake to you out of the midst of fire
15. ye saw no similitude in the day the L. spake
5. 22. these words the L. spake to your assembly
9. 10. written all the words which the L. spake
10. 4. the ten commandments which the L. spake
Josh. 14. 10. since the L. spake this word to Moses
12. this mountain whereof L. spake in that day
1 Sam. 16. 4. Samuel did that which the L. spake
1 Kings 2. 4. L. may continue his word which he sp.
27. fulfil the word of the L. which he spake
5. 5. as the L. spake to David my father, saying
8. 20. L. hath performed word he s. 2 Kings 10. 10.
12. 15. perform his saying the L. s. 2 Chr. 10. 15.
13. 26. according to the word of the L. which he spake, 14. 18. | 16. 12, 34. | 17. 16. | 22. 38. 2 Kings 10. 10. | 24. 2.
1 Kings 15. 29. according to the saying of L. which he spake by his servant Ahijah, 2 Kings 10. 17.
21. 23. and of Jezebel also spake the L. saying
2 Kings 9. 36. this is the word of L. which he spake
15. 12. the word of the L. which he spake to Jehu
21. 10. the L. spake by his servants the prophets
1 Chron. 21. 9. L. spake unto Gad, Da. seer, saying
2 Chron. 33. 10. L. spake to Manasseh and his peop.
Isa. 7. 10. moreover, the L. spake again to Ahaz
8. 5. the L. spake also unto me again, saying
11. for the L. spake thus to me with a strong hand
20. 2. at the same time spake the L. by Isaiah
Jer. 30. 4. these are the words that the L. spake
50. 1. the word that the L. spake against Babylon
51. 12. for the L. hath done that which he spake
Jonah 2. 10. the L. spake unto the fish, it vomited
Acts 18. 9. then spake the L. to Paul in the night

LORD, joined with spoken.

Gen. 12. 4. Abram departed as the L. had spoken, 21. 1. | 24. 51. Exod. 9. 12, 35. Deut. 6. 19.
Exod. 4. 30. Moses spake the words the L. had spoken
19. 8. and said, all that the L. hath spoken will we do
34. 32. gave in commandment all the L. had spoken
Lev. 10. 11. teach the statutes the L. hath spoken
Num. 1. 48. for L. had s. to Moses, saying, 15. 22.
10. 29. the L. hath spoken good concerning Israel
12. 2. hath the L. indeed spoken only by Moses?
23. 17. Balak said to him, what hath the L. spoken?
Deut. 18. 21. word which L. hath not spoken, 22.
Josh. 21. 45. failed not ought which L. had spoken
1 Sam. 25. 30. L. have done the good he hath spoken
2 Sam. 3. 18. now then do it, for the L. hath spoken
7. 29. it may continue, for thou, O L. hath spoken it
1 Kings 13. 3. this is the sign which L. hath spoken
14. 11. for the L. hath spoken it, Isa. 21. 17. | 22. 25. | 24. 3. | 25. 8. Joel 3. 8. Obad. 18.
Job 42. 7. after the L. had spoken these words to Job
Psal. 50. 1. the L. hath spoken, and called the earth
Isa. 31. 4. for thus hath the L. spoken to me, like as
38. 7. L. will do this thing that he hath spoken
Jer. 9. 12. to whom the mouth of the L. hath spoken
13. 15. give ear, be not proud, for the L. hath spoken
23. 35. and ye shall say, what hath L. spoken, 37.
27. 13. as the L. hath spoken against the nation
48. 8. shall be destroyed, as the L. hath spoken
Ezek. 5. 13. I the L. have spoken it, 15, 17. | 17. 21, 24. | 21. 32. | 22. 14. | 24. 14. | 26. 14. | 30. 12. | 34. 24. | 36. 36. | 37. 14.
22. 28. thus saith the Lord, when the L. hath not s.
26. 5. for I have spoken it, saith L. 28. 10. | 39. 5.
Amos 3. 1. hear this word that the L. hath spoken
8. the L. G. hath spoken, who can but prophesy?
Mic. 4. 4. the mouth of the L. of hosts hath spoken it
Mat. 1. 22. fulfilled which was spoken of the L. 2. 15.
Mark 16. 19. so then after the L. had spoken to them
Acts 9. 27. had seen the L. and that he had spoken
Heb. 2. 3. at the first began to be spoken by the L.

To or unto the LORD.

Gen. 14. 22. I have lift up my hands to L. most high
18. 27. I have taken on me to speak to the L. 31.
Exod. 5. 17. let us go, and do sacrifice to L. 8. 8, 29.
10. 9. we must hold a feast to L. 12. 14. Num. 29. 12.
15. 1. sing to the L. 21. Judg. 5. 3. 1 Chron. 16. 23. Psal. 13. 6. | 30. 4. | 68. 32. | 95. 1. | 96. 1, 2. | 98. 1, 5. | 104. 33. | 147. 7. | 149. 1. Isa. 12. 5. | 42. 10. Jer. 20. 13.
16. 25. for to-day is a sab. to the L. 35. 2. Lev. 25. 2.
22. 20. he that sacrificeth save unto the L. only
30. 10. it is most holy unto the L. 31. 15. Lev. 23. 20. | 27. 21, 30, 32. Num. 6. 8. Ezra 8. 28.
Num. 21. 7. said, pray to L. Jer. 29. 7. Acts 8. 24.
29. 39. these things ye shall do to the L. in feasts
Deut. 12. 31. thou shalt not do so to the L. thy God
Judg. 11. 35. I have opened my mouth to the L. 36.
17. 3. I had wholly dedicated the silver to the L.
21. 8. that came not up to the L. to Mizpeh
1 Sam. 1. 10. Hannah prayed to the L. and wept sore
8. 6. displeased Samuel, and he prayed to the L.
14. 6. there is no restraint to the L. to save by many
2 Sam. 21. 6. will hang them up to the L. in Gibeah
1 Kings 2. 27. Abiathar from being priest to the L.
2 Kings. 4. 33. Elisha shut door, prayed to L. 6. 18.
18. 6. Hezekiah clave to L. and kept his commands
20. 2. Hezekiah turned his face unto the wall, and prayed to L. 2 Chr. 32. 24. Isa. 37. 15. | 38. 2.
23. 23. this passover holden to the L. in Jerusalem
1 Chron. 11. 18. not drink it, but poured it out to L.
16. 8. give thanks to L. call on his name, 41. Ps. 92. 1.
2 Chr. 13. 11. they burn to L. morning and evening
24. 9. to bring to the L. the collection that Moses
30. 8. but yield yourselves to the L. and serve him
Psal. 3. 8. salvation belongeth to the L. thy blessing
18. 41. they cried unto the L. but he answered not
30. 8. and to the L. I made supplication, 142. 1.
89. 6. who can be compared to L. be likened to L.?
116. 12. what shall I render to the L. for benefits?
140. 6. I said to the L. thou art my God, hear voice
Prov. 3. 32. abomination to the L. 11. 1, 20. | 12. 22. | 15. 8, 9, 26. | 16. 5. | 17. 15. | 20. 10, 23.
16. 3. commit thy works to L. || 19. 17. lendeth to L.
Isa. 19. 21. shall vow a vow to the L. and perform it
22. they shall return even to the L. he shall heal
23. 18. shall be holiness to L. Jer. 2. 3. Zech. 14. 20.
55. 13. it shall be to the L. for a name, for a sign
56. 3. that hath joined himself to the L. 6.
58. 5. wilt thou call this an acceptable day to the L.
Jer. 32. 16. Jeremiah prayed to the L. saying
Hos. 4. 10. they have left off to take heed to the L.
Jonah 4. 2. Jonah prayed to the L. and said
Mic. 4. 13. I will consecrate their gain unto the L. and their substance unto the L. of the whole earth
7. 7. therefore I will look to the L. I will wait for
Zech. 14. 7. one day, which shall be known to the L.
Mat. 5. 33. but shalt perform to the L. thine oaths
Luke 2. 22. brought him to present him to the L.
23. every male shall be called holy to the L.
Acts 5. 14. believers were the more added to the L.
11. 23. exhorted that they would cleave to the L.
13. 2. as they ministered unto the L. and fasted
14. 23. had prayed, they commended them to the L.

Acts 16. 15. if ye have judged me faithful *to the L.*
Rom. 14. 6. regardeth it *to the L.* eateth *to the L.*
8. whether we live, we live *to the L.* we die *to the L.*
2 Cor. 8. 5. but first gave their own selves *to the L.*
Eph. 5. 10. proving what is acceptable *to the L.*
22. submit yourselves, as *to the L.* 6. 7. Col. 3. 23.
See Cry, Cried, Give, Turn.

LORD, as applied to *man.*

Gen. 18. 12. after I am old, my *l.* being old also
23. 11. nay, my *l.* hear me || 15. my *l.* hearken to me
24. 18. drink, my *l.* and she hasted and let down
27. 29. be *l.* over thy brethren, let thy mother's
37. Isaac answered, I have made him thy *l.*
31. 35. Rachel said, let it not displease my *l.*
32. 4. saying, thus shall ye speak to my *l.* Esau
5. I have sent to tell my *l.* that I may find grace
18. shall say, it is a present sent to my *l.* Esau
39. 16. laid up his garment, until his *l.* came home
40. 1. had offended their *l.* the king of Egypt
42. 10. nay, my *l.* but to buy food are we come
30. the man who is the *l.* of the land, 33.
44. 5. is not this it, in which my *l.* drinketh?
8. should we steal out of thy *l.* house silver or gold
9. and we also will be my *l.* bondmen
24. we came up, we told him the words of my *l.*
45. 8. and he hath made me *l.* of all his house
9. God hath made me *l.* of all Egypt, come down
47. 18. we will not hide it from my *l.* how that there
is nothing left in sight of my *l.* but our
Exod. 32. 22. let not the anger of my *l.* wax hot
Num. 11. 28. and said, my *l.* Moses forbid them
12. 11. my *l.* I beseech thee, lay not sin on us
32. 25. servants do as my *l.* commandeth, 27.
36. 2. the Lord commanded my *l.* to give land
Judg. 3. 25. their *l.* was fallen down dead on earth
4. 18. turn in, my *l.* turn in to me, fear not
19. 26. the woman fell down where her *l.* was
27. and her *l.* rose up in the morning and opened
Ruth 2. 13. let me find favour in thy sight, my *l.*
1 Sam. 1. 15. my *l.* I am of a sorrowful spirit
26. O my *l.* as thy soul liveth, my *l.* I am woman
22. 12. and he answered, here I am, my *l.*
24. 8. and cried after Saul, saying, my *l.* the king
25. 24. on me, my *l.* on me let this iniquity be
25. let not my *l.* regard this man of Belial
26. they that seek evil to my *l.* be as Nabal
27. it be given to young men that follow my *l.*
31. when the Lord shall have dealt with my *l.*
26. 15. why hast thou not kept thy *l.* the king?
17. David said, it is my voice, my *l.* O king
18. why doth my *l.* thus pursue after his servant?
29. 8. that may not fight against enemies of my *l.*
2 Sam. 1. 10. and brought them hither to my *l.*
3. 21. I will gather all Israel to my *l.* the king
9. 11. according to all that my *l.* hath commanded
11. 9. Uriah slept with all the servants of his *l.*
13. 32. let not my *l.* suppose they have slain
14. 12. let thine handmaid speak to my *l.*
17. as an angel of God, so is my *l.* the king
19. none can turn from aught my *l.* hath spoken
20. my *l.* is wise according to wisdom of an angel
16. 9. why should this dead dog curse my *l.* king
18. 31. and Cushi said, tidings, my *l.* the king
19. 19. let not my *l.* impute iniquity to me, the day
my *l.* the king went out of Jerusalem
20. I am come the first to go down to meet my *l.*
30. forasmuch as my *l.* is come again in peace
35. be a burden to my *l.* || 37. go over with my *l.*
20. 6. take thou thy *l.* servants, and pursue after
24. 3. that the eyes of my *l.* the king may see it,
but why doth my *l.* delight in this thing?
22. let my *l.* take and offer up what seemeth good
1 Kings 1. 2. that my *l.* the king may get heat
27. is this thing done by my *l.* the king?
36. the Lord God of my *l.* the king say so too
37. as the Lord hath been with my *l.* the king
2. 38. as my *l.* the king hath said, so will I do
3. 17. O my *l.* I and this woman dwell in one house
26. O my *l.* give her the living child, not slay it
11. 23. who fled from his *l.* Hadadezer king of
18. 7. Obadiah said, art thou that my *l.* Elijah?
13. was it not told my *l.* what I did, when Jezebel
14. go tell thy *l.* behold Elijah is here, he slay
20. 4. my *l.* I am thine, and all that I have
9. tell my *l.* all thou didst send for, I will do
2 Kings 2. 19. the situation is pleasant as my *l.* seeth
4. 16. nay, my *l.* do not lie to thine handmaid
28. did I desire a son of my *l.*? did I not say
5. 3. would God my *l.* were with the prophet
4. one went in and told his *l.* saying, thus said
6. 12. and one of his servants said, none, my *l.*
26. a woman cried, saying, help my *l.* O king
7. 2. then a *l.* on whose hand the king leaned, 17.
8. 5. my *l.* O king, this is the woman, and her son
12. and Hazael said, why weepeth my *l.*?
9. 11. Jehu came forth to the servants of his *l.*
18. 23. now, I pray thee, give pledges to my *l.*
2 Chr. 2. 14. with the cunning men of my *l.* David
Ezra 10. 3. according to the counsel of my *l.*
Psal. 12. 4. our lips are our own, who is *l.* over us?
Jer. 22. 18. saying, ah *l.* or ah his glory, 34. 5.
37. 20. therefore hear now, I pray thee, my *l.*
38. 9. my *l.* the king, these men have done evil
Dan. 1. 10. said to Daniel, I fear my *l.* the king
2. 10. there is no king nor *l.* that asked such things
4. 19. my *l.* the dream be to them that hate thee
24. decree which is come upon my *l.* the king
Mat. 10. 24. nor is the servant above his *l.*
25. it is enough that the servant be as his *l.*
18. 26. *l.* have patience with me, and I will pay
31. they came and told their *l.* all that was done
24. 48. my *l.* delayeth his coming, Luke 12. 45.
Luke 12. 36. and ye like men that wait for their *l.*
16. 3. my *l.* taketh away from me the stewardship
5. so he called his *l.* debtors to him, and said to
the first, how much owest thou to my *l.*?
John 15. 15. the servant knoweth not what his *l.*
doth
20. I said, the servant is not greater than his *l.*
Acts 25. 26. I have no certain thing to write to my *l.*
Gal. 4. 1. differs not from a servant, though *l.* of all
1 Pet. 3. 6. Sarah obeyed Abraham, calling him *l.*

LORDS.

Gen. 19. 2. he said, behold now my *l.* turn in
Num. 21. 28. consumed *l.* of high places of Arnon
Deut. 10. 17. is Lord of *l.* 1 Tim. 6. 15. Rev. 17. 14.
Josh. 13. 3. five *l.* of the Philistines, Judg. 3. 3.
Judg. 16. 5. *l.* of the Philistines came up to her
30. and the house fell upon the *l.* and people
1 Sam. 5. 8. they gathered *l.* of the Philistines, 11.
6. 4. one plague was on you all, and on your *l.*
12. the *l.* of the Philistines went after them
7. 7. the *l.* of the Philistines went up against Israel
29. 2. the *l.* passed on by hundreds and thousands
6. nevertheless, the *l.* favour thee not
7. return, go in peace, that thou displease not the *l.*
Ezra 8. 25. I weighed the offering which *l.* offered
Isa. 16. 8. the *l.* of the heathen have broken plants
26. 13. other *l.* have had dominion over us
Jer. 2. 31. wherefore say my people, we are *l.*?
Ezek. 23. 23. great *l.* renowned, all riding on horses
Dan. 4. 36. my counsellors and *l.* sought to me
5. 1. made a great feast to a thousand of his *l.*
23. thou and thy *l.* have drunk wine in them
6. 17. the king sealed with his own and signet of *l.*
Mark 6. 21. that Herod made a supper to his *l.*
1 Cor. 8. 5. as there be gods many, and *l.* many
1 Pet. 5. 3. nor as being *l.* over God's heritage

LORDSHIP.

Mark 10. 42. kings of Gent. exercise *l.* Luke 22. 25.

LOSE.

Judg. 18. 25. run on thee, and thou *l.* thy life
1 Kings 18. 5. mules alive, that we *l.* not all the beasts
Job 31. 39. or have caused the owners *l.* their life
Prov. 23. 8. shalt vomit up, and *l.* thy sweet words
Eccl. 3. 6. there is a time to get, and a time to *l.*
Mat. 10. 39. he that findeth his life shall *l.* it, 16.
25. Mark 8. 35. Luke 9. 24.
42. he shall in no wise *l.* his reward, Mark 9. 41.
16. 26. and *l.* his own soul, Mark 8. 36. Luke 9. 25.
Luke 15. 4. if he *l.* one sheep || 8. if she *l.* one piece
17. 33. whosoever shall *l.* his life shall preserve it
John 6. 39. the Father's will I should *l.* nothing
12. 25. he that loveth his life shall *l.* it
2 John 8. look to yourselves, we *l.* not those things

LOSETH.

Mat. 10. 39. and he that *l.* his life for my sake

LOSS.

Gen. 31. 39. that which was torn, I bare the *l.* of it
Exod. 21. 19. only he shall pay for the *l.* of time
Isa. 47. 8. nor shall I know the *l.* of children
9. come in one day *l.* of children and widowhood
Acts 27. 21. and have gained this harm and *l.*
22. there shall be no *l.* of any man's life
1 Cor. 3. 15. if work be burned he shall suffer *l.*
Phil. 3. 7. what gain, those I counted *l.* for Christ
8. yea, doubtless, and I count all things but *l.* for
Christ, for whom I suffered the *l.* of all things

LOST, *Passively.*

Exod. 22. 9. for any manner of *l.* thing, Deut. 22. 3.
Lev. 6. 3. or have found that which was *l.*
4. he shall restore the *l.* thing he found
Num. 6. 12. the days that were before shall be *l.*
1 Sam. 9. 3. the asses of Kish, Saul's father, were *l.*
20. as for thine asses that were *l.* they are found
Psal. 119. 176. I have gone astray like a *l.* sheep
Jer. 50. 6. my people hath been *l.* sheep, shepherds
Ezek. 19. 5. when she saw that her hope was *l.*
34. 4. nor have ye sought that which was *l.*
16. I will seek that which was *l.* and bring again
37. 11. they say, our hope is *l.* we are cut off
Mat. 10. 6. but go rather to the *l.* sheep of Israel
15. 24. I am not sent but to the *l.* sheep of Israel
18. 11. Son is come to save what was *l.* Luke 19. 10.
Luke 15. 4. go after that which is *l.* till he find it
6. for I have found my sheep which was *l.*
24. this my son was *l.* || 32. thy brother was *l.*
John 6. 12. gather up fragments that nothing be *l.*
17. 12. none of them is *l.* but the son of perdition
2 Cor. 4. 3. our gospel is hid, to them that are *l.*

LOST, *Actively.*

Deut. 22. 3. with any thing of thy brother's he hath *l.*
1 Kings 20. 25. number army like that thou hast *l.*
Isa. 49. 20. after thou hast *l.* the other shall say
21. seeing I have *l.* my children, and am desolate
Mat. 5. 13. if salt *l.* savour, Mark 9. 50. Luke 14. 34.
Luke 15. 9. I have found the piece which I had *l.*
John 18. 9. of them thou gavest me, I have *l.* none

LOT

Signifies, [1] *Any thing cast or drawn in order to determine any matter in debate,* Prov. 18. 18. [2] *That which falls out by lot to be one's proper share, portion, or inheritance,* Josh. 15. 1. | 16. 1. [3] *Habitations or persons,* Psal. 125. 3. [4] *Punishment,* Isa. 17. 14. [5] *Order, course, or turn,* Luke 1. 9. [6] *Fellowship,* Acts 8. 21. [7] *The object of one's worship and trust,* Isa. 57. 6. Lots were used, [1] *To find out a person,* 1 Sam. 14. 41. Jonah 1. 7. [2] *To divide lands,* Num. 26. 55, 56. [3] *To choose a church officer,* Acts 1. 26. [4] *To order and regulate the courses of men in office,* 1 Chron. 24. 5. | 25. 8. [5] *To decide a controversy,* Psal. 22. 18.

Lev. 16. 8. one *l.* for Ld. other for scape-goat, 9, 10.
Num. 26. 55. land shall be divid. by *l.* Ezek. 48. 29.
33. 54. he shall divide the land by *l.* for an inheritance, 36. 2. Josh. 13. 6. Ezek. 47. 22.
34. 13. this is the land ye shall inherit by *l.*
Deut. 32. 9. Jacob is the *l.* of his inheritance
Josh. 15. 1. this was the *l.* of the tribe of Judah
16. 1. the *l.* of Joseph || 17. 1. was a *l.* for Manasseh
17. 14. why hast thou given me but one *l.*?
17. thou shalt not have one *l.* only, but mountain
18. 11. the *l.* of the tribe of Benjamin came up
19. 1. and the second *l.* came forth to Simeon
10. the third *l.* came for the children of Zebulun
17. the fourth *l.* came out to Issachar
24. fifth *l.* to Asher || 32. sixth *l.* to Naphtali
40. the seventh *l.* came for the tribe of Dan
21. 4. *l.* for families of Kohathites, 1 Chron. 6. 54.
6. Gershon had by *l.* || 8. gave by *l.* to the Levites
Judg. 1. 3. come up with me into my *l.* to fight aga.
Canaanites, likewise go with thee into thy *l.*
20. 9. we will go up by *l.* aga. it, and take ten men
1 Sam. 14. 41. Saul said to God, give a perfect *l.*
1 Chron. 6. 63. to sons of Merari were given by *l.*
16. 18. to thee will I give the land of Canaan, the
l. of your inheritance, Psal. 105. 11.
24. 5. to thee they were divided by *l.* one sort with
7. now the first *l.* came forth to Jehoiarib
25. 9. now the first *l.* came forth for Asaph
Esth. 3. 7. they cast Pur, that is *l.* before Haman
Psal. 16. 5. portion of cup, thou maintainest my *l.*
125. 3. shall not rest on the *l.* of the righteous
Prov. 1. 14. cast in thy *l.* among us, let us all have
16. 33. *l.* is cast into lap, disposing of the Lord
18. 18. the *l.* causeth contentions to cease
Isa. 17. 14. this is the *l.* of them that rob us
34. 17. and he hath cast the *l.* for them
57. 6. the smooth stones of the stream are thy *l.*
Jer. 13. 25. this is thy *l.* from me, saith the Lord
Ezek. 24. 6. bring it out, let no *l.* fall upon it
Dan. 12. 13. shalt stand in thy *l.* at end of the days
Mic. 2. 5. shalt have none that shall cast a cord by *l.*
Luke 1. 9. his *l.* was to burn incense when he went
Acts 1. 26. the *l.* fell on Matthias, was numbered
8. 21. thou hast no *l.* or part in this matter
13. 19. he divided their land to them by *l.*

LOTS.

1 Sam. 14. 42. cast *l.* between me and Jonath. my son
1 Chron. 24. 31. these cast *l.* over against brethren
Mat. 27. 35. parted garments casting *l.* Mark 15. 24.
Acts 1. 26. gave forth their *l.* lot fell on Matthias
See Cast.

LOTHE.

Exod. 7. 18. Egypt shall *l.* to drink of the river
Job 7. 16. I *l.* it, I would not live alway
Ezek. 6. 9. shall *l.* themselves for evils have done
20. 43. ye shall *l.* yourselves in your own sight
36. 31. ye shall *l.* yourselves for your iniquities

LOTHED.

Jer. 14. 19. hath thy soul *l.* Zion? why hast thou
Zech. 11. 8. my soul *l.* them, their soul abhorred me

LOTHETH.

Num. 21. 5. and our soul *l.* this light bread
Prov. 27. 7. the full soul *l.* an honey-comb
Ezek. 16. 45. *l.* her husband and her children

LOTHING.

Ezek. 16. 5. thou wast cast out to the *l.* of thy person

LOTHSOME.

Num. 11. 20. even a whole month, till it be *l.* to you
Job 7. 5. my skin is broken and become *l.*
Psal. 38. 7. my loins are filled with a *l.* disease
Prov. 13. 5. a wicked man is *l.* and cometh to shame

LOUD.

2 Chron. 30. 21. singing with *l.* instruments to Lord
Ezra 3. 13. the people shouted with a *l.* shout
Neh. 12. 42. the singers sang *l.* with Jezrahiah
Esth. 4. 1. and Mordecai cried with a *l.* cry
Psal. 33. 3. sing to him, play skilfully with a *l.* noise
98. 4. make a *l.* noise and rejoice and sing praise
150. 5. praise him on *l.* cymbals, praise him
Prov. 7. 11. she is *l.* and stubborn, her feet abide not
Rev. 14. 18. another angel cried with a *l.* cry to him

LOUD, joined with *voice.*

Gen. 39. 14. he came to me, I cried with a *l. voice*
Exod. 19. 16. the *voice* of the trumpet exceeding *l.*
Deut. 27. 14. the Levites shall speak with a *l. voice*
2 Sam. 15. 23. all the country wept with a *l. voice*
1 Kings 8. 55. he blessed congregation with a *l. voice*
2 Chron. 15. 14. they sware to the Ld. with a *l. voice*
20. 19. to praise Lord with a *l. voice,* Luke 19. 37.
Ezra 3. 12. many wept with a *l. voice,* many shouted
10. 12. the congregation answered with a *l. voice*
Prov. 27. 14. he blesseth his friend with a *l. voice*
Ezek. 8. 18. and though they cry with a *l. voice*
9. 1. he cried with a *l. voice,* saying, cause them
Luke 1. 42. she spake out with a *l. voice,* and said
8. 28. unclean spirit cried with a *l. voice,* Acts 8. 7.
17. 15. turned back and with a *l. v.* glorified God
Acts 14. 10. said with a *l. voice* stand upright on feet
26. 24. Festus said with a *l. v.* Paul, thou art beside
Rev. 5. 2. a strong angel proclaiming with a *l. voice*
12. many angels saying with a *l. voice,* worthy is
8. 13. angel saying with a *l. v.* woe, woe, 14. 7, 9, 15.
12. 10. and I heard a *l. voice* saying in heaven

LOUD *voices.*

Luke 23. 23. and they were instant with *l. voices*

LOUDER.

Exod. 19. 19. the voice of the trumpet waxed *l.* and *l.*

LOVE

Signifies, [1] *A natural passion, inclining us to delight in an object,* Gen. 29. 20. [2] *A gracious principle or habit wrought in the soul by God, which inclines us to delight in, esteem, and earnestly desire to enjoy an interest in God's favour, and communion with him as our chief good, portion, and happiness, and the fountain of all perfection and excellency; and which likewise disposes us to do good to all, especially to such as resemble God in holiness, and bear his image,* 1 John 4. 19, 21. [3] *The effect of love,* John 15. 13. [4] *The person beloved,* Cant. 2. 2, 7. [5] *True friendship or kindness,* Prov. 15. 17. Love is, (I) Natural, *which is either, lawful,* Psal. 34. 12. *or unlawful,* John 12. 25. 2 Tim. 3. 2. (II) Conjugal, *which is,* [1] Divine, *that is God's love to his people, which is inexpressible,* John 3. 16. *Inconceivable,* Eph. 3. 19. *Everlasting,* Jer. 31. 3. *Sovereign,* Deut. 7. 8. *Free and undeserved,* Hos. 14. 4. *Immutable,* John 13. 1. *Complacential,* Prov. 8. 31. *Boundless and infinite,* 1 John 4. 16. [2] Human, *such is that between a husband and wife lawfully joined in wedlock,* Gen. 24. 67. Eph. 5. 25. [3] Idolatrous, *such is that love which idolaters have for idols and strange gods,* Jer. 2. 25. | 8. 2. (III) Parental and filial, Gen. 22. 2. | 44. 20. | 45. 11. (IV) Spiritual, as, [1] *The love of God towards his children,* John 17. 23. Rom. 5. 5, 8. [2] *Their love to God,* Psal. 116. 1. 1 John 4. 19. [3] *Of Christ, to his church,* Eph. 3. 19. | 5. 2. [4] *To some particular persons,* John 2. 2. Gal. 2. 20. [5] *The love of believers towards Christ,* Cant. 1. 4, 7. John 21. 15. [6] *To one another,* John 15. 17. Col. 1. 4. [7] *Of pastors towards their people,*

1 *Cor.* 16. 24. 2 *Cor.* 2. 4. [8] *Of hearers to their teachers*, 2 Cor. 8. 7, 8. 1 Thess. 5. 13. Tit. 3. 15. (V.) *Carnal*, 2 Sam. 13. 4. Prov. 7. 18. (VI.) *Wicked*, 2 Chron. 19. 2. Rev. 22. 15.
Gen. 29. 20. a few days for the *l.* he had to her
1 *Sam.* 20. + 17. to swear by his *l.* towards him
2 *Sam.* 1. 26. wonderful, passing the *l.* of women
13. 15. the hatred was greater than the *l.* he had
Prov. 5. 19. be thou ravished always with her *l.*
7. 18. let us take our fill of *l.* till the morning
10. 12. hatred stirreth up strifes, but *l.* covereth sins
15. 17. better is a dinner of herbs where *l.* is, than
17. 9. he that covereth a transgression seeketh *l.*
27. 5. open rebuke is better than secret *l.*
Eccl. 9. 1. no man knoweth either *l.* or hatred
6. also their *l.* and hatred is now perished
Cant. 2. 4. and his banner over me was *l.*
5. comfort me with apples, for I am sick of *l.* 5. 8.
3. 10. the midst thereof being paved with *l.*
7. 6. how pleasant art thou, O *l.* for delights!
8. 6. *l.* is strong as death, jealousy is cruel as grave
7. many waters cannot quench *l.* if a man would give all his subs. for *l.* it would be contemned
Jer. 2. 2. I remember thee, the *l.* of thy espousals
33. why trimmest thou thy way to seek *l.*?
12. + 7. I have given the *l.* of my soul to enemy
31. 3. I have loved thee with an everlasting *l.*
Ezek. 16. 8. behold, thy time was the time of *l.*
23. 11. she was more corrupt in her inordinate *l.*
17. the Babylonians came to her into bed of *l.*
33. 31. with their mouth they shew much *l.*
Dan. 1. 9. brought Daniel into tender *l.* with prince
Hos. 3. 1. according to the *l.* of Lord toward Israel
11. 4. I drew them with bands of *l.* and cords
Mat. 24. 12. the *l.* of many shall wax cold
John 13. 35. if ye have *l.* one to another
15. 13. greater *l.* hath no man than this, that he lay
17. 26. the *l.* wherewith thou hast loved me
Rom. 8. 35. who shall separate us from *l.* of Christ?
12. 9. let *l.* be without dissimulation
10. be kindly affectioned with brotherly *l.*
13. 10. *l.* worketh no ill, therefore *l.* is fulfilling
15. 30. I beseech you for the *l.* of the Spirit
2 *Cor.* 2. 4. that you may know the *l.* I have to you
8. that ye would confirm your *l.* toward him
5. 14. for the *l.* of Christ constraineth us
6. 6. by the Holy Ghost, by *l.* unfeigned
8. 8. and to prove the sincerity of your *l.*
24. shew to the churches the proof of your *l.*
13. 11. and the God of *l.* shall be with you
Gal. 5. 6. but faith which worketh by *l.*
13. but brethren, by *l.* serve one another
22. but the fruit of the Spirit is *l.* joy, peace
Eph. 1. 15. after I heard of your *l.* to all the saints
3. 19. to know the *l.* of Christ, passeth knowledge
6. 23. and *l.* with faith, from God the Father
Phil. 1. 9. this I pray, that your *l.* may abound
17. but the other of *l.* doth preach Christ
2. 1. if there be therefore any comfort of *l.*
2. that ye be like-minded, having the same *l.*
Col. 1. 4. and of the *l.* which ye have to all the saints
8. who declared to us your *l.* in the Spirit
1 *Thess.* 1. 3. remembering your labour of *l.*
4. 9. touching brotherly *l.* ye need not that I write
5. 8. putting on breast-plate of faith and *l.*
2 *Thess.* 2. 10. they received not the *l.* of the truth
1 *Tim.* 1. 14. exceeding abundant with faith and *l.*
6. 10. the *l.* of money is the root of all evil
11. follow after righteousness, *l.* patience
2 *Tim.* 1. 7. not given the spirit of fear, but of *l.*
Philem. 9. yet for *l.* sake I rather beseech thee
Heb. 6. 10. to forget your work and labour of *l.*
10. 24. to provoke unto *l.* and to good works
13. 1. let brotherly *l.* continue, entertain strangers
1 *Pet.* 1. 22. to unfeigned *l.* of the brethren
1 *John* 2. 15. the *l.* of the Father is not in him
3. 1. behold what manner of *l.* the Father hath
4. 7. let us love one another, for *l.* is of God
8. God is *l.* ‖ 10. herein is *l.* not that we loved God
16. known the *l.* that God hath to us, God is *l.*
17. herein is our *l.* made perfect, to have boldness
18. there is no fear in *l.* perfect *l.* casteth out fear
2 *John* 6. this is *l.* that we walk after his commandm.
Jude 2. mercy to you, and peace and *l.* be multiplied
Rev. 2. 4. because thou hast left thy first *l.*

LOVE *of God.*

Luke 11. 42. ye pass over judgment and the *l. of God*
John 5. 42. I know that ye have not *l. of God* in you
Rom. 5. 5. because *l. of G.* is shed abroad in our hearts
8. 39. shall be able to separate us from the *l. of God*
2 *Cor.* 13. 14. the *l. of G.* be with you all, amen
2 *Thess.* 3. 5. direct your hearts into the *l. of God*
Tit. 3. 4. after the kindness and *l. of God* appeared
1 *John* 2. 5. in him verily is the *l. of God* perfected
3. 16. hereby perceive we *l. of G.* because he laid
17. how dwelleth the *l. of God* in him?
4. 9. in this was manifested the *l. of God* towards us
5. 3. this is *l. of God* that we keep his commandm.
Jude 21. keep yourselves in the *l. of God*, looking for

His LOVE.

Deut. 7. 7. Lord did not set *his l.* upon you, because
Psal. 91. 14. because he hath set *his l.* upon me
Isa. 63. 9. in *his l.* and in his pity he redeemed them
Zeph. 3. 17. he will rest in *his l.* he will joy over
John 15. 10. I kept commandments, and abide in *h. l*
Rom. 5. 8. but God commended *his l.* toward us
1 *John* 4. 12. if love one another *his l.* is perfected

In LOVE.

1 *Kings* 11. 2. Solomon clave unto these *in l.*
Isa. 38. 17. hast *in l.* to my soul delivered it from pit
1 *Cor.* 4. 21. shall I come to you with a rod or *in l.*?
2 *Cor.* 8. 7. as ye abound *in* your *l.* to us, see that
Eph. 1. 4. we should be without blame before him *in l.*
3. 17. that ye being rooted and grounded *in l.*
4. 2. in meekness, forbearing one another *in l.*
15. but speaking the truth *in l.* may grow up to
16. maketh increase to the edifying of itself *in l.*
5. 2. walk *in l.* as Christ hath loved us and given
Col. 2. 2. hearts be comforted, being knit together *in l.*
1 *Thess.* 3. 12. the Lord make you to increase *in l.*
5. 13. esteem them highly *in l.* for work's sake

2 *Tim.* 1. 13. *in* faith and *l.* which is in Christ Jesus
1 *John* 4. 16. he that dwelleth *in l.* dwelleth in God
18. no fear *in l.* that feareth not made perfect *in l.*
2 *John* 3. Jesus the Son of the Father in truth and *l.*

My LOVE.

Psal. 109. 4. for *my l.* they are my adversaries
5. they have rewarded me hatred for *my l.*
Cant. 1. 9. I have compared thee, O *my l.* to horses
15. behold, thou art fair, *my l.* thou art fair, 4. 1.
2. 2. as lily, so is *my l.* among the daughters
7. nor awake *my l.* till he please, 3. 5. | 8. 4.
10. rise up, *m. l.* 13. ‖ 5. 2. open to me, *m. l.* my dove
4. 7. art all fair, *my l.* there is no spot in thee
6. 4. thou art beautiful, O *my l.* as Tirzah
John 15. 9. continue ye in *my l.* ‖ 10. abide in *my l.*
1 *Cor.* 16. 24. *my l.* be with you all, in Christ Jesus

Thy LOVE.

2 *Sam.* 1. 26. *thy l.* was wonderful, passing the love
Cant. 1. 2. for *thy l.* is better than wine, 4. 10.
4. we will remember *thy l.* more than wine
4. 10. how fair is *thy l.* my sister, my spouse
Philem. 5. hearing of *thy l.* and faith towards Jesus
7. we have great joy and consolation in *thy l.*
Rev. 2. 4. because thou hast left *thy* first *l.*

LOVE, *Verb.*

Lev. 19. 18. thou shalt *l.* thy neighbour as thyself, 34. *Mat.* 19. 19. | 22. 39. *Mark* 12. 31.
Deut. 6. 5. thou shalt *l.* the Lord thy God with all thy heart, 10. 12. | 11. 1, 13, 22. | 19. 9. | 30. 6.
7. 9. he is God, the faithful God, which keepeth covenant with them that *l.* him, *Dan.* 9. 4.
13. he will *l.* thee, bless thee, and multiply thee
10. 15. Lord had a delight in thy fathers to *l.* them
19. *l.* therefore the stranger, for ye were strangers
13. 3. to know whether ye *l.* the Lord your God
30. 16. in that I command thee to *l.* Lord thy God
20. that thou mayest *l.* the L. and obey his voice
Josh. 22. 5. take heed to *l.* the L. your God, 23. 11.
Judg. 5. 31. let them that *l.* him be as the sun
1 *Sam.* 18. 22. and all the king's servants *l.* thee
2 *Chr.* 19. 2. shouldest thou *l.* them that hate Lord?
Neh. 1. 5. God keepeth mercy for them that *l.* him
Psal. 4. 2. O ye sons, how long will ye *l.* vanity?
5. 11. let them that *l.* thy name be joyful in thee
18. 1. I will *l.* thee, O Lord, my strength
31. 23. O *l.* the Lord, all ye saints, Lord preserves
40. 16. let such as *l.* thy salvation say, 70. 4.
69. 36. they that *l.* his name shall dwell there
97. 10. ye that *l.* the Lord hate evil, he preserves
119. 132. usest to do to those that *l.* thy name
165. great peace have they who *l.* thy law
122. 6. they shall prosper that *l.* thee
145. 20. the Lord preserveth them that *l.* him
Prov. 1. 22. how long, ye simple, will ye *l.* simplicity
4. 6. *l.* wisdom, and she shall keep thee
8. 36. all they that hate me, *l.* death
9. 8. rebuke a wise man, and he will *l.* thee
16. 13. kings *l.* him that speaketh right
18. 21. they that *l.* it shall eat the fruit thereof
Eccl. 3. 8. a time to *l.* and a time to hate
Cant. 1. 3. therefore do the virgins *l.* thee
4. thy love more than wine, the upright *l.* thee
Isa. 56. 6. to serve and *l.* the name of the Lord
61. 8. I the Lord *l.* judgment, I hate robbery
66. 10. be glad with Jerusalem all ye that *l.* her
Jer. 5. 31. and my people *l.* to have it so
Hos. 3. 1. *l.* a woman beloved, *l.* flagons of wine
4. 18. her rulers with shame, do *l.* give ye
9. 15. drive them out, I will *l.* them no more
14. 4. I will *l.* them freely, for mine anger turned
Amos 4. + 5. publish ye free-offerings, so ye *l.*
5. 15. hate the evil, and *l.* the good, establish
Mic. 3. 2. who hate the good, and *l.* the evil
6. 8. but to *l.* mercy, and to walk humbly
Zech. 8. 17. *l.* no false oath ‖ 19. *l.* the truth
Mat. 5. 43. it hath been said, *l.* thy neighbour
44. but I say, *l.* your enemies, *Luke* 6. 27, 35.
46. if ye *l.* them which *l.* you, *Luke* 6. 32.
6. 5. they *l.* to pray standing in the synagogues
24. hate the one, and *l.* the other, *Luke* 16. 13.
22. 37. thou shalt *l.* the Lord thy God with all thy heart, *Mark* 12. 30, 33. *Luke* 10. 27.
23. 6. and *l.* the uppermost rooms at feasts
Mark 12. 38. scribes who *l.* to go in long clothing
Luke 7. 42. which of them will *l.* him most?
11. 43. ye *l.* greetings in the markets, 20. 46.
John 14. 21. I will *l.* him, and manifest myself
23. if a man *l.* me, my Father will *l.* him
15. 12. commandment that ye *l.* one another, 17.
19. if were of world, the world would *l.* his own
Rom. 8. 28. all things work for good to them *l.* God
13. 8. owe nothing to any, but to *l.* one another
9. in this saying, thou shalt *l.* thy neighbour as thyself, *Gal.* 5. 14. *Jam.* 2. 8.
1 *Cor.* 2. 9. God hath prepared for them that *l.* him
8. 3. if any man *l.* God, the same is known of him
Eph. 5. 25. husb. *l.* your wives as Christ loved the church, and gave himself, 28, 33. *Col.* 3. 19.
6. 24. grace be with all them that *l.* our Lord Jesus
1 *Thess.* 4. 9. ye are taught of God to *l.* one another
2 *Tim.* 4. 8. but to all them that *l.* his appearing
Tit. 2. 4. teach young women to *l.* their husbands
3. 15. greet them that *l.* us in the faith
Jam. 1. 12. Lord promised to them that *l.* him, 2. 5.
1 *Pet.* 1. 8. whom having not seen ye *l.* in whom
22. see ye *l.* one another with a pure heart
2. 17. honour all men, *l.* the brotherhood
3. 8. *l.* as brethren ‖ 10. he that will *l.* life
1 *John* 2. 15. *l.* not the world, if any man *l.* the world
3. 11. message ye heard from the beginning that we should *l.* one another, 4. 7, 11. 2 *John* 5.
14. from death to life, because we *l.* the brethren
23. *l.* one another, as he gave commandment
4. 12. if we *l.* one another, God dwelleth in us
19. we *l.* him, because first loved us
20. how can he *l.* God whom he hath not seen?
21 he who loveth God, *l.* his brother also
5. 2. we *l.* the children of God when we *l.* God

I LOVE.

Gen. 27. 4. make me savoury meat, such as I *l.*
Exod. 21. 5. if servant shall say, *I l.* my master
Judg. 16. 15. how canst thou say, *I l.* thee, when

2 *Sam.* 13. 4. *I l.* Tamar my brother Absalom's sister
Psal. 116. 1. *I l.* the Lord, because he hath heard
119. 97. O how *I l.* thy law ‖ 113. thy law *I l.* 163
119. therefore *I l.* thy testimonies
127. therefore *I l.* thy commands above gold
159. consider how *I l.* thy precepts, quicken me
167. thy testimonies *I. l.* exceedingly
Prov. 8. 17. *I l.* them that love me, and those that
John 14. 31. world may know that *I l.* the Father
21. 15. Lord, thou knowest that *I l.* thee, 16, 17.
2 *Cor.* 12. 15. though the more *I l.* you, the less I be
1 *John* 4. 20. if a man say, *I l.* God, and hateth
2 *John* 1. whom *I l.* in the truth, 3 *John* 1.
Rev. 3. 19. as many as *I l.* I rebuke and chasten

LOVE *me.*

Gen. 29. 32. now therefore my husband will *l. me*
Exod. 20. 6. shewing mercy to them *l. me*, *Deut.* 5. 10.
Prov. 8. 17. I love them that *l. me*, and those that seek
21. cause those that *l. me* to inherit substance
John 8. 42. if God were your Father you would *l. me*
10. 17. therefore doth my Father *l. me*, because
14. 15. if ye *l. me*, keep my commandments
23. if a man *l. me*, he will keep my words

LOVE *not.*

Prov. 20. 13. *l. not* sleep, lest thou come to poverty
1 *Cor.* 16. 22. if any man *l. not* the L. Jesus Christ
2 *Cor.* 11. 11. because I *l.* you *not*? God knoweth
1 *John* 2. 15. *l. not* the world ‖ 3. 18. let us *not l.* in word

LOVED.

Gen. 24. 67. Isaac took Rebekah to wife, and *l.* her
25. 28. Isaac *l.* Esau, but Rebekah *l.* Jacob
27. 14. his mother made such as his father *l.*
29. 18. Jacob *l.* Rachel more than Leah, 30.
34. 3. Shechem *l.* Dinah, and spake kindly to her
37. 3. Isr. *l.* Joseph more than all his children, 4.
Deut. 4. 37. and because he *l.* thy fathers, therefore
7. 8. but because the Lord *l.* you, 23. 5. | 33. 3.
Judg. 16. 4. Samson *l.* a wom. in the valley of Sorek
1 *Sam.* 1. 5. Elkanah *l.* Hannah ‖ 16. 21. Saul *l.* Dav.
18. 1. Jonathan *l.* Dav. as his own soul, 3. | 20. 17.
16. Israel and Judah *l.* David, because he went
20. and Michal, Saul's daughter, *l.* David
2 *Sam.* 12. 24. Lord *l.* Solomon, and he sent Nathan
13. 1. Amnon, the son of David, *l.* Tamar
15. hatred greater than love wherewith he *l.* her
1 *Kings* 3. 3. Solomon *l.* the L. walking in statutes
10. 9. because the Lord *l.* Israel, 2 *Chron.* 9. 8.
11. 1. king Solomon *l.* many strange women
2 *Chron.* 2. 11. the Lord *l.* his people, *Isa.* 48. 14.
11. 21. Rehoboam *l.* Maacah above all his wives
26. 10. Uzziah had husbandmen, he *l.* husbandry
Esth. 2. 17. the king *l.* Esther above all the women
Job 19. 19. they whom I *l.* are turned against me
Psal. 47. 4. the excellency of Jacob whom he *l.*
78. 68. but chose the mount Zion which he *l.*
109. 17. as he *l.* cursing, so let it come to him
Isa. 38. + 17. but thou hast *l.* me from the pit
Jer. 8. 2. all the host of heaven whom they have *l.*
14. 10. thus have they *l.* to wander, they have not
Ezek. 16. 37. I will gather all them that thou hast *l.*
Hos. 9. 1. thou hast *l.* a reward on every corn-floor
10. their abominations were according as they *l.*
11. 1. when Israel was a child, then I *l.* him
Mal. 1. 2. yet ye say, wherein hast thou *l.* us?
2. 11. Judah profaned holiness of Lord which he *l.*
Mark 10. 21. then Jesus beholding him, *l.* him
Luke 7. 47. many sins are forgiven, for she *l.* much
John 3. 16. God so *l.* the world ‖ 19. *l.* darkness
11. 5. Jesus *l.* Martha, and her sister, and Lazarus
36. then said the Jews, behold how he *l.* him
12. 43. for they *l.* praise of men more than praise
13. 1. having *l.* his own, he *l.* them to the end
23. disciple whom Jesus *l.* 19. 26. | 20. 2. | 21. 7, 20.
14. 21. he that loveth me shall be *l.* of my Father
28. if ye *l.* me, ye would rejoice, because I go to my
15. 9. as the Father *l.* me, so have I *l.* you
16. 27. Father himself loveth you, because ye *l.* me
17. 23. and hast *l.* them, as thou hast *l.* me
26. love wherewith thou hast *l.* me, may be in them
Rom. 8. 37. more than conquerors thro' him that *l.* us
2 *Cor.* 12. 15. the more I love you, the less I be *l.*
Gal. 2. 20. who *l.* me, and gave himself for me
Eph. 2. 4. for his great love wherewith he *l.* us
5. 2. as Christ also *l.* us ‖ 25. Christ *l.* the church
2 *Thess.* 2. 16. God our Father, which hath *l.* us
2 *Tim.* 4. 10. Demas having *l.* this present world
Heb. 1. 9. hast *l.* righteousness, and hated iniquity
2 *Pet.* 2. 15. Balaam *l.* the wages of unrighteousness
1 *John* 4. 10. not that we *l.* God, but that he *l.* us
11. if God so *l.* us ‖ 19. because he first *l.* us
Rev. 1. 5. to him that *l.* us and washed us from sins
12. 11. they *l.* not their lives to the death

I have LOVED.

Psal. 26. 8. *I have l.* the habitation of thy house
119. 47. delight in thy commands which *I h. l.* 48.
Isa. 43. 4. *I have l.* thee, therefore will I give men
Jer. 2. 25. *I have l.* strangers, and after them will I go
31. 3. *I have l.* thee with an everlasting love
Mal. 1. 2. *I have l.* you, yet ye say, wherein hast thou
John 13. 34. as *I have l.* you, that ye also love, 15. 12.
15. 9. as the Father loved me, so *I have l.* you
Rom. 9. 13. as it is written, Jacob *I have l.* but Esau
Rev. 3. 9. I will make them know that *I have l.* thee

LOVEDST.

Isa. 57. 8. thou *l.* their bed where thou sawest it
John 17. 24. thou *l.* me before foundation of world

LOVELY.

2 *Sam.* 1. 23. Saul and Jonathan were *l.* in their lives
Cant. 5. 16. he is altogether *l.* O daughters of Jerusal.
Ezek. 33. 32. thou art to them as a very *l.* song
Phil. 4. 8. whatsoever things are *l.* think on these

LOVER.

1 *Kings* 5. 1. for Hiram was ever a *l.* of David
Psal. 88. 18. *l.* and friend hast thou put far from me
Tit. 1. 8. a *l.* of hospitality, a *l.* of good men, sober

LOVERS.

Psal. 38. 11. my *l.* and friends stand aloof from my
Jer. 3. 1. thou hast played the harlot with many *l.*
4. 30. thy *l.* will despise thee, they will seek thy life
22. 20. go up and cry, for all thy *l.* are destroyed
22. thy *l.* shall go into captivity, shalt be ashamed
30. 14. all thy *l.* have forgotten thee, they seek

Lam. 1. 2. among all her l. hath none to comfort her
19. I called for my l. but they deceived me
Ezek. 16. 33. thou givest thy gifts to all thy l.
36. thy nakedness discovered with thy l. and idols
37. I will gather thy l. || 23. 5. doted on her l.
23. 9. I have delivered her into the hand of her l.
22. behold, I will raise up thy l. against thee
Hos. 2. 5. I will go after my l. || 7. shall follow her l.
10. I will discover her lewdness in the sight of l.
12. these rewards that my l. have given me
13. and she went after her l. and forgat me
8. 9. are gone up to Assyria, Ephraim hath hired l.
2 Tim. 3. 2. for men shall be l. of their own selves
4. heady, l. of pleasures more than l. of God

LOVES.

Prov. 7. 18. come, let us solace ourselves with l.
Cant. 7. 12. there will I give thee my l.

LOVEST.

Gen. 22. 2. take thine only son Isaac whom thou l.
Judg. 14. 16. thou dost but hate me, and l. me not
2 Sam. 19. 6. in that thou l. thine enemies, and hatest
Psal. 45. 7. thou l. righteousness, therefore God thy
52. 3. thou l. evil more than good, and lying
4. thou l. all devouring words, O thou deceitful
Eccl. 9. 9. live joyfully with the wife whom thou l.
John 11. 3. behold, he whom thou l. is sick
21. 15. Simon, son of Jonas, l. thou me? 16. 17.

LOVETH.

Gen. 27. 9. make meat for thy father, such as he l.
44. 20. a child, a little one, and his father l. him
Deut. 10. 18. Lord l. the stranger in giving him food
15. 16. I will not go away because he l. thee
Ruth 4. 15. for thy daughter-in-law who l. thee
Psal. 11. 5. and him that l. violence his soul hateth
7. for the righteous Lord l. righteousness, 33. 5.
34. 12. what man is he that l. many days?
37. 28. for the Lord l. judgment, 99. 4.
87. 2. the Ld. l. gates of Zion more than dwellings
119. 140. word is very pure, therefore thy serv. l.
146. 8. Lord openeth the eyes, Ld. l. the righteous
Prov. 3. 12. for whom the Lord l. he correcteth
12. 1. whoso l. instruction, l. knowledge
13. 24. but he that l. him, chasteneth him betimes
15. 9. he l. him that followeth after righteousness
12. a scorner l. not one that reproveth him
17. 17. a friend l. at all times, and a brother is born
19. l. transgression that l. strife, he that exalteth
19. 8. he that getteth wisdom l. his own soul
21. 17. he that l. pleasure, he that l. wine and oil
22. 11. he that l. pureness of heart, the king his
29. 3. whoso l. wisdom rejoiceth his father
Eccl. 5. 10. he that l. silver, he that l. abundance
Cant. 1. 7. tell me, O thou whom my soul l. where
3. 1. by night on my bed I sought him whom soul l.
2. I will arise and seek him whom my soul l.
3. to whom I said, saw ye him whom my soul l.?
4. I found him whom my soul l. I held him
Isa. 1. 23. every one l. gifts and follows after rewards
Hos. 10. 11. Ephraim as heifer l. to tread out corn
12. 7. he is a merchant, he l. to oppress
Mat. 10. 37. that l. father or mother, he that l. son
Luke 7. 5. he l. our nation || 47. the same l. little
John 3. 35. the Father l. the Son, hath given, 5. 20.
12. 25. he that l. his life shall lose it
14. 21. that hath my commandments, he it is that l.
me, and he that l. me shall be loved of my Fath.
24. he that l. me not, keepeth not my sayings
16. 27. the Father himself l. you, because loved me
Rom. 13. 8. he that l. another hath fulfilled the law
2 Cor. 9. 7. or of necessity, for G. l. a cheerful giver
Eph. 5. 28. he that l. his wife, l. himself
Heb. 12. 6. for whom the Lord l. he chasteneth
1 John 2. 10. he that l. his brother, abideth in light
3. 10. he that l. not his brother, is not of God
14. l. not his brother, abideth in death, 4. 8, 20.
4. 7. every one that l. is born of God, and knows G.
21. that he who l. God, l. his brother also
5. 1. that l. him that begat, l. him that is begotten
3 John 9. Diotrephes l. to have the pre-eminence
Rev. 22. 15. and whosoever l. and maketh a lie

LOVING.

2 Sam. 19. † 6. by l. thine enemies, hating friends
Prov. 5. 19. let her be as the l. hind and pleasant roe
22. 1. and l. favour rather than silver and gold
Isa. 56. 10. sleeping, lying down, l. to slumber
See KINDNESS, KINDNESSES.

LOW.

Deut. 28. 43. and thou shalt come down very l.
Judg. 1. † 9. the Canaanite that dwelt in l. countries
1 Sam. 2. 7. the Lord bringeth l. and lifteth up
2 Chron. 9. 27. as sycamore-trees in the l. plains
26. 10. Uzziah had much cattle in the l. country
28. 18. Philistines invaded cities of the l. country
Job 5. 11. to set up on high those that be l.
22. † 29. he shall save him that hath l. eyes
40. 12. look on every one proud, and bring him l.
Psal. 49. 2. both high and l. rich and poor together
62. 9. surely men of l. degree are vanity
136. 23. who remembered us in our l. estate
Prov. 29. 23. a man's pride shall bring him l.
Eccl. 10. 6. and the rich sit in l. place
12. 4. when the sound of the grinding is l.
Isa. 13. 11. I will lay l. the haughtiness of terrible
25. 12. the high fort of thy walls shall he lay l.
26. 5. the lofty city he layeth it l. to the ground
29. 4. thy speech shall be l. out of the dust
32. 19. and the city shall be l. in a l. place
Lam. 3. 55. I called on thy name out of l. dungeon
Ezek. 17. 6. it became a spreading vine of l. stature
24. trees shall know that I have exalted the l. tree
21. 26. exalt him that is l. abase him that is high
26. 20. shall set thee in the l. parts of the earth
29. † 14. and they shall be there a l. kingdom
Luke 1. 48. he regarded l. estate of his handmaiden
52. he hath exalted them of l. degree
Rom. 12. 16. but condescend to men of l. estate
Jam. 1. 9. let the brother of l. degree rejoice
10. but the rich in that he is made l.
See BROUGHT.

LOWER parts of the earth

Signify, [1] *The valleys*, Isa. 44. 23. [2] *The state of the dead*, Psal. 63. 9. [3] *The mother's womb*, Psal. 139. 15. [4] *The earth, as the lowest part of the visible world, or the grave and state of the dead*, Eph. 4. 9.

LOWER.

Gen. 6. 16. with l. second and third stories make ark
Lev. 13. 20. if rising be in sight l. than the skin
21. and if it be no l. than the skin, 26.
Neh. 4. 13. therefore I set in the l. places the people
Job 12. † 3. I fall not l. than you
Psal. 8. 5. made him little l. than angels, Heb. 2. 7, 9.
63. 9. shall go into the l. parts of the earth
Prov. 25. 7. shouldest be put l. in presence of prince
Isa. 22. 9. ye gathered the waters of the l. pool
44. 23. sing, O heavens, shout ye l. parts of earth
Ezek. 43. 14. from the bottom even to the l. settle
Eph. 4. 9. that he descended first into the l. parts

LOWEST.

Deut. 32. 22. and shall burn to the l. hell.
1 Kings 12. 31. made priests l. 13. 33. 2 Kings 17. 32.
Psal. 86. 13. hast delivered my soul from the l. hell
88. 6. thou hast laid me in the l. pit, in darkness
139. 15. curiously wrought in the l. parts of earth
Ezek. 41. 7. and so increased from the l. chamber
42. 6. the building was straitened more than the l.
Luke 14. 9. thou begin with shame to take l. room
10. but go and sit down in the l. room

LOWETH.

Job 6. 5. wild ass bray, or l. the ox over his fodder?

LOWING.

1 Sam. 6. 12. the kine went along the high-way l.
15. 14. what meaneth then the l. of the oxen?

LOWLY.

Psal. 138. 6. Lord high, yet hath he respect to l.
Prov. 3. 34. the scorners, but he giveth grace to l.
11. 2. then cometh shame, but with l. is wisdom
16. 19. better to be of humble spirit with the l.
Zech. 9. 9. he is just, l. and riding on an ass
Mat. 11. 29. learn of me, for I am meek and l.

LOWLINESS.

Eph. 4. 2. that ye walk with all l. and meekness
Phil. 2. 3. but in l. of mind, let each esteem other

LOWRING.

Mat. 16. 3. foul weather, for the sky is red and l.

LUCRE.

1 Sam. 8. 3. Samuel's sons turned after l. took bribes
1 Tim. 3. 3. a bishop not greedy of filthy l. 8.
Tit. 1. 7. a bishop must not be given to filthy l.
11. teaching things they ought not for filthy l.
1 Pet. 5. 2. feed flock not for filthy l. but ready mind

LUKEWARM.

Rev. 3. 16. so then because thou art l.

LUMP.

2 Kings 20. 7. take a l. of figs and lay, Isa. 38. 21.
Rom. 9. 21. of the same l. one vessel to honour
11. 16. if the first fruit be holy the l. is holy
1 Cor. 5. 6. a little leaven leaveneth the l. Gal. 5. 9.
7. purge out old leaven, that ye may be a new l.

LUMPS.

1 Sam. 25. † 18. Abigail took 100 l. of raisins

LUNATIC.

Mat. 4. 24. and those which were l. he healed
17. 15. Lord have mercy on my son, for he is l.

LURK.

Prov. 1. 11. come, let us l. privily for the innocent
18. they l. privily for their own lives

LURKING.

1 Sam. 23. 23. take knowledge of all the l. places
Psal. 10. 8. he sitteth in the l. places of the villages
17. 12. as it were a young lion l. in secret places

LUST

Signifies, [1] *Concupiscence, or unlawful carnal passion and desire*, 1 Pet. 2. 11. 2 Pet. 2. 10. [2] *That original corruption which inclines man to sin and evil*, Jam. 1. 14, 15. 2 Pet. 1. 4. [3] *The desiring of lawful things to support and satisfy nature*, Deut. 12. 15, 20, 21. [4] *The coveting things forbidden*, 1 Cor. 10. 6. [5] *Corrupt and inordinate desires and affections*, 1 Pet. 4. 2.

The Spirit lusteth against the flesh, Gal. 5. 17. *The Spirit of God stirs up motions and desires in the saints contrary to those of the flesh, or unrenewed part in man, and inclines them to desire and endeavour the utter destruction of it.*

Exod. 15. 9. my l. shall be satisfied on them
Num. 11. † 4. the mixed multitude lusted a l.
† 34. he called the place the graves of l.
33. † 16. and they pitched at the grave of l.
Ps. 78. 18. tempted God by asking meat for their l.
30. they were not estranged from their l.
81. 12. I gave them up to their own hearts' l.
Rom. 1. 27. burned in their l. one toward another
7. 7. I had not known l. except the law had said
Gal. 5. 16. walk in Spirit, ye shall not fulfil l. of flesh
1 Thess. 4. 5. not in l. of concupiscence as Gentiles
Jam. 1. 14. tempted, when he is drawn of his own l.
15. when l. hath conceived, it bringeth forth sin
2 Pet. 1. 4. escaped corruption that is in world thro' l.
2. 10. that walk after flesh in the l. of uncleanness
1 John 2. 16. the l. of the flesh, the l. of the eye
17. the world passeth away, and the l. thereof

LUST, *Verb*.

Prov. 6. 25. l. not after her beauty in thy heart
Mat. 5. 28. whoso looketh on a woman to l. after her
1 Cor. 10. 6. not l. after evil things as they also lusted
Jam. 4. 2. ye l. and have not, ye kill and desire to

LUSTED.

Num. 11. 34. there they buried the people that l.
Ps. 106. 14. but they l. exceedingly in the wilderness
1 Cor. 10. 6. we should not lust as they also l.
Rev. 18. 14. fruits thy soul l. after are departed

LUSTETH.

Deut. 12. 15. what thy soul l. after, 20, 21. || 14. 26.
Gal. 5. 17. the flesh l. against the Spirit, and the Spi.
Jam. 4. 5. the spirit that dwelleth in us l. to envy

LUSTING.

Num. 11. 4. and the mixed multitude fell a l.

LUSTS.

Mark 4. 19. the l. of other things choke the word
John 8. 44. and the l. of your father ye will do
Rom. 1. 24. God gave them up to uncleanness thro' l.
6. 12. that you should obey it in the l. thereof
13. 14. make no provision for the flesh, to fulfil l.
Gal. 5. 24. that are Christ's have crucified flesh with l.
Eph. 2. 3. had our conversation in the l. of the flesh
4. 22. which is corrupt according to the deceitful l.
1 Tim. 6. 9. will be rich fall into foolish and hurtful l.
2 Tim. 2. 22. flee youthful l. but follow righteousn.
3. 6. lead captive silly women led away with l.
4. 3. after their own l. shall they heap teachers
Tit. 2. 12. teaching us that denying worldly l.
3. 3. were disobedient, serving divers l. and pleas.
Jam. 4. 1. come they not hence, even of your l.?
3. ye ask that ye may consume it on your l.
1 Pet. 1. 14. not fashioning according to former l.
2. 11. beseech you abstain from fleshly l. that war
4. 2. that he no longer should live to the l. of men
3. when we walked in lasciviousness, l. excess of
2 Pet. 2. 18. they allure through the l. of the flesh
3. 3. shall come scoffers, walking after their own l.
Jude 16. murmurers, complainers, walking after l.
18. who should walk after their own ungodly l.

LUSTY.

Judg. 3. 29. they slew of Moab 10,000 men, all l.

LYAR, or LIAR.

Job 24. 25. if it be not so, who will make me a l.?
Prov. 17. 4. a l. giveth ear to a naughty tongue
19. 22. and a poor man is better than a l.
30. 6. lest he reprove thee, and thou be found a l.
Jer. 15. 18. wilt thou be altogether to me as a l.
John 8. 44. for he is a l. and the father of it
55. if I say, I know him not, I shall be a l. like to
Rom. 3. 4. let God be true, and every man a l.
1 John 1. 10. we have not sinned, we make him a l.
2. 4. keepeth not his commandments is a l. 4. 20.
22. who is a l. but he that denieth Jesus is Christ
5. 10. that believeth not God, hath made him a l.

LIARS.

Deut. 33. 29. thine enemies shall be found l. to thee
Psal. 116. 11. I said in my haste, all men are l.
Isa. 44. 25. that frustrateth the tokens of the l.
Jer. 50. 36. a sword is upon the l. they shall dote
1 Tim. 1. 10. law is made for l. for perjured persons
Tit. 1. 12. said, the Cretians are alway l. evil beasts
Rev. 2. 2. hast tried them, and hast found them l.
21. 8. all l. shall have their part in lake that burns

LYE, or LIE.

Lev. 6. 2. if a soul l. to his neighbour in that
19. 11. ye shall not steal, nor l. one to another
Num. 23. 19. God is not a man, that he should l.
1 Sam. 15. 29. Strength of Isr. will not l. nor repent
2 Kings 4. 16. my lord, do not l. to thy handmaid
Job 6. 28. look on me, for it is evident to you if I l.
34. 6. should I l. against my right, my wound is
Psal. 89. 35. once sworn that I will not l. to David
Prov. 14. 5. a faithful witness will not l. but a false
Isa. 63. 8. they are my people, child. that will not l.
Mic. 2. 11. if a man walking in falsehood do l.
Hab. 2. 3. at the end it shall speak and not l.
Acts 5. 3. why hath Satan filled thy heart to l.?
Rom. 9. 1. I say truth in Chr. I l. not, 1 Tim. 2. 7.
2 Cor. 11. 31. Father of our Lord knoweth I l. not
Gal. 1. 20. which I wrote to you, behold I l. not
Col. 3. 9. l. not one to anoth. seeing ye have put off
Tit. 1. 2. God that cannot l. promised, Heb. 6. 18.
Jam. 3. 14. glory not, and l. not against the truth
1 John 1. 6. if we say, we have fellowship with him,
and walk in darkness, we l. and do not the truth
Rev. 3. 9. which say they are Jews, but do l.

LIED.

1 Kings 13. 18. I am a prophet, but he l. unto him
Psal. 78. 36. they l. unto him with their tongues
Isa. 57. 11. of whom been afraid, that thou hast l.
Acts 5. 4. thou hast not l. unto men, but unto God

LIETH.

Lev. 6. 3. found that was lost, and l. concerning it

LIE, *Substantive*.

Signifies, [1] *A falsity or untruth*, Judg. 16. 10. [2] *False doctrine*, 1 John 2. 21. [3] *An image, or idolatrous representation of God*, Rom. 1. 25.

Psal. 62. 9. and men of high degree are a l.
119. 69. the proud have forged a l. against me
Isa. 44. 20. is there not a l. in my right hand?
Jer. 27. 10. they prophesy a l. to you to remove
you from your land, 14, 15, 16. || 29. † 9, 21.
28. 15. thou makest this people to trust in a l.
29. 31. and he caused you to trust in a l.
37. † 14. then said Jeremiah, it is a l.
Ezek. 21. 29. whilst they divine a l. to thee
Mic. 1. 14. houses of Achzib shall be a l. to kings
Zech. 10. 2. for the diviners have seen a l. and told
John 8. 44. when he speaketh a l. he speaketh of
Rom. 1. 25. who changed the truth of God into a l.
3. 7. hath more abounded thro' my l. to his glory
2 Thess. 2. 11. delusion, that they should believe a l.
1 John 2. 21. ye know that no l. is of the truth
27. anointing teach. you of all things, and is no l.
Rev. 21. 27. neither whatsoever maketh a l.
22. 15. without are whosoever lov. and mak. a l.

LIES.

Judg. 16. 10. behold, thou hast told me l. 13.
Job 11. 3. should thy l. make men hold their peace?
13. 4. ye are forgers of l. physicians of no value
Psal. 40. 4. respecteth not such as turn aside to l.
58. 3. wicked are estrang. and go astray, speak l.
62. 4. they delight in l. they curse inwardly
63. 11. the mouth that speaketh l. shall be stopped
101. 7. that telleth l. shall not tarry in my sight
Prov. 6. 19. L. hates a false witness that speaketh l.
14. 5. but a false witness will utter l.
25. but a deceitful witness speaketh l.
19. 5. and he that speaketh l. shall not escape
9. and he that speaketh l. shall perish
29. 12. if a ruler hearken to l. his servants wicked
30. 8. remove far from me vanity and l.
Isa. 9. 15. the prophet that teacheth l. he is the tail
16. 6. the pride of Moab, but his l. shall not be so
28. 15. for we have made l. our refuge
17. the hail shall sweep away the refuge of l.
59. 3. your lips have spoken l. your tongue hath
4. they trust in vanity, and speak l.
Jer. 9. 3. they bend their tongues like their bow for l.
5. they have taught their tongue to speak l.
14. 14. the prophets prophesy l. 23. 25, 26.
16. 19. surely our fathers have inherited l.

Jer. 20. 6. to whom thou hast prophesied *l.* vanity
23. 14. they commit adultery, and walk in *l.*
32. cause my peo. to err by their *l.* and lightness
48. 30. shall not be so, his *l.* shall not so effect it
Ezek. 13. 8. ye have spoken vanity and seen *l.*
9. mine hand be upon the prophets that divine *l.*
19. by your lying to my people that hear your *l.*
22. with *l.* ye have made the righteous sad
22. 28. divining *l.* unto them, saying, thus saith L.
24. 12. she hath wearied herself with *l.*
Dan. 11. 27. they shall speak *l.* at one table
Hos. 7. 3. they make the princes glad with their *l.*
13. tho' redeemed, yet they have spoken *l.* ag. me
10. 13. ye have eaten the fruit of *l.* because thou
11. 12. Ephraim compasseth me about with *l.* and the house of Isr. with deceit, but Judah faithful
12. 1. he daily increaseth *l.* and desolation
Amos 2. 4. and their *l.* caused them to err
Mic. 6. 12. the inhabitants thereof have spoken *l.*
Nah. 3. 1. woe to the bloody city, it is full of *l.*
Hab. 2. 18. the molten image, and a teacher of *l.*
Zeph. 3. 13. the remnant of Israel shall not speak *l.*
Zech. 13. 3. thou speakest *l.* in the name of the Ld.
1 *Tim.* 4. 2. speak. *l.* in hypocrisy, having conscience

LYING.

Psal. 31. 6. I have hated them that regard *l.* vanities, but I trust in the Lord
18. let the *l.* lips be put to silence, that speak things
52. 3. thou lovest *l.* rather than righteousness
59. 12. and for cursing and *l.* which they speak
109. 2. they have spoken against me with *l.* tongue
119. 29. remove from me the way of *l.* and grant
163. I hate and abhor *l.* but thy law do I love
120. 2. deliver my soul, O Lord, from *l.* lips
Prov. 6. 17. the Lord hateth a proud look, a *l.* tongue
10. 18. he that hideth hatred with *l.* lips is a fool
12. 19. but a *l.* tongue is but for a moment
22. *l.* lips are abomination to the Lord
13. 5. a righteous man hateth *l.* but a wicked man is loathsome, and cometh to shame
17. 7. much less do *l.* lips become a prince
21. 6. getting of treasures by a *l.* tongue is vanity
26. 28. a *l.* tongue hateth those afflicted by it
Isa. 30. 9. that this is a rebellious people, *l.* children
32. 7. he deviseth wicked devices with *l.* words
59. 13. in transgressing and *l.* against the Lord
Jer. 7. 4. trust ye not in *l.* words, saying, temple of L.
8. behold, ye trust in *l.* words that cannot profit
29. 23. because have spoken *l.* words in my name
Ezek. 13. 6. they have seen vanity and *l.* divination
7. have ye not spoken a *l.* divination
19. by your *l.* to my people that hear your lies
Dan. 2. 9. ye have prepared *l.* words to speak before
Hos. 4. 2. by swearing, *l.* and killing, they break out
Jonah 2. 8. they that observe *l.* vanities forsake
Eph. 4. 25. putting away *l.* speak truth, forsake
2 *Thess.* 2. 9. whose coming is with *l.* wonders

LYING *spirit.*

1 *Kings* 22. 22. I will be a *l. spirit* in the mouth of all his prophets, 2 *Chron.* 18. 21.
23. Ld. hath put a *l. s.* in prophets, 2 *Chron.* 18. 22.

LYING.

Gen. 34. 7. wrought folly in *l.* with Jacob's daughter
Num. 31. 17. kill woman that hath known man by *l.*
18. all that have not known man by *l.* with him, keep alive for yourselves, *Judg.* 21. 12.
31. 35. women had not known man by *l.* with him
Deut. 22. 22. if a man be found *l.* with a woman
Judg. 21. † 11. destroy that knoweth *l.* with man

LYING.

Gen. 29. 2. there were three flocks of sheep *l.* by it
Exod. 23. 5. the ass of him that hateth thee, *l.*
Deut. 21. 1. if one be found slain, *l.* in the field
Psal. 139. 3. thou compassest my path and *l.* down
Isa. 56. 10. sleeping, *l.* down, loving to slumber
Mat. 9. 2. brought a man sick of the palsy, *l.* on bed
Mark 5. 40. he entereth in where the damsel was *l.*
Luke 2. 12. ye shall find the babe *l.* in a manger, 16.
John 13. 25. he then *l.* on Jesus' breast saith
20. 5. he saw the linen clothes *l.* yet went not in
7. and the napkin not *l.* with the linen clothes

LYING *in wait.*

Josh. 8. † 13. there *l. in wait* on west side of the city
Judg. 9. 35. and Abimelech rose up from *l. in wait*
16. 9. now there were men *l. in wait* in the chamb.
Lam. 3. 10. he was to me as a bear *l. in wait*, as lion
Acts 20. 19. which befel me by the *l. in w.* of Jews
23. 16. when Paul's kinsmen heard of their *l. in w.*

M.

MAD

Signifies, [1] *One distracted, or deprived of reason,* Acts 26. 24. 1 Cor. 14. 23. [2] *One dissembling madness, and behaving himself foolishly,* 1 Sam. 21. 13. [3] *One furious with raging zeal in persecuting,* Acts 26. 11. [4] *One whose mind is so troubled and perplexed, that he knows not what to do, but acts irregularly and extravagantly,* Deut. 28. 34. Eccl. 7. 7. Jer. 25. 16. [5] *One who is infatuated, or impetuous and violent in his desires after idols and vanity,* Jer. 50. 38. [6] *Foolish, deceitful, and lying,* Hos. 9. 7.

Deut. 28. 34. shalt be *m.* for the sight of thine eyes
1 *Sam.* 21. 13. and David feigned himself *m.*
14. Achish said to his servants, you see man is *m.*
2 *Kings* 9. 11. wherefore came this *m.* fellow to thee?
Psal. 102. 8. they that are *m.* against me are sworn
Eccl. 2. 2. I said of laughter it is *m.* of mirth, what
7. 7. surely oppression maketh a wise man *m.*
Isa. 44. 25. and that maketh diviners *m.*
59. † 15. he that departeth from evil is accounted *m.*
Jer. 25. 16. they shall drink, be moved, and be *m.*
29. 26. for every man that is *m.* put him in prison
50. 38. and they are *m.* upon their idols
51. 7. of her wine, therefore the nations are *m.*
Hos. 9. 7. the proph. is a fool, the spiritual man is *m.*
John 10. 20. hath devil and is *m.* why hear ye him?
Acts 12. 15. and they said to Rhoda, thou art *m.*
26. 11. and being exceedingly *m.* against them

Acts 26. 24. Paul, much learning doth make thee *m.*
25. but he said, I am not *m.* most noble Festus
1 *Cor.* 14. 23. will they not say that ye are *m.?*

MADE.

Exod. 2. 14. who *m.* thee prince over us? *Acts* 7. 27.
4. 11. L. said to him, who hath *m.* man's mouth?
9. 20. *m.* his servants and cattle flee into the houses
32. 4. after he had *m.* it a molten calf, they said
25. Aaron had *m.* them naked to their shame
31. and have *m.* them gods of gold, *Hos.* 8. 4.
39. 42. so the children of Israel *m.* all the work
Num. 20. 5. why have ye *m.* us to come from Egypt?
Deut. 9. 21. I took your sin and calf which he had *m.*
Josh. 8. 15. Joshua and Isr. *m.* as if they were beaten
9. 4. went and *m.* as if they had been ambassadors
14. 8. they *m.* the heart of the people melt
22. 28. the pattern of the altar which our fathers *m.*
Judg. 16. 19. she *m.* Samson sleep upon her knees
25. Samson *m.* the Philistines sport, 27.
18. 24. ye have taken away the gods which I *m.*
1 *Sam.* 3. 13. his sons *m.* thems. vile, restrained not
8. 1. that Samuel *m.* his sons judges over Israel
12. 1. behold, I have *m.* a king over you
15. 17. wast thou not *m.* the head of Israel?
33. as thy sword hath *m.* women childless
27. 10. Achish said, whither have ye *m.* road to-day
2 *Sam.* 13. 6. Amnon lay down and *m.* himself sick
1 *Kings* 12. 32. sacrificing to calves that he had *m.*
15. 12. he removed all idols which his fathers *m.*
13. she had *m.* an idol in a grove, 2 *Chr.* 15. 16.
20. 34. shalt make streets as my father *m.* in Sama.
2 *Kings* 11. 12. they *m.* him king and anointed him
16. 11. as Ahaz sent, so Urijah the priest *m.* it
1 *Chr.* 26. 10. yet his father *m.* him the chief
2 *Chr.* 25. 16. art thou *m.* of the king's counsel?
28. 19. for Ahaz *m.* Judah naked and transgressed
33. 7. set the idol he had *m.* in the house of God
34. 33. Josiah *m.* all present to serve the Lord
Ezra 5. 14. Shesh-bazzar whom he *m.* governor
Neh. 4. 9. we *m.* our prayer unto our God
Esth. 2. 17. Ahasuerus *m.* her queen inst. of Vashti
9. 17. they *m.* it day of feasting and gladness, 18.
Job 15. 7. or wast thou *m.* before the hills?
Psal. 7. 15. he *m.* a pit, and is fallen into pit he *m.*
9. 15. the heathen are sunk into the pit they *m.*
52. 7. this is the man that *m.* not God his strength
Eccl. 2. 4. I *m.* me great works, I builded houses
5. I *m.* me gardens ‖ 6. I *m.* me pools of water
Cant. 1. 6. they *m.* me the keeper of the vineyards
3. 10. he *m.* the pillars of silver, bottom of gold
6. 12. my soul *m.* me like chariots of Amminadib
Isa. 2. 8. that which their own fingers have *m.*
14. 16. is this the man that *m.* earth to tremble?
28. 15. for we have *m.* lies our refuge, and falseh.
29. 16. shall work say of him that *m.* it, he *m.* me not
31. 7. which your hands have *m.* unto you for a sin
40. † 14. and who *m.* him understand?
59. † 2. your sins have *m.* him hide his face
8. they have *m.* them crooked paths
Jer. 10. 11. the gods that have not *m.* the heavens
12. 10. have *m.* my pleasant portion a wilderness
18. 4. the vessel that he *m.* was marred in the hand of the potter, so he *m.* it again another vessel
37. 15. for they had *m.* that the prison
41. 9. which Asa the king had *m.* for fear of Baasha
51. 34. Nebuchadnezzar *m.* me an empty vessel
Ezek. 13. 22. ye *m.* the heart of the righteous sad
17. 16. where the king dwelleth that *m.* him king
20. 28. there also they *m.* their sweet savour
21. 24. ye have *m.* your iniquity to be remembered
31. 4. waters *m.* him great, deep set him upon high
Dan. 5. 11. thy father *m.* master of the magicians
9. 13. yet *m.* we not our prayer before the Lord
Hos. 2. † 8. silver wherewith they *m.* Baal
7. 5. the princes have *m.* him sick with wine
8. 6. the workman *m.* it, therefore it is not God
Amos 5. 26. the god which ye *m.* to yourselves
Zech. 7. † 11. but they *m.* their ears heavy
12. yea, they *m.* their hearts as an adamant
Mat. 9. 22. daughter, thy faith hath *m.* thee whole, *Mark* 5. 34. | 10. 52. *Luke* 8. 48. | 17. 19.
15. 6. have *m.* commandment of G. of none effect
21. 13. called the house of prayer, but ye have *m.* it a den of thieves, *Mark* 11. 17. *Luke* 19. 46.
25. 16. traded and *m.* them other five talents
Luke 12. 14. man, who *m.* me a judge over you?
Acts 3. 16. and his name hath *m.* this man strong
8. 3. as for Saul, he *m.* havock of the church
23. 13. more than forty who had *m.* this conspiracy
27. 40. they hoised sail, and *m.* toward shore
Rom. 8. 2. hath *m.* free from law of sin and death
1 *Tim.* 1. 19. concerning faith have *m.* shipwreck
Heb. 7. 19. for the law *m.* nothing perfect
1 *John* 5. 10. he that believeth not, hath *m.* G. a liar
Rev. 7. 14. *m.* them white in the blood of the Lamb
14. 8. she *m.* all nations drink of the wine

See COVENANT, END, FIRE.

MADE, meant of *God, Lord, Christ.*

Gen. 1. 7. God *m.* the firmament and divided
16. *m.* two great lights, he *m.* stars, *Ps.* 136. 7, 9.
25. God *m.* the beast of the earth after his kind
31. God saw every thing that he had *m.* was good
2. 2. God rested from all his works he had *m.*
4. God *m.* the earth and heavens, *Exod.* 20. 11. | 31. 17. *Psal.* 146. 6. *Isa.* 45. 18. *Jer.* 10. 12.
9. *m.* to grow every tree ‖ 22. *m.* he a woman
5. 1. in the likeness of God *m.* he him, 9. 6.
6. 6. it repented the Lord he had *m.* man, 7.
8. 1. God *m.* a wind to pass over the earth
21. 6. and Sarah said, God hath *m.* me to laugh
24. 21. the Lord had *m.* his journey prosperous
26. 22. now the Lord hath *m.* room for us
39. 3. the Lord *m.* all Joseph did to prosper, 23.
41. 51. God hath *m.* me to forget all my toil
45. 8. God hath *m.* me a father to Pharaoh
9. God hath *m.* me Lord of all Egypt
Exod. 1. 21. the midwives feared God, he *m.* houses
14. 21. and the Lord *m.* the sea dry land
Lev. 23. 43. I *m.* Israel to dwell in booths
26. 13. I am L. your G. and I have *m.* you go uprig.
Num. 32. 13. he *m.* them wander in the wilderness
Deut. 2. 30. for the Lord *m.* his heart obstinate

Deut. 4. 36. out of heav. he *m.* thee to hear his voice
10. 22. the Lord hath *m.* thee as the stars
11. 4. how he *m.* the water of the Red sea to overfl.
26. 19. thee above all nations which he hath *m.*
32. 6. hath he not *m.* thee, and established thee
13. he *m.* him ride, *m.* him suck honey out of rock
15. then he forsook God which *m.* him, and rock
Josh. 22. 25. the Lord *m.* Jordan border between us
Judg. 5. 13. he *m.* him have dominion over mighty
21. 15. the Lord had *m.* a breach in the tribes
1 *Sam.* 12. 8. and *m.* them dwell in this place
15. 35. the Ld. repented that he had *m.* Saul king
2 *Sam.* 6. 8. because the Lord had *m.* a breach upon
22. 12. he *m.* darkness pavilions round about him
36. thy gentleness hath *m.* me great, *Psal.* 18. 35.
1 *Kings* 2. 24. who hath *m.* me a house as promised
10. 9. the Lord loved Israel, therefore he *m.* thee king, 14. 7. | 16. 2. 2 *Chr.* 1. 11.
1 *Chr.* 16. 26. but the Lord *m.* the heavens, *Neh.* 9. 6. *Psal.* 33. 6. | 96. 5. | 121. 2. | 124. 8. | 134. 3.
2 *Chron.* 20. 27. the Lord had *m.* them to rejoice
26. 5. he sought the Lord, God *m.* him to prosper
Ezra 6. 22. Lord had *m.* them joyful, *Neh.* 12. 43.
Job 10. 8. thy hands have *m.* me and fashioned me
16. 7. he hath *m.* me weary, thou hast *m.* desolate
17. 6. he hath *m.* me a by-word of the people
28. 26. when he *m.* a decree for the rain, and a way
31. 15. did not he that *m.* me in the womb make
33. 4. the Spirit of God *m.* me, and gave me life
40. 19. he that *m.* him can make his sword approach
Psal. 30. 1. hast not *m.* my foes to rejoice over me
46. 8. what desolations he hath *m.* in the earth
95. 5. the sea is his and he *m.* it ‖ 103. he *m.* us
105. 28. he sent darkness, and *m.* it dark
118. 24. this is the day the Lord hath *m.* will rejoice
119. 73. thy hands have *m.* me and fashioned me
136. 5. that by wisdom *m.* the heavens, *Acts* 14. 15.
14. and *m.* Israel to pass through the midst of it
148. 6. he hath *m.* a decree which shall not pass
149. 2. let Israel rejoice in him that *m.* him
Prov. 16. 4. the Lord *m.* all things for himself
20. 12. the Lord hath *m.* even both of them
Eccl. 3. 11. he hath *m.* every thing beautiful in time
7. 29. I found that God hath *m.* man upright
Isa. 27. 11. he that *m.* them will not have mercy
30. 33. he hath *m.* Tophet deep and large
44. 2. thus saith the Lord that *m.* and formed thee
53. 12. he *m.* intercession for the transgressors
66. 2. all these things hath mine hand *m.*
Jer. 8. 8. lo, certainly in vain *m.* he it
29. 26. the Lord *m.* thee priest instead of Jehoiada
32. 20. and hast *m.* thee a name as at this day
38. 16. as the Lord liveth, that *m.* us this soul
Lam. 1. 13. he hath *m.* me desolate and faint, 3. 11.
14. the Lord hath *m.* my strength to fall
3. 4. my flesh and my skin hath he *m.* old
7. hath *m.* my chain heavy ‖ 9. *m.* my paths crooked
15. he hath *m.* me drunken with wormwood
Ezek. 31. 16. I *m.* nations to shake at the sound
Jonah 1. 9. I fear God who hath *m.* sea and dry land
Zeph. 3. 6. I *m.* their streets waste, none passeth
Mat. 19. 4. he *m.* them male and female, *Mark* 10. 6.
Luke 11. 40. did not he that *m.* that which is without
John 1. 3. without him was not any thing *m.*
4. 1. Jesus *m.* more disciples ‖ 46. he *m.* water wine
5. 11. he that *m.* me whole said, take up thy bed
9. 6. he spat and *m.* clay of the spittle, 11. 14.
19. 7. because he *m.* himself the Son of God
Acts 2. 36. know that God hath *m.* that same Jesus
15. 7. ye know that God *m.* choice among us
17. 24. G. that *m.* the world and all things therein
26. hath *m.* of one blood all nations of men
20. 28. the Holy Ghost hath *m.* you overseers
1 *Cor.* 1. 20. *m.* foolish the wisdom of this world
2 *Cor.* 3. 6. hath *m.* us able ministers of New Testam.
5. 21. hath *m.* him to be sin for us who knew no sin
Gal. 5. 1. liberty wherewith Christ hath *m.* us free
Eph. 1. 6. he hath *m.* us accepted in the Beloved
2. 6. God hath *m.* us sit together in heavenly places
14. he is our peace who hath *m.* both one
Phil. 2. 7. but *m.* himself of no reputation
Col. 1. 12. who hath *m.* us meet to be partakers
2. 15. he *m.* a shew of them openly, triumphing
Heb. 1. 2. by whom also he *m.* the worlds
6. 13. for when God *m.* promise to Abraham
Rev. 1. 6. and hath *m.* us kings and priests to God
14. 7. and worship him that *m.* heaven and earth

I have, or *have* I MADE.

Gen. 7. 4. destroy every living substance *I have m.*
14. 23. lest thou say, *I have m.* Abram rich
17. 5. a father of nations *have I m.* thee, *Rom.* 4. 17.
27. 37. Isaac said, behold, *I have m.* him thy lord
Exod. 7. 1. see *I have m.* thee a god to Pharaoh
2 *Sam.* 7. 9. *I have m.* thee a great name, 1 *Chr.* 17. 8.
1 *Kings* 8. 59. wherewith *I have m.* supplication
1 *Chr.* 29. 19. for the which *I have m.* provision
Ezra 6. 11. *I* Darius *have m.* a decree, 12.
Job 17. 13. *I have m.* my bed in the darkness
31. 24. if *I have m.* gold my hope, or have said
39. 6. whose house *I have m.* the wilderness
Psal. 45. 1. I will speak of things which *I have m.*
Prov. 20. 9. who can say, *I have m.* my heart clean
Isa. 16. 10. *I have m.* their shouting to cease
21. 2. the sighing thereof *have I m.* to cease
43. 7. I have formed him, yea, *I have m.* him, 46. 4.
45. 12. *I h. m.* the earth, and creat. man, *Jer.* 27. 5.
57. 16. and the souls which *I have m.* should fail
Jer. 1. 18. behold *I have m.* thee a defenced city
49. 10. but *I have m.* Esau bare, and uncovered
Ezek. 3. 8. behold, *I have m.* thy face strong, 9.
17. *I have m.* thee a watchman to house of Israel
13. 22. ye made heart sad, whom *I have* not *m.* sad
17. 24. and *I have m.* the dry tree to flourish
22. 4. therefore *have I m.* thee a reproach
29. 3. my river is mine, *I have m.* it for myself, 9.
31. 9. *I h. m.* him fair by multitude of his branches
Dan. 3. 15. worship the image which *I have m.*
Amos 4. 10. *I have m.* the stink of camps to come up
Obad. 2. *I have m.* thee small among the heathen
Mal. 2. 9. therefore *have I m.* you contemptible
John 7. 23. because *I h. m.* a man every whit whole
1 *Cor.* 9. 19. yet *have I m.* myself servant to all

Thou hast MADE.

Exod. 15. 17. plant them in the place which th. h. m.
29. 36. when thou hast m. an atonement for it
Josh. 2. 17. this oath which thou h. m. us swear, 20.
1 Kings 3.7. t. h. m. thy servant king instead of Dav.
9. 3. I have heard thy supplication that thou h. m.
2 Kings 19. 15. O Lord God of Israel, thou hast m. heaven and earth, Isa. 37. 16. Jer. 32. 17.
1 Chr. 22. 8. word came, saying, th. h. m. great wars
Job 1. 10. t. h. m. an hedge about him and his house
10. 9. remember that thou hast m. me as the clay
16. 7. thou hast m. desolate all my company
Psal 8. 5. thou hast m. him little lower than angels
18. 43. thou hast m. me the head of the heathen
21. 6. thou hast m. him most blessed for ever
30. 7. thou hast m. my mountain to stand strong
39. 5. behold, thou h. m. my days as a hand breadth
60. 2. t. h. m. the earth to tremble, thou hast broken
3. thou hast m. us drink the wine of astonishment
74. 17. thou hast m. summer and winter
86. 9. all nations whom thou ha t m. shall worship
88. 8. thou hast m. me an abomination to them
89. 42. thou hast m. all his enemies to rejoice
44. t. h. m. his glory to cease, and cast his throne
47. wherefore hast thou m. all men in vain?
91. 9. because thou hast m. the Lord thy habitation
92. 4. thou, Ld. hast m. me glad through thy work
104. 24. thy works, in wisdom hast thou m. them all
26. Leviathan, whom thou hast m. to play therein
119. 98. thou hast m. me wiser than mine enemies
Isa. 25. 2. for thou hast m. of a city an heap, a ruin
43. 24. but thou hast m. me to serve with thy sins
63. 17. Ld. why th. h. m. us to err from thy ways?
Jer. 2. 28. but where are thy gods that t. h. m. thee?
14. 22. we wait on thee, for t. h. m. all these things
Lam. 3. 45. t. h. m. us as the offscouring and refuse
Ezek. 13. 5. nor hast t. m. up the hedge in the house
16. 24. thou h. m. thee an high place in every street
25. thou hast m. thy beauty to be abhorred
22. 4. hast defiled in thy idols which thou hast m.
13. at thy dishonest gain which t. h. m. and blood
Mat. 20.12. but one hour, and t.h.m. them equal to us
Rom. 9. 20. thing formed say, why h. t. m. me thus
Rev. 5. 10. t. h. m. us to our God kings and priests

MADE haste.

Gen. 24. 46. Rebekah m. h. and let down her pitcher
43. 30. Joseph m. h. || Exod. 34. 8. Moses m. haste
Judg. 13. 10. Manoah's wife m. haste and ran
1 Sam. 23. 26. David m. h. || 25. 18. Abigail m. haste
2 Sam. 4. 4. as Mephibosheth's nurse m. haste to flee
Psal. 119. 60. I m. haste, and delayed not to keep thy
Luke 19. 6. Zaccheus m. haste and came down
See ISRAEL, SIN, KNOWN.

MADE manifest.

Luke 8. 17. nothing secret that shall not be m. manif.
John 1. 31. but that he should be m. manif. to Israel
3. 21. to the light, that his deeds may be m. manif.
9. 3. the works of G. should be m. manif. in him
Rom. 10. 20. I was m. m. to them that asked not
16. 26. but now is m. man. to all nations for obed.
1 Cor. 3. 13. every man's work shall be m. manif.
11. 19. that they which are approved may be m. m.
14. 25. thus are the secrets of his heart m. manif.
2 Cor. 4. 10. life of Jesus should be m. manif. 11.
11. 6. we have been throughly m. m. among you
Eph. 5. 13. are approved are m. m. by the light
Col. 1. 26. but now is m. manifest to his saints
2 Tim. 1. 10. now m. m. by the appearing of Ch.
Heb. 9. 8. way into the holiest was not yet m. m.
1 John 2. 19. went out that they might be m. manif.
Rev. 15. 4. for thy judgments are m. manifest

MADE peace.

Josh. 9. 15. and Joshua m. peace with them, 10. 1. 4.
11. 19. there was not a city that m. p. with Israel
2 Sam. 10. 19. when the servants of Hadarezer were smitten, they m. peace with Israel, 1 Chron. 19. 19.
1 Kings 22. 44. Jehoshaphat m. peace with Israel

MADE ready.

Gen. 43. 25. they m. r. the present against noon
46. 29. Joseph m. ready his chariot to meet Israel
Exod. 14. 6. Pharaoh m. ready his chariot, and took
Judg. 6. 19. and Gideon went in and m. ready a kid
13. 15. Manoah said, till we have m. ready a kid
1 Kings 6. 7. m. r. before it was brought thither
2 Kings 9. 21. and Joram's chariot was m. ready
1 Chron. 28. 2. and had m. ready for the building
2 Chron. 35. 14. afterward they m. r. for themselves
Psal. 7. 12. he hath bent his bow and m. it ready
Hos. 7. 6. they have m. r. their heart like an oven
Mat. 26. 19. the disciples m. ready the passover, Mark 14. 16. Luke 22. 13.
Acts 10. 10. while they m. r. Peter fell into a trance
2 Cor. 10. 16. boast of things m. ready to our hand
Rev. 19. 7. and his wife hath m. herself ready

MADE speed.

1 Kings 12. 18. Rehoboam m. s. to get, 2 Chr. 10. 18.

MADE void.

Num. 30. 12. if her husband hath utterly m. void
Psal. 89. 39. thou hast m. v. covenant of thy serv.
119. 126. time to work, for they have m. v. thy law
Rom. 4. 14. for if they of law be heirs, faith is m. v.

MADE, passively.

Gen. 49. 24. the arms of his hands were m. strong
Lev. 22. 5. whereby he may m. be unclean
Num. 4. 26. they shall bear all that is m. for them
6. 4. he shall eat nothing that is m. of the vine-tree
1 Kings 8. 38. what supplication be m. 2 Chr. 6. 29.
2 Chr. 6. 40. ears attend to prayer m. in this place
Ezra 5. 17. let there be search m. in king's house
6. 1. and search was m. in the house of the rolls
11. let his house be m. a dunghill for this
Esth. 5. 14. let a gallows be m. of fifty cubits high
Job 7. 3. I am m. to possess months of vanity
41. 33. not his like on earth, who is m. without fear
Psal. 49. 16. be not afraid when one is m. rich
139. 14. I am fearfully and wonderfully m.
Prov. 15. 19. the way of the righteous is m. plain
21. 11. scorner is punished, the simple is m. wise
28. 25. that putteth trust in the L. shall be m. fat
Eccl. 1. 15. what is crooked cannot be m. straight
7. 3. for by sadness of count. the heart is m. better
Eccl. 10. 19. a feast is m. for laughter, wine makes
Isa. 51. 12. the son of man, which shall be m. as grass
66. 8. shall earth be m. to bring forth in one day
Jer. 19. 11. a vessel that cannot be m. whole again
20. 8. the word of the Lord was m. a reproach
Dan. 5. 21. his heart was m. like the beasts
Mat. 4. 3. command that these stones be m. bread
9. 16. and the rent is m. worse, Mark 2. 21.
18. 25. all to be sold, and payment to be m.
23. 15. when he is m. ye make him twofold more
25. 6. and at midnight there was a cry m. behold
27. 24. but that rather a tumult was m
64. command that the sepulchre be m. sure
Mark 2. 27. he said, the sabbath was m. for man
Luke 14. 12. lest a recompence be m. thee
23. 12. same day Pilate and Herod were m. friends
John 1. 3. all things were m. by him, and without him was not any thing m. that was m.
10. was in the world, the world was m. by him
14. the Word was m. flesh, and dwelt among us
2. 9. ruler had tasted the water that was m. wine
5. 6. wilt thou be m. whole? || 14. art m. whole
8. 33. ye shall be m. free || 9. 39. might be m. blind
17. 23. that they may be m. perfect in one
Acts 4. 35. distribution was m. to every man as need
12. 5. but prayer was m. without ceasing for Peter
13. 32. promise which was m. to our fathers, 26. 6.
16. 13. we went where prayer was wont to be m.
19. 26. they be no gods which are m. with hands
Rom. 1. 3. Jesus who was m. of the seed of David
20. being understood by the things that are m.
2. 25. thy circumcision is m. uncircumcision
5. 19. many were m. sinners, many m. righteous
6. 18. being m. free from sin, ye became, 22.
7. 13. was then that which is good, m. death to me?
9. † 22. vessels of wrath m. up to destruction
29. we had been m. like to Sodom and Gomorrha
10. 10. with the mouth confession is m. to salvation
11. 9. let their table be m. a snare and a trap
14. 21. nor any thing whereby thy broth. is m. weak
1 Cor. 1. 17. lest cross of Chr. be m. of none effect
30. are in Christ, who of God is m. to us wisdom
4. 9. for we are m. a spectacle to the world to ang.
13. we are m. as filth of world and offscouring
9. 22. I am m. all things to all men, that I might
12. 13. have been all m. to drink into one Spirit
15. 22. even so in Christ shall all be m. alive
45. it is written, the first man Adam was m. a living soul, last Adam was m. a quickening spirit
2 Cor. 3. 10. for even that which was m. glorious
5. 1. an house not m. with hands, eternal in heav.
21. might be m. the righteousness of God in him
12. 9. my strength is m. perfect in weakness
Gal. 3. 3. are ye now m. perfect by the flesh?
13. Christ redeemed us, being m. a curse for us
16. to Abrah. and his seed were the promises m.
19. seed should come, to whom promise was m.
4. 4. sent his Son, m. of a woman, m. under law
Eph. 2. 11. the circumcision in the flesh m. by hands
13. were far off, are m. nigh by the blood of Chr.
3. 7. whereof I was m. a minister, Col. 1. 23, 25.
Phil. 2. 7. and was m. in the likeness of men
3. 10. being m. conformable to his death
Col. 1. 20. having m. peace thro' the blood of his cross
2. 11. with the circumcision m. without hands
1 Tim. 1. 9. the law is not m. for a righteous man
2. 1. and giving of thanks be m. for all men
Tit. 3. 7. justified by his grace, we should be m. heirs
Heb. 1. 4. being m. so much better than the angels
2. 17. it behoved him to be m. like to his brethren
3. 14. for we are m. partakers of Christ, if we hold
5. 5. Christ glorified not hims. to be m. high-priest
9. being m. perfect, he became the Author of salv.
7. 3. m. like to the Son of God, abideth a priest
12. there is m. of necessity a change of the law
16. m. not after law of a carnal commandment
20. as not without an oath he was m. priest
21. for those priests were m. without an oath
22. Jesus was m. a surety of a better testament
9. 2. there was tabernacle m. wherein was candlest.
11. a perfect tabernacle not m. with hands
24. not entered into holy places m. with hands
10. 3. there is a remembrance m. of sins every year
13. expecting till his enemies be m. his footstool
33. partly whilst ye were m. a gazing-stock
11. 3. were not m. of things which do appear
34. who out of weakness were m. strong
40. that they without us should not be m. perfect
12. 23. and to the spirits of just men m. perfect
Jam. 1. 10. but the rich, in that he is m. low
2. 22. and by works was faith m. perfect
3. 9. which are m. after the similitude of God
1 Pet. 2. 7. the same is m. head of the corner
2 Pet. 2. 12. but these m. to be taken and destroyed
Rev. 8. 11. waters, because they were m. bitter
17. 2. been m. drunk with wine of her fornication

MADEST.

Psal. 8. 6. thou m. him to have dominion over works
80. 15. visit the branch that thou m. strong for thys.
17. son of man, whom thou m. strong for thyself
Ezek. 16. 17. and m. to thyself images of men
29. 7. thou m. all their loins to be at a stand
Jonah 4. 10. neither m. it grow, which came up
Acts 21. 38. art not that Egyptian which m. uproar
Heb. 2. 7. thou m. him a little lower than the angels

MAD man.

1 Sam. 21. 15. brought this fellow to play the m. man
Prov. 26. 18. as a m. man who casteth firebrands

MAD men.

1 Sam. 21. 15. have I need of m. men that ye have
Jer. 48. 2. O m. men the sword shall pursue you

MADNESS.

Deut. 28. 28. the Lord shall smite thee with m.
2 Kings 9. † 20. like Jehu, for he driveth in m.
Eccl. 1. 17. I gave my heart to know wisdom and m.
2. 12. I turned myself to behold wisdom and m.
7. 25. to know the wickedness of folly, and m.
9. 3. m. is in their heart, while they live
10. 13. the end of his talk is mischievous m.
Zech. 12. 4. I will smite every horse and rider with m.
Luke 6. 11. and they were filled with m.
2 Pet. 2. 16. dumb ass forbade the m. of the prophet

MAGICIAN.

Dan. 2. 10. that asked such things at any m.

MAGICIANS.

Gen. 41. 8. Pharaoh sent and called for the m.
24. I told this to the m. but none could declare
Exod. 7. 11. the m. of Egypt did so in like manner with their enchantments, 22. | 8. 7, 18
8. 19. the m. said to Pharaoh, this is the finger of G
9. 11. the m. could not stand before Moses
Dan. 1. 20. he found them ten times better than all m.
2. 2. then the king commanded to call the m.
27. the secret cannot the m. shew to the king
4. 7. then came in the m. but did not make known
9. O Belteshazzar, master of the m. tell me
5. 11. whom thy father made master of the m.

MAGISTRATE.

Judg. 18. 7. and there was no m. in the land
Luke 12. 58. when thou goest to the m. give diligence

MAGISTRATES.

Ezra 7. 25. set m. and judges, who may judge
Luke 12. 11. when they bring you to the m.
Acts 16. 20. they brought Paul and Silas to the m.
22. and the m. commanded to beat them
35. the m. sent the serjeants, saying, 36.
38. the serjeants told these words to the m.
Tit. 3. 1. put them in mind to obey m. and be ready

MAGNIFICAL.

1 Chron. 22. 5. the house must be exceeding m.

MAGNIFICENCE.

Acts 19. 27. and her m. should be destroyed

MAGNIFY

Signifies, [1] *To declare and show forth one's greatness and glory*, Luke 1. 46. [2] *To increase one esteem, reputation, and authority*, Josh. 3. 7. | 4. 14. 1 Chron. 29. 25.

Josh. 3. 7. Lord said, this day will I begin to m. thee
Job 7. 17. what is man that thou shouldest m. him?
19. 5. if indeed ye will m. yourselves against me
36. 24. remember that thou m. his work men behold
Psal. 34. 3. O m. the Lord with me, let us exalt
35. 26. clothed with shame that m. themselv. ag. me
38. 16. my foot slippeth they m. themselv. ag. me
55. 12. that did m. himself against me
69. 30. and will m. him with thanksgiving
Isa. 10. 15. or saw m. itself ag. him that shaketh it
42. 21. he will m. the law and make it honourable
Ezek. 38. 23. thus will I m. myself, and sanctify
Dan. 8. 25. and he shall m. himself in his heart
11. 36. the king shall m. himself above every god
37. for he shall m. himself above all
Zech. 12. 7. that they m. not themselves ag. Judah
Luke 1. 46. Mary said, my soul doth m. the Lord
Acts 10. 46. heard him speak with tongues, and m. G.
Rom. 11. 13. I am an apostle, I m. mine office

MAGNIFIED.

Gen. 19. 19. behold, thou hast m. thy mercy
Josh. 4. 14. the Lord m. Joshua in the sight of Israel
2 Sam. 7. 26. let thy name be m. 1 Chron. 17. 24.
1 Chr. 29. 25. and the Lord m. Solomon, 2 Chr. 1. 1.
2 Chron. 32. 23. Hezekiah was m. in sight of all
Psal. 35. 27. let them say, let the Lord be m.
40. 16. say continually, the Lord be m. 70. 4.
138. 2. thou hast m. thy word above all thy name
Jer. 48. 26. for he m. himself against the Lord, 42.
Ezek. 35. † 13. Dan. 8. 11.
Lam. 1. 9. behold, for the enemy hath m. himself
Zeph. 2. 8. and m. themselves against their border
10. m. themselves against people of the L.
Mal. 1. 5. Lord will be m. from the border of Israel
Acts 5. 13. but the people m. them
19. 17. and the name of the Lord Jesus was m.
Phil. 1. 20. Chr. be m. in my body by life or death

MAID.

Gen. 16. 2. I pray thee go in unto my m. Hagar
6. behold, thy m. is in thy hand, do to her as pleas.
8. Hagar, Sarai's m. whence camest thou?
29. 24. Laban gave Zilpah his m. to Leah
29. Laban gave Bilhah to be Rachel's m.
30. 3. behold my m. Bilhah, go in unto her
7. Rachel's m. conceived || 9. gave Zilpah her m.
10. Zilpah, Leah's m. bare Jacob a son, 12.
Exod. 2. 5. when she saw ark, she sent her m. to fetch
8. the m. went and called the child's mother
21. 20. if a man smite his m. with a rod
26. or the eye of his m. that it perish
22. 16. if a man entice a m. not betrothed
Lev. 25. 6. the sabb. of land shall be meat for thy m.
Deut. 22. 14. I came to her, I found her not a m. 17.
2 Kings 5. 2. had brought away captive a little m.
4. thus and thus said the m. that is of Israel
Esth. 2. 7. and the m. was fair and beautiful
Job 31. 1. why then should I think on a m.?
Prov. 30. 19. and the way of a man with a m.
Isa. 24. 2. it shall be as with m. so with her mistress
Jer. 2. 32. can a m. forget her ornaments?
51. 22. I will break the young man and the m.
Amos 2. 7. a man and his father go in to the same m.
Mat. 9. 24. give place, for the m. is not dead
25. he took her by the hand, and the m. arose
26. 71. anoth. m. saw him, Mark 14. 69. Luke 22. 56.
Luke 8. 54. and he called, saying, m. arise

MAIDS.

Esth. 2. 9. he preferred her and her m. to best place
Job 19. 15. my m. count me for a stranger
Lam. 5. 11. they ravished the m. in cities of Judah
Ezek. 9. 6. slay utterly both m. and little children
Nah. 2. 7. her m. shall lead her with voice of doves
Zech. 9. 17. make young men cheerful, new wine m.

MAID-child.

Lev. 12. 5. if she bear a m.-child unclean two weeks

MAIDEN.

Gen. 30. 18. I have given my m. to my husband
Judg. 19. 24. behold, here is my daughter a m.
2 Chron. 36. 17. no compassion on young man or m.
Esth. 2. 13. thus came every m. to the king
Psal. 123. 2. as the eyes of a m. to her mistress
Luke 8. 51. he suffered father and mother of the m.

MAIDENS.

Exod. 2. 5. her m. walked along by the river
Ruth 2. 8. but abide here fast by my m.
22. it is good that thou go out with his m.
23. so she kept fast by the m. of Boaz

Sam. 9. 11. they found *m.* going to draw water
Esth. 4. 16. I and my *m.* will fast likewise
Job 41. 5. wilt thou bind him for *thy m.?*
Psal. 78. 63. their *m.* were not given to marriage
148. 12. young men and *m.* praise the Lord
Prov. 9. 3. she hath sent forth her *m.* she crieth
27. 27. and for the maintenance for thy *m.*
31. 15. and she giveth a portion to her *m.*
Eccl. 2. 7. I got me servants and *m.* and had serv.
Ezek. 44. 22. they shall take *m.* of seed of Israel
Luke 12. 45. shall begin to beat men-servants and *m.*

MAID-SERVANT.

Exod. 11. 5. even to the first born of the *m.-servant*
20. 10. thy *m.-serv.* shall do no work, *Deut.* 5. 14.
17. shalt not covet thy neighbour's wife, nor *m.-s.*
21. 7. if a man sell his daughter to be a *m.-servant*
27. if he smite out his *m.-servant's* tooth, he shall
32. if an ox push a *m.-s.* he shall give 30 shekels
Deut. 5. 14. that thy *m.-s.* may rest as well as thou
21. neither shalt thou desire thy neighbour's *m.-s.*
12. 18. eat them, thou and thy *m.-serv.* 16. 11, 14.
15. 17. to thy *m.-servant* thou shalt do likewise
Judg. 9. 18. made Abimelech son of his *m.-s.* king
Job 31. 13. if I did despise the cause of my *m.-s.*
Jer. 34. 9. let man-servant and *m.-s.* go free, 10.

MAID-SERVANTS.

Gen. 12. 16. Abram had *m.-s.* and she-asses, 24. 35.
20. 17. God healed Abimelech's wife and *m.-s.*
30. 43. Jacob had much cattle and *m.-servants*
31. 33. Laban entered into the two *m.-s.* tents
Deut. 12. 12. ye shall rejoice, ye and your *m.-s.*
1 *Sam.* 8. 16. and he shall take your *m.-servants*
2 *Sam.* 6. 22. of the *m.-s.* shall I be had in honour
2 *Kings* 5. 26. is it a time to receive *m.-servants?*

MAJESTY

Signifies, [1] *The infinite dignity and glory of God*, Psal. 104. 1. Jude 25. [2] *The pomp, splendour, and grandeur of earthly princes*, Esth. 1. 4.
1 *Chron.* 29. 11. thine, O Lord, is the power and *m.*
25. and bestowed upon him such royal *m.*
Esth. 1. 4. when he shewed the honour of his *m.*
Job 37. 22. with God is terrible *m.*
40. 10. deck thyself now with *m.* and excellency
Psal. 21. 5. honour and *m.* hast thou laid on him
29. 4. the voice of the Lord is full of *m.*
45. 3. with thy glory and *m.* ‖ 4. in thy *m.* ride
93. 1. the Lord reigneth, he is clothed with *m.*
96. 6. honour and *m.* are before him
104. 1. thou art clothed with honour and *m.*
145. 5. I will speak of the honour of thy *m.*
12. to make known the glorious *m.* of his kingdom
Isa. 2. 10. hide thee for the glory of his *m.* 19, 21.
24. 14. they shall sing for the *m.* of the Lord
26. 10. and will not behold the *m.* of the Lord
Ezek. 7. 20. as for beauty of ornament, he set it in *m.*
Dan. 4. 30. that I built for the honour of my *m.*
36. and excellent *m.* was added unto me
5. 18. God gave Nebuchadnezzar thy father *m.*
19. for the *m.* he gave him, all people trembled
Mic. 5. 4. feed in *m.* of the name of Lord his God
Heb. 1. 3. he sat down on the right hand of *m.* 8. 1.
2 *Pet.* 1. 16. but were eye-witnesses of his *m.*
Jude 25. to the only wise God be glory and *m.*

MAIL.

1 *Sam.* 17. 5. he was armed with a coat of *m.* 38.

MAIMED.

Lev. 22. 22. blind or *m.* ye shall not offer to the Ld.
Mat. 15. 30. having with them those that were *m.*
31. wondered when they saw the *m.* to be whole
18. 8. better to enter into life *m.* *Mark* 9. 43.
Luke 14. 13. when thou makest a feast, call the *m.*
21. bring in hither the poor and *m.* halt and blind

MAIN.

Acts 27. 40. they hoised up the *m.*-sail to the wind

MAINTAIN

Signifies, [1] *To uphold and preserve*, Psal. 16. 5. [2] *To repair*, 1 Chron. 26. 27. compared with 2 Kings 12. 5. [3] *To plead*, Psal. 140. 12. [4] *To profess and practise*, Tit. 3. 8, 14. [5] *To prove or argue*, Job 13. † 15. [6] *To make*, Psal. 9. † 4.
1 *Kings* 8. 45. *m.* their cause, 49, 59. 2 *Chr.* 6. 35, 39.
1 *Chron.* 26. 27. they dedicate to *m.* the house of L.
Job 13. 15. but I will *m.* mine own ways before him
Ps. 140. 12. Lord will *m.* the cause of the afflicted
Tit. 3. 8. might be careful to *m.* good works
14. let ours also learn to *m.* good works for uses

MAINTAINED.

Psal. 9. 4. for thou hast *m.* my right and my cause

MAINTAINEST.

Psal. 16. 5. Lord is my portion, and thou *m.* my lot

MAINTENANCE.

Ezra 4. 14. because we have *m.* from the king
Prov. 27. 27. and for the *m.* for thy maidens

MAKE

Signifies, [1] *To create, frame, or fashion*, Gen. 1. 31. Exod. 32. 1. Isa. 45. 9. [2] *To choose, or bring that to be which was not so before*, 1 Sam. 12. 22. [3] *To call one to a new vocation, and fit and qualify him for the same*, Mat. 4. 19. [4] *To ordain and appoint*, Acts 26. 16. [5] *To turn*, Psal. 41. † 3. [6] *To build*, Ezra 5. † 5. [7] *To change one thing into another*, John 2. 9. [help
Gen. 1. 26. let us *m.* man ‖ 2. 18. I will *m.* him an
3. 6. and a tree to be desired to *m.* one wise
21. *m.* coats of skins ‖ 6. 14. *m.* thee an ark
11. 3. let us *m.* brick ‖ 4. let us *m.* us a name
12. 2. I will *m.* of thee a great nation, and I will bless thee, 21. 18. ‖ 46. 3. *Exod.* 32. 10.
4. let us *m.* us a name, lest we be scattered
13. 16. I will *m.* thy seed as the dust of the earth
17. 6. I will *m.* thee exceeding fruitful, 48. 4.
17. 20. I will *m.* Ishmael fruitful, I will *m.*
19. 32. let us *m.* our father drink wine, 34.
26. 4. I will *m.* thy seed as the stars of heaven
27. 4. Isa. said, *m.* me savoury meat, such as I love
28. 3. G. Almighty bless thee, and *m.* thee fruitful
32. 12. I will *m.* thy seed as the sand of the sea
34. 9. *m.* ye marriages with us, and give daughters
30. ye *m.* me to stink among the inhabitants
35. 1. go to Beth-el, and *m.* there an altar to God
3. I will *m.* there an altar unto God
40. 14. and *m.* mention of me to Pharaoh

Gen. 47. 6. in best of the land *m.* thy father to dw.
48. 20. God *m.* thee as Ephraim and Manasseh
Exod. 5. 16. no straw given, they say to us, *m.* brick
12. 4. shall *m.* your count for the lamb
18. 16. I do *m.* them know the statutes of God
20. 4. thou shalt not *m.* unto thee any graven image, or likeness, *Lev.* 26. 1. *Deut.* 5. 8.
23. ye shall not *m.* with me gods of silver
24. an altar of earth shalt thou *m.* unto me
25. if thou wilt *m.* me an altar of stones
22. 3. for he should *m.* full restitution, 5, 6, 12.
23. 13. *m.* no mention of other gods, *Josh.* 23. 7.
27. I will *m.* enemies turn their backs to thee
33. shall not dwell, lest they *m.* thee sin against me
25. 8. *m.* me a sanctuary ‖ 9. so shall ye *m.* it
28. 2. thou shalt *m.* holy garments for Aaron, 4.
4. these are the garments which they shall *m.*
40. for Aaron's sons thou shalt *m.* coats, girdles
42. thou shalt *m.* them linen breeches
30. 1. thou shalt *m.* him an altar of shittim-wood
25. thou shalt *m.* it an oil of holy ointment
37. as to perfume, you shall not *m.* like to it
31. 6. that they *m.* all that I commanded, 35. 10.
32. 1. up, *m.* us gods to go before us, 23. *Acts* 7. 40.
10. I will *m.* of thee a great nation
33. 19. I will *m.* my goodness pass before thee
34. 16. and *m.* thy sons go a whoring after their gods
17. thou shalt not *m.* molten gods, *Lev.* 19. 4.
36. 6. neither man nor woman *m.* any more
Lev. 5. 16. he shall *m.* amends for the harm done
11. 43. not *m.* yourselves abominable, 20. 25.
19. 28. not *m.* any cuttings in your flesh for dead
21. 5. they shall not *m.* baldness, *Deut.* 14. 1.
26. 9. I will *m.* you fruitful, and multiply you
19. I will *m.* your heaven as iron, earth as brass
22. beasts, which shall *m.* you few in number
27. 2. when a man shall *m.* a singular vow
Num. 5. 21. the L. *m.* thee a curse, *m.* thy thigh rot
6. 7. he shall not *m.* himself unclean for his father
25. the Lord *m.* his face to shine upon thee
8. 7. let them wash, and so *m.* themselves clean
14. 4. let us *m.* a captain, and return to Egypt
12. I will *m.* of thee a greater nation than they
16. 13. except thou *m.* thyself a prince over us
30. if the Lord *m.* a new thing and the earth open
38. let them *m.* them broad plates for the altar
17. 5. I will *m.* to cease from me the murmurings
21. 8. *m.* thee a fiery serpent, and set it on a pole
30. 8. he shall *m.* her vow of none effect
31. 23. ye shall *m.* it go through fire and water
Deut. 1. 11. Lord *m.* you a thousand times more
13. and I will *m.* them rulers over you
4. 10. I will *m.* them hear my words to fear me
16. lest ye *m.* you a graven image, 23.
7. 3. nor shalt thou *m.* marriages with them
8. 3. *m.* thee know that man liveth not by bread
20. 11. if it *m.* thee answer of peace, and open to
12. if it will *m.* no peace with thee, but war
26. 19. to *m.* thee high above all nations he made
28. 11. the Lord shall *m.* thee plenteous, 30. 9.
13. Lord shall *m.* thee the head, and not the tail
32. 26. *m.* the remembrance of them to cease
39. I kill, and I *m.* alive, I wound, and I heal
Josh. 1. 8. thou shalt *m.* thy way prosperous
6. 18. lest ye *m.* yourselves accursed, and *m.* the camp of Israel a curse, and trouble it
7. 19. and *m.* confession to him, *Ezra* 10. 11.
22. 25. so shall your children *m.* our child. cease
23. 12. and shall *m.* marriages with them
Judg. 16. 25. Samson, that he may *m.* us sport
Ruth 4. 11. L. *m.* the woman like Rachel and Leah
1 *Sam.* 1. 6. provoked her sore, to *m.* her fret
2. 8. and to *m.* them inherit the throne of glory
24. ye *m.* the Lord's people to transgress
29. to *m.* yourselves fat with chiefest offerings
6. 5. ye shall *m.* images of your emerods
7. *m.* a new cart ‖ 8. 5. *m.* us a king to judge us
8. 22. hearken to them, and *m.* them a king
12. 22. L. will not forsake, because it hath pleased the Lord to *m.* you his people, 1 *Chron.* 17. 22.
25. 28. the Lord will *m.* my lord a sure house
28. 2. I will *m.* thee keeper of mine head for ever
29. 4. *m.* this fellow return that he may go again
2 *Sam.* 7. 11. that he will *m.* thee an house
21. hast done these things, to *m.* thy servant know
23. to *m.* him a name ‖ 13. 5. and *m.* thyself sick
15. 20. should I *m.* thee go up and down with us?
23. 5. all my desire, though he *m.* it not to grow
1 *Kings* 1. 37. *m.* his throne greater than David's
47. God *m.* the name of Solomon better than
2. 42. did I not *m.* thee to swear by the Lord
8. 29. mayest hearken to the prayer which thy servant shall *m.* toward this place, 2 *Chr.* 6. 21.
33. shall confess thy name, pray, and *m.* supplication to thee in this house, 47. 2 *Chron.* 6. 24.
11. 34. I will *m.* him prince all the days of his life
12. 9. *m.* the yoke lighter, 10. 2 *Chron.* 10. 10.
16. 3. I will *m.* thy house like the house of Jeroboam the son of Nebat, 21. 22. 2 *Kings* 9. 9.
17. 13. and after *m.* for thee and for thy son
19. 2. if *m.* not thy life as the life of one of them
2 *Kings* 4. 10. let us *m.* a little chamber on the wall
5. 7. am I God to kill and to *m.* alive?
6. 2. let us *m.* a place, where we may dwell
7. 2. if Lord would *m.* windows in heaven, 19.
9. 2. *m.* him arise up, and anoint him king
10. 5. we will not *m.* any king, do that is good
18. 31. *m.* an agreement with me, *Isa.* 36. 16.
21. 8. nor will I *m.* feet of Israel move any more
23. 10. that no man might *m.* his son or daughter to pass through the fire to Molech, *Ezek.* 20. 31.
1 *Chron.* 11. 10. all Israel to *m.* him king, 12. 31, 38.
17. 21. to *m.* thee a name of greatn. and terribleness
21. 3. Lord *m.* his people 100 times so many more
28. 4. he liked me to *m.* me king over Israel
29. 12. O Lord, in thine hand it is to *m.* great
2 *Chr.* 7. 20. will *m.* it a proverb among all nations
11. 22. for he thought to *m.* him king
25. 8. God shall *m.* thee fall before the enemy
Ezra 6. 8. I *m.* a decree what ye shall do, 7. 13, 21.
Neh. 8. 15. fetch branches of thick trees to *m.* booths
Esth. 4. 8. go in to the king to *m.* supplication to him

Esth. 7. 7. Haman stood up to *m.* request for his life
9. 22. they should *m.* them days of feasting and joy
Job 5. 18. he woundeth and his hands *m.* whole
8. 5. *m.* thy supplication to the Almighty, 22. 27.
9. 30. and if I *m.* my hands never so clean
11. 3. should thy lies *m.* men hold their peace?
13. 23. *m.* me to know my transgression and sin
19. 3. that ye *m.* yourselves strange to me
24. 25. if it be not so now, who will *m.* me a liar?
31. 15. did not he that made me in womb *m.* him?
34. 29. he giveth quietness, who then can *m.* trouble?
35. 9. they *m.* the oppressed to cry, they cry out
40. 19. can *m.* his sword to approach to him
41. 3. will he *m.* many supplications to thee?
Psal. 5. 8. *m.* thy way straight before my face
† 10. *m.* them guilty, O God, let them fall
6. 6. all the night *m.* I my bed to swim
20. † 3. the Lord *m.* fat thy burnt sacrifice
21. 9. thou shalt *m.* them as a fiery oven in anger
12. therefore thou shalt *m.* them turn their back
22. 9. thou didst *m.* me hope when on breasts
25. † 14. he will *m.* them know his covenant
31. 16. *m.* thy face shine on thy servant, 119. 135.
34. 2. my soul shall *m.* her boast in the Lord
39. 4. Lord, *m.* me to know mine end and days
8. *m.* me not the reproach of the foolish
40. 17. *m.* no tarrying, 70. 5. ‖ 41. 3. will *m.* all his bed
45. 17. I will *m.* thy name to be remembered
46. 4. the streams shall *m.* glad the city of God
51. 6. in hidden part shalt *m.* me know wisdom
8. *m.* me to hear joy and gladness, that the bones
57. 1. of thy wings, will I *m.* my refuge, 61. † 4.
66. 2. sing forth his name, *m.* his praise glorious
8. ye people, *m.* the voice of his praise to be heard
83. 2. for lo, thine enemies *m.* a tumult
11. *m.* their nobles like Oreb and Zeeb
13. O my God, *m.* them like a wheel
84. 6. through the valley of Baca, *m.* it a well
89. 27. also I will *m.* him my first-born
29. his seed also will I *m.* to endure for ever
90. 15. *m.* us glad, according to the days afflicted
110. 1. until I *m.* thine enemies thy footstool, *Mat.* 22. 44. *Mark* 12. 36. *Luke* 20. 43. *Acts* 2. 35. *Heb.* 1. 13.
115. 8. they that *m.* them are like unto them, 135. 18.
119. 27. *m.* me to understand the way of thy precepts
35. *m.* me go in the path of thy commandments
132. 17. there will I *m.* the horn of David to bud
137. † 7. *m.* bare even to the foundation
139. 8. if I *m.* my bed in hell, thou art there
142. 1. to the Lord did I *m.* my supplication
Prov. 6. 3. go humble thyself, and *m.* sure thy friend
14. 9. fools *m.* a mock at sin, but among righteous
20. 18. and with good advice *m.* war
25. it is a snare after vows to *m.* enquiry
22. 21. that I might *m.* thee know the certainty
24. *m.* no friendship with an angry man
23. 5. for riches certainly *m.* themselves wings
27. 11. my son, be wise, and *m.* my heart glad
30. 26. yet *m.* they their houses in the rocks
Eccl. 7. 13. who can *m.* that straight which he
16. not right. over-much, nor *m.* thyself over-wise
Isa. 1. 15. when ye *m.* many prayers, I will not hear
16. wash you, *m.* you clean ‖ 3. 7. *m.* me not a ruler
6. 10. *m.* the heart of this people fat, ears heavy
7. 6. and let us *m.* a breach therein for us
† 11. *m.* thy petition deep, or in the height above
10. 23. the Lord of hosts shall *m.* a consumption
11. 3. and shall *m.* him of quick understanding
15. and shall *m.* men go over dry shod
12. 4. *m.* mention that his name is exalted
13. 12. I will *m.* a man more precious than gold
16. 3. *m.* thy shadow as the night in noon-day
25. 6. Lord *m.* to all people a feast of fat things
27. 5. that he may *m.* peace with me, and he shall
28. 9. whom shall he *m.* to understand doctrine?
29. 21. that *m.* a man an offender for a word
32. 6. to *m.* empty the soul of the hungry
38. 16. so wilt thou recover me and *m.* me live
40. 3. *m.* straight in the desert a highway for our God, *Mat.* 3. 3. *Mark* 1. 3. *Luke* 3. 4.
41. 18. I will *m.* the wilderness a pool of water
42. 15. I will *m.* the rivers islands, dry up pools
16. I will *m.* darkness light before them
21. he will magnify and *m.* the law honourable
43. 19. I will even *m.* a way in the wilderness
44. 9. they that *m.* a graven image are vanity
45. 2. and *m.* the crooked places straight
7. I *m.* peace and create evil, I the L. do all things
† 13. and I will *m.* straight all his ways
14. they shall *m.* supplication to thee
46. 5. to whom will ye *m.* me equal, and compare me
47. 2. *m.* bare the leg, uncover the thigh, pass over
48. 15. and he shall *m.* his way prosperous
49. 11. and I will *m.* all my mountains a way
50. 2. behold I *m.* the rivers a wilderness
51. 4. I will *m.* my judgments to rest for a light
52. 5. they that rule over them, *m.* them to howl
53. 10. when thou shalt *m.* his soul an offering
54. 12. I will *m.* thy windows of agates, thy gates
56. 7. I will *m.* them joyful in my house of prayer
57. 4. against whom *m.* ye a wide mouth?
58. 4. to *m.* your voice to be heard on high
11. and the Lord shall *m.* fat thy bones
60. 13. I will *m.* the place of my feet glorious
15. I will *m.* thee an eternal excellency
17. I will *m.* also thy officers peace and exactors
62. 7. till he *m.* Jerusalem a praise in the earth
63. 6. and I will *m.* them drunk in my fury
12. the water to *m.* himself an everlasting name
14. lead thy people to *m.* thyself a glorious name
64. 2. to *m.* thy name known to thy adversaries
66. 22. as new earth which I will *m.* shall remain
Jer. 4. 30. in vain shalt thou *m.* thyself fair
5. 14. I will *m.* my words in thy mouth fire
6. 26. *m.* thee mourning, as for an only son
7. 16. nor *m.* intercession to me for this people
9. 11. I will *m.* Jerusalem heaps and den of dragons
13. 16. he turn it, and *m.* it gross darkness
15. 20. I will *m.* thee a fenced brasen wall
16. 20. shall a man *m.* gods to himself, and no gods
18. 4. as seemed good to the potter to *m.* it

Jer. 19. 7. I will *m.* void counsel of Judah and Jeru.
12. I will even *m.* this city as Tophet
20. 4. I will *m.* thee a terror to thyself
22. 6. yet surely I will *m.* thee a wilderness
23.16. hearken not to the prophets, they *m.* you vain
26. 6. then will I *m.* this house like Shiloh
27.2.*m.* thee bonds and yokes, put them on thy neck
18. let them now *m.* intercession to the Lord
29. 17. behold, I will *m.* them like vile figs
22. the Lord *m.* thee like Zedekiah and Ahab
34. 17. I will *m.* you be removed into all kingdoms
44. 19. did we *m.* her cakes to worship her?
48. 26. *m.* ye him drunken, for he magnified himself
49. 15. I will *m.* thee small among the heathen
51. 25. I will *m.* thee a burnt mountain
36. and *m.* her springs dry ‖ 39. *m.* them drunken
57. I will *m.* drunk her princes and wise men
Lam. 3. † 21. this I *m.* to return to my heart
Ezek. 4. 9. *m.* bread thereof ‖ 7. 23. *m.* a chain
14.8. I will *m.* him a sign and a proverb, and cut off
16. 42. I will *m.* my fury toward thee to rest
18. 31. and *m.* you a new heart, and a new spirit
21. 10. it is furbished, should we then *m.* mirth?
† 27. perverted, perverted, perverted will I *m.* it
22. 30. sought a man that should *m.* up the hedge
24. 17. *m.* no mourning for the dead, bind the tire
26. 4. and *m.* her like the top of a rock, 14.
21. I will *m.* thee a terror, thou shalt be no more
32. 7. I will *m.* the stars thereof dark, 8.
34. 26. and I will *m.* them and places a blessing
37. 19. *m.* them one stick, shall be one in my hand
22. I will *m.* them one nation in the land
44. 14. I will *m.* them keepers of charge of house
Dan. 4. 25. shall *m.* thee to eat grass as oxen, 32.
8. 16. *m.* this man to understand the vision, 10. 14.
9. 24. seventy weeks to *m.* reconciliation for iniqui.
11. 35. some shall fall to *m.* them white
44. he shall go utterly to purge and *m.* away many
Hos. 2. 3. lest I *m.* her as a wilderness, and slay her
6. I will *m.* a wall, that she shall not find her path
18. and I will *m.* them to lie down safely
7. 3. they *m.* the king glad with their wickedness
10. 11. I will *m.* Ephraim ride, Judah shall plow
11.8. how shall *m.* thee as Adma, set thee as Zeboim
12. 9. I will yet *m.* thee dwell in tabernacles
Joel 2. 19. nor will I *m.* you a reproach any more
Amos 8. 4. even to *m.* the poor of the land to fail
9.14. they shall *m.* gardens, and eat fruit of them
Mic. 3. 5. the prophets that *m.* my people err
4. 7. I will *m.* her that halted a remnant
6. 13. therefore I will *m.* thee sick in smiting thee
Nah. 1. 14. I will *m.* thy grave, for thou art vile
3. 6. I will cast filth on thee, and *m.* thee vile
15.*m.* thyself many as the canker-worm, or locusts
*Hab.*2.2. write the vision,and *m.* it plain upon tables
3. 19. he will *m.* my feet like hinds' feet
Zeph. 1. 18. for he shall *m.* even a speedy riddance
3. 20. for I will *m.* you a name and a praise
Hag. 2. 23. saith the Lord, I will *m.* thee a signet
Zech. 10. 1. so the Lord shall *m.* bright clouds
12. 2. I will *m.* Jerusalem a cup of trembling
3. in that day will I *m.* Jerus. a burdensome stone
Mal. 2. 15. did not he *m.* one? yet had the residue
3. 17. in that day when I *m.* up my jewels
Mat. 1. 19. not willing to *m.* her a public example
4. 19. I will *m.* you fishers of men, *Mark* 1. 17.
5. 36. thou canst not *m.* one hair white or black
8. 2. behold, a leper said, Lord, if thou wilt, thou canst *m.* me clean, *Mark* 1. 40. *Luke* 5. 12.
12. 33. *m.* the tree good, *m.* the tree corrupt
17. 4. Peter said, Lord, if thou wilt, let us *m.* here three tabernacles, *Mark* 9. 5. *Luke* 9. 33.
23. 14. for pretence *m.* long prayers, *Mark* 12. 40.
15. to *m.* one proselyte, and when he is made
25. ye *m.* clean the outside of the cup, *Luke* 11. 39.
25. 21. I will *m.* thee ruler over many things
27. 65. go your way, *m.* it as sure as ye can
Mark 5. 39. why *m.* ye this ado and weep?
Luke 5.34. can ye *m.* children of bride-chamber fast?
11. 40. did he not *m.* that which is within also?
14. 18. all with one consent began to *m.* excuse
15. 19. *m.* me as one of thy hired servants
16. 9. *m.* friends of the mammon of unrighteousness
John 1. 23. *m.* straight the way of the Lord
2. 16. *m.* not my Father's house house of merchand.
6. 15. and take him by force to *m.* him a king
8. 32. know truth, and the truth shall *m.* you free
36. if the Son *m.* you free, ye shall be free indeed
10. 24. how long dost thou *m.* us to doubt?
14. 23. we will come and *m.* our abode with him
Acts 2. 28. *m.* me full of joy with thy countenance
9. 34. Peter said to him, arise and *m.* thy bed
26. 16. to *m.* thee a minister and a witness
24. Paul, much learning doth *m.* thee mad
Rom. 3. 3. *m.* the faith of God without effect
31. do we then *m.* void the law through faith?
9. 21. power to *m.* one vessel unto honour
28. short work will the Lord *m.* on the earth
13. 14. and *m.* not provision for the flesh
14. 4. for God is able to *m.* him stand
19. follow the things which *m.* for peace
15. 26. to *m.* a certain contribution for the poor
1 *Cor.* 6. 15. and *m.* them the members of a harlot
8. 13. if meat *m.* my brother to offend
10. 13. with temptation also *m.* a way to escape
2 *Cor.* 2. 2. if I *m.* you sorry, who then maketh glad?
9. 5. and *m.* up beforehand your bounty
8. and God is able to *m.* all grace abound
12. 17. did I *m.* gain of you by any of them?
Gal. 2. 18. I *m.* myself a transgressor
3. 17. that it should *m.* the promise of none effect
6. 12. as many as desire to *m.* a fair shew in flesh
Eph. 2. 15. to *m.* in himself of twain one new man
1 *Thess.* 3. 12. the Lord *m.* you to increase in love
2 *Thess.* 3. 9. but to *m.* ourselves an ensample to you
2 *Tim.* 3. 15. are able to *m.* thee wise to salvation
4. 5. *m.* full proof of thy ministry
Heb. 2. 10. to *m.* the Captain of their salvation perf.
17. to *m.* reconciliation for the sins of the people
7. 25. he ever liveth to *m.* intercession for them
8. 5. *m.* all things according to pattern shewed
9. 9. could not *m.* him that did service perfect
Heb. 10. 1. *m.* the comers thereunto perfect
12. 13. and *m.* straight paths for your feet
13. 21. *m.* you perfect in every good work to do will
Jam. 3. 18. is sown in peace, of them that *m.* peace
1 *Pet.* 5. 10. the God of all grace *m.* you perfect
2 *Pet.* 1. 10. *m.* your calling and election sure
1 *John* 1. 10. we *m.* him a liar, his word is not in us
Rev. 3. 9. I will *m.* them worship before thy feet
12. I will *m.* a pillar in the temple of my God
10. 9. eat it, and it shall *m.* thy belly bitter
11. 7. shall *m.* war against them, and overcome
12. 17. went to *m.* war with the remnant of her seed
13. 4. saying, who is able to *m.* war with him?
14. that they should *m.* an image to the beast
19. 11. in righteousness he doth judge and *m.* war
21. 5. behold, I *m.* all things new.
See AFRAID, ATONEMENT, COVENANT, DESOLATE, DESOLATION, END, FIRE, GOOD.

MAKE *haste.*

Deut. 32. 35. the things that come on them *m. haste*
Judg. 9. 48. and said, *m. haste* and do as I have done
1 *Sam.* 9. 12. behold, he is before you, *m. haste* now
2 *Chron.* 35. 21. for God commanded me to *m. haste*
Esth. 5. 5. king said, cause Haman to *m. haste*, 6. 10.
Job 20. 2. cause me to answer, for this I *m. haste*
Psal. 38. 22. *m. haste* to help me, O Lord, my salvation, 40. 13. | 70. 1. | 71. 12.
70. 5. I am poor and needy, *m. haste* unto me, 141. 1.
Prov. 1. 16. they *m. haste* to shed blood, *Isa.* 59. 7.
Cant. 8. 14. *m. haste*, my beloved, and be like a roe
Isa. 28. 16. he that believeth shall not *m. haste*
49. 17. thy children shall *m. haste*, thy destroyers
Jer. 9. 18. let them *m. haste*, and take up a wailing
Nah. 2. 5. they shall *m. haste* to the wall thereof
Luke 19. 5. he said, Zaccheus, *m. haste* and come down
Acts 22. 18. *m. haste* and get quickly out of Jerusalem
See KNOWN.

MAKE *manifest.*

1 *Cor.* 4. 5. will *m. manifest* the counsels of the heart
Eph. 5. 13. whatsoever doth *m. manifest* is light
Col. 4. 4. that I may *m.* it *manifest* as I ought
See MENTION, NOISE.

MAKE *ready.*

Gen. 18. 6. *m. ready* three measures of fine meal
43. 16. *m. ready*, for these men shall dine with me
2 *Kings* 9. 21. and Joram said, *m. r.* and he went out
Psal. 11. 2. they *m. ready* their arrow on the string
21. 12. when thou shalt *m. ready* thine arrows
Ezek. 7. 14. they have blown the trumpet to *m. ready*
Mark 14. 15. there *m. ready* for us, *Luke* 22. 12.
Luke 1. 17. to *m. ready* a people prepared for the [Lord
17. 8. rather say, *m. ready*, wherewith I may sup
Acts 23. 23. *m. ready* 200 soldiers to go to Cesarea

MAKE *speed.*

1 *Sam.* 20. 38. he cried, *m. speed*, haste, stay not
2 *Sam.* 15. 14. *m. speed* to depart, lest he overtake
Isa. 5. 19. that say, let him *m. speed* and hasten

MAKE *waste.*

Lev. 26. 31. I will *m.* your cities *waste*, and bring
Isa. 42. 15. I will *m. waste* mountains and hills
Ezek. 5. 14. moreover, I will *m.* Jerusalem *waste*
29. 10. I will *m.* land of Egypt utterly *waste*, 30. 12.

MAKER, or MAKERS.

Job 4. 17. shall a man be more pure than his *M.?*
32. 22. in so doing my *M.* will soon take me away
35. 10. but none saith, where is God my *M.?*
36. 3. I will ascribe righteousness to my *M.*
Psal. 95. 6. let us kneel before the Lord our *M.*
Prov. 14. 31. oppresseth the poor, reproacheth his *M.*
17. 5. whoso mocketh the poor reproacheth his *M.*
22. 2. rich and poor, the Lord is the *m.* of them all
Isa. 1. 31. and the *m.* of it as a spark
17. 7. at that day shall a man look to his *M.*
22. 11. ye have not looked to the *m.* thereof
33. † 22. the Lord is our statute *m.* he will save us
45. 9. woe to him that striveth with his *M.*
11. thus saith the holy One of Israel and his *M.*
16. they shall go to confusion that are *m.* of idols
51. 13. forgettest the Lord thy *m.* that stretched out
54. 5. thy *M.* is thy husband, and thy Redeemer
Jer. 33. 2. thus saith the Lord the *m.* thereof
Hos. 8. 14. for Israel hath forgotten his *M.*
Hab. 2. 18. what profiteth the graven image that the *m.* hath graven, *m.* of his work trusteth therein?
Heb. 11. 10. for a city, whose builder and *m.* is God

MAKEST.

Judg. 18. 3. and what *m.* thou in this place?
Job 13. 26. *m.* me possess the iniquities of my youth
22. 3. is it gain to him that thou *m.* thy ways perfect?
Psal. 4. 8. thou only *m.* me to dwell in safety
39. 11. thou *m.* his beauty to consume as a moth
44. 10. thou *m.* us to turn back from the enemy
13. thou *m.* us a reproach to our neighbours
14. thou *m.* us a by-word among the heathen
65. 8. thou *m.* the outgoings of morning to rejoice
10. thou *m.* the earth soft with showers
80. 6. thou *m.* us a strife to our neighbours
104. 20. thou *m.* darkness, and it is night
144. 3. what is man, that thou *m.* account of him?
Cant. 1. 7. where thou *m.* thy flock to rest at noon
Isa. 45. 9. to him that fashioneth it, what *m.* thou?
Jer. 22. 23. O Lebanon, that *m.* thy nest in cedars
28. 15. thou *m.* this people to trust in a lie
Ezek. 16. 31. thou *m.* thy high place in every street
Hab. 1. 14. and *m.* men as the fishes of the sea
2. 15. puttest thy bottle to him, and *m.* him drunken
Luke 14. 12. when thou *m.* a dinner or a supper
13. but when thou *m.* a feast, call the poor
John 8. 53. proph. are dead, whom *m.* thou thyself?
10. 33. because thou being a man *m.* thyself God
Rom. 2. 17. art called a Jew, and *m.* thy boast of God
23. thou that *m.* thy boast of the law

MAKETH.

Exod. 4. 11. or who *m.* the dumb, or deaf, or blind?
Lev. 7. 7. the priest that *m.* atonement clean, 14. 11.
17. 11. it is the blood that *m.* an atonement
Deut. 18. 10. that *m.* his son to pass through the fire
20. 20. against the city that *m.* war with thee
21. 16. when he *m.* his sons to inherit what he hath
24. 7. *m.* merchandise of him, or selleth him
27. 15. cursed be the man that *m.* any graven image
Deut. 27. 18. cursed be he that *m.* blind to wander
29. 12. oath which the Lord *m.* with thee this day
1 *Sam.* 2. 6. the Lord killeth and *m.* alive
7. the Lord *m.* poor and *m.* rich, he bringeth low
2 *Sam.* 22. 33. God *m.* my way perfect, *Ps.* 18. 32.
22. 34. he *m.* my feet like hinds' feet, *Psal.* 18. 33.
Job 5. 18. for he *m.* sore, and bindeth up, he wounds
9. 9. Lord *m.* Arcturus, Orion, and Pleiades
12. 17. he *m.* the judges fools ‖ 25. he *m.* to stagger
15. 27. he *m.* collops of fat on his flanks
23. 16. God *m.* my heart soft, and troubleth me
25. 2. he *m.* peace in his high places
27. 18. and as a booth that the keeper *m.*
35. 11. who *m.* us wiser than the fowls of heaven
36. 27. for he *m.* small the drops of water, they pour
41. 31. he *m.* the deep to boil like a pot
32. he *m.* a path to shine after him
Psal. 9. 12. when he *m.* inquisition for blood
23. 2. he *m.* me to lie down in green pastures
29. 9. the voice of the Lord *m.* the hinds to calve
33. 10. he *m.* the devices of people of none effect
40. 4. blessed is the man that *m.* the Ld. his trust
46. 9. he *m.* wars to cease to the end of the earth
104. 3. who *m.* the clouds his chariot, who walketh
4. who *m.* his angels spirits, *Heb.* 1. 7.
15. and wine that *m.* glad the heart of man
107. † 25. and *m.* the stormy wind to stand
29. he *m.* the storm a calm, the waters are still
36. and there he *m.* the hungry to dwell
41. and *m.* him families like a flock
113. 9. he *m.* the barren woman to keep house
135. 7. he *m.* lightnings for rain, brings the wind
147. 8. who *m.* grass to grow on the mountains
14. he *m.* peace in thy borders, and filleth thee
Prov. 10. 1. a wise son *m.* a glad father, 15. 20.
4. but the hand of the diligent *m.* rich
22. the blessing of the Lord, it *m.* rich
12. 4. she that *m.* ashamed is as rottenness in bones
25. heaviness in the heart of a man *m.* it to stoop, but a good word *m.* it glad
13. 7. that *m.* himself rich, yet hath nothing, there is that *m.* himself poor, yet hath great riches
12. hope deferred *m.* the heart sick, when desire
15. 13. a merry heart *m.* a cheerful countenance
30. and a good report *m.* the bones fat
16. 7. he *m.* even his enemies to be at peace with him
† 23. the heart of the wise *m.* wise his mouth
18. 16. a man's gift *m.* room for him, and brings
19. 4. wealth *m.* many friends, but poor is separated
31. 22. she *m.* herself coverings of tapestry
24. she *m.* fine linen, and selleth it, and girdles
Eccl. 3. 11. no man can find out the work that G. *m.*
7. 7. surely oppression *m.* a wise man mad
8. 1. a man's wisdom *m.* his face to shine
11. 5. thou knowest not works of God, who *m.* all
Isa. 24. 1. behold, the Lord *m.* the earth empty
40. 23. he *m.* the judges of the earth as vanity
43. 16. saith the Lord, which *m.* a way in the sea
44. 15. he *m.* a god, and worshippeth it, 17. | 46. 6.
24. I am the Lord that *m.* all things
25. he *m.* diviners mad ‖ 59. 15. *m.* himself a prey
55. 10. watereth earth, and *m.* it bring forth
Jer. 10. 13. he *m.* lightnings with rain, 51. 16.
17. 5. cursed be the man that *m.* flesh his arm
29. 26. every man that *m.* himself a prophet, 27.
Ezek. 22. 3. and *m.* idols against herself to defile
Dan. 6. 13. but *m.* his petition three times a day
11. 31. place abomination that *m.* desolate, 12. 11.
Amos 4. 13. that *m.* the morning darkness
5. 8. seek him that *m.* the seven stars and Orion
Nah. 1. 4. he rebuketh the sea, and *m.* it dry
Mat. 5. 45. he *m.* his sun rise on the evil and good
Mark 7. 37. he *m.* both deaf to hear, and dumb speak
John 19. 12. whosoever *m.* himself a king, speaketh
Acts 9. 34. Eneas, Jesus Christ *m.* thee whole
Rom. 5. 5. hope *m.* not ashamed, because love of G.
8. 26. the Spirit *m.* intercession for us, 27, 34.
11. 2. he *m.* intercession to God against Israel
1 *Cor.* 4. 7. who *m.* thee to differ from another?
2 *Cor.* 2. 2. who is he that *m.* me glad but the same?
14. *m.* manifest the savour of his knowledge by us
Gal. 2. 6. whatsoever they were, it *m.* no matter
Eph. 4. 16. *m.* increase of the body to the edifying
Heb. 7. 28. for the law *m.* men high-priests, but the word of the oath since the law *m.* the Son
Rev. 13. 13. he *m.* fire come down from heaven
21. 27. nor whatsoever *m.* a lie, 22. 15.

MAKETH *haste.*

Prov. 28. 20. that *m. haste* to be rich, not innocent

MAKING.

2 *Chron.* 30. 22. *m.* confession to the Lord God
Ps. 19. 7. testimony of Lord is sure, *m.* wise simple
Eccl. 12. 12. of *m.* many books there is no end
Isa. 3. 16. walking and *m.* a tinkling with their feet
Jer. 20. 15. that brought tidings, *m.* him very glad
Amos 8. 5. *m.* ephah small, and the shekel great
Mark 7. 13. *m.* the word of God of none effect
John 5. 18. *m.* himself equal with God
2 *Cor.* 6. 10. as poor, yet *m.* many rich
Eph. 1. 16. I cease not to give thanks for you, *m.* mention of you in my prayers, 1 *Thess.* 1. 2. *Philem.* 4.
2. 15. one new man, so *m.* peace, *Col.* 1. † 20.
5. 19. *m.* melody in your heart to the Lord [joy
Phil. 1. 4. in every prayer for you, *m.* request with
2 *Pet.* 2. 6. *m.* them an ensample unto those that
Jude 22. of some have compassion, *m.* a difference

MAKING.

Ezek. 27. 16. multitude of the wares of thy *m.* 18.

MALE.

Gen. 17. 23. every *m.* circumcised, 34. 15. 22, 24.
Exod. 12. 5. for the passover a *m.* of the first year
13. 12. the *m.* shall be the Lord's, 34. 19. *Luke* 2. 23.
Lev. 1. 3. a *m.* without blemish, 10. | 4. 23. | 22. 19.
7. 6. every *m.* among the priests shall eat thereof
27. 3. thy estimation shall be of the *m.* 5, 6, 7.
Num. 1. 2. every *m.* by their polls from 20 years old
20. every *m.* from 20 years old and upward
3. 15. every *m.* from a month old and upward
31. 17. now kill every *m.* among the little ones
Deut. 20. 13. thou shalt smite every *m.* thereof
Judg. 21. 11. ye shall utterly destroy every *m.*
1 *Kings* 11. 15. he had smitten every *m.* in Edom. 16.

Jer. 30. †6. see if a *m.* doth travail with child
Ezek. 16. †17. makest to thyself images of a *m.*
Mal. 1. 14. which hath in his flock a *m.*
See FEMALE.

MALE-CHILDREN.

Josh. 17. 2. these were the *m.-children* of Manasseh

MALEFACTOR.

John 18. 30. if he were not a *m.* we would not

MALEFACTORS.

Luke 23. 32. there were two *m.* led with him
33. there they crucified him, and the *m.*
39. one of the *m.* railed on him, saying

MALES.

Gen. 34. 25. Simeon and Levi slew all the *m.*
Exod. 12. 48. let all his *m.* be circumcised
13. 15. I sacrifice to the Lord all being *m.*
23. 17. three times in the year all thy *m.* shall appear before the Lord God, *Deut.* 16. 16.
Lev. 6. 18. all the *m.* of Aaron shall eat of it, 29.
Num. 3. 22. according to the number of all *m.* from a month old and upward, 28, 34. | 26. 62.
40. number all the first-born of the *m.* 43.
31. 7. warred against Midianites, and slew the *m.*
Deut. 15. 19. all firstling *m.* sanctify to the Lord
Josh. 5. 4. the *m.* that came out of Egypt died
2 *Chron.* 31. 16. beside their genealogy of *m.*
19. to give portions to all the *m.* among priests
Ezra 8. 3. were reckoned by genealogy of the *m.*

MALICE.

1 *Cor.* 5. 8. keep the feast, not with leaven of *m.*
14. 20. howbeit in *m.* be ye children
Eph. 4. 31. be put away from you with all *m.*
Col. 3. 8. but now ye also put off all these, *m.*
Tit. 3. 3. sometimes living in *m.* and envy, hateful
1 *Pet.* 2. 1. wherefore, laying aside all *m.* and guile

MALICIOUS.

3 *John* 10. prating against us with *m.* words

MALICIOUSNESS.

Rom. 1. 29. being filled with all unrighteousness, *m.*
1 *Pet.* 2. 16. not using liberty for a cloke of *m.*

MALIGNITY.

Rom. 1. 29. full of envy, murder, debate, *m.*

MALLOWS.

Job 30. 4. who cut up *m.* by the bushes for meat

MAN.

Man *was, in his original state, a very noble and exalted creature; being placed as the head and lord of this world, having all the creatures in subjection to him. The powers and operations of his mind were extensive, capacious, and perfect; capable of contemplating upon the works of God with pleasure and delight, and of performing his will without the least deviation. But by sinning against his Creator, his mind is vitiated, corrupted, and debased; and he is in a ruined, lost, miserable, and wretched state: Hence it is asked,* What is man? *Psal.* 8. 4. *The Hebrew word for* man *is* Enosh; *that is, sorry, wretched, and incurably sick, to denote his condition in his apostasy from God.*

Man *is put for,* [1] *The body,* 2 Cor. 4. 16. [2] *The sins and corruptions of human nature,* Eph. 4. 22. [3] *Strong, valiant,* 1 Cor. 16. 13. [4] *A magistrate,* Gen. 9. 6. [5] *Frail, weak,* Psal. 9. 20. [6] *The church,* Eph. 2. 15. [7] *A strong believer,* Eph. 4. 13. [8] *An angel,* Acts 1. 10. [9] *The Lord Jesus,* Gen. 32. 24. Mark 15. 39. [10] *God the Father,* Exod. 15. 3. Luke 15. 11.

To make of twain one new man, *Eph.* 2. 15. *To unite Jews and Gentiles, who formerly were at variance, into one church, or body, joining together in a new way of gospel-worship.*

The gospel is not after man, *Gal.* 1. 11. *It is no human invention, or fiction, neither doth it depend upon human authority, but is immediately revealed by God.*

I speak after the manner of men, *Gal.* 3. 15. *I make use of a comparison taken from the custom of men in their civil affairs.*

A man of God, 2 *Tim.* 3. 17. *One that is guided by the Spirit of God, and devoted to his service in a special manner.*

The inward man, *Rom.* 7. 22. *The new man, the regenerate part within me, or the principle of grace in the heart.*

The natural man, 1 *Cor.* 2. 14. *The unrenewed person, one that has no principle of grace in the heart, though he be endued with the most exquisite natural accomplishments, and has improved his reason to the highest pitch.*

Gen. 1. 26. God said, let us make *m.* in our image, after our likeness, 27. | 9. 6.
2. 7. the Lord G. formed *m.* of the dust of ground
18. it is not good that *m.* should be alone
25. they were both naked, the *m.* and his wife
3. 22. behold, the *m.* is become as one of us
6. 3. my Spirit shall not always strive with *m.*
7. I will destroy *m.* whom I have created
8. 21. I will not curse the ground for *m.* sake
9. 6. *m.* blood, by *m.* shall his blood be shed
19. 8. who have not known *m.* *Num.* 31. 35.
20. 7. restore the *m.* his wife, he is a prophet
24. 21. the *m.* wondering at her held his peace
29. Laban ran out to the *m.* to the well
65. what *m.* is this that walketh in the field?
29. 19. better than I should give her to another *m.*
38. 25. by the *m.* whose these are, am I with child
43. 13. take your brother, arise, go again to the *m.*
44. 17. the *m.* in whose hand the cup is found
Exod. 2. 20. why is it that ye have left the *m.?*
21. Moses was content to dwell with the *m.*
4. 11. the Lord said, who hath made *m.* mouth?
30. 32. upon *m.* flesh shall it not be poured
32. 1. the *m.* that brought us out of Egypt, 23.
Lev. 17. 4. blood shall be imputed to that *m.* and that *m.* shall be cut off from among the people
Num. 5. 15. then shall the *m.* bring his wife to priest
9. 13. but the *m.* that is clean, and not in a journey
12. 3. the *m.* Moses was very meek above all men
15. 35. the *m.* shall be put to death, *Deut.* 22. 25.
16. 7. the *m.* whom the Lord doth choose, be holy
19. 20. but *m.* that shall be unclean and shall not

Deut. 4. 32. since the day that God created *m.*
5. 24. God doth talk with *m.* and he liveth
8. 3. make thee know that *m.* doth not live by bread only, but by every word, *Mat.* 4. 4. *Luke* 4. 4.
20. 19. for the tree of the field is *m.* life
Josh. 7. 14. and they shall come *m.* by *m.* 17, 18.
Judg. 1. 25. but they let go the *m.* and all his family
4. 22. I will shew thee the *m.* whom thou seekest
8. 21. for as the *m.* is, so is his strength
9. 9. wherewith by me they honour God and *m.*
13. my wine which cheereth God and *m.*
10. 18. what *m.* will fight against Ammon?
13. 10. the *m.* hath appeared that came to me
11. art thou the *m.* spakest to the woman?
16. 7. I shall be weak, and as another *m.* 11, 17.
19. 22. bring forth the *m.* that came into thy house
28. then the *m.* took her on an ass and rose
Ruth 1. 2. the name of the *m.* was Elimelech, 2. 19.
3. 18. for the *m.* will not be in rest, till he hath finish.
1 *Sam.* 2. 33. the *m.* of thine whom I shall not cut off
4. 14. the *m.* came in hastily, and told Eli
9. 6. a *m.* of God, and he is an honourable *m.*
17. behold the *m.* whom I spake to thee of
10. 22. if the *m.* should yet come thither
16. 7. for the Lord seeth not as *m.* seeth
17. 26. what be done to the *m.* that killeth him?
21. 14. lo, ye see the *m.* is mad, wherefore then
2 *Sam.* 12. 5. David's anger kindled against the *m.* said to Nathan, *m.* who did this shall surely die
7. Nathan said to David, thou art the *m.*
16. 7. come out, come out, thou bloody *m.* 8.
17. 3. the *m.* thou seekest is as if all returned
21. 5. *m.* that consumed us, and devised against us
23. 1. the *m.* who was raised up on high
1 *Kings* 20. 20. and they slew every one his *m.*
2 *Kings* 5. 26. when *m.* turned again to meet thee
6. 19. I will bring you to the *m.* whom ye seek
9. 11. ye know the *m.* and his communication
22. 15. tell the *m.* that sent you, 2 *Chr.* 34. 23.
1 *Chr.* 23. 3. the Levites *m.* by *m.* were 38,000
29. 1. the palace is not for *m.* but for the L. God
2 *Chron.* 14. 11. let not *m.* prevail against thee
19. 6. for ye judge not for *m.* but for the Lord
Esth. 6. 6. what shall be done to the *m.* whom, 7, 9.
7. †6. the *m.* adversary is this wicked Haman
Job 4. 17. shall *m.* be more just than God?
5. 7. yet *m.* is born to trouble, as sparks fly upwards
17. happy is the *m.* whom God correcteth
7. 1. is there not an appointed time for *m.* on earth?
17. what is *m.* that thou shouldest magnify him? 15. 14. *Psal.* 8. 4. | 144. 3. *Heb.* 2. 6.
9. 2. but how should *m.* be just with God?
10. 4. eyes of flesh? or seest thou as *m.* seeth?
5. are thy days as days of *m.?* years as *m.* days?
11. 12. vain *m.* would be wise, tho' *m.* be born like
14. 1. *m.* that is born of a woman is of few days
10. *m.* dieth and wasteth away, *m.* giveth up ghost
12. so *m.* lieth down, and riseth not till heavens
15. 7. art thou the first *m.* that was born?
14. what is *m.* that he should be clean?
16. how much more abominable and filthy is *m.*
20. 4. since *m.* was first placed on the earth
21. 4. as for me is my complaint to *m.?*
25. 4. how then can *m.* be justified with God?
6. how much less *m.* that is a worm, and son of *m.*
32. 8. there is a spirit in *m.* inspiration of Almighty
13. God thrusteth him down, not *m.*
33. 12. I answer, that God is greater than *m.*
14. God speaketh, yet *m.* perceiveth it not
17. he opens the ears of men, that he may withdraw *m.* from purpose, and hide pride from *m.*
23. if a messenger, to shew to *m.* his uprightness
29. these things worketh God often with *m.*
34. 7. what *m.* is like Job, who drinketh scorning?
14. if he set his heart upon *m.* if he gather to hims.
23. for he will not lay on *m.* more than right
Psal. 9. 19. arise, O Lord, let not *m.* prevail
10. 18. that the *m.* of earth may no more oppress
25. 12. what *m.* is he that feareth the Lord?
34. 12. what *m.* is he that desireth life?
39. 11. when thou dost correct *m.* for iniquity
49. 12. *m.* being in honour abideth not, 20.
56. 11. I will not be afraid what *m.* can do to me
68. †18. thou hast received gifts in the *m.*
78. 25. *m.* did eat angels' food, he sent them meat
80. 17. thy hand be on the *m.* of thy right hand
89. 48. what *m.* is he that liveth, and not see death?
90. 3. thou turnest *m.* to destruction, and sayest
94. 10. that teacheth *m.* knowl. shall not he know?
103. 15. as for *m.* his days are as grass, as a flower
104. 23. *m.* goeth forth to his work and labour
118. 6. I will not fear what *m.* can do to me
8. better trust in Lord, than put confidence in *m.*
120. †7. I am a *m.* of peace, they are for war
144. 4. *m.* is like to vanity, his days as a shadow
Prov. 2. 12. from *m.* that speaketh froward things
6. 11. and thy want come as an armed *m.* 24. 34.
16. 1. the preparations of the heart in *m.*
20. 24. *m.* goings are of the Lord, how can a *m.*
26. 19. so is the *m.* that deceiveth his neighbour
Eccl. 1. 8. things full of labour, *m.* cannot utter it
2. 12. what can the *m.* do that cometh after king?
22. for what hath *m.* of all his labour?
6. 10. is named, and it is known that it is *m.*
11. what is *m.* better? || 12. what is good for *m.?*
12. 5. because *m.* goeth to his long home
Isa. 2. 22. cease from *m.* whose breath is in his nostr.
38. 11. I said, I shall behold *m.* no more
40. †13. or being the *m.* of his counsel hath taught
46. 11. the *m.* that executeth my counsel
Jer. 10. 23. it is not in *m.* to direct his steps
Lam. 3. 1. I am the *m.* that hath seen affliction
Ezek. 4. 15. I have given cows' dung for *m.* dung
18. 8. hath executed judgment between *m.* and *m.*
Dan. 4. 16. let his heart be changed from *m.*
10. 19. said, O *m.* greatly beloved, fear not
Hos. 11. 9. for I am God, and not *m.* the holy One
Amos 4. 13. and declareth to *m.* what is his thought
Mic. 5. 7. that tarrieth not for *m.* nor waiteth
6. 8. he hath shewed thee, O *m.* what is good
9. the *m.* of wisdom shall see thy name
Hab. 1. 13. the wicked devoureth *m.* more righteous

Zeph. 1. 3. I will cut off the *m.* from the land
Zech. 6. 12. the *m.* whose name is the Branch
13. 5. for *m.* taught me to keep cattle from youth
7. awake, O sword, against *m.* that is my fellow
Mal. 2. 12. Lord will cut off the *m.* that doeth this
Mat. 7. 9. what *m.* is there of you, if his son ask bread will give him a stone? 12. 11. *Luke* 15. 4.
15. 18. from the heart, and they defile the *m.*
19. 6. let not *m.* put asunder, *Mark* 10. 9.
26. 72. he denied, I do not know the *m.* 74.
Mark 2. 27. sabbath was made for *m.* not *m.* for sabb.
11. 2. shall find a colt tied, whereon never *m.* sat
Luke 5. 20. he said, *m.* thy sins are forgiven thee
12. 14. *m.* who made me a judge over you?
18. 4. though I fear not God, nor regard *m.*
22. 58. thou art of them, Peter said, *m.* I am not
60. Peter said, *m.* I know not what thou sayest
23. 6. he asked, whether the *m.* was a Galilean?
53. wherein never *m.* was laid, *John* 19. 41.
John 2. 25. for he knew what was in *m.*
5. 12. what *m.* is that which said unto thee
34. but I received not testimony from *m.*
15. 24. the works which none other *m.* did
19. 5. Pilate said unto them, behold the *m.*
Acts 4. 22. for the *m.* was above forty years old
8. 31. how can I, except some *m.* should guide me?
34. eunuch said, of himself, or of some other *m.?*
19. 16. the man in whom the evil spirit was
35. what *m.* is there that knoweth not how that
21. 11. so shall bind the *m.* that owneth this girdle
23. 30. how the Jews laid wait for the *m.*
25. 22. Agrippa said, I would also hear the *m.* mys.
Rom. 2. 1. inexcusable, O *m.* || 3. thinkest thou, O *m.*
7. 22. I delight in law of God after the inward *m.*
24. O wretched *m.* that I am, who shall deliv. me?
9. 20. but O *m.* who art thou that repliest ag. God?
10. 5. the righteousness of the law, the *m.* who doeth these things shall live by them, *Gal.* 3. 12.
10. with the heart *m.* believeth unto righteousness
1 *Cor.* 2. 11. what *m.* knoweth the things of a *m.?*
7. 16. how knowest thou, O *m.* whether thou
10. 13. no temptation but such as is common to *m.*
11. 3. and the head of the woman is the *m.*
8. *m.* is not of the woman || 9. but wom. for the *m.*
11. nor is the *m.* without the woman, nor the woman without the *m.* in the Lord
12. even so is the *m.* also by the woman
15. 21. since by *m.* came death, by *m.* came resurr.
45. the first *m.* Adam was made a living soul
47. the first *m.* is of the earth, earthy; the second *m.* is the Lord from heaven
2 *Cor.* 4. 16. but though our outward *m.* perish, yet the inward *m.* is renewed day by day
Gal. 1. 1. an apostle, not of men, neither by *m.*
11. the gospel I preached is not after *m.*
Eph. 2. 15. for to make of twain one new *m.*
3. 16. with might by his Spirit in the inner *m.*
4. 24. that ye put on new *m.* created in righteousn.
Col. 3. 10. have put on the new *m.* which is renewed
1 *Thess.* 4. 8. despiseth not *m.* but God, who hath given
1 *Tim.* 2. 5. between God and men, the *m.* C. Jesus
12. woman not to usurp authority over the *m.*
Tit. 3. 4. love of G. our Saviour toward *m.* appeared
Heb. 3. 4. for every house is built by some *m.*
8. 2. the tabernacle the Lord pitched, and not *m.*
13. 6. I will not fear what *m.* shall do to me
Jam. 1. 8. a double-minded *m.* is unstable in his ways
2. 20. wilt thou know, O vain *m.* that faith
1 *Pet.* 3. 4. let it be the hidden *m.* of the heart

A MAN.

Gen. 2. 5. there was not *a m.* to till the ground
24. therefore shall *a m.* leave his father and mother, *Mat.* 19. 5. *Mark* 10. 7. *Eph.* 5. 31.
4. 1. I have gotten *a m.* from the Lord
23. for I have slain *a m.* to my wounding
11. †3. *a m.* said to his neighbour, let us burn
13. 16. if *a m.* can number the dust of the earth
19. 31. there is not *a m.* to come in unto us
20. 3. thou art a dead man, for she is *a m.* wife
25. 27. Esau a cunning hunter, *a m.* of the field
32. 24. there wrestled *a m.* with him till breaking
41. 33. let Pharaoh look out *a m.* discreet and wise
38. *a m.* in whom the Spirit of God is
44. 15. wot ye not such *a m.* as I can certainly divine
49. 6. for in their anger they slew *a m.*
Exod. 2. †14. he said, who made thee *a m.* a prince
18. †16. I judge between *a m.* and his fellow
33. 11. face to face, as *a m.* speaketh to his friend
Lev. 13. 9. when the plague of leprosy is in *a m.*
18. 5. my judgments, which if *a m.* do he shall live in them, *Neh.* 9. 29. *Ezek.* 20. 11, 13, 21.
24. 10. and *a m.* of Israel strove together in the camp
20. as he hath caused a blemish in *a m.*
27. 28. no devoted thing *a m.* shall devote
Num. 1. 4. there shall be *a m.* of every tribe
13. 2. of every tribe shall ye send *a m.*
15. 32. they found *a m.* that gathered sticks
19. 14. this is the law when *a m.* dieth in a tent
23. 19. G. is not *a m.* that he should lie, 1 *Sam.* 15. 29.
26. 64. among these there was not *a m.* of them
65. there was not left *a m.* save Caleb and Joshua
27. 16. set *a m.* over the congregation
18. take thee Joshua, *a m.* in whom is the Spirit
Deut. 1. 31. Lord bare thee, as *a m.* doth his son
3. 11. the breadth of it, after the cubit of *a m.*
8. 5. consider, that as a *m.* chasteneth his son
19. 15. one witness shall not rise against *a m.*
Josh. 3. 12. take ye out of every tribe *a m.* 4. 2, 4.
5. 13. there stood *a m.* over against him with sword
10. 8. there shall not *a m.* of them stand before thee
14. the Lord hearkened to the voice of *a m.*
14. 15. which Arba was a great *m.* among Anakims
21. 44. stood not *a m.* of all their enemies before
Judg. 1. 24. the spies saw *a m.* come out of the city
3. 29. escaped not *a m.* || 4. 16. was not *a m.* left
7. 13. there was *a m.* that told a dream to his fellow
14. save the sword of Gideon *a m.* of Israel
10. 1. Tola *a m.* of Issachar || 16. 19. she called *a m.*
Ruth 4. 7. *a m.* plucked off his shoe and gave it
1 *Sam.* 9. 16. I will send thee *a m.* out of Benjamin
11. 13. there shall not *a m.* be put to death
13. 14. the Lord hath sought him *a m.*

1 Sam. 14. 36. and let us not leave a m. of them
16. 16. to seek out a m. who is a cunning player
17. provide me a m. that can play well, bring him
17. 8. choose you a m. for you, let him come
10. give me a m. that we may fight together
25. 17. he is such that a m. cannot speak to him
30. 17. and there escaped not a m. of them
2 Sam. 3. 34. as a m. falleth before wicked men
38. Abner a great m. is fallen this day in Israel
16. 23. as if a m. inquired at the oracle of God
18. † 20. thou shalt not be a m. of tidings
20. 1. there happened to be there a m. of Belial
1 Kings 2. 2. be strong, and shew thyself a m.
4. not fail thee a. m. on the throne, 8. 25.
20. 39. a m. turned aside, and brought a m. to me
42. a m. whom I appointed to destruction
2 Kings 1. 6. there came a m. to meet us, and said
4. 42. there came a m. from Baal-shalisha
10. 21. there was not a m. left that came not
13. 21. as they were burying a m. they spied
1 Chron. 22. 9. a son born, who shall be a m. of rest
2 Chron. 6. 16. there shall not fail thee a m. 7. 18.
Neh. 2. 10. come a m. to seek the welfare of Israel
6. 11. I said, should such a m. as I flee?
Job 2. 4. all that a m. hath will he give for his life
3. 23. why is light given to a m. whose way
4. 17. shall a m. be more pure than his Maker?
9. 32. he is not a m. as I am, that I should answer
11. 2. and should a m. full of talk be justified?
12. 14. he shutteth up a m. || 14. 14. if a m. die
16. 21. O that one might plead for a m. with God, as a m. pleadeth for his neighbour
22. 2. can a m. be profitable to G. as he that is wise?
34. 29. whether done against a nation or a m.
35. 8. thy wickedness may hurt a m. as thou art
37. 20. if a m. speak he shall be swallowed up
38. 3. gird up now thy loins like a m. 40. 7.
Psal. 38. 14. I was as a m. that heareth not
55. 13. but it was thou a m. mine equal
62. 3. how long will ye imagine mischief ag. a m.?
74. 5. a m. was famous according as he lifted up
88. 4. I am as a m. that hath no strength
105. 17. he sent a m. before them, even Joseph
147. 10. he taketh not pleasure in the legs of a m.
Prov. 3. 30. strive not with a m. without cause
6. 34. for jealousy is the rage of a m.
14. 12. a way that seemeth right to a m. 16. 25.
16. 2. all ways of a m. are clean in his own eyes
7. when a m. ways please the Lord he maketh
20. 24. how can a m. understand his own way?
23. 2. if thou be a m. given to appetite
26. 21. so a contentious m. to kindle strife
27. 8. so is a m. that wandereth from his place
21. as the furnace, so is a m. to his praise
28. 12. but when the wicked rise a m. is hidden
23. he that rebuketh a m. shall find more favour
29. † 1. a m. of reproofs || † 4. a m. of oblations
20. seest thou a m. that is hasty in words?
Eccl. 2. 21. there is a m. whose labour is in wisdom and knowledge, yet to a m. that hath not labour.
26. God giveth to a m. that is good in his sight
4. 4. for this a m. is envied of his neighbour
6. 2. a m. to whom God hath given riches
12. who can tell a m. what shall be after him?
10. 14. a m. cannot tell what shall be after him
11. 8. if a m. live many years, and rejoice in them
Cant. 8. 7. if a m. would give all his substance
Isa. 6. 5. because I am a m. of unclean lips
13. 12. I will make a m. more precious than gold
17. 7. at that day shall a m. look to his maker
28. 20. than that a. m. can stretch himself on it
29. 21. that make a m. an offender for a word
32. 2. a m. shall be an hiding-place from the wind
47. 3. and I will not meet thee as a m.
53. 3. he is a m. of sorrows and acquainted with gr.
58. 5. a day for a m. to afflict his soul?
66. 3. he that killeth an ox, is as if he slew a m.
Jer. 4. 29. forsaken, and not a m. dwell therein
5. 1. seek in broad places, if ye can find a m.
14. 9. why shouldest thou be as a m. astonied?
15. 10. that thou hast borne me a m. of strife
16. 20. shall a m. make gods to himself and no gods?
22. 30. a m. that shall not prosper in his days
23. 9. I am like a m. whom wine hath overcome
30. 6. see whether a m. doth travail with child?
31. 22. a woman shall compass a m.
33. 17. David shall never want a m. to sit on throne
18. nor shall the priests want a m. before me
35. 19. Jonadab shall not want a m. to stand bef. me
50. 42. every man put in array like a m. to battle
Lam. 3. 26. It is good for a m. to hope and wait
27. it is good for a m. that he bear the yoke
39. complain, a m. for the punishment of his sins
Ezek. 22. 30. I sought for a m. among them
28. 2. yet thou art a m. and not God, 9.
33. 2. if the people of the land take a m.
Dan. 2. 10. not a m. on earth that can shew
25. I have found a m. of the captives of Judah
5. 11. there is a m. in thy kingdom in whom
7. 4. stand as a m. and a m. heart was given to it
9. † 23. I am come, for thou art a m. of desires
10. 11. he said, O Daniel, a m. greatly beloved
Hos. 6. 9. as troops of robbers wait for a m.
9. 12. that there shall not be a m. left, woe to them
11. 4. I drew them with cords of a m. with bands
Amos 2. 7. a m. and his father go in to one maid
5. 19. as if a m. did flee from a lion, and a bear
Mic. 2. 2. oppress a m. and his house, even a m.
11. if a m. walking in spirit and falsehood
7. 6. a m. enemies are the men of his own house, the daughter against her mother, Mat. 10. 36.
Mal. 3. 17. as a m. spareth his own son that serv. him
Mat. 8. 9. I am a m. under authority, Luke 7. 8.
10. 35. I am come to set a m. at variance
12. 12. how much is a m. better than a sheep?
43. the unclean spirit is gone out of a m.
15. 11. cometh out of the mouth defileth a m.
20. to eat with unwashen hands defileth not a m.
19. 3. is it lawful for a m. to put away, Mark 10. 2.
22. 24. if a m. die, having no children
26. 18. he said, go into the city, to such a m. and say to him, Mark 14. 13. Luke 22. 10.

Luke 1. 34. how shall this be, seeing I know not a m.
5. 8. depart, for I am a sinful m. O Lord
13. 19. which a m. took and cast into his garden
19. 7. to be guest with a m. that is a sinner
John 1. 6. there was a m. sent from G. named John
30. after me cometh a m. who is preferred bef. me
3. 3. except a m. be born again, he cannot see, 5.
4. how can a m. be born when he is old?
27. a m. can receive nothing, except given him
4. 29. come, see a m. which told me all things
7. 23. angry, because I have made a m. whole
8. 40. a m. that hath told you the truth
9. 11. a m. that is called Jesus made clay
16. how can a m. a sinner, do such miracles
10. 33. thou being a m. makest thyself God
14. 23. if a m. love me, he will keep my
16. 21. for joy that a m. is born into the world
Acts 2. 22. Jesus, a m. approved of God among you
10. 26. stand up, I myself also am a m.
13. 22. I found David, a m. after mine own heart
41. not believe, though a m. declare it to you
16. 9. there stood a m. of Macedonia, prayed him
21. 39. I am a m. who am a Jew of Tarsus
Rom. 2. 21. that preachest a m. should not steal
22. sayest, a m. should not commit adultery
3. 5. I speak as a m. || 7. 1. dominion over a m.
1 Cor. 4. 1. let a m. so account of us as ministers
2. it is required, that a m. be found faithful
6. 18. every sin that a m. doeth is without the body
7. 1. it is good for a m. not to touch a woman
26. I say that it is good for a m. so to be
9. 8. say I these things as a m. or saith not law?
11. 7. a m. indeed ought not to cover his head
14. if a m. have long hair, it is a shame
28. but let a m. examine hims. and so let him eat
13. 11. but when became a m. I put away childish
2 Cor. 2. 6. sufficient to such a m. is this punishment
8. 12. it is accepted according to that a m. hath
11. 20. if a m. bring you into bondage, if a m. smite
12. 2. I knew a m. in Chr. caught up to heaven, 3.
4. which it is not lawful for a m. to utter
Gal. 2. 16. a m. is not justified by works of the law
6. 1. brethren, if a m. be overtaken in a fault
3. if a m. think himself to be something
Phil. 2. 8. and being found in fashion as a m.
1 Tim. 1. 8. the law is good, if a m. use it lawfully
3. 1. if a m. desire the office of a bishop
5. if a m. know not how to rule his house
2 Tim. 2. 5. if a m. also strive for masteries
21. if a m. therefore purge himself
Tit. 3. 10. a m. that is a heretic, reject
Jam. 1. 23. he is like a m. beholding his face
2. 2. if there come a m. with a gold ring
14. what profit, though a m. say, he hath faith
18. a m. may say, thou hast faith, I have works
24. ye see how that by works a m. is justified
5. 17. Elias was a m. subject to like passions as we
1 Pet. 2. 19. if a m. for conscience toward God
2 Pet. 2. 19. for of whom a m. is overcome
1 John 4. 20. if a m. say, I love God, and hateth
Rev. 4. 7. the third beast had a face as a m.
9. 5. as torment of a scorpion, when he striketh a m.

A certain MAN.

Gen. 37. 15. a certain m. found him, and asked him
2 Sam. 18. 10. a c. m. saw it, and told Joab, and said
1 Kings 22. 34. a c. m. drew bow at vent. 2 Chr. 18. 33.
Mat. 21. 28. a certain m. had two sons, Luke 15. 11.
Luke 10. 30. a certain m. went down from Jerusalem
12. 16. the ground of a certain rich m. brought forth
13. 6. a c. m. had a fig-tree planted in his vineyard
14. 16. a c. m. made a great supper, and bade many
16. 1. there was a certain m. which had a steward
18. 35. a c. blind m. sat by the way-side begging
19. 12. a certain noble-m. went into a far country
20. 9. a certain m. planted a vineyard, and let it out
John 4. 46. a c. noble-m. whose son was sick at Cap.
11. 1. now a c. m. was sick, named Lazar. of Betha.
Acts 3. 2. a certain m. lame from his mother's womb
5. 1. a certain m. named Ananias, sold a possession
8. 9. a certain m. called Simeon, who used sorcery
9. 33. and there he found a certain m. named Eneas
10. 1. there was a c. m. in Cesarea called Cornelius
14. 8. there sat a c. m. at Lystra, impotent in his feet
18. 7. entered into a certain m. house named Justus
19. 24. a certain m. named Demetrius, a silver-smith
25. 14. there is a certain m. left in bonds by Felix

Any MAN.

Gen. 24. 16. a virgin, nor had any m. known her
47. 6. if thou knowest any m. of activity among them
Exod. 24. 14. if any m. have any matters to do
34. 3. nor let any m. be seen through all the mount
24. nor shall any m. desire thy land, when go up
Lev. 15. 2. when any m. hath a running issue
16. if any m. seed of copulation go out from him
24. if any m. lie with her at all, he shall be unclean
24. 17. that killeth a. m. shall surely be put to death
Num. 5. 10. whatsoever any m. giveth the priest
12. if any m. wife go aside, and commit a trespass
6. 9. if any m. die very suddenly by him
19. 11. that toucheth the dead body of any m. 13.
21. 9. if a serpent had bitten any m. when beheld
Deut. 19. 11. if a. m. hate his neighbour and smite him
16. if false witness rise up against any m. to testify
22. 8. blood on thy house, if any m. fall from thence
23. 10. there be any m. among you that is not clean
Josh. 1. 5. shall not any m. be able to stand bef. thee
2. 11. nor did there remain courage in any m.
Judg. 4. 20. if any m. enquire, is there any m. here?
16. 17. I shall become weak and be like a. other m.
18. 7. and had no business with any m. 28.
1 Sam. 2. 13. that when any m. offered sacrifice
16. if any m. said, fail not to burn the fat
12. 4. nor hast thou taken aught at any m. hand
2 Sam. 15. 2. when any m. that had a controversy
5. it was so, that when any m. came nigh to him
19. 22. shall any m. be put to death this day in Isr.
21. 4. nor for us shalt thou kill any m. in Israel
1 Kings 8. 31. if any m. trespass against his neighb.
38. supplication be made by any m. 2 Chron. 6. 29.
2 Kings 4. 29. if thou meet any m. salute him not
2 Chr. 6. 5. nor choose I any m. ruler over Israel
Neh. 2. 12. nor told I any m. what G. put in my heart

Job 32. 21. let me not accept any m. person
Prov. 30. 2. surely I am more brutish than any m.
Isa. 52. 14. his visage was more marred than any m.
Jer. 44. 26. no more named in mouth of any m.
Ezek. 9. 6. come not near any m. on whom is the mark
Dan. 6. 7. shall ask a petition of any god or m. 12.
Mat. 5. 40. if any m. sue thee at law, and take thy coat
11. 27. nor know. any m. the Father, save the Son
12. 19. nor shall any m. hear his voice in the streets
16. 24. if any m. will come after me, Luke 9. 23.
21. 3. if any m. say ought to you, say, the Lord hath need of him, Mark 11. 3. Luke 19. 31.
22. 16. art true, nor carest thou for any m. for thou
46. nor durst any m. from that day ask questions
24. 23. if any m. say, lo here is Christ, Mark 13. 21.
Mark 1. 44. see thou say nothing to any m. but go
4. 23. if any m. hath ears to hear, 7. 16. Rev. 13. 9.
5. 4. neither could any m. tame him
9. 30. he would not that any m. should know it
35. if any m. desire to be first, the same shall be last
13. 5. take heed, lest any m. deceive you
16. 8. nor said any thing to any m. they were afraid
Luke 14. 8. when thou art bidden of any m. to a wed.
26. if any m. come to me, and hate not father
19. 8. if I have taken any thing from any m.
20. 28. if any m. brother die, having a wife
John 4. 33. hath any m. brought him ought to eat?
6. 46. not that any m. hath seen the Father
51. if any m. eat of this bread he shall live for ever
7. 17. if any m. do his will he shall know of doctrine
37. if any m. thirst, let him come to me and drink
51. doth our law judge any m. before it hear him?
8. 33. and we were never in bondage to any m.
9. 22. if any m. did confess that he was Christ
31. if any m. be a worshipper of God, him he hears
32. that any m. opened the eyes of one born blind
10. 9. by me if any m. enter in, he shall be saved
28. nor shall any m. pluck them out of my hand
11. 9. if any m. walk in the day, he stumbleth not
57. if any m. knew where he were, he should shew it
12. 26. if any m. serve me, let him follow me
47. if any m. hear my words and believe not
16. 30. needest not that any m. should ask thee
18. 31. it is not lawful for us to put any m. to death
Acts 10. 28. not call any m. common or unclean
47. can any m. forbid water, these be not baptized?
19. 38. if have a matter against any m. law is open
24. 12. neither found me disputing with any m.
25. 16. not manner of Romans to deliver any m.
27. 22. shall be no loss of any m. life among you
Rom. 8. 9. if any m. have not the Spirit of Christ
1 Cor. 3. 12. if any m. build on this foundation
14. if any m. work abide || 15. if any m. work be burnt
17. if any m. defile the temple of God him destroy
18. if any m. among you seemeth to be wise
5. 11. if any m. that is called a brother be a fornicat.
7. 18. is any m. called, being circumcised?
8. 2. if any m. think that he knoweth any thing
3. if any m. love G. || 11. 34. if any m. hung. let him
10. if any m. see thee which hast knowledge
9. 15. that any m. should make my glorying void
10. 28. if any m. say that this is offered
11. 16. but if any m. seem to be contentious
14. 27. if any m. speak in an unknown tongue
37. if any m. think himself to be a prophet
38. if any m. be ignorant, let him be ignorant
16. 22. if any m. love not the L. Jesus, let him be
2 Cor. 5. 17. if any m. be in C. he is a new creature
10. 7. if any m. trust to himself that he is Christ's
12. 6. lest any m. should think of me above what
Gal. 1. 9. if any m. preach any other gospel
Eph. 2. 9. not of works, lest any m. should boast
6. 8. know. that whatsoever good thing any m. doeth
Col. 2. 4. lest any m. should beguile you with words
8. beware lest any m. spoil you thro' philosophy
3. 13. if any m. have a quarrel against any
1 Thess. 5. 15. that none render evil for evil to a. m.
2 Thess. 3. 8. nor did eat any m. bread for nought
14. if any m. obey not our word, note that man
1 Tim. 6. 3. if any m. teach otherwise and consent
Heb. 4. 11. lest any m. fall after the same example
10. 38. but if any m. draw back, my soul shall have
12. 15. lest any m. fail of the grace of God
Jam. 1. 13. G. cannot be tempted, nor tempteth a. m.
26. if any m. among you seem to be religious
3. 2. if any m. offend not in word, he is perfect
1 Pet. 4. 11. if a. m. speak, let him speak as oracles
16. yet if a. m. suffer as christian, not be ashamed
1 John 2. 1. if any m. sin, we have an advocate
15. if any m. love the world, the love of Father
27. and ye need not that any m. teach you
5. 16. if any m. see his brother sin not unto death
Rev. 3. 20. if any m. hear my voice, and open door
11. 5. if any m. will hurt them, fire proceedeth
14. 9. if any m. worship the beast and his image
22. 18. if any m. shall add to these things
19. if any m. shall take away from the words

See BEAST, BLESSED, CURSED.

MAN-*child*.

Gen. 17. 10. every m.-child shall be circumcised, 12.
14. the uncircumcised m.-child shall be cut off
Lev. 12. 2. if a woman have born a m.-child, then
1 Sam. 1. 11. if wilt give to thy handmaid a m.-child
Job 3. 3. let the night perish wherein it was said, there is a m.-child conceived, Jer. 20. 15.
Isa. 66. 7. she was delivered of a m.-child, Rev. 12. 5.
Rev. 12. 13. persecuted wom. brought forth a m.-ch.

See EACH.

Every MAN.

Gen. 7. 21. all flesh died on earth, and every m.
9. 5. at hand of ev. m. brother require life of man
16. 12. his hand be ag. every m. and every m. hand
42. 25. to restore every m. money into his sack
35. behold, ev. m. money was in his sack, 43. 21.
44. 11. then they took down every m. his sack
13. and laded every m. his ass, and returned
45. 1. Joseph cried, cause e. m. to go out from me
47. 20. the Egyptians sold every m. his field
Exod. 1. 1. e. m. and his household came with Jacob
7. 12. for they cast down every m. his rod
11. 2. let every m. borrow of his neighbour jewels
12. 3. they shall take to them every m. a lamb

Exod.12. 4. e. m. accord. to his eating, 16.16. | 18. 21.
16. save that which every m. must eat, that only
16. 29. abide ye e. m. in his place, let no man go
25. 2. of every m. that giveth it willingly
30. 12. shall give every m. a ransom for his soul
32. 27. put every m. a sword by his side, slay every
m. his brother, e. m. his companion and neigh.
33. 8. stood every m. at his tent-door and looked
10. they worshipped every m. in his tent-door
36. 4. came every m. from his work that they made
38. 26. a bekah for every m. that is, half a shekel
Lev. 19. 3. fear every m. his mother and father
25. 10. ye shall return every m. to his family, 13.
Num. 1. 52. pitch every m. by his standard, 2. 2, 17.
5. 10. every m. hallowed things shall be his
7. 5. give to every m. according to his service
16. 17. take every m. his censer, and put incense in
18. they took e. m. his censer and put fire in them
17. 2. write thou every m. name on his rod
9. they looked and took every m. his rod
31. 53. men of war had taken spoil e. m. for hims.
32. 18. Israel inherited every m. his inheritance
27. servants will pass over every m. armed, 29.
Deut. 1. 16. judge righteously between every m.
3. 20. shall ye return every m. to his possession
12. 8. not do every m. what is right in his eyes
16. 17. every m. shall give as he is able
24. 16. nor children for fathers, every m. shall die
for his own sin, 2 Kings 14. 6. 2 Chron. 25. 4.
Josh. 4. 5. take up every m. of you a stone
6. 5. ascend every m. straight before him, 20.
24. 28. every m. to his inheritance, Judg. 2. 6.
Judg. 5. 30. divided to every m. a damsel or two
7. 7. let other people go every m. unto his place, 8.
16. and he put a trumpet in every m. hand
22. set e. m. sword ag. his fellow, 1 Sam. 14. 20.
8. 24. would give me every m. his ear-rings, 25.
9. 49. the people cut down every m. his bough
17. 6. e. m. did what was right in his eyes, 21. 25.
21. 21. catch you e. m. his wife of the daughters
24. every m. to his tribe, e. m. to his inheritance
1 Sam. 4. 10. and they fled every m. into his tent
8. 22. Samuel said, go ye every m. into his city
14. 34. bring hither e. m. his ox, e. m. his sheep
25. 10. that break away e. m. from his master
13. David said, gird you on every m. his sword
26. 23. the Lord render to every m. his righteousness and his faithfulness, 2 Chr. 6. 30.
30. 6. grieved every m. for his sons and daughters
22. save to every m. his wife and children
2 Sam. 13. 9. and they went out e. m. from him
29. every m. gat him upon his mule, and fled
15. 4. that every m. which hath any suit or cause
30. covered e. m. his head, and they went up
19. 8. for Israel hath fled every m. to his tent
20. 1. Sheba said, every m. to his tents, O Israel
1 Kings 4. 25. dwelt safely every m. under his vine
8. 38. which shall know e. m. the plague of his heart
39. hear, forgive, and do, and give to every m.
according to his ways, Job 34. 11. Jer. 17. 10.
10. 25. brought e. m. his present, 2 Chr. 9. 24.
12. 24. not go up, return e. m. to his house, for this
thing is from me, 22. 17, 36. 2 Chr. 11. 4.
20. 24. take the kings every m. out of his place
2 Kings 6. 2. let us go and take thence e. m. a beam
11. 8. every m. with his weapons in his hand
14. 12. Judah fled every m. to their tents
18. 31. and then eat ye every m. of his own vine
Neh. 5. 13. so God shake out e. m. from his house
Esth. 1. 8. do according to every m. pleasure
22. every m. should bear rule in his own house
Job 21. 33. and every m. shall draw after him
37. 7. he sealeth up the hand of every m. that
Ps. 39. 5. every m. at his best state is vanity, 11.
6. surely every m. walketh in a vain show
62. 12. to thee, O Lord, mercy, for thou renderest
to every m. according to his work, Prov. 24. 12.
Prov. 19. 6. every m. is a friend to him that giveth
24. 26. ev. m. shall kiss his lips that giveth right ans.
29. 26. every m. judgment cometh from the Lord
Isa. 9. 20. eat every m. the flesh of his own arm
13. 7. therefore every m. heart shall melt
31. 7. in that day every m. shall cast away his idols
Jer. 10. 14. every m. is brutish in knowledge, 51. 17.
26. 3. turn ev. m. from his evil way, 35. 15. | 36. 3.
29. 26. for every m. that is mad, and maketh hims.
31. 34. teach no more ev. m. his neigh. Heb. 8. 11.
34. 15. in proclaiming liberty ev. m. to his neigh. 17.
37. 10. they should rise up every m. in his tent
51. 45. go out and deliver ye every m. his soul
Ezek. 8. 11. with every m. his censer in his hand
12. every m. in the chambers of his imagery
9. 1. even every m. with his destroying weapon, 2.
20. 7. cast away every m. abominations of his eyes
8. they did not every m. cast away abominations
32. 10 every m. shall tremble for his own life
46. 18. not scattered every m. from his possession
Dan. 3. 10. ev. m. that shall hear the sound fall down
6. 12. that every m. that shall ask a petition
Jonah 1. 5. the mariners cried every m. to his god
Mic. 4. 4. they shall sit every m. under his vine
7. 2. they hunt every m. his brother with a net
Hag. 1. 9. and ye run every m. to his own house
Zech. 3. 10. call every m. his neighb. under the vine
8. 4. every m. with his staff in his hand for age
16. speak every m. truth to his neighb. Eph. 4. 25.
Mal. 2. 10. why do we deal treacherously every m.?
Mat. 16. 27. the Son of man shall reward every m.
according to his works, Rom. 2. 6. Rev. 22. 12.
20. 9. they received every m. a penny, 10.
25. 15. he gave to every m. according to his ability
Mark 8. 25. he was restored, and saw every m. clearly
13. 34. and gave to e. m. his work, and commanded
15. 24. casting lots what every m. should take
Luke 6. 30. give to every m. that asketh of thee
16. 16. is preached, and every m. presseth into it
19. 15. how much every m. had gained by trading
John 1. 9. the true light, which lighteth every m.
2. 10. ev. m. at beginning doth set forth good wine
6. 45. e. m. that hath heard and learned of Father
16. 32. ye shall be scattered every m. to his own
Acts 2. 8. how hear we every m. in our own tongue?

Acts 2. 45. parted to all men, as e. m. had need, 4. 35.
11. 29. e. m. determined to send relief to brethren
Rom. 2. 10. peace to every m. that worketh good
3. 4. yea, let God be true, but every m. a liar
12. 3. as God dealt to every m. the measure of faith
14. 5. let e. m. be fully persuaded in his own mind
1 Cor. 3. 5. even as the Lord gave to every m. 7. 17.
13. every m. work shall be made manifest
4. 5. then shall every m. have praise of God
7. 2. nevertheless, let every m. have his own wife
7. but every m. hath his proper gift of God
20. let every m. abide in the same calling, 24.
8. 7. there is not in every m. that knowledge
10. 24. but let every m. seek another's wealth
11. 3. know that the head of every m. is Christ
12. 7. Spirit is given to every m. to profit withal
15. 23. but every m. in his order, Christ first fruits
2 Cor. 4. 2. commend. ourselves to every m. conscience
Gal. 5. 3. I testify again to e. m. that is circumcised
6. 4. let every m. prove his own work, then shall
5. for every m. shall bear his own burden
Phil. 2. 4. look not every m. on his own things
Col. 1. 28. whom we preach, teaching every m. in all
wisdom to present every m. perfect in Christ Jes.
4. 6. may know how ye ought to answer every m.
Heb. 2. 9. that he should taste death for every m.
Jam. 1. 14. but every m. is tempted, when he is drawn
19. let every m. be swift to hear, slow to speak
1 Pet. 1. 17. who judgeth according to every m. work
3. 15. to give a reason to e. m. that asketh of hope
4. 10. as every m. hath received the gift, even so
1 John 3. 3. e. m. that hath this hope in him, purifies
Rev. 20. 13. judged e. m. according to their works
22. 18. for I testify to e. m. that heareth the words

See Evil, Foolish.

MAN of God.

Deut. 33. 1. Moses the m. of God, Josh. 14. 6.
Judg. 13. 6. woman told, say. a m. of G. came to me
8. let the m. of G. come again to us, and teach us
1 Sam. 2. 27. there came a m. of G. to Eli, and said
9. 6. behold now there is in this city a m. of God
7. there is not a present to bring the m. of God
8. that will I give to the m. of God to tell us
1 Kings 12. 22. word came to Shemaiah the m. of G.
13. 1. and there came a m. of God out of Judah
26. it is the m. of God who was disobedient
17. 18. what have I to do with thee, O m. of God?
24. now by this I know that thou art a m. of God
20. 28. there came a m. of G. and spake to Ahab
2 Kings 1. 9. thou m. of G. king said, come down, 11.
13. O m. of G. I pray thee, let my life be precious
4. 7. she came and told m. of G. || 9. this is m. of G.
16. thou m. of God, do not lie to thine handmaid
22. that I may run to m. of God, and come again
25. she came unto the m. of God to Carmel, 27.
40. O thou m. of God, there is death in the pot
42. brought the m. of God bread, of first-fruits
5. 14. dipped, according to the saying of m. of God
20. Gehazi, servant of Elisha, the m. of God, 8. 4.
6. 10. sent to place which the m. of God told him
15. when the servant of the m. of God was risen
7. 2. a lord answered the m. of God and said, 19.
17. people trod on him as the m. of God said, 18.
8. 2. the woman did after the saying of m. of God
7. m. of God is come hither || 11. the m. of God wept
8. take a present and go meet the m. of God
13. 19. and the m. of God was wroth with him
23. 16. according to the word which the m. of God
17. it is the sepulchre of m. of God which came
1 Chr. 23. 14. Moses m. of G. 2 Chr. 30. 16. Ezra 3. 2.
2 Chron. 8. 14. David the m. of God, Neh. 12. 24, 36.
25. 7. but there came a m. of God to Amaziah
9. the m. of G. answered, the Lord is able to give
Jer. 35. 4. Hanan the son of Igdaliah a m. of God
1 Tim. 6. 11. but thou, O m. of G. flee these things
2 Tim. 3. 17. that the m. of God may be perfect

See Good.

Mighty MAN.

Judg. 6. 12. the Lord is with thee, thou mighty m.
11. 1. now Jephthah was a mighty m. of valour
Ruth 2. 1. Naomi had a kinsman a migh. m. of wealth
1 Sam. 9. 1. Kish a Benjamite, a migh. m. of power
16. 18. David m. m. and man of war, 2 Sam. 17. 10.
1 Kings 11. 28. the man Jeroboam was a migh. m.
2 Kings 5. 1. Naaman was also a mighty m. in valour
1 Chr. 12. 4. Ismaiah a mighty m. among the thirty
2 Chr. 17. 17. of Benjam. Eliada a mighty m. of valour
28. 7. Zichri, a migh. m. of Ephraim, slew Maaseiah
Job 22. 8. as for the mighty m. he had the earth
Ps. 33. 16. a mighty m. is not delivered by strength
52. 1. why boastest thou in mischief, O mighty m.
78. 65. then the Lord awaked like a mighty m.
127. 4. as arrows are in the hand of a mighty m.
Isa. 3. 2. the Lord doth take away the mighty m.
5. 15. and the mighty m. shall be humbled
31. 8. shall fall with the sword, not of a mighty m.
42. 13. the Lord shall go forth as a mighty m.
Jer. 9. 23. nor let the mighty m. glory in his might
14. 9. shouldest be as a mighty m. that cannot save
46. 6. nor mighty m. escape || 12. mighty m. stumbled
Zeph. 1. 14. the mighty m. shall cry there bitterly
Zech. 9. 13. have made thee as sword of a mighty m.
10. 7. they of Ephraim shall be like a mighty m.

No MAN.

Gen. 31. 50. no m. is with us, see, God is witness
41. 44. without thee shall no m. lift his hand
45. 1. stood no m. while Joseph made hims. known
Exod. 2. 12. and when he saw that there was no m.
16. 19. let no m. leave of it till the morning
29. let no m. go out of his place on the seventh day
22. 10. be hurt or driven away, no m. seeing it
33. 4. no m. did put on him his ornaments
20. for there shall no m. see me and live
34. 3. and no m. shall come up with thee
Lev. 16. 17. there shall be no m. in the tabernacle
21. 21. no m. that hath a blemish shall come nigh
27. 26. no m. shall sanctify it, it is the Lord's
Num. 5. 19. if no m. hath lain with thee, be thou free
Deut. 7. 24. no m. able to stand before thee, 11. 25.
28. 29. oppressed, and no m. shall save thee, 68.
34. 6. but no m. knoweth of his sepulchre
Josh. 23. 9. no m. hath been able to stand before you

Judg. 11. 39. Jephthah's daughter knew no m.
19. 15. no m. that took them to his house, 18.
21. 12. young virgins that had known no m.
1 Sam. 2. 9. for by strength shall no m. prevail
11. 3. and then if there be no m. to save us
17. 32. let no m. heart fail because of him
21. 2. let no m. know any thing of the business
26. 12. and no m. saw nor knew it, nor awaked
2 Sam. 15. 3. no m. deputed of the king to hear thee
1 Kings 8. 46. is no m. that sinneth not, 2 Chr. 6. 36.
2 Kings 7. 5. behold, there was no m. in camp, 10.
23. 18. let him alone, let no m. move his bones
1 Chr. 16. 21. he suffered no m. to do them wrong,
he reproved kings for their sakes, Ps. 105. 14.
Esth. 5. 12. queen did let no m. come in with king
8. 8. may no m. reverse || 9. 2. no m. could withstand
Job 11. 3. shall no m. make thee ashamed?
15. 28. in houses which no m. inhabiteth
20. 21. therefore shall no m. look for his goods
24. 22. he riseth, and no m. is sure of his life
38. 26. where no m. is, wherein there is no m.
Ps. 22. 6. I am a worm, and no m. a reproach of men
142. 4. there was no m. Isa. 41. 28. | 59. 16. Jer. 4. 25.
143. 2. in thy sight shall no m. be justified
Prov. 1. 24. I stretched my hand, and no m. regarded
28. 1. the wicked flee when no m. pursueth
17. shall flee to the pit, let no m. stay him
Eccl. 8. 8. no m. hath power over the spirit
9. 1. no m. knoweth either love or hatred
15. no m. remembered that same poor man
Isa. 9. 19. no m. shall spare his brother
24. 10. no m. may come in || 33. 8. he regardeth no m.
50. 2. wherefore when I came, was there no m.
57. 1. and no m. layeth it to heart, Jer. 12. 11.
60. 15. so that no m. went through thee
Jer. 2. 6. and where no m. dwelt || 8. 6. no m. repent.
22. 30. for no m. of his seed shall prosper
30. 17. this is Zion, whom no m. seeketh after
36. 19. go hide, and let no m. know where ye be
38. 24. Zedekiah said, let no m. know of these words
40. 15. and no m. shall know it || 41. 4. no m. knew it
44. 2. and no m. dwelleth therein, 51. 43.
49. 18. no m. shall abide there, 33. | 50. 40.
Lam. 4. 4. ask bread, and no m. breaketh it to them
Ezek. 14. 15. that no m. may pass thro' for the beasts
44. 2. no m. shall enter in by this gate
Hos. 4. 4. yet let no m. strive or reprove another
Nah. 3. 18. is scattered, and no m. gathereth them
Zeph. 3. 6. so that there is no m. none inhabitant
Zech. 1. 21. so that no m. did lift up his head
7. 14. that no m. passed through nor returned
Mat. 6. 24. no m. can serve two masters, Luke 16. 13.
8. 4. tell no m. 16. 20. Mark 7. 36. Luke 5. 14. | 9. 21.
9. 30. Jesus charged them, saying, see that no m.
know it, Mark 5. 43. | 7. 24. | 8. 30. | 9. 9.
11. 27. no m. knoweth Son but Father, Luke 10. 22.
17. 8. they saw no m. save Jesus only
9. tell the vision to no m. till the Son be risen
22. 46. no m. was able to answer him a word
23. 9. call no m. father on the earth
24. 36. that day and hour know. no m. Mark 13. 32.
Mark 10. 29. no m. that hath left house, Luke 18. 29.
11. 14. no m. eat fruit of thee hereafter for ever
12. 14. we know that thou carest for no m.
Luke 3. 14. do violence to no m. || 10. 4. salute no m.
15. 16. with the husks, and no m. gave unto him
John 1. 18. no m. hath seen God, 1 John 4. 12.
3. 2. no m. can do these miracles, except God be
13. no m. hath ascended up to heaven
5. 22. for the Father judgeth no m. but hath
6. 44. no m. can come to me, except Fath. draw, 65.
7. 30. but no m. laid hands on him, 44. | 8. 20.
8. 11. she said, no m. Lord || 15. I judge no m.
9. 4. the night cometh when no m. can work
10. 18. no m. taketh it from me, I lay it down
29. no m. is able to pluck them out of my Father's
13. 28. no m. at the table knew why he spake this
14. 6. no m. cometh to the Father but by me
15. 13. greater love hath no m. than this
16. 22. and your joy no m. taketh from you
Acts 1. 20. and let no m. dwell therein
4. 17. that they speak to no m. in this name
5. 13. of the rest durst no m. join himself
23. we had opened, we found no m. within
9. 7. hearing a voice, but seeing no m. 8.
18. 10. no m. shall set on thee to hurt thee
28. 31. preaching king. of G. no m. forbidding him
Rom. 12. 17. recompense to no m. evil for evil
13. 8. owe no m. any thing, but to love one another
14. 7. liveth to himself, and no m. dieth to himself
13. that no m. put a stumbling-block in his way
1 Cor. 2. 11. the things of God knoweth no m.
15. yet he himself is judged of no m.
3. 11. for other foundation can no m. lay than is laid
18. let no m. deceive himself, 21.
10. 24. let no m. seek his own, but another's wealth
2 Cor. 5. 16. henceforth know we no m. after the flesh
7. 2. we have wronged no m. have corrupted no m.
Gal. 2. 6. God accepteth no m. person
3. 11. but that no m. is justified by the law
Eph. 5. 6. let no m. deceive you, 2 Thess. 2. 3.
29. for no m. ever yet hated his own flesh
Phil. 2. 20. for I have no m. like-minded, who will
Col. 2. 18. let no m. beguile you of your reward
1 Thess. 4. 6. that no m. go beyond his brother in any
1 Tim. 5. 22. lay hands suddenly on no m.
2 Tim. 4. 16. at my first answer no m. stood with me
Tit. 3. 2. put them in mind, to speak evil of no m.
Heb. 5. 4. no m. taketh this honour to himself
7. 13. of which no m. gave attendance at the altar
12. 14. without which no m. shall see the Lord
Jam. 1. 13. let no m. say when he is tempted
3. 8. the tongue can no m. tame, it is unruly
1 John 3. 7. little children, let no m. deceive you
Rev. 2. 17. a new name, which no m. knoweth
3. 7. he that shutteth, and no m. openeth
8. and no m. can shut it || 11. no m. take thy crown
5. 3. and no m. was able to open the book, 4.
7. 9. and multitude which no m. could number
13. 17. that no m. might buy or sell, save he that
14. 3. no m. could learn that song but the redeemed
15. 8. no m. was able to enter into the temple

Rev. 18. 11. no m. buyeth their merchandise any more
19. 12. he had a name written, that no m. knew

Of MAN.

Gen. 9. 5. at the hand of m. will I require life of m.
Exod. 13. 13. all the first-born of m. Num. 18. 15.
Deut. 1. 17. ye shall not be afraid of the face of m.
2 Sam. 7. 19. is this the manner of m. O Lord God?
24. 14. not fall into the hands of m. 1 Chron. 21. 13.
2 Kings 1. 7. what manner of m. was he which came
7. 10. there was no man there, nor voice of m.
Job 10. 5. are thy days as the days of m.?
14. 19. thou destroyest the hope of m.
Psal. 60. 11. for vain is the help of m. 108. 12.
76. 10. the wrath of m. shall praise thee
Prov. 5. 21. the ways of m. are before the Lord
6. † 26. the woman of a m. will hunt for life
18. 14. the spirit of m. will sustain his infirmity
19. 11. the discretion of m. deferreth his anger
22. the desire of m. is his kindness
27. 19. so the heart of m. answereth to man
29. 25. the fear of m. bringeth a snare
30. 2. and have not the understanding of m.
19. and the way of a m. with a maid
Eccl. 6. 7. all the labour of m. is for his mouth
8. 6. the misery of m. is great upon him
12. 13. for this is the whole duty of m.
Isa. 22. † 17. will carry thee with captivity of a m.
44. 13. he marketh with compass, he maketh it after the figure of m. according to the beauty of a m.
51. 12. that thou shouldest be afraid of a m.
Jer. 10. 23. I know the way of m. is not in himself
Lam. 3. 35. to turn aside the right of a m.
Ezek. 1. 10. they four had the face of a m. 10. 14.
29. 11. no foot of m. shall pass through it
32. 13. neither shall the foot of m. trouble them
Dan. 8. 15. stood as the appearance of a m. 10. 18.
Zech. 9. 1. when eyes of a m. shall be toward Lord
12. 1. who formeth the spirit of m. within him
Mat. 8. 27. what manner of m. is this, that the winds and sea obey him? Mark 4. 41. Luke 8. 25.
19. 10. if the case of m. be so with his wife
Mark 5. 8. he said, come out of the m. Luke 8. 29.
John 1. 13. nor of the will of m. but of God
2. 25. needed not that any should testify of m.
Acts 12. 22. it is the voice of a god, not of a m.
Rom. 2. 9. upon every soul of m. that doeth evil
4. 6. David describeth the blessedness of the m.
1 Cor. 2. 9. neither hath entered into the heart of m.
11. what man knoweth the things of a m. save the spirit of m. which is in him, so Spirit things of God
4. 3. should be judged of you, or of m. judgment
11. 7. but the woman is the glory of the m.
8. but the woman is of the m. 12.
Gal. 1. 12. for I neither received it of m.
Jam. 1. 20. the wrath of m. worketh not righteousn
24. forgetteth what manner of m. he was
1 Pet. 1. 24. all the glory of m. as the flower of grass
2 Pet. 1. 21. came not in old time by the will of m.
Rev. 13. 18. for it is the number of a m.
21. 17. according to the measure of a m.

See OLD.

One MAN.

Gen. 42. 11. we are all one m. sons, we are true, 13.
Exod. 16. 22. they gathered two homers for one m.
21. 35. if one m. ox hurt another's that he die
Num. 14. 15. if thou kill this people as one m.
16. 22. shall one m. sin, and wilt thou be wroth?
31. 49. and there lacketh not one m. of us
Josh. 23. 10. one m. shall chase a thousand
Judg. 6. 16. smite the Midianites as one m.
18. 19. to be a priest to the house of one m.
20. 1. the congregation was gathered as one m.
8. all the people arose as one m. saying
1 Sam. 2. 25. if one m. sin against another
2 Sam. 19. 14. even as the heart of one m.
1 Kings 22. 8. there is yet one m. Micaiah, 2 Chr. 18. 7.
Ezra 3. 1. gathered together as one m. Neh. 8. 1.
Job 13. 9. as one m. mocketh another, do ye mock
Eccl. 7. 28. one m. among a thousand have I found
8. 9. wherein one m. ruleth over another
Isa. 4. 1. seven women shall take hold of one m.
Ezek. 9. 2. one m. was clothed with linen
John 11. 50. one m. shall die for the people, 18. 14.
Rom. 5. 12. as by one m. sin entered into the world
15. the gift by grace, which is by one m. Jesus
17. if by one m. offence death reigned by one
19. as by one m. disobedience many were sinners
14. 5. one m. esteemeth one day above another
1 Tim. 5. 9. having been the wife of one m.

See POOR, RICH, RIGHTEOUS.

Son of MAN.

Num. 23. 19. nor son of m. that he should repent
Job 25. 6. and the son of m. which is a worm
35. 8. righteousness may profit the son of m.
Psal. 8. 4. and son of m. that thou visit. him, Heb. 2. 6.
80. 17. and on son of m. whom thou madest strong
144. 3. or son of m. that thou makest account of him
146. 3. put not your trust in the son of m.
Isa. 51. 12. be not afraid of the son of m. which
56. 2. blessed is the son of m. that layeth hold on it
Jer. 49. 18. nor shall son of m. dwell in it, 33. | 50. 40.
51. 43. neither doth any son of m. pass thereby
Ezek. 8. 15. hast thou seen this, O son of m. 17.
21. 6. sigh therefore, thou son of m. with bitterness
Dan. 7. 13. behold, one like the Son of m. came with the clouds of heaven, Rev. 1. 13. | 14. 14.
Mat. 8. 20. Son of m. hath not where to lay, Luke 9. 58.
9. 6. know that the Son of m. hath power on earth to forgive sins, Mark 2. 10. Luke 5. 24.
10. 23. not gone over, till the Son of m. be come
11. 19. the Son of m. came eating, Luke 7. 34.
12. 8. for the Son of m. is Lord even of the sabbath, Mark 2. 28. Luke 6. 5.
32. whosoever speaketh against Son of m. Luke 12. 10.
40. so shall Son of m. be three days and nights
13. 37. that soweth good seed is the Son of m.
41. the Son of m. shall send forth his angels
16. 13. whom do men say that I, the S. of m. am?
17. 9. until the Son of m. be risen again, Mark 9. 9.
22. the S. of m. shall be betrayed, 20. 18. | 26. 2, 45 Mark 14. 41. Luke 9. 44.

Mat. 24. 27. so shall also the coming of the Son of m. be, 37, 39. Luke 17. 26.
30. shall see S. of m. com. Mark 13. 26. Luke 21. 27.
44. hour ye think not S. of m. cometh, Luke 12. 40.
25. 31. when the Son of m. shall come in his glory
26. 24. the S. of m. goeth, Mark 14. 21. Luke 22. 22.
Mark 8. 38. of him shall the Son of m. be ashamed when he cometh in glory of the Father
9. 12. and how it is written of the Son of m.
31. the Son of m. is delivered, 10. 33. Luke 24. 7.
13. 34. Son of m. is as a man taking a far journey
Luke 6. 22. reproach you for the Son of m. sake
9. 22. the Son of m. must suffer many things, 26.
56. the S. of m. is not come to destroy men's lives
11. 30. so shall Son of m. be to this generat. 17. 24.
12. 8. him shall the Son of m. confess before angels
17. 22. desire to see one of the days of the Son of m.
18. 8. when the S. of m. cometh, shall he find faith
19. 10. the S. of m. is come to seek and to save lost
21. 36. be worthy to stand before the Son of m.
22. 48. betrayest thou the Son of m. with a kiss?
John 1. 51. ascending and descending on Son of m.
3. 13. even the Son of m. which is in heaven
14. even so must the Son of m. be lifted up
5. 27. given authority, because he is the Son of m.
6. 27. which the Son of m. shall give unto you
53. except ye eat the flesh of the Son of m.
62. what, and if ye shall see the Son of m. ascend
8. 28. when ye have lift up the Son of m. then shall
12. 23. that the Son of m. should be glorified
34. S. of m. must be lifted up, who is this S. of m.?
13. 31. Jesus said, now is the Son of m. glorified
Acts 7. 56. I see the S. of m. standing on right hand

See SON.

That MAN.

Lev. 17. 9. even t. m. shall be cut off from his peo.
20. 3. I will set my face against t. m. 5. Ezek. 14. 8.
Num. 9. 13. brought not offer. t. m. shall bear his sin
Deut. 17. 5. stone that m. or woman till they die, 12.
22. 18. elders shall take that m. and chastise him
25. 9. answer and say, so shall it be done to that m.
29. 20. his jealousy shall smoke against that m.
Josh. 22. 20. that m. perisheth not alone in iniquity
Job 1. 1. and that m. was perfect and upright
Psal. 37. 37. for the end of that m. is peace
40. 4. blessed is that m. who maketh Lord his trust
87. 5. he said, this and that m. was born in her
Prov. 28. 21. for bread that m. will transgress
Jer. 20. 16. let that m. be as cities Lord overthrew
23. 34. I will even punish that m. and his house
Mat. 12. 45. last state of t. m. is worse, Luke 11. 26.
18. 7. woe to that m. by whom the offence cometh
26. 24. woe to that m. by whom the Son of man is betrayed, Mark 14. 21. Luke 22. 22.
good were it for that m. if he had not been born
27. 19. have thou nothing to do with that just m.
Acts 17. 31. by that m. whom he hath ordained
Rom. 14. 20. evil for t. m. who eateth with offence
2 Thess. 2. 3. t. m. of sin be revealed, son of perdit.
3. 14. note that m. and have no company with him
Jam. 1. 7. let not that m. think he shall receive

This MAN.

Gen. 24. 58. wilt thou go with this m.? I will go
26. 11. he that toucheth this m. or his wife
Exod. 10. 7. how long shall t. m. be a snare to us?
Deut. 22. 16. I gave my daughter to this m. to wife
Judg. 19. 23. seeing this m. is come to my house
24. but to this m. do not so vile a thing
1 Sam. 1. 3. this m. went up yearly to worship
10. 27. but they said, how shall this m. save us?
17. 25. have you seen this m. that is come up?
25. 25. let not my lord regard this m. of Belial
1 Kings 20. 7. see how this m. seeketh mischief
39. brought a man to me, and said, keep this m.
2 Kings 5. 7. this m. sends to me to recover a man
Neh. 1. 11. grant him mercy in sight of this m.
Esth. 9. 4. for this m. Mordecai waxed greater and
Job 1. 3. this m. was the greatest of the men of east
Psal. 52. 7. lo, this m. made not God his strength
87. 4. shall be said, this m. was born there, 5, 6.
Isa. 14. 16. is this the m. that made earth tremble?
66. 2. but to this m. will I look, even to him
Jer. 22. 28. is t. m. Coniah a despised broken idol?
30. thus saith the Lord, write ye this m. childless
26. 11. saying, this m. is worthy to die, 16.
38. 4. the princes said, let this m. be put to death, this m. seeketh not the welfare of this people
Dan. 8. 16. make this m. understand the vision
Jonah 1. 14. let us not perish for this m. life
Mic. 5. 5. this m. shall be the peace when Assyrian
Mat. 8. 9. I say to t. m. go, and he goeth, to another
9. 3. scribes said, this m. blasphemeth, Mark 2. 7.
13. 54. whence hath this m. this wisdom? Mark 6. 2.
27. 47. some said, this m. calleth for Elias
Mark 14. 71. I know not this m. of whom ye speak
15. 39. truly this m. was the Son of God
Luke 7. 39. this m. if he were a prophet, would have
14. 9. come and say to thee, give this m. place
30. saying, this m. began to build and was not able
15. 2. this m. receive. sinners, and eateth with them
18. 14. I tell you, this m. went down justified rather
19. 14. we will not have this m. to reign over us
22. 56. and said, this m. was also with him
23. 4. I find no fault in t. m. 14. || 18. away with t. m.
41. but this m. hath done nothing amiss
52. this m. went to Pilate and begged the body
John 6. 52. how can this m. give us his flesh to eat?
7. 15. how knoweth this m. letters, having never
27. howbeit, we know this m. whence he is
46. answered, never man spake like this m.
9. 2. Master, who did sin, this m. or his parents?
3. neither hath this m. sinned, nor his parents
16. this m. is not of G. he keepeth not the sabbath
24. praise God, we know that this m. is a sinner
33. if this m. were not of G. he could do nothing
10. 41. all that John spake of this m. were true
11. 37. could not this m. which opened the eyes of blind, caused that this m. should not have died?
47. what do we? for this m. doeth many miracles
18. 17. art not thou one of this m. disciples?
29. what accusation bring ye against this m.?
40. not this m. but Barabbas, now he was a robber

John 19. 12. if let this m. go, art not Cæsar's friend
21. 21. Peter saith, and what shall this m. do?
Acts 1. 18. now this m. purchased a field with reward
3. 12. as though we had made this m. to walk, 16.
4. 10. even by him doth this m. stand whole
5. 28. and intend to bring this m. blood upon us
37. after this m. rose up Judas of Galilee
6. 13. this m. ceaseth not to speak blasphemous
8. 10. saying, this m. is the great power of God
9. 13. I heard of this m. how much evil hath done
13. 23. of this m. seed hath God raised Jesus
38. thro' t. m. is preached to you forgiven. of sins
18. 25. this m. was instructed in way of the Lord
21. 28. this is the m. that teacheth all men ag. law
22. 26. t. m. is a Roman || 23. 9. find no evil in t. m.
23. 27. this m. was taken of the Jews, and should
24. 5. for we have found this m. a pestilent fellow
25. 5. accuse this m. if there be any wickedness
24. ye see this m. about whom Jews dealt with me
26. 31. this m. doeth nothing worthy of death
32. this m. might have been set at liberty
28. 4. no doubt this m. is a murderer, vengeance
Heb. 3. 3. this m. was counted worthy of more glory
7. 4. now consider how great this m. was, to whom
24. but this m. because he continueth ever
8. 3. that this m. have somewhat also to offer
10. 12. this m. after he had offered one sacrifice
Jam. 1. 25. this m. shall be blessed in his deed
26. but deceiveth, this m. religion is vain

See UNDERSTANDING.

MAN of war.

Exod. 15. 3. the Lord is a m. of w. Lord is his name
Josh. 17. 1. Machir, son of Manasseh, was a m. of w.
1 Sam. 16. 18. David a m. of war, 2 Sam. 17. 8. 1 Chron. 28. 3.
17. 33. Goliah was a m. of war from his youth
Isa. 3. 2. the Lord doth take away the m. of war
42. 13. he shall stir up jealousy like a m. of war

Wicked MAN.

Deut. 25. 2. if the wicked m. be worthy to be beaten
Job 15. 20. the wicked m. travaileth with pain
20. 29. the portion of a wicked m. from God, 27. 13.
Psal. 109. 6. set thou a wicked m. over him
Prov. 6. 12. a wicked m. walketh with froward mouth
9. 7. he that rebuketh a wicked m. getteth a blot
11. 7. when a wicked m. dieth, his expectation
13. 5. a wicked m. is loathsome, and cometh to
17. 23. a wicked m. taketh a gift out of the bosom
21. 29. wicked m. hardeneth his face, but the upright
24. 15. lay not wait, O wicked m. against dwelling
Eccl. 7. 15. a wicked m. that prolongeth his days
Ezek. 3. 18. the same wicked m. shall die in iniquity
18. 24. and doth that which the wicked m. doeth
27. when a wicked m. turneth from his wickedness
33. 8. when I say to wicked, O w. m. thou shalt surely die, that wicked m. shall die in his iniquity

Wise MAN.

Gen. 41. 33. look out a m. discreet and wise, set him
1 Kings 2. 9. Solomon was w. m. and knew what to do
1 Chron. 27. 32. Jonathan David's uncle, was a w. m.
Job 15. 2. should a wise m. utter vain knowledge?
17. 10. I cannot find one wise m. among you
34. 34. and let a wise m. hearken to me
Prov. 1. 5. a wise m. will hear and increase
9. 8. rebuke a wise m. and he will love thee
9. give instruction to a wise m. he will be wiser
14. 16. a wise m. feareth, and departeth from evil
16. 14. a wise m. will pacify the wrath of a king
17. 10. a reproof entereth more into a wise m.
21. 22. a wise m. scaleth the city of the mighty
26. 12. seest thou a m. wise in his own conceit?
29. 9. if a wise m. contendeth with a foolish man
11. but a wise m. keepeth it in till afterwards
Eccl. 2. 14. the wise m. eyes are in his head
16. and how dieth the wise m.? as the fool
19. whether he shall be wise m. or a fool?
7. 7. surely oppression maketh a wise m. mad
8. 1. who is as the wise m. and who knoweth
5. a wise m. heart discerneth time and judgment
17. though a wise m. think to know it, yet not able
9. 15. now there was found in it a poor wise m.
10. 2. a wise m. heart is at his right hand
12. the words of a wise m. mouth are gracious
Jer. 9. 12. who is the wise m. that may understand?
23. let not the wise m. glory in his wisdom
Mat. 7. 24. I will liken him to a wise m. who built
1 Cor. 6. 5. that there is not a wise m. amongst you
Jam. 3. 13. who is a wise m. endued with knowledge

MAN, joined with Woman.

Gen. 3. 12. the m. said, the w. whom thou gavest me
20. 3. dead m. for the wom. thou hast is man's wife
Exod. 35. 29. every m. and wom. whose heart made
36. 6. let no m. nor woman make any more work
Lev. 13. 29. if a m. or woman have the plague
38. if m. or woman have in the skin bright spots
15. 18. the woman also with whom the m. shall lie
33. that hath an issue of the m. and woman
20. 18. if m. lie with a woman having her sickness
27. a m. or woman that hath a familiar spirit
Num. 5. 6. when m. or woman shall commit any sin
6. 2. when either m. or wom. shall separate thems.
31. 17. kill wom. that hath known m. Judg. 21. 11.
Deut. 17. 2. m. or wom. that hath wrought wickedn.
5. bring forth that m. or woman, and stone them
22. 5. the woman shall not wear that pertaineth to a m. nor shall m. put on a woman's garment
22. if a m. be found lying with a woman, both the m. that lay with the woman, and the woman
29. 18. lest there should be among you, m. or wom.
Josh. 6. 21. utterly destroyed both m. and woman
1 Sam. 15. 3. but slay both m. and woman, and infant
27. 9. David left neither m. nor woman alive, 11.
1 Chr. 16. 3. he dealt both to m. and woman a loaf
2 Chr. 15. 13. not seek Lord, m. or wom. shall die
Esth. 4. 11. whether m. or woman come to the king
Jer. 44. 7. to cut off from you, m. woman and child
51. 22. I will break in pieces m. and woman
1 Cor. 11. 3. and the head of the woman is the m.
7. but the woman is the glory of the m.
8. the m. is not of the wom. but woman of the m.
11. nor is the m. without the woman in the Lord
12. as wom. is of the m. so is the m. by the wom.

1 *Tim*. 5. 16. if any *m*. or *woman* have widows

Young MAN.

Gen. 4. 23. I have slain a *young m*. to my hurt
18. 7. Abraham gave it to a *young m*. to dress it
34. 19. the *young m*. deferred not to do the thing
41. 12. there was with us a *young m*. an Hebrew
Exod. 33. 11. Joshua a *young m*. departed not out
Num. 11. 27. and there ran *young m*. and told Moses
Deut. 32. 25. destroy both the *young m*. and virgin
Judg. 8. 14. caught a *young m*. of the men of Succoth
9. 54. Abimelech called hastily to the *young m*. and his *young m*. thrust him through, and he died
17. 7. there was a *young m*. of Bethlehem-Judah
12. the *young m*. became his priest, and was in
18. 3. knew the voice of the *young m*. the Levite
1 *Sam*. 9. 2. Saul was a choice *young m*. and goodly
14. 1. Jonathan said to the *young m*. that bare
17. 58. and Saul said, whose son art thou, *young m*.?
20. 22. but if I say thus to the *young m*. behold
30. 13. he said to David, I am *young m*. of Egypt
2 *Sam*. 1. 5. David said to the *young m*. that told, 13
14. 21. go bring the *young m*. Absalom again
18. 5. deal gently for my sake with the *young m*.
29. king said, is the *young m*. Absalom safe? 32.
32. the enemies of my lord be as that *young m*. is
1 *Kings* 11. 28. Solomon seeing *young m*. industrious
2 *Kings* 6. 17. Lord opened the eyes of the *young m*.
9. 4. so the *young m*. even *young m*. went to Ramoth
1 *Chr*. 12. 28. and Zadok, a *young m*. mighty in val.
2 *Chr*. 36. 17. and had no compassion on *young m*.
Psal. 119. 9. wherewith shall *y. m*. cleanse his way
Prov. 1. 4. to *young m*. knowledge and discretion
7. 7. I discerned a *young m*. void of understanding
Eccl. 11. 9. rejoice, O *young m*. in thy youth
Isa. 62. 5. for as *young m*. marrieth a virgin
Jer. 51. 22. break in pieces the *young m*. and maid
Zech. 2. 4. said to me, run, speak to this *young m*.
Mat. 19. 20. the *young m*. said, all these have I kept
Mark 14. 51. there followed him a certain *young m*.
16. 5. they saw a *young m*. sitting on the right side
Luke 7. 14. he said, *young m*. I say to thee, arise
Acts 7. 58. they laid their clothes at a *young m*. feet
20. 9. sat in a window a *young m*. named Eutychus
12. and they brought the *young m*. alive
23. 17. bring this *young m*. to the chief captain, 18.
22. the chief captain then let the *young m*. depart

MANDRAKES

Is a kind of plant, whose root at some distance from its upper part is generally divided into two branches, which is the reason that this root had something of the figure of a man, whose two thighs are represented by the two branches. It is said sometimes to stupify, and cause phrensy; some call it a provocative, and that therefore it was used in philtres; and that this was the reason why Rachel *so earnestly desired to obtain them from* Leah, *she being very desirous of having children. There are two sorts of* Mandrakes; *the female, whose leaves are of a very disagreeable scent: and the* male, *whose scent is said to be very pleasant and agreeable. It is reported, that in the province of* Pekin *in* China, *there is a kind of* Mandrake *so valuable, that a pound of that root is worth thrice its weight in silver: for they say it so wonderfully restores the sinking spirits of dying persons, that there is often time for the use of other means, and thereby recovering them to life and health. Those* Mandrakes *which* Reuben *brought home to his mother, are by some called* Violets, *by others* Lilies, *or* Jessamin, *by others* Citrons. *Some reckon them to be such agreeable flowers of the field, wherewith children were pleased;* Reuben *that gathered them being then only about five or six years of age.*

Gen. 30. 14. Reuben found *m*. give me of thy *m*.
15. wouldest thou take away my son's *m*. also? therefore he shall lie with thee for thy son's *m*.
16. I have hired thee with my son's *m*.
Cant. 7. 13. *m*. give a smell, and at our gates are

MANGER.

Luke 2. 7. laid him in a *m*. ‖ 12. shall find him in a *m*.
16. and they found the babe lying in a *m*.

MANIFEST, *Actively, Passively*.

Eccl. 3. 18. that God might *m*. them, and that
John 14. 21. love him, and *m*. myself to him
22. *m*. thyself to us, and not to the world?
Acts 4. 16. the miracle is *m*. to all at Jerusalem
Rom. 1. 19. what may be known of G. is *m*. in them
1 *Cor*. 4. 5. who will make *m*. counsels of hearts
15. 27. it is *m*. that he is excepted which did
2 *Cor*. 2. 14. makes *m*. the savour of his knowledge
Gal. 5. 19. now the works of the flesh are *m*.
Phil. 1. 13. so that my bonds in Christ are *m*.
Col. 4. 4. that I may make it *m*. as I ought
2 *Thess*. 1. 5. a *m*. token of righteous judgm. of God
1 *Tim*. 3. 16. God was *m*. in the flesh, justified
5. 25. the good works of some are *m*. beforehand
2 *Tim*. 3. 9. their body shall be *m*. to all men
Heb. 4. 13. there is no creature that is not *m*.
1 *Pet*. 1. 20. but was *m*. in these last times for you
1 *John* 3. 10. in this the children of God are *m*.

See MADE.

MANIFESTATION.

Rom. 8. 19. waiteth for the *m*. of the sons of God
1 *Cor*. 12. 7. the *m*. of the Sp. is given to every man
2 *Cor*. 4. 2. but by the *m*. of the truth commending

MANIFESTED.

Mark 4. 22. for nothing is hid which shall not be *m*.
John 2. 11. miracles did Jesus, and *m*. forth his glory
17. 6. I have *m*. thy name unto the men which
Rom. 3. 21. but the righteousness of God is *m*.
Tit. 1. 3. but hath in due time *m*. his word
1 *John* 1. 2. the life was *m*. and we have seen it
3. 5. that he was *m*. to take away our sins
8. for this purpose was the Son of God *m*.
4. 9. in this was *m*. the love of God toward us

MANIFESTLY.

2 *Cor*. 3. 3. are *m*. declared to be the epistle of Christ

MANIFOLD.

Neh. 9. 19. in thy *m*. mercies forsookest them not
27. according to *m*. mercies gavest them saviours
Psal. 104. 24. O Lord, how *m*. are thy works

Amos 5. 12. I know your *m*. transgressions and sins
Luke 18. 30. who shall not receive *m*. more
Eph. 3. 10. might be known the *m*. wisdom of God
1 *Pet*. 1. 6. ye are in heaviness, thro' *m*. temptations
4. 10. as good stewards of the *m*. grace of God

MANKIND.

Lev. 18. 22. shall not lie with *m*. as with woman-kind
20. 13. if a man lie with a *m*. as with a woman
Job 12. 10. in whose hand is the breath of all *m*.
1 *Tim*. 1. 10. the law for them that defile with *m*.
Jam. 3. 7. is tamed, and hath been tamed of *m*.

MANNA,

That delicious food wherewith God fed the children of Israel in the deserts of Arabia, *during their continuance there for forty years, from their eighth encampment in the wilderness of* Sin. *It was a little grain, white like hoar frost, round, and of the bigness of coriander-seed. It fell every morning upon the dew, and when the dew was exhaled by the heat of the sun, the* Manna *appeared alone lying upon the rocks or the sand,* Exodus 16. 14. Num. 11. 7. *It fell every day, except on the sabbath, and this only about the camp of the* Israelites, *Exod*. 16. 5. *It fell in so great quantities during the whole forty years of their journey in the wilderness, that it was sufficient to feed the whole multitude of above a million of souls; every one of whom gathered the quantity of an homer for his share every day, which is about three quarts of* English *measure. It maintained this vast multitude, and yet none of them found any inconvenience from the constant eating of it. Every sixth day there fell a double quantity of it; and though it putrified when it was kept any other day, yet on the sabbath it suffered no such alteration. And the same* Manna *that was melted by the heat of the sun, when it was left in the field, was of so hard a consistence when it was brought into their tents, that it was used to be beaten in mortars, and would even endure the fire, was baked in pans, made into paste, and so into cakes,* Num. 11. 8. *It is called,* Angels' food, *Psal*. 78. 25. *which may insinuate, either that it was made and prepared by their ministry; or that angels themselves, if they had need of any food, could not have any that was more agreeable than* Manna *was; it being of a heavenly original, and of singular vigour and efficacy for preserving and nourishing those who used it according to God's appointment:* Or, *as it is in the margin,* every one did eat the bread of the mighty; *that is, even the common Israelites fed upon it as delicious food, as the greatest nobles and princes did.*

To eat of the hidden Manna, *Rev*. 2. 17. *To partake of Christ, and those comforts and blessings which flow from him: It is spoken in allusion to that bread wherewith God fed the Israelites, which was a type of Christ, who is the* bread *of eternal life, and was the true* bread *which came down from heaven to give life to the world,* John 6. 32, 33, 35.

Exod. 16. 15. they said one to another, it is *m*.
33. take a pot, and put an homer full of *m*. therein
35. and Israel did eat *m*. forty years
Num. 11. 6. there is nothing besides this *m*.
7. the *m*. was as coriander-seed, and the colour
9. when the dew fell on camp the *m*. fell on it
Deut. 8. 3. he suffered thee to hunger, and fed thee with *m*. 16. *Neh*. 9. 20. *Psal*. 78. 24.
Josh. 5. 12. the *m*. ceased, they had *m*. no more
John 6. 31. our fathers did eat *m*. in the desert, 49.
58. not as your fathers did eat *m*. and are dead
Heb. 9. 4. wherein was the golden pot that had *m*.
Rev. 2. 17. to him will I give to eat of the hidden *m*.

MANNER

Signifies, [1] *Custom, practice, or fashion,* 1 Sam. 8. 9, 11. Ezek. 11. 12. [2] *Sinful behaviour, and rebellious conduct,* Acts 13. 18. [3] *Deportment and carriage in word and deed,* 1 Cor. 15. 33. [4] *Ways and means,* Heb. 1. 1. [5] *Kind or sort,* Exod. 12. 16. [6] *Order or rank,* Josh. 6. 15. [7] *The way of service or worship,* 2 Kings 17. 26, 27.

Gen. 25. 23. two *m*. of people shall be separated
40. 17. was of all *m*. of bake-meats for Pharaoh
Exod. 1. 14. made their lives bitter in all *m*. of service
12. 16. no *m*. of work shall be done in them
22. 9. all *m*. of trespass, any *m*. of lost thing
31. 3. in wisdom, and in all *m*. of workmanship, 5. | 35. 31, 33, 35. | 36. 1. 1 *Chron*. 28. 21.
Lev. 5. 10. burnt offering accord. to *m*. *Num*. 9. 14.
7. 23. shall eat no *m*. of fat of ox or sheep
26. ye shall eat no *m*. of blood, 27. | 17. 10, 14.
14. 54. the law for all *m*. of the plague of leprosy
23. 31. ye shall do no *m*. of work, it shall be a statute
24. 22. ye shall have one *m*. of law, *Num*. 15. 16.
Num. 5. 13. neither she be taken with the *m*.
15. 24. and his drink-offering according to the *m*.
28. 18. ye shall do no *m*. of servile work
Deut. 4. 15. for ye saw no *m*. of similitude in Horeb
15. 2. and this is the *m*. of the release
27. 21. cursed be he that lieth with any *m*. of beast
Judg. 6. † 26. built an altar in an orderly *m*.
8. 18. what *m*. of men were they ye slew at Tabor?
Ruth 4. 7. now this was the *m*. in former time
1 *Sam*. 8. 9. and shew them the *m*. of the king, 11.
10. 25. Samuel told the people the *m*. of the kingd.
21. 5. and the bread is in *m*. common
27. 11. and so will be his *m*. all the while
2 *Sam*. 7. 19. is this the *m*. of man, O Lord God?
2 *Kings* 1. 7. what *m*. of man was he who told you?
11. 14. the king stood by a pillar, as the *m*. was
17. 26. know not the *m*. of the God of the land
27. let him teach them the *m*. of God of the land
1 *Chron*. 23. 29. for all *m*. of measure and size
Esth. 1. 13. for so was the king's *m*. towards all
Psal. 107. 18. their soul abhorreth all *m*. of meat
144. 13. garners be full, affording all *m*. of store
Cant. 7. 13. at our gates are all *m*. of pleasant fruits
Isa. 5. 17. then the lambs shall feed after their *m*.
Jer. 22. 21. this hath been thy *m*. from thy youth
Dan. 6. 23. and no *m*. of hurt was found on him

Amos 8. 14. and the *m*. of Beer-sheba liveth
Mat. 4. 23. and healing all *m*. of sickness, 10. 1.
5. 11. shall say all *m*. of evil against you falsely
8. 27. what *m*. of man is this, that the winds and the sea obey him? *Mark* 4. 41. *Luke* 8. 25.
12. 31. all *m*. of sin shall be forgiven to men
Mark 13. 1. see what *m*. of stones are here
Luke 1. 29. what *m*. of salutation this should be
66. saying, what *m*. of child shall this be?
7. 39. having known what *m*. of woman this is
9. 55. ye know not what *m*. of spirit ye are of
11. 42. ye tithe mint, rue, and all *m*. of herbs
24. 17. what *m*. of communications are these?
John 7. 36. what *m*. of saying is this that he said
19. 40. as the *m*. of the Jews is to bury
Acts 17. 2. Paul, as his *m*. was, went in to them
20. 18. ye know after what *m*. I have been with
22. 3. taught according to the perfect *m*. of the law
25. 16. it is not *m*. of Romans to deliver any to die
26. 4. my *m*. of life from my youth, know Jews
Rom. 7. 8. wrought in me all *m*. of concupiscence
2 *Cor*. 7. 9. ye were made sorry after a godly *m*.
1 *Thess*. 1. 5. as ye know what *m*. of men we were
9. what *m*. of entering in we had unto you
2 *Tim*. 3. 10. but thou hast known my *m*. of life
Heb. 10. 25. assembling, as the *m*. of some is
Jam. 1. 24. forgetteth what *m*. of man he was
1 *Pet*. 1. 11. what *m*. of time the Spirit of Christ
15. so be ye holy in all *m*. of conversation
2 *Pet*. 3. 11. what *m*. of persons ought ye to be
1 *John* 3. 1. behold what *m*. of love the Father
Rev. 11. 5. he must in this *m*. be killed
22. 2. tree of life, which bare twelve *m*. of fruits

After the MANNER.

Gen. 18. 11. to be with Sarah *after the m*. of women
19. 31. to come in to us *after the m*. of all the earth
40. 13. *aft. the* former *m*. when thou wast his butler
Exod. 21. 9. deal with her *after the m*. of daughters
Num. 29. 18. according to the number, *after the m*.
Josh. 6. 15. compassed the city *after the* same *m*.
Judg. 18. 7. careless, *after the m*. of the Zidonians
1 *Sam*. 17. 30. he turned and spake *after the* same *m*.
2 *Kings* 17. 33. *a. the m*. of the nations, 2 *Chr*. 13. 9.
Neh. 6. 4. and I answered them *after the* same *m*.
Isa. 10. 24. *after the m*. of Egypt, 26. *Amos* 4. 10.
Ezek. 20. 30. polluted *after the m*. of your fathers
23. 15. *after the m*. of the Babylonians of Chaldea
45. *a. t. m*. of adulteresses, and *a. t. m*. of women
John 2. 6. *after the m*. of the purifying of the Jews
Acts 15. 1. ye be circumcised *after the m*. of Moses
Rom. 6. 19. I speak *after the m*. of men, 1 *Cor*. 15. 32. *Gal*. 3. 15.
1 *Cor*. 11. 25. *after the* same *m*. also he took the cup
Gal. 2. 14. being a Jew, livest *a. the m*. of the Gent.

After this MANNER.

Gen. 18. 25. that be far from thee to do *after this m*.
39. 19. saying, *after this m*. did thy servant to me
45. 23. to his father he sent *after this m*. ten asses
Num. 28. 24. *after this m*. ye shall offer daily
2 *Sam*. 17. 6. Ahithophel hath spoken *after this m*.
Jer. 13. 9. *after this m*. will I mar the pride of Judah
Mat. 6. 9. *aft. this m*. therefore pray ye, Our Father
1 *Cor*. 7. 7. one *after this m*. and another after that
1 *Pet*. 3. 5. *after this m*. in old time, women trusted

See LIKE.

On this MANNER.

Gen. 32. 19. saying, *on this m*. shall ye speak to Esau
1 *Sam*. 18. 24. told Saul, saying, *on th. m*. spake D.
2 *Sam*. 15. 6. *on this m*. did Absalom to all Israel
1 *Kings* 22. 20. one said *on this m*. 2 *Chron*. 18. 19.
2 *Chr*. 32. 15. let not Hezek. persuade you *on this m*.

MANNERS.

Lev. 20. 23. shall not walk in the *m*. of the nations
2 *Kings* 17. 34. they do after the former *m*.
Ezek. 11. 12. have done after the *m*. of the heathen
Acts 13. 18. forty years suffered he their *m*.
1 *Cor*. 15. 33. evil communications corrupt good *m*.
Heb. 1. 1. God in divers *m*. spake in time past

MAN *servant*.

Exod. 20. 10. not do work, thy *m. servant*, *Deut*. 5. 14.
17. not covet thy neighbour's *m. serv*. *Dut*. 5. 21.
21. 27. and if he smite out his *m. servant's* tooth
32. if the ox shall push a *m. servant*, he shall give
Deut. 12. 18. must eat them, thou and thy *m. serv*.
16. 11. shalt rejoice, thou and thy *m. servant*, 14.
Job 31. 13. if I did despise the cause of my *m. servant*
Jer. 34. 9. every man let his *m. servant* go free, 10.

MANSIONS.

John 14. 2. in my Father's house are many *m*.

MAN-*slayer*.

Rom. 35. 6. six cities ye shall appoint for *m.-slayer*
12. that the *m.-slayer* die not, till he stand before

MAN-*slayers*.

1 *Tim*. 1. 9. that the law was made for *m.-slayers*

MANTLE.

Judg. 4. 18. Jael covered Sisera with a *m*.
1 *Sam*. 28. 14. an old man, and covered with a *m*.
1 *Kings* 19. 13. Elijah wrapped his face in his *m*.
19. and Elijah cast his *m*. upon Elisha
2 *Kings* 2. 8. Elijah took his *m*. and smote the waters
13. Elisha took Elijah's *m*. that fell from him, 14.
Ezra 9. 3. and when I heard this, I rent my *m*. 5.
Job 1. 20. then Job arose and rent his *m*.
2. 12. and they rent every one his *m*.
Psal. 109. 29. with their confusion, as with a *m*.

MANTLES.

Isa. 3. 22. I will take away the *m*. and wimples
Dan. 3. † 21. these men were bound in their *m*.

MANY

Signifies, [1] *A great number,* Judg. 9. 40. [2] *All mankind,* Rom. 5. 19. [3] *The elect or believers only,* Mat. 26. 28. Rom. 5. 19. [4] *All the ungodly that perish,* Mat. 7. 13. [5] *Great,* Psal. 18. † 16. [6] *Very often,* Psal. 78. 38. [7] *During life,* Hos. 3. 3. [8] *A long time,* Hos. 3. 4.

Gen. 17. 4. my covenant is with thee, thou shalt be a father of *m*. nations, 5. *Rom*. 4. 17, 18.
37. 3. he made him a coat of *m*. colours, 23, 32.
Exod. 19. 21. they gaze, and *m*. of them perish
Num. 10. 36. when the ark rested, Moses said, return, O Lord, to the *m*. thousands of Israel
13. 18. and see whether they be few or *m*.

Num. 26. 54. to m. thou shalt give more inheritance
56. the possession be divided between m. and few
35. 8. from them that have m. cities, shall give m.
Deut. 7. 1. hath cast out m. nations before thee
15. 6. thou shalt lend to m. nations, 28. 12.
31. 17 and m. evils shall befall them, 21.
Josh. 11. 4. with horses and chariots very m.
Judg. 9. 40. m. were overthrown and wounded
16. 24. the destroyer which slew m. of us
1 Sam. 2. 5. she that hath m. children is feeble
14. 6. no restraint to the Lord to save by m. or few
2 Sam. 24. † 14. for his mercies are m.
1 Kings 4. 20. Judah and Israel were m. as the sand
7. 47. unweighed, because they were exceeding m.
18. 25. and dress it first, for ye are m.
2 Kings 9. 22. and her witchcrafts are so m.
1 Chron. 23. 17. the sons of Rehabiah were very m.
28. 5. for the Lord hath given me m. sons
2 Chron. 11. 23. Rehoboam desired m. wives
14. 11. nothing with thee to help with m. or few
30. 17. there were m. in congregation not sanctified
18. m. of Ephraim and Manasseh not cleansed
Ezra 10. 13. we are m. that have transgressed
Neh. 5. 2. we, our sons and our daughters are m.
6. 18. there were m. in Judah sworn to Tobiah
7. 2. he was faithful, and feared God above m.
13. 26. among m. nations was no king like him
Esth. 4. 3. and m. lay in sackcloth and ashes
Job 4. 3. behold, thou hast instructed m.
11. 19. yea, m. shall make suit unto thee
Psal. 3. 1. m. are they that rise up against me
2. there be m. that say of my soul, 4. 6.
25. 19. consider mine enemies, they are m. 56. 2.
31. 13. for I have heard the slander of m.
32. 10. m. sorrows shall be to the wicked
34. 19. m. are the afflictions of the righteous
37. 16. is better than the riches of m. wicked
40. 3. m. shall see it and fear, and trust in the Lord
55. 18. he delivered, for there were m. with me
71. 7. I am as a wonder to m. thou art my refuge
119. 157. m. are my persecutors and enemies
Prov. 4. 10. and the years of thy life shall be m.
7. 26. for she hath cast down m. wounded
10. 21. the lips of the righteous feed m.
14. 20. but the rich hath m. friends
19. 4. wealth maketh m. friends, but the poor
28. 2. for transgression m. are the princes thereof
27. he that hideth his eyes, shall have m. a curse
Eccl. 11. 8. the days of darkness shall be m.
Isa. 31. 1. and trust in chariots because they are m.
53. 11. by his knowledge shall he justify m.
12. he bare the sin of m. and made intercession
66. 16. and the slain of the Lord shall be m.
Jer. 5. 6. because their transgressions are m.
14. 7. for our backslidings are m. we sinned
42. 2. pray for us, for we are left but few of m.
46. 16. he made m. to fall, one fell on another
Lam. 1. 22. for my sighs are m. my heart is faint
Ezek. 33. 24. but we are m. the land is given us
Dan. 8. 25. and by peace shall destroy m.
11. 14. there shall m. stand up against the king
33. they that understand shall instruct m.
44. to destroy and utterly to make away m.
12. 2. m. that sleep in the dust shall awake
4. m. shall run to and fro, and knowledge be
Hos. 8. 11. Ephraim hath made m. altars to sin
Nah. 1. 12. though they be quiet, and likewise m.
Zech. 8. 20. there shall come inhabitants of m. cities
Mal. 2. 6. but did turn m. away from iniquity
Mat. 7. 13. and m. there be that go in thereat
22. m. will say to me in that day, Lord, Lord
8. 11. m. shall come from the east and west
13. 58. he did not m. mighty works there
19. 30. m. that are first shall be last, Mark 10. 31.
20. 16. for m. be called, but few chosen, 22. 14.
24. 5. for m. shall come in my name and shall deceive m. Mark 13. 6. Luke 21. 8.
12. iniquity abound, the love of m. shall wax cold
26. 28. blood shed for m. ‖ 27. 53. they appear to m.
Mark 5. 9. name is Legion, for we are m. Luke 8. 30.
Luke 1. 16. m. shall he turn to the Lord their God
2. 34. this child for the fall and rising of m. in Isr.
4. 25. m. widows, ‖ 27. m. lepers were in Israel
41. and devils also came out of m. crying out
7. 47. her sins which are m. are forgiven
14. 16. certain man made great supper, and bade m.
John 6. 9. but what are they among so m.?
60. m. therefore of his disciples said, 66.
10. 41. and m. resorted to him, and said
21. 11. for all so m. the net was not broken
Acts 9. 13. I have heard by m. of this man
12. 12. where m. were gathered together
19. 19. m. brought their books and burnt them
26. 10. m. of the saints did I shut up in prison
Rom. 5. 15. if thro' the offence of one m. be dead, the gift by grace of Jesus C. hath abounded to m.
19. m. were made sinners, m. be made righteous
12. 5. so we, being m. are one body in Christ
16. 2. she hath been a succourer of m. and of myself
1 Cor. 1. 26. not m. wise, not m. mighty are called
4. 15. yet have ye not m. fathers, for in C. Jesus
8. 5. as there be gods m. and lords m.
10. 5. but with m. God was not well pleased
17. we being m. are one bread, and one body
33. but the profit of m. that they may be saved
11. 30. for this cause m. are weak and m. sleep
12. 14. the body is not one member, but m.
16. 9. great door, and there are m. adversaries
2 Cor. 1. 11. that thanks may be given by m.
2. 6. this punishment was inflicted of m.
17. we are not as m. which corrupt the word
4. 15. thro' thanksgiving of m. redound to glory
6. 10. as poor, yet making m. rich, having nothing
9. 2. and your zeal hath provoked very m.
Gal. 1. 14. and profited above m. my equals
3. 16. he saith not, and to seeds, as of m.
Phil. 1. 14. m. breth. waxing confident by my bonds
3. 18. m. walk of whom I have told you often
Heb. 2. 10. in bringing m. sons to glory, to make
7. 23. and they truly were m. priests
9. 28. Christ was once offered to bear the sins of m.
11. 12. sprang of one so m. as the stars of the sky

Jam. 3. 1. my brethren, be not m. masters
2 Pet. 2. 2. m. shall follow pernicious ways
1 John 2. 18. even now are there m. antichrists
4. 1. because m. false prophets are gone out into

After MANY.

Exod. 23. 2. speak in a cause to decline after m.

As MANY as.

Exod. 35. 22. and as m. as were willing-hearted
Judg. 3. 1. as m. as had not known all the wars
2 Sam. 2. 23. as m. as came to the place stood still
2 Chr. 29. 31. as m. as were of free heart brought
Mat. 22. 9. as m. as ye find bid to the marriage
10. and gathered together as m. as they found
Mark 6. 56. as m. as touched him were made whole
Luke 11. 8. will rise and give as m. as he needeth
John 1. 12. but as m. as received him, to them gave
17. 2. give eternal life to as m. as hast given him
Acts 2. 39. even to as m. as the Lord shall call
3. 24. as m. as have spoken have also foretold
5. 11. fear came on as m. as heard these things
36. who was slain, and as m. as obeyed him, 37.
10. 45. were astonished, as m. as came with Peter
13. 48. as m. as were ordained to life believed
Rom. 2. 12. as m. as have sinned without law, and as m. as have sinned in the law, shall be judged
8. 14. for as m. as are led by the Spirit of God
Gal. 3. 10. as m. as are of the works of the law
6. 12. as m. as desire to make a fair shew in the flesh
16. and as m. as walk according to this rule
Phil. 3. 15. as m. as be perfect be thus minded
Col. 2. 1. and for as m. as have not seen my face
1 Tim. 6. 1. as m. servants as are under the yoke
Rev. 2. 24. but to as m. as have not this doctrine
3. 19. as m. as I love I rebuke and chasten
13. 15. cause that as m. as would not worship beast

See Believed, Days, How.

MANY people.

Exod. 5. 5. behold, the people of the land now are m.
Deut. 2. 21. people great and m. and tall as Anakims
Judg. 7. 2. the people are too m. for me ‖ 4. yet too m.
1 Sam. 6. 19. the Lord had smitten m. of the people
2 Sam. 1. 4. and m. of the people are fallen and dead
Ezra 10. 13. but the people are m. and time of rain
Esth. 8. 17. m. people of land became Jews for fear
Isa. 2. 3. m. people shall go and say, come let us go
4. he shall judge and rebuke m. people
17. 12. woe to the multitude of m. people which
Ezek. 3. 6. not to m. people of a strange speech
17. 9. shall wither without m. people to pluck it
32. 9. I will also vex the hearts of m. people when
10. I will make m. people amazed at thee
38. 9. thou, thy bands, and m. people with thee, 15.
Mic. 4. 3. he shall judge among m. people, and rebuke
13. and thou shalt beat in pieces m. people
5. 7. remn. of Jacob shall be in midst of m. people
Zech. 8. 22. m. people shall come and seek the Lord
Rev. 10. 11. thou must prophesy before m. people

MANY things.

Job 16. 2. Job said, I have heard m. such things
23. 14. and m. such things are with him
Eccl. 6. 11. there be m. things that increase vanity
Isa. 42. 20. seeing m. things, but observest not
Mat. 13. 3. he spake m. things to them in parables
16. 21. and suffer m. things of the elders and chief priests, Mark 8. 31. | 9. 12. Luke 9. 22. | 17. 25.
25. 21. I will make thee ruler over m. things, 23.
27. 13. Pilate saith, hearest thou not how m. things they witness against thee? Mark 15. 4.
19. I have suffered m. things this day in a dream
Mark 5. 26. suffered m. things of many physicians
6. 20. he did m. things, and heard him gladly
7. 4. m. things there be, as washing of cups, 8. 13.
15. 3. chief priests accused him of m. things
Luke 10. 41. thou art troubled about m. things
11. 53. to provoke him to speak of m. things
John 8. 26. I have m. things to say, and judge, 16. 12.
21. 25. there are m. other things which Jesus did
Acts 26. 9. that I ought to do m. things contrary
2 Cor. 8. 22. we have proved diligent in m. things
Gal. 3. 4. have ye suffered so m. things in vain?
2 Tim. 1. 18. in how m. things he ministered to me
Heb. 5. 11. of whom we have m. things to say
Jam. 3. 2. for in m. things we offend all
2 John 12. having m. things to write to you, 3 John 13.

MANY a time.

Ps. 78. 38. yea, m. a time turned he his anger away
129. 1. m. a time have they afflicted me, 2.

MANY times.

1 Kings 22. 16. how m. times shall I adjure thee?
Neh. 9. 28. m. times didst deliver them, Ps. 106. 43.

See Waters.

MANY years.

Lev. 25. 51. if there be yet m. years behind
Ezra 5. 11. the house that was builded m. years ago
Neh. 9. 30. yet m. years didst thou forbear them
Eccl. 6. 3. if a man beget children, and live m. years
11. 8. if a man live m. years, and rejoice in them all
Isa. 32. 10. m. days and years shall ye be troubled
Ezek. 38. 17. prophets, which prophesied m. years
Zech. 7. 3. weep, as I have done these so m. years
Luke 12. 19. thou hast goods laid up for m. years
15. 29. he said, lo, these m. years do I serve thee
Acts 24. 10. thou hast been of m. years a judge
17. now after m. years I came to bring alms
Rom. 15. 23. a great desire m. years to come to you

MAR.

Lev. 19. 27. nor m. the corners of thy beard
Ruth 4. 6. lest I m. mine own inheritance
1 Sam. 6. 5. images of your mice that m. the land
2 Kings 3. 19. and m. every good piece of land
Job 30. 13. they m. my path, they set forward
Jer. 13. 9. thus will I m. the pride of Judah

MARRED.

Isa. 52. 14. his visage was so m. more than any man
Jer. 13. 7. girdle was m. ‖ 18. 4. the vessel was m.
Nah. 2. 2. emptied, and m. their vine-branches
Mark 2. 22. wine spilled, and the bottles will be m.

MARAN-ATHA

Signifies, The Lord comes, or, The Lord is come. *It was a form of threatening, cursing, or anathematizing among the Jews*, 1 Cor. 16. 22. *If any man love not the Lord Jesus Christ, let him be* anathema, Maran-atha, *that is, Let him be accursed in, or at the coming of our Lord. Most commentators say, that the* Maran-atha *is the greatest of all anathemas among the Jews, as if the apostle Paul had said*, May he be devoted to the greatest of evils, and to the utmost severity of God's judgments; may the Lord come quickly to take vengeance on him. *Others say, that the word may be understood in an absolute sense; Let him be anathema:* The Lord is come, the Messiah has appeared, evil to him that receives him not; *the apostle particularly applying himself to the unbelieving Jews.*

MARBLE.

1 Chron. 29. 2. I have prepared m. in abundance
Esth. 1. 6. fastened to silver rings and pillars of m. pavement of red, blue, white, and black m.
Cant. 5. 15. his legs are as pillars of m. set on sockets
Rev. 18. 12. the vessels of m. no man buyeth

MARCH.

Psal. 68. 7. when thou didst m. thro' the wilderness
Isa. 27. † 4. set briars, I would m. against them
Jer. 46. 22. for they shall m. with an army
Joel 2. 7. they shall m. every one on his ways
Hab. 1. 6. which shall m. thro' the breadth of the land
3. 12. thou didst m. through the land in indignation

MARCHED.

Exod. 14. 10. behold, the Egyptians m. after them

MARCHEDST.

Judg. 5. 4. when thou m. the earth trembled

MARK, Substantive.

Gen. 4. 15. the Lord set a m. upon Cain, lest any
1 Sam. 20. 20. I will shoot, as though I shot at a m.
Job 7. 20. why hast thou set me as a m. against thee? 16. 12. Lam. 3. 12.
Ezek. 9. 4. set a m. on the men that sigh and cry
6. come not near any man on whom is the m.
Phil. 3. 14. I press toward the m. for the prize
Rev. 13. 16. he caused all to receive a m.
17. none might buy, save he that had the m.
14. 9. if any man receive his m. in his forehead
11. have no rest, whosoever receiveth his m.
15. 2. got victory over his image, and over his m.
16. 2. sore on them that had the m. of the beast
19. 20. he deceived them that received m. of beast
20. 4. nor received his m. they lived with Christ

MARK, Verb.

Ruth 3. 4. thou shalt m. the place where he shall lie
2 Sam. 13. 28. m. when Amnon's heart is merry
1 Kings 20. 7. m. how this man seeketh mischief
22. the prophet said, m. and see what thou doest
Job 18. 2. m. and afterwards we will speak
21. 5. m. me and be astonished, and lay your hand
33. 31. m. well, O Job, hearken to me, I will speak
39. 1. canst thou m. when the hinds do calve?
Psal. 37. 37. m. the perfect man, his end is peace
48. 13. m. well her bulwarks, consider her palaces
56. 6. they m. my steps, when they wait for my soul
130. 3. if thou, Lord, shouldest m. iniquities
Ezek. 44. 5. m. well, m. the entering of the house
Rom. 16. 17. m. them who cause divisions, avoid
Phil. 3. 17. m. them who walk so, as ye have us

MARKED.

1 Sam. 1. 12. as she prayed, Eli m. her mouth
Job 22. 15. hast thou m. the old way which wicked
24. 16. which they had m. in the day time
Jer. 2. 22. yet thine iniquity is m. before me
23. 18. who hath m. his word and heard it
Luke 14. 7 when he m. how they chose rooms

MARKS.

Lev. 19. 28. ye shall not print any m. upon you
Gal. 6. 17. I bear in my body the m. of the Lord

MARKEST.

Job 10. 14. if I sin, then thou m. wilt not acquit

MARKETH.

Job 33. 11. my feet in stocks, he m. all my paths
Isa. 44. 13. the carpenter m. it out with the compass

MARKET.

Ezek. 27. 13. they traded in thy m. 17, 19, 25.
Mat. 20. 3. he saw others standing idle in the m.
Mark 7. 4. and when they come from the m.
12. 38. and love salutations in the m. place
Luke 7. 32. like children sitting in the m. place
John 5. 2. there a pool at Jerusa. by the sheep m.
Acts 16. 19. and drew them into the m. place
17. 17. he disputed in the m. daily with them

MARKETS.

Mat. 11. 16. like children sitting in the m.
23. 7. love greetings in the m. Luke 11. 43. | 20. 46.

MARRIAGE

Signifies, [1] *A civil contract, by which a man and a woman are joined together, which was instituted by God for the prevention of uncleanness, the propagation of mankind, and that the parties so contracting might be mutual helps and comforts to one another*, Gen. 2. 18, 22, 23. John 2. 1. 1 Cor. 7. 2. Heb. 13. 4. [2] *That marriage covenant which is between God and his church, even the covenant of grace, wherein God graciously promises to be the God of his people, and to forgive and sanctify them through the merits of Jesus Christ and the influences of his Spirit, and so make them a willing people to himself*, Isa. 54. 5. Jer. 3. 14. Hos. 2. 19, 20. *The union between husband and wife is so near, that thereby is represented the mystical union, the sacred and spiritual marriage of Christ with his church*, Eph. 5. 30 31, 32.

Exod. 21. 10. her duty of m. shall he not diminish
Psal. 78. 63. their maidens were not given to m.
Mat. 22. 2. a king who made a m. for his son
4. come to the m. ‖ 9. all ye find, bid to the m.
30. in the resurrection not given in m. but as the angels in heaven, Mark 12. 25. Luke 20. 35.
24. 38. given in m. until the day that Noe entered
25. 10. that were ready went in with him to the m.
Luke 17. 27. they eat, they were given in m. 20. 34.
John 2. 1. there was a m. in Cana of Galilee
2. Jesus was called and his disciples to the m.
1 Cor. 7. 38. he that giveth her in m. doeth well, but he that giveth her not in m. doeth better
Heb. 13. 4. m. is honourable in all, and the bed

Rev. 19. 7. for the m. of the Lamb is come
9. blessed that are called to the m. supper of Lamb

MARRIAGES.

Gen. 34. 9. and make ye m. with us, and give
Deut. 7. 3. neither shalt thou make m. with them
Josh. 23. 12. else if he shall make m. with them

MARRY.

Gen. 38. 8. go in to thy brother's wife, and m. her
Num. 36. 6. let them m. to whom they think best, only to family of their father's tribe shall they m.
Deut. 25. 5. the wife of dead shall not m. without
Isa. 62. 5. so shall thy sons m. thee, as bridegroom
Mat. 5. 32. whosoever shall m. her that is divorced committeth adultery, 19. 9. Mark 10. 11.
19. 10. if the case be so, it is not good to m.
22. 24. his brother shall m. his wife and raise seed
30. in the resurrection they neither m. nor are given in marriage, Mark 12. 25. Luke 20. 35.
1 Cor. 7. 9. but if they cannot contain, let them m. for it is better to m. than to burn
28. if thou m. if a virgin m. she hath not sinned
36. do what he will he sinneth not, let them m.
1 Tim. 4. 3. forbidding to m. and commanding to
5. 11. they have begun to wax wanton, they will m.
14. that the younger women m. bear children

MARRIED.

Gen. 19. 14. Lot spake to them that m. his daughters
20. † 3. for the woman is m. to a husband
Exod. 21. 3. if m. his wife shall go out with him
Lev. 22. 12. if m. to a stranger, she may not eat
Num. 12. 1. the Ethiopian woman whom he had m.
36. 3. if they be m. to the sons of other tribes
11. were m. to their father's brothers' sons
Deut. 22. 22. if a man found lying with a woman m.
1 Chron. 2. 21. whom he m. when sixty years old
2 Chron. 13. 21. Abijah m. fourteen wives
Neh. 13. 23. Jews that had m. wives of Ashdod
Prov. 30. 23. an odious woman when she is m.
Isa. 54. 1. more children of desolate than of m.
62. 4. Lord delighteth in thee, thy land shall be m.
Jer. 3. 14. turn, O children, for I am m. to you
Mal. 2. 11. hath m. the daughter of a strange god
Mat. 22. 25. the first when he had m. deceased
Mark 6. 17. Philip's wife, for he had m. her
10. 12. be m. to another, committeth adultery
Luke 14. 20. I have m. a wife, and cannot come
17. 27. they did eat, they drank, they m. wives
Rom. 7. 3. if while her husband liveth she be m.
4. become dead, that ye should be m. to another
1 Cor. 7. 10. to the m. I command, yet not I
33. he that is m. ‖ 34. she that is m. careth for
39. to be m. to whom she will, only in the Lord

MARRIETH.

Isa. 62. 5. as a young man m. a virgin, so shall
Mat. 19. 9. and whoso m. her who is put away, doth commit adultery, Luke 16. 18.

MARRYING.

Neh. 13. 27. do this great evil in m. strange wives
Mat. 24. 38. they were m. and giving in marriage

MARINERS.

Ezek. 27. 8. the inhabitants of Zidon were thy m.
9. the ships of the sea with their m. were in thee
27. thy m. shall fall into the midst of the seas
29. the m. shall come down from their ships
Jonah 1. 5. then the m. were afraid, and cried

MARISHES.

Ezek. 47. 11. miry places and m. shall not be healed

MARROW

Signifies, *A soft oily substance, contained in the hollow of bones*, Job 21. 24. To which are compared, [1] *The delicate, strengthening, and comforting provisions, which God has made for his church and people in the gospel and his ordinances here, but especially in heaven hereafter*, Psal. 63. 5. Isa. 25. 6. [2] *The most secret thoughts of the heart*, Heb. 4. 12.

Job 21. 24. his bones are moistened with m.
Psal. 63. 5. my soul shall be satisfied as with m.
66. † 15. I will offer burnt sacrifices of m.
Prov. 3. 8. it shall be health and m. to thy bones
Isa. 25. 6. Lord make a feast of fat things full of m.
Heb. 4. 12. to the dividing asunder of joints and m.

MART.

Isa. 23. 3. Tyre, and she is a m. of nations

MARTYR.

Acts 22. 20. the blood of thy m. Stephen was shed
Rev. 2. 13. wherein Antipas was my faithful m.

MARTYRS.

Rev. 17. 6. woman drunken with blood of m. of J.

MARVEL.

2 Cor. 11. 14. no m. for Satan himself is transformed

MARVEL.

Eccl. 5. 8. if thou seest, m. not at the matter
Mark 5. 20. he began to publish, and all men did m.
John 3. 7. m. not that I said, ye must be born again
5. 20. shew him greater works, that ye may m.
28. m. not at this ‖ 7. 21. done one work, and ye m.
Acts 3. 12. men of Israel, why m. ye at this?
Gal. 1. 6. I m. that ye are so soon removed from
1 John 3. 13. m. not if the world hate you
Rev. 17. 7. the angel said, wherefore didst thou m.?

MARVELLED.

Gen. 43. 33. and the men m. one at another
Psal. 48. 5. they saw it, and so they m. they hasted
Mat. 8. 10. when Jesus heard it, he m. and said
27. the men m. ‖ 9. 8. m. and glorified God, 33.
21. 20. when the disciples saw it, they m. saying
22. 22. they m. at him, Mark 12. 17. Luke 20. 26.
27. 14. that the governor m. Mark 15. 5, 44.
Mark 6. 6. he m. because of their unbelief
Luke 1. 21. the people m. that he tarried so long
63. saying, his name is John, and they m. all
2. 33. Joseph and his mother m. at those things
7. 9. when Jesus heard these things he m. at him
11. 38. and when the Pharisee saw it, he m.
John 4. 27. the disciples m. he talked with the woman
7. 15. Jews m. how knoweth this man letters?
Acts 2. 7. m. saying, are not these Galileans?
4. 13. they m. and took knowledge of them

MARVELLOUS.

2 Sam. 13. † 2. it was m. in the eyes of Amnon
Job 5. 9. who doeth m. things without number
Job 10. 16. thou shewest thyself m. upon me
Psal. 17. 7. shew thy m. loving-kindness
31. 21. he hath shewed me his m. kindness
78. 12. m. things did he in the sight of their fathers
98. 1. O sing to Lord, for he hath done m. things
118. 23. this is the Lord's doing, it is m. in our eyes, Mat. 21. 42. Mark 12. 11.
Dan. 11. 36. shall speak m. things ag. God of gods
Mic. 7. 15. will I shew unto him m. things
Zech. 8. 6. if it be m. should it be m. in mine eyes?
John 9. 30. herein is a m. thing, that ye know not
1 Pet. 2. 9. called you out of darkn. into his m. light
Rev. 15. 1. another sign in heaven, great and m.

MARVELLOUS *work*.

Isa. 29. 14. behold, I will proceed to do a m. work

MARVELLOUS *works*.

1 Chr. 16. 12. remember his m. works, Ps. 105. 5.
24. declare his m. works among all nations
Psal. 9. 1. I will shew forth all thy m. works
139. 14. great and m. are thy works, Rev. 15. 3.

MARVELLOUSLY.

2 Chr. 26. 15. he was m. helped till he was strong
Job 37. 5. God thundereth m. with his voice
Hab. 1. 5. behold, and regard, and wonder m.

MARVELS.

Exod. 34. 10. I will do m. such as have not been

MASONS.

2 Sam. 5. 11. Hiram sent to David m. 1 Chr. 14. 1.
2 Kings 12. 12. they gave money to m. and hewers of stone, 22. 6. Ezra 3. 7.
1 Chron. 22. 2. he set m. to hew wrought stones
2 Chron. 24. 12. they hired m. to repair the house

MAST, S.

Prov. 23. 34. as he that lieth on the top of a m.
Isa. 30. † 17. left as a m. on the top of a hill
33. 23. they could not well strengthen their m.
Ezek. 27. 5. taken cedars from Lebanon to make m.

MASTER

Is a title applied, [1] *To Christ, who is the chief Lawgiver, and Teacher, who only can teach powerfully and inwardly, and in matters of faith and worship is only to be followed*, Mat. 23. 8, 10. [2] *To preachers and ministers of the word*, Eccl. 12. 11. [3] *To such as teach or educate disciples or scholars*, Luke 6. 40. [4] *To such as have rule over servants*, Eph. 6. 5. [5] *To such as ambitiously affect vain applause, or precedency and superiority above others*, Mat. 23. 10. [6] *To such as judge, censure, or reprove others rashly, without ground; rigidly, above the merits of the cause; uncharitably, aggravating their faults, and wresting things to the worst sense; or magisterially, out of a spirit of pride, ambition, or contradiction*, Jam. 3. 1.

Gen. 39. 20. Joseph's m. put him in prison
Exod. 21. 8. if she pleased not her m. who betrothed
32. shall give to their m. thirty shekels of silver
22. 8. the m. of the house shall be brought to judges
Deut. 15. † 2. every m. of the lending of his hand
Judg. 19. 22. and spake to the m. of the house
23. the m. of the house went out unto them
1 Sam. 25. 14. David sent messengers to salute our m.
17. for evil is determined against our m.
26. 16. because you have not kept your m.
2 Sam. 2. 7. for your m. Saul is dead and the house
1 Kings 22. 17. these have no m. 2 Chron. 18. 16.
2 Kings 6. 5. he cried, alas m. for it was borrowed
22. they may eat and drink, and go to their m.
23. sent them away, and they went to their m.
10. 2. seeing your m. sons are with you
3. look out the best of your m. sons, and set him
6. take the heads of your m. sons, and come
19. 6. thus shall ye say to your m. Isa. 37. 6.
1 Chron. 15. 27. and Chenaniah, m. of the song
Eccl. 10. † 11. a m. of the tongue is no better
Isa. 24. 2. as with the servant, so with his m.
50. † 8. who is the m. of my cause, let him come
Dan. 1. 3. the king spake to the m. of the eunuchs
4. 9. O Belteshazzar, m. of the magicians, 5. 11.
Mal. 1. 6. and if I be a m. where is my fear?
2. 12. the Lord will cut off the m. and the scholar
Mat. 8. 19. m. I will follow thee whithers. thou goest
9. 11. why eateth your m. with publicans and sinners
10. 25. if they have called the m. Beelzebub
12. 38. m. we would see a sign from thee
15. 27. the crumbs which fall from their m. table
17. 24. they said, doth not your m. pay tribute?
22. 16. m. we know that thou art true, Mark 12. 14.
23. 8. for one is your m. even Christ, 10.
26. 18. the m. saith, my time is at hand
25. m. is it I? ‖ 49. hail m. and kissed, Mark 14. 45.
Mark 5. 35. why troublest thou the m. any more?
9. 5. m. it is good for us to be here, Luke 9. 33.
10. 17. good m. what shall I do? Luke 10. 25.
13. 35. for ye know not when the m. cometh
Luke 3. 12. the publicans said, m. what shall we do?
7. 40. m. say on ‖ 8. 24. saying, m. we perish
8. 49. thy daughter is dead; trouble not the m.
13. 25. when once the m. of the house is risen
John 3. 10. art thou a m. in Israel, and knowest not
11. 28. the m. is come and calleth for thee
13. 13. ye call me m. and ye say well, for so I am
14. if I then your m. have washed your feet
Acts 27. 11. the centurion believed the m. of the ship
Eph. 6. 9. knowing your m. is in heaven, Col. 4. 1.
2 Tim. 2. 21. vessel sanctified and meet for the m. use

His MASTER.

Gen. 24. 9. put his hand under the thigh of his m.
10. took ten camels of his m. goods of his m.
39. 2. Joseph was in house of his m. the Egyptian
19. when his m. heard the words of his wife
Exod. 21. 4. if his m. have given him a wife
6. his m. shall bore his ear through with an awl
Deut. 23. 15. thou shalt not deliver to his m. the servant which is escaped from his m. unto thee
Judg. 19. 11. the servant said to his m. let us lodge
1 Sam. 20. 38. gathered the arrows and came to his m.
25. 10. servants break away every one from his m.
29. 4. wherewith should reconcile himself to his m.
2 Kings 5. 1. Naaman was a great man with his m.
25. Gehazi went in, and stood before his m.
6. 32. is not the sound of his m. feet behind him?
2 Kings 8. 14. Hazael departed and came to his m.
9. 31. she said, had Zimri peace, who slew his m.?
19. 4. his m. hath sent to reproach God, Isa. 37. 4.
1 Chron. 12. 19. saying, he will fall to his m. Saul
Job 3. 19. and the servant is free from his m.
Prov. 27. 18. so he that waiteth on his m. shall be
30. 10. accuse not a serv. to his m. lest he curse thee
Isa. 1. 3. and the ass knoweth his m. crib
Mal. 1. 6. and a servant honoureth his m.
Mat. 10. 24. the disciple is not above h. m. Luke 6. 40.
25. it is enough that the disciple be as his m.
Luke 6. 40. every one perfect shall be as his m.
Rom. 14. 4. to his own m. he standeth or falleth

My MASTER.

Gen. 24. 12. O Lord God of my m. Abraham shew kindness to my m. Abraham, 27. 42, 48.
14. know that thou hast shewed kindness to my m.
35. the Lord hath blessed my m. greatly
44. whom the Lord hath appointed for my m. son
49. if you will deal truly and kindly with my m.
54. and he said, send me away to my m. 56.
65. and the servant had said, it is my m.
39. 8. behold, my m. wotteth not what is with me
Exod. 21. 5. if the servant shall say, I love my m.
1 Sam. 24. 6. God forbid I should do this to my m.
30. 13. my m. left me because I fell sick
15. nor deliver me into the hands of my m.
2 Kings 5. 18. my m. goeth into the house of Rimmon
20. my m. hath spared Naaman this Syrian
22. my m. hath sent me, saying, behold
6. 15. and he said, alas, my m. how shall we do?
10. 9. behold, I conspired against my m. and slew
18. 24. how then wilt thou turn away one captain of the least of my m. servants, Isa. 36. 9.
27. hath my m. sent me to thy master? Isa. 36. 12.
Isa. 36. 8. give pledges, I pray thee, to my m.

Thy MASTER.

Gen. 24. 51. and let her be thy m. son's wife
1 Sam. 29. 10. rise up early with thy m. servants
2 Sam. 9. 9. I give t. m. son all that pertained to Saul
12. 8. I gave thee, thy m. house, thy m. wives
16. 3. the king said, where is thy m. son?
2 Kings 2. 3. Lord will take away thy m. to-day, 5.
16. let them go, we pray thee, and seek thy m.
9. 7. thou shalt smite the house of Ahab thy m.
18. 27. my master sent me to thy m. and to thee

MASTER-*builder*.

1 Cor. 3. 10. as wise m.-builder I have laid foundation

MASTERS.

Exod. 21. 4. the wife and her children shall be her m.
Psal. 123. 2. as the eyes of servants look to their m.
Prov. 25. 13. for he refresheth the soul of his m.
Eccl. 12. 11. as nails fastened by m. of assemblies
Jer. 27. 4. and command them to say to their m.
Amos 4. 1. which say to their m. let us drink
Zeph. 1. 9. who fill their m. houses with violence
Mat. 6. 24. no man can serve two m. Luke 16. 13.
23. 10. neither be ye called m. one is your master
Acts 16. 16. who brought her m. much gain
19. her m. saw the hope of their gains was gone
Eph. 6. 5. servants, be obedient to them that are your m. Col. 3. 22. Tit. 2. 9. 1 Pet. 2. 18.
9. ye m. do the same things to them, Col. 4. 1.
1 Tim. 6. 1. count their m. worthy of all honour
2. that have believing m. let them not despise
Jam. 3. 1. brethren, be not many m. knowing

MASTERY.

Exod. 32. 18. the voice of them that shout for m.
Dan. 6. 24. and the lions had the m. of them
1 Cor. 9. 25. that striveth for the m. is temperate

MASTERIES.

2 Tim. 2. 5. if a man also strive for m. not crowned

MATE.

Isa. 34. 15. vultures be gath. every one with her m.
16. not one shall fail, none shall want her m.

MATRIX.

Exod. 13. 12. set apart to Lord all that open m. 15.
34. 19. all that openeth the m. is mine
Num. 3. 12. instead of the first-born that open the m.
18. 15. every thing that openeth the m. is thine

MATTER.

Gen. 24. 9. and sware to him concerning that m.
30. 15. is it a small m. that thou hast taken
Exod. 5. † 13. fulfil a m. of a day in his day
18. 16. when they have a m. they come to me
22. it shall be that every great m. they shall bring to thee, but every small m. they shall judge
26. but every small m. they judged themselves
23. 7. keep thee far from a false m.
Num. 16. 49. them that died about the m. of Korah
25. 18. beguiled you in m. of Peor, in m. of Cozbi
31. 16. to commit trespass in the m. of Peor
Deut. 17. 8. if there arise a m. too hard for thee
19. 15. at mouth of three witnesses m. be established
24. † 1. he hath found a m. of nakedness in her
Judg. 19. † 24 do not the m. of this folly
Ruth 3. 18. till thou know how the m. will fall out
1 Sam. 10. 16. of the m. of the kingdom he told not
20. 23. touching the m. thou and I have spoken of
39. only Jonathan and David knew the m.
2 Sam. 1. 4. how went the m.? I pray thee tell me
18. 13. there is no m. hid from the king
20. 18. they ended the m. ‖ 21. the m. is not so
1 Kings 8. 59. at all times as the m. shall require
15. 5. save in the m. of Uriah the Hittite
1 Chr. 26. 32. for every m. pertaining to God
27. 1. their officers that served the king in any m.
2 Chr. 8. 15. departed not from command in any m.
19. † 6. who is with you in the m. of judgment
24. 5. see ye hasten the m. they hastened not
Ezra 5. 5. to cease, till the m. came to Darius
10. 16. and sat down to examine the m.
Neh. 6. 13. they might have m. for evil report
Esth. 2. 23. when inquisition was made of the m.
Job 19. 28. seeing the root of the m. is found in me
32. 18. I will answer, for I am full of m.
Psal. 45. 1. my heart is inditing a good m.
64. 5. they encourage themselves in an evil m.
Prov. 11. 13. a faithful spirit concealeth the m.
16. 20. that handleth a m. wisely shall find good
17. 9. that repeateth a m. separateth very friends
18. 13. that answereth a m. before he heareth it

Prov. 25. 2. the honour of kings is to search out a m.
Eccl. 5. 8. if seest oppression, marvel not at the m.
10. 20. that which hath wings shall tell the m.
12. 13. let us hear the conclusion of the m.
Jer. 7. † 22. concerning the m. of burnt offerings
38. 27. for the m. was not perceived
52. † 34. the m. of a day in his day, till death
Ezek. 9. 11. he that had the inkhorn, reported the m.
16. 20. is this of thy whoredoms a small m.?
Dan. 2. 10. not a man can shew the king's m.
23. thou hast made known to us the king's m.
7. 28. hitherto is the end of the m. I kept the m.
9. 23. understand the m. and consider the vision
Mark 1. 45. and began to blaze abroad the m.
10. 10. his disciples asked him again of the same m.
Acts 11. 4. Peter rehearsed the m. from beginning
15. 6. the elders came to consider of this m.
18. 14. Gallio said, if it were a m. of wrong
19. 38. if Demetrius have a m. against any
24. 22. I will know the uttermost of your m.
1 Cor. 6. 1. dare any of you having a m. go to law?
2 Cor. 9. 5. same might be ready as a m. of bounty
Gal. 2. 6. whatsoever it were, it maketh no m.
1 Thess. 4. 6. that no man defraud brother in any m.
Jam. 3. 5. how great a m. a little fire kindleth!

This MATTER.

Deut. 3. 26. L. said, speak no more to me of this m.
22. 26. as a man slayeth his neighbour, so is this m.
1 Sam. 30. 24. who will hearken to you in this m.?
2 Sam. 19. 42. wherefore be ye angry for this m.?
Ezra 5. 5. Darius returned answer concerning t. m.
17. send his pleasure to us concerning this m.
10. 4. arise, for this m. belongeth to thee
9. the people sat trembling because of this m.
15. Jonathan, Asahel, were employed about t. m.
Esth. 9. 26. they had seen concerning this m.
Dan. 1. 14. Melzar consented to them in this m.
3. 16. we are not careful to answer thee in this m.
4. 17. this m. is by the decree of the watchers
Acts 8. 21. thou hast neither part nor lot in this m.
17. 32. we will hear thee again of t. m. others said
2 Cor. 7. 11. ye approved yourselves clear in this m.

MATTERS.

Exod. 24. 14. if any have m. let him come to them
Deut. 16. † 19. a gift perverteth the m. of righteous
17. 8. if arise m. of controversy too hard for thee
1 Sam. 16. 18. a son of Jesse that is prudent in m.
2 Sam. 11. 19. hast made an end of telling the m.
15. 3. Absalom said, see thy m. are good and right
19. 29. why speakest thou any more of thy m.?
2 Chr. 19. 11. Amariah chief priest over you in m. of the Lord, and Zebadiah for all the king's m.
Neh. 6. † 19. and they uttered my m. to Tobiah
11. 24. Pethahiah in all m. concerning the people
Esth. 3. 4. whether Mordecai's m. would stand
9. 31. the m. of the fastings, and their cry, 32.
Job 33. 13. he giveth not account of his m.
Psal. 35. 20. thus devise deceitful m. against them
65. † 3. m. of iniquities prevail against me
131. 1. nor do I exercise myself in great m.
Prov. 22. † 12. he overthroweth the m. of transgressor
29. † 20. seest thou a man that is hasty in his m.?
Dan. 1. 20. in m. of wisdom he found them better
7. 1. he wrote the dream, and told the sum of the m.
Mat. 23. 23. and have omitted the weightier m.
Acts 18. 15. for I will be no judge of such m.
19. 39. if ye enquire any thing concerning other m.
25. 20. and there be judged of these m.
1 Cor. 6. 2. are ye unworthy to judge the smallest m.
1 Pet. 4. 15. or as a busy-body in other men's m.?

MATTOCK.

1 Sam. 13. 20. to sharpen every man his axe and m.
Isa. 7. 25. on all hills shall be digged with the m.

MATTOCKS.

1 Sam. 13. 21. yet they had a file for the m.
2 Chron. 34. 6. thus did Josiah with their m.

MAUL.

Prov. 25. 18. that beareth false witness, is a m.

MAW.

Deut. 18. 3. to the priest two cheeks and the m.

MAY.

2 Sam. 15. 20. seeing I go whither I m. return thou
Mat. 9. 21. she said, if I m. but touch his garment
26. 42. if this cup m. not pass away from me
Heb. 7. 9. and as I m. so say, Levi paid tithes

MAY be.

Gen. 12. 13. that it m. be well with me for thy sake
16. 2. it m. be that I may obtain children
Exod. 13. 9. that the Lord's law m. be in thy mouth
20. 20. that his fear m. be before your face
Lev. 11. 34. of all meat which m. be eaten
21. 3. for his sister a virgin he m. be defiled
23. 21. that it m. be an holy convocation
Num. 10. 10. they m. be for a memorial before God
32. 32. that the possession m. be ours
Deut. 5. 33. may live, and that it m. be well with you, 6. 3, 18. | 22. 7. Ruth 3. 1. Jer. 7. 23.
29. 13. he m. be to thee a God as he hath said
31. 26. that it m. be there for a witness against
Josh. 22. 27. that it m. be for a witness between
1 Sam. 14. 6. it m. be the Lord will work for us
18. 21. she m. be a snare, Philistines m. be ag. him
2 Sam. 14. 15. it m. be that the king will perform
16. 12. it m. be Lord will look on my affliction
2 Kings 19. 4. m. be L. thy God will hear, Isa. 37. 4.
1 Chron. 17. 27. that it m. be before thee for ever
Ezra 9. 12. that ye m. be strong, and eat the good
Job 1. 5. it m. be that my sons have sinned
Psal. 59. 13. consume them, that they m. not be
83. 4. that Israel m. be no more in remembrance
144. 12. that our sons m. be as plants grown up
13. that our garners m. be full, affording store
14. that our oxen m. be strong to labour
Prov. 22. 19. that thy trust m. be in the Lord
Eccl. 1. 10. whereof it m. be said, see this is new
Isa. 30. 8. that it m. be for the time to come
18. the Lord waiteth that he m. be gracious
46. 5. that we m. be like || 60. 21. I m. be glorified
Jer. 11. 19. that his name m. be no more remembered
36. 3. it m. be the house of Judah will hear
7. it m. be they will present their supplication
42. 6. that it m. be well with us when we obey
Jer. 51. 8. take balm, if so be she m. be healed
Lam. 3. 29. mouth in dust, if so be there m. be hope
Ezek. 12. 3. it m. be they will consider, though they
14. 11. that they m. be my people, and I their God
Dan. 4. 27. it m. be a lengthening of tranquillity
Hos. 8. 4. they made idols, that they m. be cut off
Amos 5. 15. it m. be the Lord will be gracious
Zeph. 2. 3. it m. be ye shall be hid in the day
Mat. 5. 45. that ye m. be children of your Father
6. 4. that thine alms m. be in secret, and thy Father
Luke 20. 13. it m. be they will reverence him
14. kill him, that the inheritance m. be ours
John 12. 36. that ye m. be the children of light
14. 3. that where I am, there ye m. be also
17. 11. that they m. be one, as we are one, 21. 22.
26. that the love m. be in them, and I in them
Rom. 1. † 20. that they m. be without excuse
1 Cor. 3. 18. that he m. be wise || 5. 7. ye m. be new lu.
7. 34. that she m. be holy in body and spirit
14. 10. there are, it m. be, so many kind of voices
15. 28. Son be subject, that God m. be all in all
16. 6. and it m. be that I will winter with you
10. see that he m. be with you without fear
2 Cor. 4. 7. the excellency of the power m. be of God
8. 11. so there m. be a performance also out of that
14. that your abundance m. be a supply for want
9. 3. that, as I said, you m. be ready
Eph. 6. 3. that it m. be well with thee, and thou
Phil. 2. 15. that ye m. be blameless and harmless
19. that I m. be of good comfort when I know
28. and that I m. be the less sorrowful
1 Tim. 5. 7. give charge that they m. be blameless
2 Tim. 3. 17. that the man of God m. be perfect
Tit. 1. 13. that they m. be found in the faith
Jam. 1. 4. that ye m. be perfect and entire

MAYEST.

Acts 8. 37. if thou believest with all thy heart thou m.

MAYEST be.

Gen. 28. 3. that thou m. be a multitude of people
Num. 10. 31. thou m. be to us instead of eyes
Deut. 26. 19. and that thou m. be an holy people
Neh. 6. 6. buildest, that thou m. be their king
Job 40. 8. condemn me, that thou m. be justified
Psal. 130. 4. forgiveness, that thou m. be feared
Isa. 23. 16. sing songs, that thou m. be remembered
49. 6. that thou m. be my salvation to end of earth
Jer. 4. 14. wash thy heart, that thou m. be saved
30. 13. none to plead, that thou m. be bound up
Luke 16. 2. for thou m. be no longer steward

ME.

Gen. 3. 13. the serpent beguiled me, and I did eat
22. † 1. and he said, behold me, † 7, † 11. Isa. 65. 1.
41. 10. put in ward both me and the chief baker
13. me he restored, and him he hanged
42. 36. me have ye bereaved of my children
Exod. 9. 14. there is none like me in all the earth
1 Sam. 8. 7. not thee, but they have rejected me
2 Sam. 18. 29. when Joab sent me thy servant
1 Kings 1. 26. but me, even me thy servant, not called
Isa. 57. 8. hast discovered thyself to another than me
Jer. 17. 18. be dismayed, but let not me be dismayed
50. 44. who like me, and who will appoint me time?
Hos. 13. 4. and thou shalt know no God but me
Mat. 10. 37. loveth father and mother more than me
40. he that receiveth you receiveth me, and he that receiveth me, Mark 9. 37. John 13. 20.
19. 17. why callest thou me good? Luke 18. 19.
26. 11. me ye have not always, Mark 14. 7. John 12. 8.
Luke 10. 16. that desp. me, desp. him that sent me
John 5. 46. believed Moses, ye would have bel. me
7. 7. the world cannot hate you, but me it hateth
8. 19. ye neither know me, nor my Father
10. 38. though ye believe not me, believe the works
14. 9. yet hast thou not known me, Philip?
15. 23. he that hateth me hateth my Father
24. have seen and hated both me and my Father
16. 3. they have not known the Father nor me
17. 5. O Father, glorify thou me with thyself
18. 21. why askest thou me? ask them who heard me
23. but if well, why smitest thou me?
19. 11. he that delivered me to thee hath greater sin
21. 15. Simon, son of Jonas, lovest thou me? 16, 17.
Acts 9. 4. Saul, why persecutest thou me? 22. 7.
1 Cor. 15. 32. what advantageth it me, if the dead

Above ME.

1 Sam. 2. 29. and honourest thy sons above me

About ME.

Deut. 17. 14. like the nations that are about me
Job 10. † 8. thine hands took pains about me
29. 5. when my children were about me
Psal. 3. † 3. but thou, O Lord, art a shield about me
88. 17. they came round about me daily like water
139. 11. even the night shall be light about me
Jonah 2. 6. the earth with her bars was about me
Acts 22. 6. there shone a great light about me, 26. 13.

After ME.

Gen. 31. 36. thou hast so hotly pursued after me
Judg. 3. 28. he said unto them, follow after me
1 Sam. 14. 12. said to armour-bearer, come after me
24. 21. that thou wilt not cut off my seed after me
1 Kings 1. 13. Solomon shall reign after me, 17, 30.
24. hast said, Adonijah shall reign after me
Eccl. 2. 18. unto the man that shall be after me
Isa. 43. 10. neither shall there be after me
Jer. 2. 2. when wentest after me in the wilderness
Mat. 3. 11. he that cometh after me is mightier than I, Mark 1. 7. John 1. 15, 27, 30.
10. 38. he that followeth not after me, Luke 14. 27.
16. 24. that will come a. me, Mark 8. 34. Luke 9. 23.
Acts 13. 25. there cometh one after me whose shoes
Rom. 10. 20. manifest to them that asked not a. me

Against ME.

Gen. 20. 6. I withheld thee from sinning against me
42. 36. all these things are against me
50. 20. but as for you, ye thought evil against me
Exod. 23. 33. lest they make thee sin against me
32. 33. whoso hath sinned against me him will I blot
Lev. 26. 40. which they trespassed against me
Num. 14. 27. congregation which murmur a. me, 29.
35. that are gathered together against me
22. 5. abide over ag. me || 34. thou stoodest ag. me
Deut. 32. 51. because ye trespassed against me at Meribah, Ezek. 17. 20. | 20. 27, 38. | 39. 23, 26.
Judg. 6. 39. let not thine anger be hot against me
7. 2. lest Israel vaunt themselves against me
11. 27. but thou doest me wrong to war against me
Ruth 1. 13. hand of the Lord is gone out against me
† 16. be not against me to leave thee, or to return
1 Sam. 12. 3. witness against me before the Lord
17. 35. when he arose ag. me, I caught him by beard
22. 8. that all of you have conspired against me, 13.
26. 19. if the Lord hath stirred thee up against me
2 Sam. 24. 17. let thy hand, I pray thee, be ag. me
2 Kings 5. 7. see how he seeketh a quarrel ag. me
Job 10. 17. thou renewest thy witnesses against me
13. 26. thou writest bitter things against me
16. 8. with wrinkles, which is a witness against me
19. 19. they whom I loved are turned against me
23. 6. will he plead against me with his great power
30. 21. with thy hand thou opposest thyself ag. me
31. 38. if my land cry against me, or the furrows
33. 10. behold, he findeth occasions against me
Psal. 3. 1. are many that rise up ag. me, 18. 39, 48.
22. † 13. they opened their mouths against me
27. 12. false witnesses are risen up ag. me, 54. 3.
35. 21. they opened their mouth wide against me
41. 7. ag. me do they devise my hurt, whisper ag. me
102. 8. they are mad ag. me, they are sworn ag. me
119. 23. princes also did sit and speak against me
Prov. 8. 36. but he that sinneth ag. me wrongeth
Isa. 1. 2. have rebell. ag. me, Ezek. 2. 3. | 20. 8, 13, 21.
Jer. 12. 8. it crieth out against me, therefore I hated
Lam. 3. 3. surely, ag. me he is turned, he turneth
60. hast seen all their imaginations against me
Hos. 4. 7. as they increased, so they sinned ag. me
7. 13. they transgressed ag. me, spoken lies ag. me
14. and they assemble and rebel against me
15. yet do they imagine mischief against me
Mic. 6. 3. O my people, testify against me
7. 8. rejoice not against me, O mine enemy
Mal. 3. 13. your words have been stout against me
Mat. 12. 30. that is not with me is ag. me, Luke 11. 23.
18. 21. how oft shall my brother sin against me?
John 13. 18. hath lift up his heel against me
19. 11. couldest have no power at all against me
Acts 24. 19. and object, if they had aught ag. me

At ME.

Psal. 118. 13. thou hast thrust sore at me to fall
John 7. 23. are ye angry at me because I made a man

Before ME.

Gen. 6. 13. the end of all flesh is come before me
7. 1. for thee have I seen righteous before me
17. 1. walk before me, and be thou perfect, 1 Sam. 2. 30. 1 Kings 2. 4. | 8. 25. | 9. 4. 2 Chron. 7. 17.
27. † 20. because thy God brought it before me
40. 9. in my dream, behold a vine was before me
Exod. 20. 3. shalt have no other gods b. me, Deut. 5. 7.
23. 15. none shall appear before me empty, 34. 20.
Num. 22. 32. because thy way is perverse before me
1 Sam. 9. 19. go up before me to the high place
10. 8. and thou shalt go down before me to Gilgal
16. 22. let David, I pray thee, stand before me
25. 19. go on before me, behold I come after you
2 Sam. 22. 23. for all his judgments were before me, Psal. 18. 22. | 119. 30.
1 Kings 8. 25. as thou hast walked b. me, 2 Chr. 6. 16.
11. 36. David may have a light before me in Jerus.
21. 29. how Ahab humbleth himself before me
2 Kings 22. 19. bec. hath wept b. me, 2 Chr. 34. 27.
Ezra 4. 18. letter hath been plainly read before me
Neh. 5. 15. former governors that were before me
Esth. 7. 8. will he force the queen also before me?
Job 41. 10. who then is able to stand before me?
Psal. 16. 8. I have set the Lord always before me
23. 5. thou preparest a table before me in presence
38. 17. my sorrow is continually before me
39. 1. keep my mouth while the wicked is before me
50. 8. offerings to have been continually before me
51. 3. my transgressions and my sin is ever before me
89. 36. his throne shall endure as the sun before me
Eccl. 1. 16. then all that have been before me, 2. 7, 9.
Cant. 8. 12. my vineyard which is mine, is before me
Isa. 1. 12. when ye come to appear before me, who
41. 1. keep silence before me, O islands
43. 10. b. me there was no god formed, nor after
49. 16. behold thy walls are continually before me
57. 16. for the spirit should fail before me
65. 6. behold, it is written before me, I will not
66. 22. shall remain before me, saith the Lord
Jer. 2. 22. yet thine iniquity is marked before me
6. 7. before me continually is grief and wounds
7. 10. and come and stand before me in this house
15. 1. tho' Moses and Samuel stood before me, yet
19. if thou return, thou shalt stand before me
28. 8. prophets that have been before me and thee
32. 30. for Israel have only done evil before me
33. 18. priests shall not want a man b. me, 35. 19.
34. 15. ye had made a covenant b. me in the house
49. 19. shepherd that will stand bef re me, 50. 44.
Ezek. 8. 1. and the elders of Judah sat before me
14. 1. then the elders of Israel sat before me, 20. 1.
36. 17. their way was before me as the uncleanness
44. 15. and they shall stand before me to offer
Dan. 4. 8. at the last Daniel came in before me
Jonah 1. 2. their wickedness is come up before me
Hab. 1. 3. spoiling and violence are before me
Hag. 2. 14. so is this people and nation before me
Mal. 3. 1. shall prepare the way b. me, Mat. 11. 10.
Luke 19. 27. bring hither and slay them before me
John 1. 15. preferred b. me, for he was b. me, 27. 30.
5. 7. I am coming, another steppeth down before me
10. 8. all that ever came before me are robbers
Acts 25. 9. there be judged of these things bef. me
Rom. 16. 7. who also were in Christ before me
Gal. 1. 17. to them which were apostles before me

Behind ME.

2 Kings 9. 18. Jehu said, turn thee behind me, 19.
Ezek. 3. 12. I heard behind me a voice of rushing
Mat. 16. 23. get thee behind me, Satan, thou art an offence unto me, Mark 8. 33. Luke 4. 8.

Beside, besides ME.

1 Kings 3. 20. she arose and took my son from b. m
Isa. 43. 11. bes. me there is no Saviour, Hos. 13. 4.

Isa. 44. 6. and besides me there is no God, 45. 5, 6, 21.
47. 8. that sayest, I am, and none else bes. me, 10.
Between ME.
Gen. 9. 12. covenant I make betw. me and you, 13.
15. that is betw. me and every living creature, 17.
13. 8. let there be no strife between me and thee
16. 5. L. judge betw. me and thee, 1 Sam. 24. 12, 15.
17. 2. I make my coven. b. me and thee, 7, 10, 11.
23. 15. what is that bet. me and thee? bury thy dead
31. 44. let it be for a witness betw. me and thee, 48.
49. Lord watch between me and thee when absent
50. see, God is witness between me and thee
Exod. 31. 13. my sabbath ye shall keep, for it is a sign between me and you, 17. Ezek. 20. 12, 20.
1 Sam. 14. 42. cast lots between me and Jonathan
20. 3. there is but a step between me and death
42. have sworn, saying, Lord be b. me and thee
1 Kings 15. 19. is a league b. me and thee, 2 Chr. 16. 3.
Isa. 5. 3. judge, I pray you, bet. me and my vineyard
Ezek. 43. 8. and the wall between me and them
By ME.
Gen. 48. 7. Rachel died by me in the land of Canaan
Exod. 33. 21. behold, there is a place by me
Num. 20. 18. Edom said, thou shalt not pass by me
Deut. 5. 31. as for thee, stand thou here by me
Judg. 9. 9. wherewith by me they honour God
1 Sam. 28. 17. Lord hath done, as he spake by me
2 Sam. 23. 2. the Spirit of the Lord spake by me
1 Kings 22. 28. Lord not spoken by me, 2 Chr. 18. 27.
Ezra 4. † 19. by me a decree is set, and it is found
6. † 8. by me a decree is made, Dan. 3. † 29.
Neh. 4. 18. he that sounded the trumpet was by me
Job 9. 11. lo, he goeth by me, and I see him not
Prov. 8. 15. by me kings reign ‖ 16. by me princes rule
9. 11. by me thy days shall be multiplied
Isa. 46. 3. which are borne by me ‖ 54. 15. but not by me
Hos. 8. 4. they have set up kings, but not by me
Mat. 15. 5. mightest be profited by me, Mark 7. 11.
John 6. 57. that eateth me, even he shall live by me
10. 9. I am the door, by me if any man enter in
14. 6. no man cometh to the Father but by me
Acts 27. 23. an angel stood by me this night
Rom. 15. 18. which Christ hath wrought by me
2 Cor. 1. 19. Son of God preached by me was not yea
2. 2. but the same which is made sorry by me
2 Tim. 4. 17. that by me preaching might be known
Concerneth, concerning ME.
Josh. 14. 6. Lord said to Moses conc. me and thee
1 Kings 2. 4. L. continue his word he spake conc. me
22. 8. for he doth not prophesy good conc. me, 18.
Psal. 138. 8. Lord will perfect that which conc. me
Ezek. 14. 7. cometh to a prophet to inquire conc. me
Luke 22. 37. for the things concern. me have an end
24. 44. which are written in the Psalms conc. me
Acts 22. 18. not receive thy testimony concern. me
For ME.
Gen. 23. 8. entreat for me to Ephron, Exod. 8. 28.
27. 36. hast thou not reserved a blessing for me?
30. 31. if thou wilt do this thing for me
33. so shall my righteousness answer for me
50. 5. in my grave which I have digged for me
Exod. 2. 9. take this child and nurse it for me
Num. 3. 41. thou shalt take the Levites for me
11. 14. not able, because it is too heavy for me
22. 6. for they are too mighty for me
Deut. 31. 19. this song may be a witness for me
Josh. 24. 15. as for me and my house we will serve L.
Judg. 7. 2. people are too many for me to give
11. 37. she said, let this thing be done for me
14. 2. now therefore get her for me to wife, 3.
19. 19. there is bread and wine also for me
1 Sam. 12. 23. as for me, 1 Chron. 22. 7. | 28. 2. | 29. 17. Job 21. 4. Psal. 5. 7. | 17. 15. | 35. 13.
18. 17. only be thou valiant for me, and fight
22. 3. till I know what God will do for me
8. there is none of you that is sorry for me
27. 1. nothing better for me than to escape
2 Sam. 3. 39. sons of Zeruiah be too hard for me
7. 5. shalt thou build an house for me to dwell in
10. 11. if Syrians be too strong for me, 1 Chr. 19. 12.
14. 32. good for me to have been there still
15. 34. then mayest thou for me defeat counsel
22. 18. they were too strong for me, Psal. 18. 17.
† 48. God giveth avengement for me, Psal. 18. † 47.
1 Kings 13. 6. pray for me, that my hand be restored
17. 12. may go in and dress it for me and my son
2 Kings 4. 24. drive, slack not thy riding for me
16. 15. the brazen altar be for me to inquire by
22. 13. inquire of the Lord for me, 2 Chron. 34. 21.
Neh. 5. 18. which was prepared for me daily
Job 17. 1. the graves are ready for me
23. 14. performeth the thing appointed for me
29. 23. they waited for me as for the rain
42. 3. I uttered things too wonderful for me
Psal. 3. 3. thou, O Lord, art a shield for me
7. 6. awake for me ‖ 56. 9. this I know, for G. is for me
31. 4. the net they have laid privily for me, 35. 7. | 119. 110. | 140. 5. | 141. 9. | 142. 3.
41. 12. as for me, 55. 16. | 69. 13. Isa. 59. 21. Jer. 17. 16. | 26. 14. | 40. 10. Ezek. 9. 10. Dan. 2. 30. | 7. 28. | 10. 17.
57. 2. to God, that performeth all things for me
61. 3. for thou hast been a shelter for me
73. 16. to know this, it was too painful for me
94. 16. rise up for me, who will stand up for me?
109. 21. but do thou for me, O God the Lord
119. 71. good f. me ‖ 85. the proud digged pits f. me
95. the wicked have waited for me to destroy me
131. 1. or in things too high for me
139. 6. such knowledge is too wonderful for me
Prov. 30. 8. feed me with food convenient for me
18. there be three things too wonderful for me
Isa. 38. 14. I am oppressed, undertake for me
44. 7. and who shall set it in order for me?
49. 20. the place is too strait for me, give place
23. they shall not be ashamed that wait for me
60. 9. surely the isles shall wait for me
65. 1. I am sought of them that asked not for me
Jer. 29. 13. search for me with all your heart
32. 27. is there any thing too hard for me?
Ezek. 29. 20. because they wrought for me
Hos. 3. 3. thou shalt abide for me many days

Jonah 4. 3. better for me to die than to live, 8.
Mic. 7. 9. until he execute judgment for me
Zech. 9. 13. when I have bent Judah for me
Mat. 17. 27. that take and give for me and thee
Luke 23. 28. weep not for me, but for yourselves
Acts 8. 24. Simon said, pray ye to the Lord for me
10. 29. for what intent ye have sent for me
Rom. 15. 30. strive in your prayers to God for me
1 Cor. 6. 12. all things are lawful for me, 10. 23.
9. 15. it were better for me to die, than that
Gal. 2. 20. who loved me, and gave himself for me
Eph. 6. 19. and f. me, that utterance may be given me
2 Tim. 4. 8. laid up for me a crown of righteousness
From ME.
Gen. 13. 9. separate thyself, I pray thee, from me
22. 12. hast not withheld thine only son from me
31. 27. wherefore didst thou steal away from me?
31. wouldest take by force thy daughters from me
39. 9. nor hath he kept back any thing from me
44. 28. the one went out from me, and he is torn
29. if ye take this also from me, ye shall bring
45. 1. cause every man to go out from me
Exod. 10. 28. get thee from me, see my face no more
Josh. 7. 19. tell me, hide it not from me, 1 Sam. 3. 17.
Judg. 16. 17. then my strength will go from me
1 Sam. 20. 2. why should my Fath. hide this from me?
2 Sam. 13. 9. Amnon said, have out all men from me
17. put this woman out f. me ‖ 20. 20. far be it f. me
1 Kings 12. 24. return, for this thing is from me
22. 24. went Spirit of Lord from me, 2 Chr. 18. 23.
2 Kings 4. 27. and the Lord hath hid it from me
18. 14. saying, I have offended, return from me
Neh. 13. 28. therefore I chased him from me
Job 6. 13. and is wisdom driven quite from me?
9. 34. let him take his rod away from me
13. 21. withdraw thine hand far from me
19. 13 he hath put my brethren far from me
21. 16. the counsel of the wicked is far from me
27. 5. I will not remove mine integrity from me
Ps. 13. 1. how long wilt thou hide thy face from me?
18. 22. I did not put away his statutes from me
35. 22. thou hast seen, O Lord, be not far from me
38. 10. light of mine eyes, it is gone from me
39. 10. remove thy stroke away from me
40. 11. withhold not thy tender mercies from me
51. 11. and take not thy Holy Spirit from me
66. 20. nor hath turned his mercy from me
88. 14. Lord, why hidest thou thy face from me?
102. 2. hide not thy face from me in trouble, 143. 7.
119. 19. hide not thy commandments from me
Cant. 5. 7. the keepers took away my vail from me
6. 5. turn away thine eyes from me, for they have
Isa. 22. 4. look away from me, I will weep bitterly
38. 12. mine age is removed from me as a tent
51. 4. give ear, for a law shall proceed from me
Jer. 2. 35. surely his anger shall turn from me
3. 19. and shall not turn away from me.
13. 25. this is the portion of thy measures from me
38. 14. I will ask thee, hide nothing from me
51. 53. from me shall spoilers come unto her
Ezek. 3. 17. and give them warning from me, 33. 7.
14. 5. because they are all estranged from me
7. every one that separateth himself from me
11. that Judah may go no more astray from me
44. 10. went astray from me after their idols
15. when children of Israel went astray from me
Dan. 2. 5. the king said, the thing is gone from me, 8.
Hos. 5. 3. I know Ephraim, Israel is not hid from me
7. 13. woe unto them, for they have fled from me
11. 7. my people are bent to backsliding from me
14. 8. like a fir-tree, from me is thy fruit found
Amos 5. 23. take away from me the noise of songs
Mat. 26. 39. O my Father, if it be possible, let this cup pass from me. Mark 14. 36. Luke 22. 22.
42. if this cup may not pass away from me
Luke 16. 3. my lord taketh from me the stewardship
John 10. 18. no man taketh it from me, I lay it down
2 Tim. 1. 15. all in Asia be turned away from me
See DEPART, DEPARTED.
In ME.
Gen. 41. 16. Joseph answered, it is not in me
1 Sam. 20. 8. if there be iniquity in me, 2 Sam. 14. 32.
2 Sam. 1. 9. because my life is yet whole in me
22. 20. because he delighted in me, Psal. 18. 19.
Job 6. 13. is not my help in me? is wisdom driven?
19. 28. the root of the matter is found in me
23. 6. no, but he would put strength in me
27. 3. all the while my breath is in me
28. 14. the depth saith, it is not in me
33. 9. I am clean, nor is there iniquity in me
Psal. 7. 8. according to mine integrity in me
38. 2. for thine arrows stick fast in me
42. 4. when I remember, I pour out my soul in me
5. and why art thou disquieted in me?
139. 24. see if there be any wicked way in me
Cant. 5. † 4. and my bowels were moved in me
Isa. 27. 4. fury is not in me, who would set briars
57. 13. that putteth trust in me shall possess land
Jer. 2. 5. what iniquity have fathers found in me?
39. 18. because thou hast put thy trust in me
49. 11. and let thy widows trust in me
Lam. 3. 20. my soul is humbled in me
Dan. 6. 22. before him innocency was found in me
10. 8. there remained no strength in me, 17.
Hos. 12. 8. they shall find none iniquity in me
13. 19. hast destroyed thyself, but in me is thy help
Mat. 11. 6. shall not be offended in me, Luke 7. 23.
18. 6. little ones which believe in me, Mark 9. 42.
Luke 22. 37. must yet be accomplished in me
John 6. 56. he dwelleth in me, and I in him
11. 25. he that believeth in me shall live, 26.
14. 1. believe also in me ‖ 20. you in me, and I in you
10. but the Father that dwelleth in me
30. prince cometh, and hath nothing in me
15. 2. every branch in me ‖ 4. abide in me
5. he that abideth in me ‖ 7. if ye abide in me
6. if a man abide not in me he is cast forth
16. 33. spoken, that in me ye might have peace
17. 21 as thou, Father, art in me, and I in thee
23. I in them, and thou in me, that they may
Acts 24. 20. if they have found any evil-doing in me
26. 18. which are sanctified by faith that is in me

Acts 28. 18. there was no cause of death in me
Rom. 1. 15. as much as in me is, I am ready to preach
7. 8. wrought in me all manner of concupiscence
13. sin working death in me by what is good
17. no more I, but sin that dwelleth in me, 20.
18. I know that in me dwelleth no good thing
2 Cor. 11. 10. as the truth of Christ is in me
13. 3. since ye seek a proof of Christ speaking in me
Gal. 1. 16. it pleased God to reveal his Son in me
24. and they glorified God in me
2. 8. the same was mighty in me towards Gentiles
20. yet not I, but Christ liveth in me
Phil. 1. 30. having the same conflict which ye saw in me, and now hear to be in me
4. 9. the things ye have heard and seen in me do
Col. 1. 29. working which worketh in me mightily
1 Tim. 1. 16. that in me Christ Jesus might shew
Of ME.
Gen. 20. 13. say of me, he is my brother
32. 20. peradventure he will accept of me
Judg. 9. 54. men say not of me a woman slew him
Ruth 2. 10. thou shouldest take knowledge of me
1 Sam. 27. 1. Saul shall despair of me to seek me
28. 16. wherefore then dost thou ask of me?
2 Chron. 11. 4. return, for this thing is done of me
Job 42. 7. not spoken of me the thing that is right
Psal. 2. 8. ask of me, and I shall give thee the heathen
40. 7. in thy book it is written of me, Heb. 10. 7.
41. 5. mine enemies speak evil of me
60. 8. Philistia, triumph thou because of me
81. 11. and Israel would none of me
Isa. 30. 1. but doth not take counsel of me
38. 12. from day, wilt thou make an end of me, 13.
43. 22. thou hast been weary of me, O Israel
44. 21. thou shalt not be forgotten of me
45. † 24. surely he shall say of me, in the Lord
54. 17. and their righteousness of me, saith the Lord
58. 2. they ask of me the ordinances of justice
Jer. 10. 20. my children are gone forth of me
37. 7. say to the king that sent you to enquire of me
Ezek. 20. 3. and say, are ye come to enquire of me?
49. they say of me, doth he not speak parables?
Mat. 10. 37. more than me, is not worthy of me, 37, 38.
11. 29. and learn of me, for I am meek and lowly
26. 31. be offended, because of me, Mark 14. 27.
Mark 8. 38. whoso shall be ashamed of me, Luke 9. 26.
9. 39. that can lightly speak evil of me
Luke 8. 46. I perceive that virtue is gone out of me
22. 19. saying, this do in remembrance of me
John 4. 9. thou being a Jew, askest drink of me
5. 32. another that beareth witness of me, 37.
39. and they are they which testify of me
46. have believed me, for Moses wrote of me
12. 30. this voice came not because of me
15. 26. the Comforter come, he shall testify of me
18. 34. or did others tell it thee of me?
Acts 1. 4. wait for the promise ye have heard of me
23. 11. as thou hast testified of me in Jerusalem
1 Cor. 4. 16. be ye followers of me, 11. 1. Phil. 3. 17.
11. 24. this do in remembrance of me, 25.
15. 8. last of all he was seen of me also
16. 21. the salutation of me Paul, Col. 4. 18.
2 Cor. 12. 6. lest any should think of me above that which he seeth me or heareth of me
Gal. 1. 11. that gospel which is preached of me
Phil. 4. 10. your care of me hath flourished
2 Tim. 1. 8. the testimony of me his prisoner
13. sound words, which thou hast heard of me
2. 2. things that thou hast heard of me, commit
Heb. 10. 34. he had compassion of me in my bonds
On ME, *or upon* ME.
Gen. 18. 27. I have taken upon me to speak to L. 31.
20. 9. that thou hast brought on me a great sin
27. 12. I shall bring a curse upon me, not a blessing
13. upon me be thy curse, my son, only obey me
31. 35. for the custom of women is upon me
40. 14. think on me when it shall be well with thee
Judg. 15. 12. ye will not fall upon me yourselves
19. 20. howsoever, let all thy wants lie upon me
1 Sam. 13. 12. Philistines will come down upon me
25. 24. upon me, my lord, upon me, let this iniqui. be
2 Sam. 14. 9. the iniquity be on me, and father's hou.
1 Kings 2. 15. that all Israel set their faces on me
1 Chron. 21. 17. let thy hand, I pray thee, be on me
28. 19. understand in writing by his hand upon me
Ezra 7. 28. hand of the Lord upon me, Neh. 2. 8, 18.
Neh. 5. 19. think upon me, my God, for good
Job 3. 25. which I greatly feared is come upon me
4. 14. fear came up. me ‖ 6. 28. be content, look up. me
7. 8. thine eyes are upon me, and I am not
10. 16. thou shewest thyself marvellous upon me
16. 14. he runneth upon me like a giant
19. 21. have pity upon me, O ye my friends
Psal. 4. 1. have mercy upon me, 6. 2. | 9. 13. | 25. 16. | 27. 7. | 30. 10. | 31. 9. | 51. 1. | 86. 16.
22. 17. tell my bones, they look and stare upon me
32. 4. for day and night thy hand was heavy up. me
40. 17. I am poor, yet the Lord thinketh upon me
55. 3. they cast iniquity upon me, and hate me
56. 12. thy vows are upon me, I will render praises
91. 14. because he hath set his love upon me
15. he shall call up. me ‖ 119. 132. look thou up. me
139. 5. and thou hast laid thine hand upon me
Cant. 1. 6. look not upon me, sun hath looked upon me
Isa. 43. 22. thou hast not called upon me, O Jacob
51. 5. the isles shall wait upon me, and shall trust
61. 1. Spirit of the L. God is upon me, Luke 4. 18
Jer. 13. 22. wherefore come these things upon me?
15. † 16. for thy name is called upon me, O Lord
Lam. 3. 53. and they have cast a stone upon me
Ezek. 3. 14. the hand of the Lord was strong up. me
22. was there up. me ‖ 8. 1. hand fell there up. me
11. 5. the Spirit of the Lord fell upon me, and said
33. 22. the hand of L. was upon me, 37. 1. | 40. 1.
Zeph. 3. 8. therefore wait ye upon me until the day
Zech. 6. 8. then cried he upon me and spake unto me
11. 11. the poor of the flock that waited upon me
12. 10. they shall look upon me whom they pierced
Mat. 15. 22. have mercy upon me, thou Son of Dav. Mark 10. 47, 48. Luke 18. 38, 39.
26. 10. wrought a good work upon me, Mark 14. 6.
Luke 1. 25. in the days wherein he looked on me

John 6. 35. he that believeth on me, 47. | 7. 38. | 12. 44, 46. | 14. 12.
16. 9. of sin, because they believe not on me
17. 20 who shall believe on me through their word
Acts 8. 24. that none of those things come upon me
Rom. 15. 3. that reproached thee fell on me
1 Cor 9. 16. for necessity is laid upon me
2 Cor. 11. 28. that which cometh upon me daily
12. 9. that the power of Christ may rest upon me
Phil. 2. 27. but God had mercy on me also
Rev. 1. 17. he laid his right hand upon me, saying
See CALL.

Over ME.

Exod. 8. 9. Moses said to Pharaoh, glory over me
Deut. 17. 14. shalt say, I will set a king over me
Job 7. 12. that thou settest a watch over me
Psal. 13. 2. shall mine enemy be exalted over me
19. 13. let them not have dom. over me, 119. 133.
25. 2. let not mine enemies triumph over me
41. 11. mine enemy doth not triumph over me
42. 7. thy waves and billows are gone over me
60. † 8. Philistia, triumph thou over me
88. 16. thy fierce wrath goeth over me
Cant. 2. 4. and his banner over me was love
Jonah 2. 3. thy billows and waves passed over me

To, or unto ME.

Gen. 4. 10. thy brother's blood crieth unto me
15. 3. behold, to me thou hast given no seed
20. 5. said he not u. me || 21. 23. swear u. me by G.
24. 30. saying, thus spake the man unto me
26. 27. wherefore come ye to me, seeing ye hate
27. 20. because the Lord hath brought it to me
29. 25. what is this thou hast done unto me?
31. 9. thus God hath given them to me
32. 9. L. which saidst unto me, return to thy country
34. 11. what ye shall say unto me, I will give, 12.
40. 14. shew kindness, I pray thee, unto me
46. 31. and my father's house are come unto me
Exod. 3. 9. the cry of child. of Isr. is come unto me
4. 25. surely a bloody husband art thou to me
5. 1. may hold a feast unto me in the wilderness
6. 7. and I will take you to me for a people
12. children of Israel have not hearkened unto me
13. 2. sanctify unto me all the first-born
14. 15. wherefore criest thou unto me? speak to Is.
18. 16. when they have a matter, they come unto me
19. 5. ye shall be a peculiar treasure unto me
6. ye shall be unto me a kingdom of priests
22. 23. and they cry at all unto me, I will hear, 27.
29. first-born of thy sons shalt thou give unto me
31. and ye shall be holy men unto me, nor eat
28. 1. that he may minister unto me, 3. | 29. 1. | 30. 30. | 40. 13. Jer. 33. 22. Ezek. 43. 19.
32. 26. let him come u. me || 33. 12. thou sayest u. me
34. 2. present thyself there to me in the mount
Lev. 25. 55. for unto me Israel are servants
Deut. 18. 15. of breth. like u. me, Acts 3. 22. | 7. 37.
32. 35. to me belongeth vengeance and recompence
Judg. 11. 7. why are ye come unto me now, when
15. 11. as they did u. me, so have I done to them
17. 10. and be unto me a father and a priest
Ruth 1. 17. the Lord do so to me and more also, 2 Sam. 3. 35. | 19. 13. 1 Kings 2. 23.
1 Sam. 9. 16. because their cry is come unto me
16. 3. anoint unto me him whom I name unto thee
18. 8. and to me they ascribed but thousands
2 Sam. 1. 26. very pleasant hast thou been unto me
12. 23. go to him, but he shall not return to me
15. 4. that every man might come unto me
1 Kings 2. 5. thou knowest what Joab did to me
19. 2. so let the gods do to me and more, 20. 10.
22. 14. what Lord saith unto me that will I speak
2 Kings 5. 7. send un. me to recov. a man of leprosy
8. let him come now to me || 6. 31. G. do so to me
9. 12. thus and thus spake he to me, saying
10. 6. and come to me to Jezreel by to-morrow
22. 15. tell man that sent you to me, 2 Chr. 34. 23.
1 Chron. 13. 12. how bring ark of God home to me?
2 Chron. 18. 17. he would not prophesy good u. me
Ezra 7. 28. and hath extended mercy unto me
9. 4. then were assembled unto me every one that
Neh. 1. 9. but if ye turn un. me and keep my com.
Job 3. 25. that which I was afraid of is come unto me
7. 3. and wearisome nights are appointed to me
13. 20. only do not two things u. me, then not hide
29. 21. u. me gave ear || 40. 7. declare u. me, 42. 4.
Ps. 16. 6. lines are fallen unto me in pleasant places
17. 6. O G. incline thine ear u. me, 31. 2. | 102. 2.
25. 16. turn thee un. me || 28. 1. be not silent to me
26. 11. be merciful unto me, 41. 4, 10. | 56. 1. | 57. 1. | 86. 3. | 119. 58, 132.
40. 1. he inclined un. me and heard my cry, 77. 1.
56. 4. I will not fear what flesh can do unto me
11. not be afraid what man can do unto me, 118. 6.
81. 8. O Israel, if thou wilt hearken unto me
89. 26. he shall cry unto me, thou art my father
101. 2. O when wilt thou come un. me? I will walk
122. 1. I was glad when they said un. me, let us go
139. 17. how precious are thy thoughts unto me
141. 1. Lord, I cry unto thee, make haste unto me
Prov. 1. 33. whoso hearkeneth unto me shall dwell
24. 29. I will do so to him as he hath done to me
Eccl. 2. 15. as to fool, so it happeneth even to me
Cant. 1. 13. bundle of myrrh is my bel. un. me, 14.
Isa. 1. 13. incense is an abomination unto me
14. your new moons, they are a trouble unto me
21. 11. he calleth to me out of Seir, watchman
29. 2. and it shall be unto me as Ariel
44. 22. return unto me, for I have redeemed thee
45. 22. look u. me, and be ye saved, all the ends
23. unto me every knee shall bow, every tongue
50. 8. mine adversary, let him come near to me
54. 9. for this is as the waters of Noah unto me
65. 5. come not near to me, I am holier than thou
Jer. 4. 1. if thou wilt return, return O Israel unto me
11. 11. tho' they shall cry unto me, I will not hear
12. 8. mine heritage is unto me as a lion, 9.
13. 11. that they might be unto me for a people
15. 16. thy word was unto me the joy of mine heart
18. wilt thou be altogether unto me as a liar?
23. 14. they are all of them unto me as Sodom
32. 31. this city hath been to me a provocation
Jer. 33. 9. it shall be to me a name of joy, a praise
49. 4. that trusted, saying, who shall come unto me
51. 35. the violence done to me be upon Babylon
Lam. 1. 21. and they shall be like unto me
22. and do to them as thou hast done unto me
Ezek. 16. 20. thy sons whom thou hast born unto me
22. 18. the house of Israel is to me become dross
23. 38. moreover this they have done unto me
26. 2. aha, she is broken, she is turned unto me
44. 13. to do the office of a priest unto me
15. they shall come near to me to minister unto me
Dan. 2. 30. this secret is not revealed to me
4. 36. my reason returned u. me, lords sought u. me
Hos. 2. 19. I will betroth thee unto me for ever, 20.
23. and I will sow her unto me in the earth
3. 2. so I bought her to me for fifteen pieces
4. 6. reject thee, thou shalt be no priest to me
7. 7. there is none among them that calleth unto me
14. they have not cried unto me with their hearts
8. 2. Isr. shall cry unto me, my God, we know thee
Amos 9. 7. are ye not as Ethiopians unto me?
Mic. 5. 2. out of thee shall come forth unto me
7. 8. when in darkness, L. shall be a light unto me
Hab. 2. 1. I will watch to see what he will say u. me
Hag. 2. 17. I smote you, yet ye turned not to me
Zech. 1. 3. turn ye unto me, saith the Lord of hosts
7. 5. did ye at all fast unto me, even to me?
Mat. 3. 14. baptized of thee, and comest thou to me?
7. 22. many will say to me in that day, Lord, Lord
11. 28. come unto me all ye that labour and are
14. 18. bring them to me, 17. 17. | 21. 2. Mark 9. 19.
19. 14. forbid them not to come un. me, Mark 10. 14.
25. 36. and ye came u. me || 40. ye have done it u. me
45. as ye did it not to these, ye did it not to me
28. 18. all power is given unto me in heaven
Luke 1. 38. let it be unto me according to thy word
4. 6. all this power, for that is delivered unto me
6. 47. whoso cometh to me, and heareth, 14. 26.
10. 22. all things are delivered to me of my Father
18. 13. God be merciful to me a sinner
John 5. 40. ye will not come to me to have life
6. 35. he that cometh to me shall never hunger, 37.
44. no man can come to me except Fath. draw, 65.
45. hath learned of the Father cometh unto me
7. 37. if any thirst, let him come unto me and drink
12. 32. if lifted up, I will draw all men unto me
50. even as the Father said unto me, so I speak
19. 10. Pilate said, speakest thou not unto me?
Acts 1. 8. and ye shall be witnesses unto me
2. 28. hast made known unto me the ways of life
9. 15. go thy way, for he is a chosen vessel to me
11. 5. a vessel descend, and it came even to me
22. 7. I heard a voice speaking unto me, saying
Rom. 7. 13. was that which is good made death u. me?
12. 3. through the grace given un. me, 1 Cor. 3. 10.
1 Cor. 6. 12. all things are lawful unto me, but all
9. 15. that it should be so done unto me
16. woe is unto me if I preach not the gospel
17. dispensation of the gospel is committed un. me
14. 11. and he shall be a barbarian unto me
16. 9. an effectual door is open. un. me, 2 Cor. 2. 12.
2 Cor. 11. 9. for that which was lacking to me
Gal. 2. 6. what they were, it maketh no matter to me
4. 15. plucked out eyes, and have given them to me
Eph. 3. 8. unto me who am less than least of all saints
Phil. 1. 21. for to me to live is Christ, to die is gain
3. 1. to me indeed is not grievous, but for you safe
7. but what things were gain to me, those counted
Col. 4. 11. which have been a comfort unto me
2 Tim. 4. 8. not to me only || 11. is profitable to me
Philem. 11. but now profitable to thee and to me
16. especially to me || 19. thou owest to me thyself
Heb. 10. 30. vengeance belongeth unto me, saith Ld.
13. 6. I will not fear what man shall do unto me

Toward ME.

Gen. 31. 5. countenance is not toward me as before
Psal. 86. 13. for great is thy mercy toward me
116. 12. render for all his benefits toward me
Cant. 7. 10. I am my Beloved's, his desire is tow. me
Isa. 29. 13. their fear toward me is taught by men
63. 15. and the sounding of thy bowels and mercies toward me
Dan. 4. 2. that the high God hath wrought tow. me
2 Cor. 7. 7. he told us your fervent mind toward me
Phil. 2. 30. supply your lack of service toward me

Under ME.

2 Sam. 22. 37. enlarged my steps u. me, Psal. 18. 36.
40. thou hast subdued under me, Psal. 18. 39.
48. bringeth down the people und. me, Ps. 18. 47.
Neh. 2. 14. for the beast that was under me to pass
Psal. 144. 2. who subdueth my people under me
Mat. 8. 9. having soldiers under me, Luke 7. 8.

With ME.

Gen. 12. 13. that it may be well with me for thy sake
28. 20. if G. will be w. me and keep me, Josh. 14. 12.
30. 29. thou knowest how thy cattle was with me
31. 5. the God of my father hath been with me
32. discern thou what is thine with me, and take
39. 7. and she said, lie with me, 12, 14. 2 Sam. 13. 11.
43. 8. send lad with me || 44. 34. lad be not with me
Exod. 17. 2. why chide ye with me, why tempt Ld.?
20. 23. ye shall not make with me gods of silver
33. 15. if thy presence go not with me, carry us not
Lev. 26. † 21. if ye walk at all adventures with me
Num. 11. 15. if thou deal thus with me, kill me
Deut. 32. 34. is not this laid up in store with me?
39. that I, even I, am he, and there is no G. w. me
Josh. 8. 5. I and all the people that are with me
Judg. 4. 8. if thou wilt go with me then I will go
7. 18. I and all that are with me, then blow ye
11. 12. saying, what hast thou to do with me?
16. 15. I love thee, when thy heart is not with me
17. 2. behold, the silv. is with me || 10. dwell with me
Ruth 1. 8. as ye have dealt w. me || 11. why go w. me
1 Sam. 9. 19. go up, for ye shall eat with me to-day
17. 9. if he be able to fight with me and to kill me
22. 23. but with me thou shalt be in safeguard
24. 18. how that thou hast dealt well with me
28. 19. to-morrow shalt thou and thy sons be w. me
2 Sam. 19. 25. wherefore wentest not thou with me?
33. I will feed thee with me in Jerusalem
23. 5. hath made with me an everlasting covenant
1 Chr. 4. 10. that thine hand might be with me
2 Chr. 2. 3. even so deal w. me || 7. are w. me in Judah
35. 21. from meddling with God, who is with me
Job 9. 35. and not fear, but it is not so with me
23. † 10. but he knoweth the way that is with me
28. 14. and the sea saith, it is not with me
29. 5. when the Almighty was yet with me
Ps. 7. 4. that was at peace w. me || 23. 4. thou art w. me
42. 8. in the night his song shall be with me
50. 5. those that have made a covenant with me
† 11. the wild beasts of the field are with me
55. 18. he delivered, for there were many with me
101. 6. the faithful, that they may dwell with me
119. 98. thy commands, for they are ever with me
Prov. 8. 18. riches and hon. are w. me, yea, durable
Cant. 4. 8. come with me from Lebanon, my spouse
Isa. 27. 5. and he shall make peace with me
50. 8. who will contend with me, let us stand
63. 3. of the people there was none with me
Jer. 20. 11. the Lord is with me as a mighty one
26. 14. do with me as seemeth good and meet to you
Dan. 10. 21. none holdeth with me but Michael
Hos. 2. 7. for then it was better with me than now
Joel 3. 4. yea, and what have ye to do with me?
Mal. 2. 6. he walked with me in peace and equity
Mat. 12. 30. he that is not with me is against me, he that gathereth not with me, Luke 11. 23.
18. 26. Lord, have patience with me, I will pay, 29.
20. 13. didst not thou agree with me for a penny?
26. 38. said, tarry ye here, and watch with me, 40.
Luke 11. 7. and my children are with me in bed
15. 6. saying, rejoice with me, 9. Phil. 2. 18.
31. son, thou art ever with me || 22. 21. with me on
22. 28. ye are they which have continued with me
23. 43. to day shalt thou be with me in paradise
John 8. 29. he that sent me is with me, the Father
13. 8. if I wash thee not, thou hast no part with me
18. he that eateth bread with me hath lifted up
15. 27. have been with me from the beginning
16. 32. am not alone, because the Father with me
17. 24. that they also be with me where I am
Acts 20. 34. ministered to them that were with me
22. 9. they that were with me saw the light, 11.
Rom. 7. 21. I would do good, evil is present with me
15. 30. strive with me in your prayers to God
1 Cor. 4. 3. but with me it is a very small thing
15. 10. but the grace of God that was with me
16. 4. if it be meet that I go, they shall go with me
2 Cor. 1. 17. that with me there should be yea, yea
Phil. 1. † 7. ye are all partakers with me of grace
2. 22. he hath served with me in the gospel
23. so soon as I shall see how it will go with me
4. 3. women, who laboured with me in the gospel
15. no church communicated with me but ye only
2 Tim. 4. 11. only Luke is w. me || 16. none stood w. m.
17. the Lord stood with me, and strengthened me
Philem. 13. whom I would have retained with me
Rev. 3. 4. they shall walk with me in white, for they
20. will come and sup with him, and he with me
21. will I grant to sit with me in my throne
22. 12. I come quickly, and my reward is with me

Within ME.

Job 6. 4. the arrows of the Almighty are within me
19. 27. though my reins be consumed within me
32. 18. the spirit within me constraineth me
Psal. 39. 3. heart was hot within me, while musing
42. 6. O my God, my soul is cast down within me
11. why art thou disquieted within me? 43. 5.
51. 10. O God, renew a right spirit within me
94. 19. in the multitude of my thoughts within me
103. 1. and all that is within me bless his holy name
142. 3. spirit was overwhelmed within me, 143. 4.
Isa. 26. 9. with my spirit within me will I seek thee
Jer. 23. 9. my heart within me is broken because of
Lam. 1. 20. my heart is turned within me, Hos. 11. 8.
Jonah 2. 7. when my soul fainted within me

Without ME.

Isa. 10. 4. without me they shall bow down under
John 15. 5. for without me ye can do nothing

MEADOW.

Gen. 41. 2. came out of a river, and they fed in a m.

MEADOWS.

Judg. 20. 33. came even out of the m. of Gibeah

MEAL-TIME.

Ruth 2. 14. at m.-time come thou hither and eat

MEAL.

Num. 5. 15. the tenth part of an ephah of barley m.
2 Kings 4. 41. bring m. and cast it into the pot
1 Chron. 12. 40. they that were nigh brought m.
Isa. 47. 2. take the millstones, and grind m. uncover
Hos. 8. 7. it hath no stalk, the bud shall yield no m.
See BARREL, MEASURES.

MEAN, Verb.

Gen. 21. 29. what m. these seven ewe-lambs?
Exod. 12. 26. what m. ye by this service?
Deut. 6. 20. thy son asketh what m. the testimonies?
Josh. 4. 6. ask, what m. ye by these stones? 21.
Isa. 3. 15. what m. ye that ye beat my people?
Ezek. 17. 12. know ye not what these things m.?
18. 2. what m. ye, that ye use this proverb?
Mark 9. 10. what the rising from the dead should m.
Acts 10. 17. doubted what this vision should m.
17. 20. we would know what these things m.
21. 13. what m. ye to weep and break my heart
2 Cor. 8. 13. I m. not that other men be eased

MEAN, Adjective.

Prov. 22. 29. he shall not stand before m. men
Isa. 2. 9. the m. man boweth down, the great man
5. 15. and the m. man shall be brought down
31. 8. the sword not of a m. man shall devour
Acts 21. 39. who am a citizen of no m. city
Rom. 12. † 16. but condescend to m. things

MEAN time.

Luke 12. 1. m. time when were gathered a multitude

MEAN while.

1 Kings 18. 45. m. while the heaven was black with
John 4. 31. in the m. while his disciples prayed him
Rom. 2. 15. their thoughts the m. while accusing

MEANS.

Exod. 34. 7. will by no m. clear guilty, Num. 14. 18
Judg. 5. 22. broken by the m. of the prancings
16. 5. by what m. we may prevail against him

2 *Sam.* 14. 14. yet doth he devise *m.* that his banished
1 *Kings* 20. 39. if by any *m.* he be missing, then
Ezra 4. 16. by this *m.* thou shalt have no portion
Psal. 49. 7. none can by any *m.* redeem his brother
Prov. 6. 26. for by *m.* of a whorish woman a man
Jer. 5. 31. and the priests bear rule by their *m.*
Mal. 1. 9. this hath been by your *m.*
Mat. 5. 26. thou shalt by no *m.* come out thence
Luke 5. 18. they sought *m.* to bring him in
10. 19. and nothing shall by any *m.* hurt you
John 9. 21. by what *m.* he now seeth we know not
Acts 4. 9. if be examined by what *m.* he is whole
18. 21. I must by all *m.* keep this feast in Jerusalem
27. 12. if by any *m.* they might attain to Phenice
Rom. 1. 10. if by any *m.* I might have a journey
11. 14. by any *m.* I may provoke to emulation
1 *Cor.* 8. 9. take heed, lest by any *m.* this liberty
9. 22. that I might by all *m.* save some
27. lest by any *m.* when I have preached to others
2 *Cor.* 1. 11. by *m.* of many, thanks may be given
4. † 8. yet not altogether without *m.*
11. 3. I fear, lest by any *m.* as the serpent
Gal. 2. 2. lest by any *m.* I should run in vain
Phil. 3. 11. if by any *m.* I attain to the resurrection
1 *Thess.* 3. 5. lest by some *m.* the tempter tempted
2 *Thess.* 2. 3. let no man deceive you by any *m.*
3. 16. G. of peace give you peace always by all *m.*
Heb. 9. 15. that by *m.* of death they who are called
Rev. 13. 14. deceiveth them by *m.* of those miracles

MEANEST.

Gen. 33. 8. what *m.* thou by all this drove I met?
2 *Sam.* 16. 2. what *m.* thou by these? *Ezek.* 37. 18.
Jonah 1. 6. what *m.* thou, O sleeper, arise, call on G.

MEANETH.

Deut. 29. 24. what *m.* the heat of this great anger?
1 *Sam.* 4. 6. what *m.* the noise of this shout? 14.
15. 14. what *m.* then this bleating of the sheep?
Isa. 10. 7. howbeit he *m.* not so, nor doth think so
Mat. 9. 13. but go ye, and learn what that *m.*
12. 7. but if ye had known what this *m.*
Acts 2. 12. saying one to another, what *m.* this?

MEANING.

Dan. 8. 15. when I Daniel had sought for the *m.*
1 *Cor.* 14. 11. if I know not the *m.* of the voice

MEANING.

Acts 27. 2. we launched, *m.* to sail by coasts of Asia

MEANT.

Gen. 50. 20. but God *m.* it to good, to bring to pass
Luke 15. 26. and asked what these things *m.*
18. 36. hearing multitude pass by, asked what it *m.*

MEASURE

Signifies, [1] *Some certain vessel fixed and agreed upon, whereby to estimate the quantity or capacity of things,* Prov. 20. 10. Mic. 6. 10. [2] *The height, breadth, and length of the thing measured,* Ezek. 40. 10. [3] *A stinted portion or allowance,* Ezek. 4. 11. [4] *The period or end of one's life,* Psal. 39. 4. [5] *Moderation,* Jer. 30. 11. | 46. 28. [6] *Limit, or boundary,* Jer. 51. 13. [7] *A certain proportion, resemblance, or degree,* Eph. 4. 13. [8] *To take the dimensions of land, cities, buildings, &c.* Num. 35. 5. Ezek. 40. 5. [9] *To repay, or reward,* Isa. 65. 7.

Exod. 26. 2. the curtains shall have one *m.* 8.
Lev. 19. 35. ye shall do no unrighteousness in *m.*
Deut. 25. 15. and a just *m.* shalt thou have
1 *Kings* 6. 25. cubits one *m.* || 7. 37. bases had one *m.*
2 *Kings* 7. 1. a *m.* of fine flour sold for a shek. 16, 18.
1 *Chr.* 11. † 23. he slew an Egyptian, a man of *m.*
Neh. 3. † 11. Malchijah repaired the second *m.*
Job 11. 9. the *m.* thereof is longer than the earth
28. 25. and he weigheth the waters by *m.*
Psal. 39. 4. make me to know the *m.* of my days
80. 5. thou givest them tears to drink in great *m.*
Isa. 5. 14. hell opened her mouth without *m.*
27. 8. in *m.* when it shooteth forth, wilt debate
40. 12. comprehended the dust of the earth in a *m.*
Jer. 30. 11. but I will correct thee in *m.* 46. 28.
51. 13. the end is come, and *m.* of thy covetousness
Ezek. 4. 11. thou shalt drink water by *m.* 16.
Mic. 6. 10. and scant *m.* that is abominable
Mat. 7. 2. with what *m.* you mete, it shall be measured to you again, *Mark* 4. 24. *Luke* 6. 38.
23. 32. fill ye up then the *m.* of your fathers
Mark 6. 51. and they were amazed beyond *m.*
7. 37. and were beyond *m.* astonished, 10. 26.
Luke 6. 38. good *m.* pressed down and shaken
John 3. 34. God giveth not the Spirit by *m.*
Rom. 12. 3. as God dealt to every man the *m.*
2 *Cor.* 1. 8. that were pressed out of *m.*
10. 13. we will not boast of things without our *m.* but according to the *m.* of the rule, 14, 15.
11. 23. in stripes above *m.* in prisons frequent
12. 7. and lest I should be exalted above *m.*
Gal. 1. 13. beyond *m.* I persecuted the church
Eph. 4. 7. according to the *m.* of the gift of Christ
13. to the *m.* of the stature of the fulness of Christ
16. the effectual working in the *m.* of every part
Rev. 6. 6. a voice saying, a *m.* of wheat for a penny
21. 17. according to the *m.* of a man, that is

MEASURE, *Verb.*

Num. 35. 5. ye shall *m.* from without the city
Deut. 21. 2. they shall *m.* to their cities round about
Isa. 65. 7. I will *m.* their former work into bosom
Ezek. 43. 10. and let them *m.* the pattern
Zech. 2. 2. a measuring-line to *m.* Jerusalem
Rev. 11. 1. rise and *m.* the temple of God
2. the court without leave out and *m.* not
21. 15. he had a golden reed to *m.* the city

MEASURED.

Ruth. 3. 15. he *m.* six measures of barley
2 *Sam.* 8. 2. *m.* with a line, with two lines *m.* he
1 *Kings* 17. † 21. he *m.* himself on the child
Job 7. † 4. I say, when shall the evening be *m.?*
Isa. 40. 12. who *m.* waters in hollow of his hand?
Jer. 31. 37. if heaven above can be *m.*
33. 22. as the sand of the sea cannot be *m.*
Ezek. 40. 5. he *m.* the breadth of the building
6. *m.* the threshold || 8. he *m.* also the porch, 9.
11. he *m.* the entry || 13. *m.* the gate || 24. posts
41. 5. *m.* the wall || 13. he *m.* the house
15. he *m.* the length of the building

Ezek. 42. 16. he *m.* east side with a measuring reed
17. he *m.* north side || 18. south || 19. west side
47. 3. and he *m.* a thousand cubits, 4.
Hos. 1. 10. shall be as sand of sea which cannot be *m.*
Hab. 3. 6. he stood and *m.* the earth, he beheld
Mat. 7. 2. with what measure you mete it shall be *m.* to you again, *Mark* 4. 24. *Luke* 6. 38.
Rev. 21. 16. he *m.* the city || 17. he *m.* the wall

MEASURES.

Gen. 18. 6. make ready three *m.* of fine meal
Deut. 25. 14. thou shalt not have divers *m.*
1 *Sam.* 25. 18. Abigail took five *m.* of parched corn
1 *Kings* 4. 22. Solomon's provision for one day was thirty *m.* of flour, and sixty *m.* of meal
5. 11. Solomon gave Hiram twenty thousand *m.* of wheat, and twenty *m.* of pure oil, 2 *Chron.* 2. 10.
7. 9. according to the *m.* of hewed stones, 11.
18. 32. as great as would contain two *m.* of seed
1 *Chron.* 23. 29. for all manner of *m.* and sizes
Ezra 7. 22. it be done to an hundred *m.* of wheat
Job 38. 5. who hath laid the *m.* thereof, if knowest?
Prov. 20. 10. divers *m.* are like abomination to Lord
Jer. 13. 25. this is the portion of thy *m.*
Ezek. 40. 24. the arches according to these *m.* 29.
28. he measured gate according to these *m.* 32.
43. 13. and these are the *m.* of the altar
48. 16. these are the *m.* of the profane place
Hag. 2. 16. to an heap of 20 *m.* there were but ten
Mat. 13. 33. hid in three *m.* of meal, *Luke* 13. 21.
Luke 16. 6. and he said, an hundred *m.* of oil
7. how much owest? he said, an hund. *m.* of wheat

See BARLEY.

MEASURING.

Jer. 31. 39. the *m.* line shall yet go forth on Gareb
Ezek. 40. 3. there was a man with a *m.* reed, 5.
42. 15. now when he had made an end of *m.*
16. he measured with a *m.* reed, 17, 18, 19.
Zech. 2. 1. a man with a *m.* line in his hand
2 *Cor.* 10. 12. they *m.* themselves by themselves

MEAT

Signifies, [1] *Provisions of any sort for bodily nourishment,* Luke 24. 41. [2] *Jesus Christ crucified, who, being applied by faith, is the true and real food which nourisheth the soul to eternal life,* John 6. 55. [3] *Spiritual comfort, that is sweeter, more pleasant and delightful, than food,* John 4. 32, 34. [4] *The table whereon meat is set,* Luke 22. 27. [5] *The product and fruits of the field which should be for food,* Joel 1. 16. Hab. 3. 17. [6] *The doctrines of the gospel, or mysteries of religion,* Heb. 5. 14. [7] *Ceremonial ordinances,* Heb. 13. 9.

Gen. 1. 29. to you it shall be for *m.*
30. to every beast I have given every herb for *m.*
9. 3. every moving thing shall be *m.* for you
27. 4. make me savoury *m.* such as I love, 7.
31. Esau also made savoury *m.* and brought it
45. 23. bread and *m.* for his father by the way
Lev. 11. 34. of all *m.* which may be eaten, that
22. 11. that is born in his house, shall eat of his *m.*
13. she shall eat of her father's *m.*
25. 6. the sabbath of the land shall be *m.* for you, 7.
Deut. 2. 6. ye shall buy *m.* of them for money
28. thou shalt sell me *m.* for money to eat
20. 20. thou shalt destroy trees not for *m.*
28. † 30. and shalt not use it as a common *m.*
Judg. 1. 7. kings gathered their *m.* under my table
14. 14. out of the eater came forth *m.* and out of
1 *Sam.* 20. 5. not fail to sit with the king at *m.*
34. Jonathan did eat no *m.* the second day
2 *Sam.* 3. 35. the people came to cause Dav. to eat *m.*
11. 8. there followed him a mess of *m.* from the king
12. 3. it did eat of his own *m.* and drank of his cup
13. 5. let Tamar dress the *m.* in my sight
1 *Kings* 10. 5. she saw the *m.* of his table, 2 *Chr.* 9. 4.
19. 8. he went in strength of that *m.* forty days
1 *Chron.* 12. 40. they that were nigh brought *m.*
Ezra 3. 7. they gave *m.* and drink to them of Zidon
Job 3. † 24. for my sighing cometh before my *m.*
6. 7. things my soul refused, are as my sorrowful *m.*
12. 11. doth not the mouth taste his *m.?*
20. 14. yet his *m.* in his bowels is turned
21. there shall none of his *m.* be left
30. 4. who cut juniper roots for their *m.*
33. 20. and his soul abhorreth dainty *m.*
34. 3. the ear trieth words, as the mouth tasteth *m.*
36. 31. he giveth *m.* in abundance
38. 41. cry to God, they wander for lack of *m.*
Psal. 42. 3. my tears have been my *m.* day and night
44. 11. thou hast given us like sheep for *m.*
59. 15. let them wander up and down for *m.*
69. 21. they gave me also gall for my *m.*
74. 14. thou gavest him to be *m.* to the people
78. 18. tempted God by asking *m.* for their lust
25. he sent them *m.* to the full
30. but while their *m.* was yet in their mouths
104. 21. the young lions seek their *m.* from God
27. thou mayest give them their *m.* in due season
107. 18. their soul abhorreth all manner of *m.*
111. 5. he hath given *m.* to them that fear him
145. 15. thou givest them *m.* in due season
Prov. 6. 8. the ant provideth her *m.* in the summer
23. 3. his dainties, for they are deceitful *m.*
30. 22. and a fool when he is filled with *m.*
25. yet they prepare their *m.* in the summer
31. 15. she riseth and giveth *m.* to her household
Isa. 9. † 5. this shall be with burning and *m.* of fire
62. 8. no more give thy corn to be *m.* for enemies
65. 25. and dust shall be the serpent's *m.*
Lam. 1. 11. have given their pleasant things for *m.*
19. mine elders died while they sought their *m.*
4. 10. sodden their children, they were their *m.*
Ezek. 4. 10. and thy *m.* shall be by weight
16. 19. my *m.* which I gave thee, thou hast set it
25. † 7. I will deliver thee for *m.* to the heathen
29. 5. I have given thee for *m.* to beasts, 34. 5, 8.
34. 10. that they may not be *m.* for them
47. 12. on bank shall grow trees for *m.* fruit for *m.*
Dan. 1. 8. would not defile himself with the king's *m.*
10. king who hath appointed your *m.* and drink
4. 12. the fruit much, and in it was *m.* for all, 21.
11. 26. they that feed of his *m.* shall destroy him

Hos. 11. 4. and I laid *m.* unto them
Joel 1. 16. is not the *m.* cut off before our eyes
Hab. 1. 16. because their portion is fat, *m.* plenteous
3. 17. although the fields shall yield no *m.* the flock
Hag. 2. 12. if one do touch any *m.* shall it be holy
Mal. 1. 12. in that ye say, his *m.* is contemptible
3. 10. bring all the tithes, that there may be *m.*
Mat. 3. 4. and his *m.* was locusts and wild honey
6. 25. is not the life more than *m.?* *Luke* 12. 23.
9. 10. as Jesus sat at *m.* in the house, 26. 7. *Mark* 2. 15. | 14. 3. | 16. 14. *Luke* 24. 30.
10. 10. for the workman is worthy of his *m.*
14. 9. for them which sat with him at *m.*
15. 37. and they took up of the broken *m.* *Mark* 8. 8.
24. 45. to give them *m.* in due season, *Luke* 12. 42.
25. 35. I was an hungered, and ye gave me *m.*
42. I was an hungered, and ye gave me no *m.*
Luke 3. 11. he that hath *m.* let him do likewise
8. 55. and he commanded to give her *m.*
9. 13. except we should go and buy *m.* for this peop.
14. 10. worship in presence of them that sit at *m.*
17. 7. will say to his servant, sit down to *m.*
22. 27. whether greater, he that sitteth at *m.*
24. 41. he said, have ye here any *m.?* *John* 21. 5.
John 4. 8. the disciples were gone to buy *m.*
32. I have *m.* to eat that ye know not of
34. my *m.* is to do the will of him that sent me
6. 27. labour not for the *m.* which perisheth, but for that *m.* which endureth to everlasting life
55. for my flesh is *m.* indeed, my blood is drink
Acts 2. 46. they did eat their *m.* with gladness
9. 19. when he had received *m.* he was strengthened
16. 34. the jailor set *m.* before them and rejoiced
27. 33. Paul besought them all to take *m.* 34.
36. were of good cheer, and they also took some *m.*
Rom. 14. 15. if thy brother be grieved with thy *m.* destroy not him with thy *m.* for whom Christ died
17. for the kingdom of God is not *m.* and drink
20. for *m.* destroy not the work of God
1 *Cor.* 3. 2. I have fed you with milk, and not with *m.*
8. 8. but *m.* commendeth us not to God
10. if any man see thee sit at *m.* in idol's temple
13. if *m.* make my brother to offend, I will eat no
10. 3. and did eat the same spiritual *m.*
Col. 2. 16. let no man judge you in *m.* or drink
Heb. 5. 12. such as have need of milk, not of strong *m.*
14. but strong *m.* belongeth to them of full age
12. 16. who for one morsel of *m.* sold his birth-right

See FOWLS.

MEAT *offering.*

Exod. 29. 41. according to *m. offering* of the morning
30. 9. shall offer no *m. offering* on altar of incense
40. 29. on altar of burnt offering offered *m. offering*
Lev. 2. 1. when any will offer a *m. off.* 4, 5, 7, 14.
3. remnant of *m. off.* shall be Aaron's, 10. | 5. 13.
6. 14. this is the law of the *m. offering,* 7. 37.
14. 10. three tenth deals of flour for a *m. offering*
Num. 4. 16. to Eleazar pertaineth daily *m. offering*
7. 13. mingled with oil for *m. off.* 19. | 28. 12, 13.
15. 6. for *m. off.* two tenth deals of flour, 28. 9, 12.
28. 8. as the *m. offering* of the morning, offer it
26. when ye bring a new *m. offering* to the Lord
29. 6. besides his *m. off.* and burnt off. 22, 25, 34.
Josh. 22. 23. if altar to offer *m. offering* save us not
Judg. 6. † 18. depart not, till I bring my *m. offering*
13. 19. Manoah took a kid with a *m. offering*
23. not have received a *m. offering* at our hands
2 *Kings* 3. 20. when the *m. off.* was offered, behold
1 *Chr.* 21. 23. wheat for the *m. offering* I give it all
Neh. 10. 33. for continual *m. off.* and burnt offer.
Isa. 57. 6. to them hast thou offered a *m. offering*
Ezek. 42. 13. there shall they lay the *m. offering*
44. 29. they shall eat the *m. offering* and sin offer.
45. 17. he shall prepare the *m. offering,* 24.
25. shall do the like according to the *m. offering*
46. 5. the *m. offering* shall be an ephah for a ram
7. a *m. offering* and an ephah for a bullock, 11.
15. thus shall they prepare the *m. offering* and oil
Joel 1. 9. the *m. off.* and the drink off. is cut off
13. the *m. offering* and drink offer. is withholden
2. 14. leave a blessing, even a *m. off.* to our God

MEAT *offerings.*

Num. 29. 39. these ye shall do for your *m. offerings*
Josh. 22. 29. turn to build an altar for *m. offerings*
1 *Kings* 8. 64. there Solomon offered *m. off.* altar was too little to receive *m. offerings,* 2 *Chr.* 7. 7.
Ezra 7. 17. buy speedily lambs with their *m. offer.*
Neh. 13. 5. chamber, where they laid their *m. off.*
Jer. 17. 26. come from Judah to bring *m. offerings*
33. 18. Levites not want a man to kindle *m. offer.*
Ezek. 45. 17. be the prince's part to give *m. offer.*
Amos 5. 22. tho' ye offer *m. off.* I will not accept you

MEATS.

Prov. 23. 6. neither desire thou his dainty *m.*
Mark 7. 19. into the draught, purging all *m.*
Acts 15. 29. abstain from *m.* offered to idols
Rom. 14. † 23. that putteth a difference in *m.*
1 *Cor.* 6. 13. *m.* for the belly, and the belly for *m.*
1 *Tim.* 4. 3. to abstain from *m.* God hath created
Heb. 9. 10. which stood only in *m.* and drinks
13. 9. the heart be established with grace, not *m.*

MEDDLE.

Deut. 2. 5. *m.* not with them of mount Seir
19. *m.* not with the children of Ammon
2 *Kings* 14. 10. why *m.* to thy hurt? 2 *Chr.* 25. 19.
Prov. 20. 19. *m.* not with him that flattereth
24. 21. *m.* not with them that are given to change

MEDDLED.

Prov. 17. 14. leave off contention before it be *m.* with

MEDDLETH.

Prov. 26. 17. that *m.* with strife not belonging to him

MEDDLING.

2 *Chron.* 35. 21. forbear thee from *m.* with God
Prov. 20. 3. but every fool will be *m.*

MEDIATOR

Signifies, *A person that manages, or transacts, between two contending parties, in order to reconcile them,* Gal. 3. 20. And is applied, [1] *To Jesus Christ, who is the only peace-maker and intercessor between God and men,* 1 Tim. 2. 5. [2] *To Moses, who came between the Lord and his people, to declare unto them his word,* Deut. 5. 5. Gal. 3. 19.

Gal. 3. 19. was ordained by angels in the hand of m.
20. a m. is not a m. of one, but God is one
1 Tim. 2. 5. but one m. between God and men, Jesus
Heb. 8. 6. he is the m. of a better covenant
9. 15. for this cause he is the m. of the new testament
12. 24. and to Jesus the m. of the new covenant

MEDICINE.

Prov. 3. † 8. it shall be m. to thy navel and marrow
17. 22. a merry heart doeth good like a m.
20. † 30. the blueness of a wound is a purging m.
Ezek. 47. 12. the leaf thereof shall be for m.

MEDICINES.

Jer. 30. 13. thou hast no healing m.
46. 11. in vain shalt thou use many m. not be cured

MEDITATE.

Gen. 24. 63. Isaac went out to m. in the field
Josh. 1. 8. thou shalt m. therein day and night
Judg. 5. † 10. m. ye that ride on white asses
Psal. 1. 2. in his law doth he m. day and night
2. † 1. and why do the people m. a vain thing?
63. 6. and m. on thee in the night watches
77. 12. I will m. also of all thy work
119. 15. I will m. in thy precepts, 78.
23. did m. in thy statutes || 48. I will m. in statutes
148. night-watches, that I might m. in thy word
143. 5. I m. on all thy works, I muse on the work
Isa. 33. 18. thine heart shall m. terror, where scribe
Luke 21. 14. not to m. before, what ye shall answer
1 Tim. 4. 15. m. upon these things, give thyself

MEDITATION.

1 Sam. 1. † 16. out of the abundance of my m.
Psal. 5. 1. give ear to my words, consider my m.
19. 14. let the m. of my heart be acceptable
49. 3. the m. of my heart shall be of understanding
90. † 9. we spend our years as a m.
104. 34. my m. of him shall be sweet, be glad in Ld.
119. 97. I love thy law, it is my m. all the day
99. than teachers, for thy testimonies are my m.

MEEK.

Num. 12. 3. now the man Moses was very m.
Psal. 22. 26. the m. shall eat and be satisfied
25. 9. the m. will he guide in judgment
37. 11. but the m. shall inherit the earth
69. † 32. the m. shall see this and be glad
76. 9. God arose to save all the m. of the earth
147. 6. the Lord lifteth up the m. he casteth down
149. 4. he will beautify the m. with salvation
Isa. 11. 4. reprove with equity, for the m. of earth
29. 19. the m. shall increase their joy in the Lord
61. 1. anointed to preach good tidings to the m.
Amos 2. 7. that turn aside the way of the m.
Zeph. 2. 3. seek ye the Lord, all ye m. of the earth
Mat. 5. 5. blessed are the m. || 11. 29. for I am m.
21. 5. behold, thy king cometh to thee m.
1 Pet. 3. 4. the ornament of a m. and quiet spirit

MEEKNESS

Signifies, [1] *A temper of mind that is not easily provoked, and suffers injuries without desire of revenge, and quietly submits to the will of God,* Col. 3. 12. [2] *A humble submissive frame of spirit, ready to receive and entertain the truths of God,* Jam. 1. 21.
Psal. 18. † 35. with thy m. thou hast multiplied me
45. 4. ride prosperously, because of truth and m.
Zeph. 2. 3. seek righteousness, seek m. shall be hid
1 Cor. 4. 21. shall I come in the spirit of m.?
2 Cor. 10. 1. I beseech you by the m. of Christ
Gal. 5. 23. the fruit of the Spirit is m. temperance
6. 1. restore such an one in the spirit of m.
Eph. 4. 2. that ye walk with all lowliness and m.
Col. 3. 12. put on therefore m. long-suffering
1 Tim. 6. 11. follow after faith, love, patience, m.
2 Tim. 2. 25. in m. instructing those that oppose
Tit. 3. 2. but gentle, shewing all m. to all men
Jam. 1. 21. receive with m. the ingrafted word
3. 13. let him shew his works with m. of wisdom
1 Pet. 3. 15. to give a reason of your hope with m.

MEET.

Gen. 2. 18. I will make an help m. for him
20. there was not found an help m. for Adam
Exod. 8. 26. Moses said, it is not m. so to do
Deut. 3. 18. ye pass over, all that are m. for war
Judg. 5. 30. m. for the necks of them that take
Ezra 4. 14. it was not m. to see the king's dishonour
Job 34. 31. surely it is m. to be said to God
Prov. 11. 24. that withholdeth more than is m.
Jer. 26. 14. do with me as seemeth m. to you
27. 5. have given earth to whom it seemed m. to me
Ezek. 15. 4. is it m. for any work? || 5. m. for no work
Mat. 3. 8. bring forth fruits m. for repentance
15. 26. not m. to take children's bread, Mark 7. 27.
Luke 15. 32. it was m. we should make merry
Acts 26. 20. and do works m. for repentance
Rom. 1. 27. receiving that recompence which was m.
1 Cor. 15. 9. that am not m. to be called an apostle
16. 4. if it be m. that I go also, they shall go
Phil. 1. 7. even as it is m. for me to think this
Col. 1. 12. hath made us m. to be partakers of inherit.
2 Thess. 1. 3. bound to thank G. for you as it is m.
2 Tim. 2. 21. he shall be vessel m. for master's use
Heb. 6. 7. herbs m. for them by whom it is dressed
2 Pet. 1. 13. yea, I think m. to stir you up

MEET.

Gen. 14. 17. king of Sodom went out to m. him
18. 2. Abraham saw them, and ran to m. them
19. 1. Lot seeing them rose up to m. them
24. 17. the servant ran to m. Rebekah, and said
65. what man is this that walketh to m. us?
29. 13. Laban ran to m. Jacob, and embraced him
30. 16. Leah went out to m. Jacob, and said
32. 6. thy brother Esau cometh to m. thee, 33. 4.
46. 29. Joseph went up to m. Israel his Father
Exod. 4. 14. behold, Aaron cometh forth to m. thee
27. Lord said, go into the wilderness to m. Moses
18. 7. Moses went out to m. his father-in-law
19. 17. brought forth the people to m. with God
23. 4. if thou m. thine enemy's ox going astray
25. 22. there I will m. with thee, and commune with thee, 29. 42, 43. | 30. 6, 36. Num. 17. 4.
Num. 22. 36. Balak went out to m. Balaam
23. 3. peradventure the Lord will come to m. me
15. stand here, while I m. the Lord yonder
Num. 31. 13. went forth to m. them without the camp
Josh. 2. 16. Rahab said, lest the pursuers m. you
9. 11. take victuals with you, and go to m. them
Judg. 4. 18. Jael went out to m. Sisera, 22.
6. 35. to Zebulun, and they came up to m. Gideon
11. 31. whatever cometh out of the doors to m. me
34. his daughter came to m. him with dances
19. 3. father of the damsel rejoiced to m. him
Ruth 2. 22. that they m. thee not in any other field
1 Sam. 10. 3. and there shall m. thee three men
5. thou shalt m. a company of prophets coming
13. 10. Saul went to m. Samuel to salute him
15. 12. when Samuel rose up early to m. Saul
17. 48. the Philistine drew nigh to m. David
18. 6. the women came to m. Saul with tabrets
25. 32. Lord which sent thee this day to m. me
30. 21. men went to m. David and to m. people
2 Sam. 6. 20. Michal came out to m. David
10. 5. David sent to m. the men, 1 Chron. 19. 5.
15. 32. Hushai the Archite came to m. him
19. 15. Judah || 24. Mephibosheth to m. king
1 Kings 2. 8. Shimei came down to m. me at Jordan
19. Solomon rose up to m. Bath-sheba his mother
18. 16. Obadiah went to m. Ahab, to m. Elijah
21. 18. arise, go down to m. Ahab king of Israel
2 Kings 1. 3. go up to m. messengers of king of Sam.
6. there came a man to m. us, and said to us
7. what manner of man came up to m. you?
2. 15. the sons of the prophets came to m. Elisha
4. 26. run now, I pray thee, to m. her, and say
29. if thou m. any man, salute him not
5. 21. he lighted from the chariot to m. him, 26.
8. 8. go m. the man of God || 9. Hazael went to m.
9. 17. take an horseman, and send to m. them
18. there went one on horseback to m. him
10. 15. he lighted on Jonadab coming to m. him
16. 10. Ahaz went to m. the king of Assyria
Neh. 6. 2. let us m. together in the plain, 10.
Job 5. 14. they m. with darkness in the day-time
39. 21. the horse goeth on to m. the armed men
Prov. 7. 15. therefore came I forth to m. thee
17. 12. let a bear robbed of her whelps m. a man
22. 2. the rich and poor m. together, the Lord is
29. 13. the poor and deceitful man m. together
Isa. 7. 3. go forth to m. Ahaz, thou, and thy son
14. 9. hell is moved for thee to m. thee at thy com.
34. 14. the wild beasts of the desert shall also m.
47. 3. vengeance, and I will not m. thee as a man
Jer. 41. 6. and Ishmael went forth to m. them
51. 31. one post and messenger run to m. another
Hos. 13. 8. I will m. them as a bear bereav. of whelps
Amos 4. 12. prepare to m. thy God, O Israel
Zech. 2. 3. another angel went out to m. him
Mat. 8. 34. the whole city came out to m. Jesus
25. 1. and went forth to m. the bridegroom
6. the bridegroom cometh, go ye out to m. him
Mark 14. 13. there shall m. you a man, Luke 22. 10.
Luke 14. 31. he be able with ten thousand to m. him
John 12. 13. people went forth to m. him, and cried
Acts 28. 15. they came to m. us as far as Appii-forum
1 Thess. 4. 17. in the clouds to m. the L. in the air

MEETEST.

2 Kings 10. 3. look out the m. of your master's sons
Isa. 64. 5. thou m. him that rejoic. and works right.

MEETETH.

Gen. 32. 17. when Esau my brother m. thee
Num. 35. 19. shall slay murderer when he m. him, 21.

MEETING.

Num. 24. † 1. went not to the m. of enchantments
1 Sam. 21. 1. Ahimelech was afraid at m. of David
Isa. 1. 13. it is iniquity, even the solemn m.

MELODY.

Isa. 23. 16. make sweet m. sing many songs
51. 3. joy shall be found therein, the voice of m.
Amos 5. 23. I will not hear the m. of thy viols
Eph. 5. 19. making m. in your heart to the Lord

MELONS.

Num. 11. 5. we remember the m. and the onions

MELT

Signifies, [1] *To make hard bodies liquid or fluid,* Ezek. 22. 22. [2] *To waste and be diminished,* 1 Sam. 14. 16. [3] *To faint and be discouraged,* Josh. 2. 11. 2 Sam. 17. 10.
Exod. 15. 15. the inhabitants of Canaan shall m.
Deut. 20. † 8. return, lest his brethren's heart m.
Josh. 2. † 9. the inhabitants m. because of you
11. when we heard these things, our hearts did m.
14. 8. my brethren made the heart of the people m.
2 Sam. 17. 10. is as heart of a lion, shall utterly m.
Psal. 39. † 11. thou makest his beauty to m. away
58. 7. let them m. away as waters which run
112. 10. he shall gnash with his teeth, and m. away
Isa. 13. 7. every man's heart shall m. Ezek. 21. 7.
19. 1. the heart of Egypt shall m. in midst of it
Jer. 9. 7. behold, I will m. them, and try them
Ezek. 22. 20. to m. it, I will leave you there m. you
Amos 9. 5. the L. toucheth the land, and it shall m.
13. and all the hills shall m. Nah. 1. 5.
2 Pet. 3. 10. and the elements shall m. with heat, 12.

MELTED.

Exod. 16. 21. when the sun waxed hot it m.
Deut. 1. † 28. our brethren have m. our heart
Josh. 5. 1. their heart m. || 7. 5. hearts of Israel m.
Judg. 5. 5. the mountains m. before the Lord
1 Sam. 14. 16. behold, the multitude m. away
2 Kings 22. † 9. thy servants have m. the money
Psal. 22. 14. my heart is m. in midst of my bowels
46. 6. he uttered his voice, and the earth m.
97. 5. the hills m. like wax || 107. 26. their soul m.
Isa. 34. 3. mountains shall be m. with their blood
64. † 7. hast m. us, because of our iniquities
Jer. 49. † 23. Damascus, Hamath, and Arpad, are m.
Ezek. 22. 21. ye shall be m. in the midst thereof
22. as silver is m. in the midst of the furnace

MELTETH.

Job 6. † 14. to him that m. pity be shewed
Psal. 58. 8. as a snail which m. let them pass away
68. 2. as wax m. so let wicked perish at presence
119. 28. my soul m. for heaviness, strengthen me
147. 18. he sendeth out his word and m. them
Isa. 40. 19. the workman m. a graven image
Jer. 6. 29. bellows burnt, the founder m. in vain
Nah. 2. 10. the heart of Nineveh m. the knees smite

MELTING.

Isa. 64. 2. as when the m. fire burneth, the fire

MEMBERS

Signifies, [1] *Any part of a natural body,* 1 Cor. 12. 12, 26. [2] *All the faculties of the soul, together with the parts of the body,* Rom. 6. 13, 19. *The unrenewed part of man, which is like a body consisting of many members, and putteth forth itself chiefly in and by the members of the body,* Rom. 7. 23. [4] *Every sensual and sinful affection,* Col. 3. 5. [5] *Christian or gospel believers in the church, which is Christ's mystical body,* Eph. 4. 25. | 5. 30. [6] *Thoughts,* Job 17. † 7.
1 Cor. 12. 14. the body is not one m. but many
19. if they were all one m. where were the body?
26. whether one m. suffer, one m. be honoured
Jam. 3. 5. even so the tongue is a little m.

MEMBERS.

Deut. 23. 1. he that hath his privy m. cut off
Job 17. 7. and all my m. are as a shadow
Psal. 139. 16. in thy book all my m. were written
Mat. 5. 29. that one of thy m. should perish, 30.
Rom. 6. 13. neither yield your m. instruments
19. as ye yielded your m. servants to sin
7. 5. the motions of sins did work in our m.
23. I see another law in my m. warring; into captivity to the law of sin, which is in my m.
12. 4. for as we have many m. in one body, and all m. have not the same office
5. we are every one m. one of another
1 Cor. 6. 15. know ye not, your bodies are the m. of Christ? shall I then take the m. of Christ?
12. 12. the body hath many m. all m. are one body
18. but now hath God set the m. in the body
20. but now are they many m. yet one body
22. much more those m. which seem more feeble
25. but that the m. should have the same care
26. one member suffer, all the m. suffer with it
27. ye are the body of Christ, and m. in particular
Eph. 4. 25. for we are m. one of another
5. 30. we are m. of his body, of his flesh and bones
Col. 3. 5. mortify your m. which are on the earth
Jam. 3. 6. so is the tongue among our m. that it
4. 1. even of your lusts that war in your m.

MEMORIAL.

Exod. 3. 15. this is my m. unto all generations
12. 14. this day shall be to you for a m.
13. 9. it shall be for a m. between thine eyes
17. 14. write this for a m. in a book, and rehearse
28. 12. for stones of m. to the children of Israel
29. for a m. before the Lord continually, 39. 7.
30. 16. the atonement money may be for a m.
Lev. 2. 2. the priest shall burn the m. of it on the altar, 9. 16. | 5. 12. | 6. 15. Num. 5. 26.
23. 24. a m. of blowing trumpets, Num. 10. 10.
24. 7. put pure frankincense on the bread for a m.
Num. 5. 15. for it is an offering of m. of iniquity
18. priest put the offering of m. in her hands
16. 40. took brasen censers to be a m. to Israel
31. 54. took the gold of the captains for a m.
Josh. 4. 7. and these stones shall be for a m.
Neh. 2. 20. you have no portion nor m. in Jerusalem
Esth. 9. 28. nor the m. of them perish from their seed
Psal. 9. 6. their m. is perished with them
30. † 4. at the m. of his holiness, 97. † 12.
135. 13. and thy m. throughout all generations
Isa. 66. † 3. he that maketh a m. as if he blessed
Hos. 12. 5. the Lord of hosts, the Lord is his m.
14. † 7. the m. thereof as the wine of Lebanon
Zech. 6. 14. crowns be for a m. in the temple of L.
Mat. 26. 13. this be told for a m. of her, Mark 14. 9.
Acts 10. 4. prayers and alms are come up for a m.

MEMORY

Signifies, [1] *That faculty of the mind, whereby it retains or recollects the images and remembrance of the things we have seen, imagined, or understood,* 1 Cor. 15. 2. [2] *Memorial, name, or report,* Prov. 10. 7. Isa. 26. 14.
Psal. 109. 15. that he may cut off the m. of them
145. 7. they shall utter the m. of thy great goodness
Prov. 10. 7. the m. of the just is blessed
Eccl. 9. 5. for the m. of them is forgotten
Isa. 26. 14. and made all their m. to perish
1 Cor. 15. 2. if ye keep in m. what I preached to you

MEN.

Gen. 4. 26. then began m. to call on the name of L.
6. 1. when m. began to multiply on the earth
18. 2. he looked, and lo, three m. stood by him
19. 4. the m. of the city, m. of Sodom compassed
5. where are m. which came in to thee this night?
8. only to these m. do nothing || 11. smote the m.
32. 28. power with God and m. and hast prevailed
34. 21. these m. are peaceable with us, let them
22. only herein will the m. consent to us
42. 11. we are true m. 31. || 43. 16. bring m. home
44. 4. Joseph said, up, follow after the m.
46. 32. m. are shepherds, for their trade to feed catt.
Exod. 1. 17. but saved the m. children alive, 18.
10. 11. go now, ye that are m. and serve the Lord
34. 23. thrice in the year shall m. children appear
Num. 1. 17. Moses and Aaron took these m.
13. 32. all the people are m. of great stature
14. 37. those m. that did bring evil report on land
16. 14. wilt thou put out the eyes of these m.?
29. if these m. die the common death of all men
22. 9. God said, what m. are these with thee?
35. the angel said to Balaam, go with the m.
25. 5. slay ye every one his m. that were joined
Deut. 1. 35. not one of these m. shall see good land
32. 26. make remembrance to cease from among m.
33. 6. let Reuben live, let not his m. be few
Josh. 2. 2. there came m. in hither to-night of Israel
3. bring forth the m. that are come, 1 Sam. 11. 12.
Judg. 6. 27. because he feared the m. of the city
8. 8. the m. of Penuel answered as m. of Succoth
15. should give bread to thy m. that are weary
9. 54. that m. say not of me, a woman slew him
16. 9. there were m. lying in wait in the chamber
20. 13. now therefore deliver us the m. of Belial
1 Sam. 2. 26. was in favour with the Lord and m.
† 33. all the increase of thine house shall die, m.

1 *Sam*. 5. 9. he smote the *m*. of city, small and great
12. *m*. that died not were smitten with emerods
24. 9. David said, wherefore hearest thou *m*. words?
25. 15. but the *m*. were very good unto us
2 *Sam*. 3. 39. these *m*. the sons of Zeruiah too hard
10. 12. and let us play the *m*. for our people
19. 28. were but dead *m*. before my lord the king
23. 3. he that ruleth over *m*. must be just
20. slew two lion like *m*. of Moab, 1 *Chr*. 11. 22.
1 *Kings* 10. 8. happy thy *m*. that hear thy wisdom
20. 17. there are *m*. come out of Samaria
33. now the *m*. did diligently observe whether
2 *Kings* 6. 20. Lord, open the eyes of these *m*. to see
12. 15. they reckoned not with *m*. of the money
17. 30. the *m*. of Babylon made Succoth-benoth,
m. of Cuth, Nergal, *m*. of Hamath, Ashima
18. 27. hath he not sent me to the *m*. which sit on
the wall to eat their own dung? *Isa*. 36. 12.
20. 14. said to him, what said these *m*.? *Isa*. 39. 3.
1 *Chron*. 11. 19. shall I drink the blood of these *m*.?
16. 31. let *m*. say among the nations, Lord reigns
19. 5. for the *m*. were greatly ashamed
2 *Chron*. 6. 18. will God in very deed dwell with *m*.?
28. 15. the *m*. expressed by name took the captives
34. 12. and the *m*. did the work faithfully
Ezra 1. 4. let *m*. of his place help him with silver
4. 21. give commandment to cause these *m*. cease
6. 8. I decree that expences be given to these *m*.
Neh. 4. 23. nor *m*. of the guard which followed
5. 5. other *m*. have our lands and vineyards
Job 4. 13. when deep sleep falleth on *m*. 33. 15.
19. † 19. the *m*. of my secret abhorred me
28. 4. are dried up, they are gone away from *m*.
31. 31. if the *m*. of my tabernacle said not
37. 24. *m*. do therefore fear him, he respecteth not
Psal. 9. 20. they may know themselves to be but *m*.
17. 14. from *m*. which are thy hand, from *m*.
49. 18. *m*. will praise thee when thou doest well
62. 9. *m*. of low degree are vanity, *m*. of high a lie
68. 18. ascended, thou hast received gifts for *m*.
72. 17. and *m*. shall be blessed in him, all nations
73. 5. they are not in trouble as other *m*. neither
are they plagued like other *m*.
82. 7. ye are gods, but ye shall die like *m*.
83. 18. that *m*. may know that thou art over all
107. 8. O that *m*. would praise the Lord, 15, 21, 31.
119. † 24. thy testimonies are the *m*. of my counsel
124. 2. on our side, when *m*. rose up against us
145. 6. *m*. shall speak of the might of thy acts
Prov. 6. 30. *m*. do not despise a thief, if he steal
8. 4. to you, O *m*. I call ‖ 16. 6. *m*. depart from evil
20. 6. most *m*. proclaim each his own goodness
25. 1. which the *m*. of Hezekiah copied out
27. so for *m*. to search their own glory, not glory
28. 28. when the wicked rise, *m*. hide themselves
Eccl. 3. 14. God doeth it that *m*. should fear him
Isa. 3. 25. thy *m*. shall fall by the sword, thy mighty
6. 12. and the Lord have removed *m*. far away
7. 13. is it a small thing for you to weary *m*.?
31. 3. now the Egyptians are *m*. and not God
38. 16. O Lord, by these things *m*. live
43. 4. therefore will I give *m*. for thee, and people
45. 24. even to him shall *m*. come, and all incensed
46. 8. remember this, and shew yourselves *m*.
60. 11. that *m*. may bring to thee the forces
61. 6. *m*. shall call you the ministers of our God
64. 4. *m*. have not heard, nor perceived by the ear
Jer. 5. 26. they set a trap, they catch *m*.
6. 23. horses set in array, as *m*. for war against thee
9. 10. neither can *m*. hear the voice of the cattle
18. 21. and let their *m*. be put to death
34. 18. I will give the *m*. that transgr. my covenant
38. 9. these *m*. have done evil to prophet Jeremiah
40. 8. then came to Gedaliah they and their *m*.
47. 2. then the *m*. shall cry and shall howl
49. 28. arise ye, and spoil the *m*. of the east
51. 14. surely I will fill thee with *m*. as with caterp.
Lam. 2. 15. that *m*. call the perfection of beauty
Ezek. 11. 2. these are the *m*. that devise mischief
14. 3. these *m*. set up their idols in their heart
14. tho' these three *m*. Noah, Daniel, Job, 16, 18.
23. 40. that ye have sent for *m*. to come from far
25. 4. I will deliver thee to the *m*. of the east, 10.
34. 31. ye, my flock of my pasture, are *m*. I God
35. 8. I will fill his mountains with his slain *m*.
36. 10. I will multiply *m*. upon you, 37.
Dan. 3. 12. these *m*. have not regarded thee
22. fire slew those *m*. that took up Shadrach
27. saw these *m*. on whose bodies fire had no
power
4. 25. that they shall drive thee from *m*. 32.
6. 5. then said these *m*. we shall not find occasion
26. that *m*. fear before the God of Daniel
Hos. 6. 7. but they like *m*. transgressed the covenant
Obad. 7. *m*. that were at peace deceived thee
† 7. the *m*. of thy peace have deceived thee
Mic. 2. 8. that pass securely, as *m*. averse from war
7. 6. man's enemies are the *m*. of his own house
Hab. 1. 14. and makest *m*. as the fishes of the sea
Zech. 3. 8. thy fellows, they are *m*. wondered at
7. 2. had sent their *m*. to pray before the Lord
11. 6. but lo, I will deliver the *m*. every one
Mat. 5. 16. let your light so shine before *m*.
19. and shall teach *m*. so, shall be called the least
6. 1. take heed you do not your alms before *m*.
16. their faces, that they may appear to *m*. to fast
18. anoint, that thou appear not unto *m*. to fast
7. 12. whatsoever ye would that *m*. should do to
you, do ye even so to them, *Luke* 6. 31.
9. 8. God who had given such power to *m*.
10. 32. shall confess me before *m*. *Luke* 12. 8.
33. whoso shall deny me before *m*. *Luke* 12. 9.
13. 25. but while *m*. slept, his enemy came
16. 13. whom do *m*. say that I am? *Mark* 8. 27.
23. 28. outwardly ye appear righteous to *m*.
Mark 8. 24. and said, I see *m*. as trees walking
10. 27. with *m*. it is impossible, *Luke* 18. 27.
Luke 2. 14. peace on earth, good will toward *m*.
5. 10. from henceforth thou shalt catch *m*.
11. 31. shall rise up with the *m*. of this generation
12. 48 to whom *m*. have committed much
18. 11. I thank thee, I am not as other *m*. are

John 5. 41. I receive not honour from *m*.
17. 6. I have manifested thy name to the *m*.
Acts 1. 21. of these *m*. which have companied with us
2. 13. others said, these *m*. are full of new wine
4. 16. saying, what shall we do to these *m*.?
5. 4. thou hast not lied unto *m*. but unto God
25. the *m*. ye put in prison are in the temple
29. we ought to obey God rather than *m*.
35. what ye intend to do, as touching these *m*.
38. I say unto you, refrain from these *m*.
10. 19. the Spirit said, behold three *m*. seek thee
14. 15. we also are *m*. of like passions with you
15. 26. *m*. that hazarded their lives for Jesus
16. 17. these *m*. are the servants of most high God
35. sent the serjeants, saying, let those *m*. go
19. 37. for ye have brought hither these *m*.
20. 30. also of yourselves shall *m*. arise, speaking
24. 16. conscience void of offence toward G. and *m*.
Rom. 1. 27. *m*. with *m*. working which is unseemly
12. 16. but condescend to *m*. of low estate
1 *Cor*. 4. 9. we are made a spectacle to angels and *m*.
14. 2. for he speaketh not to *m*. but to God
20. not children, but in understanding be *m*.
21. with *m*. of other tongues and lips will I speak
2 *Cor*. 5. 11. the terror of the Lord, we persuade *m*.
8. 13. for I mean not that other *m*. be eased
Gal. 1. 10. do I now persuade *m*.? or seek please *m*.?
Eph. 4. 8. he led captive, and gave gifts to *m*.
5. 28. so ought *m*. to love their wives as their own
6. 7. as to the Lord and not to *m*. *Col*. 3. 23.
1 *Thess*. 2. 4. we speak not as pleasing *m*. but God
1 *Tim*. 2. 8. I will that *m*. pray every where
2 *Tim*. 3. 2. *m*. shall be lovers of themselves, proud
Heb. 5. 1. every high-priest taken from among *m*.
6. 16. for *m*. verily swear by the greater, an oath
7. 8. and here *m*. that die receive tithes
9. 27. as it is appointed unto *m*. once to die
12. 23. to the spirits of just *m*. made perfect
Jam. 3. 9. therewith curse we *m*. which are made
1 *Pet*. 4. 6. might be judged according to *m*. in flesh
2 *Pet*. 1. 21. but holy *m*. of God spake as moved
Jude 4. for there are certain *m*. crept in unawares
Rev. 9. 4. but only those *m*. which have not the seal
10. their power was to hurt *m*. five months
14. 4. these were redeemed from among *m*.
16. 18. such as was not since *m*. were on the earth
21. 3. behold, the tabernacle of God is with *m*.

All MEN.

Gen. 17. 27. *all* the *m*. of his house were circumcised
Exod. 4. 19. *all* the *m*. are dead which sought thy life
Num. 16. 29. if these die the common death of *all m*.
Deut. 4. 3. *all* the *m*. that followed Baal-peor
2 *Sam*. 13. 9. Amnon said, have out *all m*. from me
1 *Kings* 4. 31. for Solomon was wiser than *all m*.
Job 37. 7. that *all m*. may know his work
Psal. 64. 9. *all m*. shall fear, and shall declare
89. 47. wherefore hast thou made *all m*. in vain?
116. 11. I said in my haste, *all m*. are liars
Eccl. 7. 2. for that is the end of *all m*. and living
Jer. 42. 17. so with *all* the *m*. that set their faces
Zech. 8. 10. I set *all m*. every one ag. his neighbour
Mat. 10. 22. and ye shall be hated of *all m*. for my
name's sake, *Mark* 13. 13. *Luke* 21. 17.
19. 11. *all m*. cannot receive this saying, save they
26. 33. tho' *all m*. shall be offended, yet will not I
Mark 1. 37. *all m*. seek thee ‖ 5. 20. *all m*. did marvel
11. 32. *all m*. counted John a prophet indeed
Luke 6. 26. woe to you when *all m*. speak well of you
13. 4. were sinners above *all m*. that dwell in
[Jerusalem
John 1. 7. that *all m*. through him might believe
2. 24. not commit himself, because he knew *all m*.
3. 26. the same baptizeth, and *all m*. come to him
5. 23. that *all m*. should honour the Son, even as
11. 48. if we let alone, *all m*. will believe on him
12. 32. I lifted up from earth, will draw *a. m*. to me
13. 35. by this shall *all m*. know ye are my disciples
Acts 1. 24. Lord, who knowest the hearts of *all m*.
4. 21. *all m*. glorified God for what was done
17. 30. but now commandeth *all m*. to repent
31. whereof he hath given assurance to *all m*.
19. 7. and *all* the *m*. were about twelve
19. and burned their books before *all m*.
20. 26. that I am pure from blood of *all m*.
22. 15. for thou shalt be his witness to *all m*.
Rom. 5. 12. and so death passed upon *all m*. for all
18. judgment came on *all m*. to condemnation,
the free gift came on *all m*. to justification
12. 17. provide things honest in the sight of *all m*.
18. if it be possible, live peaceably with *all m*.
16. 19. your obedience is come abroad to *all m*.
1 *Cor*. 7. 7. I would that *all m*. were even as I
9. 19. for tho' I be free from *all m*. yet servt. to all
22. I am made all things to *all m*. may save some
10. 33. even as I please *all m*. in all things
15. 19. we are of *all m*. most miserable
2 *Cor*. 3. 2. our epistle known and read of *all m*.
Gal. 6. 10. let us do good to *all m*. especially to
household of faith
Eph. 3. 9. to make *all m*. see what is the fellowship
Phil. 4. 5. let your moderation be known to *all m*.
1 *Thess*. 2. 15. please not G. and contrary to *all m*.
3. 12. make you to abound in love toward *all m*.
5. 14. support weak, be patient toward *all m*.
15. but ever follow that which is good to *all m*.
2 *Thess*. 3. 2. for *all m*. have not faith
1 *Tim*. 2. 1. that giving of thanks be made for *all m*.
4. with will have *all m*. to be saved and to come
4. 10. we trust in God, who is Saviour of *all m*.
2 *Tim*. 2. 24. but be gentle to *all m*. apt to teach
3. 9. for their folly shall be made manifest to *all m*.
4. 16. no man stood with me, but *all m*. forsook me
Tit. 2. 11. the grace of God hath appeared to *all m*.
3. 2. be gentle, shewing all meekness to *all m*.
Heb. 12. 14. follow peace with *all m*. and holiness
Jam. 1. 5. let him ask of God, that giveth to *all m*.
1 *Pet*. 2. 17. honour *all m*. love the brotherhood
3 *John* 12. Demetrius hath good report of *all m*.
See BRETHREN, CHIEF, CHOSEN, EVIL, GREAT.

In MEN.

1 *Cor*. 3. 21. therefore let no man glory *in m*.
See ISRAEL, JUDAH.

Like MEN.

1 *Sam*. 4. 9. quit yourselves *like m*. 1 *Cor*. 16. 13.
Psal. 82. 7. ye are gods, but ye shall die *like m*.
Hos. 6. 7. but they *l. m*. have transgressed covenant
Luke 12. 36. yourselves *like m*. that wait for their L.

Mighty MEN.

Gen. 6. 4. *m. m*. which were of old, men of renown
Exod. 15. 15. *m. m*. of Moab trembling shall take
Josh. 1. 14. the *mighty m*. of valour shall pass over
6. 2. I have given thee Jericho and the *mighty m*.
8. 3. Joshua chose out thirty thousand *mighty m*.
10. 2. all the *m*. of Gibeon were *mighty*
7. ascended from Gilgal with *m. m*. of valour
1 *Sam*. 2. 4. the bows of the *mighty m*. were broken
2 *Sam*. 10. 7. when David heard of it he sent Joab
and all the host of the *m*. 20. 7. 1 *Chron*. 19. 8.
16. 6. *mighty m*. were on his right hand and left
17. 8. and his *m*. that they be *mighty* and chafed
23. 8. these be the names of the *mighty m*. David had
9. Eleazar one of the three *m. m*. with David
16. the three *mighty m*. brake thro' the host, 17.
22. Benaiah had the name among three *m. m*.
1 *Kings* 1. 8. the *mighty m*. were not with Adonijah
10. the *mighty m*. and Solomon he called not
2 *Kings* 15. 20. exacted of all *mighty m*. of wealth
24. 14. he carried away all the *m. m*. of valour
1 *Chron*. 5. 24. were *m. m*. of valour, 7. 7, 9, 11, 40.
8. 40. the sons of Ulam were *mighty m*. of valour
11. 10. these also are the chief of the *m. m*. 11.
12. 1. they were among the *mighty m*. helpers
21. were all *m. m*. of valour, 25, 30. | 26. 6, 31.
29. 24. *m. m*. submitted themselves to Solomon
2 *Chron*. 13. 3. Jeroboam set battle against Abijah,
being *mighty m*. of valour, 14. 8. | 17. 13, 14, 16.
25. 6. Amaziah hired an hundred thousand *m. m*.
32. 3. Hezekiah took counsel with his *mighty m*.
21. an angel cut off all the *mighty m*. of valour
Neh. 11. 14. and their brethren *mighty m*. of valour
Job 34. 24. he shall break in pieces *mighty m*.
Eccl. 7. 19. wisdom strengtheneth more than ten *m. m*.
Cant. 4. 4. hang bucklers, all shields of *mighty m*.
Isa. 21. 17. *mighty m*. of Kedar shall be diminished
Jer. 5. 16. an open sepulchre, they are all *m. m*.
26. 21. Jehoiakim the king, with all his *mighty m*.
41. 16. Johanan recovered the *mighty m*. of war
46. 9. let *m. m*. come forth ‖ 48. 14. we are *m. m*.
48. 41. hearts of *m. m*. of Moab, as heart of woman
49. 22. heart of *mighty m*. of Edom shall be as
50. 36. a sword is upon her *m. m*. and they shall
51. 30. *m. m*. of Babylon have forborne to fight
56. her *m. m*. are taken, their bows are broken
57. I will make drunk her captains and *m. m*.
Lam. 1. 15. Lord hath trodden under foot my *m. m*.
Ezek. 39. 20. be filled at my table with *mighty m*.
Dan. 3. 20. commanded *m. m*. to bind Shadrach
Hos. 10. 13. trust in the multitude of thy *mighty m*.
Joel 2. 7. they shall run like *mighty m*. and climb
3. 9. prepare war, wake up the *mighty m*.
Obad. 9. thy *m. m*. O Teman, shall be dismayed
Nah. 2. 3. the shield of his *mighty m*. is made red
Zech. 10. 5. they shall be as *mighty m*. that tread
Rev. 6. 15. *mighty m*. hide themselves in the dens
19. 18. that ye may eat the flesh of *mighty m*.

Of MEN.

Gen. 6. 2. sons of God saw the daughters *of m*.
4. the sons of God came in to the daughters *of m*.
Lev. 27. 29. none devoted *of m*. shall be redeemed
Num. 18. 15. whether it be *of m*. or beasts, be thine
31. 11. took all the prey both *of m*. and beasts
Judg. 8. 18. what manner *of m*. were they ye slew?
1 *Sam*. 1. † 11. give to thy handmaid a seed *of m*.
10. 26. there went with him a band *of m*.
2 *Sam*. 7. 14. I will chasten him with the rod *of m*.
2 *Kings* 13. 21. behold they spied a band *of m*.
23. 14. he filled their places with the bones *of m*.
1 *Chr*. 5. 21. they took away *of m*. ten thousand
2 *Chr*. 22. 1. the band *of m*. had slain all the eldest
Job 7. 20. what shall I do, O thou Preserver *of m*.?
31. † 33. if I covered after the manner *of m*.
33. 16. then he openeth the ears *of m*. and sealeth
Psal. 17. 4. concerning the works *of m*.
22. 6. but I am a reproach *of m*. and despised
Isa. 2. 11. the haughtiness *of m*. shall be bowed down
17. the haughtiness *of m*. shall be made low
29. 13. their fear is taught by the precept *of m*.
44. 11. and the workmen, they are *of m*.
51. 7. fear ye not the reproach *of m*. nor be afraid
53. 3. he is despised and rejected *of m*. a man of
Jer. 9. 22. carcases *of m*. shall fall as dung on field
33. 5. to fill them with the dead bodies *of m*.
Ezek. 16. 17. and madest to thyself images *of m*.
24. 17. and eat not the bread *of m*. 22.
27. 13. they traded the persons *of m*. in market
36. 12. thou shalt no more bereave them *of m*.
38. the waste cities be filled with flocks *of m*.
Dan. 2. 43. they shall mingle with the seed *of m*.
4. 17. the living may know that the Most High
ruleth in the kingdom *of m*. 25, 32. | 5. 21.
and setteth up over it the basest *of m*.
Mic. 2. 12. by reason of multitude *of m*. *Zech*. 2. 4.
Mat. 4. 19. and I will make you fishers *of m*.
5. 13. to be cast out and trodden under foot *of m*.
6. 2. they may have glory *of m*. ‖ 5. seen *of m*. 23. 5.
10. 17. beware *of m*. ‖ 19. 12. made eunuchs *of m*.
15. 9. for doctrines, commandm. *of m*. *Mark* 7. 7.
16. 23. but the things that be *of m*. *Mark* 8. 33.
17. 22. shall be betrayed into the hands *of m*.
Mark 9. 31. *Luke* 9. 44. | 24. 7.
21. 25. was John's baptism of heaven or *of m*.?
26. if we say *of m*. *Mark* 11. 30, 32. *Luke* 20. 4, 6.
22. 16. regardest not persons *of m*. *Mark* 12. 14.
23. 7. love to be called *of m*. Rabbi, Rabbi
Mark 7. 21. out of the heart *of m*. proceed evil
John 1. 4. and the life was the light *of m*.
12. 43. they loved the praise *of m*. more than
18. 3. Judas having received a band *of m*.
Acts 5. 36. to whom a number *of m*. joined
38. if this work be *of m*. it will come to nought
14. 11. the gods are come down in likeness *of m*.
15. 17. the residue *of m*. might seek after God
17. 12. honourable women, and *of m*. not a few
Rom. 1. 18. against all unrighteousness *of m*.

Rom. 2. 16. when God shall judge the secrets of m.
29. whose praise is not of m. but of God
6. 19. I speak after the manner of m. because
14. 18. that serveth Christ is approved of m.
1 Cor. 2. 5. faith not stand in the wisdom of m.
4. 6. ye might learn in us not to think of m.
7. 23. ye are bought, be not the servants of m.
13. 1. though I speak with tongues of m. and angels
15. 32. if after the manner of m. I have fought
2 Cor. 8. 21. honest things in the sight of m.
Gal. 1. 1. Paul an apostle, not of m. but by Christ
3. 15. brethren, I speak after the manner of m.
Eph. 4. 14. wind of doctrine, by sleight of m.
Phil. 2. 7. and was made in the likeness of m.
Col. 2. 8. vain deceit, after the tradition of m.
22. after commandments and doctrines of m.
1 Thess. 1. 5. ye know what manner of m. we were
2. 6. nor of m. sought we glory, neither of you
13. ye received it not as the word of m.
1 Tim. 6. 5. disputings of m. of corrupt minds
Tit. 1. 14. commandments of m. that turn from truth
1 Pet. 2. 4. disallowed indeed of m. but chosen of G.
15. may put to silence ignorance of foolish m.
4. 2. he should no longer live to the lusts of m.
1 John 5. 9. if we receive the witness of m.
Rev. 9. 7. their faces were as the faces of m.
15. prepared to slay the third part of m. 18.
11. 13. in the earthquake were slain of m. 7000
13. 13. maketh fire come down in sight of m.
18. 13. merchandise of slaves and souls of m.
See CHILDREN.

Sons of MEN.

Ps. 4. 2. O ye s. of m. how long will ye turn, 58. 1.
31. 19. that trust in thee before the sons of m.
33. 13. the Lord beholdeth all the sons of m.
57. 4. I lie among the sons of m. whose teeth are
145. 12. to make known to s. of m. his mighty acts
Prov. 8. 31. and my delights were with the s. of m.
Eccl. 1. 13. travail God hath given to the sons of m.
2. 3. might see what was that good for sons of m.
8. and I gat me the delights of the sons of men
3. 10. travail which God hath given to sons of m.
18. I said concerning the estate of the sons of m.
19. for that which befalleth the sons of m.
8. 11. heart of sons of m. set in them to do evil
9. 3. also the heart of the sons of m. is full of evil
12. so are the sons of m. snared in an evil time
Isa. 52. 14. and his form more than the sons of m.
Jer. 32. 19. thine eyes are open upon the sons of m.
Dan. 5. 21. and he was driven from the sons of m.
10. 16. one like the similitude of the sons of m.
Joel 1. 12. joy is withered away from the sons of m.
Mic. 5. 7. tarrieth not, nor waiteth for the sons of m.
Mark 3. 28. all sins shall be forgiven to sons of m.
Eph. 3. 5. which was not made known to sons of m.
See OLD, RICH, RIGHTEOUS, SINGING.

MEN-servants.

Gen. 12. 16. Abram had m.-s. and maid-servants
20. 14. Abimelech gave m.-servants to Abraham
24. 35. God hath given my master m.-s. and gold
30. 43. Jacob had m.-s. and camels, and asses, 32. 5.
Exod. 21. 7. she shall not go out as m.-servants do
Deut. 12. 12. rejoice before Lord, ye and m.-serv.
1 Sam. 8. 16. the king will take you m.-servants
2 Kings 5. 26. is it a time to receive m-servants?
Luke 12. 45. and shall begin to beat the m.-servants
See TWO.

MEN of War.

Num. 31. 49. servants have taken sum of m. of war
Deut. 2. 14. till all the generation of the m. of war came out of Egypt were consumed, 16. Josh. 5. 6.
Josh. 6. 3. ye shall compass the city, ye m. of war
Judg. 20. 17. drew sword, all these were m. of war
1 Sam. 18. 5. and Saul set him over the m. of war
1 Kings 9. 22. but they were m. of war, and the chief of his captains, 2 Chron. 8. 9.
2 Kings 25. 4. and all the m. of war fled, Jer. 52. 7.
19. took an officer set over m. of war, Jer. 52. 25.
1 Chron. 12. 8. of Gadites m. of war came to David
38. all these m. of war came to Hebron to make
2 Chr. 13. 3. Abijah set battle in array with m. of w.
17. 13. and the m. of war were in Jerusalem
Jer. 38. 4. thus he weakeneth the hands of m. of war
41. 3. slew m. of war ‖ 51. 32. m. of w. are affrighted
16. Johanan took the m. of war and the women
49. 26. all the m. of war shall be cut off, 50. 30.
Ezek. 27. 10. they of Phut were thy m. of war
27. all thy m. of war that are in thee shall fall
39. 20. shall be filled at my table with m. of war
Joel 2. 7. they shall climb the wall like m. of war
3. 9. let all the m. of w. draw near, let them come
Luke 23. 11. Herod with his m. of w. set him at nought

MEN, joined with wicked.

Gen. 13. 13. but the m. of Sodom were wicked
Num. 16. 26. depart from tents of these wicked m.
1 Sam. 30. 22. then answered all the wicked m.
2 Sam. 3. 34. as a man falleth before wicked m.
4. 11. how much more when wicked m. have slain
Job 22. 15. marked old way that w. m. have trodden
34. 8. and which walketh with wicked m.
26. he striketh them as wicked m. in open sight
36. because of his answers for wicked m.
Eccl. 8. 14. there be w. m. to whom it happeneth
Jer. 5. 26. among my people are found wicked m.
Mat. 24. 41. will miserably destroy those wicked m.
2 Thess. 3. 2. that we may be delivered from w. m.

Wise MEN.

Gen. 41. 8. Pharaoh called for all w. m. Exod. 7. 11.
Exod. 36. 4. all the wise m. that wrought the work
Deut. 1. 13. take ye wise m. and understanding
15. I took the chief of your tribes, wise m.
Esth. 1. 13. king said to wise m. that knew the times
6. 13. then said Haman's wise m. and Zeresh
Job 15. 18. which w. m. have told from their fathers
34. 2. hear my words, O ye wise m. and give ear
Psal. 49. 10. he seeth that wise m. die, and the fool
Prov. 10. 14. wise m. lay up knowledge, but foolish
13. 20. he that walketh with wise m. shall be wise
29. 8. but wise m. turn away wrath
Eccl. 9. 17. the words of wise m. are heard in quiet
Isa. 19. 12. where are thy wise m. let them tell
29. 14. the wisdom of their wise m. shall perish
Isa. 44. 25. that turneth wise m. backward
Jer. 8. 9. the wise m. are ashamed and dismayed
10. 7. as among all the wise m. of the nations
50. 35. sword is upon Babylon, and on her wise m.
51. 57. and I will make drunken her wise m.
Ezek. 27. 8. thy wise m. O Tyrus, were thy pilots
9. and the wise m. thereof were thy calkers
Dan. 2. 12. to destroy all the wise m. of Babylon
27. cannot the wise m. shew unto the king
4. 6. I made a decree to bring in all the wise m.
5. 7. Belshazzar the king spake to the wise m.
Obad. 8. even destroy the wise m. out of Edom
Mat. 2. 1. came wise m. from the east to Jerusalem
7. Herod, when he had privily called the wise m.
16. was mocked of wise m. ‖ 23. 34. I send wise m.
1 Cor. 1. 26. not many wise m. not noble, are called
10. 15. speak as to wise m. judge ye what I say

MEN, joined with women.

Exod. 35. 22. both m. and women brought bracelets
Deut. 2. 34. we utterly destroyed the m. and women, and little ones, of every city, Josh. 8. 25.
Judg. 9. 49. died about a thousand m. and women
51. and thither fled all the m. and women
16. 27. now the house was full of m. and women, were upon the roof about 3000 m. and women
2 Sam. 6. 19. he dealt as well to the women as m.
Neh. 8. 2. brought the law before m. and women, 3.
Jer. 44. 20. Jeremiah said to the m. and women
Acts 5. 14. were added to Lord both m. and women
8. 3. Saul, haling m. and women, committed them
12. they were baptized, both m. and women
9. 2. whether m. or w. he might bring them bound
22. 4. delivering into prison both m. and women
MEN, Women, and Children. See CHILDREN.

Ye MEN.

Judg. 9. 7. hearken unto me, ye m. of Shechem
Job 34. 10. hearken, ye m. of understanding
Acts 1. 11. ye m. of Galilee ‖ 2. 14. ye m. of Judea
5. 35. ye m. of Israel ‖ 17. 22. ye m. of Athens
13. 15. ye m. and brethren, if ye have any word
19. 35. ye m. of Ephesus, what man is there

Young MEN.

Gen. 14. 24. that which the young m. have eaten
Exod. 24. 5. Moses sent young m. which offered burnt
Num. 11. 28. Joshua one of the young m. answered
Josh. 6. 23. the young m. that were spies went in
Judg. 14. 10. for so used the young m. to do
Ruth 2. 9. have I not charged the young m. that
3. 10. inasmuch as thou followedst not young m.
1 Sam. 2. 17. the sin of the young m. was very great
8. 16. he will take your goodliest young m.
21. 4. if the young m. kept themselves from women
5. and the vessels of the young m. are holy
25. 8. ask thy young m. and they will shew thee
25. thine handmaid saw not the young m.
26. 22. let one of the young m. come over and fetch
30. 17. save 400 young m. which rode on camels
2 Sam. 1. 15. and David called one of the young m.
2. 14. let the young m. arise and play before us
21. and lay thee hold on one of the young m.
13. 32. not suppose they have slain all the young m.
18. 15. and ten young m. that bare Joab's armour
1 Kings 12. 8. Rehoboam consulted with young m.
14. spake after counsel of y. m. 2 Chron. 10. 8, 14.
20. 14. by young m. of the princes of the provinces
2 Kings 4. 22. send, I pray thee, one of the young m.
5. 22. there be come two young m. of the prophets
8. 12. their young m. wilt thou slay with the sword
2 Chron. 36. 17. who slew their young m. with sword
Job 1. 19. it fell upon the young m. they are dead
29. 8. the young m. saw me, and hid themselves
Psal. 78. 63. the fire consumed their young m.
148. 12. praise the Lord, young m. and maidens
Prov. 20. 29. the glory of young m. is their strength
Isa. 9. 17. Lord shall have no joy in their young m
13. 18. their bows also shall dash young m. to pieces
23. 4. neither do I nourish up young m. nor virgins
31. 8. and his young m. shall be discomfited
40. 30. and the young m. shall utterly fall
42. † 22. spoiled in snaring all the young m. of
Jer. 6. 11. I will pour fury on assembly of y. m.
9. 21. to cut off the young m. from the streets
11. 22. the young m. shall die by the sword
15. 8. I brought against the mother of the y. m.
18. 21. let their young m. be slain by the sword
31. 13. both young m. and old rejoice together
48. 15. his chosen young m. are gone to slaughter
49. 26. her young m. shall fall in her streets
50. 30. therefore shall her y. m. fall in the streets
51. 3. spare ye not her young m. destroy utterly
Lam. 1. 15. called an assembly to crush my y. m.
18. my virgins and y. m. are gone into captivity
2. 21. the young m. and old lie on the ground
5. 13. they took the young m. to grind, children fell
14. the young m. have ceased from their music
Ezek. 23. 6. all of them desirable young m. 12, 23.
30. 17. young m. of Aven shall fall by the sword
Joel 2. 28. your y. m. shall see visions, Acts 2. 17.
Amos 2. 11. and of your young m. for Nazarites
4. 10. your young m. have I slain with the sword
8. 13. and your young m. shall faint for thirst
Zech. 9. 17. corn shall make the young m. cheerful
Mark 14. 51. and the young m. laid hold on him
Acts 5. 6. and the young m. arose, wound him up
10. the young m. came in and found her dead
Tit. 2. 6. young m. likewise exhort to be sober
1 John 2. 13. I write to you, young m. because, 14.

MEND.

2 Chr. 24. 12. brass to m. the house of the Lord
34. 10. they gave it to workmen to m. the house

MENDING.

Mat. 4. 21. with Zebedee m. their nets, Mark 1. 19.

MEN-pleasers.

Eph. 6. 6. not with eye-service, as m.-p. Col. 3. 22.

MEN-stealers.

1 Tim. 1. 10. the law is made for m.-stealers, for liars

MENSTRUOUS.

Isa. 30. 22. thou shalt cast them away as a m. cloth
Lam. 1. 17. Jerusalem is as a m. woman among them
Ezek. 18. 6. neither hath come near to a m. woman

MENTION.

Gen. 40. 14. and make m. of me unto Pharaoh
Exod. 23. 13. make no m. of other gods, Josh. 23. 7
1 Sam. 4. 18. when he made m. of the ark of God
Job 28. 18. no m. shall be made of coral or pearls
Psal. 71. 16. I will make m. of thy righteousness
87. 4. I will make m. of Rahab and Babylon
Isa. 12. 4. make m. that his name is exalted
19. 17. that maketh m. thereof shall be afraid
26. 13. by thee only we will make m. of thy name
48. 1. and make m. of the God of Israel, but not
49. 1. from bowels hath he made m. of my name
62. 6. ye that make m. of the Lord, keep not silence
Jer. 4. 16. make ye m. to nations, publish agst. Jerus.
20. 9. I will not make m. of him, nor speak more
Amos 6. 10. we may not make m. of name of Lord
Rom. 1. 9. without ceasing I make m. of you always in my prayers, Eph. 1. 16. 1 Thess. 1. 2.
Phil. 1. † 3. I thank my God on every m. of you
Philem. 4. making m. of thee always in my prayers
Heb. 11. 22. Joseph made m. of the departing of Isr.

MENTION.

Isa. 63. 7. I will m. the loving-kindnesses of the L.
Jer. 23. 36. burden of the Lord shall ye m. no more

MENTIONED.

Josh. 21. 9. these cities, which are m. by name
1 Chron. 4. 38. these m. by name were princes
2 Chron. 20. 34. Jehu is m. in the book of the kings
Ezek. 16. 56. for thy sister Sodom was not m.
18. 22. his transgressions shall not be m. to him
24. all his righteousness shall not be m.
33. 16. none of his sins shall be m. unto him

MERCHANDISE.

Deut. 21. 14. thou shalt not make m. of her
24. 7. stealing his brethren, and maketh m. of him
Prov. 3. 14. m. of it is better than the m. of gold
31. 18. she perceiveth that her m. is good
Isa. 23. 18. her m. shall be holiness to the Lord
45. 14. the m. of Ethiopia shall come over to thee
Jer. 14. † 18. priest make m. against a land
Ezek. 26. 12. they shall make a prey of thy m.
27. 9. the ships were in thee to occupy thy m.
15. many isles were the m. of thy hands
28. 16. by the multitude of thy m. they have filled
Mat. 22. 5. one to his farm, another to his m.
John 2. 16. make not my Father's house a house of m
2 Pet. 2. 3. with feigned words make m. of you
Rev. 18. 11. no man buyeth their m. any more
12. the m. of gold, and silver, and of pearls

MERCHANT.

Gen. 23. 16. silver current money with the m.
37. 28. then there passed by Midianites m.-men
1 Kings 10. 15. besides that he had of the m.-men
Prov. 31. 14. she is like the m. ships, she brings
24. maketh linen, and delivereth girdles to the m.
Cant. 3. 6. perfumed with all powders of the m.
Isa. 23. 11. a commandment against the m. city
Ezek. 27. 3 which art a m. of the people for isles
12. Tarshish was thy m. by reason of multitude
16. Syria ‖ 18. Damascus, ‖ 20. Dedan was m.
Hos. 12. 7. he is a m. balances of deceit in his hand
Zeph. 1. 11. for all the m. people are cut down
Mat. 13. 45. like a m.-man seeking goodly pearls

MERCHANTS.

1 Kings 10. 15. and of the traffic of spice m.
28. the king's m. received linen yarn, 2 Chr. 1. 16.
2 Chron. 9. 14. besides that which m. brought
Neh. 3. 32. repaired the goldsmiths and the m.
13. 20. so the m. lodged without Jerusalem
Job 41. 6. shall they part him among the m.?
Isa. 23. 2. whom the m. of Zidon replenished
8. the crowning city, whose m. are princes
47. 15. even thy m. they shall wander every one
Ezek. 17. 4. cropt the twigs, he set it in a city of m.
27. 13. Javan, Tubal, and Meshech, were thy m.
15. Dedan ‖ 17. Judah and Israel thy m.
21. in these were thy m. ‖ 22. m. of Sheba, 23.
24. these were thy m. in all sorts of things
36. m. shall hiss at thee ‖ 38. 13. m. of Tarshish
Nah. 3. 16. hast multiplied thy m. above the stars
Rev. 18. 3. for the m. of the earth are waxen rich
11. the m. of the earth shall weep over her
23. for thy m. were the great men of the earth

MERCY

Signifies, [1] *That essential perfection in God, whereby he pities and relieves the miseries of his creatures*, Psal. 100. 5. Tit. 3. 5. [2] *Grace, which flows from mercy as its fountain*, Jude 2. [3] *Eternal life and happiness in heaven, which is the chief fruit of mercy*, 2 Tim. 1. 18. [4] *All the blessings and benefits, whether bodily or spiritual, which proceed from the mercy of God*, Psal. 106. 7. | 119. 41. [5] *That pity and compassion which one man shews towards another that is in misery*, Luke 10. 37. [6] *Clemency and bounty*, Prov. 20. 28. [7] *All duties of charity towards our neighbour*, Mat. 9. 13. [8] *Pretended acts of mercy*, Prov. 12. 10.

Gen. 24. 27. not left destitute my master of m. truth
43. 14. and God give you m. before the man
Exod. 34. 7. keeping m. for thousands, Dan. 9. 4.
Num. 14. 18. the Lord is long-suffering and of great m. forgiving iniquity, Psal. 103. 11. | 145. 8.
Deut. 7. 9. who keepeth covenant and m. 12.
2 Sam. 7. 15. but my m. shall not depart from him, 1 Chron. 17. 13. Psal. 89. 24.
15. 20. return thou, m. and truth be with thee
1 Kings 8. 23. who keepest covenant and m. with thy servants, Neh. 1. 5. | 9. 32.
1 Chron. 16. 34. his m. endureth for ever, 41. 2 Chron. 5. 13. | 7. 3, 6. | 20. 21. Ezra 3. 11. Psal. 106. 1. | 107. 1. | 118. 1. | 136. 1. to the end, Jer. 33. 11.
Ezra 7. 28. hath extended m. to me before the king
9. 9. extended m. to us in sight of the kings of Persia
Neh. 1. 11. grant him m. in the sight of this man
Job 37. 13. whether for correction or for m.
Psal. 21. 7. and through the m. of the Most High
23. 6. surely goodness and m. shall follow me
25. 10. all the paths of the Lord are m. and truth
32. 10. that trusts in Ld. m. shall compass him about
33. † 5. the earth is full of the m. of the Lord
18. the eye of Lord is on them that hope in his m.

Psal. 52. 8. I trust in the *m.* of God for ever and ever
57. 3. God shall send forth his *m.* and truth
59. 10. the God of my *m.* shall prevent me, 17.
61. 7. O prepare *m.* and truth which may preserve
62. 12. also unto thee, O Lord, belongeth *m.*
66. 20. which hath not turned his *m.* from me
77. 8. is his *m.* clean gone for ever? doth *m.* fail?
85. 10. *m.* and truth are met together, righteousness
86. 5. thou, Lord, art plenteous in *m.* 15. | 103. 8.
89. 2. I said, *m.* shall be built up for ever
14. *m.* and truth shall go before thy face
28. my *m.* will I keep for him for evermore
98. 3. he hath remembered his *m.* toward Israel
100. 5. the Lord is good, his *m.* is everlasting
101. 1. I will sing of *m.* and judgment, to thee
103. 17. the *m.* of the Lord is from everlasting
109. 12. let there be none to extend *m.* to him
130. 7. with the Lord there is *m.* and redemption
144. † 2. Lord is my *m.* and my fortress, and tower
147. 11. takes pleasure in those that hope in his *m.*
Prov. 3. 3. let not *m.* and truth forsake thee
14. 21. he that hath *m.* on the poor, happy is he
22. *m.* and truth shall be to them that devise good
31. he that honoureth God hath *m.* on the poor
16. 6. by *m.* and truth iniquity is purged
20. 28. *m.* and truth preserve the king, and his throne is upholden by *m.* *Isa.* 16. 5.
21. 21. he that followeth after *m.* findeth life
Isa. 49. 10. he that hath *m.* on them shall lead them
54. 10. saith the Lord that hath *m.* on thee
60. 10. but in my favour have I had *m.* on thee
Jer. 6. 23. they are cruel, and have no *m.*
Hos. 1. † 6. call her name, not having obtained *m.*
2. † 1. say to brethren and sisters, having obtain. *m.*
4. 1. because there is no truth, nor *m.* in the land
6. † 4. for your *m.* is as a morning cloud, and dew
6. for I desired *m.* and not sacrifice
10. 12. reap in *m.* ‖ 12. 6. keep *m.* and wait on G.
14. 3. for in thee the fatherless findeth *m.*
Jonah 2. 8. they forsake their own *m.*
Mic. 6. 8. but to do justly, and to love *m.*
7. 18. retains not anger, because he delighteth in *m.*
20. thou wilt perform the *m.* to Abraham
Hab. 3. 2. O Lord, in wrath remember *m.*
Mat. 5. 7. blessed are the merciful, shall obtain *m.*
23. 23. and have omitted judgment and *m.*
Luke 1. 50. his *m.* is on them that fear him
54. holpen Israel in remembrance of his *m.*
72. to perform the *m.* promised to our fathers
78. by remission through the tender *m.* of our G.
Rom. 9. 23. the riches of his glory on vessels of *m.*
11. 30. have now obtained *m.* thro' their unbelief
31. that through your *m.* they also may obtain *m.*
15. 9. that Gentiles might glorify God for his *m.*
1 *Cor.* 7. 25. that hath obtained *m.* to be faithful
2 *Cor.* 4. 1. as we have received *m.* we faint not
Gal. 6. 16. peace be on them, and *m.* and on Israel
Eph. 2. 4. God who is rich in *m.* hath quickened us
Phil. 2. 27. was nigh to death, but G. had *m.* on him
1 *Tim.* 1. 2. *m.* and peace from God our Father, and J. Christ our L. 2 *Tim.* 1. 2. *Tit.* 1. 4. 2 *John* 3.
13. but I obtained *m.* because I did it ignorantly
16. howbeit, for this cause I obtained *m.*
2 *Tim.* 1. 16. L. give *m.* to the house of Onesiphorus
18. that he may find *m.* of the Lord in that day
Tit. 3. 5. but according to his *m.* he saved us
Heb. 4. 16. that we may obtain *m.* and find grace
10. 28. he that despised Moses' law died without *m.*
Jam. 2. 13. he shall have judgment without *m.* that shewed no *m.* and *m.* rejoiceth against judgment
3. 17. the wisdom that is from above is full of *m.*
5. 11. the Lord is very pitiful and of tender *m.*
1 *Pet.* 1. 3. accord. to his abundant *m.* hath begotten
2. 10. had not obtained *m.* but now have obtained *m.*
Jude 2. *m.* to you, peace and love be multiplied
21. looking for the *m.* of Lord Jesus to eternal life

Have MERCY.

Psal. 4. 1. *have m.* upon me, 6. 2. | 9. 13. | 25. 16. | 27. 7. | 30. 10. | 31. 9. | 51. 1. | 86. 16.
102. 13. shalt *h. m.* on Zion ‖ 123. 2. *h. m.* on us, 3.
Prov. 28. 13. whoso forsaketh his sins shall *have m.*
Isa. 9. 17. neither *h. m.* on their fatherless and widows
14. 1. for Lord will *have m.* on Jacob, and choose
27. 11. he that made them will not *have m.* on them
30. 18. be exalted, that he may *have m.* on you
49. 13. for God will *have m.* upon his afflicted
54. 8. with everlasting kindness will I *h. m.* on thee
55. 7. let him return, and he will *have m.* on him
Jer. 13. 14. nor *have m.* but destroy them, 21. 7.
30. 18. and I will *have m.* on his dwelling-places
31. 20. I will surely *have m.* on him, 33. 26. *Ezek.* 39. 25. *Hos.* 1. 7. | 2. 23.
42. 12. that he may *have m.* on you, and cause you
Hos. 1. 6. no more *h. m.* on the house of Israel, 2. 4.
Zech. 1. 12. O Lord, how long wilt thou not *have m.*
10. 6. I will bring them again, for I *h. m.* upon them
Mat. 9. 13. I will *have m.* and not sacrifice, 12. 7.
27. thou Son of David, *have m.* on me, 15. 22. | 20. 30, 31. *Mark* 10. 47, 48. *Luke* 18. 38, 39.
17. 15. Lord, *have m.* on my son, for he is lunatic
Luke 16. 24. father Abraham, *h. m.* on me, and send
17. 13. they said, Jesus, Master, *have m.* on us
Rom. 9. 15. I will *have m.* on whom I will *h. m.* 18.
11. 32. all in unbelief, that he might *have m.* on all

MERCY, joined with *shew, shewed, sheweth, shewing.*

Gen. 39. 21. L. was with Joseph, and *shewed* him *m.*
Exod. 20. 6. *shewing m.* to thousands, *Deut.* 5. 10.
33. 19. I will *shew m.* on whom I will *shew m.*
Deut. 7. 2. shalt make no covenant, nor *shew* them *m.*
13. 17. that the Lord may turn and *shew* thee *m.*
Judg. 1. 24. *shew* us city, and we will *shew* thee *m.*
2 *Sam.* 22. 51. *sheweth m.* to his anointed, *Ps.* 18. 50.
1 *Kings* 3. 6. Solomon said, thou hast *shewed* to thy servant David, my father, great *m.* 2 *Chron.* 1. 8.
2 *Chron.* 6. 14. and *shewest m.* to thy servants
Psal. 37. 21. but the righteous *sheweth m.* and giveth
85. 7. *shew* us thy *m.* O Lord, and grant thy salvat.
109. 16. because he remembered not to *shew m.*
Isa. 47. 6. and thou didst *shew* them no *m.*
Jer. 50. 42. they are cruel, and will not *shew m.*
Dan. 4. 27. break off thy sins, by *shewing m.*

Zech. 7. 9. execute true judgment, and *shew m.*
Luke 1. 58. how the Lord *shewed* great *m.* on her
10. 37. and he said, he that *shewed m.* on him
Rom. 9. 16. not that runs, but of God that *sheweth m.*
12. 8. he that *sheweth m.* with cheerfulness
Jam. 2. 13. judgment without *m.* that hath *shewed* [no *m.*

Thy MERCY.

Gen. 19. 19. and thou hast magnified *thy m.* to me
Exod. 15. 13. in *thy m.* hast led forth the people
Num. 14. 19. according to the greatness of *thy m.*
Neh. 13. 22. spare me according to *thy m.*
Psal. 5. 7. into thy house, in multitude of *thy m.*
6. 4. return, O L. save me for *thy m.* sake, 31. 16.
13. 5. I have trusted in *t. m.* my heart shall rejoice
25. 7. according to *thy m.* remember thou me
31. 7. I will be glad and rejoice in *thy m.* for thou
33. 22. let *thy m.* O Lord, be upon us, as we hope
36. 5. *thy m.* O Lord, is in the heavens
44. 26. arise, and redeem us, for *thy m.* sake
57. 10. for *thy m.* is great unto the heavens
59. 16. I will sing aloud of *thy m.* in the morning
69. 13. in the multitude of *thy m.* hear me
85. 7. shew us *thy m.* O L. ‖ 86. 13. great is *thy m.*
90. 14. O satisfy us early with *thy m.* to rejoice
94. 18. my foot slippeth, *thy m.* O Lord, held me up
108. 4. for *thy m.* is great above the heavens
109. 21. because *thy m.* is good, deliver thou me
26. O Lord my God, save me according to *thy m.*
115. 1. for *thy m.* and for thy truth's sake
119. 64. the earth, O Lord, is full of *thy m.*
124. deal with thy servant according to *thy m.*
138. 8. *thy m.* endureth for ever, forsake not
143. 12. and of *thy m.* cut off mine enemies

MERCIES.

Gen. 32. 10. not worthy of the least of thy *m.*
2 *Sam.* 24. 14. for his *m.* are great, 1 *Chron.* 21. 13.
2 *Chr.* 6. 42. remember the *m.* of David thy servant
Neh. 9. 19. in thy manifold *m.* forsookest them not
27. according to thy *m.* thou gavest them saviours
28. many times didst deliver according to thy *m.*
31. for thy *m.* thou didst not consume them
Ps. 51. 1. according to thy *m.* blot out my transgr.
69. 13. in the multitude of thy *m.* hear me
16. turn unto me, according to thy tender *m.*
89. 1. I will sing of the *m.* of the Lord for ever
106. 7. they remembered not multitude of thy *m.*
45. he repented according to multitude of his *m.*
119. 41. let thy *m.* come also to me, O Lord
Isa. 54. 7. with great *m.* will I gather thee
55. 3. even the sure *m.* of David, *Acts* 13. 34.
63. 7. he bestowed on them according to his *m.*
15. where is thy zeal and thy *m.* towards me?
Jer. 16. 5. I have taken away my *m.* from this peop.
42. 12. will shew *m.* to you that he may have mercy
Lam. 3. 22. it is of Lord's *m.* we are not consumed
32. have compassion according to mult. of his *m.*
Dan. 2. 18. would desire *m.* concerning this secret
9. 9. to the L. our God belong *m.* and forgivenesses
18. not for our righteousness, but thy great *m.*
Hos. 2. 19. I will betroth thee unto me in *m.*
Zech. 1. 16. I am returned to Jerusalem with *m.*
Rom. 12. 1. I beseech you by the *m.* of God
2 *Cor.* 1. 3. the Father of *m.* and God of all comfort
Phil. 2. 1. if there be any fellowship, any bowels [of *m.*
Col. 3. 12. put on therefore bowels of *m.* kindness

Tender MERCIES.

Ps. 25. 6. remember, O Lord, thy *tender. m.* 51. 1.
40. 11. withhold not thy *tender m.* from me
77. 9. hath he in anger shut up his *tender m.*
79. 8. let thy *tender m.* speedily prevent us
103. 4. bless L. who crowneth thee with *tender m.*
119. 77. let thy *tender m.* come unto me, that I may
156. great are thy *tender m.* O Lord, quicken me
145. 9. his *tender m.* are over all his works
Prov. 12. 10. the *tender m.* of the wicked are cruel

MERCIFUL.

Gen. 19. 16. the Lord being *m.* unto Lot
Exod. 34. 6. proclaimed Lord God *m.* and gracious
Deut. 21. 8. be *m.* O Lord, to thy people Israel
32. 43. and will be *m.* to his land and people
2 *Sam.* 22. 26. with the *m.* thou wilt shew thyself *m.* with upright thyself upright, *Psal.* 18. 25.
1 *Kings* 20. 31. heard that kings of Isr. are *m.* kings
2 *Chron.* 30. 9. Lord your God is gracious and *m.*
Neh. 9. 17. art G. ready to pardon, gracious and *m.*
Psal. 26. 11. redeem me, and be *m.* to me, 41. 4, 10. | 56. 1. | 57. 1. | 86. 3. | 119. 58, 132.
37. 26. the righteous is ever *m.* and lendeth
59. 5. be not *m.* to any wicked transgressors
67. 1. G. be *m.* to us, and bless us, and cause his face
103. 8. Lord is *m.* and gracious, slow to anger
117. 2. for his *m.* kindness is great toward us
119. 76. let thy *m.* kindness be for my comfort
Prov. 11. 17. the *m.* man doeth good to his own soul
Isa. 57. 1. *m.* men are taken away, none considering
Jer. 3. 12. return, for I am *m.* saith the Lord
Joel 2. 13. he is gracious and *m.* slow to anger
Jonah 4. 2. for I knew that thou art a *m.* God
Mat. 5. 7. blessed are the *m.* they shall obtain mercy
Luke 6. 36. be ye *m.* as your father also is *m.*
18. 13. publican saying, God be *m.* to me a sinner
Heb. 2. 17. that he might be a *m.* High-priest
8. 12. I will be *m.* to their unrighteousness

See God.

MERCY-SEAT,

Or Propitiatory, *was the covering of the ark of the covenant, or of the holy chest, in which the tables of the law were deposited: this cover was of gold, and at its two ends were fixed the two cherubims of the same metal, which by their wings extended forward, seemed to form a throne for the majesty of God, who in Scripture is represented as sitting between the cherubims,* Psal. 80. 1. *and the ark itself was as it were his footstool. It was an eminent type of Christ, who by his atonement covered our sins, and bore the curse for us; standing between God and the curse of the law for our sakes, that God might look on the law through Christ, as fulfilled by him on our behalf,* Gal. 3. 10, 13. *Hence Christ is called the* Propitiation, *Rom.* 3. 25.

Exod. 25. 17. and thou shalt make a *m.-seat* of gold

Exod. 25. 20. cherub. cov. *m.-s.* with wings, *Heb.* 9. 5.
22. I will commune with thee from above *m.-seat* between the cherubims, *Lev.* 16. 2. *Num.* 7. 89.
26. 34. shalt put the *m.-seat* upon the ark, 40. 20.
37. 6. and he made the *m.-seat* of pure gold
Lev. 16. 13. cloud of incense may cover the *m.-seat*
1 *Chr.* 28. 11. David gave Solom. pattern of *m.-seat*

MERRY.

Gen. 43. 34. they drank and were *m.* with him
Judg. 9. 27. they trode the grapes, and made *m.*
16. 25. their hearts were *m.* they said, call Samson
19. 6. tarry all night, and let thine heart be *m.*
9. lodge here, that thine heart may be *m.*
22. now as they were making their hearts *m.*
Ruth 3. 7. and when Boaz his heart was *m.* he went
1 *Sam.* 25. 36. Nabal's heart was *m.* within him
2 *Sam.* 13. 28. mark when Amnon's heart is *m.*
1 *Kings* 4. 20. Judah and Israel were making *m.*
21. 7. arise, eat bread, and let thine heart be *m.*
2 *Chr.* 7. 10. he sent the people away *m.* in heart
Esth. 1. 10. when the heart of the king was *m.*
Prov. 15. 13. *m.* heart maketh cheerful countenance
15. he that is of a *m.* heart hath a continual feast
17. 22. a *m.* heart doeth good like a medicine
Eccl. 8. 15. hath nothing better than to eat and be *m.*
9. 7. and drink thy wine with a *m.* heart
10. 19. feast made for laughter, wine maketh *m.*
Isa. 24. 7. vine languisheth, all the *m.* hearted do sigh
Jer. 30. 19. the voice of them that make *m.*
31. 4. in the dances of them that make *m.*
Luke 12. 19. take thine ease, eat, drink, and be *m.*
15. 23. let us eat and be *m.* 24. | 29. I might be *m.*
32. it was meet we should make *m.* and be glad
Jam. 5. 13. is any *m.*? let him sing psalms
Rev. 11. 10. shall rejoice over them and make *m*

MERRILY.

Esth. 5. 14. then go thou in *m.* with the king

MESSAGE.

Judg. 3. 20. Ehud said, I have a *m.* from G. to thee
1 *Kings* 20. 12. when Benhadad had heard this *m.*
Prov. 26. 6. he that sendeth a *m.* by fool cutteth off
Hag. 1. 13. then spake Haggai in the Lord's *m.*
Luke 19. 14. his citizens sent a *m.* after him
1 *John* 1. 5. this is the *m.* which we have heard, 3. 11.

MESSENGER

Signifies, *One who carries messages between party and party,* Gen. 32. 3. | 50. 16. It is applied, [1] *To Christ Jesus, called the* Messenger of the covenant, *Mal.* 3. 1. *Who, though he be one with the Father, yet humbled himself for our sakes, to be as a* messenger *from his Father, to declare his will to us, to confirm the covenant of grace by his death, to reveal this salvation, with the promise of the Holy Spirit to work true faith and repentance in our hearts.* [2] *To prophets or teachers, who are appointed by God to declare his will and commands to his people,* Job 33. 23. Mal. 2. 7. | 3. 1. [3] *To ambassadors sent by one prince to another,* 2 Kings 16. 7. [4] *To spies, or such as privily search into the state of places or affairs,* Josh. 6. 17. Jam. 2. 25. [5] *To any dreadful punishment which God inflicts upon the wicked for their sins,* Prov. 17. 11.

Gen. 50. 16. they sent a *m.* to Joseph, saying
Judg. 2. † 1. a *m.* of the Lord came from Gilgal
1 *Sam.* 4. 17. and the *m.* said, Israel is fled
2 *Sam.* 15. 13. there came a *m.* to David, saying
1 *Kings* 19. 2. then Jezebel sent a *m.* to Elijah
22. 13. the *m.* went to call Micaiah, 2 *Chron.* 18. 12.
2 *Kings* 6. 32. but ere the *m.* came to him, when the *m.* cometh, shut the door, hold him fast
9. 18. the *m.* came to them, but cometh not again
Job 1. 14. there came a *m.* to Job, and said
33. 23. if there be a *m.* an interpreter of a thousand
Prov. 13. 17. a wicked *m.* falleth into mischief
17. 11. a cruel *m.* shall be sent against him
25. 13. so is a faithful *m.* to them that send him
Isa. 42. 19. who is blind or deaf, as my *m.* that I sent?
Jer. 51. 31. one *m.* shall run to meet another
Ezek. 23. 40. to whom a *m.* was sent, they came
Hag. 1. 13. then spake Haggai, the Lord's *m.*
Mal. 2. 7. for he is the *m.* of the Lord of hosts
3. 1. I will send my *m.* even the *m.* of the covenant, *Mat.* 11. 10. *Mark* 1. 2. *Luke* 7. 27
2 *Cor.* 12. 7. the *m.* of Satan, to buffet me, lest I
Phil. 2. 25. my companion in labour, but your *m.*

MESSENGERS.

Gen. 32. 3. Jacob sent *m.* before him to Esau
Num. 20. 14. Moses sent *m.* from Kadesh, *Deut.* 2. 26.
21. 21. Israel sent *m.* unto Sihon, saying
22. 5. Balak sent *m.* to Balaam, the son of Peor
24. 12. spake I not also to thy *m.* sent to me?
Josh. 6. 17. Rahab hid the *m.* that we sent, 25.
7. 22. so Joshua sent *m.* to Achan's tent
Judg. 6. 35. Gideon sent *m.* through Manasseh
11. 12. Jephthah sent *m.* to the king of Ammon, 14.
1 *Sam.* 11. 4. then came the *m.* to Gibeah of Saul
16. 19. Saul sent *m.* to Jesse, and said, send David
19. 11. Saul sent *m.* to David, 14, 15, 20, 21.
25. 14. David sent *m.* to salute our master
42. Abigail went after the *m.* of David
2 *Sam.* 2. 5. David sent *m.* to Jabesh gilead
3. 12. Abner sent *m.* to David on his behalf
14. David sent *m.* to Ish-bosheth, Saul's son
26. Joab sent *m.* after Abner, which brought
5. 11. Hiram sent *m.* to David, 1 *Chron.* 14. 1.
11. 4. David sent *m.* to Bathsheba, and took her
12. 27. Joab sent *m.* to David, and said, I fought
1 *Kings* 20. 2. Benhadad sent *m.* to Ahab, king of Is.
2 *Kings* 1. 3. go up to meet the *m.* of Ahaziah
16. forasmuch as sent *m.* to inquire of Baal-zebub
14. 8. then Amaziah sent *m.* to Jehoash king of Is.
16. 7. so Ahaz sent *m.* to Tiglath pileser king of
17. 4. Hoshea had sent *m.* to So, king of Egypt
19. 9. Sennacherib sent *m.* to Hezekiah, *Isa.* 37. 9.
23. by thy *m.* hast thou reproached the Lord
1 *Chron.* 19. 2. David sent *m.* to comfort Hanun
2 *Chron.* 36. 15. the Lord sent to them by his *m.*
16. but they mocked the *m.* of God, and despised
Prov. 16. 14. the wrath of a king is as *m.* of death
Isa. 14. 32. what shall one answer *m.* of the nation?

Isa. 18. 2. go ye swift m. to nation scattered and peel.
33. † 7. behold, their m. shall cry without
37. 14. Hezekiah received letter from m. and read it
44. 26. and performeth the counsel of his m.
57. 9. and thou didst send thy m. afar off
Jer. 27. 3. send by the hand of the m. which come
Ezek. 23. 16. sent m. unto them into Chaldea
30. 9. in that day shall m. go forth from me in ships
Nah. 2. 13. the voice of thy m. be no more heard
Luke 7. 24. and when the m. of John were gone
9. 52. and sent m. before his face, they went
2 Cor. 8. 23. they are the m. of the churches
Jam. 2. 25. by works, when Rahab had received m.

MESS, or MESSES.

Gen. 43. 34. Joseph took and sent m. to them, but Benjamin's m. five times so much as theirs
2 Sam. 11. 8. there followed Uriah a m. from the king

MESSIAH

Signifies, ANOINTED. It is applied *principally, and by way of eminence, to that sovereign* Deliverer, *who was expected by the Jews, and whom they vainly expect even to this day, since he is already come at the appointed time. They used to anoint kings, high priests, and sometimes prophets.* Saul, David, Solomon, *and* Joash, *received the royal unction: Aaron and his sons received the sacerdotal; and* Elisha, *the disciple of* Elijah, *received the prophetic unction, at least God ordered* Elijah *to give it,* 1 Kings 19. 16. *and therefore the name* Messiah, *or* Anointed, *is given to the kings,* 1 Sam. 12. 3, 5. *and also to the patriarchs or prophets,* 1 Chron. 16. 22. Psal. 105. 15. *But this name chiefly belongs to* Jesus Christ, *by way of excellence, who was the object of the desire and of the expectation of the saints.* Hannah, *the mother of* Samuel, *plainly alludes to* Jesus Christ, *when at the end of her hymn, and at a time when there was no king in Israel, she says,* The Lord shall give strength to his King, and exalt the horn of his *Anointed,* 1 Sam. 2. 10. See also *Psal.* 2. 2. | 45. 7. *Dan.* 9. 25, 26. *It is not found any where, that* Jesus Christ *ever received any sensible unction; or that the apostles anointed the faithful with any particular or external oil or ointment. The unction that the prophets and the apostles speak of, when* Jesus Christ *or his disciples are understood, is the spiritual and internal unction of grace and of the Holy Ghost, of which the outward and sensible unction, with which they anciently anointed kings, priests, and prophets, was but the figure and symbol.*

Dan. 9. 25. from the commandment to build Jerusalem, unto the M. the Prince shall be seven weeks
26. and after 62 weeks shall M. be cut off
John 1. 41. we have found the M. which is Christ
4. 25. the woman saith, I know that M. cometh

MET.

Gen. 32. 1. and the angel of God m. him
33. 8. what meanest thou by this drove I m.?
Exod. 3. 18. the Lord God of the Hebrews hath m. with us, let us go to sacrifice to the Lord, 5. 3.
4. 24. the Lord m. him, and sought to kill him
27. Aaron went and m. Moses in the mount
5. 20. they m. Moses and Aaron who stood in way
Num. 23. 4. God m. Balaam, and said to him, 16.
Deut. 23. 4. because they m. you not, Neh. 13. 2.
25. 18. Amalek m. thee by way, and smote feeble
Josh. 11. 5. and when all these kings were m.
1 Sam. 10. 10. a company of prophets m. Saul
25. 20. behold, Abigail m. David and his men
2 Sam. 16. 1. Ziba m. David with asses saddled
18. 9. Absalom m. the servants of David
1 Kings 13. 24. when he was gone, a lion m. him
18. 7. Elijah m. Obadiah, and he knew him
2 Kings 9. 21. Joram and Ahaziah m. Jehu
10. 13. Jehu m. with the brethren of Ahaziah
Job 4. † 14. fear m. me that made my bones shake
Psal. 85. 10. mercy and truth are m. together
Prov. 7. 10. behold, there m. him a woman
Amos 5. 19. flee from a lion, and a bear m. him
Mat. 8. 28. there m. him two possessed with devils
28. 9. behold, Jesus m. them, saying, all hail
Mark 11. 4. in a place where two ways m.
Luke 9. 37. much people m. him, John 12. 18.
17. 12. there m. him ten men that were lepers
John 11. 20. then Martha went and m. him, 30.
Acts 10. 25. Cornelius m. him, and fell down
16. 16. a certain damsel possessed m. us
17. 17. he disputed with them that m. with him
27. 41. falling into a place where two seas m.
Heb. 7. 1. who m. Abraham returning from slaught.
10. in his father's loins, when Melchisedec m. him

METE.

Exod. 16. 18. when they did m. it with an homer
Psal. 60. 6. I will m. out valley of Succoth, 108. 7.
Mat. 7. 2. with what measure ye m. it shall be measured to you again, Mark 4. 24. Luke 6. 38.

METED.

Isa. 18. 2. go to a nation m. out, trodden down, 7.
40. 12. and m. out heaven with a span

METE-YARD.

Lev. 19. 35. ye shall do no unrighteousness in m.

MICE.

1 Sam. 6. 4. five golden m. according to number, 18.
5. ye shall make images of your emerods and m.

MID-DAY.

1 Kings 18. 29. when m. was past, Elijah said
Neh. 8. 3. read therein from morning to m. before
Acts 26. 13. at m. O king, I saw in the way a light

MIDDLE.

Judg. 7. 19. Gideon came in beginning of m. watch
9. 37. there come people by the m. of the land
16. 29. Samson took hold of the two m. pillars
1 Sam. 25. 29. sling out, as out of the m. of a sling
2 Sam. 10. 4. cut off their garments in the m.
1 Kings 8. 64. the king did hallow m. court, 2 Chr. 7. 7.
2 Kings 20. 4. afore Isaiah gone into the m. court
Jer. 39. 3. all the princes sat in the m. gate
Ezek. 1. 16. as it were a wheel in the m. of a wheel
Eph. 2. 14. broken down the m. wall of partition

MIDDLEMOST.

Ezek. 42. 5. higher than the m. of the building, 6.

MIDNIGHT.

Exod. 11. 4. at m. will I go into the midst of Egypt
12. 29. at m. the Lord smote the first-born
Judg. 16. 3. Samson lay till m. and arose at m.
Ruth 3. 8. at m. the man was afraid, and turned
1 Kings 3. 20. she arose at m. and took my son
Job 34. 20. the people shall be troubled at m.
Psal. 119. 62. at m. I will rise to give thanks
Mat. 25. 6. at m. there was a cry made, behold
Mark 13. 35. whether he shall come at even, or m.
Luke 11. 5. shall go to him at m. and say, lend me
Acts 16. 25. and at m. Paul and Silas prayed
20. 7. Paul continued his speech till m.

MIDST

Signifies, [1] *That part which is equally distant from the extremes, or the centre of a circle or sphere,* Num. 35. 5. Luke 23. 45. [2] *Among,* Deut. 18. 15. Mat. 10. 16. [3] *The thickest of a throng,* Luke 4. 30. [4] *The most open or public place,* Deut. 13. 16. [5] *The most convenient place,* Deut. 19. 2. [6] *The deepest part,* Josh. 3. 17.

Exod. 14. 16. shall go on dry ground through m. of sea, Num. 33. 8. Neh. 9. 11. Psal. 136. 14.
23. 25. I will take sickness from the m. of thee
Deut. 4. 11. the mountain burnt to the m. of heaven
13. 5. shalt put evil away from the m. of thee
18. 15. thy God will raise a Prophet from m. of thee
1 Kings 8. 51. from the m. of the furnace of iron
2 Chr. 32. 4. brook that ran thro' the m. of the land
Cant. 3. 10. the m. thereof being paved with love
Isa. 4. 4. purged blood from the m. of Jerusalem
30. 28. breath shall reach to the m. of the neck
58. 9. take away from the m. of thee the yoke
Jer. 30. 21. the governor proceed from the m. of them
48. 45. a flame shall come from the m. of Sihon
Ezek. 9. 4. go through the m. of the city and set
11. 23. the glory of Lord went up from m. of city
14. 8. I will cut him off from m. of my people, 9.
† 16. though these three were in the m. of it
15. 4. the m. of it is burnt, is it meet for work?
28. 16. have filled the m. of thee with violence
18. I will bring forth a fire from the m. of thee
Dan. 3. 26. came forth of the m. of the fire
Amos. 2. 3. I will cut off judge from the m. thereof
Luke 4. 30. but he passing through the m. of them
John 7. 14. about the m. of the feast Jesus went
8. 59. going thro' the m. of them, so passed by
Rev. 8. 13. an angel flying through the m. of heaven

In the MIDST.

Gen. 1. 6. be a firmament in the m. of heaven
2. 9. the tree of life in the m. of the garden, 3. 3.
15. 10. and Abram divided them in the m.
Exod. 3. 20. wonders I will do in the m. thereof
8. 22. I am the Lord in the m. of the earth
14. 27. overthrew Egyptians in the m. of the sea
29. walked on dry land in the m. of the sea, 15. 19.
33. 3. for I will not go up in the m. of thee, lest
Lev. 16. 16. in the m. of their uncleanness
Num. 2. 17. tabernacle set forward in the m. of camp
5. 3. defile not the camps in the m. whereof I dwell
35. 5. and the city shall be in the m. Ezek. 48. 15.
Deut. 11. 3. acts which he did in the m. of Egypt
6. swallowed them up in the m. of all Israel
19. 2. separate three cities in the m. of thy land
23. 14. God walketh in the m. of thy camp
Josh. 3. 17. priests stood firm in m. of Jordan, 4. 10.
4. 9. set up twelve stones in the m. of Jordan
7. 13. there is an accursed thing in the m. of thee
21. they are hid in the earth in the m. of my tent
1 Sam. 16. 13. anointed him in the m. of brethren
2 Sam. 18. 14. he was yet alive in the m. of the oak
23. 12. but he stood in the m. of the ground
20. slew a lion in the m. of a pit in time of snow
2 Kings 6. 20. behold, they were in the m. of Samaria
1 Chron. 19. 4. and cut off their garments in the m.
Neh. 4. 11. nor see, till we come in the m. among
Job 1. † 6. Satan came also in the m. of them
20. † 13. though he keeps in in the m. of his palate
Psal. 22. 14. it is melted in the m. of my bowels
22. I will declare thy name, in the m. of the congregation will I praise thee, Heb. 2. 12.
40. † 8. yea, thy law is in the m. of my bowels
46. 5. G. is in the m. of her, she shall not be moved
55. 10. mischief in the m. || 11. wickedness in the m.
74. 4. enemies roar in the m. of thy congregation
12. working salvation in the m. of the earth
78. 28. and he let it fall in the m. of their camp
102. 24. take me not away in the m. of my days
110. 2. rule thou in the m. of thine enemies
116. 19. pay vows in the m. of thee, O Jerusalem
138. 7. though I walk in the m. of trouble, thou wilt
Prov. 4. 21. keep them in the m. of thine heart
5. 14. I was in all evil in the m. of the congregation
8. 20. I lead in the m. of the paths of judgment
14. 33. that which is in the m. of fools is folly
23. 34. as he that lieth down in the m. of the sea
30. 19. the way of a ship in the m. of the sea
Isa. 5. 2. and I built a tower in the m. of it
6. 5. I dwell in the m. of a people of unclean lips
12. be a great forsaking in the m. of the land
7. 6. set a king in the m. of it, the son of Tabeal
12. 6. great is the Holy One in t. m. of thee, Hos. 11. 9.
16. 3. as the night in the m. of the noon day
19. 24. even a blessing in the m. of the land
41. 18. I will open fountains in the m. of thee
Jer. 6. 6. she is wholly oppression in the m. of her
9. 6. thine habitation is in the m. of deceit
14. 9. thou, O Lord, art in the m. of us, leave us not
17. 11. he shall leave them in the m. of his days
37. 12. to separate himself in the m. of the people
Lam. 4. 13. shed blood of the just in the m. of her
Ezek. 5. 5. I have set it in the m. of the nations
8. I will execute judgment in the m. of thee
6. 7. the slain shall fall in the m. of you, 11. 7.
17. 16. in the m. of Babylon he shall die
22. 3. the city sheddeth blood in the m. of it
21. and ye shall be melted in the m. thereof
22. as silver is melted in the m. of the furnace
25. they have made many widows in t. m. thereof

Ezek. 22. 27. princes in the m. thereof are like wolves
23. 39. thus have they done in the m. of my house
26. 5. for spreading of nets in the m. of the sea
28. 22. O Zidon, I will be glorified in the m. of thee
36. 23. which ye have profaned in the m. of them
37. 26. will set my sanctuary in the m. of them
28. when my sanctuary shall be in the m. of them
43. 7. where I will dwell in the m. of Israel, 9.
46. 10. and the prince in the m. shall go in
Dan. 3. 25. four men walking in the m. of the fire
9. 27. in the m. of the week, oblation shall cease
Hos. 5. 4. spirit of whoredoms is in the m. of them
Joel 2. 27. ye shall know I am in the m. of Israel
Amos 7. 10. conspired in the m. of the house of Isrl.
Mic. 5. 7. remnant be in the m. of many people, 8.
6. 14. thy casting down shall be in the m. of thee
Nah. 3. 13. thy people in the m. of thee are women
Hab. 3. 2. in the m. of the years revive thy work
Zeph. 2. 14. flocks shall lie down in the m. of her
3. 5. just Lord is in the m. thereof, will not do
12. I will leave in the m. of thee a poor people
15. king of Isr. the Lord is in the m. of thee, 17.
Zech. 2. 5. I will be the glory in the m. of her
10. rejoice, for I will dwell in the m. of thee, 11.
5. 4. the curse shall remain in the m. of his house
7. a woman that sitteth in the m. of the ephah
8. 3. and will dwell in the m. of Jerusalem, 8.
14. 4. the mount of olives shall cleave in the m.
Mat. 10. 16. I send you as sheep in the m. of wolves
14. 24. ship was in the m. of the sea, Mark 6. 47.
18. 2. set a little child in the m. of them, Mark 9. 36.
20. are gathered, there am I in the m. of them
Luke 2. 46. found him sitting in the m. of the doctors
6. 8. rise, and stand forth in the m. and he arose
21. 21. let them which are in the m. of it depart
23. 45. the vail of the temple was rent in the m.
24. 36. Jesus himself stood in t. m. John 20. 19, 26.
John 8. 3. and when they had set her in the m. 9.
19. 18. on either side one, and Jesus in the m.
Acts 1. 15. Peter stood up in the m. of the disciples
18. Judas falling burst asunder in the m.
17. 22. then Paul stood up in the m. of Mars' hill
Phil. 2. 15. blameless in the m. of a crooked generat.
Rev. 1. 13. in the m. of the seven candlesticks, 2. 1.
2. 7. which is in the m. of the Paradise of God
4. 6. and in the m. of the throne were four beasts
5. 6. lo, in the m. of the throne stood a Lamb, 7. 17.

Into the MIDST.

Exod. 14. 22. Israel went into the m. of the sea
24. 18. and Moses went into the m. of the cloud
33. 5. I will come into the m. of thee and consume
Num. 16. 47. Aaron ran into the m. of congregation
1 Kings 22. 35. blood ran into the m. of the chariot
Esth. 4. 1. Mordec. went into the m. of city and cried
Ps. 46. 2. tho' mountains be carried into the m. of sea
57. 6. into the m. whereof they are fallen themsel.
Jer. 21. 4. I will assemble them into t. m. of this city
51. 63. cast it into the m. of the river Euphrates
Ezek. 5. 4. cast them into the m. of the fire and burn
22. 19. I will gather you into the m. of Jerusalem
Dan. 3. 6. shall be cast into the m. of a fiery furnace
Zech. 5. 8. and he cast it into the m. of the ephah

Out of the MIDST.

Gen. 19. 29. sent Lot out of the m. of the overthrow
Exod. 3. 2. angel appeared out of the m. of a bush
4. God called to him out of the m. of bush, 24. 16.
Deut. 4. 12. the Lord spake unto you out of the m. of the fire, 15, 33, 36. | 5. 4, 22, 24.
34. to take him a nation out of the m. of another
Josh. 4. 3. take out of t. m. of Jordan twelve stones, 8.
7. 23. and they took them out of the m. of the tent
Isa. 24. 18. and he that cometh out of the m. of pit
52. 11. depart, go o. of m. of her, Jer. 50. 8. | 51. 6, 45.
Ezek. 11. 7. I will bring you forth out of the m. of it
29. 4. I will bring thee out of the m. of thy rivers
32. 21. shall speak to him out of the m. of hell
Amos 6. 4. that eat calves out of the m. of the stall
Mic. 5. 10. I will cut off horses out of the m. of thee
13. images || 14. pluck up groves out of m. of thee
Zeph. 3. 11. then I will take away out of t. m. of thee

MIDWIFE.

Gen. 35. 17. the m. said unto Rachel, fear not
38. 28. the m. bound on his hand a scarlet thread
Exod. 1. 16. he said, when ye do the office of a m.

MIDWIVES.

Exod. 1. 17. but the m. feared God, and did not, 21.
19. are delivered ere the m. come unto them
20. therefore God dealt well with the m.

MIGHT, *Substantive.*

Gen. 49. 3. Reuben, thou art my first born, my m.
Num. 14. 13. broughtest up this people in thy m.
Deut. 3. 24. that can do according to thy m.
6. 5. thou shalt love thy God with all thy m.
8. 17. the m. of mine hand hath gotten me wealth
28. 32. there shall be no m. in thine hand
Judg. 5. 31. as the sun goeth forth in his m.
6. 14. go in this thy m. || 16. 30. bowed with his m.
2 Sam. 6. 14. David danced with all his m.
1 Kings 15. 23. the acts of Asa and all his m.
16. 5. Baasha his m. || 27. Omri and his m.
22. 45. Jehoshaphat and his m that he shewed
2 Kings 10. 34. Jehu his m. || 13. 8. Jehoahaz his m.
13. 12. Joash || 14. 15. acts of Jehoash and his m.
14. 28. Jeroboam || 20. 20. Hezekiah and his m.
23. 25. Josiah turned to the Lord with all his m.
24. 16. the king brought captive all the men of m.
1 Chron. 12. 8. men of m. came to David to the hold
29. 2. I prepared for the house with all my m.
12. in thine hand is power and m. 2 Chron. 20. 6.
30. the acts of David with his reign and m.
2 Chr. 20. 12. we have no m. against this company
Esth. 10. 2. acts of Ahasuerus, his power and m.
Psal. 76. 5. none of the men of m. found their hands
89. † 13. thou hast an arm with m. strong is
145. 6. men shall speak of the m. of thy acts
Prov. 24. † 5. a man of knowledge strengtheneth m.
Eccl. 9. 10. thy hand findeth to do, do it with thy m.
Isa. 3. † 25. and thy m. shall fall in the war
11. 2. the spirit of counsel and m. shall rest on him
33. 13. ye that are near, acknowledge my m.
40. 26. calleth them by the greatness of his m.
29. to them that have no m. he increaseth strength

Jer. 9. 23. nor let the mighty man glory in his m.
10. 6. thou art great, and thy name is great in m.
16. 21. behold, I will cause them to know my m.
49. 35. I will break the chief of their m.
51. 30. their m. hath failed, they became as women
Ezek. 32. 30. they are ashamed of their m.
Dan. 2. 20. blessed be G. for wisdom and m. are his
23. I thank thee, O God, who hast given me m.
3. † 4. he cried with m. 4. † 14. | 5. † 7.
4. 30. that I have built by the m. of my power
Mic. 3. 8. truly I am full of judgment and of m.
7. 16. nations shall be confounded at all their m.
Zech. 4. 6. not by m. nor by power, but by my Spirit
Eph. 1. † 19. the working of the m. of his power
21. far above all m. power, and dominion
3. 16. to be strengthened with m. Col. 1. 11.
6. 10. be strong in the Lord, and in power of his m.
2 Pet. 2. 11. whereas angels that are greater in m.
Rev. 7. 12. glory and m. be unto our God for ever

MIGHT *be.*

Gen. 30. 34. I would it m. be according to thy word
Exod. 36. 18. to couple the tent, that it m. be one
39. 21. that it m. be above the curious girdle
Lev. 26. 45. brought forth that I m. be their God
Deut. 5. 29. fear me, that it m. be well with them
1 Sam. 18. 27. that he m. be the king's son-in-law
1 Kings 8. 16. that my name m. be put therein
2 Kings 7. 2. would make windows, m. this thing be
15. 19. gave silver, that his hand m. be with him
2 Chron. 6. 5. an house, that my name m. be there, 6.
Psal. 78. 8. m. not be as their fathers, a stubborn
Jer. 13. 11. that they m. be unto me a people
Ezek. 17. 8. in good soil, that it m. be a goodly vine
36. 3. that ye m. be a possession to the heathen
Hos. 6. † 5. that thy judgments m. be as the light
Mal. 2. 4. that my covenant m. be with Levi
Mark 5. 18. pray. that he m. be with him, Luke 8. 38.
Luke 8. 9. asked, saying, what m. this parable be?
John 15. 11. and that your joy m. be full
Rom. 4. 11. m. be the father of them that believe
16. that it m. be of grace || 14. 9. m. be Lord of dead
2 Thess. 3. 8. m. not be chargeable to any of you
Philem. 8. though I m. be much bold in Christ
Heb. 2. 17. that he m. be a merciful High-Priest
12. 10. that we m. be partakers of his holiness
1 Pet. 1. 21. that your faith and hope m. be in God
See FULFILLED.

MIGHTY.

Gen. 10. 9. he was a m. hunter before the Lord
18. 18. Abraham shall become a great and m. nation
23. 6. hear us, thou art a m. prince amongst us
Exod. 1. 7. the children of Israel waxed m. 20.
9. 28. that there be no more m. thunderings and hail
10. 19. the Lord turned a m. strong west wind
15. 10. they sank as lead in the m. waters
Lev. 19. 15. nor shall honour the person of the m.
Num. 22. 6. curse this people, for they are too m.
Deut. 4. 37. he brought thee out with m. power, 9. 29.
7. 23. shall destroy them with a m. destruction
26. 5. became there a great nation, m. and populous
Judg. 5. 13. L. made me have dominion over the m.
23. they came not to help of the L. against the m.
1 Sam. 4. 8. out of the hand of these m. gods
2 Sam. 1. 19. how are the m. fallen! 25.
21. the shield of the m. is vilely cast away
22. from the blood of the slain, from fat of the m.
2 Kings 24. 15. the m. of the land carried he captive
1 Chron. 1. 10. Nimrod was m. || 12. 28. Zadok m.
27. 6. Benaiah was m. || 2 Chron. 13. 21. Abijah m.
2 Chron. 26. 13. army that made war with m. power
27. 6. so Jotham became m. because he prepared
Ezra 4. 20. there have been m. kings over Jerusalem
7. 28. hath extended mercy to me before m. princes
Neh. 3. 16. Nehemiah repaired to the house of the m.
9. 11. thou threwest a stone in the m. waters
Job 5. 15. but he saveth the poor from the m.
6. 23. or redeem me from the hand of the m.?
9. 4. he is wise in heart, and m. in strength
12. 19. he leadeth princes, and he overthroweth m.
21. he weakeneth the strength of the m.
21. 7. wherefore are the wicked m. in power?
24. 22. he draweth also the m. with his power
34. 20. the m. shall be taken away without hand
35. 9. they cry out by reason of the arm of the m.
41. 25. he raiseth himself, the m. are afraid
Psal. 24. 8. Lord strong and m. Lord m. in battle
29. 1. give to the Lord, O ye m. glory and strength
45. 3. gird thy sword on thy thigh, O most m.
59. 3. for lo, the m. are gathered against me
68. 33. doth send out his voice, and that a m. voice
69. 4. being mine enemies wrongfully are m.
74. 15. thou driedst up m. rivers, the day is thine
82. 1. God standeth in the congregation of the m.
89. 6. who among sons m. can be likened to Lord?
13. thou hast a m. arm, strong is thy hand
19. I have laid help upon one that is m.
50. I bear in my bosom the reproach of the m.
93. 4. the Lord is mightier than the m. waves of sea
103. † 20. bless the Lord, ye angels m. in strength
106. 8. that he might make his m. power known
112. 2. his seed shall be m. upon the earth
120. 4. sharp arrows of the m. with coals of juniper
135. 10. who smote great nations, and slew m. kings
Prov. 16. 32. that is slow to anger is better than m.
18. 18. the lot parteth between the m.
21. 22. a wise man scaleth the city of the m.
23. 11. their Redeemer is m. shall plead their cause
Isa. 3. 25. and thy m. shall fall in the war
5. 22. woe to them that are m. to drink wine
11. 15. with his m. wind shall he shake his hand
17. 12. a rushing like the rushing of m. waters
22. 17. will carry thee away with a m. captivity
49. 24. shall the prey be taken from the m.?
63. 1. I that speak in righteousness, m. to save
Jer. 5. 15. it is a m. and an ancient nation, a nation
32. 19. great in counsel and m. in work
33. 3. and I will shew thee great and m. things
Ezek. 17. 13. he hath also taken the m. of the land
32. 12. by the swords of the m. will I make thee fall
21. the strong among the m. shall speak to him
27. they shall not lie with the m. that are fallen
38. 15. thou shalt come with a great and m. army
Ezek. 39. 18. ye shall eat the flesh of the m. and drink
Dan. 4. 3. how great and m. are his wonders!
8. 24. his power shall be m. but not by his own pow.
11. 3. a m. king shall stand up that shall rule
25. shall be stir. up with a very great and m. army
Amos 2. 14. neither shall the m. deliver himself
2. 16. he that is courageous among the m. shall flee
5. 12. I know your m. sins || 24. as a m. stream
Jonah 1. 4. there was a m. tempest in the sea
Zech. 11. 2. howl, because the m. are spoiled
Mat. 11. 20. where most of his m. works were done
21. if the m. works which were done in you, 23.
13. 54. whence hath this man these m. works?
58. he did not many m. works there, Mark 6. 5.
14. 2. this is John the Baptist, therefore m. works do shew forth themselves in him, Mark 6. 14.
Mark 6. 2. m. works are wrought by his hand
Luke 1. 49. he that is m. hath done great things
52. he hath put down the m. from their seats
9. 43. they were amazed at the m. power of God
15. 14. there arose a m. famine in that land
19. 37. praised God for the m. works they had seen
24. 19. who was a prophet m. in deed and word
Acts 2. 2. sound from heaven as of a rushing m. wind
7. 22. Moses was m. in words and in deeds
18. 24. Apollos was m. in the scriptures
Rom. 15. 19. the Gentiles obedient through m. signs
1 Cor. 1. 26. not many m. not many noble, are called
27. God hath chosen weak, to confound things m.
2 Cor. 10. 4. weapons of our warfare are m. thro' G.
13. 3. which to you is not weak, but m. in you
Gal. 2. 8. the same was m. in me toward the Gentiles
Eph. 1. 19. according to the working of his m. power
2 Thess. 1. 7. Jesus shall be reveal. with his m. angels
Rev. 6. 13. when she is shaken of a m. wind
10. 1. I saw another m. angel come down, 18. 21.
16. 18. so m. an earthquake and so great
18. 10. that m. city || 19. 6. voice of m. thunderings
See ACTS, GOD, HAND, MAN, MEN.

MIGHTY *one.*

Gen. 10. 8. Nimrod began to be a m. one in the earth
Isa. 1. 24. therefore saith Lord, Lord of hosts, the m. one of Israel, 30. 29. | 49. 26. | 60. 16.
10. 34. and Lebanon shall fall by a m. one
28. 2. behold, the Lord hath a m. and strong one
Jer. 20. 11. the Lord is with me as a m. terrible one
Ezek. 31. 11. have delivered him into hand of m. one

MIGHTY *ones.*

Exod. 15. † 11. who is like to thee among the m. ones?
Judg. 5. 22. broken by pransing of their m. ones
Isa. 13. 3. I have called my m. ones for mine anger
Jer. 46. 5. their m. ones are beaten down and fled
Joel 3. 11. thither cause thy m. ones to come down

MIGHTIER.

Gen. 26. 16. for thou art much m. than we
Exod. 1. 9. the children of Israel are m. than we
Num. 14. 12. a greater nation and m. than they Deut. 4. 38. | 7. 1. | 9. 1, 14. | 11. 23.
Psal. 93. 4. the Lord on high is m. than many waters
Eccl. 6. 10. neither contend with him that is m.
Mat. 3. 11. I baptize with water, but he that cometh after me is m. than I, Mark 1. 7. Luke 3. 16.

MIGHTIES.

1 Chron. 11. 12. Eleazar was one of the three m.
19. these things did these three m.
24. Benaiah had a name among the three m.

MIGHTILY.

Deut. 6. 3. observe to do it, that ye may increase m.
Judg. 4. 3. Jabin m. oppressed Israel twenty years
14. 6. the Spirit of L. came m. on Samson, 15. 14.
1 Sam. 14. † 48. Saul wrought m. and smote Amalek
Isa. 10. † 34. and Lebanon shall fall m.
42. † 13. the Lord shall behave himself m.
Jer. 25. 30. the Lord shall m. roar on his habitation
Jonah 3. 8. let man and beast cry m. unto God
Nah. 2. 1. watch the way, fortify thy power m.
Acts 18. 28. for he m. convinced the Jews
19. 20. so m. grew the word of God, and prevailed
Col. 1. 29. his working, which worketh in me m.
Rev. 18. 2. he cried m. saying, Babylon is fallen

MILCH.

Gen. 32. 15. thirty m. camels with their colts
1 Sam. 6. 7. make a new cart, take two m. kine, 10.

MILDEW, *See* BLASTING.

MILE.

Mat. 5. 41. shall compel thee to go a m. go twain

MILK

Signifies, *A liquid food which we have from cows, &c. wherewith babes and children are chiefly nourished,* Gen. 18. 8. Isa. 28. 9. To which are compared, [1] *The weakest spiritual food, or the most plain and easy truths of the gospel, whereby young converts are nourished and edified,* 1 Cor. 3. 2. Heb. 5. 12. 1 Pet. 2. 2. [2] *Sweet, agreeable, and edifying speech,* Cant. 4. 11. [3] *The graces, services, and obedience of the godly,* Cant. 5. 1.
A land flowing with milk and honey, Josh. 5. 6. *A country of extraordinary fertility, affording all things necessary for the support and comfort of life.*
Wine and milk, Isa. 55. 1. *All sorts of spiritual blessings and privileges.*

Gen. 18. 8. and Abraham took butter and m.
49. 12. and his teeth shall be white with m.
Deut. 32. 14. butter of kine and m. of sheep
Judg. 4. 19. Jael opened a bottle of m. and gave
5. 25. he asked water, and she gave him m.
Job 10. 10. hast thou not poured me out as m.?
21. 24. his breasts are full of m. his bones moistened
Prov. 27. 27. thou shalt have goats' m. for food
30. 33. the churning of m. bringeth forth butter
Cant. 4. 11. honey and m. are under thy tongue
5. 1. I have drunk my wine with my m.
12. his eyes washed with m. and fitly set
Isa. 7. 22. for abundance of m. that they shall give
28. 9. them that are weaned from the m.
55. 1. come, buy wine and m. without money
60. 16. thou shalt suck the m. of the Gentiles
Lam. 4. 7. her Nazarites were whiter than m.
Ezek. 25. 4. shall eat thy fruit, and drink thy m.
Joel 3. 18. the hills shall flow with m. and rivers
1 Cor. 3. 2. I have fed you with m. and not with meat
9. 7. who feedeth a flock, and eateth not of the m.?
Heb. 5. 12. ye are become such as have need of m.?
13. for every one that useth m. is a babe
1 Pet. 2. 2. new-born babes desire sincere m. of word
See FLOWING.

MILK.

Isa. 66. 11. that ye may m. out, and be delighted

MILL, S.

Exod. 11. 5. the maid-servant that is behind the m.
Num. 11. 8. the people ground the manna in m.
Mat. 24. 41. two women shall be grinding at the m.

MILLET.

Ezek. 4. 9. take lentiles, m. and make bread

MILLIONS.

Gen. 24. 60. be thou mother of thousands of m.

MILLSTONE.

Deut. 24. 6. no man shall take the m. to pledge
Judg. 9. 53. a woman cast a piece of m. 2 Sam. 11. 21.
Job 41. 24. heart as hard as a piece of the nether m.
Mat. 18. 6. it were better that a m. were hanged about his neck, Mark 9. 42. Luke 17. 2.
Rev. 18. 21. an angel took up a stone like a great m.
22. the sound of a m. shall be heard no more

MILLSTONES.

Isa. 47. 2. take the m. and grind meal, uncover
Jer. 25. 10. I will take away the sound of the m.

MINCING.

Isa. 3. 16. wanton eyes, walking and m. as they go

MIND

Signifies, [1] *The understanding, or judgment, whereby we distinguish between good and evil, lawful and unlawful,* 2 Cor. 3. 14. Tit. 1. 15. [2] *The regenerated and renewed part of man,* Rom. 7. 25. [3] *The heart,* Gen. 26. 35. Deut. 18. 6. [4] *The memory,* Psal. 31. 12. Isa. 46. 8. [5] *End, design, or intention,* Prov. 21. 27. [6] *Thought, or imagination,* Isa. 26. † 3. [7] *Wit, or soundness of mind,* Mark 5. 15. Luke 8. 35. [8] *The will,* 1 Pet. 5. 2. [9] *Affection,* Acts 17. 11.
Who hath known the mind of the Lord, 1 Cor. 2. 16. *What natural, carnal man hath been taught by the Spirit, the will, counsel, and purpose of God, and the divine mysteries of man's salvation?*
But we have the mind of Christ, 1 Cor. 2. 16. *But we who are endued with the Spirit, have an experimental knowledge of God's will, and of spiritual divine things, revealed to us by the Spirit, who is our teacher, and knows the mind of Christ, and reveals it to us,* John 16. 13. 1 Cor. 2. 10.

MIND, *Substantive.*

Gen. 26. 35. which were a grief of m. to Isaac
Lev. 24. 12. the m. of the L. might be shewed them
Deut. 18. 6. and come with all the desire of his m.
28. 65. the Lord shall give thee sorrow of m.
30. 1. shalt call them to m. among the nations
1 Chron. 28. 9. and serve him with a willing m.
Neh. 4. 6. for the people had a m. to work
Job 23. 13. but he is of one m. who can turn him?
Psal. 31. 12. am forgotten, as a dead man out of m
Prov. 21. 27. he bringeth it with a wicked m.
29. 11. a fool uttereth all his m. but a wise man
Isa. 26. 3. keep in peace, whose m. is stayed on thee
46. 8. bring it again to m. O ye transgressors
65. 17. and the former shall not come into m.
Jer. 3. 16. the ark of covenant shall not come to m.
22. † 27. the land whereunto they lift their m.
44. 21. and came it not into his m.?
Dan. 5. 20. when his m. was hardened in pride
Hab. 1. 11. then shall his m. change, and he shall
Mark 5. 15. sitting in his right m. Luke 8. 35.
14. 72. Peter called to m. the words of Jesus
Luke 1. 29. Mary cast in her m. what salutation
12. 29. neither be ye of doubtful m.
Acts 2. † 6. the multitude were troubled in m.
12. † 20. Herod bore an hostile m. against Tyre
17. 11. they received word with all readiness of m.
20. 19. serving the Lord with humility of m.
Rom. 1. 28. God gave them up to a reprobate m.
7. 25. so then, with the m. I serve the law of God
8. 7. the carnal m. is enmity against God
27. he knoweth what is the m. of the Spirit
11. 34. who hath known the m. of the Lord?
12. 16. be of the same m. one toward another
14. 5. every man be fully persuaded in his own m.
15. 6. that ye may with one m. glorify God
1 Cor. 1. 10. ye be joined together in the same m.
2. 16. for who hath known the m. of the Lord to instruct him? but we have the m. of Christ
2 Cor. 7. 7. when he told us your fervent m. tow. me
8. 12. for if there be first a willing m. it is accepted
13. 11. brethren, be of one m. Phil. 1. 27. | 2. 2.
Eph. 2. 3. fulfilling the desires of the flesh and m.
4. 17. as other Gentiles walk in vanity of their m.
Phil. 2. 3. in lowliness of m. let each esteem other
5. let this m. be in you which was in Christ Jesus
4. 2. that they be of the same m. in the Lord
Col. 2. 18. vainly puffed up by his fleshly m.
3. 12. put on kindness, humbleness of m. meekness
2 Thess. 2. 2. that they be not soon shaken in m.
2 Tim. 1. 7. God hath given us the spirit of sound m.
Tit. 1. 15. but their m. and conscience is defiled
3. 1. put them in m. to be subject to powers
Heb. 8. 10. I will put my laws into their m.
12. † 17. he found no way to change his m.
1 Pet. 3. 8. be ye all of one m. having compassion
4. 1. arm yourselves likewise with the same m.
5. 2. not for filthy lucre, but of a ready m.
Rev. 17. 9. here is the m. which hath wisdom
13. these have one m. and shall give their power
See ALIENATED.

Mine or *my* MIND.

Num. 16. 28. I have not done them of mine own m.
24. 13. I cannot do good or bad of mine own m.
1 Sam. 2. 35. according to that which is in my m.
1 Chron. 22. 7. it was in my m. to build an house
Isa. 21. † 4. my m. wandered, fearfulness affrighted
Jer. 15. 1. my m. could not be toward this people
19. 5. neither came it into my m. 32. 35.
Lam. 3. 21. this I recall to my m. therefore hope
Rom. 7. 23. another law warring ag. law of my m.

Thy MIND.

1 Sam. 9. 20. set not thy m. on asses, they are found
20. † 4. say what is thy m. and I will do it

Job 34. 33. should it be according to *thy m.*
Ezek. 38. 10. same time shall things come into *thy m.*
Dan. 2. 29. O king, thy thoughts came into *thy m.*
Mat. 22. 37. thou shalt love the Lord thy God with all *thy m.* Mark 12. 30. Luke 10. 27.
Philem. 14. without *thy m.* would I do nothing

Your MIND.

Gen. 23. 8. if it be *your m.* I should bury my dead
Jer. 51. 50. and let Jerusalem come into *your m.*
Ezek. 11. 5. I know the things that come into *your m.*
20. 32. and that which cometh into *your m.*
Rom. 12. 2. be transformed by renewing of *your m.*
2 Cor. 8. 19. and declaration of *your* ready *m.*
9. 2. for I know the forwardness of *your m.*
Eph. 4. 23. and be renewed in the spirit of *your m.*
Col. 1. 21. that were sometimes enemies in *your m.*
3. † 2. set *your m.* on things above, not on things
1 Pet. 1. 13. gird up the loins of *your m.* be sober

MIND, *Verb.*

Rom. 8. 5. that are after flesh, *m.* things of the flesh
12. 16. *m.* not high things, but condescend to men
Phil. 3. 16. nevertheless let us *m.* the same thing
19. for many walk, who *m.* earthly things

MINDED.

Ruth 1. 18. she was stedfastly *m.* to go with her
2 Chron. 24. 4. Joash was *m.* to repair the house
Ezra 7. 13. which are *m.* of their own free will
Mat. 1. 19. Joseph was *m.* to put her away privily
Rom. 8. 6. for to be carnally *m.* is death, but to be spiritually *m.* is life and peace
11. 20. be not high-*m.* but fear
15. 5. grant you to be like *m.* one toward another
2 Cor. 1. 15. in this confidence I was *m.* to come
17. when I was thus *m.* did I use lightness
Gal. 5. 10. that you will be no otherwise *m.*
Phil. 2. 2. that ye be like *m.* having the same love
20. no man like *m.* who will care for your state
3. 15. let us, as many as be perfect, be thus *m.* if in any thing ye be otherwise *m.* God will reveal
1 Thess. 5. 14. brethren, comfort the feeble *m.*
1 Tim. 6. 17. charge that the rich be not high-*m.*
2 Tim. 3. 4. for men shall be heady, high-*m.*
Tit. 2. 6 young men exhort to be sober *m.*
Jam. 1. 8. a double-*m.* man is unstable in all his ways
4. 8. and purify your hearts, ye double *m.*

MINDFUL.

1 Chron. 16. 15. be ye *m.* always of his covenant
Neh. 9. 17. our fathers were not *m.* of thy wonders
Psal. 8. 4. what is man, that thou art *m.* of him, and the son of man that thou visitest him? Heb. 2. 6.
111. 5. he will ever be *m.* of his covenant
115. 12. the Lord hath been *m.* of us, he will bless us
Isa. 17. 10. not been *m.* of the rock of thy strength
2 Tim. 1. 4. being *m.* of thy tears, to be filled
Heb. 11. 15. if they had been *m.* of that country
2 Pet. 3. 2. that ye may be *m.* of the words spoken

MINDS.

Judg. 19. 30. consider of it, and speak your *m.*
2 Sam. 17. 8. and they be chafed in their *m.*
2 Kings 9. 15. if it be your *m.* let none go forth
Ezek. 24. 25. that whereupon they set their *m.*
36. 5. with despiteful *m.* to cast it out for a prey
Acts 14. 2. and made their *m.* evil affected
28. 6. they changed their *m.* said he was a god
2 Cor. 3. 14. but their *m.* were blinded, veil untaken
4. 4. the god of this world hath blinded the *m.*
11. 3. so your *m.* should be corrupted from simplicity
Phil. 4. 7. the peace of God shall keep your *m.*
1 Tim. 6. 5. men of corrupt *m.* 2 Tim. 3. 8.
Heb. 10. 16. and in their *m.* will I write them
12. 3. lest ye be wearied and faint in your *m.*
2 Pet. 3. 1. I stir up your pure *m.* by way of rememb.

MINDING.

Acts 20. 13. Paul *m.* himself to go afoot

MINE.

Job 28. † 1. surely there is a *m.* for silver

MINE.

Gen. 31. 43. and all that thou seest is *m.*
48. 5. are *m.* as Reuben and Simeon shall be *m.*
Exod. 13. 2. sanctify to me all the first-born, both of man and beast, it is *m.* 34. 19. Num. 3. 13.
19. 5. for all the earth is *m.* Psal. 50. 12.
Lev. 20. 26. that ye should be *m.* Isa. 43. 1.
25. 23. the land is *m.* for ye are strangers
Num. 3. 12. the Levites shall be *m.* 45. | 8. 14.
8. 17. the first-born of children of Israel are *m.*
2 Sam. 14. 30. Absalom said, see, Joab's field is near *m.*
1 Kings 2. 15. knowest that the kingdom was *m.*
3. 26. let it be neither *m.* nor thine, divide it
20. 3. thy silver, and gold, and wives, are *m.*
2 Kings 10. 6. if ye will be *m.* and if ye will hearken
Job 41. 11. whatsoever is under heaven is *m.*
Psal. 18. 23. I kept myself from *m.* iniquity
50. 10. for every beast of the forest is *m.*
11. and the wild beasts of the field are *m.*
60. 7. Gilead is *m.* and Manasseh is *m.* 108. 8.
Prov. 8. 14. counsel is *m.* and sound wisdom
Cant. 2. 16. my beloved is *m.* and I am his, 6. 3.
8. 12. my vineyard, which is *m.* is before me
Jer. 44. 28. whose word shall stand, *m.* or theirs
Ezek. 16. 8. I sware to thee, thou becamest *m.*
18. 4. behold, all souls are *m.* soul of son is *m.*
23. 4. and they were *m.* || 5. when she was *m.*
29. 9. the river is *m.* || 35. 10. these countries be *m.*
Hag. 2. 8. the silver is *m.* and the gold is *m.*
Mal. 3. 17. they shall be *m.* saith the Lord
Mat. 7. 24. that heareth sayings of *m.* and doeth them
26. heareth these sayings of *m.* and doeth them not
20. 23. but to sit on my right hand and on my left, is not *m.* to give, it shall be given, Mark 10. 40.
Luke 11. 6. a friend of *m.* in his journey is come
John 2. 4. Jesus saith, *m.* hour is not yet come
7. 16. my doctrine is not *m.* || 10. 14. am known of *m.*
14. 24. the word which ye hear is not *m.*
16. 14. he shall receive of *m.* and shew it you
15. all things that the Father hath are *m.*
17. 10. all *m.* are thine, and thine are *m.*
Rom. 12. 19. vengeance is *m.* I will repay, saith Ld.
Phil. 1. 4. in every prayer of *m.* making request

MINGLE.

Isa. 5. 22. and men of strength to *m.* strong drink
9. † 11. the Lord shall *m.* his enemies together
Isa. 19. † 2. I will *m.* Egyptians with Egyptians
Dan. 2. 43. they shall *m.* with the seed of men

MINGLED.

Exod. 9. 24. there was fire *m.* with the hail
Lev. 19. 19. shalt not sow thy field with *m.* seed
Ezra 9. 2. holy seed have *m.* themselves with people
Job 24. † 6. they reap every one his *m.* corn
Psal. 102. 9. and *m.* my drink with weeping
106. 35. but were *m.* among the heathen
Prov. 9. 2. killed her beasts, she hath *m.* her wine
5. and drink of the wine which I have *m.*
Isa. 19. 14. the Lord hath *m.* a perverse spirit
Jer. 25. 20. give the cup to all the *m.* people, 24.
50. 37. a sword on all the *m.* people, Ezek. 30. 5.
Mat. 27. 34. they gave him vinegar *m.* with gall
Mark 15. 23. they gave him wine *m.* with myrrh
Luke 13. 1. whose blood Pilate had *m.* with sacrifi.
Rev. 8. 7. there followed hail and fire *m.* with blood
15. 2. I saw as it were a sea of glass *m.* with fire

MINISH, ED.

Exod. 5. 19. ye shall not *m.* ought of your task
Psal. 107. 39. again they are *m.* and brought low

MINISTER

Signifies, *One who serves, waits on, or attends another,* Exod. 24. 13. 1 Kings 10. 5. It is a word applied, [1] *To Christ, who is called,* A Minister of the sanctuary, Heb. 8. 2. that is, *Christ being now gone into heaven, typified by the* holy of holies, *he does there minister, or execute the remainder of his office in his human nature, by presenting the merit of his sacrifice, as the high-priest brought the blood of the sin offering into the most holy place once a year,* Exod. 30. 10. Lev. 16. 15. [2] *To such as are appointed to attend the service of God in his church, to dispense and give forth, faithfully and wisely, the word, sacraments, and other holy things,* 1 Cor. 4. 1. [3] *To magistrates, who are God's officers and deputies to punish such as transgress his law, and to defend the good,* Rom. 13. 6. [4] *To the holy angels, who are always ready to execute the commands of God,* Psal. 104. 4.

Exod. 24. 13. Moses rose up, and his *m.* Joshua
Josh. 1. 1. the Lord spake to Joshua, Moses' *m.*
2 Kings 6. † 15. when the *m.* of Elisha was risen
Mat. 20. 26. let him be your *m.* Mark 10. 43.
Luke 4. 20. he gave the book again to the *m.*
Acts 13. 5. and they had also John to their *m.*
26. 16. to make thee a *m.* and a witness
Rom. 13. 4. for he is the *m.* of God to thee, 6.
15. 8. Christ was a *m.* of the circumcision
16. I should be the *m.* of Jesus to the Gentiles
Gal. 2. 17. is Christ the *m.* of sin? God forbid
Eph. 3. 7. whereof I was made a *m.* Col. 1. 23, 25.
6. 21. Tychicus, a faithful *m.* of the Ld. Col. 4. 7.
Col. 1. 7. Epaphras, who is for you a faithful *m.*
1 Thess. 3. 2. Timothy our brother and *m.* of God
1 Tim. 4. 6. thou shalt be a good *m.* of Christ
Heb. 8. 2. a *m.* of the sanctuary and tabernacle

MINISTER.

Exod. 28. 1. that he may *m.* to me in the priest's office, 3, 4, 41. | 29. 1, 44. | 30. 30. | 31. 10. | 35. 19. | 39. 41. | 40. 13, 15.
35. and it shall be upon Aaron to *m.*
43. when they come to altar to *m.* 29. 30. | 30. 20.
29. 44. I will sanctify Aaron to *m.* to me
Lev. 7. 35. in the day he presented them to *m.*
16. 32. whom he shall consecrate to *m.* Num. 3. 3.
Num. 8. 26. but shall *m.* with their brethren
Deut. 10. 8. separated the tribe of Levi to *m.* to him
18. 5. to stand to *m.* in the name of the Lord, 7.
21. 5. for thy God hath chosen them to *m.*
1 Sam. 2. 11. the child did *m.* to the Lord before Eli
1 Kings 8. 11. so that the priest could not stand to *m.* because of the cloud, 2 Chron. 5. 14.
1 Chron. 15. 2. chosen to *m.* before him for ever
23. 13. to *m.* and to give thanks, 2 Chron. 31. 2.
2 Chron. 13. 10. priests which *m.* are the sons of Aaron
Psal. 9. 8. he shall *m.* judgment to the people
Isa. 60. 7. the rams of Nebaioth shall *m.* to thee
10. and their kings shall *m.* to thee
Jer. 33. 22. I will multiply the Levites that *m.*
Ezek. 40. 46. which come near to *m.* 44. 15, 16.
44. 11. they shall stand before them to *m.*
Mat. 20. 28. to be ministered to, but to *m.* Mark 10. 45.
25. 44. naked, or sick, and did not *m.* to thee?
Acts 24. 23. nor forbid his acquaintance to *m.* to him
Rom. 15. 25. but now I go to *m.* to the saints
27. their duty is to *m.* to them in carnal things
1 Cor. 9. 13. they which *m.* about holy things, live of
2 Cor. 9. 10. both *m.* bread for your food, and multip.
Eph. 4. 29. that it may *m.* grace to the hearers
1 Tim. 1. 4. which *m.* questions rather than edifying
Heb. 1. 14. angels sent to *m.* to heirs of salvation
6. 10. ye have ministered to the saints, and do *m.*
1 Pet. 1. 12. but to us they did *m.* the things
4. 10. even so *m.* the same one to another, as good
11. if any man *m.* let him do it as of the ability

MINISTERED.

Num. 3. 4. Eleazar and Ithamar *m.* Deut. 10. 6.
1 Sam. 2. 18. but Samuel *m.* before the Lord, 3. 1.
2 Sam. 13. 17. Amnon called his servant that *m.*
1 Kings 1. 4. Abishag *m.* to king David, 15.
19. 21. Elisha went after Elijah, and *m.* to him
2 Kings 25. 14. they took away the pots, snuffers, and all the vessels wherewith they *m.* Jer. 52. 18.
Ezek. 44. 12. they *m.* to them before their idols
Dan. 7. 10. thousand thousands *m.* unto him
Mat. 4. 11. angels came and *m.* to him, Mark 1. 13.
8. 15. she rose and *m.* unto them, Mark 1. 31.
Luke 8. 3. which *m.* to him of their substance
Acts 13. 2. as they *m.* and fasted, the Spirit said
20. 34. these hands have *m.* to my necessities
2 Cor. 3. 3. declared the epistle of Christ *m.* by us
Phil. 2. 25. and he that *m.* to my wants
Col. 2. 19. having nourishment *m.* increaseth with
1 Tim. 3. † 13. that have *m.* the office of deacon
2 Tim. 1. 18. in how many things he *m.* unto me
Philem. 13. that in thy stead he might have *m.*
Heb. 6. 10. that ye have *m.* to the saints, and do
2 Pet. 1. 11. for so an entrance shall be *m.* to you

MINISTERETH.

2 Cor. 9. 10. now he that *m.* seed to the sower
Gal. 3. 5. he that *m.* to you the Spirit, doeth he it

MINISTERING.

1 Chron. 9. 28. had the charge of the *m.* vessels
Ezek. 44. 11. at the gates of house, *m.* to the house
Mat. 27. 55. many women followed Jesus *m.* to him
Rom. 12. 7. let us wait on *m.* || 15. 16. *m.* the gospel
2 Cor. 8. 4. and take on us the *m.* to the saints
9. 1. for as touching *m.* to the saints, it is superfluous
Heb. 1. 14. are they not all *m.* spirits, sent minister
10. 11. every priest standeth daily *m.* and offering

MINISTERS.

1 Kings 10. 5. the attendance of his *m.* 2 Chron. 9. 4.
Ezra 7. 24. not lawful to impose toll on *m.* of house
8. 17. that they should bring unto us *m.* for house
Psal. 103. 21. ye *m.* of his that do his pleasure
104. 4. who maketh his *m.* a flaming fire, Heb. 1. 7.
Isa. 61. 6. men shall call you the *m.* of our God
Jer. 33. 21. then may also my covenant be broken with David my servant, and with my *m*
Ezek. 44. 11. they shall be *m.* in my sanctuary
45. 4. holy portion for the *m.* of the sanctuary
Joel 1. 9. the Lord's *m.* mourn || 13. howl ye *m.*
2. 17. *m.* weep between the porch and the altar
Luke 1. 2. which from beginning were *m.* of word
Rom. 13. 6. they are God's *m.* attending continually
1 Cor. 3. 5. but *m.* by whom ye believed, as Lord
4. 1. so account of us as of the *m.* of Christ
2 Cor. 3. 6. who made us able *m.* of the new testa.
6. 4. approving ourselves as the *m.* of God
11. 15. therefore it is no great thing, if his *m.* also be transformed as the *m.* of righteousness
23. are they *m.* of Christ? I am more, in labours

MINISTRATION.

Luke 1. 23. as soon as the days of his *m.* were end.
Acts 6. 1. their widows were neglected in the daily *m.*
2 Cor. 3. 7. but if the *m.* of death was glorious
8. the *m.* of the Spirit be rather glorious? 9.
9. 13. whiles by the experiment of this *m.*

MINISTRY.

Num. 4. 12. shall take all the instruments of the *m*
47. every one that came to do the service of the *m.*
2 Chron. 7. 6. when David praised by their *m.*
Hos. 12. 10. have used similitudes by *m.* of proph.
Acts 1. 17. for he had obtained part of this *m.*
25. that may take part of this *m.* and apostleship
6. 4. but we will give ourselves to *m.* of the word
12. 25. returned, when they had fulfilled their *m.*
20. 24. so that I might finish my course, and *m.*
21. 19. what things God had wrought by his *m.*
Rom. 12. 7. or *m.* let us wait on our ministering
1 Cor. 16. 15. addicted themselves to the *m.* of saints
2 Cor. 4. 1. seeing we have this *m.* we faint not
5. 18. hath given to us the *m.* of reconciliation
6. 3. giving no offence, that the *m.* be not blamed
Eph. 4. 12. for work of the *m.* for edifying the body
Col. 4. 17. take heed to the *m.* thou hast received
1 Tim. 1. 12. putting me into the *m.* who was before
2 Tim. 4. 5. watch thou, make full proof of thy *m.*
11. for he is profitable to me for the *m.*
Heb. 8. 6. now hath he obtained a more excellent *m.*
9. 21. he sprinkled with blood the vessels of the *m.*

MINSTREL, S.

2 Kings 3. 15. but now bring me a *m.* when *m.* played
Mat. 9. 23. when Jesus saw the *m.* and the people

MINT.

Mat. 23. 23. ye pay tithe of *m.* anise, and cummin
Luke 11. 42. ye tithe *m.* and all manner of herbs

MIRACLE

Is a supernatural operation performed alone by the power of God, John 3. 2. | 9. 16. Acts 2. 22. | 15. 12. *Our Saviour confirmed the doctrine which he taught by a train of incontestable miracles: They were so great in their nature, so real and solid in their proof, so divine in the manner of performing them, by the power of his will; so holy in their end, to confirm a doctrine most becoming the wisdom and other glorious attributes of God, and for the accomplishment of the prophecies concerning the Messiah, whose coming was foretold to be with miraculous healing benefits; that there was the greatest assurance, that none without the omnipotent hand of God could do them. The magicians performed divers wonders in Egypt, but they were outdone by Moses, to convince the spectators, that he was sent from a power infinitely superior to that of evil spirits. Real miracles that are contrary to the order, and exceed the power of nature, can only be produced by creating power, and are wrought to give credit to those who are sent from God; and when God permits false miracles to be done by seducers, that would thereby obtain authority and credit among men, the deception is not invincible; for it is foretold expressly, to give us warning, that the man of sin shall come with lying wonders after the working of Satan,* 2 Thess. 2. 9. *but the heavenly doctrine of the gospel has been confirmed by real miracles, incomparably greater than all the strange things done to give credit to doctrines opposed to it.*

Exod. 7. 9. when Pharaoh shall speak, saying, shew a *m.*
2 Chron. 32. † 24. and he wrought a *m.* for him
Mark 6. 52. they considered not the *m.* of the loaves
9. 39. no man which shall do a *m.* in my name
Luke 23. 8. hoped to have seen some *m.* done by him
John 4. 54. this is the second *m.* that Jesus did
10. 41. many resorted and said, John did no *m.*
Acts 4. 16. a notable *m.* hath been done by them
22. above forty years on whom this *m.* was wrought

MIRACLES.

Num. 14. 22. which have seen *m.* which I have done
Deut. 11. 3. your children, that have not seen his *m.*
29. 3. thine eyes have seen those signs and great *m.*
Judg. 6. 13. where be all his *m.* our fathers told us
John 2. 11. this beginning of *m.* did Jesus in Cana
23. many believed, when they saw the *m.* he did
3. 2. no man can do these *m.* except G. be with him
6. 2. a multit. followed him, because they saw his *m.*
26. ye seek me, not because ye saw the *m.*
7. 31. will he do more *m.* than this man doeth

John 9. 16. can a man that is a sinner do such *m.?*
11. 47. what do we? for this man doeth many *m.*
12. 37. though he had done so many *m.* bef. them
Acts 2. 22. a man approved of God by *m.* and signs
6. 8. Stephen did great *m.* among the people
8. 6. hearing and seeing the *m.* which he did
13. wondered, beholding the *m.* which were done
15. 12. declaring what *m.* God had wrought
19. 11. God wrought special *m.* by hands of Paul
1 *Cor.* 12. 10. to another the working of *m.*
28. after that *m.* ‖ 29. are all workers of *m.?*
Gal. 3. 5. he that worketh *m.* doeth he it by works
Heb. 2. 4. God also bearing them witness with *m.*
Rev. 13. 14. deceiveth them by the means of those *m.*
16. 14. for they are the spirits of devils working *m.*
19. 20. the false prophet that wrought *m.* before him

MIRE

Signifies, *Mud or dirt trodden under foot*, 2 Sam. 22. 43.
He hath cast me into the mire, *Job* 30. 19. *He hath made me contemptible, filthy, and loathsome, by reason of my sores, my whole body being a kind of mire in regard of the filth breaking forth in all its parts.*
The sow that was washed turned to her wallowing in the mire, 2 *Pet.* 2. 22. *As swine that naturally love the dirt and mire, if sometimes they be washed from it, yet still retaining their former dispositions, return to it again: So likewise these persons here mentioned, however they be washed from the pollutions of the world, and by the preaching of the gospel brought off from their former sinful courses, and brought to a profession of holiness; yet still retaining their old nature and corrupt dispositions, they are easily prevailed upon and enticed, and they relapse into their former abominations.*
2 *Sam.* 22. 43. I did stamp them as *m.* of the street, and spread them abroad, *Isa.* 10. 6. *Mic.* 7. 10.
Job 8. 11. can the rush grow up without *m.?*
30. 19. he hath cast me into the *m.* I am like dust
38. † 38. when the dust is turned into *m.*
41. 30. he spreadeth sharp-pointed things on the *m.*
Psal. 69. 2. I sink in deep *m.* where is no standing
14. deliver me out of the *m.* let me not sink
Isa. 57. 20. whose waters cast up *m.* and dirt
Jer. 38. 6. in the dungeon was no water, but *m.*
22. thy feet are sunk in the *m.* and turned
Zech. 9. 3. and fine gold as the *m.* of the streets
10. 5. which tread their enemies in *m.* of the streets
2 *Pet.* 2. 22. the sow to her wallowing in the *m.*

MIRY.

Psal. 40. 2. he brought me out of the *m.* clay
Ezek. 47. 11. the *m.* places shall not be healed
Dan. 2. 41. thou sawest iron mixed with *m.* clay, 43.

MIRTH.

Gen. 31. 27. I might have sent thee away with *m.*
Neh. 8. 12. the people went away to make great *m.*
Job 21. † 13. they spend their days in *m.*
Psal. 137. 3. they that wasted us desired of us *m.*
Prov. 14. 13. and the end of that *m.* is heaviness
Eccl. 2. 1. I said, go to, I will prove thee with *m.*
2. I said of *m.* what doeth it?
7. 4. the heart of fools is in the house of *m.*
8. 15. then I commended *m.* because a man hath
Isa. 24. 8. *m.* of tabrets, the joy of the harp ceaseth
11. joy is darkened, the *m.* of the land is gone
Jer. 7. 34. I will cause to cease the voice of *m.* from Judah and Jerusalem, 16. 9. | 25. 10. *Hos.* 2. 11.
Ezek. 21. 10. it is furbished, should we then make *m.?*

MISCARRYING.

Hos. 9. 14. give them a *m.* womb and dry breasts

MISCHIEF.

Gen. 42. 4. for he said, lest some *m.* befall him
38. if *m.* befall him by the way ye go in, 44. 29.
Exod. 21. 22. her fruit depart, and yet no *m.* follow
32. 12. for *m.* did he bring them out to slay them
22. thou knowest the people that are set on *m.*
1 *Sam.* 23. 9. David knew that Saul practised *m.*
2 *Sam.* 16. 8. behold, thou art taken in thy *m.*
1 *Kings* 11. 25. besides the *m.* that Hadad did
20. 7. mark and see how this man seeketh *m.*
2 *Kings* 7. 9. if we tarry, some *m.* will befall us
Neh. 6. 2. but they thought to do me *m.*
Esth. 8. 3. Esther besought to put away *m.* of Haman
Job 15. 35. they conceive *m.* and bring forth vanity
Ps. 7. 14. he conceived *m.* brought forth falsehood
16. his *m.* shall return upon his own head
10. 7. under his tongue is *m.* and vanity
14. thou beholdest *m.* and spite, to requite it
26. 10. in whose hands is *m.* their hand is full
28. 3. which speak peace, but *m.* is in their hearts
36. 4. the wicked deviseth *m.* upon his bed
52. 1. why boastest thyself in *m.* O mighty man?
55. 10. *m.* and sorrow are in the midst of it
62. 3. how long will ye imagine *m.* ag. a man?
94. 20. the throne, which frameth *m.* by a law
119. 150. they draw nigh that follow after *m.*
140. 9. let the *m.* of their own lips cover them
Prov. 4. 16. sleep not, except they have done *m.*
6. 14. he deviseth *m.* continually, he soweth
18. feet that be swift in running to *m.*
10. 23. it is as sport to a fool to do *m.*
11. 27. he that seeketh *m.* it shall come to him
12. 21. but the wicked shall be filled with *m.*
13. 17. a wicked messenger falleth into *m.*
17. 20. that hath a perverse tongue falleth into *m.*
24. 2. their heart studieth and their lips talk of *m.*
16. but the wicked shall fall into *m.* 28. 14.
Isa. 47. 11. therefore *m.* shall fall upon thee
59. 4. they trust in vanity, they conceive *m.*
Ezek. 7. 26. *m.* shall come upon *m.* and rumour
11. 2. said he, these are the men that devise *m.*
Dan. 11. 27. both these kings' hearts shall be to do *m.*
Hos. 7. 15. yet do they imagine *m.* against me
Mic. 7. † 3. the great man uttereth the *m.* of his soul
Acts 13. 10. O full of all *m.* thou child of the devil

MISCHIEFS.

Deut. 32. 23. I will heap *m.* on them, I will spend
Psal. 52. 2. thy tongue deviseth *m.* like a razor
140. 2. which imagine *m.* in their heart

MISCHIEVOUS.

Psal. 21. 11. they imagined a *m.* device, not able to

Ps. 38. 12. they that seek my hurt, speak *m.* things
Prov. 24. 8. he shall be called a *m.* person
Eccl. 10. 13. the end of his talk is *m.* madness
Ezek. 38. † 10. thou shalt conceive a *m.* purpose
Mic. 7. 3. the great man uttereth his *m.* desire

MISERABLE.

Job 16. 2. Job said, *m.* comforters are ye all
1 *Cor.* 15. 19. we are of all men most *m.*
Rev. 3. 17. and knowest not that thou art *m.*

MISERABLY.

Mat. 21. 41. he will *m.* destroy those wicked men

MISERY.

Judg. 10. 16. his soul was grieved for the *m.* of Israel
Job 3. 20. why is light given to him that is in *m.?*
11. 16. because thou shalt forget thy *m.*
Prov. 31. 7. drink, and remember his *m.* no more
Eccl. 8. 6. the *m.* of a man is great on him
Lam. 3. 19. remembering mine affliction and *m.*
Rom. 3. 16. destruction and *m.* are in their ways

MISERIES.

Lam. 1. 7. Jerusalem remembered in days of her *m.*
Jam. 5. 1. howl for your *m.* that shall come on you

MISS.

Judg. 20. 16. sling at an hair-breadth and not *m.*
1 *Sam.* 20. 6. if thy father at all *m.* me, then say

MISSED.

1 *Sam.* 20. 18. thou shalt be *m.* † thy seat will be *m.*
25. 15. neither *m.* any thing as long as conversant
21. nothing was *m.* of all that pertained to him

MISSING.

1 *Sam.* 25. 7. neither was there ought *m.* unto them
1 *Kings* 20. 39. if by any means he be *m.* then thy life

MIST.

Gen. 2. 6. but there went up a *m.* from the earth
Acts 13. 11. immediately there fell on him a *m.*
2 *Pet.* 2. 17. to whom the *m.* of darkness is reserved

MISTRESS.

Gen. 16. 4. Sarah her *m.* was despised in her eyes
8. I flee from my *m.* Sarai ‖ 9. return to thy *m.*
1 *Kings* 17. 17. son of the *m.* of the house fell sick
2 *Kings* 5. 3. said to her *m.* would G. my lord were
Psal. 123. 2. as eyes of a maiden to hand of her *m.*
Prov. 30. 23. and handmaid that is heir to her *m.*
Isa. 24. 2. shall be as with the maid so with her *m.*
Nah. 3. 4. *m.* of witchcrafts, that selleth nations

MISUSED.

2 *Chr.* 36. 16. but they despised and *m.* his prophets

MITE, S.

Mark 12. 42. a widow threw in two *m.* *Luke* 21. 2.
Luke 12. 59. till thou hast paid the very last *m.*

MITRE.

Exod. 28. 4. they shall make a *m.* 39. | 39. 28.
37. a blue lace upon the *m.* 39. 31.
29. 6. and thou shalt put the *m.* upon his head
Lev. 8. 9. he put also the holy crown on the *m.*
16. 4. with the linen *m.* shall he be attired
Zech. 3. 5. a fair *m.* on his head, so they set a fair *m.*

MIXED.

Exod. 12. 38. a *m.* multitude went up with them
Num. 11. 4. the *m.* multitude fell a lusting
Neh. 13. 3. they separated from Isr. all *m.* multitude
Prov. 23. 30. they that go to seek *m.* wine
Isa. 1. 22. thy silver is dross, thy wine *m.* with water
Dan. 2. 41. thou sawest the iron *m.* with miry clay
Hos. 7. 8. Ephraim *m.* himself among the people
Heb. 4. 2. not being *m.* with faith in them heard it

MIXTURE.

Exod. 8. † 21. I will send a *m.* of noisome beasts
12. † 38. a great *m.* went up also with them
Psal. 75. 8. there is a cup, wine red, it is full of *m.*
John 19. 39. there came also Nicodemus, and brought a *m.* of myrrh and aloes
Rev. 14. 10. is poured out without *m.* into the cup

MOCK.

Prov. 14. 9. fools make a *m.* at sin; but among

MOCK

Signifies, [1] *To deride, scoff, or laugh at*, 2 Chron. 30. 10. [2] *To speak merrily, or in jest*, Gen. 19. 14. [3] *To deceive one's expectation, by departing from wonted obedience*, Num. 22. 29. [4] *To beguile with words*, Judg. 16. 10, 13. [5] *To ravish, force, or abuse*, Gen. 39. 17.
Gen. 39. 14. he brought in an Hebrew to *m.* us, 17.
1 *Sam.* 31. † 4. lest these uncircumcised come and thrust me through, and *m.* me, 1 *Chron.* 10. † 4.
Job 13. 9. as one that mocketh, do ye so *m.* him
21. 3. and after that I have spoken, *m.* on
Prov. 1. 26. I will *m.* when your fear cometh
Jer. 9. † 5. they will *m.* every one his neighbour
38. 19. lest they deliver me, and they *m.* me
Lam. 1. 7. the adversary did *m.* at her sabbaths
Ezek. 22. 5. shall *m.* thee who art infamous and vexed
Mat. 20. 19. shall deliver him to Gentiles to *m.* him
Mark 10. 34. they shall *m.* him and scourge him
Luke 14. 29. lest they that behold, begin to *m.* him

MOCKED.

Gen. 19. 14. he seemed as one that *m.* to his sons
Num. 22. 29. Balaam said, because thou hast *m.* me
Judg. 16. 10. hast *m.* me, and told me lies, 13. 15.
1 *Kings* 18. 27. at noon, Elijah *m.* them, and said
2 *Kings* 2. 23. little children out of the city *m.* Elisha
2 *Chron.* 30. 10. they laughed them to scorn and *m.*
36. 16. but they *m.* the messengers of God
Neh. 4. 1. Sanballat was wroth, and *m.* the Jews
Job 12. 4. I am as one *m.* of his neighbour
Mat. 2. 16. when Herod saw that he was *m.* he was
27. 29. they bowed the knee and *m.* 31. *Mark* 15. 20.
Luke 18. 32. shall be *m.* and spitefully entreated
22. 63. and the men that held Jesus *m.* him
23. 11. Herod *m.* him ‖ 36. the soldiers also *m.* him
Acts 17. 32. when heard of the resurrection, some *m.*
Gal. 6. 7. be not deceived, God is not *m.*

MOCKER.

Prov. 20. 1. wine is a *m.* strong drink is raging

MOCKERS.

Job 17. 2. are there not *m.* with me? and doth not
Psal. 35. 16. with hypocritical *m.* in feasts
Isa. 28. 22. be not *m.* lest bands be made strong
Jer. 15. 17. I sat not in the assembly of *m.*
Jude 18. there should be *m.* in the latter times

MOCKEST.

Job 11. 3. when thou *m.* shall no man make asham.?

MOCKETH.

Job 13. 9. as one *m.* another, do ye so mock him?
39. 22. he *m.* at fear, and is not affrighted
Prov. 17. 5. who *m.* poor reproacheth his Maker
30. 17. eye that *m.* at his father, eagles shall eat it
Jer. 20. 7. I am a derision, every one *m.* me

MOCKING.

Gen. 21. 9. and Sarah saw the son of Hagar *m.*
Mat. 27. 41. the chief priests *m.* *Mark* 15. 31.
Acts 2. 13. others *m.* said, these men are full

MOCKING.

Ezek. 22. 4. therefore I made thee a *m.* to all

MOCKINGS.

Heb. 11. 36. others had trial of cruel *m.*

MODERATE.

1 *Cor.* 10. † 13. no temptation but such as is *m.*

MODERATING.

Eph. 6. † 9. ye masters, do the same, *m.* threatening

MODERATION.

Phil. 4. 5. let your *m.* be known to all men

MODERATELY.

Joel 2. 23. he hath given you the former rain *m.*

MODEST.

1 *Tim.* 2. 9. women adorn themselves in *m.* apparel

MOE, *See* MORE.

MOIST.

Num. 6. 3. nor shall he eat *m.* grapes, or dried

MOISTENED.

Job 21. 24. and his bones are *m.* with marrow

MOISTURE.

Ps. 32. 4. my *m.* is turned into drought of summer
Luke 8. 6. it withered away, because it lacked *m.*

MOLE.

Lev. 11. 30. lizard, snail, and *m.* are unclean

MOLES, *See* BATS.

MOLLIFIED.

Isa. 1. 6. neither bound up, nor *m.* with ointment

MOLTEN.

Exod. 32. 4. he fashioned it after he had made a *m.* calf, 8. *Deut.* 9. 12, 16. *Neh.* 9. 18.
34. 17. shalt make thee no *m.* gods, *Lev.* 19. 4.
1 *Kings* 7. 16. he made two chapiters of *m.* brass
23. he made a *m.* sea ‖ 30. undersetters *m.*
33. their felloes and their spokes were all *m.*
Job 28. 2. and brass is *m.* out of the stone
37. 18. sky is strong, and as a *m.* looking-glass
Ezek. 24. 11. the filthiness of it may be *m.* in it
Mic. 1. 4. the mountains shall be *m.* under him
Nah. 2. † 6. the palace of Nineveh shall be *m.*
See IMAGE.

MOMENT.

Exod. 33. 5. will come into the midst of thee in a *m.*
Num. 16. 21. that I may consume them in a *m.* 45.
Ezra 9. † 8. for a *m.* grace hath been shewed
Job 7. 18. that thou shouldest try him every *m.*
20. 5. the joy of the hypocrite is but for a *m.*
21. 13. and in a *m.* they go down to the grave
34. 20. in a *m.* shall they die, people be troubled
Psal. 30. 5. for his anger endureth but a *m.*
73. 19. the wicked brought into desolat. as in a *m.*
Prov. 12. 19. a lying tongue is but for a *m.*
Isa. 26. 20. hide thyself as it were for a *m.*
27. 3. I the L. do keep it, I will water it every *m.*
47. 9. but these two things shall come in a *m.*
54. 7. for a small *m.* have I forsaken thee
8. I hid my face from thee for a *m.* but with
Jer. 4. 20. my tents spoiled, and my curtains in a *m.*
Lam. 4. 6. Sodom that was overthrown in a *m.*
Ezek. 26. 16. and shall tremble at every *m.* 32. 10.
Luke 4. 5. devil shew. the kingdoms of world in a *m.*
1 *Cor.* 15. 52. we shall all be changed in a *m.*
2 *Cor.* 4. 17. our affliction, which is but for a *m.*

MONEY.

Gen. 23. 9. give it for as much *m.* as it is worth
13. I will give thee *m.* for the field, take it
31. 15. and he hath quite devoured also our *m.*
42. 25. Joseph command. to restore every man's *m.*
27. he espied his *m.* ‖ 28. my *m.* is restored
43. 12. and take double *m.* in your hand, 15.
23. peace be to you, fear not, I had your *m.*
44. 1. and put every man's *m.* in his sack's mouth
47. 14. Joseph gathered all the *m.* in Egypt
15. for *m.* faileth ‖ 18. how that our *m.* is spent
Exod. 21. 11. she shall go out free without *m.*
21. for he is his *m.* ‖ 35. and divide the *m.*
30. if there be laid on him a sum of *m.* then he
22. 7. if a man deliver to his neighbour *m.* to keep
25. if thou lend *m.* to any of my people
30. 16. thou shalt take the atonement *m.* of Israel
Lev. 25. 37. not give him *m.* on usury, *Deut.* 23. 19.
Num. 3. 49. and Moses took the redemption *m.*
Deut. 2. 6. ye shall buy meat and water for *m.* 28.
14. 25. turn it into *m.* ‖ 26. shalt bestow that *m.*
21. 14. thou shalt not sell her at all for *m.*
Judg. 5. 19. they fought, they took no gain of *m.*
16. 18. lords of Philistines brought *m.* to Dalilah
17. 4. yet he restored the *m.* to his mother
1 *Kings* 21. 2. I will give thee the worth of it in *m.*
2 *Kings* 5. 26. is it a time to receive *m.* and oxen?
12. 4. all the *m.* of the dedicated things brought
12. 7. now therefore receive no more *m.* 8.
10. they saw there was much *m.* in the chest, and told the *m.* that was found, 2 *Chron.* 24. 11.
16. the trespass *m.* and sin *m.* was not brought
15. 20. Menahem exacted the *m.* of Israel
23. 35. Jehoiakim gave *m.* to Pharaoh
Ezra 3. 7. gave *m.* also to masons and carpenters
7. 17. buy speedily with this *m.* bullocks, rams
Neh. 5. 4. we have borrowed *m.* for the king
10. I and my servants might exact of them *m.*
Esth. 4. 7. of the sum of *m.* Haman had promised
Job 31. 39. if I have eaten the fruits without *m.*
42. 11. every man also gave him a piece of *m.*
Psal. 15. 5. he that putteth not out his *m.* to usury
Prov. 7. 20. he hath taken a bag of *m.* with him
Eccl. 7. 12. for wisdom and *m.* is a defence
10. 19. wine makes merry, but *m.* answers all things
Isa. 52. 3. ye shall be redeemed without *m.*
55. 1. he that hath no *m.* come, buy without *m.*
2. wherefore spend ye *m.* for what is not bread?

er. 32. 9. I weighed him the *m.* 17 shekels, 10.
44. men shall buy fields for *m.* and subscribe
Lam. 5. 4. we have drunken our water for *m.*
Mic. 3. 11. the prophets thereof divine for *m.*
Mat. 17. 24. they that received the tribute *m.* came
27. thou shalt find a piece of *m.* that take and give
22. 19. why tempt ye me? shew me the tribute *m.*
25. 18. digged in the earth, and hid his lord's *m.*
27. thou oughtest therefore to have put my *m.* to the exchangers, and at my coming, *Luke* 19. 23.
28. 12. they gave large *m.* to the soldiers
15. so they took *m.* and did as they were taught
Mark 6. 8. they take no *m.* in their purse, *Luke* 9. 3.
12. 41. the people cast *m.* into the treasury
14. 11. and promised to give him *m.* *Luke* 22. 5.
Acts 4. 37. brought the *m.* and laid it at apostles' feet
8. 18. Simon the sorcerer offered them *m.*
20. but Peter said, thy *m.* perish with thee
24. 26. he hoped that *m.* should have been given
1 *Tim.* 6. 10. the love of *m.* is the root of all evil
See Bought.

MONEY-CHANGERS.

Mat. 21. 12. Jesus overthrew tables of *m.-changers*, and seats of them that sold doves, *Mark* 11. 15.
John 2. 14. Jesus found in temple *m.-changers* sitting
15. he poured out *m.-chang.* overthrew their tables

MONSTERS.

Lam. 4. 3. even the sea *m.* draw out the breast

MONTH.

The Hebrews *had their* Sacred *and* Civil *year; the former for the celebration of their feasts and religious ceremonies, which began with the month* Nisan, *or* March; *the latter for the ordering of their political or civil affairs, which began in* Tisri, *or* September. *The ancient* Hebrews *had no particular names to express their* Months; *they said, the first, second, third, and so on. In* Exod. 13. 4. *we find* Moses *makes mention of the month* Abib, *or the month of the* young ears of corn, *or of the* new fruits, *which is probably the name that the* Egyptians *gave to the month which the* Hebrews *afterwards called* Nisan, *and which was the first of the holy year; every where else* Moses *marks out the months only by their order of succession, which method is continued in the books of* Joshua, Judges, and Samuel. *Under* Solomon, 1 Kings 6. 1. *we read of the month Zif, which is the second month of the holy year, and which answers to that which afterwards had the name of* Jiar, *or* April. *In the same chapter, verse* 38. *we read of the month* Bul, *which is the eighth of the holy year, and answers to* Marchesvan, *or* October. *Lastly, in* 1 Kings 8. 2. *we read of the month* Ethanim, *which answers to* Tisri, *or the seventh of the holy year. The critics are not agreed about the origin of these names of the months, or from whom they were borrowed. But after the captivity of* Babylon, *the* Hebrews *took the names of the months, as they found them among the* Chaldeans *and* Persians, *among whom they had lived so long a time. Here follow the names of these months, and the order in which they follow one another.*

The names of the *Hebrew* months, according to the order of the holy year.

1. Nisan,	Answering to our	*March.*
2. Jiar,		*April.*
3. Sivan,		*May.*
4. Thammuz,		*June.*
5. Ab,		*July.*
6. Elul,		*August.*
7. Tisri,		*September.*
8. Marchesvan,		*October.*
9. Chisleu,		*November.*
10. Thebet,		*December.*
11. Sebat,		*January.*
12. Adar,		*February.*

The names and order of the months in the Civil year are the same as in the preceding table, only beginning the year with Tisri, *or* September, *and ending with* Elul, *or* August.

At first they measured their months according to the sun, and then every month consisted of thirty days, which appears by the enumeration of the days the flood was upon the earth, namely, a hundred and fifty days, which made five months, Gen. 7. 11. | 8. 4. *But after they came out of* Egypt, *they measured their months by the course of the moon, and then the first month was of thirty days, the next of twenty-nine, and so on alternately: That which had thirty days was called a full or complete month: and that which had but twenty-nine days was called incomplete, or deficient. The new moon was always the beginning of the month, and that day they called* Neomenia, *new Moon, or new Month.*

When it is said, that the Hebrew *months answered to ours, that* Nisan, *for example, answered to* March, *it must be understood with some latitude: for the lunar months can never be reduced exactly to solar ones. The vernal equinox falls in the month of* March, *according to the course of the solar year. But in the lunar year, the new moon will fall in the month of* March, *and the full moon in the month of* April. *So that the* Hebrew *months will commonly answer to two of our months, and partake of both.*

The twelve lunar months making but three hundred and fifty-four days, and six hours, the Jewish *year was short of the* Roman *by twelve days. But to recover the equinoctial points again, from which this difference of the solar and lunar year would separate the new moon of the first month, the Jews took care every three years to intercalate a thirteenth month into their year, which they called* Ve-adar, *or the second* Adar: *And by this means their lunar year equalled the solar: because in thirty-six months, according to the sun, there would be thirty-seven according to the moon.*

Gen. 29. 14. Jacob abode with Laban space of a *m.*
Exod. 13. 4. this day came ye out in the *m.* Abib
Exod. 23. 15. thou shalt keep the feast in the *m.* Abib
34. 18. for in the *m.* Abib thou camest out from Egypt, 34. 18. *Deut.* 16. 1. *Josh.* 5. 10.
Lev. 27. 6. if it be from a *m.* old to five years
Num. 3. 15. number of the children of Levi, every male from a *m.* old, 22, 28, 34, 39, 40, 43. | 26. 62.
9. 22. or a *m.* or year that the cloud tarried
11. 20. ye shall eat flesh, even a whole *m.* 21.
18. 16. from a *m.* old shalt thou redeem
28. 14. the burnt offering of every *m.* 29. 6.
Deut. 21. 13. remain in thine house a full *m.*
1 *Kings* 4. 7. each man his *m.* made provision, 27.
5. 14. a *m.* they were in Lebanon, two at home
6. 37. in the *m.* Zif || 38. in the *m.* Bul
8. 2. feast in *m.* Ethanim || *Neh.* 1. 1. in *m.* Chisleu
Neh. 2. 1. in *m.* Nisan, *Esth.* 3. 7. || 6. 15. *m.* Elul
Esth. 9. 15. Jews gathered in *m.* Adar, 17, 19, 21.
22. *m.* which was turned from sorrow to joy
Jer. 2. 24. in her *m.* they shall find her
Hos. 5. 7. now shall a *m.* devour them with portions
Zech. 11. 8. three shepherds I cut off in one *m.*
Rev. 9. 15. which were prepared for a day and a *m.*
22. 2. the tree of life yielded her fruit every *m.*
See First.

Second MONTH.

Gen. 7. 11. in *second m.* the fountains were broken up
8. 14. and in the *second m.* was the earth dried
Exod. 16. 1. came to the wildern. of Sin in *second m.*
Num. 1. 1. in *second m.* take sum of the congregation
9. 11. on *sec. m.* shall keep passover, 2 *Chr.* 30. 2.
10. 11. on *sec. m.* cloud was taken up from tabern.
1 *Kings* 6. 1. *sec. m.* Sol. began to build, 2 *Chr.* 3. 2.
1 *Chron.* 27. 4. over the course of *sec. m.* was Dodai
Ezra 3. 8. in *second m.* began Zerubbabel to appoint

Third MONTH.

Exod. 19. 1. in *third m.* came into wilderness of Sinai
1 *Chr.* 27. 5. third captain for *third m.* was Benaiah
2 *Chr.* 15. 10. gathered at Jerusalem in the *third m.*
31. 7. in *third m.* they began to lay the foundation
Esth. 8. 9. the king's scribes were called in *third m.*
Ezek. 31. 1. in *th. m.* word of Lord came to Ezekiel

Fourth MONTH.

2 *Kings* 25. 3. in the *fourth m.* the famine prevailed
1 *Chr.* 27. 7. fourth captain for *fourth m.* was Asahel
Jer. 39. 2. in the *fourth m.* the city was broken up
52. 6. in *fourth m.* the famine was sore in the city
Ezek. 1. 1. in *fourth m.* Ezekiel saw visions of God
Zech. 8. 19. the fast of the *fourth m.* shall be joy
See Fifth.

Sixth MONTH.

1 *Chr.* 27. 9. the sixth captain for *sixth m.* was Ira
Ezek. 8. 1. in *sixth m.* the elders of Jud. sat before me
Hag. 1. 1. in *sixth m.* word of Lord came by Haggai
15. in *sixth m.* they did work in house of the L.
Luke 1. 26. in *sixth m.* the angel Gabriel was sent
36. this is *sixth m.* with her that was called barren
See Seventh.

Eighth MONTH.

Zech. 1. 1. in *eighth m.* came the word to Zechariah

Ninth MONTH.

Ezra 10. 9. in the *ninth m.* the people sat trembling
Jer. 36. 9. in the *ninth m.* they proclaimed a fast
22. the king sat in winter house in the *ninth m.*
Hag. 2. 10. in *ninth m.* came word of L. by Haggai
18. even from the *ninth m.* consider it
Zech. 7. 1. the word came to Zechariah in *ninth m.*

Tenth MONTH.

Gen. 8. 5. the waters decreased until the *tenth m.*
Ezra 10. 16. and sat down in *tenth m.* to examine
Esth. 2. 16. Esther was taken to the king in *tenth m.*
Jer. 39. 1. *tenth m.* came Neb. against Jerusal. 52. 4.
Ezek. 24. 1. in *tenth m.* came word of L. to me, 29. 1.
33. 21. in the *tenth m.* one that had escaped told me

Eleventh MONTH.

Deut. 1. 3. in the *eleventh m.* Moses spake to Israel
Zech. 1. 7. in *elev. m.* came the word to Zechariah

Twelfth MONTH.

Esth. 3. 7. cast lots before Haman to the *twelfth m.*
13. on the thirteenth day of *twel. m.* 8. 12. | 9. 1.
Jer. 52. 31. in *twelfth m.* Evil-merodach lifted head
Ezek. 32. 1. in *twelfth m.* the word of L. came to me

This MONTH.

Exod. 12. 2. *this m.* shall be the beginning of months
3. *this m.* they shall take every man a lamb
13. 5. keep this service in *this m.* *Num.* 9. 3. | 28. 17.
Num. 29. 7. on tenth day of *t. m.* an holy convocation
Neh. 9. 1. *this m.* Israel assembled with fasting

MONTHLY.

Isa. 47. 13. let the *m.* prognosticators stand up

MONTHS.

Num. 10. 10. in beginnings of your *m.* blow trumpets
28. 11. in beginnings of *m.* offer a burnt offering
14. this is the burnt-offering through the *m.*
Judg. 11. 37. let me alone two *m.* that I may bewail
39. at the end of two *m.* she returned to Jephthah
19. 2. his concubine was with her father four *m.*
20. 47. and abode in the rock Rimmon four *m.*
1 *Sam.* 6. 1. ark was in coun. of Philistines seven *m.*
27. 7. Dav. was with Philistines a year and four *m.*
2 *Sam.* 2. 11. David reigned in Hebron over Judah seven years and six *m.* 5. 5. 1 *Chron.* 3. 4.
6. 11. the ark was with Obed-edom three *m.*
24. 8. they came to Jerusalem at the end of nine *m.*
1 *Kings* 5. 14. and two *m.* they were at home
11. 16. for six *m.* did Joab remain in Edom
2 *Kings* 15. 8. Zachariah reigned over Israel six *m.*
1 *Chr.* 27. 1. month by month thro' the *m.* of the year
Esth. 2. 12. after she had been twelve *m.* purified, six *m.* with oil of myrrh, six *m.* with sweet odours
Job 3. 6. let it not come into the number of the *m.*
7. 3. so am I made to possess *m.* of vanity
14. 5. the number of his *m.* are with thee
21. 21. when the number of his *m.* is cut off
29. 2. O that I were as in *m.* past, as in the days
39. 2. canst thou number the *m.* that they fulfil?
Ezek. 39. 12. seven *m.* Israel shall be burying of Gog
14. after the end of seven *m.* shall they search
47. 12. shall bring new fruit according to his *m.*
Dan. 4. 29. at the end of twelve *m.* Nebuch. walked
Luke 1. 24. Elizabeth conceiv. and hid herself five *m.*
4. 25. many widows in days of Elias, when heaven was shut up three years and six *m.* *Jam.* 5. 17.
John 4. 35. are yet four *m.* then cometh harvest
Acts 18. 11. Paul continued there a year and six *m.*
Gal. 4. 10. ye observe days, and *m.* and times
Rev. 9. 5. they shall be tormented five *m.* 10.
11. 2. holy city they tread under foot forty-two *m.*
13. 5. power was given him to continue forty-two *m.*
See Three.

MONUMENTS.

Isa. 65. 4. a provok. people which lodge in the *m.*

MOON

Is a secondary planet, which attends on the earth to give light by night, and which furnishes the fruits of the earth with the moisture and juices that nourish them, Gen. 1. 16. Deut. 33. 14. Jer. 31. 35. To which are compared, [1] *The church of God, because of her splendour and brightness, which she derives from Christ, the* Sun of righteousness, *as the moon does her light from the sun; and withal to intimate that the church, like the moon, may have her eclipses, and be in darkness for a time,* Cant. 6. 10. [2] *The world, and all earthly things, because of their changeableness and uncertainty,* Rev. 12. 1.

Deut. 33. 14. precious things put forth by the *m.*
Josh. 10. 12. stand, thou *m.* in the valley of Ajalon
Judg. 8. † 21. took ornaments from them like *m.*
Job 25. 5. behold the *m.* and it shineth not
Psal. 8. 3. when I consider the *m.* thou ordained
72. 7. and peace so long as the *m.* endureth
89. 37. it shall be established for ever as the *m.*
104. 19. he appointeth the *m.* for seasons
Eccl. 12. 2. while the sun, *m.* or stars, be not darken.
Cant. 6. 10. fair as *m.* clear as the sun, and terrible
Isa. 3. 18. and their round tires like the *m.*
See Sun.

New MOON.

1 *Sam.* 20. 5. behold, to-morrow is the *new m.* 18.
2 *Kings* 4. 23. it is neither *new m.* nor sabbath
Psal. 81. 3. blow up the trumpet in the *new m.*
Prov. 7. † 20. and will come home at the *new m.*
Isa. 66. 23. that from one *new m.* to another
Ezek. 46. 1. in the day of *new m.* it shall be opened
6. in the day of *new m.* offer a young bullock
Amos 8. 5. saying, when will the *new m.* be gone?
Col. 2. 16. no man judge you in respect of the *new m.*

New MOONS.

1 *Chron.* 23. 31. to offer burnt sacrifices in the *new m.* 2 *Chron.* 2. 4. | 31. 3. *Ezra* 3. 5. *Neh.* 10. 33. *Ezek.* 46. 3.
Isa. 1. 13. *new m.* and sabbaths I cannot away with
14. your *new m.* and feasts my soul hateth
Ezek. 45. 17. and drink offerings in the *new m.*
Hos. 2. 11. I will cause to cease her *new m.*

MORE.

Gen. 29. 30. Jacob loved Rachel *m.* than Leah
36. 7. riches *m.* than that they might dwell together
37. 3. Israel loved Joseph *m.* than all his children
5. and his brethren hated him yet the *m.* 8.
Exod. 1. 9. the children of Israel are *m.* than we
12. the *m.* they afflicted them, the *m.* they grew
5. 9. let there *m.* work be laid upon the men
9. 34. Pharaoh sinned yet *m.* and hardened his heart
11. 1. yet will I bring one plague *m.* on Pharaoh
16. 17. they gathered some *m.* some less
30. 15. the rich shall not give *m.* nor poor less
Lev. 6. 5. and shall add the fifth part *m.* thereto
13. 5. priest shall shut him seven days *m.* 33, 54.
26. 18. I will punish you seven times *m.* 21.
Num. 3. 46. first-born which are *m.* than Levites
22. 15. sent again princes *m.* honourable than they
18. beyond the word of the Lord, to do less or *m.*
19. I may know what the Lord will say to me *m.*
26. 54. to many thou shalt give the *m.* 33. 54.
Deut. 1. 11. the L. make you a thousand times *m.*
7. 7. Lord did not set his love on you, because *m.*
17. if thou say, nations are *m.* than I, 20. 1.
19. 9. then shalt thou add three cities *m.* for thee
Josh. 10. 11. they were *m.* which died with hail
Judg. 2. 19. they corrupted themselves *m.* than
16. 30. *m.* than they which he slew in his life
18. 24. ye are gone away, and what have I *m.?*
Ruth 1. 17. Ruth said, the Lord do so to me and *m.* also, 1 *Sam.* 14. 44. 2 *Sam.* 3. 35. | 19. 13.
3. 10. thou hast shewed *m.* kindn. in the latter end
1 *Sam.* 3. 17. God do so to thee and *m.* also
18. 8. what can ye have *m.* but the kingdom?
20. 13. the Lord do so and much *m.* to Jonathan
22. 15. thy servant knew nothing less or *m.*
24. 17. he said, thou art *m.* righteous than I
25. 22. so and *m.* do God to the enemies of David
36. she told him nothing less or *m.* until morning
2 *Sam.* 3. 9. so do God to Abner, and *m.* also
5. 13. David took him *m.* concubines and wives
6. 22. and I will yet be *m.* vile than thus
7. 20. and what can David say *m.* unto thee?
19. 43. we have also *m.* right in David than ye
1 *Kings* 2. 23. God do so, *m.* also, 20. 10. 2 *Kings* 6. 31.
16. 33. Ahab did *m.* to provoke God to anger
19. 2. so let the gods do to me, and *m.* also
2 *Kings* 4. 6. he said, there is not a vessel *m.*
6. 16. *m.* than they that be with them, 2 *Chr.* 32. 7.
21. 9. Manasseh seduced them to do *m.* evil
1 *Chron.* 21. 3. Lord make his people so many *m.*
24. 4. and there were *m.* chief men found
2 *Chron.* 10. 11. I will put *m.* to your yoke
20. 25. found *m.* spoil than they could carry away
25. 9. the Lord is able to give thee *m.* than this
28. 13. ye intend to add *m.* to our sins and trespass
22. Ahaz did trespass yet *m.* against the Lord
29. 34. the Levites were *m.* upright in heart
32. 16. his servants spake *m.* against the Lord
33. 23. but Amon trespassed *m.* and *m.*
Ezra 7. 20. whatsoever *m.* shall be needful
Neh. 13. 18. yet ye bring *m.* wrath upon Israel
Esth. 2. 17. Esther obtained favour *m.* than all
6. 6. delight to do honour *m.* than to myself?
Job 3. 21. and dig for it *m.* than hid treasures
23. 12. his words *m.* than my necessary food
34. 19. nor regardeth the rich *m.* than the poor
23. for he will not lay on man *m.* than right
35. 2. saidst, my righteousness is *m.* than God's
11. who teacheth us *m.* than the beasts of earth

Job 42. 12. Lord blessed the latter end of Job *m.* than
Ps. 4. 7. *m.* than when their corn and wine increas.
19. 10. *m.* to be desired are they than gold
40. 5. thy thoughts are *m.* than can be numbered
12. iniquities are *m.* than hairs of mine head
52. 3. thou lovest evil *m.* than good, and lying
69. 4. that hate me are *m.* than hairs of mine head
71. 14. and I will yet praise thee *m.* and *m.*
73. 7. they have *m.* than heart could wish
78. 17. and they sinned yet *m.* against him
87. 2. gates of Zion *m.* than all dwellings of Jacob
115. 14. the Lord shall increase you *m.* and *m.*
119. 99. I have *m.* understanding than my teachers
100. I understand *m.* than the ancients
130. 6. *m.* than they that watch for the morning
Prov. 3. 15. wisdom is *m.* precious than rubies
4. 18. that shineth *m.* and *m.* to the perfect day
11. 24. there is that withholdeth *m.* than is meet
17. 10. a reproof entereth *m.* into a wise man
26. 12. there is *m.* hope of a fool than of him, 29. 20.
Eccl. 2. 9. I increased *m.* than all before me
16. there is no remembrance of wise *m.* than fool
25. or who can hasten hereunto *m.* than I?
4. 2. the dead *m.* than the living that are yet alive
5. 1. and be *m.* ready to hear than to give sacrifice
Cant. 1. 4. we will remember thy love *m.* than wine
5. 9. what is thy beloved *m.* than another? 9.
Isa. 5. 4. what could been done *m.* to my vineyard?
9. 1. afterward did *m.* grievously afflict her
15. 9. for I will bring *m.* upon Dimon, lions
52. 14. his visage so marred *m.* than any man
54. 1. for *m.* are the children of the desolate than
Jer. 3. 11. Israel justified herself *m.* than Judah
46. 23. because they are *m.* than the grasshoppers
Ezek. 5. 6. changed my judgments into wicked. *m.*
7. because he multiplied *m.* than the nations
16. 47. thou wast corrupted *m.* than they in all thy
ways, 51, 52. | 23. 11.
Dan. 2. 30. not for any wisdom that I have *m.* than
3. 19. they should heat the furnace seven times *m.*
11. 8. he shall continue *m.* years than the king
Hos. 6. 6. knowledge of God *m.* than burnt offering
13. 2. now they sin *m.* and *m.* and have made idols
Jonah 1. †11. the sea grew *m.* and *m.* tempestuous
Hab. 1. 13. wicked devoureth man *m.* righteous than
2. †16. art filled *m.* with shame than glory
Mat. 5. 37. what is *m.* than these cometh of evil
47. brethren only, what do you *m.* than others?
6. 25. is not the life *m.* than meat? *Luke* 12. 23.
10. 31. of *m.* value than many sparrows, *Luke* 12. 7.
37. he that loveth father or mother *m.* than me
11. 9. I say unto you, and *m.* than a prophet
12. 45. taketh seven spirits *m.* wicked than himself
13. 12. and he shall have *m.* abundance
18. 13. he rejoiceth *m.* of that sheep than of 99
16. then take with thee one or two *m.*
20. 10. they supposed they should have received *m.*
31. but they cried the *m.* have mercy on us, 27. 23.
Mark 10. 48. | 15. 14. *Luke* 18. 39.
26. 53. give me *m.* than twelve legions of angels
Mark 4. 24. to you that hear shall *m.* be given
7. 36. the *m.* he charged them, so much the *m.*
12. 43. poor widow cast in *m.* than all, *Luke* 21. 3.
14. 5. the ointment might have been sold for *m.*
Luke 10. 35. what thou spendest *m.* I will repay
12. 48. committed much, of him they will ask *m.*
18. 30. who shall not receive manifold *m.*
John 4. 41. many *m.* believed, because of his word
5. 18. the Jews sought the *m.* to kill him
7. 31. will he do *m.* miracles than these?
12. 43. they loved the praise of men *m.* than
15. 2. purgeth it, that it may bring forth *m.* fruit
21. 15. Simon, lovest thou me *m.* than these?
Acts 4. 19. to hearken to you *m.* than to God
5. 14. believers were the *m.* added to the Lord
9. 22. but Saul increased the *m.* in strength
19. 32. the *m.* part knew not why they came
20. 35. it is *m.* blessed to give, than to receive
23. 13. there were *m.* than forty who conspired, 21.
27. 11. believed the master *m.* than Paul
Rom. 1. 25. who served the creature *m.* than Creator
3. 7. if the truth of God hath *m.* abounded
8. 37. in all these we are *m.* than conquerors
1 *Cor.* 8. †8. neither if we eat, have we the *m.*
9. 19. myself servant to all, that I might gain the *m.*
14. 18. I speak with tongues *m.* than you all
2 *Cor.* 7. 7. so I rejoiced the *m.* || 10. 8. I boast the *m.*
11. 23. I am *m.* in prisons *m.* frequent, in deaths oft
Gal. 4. 27. the desolate hath many *m.* children
Phil. 1. 9. love may abound *m.* and *m.* 1 *Thess.* 4. 10.
3. 4. if he might trust in the flesh, I *m.*
1 *Thess.* 4. 1. in pleasing God, abound *m.* and *m.*
2 *Tim.* 3. 4. lovers of pleasure *m.* than lovers of God
Philem. 21. that thou wilt also do *m.* than I say
Heb. 11. 32. what shall I say *m.* time would fail
12. 25. much *m.* shall not we escape, if we turn
26. yet once *m.* I shake not the earth only, 27.
Jam. 4. 6. he giveth *m.* grace, wherefore he saith
2 *Pet.* 1. 19. we have a *m.* sure word of prophecy
Rev. 2. 19. and the last to be *m.* than the first
9. 12. behold, there come two woes *m.* hereafter
See ABUNDANTLY.

Any MORE.

Gen. 8. 12. the dove returned not again *any m.*
21. I will not curse the ground *any m.* 9. 11.
17. 5. nor shall thy name *any m.* be called Abram
35. 10. not *any m.* be called Jacob, but Israel
Exod. 8. 29. let not Pharaoh deal deceitfully *any m.*
9. 29. neither shall there be *any m.* hail
11. 6. nor shall there a cry be like it *any m.*
36. 6. let neither man nor woman make *any m.*
Lev. 27. 20. it shall not be redeemed *any m.*
Num. 18. 5. that there be no wrath *any m.* on Israel
Deut. 5. 25. if we hear the voice of the Ld. *any m.*
18. 16. neither let me see this great fire *any m.*
Josh. 5. 12. neither had Israel manna *any m.*
7. 12. neither will I be with you *any m.*
Ruth 1. 11. are there *any m.* sons in my womb?
1 *Sam.* 27. 1. Saul shall despair to seek me *any m.*
2 *Sam.* 7. 10. nor children of wickedn. afflict *any m.*
10. 19. feared to help Ammon *any m.* 1 *Chr.* 19. 19.
19. 29. why speakest thou *any m.* of thy matters?

2 *Kings* 21. 8. neither will I make the feet of Israel
move *any m.* out of the land, 2 *Chr.* 33. 8.
Job 7. 10. nor shall his place know him *any m.* 20. 9.
34. 31. it is meet to say, I will not offend *any m.*
Eccl. 9. 5. neither have they *any m.* a reward
Isa. 1. 5. why should ye be stricken *any m.*?
2. 4. nor shall they learn war *any m.* *Mic.* 4. 3.
30. 20. nor shall thy teachers be removed *any m.*
62. 4. nor shall thy land be termed desolate *any m.*
Jer. 3. 16. neither shall that be done *any m.*
17. nor walk *any m.* after imagination of heart
10. 20. there is none to stretch forth my tent *any m.*
20. 9. I said, I will not speak *any m.* in his name
22. 11. he shall not return thither *any m.*
30. no man shall prosper, ruling *any m.* in Judah
31. 12. they shall not sorrow *any m.* at all
40. it shall not be thrown down *any m.* for ever
34. 10. should not serve themselves of them *any m.*
Ezek. 5. 9. whereunto I will not do *any m.* the like
12. 28. none of my words be prolonged *any m.*
16. 41. thou also shalt give no hire *any m.*
63. thou mayest never open thy mouth *any m.*
21. 5. my sword shall not return *any m.*
23. 27. thou shalt not remember Egypt *any m.*
24. 13. not be purged from thy filthiness *any m.*
27. 36. be a terror, and never shalt be *any m.* 28. 19.
29. 15. neither shall it exalt itself *any m.*
32. 13. nor foot of man trouble them *any m.* 37. 23.
39. 28. but I have left none of them *any m.* there
29. nor will I hide my face *any m.* from them
Hos. 14. 3. nor say *any m.* to the work of our hands
8. what have I to do *any m.* with idols?
Joel 3. 17. no strangers pass through her *any m.*
Amos 7. 8. I will not again pass by them *a. m.* 8. 2.
13. but prophesy not again *any m.* at Beth-el
Zeph. 3. 15. thou shalt not see evil *any m.*
Mat. 22. 46. nor durst any ask him *any m.* questions
Mark 8. 14. they had not *any m.* than one loaf
9. 8. they saw no man *any m.* save Jesus only
Luke 20. 36. neither can they die *any m.* for they
22. 16. I will not eat *any m.* thereof, until it be
Rom. 14. 13. let us not judge one another *any m.*
Heb. 12. 19. word should not be spoken to them *a. m.*
Rev. 7. 16. neither shall they thirst *any m.*
12. 8. nor was their place in heaven found *any m.*
18. 11. no man buyeth her merchandise *any m.*
21. 4. neither shall there be *any m.* pain

No MORE.

Gen. 9. 15. the waters shall *no m.* become a flood
32. 28. thy name shall be called *no m.* Jacob
38. 26. and Judah knew her again *no m.*
44. 23. ye shall see my face *no m.* *Exod.* 10. 28.
Exod. 5. 7. ye shall *no m.* give the people straw
10. 29. he said, I will see thy face again *no m.*
14. 13. ye shall see them again *no m.* for ever
Lev. 17. 7. shall *no m.* offer their sacrifices to devils
Num. 8. 25. from age of fifty they shall serve *no m.*
Deut. 3. 26. speak *no m.* to me of this matter
5. 22. these words the Lord spake, and added *no m.*
10. 16. circumcise, and be *no m.* stiff-necked
13. 11. shall do *no m.* such wickedness, 17. 13.
17. 16. henceforth return *no m.* that way
28. 68. thou shalt see it *no m.* again, and be sold
31. 2. I am 120 years, I can *no m.* go out and come in
Josh. 23. 13. God will *no m.* drive out these nations
Judg. 8. 28. so they lifted up their heads *no m.*
10. 13. wherefore I will deliver you *no m.*
1 *Sam.* 1. 18. her countenance was *no m.* sad
2. 3. talk *no m.* so exceeding proudly
7. 13. they came *no m.* into the coast of Israel
15. 35. and Samuel came *no m.* to see Saul
18. 2. let him go *no m.* home to his father's house
26. 21. return, for I will *no m.* do thee harm
27. 4. and he sought *no m.* again for him
28. 15. and answereth me *no m.* by prophets
2 *Sam.* 2. 28. and pursued after Israel *no m.*
7. 10. I will plant Israel, that they may dwell in a
place of their own, and move *no m.* 1 *Chr.* 17. 9.
21. 17. thou shalt go *no m.* out with us to battle
1 *Kings* 10. 5. there was *no m.* spirit in her, 2 *Chr.* 9. 4.
2 *Kings* 2. 12. and Elisha saw Elijah *no m.*
6. 23. the bands of Syria came *no m.* into the land
9. 35. they found *no m.* of her than the skull
1 *Chron.* 23. 26. shall *no m.* carry the tabernacle
Neh. 2. 17. let us build, that we be *no m.* a reproach
13. 21. they came *no m.* on the sabbath
Esth. 1. 19. Vashti come *no m.* before the king
2. 14. she came *no m.* in to the king, except
Job 7. 7. mine eyes shall *no m.* see good
8. shall see me *no m.* || 9. shall come up *no m.*
10. he shall return *no m.* to his house
14. 12. man riseth not, till the heavens be *no m.*
20. 9. the eye that saw him shall see him *no m.*
24. 20. he shall be *no m.* remembered
32. 15. they were amazed, they answered *no m.* 16.
34. 32. if I have done iniquity, I will do *no m.*
41. 8. remember the battle, do *no m.*
Psal. 10. 18. that man of earth may *no m.* oppress
39. 13. spare me, before I go hence, and be *no m.*
41. 8. now that he lieth, he shall rise up *no m.*
74. 9. see not signs, there is *no m.* any prophet
77. 7. will he cast off, and be favourable *no m.*
83. 4. that name of Isr. be *no m.* in remembrance
88. 5. the slain whom thou rememberest *no m.*
103. 16. the place thereof shall know it *no m.*
104. 35. and let the wicked be *no m.*
Prov. 10. 25. as the whirlwind, so is the wicked *no m.*
31. 7. and remember his misery *no m.*
Eccl. 4. 13. king, who will *no m.* be admonished
Isa. 1. 13. bring *no m.* vain oblat. incense abomin.
10. 20. shall *no m.* stay on him that smote them
19. 7. shall wither, be driven away, and be *no m.*
23. 10. there is *no m.* strength || 12. *no m.* rejoice
26. 21. the earth shall *no m.* cover her slain
30. 19. shalt weep *no m.* || 38. 11. behold man *no m.*
32. 5. the vile person shall be *no m.* called liberal
47. 1. thou shalt *no m.* be called tender and delic.
5. shalt *no m.* be called the lady of kingdoms
51. 22. thou shalt *no m.* drink it again
52. 1. *no m.* come into the uncircumcised
60. 18. violence shall *no m.* be heard in thy land
19. the sun shall be *no m.* thy light by day

Isa. 60. 20. thy sun shall *no m.* go down, nor moon
62. 4. thou shalt *no m.* be termed Forsaken
8. I will *no m.* give thy corn to thine enemies
65. 19. the voice of weeping shall be *no m.* heard
20. there shall be *no m.* thence an infant of days
Jer. 2. 31. we are lords, we will come *no m.* to thee
3. 16. they shall say *no m.* the ark of the covenant
7. 32. it shall *no m.* be called Tophet, 19. 6.
11. 19. that his name may be *no m.* remembered
16. 14. shall be *no m.* said, the Lord liveth, 23. 7.
22. 10. shall return *no m.* || 12. see this land *no m.*
23. 4. they shall fear *no m.* nor be dismayed
36. the burden of the L. shall ye mention *no m.*
25. 27. fall, and rise *no m.* because of the sword
31. 34. and they shall teach *no m.* every man his
neighbour, and I will remember their sin *no m.*
33. 24. they should be *no m.* a nation before them
42. 18. and ye shall see this place *no m.*
44. 26. my name shall be *no m.* named in Egypt
49. 7. thus saith Lord, is wisdom *no m.* in Teman?
50. 39. it shall *no m.* be inhabited for ever
Lam. 2. 9. law is *no m.* her prophets find no vision
4. 22. he will *no m.* carry thee away into captivity
Ezek. 12. 24. there shall be *no m.* any vain vision
25. and my word shall be *no m.* prolonged
13. 15. the wall is *no m.* || 14. 11. go *no m.* astray
21. and they shall be *no m.* in your hand
23. therefore ye shall see *no m.* vanity
16. 42. I will be quiet, and will be *no m.* angry
19. 9. that his voice should be *no m.* heard
20. 39. but pollute ye my holy name *no m.*
21. 13. it shall be *no m.* saith the Lord, 27.
32. thou shalt be *no m.* remembered, L. spoken it
24. 27. and thou shalt speak, and be *no m.* dumb
26. 14. thou shalt be *no m.* built || 21. shall be *no m.*
28. 24. there shall be *no m.* a pricking briar to Isr
29. 15. they shall *no m.* rule over the nations
16. shall be *no m.* the confidence of Israel
30. 13. there shall be *no m.* a prince of Egypt
34. 22. and they shall be *no m.* a prey, 28, 29.
36. 14. therefore thou shalt devour men *no m.*
37. 22. and they shall be *no m.* two nations
43. 7. my name shall house of Israel *no m.* defile
45. 8. my princes shall *no m.* oppress my people
Hos. 1. 6. I will *no m.* have mercy upon Israel
2. 16. and thou shalt call me *no m.* Baali
17. they shall *no m.* be remembered by their name
9. 15. I will drive them out, I will love them *no m.*
Joel 2. 19. I will *no m.* make you a reproach
Amos 5. 2. the virgin is fallen, she shall *no m.* rise
9. 15. they shall *no m.* be pulled out of their land
Mic. 5. 12. thou shalt have *no m.* soothsayers
13. thou shalt *no m.* worship work of thine hands
Nah. 1. 12. I will afflict thee *no m.* saith the Lord
14. a command that *no m.* of thy name be sown
15. the wicked shall *no m.* pass through thee
2. 13. voice of thy messengers shall *no m.* be heard
Zeph. 3. 11. and thou shalt *no m.* be haughty
Zech. 11. 6. I will *no m.* pity the inhabitants
13. 2. and they shall *no m.* be remembered
14. 11. there shall be *no m.* utter destruction
21. be *no m.* the Canaanite in the house of Lord
Mat. 19. 6. they are *no m.* twain, but one, *Mark* 10. 8.
Mark 7. 12. and ye suffer him *no m.* to do ought
9. 25. come out of him, and enter *no m.* into him
14. 25. I will drink *no m.* of the fruit of the vine
Luke 3. 13. exact *no m.* than that is appointed
9. 13. we have *no m.* but five loaves and two fishes
12. 4. after that have *no m.* that they can do
John 5. 14. thou art made whole, sin *no m.* 8. 11.
6. 66. many went back, and walked *no m.* with him
14. 19. a little while the world seeth me *no m.*
15. 4. *no m.* can ye, except ye abide in me
16. 10. I go to my Father, and ye see me *no m.*
21. she remembereth *no m.* the anguish, for joy
25. when I shall *no m.* speak in parables
17. 11. now I am *no m.* in the world, but these are
Acts 8. 39. that the eunuch saw him *no m.*
13. 34. now *no m.* to return to corruption
20. 25. I know that ye shall see my face *no m.* 38.
Rom. 6. 9. dieth *no m.* death hath *no m.* dominion
7. 17. now then it is *no m.* I that do it, but sin, 20.
11. 6. it is *no m.* of works, else grace is *no m.* grace,
but if it be of works, grace is *no m.* grace
2 *Cor.* 5. 16. yet henceforth know we him *no m.*
Gal. 3. 18. if of the law, it is *no m.* of promise
4. 7. thou art *no m.* a servant, but a son
Eph. 2. 19. ye are *no m.* strangers and foreigners
4. 14. we be *no m.* children tossed to and fro
28. let him that stole steal *no m.* but labour
Heb. 8. 12. their iniq. I will remember *no m.* 10. 17.
10. 2. should have *no m.* conscience of sins
18. there is *no m.* offering for sin, 26.
Rev. 3. 12. he that overcometh shall go *no m.* out
7. 16. shall hunger *no m.* neither thirst any more
18. 14. thou shalt find them *no m.* at all
22. musicians shall be heard *no m.* in thee, 23.
20. 3. that he should deceive the nations *no m.*
21. 1. *no m.* sea || 4. *no m.* death || 22. 3. *no m.* curses

Much MORE.

Exod. 36. 5. the people bring *much m.* than enough
Prov. 11. 31. *much m.* the wicked and the sinner
Isa. 56. 12. as this day, and *much m.* abundant
Mat. 6. 30. shall he not *much m.* clothe you?
Luke 5. 15. so *much m.* went a fame of him abroad
7. 26. I say unto you, and *much m.* than a prophet
Rom. 5. 9. *much m.* being now justified by his blood
10. *much m.* being reconciled, we shall be saved
17. *much m.* they that receive abundance of grace
20. where sin abounded, grace *much m.* abound
2 *Cor.* 3. 9. *much m.* doth ministration of righteousn.
11. *much m.* that which remaineth is glorious
8. 22. but now we have proved *much m.* diligent
Phil. 1. 14. are *much m.* bold to speak thereof
2. 12. have obeyed, now *much m.* in my absence
Heb. 10. 25. so *much m.* as you see day approaching
12. 25. *much m.* shall not we escape, if we turn
1 *Pet.* 1. 7. being *much m.* precious than of gold

MOREOVER.

Psal. 19. 11. *m.* by them is thy servant warned
Isa. 39. 8. he said, *m.* there shall be peace and truth
Ezek. 16. 29. thou hast *m.* multiplied fornication

Zech. 5. 6. *m.* this is their resemblance through earth
Heb. 11. 36. of mockings, *m.* of bonds and imprison.

MORNING

Signifies, [1] *The beginning of the day, or the time of the sun's rising,* Mark 16. 2. Luke 24. 1. [2] *The one part of a natural day,* Gen. 1. 5. *The evening and the morning make the day, according to* Moses, *because the ancient Hebrews began their day in the evening.* [3] *The general resurrection, when the dead shall be raised,* Psal. 49. 14. *Death being called the* night, *John* 9. 4. *and compared to sleep,* John 11. 11. *that day is fitly compared to the morning, when men awake out of sleep, and enter upon that everlasting day.* [4] *Early or seasonably,* Psal. 5. 3. [5] *Unseasonably,* Eccl. 10. 16. [6] *Suddenly, or quickly, or in a short time,* Psal. 30. 5. [7] *Daily,* Psal. 73. 14. [8] *The light,* Joel 2. 2.

Wings of the morning, *Psal.* 139. 9. denote *a rapid flight; there being no motion we know of so rapid as the diffusion of the beams of the sun at the breaking of the day.*

*Gen.*19.15.when the *m.* arose, the angel hastened Lot
24. 54. Abraham and servants rose up in the *m.*
26. 31. they rose betimes in the *m.* and sware
29. 25. that in the *m.* behold it was Leah
32. † 24. wrestled with him till ascending of the *m.*
40. 6. Joseph came into them in the *m.* were sad
49. 27. in the *m.* he shall devour the prey
Exod. 7. 15. get thee to Pharaoh in the *m.*
10. 13. in the *m.* the east wind brought locusts
14. 27. the sea returned to his strength in the *m.*
16. 7. in the *m.* ye shall see the glory of the Lord
8. shall give you in the *m.* bread to the full, 12.
13. in the *m.* the dew lay round about the host
29. 39. one lamb thou shalt offer in *m.* *Num.* 28. 4.
41. according to the meat offering of the *m.*
34. 2. be ready in the *m.* and come up in the *m.*
25. nor shall the passover be left to the *m.*
Lev. 6. 9. the burning on the altar all night to the *m.*
Num. 9. 21. the cloud was taken up in the *m.*
22.21. Balaam rose in the *m.* and saddled his ass,22.
Deut. 28. 67. in the *m.* would God it were even
Judg. 6. 31. let him be put to death whilst it is yet *m.*
16. 2. in the *m.* when it is day, we shall kill him
19. 27. her lord rose in the *m.* and opened the doors
20. 19. the children of Israel rose up in the *m.*
2 *Sam.* 13. † 4. why art thou lean *m.* by *m.?*
23. 4. and he shall be as the light of the *m.* when the sun riseth, even a *m.* without clouds
24. 11. for when David was up in the *m.* word came
1 *Kings* 3. 21. when I had considered it in the *m.*
18. 26. and called on name of Baal from *m.* to noon
Neh. 4. 21. some laboured from *m.* till stars appear
8. 3. he read therein from *m.* to mid-day
Job 3. † 9. nor let it see the eye-lids of the *m.*
7. 21. thou shalt seek me in the *m.* but I shall not be
11. 17. thou shalt shine forth, and be as the *m.*
24. 17. for the *m.* is to them as the shadow of death
38. 12. hast thou commanded the *m.* since thy days
41. 18. his eyes are like eyelids of the *m.*
Psal. 5. 3. my voice shalt thou hear in the *m.* O Ld. in the *m.* will I direct my prayer to thee
30. 5. weeping for a night, but joy cometh in the *m.*
46. † 5. God shall help her when the *m.* appeareth
49. 14. shall have dominion over them in the *m.*
59. 16. I will sing of thy mercy in the *m.*
88. 13. in the *m.* shall my prayer prevent thee
90. 5. in the *m.* they are like grass which grows up
6. in the *m.* it flourisheth and groweth up
119. 147. I prevented the dawning of the *m.*
130. 6. waits more than they that watch for the *m.*
139. 9. if I take the wings of the *m.* and dwell
143. 8. to hear thy loving-kindness in the *m.*
Eccl. 10.16.thy king, a child and princes eat in the *m.*
11. 6. in the *m.* sow thy seed, and in the evening
Cant. 6. 10. who is she that looketh forth as the *m.*
Isa. 14. 12. how art fallen, O Lucifer, son of the *m.!*
17. 14. and behold, before the *m.* he is not
21. 12. the watchman said, the *m.* cometh
28. 19. for *m.* by *m.* shall it pass over, by day and n.
50. 4. he wakeneth *m.* by *m.* he wakeneth my ear
58. 8. then shall thy light break forth as the *m.*
Jer. 5. 8. they were as fed horses in the *m.* every one
20. 16. and let him hear the cry in the *m.*
21. 12. execute judgment in the *m.* and deliver
Ezek. 7. 7. the *m.* is come on thee, O thou that dwell.
10. the *m.* is gone forth, the rod hath blossomed
12. 8. in the *m.* came the word of the Lord
24. 18. I spake to the people in the *m.* at even my wife died, I did in the *m.* as I was commanded
33. 22. opened my mouth until came to me in the *m.*
Hos. 6. 3. his going forth is prepared as the *m.*
4. for your goodness is as a *m.* cloud, as early dew
7. 6. in the *m.* it burneth as a flaming fire
10. 15. in a *m.* shall the king of Israel be cut off
Joel 2. 2. as the *m.* spread upon the mountains
Amos 4. 13. that maketh the *m.* darkn. and treadeth
5. 8. and turneth the shadow of death into the *m.*
Jonah 4. 7. God prepared a worm when the *m.* rose
Mic. 2. 1. when the *m.* is light, they practise it
Mat. 16. 3. in the *m.* it will be foul weather
27. 1. when *m.* was come, the elders took counsel
Mark 11. 20. in the *m.* as they passed by, they saw
13. 35. watch, or at the cock-crowing, or in the *m.*

Early in the MORNING.

Gen. 19. 27. Abrah. gat up *early in m.* 21. 14. | 22. 3.
20. 8. therefore Abimelech rose *early in the m.*
28. 18. Jacob rose up *early in m.* and set up a pillar
31. 55. Laban rose *early in m.* kissed sons, daught.
Exod. 8. 20. Ld. said, rise up *early in m.* stand, 9. 13.
24. 4. Moses rose *early in m.* built an altar, 34. 4.
Josh. 3. 1. Josh. rose *early in m.* 6. 12. | 7. 16. | 8. 10.
Judg. 6. 28. the men of the city rose *early in the m.*
38. Gid. rose *ear. in m.* || 19. 5. Levite *ear. in m.* 8.
1 *Sam.* 1. 19. they rose up *early in the m.* 29. 11.
2 *Kings* 3. 22. | 19. 35. 2 *Chr.* 20. 20. *Isa.* 37. 36.
15. 12. Sam. rose *early in m.* || 17. 20. Dav. *ear. in m.*
29. 10. wherefore rise up *early in m.* and depart
Job 1. 5. Job rose up *early in the m.* and offered
Prov. 27. 14. blesseth his friend, rising *early in m.*
Isa. 5. 11. woe to them that rise *early in m.* to follow
Isa. 37. 36. arose *e. in m.* they were all dead corpses
Dan. 6. 19. then king Darius rose very *early in m.*
Mat. 20. 1. who went *early in m.* to hire labourers
Mark 16. 2. *early in m.* came to sepulchre, *Luke* 24. 1.
Luke 21. 38. the people came *early in m.* *John* 8. 2.
Acts 5. 21. they entered into the temple *early in m.*

See EVENING.

Every MORNING.

Exod. 16. 21. and they gathered manna *every m.*
30. 7. shalt burn thereon sweet incense *every m.*
36. 3. brought unto him free offerings *every m.*
Lev. 6. 12. the priest shall burn wood on it *every m.*
1 *Chr.* 9. 27. opening *every m.* pertaineth to porters
23. 30. to stand *every m.* to thank and praise Lord
2 *Chron.* 13. 11. they burn to the Lord *every m.*
Job 7. 18. that thou shouldest visit him *every m.*
Psal. 73. 14. and I have been chastened *every m.*
Isa. 33. 2. O Lord, be thou our arm *every m.*
Lam. 3. 23. the Lord's mercies are new *every m.*
Ezek. 46. 13. thou shalt prepare a lamb *every m.*
14. meat off. *every m.* || 15. *every m.* a burnt off.
Amos 4. 4. and bring your sacrifices *every m.*
Zeph. 3. 5. *every m.* doth he bring judgment to light

Until the MORNING.

Exod. 12. 10. let nothing of it remain *until the m.* 16. 19. | 23. 18. | 29. 34. *Lev.* 7. 15. *Num.* 9. 12.
22. none of you shall go out at the door *u. t. m.*
16. 20. but some of them left of it *until the m.*
23. lay up for you to be kept *until the m.*
Lev. 19. 13. the wages shall not abide *until the m.*
Deut. 16. 4. nor any of the flesh remain *until the m.*
Judg. 19. 25. they abused her all night *until the m.*
Ruth 3. 13. lie down *u. the m.* || 14. she lay *u. t. m.*
1 *Sam.* 3. 15. and Samuel lay *u. t. m.* and opened
19. 2. therefore take heed to thyself *until the m.*
2 *Kings* 10. 8. lay heads of kings in two heaps *u. m.*
Prov. 7. 18. let us take our fill of love *until the m.*
Isa. 38. 13. I reckoned *until the m.* that as a lion

MORNING *light.*

1 *Sam.* 14. 36. and let us spoil them until *m. light*
25. 22. all that pertain to him by *m. light*
36. Abigail told him nothing until *m. light*
2 *Sam.* 17. 22. they passed over Jordan by *m. light*
2 *Kings* 7. 9. they said, if we tarry until *m. light*

See CLOUD.

MORNING *star* and *stars.*

Job 38. 7. when *m. stars* sang together, sons of God
Rev. 2. 28. and I will give him the *m. star*
22. 16. I Jesus am the bright and *m. star*

MORNING *watch.*

Exod. 14. 24. in *m. watch* the Lord said to Moses
1 *Sam.* 11. 11. came into middle of host in *m. watch*

MORROW.

Gen. 30. † 33. my righteousness answer for me to *m.*
Exod. 8. 23. to *m.* shall this sign be, the Lord did so
9. 5. to *m.* the Lord shall do this thing in the land
6. the Lord did that thing, on the *m.* cattle died
13. † 14. asketh thee to *m.* *Deut.* 6. † 20. *Josh.* 4. † 6.
16. 23. to *m.* is the rest of the holy sabbath to Lord
19. 10. go, and sanctify them to day and to *m.*
32. 5. Aaron said, to *m.* is a feast to the Lord
Lev. 7. 16. on the *m.* the remainder shall be eaten, 19. 6.
22. 30. ye shall leave none of it till the *m.*
23. 11. on *m.* after sabbath priest shall wave it
15. ye shall count from the *m.* after the sabbath
Num. 11. 18. say thou to the people, sanctify yourselves against to *m.* ye shall eat, *Josh.* 7. 13.
16. 5. to *m.* the Lord will shew who are his
16. be thou, they and Aaron to *m.* before Lord
41. on the *m.* the congregation murmured
Josh. 3. 5. to *m.* Lord will do wonders among you
5. 12. manna ceased on the *m.* after they had eaten
22. 18. to *m.* he will be wroth with congregation
† 24. to *m.* your children might speak to our child.
Judg. 19. 9. to *m.* get you early on your way
20. 28. go up, for to *m.* I will deliver them
1 *Sam.* 11. 9. to *m.* by that time the sun be hot
20. 5. behold, to *m.* is the new moon, 18.
28. 19. to *m.* shalt thou and thy sons be with me
1 *Kings* 20. 6. I will send my servants to thee to *m.*
2 *Kings* 6. 28. thy son to day, we will eat my son to *m.*
7. 1. to *m.* a measure of fine flour be sold for a shekel
8. 15. on the *m.* he took a thick cloth, and dipt
10. 6. come to me to Jezreel by to *m.* this time
2 *Chron.* 20. 16. to *m.* go ye down against them, 17.
Esth. 5. 8. I will do to *m.* as the king hath said
12. to *m.* am I invited to her with the king
Prov. 3. 28. to *m.* I will give, when thou hast it by thee
27. 1. boast not thyself to *m.* thou knowest not
Isa. 22. 13. let us eat, for to *m.* we die, 1 *Cor.* 15. 32.
56. 12. and to *m.* shall be as this day, much more
Zeph. 3. 3. they gnaw not the bones till the *m.*
Mat. 6. 30. to *m.* is cast into the oven, *Luke* 12. 28.
34. take therefore no thought for the *m.* for the *m.* shall take thought for the things of itself
Luke 13. 32. and I do cures to day, and to *m.*
33. nevertheless, I must walk to day and to *m.*
Acts 20. 7. Paul preached; ready to depart on *m.*
25. 22. to *m.* said he, thou shalt hear him
Jam. 4. 13. to day or to *m.* we will go into such a city
14. whereas, ye know not what shall be on the *m.*

MORSEL.

Gen. 18. 5. I will fetch a *m.* of bread, comfort ye
Judg. 19. 5. comfort thine heart with a *m.* of bread
Ruth 2. 14. eat bread, and dip thy *m.* in the vinegar
2 *Sam.* 12. † 3. it did eat of his own *m.* and drank
Job 31. 17. or have eaten my *m.* myself alone
Prov. 17. 1. better is a dry *m.* and quietness therewith
23. 8. the *m.* thou hast eaten shalt thou vomit up
John 13. † 26. he it is to whom I shall give a *m.*
Heb. 12. 16. who for one *m.* sold his birth-right

See BREAD.

MORSELS.

Psal. 147. 17. he casteth forth his ice like *m.*

MORTAL.

2 *Chron.* 14. † 11. let not *m.* man prevail against thee
Job 4. 17. shall *m.* man be more just than God?
Rom. 6. 12. let not sin reign in your *m.* body
8. 11. shall also quicken your *m.* bodies by his Spirit
1 *Cor.* 15. 53. this *m.* must put on immortality, 54.
2 *Cor.* 4. 11. life of Jesus be manifest in our *m.* flesh

MORTALITY.

2 *Cor.* 5. 4. that *m.* might be swallowed up of life

MORTALLY.

Deut. 19. 11. and smite his neighbour *m.* that he die

MORTAR.

Gen. 11. 3. brick for stone, and slime had they for *m.*
Exod. 1. 14. they made them serve in *m.* and brick
Lev. 14. 42. shall take other *m.* and plaster the house
45. and shall break down the *m.* of the house
Isa. 41. 25. he shall come upon princes as upon *m.*
Ezek. 13. 10. one built a wall, and lo others daubed it with untempered *m.* 11, 14, 15. | 22. 28.
Nah. 3. 14. go into clay, and tread the *m.*

MORTAR.

Num. 11. 8. ground it in mills, or beat it in a *m.*
Prov. 27. 22. tho' thou shouldest bray a fool in a *m.*

MORTGAGED.

Neh. 5. 3. some also said, we have *m.* our lands

MORTIFY.

Rom. 8. 13. but if ye *m.* deeds of body ye shall live
Col. 3. 5. *m.* your members which are on the earth

MOST.

Prov. 20. 6. *m.* men proclaim every one his goodness
Mat. 11. 20. wherein *m.* of mighty works were done
Luke 7. 42. which of them will love him *m.?*
43. I suppose that he to whom he forgave *m.*
Acts 20. 38. sorrowing *m.* of all for words he spake
1 *Cor.* 14. 27. let it be by two, or at *m.* by three

MOTE.

Mat. 7. 3. why beholdest thou *m.* that is in thy brother's eye, but not beam in thy own? *Luke* 6. 41.
4. let me pull out the *m.* out of thine eye
5. first cast, and then shalt thou see clearly to cast out the *m.* out of thy brother's eye, *Luke* 6. 42.

MOTH

Signifies, [1] *A sort of fly which eats cloth,* Job 4. 19. | 13. 28. [2] *Some secret curse and judgment from God,* Isa. 50. 9.

Job 4. 19. in them which are crushed before the *m.*
27. 18. he buildeth his house as a *m.* and booth
Psal. 39. 11. thou makest his beauty consume like *m.*
Isa. 50. 9. the *m.* shall eat them up, 51. 8.
Hos. 5. 12. therefore will I be to Ephraim as a *m.*
Mat. 6. 19. treasures, where *m.* and rust doth corrupt
20. where neither *m.* nor rust corrupt, *Luke* 12. 33.

MOTH-EATEN.

Job 13. 28. consumeth as garment that is *m.-eaten*
Jam. 5. 2. riches corrupted, your garments *m.-eaten*

MOTHER

Signifies, [1] *A woman who has brought forth a child,* Exod. 2. 8. [2] *The dam of the beast,* Exod. 23. 19. It is applied, [1] *To the true church, in which true gospel believers are begotten to, and nourished up in, the faith, by the dispensation of the word and ordinances,* Gal. 4. 26. *It is said to be from above, because its original is from heaven, and its members have their conversation there,* Phil. 3. 20. [2] *To a valiant woman, of whom God made use to deliver his people, to instruct and take care of them with a tender affection,* Judg. 5. 7. [3] *To matrons or aged women, to whom we ought to carry ourselves respectfully, because of their age, as dutiful children do to their mothers,* 1 Tim. 5. 2. [4] *To all true believers who are more dear and near to Christ, than the nearest relations are to any person,* Mat. 12. 49, 50. [5] *To one who tenders and loves another, as a mother does her son,* Rom. 16. 13. [6] *To a female superior, whether a mother, mother-in-law, one advanced in age, a teacher or governess,* Exod. 20. 12. [7] *To the kingdom of Judah, the city of Jerusalem, or the family of David,* Ezek. 19. 2, 10. [8] *To a metropolis, or the capital city of a country or of a tribe,* 2 Sam. 20. 19.

Gen. 3. 20. because she was the *m.* of all living
17. 16. I will bless her, she shall be a *m.* of nations
24. 28. the damsel told them of her *m.* house
53. he gave to her brother and *m.* precious things
60. be thou the *m.* of thousands of millions
32. 11. lest he smite the *m.* with the children
Exod. 2. 8. the maid went and called the child's *m.*
Lev. 20. 14. to take a wife and her *m.* is wickedness
Judg. 5. 7. till that I Deborah arose a *m.* in Israel
28. the *m.* of Sisera looked out at a window
Ruth 1. 8. go, return each to her *m.* house
2 *Sam.* 17. 25. Abigail, sister to Zeruiah, Joab's *m.*
20. 19. thou seekest to destroy a *m.* in Israel
1 *Kings* 2. 19. caused a seat to be set for the king's *m.*
3. 27. give her the child, she is the *m.* thereof
2 *Kings* 24. 15. he carried away the king's *m.*
Psal. 113. 9. and to be a joyful *m.* of children
Prov. 30. 11. a generation doth not bless their *m.*
Cant. 6. 9. my dove, she is the only one of her *m.*
Isa. 50. 1. where is the bill of your *m.* divorce?
Jer. 50. 12. your *m.* shall be sore confounded
Ezek. 16. 44. as is the *m.* so is the daughter
45. your *m.* was an Hittite, father an Amorite
21. † 21. king stood at the *m.* of the way
23. 2. were two women the daughters of one *m.*
Hos. 2. 2. plead with your *m.* for she is not my wife
5. for their *m.* hath played the harlot
10. 14. *m.* was dashed in pieces upon her children
Mic. 7. 6. daughter riseth up against her *m.* a man's enemies of his house, *Mat.* 10. 35. *Luke* 12. 53.
Mat. 8. 14. saw Peter's wife's *m.* sick, *Luke* 4. 38.
14. 8. she being before instructed of her *m.*
11. and she brought it to her *m.* *Mark* 6. 28.
19. 12. eunuchs were so born from their *m.* womb
20. 20. then came the *m.* of Zebedee's children
Luke 1. 43. the *m.* of my Lord should come to me?
John 2. 1. the *m.* of Jesus was there, *Acts* 1. 14.
Acts 12. 12. he came to house of Mary *m.* of John
Gal. 4. 26. Jerusalem which is the *m.* of us all
Rev. 17. 5. the *m.* of harlots and abominations

See FATHER.

His MOTHER.

Gen. 21. 21. *his m.* took him a wife out of Egypt
24. 67. Isaac brought Rebekah into his *m.* Sarah's tent, and was comforted after the death of *his m.*
27. 14. Jacob went and brought them to *his m.*
30. 14. Reuben brought mandrakes to *his m.*

Gen. 43. 29. he saw his brother Benjamin, *his m* son
44. 20. he alone is left of *h. m.* his father loves him
Exod. 23. 19. thou shalt not seethe the kid in *his m.* milk, 34. 26. Deut. 14. 21.
Lev. 20. 17. shall take *his m.* daughter and see her
24. 11. *his m.* name was Shelomith, tribe of Dan
Num. 12. 12. when he cometh out of *his m.* womb
Deut. 27. 22. that lieth with the daughter of *his m.*
Judg. 9. 1. Abimelech went to *his m.* brethren
17. 2. he said to *his m.* ‖ 3. he restored it to *his m.*
1 Sam. 2. 19. *his m.* made him a little coat
1 Kings 1. 6. and *his m.* bare him after Absalom
15. 13. *his m.* he removed from being queen
17. 23. Elijah delivered him to *his m.* and said
22. 52. Ahaziah walked in the way of *his m.*
2 Kings 4. 19. he said to a lad, carry him to *his m.*
1 Chron. 4. 9. *his m.* called his name Jabez
2 Chr. 22. 3. *his m.* was his counsellor to do wickedly
Psal. 35. 14. as one that mourneth for *his m.*
109. 14. let not the sin of *his m.* be blotted out
131. 2. as a child that is weaned of *his m.*
Prov. 10. 1. a foolish son is the heaviness of *his m.*
15. 20. but a foolish man despiseth *his m.*
29. 15. a child left bringeth *his m.* to shame
31. 1. the prophecy that *his m.* taught him
Eccl. 5. 15. as he came forth of *his m.* womb, naked
Cant. 3. 11. crown wherewith *his m.* crowned him
Isa. 66. 13. as one whom *his m.* comforteth
Mat. 1. 18. when *his m.* was espoused to Joseph
2. 13. take the young child and *his m.* and flee, 20.
12. 46. *his m.* stood without, Mark 3. 31. Luke 8. 19.
13. 55. carpenter's son, is not *his m.* called Mary?
Luke 1. 15. filled with Holy Ghost from *his m.* womb
60. *his m.* said, he shall be called John
2. 43. but Joseph and *his m.* knew not of it
51. but *his m.* kept these sayings in her heart
7. 12. the only son of *his m.* and she was a widow
15. he sat up, and he delivered him to *his m.*
John 3. 4. can he enter second time into *his m.* womb?
19. 25. *his m.* stood by the cross of Jesus
26. when Jesus saw *his m.* he saith to *his m.*
Acts 3. 2. certain man lame from *his m.* womb, 14. 8.
Rom. 16. 13. salute Rufus and *his m.* and mine

MOTHER-*in-law.*

Deut. 27. 23. cursed be that lieth with his *m.-in-law*
Ruth 1. 14. and Orpah kissed her *m.-in-law*
2. 11. all that thou hast done to thy *m.-in-law*
23. and Ruth dwelt with her *m.-in-law*
3. 6. according to all that her *m.-in-law* bade her
17. for he said, go not empty to thy *m.-in-law*
Mic. 7. 6. the daughter-in-law riseth up against the *m.-in-law*, Mat. 10. 35. Luke 12. 53.

My MOTHER.

Gen. 20. 12. she is not the daughter of *my m.*
Judg. 8. 19. my brethren, even the sons of *my m.*
16. 17. I have been a Nazarite from *my m.* womb
1 Kings 2. 20. the king said to her, ask on, *my m.*
Job 1. 21. naked came I out of *my m.* womb
3. 10. it shut not up the doors of *my m.* womb
17. 14. I have said to the worm, thou art *my m.*
31. 18. and I have guided her from *my m.* womb
Psal. 22. 9. make me hope, when on *my m.* breasts
10. thou art my God from *my m.* belly
51. 5. and in sin did *my m.* conceive me
69. 8. I am become an alien to *my m.* children
71. 6. thou art he that took me out of *my m.* bowels
139. 13. thou hast covered me in *my m.* womb
Prov. 4. 3. tender and beloved in the sight of *my m.*
Cant. 1. 6. *my m.* children were angry with me
3. 4. until I had brought him to *my m.* house
8. 1. my brother that sucked the breasts of *my m.*
2. and I would bring thee into *my m.* house
Isa. 49. 1. from the bowels of *my m.* he made mention
Jer. 15. 10. woe is me *my m.* that thou hast borne me
20. 14. let not the day wherein *my m.* bare me
17. or that *my m.* might have been my grave
Mat. 12. 48. Jesus said, who is *my m.?* Mark 3. 33.
49. behold *my m.* and my brethren, Mark 3. 34.
Luke 8. 21. *my m.* and my brethren are these
Gal. 1. 15. God, who separated me from *my m.* womb

Thy MOTHER.

Gen. 27. 29. and let *thy m.* sons bow down to thee
37. 10. shall I and *thy m.* come to bow to thee?
Lev. 18. 7. nakedness of *thy m.* shalt thou not uncover
9. not uncover nakedness of daughter of *thy m.*
13. not uncover naked. of sister of *thy m.* 20. 19.
Deut. 13. 6. brother, the son of *thy m.* entice thee
1 Sam. 15. 33. so shall *thy m.* be childless among wom.
20. 30. to the confusion of *thy m.* nakedness
2 Kings 9. 22. as whoredoms of *thy m.* are so many
Psal. 50. 20. thou slanderest *thine* own *m.* son
Prov. 1. 8. and forsake not the law of *thy m.* 6. 20.
23. 22. and despise not *thy m.* when she is old
Cant. 8. 5. there *thy m.* brought thee forth
Jer. 22. 26. cast thee out, and *thy m.* that bare thee
Ezek. 16. 3. thy father an Amorite, *thy m.* an Hittite
45. thou art *thy m.* daughter that loatheth her husb.
19. 2. and say, what is *thy m.?* a lioness
10. *thy m.* is like a vine in thy blood, planted
Hos. 4. 5. thou shalt fall, and I will destroy *thy m.*
Mat. 12. 47. one said to him, behold *thy m.* and thy brethren, Mark 3. 32. Luke 8. 20. John 19. 27.
2 Tim. 1. 5. faith, which dwelt in *thy m.* Eunice

MOTHERS.

Isa. 49. 23. and queens shall be thy nursing *m.*
Jer. 16. 3. saith the Lord, concerning their *m.*
Lam. 2. 12. they say to their *m.* where is corn and wine? soul was poured out into their *m.* bosom
5. 3. we are fatherless, our *m.* are as widows
Mark 10. 30. receive an hundred-fold, sisters, *m.*
1 Tim. 1. 9. the law is made for murderers of *m.*
5. 2. but entreat the elder women as *m.* the younger

MOTIONS.

Rom. 7. 5. the *m.* of sins did work in our members

MOVE

Signifies, [1] *To stir out of a place*, 2 Kings 21. 8. [2] *To provoke*, Deut. 32. 21. [3] *To persuade*, Josh. 15. 18. [4] *To excite, enable, and strengthen*, Judg. 13. 25. [5] *To set or raise up*, Job 40. † 17. [6] *To tremble and shake*, Psal. 18. 7. [7] *To touch*, Mat. 23. 4. [8] *To deter, or discourage one from doing a thing*, Acts 20. 24. [9] *To be sensibly affected both with wonder at, and compassion towards, a person under affliction*, Ruth 1. 19.

Exod. 11. 7. not a dog *m.* his tongue against man
Lev. 11. 10. of all that *m.* in the waters
Deut. 23. 25. not *m.* a sickle into neighbour's corn
32. 21. and I will *m.* them to jealousy with those
Judg. 13. 25 the Spirit of the Lord began to *m.* him
2 Sam. 7. 10. may dwell and *m.* no more, 2 Kings 21. 8.
2 Kings 5. † 11. he will *m.* his hand up and down
23. 18. let him alone, let no man *m.* his bones
Jer. 10. 4. they fasten it with nails that it *m.* not
Amos 9. † 9. I will cause to *m.* the house of Israel
Mic. 7. 17. they sh. *m.* out of their holes like worms
Mat. 23. 4. they themselves will not *m.* them
Acts 17. 28. for in him we live, *m.* have our being
20. 24. none of these things *m.* me, nor count I

MOVEABLE.

Prov. 5. 6. her ways are *m.* canst not know them

MOVED.

Gen. 1. 2. the Spirit of God *m.* on face of the waters
7. 21. all flesh died that *m.* on the earth, of fowl
Deut. 32. 21. they have *m.* me to jealousy with that
Josh. 10. 21. none *m.* his tongue against Israel
15. 18. *m.* him to ask of father a field, Judg. 1. 14.
Ruth 1. 19. that all the city was *m.* about them
1 Sam. 1. 13. she spake in her heart, only her lips *m.*
2 Sam. 18. 33. the king was much *m.* and wept
22. 8. the foundations of heaven *m.* and shook
24. 1. he *m.* David against them, to say, go number
1 Chron. 16. 30. fear before him, the world shall be stable, that it be not *m.* Psal. 93. 1. | 96. 10.
17. 9. they shall dwell, and shall be *m.* no more
2 Chron. 18. 31. God *m.* them to depart from him
Ezra 4. 15. they have *m.* sedition of old time
Esth. 5. 9. Haman saw that Mordecai *m.* not for him
Job 37. 1. at this my heart is *m.* out of his place
41. 23. the flakes of his flesh, they cannot be *m.*
Psal. 10. 6. I shall not be *m.* 16. 8. | 30. 6. | 62. 2, 6.
13. 4. those that trouble me rejoice when I am *m.*
15. 5. he that doeth these things shall never be *m.*
17. † 5. hold up, that my footsteps be not *m.*
18. 7. foundations of the hills *m.* and were shaken
21. 7. the king trusteth in Lord, and shall not be *m.*
46. 5. she shall not be *m.* God shall help her
6. the heathen raged, the kingdoms were *m.*
55. 22. he shall never suffer the righteous to be *m.*
66. 9. and suffereth not our feet to be *m.*
68. 8. Sinai was *m.* at the presence of God
78. 58. they *m.* him to jealousy with graven images
82. † 5. the foundations of the earth are *m.*
99. 1. the Lord reigneth, let the earth be *m.*
112. 6. surely he shall not be *m.* for ever
121. 3. he will not suffer thy foot to be *m.*
Prov. 12. 3. the root of the righteous shall not be *m.*
Cant. 5. 4. and my bowels were *m.* for him
Isa. 6. 4. the posts of the door *m.* at the voice of him
7. 2. his heart was *m.* as trees are *m.* with wind
10. 14. and there was none that *m.* the wing
14. 9. hell from beneath is *m.* for thee to meet thee
19. 1. the idols of Egypt shall be *m.* at his presence
24. 19. earth is broken down, and *m.* exceedingly
40. 20. a graven image that shall not be *m.* 41. 7.
Jer. 4. 24. they trembled, and all the hills *m.* lightly
25. 16. they shall drink, and be *m.* and be mad
46. 7. whose waters are *m.* as the rivers, 8.
49. 21. the earth is *m.* at the noise of Edom's fall
50. 46. at the taking of Babylon the earth is *m.*
Dan. 8. 7. he was *m.* with choler against him
10. † 10. touched me, which *m.* me on my knees
11. 11. the king of the south shall be *m.* with choler
Mat. 9. 36. he was *m.* with compassion on them, 14. 14. | 18. 27. Mark 1. 41. | 6. 34.
20. 24. were *m.* with indignation against brethren
21. 10. all the city was *m.* saying, who is this?
Mark 15. 11. but the chief priests *m.* the people
Acts 2. 25. on my right hand, that I should not be *m.*
7. 9. patriarchs, *m.* with envy, sold Jos. into Egypt
17. 5. but the Jews *m.* with envy, took lewd fellows
21. 30. the city was *m.* and people ran together
Col. 1. 23. be not *m.* from the hope of the gospel
1 Thess. 3. 3. that no man be *m.* by these afflictions
Heb. 11. 7. Noah, *m.* with fear, prepared an ark
12. 28. we receiving a kingdom which cannot be *m.*
2 Pet. 1. 21. they spake as *m.* by the Holy Ghost
Rev. 6. 14. every mountain and island *m.* out of place

MOVEDST.

Job 2. 3. tho' thou *m.* me against him without cause
Jer. 48. † 27. since thou spakest, thou *m.* thyself

MOVER.

Acts 24. 5. have found this fellow a *m.* of sedition

MOVETH.

Gen. 1. 21. God created every living creature that *m.*
28. dominion over every thing that *m.* on earth
9. 2. the fear of you shall be on all that *m.* on earth
Lev. 11. 46. this is the law of every creature that *m.*
20. † 25. abominable by any thing that *m.*
Job 40. 17. Behemoth *m.* his tail like a cedar
Psal. 69. 34. let every thing that *m.* praise him
Prov. 23. 31. not on wine when it *m.* itself aright
Ezek. 47. 9. that *m.* whithersoever the rivers come

MOVING.

Gen. 1. 20. let the waters bring forth *m.* creatures
9. 3. every *m.* thing shall be meat for you
Prov. 16. 30. *m.* his lips, he bringeth evil to pass
Hab. 1. † 14. makest men as the *m.* things, no ruler

MOVING, *Substantive.*

Job 16. 5. the *m.* of my lips should assuage grief
John 5. 3. blind, waiting for the *m.* of the water

MOULDY.

Josh. 9. 5. the bread of provision was dry and *m.* 12.

MOUNT, ING.

Job 20. 6. though his excellency *m.* up to the heavens
39. 27. doth the eagle *m.* up at thy command?
Psal. 107. 26. they *m.* up to heaven, they go down
Isa. 9. 18. they shall *m.* up as the lifting up of smoke
15. 5. by the *m.* up of Luhith shall they go up
40. 31. they shall *m.* up with wings, as eagles
Jer. 51. 53. though Babylon should *m.* up to heaven
Ezek. 10. 16. when the cherubims lift up to *m.* up, 19.

MOUNT.

Gen. 31. 54. Jacob offered sacrifice on the *m.*
Exod. 18. 5. where he encamped at the *m.* of God
19. 12. whoso toucheth the *m.* shall be put to death
14. Moses went down from the *m.* 32. 15. | 34. 29.
16. a thick cloud upon the *m.* 24. 15.
18. *m.* Sinai on a smoke ‖ 23. bounds about the *m.*
24. 16. the glory of the Lord abode upon *m.* Sinai
17. was like devouring fire on the top of *m.*
31. 18. the Lord gave Moses on *m.* Sinai two tables
32. 19. and Moses brake them beneath the *m.*
34. 2. and come up in the morning to *m.* Sinai
3. nor let any man be seen through all the *m.*
Num. 10. 33. they departed from the *m.* of the Lord
20. 22. from Kadesh, and came unto *m.* Hor
25. bring up to *m.* Hor ‖ 28. Aaron died in *m.* Hor
34. 7. you shall point out for you *m.* Hor
Deut. 1. 6. ye have dwelt long enough in this *m.*
7. turn you, and go to the *m.* of the Amorites
9. 15. I came down, and the *m.* burned with fire
27. 13. and these shall stand upon *m.* Ebal
32. 49. get thee to *m.* Nebo, which is in Moab
33. 2. the Lord shined forth from *m.* Paran
Judg. 4. 6. go and draw towards *m.* Tabor
7. 3. let him depart early from *m.* Gilead
9. 48. Abimelech gat him up to *m.* Zalmon
2 Sam. 15. 30. David went up by the ascent of *m.*
32. the top of the *m.* where he worshipped God
1 Kings 19. 8. Elijah went to Horeb, the *m.* of God
11. go and stand on the *m.* before the Lord
2 Kings 23. 13. on right hand the *m.* of corruption
Neh. 8. 15. go to the *m.* and fetch olive branches
9. 13. thou camest down also on *m.* Sinai
Cant. 4. 1. is as a flock of goats from *m.* Gilead
Isa. 10. 32. the *m.* of the daughter of Zion, 16. 1.
14. 13. I will sit on the *m.* of the congregation
27. 13. shall worship in the holy *m.* at Jerusalem
29. 3. and will lay siege against thee with a *m.*
Jer. 6. 6. hew ye down trees, and cast a *m.* against Jerusalem, Ezek. 4. 2. | 21. 22. | 26. 8.
Dan. 11. 15. the king of the north shall cast up a *m.*
Obad. 8. even destroy understanding out of *m.* Esau
21. saviours shall come to judge the *m.* of Esau
Hab. 3. 3. and the Holy One from *m.* Paran
Acts 7. 30. there appeared in wilderness of *m.* Sinai
Gal. 4. 24. the one from the *m.* Sinai, which is Agar
25. for this Agar is *m.* Sinai in Arabia
Heb. 12. 18. not come to the *m.* might be touched

See CARMEL, GERIZIM.

Before the MOUNT.

Exod. 19. 2. and there Israel camped *before the m.*
31. 3. neither let the flocks feed *before the m.*

See EPHRAIM.

In, or *into the* MOUNT.

Gen. 22. 14. *in the m.* of the Lord it shall be seen
31. 23. and they overtook Jacob *in the m.* Gilead
54. they did eat, and tarried all night *in the m.*
Exod. 4. 27. he went and met him *in the m.* of God
19. 12. take heed ye go not up *into the m.* or
24. 12. L. said to Moses, come *into m.* Deut. 10. 1.
13. Moses went up *into the m.* of God, 15, 18.
18. Moses was *in the m.* forty days and forty nights, Deut. 9. 9. | 10. 10.
25. 40. look thou make them after their pattern shewed thee *in the m.* 26. 30. | 27. 8. Heb. 8. 5.
Num. 27. 12. get thee up *into m.* Abarim, and see
Deut. 32. 50. die *in the m.* as Aaron died *in m.* Hor
Josh. 8. 30. Joshua built an altar to Lord *in m.* Ebal
2 Kings 23. 16. Josiah spied the sepulchres *in the m.*
2 Chr. 3. 1. to build the house of Lord *in m.* Moriah
Isa. 28. 21 for the L. shall rise up as *in m.* Perazim
Acts 7. 38. the angel who spake to him *in m.* Sinai
2 Pet. 1. 18. when we were with him *in the* holy *m.*

See GILBOA.

MOUNT *of Olives.*

Zech. 14. 4. his feet shall stand on the *m. of Olives*, the *m. of Olives* shall cleave in the midst thereof
Mat. 21. 1. they were come to *m. of Ol.* Luke 19. 29.
24. 3. and as he sat upon *m. of Olives*, Mark 13. 3.
26. 30. and when he had sung an hymn, they went out *into m. of Olives*, Mark 14. 26. Luke 22. 39.
Luke 19. 37. he was at the descent of *m. of Olives*
21. 37. at night he went out, and abode in *m. of Ol.*
John 8. 1. Jesus went unto the *m. of Olives*
Acts 1. 12. then they returned from the *m. of Olives*

See SEIR, ZION.

MOUNTS.

Jer. 32. 24. the *m.* are come to the city to take it
33. 4. the houses which are thrown down by the *m.*
Ezek. 17. 17. nor make for him, by casting up *m.*

MOUNTAIN

Signifies [1] *A vast heap of earth raised to a great height, either by nature or art*, Prov. 8. 25. [2] *The church of God, whereof the temple built on mount* Sion *was a type*, Isa. 2. 2. [3] *The idolatrous inhabitants of the mountains*, Ezek. 6. 2. [4] *Places of power and authority in a kingdom*, Amos 4. 1. [5] *High places, whereon idols were worshipped*, Isa. 57. 7. Ezek. 18. 6. [6] *Such powerful obstacles as hinder the progress of the gospel*, Isa. 40. 4. | 49. 11. [7] *Idols that were worshipped in mountains, or high places*, Jer. 3. 23. [8] *The most lofty and powerful enemies*, Isa. 41. 15.

A Catalogue of the most famous mountains mentioned in Scripture.

Mount Amalek, *in the tribe of* Ephraim, *Judg.* 12. 15.
Mount Calvary, *whereon our Lord* Jesus Christ *was crucified, north-west from* Jerusalem, *Luke* 23. 33.
Mount Carmel, *near the* Mediterranean sea, *between* Dora *and* Ptolemais, *Josh.* 19. 26.
Mount Ebal, *near to* Gerizim, *Josh.* 8. 30.
The mountain of Engedi, *near the* Dead sea, *Josh.* 15. 62.
Mount Gaash *in tribe of* Ephraim, *Josh.* 24. 30.
Mount Gilboa, *to the south of the valley of* Israel, 2 *Sam.* 1. 21.
Mount Gilead, *beyond* Jordan, *Gen.* 31. 21, 23, 25.
Mount Gerizim, *whereon was afterwards the temple of the* Samaritans, *Judg.* 9. 7.
Mount Hermon, *beyond* Jordan, *Josh.* 11. 3.
Mount Hor, *in* Idumea, *Num.* 20. 22.

Mount Horeb, *near to* Sinai, *in* Arabia Petræa, *Deut.* 1. 2.

Mount Lebanon, *which separates* Syria *from* Palestine, *Deut.* 3. 25.

Mount Moriah, *where the temple was built,* 2 Chron. 3. 1.

Mount Nebo, *part of the mountains of* Abarim, *Num.* 32. 3.

The mount of Olives, *which stood to the east of* Jerusalem, *and was parted from the city only by the brook* Kidron, *and the valley of* Jehoshaphat. *It was otherwise called,* The mount of Corruption, 2 *Kings* 23. 13. *because on it* Solomon *built high places to the gods of the* Ammonites *and* Moabites, *out of complaisance to his idolatrous wives, natives of these nations,* 1 Kings 11. 1. 7. *It was from this mountain our Saviour ascended into heaven,* Acts 1. 12.

Mount of Paran, *in* Arabia Petræa, *Gen.* 14. 6. *Deut.* 1. 1.

Mount Pisgah, *beyond* Jordan, *in the country of* Moab, *Num.* 21. 20. *Deut.* 34. 1.

Mount Seir, *in* Idumea, *Gen.* 14. 6.

Mount Sinai, *in* Arabia Petræa, *Exod.* 19. 2. *Deut.* 33. 2.

Mount Sion, *near to mount* Moriah, 2 *Sam.* 5. 7.

Mount Tabor, *in the lower* Galilee, *to the north of the great plain,* Judg. 4. 6.

Gen. 14. 10. and they that remained fled to the *m.*
19. 17. escape to the *m.* ‖ 19. I cannot escape to *m.*
Exod. 3. 1. and came to the *m.* of G. even to Horeb
12. people from Egypt, shall serve G. on this *m.*
19. 3. the Lord called to him out of the *m.* saying
20. 18. all the people saw the *m.* smoking
Num. 14. 40. they gat them up into top of the *m.*
Deut. 1. 20. ye are come to the *m.* of the Amorites
2. 3. ye have compassed this *m.* long enough
3. 25. let me see that goodly *m.* and Lebanon
4. 11. the *m.* burnt with fire to heaven, 5. 23.
33. 19. they shall call the people to the *m.*
Josh. 2. 16. get ye to the *m.* and hide yourselves
11. 16. Joshua took the plain and the *m.* of Israel
14. 12. give me this *m.* ‖ 17. 18. the *m.* shall be thine
Judg. 1. 19. he drave out the inhabitants of the *m.*
34. Amorites forced children of Dan into the *m.*
1 *Sam.* 17. 3. the Philistines stood on a *m.* on the one side, and Israel stood on a *m.* on other side
23. 26. Saul went on this side of the *m.* and David and his men on that side of the *m.*
2 *Kings* 2. 16. the Spirit hath cast him on some *m.*
6. 17. the *m.* was full of horses and chariots
Job 14. 18. surely the *m.* falling cometh to nought
Psal. 11. 1. how say ye, flee as a bird to your *m.?*
30. 7. thou hast made my *m.* to stand strong
78. 54. brought to this *m.* his right hand purchased
Isa. 2. 2. the *m.* of L. house established, *Mic.* 4. 1.
3. let us go up to the *m.* of the Lord, *Mic.* 4. 2.
30. 17. until ye be left as a beacon on the top of a *m.*
29. as when one goeth with a pipe to *m.* of Lord
40. 4. every *m.* shall be made low, *Luke* 3. 5.
Jer. 16. 16. they shall hunt them from every *m.*
17. 3. O my *m.* in the field, I will give thy substance
26. 18. Zion plowed like a field, and the *m.* of the house as high places of the forest, *Mic.* 3. 12.
50. 6. my people have gone from *m.* to hill
51. 25. I am against thee, O destroying *m.* saith the Lord, and I will make thee a burnt *m.*
Lam. 5. 18. our eyes are dim, because of *m.* of Zion
Ezek. 11. 23. the glory of the Lord stood on the *m.*
28. 16. I will cast thee as profane out of *m.* of God
43. 12. this is the law of the house on top of the *m.*
† 15. Hariel, the *m.* of God, shall be four cubits
Dan. 2. 35. and the stone became a great *m.*
45. the stone was cut out of the *m.* without hands
Mic. 7. 12. he shall come to thee from *m.* to *m.*
Hag. 1. 8. go up to *m.* bring wood and build house
Zeph. 4. 7. who art thou, O great *m.* before Zerubb.
8. 3. be called the *m.* of the Lord, the holy *m.*
14. 4. half of *m.* shall remove towards the north
Mat. 5. 1. and seeing the multitudes, he went up into a *m.* 14. 23. | 15. 29. *Mark* 3. 13. | 6. 46. *Luke* 6. 12. | 9. 28. *John* 6. 3, 15.
8. 1. when he was come down from the *m.*
17. 1. Jesus bringeth them into an high *m.* apart
9. and as they came down from the *m.* *Mark* 9. 9.
20. if ye have faith, as a grain of mustard, shall say to this *m.* remove hence, 21. 21. *Mark* 11. 23.
28. 16. went into a *m.* where Jesus had appointed
Luke 8. 32. an herd of many swine feeding on *m.*
Heb. 12. 20. if so much as a beast touch the *m.*
Rev. 6. 14. every *m.* and island were removed from
8. 8. as it were a great *m.* burning with fire

High MOUNTAIN.

Isa. 13. 2. lift ye up a banner upon the *high m.*
30. 25. there shall be upon every *high m.* rivers
40. 9. O Zion, get thee up into the *high m.*
57. 7. on a lofty and *high m.* hast thou set thy bed
Jer. 3. 6. Israel is gone up upon every *high m.*
Ezek. 17. 22. and I will plant it on a *high m.*
40. 2. he brought me, and set me on a very *high m.*
Mat. 4. 8. the devil taketh him up into an exceeding *h. m.* and sheweth kingdoms of world, *Luke* 4. 5.
17. 1. Jesus taketh Peter, James, and John, and bringeth into an *high m.* apart, *Mark* 9. 2.
Rev. 21. 10. he carried me in the Spirit to *high m.*
See HOLY.

In the, or *in this* MOUNTAIN.

Gen. 19. 30. Lot went from Zoar, and dwelt *in the m.*
Exod. 15. 17. plant them *in the m.* of thine inheritance
Num. 13. 17. Moses said unto them, go up *into the m.*
Deut. 32. 49. get thee up *in this m.* Abarim, to Nebo
Judg. 3. 27. he blew a trumpet *in the m.* of Ephraim
1 *Sam.* 23. 14. David remained *in a m.* of Ziph
2 *Chron.* 2. 2. Solomon told 80,000 to hew *in the m.*
Psal. 48. 1. God is to be praised *in the m.* of holiness
Isa. 25. 6. *in this m.* shall the Lord make a feast
7. he will destroy *in this m.* the face of covering
10. *in this m.* shall the hand of the Lord rest
Ezek. 17. 23. *in the m.* of Israel I will plant it
Amos 4. 1. ye kine, that are *in the m.* of Samaria
6. 1. woe to them that trust *in the m.* of Samaria
John 4. 20. our fathers worshipped *in this m.*
John 4. 21. neither *in this m.* nor Jerusalem, worship [the Father

MOUNTAINS.

Gen. 7. 20. *m.* were cover. ‖ 8. 4. ark rested on the *m.*
8. 5. in tenth month tops of the *m.* were seen
Num. 33. 48. they departed from the *m.* of Abarim
Deut. 12. 2. ye shall destroy places on the high *m.*
Josh. 11. 21. Joshua cut off the Anakims from the *m.*
Judg. 5. 5. the *m.* melted from before the Lord
11. 37. that I may go up and down on the *m.*
38. she bewailed her virginity on the *m.*
2 *Sam.* 1. 21. ye *m.* of Gilboa, let there be no dew
1 *Kings* 19. 11. a great and strong wind rent the *m.*
1 *Chron.* 12. 8. were as swift as the roes on the *m.*
2 *Chr.* 18. 16. I did see all Isr. scattered on the *m.*
Job 9. 5. which removeth the *m.* and they know not
28. 9. he overturneth the *m.* by the roots
40. 20. surely the *m.* bring him forth food
Psal. 36. 6. thy righteousness is like the great *m.*
46. 2. tho' the *m.* be carried into the midst of the sea
3. though the *m.* shake with the swelling thereof
65. 6. by his strength setteth fast the *m.*
72. 3. the *m.* shall bring peace to the people
76. 4. thou art more glorious than the *m.* of prey
83. 14. as the flames setteth the *m.* on fire
90. 2. before the *m.* were brought forth
104. 6. the waters stood above the *m.*
8. they go up by the *m.* down by the valleys
114. 4. *m.* skipped like rams, little hills as lambs, 6.
125. 2. as the *m.* are round about Jerusalem
133. 3. as the dew that descended on the *m.*
144. 5. touch the *m.* and they shall smoke
147. 8. who maketh grass to grow on the *m.*
148. 9. *m.* and all hills praise the Lord
Prov. 8. 25. before the *m.* were settled, before the hills was I brought forth
Cant. 2. 8. behold, he cometh leaping on the *m.*
17. turn, and be thou like a roe on the *m.* 8. 14.
4. 8. look from Amana and the *m.* of the leopards
Isa. 2. 14. the day of the Lord shall be on high *m.*
14. 25. and on my *m.* tread him under foot
18. 3. when he lifteth up an ensign on the *m.*
34. 3. the *m.* shall be melted with their blood
40. 12. who hath weighed the *m.* in scales
41. 15. thou shalt thresh the *m.* and beat small
42. 15. and I will make waste *m.* and hills
44. 23. break forth into singing, ye *m.* 49. 13.
49. 11. and I will make all my *m.* a way
52. 7. how beautiful on the *m.* are feet, *Nah.* 1. 15.
54. 10. for the *m.* shall depart, the hills be removed
55. 12. *m.* shall break forth before you into singing
64. 1. the *m.* might flow down at thy presence, 3.
65. 7. which have burnt incense on the *m.*
9. will bring out of Judah an inheritor of my *m.*
Jer. 4. 24. I beheld the *m.* and they trembled
9. 10. for the *m.* will I take up a weeping
13. 16. before your feet stumble on the dark *m.*
17. 26. shall come from the *m.* bringing offerings
31. 5. shall plant vines on the *m.* of Samaria
46. 18. as Tabor among the *m.* so shall ye come
50. 6. they have turned them away on the *m.*
Lam. 4. 19. our persecutors pursued us on the *m.*
Ezek. 6. 2. set thy face toward the *m.* of Israel
3. and say, ye *m.* of Israel, hear the word of Ld.
7. 16. they shall be on the *m.* like doves of valleys
18. 6. and hath not eaten upon the *m.* 15.
11. but hath eaten on the *m.* and defiled
19. 9. his voice should no more be heard on the *m.*
22. 9. and in thee they eat upon the *m.*
31. 12. upon the *m.* his branches are fallen
32. 5. I will lay thy flesh on the *m.* and fill valleys
33. 28. the *m.* of Israel shall be desolate
34. 6. my sheep wandered through all the *m.*
13. I will feed them on the *m.* of Israel, 14.
35. 8. I will fill his *m.* with his slain men
12. which thou hast spoken against the *m.* of Israel
36. 1. prophesy unto the *m.* of Israel, and say, ye *m.* of Israel, hear the word of the Lord, 4.
8. but ye, O *m.* of Isr. shall shoot forth branches
37. 22. I will make one nation on the *m.* of Israel
38. 8. and is gathered out against the *m.* of Israel
20. and the *m.* shall be thrown down
21. I will call a sword against him thro' all my *m.*
39. 2. and I will bring thee on the *m.* of Israel
4. thou shalt fall on the *m.* of Israel, and all bands
17. even a great sacrifice on the *m.* of Israel
Joel 2. 2. as the morning spread upon the *m.*
3. 18. that the *m.* shall drop down new wine
Amos 1. † 13. because they divided the *m.*
3. 9. assemble yourselves on the *m.* of Samaria
4. 13. he that formeth the *m.* the Lord is his name
9. 13. and the *m.* shall drop sweet wine
Mic. 1. 4. the *m.* shall be molten under him
6. 1. arise, contend thou before the *m.* let the hills
2. hear ye, O ye *m.* the Lord's controversy
Nah. 1. 5. the *m.* quake at him, the hills melt
3. 18. thy people is scattered on the *m.* no man
Hab. 3. 6. the everlasting *m.* were scattered, the hills
10. the *m.* saw thee, and they trembled
Hag. 1. 11. I called for a drought on the *m.*
Zech. 6. 1. four chariots between the *m.* of brass
Mal. 1. 3. I hated Esau, and laid his *m.* waste
Mat. 18. 12. and goeth into the *m.* and seeketh
24. 16. let them which be in Judea flee into the *m.*
1 *Cor.* 13. 2. all faith, so that I could remove *m.*
Rev. 16. 20. every island, and the *m.* were not found
17. 9. the seven heads are seven *m.* on which

In the MOUNTAINS.

Exod. 32. 12. bring them out to slay them *in the m.*
Num. 33. 47. pitched *in t. m.* of Abarim, before Nebo
Deut. 2. 37. thou camest not to the cities *in the m.*
Josh. 10. 6. the kings that dwell *in t. m.* are gathered
Judg. 6. 2. Israel made them dens *in the m.* and caves
1 *Sam.* 26. 20. as one doth hunt a partridge *in the m.*
1 *Kings* 5. 15. eighty thousand hewers *in the m.*
2 *Chr.* 21. 11. he made high places *in m.* of Judah
26. 10. Uzziah had vine dressers *in the m.*
Isa. 13. 4. the noise of a multitude *in the m.* like
Mark 5. 5. night and day he was *in the m.* and tombs
Heb. 11. 38. they wandered in deserts and *in the m.*

Of the MOUNTAINS.

Gen. 8. 5. tops *of the m.* were seen in the tenth month
22. 2. offer him on one of *m.* I will tell thee of
Num. 23. 7. Balak brought me out of *m. of the* east
Deut. 32. 22. set on fire the foundations *of the m.*
33. 15. for the chief things *of the* ancient *m.*
Judg. 9. 25. set liers in wait for him in top *of the m.*
36. there come people down from the top *of the m.*
thou seest the shadow *of the m.* as if they were men
2 *Kin.* 19. 23. I am come up to height *of m.* *Isa.* 37. 24
Job 24. 8. they are wet with the showers *of the m.*
39. 8. the range *of the m.* is his pasture
Ps. 50. 11. I know all the fowls *of the m.* and beasts
72. 16. shall be an handful of corn on top *of the m.*
Prov. 27. 25. and herbs *of the m.* are gathered
Isa. 2. 2. shall be established in top *of m.* *Mic.* 4. 1.
17. 13. and shall be chased as the chaff *of the m.*
18. 6. they shall be left to the fowls *of the m.*
42. 11. let them shout from the top *of the m.*
Jer. 3. 23. hoped for from the multitude *of the m.*
32. 44. shall take witnesses in the cities *of the m.*
33. 13. in cities *of the m.* shall flocks pass again
Ezek. 6. 13. their slain shall be in the tops *of the m.*
7. 7. and not the sounding again *of the m.*
Hos. 4. 13. they sacrifice on the tops *of the m.*
Joel 2. 5. like the noise of chariots on tops *of the m.*
Jonah 2. 6. I went down to the bottom *of the m.*
Zech. 14. 5. and ye shall flee to the valley *of the m.*
Rev. 6. 15. hid themselves in the rocks *of the m.*

To the MOUNTAINS.

Cant. 4. 6. I will get me *to the m.* of myrrh
Isa. 22. 5. it is a day of trouble and crying *to the m.*
Ezek. 6. 3. thus saith the L. *to the m.* and hills, 36. 4.
32. 6. I will water with thy blood even *to the m.*
36. 1. son of man, prophesy *to the m.* of Israel, 6.
Hos. 10. 8. and they shall say *to the m.* cover us
Mark 5. 11. there was nigh *to the m.* a herd of swine
13. 14. that be in Judea flee *to the m.* *Luke* 21. 21.
Luke 23. 30. begin to say *to m.* fall on us, *Rev.* 6. 16.

MOURN.

Gen. 23. 2. Abraham came to *m.* for Sarah
1 *Sam.* 16. 1. how long wilt thou *m.* for Saul?
2 *Sam.* 3. 31. rend clothes, and *m.* before Abner
1 *Kings* 13. 29. old prophet came into the city to *m.*
14. 13. all Israel shall *m.* for him, and bury him
Neh. 8. 9. this day is holy to the Lord, *m.* not
Job 2. 11. he made an appointment to *m.* with him
5. 11. that those which *m.* may be exalted to safety
14. 22. and his soul within him shall *m.*
Psal. 55. 2. I *m.* in my complaint, and make a noise
Prov. 5. 11. and thou *m.* at the last, when thy flesh
29. 2. when the wicked bear rule, the people *m.*
Eccl. 3. 4. a time to *m.* and a time to dance
Isa. 3. 26. and her gates shall lament and *m.*
16. 7. for foundations of Kir-hareseth shall ye *m.*
19. 8. fishers shall *m.* ‖ 38. 14. I did *m.* as a do e
59. 11. we roar like bears, we *m.* sore like doves
61. 2. he hath sent me to comfort all that *m.*
3. to appoint them that *m.* in Zion beauty for ashes
66. 10. rejoice for joy, all ye that *m.* for her
Jer. 4. 28. for this shall earth *m.* and heavens black
12. 4. how long shall the land *m.* herbs wither?
48. 31. my heart shall *m.* for men of Kir-heresêth
Lam. 1. 4. ways of Zion do *m.* because none come
Ezek. 7. 12. the time is come, let not the seller *m.*
27. the king shall *m.* and the prince be clothed
24. 16. yet neither shalt thou *m.* nor weep
23. ye shall pine away and *m.* one towards another
31. 15. I caused Lebanon to *m.* for him
Hos. 4. 3. therefore shall the land *m.* and languish
10. 5. for the people shall *m.* over Samaria
Joel 1. 9. the priests, the Lord's ministers, *m.*
Amos 1. 2. the habitations of the shepherds shall *m.*
8. 8. and every one *m.* that dwelleth therein, 9. 5.
Zech. 12. 10. and shall *m.* for him as one mourneth
12. and the land shall *m.* every family apart
Mat. 5. 4. blessed are they that *m.* for they shall
9. 15. can the children of the bride-chamber *m.?*
24. 30. then shall all the tribes of the earth *m.*
Luke 6. 25. woe to you that laugh, for ye shall *m.*
Jam. 4. 9. be afflicted, and *m.* and weep
Rev. 18. 11. the merchants shall weep and *m.*

MOURNED.

Gen. 37. 34. Jacob *m.* for his son many days
50. 3. Egyptians *m.* for Jacob seventy days, 10.
Exod. 33. 4. and when the people heard these evil tidings, they *m.* *Num.* 14. 39.
Num. 20. 29. the congregation *m.* for Aaron
1 *Sam.* 15. 35. nevertheless Samuel *m.* for Saul
2 *Sam.* 1. 12. and they *m.* for Saul and Jonathan
11. 26. Bath-sheba *m.* for Uriah her husband
13. 37. David *m.* for his son Absalom every day
14. 2. as one that had long time *m.* for the dead
1 *Kings* 13. 30. and they *m.* over the man of God
14. 18. all Israel *m.* for Jeroboam's son
1 *Chron.* 7. 22. Ephraim their father *m.* many days
2 *Chron.* 35. 24. and all Judah *m.* for Josiah
Ezra 10. 6. he *m.* for the transgression of them
Neh. 1. 4. I sat down and *m.* certain days
Zech. 7. 5. when ye *m.* and fasted, did ye fast to me?
Mat. 11. 17. and saying, we have *m.* unto you, and ye have not lamented, *Luke* 7. 32.
Mark 16. 10. and she told them as they *m.* and wept
1 *Cor.* 5. 2. are puffed up, and have not rather *m.*

MOURNER.

2 *Sam.* 14. 2. I pray thee, feign thyself to be a *m.*

MOURNERS.

Job 29. 25. I dwelt as one that comforteth the *m.*
Eccl. 12. 5. and the *m.* go about the streets
Isa. 57. 18. I will restore comforts to him and his *m.*
Hos. 9. 4. sacrifices shall be to them as bread of *m.*

MOURNETH.

2 *Sam.* 19. 1. behold, the king *m.* for Absalom
Psal. 35. 14. I bowed as one that *m.* for his mother
88. 9. mine eye *m.* by reason of affliction
Isa. 24. 4. the earth *m.* 33. 9. ‖ 7. the new wine *m.*
Jer. 12. 11. my vineyard being desolate *m.* to me
14. 2. Judah *m.* and the gates thereof languish
23. 10. for because of swearing the land *m.*
Joel 1. 10. the land *m.* for the corn is wasted
Zech. 12. 10. as one that *m.* for his first-born

MOURNFULLY.

Mal. 3. 14. what profit that we have walked *m.*

MOURNING

Signifies, [1] *A godly sorrow for our own, or for*

the sins of others, Mat. 5. 4. [2] *A moderate sorrow and concern for the afflictions and worldly losses that befall ourselves or others*, Gen. 23. 2. | 50. 3. [3] *Exceeding great and most grievous lamentation*, Mat. 24. 30. [4] *Judgments and calamities, which should cause most bitter mourning*, Ezek. 2. 10.

The Hebrews, *at the death of their near friends and relations, used great signs of grief and mourning. They wept, tore their clothes, smote their breasts, fasted, and lay upon the ground, and went barefoot. The time of mourning was commonly seven days; but sometimes this was lengthened or shortened, according to the state or circumstances in which they found themselves: the mourning for* Saul *lasted but seven days*, 1 Sam. 31. 13. *but those for* Moses *and* Aaron *were prolonged to thirty days*, Num. 20. 29. Deut. 34. 8. *The whole time of their mourning, the near relations of the deceased continued sitting in their houses, and ate upon the ground; the food they took was thought unclean, and even themselves were judged impure.* Their sacrifices shall be to them as the bread of mourners, all that eat thereof shall be polluted, *Hos.* 9. 4. *Their faces were covered, and for all that time they could not apply themselves to any labour. They did not dress themselves, nor make their beds, nor uncover their heads, nor shave themselves, nor cut their nails, nor saluted any body.*

Gen. 27. 41. the days of *m.* for my father are at hand
50. 4. and when the days of his *m.* were past
10. he made a *m.* for his father Jacob seven days
11. the Canaanites saw the *m.* this is a grievous *m.*
Deut. 26. 14. I have not eaten thereof in my *m.*
34. 8. so the days of *m.* for Moses were ended
2 *Sam.* 11. 27. when the *m.* was past David sent
19. 2. the victory that day was turned into *m.*
Esth. 4. 3. there was great *m.* among the Jews
9. 22. was turned to them from *m.* into a good day
Job 3. 8. who are ready to raise up their *m.*
30. 31. my harp also is turned to *m.* and my organ
Psal. 30. 11. thou hast turned my *m.* into dancing
Eccl. 7. 2. it is better to go to the house of *m.*
4. the heart of the wise is in the house of *m.*
Isa. 22. 12. in that day the Lord did call to *m.*
51. 11. and sorrow and *m.* shall flee away
60. 20. and the days of thy *m.* shall be ended
61. 3. to give to them the oil of joy for *m.*
Jer. 6. 26. make thee *m.* as for an only son
16. 5. enter not into the house of *m.* neither go
31. 13. for I will turn their *m.* into joy
Lam. 2. 5. increased in the daughter of Judah *m.*
5. 15. joy is ceased, our dance is turned into *m.*
Ezek. 2. 10. was written lamentations, *m.* and woe
24. 17. no *m.* for the dead || 31. 15. I caused a *m.*
Joel 2. 12. turn ye to me with weeping and *m.*
Amos 5. 16. they shall call the husbandmen to *m.*
8. 10. and I will turn your feasts into *m.* and I will make it as the *m.* of an only son
Mic. 1. 11. came not forth in the *m.* of Beth-ezel
Zech. 12. 11. *m.* in Jerusalem, as *m.* of Hadadrimmon
Mat. 2. 18. was heard great *m.* Rachel weeping
2 *Cor.* 7. 7. when he told us your desire, your *m.*
Jam. 4. 9. let your laughter be turned into *m.*
Rev. 18. 8. in one day death and *m.* and famine

MOURNING.

Gen. 37. 35. will go down to the grave to my son *m.*
2 *Sam.* 14. 2. I pray thee, put on *m.* apparel
Esth. 6. 12. but Haman hasted to his house *m.*
Job 30. 28. I went *m.* without the sun, I stood up
Psal. 38. 6. I am troubled, I go *m.* all day long
42. 9. why go I *m.* bec. of oppression of enemy, 43. 2.
Jer. 9. 17. consider ye, and call for the *m.* women
16. 7. in *m.* to comfort them for the dead
Ezek. 7. 16. all of them *m.* for their iniquities
Dan. 10. 2. in those days I Daniel was *m.* 3 weeks
Mic. 1. 8. I will make a *m.* as the owls

MOUSE.

Lev. 11. 29. the weasel and *m.* shall be unclean
Isa. 66. 17. eating the abomination, and the *m.*

MOUTH

Signifies [1] *The part of the body so called, which is an instrument of speech*, Psal. 115. 5. | 135. 17. [2] *Speech, or words uttered by the mouth*, Job 19. 16. Psal. 73. 9. Isa. 49. 2. [3] *Just desires and necessities*, Psal. 103. 5. [4] *The palate*, Job 12. 11. [5] *The throat*, Psalm 149. † 6. [6] *A door*, Daniel 3. † 26. [7] *Freedom and boldness of speech*, Luke 21. 15. [8] *Boasting*, Judg. 9. 38. [9] *Reproaches and calumnies*, Job 5. 15. [10] *A testimony*, Deut. 17. 6.

If my mouth hath kissed my hand, *Job* 31. 27. *This was a mark or token of worship and adoration*, 1 Kings 19. 18. Hos. 13. 2. *and when the idols were out of the reach of idolaters, they could not kiss them, they used to kiss their hands, and as it were to throw kisses at them: Job here insinuates, that he had used no such idolatrous practice, while he beheld the sun or moon.* To ask counsel at the mouth of the Lord, *Josh.* 9. 14. *is to consult him.* They set their mouth against the heavens, *Psal.* 73. 9. *They speak arrogantly, insolently, and without the fear of God; they bid defiance both to God and man, blaspheming God's name, denying or deriding his providence, reviling his servants, &c. God appoints, that* his law may be always in the mouth of his people, Josh. 1. 8. that is, *That the* Israelites *may commune frequently with one another about it, and that the sentence which should come out of their mouth, might in all things be given according to that rule.* Moses *tells us, that* God opened the mouth of *Balaam's* ass, *Num.* 22. 28. *He made her speak to her master, and reason the matter with him for a time.* Out of the abundance of the heart the mouth speaketh, *Mat.* 12. 34. *Men's discourses are the echo of the sentiments of their hearts; your speech bewrays the wickedness of your hearts.* Not that which goeth into the mouth defileth a man, *Mat.* 15. 11. *It is neither meat nor drink that makes a man unclean in the sight of God.*

Gen. 8. 11. and lo, in her *m.* was an olive-leaf
24. 57. call the damsel, and inquire at her *m.*
29. 2. and a great stone was upon the well's *m.*
3. they rolled the stone from the well's *m.* 10.
34. † 26. slew Hamor with the *m.* of the sword
42. 27. his money was in his sack's *m.* 43. 12, 21.
43. † 7. we told according to the *m.* of these words
45. † 21. gave waggons, according to *m.* of Pharaoh
Exod. 4. 11. Lord said, who hath made man's *m.?*
16. even he shall be to thee instead of a *m.*
Num. 12. 8. with him will I speak *m.* to *m.*
16. 30. the earth open her *m.* and swallow them up
23. 5. the Lord put a word in Balaam's *m.*
35. 30. whoso kills any person, shall be put to death by the *m.* of witnesses, *Deut.* 17. 6. | 19. 15.
Josh. 9. † 2. they gathered together with one *m.*
10. 18. roll great stones on the *m.* of the cave, 27.
22. open *m.* of cave, and bring out the five kings
1 *Sam.* 1. 12. as she prayed, Eli marked her *m.*
2 *Sam.* 14. 3. so Joab put the words in her *m.* 19.
17. 19. she spread a covering over the well's *m.*
1 *Kings* 19. 18. every *m.* that hath not kissed him
22. 13. the words of the prophets declare good to the king with one *m.* 2 *Chron.* 18. † 12.
22. I will go forth and be a lying spirit in the *m.* of his prophets, 23. 2 *Chron.* 18. 21, 22.
2 *Kings* 10. † 21. was so full, that they stood *m.* to *m.*
21. † 16. till he filled Jerusalem from *m.* to *m.*
2 *Chron.* 35. 22. heark. not to Necho from *m.* of God
36. 21. to fulfil the word of the Lord by the *m.* of Jeremiah, 22. *Ezra* 1. 1.
Esth. 7. 8. as the word went out of the king's *m.*
Job 5. 16. poor hath hope, iniquity stoppeth her *m.*
12. 11. doth not the *m.* taste his *m.?* 34. 3.
32. 5. there was no answer in the *m.* of these men
Psal. 8. 2. out of *m.* of babes hast ordained strength
22. 21. save me from the lion's *m.* for thou heardest
32. 9. whose *m.* must be held in with bit and bridle
37. 30. the *m.* of the righteous speaketh wisdom
38. 14. and in whose *m.* are no reproofs
63. 11. but *m.* that speaketh lies shall be stopped
69. 15. let not the pit shut her *m.* upon me
107. 42. and all iniquity shall stop her *m.*
109. 2. *m.* of wicked, *m.* of deceitful are opened
126. 2. then was our *m.* filled with laughter
141. 7. our bones are scattered at the grave's *m.*
144. 8. whose *m.* speaketh vanity, 11.
Prov. 4. 24. put away from thee a froward *m.*
5. 3. and her *m.* is smoother than oil
6. 12. wicked man walketh with froward *m.* 10. 32.
8. 13. proud, and the froward *m.* do I hate
10. 6. violence covereth the *m.* of the wicked, 11.
14. the *m.* of the foolish is near destruction
31. the *m.* of the just bringeth forth wisdom
11. 11. the city is overthrown by *m.* of the wicked
12. 6. the *m.* of the upright shall deliver them
14. 3. in the *m.* of the foolish is a rod of pride
15. 2. the *m.* of fools poureth out foolishness
14. the *m.* of fools feedeth on foolishness
28. the *m.* of the wicked poureth out evil things
18. 4. the words of a man's *m.* are as deep waters
7. a fool's *m.* is his destruction, and his lips
19. 28. the *m.* of the wicked devoureth iniquity
22. 14. the *m.* of a strange woman is a deep pit
26. 7. so is a parable in the *m.* of fools, 9.
28. and a flattering *m.* worketh ruin
30. 20. she eateth, and wipeth her *m.* and saith
Eccl. 10. 12. words of a wise man's *m.* are gracious
Isa. 9. 12. they shall devour Israel with open *m.*
17. an evil doer, and every *m.* speaketh folly
57. 4. against whom make ye a wide *m.?*
59. 21. my Spirit not depart out of *m.* of thy seed
Jer. 32. 4. shall speak with him *m.* to *m.* 34. 3.
36. 4. Baruch wrote from *m.* of Jerem. 27, 32. | 45. 1.
44. 17. what thing goeth forth out of our *m.*
26. no more named in *m.* of any man of Judah
Lam. 3. 38. out of the *m.* of Most High proceedeth
Ezek. 21. 22. to open the *m.* in the slaughter
29. 21. I will give thee the opening of the *m.*
Dan. 3. 26. came near to the *m.* of the furnace
4. 31. while the word was in the king's *m.*
6. 17. a stone brought, and laid on the *m.* of the den
7. 5. it had three ribs in *m.* of it between teeth
8. there was a *m.* speaking great things, 20.
Hos. 2. 17. take the names of Baalim out of her *m.*
Amos 3. 12. as a shepherd taketh out of the *m.*
Nah. 3. 12. shall even fall into the *m.* of the eater
Zech. 5. 8. cast the weight of lead on the *m.* of it
Mat. 4. 4. that proceedeth out of the *m.* of God
12. 34. abundance of the heart the *m.* speaketh
15. 11. what goeth into the *m.* defileth not
18. 16. that in the *m.* of two or three witnesses every word may be established, 2 *Cor.* 13. 1.
21. 16. out of the *m.* of babes hast perfected praise
Luke 1. 70. as he spake by *m.* of his holy prophets
21. 15. for I will give you a *m.* and wisdom
Acts 1. 16. Holy Ghost spake by *m.* of David, 4. 25.
3. 18. God shewed by *m.* of all his prophets, 21.
15. 27. who shall tell you the same things by *m.*
23. 2. commanded them to smite him on the *m.*
Rom. 3. 14. whose *m.* is full of cursing and bittern.
19. that every *m.* may be stopped, and all world
10. 10. with the *m.* confession is made to salvation
15. 6. that ye may with one *m.* glorify God
1 *Cor.* 9. 9. thou shalt not muzzle the *m.* of the ox
2 *Tim.* 4. 17. I was delivered out of *m.* of the lion
Jam. 3. 10. out of the same *m.* proceedeth blessing
Rev. 13. 5. given to him a *m.* speaking blasphemies
16. 13. the spirits came out of *m.* of the dragon

His MOUTH.

Gen. 25. † 28. loved Esau, for venison was in *his m.*
Exod. 4. 15. put words in *his m.* I will be with *his m.*
Num. 23. 16. God put a word in *his m.* and said, go
30. 2. accord. to all that proceedeth out of *his m.*
Deut. 18. 18. and I will put my words in *his m.*
1 *Sam.* 14. 26. but no *m.* put his hand to *his m.* 27.
17. 35. I went and delivered it out of *his m.*
2 *Sam.* 17. † 5. and let us hear what is in *his m.*
18. 25. if he be alone, there is tidings in *his m.*
22. 9. and fire out of *his m.* devoured, *Psal.* 18. 8.
1 *Kings* 8. 15. spake with *his m.* to Dav. 2 *Chr.* 6. 4.
2 *Kings* 4. 34. and he put *his m.* on *his m.*

1 *Chr.* 16. 12. remember the judgments of *his m.*
Job 15. 30. by the breath of *his m.* he shall go away
20. 12. though wickedness be sweet in *his m.*
13. though he keep it still within *his m.*
22. 22. receive, I pray thee, the law from *his m.*
23. 12. I have esteemed the words of *his m.* more
37. 2. and the sound that goeth out of *his m.*
40. 23. that he can draw up Jordan into *his m.*
41. 19. out of *his m.* go burning lamps and sparks
21. and a flame goeth out of *his m.*
Psal. 10. 7. *his m.* is full of cursing and deceit
33. 6. the host of them made by breath of *his m.*
36. 3. the words of *his m.* are iniquity and deceit
38. 13. as a dumb man that openeth not *his m.*
55. 21. words of *his m.* are smoother than butter
105. 5. remember the judgments of *his m.*
Prov. 2. 6. out of *his m.* cometh knowledge
11. 9. hypocrite with *his m.* destroyeth neighbour
12. 14. satisfied with good by the fruit of *his m.*
13. 2. a man shall eat good by the fruit of *his m.*
3. he that keepeth *his m.* keepeth his life
15. 23. a man hath joy by the answer of *his m.*
16. 10. *his m.* transgresseth not in judgment
23. the heart of the wise teacheth *his m.*
26. for himself, for *his m.* craveth it of him
18. 6. and *his m.* calleth for strokes
20. shall be satisfied with the fruit of *his m.*
19. 24. will not so much as bring it to *his m.* 26. 15.
20. 17. but *his m.* shall be filled with gravel
21. 23. whoso keepeth *his m.* keepeth his soul
Eccl. 6. 7. all the labour of a man is for *his m.*
10. 13. beginning of words of *his m.* is foolishness
Cant. 1. 2. let him kiss me with the kisses of *his m.*
5. 16. *his m.* is most sweet, this is my beloved
Isa. 11. 4. smite the earth with the rod of *his m.*
53. 9. neither was any deceit in *his m.*
Jer. 9. 8. one speaketh peaceably with *his m.*
20. and let your ear receive the word of *his m.*
36. 17. how didst thou write all these words at *his m.*
51. 44. bring out of *his m.* that which he swallowed
Lam. 1. † 18. for I have rebelled against *his m.*
3. 29. he putteth *his m.* in the dust, if so be there
4. 4. the tongue cleaveth to the roof of *his m.*
Zech. 9. 7. I will take away his blood out of *his m.*
Mal. 2. 6. the law of truth was in *his m.*
7. and they should seek the law at *his m.*
Luke 1. 64. and *his m.* was opened immediately
4. 22. gracious words proceeded out of *his m.*
6. 45. of the abundance of heart *his m.* speaketh
11. 54. seeking to catch somewhat out of *his m*
22. 71. ourselves have heard of *his* own *m.*
John 19. 29. filled a spunge and put it to *his m.*
Acts 22. 14. and shouldest hear the voice of *his m.*
2 *Thess.* 2. 8. shall consume with the spirit of *his m.*
1 *Pet.* 2. 22. neither was guile found in *his m.*
Rev. 1. 16. out of *his m.* went a sharp sword, 19. 15, 21.
12. 15. the serpent cast out of *his m.* water
16. the flood which the dragon cast out of *his m.*
13. 2. and *his m.* was as the mouth of a lion

See LORD.

My MOUTH.

Gen. 45. 12. that it is *my m.* that speaketh to you
Num. 22. 38. the word G. putteth in *my m.* 23. 12.
Deut. 32. 1. hear, O earth, the words of *my m.*
1 *Sam.* 2. 1. *my m.* is enlarged over mine enemies
Job 7. 11. therefore I will not refrain *my m.*
9. 20. *mine* own *m.* shall condemn me
16. 5. I would strengthen you with *my m.*
19. 16. I entreated my servant with *my m.*
23. 4. I would fill *my m.* with arguments
31. 27. or *my m.* hath kissed my hand
30. neither have I suffered *my m.* to sin
33. 2. behold my tongue hath spoken in *my m.*
40. 4. I am vile, I will lay my hand upon *my m.*
Ps. 17. 3. purposed that *my m.* shall not transgress
19. 14. let the words of *my m.* be acceptable
34. 1. his praise shall continually be in *my m.*
39. 1. I said, I will keep *my m.* with a bridle
40. 3. he hath put a new song in *my m.* even praise
49. 3. hear this, *my m.* shall speak of wisdom
51. 15. and *my m.* shall shew forth thy praise
54. 2. hear and give ear to the words of *my m.*
63. 5. *my m.* shall praise thee with joyful lips
66. 14. *my m.* hath spoken when I was in trouble
17. I cried to him with *my m.* he was extolled
71. 8. let *my m.* be filled with thy praise
15. *my m.* shall shew forth thy righteousness
78. 1. incline your ears to the words of *my m.*
2. I will open *my m.* in a parable, I will utter
89. 1. with *my m.* will I make known thy faithfuln.
109. 30. I will greatly praise the Lord with *my m.*
119. 43. take not the word of truth out of *my m.*
103. thy words are sweeter than honey to *my m.*
108. accept the free-will offerings of *my m.*
137. 6. let my tongue cleave to the roof of *my m.*
141. 3. set a watch, O Lord, before *my m.*
145. 21. *my m.* shall speak the praise of the Lord
Prov. 4. 5. nor decline from the words of *my m.* 5. 7.
7. 24. O children, attend to the words of *my m.*
8. 7. for *my m.* shall speak truth, and wickedness
8. the words of *my m.* are in righteousness
Isa. 6. 7. and he laid the coal on *my m.* and said
30. 2. go to Egypt, and have not asked at *my m.*
34. 16. for *my m.* it hath commanded
45. 23. word is gone out of *my m.* in righteousness
48. 3. the former things went forth out of *my m.*
49. 2. he hath made *my m.* like a sharp sword
55. 11. so shall my word be that goeth out of *my m.*
Jer. 1. 9. Ld. put forth his hand and touched *my m.*
15. 19. shalt be as *my m.* || 36. 6. written from *my m.*
Ezek. 3. 3. it was in *my m.* like honey for sweetness
17. therefore hear the word at *my m.* 33. 7.
4. 14. nor came there abominable flesh into *my m.*
Dan. 10. 3. neither came flesh nor wine in *my m.*
Hos. 6. 5. I have slain them by the words of *my m.*
Mat. 13. 35. I will open *my m.* in parables
Acts 11. 8. hath at any time entered into *my m.*
15. 7. the Gentiles by *my m.* should hear the word
Eph. 6. 19. praying that I may open *my m.* boldly
Rev. 2. 16. I will fight with the sword of *my m.*
3. 16. nor cold nor hot, I will spue thee out of *my m.*
10. 10. the book was in *my m.* sweet as honey

MOUTH with *opened*.
Gen. 4. 11. earth *open.* her *m.* to receive broth. blood
Num. 16. 32. the earth *opened* her *m.* and swallowed
them up, and their houses, 26. 10. Deut. 11. 6.
22. 28. Lord *opened* the *m.* of the ass, and she said
Judg. 11. 35. I have *opened* my *m.* to the Lord, 36.
Job 3. 1. *opened* Job his *m.* and cursed his day
29. 23. and they *opened* their *m.* wide, Psal. 35. 21.
33. 2. I pray, hear, behold now I have *open.* my *m.*
Psal. 39. 9. I was dumb, I *opened* not my *m.* because
109. 2. *m.* of the deceitful are *opened* against me
119. 131. I *opened* my *m.* and panted, for I longed
Isa. 5. 14. hell hath *opened* her *m.* without measure
10. 14. there was none that *opened m.* or peeped
53. 7. he was oppressed, yet he *opened* not his *m.*
Ezek. 3. 2. I *open.* my *m.* and he caused me to eat it
24. 27. thy *m.* be *o.* to him which is escaped, 33. 22.
Dan. 10. 16. then I *opened* my *m.* and spake, and said
Mat. 5. 2. he *opened* his *m.* and taught them, saying
17. 27. when thou hast *opened* his *m.* thou shalt find
Luke 1. 64. his *m.* was *opened* immediately, and spake
Acts 8. 32. like a lamb dumb, so *opened* he not his *m.*
35. Philip *opened m.* ‖ 10. 34. Peter *opened m.* said
2 Cor. 6. 11. O Corinthians, our *m.* is *opened* to you
Rev. 12. 16. earth *opened* her *m.* and helped woman
13. 6. he *opened* his *m.* in blasphemy against God
MOUTH with *openeth*.
Psal. 38. 13. as a dumb man that *openeth* not his *m.*
Prov. 24. 7. a fool *openeth* not his *m.* in the gate
31. 26. she *openeth* her *m.* with wisdom
Their MOUTH.
Deut. 21. † 5. by *their m.* every controversy be tried
Judg. 7. 6. lapped, putting their hand to *their m.*
Ezra 8. † 17. I sent them, and put words in *their m.*
Neh. 9. 20. withheldest not thy manna from *their m.*
Job 5. 15. but he saveth the poor from *their m.*
16. 10. they have gaped upon me with *their m.*
29. 9. the princes laid their hand on *their m.*
10. their tongue cleaved to the roof of *their m.*
Psal. 5. 9. there is no faithfulness in *their m.*
17. 10. with *their m.* they speak proudly
49. † 13. their posterity delight in *their m.*
58. 6. break their teeth, O G. in *their m.* break out
59. 7. behold they belch out with *their m.*
12. for the sin of *their m.* and words of their lips
62. 4. they bless with *their m.* but curse inwardly
73. 9. they set *their m.* against the heavens
78. 36. they did flatter him with *their m.* and lied
149. 6. let the high praises of God be in *their m.*
Isa. 29. 13. this people draw near me with *their m.*
Jer. 7. 28. and truth is cut off from *their m.*
12. 2. thou art near in *their m.* far from their reins
Lam. 2. 16. enemies have open. *their m.* against thee
Ezek. 33. 31. with *their m.* they shew much love
34. 10. I will deliver my flock from *their m.*
Mic. 6. 12. their tongue is deceitful in *their m.*
7. 16. they shall lay their hand on *their m.*
Zeph. 3. 13. nor a deceitful tongue found in *their m.*
Zech. 14. 12. tongue shall consume away in *their m.*
Mat. 15. 8. this peop. draweth nigh to me with *th. m.*
Jude 16. *their m.* speaketh great swelling words
Rev. 9. 19. their power is in *their m.* and tails
11. 5. if any hurt them, fire proceedeth out of *th. m.*
14. 5. and in *their m.* was found no guile
Thy MOUTH.
Exod. 4. 12. I will be with *thy m.* and teach thee, 15.
13. 9. that the Lord's law may be in *thy m.*
23. 13. make no mention of other gods out of *thy m.*
Deut. 23. 23. keep that hast promised with *thy m.*
30. 14. word is nigh to thee, in *thy m.* Rom. 10. 8.
Josh. 1. 8. book of the law not depart out of *thy m.*
Judg. 9. 38. then said Zebul, where is now *thy m.*?
11. 36. if thou hast opened *thy m.* to the Lord
18. 19. lay thine hand upon *thy m.* Prov. 30. 32.
2 Sam. 1. 16. *thy m.* hath testified against thee
1 Kings 8. 24. thou spakest with *thy m.* 2 Chr. 6. 15.
17. 24. the word of the Lord in *thy m.* is truth
Job 8. 2. the words of *thy m.* be like a strong wind
21. till he fill *thy m.* with laughing, and thy lips
15. 5. for *thy m.* uttereth thine iniquity
6. thine own *m.* condemneth thee, and not I
13. that thou lettest such words go out of *thy m.*
33. † 6. behold, I am according to *thy m.*
39. † 27. doth the eagle mount up by *thy m.*?
Psal. 50. 16. shouldest take my covenant in *thy m.*
19. thou givest *thy m.* to evil ‖ 81. 10. open *thy m.*
103. 5. who satisfieth *thy m.* with good things
119. 13. have declared all the judments of *thy m.*
72. the law of *thy m.* is better to me than gold
88. so shall I keep the testimony of *thy m.*
138. 4. when they hear the words of *thy m.*
Prov. 6. 2. thou art snared with the words of *thy m.*
27. 2. let another praise thee, and not *thine* own *m.*
31. 8. open *thy m.* for the dumb, in the cause of all
9. open *thy m.* judge righteously, and plead cause
Eccl. 5. 2. be not rash with *thy m.* to utter any thing
6. suffer not *thy m.* to cause thy flesh to sin
Cant. 7. 9. the roof of *thy m.* like the best wine
Isa. 51. 16. I have put my words in *thy m.* Jer. 1. 9.
59. 21. which I put in *thy m.* not depart out of *t. m.*
Jer. 5. 14. I will make my words in *thy m.* fire
Ezek. 2. 8. open *thy m.* and eat that I give thee
3. 26. make thy tongue cleave to roof of *thy m.*
27. I will open *thy m.* and thou shalt say to them
16. 56. sister Sodom was not mentioned by *thy m.*
63. that thou mayest never open *thy m.* any more
Hos. 8. 1. set the trumpet to *thy m.* he shall come
Mic. 7. 5. keep doors of *thy m.* from her that lieth
Luke 19. 22. out of *thine* own *m.* will I judge thee
Rom. 10. 9. if confess with *thy m.* the Lord Jesus
Rev. 10. 9. it shall be in *thy m.* sweet as honey
Your MOUTH.
Num. 32. 24. do that which proceeded out of *your m.*
1 Sam. 2. 3. let not arrogancy come out of *your m.*
Job 21. 5. mark me, and lay your hand on *your m.*
Ezek. 35. 13. thus with *your m.* ye have boasted
Joel 1. 5. for the wine is cut off from *your m.*
Eph. 4. 29. let no corrupt communication proceed
out of *your m.* but what is edifying, Col. 3. 8.
MOUTHS.
Deut. 31. 19. write this song, put it in their *m.*
21. not be forgotten out of *m.* of their seed

1 Sam. 13. † 21. yet they had a file with *m.*
Psal. 22. 13. they gaped upon me with their *m.*
78. 30. while their meat was yet in their *m.*
115. 5. they have *m.* but they speak not, 135. 16.
135. 17. neither is there any breath in their *m.*
Isa. 41. † 15. a new threshing instrument having *m.*
52. 15. the kings shall shut their *m.* at him
Jer. 44. 25. ye and wives have spoken with your *m.*
Lam. 3. 46. our enemies opened their *m.* against us
Dan. 6. 22. my God hath shut the lions' *m.*
Mic. 3. 5. and he that putteth not into their *m.*
Tit. 1. 11. deceivers, whose *m.* must be stopped
Heb. 11. 33. who stopped the *m.* of lions
Jam. 3. 3. behold, we put bits in the horses' *m.*
Rev. 9. 17. out of their *m.* issued fire and smoke, 18.
MOWER.
Psal. 129. 7. wherewith the *m.* filleth not his hand
MOWINGS.
Amos 7. 1. the latter growth after the king's *m.*
MOWN.
Psal. 72. 6. come down like rain upon the *m.* grass
MUCH.
Gen. 26. 16. for thou art *m.* mightier than we
Exod. 12. 42. it is a night to be *m.* observed
16. 18. he that gathered *m.* 2 Cor. 8. 15.
Lev. 13. 7. if the scab spread *m.* abroad, 22. 27, 35.
Num. 21. 4. soul of the people was *m.* discouraged
Deut. 28. 38. shall carry *m.* seed out into the field
Josh. 22. 8. return with *m.* riches to your tents
Ruth 1. 13. it grieveth me *m.* for your sakes
1 Sam. 14. 30. had there been a *m.* greater slaughter
18. 30. so that his name was *m.* set by
19. 2. but Jonathan delighted *m.* in David
26. 24. as thy life was *m.* set by this day, so let
my life be *m.* set by in the eyes of the Lord
1 Kings 4. 29. Solom. had understand. exceeding *m.*
2 Kings 10. 18. but Jehu shall serve him *m.*
21. 6. Ahab wrought *m.* wickedness in sight of Ld.
2 Chron. 27. 3. on the wall of Ophel he built *m.*
33. 6. Manasseh wrought *m.* evil in sight of Lord
Ezra 10. 13. and it is a time of *m.* rain, not able
Neh. 9. 37. it yieldeth *m.* increase unto the kings
Job 5. † 25. know that thy seed shall be *m.*
31. 25. because mine hand had gotten *m.*
Psal. 19. † 13. shall be innocent from *m.* transgress.
129. † 1. *m.* have they afflicted me from my youth
Prov. 17. 7. *m.* less do lying lips become a prince
19. 10. *m.* less for a servant to have rule over
Eccl. 5. 12. sleep is sweet, whether he eat little or *m.*
17. he hath *m.* sorrow and wrath with sickness
9. 18. but one sinner destroyeth *m.* good
Jer. 2. 22. for though thou take thee *m.* sope
Ezek. 23. 32. containeth *m.* ‖ 33. 31. shew *m.* love
Dan. 4. 12. and the fruit thereof was *m.* 21.
Mic. 6. † 16. doth *m.* keep the statutes of Omri
Hag. 1. 6. ye have sown *m.* ‖ 9. ye looked for *m.*
Mat. 6. 26. are ye not *m.* better than they?
26. 9. this ointment might have been sold for *m.*
Mark 4. 5. where it had not *m.* earth, Mat. 13. 5.
Luke 1. † 28. hail, thou that art *m.* graced
7. 47. her many sins are forgiven, for she loved *m.*
12. 48. for to whom *m.* is given, of him shall *m.*
be required, to whom men have committed *m.*
16. 10. he that is faithful also in *m.* is unjust in *m.*
John 12. 24. it bringeth forth *m.* fruit, 15. 5.
14. 30. hereafter I will not talk *m.* with you
Acts 16. 16. which brought her masters *m.* gain
18. 27. who helped them *m.* which had believed
26. 24. Festus said, *m.* learning doth make thee mad
Rom. 3. 2. *m.* every way ‖ 16. 12. laboured *m.* in L.
2 Cor. 2. 4. out of *m.* affliction I wrote to you
Heb. 12. 9. *m.* rather be in subjection and live
25. *m.* more shall not we escape, if we turn away
Jam. 5. 16. the prayer of the righteous availeth *m.*
Rev. 5. 4. I wept *m.* because no man was found
As MUCH.
Gen. 23. 9. give it for *as m.* money as it is worth
43. 34. mess was five times *as m.* as any of theirs
44. 1. fill sacks with food *as m.* as they can carry
Exod. 16. 5. twice *as m.* as they gather daily, 22.
Lev. 7. 10. Aaron's sons have one *as m.* as another
Josh. 17. 14. for *as m.* as the Lord hath blessed me
1 Sam. 2. 16. then take *as m.* as thy soul desireth
2 Chron. 2. 16. cut wood *as m.* as thou shalt need
Job 42. 10. the Ld. gave Job twice *as m.* as he had
Ps. 119. 14. joy in testimonies, *as m.* as in all riches
Luke 6. 34. sinners lend, to receive *as m.* again
John 6. 11. likewise of fishes *as m.* as they would
Rom. 1. 15. *as m.* as in me is, I am ready to preach
11. 13. in *as m.* as I am the apostle of the Gentiles
12. 18. *as m.* as lieth in you, live peaceably with all
Phil. 1. 7. in *as m.* as both in bonds, and in defence
Heb. 3. 3. in *as m.* as he who builded the house
7. 20. in *as m.* as not without an oath was priest
1 Pet. 4. 13. in *as m.* as ye are partakers of sufferings
See How *much*, How *much less*, How *much more*, *Much* More, People.
So MUCH.
Exod. 14. 28. remained not *so m.* as one of them
30. 23. and of sweet cinnamon half *so m.*
Lev. 14. 21. if he be poor and cannot get *so m.*
Deut. 2. 5. not give you *so m.* as a foot-breadth
2 Sam. 14. 25. none to be *so m.* praised as Absalom
17. 12. there shall not be left *so m.* as one
2 Chron. 20. 25. in gathering the spoil, it was *so m.*
Prov. 19. 24. will not *so m.* as bring it to his mouth
25. 16. eat *so m.* as is sufficient for thee, lest filled
Jer. 2. 36. why gaddest thou *so m.* to change thy way?
Mal. 3. 13. what have we spoken *so m.* against thee?
Mat. 15. 33. whence should we have *so m.* bread?
Mark 2. 2. was no room, no not *so m.* as about door
3. 20. so that they could not *so m.* as eat, 6. 31.
7. 36. *so m.* more a great deal they published it
Luke 5. 15. *so m.* the more went there a fame abroad
6. 3. have ye not read *so m.* as this what David did?
18. 13. would not lift up *so m.* as his eyes to heaven
39. he cried *so m.* the more, have mercy on me
Acts 5. 8. if ye sold it for *so m.* she said, yea, for *so m.*
7. 5. no inheritance, not *so m.* as to set his foot on
19. 2. not *so m.* as heard whether any Holy Ghost
1 Cor. 5. 1. not *so m.* as named among the Gentiles
2 Cor. 9. † 5. bounty hath been *so m.* spoken of before

Heb. 1. 4. being made *so m.* better than the angels
7. 22. by *so m.* Jesus made surety of better testam
10. 25. and *so m.* more, as ye see day approaching
12. 20. if *so m.* as a beast touch the mountain
Rev. 18. 7. *so m.* torment and sorrow give her
Too MUCH.
Exod. 36. 7. the stuff was sufficient, and *too m.*
Num. 16. 3. said to them, ye take *too m.* upon you, 7.
Josh. 19. 9. part of children of Judah was *too m.*
1 Kings 12. 28. *too m.* for you to go up to Jerusalem
Esth. 1. 18. thus shall there arise *too m.* contempt
Very MUCH.
Gen. 41. 49. Joseph gathered corn as sand, *very m.*
Exod. 12. 38. *very m.* cattle went up with them
Josh. 13. 1. remaineth *very m.* land to be possessed
22. 8. return with *very m.* cattle, *very m.* raiment
1 Kings 10. 2. queen of Sheba came with *very m.* gold
2 Kings. 21. 16. Manasseh shed innoc. blood. *very m.*
1 Chr. 18. 8. from Chun brought David *very m.* brass
2 Chron. 14. 13. they carried away *very m.* spoil
32. 29. for God hath given him substance *very m.*
36. 14. the priests and people transgressed *very m.*
Psal. 119. 107. I am afflicted *very m.* quicken me
Jer. 40. 12. and gathered summer-fruits *very m.*
MUFFLERS.
Isa. 3. 19. I will take away the chains, the *m.*
MULBERRY-*trees*.
2 Sam. 5. 23. thou shalt not go up, but come upon
them over-against the *m.-trees*, 1 Chron. 14. 14.
24. when thou hearest the sound in tops of the *m.-trees*, then bestir thyself, 1 Chron. 14. 15.
Ps. 84. † 6. who passing thro' the valley of *m.-trees*
MULE.
2 Sam. 13. 29. every man gat him upon his *m.*
18. 9. Absalom rode on a *m.* the *m.* went away
1 Kings 1. 33. cause Solom. to ride on my *m.* 38. 44.
Psal. 32. 9. be not as the horse or *m.* which have
Zech. 14. 15. so shall be plague of the horse, of the *m.*
MULES.
Gen. 36. 24. Anah that found *m.* in the wilderness
1 Kings 4. † 28. they brought barley for the *m.*
10. 25. brought *m.* a rate year by year, 2 Chr. 9. 24.
18. 5. we may find grass to save the *m.* alive
2 Kings 5. 17. be given to thy servant two *m.* burden
1 Chron. 12. 40. brought bread on camels and on *m.*
Ezra 2. 66. their *m.* were 245, Neh. 7. 68.
Esth. 8. 10. he sent letters by riders on *m.* 14.
Isa. 66. 20. they shall bring your brethren on *m.*
Ezek. 27. 14. Togarmah traded in thy fairs with *m.*
MULTIPLY.
Gen. 1. 22. be fruitf. and *m.* 28. ‖ 8. 17. ‖ 9. 7. ‖ 35. 11.
3. 16. I will *m.* thy sorrow and conception
6. 1. when men began to *m.* on the face of the earth
16. 10. I will *m.* Hagar's seed exceedingly, 17. 20.
17. 2. and I will *m.* thee exceedingly, 48. 4.
22. 17. I will *m.* thy seed, 26. 4, 24. Heb. 6. 14.
28. 3. God Almighty bless thee, and *m.* thee
Exod. 1. 10. let us deal wisely with them, lest they *m.*
7. 3. I will *m.* my signs and wonders in Egypt
23. 29. lest the beast of the field *m.* against thee
30. † 15. the rich shall not *m.* half a shekel
32. 13. to whom thou saidst, I will *m.* your seed,
Lev. 26. 9. Deut. 7. 13. ‖ 13. 17. ‖ 28. 63. ‖ 30. 5.
Lev. 11. † 42. whatsoever doth *m.* feet, not eat
Num. 26. † 54. to many *m.* his inheritance, 33. † 54.
Deut. 8. 1. that ye may live and *m.* and go in, 30. 16.
17. 16. the king shall not *m.* horses to himself
17. neither shall he *m.* wives, nor silver, and gold
2 Sam. 14. † 11. revengers do not *m.* to destroy
1 Chron. 4. 27. neither did all their family *m.*
Job 29. 18. I shall *m.* my days as the sand
Isa. 1. † 15. when ye *m.* prayer, I will not hear
55. † 7. return to God, for he will *m.* to pardon
Jer. 30. 19. I will *m.* them, they shall not be few
33. 22. so will I *m.* the seed of David my servant
Ezek. 16. 7. I have caused thee to *m.* as the bud
36. 10. I will *m.* men ‖ 11. *m.* man and beast
30. I will *m.* the fruit of the tree, and increase
37. 26. and I will place them and *m.* them
Amos 4. 4. come to Bethel, at Gilgal *m.* transgression
2 Cor. 9. 10. and *m.* your seed sown, and increase
MULTIPLIED.
Gen. 47. 27. Israel grew and *m.* Exod. 1. 7, 20.
Exod. 1. 12. the more afflicted, they *m.* and grew
11. 9. that my wonders may be *m.* in Egypt
Deut. 1. 10. the Lord your God hath *m.* you
8. 13. thy gold is *m.* and all that thou hast is *m.*
11. 21. that your days may be *m.* in the land
Josh. 24. 3. I *m.* his seed, and gave him Isaac
Judg. 16. † 24. our enemy, who *m.* our slain
1 Sam. 1. † 12. as she *m.* to pray, Eli marked
2 Sam. 22. † 36. and thy gentleness hath *m.* me
1 Chron. 5. 9. because their cattle were *m.* in Gilead
2 Chron. 33. † 23. but Amon *m.* trespass
Neh. 6. † 17. the nobles *m.* letters to Tobiah
Job 27. 14. if his children be *m.* it is for sword
35. 6. if thy transgressions be *m.* what doest to him?
Psal. 16. 4. their sorrows shall be *m.* that hasten
38. 19. they that hate me wrongfully are *m.*
107. 38. he blesseth them, so that they are *m.*
Prov. 9. 11. for by me thy days shall be *m.*
29. 16. when wicked are *m.* transgression increaseth
Isa. 9. 3. thou hast *m.* the nation, and not increased
59. 12. for our transgressions are *m.* before thee
Jer. 3. 16. when ye be *m.* they shall say no more
46. † 16. he *m.* the faller, one fell on another
Ezek. 5. 7. ye *m.* more than the nations about you
11. 6. ye have *m.* your slain in this city
16. 25. thou hast *m.* thy whoredoms, 23. 19.
29. *m.* fornication ‖ 51. *m.* abominations
21. 15. that their heart may faint, and ruins be *m.*
31. 5. his boughs were *m.* ‖ 35. 13. *m.* your words
Dan. 4. 1. peace be *m.* to you, 6. 25. 1 Pet. 1. 2. 2 Pet. 1. 2. Jude 2.
Hos. 2. 8. did not know that I *m.* her silver and gold
8. 14. and Judah hath *m.* fenced cities
12. 10. I have *m.* visions, and used similitudes
Nah. 3. 16. thou hast *m.* thy merchants above stars
Acts 6. 1. when the number of disciples was *m.* 7.
7. 17. the people grew and *m.* in Egypt
9. 31. walking in the fear of the Lord were *m.*
12. 24. but the word of God grew and *m.*

MULTIPLIEDST.
Neh. 9. 23. their children also *m.* thou as the stars
MULTIPLIETH.
Job 9. 17. he *m.* my wounds without cause
34. 37. he *m.* his words against God
35. 16. he *m.* words without knowledge
Eccl. 10. † 14. a fool also *m.* words, man cannot tell
MULTIPLYING.
Gen. 22. 17. in *m.* I will multiply, *Heb.* 6. 14.
MULTITUDE
Signifies, [1] *A great company or number of persons or things*, Gen. 30. 30. | 48. 4. [2] *The common people*, Mat. 9. 33. [3] *The whole assembly, both common people and senators*, Acts 23. 7. [4] *The church, or a company of the faithful*, Acts 15. 12, 22. | 21. 22. [5] *Great store, or plenty*, Jer. 10. 13. [6] *Much variety*, Eccl. 5. 3, 7. [7] *Infinite*, Psal. 51. 1.
Gen. 16. 10. not numbered for *m.* 32. 12. 1 *Kings* 3. 8.
17. † 4. thou shalt be a father of *m.* of nations
28. 3. God Almighty make thee a *m.* of people
30. 30. and it is now increased unto a *m.*
48. 4. I will make of thee a *m.* of people, 16. 19.
Exod. 12. 38. a mixed *m.* went up also with them
23. 2. thou shalt not follow a *m.* to do evil
Lev. 25. 16. according to the *m.* of years increase
Num. 11. 4. and the mixed *m.* fell a lusting
Deut. 1. 10. behold, ye are this day as the stars for *m.* 10. 22. | 28. 62. *Heb.* 11. 12.
Josh. 11. 4. as sand on sea-shore for *m.* *Judg.* 7. 12. 1 *Sam.* 13. 5. 2 *Sam.* 17. 11. 1 *Kings* 4. 20.
Judg. 6. 5. Midianites as grasshoppers for *m.* 7. 12.
1 *Sam.* 14. 16. behold, the *m.* melted away
2 *Sam.* 6. 19. he dealt among the whole *m.* of Israel
1 *Kings* 7. † 47. unweighed for the exceeding *m.*
8. 5. and oxen that could not be told for *m.*
2 *Kings* 7. 13. they are as all the *m.* that are left
19. 23. hast said, with the *m.* of my chariots I am come up to the sides of Lebanon, *Isa.* 37. 24.
2 *Chron.* 1. 9. over a people like the dust for *m.*
14. 11. in thy name we go against this *m.*
20. 24. and behold, the *m.* were dead bodies
30. 18. for a *m.* had not cleansed themselves
32. 7. be not afraid of all the *m.* with him
Neh. 13. 3. they separated from Israel the mixed *m.*
† 22. spare me, according to *m.* of thy mercy
Esth. 5. 11. Haman told of the *m.* of his children
10. 3. Mordecai accepted of the *m.* of brethren
Job 4. † 14. made the *m.* of my bones to shake
11. 2. should not the *m.* of words be answered?
32. 7. and *m.* of years should teach wisdom
35. 9. by reason of the *m.* of oppressions they make
39. 7. he scorneth the *m.* of the city, nor regardeth
Psal. 5. 7. I will come in the *m.* of thy mercy
10. cast them out in *m.* of their transgressions
33. 16. there is no king saved by the *m.* of an host
42. 4. I had gone with the *m.* to the house of God
49. 6. that boast themselves in *m.* of their riches
51. 1. according to the *m.* of thy mercies blot out
68. 30. rebuke the *m.* of bulls, with calves
69. 13. O God, in the *m.* of thy mercy, hear me!
16. turn to me, according to *m.* of thy mercies
74. 19. deliver me not to the *m.* of the wicked
94. 19. in the *m.* of my thoughts within me
106. 7. they remembered not *m.* of thy mercies
45. and repented, according to *m.* of his mercies
109. 30. I will praise him among the *m.*
Prov. 10. 19. in the *m.* of words wanteth not sin
11. 14. in the *m.* of counsellors is safety, 24. 6.
14. 28. in the *m.* of people is the king's honour
15. 22. in *m.* of counsellors they are established
20. 15. there is gold, and a *m.* of rubies
Eccl. 5. 3. for a dream cometh through the *m.* of business, a fool's voice is known by the *m.* of words
7. in the *m.* of dreams there are divers vanities
Isa. 1. 11. to what purpose is the *m.* of sacrifices?
5. 13. and their *m.* dried up with thirst
14. their *m.* and pomp shall descend into hell
17. 12. woe to *m.* of many people which make noise
29. 8. so *m.* of nations be that fight against Zion
31. 4. when *m.* of shepherds is called against him
47. 9. shall come on thee for *m.* of thy sorceries
12. stand now with the *m.* of thy sorceries
13. thou art wearied in the *m.* of thy counsels
60. 6. the *m.* of camels shall cover thee
63. 7. according to *m.* of his loving-kindnesses
† 15. the *m.* of thy bowels, are they restrained?
Jer. 10. 13. is a *m.* of waters in heavens, 51. 16.
12. 6. yea, they have called a *m.* after thee
30. 14. I have wounded thee for *m.* of thine iniquity
46. 25. behold, I will punish the *m.* of No
Lam. 1. 5. afflicted her, for *m.* of her transgressions
3. 32. compassion according to *m.* of his mercies
Ezek. 7. 12. wrath is on all the *m.* thereof, 14.
13. for the vision is touching the whole *m.* thereof
14. 4. answer him according to the *m.* of his idols
27. 12. by reason of the *m.* of riches, 18. 33.
16. by reason of the *m.* of the wares, 18.
31. 18. this is Pharaoh and all his *m.* 32. 32.
32. 24. Elam and her *m.* || 26. Tubal and all her *m.*
39. 11. they shall bury Gog, and all his *m.*
Dan. 10. 6. voice of his words like the voice of a *m.*
11. 13. the king of the north shall set forth a *m.*
Hos. 9. 7. days of recompence, for *m.* of thine iniq.
10. 13. thou didst trust in the *m.* of mighty men
Nah. 3. 3. there is a *m.* of slain, they stumble
4. because of the *m.* of the whoredoms of harlot
Zech. 8. † 4. with his staff for *m.* of days
Mat. 14. 5. put to death, he feared the *m.* 21. 46.
15. 32. I have compassion on the *m.* *Mark* 8. 2.
Mark 5. 31. seest the *m.* thronging thee, *Luke* 8. 45.
Luke 2. 13. there was with the angel a *m.* of the host
12. 1. were gathered together an innumerable *m.*
22. 6. to betray him in the absence of the *m.*
47. and while he yet spake, behold, a *m.*
23. 1. whole *m.* of them arose, and led him to Pilate
John 5. 13. a *m.* being present in that place
21. 6. not able to draw it for the *m.* of fishes
Acts 4. 32. the *m.* that believed were of one heart
6. 5. and the saying pleased the whole *m.*
16. 22. the *m.* rose up together against them
21. 22. the *m.* must needs come together

Eph. 4. † 8. he ascended, he led a *m.* of captives
Jam. 5. 20. shall save a soul from death, and shall hide a *m.* of sins
1 *Pet.* 4. 8. for charity shall cover the *m.* of sins
See GREAT.
MULTITUDES.
Ezek. 32. 20. draw her and all her *m.*
Joel 3. 14. *m. m.* in the valley of decision
Mat. 9. 33. the dumb spake; and the *m.* marvelled
36. when he saw the *m.* he was moved
21. 9. the *m.* cried, saying, Hosanna to Son of D.
Acts 5. 14. *m.* were added both of men and women
13. 45. Jews saw *m.* they were filled with envy
Rev. 17. 15. the waters are *m.* and nations
See GREAT.
MUNITION.
Isa. 29. 7. all that fight against her and her *m.*
Nah. 2. 1. keep the *m.* watch the way, fortify
MUNITIONS.
Isa. 33. 16. his defence shall be the *m.* of rocks
Dan. 11. † 15. the king shall take the city of *m.*
† 38. in his estate he shall honour the God of *m.*
† 39. thus shall he do in the fortresses of *m.*
MURDER
Signifies, [1] *The taking away of a man's life unlawfully*, Mark 15. 7. [2] *All cruelty in thought, word, or deed*, Mat. 19. 18. 1 John 3. 15.
Voluntary murder *was always punished with death, but involuntary or accidental* murder, *among the* Hebrews, *was only punished by banishment. Cities of refuge were appointed for involuntary manslaughter, whither they might retire, and continue in safety, till the death of the high priest; then the offender was at liberty to return to his own city, and his own house, if he pleased. But as for the voluntary murderer, he was put to death without any remission, and the kinsmen of the murdered person might kill him with impunity: money could not redeem his life; he was dragged away, even from the altar, if he had taken refuge there*, Num. 35. 27, 28, 31. *The ceremony used by the* Israelites, *when a dead body was found in the fields slain by a murderer unknown, as it is recorded*, Deut. 21. *from verse* 1 *to* 9. *may inform us what idea they had of the heinousness of murder, and how much horror they conceived at this crime; and also the fear they were in, that God might take vengeance for it on the whole country; and of the pollution that the country was supposed to contract, by the blood that was spilt in it, unless it were expiated, or revenged upon him that was the occasion of it, if he could by any means be discovered.*
Psal. 10. 8. in secret doth he *m.* the innocent
94. 6. they slay the widow, and *m.* the fatherless
Jer. 7. 9. will ye steal, *m.* and commit adultery?
Hos. 6. 9. so priests *m.* in the way by consent
MURDER.
Mat. 19. 18. Jesus said, thou shalt do no *m.*
Mark 15. 7. one Barabbas, who had committed *m.*
Luke 23. 19. and for *m.* was cast into prison, 25.
Rom. 1. 29. full of envy, *m.* debate, deceit
MURDERER.
Num. 35. 16. if he smite him he is a *m.* the *m.* shall surely be put to death, 17. 18, 21.
19. the revenger of blood shall slay the *m.* 21.
30. *m.* shall be put to death by mouth of witnesses
31. shall take no satisfaction for the life of a *m.*
2 *Kings* 6. 32. see how this son of *m.* hath sent to take
Job 24. 14. *m.* rising with the light, killeth the poor
Hos. 9. 13. Ephraim bring forth his children to the *m.*
John 8. 44. he was a *m.* from the beginning
Acts 3. 14. ye desired a *m.* to be granted to you
28. 4. they said, no doubt this man is a *m.*
1 *Pet.* 4. 15. but let none of you suffer as a *m.*
1 *John* 3. 15. whoso hateth his brother is a *m.* ye know that no *m.* hath eternal life abiding in him
MURDERERS.
2 *Kings* 14. 6. the children of the *m.* he slew not
Isa. 1. 21. righteousness lodged in it, but now *m.*
Jer. 4. 31. for my soul is wearied, because of *m.*
Mat. 22. 7. he sent forth and destroyed those *m.*
Acts 7. 52. of whom ye have been now the *m.*
21. 38. and leddest out 4000 men that were *m.*
1 *Tim.* 1. 9. law made for *m.* of fathers and mothers
Rev. 21. 8. *m.* shall have their part in the lake
22. 15. for without are whoremongers and *m.*
MURDERS.
Mat. 15. 19. out of the heart proceed *m.* *Mark* 7. 21.
Gal. 5. 21. the works of the flesh are envyings, *m.*
Rev. 9. 21. nor repented they of their *m.* nor fornica.
MURMUR
Signifies, *To repine at or complain of some wrong pretended to have been received*, Exod. 16. 2. St. Paul *forbids all murmuring, which was so fatal to the* Israelites *that murmured in the wilderness*, 1 Cor. 10. 10. *and for which God punished them severely. They murmured at the* Graves of Lust, *and God sent them quails for food; but hardly was this meat out of their mouths, before the wrath of the Lord was kindled against them, and he destroyed three and twenty thousand of them*, Num. 11. 33, 34. Psal. 78. 30, 31. *They murmured again after the return of the spies that were sent to search out and view the promised land; and God punished them by depriving them of the happiness of ever seeing that land, and condemned them to die in the wilderness*, Num. 14. 29, 30. *They were again punished for murmuring, by the fiery serpents that God sent among them, which killed a great number of them*, Num. 21. 4, 5, 6. *The murmuring of* Miriam *the sister of Moses, was chastised by a leprosy that seized her whole body, and obliged her to abide seven days without the camp*, Num. 12. 1, 2, 10, 15. *And the murmuring and rebellion of* Korah, Dathan, *and* Abiram, *was punished in a still more terrible manner, the earth opening and swallowing up the authors of the sedition, and fire consuming their accomplices*, Num. 16. 3, 31, 32, 35.
Exod. 16. 7. what are we, that ye *m.* against us?

Exod. 16. 8. Lord heareth murmur. ye *m.* *Num.* 14. 27.
Num. 14. 36. the spies made the congregation to *m.*
16. 11. what is Aaron, that ye *m.* against him?
17. 5. of Israel, whereby they *m.* against you
Lam. 3. † 39. wherefore doth a living man *m.*?
John 6. 43. Jesus said, *m.* not among yourselves
1 *Cor.* 10. 10. neither *m.* as some of them murmured
MURMURED.
Exod. 15. 24. the people *m.* against Moses, 17. 3.
16. 2. the whole congregation of Israel *m.* against Moses and Aaron, *Num.* 14. 2. | 16. 41.
Num. 14. 29. from twenty years old, which have *m.*
Deut. 1. 27. and ye *m.* in your tents, and said
Josh. 9. 18. all the congregation *m.* against princes
Psal. 106. 25. they believed not, but *m.* in their tents
Isa. 29. 24. they that *m.* shall learn doctrine
Mat. 20. 11. when they had received a penny, they *m.*
Mark 14. 5. and they *m.* against her
Luke 5. 30. but the Scribes and Pharisees *m.*
15. 2. they *m.* saying, this man receiveth sinners
19. 7. *m.* that he was gone to be guest to Zaccheus
John 6. 41. the Jews, *m.* at him, because he said
61. he knew that his disciples *m.* at it
7. 32. the Pharisees heard that the people *m.*
1 *Cor.* 10. 10. neither murmur as some of them *m.*
MURMURERS.
Jude 16. these are *m.* complainers, walking after lusts
MURMURING.
John 7. 12. there was much *m.* among the people
Acts 6. 1. a *m.* of Grecians against the Hebrews
MURMURINGS.
Exod. 16. 7. he heareth your *m.* 8, 9, 12. *Num.* 14. 27.
8. your *m.* are not against us, but the Lord
Num. 17. 5. I will make to cease the *m.* of Israel
10. thou shalt quite take away their *m.* from me
Phil. 2. 14. do all things without *m.* and disputings
MURRAIN.
Exod. 9. 3. therefore there shall be a very grievous *m.*
Psal. 78. † 50. he gave their beasts to the *m.*
MUSE.
Psal. 143. 5. I *m.* on the work of thy hands
MUSED.
Luke 3. 15. all men *m.* in their hearts of John
MUSING.
Psal. 39. 3. while I was *m.* the fire burned
MUSICAL.
1 *Chron.* 16. 42. with *m.* instruments of God
Neh. 12. 36. with the *m.* instruments of David
Eccl. 2. 8. as *m.* instruments, and that of all sorts
MUSICIANS.
Rev. 18. 22. voice of *m.* shall be heard no more in thee
MUSIC.
1 *Sam.* 18. 6. women came to meet king Saul with *m.*
1 *Chr.* 15. 16. to be the singers with instruments of *m.* 2 *Chron.* 5. 13. | 23. 13. | 34. 1.
2 *Chr.* 7. 6. Levites with instruments of *m.*
Eccl. 12. 4. daughters of *m.* shall be brought low
Lam. 3. 63. sitting and rising, I am their *m.*
5. 14. young men have ceased from their *m.*
Dan. 3. 5. when ye hear all kinds of *m.* 7. 10, 15.
6. 18. neither were instruments of *m.* brought
Amos. 6. 5. that invent instruments of *m.* like David
Luke 15. 25. his elder son heard *m.* and dancing
MUST
Denotes, (I) *A necessity of that thing to which it is applied*, Heb. 9. 16. [1] *Of a good thing, in respect either of God's commandment or promise*, Mark 9. 11. Rom. 13. 5. [2] *Of moral evil, or sin, in respect of God's permission of it, man's propension to it, and Satan's suggestions of it*, Mat. 18. 7. (II) *A duty, and that which ought to be*, 2 Tim. 2. 6.
Gen. 24. 5. *m.* I needs bring thy son again to the land?
29. 26. it *m.* not be so done in our country
30. 16. thou *m.* come in to me || 43. 11. if it *m.* be so
Lev. 11. 32. it *m.* be put in water, so be cleansed
23. 6. seven days ye *m.* eat unleavened bread
Num. 6. 21. so he *m.* do after the law of separation
20. 10. *m.* we fetch you water out of this rock?
23. 12. *m.* I not take heed to speak that the Lord
26. all that the Lord speaketh that I *m.* do
Deut. 1. 22. bring us word by what way we *m.* go
4. 22. I *m.* die in this land, I *m.* not go over
12. 18. thou *m.* eat them before the Lord thy God
31. 14. thy days approach that thou *m.* die
Josh. 3. 4. may know the way by which ye *m.* go
Judg. 13. 16. thou *m.* offer it to the Lord
21. 17. there *m.* be an inheritance for them
1 *Sam.* 14. 43. I did but taste a little, and lo I *m.* die
2 *Sam.* 23. 3. he that ruleth over men *m.* be just
7. that shall touch them *m.* be fenced with iron
1 *Kings* 18. 27. he sleepeth, and *m.* be awaked
Ezra 10. 12. as thou hast said, so *m.* we do
Jer. 10. 5. they *m.* needs be borne, they cannot go
Mat. 26. 54. scriptures be fulfilled, that thus it *m.* be
Mark 2. 22. else the bottles will be marred, but new wine *m.* be put into new bottles, *Luke* 5. 38.
8. 31. Son of man *m.* suffer many things, 9. 12.
9. 11. why say the scribes that Elias *m.* first come?
13. 7. when ye shall hear of wars, be ye not troubled, for such things *m.* be, *Luke* 21. 9.
10. gospel *m.* first be published among all nations
Luke 2. 49. I *m.* be about my Father's business
4. 43. I *m.* preach kingdom of God, for I am sent
14. 18. I bought ground, and *m.* go and see it
19. 5. Zaccheus, to-day I *m.* abide at thy house
22. 7. the day when the passover *m.* be killed
37. the things written *m.* be accomplished, 24. 44.
23. 17. he *m.* release one to them at the feast
24. 7. Son of man *m.* be delivered to sinful men
John 3. 7. marvel not I said, ye *m.* be born again
14. the serpent, so *m.* the Son of man be lifted up
30. he *m.* increase, but I *m.* decrease
4. 4. and he *m.* needs go through Samaria
24. G. is a Spirit, *m.* worship him in spirit, truth
9. 4. I *m.* work the works of him that sent me
10. 16. other sheep I have, them also I *m.* bring
20. 9. knew not he *m.* rise again from the dead
Acts 1. 16. this scripture *m.* have been fulfilled
22. *m.* one be ordained to be a witness with us
4. 12. none other name whereby we *m.* be saved
9. 6. it shall be told thee what thou *m.* do

Acts 14.22. we m. thro' much tribulat. enter kingdom
15. 24. ye m. be circumcised and keep the law
16. 30. said, sirs, what m. I do to be saved
18. 21. I m. by all means keep this feast in Jerus.
21. 22. the multitude m. needs come together
23. 11. so m. thou bear witness also at Rome
27. 24. fear not, thou m. be brought before Cæsar
26. howbeit we m. be cast on a certain island
Rom. 13. 5. wherefore ye m. needs be subject
1 Cor. 5. 10. then m. ye needs go out of the world
11. 19. there m. also be heresies among you
15. 25. for he m. reign till he hath put under
2 Cor. 5. 10. for we m. all appear before the judgm.
11. 30. if I m. needs glory, I will glory of things
1 Tim. 3. 2. a bishop then m be blameless, Tit. 1. 7.
7. he m. have a good report of them without
8. likewise m. deacons be grave, not double tong.
2 Tim. 2. 6. husbandman m. be first partaker of fruits
24. the servant of the Lord m. not strive
Heb. 4. 6. it remaineth that some m. enter therein
9. 16. there m. be the death of the testator
11. 6. he that cometh to God, m. believe that he is
13. 17. they watch, as they that m. give account
Rev. 4. 1. shew thee things which m. be hereafter
11. 5. if any be hurt he m. in this manner be killed
20. 3. after that he m. be loosed a little season
22. 6. to shew things which m. shortly be done

MUSTARD-SEED; see GRAIN.

MUSTERED.

2 Kings 25. 19. took the scribe which m. Jer. 52. 25.

MUSTERETH.

Isa. 13. 4. the Lord m. the host of the battle

MUTTER.

Isa. 8. 19. to wizards that peep, and that m.
16. † 7. for Kirhareseth shall ye m.

MUTTERED.

Isa. 59. 3. your tongue hath m. perverseness

MUTUAL.

Rom. 1. 12. I may be comforted by the m. faith

MUZZLE.

Deut. 25. 4. thou shalt not m. the ox when he treadeth out the corn. 1 Cor. 9. 9. 1 Tim. 5. 18.

MYRRH.

Gen. 37. 25. Ishmaelites came bearing balm and m.
43. 11. carry down the man a present, m. nuts
Exod. 30. 23. of pure m. five hundred shekels
Esth. 2. 12. to wit, six months with oil of m.
Psal. 45. 8. thy garments smell of m. aloes and cassia
Prov. 7. 17. I have perfumed my bed with m.
Cant. 1. 13. a bundle of m. is my beloved to me
3. 6. perfumed with m. and frankincense
4. 6. I will get me to the mountain of m. and aloes
14. m. and aloes with all the chief spices
5. 1. I have gathered my m. with my spice
5. my hands dropped with m. fingers with sweet m.
13. his lips like lilies, dropping sweet-smelling m.
Mat. 2. 11. they presented to him gifts, gold and m.
Mark 15. 23. to drink wine mingled with m.
John 19. 39. brought a mixture of m. and aloes

MYRTLE.

Neh. 8. 15. go forth and fetch m. olive branches
Isa. 41. 19. I will plant in the wilderness the m.
55. 13. instead of brier shall come the m. tree

MYRTLE-TREES.

Zech. 1. 8. and he stood among the m. 10. 11.

MYSTERY.

The word signifies, a secret, a mystery *being a thing kept secret and hid from our understanding, till it be revealed to us.* 1 Cor. 2. 7. We speak the wisdom of God in a mystery, even the hidden wisdom. Mysteries *are said to be of two sorts:* one sort *are such as would never have been known without revelation; but when revealed, may be in a good measure explained and understood. Such is the doctrine of the satisfaction of* Christ, *of the resurrection from the dead, of the forgiveness of sins for the sake of* Christ's *sufferings, and of eternal life in a future world.* The other sort *of mysteries are those, which when revealed to us, we know the existence, or reality and certainty of them, but cannot comprehend the manner and mode how they are. These are the mystery of the blessed Trinity, and the mystery of the incarnation of* Christ; *or the union of the divine and human natures in one person. The calling of the* Gentiles, *which was hid and kept secret for many ages, is called a* mystery, Rom. 16. 25. Col. 1. 26, 27. *The spiritual union between* Christ *and his church is called a* mystery, *because it exceeds human understanding, and is revealed only to the children of God,* Eph. 5. 32. Mark 4. 11. *The gospel is called* the mystery of godliness, 1 Tim. 3. 16.

The prophecies concerning the person, the coming, the characters, the death and passion, of the Messiah, *are to be found in a multitude of places in the Old Testament, but after a figurative and mysterious manner. The actions, the words, the life of the prophets were a continual and general prophecy, which was concealed from the eyes of the people, and sometimes from the prophets themselves, and was not explained or discovered, till after the birth and death of* Christ; *and these mysteries were dispensed in so wonderful a method, and by so wise a providence, that the first served as a foundation for the second, and the succeeding gave new light to those that went before. They still improved in clearness and evidence, and the Holy Ghost dispensed them by measure, and in due degrees.* Daniel *is more explicit than the prophets before him;* Haggai, Zechariah, *and* Malachi, *speak of the coming, of the death, and of the priesthood of* Jesus Christ, *and of the calling of the Gentiles, after a more plain and distinct manner than the other prophets before them.*

The mysteries *of the Christian religion, is that of the blessed* Trinity, *the incarnation of* Christ, *his hypostatical union with his human nature, his miraculous birth, his death, resurrection, and ascension, the predestination, and reprobation of men; the grace of* Jesus Christ, *and the manner of its operation in our hearts; the resurrection of the dead, with all the other mysteries revealed to us both in the Old and New Testament, are the objects of the faith of all true Christians; and the doctrine of the gospel, and these tenets of christianity were called* mysteries, *not only because they were secrets which would not have been known, if the Son of God, and his Holy Spirit, had not revealed them to believers, but also because they were not revealed indifferently to every body. The command of our Lord* Jesus Christ *to his apostles was in this case put in practice,* Give not that which is holy unto dogs, neither cast ye your pearls before swine, *Mat.* 7. 6. *They preached the gospel only to those who seriously desired to be instructed in it; nor did they presently discover to them all the mysteries of religion; but in proportion as they became capable to receive them.*

Mark 4. 11. to you given to know the m. of kingdom
Rom. 11. 25. that ye should be ignorant of this m.
16. 25. according to the revelation of the m.
1 Cor. 2. 7. we speak the wisdom of God in a m.
15. 51. I shew you a m. we shall not all sleep
Eph. 1. 9. made known to us the m. of his will
3. 3. how that he made known to me the m.
4. understand my knowledge in the m. of Christ
9. make all see what is the fellowship of the m.
5. 32. this is a great m. but I speak of Christ
6. 19. may open my mouth boldly, to make known the m. of the gospel, Col. 1. 26, 27. | 4. 3.
Col. 2. 2. to the acknowledgment of the m. of God
2 Thess. 2. 7. the m. of iniquity doth already work
1 Tim. 3. 9. holding m. of faith in pure conscience
16. great is m. of godliness, God was manifest in flesh
Rev. 1. 20. the m. of the seven stars thou sawest
10. 7. the m. of God should be finished, as declared
17. 5. m. Babylon the great ‖ 7. m. of the woman

MYSTERIES.

Mat. 13. 11. it is given to you to know the m. of the kingdom, but to them not given, Luke 8. 10.
1 Cor. 4. 1. and as stewards of the m. of God
13. 2. and tho' I understand all m. and knowledge
14. 2. howbeit, in the Spirit he speaketh m.

N.

NAIL.

Lev. 1. † 15. shall pinch off his head with the n.
Judg. 4. 21. Jael took a n. of tent, and smote the n.
22. Sisera lay dead, the n. was in his temples
5. 26. she put her hand to the n. and hammer
Ezra 9. 8. to give us a n. in his holy place
Isa. 22. 23. I will fasten him as a n. in a sure place
25. shall the n. that is fastened be removed
Zech. 10. 4. of him came the n. the battle-bow

NAILS.

Deut. 21. 12. she shall shave her head, and pare her n.
1 Chron. 22. 3. prepared iron in abundance for n.
2 Chron. 3. 9. the weight of the n. was fifty shekels
Eccl. 12. 11. n. fastened by the masters of assemblies
Isa. 41. 7. he fastened his idol with n. Jer. 10. 4.
Dan. 4. 33. his n. were grown like bird's claws
7. 19. the fourth beast, whose n. were of brass
John 20. 25. put my finger into the print of the n.

NAILING.

Col. 2. 14. he took it out of the way, n. it to his cross

NAKED

Signifies, [1] *One altogether unclothed or uncovered,* Gen. 2. 25. | 3. 7. [2.] *Such as have but few clothes on, having put off the greatest part of them,* 1 Sam. 19. 24. John 21. 7. [3] *One void of grace, that is not clothed with the righteousness of Christ, and so is exposed to the wrath of God for his sins,* Rev. 3. 17. [4] *Such as had heinously sinned and were deprived of the favour and protection of God, and so might be easily surprised by their enemies,* Exod. 32. 25. [5] *One destitute of all worldly goods,* Job 1. 21. [6] *That which is discovered, known, and manifest,* Job 26. 6. Heb. 4. 13.

The nakedness of a land, *Gen.* 42. 9. *The weak and ruined parts of it, where the country lies most open and exposed to danger, and may most easily be assaulted or surprised.*

To uncover the nakedness of any one, *denotes a shameful and unlawful conjunction, or an incestuous marriage,* Lev. 20. 19.

The nakedness *of* Adam *and* Eve *was unknown to them before they sinned,* Gen. 2. 25. *They were not ashamed at it, because concupiscence and irregular desires had not yet made the flesh rebel against the spirit; and their nakedness excited no disorder in their imaginations, nor any thing that was irregular or contrary to reason. They were exempt from whatever indecency might happen among us, upon the occasion of the nakedness of the body.*

Gen. 2. 25. they were n. and were not ashamed
3. 7. and they knew that they were n. 10, 11.
Exod. 32. 25. when Moses saw that the people were n. for Aaron had made them n. to their shame
Lev. 20. † 18. he hath made n. her fountain
1 Sam. 19. 24. Saul lay down n. all that day
2 Chron. 28. 15. with the spoil clothed all the n.
19. Ahaz made Judah n. and transgressed ag. Ld.
Job 1. 21. Job said, n. came I out of my mother's womb, and n. shall I return thither
22. 6. thou hast stripped the n. of their clothing
24. 7. they cause the n. to lodge without, 10.
26. 6. hell is n. before him and destruction
Prov. 29. † 18. where no vision, the people is made n.
Eccl. 5. 15. n. shall he return, to go as he came
Isa. 22. † 6. and Kir made n. the shield
58. 7. when thou seest the n. that thou cover him
Jer. 48. † 6. be like a n. tree in the wilderness
51. † 58. the walls of Babylon shall be made n.
Lam. 4. 21. O Edom, thou shalt make thyself n.
Ezek. 18. 7. if he hath covered the n. 16.
Hos. 2. 3. lest I strip her n. and set her as in the day
Amos 2. 16. shall flee away n. in that day, saith L.
Mic. 1. 8. therefore I will wail, will go strip. and n
11. pass ye away, having thy shame n.
5. † 6. shall waste with her own n. swords
Hab. 3. 9. thy bow was made quite n. according
Mat. 25. 36. I was n. and ye clothed me not, 43.
38. when saw we thee n. and clothed thee? 44.
Mark 14. 51. having a linen cloth about his n. body
52. he left the linen cloth, and fled from them n.
John 21. 7. Peter was n. and cast himself into the sea
Acts 19. 16. they fled out of that house n. wounded
1 Cor. 4. 11. to this present hour we are n.
2 Cor. 5. 3. being clothed, we shall not be found n.
Heb. 4. 13. but all things are n. to the eyes of him
Jam. 2. 15. if a brother or sister be n. and destitute
Rev. 3. 17. miserable, poor, and blind, and n.
16. 15. keepeth his garments, lest he walk n.
17. 16. and shall make her desolate and n. and eat

See BARE.

NAKEDNESS.

Gen. 9. 22. and Ham saw the n. of his father
23. and covered n. they saw not their father's n.
42. 9. to see the n. of the land ye are come, 12.
Exod. 20. 26. that thy n. be not discovered thereon
28. 42. shalt make linen breeches to cover their n.
Lev. 18. 6. none of you shall uncover their n.
7. the n. of father or mother, 8. 11, 15. | 20. 11.
9. the n. of thy sister ‖ 10. n. of thy son's daughter
11. n. of father's wife's daughter shalt not uncover
12. n. of father's sister ‖ 13. mother's sister, 20. 19.
14. father's brother ‖ 15. n. of daughter-in-law
16. n. of thy brother's wife, it is thy brother's n.
17. n. of a woman and her daughter not uncover
19. n. of a woman as long as put apart, 20. 18.
20. 17. and see his sister's n. and she see his n.
20. uncovered his uncle's n. ‖ 21. brother's n.
Deut. 23. † 14. camp be holy, that he see no n. in thee
24. † 1. if found matter of n. in her, write a bill
28. 48. shalt serve thine enemies in n. and want
1 Sam. 20. 30. to the confusion of thy mother's n.
Isa. 20. † 4. buttocks uncovered to the n. of Egypt
47. 3. thy n. shall be uncovered, yea, thy shame
Lam. 1. 8. because they have seen her n.
Ezek. 16. 8. I covered thy n. yea, I sware to thee
36. thy n. discovered thro' thy whoredoms, 23. 18.
16. 37. and will discover thy n. to them
22. 10. in thee they discovered their father's n.
23. 10. these discovered her n. and slew her
29. the n. of thy whoredom shall be discovered
Hos. 2. 9. my wool and flax given to cover her n.
Nah. 3. 5. and I will shew the nations thy n.
Hab. 2. 15. that thou mayest look on their n.
Rom. 8. 35. shall n. separate us from love of God?
2 Cor. 11. 27. in fastings often, in cold and n.
Rev. 3. 18. that the shame of thy n. do not appear

NAME

Is referred (I) *To God,* and signifies, *any thing whereby his nature and will is made better known to us,* as, [1] *His titles,* Exod. 3. 13, 14. | 6. 3. [2] *His attributes, or properties,* Exod. 33. 19. | 34. 6, 7. 1 Tim. 6. 1. [3] *His will and purpose concerning salvation by Christ,* John 17. 6, 26. [4] *His help and assistance,* 1 Sam. 17. 45. Psal. 44. 5. [5] *His honour, renown, and glory,* Psal. 76. 1. [6] *His word,* Psal. 5. 11. Acts 9. 15. [7] *His grace, mercy, and love to sinners, in sending Christ into the world to save them,* Psal. 22. 22. John 17. 26. [8] *His wisdom, power, and goodness, as displayed in the works of creation and providence,* Psal. 8. 1, 9. [9] *His grace, power, and providence,* Psal. 20. 1, 7. [10] *His worship and service,* 1 Kings 5. 5. Mal. 1. 6. [11] *God himself,* Psal. 29. 2. | 34. 3. | 61. 5. (II) *To Christ,* and signifies, [1] *His deity and perfections, that which he really is, and is acknowledged to be,* Isa. 9. 6. Mat. 1. 23. Rev. 19. 13. *His name shall be called Wonderful, the mighty God; that is,* he is wonderful, he is the mighty God. [2] *His authority and commission,* Mat. 7. 22. Acts 4. 7. [3] *The preaching, or professing of his gospel,* Mat. 10. 22. | 19. 29. Rev. 2. 13. [4] *His advancement above all principality and power, to the highest degree of glory, honour, majesty, and dominion,* Phil. 2. 9. compared with Eph. 1. 20, 21. (III) *To man,* and signifies, [1] *That particular name by which any person is called,* Luke 1. 60, 63. [2] *The whole person,* Luke 10. 20. Rev. 3. 4. [3] *Reputation or character, whether good or evil,* Deut. 22. 14. Prov. 22. 1. [4] *Honour, glory, and renown,* Deut. 26. 19. Zeph. 3. 20. [5] *An appearance and shew of religion in the opinion of men,* Rev. 3. 1. [6] *The memory, or remembrance,* Deut. 29. 20. [7] *Posterity, or issue,* Deut. 25. 7. Isa. 66. 22. [8] *Fame or renown,* 2 Chron. 26. 8. 15.

To take the name of God in vain, *Exod.* 20. 7. *To swear falsely, or without occasion, and to mingle the name of God in our discourses, or our oaths, either falsely, or rashly, or wantonly, or unnecessarily, or presumptuously. God forbids* to make mention of the names of other gods, *Exod.* 23. 13. *He would not so much as have them named, or their names pronounced. The gods of the heathen are nothing at all, therefore the* Israelites *were to shew nothing but contempt for them: they hardly ever pronounced the name* Baal, *they disfigured it, for example, by saying,* Mephibosheth, *or* Meribosheth, *instead of* Mephibaal, *or* Meribaal; *where* Bosheth *signifies something shameful, or contemptible.*

To give a name, *is a token of command and authority. The father gives names to his children and slaves. It is said, that* Adam *gave a name to his wife, and to all the animals, and that the name he gave them became their true name. God changed the name of* Abram, Jacob, *and* Sarai; *which expresses his absolute dominion over all men, and his particular benevolence towards those whom he receives more especially into the number of his own: hence it was that he gave a name, even before their birth, to some persons whom*

he appointed for great purposes, and who belonged to him in a particular manner; such as to Jedidiah, *or* Solomon, *son of* David; *to the* Messiah, *to* John *the Baptist, &c.*
To know any one by his name, I know thee by name, *Exod.* 33. 12. *expresses a distinction, a friendship, a particular familiarity. It is spoken perhaps in allusion to the manner of the kings of the east, who had very little conversation with their subjects; they saw them but seldom, and hardly ever appeared in public: so that when they knew any one of their servants by name, when they vouchsafed to speak to them, to call them, and to admit them into their presence, it was esteemed as a very great mark of favour.*
Gen. 2. 19. what Adam called, that was *n.* thereof
4. 17. call the *n.* of the city after the *n.* of his son
5. 2. he blessed them, and called their *n.* Adam
11. 4. let us make us a *n.* lest we be scattered
19. 22. therefore the *n.* of the city is Zoar
28. 19. the *n.* of the city was Luz at the first
48. 6. shall be called after the *n.* of their brethren
Exod. 34. 14. the Lord, whose *n.* is Jealous, is jealous
Lev. 18. 21. neither shalt thou profane the *n.* of thy God, saith the Lord, 19. 12. | 21. 6. | 22. 2, 32.
Num. 11. 26. *n.* of one Eldad, of the other Medad
17. 2. write thou every man's *n.* upon his rod
25. 14. the *n.* of the Israelite that was slain
15. *n.* of Midianitish woman slain was Cozbi
27. 4. why should *n.* of our father be done away?
32. 42. and called it Nobah, after his own *n.*
Deut. 7. 24. shalt destroy their *n.* from under heaven
9. 14. and blot out their *n.* from under heaven
22. 14. bring up an evil *n.* on her, and say
19. he hath brought up an evil *n.* on a virgin
25. 6. first born shall succeed in *n.* of his brother
7. to raise up to his brother a *n.* in Israel
26. 19. to make thee high in *n.* and in honour
28. 58. thou mayest fear this glorious and fearful *n.*
Josh. 23. 7. nor make mention of *n.* of their gods
Ruth 2. 19. man's *n.* with whom I wrought is Boaz
4. 5. to raise up the *n.* of the dead, 10.
17. the women her neighbours gave it a *n.*
1 *Sam.* 25. 3. the *n.* of the man was Nabal
9. they spake to Nabal in the *n.* of David
2 *Sam.* 6. 2. whose *n.* is called by the *n.* of the Lord
7. 9. I have made thee a great *n.* like the *n.* of the great men in the earth, 1 *Chron.* 17. 8.
23. God redeemed to make him a *n.* 1 *Chr.* 17. 21.
8. 13. David gat him a *n.* when he returned
14. 7. shall not leave to my husband neither *n.* nor
23. 18. Abishai had the *n.* among three
22. these things did Benaiah, and had the *n.* among three mighty men, 1 *Chron.* 11. 20, 24.
1 *Kings* 1. 47. God make the *n.* of Solomon better than thy *n.* and his throne greater than thy
14. 21. chose to put his *n.* there, 2 *Chron.* 12. 13.
18. 24. call ye on the *n.* of your gods, 25.
21. 8. so Jezebel wrote letters in Ahab's *n.*
2 *Kings* 14. 27. would not blot out the *n.* of Israel
Ezra 2. 61. and was called after their *n.* *Neh.* 7. 63.
5. 1. prophesied in the *n.* of the God of Israel
Neh. 9. 7. and gavest him the *n.* of Abraham
10. so didst thou get thee a *n.* as it is this day
Esth. 2. 22. Esther certified the king in Mordecai's *n.*
8. 8. write ye also for the Jews in the king's *n.*
Job 18. 17. he shall have no *n.* in the street
30. † 8. they were children of men and of no *n.*
Psal. 9. 5. thou hast put out their *n.* for ever
20. 1. the *n.* of the God of Jacob defend thee
5. in the *n.* of God we will set up our banners
44. 20. if we have forgotten the *n.* of our God
69. 30. I will praise the *n.* of God with a song
83. 4. the *n.* of Israel be no more in remembrance
18. whose *n.* alone is JEHOVAH, art most high
99. 3. let them praise thy great *n.* for it is holy
109. 13. and let their *n.* be blotted out
113. 3. the Lord's *n.* is to be praised
Prov. 10. 7. but the *n.* of the wicked shall rot
18. 10. the *n.* of the Lord is a strong tower
22. 1. a good *n.* is rather to be chosen than riches
30. 9. lest I take the *n.* of my God in vain
Eccl. 7. 1. a good *n.* better than precious ointment
Isa. 14. 22. I will cut off from Babylon the *n.*
55. 13. it shall be to the Lord for a *n.* for a sign
56. 5. I will give them a *n.* an everlasting *n.*
57. 15. whose *n.* is holy || 62. 2. called by a new *n.*
63. 12. to make himself an everlasting *n.*
14. lead thy people, to make thyself a glorious *n.*
65. 15. ye shall leave your *n.* for a curse to my chosen, and call his servants by another *n.*
66. 22. so shall your seed and your *n.* remain
Jer. 13. 11. that they might be to me for a *n.* 33. 9.
32. 20. which hast made thee a *n.* *Dan.* 9. † 15.
33. 16. this is the *n.* wherewith she shall be called
46. 18. as I live, saith the King, whose *n.* is the Lord of hosts, 48. 15. | 51. 57.
Ezek. 20. 29. and the *n.* thereof is called Bamah
22. † 5. mock thee which art polluted of *n.*
23. † 10. and she became a *n.* among women
24. 2. son of man, write thee the *n.* of the day
48. 35. the *n.* of the city shall be, The Lord is there
Dan. 2. 20. blessed be the *n.* of God for ever and ever
4. 8. Daniel came, according to the *n.* of my God
Hos. 1. 6. God said to him, call her *n.* Lo-ruhamah
2. 17. they shall no more be remembered by their *n.*
Amos 5. 27. saith Lord, whose *n.* is the God of hosts
Mic. 4. 5. for all people walk every one in the *n.* of his god, we will walk in the *n.* of our God
Zeph. 1. 4. I will cut off the *n.* of the Chemarims
3. 20. I will make you a *n.* and a praise
Zech. 6. 12. the man whose *n.* is the BRANCH
Mat. 10. 41. receiveth prophet in the *n.* of a prophet, a righteous man in *n.* of a righteous man
42. shall give a cup of water only in *n.* of disciple
28. 19. baptizing them in the *n.* of the Father
Luke 1. 61. none of thy kindred is called by this *n.*
63. and he wrote, saying, his *n.* is John
6. 22. blessed, when shall cast out your *n.* as evil
John 1. 6. a man sent from God, whose *n.* was John
3. 18. not believed in the *n.* of the only begotten
5. 43. I am come in my Father's *n.* and ye receive

John 10. 25. the works that I do in my Father's *n.*
Acts 2. 38. be baptized in the *n.* of the Lord Jesus
3. 6. in the *n.* of Jesus Christ, rise up and walk
4. 7. by what power or *n.* have ye done this?
12. there is none other *n.* under heaven given
17. speak henceforth to no man in this *n.* 18.
30. that wonders may be done by the *n.* of Jesus
5. 28. that you should not teach in this *n.* 40.
8. 12. preaching, concerning the *n.* of Jesus
9. 21. that destroyed them that called on this *n.*
27. he had preached boldly in the *n.* of Jesus
15. 26. have hazarded their lives for the *n.* of Jesus
16. 18. said, in the *n.* of Jesus come out of her
19. 5. they were baptized in the *n.* of Jesus
26. 9. to do contrary to the *n.* of Jesus of Nazareth
Rom. 2. 24. for the *n.* of God is blasphemed
1 *Cor.* 1. 13. were ye baptized in the *n.* of Paul?
5. 4. in the *n.* of our Lord Jesus, *Eph.* 5. 20.
6. 11. are justified in the *n.* of the Lord Jesus
Eph. 1. 21. far above every *n.* that is named
Phil. 2. 9. hath given him a *n.* above every *n.*
10. at the *n.* of Jesus every knee should bow
Col. 3. 17. do all in the *n.* of the Lord Jesus
1 *Tim.* 6. 1. that the *n.* of God be not blasphemed
2 *Tim.* 2. 19. the *n.* of Christ, depart from iniquity
Heb. 1. 4. he hath obtained a more excellent *n.*
Jam. 2. 7. do not they blaspheme that worthy *n.*?
1 *Pet.* 4. 14. if reproached for the *n.* of Christ
1 *John* 3. 23. should believe on *n.* of his Son, 5. 13.
Rev. 2. 17. a *n.* written, which no man knoweth
3. 1. thou hast a *n.* that thou livest, and art dead
12. I will write on him the *n.* of my God
8. 11. the *n.* of the star is called Wormwood
9. 11. whose *n.* in the Hebrew tongue is Abaddon
13. 1. and on his heads the *n.* of blasphemy
14. 1. his Father's *n.* written in their foreheads
16. 9. and men blasphemed the *n.* of God
17. 5. on her forehead was a *n.* written, Mystery
19. 12. a *n.* written no man knew but himself
16. on his thigh a *n.* written, King of kings
See CALLED.

By NAME, *or by the* NAME.

Exod. 6. 3. I appeared *by the n.* of God Almighty
31. 2. I have called *by n.* Bezaleel, 35. 30.
33. 12. yet thou hast said, I know thee *by n.* 17.
Num. 4. 32. *by n.* ye shall reckon the instruments
Josh. 21. 9. they gave these cities mentioned *by n.*
1 *Sam.* 17. 23. Philistine of Gath, Goliath *by n.*
2 *Sam.* 20. 21. Sheba, son of Bichri *by n.* hath lifted
1 *Kings* 13. 2. a child shall be born, Josiah *by n.*
1 *Chr.* 4. 41. these written *by n.* came and smote
12. 31. expressed *by n.* 16. 41. 2 *Chr.* 28. 15. | 31. 19.
Esth. 2. 14. except that she were called *by n.*
Isa. 44. 5. shall call himself *by the n.* of Jacob, and surname himself *by the n.* of Israel, 48. 1.
45. 3. I the Lord which call thee *by* thy *n.*
John 10. 3. and he calleth his own sheep *by n.*
Acts 4. 10. *by the n.* of Jesus this man is whole
1 *Cor.* 1. 10. I beseech you *by the n.* of our Lord
3 *John* 14. our friends salute thee, greet friends *by n.*
See EXPRESSED.

His NAME.

Exod. 3. 13. shall say, what is *his n.?* *Prov.* 30. 4.
15. 3. the Ld. is *his n.* *Jer.* 33. 2. *Amos* 5. 8. | 9. 6.
20. 7. guiltless that taketh *his n.* in vain, *Deut.* 5. 11.
28. 21. every stone with *his n.* shall they be, 39. 14.
Deut. 3. 14. Jair called them after *his* own *n.*
6. 13. shalt serve him, and shalt swear by *his n.*
10. 8. to bless in *his n.* to this day, 1 *Chr.* 23. 13.
12. 5. the Lord your God shall choose to put *his n.* there, 21. 1 *Kings* 14. 21. 2 *Chron.* 12. 13.
11. shall choose to cause *his n.* to dwell there
14. 23. choose to place *his n.* there, 16. 6, 11. | 26. 2.
24. the Lord shall choose to set *his n.* there
25. 6. that *his n.* be not put out of Israel
10. and *his n.* shall be called in Israel
29. 20. L. shall blot out *his n.* from under heaven
Judg. 13. 6. I asked not, neither told he me *his n.*
Ruth 4. 14. that *his n.* may be famous in Israel
1 *Sam.* 12. 22. for *his n.* sake, *Psal.* 23. 3. | 106. 8. 1 *John* 2. 12. 3 *John* 7.
18. 30. so that *his n.* was much set by
25. 25. as *his n.* is, so is he, Nabal is *his n.*
1 *Chr.* 16. 8. give thanks to Lord, call upon *his n.* make known his deeds, *Ps.* 105. 1. *Isa.* 12. 4.
29. give the glory due to *his n.* *Ps.* 29. 2. | 96. 8.
Ezra 6. 12. God that caused *his n.* dwell there
Psal. 34. 3. let us exalt *his n.* together, 66. 2.
41. 5. when shall he die and *his n.* perish?
68. 4. that rideth on the heavens by *his n.* JAH
69. 36. they that love *his n.* shall dwell therein
72. 17. *his n.* shall endure for ever, as long as sun
19. and blessed be *his* glorious *n.* for ever
76. 1. *his n.* is great in Isr. || 96. 2. bless *his n.* 100. 4.
99. 6. Samuel among them that call on *his n.*
111. 9. holy and reverend is *his n.*
135. 3. sing praises to *his n.* for it is pleasant
148. 13. praise *his n.* for *his n.* alone is excellent
149. 3. let them praise *his n.* in the dance
Prov. 21. 24. proud and haughty scorner is *his n.*
Eccl. 6. 4. *his n.* shall be covered with darkness
Isa. 7. 14. shall call *his n.* Immanuel, *Mat.* 1. 23.
9. 6. and *his n.* shall be called, Wonderful
12. 4. make mention that *his n.* is exalted
47. 4. the Lord of hosts is *his n.* the Holy One of Israel, 48. 2. | 51. 15. | 54. 5. *Jer.* 10. 16. | 31. 35. | 32. 18. | 50. 34. | 51. 19.
48. 19. *his n.* should not have been cut off
Jer. 11. 19. *his n.* may be no more remembered
20. 9. I will not speak any more in *his n.*
23. 6. this is *his n.* whereby he shall be called
48. 17. all ye that know *his n.* say, how is staff
Amos 4. 13. the Lord, the God of hosts is *his n.*
Zech. 10. 12. they shall walk up and down in *his n.*
14. 9. in that day shall be one Lord, and *his n.* one
Mal. 3. 16. for them that thought on *his n.* a book
Mat. 1. 23. shalt call *his n.* Jes. *Luke* 1. 31. | 2. 21.
12. 21. in *his n.* shall the Gentiles trust
Mark 6. 14. for *his n.* was spread abroad
Luke 1. 13. and thou shalt call *his n.* John
24. 47. remission of sins should be preached in *his n.*
John 1. 12. even to them that believe on *his n.*

John 2. 23. many believed in *his n.* when they saw
5. 43. if another shall come in *his* own *n.*
20. 31. that believing ye might have life thro' *his n.*
Acts 3. 16. *his n.* through faith in *his n.* hath made
5. 41. they were counted worthy to suffer for *his n.*
10. 43. thro' *his n.* shall receive remission of sins
13. 8. Elymas the sorcerer, for so is *his n.*
15. 14. to take out of them a people for *his n.*
Rom. 1. 5. to the faith among all nations for *his n.*
Heb. 6. 10. of love which ye shewed towards *his n.*
13. 15. let us offer praise, giving thanks to *his n.*
Rev. 3. 5. not blot out *his n.* but will confess *his n.*
6. 8. and *his n.* that sat on him was Death
9. 11. in the Greek tongue hath *his n.* Apollyon
13. 6. to blaspheme *his n.* || 17. number of *h. n.* 15. 2.
14. 11. whosoever receiveth the mark of *his n.*
22. 4. and *his n.* shall be in their foreheads
See HOLY, LORD.

My NAME.

Gen. 32. 29. why is it that thou dost ask after *my n.?*
48. 16. let *my n.* be named on them, let them grow
Exod. 3. 15. this is *my n.* for ever, and my memorial
9. 16. raised thee up, that *my n.* may be declared
20. 24. where I record *my n.* I will come unto thee
23. 21. provoke him not, for *my n.* is in him
Lev. 19. 12. ye shall not swear by *my n.* falsely
20. 3. his seed unto Molech, to profane *my* holy *n.*
Num. 6. 27. put *my n.* on the children of Israel
Deut. 18. 19. which he shall speak in *my n.* 20.
Judg. 13. 18. why askest thou thus after *my n.?*
1 *Sam.* 24. 21. swear thou wilt not destroy *my n.*
25. 5. and go to Nabal, and greet him in *my n.*
2 *Sam.* 7. 13. he shall build an house for *my n.* 1 *Kings* 5. 5. | 8. 18, 19. 1 *Chron.* 22. 10.
12. 28. lest the city be called after *my n.*
18. 18. I have no son to keep *my n.* in remembrance
1 *Kings* 8. 16. that *my n.* might be therein, 29. | 11. 36. 2 *Kings* 21. 4, 7. 2 *Chron.* 6. 5, 6. | 7. 16. | 33. 4, 7.
9. 7. this house which I have hallowed for *my n.*
1 *Chr.* 22. 8. shall not build an house to *my n.* 28. 3.
2 *Chr.* 6. 8. in heart to build an house for *my n.*
9. Solomon shall build the house for *my n.*
7. 20. this house which I have sanctified for *my n.*
Neh. 1. 9. I have chosen to set *my n.* there, *Jer.* 7. 12.
Psal. 89. 24. in *my n.* shall his horn be exalted
91. 14. because he hath known *my n.*
Isa. 29. 23. they shall sanctify *my n.* and fear
41. 25. from rising of the sun shall he call on *my n.*
42. 8. I am the Lord, that is *my n.* and my glory
48. 9. for *my n.* sake will I defer mine anger
11. for how should *my n.* be polluted?
49. 1. hath he made mention of *my n.*
52. 5. *my n.* continually every day is blasphemed
6. therefore my people shall know *my n.*
66. 5. brethren that cast you out for *my n.* sake
Jer. 14. 14. they prophesy lies in *my n.* 15. | 23. 25.
16. 21. they shall know that *my n.* is the Lord
23. 27. they think to cause my people to forget *my n.* as their fathers have forgotten *my n.* for Baal
27. 15. they prophesy a lie in *my n.* 29. 9, 21, 23.
34. 16. but ye turned and polluted *my n.*
44. 26. sworn by *my* great *n.* *my n.* no more named
Ezek. 20. 9. but I wrought for *my n.* 14. 22, 44.
36. 23. and I will sanctify *my* great *n.*
Zech. 13. 9. they shall call on *my n.* I will hear
Mal. 1. 6. to you, O priests, that despise *my n.*
11. for *my n.* shall be great among Gentiles, and in every place incense shall be offered to *my n.*
14. *my n.* is dreadful among the heathen
2. 2. lay it to heart, to give glory unto *my n.*
5. he feared me, and was afraid before *my n.*
4. 2. to you that fear *my n.* shall the sun of right.
Mat. 10. 22. ye shall be hated of all men for *my n.* sake, 24. 9. *Mark* 13. 13. *Luke* 21. 17.
18. 5. rec. a child in *my n.*, *Mark* 9. 37. *Luke* 9. 48.
20. two or three are gathered together in *my n.*
19. 29. that hath forsaken houses for *my n.* sake
24. 5. for many shall come in *my n.* and shall deceive many, *Mark* 13. 6. *Luke* 21. 8.
Mark 5. 9. he answered, saying, *my n.* is Legion
9. 39. no man which shall do a miracle in *my n.*
41. give you a cup of water to drink in *my n.*
16. 17. in *my n.* shall they cast out devils
Luke 21. 12. brought before rulers for *my n.* sake
John 14. 13. whatsoever ye shall ask in *my n.* that will I do, 14. | 15. 16. | 16. 23, 24, 26.
26. the Comforter whom he will send in *my n.*
15. 21. these things will they do for *my n.* sake
Acts 9. 15. he is a chosen vessel to bear *my n.*
16. great things he must suffer for *my n.* sake
15. 17. the Gentiles upon whom *my n.* is called
Rom. 9. 17. and that *my n.* might be declared
1 *Cor.* 1. 15. lest any say, I baptized in *mine* own *n.*
Rev. 2. 3. and for *my n.* sake hast laboured
13. thou holdest fast *my n.* and hast not denied
3. 8. hast kept my word, and hast not denied *my n.*
See CALLED.

Thy NAME.

Gen. 12. 2. I will bless thee, and make *thy n.* great
17. 5. *thy n.* Abram, but *thy n.* shall be Abraham
32. 27. said to him, what is *thy n.?* 29. *Judg.* 13. 17.
28. he said, *thy n.* shall be no more called Jacob, but Israel, 35. 10. 1 *Kings* 18. 31.
Exod. 5. 23. since came to Pharaoh to speak in *thy n.*
Josh. 7. 9. what wilt thou do to *thy* great *n.?*
2 *Sam.* 7. 26. let *thy n.* be magnified for ever
22. 50. I will sing praise to *thy n.* *Psal.* 9. 2. | 18. 49. | 61. 8. | 66. 4. | 92. 1.
1 *Kings* 1. 47. name of Solomon better than *thy n.*
8. 33. turn and confess *thy n.* 2 *Chron.* 6. 24, 26.
41. but cometh for *thy n.* sake, 2 *Chron* 6. 32.
42. for they shall hear of *thy* great *n.*
43. that all people of the earth may know *thy n.* this house is called by *thy n.* 2 *Chr.* 6. 33.
44. house I built for *thy n.* 48. 2 *Chr.* 6. 34, 38.
1 *Chron.* 17. 24. *thy n.* may be magnified for ever
29. 13. we thank and praise *thy n.* *Psal.* 44. 8.
2 *Chr.* 6. 20. that thou wouldest put *thy n.* there
14. 11. in *thy n.* we go against this multitude
20. 8. have built thee a sanctuary for *thy n.*
9. before this house, for *thy n.* is in this house

Neh. 1. 11. servants, who desire to fear thy n.
9. 5. blessed be thy glorious n. which is exalted
Psal. 5. 11. let them that love thy n. be joyful
8. 1. how excellent is thy n. in all the earth! 9.
9. 10. they that know thy n. will trust in thee
22. 22. I will declare thy n. to brethren, Heb. 2. 12.
25. 11. for thy n. sake pardon mine iniquity
31. 3. for thy n. sake lead me and guide me
44. 5. through thy n. will we tread them under
45. 17. I will make thy n. to be remembered
48. 10. according to thy n. so is thy praise
52. 9. I will wait on thy n. || 54. 1. save me by thy n.
61. 5. given the heritage of those that fear thy n.
63. 4. will bless, I will lift up my hands in thy n.
74. 7. they have defiled the dwelling-place of thy n.
10. shall the enemy blaspheme thy n. for ever?
18. the foolish people have blasphemed thy n.
21. let the poor and needy praise thy n.
75. 1. for that thy n. is near thy works declare
79. 6. that have not called on thy n. Jer. 10. 25.
9. help us, O G. of salvation, for the glory of thy n. and purge away our sins for thy n. sake
80. 18. quicken us, and we will call upon thy n.
83. 16. that they may seek thy n. O Lord
86. 9. all nations shall come and glorify thy n. 12.
11. teach me, unite my heart to fear thy n.
89. 12. Hermon shall rejoice in thy n. 16.
109. 21. do thou for me, O Lord, for thy n. sake
115. 1. not unto us, but unto thy n. give glory
119. 55. I have remembered thy n. in the night
132. as thou usest to do to those that love thy n.
135. 13. thy n. O Lord, endureth for ever
138. 2. I will praise thy n. for thy loving-kindness, thou hast magnified thy word above all thy n.
139. 20. and thine enemies take thy n. in vain
140. 13. the righteous shall give thanks to thy n.
142. 7. out of prison, that I may praise thy n.
143. 11. quicken me, O Lord, for thy n. sake
145. 1. I will bless thy n. for ever and ever, 2.
2. and I will praise thy n. for ever, Isa. 25. 1.
Cant. 1. 3. thy n. is as ointment poured forth
Isa. 26. 8. the desire of our soul is to thy n.
13. by thee we will make mention of thy n.
63. 16. O Lord, thy n. is from everlasting
64. 2. make thy n. known to thine adversaries
7. there is none that calleth on thy n.
Jer. 10. 6. thou art great and thy n. is great in might
11. 16. the Lord calleth thy n. a green olive-tree
14. 7. do thou it for thy n. sake, we have sinned
21. do not abhor us for thy n. sake, remember
29. 25. sent letters in thy n. to all people at Jerus.
Lam. 3. 55. I called upon thy n. out of the dungeon
Dan. 9. 6. the prophets spake in thy n. to our kings
Mic. 6. 9. and the man of wisdom shall see thy n.
Nah. 1. 14. that no more of thy n. be sown
Mal. 1. 6. wherein have we despised thy n.?
Mat. 6. 9. hallowed be thy n. Luke 11. 2.
7. 22. in thy n. have we not cast out devils
Mark 5. 9. he asked him, what is thy n.? Luke 8. 30.
9. 38. casting out devils in thy n. Luke 9. 49.
Luke 10. 17. the devils are subject through thy n.
John 12. 28. Fath. glorify thy n. then came a voice
17. 6. I have manifested thy n. to the men, 26.
11. holy Father, keep through thine own, n. 12.
Acts 9. 14. authority to bind all that call on thy n.
Rom. 15. 9. I will confess, and sing unto thy n.
Rev. 11. 18. give reward to them that fear thy n.
15. 4. who shall not fear and glorify thy n.?

See CALLED.

NAME, Verb.

1 Sam. 16. 3. thou shalt anoint to me him whom I n.
28. 8. bring him up whom I shall n. unto thee
Isa. 62. 2. which the mouth of the Lord shall n.

NAMED, ETH.

Gen. 23. 16. Abrah. weighed silver which he had n.
27. 36. he said, is not he rightly n. Jacob?
48. 16. and let my name be n. on them
1 Sam. 4. 21. she n. the child I-chabod, saying
2 Kings 17. 34. the children of Jac. whom he n. Isr.
1 Chron. 23. 14. Moses' sons n. of the tribe of Levi
Eccl. 6. 10. what hath been, is n. already
Isa. 61. 6. ye shall be n. the priests of the Lord
Jer. 44. 26. my name shall no more be n. in mouth
Amos 6. 1. which are n. chief of the nations
Mic. 2. 7. O thou that art n. of the house of Jacob
Luke 2. 21. Jesus was so n. of the angel before conc.
6. 13. he chose twelve, whom he n. apostles
Rom. 15. 20. to preach, not where Christ was n.
1 Cor. 5. 1. such fornication not n. among Gentiles
Eph. 1. 21. far above every name that is n.
3. 15. the whole family in heaven and earth is n.
5. 3. covetousness, let it not be once n. among you
2 Tim. 2. 19. let every one that n. the name of Chr.

NAMELY.

Eccl. 5. 13. sore evil, n. riches kept for the owners
Isa. 7. 20. Lord shave with a razor, n. by Assyria
Mark 12. 31. the second is like, n. this, shalt love

NAMES.

Gen. 2. 20. Adam gave n. to all cattle, and to fowl
26. 18. called their n. after n. his father called them
Exod. 23. 13. be circumspect and make no mention of the n. of other gods, Deut. 12. 3.
28. 9. grave on them the n. of children of Isr. 21.
12. Aaron shall bear their n. before the Lord, 29.
Num. 1. 2. the number of their n. by their poll
5. the n. of the men that shall stand with you
3. 43. numb. of n. of the Levites from a month old
13. 16. the n. of the men which Moses sent to spy
34. 17. n. of men which shall divide the land
2 Sam. 23. 8. the n. of mighty men whom David had
Ezra 5. 4. what are their n. who make this building
Psal. 16. 4. nor take up their n. into my lips
49. 11. they call their lands after their own n.
147. 4. the stars he calleth them by n. Isa. 40. 26.
Ezek. 23. 4. the n. of them were Aholah the elder
Hos. 2. 17. for I will take away the n. of Baalim
Zech. 13. 2. cut off the n. of the idols out of the land
Luke 10. 20. rejoice, your n. are written in heaven
Acts 1. 15. the number of the n. together were 120
18. 15. if it be a question of words and n. look to it
Phil. 4. 3. whose n. are in the book of life
Rev. 3. 4. thou hast a few n. in Sardis, not defiled
Rev. 11. † 13. were slain n. of men seven thousand
13. † 1. and on his heads the n. of blasphemy
8. whose n. are not written in book, 17. 8.
17. 3. I saw a woman full of n. of blasphemy
21. 12. n. written thereon, n. of the twelve tribes
14. in them the n. of twelve apostles of the Lamb

NAPKIN.

Luke 19. 20. thy pound which I have kept in a n.
John 11. 44. his face was bound about with a n.
20. 7. the n. that was about his head not lying

NARD.

Mark. 14. † 3. a woman having a box of pure n.

NARROW.

Num. 22. 26. angel of the Lord stood in a n. way
Josh. 17. 15. cut down, if mount Ephraim be too n.
1 Kings 6. 4. for house he made windows of n. lights
Prov. 23. 27. and a strange woman is a n. pit
24. † 10. if thou faint, thy strength is n.
Isa. 49. 19. the land of thy destruction shall be too n.
Mat. 7. 14. n. is the way which leadeth to life

NARROWED.

1 Kings 6. 6. in wall of house made n. rests round

NARROWER.

Isa 28. 20. the covering n. than he can wrap himself

NARROWLY.

Job 13. 27. thou lookest n. to all my paths
Isa. 14. 16. that see thee, shall n. look upon thee

NATION

Signifies, [1] All the inhabitants of a particular country, Deut. 4. 34. [2] A country or kingdom, Exod. 34. 10. Rev. 7. 9. [3] Countrymen, natives of the same stock, Acts 26. 4. [4] The father, head, and original of a nation or people, Gen. 25. 23. [5] The heathen or Gentiles, Isa. 55. 5.

Gen. 15. 14. and also that n. they serve will I judge
20. 4. Lord, wilt thou slay also a righteous n.?
21. 13. of the bond-woman I will make a n.
35. 11. a n. and kings shall come of thee
Exod. 9. 24. in all Egypt, since it became a n.
19. 6. ye shall be unto me an holy n. 1 Pet. 2. 9.
21. 8. to sell her to a strange n. have no power
33. 13. and consider that this n. is thy people
34. 10. have not been done in any n. do with thee
Lev. 18. 26. nor any of your n. commit abominations
20. 23. shall not walk in the manners of the n.
Num. 14. 12. I will make of thee a great n. Deut. 9. 14.
Deut. 4. 34. or hath God assayed to take him a n. from the midst of another n. by wonders?
28. 33. the fruit of thy land shall a n. eat up
36. the Lord shall bring thee and thy king to a n.
49. Lord shall bring a n. against thee from far
50. a n. of fierce countenance shall not regard
32. 28. are a n. void of counsel, no understanding
2 Sam. 7. 23. what n. like thy people? 1 Chr. 17. 21.
1 Kings 18. 10. there is no n. whither my Lord hath not sent to seek thee, he took an oath of that n.
2 Kings 17. 29. every n. made gods of their own
1 Chr. 16. 20. and when they went from n. to n.
2 Chr. 15. 6. n. was destroyed of n. and city of city
32. 15. no god of any n. or kingdom was able
Job 34. 29. it be done against a n. or a man only
Ps. 33. 12. blessed is the n. whose God is the Lord
43. 1. O God plead my cause against an ungodly n.
83. 4. come, let us cut them off from being a n.
105. 13. they went from one n. to another
106. 5. that I may rejoice in the gladness of thy n.
147. 20. he hath not dealt so with any n.
Prov. 14. 34. righteousness exalteth a n. but sin is
Isa. 1. 4. ah sinful n. a people laden with iniquity
2. 4. n. shall not lift up sword against n. Mic. 4. 3.
9. 3. thou hast multiplied the n. not increased joy
10. 6. I will send him against an hypocritical n.
14. 32. what answer the messengers of the n.?
18. 2. go, ye swift messengers, to a n. scattered and peeled, a n. meted out and trodden down, 7.
26. 2. open that the righteous n. may enter in
15. thou hast increased the n. O Lord, the n.
49. 7. saith the Lord to him whom the n. abhorreth
51. 4. hearken and give ear to me, O my n.
55. 5. thou shalt call a n. thou knowest not
58. 2. seek me, as a n. that did righteousness
60. 12. the n. that will not serve thee shall perish
22. and a small one shall become a strong n.
65. 1. a n. that was not called by my name
66. 8. or shall a n. be born at once?
Jer. 2. 11. hath a n. changed their gods?
5. 9. my soul be avenged on such a n. 29. | 9. 9.
15. I will bring a n. on you from far, O house of Israel, it is a mighty n. it is an ancient n.
7. 28. a n. that obeyeth not the voice of the Lord
12. 17. I will utterly pluck up and destroy that n.
18. 7. speak concerning a n. to pluck it up, 9.
8. if that n. against whom I have pronounced
25. 12. punish that n. for their iniquity, 27. 8.
32. behold, evil shall go forth from n. to n.
27. 8. n. which will not serve Nebuchadnezzar, 13.
31. 36. then Israel cease from being a n. 33. 24.
48. 2. let us cut off Moab from being a n.
49. 31. arise, get you up to the wealthy n.
36. shall be no n. whither Elam shall not come
50. 3. out of the north cometh a n. against her
Lam. 4. 17. have watched for a n. that could not save
Ezek. 2. 3. I send thee to Israel, a rebellious n.
37. 22. I will make them one n. in the land
Dan. 8. 22. four kingd. shall stand up out of the n.
12. 1. trouble, such as never was since was a n.
Joel 1. 6. for a n. is come up upon my land
Amos 6. 14. behold, I will raise up against you a n.
Mic. 4. 7. I will make her that was cast off a strong n.
Hab. 1. 6. the Chaldeans, that bitter and hasty n.
Zeph. 2. 1. gather together, O n. not desired
5. woe to the n. of the Cherethites
Hag. 2. 14. so is this people and n. before me
Mal. 3. 9. even this whole n. have robbed me
Mat. 21. 43. the kingdom of God given to a n.
24. 7. n. shall rise ag. n. Mark 13. 8. Luke 21. 10.
Luke 7. 5. for he loveth our n. and hath built us
23. 2. we found this fellow perverting the n.
John 11. 48. the Romans shall come and take our n.
50. one man die, that the whole n. perish not
51. prophesied that Jesus should die for that n.
John 11. 52. and not for that n. only, but that also
18. 35. thine own n. hath delivered thee to me
Acts 2. 5. Jews, devout men out of every n.
7. 7. the n. to whom they shall be in bondage
10. 22. of good report among all the n. of the Jews
28. it is unlawful to come to one of another n.
35. but in every n. he that feareth him
24. 2. that very worthy deeds are done to this n.
10. I know that thou hast been a judge to this n.
17. I came to bring alms to my n. and offerings
26. 4. my life was at first among mine own n.
28. 19. not that I had aught to accuse my n. of
Gal. 1. 14. profited above my equals in my own n.
Phil. 2. 15. in midst of a crooked and perverse n.
Rev. 5. 9. thou hast redeemed us out of every n.
14. 6. having the gospel to preach to every n.

See FOOLISH.

NATIONS.

Gen. 10. 32. and by these were the n. divided
14. 1. Tidal king of n. made war with Bera, 9.
17. 4. shalt be a father of many n. 5. Rom. 4. 17, 18
6. and I will make n. of thee, 35. 11. | 48. 19.
16. I will bless Sarah, she shall be a mother of n.
25. 23. the Lord said, two n. are in thy womb
27. 29. and let n. bow down to thee
Exod. 34. 24. I will cast out the n. before thee, and enlarge thy borders, Deut. 4. 38. | 7. 22. | 8. 20.
Lev. 18. 24. the n. are defiled || 28. as it spued out n
Num. 23. 9. and shall not be reckoned among the n.
24. 8. Israel shall eat up the n. his enemies
20. Amalek was the first of the n. but latter end
Deut. 2. 25. I will put the fear of thee on the n.
4. 6. this is your wisdom in sight of the n.
27. Lord shall scatter you among the n. Neh. 1. 8
7. 1. Lord hath cast out many n. before thee
9. 1. to possess n. greater than thyself, 11. 23.
12. 29. when God shall cut off the n. 19. 1.
15. 6. thou shalt lend to many n. 28. 12.
28. 1. the Lord will set thee on high above all n.
32. 8. Most High divided to the n. their inheritance
43. rejoice, O ye n. with his people, he will avenge
Judg. 2. 23. therefore the Lord left those n.
2 Sam. 7. 23. which thou redeemedst from the n.
1 Kings 11. 2. of the n. concerning which the L. said
2 Kings 17. 33. served gods after the manner of n.
18. 33. hath any of the gods of the n. delivered, 19. 12. 2 Chron. 32. 13, 14. Isa. 36. 18.
1 Chr. 16. 31. say among the n. the Lord reigneth
17. 21. by driving out n. from before thy people
2 Chr. 13. 9. made priests after the manner of n.
Neh. 13. 26. among many n. was no king like him
Job 12. 23. he increaseth the n. he enlargeth the n.
Psal. 9. 20. that the n. may know themselves
22. 27. all the kindreds of n. shall worship thee
28. the Lord is governor among the n.
47. 3. he shall subdue the n. under our feet
57. 9. I will sing to thee among the n. 108. 3.
66. 7. his eyes behold the n. || 67. 4. let the n. be glad
96. 5. for all the gods of the n. are idols
106. 27. to overthrow their seed among the n.
34. they did not destroy the n. Lord commanded
Prov. 24. 24. the people curse, n. shall abhor him
Isa. 2. 4. and he shall judge among the n.
5. 26. he will lift up an ensign to the n. from far
10. 7. it is in his heart to cut off n. not a few
11. 12. he shall set up an ensign for the n.
14. 6. he that ruled the n. in anger, is persecuted
12. how cut down, which didst weaken the n.
18. all the kings of the n. lie in glory
23. 3. the seed of Sihor, she is a mart of n.
33. 3. at the lifting up the n. were scattered
34. 1. come near, ye n. to hear, Jer. 31. 10.
40. 15. behold, the n. are as a drop of a bucket
52. 15. so shall he sprinkle many n.
55. 5. n. that knew not thee, shall run to thee
60. 12. yea, those n. shall be utterly wasted
64. 2. that the n. may tremble at thy presence
66. 19. I will send those that escape to the n.
Jer. 1. 5. and ordained thee a prophet to the n.
10. see, I have this day set thee over the n.
4. 2. n. shall bless themselves in him, and glory
16. make ye mention to n. publish against Jerusa.
6. 18. therefore hear ye n. and know, 31. 10.
10. 7. who would not fear thee, O King of n.?
10. the n. shall not be able to abide his indignation
22. 8. many n. shall pass by this city, and say
25. 14. n. shall serve themselves of them, 27. 7.
31. the Lord hath a controversy with the n.
46. 12. the n. have heard of thy shame, they cry
50. 2. declare ye among the n. Babylon is taken
12. hindermost of the n. shall be a wilderness
46. and the cry is heard among the n.
51. 7. the n. have drunken of her wine, n. are mad
20. with thee will I break in pieces the n.
27. prepare the n. against her, call together
41. Babylon is an astonishment among the n.
44. the n. shall not flow together any more
Lam. 1. 1. the city that was great among the n.
Ezek. 5. 6. into wickedness, more than the n. 7.
14. I will make thee a reproach among the n.
6. 8. the remnant shall escape among the n.
9. that escape shall remember me among the n.
12. 15. when I shall scatter them among the n.
19. 4. the n. also heard of him, he was taken
8. then the n. set against him on every side
26. 3. I will cause many n. to come against thee
5. and it shall become a spoil to the n.
28. 7. behold, therefore, I will bring strangers upon thee, the terrible of the n. 30. 11. | 31. 12.
29. 12. I will scatter Egyptians among n. 30. 23.
15. that they shall no more rule over the n.
31. 16. I made n. shake at the sound of his fall
32. 2. thou art like a lion of the n. as a whale
16. the daughters of the n. shall lament her, 18.
35. 10. thou hast said, these two n. shall be mine
36. 13. thou land hast bereaved thy n.
37. 22. and they shall be no more two n.
38. 8. it is brought forth out of the n. 12.
23. I will be known in the eyes of many n.
39. 27. and am sanctified in the sight of many n.
Hos. 8. 10. though they have hired among the n.
9. 17. they shall be wanderers among the n.

Joel 3. 2. whom they have scattered among the n.
Amos 6. 1. woe to them which are named chief of n.
Mic. 4. 2. many n. shall come and say, let us go
3. he shall rebuke strong n. afar off, and beat
11. now also many n. are gathered against thee
7. 16. the n. shall see, be confounded at their might
Nah. 3. 4. that selleth n. through her whoredoms
5. I will shew the n. thy nakedness and shame
Hab. 1. 17. shall they not spare continually to slay n.
2. 8. because thou hast spoiled many n.
3. 6. he beheld, and drove asunder the n.
Zeph. 3. 6. I have cut off the n. their towers desolate
8. for my determination is to gather the n.
Zech. 2. 11. many n. shall be joined to the Lord
8. 22. and strong n. shall come to seek the Lord
23. take hold out of all the languages of the n.
Luke 12. 30. these things do the n. seek after
21. 25. and upon the earth shall be distress of n.
Acts 13. 19. when he had destr. seven n. in Chanaan
Rev. 2. 26. to him will I give power over the n.
10. 11. thou must prophesy before many n.
11. 9. n. shall see their dead bodies three days
18. and the n. were angry, thy wrath is come
13. 7. and power was given him over all n.
16. 19. cities of the n. fell || 17. 15. waters are n.
20. 3. that he should deceive the n. no more
21. 24. the n. of them which are saved shall walk
26. they shall bring the honour of the n. into it
22. 2. the leaves were for the healing of the n.

See GREAT.

All NATIONS.

Deut. 4. 19. which the Lord hath divided to all n.
26. 19. and to make thee high above all n. 28. 1.
28. 37. shall become a by-word among all n.
1 Kings 4. 31. his fame was in all n. round about
1 Chron. 14. 17. brought the fear of David on all n.
16. 24. declare his marvellous works among all n.
2 Chr. 32. 23. Hezekiah magnified in sight of all n.
Psal. 67. 2. thy saving health among all n.
72. 11. kings fall down, all n. shall serve him
17. men blessed in him, all n. shall call him blessed
82. 8. arise, O God, for thou shalt inherit all n.
86. 9. all n. shall come and worship before thee
113. 4. L. is high above all n. glory above heaven
117. 1. praise the Lord, all ye n. praise him
118. 10. all n. compassed me about, but in name
Isa. 2. 2. and all n. shall flow unto it
25. 7. he will destroy the vail that is over all n.
34. 2. the indignation of the Lord is on all n.
40. 17. all n. before him are as nothing, and vanity
66. 18. I will gather all n. and languages, Joel 3. 2.
20. they shall bring your brethren out of all n.
Jer. 27. 7. and all n. shall serve him, Dan. 7. 14.
Amos 9. 9. I will sift the house of Israel among a. n.
Hab. 2. 5. but gathereth to him all n. and people
Hag. 2. 7. I will shake all n. and the desire of all n.
shall come; and I will fill this house with glory
Zech. 14. 2. I will gather all n. against Jerusalem
19. the punishment of all n. that come not up
Mal. 3. 12. and all n. shall call you blessed
Mat. 24. 9. ye shall be hated of all n. for my sake
14. this gospel of kingdom shall be preached to
all n. Mark 13. 10. Luke 24. 47. Rom. 16. 26.
25. 32. before him shall be gathered all n.
28. 19. go ye, and teach all n. baptizing them
Mark 11. 17. be called of all n. the house of prayer
Luke 21. 24. shall be led away captive into all n.
Acts 14. 16. who suffered all n. to walk in their ways
17. 26. hath made of one blood all n. of men
Rom. 1. 5. for obedience to the faith among all n.
16. 26. made known to all n. for obedience of faith
Gal. 3. 8. saying, in thee shall all n. be blessed
Rev. 7. 9. a multitude of all n. stood before throne
12. 5. a man-child, who was to rule all n. with a rod
14. 8. she made all n. drink of the wine, 18. 3.
15. 4. for all n. shall come and worship before thee
18. 23. for by thy sorceries were all n. deceived

All the NATIONS.

Gen. 18. 18. all t. n. of earth be blessed. 22. 18. | 26. 4.
Deut. 14. 2. chosen above all the n. on earth
17. 14. set a king over me, as all t. n. 1 Sam. 8. 5, 20.
30. 1. thou shalt call them to mind among all t. n.
3. the Lord will gather thee from all the n.
Psal. 9. 17. into hell, and all the n. that forget God
Isa. 14. 26. hand that is stretched out on all the n.
29. 7. the multitude of all the n. that fight, 8.
37. 18. laid waste all the n. and their countries
43. 9. let all the n. be gathered together, and let
52. 10. L. made bare his holy arm in eyes of all t. n.
61. 11. cause praise to spring forth before all the n.
Jer. 3. 17. and all the n. shall be gathered unto it
25. 13. Jeremiah prophesied against all the n.
15. cause all n. to drink it || 17. made all n. drink
26. 6. make this city a curse to all t. n. of the earth
29. 14. I will gather you from all the n. and places
18. a reproach among all t. n. of the earth, 44. 8.
33. 9. name of joy and honour before all the n.
46. 28. for I will make a full end of all the n.
Zech. 7. 14. but I scattered them among all the n.
12. 9. destroy all the n. that come against Jerusal.
14. 16. left of all the n. that came against Jerusal.

These NATIONS.

Deut. 7. 17. if thou say, these n. are more than I
9. 4. for wickedness of these n. Lord doth drive, 5.
11. 23. then will the Lord drive out all these n.
12. 30. saying, how did these n. serve their gods
18. 14. these n. hearkened to observers of times
20. 15. thus do to the cities which are not of t. n.
28. 65. among these n. shalt thou find no ease
29. 18. lest any among you serve the gods of t. n.
31. 3. the Lord will destroy these n. before thee
Josh. 23. 3. seen what the Lord hath done to t. n.
4. I have divided to you by lot t. n. that remain
7. that ye come not among these n. that remain
12. if ye cleave to the remnant of these n.
13. God will no more drive out any of these n.
Judg. 3. 1. these n. the Lord left to prove Israel
2 Kings 17. 41. so t. n. feared L. and served images
Jer. 9. 26. for all these n. are uncircumcised
25. 9. bring them against these n. round about
11. these n. shall serve the king of Babylon
28. 14. I have put yoke of iron on neck of these n.

NATIVE.

Jer. 22. 10. he shall no more see his n. country

NATIVITY.

Gen. 11. 28. Haran died in the land of his n.
Ruth 2. 11. how thou hast left the land of thy n.
Jer. 46. 16. arise, let us go the land of our n.
Ezek. 16. 3. thy n. is of the land of Canaan
4. as for thy n. in the day thou wast born
21. 30. I will judge thee in the land of thy n.
23. 15. the manner of Chaldea, the land of their n.

NATURE

Signifies, [1] *The natural method and course of things established in the world by God its Creator*, Rom. 1. 26, 27. [2] *Reason, or the light implanted in the mind*, Rom. 2. 14. [3] *Birth, or natural descent*, Gal. 2. 15. [4] *Common sense, and the custom of all nations*, 1 Cor. 11. 14. [5] *Substance, or essence*, Heb. 2. 16. [6] *Our corrupt and sinful estate by our birth, being naturally inclined to all sorts of evil*, Eph. 2. 3. [7] *Holy and divine qualities and dispositions, which express and resemble the perfections of God*, 2 Pet. 1. 4. [8] *In truth and very deed*, Gal. 4. 8.

A natural body, 1 Cor. 15. 44. *A body which has nothing but what its soul can bestow upon it in a natural way, which is maintained in life by natural and ordinary means, as meat, drink, sleep, &c. and is subject to natural affections and operation, as generation, augmentation, motion, &c.* A spiritual body, *ibid.* Spiritual, *not as to the substance of it, but in respect of the qualities and conditions of it; a body that is beautiful, incorruptible, free from infirmities, not subject to hunger or thirst, or injuries from cold, heat, &c. not using meat, drink, clothes, physic; but free, active, and nimble, as spirits; it is likewise a* spiritual body, *as it is perfectly subject to the Spirit of God, without any rebellious motions; it is immediately supported by the Spirit, without any corporeal means; and does most wonderfully contribute to the most lively, divine, and enlarged vital operations of the soul herself.*

The natural man, 1 Cor. 2. 14. *The unrenewed person; one that hath nothing but a principle of reason, though he be one of the most exquisite natural accomplishments, and has improved his reason to the highest pitch.*

Rom. 1. 26. women did change to that against n.
2. 14. do by n. the things contained in the law
27. shall not uncircumcision by n. judge thee?
11. 24. if thou wert cut out of the olive-tree, which
is wild by n. and wert graffed contrary to n.
1 Cor. 11. 14. doth not even n. itself teach you?
Gal. 2. 15. who are Jews by n. and not sinners of
4. 8. did service unto them, which by n. are no gods
Eph. 2. 3. and were by n. children of wrath
Heb. 2. 16. he took not on him the n. of angels
Jam. 3. 6. tongue setteth on fire the course of n.
† 7. n. of beasts hath been tamed by n. of men
2 Pet. 1. 4. ye might be partakers of the divine n.

NATURAL.

Deut. 34. 7. eye not dim, nor his n. force abated
Rom. 1. 26. even women did change the n. use
27. also men leaving the n. use of the woman
31. without n. affection, 2 Tim. 3. 3.
11. 21. if God spared not the n. branches, 24.
1 Cor. 2. 14. n. man receiveth not things of Sp. of G.
15. 44. it is sown a n. body, there is a n. body
46. but that which is n. was first, and afterward
Jam. 1. 23. a man beholding his n. face in a glass
3. † 15. this wisdom is earthly, n. devilish
2 Pet. 2. 12. these as n. brute beasts speak evil

NATURALLY.

Phil. 2. 20. who will n. care for your state
Jude 10. but what they know n. as brute beasts

NAVEL.

Judg. 9. † 37. come down by the n. of the land
Job 40. 16. his force is in the n. of his belly
Prov. 3. 8. it shall be health to thy n. and marrow
Cant. 7. 2. thy n. is like a round goblet
Ezek. 16. 4. when thou wast born, thy n. was not cut

NAVES.

1 Kings 7. 33. their n. and spokes were all molten

NAUGHT, or NOUGHT.

Gen 29. 15. shouldest thou theref. serve me for n.?
Deut. 13. 17. shall cleave n. of the cursed thing
15. 9. thy poor brother, and thou givest him n.
28. 63. the Lord will rejoice to bring you to n.
2 Kings 2. 19. the city is pleasant, but the water n.
Neh. 4. 15. God brought their counsel to n.
Job 1. 9. Satan said, doth Job fear God for n.?
8. 22. the place of the wicked shall come to n.
14. 18. surely the mountain falling cometh to n.
22. 6. hast taken a pledge from thy brother for n.
Psal. 33. 10. Lord bringeth counsel of heathen to n.
44. 12. thou sellest thy people for n.
Prov. 1. 25. but ye have set at n. all my counsel
20. 14. it is n. it is n. saith the buyer
Isa. 8. 10. take counsel, it shall come to n.
29. 20. for the terrible one is brought to n.
21. that turn aside the just for a thing of n.
41. 12. they shall be as nothing, as a thing of n.
24. ye are of nothing, and your work of n.
49. 4. I have spent my strength for n. and in vain
52. 3. saith the Lord, ye have sold yourselves for n.
5. that my people is taken away for n.
Jer. 14. 14. a false vision, and a thing of n.
Amos 5. 5. and Beth el shall come to n.
6. 13. ye which rejoice in a thing of n. who say
Mal. 1. 10. who is there, would shut the doors for n.?
neither do ye kindle fire on mine altar for n.
Mark 9. 12. must suffer, and be set at n. Luke 23. 11.
Acts 4. 11. this is the stone set at n. of you builders
5. 36. all were scattered and brought to n.
38. if this work be of men, it will come to n.
19. 27. our craft is in danger to be set at n.
Rom. 14. 10. why dost thou set at n. thy brother?
1 Cor. 1. 28. to bring to n. things that are
2. 6. the wisdom of this world that cometh to n.
2 Thess. 3. 8. nor did we eat any man's bread for n.
Rev. 18. 17. in one hour so great riches come to n.

NAUGHTY.

Prov. 6. 12. a n. person walketh with froward mouth
17. 4. and a liar giveth ear to a n. tongue
Jer. 24. 2. the other basket had very n. figs

NAUGHTINESS.

1 Sam. 17. 28. I know thy pride, and the n. of thy [heart
Prov. 11. 6. transgressors be taken in their own n.
Jam. 1. 21. lay apart all filthin. and superfluity of n.

NAVY.

1 Kings 9. 26. Solom. made a n. of ships in Ezion-g.
27. Hiram sent in the n. his servants, shipmen
10. 11. the n. of Hiram brought gold from Ophir
22. king Solomon had at sea a n. of Tarshish

NAY.

1 Kings 2. 17. speak, for he will not say thee n.
20. say me not n. for I will not say thee n.
Mat. 5. 37. but let your communication be yea, yea,
n. n. more cometh of evil, Jam. 5. 12.
Luke 12. 51. I tell you n. but rather division
13. 3. I tell you n. but except ye repent, 5.
16. 30. and he said, n. father Abraham, but if one
Acts 16. 37. n. verily, but let them come and fetch
Rom. 3. 27. by law of works? n. but by law of faith
9. 20. n. but O man, who art thou that repliest?
2 Cor. 1. 17. with me there should be yea, yea, n. n.
18. our word toward you was not yea and n.
19. the Son of God Jesus Christ was not yea, n.

NAZARITE

Denotes, *A man or woman who engaged themselves by a vow to abstain from wine and all intoxicating liquors; to let their hair grow without cutting, or shaving; not to enter into any house that was polluted by having a dead corpse in it, nor to be present at any funeral: and if any one should have died very suddenly in their presence, they began again the whole ceremony of their consecration and Nazariteship, which ceremony lasted generally eight days. When the time of their Nazariteship was accomplished, the priest brought the person to the door of the tabernacle; who there offered to the Lord a he-lamb for a burnt offering, a she-lamb for an expiatory sacrifice, and a ram for a peace offering; by which sacrifices they not only gave thanks to God who had given them grace to make, and in some measure to keep, such a vow; but also confessed and bewailed their frailties and miscarriages, notwithstanding the strictness of their vow, and all the diligence and care they could use, and consequently acknowledged their need of the grace of God in* Christ Jesus, *the true* Nazarite. *After these sacrifices were offered to the Lord, the priest, or some other, shaved the head of the* Nazarite *at the door of the tabernacle; which was done so publicly, that it might be known that his vow was ended, and therefore he was at liberty as to those things from which he had restrained himself for a season, otherwise some might have been scandalized at his liberty; after which his hair was burnt, being thrown upon the fire on which the flesh of the peace offering was boiled; then the priest put into the hands of the* Nazarite *the shoulder of the ram boiled, with a loaf and a cake, which the* Nazarite *returning into the hands of the priest, he offered them to the Lord, lifting them up in the presence of the* Nazarite: *and from this time he might again drink wine, his Nazariteship being now accomplished.*

Some obliged themselves only for a time, as those mentioned in Num. 6. 13. *others for their whole life, as* Samson, John *the Baptist, &c.* Judg. 16. 17. Luke 1. 15. *Their principal design was to sequester themselves in a great part from worldly employments and enjoyments, that they might devote themselves to the service of God.* Nazarite *signifies, sanctified, or consecrated.*

Num. 6. 2. a vow of a n. to separate themselves
13. and this is the law of the n. when, 21.
18. the n. shall shave the head of his separation
19. and shall put them on the hands of the n.
20. and after that the n. may drink wine
Judg. 13. 5. the child shall be a n. to God, 7. | 16. 17.

NAZARITES.

Lam. 4. 7. her n. purer than snow, whiter than milk
Amos 2. 11. I raised up of your young men for n.
12. but ye gave the n. wine to drink, and prophets

NEAR.

Gen. 19. 20. this city is n. to flee to, it is a little one
27. 22. Jacob went n. to Isaac his father
25. bring it n. he brought it n. and he did eat
29. 10. Jacob went n. and rolled the stone
45. 10. thou shalt be n. to me, thou and thy children
48. 10. he brought them n. and kissed them
Exod. 13. 17. the land of Philistines, altho' that was n.
Lev. 18. 6. not approach to any that is n. of kin
12. she is thy father's n. kinswoman
13. for she is thy mother's n. kinswoman, 17.
20. 19. for he uncovereth his n. kin
21. 2. but for his kin n. to him he may be defiled
Num. 3. 6. bring the tribe of Levi n. and present
5. 16. bring her n. and set her before the Lord
16. 9. to bring you n. to himself, 10.
17. 13. whoso cometh n. the tabernacle shall die
26. 3. Moses spake in plains of Moab, n. Jericho
Deut. 5. 27. go thou n. and hear all God shall say
16. 21. not plant a grove of trees n. altar of Lord
Judg. 18. 22. the men n. Micah's house gathered
20. 34. they knew not that evil was n. them
Ruth 2. 20. the man is n. of kin to us, next kinsman
3. 9. spread skirt, for thou art a n. kinsman, 12.
2 Sam. 14. 30. see, Joab's field is n. mine, set on fire
19. 42. because the king is n. of kin to us
1 Kings 8. 46. land of enemy far or n. 2 Chr. 6. 36.
21. 2. thy vineyard, because it is n. to my house
Job 41. 16. one is so n. another, no air can come
Psal. 22. 11. for trouble is n. || 75. 1. thy name is n.
119. 151. thou art n. O Lord, thy comm. are truth
148. 14. the horn of Israel, a people n. to him
Prov. 7. 8. passing through the street, n. her corner
10. 14. but the mouth of the foolish is n. destruction
27. 10. better is a neighbour that is n. than a brother
Isa. 33. 13. ye that are n. acknowledge my might
45. 21. tell ye, and bring them n. yea, let them

Isa. 46. 13. I bring *n.* my righteousness, not far off
50. 8. he is *n.* that justifieth me, who will contend?
51. 5. my righteousness is *n.* my salvation
55. 6. call upon the Lord while he is *n.*
56. 1. my salvation is *n.* to come, and my righteous.
57. 19. peace be to him that is *n.* saith the Lord
Jer. 12. 2. thou art *n.* in their mouth, and far
25. 26. all kings of the north far and *n.* shall drink
Lam. 4. 18. our end is *n.* our days are fulfilled
Ezek. 6. 12. he that is *n.* shall fall by the sword
7. 7. the time is come, the day of trouble is *n.* 30. 3.
11. 3. who say, it is not *n.* let us build houses
22. 5. those that be *n.* and far shall mock thee
Dan. 9. 7. confusion belongs to Israel that are *n.*
Obad. 15. the day of the Lord is *n.* *Zech.* 1. 14.
Mat. 24. 33. know that it is *n.* even at the doors
Mark 13. 28. ye know that summer is *n.*
Acts 10. 24. Cornelius called together his *n.* friends
See CAME, COME, DRAW, DREW.

NEARER.

Ruth 3. 12. howbeit, there is a kinsman *n.* than I
Rom. 13. 11. our salvation *n.* than when we believed

NECESSARY.

Job 23. 12. I esteemed his words more than *n.* food
Acts 13. 46. was *n.* the word first be spoken to you
15. 28. to lay no greater burden than these *n.* things
28. 10. they laded us with such things as were *n.*
1 *Cor.* 12. 22. the members which seem feeble are *n.*
2 *Cor.* 9. 5. I thought it *n.* to exhort the brethren
Phil. 2. 25. I supposed it *n.* to send Epaphras
Tit. 3. 14. to maintain good works for *n.* uses
Heb. 9. 23. *n.* patterns should be purified with these

NECESSITY

Signifies, [1] *The state of a thing that must needs be, when it is contrary to its very nature and principles to be otherwise,* Heb. 9. 16. [2] *Poverty, or want of temporal good things,* Rom. 12. 13. [3] *Force or constraint,* 2 Cor. 9. 7.
The word necessary, *or such as are equivalent to it, as* must, must needs, *do not always denote an absolute necessity, but a necessity of decency; or of duty, or merely something useful and advantageous; as for example,* Luke 14. 18. I have bought a piece of ground, and I must needs go and see it; *that is, It is convenient that I go and see it.* Rom. 13. 5. Ye must needs be subject; *that is, it is your duty, as well as interest, so to be. And,* Luke 23. 17. Of necessity he must release one at the feast; *that is, it has been a custom observed among us for a long time, and it is proper to have it continued.*
Luke 23. 17. for of *n.* he must release one at the feast
Rom. 12. 13. distributing to the *n.* of saints
1 *Cor.* 7. 37. having no *n.* and hath so decreed
9. 16. for *n.* is laid upon me, yea, woe is to me
2 *Cor.* 9. 7. so let him give, not grudgingly, or of *n.*
Phil. 4. 16. ye sent once and again to my *n.*
Philem. 14. not be as it were of *n.* but willingly
Heb. 7. 12. there is made of *n.* a change of the law
8. 3. it is of *n.* this man have somewhat to offer
9. 16. there must of *n.* be the death of the testator

NECESSITIES.

Acts 20. 34. these hands have ministered to my *n.*
2 *Cor.* 6. 4. as the ministers of God in *n.*
12. 10. I take pleasure in *n.* in persecutions

NECK

Signifies, [1] *That part of the body between the head and shoulders,* Gen. 27. 16. [2] *The head,* Deut. 21. 4. [3] *The whole man,* Deut. 28. 48. Jer. 27. 8, 11. [4] *The heart,* Neh. 9. 29. Prov. 29. 1. [5] *The hand or body,* Neh. 3. 5.
Gen. 27. 16. put the skins on the smooth of his *n.*
40. thou shalt break the yoke from off thy *n.*
33. 4. Esau fell on his *n.* and kissed him
41. 42. Pharaoh put a gold chain about Joseph's *n.*
Ezek. 16. 11. *Dan.* 5. 7, 16, 29.
45. 14. Joseph fell on Benjamin's *n.* and wept
46. 29. he fell on Jacob's *n.* he wept on his *n.*
49. 8. thy hand shall be on the *n.* of thine enemies
Exod. 13. 13. if not redeem it, break his *n.* 34. 20.
Lev. 5. 8. and wring off his head from his *n.*
Deut. 21. 4. strike off the heifer's *n.* in the valley
28. 48. he shall put a yoke of iron upon thy *n.*
1 *Sam.* 4. 18. and his *n.* brake, and he died
2 *Chron.* 29. † 6. our fathers have given the *n.*
36. 13. Zedekiah stiffened his *n.* hardened his heart
Neh. 9. 29. hardened their *n.* and would not hear
Job 15. 26. he runneth on him, even on his *n.*
16. 12. he hath taken me by the *n.* and shaken me
39. 19. hast thou clothed his *n.* with thunder?
41. 22. in his *n.* remaineth strength, and sorrow
Psal. 75. 5. lift not up, speak not with a stiff *n.*
Prov. 1. 9. for they shall be chains about thy *n.*
3. 3. bind them about thy *n.* write them, 6. 21.
22. so shall they be life and grace to thy *n.*
Cant. 1. 10. thy *n.* is comely with chains of gold
4. 4. thy *n.* is like the tower of David
9. hast ravished my heart with one chain of thy *n.*
7. 4. thy *n.* is a tower of ivory, thine eyes
Isa. 8. 8. he shall reach even to the *n.*
10. 27. his yoke shall be taken from off thy *n.*
30. 28. shall reach to the midst of the *n.*
48. 4. thy *n.* is an iron sinew, thy brow brass
52. 2. loose thyself from the bands of thy *n.*
66. 3. that sacrificeth, as if he cut off a dog's *n.*
Jer. 2. † 27. turned the hinder part of the *n.* to me
17. 23. but they obeyed not, made their *n.* stiff
27. 2. make thee yokes, and put them on thy *n.*
8. will not put *n.* under yoke of king of Babyl. 11.
28. 10. took the yoke from off Jeremiah's *n.* 12.
14. I have put a yoke on the *n.* of these nations
30. 8. I will break his yoke from off thy *n.*
48. † 39. Moab hath turned the *n.* with shame
Lam. 1. 14. my transgressions are come upon my *n.*
Hos. 10. 11. but I passed over on her fair *n.*
Hab. 3. 13. discovering the foundation to the *n.*
Mat. 18. 6. it were better that a millstone were hanged about his *n.* *Mark* 9. 42. *Luke* 17. 2.
Luke 15. 20. his father fell on his *n.* and kissed him
Acts 15. 10. put a yoke on the *n.* of the disciples
20. 37. they fell on Paul's *n.* and kissed him
See HARDEN.

NECKS.

Josh. 7. † 8. when Israel turneth their *n.*
10. 24. put your feet on the *n.* of these kings
Judg. 5. 30. for the *n.* of them that take the spoil
8. 21. ornaments that were on their camel's *n.* 26.
2 *Sam.* 22. 41. given me *n.* of enemies, *Psal.* 18. 40.
2 *Chron.* 30. † 8. harden not your *n.* as your fathers
Neh. 3. 5. the nobles put not their *n.* to the work
Isa. 3. 16. and walk with stretched-forth *n.*
Jer. 27. 12. bring your *n.* under yoke of Babylon
Lam. 5. 5. our *n.* are under persecution, we labour
Ezek. 21. 29. to bring thee on the *n.* of the slain
Mic. 2. 3. from which ye shall not remove your *n.*
Rom. 16. 4. who for my life laid down their own *n.*

NECROMANCER.

Deut. 18. 11. there shall not be found among you a *n.*

NEED.

Deut. 15. 8. thou shalt lend him sufficient for his *n.*
1 *Sam.* 21. 15. have I *n.* of madmen, that ye brought
2 *Chron.* 2. 16. cut wood as much as thou shalt *n.*
20. 17. ye shall not *n.* to fight in this battle
Ezra 6. 9. and let what they have *n.* of be given
Prov. 31. 11. so he shall have no *n.* of spoil
Mat. 3. 14. I have *n.* to be baptized of thee
6. 8. for your father knoweth what things ye have *n.* of before ye ask him, 32. *Luke* 12. 30.
9. 12. they that be whole *n.* not a physician, but they that are sick, *Mark* 2. 17. *Luke* 5. 31.
14. 16. they *n.* not depart, give ye them to eat
21. 3. the Lord hath *n.* of them, and he will send them, *Mark* 11. 3. *Luke* 19. 31, 34.
26. 65. the high priest said, what further *n.* have we of witnesses? *Mark* 14. 63. *Luke* 22. 71.
Mark 2. 25. read what David did when he had *n.*
Luke 9. 11. and healed them that had *n.* of healing
15. 7. over just persons which *n.* no repentance
John 13. 29. buy those things we have *n.* of
Acts 2. 45. parted them as every man had *n.* 4. 35.
Rom. 16. 2. that ye assist her in what she hath *n.*
1 *Cor.* 7. 36. if *n.* so require, let him do what he will
12. 21. cannot say to the hand, I have no *n.* of thee
24. for our comely parts have no *n.* but God
2 *Cor.* 3. 1. or *n.* we epistles of commendation to you?
Phil. 4. 12. I know how to abound and to suffer *n.*
19. my God shall supply all your *n.* by Christ J.
1 *Thess.* 1. 8. so that we *n.* not to speak any thing
4. 9. of brotherly love ye *n.* not that I write
5. 1. of the times ye have no *n.* that I write
Heb. 4. 16. and find grace to help in time of *n.*
5. 12. *n.* one teach you, such as have *n.* of milk
7. 11. what *n.* that another priest should rise
10. 36. for ye have *n.* of patience, that after
1 *Pet.* 1. 6. though now, if *n.* be, ye are in heaviness
1 *John* 2. 27. ye *n.* not that any man teach you
3. 17. whoso had goods, and see his brother have *n.*
Rev. 3. 17. I am rich, and have *n.* of nothing
21. 23. the city hath no *n.* of sun or moon
22. 5. and they *n.* no candle, nor light of the sun

NEEDED.

John 2. 25. he *n.* not that any should testify of man
Acts 17. 25. as tho' he *n.* any thing, seeing he gives

NEEDEST, ETH.

Gen. 33. 15. Jacob said, what *n.* it, let me find grace
Luke 11. 8. he will give him as many as he *n.*
John 13. 10. is washed, *n.* not save to wash his feet
16. 30. and *n.* not that any man should ask thee
Eph. 4. 28. that he may have to give to him that *n.*
2 *Tim.* 2. 15. a workman that *n.* not to be ashamed
Heb. 7. 27. who *n.* not daily to offer up sacrifice

NEEDFUL.

Ezra 7. 20. shall be *n.* for the house of thy God
Luke 10. 42. one thing is *n.* and Mary hath chosen
Acts 15. 5. that it was *n.* to circumcise them
Phil. 1. 24. to abide in the flesh is more *n.* for you
Jam. 2. 16. these things which are *n.* for the body
Jude 3. beloved, it was *n.* for me to write to you

NEEDLE.

Mat. 19. 24. it is easier for a camel to go through the eye of a *n.* *Mark* 10. 25. *Luke* 18. 25.

NEEDLE-WORK.

Exod. 26. 36. thou shalt make an hanging wrought with *n.* 27. 16. | 36. 37. | 38. 18.
28. 39. thou shalt make the girdle of *n.* 39. 29.
Judg. 5. 30. to Sisera, a prey of divers colours of *n.*
Psal. 45. 14. she shall be brought in raiment of *n.*

NEEDS.

Gen. 17. 13. he must *n.* be circumcised
19. 9. they said, this one fellow will *n.* be a judge
24. 5. must I *n.* bring thy son again to the land?
31. 30. and now though thou wouldest *n.* be gone
2 *Sam.* 14. 14. we must *n.* die, and are as water spilt on the ground
Jer. 10. 5. must *n.* be born, because they cannot go
Mat. 18. 7. it must *n.* be that offences come
Mark 13. 7. for such things must *n.* be, and not yet
Luke 14. 18. bought ground, and I must *n.* go and see
John 4. 4. and he must *n.* go through Samaria
Acts 1. 16. this scripture must *n.* have been fulfilled
17. 3. that Christ must *n.* have suffered
21. 22. the multitude must *n.* come together
Rom. 13. 5. wherefore ye must *n.* be subject
1 *Cor.* 5. 10. then must ye *n.* go out of the world
2 *Cor.* 11. 30. if I must *n.* glory, I will glory

NEEDY.

Deut. 15. 11. thou shalt open thy hand to the *n.*
24. 14. an hired servant that is poor and *n.*
Job 24. 4. they turn the *n.* out of the way
14. the murderer killeth the poor and *n.*
Psal. 9. 18. the *n.* shall not alway be forgotten
12. 5. for the sighing of the *n.* now will I arise
35. 10. which deliverest the poor and *n.* 72. 4, 13.
37. 14. have bent their bow to cast down the *n.*
40. 17. I am poor and *n.* make no tarrying, 70. 5.
72. 12. for he shall deliver the *n.* 82. 4.
13. he shall spare the poor and *n.* save the *n.*
74. 21. let the poor and *n.* praise thy name
82. 3. do justice to the afflicted and *n.*
4. deliver the poor and *n.* rid from the wicked
86. 1. hear me, for I am poor and *n.* 109. 22.
109. 16. but persecuted the poor and *n.* man
113. 7. he lifteth the *n.* out of the dunghill
Prov. 30. 14. devour the *n.* from among men
Prov. 31. 9. and plead the cause of the poor and *n.*
20. she reacheth forth her hands to the *n.*
Isa. 10. 2. to turn aside the *n.* from judgment
14. 30. and the *n.* shall lie down in safety
25. 4. been a strength to the *n.* in his distress
26. 6. the steps of the *n.* shall tread it down
32. 7. even when the *n.* speaketh right
41. 17. when the poor and *n.* seek water
Jer. 5. 28. and the right of *n.* do they not judge
22. 16. he judged the cause of the poor and *n.*
Ezek. 16. 49. nor strengthen the hands of the *n.*
18. 12. he hath oppressed the poor and *n.*
22. 29. the people have vexed the poor and *n.*
Amos 4. 1. ye kine of Bashan, which crush the *n.*
8. 4. hear this, O ye that swallow up the *n.*
6. that we may buy the *n.* for a pair of shoes

NEESED, or SNEEZED.

2 *Kings* 4. 35. the child *n.* seven times, and opened

NEESINGS.

Job 41. 18. by his *n.* a light doth shine, his eyes

NEGLECT.

Mat. 18. 17. and if he shall *n.* to hear them, tell it to the church, but if he *n.* to hear the church
1 *Tim.* 4. 14. *n.* not the gift that is in thee
Heb. 2. 3. how shall escape, if *n.* so great salvation?

NEGLECTED.

Acts 6. 1. their widows were *n.* in the ministration

NEGLECTING.

Col. 2. 23. *n.* the body, not in any honour to the

NEGLIGENT.

2 *Chr.* 29. 11. my sons, be not now *n.* for Lord
2 *Pet.* 1. 12. not be *n.* to put you in remembrance

NEIGHBOUR

Signifies, [1] *One who dwells or is seated near to another,* 2 Kings 4. 3. [2] *Every man, to whom we have an opportunity of doing good,* Mat. 22. 39. [3] *A fellow-labourer, of one and the same people,* Acts 7. 27. [4] *One who does us good, and who pities and relieves us in distress, though at a distance from us,* Luke 10. 36. [5] *One that stands in need of help,* Prov. 3. 28. [6] *A friend,* Job 16. † 21.
At the time of our Saviour, the Pharisees had restrained the word Neighbour *to signify those of their own nation only, or their own friends; being of opinion, that to hate their enemy was not forbidden by their law: but our Saviour informed them, that the whole world were their neighbours; that they ought not to do to another what they would not have done to themselves; and that this charity ought to be extended even to their enemies,* Mat. 5. 43. Luke 10. 29, &c.
Exod. 3. 22. every woman borrow of her *n.* 11. 2.
1 *Sam.* 15. 28. and hath given it to a *n.* of thine
Prov. 27. 10. better is a *n.* that is near, than a brother
Jer. 6. 21. the *n.* and his friends shall perish
9. 20. and teach every one her *n.* lamentation
Luke 10. 36. was *n.* to him that fell among thieves

NEIGHBOUR, *Adjective.*

Jer. 49. 18. as in the overthrow of Sodom and Gomorrah and the *n.* cities thereof, 50. 40.

His NEIGHBOUR.

Exod. 12. 4. let him and *his n.* take a lamb
21. 14. but if a man come on *his n.* to slay him
22. 7. if a man deliver to *his n.* money or stuff
8. whether he put his hand to *his n.* goods, 11.
10. if a man deliver to *his n.* an ass or ox
14. if borrow ought of *his n.* and it be hurt or die
32. 27. go through the camp, slay every man *his n.*
Lev. 6. 2. and lie unto or hath deceived *his n.*
20. 10. he that committeth adultery with *his n.* wife, shall surely be put to death, *Deut.* 22. 24.
24. 19. and if a man cause a blemish in *his n.*
Deut. 4. 42. which should kill *his n.* unawares, 19. 4.
15. 2. every creditor that lendeth aught to *his n.* he shall not exact of *his n.* or his brother
19. 11. if any hate *his n.* and lie in wait for him
22. 26. a man riseth against *his n.* and slayeth him
27. 17. cursed be he that removeth *his n.* land-mark
24. cursed be he that smiteth *his n.* secretly
Ruth 4. 7. man plucked off his shoe, and gave to *h. n.*
1 *Kings* 8. 31. if a man trespass ag. *his n.* an oath
2 *Chr.* 6. 22. if a man sin against *his n.* and an oath
Job 12. 4. I am as one mocked of *his n.*
16. 21. plead with G. as a man pleadeth for *his n.*
Psal. 12. 2. they speak vanity each with *his n.*
15. 3. nor doeth evil to *his n.* taketh up a reproach
101. 5. whoso privily slandereth *his n.* will cut off
Prov. 6. 29. so he that goeth into *his n.* wife
11. 9. an hypocrite with his mouth destroyeth *his n.*
12. who is void of wisdom despiseth *his n.* 14. 21.
12. 26. the righteous is more excellent than *his n.*
14. 20. the poor is hated even of *his n.*
16. 29. a violent man enticeth *his n.* and leadeth
18. 17. but *his n.* cometh and searcheth him
19. 4. but the poor is separated from *his n.*
21. 10. *his n.* findeth no favour in his eyes
25. 18. man that beareth false witness against *his n.*
26. 19. so is the man that deceiveth *his n.*
29. 5. that flattereth *his n.* spread. a net for his feet
Eccl. 4. 4. that for this a man is envied of *his n.*
Isa. 3. 5. shall be oppressed every one by *his n.*
19. 2. they shall fight every one against *his n.*
41. 6. they helped every one *his n.* and said
Jer. 5. 8. every one neighed after *his n.* wife
7. 5. execute judgment between a man and *his n.*
9. 4. take ye heed every one of *his n.* trust not
5. and they will deceive every one *his n.*
8. speak peaceably to *his n.* with his mouth
22. 8. they shall say every man to *his n.* 23. 35.
13. that useth *his n.* service without wages
Jer. 23. 27. dreams they tell every one to *his n.*
30. that steal my word, every one from *his n.*
31. 34. teach no more every man *his n.* *Heb.* 8. 11.
34. 15. in proclaiming liberty to *his n.* 17.
Ezek. 18. 6. neither hath defiled *his n.* wife, 15.
11. hath defiled *his n.* wife, 22. 11. | 33. 26.
Hab. 2. 15. woe to him that giveth *his n.* drink
Zech. 3. 10. shall call every man *his n.* under the vine
8. 10. for I set all men, every one against *his n.*
16. speak ye every man the truth to *his n.*
17. let none of you imagine evil against *his n.*

Mark 12. 33. and to love *his n.* as himself, is more
Acts 7. 27. he that did *his n.* wrong, thrust him
Rom. 13. 10. love worketh no evil to *his n.*
15. 2. let every one please *his n.* for his good
Eph. 4. 25. speak every man truth with *his n.*

My NEIGHBOUR.

Job 31. 9. or if I have laid wait at *my n.* door
Luke 10. 29. but he said to Jesus, who is *my n.?*

Thy NEIGHBOUR.

Exod. 20. 16. thou shalt not bear false witness against *thy n.* *Deut.* 5. 20.
22. 26. if thou take *thy n.* raiment to pledge
Lev. 18. 20. shalt not lie carnally with *thy n.* wife
19. 13. thou shalt not defraud *thy n.* nor rob him
15. in righteousness shalt thou judge *thy n.*
16. nor shalt thou stand against the blood of *thy n.*
17. thou shalt in any wise rebuke *thy n.*
18. but thou shalt love *thy n.* as thyself
25. 14. if sell to, or buyest ought of *thy n.* 15.
Deut. 5. 21. thou shalt not desire or covet *thy n.* wife
19. 14. thou shalt not remove *thy n.* land-mark
23. 24. when thou comest into *thy n.* vineyard
1 *Sam.* 28. 17. rent kingdom, and given it to *thy n.*
2 *Sam.* 12. 11. take wives, and give them to *thy n.*
Prov. 3. 28. say not to *thy n.* go, and come again
29. devise not evil against *thy n.* seeing he dwells
24. 28. be not witness against *thy n.* without cause
25. 8. when *thy n.* hath put thee to shame
9. debate thy cause with *thy n.* himself
17. withdraw thy foot from *thy n.* house
Mat. 5. 43. thou shalt love *thy n.* 19. 19. | 22. 39. *Mark* 12. 31. *Luke* 10. 27. *Rom.* 13. 9. *Gal.* 5. 14. *Jam.* 2. 8.

NEIGHBOURS.

Josh. 9. 16. they heard that they were their *n.*
Ruth 4. 17. the women her *n.* gave it a name
2 *Kings* 4. 3. go borrow vessels abroad of all thy *n.*
Psal. 28. 3. who speak peace to their *n.* but mischief
31. 11. I was a reproach among all my *n.*
44. 13. thou makest us a reproach to our *n.*
79. 4. we are become a reproach to our *n.*
12. render to our *n.* seven-fold into their bosom
80. 6. thou makest us a strife to our *n.*
89. 41. spoil him he is a reproach to his *n.*
Jer. 12. 14. thus saith the Lord, again, all my evil *n.*
29. 23. have committed adultery with their *n.* wives
49. 10. his seed is spoiled and his *n.* and he is not
Ezek. 16. 26. commit fornication with Egypt, thy *n.*
22. 12. thou hast gained of thy *n.* by extortion
23. 5. she doted on the Assyrians her *n.* 12.
Luke 1. 58. her *n.* and her cousins heard how Lord
14. 12. when makest a supper, call not thy rich *n.*
15. 6. he calleth together his friends and *n.* 9.
John 9. 8. *n.* and they who before had seen him blind

NEIGHED.

Jer. 5. 8. every one *n.* after his neighbour's wife

NEIGHING.

Jer. 8. 16. land trembled at the *n.* of his strong ones

NEIGHINGS.

Jer. 13. 27. I have seen thine adulteries and *n.*

NEITHER.

Gen. 3. 3. the tree, *n.* shall ye touch it, lest ye die
1 *Kings* 22. 31. fight *n.* with small nor great, but with
Mat. 21. 27. *n.* tell I you by what authority I do

NEPHEW.

Job 18. 19. he shall neither have son nor *n.*
Isa. 14. 22. I will cut off from Babylon son and *n.*

NEPHEWS.

Judg. 12. 14. Abdon had forty sons and thirty *n.*
1 *Tim.* 5. 4. if any widow have children or *n.*

NEST

Signifies, [1] *A little lodgment in which birds hatch and breed their young*, Psal. 84. 3. [2] *The birds in the nest*, Deut. 32. 11. Isa. 10. 14. [3] *A very high habitation, seemingly secure, and without disturbance*, Obad. 4. Hab. 2. 9.

Num. 24. 21. and thou puttest thy *n.* in a rock
Deut. 22. 6. if a bird's *n.* chance to be before thee
32. 11. as an eagle stirreth up her *n.*
Job 29. 18. then I said, I shall die in my *n.*
39. 27. doth eagle at thy command make *n.* on high?
Psal. 84. 3. the swallow hath found a *n.* for herself
Prov. 27. 8. as a bird that wandereth from her *n.*
Isa. 10. 14. hath found as *n.* the riches of the people
16. 2. as a wandering bird cast out of the *n.*
34. 15. there shall the great owl make her *n.*
Jer. 22. 23. that makest thy *n.* in the cedars
48. 28. the dove makes her *n.* in the sides of holes
49. 16. tho' thou make thy *n.* as high as the eagle
Obad. 4. though thou set thy *n.* among the stars
Hab. 2. 9. that he may set his *n.* on high

NESTS.

Gen. 6. † 14. *n.* shalt thou make in the ark
Psal. 104. 17. where the birds make their *n.*
Ezek. 31. 6. all the fowls of heaven made their *n.*
Mat. 8. 20. and the birds of the air have *n.* *Luke* 9. 58.

NET

Signifies, [1] *An instrument for catching fish, birds, or wild beasts*, Isa. 51. 20. Mat. 4. 18. [2] *Artificial work wrought like a net*, 1 Kings 7. 17. [3] *Mischief cunningly devised*, Psal. 9. 15. Mic. 7. 2. [4] *A fortress*, Prov. 12. † 12. [5] *Inextricable difficulties*, Job 18. 8. [6] *Trying afflictions, wherewith God chastiseth his people*, Job 19. 6.

They sacrifice unto their net, *Hab.* 1. 16. *They ascribe the praise of their victories and acquired glory to their own contrivances, diligence, and power; as if the fisherman should make his net his god, and offer sacrifices thereto, because it had enclosed a good draught of fishes.*

Job 18. 8. he is cast into a *n.* by his own feet
19. 6. God hath compassed me with his *n.*
Psal. 9. 15. in the *n.* they hid, is their foot taken
10. 9. when he draweth him into his *n.*
25. 15. he shall pluck my feet out of the *n.* 31. 4.
35. 7. they have hid for me their *n.* in a pit
8. let his *n.* that he hath hid catch himself
57. 6. they have prepared a *n.* for my steps
66. 11. thou broughtest us into the *n.*
140. 5. they have spread a *n.* by the way-side
Prov. 1. 17. surely in vain the *n.* is spread in sight
12. 12. the wicked desireth the *n.* of evil men
29. 5. a man that flattereth spreadeth a *n.*
Eccl. 9. 12. as the fishes are taken in an evil *n.*
Isa. 51. 20. thy sons lie, as a wild bull in a *n.*
Lam. 1. 13. he hath spread a *n.* for my feet
Ezek. 12. 13. my *n.* will I spread on him, 17. 20.
19. 8. the nations shall spread their *n.* over him
32. 3. I will spread out my *n.* over thee
Hos. 5. 1. ye have been a *n.* spread upon Tabor
7. 12. when they go, I will spread my *n.* upon them
Mic. 7. 2. hunt every man his brother with a *n.*
Hab. 1. 15. they catch them in their *n.*
16. therefore they sacrifice to their *n.* and burn
17. shall they therefore empty their *n.!*
Mat. 4. 18. casting *n.* into the sea, *Mark* 1. 16.
13. 47. the kingdom of heaven is like a *n.* cast
Luke 5. 5. at thy word I will let down the *n.*
6. a great multitude of fishes, and their *n.* brake
John 21. 6. cast the *n.* on the right side of the ship
8. came in a ship, dragging the *n.* with the fishes
11. drew the *n.* to land, yet was not the *n.* broken

NETS.

1 *Kings* 7. 17. *n.* of checker-work and wreaths
Psal. 141. 10. let the wicked fall into their own *n.*
Eccl. 7. 26. the woman whose heart is snares and *n.*
Isa. 19. 8. they that spread *n.* shall languish
Ezek. 26. 5. spreading of *n.* in the midst of the sea
14. it shall be a place to spread *n.* on, 47. 10.
Mat. 4. 21. he saw James and John mending their *n.* and he called them, *Mark* 1. 19. *Luke* 5. 2.
Mark 1. 18. they forsook their *n.* and followed him
Luke 5. 4. and let down your *n.* for a draught

NETHER.

Exod. 19. 17. they stood at the *n.* part of the mount
Deut. 24. 6. no man shall take *n.* millstone to pledge
Josh. 15. 19. and he gave her the upper springs and the *n.* springs, *Judg.* 1. 15.
1 *Kings* 9. 17. and Solomon built Gezer and Beth-horon the *n.* 1 *Chron.* 7. 24.
Job 41. 24. his heart hard as a piece of *n.* millstone
Ezek. 31. 14. they are delivered to death to *n.* parts
16. shall be comforted in the *n.* parts of the earth
18. shalt be brought down to *n.* parts of the earth
32. 18. cast them down to the *n.* parts of the earth
24. Elam gone down to the *n.* parts of the earth

NETHERMOST.

1 *Kings* 6. 6. the *n.* chamber was five cubits broad

NETTLES.

Job 30. 7. under the *n.* they were gathered together
Prov. 24. 31. and *n.* had covered the face thereof
Isa. 34. 13. *n.* and brambles in the fortresses thereof
Hos. 9. 6. *n.* shall possess the pleasant places for silv.
Zeph. 2. 9. surely Moab shall be the breeding of *n.*

NET-WORK.

Exod. 27. 4. shalt make a grate of *n.* of brass, 38. 4.
1 *Kings* 7. 18. two rows round about on *n.* 42.
Jer. 52. 22. with *n.* on the chapiters round about
23. all the pomegranates on *n.* were an hundred

NET-WORKS.

1 *Kings* 7. 41. the two *n.* upon the chapiters
42. four hundred pomegranates for the two *n.*
Isa. 3. † 18. the Lord will take away their *n.*
19. 9. they that weave *n.* shall be confounded

NEVER.

Gen. 41. 19. kine, such as I *n.* saw in all Egypt
Lev. 6. 13. the fire on the altar shall *n.* go out
Num. 19. 2. a red heifer, upon which *n.* came yoke
Deut. 15. 11. the poor shall *n.* cease out of the land
Judg. 2. 1. I will *n.* break my covenant with you
14. 3. is there *n.* a woman among all my people?
16. 7. with seven green withs that were *n.* dried
11. if bind with new ropes that *n.* were occupied
2 *Sam.* 12. 10. the sword shall *n.* depart from thy house
2 *Chron.* 18. 7. he *n.* prophesied good unto me
21. 17. there was *n.* a son left him, save Jehoahaz
Job 3. 16. as infants which *n.* saw light
9. 30. and if I make my hands *n.* so clean
21. 25. another *n.* eateth with pleasure
Psal. 10. 6. hath said, for I shall *n.* be in adversity
11. he hideth his face, he will *n.* see it
15. 5. he that doeth these things shall *n.* be moved
30. 6. in prosperity I said, I shall *n.* be moved
31. 1. in thee do I trust, let me *n.* be ashamed
49. 19. shall go up to fathers; they shall *n.* see
55. 22. Lord will *n.* suffer the righteous to be moved
71. 1. O Lord, let me *n.* be put to confusion
119. 93. I will *n.* forget thy precepts, for with them
Prov. 10. 30. the righteous shall *n.* be removed
27. 20. hell and destruction are *n.* full, so the eyes of a man are *n.* satisfied
30. 15. there are three things that are *n.* satisfied
Isa. 13. 20. Babylon *n.* be inhabited nor dwelt in
14. 20. the seed of evil doers shall *n.* be renowned
25. 2. to be no city, it shall *n.* be built
56. 11. are greedy dogs which can *n.* have enough
62. 6. watchmen that shall *n.* hold their peace
63. 19. we are thine, thou *n.* barest rule over them
Jer. 20. 11. their confusion shall *n.* be forgotten
33. 17. David shall *n.* want a man to sit on throne
Ezek. 16. 63. and *n.* open thy mouth any more
26. 21. Tyrus shall *n.* be found again, saith Lord
27. 36. a terror and *n.* shalt be any more, 28. 19.
Dan. 2. 44. a kingdom that shall *n.* be destroyed
12. 1. there shall be trouble, such as *n.* was
Joel 2. 26. and my people shall *n.* be ashamed, 27.
Amos 8. 7. I will *n.* forget any of their works
14. even they shall fall and *n.* rise up again
Hab. 1. 4. and judgment doth *n.* go forth
Mat. 7. 23. I will profess unto them I *n.* knew you
9. 33. saying, it was *n.* so seen in Israel
21. 16. Jesus saith, have ye *n.* read, out of the mouth of babes hast perfected praise, 42. *Mark* 2. 25.
26. 33. Peter said, yet will I *n.* be offended
27. 14. and he answered him to *n.* a word
Mark 2. 12. saying, we *n.* saw it on this fashion
3. 29. shall blaspheme ag. Holy Ghost, hath *n.* forg.
9. 43. into fire that *n.* shall be quenched, 45.
11. 2. colt tied, whereon *n.* man sat, *Luke* 19. 30.
14. 21. good for that man if he had *n.* been born
Luke 15. 29. yet thou *n.* gavest me a kid to make
23. 29. blessed are the wombs that *n.* bare
53. wherein *n.* man before was laid, *John* 19. 41.
John 4. 14. who drinks of water I give, shall *n.* thirst
6. 35. he that cometh to me shall *n.* hunger, and he that believeth on me shall *n.* thirst
7. 15. how knoweth this man, having *n.* learned?
46. the officers said, *n.* man spake like this man
8. 33. and we were *n.* in bondage to any
51. he shall *n.* see death, 52. | 10. 28. | 11. 26.
13. 8. Peter saith, thou shalt *n.* wash my feet
Acts 10. 14. I have *n.* eaten any thing common
14. 8. being a cripple, who *n.* had walked
1 *Cor.* 13. 8. charity *n.* faileth, but whether prophec.
2 *Tim.* 3. 7. *n.* able to come to knowledge of truth
Heb. 10. 1. can *n.* with those sacrifices make perfect
11. the same sacrifices which can *n.* take away sins
13. 5. I will *n.* leave thee, nor forsake thee
2 *Pet.* 1. 10. if ye do these things, ye shall *n.* fall

NEVER *so.*

Psal. 58. 5. to charmers, charming *n. so* wisely

NEVER *so much.*

Gen. 34. 12. ask me *n. so m.* dowry, and I will give

NEVERTHELESS.

Exod. 32. 34. *n.* in the day when I visit, I will visit
Lev. 11. 4. *n.* these ye shall not eat, *Deut.* 14. 7.
36. *n.* a fountain or pit shall be clean
Num. 13. 28. *n.* the people be strong that dwell
14. 44. *n.* the ark of the covenant departed not
18. 15. *n.* the first-born of man shalt thou redeem
24. 22. *n.* the Kenite shall be wasted, until Asshur
31. 23. *n.* it shall be purified with water of separat.
Deut. 23. 5. *n.* the L. thy God would not hearken
Josh. 13. 13. *n.* children of Isr. expelled not Geshur
14. 8. *n.* my brethren that went up with me
Judg. 1. 33. *n.* the inhabitants of Beth-shemesh
2. 16. *n.* the Lord raised up judges to deliver them
1 *Sam.* 8. 19. *n.* the people refused to obey Samuel
15. 35. to see Saul, *n.* Samuel mourned for Saul
20. 26. *n.* Saul spake not any thing that day
29. 6. said to David, *n.* the lords favour thee not
2 *Sam.* 5. 7. *n.* David took the strong-hold of Zion
17. 18. *n.* a lad saw them, and told Absalom
23. 16. *n.* he would not drink thereof, poured out
1 *Kings* 8. 19. *n.* thou shalt not build the house
15. 4. *n.* for David's sake did the Lord give
14. *n.* Asa his heart was perfect with the Lord
23. *n.* in his old age he was diseased in his feet
22. 43. *n.* the high places were not taken away
2 *Kings* 2. 10. *n.* if thou see me when I am taken
3. 3. *n.* he cleaved to the sins of Jeroboam
13. 6. *n.* they departed not from the sins of Jerob.
23. 9. *n.* the priests of the high places came not
1 *Chron.* 11. 5. *n.* David took the castle of Zion
21. 4. *n.* the king's word prevailed against Joab
2 *Chron.* 12. 8. *n.* they shall be his servants
15. 17. *n.* the heart of Asa was perfect all his days
19. 3. *n.* there are good things found in thee
30. 11. *n.* divers of Asher humbled themselves
33. 17. *n.* the people did sacrifice in the high places
35. 22. *n.* Josiah would not turn from him
Neh. 4. 9. *n.* we made our prayer to our God
9. 26. *n.* they were disobed. and rebelled ag. thee
31. *n.* for thy mercies' sake thou didst not consume
13. 26. *n.* him did outlandish women cause to sin
Esth. 5. 10. *n.* Haman refrained himself
Psal. 31. 22. *n.* thou heardest my supplication
49. 12. *n.* man being in honour, abideth not
73. 23. *n.* I am continually with thee, hast holden
78. 36. *n.* they did flatter him with their mouth
89. 33. *n.* my loving-kindness not take from him
106. 8. *n.* he saved them for his name's sake
44. *n.* he regarded their affliction, heard their cry
Prov. 19. 21. *n.* the counsel of the Lord shall stand
Eccl. 9. 16. *n.* the poor man's wisdom is despised
Isa. 9. 1. *n.* the dimness shall not be such as was
Jer. 5. 18. *n.* in those days I will make a full end
26. 24. *n.* the hand of Ahikam was with Jeremiah
28. 7. *n.* hear thou this word that I speak in thy ears
36. 25. *n.* Elnathan and Delaiah made intercession
Ezek. 3. 21. *n.* if thou warn the righteous man
16. 60. *n.* I will remember my covenant with thee
20. 17. *n.* mine eye spared them from destroying
22. *n.* I withdrew my hand, and wrought for my
33. 9. *n.* if thou warn the wicked of his way
Dan. 4. 15. *n.* leave the stump of his roots in earth
Jonah 1. 13. *n.* the men rowed hard to bring to land
Mat. 14. 9. *n.* for the oath's sake he commanded it
26. 39. from me, *n.* not as I will, but as thou wilt
64. *n.* hereafter ye shall see the Son of man com.
Mark 14. 36. *n.* not what I will, *Luke* 22. 42.
Luke 5. 5. *n.* at thy word I will let down the net
13. 33. *n.* I must walk to-day and to-morrow
18. 8. *n.* when Son of man cometh shall he find faith
John 11. 15. Lazarus is dead, *n.* let us go to him
12. 42. *n.* among the chief rulers many believed
16. 7. *n.* I tell you the truth, it is expedient for you
Acts 14. 17. *n.* he left not himself without witness
27. 11. *n.* the centurion believed the master of ship
Rom. 5. 14. *n.* death reigned from Adam to Moses
15. 15. *n.* I have written more boldly to you
1 *Cor.* 7. 2. *n.* to avoid fornicat. let every man have
28. *n.* such shall have trouble in the flesh
37. *n.* he that standeth stedfast in his heart
9. 12. *n.* we have not used this power
11. 11. *n.* neither is the man without the woman
2 *Cor.* 3. 16. *n.* when it shall turn to the Lord
7. 6. *n.* G. that comforteth those that are cast down
12. 16. *n.* being crafty, I caught you with guile
Gal. 2. 20. *n.* I live, yet not I, but Christ in me
4. 30. *n.* what saith scripture, cast out bond-wom.
Eph. 5. 33. *n.* let every man so love his wife as hims.
Phil. 1. 24. *n.* to abide in the flesh is more needful
3. 16. *n.* whereto we have already attained
2 *Tim.* 1. 12. *n.* I am not ashamed, for I know whom
2. 19. *n.* the foundation of God standeth sure
Heb. 12. 11. *n.* it yieldeth peaceable fruit of right.
2 *Pet.* 3. 13. *n.* we look for new heavens and earth
Rev. 2. 4. *n.* I have somewhat against thee

NEW

Signifies, [1] *That which is fresh, or of late date*, Josh. 9. 13. [2] *That which was never used or worn before*, 1 Kings 11. 29. [3] *That which is extraordinary and unusual*, Num. 16. 30. [4] *One who is regenerated, and endued with new qualities,*

new apprehensions and inclinations, 2 Cor. 5. 17.
Gal. 6. 15. [5] *Strange and unknown*, Mark 16.
17. [6] *Another*, Exod. 1. 8.
Exod. 1. 8. there arose up a n. king over Egypt
Lev. 23. 16. offer a n. meat offering, Num. 28. 26.
26. 10. shall bring forth the old, because of the n.
Num. 16. 30. but if the Lord make a n. thing
Deut. 20. 5. what man hath built a n. house, 22. 8.
24. 5. when taken a n. wife, he shall not go to war
32. 17. they sacrificed to devils, to n. gods
Josh. 9. 13. and these bottles of wine were n.
Judg. 5. 8. they chose n. gods, then was war in gates
15. 13. they bound him with n. cords, 16. 11, 12.
1 Sam. 6. 7. make a n. cart, and take two kine
2 Sam. 6. 3. set the ark on a n. cart, 1 Chron. 13. 7.
21. 16. he being girded with a n. sword thought
1 Kings 11. 29. Jeroboam clad with a n. garment
30. Ahijah caught the n. garment, and rent it
2 Kings 2. 20. bring a n. cruse, and put salt therein
2 Chron. 20. 5. Jehoshaphat stood in the n. court
Job 32. 19. it is ready to burst like n. bottles
Psal. 33. 3. sing to him a n. song, 96. 1. | 98. 1.
| 144. 9. | 149. 1. Isa. 42. 10.
40. 3. he hath put a n. song in my mouth, even praise
Eccl. 1. 9. there is no n. thing under the sun
10. is any thing whereof may be said, this is n.?
Cant. 7. 13. are all pleasant fruits, n. and old
Isa. 42. 9. behold, n. things do I declare, 48. 6.
43. 19. behold, I will do a n. thing, make a way
62. 2. and thou shalt be called by a n. name
65. 17. I create n. heavens and a n. earth, 66. 22.
Jer. 26. 10. the n. gate of the Lord's house, 36. 10.
31. 22. the L. hath created a n. thing in the earth
Lam. 3. 23. the Lord's mercies are n. every morning
Ezek. 11. 19. I will put a n. spirit within you, 36. 26.
18. 31. and make you a n. heart and a n. spirit
47. 12. trees which shall bring forth n. fruit
Mat. 9. 16. no man putteth a piece of n. cloth to
an old garment, Mark 2. 21. Luke 5. 36.
17. but they put n. wine into n. bottles, and both
are preserved, Mark 2. 22. Luke 5. 38.
13. 52. bringeth out of his treasure things n. and old
26. 28. for this is my blood of the n. testament,
Mark 14. 24. Luke 22. 20. 1 Cor. 11. 25.
29. until I drink it n. with you, Mark 14. 25.
27. 60. Joseph laid the body in his own n. tomb
Mark 1. 27. saying, what n. doctrine is this?
16. 17. they shall speak with n. tongues
John 13. 34. a n. commandment I give unto you
19. 41. a n. sepulchre, wherein was never man laid
Acts 17. 19. may we know what this n. doctrine is?
21. but either to tell or to hear some n. thing.
1 Cor. 5. 7. purge out, that ye may be a n. lump
2 Cor. 3. 6. made us able ministers of the n. testament
5. 17. if any man be in Christ, he is a n. creature;
behold, all things are become n.
Gal. 6. 15. nor uncircumcision, but a n. creature
Eph. 2. 15. of twain, one n. man, so making peace
4. 24. and that ye put on the n. man. Col. 3. 10.
Heb. 9. 15. he is the Mediator of the n. testament
10. 20. by a n. and living way hath consecrated
1 Pet. 2. 2. as n. born babes desire the milk of word
2 Pet. 3. 13. we look for n. heavens and a n. earth
1 John 2. 7. I write no n. commandment unto you
8. a n. commandment I write unto you
2 John 5. not as though I wrote a n. commandment
Rev. 2. 17. n. name written, which no man knoweth
3. 12. n. Jerusalem, 21. 2. || 3. 12. write my n. name
5. 9. and they sung a n. song, saying, 14. 3.
21. 1. I saw a n. heaven and a n. earth
5. he said, behold, I make all things n.
See COVENANT, MOON.

NEW *Wine*.

Neh. 10. 39. shall bring offering of the n. wine
13. 5. prepar. a chamber where the n. wine was laid
12. brought tithe of n. wine unto the treasuries
Prov. 3. 10. thy presses shall burst out with n. wine
Isa. 24. 7. the n. wine mourneth, the vine languisheth
49. † 26. drunken with their blood as with n. wine
65. 8. as the n. wine is found in the cluster
Hos. 4. 11. wine and n. wine take away the heart
9. 2. and the n. wine shall fail in her
Joel 1. 5. the n. wine is cut off || 10. n. wine is dried up
3. 18. mountains shall drop n. wine, Amos 9. † 13.
Hag. 1. 11. I called for a drought on the n. wine
Zech. 9. 17. n. wine shall make the maids cheerful
Mat. 9. 17. do men put n. wine into old bottles, but
n. wine into new bottles, Mark 2. 22. Luke 5. 37.
Acts 2. 13. others said, these men are full of n. wine

NEWS.

Prov. 25. 25. so is good n. from a far country

NEWLY.

Deut. 32. 17. sacrificed to new gods that came n. up
Judg. 7. 19. they had but n. set the watch
2 Sam. 24. † 6. they came to the land n. inhabited
1 Tim. 3. † 6. not one n. come to the faith

NEWNESS.

Rom. 6. 4. even so we also should walk in n. of life
7. 6. that we should serve in n. of spirit, not oldness

NEXT.

Gen. 17. 21. Sarah shall bear at this set time n. year
Exod. 12. 4. let him and his neighbour n. take a lamb
Num. 11. 32. stood up all the n. day and gathered
27. 11. ye shall give inheritance to his kinsman n.
Deut. 21. 3. the city which is n. to the slain man
6. the elders of the city n. to the slain man
25. † 5. her n. kinsman shall take her to wife
Ruth 2. 20. the man is one of our n. kinsmen
1 Sam. 23. 17. thou king, and I shall be n. to thee
30. 17. David smote them to the evening of n. day
2 Chron. 28. 7. Elkanah that was n. to the king
Esth. 10. 3. Mordecai was n. to king Ahasuerus
Jonah 4. 7. a worm the n. day smote the gourd
Mat. 27. 62. the n. day that followed the preparation
Mark 1. 38. he said, let us go into the n. towns
John 1. 29. the n. day John seeth Jesus coming
Acts 4. 3. they put them in hold unto the n. day
7. 26. the n. day Moses shewed himself to them
13. 42. that these words be preached n. sabbath, 44.

NIGH.

Lev. 21. 3. for his sister a virgin that is n. to him
25. 49. any that is n. of kin may redeem him
Num. 24. 17. I shall behold him, but not n. a star
Deut. 4. 7. what nation, who hath God so n. to them?
13. 7. entice thee to gods of the people n. to thee
22. 2. if thy brother be not n. unto thee
30. 14. the word is n. unto thee, Rom. 10. 8.
2 Sam. 11. 20. wherefore approached ye so n.? 21.
1 Kings 8. 59. let these my words be n. to the Lord
Psal. 34. 18. L. is n. them who are of broken heart
85. 9. his salvation is n. them that fear him
145. 18. the Lord is n. to all that call on him
Joel 2. 1. the day of the Lord is n. at hand
Mat. 24. 32. ye know that summer is n. Luke 21. 30.
Mark 13. 29. know that it is n. even at the doors
Luke 21. 20. know that the desolation thereof is n.
28. look up, for your redemption draweth n.
31. know that the kingdom of God is n. at hand
John 6. 4. and the passover, a feast of Jews, was n.
11. 55. the Jews' passover was n. at hand
19. 42. for the sepulchre was n. at hand
Eph. 2. 13. ye are made n. by the blood of Christ
17. came and preached peace to them that were n.
Phil. 2. 27. for he was sick, n. unto death, 30.
Heb. 6. 8. is rejected, is n. unto cursing, to be burned
See CAME, DRAW.

NIGHT

Signifies, [1] *That time while the sun is absent and below our horizon*, Exod. 12. 30, 31. Matt. 27. 64. [2] *Suddenly and unexpectedly*, Isa. 15. 1. Luke 12. 20. [3] *A time of ignorance and unbelief*, Rom. 13. 12. [4] *Adversity and affliction*, Isa. 21. 12. [5] *Death*, John 9. 4.

Gen. 1. 5. the light day, and the darkness he called n.
14. let there be lights, to divide the day from n.
16. he made the lesser light to rule the n.
19. 2. tarry all n. Num. 22. 19. Judg. 19. 6, 9.
5. where are men which came in to thee this n.?
33. they made him drink wine that n. 34, 35.
24. 54. tarried all n. 28. 11. | 31. 54. | 32. 13, 21.
26. 24. the Lord appeared to Isaac the same n.
30. 15. Rachel said, he shall lie with thee to n. 16.
40. 5. dreamed each man his dream in one n. 41. 11.
46. 2. God spake to Israel in visions of the n.
49. 27. and at n. he shall divide the spoil
Exod. 12. 8. eat the flesh in that n. roast with fire
12. I will pass through the land of Egypt this n.
42. it is a n. to be much observed to the Lord,
this is that n. of the L. to be observed of Israel
14. 20. the one came not near the other all n.
Lev. 6. 9. the burning on the altar all n.
19. 13. the wages shall not abide with thee all n.
Num. 11. 32. the people stood up all that n.
14. 1. and the people wept that n. and murmured
22. 8. he said to them, lodge here this n. 19.
20. God came to Balaam at n. and said to him
Deut. 16. 4. there shall no leav. bread remain all n.
21. 23. his body shall not remain all n. on the tree
Josh. 2. 2. there came men in hither to n. of Israel
Judg. 6. 40. G. did so that n. for it was dry on fleece
16. 2. laid wait for him all n. and were quiet all n.
19. 10. but the man would not tarry that n.
25. and abused her all the n. until the morning
Ruth 1. 12. if I should have an husband also to n.
3. 2. behold, Boaz winnoweth barley to n.
1 Sam. 15. 11. and Samuel cried to the Lord all n.
16. tell what the Lord hath said to me this n.
19. 10. and David fled and escaped that n.
11. saying, if thou save not thy life to n.
28. 25. Saul rose up and went away that n.
31. 12. the men of Jabesh went all n. and took
2 Sam. 2. 29. Abner and his men walked all n.
32. Joab and his men went all n. and came
4. 7. and gat them away through the plain all n.
12. 16. David went and lay all n. on the earth
17. 1. I will arise and pursue after David this n.
16. saying, lodge not this n. in the plain
19. 7. there will not tarry one with thee this n.
2 Kings 19. 35. that n. the angel of the Lord smote
2 Chron. 1. 7. that n. did God appear to Solomon
Esth. 6. 1. on that n. could not the king sleep
Job 3. 3. let the n. perish in which it was said
7. let that n. be solitary || 4. 13. the visions of the n.
7. 4. when shall I arise, and the n. be gone?
29. 19. and the dew lay all n. on my branch
30. † 3. for want and famine they were dark as n.
36. 20. desire not the n. when people are cut off
Psal. 6. 6. all the n. make I my bed to swim
19. 2. and n. unto n. sheweth knowledge
30. 5. weeping may endure for a n. but joy
59. † 15. if they be not satisfied they will stay all n.
78. 14. he led them all n. with a light of fire
92. 2. to shew forth thy faithfulness every n.
104. 20. thou makest darkness, and it is n.
139. 11. even the n. shall be light about me
Prov. 7. 9. passing in the black and dark n.
31. 15. she ariseth also while it is yet n.
Cant. 1. 13. he shall lie all n. between my breasts
5. 2. and my locks with the drops of the n.
Isa. 5. 11. continue until n. till wine inflame them
16. 3. take counsel, make thy shadow as the n.
21. 4. the n. of my pleasure he turned into fear
† 8. and I am set in my ward every n.
11. watchman, what of the n.? what of the n.?
12. the morning cometh, and also the n.
29. 7. shall be as a dream of a n. vision
Jer. 14. 8. that turneth aside to tarry for a n.
Dan. 2. 19. the secret was revealed in a n. vision
5. 30. in that n. was Belshazzar the king slain
6. 18. then the king passed the n. fasting
Hos. 7. 6. their baker sleepeth all the n.
Joel 1. 13. howl, come, lie all n. in sackcloth
Amos 5. 8. that maketh the day dark with n.
Jonah 4. 10. which came up in a n. perished in a n.
Mic. 3. 6. therefore n. shall be to you, shall be dark
Mat. 14. 25. in the fourth watch of n. Jesus went
to them walking on the sea, Mark 6. 48.
26. 31. then Jesus saith to them, all ye shall be
offended because of me this n. Mark 14. 27.
34. this n. before cock-crow, thou shalt deny me
Luke 5. 5. we have toiled all n. and taken nothing
6. 12. he continued all n. in prayer to God
12. 20. this n. thy soul shall be required of thee
17. 34. in that n. two shall be in one bed
Luke 21. 37. at n. he went out and abode in mount
John 9. 4. the n. cometh when no man can work
13. 30. he immediately went out, and it was n.
21. 3. and that n. they caught nothing
Acts 12. 6. the same n. Peter was sleeping, bound
16. 33. he took them the same hour of the n.
23. 11. the n. following the Lord stood by him
23. make ready soldiers at third hour of the n.
27. 23. stood by me this n. the angel of God
Rom. 13. 12. the n. is far spent, the day is at hand
1 Cor. 11. 23. the same n. in which he was betrayed
1 Thess. 5. 5. we are not of the n. nor of darkness
Rev. 21. 25. there shall be no n. there, 22. 5.

By NIGHT.

Gen. 20. 3. God came to Abimelech in a dream by n.
31. 24. God came to Laban in a dream by n.
39. whether stolen by day, or stolen by n.
40. the drought consumed me, and the frost by n.
Exod. 12. 31. he called for Moses and Aaron by n.
13. 21. the Lord went before them by n. in a pillar
of fire, 22. | 14. 20. | 40. 38. Neh. 9. 12.
Num. 9. 16. and the appearance of fire by n.
21. whether cloud was taken up by day or by n.
Deut. 1. 33. in fire by n. to shew you the way
16. 1. God brought you forth out of Egypt by n.
23. 10. by uncleanness that chanceth him by n.
Josh. 8. 3. and Joshua sent them away by n.
Judg. 6. 27. and so it was that he did it by n.
9. 32. up by n. thou and thy people with thee
20. 5. and beset the house round about by n.
1 Sam. 14. 36. go down after the Philistines by n.
26. 7. David and Abishai came to the people by n.
28. 8. Saul came to the woman by n. and said
2 Sam. 21. 10. nor the beasts of the field by n.
1 Kings 3. 5. Ld. appeared to Sol. by n. 2 Chr. 7. 12.
2 Kings 6. 14. came by n. and compassed the city
8. 21. rose by n. and smote Edomites, 2 Chr. 21. 9.
25. 4. all the men of war fled by n. Jer. 52. 7.
Psal. 91. 5. thou shalt not be afraid of terror by n.
121. 6. nor shall the moon smite thee by n.
134. 1. that by n. stand in the house of the Lord
136. 9. moon and stars to rule by n. Jer. 31. 35.
Prov. 31. 18. her candle goeth not out by n.
Cant. 3. 1. by n. on my bed I sought him whom
Isa. 4. 5. the shining of a flaming fire by n.
Jer. 6. 5. let us go by n. and destroy her palaces
39. 4. they fled, and went forth out of the city by n.
49. 9. if thieves by n. they will destroy till have
Dan. 7. 2. I saw in my vision by n. and behold
Obad. 5. if thieves came to thee, if robbers by n. would
they not have stolen till they had enough?
Mat. 2. 14. took the young child and his mother by n.
27. 64. lest his disciples come by n. and steal, 28. 13.
Luke 2. 8. keeping watch over their flock by n.
John 3. 2. Nicodemus came to Jesus by n. 19. 39.
Acts 5. 19. the angel by n. opened the prison-doors
9. 25. they took Paul by n. and let him down
17. 10. sent away Paul and Silas by n. to Berea
See DAY.

In the NIGHT.

Exod. 12. 30. Pharaoh and his servants rose in the n.
Num. 11. 9. when the dew fell on the camp in the n.
1 Kings 3. 19. and this woman's child died in the n.
2 Kings 7. 12. and the king arose in the n. and said
Neh. 2. 12. I arose in the n. || 15. I went up in the n.
4. 22. that in the n. they may be a guard to us
6. 10. yea, in the n. will they come to slay thee
Job 5. 14. and grope in the noon-day, as in the n.
24. 14. in the n. the murderer is as a thief
27. 20. a tempest stealeth him away in the n.
34. 25. and he overturneth them in the n.
35. 10. where is God, who giveth songs in the n.?
Psal. 16. 7. my reins instruct me in the n. seasons
17. 3. thou hast visited me in the n. and tried me
22. 2. I cry in the n. season, and am not silent
42. 8. and in the n. his song shall be with me
77. 2. my sore ran in the n. and ceased not
6. I call to remembrance my song in the n.
90. 4. a thousand years are but as a watch in the n.
105. 39. he spread a fire to give light in the n.
119. 55. I have remembered thy name in the n.
Eccl. 2. 23. his heart taketh not rest in the n.
Cant. 3. 8. hath his sword because of fear in the n.
Isa. 15. 1. in the n. Ar and Kir of Moab is laid waste
26. 9. with my soul have I desired thee in the n.
30. 29. ye shall have a song as in the n.
59. 10. we stumble at noon-day as in the n.
Jer. 36. 30. shall be cast out in the n. to the frost
Lam. 1. 2. she weep. sore in the n. || 2. 19. cry out in n.
Hos 4. 5. the prophet shall fall with thee in the n.
John 11. 10. if a man walk in the n. he stumbleth
Acts 16. 9. a vision appeared to Paul in the n. 18. 9.
1 Thess. 5. 2. day cometh as a thief in the n. 2 Pet. 3. 10.
7. they that sleep, sleep in the n. are drunk. in the n.

NIGHTS.

Gen. 7. 4. I will cause it rain forty days, forty n. 12.
Job 7. 3. wearisome n. are appointed to me
Isa. 21. 8. and I am set in my ward whole n.
See DAYS.

NIGHT-*hawk*.

Lev. 11. 16. owl and n. ye shall not eat, Deut. 14. 15.

NIGHT-*watches*.

Psal. 63. 6. when I meditate on thee in the n.-w.
119. 148. mine eyes prevent the n.-w. to meditate

NINE.

Num. 29. 26. on fifth day n. bullocks, two rams
34. 13. which the Lord commanded to give to the n.
tribes and half tribe, Josh. 13. 7. | 14. 2.
Deut. 3. 11. Og's bedstead was n. cubits in length
2 Sam. 24. 8. Joab came to Jerus. at end of n. months
Neh. 11. 1. and n. parts to dwell in other cities
Luke 17. 17. ten cleansed, but where are the n.?
See HUNDRED.

NINETEEN.

2 Sam. 2. 30. there lacked of David's servants n. men

NINETEENTH.

2 Kings 25. 8. in the n. year of Nebuchadnezzar the
house of the Lord was burnt, Jer. 52. 12.

NINETY.

Gen. 5. 9. Enos lived n. years, and begat Cainan
17. 17. shall Sarah, that is n. years old, bear?
Ezek. 41. 12. the length of the building n. cubits

NINETY-FIVE.

Ezra 2. 20. the children of Gibbar *n.-five*
Neh. 7. 25. the children of Gibeon *n.-five*

NINETY-SIX.

Ezra 8. 35. offered for all Israel *n.-six* rams
Jer. 52. 23. were *n.-six* pomegranates on a side

NINETY-EIGHT.

1 *Sam.* 4. 15. now Eli was *n.-eight* years old
Ezra 2. 16. the children of Ater *n.-eight*, *Neh.* 7. 21.

NINETY-NINE.

Gen. 17. 1. Abram was *n.-nine* years ol l, L. appeared
24. was *n.-nine* years old when he was circumcised
Mat. 18. 12. doth he not leave the *n.-nine*, and seeketh that which is gone astray? 13. *Luke* 15. 4, 7.

NINTH.

Lev. 25. 22. ye shall eat of old fruit till the *n.* year
2 *Kings* 17. 6. in *n.* of Hosh. Samaria taken, 18. 10.
25. 1. in the *n.* year of Zedekiah, Nebuchadnezzar came up, *Jer.* 39. 1. | 52. 4. *Ezek.* 24. 1.
1 *Chr.* 12. 12. Elzabad the *n.* captain of the Gadites
24. 11. the *n.* lot came forth to Jeshuah
27. 12. *n.* captain for the *n.* month was Abiezer
Mat. 20. 5. he went out about the sixth and *n.* hour
27. 45. from sixth hour there was darkness over all the land unto the *n.* hour, *Mark* 15. 33.
46. *n.* hour Jesus gave up the ghost, *Mark* 15. 34.
Acts 3. 1. at the hour of prayer, being the *n.* hour
10. 3. Cornelius saw a vision about the *n.* hour, 30.
Rev. 21. 20. the *n.* foundation was a topaz
See DAY, MONTH.

NITRE.

Prov. 25. 20. as vinegar upon *n.* so is he singing songs
Jer. 2. 22. though thou wash thee with *n.* and soap

NO.

Gen. 13. 8. let there be *no* strife betw. me and thee
15. 3. behold, to me thou hast given *no* seed
26. 29. be an oath that thou wilt do us *no* hurt
37. 22. shed *no* blood, and lay *no* hand upon him
38. 21. there was *no* harlot in this place, 22.
40. 8. *no* interpreter || 42. 11. we are *no* spies, 31, 34.
47. 4. thy servants have *no* pasture, *Lam.* 1. 6.
Exod. 5. 16. is *no* straw given to thy servants, 18.
8. 22. that *no* swarms of flies shall be there
12. 16. *no* work shall be done, *Lev.* 16. 29. | 23. 3, 7, 21, 28, 31. *Num.* 29. 1. *Deut.* 16. 8.
19. seven days *no* leaven shall be found, 13. 3, 7.
14. 11. because there were *no* graves in Egypt
16. 18. he that gathered little had *no* lack
21. 22. hurt a woman, and *no* mischief follow
22. 2. there shall *no* blood be shed for him
23. 8. thou shalt take *no* gift, gift blindeth the wise
32. thou shalt make *no* covenant with them
30. 9. ye shall offer *no* strange incense thereon
12. that there be *no* plague amongst them
34. 14. for thou shalt worship *no* other god
17. thou shalt make thee *no* molten gods
35. 3. ye shall kindle *no* fire in your habitations
Lev. 2. 11. ye shall burn *no* leaven in any offering
5. 11. put *no* oil upon it || 7. 23. ye shall eat *no* fat
7. 26. ye shall eat *no* manner of blood, 17. 12, 14.
12. 4. ye shall touch *no* hallowed thing
13. 21. and there be *no* white hairs therein, 26.
31. *no* black hair || 32. there be *no* yellow hair
19. 15. do *no* unrighteousness in judgment, 35.
20. 14. that there be *no* wickedness among you
22. 13. but there shall *no* stranger eat thereof
21. there shall be *no* blemish therein
25. 31. the houses which have *no* walls round about
36. take thou *no* usury of him, or increase
26. 1. ye shall make you *no* idols nor graven image
27. 28. *no* devoted thing shall be sold or redeem.
Num. 5. 8. if the man have *no* kinsman to recompense
13. and there be *no* witness against her
6. 3. and shall drink *no* vinegar of wine
5. there shall *no* razor come upon his head
6. he shall come at *no* dead body
16. 40. that *no* stranger come near to offer incense
26. 33. Zelophehad had *no* sons, but daughters, 27. 3, 4. *Josh.* 17. 3. 1 *Chron.* 23. 22. | 24. 28.
27. 8. if a man die and have *no* son then cause
9. and if he have *no* daughter, ye shall give
17. congregation of Lord be not as sheep that have *no* shepherd, *Ezek.* 34. 5. *Mat.* 9. 36.
35. 31. *no* satisfaction for the life of a murderer, 32.
Deut. 4. 12. ye heard, but saw *no* similitude, 15.
7. 16. thine eye shall have *no* pity on them
10. 9. Levi hath *no* part with his brethren, 14. 27, 29. | 18. 1. *Josh.* 14. 4. | 18. 7.
15. 4. when there shall be *no* poor among you
20. 12. if it will make *no* peace with thee
28. 32. there shall be *no* might in thy hand
65. among these nations thou shalt find *no* ease
32. 20. they are children in whom is *no* faith
Josh. 10. 14. there was *no* day like that before
22. 25. ye have *no* part in the Lord, 27.
Judg. 17. 6. there was *no* king in Israel, 18. 1. | 21. 25.
18. 7. there was *no* magistrate || 28. *no* deliverer
10. where there is *no* want of any thing, 19. 19.
1 *Sam.* 2. 24. for it is *no* good report that I hear
3. 1. word was precious, there was *no* open vision
21. 9. take it, for there is *no* other, save that here
2 *Sam.* 12. 6. shall restore, because he had *no* pity
13. 12. *no* such thing ought to be done in Israel
15. 26. if he say, I have *no* delight in thee
18. 18. I have *no* son to keep my name in remembr.
20. 1. Sheba said, we have *no* part in David
1 *Kings* 8. 23. there is *no* God like thee in heaven
22. 18. he would prophesy *no* good concerning me
2 *Kings* 1. 16. is it not because there is *no* God in Isr.
17. because Ahaziah had *no* son
10. 31. Jehu took *no* heed to walk in the law
1 *Chron.* 2. 34. now Sheshan had *no* sons, but daugh.
16. 22. do my prophets *no* harm, *Psal.* 105. 15.
2 *Chron.* 18. 16. that have *no* shepherd, *Zech.* 10. 2.
19. 7. there is *no* iniquity with the Lord
20. 12. we have *no* might against this company
21. 19. his people made *no* burning for him
35. 18. there was *no* passover like to that
36. 16. they mocked till there was *no* remedy
Ezra 9. 14. so that there should be *no* remnant
Neh. 2. 20. ye have *no* portion in Jerusalem
13. 26. there was *no* king like Solomon

Job 4. 18. he put *no* trust in his servants
5. 19. in seven there shall *no* evil touch thee
9. 25. see *no* good || 10. 18. that *no* eye had seen me
12. 14. he shutteth, and there can be *no* opening
24. causeth to wander where there is *no* way
13. 4. ye are all physicians of *no* value
16. 18. O earth, let my cry have *no* place
18. 17. he shall have *no* name in the street
19. 16. I called my servant, he gave me *no* answer
24. 15. *no* eye shall see me || 30. 13. have *no* helper
Psal. 3. 2. there is *no* help for him in God
32. 2. in whose spirit there is *no* guile
34. 9. there is *no* want to them that fear him
36. 1. there is *no* fear of God before his eyes
53. 5. they were in fear where *no* fear was
55. 19. because they have *no* changes
84. 11. *no* good will he withhold from them
91. 10. there shall *no* evil befall thee
92. 15. there is *no* unrighteousness in him
119. 3. they do *no* iniquity, they walk in his ways
146. 3. son of man, in whom there is *no* help
Prov. 12. 21. there shall *no* evil happen to the just
17. 16. to get wisdom, seeing he hath *no* heart to it
21. 30. there is *no* wisdom against the Lord
Eccl. 4. 1. were oppressed, and they had *no* comforter
9. 10. for there is *no* work in the grave
Cant. 4. 7. my love, there is *no* spot in thee
8. 8. we have a little sister, and she hath *no* breasts
Isa. 1. 6. there is *no* soundness in it, but wounds
5. 8. join field to field, till there be *no* place
8. 20. it is because there is *no* light in them
9. 7. of his government there shall be *no* end
34. 16. *no* one of these shall fail, none shall want
40. 29. and to them that have *no* might
43. 11. and besides me there is *no* Saviour
48. 22. there is *no* peace to the wicked, 57. 21.
50. 10. that walketh in darkness, and hath *no* light
53. 2. he hath *no* form, nor comeliness, nor beauty
54. 17. *no* weapon formed against thee shall prosper
55. 1. and he that hath *no* money, come ye, buy
57. 10. thou saidst not, there is *no* hope, *Jer.* 2. 25.
59. 8. there is *no* judgment in their goings
16. he wondered that there was *no* intercessor
Jer. 2. 11. changed their gods, which are yet *no* gods
30. your children received *no* correction
6. 14. peace, peace, when there is *no* peace, 8. 11.
23. they are cruel, and have *no* mercy
8. 15. we looked for peace, but *no* good came, 14. 19.
10. 14. and there is *no* breath in them, 51. 17.
22. 28. a vessel wherein is *no* pleasure, 48. 38.
25. 6. provoke me not, I will do you *no* hurt
39. 12. do him *no* harm || 42. 14. shall see *no* war
48. 8. spoiler shall come, and *no* city shall escape
49. 1. hath Israel *no* sons? hath he *no* heir?
Lam. 1. 9. she came down, she had *no* comforter
Ezek. 13. 10. peace, and there was *no* peace, 16.
18. 32. I have *no* pleasure in death of him, 33. 11.
29. 18. yet had he *no* wages, nor his army
Dan. 3. 29. because there is *no* other god can deliver
Hos. 4. 1. because there is *no* truth nor mercy
6. reject thee, that thou shalt be *no* priest to me
10. 3. now they shall say, we have *no* king
Amos 7. 14. I was *no* prophet, neither prophet's son
Mic. 3. 7. their lips, for there is *no* answer of God
4. 9. why dost thou cry out? is there *no* king in thee?
Nah. 3. 19. there is *no* healing of thy bruise
Hab. 1. 14. as the creeping things that have *no* ruler
Zeph. 3. 5. but the unjust knoweth *no* shame
Zech. 8. 17. love *no* false oath || 9. 8. *no* oppressor
Mal. 1. 10. I have *no* pleasure in you, saith the L.
Mat. 5. 20. ye shall in *no* case enter into heaven
26. thou shalt by *no* means come out thence
6. 34. take therefore *no* thought for the morrow, 10. 19. *Mark* 13. 11. *Luke* 12. 11, 22.
22. 23. which say that there is *no* resurrection, *Mark* 12. 18. *Acts* 23. 8. 1 *Cor.* 15. 12, 13.
Mark 13. 20. shortened those days, *no* flesh be saved
Luke 15. 7. just persons, which need *no* repentance
23. 4. I find *no* fault in him, 14. *John* 18. 38. | 19. 4, 6.
John 4. 17. I have *no* husband || 6. 53. ye have *no* life
7. 52. search, for out of Galilee ariseth *no* prophet
9. 41. if ye were blind, ye should have *no* sin
11. 10. he stumbleth, because there is *no* light in him
13. 8. if I wash thee not, thou hast *no* part with me
15. 22. now they have *no* cloak for their sin
19. 15. priests answered, we have *no* king but Cesar
Acts 15. 9. put *no* difference between us and them
18. 15. for I will be *no* judge of such matters
21. 25. written that they observe *no* such thing
25. 10. to the Jews have I done *no* wrong
28. 2. the people shewed us *no* little kindness
Rom. 3. 22. all that believe, for there is *no* difference
4. 15. for where *no* law is, *no* transgression
5. 13. sin is not imputed where there is *no* law
7. 18. that in my flesh dwelleth *no* good thing
10. 19. to jealousy by them that are *no* people
13. 10. love worketh *no* ill to his neighbour
1 *Cor.* 1. 29. that *no* flesh glory in his presence
4. 11. and have *no* certain dwelling-place
8. 13. I will eat *no* flesh while the world standeth
10. 13. there hath *no* temptation taken you but such
11. 16. we have *no* such custom, nor the churches
12. 21. I have *no* need of thee || 13. 2. *no* charity
14. 28. if there be *no* interpreter, let him keep
2 *Cor.* 5. 21. made him sin for us, who knew *no* sin
6. 3. giving *no* offence in any thing, that ministry
13. 7. now I pray to God that ye do *no* evil
Gal. 5. 23. meekness, against such there is *no* law
Eph. 5. 11. have *no* fellowsh. with works of darkness
Phil. 2. 7. but made himself of *no* reputation
3. 3. and have *no* confidence in the flesh
1 *Thess.* 4. 13. even as others which have *no* hope
2 *Thess.* 3. 14. and have *no* company with him
2 *Tim.* 3. 9. but they shall proceed *no* further
Heb. 6. 13. because he could swear by *no* greater
8. 7. *no* place have been sought for the second
9. 22. without shedding of blood is *no* remission
10. 38. my soul shall have *no* pleasure in him
12. 11. *no* chastening for the present seemeth joyous
17. for he found *no* place of repentance, though he
13. 14. here have we *no* continuing city, but seek
Jam. 1. 17. with whom is *no* variableness, nor shad.

1 *Pet.* 2. 22. who did *no* sin, nor was guile found
2 *Pet.* 1. 20. *no* prophecy of private interpretation
1 *John* 1. 5. and in him is *no* darkness at all
8. if we say, we have *no* sin, we deceive ourselves
3. 5. in him is *no* sin, || 4. 18. there is *no* fear in love
3 *John* 4. I have *no* greater joy than to hear
Rev. 14. 5. in their mouth was found *no* guile
17. 12. which have received *no* kingdom as yet
18. 7. I am *no* widow, and shall see *no* sorrow
20. 11. and there was found *no* place for them
21. 22. *no* temple therein || 23. *no* need of the sun
25. *no* night there, they need *no* candle, 22. 5.
See BREAD, CHILD, CHILDREN, INHERITANCE, KNOWLEDGE, MAN, POWER.

No RAIN.

Deut. 11. 17. he shut up the heaven, that there be *no rain*, 1 *Kings* 8. 35. 2 *Chron.* 6. 26. | 7. 13.
1 *Kings* 17. 7. there had been *no rain* in the land, *Jer.* 14. 4.
Isa. 5. 6. clouds, that they rain *no rain* upon it
Jer. 3. 3. and there hath been *no* latter *rain*
Zech. 14. 17. even upon them there shall be *no rain*
18. and if Egypt that have *no rain* come not

NO *rest.*

Gen. 8. 9. but the dove found *no rest* for her foot
Job 30. 17. and my sinews take *no rest*
Prov. 29. 9. whether he rage or laugh there is *no r.*
Isa. 23. 12. there also shalt thou have *no rest*
62. 7. and give him *no r.* till he establish Jerusalem
Jer. 45. 3. I fainted in sighing, and find *no rest*
Lam. 1. 3. among the heathen she findeth *no rest*
2. 18. give thyself *no rest* || 5. 5. we have *no rest*
2 *Cor.* 2. 13. I had *no rest* in my spirit, because
7. 5. when come into Macedonia, our flesh had *no r.*
Rev. 14. 11. they have *no rest* day nor night

NO *strength.*

1 *Sam.* 28. 20. and there was *no strength* in Saul
Job 26. 2. how savest thou arm that hath *no strength*
Psal. 88. 4. I am as a man that hath *no strength*
Dan. 10. 8. and there remained *no str.* in me, 17.
16. are turned on me, I have retained *no strength*
Heb. 9. 17. otherwise it is of *no strength* at all
See WATER, WRATH.

NO, *Adverb.*

Exod. 3. 19. not let you go, *no*, not by mighty hand
16. 4. whether walk in my law, or *no*, *Deut.* 8. 2.
Judg. 4. 20. is any man here, thou shalt say, *no*
15. 13. *no*, but we will bind thee, and deliver thee
1 *Sam.* 1. 15. *no*, my lord, I am of a sorrowful spir.
20. 15. *no*, not when the Lord hath cut off enemies
Job 23. 6. *no*, but he would put strength in me
36. 19. *no*, not gold, nor the forces of strength
Psal. 14. 3. that doeth good, *no*, not one, 53. 3.
Eccl. 10. 20. curse not king, *no*, not in thy thought
Isa. 30. 16. *no*, for we will flee upon horses
Jer. 2. 25. *no*, for I have loved strangers, after them
42. 14. *no*, but we will go into the land of Egypt
Amos 6. 10. is there any with thee? he shall say, *no*
Hag. 2. 12. the priests answered and said, *no*
Zech. 4. 5. knowest what these be, I said, *no*, 13.
Mat. 8. 10. so great faith, *no*, not in Isr. *Luke* 7. 9.
24. 21. to this time, *no*, nor ever shall be
36. *no* not the angels, but my Father only
Mark 2. 2. no room, *no* not so much as about the door
5. 3. no man could bind him, *no*, not with chains
Luke 20. 22. for us to give tribute to Cesar, or *no?*
23. 15. *no*, nor yet Herod; for I sent you to him
John 1. 21. art thou that prophet? he said, *no*
9. 25. whether he be a sinner or *no*, I know not
21. 5. have ye any meat? they answered, *no*
Acts 7. 5. *no*, not so much as to set his foot on
Rom. 3. 9. are we better than they? *no*, in no wise
10. there is none righteous, *no*, not one, 12.
1 *Cor.* 5. 11. with such a one, *no*, not to eat
6. 5. *no*, not one that shall be able to judge between
Gal. 2. 5. place by subjection, *no*, not for an hour

NO *where.*

1 *Sam.* 10. 14. when we saw that they were *no where*
See MORE, WISE.

NOBLE

Signifies, [1] *A person honourable, either by his birth or merit*, Neh. 6. 17. Acts 24. 3. [2] *Such as are of a more tractable disposition, of a more excellent, divine, commendable temper than others*, Acts 17. 11. [3] *Valiant ones*, Nah. 3. † 18. [4] *A courtier, or ruler*, John 4. † 46.
Ezra 4. 10. whom the *n.* Asnapper brought over
Esth. 6. 9. one of the king's most *n.* princes
Jer. 2. 21. I had planted thee a *n.* vine
Luke 19. 12. a *n.* man went into a far country
John 4. 46. there was a *n.* man whose son was sick
49. *n.* man saith, sir, come down ere my child die
Acts 17. 11. the Bereans more *n.* than Thessalonians
24. 3. we accept it always, most *n.* Felix, 26. 25.
1 *Cor.* 1. 26. how that not many *n.* are called

NOBLES.

Exod. 24. 11. on the *n.* of Israel he laid not his hand
Num. 21. 18. the *n.* of the people digged it
Judg. 5. 13. dominion over the *n.* among the people
1 *Kings* 21. 8. Jezebel sent letters to the *n.* in his city
2 *Chron.* 23. 20. Jehoiada took the *n.* of the people
Neh. 2. 16. nor had I as yet told it to the *n.*
3. 5. the *n.* put not their necks to the work
5. 7. and I rebuked the *n.* and the rulers
6. 17. the *n.* of Judah sent letters to Tobiah
7. 5. God put into mine heart to gather the *n.*
10. 29. they clave to their brethren, their *n.*
13. 17. I contended with the *n.* of Judah
Job 29. 10. the *n.* held their peace
Psal. 83. 11. make their *n.* like Oreb and Zeeb
149. 8. to bind their *n.* with fetters of iron
Prov. 8. 16. by me princes rule, and *n.* all judges
Eccl. 10. 17. when thy king is the son of *n.*
Isa. 13. 2. they may go into the gates of the *n.*
34. 12. they shall call the *n.* to the kingdom
43. 14. and have brought down all their *n.*
Jer. 14. 3. the *n.* sent their little ones to the waters
27. 20. Nebuchadnezzar carried captive *n.* of Judah
30. 21. and their *n.* shall be of themselves
39. 6. the king of Babylon slew all the *n.* of Judah
Jonah 3. 7. by the decree of the king and his *n.*
Nah. 3. 18. Assyria, thy *n.* shall dwell in the dust

NOISE.

Exod. 20. 18. people heard the n. of the trumpet
32. 17. he said, there is a n. of war in the camp
18. but the n. of them that sing do I hear
Josh. 6. 10. ye shall not shout nor make any n.
Judg. 5. 11. are delivered from the n. of archers
1 Sam. 4. 6. what meaneth the n. of this shout? 14.
14. 19. the n. in the host of Philistines increased
1 Kings 1. 41. wherefore is this n. of the city?
45. this is the n. that ye have heard
18. †41. there is a n. of abundance of rain
2 Kings 7. 6. the n. of chariots, and a n. of horses
11. 13. Athaliah heard n. of guard, 2 Chron. 23. 12.
1 Chron. 15. 28. making a n. with psalteries
Ezra 3. 13. not discern n. of joy, from n. of weeping
Job 36. 29. any understand the n. of his tabernacle
33. the n. thereof sheweth concerning it
37. 2. hear attentively the n. of his voice
Psal. 33. 3. play skilfully with a loud n.
40. †2. he brought me up out of a pit of n.
42. 7. deep calleth at the n. of thy water-spouts
55. 2. I mourn in my complaint, and make a n.
59. 6. they make a n. like a dog, 14.
65. 7. who stilleth the n. of the seas, n. of waves
66. 1. make a joyful n. to God, all ye lands, 81. 1. | 95. 1, 2. | 98. 4, 6. | 100. 1.
93. 4. the Lord is mightier than the n. of waters
Isa. 9. 5. for every battle is with confused n.
13. 4. the n. of a multitude in the mountains, a tumultuous n. of the kingdoms of nations
14. 11. the n. of thy viols is brought down
17. 12. which make a n. like the n. of the seas
24. 8. the n. of them that rejoice endeth
18. he who fleeth from the n. of fear
25. 5. thou shalt bring down the n. of strangers
29. 6. shall be visited of the Lord with great n.
31. 4. nor abase himself for the n. of them
33. 3. at the n. of the tumult the people fled
60. †5. the n. of sea shall be turned toward thee
66. 6. a voice of n. from the city and temple
Jer. 4. 19. my heart maketh a n. in me
29. the city shall flee for the n. of horsemen
10. 22. behold, the n. of the bruit is come
11. 16. with the n. of great tumult he kindled
25. 31. a n. shall come to the ends of the earth
46. 17. Pharaoh king of Egypt is but a n.
47. 3. at the n. of the stamping of his horses
49. 21. the earth is moved at the n. of their fall, at the cry the n. was heard in the Red sea
50. 46. at the n. of taking of Babylon
51. 55. a n. of their voice is uttered
Lam. 2. 7. the enemy made n. in house of the Lord
Ezek. 1. 24. when they went, I heard the n. of their wings, like the n. of great waters, 43. 2.
3. 13. the n. of the wheels, the n. of a great rushing
19. 7. the land was desolate by the n. of his roaring
26. 10. thy walls shall shake at the n. of horsemen
13. I will cause the n. of my songs to cease
37. 7. and as I prophesied, there was a n.
Joel 2. 5. like the n. of chariots, like the n. of fire
Amos 5. 23. take from me the n. of thy songs
Mic. 2. 12. they shall make a great n. by reason
Nah. 3. 2. the n. of a whip, n. of rattling wheels
Zeph. 1. 10. the n. of a cry from the fish gate
Zech. 9. 15. they shall drink and make a n.
Mat. 9. 23. he saw the people making a n.
2 Pet. 3. 10. heavens shall pass away with great n.
Rev. 6. 1. I heard as it were the n. of thunder

NOISED.

Josh. 6. 27. Joshua, his fame was n. thro' the country
Mark 2. 1. it was n. that he was in the house
Luke 1. 65. all these sayings were n. abroad
Acts 2. 6. now when this was n. abroad

NOISOME.

Exod. 8. †21. I will send a mixture of n. beasts
Job 31. †40. n. weeds grow instead of barley
Psal. 91. 3. shall deliver thee from the n. pestilence
Ezek. 14. 21. when I send the sword and n. beast
Rev. 16. 2. fell a n. and grievous sore on the men

NONE.

Gen. 28. 17. this is n. other but the house of God
Exod. 12. 22. n. of you shall go out at the door
15. 26. I will put n. of these diseases upon thee
16. 26. on the seventh day, in it there shall be n.
27. some went to gather, and they found n.
20. 3. shalt have n. other gods before me, Deut. 5. 7.
23. 15. n. shall appear before me empty, 34. 20.
Lev. 18. 6. n. shall approach to any near of kin
21. 1. there shall n. be defiled for the dead
22. 30. shall leave n. of it until morrow, Num. 9. 12.
25. 26. and if the man have n. to redeem it
26. 6. shall lie down, and n. shall make you afraid
17. ye shall flee when n. pursueth, 36, 37.
Num. 7. 9. but to the sons of Kohath he gave n.
32. 11. n. that came out of Egypt shall see the land
Deut. 2. 34. we destroyed, and left n. to remain, 3. 3. Josh. 8. 22. | 10. 28, 30, 33. | 11. 8.
7. 15. will put n. of the diseases of Egypt on you
28. 31. thy sheep shall be given, and n. to rescue
66. thou shalt have n. assurance of thy life
Josh. 6. 1. n. went out of Jericho, n. came in
9. 23. n. of you be freed from being bond-men
10. 21. n. moved his tongue against any of Israel
Judg. 21. 8. there came n. to the camp from Jabesh
1 Sam. 2. 2. there is n. holy as the Lord
3. 19. let n. of his words fall to the ground
2 Sam. 18. 12. beware that n. touch the young man
1 Kings 10. 21. n. were of silver, 2 Chron. 9. 20.
15. 22. Asa made a proclamation, n. was exempted
2 Kings 5. 16. as the Lord liveth, I will receive n.
6. 12. n. but Elisha tells the king of Israel
9. 10. and there shall be n. to bury Jezebel
15. let n. go forth or escape out of the city, 10. 25.
10. 11. till Jehu left Ahab n. remaining
19. the prophets of Baal, let n. be wanting
23. look there be n. of the servants of God there
1 Chron. 15. 2. n. ought to carry ark of G. but Levites
2 Chron. 1. 12. honour, such as n. of the kings had
16. 1. he might let n. go out or come in to Asa
20. 6. so that n. is able to withstand thee
24. they were dead bodies fallen, n. escaped
23. 19. n. which was unclean should enter in
Ezra 8. 15. I found there n. of the sons of Levi
Neh. 4. 23. n. of us put off our clothes, saving that
Esth. 1. 8. drinking according to law, n. did compel
4. 2. n. might enter the king's gate in sackcloth
Job 2. 13. sat down, and n. spake a word to him
3. 9. let it look for light but have n.
11. 19. shalt lie down, and n. shall make thee afraid
18. 15. in his tabernacle, because it is n. of his
20. 21. there shall n. of his meat be left
29. 12. delivered him that had n. to help him
35. 10. but n. saith, where is God my Maker?
12. there they cry, but n. giveth answer
Ps. 10. 15. seek out his wickedness till thou find n.
22. 29. and n. can keep alive his own soul
25. 3. let n. that wait on thee be ashamed
34. 22. n. that trust in him shall be desolate
37. 31. law in his heart, n. of his steps shall slide
49. 7. n. of them can redeem his brother
50. 22. lest I tear you, and there be n. to deliver
69. 20. I looked for comforters, but found n.
25. and let n. dwell in their tents
76. 5. n. of the men of might found their hands
81. 11. not hearken, Israel would n. of me
109. 12. let there be n. to extend mercy to him
Prov. 1. 25. and ye would n. of my reproof
30. they would n. of my counsel, they despised
2. 19. n. that go unto her return again, nor take
3. 31. envy not, and choose n. of his ways
Cant. 4. 2. bear twins, and n. is barren among them
Isa. 1. 31. they shall burn and n. shall quench them
5. 27. n. shall be weary, n. shall slumber
29. carry it away safe, and n. shall deliver it
14. 6. he is persecuted, and n. hindereth
31. n. shall be alone in his appointed times
17. 2. n. shall make them afraid, Zeph. 3. 13.
22. 22. he shall open, and n. shall shut, n. open
34. 10. n. shall pass through it for ever and ever
12. they shall call the nobles but n. shall be there
16. no one shall fail, n. shall want her mate
42. 22. n. delivereth, and n. saith, restore
44. 19. n. considereth in his heart, nor is there
47. 8. that sayest, I am, and n. else besides me, 10.
10. n. seeth me, || 15. n. shall save thee
57. 1. n. considering that righteous is taken away
59. 4. n. calleth for justice, nor pleadeth for truth
66. 4. because when I called, n. did answer
Jer. 4. 4. and burn, that n. can quench it, 21. 12.
7. 33. for the beasts, and n. shall fray them away
9. 10. burnt up, so that n. can pass through them
12. burnt like a wilderness that n. passeth through
22. shall fall as dung, and n. shall gather them
13. 19. cities shall be shut, and n. shall open them
14. 16. cast out, and shall have n. to bury them
23. 14. that n. doth return from his wickedness
30. 10. and n. shall make him afraid, 46. 27.
34. 9. that n. should serve himself of them
10. that n. should serve themselves of them
35. 14. to this day they drink n. but obey father's
36. 30. shall have n. to sit on the throne of David
42. 17. n. shall remain or escape
44. 14. n. shall return, but such as escape
48. 33. n. shall tread with shouting, no shouting
49. 5. n. shall gather up him that wandereth
50. 3. land desolate, and n. shall dwell therein
9. their arrows, n. shall return in vain
20. iniquity sought for, and there shall be n.
29. camp against it, let n. thereof escape
32. the proud shall fall, and n. shall raise him up
51. 62. that n. shall remain in it, Ezek. 7. 11.
Lam. 1. 2. she hath n. to comfort her, 17.
4. because n. come to the solemn feasts
7. when her people fell, and n. did help her
21. heard that I sigh, there is n. to comfort me
Ezek. 7. 14. but n. goeth to the battle
25. they shall seek peace, and there shall be n.
12. 28. n. of my words shall be prolonged any more
16. 34. n. followeth thee to commit whoredoms
18. 7. hath spoiled n. by violence, given bread
22. 30. I sought for a man, but I found n.
33. 16. n. of his sins shall be mentioned to him
28. mountains desolate, that n. shall pass through
34. 6. and n. did search or seek after them
28. shall dwell safely, and n. shall make them afraid, 39. 26. Mic. 4. 4. Nah. 2. 11.
39. 28. and have left n. of them any more there
Dan. 1. 19. n. found like Daniel among them all
4. 35. n. stay hand, or say to him, what doest thou?
8. 27. astonished at the vision, but n. understood it
11. 16. n. shall stand before him, he shall stand
45. shall come to his end, and n. shall help him
12. 10. n. of the wicked sh. understand, but the wise
Hos. 2. 10. n. shall deliver her out of my hands, 5. 14.
11. 7. though they called, n. at all would exalt him
Joel 2. 27. I am the Lord your God, and n. else
Amos 5. 6. there be n. to quench it in Bethel
Mic. 2. 5. shalt have n. that shall cast a cord by lot
3. 11. they will say, n. evil can come upon us
5. 8. he teareth in pieces, and n. can deliver
Nah. 2. 8. they cry, stand, but n. shall look back
Zech. 7. 10. let n. of you imagine evil, 8. 17.
Mal. 2. 15. let n. deal treacherously against the wife
Mat. 12. 43. unclean spirit walketh thro' dry places seeking rest and findeth n. Luke 11. 24.
26. 60. witnesses came, yet found n. Mark 14. 55.
Luke 3. 11. let him impart to him that hath n.
4. 26. to n. of them was Elias sent, save to Sarepta
27. n. of them was cleansed save Naaman the Syr.
14. 24. n. of them shall taste of my supper
18. 19. n. is good, save one, that is God
John 7. 19. and yet n. of you keepeth the law
15. 24. if I had not done the works n. other did
17. 12. n. is lost but the son of perdition
18. 9. of them thou gavest me, I have lost n.
Acts 3. 6. Peter said, silver and gold have I n.
8. 16. for as yet he was fallen on n. of them
24. pray, that n. of these things come on me
11. 19. preaching the word to n. but to the Jews
18. 17. Gallio cared for n. of these things
20. 24. but n. of these things move me
24. 23. he should forbid n. of his acquaintance
25. 11. if there be n. of these things they accuse
26. 22. saying n. other than the prophets did say
Rom. 8. 9. if any have not the Spirit, he is n. of his
14. 7. n. of us liveth, and n. dieth to himself
1 Cor. 1. 14. I thank God, I baptized n. of you
2. 8. whom n. of the princes of this world knew
7. 29. they that have wives be as tho' they had n.
9. 15. but I have used n. of these things
10. 32. give n. offence to the Jews nor Gentiles
14. 10. and n. of them is without signification
Gal. 1. 19. but other of the apostles saw I n.
1 Thess. 5. 15. see that n. render evil for evil
1 Tim. 5. 14. give n. occasion to the adversary
1 Pet. 4. 15. let n. of you suffer as a murderer
Rev. 2. 10. fear n. of these things thou shalt suffer
See Effect, Like.

There is NONE.

Gen. 39. 9. there is n. greater in this house than I
41. 15. and there is n. that can interpret it
39. there is n. so discreet and wise as thou art
Deut. 4. 35. the Lord is God, there is n. else, 39. 1 Kings 8. 60. Isa. 45. 5, 6, 14, 18, 22. | 46. 9. Mark 12. 32.
Ruth 4. 4. for there is n. to redeem it besides thee
1 Sam. 2. 2. there is n. holy as the L. there is n. besides
22. 8. there is n. sheweth me, there is n. that is sorry
1 Chr. 29. 15. days are as a shadow, there is n. abiding
Job 10. 7. there is n. that can deliver, Ps. 7. 2. | 71. 11.
Psal. 14. 1. they are corrupt, there is n. that doeth good, 3. | 53. 1, 3. Rom. 3. 12.
22. 11. for trouble is near, for there is n. to help
73. 25. there is n. on earth I desire beside thee
Isa. 41. 17. when the needy seek water, there is n.
26. there is n. sheweth, there is n. that declareth
43. 13. there is n. that can deliver out of my hand
51. 18. and there is n. to guide her among her sons
59. 11. we look for judgment, but there is n.
64. 7. and there is n. that calleth on thy name
Jer. 10. 20. there is n. to stretch forth my tent
30. 13. there is n. to plead thy cause, that thou
Lam. 5. 8. there is n. that doth deliver us from hand
Dan. 10. 21. there is n. that holdeth with me in these
Hos. 7. 7. there is n. of them that calleth on me
Amos 5. 2. she is forsaken, there is n. to raise her up
Mic. 7. 2. there is n. upright among men, they all lie
Zeph. 2. 15. that said, I am, and there is n. besides me
Hag. 1. 6. ye clothe you, but there is n. warm
Mat. 19. 17. there is n. good but one, that is God, Mark 10. 18.
Mark 12. 31. there is n. other commandment greater
Luke 1. 61. there is n. of thy kindred that is called
Acts 4. 12. there is n. other name under heaven given
Rom. 3. 10. there is n. righteous, no, not one
11. there is n. understandeth, there is n. seeketh G.
1 Cor. 8. 4. and there is n. other God but one

There was NONE.

Gen. 39. 11. there was n. of men of the house within
41. 8. there was n. that could interpret them
24. but there was n. that could declare it to me
Num. 21. 35. until there was n. left him alive
Deut. 22. 27. damsel cried, and there was n. to save
2 Sam. 14. 6. they strove, and th. was n. to part them
25. there was n. to be so much praised as Absalom
22. 42. looked, but there was n. to save, Psal. 18. 41.
1 Kings 12. 20. there was n. that followed the house of Dav. but tribe of Judah only, 2 Kings 17. 18.
Ps. 69. 20. looked some to have pity, but there was n.
79. 3. shed their blood, and there was n. to bury them
107. 12. they fell down, and there was n. to help
139. 16. when as yet there was n. of them
Isa. 10. 14. there was n. moved the wing or peeped
50. 2. when I called, there was n. to answer
63. 3. I have trodden the wine-press alone, and of the people there was n. with me, I will tread
5. and I wondered that there was n. to uphold
Dan. 8. 7. there was n. that could deliver the ram

NOON

Signifies, [1] *The mid day between morning and night*, 1 Kings 18. 26, 27. Psal. 55. 17. [2] *A time of clear light*, Job 5. 14. [3] *Clearly and manifestly*, Psal. 37. 6. [4] *Without delay, or fear*, Jer. 6. 4. | 15. 8. [5] *A time of great prosperity and imaginary security*, Amos 8. 9.

Tell me where thou makest thy flock to rest at noon, Cant. 1. 7. *Discover to me by thy word and Spirit, which are those assemblies where thou art present, and to whom thou affordest comfort and refreshing under scorching persecutions and trials.* It is spoken *in allusion to the custom of shepherds in hot countries, who, in the heat of the day, used to carry their flocks into shadowy places.*

Gen. 43. 16. these men shall dine with me at n.
25. the present against Joseph came at n.
Judg. 19. 8. and they tarried until after n.
2 Sam. 4. 5. Ish-bosheth, who lay on a bed at n.
1 Kings 18. 26. they called on Baal even until n.
27. at n. Elijah mocked them, and said, cry aloud
20. 16. he numbered them, and they went out at n.
2 Kings 4. 20. he sat on her knees till n. and died
Psal. 55. 17. at n. will I pray, and he shall hear
Cant. 1. 7. thou makest thy flock to rest at n.
Jer. 6. 4. prepare war, arise, let us go up at n.
Amos 8. 9. I will cause the sun to go down at n.
Acts 22. 6. about n. there shone great light round me

NOON *day*.

Deut. 28. 29. thou shalt grope at n.-day as the blind
Job 5. 14. they grope in the n.-day as in the night
11. 17. thine age shall be clearer than the n.-day
Psal. 37. 6. he shall bring forth judgment as n.-day
91. 6. for the destruction that wasteth at n.-day
Isa. 16. 3. shadow as the night, in midst of n.-day
58. 10. thy darkness shall be as the n.-day
59. 10. we stumble at n.-day as in the night
Jer. 15. 8. I have brought a spoiler at n.-day
Zeph. 2. 4. they shall drive out Ashdod at n.-day

NOON-*tide*.

Jer. 20. 16. let him hear the shouting at n.-tide

NORTH.

Gen. 28. 14. thou shalt spread abroad to the n.
1 Kings 7. 25. a molten sea stood upon twelve oxen, three oxen looking toward the n. 2 Chron. 4. 4.
1 Chron. 9. 24. the porters were toward the n.
Job 26. 7. he stretcheth out the n. over empty place
37. 9. and cold cometh out of the n.

Job 37. 22. fair weather cometh out of the n. with G. is
Psal. 48. 2. on the sides of n. the city of great King
89. 12. n. and south, thou hast created them
Eccl. 1. 6. the wind turneth about to the n.
11. 3. if the tree fall toward the n. there it shall be
Isa. 14. 13. I will sit in the sides of the n.
43. 6. I will say to the n. give up; and to the south
Jer. 1. 13. the pot's face is toward the n.
14. out of n. an evil break forth, 4. 6. | 46. 20.
15. all the families of the kingdoms of the n.
3. 12. go and proclaim these words toward the n.
18. shall come together out of the land of the n.
6. 1. for evil appeareth out of the n. and great
23. 8. which led Israel out of the n. country, 31. 8.
25. 9. I will send and take all the families of the n.
26. all the kings of the n. far and near, shall drink
46. 6. they shall stumble and fall toward the n.
10. Ld. of hosts hath a sacrifice in the n. country
24. she shall be delivered to the people of the n.
47. 2. behold, waters rise up out of the n.
50. 3. out of the n. cometh up a nation against her
Ezek. 1. 4. behold, a whirlwind came out of the n.
8. 5. so I lifted up mine eyes the way toward the n.
14. toward the n. sat women weeping for Tammuz
20. 47. all faces from south to n. shall be burnt
21. 4. all flesh from south to n. will I cut off
32. 30. the princes of the n. all of them be there
40. 44. having the prospect toward the n. 46.
41. 11. one door was toward the n. 42. 4.
42. 1. brought into court and building toward the n.
4. their doors n. || 11. chambers toward the n. 13.
46. 19. the holy chambers looked toward the n.
48. 10. for priests be this holy oblation toward n.
17. the suburbs of the city shall be toward the n.
Dan. 11. 6. of south shall come to the king of the n.
8. continue more years than the king of the n.
11. shall come and fight with the king of the n.
13. for the king of the n. shall return and set forth
15. the king of the n. shall cast up a mount, 40.
44. but tidings out of the n. shall trouble him
Zeph. 2. 13. he will stretch his hand against the n.
Zech. 6. 6. black horses go into the n. country
8. have quieted my spirit in the n. country
14. 4. the mountain shall remove toward the n.
Rev. 21. 13. and on the n. were three gates

From the NORTH.

Psal. 107. 3. gathered *from the n.* and the south, Isa. 49. 12. Jer. 16. 15. | 23. 8.
Isa. 14. 31. for there shall come *from the n.* a smoke
41. 25. I raised up one *from the n.* he shall come
Jer. 4. 6. I will bring evil *from the n.* and great destruction, 6. 22. | 10. 22. | 50. 9, 41. | 51. 48.
Ezek. 26. 7. I will bring a king of kings *from the n.*
39. 2. I will cause thee to come up *from the n.* parts
Amos 8. 12. they shall wander *from the n.* to the east
Zech. 2. 6. and flee *from* the land of *the n.*
Luke 13. 29. come *from the n.* and sit down in kingd.

NORTH *border*.

Num. 34. 7. and this shall be your *n. border*, 9.

NORTH *quarter*.

Josh. 15. 5. Judah's border in *n. quarter* was from sea
Ezek. 38. 6. Togarmah of *n. quarter* and his bands

NORTH *side*.

Exod. 26. 20. tabernacle on the *n. side* twenty boards
35. thou shalt put the table on the *n. side*
27. 11. for *n. side* hangings of 100 cubits, 38. 11.
Num. 2. 25. the camp of Dan shall be on the *n. side*
Josh. 8. 11. people of war pitched on the *n. side* of Ai
Judg. 7. 1. Midianites were on the *n. side* of them
21. 19. there is a feast on the *n. side* of Beth-el
2 Kings 16. 14. put brasen altar on *n. side* of altar
Ezek. 42. 17. he measured the *n. side* 500 reeds
48. 30. the goings out of the city on the *n. side*

NORTHERN.

Jer. 15. 12. break the n. iron, and the steel
Joel 2. 20. I will remove from you the n. army

NORTHWARD.

Gen. 13. 14. look n. and eastward, Deut. 3. 27.
Exod. 40. 22. tabernacle n. without the vail
Lev. 1. 11. kill it on the side of the altar n.
Deut. 2. 3. ye compassed mountain, turn you n.
1 Sam. 14. 5. front of one rock was situate n.
1 Chron. 26. 14. Zecharias' lot came out n.
17. and n. were four Levites a day
Ezek. 8. 5. n. was this image of jealousy
47. 2. then he brought me out of the gate n.
48. 31. three gates n. one gate of Reuben

NOSE.

The Hebrews commonly place anger in the nose. There went up a smoke out of his nostrils, 2 Sam. 22. 9. *And*, Job 41. 20. Out of his nostrils goeth smoke. *The eastern women, in several places, put golden rings to one of their nostrils:* Solomon *alludes to this custom*, Prov. 11. 22. As a jewel of gold in a swine's snout, so is a fair woman without discretion. *They also put rings in the nostrils of oxen and camels, to guide them by; hence is that metaphorical speech borrowed*, 2 Kings 19. 28. I will put my hook in thy nose, and my bridle in thy lips, and I will turn thee back.

Lev. 21. 18. that hath a flat n. shall not offer
Deut. 33. +10. they shall put incense at thy n.
2 Kings 19. 28. put my hook in thy n. Isa. 37. 29.
Job 40. 24. his n. pierceth through snares
41. 2. canst thou put a hook into his n.?
Prov. 30. 33. the wringing of the n. bringeth blood
Cant. 7. 4. thy n. is as the tower of Lebanon
8. and the smell of thy n. like apples
Isa. 65. 5. these are a smoke in my n. a fire that burns
Ezek. 8. 17. they put the branch to their n.
23. 25. they shall take away thy n. and ears

NOSES.

Psal. 115. 6. n. have they, but they smell not
Ezek. 39. 11. it shall stop the n. of the passengers

NOSE-*jewels*.

Isa. 3. 21. in that day the Lord will take away their tinkling ornaments, the rings and *n.-jewels*

NOSTRILS.

Gen. 2. 7. God breathed into man's n. the breath
7. 22. all in whose n. was breath of life, died
Exod. 15. 8. with blast of thy n. waters gathered
Num. 11. 20. eat till it come out at your n.
2 Sam. 22. 9. went a smoke of his n. Psal. 18. 8.
16. the blast of the breath of his n. Psal. 18. 15.
Job 4. 9. by breath of his n. they are consumed
27. 3. and the Spirit of God is in my n.
39. 20. the glory of his n. is terrible
41. 20. out of his n. goeth smoke, as out of a pot
Isa. 2. 22. from man, whose breath is in his n.
Lam. 4. 20. the breath of our n. was taken
Amos 4. 10. stink of your camps to come into your n.

NOT

Is a particle *of denying*, [1] *Absolutely*, Exod. 20. 13, 17. [2] *Conditionally*, Gal. 5. 21. [3] *Comparatively*, 1 Cor. 1. 17.

1 Kings 11. 39. I will afflict, but n. for ever
Job 7. 8. thine eyes are upon me, and I am n.
14. 21. come to honour, he knoweth it n. 35. 15.
Psal. 115. 1. n. unto us, O Lord, n. to us be glory
119. 36. to thy testimonies, and n. to covetousness
Prov. 12. 7. the wicked are n. || 23. 23. sell it n.
27. 24. for riches are n. for ever, doth crown endure
Isa. 3. 7. I will n. be an healer, make me n. a ruler
10. 11. shall I n. as I have done to Samaria, so do
16. 6. pride of Moab, but his lies shall n. be so
30. 1. take counsel, but n. of me, n. of my Spirit
41. 9. I have chosen thee, and n. cast thee away
44. 21. thou shalt n. be forgotten of me
45. 13. let go my captives, n. for a price nor reward
48. 1. but n. in truth and righteousness
49. 15. they may forget, yet will I n. forget thee
57. 11. I held my peace, and thou fearest me n.
65. 1. I am found of them that sought me n.
Jer. 4. 11. a wind, n. to fan || 10. 20. and they are n.
11. 8. I commanded, but they did them n.
14. 9. leave us n. || 21. 10. and n. for good, 39. 16.
14. I sent them n. neither have commanded them, 15. | 23. 32. | 29. 9, 31. Ezek. 13. 6.
23. 16. and n. out of the mouth of the Lord
29. 11. of peace, and n. of evil || 30. 5. n. of peace
31. 15. because they were n. Mat. 2. 18.
Lam. 3. 2. brought into darkness, but n. into light
5. 7. our fathers have sinned, and are n.
Ezek. 16. 16. the like things shall n. come
61. I will give them, but n. by thy covenant
20. 44. n. according to your wicked ways
28. 2. yet thou art a man, and n. God
33. 31. they hear, but they will n. do them, 32.
36. 22. I do n. this for your sakes, O Israel, 32.
Dan. 8. 24. shall be mighty, but n. by his power
9. 26. but n. for himself || 11. 25. shall n. stand
Hos. 1. 9. ye are n. my people, I will n. be your G.
7. 16. they return, but n. to the Most High
Amos 7. 3. it shall n. be, saith the Lord, 6.
Hab. 2. 3. at the end it shall speak, and n. lie
Zech. 1. 4. be ye n. as your fathers, to whom
4. 6. n. by might nor power, but by my Spirit
Mal. 3. 6. for I am the Lord, I change n.
Mat. 6. 5. be n. like the hypocrites, 8, 16.
7. 25. and it fell n. || 26. and doeth them n.
29. for he taught n. as the scribes, Mark 1. 22.
9. 13. I will have mercy, and n. sacrifice, 12. 7.
12. 31. shall n. be forgiven to men, 32. Luke 12. 10.
16. 22. saying, Lord, this shall n. be unto thee
20. 26. but it shall n. be so among you, whoso will
28. the Son of man came, n. to be ministered unto
21. 30. the second said, I go, sir, and went n.
23. 3. but do n. ye after their works
23. to have done, and n. to leave the other undone
24. 6. the end is n. yet || 17. let him n. come down
25. 43. ye clothed me n. ye visited me n.
45. did it n. to one of these, did it n. to me
26. 5. n. on the feast day, lest there be an uproar
39. n. as I will, but as thou wilt, Mark 14. 36.
Mark 8. 18. see ye n.? hear ye n.? do ye n. rememb.?
10. 43. but so it shall n. be among you
14. 7. the poor ye have, but me ye have n. always
Luke 3. 15. whether he were the Christ or n.
13. 14. be healed, and n. on the sabbath-day
18. 11. that I am n. as other men are
22. 57. woman, I know him n. || 58. man, I am n.
John 1. 20. he confessed, I am n. the Christ, 3. 28.
4. 42. we believe, n. because of thy saying
5. 40. ye will n. come to me, that ye might have life
42. I know ye have n. the love of God in you
6. 26. ye seek me n. because ye saw the miracles
38. I came down, n. to do mine own will
8. 16. my judgment is true, for I am n. alone, but I and the Father that sent me, 16. 32.
23. I am n. of this world || 10. 12. n. the shepherd
10. 26. ye believe n. because ye are n. of my sheep
11. 40. said I n. unto thee, if thou wouldest believe
51. this spake he, n. of himself, but being high-pr.
52. and n. for that nation only, but that also
12. 6. this he said, n. that he cared for the poor
47. I judge him n. for I came n. to judge world
13. 9. Lord, n. my feet only, but also my hands
10. ye are clean, but n. all || 14. 2. if it were n. so
14. 22. Judas, n. Iscariot, and n. to the world
27. n. as the world giveth, give I unto you
15. 15. I call you n. servants, but friends
16. 7. if I go n. away, the Comforter will n. come
13. for he shall n. speak of himself
18. 40. saying, n. this man || 20. 17. touch me n.
Acts 4. 18. n. to speak at all in the name of Jesus
7. 53. have n. kept it || 8. 32. he opened n. his mouth
10. 41. and shewed him, n. to all the people
12. 22. it is the voice of a god, and n. of a man
13. 25. I am n. he || 18. 9. hold n. thy peace
17. 27. though he be n. far from every one of us
20. 22. n. knowing the things that shall befall
29. shall wolves enter in, n. sparing the flock
21. 13. for I am ready n. to be bound only
23. 5. I wist n. that he was the high-priest
Rom. 2. 13. n. the hearers of the law are just
14. these having n. the law, are a law to themselves
29. and n. in the letter || 4. 2. but n. before God
4. 5. but to him that worketh n. but believeth
10. n. in circumcision, but uncircumcision
5. 16. and n. as it was by one that sinned
7. 15. I allow n. what I would, that do I n.
8. 9. but ye are n. in the flesh, but in the Spirit
32. how shall he n. with him give us all things?
Rom. 9. 24. n. of the Jews only, but of the Gentiles
26. where it was said, ye are n. my people
10. 18. have they n. heard? yes, verily
12. 3. n. to think of himself more highly than
15. 1. ought to bear, and n. to please ourselves
20. to preach, n. where Christ was named
16. 4. to whom n. only I give thanks, but also
1 Cor. 1. 28. hath chosen the things which are n.
2. 9. eye hath n. seen, nor ear heard, nor entered
3. 2. n. with meat || 7. 10. yet n. I, but the Lord
3. are ye n. carnal, and walk as men, 4.
4. 6. n. to think of men above that is written
19. and I will know, n. the speech of them which
5. 8. n. with old leaven || 6. 1. n. before the saints
7. 12. but to the rest speak I, n. the Lord
9. 1. am I n. an apostle? am I n. free? have I n. seen
26. I therefore so run, n. as uncertainly
10. 29. conscience, I say, n. thine own, but of others
11. 22. have ye n. houses to eat and drink in?
12. 16. because n. the eye, I am n. of the body
15. 10. yet n. I, but the grace of God with me
2 Cor. 2. 17. for we are n. as many, which corrupt
3. 3. n. with ink, n. in tables of stone
5. n. that we are sufficient of ourselves
13. n. as Moses, which put a vail over his face
4. 1. we faint n. 16. || 7. may be of God, and n. of us
9. n. forsaken, cast down, but n. destroyed
5. 1. we have an house n. made with hands
7. we walk by faith, n. by sight || 12. n. in heart
7. 7. God comforteth us, n. by his coming only
9. I rejoice, n. that ye were made sorry
12. I did it n. for his cause that had done wrong
8. 5. and this they did, n. as we hoped, but first
12. and n. according to that he hath n.
10. 12. we dare n. make ourselves of the number
12. 18. walked we n. in the same spirit, same steps?
Gal. 1. 1. Paul an apostle, n. of men, nor by man
2. 20. I live, yet n. I || 6. 4. and n. in another
Eph. 2. 8. through faith, and that n. of yourselves
9. n. of works || 5. 15. n. as fools, but as wise
6. 7. doing service as to the Lord, and n. to men
12. for we wrestle n. against flesh and blood
Phil. 1. 29. it is given to you, n. only to believe
2. 12. have obeyed, n. as in my presence only
27. and n. on him only, but on me also
3. 9. found in him, n. having mine own righteousn.
12. n. as tho' I had already attained, or perfect
Col. 2. 19. n. holding the head, from which the body
21. touch n. taste n. handle n. all to perish
3. 2. on things above, n. on things on the earth
23. do heartily, as to the Lord, and n. to men
1 Thess. 2. 1. our entrance, that it was n. in vain
13. ye received it, n. as word of men, but w. of G.
5. 6. therefore let us n. sleep, as do others
2 Thess. 3. 2. for all men have n. faith
9. n. because we have n. power, but to make
1 Tim. 3. 3. n. given to wine, n. greedy of lucre
2 Tim. 1. 9. n. according to our works, Tit. 3. 5.
4. 8. and n. to me only, but to them that love
Tit. 2. 9. to please them, n. answering again
Philem. 16. n. now as a servant, but above a servant
Heb. 7. 20. n. without an oath, he was made priest
8. 2. which the Lord pitched, and n. man
9. 7. n. without blood, which he offered for himself
11. n. made with hands, n. of this building
11. 1. faith is the evidence of things n. seen
13. died, n. having received the promises
40. they without us should n. be made perfect
12. 8. bastards, n. sons || 13. 7. n. with grief
Jam. 1. 23. if any man be a hearer, and n. a doer
2. 14. and have n works, can faith save him?
2. 24. n. by faith only || 3. 2. offend n. in word
4. 2. yet ye have n. || 17. and doeth it n. it is sin
1 Pet. 2. 10. n. a people, had n. obtained mercy
18. be subject, n. only to the good and gentle
23. who reviled n. again, he threatened n.
2 Pet. 2. 21. better for them n. to have known
1 John 2. 23. the same hath n. the Father
3. 12. n. as Cain || 4. 10. n. that we loved God
5. 12. he that hath n. the Son, hath n. life
17. and there is a sin n. unto death
Jude 19. these be sensual, having n. the Spirit
Rev. 2. 2. which say they are apostles, and are n. 9.
19. 10. he said unto me, see thou do it n. 22. 9.
See Able, Afraid, Ashamed, Answered, Believe, Confounded, Departed, Destroy, Die, Eat, Enter, Fear, Few, Find, Forsaken, Give, Given, Hear, Hearken, Hid.

If NOT.

Gen. 18. 21. I will go down, and *if n.* I will know
24. 49. and *if n.* tell me, that I may know
Exod. 32. 32. *if n.* blot me, I pray, out of thy book
Judg. 9. 15. *if n.* let fire come out of bramble, 20.
1 Sam. 2. 16. and *if n.* I will take it by force
6. 9. but *if n.* then we shall know that it is not
2 Sam. 13. 26. *if n.* let Amnon go || 17. 6. *if n.* speak
2 Kings 2. 10. but *if n.* it shall not be so
Job 9. 24. *if n.* where, and who is he?
33. 33. if n. hearken to me, hold thy peace
Zech. 11. 12. give me my price, and *if n.* forbear
Luke 10. 6. *if n.* it shall turn to you again
13. 9. and *if n.* then thou shalt cut it down
See Is, Knew, Know, No, Obey, Obeyed, Passed, See, Seek, So, Will, Would.

Or NOT.

Gen. 24. 21. L. made his journey prosperous, *or n.*
Exod. 17. 7. saying, is the Lord among us, *or n.?*
Num. 11. 23. whether my word come to pass, *or n.*
13. 20. whether there be wood therein, *or n.*
Judg. 2. 22. as their fathers did keep it, *or n.*

NOTABLE

Signifies, [1] *Conspicuous, or sightly*, Dan. 8. 5. [2] *Notorious*, Mat. 27. 16. [3] *Terrible*, Acts 2. 20. [4] *Known, or apparent*, Acts 4. 16.

Dan. 8. 5. the goat had a n. horn between his eyes
8. for it came up four n. ones, toward four winds
Mat. 27. 16. and they had then a n. prisoner
Acts 2. 20. before that n. day of the Lord come
4. 16. a n. miracle hath been done by them

NOTE, ED.

Isa. 30. 8. now go, write it, and n. it in a book

Dan. 10. 21. that is n in the scripture of truth
2 Thess. 3. 14. n. that man, and have no company

NOTE.

Rom. 16. 7. who are of n. among the apostles

NOTHING.

Signifies, [1] Not any thing, Gen. 19. 8. [2] For no use or service, Mat. 5. 13. [3] Of no force to bind or oblige, Mat. 23. 16, 18. [4] No good works that are acceptable to God, John 15. 5. [5] False and groundless, Acts 21. 24. [6] No other means, Mark 9. 29. [7] No reward or wages, 3 John 7. [8] No new doctrine pertaining to salvation, Gal. 2. 6. [9] No sin or guilt, John 14. 30. [10] No divine power, no God, 1 Cor. 8. 4.

It is taken, [1] Absolutely, Job 26. 7. Psal. 49. 17. [2] Comparatively, Psal. 39. 5. Isa. 40. 17. [3] In a person's estimation of himself, 2 Cor. 12. 11. [4] Not in the matter, but in the manner, as being of no use or service, 1 Cor. 7. 19. Thus circumcision is called nothing, because it avails nothing, in point of acceptation with God now in gospel-times.

Gen. 11. 6. now n. will be restrained from them
19. 8. only unto these men do n. for they came
26. 29. as we have done to thee n. but good
40. 15. and here also have I done n. to put me
Exod. 9. 4. n. die that is the children's of Israel
12. 10. let n. of it remain until morning
20. ye shall eat n. leavened in your habitations
16. 18. gathered much, had n. over, 2 Cor. 8. 15.
22. 3. if he have n. then he shall be sold for his theft
23. 26. there shall n. cast their young
Num. 6. 4. eat n. that is made of the vine-tree
16. 26. touch n. of theirs, lest ye be consumed
22. 16. let n. hinder thee from coming
Deut. 2. 7. thou hast lacked n. Neh. 9. 21.
20. 16. thou shalt save alive n. that breatheth
22. 26. to the damsel thou shalt do n.
28. 55. because he hath n. left him in the siege
Josh. 11. 15. Joshua left n. commanded undone
Judg. 2. † 19. let n. fall of their own doings
3. 2. at least such as before knew n. thereof
14. 6. he rent him, and had n. in his hand
1 Sam. 3. 18. Samuel told, and hid n. from him
20. 2. my father will do n. but will shew it me
22. 15. thy servant knew n. of all this
25. 21. so that n. was missed of all, 30. 19.
36. she told him n. less or more until morning
2 Sam. 12. 3. the poor man had n. save one ewe-lamb
24. 24. not offer of that which doth cost me n.
1 Kings 4. 27. provided victuals, they lacked n.
8. 9. there was n. in the ark save the two tables
10. 21. silver was n. accounted of in days of Solom.
11. 22. and he answered n. Luke 22. 35.
22. 16. tell me n. but truth, 2 Chron. 18. 15.
2 Kings 10. 10. fall n. to earth of word of the Lord
20. 13. n. in his house that he shewed not
17. be carried away, n. shall be left, Isa. 39. 2, 6.
2 Chr. 9. 2. n. hid from Solom. which he told her not
Ezra 4. 3. ye have n. to do with us in building
Neh. 5. 8. then they found n. to answer
12. we will restore, and require n. of them
8. 10. send portions for whom n. is prepared
9. 21. sustained them, so that they lacked n.
Esth. 2. 15. now Esther required n. but what
5. 13. yet all this availeth me n. so long as I see
6. 10. let n. fail of all that thou hast spoken
Job 6. 18. they go to n. and perish || 21. for ye are n.
8. 9. we are but of yesterday, and know n.
24. 25. who will make my speech n. worth
26. 7. and he hangeth the earth upon n.
34. 9. for he hath said, it profiteth a man n. that he should delight himself with God
Psal. 17. 3. thou hast tried me and shalt find n.
39. 5. and mine age is as n. before thee
49. 17. when he dieth, he shall carry n. away
119. 165. who love thy law, and n. shall offend them
Prov. 9. 13. a foolish woman is simple, and knoweth n.
10. 2. treasures of wickedness profit n.
13. 4. the sluggard desireth, and hath n. 20. 4.
7. there is that maketh himself rich, yet hath n.
22. 27. if thou hast n. to pay, why should he take
Eccl. 3. 14. whatsoever God doeth, n. can be put to it
5. 15. and he shall take n. of his labour
6. 2. so that he wanteth n. for his soul of all
7. 14. to the end that man should find n. after him
Isa. 34. 12. none there, and all her princes shall be n.
40. 17. all nations before him are as n. they are counted to him less than n. and vanity, 41. 29.
23. that bringeth the princes to n. 41. 11, 12.
43. † 10. before me there was n. God formed
Jer. 10. 24. not in anger, lest thou bring me to n.
32. 23. done n. of all that thou commandest them
38. 14. I will ask thee a thing, hide n. from me
39. 10. left of the poor which had n. in Judah
42. 4. I will keep n. back from you
50. 26. destroy her utterly, let n. of her be left
Lam. 1. 12. is it n. to you, all ye that pass by?
Ezek. 13. 3. woe to the prophets that have seen n.
Dan. 4. 35. all the inhabitants of earth reputed as n.
9. † 26. Messiah be cut off, but shall have n.
Joel 2. 3. a wilderness, yea, and n. shall escape them
Amos 3. 4. will young lion cry if he have taken n.?
5. taken up snare, and taken n. || 7. Ld. will do n.
Hag. 2. 3. it is not in comparison of it as n.?
Zech. 8. † 10. the hire of a man became n.
Mat. 15. 32. they have n. to eat, Mark 6. 36. | 8. 1, 2.
17. 20. n. shall be impossible to you, Luke 1. 37.
21. 19. he found n. thereon but leaves, Mark 11. 13.
26. 62. answerest thou n.? what is it these witness?
27. 12. he answered n. Mark 14. 60, 61. | 15. 3, 4, 5.
19. have thou n. to do with that just man
24. when Pilate saw that he could prevail n.
Mark 1. 44. see thou say n. to any man, but go
5. 26. and had spent all, and was n. bettered
6. 8. they should take n. for their journey, Luke 9. 3.
9. 29. this kind can come forth by n. but by prayer
Luke 4. 2. and in those days he did eat n.
5. 5. have toiled all night and taken n. John 21. 3.
7. 42. they had n. to pay, he frankly forgave them
10. 19. and n. shall by any means hurt you
11. 6. and I have n. to set before him
Luke 23. 15. and lo, n. worthy of death is done to him, Acts 23. 29. | 25. 25. | 26. 31.
41. but this man hath done n. amiss
John 3. 27. man can receive n. except it be given him
5. 19. verily the Son can do n. of himself, 30.
6. 12. gather, that n. be lost || 39. I should lose n.
63. the Spirit quickeneth, the flesh profiteth n.
7. 26. they say n. || 8. 28. I do n. of myself
9. 33. he could do n. || 11. 49. ye know n. at all
12. 19. perceive ye how ye prevail n.? behold
14. 30. the prince of this world hath n. in me
15. 5. I am the vine, for without me ye can do n.
16. 23. and in that day ye shall ask me n.
24. hitherto have ye asked n. in my name
18. 20. I spake openly, in secret have I said n.
Acts 4. 14. they could say n. against it
21. finding n. how they might punish them
10. 20. and go with them, doubting n. 11. 12.
19. 36. ye ought to be quiet, and do n. rashly
20. 20. I kept back n. that was profitable to you
21. 24. all may know, that those things are n.
23. 14. we will eat n. until we have slain Paul
27. 33. ye have continued fasting, having taken n.
1 Cor. 1. 19. bring to n. the understand. of prudent
4. 4. I know n. by mys. || 5. judge n. before the time
8. 2. he knoweth n. yet as he ought to know
9. 16. for though I preach, I have n. to glory of
13. 2. and have no charity, I am n. 2 Cor. 12. 11.
3. and have not charity, it profiteth me n.
2 Cor. 6. 10. as having n. yet possessing all things
13. 8. for we can do n. against the truth
Gal. 2. 6. they in conference added n. to me
4. 1. heir when a child, differeth n. from a servant
5. 2. I say unto you, Christ shall profit you n.
Phil. 2. 3. let n. be done through strife or vain-glory
1 Tim. 4. 4. every creature is good, n. to be refused
5. 21. doing n. by partiality || 6. 4. proud, knowing n.
6. 7. for we brought n. and we can carry n. out
Tit. 3. 13. that n. be wanting unto them
Philem. 14. without thy mind would I do n.
Heb. 2. 8. he left n. that is not put under him
7. 14. Moses spake n. concerning priesthood
19. for the law made n. perfect, but bringing in
Jam. 1. 4. be perfect and entire, wanting n.
6. but let him ask in faith, n. wavering
3 John 7. they went forth, taking n. of the Gentiles

For NOTHING.

Exod. 21. 2. in the seventh he shall go out free for n.
Isa. 44. 10. an image that is profitable for n.
Jer. 13. 7. the girdle was profitable for n. 10.
Mat. 5. 13. unsavoury salt is good f. n. to be cast out
Luke 6. 35. do good and lend, hoping for n. again
Phil. 4. 6. be careful for n. but by prayer and suppl.

In NOTHING.

Acts 17. 21. Athenians spent their time in n. else
2 Cor. 7. 9. ye might receive damage by us in n.
12. 11. in n. am I behind chiefest, though I be n.
Phil. 1. 20. and my hope, that in n. I shall be ash.
28. and in n. terrified by your adversaries

Is NOTHING.

Num. 11. 6. there is n. at all besides this manna
Judg. 7. 14. this is n. else save the sword of Gideon
1 Sam. 27. 1. there is n. better than to go to Philist.
1 Kings 18. 43. he looked, and said, there is n.
2 Kings 20. 15. there is n. among my treas. Isa. 39. 4.
2 Chr. 14. 11. it is n. with thee to help with many
Neh. 2. 2. this is n. else but sorrow of heart
Esth. 6. 3. they said, there is n. done for him
Psal. 19. 6. there is n. hid from the heat thereof
Prov. 8. 8. there is n. froward or perverse in them
Eccl. 2. 24. there is n. better for a man, 3. 22.
5. 14. begetteth a son, and there is n. in his hand
Jer. 32. 17. there is n. too hard for thee
Mat. 10. 26. for there is n. covered that shall not be revealed, Mark 4. 22. Luke 12. 2.
23. 16. whoso shall swear by the temple, it is n.
18. whoso shall swear by the altar, it is n.
Mark 7. 15. there is n. from without a man defileth
John 8. 54. if I honour myself, my honour is n.
Rom. 14. 14. that there is n. unclean of itself
1 Cor. 7. 19. circumcision is n. uncircumcision is n.
8. 4. we know that an idol is n. in the world
Gal. 6. 3. when he is n. he deceiveth himself
Tit. 1. 15. to them that are defiled is n. pure

Of NOTHING.

Isa. 41. 24. behold, ye are of n. your work nought
1 Thess. 4. 12. and that ye may have lack of n.
Rev. 3. 17. I am rich, increased, and have need of n.

NOTWITHSTANDING.

Exod. 16. 20. n. they hearkened not to Moses, but some left of it, 1 Sam. 2. 25. 2 Kings 17. 14.
21. 21. n. if he continue a day or two not punished
Deut. 1. 26. n. ye would not go up, but rebelled
1 Kings 11. 12. n. in thy days I will not do it
Jer. 35. 14. n. I have spoken unto you, rising early
Mat. 2. 22. n. being warned of God in a dream
11. 11. n. he that is least in kingdom is greater
17. 27. n. lest we should offend, go to the sea
Luke 10. 11. n. be sure of this that kingdom is come
20. n. in this rejoice not, that spirits are subject
Phil. 1. 18. n. whether in pretence or truth Christ is
4. 14. n. have well done, that ye communicate with
1 Tim. 2. 15. n. she shall be saved in child-bearing
2 Tim. 4. 17. n. L. stood with me, and strengthened
Jam. 2. 16. n. ye give them not those things needful
Rev. 2. 20. n. I have a few things against thee

NOUGHT, see NAUGHT.

NOVICE.

1 Tim. 3. 6. not a n. lest being lifted up with pride

NOURISH

Signifies, [1] To feed or maintain, Gen. 47. 12. [2] To educate or bring up, Acts 7. 21. [3] To cause to grow, Isa. 44. 14. [4] To instruct, 1 Tim. 4. 6. [5] To cherish and comfort, Ruth 4. 15. Jam. 5. 5.

Gen. 45. 11. and there will I n. thee, 50. 21.
Isa. 7. 21. that man shall n. young cow and two sheep
23. 4. nor do I n. up young men, nor bring up virgins
44. 14. he planteth an ash, the rain doth n. it

NOURISHED.

Gen. 47. 12. Joseph n. his father and brethren
2 Sam. 12. 3. a lamb which he bought and n. up
Isa. 1. 2. I have n. and brought up children, and they
Ezek. 19. 2. she n. her whelps among young lions
Acts 7. 20. and n. in his father's house three months
21. Pharaoh's daughter n. him for her own son
12. 20. their country was n. by the king's country
1 Tim. 4. 6. n. up in words of faith and good doctr.
Jam. 5. 5. have n. your hearts as in day of slaughter
Rev. 12. 14. n. for a time, times, and half a time

NOURISHER, S.

Ruth 4. 15. women said, he shall be n. of thy old age
2 Kings 10. † 1. Jehu sent to the n. of Ahab's childr.
Isa. 49. † 23. and kings shall be thy n. and queens
Jer. 46. † 25. I will punish the n. of No.

NOURISHETH.

Eph. 5. 29. but n. his flesh, as the Lord the church

NOURISHING.

Dan. 1. 5. so n. them three years to stand before king
Nah. 3. † 8. art thou better than n. No

NOURISHMENT.

Col. 2. 19. all the body by joints and bands having n.

NOW.

Gen. 2. 23. Adam said, this is n. bone of my bones
18. 21. I will go down n. and see whether they
19. 9. n. will we deal worse with thee than
22. 12. for n. I know that thou fearest God
26. 29. thou art n. the blessed of the Lord
27. 37. what shall I do n. to thee, my son?
29. 35. she said, n. will I praise the Lord
32. 4. sojourned with Laban, and stayed there till n.
43. 11. Israel said to them, if it be so n. do this
45. 8. so n. it was not you that sent me hither
46. 34. trade hath been about catt. from youth till n.
Exod. 9. 18. not such hail been in Egypt even till n.
10. 11. go n. ye that are men, and serve the Lord
32. 32. yet n. if thou wilt forgive their sin
Num. 12. 13. heal her n. O God, I beseech thee
14. 19. has forgiven this people from Egypt till n.
24. 17. I shall see him, but not n. shall behold him
Josh. 5. 14. but as captain of Lord's host am I n. come
7. 19. tell me n. what thou hast done, hide it not
Judg. 11. 7. why are ye come to me n. in distress?
17. 13. n. I know that the Lord will do me good
1 Sam. 2. 16. nay, but thou shalt give it me n.
30. but n. the Lord saith, be it far from me
15. 30. honour me n. I pray thee, before the elders
17. 29. what have I n. done? is there not a cause?
2 Sam. 13. 25. nay, my son, let us not all n. go
15. 34. so will I n. also be thy servant
24. 14. let us n. fall into the hand of the Lord
1 Kings 14. 14. who shall cut off, but what? even n.
19. 4. it is enough, n. O Lord, take away my life
2 Kings 1. 5. he said, why are ye n. turned back?
8. 6. restore all that was her's since she went till n.
10. 10. know n. there shall fall to earth nothing
18. 25. am I n. come up without Lord, Isa. 36. 10.
19. 25. n. have I brought it to pass, Isa. 37. 26.
20. 3. remember n. how I have walked, Isa. 38. 3.
Ezra 4. 13. be it n. known to the king, if city built
5. 16. even till n. hath it been building, not finished
9. 8. n. for little space grace been shewed from Lord
10. 2. n. there is hope in Isr. concerning this thing
Job 1. 11. put forth thy hand n. and touch, 2. 5.
4. 5. n. it is come upon thee, and thou faintest
6. 21. for n. ye are nothing, ye see my casting down
17. 3. lay down n. || 24. 25. and if it be not so n.
15. where is n. my hope? || 30. 9. n. I am their song
42. 5. have heard of thee, but n. my eye seeth thee
Psal. 12. 5. n. will I arise, saith the Lord
20. 6. n. know I that the Lord saveth his anointed
39. 7. n. Lord, what wait I for, my hope is in thee
115. 2. why heathen say, where is n. their God?
118. 25. save n. I beseech thee, O Lord, send now
119. 67. but n. have I kept thy word
Prov. 6. 3. do this n. my son, and deliver thyself
7. 12. n. she is without, n. in the streets, and lieth
Eccl. 2. 1. go to n. || 3. 15. what hath been is n.
16. that which n. is shall all be forgotten
Cant. 3. 2. I will rise n. and go about the city
Isa. 5. 5. n. go to, I will tell you what I will do
16. 14. but n. the Lord hath spoken, saying
19. 12. thy wise men, let them tell thee n.
22. 1. what aileth thee n. that thou art wholly gone
33. 10. n. will I rise, n. will I lift up myself
64. 8. but n. O Lord, thou art our Father
Jer. 2. 18. n. what hast thou to do in way of Egypt?
4. 12. n. will I give sentence against them
17. 15. the word of the Lord let it n. come
25. 5. turn n. every one from his evil way
30. 6. ask ye n. and see whether a man doth travail
34. 15. ye were n. turned, and had done right
35. 15. return ye n. every man from his evil way
45. 3. woe is me n. the Lord hath added grief
Dan. 10. 11. O Daniel, to thee am I n. sent
Hos. 2. 7. for then was it better with me than n.
13. 2. and n. they sin more and more, and made
Zech. 1. 4. turn ye n. from your evil ways and doings
9. 8. for n. have I seen with mine eyes
Mal. 3. 10. prove me n. herewith, saith the Lord
Mat. 1. 22. n. all this was done, that it might be
11. 12. from the days of John the Baptist, till n.
26. 45. sleep on n. || 27. 43. let him deliver him n.
53. thinkest that I cannot n. pray to my Father?
27. 42. let him n. come down from the cross
Mark 4. 37. so that the ship was n. full of waves
Luke 2. 29. Lord, n. lettest thy serv. depart in peace
10. 36. which n. these three was neighbour to him?
14. 17. come, for all things are n. ready
22. 36. but n. he that hath a purse, let him take it
John 2. 8. draw out n. and bear to governor of feast
10. but thou hast kept the good wine until n.
4. 18. he whom thou n. hast is not thy husband
23. but the hour cometh, and n. is, 5. 25.
9. 19. who was born blind, how then doth he n. see?
13. 7. what I do thou knowest not n. but shalt know
16. 12. many things, but ye cannot bear them n.
22. ye n. therefore have sorrow, but I will see you
29. lo, n. speakest thou plainly, and no proverb
30. n. we are sure, || 31. do ye n. believe?
17. 13. I kept them, and n. come I to thee
21. 14. this is n. the third time that Jesus shewed
Acts 2. 33. shed forth this which ye n. see and hear
37. n. when they heard this, were pricked in heart

Acts 4. 29. and *n.* Lord, behold their threatenings
12. 11. *n.* I know of a surety Lord sent his angel
18. *n.* as soon as it was day, there was a stir
22. 16. and *n.* why tarriest thou, arise, be baptized
26. 17. the Gentiles, to whom *n.* I send thee
Rom. 6. 22. but *n.* being made free from sin
7. 17. *n.* then it is no more I that do it, but sin
13. 11. *n.* it is high time to awake out of sleep
1 *Cor.* 4. 8. *n.* ye are full, *n.* ye are rich
7. 14. *n.* are they holy ‖ 13. 12. *n.* I know in part
16. 7. for I will not see you *n.* by the way
Gal. 1. 9. as we said before, so say I *n.* again
10. for do I *n.* persuade men or God?
2. 20. the life which I *n.* live in the flesh, I live by
3. 3. are ye *n.* made perfect by the flesh?
4. 20. I desire to be present with you *n.* and change
29. but as then, even so it is *n.*
Eph. 3. 10. to the intent that *n.* to principalities
5. 8. were darkness, but *n.* are ye light in the Ld.
Phil. 1. 5. your fellowship from the first day until *n.*
2. 12. obeyed, but *n.* much more in my absence
Col. 3. 8. but *n.* ye also put off all these, anger
1 *Thess.* 3. 8. *n.* we live, if ye stand fast in the Lord
1 *Tim.* 4. 8. having the promise of the life that *n.* is
2 *Tim.* 4. 6. for I am *n.* ready to be offered
Philem. 16. not *n.* as a servant, but above a servant
Heb. 2. 8. *n.* we see not yet all things put under him
Jam. 4. 13. go to, *n.* ye that say, to-day or to-morrow
5. 1. go to, *n.* rich men, weep and howl for miseries
1 *Pet.* 1. 8. though *n.* ye see him not, yet believing
2. 10. but are *n.* the people of G. had not obtained
1 *John* 2. 8. because the true light *n.* shineth
3. 2. *n.* are we the sons of God, it doth not appear
4. 3. and even *n.* already is it in the world
See Behold, Hear, If.

NOW *therefore.*

Gen. 20. 7. *n. therefore* restore the man his wife
29. 32. *n. therefore* my husband will love me
37. 20. come *n. theref.* and let us slay him, and cast
Josh. 24. 14. *n. therefore* fear Lord, and serve him
1 *Sam.* 12. 13. *n. theref.* behold king ye have chosen
16. *n. therefore* stand and see this great thing
2 *Sam.* 4. 11. shall I not *th. n.* require his blood?
2 *Kings* 1. 14. *n. therefore* let my life be precious
1 *Chr.* 21. 12. *n. theref.* advise thyself what word
2 *Chr.* 2. 7. send me *n. theref.* man cunning to work
Neh. 6. 9. *n. theref.* O God, strengthen my hands
Job 6. 28. *n. therefore* be content, look upon me
Psal. 2. 10. be wise, *n. th.* O ye kings, be instructed
Isa. 28. 22. *n. th.* be not mockers, lest your bands
52. 5. *n. theref.* what have I here, saith the Lord
Jer. 26. 13. *n. theref.* amend your ways and doings
29. 27. *n. therefore* why hast thou not reproved?
42. 22. *n. therefore* know certainly that ye shall die
Dan. 9. 17. *n. theref.* O our God, hear the prayer
Joel 2. 12. *therefore* also *n.* saith the Lord, turn ye
Amos 6. 7. *therefore n.* shall they go captive first
7. 16. *n. therefore* hear thou word of the Lord
Acts 10. 33. *n. theref.* are we all present before God
15. 10. *n. theref.* why tempt ye God to put a yoke
16. 36. *n. therefore* depart, and go in peace
1 *Cor.* 6. 7. *n. therefore* there is a fault among you
2 *Cor.* 8. 11. *n. therefore* perform the doing of it
Eph. 2. 19. *n. therefore* ye are no more strangers

NUMBER, *Substantive,*

Signifies, [1] *A small number, such as is easy to reckon,* Gen. 34. 30. Deut. 4. 27. [2] *A great number, or multitude, which no man can reckon or number,* Psal. 147. 4. [3] *Society, or company,* Luke 22. 3. Acts 1. 17. *The number of the beast, or the number of the name of the beast,* Rev. 13. 17, 18. *stands for the numerical value of the letters that compose his name.*

Gen. 34. 30. I being few in *n.* they shall slay me
41. 49. very much, for it was without *n.*
Exod. 12. 4. take the lamb according to *n.* of souls
16. 16. gather manna, according to *n.* of persons
23. 26. nothing barren, *n.* of thy days I will fulfil
Lev. 25. 15. the *n.* of years after the jubilee, the *n.* of years of the fruits he shall sell, 16. 50.
26. 22. beasts, which shall make you few in *n.*
Num. 1. 2. with the *n.* of their names, 18. 22.
3. 22. *n.* of males from a month old, 28, 34, 40, 43.
48. odd *n.* of them is to be redeemed to Aaron
14. 29. your whole *n.* from twenty years old
34. after the *n.* of days ye searched the land
15. 12. according to *n.* ye shall prepare, so shall ye do to every one according to their *n.*
23. 10. who can count the *n.* of fourth part of Isr.?
29. 18. their offerings shall be according to their *n.* 21. 24, 27, 30, 33, 37.
31. 36. the half of their portion was in *n.*
Deut. 4. 27. left few in *n.* among heathen, 28. 62.
7. 7. because ye were more in *n.* than any people
25. 2. judge cause him to be beaten by a certain *n.*
32. 8. he set bounds according to the *n.* of Israel
Josh. 4. 5. every man of you a stone accord. to *n.* 8.
Judg. 6. 5. they and their camels without *n.* 7. 12.
7. 6. the *n.* of them that lapped were 300 men
21. 23. according to the *n.* of them that danced
1 *Sam.* 6. 4. the *n.* of the lords of the Philistines
18. to the *n.* of all the cities of the Philistines
27. † 7. *n.* of days David dwelt in country of Phil.
2 *Sam.* 2. 15. there arose and went over by *n.* twelve
21. 20. had fingers and toes twenty-four in *n.*
24. 2. that I may know the *n.* of the people
9. Joab gave up the sum of the *n.* of the people
1 *Kings* 18. 31. Elijah took 12 stones according to *n.*
1 *Chron.* 7. 2. whose *n.* was in the days of David
9. the *n.* of them after their genealogy, 40.
11. 11. the *n.* of mighty men whom David had
16. † 19. when ye were but men of *n.* even a few
22. 16. of the gold and silver there is no *n.*
23. 3. their *n.* by their polls, man by man
† 27. the Levites *n.* from twenty and above
31. set feasts by *n.* ‖ 25. 1. *n.* of the workmen
25. 7. the *n.* that were instructed in the songs
27. 23. but David took not the *n.* of them
2 *Chr.* 12. 3. the people were without *n.* that came
26. 12. the whole *n.* of the chief of the fathers
29. 32. the *n.* of the burnt offerings, bullocks
30. 24. a great *n.* of priests sanctified themselves

Ezra 1. 9. and this is the *n.* of the vessels
2. 2. the *n.* of the men of the people of Israel
3. 4. and offered the daily burnt offerings by *n.*
6. 17. twelve he-goats, according to the *n.* of tribes
8. 34. by *n.* and by weight of every one
Esth. 9. 11. the *n.* of those slain in Shushan the palace
Job 1. 5. Job offered according to the *n.* of them all
3. 6. let it not come into the *n.* of the months
5. 9. marvellous things without *n.* 9. 10.
14. 5. the *n.* of his months are with thee
15. 20. the *n.* of years is hidden to the oppressor
16. † 22. when years of *n.* are come, I shall go
25. 3. is there any *n.* of his armies?
31. 37. I would declare to him the *n.* of my steps
34. 24. shall break in pieces mighty men without *n.*
36. 26. neither can the *n.* of his years be searched
38. 21. because the *n.* of thy days is great
Psal. 105. 12. when they were but a few men in *n.*
34. caterpillars, and that without *n.*
139. 18. they are more in *n.* than the sand
147. 4. he telleth the *n.* of the stars, calleth them
† 5. of his understanding there is no *n.*
Eccl. 2. † 3. *n.* of days of their life, 5. † 18. ‖ 6. † 12.
Cant. 6. 8. there are queens and virgins without *n.*
Isa. 10. † 19. the rest of the trees shall be *n.*
21. 17. the residue of the *n.* of archers, mighty men
40. 26. that bringeth out their host by *n.*
65. 11. that furnish the drink offering to that *n.*
Jer. 2. 28. as *n.* of thy cities are thy gods, O Judah
32. my people have forgotten me days without *n.*
11. 13. according to the *n.* of thy cities, *n.* of streets
44. 28. yet a small *n.* that escape sword shall return
Ezek. 4. 4. according to the *n.* of the days, 5, 9.
5. 3. thou shalt take a few in *n.* and bind them
12. † 16. I will leave men in *n.* from the sword
43. † 10. and let them measure the *n.*
Dan. 9. 2. I understood by books the *n.* of years
Hos. 1. 10. *n.* of Isr. shall be as the sand, *Rom.* 9. 27.
Joel 1. 6. a nation is come up strong and without *n.*
Nah. 3. 3. there is a great *n.* of carcases, they stumble
Luke 22. 3. Judas, being of the *n.* of the twelve
John 6. 10. the men sat down, in *n.* 5000, *Acts* 4. 4.
Acts 1. 15. the *n.* of the names together were 120.
5. 36. to Theudas a *n.* of men joined
6. 1. when the *n.* of disciples was multiplied, 7.
11. 21. a great *n.* believed and turned to the Lord
16. 5. the churches were increased in *n.* daily
2 *Cor.* 10. 12. for we dare not make ourselv. of the *n.*
1 *Tim.* 5. 9. let not a widow be taken into the *n.*
Rev. 5. 11. the *n.* of them was 10,000 times 10,000
7. 4. I heard the *n.* of them which were sealed
9. 16. the *n.* of the army of the horsemen
13. 17. *n.* of his name ‖ 18. count the *n.*
18. it is the *n.* of a man, and his *n.* is 666
15. 2. I saw them that had victory over *n.* of beast
20. 8. *n.* of Gog is as the sand of the sea

NUMBER, *Verb.*

Gen. 13. 16. if a man can *n.* the dust of the earth
15. 5. tell the stars, if thou be able to *n.* them
Lev. 15. 13. he shall *n.* seven days for his cleansing
28. then she shall *n.* to herself seven days
23. 16. after the seventh sabb. shall ye *n.* fifty days
25. 8. thou shalt *n.* seven sabbaths of years to thee
Num. 1. 3. Aaron shall *n.* them by their armies
49. only thou shalt not *n.* the tribe of Levi
3. 15. *n.* the children of Levi from a month old
40. *n.* all the first-born of the males of Israel
4. 23. until fifty years old shalt thou *n.* them, 30.
29. as for the sons of Merari thou shalt *n.* them
37. which Moses and Aaron did *n.* 41.
Deut. 16. 9. seven weeks shalt thou *n.* begin to *n.*
1 *Sam.* 14. 17. *n.* and see who is gone from us
2 *Sam.* 24. 1. to say, go *n.* Israel and Judah
2. go now and *n.* the people, 4. 1 *Chron.* 21. 2.
1 *Kings* 20. 25. *n.* thee an army like the army lost
1 *Chron.* 21. 1. Satan provoked David to *n.* Israel
27. 24. Joab began to *n.* but he finished not
Job 38. 37. who can *n.* the clouds in wisdom?
39. 2. canst thou *n.* the months that they fulfil?
Ps. 90. 12. so teach us to *n.* our days, that we may
Isa 65. 12. therefore will I *n.* you to the sword
Rev. 7. 9. a great multitude which no man could *n.*

NUMBERS.

1 *Chron.* 12. 23. these are the *n.* of the bands
2 *Chron.* 17. 14. these are the *n.* of them, accord.
Psal. 71. 15. for I know not the *n.* thereof

NUMBERED.

Gen. 13. 16. then shall thy seed also be *n.*
16. 10. it shall not be *n.* for multitude, 32. 12.
Exod. 30. 13. that passeth among them that are *n.* 14.
38. 25. them that were *n.* of the congregation, 26.
Num. 1. 19. he *n.* them in the wilderness of Sinai
21. those that were *n.* of them, 23, 44, 46. ‖ 2. 4, 13, 15, 19, 21, 23, 26, 28, 30.
47. the Levites were not *n.* among them, 2. 33.
2. 9. all that were *n.* in the camp of Judah
16. were *n.* in camp of Reuben ‖ 24. *n.* of Ephraim
31. *n.* in camp of Dan ‖ 3. 16. Moses *n.* them, 42.
3. 39. all that were *n.* of the Levites were 22,000
4. 34. they *n.* of the sons of the Kohathites, 37.
38. those that were *n.* of the Gershonites, 41.
42. those that were *n.* of the sons of Merari, 45.
45. these whom Moses and Aaron *n.* 46.
7. 2. who were princes and over them that were *n.*
14. 29. carcases fell in wilderness, all that were *n.*
26. 51. these were *n.* of the children of Israel
57. *n.* of the Levites ‖ 63. Moses and Eleazar *n.*
Josh. 8. 10. Joshua rose early and *n.* the people
Judg. 20. 15. the children of Benjamin were *n.*
1 *Sam.* 11. 8. and when he *n.* them in Bezek
15. 4. Saul *n.* people in Telaim, 200,000 footmen
2 *Sam.* 18. 1. David *n.* the people that were with him
24. 10. David's heart smote him after he had *n.*
1 *Kings* 3. 8. a great people that cannot be *n.*
8. 5. sheep and oxen that could not be *n.* 2 *Chr.* 5. 6.
20. 15. then he *n.* the princes of the provinces
26. at return of the year Ben-hadad *n.* the Syrians
27. Israel were *n.* and were like two flocks
2 *Kings* 3. 6. and king Jehoram *n.* all Israel
1 *Chron.* 21. 17. I commanded the people to be *n.*
23. 3. now the Levites were *n.* from thirty years, 27.
2 *Chr.* 2. 17. Solomon *n.* all the strangers in Israel

2 *Chr.* 25. 5. he *n.* them from twenty years old and
Ezra 1. 8. Cyrus *n.* the vessels to Sheshbazzar
Psal. 40. 5. they are more than can be *n.*
Eccl. 1. 15. that which is wanting cannot be *n.*
Isa. 22. 10. ye have *n.* the houses of Jerusalem
53. 12. he was *n.* with transgressors, *Mark* 15. 28.
Jer. 33. 22. as the host of heaven, cannot be *n.*
Dan. 5. 26. God hath *n.* thy kingdom, and finished it
Hos. 1. 10. as the sand of the sea, which cannot be *n.*
Mat. 10. 30. hairs of your head are all *n.* *Luke* 12. 7.
Acts 1. 17. for he was *n.* with us, and obtained part
26. Matthias was *n.* with the eleven apostles

NUMBEREST.

Exod. 30. 12. shall give every man a ransom when thou *n.* that there be no plague when thou *n.*
Job 14. 16. for now thou *n.* my steps, dost not thou

NUMBERING.

Gen. 41. 49. Joseph gathered corn until he left *n.*
2 *Chron.* 2. 17. after the *n.* wherewith David numb.

NURSE

Signifies, [1] *A woman who suckles a child,* Exod. 2. 7. [2] *One that assists in bringing up of children,* Ruth 4. 16. It is applied, [1] *To godly kings and queens, who have a sincere affection and tender regard to the church,* Isa. 49. 23. [2] *To faithful ministers of the gospel, who are mild and obliging, using all kind and winning expressions, as nurses do to please children,* 1 Thess. 2. 7.

Gen. 24. 59. they sent away Rebekah and her *n.*
35. 8. but Deborah, Rebekah's *n.* died, and was b.
Exod. 2. 7. shall I call to thee a *n.* of Hebr. women?
Ruth 4. 16. Naomi took the child, and became *n.*
2 *Sam.* 4. 4. his *n.* took him up and fled, and he fell
2 *Kings* 11. 2. they hid him and his *n.* 2 *Chr.* 22. 11.
Acts 13. † 18. he suffered, as a *n.* beareth the child
1 *Thess.* 2. 7. were gentle, as a *n.* cherish. her childr.

NURSE.

Exod. 2. 7. that she may *n.* the child for thee
9. take this child away, and *n.* it for me, I will give

NURSED.

Exod. 2. 9. the woman took the child, and *n.* it
Isa. 60. 4. thy daughters shall be *n.* at thy side

NURSING.

Num. 11. 12. carry them in thy bosom, as a *n.* father
Isa. 49. 23. kings be *n.* fathers, queens thy *n.* mothers

NURTURE.

Eph. 6. 4. bring them up in the *n.* of the Lord

NUTS.

Gen. 43. 11. carry down a present, *n.* and almonds
Cant. 6. 11. I went down into the garden of *n.*

O.

OAK.

Gen. 35. 4. Jacob hid the gods under the *o.* by Shec.
8. Debor. Rebekah's nurse, was buried under an *o.*
Josh. 24. 26. and set it up there under an *o.*
Judg. 6. 11. an angel of the Lord sat under an *o.*
9. † 6. made Abimelech king by the *o.* of the pillar
2 *Sam.* 18. 9. Absalom's mule went under an *o.*
10. Absalom hanged in an *o.* ‖ 14. alive in the *o.*
1 *Kings* 13. 14. he found the man of God under an *o.*
1 *Chr.* 10. 12. buried their bones under *o.* in Jabesh
Isa. 1. 30. ye shall be as an *o.* whose leaf fadeth
6. 13. as teil tree, or *o.* whose substance is in them
44. 14. he taketh the cypress and *o.* to make a god
Ezek. 6. 13. among their idols under every thick *o.*

OAKS.

Isa. 1. 29. shall be ashamed of the *o.* which ye desir.
2. 13. the day of the Lord on all the *o.* of Bashan
57. † 5. inflaming yourselves among the *o.*
Ezek. 27. 6. of *o.* of Bashan have they made thine oars
Hos. 4. 13. and burn incense upon the hills under *o.*
Amos 2. 9. the Amorite was strong as the *o.*
Zech. 11. 2. howl, fir-tree, howl, O ye *o.* of Bashan

OAR.

Ezek. 27. 29. all that handle the *o.* shall cry

OARS

Isa. 33. 21. wherein shall go no galley with *o.*
Ezek. 27. 6. of the oaks of Bashan they made thy *o.*

OATH

Is a solemn action, whereby we call upon God, the searcher of hearts, to witness the truth of what we affirm, for the ending of strife or controversies, Heb. 6. 16. It is spoken, (I) *Of God the Father, who sware,* [1] *To his Son, the Lord Messiah, the Mediator of the new covenant, that Christ should be his only and eternal Priest, hereby honouring his Son, and giving strong consolation to his people, in such a Royal High Priest, who should effectually manage all their concerns with him for ever,* Psal. 110. 4. Heb. 7. 21. [2] *To men, either in love or wrath, hereby assuring them of the immutability of his purposes, that the blessings he promised should be bestowed, and that the judgments he threatened should be inflicted,* Gen. 22. 16, 17. Psal. 95. 11. Heb. 6. 17. (II) *Of men, who when necessity, or the importance of a matter, requires it, ought to swear,* [1] *Religiously, by God only,* Deut. 6. 13. ‖ 10. 20. [2] *Reverently, and with fear,* Eccl. 9. 2. [3] *Cautiously,* Gen. 24. 5, 8. Josh. 2. 17. [4] *Sincerely, faithfully, and justly,* Jer. 4. 2.

Men must not swear, [1] *Idolatrously, in the name of any false gods, or in the name of inanimate things,* Josh. 23. 7. Jam. 5. 12. [2] *Deceitfully,* Jer. 42. 5, 20. [3] *Falsely,* Lev. 6. 3. ‖ 19. 12. [4] *Rashly,* Lev. 5. 4. Mat. 14. 7.

Gen. 24. 8. thou shalt be clear from this my *o.* 41.
26. 3. I will perform the *o.* which I swear to Abraham, *Deut.* 7. 8. *Psal.* 105. 9. *Jer.* 11. 5.
28. let there be now an *o.* betwixt us and thee
50. 25. Joseph took an *o.* of the children of Israel
Exod. 22. 11. an *o.* of the Lord shall be between us
Lev. 5. 4. that a man shall pronounce with an *o.*
Num. 5. 19. the priest shall charge her by an *o.*
21. L. make thee a curse and an *o.* among people
30. 2. if a man swear an *o.* to bind his soul, 10.
13. every vow, and every binding *o.* to afflict soul
Deut. 29. 12. his *o.* which the Lord maketh with thee

Deut. 29. 14. neither with you only do I make this o.
Josh. 2. 17. we will be blameless of this thine o.
9. 20. lest wrath be on us, because of the o.
Judg. 21. 5. for Israel had made a great o.
1 Sam. 14. 26. for the people feared the o.
27. when Saul charged them with the o. 28.
2 Sam. 21. 7. king spared Mephibosheth, bec. of o.
1 Kings 2. 43. why then hast thou not kept the o.?
8. 31. and an o. be laid on him, and the o. come before thine altar in this house, 2 Chr. 6. 22.
18. 10. he took an o. of the kingdom and nation
2 Kings 11. 4. Jehoiada took an o. of them in house
1 Chr. 16. 16. be mindful of his o. to Isaac
2 Chr. 15. 15. all Judah rejoiced at the o.
Neh. 5. 12. and Nehemiah took an o. of the priests
10. 29. they entered into an o. to walk in God's law
Eccl. 8. 2. and that in regard of the o. of God
9. 2. he that sweareth, as he that feareth an o.
Ezek. 16. 59. which hast despised the o. 17, 18, 19.
17. 13. a covenant, and hath taken an o. of him
16. that made him king, whose o. he despised
Dan. 9. 11. curse is poured on us, and o. writt. in law
Zech. 8. 17. love no false o. for this I hate
Mat. 14. 7. he promised with an o. to give her
9. nevertheless, for the o. sake, Mark 6. 26.
26. 72. again he denied with an o. I know not man
Luke 1. 73. the o. which he sware to our father
Acts 2. 30. that God hath sworn with an o. to him
23. 21. which have bound themselves with an o.
Heb. 6. 16. an o. for confirmation is an end of all strife
17. God confirmed it by an o. that by two things
7. 20. as not without an o. he was made priest, 21.
28. the o. which was since the law, maketh the Son
Jam. 5. 12. swear not by the earth, nor any other o.

OATHS.

Ezek. 21. 23. divination to them that have sworn o.
Hab. 3. 9. the bow made naked, according to the o.
Mat. 5. 33. shalt perform to the Lord thine o.

OBEDIENCE

Is twofold, (I) *That which is given to God*, and is spoken, [1] *Of Christ the great Redeemer's perfect obedience to the will of his Father, both in doing and suffering, by the merit of which sinners are justified before God*, Rom. 5. 19. [2] *Of that voluntary, free, and cheerful obedience, which the angels in heaven yield to the commands of God*, Psal. 103. 20. Mat. 6. 10. [3] *Of that involuntary obedience which devils and wicked men are forced to yield to the commands of God*, Exod. 11. 1. | 12. 31. Mark 1. 27. Luke 4. 36. [4] *Of the obedience of good men, which consists*, [1] *In believing and embracing the gospel, and subjecting themselves thereunto; whence it is, that* obedience *is put for* faith, Rom. 16. 19. compared with Rom. 1. 8. [2] *In a conformity of our affections and actions unto the will of God revealed in his word, which is begun in this life, but is to be perfected in heaven*, Rom. 6. 16. 1 Pet. 1. 14. [5] *Of the subjection of all creatures to the command of God*, Psal. 105. 30, 31. *At his command the ravens did feed* Elijah, 1 Kings 17. 4, 6. *The fish vomited out* Jonah, *chap.* 2. 10. *The tempestuous sea became calm*, Mat. 8. 26, 27. *He spake, and there came frogs, flies, lice, hail, locusts, &c. upon* Egypt, Psal. 105. 30, 31, 32, 34. (II) *That which is due, or performed to man, either*, [1] *By the unreasonable creatures*, Jam. 3. 3. *Or*, [2] *By inferiors to their superiors: as, by* wives *unto their* husbands, Tit. 2. 5. Children *to their* parents, Eph. 6. 1. Servants *to their* masters, Eph. 6. 5. Subjects *to their* princes *or* magistrates, Rom. 13. 1. *And by* people *to their* pastors, Heb. 13. 17.

2 Sam. 22. † 45. strangers shall yield feigned o. unto me as soon as they hear, Psal. 18. † 44. | 66. † 3.
Rom. 1. 5. for o. to the faith among all nations
5. 19. by the o. of one shall many be made righteous
6. 16. of sin to death, or of o. unto righteousness
16. 19. your o. is come abroad unto all men
26. made known to all nations for the o. of faith
1 Cor. 14. 34. women are commanded to be under o.
2 Cor. 7. 15. he remembereth the o. of you all
10. 5. bringing every thought to the o. of Christ
6. all disobedience, when your o. is fulfilled
Philem. 21. having confidence in thy o. I wrote
Heb. 5. 8. yet learned he o. by the things he suffered
1 Pet. 1. 2. through sanctification of the Spirit to o.

OBEDIENT.

Exod. 24. 7. Lord hath said, we will do, and be o.
Num. 27. 20. put honour on him, that Isr. may be o.
Deut. 4. 30. if turn to L. and shall be o. to his voice
8. 20. ye shall perish, because ye would not be o.
2 Sam. 22. 45. strangers shall be o. unto me
Prov. 25. 12. so is a wise reprover upon an o. ear
Isa. 1. 19. if o. ye shall eat the good of the land
42. 24. neither were they o. to his law
Acts 6. 7. the priests were o. to the faith
Rom. 15. 18. to make Gentiles o. by word and deed
2 Cor. 2. 9. might know whether ye be o. in all things
Eph. 6. 5. servants, be o. to your masters, Tit. 2. 9.
Phil. 2. 8. Christ became o. unto death of the cross
Tit. 2. 5. wives, be o. || 1 Pet. 1. 14. children, be o.

OBEY.

Gen. 27. 8. therefore, my son, o. my voice, 13. 43.
Exod. 5. 2. who is the Lord, that I should o. him?
19. 5. now if ye will o. my voice indeed
23. 21. o. his voice || 22. if shalt indeed o. his voice
Deut. 11. 27. a blessing, if ye o. commands of Lord
13. 4. o. his voice, 27. 10. 30. 2, 8. 1 Sam. 12. 14.
30. 20. and that thou mayest o. his voice
Josh. 24. 24. the Lord's voice will we o.
1 Sam. 8. 19. the people refused to o. voice of Samuel
15. 22. behold, to o. is better than sacrifice
Neh. 9. 17. and refused to o. neither were mindful
Job 36. 11. if they o. and serve him they shall spend
Psal. 18. 44. as soon as they hear, they shall o. me
Prov. 30. 17. the eye that despiseth, to o. his mother
Isa. 11. 14. the children of Ammon shall o. them
Jer. 7. 23. o. my voice, and I will be your God, and ye shall be my people, 11. 4, 7.
26. 13. amend your ways, and o. the voice of the Lord your God, 38. 20. Zech. 6. 15.
Jer. 35. 14. Rechabites o. their father's commandm.
42. 6. we will o. the voice of Lord our God, that it may be well with us when we o. the Lord
Dan. 7. 27. and all dominions shall serve and o. him
Mat. 8. 27. what manner of man is this, that even winds and sea o. him? Mark 4. 41. Luke 8. 25.
Mark 1. 27. even the unclean spirits o. him
Luke 17. 6. be thou plucked up, and it shall o. you
Acts 5. 29. we ought to o. God rather than men
32. whom God hath given to them that o. him
Rom. 2. 8. but to them that o. unrighteousness
6. 12. that ye should o. it in the lusts thereof
16. know ye not, to whom ye yield yourselves servants to o. his servants ye are to whom ye o.
Eph. 6. 1. children, o. your parents, Col. 3. 20.
Col. 3. 22. servants, o. in all things your masters
Tit. 3. 1. put them in mind to o. magistrates
Heb. 5. 9. author of eternal salvat. to all that o. him
13. 17. o. them that have the rule over you
Jam. 3. 3. put bits in horses' mouths, that they may o.

Not OBEY, OBEY not.

Deut. 11. 28. a curse, if ye will not o. the commandments of Lord your God, 28. 62. 1 Sam. 12. 15. Job 36. 12. Jer. 12. 17. | 18. 10.
21. 18. who will not o. the voice of his father, 20.
1 Sam. 15. 19. wherefore then didst thou not o.?
Jer. 42. 13. but if ye say, we will not o. the Lord
Dan. 9. 11. that they might not o. thy voice
Acts 7. 39. to whom our fathers would not o.
Rom. 2. 8. that are contentious, and do not o. truth
Gal. 3. 1. who bewitcheth you, that should not o.? 5. 7.
2 Thess. 1. 8. taking veng. on them that o. not gospel
3. 14. if any man o. not our word, note that man
1 Pet. 3. 1. if any o. not the word, they may be won
4. 17. what shall end be of them that o. not gospel?

OBEYED.

Gen. 22. 18. be blessed, because thou hast o. 26. 5.
28. 7. that Jacob o. his father and his mother
Josh. 22. 2. have o. my voice in all I command. you
1 Sam. 15. 20. Saul said, I have o. the voice of Lord
24. because I feared the people, and o. their voice
28. 21. behold, thine handmaid hath o. thy voice
1 Chron. 29. 23. then all Israel o. Solomon
2 Chron. 11. 4. they o. the words of the Lord
Jer. 34. 10. then they o. and let them go
35. 8. thus have we o. the voice of Jonadab, 10.
18. because ye o. the commandment of your fath.
Dan. 9. 10. neither have we o. the voice of the Lord
Hag. 1. 12. the people o. the voice of the Lord
Acts 5. 36. many as o. Theudas were scattered, 37.
Rom. 6. 17. have o. from heart that form of doctrine
Phil. 2. 12. ye have o. not in my presence only
Heb. 11. 8. by faith Abraham o. and went out
1 Pet. 3. 6. Sarah o. Abraham, calling him, Lord

Not OBEYED.

Josh. 5. 6. were consumed, because they o. not
Judg. 2. 2. but ye have not o. my voice, 6. 10.
1 Kings 20. 36. thou hast not o. the voice of Lord
2 Kings 18. 12. because they o. not the voice of Lord
Prov. 5. 13. and have not o. the voice of my teachers
Jer. 3. 13. ye have not o. my voice, saith the Lord, 25. | 42. 21. | 43. 4, 7. | 44. 23.
9. 13. they have not o. my voice, 11. 8. | 17. 23. | 32. 23. | 40. 3. Dan. 9. 10. 14.
Zeph. 3. 2. she o. not the voice, she drew not near
Rom. 10. 16. but they have not all o. the gospel

OBEYEDST.

1 Sam. 28. 18. because thou o. not the voice of Lord
Jer. 22. 21. thy manner that thou o. not my voice

OBEYETH.

Prov. 15. † 32. that o. reproof getteth understanding
Isa. 50. 10. who that o. the voice of his servant?
Jer. 7. 28. this is a nation that o. not the Lord
11. 3. cursed be the man that o. not the words of

OBEYING.

Judg. 2. 17. your fathers o. but they did not so
1 Sam. 15. 22. in sacrifice, as in o. the voice of Lord
1 Pet. 1. 22. have purified your souls in o. the truth

OBEISANCE.

Gen. 37. 7. your sheaves made o. to my sheaf
9. the sun, moon, and eleven stars made o. to me
43. 28. they bowed and made o. to Joseph
Exod. 18. 7. Moses did o. to his father-in-law
2 Sam. 1. 2. the Amalekite did o. to David
14. 4. the woman of Tekoah did o. to the king
15. 5. when any man came nigh to do him o.
1 Kings 1. 16. Bath-sheba did o. to king David
2 Chron. 24. 17. princes of Judah made o. to the king

OBJECT.

Acts 24. 19. and o. if they had ought against me

OBLATION.

Lev. 2. 4. an o. of a meat offering baken, 5, 7, 13.
12. as for o. of the first-fruits, ye shall offer them
3. 1. if his o. be a sacrifice of peace offering
7. 14. he shall offer one out of the whole o.
29. he shall bring his o. to the Lord, of sacrifices
22. 18. that will offer his o. for all his vows
Num. 18. 9. every o. of theirs shall be most holy
31. 50. we have brought an o. for the Lord
Isa. 19. 21. the Egyptians shall do o. to the Lord
40. 20. that is so impoverished that he hath no o.
66. 3. that offereth an o. as if he offered swine's flesh
Jer. 14. 12. when they offer an o. I will not accept
Ezek. 44. 30. and every o. shall be the priest's
45. 1. when ye shall divide the land, offer an o.
13. this is the o. ye shall offer, 48. 9, 20, 21.
16. shall give this o. for the prince in Israel
Dan. 2. 46. that they should offer an o. to Daniel
9. 21. time of the even o. || 27. shall cause o. to cease

OBLATIONS.

Lev. 7. 38. he commanded Israel to offer their o.
2 Chron. 31. 14. to distribute the o. of the Lord
Prov. 29. † 4. but a man of o. overthroweth it
Isa. 1. 13. bring no more vain o. unto me
Ezek. 20. 40. I will require the first-fruits of your o.
44. 30. every sort of your o. shall be the priest's

OBSCURE.

Prov. 20. 20. his lamp shall be put out in o. darkness

OBSCURITY.

By obscurity, *or* darkness, *all kinds of adversity and calamity are resembled, as happiness and prosperity are by* light, Isa. 58. 10. *It is said, that the Jews, after they were delivered from their dark and calamitous condition in the* Babylonish *captivity, observed a feast, which they called,* The feast of lights; *because so great a happiness of being delivered from bondage, and of having the service of the temple re-established, broke forth upon them beyond their hope, as the rays of the sun dart themselves through the clouds.* Obscurity *also signifies spiritual ignorance and blindness, from which God delivers his people, when he bestows upon them the clear and saving knowledge of the truth*, Isa. 29. 18.

Isa. 29. 18. the eyes of the blind shall see out of o.
58. 10. then shall thy light rise in o. and darkness
59. 9. we wait for light, but behold o. for brightness

OBSERVATION.

The kingdom of God cometh not with observation, Luke 17. 20. *That kingdom which God will set up in the world, will not become conspicuous and remarkable by any outward splendour, or worldly pomp, but by its inward power and efficacy upon the hearts and minds of men.*

Mal. 3. † 14. what profit that we have kept his o.?
Luke 17. 20. the kingdom of God cometh not with o.

OBSERVATIONS.

Exod. 12. † 42. it is a night of o. unto the Lord
Neh. 13. † 14. my deeds done for the o. thereof

OBSERVE.

Exod. 12. 17. ye shall o. the feast of unleaven. bread, for I brought armies out of Egypt, 24. Deut. 16. 1.
31. 16. o. the sabbath || 34. 22. o. feast of weeks
34. 11. o. thou that which I command thee this day, Deut. 12. 28. | 24. 8.
Lev. 19. 26. nor shall ye use enchantments, o. times
37. ye shall o. all my statutes, 2 Chron. 7. 17. Neh. 1. 5. Psal. 105. 45. Ezek. 37. 24.
Num. 28. 2. my sacrifice shall ye o. to offer me
Deut. 16. 13. o. the feast of tabernacles seven days
1 Kings 20. 33. now the men did diligently o.
Ps. 5. † 8. because of those which o. me, 27. † 11.
54. † 5. he shall reward evil to those that o. me
71. † 10. they that o. my soul take counsel together
107. 43. whoso is wise, and will o. these things
119. 34. I shall o. it with my whole heart
Prov. 23. 26. and let thine eyes o. my ways
Jer. 8. 7. the crane and swallow o. the time
Ezek. 20. 18. neither o. their judgments nor defile
Hos. 13. 7. as a leopard by the way will I o. them
Jonah 2. 8. that o. lying vanities, forsake their mercies
Mat. 28. 20. teaching them to o. all things whatever
Acts 16. 21. customs not lawful to o. being Romans
21. 25. concluded that the Gentiles o. no such thing
Gal. 4. 10. ye o. days, and months, and times
1 Tim. 5. 21. then o. these things without preferring
See Do.

OBSERVED.

Gen. 37. 11. but his father o. the saying
Exod. 12. 42. it is a night to be much o. to the Lord
Num. 15. 22. have erred, and not o. commandments
Deut. 33. 9. Levi o. thy word, kept thy covenant
2 Sam. 11. 16. when Joab o. city, he assigned Uriah
2 Kings 21. 6. Manasseh o. times, 2 Chron. 33. 6.
Hos. 14. 8. I have heard him, and o. him
Mark 6. 20. for Herod feared John and o. him
10. 20. all these have I o. from my youth

OBSERVER.

Deut. 18. 10. there shall not be found an o. of times

OBSERVERS.

Deut. 18. 14. these nations hearkened to o. of times
Ps. 59. † 10. God shall let me see my desire on my o.

OBSERVEST.

Job 10. † 27. thou o. all my paths, settest a print
Isa. 42. 20. seeing many things, but thou o. not

OBSERVETH.

Eccl. 11. 4. he that o. the wind shall not sow

OBSTINATE.

Deut. 2. 30. the Lord thy God made his heart o.
Isa. 48. 4. because I knew that thou art o.

OBTAIN.

Gen. 16. 2. it may be I may o. children by her
1 Chron. 29. † 14. that we should o. strength to offer
Prov. 8. 35. and shall o. favour of the Lord
Isa. 35. 10. they shall o. joy and gladness, 51. 11.
Dan. 11. 21. he shall o. the kingdom by flatteries
Luke 20. 35. be accounted worthy to o. that world
Rom. 11. 31. thro' your mercy they may o. mercy
1 Cor. 9. 24. so run that ye may o.
25. they do it to o. a corruptible crown, but we
1 Thess. 5. 9. but to o. salvation by our L. Jes. Chr.
2 Tim. 2. 10. may o. salvation which is in Chr. Jes.
Heb. 4. 16. that we may o. mercy, and find grace
11. 35. that they might o. a better resurrection
Jam. 4. 2. ye kill, ye desire to have, and cannot o.

OBTAINED.

2 Chron. 2. † 6. but who hath o. strength to build
Neh. 13. 6. after certain days I o. leave of the king
Esth. 2. 9. Esther o. kindness, || 17. she o. grace
Hos. 2. 23. have mercy on her that had not o. mercy
Acts 1. 17. and had o. part of this ministry
22. 28. with a great sum o. I this freedom
26. 22. having o. help of G. I continue to this day
27. 13. supposing that they had o. their purpose
Rom. 11. 7. what then? Israel hath not o. what he seeketh for, but the election hath o. it
30. ye have now o. mercy through their unbelief
1 Cor. 7. 25. as one that hath o. mercy of the Lord
Eph. 1. 11. in whom we have o. an inheritance
1 Tim. 1. 13. I o. mercy, because I did it ignorantly, 16.
Heb. 1. 4. o. a more excellent name than they
6. 15. he had patiently endured, he o. the promises
8. 6. he hath o. a more excellent ministry than they
9. 12. having o. eternal redemption for us
11. 2. by it the elders o. a good report, 39.
4. Abel o. witness that he was righteous
33. who o. promises, stopped mouths of lions
1 Pet. 2. 10. which had not o. mercy, but now have o.
2 Pet. 1. 1. that have o. like precious faith with us
See Favour.

OBTAINING.

2 Thess. 2. 14. to o. of the glory of our L. Jes. Chr.

OCCASION.

Gen. 43. 18. that he may seek *o.* against us and fall
Judg. 9.33. mayest do as thou shalt find *o.* 1 *Sam.* 10.7.
14. 4. Samson sought *o.* against the Philistines
2 *Sam.* 12. 14. given great *o.* to enemies to blaspheme
Ezra 7. 20. which thou shalt have *o.* to bestow
Jer. 2. 24. in her *o.* who can turn her away?
Ezek. 18. 3. shall not have *o.* any more to use prov.
Dan. 6. 4. sought to find *o.* and could find none *o.* 5.
Rom. 7. 8. sin taking *o.* by the commandment, 11.
14. 13. put not an *o.* to fall in his brother's way
2 *Cor.* 5. 12. we give you *o.* to glory on our behalf
8. 8. I speak by *o.* of the forwardness of others
11.12. that I may cut off *o.* from them which desire *o.*
Gal. 5. 13. only use not liberty for an *o.* to the flesh
1 *Tim.* 5. 14. younger give none *o.* to the adversary
1 *John* 2. 10. there is none *o.* of stumbling in him

OCCASIONED.

1 *Sam.* 22. 22. I have *o.* the death of all the persons

OCCASIONS.

Deut. 22. 14. and give *o.* of speech against her, 17.
Job 33. 10. behold, he findeth *o.* against me

OCCUPATION.

Gen. 46. 33. shall say, what is your *o.*? 47. 3. *Jon.* 1. 8.
Acts 18. 3. for by *o.* they were tent-makers
19. 25. whom he called, with the workmen of like *o.*

OCCUPY.

Ezek. 27. 9. with mariners to *o.* thy merchandise
Luke 19. 13. he said to his servants, *o.* till I come

OCCUPIED.

Exod. 38. 24. the gold that was *o.* for the work
Judg. 16. 11. if bind with new ropes that never were *o.*
Ezek. 27. 16. Syria *o.* ‖ 19. Dan and Javan *o.*
21. Arabia *o.* ‖ 22. Sheba *o.* in thy fairs
Heb. 13. 9. meats not profited them that have *o.*

OCCUPIERS.

Ezek. 27. 27. the *o.* of thy merchandise shall fall

OCCUPIETH.

1 *Cor.* 14. 16. he that *o.* the room of the unlearned

OCCURRENT.

1 *Kings* 5. 4. there is neither adversary nor evil *o.*

ODD.

Num. 3. 48. the *o.* number of them is to be redeemed

ODIOUS.

1 *Chron.* 19. 6. the Ammonites made themselves *o.*
Prov. 30. 23. for an *o.* woman when she is married

ODOUR.

John 12. 3. house was filled with *o.* of the ointment
Phil. 4. 18. an *o.* of a sweet smell, a sacrifice

ODOURS.

Lev. 26. 31. will not smell the savour of your sweet *o.*
2 *Chron.* 16. 14. Asa was laid in a bed of sweet *o.*
Esth. 2. 12. six months with oil of myrrh and sweet *o.*
Jer. 34. 5. so shall they burn *o.* for thee and lament
Dan. 2. 46. that they should offer sweet *o.* to Daniel
Rev. 5. 8. having harps and golden vials full of *o.*
18. 13. no man buyeth their *o.* and ointments

OFFENCE

Signifies, *Any thing that a man finds in his way, that may occasion him to stumble or fall: thus* Moses *forbids,* To put a stumbling-block (*or an offence*) before the blind, *Lev.* 19. 14. *that is, neither wood, stone, nor any thing else that may make him stumble or fall. It was prophesied,* That Christ Jesus should be for a stone of stumbling and rock of offence to both the houses of Israel, *Isa.* 8. 14. *His humiliation, his poverty, his birth, death, and cross, were rocks against which the* Jews *struck, and upon which they have fallen and are broken; because they could not be convinced, that such humble qualifications could belong to the* Messiah *they expected. And the apostle* Paul *exhorts the* Corinthians, To give none offence to Jews or Gentiles, 1 *Cor.* 10. 32. *that is, not to hinder them in their way to heaven, or induce them to act with a doubting conscience, by an unseasonable use of christian liberty.*

In a moral sense, there is an active and passive scandal *or* offence. *The first is that which we give to others by our words or actions; and the second is taken from others, by seeing their evil words or actions. It signifies,* [1] *An impediment,* Mat. 16. 23. [2] *Sin,* Rom. 4. 25. [3] *Contempt,* Mat. 18. 7.

1 *Sam.* 25. 31. this shall be no *o.* of heart to my lord
Isa. 8. 14. but a rock of *o.* to both the houses of Isr.
Hos. 5. 15. till they acknowledge their *o.* and seek me
Mat. 16. 23. get behind me, Satan, thou art *o.* to me
18. 7. woe to that man by whom the *o.* cometh
Acts 24. 16. a conscience void of *o.* towards God
Rom. 5. 15. but not as the *o.* so also is the free gift, for if through the *o.* of one many be dead, 18.
17. for if by one man's *o.* death reigned by one
20. the law entered that the *o.* might abound
9. 33. I lay in Sion a stumbling-stone, and rock of *o.*
14. 20. it is evil for that man who eateth with *o.*
1 *Cor.* 10. 32. give none *o.* in any thing, 2 *Cor.* 6. 3.
2 *Cor.* 11. 7. have I commit. an *o.* in abasing myself?
Gal. 5. 11. then is the *o.* of the cross ceased
Phil. 1. 10. may be without *o.* till the day of Christ
1 *Pet.* 2. 8. a rock of *o.* to them which stumble

OFFENCES.

Eccl. 10. 4. for yielding pacifieth great *o.*
Mat. 18. 7. woe to the world because of *o.* for it must needs be that *o.* come, *Luke* 17. 1.
Rom. 4. 25. who was delivered for our *o.* and raised
5. 16. but the free gift is of many *o.* to justification
16. 17. I beseech you, mark them which cause *o.*

OFFEND

Signifies, [1] *To commit any sin in thought, word, or deed,* Jam. 3. 2. [2] *To draw one to evil, or be a let and hinderance to that which is good,* Mat. 5. 29, 30. [3] *To take occasion of sinning when none is given, thus the Pharisees were offended at Christ,* Mat. 15. 12. *that is, they were more alienated from his person and doctrine.* [4] *To be scandalized, or stumbled by the example of another,* 1 Cor. 8. 13. [5] *To act unjustly, or injuriously,* Acts 25. 8. [6] *To wrong,* Psal. 73. 15.

Job 34. 31. it is meet to say, I will not *o.* any more
Ps. 73. 15. I should *o.* against generat. of thy childr.
119. 165. that love thy law, nothing shall *o.* them
Jer. 2. 3. all that devour him shall *o.* evil shall come
50. 7. and their adversaries said, we *o.* not
Hos. 4. 15. tho' Isr. play the harlot, let not Judah *o.*
Hab. 1. 11. and he shall pass over and *o.* imputing
Mat. 5. 29. if thy right eye *o.* thee, pluck it out
30. if thy hand *o.* thee, 18. 8, 9. *Mark* 9. 43, 45, 47.
13. 41. they shall gather all things that *o.*
17. 27. lest we should *o.* them, go to the sea
18. 6. whoso *o.* one of these, *Mark* 9. 42. *Luke* 17. 2.
John 6. 61. he said to them, doth this *o.* you?
1 *Cor.* 8. 13. if meat make thy brother *o.* lest he *o.*
Jam. 2. 10. yet *o.* in one point, he is guilty of all
3. 2. in many things we *o.* all, if any man *o.* not

OFFENDED.

Gen. 20. 9. and what have I *o.* thee? *Jer.* 37. 18.
40. 1. the butler and baker had *o.* their lord
2 *Kings* 18. 14. saying, I have *o.* return from me
2 *Chr.* 28. 13. we have *o.* against the Lord already
Ezra 10. † 13. for we have greatly *o.* in this
Prov. 18. 19. a brother *o.* is harder to be won than
Ezek. 25. 12. because Edom hath greatly *o.*
Hos. 13. 1. when Ephraim *o.* in Baal, he died
Mat. 11. 6. bless. is he who shall not be *o.* *Luke* 7. 23.
13. 21. when tribulation or persecution ariseth because of the word, by and by he is *o.* *Mark* 4. 17.
57. and they were *o.* in him, *Mark* 6. 3.
15. 12. the Pharisees were *o.* after they heard
24. 10. then shall many be *o.* and betray one anoth.
26. 31. all ye shall be *o.* because of me this night
33. Peter said, though all men shall be *o.* because of thee, yet will I never be *o.* *Mark* 14. 29.
John 16. 1. I have spoken, that ye should not be *o.*
Acts 25. 8. nor yet against Cesar have I *o.* at all
Rom. 14. 21. whereby thy brother is *o.* or made weak
2 *Cor.* 11. 29. who is *o.* and I burn not?

OFFENDER.

Isa. 29. 21. that make a man an *o.* for a word
Acts 25. 11. if I be an *o.* or have committed any thing

OFFENDERS.

1 *Kings* 1. 21. I and my son Sol. shall be counted *o.*

OFFER.

Exod. 22. 29. not delay to *o.* the first of the fruits
23. 18. thou shalt not *o.* the blood, 34. 25.
29. 36. thou shalt *o.* every day a bullock for atonem.
38. thou shalt *o.* on altar two lambs of first year
39. one lamb thou shalt *o.* in the morning, and the other lamb at even, 41. *Num.* 28. 4, 8.
30. 9. ye shall *o.* no strange incense thereon
35. 24. every one that did *o.* silver and brass
Lev. 1. 3. *o.* male without blemish, 3. 6. | 22. 19, 20.
2. 1. and when any will *o.* a meat offering to the Lord, 14. | 23. 16. *Num.* 6. 17.
13. with all thine offerings thou shalt *o.* salt
3. 1. if he *o.* a peace offering, he shall *o.* it without blemish before the Lord, 6. | 9. 2. | 19. 5.
7. if he *o.* a lamb for his offering, 14. 12.
12. the goat he shall *o.* before the Lord
4. 14. congregation *o.* a young bullock, *Num.* 15. 24.
5. 8. *o.* that for the sin offering first, 9. 7.
6. 14. the sons of Aaron shall *o.* it before the Lord, 22. | 14. 19. | 15. 15, 30. *Num.* 6. 11.
7. 3. he shall *o.* of it all the fat thereof
12. if he *o.* it for a thanksgiving, 22. 29.
38. Israel to *o.* their oblations to the Lord
17. 7. they shall no more *o.* their sacrifices to devils
9. bringeth it not to the door to *o.* it to the Lord
19. 6. it shall be eaten the same day ye *o.* it
21. 6. and the bread of their God they do *o.*
21. that hath a blemish shall not come nigh to *o.*
22. 23. thou mayest *o.* for a free-will offering
Num. 7. 11. they *o.* their offering each prince
8. 11. Aaron shall *o.* the Levites, 13. 15.
9. 7. why are we kept back, that we may not *o.*?
15. 7. shalt *o.* the third part of an hin of wine
14. if a stranger will *o.* an offering made by fire
19. shall *o.* an heave-offering, 18. 24, 26, 28, 29.
16. 40. that no stranger come near to *o.* incense
28. 2. shall ye observe to *o.* to me in their season
11. in the beginnings of your months ye shall *o.*
24. after this manner ye shall *o.* daily the meat
Deut. 12. 14. the place the L. shall choose, there *o.*
18. 3. shall be the priest's due from them that *o.*
33. 19. shall *o.* sacrifices of righteousness. *Ps.* 4. 5.
Judg. 3. 18. when he made an end to *o.* the present
16. 23. to *o.* a great sacrifice to Dagon their God
1 *Sam.* 1. 21. Elkanah went up to *o.* to the Lord
2. 19. Hannah came with her husband to *o.* sacrifice
28. did I choose him my priest to *o.* on mine altar
2 *Sam.* 24. 12. I *o.* thee three things, 1 *Chr.* 21. 10.
1 *Kings* 13. 2. on thee shall *o.* priests of high places
1 *Chr.* 29. 14. should be able to *o.* so willingly, 17.
2 *Chr.* 24. 14. whereof were made vessels to *o.* withal
Ezra 6. 10. to *o.* sacrifices of sweet savours to God
Psal. 16. 4. drink offerings of blood will I not *o.*
27. 6. therefore will I *o.* in his tabernacle sacrifices
50. 14. *o.* to God thanksgiving, pay thy vows to L.
51. 19. then shall they *o.* bullocks on thine altar
66. 15. I will *o.* to thee burnt sacrifices and fatlings
72. 10. the kings of Sheba and Seba shall *o.* gifts
116. 17. I will *o.* the sacrifice of thanksgiving
Isa. 57. 7. thither wentest thou up to *o.* sacrifice
Jer. 11. 12. cry to the gods to whom they *o.* incense
Ezek. 20. 31. when ye *o.* your gifts, ye pollute
44. 7. when ye *o.* my bread, the fat and the blood
15. they shall *o.* to me the fat and the blood
45. 1. ye shall *o.* an oblation to the Ld. 13. | 48. 9.
Dan. 2. 46. that they should *o.* an oblation to Daniel
Hos. 9. 4. they shall not *o.* wine-offerings to Lord
Amos 4. 5. *o.* a sacrifice of thanksgiving with leaven
Hag. 2. 14. that which they *o.* there is unclean
Mal. 1. 7. ye *o.* polluted bread upon mine altar
8. if ye *o.* the blind, *o.* it now to thy governor
3. 3. *o.* to the Lord an offering in righteousness
Mat. 5. 24. and then come and *o.* thy gift
8. 4. *o.* gift Moses commanded, *Mark* 1. 44. *Luke* 5. 14.
Luke 6. 29. smiteth on one cheek, *o.* also the other
11. 12. if shall ask an egg, will he *o.* him a scorpion?
1 *Tim.* 3. † 3. not ready to *o.* wrong, as one in wine
Heb. 5. 1. that he may *o.* both gifts and sacrifi. for sin
3. he ought for himself to *o.* for sins
7. 27. needeth not to *o.* sacrifice, first for his own sins
Heb. 8. 3. every high priest is ordained to *o.* it is of necessity that this man have somewhat also to *o.*
9. 25. nor yet that he should *o.* himself often
13. 15. by him let us *o.* sacrifice of praise to God
1 *Pet.* 2. 5. by Jesus Christ to *o.* spiritual sacrifices
Rev. 8. 3. he should *o.* it with prayers of all saints

See Burnt Offerings.

OFFERED.

Gen. 31. 54. Jacob *o.* sacrifice on the mount, 46. 1.
Exod. 35. 22. every man *o.* an offering of gold
Lev. 9. 15. he slew the goat, and *o.* it for sin
10. 1. Nadab and Abihu *o.* strange fire, and fire devoured them and they died, 16. 1. *Num.* 3. 4. | 26. 61.
Num. 7. 2. the princes *o.* for the dedication, 10.
8. 21. Aaron *o.* them as an offering before the Lord
16. 35. two hundred and fifty men that *o.* incense
22. 40. Balak *o.* oxen and sheep, 23. 2, 4, 14, 30.
Judg. 5. 2. the people willingly *o.* themselves, 9.
13. 19. Manoah took a kid and *o.* it on a rock
1 *Sam.* 1. 4. when the time was that Elkanah *o.*
2. 13. when any *o.* the priest's servant came
2 *Sam.* 6. 17. David *o.* peace offerings, 24. 25.
1 *Kings* 8. 62. Solomon and all Israel *o.* 63.
12. 32. Jeroboam *o.* in Beth-el to the calves, 33.
22. 43. the people *o.* yet in the high places
2 *Kings* 3. 20. when meat offering was *o.* came water
16. 12. Ahaz approached to the altar and *o.*
1 *Chron.* 29. 6. the captains with the rulers *o.*
9. the people rejoiced for that they *o.* willingly
2 *Chron.* 15. 11. Asa *o.* to the Lord of the spoil
17. 16. Amaziah willingly *o.* himself to the Lord
Ezra 1. 6. besides all that was willingly *o.*
2. 68. some of fathers *o.* freely for the house of God
6. 17. *o.* at the dedication of this house of God
7. 15. his counsellors freely *o.* to the God of Israel
8. 25. the king and all Israel there present had *o.*
10. 19. they *o.* a ram of the flock for their trespass
Neh. 11. 2. willingly *o.* themselves to dwell at Jeru.
12. 43. that day they *o.* great sacrifices and rejoiced
Isa. 57. 6. to them thou hast *o.* a meat offering
66. 3. offereth an oblation, as if he *o.* swine's blood
Jer. 32. 29. they have *o.* incense unto Baal
Ezek. 20. 28. they *o.* there their sacrifices
Dan. 11. 18. cause the reproach *o.* by him to cease
Amos 5. 25. have ye *o.* to me sacrifices and offerings?
Jonah 1. 16. the men feared, and *o.* a sacrifice to L.
Mal. 1. 11. in every place incense be *o.* to my name
Acts 8. 18. Simon *o.* them money, saying, give me
15. 29. abstain from meats *o.* to idols, 21. 25.
21. 26. an offering should be *o.* for every one of them
1 *Cor.* 8. 1. things *o.* to idols, 4. 7, 10. | 10. 19, 28.
Phil. 2. 17. if I be *o.* on the service of your faith
2 *Tim.* 4. 6. for I am now ready to be *o.* the time
Heb. 5. 7. when he had *o.* up prayers and supplicat.
7. 27. this he did once, when he *o.* up himself
9. 7. not without blood, which he *o.* for himself
9. were *o.* gifts ‖ 14. *o.* himself without spot to G.
28. Christ was once *o.* to bear the sins of many
11. 4. by faith Abel *o.* to G. a more excellent sacr.
17. by faith Abraham, when tried, *o.* up Isaac
Jam. 2. 21. Abraham justified by works when he *o.*

OFFERETH.

Lev. 6. 26. the priest that *o.* it for sin shall eat it
7. 18. neither shall it be imputed to him that *o.* it
21. 8. for he *o.* the bread of thy God, shall be holy
Psal. 50. 23. whoso *o.* praise glorifieth me, to him
Isa. 66. 3. he that *o.* oblation as if offered swine's flesh

OFFERING.

The Hebrews *had several kinds of* offerings, *which they presented at the tabernacle and temple. Some were free-will offerings, and others were of obligation. The First-fruits, the Tenths, the Sin offerings, were of obligation; the Peace offerings, Vows, offerings of wine, oil, bread, and other things which were made to the temple, or to the ministers of the Lord, were offerings of devotion. The* Hebrews *called all offerings in general,* Corban. *But the offerings of bread, salt, fruits, and liquors, as wine and oil, which were presented to the temple, they called* Mincha. *The offerings of grain, meal, bread, cakes, fruits, wine, salt, oil, were common in the temple and tabernacle. Sometimes these offerings were alone, and sometimes they accompanied the sacrifices. There were five sorts of these offerings, called in* Hebrew, Mincha. 1. *Fine flour or meal.* 2. *Cakes of several sorts, baked in an oven.* 3. *Cakes baked upon a plate.* 4. *Another sort of cakes baked upon a gridiron, or plate with holes in it.* 5. *The first-fruits of the new corn, which were offered either pure and without mixture, or roasted or parched in the ear, or out of the ear.*

The cakes were kneaded with oil-olive, or fried in oil in a pan, or only dipped in oil after they were baked. The bread offered to be presented upon the altar, was to be without leaven, for leaven was never offered upon the altar, nor with the sacrifices; partly to put them in mind of their deliverance out of Egypt, *when they were forced through haste to take away their meal unleavened; partly to signify what* Christ *would be, and what they should be, pure and free from all error in the faith and worship of God, and from all hypocrisy and malice, or wickedness, all which are signified by* leaven, *Mat.* 16. 12. *Mark* 8. 15. 1 *Cor.* 5. 8. *Gal.* 5. 9.

The offerings now mentioned were appointed in favour of the poorer sort, who could not go to the charge of sacrificing animals: and even those that offered living victims were not excused from giving meal, wine, and salt, which was to go along with the greater sacrifices: and also those that offered only oblations of bread, or of meal, offered also oil, incense, salt, and wine, which were in a manner the seasoning of it; In all thy offerings thou shalt offer salt, *Lev.* 2. 13. *noting, incorruption, or soundness of mind, and sincerity of grace, which in Scripture is signified by salt, Mark* 9. 49. *Col.* 4. 6. *and which is necessary in all them that would offer an acceptable offering to God, or in testimony of that communion which they had with God in these exercises of his worship; salt being the great symbol of friendship in all nations and ages.* The priest in waiting received the offerings from the hand of him that offered them, laid a part of them upon the altar, and reserved the rest for his own subsistence: that was his right as a minister of the Lord: nothing was quite burnt up but the incense, of which the priest kept back nothing for his own share.

When an Israelite offered a loaf to the priest, or a whole cake, the priest broke the loaf or cake into two parts, setting that part aside that he reserved to himself, and broke the other into crumbs, poured oil upon it, salt, wine, and incense, and spread the whole upon the fire of the altar: If these offerings were accompanied by an animal for a sacrifice, it was all thrown upon the victim, to be consumed along with it.

If these offerings were the ears of new corn, either of wheat or barley, these ears were parched at the fire, or in the flame, and rubbed in the hand, and then offered to the priest in a vessel; over which he put oil, incense, wine, and salt, and then burnt it upon the altar, first having taken as much of it as of right belonged to himself.

The greatest part of these offerings were voluntary, and of pure devotion. But when an animal was offered in sacrifice, they were not at liberty to omit these offerings: every thing was to be supplied that was to accompany the sacrifice, and which served as a seasoning to the victim.

The Hebrews had properly but three sorts of sacrifices, which were the Burnt offering, or Holocaust; the Sacrifice for Sin, or the Sacrifice of Expiation; and the Pacific Sacrifice, or Sacrifice of Thanksgiving.

The Holocaust was offered and quite burnt up on the altar of burnt offerings, without any reserve to the person that gave the victim, or to the priest that killed and sacrificed it; only the priest had the benefit of the skin; for before the sacrifices were offered to the Lord, their skins were flayed off, and their feet and entrails were washed, Lev. 7. 8.

The sacrifice for sin, or for expiation, or the purification of a man who had fallen into any offence against the law, was not entirely consumed upon the fire of the altar. Nothing of it returned to him that had given it, but the sacrificing priest had a share in it, and these are the particulars that were observed in this case. If it were the high-priest who had offended through ignorance, he offered a calf without blemish: he brought it to the door of the tabernacle, put his hand upon the head of the sacrifice, confessed his sin, asked pardon for it, killed and stuck the calf, carried its blood into the tabernacle, with his finger made seven aspersions towards the veil that separated the holy place from the sanctuary, put a little of this blood upon the altar of incense, and afterwards poured out all the rest at the foot of the altar of burnt offerings. After this he took away the fat that covered the kidneys, the liver, and the bowels; he put the whole upon the fire of the altar of burnt sacrifices; and as to the skin, the feet, the bowels, and the flesh of the sacrifice, he caused them to be burnt out of the camp, in a clean place, where they used to put the ashes that were taken away from the altar of burnt sacrifices, Lev. 4. 3, 4, &c.

If it were the whole people that had offended, they were to offer a calf in like manner. The elders brought it to the door of the tabernacle, put their hands upon its head, and confessed their offence; after which the priest stuck the victim, and did with it as has been said of the sin offering of the high-priest, Lev. 4. 13, 14, &c.

If a prince or ruler had offended, he offered a goat, brought it to the door of the tabernacle, put his hand upon its head, and confessed his sin. The priest sacrificed it, put of the blood of the victim upon the horns of the altar of burnt offerings, poured out the rest of the blood at the bottom of the same altar, and the rest of the sacrifice was for himself: he was obliged to eat it in the tabernacle, and was not allowed to carry any of it without, Lev. 4. 22, 23, &c.

If it was only a private person who had committed an offence, he offered a sheep, or a she-goat without blemish. If he was not of ability to offer a sheep or a she-goat, he offered two turtles, or two young pigeons, one for his sin, the other for a burnt offering. But if he was so poor, as that he could not afford to offer either of these, he might offer the tenth part of an ephah of meal, that is, a little more than a gallon, without oil or spice. He presented it to the priest, who took a handful of it, and threw it upon the fire, and the rest was for himself, Lev. 5. 6, 7, &c.

The Peace offering was offered to return thanks to God for his benefits, or to ask favours from him, or to satisfy any one's private devotion, or for the honour of God only. The Israelites offered them when they pleased, and there was no law that obliged them to it. It was free to them to present what animals they would, provided they were such as it was allowed them to sacrifice. In these sacrifices no distinction was observed either of the age or sex of the victim, as was required in the burnt sacrifices, and the sacrifices for sin, the law only required that their victims should be without blemish, Lev. 3. 1. He that presented them came to the door of the tabernacle, put his hand upon the head of the victim and killed it. The priest poured out the blood about the altar of burnt offerings; burnt upon the fire of the altar the fat which covers the kidneys, the liver, and bowels; and if it were a lamb, or a ram, he added to it the rump of the animal, which in that country is always very fat. Before these things were set in order upon the fire of the altar, the priest put them into the hands of the person that provided the victim, then made them lift them up on high, and wave them towards the four quarters of the world, the priest supporting and directing his hands The breast and the right shoulder belonged to the priest that performed the service; all the rest of the sacrifice belonged to him that presented it to the priest, and he might eat it with his family and friends, as any other meat.

Those sacrifices, in which they set at liberty a bird, or goat, were not properly sacrifices; because there was no shedding of blood, and the victim remained alive and sound. It was thus they set at liberty the sparrow that was offered for the purification of a leper, or of a house spotted with leprosy. They presented to the priest a couple of sparrows, or two clean birds, with a bundle made up of cedar-wood and hyssop, and tied with a scarlet string: The priest killed one of the birds over running water, which was in a clean vessel of fresh earth; afterwards, tying the living sparrow to the bundle of cedar and hyssop, with the tail turned towards the handle of the vessel, he plunged it in the water drenched with the blood of the first sparrow, sprinkled the leper or the house with it, then set the living sparrow at liberty, and let it go where it pleased, Lev. 14. 4, 5, &c.

The other sort of animal that was set at liberty was a goat; and this is the occasion upon which it was done: On the day of solemn expiation, the multitude of the children of Israel presented to the high-priest at the door of the tabernacle two goats for a sin offering. The high priest then cast lots upon the two goats which should be sacrificed to the Lord, and which should be set at liberty, or be the scape-goat, the Azazel, as the Hebrews call it. He that was determined by lot to be sacrificed, was put to death, and offered for the sins of the people: He that was to be set at liberty was brought alive before the Lord. The high priest said over him certain prayers, laid his two hands upon his head, confessed the sins of the whole congregation, charged therewith the head of the goat with imprecations, then sent him into the wilderness by a man appointed for that office, Lev. 16. 5, &c. The scape-goat did bear upon him all their iniquities, to a land not inhabited. Both the birds and goats typified Christ; those that were killed prefigured his death, and those that were saved alive his resurrection.

Such were the sacrifices of the Hebrews: Sacrifices very imperfect, and altogether incapable of themselves to purify the defilements of the soul. The apostle Paul has comprehended the sacrifices, and the other ceremonies of the law, under the character of weak and beggarly elements, Gal. 4. 9. They represented grace and purity, but they did not communicate it. They convinced the sinner of the necessity that was incumbent on him, to purify himself, and of a satisfaction to be made to God; but they did not impart grace to him. But all these Sacrifices were no other than prophecies and figures of Christ Jesus the true Christian sacrifice, which eminently includes all the virtues and qualities of the other sacrifices; being at the same time an Holocaust, a Sacrifice for Sin, and a Sacrifice of Thanksgiving; but with this difference, that it contains the whole substance and efficacy, of which the ancient sacrifices were only the shadow and representation.

Gen. 4. 3. Cain brought an o. unto the Lord
4. the Lord had respect to Abel and to his o.
Exod. 25. 2. bring me an o. of every man, take my o.
3. this is the o. which ye shall take, 35. 5.
30. 13. an half shekel shall be the o. of the Lord
15. an o. to the L. to make atonement for your souls
Lev. 1. 2. ye shall bring your o. of the cattle
14. o. to Lord be of fowls ‖ 2. 1. o. of fine flour
2. 11. no meat o. shall be made with leaven
3. 2. he shall lay his hand on the head of his o. 8.
7. if he offer a lamb for his o. Num. 6. 14.
12. and if his o. be a goat, 4. 23, 28.
6. 20. this is the o. of Aaron and of his sons
7. 16. if his o. be a vow, or a voluntary o.
Num. 5. 15. an o. of jealousy, an o. of memorial
7. 10. the princes offered their o. before the altar
11. they shall offer their o. each prince on his day
8. 11. shall offer Levites before the L. for an o. 21.
9. 13. the o. of the Lord in his appointed season
16. 15. Moses said, respect not thou their o.
1 Sam. 2. 29. wherefore kick ye at mine o.?
3. 14. shall not be purged with sacrifice nor o.
26. 19. hear the words of thy servant, if the Lord have stirred thee up ag. me, let him accept an o.
1 Kings 18. 29. prophesied till o. of evening sacrifice
1 Chron. 16. 29. bring an o. and come, Psal. 96. 8.
Neh. 10. 39. Israel shall bring the o. of the corn
Isa. 43. 23. I have not caused thee to serve with an o.
53. 10. thou shalt make his soul an o. for sin
66. 20. they shall bring your brethren for an o.
Ezek. 20. 28. they presented provocation of their o.
Zeph. 3. 10. the daughter of my dispersed bring my o.
Mal. 1. 10. nor will I accept an o. at your hand
13. thus ye brought an o. should I accept this?
2. 13. that he regardeth not the o. any more
3. 3. offer to the Lord an o. in righteousness
Rom. 15. 16. that the o. up of Gentiles be acceptable
Eph. 5. 2. an o. and a sacrifice to God for us
Heb. 10. 5. sacrifice and o. thou wouldest not, 8.
10. through the o. of the body of Jesus once for all
14. by one o. he hath perfected for ever sanctified
18. where remission is, there is no more o. for sin
See Burnt, Drink, Free.

Heave OFFERING.

Exod. 29. 27. sanctify the shoulder of the heave o.
Lev. 7. 14. out of the whole oblation for an heave o.
Num. 15. 19. ye shall offer up an heave o. 20.
21. of the first dough give an heave o. to the Lord
18. 24. the tithes which they offer as an heave o.
28. give the Lord's heave o. to Aaron the priest
31. 29. give it to Eleazar for an heave o. of the Lord
41. the tribute which was the Lord's heave o.
See Made, Make, Fire, Burnt Offering.

Peace OFFERING.

Lev. 3. 1. if oblation be sacrifice of peace o. 3, 6, 9.

Sin OFFERING.

Exod. 29. 14. the flesh of bullock shalt thou burn, it is a sin o. Lev. 4. 21, 24. | 5. 9, 11, 12.
30. 10. the blood of the sin o. of atonements
Lev. 4. 3. let him bring a young bullock without blemish for a sin o. 16. 3, 27. Num. 8. 8.
25. the priest shall take of the blood of sin o. 5. 9.
29. shall lay his hand on the head of the sin o. 33. slay the sin o. in the place of the burnt offering
32. if he bring a lamb for a sin o. Num. 6. 14.
5. 6. he shall bring a lamb or a kid of goats for a sin o. 9. 3. | 16. 5, 15, 27. | 23. 19.
8. priest shall offer that which is for the sin o. first
11. he shall bring fine flour for a sin o.
6. 25. saying, this is the law of the sin o. 7. 37.
7. 7. as the sin o. is, so is trespass offering, 14. 13.
9. 2. take thee a young calf for a sin o. and a ram
10. 16. Moses sought the goat of the sin o.
17. why have ye not eaten sin o. in the holy place
12. 6. she shall bring a turtle-dove for a sin o.
16. 25. fat of the sin o. shall be burnt on the altar
Num. 7. 16. one kid of the goats for a sin o. 22, 28. | 15. 24. | 28. 15. | 29. 5.
2 Chr. 29. 24. the sin o. should be made for all Israel
Ezra 8. 35. offered twelve he-goats for a sin o.
Psal. 40. 6. and sin o. hast thou not required
Ezek. 43. 19. give the priest a bullock for a sin o.
22. on the second day offer a kid for a sin o.
25. prepare every day a goat for a sin o.
44. 27. into sanctuary, he shall offer his sin o.
29. they shall eat the meat offering and sin o.
46. 20. this is the place where priest shall boil sin o.

Trespass OFFERING.

Lev. 5. 6. he shall bring his trespass o. to the Lord
15. shall bring lamb without blem. for trespass o.
16. atonem. with ram t. o. 18. | 6. 6. | 19. 21, 22.
6. 5. he shall give it, in the day of his trespass o.
7. 37. law of tres. o. ‖ 14. 13. tres. o. is most holy
14. 12. he-lamb for tres. o. 21, 24, 25. Num. 6. 12.
1 Sam. 6. 3. but in any wise return him a trespass o.
4. they said, what shall be the trespass o.? 8. 17.
Ezek. 40. 39. two tables to slay the tres. o. on, 42. 13.
44. 29. eat the trespass o. and every dedicated thing
46. 20. where the priests shall boil the trespass o.

Wave OFFERING.

Exod. 29. 24. wave them for a wave o. 26. Lev. 7. 30. | 8. 27, 29. | 9. 21. | 10. 15. | 14. 12, 24. | 23. 20. Num. 6. 20.
27. thou shalt sanctify the breast of the wave o.
Lev. 23. 15. ye brought the sheaf of the wave o.

Wood OFFERING.

Neh. 10. 34. cast lots for the wood o. to bring it
13. 31. and for the wood o. at the times appointed

OFFERING.

1 Sam. 7. 10. as Samuel was o. the burnt offering
2 Sam. 6. 18. David made an end of o. 1 Chron. 16. 2.
2 Kings 10. 25. as soon as Jehu had made an end of o.
2 Chr. 8. 13. o. according to commandment of Moses
29. 29. made an end of o. the king, and all bowed
30. 22. they did eat seven days, o. peace offerings
35. 14. the sons of Aaron were busied in o.
Ezra 7. 16. priests o. willingly for the house of God
Jer. 11. 17. to provoke me to anger in o. to Baal
Luke 23. 36. coming to him and o. him vinegar
Heb. 10. 11. every priest o. often the same sacrifices

OFFERINGS.

Lev. 1. 10. if his o. be of the flocks, sheep, or goats
2. 13. with all thy o. thou shalt offer salt
1 Sam. 2. 29. to make fat with chief of all the o.
2 Sam. 1. 21. let there be no dew nor fields of o.
2 Chron. 31. 12. the people brought in the o.
35. 8. people gave to the priests for passover, o. 9.
13. but the other holy o. sod they in pots
Neh. 10. 37. should bring the first-fruits of o. 12. 44.
Psal. 20. 3. the Lord remember all thy o.
Jer. 41. 5. with o. and incense in their hands
Ezek. 20. 40. there will I require your o.
Hos. 8. 13. they sacrifice flesh for mine o.
Amos 5. 25. have ye offered me o. forty years?
Mal. 3. 4. then o. of Judah and Jerusalem be pleasant
8. wherein have we robbed thee? in tithes and o.
Luke 21. 4. of their abundance cast in unto the o.
Acts 24. 17. I came to bring alms to my nation and o.
See Burnt, Drink, Free.
Made by Fire.

Heave OFFERINGS.

Num. 18. 8. given the charge of mine heave o.
Deut. 12. 6. thither ye shall bring your heave o.

OFFERINGS of the Lord.

1 Sam. 2. 17. for men abhorred the o. of the Lord
See Meat.

Peace OFFERINGS.

Exod. 20. 24. shalt sacrifice thereon thy peace o.
24. 5. sacrificed peace o. of oxen to the Lord
29. 28. it is an heave offering of the peace o.
32. 6. people brought peace o. and sat down to eat
Lev. 4. 10. as taken from the bullock of peace o.
26. shall burn as fat of peace o. 31, 35. | 6. 12.
7. 11. this is the law of sacrifice of peace o. 13, 37.
9. 4. also a bullock and a ram for peace o. 18.
10. 14. are given out of the sacrifice of peace o.
17. 5. offer them for peace o. to the Lord, 23. 19.
19. 5. if ye offer a sacrifice of peace o. 22. 21.
Num. 6. 14. a lamb for peace o. ‖ 17. a ram for p. o.
7. 17. for sacrifice of peace o. two oxen, five lambs of the first year, 23, 29, 35, 41. | 29. 39
10. 10. blow over the sacrifice of your peace o.
Josh. 8. 31. Joshua sacrificed peace o. to the Lord
22. 23. if to offer peace o. let the Lord require it
Judg. 20. 26. all Israel offered peace o. 21. 4.
1 Sam. 10. 8. I will come and offer peace o. 11. 15.
2 Sam. 6. 17. David offered p. o. 24. 25. 1 Chr. 21. 26.
1 Kings 3. 15. Solomon offered peace o. 8. 63.
9. 25. thrice in a year Solomon offered peace o.
2 Chron. 31. 2. Hezekiah appointed priests for p. o.
33. 16. Manasseh offered peace o. on the altar
Prov. 7. 14. she said to him, I have peace o. with me
Ezek. 45. 15. peace o. to make reconciliation, 17.
46. 2. priest prepare peace o. ‖ 12. prince his peace o.
Amos 5. 22. not regard peace o. of your fat things

Sin OFFERINGS.
Neh. 10. 33. *sin o.* to make an atonement for Israel
Thank OFFERINGS.
2 Chr. 29. 31. come near and bring *thank o.* to house
33. 16. the altar, and sacrificed thereon *thank o.*
Wave OFFERINGS.
Num. 18. 11. all the *wave o.* I have given to thee
Wine OFFERINGS.
Hos. 9. 4. not offer *wine o.* to be pleasing to God
OFFICE.
Gen. 41. 13. me he restored to mine *o.* him he hanged
Exod. 1. 16. when ye do the *o.* of a midwife
Num. 3. † 36. under the *o.* of the sons of Merari
4. 16. to the *o.* of Eleazar the son of Aaron
1 *Chron.* 6. 32. and then they waited on their *o.*
9. 22. whom David did ordain in their set *o.*
26. the four chief porters were in their set *o.*
2 *Chron.* 24. 11. chest was brought to the king's *o.*
31. 18. in their set *o.* they sanctified themselves
Neh. 13. 13. their *o.* was to distribute to brethren
Psal. 109. 8. and let another take his *o.*
Ezek. 44. 13. shall not come near to do *o.* of priest
Rom. 11. 13. I am apos. of Gentiles, I magnify my *o.*
12. 4. all members have not the same *o.*
1 *Tim.* 3. 1. if a man desire the *o.* of a bishop
10. let them use the *o.* of a deacon, 13.
Heb. 7. 5. who receive the *o.* of the priesthood
Priest's OFFICE.
Exod. 28. 1. that he may minister to me in the *priest's o.* 3, 4, 41. | 29. 1, 44. | 30. 30. | 35. 19. | 40. 13, 15. *Lev.* 7. 35. | 16. 32. *Num.* 3. 3.
29. 9. the *priest's o.* shall be theirs for a statute
31. 10. to minister in the *priest's o.* 39. 41.
Num. 3. 4. Ithamar ministered in the *priest's o.*
18. 7. thou and thy sons keep your *priests' o.*
Deut. 10. 6. Eleazar his son ministered in the *p.'s o.*
1 *Chr.* 6. 10. Azariah executed *priest's o.* in temple
2 *Chr.* 11. 14. cast them off from executing *p.'s o.*
Luke 1. 8. while Zacharias executed the *priest's o.*
OFFICES.
1 *Sam.* 2. 36. put me into one of the priests' *o.*
1 *Chr.* 24. 3. Dav. distributed priests according to *o.*
2 *Chron.* 7. 6. and the priests waited on their *o.*
Neh. 13. 14. wipe not out my good deeds for *o.*
OFFICER.
Gen. 37. 36. Potiphar an *o.* of Pharaoh, 39. 1.
Judg. 9. 28. is not he son Jerubbaal, and Zebul his *o.?*
1 *Kings* 4. † 2. Azariah son of Zadok, the chief *o.*
5. Zabud, son of Nathan, was the principal *o.*
19. Geber, son of Uri, was the only *o.* in the land
22. 9. Ahab called an *o.* and said, hasten hither
2 *Kings* 8. 6. the king appointed an *o.* to restore
25. 19. Nebuzaradan took an *o.* out of the city
Mat. 5. 25. the judge deliver thee to the *o.* and the *o.* cast thee into prison, *Luke* 12. 58.
OFFICERS.
Gen. 40. 2. Pharaoh was wroth with two of his *o.*
7. Joseph asked Pharaoh's *o.* why look ye sad?
41. 34. let Pharaoh appoint *o.* over the land
Exod. 5. 15. the *o.* of Israel cried to Pharaoh
19. the *o.* did see that they were in evil case
Num. 11. 16. gather unto me the *o.* *Deut.* 31. 28.
Deut. 1. 15. I made them *o.* among your tribes
16. 18. judges and *o.* shalt thou make thee in gates
20. 5. the *o.* shall speak to the people, 8.
1 *Sam.* 8. 15. take vineyards and give to his *o.*
1 *Kings* 4. 5. Azariah, son of Nathan, over the *o.*
7. Solomon had twelve *o.* over all Israel
28. brought they to the place where the *o.* were
5. 16. besides the chief of Solomon's *o.* 9. 23.
2 *Kings* 11. 15. Jehoiada commanded the *o.*
18. appointed *o.* over the house, 2 *Chron.* 23. 18.
24. 12. Jehoiachin went out with his *o.*
15. the *o.* and mighty men carried he away
1 *Chron.* 23. 4. six thousand were *o.* and judges
26. 29. Chenaniah and his sons were for *o.* and judg.
2 *Chron.* 8. 10. Solomon's *o.* 250 that bare rule
19. 11. also the Levites shall be *o.* before you
Esth. 9. 3. the *o.* of the king helped the Jews
Isa. 60. 17. I will make thine *o.* peace, and exact.
Jer. 29. 26. should be *o.* in the house of the Lord
John 7. 32. the chief priests sent *o.* to take him
46. the *o.* answered, never man spake like this man
18. 3. Judas having received *o.* cometh with lant.
12. *o.* took Jesus || 22. one of the *o.* struck Jesus
Acts 5. 22. the *o.* found them not in the prison
OFF-SCOURING.
Lam. 3. 45. thou hast made us as the *o.* and refuse
1 *Cor.* 4. 13. and are the *o.* of all things to this day
OFFSPRING
Signifies, *That which is sprung of or produced by another, as children, plants, and fruits,* Job 31. 8. Isa. 48. 19.
I am the Root and Offspring of David, *Rev.* 22. 16. I *am* David's *Lord, and yet his Son: his* Root, *as I am God, and gave a being to his family, and to all the families of the earth; and yet, as to my human nature, I am his* Son, *a* Branch *out of the root of* Jesse.
Job 5. 25. and thy *o.* as the grass of the earth
21. 8. their *o.* is established before their eyes
27. 14. and his *o.* shall not be satisfied with bread
31. 8. yea, let my *o.* be rooted out
Isa. 22. 24. they shall hang on him the *o.* and issue
44. 3. I will pour my blessing upon thine *o.*
48. 19. the *o.* of thy bowels like the gravel thereof
61. 9. their *o.* shall be known among the people
65. 23. the seed of the blessed, and *o.* with them
Acts 17. 28. for we are also his *o.* 29.
Rev. 22. 16. I am the Root and the *O.* of David
OFT.
2 *Kings* 4. 8. as *o.* as he passed by, he turned in
Job 21. 17. how *o.* cometh their destruction on them?
Ps. 78. 40. how *o.* did provoke him in wilderness?
Mat. 9. 14. why do we and the Pharisees fast *o.?*
17. 15. my son is sore vexed, for *o.* times he falleth into the fire, and *o.* into the water, *Mark* 9. 22.
18. 21. how *o.* shall my brother sin against me?
Mark 7. 3. the Jews, except they wash *o.* eat not
Acts 26. 11. I punished them *o.* in every synagogue
1 *Cor.* 11. 25. this do ye as *o.* as ye drink it in remem.
2 *Cor.* 11. 23. in prisons frequent, in deaths *o.*

2 *Tim.* 1. 16. for *o.* refreshed me, not ashamed of bonds
Heb. 6. 7. the earth drinketh up rain that cometh *o.*
OFTEN.
Prov. 29. 1. he that being *o.* reproved, hardeneth
Mal. 3. 16. they that feared the Lord spake *o.*
Mat. 23. 37. how *o.* would I have gathered thy children as a hen gathereth, *Luke* 13. 34.
Mark 5. 4. had been *o.* bound with fetters and chains
Luke 5. 33. why do the disciples of John fast *o.?*
1 *Cor.* 11. 26. for as *o.* as ye eat this bread and drink
2 *Cor.* 11. 26. in journeyings *o.* in perils
27. I have been in watchings *o.* in fastings *o.*
Phil. 3. 18. many walk, of whom I have told you *o.*
1 *Tim.* 5. 23. use a little wine for thy *o.* infirmities
Heb. 9. 25. nor yet that he should offer himself *o.*
26. then he must *o.* have suffered since foundat.
Rev. 11. 6. to smite the earth as *o.* as they will
OFTENTIMES.
Job 33. 29. these things worketh God *o.* with man
Eccl. 7. 22. for *o.* also thine own heart knoweth
Luke 8. 29. for *o.* it had caught him, was kept bound
John 18. 2. for Jesus *o.* resorted thither with discip.
Rom. 1. 13. that *o.* I purposed to come to you
2 *Cor.* 8. 22. have *o.* proved diligent in many things
Heb. 10. 11. and *o.* offering the same sacrifices
OFTENER.
Acts 24. 26. Felix sent for him *o.* to commune with
OIL
Signifies, [1] *The juice of olives, &c.* Psal. 104. 15. [2] *That oil confected by God's appointment,* Exod. 30. 25. *to anoint the priests, their garments, and holy things about the tabernacle, which signified the separation of those things to the service of God, and the inward qualifications requisite for the office of the high priest, namely, the gifts and graces of the Holy Spirit, which elsewhere in scripture are set forth by* oil, *Mat.* 25. 4. *It was also typical of those gifts with which our Lord Jesus Christ beyond measure, and by him his members in measure, should be furnished.*
God hath anointed thee with the oil of gladness, *Psal.* 45. 7. *God hath raised and advanced thee far above all men and angels, to a state of joy and endless glory at his right hand: Thus* anointing *signifies the designation or inauguration of a person to some high dignity or employment,* Ezek. 28. 14. *Or, God hath endowed thee with all the gifts and graces of the Holy Spirit in an eminent and peculiar manner, to the comfort and refreshment of thine own, and all thy people's hearts; and hath solemnly called thee to be the Priest, Prophet, and King of his church.*
Gen. 28. 18. Jacob poured *o.* on the top of it, 35. 14.
Exod. 25. 6. take *o.* for the light, 35. 14. | 39. 37.
29. 2. cakes unleavened, tempered with *o.* 40.
30. 25. shalt make it an *o.* of holy ointment
Lev. 2. 1. and he shall pour *o.* upon it, 6.
4. cakes of fine flour mingled with *o.* 5. | 14. 10, 21. | 23. 13. *Num.* 6. 15. | 7, 13, 19, 25, 31, 37, 43, 49, 55, 61, 67, 73, 79. | 8. 8. | 28. 13. | 29. 3, 9, 14.
15. thy meat offering put *o.* upon it, 6. 21.
16. the priest shall burn part of the *o.* thereof
5. 11. he shall put no *o.* on it, *Num.* 5. 15.
7. 10. meat offering mingled with *o.* 9. 4. | 14. 10.
12. shall offer cakes mingled with *o.* *Num.* 6. 15.
14. 16. the priest shall dip his right finger in the *o.*
17. rest of the *o.* that is in his hand, 18, 29.
Num. 4. 9. all the *o.* vessels wherewith they minister
11. 8. the taste of it was as the taste of fresh *o.*
15. 4. mingled with fourth part of an hin of *o.*
6. mingled with the third part of an hin of *o.*
28. 12. *o.* for one bullock, and *o.* for one ram
Deut. 28. 40. shalt have olive trees, but shalt not anoint thyself with *o.* 2 *Sam.* 14. 2. *Mic.* 6. 15.
32. 13. made him suck *o.* out of the flinty rock
33. 24. let Asher be acceptable, and dip his foot in *o.*
1 *Sam.* 10. 1. Samuel took a vial of *o.* and poured it
16. 1. fill thy horn with *o.* and go, 13.
1 *Kings* 1. 39. Zadok the priest took an horn of *o.*
5. 11. Solomon gave Hiram twenty measures of *o.*
17. 12. *o.* in a cruse || 14. nor cruse of *o.* fail, 16.
2 *Kings* 4. 2. nothing in the house save a pot of *o.*
6. the *o.* stayed || 7. go sell the *o.* and pay thy debt
9. 1. take this box of *o.* go to Ramoth Gilead, 3.
6. he poured the *o.* on his head and said to him
1 *Chron* 27. 28. over the cellars of *o.* was Joash
Ezra 3. 7. gave drink and *o.* to them of Zidon
Esth. 2. 12. six months with *o.* of myrrh
Job 24. 11. which make *o.* within their walls
29. 6. and the rock poured me out rivers of *o.*
Psal. 23. 5. thou anointest my head with *o.*
55. 21. words were softer than *o.* yet drawn swords
104. 15. and *o.* to make his face to shine
109. 18. let it come like *o.* into his bones
141. 5. it shall be a kindness, an excellent *o.*
Prov. 5. 3. her mouth is smoother than *o.*
21. 20. and *o.* in the dwelling of the wise
Isa. 5. † 1. a vineyard in the horn of the son of *o.*
61. 3. to give to them the *o.* of joy for mourning
Jer. 41. 8. slay us not, we have treasures of *o.*
Ezek. 16. 13. thou didst eat flour, honey, and *o.* 19.
18. hast set mine *o.* and incense before them
27. 17. Judah traded in honey and *o.* and balm
32. 14. I will cause their rivers to run like *o.*
45. 14. concerning the ordinance of *o.* bath of *o.*
24. ephah for a ram, an hin of *o.* for an ephah
Hos. 2. 5. my lovers that give me my bread and *o.*
12. 1. with Assyrians, and *o.* is carried into Egypt
Mic. 6. 7. will L. be pleased with 10,000 rivers of *o.?*
Zech. 4. 12. empty the golden *o.* out of themselves
† 14. the two sons of *o.* stand by the Lord
Mat. 25. 3. the foolish took no *o.* with them
4. the wise took *o.* || 8. give us of your *o.*
Luke 7. 46. my head with *o.* thou didst not anoint
16. 6. he said, an hundred measures of *o.*
See ANOINTED, ANOINTING, BEATEN, LOG.
Wine with OIL.
Num. 18. 12. best of the *o.* and *w.* they shall offer
Deut. 7. 13. the Lord will bless thy *w.* and thy *o.*
11. 14. that thou mayest gather thy *wine* and *o.*

Deut. 12. 17. not eat the tithe of thy *wine* and *o.* 14. 23.
18. 4. the first-fruits of *wine* and *o.* 2 *Chron.* 31. 5.
28. 51. who shall not leave thee either *wine* or *o.*
1 *Chron.* 9. 29. some to oversee the *wine* and *o.*
12. 40. they that were nigh brought *wine* and *o.*
2 *Chr.* 2. 10. give serv. 20,000 baths of *w.* and *o.* 15.
11. 11. Rehoboam put in strong holds *o.* and *wine*
32. 28. Hezekiah made store-houses for *wine* and *o.*
Ezra 6. 9. give *wine* and *o.* according to appointment
7. 22. to 100 baths of *wine*, and 100 baths of *o.*
Neh. 5. 11. restore *wine* and *o.* that ye exact of them
10. 37. should bring the first-fruits of *wine* and *o.*
39. offering of the corn, new *wine* and *o.*
13. 5. laid the tithes of corn, new *wine* and *o.* 12.
Prov. 21. 17. that loveth *wine* and *o.* shall not be rich
Jer. 31. 12. they shall flow to Lord for *wine* and *o.*
40. 10. gather ye *wine* and summer-fruits and *o.*
Hag. 1. 11. I called for a drought on new *wine* and *o.*
2. 12. touch bread, *wine* or *o.* shall it be holy?
Luke 10. 34. bound up his wounds, pour. in *o.* and *w.*
Rev. 6. 6. see thou hurt not the *wine* and the *o.*
18. 13. no man buyeth their *wine* and *o.* any more
OILED.
Exod. 29. 23. one cake of *o.* bread, *Lev.* 8. 26.
OIL-*olive.*
Exod. 27. 20. pure *o.-olive* beaten for the light
30. 24. take thou unto thee of *o.-olive* an hin
Lev. 24. 2. that they bring unto thee pure *o.-olive*
Deut. 8. 8. land of *o.-ol.* and honey, 2 *Kings* 18. 32.
OIL-*tree.*
Isa. 41. 19. I will plant in the wilderness, the *o.-tree*
OINTMENT.
Exod. 30. 25. make oil of holy *o.* and *o.* compound
2 *Kings* 20. 13. Hezekiah shewed them the house of his precious things and precious *o.* *Isa.* 39. 2.
1 *Chron.* 9. 30. the priest made the *o.* of the spices
Job 41. 31. he maketh the sea to boil like pot of *o.*
Psal. 133. 2. it is like the precious *o.* on the head
Prov. 27. 9. *o.* and perfume rejoice the heart
16. the *o.* of his right hand bewrayeth itself
Eccl. 7. 1. a good name is better than precious *o.*
9. 8. garments be white, and let thy head lack no *o.*
10. 1. dead flies cause the *o.* of apothecary to stink
Cant. 1. 3. thy name is as *o.* poured forth, virgins love
Isa. 1. 6. nor bound up, nor mollified with *o.*
57. 9. thou wentest to the king with *o.* and increased
Mat. 26. 7. a box of prec. *o.* *Mark* 14. 3. *Luke* 7. 37.
9. this *o.* might have been sold for much, *John* 12. 5.
12. in that she hath poured out this *o.* on my body
Mark 14. 4. why was this waste of the *o.* made?
Luke 7. 38. and anointed his feet with *o.* 46.
John 11. 2. Mary anointed the Lord with *o.*
12. 3. Mary took pound of *o.* and anointed the feet of Jesus, house was filled with the odour of the *o.*
OINTMENTS.
Cant. 1. 3. because of the savour of thy good *o.*
4. 10. the smell of thine *o.* is better than all spices
Amos 6. 6. and anoint themselves with the chief *o.*
Luke 23. 56. they returned, prepared spices and *o.*
Rev. 18. 13. no man buyeth their odours and *o.*
OKE, *See* OAK.
OLD.
Gen. 5. 32. Noah was 500 years *o.* and begat Shem
7. 6. Noah was 600 years *o.* when the flood came
11. 10. Shem was 100 years *o.* and begat Arphaxad
12. 4. Abr. 75 years *o.* when departed from Har.
15. 9. take a heifer and a ram of three years *o.*
16. 16. and Abram was fourscore and six years *o.* when Hagar bare Ishmael to Abram
17. 12. he that is eight days *o.* shall be circumcised
17. a child born to him that is an hundred years *o.*
24. Abraham 99 years *o.* when he was circumcised
25. Ishmael thirteen years *o.* when circumcised
18. 11. now Abraham and Sarah were *o.*
12. after I am waxed *o.* my Lord being *o.* also
13. Sar. said, shall of surety bear child, who am *o.?*
19. 4. men of city compass. the house, *o.* and young
31. our father is *o.* || 24. 1. Abraham was *o.*
21. 4. Abr. circumcised Isaac when eight days *o.*
5. Abraham 100 years *o.* when Isaac was born
23. 1. Sarah was 127 years *o.* the years of her life
25. 20. Isaac 40 years *o.* when took Rebek. to wife
26. Isaac was 60 years *o.* when she bare them
26. 34. Esau 40 years *o.* when he took Judith
27. 1. it came to pass when Isaac was *o.* 2. | 35. 29.
37. 2. Joseph being 17 years *o.* was feeding flock
47. 8. Pharaoh said to Jacob, how *o.* art thou?
49. 9. couch. as an *o.* lion, who shall rouse him up?
50. 26. Joseph died, being 110 years *o.*
Exod. 7. 7. Moses was eighty yrs. *o.* and Aar. eighty-three years *o.* when they spake to Pharaoh
10. 9. we will go with our young our *o.* with sons
30. 14. every one that are numbered from twenty years *o.* and above, 38. 26. *Num.* 1. 3, 18. | 14. 29. 1 *Chron.* 23. 27. 2 *Chron.* 25. 5. | 31. 17. *Ezra* 3. 8.
Lev. 13. 11. it is an *o.* leprosy in the skin of his flesh
25. 22. shall eat *o.* fruit || 26. 10. shall eat *o.* store
27. 3. the male from 20 years *o.* even to 60 years
5. and if it be from five even to twenty years *o.*
6. if it be from a month *o.* to five years *o.*
Num. 3. 15. every male from a month *o.* and upward shalt thou number, 22, 28, 34, 39, 40, 43.
4. 3. from thirty years *o.* to fifty from among the son of Levi, 23. 30. 1 *Chron.* 23. 3.
8. 24. the Levites from 25 years *o.* and upward
18. 16. to be redeemed, from month *o.* shalt redeem
26. 62. numbered 23000 from a month *o.* and upw.
33. 39. Aaron was 123 years *o.* when he died
Deut. 8. 4. thy raiment waxed not *o.* 29. 5. *Neh.* 9. 21.
28. 50. which shall not regard the person of the *o.*
31. 2. Moses said, I am 120 years *o.* this day
34. 7. Moses was an 120 years *o.* when he died
Josh. 5. 11. and they did eat of the *o.* corn, 12.
6. 21. utterly destroy. men and wom. young and *o.*
9. 4. they took *o.* sacks || 5. *o.* shoes on their feet, 13.
13. 1. Joshua was *o.* and stricken in years, 23. 1, 2.
14. 7. forty years *o.* was I, when Moses sent me
10. and now, lo, I am this day eighty-five years *o.*
24. 29. Joshua died, being 110 years *o.* *Judg.* 2. 8.
Ruth 1. 12. for I am too *o.* to have a husband
1 *Sam.* 2. 22. now Eli was very *o.* and heard all

1 *Sam.* 4. 15. Eli was ninety and eight yrs. *o.* his eyes
8. 1. when Samuel was *o.* he made, 5. | 12. 2.
2 *Sam.* 2. 10. Saul's son was forty years *o.* when
4. 4. Mephibosheth was lame, and five years *o.*
5. 4. David thirty years *o.* when he began to reign
19. 32. now Barzillai was eighty years *o.* 35.
1 *Kings* 1. 1. king David was *o.* 15. 1 *Chron.* 23. 1.
11. 4. when Sol. was *o.* his wives turned his heart
13. 11. there dwelt an *o.* prophet in Beth-el
2 *Kings* 4. 14. she hath no child, and her husb. is *o.*
1 *Chron.* 2. 21. Hezron married when sixty years *o.*
2 *Chr.* 31. 16. males from three years *o.* and upward
Esth. 3. 13. sent to destroy all the Jews, young and *o.*
Job 21. 7. why do the wicked live, become *o.?*
32. 6. Elihu said, I am young, and ye are very *o.*
Psal. 32. 3. my bones waxed *o.* through my roaring
37. 25. I have been young, and now am *o.*
71. 18. now when I am *o.* O God, forsake me not
Prov. 22. 6. when *o.* he will not depart from it
23. 10. remove not *o.* land-mark, enter not fields
22. and despise not thy mother when she is *o.*
Eccl. 4. 13. better is a wise child than an *o.* king
Cant. 7. 13. all manner of pleasant fruits new and *o.*
Isa. 15. 5. an heifer of three years *o.* *Jer.* 48. 34.
20. 4. captives, young and *o.* naked and barefoot
50. 9. they shall wax *o.* as garment, moth eat them
58. 12. they shall build the *o.* waste places, 61. 4.
65. 20. for the child shall die 100 years *o.* but the
sinner being 100 years *o.* shall be accursed
Jer. 6. 16. Lord said, see and ask for the *o.* paths
38. 11. Ebedmel. took thence *o.* clouts, *o.* rags, 12.
51. 22. with thee I will break in pieces young and *o.*
Lam. 2. 21. the young and *o.* lie on the ground
3. 4. my flesh and my skin hath he made *o.*
Ezek. 9. 6. slay utterly *o.* and young, maids and chil.
23. 43. then I said to her that was *o.* in adulteries
25. 15. vengeance to destroy it for the *o.* hatred
36. 11. I will settle you after your *o.* estates
Dan. 5. 31. Darius took kingdom, being 62 years *o.*
Mic. 6. 6. shall I come before him with calves of yr. *o.*
Mat. 2. 16. Herod slew the children from two yrs. *o.*
9. 16. no man putteth new cloth to on *o.* garment
17. neither do men put new wine into *o.* bottles,
Mark 2. 21, 22. *Luke* 5. 36, 37.
13. 52. bringeth forth of treasure things new and *o.*
Luke 2. 42. Jesus twelve years *o.* went to Jerusalem
5. 39. for he saith, the *o.* wine is better
9. 8. it was said, that one of the *o.* prophets is risen
John 3. 4. how can a man be born when he is *o.?*
8. 57. thou art not yet fifty years *o.* hast seen Abr.?
21. 18. when thou shalt be *o.* another shall lead thee
Acts 4. 22. the man was above forty years *o.*
7. 23. when Moses was full forty years *o.*
21. 16. brought Mnason of Cyprus, an *o.* disciple
Rom. 4. 19. Abraham when about 100 years *o.*
1 *Cor.* 5. 7. purge out therefore the *o.* leaven
8. let us keep the feast, not with *o.* leaven
2 *Cor.* 3. 14. in the reading of the *O.* Testament
5. 17. *o.* things are past away, all things are new
1 *Tim.* 4. 7. refuse profane and *o.* wives' fables
5. 9. widow not be taken under sixty years *o.*
Heb. 8. 13. a new covenant, he hath made the first *o.*
what decayeth and wax. *o.* is ready to vanish away
2 *Pet.* 1. 9. that he was purged from his *o.* sins
2. 5. if God spared not the *o.* world, but saved Noe
1 *John* 2. 7. *o.* commandm. is word from beginning
Rev. 12. 9. that *o.* serpent, called the devil and Satan
20. 2. he laid hold on the dragon, that *o.* serpent

OLD *Age.*

Gen. 15. 15. thou shalt be buried in a good *o. age*
21. 2. Sarah bare Abraham a son of his *o. age*, 7.
25. 8. Abraham died in a good *o. age*, an old man
37. 3. Joseph was the son of his *o. age*, 44. 20.
Judg. 8. 32. and Gideon died in a good *o. age*
Ruth 4. 15. he shall be a nourisher in thine *o. age*
1 *Kings* 15. 23. Asa in *o. age* was diseased in his feet
1 *Chr.* 29. 28. Dav. died in good *o. age*, full of days
Job 30. 2. in whom *o. age* was perished
Psal. 71. 9. cast me not off in the time of *o. age*
92. 14. they shall bring forth fruit in *o. age*
Isa. 46. 4. and even to your *o. age* I am he
Luke 1. 36. Elizabeth conceived a son in her *o. age*
Days of OLD; *see Of* OLD.
OLD *Gate, see* GATE.

OLD *Man.*

Gen. 25. 8. Abraham died an *o. man* full of years
43. 27. the *o. man* of whom ye spake, is he alive?
44. 20. and we said, we have a father, an *o. man*
Lev. 19. 32. thou shalt honour the face of the *o. man*
Judg. 19. 16. there came an *o. man* from his work
17. the *o. man* said, 20. || 22. spake to the *o. man*
1 *Sam.* 2. 31. shall not be an *o. m.* in thy house, 32.
4. 18. Eli was an *o. m.* || 17. 12. Jesse was an *o. m.*
28. 14. an *o. man* cometh up, and is covered
2 *Chron.* 36. 17. and had no compassion on *o. man*
Isa. 65. 20. nor *o. man* that hath not filled his days
Luke 1. 18. I am an *o. man*, my wife strick. in years
Rom. 6. 6. our *o. man* is crucified with him
Eph. 4. 22. put off the *o. man* which is corrupt
Col. 3. 9. ye have put off the *o. man* with his deeds

OLD *men.*

1 *Kings* 12. 6. Rehoboam consulted with the *o. men*
8. forsook counsel of *o. m.* 13. 2 *Chr.* 10. 6, 8, 13.
Psal. 148. 12. *o. men* and children, praise the Lord
Prov. 17. 6. children's children the crown of *o. men*
20. 29. the beauty of *o. men* is the grey head
Jer. 31. 13. rejoice in the dance, young *men* and *o.*
Joel 1. 2. hear this ye *o. men*, and give ear all ye
2. 28. *o. men* shall dream dreams, *Acts* 2. 17.
Zech. 8. 4. *o. men* and women dwell in the streets

Of OLD.

Gen. 6. 4. which were *of o.* men of renown
1 *Sam.* 27. 8. those nations were *of o.* the inhabitants
1 *Chron.* 4. 40. they of Ham had dwelt there *of o.*
Neh. 12. 46. *of o.* there were chief of the singers
Job 20. 4. knowest thou not this *of o.* since man
Psal. 25. 6. thy tender mercies have been ever *of o.*
44. 1. what work thou didst in the times *of o.*
55. 19. afflict them, even he that abideth *of o.*
68. 33. upon heavens of heavens which were *of o.*
74. 2. thy congregation which hast purchased *of o.*
12. for God is my king *of o.* working salvation
Ps. 77. 5. I have considered the days *of o.* the years
11. surely I will remember thy wonders *of o.*
78. 2. I will utter dark sayings *of o.*
93. 2. thy throne is established *of o.* from everlast.
102. 25. *of o.* hast laid the foundation of the earth
119. 52. I remembered thy judgments *of o.* O Ld.
152. thy testimonies I have known *of o.*
143. 5. I remember the days *of o.* *Isa.* 63. 11.
Prov. 8. 22. Lord possessed me before his works *of o.*
Isa. 25. 1. thy counsels *of o.* are faithfuln. and truth
30. 33. for Tophet is ordained *of o.* he hath made
43. 18. neither consider the things *of o.*
46. 9. remember the former things *of o.* I am God
51. 9. awake, awake, as in the generations *of o.*
57. 11. have not I held my peace even *of o.?*
63. 9. and carried them all the days *of o.*
Jer. 28. 8. the prophets before me and thee *of o.*
31. 3. the Lord hath appeared *of o.* to me
46. 26. afterwards shall be inhabited as in days *of o.*
Lam. 1. 7. pleasant things she had in the days *of o.*
2. 17. word that he commanded in days *of o.*
3. 6. set me in dark places, as they that be dead *of o.*
5. 21. turn us, O Lord, renew our days as *of o.*
Ezek. 26. 20. shall bring thee down with people *of o.*
35. † 5. because thou hast had hatred *of o.*
Amos 9. 11. I will build it as in the days *of o.*
Mic. 5. 2. whose goings forth have been from *of o.*
7. 14. let them feed in Bashan, as in the days *of o.*
20. hast sworn to our fathers from the days *of o.*
Nah. 2. 8. Nineveh is *of o.* like a pool of water
Mal. 3. 4. be pleasant to the Lord, as in the days *of o.*
2 *Pet.* 3. 5. by word of God the heavens were *of o.*
Jude 4. who were *of o.* ordained to condemnation

OLD *time.*

Deut. 2. 20. giants dwelt there in *o. t.* Zamzummims
19. 14. they of *o. time* set in thy inheritance
Josh. 24. 2. your fathers dwelt on other side in *o. t.*
2 *Sam.* 20. 18. they were wont to speak in *o. time*
Ezra 4. 15. they have moved sedition of *o. time*
Eccl. 1. 10. it hath been already of *o. time*
Jer. 2. 20. for of *o. time* I have broken thy yoke
Ezek. 26. 20. bring thee down with people of *o. time*
38. 17. he of whom I have spoken in *o. time*
Mat. 5. 21. it was said by them of *o. time*, 27, 33.
Acts 15. 21. Moses of *o. time* hath in every city
1 *Pet.* 3. 5. in *o. time* holy women also adorned
2 *Pet.* 1. 21. the prophecy came not in *o. time* by man
See WAX.

OLD *Way.*

Job 22. 15. the *o. w.* which wicked men have trodden

OLDNESS.

Rom. 7. 6. that we should not serve in *o.* of the letter

OLIVE

Is *a tree full of fatness, which yields plenty of oil. The church of the* Jews *is compared to an* olive-tree, *Jer.* 11. 16. *When God brought them into* Canaan, *he fixed them in a flourishing and prosperous state and condition, so that they were in a capacity both to have done much good to themselves, and to have brought him much glory, like a beautiful green* olive-tree, *fit to bear fair and goodly fruit.*

There are two kinds of olive-trees, *the wild and natural, and those that require care and culture. The cultivated* olive-tree *is of a moderate height, its trunk is knotty, its bark smooth, and of an ash-colour, its wood is solid and yellowish, the leaves are oblong, and almost like those of the* willow, *of a green colour, dark on the upper side, and white on the under side. In the month of* June *it puts out white flowers that grow in bunches: Each flower is of one piece, widening upwards, and dividing into four parts. After the flower succeeds the fruit, which is also oblong and plump: It is first green, then pale, and lastly black, when it is quite ripe: In the flesh of it is inclosed a hard stone, full of an oblong seed. The wild* olive *differs from this, in that it is smaller in all its parts.*

Gen. 8. 11. and lo, in her mouth was an *o.* leaf
Deut. 28. 40. for thine *o.* shall cast her fruit
Neh. 8. 15. go to the mount, and fetch *o.* branches
Job 15. 33. he shall cast off his flower as the *o.*
Ps. 128. 3. thy children like *o.* plants round thy table
Hab. 3. 17. although the labour of the *o.* shall fail
Zech. 4. 12. I said, what be these two *o.* branches?
Jam. 3. 12. can fig-tree, my brethren, bear *o.* berries?
See OIL.

OLIVES.

Judg. 15. 5. the foxes burnt up the vineyards and *o.*
Mic. 6. 15. shalt tread the *o.* but shalt not anoint thee
See MOUNT.

OLIVET.

2 *Sam.* 15. 30. David went up by ascent to mount *O.*
Acts 1. 12. they returned from the mount called *O.*

OLIVE-*tree.*

Deut. 24. 20. when thou beatest thine *o.-tree*
Judg. 9. 8. they said to the *o.-tree*, reign over us
9. the *o.-tree* said, should I leave my fatness?
1 *Kings* 6. 23. he made two cherubims of *o.-tree*
31. two doors were of *o.-tree*, 32. || 33. posts of *o.-tree*
Psal. 52. 8. like a green *o.-tree* in the house of God
Isa. 17. 6. as the shaking of an *o.-tree*, 24. 13.
Jer. 11. 16. the Lord called thy name a green *o.-tree*
Hos. 14. 6. his beauty shall be as the *o.-tree*
Hag. 2. 19. as yet the *o.-tree* hath not brought forth
Rom. 11. 17. thou partakest of the fatness of *o.-tree*
24. cut out of the *o.-tree*, graffed in a good *o.-tree*

OLIVE-*trees.*

Exod. 23. † 11. thus shalt thou do with thine *o.-trees*
Deut. 6. 11. and *o.-trees*, which thou plantest not
8. † 8. a land of vines and *o.-trees*, of oil, and honey
28. 40. thou shalt have *o.-trees*, but shalt not anoint
1 *Chron.* 27. 28. over the *o.-trees* was Baal-hanan
Amos 4. 9. *o.-trees* increased, palmer-worm devoured
Zech. 4. 3. two *o.-trees* by it on the right and left
Rev. 11. 4. these are the two *o.-trees* standing before

Wild OLIVE-TREE.

Rom. 11. 17. thou being *wild o.-tree* wert graffed in

OLIVE-YARD.

Exod. 23. 11. thus shalt thou do with thy *o.-yard*

OLIVE-YARDS.

Josh. 24. 13. cities ye built not, of vineyards and *o.-y.* which ye planted not, do ye eat, *Neh.* 9. 25.
1 *Sam.* 8. 14. the king shall take your *o.-yards*
2 *Kings* 5. 26. a time to receive money and *o.-yards*
Neh. 5. 11. restore, I pray, to them their *o.-yards*

OMITTED.

Mat. 23. 23. have *o.* weightier matters of the law

OMNIPOTENT.

Rev. 19. 6. Alleluia, for the Lord God *o.* reigneth

ONCE.

Gen. 18. 32. he said, I will speak yet but this *o.*
Exod. 10. 17. forgive my sin only this *o.* entreat L.
30. 10. Aaron shall make an atonement on horns of altar of incense *o.* year, *Lev.* 16. 34. *Heb.* 9. 7, 12.
Num. 13. 30. let us go up at *o.* and possess it
Deut. 7. 22. thou mayest not consume them at *o.*
Josh. 6. 3. ye shall go round the city *o.* 11, 14.
Judg. 6. 39. I will speak but this *o.* prove but this *o.*
16. 18. come up *o.* || 28. strengthen me this *o.*
1 *Sam.* 26. 8. let me smite him to the earth at *o.*
1 *Kings* 10. 22. *o.* in three years came the navy of Tarshish, bringing gold and silver, 2 *Chr.* 9. 21.
2 *Kings* 6. 10. he saved himself not *o.* or twice
Neh. 5. 18. *o.* in ten days all store of wine was prep.
13. 20. lodged without Jerusalem *o.* or twice
Job 33. 14. G. speaks *o.* yea twice, man perceives not
40. 5. *o.* have I spoken, but I will not answer
Ps. 62. 11. God hath spoken *o.* twice I have heard
74. 6. they break down the carved work at *o.*
76. 7. who may stand in sight when *o.* art angry?
89. 35. *o.* have I sworn by my holiness, I will not
Prov. 28. 18. he that is perverse shall fall at *o.*
Isa. 42. 14. I will destroy and devour at *o.*
66. 8. in one day, or shall a nation be born at *o.?*
Jer. 10. 18. I will sling out the inhabitants at *o.*
13. 27. wilt thou not be clean, when shall it *o.* be?
16. 21. behold, I will this *o.* cause them to know
Hag. 2. 6. yet *o.* it is a little while, and I will shake the heavens and the earth, and sea, *Heb.* 12. 26.
Luke 13. 25. when *o.* the master of house is risen up
23. 18. they cried all at *o.* saying, not this man
Rom. 6. 10. in that he died, he died unto sin *o.*
7. 9. for I was alive without the law *o.* but when
1 *Cor.* 15. 6. was seen of above 500 brethren at *o.*
2 *Cor.* 11. 25. thrice beaten with rods, *o.* was I stoned
Gal. 1. 23. now preacheth the faith he *o.* destroyed
Eph. 5. 3. but fornication, let it not be *o.* named
Phil. 4. 16. ye sent *o.* and again to my necessity
1 *Thess.* 2. 18. would have come to you *o.* and again
Heb. 6. 4. those who were *o.* enlightened, and tasted
7. 27. for this he did *o.* when he offered up himself
9. 26. but now *o.* in end of the world he appeared
27. as it is appointed to men *o.* to die, after this
28. Chr. was *o.* offered to bear sins of many, 10. 10
10. 2. because that the worshippers *o.* purged
12. 27. yet *o.* more, signifieth the removing of those
1 *Pet.* 3. 18. for Christ hath suffered *o.* for our sins
20. *o.* long-suffering of God waited in days of Noe
Jude 3. contend for the faith *o.* delivered to saints
5. put you in remembrance, tho' ye *o.* knew this

ONE

Signifies, [1] *One only, so that there is no other of that kind,* 1 Tim. 2. 5. Heb. 10. 14. [2] *The very same,* Gen. 11. 1. | 40. 5. [3] *Very few,* Deut. 32. 30. Josh. 23. 10. [4] *The like,* 1 Sam. 6. 4. [5] *Some body, any one,* 2 Sam. 23. 15.

That they all may be one, *John* 17. 21. *May be one in mind, love, design, and interest; being first united by faith to me, and by me to thee, that so their union may in some sort resemble that inexpressible union between thyself and me.*

That they may be one in us, [1] *By the communication and inhabitation of the Spirit that proceeds from us.* [2] *In ways of holiness.* [3] *By keeping communion with us.* [4] *By following our example.* [5] *Being united to us by faith, they may be united to one another by love.*

In one day, *Rev.* 18. 8. *that is, suddenly and unexpectedly.*

One thing is needful, *Luke* 10. 42. *Attendance upon the means of grace, and a right use of them, is absolutely necessary in order to the salvation of the soul. Mary chose to take the advantage of Christ's company, and rather to spend an hour or two in hearing him, than in preparing a supper for him; she was taking care of her soul with reference to eternity, which is the one thing needful.*

Gen. 2. 24. a man shall cleave to his wife, and they shall be *o.* flesh, *Mat.* 19. 5. *Mark* 10. 8. 1 *Cor.* 6. 16.
27. 38. hast thou but *o.* blessing, my father?
34. 14. not give our sister to *o.* that is uncircumcised
42. 13. *o.* is not, 32. || 44. 28. *o.* went out from me
Exod. 11. 1. yet will bring *o.* plague more on Phar.
12. 46. in *o.* house shall it be eaten, not carry forth
49. *o.* law shall be to him that is home-born and stranger, *Lev.* 24. 22. *Num.* 15. 16, 29.
23. 29. I will not drive them out in *o.* year
26. 2. every curtain shall have *o.* measure, 36. 9, 15
6. and it shall be *o.* tabernacle, 36. 13.
29. 23. *o.* loaf of bread, *o.* cake, and *o.* wafer
Lev. 5. 4. he shall be guilty in *o.* of these, 5, 13.
16. 29. whether *o.* of your own country, 17. 15.
26. 26. ten women shall bake your bread in *o.* oven
Num. 10. 4. if they blow but with *o.* trumpet
16. 15. I have not taken *o.* as from them
17. 3. *o.* rod shall be for the head of the house
36. 8. of the tribe shall be wife to *o.* of the family
Deut. 1. 23. I took twelve men, *o.* of a tribe
4. 42. that fleeing to *o.* of these cities, 19. 5, 11.
19. 15. *o.* witness shall not rise up against a man
24. 5. but he shall be free at home *o.* year
32. 30. how should *o.* chase a thousand?
Josh. 10. 42. all these Joshua took at *o.* time
12. 9. the king of Jericho *o.* the king of Ai *o.*
10. the king of Jerusalem *o.* king of Hebron *o.*
17. 14. why hast given me but *o.* lot and *o.* portion?
17. a great people, thou shalt not have *o.* lot only
Judg. 9. 2. whether is better, that *o.* reign over you?
21. 8. what *o.* is there of the tribes of Israel?
1 *Sam.* 6. 4. for *o.* plague was on you all and lords
17. for Ashdod *o.* for Gaza *o.* for Ashkelon *o.*

1 Sam. 11. 7. and they came out with o. consent
18. 21. this day my son-in-law in o. of the twain
2 Sam. 7. 23. what o. nation is like thy people?
8. 2. and with o. full line to keep alive
19. 7. there will not tarry o. with thee this night
23. 8. whom he slew at o. time, 1 Chron. 11. 11.
15. O that o. would give me to drink of the water
of the well of Bethlehem, 1 Chron. 11. 17.
1 Kings 1. 48. given me o. to sit on my throne
2. 16. I ask o. petition of thee, deny me not
6. 25. the cherubims were of o. measure, o. size
8. 56. there hath not failed o. word of his promise
11. 13. I will give o. tribe to thy son, 32, 36.
22. 13. behold now words of the prophets declare
good to the king with o. mouth, 2 Chron. 18. 12.
2 Kings 17. 27. carry thither o. of the priests
28. o. of the priests came and dwelt in Bethel
18. 24. will turn away face of o. captain, Isa. 36. 9.
1 Chron. 10. 13. for asking counsel of o. that had fame
12. 14. o. of the least was over an hundred
2 Chron. 32. 12. he shall worship before o. altar
Neh. 1. 2. Hanani, o. of my brethren, came
11. 1. bring o. of ten to dwell in Jerusalem
Job 9. 3. he cannot answer him o. of a thousand
† 33. neither is there o. that should argue
21. 23. o. dieth in his full strength, at ease
23. 13. he is in o. mind, and who can turn him?
33. 23. if an interpreter o. among a thousand
Psal. 22. † 20. deliver my only o. from the dog
35. † 17. rescue my only o. from the lions
49. 16. be not afraid when o. is made rich
72. † 15. o. shall give him of the gold of Sheba
82. 7. and shall fall like o. of the princes
86. † 2. for I am o. whom thou favourest
89. 19. I have laid help on o. that is mighty.
137. 3. saying, sing us o. of the songs of Zion
Prov. 1. 14. cast in thy lot, let us all have o. purse
26. 17. is like o. that taketh a dog by the ears
Eccl. 1. 4. o. generat. passeth away, another cometh
2. 14. I perceived that o. event happen. to them all
3. 19. yea, they have all o. breath, all is vanity
20. all go unto o. place, all are dust, 6. 6.
4. 9. two better than o. ‖ 11. how can o. be warm?
12. if o. prevail against him, two shall withstand
7. 27. counting o. by o. to find out the account
9. 18. but o. sinner destroyeth much good
12. 11. words, which are given from o. shepherd
Cant. 4. 9. thou hast ravish. my heart, my sister, my
spouse, with o. of thy eyes, with o. chain of thy neck
6. 9. my undefiled is but o. she is the only o.
Isa. 5. 10. ten acres of vineyard shall yield o. bath
14. 32. what shall o. answer messengers of nation?
19. 18. o. shall be called the city of destruction
23. 15. according to the days of o. king
27. 12. ye shall be gathered o. by o. O Israel
30. 17. o. thousand shall flee at the rebuke of o.
34. 16. no o. of these shall fail, none want her mate
41. 25. I have raised up o. from the north
27. I will give Jerus. o. that bringeth good tidings
44. 5. o. shall say, I am the Lord's, and another
45. 24. surely shall o. say, in L. have I righteous.
65. 8. o. saith, destroy it not, a blessing is in it
Ezek. 1. 16. they four had o. likeness, and a wheel
19. 3. she brought up o. of her whelps, it became
21. 19. both twain shall come forth out of o. land
23. 13. then I saw that they took both o. way
33. 21. that o. that had escaped came unto me
24. Abraham was o. ‖ 32. as a lovely song of o.
34. 23. I will set up o. shepherd over them, 37. 24.
37. 17. and they shall become o. in thy hand
19. make them o. stick ‖ 22. o. nation, o. king
48. 31. o. gate of Reuben ‖ 32. o. gate of Joseph
Dan. 2. 9. there is but o. decree for you
4. 19. then Daniel was astonied for o. hour
7. 13. behold, o. like the Son of man, 10. 16, 18.
9. 27. he shall confirm the covenant for o. week
11. 7. out of a branch of her roots shall o. stand
10. o. shall certainly come and overflow, and pass
27. they shall speak lies at o. table, not prosper
Hos. 1. 11. Israel shall appoint themselves o. head
Amos 4. 8. two or three cities wandered to o. city
6. 9. if there remain ten men in o. house
Zeph. 3. 9. to serve the Lord with o. consent
Zech. 3. 9. behold, o. stone shall be seven eyes
11. 8. I will cut off three shepherds in o. month
14. 9. there shall be o. Lord, and his name o.
Mal. 2. 15. did he not make o.? and wherefore o.?
Mat. 3. 3. the voice of o. crying in the wilderness,
Mark 1. 3. Luke 3. 4. John 1. 23.
5. 18. o. jot, or o. tittle shall not pass from the law
19. whoso shall break o. of these least commandm.
29. that o. of thy members should perish, 30.
36. thou canst not make o. hair white or black
6. 27. which of you can add o. cubit to his stature?
29. was not arrayed like o. of these, Luke 12. 27.
10. 42. shall give to drink to o. of these little ones
12. 11. what man among you shall have o. sheep?
16. 14. Elias and Jeremias, or o. of the prophets,
Mark 6. 15. | 8. 28. Luke 9. 8, 19.
17. 4. three tabernacles, o. for thee, o. for Moses,
and o. for Elias, Mark 9. 5. Luke 9. 33.
18. 6. shall offend o. of these, Mark 9. 42. Luke 17. 2.
10. take heed ye despise not o. of these little ones
14. that o. of these little ones should perish
16. if not hear, then take with thee o. or two more
19. 17. none good but o. Mark 10. 18. Luke 18. 19.
20. 12. saying, these last have wrought but o. hour
21. 35. they beat o. and killed another, and stoned
22. 5. they went their ways, o. to his farm, another
23. 4. but they themselves will not move them
with o. of their fingers, Luke 11. 46.
8. for o. is your Master, even Christ, 10.
9. o. is your Father ‖ 25. 40. as ye have done it to o.
25. 15. he gave to o. five talents, to another two
18. but he that had received the o. 24.
45. as ye did it not to o. of the least of these
26. 21. Jesus said, verily I say to you, that o. of
you shall betray me, Mark 14. 18. John 13. 21.
40. could ye not watch o. hour? Mark 14. 37.
Mark 8. 14. nor had they more than o. loaf
9. 37. whoever shall receive o. of such children
38. we saw o. casting out devils, Luke 9. 49.

Mark 11. 29. I will also ask of you o. quest. ans. me
12. 6. having yet o. son, he sent him also to them
14. 19. and they began to say, o. by o. is it I?
15. 6. at the feast he released o. Luke 23. 17.
Luke 3. 16. John said, but o. mightier than I cometh
7. 8. I say to o. go, and he goeth, and to another
8. 42. he had o. only daughter, and she lay a dying
12. 52. there shall be five in o. house divided
15. 7. joy in heaven over o. sinner that repenteth, 10.
16. 17. to pass, than o. tittle of the law to fail
30. nay, but if o. went from the dead, 31.
17. 22. to see o. of the days of the Son of man
22. 36. let him sell his garment, and buy o.
John 1. 26. but there standeth o. among you
6. 70. o. of you is a devil ‖ 7. 21. have done o. work
8. 9. went out o. by o. beginning at the eldest
18. I am o. that bear witness of myself
41. they said, we have o. Father, even God
10. 16. and there shall be o. fold, and o. shepherd
30. I and my Father are o.
11. 52. should gather in o. the children of God
12. 48. he hath o. that judgeth him, the word
17. 11. that they may be o. as we are, 21, 22.
23. that they may be made perfect in o.
18. 17. art not thou o. of this man's disciples? 25.
Acts 1. 22. must o. be ordained to be witness of resur.
4. 32. believed, were of o. heart and of o. soul
9. 11. go and enquire for o. Saul of Tarsus
13. 25. there cometh o. after me, whose shoes
17. 7. saying, that there is another king, o. Jesus
26. God hath made of o. blood all nations
24. 21. except it be for this o. voice, of resurrection
25. 19. had questions of o. Jesus, who was dead
28. 25. after that Paul had spoken o. word
Rom. 5. 7. for scarcely for a righteous man will o. die
15. for if through the offence of o. many be dead
16. and not as it was by o. that sinned, for the
judgment was by o. to condemnation
17. death reigned by o. shall reign in life by o. J. C.
18. by the offence of o. so by righteousness of o.
19. so by obedience of o. shall many be righteous
9. 10. but when Rebekah also had conceived by o.
1 Cor. 3. 4. for while o. saith, I am Paul of
8. now he that planteth and that watereth are o.
5. 1. such fornication, that o. have his father's wife
8. 4. and that there is none other God but o.
6. to us there is but o. God, and o. Lord Jesus
9. 24. all run, but o. receiveth the prize
10. 17. we being many are o. bread and o. body
11. 21. o. is hungry ‖ 14. 27. let o. interpret
12. 8. to o. is given by Spirit the word of wisdom
13. by o. Spirit we are baptized into o. body
14. 24. there come in o. that believeth not, or o. unlearned, he is convinced of all, judged of all
31. for ye may all prophesy o. by o. that all may
15. 8. was seen of me as of o. born out of due time
2 Cor. 5. 14. if o. died for all, then were all dead
11. 2. for I have espoused you to o. husband
24. five times received I forty stripes save o.
13. 11. be perfect, be of good comfort, be of o. mind,
Phil. 2. 2. 1 Pet. 3. 8. Rev. 17. 13.
Gal. 3. 16. but as of o. ‖ 28. ye are all o. in Christ
5. 14. for all the law is fulfilled in o. word
Eph. 1. 10. he might gather together in o. all things
2. 14. who hath made both o. ‖ 15. o. new man
18. through him we both have access by o. Spirit
4. 4. as ye are called in o. hope of your calling
5. o. faith, o. Lord, o. baptism ‖ 6. o. God
Phil. 1. 27. that stand fast with o. spirit, with o. mind
1 Tim. 3. 2. the husband of o. wife, Tit. 1. 6.
4. a bishop, o. that ruleth well his own house
1 Tim. 3. 12. the deacons be the husbands of o. wife
Tit. 1. 12. o. of themselves, even a prophet, said
Heb. 2. 6. but o. in a certain place testifieth
11. and they that are sanctified are all of o.
5. 12. ye have need that o. teach you again
10. 12. but this man after he had offered o. sacrifice
14. for by o. offering he hath perfected for ever
11. 12. therefore sprang there even of o. so many
12. 16. for o. morsel of meat sold his birth right
13. 14. here we have no city, but we seek o. to come
Jam. 2. 10. yet offend in o. point, he is guilty of all
5. 19. if any of you err, and o. convert him
1 John 5. 7. these three are o. ‖ 8. these agree in o.
Rev. 9. 12. o. woe is past, there come two woes more
13. 3. I saw o. of his heads as wounded to death
14. 14. on the cloud o. sat like unto the Son of man
17. 12. receive power as kings o. hour with the beast
18. 10. for in o. hour is thy judgment come
17. in o. hour so great riches come to nought
19. that great city, for in o. hour is she made desol.
21. 21. every several gate was of o. pearl
See ACCORD, ANOTHER, MAN, GOD.

As ONE.

Gen. 3. 22. behold, the man is become as o. of us
19. 14. but he seemed as o. that mocked to his sons
49. 16. Dan shall judge as o. of the tribes of Israel
Exod. 12. 48. be circumcised, and he shall be as o.
that is born in the land, Lev. 19. 34. | 24. 22.
Num. 12. 12. let her not be as o. dead, of whom
Josh. 10. 2. Gibeon a great city, as o. of royal cities
Judg. 17. 11. young man was to him as o. of his sons
1 Sam. 17. 36. uncircum. Philistine be as o. of them
26. 20. as when o. doth hunt a partridge in mount.
2 Sam. 6. 20. uncovered as o. of the vain fellows
9. 11. he shall eat at my table as o. of king's sons
13. 13. thou shalt be as o. of the fools in Israel
14. 13. the king speaketh this as o. that is faulty
17. 12. there shall not be left so much as o.
2 Kings 6. 5. but as o. was felling a beam, axe head fell
2 Chron. 5. 13. the trumpeters and singers were as o.
Job 2. 10. thou speakest as o. of the foolish women
12. 4. I am as o. mocked of his neighbour
19. 11. he counteth me to him as o. of his enemies
Psal. 35. 14. as o. that mourneth for his mother
78. 65. then the Lord awaked as o. out of sleep
89. 10. thou hast broken Rahab, as o. that is slain
119. 162. I rejoice as o. that findeth great spoil
Prov. 6. 11. thy poverty as o. that travaileth, 24. 3.
Eccl. 3. 19. as the o. dieth, so dieth the other
Cant. 1. 7. for why should I be as o. turneth aside?
8. 10. then I was in his eyes as o. that found favour

Isa. 10. 14. as o. that gathereth eggs that are left
29. 4. thy voice as o. that hath a familiar spirit
66. 13. as o. whom his mother comforteth
Jer. 19. 11. I will break as o. breaketh potter's vessel
Zech. 12. 10. mourn as o. in bitterness for first-born
Mat. 7. 29. as o. having authority, Mark 1. 22.
Mark 6. 15. or as o. of the prophets ‖ 9. 26. as o. dead
Luke 15. 19. make me as o. of thy hired servants
23. 14. this man as o. that perverteth the people
1 Cor. 7. 25. as o. that hath obtained mercy of Lord
9. 26. so fight I, not as o. that beateth the air
See DAY, HEART, EVERY.

Is ONE.

Gen. 11. 6. the people is o. ‖ 41. 25. the dream is o. 26.
Exod. 2. 6. this is o. of the Hebrew children
Deut. 6. 4. the Lord our God is o. Lord, Mark 12. 29.
Ruth 2. 20. Boaz is o. of our next kinsmen
Mat. 12. 6. in this place is o. greater than the temple
Mark 14. 20. it is o. of the twelve that dippeth
Rom. 2. 28. he is not a Jew that is o. outwardly
29. but he is a Jew who is o. inwardly
3. 30. seeing it is o. God who shall justify
1 Cor. 6. 17. that is joined to the Lord is o. spirit
12. 12. for as body is o. and hath many members
15. 40. but the glory of the celestial is o. and glory
Gal. 3. 20. is not a mediator of one, but God is o.
Col. 4. 9. with Onesimus, who is o. of you, 12.
See LITTLE, MAN.

Not ONE.

Gen. 24. 41. if they give not thee o. shall be clear
Exod. 8. 31. there remained not o. 10. 19.
9. 6. but of the cattle of Israel died not o. 7.
12. 30. not a house where there was not o. dead
Deut. 1. 35. shall n. o. of these men see that good land
2. 36. there was not o. city too strong for us
2 Sam. 13. 30. and there is not o. of them left
17. 13. till there be not o. small stone found there
1 Kings 16. 11. he left him n. o. that pisseth ag. wall
Job 14. 4. a clean thing out of an unclean, not o.
31. 15. and did not o. fashion us in the womb?
41. 9. shall n. o. be cast down at the sight of him?
Psal. 14. 3. are altogether become filthy, there is
none that doeth good, not o. 53. 3. Rom. 3. 12.
105. 37. there was n. o. feeble person among them
Isa. 40. 26. for that he is strong in power, n. o. faileth
Mat. 18. 10. take heed ye desp. n. o. of these little ones
Rom. 3. 10. there is none righteous, no not o.
1 Cor. 6. 5. no not o. that shall be able to judge
12. 14. for the body is not o. member, but many
See MIGHTY.

ONE, in reference to other.

Gen. 4. 19. the name of o. was Adah, of other Zillah
13. 11. they separated the o. from the other
47. 21. from the o. end of Egypt to the other
Exod. 1. 15. name of o. Shiphrah, of the other Puah
14. 20. so that the o. came not near the other
17. 12. stayed up his hands on o. side, and the oth.
18. 3. name of the o. Gershom, of the other Eliezer
Lev. 5. 7. two pigeons, o. for a sin offering, the other
for a burnt offering, 12. 8. Num. 6. 11. | 8. 12
16. 8. o. lot for the Lord, other for the scape-goat
Num. 11. 26. name of the o. Eldad, the other Medad
28. 4. o. lamb in the morning, the other at even
Deut. 4. 32. ask from o. side of heaven to the other
13. 7. from the o. end of the earth to other, 28. 64.
Judg. 16. 29. took hold of o. pillar and of the other
Ruth 1. 4. name of the o. was Orpah, of other Ruth
1 Sam. 1. 2. name of o. Hannah, the other Peninnah
2 Sam. 4. 2. name of o. Baanah, of the oth. Rechab
12. 1. there were two men, o. rich, the other poor
1 Kings 3. 23. o. saith, this is my son, the other saith
25. give half to the o. and half to the other
20. 29. they pitched o. against the other seven days
Neh. 4. 17. o. hand wrought, with oth. held weapon
Eccl. 3. 19. as the o. dieth, so dieth the other
7. 14. God hath set the o. over-against the other
Jer. 12. 12. for the sword of the Lord shall devour
from o. end of the land to the other end, 25. 33.
24. 2. o. basket had good figs, other basket had bad
Ezek. 21. 16. go the o. way or oth. on right or left
Dan. 8. 3. but o. horn was higher than the other
12. 5. o. on this side of river, the other on that side
Zech. 11. 7. the o. I called Beauty, the other Bands
Mat. 6. 24. he will hate the o. and love the other, or
hold to the o. and despise the other, Luke 16. 13.
20. 21. my two sons may sit, the o. on thy right
hand, and the other on thy left, Mark 10. 37.
24. 31. gather from o. end of heaven to the other
40. o. taken, the oth. left, 41. Luke 17. 34, 35, 36.
Mark 15. 27. they crucify two thieves, the o. on his
right hand, the other on his left, Luke 23. 33.
Luke 6. 29. if smite thee on o. cheek, offer the other
7. 41. the o. owed 500 pence, the other fifty
17. 24. lightning out of o. part, shineth to the other
18. 10. the o. a Pharisee, the other a publican
John 20. 12. o. angel at the head, other at the feet
Acts 15. 39. that they departed asunder o. from oth.
23. 6. the o. part Sadducees, the other Pharisees
1 Cor. 7. 5. defraud ye not o. the other, except it be
2 Cor. 2. 16. to o. the savour of life, to oth. of death
Gal. 4. 22. o. by bond-maid, other by a free-woman
5. 17. and these are contrary, the o. to the other
Rev. 17. 10. and o. is, the other is not yet come
See PEOPLE.

There is ONE.

Lev. 7. 7. trespass offering, there is o. law for them
Judg. 21. 6. there is o. tribe cut off from Israel
Esth. 4. 11. there is o. law of his to put him to death
Eccl. 4. 8. there is o. alone, and there is not a second
9. 2. there is o. event to righteous and the wicked
3. this is an evil, that there is o. event to all
Dan. 2. 9. if ye will not, there is o. decree for you
Nah. 1. 11. th. is o. come out of thee imagineth evil
Mark 12. 32. th. is o. God, 1 Tim. 2. 5. Jam. 2. 19.
John 5. 45. there is o. that accuseth you, even Mos.
8. 50. there is o. that seeketh and judgeth
1 Cor. 15. 39. th. is o. kind of flesh of men, anoth. of
41. there is o. glory of sun, another of moon
Jam. 4. 12. there is o. lawgiver, who is able to save

ONE of them.

Gen. 42. 27. as o. of them opened his sack in the inn
Exod. 14. 28. there remained not so much as o. of th.

Num. 16. 15. neither have I hurt *o. of them*
Deut. 25. 5. if *o. of them* die, and have no child
Judg. 11. 35. thou art *o. of them* that trouble me
1 *Sam.* 17. 36. this Philistine shall be as *o. of them*
2 *Sam.* 17. 22. lacked not *o. of th.* was not over Jord.
20. 19. I am *o. of them* that are peaceable in Isr.
24. 12. three things choose *o. of them*, 1 *Chr.* 21. 10.
1 *Kings* 18. 40. prophets of Baal, let not *o. of t.* escape
19. 2. if I make not thy life as the life of *o. of them*
22. 13. let thy word be like the word of *o. of them*
Ps. 34. 20. keep. his bones, not *o. of them* is broken
53. 3. every *o. of th.* is gone back, none doth good
58. 8. as a snail let every *o. of them* pass away
64. 6. inward thought of every *o. of them* is deep
84. 7. every *o. of them* in Zion appeareth before G.
106. 11. their enemies, there was not *o. of them* left
Prov. 22. 26. be not thou *o. of them* that strike hands
Eccl. 10. 15. labour of foolish wearieth every *o. of th.*
Jer. 15. 10. yet every *o. of them* doth curse me
Ezek. 11. 5. for I know the things, every *o. of them*
Dan. 8. 9. out of *o. of them* came forth a little horn
Obad. 11. and cast lots, even thou wast as *o. of them*
Mat. 10. 29. *o. of them* sold for a farthing, shall not fall to the ground without your Father, *Luke* 12. 6.
18. 12. have sheep, *o. of t.* be gone astray, *Luke* 15. 4.
26. 73. surely thou art *o. of them*, *Mark* 14. 69, 70.
Luke 17. 15. *o. of th.* when he saw that he was healed
John 6. 7. that every *o. of them* may take a little
7. 50. that came to Jesus by night, being *o. of them*
12. 2. Lazarus was *o. of them* that sat at the table
Acts 7. 24. and seeing *o. of them* suffer wrong
11. 28. and there stood up *o. of them* named Agab.

ONE *thing.*

Josh. 23. 14. not *o. thing* hath failed of all the good
Job 9. 22. this is *o. thing*, therefore I said it
Psal. 27. 4. *o. thing* have I desired of the Lord
Eccl. 3. 19. even *o. thing* befalleth them
Mat. 21. 24. I will ask you *o. thing*, *Luke* 6. 9. | 20. 3.
Mark 10. 21. *o. thing* thou lackest, *Luke* 18. 22.
Luke 10. 42. thou art careful, but *o. thing* is needful
John 9. 25. *o. thing* I know, that whereas I was blind
Acts 19. 32. some cried *o. th.* some another, 21. 34.
Phil. 3. 13. but this *o. th.* I do, I press toward mark
2 *Pet.* 3. 8. but be not ignorant of this *o. thing*

Wicked ONE.

Mat. 13. 19. then cometh the *wicked o.* and catcheth
38. the tares are the children of the *wicked o.*
1 *John* 2. 13. because ye have overcome *wicked o.* 14.
3. 12. not as Cain, who was of that *wicked o.*
5. 18. and that *wicked o.* toucheth him not

ONES.

Isa. 13. 3. I have commanded my sanctified *o.* I have also called my mighty *o.* for mine anger
Dan. 8. 8. and for it came up four notable *o.*
11. 17. set his face to enter, and upright *o.* with him

ONLY.

Gen. 6. 5. thoughts of his heart are *o.* evil continually
7. 23. Noah *o.* remained alive, and those in the ark
19. 8. *o.* to these men do nothing
22. 2. take now thy son, thine *o.* son Isaac, thou lov.
12. thou hast not withheld thy son, thine *o.* son, 16.
24. 8. *o.* bring not my son thither again
27. 13. *o.* obey my voice, and go fetch me them
34. 22. *o.* herein will the men consent to us, 23.
41. 40. *o.* in the throne will I be greater than thou
47. 22. *o.* the land of priests bought he not, 26.
Exod. 8. 9. they may remain in the river *o.* 11.
28. I will let you go, *o.* you shall not go far away
10. 17. now forgive my sin, I pray thee, *o.* this once that he may take away from me this death *o.*
24. *o.* let your flocks and your herds be stayed
12. 16. ev. man must eat, that *o.* may be done of you
21. 19. *o.* he shall pay for the loss of his time
22. 20. that sacrificeth to any, save to the Lord *o.*
27. for that is his covering, *o.* it is his raiment
Lev. 21. 23. *o.* he shall not go in unto the vail
27. 26. *o.* the firstling of the beasts, it is the Lord's
Num. 1. 49. *o.* thou shalt not number tribe of Levi
12. 2. hath the Lord indeed *o.* spoken by Moses?
14. 9. rebel not ye against the Lord *o.*
18. 3. *o.* they shall not come nigh the vessels
20. 19. I will *o.* go through on my feet, *Deut.* 2. 28.
22. 35. *o.* the word that I shall speak to thee
31. 22. *o.* the gold and the silver, the brass
36. 6. *o.* marry to the family of their father's tribe
Deut. 4. 9. *o.* take heed to thyself, keep thy soul
12. ye saw no similitude, *o.* ye heard a voice
8. 3. know that man doth not live by bread *o.*
10. 15. *o.* the Lord had a delight in thy fathers
12. 16. *o.* ye shall not eat the blood, 23. | 15. 23.
22. 25. the man *o.* that lay with her shall die
28. 13. thou shalt be above *o.* not be beneath
29. thou shalt be *o.* oppressed and spoiled, 33.
29. 14. nor with you *o.* do I make this covenant
Josh. 1. 7. *o.* be thou strong and very courageous, 18.
17. *o.* Lord thy God be with thee as with Moses
6. 15. *o.* that day compassed the city seven times
17. *o.* Rahab shall live || 11. 13. burned Hazor *o.*
17. 17. thou shalt not have one lot *o.*
Judg. 3. 2. they might *o.* know to teach them war
6. 37. if dew be on the fleece *o.* and dry on earth
39. let it not be dry *o.* upon the fleece, 40.
10. 15. deliver us *o.* we pray thee, this day
11. 34. came to meet him, and she was his *o.* child
16. 28. strengthen me, I pray thee, *o.* this once
19. 20. the man said, *o.* lodge not in the street
1 *Sam.* 1. 13. Han. *o.* moved her lips, voice not heard
23. *o.* the Lord establish his word
5. 4. *o.* the stump of Dagon was left to him
7. 3. and serve him *o.* 4. *Mat.* 4. 10. *Luke* 4. 8.
12. 24. *o.* fear the Lord, and serve him in truth
18. 17. *o.* be thou valiant for me, and fight battles
20. 14. not *o.* while I live, shew me kindness
39. *o.* Jonathan and David knew the matter
2 *Sam.* 13. 32. Jonadab said, *o.* Amnon is dead, 33.
17. 2. the people flee, and I will smite the king *o.*
20. 21. deliver him *o.* and I will depart from city
23. 10. the people returned after him *o.* to spoil
1 *Kings* 3. 2. *o.* the people sacrificed in high places, 3.
4. 19. Gebar was the *o.* officer who was in the land
12. 20. none followed David, but Judah *o.*
14. 8. David did that *o.* which was right in my eyes
1 *Kings* 14. 13. he *o.* of Jeroboam shall come to grave
15. 5. save *o.* in the matter of Uriah the Hittite
19. 10. I *o.* am left, and they seek my life, 14.
22. 31. fight not, save *o.* with the king of Israel
2 *Kings* 10. 23. but the worshippers of Baal *o.*
17. 18. there was none left but the tribe of Judah *o.*
19. 19. thou art the Lord, even thou *o.* *Isa.* 37. 20.
1 *Chron.* 22. 12. *o.* the Lord give thee wisdom
2 *Chron.* 2. 6. save *o.* to burn sacrifice before him
6. 30. thou *o.* knowest the hearts of children of men
33. 17. did sacrifice, yet to the Lord their God *o.*
Esth. 1. 16. the queen hath not done wrong to king *o.*
Job 1. 12. *o.* on himself put not forth thy hand
15. I *o.* am escaped to tell thee, 16, 17, 19.
13. 20. *o.* do not two things to me, then will I not
34. 29. whether done against a nation, or a man *o.*
Psal. 4. 8. thou Lord, *o.* makest me dwell in safety
51. 4. against thee, thee *o.* have I sinned
62. 2. he *o.* is my rock and my salvation, 6.
4. *o.* consult to cast him down from excellency
5. my soul, wait thou *o.* upon God
71. 16. mention thy righteousness, even thine *o.*
72. 18. God of Israel *o.* doth wondrous things
91. 8. *o.* with thine eyes shalt thou behold and see
Prov. 4. 3. tender and *o.* beloved in sight of mother
5. 17. let them be *o.* thine own, and not strangers
11. 23. the desire of the righteous is *o.* good
13. 10. *o.* by pride cometh contention
14. 23. the talk of the lips tendeth *o.* to penury
17. 11. an evil man seeketh *o.* rebellion
21. 5. tend *o.* to plenteousness, *o.* to want
Eccl. 7. 29. this *o.* have I found, that God made man
Cant. 6. 9. she is the *o.* one of her mother
Isa. 4. 1. *o.* let us be called by thy name
26. 13. we will *o.* make mention of thy name
28. 19. it shall be a vexation *o.* to understand report
Jer. 3. 13. *o.* acknowledge thine iniquity
6. 26. make mourning as for an *o.* son, *Amos* 8. 10.
32. 30. *o.* done evil, *o.* provoked me to anger
Ezek. 7. 5. and evil, an *o.* evil, behold, is come
14. 16. they *o.* shall be delivered, 18.
44. 20. they shall *o.* poll their heads
Amos 3. 2. you *o.* have I known of all famil. of earth
Mat. 5. 47. if ye salute your brethren *o.* what do you
8. 8. the centurion said, Lord, speak the word *o.*
10. 42. shall give a cup of cold water *o.* in name
12. 4. not lawful for him to eat, but *o.* for priests
14. 36. they might *o.* touch hem of his garment
17. 8. they saw no man, save Jesus *o.* *Mark* 9. 8.
21. 19. they found nothing thereon but leaves *o.*
21. shall not *o.* do this which is done to fig-tree
24. 36. not the angels in heaven, but my Father *o.*
Mark 2. 7. who can forgive sins, but God *o.*?
5. 36. Jes. saith, be not afraid, *o.* believe, *Luke* 8. 50.
6. 8. should take nothing for journey, save a staff *o.*
Luke 7. 12. was a dead man, *o.* son of his mother
8. 42. one *o.* daughter || 9. 38. he is my *o.* child
24. 18. art thou *o.* a stranger in Jerusal. not known
John 5. 18. not *o.* because he had broken sabbath
44. and seek not honour that cometh from God *o.*
11. 52. that Jesus should die, not for that nation *o.*
12. 9. came not for Jesus' sake *o.* but to see Lazarus
13. 9. Lord, not my feet *o.* but also my hands
17. 3. that they might know thee the *o.* true God
Acts 8. 16. *o.* they were baptized in name of Jesus
11. 19. preaching the word to none but Jews *o.*
18. 25. Apollos taught, knowing *o.* bapt. of John
19. 27. not *o.* our craft is in danger to be at nought
21. 13. ready not to be bound *o.* but to die for Jes.
25. *o.* that they keep thems. from things offered
26. 29. I would to God that not *o.* thou, but all
Rom. 1. 32. not *o.* do same, but have pleas. in them
3. 29. is he God of Jews *o.*? is he not of Gentiles?
4. 9. cometh this blessedn. on circumcision *o.*? 12.
16. not to that *o.* which is of law, but to faith
5. 3. not *o.* so, 11. || 8. 23. not *o.* they, but ourselves
9. 24. whom he called, not of Jews *o.* but of Gentiles
13. 5. ye must be subject, not *o.* for wrath, but also
16. 4. to whom not *o.* I give thanks, but churches
27. to God *o.* wise be glory, 1 *Tim.* 1. 17. *Jude* 25.
1 *Cor.* 7. 39. *o.* in the Ld. || 9. 6. I *o.* and Barnabas
14. 36. came word of God from you *o.* or to you *o.*?
15. 19. if in this life *o.* we have hope, most miserable
2 *Cor.* 7. 7. God comforted us, not by his coming *o.*
8. 10. have begun not *o.* to do || 19. not that *o.*
21. not *o.* in sight of Lord, but in sight of men
Gal. 1. 23. heard *o.* he who persecuted in times past
2. 10. *o.* would that we should remember the poor
3. 2. this *o.* would I learn of you, received ye Spir.?
4. 18. and not *o.* when I am present with you
5. 13. *o.* use not liberty for an occasion to the flesh
6. 12. *o.* lest they should suffer persecut. for Christ
Eph. 1. 21. every name named, not *o.* in this world
Phil. 1. 27. *o.* let your convers. be as becomes gosp.
29. is given not *o.* to believe on him, but to suffer
2. 12. as ye obeyed, not as in my presence *o.* but in absence
27. God had mercy not on him *o.* but on me
4. 15. no church communicated with me, but ye *o.*
Col. 4. 11. these *o.* are my fellow-workers to kingd.
1 *Thess.* 1. 5. gosp. came not in word *o.* but in power
2. 8. to have imparted to you not gospel of God *o.*
2 *Thess.* 2. 7. *o.* he who now letteth will let, till taken
1 *Tim.* 5. 13. not *o.* idle, but tatlers and busy-bodies
6. 15. is blessed and *o.* Potentate, King of kings
16. who *o.* hath immortality, dwelling in light
2 *Tim.* 4. 8. not to me *o.* || 11. *o.* Luke is with me
Heb. 9. 10. which stood *o.* in meats and drinks
12. 26. once more I shake not earth *o.* but heaven
Jam. 1. 22. be ye doers of word, and not hearers *o.*
2. 24. a man is justified by works, and not faith *o.*
1 *Pet.* 2. 18. not *o.* to good and gentle, but froward
1 *John.* 2. 2. not for our sins *o.* || 5. 6. not by water *o.*
2 *John* 1. whom I love in the truth, and not I *o.*
Jude 4. denying the *o.* Lord God and our Lord Jesus
Rev. 9. 4. but *o.* those which have not seal of God
15. 4. who shall not fear thee? for thou *o.* art holy

See BEGOTTEN.

ONIONS.

Num. 11. 5. we remember the *o.* and the garlic

ONWARD.

Exod. 40. 36. when cloud was taken up, Isr. went *o.*

ONYCHA.

Exod. 30. 34. take thee spices, *o.* and galbanum

ONYX.

Exod. 28. 20. fourth row a beryl and an *o.* 39. 13.
Job 28. 16. wisdom cannot be valued with the *o.*
Ezek. 28. 13. the topaz and the *o.* was thy covering

See STONES.

OPEN, *Adjective.*

Gen. 1. 20. and fowl that may fly in *o.* firmament
38. 14. Tamar sat in an *o.* place by way of Timnath
Num. 19. 15. every *o.* vessel not covered is unclean
24. 3. the man whose eyes are *o.* hath said, 4. 15.
Josh. 8. 17. they left Ai *o.* and pursued after Israel
1 *Sam.* 3. 1. word of Lord precious, was no *o.* vision
1 *Kings* 6. 18. cedar carved with *o.* flowers, 29. 32, 35.
8. 29. that thine eyes may be *o.* towards this house night and day, 52. 2 *Chron.* 6. 20, 40. | 7. 15.
Neh. 1. 6. let thine eyes be *o.* ear attentive to hear
6. 5. Sanballat with an *o.* letter sent his servant
Job 34. 26. as wicked men in the *o.* sight of others
Psal. 5. 9. their throat is an *o.* sepulchre, *Rom.* 3. 13.
34. 15. the righteous, his ears are *o.* to their cry
Prov. 13. 16. but a fool layeth *o.* his folly
27. 5. *o.* rebuke is better than secret love
Isa. 9. 12. they shall devour Israel with *o.* mouth
24. 18. for the windows from on high are *o.*
60. 11. thy gates shall be *o.* continually, not shut
Jer. 5. 16. quiver is an *o.* sepulchre, are mighty men
32. 11. took evidence, both what was sealed and *o.*
19. thine eyes are *o.* on all the ways of men
Ezek. 37. 2. there were many bones in the *o.* valley
Dan. 6. 10. his windows being *o.* in chamber to Jerus.
Nah. 3. 13. gates of thy land shall be set wide *o.*
John 1. 51. hereafter ye shall see heaven *o.* angels
Acts 16. 27. seeing prison-doors *o.* drew his sword
19. 38. the law is *o.* and there are deputies
2 *Cor.* 3. 18. we all with *o.* face beholding as in glass
6. 11. our mouth is *o.* to you, our heart is enlarged
1 *Tim.* 5. 24. some men's sins are *o.* beforehand
Heb. 6. 6. seeing they put him to an *o.* shame
1 *Pet.* 3. 12. his ears are *o.* to their prayers
Rev. 3. 8. behold I have set before thee an *o.* door
10. 2. he had in his hand a little book *o.* 8.

See FIELD, FIELDS.

OPEN, *Verb,*

Signifies, [1] *To unlock that which is fastened and made sure*, Acts 16. 26. [2] *To interpret, unfold, or explain*, Luke 24. 32. [3] *To receive an answer to our prayers*, Mat. 7. 7. [4] *To receive Christ into the heart by faith and love*, Cant. 5. 2. Rev. 3. 20. [5] *To uncover or lay open*, Exod. 21. 33. [6] *To cleave, rend, or divide*, Num. 16. 32. Ezek. 1. 1.

To open the book, *Rev.* 5. 3, 9. *To unseal the book, by declaring and revealing to* John, *and by him to the church, such secret mysteries as were before hidden in God's counsel: this no creature could do; Christ the Mediator of the new covenant was only able to do it, for he came out of the Father's bosom to reveal his will to us.*

To open their eyes, *Acts* 26. 18. *To preach the gospel to them, whereby they may attain to a spiritual understanding, and embrace the gospel.*

To open the heart, *Acts* 16. 14. *To enlighten the understanding, renew the will and affections, and incline a person to embrace the gospel.*

To open the lips, *Psal.* 51. 15. *To give occasion and ability, both of heart and tongue, to praise God.*

Exod. 21. 33. if a man shall *o.* a pit or dig a pit
Num. 8. 16. given instead of such as *o.* every womb
16. 30. if earth *o.* her mouth and swallow them
Deut. 15. 8. thou shalt *o.* thy hand wide to him, 11.
20. 11. if it make answer of peace, and *o.* to thee
28. 12. Lord shall *o.* to thee his good treasure
Josh. 10. 22. *o.* mouth of cave and bring out 5 kings
2 *Kings* 9. 3. then *o.* door, and flee, and tarry not
13. 17. and he said, *o.* the window eastward
Job 11. 5. oh that God would *o.* his lips against thee
32. 20. I will *o.* my lips, and answer
35. 16. therefore doth Job *o.* his mouth in vain
41. 14. who can *o.* the doors of his face?
Psal. 22. † 7. all they that see me, *o.* the lip
49. 4. I will *o.* my dark saying upon the harp
78. 2. I will *o.* mouth in parable, utter dark sayings
81. 10. *o.* thy mouth wide and I will fill it
118. 19. *o.* to me the gates of righteousness
Prov. 31. 8. *o.* thy mouth for dumb in the cause
9. *o.* thy mouth, judge righteously, plead cause
Cant. 5. 2. *o.* to me, my sister, my love, my dove
5. I rose up to *o.* to my belov. hands dropt myrrh
Isa. 22. 22. *o.* none shall shut, shut and none shall *o.*
26. 2. *o.* the gates, that the righteous nation enter
28. 24. doth he *o.* and break clods of his ground?
41. 18. I will *o.* rivers in high places, and fountains
42. 7. to *o.* blind eyes, to bring out the prisoners
45. 1. to *o.* before him the two-leaved gates
8. let the earth *o.* let them bring forth salvation
Jer. 13. 19. the cities shall be shut up, none shall *o.*
50. 26. *o.* her store-houses, cast her up as heaps
Ezek. 2. 8. *o.* thy mouth and eat that I give thee
3. 27. when I speak with thee, I will *o.* thy mouth
16. 63. mayest be confounded and never *o.* mouth
21. 22. to *o.* the mouth in the slaughter to lift up
25. 9. behold, I will *o.* side of Moab from cities
37. 12. I will *o.* your graves, cause you come up
46. 12. one shall *o.* him the gate toward the east
Amos 8. † 5. and the sabbath, that we may *o.* wheat
Zech. 11. 1. *o.* thy doors, O Lebanon, that fire devour
Mal. 3. 10. if I will not *o.* you windows of heaven
Mat. 13. 35. I will *o.* my mouth in parables
25. 11. saying, Lord, Lord, *o.* to us, *Luke* 13. 25.
Luke 12. 36. when he cometh and knocketh may *o.*
Acts 18. 14. when Paul was about to *o.* his mouth
Eph. 6. 19. praying, that I may *o.* my mouth boldly
Col. 4. 3. that God would *o.* to us door of utterance
Rev. 5. 2. who is worthy to *o.* the book and seals?
3. no man in heaven or earth was able to *o.* book
4. no man was found worthy to *o.* and read book
5. behold, the Root of David prevailed to *o.* book
9. thou art worthy to take book, and *o.* seals

See EYES.

OPENED.

Gen. 7. 11. the same day windows of heaven were *o.*
8. 6. Noah *o.* the window of the ark he had made
29. 31. God *o.* Leah's womb ‖ 30. 22. he *o.* Rachel's
41. 56. Joseph *o.* all storehouses and sold to Egypt
42. 27. one of them *o.* his sack, 43. 21. | 44. 11.
Exod. 2. 6. when she had *o.* ark she saw the child
Num. 16. 32. the earth *o.* her mouth, and swallowed up Korah, Dathan, and Abiram, *Psal.* 106. 17.
Judg. 3. 25. he *o.* not the doors, they *o.* them
4. 19. she *o.* a bottle of milk and gave him drink
19. 27. her lord *o.* doors, went out to go his way
2 Sam. 7. † 27. thou, O Lord, hast *o.* ear of thy serv.
2 Kings 9. 10. and Elisha *o.* the door and fled
15. 16. they *o.* not to him, therefore he smote them
2 Chron. 29. 3. Hezekiah *o.* doors of Lord's house
Neh. 7. 3. I said, let not gates of Jerusalem be *o.*
8. 5. Ezra *o.* book, when he *o.* it people stood up
13. 19. charged gates not to be *o.* till after sabbath
Job 29. † 19. my root was *o.* by the waters
31. 32. but I *o.* my doors to the traveller
32. † 19. behold, my belly as wine which is not *o.*
38. 17. have the gates of death been *o.* to thee?
Psal. 22. † 13. they *o.* their mouths against me
40. 6. sacrifice not desire, mine ears hast thou *o.*
66. † 14. I will pay my vows that my lips have *o.*
78. 23. though he had *o.* the doors of heaven
105. 41. he *o.* the rock, and the waters gushed out
Cant. 5. 6. I *o.* to my beloved, but he was gone
Isa. 14. 17. that *o.* not the house of his prisoners
48. 8. from that time that thine ear was not *o.*
50. 5. Lord God hath *o.* mine ear, not rebellious
Jer. 1. † 14. out of the north an evil shall be *o.*
20. 12. for to thee have I *o.* my cause
50. 25. Lord hath *o.* his armoury and brought forth
Ezek. 1. 1. that the heavens were *o.* *Mat.* 3. 16. *Mark* 1. 10. *Luke* 3. 21. *Acts* 7. 56.
16. 25. thou hast *o.* thy feet to every one passed by
37. 13. when I have *o.* your graves, O my people
44. 2. gate shall not be *o.* no man enter by it
46. 1. but on sabbath and new moon it shall be *o.*
Dan. 7. 10. the judgment was set, the books were *o.*
Nah. 2. 6. gates of the rivers shall be *o.* palace be
Zech. 13. 1. fountain shall be *o.* to house of David
Mat. 2. 11. when they had *o.* their treasures
7. 7. knock, it shall be *o.* to you, *Luke* 11. 9, 10.
27. 52. graves were *o.* many bodies of saints arose
Mark 7. 34. that is, be *o.* ‖ 35. his ears were *o.*
Luke 4. 17. when he had *o.* book he found the place
24. 32. while he *o.* to us the scriptures
45. then *o.* he their understand. to underst. script.
Acts 5. 19. the angel by night *o.* the prison doors
23. but when we had *o.* we found no man within
10. 11. Peter saw heaven *o.* and a vessel descending
12. 10. iron gate *o.* ‖ 14. *o.* not the gate, but ran in
16. when they had *o.* the door and saw him
14. 27. how he had *o.* the door of faith to Gentiles
16. 14. Lydia, whose heart Lord *o.* she attended
26. the prison doors were *o.* bands were loosed
1 Cor. 16. 9. for a great door and effectual is *o.* unto me, there are many adversaries, *2 Cor.* 2. 12.
Heb. 4. 13. all things are naked and *o.* to him
Rev. 4. 1. behold, a door was *o.* in heaven
6. 1. I saw when the Lamb *o.* one of the seals
3. had *o.* the second ‖ 5. the third ‖ 7. the fourth
9. *o.* the fifth seal ‖ 12. the sixth ‖ 8. 1. the seventh
9. 2. he *o.* the bottomless pit, and there arose
11. 19. the temple of God was *o.* in heaven
15. 5. the tabernacle of the testimony was *o.*
19. 11. I saw heaven *o.* and behold a white horse
20. 12. the books were *o.* the book of life was *o.*
See DAYS, MOUTH.

OPENEST.

Psal. 104. 28. thou *o.* thy hand, are filled with good
145. 16. thou *o.* thine hand and satisfiest the desire

OPENETH.

Exod. 13. 2. sanctify to me whatsoever *o.* the womb
12. thou shalt set apart all that *o.* the matrix, 15. | 34. 19. *Num.* 3. 12. | 18. 15. *Luke* 2. 23.
Job 27. 19. the rich man *o.* his eyes, and he is not
33. 16. he *o.* ears of men, and sealeth instruction
36. 10. he *o.* their ear to discipline and commands
15. he delivers poor, *o.* their ears in oppression
Psal. 38. 13. I as a dumb man that *o.* not his mouth
Prov. 13. 3. he that *o.* wide his lips have destruction
24. 7. he *o.* not his mouth in the gate
31. 26. she *o.* her mouth with wisdom, in her tongue
Isa. 53. 7. brought as a lamb, so he *o.* not his mouth
Ezek. 20. 26. to pass thro' the fire, all that *o.* womb
John 10. 3. to him the porter *o.* sheep hear his voice
Rev. 3. 7. he that hath key of David, he that *o.* and no man shutteth, and shutteth and no man *o.*

OPENING.

Isa. 42. 20. *o.* the ears, but he heareth not
Acts 17. 3. *o.* and alleging Christ must have suffer.

OPENING, S.

1 Chron. 9. 27. *o.* of house of God pertained to them
Job 12. 14. he shutteth up a man, there can be no *o.*
Prov. 1. 21. in the *o.* of the gates wisdom crieth
8. 6. and the *o.* of my lips shall be right things
Isa. 61. 1. proclaim the *o.* of the prison to the bound
Ezek. 29. 21. I will give thee the *o.* of the mouth

OPENLY.

Gen. 38. 21. where harlot that was *o.* by way-side?
2 Sam. 6. † 20. as a vain fellow *o.* uncovers himself
Psal. 98. 2. his righteousness hath he *o.* shewed
Mat. 6. 4. thy Father shall reward thee *o.* 6. 18.
Mark 8. 32. and he spake that saying *o.*
John 7. 4. he himself seeketh to be known *o.*
10. then went he to the feast, not *o.* but in secret
13. no man spake of him *o.* for fear of the Jews
11. 54. Jesus walked no more *o.* among the Jews
18. 20. Jesus said, I spake *o.* to the world
Acts 10. 40. him God raised up, and shewed him *o.*
16. 37. they have beaten us *o.* uncondemned
Col. 2. 15. he made a shew of them *o.* triumphing

OPERATION.

Psal. 28. 5. they regard not the *o.* of his hands
Isa. 5. 12. nor consider the *o.* of his hands
Col. 2. 12. risen through the faith of the *o.* of God

OPERATIONS.

Cor. 12. 6. there are diversity of *o.* but same God

OPINION.

Job 32. 6. was afraid, and durst not shew you mine *o.*
10. hearken to me, I also will shew you mine *o.* 17.

OPINIONS.

1 Kings 18. 21. how long halt ye between two *o.?*

OPPORTUNITY.

Lev. 16. † 21. send the scape-goat by a man of *o.*
Mat. 26. 16. he sought to betray him, *Luke* 22. 6.
Gal. 6. 10. as we have *o.* let us do good to all, but
Phil. 4. 10. ye were also careful, but ye lacked *o.*
Heb. 11. 15. they might have had *o.* to have returned

OPPOSE.

2 Tim. 2. 25. instructing those that *o.* themselves

OPPOSED.

Acts 18. 6. when they *o.* themselves and blasphemed

OPPOSEST.

Job 30. 21. with thy strong hand thou *o.* thyself

OPPOSETH.

2 Thess. 2. 4. who *o.* and exalteth himself above all

OPPOSITIONS.

1 Tim. 6. 20. avoiding *o.* of science falsely so called

OPPRESS.

Exod. 3. 9. wherewith the Egyptians *o.* them
22. 21. neither vex nor *o.* a stranger, 23. 9.
Lev. 25. 14. ye shall not *o.* one another, 17.
Deut. 23. 16. shalt not *o.* servant that is escaped
24. 14. thou shalt not *o.* an hired servant, poor
Judg. 10. 12. Moabites did *o.* you, and ye cried
Job 10. 3. is it good to thee that thou shouldest *o.?*
Psal. 10. 18. that the man of earth may no more *o.*
17. 9. hide me from the wicked that *o.* me
119. 122. be surety for good, let not proud *o.* me
Prov. 22. 22. nor *o.* the afflicted in the gate
Isa. 49. 26. will feed them that *o.* thee with their flesh
Jer. 7. 6. if ye *o.* not the stranger and the widow
30. 20. and I will punish all that *o.* them
Ezek. 45. 8. princes shall no more *o.* my people
Hos. 12. 7. he is a merchant, he loveth to *o.*
Amos 4. 1. ye kine of Bashan which *o.* the poor
Mic. 2. 2. they *o.* a man and his house, even a man
Zech. 7. 10. *o.* not the widow nor the fatherless
Mal. 3. 5. will be swift witness against those that *o.*
1 Thess. 4. † 6. no man *o.* his brother in any matter
Jam. 2. 6. do not rich men *o.* you and draw you?

OPPRESSED.

Deut. 28. 29. thou shalt be only *o.* and spoiled, 33.
Judg. 2. 18. by reason of them that *o.* and vexed
4. 3. Jabin *o.* Israel ‖ 10. 8. Philist. and Ammon *o.*
6. 9. I delivered you out of the hand of the Egyptians, and of all that *o.* you, *1 Sam.* 10. 18.
1 Sam. 12. 3. whose ox have I taken? whom have I *o.?*
4. thou hast not defrauded, nor *o.* us, nor taken
2 Kings 13. 4. Assyria *o.* them ‖ 22. king of Syria *o.*
2 Chron. 16. 10. Asa *o.* some of the people same time
Job 20. 19. because he hath *o.* and forsaken the poor
35. 9. by oppressions they make the *o.* to cry
Psal. 9. 9. the Lord will be a refuge for the *o.*
10. 18. judge the fatherless and *o.* 103. 6. | 146. 7.
74. 21. O let not the *o.* return ashamed
106. 42. their enemies *o.* them, brought to subject.
Eccl. 4. 1. and, behold, the tears of such as were *o.*
Isa. 1. 17. learn to do well, seek judgment, relieve *o.*
3. 5. the people shall be *o.* every one by another
23. 12. O thou, *o.* virgin, daughter of Zidon, arise
38. 14. O Lord, I am *o.* undertake for me
52. 4. the Assyrian *o.* them without cause
53. 7. he was *o.* and afflicted, yet he opened not
58. 6. is not this the fast? to let the *o.* go free
Jer. 50. 33. Israel and Judah were *o.* together
Ezek. 18. 7. hath not *o.* any, but hath restored, 16.
12. because he hath *o.* ‖ 18. he cruelly *o.*
22. 29. they have *o.* the stranger wrongfully
Hos. 5. 11. Ephraim is *o.* and broken in judgment
Amos 3. 9. behold the *o.* in the midst thereof
Acts 7. 24. Moses avenged him that was *o.*
10. 38. Jesus healed all that were *o.* of the devil

OPPRESSETH.

Num. 10. 9. if ye go to war against him that *o.* you
Job 40. † 23. behold, Behemoth *o.* a river, hasteth not
Psal. 56. 1. be merciful, he fighting daily *o.* me
Prov. 14. 31. he that *o.* the poor reproacheth, 22. 16.
28. 3. a poor man that *o.* the poor, is like rain

OPPRESSING.

Jer. 46. 16. arise, let us go from the *o.* sword
50. 16. for fear of the *o.* sword, they shall turn
Zeph. 3. 1. woe to *o.* city, she obeyed not the voice

OPPRESSION

Is *the spoiling or taking away of men's goods or estates by constraint, terror, or force, without having any right thereto; working upon the ignorance, weakness, or fearfulness of the oppressed. Men are guilty of* Oppression, *when they offer any violence to men's bodies, estates, or consciences; when they crush or overburden others, as the Egyptians did the Hebrews,* Exod. 3. 9. *when they impose upon the consciences of men, and persecute them merely because they are of a persuasion different from theirs: St.* Paul *acknowledges that he had been one of this sort of oppressors,* 1 Tim. 1. 13. *And when they commit adultery or fornication, whereby the innocent is robbed of his right in his wife, daughter, &c.* 1 Thess. 4. 6.

Exod. 3. 9. I have seen *o.* wherewith the Egyptians
Deut. 26. 7. the Lord heard and looked on our *o.*
2 Kings 13. 4. the Lord saw the *o.* of Israel
Job 36. 15. and he openeth their ears in *o.*
Psal. 12. 5. for the *o.* of the poor will I arise
42. 9. because of the *o.* of the enemy, 43. 2. | 55. 3.
44. 24. forgettest our *o.* ‖ 62. 10. trust not in *o.*
73. 8. and they speak wickedly concerning *o.*
107. 39. again they are brought low through *o.*
119. 134. deliver me from the *o.* of man
Eccl. 5. 8. if thou seest the *o.* of the poor, and violent
7. 7. surely *o.* maketh a wise man mad, and a gift
Isa. 5. 7. but behold *o.* ‖ 30. 12. because ye trust in *o.*
30. † 20. though the Lord give you the water of *o.*
54. 14. thou shalt be far from *o.* ‖ 59. 13. speak. *o.*
Jer. 6. 6. she is wholly *o.* in the midst of her
22. 17. but thine eyes and heart are for *o.*
Ezek. 22. 7. they dealt by *o.* with the stranger
29. the people of the land have used *o.*

Ezek. 46. 18. the prince shall not take inherit. by *o.*

OPPRESSIONS.

Job 35. 9. by reason of the multitude of *o.*
Eccl. 4. 1. I considered the *o.* done under the sun
Isa. 33. 15. he that despiseth the gain of *o.*
Amos 3. † 9. behold the *o.* in the midst thereof

OPPRESSOR.

Esth. 3. † 10. the king gave his ring to the Jews' *o.*
Job 3. 18. they hear not the voice of the *o.*
15. 20. the number of years is hidden to the *o.*
Psal. 72. 4. he shall break in pieces the *o.*
Prov. 3. 31. envy not *o.* choose none of his ways
28. 16. prince that wanteth understanding is an *o.*
Isa. 9. 4. for thou hast broken the rod of his *o.*
14. 4. and say, how hath the *o.* ceased!
51. 13. hast feared because of the fury of the *o.*
Jer. 21. 12. O house of David, deliver him that is spoiled out of the hand of the *o.* 22. 3.
25. 38. because of the fierceness of the *o.*
Zech. 9. 8. no *o.* shall pass through them any more
10. 4. out of him came every *o.* together

OPPRESSORS.

Job 27. 13. this is heritage of *o.* they shall receive
Psal. 54. 3. strangers risen and *o.* seek after my soul
119. 121. have done judg. leave me not to mine *o.*
Eccl. 4. 1. on the side of their *o.* there was power
Isa. 3. 12. children are their *o.* women rule over them
14. 2. and they shall rule over their *o.*
16. 4. the *o.* are consumed out of the land
19. 20. they shall cry to the Lord because of the *o.*

ORACLE

Is by some taken for the Propitiatory, *or* Mercy-seat, *by translating the* Hebrew *word* Caphoreth, *Exod.* 25. 18, 20. *by* Oracle. *This word comes from the verb* Caphar, *which signifies to expiate, to pardon sins, to cover. It may be rendered by a* Covering, *for it was the cover of the ark of the covenant, or of the sacred chest in which the laws of the covenant were shut up. And perhaps by translating* Caphoreth *by* propitiatory *or* mercy-seat, *it may be insinuated that from thence the Lord heard the vows and prayers of his people, and pardoned them their sins. And by translating it* Oracle *they would shew, that it was from thence that God manifested his will and pleasure, and gave responses to* Moses.

Oracle *is taken for the* sanctuary, *or for the* most holy place, *wherein the ark of the covenant was deposited,* 1 Kings 6. 5, 16, 17.

It is taken also for the Oracles *of false gods; the most famous of which in* Palestine *was that of* Baal-zebub, *the god of* Ekron, *which the* Jews *themselves often went to consult,* 2 Kings 1. 2, 3, 6, 16. *There were also* Teraphims, *as that of* Micah, *mentioned,* Judg. 17. 5. *and the false gods adored in the kingdom of* Samaria, *which had their false prophets, and consequently their* oracles, *whether these* oracles *were really delivered by the assistance of the devil, or that the priests and false prophets imposed upon the people, making them believe they were inspired, though they only spoke by their own seducing spirit.*

Some have ascribed to Demons, all the oracles *of antiquity; others have imputed them to the knavery of the priests; and others have pretended, that there were several kinds of* oracles: *some were illusions and tricks of the devil; others were the effects of the juggling and contrivance of the priests. The Scripture affords examples of these sorts of* oracles. Balaam, *at the instigation of his own spirit, and urged on by his avarice, fearing to lose the recompence that he was promised by* Balak, *king of the* Moabites, *suggests a diabolical expedient to this prince, of making the* Israelites *to fall into idolatry and fornication, by which he assures him of a certain victory, or at least of a considerable advantage against the people of God,* Num. 24. 14. | 31. 16.

Micaiah, *the son of* Imlah, *a prophet of the Lord, says, "That he saw the Almighty sitting upon his throne, and all the hosts of heaven round about him; and the Lord said, who shall tempt* Ahab, *king of* Israel, *that he may go to war against* Ramoth-gilead, *and fall in the battle? One answered after one manner, and another in another. At the same time an evil spirit presented himself before the Lord, and said, I will seduce him: and the Lord asked him, how? To which Satan answered, I will go and be a lying spirit in the mouth of his prophets. And the Lord said, Go, and thou shalt prevail,"* 1 Kings 22. *This dialogue proves these two things:* First, *that the devil could do nothing by his own power; and* secondly, *that with the permission of God he could inspire the false prophets, sorcerers, and magicians, and make them deliver false* oracles.

Among the Jews *there were several sorts of real* oracles. [1] *They had* oracles *that were delivered* vivâ voce, *as when God spake to* Moses *face to face, and as one friend speaks to another,* Num. 12. 8. [2] *Prophetical dreams sent by God; as the dreams which God sent to* Joseph, *and which foretold his future greatness,* Gen. 37. 5, 6. [3] *Visions: as when a prophet in an ecstasy, being neither properly asleep nor awake, had supernatural revelations,* Gen. 15. 1. | 46. 2. Num. 12. 6. [4] *The* oracles *of* Urim *and* Thummim, *which was in the* Ephod, *or* Pectoral, *worn by the high priest, and which God endued with the gift of foretelling things to come. This manner of inquiring of the Lord was often made use of, from* Joshua's *time, to the erection of the temple at Jerusalem,* 1 Sam. 23. 9. | 30. 7. [5] *After the building of the temple, they generally consulted the prophets, who were frequent in the kingdoms of* Judah *and* Israel. *These oracles of truth had no necessary connexion either with time, or place, or any other circumstance, or with the personal qualifications and merit of the person by whom they were uttered: the high priest clothed with the*

Ephod and Pectoral gave a true answer, whatever was the manner of his life. Sometimes he gave an answer without knowing clearly himself what was the subject of the question he was consulted about. Caiaphas *pronounces an oracle relating to our* Lord Jesus Christ, *whom he hated, and whose destruction he desired, and an oracle which he understood not himself.* John 11. 49, 50, 51. Ye know nothing at all, nor consider that it is expedient for us that one man should die for the people, and that the whole nation perish not. *To which is added,* And this spake he not of himself, but being high priest that year, he prophesied that *Jesus* should die for that nation.

At the time of the planting of the Christian church, the gifts of prophecy and inspiration were very common. Christ Jesus, *our great Prophet and High Priest, has himself taught us the mind and will of God about the way of our salvation, and by his Holy Spirit has inspired persons, chosen on purpose, to pen the doctrine which he taught in the Scriptures of the New Testament, and to open and unfold the mysteries of the Old. These revelations are the* oracles, *which Christians are to consult at all times, especially in all matters of moment and difficulty, and in the great affairs relating to their souls and another life,* Heb. 5. 12.

2 *Sam.* 16.23. as if man had inquired at the *o.* of God
1 *Kings* 6. 16. he built them for it within, for the *o.*
8. 6. the priests brought the ark of Lord into the *o.*
2 *Chr.* 4. 20. should burn before the *o.* of pure gold
*Ps.*28.2. when I lift up my hands towards thy holy *o.*

ORACLES.

Acts 7. 38. who received the lively *o.* to give to us
Rom. 3. 2. to them were committed the *o.* of God
Heb. 5. 12. the first principles of the *o.* of God
1 *Pet.* 4. 11. if speak, let him speak as the *o.* of God

ORATION.

Acts 12. 21. upon a set day Herod made an *o.* to them

ORATOR.

Isa. 3. 3. L. taketh away from Judah the eloquent *o.*
Acts 24. 1. and with a certain *o.* named Tertullus

ORCHARD.

Cant. 4. 13. thy plants are an *o.* of pomegranates

ORCHARDS.

*Eccl.*2.5. I made me gardens and *o.* and planted trees

ORDAIN

Signifies, [1] *To command or enjoin,* 1 Cor. 9. 14. [2] *To appoint or design to a certain end or use,* Rom. 7. 10. [3] *To choose or set apart for an office or employment,* Mark 3. 14. [4] *To fore-ordain,* Acts 10. 42. | 13. 48. [5] *To found,* 1 Chron. 9. † 22. Psal. 8. † 2. [6] *To give,* Jer. 1. † 5. [7] *To order,* Rom. 13. † 1. [8] *To prepare,* Isa. 30. 33. Ephes. 2. † 10.

1 *Chr.* 9. 22. Dav. and Sam. did *o.* in their set office
17. 9. I will *o.* a place for my people Israel
Isa. 26. 12. Lord, thou wilt *o.* peace for us, for thou
1 *Cor.* 7. 17. and so *o.* I in all churches
Tit. 1. 5. that thou shouldest *o.* elders in every city

ORDAINED.

Num. 28. 6. an offering that was *o.* in mount Sinai
1 *Kings* 12. 32. and Jeroboam *o.* a feast, 33.
2 *Kings* 23. 5. and he put down idolatrous priests *o.*
2 *Chron.* 11. 15. Jeroboam *o.* priests for high places
23. 18. to offer the offerings as it was *o.* by David
29. 27. the instruments *o.* by David, king of Israel
Esth. 9. 27. the Jews *o.* the feast of Purim
Psal. 8. 2. out of the mouth of babes hast *o.* strength
3. the moon and the stars which thou hast *o.*
81. 5. this he *o.* in Joseph for a testimony
132. 17. I have *o.* a lamp for mine anointed
Isa. 30. 33. Tophet is *o.* of old, he made it deep
Jer. 1. 5. I *o.* thee to be a prophet to the nations
Dan. 2. 24. the king had *o.* to destroy the wise men
Hab. 1. 12. O Lord, thou hast *o.* them for judgment
Mark 3. 14. Jesus *o.* twelve to be with him
John 15. 16. I have *o.* that ye should bring forth fruit
Acts 1. 22. one *o.* to be witness with us of resurrection
10. 42. *o.* of God to be the judge of quick and dead
13. 48. as many as were *o.* to eternal life believed
14. 23. when they had *o.* them elders in every church
16. 4. the decrees that were *o.* of apostles and elders
17. 31. will judge world by that man whom hath *o.*
Rom. 7. 10. the commandment which was *o.* to life
13. 1. the powers that be, are *o.* of God
1 *Cor.* 2. 7. we speak hidden wisdom which God *o.*
9. 14. the Lord hath *o.* that they which preach
Gal. 3. 19. the law was *o.* by angels, in the hand
Eph. 2. 10. to good works, which God hath before *o.*
1 *Tim.* 2. 7. I am *o.* preacher and apostle to Gentiles
Heb. 5. 1. for every high priest is *o.* for men, 8. 3.
9. 6. now when these things were thus *o.* priests
Jude 4. who were of old *o.* to this condemnation

ORDAINED.

Psal. 7. 13. he *o.* his arrows against the persecutors

ORDER.

Judg. 17. † 10. I will give thee an *o.* of garments
2 *Kings* 23. 4. king commanded priests of second *o.*
1 *Chron.* 6. 32. they waited according to their *o.*
15. 13. for we sought him not after the due *o.*
23. 31. the *o.* commanded to them before the L.
25. 2. accord. to the *o.* of David, 6. 2 *Chron.* 8. 14.
Job 10. 22. a land of darkness, without any *o.*
Psal. 110. 4. thou art a priest for ever, after the *o.* of Melchizedek, *Heb.* 5. 6, 10. | 6. 20. | 7. 11, 17, 21.
1 *Cor.* 16. 1. I have given *o.* to churches of Galatia
Col. 2. 5. joying and beholding your *o.* and stedfast.
Heb. 7. 11. and not be called after the *o.* of Aaron

In ORDER.

Gen. 22. 9. Abraham laid wood *in o.* and bound Isaac
Exod. 26. 17. two tenons *in o.* || 39. 37. lamps set *in o.*
40. 4. thou shalt set *in o.* the things that are to be set *in o. Lev.* 1. 7, 8, 12. | 6. 12. | 24. 8.
23. and he set bread *in o.* upon it before the Lord
Josh. 2. 6. stalks of flax she had laid *in o.* upon roof
2 *Sam.* 17. 23. Ahithophel put his house *in o.*
1 *Kings* 18. 33. Elijah put wood *in o.* and cut bullock
2 *Kings* 20. 1. set thine house *in o. Isa.* 38. 1.
2 *Chron.* 13. 11. the shew bread also set they *in o.*
2 *Chr.* 29. 35. the service of house of Lord set *in o.*
Job 33. 5. set thy words *in o.* before me, stand up
Psal. 40. 5. they cannot be reckoned up *in o.* to thee
50. 21. I will set them *in o.* before thine eyes
Eccl. 12. 9. the preacher set *in o.* many proverbs
Isa. 44. 7. who declare it, and set it *in o.* before me?
Ezek. 41. 6. the side chambers were thirty *in o.*
Luke 1. 1. have taken in hand to set forth *in o.* 3.
8. Zacharias served before God *in* his *o.*
Acts 18. 23. he went over country of Phrygia *in o.*
1 *Cor.* 11. 34. the rest will I set *in o.* when I come
14. 40. let all things be done decently and *in o.*
15. 23. but every man shall rise *in* his *o.* Christ
Tit. 1. 5. I left thee to set *in o.* the things wanting

ORDER.

Exod. 27. 21. Aaron and sons shall *o.* it, *Lev.* 24. 3, 4.
Judg. 13. 12. he said, how shall we *o.* the child?
1 *Kings* 20. 14. then he said, who shall *o.* the battle?
Job 23. 4. I would *o.* my cause before him
37. 19. teach us, for we cannot *o.* our speech
Psal. 40. † 5. thy thoughts none can *o.* them to thee
78. † 19. can God *o.* a table in the wilderness?
119. 133. *o.* my steps in thy word, let not iniquity
Isa. 9. 7. on throne, and upon his kingdom to *o.* it
Jer. 46. 3. *o.* ye the buckler and the shield, and draw

ORDERED, ETH.

Judg. 6. 26. build an altar to Lord in the *o.* place
2 *Sam.* 23. 5. made everlasting covenant *o.* and sure
Job 13. 18. behold now, I have *o.* my cause, I know
32. † 14. he hath not *o.* his words against me
Psal. 37. 23. steps of a good men are *o.* by the Lord
50. 23. to him who *o.* his conversation aright
Prov. 4. † 26. let all thy ways be *o.* aright

ORDERINGS.

1 *Chr.* 24. 19. these were their *o.* under Aaron

ORDERLY.

Acts 21. 24. thou walkest *o.* and keepest the law

ORDINANCE

Signifies, [1] *Any decree, statute, or law, made by civil governors,* 1 Pet. 2. 13. [2] *The laws, statutes, and commandments of God,* Lev. 18. 4. [3] *Appointment, decree, and determination,* Psal. 119. 91. [4] *Laws, directions, rites, institutions, and constitutions, in the worship of God,* Heb. 9. 1, 10.

Exod. 12. 14. ye shall keep to Lord the feast of the passover, for an *o.* for ever, 24, 43. | 13. 10.
15. 25. there he made for them a statute and an *o.*
Lev. 5. † 10. offer according to the *o.* 9. † 16.
Num. 9. 14. according to *o.* of passover, 2 *Chr.* 35. 13.
10. 8. they shall be to you for an *o.* for ever
15. 15. one *o.* shall be for you in your generations
18. 8. and to thy sons by an *o.* for ever, 2 *Chr.* 2. 4.
19. 2. *o.* of the law the Lord commanded, 31. 21.
Josh. 24. 25. and he set them an *o.* in Shechem
1 *Sam.* 30. 25. he made it an *o.* for ever to this day
1 *Kings* 6. † 38. house was finished with all the *o.*
2 *Chr.* 35. 25. and made them an *o.* in Israel
Ezra 3. 10. after the *o.* of David king of Israel
Neh. 11. † 23. that a sure *o.* be for the singers
Isa. 24. 5. have transgressed the law, changed the *o.*
58. 2. and forsook not the *o.* of their God
Ezek. 40. † 45. for the priests that keep the *o.*
45. 14. concerning the *o.* of oil, the bath of oil
46. 14. an offering by a perpetual *o.* unto the Lord
Mal. 3. 14. what profit is it that we have kept his *o.*?
Rom. 13. 2. whoso resisteth the power resists *o.* of G.
1 *Pet.* 2. 13. submit yourselves to every *o.* of man

ORDINANCES.

Exod. 18. 20. thou shalt teach them *o.* and laws
Lev. 18. 3. neither shall ye walk in their *o.*
4. ye shall keep mine *o.* 30. | 22. 9. 2 *Chron.* 33. 8. *Ezek.* 11. 20. | 43. 11. 1 *Cor.* 11. 2.
Num. 9. 12. according to the *o.* of the passover, 14.
2 *Kings* 17. 34. neither do they after their *o.*
37. the *o.* which he wrote for you, observe
Neh. 10. 32. also we made *o.* for us to charge oursel.
Job 38. 33. canst thou guide Arcturus? knowest thou the *o.* of heaven? *Jer.* 31. 35. | 33. 25.
Psal. 99. 7. they kept the *o.* that he gave them
119. 91. they continue according to thine *o.*
Isa. 58. 2. they ask of me the *o.* of justice, delight
Jer. 10. † 3 the *o.* of the people are vanity
31. 36. if those *o.* depart from before me, saith Lord
Ezek. 43. 18. he said, these are the *o.* of the altar
44. 5. concerning the *o.* of the house of the Lord
Mal. 3. 7. ye are gone away from mine *o.* not kept
Luke 1. 6. Zacharias and Elisabeth walking in all the commandments and *o.* of the Lord, blameless
Eph. 2. 15. law of commandments contained in *o.*
Col. 2. 14. blotting out the hand-writing of *o.*
20. why, as though in world, are ye subject to *o.*?
Heb. 9. 1. the first covenant had *o.* of divine service
10. which stood in carnal *o.* imposed on them

ORDINARY.

Ezek. 16. 27. I have diminished thine *o.* food
Acts 19. † 39. it shall be determined in an *o.* assembly

ORGAN, S.

Gen. 4. 21. Jubal, the father of such as handle the *o.*
Job 21. 12. they rejoice at the sound of the *o.*
30. 31. my *o.* turned into voice of them that weep
Psal. 150. 4. praise him with the timbrel and *o.*

ORNAMENT.

Prov. 1. 9. they shall be an *o.* of grace to thy head
4. 9. she shall give to thine head an *o.* of grace
25. 12. as an *o.* of fine gold, so is a wise reprover
Isa. 30. 22. ye shall defile *o.* of thy molten images
49. 18. shall clothe thee with them all as with an *o.*
Ezek. 7. 20. the beauty of his *o.* he set it in majesty
Dan. 11. † 16. he shall stand in the land of *o.*
1 *Pet.* 3. 4. even the *o.* of a meek and quiet spirit

ORNAMENTS.

Exod. 33. 4. and no man did put on him his *o.*
5. therefore now put off thy *o.* from thee, 6.
Judg. 8. 21. Gideon took *o.* that were on camels' necks
26. golden ear-rings that he requested, beside *o.*
2 *Sam.* 1. 24. weep over Saul, who put *o.* on your
Isa. 3. 18. shall take away tinkling *o.* about their feet
† 19. the chains, the bracelets, and the spangled *o.*
20. bonnets, and the *o.* of the legs, head-bands
61. 10. as a bridegroom decketh himself with *o.*
Jer. 2. 32. can maid forget her *o.* or bride her attire?
Jer. 4. 30. though thou deckest thee with *o.* of gold
Ezek. 16. 7. and thou art come to excellent *o.*
11. decked thee with *o.* put bracelets on thy hands
† 39. and shall take instruments of thy *o.*
23. 40. for whom thou deckedst thyself with *o.*

ORPHANS.

Lam. 5. 3. we are *o.* our mothers are as widows

OSPREY, OSSIFRAGE.

Lev. 11. 13. eagle, *osp.* and *ossif.* not eat, *Deut.* 14. 12.

OSTRICH.

This animal is ranged among birds: Moses *forbids the use of it to the* Hebrews, *Lev.* 11. † 16. *It is very large, has very long legs, its wings very short, the neck about the length of four or five spans. The feathers of its wings are in great esteem, and are used as an ornament for hats, beds, and canopies: they are stained of several colours, and made into very pretty tufts: they are hunted by way of course, for they never fly; but they use their wings to assist them in running more swiftly.*

This bird is made the symbol of cruelty and forgetfulness, Job 39. 13, 14, &c. Lam. 4. 3. *We are told of it, that it lays its eggs upon the ground, hides them under the sand, and the sun hatches them. As the* Ostrich *is extremely large and heavy, she would break her eggs if she were to sit upon them like other birds; she therefore hides them in the sand, watches them, and hatches them, as it were, with her eye. The male and female stay with them alternately, and while one of them goes to seek its provision, the other does not leave sight of them: however, if either of them should be driven away, or go too far from their nest, they could not find their eggs again: and it is probably this, that has given occasion to what is said of their* cruelty *and* forgetfulness.

Job 39. 13. gavest thou wings and feathers to *o.*?

OSTRICHES.

Job 30. † 29. and I am a companion to *o.*
Lam. 4. 3. become cruel, like *o.* in the wilderness

OTHER.

Gen. 8. 10. Noah stayed yet *o.* seven days, 12.
28. 17. this is none *o.* but the house of God
29. 27. shalt serve with me yet *o.* seven years, 30.
31. 50. if shalt take *o.* wives besides my daughters
32. 8. then the *o.* company that is left shall escape
41. 3. behold, seven *o.* kine came up, 19.
43. 14. that he may send away your *o.* brother
22. *o.* money have we brought down to buy food
Exod. 4. 7. behold, it was turned again as his *o.* flesh
18. 7. they asked each *o.* of their welfare
29. 41. the *o.* lamb offer thou at even, *Num.* 28. 8.
30. 32. ye shall not make any *o.* like that oil
Lev. 6. 11. and he shall put off his garments, and put on *o.* garments, *Ezek.* 42. 14. | 44. 19.
7. 24. and the fat may be used in any *o.* use
14. 42. they shall take *o.* stones and *o.* mortar
18. 18. nor take a wife besides the *o.* in her life
20. 24. I have separated you from *o.* people, 26.
Num. 10. 21. and the *o.* did set up the tabernacle
24. 1. he went not as at *o.* times to seek enchantm.
32. 38. they gave *o.* names to the cities they built
36. 3. if they be married to any of the *o.* tribes
Josh. 11. 19. all *o.* cities they took in battle
Judg. 13. 10. the man that came to me the *o.* day
16. 17. and be like any *o.* man || 20. as at *o.* times
20. 31. and they began to kill as at *o.* times
1 *Sam.* 3. 10. the Lord called as at *o.* times, Sam.
18. 10. David played with his hand as at *o.* times
20. 25. Saul sat on his seat as at *o.* times by wall
21. 9. take it, for there is no *o.* save that here
2 *Sam.* 13. 16. this evil is greater than *o.* thou didst
2 *Chron.* 30. 23. took counsel, to keep *o.* seven days
32. 22. Lord saved Hezekiah from hand of all *o.*
Neh. 4. 16. the *o.* half of them held both the spears
5. 5. for *o.* men have our lands and vineyards
Job 8. 12. the flag withereth before any *o.* herb
24. 24. they are taken out of the way, as all *o.*
Psal. 73. 5. the wicked are not in trouble as *o.* men, neither are they plagued like *o.* men
85. 10. righteousness and peace kissed each *o.*
Eccl. 6. 5. this hath more rest than the *o.*
Isa. 26. 13. *o.* lords have had dominion over us
49. 20. thou shalt have, after thou hast lost the *o.*
Ezek. 16. 34. the contrary is in thee from *o.* women
Dan. 2. 11. none *o.* can shew it before the king
44. the kingdom shall not be left to *o.* people
Hos. 9. 1. rejoice not for joy, O Israel, as *o.* people
13. 10. where is any *o.* to save thee in thy cities?
Mat. 4. 21. and going on he saw *o.* two brethren
5. 39. on the right cheek, turn to him the *o.* also
12. 13. restored whole as *o. Mark* 3. 5. *Luke* 6. 10.
45. then he taketh seven *o.* spirits, *Luke* 11. 26.
13. 8. *o.* fell into good ground, *Mark* 4. 8. *Luke* 8. 8.
21. 36. again he sent *o.* servants more, 22. 4.
41. he will let out his vineyard to *o.* husbandmen
23. 23. and not to leave *o.* undone, *Luke* 11. 42.
25. 11. afterward came also the *o.* virgins, saying
16. he traded, and made them *o.* five talents
Mark 4. 19. and the lusts of *o.* things entering in
7. 4. and many *o.* things there be they hold, 8.
12. 31. none *o.* commandment is greater than these
32. there is one God, and there is none *o.* but he
Luke 4. 43. I must preach kingd. of God to *o.* cities
10. 1. the Lord appointed *o.* seventy also, and sent
14. 32. or else while the *o.* is yet a great way off
18. 11. I thank thee, that I am not as *o.* men
14. he went down justified rather than the *o.*
22. 65. *o.* things blasphemously spake they ag. him
John 4. 38. *o.* men laboured || 10. 16. *o.* sheep I have
15. 24. if I had not done works none *o.* man did
18. 16. then went out that *o.* disciple, spake to her
21. 25. there are many *o.* things which Jesus did
Acts 2. 4. they began to speak with *o.* tongues
40. and with many *o.* words did he testify
4. 12. neither is there salvation in any *o.* none *o.* name under heaven whereby we must be saved
8. 34. speaketh he of himself, or of some *o.* man?
Rom. 8. 39. nor *o.* creature shall be able to separate
13. 9. and if there be any *o.* commandment, it is
1 *Cor.* 1. 16. I know not whether I baptized any *o.*
3. 11. *o.* foundation can no man lay than is laid

1 Cor. 9. 5. power to lead about sist. well as o. apost.
11. 21. for in eating every one taketh before o.
14. 17. thou givest thanks, but the o. is not edified
21. with men of o. tongues and o. lips I will speak
29. let the prophets speak, and let the o. judge
15. 37. it may chance of wheat, or some o. grain
2 Cor. 8. 13. for I mean not that o. men be eased
10. 15. not boasting of o. men's labours
11. 8. I robbed o. churches to do you service
13. 2. I write to them and to all o. that if I come
Gal. 1. 19. o. apostles saw I none, save James
2. 13. and the o. Jews dissembled likewise with him
Eph. 3. 5. which in o. ages was not made known
4. 17. that ye walk not as o. Gentiles walk
Phil. 1. 17. but the o. preach Christ of love
2. 3. let each esteem o. better than themselves
3. 4. if any o. thinketh that he might trust in flesh
4. 3. with Clement and o. my fellow-labourers
2 Thess. 1. 3. and charity toward each o. aboundeth
1 Tim. 1. 3. charge that they teach no o. doctrine
10. be any o. thing contrary to sound doctrine
5. 22. neither be partaker of o. men's sins
Jam. 5. 12. neither swear by any o. oath, but let
1 Pet. 4. 15. as a busy-body in o. men's matters
2 Pet. 3. 16. they wrest, as they do o. scriptures
Rev. 2. 24. I will put on you none o. burden
8. 13. by reason of o. the o. voices of the trumpet
See GOD, GODS, ONE, SIDE.

OTHERS.

Job 8. 19. and out of the earth shall o. grow
31. 10. and let o. bow down upon her
34. 24. and he shall set o. in their stead
26. he striketh them in the open sight of o.
Psal. 49. 10. they die, and leave their wealth to o.
Prov. 5. 9. lest thou give thine honour to o.
Eccl. 7. 22. that thou thyself likewise hast cursed o.
Isa. 56. 8. yet will I gather o. to him, besides those
Jer. 6. 12. their houses shall be turned to o.
8. 10. I will give their wives unto o. and fields
Ezek. 13. 6. and they have made o. to hope
10. and o. daubed it with untempered mortar
Dan. 7. 19. fourth beast which was diverse from all o.
11. 4. for his kingdom shall be plucked up for o.
Mat. 5. 47. what do ye more than o.?
16. 14. o. say that thou art Jeremias, or one of the old prophets, Mark 6. 15. | 8. 28. Luke 9. 8, 19.
20. 3. he saw o. standing idle in the market
21. 8. o. cut down branches from trees, Mark 11. 8.
26. 67. o. smote him with the palms of their hands
Mark 12. 9. will give vineyard to o. Luke 20. 16.
15. 31. saved o. himself he cannot, Luke 23. 35.
Luke 8. 3. and many o. which ministered to him
John 18. 34. or did o. tell it thee of me?
1 Cor. 9. 2. if I be not an apostle to o. yet to you
12. if o. be partakers of this power over you
27. lest when I have preached to o. I be cast-away
10. 29. conscience, not thine own, but of the o.
14. 19. that by my voice I might teach o. also
2 Cor. 3. 1. or need we, as some o. epist. of commend.
8. 8. but by occasion of the forwardness of o.
Eph. 2. 3. we were children of wrath, even as o.
Phil. 2. 4. but every man also on the things of o.
1 Thess. 2. 6. neither of you, nor yet of o. sought we
4. 13. that ye sorrow not as o. which have no hope
5. 6. let us not sleep as do o. but let us watch
1 Tim. 5. 20. them that sin rebuke, that o. may fear
2 Tim. 2. 2. who shall be able to teach o. also
Heb. 9. 25. entered every year with the blood of o.
11. 35. o. were tortured, not accepting deliverance
36. o. had trial of cruel mockings and scourgings
Jude 23. o. save with fear, pulling them out of fire

OTHERWISE.

2 Sam. 18. 13. o. I should have wrought falsh. against mine own life, for no matter is hid from the king
1 Kings 1. 21. o. I and my son Solomon be counted offenders
2 Chr. 30. 18. they eat passover o. than was written
Psal. 38. 16. hear me, lest o. should rejoice over me
Mat. 6. 1. o. have no reward of your Father in heav.
Rom. 11. 6. not of works, o. grace is no more grace; then no more of grace, o. work is no more work
22. toward thee goodn. o. thou shalt also be cut off
2 Cor. 11. 16. if o. yet as a fool receive me to boast
Gal. 5. 10. that you will be none o. minded
Phil. 3. 15. and if in any thing you be o. minded
1 Tim. 5. 25. and they that are o. cannot be hid
6. 3. if any man teach o. and consent not to words
Heb. 9. 17. o. it is of no strength at all whilst testator

OUCHES.

Exod. 28. 11. set the stones in o. of gold, 39. 6, 13.
13. shalt make o. of gold || 25. fasten in the two o.
14. and fasten wreathen chains to the o. 39. 18.

OVEN

Is *a place for baking*, Lev. 2. 4. To which are compared, [1] *Persons inflamed with lust; who, by yielding to the temptations of Satan, and encouraging them, suffer sin to seize upon the whole man, both the understanding, will, affections, and members; as a baker doth by a continual supply of fuel heat his oven to the highest degree*, Hos. 7. 4. [2] *Such as are enemies to God, upon whom he will bring unavoidable destruction: as wood, when it is cast into the fire, is quickly dissolved*, Psal. 21. 9. [3] *The day of judgment, when the judgment of God will fall dreadfully and terribly upon the wicked and ungodly*, Mal. 4. 1.
Lev. 2. 4. of a meat-offering baken in the o. 7. 9.
11. 35. be unclean, whether it be o. or ranges
26. 26. ten women shall bake your bread in one o.
Psal. 21. 9. thou shalt make them as a fiery o.
Lam. 5. 10. our skin was black like an o. for famine
Hos. 7. 4. adulterers, as an o. heated by the baker
6. they have made ready their heart like an o.
7. are all hot as an o. have devoured their judges
Mal. 4. 1. the day cometh that shall burn as an o.
Mat. 6. 30. to-morrow is cast into o. Luke 12. 28.

OVENS.

Exod. 8. 3. the frogs shall come into thine o.

OVER.

Gen. 25. 25. first red, all o. like an hairy garment
27. 29. be lord o. thy brethren, let them bow to thee
41. 40. Pharaoh said, thou shalt be o. my house

Exod. 16. 18. gathered much had noth. o. 2 Cor. 8. 15.
23. what remaineth o. lay up until the morning
30. 6. the mercy-seat, o. the testimony, Heb. 9. 5.
37. 9. the cherubims covered o. the mercy-seat
40. 36. the cloud was taken up from o. the tabern.
Lev. 14. 5. one be killed o. running water, 6. 50.
Num. 1. 50. thou shalt appoint Levites o. tabernacle
3. 49. o. and above them that were redeemed
10. 10. blow with trumpets o. the burnt offerings
27. 16. let the Lord set a man o. the congregation
Judg. 5. 13. dominion o. the nobles, o. the mighty
9. 9. and go to be promoted o. the trees, 11. 13.
2 Sam. 1. 17. o. Saul and Jonathan his son, 24.
2. 9. he made Ish-bosheth king o. Gilead, o. Ashurites o. Jezreel, o. Ephraim, and o. Benjamin
2 Kings 8. 20. Edom made a king o. themselves
1 Chron. 29. 3. o. and above all I have prepared
Ezra 9. 6. our iniquities are increased o. our heads
Job 14. 16. dost thou not watch o. my sin?
41. 34. he is a king o. the children of pride
Psal. 23. 5. anointest my head, my cup runneth o.
27. 12. deliver me not o. to the will of mine enemies
118. 18. but he hath not given me o. to death
145. 9. his tender mercies are o. all his works
Cant. 2. 11. for lo, winter is past, rain is o. and gone
Jer. 1. 10. set thee o. the nations and o. kingdoms
Dan. 4. 17. he setteth up o. it the basest of men
6. 3. king thought to set him o. the whole realm
Hos. 10. 5. for the people shall mourn o. it and priest
Mic. 3. 6. and the day shall be dark o. them
Mat. 25. 21. I will make thee ruler o. many, 23.
Luke 6. 38. measure shaken together, and running o.
15. 7. more joy o. one sinner that repenteth, 10.
19. 14. we will not have this man to reign o. us
17. been faithful, have thou authority o. ten cities
41. come near, he beheld city, and wept o. it
Acts 6. 3. whom we may appoint o. this business
Rom. 7. 1. that the law hath dominion o. a man
9. 21. hath not the potter power o. the clay?
Eph. 4. 19. have given themselves o. to lasciviousness
1 Tim. 2. 12. not usurp authority o. the man
1 Pet. 3. 12. eyes of the Lord are o. the righteous
Rev. 2. 26. to him will I give power o. the nations

OVER *against*.

Exod. 26. 35. candlestick o. *against* table, 40. 24.
Num. 8. 2. lamps give light o. *against* candlestick, 3.
2 Sam. 5. 23. fetch a compass behind them, come on them o. *against* mulberry-trees, 1 Chr. 14. 14.
1 Kings 20. 29. they pitched one o. *against* the other
Neh. 7. 3. appoint every one to be o. *against* house
Eccl. 7. 14. God hath set one o. *against* the other
Jer. 31. 39. the line shall yet go forth o. *against* it
Mat. 21. 2. go into village o. *against* you, and ye shall find an ass tied, Mark 11. 2. Luke 19. 30.
27. 61. and Mary sitting o. *against* the sepulchre
See ALL, HIM, JORDAN, ISRAEL, ME, THEE, THEM, US, YOU.

OVERCAME.

Acts 19. 16. man in whom the evil spirit was, o. them
Rev. 3. 21. even as I also o. and am set down at
12. 11. and they o. him by the blood of the Lamb

OVERCHARGE.

2 Cor. 2. 5. but in part, that I may not o. you all

OVERCHARGED.

Luke 21. 34. lest your hearts be o. with surfeiting

OVERCOME.

Exod. 32. 18. voice of them that cry for being o.
Isa. 28. 1. the head of them that are o. with wine
Eph. 6. † 13. withstand, and having o. all to stand
2 Pet. 2. 19. of whom man is o. of same is he brought
20. for if they are again entangled therein and o.

OVERCOME.

Gen. 49. 19. troop shall o. him, but he shall o. at last
Num. 13. 30. go up, for we are well able to o. it
22. 11. peradventure I shall be able to o. them
2 Kings 16. 5. they besieged Ahaz, could not o. him
Cant. 6. 5. turn away thine eyes, for they have o. me
Jer. 23. 9. like a man whom wine hath o.
Luke 11. 22. but when a stronger shall o. him
John 16. 33. be of good cheer, I have o. the world
Rom. 3. 4. that mightest o. when thou art judged
12. 21. be not o. of evil, but o. evil with good
1 John 2. 13. because ye have o. the wicked one, 14.
4. 4. ye are of God and have o. them, because
Rev. 11. 7. beast shall o. the witnesses and kill them
13. 7. to make war with the saints, and to o. them
17. 14. shall make war, and Lamb shall o. them

OVERCOMETH.

1 John 5. 4. whosoever is born of God, o. the world, this is victory that o. world, even our faith
5. who is he that o. world, but he that believeth
Rev. 2. 7. to him that o. will I give of tree of life
11. he that o. shall not be hurt of second death
17. to him that o. will I give to eat hidden manna
26. to him that o. will I give power over nations
3. 5. he that o. shall be clothed in white raiment
12. him that o. will I make pillar in temple of G.
21. to him that o. will I grant to sit with me
21. 7. he that o. shall inherit all things, I his God

OVERDRIVE.

Gen. 33. 13. if men should o. them all flock will die

OVERFLOW.

Deut. 11. 4. he made water of Red sea to o. them
Psal. 69. 2. I am come where the floods o. me
15. let not waterfloods o. me, nor deep swallow
Isa. 8. 8. he shall pass through Judah, o. and go over
10. 22. consumption decreed shall o. with righteo.
28. 17. the waters shall o. the hiding-place
43. 2. and through the rivers they shall not o. thee
Jer. 47. 2. waters of the north shall o. the land
Dan. 11. 10. one shall certainly come and o. 26. 40.
Joel 2. 24. fats shall o. with wine and oil, 3. 13.

OVERFLOWED.

Psal. 78. 20. he smote the rock, and streams o.
2 Pet. 3. 6. world being o. with water, perished

OVERFLOWETH.

Josh 3. 15. in harvest Jordan o. all its banks

OVERFLOWING.

Job 28. 11. he bindeth the floods from o.
38. 25. who divided a water-course for o. of waters
Isa. 28. 2. which as a flood of mighty waters o.
15. when the o. scourge shall pass through, 18.

Isa. 30. 28. his breath as an o. stream shall reach
Jer. 47. 2. out of the north shall be an o. flood
Ezek. 13. 11. there shall be an o. shower, 13.
38. 22. I will rain on him an o. rain and hailstones
Hab. 3. 10. the o. of the water passed by the deep

OVERFLOWN.

1 Chron. 12. 15. went over Jordan when it had o.
Job 22. 16. whose foundation was o. with a flood
Dan. 11. 22. with arms of a flood shall they be o.

OVERLAY.

Exod. 25. 11. shalt o. ark with pure gold, 24. | 30. 3.
27. 2. o. the horns of the altar with brass, 38. 2.

OVERLAID.

Exod. 26. 32. pillars of shittim-wood o. with gold
38. 6. he o. the staves of shittim-wood with brass
1 Kings 3. 19. her child died, because she o. it
2 Chron. 4. 9. he o. the doors of them with brass
Cant. 5. 14. belly is as bright ivory o. with sapphires
See GOLD.

OVERLAYING.

Exod. 38. 17. the o. of their chapiters of silver
19. and o. of their chapiters and fillets of silver

OVERLIVED.

Josh. 24. 31. the days of the elders that o. Joshua

OVERMUCH.

Eccl. 7. 16. be not righteous o. || 17. be not o. wicked
2 Cor. 2. 7. lest such be swallowed up with o. sorrow

OVERPASS.

Jer. 5. 28. they shine, they o. the deeds of wicked

OVERPAST.

Psal. 57. 1. make refuge until these calamities be o.
Isa. 26. 20. hide thyself until indignation be o.

OVERPLUS.

Lev. 25. 27. let him restore the o. to the man

OVERRAN.

2 Sam. 18. 23. Ahimaaz ran by plain and o. Cushi

OVERRUNNING.

Nah. 1. 8. with an o. flood he will make an end

OVERSEE.

1 Chron. 9. 29. some appointed to o. the vessels
15. † 21. with harps on the eighth to o.
23. † 4. of which 24,000 were to o. the work
2 Chron. 2. 2. three thousand six hundred to o. them

OVERSEER.

Gen. 39. 4. he made him o. over his house, 5.
Neh. 11. 9. Joel was their o. || 14. Zabdiel was o.
22. o. of Levites was Uzzi || 12. 42. Jezrahiah o.
Prov. 6. 7. the ant having no guide o. or ruler

OVERSEERS.

Gen. 41. 34. let Pharaoh appoint o. in the land
2 Chron. 2. 18. Solomon set 3,600 o. of the work
31. 13. they were o. under hand of Cononiah
34. 12. the o. of all them that wrought, 13.
17. have delivered money into the hand of o.
Acts 20. 28. the Holy Ghost hath made you o.

OVERSHADOW.

Luke 1. 35. the power of the Highest shall o. thee
Acts 5. 15. that shadow of Peter might o. them

OVERSHADOWED.

Mat. 17. 5. a cloud o. them, Mark 9. 7. Luke 9. 34.

OVERSIGHT.

Gen. 43. 12. carry it again, peradventure it was an o.
Num. 3. 32. have the o. of them that keep charge
4. 16. pertaineth the o. of all the tabernacle
2 Kings 12. 11. of them that had the o. of the house of the Lord, 22. 5, 9. 2 Chron. 34. 10.
1 Chron. 9. 23. had the o. of the gates of the house
Neh. 11. 16. had the o. of the outward business
13. 4. the o. of the chamber of the house of God
1 Pet. 5. 2. taking o. not by constraint, but willingly

OVERSPREAD.

Gen. 9. 19. and of them was the whole earth o.

OVERSPREADING.

Dan. 9. 27. for the o. of abominations be desolate

OVERTAKE.

Gen. 44. 4. up, when thou dost o. them, say to them
Exod. 15. 9. enemy said, I will pursue, I will o.
Deut. 19. 6. lest the avenger of blood o. the slayer
28. 2. all these blessings shall come and o. thee
15. that all these curses shall o. thee, 45.
Josh. 2. 5. pursue after them, for ye shall o. them
1 Sam. 30. 8. shall I o. them, thou shalt surely o. them
2 Sam. 15. 14. lest Absalom o. us suddenly, and bring
Isa. 59. 9. judgment is far, neither doth justice o. us
Jer. 42. 16. the sword ye feared shall o. you
Hos. 2. 7. shall follow, but she shall not o. her lovers
10. 9. the battle in Gibeah did not o. them
Amos 9. 10. the evil shall not o. nor prevent us
13. behold, the plowman shall o. the reaper
Zech. 1. † 6. my words, did they not o. your fathers?
1 Thess. 5. 4. that that day should o. you as a thief

OVERTAKEN.

Ps. 18. 37. I have pursued mine enemies and o. them
Gal. 6. 1. brethren, if a man be o. in a fault

OVERTAKETH.

1 Chron. 21. 12. flee three months, till sword o. thee

OVERTHREW.

Gen. 19. 25. God o. these cities and the plain, 29.
Exod. 14. 27. Lord o. the Egyptians, Psal. 136. 15.
Deut. 29. 23. which Lord o. in his anger and wrath
Isa. 13. 19. Babylon shall be, as when God o. Sodom and Gomorrah, Jer. 50. 40. Amos 4. 11.
Jer. 20. 16. let that man be as the cities Lord o.
Mat. 21. 12. Jesus o. tables of the money-changers in the temple, Mark 11. 15. John 2. 15.

OVERTHROW.

Gen. 19. 21. I have accepted thee, will not o. this city
Exod. 23. 24. but thou shalt utterly o. their gods
Deut. 12. 3. ye shall o. their altars, and break pillars
2 Sam. 10. 3. hath not David sent to spy it out and o.
11. 25. make thy battle more strong, and o. it
1 Chr. 19. 3. David hath sent to o. and spy the land
Psal. 106. 26. his hand to o. them in the wilderness
27. to o. their seed also among the nations
140. 4. who have purposed to o. my goings
11. evil shall hunt the violent man to o. him
Prov. 18. 5. not good to o. righteous in judgment
Hag. 2. 22. I will o. the throne of kingdoms, I will o. the chariots and those that ride in them
Acts 5. 39. but if it be of God, ye cannot o. it
2 Tim. 2. 18. have erred, and o. the faith of some

OVERTHROW.
Gen. 19. 29. God sent Lot out of the midst of the o.
Deut. 29. 23. as in the o. of Sodom, Jer. 49. 18.
2 Pet. 2. 6. condemned the cities with an o. making
OVERTHROWETH.
Job 12. 19. he leadeth princes, and o. the mighty
Prov. 13. 6. but wickedness o. the sinner
21. 12. God o. the wicked for their wickedness
22. 12. he o. the words of the transgressor
29. 4. but he that receiveth gifts o. the land
OVERTHROWN.
Exod. 15. 7. hast o. them that rose up against thee
Judg. 9. 40. and many were o. and wounded
2 Sam. 17. 9. when some of them be o. at the first
2 Chron. 14. 13. and the Ethiopians were o.
Job 19. 6. know now that God hath o. me
Psal. 141. 6. when their judges are o. in stony places
Prov. 11. 11. city is o. by the mouth of the wicked
12. 7. wicked are o. || 14. 11. house of wicked o.
Isa. 1. 7. your land is desolate as o. by strangers
Jer. 18. 23. but let them be o. before thee
Lam. 4. 6. sin of Sodom, that was o. as in a moment
Dan. 11. 41. and many countries shall be o.
Amos 4. 11. I have o. some of you, as Sodom
Jonah 3. 4. yet forty days and Nineveh shall be o.
1 Cor. 10. 5. for they were o. in the wilderness
OVERTOOK.
Gen. 31. 23. they o. Jacob in the mount Gilead
25. Laban o. Jacob || 44. 6. the steward o. them
Exod. 14. 9. Egyptians o. them encamping by sea
Judg. 18. 22. Micah o. the children of Dan
20. 42. but the battle o. the men of Benjamin
2 Kings 25. 5. the army of Chaldees o. Zedekiah in
the plains of Jericho, Jer. 39. 5. | 52. 8.
Lam. 1. 3. all her persecutors o. her between straits
OVERTURN.
Job 12. 15. he sendeth out waters, they o. earth
Ezek. 21. 27. I will o. o. o. it, until he come whose
OVERTURNETH.
Job 9. 5. which o. the mountains in his anger
28. 9. he o. the mountains by the roots
34. 25. knows their works and o. them in night
OVERTURNED.
Judg. 7. 13. smote the tent that it fell and o. it
OVERWHELM.
Job 6. 27. ye o. fatherless, dig a pit for your friend
OVERWHELMED.
Psal. 55. 5. trembling come, and horror hath o. me
61. 2. when my heart is o. lead me to the rock
77. 3. and my spirit was o. 142. 3. | 143. 4.
78. 53. he led them on, but the sea o. their enemies
124. 4. then the waters had o. us stream gone over
OVERWISE.
Eccl. 7. 16. not right. overmuch, nor make thyself o.
OUGHT; *see* OWED.
OUGHT.
Gen. 20. 9. that o. not be done, 34. 7. Lev. 4. 2, 27.
2 Sam. 13. 12. no such thing o. to be done in Israel
1 Chron. 12. 32. to know what Israel o. to do
15. 2. none o. to carry the ark but the Levites
2 Chr. 13. 5. o. ye not to know Lord gave kingdom
Neh. 5. 9. o. ye not to walk in the fear of God?
Psal. 76. 11. bring presents to him who o. be feared
Mat. 23. 23. these o. ye to have done, Luke 11. 42.
Mark 13. 14. desolation standing where it o. not
Luke 12. 12. in the same hour what ye o. to say
13. 14. there are six days in which men o. to work
16. o. not this woman to be loosed from this bond
18. 1. that men o. always to pray, and not to faint
24. 26. O fools, o. not Christ to have suffered?
John 4. 20. the place where men o. to worship
13. 14. ye also o. to wash one another's feet
19. 7. we have a law, and by our law he o. to die
Acts 5. 29. we o. to obey God rather than men
17. 29. we o. not to think the Godhead like gold
19. 36. ye o. to be quiet, and to do nothing rashly
20. 35. how so labouring ye o. to support the weak
21. 21. that they o. not to circumcise their children
24. 19. who o. to have been here before thee
25. 10. judgment-seat, where I o. to be judged
24. crying, that he o. not to live any longer
26. 9. that I o. to do many things contrary to Jesus
Rom. 8. 26. we know not what to pray for as we o.
12. 3. not think of himself more highly than he o.
15. 1. we o. to bear the infirmities of the weak
1 Cor. 8. 2. he knoweth nothing as he o. to know
11. 7. for a man indeed o. not to cover his head
10. the woman o. to have power on her head
2 Cor. 2. 3. sorrow from them, of whom I o. to rejoice
7. ye o. rather to forgive him and comfort him
12. 11. for I o. to have been commended of you
14. the children o. not to lay up for the parents
Eph. 5. 28. so o. men to love their wives as their bodies
6. 20. may speak boldly, as I o. to speak, Col. 4. 4.
Col. 4. 6. know how ye o. to answer every man
1 Thess. 4. 1. ye received of us how ye o. to walk
2 Thess. 3. 7. yourselves know how ye o. to follow us
1 Tim. 5. 13. speaking things which they o. not
Tit. 1. 11. teaching things which they o. not
Heb. 2. 1. we o. to give the more earnest heed
5. 3. he o. for people and for himself, to offer for sins
12. for when for the time ye o. to be teachers
Jam. 3. 10. my brethren, these things o. not so to be
4. 15. for that ye o. to say, if the Lord will
2 Pet. 3. 11. what manner of persons o. ye to be
1 John 2. 6. o. himself also to walk as he walked
3. 16. o. to lay down our lives for the brethren
4. 11. if God loved us, we o. also love one another
3 John 8. we therefore o. to receive such
OUGHT, *Substantive*.
Gen. 39. 6. he knew not o. that he had, save bread
47. 18. there is not o. left, but our bodies and lands
Exod. 5. 8. ye shall not diminish o. thereof, 11. 19.
12. 46. thou shalt not carry forth o. of the flesh
22. 14. if a man borrow o. of his neighbour
29. 34. if o. of flesh of the consecrations remain
Lev. 11. 25. whoso beareth o. of carcase is unclean
19. 6. if o. remain unto third day, shall be burnt
25. 14. if thou sellest o. or buyest o. from thy neigh.
27. 31. if a man will redeem o. of his tithes
Num. 15. 24. if o. be committed by ignorance
30. the soul that doeth o. presumptuously

Num. 30. 6. when she vowed, or utt. o. out of her lips
Deut. 4. 2. ye shall not add or diminish o. from it
15. 2. creditor that lendeth o. to his neighbour
26. 14. neither have I taken o. in my mourning for
any unclean use, nor given o. thereof for dead
Josh. 21. 45. there failed not o. of any good thing
Ruth 1. 17. if o. but death part thee and me
1 Sam. 12. 4. nor hast thou taken o. of any man's hand
5. that ye have not found o. in my hand
25. 7. neither was there o. missing to them
30. 22. we will not give them o. of the spoil
2 Sam. 3. 35. if I taste bread or o. else, till sun be down
14. 10. whoso saith o. to thee, bring him to me
19. none can turn from o. my lord hath spoken
Mat. 5. 23. that thy brother hath o. against thee
21. 3. if any man say o. to you, ye shall say
Mark 7. 12. and ye suffer him no more to do o.
8. 23. he took blind man and asked him if he saw o.
11. 25. forgive, if ye have o. against any
John 4. 33. hath any man brought him o. to eat?
Acts 4. 32. neither said any that o. was his own
24. 19. and object, if they had o. against me
28. 19. that I had o. to accuse my nation of
Philem. 18. if he oweth thee o. put to my account
OUGHTEST.
1 Kings 2. 9. and knowest what thou o. to do to him
Mat. 25. 27. thou o. to have put my money to
Acts 10. 6. he shall tell thee what thou o. to do
1 Tim. 3. 15. how thou o. to behave thyself
OUR; *see* BROTHER, FATHER, LORD.
OURS.
Gen. 26. 20. did strive, saying, the water is o.
31. 16. God hath taken from our father that is o.
34. 23. shall not every beast of theirs be o.?
Num. 32. 32. possession on this side Jordan may be o.
1 Kings 22. 3. know that Ramoth in Gilead is o.
Ezek. 36. 2. ancient high places are o. in possession
Mark 12. 7. and inheritance shall be o. Luke 20. 14.
1 Cor. 1. 2. all that call on Jesus, both theirs and o.
2 Cor. 1. 14. as ye also are o. in the day of the Lord
Tit. 3. 14. let o. learn to maintain good works
OUT.
Gen. 2. 9. o. of ground made Lord to grow every tree
23. woman, because she was taken o. of man
3. 19. for o. of it wast thou taken; dust thou art
Num. 32. 23. and be sure your sin will find you o.
Job 28. 5. as for the earth o. of it cometh bread
Psal. 8. 2. o. of the mouth of babes and sucklings
82. 5. foundations of the earth are o. of course
94. 12. blessed, whom thou teachest o. of thy law
118. 26. we have blessed you o. of house of Lord
Prov. 4. 23. keep heart, for o. of it are issues of life
31. 18. her candle goeth not o. by night
Isa. 13. 9. he shall destroy sinners thereof o. of it
29. 18. eyes shall see o. of obscurity, o. of darkness
Jer. 30. 7. but he shall be saved o. of it
19. and o. of them shall proceed thanksgiving
Ezek. 34. 11. behold I will seek o. my sheep
46. 20. that they bear them not o. into the court
Mic. 5. 2. yet o. of thee shall he come forth to me
that is to be ruler in Israel, Mat. 2. 6.
Zech. 10. 4. o. of him came forth the corner
Mat. 12. 34. o. of the abundance of the heart
35. o. of good treasure, o. of the evil treasure
15. 19. o. of the heart proceed evil thoughts
Mark 10. 26. they were astonished o. of measure
13. 15. nor enter to take any thing o. of his house
16. 9. o. of whom he had cast seven devils
Luke 19. 22. o. of thy own mouth will I judge thee
John 15. 19. but I have chosen you o. of the world
Acts 2. 5. devout men, o. of every nation under hea.
28. 23. both o. of the law, and o. of the prophets
1 Cor. 15. 8. seen of me, as of one born o. of due time
2 Cor. 2. 4. for o. of much affliction I wrote to you
8. 11. be a performance o. of that which ye have
2 Tim. 2. 26. recover themselves o. of snare of devil
3. 11. but o. of them all the Lord delivered me
4. 2. be instant in season, o. of season, reprove
Jam. 3. 10. o. of same mouth proceedeth blessing
See CAMP, CAPTIVITY, CITY, DARKNESS, WAY, ZION.
OUTCAST.
Jer. 30. 17. saith Lord, because they called thee an o.
OUTCASTS.
Psal. 147. 2. he gathereth o. of Israel, Isa. 56. 8.
Isa. 11. 12. he shall assemble the o. of Israel
16. 3. hide the o. || 4. let my o. dwell with thee
27. 13. the o. in the land of Egypt shall worship
Jer. 49. 36. whither the o. of Elam shall not come
OUTER.
Ezek. 46. 21. he brought me into the o. court
47. 2. he led me the way without to the o. gate
Mat. 8. 12. be cast into o. darkness, 22. 13. | 25. 30.
OUT-GOINGS.
Josh. 17. 9. the o. it were at the sea, 19. 29.
18. and the o. of it shall be thine
18. 19. the o. of the border were at the north
19. 14. the o. thereof are in the valley of Jiphthah-el
22. the o. of their border were at Jordan, 33.
Psal. 65. 8. thou makest the o. of the morning
OUTLANDISH.
Neh. 13. 26. even o. women caused Solomon to sin
OUTLIVED.
Judg. 2. 7. all the days of the elders that o. Joshua
OUTRAGEOUS.
Prov. 27. 4. wrath is cruel and anger is o.
OUTRUN.
John 20. 4. they ran, and other disciple did o. Peter
OUTSIDE.
Judg. 7. 11. Gideon went to o. of the armed men
17. and when I come to the o. of the camp
19. so they came to the o. of the camp
1 Kings 7. 9. and so on o. toward the great court
Ezek. 40. 5. behold a wall on the o. of the house
Mat. 23. 25. make clean o. of the cup, Luke 11. 39.
26. that the o. of them may be clean also
OUTSTRETCHED.
Deut. 26. 8. Lord brought us out with an o. arm
Jer. 21. 5. I will fight against you with an o. hand
27. 5. I have made the earth by my o. arm
OUTWARD.
1 Sam. 16. 7. for man looketh on o. appearance

1 Chron. 26. 29. Chenaniah for the o. business
Neh. 11. 16. the chief of the Levites for o. business
Esth. 6. 4. Haman was come into the o. court
Ezek. 40. 17. he brought me into the o. court
Mat. 23. 27. which indeed appear beautiful o.
Rom. 2. 28. nor circumcision, which is o. in the flesh
2 Cor. 4. 16. but though our o. man perish, yet our
10. † 1. who in o. appearance am base among you
7. do ye look on things after the o. appearance?
1 Pet. 3. 3. not that o. adorning of plaiting hair
OUTWARDLY.
Mat. 23. 28. ye o. appear righteous unto men
Rom. 2. 28. for he is not a Jew which is one o.
OUTWENT.
Mark 6. 33. many ran afoot thither, and o. them
OWE.
Rom. 13. 8. o. no man any thing, but to love
OWED.
Mat. 18. 24. one which o. him 10,000 talents
28. and found one which o. him an hundred pence
Luke 7. 41. the one o. 500 pence, and the other 50
OWEST.
Mat. 18. 28. he took him, saying, pay me that thou o.
Luke 16. 5. how much o. thou unto my lord? 7.
Philem. 19. thou o. to me even thine own self besides
OWETH.
Philem. 18. if he hath wronged thee, or o. thee ought
OWL.
Lev. 11. 16. o. and cuckow unclean, Deut. 14. 15, 16.
17. the little o. and cormorant, Isa. 34. 11, 15.
Psal. 102. 6. I am like an o. of the desert
OWLS.
Job 30. 29. I am a companion to o. a brother to drag.
Isa. 13. 21. the wild beasts shall lie there, and o.
shall dwell there, 34. 13. Jer. 50. 39.
43. 20. the dragons and o. shall honour me
Mic. 1. 8. I will make a mourning as the o.
OWN.
Gen. 1. 27. God created man in his o. image
5. 3. Adam begat a son in his o. likeness
15. 4. shall come of thine o. bowels shall be heir
30. 25. send me, that I may go to mine o. place
47. 24. four parts shall be your o. for seed of field
Exod. 21. 36. ox for ox, and dead shall be his o.
22. 5. of best of his o. field shall make restitution
Lev. 1. 3. he shall offer it of his o. voluntary will
7. 30. his o. hands shall bring the offering of Lord
14. 15. pour it into palm of his o. left hand, 26.
18. 10. for theirs is thine o. nakedness
26. nor any of your o. nation, nor strangers among
you, shall commit any of these abominations
25. 5. that which groweth of its o. accord
41. and he shall return to his o. family
Num. 1. 52. each by his o. camp, by his o. standard
16. 28. have not done them of mine o. mind, 24. 13.
38. these censers of sinners against their o. souls
32. 42. he called it after his o. name, Deut. 3. 14.
36. 9. shall keep himself to his o. inheritance
Deut. 23. 24. mayest eat grapes at thine o. pleasure
24. 13. that he may sleep in his o. raiment, and bless
16. not children for fathers, every man shall be
put to death for o. sin, 2 Kings 14. 6. 2 Chr. 25. 4.
28. 53. thou shalt eat the fruit of thine o. body
33. 9. nor knew he his o. children
Josh. 7. 11. they have put it even among their o. stuff
Judg. 2. 19. they ceased not from their o. doings
7. 2. saying, mine o. hand hath saved me
1 Sam. 2. 20. and they went to their o. home
5. 11. let the ark go again to his o. place
15. 17. when thou wast little in thine o. sight
25. 26. from avenging with thine o. hand
2 Sam. 6. 22. I will be base in mine o. sight
7. 10. that they may dwell in a place of their o.
12. 3. did eat of his o. meat, and drink of his o. cup
17. 11. that thou go to battle in thine o. person
18. 13. have wrought falsehood against mine o. life
1 Kings 2. 23. spoken this word against his o. life
32. shall return his blood on his o. head, 37.
13. 30. he laid his carcase in his o. grave
17. 19. and Elijah laid him upon his o. bed
2 Kings 17. 29. every nation made gods of their o.
1 Chr. 29. 14. and of thine o. have we given thee
16. all this store we prepared, is all thine o.
2 Chr. 6. 23. recompensing his way on his o. head
Neh. 4. 4. turn their reproach on their o. head
Esth. 9. 25. wicked devise should return on o. head
Job 20. 7. he shall perish for ever like his o. dung
Psal. 5. 10. let them fall by their o. counsel
12. 4. our lips are our o: who is lord over us?
67. 6. God, even our o. God, shall bless us
78. 29. were filled, for he gave them their o. desire
81. 12. I gave them up to their o. hearts' lust
94. 23. he shall bring on them their o. iniquity, and
shall cut them off in their o. wickedness
Prov. 5. 17. let them be only thy o. not strangers
Isa. 37. 35. for mine o. sake, 43. 25. | 48. 11.
58. 13. not finding thine o. pleasure, nor o. words
Ezek. 29. 3. which hath said, my river is mine o.
33. 13. if he trust to his o. righteousness
Hos. 7. 2. now their o. doings have beset them about
Jonah 2. 8. they forsake their o. mercy
Mat. 20. 15. lawful to do what I will with mine o.
Luke 14. 26. if any man hate not his o. life also
16. 12. who shall give you that which is your o.?
John 1. 11. he came to his o. his o. received him not
8. 44. when he speaketh a lie, he speaketh of his o.
10. 12. an hireling, whose o. the sheep are not
13. 1. having loved his o. that were in the world
15. 19. if of the world, world would love his o.
16. 32. ye shall be scattered every man to his o.
Acts 3. 12. as though by our o. power or holiness
5. 4. was it not thine o.? was it not in thine o. power?
20. 28. which he purchased with his o. blood
Rom. 4. 19. he considered not his o. body now dead
8. 32. he that spared not his o. Son, but delivered
14. 4. to his o. master he standeth or falleth
1 Cor. 6. 19. ye are not your o. for ye are bought
7. 2. nevertheless, let every man have his o. wife
10. 24. let no man seek his o. but another's wealth
29. conscience, I say, not thine o. but others
13. 5. charity seeketh not her o. is not easily
Phil. 2. 21. for all seek their o. things, not Christ's

Phil. 3. 9. found in him, not having mine *o.* right.
1 Tim. 5. 8. but if any provide not for his *o.* his *o.*
Tit. 1. 12. a prophet of their *o.* said, the Cretians
Heb. 9. 12. but by his *o.* blood he entered in once
Rev. 1. 5. washed us from our sins in his *o.* blood
See COUNSEL, COUNTRY, EYES, HEART, HOUSE, LAND, PEOPLE, SELF, SELVES, SOUL, WAY, WAYS, WILL.

OWNER.

Exod. 21. 28. but the *o.* of the ox shall be quit
29. it hath been testified to his *o.* his *o.* shall
34. the *o.* of the pit shall make it good
36. and his *o.* hath not kept him in, ox for ox
22. 11. *o.* of it shall accept thereof, not make good
12. he shall make restitution to the *o.* thereof
14. *o.* thereof not being with it, make it good
15. but if *o.* thereof be with it, not make it good
1 Kings 16. 24. after name of Shemer, *o.* of the hill
Prov. 3. + 27. withhold not good from the *o.*
Isa. 1. 3. the ox knoweth his *o.* the ass his crib
Acts 27. 11. centurion believed the *o.* of the ship

OWNERS.

Job 31. 39. or have caused the *o.* to lose their lives
Prov. 1. 19. which taketh away life of *o.* thereof
Eccl. 5. 11. what good is there to the *o.* thereof?
13. a sore evil, riches kept for *o.* to their hurt
Luke 19. 33. the *o.* said, why loose ye the colt?

OWNETH.

Lev. 14. 35. he that *o.* the house shall tell priest
Acts 21. 11. Jews shall bind man that *o.* this girdle

OX.

Exod. 20. 17. shalt not cov. thy neigh. *ox*, Deut. 5. 21.
21. 28. if *ox* gore a man, he shall be stoned, 29, 32.
29. if *ox* were wont to push with his horns, 36.
32. if *ox* push a man-servant or maid-servant
33. if an *ox* or ass shall fall into a pit, the owner
22. 1. if a man shall steal an *ox* or a sheep
4. whether it be *ox* or ass, he shall restore double
9. trespass for an *ox* ‖ 10. deliver an *ox* to keep
23. 4. if thou meet thine enemy's *ox* going astray
12. that thine *ox* and thine ass may rest
34. 19. every firstling of an *ox* or sheep is mine
Lev. 7. 23. shall eat no manner of fat of *ox* or sheep
17. 3. what man soever killeth an *ox* or lamb
Num. 7. 3. they brought for each of princes an *ox*
22. 4. as the *ox* licketh up the grass of the field
Deut. 5. 14. thine *ox* shall do no work on sabbath
14. 4. the *ox*, the sheep, and goat ye may eat
18. 3. the priest's due, whether it be *ox* or sheep
22. 1. thou shalt not see thy brother's *ox* go astray
4. thou shalt not see thy brother's *ox* fall down
10. shalt not plough with an *ox* and ass together
25. 4. thou shalt not muzzle the *ox* when he treadeth out the corn, 1 Cor. 9. 9. 1 Tim. 5. 18.
28. 31. thine *ox* shall be slain before thine eyes
Josh. 6. 21. they destroy. *ox* and sheep, 1 Sam. 15. 15.
Judg. 3. 31. Shamgar slew 600 men with an *ox*-goad
6. 4. they left neither sheep nor *ox* for Israel
1 Sam. 12. 3. Sam. said, whose *ox* or ass have I taken?
14. 34. bring me hither every man his *ox* and sheep
Neh. 5. 18. prepared for me daily one *ox*, six sheep
Job 6. 5. or loweth the *ox* over his fodder?
24. 3. they take the widow's *ox* for a pledge
40. 15. behold, Behemoth eateth grass as an *ox*
Psal. 69. 31. this shall please L. better than an *ox*
106. 20. changed their glory into similitude of an *ox*
Prov. 7. 22. goeth after her as an *ox* goeth to slaught.
14. 4. but increase is by the strength of the *ox*
15. 17. better than a stalled *ox*, and hatred therewith
Isa. 1. 3. the *ox* knoweth his owner, ass his crib
11. 7. and the lion shall eat straw like the *ox*
32. 20. that send forth thither the feet of the *ox*
66. 3. that killeth an *ox* as if he slew a man
Jer. 11. 19. but I was like a lamb or an *ox* brought
Ezek. 1. 10. they four had the face of an *ox*
Luke 13. 15. doth not each of you loose his *ox* on sab.
14. 5. shall have an *ox* or an ass fallen into a pit

Wild OX.

Deut. 14. 5. the *wild ox* and chamois ye may eat

OXEN.

Gen. 12. 16. Abram had sheep and *o.* and asses
20. 14. Abimelech gave Abraham sheep and *o.*
21. 27. Abraham gave Abimelech sheep and *o.*
32. 5. Jacob said thus, I have *o.* and asses
34. 28. the sons of Jacob took Shechem's *o.*
Exod. 9. 3. the hand of the Lord is upon the *o.*
20. 24. thou shalt sacrifice thereon thine *o.*
22. 1. he shall restore five *o.* for one ox, and four
30. likewise shalt thou do with thine *o.* and sheep
Num. 7. 3. and the princes brought twelve *o.*
7. four *o.* he gave to the sons of Gershom
8. and eight *o.* he gave to the sons of Merari
22. 40. Balak offered *o.* and sheep, and sent to Bal.
23. 1. prepare me here seven *o.* and seven rams
Deut. 14. 26. shalt bestow that money for *o.* or sheep
Josh. 7. 24. Joshua took Achan, his *o.* and sheep
1 Sam. 11. 7. Saul hewed a yoke of *o.* in pieces, and sent them thro' Israel, so shall it be done to his *o.*
14. 14. acre of land, which yoke of *o.* might plow
32. the people took sheep and *o.* and slew them
15. 9. Saul spared Agag and the best of the *o.*
14. what meaneth lowing of *o.* which I hear?
15. the people spared the best of the sheep and *o.*
22. 19. Doeg smote the *o.* and sheep and asses
27. 9. David took away the sheep and *o.* and asses
2 Sam. 6. 6. Uzza took hold of it, for *o.* shook it
13. David sacrificed *o.* and fatlings
24. 22. behold, here be *o.* for burnt sacrifice
24. so David bought the threshing-floor and *o.*
1 Kings 1. 9. Adonijah slew sheep and *o.* 19, 25.
4. 23. Solomon's daily provision, 10 fat *o.* 100 sheep
7. 25. one sea, 12 *o.* under it, 44. 2 Chr. 4. 4, 15.
8. 5. with him before ark, sacrificing sheep and *o.*
63. Solomon offered a sacrifice to the Lord of 22,000 *o.* and 120,000 sheep, 2 Chron. 7. 5.
19. 19. Elisha was plowing with twelve yoke of *o.*
20. Elisha left the *o.* and ran after Elijah
21. he took a yoke of *o.* and slew them
2 Kings 5. 26. is it a time to receive sheep and *o.*?
1 Chron. 12. 40. brought bread on mules and on *o.*
2 Chron. 15. 11. they offered of the spoil 700 *o.*
18. 2. Ahab killed sheep and *o.* for him and people
2 Chron. 29. 33. consec. things were 600 *o.* 3000 sheep
31. 6. they brought in the tithes of *o.* and sheep
35. 8. princes gave for passover three hundred *o.*
Job 1. 3. his substance was 3000 camels, 500 yoke of *o.*
14. the *o.* were plowing, and the asses feeding
42. 12. Lord gave him 1000 yoke of *o.* 1000 asses
Psal. 8. 7. thou madest him to have dominion over *o.*
144. 14. that our *o.* may be strong to labour
Prov. 14. 4. where no *o.* are the crib is clean
Isa. 7. 25. but it shall be for the sending forth of *o.*
22. 13. and behold, joy and gladness, slaying *o.*
30. 24. the *o.* and asses shall eat clean provender
Jer. 51. 23. I will break the husbandman and his *o.*
Dan. 4. 25. make thee eat grass as *o.* 32, 33. | 5. 21.
Amos 6. 12. will one plow there with *o.*?
Mat. 22. 4. my *o.* and my fatlings are killed
Luke 14. 19. I have bought five yoke of *o.*
John 2. 14. found in the temple those that sold *o.*
15. he drove them all out, the sheep and the *o.*
Acts 14. 13. priest of Jupiter brought *o.* and garlands
1 Cor. 9. 9. doth God take care for *o.*?

OYL, *see* OIL.

P.

PACES.

2 Sam. 6. 13. when gone six *p.* he sacrificed oxen

PACIFY, ED, ETH.

Esth. 7. 10. hanged Haman, then was king's wrath *p.*
Prov. 16. 14. a wise man will *p.* the wrath of a king
21. 14. a gift in secret *p.* anger, and a reward
Eccl. 10. 4. for yielding *p.* great offences
Ezek. 16. 63. for thy shame, when I am *p.* toward

PADDLE.

Deut. 23. 13. thou shalt have a *p.* on thy weapon

PAID, *see after* PAY.

PAIN

Signifies, [1] *Any bodily disease or distemper*, Job 33. 19. [2] *Disquiet, or uneasiness of mind*, Psal. 25. 18. | 55. 4. [3] *Travail in child-birth*, 1 Sam. 4. 19. [4] *Fear*, Ezek. 30. 4.

The wicked man travaileth with pain all his days, Job 15. 20. *He lives a life of care, fear, and grief, by reason of God's wrath, and the torments of his own mind, and his manifold and dreadful outward calamities.*

They blasphemed the God of heaven, because of their pains, Rev. 16. 11. *Some observe from hence the contrary effects that trouble produces in the godly and in the wicked; the one blesseth, the other blasphemeth, the Lord. In tribulation the godly rejoice, the wicked rage; for the one in suffering communicates with the cross of Christ, the other with the curse of* Adam. *Stars shine in the night, which in the day are not seen; and grace is manifested by trouble, which in prosperity lies secret. Trouble tries true religion from false, and discerns grace from nature.*

Job 14. 22. but his flesh on him shall have *p.*
15. 20. the wicked man travaileth with *p.*
33. 19. he is chastened also with *p.* on his bed
Psal. 25. 18. look on mine affliction and my *p.*
48. 6. *p.* as a woman in travail, Isa. 13. 8. | 26. 17.
139. + 24. see if there be any way of *p.* in me
Isa. 21. 3. therefore are my loins filled with *p.*
26. 18. we have been with child, we have been in *p.*
66. 7. before her *p.* came, she was delivered
Jer. 6. 24. anguish hath taken hold of us, and *p.* as of a woman in travail, 22. 23. Mark 13. + 8.
12. 13. put themselves to *p.* but shall not profit
15. 18. why is my *p.* perpetual, wound incurable
30. 23. it shall fall with *p.* on head of the wicked
51. 8. howl for Babylon, take balm for her *p.*
Ezek. 30. 4. great *p.* shall be in Ethiopia, 9.
16. Sin shall have great *p.* No shall be rent asund.
Mic. 4. 10. be in *p.* and labour to bring forth, O Zion
Nah. 2. 10. much *p.* is in all loins, faces gather black.
Rom. 8. 22. the whole creation travaileth in *p.*
Rev. 16. 10. they gnawed their tongues for *p.*
21. 4. nor sorrow, nor shall there be any more *p.*
See PANGS.

PAINED.

Psal. 55. 4. my heart is sore *p.* within me, and terror
Isa. 23. 5. they shall be sorely *p.* at report of Tyre
Jer. 4. 19. my bowels, I am *p.* at my very heart
Joel 2. 6. before their face, people shall be much *p.*
Rev. 12. 2. travailing in birth, and *p.* to be delivered

PAINS.

1 Sam. 4. 19. she travailed, for her *p.* came upon her
Psal. 116. 3. and the *p.* of hell gat hold on me
Acts 2. 24. God raised up, having loosed *p.* of death
Rev. 16. 11. they blasphemed, because of their *p.*

PAINFUL.

Psal. 73. 16. to know this, it was too *p.* for me

PAINFULNESS.

2 Cor. 11. 27. in weariness and *p.* in watchings often

PAINTED.

2 Kings 9. 30. Jezebel *p.* her face, and tired her head
Jer. 22. 14. ceiled with cedar, and *p.* with vermilion

PAINTEDST.

Ezek. 23. 40. thou *p.* thy eyes, and deckedst thyself

PAINTING.

2 Kings 9. + 30. Jezebel put her eyes in *p.* tired head
Jer. 4. 30. though thou rentest thy face with *p.* in vain

PAIR.

Luke 2. 24. to offer a *p.* of turtle doves or pigeons
Rev. 6. 5. he had a *p.* of balances in his hand

PALACE

Signifies, [1] *A royal dwelling or mansion-house*, Isa. 39. 7. [2] *The temple of God at* Jerusalem, 1 Chron. 29. 1, 19. [3] *Stately and magnificent buildings*, 2 Chron. 36. 19. [4] *The high priest's house*, Mat. 26. 58. [5] *The church*, Psal. 48. 13.

1 Kings 16. 18. Zimri burnt the king's *p.* and died
21. 1. Naboth had a vineyard hard by the *p.*
2 Kings 15. 25. Pekah smote Pekaiah in the *p.*
20. 18. they shall be eunuchs in *p.* of king of Babylon
1 Chron. 29. 1. *p.* is not for man, but for Lord God
19. give Solomon a perfect heart to build the *p.*
2 Chr. 9. 11. he made terraces to the king's *p.*
Ezra 4. 14. we have maintenance from the *p.*
6. 2. there was found at Achmetha, in *p.* a roll
Neh. 1. 1. it came to pass, as I was in Shushan the *p.*
2. 8. timber to make beams for the gates of *p.*
7. 2. I gave Hanani, ruler of *p.* charge over Jerus.
Esth. 2. 3. may gather all young virgins to the *p.*
3. 15. decree was given in Shushan the *p.* 8. 14.
9. 12. Jews destroyed 500 men in Shushan the *p.*
Psal. 45. 15. they shall enter into the king's *p.*
69. + 25. let their *p.* be desolate, let none dwell
144. 12. polished after the similitude of a *p.*
Cant. 8. 9. we will build on her a *p.* of silver
Isa. 25. 2. hast made a *p.* of strangers to be no city
Dan. 4. 4. I was at rest, and flourishing in my *p.*
6. 18. king went to his *p.* passed the night fasting
11. 45. he shall plant his *p.* between the seas
Amos 4. 3. ye shall cast them into *p.* saith the Lord
Nah. 2. 6. gates opened, and *p.* shall be dissolved
Mat. 26. 58. Peter followed Jesus afar off to the high priest's *p.* and went in, Mark 14. 54.
Luke 11. 21. when a strong man keepeth his *p.*
Phil. 1. 13. my bonds are manifest in all the *p.*

PALACES.

2 Chron. 36. 19. and burnt all the *p.* with fire
Ps. 45. 8. garments smell of myrrh, out of ivory *p.*
48. 3. God is known in her *p.* for a refuge
13. mark well her bulwarks, consider her *p.*
78. 69. he built his sanctuary like high *p.*
122. 7. peace and prosperity within thy *p.*
Prov. 30. 28. spider takes hold, and is in king's *p.*
Isa. 13. 22. dragons shall cry in thy pleasant *p.*
32. 14. because the *p.* shall be forsaken
34. 13. thorns shall come up in her *p.* nettles
Jer. 6. 5. arise, and let us destroy her *p.*
9. 21. for death is come and is entered into our *p.*
17. 27. fire shall devour the *p.* of Jerusalem
49. 27. it shall consume the *p.* of Benhadad
Lam. 2. 5. he hath swallowed up all her *p.*
Ezek. 19. 7. and he knew their desolate *p.*
25. 4. they shall set their *p.* in thee, and make
Amos 3. 9. publish in *p.* at Ashdod, in *p.* of Egypt
10. who store up violence and robbery in their *p.*
11. thy *p.* shall be spoiled ‖ 6. 8. I hate his *p.*
Mic. 5. 5. when he shall tread in our *p.* then shall raise
See DEVOUR.

PALE.

Isa. 29. 22. neither shall his face now wax *p.*
Rev. 6. 8. I looked, and behold a *p.* horse, name Death

PALENESS.

Jer. 30. 6. as a woman, and all faces turned into *p.*

PALM.

Lev. 14. 15. pour it into *p.* of his left hand, 26.
Isa. 48. + 13. *p.* of my hand spread out heavens
John 18. 22. struck Jesus with the *p.* of his hand

PALM-BRANCHES.

Neh. 8. 15. go forth to the mount and fetch *p.*

PALMER-WORM.

Joel 1. 4. what the *p.* left, the locust hath eaten
2. 25. I will restore the years that *p.* hath eaten
Amos 4. 9. your fig-trees, the *p.* devoured them

PALMS.

1 Sam. 5. 4. both the *p.* of his hands were cut off
2 Kings 9. 35. they found skull and *p.* of her hands
Isa. 49. 16. I have graven thee on *p.* of my hands
Dan. 10. 10. which set me on the *p.* of my hands
Mat. 26. 67. they spit in his face, others smote him with the *p.* of their hands, Mark 14. 65.
Rev. 7. 9. with white robes, and *p.* in their hands

PALM-TREE

Is an upright, tall, fruit-bearing, flourishing, and shadowy tree, Psal. 92. 12. Cant. 7. 7, 8. Jer. 10. 5. *It grows by the sweet springs of waters, and continues long. It will not be pressed or bound downward, or grow crooked, though heavy weights be laid on it. This tree is one of the most famous of all the forest, and is the usual emblem of constancy, fruitfulness, patience, and victory; which the more it is oppressed, the more it flourisheth; the higher it grows, the stronger and broader it is in the top. Some think it is the same with the Date-tree, which is not only of a beautiful aspect, but of a delightful taste, and is fit both for food and drink; and this was perhaps the reason why the children of Israel pitched their camp at Elim*, Num. 32. 9. *because there were not only* twelve fountains of water *there, but also three-score and ten Palm-trees. The Hebrews called it* Thamar, *and the* Greeks, Φοινιξ. *The finest and best Palm-trees were about* Jericho, En-gedi, *and along the banks of* Jordan. *Palm-trees, from the same root, produce a great number of suckers, which form upwards a kind of forest by their spreading. It was under a little wood of Palm-trees of this kind that the prophetess* Deborah *dwelt between* Ramah *and* Beth-el, Judg. 4. 5.

It was probably to this multiplication of the Palm-tree that the prophet makes allusion, when he says, The righteous shall flourish like the Palm-tree, Psal. 92. 12. *Or, it is made an emblem of a just man's person and condition, because it is constantly green, flourishing, and fruitful.*

The Palm-tree *is a symbol of victory*, Rev. 7. 9. *And the spouse is compared to a palm-tree*, Cant. 7. 7. *because it is tall, and grows directly upward and in spite of all pressures.*

Judg. 4. 5. she dwelt under the *p.* of Deborah
Psal. 92. 12. the righteous shall flourish like the *p.*
Cant. 7. 7. this thy stature is like to a *p.* thy breasts
8. I said, I will go up to the *p.* I will take hold
Jer. 10. 5. they are upright as the *p.* but speak not
Ezek. 41. 19. the face of a man was toward the *p.*
Joel 1. 12. the *p.* and the apple-tree are withered

PALM-TREES.

Exod. 15. 27. came to Elim, where were seventy *p.*
Lev. 23. 40. ye shall take your branches of *p.*
Deut. 34. 3. Lord shewed him city of *p.* unto Zoar
Judg. 1. 16. the Kenite went out of the city of *p.*
3. 13. Moab smote Israel, and possessed city of *p.*
1 Kings 6. 29. he carved with carved figures of *p.* 32. 35. | 7. 36. 2 Chron. 3. 5. Ezek. 40. 16.
2 Chron. 28. 15. and brought them to the city of *p.*

John 12. 13. people took branches of *p.* went forth

PALSY.

This distemper is a preclusion or stoppage in one or more of the limbs, which deprives them of motion, and makes them useless to the patient. There are some Palsies *that are very painful, and others not so much, from the nature of the humours that cause them. Our Saviour cured several Paralytics by his word alone,* Mat. 4. 24. | 8. 6, 7. | 9. 2. *The word* Paralytic *is derived from the* Greek *word,* παραλυω, *which signifies to resolve, or relax; as if it was to shew, that the* Palsy *is a relaxation of the nerves: but it may be produced by other causes.*

Mat. 4. 24. they brought to him those that had the *p.*
he healed them, 9. 2. *Mark* 2. 3. *Luke* 5. 18.
8. 6. my servant lieth at home sick of the *p.*
9. 2. Jesus seeing their faith, said to the sick of the
p. son, thy sins be forgiven thee, *Mark* 2. 5.
Mark 2. 10. Jesus saith to sick of *p.* arise, *Luke* 5. 24.
Acts 9. 33. he found Eneas, who was sick of the *p.*

PALSIES.

Acts 8. 7. many taken with *p.* and lame were healed

PAN.

Lev. 2. 5. if it be a meat offering baken in a *p.*
6. 21. in a *p.* it shall be made with oil, when baken
7. 9. all that is dressed in *p.* shall be the priest's
1 *Sam.* 2. 14. the priest's servant stuck it into the *p.*
2 *Sam.* 13. 9. Tamar took a *p.* and poured them out
Ezek. 4. 3. take unto thee an iron *p.* set it for a wall

PANS.

Exod. 27. 3. thou shalt make *p.* to receive his ashes
Num. 11. 8. they baked manna in *p.* and made cakes
1 *Chron.* 9. 31. over the things made in the *p.* 23. 29.
2 *Chron.* 35. 13. other holy offerings sod they in *p.*

PANGS.

2 *Sam.* 22. † 5. when the *p.* of death compassed me
Isa. 13. 8. *p.* and sorrows shall take hold of them
21. 3. *p.* have taken hold on me, as *p.* of a woman
26. 17. as a woman crieth out in her *p.* so have we
Jer. 22. 23. gracious shalt thou be when *p.* come
48. 41. as the heart of a woman in her *p.* 49. 22.
50. 43. and *p.* as of a woman in travail, *Mic.* 4. 9.

PANNAG.

Ezek. 27. 17. Jud. traded in thy market, *p.* and honey

PANT.

Amos 2. 7. that *p.* after the dust of the earth

PANTED.

Psal. 119. 131. I opened my mouth and *p.* I longed
Isa. 21. 4. at the grievous vision my heart *p.*

PANTETH.

Psal. 38. 10. my heart *p.* my strength faileth me
42. 1. as hart *p.* so *p.* my soul after thee, O God

PAPER

Is a plant, or kind of bulrush, which grows in Egypt, *upon the banks of the* Nile. *The* Egyptians *applied it to several uses, as to make baskets, shoes, clothes, little boats to swim in upon the* Nile, *and paper to write on; it was of this that the little ark was made, in which the parents of* Moses *exposed him upon the banks of the* Nile.

As to the writing-paper made use of by the ancients, it was very different from that in use amongst us, and was composed of the leaves of the paper reeds, *from whence it has its name. This is said to be their manner of working it. The trunk of this plant is composed of several leaves or films placed one over another, which were peeled off, and separated with a needle: they were afterwards stretched out upon a wet table, to the length and breadth of the intended leaf of paper: over the first layer of the leaves of paper they put some thin paste, or only some of the muddy water of the* Nile *a little warmed, upon which they spread a second layer of the leaves of the plant: then they let it dry by the sun. The* Egyptians *applied the paper reeds to several uses, as to make baskets, shoes, clothes, little boats to swim in, and paper to write on.*

Isa. 19. 7. the *p.* reeds by the brooks shall wither
2 *John* 12. I would not write with *p.* and ink

PAPS.

Ezek. 23. 21. lewdness, for the *p.* of thy youth
Luke 11. 27. blessed are *p.* which thou hast sucked
23. 29. blessed are the *p.* which never gave suck
Rev. 1. 13. and girt about *p.* with a golden girdle

PARABLE.

This word is formed from the Greek, παραβολη, *which comes from the verb* παραβελλειν, *signifying to compare things together. It is a similitude taken from natural things, to instruct us in the knowledge of things spiritual. The parabolical, enigmatical, figurative, and sententious way of speaking, was the language of the eastern sages, and learned men; and nothing was more insupportable than to hear a fool utter* Parables, *Prov.* 26. 7. The legs of the lame are not equal, so is a parable in the mouth of fools; *that is, As it is uncomely and ridiculous to see a lame man dancing: no less absurd and indecent are wise and pious speeches from a foolish and ungodly man, whose actions grossly contradict them, whereby he makes them contemptible, and himself ridiculous.*

The prophets made use of Parables, *to give a stronger impression to prince and people, of the threatenings or of the promises they made to them.* Nathan *reproved* David *under the parable of a rich man that had taken away and killed the lamb of a poor man,* 2 Sam. 12. 2, 3, &c. *The woman of* Tekoah, *that was hired by* Joab *to reconcile the mind of the same prince towards his son* Absalom, *proposed to him the parable of her two sons that fought together in the field, and one of which having killed the other, they were going to put the murderer to death, and so to deprive her of both her sons at once,* 2 Sam. 14. 2, 3, &c. Jotham, *son of* Gideon, *proposed to the men of* Shechem, *the parable of the bramble, whom the trees had a mind to choose for their king,* Judg. 9. 7, 8, &c. *The prophets often reprove the infidelity of* Jerusalem *under the parable of an adulterous wife. They describe the violence of such princes as are enemies to the people of God, under the representations of lions, eagles, bears, &c.*

Our Saviour in the gospel often speaks to the people in parables, Mat. 13. 10, 13, &c. *He made use of them to verify the prophecy of* Isaiah, *who foretold, that the people should see without knowing, and hear without understanding, and should continue in their blindness and hardness of heart, in the midst of the instructions they should receive,* Isa. 6. 9, 10. *There are some parables in the New Testament, which are supposed to be true histories; there are others in which our Saviour seems to allude to some particular things of those times.*

Num. 23. 7. Baalam took up his *p.* and said, Balak,
king of Moab, 24. 3, 15, 20, 21, 23.
18. took up his *p.* rise up, Balak, and hear
Job 27. 1. Job continued his *p.* and said, 29. 1.
Psal. 49. 4. I will incline mine ear to a *p.*
78. 2. I will open my mouth, in a *p.* I will utter
Prov. 26. 7. so is a *p.* in the mouth of fools, 9.
Ezek. 17. 2. and speak a *p.* to the house of Israel
24. 3. utter a *p.* to the rebellious house, and say
Mic. 2. 4. one shall take up a *p.* against you
Hab. 2. 6. shall not all these take up a *p.* against him
Mat. 13. 18. hear ye therefore the *p.* of the sower
24. another *p.* put he forth, 31, 33. | 21. 33.
34. without a *p.* spake he not to them, *Mark* 4. 34.
36. declare to us the *p.* of the tares, 15. 15.
24. 32. now learn a *p.* of the fig-tree, when branch
putteth forth leaves, *Mark* 13. 28. *Luke* 21. 29.
Mark 4. 10. they asked him of *p.* 7. 17. *Luke* 8. 9.
13. he said to them, know ye not this *p.?*
12. 12. he had spoken *p.* against them, *Luke* 20. 19.
Luke 5. 36. he spake a *p.* to them, 6. 39. | 8. 4. | 12.
16. | 13. 6. | 14. 7. | 15. 3. | 18. 1, 9. | 19. 11. |
20. 9. | 21. 29. *John* 10. 6.
12. 41. Lord, spakest thou this *p.* to us, or to all?

PARABLES.

Ezek. 20. 49. they say of me, doth he not speak *p.?*
Mat. 13. 3. he spake many things to them in *p.* 13.
34. | 22. 1. *Mark* 3. 23. | 4. 2, 13, 33. | 12. 1.
Mark 4. 13. how then will ye know all *p.?*
Luke 8. 10. but others in *p.* that seeing might not see
John 16. † 25. when I shall no more speak in *p.*

PARADISE.

Luke 23. 43. to-day shalt thou be with me in *p.*
2 *Cor.* 12. 4. how that he was caught up into *p.*
Rev. 2. 7. which is in the midst of the *p.* of God

PARAMOURS.

Ezek. 23. 20. for she doted upon their *p.* whose flesh

PARCEL.

Gen. 33. 19. Jacob brought a *p.* of a field of the
children of Hamor, *Josh.* 24. 32. *John* 4. 5.
Ruth 4. 3. Naomi selleth a *p.* of land, Elimelech's
1 *Chr.* 11. 13. was a *p.* of ground full of barley, 14.

PARCHED.

Isa. 35. 7. the *p.* ground shall become a pool
Jer. 17. 6. but he shall inhabit the *p.* places

See CORN.

PARCHMENTS.

2 *Tim.* 4. 13. bring the books, but especially the *p.*

PARDON.

Exod. 23. 21. he will not *p.* your transgressions
34. 9. *p.* our iniquity and our sin, *Num.* 14. 19.
1 *Sam.* 15. 25. therefore, I pray thee, *p.* my sin
2 *Kings* 5. 18. in this the Lord *p.* thy servant
24. 4. innocent blood, which Lord would not *p.*
2 *Chron.* 30. 18. the good Lord *p.* every one
Neh. 9. 17. but thou art a God ready to *p.* gracious
Job 7. 21. why dost thou not *p.* my transgression?
Psal. 25. 11. for thy name's sake *p.* mine iniquity
Isa. 55. 7. return to Lord, for he will abundantly *p.*
Jer. 5. 1. and I will *p.* it ‖ 7. how shall I *p.* thee
33. 8. I will *p.* all their iniquities, whereby sinned
50. 20. for I will *p.* them whom I reserve

PARDONED.

Num. 14. 20. I. said, I have *p.* according to thy word
Isa. 40. 2. tell her that her iniquity is *p.*
Lam. 3. 42. we have rebelled, thou hast not *p.*

PARDONETH.

Mic. 7. 18. who is a God like to thee, that *p.* iniquity?

PARDONS.

Neh. 9. † 17. thou art a God of *p.* slow to anger

PARE.

Deut. 21. 12. he shall shave her head and *p.* her nails

PARENTS.

Mat. 10. 21. children shall rise up against their *p.*
and cause them to be put to death, *Mark* 13. 12.
Luke 2. 27. when the *p.* brought in the child Jesus
8. 56. her *p.* were astonished, but he charged them
18. 29. there is no man that hath left *p.* or wife
21. 16. ye shall be betrayed both by *p.* and brethren
John 9. 2. Master, who did sin, this man or his *p.?*
22. these words spake *p.* because feared Jews, 23.
Rom. 1. 30. proud, disobedient to *p.* 2 *Tim.* 3. 2.
2 *Cor.* 12. 14. children ought not to lay up for the *p.*
Eph. 6. 1. children, obey your *p.* *Col.* 3. 20.
1 *Tim.* 5. 4. let them learn to requite their *p.*
Heb. 11. 23. Moses was hid three months of his *p.*

PARLOUR.

Judg. 3. 20. Eglon was sitting in a summer *p.*
23. Ehud shut the doors of the *p.* upon him
1 *Sam.* 9. 22. Samuel brought them into the *p.*

PARLOURS.

1 *Chron.* 28. 11. David gave Solomon a pattern of *p.*

PART.

Exod. 19. 17. they stood at nether *p.* of mountain
29. 26. thou shalt take the breast, it shall be thy *p.*
Lev. 2. 16. *p.* of the beaten corn, *p.* of oil thereof
7. 33. he shall have the right shoulder for his *p.*
8. 29. the breast of consecration was Moses' *p.*
11. 37. if any *p.* of their carcase fall thereon, 38.
13. 41. his hair fallen off from the *p.* of his head
Num. 18. 20. neither shalt thou have any *p.* among
them, *Deut.* 10. 9. | 12. 21. | 14. 27. 29. |
18. 1. *Josh.* 14. 4. | 18. 7.
I am thy *p.* and thine inheritance in Israel
22. 41. might see utmost *p.* of the people, 23. 13.
Deut. 33. 21. he provided the first *p.* for himself
Josh. 19. 9. the *p.* of Judah was too much for them
22. 25. ye have no *p.* in the Lord, 27.
Ruth 2. 3. her hap was to light on a *p.* of the field
Ruth 3. 13. if he will perform to thee *p.* of a kinsm.
1 *Sam.* 5. † 4. only the fishy *p.* was left to Dagon
14. 2. Saul tarried in the utmost *p.* of the camp
23. 20. our *p.* shall be to del. him into king's hand
30. 24. as his *p.* is that goeth down to battle, so shall
his *p.* be that tarrieth by stuff, shall part alike
2 *Sam.* 20. 1. Sheba said, we have no *p.* in David
2 *Kings* 7. 5. the lepers were come to uttermost *p.* 8.
18. 23. if able on thy *p.* to set riders, *Isa.* 36. 8.
22. † 14. dwelt in the second *p.* 2 *Chron.* 34. † 22.
1 *Chron.* 12. 29. greatest *p.* had kept house of Saul
2 *Chron.* 29. 16. the priests went into the inner *p.*
Neh. 1. 9. cast out to the uttermost *p.* of heaven
5. 11. restore the hundredth *p.* of the money
Job 32. 17. I will answer my *p.* will shew my opinion
Psal. 5. 9. their inward *p.* is very wickedness
16. † 5. the Lord is the portion of my *p.*
51. 6. in hidden *p.* shalt make me know wisdom
118. 7. Lord takes my *p.* with them that help me
Prov. 8. 26. nor highest *p.* of the dust of the world
31. rejoicing in the habitable *p.* of his earth
17. 2. shall have *p.* of inheritance among brethren
Isa. 7. 18. hiss for the fly that is in the utmost *p.*
24. 16. from utmost *p.* of earth we heard songs
44. 16. he burneth *p.* thereof in the fire, with *p.*
thereof he eateth flesh, he warmeth himself, 19.
Ezek. 4. 11. thou shalt drink the sixth *p.* of an hin
39. 2. leave but the sixth *p.* of thee, and cause thee
45. 13. sixth *p.* of an ephah of an homer of wheat
17. it shall be the prince's *p.* to give offerings
46. 14. a meat offering the sixth *p.* of an ephah
Dan. 2. 33. his feet *p.* of iron, and *p.* of clay, 41. 42.
5. 5. the king saw *p.* of the hand that wrote, 24.
11. 31. arms shall stand on his *p.* they shall pollute
Amos 7. 4. it devoured great deep, did eat up a *p.*
Mark 4. 38. he was in the hinder *p.* of the ship
9. 40. he that is not against us, is on our *p.*
Luke 10. 42. and Mary hath chosen that good *p.*
11. 39. your inward *p.* is full of ravening and wick.
17. 24. as lightning that lighteneth out of one *p.*
shining to other *p.* under heaven, so Son of man
John 13. 8. if I wash thee not, hast no *p.* with me
19. 23. soldiers made four parts, every soldier a *p.*
Acts 1. 17. and had obtained *p.* of this ministry
25. that he may take *p.* of this ministry
5. 2. but Ananias kept back *p.* of the price, and
brought a certain *p.* and laid it at apostles' feet, 3.
8. 21. thou hast neither *p.* nor lot in this matter
14. 4. *p.* held with the Jews, *p.* with the apostles
16. 12. the chief city of that *p.* of Macedonia
19. 32. more *p.* knew not wherefore they came
23. 6. perceived that the one *p.* were Sadducees
27. 12. the more *p.* advised to depart thence
1 *Cor.* 12. 24. honour to that *p.* which lacked
15. 6. of whom the greater *p.* remain to this day
16. 17. what was lacking on your *p.* they supplied
2 *Cor.* 6. 15. what *p.* he that believeth with infidel?
Eph. 4. 16. the working in the measure of every *p.*
Tit. 2. 8. that he of the contrary *p.* may be ashamed
Heb. 2. 14. himself likewise took *p.* of the same
1 *Pet.* 4. 14. Spirit of God rests on you; on their *p.* he
is evil spoken of, but on your *p.* he is glorified
Rev. 20. 6. holy that hath *p.* in the first resurrection
21. 8. all liars shall have their *p.* in the lake
22. 19. God shall take away his *p.* out of book

In PART.

Rom. 11. 25. blindness *in p.* is happened to Israel
1 *Cor.* 13. 9. we know *in p.* and we prophesy *in p.*
10. then that which is *in p.* shall be done away
12. I know *in p.* but then shall I know as I am
2 *Cor.* 1. 14. as also ye have acknowledged us *in p.*
2. 5. caused grief, it hath not grieved me but *in p.*

Third PART.

Num. 15. 6. for a ram, flour mingled with the *third*
p. of an hin of oil, 28. 14. *Ezek.* 46. 14.
7. thou shalt offer the *third p.* of an hin of wine
2 *Sam.* 18. 2. David sent a *third p.* of the people
2 *Kings* 11. 5. a *third p.* that enter in on the sabbath
2 *Chron.* 23. 4. a *third p.* of you shall be porters
Neh. 10. 32. charge ourselves with *third p.* of shekel
Ezek. 5. 2. burn with fire a *third p.* a *third p.* smite
about it, a *third p.* scatter in the wind, 12.
Zech. 13. 8. but the *third p.* shall be left therein
9. I will bring the *third p.* through the fire
Rev. 8. 7. *third p.* of the trees was burnt up
8. and the *third p.* of the sea became blood
9. *third p.* of the creatures died, *third p.* of ships
10. and it fell upon the *third p.* of the rivers
11. the *third p.* of the waters became wormwood
12. the *third p.* of the sun, moon, and stars, was
smitten, the day shone not for a *third p.* of it
9. 15. were prepared for to slay the *third p.* of men
18. by these three was the *third p.* of men killed
12. 4. his tail drew *third p.* of the stars of heaven

Fourth PART.

Exod. 29. 40. flour mingled with the *fourth p.* of an
hin of beaten oil, *Num.* 15. 4. | 28. 5.
fourth p. of an hin of wine for a drink offering,
Lev. 23. 13. *Num.* 15. 5. | 28. 7, 14.
1 *Sam.* 9. 8. I have here the *fourth p.* of a shekel
1 *Kings* 6. 33. posts of olive-tree *fourth p.* of wall
2 *Kings* 6. 25. the *fourth p.* of a cab of doves' dung
Neh. 9. 3. read one *fourth p.* another *fourth p.* they
Rev. 6. 8. power was given over *fourth p.* of earth

Fifth PART.

Gen. 41. 34. take up *fifth p.* of the land of Egypt
47. 24. ye shall give the *fifth p.* to Pharaoh, 26.
Lev. 5. 16. and shall add the *fifth p.* thereto, 6. 5.
| 22. 14. | 27. 13, 19, 27, 31. *Num.* 5. 7.
1 *Kings* 6. 31. lintel and side posts were a *fifth p.*

Tenth PART.

Exod. 16. 36. an homer is the *tenth p.* of an ephah
Lev. 5. 11. shall bring for his offering the *tenth p.*
of an ephah of fine flour, 6. 20. *Num.* 28. 5.
Num. 5. 15. the *tenth p.* of an ephah of barley-meal
18. 26. ye shall offer even the *tenth p.* of the tithe
Ezek. 45. 11. bath and ephah may contain *tenth p.*
14. ye shall offer the *tenth p.* of a bath of oil
Heb. 7. 2. to whom Abraham gave a *tenth p.* of all
Rev. 11. 13. and the *tenth p.* of the city fell

PARTS.

Gen. 47. 24. and four *p.* shall be your own

Lev. 1. 8. Aaron's sons shall lay the p. in order
22. 23. that hath any thing lacking in his p.
Num. 31. 27. and divide the prey into two p.
Deut. 19. 3. divide coasts of the land into three p.
30. 4. if any be driven to the utmost p. of heaven
Josh. 18. 5. they shall divide it into seven p. 6, 9.
1 Sam. 5. 9. they had emerods in their secret p.
2 Sam. 19. 43. we have ten p. in the king
1 Kings 16. 21. Israel were divided into two p.
2 Kings 11. 7. two p. keep watch about the king
Neh. 11. 1. and nine p. to dwell in other cities
Job 26. 14. lo, these are p. of his ways, how little
41. 12. I will not conceal his p. nor his power
Psal. 2. 8. uttermost p. of earth for thy possession
63. 9. shall go into lower p. of the earth
65. 8. that dwell in utmost p. afraid at thy tokens
136. 13. which divided the Red sea into p.
139. 9. if I dwell in the utmost p. of the sea
Prov. 18. 8. they go down into innermost p. 26. 22.
Isa. 3. 17. and the Lord will discover their secret p.
44. 23. shout, ye lower p. of the earth
Jer. 34. 18. and passed between the p. thereof, 19.
Ezek. 26. 20. and set thee in the low p. of the earth
31. 14. are delivered to the nether p. of earth, 18.
16. comforted in nether p. of earth, 32. 18, 24.
37. 11. hope is lost, we are cut off for our p.
38. 15. from thy place out of the north p. 39. 2.
48. 8. offering in length as one of the other p.
Zech. 13. 8. said Lord, two p. therein shall be cut off
Mat. 2. 22. he turned aside into the p. of Galilee
12. 42. she came from uttermost p. Luke 11. 31.
John 19. 23. took his garments and made four p.
Acts 20. 2. when he had gone over those p. he came
Rom. 15. 23. having no more place in those p.
1 Cor. 12. 23. uncomely p. have more comeliness
24. for our comely p. have no need, but God
Eph. 4. 9. he descended first into lower p. of earth
Rev. 16. 19. the great city was divided into three p.
See BACK, HINDER, INWARD.

PART, *Verb*.

Lev. 2. 6. thou shalt p. the meat offering in pieces
Ruth 1. 17. if ought but death p. thee and me
1 Sam. 30. 24. they shall p. alike, and it was so
2 Sam. 14. 6. and there was none to p. them
Job 41. 6. shall they p. him among the merchants?
Psal. 22. 18. they p. my garments among them

PARTED.

Gen. 2. 10. the river was p. into four heads
2 Kings 2. 11. the chariot p. them both asunder
14. the waters p. hither and thither, he went over
Job 38. 24. by what way is the light p.?
Joel 3. 2. whom they scattered, and p. my land
Mat. 27. 35. they crucified him, and p. his garments, Mark 15. 24. Luke 23. 34. John 19. 24.
Luke 24. 51. while he blessed them, was p. from
Acts 2. 45. p. them to all men, as each had need

PARTETH.

Lev. 11. 3. whatsoever p. the hoof, Deut. 14. 6.
Prov. 18. 18. the lot p. between the mighty

PARTAKER.

Psal. 50. 18. and hast been p. with adulterers
1 Cor. 9. 10. that he should be p. of his hope
23. that I might be p. thereof with you
10. 30. if I by grace be p. why am I evil spoken of?
1 Tim. 5. 22. neither be p. of other men's sins
2 Tim. 1. 8. but be thou p. of afflictions of gospel
2. 6. the husbandman be first p. of the fruits
1 Pet. 5. 1. who am also a p. of the glory which
2 John 11. biddeth God speed is p. of his evil deeds

PARTAKERS.

Mat. 23. 30. would not been p. in blood of prophets
Rom. 15. 27. if Gentiles have been made p. of their spiritual things, their duty to minister in carnal
1 Cor. 9. 12. if others be p. of this power over you
13. who wait at the altar, are p. with the altar
10. 17. for we are all p. of that one bread
18. are not they which eat p. of the altar?
21. cannot be p. of the Lord's table, and devils'
2 Cor. 1. 7. as you are p. of the sufferings, so shall be
Eph. 3. 6. and p. of his promise in Christ by gospel
5. 7. be not ye therefore p. with them
Phil. 1. 7. in defence of gosp. ye all are p. of my grace
Col. 1. 12. hath made us meet to be p. of inheritance
1 Tim. 6. 2. because they are p. of the benefit
Heb. 2. 14. as the children are p. of flesh and blood
3. 1. holy brethren, p. of the heavenly calling
14. for we are made p. of Christ, if we hold
6. 4. and were made p. of the Holy Ghost
12. 8. if without chastisement, whereof all are p.
10. that we might be p. of his holiness
1 Pet. 4. 13. as ye are p. of Christ's sufferings
2 Pet. 1. 4. ye might be p. of the divine nature
Rev. 18. 4. come out of her, that ye be not p. of her

PARTAKEST.

Rom. 11. 17. and with them p. of root and fatness

PARTIAL.

Mal. 2. 9. not keep my ways, but have been p. in law
Jam. 2. 4. are ye not then p. in yourselves?

PARTIALITY.

1 Tim. 5. 21. observe these things, doing noth. by p.
Jam. 3. 17. without p. and without hypocrisy

PARTICULAR.

1 Cor 12. 27. ye are body of Christ, members in p.
Eph. 5. 33. let every one of you in p. so love his wife

PARTICULARLY.

Acts 21. 19. Paul declar. p. what things G. wrought
Heb. 9. 5. mercy-seat, which we cannot now speak p.

PARTIES.

Exod. 22. 9. cause of both p. shall come before judges

PARTING.

Exod. 21. 21. king of Babylon stood at p. of the way

PARTITION.

1 Kings 6. 21. and he made a p. by chains of gold
Eph. 2. 14. who hath broken down middle wall of p.

PARTLY.

Dan. 2. 42. the kingdom shall be p. strong, p. broken
1 Cor. 11. 18. I hear there be divisions, I p. believe it
Heb. 10. 33. p. whilst ye were made a gazing-stock by afflictions, p. whilst ye became companions

PARTNER.

Prov. 29. 24. whoso is p. with thief hateth his soul
2 Cor. 8. 23. Titus, he is my p. and fellow-helper

Philem. 17. if count me a p. receive him as myself

PARTNERS.

Luke 5. 7. they beckoned to their p. to help them
10. James and John who were p. with Simon

PARTRIDGE.

1 Sam. 26. 20. as when one doth hunt a p. in mount.
Jer. 17. 11. as p. sitteth on eggs, hatcheth them not

PASSAGE.

Num. 20. 21. Edom refused to give Isr. p. thro' border
Josh. 22. 11. have built an altar at the p. of Isr.
1 Sam. 13. 23. garrison of Philistines went out to p.
Isa. 10. 29. they are gone over p. Ramah is afraid

PASSAGES.

Judg. 12. 6. took and slew him at the p. of Jordan
1 Sam. 14. 4. between the p. there were sharp rocks
Jer. 22. 20. lift up thy voice, and cry from the p.
51. 32. to shew Babylon that the p. are stopped

PASS.

Gen. 18. 5. I will fetch bread, after that ye shall p. on
41. 32. and God will shortly bring it to p.
Exod. 33. 19. I will make my goodness p. before thee
Num. 27. 7. inherit. of their father to p. to them, 8.
Josh. 1. 14. ye shall p. before your brethren armed
6. 7. he said to people, p. on, and compass the city
1 Sam. 9. 27. bid the servants p. on before us
16. 8. Jesse made Abinadab p. before Samuel
10. Jesse made seven of his sons p. before him
Neh. 2. 14. there was no place for the beast to p.
Job 6. 15. as a stream of brooks they p. away
11. 16. and remember it as waters that p. away
34. 20. and people shall be troubled, and p. away
Psal. 58. 8. as snail which melteth let them p. away
73. † 7. they p. the thoughts of the heart
119. † 37. make to p. mine eyes from beholding van.
Prov. 16. 30. moving his lips he bringeth evil to p.
22. 3. the simple p. on and are punished, 27. 12.
Isa. 2. † 18. the idols shall utterly p. away
30. 32. in every place where grounded staff shall p.
31. † 9. his rock shall p. away for fear
33. 21. no galley nor gallant ship shall p. thereby
37. 26. dried up rivers, now have I brought it to p.
Jer. 8. 13. the things I have given shall p. away
15. 14. I will make thee to p. with thine enemies
33. 13. the flocks shall p. again under the hands of him that telleth them, saith the Lord
51. 43. nor doth any son of man p. thereby
Ezek. 5. 1. cause a barber's razor to p. on thine head
20. 37. I will cause you to p. under rod, and bring
32. 19. whom dost thou p. in beauty? go down
Amos 6. 2. p. ye unto Calneh and see, go to Hamath
Mic. 1. 11. p. ye away, thou inhabitant of Saphir
2. 13. and their king shall p. before them
Zeph. 2. 2. before decree bring forth, the day p. as
Zech. 3. 4. I have caused thy iniquity to p. from thee
Mat. 5. 18. heaven and earth shall p. one tittle not p.
26. 39. Father, let this cup p. from me, Mark 14. 35.
Luke 16. 26. so that they which would p. from hence to you cannot; nor can they p. to us from you
19. 4. he ran to see him, for he was to p. that way
1 Cor. 7. 36. if she p. the flower of her age, and need
Jam. 1. 10. as flower of the grass he shall p. away
1 Pet. 1. 17. p. time of your sojourning here in fear
2 Pet. 3. 10. in which the heavens shall p. away

PASS *by*.

Exod. 33. 22. cover thee with my hand while I p. by
Deut. 2. 30. Sihon would not let us p. by him
1 Sam. 16. 9. then Jesse made Shammah to p. by
Psal. 80. 12. all they that p. by the way do pluck her
89. 41. all that p. by the way spoil him, he is at
Jer. 22. 8. many nations shall p. by this city
Lam. 1. 12. all ye that p. by behold and see
2. 15. all that p. by clap their hands at thee
Ezek. 5. 14. a reproach in sight of all that p. by
37. 2. and caused me to p. by them round about
46. 21. caused me to p. by four corners of the earth
Amos 7. 8. I will not again p. by them any more, 8. 2.
Mic. 2. 8. ye pull off garments of them that p. by
Mat. 8. 28. that no man might p. by that way
Luke 18. 36. hearing the multitude p. by he asked
2 Cor. 1. 16. and to p. by you into Macedonia
See CAME, COME.

Not PASS.

Num. 20. 17. we will *not* p. through the fields or vine.
18. and Edom said, thou shalt *not* p. by me
Deut. 24. † 5. when a man hath taken a new wife, he shall not go out to war, *not* any thing p. on him
Job 14. 5. hast appointed his bounds he *cannot* p.
19. 8. he hath fenced my way, that I *cannot* p.
Psal. 148. 6. he made a decree, which shall *not* p.
Prov. 8. 29. waters should *not* p. his commandment
Jer. 5. 22. by a perpetual decree, that it *cannot* p.
Dan. 7. 14. everlast. dominion, that shall *not* p. away
Mat. 24. 34. this generation shall *not* p. away, till all these things be fulfilled, Mark 13. 30. Luke 21. 32.
35. heaven and earth shall pass away, but my word shall *not* p. away, Mark 13. 31. Luke 21. 33.

PASS *not*.

Gen. 18. 3. my lord, p. *not* away from thy servant
2 Kings 6. 9. beware that thou p. *not* such a place
Prov. 4. 15. avoid it, p. *not* by it, turn aside
Amos 5 5. seek not Beth-el, p. *not* to Beer-sheba

PASS *over*.

Gen. 8. 1. God made a wind to p. *over* the earth
31. 52. that I will not p. *over* this heap to thee
32. 16. p. *over* before me, and put a space betwixt
† 23. he caused them to p. *over* the brook
33. 14. let my lord p. *over* before thy servant
Exod. 12. 13. when I see blood, I will p. *over* you, 23.
13. † 12. cause to p. *over* to the Lord all that open
15. 16. as still as a stone, till thy people p. *over*
Num. 32. 27. but thy servants will p. *over*, 29. 32.
30. if they will not p. *over* with you armed
Deut. 2. 18. thou art to p. *over* through Ar this day
24. p. *over* Arnon ‖ 29. until I shall p. *over* Jordan
3. 18. ye shall p. *over* armed before your brethren
6. † 1. might do them in land whither ye p. *over*
9. 1. thou art to p. *over* Jordan this day, 11. 31. | 27. 2. Josh. 1. 11. | 3. 6, 14. | 4, 5.
Josh. 22. 19. then p. *over* into the land of possession
Judg. 3. 28. and suffered not a man to p. *over*
19. 12. his master said, we will p. *over* to Gibeah
1 Sam. 14. 8. behold, we will p. *over* to these men

2 Sam. 15. 22. David said to Ittai, go and p. *over*
17. 16. lodge not in plains, but speedily p. *over*
Psal. 104. 9. set a bound, that they may not p. *over*
141. † 10. let the wicked fall, whilst that I p. *over*
Prov. 19. 11. it is a glory to p. *over* a transgression
Isa. 23. 6. p. *over* to Tarshish, howl ye inhabitants
12. p. o. to Chittim ‖ 28. 19. by morning shall p. o.
31. 9. he shall p. *over* to his strong-hold for fear
35. 8. the way of holiness, unclean shall not p. o.
47. 2. uncover the thigh, p. *over* the rivers
51. 10. the depths, a way for ransomed to p. *over*
Jer. 2. 10. for p. *over* the isles of Chittim and see
5. 22. though they roar, yet can thy not p. o. it
Ezek. 47. 5. it was a river that I could not p. *over*
Dan. 4. 16. and let seven times p. *over* him, 25.
11. † 20. one that causeth an exactor to p. *over*
40. the king of the north shall p. *over*
Hab. 1. 11. his mind shall change, he shall p. *over*
Luke 11. 42. and p. o. judgment, and love of God

PASS *through*.

Gen. 30. 32. I will p. *through* all thy flock to-day
Exod. 12. 12. I will p. *thro'* land of Egypt this night
23. the Lord will p. *thro'* to smite the Egyptians
Lev. 18. 21. shalt not let any of thy seed p. *through* the fire to Molech, Deut. 18. 10. 2 Kings 17. 17.
Num. 20. 17. let us I pray thee p. *thro* thy country
21. 22. let me p. *through* thy land, Deut. 2. 27.
23. Sihon not suffer Israel to p. t. Judg. 11. 20.
Deut. 2. 4. ye are to p. *thro'* the coasts of Edom
28. water to drink, only I will p. *thro'* on my feet
Josh. 1. 11. p. t. the host and command the people
2 Sam. 12. 31. and made them p. *thro'* brick-kiln
1 Kings 18. 6. they divided the land to p. *thro'* it
2 Kings 16. 3. to p. *thro'* the fire, 21. 6. | 23. 10. 2 Chr. 33. 6. Jer. 32. 35. Ezek. 20. 26, 31.
Psal. 78. 13. caused them to p. t. the sea, 136. 14.
Isa. 8. 8. he shall p. *through* Judah, and go over
21. shall p. *thro'* it hardly bestead and hungry
21. 1. as whirlwinds in the south p. *thro'*, so it
23. 10. p. *thro'* thy land as a river, O Tarshish
28. 15. the overflowing scourge shall p. *thro'*, 18.
34. 10. none shall p. *through* it for ever and ever
Jer. 9. 10. burnt up, so that none can p. *thro'* them
Lam. 3. 44. that our prayers should not p. *through*
4. 21. the cup also shall p. *through* to thee
Ezek. 5. 17. pestilence and blood shall p. *thro'* thee
14. 15. if I cause noisome beasts p. *thro'* land that no man may p. *thro'* for beasts, 29. 11. | 33. 28.
39. 15. the passengers that p. *through* the land
Dan. 11. 10. one shall come, p. *thro'*, and overflow
Joel 3. 17. no stranger shall p. *thro'* her any more
Amos 5. 17. I will p. *through* thee, saith the Lord
Nah. 1. 12. shall he cut down, when he shall p. t.
15. the wicked shall no more p. *through* thee
Zech. 9. 8. and no oppressor shall p. *through* them
1 Cor. 16. 5. when I shall p. *through* Macedonia

PASSED.

Gen. 15. 17. a lamp that p. between those pieces
Num. 20. 17. until we have p. thy borders
Josh. 3. 4. ye have not p. this way heretofore
6. 8. the seven priests p. on before and blew
24. 17. Lord our God preserved us in all the way we went, among all people through whom we p.
Judg. 3. 26. Ehud escaped and p. beyond quarries
1 Sam. 15. 12. Saul is gone about and p. on
29. 2. the lords of Philistines p. on by hundreds
2 Sam. 15. 18. David's servants p. on beside him
2 Kings 4. 8. it fell, that Elisha p. to Shunem
31. Gehazi p. on before them, and laid the staff
2 Chron. 9. 22. Solomon p. all the kings in wisdom
Job 4. 15. then a spirit p. before my face
9. 26. my days are p. away, as the swift ships
15. 19. and no stranger p. among them
Psal. 18. 12. at the brightness, his thick clouds p.
37. 36. yet he p. away, and lo, he was not
81. † 6. his hands p. away from the pots
90. 9. all our days are p. away in thy wrath
Cant. 3. 4. it was but a little that I p. from them
Isa. 10. 28. he is come to Aiath, he is p. to Migron
41. 3. he pursued them, and p. safely
Jer. 11. 15. and the holy flesh is p. from thee
34. 18. and p. between the parts thereof, 19.
46. 17. he hath p. the time appointed
Dan. 3. 27. nor the smell of fire had p. on them
6. 18. the king went and p. the night fasting
Nah. 3. 19. hath not thy wickedness p. continually?
Mark 6. 35. a desert place, now the time is far p.
John 5. 24. but is p. from death to life, 1 John 3. 14.
Rom. 5. 12. so death p. on all men, all have sinned
Heb. 4. 14. great High Priest that is p. into heavens
Rev. 21. 1. first heaven and first earth were p. away
4. for the former things are p. away

PASSED *by*.

Gen. 37. 28. there p. by Midianites, merchantmen
Exod. 34. 6. Lord p. by before him, and proclaimed
Deut. 29. 16. through the nations which ye p. by
1 Kings 13. 25. behold, men p. by and saw the lion
19. 11. the Lord p. by ‖ 19. Elijah p. by Elisha
20. 39. as the king p. by he cried to the king
2 Kings 4. 8. that as oft as he p. by he turned in
6. 30. the king p. by on the wall, people looked
14. 9. and there p. by a wild beast, 2 Chron. 25. 18.
Job 28. 8. nor hath the fierce lion p. by it
Psal. 48. 4. for lo, the kings p. by together
Ezek. 16. 6. when I p. by and saw thee polluted, 8.
15. poured fornicat. on every one that p. by, 25.
36. 34. it lay desolate in sight of all that p. by
Hab. 3. 10. the overflowing of the waters p. by
Mat. 20. 30. when heard that Jesus p. by, they cried
27. 39. they that p. by reviled him, Mark 15. 29.
Mark 2. 14. as he p. by he saw Levi sitting at receipt
6. 48. he cometh, and would have p. by them
11. 20. in morning as they p. by they saw fig-tree
15. 21. they compel one Simon who p. by to bear
Luke 10. 31. he p. by on the other side, 32.
John 8. 59. going thro' midst of them, and so p. by
Acts 17. 23. as I p. by and beheld your devotion

PASSED *over*.

Gen. 31. 21. Jacob rose up, and p. *over* the river
32. 10. for with my staff I p. *over* this Jordan
Exod. 12. 27. who p. *over* houses of Israel in Egypt
Num. 33. 51. when ye are p. *over* Jordan, Deut. 27. 3.

Josh. 3. 16. they p. over right against Jericho
17. all the Israelites p. over on dry ground
4. 1. when all people were clean p. over, 11.
10. people hasted and p. over || 11. the ark p. over
12. Reubenites and Gadites p. over armed before
Judg. 8. 4. Gideon p. over and 300 men with him
10. 9. the children of Ammon p. over Jordan
11. 29. Jephthah p. over to fight with Ammon, 32.
1 Sam. 14. 23. the battle p. over to Beth-aven
27. 2. David p. over with 600 men unto Achish
2 Sam. 2. 29. Abner and his men p. over Jordan
15. 22. Ittai p. over || 23. king and people p. over
Isa. 40. 27. my judgment is p. over from my God
Ezek. 47. 5. a river that could not be p. over
Hos. 10. 11. but I p. over upon her fair neck
Jonah 2. 3. all thy billows and waves p. over me

PASSED *through*.

Gen. 12. 6. Abram p. through the land to Sichem
Num. 14. 7. land which we p. thro' to search is good
33. 8. they p. thro' midst of the sea into wilderness
1 Sam. 9. 4. Saul p. t. mount Ephraim and Shalisha
2 Chron. 30. 10. posts p. thro' country of Ephraim
Mic. 2. 13. breaker is come, they p. through the gate
Zech. 7. 14. land was desolate, that no man p. thro'
Luke 17. 11. that he p. thro' the midst of Samaria
Acts 9. 32. as Peter p. thro' all quarters, came down
12. 10. they went out, and p. through one street
1 Cor. 10. 1. all our fathers p. through the sea
Heb 11. 29. by faith they p. through the Red sea

PASSEDST.

Judg. 12. 1. why p. thou over to fight ag. Ammon?

PASSENGERS.

Prov. 9. 15. she standeth to call p. who go right on
Ezek. 39. 11. I will give Gog valley of p. it shall stop noses of the p. there shall they bury Gog
14. to bury with p. those that remain on earth
15. when p. see a man's bone, they set a sign by it

PASSEST.

Deut. 3. 21. so L. do to all kingdoms whither thou p.
30. 18. on land whither thou p. over to possess
2 Sam. 15. 33. if p. on, thou shalt be a burden
1 Kings 2. 37. day thou p. over the brook Kidron
Isa. 43. 2. when p. thro' waters, I will be with thee

PASSETH.

Exod. 30. 13. every one that p. among them, 14.
33. 22. I will cover thee, while my glory p. by
Lev. 27. 32. whatsoever p. under the rod, the tenth
Josh. 3. 11. even the Lord p. over before you
1 Kings 9. 8. at this house every one that p. by it shall be astonished, and shall hiss, 2 Chr. 7. 21.
2 Kings 4. 9. is an holy man of God, which p. by us
12. 4. money of every one that p. the account
Job 9. 11. he p. on also, but I perceive him not
14. 20. thou prevailest against him, and he p.
30. 15. and my welfare p. away as a cloud
37. 21. but the wind p. and cleanseth them
Psal. 8. 8. dominion over whatever p. thro' the seas
78. 39. are a wind that p. away, comes not again
103. 16. for the wind p. over it, and it is gone
144. 4. his days are as a shadow that p. away
Prov. 10. 25. as whirlwind p. so is wicked no more
26. 17. he that p. by and meddleth with strife
Eccl. 1. 4. one generat. p. away, and another cometh
Isa. 29. 5. the terrible shall be as chaff that p. away
Jer. 2. 6. a land that no man p. through, 9. 12.
13. 24. scatter them as stubble that p. away
18. 16. every one that p. shall be astonished, 19. 8.
Ezek. 35. 7. I will cut off from it him that p. out
Hos. 13. 3. they shall be as early dew that p. away
Mic. 7. 18. G that p. by transgression of remnant
Zeph. 2. 15. every one that p. by her shall hiss
3. 6. I made their streets waste, that none p. by
Zech. 9. 8. I will encamp, because of him that p. by
Luke 18. 37. they told him that Jesus p. by
1 Cor. 7. 31. fashion of this world p. away, 1 John 2. 17.
Eph. 3. 19. the love of Christ which p. knowledge
Phil. 4. 7. the peace of God which p. understanding

PASSING.

Judg. 19. 18. we are p. from Beth-lehem-judah
2 Sam. 1. 26. thy love to me p. love of women
15. 24. the people had done p. out of the city
2 Kings 6. 26. as king of Israel was p. by on wall
Psal. 84. 6. p. thro' the valley of Baca make a well
Prov. 7. 8. p. through the street near the corner
Isa. 31. 5. and p. over he will preserve Jerusalem
Ezek. 39. 14. p. thro' land to bury those that remain
Luke 4. 30. he p. thro' midst of them, went his way
Acts 5. 15. at the least the shadow of Peter p. by
8. 40. Philip p. through, preached in all the cities
16. 8. they p. by Mysia, came down to Troas
27. 8. and hardly p. Crete we came to fair havens

PASSION

Signifies, [1] *The sufferings and death of Christ,* Acts 1. 3. 1 Pet. 1. 11. [2] *The sufferings which Christ's members endure for his sake,* Col. 1. 24. Heb. 10. 32. 1 Pet. 4. 13. [3] *Natural and sinful infirmities,* Acts 14. 15. Jam. 5. 17. [4] *Shameful passions, to which persons are given up, whom God abandons to their own desires,* Rom. 1. 26. [5] *The passions, or motions of sin which act in our members, to bring forth the fruit of death,* Rom. 7. 5. [6] *The passions, or desires, our evil inclinations, the motions of concupiscence, to which the heathen, without any scruple, abandoned themselves,* 1 Thess. 4. 5.

Most of the passages of Scripture here cited are otherwise rendered in our translation, but the words in the original are, Παθος *and* Παθημα, *which words are often translated by* passions.

Acts 1. 3. to whom he shewed himself alive after p.

PASSIONS.

Acts 14. 15. we also are men of like p. with you
Jam. 5. 17. Elias was a man subject to like p. as we

PASSOVER.

This word comes from the Hebrew *verb,* pasach, *which signifies* to pass, to leap, or skip over. *They gave the name of* Passover *to the feast which was established in commemoration of the coming forth out of* Egypt, *because the night before their departure, the destroying angel, who slew the first-born of the* Egyptians, *passed over the* Israelites, *because they were marked with the blood of the lamb which was killed the evening before; and which for this reason was called the* Paschal Lamb.

It *was typical of the justice of God's passing over and sparing such who are sprinkled with the blood of* Christ, 1 Cor. 5. 7. *As the destroying angel passed over the houses marked with the blood of the paschal lamb, so the wrath of God passes over them whose souls are sprinkled with the blood of* Christ. *As the paschal lamb was killed before* Israel *was delivered; so it was necessary Christ should suffer before we could be redeemed. It was killed before* Moses' *law, or* Aaron's *sacrifices, were enjoined; to shew, that deliverance comes to mankind by none of them, but only by the true* Passover, *that* Lamb of God, *slain from the foundation of the world,* Rom. 3. 25. Heb. 9. 14. *It was killed the first month of the year, which prefigured that* Christ *should suffer death in that month,* John 18. 28. *It was killed in the evening,* Exod. 12. 6. *So* Christ *suffered in the last days, and at that time of the day,* Mat. 27. 46. Heb. 1. 2. *At even also the sun sets, which shews, that it was the* Sun of righteousness *who was to suffer and die; and that at his passion universal darkness should be upon the whole earth.* Luke 23. 44. *The passover was roast with fire, to note the sharp and dreadful pains which* Christ *should suffer, not only from men, but from God also. It was to be eaten with bitter herbs,* Exod. 12. 8. *not only to put them in remembrance of their bitter bondage in* Egypt, *but also to testify our mortification to sin, and readiness to undergo afflictions for* Christ, *Col.* 1. 24. *and likewise to teach us the absolute necessity of true repentance in all that would profitably feed on* Christ.

Exod. 12. 11. it is Lord's p. ye shall eat it with your loins girded, 27. Lev. 23. 5. Num. 28. 16.
21. kill the p. || 43. this is the ordinance of the p.
Num. 9. 5. they kept the p. at even, Josh. 5. 10.
33. 3. on the morrow of the p. Josh. 5. 11.
Deut. 16. 2. thou shalt sacrifice the p. to Lord, 6.
5. thou mayest not sacrifice p. within thy gates
2 Kings 23. 22. was not holden such a p. from days of judges, nor in days of kings of Israel or Jud.
23. wherein this p. was holden to the Lord
2 Chr. 30. 15. then they killed p. in second month, 35. 1, 11. Ezra 6. 20. Mark 14. 12. Luke 22. 7.
18. yet did they eat p. otherwise than written
35. 1. Josiah kept a p. to Ld. 17. 19. Ezra 6. 19.
7. Josiah gave all for the p. offerings, 8, 9.
13. they roasted p. with fire, accord. to ordinance
Ezek. 45. 21. ye shall have p. a feast of seven days
Mat. 26. 17. where wilt thou that we prepare for thee to eat p.? Mark 14. 12. Luke 22. 8, 11.
19. disciples did as Jesus appointed them, and they made ready p. Mark 14. 16. Luke 22. 13.
Luke 22. 15. with desire I have desired to eat this p.
John 2. 13. and the Jews' p. was at hand, 11. 55.
23. now when he was in Jerusalem at the p.
11. 55. many went to Jerusalem before p. to purify
12. 1. Jesus came six days before p. to Bethany
18. 28. lest defiled, but that they might eat the p.
39. that I should release to you one at the p.
19. 14. and it was the preparation of the p.
1 Cor. 5. 7. Christ our p. is sacrificed for us
Heb. 11. 28. through faith he kept the p. lest he that
See Feast, Keep.

PASSOVERS.

2 Chron. 30. 17. Levites had charge of killing of p.

PAST.

Gen. 50. 4. days of mourning were p. 2 Sam. 11. 27.
Exod. 21. 29. if ox wont push with horn in time p. 36.
Num. 21. 22. go along, until we be p. thy borders
Deut. 2. 10. the Emims dwelt therein in times p.
4. 32. for ask now of the days which are p.
42. and hated him not in times p. 19. 4, 6.
1 Sam. 15. 32. Agag said, bitterness of death is p.
19. 7. he was in his presence as in times p.
2 Sam. 3. 17. ye sought for Dav. in time p. to be king
5. 2. also in time p. when Saul was king over us
16. 1. David was a little p. the top of the hill
1 Kings 18. 29. when mid-day was p. was no voice
1 Chron. 9. 20. Phinehas was ruler in time p.
Job 9. 10. which doeth great things p. finding out
14. 13. keep me in secret, until thy wrath be p.
17. 11. my days are p. my purposes broken off
29. 2. O that I were as in months p. in the days
Psal. 90. 4. years are but as yesterday when it is p.
Eccl. 3. 15. and God requireth that which is p.
Cant. 2. 11. for lo the winter is p. the rain is over
Jer. 8. 20. the harvest is p. the summer is ended
Mat. 14. 15. the time is now p. send them away
Mark 16. 1. and when the sabbath was p. Mary
Luke 9. 36. when the voice was p. Jesus was alone
Acts 12. 10. when they were p. first and second ward
14. 16. who in times p. suffered all nations to walk
27. 9. because the fast was now already p. Paul
Rom. 3. 25. his right. for remission of sins that are p.
11. 30. for as ye in times p. have not believed God
33. his judgments and his ways are p. finding out
2 Cor. 5. 17. old things p. away; all things are new
Gal. 1. 13. have heard of my conversation in time p.
23. he which persecuted us in times p. preacheth
5. 21. I tell you, as I have also told you in time p.
Eph. 2. 2. wherein in time p. ye walked after course
3. we all had our conversation in times p.
4. 19. who being p. feeling have given themselves
2 Tim. 2. 18. saying that resurrection is p. already
Philem. 11. who in time p. was to thee unprofitable
Heb. 1. 1. who spake in time p. to the fathers
11. 11. strength to conceive seed, when she was p.
1 Pet. 2. 10. which in time p. were not a people
4. 3. for the time p. of our life may suffice us
1 John 2. 8. because darkness is p. true light shineth
Rev. 9. 12. one woe is p. || 11. 14. the second woe is p.

PASTE.

2 Sam. 13. † 8. Tamar took p. and kneaded it

PASTOR, or SHEPHERD,

Signifies, *One who takes care of a flock of sheep, not only that they feed in good pasture, but also that they be not torn by wild beasts, or hurt any other way,* Gen. 47. 3. Luke 2. 8. It is spoken, [1] *Of God, who performs the office of a faithful shepherd to his people, by leading, feeding, preserving, and healing them,* Psal. 23. 1. [2] *Of Christ who not only exposed and adventured his life, but also willingly laid it down, for his sheep, and who takes the charge, care, and oversight of them, to dispense all things necessary for their welfare,* John 10. 11. 1 Pet. 2. 25. [3] *Of ministers of the gospel, who should feed their people with knowledge and understanding,* Jer. 3. 15. Eph. 4. 11. [4] *Of civil and political rulers,* Jer. 12. 10, 25. 34.

Jer. 17. 16. I have not hastened from being a p.

PASTORS.

Jer. 2. 8. p. also transgressed against me, and proph.
3. 15. I will give you p. according to mine heart
10. 21. for p. are become brutish, not sought Lord
12. 10. many p. have destroyed my vineyard
22. 22. wind shall eat up all thy p. and thy lovers
23. 1. woe to the p. that destroy and scatter sheep
2. thus saith Lord against p. that feed my sheep
Eph. 4. 11. and he gave some p. and teachers

PASTURE

Signifies, [1] *Unplowed land, kept for feeding of cattle,* 1 Chron. 4. 40. Job 39. 8. [2] *The land of* Canaan, *in which God placed his people, as sheep in a pasture,* Hos. 13. 6. [3] *All necessary and delightful provisions both for soul and body,* Psal. 23. 2. John 10. 9.

Gen. 47. 4. thy servants have no p. for their flocks
1 Chron. 4. 39. they went to seek p. for their flocks
40. they found fat p. || 41. because there was p.
Job 39. 8. the range of the mountains is his p.
Psal. 74. 1. thy anger smoke against sheep of thy p.
79. 13. so we sheep of thy p. will give thee thanks
95. 7. we are the people of his p. 100. 3.
Isa. 32. 14. a joy of wild asses, a p. of flocks
Jer. 23. 1. woe to pastors that scatter sheep of my p.
25. 36. for the Lord hath spoiled their p.
Lam. 1. 6. princes become like harts that find no p.
Ezek. 34. 14. I will feed them in a good p. a fat p.
18. seemeth it a small thing to have eaten good p.
31. ye my flock, flock of my p. are men, I God
Hos. 13. 6. according to their p. so were they filled
Joel 1. 18. beasts groan, because they have no p.
John 10. 9. he shall go in and out, and find p.

PASTURES.

1 Kings 4. 23. Solomon had twenty oxen out of p.
Psal. 23. 2. he maketh me to lie down in green p.
65. 12. they drop upon the p. of the wilderness
13. p. are clothed with flocks, valleys covered
Isa. 30. 23. in that day thy cattle shall feed in large p.
49. 9. and their p. shall be in all high places
Ezek. 34. 18. but ye tread down residue of your p.
45. 15. one lamb out of flock of fat p. of Israel
Joel 1. 19. for fire hath devoured p. of wilderness, 20.
2. 22. for the p. of the wilderness do spring

PATE.

Ps. 7. 16. his dealing shall come down upon own p.

PATERN. *See* Pattern.

PATH

Is spoken, (I.) *Of God, and* signifies, [1] *His precepts,* Psal. 17. 5. [2] *His dealings and dispensations,* Psal. 25. 10. [3] *The clouds which distil the rain,* Psal. 65. 11. (II.) *Of good men,* and signifies, [1] *Their holy conversation and good example,* Prov. 2. 20. [2] *The affairs they undertake,* Prov. 3. 6. [3] *Their actions and course of life,* Job 13. 27. | 33. 11. (III.) *Of wicked men, signifying their ungodly practices,* Isa. 59. 7.

Gen. 49. 17. Dan a serpent, an adder in p. that biteth
Num. 22. 24. the angel of the Lord stood in a p.
Job 28. 7. there is a p. which no fowl knoweth
30. 13. mar my p. they set forward my calamity
41. 32. he maketh a p. to shine after him
Psal. 16. 11. thou wilt shew me the p. of life
27. 11. teach me thy way, lead me in a plain p.
77. 19. thy way in sea, thy p. is in great waters
78. † 50. he weighed a p. to his anger
119. 35. make me to go in p. of thy commands
105. thy word is a lamp, and a light to my p.
139. 3. thou compassest my p. and lying down
142. 3. spirit overwhelmed, then thou knewest my p.
Prov. 1. 15. my son, refrain thy foot from their p.
2. 9. then thou shalt understand every good p.
4. 14. enter not into the p. of the wicked
18. the p. of the just is as the shining light
26. ponder the p. of thy feet, and let thy ways
5. 6. lest thou shouldest ponder the p. of life
Isa. 26. 7. thou dost weigh the p. of the just
30. 11. get ye out of the way, turn aside out of p.
40. 14. and taught him in the p. of judgment
43. 16. which maketh a p. in the mighty waters
Joel 2. 8. they shall walk every one in his p.

PATH-WAY.

Prov. 12. 28. in the p. thereof there is no death

PATHS.

Job 6. 18. the p. of their way are turned aside
8. 13. so are the p. of all that forget God
13. 27. thou lookest narrowly to all my p.
19. 8. he hath set darkness in my p.
24. 13. neither abide they in the p. thereof
33. 11. putteth my feet in stocks, marketh all my p.
38. 20. that thou shouldest keep the p. of house
Psal. 8. 8. whatsoever passeth thro' the p. of seas
17. 4. I have kept me from the p. of destroyer
5. hold up my goings in p. that footsteps slip not
23. 3. he leadeth me in the p. of righteousness
25. 4. shew me thy ways, O Lord, teach me thy p.
10. all the p. of the Lord are mercy and truth
65. 11. and thy p. drop fatness upon the pastures
Prov. 2. 8. he keepeth p. of judgment, and preserveth
13. who leave p. of uprightness to walk in darkn.
15. ways crooked, and they froward in their p.
18. and her p. incline unto the dead
19. neither take they hold of the p. of life
20. thou mayest keep the p. of the righteous
3. 6. he shall direct thy p. || 17. all her p. are peace
4. 11. I taught thee, I have led thee in right p.
7. 25. go not astray in her p. || 8. 2. in places of p.

Prov. 8. 20. I lead in the midst of the *p.* of judgm.
Isa. 2. 3. and we will walk in his *p.* *Mic.* 4. 2.
3. 12. they destroy the way of thy *p.*
42. 16. I will lead them in *p.* they have not known
58. 12. be called, the restorer of *p.* to dwell in
59. 7. wasting and destruction are in their *p.*
8. they have made them crooked *p.*
Jer. 6. 16. stand ye in the way, and ask for old *p.*
18. 15. from ancient *p.* to walk in *p.* in a way not
Lam. 3. 9. he hath made my *p.* crooked
Hos. 2. 6. I will make a wall, she shall not find *p.*
Mat. 3. 3. make his *p.* straight, *Mark* 1. 3. *Luke* 3. 4.
Heb. 12. 13. and make straight *p.* for your feet

PATIENCE

Signifies, [1] *That grace which enables us to bear afflictions and calamities with constancy and calmness of mind, and with a ready submission to the will of God,* Rom. 5. 3. 2 Tim. 3. 10. [2] *A bearing long with such as have greatly transgressed, expecting their reformation,* Mat. 18. 26, 29. [3] *An humble and submissive waiting for, and expectation of, eternal life, and the accomplishment of God's promises,* Rom. 8. 25. Heb. 10. 36. [4] *Perseverance,* James 5. 7, 9, 10.
Mat. 18. 26. servant worshipped him, saying, Lord have *p.* with me, and I will pay thee all, 29.
Luke 8. 15. are they who bring forth fruit with *p.*
21. 19. in your *p.* possess ye your souls
Rom. 5. 3. knowing that tribulation worketh *p.*
4. and *p.* experience, and experience hope
8. 25. we see not, then do we with *p.* wait for it
15. 4. that we thro' *p.* and comf. might have hope
5. the God of *p.* grant you to be like minded
2 *Cor.* 6. 4. ourselves as ministers of God in much *p.*
12. 12. signs were wrought among you in all *p.*
Col. 1. 11. strengthened with all might to all *p.*
1 *Thess.* 1. 3. remembering your *p.* of hope in Jesus
2 *Thess.* 1. 4. so that we glory in you for your *p.*
3. † 5. Lord direct your hearts into the *p.* of Christ
1 *Tim.* 6. 11. and follow after love, *p.* meekness
2 *Tim.* 3. 10. but thou hast fully known my *p.*
Tit. 2. 2. that aged men be sound in faith, in *p.*
Heb. 6. 12. who through faith and *p.* inherit promises
10. 36. ye have need of *p.* that after ye have done
12. 1. let us run with *p.* the race set before us
Jam. 1. 3. that the trying of your faith worketh *p.*
4. but let *p.* have her perfect work, that ye may
5. 7. behold, the husbandman hath long *p.* for it
10. for an exam. of *p.* ‖ 11. have heard of *p.* of Job
2 *Pet.* 1. 6. add to temperance *p.* to *p.* godliness
Rev. 1. 9. who am your companion in *p.* of Jesus
2. 2. I know thy *p.* 19. ‖ 3. and thou hast *p.*
3. 10. because thou hast kept word of my *p.*
13. 10. here is the *p.* of the saints, 14. 12.

PATIENT.

Eccl. 7. 8. *p.* in spirit is better than proud in spirit
Rom. 2. 7. who by *p.* continuance in well-doing
12. 12. rejoicing in hope, *p.* in tribulation
1 *Thess.* 5. 14. brethren, be *p.* toward all men
2 *Thess.* 3. 5. and into the *p.* waiting for Christ
1 *Tim.* 3. 3. not greedy of lucre, but *p.* 2 *Tim.* 2. 24.
Jam. 5. 7. be *p.* brethren ‖ 8. be ye also *p.*

PATIENTLY.

Psal. 37. 7. rest in the Lord, and wait *p.* for him
40. 1. I waited *p.* for the Lord, and he heard me
Acts 26. 3. wherefore I beseech thee to hear me *p.*
Heb. 6. 15. after he had *p.* endured, obtained prom.
1 *Pet.* 2. 20. if when ye be buffeted for faults ye take it *p.* but if ye do well and suffer, ye take it *p.*

PATRIARCH.

This name is given to the heads or princes of the family, chiefly to those that then lived before Moses, *as* Adam, Lamech, Noah, Shem, Phaleg, Heber, Abraham, Isaac, Jacob, Judah, Levi, *and the other sons of* Jacob, *and the heads of the twelve tribes. The* Hebrews *call them Princes of the tribes, or heads of the fathers,* Roshe Aboth. *The name* Patriarch *comes from the* Greek *word,* πατριαρχα, *which signifies* Head of a family.
Acts 2. 29. let me freely speak of the *p.* David
Heb. 7. 4. to whom the *p.* Abraham paid tithes

PATRIARCHS.

Acts 7. 8. and Jacob begat the twelve *p.*
9. *p.* moved with envy sold Joseph into Egypt

PATRIMONY.

Deut. 18. 8. beside that cometh of sale of his *p.*

PATTERN.

Exod. 25. 9. after the *p.* of all the instruments
40. look that thou make them after their *p.*
Num. 8. 4. the candlestick was made after the *p.*
Josh. 22. 28. behold the *p.* of the altar of the Lord
2 *Kings* 16. 10. Ahaz sent to Urijah the *p.* of altar
1 *Chr.* 28. 11. David gave Solomon *p.* 12, 18, 19.
Ezek. 43. 10. let them measure the *p.*
1 *Tim.* 1. 16. that in me first J. Christ might shew *p.*
Tit. 2. 7. shewing thyself a *p.* of good works
Heb. 8. 5. according to *p.* I shewed thee in mount

PATTERNS.

Heb. 9. 23. it was necessary that the *p.* of things

PAVED.

Exod. 24. 10. under his feet as it were a *p.* work
Cant. 3. 10. the midst thereof being *p.* with love

PAVEMENT.

2 *Kings* 16. 17. he put the sea on a *p.* of stones
2 *Chron.* 7. 3. all Israel bowed themselves upon *p.*
Esth. 1. 6. the beds were on a *p.* of red and blue
Ezek. 40. 17. there were chambers and a *p.* made for the court, thirty chambers were upon the *p.*
18. *p.* by the side of the gates, was the lower *p.*
42. 3. over against *p.* was gallery against gallery
John 19. 13. Pilate sat in a place called the *p.*

PAVILION, S.

2 *Sam.* 22. 12. he made darkness his *p.* *Psal.* 18. 11.
1 *Kings* 20. 12. Benhadad and kings drinking in *p.*
16. Benhadad was drinking himself drunk in *p.*
Psal. 27. 5. in secret of his tab. he shall hide me in *p.*
31. 20. thou shalt keep them secretly in a *p.*
Jer. 43. 10. Nebuchadnezzar spread his royal *p.*

PAW.

1 *Sam.* 17. 37. Lord delivered me out of *p.* of the lion

PAWS.

Lev. 11. 27. whatsoever goeth on *p.* these are unclean

PAWETH.

Job 39. 21. the horse *p.* in the valley and rejoiceth

PAY.

Exod. 21. 19. only he shall *p.* for loss of his time
22. and he shall *p.* as the judges determine
36. he shall surely *p.* ox for ox, the dead his own
22. 7. if thief be found, let him *p.* double, 9.
17. he shall *p.* according to the dowry of virgins
Num. 20. 19. if I drink thy water I will *p.* for it
Deut. 23. 21. shall vow a vow, shall not slack to *p.*
2 *Sam.* 15. 7. let me go and *p.* my vow in Hebron
1 *Kings* 20. 39. else thou shalt *p.* a talent of silver
2 *Kings* 4. 7. he said, go sell oil, and *p.* thy debt
2 *Chron.* 8. 8. them did Solomon make to *p.* tribute
27. 5. so much did children of Ammon *p.* to him
Ezra 4. 13. then will they not *p.* toll and custom
Esth. 3. 9. I will *p.* 10,000 talents of silver, 4. 7.
Job 22. 27. shalt make prayer, and shalt *p.* thy vows
Psal. 22. 25. I will *p.* my vows, 66. 13. | 116. 14, 18.
50. 14. and *p.* thy vows to the Most High
76. 11. vow and *p.* to the Lord your God
Prov. 19. 17. that he hath given, will he *p.* again
22. 27. if hast nothing to *p.* why should he take
Eccl. 5. 4. defer not to *p.* it, *p.* that hast vowed
5. not vow, than thou shouldest vow and not *p.*
Jonah 2. 9. I will *p.* that which I have vowed
Mat. 17. 24. doth not your master *p.* tribute?
18. 25. had not to *p.* he forgave him, *Luke* 7. 42.
26. I will *p.* thee all, 29. ‖ 28. *p.* that thou owest
30. but cast into prison, till he should *p.* debt
34. till he should *p.* all that was due to him
23. 23. for ye *p.* tithe of mint, anise, and cummin
Rom. 13. 6. for this cause *p.* ye tribute also

PAYED, or PAID.

Ezra 4. 20. toll, tribute, and custom, was *p.* them
Prov. 7. 14. peace-offerings, this day have I *p.* vows
Jonah 1. 3. so he *p.* fare thereof, and went into it
Mat. 5. 26. thou shalt not come out thence till thou hast *p.* the uttermost farthing, *Luke* 12. 59.
Heb. 7. 9. Levi, who received tithes, *p.* tithes in Abr.

PAYETH.

Psal. 37. 21. the wicked borroweth and *p.* not

PAYMENT.

Mat. 18. 25. all to be sold, and *p.* to be made

PEACE.

Mark. 4. 39. he arose and said to the sea, *p.* be still

PEACE.

This word is used in the Scripture in different ways, as, (I.) *There is peace, or reconciliation with God:* [1] *By satisfaction for sins committed against him: this is done by the sufferings and merits of Christ,* Eph. 2. 14. (II.) *There is peace with ourselves or our own consciences: this arises from a sense of our reconciliation to God, which is the gift of* Christ, *and wrought in us by his Spirit,* Rom. 14. 17. Phil. 4. 7. [2] *Submission to the will of God,* Job 22. 21. (III.) *Peace with men;* [1] *Mutual concord and agreement with Christian brethren,* Psal. 34. 14. Gal. 5. 22. [2] *Deliverance or safety from such as are our enemies,* Prov. 16. 7.
Peace *is opposed to war, when a state or kingdom enjoys a public tranquillity, when they are free from foreign and civil wars,* 2 Kings 20. 19. *It is likewise taken for the public tranquillity, and quiet state of the church, when it is not troubled within, by schisms and heresies, or without, by persecuting tyrants, filling all with tumults, slaughters, and bloody wars,* Psal. 122. 6. Acts 9. 31. Rev. 6. 4. *Sometimes it signifies a league or covenant between one prince and another,* 1 Kings 5. 12. *and sometimes only a cessation of hostilities,* Judg. 4. 17. *The apostle* Paul, *in the titles of his epistles, generally wisheth for grace and peace to the faithful to whom he writes,* Rom. 1. 7. 1 Cor. 1. 3. *This is both a christian salutation, and an apostolical ministerial benediction: that is, I wish that the free, undeserved love and favour of God, and a lively sense thereof in your souls, may be continued to, and increased in, you; and that as a fruit of this, you may enjoy all blessings, both inward and outward, especially peace of conscience, and a secure enjoyment of the love of God. Lastly,* peace *is put for that perfect rest, joy, and felicity, which the saints enjoy in heaven, where they are out of the reach of enemies, to disturb or molest them,* Isa. 57. 2. 2 Pet. 3. 14.
Gen. 29. † 6. he said to them, is there *p.* to him?
37. † 14. go see the *p.* of thy brethren
41. 16. God shall give Pharaoh an answer of *p.*
Exod. 18. † 7. they asked each other of their *p.*
Lev. 26. 6. I will give *p.* in land, none make afraid
Num. 6. 26. Lord lift up counten. and give thee *p.*
25. 12. behold, I give to him my covenant of *p.*
Deut. 2. 26. sent a messeng. to Sihon with words of *p.*
20. 10. when comest nigh city, proclaim *p.* to it
11. if it make thee answer of *p.* and open to thee
12. if it will make no *p.* with thee, then besiege
23. 6. thou shalt not seek their *p.* nor prosperity
29. 19. I shall have *p.* though walk in imag. of heart
Judg. 4. 17. there was *p.* between Jabin and Heber
6. † 24. Gideon called the altar, the Lord sent *p.*
18. † 15. they came and asked the Levite of *p.*
1 *Sam.* 7. 14. there was *p.* between Isr. and Amorites
10. † 4. they will ask of thee *p.* and give thee loaves
17. † 22. David came and asked his brethren of *p.*
20. 7. if he say, it is well, servant shall have *p.*
21. come thou, for there is *p.* to thee, no hurt
25. † 5. go and ask Nabal, of *p.* in my name
1 *Kings* 2. 33. but on his throne shall there be *p.*
4. 24. Solomon had *p.* on all sides round about
5. 12. there was *p.* between Hiram and Solomon
20. 18. whether they be come for *p.* take them alive
2 *Kings* 9. 17. and let him say, is it *p.* Jehu? 18.
19. what hast thou to do with *p.*? turn, 22.
22. what *p.* so long as her witchcrafts are so many?
31. she said, had Zimri *p.* who slew his master?
20. 19. is it not good, if *p.* be in my days? *Isa.* 39. 8.
1 *Chr.* 22. 9. I will give *p.* to Israel in his days
2 *Chr.* 15. 5. in those times there was no *p.* to him
Ezra 4. 17. and to the rest beyond the river, *p.*
5. 7. to Darius king, all *p.* ‖ 7. 12. to Ezra perf. *p.*
Ezra 9. 12. nor seek their *p.* or their wealth for ever
Esth. 2. † 11. Mordecai walked to know *p.* of Esther
9. 30. Mord. sent letters with words of *p.* and truth
10. 3. Mordecai speaking *p.* to all his seed
Job 5. 23. beasts of field shall be at *p.* with thee
21. † 9. houses are *p.* from fear, nor rod on them
22. 21. acquaint thyself with him, and be at *p.*
25. 2. he maketh *p.* in his high places
Psal. 7. 4. if I have evil to him that was at *p.* with
28. 3. which speak *p.* to neighbours, but mischief
29. 11. the Lord will bless his people with *p.*
34. 14. do good, seek *p.* and pursue it, 1 *Pet.* 3. 11.
35. 20. they speak not *p.* but they devise matters
37. 11. meek delight themselves in abundance of *p.*
37. for the end of the upright man is *p.*
41. † 9. man of my *p.* hath lift up heel against me
55. 20. put forth against such as be at *p.* with him
72. 3. the mountains shall bring *p.* to the people
7. in days abundance of *p.* so long as moon endur.
85. 8. he will speak *p.* to his people and his saints
10. righteousness and *p.* have kissed each other
119. 165. great *p.* have they which love thy law
120. 6. hath long dwelt with him that hateth *p.*
7. I am for *p.* but when I speak they are for war
122. 6. pray for *p.* of Jerusalem, prosper that love
125. 5. but *p.* shall be upon Israel
128. 6. yea, thou shalt see *p.* upon Israel
147. 14. he maketh *p.* in thy borders, and filleth
Prov. 3. 17. wisdom's ways pleasantness, and paths *p.*
12. 20. but to the counsellors of *p.* is joy
16. 7. he maketh his enemies to be at *p.* with him
Eccl. 3. 8. a time of war, and a time of *p.*
Isa. 9. 6. Prince of *p.* ‖ 7. increase of his *p.* no end
26. 12. Lord, thou wilt ordain *p.* for us, for thou
27. 5. he make *p.* with me, and he shall make *p.*
32. 17. the work of righteousness shall be *p.*
33. 7. the ambassadors of *p.* shall weep bitterly
38. 17. behold, for *p.* I had great bitterness
45. 7. make *p.* and create evil, I do all these things
48. 18. then had thy *p.* been as river, righteousness
22. there is no *p.* to the wicked, 57. 21.
52. 7. feet of him that publisheth *p.* *Nah.* 1. 15.
53. 5. the chastisement of our *p.* was upon him
54. 10. nor shall covenant of my *p.* be removed
13. and great shall be the *p.* of thy children
55. 12. ye shall go out with joy, led forth with *p.*
57. 2. he shall enter into *p.* they shall rest in beds
19. I create the fruit of the lips, *p.* *p.* to him
59. 8. the way of *p.* they know not, *Rom.* 3. 17.
60. 17. I will make thine officers *p.* and exactors
66. 12. behold, I will extend *p.* to her like river
Jer. 4. 10. ye shall have *p.* whereas sword reaches
6. 14. saying, *p.* *p.* when there is no *p.* 8. 11.
8. 15. we looked for *p.* but no good came, 14. 19.
12. 5. if in land of *p.* they wearied thee, then
12. for sword shall devour, no flesh shall have *p.*
14. 13. but I will give you assured *p.* in this place
15. † 5. who shall go aside to ask of thy *p.*
16. 5. I have taken away my *p.* from this people
20. † 10. every man of *p.* watched for my halting
28. 9. the prophet which prophesied of *p.*
29. 7. and seek *p.* of the city whither I caused
11. I think toward you thoughts of *p.* not evil
30. 5. we have heard a voice of fear, and not of *p.*
33. 6. reveal to them abundance of *p.* and truth
38. † 22. men of thy *p.* have prevailed against thee
Lam. 3. 17. thou hast removed my soul far from *p.*
Ezek. 7. 25. they shall seek *p.* there shall be none
13. 10. saying *p.* and there was no *p.* 16.
34. 25. will make with them a covenant of *p.* 37. 26.
Dan. 8. 25. and by *p.* he shall destroy many
Obad. 7. men at *p.* with thee have deceived thee
Mic. 3. 5. that bite with their teeth and cry *p.*
5. 5. this man shall be *p.* when Assyrian come
Hag. 2. 9. and in this place I will give *p.* saith Lord
Zech. 6. 13. the counsel of *p.* be between them both
8. 10. nor was there any *p.* to him that came in
† 12. for seed shall be of *p.* vine give her fruit
16. execute judgment of truth and *p.* ‖ 19. love *p.*
9. 10. and he shall speak *p.* to the heathen
Mal. 2. 5. my covenant was with him of life and *p.*
Mat. 10. 13. and if house be worthy, let your *p.* come upon it; if not, let your *p.* return to you
34. think not that I am come to send *p.* on earth
Mark 9. 50. and have *p.* one with another
Luke 1. 79. to guide our feet into the way of *p.*
2. 14. and on earth *p.* good will toward men
10. 6. if son of *p.* be there, your *p.* shall rest on it
12. 51. that I am come to give *p.* on the earth?
14. 32. he sendeth and desireth conditions of *p.*
19. 38. *p.* in heaven, and glory in the highest
42. if known the things that belong to thy *p.*
John 14. 27. *p.* I leave with you, my *p.* I give you
16. 33. that in me ye might have *p.* in world trib.
Acts 10. 36. preaching *p.* by Jesus Chr. he L. of all
12. 20. having made Blastus their friend desired *p.*
Rom. 1. 7. *p.* from God the Father, 1 *Cor.* 1. 3. 2 *Cor.* 1. 2. *Gal.* 1. 3. *Eph.* 1. 2. *Phil.* 1. 2.
2. 10. but *p.* to every man that worketh good
5. 1. justified, we have *p.* with God, through Christ
8. 6. but to be spiritually minded is life and *p.*
10. 15. feet of them that preach the gospel of *p.*
14. 17. for the kingdom of God is joy and *p.*
19. let us follow the things that make for *p.*
15. 13. fill you with all joy and *p.* in believing
1 *Cor.* 7. 15. but God hath called us to *p.*
14. 33. but author of *p.* as in churches of saints
Gal. 5. 22. the fruit of the Spirit is love, joy, *p.*
Eph. 2. 14. for he is our *p.* ‖ 15. so making *p.*
17. Christ came and preached *p.* to you afar off
4. 3. to keep unity of the Spirit in the bond of *p.*
6. 15. feet shod with preparation of gospel of *p.*
Phil. 4. 7. *p.* of God, which passeth understanding
Col. 1. 2. grace and *p.* from God our Father, 1 *Thess.* 1. 1. 2 *Thess.* 1. 2. 1 *Tim.* 1. 2. 2 *Tim.* 1. 2. *Tit.* 1. 4. *Philem.* 3. 2 *John* 3.
3. 15. let the *p.* of God rule in your hearts
1 *Thess.* 5. 3. for when they shall say *p.* and safety
13. and be at *p.* among yourselves
2 *Thess.* 3. 16. now Lord of *p.* give you *p.* always
2 *Tim.* 2. 22. follow *p.* with all men, *Heb.* 12. 14.
Heb. 7. 2. the king of Salem, that is, king of *p.*

Heb. 11. 31. Rahab believed and received spies in p.
Jam. 3. 18. is sown in p. of them that make p.?
Rev. 1. 4. p. from him that is, was, and is to come
6. 4. power was given to him to take p. from earth

PEACE be.

Gen. 43. 23. and he said, p. be to you, fear not
Judg. 6. 23. the Lord said, p. be to thee, fear not
19. 20. and the old man said, p. be with thee
1 Sam. 25. 6. p. be to thee, p. be to house, p. be to all
2 Sam. 18. † 28. Ahimaaz said, p. be to thee
1 Chr. 12. 18. p. be to thee, and p. be to thy helpers
Psal. 122. 7. p. be within thy walls, and prosperity
8. I will now say, p. be within thee
Dan. 4. 1. p. be multiplied to you, 6. 25. 1 Pet. 1. 2. 2 Pet. 1. 2. Jude 2.
10. 19. p. be to thee, be strong, yea, be strong
Luke 10. 5. first say, p. be to this house
24. 36. he saith, p. be to you, John 20. 19, 21, 26.
Gal. 6. 16. p. be on them, and mercy on Isr. of God
Eph. 6. 23. p. be to brethren, and love with faith
1 Pet. 5. 14. p. be with you all that are in Christ
3 John 14. p. be to thee, our friends salute thee

God of PEACE.

Rom. 15. 33. the God of p. be with you all, amen
16. 20. the God of p. shall bruise Satan shortly
2 Cor. 13. 11. God of p. shall be with you, Phil. 4. 9.
1 Thess. 5. 23. very God of p. sanctify you wholly
Heb. 13. 20. now the God of p. make you perfect
See Held, Hold.

In PEACE.

Gen. 26. 29. and we have sent thee away in p.
31. and they departed from Isaac in p.
28. 21. so that I come to my father's house in p.
44. 17. as for you, get you up in p. to your father
Josh. 10. 21. came to Joshua, at Makkedah, in p.
Judg. 8. 9. when I come again in p. will break down
11. 31. when I return in p. whatever meet me
2 Sam. 3. 21. Abner went in p. 22. ‖ 23. he is gone in p.
15. 27. return to the city in p. and your two sons
17. 3. so all the people shall be in p.
19. 24. king departed, until the day he came in p.
30. as my lord the king is come again in p.
1 Kings 2. 5. Joab shed the blood of war in p.
22. 17. return every man in p. 2 Chron. 18. 16.
27. in prison until I come in p. 2 Chron. 18. 26.
28. if thou return at all in p. 2 Chron. 18. 27.
2 Kings 22. 20. behold therefore shalt be gathered to thy grave in p. not see evil, 2 Chron. 34. 28.
2 Chron. 19. 1. and Jehoshaphat returned in p.
Job 5. 24. shalt know thy tabernacle shall be in p.
Psal. 4. 8. I will lay me down in p. and sleep
55. 18. he hath delivered my soul in p. from the batt.
Prov. 13. † 13. feareth commandment shall be in p.
Isa. 26. 3. thou wilt keep him in perfect p.
41. † 3. he pursued them, and passed in p.
Jer. 29. 7. in the p. thereof shall ye have peace
34. 5. but thou shalt die in p. they will lament
Mal. 2. 6. he walked with me in p. and equity
Luke 2. 29. now lettest thou thy servant depart in p.
11. 21. keepeth his palace his goods are in p.
1 Cor. 16. 11. but conduct him forth in p. may come
2 Cor. 13. 11. be perfect, be of one mind, live in p.
Jam. 2. 16. depart in p. be ye warmed and filled
3. 18. the fruit of righteousness is sown in p.
2 Pet. 3. 14. that ye may be found of him in p.
See Go, Made, Offerings.

PEACEABLE.

Gen. 34. 21. saying, these men are p. with us
2 Sam. 20. 19. I am one of them that are p. in Israel
1 Chron. 4. 40. the land was wide, quiet, and p.
22. † 9. a man of rest, for his name shall be p.
Isa. 32. 18. my people dwell in a p. habitation
Jer. 25. 37. the p. habitations are cut down
1 Tim. 2. 2. that we may lead a quiet and p. life
Heb. 12. 11. it yieldeth the p. fruit of righteousness
Jam. 3. 17. wisdom from above is pure, p. gentle

PEACEABLY.

Gen. 37. 4. they could not speak p. to him
Judg. 11. 13. therefore restore those lands again p.
21. 13. send some to call p. to the Benjamites
1 Sam. 16. 4. com. thou p.? ‖ 5. he said, p. 1 Kings 2. 13.
2 Sam. 3. † 27. Joab took Abner aside to speak p.
1 Chron. 12. 17. if ye be come p. to me, to help me
Jer. 9. 8. one speaketh p. to his neighbour
Dan. 11. 21. he shall come in p. and obtain, 24.
Rom. 12. 18. if possible, live p. with all men

PEACE-MAKERS.

Mat. 5. 9. blessed are p. for they shall be children

PEACOCKS.

1 Kings 10. 22. navy came, bringing p. 2 Chr. 9. 21.
Job 39. 13. gavest thou the goodly wings to p.?

PEARL

Is a gem or jewel found in a testaceous fish. The finest pearls are fished up in the Persian gulf, now called the sea of Catif. They fish for them also in the island of Kis, and upon the coast of Bahrein, so called from the city of that name, which lies upon the borders of Arabia. Idumæa, and Palestine, being not far from this sea, it is not to be wondered at, that Pearls were so well known to Job and the Hebrews, Job 28. 18.

Christ Jesus forbids his apostles to cast their pearls before swine, Mat. 7. 6. That is to say, expose not the sacred truths and mysteries of the gospel to the raillery of profane libertines and hardened atheists: preach not the gospel to those that persecute you for your message; and apply not the promises to the profane. The transcendent excellency of Christ and his grace made known and offered in the gospel, is compared to a pearl of great price, Mat. 13. 46. And the glorious state of the saints in heaven, which will yield unspeakable satisfaction to such as shall be admitted into them, is shadowed out by pearls, and other rich things in the world, which please the outward senses, Rev. 21. 19.

Mat. 13. 46. when he found one p. of great price
Rev. 21. 21. every several gate was of one p.

PEARLS.

Job 28. 18. no mention shall be made of coral or p.
Mat. 7. 6. neither cast ye your p. before swine
Mat. 13. 45. like a merchant-man seeking goodly p.
1 Tim. 2. 9. not with gold, or p. or costly array
Rev. 17. 4. the woman was decked with gold and p.
18. 12. no man buyeth the merchandise of p. 16.
21. 21. and the twelve gates were twelve p.

PECULIAR.

Exod. 19. 5. then ye shall be a p. treasure to me
Deut. 14. 2. to be a p. people, 26. 18. 1 Pet. 2. 9.
Ps. 135. 4. Lord hath chosen Israel for his p. treas.
Eccl. 2. 8. I gathered the p. treasure of kings
Tit. 2. 14. that he might purify to himself p. people

PEDIGREE, S.

Num. 1. 18. they declared their p. after their families
Ezra 2. † 59. could not shew their p. Neh. 7. † 61.
Heb. 7. † 3. without father, mother, without p.
† 6. he whose p. is not counted from them

PEELED.

Isa. 18. 2. go ye to a nation scattered and p. 7.
Ezek. 29. 18. head bald, and every shoulder was p.

PEEP.

Isa. 8. 19. to wizards that p. and that mutter

PEEPED.

Isa. 10. 14. none that opened the mouth or p.

PELICAN.

Lev. 11. 18. swan and p. unclean, Deut. 14. 17.
Psal. 102. 6. I am like a p. of the wilderness
Isa. 34. † 11. the p. shall possess it, Zeph. 2. † 14.

PEN.

Judg. 5. 14. of Zebulun, they that handle the p.
Job 19. 24. they were graven with an iron p.
Psal. 45. 1. my tongue is the p. of a ready writer
Isa. 8. 1. take a roll, and write in it with a man's p.
Jer. 8. 8. he made it p. of the scribes is in vain
17. 1. the sin of Judah is written with a p. of iron
3 John 13. I will not with ink and p. write to thee

PENCE.

Mat. 18. 28. one who owed him an hundred p.
Mark 14. 5. sold for more than 300 p. John 12. 5.
Luke 7. 41. the one owed 500 p. the other fifty
10. 35. on morrow he took out two p. and gave

PENKNIFE.

Jer. 36. 23. Jehudi cut roll with a p. and cast it

PENTECOST.

This word is derived from the Greek word Πεντεκοστη, which signifies the fiftieth, because the feast of Pentecost was celebrated the fiftieth day after the sixteenth of Nisan, which was the second day of the feast of the passover. The Hebrews call it the Feast of Weeks, Exod. 34. 22. because it was kept seven weeks after the passover.

On the sixteenth day of the month Nisan, or March, the wave-offering of the first sheaf was to be made, to implore the divine blessing upon the ensuing harvest, which began about that time; that climate being so much warmer and forwarder than ours. And fifty days being allowed with that for the getting in all their corn; that is, the remaining fifteen in Nisan, (March,) and twenty-nine in Jair or Zif, (April,) the sixth of Sivan (May) would be the day of Pentecost: when they were to hold the solemn festival of thanksgiving, for their participation of the harvest, together with a grateful commemoration of their being delivered from Egyptian servitude, and enjoying their property, by reaping the fruits of their labours, Lev. 23. 10, 11, &c. The learned have observed, that the very day of Pentecost was the same day on which God delivered the law from mount Sinai, Exod. 19. 11. as it was that, on which the apostles were filled with the Holy Ghost, and the gospel was attended with remarkable success, Acts 2. 1.

Acts 2. 1. when the day of p. was fully come
20. 16. he hasted to be at Jerusalem the day of p.
1 Cor. 16. 8. but I will tarry at Ephesus until p.

PENURY.

Prov. 14. 23. talk of the lips tendeth only to p.
Luke 21. 4. but she of her p. hath cast in all she had

PENNY.

Mat. 20. 2. when had agreed with labourers for a p.
9. when they came, they received every man a p.
13. friend, didst thou not agree with me for a p.?
22. 19. and they brought unto him a p.
Mark 12. 15. he said, bring me a p. Luke 20. 24.
Rev. 6. 6. I heard a voice say, a measure of wheat for a p. and three measures of barley for a p.

PENNY-worth.

Mark 6. 37. and buy two hundred p.-worth of bread
John 6. 7. two hundred p.-worth is not sufficient

PEOPLE

Signifies, [1] The whole body of persons that make up a nation, being governed by a certain magistrate, and regulated by the same laws, Gen. 41. 40. 1 Sam. 15. 30. [2] Godly progenitors and forefathers departed this life, Gen. 25. 8. Deut. 32. 50. [3] The vulgar, or inferior sort of persons in a city, or nation, Mark 12. 37. Luke 23. 14. [4] Jacob's children and posterity, Gen. 50. 20. [5] The Gentiles, Psal. 117. 1. [6] Both Jews and Gentiles, Luke 2. 10. [7] The army, or soldiers of the Romans, Dan. 9. 26. It is also applied to unreasonable creatures, Prov. 30. 25.

Gen. 27. 29. let p. serve thee, and nations bow to thee
48. 19. he also shall become a p. and be great
Exod. 6. 7. I will take you to me for a p. and be to you a God, Deut. 4. 20. 2 Sam. 7. 24. Jer. 13. 11.
33. 3. thou art a stiff-necked p. 5. ‖ 34. 9. Deut. 9. 6.
Lev. 20. 24. I separated you from other p. 26.
Num. 21. 29. thou art undone, O p. of Chemosh
22. 5. behold, there is a p. come out from Egypt, 11.
25. 15. he was head over a p. in Midian
Deut. 4. 33. did ever p. hear voice of God out of fire?
7. 6. L. thy God hath chosen thee to be a special p.
14. 2. the Lord hath chosen thee to be a peculiar p.
20. 1. a p. more than thou, be not afraid of them
28. 32. thy sons shall be given to another p.
29. 13. that he may establish thee for p. to himself
32. 21. will move them with those that are not a p.
33. 29. who is like to thee, O p. saved by Lord?
Ruth 1. 15. thy sister is gone back to her p.
1 Sam. 2. 24. ye make the Lord's p. to transgress
1 Sam. 5. 10. brought ark to us, to slay us and our p
11. let it go, that it slay us not, and our p.
2 Sam. 7. 23. whom God went to redeem for a p.
22. 28. afflicted p. thou wilt save, Psal. 18. 27.
44. a p. I knew not shall serve me, Psal. 18. 43.
1 Kings 22. 28. hearken, O p. every one of you
2 Kings 11. 17. shalt be Lord's p. 2 Chr. 23. 16.
1 Chr. 16. 20. they went from nation to nation, from one kingdom to another p. Psal. 105. 13.
19. 13. let us behave ourselves valiantly for our p.
2 Chron. 1. 9. thou hast made me king over a p.
Esth. 1. 22. for he sent letters to every p. after their language, 3. 12. ‖ 8. 9. Neh. 13 24.
2. 10. Esther had not shewed her p. nor kindred
3. 8. there is a certain p. scattered abroad
4. 8. go in to make request before him for her p.
Job 36. 20. when p. are cut off in their place
Psal. 62. 8. ye p. pour out your hearts before him
66. 8. bless our God, ye p. ‖ 95. 10. a p. that do err
114. 1. went out from a p. of a strange language
144. 15. happy is that p. ‖ 148. 14. a p. near to him
Prov. 14. 34. but sin is a reproach to any p.
28. 15. so is a wicked ruler over the poor p.
30. 25. ants are a p. not strong, yet prepare meat
Isa. 1. 4. a p. laden with iniquity, a seed of evil doers
10. give ear to the law, ye p. of Gomorrah
7. 8. Ephraim shall be broken, that it be not a p.
8. 19. should not a p. seek unto their God?
27. 11. for it is a p. of no understanding, therefore
30. 9. write, that this is a rebellious p. 65. 2.
43. 4. therefore I will give p. for thy life
8. bring forth the blind p. that have eyes
65. 3. a p. that provoketh me to anger to my face
18. I create Jerusalem a rejoicing, and her p. a joy
Jer. 6. 22. a p. cometh from the north, 50. 41.
48. 42. Moab shall be destroyed from being a p.
Lam. 1. 7. her p. fell into the hand of the enemy
Hos. 4. 9. and there shall be like p. like priest
9. 1. rejoice not, O Israel, for joy as other p.
Jonah 1. 8. tell us, of what p. art thou?
Mic. 4. 1. it shall be exalted, and p. shall flow unto it
Zech. 8. 20. there shall come p. and inhabitants
Luke 1. 17. to make ready a p. prepared for Lord
Acts 15. 14. to take out of them a p. for his name
Rom. 10. 19. provoke to jeal. by them that are no p.
Tit. 2. 14. he might purify to himself a peculiar p.
Heb. 8. 10. to them a God, and they shall be to me a p.
1 Pet. 2. 9. but ye are a peculiar p. to shew forth
10. p. of God, in time past were not a p. now
Rev. 5. 9. thou hast redeemed us out of every p.

All PEOPLE.

Exod. 19. 5. ye shall be a peculiar treasure above all p. Deut. 7. 6, 14. ‖ 10. 15. Psal. 99. 2.
Deut. 7. 7. for ye were the fewest of all p.
28. 64. the Lord shall scatter thee among all p.
1 Kings 4. 34. came of all p. to hear wisdom of Sol.
8. 43. all p. may know thy name, 2 Chron. 6. 33.
9. 7. shall be a proverb and by-word among all p.
Esth. 3. 8. and their laws are diverse from all p.
14. copy of writing was published to all p. 8. 13.
9. 2. for the fear of them fell upon all p.
Ps. 47. 1. O clap your hands, all ye p. shout to G.
96. 3. declare his wonders among all p.
117. 1. O praise L. all ye nations, praise him, all ye p. for his kindness, 148. 11. Rom. 15. 11.
Isa. 25. 6. Lord make to all p. a feast of fat things
7. the face of the covering cast over all p.
56. 7. my house be called house of prayer for all p.
Lam. 1. 11. all her p. sigh, they seek bread
18. hear, I pray you, all p. behold, Mic. 1. 2.
Dan. 5. 19. all p. and nations feared before him
7. 14. that all p. and nations should serve him
Mic. 4. 5. all p. will walk each in name of his god
Hab. 2. 5. because he heapeth unto him all p.
Zeph. 3. 20. make you a praise among all p. of earth
Zech. 12. 3. make Jeru. a burdensome stone for all p.
Luke 2. 10. tidings of joy, which shall be to all p.
31. thou hast prepared before the face of all p.

All the PEOPLE.

Gen. 19. 4. all the p. of Sodom compass. Lot's house
35. 6. Jacob came to Luz, he and all the p. with him
42. 6. Joseph, he it was that sold to all the p. of Eg.
Exod. 11. 8. get thee out, and all t. p. that follow thee
18. 14. all the p. stand by thee from morn. to evening
21. thou shalt provide out of all the p. able men
19. 8. all the p. answered together and said, 24. 3.
11. Lord will come down in sight of all the p.
20. 18. all the p. saw thunderings and lightnings
Lev. 9. 23. glory of the Lord appeared to all the p.
10. 3. and before all the p. I will be glorified
Num. 11. 29. that all the Lord's p. were prophets
13. 32. and all t. p. we saw are men of great stature
15. 26. seeing all the p. were in ignorance
Deut. 13. 9. afterwards the hand of all the p. 17. 7.
17. 13. all t. p. shall hear and fear, and do no more
27. 15. all the p. shall say, amen, 16, 17, 18, 19, 20, 21.
28. 10. all the p. of the earth shall see that thou
Josh. 4. 24. that all the p. of the earth might know
5. 4. all the p. that came out were circumcised, 5.
6. 5. all the p. shall shout ‖ 7. 3. let not all the p. go
24. 18. Lord drave out from before us all the p.
Judg. 16. 30. the house fell upon all the p. therein
20. 8. and all the p. arose as one man, saying
1 Sam. 10. 24. there is none like him among all the p.
11. 4. all the p. wept ‖ 12. 18. all the p. feared greatly
30. 6. because the soul of all the p. was grieved
2 Sam. 2. 28. all the p. stood, and pursued no more
3. 32. king wept at Abner's grave, and all p. wept, 34.
36. and all the p. took notice of it, it pleased
17. 3. and I will bring back all the p. unto thee, so all the p. shall be in peace
19. 9. and all the p. were at strife through all Isr
20. 22. woman went to all the p. in her wisdom
1 Kings 8. 53. didst separate them from all the p.
60. that all the p. of the earth may know that
20. 10. not suffice for handfuls for all the p.
2 Kings 23. 3. and all the p. stood to the covenant
1 Chron. 16. 36. and all the p. said, amen, and praised
28. 21. all the p. will be wholly at thy command
2 Chron. 7. 4. king and all the p. offered sacrifices
Ezra 7. 25. set judges, which may judge all the p.

Neh. 8. 5. in sight of *all the p.* for he was above *all p.*
11. so the Levites stilled *all the p.* saying, hold
Psal. 67. 3. O God, let *all the p.* praise thee, 5.
97. 6. heavens declare right. and *all p.* see his glory
106. 48. blessed be L. God, let *all the p.* say, amen
Eccl. 4. 16. there is no end of *all the p.* even of all
Jer. 26. 8. L. commanded him to speak to *all the p.*
9. *all the p.* were gathered against Jeremiah
34. 1. and *all the p.* fought against Jerusalem
8. Zedekiah made a covenant with *all the p.* 10.
38. 4. thus he weakeneth the hands of *all the p.*
43. 4. *all the p.* obeyed not the voice of the Lord
Ezek. 31. 12. *all the p.* are gone from his shadow
Dan. 3. 7. when *all the p.* heard the sound of cornet
Zech. 11. 10. break my covenant I made with *all t. p.*
12. 2. Jerusalem a cup of trembling to *all the p.*
14. 12. the Lord will smite *all the p.* that fought
Mal. 2. 9. I also made you base before *all the p.*
Luke 8. 47. she declared unto him before *all the p.*
13. 17. *all the p.* rejoiced for the glorious things
18. 43. *all the p.* when they saw, gave praise to God
19. 48. *all the p.* were very attentive to hear him
20. 6. but if we say, of men, *all the p.* will stone us
Acts 2. 47. and having favour with *all the p.*
5. 34. Gamaliel had in reputation among *all the p.*
10. 41. not to *all the p.* but unto witnesses chosen
13. 24. the baptism of repentance to *all the p.*
21. 27. stirred up *all the p.* and laid hands on him
Heb. 9. 19. when Moses had spoken every precept
to *all the p.* he sprinkled both book and *all the p.*

Among the PEOPLE.

Lev. 18. 29. shall be cut off from *among the p.*
Num. 5. 27. woman shall be a curse *among the p.*
1 *Sam.* 14. 34. disperse yourselves *among the p.*
Psal. 94. 8. understand, ye brutish *among the p.*
Ezek. 28. 19. all that know thee *among the p.* shall be
Dan. 11. 33. and they that understand *among the p.*
Joel 2. 17. wherefore should they say *among the p.*
Zech. 10. 9. and I will sow them *among the p.*
Mat. 4. 23. all manner of disease *among the p.* 9. 35.
26. 5. feast day, lest there be an uproar *among the p.*
John 7. 12. there was much murmuring *among t. p.*
43. was a division *among the p.* because of him
Acts 3. 23. shall be destroyed from *among the p.*
4. 17. that it spread no further *among the p.*
5. 12. many wonders were wrought *am. the p.* 6. 8.
14. 14. Barnabas and Paul ran in *among the p.*
2 *Pet.* 2. 1. there were false prophets also *am. the p.*
See COMMON, FOOLISH.

PEOPLE *of God.*

Judg. 20. 2. presently in assembly of the *p. of God*
2 *Sam.* 14. 13. thought such a thing against *p. of G.*
Psal. 47. 9. even *p. of the God* of Abraham, gathered
Heb. 4. 9. there remaineth a rest to the *p. of God*
11. 25. choosing to suffer affliction with *p. of God*
1 *Pet.* 2. 10. was not a people, but are now *p. of G.*
See GREAT.

His PEOPLE.

Gen. 17. 14. be cut off from *his p. Exod.* 30. 33, 38.
| 31. 14. *Lev.* 7. 20, 21, 25, 27. | 17. 4, 9. |
19. 8. | 23. 29. *Num.* 9. 13. | 15. 30.
25. 8. then Abraham was gathered to *his p.*
17. Ishmael was gathered to *his p.* || 35. 29. Isaac
49. 16. Dan shall judge *his p.* as one of tribes, 33.
Exod. 8. 29. that flies may depart from *his p.* 31.
17. 13. Joshua discomfited Amalek and *his p.*
18. 1. God had done for Moses and for Israel *his p.*
Lev. 17. 10. that soul that eateth blood, I will cut
him off from among *his p.* 20. 3, 6. | 23. 30.
21. 1. none be defiled for the dead among *his p.*
15. nor shall he profane his seed among *his p.*
Num. 20. 24. Aaron shall be gathered to *his p.* 26.
21. 34. fear not Og of Bashan, I have delivered him
into thy hand, and all *his p.* 35. *Deut.* 2. 33.
Deut. 3. 2. I will deliver Og and all *his p.* 3.
26. 18. Lord avouched thee to be *his* peculiar *p.*
32. 9. for Lord's portion is *his p.* Jacob the lot
36. the Lord shall judge *his p. Psal.* 135. 14.
43. rejoice, O ye nations, with *his p.* he will be
merciful to his land and *his p. Rom.* 15. 10.
50. Aaron died in mount Hor, was gather. to *his p.*
33. 7. hear, Lord, and bring Judah to *his p.*
Josh. 8. 1. I have given thee Ai, the king and *his p.*
Judg. 11. 23. hath dispossess. Amorites before *his p.*
Ruth 1. 6. heard how the Lord had visited *his p.*
1 *Sam.* 12. 22. L. will not forsake *his p.* for his great
name's sake, pleased the Ld. to make you *his p.*
15. 1. to anoint thee to be king over all *his p.*
27. 12. made *his p.* Israel utterly to abhor him
2 *Sam.* 8. 15. David reigned over all Israel, David
executed justice to all *his p.* 1 *Chron.* 18. 14.
1 *Kings* 20. 42. and thy people shall go for *his p.*
1 *Chr.* 21. 3. Joab answered, the Lord make *his p.* a
hundred times so many more as they be
22. 18. the land is subdued before Lord and *his p.*
23. 25. the God of Israel hath given rest to *his p.*
2 *Chr.* 2. 11. because the Lord hath loved *his p.*
31. 10. for the Lord hath blessed *his p.*
32. 14. who was there that could deliver *his p.?* 15.
33. 10. the Lord spake to Manasseh and *his p.*
36. 15. because he had compassion on *his p.*
16. mocked, until wrath of Lord rose against *his p.*
23. who among you of all *his p.* go up, *Ezra* 1. 3.
Esth. 10. 3. Mordecai seeking the wealth of *his p.*
Job 18. 19. not have son nor nephew among *his p.*
Psal. 14. 7. bringeth back captivity of *his p.* 53. 6.
29. 11. the Lord will give strength to *his p.* the
Lord will bless *his p.* with peace, 68. 35.
50. 4. he shall call, that he may judge *his p.*
73. 10. therefore *his p.* return hither, and waters
78. 20. they said, can he provide flesh for *his p.?*
62. he gave *his p.* over also to the sword
71. he brought him to feed Jacob *his p.*
85. 8. for he will speak peace to *his p.* and saints
94. 14. for the Lord will not cast off *his p.*
100. 3. we are *his p.* || 105. 43. brought forth *his p.*
105. 24. he increased *his p.* greatly, made them
25. he turned their heart to hate *his p.* to deal
106. 40. the wrath of the Lord kindled against *his
p.* that he abhorred his inheritance, *Isa.* 5. 25.
111. 6. he shewed *his p.* the power of his works
9. he sent redemption to *his p.* holy is his name

Psal. 113. 8. he may set him with the princes of *his p.*
116. 14. now in the presence of all *his p.* 18.
125. 2. so is the Lord round about *his p.* henceforth
136. 16. him who led *his p.* through the wilderness
148. 14. he also exalteth the horn of *his p.*
149. 4. Lord taketh pleasure in *his p.* beautify
Isa. 3. 14. into judgment with the ancients of *his p.*
7. 2. his heart was moved, and the heart of *his p.*
11. 11. to recover the remnant of *his p.* left
16. be an highway for the remnant of *his p.*
14. 32. the poor of *his p.* shall trust in him
25. 8. the rebuke of *his p.* shall he take away
28. 5. for a diadem of beauty to residue of *his p.*
30. 26. in day Lord bindeth up breach of *his p.*
49. 13. for God hath comforted *his p.* 52. 9.
51. 22. thy God that pleadeth the cause of *his p.*
56. 3. the Lord hath separated me from *his p.*
63. 11. he remembered days of old, Moses and *his p.*
Jer. 27. 12. and serve him and *his p.* and live
50. 16. they shall return every one to *his p.*
Ezek. 18. 18. and did what is not good among *his p.*
30. 11. he and *his p.* with him shall be brought
Joel 2. 18. then will Lord be jealous and pity *his p.*
19. the Lord will answer and say to *his p.*
3. 16. the Lord will be the hope of *his p.*
Mic. 6. 2. the Lord hath a controversy with *his p.*
Zech. 9. 16. Lord shall save them as flock of *his p.*
Mat. 1. 21. Jesus, he shall save *his p.* from their sins
Luke 1. 68. for he hath visited and redeemed *his p.*
77. give knowl. of salvation to *his p.* by remission
7. 16. prophet risen, and that God hath visited *his p.*
Rom. 11. 1. hath God cast away *his p.?* God forbid
2. God hath not cast away *his p.* he foreknew
Heb. 10. 30. again, the Lord shall judge *his p.*
Rev. 21. 3. they shall be *his p.* God himself their G.
See HOLY, ISRAEL, MANY, MEN.

PEOPLE *of the land.*

Gen. 23. 7. Abrah. bowed himself to *p. of the l.* 12.
42. 6. it was Joseph that sold to all *p. of the land*
Exod. 5. 5. *p. of the l.* are many, ye make them rest
Lev. 20. 2. *p. of the l.* shall stone him with stones
4. if *p. of the land* do hide their eyes from him
Num. 14. 9. rebel not, neither fear ye *p. of the l.*
2 *Kings* 11. 14. all *p. of the l.* rejoiced and blew, 20.
15. 5. Jotham judged *p. of the land,* 2 *Chr.* 26. 21.
21. 24. *p. of the l.* slew that had killed Amon, and
p. of the l. made Josiah king, 2 *Chr.* 33. 25.
23. 30. *p. of l.* took Jehoahaz his son, 2 *Chr.* 36. 1.
25. 3. there was no bread for *p. of the l. Jer.* 52. 6.
19. Nebuchadn. took him that mustered *p. of the l.*
and sixty men of *p. of the land, Jer.* 52. 25.
1 *Chr.* 5. 25. went after the gods of *p. of the land*
Ezra 4. 4. *p. of the l.* weakened hands of builders
10. 2. and taken strange wives of the *p. of the land*
11. separate yourselves from the *p. of the land*
Neh. 10. 30. not give our daughters to *p. of the l.*
31. if the *p. of the l.* bring ware, or any victuals
Esth. 8. 17. many of the *p. of the land* became Jews
Jer. 1. 18. made thee an iron pillar against *p. of the l.*
34. 19. all the *p. of the land* which passed between
Ezek. 7. 27. hands of *p. of the land* shall be troubled
22. 29. *p. of the l.* have used oppression and robbery
33. 2. if *p. of the land* take man to be a watchman
39. 13. and all the *p. of the land* shall bury them
45. 16. all the *p. of the land* shall give this oblation
22. that day the prince prepare for *p. of the land*
46. 3. *p. of the l.* shall worship at door of this gate
9. when *p. of the land* shall come in solemn feasts
Dan. 9. 6. prophets which spake to the *p. of the land*
Hag. 2. 4. be strong, all ye *p. of the land,* and work
Zech. 7. 5. speak to all the *p. of the land* and priests

Much PEOPLE.

Num. 20. 20. Edom came out ag. him with *much p.*
Josh. 11. 4. they went with *much p.* even as the sand
2 *Sam.* 13. 34. there came *much p.* by way of the hill
2 *Chr.* 30. 13. there assembled at Jerusal. *much p.*
32. 4. so there was gathered *much p.* together
Psal. 35. 18. I will praise thee among *much p.*
Mark 5. 21. *much p.* gathered unto him nigh the sea
24. Jesus went with him, and *much p.* followed him
6. 34. Jesus saw *much p.* was moved with compass.
John 12. 9. *much p.* of Jews knew that he was there
12. next day *much p.* took branches of palm-trees
Acts 5. 37. and drew away *much p.* after him
11. 24. and *much p.* was added unto the Lord
18. 10. I am with thee, for I have *m. p.* in this city
19. 26. this Paul hath turned away *much p.*
Rev 19. 1. I heard a voice of *much p.* in heaven

My PEOPLE.

Gen. 23. 11. in presence of the sons of *m. p.* give I it
41. 40. to thy word shall all *my p.* be ruled
49. 29. I am to be gathered to *my p.* bury me
Exod. 3. 7. I have seen affliction of *m. p. Acts* 7. 34.
10. that thou mayest bring forth *my p.* 7. 4.
5. 1. let *my p.* go, 7. 16. | 8. 1, 20. | 9. 1, 13. | 10. 3.
8. 8. take away the frogs from me and from *my p.*
21. else if thou wilt not let *my p.* go, 10. 4.
22. I will sever the land in which *my p.* are, 23.
9. 17. as yet exaltest thou thyself against *my p.*
27. Lord is righteous, I and *my p.* are wicked
12. 31. and get you forth from among *my p.*
22. 25. if thou lend money to any of *my p.*
Lev. 26. 12. ye shall be *my p. Jer.* 11. 4. | 30. 22.
Num. 24. 14. and now behold I go unto *my p.*
Judg. 12. 2. I and *my p.* were at great strife
14. 3. is there never a woman among all *my p.?*
16. hast put forth a riddle to children of *my p.*
Ruth 1. 16. thy people shall be *my p.* God my God
3. 11. for all the city of *my p.* doth know that
1 *Sam.* 9. 16. shalt anoint him to be captain over
my p. that he may serve *my p.* I looked on *my p.*
2 *Sam.* 3. 18. by the hand of David I will save *my p.*
7. 8. I took thee to be a ruler over *my p.* 2 *Chr.* 6. 5.
1 *Kings* 22. 4. I am as thou art, *my p.* as thy people,
my horses as thy horses, 2 *Kings* 3. 7. 2 *Chr.* 18. 3.
2 *Kings* 20. 5. tell Hezekiah, the captain of *my p.*
1 *Chr.* 17. 6. whom I commanded to feed *my p.*
28. 2. David stood and said, hear me, *my p.*
29. 14. who am I, and what *my p.* to be able to offer
2 *Chr.* 1. 11. wisdom, that thou mayest judge *my p.*
6. 5. since day I brought forth *my p.* out of Egypt
7. 13. or if I send pestilence among *my p.*

2 *Chr.* 7. 14. if *my p.* shall humble thems. and pray
Esth. 7. 3. let *my p.* be given me at my request
4. for we are sold, I and *my p.* to be destroyed
8. 6. how endure to see evil shall come to *my p.?*
Psal. 14. 4. who eat up *my p.* as they eat bread, 53. 4.
50. 7. hear, O *my p.* I will speak and testify, 81. 8.
59. 11. slay them not, least *my p.* forget, scatter them
68. 22. I will bring *my p.* again from Bashan
78. 1. give ear, O *my p.* to my law, incline your ears
81. 11. but *my p.* would not hearken to my voice
13. O that *my p.* had hearkened unto me
144. 2. my shield, who subdueth *my p.* under me
Isa. 1. 3. but Israel not know, *my p.* doth not consid.
3. 12. as for *my p.* children are their oppressors, O
my p. they which lead thee cause thee to err
15. what mean ye that ye beat *my p.* to pieces?
5. 13. *my p.* are gone into captivity, because
10. 2. to take away the right from poor of *my p.*
24. O *my p.* that dwellest in Zion, be not afraid
19. 25. blessed be Egypt, *my p.* and Assyria, Israel
26. 20. come, *my p.* enter thou into thy chambers
32. 18. *my p.* shall dwell in a peaceable habitation
40. 1. comfort ye, comfort ye *my p.* saith your God
43. 20. to give drink to *my p.* my chosen
47. 6. I was wroth with *my p.* I have polluted
51. 4. hearken unto me, *my p.* and give ear to me
16. and say to Zion, thou art *my p.*
52. 4. *my p.* went down into Egypt to sojourn there
5. saith Lord, that *my p.* is taken away for nought
6. therefore *my p.* shall know my name
53. 8. for transgression of *my p.* was he stricken
57. 14. take stumbling-block out of the way of *my p.*
58. 1. and shew *my p.* their transgression, and Jacob
63. 8. for he said, surely they are *my p.* children
65. 10. Sharon a fold for *my p.* that have sought me
19. I will rejoice in Jerusalem, and joy in *my p.*
22. for as the days of a tree, are the days of *my p.*
Jer. 2. 11. but *my p.* have changed their glory for
13. for *my p.* have committed two evils, forsaken
31. why say *my p.* we are lords, will come no more
32. yet *my p.* have forgotten me, 18. 15.
4. 22. for *my p.* is foolish, they have not known me
5. 26. for among *my p.* are found wicked men
31. *my p.* love to have it so, what will ye do?
6. 27. I have set thee for a fortress among *my p.*
7. 23. obey my voice, and ye shall be *my p.*
8. 7. *my p.* know not the judgment of the Lord
9. 2. that I might leave *my p.* and go from them
12. 16. if they will diligently learn the ways of *my p.*
as they taught *my p.* to swear by Baal
15. 7. I will destroy *my p.* since they return not
23. 2. saith Ld. against the pastors that feed *my p.*
22. if they had caused *my p.* to hear my words
27. who think to cause *my p.* to forget my name
32. cause *my p.* to err by their lies and lightness
24. 7. they shall be *my p.* 31. 1, 33. | 32. 38. *Ezek.*
11. 20. | 36. 28. | 37. 23, 27. *Zech.* 8. 8.
29. 32. nor behold good that I will do for *my p.*
31. 14. *my p.* shall be satisfied with my goodness
33. 24. thus they have despised *my p.* not a nation
50. 6. *my p.* hath been lost sheep, they have gone
51. 45. *my p.* go ye out of midst of her, *Rev.* 18. 4.
Lam. 3. 14. I was a derision to all *my p.* and song
Ezek. 13. 9. they shall not be in assembly of *my p.*
10. have seduced *my p.* || 18. hunt souls of *my p.*
19. ye pollute me among *my p.* by lying to *my p.*
21. I will deliver *my p.* out of your hand, 23.
14. 8. I will cut him off from the midst of *my p.*
11. but that they may be *my p.* and I their God
21. 12. terrors by the sword shall be upon *my p.*
34. 30. even house of Israel are *my p.* saith Lord
37. 12. behold, O *my p.* I will open your graves, 13.
38. 16. thou shalt come up against *my p.* Israel
44. 23. they shall teach *my p.* the difference
45. 8. my princes shall no more oppress *my p.*
9. take away your exactions from *my p.* saith Lord
46. 18. that *my p.* be not scattered from possession
Hos. 1. 9. then said God, are ye not *my p.?* 10.
2. †1. say unto your brethren, *my. p.* and sisters
2. 23. say to them which were not *my p.*
4. 6. *my p.* are destroyed for lack of knowledge
8. they eat up the sin of *my p.* and they set
12. *my p.* ask counsel at their stocks, and staff
6. 11. when I returned the captivity of *my p.*
11. 7. *my p.* are bent to backsliding from me
Joel 2. 26. *my p.* shall never be ashamed, 27.
3. 2. and will plead with them there for *my p.*
3. and they have cast lots for *my p.* and sold
Amos 9. 10. sinners of *my p.* shall die by the sword
Obad. 13. not have entered into the gate of *my p.*
Mic. 1. 9. he is come to the gate of *my p.* even
2. 4. he hath changed the portion of *my p.*
8. of late *my p.* is risen up as an enemy
9. the women of *my p.* have ye cast out
3. 3. who also eat the flesh of *my p.* and flay
5. concerning prophets that make *my p.* err
6. 3. O *my p.* what have I done unto thee? 5.
16. therefore ye shall bear the reproach of *my p.*
Zeph. 2. 8. whereby they reproached *my p.*
9. the residue of *my p.* shall spoil them
Zech. 2. 11. and many nations shall be *my p.*
8. 7. I will save *my p.* from the east country
13. 9. I will say, it is *my p.* and they shall say
Rom. 9. 25. call them *my p.* which were not *my p.*
26. in the place where it was said, ye are not *my p.*
2 *Cor.* 6. 16. I will be their God, they shall be *my p.*
See DAUGHTER.

Of the PEOPLE.

Gen. 25. 23. two manner *of the p.* shall be separated
26. 10. one *of the p.* might lightly have lien
49. 10. to him shall the gathering *of the p.* be
Num. 25. 4. take all the heads *of the p.* and hang
26. 4. take the sum *of the p.* from 20 years old
Josh. 4. 2. take you twelve men out *of the p.*
1 *Sam.* 9. 2. he was higher than any *of the p.* 10. 23.
12. for there is a sacrifice *of the p.* to-day
14. 24. so none *of the p.* tasted any food
28. then answered one *of the p.* and said
26. 15. there came one *of the p.* to destroy king
2 *Kings* 13. 7. nor did he leave *of the p.* to Jehoahaz
Ezra 3. 3. because *of the p.* of those countries
Neh. 5. 1. there was great cry *of t. p.* and their wives

Neh. 7. 73. and some *of the p.* dwelt in their cities
Psal. 65. 7. which stilleth the tumult *of the p.*
72. 4. he shall judge the poor *of the p.* and save
89. 19. I have exalted one chosen out *of the p.*
Isa. 18. 7. a present *of a p.* scattered and peeled
42. 6. I will give thee for a covenant *of the p.*
51. 4. my judgment to rest for a light *of the p.*
63. 3. and *of the p.* there was none with me
Ezek. 46. 18. prince not take *of the p.* inheritance
24. the ministers shall boil the sacrifice *of the p.*
John 7. 31. and many *of the p.* believed on him
11. 42. because *of the p.* that stand by I said it
Acts 4. 21. how they might punish, because *of the p.*
Heb. 9. 7. he offered for himself, and errors *of the p.*
Rev. 11. 9. they *of the p.* shall see their dead bodies
See EARS, ELDERS.

One PEOPLE.

Gen. 25. 23. *one p.* shall be stronger than the other
34. 16. we will dwell with you, and become *one p.*
22. will consent to dwell with us, to be *one p.*

Own PEOPLE.

Exod. 5. 16. but the fault is in thine *own p.*
Lev. 21. 14. he shall take a virgin of his *own p.*
1 *Chron.* 17. 21. God went to redeem to be his *own p.*
2 *Chron.* 25. 15. that could not deliver their *own p.*
Psal. 45. 10. O daughter, forget also thy *own p.*
78. 52. but made his *own p.* to go forth like sheep
Isa. 13. 14. shall every man turn to his *own p.*
Jer. 46. 16. arise, let us go again to our *own p.*

The PEOPLE.

Gen. 11. 6. the Lord said, behold *the p.* is one
Exod. 5. 4. why do ye let *the p.* from their work?
5. behold, *the p.* of the land now are many
12. 27. and *the p.* bowed the head and worshipped
13. 18. God led *the p.* ‖ 14. 5. was told that *the p.* fled
14. 31. *the p.* feared Lord, and believed the Lord
15. 14. *the p.* shall hear and be afraid, sorrow take
16. till *the p.* pass over which thou hast purchased
24. *the p.* murmured, saying, what shall we drink?
16. 30. so *the p.* rested on the seventh day
17. 1. there was no water for *the p.* to drink
2. *the p.* did chide with Moses, *Num.* 20. 3.
6. shall come water out of it, that *the p.* may drink
18. 19. be thou for *the p.* to God-ward, to bring
19. 9. that *the p.* may hear when I speak with thee
17. Moses brought forth *the p.* out of the camp
21. charge *the p.* ‖ 24. let not *the p.* break through
20. 18. when *the p.* saw it, they stood afar off, 21.
24. 2. neither shall *the p.* go up with him
8. Moses took blood and sprinkled it on *the p.*
Lev. 9. 7. make an atonement for thyself and *the p.*
15. the sin offering for *the p.* 18. ‖ 16. 15.
23. blessed *the p.* ‖ *Num.* 11. 1. *the p.* complained
Num. 11. 2. *the p.* cried to Moses, and he prayed
13. 18. and see *the p.* that dwelleth therein
28. *the p.* be strong ‖ 30. Caleb stilled *the p.*
14. 1. *the p.* wept that night ‖ 39. *the p.* mourned
21. 5. *the p.* spake against God and against Moses
23. 9. lo, *the p.* shall dwell alone, not reckoned
24. behold, *the p.* shall rise up as a great lion
Deut. 4. 10. the Lord said, gather me *the p.* together
18. 3. this shall be the priest's due from *the p.*
33. 3. yea, he loved *the p.* ‖ 17. he shall push *the p.*
19. they shall call *the p.* to the mountain
Josh. 4. 10. and *the p.* hasted and passed over
6. 20. so *the p.* shouted ‖ 24. 28. let *the p.* depart
Judg. 7. 2. *the p.* that are with thee are too many, 4.
9. 32. up thou, and *the p.* that are with thee
1 *Sam.* 2. 13. the priest's custom with *the p.* was
4. 4. so *the p.* sent to Shiloh to bring the ark
6. 6. did they not let *the p.* go, and they departed
8. 19. *the p.* refused to obey the voice of Samuel
9. 13. for *the p.* will not eat until he come
14. 45. *the p.* said to Saul, shall Jonathan die? so
the p. rescued Jonathan, that he died not
15. 15. for *the p.* spared the best of the sheep
21. but *the p.* took of the spoil sheep and oxen
17. 27. *the p.* answered after this manner, 30.
30. 6. Dav. distressed, for *the p.* spake of ston. him
2 *Sam.* 1. 4. that *the p.* are fled from the battle
14. 15. it is because *the p.* have made me afraid
15. 12. for *the p.* increased with Absalom
1 *Kings* 1. 40. and *the p.* piped with pipes and rejoic.
12. 30. for *the p.* went to worship before the one
16. 22. *the p.* that followed Omri prevailed against
the p. that followed Tibni, son of Ginath
18. 21. and *the p.* answered him not a word
2 *Kings* 4. 41. pour out for *the p.* that they may eat
43. he said, give *the p.* that they may eat
7. 17. and *the p.* trode upon him in the gate
11. 17. made a covenant between king and *the p.*
12. 3. as yet *the p.* did sacrifice, 14. 4. ‖ 15. 4, 35.
18. 36. *the p.* held their peace, and answered not
22. 13. inquire of the Lord for me and for *the p.*
2 *Chr.* 12. 3. *the p.* were without number that came
20. 33. as yet *the p.* had not prepared, 30. 3.
27. 2. and *the p.* did yet corruptly
30. 20. Ld. hearkened to Hezek. and healed *the p.*
31. 10. since *the p.* began to bring offerings
32. 8. *the p.* rested on the words of Hezekiah
36. 14. and *the p.* transgressed very much
Ezra 10. 13. but *the p.* are many, and it is rain
Neh. 4. 6. for *the p.* had a mind to work
5. 13. and *the p.* did according to this promise
7. 4. city was large, but *the p.* were few therein
8. 7. and *the p.* stood in their place
16. so *the p.* went and brought palm-branches
11. 2. *the p.* blessed all that offered willingly
Esth. 3. 6. they had shewed him *the p.* of Mordecai
11. *the p.* also, to do with them as seemeth to thee
4. 11. *the p.* of the king's provinces do know
Job 12. 2. Job said, no doubt but ye are *the p.*
34. 30. hypocrite reign not, lest *the p.* be ensnared
Psal. 2. 1. why do *the p.* imagine a vain thing?
33. 12. blessed are *the p.* whom he hath chosen
44. 2. we heard, how thou didst afflict *the p.*
45. 5. arrows, whereby *the p.* fall under thee
17. therefore shall *the p.* praise thee for ever
56. 7. in thine anger cast down *the p.* O God
67. 3. let *the p.* praise thee, O God, 5.
89. 15. blessed is *the p.* that know the joyful sound
95. 7. and we are *the p.* of his pasture

Psal. 96. 13. he shall judge *the p.* with his truth
98. 9. and he shall judge *the p.* with equity
99. 1. the Lord reigneth, let *the p.* tremble
105. 1. make known his deeds among *the p.*
Prov. 11. 14. where no counsel is *the p.* fall
26. withholds corn, *the p.* shall curse him, 24. 24.
29. 2. in authority, *the p.* rejoiced, *the p.* mourn
18. where there is no vision, *the p.* perish
Isa. 3. 5. *the p.* shall be oppressed, every one by ano.
9. 2. *the p.* that walked in darkness have seen light
13. *the p.* turneth not to him that smiteth them
19. and *the p.* shall be as the fuel of the fire
10. 6. and against *the p.* of my wrath will I give
14. 2. and *the p.* shall take them and bring them
24. 2. it shall be as with *the p.* so with the priest
30. 19. for *the p.* shall dwell in Zion at Jerusalem
33. 24. *the p.* shall be forgiven their iniquity
34. 5. my sword shall come on *the p.* of my curse
40. 7. surely *the p.* is grass, the grass withereth
51. 7. *the p.* in whose heart is my law, fear ye not
63. 6. I will tread down *the p.* in mine anger
18. *the p.* of thy holiness have possessed it
Jer. 23. 34. *the p.* that shall say, the burthen of Ld.
31. 2. *the p.* which were left of sword found grace
37. 4. Jeremiah came in and went out among *the p.*
39. 14. carry him home, so he dwelt among *the p.*
40. 5. go back and dwell with him among *the p.* 6.
48. 46. woe to thee, O Moab, *t. p.* of Chemosh perish
51. 58. and *the p.* shall labour in vain, and be weary
Ezek. 11. 17. I will even gather you from *the p.*
20. 34. I will bring you out from *the p.* 34. 13.
25. 7. and I will cut thee off from *the p.*
26. 20. will bring thee down with *the p.* of old time
33. 6. see sword come, and *the p.* be not warned
31. and they come unto thee as *the p.* cometh
36. 20. they said, these are *the p.* of the Lord
39. 4. thou shalt fall, and *the p.* that is with thee
42. 14. approach to those things which are for *the p.*
44. 11. they shall slay the sacrifice for *the p.*
19. shall not sanctify *the p.* with their garments
Dan. 9. 26. *the p.* of the prince that shall come
11. 32. *the p.* that know their God shall be strong
Hos. 4. 14. *the p.* that doth not understand, shall fall
10. 5. for *the p.* thereof shall mourn over it
10. and *the p.* shall be gathered against them
Joel 2. 6. before them *the p.* shall be much pained
Amos 1. 5. *the p.* of Syria shall go into captivity
3. 6. shall trumpet be blown, and *the p.* not afraid?
Jonah 3. 5. so *the p.* of Nineveh believed God
Hab. 2. 13. that *the p.* shall labour in the fire, and
the p. shall weary themselves for very vanity
Zeph. 2. 10. magnified themselves ag. *the p.* of Lord
Hag. 1. 12. and *the p.* did fear before the Lord
Mal. 1. 4. *the p.* against whom Lord hath indignation
Mat. 4. 16. *the p.* that sat in darkness saw light
21. 26. if we shall say, of men, we fear *the p.* for
all hold John as a prophet, *Mark* 11. 32.
Luke 1. 21. and *the p.* waited for Zacharias
3. 15. as *the p.* were in expectat. and all men mused
4. 42. *the p.* sought him ‖ 5. 1. *the p.* pressed on
8. 40. when returned, *the p.* gladly received him
9. 18. he asked them, whom say *the p.* that I am?
20. 19. feared *the p.* 22. 2. ‖ 23. 5. stirreth up *the p.*
23. 14. brought this man, one that perverteth *the p.*
John 6. 24. when *the p.* saw that Jesus was not there
7. 12. others said, nay, but he deceiveth *the p.*
11. 50. that one man should die for *the p.* 18. 14.
Acts 5. 13. but *the p.* magnified them
8. 6. *the p.* with one accord gave heed to those things
12. 22. *the p.* gave shout, saying, it is voice of God
14. 11. and when *the p.* saw what Paul had done
18. with these sayings scarce restrained they *t. p.*
19. who persuaded *the p.* and stoned Paul
26. 17. delivering thee from *the p.* and the Gentiles
28. 17. though I committed nothing against *the p.*
Heb. 5. 3. as for *the p.* so also for himself, 7. 27.
7. 11. for under it *the p.* received the law
13. 12. that he might sanctify *the p.* with his blood
Jude 5. how that the Lord having saved *the p.*

This PEOPLE.

Exod. 3. 21. I will give *this p.* favour in sight of
5. 22. why hast thou so evil entreated *this p.?*
23. for Pharaoh hath done evil to *this p.*
17. 4. Moses cried, saying, what shall I do to *this p.?*
18. 18. thou wilt wear away, both thou and *this p.*
23. all *this p.* shall also go to their place in peace
32. 9. I have seen *this p.* ‖ 21. what did *this p.* to thee
32. 31. oh, *this p.* have sinned a great sin
33. 12. see, thou sayest to me, bring up *this p.*
Num. 11. 11. layest the burden of all *this p.* on me
12. have I conceiv. all *this p.?* ‖ 13. flesh to *this p.*
14. I am not able to bear all *this p.* alone
14. 11. Lord said, how long will *this p.* provoke me?
14. they heard that thou art among *this p.*
15. if thou shalt kill all *this p.* as one man
16. was not able to bring *this p.* into the land
19. pardon *this p.* as thou hast forgiven *this p.*
21. 2. if thou wilt indeed deliver *this p.*
22. 6. come now, I pray thee, curse *this p.* 17.
24. 14. what *this p.* shall do to thy people
32. 15. and ye shall destroy all *this p.*
Deut. 3. 28. Joshua shall go over before *this p.*
5. 28. I have heard voice of the words of *this p.*
9. 13. the Lord spake, saying, I have seen *this p.*
27. look not to the stubbornness of *this p.*
31. 7. be strong, for thou must go with *this p.*
16. *this p.* will rise up and go whoring after gods
Josh. 1. 6. to *this p.* thou shalt divide the land
Judg. 2. 20. because *this p.* have transgressed
9. 29. would to God *this p.* were under my hand
38. is not *this* the *p.* thou hast despised? go out
1 *Sam.* 2. 23. I hear of your evil doings by *this p.*
2 *Sam.* 16. 18. but whom Lord and *this p.* choose
1 *Kings* 12. 6. that I may ans. *this p.* 9. 2 *Chr.* 10. 6, 9.
7. if thou wilt be a servant to *this p.* this day
27. if *this p.* go up to do sacrifice at Jerusalem, then
the heart of *this p.* shall turn again to Rehoboam
14. 2. who told me that I should be king over *t. p.*
18. 37. hear me, O Lord, that *this p.* may know
2 *Kings* 6. 18. I pray, smite *this p.* with blindness
2 *Chr.* 1. 10. I may go out and come in before *this p.*
Neh. 5. 18. the bondage was heavy on *this p.*

Neh. 5. 19. accord. to all that I have done for *this p.*
Isa. 6. 9. go and tell *this p.* hear ye indeed, but not
10. make the heart of *this p.* fat, ears heavy, and
shut their eyes, *Mat.* 13. 15. *Acts* 28. 26, 27.
8. 6. *this p.* refuseth the waters of Shiloah
11. I should not walk in the way of *this p.*
12. to whom *this p.* shall say, a confederacy
9. 16. the leaders of *this p.* cause them to err
23. 13. *this p.* was not till the Assyrian founded it
28. 11. with another tongue will speak to *this p.*
14. hear, ye scornful men that rule *this p.*
29. 13. *this p.* draw near me with their mouth
14. to do a marvellous work among *this p.*
42. 22. but *this* is a *p.* robbed and spoiled
43. 21. *this p.* have I formed for myself
Jer. 4. 10. thou hast greatly deceived *this p.*
5. 14. will make my words fire, and *this p.* wood
23. but *this p.* hath a revolting heart
6. 19. behold, I will bring evil on *this p.*
21. I will lay stumbling-blocks before *this p.*
7. 16. pray not thou for *this p.* 11. 14. ‖ 14. 11.
33. carcasses of *this p.* meat for fowls of heaven
8. 5. why is *this p.* of Jerusalem slidden back?
9. 15. I will feed even *this p.* with wormwood
13. 10. *this* evil *p.* who refuse to hear my words
15. 1. yet my mind could not be toward *this p.*
16. 5. I have taken away my peace from *this p.*
19. 11. even so will I break *this p.* and this city
23. 32. they shall not profit *this p.* at all
33. and when *this p.* shall ask thee, saying
28. 15. thou makest *this p.* to trust in a lie
29. 32. shall not have a man to dwell among *this p.*
32. 42. brought all this great evil upon *this p.*
33. 24. considerest not what *this p.* have spoken
35. 16. but *this p.* have not hearkened unto me
36. 7. great is the anger pronounced against *this p.*
37. 18. what have I offended against *this p.?*
38. 4. this man seeketh not the welfare of *this p.*
Mic. 2. 11. he shall be the prophet of *this p.*
Hag. 1. 2. *this p.* say, the time is not come
2. 14. Haggai said, so is *this p.* before me
Zech. 8. 6. in the eyes of the remnant of *this p.*
11. I will not be to *this p.* as in former days
12. I will cause the remnant of *this p.* to possess
Mat. 15. 8. *this p.* draweth nigh with their mouth
Mark 7. 6. *this p.* honoureth me with their lips
Luke 9. 13. except we should buy meat for *this p.*
21. 23. for there shall be wrath upon *this p.*
John 7. 49. but *this p.* who knoweth not the law
Acts 13. 17. the God of *this p.* chose our fathers
1 *Cor.* 14. 21. with other lips I will speak to *this p.*

Thy PEOPLE.

Exod. 5. 23. neither hast thou delivered *thy p.*
8. 3. frogs on *thy p.* 4. ‖ 21. swarms of flies on *thy p.*
9. 14. for I will send all my plagues on *thy p.*
15. that I may smite thee and *thy p.* with pestilen.
15. 16. they shall be still, till *thy p.* pass over, O Ld.
22. 28. nor shalt curse ruler of *thy p.* *Acts* 23. 5.
23. 11. let it rest, that the poor of *thy p.* may eat
33. 13. and consider that this nation is *thy p.*
16. I and *thy p.* have found grace in thy sight
34. 10. I make a covenant before all *thy p.*
Lev. 19. 16. shalt not go as a tale-bearer among *thy p.*
Num. 5. 21. make thee a curse and oath among *thy p.*
24. 14. what this peo. shall do *thy p.* in latter days
27. 13. shalt be gathered to *thy p.* 31. 2. *Deut.* 32. 50.
Deut. 9. 12. for *thy p.* have corrupted themselves
26. destroy not *thy p.* ‖ *Ruth* 1. 16. *thy p.* my peo.
29. yet they are *thy p.* and inheritance, *Neh.* 1. 10.
Ruth 1. 10. we will return with thee to *thy p.*
2 *Sam.* 7. 23. what nation like *thy p.?* 1 *Chr.* 17. 21.
before *thy p.* which thou redeemedst from Egypt
1 *Kings* 3. 8. thy servant is in the midst of *thy p.*
9. understanding heart to judge *thy p.* 2 *Chr.* 1. 10.
8. 44. if *thy p.* go out to battle, and shall pray
50. forgive *thy p.* that have sinned, 2 *Chr.* 6. 34, 39.
51. they be *thy p.* ‖ 20. 42. *thy p.* for his people
22. 4. he said, I am as thou art, my people as *thy*
p. my horses as thy horses, 2 *Kings* 3. 7.
1 *Chron.* 21. 17. but let not thy hand be on *thy p.*
29. 18. keep this in the thoughts of heart of *thy p.*
2 *Chron.* 21. 14. with a plague will the Lord smite
thy p. thy children, thy wives, and thy goods
Ps. 3. 8. salvation to L. thy blessing is upon *thy p.*
28. 9. save *thy p.* and bless thine inherit. *Jer.* 31. 7.
44. 12. thou sellest *thy p.* for nought
60. 3. thou hast shewed *thy p.* hard things
68. 7. when thou wentest forth before *thy p.*
72. 2. he shall judge *thy p.* with righteousness
77. 15. thou hast with thine arm redeemed *thy p.*
20. thou leddest *thy p.* as flock by Moses and Aar.
79. 13. so we *thy p.* will give thee thanks
80. 4. how long be angry against prayer of *thy p.?*
83. 3. they have taken crafty counsel against *thy p.*
85. 2. thou hast forgiven the iniquity of *thy p.*
6. revive us, that *thy p.* may rejoice in thee
94. 5. they break in pieces *thy p.* O Lord
106. 4. the favour that thou bearest to *thy p.*
110. 3. *thy p.* shall be willing in the day of power
Isa. 2. 6. therefore thou hast forsaken *thy p.*
7. 17. the Lord shall bring on thee and *thy p.* days
14. 20. thou hast destroyed thy land and *thy p.*
60. 21. *thy p.* shall be all righteous, shall inherit
63. 14. so didst thou lead *thy p.* ‖ 64. 9. we are *thy p.*
Jer. 22. 2. hear, thou and *thy p.* that enter in
27. 13. why will ye die, thou and *thy p.* by sword?
Ezek. 3. 11. get thee to *thy p.* and speak to them
13. 17. set thy face against the daughters of *thy p.*
26. 11. he shall slay *thy p.* with the sword
33. 2. speak to the children of *thy p.* and say, 12.
17. yet children of *thy p.* say, way is not equal
30. the children of *thy p.* still are talking
37. 18. when the children of *thy p.* shall speak
Dan. 9. 16. *thy p.* are become a reproach to all
19. thy city and *thy p.* are called by thy name
24. seventy weeks are determined upon *thy p.*
10. 14. to understand what shall befall *thy p.*
12. 1. Michael, who standeth for the children of *thy*
p. and at that time *thy p.* shall be delivered
Hos. 4. 4. *thy p.* as they that strive with the priest
10. 14. shall a tumult arise among *thy p.*
Joel 2. 17. spare *thy p.* ‖ *Mic.* 7. 14. feed *thy p.*

Nah. 3. 13. *thy p.* in the midst of thee are women
18. *thy p.* is scattered on the mountains
Hab. 3. 13. thou wentest forth for salvation of *thy p.*
To or *unto the* PEOPLE.
Exod. 4. 16. and he shall be spokesman *to the p.*
18. 14. when Jethro saw all that he did *to the p.*
what is this thing that thou doest *to the p?*
19. 10. go *to the p.* ‖ 12. thou shalt set bounds *to the p.*
14. Moses went down from mount *to the p.* 25.
Deut. 20. 2. that the priest shall speak *to the p.*
5. and the officers shall speak *to the p.* 8.
Judg. 8. 5. give, I pray, loaves of bread *to the p.*
18. 10. when ye go, ye shall come *to a p.* secure, 27.
Ruth 2. 11. and art come *to a. p.* thou knewest not
1 *Sam.* 8. 10. Samuel told all the words *to the p.*
26. 7. David and Abishai came *to the p.* by night
14. David cried *to the p.* and to Abner, saying
30. 21. when David came near *to the p.* he saluted
2 *Sam.* 24. 3. now the Lord thy God add *to the p.*
1 *Kings* 12. 15. the king hearkened not *to the p.*
18. 21. Elijah came *to the p.* and said, how long
19. 21. Elisha gave *to the p.* and they did eat
2 *Kings* 4. 42. he said, give *to p.* that they may eat
11. 13. Athaliah came *to the p.* 2 *Chron.* 23. 12.
1 *Chron.* 10. 9. Philist. sent to carry tidings *to the p.*
2 *Chron.* 35. 7. Josiah gave *to the p.* lambs and kids
8. his princes gave willingly *to the p.* to priests
Neh. 4. 22. at the same time said I *to the p.* lodge
5. 15. former governors were chargeable *to the p.*
Psal. 9. 8. he shall minister judgment *to the p.*
72. 3. the mountains shall bring peace *to the p.*
Isa. 42. 5. he that giveth breath *to the p.* upon it
49. 22. and I will set up my standard *to the p.*
55. 4. behold, I have given him for a witness *to the p.* a leader and commander *to the p.*
Ezek. 24. 18. so I spake *to the p.* in the morning
Dan. 7. 27. kingdom be given *to the p.* of the saints
Joel 3. 8. they shall sell them *to the p.* far off
Hab. 3. 16. when he cometh up to *t. p.* he will invade
Zeph. 3. 9. I will turn *to the p.* a pure language
Hag. 1. 13. then spake Haggai the Lord's message *to the p.*
Mat. 12. 46. while he yet talked *to the p.* behold
27. 15. was wont to release *to the p.* a prisoner
Luke 7. 24. he began to speak *to the p.* concern. John
Acts 4. 1. as they spake *to the p.* the priests came
5. 20. speak in the temple *to the p.* all the words
10. 2. which gave alms *to the p.* and prayed to God
42. and he commanded us to preach *to the p.*
12. 4. intending to bring Peter forth *to the p.*
13. 31. seen of them who are his witnesses *to the p.*
17. 5. the Jews sought to bring them out *to the p.*
19. 30. when Paul would have entered in *to the p.*
33. and would have made his defence *to the p.*
21. 39. I beseech thee suffer me to speak *to the p.*
40. Paul beckoned with the hand *to the p.*
26. 23. Christ should suffer, and shew light *to the p.*
PEOPLES.
Rev. 10. 11. thou must prophesy before many *p.*
17. 15. waters thou sawest are *p.* and multitudes
PERADVENTURE.
Gen. 18. 24. *p.* there be fifty righteous within city
28. *p.* there shall lack five of the fifty righteous
29. *p.* there be forty ‖ 30. thirty ‖ 31. twenty
32. I will speak this once, *p.* ten shall be found
24. 5. *p.* the woman shall not be willing, 39.
27. 12. Jacob said, my father *p.* will feel me
31. 31. *p.* thou wouldest take by force thy daughters
32. 20. I will see his face, *p.* he will accept of me
42. 4. for he said, lest *p.* mischief befall him
43. 12. carry it again, *p.* it was an oversight
44. 34. lest *p.* I see evil shall come on my father
50. 15. Joseph will *p.* hate us, and will requite us
Exod. 13. 17. lest *p.* the people repent when see war
32. 30. *p.* I shall make an atonement for your sin
Num. 22. 6. curse this people, *p.* I shall prevail, 11.
23. 3. *p.* the Lord will come to meet me
27. *p.* it will please God that thou curse me them
Josh. 9. 7. men of Israel said, *p.* ye dwell among us
1 *Sam.* 6. 5. *p.* he will lighten his hand from off you
9. 6. *p.* he can shew us our way that we should go
1 *Kings* 18. 5. *p.* we may find grass to save horses
27. or *p.* he sleepeth, and must be awaked
20. 31. go to the king, *p.* he will save thy life
2 *Kings* 2. 16. lest *p.* Spirit of Lord hath cast him
Jer. 20. 10. watched for halting, *p.* he will be enticed
Rom. 5. 7. *p.* for a good man some would dare to die
2 *Tim.* 2. 25. *p.* God will give them repentance
PERCEIVE
Signifies, [1] *To discover, or find out,* 2 Sam. 14. 1. Jer. 38. 27. [2] *Spiritually to discern and consider things, so as to make a good use and improvement of them,* Deut. 29. 4. [3] *To know,* 2 Kings 4. 9.
He passeth on, but I perceive him not, *Job* 9. 11. *God continues to work by his providence in ways of mercy or judgment: but though I see the effects, I cannot understand the causes or grounds of his actions, because they are incomprehensible by me, or by any other man.*
Deut. 29. 4. Lord hath not given you a heart to *p.*
Josh. 22. 31. this day we *p.* the Lord is among us
1 *Sam.* 12. 17. that ye may *p.* your wickedness
2 *Sam.* 19. 6. I *p.* if Absalom had lived, and we died
2 *Kings* 4. 9. I *p.* that this is an holy man of God
Job 9. 11. but I *p.* him not ‖ 23. 8. I cannot *p.* him
Prov. 1. 2. to *p.* the words of understanding
Eccl. 3. 22. I *p.* that there is nothing better than
Isa. 6. 9. and see ye indeed, but *p.* not
33. 19. of a deeper speech than thou canst *p.*
Mat. 13. 14. shall hear and not understand, seeing, ye shall see, and shall not *p. Mark* 4. 12. *Acts* 28. 26.
Mark 7. 18. do ye not *p.* that whatsoever entereth in
8. 17. he said, *p.* ye not yet, neither understand?
Luke 8. 46. I *p.* that virtue is gone out of me
John 4. 19. woman saith, I *p.* that thou art a proph.
12. 19. Pharisees said, *p.* ye how prevail nothing?
Acts 8. 23. I *p.* thou art in the gall of bitterness
10. 34. of a truth I *p.* God is no respecter of persons
17. 22. I *p.* in all things ye are too superstitious
2 *Cor.* 7. 8. I *p.* the same epistle made you sorry
1 *John* 3. 16. hereby *p.* we the love of God

PERCEIVED.
Gen. 19. 33. he *p.* not when she lay down, 35.
Judg. 6. 22. when Gideon *p.* he was an angel
1 *Sam.* 3. 8. Eli *p.* that Lord had called child
28. 14. and Saul *p.* that it was Samuel, and stooped
2 *Sam.* 5. 12. and David *p.* that the Lord had established him king over Israel, 1 *Chron.* 14. 2.
12. 19. David *p.* that the child was dead
14. 1. Joab *p.* the king's heart was to Absalom
1 *Kings* 22. 33. when the captains of chariots *p.* that it was not king of Israel, 2 *Chron.* 18. 32.
Neh. 6. 12. lo, I *p.* that God had not sent him
16. they *p.* that this work was wrought of God
13. 10. I *p.* portions of Levites had not been given
Esth. 4. 1. when Mordecai *p.* all that was done
Job 38. 18. hast thou *p.* the breadth of the earth?
Eccl. 1. 17. I *p.* that this also is vexation of spirit
2. 14. I myself *p.* that one event happeneth to all
Isa. 64. 4. nor *p.* by the ear what God hath prepared
Jer. 23. 18. and who hath *p.* and heard his word
38. 27. they left off, for the matter was not *p.*
Mat. 21. 45. *p.* that he spake of them, *Luke* 20. 19.
22. 18. but Jesus *p.* their wickedness and said
Mark 2. 8. Jes. *p.* in spirit that they reasoned among
Luke 1. 22. they *p.* that he had seen a vision
5. 22. but when Jesus *p.* their thoughts
9. 45. the saying was hid, that they *p.* it not
20. 23. but he *p.* their craftiness, and said to them
John 6. 15. Jesus *p.* they would make him a king
Acts 4. 13. when they *p.* that they were unlearned
23. 6. when Paul *p.* that one part were Pharisees
Gal. 2. 9. when James *p.* the grace given to me
PERCEIVEST.
Prov. 14. 7. when thou *p.* not in him lips of knowl.
Luke 6. 41. but *p.* not beam that is in thine own eye
PERCEIVETH.
Job 14. 21. are brought low, but he *p.* it not of them
33. 14. God speaketh once, yet man *p.* it not
Prov. 31. 18. she *p.* that her merchandise is good
PERCEIVING.
Mark 12. 28. *p.* that he had answered them well
Luke 9. 47. Jesus *p.* the thought of their heart
Acts 14. 9. and *p.* he had faith to be healed
PERDITION
Signifies, *Utter ruin or destruction,* Rev. 17. 8. The son of perdition. Judas *is called by this name,* John 17. 12. *because* [1] *He was most worthy to be destroyed, having brought himself into a state of destruction.* [2] *He was ordained and appointed by God to destruction for his sins.* [3] *He was one, who by reason of the horridness of his crime, is mentioned as the most dreadful instance of God's irrevocable doom to eternal perdition.* Antichrist *is likewise called by this name,* 2 Thess. 2. 3. *because he brings destruction upon others, and is himself devoted to perdition.*
John 17. 12. none of them lost but the son of *p.*
Phil. 1. 28. which is to them an evident token of *p.*
2 *Thess.* 2. 3. that man of sin be revealed, son of *p.*
1 *Tim.* 6. 9. which drown men in destruction and *p.*
Heb. 10. 39. are not of them who draw back to *p.*
2 *Pet.* 3. 7. day of judgment, and *p.* of ungodly men
Rev. 17. 8. beast was and is not, and goeth into *p.* 11.
11. beast is eighth, and of seven, goeth into *p.*
PERFECT
Is applied, [I.] *To God, who is absolutely perfect,* Mat. 5. 48. [II.] *To things, as weight, measure, &c.* Deut. 25. 15. [III.] *To man, who is accounted so,* [1] *By Christ's righteousness being imputed,* Col. 1. 28. [2] *Comparatively, when compared with others who are partial in their obedience to God's commands,* Job 8. 20. | 9. 22. [3] *As being upright and sincere in heart, and unblamable in the course of his life,* Gen. 6. 9. | 17. 1. [4] *As carrying himself innocently and harmlessly towards his enemies,* Psal. 64. 4. [5] *As imitating God, in loving and doing good to others,* Mat. 5. 48. [6] *As being joined together in judgment, affections, and conversations, laying aside all factions and divisions,* 2 Cor. 13. 11. [7] *As having a good degree of understanding,* 1 Cor. 2. 6.
Gen. 6. 9. Noah was *p.* ‖ 17. 1. and be thou *p.*
Lev. 22. 21. the free-will offering shall be *p.*
Deut. 18. 13. thou shalt be *p.* with the Lord thy G.
25. 15. thou shalt have a *p.* weight, a *p.* measure
1 *Sam.* 14. 41. Saul said to the Lord, give a *p.* lot
2 *Sam.* 22. 33. he maketh my way *p. Psal.* 18. 32.
2 *Chr.* 4. 21. lamps and tongs made he of *p.* gold
Ezra 7. 12. Artax. king of kings, to Ezra, *p.* peace
Job 1. 1. that man was *p.* and upright, 8. | 2. 3.
8. 20. God will not cast away a *p.* man
9. 20. if I say, I am *p.* ‖ 21. though I were *p.*
22. he destroyeth the *p.* and the wicked
22. 3. is it gain to him, thou makest thy ways *p.?*
Psal. 37. 37. mark the *p.* man, his end is peace
64. 4. that they may shoot in secret at the *p.*
101. 2. I will behave myself wisely in a *p.* way
6. he that walketh in a *p.* way shall serve me
119. † 1. blessed are the *p.* in the way
139. 22. I hate them with *p.* hatred
Prov. 2. 21. and the *p.* shall remain in it
4. 18. path of just shineth more and more to *p.* day
11. 5. righteousness of the *p.* shall direct his way
Isa. 26. 3. thou wilt keep him in *p.* peace, whose
Ezek. 16. 14. for it was *p.* through my comeliness
27. 3. thou hast said, I am of *p.* beauty
11. they have made thy beauty, *p.* 28. 12.
28. 15. thou wast *p.* in thy ways, from the day
Mat. 5. 48. be ye *p.* even as your father is *p.*
19. 21. thou wilt be *p.* go and sell that thou hast
Luke 1. 3. having had *p.* understanding of things
John 17. 23. that they may be made *p.* in one
Acts 3. 16. hath given him this *p.* soundness
22. 3. taught according to the *p.* manner of law
24. 22. having more *p.* knowledge of that way
Rom. 12. 2. may prove what is that *p.* will of God
1 *Cor.* 2. 6. speak wisdom among them that are *p.*
14. † 20. but in understanding be *p.*
2 *Cor.* 12. 9. my strength is made *p.* in weakness
13. 11. be *p.* be of good comfort, be of one mind
Gal. 3. 3. begun in Spirit, are ye made *p.* by flesh?
Eph. 4. 13. till we come to *p.* man, to fulness of C.

Phil. 3. 12. not as though I were already *p.*
15. let us, as many as be *p.* be thus minded
Col. 1. 28. we may present every man *p.* in Christ
4. 12. may stand *p.* and complete in will of God
1 *Thess.* 3. 10. might *p.* which is lacking in your
2 *Tim.* 3. 17. that the man of God may be *p.*
Heb. 2. 10. to make Captain of their salvation *p.*
5. 9. being made *p.* he became Author of salvation
7. 19. for law made nothing *p.* but bringing in
9. 9. could not make him that did the service *p.*
11. by a greater and more *p.* tabernacle not made
10. 1. law can never make the comers thereunto *p.*
11. 40. they without us should not be made *p.*
12. 23. and to the spirits of just men made *p.*
13. 21. God make you *p.* in every good work
Jam. 1. 4. but let patience have her *p.* work, that ye may be *p.* and entire, wanting nothing
17. every good and *p.* gift is from above
25. whoso looketh into the *p.* law of liberty
2. 22. and by works was faith made *p.*
3. 2. if any offend not in word, same is a *p.* man
1 *Pet.* 5. 10. after ye have suffered, make you *p.*
1 *John* 4. 17. herein is our love made *p.* that we
18. but *p.* love casteth out fear, because fear hath torment; he that feareth is not made *p.* in love
See HEART.
Is PERFECT.
Deut. 32. 4. is the rock, his work *is p.* his ways
2 *Sam.* 22. 31. as for God, his way *is p. Psal.* 18. 30.
Job 36. 4. he that *is p.* in knowledge, 37. 16.
Psal. 19. 7. law of the Lord *is p.* converting soul
Isa. 18. 5. behold the harvest, when the bud *is p.*
42. 19. who is blind as he that *is p.* as Lord's serv.
Mat. 5. 48. as your Father which is in heaven *is p.*
Luke 6. 40. every one that *is p.* shall be as his master
1 *Cor.* 13. 10. when that which *is p.* is come, then
PERFECTED.
2 *Chron.* 8. 16. so the house of God was *p.*
24. 13. workm. wrought, and work was *p.* by them
Ezek. 27. 4. thy builders have *p.* thy beauty
Mat. 21. 16. out of mouth of babes thou hast *p.* praise
Luke 6. † 40. every one shall be *p.* as his master
13. 32. and the third day I shall be *p.*
Heb. 7. † 28. maketh Son, who is *p.* for evermore
10. 14. by one offering he hath *p.* for ever sanctified
1 *John* 2. 5. in him verily is the love of God *p.*
4. 12. if we love one another, his love is *p.* in us
PERFECTING.
2 *Cor.* 7. 1. *p.* holiness in the fear of God
Eph. 4. 12. for *p.* of the saints, for edifying of body
PERFECTION
Signifies, [1] *The highest degree, or greatest accomplishment of, a thing,* Job 11. 7. Canst thou find out the Almighty unto perfection? *that is, Canst thou know him and his counsels perfectly? Canst thou throughly understand what he aims at in afflicting thee?* [2] *Full growth, maturity, or ripeness,* Luke 8. 14. [3] *That good order which by the word of God is settled in any church, when all the members thereof keep their due place, and perform their office duly,* 2 Cor. 13. 9. [4] *The deep mysteries of the gospel, or greater degrees of knowledge and grace,* Heb. 6. 1. [5] *Justification, sanctification, and consequently salvation,* Heb. 7. 11.
I have seen an end of all perfection, *Psal.* 119. 96. *I have observed by my experience, that the greatest and most perfect accomplishments and enjoyments in this world, the greatest glory and riches, power and wisdom, are too narrow and short-lived to make men happy.*
Job 11. 7. canst thou find out the Almighty to *p.?*
15. 29. nor shall he prolong the *p.* thereof on earth
21. † 23. one dieth in the strength of his *p.*
28. 3. setteth an end to dark. he searcheth out all *p.*
Psal. 50. 2. out of Zion, *p.* of beauty, God shined
119. 96. I have seen an end of *p.* but thy comma.
Isa. 47. 9. they shall come upon thee in their *p.*
Lam. 2. 15. the city that men call the *p.* of beauty
Luke 8. 14. are choked, and bring no fruit to *p.*
2 *Cor.* 13. 9. and this also we wish, even your *p.*
Heb. 6. 1. leaving the principles, let us go on to *p.*
7. 11. if *p.* were by the Levitical priesthood
PERFECTLY.
Jer. 23. 20. in the latter days ye shall consider it *p.*
Mat. 14. 36. as many as touched were made *p.* whole
Acts 18. 26. and expounded way of God more *p.*
23. 15. ye would inquire something more *p.* 20.
1 *Cor.* 1. 10. but be *p.* joined together in same mind
1 *Thess.* 5. 2. for yourselves know *p.* that day of Ld.
PERFECT, *Verb.*
Psal. 138. 8. the Lord will *p.* which concerneth me
PERFECTNESS.
Col. 3. 14. put on charity, which is the bond of *p.*
PERFORMANCE.
Luke 1. 45. for there shall be a *p.* of those things
2 *Cor.* 8. 11. so may be a *p.* also out of that ye have
PERFORM
Signifies, [1] *To put in execution,* Job 5. 12. [2] *To fulfil or make good,* Deut. 9. 5. Jer. 28. 6. [3] *To grant or yield to,* Esth. 5. 8. [4] *To keep and observe,* Psal. 119. 112. [5] *To finish,* Phil. 1. † 6.
Gen. 26. 3. I will *p.* the oath which I sware to Abraham thy father, *Deut.* 9. 5. *Luke* 1. 72.
Exod. 18. 18. thou art not able to *p.* it thyself alone
Num. 4. 23. all that enter in to *p.* the service
Deut. 4. 13. his covenant he commanded you to *p.*
23. 23. that which is gone out of thy lips shalt *p.*
25. 5. and *p.* duty of a husband's brother to her
7. he will not *p.* duty of my husband's brother
Ruth 3. 13. if he will *p.* the part of a kinsman
1 *Sam.* 3. 12. in that day I will *p.* ag. Eli things spok.
2 *Sam.* 14. 15. that the king will *p.* the request
1 *Kings* 6. 12. then I will *p.* my word with thee
12. 15. that he might *p.* his saying, 2 *Chron.* 10. 15.
2 *Kings* 23. 3. to *p.* the words of this covenant, to keep God's commandments, 24. 2 *Chron.* 34. 31.
Esth. 5. 8. if it please the king to *p.* my request
Job 5. 12. their hands cannot *p.* their enterprise
Psal. 21. 11. a device which they are not able to *p.*
61. 8. I will sing praise, that I may daily *p.* vows

Ps. 119. 106. I have sworn, and I will *p.* it, to keep
112. I have inclined my heart to *p.* thy statutes
Isa. 9. 7. the zeal of the Lord of hosts will *p.* this
19. 21. they shall pay a vow to the Lord, and *p.* it
44. 28. Cyrus my shepherd shall *p.* all my pleasure
Jer. 1. 12. for I will hasten my word to *p.* it
11. 5. I may *p.* the oath which I have sworn
28. 6. Lord *p.* thy words thou hast prophesied
29. 10. I will *p.* my good word toward you, 33. 14.
44. 25. ye will surely accomplish and *p.* your vows
Ezek. 12. 25. I will say the word, and will *p.* it
Mic. 7. 20. thou wilt *p.* the truth to Jacob
Nah. 1. 15. keep thy solemn feasts, *p.* thy vows
Mat. 5. 33. thou shalt *p.* to the Lord thine oaths
Rom. 4. 21. what he promised, he was able also to *p.*
7. 18. how to *p.* that which is good, I find not
2 *Cor.* 8. 11. now therefore *p.* the doing of it
Phil. 1. 6. he will *p.* it until the day of Jesus Christ

PERFORMED.

1 *Sam.* 15. 11. Saul hath not *p.* my commandments
13. I have *p.* the commandment of the Lord
2 *Sam.* 21. 14. they *p.* all that the king commanded
1 *Kings* 8. 20. Lord hath *p.* his word, and I am risen
up in room of David, 2 *Chr.* 6. 10. *Neh.* 9. 8.
Esth. 1. 15. Vashti hath not *p.* command. of king
5. 6. to half of the kingdom it shall be *p.* 7. 2.
Psal. 65. 1. and unto thee shall the vow be *p.*
Isa. 10. 12. when Lord hath *p.* his whole work
Jer. 23. 20. till he have *p.* the thoughts, 30. 24.
34. 18. who have not *p.* words of the covenant
35. 14. the words of Jonadab are *p.* 16.
51. 29. for every purpose of the Lord shall be *p.*
Ezek. 37. 14. having spoken and *p.* it saith Lord
Luke 1. 20. till the day that these things shall be *p.*
2. 39. when they had *p.* all things to law of Lord
Rom. 15. 28. when I have *p.* this, I will come to Spain

PERFORMETH.

Neh. 5. 13. every man that *p.* not this promise
Job 23. 14. he *p.* thing that is appointed for me
Psal. 57. 2. I will cry to G. that *p.* all things for me
Isa. 44. 26. that *p.* the counsel of his messengers

PERFORMING.

Num. 15. 3. an offering or sacrifice in *p.* a vow, 8.

PERFUME, S.

Exod. 30. 35. and thou shalt make it a *p.* 37.
Prov. 27. 9. ointment and *p.* rejoice the heart
Cant. 5. † 13. his cheeks are as towers of *p.*
Isa. 57. 9. thou didst increase thy *p.* and send

PERFUMED.

Prov. 7. 17. I have *p.* my bed with myrrh, aloes
Cant. 3. 6. who is this that cometh *p.* with myrrh?

PERHAPS.

Acts 8. 22. if *p.* thy thought may be forgiven thee
2 *Cor.* 2. 7. lest *p.* such a one be swallowed up
Philem. 15. for *p.* he therefore departed for a season

PERIL.

Lam. 5. 9. we get our bread with the *p.* of our lives
Rom. 8. 35. shall famine, *p.* or sword, separate us?

PERILS.

2 *Cor.* 11. 26. in *p.* of waters, in *p.* of robbers, in *p.*
by countrymen, in *p.* by heathen, in *p.*
in city, in *p.* in wilderness, in *p.* in sea,
in *p.* among false brethren

PERILOUS.

2 *Tim.* 3. 1. in the last days *p.* times shall come

PERISH

Signifies, [1] *To die, or lose life,* Jonah 1. 6. [2] *To be rooted out,* 2 Kings 9. 8. [3] *To starve,* Luke 15. 17. [4] *To be damned,* 2 Cor. 2. 15. 2 Pet. 2. 12. [5] *To be taken away,* Mic. 7. 2. [6] *To be deprived of being,* 1 Cor. 15. 18.

Gen. 41. 36. that the land *p.* not through famine
Exod. 19. 21. lest they gaze, and many of them *p.*
21. 26. if a man smite eye of his maid, that it *p.*
Num. 17. 12. behold, we die, we *p.* we all *p.*
24. 20. but his latter end shall be that *p.* for ever
Deut. 11. 17. lest ye *p.* quickly from the land
26. 5. a Syrian ready to *p.* was my father
28. 20. until thou *p.* quickly, 22. *Josh.* 23. 13.
Judg. 5. 31. let all thine enemies *p.* O Lord
1 *Sam.* 26. 10. he shall descend into battle, and *p.*
Esth. 3. 13. and to cause to *p.* all the Jews, 7. 4.
4. 16. and if I *p.* I *p.* ‖ 8. 11. to cause to *p.* all power
9. 28. nor the memorial of them *p.* from their seed
Job 3. 3. let the day *p.* wherein I was born
4. 9. by the blast of God they *p.* by the breath
20. they *p.* for ever, without any regarding it
6. 18. paths of their way go to nothing and *p.*
29. 13. the blessing of him that was ready to *p.*
31. 19. if I have seen any *p.* for want of clothing
Psal. 2. 12. lest he be angry, and ye *p.* from way
9. 18. the expectation of the poor shall not *p.*
49. 10. likewise the fool and the brutish person *p.*
12. man in honour is like the beasts that *p.* 20.
68. 2. as wax melteth, so let wicked *p.* 83. 17.
80. 16. they *p.* at the rebuke of thy countenance
146. 4. not trust, in that very day his thoughts *p.*
Prov. 11. 10. when the wicked *p.* 28. 28.
29. 18. where there is no vision, the people *p.*
31. 6. give strong drink to him that is ready to *p.*
Eccl. 5. 14. but those riches *p.* by evil travail
Isa. 26. 14. and made all their memory to *p.*
27. 13. they shall come which were ready to *p.*
Jer. 18. 18. the law shall not *p.* from the priest
25. † 10. I will cause to *p.* the voice of mirth
27. 10. that I drive you out, and ye should *p.* 15.
40. 15. that the remnant in Judah should *p.*
Ezek. 25. 7. I will cause thee to *p.* out of countries
Dan. 2. 18. that Daniel and fellows should not *p.*
Jonah 1. 6. God will think on us that we *p.* not, 3. 9.
14. O Lord, let us not *p.* for this man's life
Mat. 5. 29. that one of thy members should *p.* 30.
8. 25. saying, Lord, save us, we *p.* *Luke* 8. 24.
9. 17. the wine runneth out, and the bottles *p.*
18. 14. that one of these little ones should *p.*
Mark 4. 38. Master, carest thou not that we *p.*?
Luke 13. 33. that a prophet *p.* out of Jerusalem
15. 17. have bread enough, and I *p.* with hunger
21. 18. there shall not an hair of your head *p.*
John 3. 15. whoso believeth in him should not *p.* 16.
11. 50. and that the whole nation *p.* not
Acts 8. 20. thy money *p.* with thee, because thou
Acts 13. 41. behold, ye despisers, and wonder, and *p.*
1 *Cor.* 1. 18. for preaching of the cross is to them that
p. foolishness, but to us saved power of God
2 *Cor.* 2. 15. a savour of Christ in them that *p.*
4. 16. but tho' our outward man *p.* inward is renew.
Col. 2. 22. which all are to *p.* with the using
2 *Thess.* 2. 10. of unrighteousness in them that *p.*
2 *Pet.* 3. 9. not willing that any should *p.* but that all

Shall PERISH.

Lev. 26. 38. and ye *shall p.* among the heathen
Num. 24. 24. and he also *shall p.* for ever
Deut. 4. 26. ye *shall* soon utterly *p.* ye shall not pro
long your days, 8. 19, 20. | 30. 18. *Josh.* 23. 16.
1 *Sam.* 27. 1. I *shall* one day *p.* by the hand of Saul
2 *Kings* 9. 8. the whole house of Ahab *shall p.*
Job 8. 13. and the hypocrite's hope *shall p.*
11. † 20. and flight *shall p.* from the wicked
18. 17. his remembrance *shall p.* 20. 7. | 36. 12.
34. 15. all flesh *shall p.* together, and man return
Psal. 1. 6. but the way of the ungodly *shall p.*
37. 20. wicked *shall p.* ‖ 92. 9. thine enemies *shall p.*
73. 27. they that are far from thee *shall p.*
102. 26. they *shall p.* but thou shalt endure
112. 10. the desire of the wicked *shall p.*
Prov. 10. 28. expectation of wicked *shall p.* 11. 7.
19. 9. and he that speaketh lies *shall p.*
21. 28. a false witness *shall p.* but the man
Isa. 29. 14. the wisdom of their wise men *shall p.*
41. 11. they that strive with thee *shall p.*
60. 12. kingdom that will not serve thee *shall p.*
Jer. 4. 9. that the heart of the king *shall p.*
6. 21. friend *shall p.* ‖ 10. 11. gods *shall p.* 15. | 51. 18.
25. † 35. and flight *shall p.* from the shepherds
48. 8. valley also *shall p.* and the plain destroyed
Ezek. 7. 26. but the law *shall p.* from the priest
Amos 1. 8. the remnant of the Philistines *shall p.*
2. 14. therefore the flight *shall p.* from the swift
3. 15. and the houses of ivory *shall p.* great houses
Zech. 9. 5. and the king *shall p.* from Gaza
Mat. 26. 52. that take the sword, *shall p.* with sword
Luke 5. 37. new wine be spilled, and bottles *shall p.*
13. 3. except ye repent, ye *shall* all likewise *p.* 5.
John 10. 28. sheep *shall* never *p.* nor any pluck them
Rom. 2. 12. sinned without law, *shall p.* without law
1 *Cor.* 8. 11. *shall* weak brother *p.* for whom Chr. died
Heb. 1. 11. they *shall p.* but thou remainest
2 *Pet.* 2. 12. and *shall p.* in their own corruption

PERISHED.

Num. 16. 33. and they *p.* from the congregation
21. 30. Heshbon is *p.* even to Dibon, laid waste
Josh. 22. 20. that man *p.* not alone in his iniquity
2 *Sam.* 1. 27. and how are the weapons of war *p.*!
Job 4. 7. remember, who ever *p.* being innocent
30. 2. might profit me, in whom old age was *p.*
Psal. 9. 6. their memorial is *p.* with them
10. 16. the heathen are *p.* out of his land
83. 10. as Sisera and Jabin, which *p.* at En-dor
119. 92. I should have *p.* in mine affliction
142. † 4. none would know me, refuge *p.* from me
Eccl. 9. 6. their envy is *p.* ‖ *Jer.* 7. 28. truth is *p.*
Jer. 48. 36. the riches that he hath gotten are *p.*
49. 7. is counsel *p.* from the prudent? is wisdom
Lam. 3. 18. I said, my strength and hope is *p.*
Joel 1. 11. because the harvest of the field is *p.*
Jonah 4. 10. which came up and *p.* in a night
Mic. 4. 9. why dost thou cry? is thy counsellor *p.*
7. 2. the good man is *p.* out of the earth
Mat. 8. 32. herd of swine ran and *p.* in the waters
Luke 11. 51. which *p.* between the altar and temple
Acts 5. 37. he also *p.* and as many as obeyed him
1 *Cor.* 15. 18. then they fallen asleep in Christ are *p.*
Heb. 11. 31. by faith the harlot Rahab *p.* not
2 *Pet.* 3. 6. world being overflowed with water *p.*
Jude 11. and *p.* in the gain-saying of Core

PERISHETH.

Job 4. 11. the old lion *p.* for lack of prey
Psal. 31. † 12. I am like a vessel that *p.*
Prov. 11. 7. and the hope of unjust men *p.*
Eccl. 7. 15. there is a just man that *p.* in his right.
Isa. 57. 1. righteous *p.* and no man layeth it to heart
Jer. 9. 12. for what the land *p.* and is burnt up
48. 46. O Moab, the people of Chemosh *p.*
John 6. 27. labour not for the meat which *p.*
Jam. 1. 11. and the grace of the fashion of it *p.*
1 *Pet.* 1. 7. trial of faith more precious than gold *p.*

PERISHING.

Job 33. 18. and his life from *p.* by the sword

PERJURED.

1 *Tim.* 1. 10. law is made for liars and *p.* persons

PERMISSION.

1 *Cor.* 7. 6. I speak this by *p.* not by commandment

PERMIT.

1 *Cor.* 16. 7. I trust to tarry awhile, if the Lord *p.*
Heb. 6. 3. and this will we do, if God *p.*

PERMITTED.

Acts 26. 1. Agrippa said, thou art *p.* to speak for thy.
1 *Cor.* 14. 34. for it is not *p.* to women to speak

PERNICIOUS.

2 *Pet.* 2. 2. and many shall follow their *p.* ways

PERPETUAL

Signifies, [1] *Continual, or uninterrupted,* Ezek. 35. 5. [2] *Everlasting, or endless,* Psal. 9. 6. [3] *The duration of time to the end of the world,* Gen. 9. 12. [4] *During the continuance of the legal dispensation,* Exod. 29. 9. | 30. 8. [5] *A set space of time,* Jer. 25. 9, 12.

Gen. 9. 12. token of the covenant for *p.* generations
Exod. 29. 9. the priest's office be theirs for *p.* statute
30. 8. a *p.* incense before the Lord for generations
31. 16. keep the sabbath for a *p.* covenant
Lev. 3. 17. a *p.* statute not to eat fat or blood
6. 20. a *p.* meat-offering for Aaron and his sons
24. 9. the shew-bread be Aaron's by a *p.* statute
25. 34. may not be sold, for it is their *p.* possession
Num. 19. 21. a *p.* statute, that he that sprinkleth
Psal. 9. 6. destructions are come to a *p.* end
74. 3. lift up thy feet to the *p.* desolations
78. 66. he put them to a *p.* reproach
Jer. 5. 22. by a *p.* decree, that it cannot pass it
8. 5. why peo. slidden back by a *p.* backsliding?
15. 18. why is my pain *p.* and my wound incurable?
18. 16. to make their land desolate, and *p.* hissing
Jer. 23. 40. and I will bring upon you a *p.* shame
25. 9. and make them *p.* desolations, 12.
49. 13. the cities thereof shall be *p.* wastes
50. 5. let us join to the Lord in a *p.* covenant
51. 39. that they may sleep a *p.* sleep, 57.
Ezek. 35. 5. because thou hast had a *p.* hatred
9. I will make thee *p.* desolations, *Zeph.* 2. 9.
46. 14. by a *p.* ordinance to the Lord
Hab. 3. 6. he beheld, and the *p.* hills did bow

PERPETUALLY.

1 *Kings* 9. 3. my heart shall be there *p.* 2 *Chr.* 7. 16.
Amos 1. 11. his anger did tear *p.* and kept wrath

PERPLEXED.

Esth. 3. 15. but the city Shushan was *p.*
Joel 1. 18. the herds of cattle are *p.* no pasture
Luke 9. 7. Herod was *p.* ‖ 24. 4. as they were *p.*
2 *Cor.* 4. 8. we are *p.* but not in despair

PERPLEXITY.

Isa. 22. 5. for it is a day of *p.* by the Lord God
Mic. 7. 4. the day cometh, now shall be their *p.*
Luke 21. 25. on earth distress of nations, with *p.*

PERSECUTE.

Job 19. 22. why do ye *p.* me as God, and are not
28. why *p.* ye him, seeing the root is in me?
Psal. 7. 1. save me from all them that *p.* me
5. let the enemy *p.* my soul, and take it
10. 2. the wicked in his pride doth *p.* the poor
31. 15. deliver me from them that *p.* me
35. 3. stop the way against them that *p.* me
6. and let the angel of the Lord *p.* them
69. 26. they *p.* him whom thou hast smitten
71. 11. *p.* and take him, there is none to deliver
83. 15. so *p.* them with thy tempest, and make
119. 84. execute judgment on them that *p.* me
86. they *p.* me wrongfully, help thou me
Jer. 17. 18. let them be confounded that *p.* me
29. 18. I will *p.* them with the sword
Lam. 3. 66. *p.* and destroy them in anger
Mat. 5. 11. blessed are ye, when men shall *p.* you
44. and pray for them which *p.* you
10. 23. when they *p.* you in one city, flee to another
23. 34. ye shall *p.* them from city to city
Luke 11. 49. some of them they shall *p.* 21. 12.
John 5. 16. and therefore did the Jews *p.* Jesus
15. 20. if they have persecuted me, they will also *p.* you
Rom. 12. 14. bless them which *p.* you, curse not

PERSECUTED.

Deut. 30. 7. will put curses on them that *p.* thee
Psal. 109. 16. because he *p.* the poor and needy
119. 161. princes have *p.* me without cause
143. 3. for the enemy hath *p.* my soul
Isa. 14. 6. he that ruleth nations in anger is *p.*
Lam. 3. 43. thou hast covered with anger, and *p.* us
Mat. 5. 10. blessed which are *p.* for righteousness
12. so *p.* they the prophets before you
John 15. 20. if they have *p.* me, they will *p.* you
Acts 7. 52. which prophets have not your fathers *p.*
22. 4. and I *p.* this way unto the death
26. 11. I *p.* them even to strange cities
1 *Cor.* 4. 12. reviled, we bless; being *p.* we suffer it
15. 9. because I *p.* the church of God, *Gal.* 1. 13.
2 *Cor.* 4. 9. we are *p.* but not forsaken, cast down
Gal. 1. 23. that he which *p.* us in times past
4. 29. he that was born after the flesh *p.* him
1 *Thess.* 2. 15. who have killed the Lord and *p.* us
Rev. 12. 13. dragon *p.* woman that brought forth

PERSECUTEST.

Acts 9. 4. Saul, Saul, why *p.* thou me? 22. 7. | 26. 14.
5. I am Jesus, whom thou *p.* 22. 8. | 26. 15.

PERSECUTING.

Phil. 3. 6. concerning zeal, *p.* the church

PERSECUTION.

Lam. 5. 5. our necks are under *p.* we have no rest
Mat. 13. 21. for when *p.* ariseth, *Mark* 4. 17.
Acts 8. 1. at that time there was great *p.* ag. church
11. 19. they which were scattered abroad on the *p.*
13. 50. and raised *p.* against Paul and Barnabas
Rom. 8. 35. shall *p.* or sword, separate us from Chr.?
Gal. 5. 11. if I preach circum. why do I yet suffer *p.*?
6. 12. lest they should suffer *p.* for cross of Christ
2 *Tim.* 3. 12. all that will live godly shall suffer *p.*

PERSECUTIONS.

Mark 10. 30. shall have in this world lands with *p.*
2 *Cor.* 12. 10. I take pleasure in *p.* for Christ's sake
2 *Thess.* 1. 4. we glory for your faith in all your *p.*
2 *Tim.* 3. 11. know my *p.* at Antioch, what *p.* endured

PERSECUTOR.

1 *Tim.* 1. 13. who was before a *p.* and injurious

PERSECUTORS.

Neh. 9. 11. their *p.* thou threwest into the deeps
Psal. 7. 13. he ordaineth his arrows against the *p.*
119. 157. many are my *p.* ‖ 142. 6. deliver from *p.*
Jer. 15. 15. O L. visit me, and revenge me of my *p.*
20. 11. therefore my *p.* shall stumble, not prevail
Lam. 1. 3. all her *p.* overtook her between straits
4. 19. our *p.* are swifter than the eagles of heaven

PERSEVERANCE.

Eph. 6. 18. and watching thereunto with all *p.*

PERSON

Signifies, [1] *A particular individual man or woman,* Gen. 14. 21. Job 22. 29. [2] *The outward qualities and conditions of men; such as country, riches, friends, poverty, and the like,* Luke 20. 21. Acts 10. 34. Rom. 2. 11. [3] *Sight, name, or authority,* 2 Cor. 2. 10.

Gen. 39. 6. Joseph was a goodly *p.* and well favour.
Exod. 12. 48. no uncircumcised *p.* shall eat thereof
Lev. 19. 15. nor honour the *p.* of the mighty
Num. 5. 6. when commit any sin that *p.* be guilty
19. 17. for an unclean *p.* shall take of the ashes
18. clean *p.* shall take hyssop and dip it in water
22. whatsoever unclean *p.* toucheth, be unclean
31. 19. whosoever hath killed any *p.* or touched
any slain, 35. 11, 15, 30. *Josh.* 20. 3, 9.
35. 30. one witness shall not testify against any *p.*
Deut. 15. 22. unclean and clean *p.* shall eat it alike
27. 25. that taketh reward to slay an innocent *p.*
28. 50. shall not regard the *p.* of old or young
1 *Sam.* 9. 2. there was not a goodlier *p.* than he
16. 18. David a comely *p.* ‖ 25. 35. accepted thy *p.*
2 *Sam.* 4. 11. have slain a righteous *p.* in his house
14. 14. neither doth God respect any *p.*

2 *Sam.* 17. 11. that thou go to battle in thine own *p.*
Job 22. 29. and he shall save the humble *p.*
Psal. 15. 4. in whose eyes a vile *p.* is contemned
49. 10. likewise the fool and the brutish *p.* perish
101. 4. I will not know a wicked *p.*
105. 37. was not one feeble *p.* among their tribes
Prov. 6. 12. naughty *p.* walks with froward mouth
24. 8. deviseth evil, shall be called mischievous *p.*
28. 17. that doeth violence to the blood of any *p.*
Isa. 32. 5. the vile *p.* shall be no more called liberal
6. for the vile *p.* will speak villany, and his
43. † 4. therefore I will give people for thy *p.*
Jer. 43. 6. Johanan took every *p.* that was left
52. 25. he took seven that were near the king's *p.*
Ezek. 16. 5. was cast out to the loathing of thy *p.*
33. 6. if sword come and take any *p.* among them
44. 25. the priests shall come at no dead *p.*
Dan. 11. 21. in his estate shall stand up a vile *p.*
Mat. 22. 16. regardest not *p.* of men, *Mark* 12. 14.
27. 24. I am innocent of the blood of this just *p.*
1 *Cor.* 5. 13. put away from you that wicked *p.*
2 *Cor.* 2. 10. forgave I it in the *p.* of Christ
Eph. 5. 5. nor unclean *p.* hath inheritance in kingd.
Heb. 1. 3. and the express image of his *p.*
12. 16. or profane *p.* as Esau, who sold his birthright
2 *Pet.* 2. 5. but saved Noah, the eighth *p.* a preacher

PERSONS.

Gen. 14. 21. give me *p.* and take the goods to thyself
Exod. 16. 16. gather according to number of your *p.*
Lev. 27. 2. *p.* shall be for the Lord by estimation
Num. 19. 18. clean person shall sprinkle it upon *p.*
31. 28. both of the *p.* beeves, asses, and sheep
35. thirty and two thousand *p.* in all, of women
Deut. 10. 17. God of gods, which regardeth not *p.*
22. fathers went down into Egypt with seventy *p.*
Judg. 9. 2. the sons of Jerubbaal which were 70 *p.*
4. Abimelech hired vain and light *p.* followed
5. he went and slew threescore and ten *p.* 18.
20. 39. Benjamin began to kill of Israel about 30 *p.*
1 *Sam.* 9. 22. those bidden, which were about 30 *p.*
22. 18. and Doeg slew on that day 85 *p.*
22. I have occasioned the death of all the *p.*
2 *Kings* 10. 6. now the king's sons being 70 *p.*
7. they took the king's sons and slew 70 *p.*
Ps. 26. 4. I have not sat with vain *p.* nor dissemblers
Prov. 12. 11. he that followeth vain *p.* 28. 19.
Jer. 52. 29. he carried captive from Jerusalem 832 *p.*
30. he carried away captive of Jews 745 *p.*
Ezek. 7. † 11. none of their tumultuous *p.*
17. 17. and building forts to cut off many *p.*
27. 13. they traded the *p.* of men in thy market
Jonah 4. 11. wherein are more than 120,000 *p.*
Zeph. 3. 4. her prophets are treacherous *p.*
Luke 15. 7. joy more than over ninety-nine just *p.*
Acts 17. 17. Paul disputed with the devout *p.*
2 *Cor.* 1. 11. gift bestowed on us by means of many *p.*
1 *Tim.* 1. 10. the law is made for perjured *p.*
2 *Pet.* 3. 11. what manner of *p.* ought ye to be
Jude 16. having men's *p.* in admiration of advantage
See RESPECT.

PERSUADE

Signifies, [1] *To convince and convert*, Gen. 9. † 27. Luke 16. 31. [2] *To be assured or satisfied*, Rom. 8. 38. | 14. † 5. [3] *To advise, or put one upon doing any thing*, 2 Chron. 32. 11. [4] *To deceive*, 1 Kings 22. 20. [5] *To pacify*, Prov. 25. 15. [6] *To trust or hope for*, Heb. 6. 9. [7] *To provoke, or stir up*, Acts 14. 19.
Gen. 9. † 27. God shall *p.* Japhet, and dwell in tents
1 *Kings* 22. 20. who shall *p.* Ahab, to go up and fall
21. I will *p.* him ‖ 22. thou shalt *p.* him and prevail
2 *Chron.* 32. 11. doth not Hezekiah *p.* you to give
Isa. 36. 18. beware, lest Hezekiah *p.* you, saying
Mat. 28. 14. we will *p.* him and secure you
2 *Cor.* 5. 11. we *p.* men ‖ *Gal.* 1. 10. do I now *p.* men?
1 *John* 3. † 19. and shall *p.* our hearts before him

PERSUADED.

2 *Chr.* 18. 2. Ahab *p.* Jehoshaphat to go with him
Prov. 25. 15. by long forbearing is a prince *p.*
Mat. 27. 20. the chief priests *p.* the multitude
Luke 16. 31. will not be *p.* if one rose from dead
20. 6. for they be *p.* that John was a prophet
Acts 13. 43. *p.* them to continue in grace of God
14. 19. who *p.* the people, and having stoned Paul
18. 4. Paul *p.* the Jews and the Greeks
19. 26. this Paul hath *p.* turned away much people
21. 14. when he would not be *p.* we ceased
26. 26. I am *p.* none of these things are hid from
Rom. 4. 21. being *p.* that what he had promised
8. 38. I am *p.* that nothing can separate us from
14. 5. let every man be fully *p.* in his mind
14. I know and am *p.* there is nothing unclean
15. 14. I myself also am *p.* of you, my brethren
2 *Tim.* 1. 5. and I am *p.* that in thee also
12. I am *p.* that he is able to keep what I comm.
Heb. 6. 9. we are *p.* better things of you, though thus
11. 13. having seen them afar off, were *p.* of them

PERSUADEST.

Acts 26. 28. almost thou *p.* me to be a christian

PERSUADETH.

2 *Kings* 18. 32. when Hezekiah *p.* you, saying
Acts 18. 13. Paul *p.* men to worship contrary to law

PERSUADING.

Acts 19. 8. *p.* things concerning kingdom of God
28. 23. *p.* them concern. Jesus from law and proph.

PERSUASION.

Gal. 5. 8. this *p.* cometh not of him that calleth you

PERTAIN.

Lev. 7. 20. sacrifice of peace offerings *p.* to Lord
21. and eat of the sacrifice which *p.* to the Lord
1 *Sam.* 25. 22. if I leave all that *p.* to him
Rom. 15. 17. in those things which *p.* to God
1 *Cor.* 6. 3. how much more things *p.* to this life
2 *Pet.* 1. 3. hath given us all things that *p.* to life

PERTAINED.

Num. 31. 43. the half that *p.* to the congregation
Josh. 24. 33. Eleazar was buried in a hill that *p.*
Judg. 6. 11. angel sat under an oak that *p.* to Joash
1 *Sam.* 25. 21. nothing missed of all that *p.* to Nabal
2 *Sam.* 2. 15. which *p.* to Ish-bosheth, son of Saul
6. 12. God blessed all that *p.* to Obed edom
9. 9. have given master's son all that *p.* to Saul

2 *Sam.* 16. 4. thine are all that *p.* to Mephibosheth
1 *Kings* 7. 48. Solomon made vessels that *p.* to house
2 *Kings* 24. 7. all that *p.* to the king of Egypt
1 *Chron.* 9. 27. opening every morning *p.* to them
2 *Chron.* 12. 4. he took the cities which *p.* to Judah
34. 33. Josiah took away abominations *p.* to Israel

PERTAINETH.

Lev. 14. 32. to get that which *p.* to cleansing
Num. 4. 16. to the office of Eleazar *p.* the oil
Deut. 22. 5. woman shall not wear what *p.* to a man
1 *Sam.* 27. 6. Ziklag *p.* to the kings of Judah
2 *Chron.* 26. 18. it *p.* not to thee, Uzziah, to burn
Rom. 9. 4. to whom *p.* the adoption and the glory
Heb. 7. 13. he *p.* to another tribe, of which no man

PERTAINING.

Josh. 13. 31. half Gilead and cities *p.* to Machir
1 *Chron.* 26. 32. rulers for every matter *p.* to God
Acts 1. 3. speaking of things *p.* to kingdom of God
1 *Cor.* 6. 4. have judgment of things, *p.* to this life
Heb. 2. 17. merciful High Priest in things *p.* to God
5. 1. is ordained for men in things *p.* to God
9. 9. not make him perfect, as *p.* to conscience

PERVERSE.

Num. 22. 32. because thy way is *p.* before me
Deut. 32. 5. they are a *p.* and crooked generation
1 *Sam.* 20. 30. thou son of the *p.* rebellious woman
Job 6. 30. cannot my taste discern *p.* things?
9. 20. my mouth shall also prove me *p.*
Prov. 4. 24. and *p.* lips put far from thee
8. 8. there is nothing froward or *p.* in them
12. 8. he that is of a *p.* heart shall be despised
14. 2. he that is *p.* in his ways despiseth him
17. 20. that hath *p.* tongue falleth into mischief
19. 1. than he that is *p.* in his lips, and a fool
23. 33. and thine heart shall utter *p.* things
28. 6. than he that is *p.* in his ways, though rich
18. he that is *p.* in his ways shall fall at once
Isa. 19. 14. the Lord hath mingled a *p.* spirit
Mat. 17. 17. O *p.* generation, *Luke* 9. 41.
Acts 20. 30. shall men arise, speaking *p.* things
Phil. 2. 15. blameless in the midst of a *p.* nation
1 *Tim.* 6. 5. *p.* disputings of men of corrupt minds

PERVERSELY.

2 *Sam.* 19. 19. nor remember what servant did *p.*
1 *Kings* 8. 47. we have sinned and have done *p.*
Psal. 119. 78. they dealt *p.* with me without cause

PERVERSENESS.

Num. 23. 21. neither hath he seen *p.* in Israel
Prov. 11. 3. but *p.* of transgressors shall destroy them
15. 4. but *p.* therein as a breach in the spirit
Isa. 30. 12. ye trust in *p.* and stay thereon
59. 3. lips have spoken lies, your tongue hath muttered *p.*
Ezek. 9. 9. the land is full of blood, and city of *p.*

PERVERT.

Deut. 16. 19. a gift doth *p.* words of the righteous
24. 17. thou shalt not *p.* the judgment of stranger
Job 8. 3. doth God *p.* judgment or justice?
34. 12. nor will the Almighty *p.* judgment
Prov. 17. 23. to *p.* the ways of judgment
31. 5. and *p.* the judgment of any of the afflicted
Mic. 3. 9. hear this, I pray you, ye that *p.* equity
Acts 13. 10. wilt not cease to *p.* right ways of Lord?
Gal. 1. 7. and would *p.* the gospel of Christ

PERVERTED.

1 *Sam.* 8. 3. Samuel's sons took bribes, *p.* judgment
Job 33. 27. if any say, I have *p.* what was right
Isa. 47. 10. thy wisdom and knowledge, it hath *p.*
Jer. 3. 21. they have *p.* their way, and forgotten L.
23. 36. ye have *p.* the words of the living God

PERVERTETH.

Exod. 23. 8. the gift *p.* the words of the righteous
Deut. 27. 19. cursed be he that *p.* judgm. of stranger
Prov. 10. 9. but he that *p.* his ways shall be known
19. 3. the foolishness of a man *p.* his way
Isa. 24. † 1. the Lord *p.* the face of the earth
Luke 23. 14. brought this man as one that *p.* people

PERVERTING.

Eccl. 5. 8. if thou seest the violent *p.* of judgment
Luke 23. 2. found this fellow *p.* the nation

PESTILENCE.

Exod. 5. 3. lest he fall on us with *p.* or sword
9. 15. that I may smite thee and thy peop. with *p.*
Lev. 26. 25. I will send the *p.* among you
Num. 14. 12. I will smite them with the *p.*
Deut. 28. 21. the Lord shall make *p.* cleave to thee
2 *Sam.* 24. 13. there be three days' *p.* 1 *Chr.* 21. 12.
15. the Lord sent a *p.* on Israel, 1 *Chr.* 21. 14.
1 *Kings* 8. 37. if there be in the land famine, *p.* blasting locust, 2 *Chr.* 6. 28. | 7. 13. | 20. 9.
Psal. 78. 50. he gave their life over to the *p.*
91. 3. he shall deliver thee from the noisome *p.*
6. nor for the *p.* that walketh in darkness
Jer. 14. 12. I will consume them by *p.* 24. 10. | 27. 8.
21. 6. the inhabitants of this city shall die by *p.*
7. I will deliver Zedekiah from the *p.*
9. he that abideth in city shall die by *p.* 38. 2.
27. 13. why will ye die by the sword and *p.*?
28. 8. prophets of old prophesied of war and of *p.*
29. 17. behold, I will send upon them the *p.*
18. I will persecute them with the famine and *p.*
32. 24. the city is given because of the *p.* 36.
34. 17. I proclaim a liberty for you to the *p.*
42. 17. they that go to Egypt shall die by the *p.* 22.
44. 13. as I have punished Jerusalem by the *p.*
Ezek. 5. 12. a third part shall die with the *p.*
17. *p.* and blood shall pass thro' thee, L. spoken it
6. 11. they shall fall by sword, famine, and the *p.*
12. he that is far off shall die by the *p.*
7. 15. a sword without, *p.* and famine within
12. 16. I will leave a few men of them from the *p.*
14. 19. or if I send a *p.* into that land, and pour out
21. when I send the *p.* to cut off man and beast
28. 23. I will send to her *p.* and blood into streets
33. 27. they that be in caves shall die of the *p.*
38. 22. I will plead against him with *p.* and blood
Amos 4. 10. I have sent among you the *p.*
Hab 3. 5. before him went the *p.* and burning

PESTILENCES.

Mat. 24. 7. and there shall be *p.* *Luke* 21. 11.

PESTILENT.

Acts 24. 5. we have found this man a *p.* fellow

PESTLE.

Prov. 27. 22. bray a fool in a mortar with a *p.*

PETITION.

1 *Sam.* 1. 17. the God of Israel grant thee thy *p.*
27. Lord hath given me my *p.* which I asked
† 28. he whom I obtained by *p.* shall be returned
2. † 20. Lord give thee seed, for the *p.* she asked
1 *Kings* 2. 16. now I ask one *p.* of thee, deny me not
20. I desire one small *p.* of thee, say me not nay
Esth. 5. 6. the king said, what is thy *p.*? 7. 2. | 9. 12.
7. then Esther said, my *p.* and request is
8. if it please the king to grant my *p.* and request
7. 3. let my life be given me at my *p.* and my peo
Isa. 7. † 11. ask thee a sign, make thy *p.* deep
Dan. 6. 7. whosoever shall ask a *p.* of any god, 12.
13. but maketh his *p.* three times a day

PETITIONS.

Psal. 20. 5. the Lord fulfil all thy *p.*
1 *John* 5. 15. we know we have the *p.* we desired

PHARISEE.

This sect was one of the most ancient and most considerable among the Jews, *and its original is not very well known, some placing the beginning of the* Pharisees *sooner, others later. They take their name from a* Hebrew *word, which signifies* Division, *or* Separation, *because they distinguished themselves from the other* Israelites, *by a more strict manner of life, of which they made profession: they were very numerous, and far extended: they substituted human traditions in the room of God's word, affected to make a great shew of religion in outward things; but were proud, covetous, unjust, superstitious, and hypocritical.*

When our Saviour Jesus Christ *appeared in* Judea, *the* Pharisees *were then in great credit among the people, because of the opinion they had conceived of their great learning, sanctity of manners, and exact observance of the law. They fasted often, made long prayers, paid their tithes scrupulously, distributed much alms. But all this was vitiated and corrupted by a spirit of pride, ostentation, hypocrisy, and self-love. Like to whitened sepulchres, they appeared beautiful without, whilst within was nothing but corruption and deformity,* Mat. 23. 27. *They wore large rolls of parchment upon their foreheads and wrists, on which were written certain words of the law; and affected to have fringes and borders at the corners and hems of their garments, broader than the other Jews wore, as a badge of distinction, and as greater observers of the law than others.*

In matters of religion, the traditions of the ancients were the chief subject of their studies; and to these they made additions of their own, as they thought fit, making their own opinion to pass for traditions of the ancients. By this means they had overburdened the law of God with a vast number of trifling observances, that were useless and disgustful, and which made it a heavy and insupportable yoke. They had even altered and corrupted it in important articles, by their own perverse interpretations of it, as our Saviour in his gospel reproaches them with. For example, the law commands us to honour our father and mother: the Pharisees taught, that if we say to our parents that are in necessity; "Father, or mother, the thing you ask of me is dedicated to God, it is no longer in my power, but you shall have a part in the merit of my offering, which will do you as much good as if I had given it to you;" they were then freed from the obligation of succouring their parents, Mat. 15. 4, 5, 6.

The observation of the sabbath is another point they had refined upon, and our Saviour often argued with them upon this head. They maintained, that upon this day it was not so much as allowed to heal a sick person, though Christ *did it only with a word speaking,* Luke 6. 7, 8. *They found fault, that upon this day the people brought their sick to be healed. They were scandalized, that a man carried away his bed upon the sabbath-day, after he had been cured of a palsy,* John 5. 8, 9, 10. *From all which they concluded, that our* Lord *and* Saviour Jesus Christ *could not be a man sent from God, because he so little observed that profound rest, that they thought was to be kept on this day,* John 9. 16.

Our Saviour upbraids them with making long prayers, standing up in the synagogues, or at the corners of the streets, and under pretence of prayer to consume widows' houses, either by entertaining them on account of their prayers, or by persuading these shallow widows to intrust them with their estates, and then defrauding them of the same, Mat. 23. 14. *He also reproaches them with compassing sea and land to make a proselyte, or to convert a Gentile: and after that to make him still a greater sinner than he was before, by teaching him a pernicious doctrine, and making him more opposite to the gospel, instead of shewing him the true paths to piety,* Mat. 23. 15. *He says, they affect to build up the tombs of the old prophets, and openly to declare, that they disapprove of the actions of their forefathers who persecuted them, while they themselves were actuated by the same spirit, and oppose all those that would reclaim them from their enormities,* Mat. 23. 29. Luke 11. 47, 48.

The Pharisees *believed the soul to be immortal, and acknowledged the existence of angels and spirits,* Acts 23. 8. *They likewise admitted a kind of transmigration of the souls of good men, which might pass from one body to another; whereas those of wicked men were condemned to dwell for ever in prisons of darkness. It was in consequence of these principles, that some of the Pharisees said, that* Jesus Christ *was* John *the Baptist, or* Elias, *or some one of the old prophets,* Mat. 16. 14. *that is, that the soul of one of these great men had passed into the body of our Saviour. They believed also the resurrection of the dead, and admitted of all the consequences of it, against the Sadducees who rejected it.* Mat. 22. 23. Acts 23. 8.

Mat. 23. 26. thou blind *p.* cleanse first within
Luke 11. 37. a certain *p.* besought him to dine
18. 10. went to pray, one a *p.* the other a publican
11. the *p.* stood and prayed thus with himself
Acts 5. 34. then stood up one in the council, a *p.*
23. 6. Paul cried out, I am a *p.* the son of a *p.*
26. 5. after strictest sect of our religion I lived a *p.*
Phil. 3. 5. Hebrew of Hebrews, as touching law, a *p.*

PHARISEES.

Mat. 5. 20. exceed the righteousness of the *p.*
9. 14. why do we and the *p.* fast oft? *Mark* 2. 18.
34. *p.* said, he casteth out devils by prince of dev.
15. 12. knowest thou that the *p.* were offended
16. 6. take heed and beware of the leaven of the *p.* and Sadducees, 11. *Mark* 8. 15. *Luke* 12. 1.
19. 3. the *p.* also came to him, tempting him
23. 2. saying, the scribes and *p.* sit in Moses' seat
13. woe to you scribes and *p.* hypocrites, 14, 15, 23, 25, 27, 29. *Luke* 11. 42, 43, 44.
Luke 5. 30. the scribes and *p.* murmured, 15. 2.
6. 7. the scribes and *p.* watched him, whether
7. 30. but the *p.* rejected the counsel of God
11. 39. now do ye *p.* make clean outside of the cup
16. 14. *p.* who were covetous, heard these things
John 1. 24. they which were sent were of the *p.*
3. 1. there was a man of the *p.* named Nicodemus
7. 32. the *p.* and priests sent officers to take him
48. have any of the rulers or *p.* believed on him?
11. 47. then the *p.* gathered a council, and said
57. now the *p.* had given a commandment
Acts 15. 5. there rose up certain of sect of the *p.*
23. 7. there arose a dissension between *p.* and Sad.
8. there is no resurrection, but the *p.* confess both

PHILOSOPHY,

The love of wisdom. It comes from the Greek *word* φιλος, *a lover, and* σοφια, *wisdom. The apostle* Paul *bids the* Colossians *beware,* lest any man spoil them through philosophy, *Col.* 2. 8. *And in the* Acts, *St.* Luke *relates, that when St.* Paul *came to* Athens, *he there found* Epicurean *and* Stoic *philosophers, who made a jest of his discourses; and no wonder, seeing they placed the chief happiness in pleasure, and denied the providence of God,* Acts 17. 18. *The same apostle, in many places of his epistles, opposes the false wisdom, and wise men of the age, which is nothing else but the pagan philosophy, always contrary to the wisdom of* Christ, *and the true religion; which in the notion of the philosophers and sophists of this world seemed to be mere folly, being built neither upon evidence, nor the eloquence and subtilty of those that preached it, but upon the power of God, and his single authority, upon the operation of the Holy Ghost, which influenced the hearts and minds of those whom he called to the faith.*
Col. 2. 8. beware, lest any man spoil you through *p.*

PHILOSOPHERS.

Acts 17. 18. then certain *p.* encountered him, and said

PHYLACTERIES.

This word comes from the Greek, *and signifies,* Things to be especially observed. *These* Phylacteries *were certain little boxes, or certain rolls of parchment, wherein were written certain words of the law. These the* Jews *wore upon their foreheads, upon their wrists, and the hem of their garments, which custom is founded upon what you read in* Exod. 13. 9, 16. *and in* Num. 15. 38, 39. *The Pharisees affected to have their phylacteries broader than the other* Jews *wore, as a badge of distinction, and through ostentation, which is that our Saviour reprehends them for.*
Mat. 23. 5. they make broad their *p.* and enlarge

PHYSICIAN

Signifies, [1] *One who professes and practises the art of physic,* Mark 5. 26. [2] *Embalmers of dead bodies,* Gen. 50. 2. [3] *Comforters or healers by advice and counsel,* Job 13. 4. [4] *Prophets and teachers, as instruments of curing hard-hearted sinners,* Jer. 8. 22. [5] Jesus Christ, *the great Physician of value, the only sovereign Physician of the soul, who by his blood and Spirit cures all our spiritual sicknesses,* Mat. 9. 12.
Jer. 8. 22. is no balm in Gilead? is there no *p.* there?
Mat. 9. 12. Jesus said, they that be whole need not a *p.* but the sick, *Mark* 2. 17. *Luke* 5. 31.
Luke 4. 23. *p.* heal thyself ‖ *Col.* 4. 14. Luke the *p.*

PHYSICIANS.

Gen. 50. 2. Joseph commanded the *p.* his servants, to embalm his father; the *p.* embalmed Israel
2 *Chr.* 16. 12. Asa sought not to the Lord, but *p.*
Job 13. 4. forgers of lies, ye are all *p.* of no value
Mark 5. 26. had suffer. many things of *p.* *Luke* 8. 43.

PICK.

Prov. 30. 17. the ravens of the valley shall *p.* it out

PICTURES.

Num. 33. 52. shall destroy all their *p.* and images
Prov. 25. 11. like apples of gold in *p.* of silver
Isa. 2. 16. the day of the Lord on all pleasant *p.*

PIECE.

Gen. 15. 10. he laid one *p.* against another
Exod. 37. 7. made two cherubims beaten out of one *p.*
Num. 10. 2. make thee two trumpets of a whole *p.*
Judg. 9. 53. a certain woman cast a *p.* of a millstone upon Abimelech's head, 2 *Sam.* 11. 21.
1 *Sam.* 2. 36. shall come and crouch to him for a *p.* of silver, that I may eat a *p.* of bread
30. 12. they gave him a *p.* of a cake of figs
2 *Sam.* 6. 19. to every one a *p.* of flesh, 1 *Chr.* 16. 3.
23. 11. where was a *p.* of ground full of lentiles
2 *Kings* 3. 19. and mar every good *p.* of land, 25.
5. † 19. Naaman departed a little *p.* of ground
Neh. 3. 11. and Hashub repaired the other *p.*
19. next Ezer another *p.* 20, 21, 24, 27, 30.
Job 41. 24. as hard as a *p.* of the nether millstone
42. 11. every man also gave him a *p.* of money
Prov. 6. 26. a man is brought to a *p.* of bread
28. 21. for a *p.* of bread that man will transgress
Cant. 4. 3. thy temples are a *p.* of pomegranate, 6. 7.
Jer. 37. 21. should give him daily a *p.* of bread
Ezek. 24. 4. every good *p.* the thigh and the shoulder
6. bring it out *p.* by *p.* let no lot fall upon it
Amos 3. 12. out of the mouth of lion a *p.* of an ear
Amos 4. 7. one *p.* was rained on, and the *p.* whereon
Zech. 5. † 7. there was lift up a weighty *p.* of lead
Mat. 9. 16. no man putteth a *p.* of new cloth to an old garment, *Mark* 2. 21. *Luke* 5. 36.
17. 27. thou shalt find a *p.* of money, that take
Luke 14. 18. I have bought a *p.* of ground
15. 8. if she lose one *p.* she doth light a candle
9. for I have found the *p.* that I had lost
24. 42. they gave him a *p.* of a broiled fish

PIECES.

Gen. 15. 17. a burning lamp passed between those *p.*
20. 16. I have given thy brother 1000 *p.* of silver
33. 19. bought for 100 *p.* of money, *Josh.* 24. 32.
37. † 23. they stripped Joseph of his coat of many *p.*
28. they sold Joseph for twenty *p.* of silver
33. Joseph without doubt is rent in *p.* 44. 28.
45. 22. he gave to Benjamin thirty *p.* of silver
Exod. 22. 13. if it be torn in *p.* let him bring it
28. 7. the ephod shall have the two shoulder *p.*
25. put two chains on the shoulder *p.* 39. 4, 18.
Lev. 2. 6. thou shalt part the meat offering in *p.*
8. 20. Moses burnt the *p.* and fat of the ram
9. 13. they presented burnt offering with the *p.*
Judg. 9. 4. they gave Abimelech seventy *p.* of silver
16. 5. we will give thee 1100 *p.* of silver
19. 29. he divided his concubine into twelve *p.*
1 *Sam.* 11. 7. Saul hewed a yoke of oxen in *p.*
15. 33. Samuel hewed Agag in *p.* before the Lord
1 *Kings* 11. 30. Ahijah rent new garment in twelve *p.*
31. Ahijah said to Jeroboam, take thee ten *p.*
19. 11. a strong wind brake in *p.* the rocks
2 *Kings* 2. 12. Elisha rent his clothes in two *p.*
5. 5. Naaman took with him 6000 *p.* of gold
6. 25. an ass's head was sold for eighty *p.* of silver
11. 18. and brake the images of Baal in *p.* 23. 14.
18. 4. brake in *p.* the brasen serpent Moses made
2 *Chr.* 23. 17. went to the house of Baal, and brake the images in *p.* 38. 1. | 34. 4. *Mic.* 1. 7.
Job 4. † 20. they are beaten in *p.* from morning
16. 12. and he hath also shaken me in *p.*
40. 18. his bones as strong *p.* of brass, as bars of iron
41. † 15. strong *p.* of shields are his pride
† 30. sharp *p.* of the potsherd are under him
Psal. 7. 2. rending in *p.* while none to deliver
50. 22. consider this, lest I tear you in *p.*
68. 30. till every one submit with *p.* of silver
74. 14. thou brakest the heads of Leviathan in *p.*
Cant. 8. 11. every one for the fruit bring 1000 *p.*
Isa. 3. 15. what mean ye that ye beat my people to *p.*?
Jer. 5. 6. every one that goeth out shall be torn in *p.*?
23. 29. a hammer that breaketh the rock in *p.*
Lam. 3. 11. he hath turned aside and pulled me in *p.*
Ezek. 4. 14. have not eaten that which is torn in *p.*
9. † 2. every man a weapon of his breaking in *p.*
13. 19. and will ye pollute me for *p.* of bread?
24. 4. gather the *p.* thereof into the pot
Dan. 2. 34. which brake the image in *p.* 45.
40. forasmuch as iron breaketh in *p.* and subdueth
6. 24. the lions brake all their bones in *p.*
7. 7. the fourth beast devoured and brake in *p.* 19.
Hos. 3. 2. I bought her to me for fifteen *p.* of silver
Mic. 3. 3. who chop my people in *p.* as for the pot
4. 13. and thou shalt beat in *p.* many people
5. 8. as a lion teareth in *p.* and none can deliver
Nah. 2. 12. lion did tear in *p.* enough for his whelps
Zech. 11. 12. they weighed for my price thirty *p.*
13. I took the thirty *p.* of silver, *Mat.* 27. 6, 9.
Luke 15. 8. what woman having ten *p.* of silver
Acts 19. 19. they found the price 50,000 *p.* of silver
23. 10. lest Paul should be pulled in *p.* of them
27. 44. and some on broken *p.* of the ship
See Break, Broken, Cut, Dash, Dashed.

PIERCE.

Num. 24. 8. he shall *p.* them through with arrows
2 *Kings* 18. 21. on which if a man lean, it will go into his hand and *p.* it. *Isa.* 36. 6.
Luke 2. 35. a sword shall *p.* through thy own soul

PIERCED.

Judg. 5. 26. when she had *p.* through his temples
Job 30. 17. my bones are *p.* in me in the night
Psal. 22. 16. they *p.* my hands and my feet
Hag. 1. † 6. earneth wages, to put it into bag *p.* thro'
Zech. 12. 10. they shall look on me whom they have *p.* and shall mourn for him, *John* 19. 37.
John 19. 34. one of the soldiers *p.* his side
1 *Tim.* 6. 10. and *p.* themselves with many sorrows
Rev. 1. 7. they also which *p.* him shall see him

PIERCETH.

Job 40. 24. Behemoth's nose *p.* through snares

PIERCING.

Isa. 27. 1. the Lord shall punish the *p.* serpent
Heb. 4. 12. word of God is quick, *p.* to the dividing

PIERCINGS.

Prov. 12. 18. that speaketh like the *p.* of a sword

PIETY.

1 *Tim.* 5. 4. let them learn to shew *p.* at home

PIGEON, *see* Young.

PILE.

Isa. 30. 33. the *p.* of it is fire and much wood
Ezek. 24. 9. I will even make the *p.* for fire great

PILGRIMAGE.

Gen. 47. 9. the days of years of my *p.* are 130 years, I have not attained to years in the days of their *p.*
Exod. 6. 4. to give them the land of their *p.*
Ps. 119. 54. been my songs in the house of my *p.*

PILGRIMS.

Heb. 11. 13. confessed they were strangers and *p.*
1 *Pet.* 2. 11. I beseech you, as *p.* abstain from lusts

PILLAR

Signifies, [1] *That which supporteth an house or building,* Judg. 16. 25, 26, 29. [2] *A monument raised in memory of some person or action,* Gen. 35. 20. 2 Sam. 18. 18. [3] *The cloud in the wilderness, which resembled a pillar,* Exod. 13. 21.
A pillar of cloud, a pillar of fire, a pillar of smoke, Exod. 13. 21. *Judg.* 20. 40. signify, *a cloud, a fire, a smoke, which are raised up towards heaven in the form of an irregular pillar.*
The pillars of heaven, *Job* 26. 11. *and* the pillars of the earth, *Job* 9. 6. *are metaphorical expressions, that suppose the heavens and the earth to be as an edifice, raised by the hand of God, and founded upon its basis, or foundation; which appears from those words in* Job 38. 4, 5, 6. Where wast thou when I laid the foundations of the earth? declare, if thou hast understanding. *The ancients imagined the earth to lie upon a flat, and that the heavens rested upon its extremities.*
The church is called the pillar of truth, 1 *Tim.* 3. 15. *It holds forth the mind of* Christ, *as a pillar does an edict, or proclamation, that all may take notice of it, so that the truths of God are published, supported, and kept from sinking by it, but do not derive their authority from it. In which sense teachers, prophets, and apostles, are likewise called* pillars, *Prov.* 9. 1. *Jer.* 1. 18. *Gal.* 2. 9.
Gen. 19. 26. she looked back, and became a *p.* of salt
28. 18. Jacob set it up for a *p.* 22. | 35. 14.
31. 13. Beth-el, where thou anointedst the *p.*
51. behold this *p.* ‖ 52. and this *p.* be witness
35. 20. Jacob set *p.* on Rachel's grave, that is the *p.*
Exod. 33. 9. cloudy *p.* descended and stood at door
10. the people saw the cloudy *p.* stand at door of
Lev. 26. † 1. ye shall not rear up a *p.* *Deut.* 16. † 22.
Judg. 9. 6. made Abimelech king by plain of the *p.*
20. 40. the flame arose with a *p.* of smoke
2 *Sam.* 18. 18. Absalom reared up a *p.* called the *p.*
1 *Kings* 7. 21. Solomon set up the right *p.* the left *p.*
2 *Kings* 11. 14. king stood by *p.* 23. 3. 2 *Chr.* 23. 13.
Neh. 9. 12. thou leddest them in day by a cloudy *p.*
Psal. 99. 7. he spake to them in the cloudy *p.*
Isa. 19. 19. and a *p.* at the border thereof to Lord
Jer. 1. 18. I have made thee this day an iron *p.*
52. 21. the height of one *p.* was eighteen cubits
1 *Tim.* 3. 15. church, the *p.* and ground of the truth
Rev. 3. 12. him that overcometh will I make a *p.*
See Cloud, Fire.

PILLARS.

Exod. 24. 4. Moses built an altar and twelve *p.*
26. 32. thou shalt hang the vail upon four *p.*
37. thou shalt make for the hanging five *p.* 36. 38.
27. 10. twenty *p.* thereof brass hooks of the *p.* silver 11. | 38. 10, 11, 12, 17.
12. ten *p.* ‖ 14. their *p.* three, 15. | 38. 14, 15.
16. *p.* four ‖ 38. 17. sockets for *p.* were of brass
Deut. 7. † 5. ye shall break down their *p.* 12. 3.
Judg. 16. 25. they set Samson between the *p.*
1 *Sam.* 2. 8. the *p.* of the earth are the Lord's
1 *Kings* 7. 15. he cast two *p.* of brass of 18 cubits
10. 12. the king made of the almug-trees *p.*
2 *Kings* 18. 16. Hezekiah cut off gold from the *p.*
25. 13. the Chaldees brake in pieces the *p.* of brass, and carried brass to Babylon, 16. *Jer.* 52. 17, 20.
Esth. 1. 6. hangings fastened to rings and *p.* of marb.
Job 9. 6. and the *p.* thereof tremble, 26. 11.
Psal. 75. 3. earth is dissolved, I bear up the *p.* of it
Prov. 9. 1. she hath hewn out her seven *p.*
Cant. 3. 6. that cometh like a *p.* of smoke perfumed
10. made *p.* thereof of silver, bottom of gold
5. 15. legs are as *p.* of marble set on sockets of gold
Joel 2. 30. I will shew blood, fire, and *p.* of smoke
Gal. 2. 9. John and Cephas who seemed to be *p.*
Rev. 10. 1. face as the sun, his feet were as *p.* of fire

PILLED.

Gen. 30. 37. Jacob *p.* white strakes in the rods
38. he set rods which he had *p.* before the flocks

PILLOW, S.

It signifies, [1] Properly, *a sort of cushion to lie under one's head in bed,* Mark 4. 38. [2] Figuratively, *it betokens ease, rest, and quietness; such did the false prophetesses make, that they might be signs to the people of ease and rest; and they thus endeavoured to render them secure.* Ezek. 13. 18, 20.
Gen. 28. 11. and Jacob put stones for his *p.*
18. Jacob took the stone that he had put for his *p.*
1 *Sam.* 19. 13. Michal put a *p.* of goats' hair, 16.
Ezek. 13. 18. woe to the women that sew *p.* and make
20. wherefore, behold, I am against your *p.*
Mark 4. 38. Jesus was in the ship asleep on a *p.*

PILOTS.

Ezek. 27. 8. thy wise men, O Tyrus, were thy *p.*
28. suburbs shake at the sound of the cry of thy *p.*

PINE.

Lev. 26. 39. they that are left of you shall *p.* away, in iniquities of their fathers shall they *p.* away
Lam. 4. 9. these *p.* away, stricken through for want
Ezek. 24. 23. ye shall *p.* away for your iniquities
33. 10. if sins be upon us, and we *p.* away in them

PINE.

Neh. 8. 15. fetch olive and *p.* branches for booths

PINE-TREE.

Isa. 41. 19. I will plant *p.* and box-tree together
60. 13. the *p.* and box-tree shall come to thee

PINETH.

Mark 9. 18. gnasheth with his teeth, and *p.* away

PINING.

Isa. 38. 12. he will cut me off with *p.* sickness

PIN.

Judg. 16. 14. Delilah fastened it with a *p.* Samson awaked and went away with the *p.* of the beam
Ezra 9. † 8. and to give us a *p.* in his holy place
Ezek. 15. 3. will men take a *p.* of the vine-tree?

PINNACLE.

Mat. 4. 5. setteth him on a *p.* of temple, *Luke* 4. 9.

PINS.

Exod. 27. 19. make all the *p.* of the tabernacle and court of brass, 35. 18. | 38. 20, 31. | 39. 40.
Num. 3. 37. under the custody of Merari, *p.* 4. 32.

PIPE, S.

1 *Sam.* 10. 5. shalt meet company of prophets with *p.*
1 *Kings* 1. 40. the people piped with *p.* and rejoiced
Psal. 149. † 3. praise his name with a *p.* 150. † 4.
Isa. 5. 12. the harp and *p.* are in their feasts
30. 29. have a song, as when one goeth with a *p.*
Jer. 48. 36. mine heart shall sound for Moab like *p.*
Ezek. 28. 13. workmanship of thy *p.* was prepared
Zech. 4. 2. and seven *p.* to the seven lamps
12. which through the golden *p.* empty themselves
1 *Cor.* 14. 7. things without life, whether *p.* or harp

PIPED.

1 *Kings* 1. 40. people *p.* with pipes, and rejoiced
Mat. 11. 17. saying, we have *p.* unto you, *Luke* 7. 32.
1 *Cor.* 14. 7. how shall it be known what is *p.*?

PIPERS.
Rev. 18. 22. voice of *p.* shall be heard no more
PISS.
2 *Kings* 18. 27. drink own *p.* with you, *Isa.* 36. 12.
PISSETH. *See* WALL.
PIT, S.
Signifies, [1] *A hole in the earth,* Isa. 30. 14. [2] *Any mischief, or evil, for insnaring a person,* Psal. 7. 15. [3] *The grave,* Psal. 28. 1. | 30. 3. [4] *Trouble,* Psal. 40. 2. [5] Abraham *and* Sarah, *from whom the* Israelites *sprang, even when their bodies were like a rock, or pit,* Isa. 51. 1, 2. [6] *Hell,* Rev. 9. 2. | 20. 1.
Gen. 14. 10. the vale of Siddim was full of slime *p.*
37. 20. come, let us cast him into some *p.* 24.
Exod. 21. 34. owner of the *p.* shall make it good
Lev. 11. 36. a *p.* wherein is water, shall be clean
Num. 16. 30. they go down quick into the *p.* 33.
1 *Sam.* 13. 6. the Israelites hid themselves in *p.*
2 *Sam.* 17. 9. behold, he is now hid in some *p.*
18. 17. cast Absalom in a great *p.* in the wood
23. 20. Benaiah slew a lion in a *p.* 1 *Chron.* 11. 22.
2 *Kings* 10. 14. and Jehu slew them at the *p.*
18. † 31. drink every one the waters of his *p.*
Job 17. 16. they shall go down to the bars of the *p.*
33. 18. he keepeth back his soul from the *p.* 30.
24. deliver him from going down into the *p.* 28.
Psal. 9. 15. heathen are sunk down into the *p.*
28 1. become like them that go down into the *p.*
30. 3. that I should not go down to the *p.*
9. what profit in my blood, when I go down to *p.?*
35. 7. they have hid from me their net in a *p.*
40. 2. he brought me up out of an horrible *p.*
55. 23. bring them to the *p.* of destruction
69. 15. let not the *p.* shut her mouth on me
88. 4. I am counted with them that go into *p.*
6. thou hast laid me in the lowest *p.*
119. 85. the proud have digged *p.* for me
140. 10. let them be cast into deep *p.* not to rise
143. 7. like them that go down into *p.* *Prov.* 1. 12.
Prov. 22. 14. mouth of strange women is a deep *p.*
23. 27. and a strange woman is a narrow *p.*
28. 10. he shall fall himself into his own *p.*
17. he shall flee to the *p.* let no man stay him
Isa. 14. 15. be brought down to the sides of the *p.*
19. that go down to the stones of the *p.*
24. 17. fear, and the *p.* and the snare are on thee
18. cometh out of midst of *p.* *Jer.* 48. 43, 44.
22. be gathered, as prisoners are gathered in *p.*
30. 14. a sherd to take water withal out of the *p.*
38. 17. hast delivered it from the *p.* of corruption
38. 18. they that go down to *p.* cannot hope
51. 14. hasteneth, that he should not die in the *p.*
Jer. 2. 6. the Lord that led us through a land of *p.*
14. 3. they came to the *p.* and found no water
41. 7. and cast them into the midst of the *p.*
9. the *p.* which Asa made for fear of Baasha
Lam. 4. 20. anointed of Lord was taken in their *p.*
Ezek. 19. 4. nations heard, he was taken in *p.* 8.
26. 20. with them that descend into the *p.* 28. 8.
| 31. 14, 16. | 32. 18, 24, 25, 29, 30.
32. 23. whose graves are set in the sides of the *p.*
Jonah 2. † 6. hast thou brought my life from *p.*
Zeph. 2. 9. even the breeding of nettles and salt *p.*
Zech. 9. 11. I have sent thy prisoners out of the *p.*
Mat. 12. 11. if it fall into a *p.* on sabbath, *Luke* 14. 5.
See BOTTOMLESS, DIG, DIGGED.
PITCH.
Gen. 6. 14. pitch it within and without with *p.*
Exod. 2. 3. she daubed it with slime and with *p.*
Isa. 34. 9. streams thereof shall be turned to *p.* and the land thereof shall become burning *p.*
PITCH.
Num. 1. 52. Israel shall *p.* every man by his camp
53. the Levites shall *p.* round the tabernacle
2. 2. every man shall *p.* by his own standard
3. camp of Judah *p.* ‖ 3. 23. the Gershonites *p.*
3. 29. sons of Kohath *p.* ‖ 35. Merari shall *p.*
Deut. 1. 33. to search you out a place to *p.* in
Josh. 4. 20. Joshua did *p.* twelve stones in Gilgal
Isa. 13. 20. neither shall the Arabian *p.* tent there
Jer. 6. 3. shepherds shall *p.* their tents against her
PITCHED.
Gen. 12. 8. Abram *p.* his tent, and built an altar
13. 12. Lot *p.* ‖ 26. 17. Isaac *p.* in valley, 25.
31. 25. Jacob *p.* in mount, Laban *p.* in Gilead
33. 18. Jacob *p.* his tent before the city Shalem
Exod. 17. 1. from Sin, Israel *p.* in Rephidim
19. 2. were come to desert, and had *p.* in wildern.
33. 7. Moses took tabernacle, *p.* it without camp
Num. 1. 51. when tabern. is *p.* Levites shall set it up
2. 34. so they *p.* by their standards and set forward
9. 18. at the commandment of the Lord they *p.*
12. 16. the people *p.* in the wilderness of Paran
21. 10. Israel *p.* in Oboth ‖ 11. *p.* in Ije-abarim
33. 5. Israel *p.* in Succoth ‖ 6. they *p.* in Etham
Josh. 8. 11. the ambush *p.* on the north side of Ai
2 *Sam.* 6. 17. set ark in tabernacle David had *p.*
17. 26. Israel and Absalom *p.* in land of Gilead
1 *Kings* 20. 27. and Israel *p.* before them, 29.
2 *Kings* 25. 1. Nebuchadn. *p.* against it, *Jer.* 52. 4.
1 *Chron.* 15. 1. David prepared a place for the ark, and *p.* for it a tent, 16. 1. 2 *Chron.* 1. 4.
Ezra 8. † 15. there *p.* we by the river Ahava
Heb. 8. 2. of the true tabernacle which Lord *p.*
PITCHER, S,
Signifies, [1] *A vessel with a handle, for containing liquors,* Gen. 24. 14, 15. [2] *Such vessels in the human body as convey vital supplies into the several parts of it, as the veins and arteries; especially the arterious vein, by which the blood is conveyed to the lungs, and thence to the left ventricle of the heart, and then by the pulse thrust out into the great artery, called* Arteria aorta; *and by its branches dispersed into all the parts of the body; which being done, the residue of the blood is carried back into the right ventricle, whence it is disposed as has been mentioned, and so runs a perpetual round,* Eccl. 12. 6. *which may be said to be broken, when they become useless and insufficient for the performance of their several functions.*

Gen. 24. 14. let down *p.* I pray thee, that I may drink
15. behold, Rebekah came with her *p.* 45.
Judg. 7. 16. with empty *p.* and lamps within the *p.*
19. they brake *p.* that were in their hands, 20.
Eccl. 12. 6. or the *p.* be broken at the fountain
Lam. 4. 2. how are they esteemed as earthen *p.?*
Mark 14. 13. man bear. a *p.* of water, *Luke* 22. 10.
PITY.
Deut. 7. 16. thine eye shall have no *p.* on them
2 *Sam.* 12. 6. restore the lamb, because he had no *p.*
Job 6. 14. to the afflicted *p.* should be shewed
19. 21. have *p.* on me, *p.* on me, O my friends
Ps. 69. 20. looked for some to take *p.* but was none
Prov. 19. 17. that hath *p.* on poor, lendeth to Lord
Isa. 13. 18. they shall have no *p.* on fruit of womb
63. 9. in his love and in his *p.* he redeemed them
Jer. 15. 5. for who shall have *p.* on thee O Jerusalem
21. 7. he shall not spare, nor have *p.* nor mercy
Ezek. 5. 11. nor will I have *p.* 7. 4, 9. | 8. 18. | 9. 10.
9. 5. let not your eye spare, neither have ye *p.*
24. † 21. behold, I will profane *p.* of your soul
36. 21. but I had *p.* for mine holy name
Amos 1. 11. because Edom did cast off all *p.*
Jonah 4. 10. thou hast had *p.* on the gourd
Mat. 18. 33. have had compassion, as I had *p.* on thee
PITY.
Deut. 13. 8. nor shall thine eye *p.* him, 19. 13, 21.
25. 12. shalt cut off her hand, thine eye shall not *p.*
Prov. 28. 8. shall gather for him that will *p.* poor
Jer. 13. 14. I will not *p.* nor spare, but destroy
Joel 2. 18. then the Lord will *p.* his people
Zech. 11. 5. their own shepherds *p.* them not
6. for I will no more *p.* inhabitants of the land
PITIED.
Psal. 106. 46. he made them also to be *p.* of all
Lam. 2. 2. and the Lord hath not *p.* 17. 21. | 3. 43.
Ezek. 16. 5. none eye *p.* thee, to do any of these
PITIETH.
Psal. 103. 13. like as a father *p.* his children, so the Lord *p.* them that fear him
Ezek. 24. 21. I will profane what your soul *p.*
PITIFUL.
Lam. 4. 10. hands of *p.* women have sodden children
Jam. 5. 11. ye have seen that the Lord is very *p.*
1 *Pet.* 3. 8. love as brethren, be *p.* be courteous
PLACE
Signifies, [1] *The space or room in which a person or thing is,* Gen. 40. 3. [2] *A city, tent, or dwelling,* Gen. 18. 26, 33. [3] *Lot, state, or condition,* Job 18. 21. [4] *Room, or stead,* Gen. 50. 19. [5] *Acceptation, kind welcome, or entertainment,* John 8. 37. [6] *A portion or text of scripture,* Acts 8. 32. [7] *Advantage, occasion, or opportunity,* Eph. 4. 27. [8] *An office, or employment,* Gen. 40. 13.
Gen. 13. 14. Lord said, look from *p.* where thou art
18. 24. wilt thou destroy and not spare the *p.?*
26. I will spare the *p.* for their sakes
20. 13. the kindness thou shalt shew at every *p.*
22. 4. the third day Abraham saw the *p.* afar off
30. 25. send me away, I may go to mine own *p.*
40. 3. into prison, the *p.* where Joseph was bound
Exod. 3. 5. *p.* where thou standest is holy, *Josh.* 5. 15.
18. 23. this people shall go to their *p.* in peace
23. 20. to bring thee into the *p.* I have prepared
Lev. 1. 16. he shall cast it by the *p.* of the ashes
Num. 10. 14. in the first *p.* went standard of Judah
18. 31. ye shall eat in every *p.* ye and households
Deut. 11. 24. every *p.* whereon the soles of your feet shall tread shall be yours, *Josh.* 1. 3.
12. 5. *p.* the Lord God shall choose, 14. | 16. 16.
13. offer not thy burnt-offering in every *p.*
21. if the *p.* be too far from thee, 14. 24.
Judg. 11. 19. let us pass through thy land to my *p.*
20. 36. men of Israel gave *p.* to the Benjamites
Ruth 3. 4. thou shalt mark the *p.* where he lieth
1 *Sam.* 10. 12. and one of the same *p.* answered
14. 46. the Philistines went to their own *p.*
20. 25. and David's *p.* was empty, 27.
2 *Sam.* 2. 23. he fell down and died in the same *p.*
15. 21. in what *p.* my lord the king shall be
17. 9. he is hid in some pit, or in some other *p.*
12. so shall we come upon him in some *p.*
18. 18. it is called to this day Absalom's *p.*
1 *Kings* 8. 29. thine eyes may be open toward *p.*
2 *Kings* 5. 11. and strike his hand over the *p.*
6. 1. behold, *p.* where we dwell is too strait for us
1 *Chron.* 21. 22. grant me the *p.* of threshing-floor
25. David gave to Ornan for the *p.* 600 shekels
2 *Chron.* 30. 16. the priests stood in their *p.* 35. 10.
35. 15. singers, sons of Asaph, were in their *p.*
Neh. 2. 3. *p.* of my father's sepulchre lieth waste
14. there was no *p.* for beast under me to pass
4. 20. in what *p.* ye hear sound of the trumpet
13. 11. I set singers and Levites in their *p.*
Esth. 2. 9. Esther and her maids to the best *p.*
4. 14. shall deliverance arise from another *p.*
Job 6. 17. they are consumed out of their *p.*
9. 6. which shake the earth out of her *p.*
16. 18. cover not my blood, let my cry have no *p.*
28. 12. where is the *p.* of understanding? 20.
23. and he knoweth the *p.* thereof
36. 20. when people are cut off in their *p.*
38. 19. as for darkness, where is the *p.* thereof?
40. 12. and tread down the wicked in their *p.*
Psal. 26. 8. the *p.* where thine honour dwelleth
12. my foot standeth in an even *p.*
32. 7. thou art my hiding *p.* 119. 114.
33. 14. from the *p.* of his habitation he looketh
103. 16. the *p.* thereof shall know it no more
Eccl. 3. 16. the *p.* of judgment the *p.* of righteousness
20. all go to one *p.* all are of the dust, 6. 6.
Isa. 5. 8. that lay field to field, till there be no *p.*
13. 13. the earth shall remove out of her *p.*
14. 2. shall take them, and bring them to their *p.*
28. 8. full of filthiness, so that there is no *p.* clean
25. the appointed barley and rye in their *p.*
30. 32. in every *p.* where grounded staff shall pass
49. 20. the *p.* is too strait for me, give *p.* to me
54. 2. enlarge the *p.* of thy tent, spare not
60. 13. I will make the *p.* of my feet glorious
66. 1. and where is the *p.* of my rest?

Jer. 7. 12. go to my *p.* ‖ 32. till there be no *p.* 19. 11.
17. 12. glorious throne is the *p.* of our sanctuary
18. 14. the flowing waters come from another *p.*
Ezek. 6. 13. there slain be on *p.* where they offered
43. 7. *p.* of my throne shall Israel no more defile
21. he shall burn it in the appointed *p.* of house
Dan. 2. 35. that no *p.* was found for them
8. 11. the *p.* of his sanctuary was cast down
Hos. 5. 15. I will go and return to my *p.* till they
Joel 3. † 16. the Lord will be the *p.* of repair
Amos 2. † 13. press your *p.* as a cart is pressed
8. 3. there shall be many dead bodies in every *p.*
Nah. 3. 17. their *p.* is not known where they are
Zech. 10. 10. and *p.* shall not be found for them
12. 6. shall be inhabited again in her own *p.* 14. 10.
Mal. 1. 11. incense shall be offered in every *p.*
Mat. 28. 6. see the *p.* where Lord lay, *Mark* 16. 16.
Mark 6. 10. in what *p.* soever ye enter into an house
Luke 4. 17. he found the *p.* where it was written
10. 1. Lord sent them two and two unto every *p.*
32. a Levite, when he was at the *p.* passed by
14. 9. and say to thee, give this man *p.*
John 4. 20. Jerusalem is the *p.* of worship
8. 37. because my word hath no *p.* in you
11. 6. he abode two days still in the same *p.*
48. Romans shall take away our *p.* and nation
18. 2. Judas which betrayed him, knew the *p.*
Acts 2. 1. they were with one accord in one *p.*
4. 31. when they had prayed, the *p.* was shaken
7. 33. the *p.* whereon thou standest is holy
49. or what is the *p.* of my rest?
8. 32. the *p.* of scripture which he read was this
Rom. 12. 19. avenge not, but rather give *p.* to wrath
15. 23. but now having no more *p.* in these parts
1 *Cor.* 1. 2. with all that in every *p.* call on Jes. Chr.
11. 20. when ye come together into one *p.*
14. 23. the whole church be come into one *p.*
2 *Cor.* 2. 14. the savour of his knowledge in every *p.*
Gal. 2. 5. to whom gave *p.* by subjection not an hour
Eph. 4. 27. neither give *p.* to the devil
1 *Thess.* 1. 8. in every *p.* your faith G.-ward is spread
1 *Tim.* 2. † 2. prayers for kings and all in eminent *p.*
Heb. 5. 6. as he saith also in another *p.* thou a priest
8. 7. no *p.* should have been sought for the second
12. 17. he found no *p.* of repentance though sought
Jam. 3. 11. at the same *p.* sweet water and bitter
Rev. 12. 8. nor was there *p.* found any more in heav.
14. that she might fly into wilderness to her *p.*
20. 11. and there was found no *p.* for them
A PLACE.
Gen. 39. 20. *a p.* where king's prisoners were bound
Exod. 21. 13. then I will appoint thee *a p.* to flee
33. 21. the Lord said, behold, there is *a p.* by me
Num. 32. 1. behold, the place was *a p.* for cattle
Deut. 1. 33. search you out *a p.* to pitch your tents in
23. 12. thou shalt have *a p.* without the camp
Josh. 20. 4. they shall give him *a p.* in the city
Judg. 17. 8. to sojourn where he could find *a p.* 9.
18. 10. *a p.* where is no want of any thing
1 *Sam.* 15. 12. Saul set him up *a p.* and is gone
21. 2. I have appointed my servants to such *a p.*
27. 5. let them give me *a p.* in some town
2 *Sam.* 7. 10. I will appoint *a p.* for Israel, they may dwell in *a p.* of th. own, move no more, 1 *Chr.* 17. 9.
11. 16. Joab assigned Uriah to *a p.* where valiant
1 *Kings* 8. 21. I set there *a p.* for ark, 1 *Chron.* 15. 1.
2 *Kings* 6. 2. let us make *a p.* where we may dwell
8. in such and such *a p.* shall be my camp
9. man of God said, beware thou pass not such *a p.*
2 *Chron.* 6. 2. I have built *a p.* for thy dwelling
Job 28. 1. there is *a p.* for gold where they fine it
Psal. 132. 5. until I find out *a p.* for the Lord
Prov. 14. 26. and his children have *a p.* of refuge
Isa. 4. 6. shall be for *a p.* of refuge from rain
33. 21. the Lord will be to us *a p.* of broad rivers
34. 14. and find for herself *a p.* of rest
56. 5. and within my walls *a p.* and a name
65. 10. Achor *a p.* for the herds to lie down in
Ezek. 26. 5. *a p.* for the spreading of nets, 14.
39. 11. I will give to Gog, *a p.* of graves in Israel
Zeph. 2. 15. she is become *a p.* for beasts to lie down
Mat. 27. 33. that is *a p.* of a scull, *John* 19. 17.
Mark 11. 4. found colt in *a p.* where two ways met
John 14. 2. I go to prepare *a p.* for you, 3.
Heb. 2. 6. one in *a* certain *p.* testified, saying
4. 4. he spake in *a* certain *p.* of the seventh day
11. 8. when called to go out into *a p.* he obeyed
Rev. 12. 6. where she hath *a p.* prepared of God
16. 16. gathered them into *a p.* called Armageddon
See CHOOSE, DWELLING.
High PLACE.
Num. 23. 3. and Balaam went up to an *high p.*
1 *Sam.* 9. 12. there is a sacrifice to-day in *high p.*
10. 5. shalt meet prophets coming from *high p.*
13. when had made an end, Saul came to *high p.*
1 *Kings* 3. 4. that was great *high p.* 1 *Chron.* 16. 39.
11. 7. Solomon built an *high p.* for Chemosh
2 *Kings* 23. 15. *high p.* that Jeroboam had made, Josiah brake down the *high p.* burnt the *high p.*
2 *Chron.* 1. 3. so Solomon went to the *high p.*
13. come from his journey to *high p.* at Gibeon
Psal. 9. † 9. Lord will be an *high p.* for the oppressed
20. † 1. name of God of Jacob set thee on a *high p*
46. † 7. the God of Jacob is an *high p.* for us
Isa. 16. 12. that Moab is weary on the *high p.*
Ezek. 16. 24. made *high p.* in every street, 25. 31.
20. 29. what is the *high p.* whereunto ye go?
His PLACE.
Gen. 18. 33. and Abraham returned to *his p.*
31. 55. Laban rose up and returned to *his p.*
Exod. 10. 23. neither rose from *his p.* for three days
16. 29. abide ev. man in *his p.* none go out of *his p.*
Lev. 13. 23. but if the bright spot stay in *his p.*
Num. 2. 17. every man in *his p.* by their standards
24. 25. Balaam rose up and returned to *his p.*
Deut. 21. 19. and bring him to the gate of *his p.*
Ruth 4. 10. name of dead be not cut off from *his p.*
1 *Sam.* 3. 2. when Eli was laid down in *his p.*
9. so Samuel went and lay down in *his p.*
5. 3. and they set Dagon in *his p.* again
11. let the ark go down to *his* own *p.* 6. 2.
23. 22. go and see *his p.* where his haunt is

1 Sam. 26. 25. Dav. went on, Saul returned to his p.
29. 4. send David, that he may go again to his p.
2 Sam. 6. 17. they set the ark of the Lord in his p.
19. 39. Barzillai returned to his own p.
1 Kings 8. 6. priests brought ark to his p. 2 Chron. 5. 7.
20. 24. take kings away, every man out of his p.
1 Chron. 15. 3. to bring the ark of the Lord to his p.
16. 27. strength and gladness are in his p.
2 Chron. 24. 11. carried the chest to his p. again
34. 31. king stood in his p. and made a covenant
Ezra 1. 4. let men of his p. help him with silver
2. 68. for house of G. to set it in his p. 5. 15. | 6. 7.
Job 2. 11. they came every one from his own p.
7. 10. neither shall his p. know him any more
8. 18. if he destroy him from his p. it shall deny
14. 18. and the rock is removed out of his p.
18. 4. and shall the rock be removed out of his p.?
20. 9. nor shall his p. any more behold him
27. 21. and as a storm hurleth him out of his p.
23. men shall clap hands and hiss him out of his p.
37. 1. and my heart is removed out of his p.
38. 12. and caused the day-spring to know his p.
Psal. 37. 10. thou shalt diligently consider his p.
Prov. 27. 8. so is a man that wandereth from his p.
Eccl. 1. 5. the sun hasteth to his p. where he arose
Isa. 26. 21. Lord cometh out of his p. to punish
33. 16. his p. of defence shall be munition of rocks
46. 7. set him in his p. shall not remove from his p.
Jer. 4. 7. he is gone from his p. to make desolate
6. 3. they shall feed every one in his p.
Ezek. 3. 12. blessed be the glory of Lord from his p.
Mic. 1. 3. behold, the Lord cometh out of his p.
Zeph. 2. 11. men shall worship every one from his p.
Zech. 6. 12. and he shall grow up out of his p.
Mat. 26. 52. put up again thy sword into his p.
Acts 1. 25. that he might go to his own p.
Rev. 2. 5. remove thy candlestick out of his p.
See HOLY, Most HOLY.

In the PLACE.

Gen. 50. 19. Jos. said, fear not, I am in the p. of God
Exod. 15. 17. plant them in the p. thou hast made
Lev. 4. 24. kill it in the p. where they kill burnt offering before the Lord, 29, 33. | 6. 25. | 7. 2.
13. 19. in the p. of the boil there be white rising
Num. 9. 17. in the p. where cloud abode, there Israel
33. 54. inheritance be in the p. where his lot falleth
Josh. 4. 9. Joshua set up twelve stones in the p.
1 Kings 13. 22. because hast drunk water in the p.
21. 19. in the p. where dogs licked blood of Naboth
2 Chron. 3. 1. in the p. that David had prepared
Job 34. † 26. striketh them in the p. of beholders
Psal. 44. 19. hast sore broken us in the p. of dragons
Prov. 25. 6. and stand not in the p. of great men
Eccl. 11. 3. in the p. where the tree falleth it shall be
Jer. 22. 12. but he shall die in the p. 38. 9. | 42. 22.
Ezek. 17. 16. in the p. where the king dwelleth
21. 30. judge thee in the p. where thou wast created
Hos. 1. 10. that in the p. where it was said, ye are not my people, shall be sons of God, Rom. 9. 26.
13. 13. not stay long in the p. of breaking forth
John 19. 41. in the p. where crucified, was a garden

Of the PLACE.

Gen. 26. 7. men of p. asked him, lest men of p. kill
29. 22. Laban gathered all the men of the p.
32. 30. Jacob called the name of the p. Peniel
33. 17. name of p. Succoth || 35. 15. na. of p. Beth-el
Exod. 17. 7. and he called name of the p. Massah
Num. 11. 3. name of the p. Taberah || 21. 3. Hormah
Josh. 4. 3. take ye out of the p. twelve stones
5. 9. name of the p. Gilgal || 7. 26. valley of Achor
Judg. 19. 16. the men of the p. were Benjamites
Ruth 1. 7. Naomi went forth out of the p. where
2 Sam. 6. 8. David called name of the p. Perez-uzzah
1 Chron. 28. 11. pattern of the p. of the mercy seat
2 Chron. 20. 26. name of the p. valley of Berachah
Ezek. 41. 11. breadth of the p. left was five cubits
Joel 3. 7. raise them out of the p. whither ye sold
Nah. 1. 8. make an utter end of the p. thereof

That PLACE.

Gen. 21. 31. Abraham called that p. Beer-sheba
22. 14. that p. Jehovah-jireh || 28. 19. Beth-el
32. 2. Mahanaim || 38. 21. asked men of that p.
Num. 11. 34. name of that p. Kibroth-hattaavah
Deut. 12. 3. destroy names of them out of that p.
17. 10. the sentence they of that p. shall shew
Judg. 2. 5. they called name of that p. Bochim
15. 17. that p. Ramath-lehi || 18. 12. Mahaneh-dan
1 Sam. 23. 28. called that p. Selah hammah-lekoth
2 Sam. 2. 16. that p. was called Helkath-hazzurim
5. 20. called that p. Baal-perazim, 1 Chron. 14. 11.
1 Chron. 13. 11. that p. is called Perez-uzzah
Mat. 14. 35. men of that p. had knowledge of him
Mark 6. 10. there abide till ye depart from that p.
John 5. 13. a multitude being in that p.
11. 30. but was in that p. where Martha met him
Acts 21. 12. both we and they of that p. besought

This PLACE.

Gen. 19. 12. thy sons bring them out of this p.
13. we will destroy this p. || 14. get out of this p.
20. 11. surely the fear of God is not in this p.
28. 16. Lord is in this p. || 17. dreadful is this p.
38. 21. there was no harlot in this p. 22.
48. 9. are sons, whom God hath given me in this p.
Exod. 13. 3. the Lord brought you out from this p.
Num. 20. 5. to bring us unto this evil p.
Deut. 1. 31. bare thee till ye came to this p. 9. 7. | 11. 5.
26. 9. and he hath brought us into this p.
29. 7. when ye came unto this p. Sihon came out
Judg. 18. 3. and what makest thou in this p.?
1 Kings 8. 29. hearken to prayer toward this p. 30. 35. 2 Chron. 6. 20, 21, 26, 40. | 7. 15.
13. 8. nor eat bread, nor drink water in this p. 16.
2 Kings 18. 25. come not without L. against this p.
22. 16. I will bring evil on this p. and inhabitants thereof, 17, 20. 2 Chron. 34. 24, 25, 28.
2 Chron. 7. 12. and have chosen this p. to myself
Job 18. 21. this the p. of him that knows not God
Jer. 7. 6. and shed not innocent blood in this p.
20. my fury shall be poured out on this p.
14. 13. I will give you assured peace in this p.
16. 2. neither have sons nor daughters in this p.
9. cause to cease out of this p. the voice of mirth
Jer. 19. 3. behold, I will bring evil upon this p.
4. they estranged this p. filled this p. with blood
6. that this p. shall no more be called Tophet
12. thus will I do to this p. saith the Lord, 40. 2.
22. 11. which went forth out of this p. 24. 5.
27. 22. and I will restore them to this p. 32. 37.
28. 3. I will bring to this p. all the vessels, 6.
4. I will bring again to this p. Jeconiah
29. 10. in causing you to return to this p.
33. 10. again be heard in this p. the voice of joy
42. 18. and ye shall see this p. no more
44. 29. that I will punish you in this p.
51. 62. O Lord, thou hast spoken against this p.
Ezek. 46. 20. this is p. where the priests shall boil
Zeph. 1. 4. cut off the remnant of Baal from this p.
Hag. 2. 9. in t. p. will I give peace, saith the Lord
Mat. 12. 6. in this p. one greater than the temple
Luke 16. 28. lest they come into this p. of torment
23. 5. teaching, beginning from Galilee to this p.
Acts 6. 14. Jesus of Nazareth shall destroy this p.
7. 7. they shall come forth and serve me in this p.
21. 28. that teacheth against the law and this p.
Heb. 4. 5. and in this p. again, if they shall enter

Thy PLACE.

Gen. 40. 13. Pharaoh shall restore thee to thy p.
Num. 24. 11. therefore now flee thou to thy p.
2 Sam. 15. 19. return to thy p. and abide with king
Eccl. 10. 4. if ruler rise against thee, leave not t. p.
Ezek. 12. 3. thou shalt remove from thy p. 38. 15.

To or unto the PLACE.

Gen. 13. 3. Abram went unto t. p. where his tent, 4.
22. 3. went unto the p. of which God told him, 9.
Exod. 3. 8. to bring you unto t. p. of the Canaanite
32. 34. lead people unto the p. of which I spake
Num. 10. 29. we are journeying to the p. of which
14. 40. go up to the p. which Lord hath promised
Josh. 4. 8. carried stones to t. p. where they lodged
1 Sam. 20. 19. come to t. p. where thou hide thyself
2 Sam. 2. 23. as many as came to the p. stood still
2 Kings 6. 10. sent to the p. which man of God told
1 Chr. 15. 12. bring ark to the p. that I prepared
Neh. 1. 9. I will bring them to the p. I have chosen
Psal. 104. 8. they go to t. p. that thou hast founded
Isa. 18. 7. present brought to the p. of name of L.
Jer. 7. 14. I will do to the p. which I gave to you
29. 14. will bring you again to t. p. whence I caused
Acts 25. 23. and was entered into the p. of hearing

PLACE, Verb.

Gen. 33. † 15. let me p. some of the folk with thee
Exod. 18. 21. and p. such over them to be rulers
Deut. 14. 23. in the place which he shall choose, to p. his name there, 16. 2, 6, 11. | 26. 2.
1 Kings 20. † 12. Benhadad said, p. the engines
Ezra 6. 5. and p. them in the house of God
Isa. 46. 13. and I will p. salvation in Zion for Israel
Ezek. 37. 14. I shall p. you in your own land, 26.
Dan. 11. 31. and they shall p. the abomination
Hos. 11. 11. I will p. them in their houses, saith L.
Zech. 10. 6. I will bring them again to p. them

PLACED.

Gen. 3. 24. God p. at east of the garden cherubims
47. 11. Joseph p. his father and his brethren
1 Kings 12. 32. Jeroboam p. in Beth-el the priests
2 Kings 17. 6. and p. them in Halah and in Habor
24. and p. them in the cities of Samaria, 26.
2 Chron. 1. 14. which he p. in the chariot cities
4. 8. he made tables, p. them in the temple
17. 2. he p. forces in all the fenced cities of Judah
Job 20. 4. of old, since man was p. upon earth
Psal. 78. 60. the tent which he had p. among men
Cant. 5. † 12. his eyes as the eyes of doves fitly p.
Isa. 5. 8. that they may be p. alone in the midst
Jer. 5. 22. which p. sand for the bound of the sea
Ezek. 17. 5. the eagle p. it by the great waters

PLACES.

Gen. 28. 15. I am with thee, will keep thee in all p.
Exod. 20. 24. in all p. where I record my name
Deut. 12. 2. shall utterly destroy all the p. wherein
Josh. 5. 8. abode in their p. till they were whole
Judg. 5. 11. delivered in the p. of drawing water
19. 13. let us draw near to one of these p. to lodge
1 Sam. 7. 16. Samuel judged Israel in all those p.
30. 31. David sent presents to all the p.
2 Sam. 7. 7. in all the p. I spake I a word with any
2 Kings 23. 5. put down priests in p. about Jerusal.
14. he filled their p. with the bones of men
Neh. 4. 12. from all p. whence ye shall return
13. I set the people in lower p. and on higher p.
12. 27. they sought Levites out of all their p.
Job 21. 28. where are dwelling p. of the wicked
37. 8. beasts go into dens and remain in their p.
Psal. 10. 8. he sitteth in lurking p. of the villages
16. 6. the lines are fallen to me in pleasant p.
18. 45. and be afraid out of their close p.
73. 18. thou didst set them in slippery p.
74. 20. the dark p. of the earth are full of cruelty
103. 22. bless the Lord, all his works, in all p.
105. 41. they ran in the dry p. like a river
110. 6. he shall fill the p. with the dead bodies
Prov. 8. 2. she standeth in the p. of the paths
Cant. 2. 14. O my dove, that art in the secret p.
Isa. 32. 18. my people shall dwell in quiet resting p.
40. 4. crooked made straight, and rough p. plain
45. 2. I will make the crooked p. straight
Jer. 4. 12. a wind from those p. shall come to me
8. 3. in all p. whither I have driven them, 29. 14.
17. 26. they shall come from p. about Jerusalem
24. 9. to be a taunt and a curse in all p. I drive
32. 44. take witnesses in the p. about Jerusalem
40. 12. all the Jews returned out of all p. whither
45. 5. thy life I will give for a prey in all p.
Lam. 2. 6. he hath destroyed his p. of the assembly
Ezek. 34. 12. I will deliver them out of all p.
26. I will make the p. round my hill a blessing
46. 24. he said these are the p. of them that boil
47. 11. but the miry p. thereof shall not be healed
Amos 4. 6. and want of bread in all your p.
Zech. 3. 7. I will give thee p. to walk among these
Mat. 12. 43. he walketh through dry p. Luke 11. 24.
13. 5. some fell on stony p. and sprung up, 20.
24. 7. and there shall be famines and earthquakes in divers p. Mark 13. 8. Luke 21. 11.
Acts 24. 3. we accept it in all p. most noble Felix
Eph. 1. 3. who hath blessed us in heavenly p.
20. set him at his own right hand in heavenly p.
2. 6. made us sit together in heavenly p. in Chr. J.
3. 10. to powers in heavenly p. might be known
Phil. 1. 13. my bonds in Chr. are manifest in all p.
Rev. 6. 14. mountain and island mov. out of their p.
See DESOLATE, HOLY.

High PLACES.

Lev. 26. 30. I will destroy your high p. and images
Num. 21. 28. consumed lords of high p. of Arnon
22. 41. brought him up into the high p. of Baal
33. 52. and quite pluck down all their high p.
Deut. 32. 13. made him ride on high p. of the earth
33. 29. and thou shalt tread upon their high p.
Judg. 5. 18. jeoparded their lives in the high p.
1 Sam. 13. 6. the people hide themselves in high p.
2 Sam. 1. 19. the beauty of Israel slain in high p.
25. Jonathan, thou wast slain in thy high p.
22. 34. and setteth me on my high p. Psal. 18. 33.
1 Kings 3. 2. only the people sacrificed in high p. 2 Kings 17. 32. 2 Chr. 33. 17.
3. sacrificed and burnt incense in high p. 22. 43. 2 Kings 12. 3. | 15. 4, 35. | 16. 4. | 17. 11.
12. 31. Jeroboam made an house of high p.
32. he placed in Beth-el the priests of high p.
13. 2. he shall offer the priests of the high p.
32. he cried against all the houses of the high p.
1 Kings 13. 33. Jeroboam made of the lowest of the people priests of the high p. 2 Kings 17. 32.
15. 14. but the high p. were not removed, 22. 43. 2 Kings 12. 3. | 14. 4. | 15. 4, 35.
2 Kings 17. 29. put their gods in houses of high p.
18. 4. Hezekiah removed the high p. 22.
23. 5. had ordained to burn incense in the high p.
8. defiled the high p. and brake down the high p. 13. 2 Chron. 31. 1. | 32. 12. Isa. 36. 7.
9. priests of high p. came not up to altar of Lord
20. he slew all the priests of the high p.
2 Chr. 11. 15. Rehoboam ordained priests for high p.
14. 3. Asa took away the high p. and images, 5.
15. 17. the high p. were not taken away, 20. 33.
17. 6. Jehoshaphat took away the high p.
21. 11. Jehor. made high p. || 28. 25. Ahaz high p.
34. 3. Josiah did purge Jerusalem from the high p.
Job 25. 2. he maketh peace in his high p.
Psal. 78. 58. they provoked him with their high p.
Prov. 8. 2. she standeth on the top of the high p.
9. 14. sitteth on a seat in the high p. of the city
Isa. 15. 2. he is gone up to the high p. to weep
41. 18. I will open rivers in high p. and fountains
49. 9. their pastures shall be in all high p.
58. 14. cause thee to ride on high p. of the earth
Jer. 3. 2. lift up thine eyes to the high p. and see
21. a voice was heard on the high p. weeping
4. 11. a dry wind in the high p. of the wilderness
7. 29. and take up a lamentation in the high p.
12. 12. the spoilers are come up on all the high p.
14. 6. the wild asses did stand in the high p.
17. 3. I will give thy high p. for sin, thro' borders
26. 18. and the mountain of the house shall become as the high p. of the forest, Mic. 3. 12.
48. 35. to cease in Moab him that offereth in high p.
Ezek. 6. 3. behold, I will destroy your high p.
16. 16. deckedst thy high p. with divers colours
39. and they shall break down thy high p.
36. 2. the ancient high p. are ours in possession
Hos. 10. 8. the high p. of Aven shall be destroyed
Amos 4. 13. treadeth on high p. of earth, Mic. 1. 3.
7. 9. the high p. of Isaac shall be desolate
Mic. 1. 5. and what are the high p. of Judah?
Hab. 3. 19. will make me to walk on mine high p.
Eph. 6. 12. against spiritual wickedness in high p.
See BUILT.

Waste PLACES.

Isa. 5. 17. waste p. of fat ones shall strangers eat
51. 3. the Lord will comfort all her waste p.
52. 9. sing together, ye waste p. of Jerusalem
58. 12. and they shall build the old waste p.

PLAGUE.

Psal. 89. 23. and I will p. them that hate him

PLAGUE, Substantive.

Exod. 11. 1. yet I will bring one p. on Pharaoh
12. 13. the p. shall not be on you to destroy you
30. 12. that there be no p. among them
Lev. 13. 3. when hair in the p. is turned white, 17.
5. if the p. spread not in the skin, 6. | 14. 48.
30. if a man or woman hath a p. then priest shall see the p. 31, 32, 50, 51, 55. | 14. 37.
44. he is a leprous man, his p. is in his head
50. and shut up it that hath the p. seven days
57. if it app. in warp or woof, it is a spreading p.
58. if p. be departed from them, it be washed
14. 35. there is as it were a p. in the house
Num. 8. 19. that there be no p. among Israel
11. 33. Lord smote people with a very great p.
14. 37. those men died by the p. before the Lord
16. 46. wrath is gone out, the p. is begun, 47.
48. and the p. was stayed, 50. | 25. 8.
49. now they that died in the p. were, 25. 9.
Deut. 28. 61. every p. which is not written in book
Josh. 22. 17. we are not cleansed, altho' there was p.
1 Sam. 6. 4. one p. was on you all and your lords
2 Sam. 24. 21. that p. may be stayed, 1 Chr. 21. 22.
1 Kings 8. 37. whatever p. or sickness there be
38. shall know every man the p. of his own heart
2 Chron. 21. 14. with a great p. will the Lord smite
Psal. 91. 10. nor any p. come nigh thy dwelling
106. 29. and the p. brake in upon them
30. Phinehas executed judgment, so p. was stayed
Zech. 14. 12. this shall be p. the Lord will smite, 18.
Mark 5. 29. she felt that she was healed of that p.
34. go in peace, and be whole of thy p.
Rev. 16. 21. blasphemed because of the p. of hail

PLAGUED.

Gen. 12. 17. the Lord p. Pharaoh and his house
Exod. 32. 35. Lord p. the people for making calf
Josh. 24. 5. p. Egypt, and afterwards brought you
1 Chr. 21. 17. not on people, that they should be p.
Psal. 73. 5. nor are they p. like other men
14. all the day have I been p. and chastened

PLAGUES.

Gen. 12. 17. Lord plagued Pharaoh with great *p.*
Exod. 9. 14. I will at this time send all my *p.*
Lev. 26. 21. I will bring seven times more *p.* on you
Deut. 28. 59. the Lord will make thy *p.* wonderful
29. 22. when they see the *p.* of that land
1 *Sam.* 4. 8. gods that smote the Egyptians with *p.*
Job 10. † 17. thou renewest thy *p.* against me
Jer. 19. 8. hiss, because of the *p.* 49. 17. | 50. 13.
Ezek. 39. † 2. I will strike thee with six *p.*
Hos. 13. 14. O death, I will be thy *p.* O grave
Mark 3. 10. pressed to touch him as many as had *p.*
Luke 7. 21. same hour he cured many of their *p.*
Rev. 9. 20. rest which were not killed by these *p.*
11. 6. these have power to smite earth with *p.*
16. 9. name of God, who hath power over these *p.*
18. 4. and that ye receive not of her *p.*
8. therefore shall her *p.* come in one day, death
22. 18. God shall add to him the *p.* written
See SEVEN.

PLAIN.

Gen. 25. 27. Jacob was a *p.* man, dwelling in tents
Psal. 27. 11. teach me, and lead me in a *p.* path
Prov. 8. 9. they are *p.* to him that understandeth
15. 19. but the way of the righteous is made *p.*
Isa. 28. 25. when he made *p.* the face thereof
40. 4. crooked made straight, and rough places *p.*
Jer. 48. 21. judgment is come on the *p.* country
Hab. 2. 2. write the vision, make it *p.* upon tables
Mark 7. 35. tongue was loosed, and he spake *p.*

PLAIN.

Gen. 11. 2. they found a *p.* in the land of Shinar
13. 10. and Lot beheld all the *p.* of Jordan
11. then Lot chose him all the *p.* of Jordan
12. Lot dwelled in cities of the *p.* toward Sodom
18. Abram came and dwelt in the *p.* 14. 13.
19. 17. nor stay thou in all *p.* escape to mountain
25. he overthrew those cities in all the *p.*
Josh. 11. 16. Joshua took the valley and the *p.*
Judg. 9. 6. made Abimelech king by *p.* of pillar
11. 33. Jephthah smote the Ammonites to the *p.*
1 *Sam.* 10. 3. thou shalt come to the *p.* of Tabor
23. 24. David and his men were in the *p.*
2 *Sam.* 2. 29. Abner and his men walked through *p.*
4. 7. Baanah and Rechab gat them through the *p.*
5. † 20. he called that place the *p.* of breaches
15. 28. I will tarry in the *p.* till I hear from you
18. 23. then Ahimaaz ran by the way of the *p.*
1 *Kings* 7. 46. in *p.* of Jordan did king cast them
20. 23. let us fight against them in the *p.* 25.
2 *Kings* 25. 4. king went towards the *p. Jer.* 52. 7.
Neh. 3. 22. after him repaired the priests of the *p.*
Jer. 17. 26. shall come from *p.* bringing offerings
21. 13. I am against thee, O rock of the *p.*
48. 8. *p.* shall be destroyed, as Lord hath spoken
Ezek. 3. 22. he said, arise, go forth in the *p.* 23.
8. 4. according to the vision that I saw in the *p.*

PLAINS.

Gen. 18. 1. the Lord appeared in the *p.* of Mamre
Num. 22. 1. Israel pitched in *p.* of Moab, 33. 48.
26. 63. who numbered Israel in the *p.* of Moab
31. 12. they brought spoil to the camp in the *p.*
33. 50. the Lord spake to Moses in the *p.* 35. 1.
36. 13. the Lord commanded in the *p.* of Moab
Deut. 34. 1. Moses went up from the *p.* of Moab
8. Israel wept for Moses in the *p.* forty days
2 *Sam.* 17. 16. lodge not in the *p.* of the wilderness
2 *Kings* 25. 5. the army of the Chaldees overtook him in the *p.* of Jericho, *Jer.* 39. 5. | 52. 8.
1 *Chron.* 27. 28. over sycamore-trees in the low *p.*
2 *Chron.* 9. 27. made cedars as sycamores in low *p.*
26. 10. Uzziah had much cattle in the *p.*

PLAINLY.

Exod. 21. 5. if the servant *p.* say, I love my master
Deut. 27. 8. write the words of this law very *p.*
1 *Sam.* 2. 27. did I *p.* appear to house of thy father?
10. 16. he told us *p.* that the asses were found
2 *Sam.* 20. † 18. they *p.* spake in the beginning
Ezra 4. 18. the letter hath been *p.* read before me
Isa. 32. 4. tongue of the stammerers shall speak *p.*
John 10. 24. if thou be the Christ, tell us *p.*
11. 14. then Jesus said to them *p.* Lazarus is dead
16. 25. but I shall shew you *p.* of the Father
29. now speakest thou *p.* and speakest no proverb
Heb. 11. 14. for they that say such things declare *p.*

PLAINNESS.

2 *Cor.* 3. 12. have such hope, we use great *p.* of speech

PLAISTER.

Isa. 38. 21. a lump of figs, lay it for a *p.* on boil

PLAISTER.

Lev. 14. 42. shall take mortar and shall *p.* house
Deut. 27. 2. great stones, and *p.* them with *p.* 4.
Dan. 5. 5. wrote on the *p.* of the wall of palace

PLAISTERED.

Lev. 14. 43. if the plague come again after it is *p.*
48. plague hath not spread after the house was *p.*

PLAITING.

1 *Pet.* 3. 3. whose adorning let it not be *p.* of hair

PLANES.

Isa. 44. 13. the carpenter fitteth the image with *p.*

PLANETS.

2 *Kings* 23. 5. that burnt incense to sun, moon, *p.*

PLANKS.

1 *Kings* 6. 15. he covered the floor with *p.* of fir
Ezek. 41. 25. were thick *p.* on face of the porch
26. on the side chambers of house, and thick *p.*

PLANT, *Substantive.*

Gen. 2. 5. the Lord God made every *p.* of the field
Job 14. 9. will bud and bring forth boughs like *p.*
Isa. 5. 7. and the men of Judah his pleasant *p.*
17. 11. in the day thou shalt make thy *p.* grow
53. 2. he shall grow before him as a tender *p.*
Jer. 2. 21. how art thou turned into degenerate *p.*
Ezek. 34. 29. raise up for them a *p.* of renown
Mat. 15. 13. every *p.* my Father hath not planted

PLANTS.

1 *Chr.* 4. 23. those that dwell among *p.* and hedges
Psal. 128. 3. thy children like olive *p.* round table
144. 12. that our sons may be as *p.* grown up
Cant. 4. 13. thy *p.* as an orchard of pomegranates
Isa. 16. 8. have broken down principal *p.* thereof
17. 10. therefore shalt thou plant pleasant *p.*

Jer. 48. 32. thy *p.* are gone over sea, they reach
Ezek. 31. 4. with rivers running round about his *p.*

PLANT

Signifies, [1] *To set trees or herbs*, Gen. 9. 20. [2] *To bring a people from one country into another, there to place and settle them*, Psal. 44. 2. | 80. 8. [3] *To be made real and living members of the church of God*, Psal. 92. 13. [4] *To lay the first foundation of Christianity among a people, and be instrumental, by the preaching of the gospel, in converting them to Christ*, 1 Cor. 3. 6.

Exod. 15. 17. *p.* them in mount of thy inheritance
Deut. 16. 21. thou shalt not *p.* a grove of any trees
28. 30. thou shalt *p.* a vineyard, and not eat, 39.
2 *Sam.* 7. 10. moreover, I will *p.* them, 1 *Chr.* 17. 9.
2 *Kings* 19. 29. *p.* vineyards and eat, *Isa.* 37. 30.
Psal. 107. 37. sow the fields, and *p.* vineyards
Isa. 17. 10. therefore thou shalt *p.* pleasant plants
41. 19. I will *p.* in the wilderness the cedar
51. 16. that I may *p.* heavens, and lay foundations
65. 21. they shall *p.* vineyards, eat fruit of them
22. they shall not *p.* and another eat
Jer. 1. 10. I have set thee to build and to *p.*
18. 9. concerning a kingdom to build and to *p.*
24. 6. I will *p.* and not pluck them up, 42. 10.
29. 5. *p.* gardens, and eat the fruit of them, 28.
31. 5. shall *p.* vines on the mountains of Samaria
28. I will watch over them to build and to *p.*
32. 41. I will *p.* them in this land assuredly
35. 7. nor shall you sow seed, nor *p.* vineyard
Ezek. 17. 22. I will *p.* it on a high mountain, 23.
28. 26. they shall *p.* vineyards, and dwell safely
36. 36. Lord build and *p.* that that was desolate
Dan. 11. 45. he shall *p.* tabernacles of his palace
Amos 9. 14. they shall *p.* vineyards and drink wine
15. I will *p.* them upon their land, saith Lord
Zeph. 1. 13. they shall *p.* viney. but not drink wine

PLANTATION.

Ezek. 17. 7. might water it by furrows of her *p.*

PLANTED.

Gen. 2. 8. the Lord God *p.* a garden eastward
9. 20. Noah *p.* vineyard || 21. 33. Abram *p.* a grove
Num. 24. 6. as trees which the Lord hath *p.*
Deut. 20. 6. what man is he that hath *p.* a vineyard
Josh. 24. 13. of olive-yards ye *p.* not, do ye eat
Psal. 1. 3. like a tree *p.* by the rivers, *Jer.* 17. 8.
80. 8. thou hast cast out heathen, and *p.* the vine
15. the vineyard which thy right hand hath *p.*
92. 13. those that be *p.* in the house of the Lord
94. 9. he that *p.* the ear, shall he not hear?
104. 16. the cedars of Lebanon which he hath *p.*
Eccl. 2. 4. I *p.* me vineyards || 5. I *p.* trees
3. 2. and a time to pluck up that which is *p.*
Isa. 5. 2. and *p.* it with the choicest vine
40. 24. yea, they shall not be *p.* nor be sown
Jer. 2. 21. yet I had *p.* thee a noble vine
11. 17. for the Lord of hosts that *p.* thee
12. 2. thou hast *p.* them, they have taken root
45. 4. what I have *p.* I will pluck up
Ezek. 17. 5. and *p.* it in a fruitful field, 8.
10. yea, behold, being *p.* shall it prosper?
19. 10. *p.* by the waters she was fruitful
13. and now she is *p.* in the wilderness
Hos. 9. 13. Ephraim is *p.* in a pleasant place
Amos 5. 11. ye have *p.* pleasant vineyards
Mat. 15. 13. plant my heavenly Father hath not *p.*
21. 33. man *p.* a vineyard, *Mark* 12. 1. *Luke* 20. 9.
Luke 13. 6. certain man had a fig-tree *p.* in vineyard
17. 6. be plucked up, and be thou *p.* in the sea
28. they bought, they sold, they *p.* they builded
Rom. 6. 5. if we have been *p.* together in his death
1 *Cor.* 3. 6. I have *p.* Apollos watered, God increase

PLANTEDST.

Deut. 6. 11. and olive-trees which thou *p.* not
Psal. 44. 2. didst drive out heathen and *p.* them

PLANTERS.

Jer. 31. 5. *p.* shall plant, and eat them as common

PLANTETH.

Prov. 31. 16. with fruit of her hands she *p.* vineyard
Isa. 44. 14. he *p.* an ash, and the rain doth nourish
1 *Cor.* 3. 7. neither is he that *p.* any thing
8. he that *p.* and he that watereth are one
9. 7. who *p.* a vineyard and eateth not the fruit

PLANTING.

Isa. 60. 21. branch of my *p.* work of my hands
61. 3. they might be called the *p.* of the Lord

PLANTINGS.

Mic. 1. 6. I will make Samaria as *p.* of a vineyard

PLAT.

2 *Kings* 9. 26. I will requite thee in this *p.* now take and cast him into the *p.* of ground

PLATE.

Exod. 28. 36. thou shalt make a *p.* of pure gold
39. 30. they made the *p.* of holy crown of gold
Lev. 2. † 5. meat offering taken in a *p.* 7. † 9.
8. 9. on his fore-front he put the golden *p.*
Ezek. 4. † 3. take a flat *p.* set it for a wall

PLATES.

Exod. 39. 3. they did beat gold into thin *p.*
Num. 16. 38. let them make of censers broad *p.*
39. were made broad *p.* for a covering of altar
1 *Kings* 7. 30. and every base had *p.* of brass
Jer. 10. 9. silver spread into *p.* is brought from Tars.

PLATTED.

Mat. 27. 29. when they had *p.* a crown of thorns, they put it on his head, *Mark* 15. 17. *John* 19. 2.

PLATTER.

Mat. 23. 25. ye make clean outside of the *p.* but within full of extortion and excess, *Luke* 11. 39.

PLAY

The Hebrew *word*, Zachak, *which signifies*, to play, *is also commonly used for* laughing, mocking, insulting. *When* Sarah *saw* Ishmael *play with her son* Isaac, *she was offended at it*, Gen. 21. 9. *It was a play of mockery, or insult, or perhaps of squabbling, as the word is used*, 2 Sam. 2. 14. Let the young men now arise and play before us; *let them fight as it were by way of play. But the event shews that they fought in good earnest, since they were all killed. We find* play *taken in another sense in* Exod. 32. 6. *When the* Israelites *had set up the golden calf, they began to shout, to sing, and dance about it, and to divert themselves*, The people sat down to eat and drink, and rose up to play.

Exod. 32. 6. the people rose up to *p.* 1 *Cor.* 10. 7.
Deut. 22. 21. to *p.* the whore in her father's house
1 *Sam.* 16. 16. that he shall *p.* with his hand
17. provide me now a man that can *p.* well
21. 15. have brought this fellow to *p.* madman
2 *Sam.* 2. 14. let young men arise and *p.* before us
6. 21. therefore will I *p.* before the Lord
10. 12. and let us *p.* the men for our people
Job 40. 20. where all the beasts of the field *p.*
41. 5. wilt thou *p.* with him as with a bird?
Psal. 33. 3. *p.* skilfully with a loud noise
104. 26. leviathan whom thou made to *p.* therein
Isa. 11. 8. sucking child shall *p.* on hole of the asp
Ezek. 33. 32. and can *p.* well on an instrument

PLAYED.

Judg. 19. 2. and his concubine *p.* the whore
1 *Sam.* 16. 23. David *p.* with his hand, 18. 10. | 19. 9.
18. 7. the women answered one another as they *p.*
26. 21. I have *p.* fool, and have erred exceedingly
2 *Sam.* 6. 5. David and all Israel *p.* 1 *Chr.* 13. 8.
2 *Kings* 3. 15. it came to pass when the minstrel *p.*
Ezek. 16. 28. hast *p.* the whore with the Assyrians
See HARLOT.

PLAYER.

1 *Sam.* 16. 16. who is a cunning *p.* on an harp

PLAYERS.

Psal. 68. 25. the *p.* on instruments followed after
87. 7. as well the singers as the *p.* on instruments

PLAYETH.

1 *Sam.* 21. † 14. you see the man *p.* the madman
Ezek. 23. 44. as to a woman that *p.* the harlot

PLAYING.

1 *Sam.* 16. 18. have seen a son of Jesse cunning in *p.*
1 *Chron.* 15. 29. Michal saw David dancing and *p.*
Psal. 68. 25. amongst them were the damsels *p.*
Zech. 8. 5. boys and girls *p.* in the streets thereof

PLEA.

Deut. 17. 8. if a matter too hard between *p.* and *p.*

PLEAD.

Judg. 6. 31. will ye *p.* for Baal? he that will *p.* for him
32. saying, let Baal *p.* against him, because he
Job 9. 19. if of judgm. who shall set me a time to *p.*?
13. 19. who is he that will *p.* with me?
16. 21. O that one might *p.* for a man with God
19. 5. if he will *p.* against me my reproach
23. 6. will he *p.* against me with his great power?
Isa. 1. 17. seek judgment, *p.* for the widow
3. 13. Lord standeth up to *p.* and judge the people
43. 26. let us *p.* together, declare thou to be justified
66. 16. by fire will the Lord *p.* with all flesh
Jer. 2. 9. wherefore, I will yet *p.* with you, 35. and with your children's children will I *p.*
29. wherefore will ye *p.* with me? all transgressed
12. 1. righteous art thou, O Ld. when I *p.* with thee
25. 31. Lord will *p.* with all flesh, saith the Lord
50. † 44. and who will covenant me to *p.*?
Ezek. 17. 20. and I will *p.* with him there
20. † 4. wilt thou *p.* for them? 22. † 2. | 23. † 36.
35. and there will I *p.* with you face to face
36. so will I *p.* with you, saith the Lord God
38. 22. I will *p.* against him with pestilence
Hos. 2. 2. *p.* with your mother, *p.* she is not my wife
5. † 13. Ephraim sent to the king that should *p.*
Joel 3. 2. and I will *p.* with them for my people
Mic. 6. 2. and the Lord will *p.* with Israel
See CAUSE.

PLEADED.

1 *Sam.* 25. 39. blessed be the Lord that *p.* the cause
Lam. 3. 58. O Lord, thou hast *p.* causes of my soul
Ezek. 20. 36. like as I *p.* with your fathers in wilder.

PLEADETH.

Job 16. 21. with God, as a man *p.* for his neighbour
Isa. 51. 22. saith thy God, that *p.* cause of his people
59. 4. none calleth for justice, nor any *p.* for truth

PLEADING.

Job 13. 6. hear and hearken to the *p.* of my lips

PLEASANT.

Gen. 2. 9. God made every tree grow that is *p.*
3. 6. was *p.* to the eyes, and a tree to be desired
49. 15. Issachar saw the land that it was *p.*
2 *Sam.* 1. 23. Saul and Jonathan were *p.* in their lives
26. Jonathan, very *p.* hast thou been to me
1 *Kings* 20. 6. whatever is *p.* they shall take away
2 *Kings* 2. 19. behold, the situation of this city is *p.*
2 *Chron.* 32. 27. he made treasuries for *p.* jewels
Psal. 16. 6. the lines are fallen to me in *p.* places
81. 2. bring hither the *p.* harp with the psaltery
106. 24. yea, they despised the *p.* land, believed not
133. 1. how *p.* for brethren to dwell together in unity
135. 3. sing praises to his name, for it is *p.* 147. 1.
Prov. 2. 10. when knowledge is *p.* to thy soul
5. 19. let her be as the loving hind and *p.* roe
9. 17. stolen waters sweet, bread eaten in secret is *p.*
15. 26. but the words of the pure are *p.* words
16. 24. *p.* words are as honey-comb, sweet to soul
22. 18. for it is *p.* if thou keep them within thee
24. 4. the chambers shall be filled with all *p.* riches
Eccl. 11. 7. *p.* it is for the eyes to behold the sun
Cant. 1. 16. thou art fair, my beloved, yea *p.*
4. 13. thy plants are an orchard with *p.* fruits
16. let my beloved come and eat his *p.* fruits
7. 6. how fair and *p.* art thou, O love, for delights
13. at our gates are all manner of *p.* fruits
Isa. 2. 16. the day of the Lord upon all *p.* pictures
5. 7. and the men of Judah his *p.* plant
13. 22. and dragons shall cry in their *p.* palaces
17. 10. therefore shalt thou plant *p.* plants
32. 12. they lament for *p.* fields, for fruitful vine
54. 12. I will make all thy borders of *p.* stones
64. 11. and all our *p.* things are laid waste
Jer. 3. 19. how shall I give thee a *p.* land?
12. 10. made my *p.* portion a desolate wilderness
23. 10. *p.* places of the wilderness are dried up
25. 34. and ye shall fall like a *p.* vessel
31. 20. is Ephraim my dear son? is he a *p.* child?
Lam. 1. 7. she remembered all her *p.* things of old
10. advers. hath spread his hand on her *p.* things
11. they have given their *p.* things for meat

Lam. 2. 4. slew all that were p. to the eye in tabern.
Ezek. 26. 12. they shall destroy thy p. houses
33. 32. very lively song of one that hath p. voice
Dan. 8. 9. waxed exceeding great toward the p. land
10. 3. I ate no p. bread, nor came flesh in my mouth
11. 38. he shall honour a god with p. things
Hos. 9. 6. the p. places nettles shall possess them
13. Ephraim is planted in a p. place, but Ephraim
Joel 3. 5. have carried into your temp. my p. things
Amos 5. 11. ye planted p. vineyards, shall not drink
Mic. 2. 9. women have ye cast out from p. houses
Nah. 2. 9. and glory out of all the p. furniture
Zech. 7. 14. for they laid the p. land desolate
Mal. 3. 4. offering of Jerusalem be p. to the Lord

PLEASANTNESS.

Prov. 3. 17. her ways are ways of p. her paths peace
15. † 26. the words of the pure are words of p.

PLEASE

Is spoken, (I) *Of God, pleasing himself*, and denotes, [1] *His will and good pleasure*, Isa. 55. 11. 1 Cor. 1. 21. [2] *His decree and purpose*, Psal. 115. 3. | 135. 6. (II) *Of Christ pleasing God*, and signifies, *That God the Father did perfectly accept of Christ as Mediator, and had a singular complacency and satisfaction in his undertaking, and in all he should do or suffer in the accomplishment of man's redemption*, Mat. 3. 17. | 17. 5. John 8. 29. (III) *Of man, who pleases*, [1] *God*, denoting *a being approved and accepted of God*, Heb. 11. 5. | 13. 16. [2] *Himself*, 1. *In things sinful*, Isa. 2. 6. 2. *In things lawful*, Acts 15. 34. [3] *His neighbour, which is*, first, *Lawful, to endeavour to comply with his weakness in things indifferent, or that tend to edification*, Rom. 15. 2. 1 Cor. 10. 33. Secondly, *Sinful to flatter him, or suit one's doctrine to his humour, concealing some necessary truth*, Gal. 1. 10.

Exod. 21. 8. if she p. not her master, who betrothed
Num. 23. 27. peradventure it will p. God thou curse
1 Sam. 20. 13. if it p. my father to do thee evil
2 Sam. 7. 29. let it p. thee to bless the house of thy servant, that it may continue, 1 Chron. 17. 27.
1 Kings 21. 6. if it p. I will give thee another viney.
2 Chron. 10. 7. if thou p. they will be thy servants
Neh. 2. 5. if it p. king, and thy servant found favour, 7. Esth. 1. 19. | 3. 9. | 5. 8. | 7. 3. | 8. 5. | 9. 13.
Job 6. 9. that it would p. God to destroy me
20. 10. his children shall seek to p. the poor
Psal. 69. 31. this also shall p. the Lord better
Prov. 16. 7. when a man's ways p. the Lord
Cant. 2. 7. nor awake my love till he p. 3. 5. | 8. 4.
Isa. 2. 6. they p. themselves in children of strangers
55. 11. it shall accomplish that which I p.
56. 4. and choose the things that p. me
John 8. 29. I do always those things that p. him
Rom. 8. 8. they that are in the flesh cannot p. God
15. 1. we ought to bear, and not to p. ourselves
2. let every one p. his neighbour for his good
1 Cor. 7. 32. careth how he may p. the Lord
33. p. his wife || 34. how she may p. her husband
10. 33. even as I p. all men in all things
Gal. 1. 10. do I persuade men? do I seek to p. men?
1 Thess. 2. 15. they p. not G. are contrary to all men
4. 1. how ye ought to walk and to p. God
2 Tim. 2. 4. that may p. him who hath chosen him
Tit. 2. 9. and to p. them well in all things
Heb. 11. 6. without faith it is impossible to p. God

PLEASED.

Gen. 28. 8. Esau seeing daugh. Canaan p. not Isaac
33. 10. have seen thy face, thou wast p. with me
34. 18. and their words p. Hamor and Shechem
45. 16. it p. Pharaoh well and his servants
Num. 24. 1. Balaam saw it p. Lord to bless Israel
Deut. 1. 23. the saying p. me well, I took 12 men
Josh. 22. 30. what children of Gad spake it p. them
Judg. 13. 23. if the Lord were p. to kill us
14. 7. he talked with her, and she p. Samson well
1 Sam. 12. 22. it p. Lord to make you his people
18. 20. it p. Saul that Michal loved David
26. it p. David to be the king's son-in-law
2 Sam. 3. 36. what the king did p. all the people
17. 4. saying p. Absalom well, and elders of Israel
19. 6. if all we had died, then it had p. thee well
1 Kings 3. 10. Solomon's speech p. the Lord
9. 12. the cities Solomon gave p. not Hiram
2 Chron. 30. 4. the thing p. the king and all the congregation, Neh. 2. 6. Esth. 1. 21. | 2. 4.
Esth. 2. 9. the maiden p. the king, and she obtained
5. 14. the thing p. Haman, he caused the gallows
Psal. 40. 13. be p. O Lord, to deliver me
51. 19. then shalt thou be p. with sacrifices
115. 3. our God is in the heavens, he hath done whatsoever he p. 135. 6. Jonah 1. 14.
Isa. 53. 10. yet it p. the Lord to bruise him
Dan. 6. 1. it p. Darius to set over the kingdom
Mic. 6. 7. will Lord be p. with thousands of rams?
Mal. 1. 8. offer it, will he be p. with thee?
Mat. 14. 6. on Herod's birth-day daugh. of Herodias danced before them, and p. Herod, Mark 6. 22.
Acts 6. 5. the saying p. the whole multitude
12. 3. because Herod saw it p. the Jews
Rom. 15. 3. for even Christ p. not himself
26. for it hath p. them of Macedonia, 27.
1 Cor. 1. 21. it p. God by foolishness of preaching
7. 12. and she be p. to dwell with him, let him not
13. and if he be p. to dwell with her, let her not
12. 18. God hath set members as it hath p. him
15. 38. God giveth it a body as it hath p. him
Gal. 1. 10. for if I yet p. men, I should not be serv.
15. when it p. God to reveal his Son in me
Col. 1. 19. it p. Father that in him all fulness dwell
Heb. 11. 5. he had this testimony, that he p. God

Well PLEASED.

Psal. 81. † 5. thou hast been *well* p. with thy land
Isa. 42. 21. L. is *well* p. for his righteousness' sake
Mat. 3. 17. beloved Son, in whom I am *well* p. 12. 18. | 17. 5. Mark 1. 11. Luke 3. 22. 2 Pet. 1. 17.
1 Cor. 10. 5. with many of them G. was not *well* p.
Heb. 13. 16. with such sacrifices God is *well* p.

Men PLEASERS.

Eph. 6. 6. not with eye-service, as *men* p. Col. 3. 22.

PLEASETH.

Gen. 16. 6. Abraham said, do to her as it p. thee
20. 15. behold my land, dwell where it p. thee
Judg. 14. 3. get her for me, for she p. me well
Esth. 2. 4. let maiden which p. the king be queen
Eccl. 7. 26. whoso p. God shall escape from her
8. 3. stand not in evil, he doeth whatsoever p. him

PLEASING.

Esth. 8. 5. and if I be p. in his eyes let it be written
Hos. 9. 4. neither shall they be p. to him
Col. 1. 10. might walk worthy of the Lord to all p.
1 Thess. 2. 4. so we speak, not as p. men, but God
1 John 3. 22. do those things that are p. in his sight

Well-PLEASING.

Phil. 4. 18. a sacrifice acceptable, *well-p.* to God
Col. 3. 20. obey, for this is *well-p.* to the Lord
Heb. 13. 21. working in you what is *w.-p.* in his sight

PLEASURE

Signifies, [1] *Delight or joy*, Psal. 102. 14. [2] *Purpose, intention, or resolution*, Ezra 5. 17. [3] *Commands*, Psal. 103. 21. [4] *Lawful delights*, Eccl. 2. 1. [5] *A kindness, or favour*, Acts 25. 9. [6] *Voluptuous and sinful ways*, 1 Tim. 5. 6.

Gen. 18. 12. after I am waxed old, shall I have p.?
Deut. 23. 24. mayest eat grapes thy fill at own p.
1 Chron. 29. 17. I know thou hast p. in uprightness
Ezra 5. 17. and let the king send his p. to us
10. 11. make confession to Lord God, and do his p.
Neh. 9. 37. have dominion over our cattle at their p.
Esth. 1. 8. should drink according to every man's p.
Job 21. 21. what p. hath he in his house after him?
25. another dieth, and never eateth with p.
22. 3. is it any p. to Almighty that thou art right.
Psal. 5. 4. art not a God that hath p. in wickedness
35. 27. which hath p. in the prosperity of his serv.
51. 18. do good in thy good p. to Zion, build walls
102. 14. for thy servants take p. in her stones
103. 21. bless L. ye ministers of his, that do his p.
105. 22. to bind his princes at his p. and teach
111. 2. sought out of all them that have p. therein
147. 10. he taketh not p. in the legs of a man
11. the Lord taketh p. in them that fear him
149. 4. for the Lord taketh p. in his people
Prov. 21. 17. he that loveth p. shall be a poor man
Eccl. 2. 1. enjoy p. || 5. 4. he hath no p. in fools
12. 1. thou shalt say, I have no p. in them
Isa. 21. 4. the night of my p. he turned to fear
29. † 9. stay and wonder, take your p. and riot
44. 28. Cyrus my shepherd shall perform all my p.
46. 10. my counsel shall stand, I will do all my p.
48. 14. he will do his p. on Babylon, and his arm
53. 10. and p. of the Lord shall prosper in his hand
58. 3. behold, in the day of your fast ye find p.
13. from doing thy p. on my holy day, and call the sabbath a delight, not finding thine own p.
Jer. 2. 24. she snuffeth up the wind at her p.
22. 28. is he a vessel wherein is no p.?
34. 16. whom had set at liberty at their p. to return
48. 38. broken Moab like a vessel wherein is no p.
Ezek. 16. 37. with whom thou hast taken p.
18. 23. have I any p. that wicked die, saith Lord, and not that he should return? 32. | 33. 11.
Hos. 8. 8. Israel as a vessel wherein is no p.
Hag. 1. 8. build the house, and I will take p. in it
Mal. 1. 10. I have no p. in you saith the Lord
Luke 12. 32. Father's good p. to give you the kingd.
Acts 24. 27. Felix, willing to do the Jews a p. left Paul bound
25. 9. but Festus willing to do the Jews a p. said
Rom. 1. 32. but have p. in them that do them
2 Cor. 12. 10. therefore I take p. in infirmities
Eph. 1. 5. according to the good p. of his will, 9.
Phil. 2. 13. both to will and to do of his good p.
2 Thess. 1. 11. fulfil the good p. of his goodness
2. 12. believed not, but had p. in unrighteousness
1 Tim. 5. 6. but she that liveth in p. is dead
Heb. 10. 6. in sacrifices thou hast had no p. 8.
38. if draw back, my soul shall have no p. in him
12. 10. they chastened us after their own p.
Jam. 5. 5. ye have lived in p. on earth, in day time
2 Pet. 2. 13. as they that count it p. to riot in day time
Rev. 4. 11. for thy p. they are and were created

PLEASURES.

Job 36. 11. they shall spend their years in p.
Psal. 16. 11. at thy right hand are p. for evermore
36. 8. shalt make them drink of river of thy p.
Isa. 47. 8. hear this, thou that art given to p.
Luke 8. 14. are choked with the p. of this life
2 Tim. 3. 4. lovers of p. more than lovers of God
Tit. 3. 3. deceived, serving divers lusts and p.
Heb. 11. 25. than to enjoy the p. of sin for a season

PLEDGE.

Gen. 38. 17. Tamar said, wilt thou give me a p.?
18. what p.? || 20. Judah sent to receive his p.
Exod. 22. 26. if thou take a neighbour's raiment to p.
Deut. 24. 6. no man shall take the nether or upper millstone to p. for he taketh a man's life to p.
10. shalt not go into his house to fetch his p. 11.
12. if poor, thou shalt not sleep with his p. 13.
17. nor shalt take a widow's raiment to p.
1 Sam. 17. 18. how thy brethren fare, take their p.
Job 22. 6. thou hast taken a p. from thy brother
24. 3. they take the widow's ox for a p.
9. and they take a p. of the poor
Prov. 20. 16. take p. for a strange woman, 27. 13.
Ezek. 18. 7. hath restored to the debtor his p. 16.
12. hath not restored the p. shall he then live?
33. 15. if wicked restore the p. he shall not die
Amos 2. 8. on clothes laid to p. by every altar

PLEDGES.

2 Kings 18. 23. I say, give p. king of Assy. Isa. 36. 8.

PLEIADES.

They are seven stars beyond the Bull, *which appear at the beginning of the spring.* The Hebrew *reads*, Chima, Job 38. 31. Canst thou bind the sweet influences of the *Pleiades, or Chima? Canst thou hinder them from rising in their season; or canst thou hinder or shut up the earth when they open it?*

Job 9. 9. which maketh Arcturus, Orion, and P.
38. 31. canst thou bind the sweet influences of P.?

PLENTEOUS.

Gen. 41. 34. take the fifth part in the p. years
47. in the p. years the earth brought forth
Deut. 28. 11. the Lord shall make thee p. 30. 9.
2 Chron. 1. 15. Solomon made gold as p. as stones
Psal. 86. 5. art p. in mercy to all call on thee, 15.
103. 8. Lord is merciful, gracious, and p. in mercy
130. 7. and with him is p. redemption
Isa. 30. 23. the bread shall be fat and p. in that day
Hab. 1. 16. their portion is fat, and their meat p.
Mat. 9. 37. the harvest truly is p. but labourers few

PLENTEOUSNESS.

Gen. 41. 53. the seven years of p. were ended
Prov. 21. 5. the thoughts of the diligent tend to p.

PLENTY.

Gen. 27. 28. God give thee p. of corn and wine
41. 29. behold, there come seven years of great p.
30. all the p. shall be forgotten in land of Egypt
31. and the p. shall not be known in the land
Lev. 11. 36. a pit, wherein there is p. of water
1 Kings 10. 11. brought in from Ophir p. of almug-tr.
2 Chron. 31. 10. we had enough to eat, have left p.
Job 22. 25. and thou shalt have p. of silver
37. 23. he is excellent in power and p. of justice
Prov. 3. 10. so shall thy barns be filled with p.
28. 19. he that tilleth his land shall have p. of bread
Jer. 44. 17. for then had we p. of victuals, and well
Joel 2. 26. shall eat in p. and praise Lord your God

PLENTIFUL.

Psal. 68. 9. thou, O God, didst send a p. rain
Isa. 16. 10. joy is taken out of the p. field
Jer. 2. 7. and I brought you to a p. country
48. 33. joy and gladness is taken from the p. field

PLENTIFULLY.

Job 26. 3. how hast p. declared the thing as it is?
Psal. 31. 23. and p. rewardeth the proud doer
Luke 12. 16. ground of a rich man brought forth p.

PLOTTETH.

Psal. 37. 12. the wicked p. against the just, gnasheth

PLOUGH.

Luke 9. 62. no man having put his hand to the p.

PLOW

Signifies, [1] *To till and break up ground with a plow*, Deut. 22. 10. [2] *To labour in any calling*, 1 Cor. 9. 10. [3] *To contrive, plot, and practise*, Job 4. 8. Hos. 10. 13. [4] *Cruelly to torment, wound, and mangle*, Psal. 129. 3.
To put the hand to the plough, Luke 9. 62. *To engage oneself in the service of God, or work of the ministry, or preaching the gospel.*

Deut. 22. 10. shalt not p. with an ox and ass together
1 Sam. 14. 14. which a yoke of oxen might p.
Job 4. 8. they that p. iniquity, reap the same
Prov. 20. 4. sluggard will not p. by reason of cold
Isa. 28. 24. doth the plowman p. all day to sow
Hos. 10. 11. Judah shall p. Jacob break his clods
Amos 6. 12. will one p. there with oxen?
1 Cor. 9. 10. he that ploweth should p. in hope

PLOWED.

Judg. 14. 18. if ye had not p. with my heifer
Psal. 129. 3. the plowers p. on my back
Jer. 26. 18. Zion shall be p. as a field, Mic. 3. 12.
Hos. 10. 13. ye have p. wickedness, reaped iniquity

PLOWETH.

1 Cor. 9. 10. that he that p. should plow in hope

PLOWING.

1 Kings 19. 19. Elijah found Elisha, who was p.
Job 1. 14. the oxen were p. and the asses feeding
Luke 17. 7. which of you having a servant p.

PLOWING.

Prov. 21. 4. and the p. of the wicked is sin

PLOWMAN.

Isa. 28. 24. doth the p. plow all day to sow?
Amos 9. 13. the p. shall overtake the reaper

PLOWMEN.

Isa. 61. 5. the sons of the alien shall be your p.
Jer. 14. 4. the p. were ashamed, they covered

PLOW-SHARES.

Isa. 2. 4. shall beat their swords into p. Mic. 4. 3.
Joel 3. 10. beat your p. into swords, hooks into spears

PLUCK.

Lev. 1. 16. shall p. away his crop with his feathers
Num. 33. 52. and quite p. down their high places
Deut. 7. † 22. thy God will p. off those nations
23. 25. then thou mayest p. the ears with thy hand
2 Chron. 7. 20. then will I p. them up by the roots
Job 24. 9. they p. the fatherless from the breast
Psal. 25. 15. he shall p. my feet out of the net
52. 5. and p. thee out of thy dwelling-place
74. 11. thy right hand, p. it out of thy bosom
80. 12. they which pass by the way do p. her
Eccl. 3. 2. and a time to p. up what is planted
Jer. 12. 14. p. out the house of Judah from them
17. I will utterly p. up and destroy that nation
18. 7. I speak concerning a kingdom, to p. it up
22. 24. on my hand, yet would I p. thee thence
24. 6. will plant them, and not p. them up, 42. 10.
31. 28. as I have watched over them to p. up
45. 4. that which I have planted I will p. up
Ezek. 17. 9. without many people to p. it up by roots
23. 34. thou shalt p. off thine own breasts
Mic. 3. 2. who p. off the skin from off them
5. 14. I will p. up thy groves out of thee
Mat. 5. 29. if thy right eye offend thee, p. it out, and cast it from thee, 18. 9. Mark 9. 47.
12. 1. began to p. the ears of corn, Mark 2. 23.
John 10. 28. nor shall any p. them out of my hand
29. no man is able to p. them out of Father's hand

PLUCKED.

Gen. 8. 11. in her mouth was an olive-leaf p. off
Exod. 4. 7. and he p. his hand out of his bosom
Deut. 28. 63. ye shall be p. from off the land
Josh. 4. † 18. the soles of the priests' feet were p. up
Ruth 4. 7. a man p. off his shoe, and gave it
2 Sam. 23. 21. p. the spear out of Egyptian's hand and slew him with his spear, 1 Chron. 11. 23
Ezra 9. 3. I p. off the hair of my head and beard
Neh. 13. 25. I cursed them, and p. off their hair
Job 29. 17. and p. the spoil out of his teeth
Prov. 2. † 22. the transgressors shall be p. up
Isa. 50. 6. my cheeks to them that p. off the hair
Jer. 6. 29. for the wicked are not p. away

Jer. 12. 15. after I have p. them out, I will return
31. 40. it shall not be p. up nor thrown down
Ezek. 19. 12. but she was p. up in fury, and cast
Dan. 7. 4. I beheld till the wings thereof were p.
8. three of the first horns p. up by the roots
11. 4. for his kingdom shall be p. up for others
Amos 4. 11. as a fire-brand p. out of the burning
Zech. 3. 2. is not this a fire-brand p. out of the fire ?
Mark 5. 4. the chains had been p. asunder by him
Luke 6. 1. his disciples p. ears of corn, and did eat
17. 6. be thou p. up by the root, it should obey
Gal. 4. 15. ye would have p. out your own eyes
Jude 12. twice dead, p. up by the roots

PLUCKETH.

Prov. 14. 1. the foolish p. it down with her hands

PLUMB-LINE.

Amos 7. 7. he shewed me, and behold the Ld. stood on a wall made by a p. with a p. in his hand
8. Amos, what seest thou ? and I said, a p. behold, I will set a p. in the midst of my people Israel

PLUMMET.

2 Kings 21. 13. I will stretch over Jerusalem the p.
Isa. 28. 17. I will lay righteousness to the p.
Zech. 4. 10. shall see the p. in hand of Zerubbabel

PLUNGE.

Job 9. 31. yet shalt thou p. me in the ditch and my

POETS.

Acts 17. 28. as certain also of your own p. said

POINT.

Num. 34. 7. ye shall p. out for you mount Hor
8. p. out your border || 10. p. out your east border

POINT.

Gen. 25. 32. Esau said, behold, I am at the p. to die
Jer. 17. 1. is written with the p. of a diamond
Mark 5. 23. my daughter lieth at the p. of death
John 4. 47. for he was at the p. of death
Jam. 2. 10. and yet offend in one p. is guilty

POINTS.

Eccl. 5. 16. in all p. as he came, so shall he go
Heb. 4. 15. but was in all p. tempted like as we are

POINTED.

Job 41. 30. he spreadeth sharp p. things on the mire

POISON.

Deut. 32. 24. with the p. of serpents of the dust
33. their wine is p. of dragons and venom of asps
Job 6. 4. the p. whereof drinketh up my spirit
20. 16. he shall suck p. of asps, viper's tongue slay
Psal. 58. 4. their p. is like the p. of serpents
140. 3. like a serpent, adders' p. is under their lips
Jer. 8. † 14. he hath given us p. to drink
Zech. 12. † 2. I will make Jerusalem a cup of p.
Rom. 3. 13. the p. of asps is under their lips
Jam. 3. 8. their tongue is an evil, full of deadly p.

POLE.

Num. 21. 8. set it upon a p. || 9. Moses put it on a p.

POLICY.

Dan. 8. 25. thro' his p. shall cause craft to prosper

POLISHED.

Psal. 144. 12. p. after the similitude of a palace
Isa. 18. † 2. to a nation outspread and p. † 7.
49. 2. he hath made me a p. shaft, he hid me
Dan. 10. 6. his feet like in colour to p. brass

POLISHING.

Lam. 4. 7. Nazarites purer, their p. was of sapphire

POLL, S.

Exod. 16. † 16. gather of it an homer for every p.
Num. 1. 2. with the number of their names every male by their p. 18. 20, 22. 1 Chron. 23. 3, 24.
3. 47. thou shalt take five shekels a piece by their p.

POLL.

Ezek. 44. 20. they shall only p. their heads
Mic. 1. 16. make thee bald, and p. thee for children

POLLED.

2 Sam. 14. 26. when he p. his head, at year's end he p.
Jer. 9. † 26. having corners of their hair p. that dwell in the wilderness, 25. † 23. | 49. † 32.

POLLUTE.

Num. 18. 32. neither shall ye p. the holy things
35. 33. so shall ye not p. the land wherein ye are
Isa. 23. † 9. L. purposed to p. the pride of all glory
Jer. 7. 30. in the house called by name, to p. it
Ezek. 7. 21. they shall p. my secret place, 22.
13. 19. will ye p. me among my peo. for handfuls
20. 31. ye p. yourselves with idols, 23. 30. | 36. 18.
39. but p. ye my holy name no more, 39. 7.
44. 7. strangers to be in my sanctuary to p. it
Dan. 11. 31. they shall p. the sanctuary of strength

POLLUTED.

Exod. 20. 25. if lift thy tool upon it, thou hast p. it
2 Kings 23. 16. Josiah p. the altar at Beth-el
2 Chr. 36. 14. the priests p. the house of the Lord
Ezra 2. 62. therefore were they as p. Neh. 7. 64.
Psal. 106. 38. and the land was p. with blood
Isa. 47. 6. I was wroth, I have p. mine inheritance
48. 11. for how should my name be p.
Jer. 2. 23. how canst thou say, I am not p. ?
3. 1. shall not that land be greatly p. ? 2.
34. 16. but ye turned and p. my name
Lam. 2. 2. he hath p. the kingdom and princes
4. 14. they have p. themselves with blood
† 15. they cried, depart, ye p. depart, touch not
Ezek. 4. 14. behold, my soul hath not been p.
14. 11. nor be p. with all their transgressions
16. 6. I saw thee p. in thine own blood, 22.
20. 9. my name's sake, that it should not be p. 14, 22.
13. my sabbaths they greatly p. 16, 21, 24.
26. and I p. them in their own gifts
30. are ye p. after the manner of your fathers?
22. † 5. shall mock thee which art p. in name
23. 17. and she was p. with the Babylonians
Hos. 6. 8. Gilead is a city that is p. with blood
9. 4. all that eat thereof shall be p.
Amos 7. 17. and thou shalt die in a p. land
Mic. 2. 10. this is not your rest, because it is p.
Zeph. 3. 1. woe to her that is filthy and p.
4. her priests have p. sanctuary, done violence
Mal. 1. 7. ye offered p. bread upon mine altar, and ye say, wherein have we p. thee ?
12. that ye say, the table of the Lord is p.
Acts 21. 28. and hath p. this holy place

POLLUTING.

Isa. 56. 2. that keepeth the sabbath from p. it, 6.

POLLUTION.

Ezek. 22. 10. have humbled her that was apart for p.

POLLUTIONS.

Acts 15. 20. will that they abstain from p. of idols
2 Pet. 2. 20. if after having escaped p. of the world

POLLUX, see SIGN.

POMEGRANATE

Is *a kind of apple, covered without with a reddish rind, and red within, which opens length-ways, and shews red grains within, full of juice like wine, with little kernels. God gave orders to* Moses *to put embroidered pomegranates, with golden bells between, at the bottom of the high priest's blue robe or ephod,* Exod. 28. 33, 34. Pomegranates *being very common in* Palestine, *and being a very beautiful fruit, the Scriptures make use of similitudes taken from the* pomegranate. *The blossoms of the tree or shrub that bears this fruit, are called* Balausts *by the apothecaries. They are astringent, and very good in a Dysentery, Diarrhœa, and Lientery.*

Exod. 28. 34. a golden bell and a p. upon the hem of the robe round about, 39. 26.
1 Sam. 14. 2. Saul tarried under a p. tree
Cant. 4. 3. thy temples are like a piece of p. 6. 7.
8. 2. would cause thee to drink of juice of my p.
Joel. 1. 12. the p. tree and all trees are withered
Hag. 2. 19. as yet the p. hath not brought forth

POMEGRANATES.

Exod. 28. 33. thou shalt make p. of blue, 39. 24, 25.
Num. 13. 23. they brought of the p. and figs
20. 5. it is no place of seed, figs, vines, or p.
Deut. 8. 8. into a land of p. oil-olive, and honey
1 Kings 7. 18. to cover the chapiters on top with p. 2 Kings 25. 17. 2 Chron. 3. 16. Jer. 52. 22.
Cant. 4. 13. thy plants are an orchard of p. with fruits
6. 11. I went to see whether the p. budded, 7. 12.

POMMELS.

2 Chr. 4. 12. the pillars and p. of the chapiters

POMP.

Isa. 5. 14. and their p. shall descend into hell
14. 11. thy p. is brought down to the grave
Ezek. 7. 24. I will make the p. of the strong to cease
30. 18. the p. of her strength shall cease, 33. 28.
32. 12. and they shall spoil the p. of Egypt
Acts 25. 23. Agrippa and Bernice come with great p.

PONDER.

Prov. 4. 26. p. the path of thy feet, and let thy ways
5. 6. lest thou shouldest p. the path of life, her ways

PONDERED.

Luke 2. 19. but Mary p. them in her heart, and kept

PONDERETH.

Prov. 5. 21. ways of man, the Lord p. all his goings
21. 2. Lord p. the heart || 24. 12. he that p. the heart

PONDS.

Exod. 7. 19. stretch out thy hand on their p. 8. 5.
Isa. 19. 10. be broken in purposes, that make p.

POOL.

2 Sam. 2. 13. the one set on the one side of the p.
4. 12. they hanged them up over the p. at Hebron
1 Kings 22. 38. one washed chariot in p. of Samaria
2 Kings 18. 17. when come up they came and stood by the conduit of the upper p. Isa. 7. 3. | 36. 2.
20. 20. and how he made a p. and conduit
Neh. 2. 14. then I went on to the king's p.
3. 15. Shallum repaired the wall of the p.
Isa. 22. 9. ye gathered the waters of the lower p.
11. ye made a ditch for the water of the old p.
35. 7. the parched ground shall become a p.
41. 18. I will make the wilderness a p. of water
Nah. 2. 8. Nineveh of old is like a p. of water
John 5. 2. there is at Jerusal. by sheep market a p.
4. an angel went down into the p. and troubled
7. he said, I have no man to put me into the p.
9. 7. he said, go wash in the p. of Siloam, 11.

POOLS.

Exod. 7. 19. take rod, stretch thy hand on all their p.
Psal. 84. 6. make it a well, rain also filleth the p.
Eccl. 2. 6. I made me p. of water to water the wood
Isa. 14. 23. I will also make it for the p. of water
42. 15. and I will dry up the p. and herbs

POOR

Signifies, [1] *Indigent, needy, or necessitous,* Mat. 26. 11. [2] *Such as are sensible of their lost and undone condition by sin, and discern their poverty and inability in spiritual things, and fly to the free grace of God, and the righteousness of Christ, for pardon and acceptance,* Mat. 5. 3. Luke 6. 20. [3] *Such as are void of true saving grace, or spiritually poor,* Rev. 3. 17.

Gen. 41. 19. came up after them seven p. kine
Exod. 23. 11. that the p. of thy people may eat
30. 15. the p. shall not give less than half a shekel
Lev. 14. 21. if he be p. and cannot get so much
19. 10. thou shalt leave them for the p. and stranger
15. thou shalt not respect the person of the p.
25. 25. if thy brother be waxen p. 35, 39, 47.
Deut. 15. 4. save when there be no p. among you
11. for the p. shall never cease out of the land
Ruth 3. 10. thou followedst not young men, p. or rich
1 Sam. 2. 7. the Lord maketh p. and maketh rich
8. he raiseth up the p. out of the dust, Ps. 113. 7.
2 Sam. 12. 1. two men, one rich, and the other p.
2 Kings 25. 12. but the captain of the guard left of the p. of the land, Jer. 39. 10. | 40. 7. | 52. 15, 16.
Job 5. 15. but he saveth the p. from the sword
16. so the p. hath hope, and iniquity stoppeth
20. 10. his children shall seek to please the p.
19. because he hath oppressed and forsaken the p.
24. 4. the p. of the earth hide themselves together
9. and they take a pledge of the p.
14. the murderer killeth the p. and needy
29. 12. because I delivered the p. that cried
30. 25. was not my soul grieved for the p. ?
31. 16. if I withheld the p. from their desire
19. or if I have seen any p. without covering
34. 19. nor regardeth the rich more than the p.
28. they cause the cry of the p. to come to him
36. 15. he delivereth the p. in affliction, Ps. 72. 12.
Ps. 9. 18. the expectation of the p. shall not perish
10. 2. the wicked in his pride doth persecute the p.
8. his eyes are privily set against the p
Psal. 10. 9. he lieth in wait secretly to catch the p.
10. that the p. may fall by his strong ones
14. the p. committeth himself to thee, thou art
12. 5. for the oppression of the p. I will arise
14. 6. ye have shamed the counsel of the p.
35. 10. who deliverest the p. from him that spoileth
37. 14. have bent their bow to cast down the p.
40. 17. but I am p. 69. 29. | 70. 5. | 86. 1. | 109. 22.
41. 1. blessed is he that considereth the p.
49. 2. both low and high, rich and p. together
68. 10. hast prepared of thy goodness for the p.
69. 33. Lord heareth p. and despiseth not prisoners
72. 4. he shall judge the p. of the people
13. he shall spare the p. || 82. 3. defend the p.
74. 21. let the p. and needy praise thy name
82. 4. deliver the p. and needy, rid them out of
107. 41. yet setteth he p. on high from affliction
109. 31. he shall stand at the right hand of the p.
132. 15. will satisfy her p. with bread, will clothe
140. 12. and will maintain the right of the p.
Prov. 10. 4. he becometh p. that dealeth with a slack
15. the destruction of the p. is their poverty
13. 7. there is that maketh himself p. hath riches
8. his riches, but the p. heareth not rebuke
23. much food is in the tillage of the p. but there
14. 20. the p. is hated even of his neighbour
21. he that hath mercy on the p. happy is he
31. he that oppresseth the p. reproacheth his Maker; he that honoureth him hath mercy on the p.
17. 5. whoso mocketh the p. reproacheth his Maker
18. 23. the p. useth entreaties, but the rich
19. 4. the p. is separated from his own neighbour
7. all brethren of the p. do hate him, how much
21. 13. whoso stoppeth his ears at the cry of the p.
22. 2. the rich and p. meet together, Lord is maker
7. the rich ruleth over the p. and the borrower is
16. he that oppresseth the p. to increase his riches
28. 8. shall gather it for him that will pity the p.
11. the p. that hath understanding searcheth him
15. so is a wicked ruler over the p. people
29. 7. righteous considereth the cause of the p. 13.
14. the king that faithfully judgeth the p.
30. 9. lest I be p. and steal, and take name of God
14. whose teeth are as swords, to devour the p.
31. 9. and plead the cause of the p. and needy
Eccl. 4. 14. that is born in his kingdom, becometh p
5. 8. if thou seest the oppression of the p.
6. 8. what hath the p. that knoweth to walk
Isa. 3. 14. the spoil of the p. is in your houses
15. what mean ye that ye grind faces of the p. ?
10. 2. and to take away the right from the p.
30. cause it to be heard to Laish, O p. Anathoth
11. 4. with righteousness shall he judge the p.
14. 30. the first-born of the p. shall feed in it
32. and the p. of his people shall trust in it
26. 6. even the feet of the p. shall tread it down
29. 19. even p. among men shall rejoice in Holy One
32. 7. to destroy the p. with lying words
41. 17. when the p. and needy seek water
58. 7. that thou bring the p. that are cast out
Jer. 2. 34. is found the blood of the p. innocents
5. 4. I said, surely these are p. they are foolish
20. 13. for he hath delivered the soul of the p.
22. 16. he judged the cause of the p. and needy
Ezek. 16. 49. nor did she strengthen hand of the p.
18. 12. hath oppressed p. and needy, hath spoiled
17. that hath taken off his hand from the p.
22. 29. and they have vexed the p. and needy
Amos 2. 6. they sold the p. for a pair of shoes
7. that pant after the dust on the head of the p.
4. 1. which oppress the p. and crush the needy
5. 11. forasmuch as your treading is on the p.
12. and they turn aside the p. in the gate
8. 4. even to make the p. of the land to fail
6. that we may buy the p. for silver, and needy
Hab. 3. 14. their rejoicing was to devour the p.
Zeph. 3. 12. the p. people shall trust in the Lord
Zech. 7. 10. and oppress not the widow nor p.
11. 7. I will feed even you, O p. of the flock
11. the p. of the flock that waited upon me
Mat. 5. 3. blessed are the p. in spirit, for theirs is
11. 5. the p. have the gospel preached to them
26. 11. for ye have the p. always with you, but me ye have not always, Mark 14. 7. John 12. 8.
Mark 12. 42. there came a certain p. widow
43. this p. widow cast more in, Luke 21. 3.
Luke 6. 20. blessed be ye p. your's is the kingdom
14. 13. call the p. the maimed, the lame, 21.
John 12. 6. this he said, not that he cared for the p.
Rom. 15. 26. to make a contribution for the p.
2 Cor. 6. 10. as p. yet making many rich
8. 9. though rich, yet for your sakes he became p.
Gal. 2. 10. that we should remember the p.
Jam. 2. 5. hath not God chosen the p. of this world
6. but ye have despised the p. rich oppress you
Rev. 3. 17. and knowest not that thou art p.
13. 16. he causeth rich and p. to receive a mark

Is POOR.

Exod. 22. 25. if lend to any of my people that *is* p.
Deut. 24. 14. shalt not oppress hired servt. that *is* p.
15. for he *is* p. and setteth his heart upon it
Judg. 6. 15. behold, my family *is* p. in Manasseh
Prov. 19. 1. better *is* the p. that walketh in his integrity, than he that is perverse in his lips, 28. 6.
22. 22. rob not poor because he *is* p. nor oppress
Eccl. 4. 13. better *is* a p. and wise child, than an old
Isa. 66. 2. to him that *is* p. and of a contrite heart

POOR *man.*

Exod. 23. 3. nor countenance a p. *man* in his cause
Deut. 15. 7. if a p. *man*, harden not thy heart
24. 12. if a p. *man* sleep not with his pledge
1 Sam. 18. 23. to be king's son, seeing I am a p. *man*
2 Sam. 12. 3. p. *man* had nothing, save one ewe lamb
4. but took the p. *man's* ewe-lamb and dressed it
Psal. 34. 6. this p. *man* cried, and the Lord heard
109. 16. but persecuted the p. and needy *man*
Prov. 19. 22. and a p. *man* is better than a liar
21. 17. he that loveth pleasure shall be a p. *man*
28. 3. a p. *man* that oppresseth the poor is like
29. 13. the p. and deceitful *man* meet together
Eccl. 9. 15. now there was found in it a p. wise *man*, yet no man remembered that same p. *man*

Eccl. 9. 16. the p. man's wisd. is desp. and not heard
Jam. 2. 2. there come in a p. man in vile raiment

To the POOR.

Lev. 23. 22. thou shalt leave them to the p. and stran.
Esth. 9. 22. make them days of sending gifts to the p.
Job 29. 16. I was a father to the p. and feet to lame
36. 6. of the wicked, but he giveth right to the p.
Psal. 112. 9. he hath given to the p. 2 Cor. 9. 9.
Prov. 22. 9. for he giveth of his bread to the p.
28. 27. he that giveth to the p. shall not lack
31. 20. she stretcheth out her hand to the p.
Isa. 25. 4. thou hast been a strength to the p.
Dan. 4. 27. break off sins, by shewing mercy to the p.
Mat. 19. 21. sell all, and give to the p. Mark 10. 21.
26. 9. this ointment might have been sold for much, and given to the p. Mark 14. 5. John 12. 5.
Luke 4. 18. to preach the gospel to the p. 7. 22.
18. 22. sell all thou hast and distribute to the p.
19. 8. behold, the half of my goods I give to the p.
John 13. 29. that he should give something to the p.
1 Cor. 13. 3. I bestow all my goods to feed the p.
Jam. 2. 3. and say to the p. stand thou there, or sit h.

Thy POOR.

Exod. 23. 6. shalt not wrest the judgment of thy p.
Deut. 15. 7. nor shut thine hand from thy p. brother
9. and thine eye be evil against thy p. brother
11. thou shalt open thine hand wide to thy p.
Psal. 72. 2. he shall judge thy p. with judgment
74. 19. forget not the congregation of thy p. for ever

POORER.

Lev. 27. 8. if he be p. than thy estimat. shall present

POOREST.

2 Kings 24. 14. none remained, save p. sort of people

POPLAR, S.

Gen. 30. 37. Jacob took rods of green p. and of hasel
Hos. 4. 13. and they burn incense under oaks and p.

POPULOUS.

Deut. 26. 5. became a nation great, mighty, and p.
Nah. 3. 8. art thou better than p. No?

PORCH.

Judg. 3. 23. then Ehud went forth through the p.
1 Chron. 28. 11. David gave Solomon pattern of p.
2 Chron. 29. 7. they have shut up the doors of the p.
17. eighth day of the month came they to the p.
Ezek. 8. 16. between the p. and altar were 25 men
44. 3. shall enter by way of p. of the gate, 46. 2, 8.
Joel 2. 17. let priests weep between p. and the altar
Mat. 26. 71. when he was gone out into the p.
Mark 14. 68. he went out into the p. and cock crew
John 10. 23. Jesus walked in temple in Solomon's p.
Acts 3. 11. the people ran together in Solomon's p.
5. 12. they were all with one accord in Solomon's p.

PORCHES.

Ezek. 41. 15. with the temple and p. of the court
John 5. 2. a pool called Bethesda, having five p.

PORTER.

2 Sam. 18. 26. watchmen called to the p. and said
2 Kings 7. 10. lepers called to the p. of the city
1 Chron. 9. 21. Zechariah was p. of door of tabern.
2 Chron. 31. 14. and Kore the p. toward the east
Mark 13. 34. and commanded the p. to watch
John 10. 3. to him the p. openeth, the sheep hear

PORTERS.

1 Chron. 9. 17. the p. were Shallum, Akkub, Talmon
15. 18. and Obed-edom, and Jehiel the p.
16. 38. Hosah ‖ 42. the sons of Jeduthun were p.
23. 5. moreover, four thousand were p.
26. 1. concerning the divisions of the p. 12, 19.
2 Chron. 8. 14. the p. by their courses at every gate
35. 15. and the p. waited at every gate
Ezra 7. 7. p. and Nethinims went up to Jerusalem
Neh. 7. 73. the Levites and p. dwelt in their cities

PORTION.

Gen. 14. 24. Aner, Eshcol, let them take their p.
31. 14. is there yet any p. or inheritance for us?
47. 22. priest had a p. assigned, and did eat their p.
48. 22. I have given thee one p. above thy brethren
Exod. 16. †4. shall gather the p. of a day in his day
†15. what is this? it is a p. for they wist not
Lev. 6. 17. have given them it for p. of my offerings
7. 35. this is the p. of the anointing of Aaron
Num. 31. 30. of Israel's half take thou one p. 36.
47. Moses took one p. of fifty for the Levites
Deut. 21. 17. by giving him a double p. of all he hath
32. 9. for Lord's p. is his people, Jacob is the lot
33. 21. in a p. of the lawgiver was he seated
Josh. 17. 14. why hast thou given me but one p.?
1 Sam. 1. 5. but to Hannah he gave a worthy p.
9. 23. Samuel said, bring the p. which I gave thee
1 Kings 12. 16. what p. have we in David, nor inheritance in the son of Jesse, 2 Chron. 10. 16.
2 Kings 2. 9. let a double p. of thy spirit be on me
9. 10. dogs shall eat Jezebel in p. of Jezreel, 36, 37.
21. Joram met him in p. of Naboth the Jezreelite
25. take up, cast him in the p. of Naboth's field
†26. I will requite thee in this p. saith the Lord
2 Chron. 28. 21. Ahaz took a p. out of house of Lord
31. 3. Hezekiah appointed king's p. for offerings
4. to give the p. of the priests and Levites, 16.
Ezra 4. 16. shalt have no p. on this side the river
Neh. 2. 20. but ye have no p. nor right in Jerusalem
11. 23. that a certain p. should be for the singers
12. 47. gave singers and porters every day his p.
Job 20. 29. this is the p. of a wicked man from God
23. †12. his words more than my appointed p.
24. 18. their p. is cursed in the earth
26. 14. but how little a p. is heard of him? 27. 13.
31. 2. for what p. of God is there from above?
Psal. 11. 6. this shall be the p. of their cup
16. 5. the Lord is the p. of mine inheritance
17. 14. from men who have their p. in this life
63. 10. shall be a p. for foxes ‖ 73. 26. God is my p.
119. 57. thou art my p. O Lord, 142. 5.
Prov. 31. 15. and giveth a p. to her maidens
Eccl. 2. 10. and this was my p. of all my labour
21. yet to a man shall he leave it for his p.
3. 22. should rejoice, for that is his p. 5. 18. | 9. 9.
5. 19. God hath given him power to take his p.
9. 6. nor have they any more p. for ever in any thing
11. 2. give a p. to seven, and also to eight
Isa. 17. 14. this is the p. of them that spoil us
53. 12. I will divide him a p. with the great

Isa. 57. 6. among smooth stones of stream is thy p.
61. 7. for confusion, they shall rejoice in their p.
Jer. 10. 16. the p. of Jacob is not like them, 51. 19.
12. 10. they have trodden my p. under foot, they have made my pleasant p. a desolate wilderness
13. 25. this is the p. of thy measures from me
52. 34. every day a p. until the day of his death
Lam. 3. 24. the Lord is my p. saith my soul
Ezek. 45. 1. shall offer an holy p. of the land, 4.
7. a p. shall be for prince on one side and other
48. 1. to the coast of Hethlon, a p. for Dan
2. by the border of Dan a p. for Asher
3. a p. for Naphtali ‖ 4. a p. for Manasseh
Dan. 1. 8. not defile himself with p. of king's meat
4. 15. and let his p. be with the beasts, 23.
11. 26. yea, they that feed of the p. of his meat
Mic. 2. 4. he hath changed the p. of my people
Hab. 1. 16. because by them their p. is fat, and meat
Zech. 2. 12. the Lord shall inherit Judah his p.
Mat. 24. 51. shall appoint him his p. with hypocrites
Luke 12. 42. to give them their p. in due season
46. will appoint him his p. with unbelievers
15. 12. give me the p. of goods that falleth to me

PORTIONS.

Deut. 18. 8. they shall have like p. to eat besides that
Josh. 17. 5. there fell ten p. to Manasseh
1 Sam. 1. 4. he gave her sons and daughters p.
2 Chron. 31. 19. to give p. to all the males
Neh. 8. 10. eat the fat, and send p. to them, 12.
12. 44. p. for the priests ‖ 47. p. of the singers
13. 10. that the p. of the Levites had not been given
Esth. 9. 19. a day of sending p. to one another, 22.
Ezek. 47. 13. Joseph shall have two p.
48. 21. over against the p. for the prince
Hos. 5. 7. a month shall devour them with their p.

POSSESS.

Gen. 22. 17. thy seed shall p. the gate, 24. 60.
Num. 13. 30. let us go up at once and p. it, for we are well able to overcome it, Deut. 1. 21.
27. 11. and his next kinsman shall p. it
Deut. 1. 39. to them will I give it, they shall p. it
2. 31. begin to p. that thou mayest inherit his land
11. 23. ye shall p. greater nations, and mightier than yourselves, 12. 2, 29. | 18. 14. | 31. 3.
28. †42. the fruit of thy land shall locusts p.
30. 18. thou passest over Jordan to p. it, 31. 13.
Josh. 24. 4. I gave to Esau mount Seir to p. it
Judg. 11. 23. and shouldest thou p. it?
24. wilt not thou p. what Chemosh giveth thee?
14. †15. have ye called us to p. us? is it not so
1 Kings 21. 18. he is gone down to p. the vineyard
Job 7. 3. I am made to p. months of vanity
13. 26. thou makest me p. iniquities of my youth
Isa. 34. 11. the cormorant and bittern shall p. it, 17.
Ezek. 7. 24. and they shall p. their houses
35. 10. these two countries shall be mine, we will p.
36. 12. I will cause my people Israel to p. thee
Dan. 7. 18. the saints shall p. the kingdom for ever
Hos. 9. 6. pleasant places for silver, nettles shall p.
Amos 9. 12. that they may p. the remnant of Edom
Obad. 17. the house of Jac. shall p. their possessions
19. shall p. mount Esau, and Benjamin p. Gilead
20. captivity of Isr. shall p. that of Canaanites; and Jerusalem shall p. the cities of the south
Hab. 1. 6. the Chaldeans to p. that is not theirs
Zeph. 2. 9. the remnant of my people shall p. them
Zech. 8. 12. I will cause remn. to p. all these things
Luke 18. 12. I fast, I give tithes of all that I p.
21. 19. in your patience p. ye your souls
1 Thess. 4. 4. every one should know how to p. vessel

POSSESS, with land.

Lev. 20. 24. I will give you their land to p. Num. 33. 53. Deut. 3. 18. | 5. 31. | 17. 14.
Num. 14. 24. seed shall p. it, I will bring into land
Deut. 1. 8. go in and p. the land, 4. 1. | 6. 18. | 8. 1. | 9. 5, 23. | 10. 11. | 11. 31. Josh. 1. 11.
4. 5. land whither ye go to p. it, 14, 26. | 5. 33. | 6. 1. | 7. 1. | 11. 10, 11, 29. | 23. 20.
22. but ye shall go over and p. that good land
9. 4. the Lord hath brought me to p. this land
6. gives not this land to p. for thy righteousness
11. 8. that ye may be strong and p. the land
12. 1. land which Lord God of thy fathers giveth thee to p. 15. 4. | 19. 2, 14. | 21. 1. | 25. 19.
28. 21. have consumed from off l. thou goest to p.
63. plucked from off the land thou goest to p.
Josh. 18. 3. how long are ye slack to p. the land
23. 5. drive them out, and ye shall p. their land
24. 8. I gave them, that ye might p. their land
Judg. 2. 6. Israel went every man to p. the land
18. 9. be not slothful to enter to p. the land
1 Chron. 28. 8. that ye may p. this good land
Ezra 9. 11. the land ye go to p. is an unclean land
Neh. 9. 15. promisedst that they should p. the land
23. thou broughtest them in to p. the land
Isa. 14. 2. Israel shall p. them in the land of the L.
21. that they do not rise nor p. the land
57. 13. that putteth trust in me shall p. the land
61. 7. in their land shall they p. the double
Jer. 30. 3. cause them to return to land and p. it
Ezek. 33. 25. ye shed blood, shall ye p. the land? 26.
Amos 2. 10. I brought you to p. land of Amorite

POSSESSED.

Num. 21. 24. Israel p. Sihon's land from Arnon to
35. they smote Og, his sons, and people, and have p. the land, Deut. 3. 12. | 4. 47. Neh. 9. 22.
Deut. 30. 5. will bring thee to land thy fathers p.
Josh. 1. 15. until your brethren have p. the land
12. 1. they p. their land on the other side Jordan
13. 1. there remaineth yet very much land to be p.
19. 47. the children of Dan took Leshem and p. it
21. 43. they p. it and dwelt therein, 22. 9.
Judg. 1. †19. and Judah p. the mountain
3. 13. Eglon king of Moab p. city of palm-trees
11. 21. Israel p. all the land of the Amorites, 22.
2 Kings 17. 24. men of Ava p. Samaria and dwelt
Psal. 139. 13. for thou hast p. my reins, thou hast
Prov. 8. 22. Lord p. me in the beginning of his way
Isa. 63. 18. people of thy holiness hath p. it a little
Jer. 32. 15. vineyards shall be p. again in this land
23. they came in and p. it, but obeyed not
Dan. 7. 22. time came that saints p. the kingdom

Luke 8. 36. by what means he that was p. was cured
Acts 4. 32. none said that aught he p. was his own
16. 16. a damsel p. with a spirit of divination
1 Cor. 7. 30. they that buy as though they p. not

See DEVILS.

POSSESSEST.

Deut. 26. 1. when thou comest into land and p. it

POSSESSETH.

Num. 36. 8. every daughter that p. an inheritance
Luke 12. 15. a man's life consists not in things he p.

POSSESSING.

2 Cor. 6. 10. as having nothing, yet p. all things

POSSESSION

Signifies, [1] *The possessing or actual enjoyment of any thing*, 1 Kings 21. 19. [2] *Lands, houses, or habitations*, Obad. 17. [3] *Kingdom, or dominion*, Gen. 36. 43. [4] *Riches, whether in lands, goods, servants, or cattle*, Eccl. 2. 7. Mat. 19. 22. [5] *The land of* Canaan, *which was possessed by the* Gentiles, *Acts* 7. 45. [6] *That people which* Christ *has purchased with his blood, to be his peculiar possession*, Eph. 1. 14.

I am their possession, *Ezek.* 44. 28. *That portion which I have reserved for myself out of the offerings I have bestowed on them; or, I have appointed them a liberal maintenance out of my oblations.*

Gen. 17. 8. I will give all the land of Canaan for an everlasting p. and I will be their God, 48. 4.
23. 4. give me a p. of a burying-place to bury my dead out of my sight, 9, 18, 20. | 49. 30. | 50. 13.
26. 14. Isaac had p. of flocks, of herds, and servants
36. 43. the dukes of Edom in the land of their p.
47. 11. and gave them a p. in the land of Egypt
Lev. 14. 34. Canaan, which I give to you for a p.
25. 10. it shall be a jubilee to you, and ye shall return every man to his p. 13, 27, 28, 41. Deut. 3. 20.
25. if thy brother hath sold away some of his p.
33. the Levites' p. shall go out in the jubilee
45. the strangers shall be your p. 46.
27. 16. if a man shall sanctify some part of his p.
21. the p. thereof shall be the priest's
24. return to whom the p. of the land did belong
Num. 24. 18. Edom shall be a p. Seir also a p.
26. 56. according to the lot shall the p. be
27. 4. give us a p. among brethren of our fathers
7. to the daughters of Zelophehad give a p.
32. 5. let this land be given to thy servants for p.
22. this land shall be your p. before the Lord
35. 2. give to the Levites of their p. cities, 8.
28. the slayer shall return to the land of his p.
Deut. 2. 5. I have given mount Seir to Esau for a p.
9. because I have given Ar to Lot for a p. 19.
12. as Israel did in land of his p. Lord gave them
11. 6. the earth swallowed up all in their p.
32. 49. Canaan, which I gave Israel for a p.
Josh. 12. 6. Moses gave it for a p. to Reubenites
22. 4. return ye, get ye unto the land of your p.
7. to half tribe of Manasseh Moses had given a p.
9. they returned to the land of their p.
19. if your p. be unclean, take p. among us
1 Kings 21. 15. take p. of the vineyard of Naboth
19. hast thou killed, and also taken p.?
2 Chron. 20. 11. to come to cast us out of thy p.
Neh. 11. 3. in Judah dwelt every one in his p.
Psal. 2. 8. the uttermost parts of earth for thy p.
44. 3. got not the land in p. by their own sword
69. 35. that they may dwell and have it in p.
83. 12. let us take the houses of God in p.
Prov. 28. 10. the upright have good things in p.
Isa. 14. 23. I will make it a p. for the bittern
Ezek. 11. 15. to us is this land given in p.
25. 4. I will deliver thee to men of the east for p.
36. 2. even the ancient high places are ours in p.
5. which have appointed my land into their p.
44. 28. give them no p. in Israel, I am their p.
46. 18. his son's inheritance out of his own p.
Acts 5. 1. Ananias with Sapphira sold a p.
7. 5. that he would give it to him for a p.
45. brought in with Jesus into p. of Gentiles
Eph. 1. 14. till the redemption of the purchased p.

POSSESSIONS.

Gen. 34. 10. dwell and trade, and get you p. therein
47. 27. Israel had p. therein, and multiplied
Num. 32. 30. they shall have p. among you
Josh. 22. 4. get you to the land of your p.
1 Sam. 25. 2. a man in Maon, whose p. were in Carmel
1 Chron. 9. 2. the inhabitants that dwelt in their p.
2 Chron. 11. 14. for the Levites left their p.
32. 29. Hezekiah provided p. of flocks and herds
Eccl. 2. 7. I had great p. of great and small cattle
Obad. 17. the house of Jacob shall possess their p.
Mat. 19. 22. for he had great p. Mark 10. 22.
Acts 2. 45. and sold their p. and parted them
28. 7. in the same quarters were p. of Publius

POSSESSOR.

Gen. 14. 19. most high G. p. of heav. and earth, 22.
Judg. 18. †7. and there was no p. in the land

POSSESSORS.

Zech. 11. 5. whose p. slay them, and hold themselves
Acts 4. 34. as many as were p. of lands sold them

POSSIBLE

Signifies, [1] *That which may be done, or effected*, Mark 9. 23. Rom. 12. 18. [2] *Profitable or necessary*, Gal. 4. 15. [3] *Agreeable to the will of God*, Mat. 26. 39. Acts 20. 16.

Mat. 19. 26. with God all things are p. Mark 10. 27.
24. 24. if p. shall deceive the elect, Mark 13. 22.
26. 39. if p. let this cup pass from me, Mark 14. 35.
Mark 9. 23. all things are p. to him that believeth
14. 36. all things are p. to thee, Luke 18. 27.
Acts 2. 24. was not p. he should be holden of it
20. 16. if p. be at Jerusalem the day of Pentecost
Rom. 12. 18. if it be p. live peaceably with all men
2 Cor. 12. †4. which is not p. for a man to utter
Gal. 4. 15. if p. ye would have plucked out your eyes
Heb. 10. 4. not p. the blood of bulls take away sins

POST.

Job 9. 25. now my days are swifter than a p.
Jer. 51. 31. one p. shall run to meet another

POSTS.

2 *Chron.* 30. 6. so the *p.* went with the letters from the king and his princes, *Esth.* 3. 13, 15. | 8. 10.
Esth. 8. 14. *p.* rode on mules and camels went out

POST.

1 *Sam.* 1. 9. Eli sat on a seat by a *p.* of the temple
Ezek. 40. 16. and on each *p.* were palm trees

POSTS.

Deut. 6. 9. shall write them on the *p.* of thy house
Judg. 16. 3. Samson took the two *p.* and went away
1 *Kings* 7. 5. all the doors and *p.* were square
Prov. 8. 34. waiting at the *p.* of my doors
Isa. 6. 4. the *p.* of the door moved at the voice
57. 8. behind the *p.* thou set up thy remembrance
Ezek. 40. 10. the *p.* had one measure on this side
43. 8. in their setting of their *p.* by my *p.*
Amos 9. 1. smite the lintel, that the *p.* may shake

See DOOR.

Side-POSTS.

Exod. 12. 7. strike the blood on the two *side-p.* 22.
23. when he seeth the blood on the *side-p.*
1 *Kings* 6. 31. lintel and *side-p.* were a fifth part

POSTERITY.

Gen. 45. 7. to preserve you a *p.* in the earth
Num. 9. 10. or if any of your *p.* be unclean
1 *Kings* 16. 3. I will take away the *p.* of Baasha
21. 21. will take away the *p.* of Ahab
Psal. 49. 13. yet their *p.* approve their sayings
109. 13. let his *p.* be cut off and blotted out
Dan. 11. 4. kingdom shall not be divided to his *p.*
Amos 4. 2. and take your *p.* with fish-hooks

POT

Is *a vessel of earth or metal for uses in a family,* 2 Kings 4. 38.

Though ye have lien among the pots, *Psal.* 68. 13. *Though ye have endured great hardships in* Egypt, *and have been in an afflicted contemptible condition there. It is a metaphor taken from scullions that commonly lie down in the kitchen among the pots, or upon the hearth-stones, whereby they are very much discoloured and deformed. In* Psal. 81. 6. *it is said,* His hands were delivered from the pots; *where pots may note all those vessels wherein they carried water, lime, straw, bricks, &c. The meaning is,* I delivered him *from his slavery and bondage in* Egypt. *And in* Ezek. 24. 3, 6. *by the similitude of a boiling pot, are shewed the miseries and calamities wherewith the inhabitants of* Jerusalem *should be afflicted and consumed.*

Exod. 16. 33. take a *p.* and put an homer of manna
Lev. 6. 28. and if it be sodden in a brazen *p.*
Judg. 6. 19. Gideon put the broth in a *p.*
1 *Sam.* 2. 14. he struck it into the caldron or *p.*
2 *Kings* 4. 2. hath not any thing, save a *p.* of oil
38. set on great *p.* || 40. there is death in the *p.*
41. he cast meal into the *p.* no harm in the *p.*
Job 41. 20. goeth smoke, as out of a seething *p.*
31. he maketh the deep to boil like a *p.*
Prov. 17. 3. the fining *p.* is for silver, 27. 21.
Jer. 1. 13. what seest thou? I see a seething *p.*
Ezek. 24. 3. thus saith the Lord, set on a *p.*
6. woe to bloody city, to *p.* whose scum is therein
Joel 2. † 6. all faces shall gather *p.*
Mic. 3. 3. they chop them in pieces, as for the *p.*
Zech. 14. 21. every *p.* in Jerusalem shall be holiness
Heb. 9. 4. wherein was the golden *p.* with manna

Water-POT.

John 4. 28. the woman then left her *water-p.*

POTS.

Exod. 38. 3. Bezaleel made the *p.* and shovels
Lev. 11. 35. whether it be oven, or ranges for *p.*
1 *Kings* 7. 45. *p.* and shovels of brass, 2 *Chron.* 4. 16.
2 *Chron.* 4. 11. Huram made the *p.* and shovels
35. 13. but the other holy offerings sod they in *p.*
Psal. 58. 9. before your *p.* can feel the thorns
68. 13. though ye have lien among the *p.*
81. 6. his hands were delivered from the *p.*
Jer. 35. 5. I set before the Rechabites *p.* full of wine
Mark 7. 4. as the washing of cups and *p.* 8.

See FLESH.

Water-POTS.

John 2. 6. there was set there six *water-p.*
7. Jesus saith to them, fill *water-p.* with water

POTENTATE.

1 *Tim.* 6. 15. who is the blessed and only *P.*

POTSHERD, S.

Job 2. 8. he took him a *p.* to scrape himself
41. † 30. sharp pieces of *p.* are under him
Psal. 22. 15. my strength is dried up like a *p.*
Prov. 26. 23. are like a *p.* covered with silver dross
Isa. 45. 9. let the *p.* strive with *p.* of the earth

POTTAGE.

Gen. 25. 29. Jacob sod *p.* and Esau came from field
30. feed me with *p.* || 34. Jacob gave Esau *p.*
2 *Kings* 4. 38. seethe *p.* for sons of the prophets
39. and came and shred them into the pot of *p.*
40. as they were eating the *p.* they cried out
Hag. 2. 12. if one with his skirt do touch bread or *p.*

POTTER.

Frequent mention is made of the Potter *in Scripture. When God would shew his absolute dominion over men, and his irresistible power over their hearts, he has often recourse to the similitude of a* Potter, *who makes what he pleases of his clay; sometimes a vessel of honour, and sometimes of dishonour; now forming it, and then breaking it; now preserving it, and then rejecting it.* Psal. 2. 9. Rom. 9. 21.

Psal. 2. 9. shalt dash them in pieces like a *p.* vessel
Isa. 30. 14. he shall break it as the breaking of a *p.* vessel, *Jer.* 19. 11. *Rev.* 2. 27.
Jer. 18. 2. arise, go down to the *p.* house
19. 1. go and get a *p.* earthen bottle and take
Lam. 4. 2. the work of the hands of the *p.*
Zech. 11. 13. the Lord said, cast it unto the *p.*
Mat. 27. 10. and gave them for the *p.* field

POTTERS.

1 *Chron.* 4. 23. these were the *p.* and those that dwelt

See CLAY.

POVERTY.

Gen. 45. 11. lest thou and all thou hast come to *p.*

1 *Chr.* 22. † 14. in my *p.* I prepared for the house
Prov. 6. 11. so thy *p.* come as an armed man, 24. 34.
10. 15. the destruction of the poor is their *p.*
11. 24. that withholdeth, but it tendeth to *p.*
13. 18. *p.* be to him that refuseth instruction
20. 13. love not sleep, lest thou come to *p.*
23. 21. the drunkard and glutton come to *p.*
28. 19. followeth vain persons, shall have *p.* enough
22. considereth not that *p.* shall come upon him
30. 8. give me neither *p.* nor riches, feed me with
31. 7. let him drink and forget his *p.* and remember
2 *Cor.* 8. 2. their deep *p.* abounded to riches of liberality
9. became poor, that ye thro' his *p.* might be rich
Rev. 2. 9. I know thy works and *p.* thou art rich

POUND, S.

1 *Kings* 10. 17. three *p.* of gold went to one shield
Ezra 2. 69. they gave to treasure 5000 *p.* of silver
Neh. 7. 71. gave to the treasure 2200 *p.* of silver
72. the rest gave 2000 *p.* of silver and gold
Luke 19. 13. and delivered to his servants ten *p.*
16. second said, Lord, thy *p.* hath gained ten *p.*
18. hath gained five *p.* || 20. behold, here is thy *p.*
24. take from him the *p.* || 25. he hath ten *p.*
John 12. 3. then Mary took a *p.* of ointment
19. 39. and of aloes about 100 *p.* weight

POURTRAY.

Ezek. 4. 1. and *p.* upon it the city Jerusalem

POURTRAYED.

Ezek. 8. 10. all the idols of Israel *p.* on the wall
23. 14. for when she saw men *p.* on the wall, the images of the Chaldeans *p.* with vermilion

POWDER.

Exod. 32. 20. Moses burnt calf and ground it to *p.*
Deut. 28. 24. Lord shall make rain of thy land *p.*
2 *Kings* 23. 6. stamped the grove to *p.* cast the *p.*
15. he stamped the altar to *p.* 2 *Chron.* 34. 7.
Mat. 21. 44. it will grind him to *p.* *Luke* 20. 18.

POWDERS.

Cant. 3. 6. perfumed with all the *p.* of the merchant

POWER

Signifies, [1] *That attribute, or perfection of God, whereby he can do whatsoever he hath purposed to do, and hinder what he will not have done,* Mat. 6. 13. [2] *Absolute right and authority,* Mat. 9. 6. The Son of man hath power on earth to forgive sins; *that is, he that is the Son of man, being God, hath this power.* [3] *Right, or privilege,* John 1. † 12. [4] *Force, violence, or compulsion,* Ezra 4. 23. [5] *Liberty, or freedom,* 1 Cor. 9. 4, 5. [6] *The effectual and powerful work of the Holy Spirit, in regenerating and carrying on the work of grace in believers, against all opposition, from one degree to another, till it be perfected in glory,* Eph. 1. 19. [7] *The means, or instrument, which by God's power is made effectual to bring to salvation,* Rom. 1. 16. 1 Cor. 1. 18. [8] *A veil, or covering, in token that one is under the power of a superior.* 1 Cor. 11. 10. The woman ought to have power on her head; *that is, she ought to wear a covering, or veil, in token that she is under the power of her husband: or she ought to reckon and acknowledge power to be in her head, that is, in her husband, who is her head,* Eph. 5. 23. [9] *Good or evil angels,* Col. 1. 16. Eph. 6. 12. [10] *Civil governors, or magistrates,* Rom. 13. 1. [11] *Excellency, beauty, and glory,* 1 Cor. 15. 43.

All power is given unto me in heaven and in earth, *Mat.* 28. 18. *Supreme and absolute authority and ability is given me* in heaven, *so as,* [1] *To prevail with God to be reconciled to man.* [2] *To send the Holy Ghost,* Acts 2. 33. [3] *Over angels,* Col. 1. 16. Heb. 1. 4. [4] *To give heaven to all that believe in me,* Mat. 25. 34. *Power is also given me* in earth, *to prevail with men to be reconciled to God, and so to gather a church out of all nations,* Mark 16. 15, 16. *and to rule, govern, and defend the same against all its enemies,* Acts 10. 36, 38, 42. Eph. 1. 2 , 21.

The body is raised in power, 1 *Cor.* 15. 43. *It will be able,* [1] *To attend the soul in the highest operations.* [2] *To be continually exercised in the highest employments without weariness.* [3] *To bear the weight of glory.* [4] *To do whatsoever the soul would have it.* [5] *It will be above the reach of inward infirmities, or outward dangers.*

Gen. 32. 28. as a prince hast thou *p.* with God
49. 3. the excellency of dignity, excellency of *p.*
Lev. 26. 19. I will break the pride of your *p.*
Num. 22. 38. have I now any *p.* to say any thing?
Deut. 3. † 18. ye shall pass over all that are sons of *p.*
4. 37. brought thee with his mighty *p.* out of Egypt
8. 18. it is he that giveth thee *p.* to get wealth
32. 36. when he seeth that their *p.* is gone
Ruth 4. † 11. and get thee *p.* in Ephratah
2 *Sam.* 22. 33. God is my strength and *p.*
2 *Kings* 19. 26. the inhabitants were of small *p.*
1 *Chron.* 20. 1. Joab led forth the *p.* of the army
29. 11. thine is the *p.* and the glory, *Mat.* 6. 13.
12. in thine hand is *p.* and might, 2 *Chron.* 20. 6.
2 *Chron.* 25. 8. God hath *p.* to help, and cast down
32. 9. Sennacherib laid siege, and all his *p.* with him
Ezra 4. 23. and made them cease by force and *p.*
8. 22. his *p.* and wrath against all that forsake him
Neh. 5. 5. nor is it in our *p.* to redeem them
Esth. 1. 3. he made a feast to *p.* of Persia and Media
8. 11. to cause to perish the *p.* of the people
9. 1. the Jews hoped to have *p.* over them
Job 5. 20. redeem in war from the *p.* of the sword
24. 22. he draweth also the mighty with his *p.*
26. 2. how hast thou helped him that is without *p.*
12. he divided the sea with his *p.*
14. the thunder of his *p.* who can understand?
36. 22. behold, God exalteth by his *p.*
41. 12. I will not conceal his parts nor his *p.*
Psal. 22. 20. my darling from the *p.* of the dog
49. 15. redeem my soul from the *p.* of the grave
62. 11. I heard, that *p.* belongeth unto God
65. 6. who setteth fast mountains girded with *p.*
66. 7. he ruleth by his *p.* for ever, his eyes behold
68. 35. he giveth strength and *p.* to his people
78. 26. by his *p.* he brought in the south wind

Psal. 90. 11. who knoweth the *p.* of thine anger
106. 8. might make his mighty *p.* to be known
111. 6. he shewed his people the *p.* of his works
150. 1. praise him in the firmament of his *p.*
Eccl. 4. 1. on the side of oppressors there was *p.*
5. 19. and hath given him *p.* to eat thereof
6. 2. God giveth him not *p.* to eat thereof
8. 4. where the word of a king is, there is *p.*
8. there is no man hath *p.* over the spirit
Isa. 37. 27. their inhabitants were of small *p.*
40. 29. he giveth *p.* to the faint, and to them
43. 17. which bringeth forth the army and *p.*
47. 14. shall not deliver from the *p.* of the flame
Jer. 10. 12. he made the earth by his *p.* 51. 15.
Ezek. 22. 6. were in thee to their *p.* to shed blood
30. 6. and the pride of her *p.* shall come down
Dan. 2. 37. God hath given thee *p.* and glory
6. 27. who delivered Daniel from the *p.* of lions
8. 6. ran in fury of his *p.* || 22. but not in his *p.*
24. his *p.* shall be mighty, but not by his *p.*
11. 6. but she shall not retain the *p.* of the arm
25. he shall stir up his *p.* and his courage
43. but he shall have *p.* over the treasures of gold
12. 7. to scatter the *p.* of the holy people
Hos. 12. 3. by his strength he had *p.* with God
4. yea, he had *p.* over the angel, and prevailed
13. 14. I will ransom them from the *p.* of the grave
Mic. 2. 1. because it is in the *p.* of their hand
3. 8. I am full of *p.* by the Spirit of the Lord
Hab. 1. 11. imputing this his *p.* to his god
2. 9. that he may be delivered from the *p.* of evil
3. 4. and there was the hiding of his *p.*
Zech. 4. 6. not by might, nor by my *p.* but by my Sp.
9. 4. behold, the Lord will smite her *p.* in the sea
Mat. 9. 6. may know Son of man hath *p.* on earth to forgive sins, *Mark* 2. 10. *Luke* 5. 24.
8. glorified God, who had given such *p.* to men
10. 1. give *p.* against unclean spirits, *Luke* 9. 1.
24. 30. coming in the clouds with *p.* *Luke* 21. 27.
26. 64. sitting on right hand with *p.* *Mark* 14. 62.
28. 18. all *p.* is given to me in heaven and earth
Mark 3. 15. and to have *p.* to heal sicknesses
9. 1. have seen the kingdom of God come with *p.*
Luke 1. 35. *p.* of the Highest shall overshadow thee
4. 6. the devil said, all this *p.* will I give thee
32. they were astonished for his word was with *p.*
4. 36. with *p.* he commandeth unclean spirits
5. 17. the *p.* of the Lord was present to heal them
10. 19. I give you *p.* to tread on serpents, and over all the *p.* of the enemy, nothing shall hurt you
12. 5. fear him that hath *p.* to cast into hell
20. 20. they might deliver him to *p.* of governor
22. 53. this is your hour, and the *p.* of darkness
24. 49. until ye be endued with *p.* from on high
John 1. 12. to them gave he *p.* to become sons of G.
10. 18. I have *p.* to lay it down, and *p.* to take it
17. 2. thou hast given him *p.* over all flesh
19. 10. I have *p.* to crucify thee, *p.* to release thee
Acts 1. 7. seasons the Father hath put in his own *p.*
8. shall receive *p.* after H. Ghost is come on you
3. 12. as though by our own *p.* or holiness we made
4. 7. they asked, by what *p.* have ye done this?
5. 4. after it was sold, was it not in thine own *p.?*
6. 8. Stephen full of faith and *p.* did great wonders
8. 19. saying, give me also this *p.* on whom lay han.
10. 38. how G. anointed Jesus with H. Ghost and *p.*
26. 18. to turn them from the *p.* of Satan to God
Rom. 1. 4. and declared to be the Son of God with *p.*
20. clearly seen, even his eternal *p.* and Godhead
9. 21. hath not the potter *p.* over the clay?
22. what if God, willing to make his *p.* known
13. 2. whosoever therefore resisteth the *p.* resisteth
3. wilt thou then not be afraid of the *p.?*
15. 13. abound in hope, thro' *p.* of the Holy Ghost
19. wonders, by the *p.* of the Spirit of God
16. 25. now to him that is of *p.* to establish you
1 *Cor.* 2. 4. in demonstration of the Spirit and *p.*
4. 19. I will not know their speech, but the *p.*
5. 4. with the *p.* of our Lord Jesus Christ
6. 12. I will not be brought under the *p.* of any
14. and will also raise us up by his own *p.*
7. 4. the wife and husband have not *p.* of their body
37. but hath *p.* over his own will, so decreed
9. 4. have we not *p.* to eat and to drink?
5. have we not *p.* to lead about a sister, a wife?
6. have we not *p.* to forbear working?
12. if others be partakers of this *p.* over you, we have not used this *p.* but suffer all things
11. 10. the woman ought to have *p.* on her head
15. 24. he hath put down all authority and *p.*
2 *Cor.* 4. 7. that the excellency of *p.* may be of God
8. 3. to their *p.* yea, and beyond their *p.*
12. 9. that the *p.* of Christ may rest upon me
13. 10. according to the *p.* God hath given me
Eph. 1. 19. the exceeding greatness of his *p.* toward us, according to the working of his mighty *p.*
21. far above all principality, *p.* and might
2. 2. according to the prince of the *p.* of the air
3. 7. given to me, by the effectual working of his *p.*
20. according to the *p.* that worketh in us
Phil. 3. 10. I may know the *p.* of his resurrection
Col. 1. 11. strengthened according to his glorious *p.*
13. who hath delivered us from the *p.* of darkness
2. 10. who is head of all principality and *p.*
2 *Thess.* 1. 9. be punished from the glory of his *p.*
11. and fulfil the work of faith with *p.*
2. 9. after the working of Satan with all *p.*
3. 9. not because we have not *p.* but to make oursel.
1 *Tim.* 6. 16. whom be honour and *p.* everlast. amen
2 *Tim.* 1. 7. God hath given us spirit of *p.* and love
3. 5. having a form of godliness, but denying the *p.*
Heb. 1. 3. upholding all things by word of his *p.*
2. 14. he might destroy him that had *p.* of death
7. 16. but after the *p.* of an endless life
2 *Pet.* 1. 3. as his divine *p.* hath given us all things
16. when we made known the *p.* of our Lord
Jude 25. to only wise G. our Saviour be glory and *p.*
Rev. 2. 26. to him will I give *p.* over the nations
4. 11. thou art worthy to receive honour and *p.* 5. 12.
5. 13. blessing, glory, honour, and *p.* be to him
6. 4. *p.* was given to him that sat on the red horse
8. *p.* was given them over fourth part of earth

Rev. 7. 12. honour, p. and might be given to our G.
9. 3. to them was given p. as scorpions have p.
10. and their p. was to hurt men five months
19. for their p. is in their mouth and their tails
11. 3. I will give p. to my two witnesses
6. these have p. to shut heaven, p. over waters
12. 10. now is the p. of his Christ come
13. 2. the dragon gave him p. and his seat, 4.
5. p. was given to him to continue, 7.
12. he exerciseth all the p. of the first beast
15. had p. to give life ‖ 14. 18. had p. over fire
15. 8. the temple was filled with smoke from his p.
16. 8. p. was given him to scorch men with fire
9. blasphemed God who hath p. over these plagues
17. 12. but receive p. as kings one hour with beast
13. shall give their p. and strength to the beast
19. 1. glory, honour, and p. to the Lord our God

POWER of God.

Mat. 22. 29. Jesus said, ye do err, not knowing the scriptures, nor the p. of God, Mark 12. 24.
Luke 9. 43. were all amazed at the mighty p. of God
22. 69. the Son sit on the right hand of p. of God
Acts 8. 10. saying, this man is the great p. of God
Rom. 1. 16. the gospel is the p. of God to salvation
1 Cor. 1. 18. to us which are saved, it is the p. of God
24. Christ the p. of God, and wisdom of God
2. 5. faith should not stand but by the p. of God
2 Cor. 6. 7. by the word of truth, by the p. of God
13. 4. tho' crucified thro' weakness, yet he liveth by p. of G. but we shall live with him by p. of God
2 Tim. 1. 8. but be thou partaker of the afflictions of the gospel, according to the p. of God
1 Pet. 1. 5. who are kept by the p. of God thro' faith
See GREAT.

In POWER.

Gen. 31. 29. it is in p. of my hand to do you hurt
Exod. 15. 6. thy right hand is become glorious in p.
Job 21. 7. why are the wicked mighty in p.?
37. 23. he is excellent in p. and in judgment
Psal. 29. † 4. the voice of the Lord is in p.
Prov. 3. 27. when it is in p. of thy hand to do it
18. 21. death and life are in the p. of the tongue
Isa. 40. 26. that he is strong in p. not one faileth
Nah. 1. 3. the Lord is slow to anger, great in p.
Luke 1. 17. shall go before him in the p. of Elias
4. 14. Jesus returned in the p. of the Spirit
1 Cor. 4. 20. kingdom of God not in word, but in p.
15. 43. it is sown in weakness, it is raised in p.
Eph. 6. 10. be strong in the Lord and p. of his might
1 Thess. 1. 5. but our gos. came in word, and also in p.
2 Pet. 2. 11. angels who are greater in p. and might

My POWER.

Gen. 31. 6. with all my p. I have served your father
Exod. 9. 16. I raised thee to shew in thee my p.
Deut. 8. 17. sayest, my p. hath gotten me this wealth
Dan. 4. 30. Babylon built by the might of my p.
Rom. 9. 17. that I might shew my p. in thee
1 Cor. 9. 18. that I abuse not my p. in the gospel

No POWER.

Exod. 21. 8. to sell her, he shall have no p.
Lev. 26. 37. shall have no p. to stand before enemies
Josh. 8. 20. men of Ai had no p. to flee this way
1 Sam. 30. 4. till David and peo. had no p. to weep
2 Chron. 14. 11. to help with them that have no p.
22. 9. house of Ahaziah had no p. to keep kingdom
Isa. 50. 2. or have I no p. to deliver? behold I dry up
Dan. 3. 27. on whose bodies the fire had no p.
8. 7. there was no p. in the ram to stand before him
John 19. 11. no p. against me, except it were given
Rom. 13. 1. for there is no p. but of God
Rev. 20. 6. on such the second death hath no p.

Thy POWER.

Deut. 9. 29. thou broughtest out by thy mighty p.
Job 1. 12. behold, all that he hath is in thy p.
Psal. 21. 13. so will we sing, and praise thy p.
59. 11. scatter them by thy p. ‖ 16. will sing of thy p.
63. 2. to see thy p. and thy glory, as I have seen
66. 3. through greatness of thy p. enemies submit
71. 18. and thy p. to every one that is to come
79. 11. according to the greatness of thy p.
110. 3. thy people shall be willing in day of thy p.
145. 11. and they shall talk of thy p.
Nah. 2. 1. watch the way, fortify thy p. mightily

POWERFUL.

Psal. 29. 4. the voice of the Lord is p. full of majesty
2 Cor. 10. 10. for his letters, say they, are p.
Heb. 4. 12. the word of God is quick, p. and sharp.

POWERS.

Mat. 24. 29. the stars shall fall from heaven, p. of heaven shall be shaken, Mark 13. 25. Luke 21. 26.
Luke 12. 11. when brought before p. take no thought
Rom. 8. 38. nor p. can separate from love of God
13. 1. the p. that be are ordained of God
1 Cor. 12. † 29. are all teachers? are all p.?
Eph. 3. 10. that now to p. in heavenly places
6. 12. we wrestle against principalities and p.
Col. 1. 16. p. were created by him and for him
2. 15. having spoiled p. he made a shew openly
Tit. 3. 1. put them in mind to be subject to p.
Heb. 6. 5. tasted the p. of the world to come
1 Pet. 3. 22. who is on the right hand of God, p.

POUR.

Exod. 4. 9. shall take and p. water on the dry land
29. 7. shall p. the anointing oil on his head
12. thou shalt p. the blood of the bullock beside the bottom of altar, Lev. 4. 7, 18, 25, 30, 34.
30. 9. neither shall ye p. drink offerings thereon
Lev. 2. 1. he shall p. oil on the meat offerings, 6.
14. 15. p. it into the palm of his own left hand, 26.
18. p. it on head of him that is to be cleansed
41. they shall p. out the dust that they scrape off
17. 13. he shall p. out blood thereof and cover it
Num. 5. 15. he shall p. no oil upon her offering
24. 7. he shall p. water out of his buckets
Deut. 12. 16. p. blood out as water, 24. ‖ 15. 23.
Judg. 6. 20. take the flesh, and p. out the broth
1 Kings 18. 33. p. water on the burnt sacrifice
2 Kings 4. 4. p. out the oil into those vessels
41. p. out for the people, that they may eat
9. 3. and p. the oil on Jehu's head, and say
Job 36. 27. they p. down rain according to vapour
Psal. 42. 4. when I remember I p. out my soul
62. 8. ye people, p. out your heart before him
69. 24. p. out thine indignation on them
79. 6. p. out thy wrath on the heathen, not known
Prov. 1. 23. I will p. out my spirit unto you, Isa. 44. 3. Joel 2. 28, 29. Acts 2. 17, 18.
Isa. 44. 3. I will p. water on him that is thirsty
45. 8. let the skies p. down righteousness
Jer. 6. † 6. p. out engine of shot against Jerusalem
6. 11. I will p. it out on the children abroad
7. 18. and to p. out drink offerings to other gods
10. 25. p. out thy fury on heathen, know thee not
14. 16. I will p. their wickedness upon them
18. 21. p. out their blood by force of the sword
44. 17. to p. out drink offerings to the queen of heaven, as we and fathers have done, 18, 19, 25.
Lam. 2. 19. p. out thine heart like water before Ld.
Ezek. 7. 8. now will I shortly p. out my fury upon thee, 14. 19. ‖ 20. 8, 13, 21. ‖ 30. 15.
21. 31. I will p. out mine indignation, Zeph. 3. 8.
24. 3. set on the pot, and p. water into it
Hos. 5. 10. I will p. out my wrath like water
Mic. 1. 6. I will p. down the stones thereof into
Zech. 12. 10. I will p. on house of David the Spirit
Mal. 3. 10. if I will not p. you out a blessing
Rev. 16. 1. p. out the vials of wrath of God on earth

POURED.

Gen. 28. 18. Jacob p. oil on the top of the stone
35. 14. Jacob p. a drink offering thereon
Exod. 9. 33. the rain was not p. on the earth
30. 32. upon man's flesh shall it not be p.
Lev. 4. 12. where ashes are p. he shall be burnt
8. 12. Moses p. anointing oil on Aaron's head
15. he p. the blood at the bottom of altar, 9. 9.
21. 10. on whose head the anointing oil was p.
Num. 28. 7. to be p. to the Ld. for a drink offering
Deut. 12. 27. blood of thy sacrifices shall be p. out
Josh. 7. † 23. and p. them out before the Lord
1 Sam. 1. 15. but I have p. out my soul before Ld.
7. 6. drew water, and p. it out before the Lord
10. 1. Samuel p. oil on Saul's head, and kissed him
2 Sam. 13. 9. Tamar p. them out before him
23. 16. nevertheless, Dav. would not drink thereof, but p. it out unto the Lord, 1 Chron. 11. 18.
1 Kings 13. 3. altar shall be rent, and ashes p. out, 5.
2 Kings 3. 11. who p. water on the hands of Elijah
4. 5. who brought the vessels to her, and she p. out
40. so they p. out for the men to eat
16. 13. and Ahaz p. his drink offering
2 Chr. 12. 7. my wrath not be p. out on Jerusalem
34. 21. great is the wrath of Lord p. out on us
25. therefore my wrath shall be p. out on this place
Job 3. 24. my roarings are p. out like the waters
10. 10. hast not thou p. me out as milk, and curdled
22. † 16. flood was p. on their foundation
29. 6. when the rock p. me out rivers of oil
30. 16. and now my soul is p. out upon me
Psal. 22. 14. I am p. like water, bones out of joint
45. 2. grace is p. into thy lips, therefore God blessed
77. 17. clouds p. out water, skies sent out a sound
142. 2. I p. out my complaint before him
Cant. 1. 3. thy name is as ointment p. forth
Isa. 26. 16. p. out a prayer, when chastening on them
29. 10. Lord hath p. on you the spirit of deep sleep
32. 15. till the Spirit be p. on us from on high
42. 25. he hath p. on him the fury of his anger
53. 12. because he hath p. out his soul to death
57. 6. to them thou hast p. out a drink offering
Jer. 7. 20. my fury shall be p. out on this place
19. 13. they have p. out drink offerings, 32. 29.
42. 18. as fury hath been, so shall it be p. out
44. 6. my fury and mine anger was p. forth
19. when we p. drink offerings to queen of heaven
Lam. 2. 4. he p. out his fury like fire, 4. 11.
11. my liver is p. on earth ‖ 12. their soul p. out
4. 1. the stones of the sanctuary are p. out
Ezek. 16. 36. because thy filthiness was p. out
20. 28. and p. out there their drink offerings
33. with fury p. out will I rule over them, 34.
22. 22. that I the Lord have p. out my fury
31. therefore I p. out mine indignation on them
23. 8. they p. their whoredom upon her
24. 7. she p. it not on the ground to cover it
36. 18. wherefore I p. out my fury upon them
39. 29. I p. out my Spirit on the house of Israel
Dan. 9. 11. therefore the curse is p. on us, and oath
27. and that determined shall be p. on desolate
Mic. 1. 4. as waters that are p. down a steep place
Nah. 1. 6. fury is p. out like fire, rocks thrown down
Zeph. 1. 17. their blood shall be p. out as dust
Mat. 26. 7. p. ointment on his head, 12. Mark 14. 3.
John 2. 15. and he p. out the changers' money
Acts 10. 45. on the Gentiles was p. out the gift
Phil. 2. † 17. if I be p. forth on service of your faith
Rev. 14. 10. wine of wrath of G. p. without measure
16. 2. went and p. out his vial, 3, 4, 8, 10, 12, 17.

POUREDST.

Ezek. 16. 15. p. out thy fornications on every one

POURETH.

Job 12. 21. he p. contempt on princes, Psal. 107. 40.
16. 13. he p. out my gall upon the ground
20. but mine eye p. out tears unto God
Psal. 75. 8. wine is red, and he p. out of the same
Prov. 15. 2. but mouth of fools p. out foolishness
28. the mouth of the wicked p. out evil things
Amos 5. 8. p. out waters on the face of earth, 9. 6.
John 13. 5. after that, he p. water into a basin

POURING.

Lev. 4. † 12. he shall be burnt at the p. out of ashes
Ezek. 9. 8. wilt thou destroy all in p. thy fury on Jerusalem?
Luke 10. 34. he bound up his wounds, p. in oil

PRACTICES.

2 Pet. 2. 14. an heart exercised with covetous p.

PRACTISE.

Psal. 141. 4. not to p. wicked works with men
Prov. 3. † 29. p. no evil against thy neighbour
Isa. 32. 6. the vile person shall p. hypocrisy
Dan. 8. 24. a king shall destroy, prosper, and p.
Mic. 2. 1. when the morning is light, they p. it [mischief

PRACTISED.

1 Sam. 23. 9. David knew that Saul secretly p.
Dan. 8. 12. the little horn p. and prospered

PRAISE

Signifies, [1] A confession and due acknowledgment of the great and wonderful excellences and perfections that be in God, Psal. 138. 1. Rev. 19. 5. [2] A speaking forth and commending the good qualifications that be in others, Prov. 27. 2. [3] The object, matter, and ground of praise, Deut. 10. 20. Psal. 118. 14. [4] Commendation, encouragement, and protection, Rom. 13. 3. 1 Pet. 2. 14. [5] Great and praiseworthy actions, Psal 106. 2.

Gen. 29. † 35. therefore she called his name P.
Deut. 10. 21. he is thy p. and he is thy God
26. 19. to make thee high in p. and in name
Judg. 5. 3. I will sing p. to the Lord God of Israel, Psal. 7. 17. ‖ 9. 2. ‖ 57. 7. ‖ 61. 8. ‖ 104. 33.
1 Chron. 16. 35. deliver, that we may glory in thy p.
2 Chr. 23. 13. and such as taught to sing p.
Neh. 9. 5. who is exalted above all blessing and p.
12. 46. in the days of David were songs of p.
Psal. 9. 14. that I may shew forth all thy p.
22. 25. my p. shall be of thee in the congregation
30. 12. that my glory may sing p. to thee
33. 1. for p. is comely for the upright
34. 1. his p. shall be continually in my mouth
35. 28. my tongue shall speak of thy p. all day long
40. 3. even p. to our God ‖ 42. 4. with voice of p.
48. 10. so is thy p. to the ends of the earth
50. 23. whoso offereth p. glorifieth me
51. 15. and my mouth shall shew forth thy p.
65. 1. p. waiteth for thee, O God, in Sion
66. 2. sing forth his honour, make his p. glorious
8. and make the voice of his p. to be heard
71. 6. my p. shall be continually of thee
8. let my mouth be filled with thy p. and honour
79. 13. we will shew forth thy p. ‖ 98. 4. sing p.
100. 4. and enter into his courts with p.
102. 21. and to declare his p. in Jerusalem
106. 2. who can shew forth all his p.?
12. then they sang his p. ‖ 47. triumph in thy p.
108. 1. I will sing and give p. with my glory
109. 1. O God of my p. ‖ 111. 10. his p. endureth
119. 171. lips shall utter p. when thou hast taught
138. 1. before the gods will I sing p. to thee
145. 21. my mouth shall speak the p. of the Lord
147. 1. p. is comely ‖ 7. sing p. on the harp
148. 14. he exalteth the p. of all his saints
149. 1. sing his p. in the congregation of saints
Prov. 27. 21. as the furnace, so is a man to his p.
Isa. 42. 8. I will not give my p. to graven images
10. sing his p. from the end of the earth
12. let them declare his p. in the islands
43. 21. this people, they shall shew forth my p.
48. 9. and for my p. will I refrain for thee
60. 18. but thou shalt call thy gates P.
61. 3. the garment of p. for the spirit of heaviness
11. L. will cause righteousn. and p. to spring forth
62. 7. till he make Jerusalem a p. in the earth
Jer. 13. 11. that they might be to me for a p.
17. 14. save me, O Lord, for thou art my p.
26. bringing sacrifices of p. to house of L. 33. 11.
33. 9. it shall be to me a joy, a p. and an honour
48. 2. there shall be no more p. of Moab
49. 25. how is the city of p. not left, city of joy?
51. 41. how is the p. of whole earth surprised?
Hab. 3. 3. and the earth was full of his p.
Zeph. 3. 19. I will get them p. and fame in every land
20. make you a p. among all people of the earth
Mat. 21. 16. of sucklings, thou hast perfected p.
Luke 18. 43. people, when they saw it, gave p. to G.
John 9. 24. give God the p. this man is a sinner
12. 43. they loved p. of men more than p. of God
Rom. 2. 29. whose p. is not of men, but of God
13. 3. do what is good, thou shalt have p. of same
1 Cor. 4. 5. then shall every man have p. of God
2 Cor. 8. 18. the brother, whose p. is in the gospel
Eph. 1. 6. predestinated to p. of glory of his grace
12. to p. of glory who first trusted in Christ, 14.
Phil. 1. 11. by Jesus Christ, to p. and glory of God
4. 8. if there be any p. think on these things
Heb. 2. 12. in midst of the church will I sing p.
13. 15. by him let us offer sacrifice of p. continually
1 Pet. 1. 7. trial of your faith might be found to p.
2. 14. and for the p. of them that do well
4. 11. to whom be p. and dominion for ever

PRAISE, Verb.

Gen. 49. 8. thou art he whom thy brethren shall p.
Lev. 19. 24. the fruit thereof holy to p. the Lord
Deut. 32. † 43. p. his people, ye nations
2 Sam. 14. † 25. as Absalom, not a man to p. greatly
1 Chr. 23. 5. instruments I made to p. therewith
29. 13. we thank and p. thy glorious name
2 Chron. 8. 14. Levites to p. before the priests
20. 21. that should p. the beauty of holiness
22. and when they began to sing and to p.
31. 2. and to p. in the gates of the tents of Lord
Psal. 21. 13. so will we sing and p. thy power
22. 23. ye that fear the Lord, p. him, seed of Jacob
30. 9. when I go to the pit, shall the dust p. thee?
42. 5. hope in God, for I shall yet p. him, 11. ‖ 43. 5.
44. 8. in God we boast, and p. thy name for ever
45. 17. therefore shall the people p. thee
49. 18. men will p. thee, when doest well to thyself
63. 3. my lips shall p. thee ‖ 5. mouth shall p. thee
67. 3. let people p. thee ‖ 5. let all people p. thee
69. 34. let the heaven and earth p. him
71. 14. I will yet p. thee more and more
74. 21. let the poor and needy p. thy name
76. 10. surely the wrath of man shall p. thee
88. 10. shall the dead arise and p. thee?
89. 5. the heavens shall p. thy wonders, O Lord
99. 3. let them p. thy great and terrible name
107. 32. p. him in the assembly of the elders
113. 1. p. him, O ye servants of the Lord, 135. 1.
115. 17. the dead p. not the Lord, nor any that
119. 164. seven times a day do I p. thee
175. let my soul live and it shall p. thee
138. 2. I will p. thy name for thy loving kindness
4. all the kings of the earth shall p. thee
142. 7. bring out of prison that I may p. thy name
145. 4. one generation shall p. thy works to another
10. all thy works shall p. thee, O Lord

Ps. 147 12. *p.* the L. Jerusalem, *p.* thy God, O Zion
148. 1. *p.* ye the Lord, *p.* him in the heights
2. *p.* him, all his angels, *p.* him, ye his hosts
3. *p.* him, sun and moon, *p.* him, all ye stars
4. *p.* him, ye heavens of heavens, and waters
149. 3. let them *p.* his name in the dance
150. 1. *p.* God in his sanctuary, *p.* him in firmam.
2. *p.* him for his mighty acts, *p.* him for greatness
3. *p.* him with trumpet ‖ 4. *p.* him with timbrel
5. *p.* him upon the loud and sounding cymbals
Prov. 27. 2. let another man *p.* thee, a stranger
28. 4. they that forsake the law *p.* the wicked
31. 31. let her own works *p.* her in the gates
Isa. 38. 18. the grave cannot *p.* thee, death cannot
19. the living he shall *p.* thee, as I do this day
Jer. 31. 7. publish, *p.* ye and say, O L. save people
Dan. 2. 23. I thank and *p.* thee, O God of my fathers
4. 37. I *p.* extol, and honour the king of heaven
Joel 2. 26. *p.* the name of the Lord your God
Luke 19. 37. disciples began to *p.* G. with loud voice
1 *Cor.* 11. 2. now I *p.* you that ye remember me
17. in this that I declare, I *p.* you not, 22.
Rev. 19. 5. saying, *p.* our God, all ye his servants

I will, or *will I* PRAISE.

Gen. 29. 35. Leah said, now *will I p.* the Lord
Psal. 7. 17. *I will p.* Ld. according to his righteous.
9. 1. *I will p.* thee, O Lord, with my whole heart, will shew forth thy works, 111. 1. | 138. 1.
22. 22. in midst of the congregation *will I p.* thee
28. 7. therefore with my song *will I p.* him
35. 18. I will give thee thanks, *I will p.* thee among much people, 57. 9. | 108. 3. | 109. 30.
43. 4. on the harp *will I p.* thee, O God
52. 9. *I will p.* thee for ever, because thou hast done
54. 6. *I will p.* thy name, O Lord, for it is good
56. 4. in God *I will p.* his word, in God I trust, 10.
69. 30. *I will p.* the name of God with a song
71. 22. *I will* also *p.* thee with the psaltery
86. 12. *I will p.* thee, O Lord my G. with my heart
118. 19. *I will* go into them, and will *p.* the Lord
21. *I will p.* thee, for thou hast heard me
28. thou art my God, and *I will p.* thee
119. 7. *I will p.* thee with uprightness of heart
139. 14. *I will p.* thee, for I am wonderfully made
145. 2. *I will p.* thy name for ever and ever
Isa. 12. 1. *I will p.* thee, though thou wast angry
25. 1. *I will p.* thy name, thou hast done wonders

PRAISE *ye the Lord*, or PRAISE *the Lord.*

Judg. 5. 2. *p. ye the Lord*, for the avenging of Israel
1 *Chr.* 16. 4. he appointed Levites to *p. the Lord*
23. 30. to stand every morning to *p. the Lord*
25. 3. who prophesied with a harp to *p. the Lord*
2 *Chr.* 20. 19. the Levites stood up to *p. the Lord*
21. *p. the Lord*, for his mercy endureth for ever
Ezra 3. 10. set Levites with cymbals to *p. the Lord*
Psal. 22. 26. they shall *p. the Lord* that seek him
33. 2. *p. the Lord* with harp, sing unto him
102. 18. people that shall be created shall *p. the L.*
104. 35. *p. ye L.* 106. 1, 48. | 111. 1. | 112. 1. | 113. 1, 9. | 115. 18. | 116. 19. | 117. 2. | 135. 1. | 146. 1, 10. | 147. 20. | 148. 1, 14. | 149. 1, 9. | 150. 1, 6. *Jer.* 20. 13.
107. 8. oh that men would *p. the Lord*, 15, 21, 31.
109. 30. I will greatly *p. the Lord* with my mouth
118. 19. I will *p. the L.* ‖ 135. 3. *p. L.* for he is good
146. 2. while I live will I *p. the Lord*, I will sing
147. 1. *p. ye the Lord*, for it is good to sing praise
12. *p. the L.* O Jerusalem, praise thy God, O Zion
148. 7. *p. the Lord* from the earth, ye dragons
Isa. 12. 4. shall say, *p. the Lord*, call upon his name
62. 9. but they shall eat it, and *p. the Lord*
Jer. 33. 11. *p. the Lord* of hosts, for the Lord is good
Rom. 15. 11. and again, *p. the Lord*, all ye Gentiles

PRAISED.

Judg. 16. 24. the people *p.* their god Dagon
2 *Sam.* 14. 25. none to be so much *p.* as Absalom
22. 4. the Lord is worthy to be *p. Psal.* 18. 3.
1 *Chron.* 16. 25. for the Lord is great, and greatly to be *p. Psal.* 48. 1. | 96. 4. | 145. 3.
36. all the people *p.* the Lord, and said, amen
23. 5. four thousand were porters, and four thousand *p.* the Lord, 2 *Chron.* 7. 3. *Neh.* 5. 13.
2 *Chron.* 5. 13. with instruments of music *p.* Lord
7. 6. when David *p.* by their ministry
30. 21. Levites and priests *p.* the Lord day by day
Ezra 3. 11. a great shout when they *p.* the Lord
Psal. 72. 15. prayer for him, and daily shall he be *p.*
113. 3. from rising of sun Lord's name is to be *p.*
Prov. 31. 30. a woman that feareth Lord shall be *p.*
Eccl. 4. 2. wherefore I *p.* the dead more than living
Cant. 6. 9. yea, the queens and concubines *p.* her
Isa. 64. 11. our house, where our fathers *p.* thee
Dan. 4. 34. I *p.* and honoured him that liveth for ev.
5. 4. and they *p.* the gods of gold and silver, 23.
Luke 1. 64. and Zacharias spake and *p.* God

PRAISES.

Exod. 15. 11. who is like thee, fearful in *p.?*
2 *Sam.* 22. 50. I will give thanks and sing *p.* to thy name, *Psal.* 18. 49. | 92. 1. | 135. 3.
2 *Chron.* 29. 30. commanded the Levites to sing *p.* to the Lord, and they sang *p.* with gladness
Psal. 9. 11. sing *p.* to Lord that dwelleth in Zion
22. 3. art holy, O thou that inhabitest *p.* of Israel
27. 6. I will sing, yea, I will sing *p.* to God, 47. 6. | 68. 32. | 75. 9. | 108. 3.
47. 7. God is king, sing ye *p.* with understanding
56. 12. I will render *p.* unto thee, 144. 9.
68. 4. sing to God, sing *p.* to his name, extol him
78. 4. shewing to generation to come *p.* of Lord
146. 2. I will sing *p.* to my God while I have being
147. 1. for it is good to sing *p.* to our God
149. 3. let them sing *p.* to him with the timbrel
6. let the high *p.* of God be in their mouths
Isa. 60. 6. they shall shew forth the *p.* of the Lord
63. 7. I will make mention of the *p.* of the Lord
Acts 16. 25. Paul and Silas prayed and sang *p.* to G.
1 *Pet.* 2. 9. shew forth the *p.* of him who called you

PRAISETH.

Prov. 31. 28. her husband also, and he *p.* her

PRAISING.

2 *Chr.* 5. 13. to make one sound to be heard in *p.* L.
23. 12. Athaliah heard the people *p.* the king

Ezra 3. 11. they sang by course in *p.* the Lord
Psal. 84. 4. they will be still *p.* thee
Luke 2. 13. a multitude of the heavenly host *p.* God
20. the shepherds returned *p.* God for all things
24. 53. they were continually in the temple *p.* God
Acts 2. 46. they did eat with gladness, *p.* God
3. 8. walking, and leaping, and *p.* God, 9.

PRANCING.

Nah. 3. 2. the noise of the *p.* horses and chariots

PRANCINGS.

Judg. 5. 22. horse-hoofs broken by means of *p.*

PRATING.

Prov. 10. 8. but a *p.* fool shall fall, 10.
3 *John* 10. *p.* against us with malicious words

PRAY.

Gen. 20. 7. he is a prophet, and shall *p.* for thee
24. † 63. Isaac went out to *p.* in the field
1 *Sam.* 1. † 12. as Hannah multiplied to *p.* before L.
7. 5. Samuel said, I will *p.* for you to the Lord
12. 19. *p.* for thy servants to the Lord thy God
23. that I should sin in ceasing to *p.* for you
2 *Sam.* 7. 27. found in his heart to *p.* 1 *Chr.* 17. 25.
1 *Kings* 8. 30. hearken thou when they shall *p.* toward this place, 35, 42, 44, 48. 2 *Chron.* 6. 26, 34, 38.
13. 6. *p.* that my hand may be restored again
2 *Chron.* 6. 24. shall *p.* and make supplication, 32.
37. and turn and *p.* in the land of their captivity
7. 14. if my people shall *p.* and seek my face
Ezra 6. 10. and *p.* for the life of the king and sons
Neh. 1. 6. hear the prayer which I *p.* before thee
Job 21. 15. what profit should we have if *p.* to him
33. 26. *p.* to God, and he will be favourable to him
42. 8. my serv. Job shall *p.* for you, him will accept
Ps. 5. 2. my King, my God, for to thee will I *p.*
55. 17. evening, morning, and at noon will I *p.*
122. 6. *p.* for peace of Jerus. prosper that love thee
Isa. 16. 12. he shall come to his sanctuary to *p.*
45. 20. and *p.* to a god that cannot save
Jer. 7. 16. *p.* not thou for this people, 11. 14. | 14. 11.
29. 7. seek peace of the city, *p.* to the Lord for it
12. ye shall *p.* to me, and I will hearken to you
37. 3. *p.* now to the Lord our God for us, 42. 2, 20.
42. 4. behold, I will *p.* to the Lord your God
Zech. 7. 2. they sent men to *p.* before the Lord
8. 21. go speedily to *p.* before the Lord, 22.
Mat. 5. 44. and *p.* for them which despitefully use you and persecute you, *Luke* 16. 27.
6. 5. for they love to *p.* standing in the synagogue
6. *p.* to thy Father which is in secret, shall reward
7. when ye *p.* use not vain repetitions as heathen do
9. after this manner *p.* ye, Our Father who art
9. 38. *p.* the Lord of the harvest, *Luke* 10. 2.
14. 23. he went up into a mountain apart to *p.* and was alone, *Mark* 6. 46. *Luke* 6. 12. | 9. 28.
19. 13. that he should put his hands on them and *p.*
24. 20. *p.* your flight be not in winter, *Mark* 13. 18.
26. 36. Jesus saith to the disciples, sit ye here while I go and *p.* yonder, *Mark* 14. 32.
41. watch and *p.* that ye enter not into temptation, *Mark* 13. 33. | 14. 38. *Luke* 21. 36. | 22. 40, 46.
53. thinkest thou that I cannot *p.* to my Father?
Mark 5. 17. and they began to *p.* him to depart
11. 24. what things soever ye desire when ye *p.*
Luke 11. 1. Lord, teach us to *p.* as John taught his
2. he said to them, when ye *p.* say, Our Father
18. 1. that men ought always to *p.* and not to faint
10. two men went up into the temple to *p.*
John 14. 16. and I will *p.* the Father, 16. 26.
17. 9. I *p.* for them, I *p.* not for the world
15. I *p.* not that thou take them out of the worl
20. nor *p.* I for these alone, but for them also
Acts 8. 22. *p.* God, if perhaps the thought of heart
24. Simon said, *p.* ye to the Lord for me
10. 9. Peter went up on the house top to *p.*
Rom. 8. 26. for we know not what we should *p.* for
1 *Cor.* 11. 13. is it comely that woman *p.* uncovered?
14. 13. wherefore let him *p.* that he may interpret
14. for if I *p.* in unknown tongue, spirit prayeth
15. I will *p.* with Spirit, *p.* with understanding
2 *Cor.* 5. 20. we are ambassadors for Christ, we *p.* you in Christ's stead, be ye reconciled to God
13. 7. now I *p.* to God, that ye do no evil
Phil. 1. 9. this I *p.* that your love may abound
Col. 1. 9. for this cause we do not cease to *p.* for you
1 *Thess.* 5. 17. rejoice evermore, *p.* without ceasing
23. I *p.* God your whole spirit be preserved
25. brethren, *p.* for us, 2 *Thess.* 3. 1. *Heb.* 13. 18.
2 *Thess.* 1. 11. wherefore we *p.* always for you
1 *Tim.* 2. 8. I will that men *p.* every where
2 *Tim.* 4. 16. I *p.* God it be not laid to their charge
Jam. 5. 13. is any among you afflicted? let him *p.*
14. and let them *p.* over him, anointing him
16. confess your faults, and *p.* one for another
1 *John* 5. 16. I do not say that he shall *p.* for it
3 *John* † 2. I *p.* that thou mayest prosper and in health

PRAYED.

Gen. 20. 17. Abraham *p.* and God healed Abimelech
Num. 11. 2. when Moses *p.* the fire was quenched
21. 7. and Moses *p.* for the people, *Deut.* 9. 26.
Deut. 9. 20. I *p.* for Aaron also the same time
1 *Sam.* 1. 10. Hannah *p.* to Lord and wept sore, 21.
27. for this child I *p.* ‖ 8. 6. Samuel *p.* to the Lord
2 *Kings* 4. 33. Elisha *p.* to the Lord, 6. 17, 18.
19. 15. Hezekiah *p.* 20. 2. 2 *Chron.* 30. 18. | 32. 24.
20. that which thou hast *p.* to me, *Isa.* 37. 21.
2 *Chron.* 32. 20. Isaiah *p.* ‖ 33. 13. Manasseh *p.*
Ezra 10. 1. now when Ezra had *p. Neh.* 1. 4. | 2. 4.
Job 42. 10. Lord turned the captivity when Job *p.*
Jer. 32. 16. Jeremiah *p.* ‖ *Jonah* 2. 1. Jonah *p.* 4. 2.
Dan. 6. 10. Daniel *p.* three times a day, 9. 4.
Mat. 26. 39. Jesus fell on his face and *p.* let this cup pass from me, 42, 44. *Mark* 14. 35, 39. *Luke* 22. 41.
Mark 1. 35. he went into a solitary place and *p.*
5. 18. he *p.* him that he might be with him
Luke 5. 3. Jesus *p.* him he would thrust out a little
16. he withdrew into the wilderness and *p.*
9. 29. as he *p.* his countenance was altered
18. 11. the Pharisee stood and *p.* thus, I thank thee
22. 32. but I have *p.* that thy faith fail not
44. being in an agony he *p.* more earnestly
John 4. 31. his disciples *p.* him, Master, eat
Acts 1. 24. the disciples *p.* and said, thou Lord

Acts 4. 31. when they *p.* they laid their hands on th.
8. 15. Peter and John when come *p.* for them
9. 40. Peter *p.* ‖ 10. 2. Cornelius *p.* always, 30.
10. 48. then they *p.* him to tarry certain days
13. 3. and when they had fasted and *p.* 14. 23.
16. 9. *p.* him, saying, come over into Macedonia
25. at midnight Paul and Silas *p.* and sang
20. 36. Paul kneeled down and *p.* with them all
21. 5. we kneeled down on the shore and *p.*
22. 17. while I *p.* in the temple, I was in a trance
23. 18. Paul *p.* me to bring this young man to thee
28. 8. to whom Paul entered in and *p.*
Jam. 5. 17. Elias *p.* that it might not rain
18. and he *p.* again, and the heaven gave rain

PRAYER

Is *an offering up of our desires to God for things lawful and needful, with an humble confidence to obtain them through the alone mediation of Christ, to the praise of the mercy, truth, and power of God*, Mat. 6. 6. John 16. 23, 24, 26. *It is either mental or vocal, ejaculatory or occasional, either private or public; for ourselves or others; for the procuring of good things, or the removing, or preventing, of things evil*, 1 Tim. 2. 1, 2. *As God is the only object of* prayer, *Psal.* 50. 15. *and as we must pray for others, as well as for ourselves*, Jam. 5. 16. *so we are to pray fervently*, Col. 4. 12. *sincerely*, Psal. 17. 1. *constantly*, Col. 4. 2. *with faith*, Jam. 5. 15. *and not without repentance*, Psal. 66. 18. Jer. 36. 7. *and by the help of the Holy Spirit*, Rom. 8. 26.

Prayer *comes from a word in the* Hebrew, *which signifies* appeal, interpellation, intercession; *whereby we refer our own cause, and that of others, unto God as judge, calling upon him, appealing to him for right, presenting ourselves and our cause unto him. The prayers that we direct to God, are the ordinary conveyance of the graces that we receive from him:* Christ *himself, the great example of the righteous, and of the elect, taught us to pray, to inform us, that it is by that we honour God, and draw down upon ourselves his favours and graces.*

The parts of Prayer *are said to be invocation, adoration, confession, petition, pleading, dedication, thanksgiving, and blessing.*

2 *Sam.* 7. 27. found in his heart to pray this *p.* to thee
1 *Kings* 8. 28. have respect to the *p.* of thy servant
29. mayest hearken to the *p.* 2 *Chron.* 6. 19, 20.
38. *p.* shall be made by any man, 2 *Chron.* 6. 29.
45. hear their *p.* 49. 2 *Chron.* 6. 35, 39, 40.
54. Solomon made an end of praying this *p.*
2 *Kings* 19. 4. lift up thy *p.* for remnant, *Isa.* 37. 4.
2 *Chron.* 7. 15. my ears shall be attent to the *p.*
30. 27. their *p.* came to his holy dwelling
33. 18. Manasseh's *p.* how God was intreated, 19.
Neh. 1. 6. thou mayest hear the *p.* of thy servant
4. 9. nevertheless we made our *p.* to our God
Job 15. 4. yea thou restrainest *p.* before God
22. 27. thou shalt make thy *p.* to him, shall hear
Psal. 65. 2. O thou that hearest *p.* to thee shall all
72. 15. *p.* shalt be made for him continually
80. 4. how long be angry against *p.* of thy people
102. 17. shall appear in his glory, he will regard the *p.* of the destitute, and not despise their *p.*
109. 4. my adversaries, but I give myself unto *p.*
7. let him be condemned, and let his *p.* become sin
Prov. 15. 8. the *p.* of the upright is his delight
29. but he heareth the *p.* of the righteous
28. 9. even his *p.* shall be abomination
Isa. 26. 16. poured out a *p.* when thy chastening
56. 7. I will make them joyful in my house of *p.* for my house shall be called an house of *p.* *Mat.* 21. 13. *Mark* 11. 17. *Luke* 19. 46.
Jer. 7. 16. nor lift up my cry nor *p.* for them, 11. 14.
Lam. 3. 44. that our *p.* should not pass through
Dan. 9. 3. I set my face to the Lord, to seek by *p.*
13. yet made we not our *p.* before Lord our God
17. now, O our God, hear the *p.* of thy servant
Hab. 3. 1. a *p.* of Habakkuk the prophet
Mat. 17. 21. nothing impossible, howbeit, this kind goeth not out but by *p.* and fasting, *Mark* 9. 29.
Luke 1. 13. fear not, Zacharias, thy *p.* is heard
Acts 3. 1. went into the temple at the hour of *p.*
6. 4. but we will give ourselves continually to *p.*
10. 31. Cornelius, thy *p.* is heard, and thy alms
12. 5. *p.* was made without ceasing to God for him
16. 13. we went out where *p.* was wont to be made
16. as we went to *p.* a certain damsel met us
1 *Cor.* 7. 5. that ye may give yourselves to *p.*
2 *Cor.* 1. 11. ye also helping together by *p.* for us
9. 14. by their *p.* for you, which long after you
Eph. 6. 18. praying always with all *p.* and supplicat.
Phil. 1. 4. always in every *p.* of mine for you all
19. this shall turn to my salvation through your *p.*
4. 6. in every thing by *p.* let requ. be made known
1 *Tim.* 4. 5. for it is sanctified by the word and *p.*
Jam. 5. 15. the *p.* of faith shall save the sick
16. the effectual *p.* of a righteous man availeth
† 17. he prayed in his *p.* that it might not rain
1 *Pet.* 4. 7. be therefore sober, and watch unto *p.*

See HEARD.

In PRAYER.

Neh. 11. 17. Mattaniah began the thanksgiving *in p.*
Dan. 9. 21. yea, while I was speaking *in p.* Gabriel
Mat. 21. 22. whatever ye ask *in p.* believing
Luke 6. 12. he continued all night *in p.* to God
Acts 1. 14. they continued with one accord *in p.*
Rom. 12. 12. patient in tribu. continuing instant *in p.*
Col. 4. 2. continue *in p.* and watch in the same

My PRAYER.

Job 16. 17. not for any injustice, also *my p.* is pure
Ps. 4. 1. have mercy, hear *my p.* 17. 1. | 39. 12. | 54. 2.
5. 3. in the morning will I direct *my p.* to thee
6. 9. the Lord heard, the Lord will receive *my p.*
35. 13. and *my p.* returned to mine own bosom
42. 8. his song, and *my p.* to the God of my life
55. 1. give ear unto *my p.* O God, and hide not
61. 1. hear my cry, O God, attend to *my p.* 64. 1. | 84. 8. | 86. 6. | 102. 1. | 143. 1.
66. 19. he hath attended to the voice of *my p.*

Ps. 66. 20. God which hath not turned away *my p.*
69. 13. *my p.* is to thee in an acceptable time
88. 2. let *my p.* come before thee, incline thine ear
13. in the morning shall *my p.* prevent thee
141. 2. let *my p.* be set forth before thee as incense
5. for yet *my p.* shall be in their calamities
Lam. 3. 8. when I cry and shout, he shutt. out *my p.*
Jon. 2. 7. *my p.* came in to thee into thy holy temple
Rom. 10. 1. brethren, *my p.* to God for Israel is

PRAYERS.

Psal. 72. 20. *p.* of David, son of Jesse, are ended
Isa. 1. 15. when ye make many *p.* I will not hear
Mat. 23. 14. for pretence make long *p.* therefore have greater damnation, *Mark* 12. 40. *Luke* 20. 47.
Luke 2. 37. Anna continued in *p.* day and night
5. 33. why do the disciples of John make *p.?*
Acts 2. 42. continued in breaking of bread and in *p.*
10. 4. thy *p.* and alms are come up before God
Rom. 1. 9. I make mention of you always in my *p.*
Eph. 1. 16. 1 *Thess.* 1. 2. 2 *Tim.* 1. 3. *Philem.* 4.
15. 30. strive with me in your *p.* to God for me
Col. 4. 12. Epaphras labouring fervently for you in *p.*
1 *Tim.* 2. 1. I exhort that *p.* be made for all men
5. 5. widow indeed continueth in *p.* night and day
Philem. 22. I trust thro' your *p.* I shall be given to y.
Heb. 5. 7. when he had offered up *p.* with tears
1 *Pet.* 3. 7. as heirs of life, that your *p.* be not hinder.
12. his ears are open to their *p.* but face of Lord
Rev. 5. 8. full of odours, which are *p.* of the saints
8. 3. he should offer it with the *p.* of the saints
4. the smoke which came from the *p.* of the saints

PRAYEST.

Mat. 6. 5. when thou *p.* be not as the hypocrites, 6.

PRAYETH, ING.

1 *Sam.* 1. 12. as Hannah continued *p.* before Lord
26. my lord, I am woman that stood *p.* by thee
1 *Kings* 8. 28. hearken to prayer which thy servant *p.* before thee this day, 2 *Chron.* 6. 19, 20.
54. Solomon had made an end of *p.* 2 *Chron.* 7. 1.
Isa. 44. 17. he worshippeth it and *p.* to it
Dan. 6. 11. these assembled and found Daniel *p.*
9. 20. while I was speaking and *p.* and confessing
Mark 11. 25. when ye stand *p.* forgive aught ag. any
Luke 1. 10. multitude of the people were *p.* without
3. 21. and Jesus *p.* the heaven was opened
9. 18. and was alone *p.* his disciples were with him
11. 1. as he was *p.* in certain place, when he ceased
Acts 9. 11. behold he *p.* ‖ 11. 5. I was at Joppa *p.*
12. 12. where many were gathered together *p.*
1 *Cor.* 11. 4. every man *p.* with his head covered
5. but every woman that *p.* with head uncovered
14. 14. my spirit *p.* but my understand. is unfruitf.
2 *Cor.* 8. 4. *p.* us with much entreaty to receive gift
Eph. 6. 18. *p.* always with all prayer in the Spirit
Col. 1. 3. *p.* always for you ‖ 4. 3. *p.* also for us
1 *Thess.* 3. 10. night and day *p.* exceed. to see your
Jude 20. but ye, beloved, *p.* in the Holy Ghost

PREACH.

Neh. 6. 7. thou hast appointed prophets to *p.* of thee
Isa. 61. 1. Ld. hath anointed me to *p.* good tidings
Jonah 3. 2. *p.* to it the preaching that I bid thee
Mat. 4. 17. from that time Jesus began to *p.*
10. 7. *p.* saying, the kingdom of God is at hand
27. what ye hear, that *p.* ye upon the house-tops
11. 1. he departed thence to *p.* in their cities
Mark 1. 4. John did *p.* the baptism of repentance
38. that I may *p.* there also, *Luke* 4. 43.
3. 14. that he might send them forth to *p.* *Luke* 9. 2.
Luke 4. 18. to *p.* deliverance to the captives, 19.
9. 60. but go thou and *p.* the kingdom of God
Acts 5. 42. they ceased not to *p.* Jesus Christ
10. 42. he commanded us to *p.* to the people
14. 15. and *p.* unto you that ye should turn to God
15. 21. Moses hath in every city them that *p.* him
16. 6. forbidden by Holy Ghost to *p.* word in Asia
17. 3. that this Jesus whom I *p.* to you is Christ
Rom. 10. 8. that is the word of faith which we *p.*
15. and how shall they *p.* except they be sent?
1 *Cor.* 1. 23. but we *p.* Christ crucified
9. 16. tho' I *p.* gospel, I have nothing to glory, woe is to me if I *p.* not gospel, necessity is laid on me
15. 11. I or they, so we *p.* and so ye believed
2 *Cor.* 4. 5. we *p.* not ourselves, but Christ Jesus
Gal. 1. 16. that I might *p.* him among the heathen
2. 2. the gospel which I *p.* among the Gentiles
5. 11. and I, brethren, if I yet *p.* circumcision
Eph. 3. 8. that I should *p.* among the Gentiles
Phil. 1. 15. some indeed *p.* Christ of envy and strife
16. the one *p.* Christ of contention, not sincerely
Col. 1. † 25. dispensation given me fully to *p.* word
28. whom we *p.* warning every man, in all wisdom
2 *Tim.* 4. 2. *p.* the word, be instant in season

PREACHED.

Ps. 40. 9. I have *p.* righteousness in great congregat.
Mat. 11. 5. the poor have the gospel *p.* to them
Mark 1. 7. John *p.* saying, there cometh one after me
39. he *p.* in their synagogues through Galilee
2. 2. many were gathered, he *p.* the word to them
6. 12. they went and *p.* that men should repent
16. 20. they went forth and *p.* every where
Luke 3. 18. many other things *p.* he to the people
4. 44. he *p.* in the synagogues of Galilee
16. 16 since that time the kingdom of God is *p.*
24. 47. that remission of sin should be *p.* in his name
Acts 3. 20. Jesus Christ, who before was *p.* to you
4. 2. *p.* through Jesus the resurrection from dead
8. 5. *p.* Christ to Samaria ‖ 35. *p.* Jesus to eunuch
25. they *p.* the word of the Lord, *p.* the gospel
40. Philip *p.* in all cities till he came to Cesarea
9. 20. Saul *p.* Christ in synagogues to be Son of G.
27. Barnabas told how Saul had *p.* boldly at Dam.
10. 37. that word, after the baptism which John *p.*
13. 5. they *p.* the word of God in their synagogues
24. when John had first *p.* before his coming
38. through this man is *p.* to you forgiveness of sins
42. that these words might be *p.* the next sabbath
14. 25. when they had *p.* the word in Perga
15. 36. let us go and visit where we have *p.*
17. 13. the word of God was *p.* of Paul at Berea
18. because he *p.* Jesus and the resurrection
20. 7. Paul *p.* ready to depart on the morrow
1 *Cor.* 9. 27. lest when I have *p.* to others, I myself

1 *Cor.* 15. 2. if ye keep in memory what I *p.* to you
12. if Christ be *p.* that he rose from the dead
2 *Cor.* 1. 19. Jesus who was *p.* among you by us
11. 4. if preach another Jesus whom we have not *p.*
Gal. 1. 8. other gospel than that we have *p.* to you
Eph. 2. 17. came and *p.* peace to you who were afar
Phil. 1. 18. Christ is *p.* and I therein do rejoice
Col. 1. 23. which was *p.* to every creat. under heaven
1 *Tim.* 3. 16. *p.* to Gentiles, believed on in the world
Heb. 4. 2. but the word *p.* did not profit them
6. they to whom it was first *p.* entered not in
1 *Pet.* 3. 19. he went and *p.* to the spirits in prison

See GOSPEL.

PREACHER.

Eccl. 1. 1. the words of the *p.* the son of David
2. vanity of vanities, saith the *p.* all vanity, 12. 8.
12. I the *p.* was king over Israel in Jerusalem
7. 27. behold, this have I found, saith the *p.*
12. 9. because *p.* was wise, he still taught the people
10. the *p.* sought to find out acceptable words
Rom. 10. 14. how shall they hear without a *p.?*
1 *Tim.* 2. 7. whereto I am ordained a *p.* 2 *Tim.* 1. 11.
2 *Pet.* 2. 5. but saved Noah, a *p.* of righteousness

PREACHEST, ETH, ING.

Jonah 3. 2. preach to it the *p.* that I bid thee
Mat. 3. 1. in those days came John *p.* *Luke* 3. 3.
4. 23. *p.* the gospel of the kingdom, 9. 35.
12. 41. rise in judgment, because they repented at the *p.* of Jonas, and a greater is here, *Luke* 11. 32.
Mark 1. 14. Jesus came into Galilee *p.* the gospel
Luke 8. 1. *p.* and shewing glad tidings of the kingd.
9. 6. they went through the towns *p.* the gospel
Acts 8. 4. they went every where *p.* the word
12. *p.* the things concerning the kingdom of God
10. 36. *p.* peace by Jesus Christ, he is Lord of all
11. 19. *p.* the word to none but to the Jews only
20. spake to the Greeks, *p.* the Lord Jesus
15. 35. Paul and Barnabas continued in Antioch *p.*
19. 13. we adjure you by Jesus, whom Paul *p.*
20. 9. as Paul was long *p.* Eutychus sunk with sleep
25. ye all, among whom I have gone *p.* shall see
28. 31. *p.* the kingdom of God, and teaching
Rom. 2. 21. thou that *p.* a man should not steal
10. † 16. Lord, who hath believed our *p.?*
16. 25. to establish you according to the *p.* of Jesus
1 *Cor.* 1. 18. for the *p.* of the cross is foolishness
21. by the foolishness of *p.* to save them that
2. 4. my *p.* was not with enticing words
15. 14. if Christ be not risen, then is our *p.* vain
2 *Cor.* 1. † 18. our *p.* toward you was not yea
10. 14. come as far as to you, *p.* gospel of Christ
11. 4. if he that cometh *p.* another Jesus
Gal. 1. 23. he *p.* the faith which once he destroyed
2 *Tim.* 4. 17. that by me *p.* might be fully known
Tit. 1. 3. hath in due times manifes. his word thro' *p.*

PRECEPT, S.

Neh. 9. 14. commandedst them *p.* and statutes
Psal. 119. 4. thou hast commanded us to keep thy *p.*
15. I will meditate in thy *p.* 78.
27. make me to understand the way of thy *p.*
40. behold, I have longed after thy *p.* quicken me
45. for I seek thy *p.* ‖ 87. I forsook not thy *p.*
56. this I had, because I kept thy *p.* 100, 168.
63. keep thy *p.* 69, 134. ‖ 93. never forget thy *p.*
94. I am thine, save me, for I have sought thy *p.*
104. through thy *p.* I get understanding, and hate
110. wicked laid snare, yet I erred not from thy *p.*
128. therefore I esteem all thy *p.* to be right
141. I am small, yet do not I forget thy *p.*
159. consider how I love thy *p.* quicken me
173. help me, for I have chosen thy *p.*
Isa. 28. 10. for *p.* must be upon *p.* on *p.* 13.
29. 13. their fear is taught by the *p.* of men
Jer. 35. 18. because ye have kept all Jonadab's *p.*
Dan. 9. 5. we have rebelled by depart. from thy *p.*
Mark 10. 5. for hardn. of heart he wrote you this *p.*
Heb. 9. 19. for when Moses had spoken every *p.*

PRECIOUS.

Gen. 24. 53. he gave to Rebekah's mother *p.* things
Deut. 33. 13. blessed, for the *p.* things of heaven
14. for *p.* fruits brought forth by sun and moon
15. and for the *p.* things of the lasting hills
16. for *p.* things of the earth, and fulness thereof
1 *Sam.* 3. 1. the word of the Ld. was *p.* in those days
18. † 30. David behaved so that his name was *p.*
26. 21. because my soul was *p.* in thine eyes
2 *Kings* 1. 13. let my life be *p.* in thy sight, 14.
20. 13. Hezekiah shewed them *p.* things, *Isa.* 39. 2.
2 *Chr.* 20. 25. and *p.* jewels which they stripped off
21. 3. Jehoshaphat gave them gifts of *p.* things
32. † 23. many brought *p.* things to Hezekiah
Ezra 1. 6. strengthened their hands with *p.* things
8. 27. two vessels of fine copper, *p.* as gold
Job 28. 10. and his eye seeth every *p.* thing
16. cannot be valued with the *p.* onyx or sapphire
Psal. 36. † 7. how *p.* is thy loving kindness!
49. 8. for the redemption of their soul is *p.*
72. 14. and *p.* shall their blood be in his sight
116. 15. *p.* in sight of Ld. is the death of his saints
126. 6. he that goeth forth bearing *p.* seed
133. 2. it is like the *p.* ointment on the head
139. 17. how *p.* also are thy thoughts to me, O God
141. † 5. let not their *p.* oil break my head
Prov. 1. 13. we shall find all *p.* substance
3. 15. wisdom is more *p.* than rubies, and all things
6. 26. the adulteress will hunt for the *p.* life
12. 27. but the substance of a diligent man is *p.*
20. 15. but lips of knowledge are a *p.* jewel
24. 4. chambers filled with all *p.* and pleasant riches
Eccl. 7. 1. a good name is better than *p.* ointment
Isa. 13. 12. I will make a man more *p.* than fine gold
28. 16. I lay in Zion a *p.* corner-stone, 1 *Pet.* 2. 6.
43. 4. since thou wast *p.* in my sight been honour.
Jer. 15. 19. if thou take the *p.* from the vile
20. 5. I will deliver all the *p.* things thereof
Lam. 4. 2. the *p.* sons of Zion, comparable to gold
Ezek. 22. 25. have taken the treasure and *p.* things
27. 20. Dedan was merch. in *p.* clothes for chariots
Dan. 11. 8. and shall carry away their *p.* vessels
43. he shall have power over all *p.* things
Zech. 14. † 6. in that day light shall not be *p.*

Mat. 26. 7. there came to him a woman, having an alabaster box of very *p.* ointment, *Mark* 14. 3.
Jam. 5. 7. the husbandman waiteth for the *p.* fruit
1 *Pet.* 1. 7. trial of your faith much more *p.* than gold
19. but with the *p.* blood of Christ, as of a lamb
2. 4. as to a living stone, chosen of God, and *p.*
7. to you therefore which believe he is *p.*
2 *Pet.* 1. 1. that have obtained like *p.* faith with us
4. are given to us exceeding great and *p.* promises
Rev. 18. 12. for no man buyeth their *p.* vessels
21. 11. her light was like to a stone most *p.*

PRECIOUSNESS.

Psal. 37. † 20. enemies of the Lord as the *p.* of lambs

PREDESTINATE.

This word is taken for the design that God has been pleased to have from all eternity, of bringing by his free grace to faith and eternal salvation, some certain persons, whom he loved in Christ; *whilst he leaves others to continue in their infidelity, or in their corruptions: Those that are so left are the* Reprobate, *and the others are the* Elect, *or* Predestinated.

Rom. 8. 29. for whom he did foreknow, he did *p.*
30. and whom he did *p.* them he also called

PREDESTINATED.

Eph. 1. 5. having *p.* us to the adoption of sons
11. being *p.* according to the purpose of him

PRE-EMINENCE.

Eccl. 3. 19. a man hath no *p.* above a beast
Col. 1. 18. that in all things he might have the *p.*
3 *John* 9. Diotrephes, who loveth to have the *p.*

PREFER.

Ps. 137. 6. if I *p.* not Jerusalem above my chief joy

PREFERRED, ING.

Esth. 2. 9. and he *p.* her and her maidens
Dan. 6. 3. Daniel was *p.* above the presidents
John 1. 15. he that cometh after me is *p.* before me, 27.
30. who is *p.* before me, for he was before me
Rom. 12. 10. in honour *p.* one another
1 *Tim.* 5. 21. observe, without *p.* one before another

PREJUDICE.

1 *Tim.* 5. † 21. observe these things without *p.*

PRE-MEDITATE.

Mark 13. 11. neither *p.* but whatsoever is given

PREPARATION.

1 *Chron.* 22. 5. I will therefore now make *p.* for it
Nah. 2. 3. with flaming torches in the day of *p.*
Mat. 27. 62. the next day that followed the day of *p.*
Mark 15. 42. *Luke* 23. 54. *John* 19. 14, 31, 42.
Eph. 6. 15. feet shod with *p.* of the gospel of peace

PREPARATIONS.

Prov. 16. 1. *p.* of the heart of man from the Lord

PREPARE

Signifies, [1] *To get or make ready,* Josh. 1. 11. [2] *To fit and qualify,* Rom. 9. 23. [3] *To appoint,* Mat. 20. 23. [4] *To be fixed,* Psal. 57. † 7. [5] *To direct, guide, and establish,* 1 Chron. 29. 18.

Exod. 15. 2. my God, and I will *p.* him a habitation
16. 5. on sixth day they shall *p.* that they bring in
Lev. 14. † 36. priest shall command they *p.* the house
Num. 15. 5. for a drink offering *p.* the fourth part
6. or for a ram *p.* thou for a meat offering
12. according to the number that ye shall *p.*
23. 1. Balaam said, *p.* me seven oxen, five rams
29. build me seven altars, and *p.* seven bullocks
Deut. 19. 3. thou shalt *p.* thee a way, divide coasts
Josh. 1. 11. *p.* you victuals to pass over Jordan
22. 26. we said, let us now *p.* to build us an altar
1 *Sam.* 7. 3. *p.* your hearts to the Lord, and serve him
1 *Kings* 18. 44. say to Ahab, *p.* chariot, get thee down
1 *Chron.* 9. 32. to *p.* shew-bread every sabbath
29. 18. O Lord God, *p.* their heart unto thee
2 *Chron.* 2. 9. to *p.* me timber in abundance
31. 11. *p.* chambers ‖ 35. 4. and *p.* yourselves
35. 6. sanctify yourselves, and *p.* your brethren
Esth. 5. 8. come to banquet that I shall *p.* for them
Job 8. 8. and *p.* thyself to the search of their fathers
11. 13. if thou *p.* thine heart toward him
27. 16. tho' he *p.* raiment as clay ‖ 17. he may *p.* it
Psal. 10. 17. Lord, thou wilt *p.* their heart
59. 4. they *p.* themselves without my fault
61. 7. O *p.* mercy and truth, which may preserve
107. 36. that they may *p.* a city for habitation
Prov. 24. 27. *p.* thy work without, and make it fit
30. 25. yet they *p.* their meat in the summer
Isa. 14. 21. *p.* slaughter for his children for iniquity
21. 5. *p.* the table, watch in the watch-tower
40. 3. of him that crieth, *p.* ye way of Lord, *Mal.* 3. 1. *Mat.* 3. 3. *Mark* 1. 2, 3. *Luke* 1. 76.
20. he seeketh a workman to *p.* a graven image
57. 14. and shall say, cast ye up, *p.* the way
62. 10. *p.* ye the way of the people, cast up
65. 11. they that *p.* a table for that troop
Jer. 6. 4. *p.* ye war against her, arise, let us go up
12. 3. and *p.* them for the day of slaughter
22. 7. I will *p.* destroyers against thee
46. 14. say ye, stand fast and *p.* thee, sword shall
51. 12. set up watchmen, *p.* the ambushes
27. blow the trumpet, *p.* nations against her, 28.
Ezek. 4. 15. and thou shalt *p.* thy bread therewith
12. 3. *p.* thee stuff for removing, and remove
35. 6. I will *p.* thee to blood, blood shall pursue
38. 7. *p.* for thyself, thou and all thy company
43. 25. *p.* every day a goat, they shall also *p.*
45. 17. the prince shall *p.* the sin offering
22. on that day prince shall *p.* for himself, 46. 12.
24. he shall *p.* a meat offering, 46. 7, 14.
46. 2. the priest shall *p.* his burnt offering, 13.
15. they shall *p.* the lamb and meat offering
Joel 3. 9. *p.* war ‖ *Amos* 4. 12. *p.* to meet thy God
Mic. 3. 5. they even *p.* war against him
Mat. 11. 10. messenger, who shall *p.* way before thee
26. 17. where wilt thou that we *p.* for thee to eat the passover? *Mark* 14. 12. *Luke* 22. 8, 9.
Luke 3. 4. saying, *p.* ye the way of the Lord, 7. 27.
John 14. 2. I go to *p.* a place for you
3. if I go and *p.* a place for you, I will come ag.
1 *Cor.* 14. 8. who shall *p.* himself to the battle?
Philem. 22. but withal *p.* me also a lodging

PREPARED.

Gen. 24. 31. I *p.* the house and room for camels

Gen. 41. † 32. dream doubled, for the thing is *p.* of G.
Exod. 12. 39. neither had they *p.* any victual
23. 20. to bring thee into the place I have *p.*
Num. 21. 27. let the city of Sihon be built and *p.*
23. 4. I have *p.* seven altars, and have offered
2 *Sam.* 15. 1. Absalom *p.* chariots and horses
1 *Kings* 1. 5. Adonijah *p.* ‖ 5. 18. they *p.* timber
6. 19. the oracle he *p.* in the house within
2 *Kings* 6. 23. he *p.* provision and sent them away
1 *Chr.* 12. 39. for their brethren had *p.* for them
15. 1. David *p.* a place for ark of God, and pitched for it a tent, 3, 12. 2 *Chron.* 1. 4. | 3. 1.
22. 3. David *p.* iron in abundance for the nails
5. David *p.* abund. before his death, 14. | 29. 2.
2 *Chron.* 8. 16. all the work of Solomon was *p.*
12. 14. Rehoboam *p.* not his heart to seek the Ld.
19. 3. Jehoshaphat *p.* his heart to seek God
20. 33. for as yet the people had not *p.* their heart
26. 14. Uzziah *p.* shields and spears for them
27. 6. Jotham *p.* his ways before the Lord
29. 19. the vessels Ahaz cast away we have *p.*
36. he rejoiced that God had *p.* the people
31. 11. they *p.* chambers in the house of the Lord
35. 10. the service was *p.* the priests stood, 16.
20. after this, when Josiah had *p.* the temple
Ezra 7. 10. Ezra had *p.* his heart to the law
Neh. 5. 18. now that which was *p.* for me daily
8. 10. and send to them for whom nothing is *p.*
13. 5. he had *p.* for him a great chamber
Esth. 5. 4. to the banquet that I have *p.* 12. | 6. 14.
6. 4. to hang Mordecai on gallows Haman *p.* 7. 10.
Job 28. 27. he *p.* it, yea, and searched it out
29. 7. when I *p.* my seat in the street
Psal. 7. 13. he *p.* for him the instruments of death
9. 7. he hath *p.* his throne for judgment
57. 6. they have *p.* a net for my steps
† 7. my heart is *p.* I will sing and give praise
68. 10. thou hast *p.* of thy goodness for the poor
74. 16. thou hast *p.* the light and the sun
78. † 8. a generation that *p.* not their hearts
103. 19. the Lord hath *p.* his throne in the heavens
Prov. 3. † 19. by understanding he *p.* the heavens
8. 27. when he *p.* the heavens, I was there
19. 29. judgments are *p.* for scorners, and stripes
21. 31. the horse is *p.* against the day of battle
Isa. 2. † 2. mountain of the Lord's house shall be *p.*
16. † 5. in mercy shall the throne be *p.*
30. 33. Tophet of old, for the king it is *p.*
64. 4. neither hath the eye seen what he hath *p.*
Ezek. 23. 41. a stately bed, and a table *p.* before it
28. 13. workmanship of the pipes was *p.* in thee
38. 7. be thou *p.* and prepare for thyself
Dan. 2. 9. for ye have *p.* lying words to speak
Hos. 2. 8. her silver and gold which they *p.* for Baal
6. 3. his going forth is *p.* as the morning
Jonah 1. 17. now the Lord had *p.* a great fish
4. 6. God *p.* a gourd ‖ 7. a worm ‖ 8. an east wind
Nah. 2. 5. make haste, and the defence shall be *p.*
Zeph. 1. 7. for the Lord hath *p.* a sacrifice
Mat. 20. 23. it is not mine to give, but it shall be given to them for whom it is *p.* *Mark* 10. 40.
22. 4. tell them, behold, I have *p.* my dinner
25. 34. inherit the kingdom *p.* ‖ 41. into fire *p.*
Mark 14. 15. will shew you a large upper room *p.*
Luke 1. 17. to make ready a people *p.* for the Lord
2. 31. which thou hast *p.* before face of all people
12. 47. which knew his Lord's will, but *p.* not
23. 56. they *p.* spices, and rested the sabbath, 24. 1.
Rom. 9. 23. the vessels of mercy afore *p.* to glory
1 *Cor.* 2. 9. things G. hath *p.* for them that love him
Eph. 2. † 10. good works God hath *p.* to walk in
2 *Tim.* 2. 21. be a vessel *p.* to every good work
Heb. 10. 5. but a body hast thou *p.* me
11. 7. Noah *p.* an ark to the saving of his house
16. their God, for he hath *p.* for them a city
Rev. 8. 6. and the seven angels *p.* to sound
9. 7. the locusts were like to horses *p.* for battle
15. which were *p.* for an hour, a day, and a month
12. 6. and the woman hath a place *p.* of God
16. 12. that the way of kings of east may be *p.*
21. 2. the holy city *p.* as a bride for her husband

PREPAREDST.

Psal. 80. 9. thou *p.* room before it, to take deep root

PREPAREST.

Num. 15. 8. when thou *p.* a bullock for an offering
Psal. 23. 5. thou *p.* a table before me in presence
65. 9. thou waterest the earth, thou *p.* them corn when thou hast so prepared for it

PREPARETH.

2 *Chron.* 30. 19. that *p.* his heart to seek God
Job 15. 35. bring forth vanity, their belly *p.* deceit
Psal. 147. 8. who *p.* rain for earth, maketh grass grow

PREPARING.

Neh. 13. 7. *p.* him a chamber in courts of house of G.
1 *Pet.* 3. 20. in days of Noah, while the ark was *p.*

PRESBYTERY.

1 *Tim.* 4. 14. with laying on of the hands of the *p.*

PRESCRIBED, ING.

Ezra 7. 22. and salt without *p.* how much
Isa. 10. 1. that write grievousness which they have *p.*

PRESENCE.

Gen. 3. 8. hid themselves from the *p.* of the Lord
4. 16. Cain went out from the *p.* of the Lord
27. 30. Jacob was scarce gone from the *p.* of Isaac
45. 3. for Joseph's brethren were troubled at his *p.*
47. 15. for why should we die in thy *p.*? money fails
Exod. 10. 11. they were driven out from Pharaoh's *p.*
33. 14. he said, my *p.* shall go with thee
15. if thy *p.* go not with me, carry us not up hence
35. 20. all Israel departed from the *p.* of Moses
Lev. 22. 3. that soul shall be cut off from my *p.*
Num. 20. 6. Moses went from the *p.* of assembly
1 *Sam.* 18. 11. David avoided out of his *p.* twice
19. 10. but he slipped away out of Saul's *p.* and fled
21. 15. this fellow to play the madman in my *p.*
2 *Sam.* 16. 19. whom should I serve? as I have served in thy father's *p.* so will I be in thy *p.*
17. † 11. I counsel that thy *p.* go to battle
1 *Kings* 12. 2. Jeroboam fled from the *p.* of Solomon
2 *Kings* 3. 14. were it not I regard *p.* of Jehoshaphat
5. 27. and he went out from his *p.* a leper
13. 23. neither cast he them from his *p.* as yet

2 *Kings* 24. 20. till he had cast them out from his *p.*
25. 19. five of them that were in the king's *p.*
1 *Chron.* 16. 27. glory and honour are in his *p.*
33. then shall the trees sing at the *p.* of God
2 *Chron.* 9. 23. the king sought the *p.* of Solomon
20. 9. when we stand before this house in thy *p.*
34. 4. they brake the altars of Baalim in his *p.*
Neh. 2. 1. I had not been before sad in his *p.*
Esth. 7. 6. Haman was afraid at the *p.* of the king
8. 15. Mordecai went from the *p.* of king in apparel
Job 1. 12. Satan went from the *p.* of the Lord, 2. 7.
23. 15. therefore I am troubled at his *p.*
Psal. 9. 3. they shall fall and perish at thy *p.*
16. 11. in thy *p.* fulness of joy, right hand pleasures
17. 2. let my sentence come forth from thy *p.*
31. 20. thou shalt hide them in the secret of thy *p.*
42. † 5. I shall praise him, his *p.* is salvation
51. 11. cast me not away from thy *p.* take not thy
68. 2. let the wicked perish at the *p.* of God
8. heavens dropped, Sinai moved at the *p.* of God
95. 2. come before his *p.* with thanksgiving
97. 5. the hills melted like wax at the *p.* of God
100. 2. come before his *p.* with singing
114. 7. tremble, thou earth, at the *p.* of the Lord
139. 7. whither shall I flee from thy *p.*?
140. 13. the upright shall dwell in thy *p.*
Prov. 14. 7. go from the *p.* of a foolish man
Isa. 1. 7. strangers shall devour your land in your *p.*
19. 1. the idols of Egypt shall be moved at his *p.*
63. 9. and the angel of his *p.* saved them
64. 1. that mountains might flow down at thy *p.*
2. that the nations may tremble at thy *p.*
3. the mountains flowed down at thy *p.*
Jer. 4. 26. all the cities broken down at *p.* of Lord
5. 22. will ye not tremble at my *p.* which have
23. 39. and I will cast you out of my *p.* 52. 3.
Ezek. 38. 20. all the men shall shake at my *p.*
Jonah 1. 3. Jonah rose to flee from the *p.* of the L.
10. men knew he fled from the *p.* of the Lord
Nah. 1. 5. and the earth is burnt at his *p.*
Zeph. 1. 7. hold thy peace at the *p.* of the Lord
Luke 13. 26. we have eaten and drunk in thy *p.*
Acts 3. 19. the times of refreshing come from the *p.*
5. 41. they departed from the *p.* of the council
1 *Cor.* 1. 29. that no flesh should glory in his *p.*
2 *Cor.* 10. 1. who in *p.* am base among you
10. his letters weighty, but his bodily *p.* is weak
Phil. 2. 12. ye have obeyed, not as in my *p.* only
1 *Thess.* 2. 17. being taken from you in *p.* not in heart
2 *Thess.* 1. 9. with destruction from the *p.* of the L.
Jude 24. present you faultless before *p.* of his glory

In the PRESENCE.

Gen. 16. 12. he shall dwell *in the p.* of his brethren
23. 11. *in the p.* of my people I give it thee
18. made sure *in the p.* of the children of Heth
25. 18. Ishmael died *in the p.* of all his brethren
Deut. 25. 9. his brother's wife come *in t. p.* of elders
2 *Sam.* 16. 19. should I not serve *in the p.* of his son
1 *Kings* 8. 22. Solomon stood *in t. p.* of congregation
21. 13. against Naboth, *in the p.* of the people
1 *Chron.* 24. 31. these cast lots *in the p.* of David
Psal. 23. 5. a table *in the p.* of mine enemies
116. 14. now *in the p.* of all his people, 18.
Prov. 17. 18. become surety *in the p.* of his friend
25. 6. put not forth thyself *in the p.* of the king
7. than be put lower *in the p.* of the prince
Jer. 28. 1. Hananiah spake *in the p.* of the princes
11. *in the p.* of people ‖ 32. 12. *in p.* of witnesses
Luke 1. 19. I am Gabriel, that stand *in the p.* of G.
14. 10. thou shalt have worship *in the p.* of them
15. 10. there is joy *in the p.* of the angels of God
John 20. 30. signs did Jesus *in the p.* of his disciples
Acts 3. 13. and denied him *in the p.* of Pilate
16. given him perfect soundness *in the p.* of you all
27. 35. he gave thanks to God *in the p.* of them all
1 *Thess.* 2. 19. are not even ye *in t. p.* of our L. Jes.
Heb. 9. 24. now to appear *in the p.* of God for us
Rev. 14. 10. *in the p.* of holy angels, *in t. p.* of Lamb

PRESENT, *Substantive.*

Gen. 32. 13. he took a *p.* for Esau his brother, 18.
20. for he said, I will appease him with the *p.*
21. so went the *p.* over before him, himself lodged
33. 10. if found grace, then rec. my *p.* at my hand
43. 11. Israel said, carry down the man a *p.*
15. men took the *p.* ‖ 25. they made ready the *p.*
26. they brought him the *p.* in their hand
Judg. 3. 15. by Ehud Israel sent a *p.* to Eglon
17. he brought the *p.* ‖ 18. an end to offer the *p.*
6. 18. depart not till I come and bring forth my *p.*
1 *Sam.* 9. 7. there is not a *p.* for the man of God
25. † 27. let this *p.* be for the young men
30. 26. behold, a *p.* of the spoil of the enemies
1 *Kings* 9. 16. had given it for a *p.* to his daughter
10. 25. they brought every man his *p.* 2 *Chr.* 9. 24.
15. 19. I have sent thee a *p.* of silver and gold
2 *Kings* 8. 8. the king said, take a *p.* in thine hand
9. so Hazael went to meet him, and took a *p.*
16. 8. and sent it for a *p.* to the king of Assyria
17. 4. and brought no *p.* to the king of Assyria
18. 31. make an agreement by a *p.* *Isa.* 36. 16.
20. 12. sent letters and a *p.* to Hezekiah, *Isa.* 39. 1.
Isa. 18. 7. *p.* brought to Lord of hosts for a people
Ezek. 27. 15. they brought for a *p.* horns of ivory
Hos. 10. 6. be carried to Assyria for *p.* to king Jareb

PRESENT, *Participle.*

1 *Sam.* 13. 15. Saul numbered the people *p.* with him
21. 3. give me five loaves, or what there is *p.*
2 *Sam.* 20. 4. assemble Judah, and be thou here *p.*
1 *Kings* 20. 27. Isr. were numbered, and were all *p.*
1 *Chr.* 29. 17. have seen thy people *p.* to offer will.
2 *Chron.* 5. 11. all the priests *p.* were sanctified
30. 21. Israel *p.* at Jerusalem, kept the feast
31. 1. all *p.* went out and brake the images
34. 32. he caused all that were *p.* to stand to it
Ezra 8. 25. king, lords, and all Israel *p.* offered
Esth. 4. 16. gather all the Jews *p.* in Shushan
Psal. 46. 1. God is a very *p.* help in time of trouble
Luke 5. 17. power of the Lord was *p.* to heal them
13. 1. there were *p.* at that season some that told him
18. 30. shall receive manifold more in this *p.* life
John 14. 25. I have spoken, being yet *p.* with you
Acts 10. 33. now are we all *p.* before God, to hear

Acts 21. 18. Paul went with us, all the elders were *p.*
28. 2. kindled a fire, received us because of *p.* rain
Rom. 7. 18. to will is *p.* with me, but how to perform
21. when I would do good, evil is *p.* with me
8. 18. I reckon that the sufferings of this *p.* time
38. nor things *p.* are able to separate us from love
11. 5. even at this *p.* time, there is a remnant
1 *Cor.* 3. 22. things *p.* or things to come, all are yours
4. 11. even to this *p.* hour we both hunger and thirst
5. 3. but *p.* in spirit, have judged as tho' I were *p.*
7. 26. that this is good for the *p.* distress
15. 6. of whom the greater part remain to this *p.*
2 *Cor.* 5. 8. willing rather to be *p.* with the Lord
9. we labour, that whether *p.* or absent
10. 2. I beseech you, that I may not be bold when *p.*
11. 9. when I was *p.* with you and wanted
13. 2. I foretell, as if I were *p.* the second time
10. I write, lest being *p.* I should use sharpness
Gal. 1. 4. that he might deliver us from this *p.* world
4. 18. and not only when I am *p.* with you
20. I desire to be *p.* with you, and to change
2 *Tim.* 4. 10. forsaken me, having lov. this *p.* world
Tit. 2. 12. we should live godly in this *p.* world
Heb. 9. 9. which was a figure for the time the *p.*
12. 11. no chastening for the *p.* seemeth joyous
2 *Pet.* 1. 12. and be established in the *p.* truth

PRESENT, ED.

Gen. 46. 29. Joseph *p.* himself to his father
47. 2. he *p.* five of his brethren to Pharaoh
Exod. 34. 2. and *p.* thyself there to me in the mount
Lev. 2. 8. the meat offering, when it is *p.* to the priest
7. 35. in the day when he *p.* them to minister
9. 12. Aaron's sons *p.* to him the blood, 18.
13. and they *p.* the burnt offering to him
14. 11. the priest shall *p.* the man to be made clean
16. 7. the two goats, and *p.* them before the Lord
10. the scape-goat shall be *p.* before the Lord
27. 8. then he shall *p.* himself before the priest
11. then he shall *p.* the beast before the priest
Num. 3. 6. and *p.* the tribe of Levi before Aaron
Deut. 31. 14. *p.* yourselves before the tabernacle
Josh. 24. 1. they *p.* themselves before God
Judg. 6. 19. Gideon brought it under oak, and *p.* it
20. 2. the tribes of Israel *p.* themselves
1 *Sam.* 10. 19. now *p.* yourselves before the Lord
17. 16. Goliath the Philistine *p.* himself forty days
2 *Chron.* 11. † 13. the Levites *p.* themselves to him
Job 1. 6. the sons of God came to *p.* themselves
2. 1. Satan came to *p.* himself before the Lord
Jer. 36. 7. it may be they will *p.* their supplication
38. 26. I *p.* my supplication before the king
42. 9. ye sent to *p.* your supplication before him
Ezek. 20. 28. they *p.* the provocation of offering
Dan. 9. 18. for we do not *p.* our supplications
Mat. 2. 11. they *p.* to him gifts, gold and myrrh
Luke 2. 22. they brought him to *p.* to the Lord
Acts 9. 41. when he had called the saints, *p.* her alive
23. 33. they *p.* Paul also before the governor
Rom. 12. 1. that ye *p.* your bodies a living sacrifice
2 *Cor.* 4. 14. shall raise us up by Jes. and *p.* us with
11. 2. that I may *p.* you as a chaste virgin to Christ
Eph. 5. 27. he might *p.* it to hims. a glorious church
Col. 1. 22. to *p.* you holy and unblameable
28. that we may *p.* every man perfect in Christ
Jude 24. to him that is able to *p.* you faultless

PRESENTING.

Dan. 9. 20. *p.* my supplication before the Lord

PRESENTLY.

1 *Sam.* 2. 16. let them not fail to burn the fat *p.*
Prov. 12. 16. a fool's wrath is *p.* known
Mat. 21. 19. and *p.* the fig-tree withered away
26. 53. he shall *p.* give me more than twelve legions
Phil. 2. 23. him therefore I hope to send *p.*

PRESENTS.

1 *Sam.* 10. 27. and they brought him no *p.*
1 *Kings* 4. 21. they brought *p.* and served Solomon
2 *Kings* 17. 3. Hoshea gave Shalmanezer *p.*
2 *Chron.* 17. 5. *p.* to Jehosh. 11. ‖ 32. 23. to Hezek.
Psal. 68. 29. kings shall bring *p.* unto thee
72. 10. kings of Tarsh. and the isles shall bring *p.*
76. 11. let all bring *p.* to him that ought to be feared
Mic. 1. 14. therefore shalt give *p.* to Moresheth-gath

PRESERVE

Signifies, [1] *To keep safe or defend,* Psal. 16. 1. [2] *To sustain or uphold,* Psal. 36. 6. [3] *To reserve, save, or keep alive,* Gen. 45. 7.

O thou Preserver of men, *Job* 7. 20. *O thou who, as thou wast the Creator of man, delightest to be, and to be called, the Preserver and Saviour of men: and that waitest to be kind and gracious to men from day to day, as occasion requires; do not deal with me in a way contrary to thine own nature and name, and to the manner of thy dealing with all the rest of mankind. Or,* thou Observer of men, *thou who didst exactly know and diligently observe all the inward motions and outward actions of men;* I have sinned; *and therefore if thou shalt be severe to mark mine iniquities, as thou seemest to be,* I have not what to say or do unto thee.

Gen. 19. 32. that we may *p.* seed of our father, 34.
45. 5. for God did send me before you to *p.* life
7. God sent me to *p.* you a posterity in the earth
Deut. 6. 24. that he might *p.* us alive, as at this day
Psal. 12. 7. thou shalt *p.* them from this generation
16. 1. *p.* me, O God, for in thee do I put my trust
25. 21. let integrity and uprightness *p.* me
32. 7. my hiding place, shalt *p.* me from trouble
40. 11. let thy loving kindness continually *p.* me
41. 2. the Lord will *p.* him and keep him alive
61. 7. prepare mercy and truth which may *p.* him
64. 1. hear me, *p.* my life from fear of the enemy
79. 11. *p.* thou those that are appointed to die
86. 2. *p.* my soul, for I am holy, O thou my God
121. 7. L. *p.* thee from all evil, he shall *p.* thy soul
8. the Lord shall *p.* thy going out and coming in
140. 1. O Lord, *p.* me from the violent man, 4.
Prov. 2. 11. discretion shall *p.* thee, unders. keep thee
4. 6. forsake her not, and she shall *p.* thee
14. 3. but the lips of the wise shall *p.* them
20. 28. mercy and truth *p.* the king, his throne
22. 12. the eyes of the Lord *p.* knowledge

Isa. 31. 5. and passing over he will *p.* Jerusalem
49. 8. I will *p.* thee, and give thee for a covenant
Jer. 49. 11. thy children, I will *p.* them alive
Hab. 3. † 2. *p.* alive thy work in midst of the years
Luke 17. 33. whoso shall lose his life shall *p.* it
2 *Tim.* 4. 18. Lord will *p.* to his heavenly kingdom

PRESERVED, ETH.

Gen. 32. 30. I have seen God, and my life is *p.*
Josh. 24. 17. and *p.* us in all the way we went
1 *Sam.* 30. 23. Lord hath given us, who hath *p.* us
2 *Sam.* 8. 6. Syrians David's servants, Lord *p.* Dav. whithersoever he went, 1 *Chron.* 18. 6, 13.
Job 10. 12. thy visitation hath *p.* my spirit
29. 2. that I were as in the days when God *p.* me
36. 6. he *p.* not the life of the wicked, gives right
Psal. 31. 23. love Lord, for the Lord *p.* the faithful
37. 28. forsakes not his saints, they are *p.* for ever
97. 10. hate evil, he *p.* the souls of his saints
116. 6. the Lord *p.* the simple, I was brought low
145. 20. the Lord *p.* all them that love him
146. 9. the Lord *p.* the strangers, he relieveth
Prov. 2. 8. he *p.* the way of his saints
16. 17. he that keepeth his way *p.* his soul
Isa. 49. 6. and to restore the *p.* of Israel
Hos. 12. 13. and by a prophet was he *p.*
Mat. 9. 17. but they put new wine into new bottles, and both are *p.* *Luke* 5. 38.
1 *Thess.* 5. 23. your spirit soul and body *p.* blameless
Jude 1. sanctified, and *p.* in Jesus Christ, and called

PRESERVER.

Job 7. 20. what shall I do to thee, O thou *P.* of men?

PRESERVEST.

Neh. 9. 6. thou Lord hast made and *p.* them all
Psal. 36. 6. O Lord, thou *p.* man and beast

PRESIDENTS.

Dan. 6. 2. and over these three *p.* Daniel was first
3. this Daniel was preferred above *p.* and princes
4. the *p.* sought to find occasion against Daniel
6. these *p.* and princes assembled to the king, 7.

PRESS

Signifies, [1] *To squeeze close together*, Gen. 40. 11. [2] *To throng or crowd*, Luke 8. 45. [3] *To urge, or be instant*, Gen. 19. 3. [4] *To pursue and seek after salvation and happiness with a holy boldness, resolution, zeal, and fervency*, Luke 16. 16. Phil. 3. 14. [5] *A crowd or throng*, Luke 19. 3.

The *word* Press *is likewise used, not only for the instrument or machine by which grapes are squeezed*, Isa. 16. 10. *but also for the vessel or vat, wherein the wine runs from the* Press, *and in which it is received and preserved: Whence are these expressions;* He digged a wine press *in his vineyard*, Mat. 21. 33. Thy presses shall burst out with new wine, *Prov.* 3. 10. To draw out of the press, *Hag.* 2. 16. *It was a kind of subterraneous cistern; in which the wine was received and kept, till it was put into jars or vessels of earth or wood.*

Mark 2. 4. could not come nigh for the *p.* *Luke* 8. 19.
5. 27. came in *p.* behind him, touched his garment
30. Jesus turned him about in the *p.* and said
Luke 19. 3. Zaccheus could not see Jesus for the *p.*

PRESS.

Joel 3. 13. for the *p.* is full, the fats overflow
Hag. 2. 16. to draw out fifty vessels out of the *p.*
See WINE.

PRESS-FAT.

Hag. 2. 16. when one came to the *p.* to draw vessels

PRESS, ED, ETH.

Gen. 19. 3. Lot *p.* on the two angels at Sodom greatly
9. they *p.* sore on Lot, and came near the door
40. 11. and I took the grapes and *p.* them
Judg. 16. 16. Delilah *p.* him daily with her words
2 *Sam.* 13. 25. Absalom *p.* him, he would not go, 27.
Esth. 8. 14. posts *p.* on by the king's command
Psal. 38. 2. arrows stick fast, and thy hand *p.* me sore
Ezek. 23. 3. there were their breasts *p.* they bruised
Amos 2. 13. behold, I am *p.* under you as a cart is *p.*
Mark 3. 10. they *p.* on him for to touch him
Luke 5. 1. as the people *p.* to hear the word of God
6. 38. good measure, *p.* down and shaken together
8. 45. the multitude throng thee and *p.* thee
16. 16. kingdom preached, every man *p.* into it
Acts 18. 5. Paul was *p.* in spirit, and testified to Jews
2 *Cor.* 1. 8. that we were *p.* above measure
Phil. 3. 14. I *p.* toward the mark for the prize

PRESSES.

Prov. 3. 10. thy *p.* shall burst with new wine
Isa. 16. 10. treaders shall tread out no wine in their *p.*

PRESUME.

Deut. 18. 20. the prophet who shall *p.* to speak
Esth. 7. 5. where is he that durst *p.* in his heart to do

PRESUMED.

Num. 14. 44. but they *p.* to go up to the hill top

PRESUMPTUOUS.

Deut. 1. † 43. ye were *p.* and went up the hill
Psal. 19. 13. keep thy servant also from *p.* sins
2 *Pet.* 2. 10. *p.* are they, self-willed, not afraid to sp.

PRESUMPTUOUSLY.

Exod. 21. 14. if a man come *p.* on his neighbour
Num. 15. 30. the soul that doth aught *p.* *Deut.* 17. 12.
Deut. 1. 43. and went *p.* up into the hill
17. 13. the people shall hear, and do no more *p.*
18. 22. but the prophet hath spoken it *p.*

PRETENCE.

Mat. 23. 14. for a *p.* make long prayers, *Mark* 12. 40.
Phil. 1. 18. whether in *p.* or in truth C. is preached

PREVAIL

Signifies, [1] *To have the advantage over, or the better of*, Judg. 16. 5. [2] *To be raised or lifted up*, Gen. 7. 20.

The blessings of thy father have prevailed above the blessings of my progenitors, *Gen.* 49. 26. *The blessings which I thy father have conferred upon thee, are much more considerable than those which I received either from my father* Isaac, *or from my grandfather* Abraham; *and that,* (1) *In the extent of the blessings:* Ishmael *was excluded in one, and* Esau *in the other's blessings; but I have included both* Ephraim *and* Manasseh *in my blessing.* (2) *In the distinctness and clearness of them: For that land of* Canaan, *which was transmitted to* Isaac *and* Jacob *only in the general, was now in some sort particularly distributed to* Joseph *and to the rest of his brethren; and,* (3) *In the nearness of the accomplishment: Now there was a more likely prospect of the multiplication of their seed, than to* Abraham *or* Isaac; *and soon after they multiplied to astonishment, and drew near to the possession of the promised land.*

Gen. 7. 20. fifteen cubits upward did the waters *p.*
Num. 22. 6. peradventure I shall *p.* † 11.
Judg. 16. 5. and see by what means we may *p.*
1 *Sam.* 2. 9. for by strength shall no man *p.*
17. 9. if I *p.* ag. him, then ye shall be our servants
26. 25. thou shalt do great things and shalt still *p.*
1 *Kings* 22. 22. he said, thou shalt persuade him, and *p.* also, go forth and do so, 2 *Chr.* 18. 21.
2 *Chron.* 14. 11. O Lord, let not man *p.* against thee
Esth. 6. 13. thou shalt not *p.* against him
Job 15. 24. they shall *p.* against him, as a king
18. 9. and the robber shall *p.* against him
Psal. 9. 19. arise, O Lord, let not man *p.*
12. 4. who said, with our tongue will we *p.* our lips
65. 3. iniquities *p.* ag. me, as for our transgressions
Prov. 6. † 3. so shalt thou *p.* with thy friend
Eccl. 4. 12. if one *p.* against him, two shall withstand
Isa. 7. 1. to war, but could not *p.* against it
16. 12. Moab shall come to pray, but he shall not *p.*
42. 13. he shall cry, he shall *p.* against his enemies
47. 12. stand now, if so be thou mayest *p.*
Jer. 1. 19. they shall not *p.* against thee, for I am with thee, saith L. of hosts, 15. 20. | 20. 11.
5. 22. though the waves toss, yet can they not *p.*
20. 10. will be enticed, and we shall *p.* against him
Dan. 11. 7. who shall deal against him and shall *p.*
Mat. 16. 18. the gates of hell shall not *p.* against it
27. 24. when Pilate saw he could *p.* nothing
John 12. 19. perceive ye how ye *p.* nothing

PREVAILED.

Gen. 7. 18. the waters *p.* and increased, 19.
24. the waters *p.* on the earth 150 days
30. 8. I have wrestled with my sister and have *p.*
32. 25. when he saw he *p.* not against him
28. thou hast power with God and men, hast *p.*
47. 20. because the famine *p.* over them
49. 26. the blessings of thy father have *p.*
Exod. 17. 11. when Moses held up his hand, Israel *p.* when he let down his hand, Amalek *p.*
Judg. 1. 35. the hand of the house of Joseph *p.*
3. 10. Othniel's hand *p.* against Chushan
4. 24. the children of Israel *p.* against Jabin
6. 2. the hand of Midian *p.* against Israel
1 *Sam.* 17. 50. so David *p.* over Goliath
2 *Sam.* 11. 23. surely the men *p.* against us
24. 4. the king's word *p.* against Joab
1 *Kings* 16. 22. the people that followed Omri *p.*
2 *Kings* 25. 3. the famine *p.* in the city, no bread
1 *Chron.* 5. 2. for Judah *p.* above his brethren
2 *Chr.* 8. 3. Solomon *p.* against Hamath-zobah
13. 18. Judah *p.* because they relied on the Lord
27. 5. Jotham *p.* against the Ammonites
Ps. 13. 4. lest mine enemy say, I have *p.* against thee
129. 2. yet they have not *p.* against me
Jer. 20. 7. thou art stronger than I, and hast *p.*
38. 22. thy friends have *p.* against thee
Lam. 1. 16. I weep because the enemy *p.*
Dan. 7. 21. the same horn *p.* against the saints
Hos. 12. 4. he had power over the angel and *p.*
Obad. 7. the men at peace have deceived thee and *p.*
Luke 23. 23. the voices of the chief priests *p.*
Acts 19. 16. the man in whom the evil spirit was *p.*
20. so mightily grew the word of God and *p.*
Rev. 5. 5. the root of David hath *p.* to open the book
12. 8. the dragon and his angels *p.* not

PREVAILEST.

Job 14. 20. thou *p.* for ever against him, he passeth

PREVAILETH.

Lam. 1. 13. he sent fire into my bones, and it *p.*

PREVENT.

Job 3. 12. why did the knees *p.* me? or the breasts
Psal. 17. † 13. arise, O Lord, *p.* his face
59. 10. the God of my mercy shall *p.* me
79. 8. let thy tender mercies speedily *p.* us
88. 13. in the morning shall my prayer *p.* thee
95. † 2. let us *p.* his face with thanksgiving
119. 148. mine eyes *p.* the night-watches
Amos 9. 10. which say, the evil shall not *p.* us
1 *Thess.* 4. 15. we shall not *p.* them who are asleep

PREVENTED.

2 *Sam.* 22. 6. the snares of death *p.* me, *Psal.* 18. 5.
19. they *p.* me in the day of my calamities, but the Lord was my stay, *Psal.* 18. 18.
Job 30. 27. the days of affliction *p.* me
41. 11. who hath *p.* me that I should repay him?
Psal. 119. 147. I *p.* the dawning of the morning
Isa. 21. 14. they *p.* with their bread him that fled
Mat. 17. 25. Jesus *p.* him, saying, Simon, of whom

PREVENTEST.

Ps. 21. 3. for thou *p.* him with blessings of goodness

PREY.

Jer. 30. 16. and all that *p.* on thee will I give for a *p.*

PREY.

Gen. 49. 9. from the *p.* my son, thou art gone up
27. in the morning he shall devour the *p.*
Num. 14. 3. why brought to this land, that our wives and children shall be a *p.*? 31. *Deut.* 1. 39.
23. 24. Israel not lie down till he eat of the *p.*
31. 12. they brought the captives and *p.* to Moses
26. take the sum of the *p.* that was taken
27. and divide the *p.* into two parts between them
32. and the booty being the rest of the *p.*
Deut. 2. 35. only the cattle we took for a *p.* to ourselves and the spoil, 3. 7. *Josh.* 8. 2, 27. | 11. 14.
Judg. 5. 30. divided the *p.* a *p.* of divers colours
8. 24. that ye would give me the ear-rings of his *p.*
25. did cast every man the ear-rings of his *p.*
2 *Kings* 21. 14. Judah shall become a *p.* and a spoil
Neh. 4. 4. give them for a *p.* in the land of captivity
Esth. 3. 13. take the spoil of them for a *p.* 8. 11.
9. 15. on the *p.* they laid not their hand, 16.
Job 4. 11. the old lion perisheth for lack of *p.*
9. 26. as the eagle that hasteth to the *p.*
Job 24. 5. behold, as wild asses rising betimes for *p*
38. 39. wilt thou hunt the *p.* for the lion?
39. 29. from thence she seeketh the *p.* and her eyes
Psal. 17. 12. like a lion that is greedy of his *p.*
76. 4. more excellent than the mountains of *p.*
104. 21. the young lions roar after their *p.*
111. † 5. he hath given *p.* to them that fear him
124. 6. who hath not given us for a *p.* to their teeth
Prov. 23. 28. she also lieth in wait as for a *p.*
Isa. 5. 29. yea, they shall roar and lay hold of the *p.*
10. 2. that widows may be their *p.* and rob fatherless
6. to take the *p.* of an hypocritical nation
31. 4. as the lion and young lion roaring on his *p.*
33. 23. then is the *p.* of a great spoil divided
42. 22. they are for a *p.* and none delivereth
49. 24. shall the *p.* be taken from the mighty?
25. the *p.* of the terrible shall be delivered
59. 15. that departeth from evil maketh himself a *p.*
Jer. 21. 9. he shall live, and his life shall be to him for a *p.* 38. 2. | 39. 18. | 45. 5.
30. 16. and all that *p.* on thee I will give for a *p.*
Ezek. 7. 21. I will give it to hands of strangers for *p.*
19. 3. a young lion, it learned to catch the *p.*
22. 27. her princes are like wolves ravening the *p.*
26. 12. they shall make a *p.* of thy merchandise
29. 19. he shall take her spoil, and take her *p.*
34. 8. because my flock became a *p.* and meat
22. and my flock shall no more be a *p.* 28.
36. 4. saith the Lord, to the cities that became a *p.*
5. with despiteful minds to cast it out for a *p.*
38. 12. I will go up to take a spoil and a *p.* 13.
Dan. 11. 24. he shall scatter among them the *p.*
Amos 3. 4. will a lion roar when he hath no *p.*?
Nah. 2. 12. the lion filled his holes with *p.* and dens
13. I will cut off thy *p.* from the earth
3. 1. woe to the bloody city, the *p.* departeth not
Zeph. 3. 8. till the day that I rise up to the *p.*

PRICE

Signifies, [1] *The rate of any thing that is bought or sold*, 2 Chron. 1. 16. [2] *Worth or value*, Prov. 31. 10. [3] *Esteem*, 1 Pet. 3. 4. [4] *An opportunity or advantage*, Prov. 17. 16.

Ye are bought with a price, 1 *Cor.* 6. 20. *Ye are redeemed out of the hands of divine justice, and rescued out of the bondage of sin and Satan, by the blood of* Christ, *paid to God, the Supreme Judge, for your ransom, whereby* Christ *has got an everlasting dominion over you.*

Lev. 25. 16. according to years thou shalt increase the *p.* to fewness thou shalt diminish the *p.* 50.
52. shall give him again the *p.* of his redemption
Deut. 23. 18. not bring *p.* of a dog to house of Lord
2 *Sam.* 24. 24. I will buy it at a *p.* 1 *Chr.* 21. 22, 24.
1 *Kings* 10. 28. king Solomon's merchants received the linen yarn at a *p.* 2 *Chron.* 1. 16.
Job 28. 13. man knoweth not the *p.* thereof, 15.
18. for the *p.* of wisdom is above rubies
Ps. 44. 12. thou dost not increase wealth by their *p.*
Prov. 17. 16. why is there a *p.* in hand of a fool?
26. and the goats are the *p.* of the field
31. 10. virtuous woman, for her *p.* far above rubies
Isa. 45. 13. shall let go my capt. not for *p.* nor reward
55. 1. yea, come, buy wine and milk without *p.*
Jer. 15. 13. thy substance to the spoil without *p.*
Lam. 5. † 4. our wood cometh for *p.* unto us
Zech. 11. 12. give me my *p.* weighed for me my *p.*
13. a goodly *p.* that I was prized at of them
Mat. 13. 46. when he had found one pearl of great *p.*
27. 6. not into treasury, because it is the *p.* of blood
9. they took the *p.* of him that was valued
Acts 5. 2. and kept back part of the *p.* 3.
19. 19. they counted the *p.* of the books burnt
1 *Cor.* 6. 20. for ye are bought with a *p.* 7. 23.
1 *Pet.* 3. 4. meek spirit is in sight of God of great *p.*

PRICES.

Acts 4. 34. brought *p.* of the things that were sold

PRICKED.

Psal. 73. 21. thus heart grieved, I was *p.* in my reins
Acts 2. 37. they were *p.* in their heart, and said

PRICKING.

Ezek. 28. 24. shall be no more a *p.* briar to Israel

PRICKS.

Num. 33. 55. those that remain be *p.* in your eyes
Acts 9. 5. it is hard to kick against the *p.* 26. 14.

PRIDE.

Lev. 26. 19. I will break the *p.* of your power
1 *Sam.* 17. 28. I know thy *p.* and naughtiness
2 *Chron.* 32. 26. Hezekiah humbled himself for *p.*
Job 9. † 13. the helpers of *p.* do stoop under him
26. † 12. by understanding he smiteth through *p.*
33. 17. and that he may hide *p.* from man
35. 12. they cry because of the *p.* of evil men
38. † 11. the *p.* of thy waves shall be stayed
41. 15. his scales are his *p.* shut up together
34. he is a king over all the children of *p.*
Psal. 10. 2. the wicked in his *p.* doth persecute
4. through *p.* of his countenance will not seek God
31. 20. thou shalt hide them from the *p.* of man
36. 11. let not the foot of *p.* come against me
59. 12. let them even be taken in their *p.*
73. 6. therefore *p.* compasseth them about as chain
Prov. 8. 13. *p.* do I hate || 11. 2. when *p.* cometh
13. 10. only by *p.* cometh contention
14. 3. in the mouth of the foolish is a rod of *p.*
16. 18. *p.* goeth before destruction, before a fall
21. † 24. who dealeth in the wrath of *p.*
29. 23. a man's *p.* shall bring him low
Isa. 9. 9. that say in the *p.* of their hearts
16. 6. we have heard of the *p.* of Moab, even of his haughtiness and his *p.* *Jer.* 48. 29.
23. 9. hath purposed to stain the *p.* of all glory
25. 11. and he shall bring down their *p.*
28. 1. woe to the crown of *p.* to the drunkards, 3.
Jer. 13. 9. I will mar the *p.* of Judah and Jerusalem
17. my soul shall weep in secret places for your *p.*
49. 16. the *p.* of thy heart hath deceived thee
50. † 31. behold, I am against thee, O thou *p.*
† 32. *p.* shall stumble and fall, none shall raise
Ezek. 7. 10. the rod hath blossomed, *p.* hath budded
16. 49. iniquity of thy sister Sodom *p.* fuln. of bread
56. Sodom was not mentioned in the day of thy *p.*
30. 6. and the *p.* of her power shall come down

Dan. 4. 37. those that walk in *p.* he is able to abase
5. 20. but when his mind was hardened in *p.*
Hos. 5. 5. the *p.* of Israel doth testify, 7. 10.
bad. 3. the *p.* of thy heart hath deceived thee
Nah. 2. † 2. for the Lord hath turned away the *p.* of Jacob and the *p.* of Israel
Zeph. 2. 10. this shall they have for their *p.*
3. 11. I will take them away that rejoice in thy *p.*
Zech. 9. 6. I will cut off the *p.* of the Philistines
10. 11. the *p.* of Assyria shall be brought down
11. 3. roaring of lions, for the *p.* of Jordan is spoiled
Mark. 7. 22. for out of the heart proceedeth *p.*
1 *Tim.* 3. 6. lest being lifted up with *p.* he fall into
1 *John* 2. 16. the *p.* of life, is not of the Father

PRIEST.

The Priest *under the law was a person consecrated and ordained of God, not only to teach the people, and pray for them, but also to offer up sacrifices for his own sins, and those of the people,* Lev. 4. 5, 6.

The Priesthood *was not annexed to a certain family, till after the promulgation of the law of* Moses. *Before that time the first-born of every family, the fathers, the princes, the kings, were priests, born in their city and in their house.* Cain *and* Abel, Noah, Abraham, *and* Job, Abimelech *and* Laban, Isaac *and* Jacob, *offered themselves their own sacrifices. In the solemnity of the covenant that the Lord made with his people at the foot of mount* Sinai, *Moses performed the office of mediator, and young men were chosen from among the children of Israel, to perform the office of priests,* Exod. 24. 5, 6. *But after that the Lord had chosen the tribe of* Levi *to serve him in his tabernacle, and that the priesthood was annexed to the family of* Aaron, *then the right of offering sacrifices to God was reserved to the priests alone of his family,* Num. 16. 40.

The ordinary priests served immediately at the altar, offered the sacrifices, killed and flayed them, and poured their blood at the foot of the altar, 2 Chron. 29. 34. | 35. 11. *They kept up a continual fire upon the altar of burnt sacrifices, and in the lamps of the golden candlestick that was in the holy place; they kneaded the loaves of the shew-bread, baked them, offered them upon the golden altar, and changed them every sabbath day.*

One of the chief employments of the priests, next to attending upon the sacrifices and the service of the temple, was the instruction of the people; the distinguishing the several sorts of leprosy, the causes of divorce, the waters of jealousy, vows, the uncleannesses that were contracted several ways; all these were brought before the priests, Lev. 13. 13. Num. 5. 14, 15. Hos. 4. 6. Mal. 2. 7.

The high priest only had the privilege of entering into the sanctuary once a year, which was the day of solemn expiation, to make atonement for the sins of the whole people, Lev. 16. 2, 3, 4, &c. *God had also appropriated to his person the oracle of his truth; so that when he was habited with the proper ornaments of his dignity, and with the* Urim *and* Thummim, *he gave answers to the questions made to him, and God discovered to him secret and future things,* Exod. 28. 30.

The term Priest *is most properly given to* Christ, *of whom the high priests under the law were types and figures, he being the* High priest, *especially ordained of God, who, by the sacrifice of himself, once offered by himself, and also by his intercession, might reconcile unto, and for ever keep in favour with God, all true believers,* Heb. 7. 17. | 9. 11, 12, 24, 25.

The word is also applied to every true believer, who is enabled to offer up himself spiritual sacrifices of prayer and praise to God, through Jesus Christ, 1 Pet. 2. 5. Rev. 1. 6.

Gen. 14. 18. the *p.* of the most high God, *Heb.* 7. 1.
Exod. 2. 16. the *p.* of Midian had seven daughters
29. 30. that son that is *p.* in his stead, *Lev.* 16. 32.
Lev. 1. 9. the *p.* shall burn it all on the altar, 13, 17. | 2. 2, 9, 16. | 3. 11, 16. | 4. 10. | 31. 35. | 7. 5, 31.
12. the *p.* shall lay them in order on the wood
2. 8. when it is presented to the *p.* he shall bring it
4. 3. if the *p.* that is anointed do sin as the people
6. the *p.* shall dip his finger in the blood, 17.
20. *p.* shall make an atonement for them, 26. | 5. 6. | 6. 7. | 12. 8. | 15. 15, 30. | 16. 30. | 19. 22.
25. and the *p.* shall take of the blood, 30, 34.
5. 8. he shall bring them to the *p.* who shall offer
6. 10. the *p.* shall put on his linen garment
7. 8. the *p.* shall have to himself the skin of offering
9. it shall be the *p.* that offereth it, 14. | 14. 13.
13. 3. the *p.* shall look on the plague in the skin, 5, 6, 17, 20, 21, 25, 26, 27, 30, 31, 32. the *p.* shall look on him, and pronounce him unclean, 8, 11, 20, 22, 25, 30, 44.
4. the *p.* shall shut him up seven days, 5. 31, 33.
6. *p.* shall pronounce him clean, 17. 23, 28, 34.
9. brought to the *p.* ‖ 16. come to the *p.* 14. 2.
14. 11. *p.* that maketh him clean shall present
16. the *p.* shall dip his right finger in the oil
35. that owneth the house shall come and tell *p.*
48. the *p.* shall pronounce the house clean
21. 9. if the daughter of a *p.* profane herself
22. 11. if the *p.* buy any soul with his money
23. 10. ye shall bring a sheaf of first-fruits to the *p.*
11. the *p.* shall wave it before the Lord
27. 8. the *p.* shall value him, according to ability
Num. 5. 8. let the trespass be recompensed to the *p.*
15. then the man shall bring his wife to the *p.*
30. the *p.* shall execute upon her all this law
6. 20. this is holy for the *p.* with the wave-breast
19. 7. the *p.* shall wash and be unclean until even
35. 32. shall not dwell in land till death of high *p.*
Deut. 17. 12. the man that will not hearken to *p.*
20. 2. are come nigh to battle, the *p.* shall approach
26. 3. thou shalt go to the *p.* in those days
Judg. 17. 5. one of his sons, who became his *p.*
10. dwell with me, and be to me a father and a *p.*
13. L. do me good, seeing I have Levite to my *p.*

Judg. 18. 4. Micah hath hired me, and I am his *p.*
19. be to us a *p.* and a father, better be a *p.*
1 *Sam.* 2. 14. all that the *p.* took for himself
15. and said, give flesh to roast for the *p.*
28. did I choose him out of Israel to be my *p.*?
35. and I will raise me up a faithful *p.*
14. 19. while Saul talked to the *p.* the noise
36. then said the *p.* let us draw near to God
21. 4. the *p.* answered, there is no common bread
6. so the *p.* gave him hallowed bread
1 *Kings* 2. 27. Solom. thrust Abiathar from being *p.*
2 *Kings* 11. 15. the *p.* had said, let her not be slain
2 *Chron.* 13. 9. the same may be a *p.* of them that are no gods, but as for us, the Lord is our God
15. 3. Israel hath been without a teaching *p.*
Ezra 2. 63. till there stood up a *p.* *Neh.* 7. 65.
Psal. 110. 4. L. hath sworn, thou art a *p.* for ever after the order of Melchis. *Heb.* 5. 6. | 7. 17, 21.
Isa. 8. 2. I took faithful witnesses, Uriah the *p.*
24. 2. as with the people, so with the *p.*
28. 7. the *p.* and the prophet have erred thro' wine
Jer. 6. 13. to the *p.* every one dealeth falsely, 8. 10.
14. 18. prophet and *p.* go to a land they know not
18. 18. the law shall not perish from the *p.*
23. 11. for both prophet and *p.* are profane
33. when a prophet and *p.* shall ask thee, 34.
29. 26. the Lord made thee *p.* instead of Jehoiada
Lam. 2. 6. and hath despised the king and the *p.*
20. shall the *p.* and prophet be slain in sanctuary
Ezek. 7. 26. but the law shall perish from the *p.*
44. 13. shall not come near to do the office of a *p.*
21. nor shall any *p.* drink wine when they enter
22. or shall take a widow that had a *p.* before
30. ye give to the *p.* the first of your dough
31. the *p.* shall not eat of any thing that is torn
Hos. 4. 4. this people, as they that strive with the *p.*
6. I will reject thee, thou shalt be no *p.* to me
9. and there shall be like people like *p.*
Amos 7. 10. the *p.* of Bethel sent to Jeroboam
Zech. 6. 13. and he shall be a *p.* on his throne
Mal. 2. 7. the *p.* lips should keep knowledge
Mat. 8. 4. see thou tell no man, but go thy way, shew thyself to the *p.* *Mark* 1. 44. *Luke* 5. 14.
Luke 1. 5. a certain *p.* named Zacharias, and his wife
10. 31. by chance there came down a certain *p.*
Acts 14. 13. *p.* of Jupiter brought oxen and garlands
Heb. 7. 3. like Son of God, abideth a *p.* continually
11. what need another *p.* should rise after order
15. after similitude Melchisedec ariseth anoth. *p.*
20. as not without an oath he was made *p.*
8. 4. if he were on earth, he should not be a *p.*
10. 11. every *p.* standeth daily ministering

See Chief.

High PRIEST.

Lev. 21. 10. the *high p.* shall not uncover his head
Num. 35. 25. he shall abide in the city of refuge till the death of the *high p.* *Josh.* 20. 6.
2 *Kings* 12. 10. when much money in chest, the *high p.* came and put it in bags, 2 *Chr.* 24. 11.
22. 4. go to Hilkiah the *high p.* that he may sum
Neh. 3. 1. Eliashib the *high p.* rose up with brethren
Zech. 3. 1. Joshua the *high p.* standing, 8. | 6. 11.
Mat. 26. 3. to the palace of the *high p.* *Luke* 22. 54.
51. one of them struck a servant of the *high p.* and smote off his ear, *Luke* 22. 50. *John* 18. 10.
57. led him to Caiaphas the *high p.* *John* 18. 24.
65. the *high p.* rent his clothes, *Mark* 14. 63.
Mark 2. 26. in the days of Abiathar the *high p.*
John 11. 49. Caiaphas being *high p.* 51. | 18. 13.
18. 15. that disciple was known to the *high p.*
22. saying, answerest thou the *high p.* so?
Acts 4. 6. as many as were of the kindred of *high p.*
7. 1. then said the *high p.* are these things so?
9. 1. Saul went to the *high p.* and desired letters
22. 5. as also the *high p.* doth bear me witness
23. 4. they said, revilest thou God's *high p.*?
Heb. 2. 17. that he might be a faithful *high p.*
3. 1. consider Apostle *High P.* of our profession
4. 14. we have great *h. p.* that is passed into heav.
15. we have not a *h. p.* which cannot be touched
5. 1. for every *high p.* taken from among men
5. Christ glorified not himself to be a *high p.*
10. called an *high p.* after order of Melch. 6. 20.
7. 26. such an *h. p.* became us, who is holy, harml.
8. 1. we have such an *high p.* who is set on throne
3. every *high p.* is ordained to offer gifts and sacr.
9. 7. but into the second went the *high p.* alone
11. Christ being come an *high p.* of good things
25. as the *high p.* entereth into the holy place
10. 21. having an *high p.* over the house of God
13. 11. blood is brought into sanctuary by *high p.*

See Office.

PRIESTS.

Gen. 47. 22. the land of the *p.* bought he not, for the *p.* had a portion assigned them of Pharaoh
26. except the land of the *p.* only, not Pharaoh's
Exod. 19. 6. ye shall be to me a kingdom of *p.*
Lev. 1. 11. the *p.* shall sprinkle the blood, 3. 2.
5. 13. and the remnant shall be the *p.* as an offering
6. 29. all the males among the *p.* shall eat thereof
13. 2. or brought to one of his sons the *p.*
16. 33. he shall make an atonement for the *p.*
22. 10. a sojourner of the *p.* shall not eat
12. if *p.* daughter be married ‖ 13. if widow
23. 20. they shall be holy to the Lord for the *p.*
27. 21. the possession thereof shall be the *p.*
Deut. 18. 3. this shall be the *p.* due from the people
19. 17. shall stand before *p.* and judges that shall be
Josh. 3. 17. the *p.* that bare the ark stood firm
4. 3. take you out where the *p.* feet stood, 9.
6. 4. the *p.* bare seven trumpets of rams' horns, 13.
12. and the *p.* took up the ark of the Lord
Judg. 18. 30. he and his sons were *p.* to tribe of Dan
1 *Sam.* 1. 3. Hophni and Phinehas the *p.* were there
5. 5. nor the *p.* of Dagon tread on the threshold
6. 2. the Philistines called for the *p.* and diviners
22. 17. king said, turn and slay the *p.* of the Lord
18. said to Doeg, turn thou and fall on the *p.*
21. shewed David, that Saul had slain Lord's *p.*
1 *Kings* 8. 3. the elders and the *p.* took up the ark
12. 31. Jeroboam made *p.* of the lowest of the people who were not of the sons of Levi, 13. 33.

1 *Kin.* 13. 2. on thee shall he offer the *p.* of high plac.
2 *Kings* 10. 11. Jehu slew Ahab's *p.* he left him none
19. call me all Baal's *p.* let none be wanting
12. 6. *p.* had not repaired breaches of the house
17. 27. carry thither one of the *p.* ye brought
23. 5. he put down idolatrous *p.* of king of Judah
20. and he slew all the *p.* of the high places
2 *Chron.* 4. 6. the sea was for the *p.* to wash in
5. 12. an hund. twenty *p.* sounding with trumpets
14. the *p.* could not stand to minister for the cloud
6. 41. let thy *p.* be clothed with salvation
8. 14. he appointed the courses of the *p.*
11. 15. he ordained him *p.* for the high places
13. 9. have ye not cast out the *p.* of the Lord?
12. and his *p.* with trumpets to cry alarm
23. 6. none came into the house of Lord save the *p.*
26. 17. with him fourscore *p.* of the Lord
19. while Uzziah was wroth with the *p.*
29. 34. but the *p.* were too few, they could not slay
30. 3. *p.* had not sanctified themselves sufficiently
34. 5. Josiah burnt the bones of the *p.*
35. 2. Josiah set the *p.* in their charges
8. gave it to the *p.* for the passover-offerings
Ezra 6. 18. they set the *p.* in their divisions
20. *p.* were purified, and killed the passover for *p.*
7. 16. of the people and *p.* offering willingly
9. 7. and our *p.* been delivered into hand of kings
Neh. 2. 16. nor had I as yet told it to the *p.*
3. 22. after him repaired the *p.* men of the plain
9. 32. the trouble that hath come on us and our *p.*
34. neither have we nor our *p.* kept thy law
13. 5. where they laid the offerings of the *p.*
Psal. 78. 64. their *p.* fell by the sword, their widows
99. 6. Moses and Aaron among his *p.* and Samuel
132. 9. let thy *p.* be clothed with righteousness
16. I will clothe her *p.* with salvation
Isa. 37. 2. he sent elders of *p.* covered with sackcloth
61. 6. but ye shall be named the *p.* of the Lord
Jer. 1. 18. against the *p.* thereof and people of land
2. 8. the *p.* said not, where is the Lord?
26. their *p.* ashamed ‖ 4. 9. their *p.* astonished
5. 31. and the *p.* bare rule by their means
8. 1. the bones of the *p.* they shall bring out
13. 13. I will fill the *p.* with drunkenness
31. 14. I will satiate the souls of the *p.* with fatness
32. 32. to provoke me to anger, they and their *p.*
48. 7. shall go into captivity with his *p.* 49. 3.
Lam. 1. 4. her *p.* sigh, her virgins are afflicted
19. my *p.* and mine elders gave up the ghost
4. 13. for the iniquities of her *p.* that shed blood
16. they respected not the persons of the *p.*
Ezek. 22. 26. her *p.* violated my law, and profaned
40. 45. he said, this chamber is for the *p.*
44. 30. shall be for the *p.* 45. 4. | 48. 10, 11.
Hos. 5. 1. hear this, O *p.* and hearken, O Israel
6. 9. company of *p.* murder in the way by consent
Joel 1. 9. the *p.* the Lord's ministers mourn, 13. | 2. 17.
Mic. 3. 11. the *p.* thereof teach for hire
Zeph. 1. 4. I will cut off the names of the *p.*
3. 4. her *p.* have polluted the sanctuary
Hag. 2. 11. ask now the *p.* concerning the law
Mal. 1. 6. to you, O *p.* that despise my name
2. 1. and now, O *p.* this commandment is for you
Mat. 12. 4. not lawful but only for the *p.* to eat
5. the *p.* in the temple profane the sabbath, and are blameless, *Mark* 2. 26. *Luke* 6. 4.
Mark 2. 26. which is not lawful to eat but for the *p.*
Luke 17. 14. go shew yourselves to the *p.*
Acts 4. 1. the *p.* and captain came upon them
6. 7. a company of *p.* were obedient to the faith
19. 14. the sons of Sceva chief of the *p.* did so
Heb. 7. 21. those *p.* were made without an oath
23. they truly were many *p.* not suffered to continue
8. 4. seeing there are *p.* that offer gifts by law
9. 6. the *p.* went always into the first tabernacle
Rev. 1. 6. hath made us kings and *p.* to God, 5. 10.
20. 6. shall be *p.* of God and of Christ, and reign

See Chief, Levites, Office.

High PRIESTS.

Luke 3. 2. Annas and Caiaphas were *high p.*
Heb. 7. 27. needeth not daily as those *high p.* to offer
28. for the law maketh men *high p.* which have

PRIESTHOOD.

Exod. 40. 15. for their anointing shall be an everlasting *p.* throughout their generations, *Num.* 25. 13.
Num. 16. 10. and seek ye the *p.* also?
18. 1. thou and sons shall bear iniquity of your *p.*
Josh. 18. 7. for *p.* of the Lord is their inheritance
1 *Sam.* 2. † 36. put me into somewhat about the *p.*
Ezra 2. 62. as polluted from the *p.* *Neh.* 7. 64.
Neh. 13. 29. they defiled the *p.* the covenant of *p.*
Heb. 7. 5. they of Levi, who receive the office of *p.*
11. if perfection were by the Levitical *p.*
12. for the *p.* being changed, there is made
14. Moses spake nothing concerning the *p.*
24. but this man hath an unchangeable *p.*
1 *Pet.* 2. 5. an holy *p.* ‖ 9. ye are a royal *p.*

PRINCE.

This name is given, [1] *To God, who is the supreme Ruler and Governor,* Dan. 8. 11. [2] *To Christ, who is called the* Prince of Peace, *Isa.* 9. 6. *He is the only purchaser and procurer of peace between* God *and* men, Isa. 53. 5. *and of peace between men and men, between* Jews *and* Gentiles, *Eph.* 2. 15. *and he left peace as his legacy to his disciples,* John 14. 27. *He is called the* Prince of Life, *Acts* 3. 15. *As God, he is the author of our temporal life, in whom we live and move, and in whose hands is our breath; and as Mediator, he is the guide and way to eternal life,* John 14. 6. *He is also called,* the Prince of the kings of the earth, *Rev.* 1. 5. *He, as King, rules over all, even his greatest and most powerful enemies.* [3] *To the chief of the priests, called the* princes of the sanctuary, Isa. 43. 28. [4] *To the Roman emperor,* Dan. 9. 26. [5] *To men of princely excellency and worth,* Eccl. 10. 7. [6] *To the nobles, counsellors, and officers in a kingdom,* Isa. 10. 8. [7] *To the chief, or principal men of families, or tribes,* Num. 17. 2. [8] *To the devil, called the* prince of this world, *John* 12. 31. *who boasts of having all the kingdoms of the earth at his disposal,* Mat. 4. 9.

Gen. 23. 6. thou art a mighty p. amongst us
32. 28. as a p. hast thou power with God and men
34. 2. when Shechem, p. of the country, saw her
41. † 45. he gave him to wife Asenath the daughter of Potipherah, p. of On, † 50. | 46. † 20.
Exod. 2. 14. who made thee a man, a p. over us?
† 16. the p. of Midian had seven daughters
Num. 7. 11. each p. shall offer on his day
16. 13. except make thyself altogether a p. over us
17. 6. for each p. a rod, even twelve rods
25. 18. Cozbi the daughter of a p. of Midian
34. 18. take one p. of every tribe to divide the land
Josh. 5. † 14. as a p. of host of the Lord am I come
22. 14. of each chief house a p. through all Israel
2 Sam. 3. 38. know ye not there is a p. fallen in Israel
20. † 26. Ira the Jairite was a p. about David
1 Kings 11. 34. I will make him p. all his days
14. 7. and made thee a p. over my people, 16. 2.
Ezra 1. 8. numbered to Sheshbazzar the p. of Judah
Job 21. 28. for ye say, where is the house of the p.?
31. 37. as a p. would I go near to him
Prov. 14. 28. but in want of people is destruct. of p.
17. 7. much less do lying lips become a p.
25. 7. shouldest be put lower in presence of the p.
15. by long forbearing is a p. persuaded
28. 16. p. that wanteth understand. is an oppressor
Cant. 7. 1. how beautiful are thy feet, O p. daughter!
Isa. 9. 6. the P. of peace || 24. † 2. so with the p.
Jer. 51. 59. and this Seraiah was a quiet p.
Ezek. 7. 27. the p. shall be clothed with desolation
12. 10. this burden concerneth the p. in Jerusalem
12. and p. shall bear on his shoulder in twilight
21. 25. thou profane wicked p. of Isr. day is come
28. 2. son of man, say to the p. of Tyrus
30. 13. be no more a p. of the land of Egypt
34. 24. and my servant David a p. among them
37. 25. my servant David shall be their p. for ever
38. 2. son of man, prophesy against Gog, Magog, the chief p. of Meshech and Tubal, 3. | 39. 1.
44. 3. this gate is for the p. the p. shall sit in it
45. 7. and a portion shall be for the p. on one side
17. it shall be the p. part to give burnt offerings
22. on that day shall the p. prepare a bullock
46. 2. the p. shall enter by the way of the porch
4. the burnt offering that the p. shall offer
8. and when the p. shall enter he shall go in
10. and the p. in the midst of them, shall go in
12. when p. prepares a voluntary burnt offering
16. if the p. give a gift to any of his sons
17. after, it shall return to the p. but inheritance
18. p. shall not take of the people's inheritance
48. 21. residue shall be for the p. on the one side
Dan. 1. 7. to whom p. of the eunuchs gave names
8. he requested of p. of the eunuchs not to defile
9. Daniel in favour with the p. of the eunuchs
8. 11. he magnified himself even to p. of the host
25. he shall also stand up ag. the p. of princes
9. 25. to build Jerusalem, unto the Messiah, the P.
26. people of the p. that shall come shall destroy
10. 13. but the p. of Persia withstood me
20. to fight with p. of Persia, p. of Grecia come
21. none holdeth with me, but Michael your p.
11. 18. but a p. for his own behalf shall cause
22. shall be broken, also the p. of the covenant
12. 1. then shall Michael stand up, the great p.
Hos. 3. 4. Israel shall abide many days without a p.
12. † 3. Jacob by his strength was a p. with God
Mic. 7. 3. the p. and the judge ask for a reward
Mat. 9. 34. the Pharisees said, he casteth out devils by the p. of devils, 12. 24. Mark 3. 22.
John 12. 31. the p. of this world shall be cast out
14. 30. for the p. of this world cometh, and hath
16. 11. because the p. of this world is judged
Acts 3. 15. and killed P. of life whom God raised
5. 31. him hath God exalted to be a P. and Saviour
Eph. 2. 2. according to p. of the power of the air
Rev. 1. 5. Jesus Christ the P. of kings of the earth

PRINCES.

Gen. 12. 15. the p. also of Pharaoh saw Sarai
17. 20. twelve p. shall Ishmael beget, 25. 16.
47. † 22. the land of the p. bought he not, † 26.
Exod. 12. † 12. and against all the p. of Egypt will I execute judgment, I am the Lord
Num. 7. 3. a waggon for two p. || 10. the p. offered
16. 2. rose up 250 p. || 21. 18. the p. digged a well
22. 8. and the p. of Moab abode with Balaam
15. Balak sent yet again p. more honourable than
24. † 17. sceptre out of Israel shall smite p. of Moab
Josh. 9. 15. p. of the congregation sware to them
13. 21. whom Moses smote with the p. of Midian
22. 14. with Phinehas ten p. sent to Reuben
Judg. 5. 3. hear, O ye kings, give ear, O ye p.
15. and the p. of Issachar were with Deborah
7. 25. they took the two p. of the Midianites
8. 14. he described to him the p. of Succoth
1 Sam. 2. 8. he raiseth the poor, to set them among p.
29. 4. the p. of the Philistines were wroth
2 Sam. 8. † 18. and David's sons were p.
19. † 6. that p. or servants are not to thee
1 Kings 20. 14. even by the young men of the p.
1 Chron. 4. 38. these were p. in their families
28. 21. p. and people will be at thy command
2 Chron. 28. 14. armed men left spoil before the p.
30. 12. one heart to do the commandment of p.
24. and the p. gave a thousand bullocks
35. 8. his p. gave willingly to the people to priests
36. 18. treasures of his p. brought to Babylon
Ezra 7. 28. and before all the king's mighty p.
9. 2. yea, the hand of the p. hath been chief
10. 8. come according to the counsel of the p.
Neh. 9. 34. neither have our p. kept thy law
38. our p. Levites, and priests seal to it
Esth. 1. 3. he made a feast to all his p. 2. 18.
5. 11. how he had advanced him above the p.
6. 9. to the hand of one of the king's noble p.
Job 3. 15. had been at rest with p. that had gold
12. 19. leadeth p. away spoiled, overthrows mighty
21. he poureth contempt on p. and weakeneth
29. 9. the p. refrained talking, and laid their hands
34. 18. is it fit to say to p. ye are ungodly?
19. to him that accepteth not the persons of p.
Psal. 45. 16. thou mayest make p. in all the earth
47. 9. the p. of the people are gathered toge.
68. 27. the p. of Zebulun, the p. of Naphtali
31. p. shall come out of Egypt, Ethiopia stretch
76. 12. he shall cut off the spirit of p. he is terrible
82. 7. die like men, and fall like one of the p.
105. 22. to bind his p. at his pleasure, and teach
107. 40. he poureth contempt upon p. and causeth
113. 8. he may set him with p. even with the p.
118. 9. to trust in Lord, than to put confidence in p.
119. 23. p. also did sit and speak against me
161. p. have persecuted me without a cause
146. 3. put not your trust in p. nor in son of man
148. 11. p. and all judges of the earth, praise
Prov. 8. 15. by me p. decree justice || 16. p. rule
17. 26. it is not good to strike p. for equity
19. 10. much less for a servant to rule over p.
28. 2. for transgression, many are the p. thereof
31. 4. it is not for p. to drink strong drink
Eccl. 10. 7. p. walking as servants on the earth
16. O land, when thy p. eat in the morning
17. blessed art thou, when thy p. eat in due season
Isa. 1. 23. thy p. are rebellious and thieves
3. 4. and I will give children to be their p.
14. the Lord will enter into judgment with the p.
10. 8. are not my p. altogether kings?
19. 11. p. of Zoan fools, p. of Noah deceived, 13.
21. 5. arise, ye p. and anoint the shield
23. 8. against Tyre, whose merchants are p.
30. 4. his p. were at Zoan, his ambassadors came
31. 9. his p. shall be afraid of the ensign
32. 1. and p. shall rule in judgment
34. 12. and all her p. shall be nothing
40. 23. that bringeth the p. to nothing
41. 25. and he shall come upon p. as on mortar
43. 28. I have profaned the p. of the sanctuary
49. 7. p. also shall worship because of the Lord
Jer. 1. 18. made thee brasen walls against the p.
2. 26. they, their kings and p. are ashamed
4. 9. the heart of the p. shall be astonished
8. 1. they shall bring out the bones of his p.
17. 25. kings and p. sitting on the throne of David
24. 8. so will I give the king of Judah and his p.
26. 16. the p. said, this man is not worthy to die
32. 32. they and their kings and p. provoke me
34. 21. his p. I will give to their enemies
37. 15. the p. were wroth with Jeremiah
38. 17. if thou go forth to the king of Babylon's p.
25. if the p. hear that I have talked with thee
44. 21. the incense that ye and your p. burn
48. 7. Chemosh and his p. go into captivity, 49. 3.
49. 38. I will destroy from thence the p.
50. 35. a sword is on her p. and her wise men
51. 57. I will make drunk her p. and wise men
Lam. 1. 6. her p. are become like harts that find
2. 2. he hath polluted the kingdom and p. thereof
9. her kings and p. are among the Gentiles
5. 12. p. are hanged up by their hand
Ezek. 22. 27. her p. like wolves ravening the prey
23. 15. in dyed attire, all of them p. to look to
32. 29. Edom and her p. with their might
30. there the p. of the north, all of them
39. 18. and ye shall drink the blood of the p.
45. 8. my p. shall no more oppress my people
Dan. 3. 2. the king sent to gather together the p.
6. 1. pleased to set over the kingdom 120 p.
3. this Daniel was preferred above the p.
4. the p. sought to find occasion against Daniel
8. 25. he shall stand up against the prince of p.
9. 6. the prophets who spake in thy name to our p.
8. confusion of face to our p. and fathers
10. 13. Michael one of the chief p. came to me
11. 5. one of his p. shall be strong above him
Hos. 7. 3. they make p. glad with their lies
5. the p. have made him sick with wine
16. their p. shall fall by the sword for rage
8. 4. they have made p. and I knew it not
10. shall sorrow for the burthen of the king of p.
9. 15. I love them no more, all their p. are revolters
13. 10. of whom thou saidst, give me a king and p.
Amos 1. 15. their king go into captivity, he and his p.
Mic. 3. 1. hear, ye p. of the house of Israel, 9.
5. † 5. shall raise against him eight p. of men
Hab. 1. 10. the p. shall be a scorn unto them
Zeph. 1. 8. I will punish the p. and king's children
3. 3. her p. within her are roaring lions
Mat. 20. 25. the p. of Gentiles exercise dominion
1 Cor. 2. 6. nor the wisdom of the p. of this world
8. which none of the p. of this world knew

All the PRINCES.

2 Kings 24. 14. carried away a. t. p. and migh. men
1 Chron. 29. 24. and all the p. submitted themselves
2 Chron. 24. 23. and destroyed all the p. of people
Esth. 1. 16. hath done wrong to all the p. and peo.
3. 1. set his seat above all the p. that were with him
Psal. 83. 11. all their p. as Zebah and Zalmunna
Jer. 26. 12. Jeremiah spake to all the p. and people
36. 21. Jehudi read it in the ears of all the p.
Ezek. 26. 16. then all the p. of the sea came down
Amos 2. 3. and will slay all the p. thereof with him
See ISRAEL.

PRINCES of Judah.

Neh. 12. 31. then I brought up p. of Judah on wall
Psal. 68. 27. there is p. of Judah, and their counsel.
Jer. 52. 10. he slew all the p. of Judah in Riblah
Hos. 5. 10. p. of Judah are like to them that remove
Mat. 2. 6. thou art not the least among p. of Judah

PRINCESS.

Lam. 1. 1. she that was p. among the provinces

PRINCESSES.

1 Kings 11. 3. Solomon had 700 wives p.
Isa. 49. † 23. p. shall be thy nursing mothers

PRINCIPAL.

Exod. 30. 23. take thou also unto thee p. spices
Lev. 6. 5. he shall even restore it in the p.
Num. 5. 7. recompense his trespass with the p.
1 Kings 4. 5. Zabud son of Nathan was p. officer
2 Kings 25. 19. the p. scribe of the host, Jer. 52. 25.
1 Chron. 24. 6. one p. household taken for Eleazar
31. the priests even p. fathers cast lots
27. † 5. Benaiah son of Jehoiada was a p. officer
Neh. 11. 17. Mattaniah p. to begin thanksgiving
Job 30. † 15. they pursue my p. one as the wind
Prov. 1. † 7. fear of the L. is the p. part of wisdom
4. 7. wisdom is the p. thing, therefore get wisdom
Isa. 16. 8. have broken down the p. plants thereof
28. 25. and cast in the p. wheat and barley
Jer. 25. 34. wallow in the ashes, ye p. of the flock
35. no way to fly, nor the p. of the flock escape
38. † 14. the king took Jeremiah into the p. entry
Ezek. 47. † 12. it shall bring forth p. fruit
Mic. 5. 5. there we shall raise ag. him eight p. men
Acts 25. 23. p. men of the city entered with Agrippa

PRINCIPALITY, TIES.

Jer. 13. 18. for your p. shall come down, the crown
Rom. 8. 38. angels, p. nor powers be able to separate
Eph. 1. 21. far above all p. power, and might
3. 10. that now to the p. might be known wisdom
6. 12. we wrestle against p. and against powers
Col. 1. 16. p. were created by him and for him
2. 10. which is the head of all p. and power
15. having spoiled p. he made a shew of them
Tit. 3. 1. put them in mind to be subject to p.
Jude. † 6. the angels which kept not their p.

PRINCIPLES.

Heb. 5. 12. have need that one teach you the first p.
6. 1. leaving the p. of the doctrine of Christ

PRINT.

Lev. 19. 28. ye shall not p. any marks upon you

PRINT.

Job 13. 27. thou settest a p. on the heels of my feet
John 20. 25. except I see in his hands the p. of the nails, and put my finger into the p. of the nails

PRINTED.

Job 19. 23. O that my words were p. in a book!

PRISON

Signifies, [1] *A place to confine debtors or malefactors*, Mat. 18. 30. Luke 23. 19. [2] *A low, obscure, and base condition*, Eccl. 4. 14. [3] *The cave wherein, as in a prison, David hid himself*, Psal. 142. 7. [4] *That spiritual thraldom and bondage in which sinners are kept by* Satan, *and their own lusts*, Isa. 42. 7. [5] *The grave*, Isa. 53. 8. [6] *That powerful restraint by which God keeps in and bridles* Satan, *Rev.* 20. 7.

He preached to the spirits in prison, 1 Pet. 3. 19. Christ *preached to the sinners of the old world by* Noah, *whom he inspired, that he might be a preacher of righteousness, to warn that wicked generation of approaching judgments, and exhort them to repentance; whose souls, because of their disobedience, are reserved in the infernal prison of hell, and were so at the time when the apostle* Peter *wrote this epistle.*

Gen. 39. 20. Potiphar put Joseph in p.
22. the keeper of the p. committed to Joseph
40. 3. put butler and baker in p. where Joseph was
42. 19. let one be bound in the house of your p.
1 Kings 22. 27. put this fellow in p. 2 Chr. 18. 26.
2 Kings 17. 4. king of Assyria bound Hoshea in p.
25. 27. he brought Jehoiachin out of p.
29. and changed his p. garments, Jer. 52. 31, 33.
Neh. 3. 25. Palal repaired by the court of the p.
Ps. 142. 7. bring my soul out of p. to praise thy name
Eccl. 4. 14. for out of p. he cometh to reign
Isa. 24. 22. and they shall be shut up in the p.
42. 7. to bring out the prisoners from the p.
22. they are all of them hid in p. houses
53. 8. he was taken from p. and from judgment
61. 1. to proclaim opening of the p. to the bound
Jer. 29. 26. that thou shouldest put him in p.
32. 2. Jeremiah was shut up in the court of the p.
12. before Jews that sat in the court of the p.
33. 1. word came to Jeremiah while he was shut up in court of the p. 37. 21. | 38. 6, 28. | 39. 15.
37. 4. for they had not put him into p.
15. they put him in p. in Jonathan's house
39. 14. they took Jeremiah out of the p.
52. 11. he put Zedekiah in p. till his death
Mat. 4. 12. Jesus heard that John was cast into p.
5. 25. and thou be cast into p. Luke 12. 58.
11. 2. when John heard in p. the works of Christ
14. 3. Herod put him in p. for Herodias' sake
10. he sent and beheaded John in p. Mark 6. 27.
18. 30. he cast him into p. till he should pay debt
25. 36. I was in p. and ye came unto me
39. when saw we thee in p. and came to thee? 44.
Mark 1. 14. now after that John was put in p.
6. 17. Herod had sent and bound John in p.
Luke 3. 20. added this, that he shut up John in p.
22. 33. to go with thee both into p. and to death
23. 19. and for murder was cast into p. 25.
John 3. 24. for John was not yet cast into p.
Acts 5. 18. and put the apostles in the common p.
19. the angel by night opened the p. doors
21. sent to the p. || 22. found them not in the p.
8. 3. haling men and women, committed them to p.
12. 4. Peter was put in p. || 5. he was kept in p.
7. light shined || 17. Lord brought him out of p.
16. 23. Paul and Silas were cast into p.
24. the inner p. || 27. seeing the p. doors open
26. 10. many of the saints did I shut up in p.
1 Pet. 3. 19. he went and preached to the spirits in p.
Rev. 2. 10. the devil shall cast some of you into p.
20. 7. Satan shall be loosed out of his p.
See GATE.

PRISON-HOUSE.

Judg. 16. 21. and Samson did grind in the p.
25. and they called for Samson out of the p.
2 Chron. 16. 10. then Asa put Hanani in a p.
Isa. 42. 7. to bring them in darkness out of the p.

PRISONER.

Psal. 79. 11. let sighing of the p. come before thee
102. 20. to hear groaning of the p. to loose those
Mat. 27. 15. was wont to release to the people a p.
16. they had then a notable p. Mark 15. 6.
Acts 23. 18. Paul p. called me to him, and prayed
25. 27. it seemeth unreasonable to send a p.
28. 17. yet was I delivered p. to the Romans
Eph. 3. 1. I Paul the p. of Jesus, 4. 1. Philem. 1. 9.
2 Tim. 1. 8. be not thou ashamed of me his p.
See FELLOW.

PRISONERS.

Gen. 39. 20. a place where king's p. were bound
22. the keeper committed to Joseph all the p.

Num. 21. 1. king Arad took some of Israel p.
Job 3. 18. there the p. rest together, they hear not
Psal. 69. 33. the Lord despiseth not his p.
146. 7. the Lord looseth the p. opens eyes of blind
Isa. 10. 4. they shall bow down under the p.
14. 17. that opened not the house of his p.
20. 4. Assyria shall lead the Egyptians p.
24. 22. they shall be gathered together as p.
42. 7. to bring out the p. from the prison
49. 9. that thou mayest say to the p. go forth
Lam. 3. 34. to crush under feet the p. of the earth
Zech. 9. 11. I have sent forth thy p. out of the pit
12. turn ye to the strong hold, ye p. of hope
Acts 16. 25. sang praises, and the p. heard them
27. supposing that the p. had been fled
27. 1. they delivered Paul and certain other p.
42. the soldiers' counsel was to kill the p.
28. 16. the centurion delivered the p. to captain

PRISONS.

Luke 21. 12. persecute you, delivering you into p.
Acts 22. 4. bind and deliver into p. men and wom.
2 Cor. 11. 23. in p. more frequent, in deaths oft

PRIVATE.

2 Pet. 1. 20. no prophecy of any p. interpretation

PRIVATELY.

Mat. 24. 3. the disciples came to Christ p. saying
Mark 6. 32. Jesus went into a ship p. Luke 9. 10.
9. 28. disciples John and Andrew ask him p. 13. 3.
Luke 10. 23. he turned to his disciples and said p.
Acts 23. 19. went aside with Paul's kinsman p.
Gal. 2. 2. but p. to them that were of reputation

PRIVILEGE.

John 1. † 12. to as many as received him gave he p.

PRIVILY.

Judg. 9. 31. he sent messengers to Abimelech p.
1 Sam. 24. 4. David cut off Saul's skirt p.
Psal. 10. 8. his eyes are p. set against the poor
11. 2. that they may p. shoot at the upright
31. 4. pull me out of net laid p. for me, 142. 3.
64. 5. they commune of laying snares p.
101. 5. whoso p. slanders his neighbour will cut off
Prov. 1. 11. let us lurk p. for the innocent
18. they lurk p. for their own lives
Mat. 1. 19. Joseph was minded to put her away p.
2. 7. Herod, when he had p. called the wise men
Acts 16. 37. and now do they thrust us out p.?
Gal. 2. 4. who came in p. to spy out our liberty
2 Pet. 2. 1. who shall p. bring in damnable heresies

PRIVY.

Deut. 23. 1. he that hath his p. member cut off
1 Kings 2. 44. the wickedness thy heart is p. to
Ezek. 21. 14. the sword enters into their p. chambers
Acts 5. 2. part of price, his wife also being p. to it

PRIZE.

1 Cor. 9. 24. all run, but one receiveth the p.
Phil. 3. 14. I press toward the mark for the p.

PRIZED.

Zech. 11. 13. a goodly price that I was p. at of them

PROCEED.

Exod. 25. 35. according to the six branches that p.
Josh. 6. 10. nor any word p. out of your mouth
2 Sam. 7. 12. seed which shall p. out of thy bowels
Job 40. 5. twice spoken, but I will p. no further
Isa. 29. 14. I will p. to do a marvellous work
51. 4. give ear, for a law shall p. from me
Jer. 9. 3. for they p. from evil to evil, know not me
30. 19. and out of them shall p. thanksgiving
21. their governor shall p. from midst of them
Hab. 1. 7. their judgm. and dignity shall p. of thems.
Mat. 15. 18. p. out of the mouth defile the man
19. out of the heart p. murders, Mark 7. 21.
Eph. 4. 29. let no corrupt communication p.
2 Tim. 3. 9. they shall p. no further, folly manifest

PROCEEDED.

Num. 30. 12. whatever p. out of her lips, not stand
32. 24. do that which hath p. out of your mouth
Judg. 11. 36. do that which p. out of thy mouth
Job 36. 1. Elihu also p. and said, suffer me
Luke 4. 22. wondered at the gracious words which p.
John 8. 42. for I p. forth and came from God
Acts 12. 3. he p. further to take Peter also
Rev. 19. 21. which sword p. out of his mouth

PROCEEDETH.

Gen. 24. 50. the thing p. from the Lord
Num. 30. 2. according to all that p. out of his mouth
Deut. 8. 3. but by every word that p. out of the
mouth of God doth man live, Mat. 4. 4.
1 Sam. 24. 13. wickedness p. from the wicked
Eccl. 10. 5. as an error which p. from the ruler
Lam. 3. 38. out of Most High p. not evil and good
Hab. 1. 4. therefore wrong judgment p.
John 15. 26. Spirit of truth which p. from Father
Jam. 3. 10. out of the same mouth p. blessing
Rev. 11. 5. fire p. out of their mouth and devours

PROCEEDING.

Rev. 22. 1. water of life p. out of throne of God

PROCESS.

Gen. 4. 3. in p. of time Cain brought an offering
38. 12. in p. of time Shuah Judah's wife died
Exod. 2. 23. in p. of time the king of Egypt died
Judg. 11. 4. in p. children of Ammon made war
2 Chron. 21. 19. in p. Jehoram's bowels fell out

PROCLAMATION.

Exod. 32. 5. Aaron made p. and said, to morrow
1 Kings 15. 22. king Asa made a p. through all Jud.
22. 36. and there went a p. throughout the host
2 Chr. 24. 9. Joash made a p. thro' Judah and Jerus.
30. 5. to make p. throughout all Israel
36. 22. Cyrus made p. through kingdom, Ezra 1. 1.
Ezra 10. 7. Ezra and princes made p. through Judah
Dan. 5. 29. Belshazzar made p. concerning Daniel

PROCLAIM.

Exod. 33. 19. and I will p. the name of the Lord
Lev. 23. 2. feast of the Lord ye shall p. 4, 21, 37.
25. 10. p. liberty || Deut. 20. 10. p. peace unto it
Judg. 7. 3. go to p. in the ears of the people
21. † 13. they sent to p. peace to Benjamin
Ruth 4. † 11. and p. thy name in Beth-lehem
1 Kings 21. 9. p. a fast, and set Naboth on high
2 Kings 10. 20. Jehu said, p. a solemn assembly
Neh. 8. 15. p. that they fetch pine-branches
Esth. 6. 9. p. before him, thus shall it be done
Prov. 20. 6. most men p. their own goodness
Isa. 12. † 4. praise the Lord, p. his name
61. 1. he hath sent me to p. liberty to the captives
2. to p. the acceptable year of the Lord
Jer. 3. 12. go and p. these words, 11. 6. | 19. 2.
7. 2. stand in gate of Lord, and p. there this word
34. 8. had made a covenant to p. liberty to them
17. I p. a liberty for you to sword, to pestilence
Joel 3. 9. p. ye this among the Gentiles, prepare war
Amos 4. 5. and p. and publish the free offerings

PROCLAIMED.

Exod. 34. 5. and p. the name of the Lord, 6.
36. 6. they caused it to be p. through the camp
1 Kings 21. 12. they p. a fast, set Naboth on high
2 Kings 10. 20. a solemn assembly, and they p. it
23. 16. the man of God p. who p. these words, 17.
2 Chron. 20. 3. Jehoshaphat feared and p. a fast
Ezra 8. 21. I p. a fast there at the river Ahava
Esth. 6. 11. Haman p. before him, thus shall be done
Isa. 62. 11. Lord hath p. thy salvation cometh
Jer. 36. 9. they p. a fast before Lord to Jerusalem
Lam. 1. † 21. thou wilt bring the day thou hast p.
Jonah 3. 5. they p. a fast, and put on sackcloth
7. caused it to be p. and published thro' Nineveh
Luke 12. 3. shall be p. upon the house-tops

PROCLAIMETH, ING.

Prov. 12. 23. the heart of fools p. foolishness
Jer. 34. 15. in p. liberty every man to neighbour, 17.
Rev. 5. 2. I saw a strong angel p. with a loud voice

PROCURE.

Jer. 26. 19. thus might we p. great evil ag. our souls
33. 9. they shall fear for all posterity I p. to it

PROCURED.

Jer. 2. 17. hast thou not p. this to thyself?
4. 18. thy doings have p. these things to thee

PROCURETH.

Prov. 11. 27. that diligently seeketh good p. favour
17. † 9. he that covereth a transgression p. love

PRODUCE.

Isa. 41. 21. p. your cause, saith Lord, bring forth

PROFANE.

This is said of the contempt and abuse of holy things: A man who is defiled, and touches any sacred thing pollutes or profanes *it. A profane person is one openly wicked. He that makes a jest of sacred things, who defiles himself by impure and shameful actions, is a* profane person, Lev. 21. 9, 12. *The Scripture calls* Esau, profane, *because he sold his birthright, which was considered as an holy thing, not only because the priesthood was annexed to it, but also because it was a privilege leading to* Christ, *and a type of his title to the heavenly inheritance,* Heb. 12. 16. *The priests of the race of* Aaron *were enjoined to distinguish between sacred and* profane, *between pure and defiled,* Lev. 10. 10. *and for this reason the use of wine was forbid them in the temple, during their time of waiting. It was forbid them to keep the flesh of the peace-offerings above two days: if they eat of it on the third day, they were punished as* profaners *of holy things,* Lev. 19. 7, 8.

To profane *the temple, to* profane *the sabbath, to* profane *the altar, are expressions to denote the violation of the holy rest of the sabbath, the entering of foreigners into the temple, the irreverences that are committed there, the impious sacrifices that are offered on the altar of the Lord.* To profane *a vine, or a tree, is to make them common, and proper to be employed in ordinary uses,* Deut. 20. 6. What man is he that hath planted a vineyard, and hath not eaten of it? *The* Hebrew *says, who hath not yet* profaned *it. In* Lev. 19. 23, 24, &c. *where* Moses *passes a law concerning the fruit of trees newly planted, he expressed the impurity of the first-fruits, by calling them uncircumcised. For the three first years these fruits were cut off as impure: the fourth year they offered what was produced in the temple: and in the fifth year the owner had the liberty of making use of the fruit as his own, which then became* profane, *or common.* Jeremiah *promises the* Israelites *that they should return again into their own country, that they should plant vineyards on the mountains of* Samaria, *and should* profane *them; that is, should eat of the fruit thereof,* Jer. 31. † 5.

Lev. 21. 7. they shall not take a wife that is p. 14.
Jer. 23. 11. both prophet and priests are p.
Ezek. 21. 25. and thou p. wicked prince of Israel
22. 26. and put no difference between holy and p.
28. 16. I will cast thee as p. out of mountain of God
42. 20. between the sanctuary and the p. place
44. 23. shall teach difference between holy and p.
48. 15. shall be a p. place for the city, for suburbs
1 Tim. 1. 9. the law is made for the unholy and p.
4. 7. refuse p. and old wives' fables, exercise thys.
6. 20. avoid p. and vain babblings, 2 Tim. 2. 16.
Heb. 12. 16. lest there be any p. person, as Esau

PROFANE.

Lev. 18. 21. neither shalt thou p. name of thy God,
I am Lord, 19. 12. | 20. 3. | 21. 6. | 22. 2, 32.
19. † 29. do not thou p. thy daughter to cause
21. 4. being chief among his people to p. himself
9. the daughter of any priest, if she p. herself
12. he shall not p. the sanctuary of his God, 23.
15. nor shall he p. his seed among his people
22. 9. and die therefore, if they do p. my ordinance
15. they shall not p. the holy things of Israel
Num. 30. † 2. if a man vow he shall not p. his word
Deut. 28. † 30. plant a vineyard, and not p. it
Neh. 13. 17. evil that ye do, and p. the sabbath day
Psal. 89. † 31. if they p. my statutes, and keep not
Jer. 31. † 5. the planters shall plant and p. them
Ezek. 23. 39. they came to my sanctuary to p. it
24. 21. behold, I will p. my sanctuary
Amos 2. 7. go in to same maid, to p. my holy name
Mat. 12. 5. the priests in the temple p. the sabbath
Acts 24. 6. who hath gone about to p. the temple

PROFANED.

Lev. 19. 8. he hath p. the hallowed things
Psal. 55. † 20. he hath p. his covenant
89. 39. thou hast p. his crown to the ground
Isa. 43. 28. therefore I have p. the princes of sanc.
Ezek. 22. 8. thou hast p. my sabbaths, 23. 38.
† 16. thou shalt be p. in sight of the heathen
26. p. my holy things, I am p. among them
25. 3. aha, against my sanctuary, when it was p.
36. 20. they p. my holy name, when they said
21. pity for my name which Israel had p. 22, 23.
Mal. 1. 12. but ye have p. it, in that ye say
2. 11. Judah hath p. the holiness of the Lord

PROFANENESS.

Jer. 23. 15. from the prophets of Jerusalem is p.

PROFANETH.

Lev. 21. 9. she p. her father, she shall be burnt

PROFANING.

Neh. 13. 18. bring more wrath by p. the sabbath
Mal. 2. 10. by p. the covenant of our fathers

PROFESS.

Deut. 26. 3. I p. this day to the Lord thy God
Mat. 7. 23. then will I p. I never knew you
Tit. 1. 16. they p. that they know God, but deny him
3. † 14. let ours learn to p. honest trades

PROFESSED, ING.

Rom. 1. 22. p. themselves to be wise, they became
2 Cor. 9. 13. glorify God for your p. subject. to gosp.
1 Tim. 2. 10. which becometh women p. godliness
6. 12. hast p. a good profession before many
21. some p. have erred concerning the faith

PROFESSION.

1 Tim. 6. 12. hast professed a good p. before many
† 13. who before Pontius Pilate witnessed good p.
Heb. 3. 1. the high priest of our p. Christ Jesus
4. 14. an high priest, let us hold fast our p. 10. 23.

PROFIT, *Substantive.*

Gen. 25. 32. what p. shall this birth-right do me?
37. 26. what p. is it if we slay our brother?
Esth. 3. 8. it is not for the king's p. to suffer
Job 21. 15. what p. should have if we pray to him?
30. 2. whereto might their strength p. me?
35. 3. and what p. if I be cleansed from my sin?
Psal. 30. 9. what p. is there in my blood?
Prov. 14. 23. in all labour there is p. but talk of lips
Eccl. 1. 3. all is vanity, what p. hath a man of all
his labour under the sun? 3. 9. | 5. 16.
2. 11. and there was no p. under the sun
5. 9. moreover the p. of the earth is for all
7. 11. by wisdom there is p. to them that see sun
Isa. 30. 5. nor be any help nor p. but a shame
Jer. 16. 19. have inherited things wherein is no p.
Mal. 3. 14. what p. that we have kept ordinance?
Rom. 3. 1. what p. is there of circumcision?
1 Cor. 7. 35. and this I speak for your own p.
10. 33. not seeking mine own p. but the p. of many
2 Tim. 2. 14. they strive not about words to no p.
Heb. 12. 10. but he chasteneth us for our p.

PROFIT, *Verb.*

1 Sam. 12. 21. after vain things which cannot p.
Job 35. 8. thy righteousness may p. the son of man
Psal. 120. † 3. what shall it p. thee, false tongue?
Prov. 10. 2. treasures of wickedness p. nothing
11. 4. riches p. not in the day of wrath
Isa. 30. 5. were ashamed of people that could not p. 6.
44. 9. their delectable things shall not p.
47. 12. if so be thou shalt be able to p.
48. 17. I am the Lord which teacheth thee to p.
57. 12. and thy works, for they shall not p. thee
Jer. 2. 8. and walked after things that do not p.
11. people changed, for that which doth not p.
7. 8. behold, ye trust in lying words that cannot p.
12. 13. put themselves to pain, but shall not p.
23. 32. they shall not p. this people, saith the Lord
Mark 8. 36. what p. if he gain the whole world
1 Cor. 12. 7. is given to every man to p. withal
14. 6. speaking with tongues, what shall I p. you
Gal. 5. 2. Christ shall p. you nothing
Heb. 4. 2. the word preached did not p. them
Jam. 2. 14. what doth it p. my brethren, though
16. if ye give not things needful, what doth it p.?

PROFITABLE.

Job 22. 2. can a man be p. to God, as p. to himself
Eccl. 10. 10. but wisdom is p. to direct
Isa. 44. 10. a graven image that is p. for nothing
Jer. 13. 7. the girdle was p. for nothing
Mat. 5. 29. that one of thy members perish, 30.
Acts 20. 20. I kept back nothing p. to you
1 Cor. 6. † 12. all things are lawful, but not p.
1 Tim. 4. 8. but godliness is p. to all things
2 Tim. 3. 16. the scripture is p. for doctrine
4. 11. Mark is p. to me for the ministry
Tit. 3. 8. these things are good and p. to men
Philem. 11. but now p. to thee and to me

PROFITABLY.

Eph. 4. † 29. but that which is good to edify p.

PROFITED, ETH.

Job 33. 27. if any say I have sinned, and it p. not
34. 9. he said, it p. nothing to delight in God
Hab. 2. 18. what p. the graven and molten image
Mat. 15. 5. whoso shall say to father or mother, it is a
gift by whatever thou mightest be p. Mark 7. 11.
16. 26. what is a man p. if he gain whole world
John 6. 63. the spirit quickeneth, flesh p. nothing
Rom. 2. 25. circumcision p. if thou keep the law
1 Cor. 13. 3. and have not charity, it p. nothing
Gal. 1. 14. I p. in the Jews' religion above many
1 Tim. 4. 8. for bodily exercise p. little, but godliness
Heb. 13. 9. not p. them that have been occupied

PROFITING.

1 Tim. 4. 15. that thy p. may appear to all

PROFOUND.

Hos. 5. 2. the revolters are p. to make slaughter

PROGENITORS.

Gen. 49. 26. prevailed above the blessings of my p.

PROGNOSTICATORS.

Isa. 47. 13. let monthly p. stand up and save thee

PROLONG, ED.

Num. 9. † 19. when cloud p. they journeyed not
Deut. 4. 26. ye shall not p. your days, 30. 18.
40. thou shalt keep his statutes, that thou mayest
p. thy days upon the earth, 5. 16, 33. | 6. 2.
| 11. 9. | 17. 20. | 22. 7.
32. 47. through this thing ye shall p. your days
Josh. 24. † 31. Israel served all the days of the elders
that p. after Joshua, Judg. 2. † 7.

Job 6. 11. what is my end, that I should p. my life?
15. 29. the wicked shall not p. the perfection
Psal. 61. 6. thou wilt p. the king's life and years
Prov. 28. 2. by knowledge the state shall be p.
16. he that hateth covetousness shall p. his days
Eccl. 8. 12. though a sinner's days be p. yet surely
13. neither shall the wicked p. his days
Isa. 13. 22. and her days shall not be p.
53. 10. he shall see his seed, he shall p. his days
Ezek. 12. 22. the days are p. and vision faileth
25. I am the Lord, I will speak, and the word shall come to pass, it shall be no more p.
28. there shall none of my words be p. any more
Dan. 7. 12. yet their lives were p. for season and time

PROLONGETH.

Prov. 10. 27. the fear of the Lord p. days
Eccl. 7. 15. there is a wicked man that p. his life

PROMISE.

It is an assurance that God has given in his word of bestowing blessings upon his people, 2 Pet. 1. 4. *The word in the New Testament is often taken for those promises that God heretofore made to* Abraham *and the other patriarchs, of sending the* Messiah. *It is in this sense that the apostle* Paul *commonly uses the word* promise, Rom. 4. 13, 14. Gal. 3. 16. *The* promises *of the new covenant are called better than those of the old,* Heb. 8. 6. *because they are more spiritual, clear, extensive, and universal, than those in the Mosaical covenant were. The time of the* promise, Acts 7. 17. *is the time of the fulfilling of the promise. God had told* Abram, Gen. 15. 13, 14. *that his seed should be a stranger in a strange land, but that after four hundred years he would bring them out thence; the time of the promise came, when these four hundred years were expired. The children of the* promise *are,* [1] *The Israelites descended from* Isaac, *in opposition to the* Ishmaelites *descended from* Ishmael *and* Hagar. [2] *The* Jews *converted to Christianity, in opposition to the incredulous* Jews, *who will not believe in* Christ: *and* [3] *All true believers who are born again by the supernatural power of God's Spirit, and by faith lay hold on the promise of salvation made in Christ; these are the spiritual seed of* Abraham, *to whom the spiritual blessings contained in the covenant and the inheritance do belong,* Rom. 9. 8. Gal. 4. 28. *The Holy Spirit of promise,* Eph. 1. 13. signifies, *the Holy Ghost, which God has promised to those that shall believe in him, which is the pledge of a believer's everlasting happiness. The first commandment to which God has annexed a* promise, *is that,* Honour thy father and mother, *Eph.* 6. 2. *To which God has subjoined this* promise, *that their days shall be multiplied upon the earth,* Exod. 20. 12. Promises *also denote eternal life, or the blessedness promised, which is the object of the Christian's hope,* Heb. 6. 12.

Num. 14. 34. and ye shall know my breach of p.
1 Kings 8. 56. hath not failed one word of good p.
2 Chron. 1. 9. let thy p. to David be established
Neh. 5. 12. they should do according to this p.
13. that performeth not this p. even thus be he shaken out, and emptied people did accord. to p.
Psal. 77. 8. doth his p. fail for evermore?
105. 42. for he remembered his holy p. and Abram
Luke 24. 49. behold, I send p. of my Father on you
Acts 1. 4. but wait for the p. of the Father
2. 33. received of Father the p. of the Holy Ghost
39. for the p. is to you and to your children
7. 17. but when the time of the p. drew nigh
13. 23. God accord. to his p. hath raised a Saviour
32. the p. made to fathers God hath fulfilled
23. 21. now are ready, looking for a p. from thee
26. 6. for hope of the p. made of God to fathers
7. to which p. our tribes serving G. day and night
Rom. 4. 13. the p. that he shall be the heir of world
14. and the p. is made of none effect
16. to the end the p. might be sure to the seed
20. he staggered not at the p. through unbelief
9. 8. but children of the p. counted for the seed
9. for this is word of p. at this time I will come
Gal. 3. 14. that we might receive p. of the Spirit
17. that it should make the p. of none effect
18. for if the inheritance be of the law, it is no more of p. but God gave it to Abraham by p.
19. seed shall come, to whom the p. was made
22. that the p. by faith of Jesus Christ might be
29. then are ye heirs according to the p.
4. 23. but he of the free woman was by p.
28. we, as Isaac was, are the children of p.
Eph. 1. 13. ye were sealed with that Holy Spirit of p.
2. 12. and strangers from the covenants of p.
3. 6. the Gentiles be partakers of his p. in Christ
6. 2. which is the first commandment with p.
1 Tim. 4. 8. having the p. of the life that now is
2 Tim. 1. 1. according to the p. of life in Christ Jes.
Heb. 4. 1. fear, lest a p. left us of entering into rest
6. 13. for when God made p. to Abraham
15. after he had patiently endured, he obtain. p.
17. God willing to shew unto the heirs of p.
9. 15. might receive the p. of eternal life, 10. 36.
11. 9. by faith he sojourned in the land of p. in a strange country, heirs with him of the same p.
39. and these all received not the p.
2 Pet. 3. 4. saying, where is the p. of his coming?
9. the Lord is not slack concerning his p.
13. according to his p. we look for new heavens
1 John 2. 25. this is the p. that he hath promised us

PROMISE, Verb.

2 Pet. 2. 19. while they p. them liberty, they are

PROMISED.

Exod. 12. 25. will give you according as he hath p.
Num. 14. 40. we will go to the place the Lord p.
Deut. 1. 11. the Lord bless you as he hath p. 15. 6.
6. 3. that ye may increase as the Lord p. thee
9. 28. not able to bring them to the land he p.
10. 9. the Lord is his inheritance, as he p.
12. 20. the Lord shall enlarge thy border, as he p.
19. 8. and give thee the land he p. to give, 27. 3.
23. 23. shall keep that which thou hast p. to God
Deut. 26. 18. to be his peculiar people, as he p. thee
Josh. 9. 21. let them live, as the princes had p.
22. 4. given rest to your brethren, as he p. them
23. 5. ye shall possess their land, as the L. p. you
10. God fighteth for you, as he hath p. you
15. as all good things are come the Lord p. you
2 Sam. 7. 28. hast p. this goodness to thy servant
1 Kings 2. 24. and hath made me an house, as he p.
5. 12. Lord gave Solomon wisdom, as he p. him
8. 20. I sit on the throne of Israel as the Lord p.
56. hath given rest to people, as he p. by Moses
9. 5. as I p. to David thy father, saying
2 Kings 8. 19. as he p. to give a light, 2 Chron. 21. 7.
1 Chron. 17. 26. and thou hast p. this goodness
2 Chron. 6. 10. I am set on the throne as the Lord p.
15. hast kept that which thou hast p. David, 16.
Neh. 9. 23. concerning which thou hadst p. to father
Esth. 4. 7. of the sum that Haman had p. to pay
Jer. 32. 42. will bring on them all good I p. 33. 14.
Mat. 14. 7. Herod p. with oath to give her whatever
Mark 14. 11. they were glad, p. to give him money
Luke 1. 72. to perform the mercy p. to our fathers
22. 6. he p. to betray him unto them in absence
Acts 7. 5. yet he p. to give it to him for a possession
Rom. 1. 2. gospel of God, which he had p. afore
4. 21. that what he p. he was also able to perform
Tit. 1. 2. in hope of eternal life, p. before world began
Heb. 10. 23. hold fast profession, he is faithful that p.
11. 11. because they judged him faithful that had p.
12. 26. now he hath p. saying, once more I shake
Jam. 1. 12. which Lord p. to them that love him, 2. 5.
1 John 2. 25. this is promise he hath p. us eternal life

PROMISEDST.

1 Kings 8. 24. keep with David that thou p. him, 25.
Neh. 9. 15. and p. that they should go into the land

PROMISES.

Rom. 9. 4. are Israelites, to whom pertain the p.
15. 8. to confirm the p. made to the fathers
2 Cor. 1. 20. all p. of God in him are yea and amen
7. 1. having therefore these p. dearly beloved
Gal. 3. 16. to Abraham and his seed were p. made
21. is the law then against the p. of God?
Heb. 6. 12. who through faith and patience inherit p.
7. 6. Melchisedec blessed him that had the p.
8. 6. covenant which was established upon better p.
11. 13. these all died in faith, not having received p.
17. he that had received the p. offered up his son
33. who thro' faith obtained p. and stopped mouths
2 Pet. 1. 4. given us exceeding great and precious p.

PROMISING.

Ezek. 13. 22. not return from his wick. way by p. life

PROMOTE.

Num. 22. 17. I will p. thee to great honour, 24. 11.
37. am I not able indeed to p. thee to honour?
Prov. 4. 8. exalt her, and she shall p. thee

PROMOTED.

Judg. 9. 9. and go to be p. over the trees, 11, 13.
Esth. 5. 11. told wherein the king had p. him
Dan. 3. 30. then the king p. Shadrach, Meshach

PROMOTION.

Psal. 75. 6. p. cometh not from the east nor west
Prov. 3. 35. but shame shall be the p. of fools

PRONOUNCE.

Lev. 5. 4. that a man shall p. with an oath
13. 3. the priest shall look on him and p. him unclean, 6, 8, 11, 15, 20, 22, 25, 27, 30, 44.
13. shall p. him clean, 17, 23, 28, 34, 37. | 14. 7.
59. this is the law, to p. it clean or unclean
14. 48. then the priest shall p. the house clean
Judg. 12. 6. for he could not frame to p. it right

PRONOUNCED.

Neh. 6. 12. but he p. this prophecy against me
Jer. 11. 17. the Lord hath p. evil against thee
16. 10. p. this great evil, 19. 15. | 35. 17. | 40. 2.
18. 8. if that nation against whom I p. turn
25. 13. the word which I have p. against it
26. 13. Lord will repent of the evil that he p.
19. the Lord repented of the evil he had p.
34. 5. for I have p. the word, saith the Lord
36. 7. that the Lord hath p. against this people
18. Jeremiah p. all these words unto me, 31.

PRONOUNCING.

Lev. 5. 4. if a soul swear, p. to do evil or good

PROOF.

2 Cor. 2. 9. that I might know the p. of you
8. 24. shew ye to them the p. of your love
13. 3. since ye seek a p. of Christ speaking in me
Phil. 2. 22. but ye know the p. of him
2 Tim. 4. 5. make full p. of thy ministry

PROOFS.

Acts 1. 3. shewed himself alive by many infallible p.

PROPER.

1 Chr. 29. 3. I have of mine own p. good, of gold
Acts 1. 19. field is called in their p. tongue, Aceldama
1 Cor. 7. 7. but every man hath his p. gift of God
Heb. 11. 23. because they saw he was a p. child

PROPHANE, See PROFANE.

PROPHECY.

2 Chron. 9. 29. Solomon's acts in the p. of Ahijah
15. 8. when Asa heard p. of Obed he took courage
Neh. 6. 12. he pronounced this p. against me
Prov. 30. 1. the p. man spake to Ithiel and Ucal
31. 1. and the p. that his mother taught him
Mat. 13. 14. in them is fulfilled the p. of Esaias
1 Cor. 12. 10 to another p. by the same Spirit
13. 2. though I have the gift of p. and not charity
1 Tim. 4. 14. neglect not the gift given thee by p.
2 Pet. 1. 19. we have also a more sure word of p.
20. no p. of scripture is of private interpretation
21. p. came not in old time by the will of man
Rev. 1. 3. blessed that hear the words of this p.
11. 6. that it rain not in the days of their p.
19. 10. for the testimony of Jesus is spirit of p.
22. 7. blessed that keepeth the sayings of this p.
10. seal not the sayings of the p. of this book
18. that heareth words of the p. of this book
19. if any man take from the words of this p.

PROPHECIES.

1 Cor. 13. 8. but whether p. they shall cease
1 Tim. 1. 18. according to the p. that went before

PROPHESY, Verb.

Num. 11. 27. Eldad and Medad do p. in the camp
1 Sam. 10. 5. they shall p. || 6. thou shalt p.
1 Kings 22. 8. he doth not p. good of me, but evil
18. that he would not p. good, 2 Chron. 18. 17.
1 Chr. 25. 1. who should p. with harps and cymbals
Isa. 30. 10. p. not to us right things, p. deceits
Jer. 5. 31. the prophets p. falsely, and priests
11. 21. saying, p. not in the name of the Lord
14. 14. prophets p. lies, they p. false visions
15. concerning the prophets that p. in my name
16. the people to whom they p. shall be cast out
19. 14. Jeremiah came from where Lord sent to p.
23. 16. hearken not to the prophets that p.
25. what the prophets said, that p. lies in my name, 26, 32. | 27. 10, 14, 15, 16. | 29. 9, 21.
25. 30. p. against the inhabitants of the earth
26. 12. Lord sent me to p. against this house
32. 3. why dost thou p. and say, will give this city?
Ezek. 4. 7. thou shalt p. against Jerusalem
6. 2. p. against the mountains of Israel, 36. 1.
11. 4. p. against Jaazaniah and Pelatiah, p.
13. 2. p. against the prophets that p. 17.
20. 46. p. against the forest of the south field
21. 2. p. against land of Israel || 9. Jerusalem
14. son of man, p. and smite thy hands together
28. p. and say concerning the Ammonites, 25. 2.
28. 21. p. against Zidon || 29. 2. p. against Pharaoh
30. 2. p. against Egypt || 35. 2. p. against mount Seir
34. 2. son of man, p. against the shepherds of Isr.
36. 6. p. concerning the land of Israel, and say
37. 4. p. on these bones || 9. p. to the wind
38. 2. son of man, p. against Gog, 14. | 39. 1.
43. †3. when I came to p. city should be destroyed
Joel 2. 28. your sons shall p. Acts 2. 17, 18.
Amos 2. 12. ye gave the Nazarites wine, and commanded the prophets, saying, p. not, Mic. 2. 6.
3. 8. who can but p.? || 7. 12. eat bread and p.
7. 13. but p. not again any more at Beth-el
15. Lord said to me, go p. to my people Israel
16. p. not against Israel and the house of Isaac
Mic. 2. 11. I will p. to thee of wine and strong drink
Zech. 13. 3. that when any shall yet p. then his father
Mat. 15. 7. well did Esaias p. of you, saying
26. 68. p. thou Christ, Mark 14. 65. Luke 22. 64.
Acts 21. 9. had four daughters, virgins, which did p.
Rom. 12. 6. whether p. let us p. to the proportion
1 Cor. 13. 9. we know in part, and we p. in part
14. 1. rather that ye may p. || 39. covet to p.
24. if all p. || 31. we may all p. one by one
Rev. 10. 11. thou must p. ag. before nations and kings
11. 3. my two witnesses shall p. 1260 days

PROPHESIED.

Num. 11. 25. they p. and did not cease
26. Eldad and Medad they p. in the camp
1 Sam. 10. 10. Spirit of God came upon Saul, and he p. among them, 11. | 18. 10. | 19. 23, 24.
19. 20. the messengers of Saul also p. 21.
1 Kings 18. 29. they p. until the evening sacrifice
22. 10. prophets p. before them, 12. 2 Chron. 18. 9.
1 Chron. 25. 2. sons of Asaph p. according to order
3. the sons of Jeduthun who p. with a harp
2 Chron. 20. 37. Eliezer p. against Jehoshaphat
Ezra 5. 1. Haggai and Zechariah p. to the Jews
Jer. 2. 8. pastors transgressed, prophets p. by Baal
20. 1. Pashur heard that Jeremiah p. these things
6. Pashur shall die, and all to whom thou p. lies
23. 13. the prophets of Samaria p. in Baal
21. I have not spoken to them, yet they p.
25. 13. bring on Babylon all that Jeremiah hath p.
26. 9. why hast thou p. in the name of the Lord?
11. for he hath p. against this city, 20.
18. Micah p. in days of Hezekiah king of Judah
20. Urijah p. || 28. 8. p. against many countries
28. 6. the Lord perform the words thou hast p.
29. 31. because Shemaiah hath p. to you a lie
37. 19. where are your prophets which p. to you?
Ezek. 11. 13. when I p. Pelatiah son of Benaiah died
37. 7. so I p. as I was commanded, and as I p. 10.
38. 17. who p. I would bring thee against them
Zech. 13. 4. prophets shall be ashamed when they p.
Mat. 7. 22. Lord, have we not p. in thy name?
11. 13. the prophets and the law p. until John
Mark 7. 6. he said, well hath Esaias p. of you
Luke 1. 67. his father Zacharias p. saying, blessed
John 11. 51. Caiaphas p. that Jesus should die
Acts 19. 6. they spake with tongues and p.
1 Cor. 14. 5. I would rather that ye p. greater is he
1 Pet. 1. †. 10. of which salvation they p. who p. of the grace which should come unto you
Jude 14. Enoch also p. of these things, saying

PROPHESIETH.

2 Chr. 18. 7. for he never p. good to me, but evil
Jer. 28. 9. the prophet which p. of peace
Ezek. 12. 27. he p. of the times that are far off
Zech. 13. 3. shall thrust him through when he p.
1 Cor. 11. 5. that p. with her head uncovered
14. 3. he that p. speaketh unto men to edification
4. but he that p. edifieth the church
5. greater is he that p. than he that speaketh

PROPHESYING, S.

1 Sam. 10. 13. when he had made an end of p.
19. 20. they saw the company of the prophets p.
Ezra 6. 14. they prospered through p. of Haggai
1 Cor. 11. 4. every man p. having his head covered
14. 6. except I shall speak to you by p. or doctrine
22. but p. serveth not for them that believe not
1 Thess. 5. 20. despise not p. prove all things

PROPHET.

This word comes from the Greek, προφητης, *which signifies,* one that foretells future events. *The* Hebrews *at the beginning called them* Seers, ראה videns. *Afterwards they called them* Nabi, *which comes from the root* נבא Nibba, *to foretell, to divine. Also the scripture often gives them the name of* Men of God, *and of* Angels, *or* Messengers of the Lord. *The verb* Nibba, *to prophesy, is of great extent. Sometimes it signifies to foretell what is to come: at other times, to be inspired, to speak from God. It is said,* Exod. 7. 1. *Aaron* thy brother shall be thy prophet: *that is, he shall explain and interpret thy sentiments and commands to* Pharaoh *and the people. The apostle* Paul, *in his epistle to* Titus, 1. 12. *quoting a profane poet, calls him*

Prophet; because the Pagans thought their poets inspired by the gods. The Scripture often gives the name of Prophet to impostors, who falsely boasted of inspiration, 1 Kings 18. 22.

As the true Prophets, at the time that they were transported by the motions of God's Spirit, were sometimes agitated in a violent manner; those motions were called prophesying, which persons exhibited, who were filled with a good or evil spirit. For example, Saul, being moved by an evil spirit, prophesied in his house, 1 Sam. 18. 10. that is, he was agitated with violence, and used strange and unusual gestures, signs, and speeches, as the Prophets did. To prophesy is also put for to make or sing psalms, or songs of praise to God, 1 Sam. 10. 5, 6. 1 Chron. 25. 1. This term is also used by St. Paul, for explaining Scripture, preaching, or speaking to the church in public, 1 Cor. 14. 1, 3, 4.

The most usual way by which God communicated himself to the Prophets was by inspiration, which consisted in illuminating the mind of the prophet, and exciting his will to proclaim what the Lord dictated to him from within. It is in this sense that all the authors of the canonical books of Scripture, both of the Old and New Testament, are acknowledged as Prophets. God also communicated himself to the prophets by dreams and nocturnal visions. In Acts 10. 11, 12. it is said, that Peter fell into an ecstasy at noon-day, and had a revelation concerning the call of the Gentiles to the faith. The Lord appeared to Job and to Moses in a cloud, and discovered his will to them, Num. 11. 25. Job 38. 1. He has often made his voice to be heard in an articulate manner; thus he spake to Moses in the burning bush, and upon mount Sinai, and to Samuel in the night, 1 Sam. 3. 4.

We have in the Old Testament the writings of the sixteen Prophets; that is, of four greater, and twelve lesser Prophets. The four great Prophets are Isaiah, Jeremiah, Ezekiel, and Daniel. The twelve lesser Prophets are, Hosea, Joel, Amos, Obadiah, Jonah, Micah, Nahum, Habakkuk, Zephaniah, Haggai, Zechariah, and Malachi.

This is nearly the chronological order in which they may be ranged.

1. Hosea prophesied under Uzziah, Jotham, Ahaz, and Hezekiah, kings of Judah, and under Jeroboam II. king of Israel, and his successors, to the destruction of Samaria. Some think, that the title of Hosea's prophecy, wherein mention is made of his having prophesied under so many kings, is not his own, but some ancient transcriber's; and that the true beginning of this Prophet's work is at verse 2. The beginning of the word of the Lord: For, say they, if he had prophesied under the reign of all these princes, he must have lived a very long time; by a moderate calculation, for the space of one hundred and twelve years.
2. Amos began to prophesy the second year before the earthquake, which was in the reign of king Uzziah, about six years before the death of Jeroboam II. king of Israel.
3. Isaiah began to prophesy at the death of Uzziah, and at the beginning of the reign of Jotham king of Judah. He continued to prophesy to the reign of Manasseh, who caused him to be put to death.
4. Jonah lived in the kingdom of Israel under the kings Joash and Jeroboam II. about the same time as Hosea, Isaiah, and Amos.
5. Micah lived under Jotham, Ahaz, and Hezekiah, kings of Judah; he was contemporary with Isaiah, but began later to prophesy.
6. Nahum appeared in Judah under the reign of Hezekiah, and after the expedition of Sennacherib.
7. Jeremiah began in the thirteenth year of the reign of Josiah king of Judah. He continued to prophesy under the reigns of Shallum, Jehoiakim, Jeconiah, and Zedekiah, to the taking of Jerusalem by the Chaldeans; and it is thought he died two years after in Egypt; Baruch was his disciple and amanuensis.
8. Zephaniah appeared at the beginning of the reign of Josiah, and before the twenty-eighth year of this prince; he was contemporary with Jeremiah.
9. Joel prophesied under Josiah about the same time as Jeremiah and Zephaniah.
10. Daniel was taken into Chaldea in the fourth year of Jehoiakim, king of Judah, and prophesied at Babylon to the end of the captivity.
11. Ezekiel was carried captive to Babylon, along with Jeconiah king of Judah, in the year of the world 3405. He began to prophesy in the year 3409. He continued till towards the end of the reign of Nebuchadnezzar, who died in the year of the world 3442.
12. Habakkuk lived in Judea at the beginning of the reign of Jehoiakim, about the year 3394, and before the coming of Nebuchadnezzar into the country in 3398. He dwelt in Judea during the captivity.
13. Obadiah lived in Judea after the taking of Jerusalem, and before the desolation of Idumea.
14. Haggai was born in all probability at Babylon, from whence he returned with Zerubbabel. In the second year of Darius son of Hystaspes, he was excited by God to exhort Zerubbabel, the prince of Judah, and the high priest Joshua, to resume the work of the temple, which had been interrupted for so long time, by the envy of those who were enemies to the Jews, who prevailed with Cyrus to revoke that permission whereby he had empowered the Jews to rebuild their temple. And Cambyses the son of Cyrus coming to the crown, renewed the same prohibition: so that the temple for fourteen years continued in the same state wherein the Jews had put it immediately after their return.
15. Zechariah prophesied in Judea at the same time as Haggai, and he seems to have continued to prophesy after him.
16. Malachi, the last prophet, has not put any date to his prophecies. If he was the same as Ezra, as some think, he may have prophesied under Nehemiah, who returned into Judah in 3550.

Besides these, there are found the names of a great many more prophets in Scripture, such as Abraham, Isaac, Jacob, Moses, Joshua, Samuel, Nathan, David, Solomon, &c. Christ Jesus is the great Prophet of his church; Moses prophesying of him, Deut. 18. 15. says, God will raise up a Prophet like unto me; that is, such a prophet as I am, resembling me in nature and office, being a man and mediator, as I am, though more excellent, and in a more singular sort; I as a servant, he as a Son and Lord of his church, who will teach them the will of God, not only in his own person on earth, but by his word and Spirit when exalted to the right hand of power in heaven.

Exod. 7. 1. and Aaron thy brother shall be thy p.
Deut. 18. 20. but the p. which shall presume, 22.
1 Sam. 22. 5. the p. Gad said to David, abide not
2 Sam. 24. 11. the word of the Lord came to the p.
1 Kings 1. 32. David said, call me Nathan the p.
44. the king hath sent with him Nathan the p.
11. 29. Ahijah the p. found Jeroboam in the way
13. 11. there dwelt an old p. in Bethel, 25.
23. for the p. whom he had brought back
29. p. took up the carcase of the man of God, and the old p. came to mourn and bury him
16. 7. by hand of the p. Jehu came the word, 12.
18. 36. Elijah p. came near and said, God of Abr.
20. 22. p. came to king of Israel, and said to him
2 Kings 5. 3. would God my lord were with the p.
13. if the p. had bid thee do some great thing
6. 12. Elisha the p. telleth what thou speakest
9. 4. young man the p. went to Ramoth-gilead
20. 11. Isaiah the p. cried to Lord, he brought
23. 18. with bones of p. that came out of Samaria
2 Chron. 12. 5. came Shemaiah the p. to Rehoboam
13. 22. are written in the story of the p. Iddo
15. 8. when Asa heard the prophecy of the p. Oded
21. 12. there came a writing from Elijah the p.
25. 16. then the p. forbare, and said, I know
32. 20. the p. Isaiah prayed and cried to heaven
35. 18. none like it from the days of Samuel the p.
36. 12. humbled not himself before Jeremiah the p.
Ezra 5. 1. then Haggai the p. prophesied
6. 14. through the prophesying of Haggai the p.
Psal. 74. 9. there is no more any p. among you
Isa. 3. 2. Lord doth take away the p. and prudent
9. 15. the p. that teacheth lies, he is the tail
28. 7. priest and p. have erred thro' strong drink
Jer. 6. 13. from p. to the priests deal falsely, 8. 10.
18. 18. nor shall the word perish from the p.
23. 11. for both p. and priests are profane
28. the p. that hath a dream let him tell
28. 6. the p. Jeremiah said, amen, the Lord do so
9. p. which prophesieth of peace, when the word of the p. shall come to pass then p. be known
17. so Hananiah the p. died the same year
36. 26. to take Baruch and Jeremiah the p.
37. 2. nor he nor his servants hearken to the p.
38. 10. take up Jeremiah the p. out of dungeon
Lam. 2. 20. shall the p. be slain in the sanctuary?
Ezek. 7. 26. then shall they seek a vision of p.
14. 4. and cometh to the p. I will answer him
9. if the p. be deceived, I have deceived that p.
10. the punishment of the p. shall be even as
Hos. 4. 5. the p. also shall fall with thee in the night
9. 7. the p. is a fool ‖ 8. p. is a snare of a fowler
Amos 7. 14. then he said, I was no p. nor p. son
Hab. 3. 1. a prayer of Habakkuk the p. on Shigionoth
Zech. 13. 5. he shall say, I am no p. an husbandman
Mal. 4. 5. behold, I will send you Elijah the p.
Mat. 1. 22. which was spoken by the p. Isaiah, 2. 15. | 3. 3. | 4. 14. | 8. 17. | 21. 4. Luke 3. 4. John 1. 23. | 12. 38. Acts 28. 25.
2. 5. in Bethlehem, for thus it is written by the p.
17. that which was spoken by Jeremy p. 27. 9.
12. 39. but the sign of the p. Jonas, Luke 11. 29.
13. 35. which was spoken by p. David, 27. 35.
21. 11. this is Jesus the p. of Nazareth of Galilee
24. 15. spoken of by Daniel the p. Mark 13. 14.
Luke 1. 76. thou child be called p. of the Highest
4. 17. delivered to him the book of the p. Esaias
24. no p. is accepted in his own country
27. many lepers in the time of Eliseus the p.
7. 28. not a greater p. than John the Baptist
John 7. 40. the people said, of a truth this is the p.
52. look, for out of Galilee ariseth no p.
Acts 2. 16. this is what was spoken by the p. Joel
7. 48. not in temples made with hands, as saith p.
8. 28. in his chariot he read Esaias the p. 30.
34. I pray thee, of whom speaketh the p. this?
13. 20. he gave them judges until Samuel the p.
2 Pet. 2. 16. the ass forbade the madness of the p.
See PRIEST.

A PROPHET.

Gen. 20. 7. now restore man his wife, for he is a p.
Num. 12. 6. if there be a p. among you, I the Lord
Deut. 13. 1. if there arise a p. or dreamer of dreams
18. 15. I will raise up a p. from among brethren, to him ye shall hearken, 18. Acts 3. 22. | 7. 37.
22. when a p. speaketh in the name of the Lord
34. 10. there arose not a p. in Israel like Moses
Judg. 6. 8. Lord sent a p. to the children of Israel
1 Sam. 3. 20. Samuel was established to be a p.
9. 9. he that is now called a p. was called a seer
1 Kings 13. 18. he said, I am a p. also as thou art
18. 22. I, even I only remain a p. of the Lord
19. 16. shalt anoint Elisha to be a p. in thy room
20. 13. there came a p. unto Ahab, saying
22. 7. is there not here a p. of the Lord besides, to inquire of him? 2 Kings 3. 11. 2 Chron. 18. 6.
2 Kings 5. 8. he shall know there is a p. in Israel
2 Chron. 25. 15. the Lord sent a p. to Amaziah
28. 9. but a p. of the Lord was there, Oded
Jer. 1. 5. I ordained thee a p. to the nations
29. 26. that is mad and maketh himself a p. 27.
Ezek. 2. 5. there hath been a p. among them, 33. 33.
14. 7. cometh to a p. to inquire of him about me
Hos. 12. 13. by a p. the Lord brought Israel out of Egypt, and by a p. was he preserved
Mic. 2. 11. he shall even be the p. of his people
Mat. 10. 41. he that receiveth a p. in the name of a p. shall receive a p. reward
11. 9. but what went ye out for to see? a p.?
13. 57. a p. is not without honour save in his own country and house, Mark 6. 4. John 4. 44.
14. 5. he feared multitude, because they accounted him as a p. 21. 26. Mark 11. 32. Luke 20. 6.
21. 46. the multitude, they took him for a p.
Mark 6. 15. that it is a p. or as one of the prophets
Luke 7. 16. saying, a great p. is risen up among us
39. this man, if he were a p. would have known
13. 33. for it cannot be that a p. perish out of Jerus
24. 19. concerning Jesus, who was a p. mighty
John 4. 19. she said, I perceive that thou art a p.
9. 17. the blind man said, he is a p.
Acts 2. 30. David being a p. and knowing that God
21. 10. there came a certain p. named Agabus
1 Cor. 14. 37. if any man think himself to be a p.
Tit. 1. 12. one, even a p. of their own land

False PROPHET.

Acts 13. 6. found a false p. a Jew named Barjesus
Rev. 16. 13. like frogs out of mouth of false p.
19. 20. the beast was taken, with him the false p.
20. 10. devil was cast where beast and false p. are
See LORD.

That PROPHET.

Deut. 13. 3. not hearken to the words of that p.
5. and that p. or that dreamer shall die, 18. 20.
Ezek. 14. 9. I the Lord have deceived that p.
John 1. 21. they asked him, art thou that p.? 25.
6. 14. this is of a truth that p. that should come
Acts 3. 23. every soul which will not hear that p.

PROPHETS.

Num. 11. 29. that all the Lord's people were p.
1 Sam. 10. 5. thou shalt meet a company of p.
10. p. met him ‖ 11. prophesied among the p.
12. is Saul also among the p.? 19. 24.
28. 6. the Lord answered him not by p. 15.
1 Kings 18. 4. Obadiah hid 100 p. by 50 in a cave
13. Jezebel slew the p. ‖ 19. p. of Baal 450. ‖ 22.
40. take the p. of Baal, let none of them escape
19. 10. Israel have forsaken thy covenant, have slain thy p. with the sword, 14. Neh. 9. 26.
22. 6. the king of Israel gathered the p. together
22. I will be a lying spirit in p. 2 Chron. 18. 21.
2 Kings 3. 13. to p. of thy father, and p. of mother
23. 2. Josiah went and the p. to the house of Lord
2 Chron. 20. 20. believe his p. so shall ye prosper
24. 19. he sent p. ‖ 36. 16. they misused his p.
Ezra 5. 2. with them were the p. of God helping
Neh. 6. 7. and thou hast appointed p. to preach
9. 30. thou testifiedst by thy Spirit in thy p.
32. the trouble that hath come on our p.
Isa. 29. 10. the p. and seers hath he covered
30. 10. say to the p. prophesy not, Amos 2. 12.
Jer. 2. 8. and p. prophesied by Baal, and walked
26. their princes, their priests and p. are ashamed
30. your own sword hath devoured your p.
4. 9. the p. shall wonder ‖ 5. 13. p. become wind
5. 31. the p. prophesy falsely, and priests bear rule
8. 1. they shall bring out the bones of the p.
13. 13. I will fill the p. with drunkenness
14. 13. the p. say, ye shall not see the sword
14. p. prophesy lies in my name, sent them not
15. by sword and famine shall those p. be cons.
23. 13. I have seen folly in the p. of Samaria
14. I have seen in the p. an horrible thing
15. from p. is profaneness gone forth into land
21. I have not sent these p. yet they ran
25. I have heard what the p. said, that prophesy
26. they are p. of the deceit of their own heart
30. I am against the p. that steal my word, 31.
26. 7. so priests and p. heard Jeremiah speaking
8. the p. and all the people took Jeremiah
11. then spake the p. this man is worthy to die
27. 9. therefore hearken not to your p. 16.
15. and that ye and the p. might perish
18. if they be p. and word of Lord be with them
28. 8. the p. that have been before me and thee
29. 1. words of the letter Jeremiah sent to the p.
8. saith the Lord, let not your p. deceive you
15. the Lord hath raised us up p. in Babylon
32. 32. they and their p. provoke me to anger
37. 19. where are now your p. which prophesied
Lam. 2. 9. her p. also find no vision from the Lord
14. thy p. have seen vain things for thee
4. 13. for the sins of her p. that hath shed blood
Ezek. 13. 2. prophesy against the p. of Israel
3. thus saith the Lord, woe unto the foolish p.
4. O Israel, thy p. are like foxes in deserts
9. my hand shall be upon the p. that see vanity
22. 25. there is a conspiracy of her p. in midst
28. her p. daubed them with untempered mortar
Hos. 6. 5. I have hewed them by the p. have slain
12. 10. I have spoken by p. and multiplied visions
Amos 2. 11. I have raised up of your sons p.
12. and commanded the p. saying, prophesy not
Mic. 3. 6. the sun shall go down over the p.
11. and the p. thereof divine for money
Zeph. 3. 4. her p. are light and treacherous persons
Zech. 1. 4. to whom the former p. have cried
5. and the p. do they live for ever?
7. 7. the words the Lord hath cried by former p.
12. word Lord sent in his Spirit by former p.
13. 2. I will cause the p. to pass out of the land
4. the p. shall be ashamed, each of his vision
Mat. 5. 12. so persecuted they the p. Luke 6. 23.
17. think not that I am come to destroy the p.
7. 12. do so to them, for this is the law and the p.
13. 17. many p. have desired to see, Luke 10. 24.
22. 40. on these two hang all the law and the p.
23. 31. the children of them who killed the p.
34. I send unto you p. and wise men, Luke 11. 49.
37. O Jerusalem, thou that killest the p.
Mark 1. 2. as it is written in the p. I send my messenger, Luke 18. 31. | 24. 25. John 6. 45.
Luke 1. 70. as he spake by his holy p. 2 Pet. 3. 2.
16. 16. the law and the p. were until John
29. Abraham said, they have Moses and p. 31

Luke 24. 25. slow to believe what the *p*. have spoken
John 1. 45. we found him of whom the *p*. did write
8. 52. Abraham and the *p*. are dead, 53.
Acts 3. 18. God shewed by the mouth of his *p*. 21.
11. 27. *p*. came from Jerusalem to Antioch
13. 1. in church at Antioch certain *p*. and teachers
15. after the reading of the law and the *p*.
40. that come on you which is spoken in the *p*.
15. 32. Judas and Silas being *p*. also themselves
24. 14. believing all things written in the *p*.
26. 22. saying none other things than *p*. did say
27. king Agrippa, believest thou the *p*.?
Rom. 1. 2. which he promised afore by his *p*.
3. 21. being witnessed by the law and the *p*.
11. 3. Lord, they have killed *p*. and digged down
1 *Cor*. 12. 28. secondarily, *p*. thirdly, teachers
29. are all *p*.? ‖ 14. 29. let *p*. speak two or three
Eph. 2. 20. built on the foundation of the *p*.
3. 5. as it is now revealed to his *p*. by the Spirit
4. 11. and he gave some *p*. and teachers
1 *Thess*. 2. 15. who killed the Lord and their own *p*.
Heb. 1. 1. who spake to the fathers by the *p*.
Jam. 5. 10. take, my brethren, *p*. who have spoken
1 *Pet*. 1. 10. of which salvation the *p*. inquired
Rev. 11. 10. because these two *p*. tormented them
18. 20. rejoice over her, ye holy apostles and *p*.
24. in her was found blood of *p*. and of saints
22. 9. do it not, for I am of thy brethren the *p*.

All the PROPHETS.

1 *Kings* 19. 1. told Jezebel how he had slain *all the p*.
22. 10. kings of Israel and Judah on their throne, and *all the p*. prophesied, 12. 2 *Chron*. 18. 9, 11.
2 *Kings* 10. 19. now call to me *all the p*. of Baal
17. 13. Lord testified against Israel by *all the p*.
Mat. 11. 13. *all the p*. prophesied until John
Luke 11. 50. that blood of *all the p*. may be required
13. 28. when ye see *all the p*. in kingdom of God
24. 27. and beginning at *all the p*. he expounded
Acts 3. 24. yea, and *all the p*. from Samuel foretold
10. 43. to him give *all the p*. witness thro' his name

False PROPHETS.

Mat. 7. 15. beware of *false p*. in sheep's clothing
24. 11. many *false p*. shall rise, 24. *Mark* 13. 22.
Luke 6. 26. for so did their fathers to the *false p*.
2 *Pet*. 2. 1. there were *false p*. also among them
1 *John* 4. 1. because many *false p*. are gone out

My PROPHETS.

1 *Chron*. 16. 22. saying, touch not mine anointed, and do *my p*. no harm, *Psal*. 105. 15.

Of the PROPHETS.

1 *Sam*. 10. 10. behold, a company *of the p*. met him
19. 20. when they saw the company *of the p*.
1 *Kings* 20. 35. a certain man of the sons *of the p*.
41. the king discerned him that he was *of the p*.
22. 13. words *of the p*. declare good, 2 *Chr*. 18. 12.
2 *Kings* 2. 3. sons *of the p*. that were at Beth-el came
5. the sons *of the p*. at Jericho came to Elisha
7. fifty sons *of the p*. went to view afar off
15. the sons *of the p*. said, the spirit of Elijah
4. 1. a woman of the wives of sons *of the p*. cried
38. and seethe pottage for the sons *of the p*.
Neh. 6. 14. my God, think thou of the rest *of the p*.
Jer. 23. 9. because *of the p*. all my bones shake
16. hearken not to the words *of the p*. 27. 14.
26. how long shall this be in the heart *of the p*.?
Hos. 12. 10. used similitudes by ministry *of the p*.
Zech. 8. 9. that hear these by the mouth *of the p*.
Mat. 16. 14. Elias or one *of the p*. *Mark* 6. 15. | 8. 28.
23. 29. ye build the tombs *of the p*. *Luke* 11. 47.
30. partakers with them in the blood *of the p*.
26. 56. that scriptures *of the p*. might be fulfilled
Luke 9. 8. that one *of the p*. was risen again, 19.
Acts 3. 25. ye are children *of the p*. and of covenant
7. 42. as it is written in the book *of the p*.
52. which *of p*. have not your fathers persecuted?
13. 15. after the reading *of the* law and *the p*.
27. because they knew not the voice *of the p*.
15. 15. and to this agree the words *of the p*.
28. 23. persuading them of Jesus out *of the p*.
Rom. 16. 26. made manifest by scriptures *of the p*.
1 *Cor*. 14. 32. spirits *of the p*. are subjects to the *p*.
Eph. 2. 20. built on the foundation *of the p*.
Heb. 11. 32. time would fail me to tell *of the p*.
Rev. 16. 6. for they have shed the blood *of the p*.
22. 6. the Lord God *of the* holy *p*. sent his angel

Servants the PROPHETS.

2 *Kings* 9. 7. I may avenge blood of my *serv. the p*.
17. 13. law which I sent to you by my *serv. the p*.
23. as the Lord had said by all his *servants the p*.
21. 10. and Lord spake by his *servants the p*. 24. 2.
Ezra 9. 11. which thou hast commanded by *serv. p*.
Jer. 7. 25. sent you my *s. p*. 25. 4. | 29. 19. | 35. 15.
26. 5. hearken to the words of my *servants the p*.
Ezek. 38. 17. I have spoken in old time by my *servants the p*.
Dan. 9. 6. neither have we hearkened to *servants p*.
10. laws which he set before us by his *servants p*.
Amos 3. 7. he revealeth his secret to his *servants p*.
Zech. 1. 6. words which I commanded my *serv. p*.
Rev. 10. 7. he finished, as he declared to his *serv. p*.
11. 18. that thou shouldest give reward to *servants the p*.

PROPHETESS.

Exod. 15. 20. Miriam *p*. took a timbrel in her hand
Judg. 4. 4. and Deborah a *p*. judged Israel
2 *Kings* 22. 14. went to Huldah *p*. 2 *Chron*. 34. 22.
Neh. 6. 14. my God, think on the *p*. Noadiah
Isa. 8. 3. I went to the *p*. and she conceived a son
Luke 2. 36. there was one Anna a *p*. of great age
Rev. 2. 20. woman Jezebel, who calleth herself a *p*.

PROPITIATION.

Rom. 3. 25. whom God hath set forth to be a *p*.
1 *John* 2. 2. and he is the *p*. for our sins, 4. 10.

PROPORTION.

1 *Kings* 7. 36. according to the *p*. of every one
Job 41. 12. I will not conceal his comely *p*.
Rom. 12. 6. let us prophesy according to *p*. of faith

PROSELYTE.

This term comes from the Greek *word* προσελυτος, *which signifies a* stranger, *one that comes from abroad, or from another place.* *The* Hebrew *word* Ger *or* Necher, *has the same signification. In the language of the Jews, they go by this name, who come to dwell in their country, or who embrace their religion, though they are not* Jews *by birth.*

The Hebrews *distinguish two kinds of* Proselytes. *The first are called* Proselytes of the Gate, *and the others* Proselytes of Justice. *The first are those who dwell in the land of* Israel, *or even out of that country, and who, without obliging themselves to circumcision, or to any other ceremony of the law, feared and worshipped the true God, observing the rules that were imposed upon the children of* Noah: *these precepts are seven in number,* [1] De Judiciis. *Obedience is due to judges, magistrates, and princes.* [2] De cultu extraneo. *The worship of false gods, superstition, and sacrilege, are absolutely forbidden.* [3] De maledictione nominis sanctissimi. *As also cursing the name of God, blasphemies, and false oaths.* [4] De revelatione turpitudinum. *Likewise all incestuous and unlawful conjunctions or copulations, as sodomy, bestiality, crimes against nature.* [5] De sanguinis effusione. *The effusion of the blood of all sorts of animals, murder, wounds, and mutilations.* [6] De rapina. *Thefts, cheats, lying, &c.* [7] De membro animalis viventis. *The parts of an animal still alive are not to be eaten, as was practised by some pagans. Of this number was* Naaman, *the* Syrian, Cornelius *the centurion, the eunuch of queen* Candace, *and others. Such as would enter themselves as* Proselytes of habitation, *or of the* gate, *promised with an oath, in the presence of three witnesses, to keep those seven precepts. Their privileges were said to be,* First, *that by the observation of the rules of natural justice, and by exemption from idolatry, blasphemy, incest, adultery, and murder, they thought they were in the path to eternal life.* Secondly, *they might dwell in the land of* Israel, *and have a share in the outward prosperities of the people of God.*

The Proselytes of Justice *are those that were converted to* Judaism, *who had engaged themselves to receive circumcision, and to observe the whole law of Moses. Thus were they admitted to all the prerogatives of the people of God, as well in this life as in the other. The Rabbins say, that before circumcision was administered to them, and before they were admitted into the religion of the* Hebrews, *they were examined about the motives of their conversion; to know whether their change was voluntary, or whether it proceeded from any reasons of interest, fear, ambition, or such like. Three things were required in a complete* Proselyte, *which were, washing, or plunging his body in a cistern of water, circumcision, and sacrifice; but for women, only washing and sacrifice.*

Mat. 23. 15. compass sea and land to make one *p*.
Acts 6. 5. they chose Nicholas a *p*. of Antioch

PROSELYTES.

Acts 2. 10. Jews and *p*. we hear in our tongues
13. 43. many Jews and religious *p*. followed Paul

PROSPECT.

1 *Kings* 7. † 5. doors and posts were square in *p*.
Ezek. 40. 44. chambers whose *p*. was to the south
46. *p*. to the north ‖ 42. 15. *p*. to the east, 43. 4.

PROSPER.

Gen. 24. 40. God will send his angel, and *p*. thee
42. if now thou do *p*. my way which I go
39. 3. Lord made all which Joseph did to *p*. 23.
Num. 14. 41. you transgress, but it shall not *p*.
Deut. 28. 29. thou shalt not *p*. in thy ways
29. 9. that ye may *p*. *Josh*. 1. 7. 1 *Kings* 2. 3.
1 *Kings* 22. 12. the prophets prophesied, saying, go up to Ramoth-gilead and *p*. 15. 2 *Chr*. 18. 11, 14.
1 *Chron*. 22. 11. now, my son, the Lord *p*. thee
13. then shalt thou *p*. if thou takest heed
2 *Chron*. 13. 12. fight ye not, for ye shall not *p*.
20. 20. believe his prophets, so shall ye *p*.
24. 20. why transgress ye, that ye cannot *p*.?
26. 5. as he sought the Lord, God made him to *p*.
Neh. 1. 11. *p*. I pray thee, thy servant this day
2. 20. I said, the God of heaven, he will *p*. us
Job 12. 6. the tabernacles of robbers *p*.
Psal. 1. 3. and whatsoever he doeth shall *p*.
45. † 4. and in thy majesty *p*. thou, ride thou
73. 12. these are the ungodly who *p*. in the world
122. 6. they shall *p*. that love thee
Prov. 28. 13. he that covereth his sins shall not *p*.
Eccl. 11. 6. thou knowest not whether shall *p*.
Isa. 52. † 13. behold my servant shall *p*.
53. 10. pleasure of the Lord shall *p*. in his hand
54. 17. no weapon formed against thee shall *p*.
55. 11. it shall *p*. in the thing whereto I sent it
Jer. 2. 37. and thou shalt not *p*. in them
5. 28. yet they *p*. ‖ 10. 21. they shall not *p*. 20. 11.
12. 1. wherefore doth the way of the wicked *p*.?
22. 30. write this man childless, a man that shall not *p*. in his days, for no man of his seed shall *p*.
23. 5. a king shall reign and *p*. and execute
32. 5. tho' ye fight with Chaldeans, ye shall not *p*.
Lam. 1. 5. her adversaries are chief, her enemies *p*.
Ezek. 15. † 4. the vine when burnt, will it *p*.?
16. 13. thou didst *p*. ‖ 17. 9. shall it *p*.? 10.
17. 15. shall he *p*. shall he escape?
Dan. 3. † 30. king made Shadrach to *p*. in Babylon
8. 24. he shall destroy wonderfully and *p*.
25. through his policy he shall cause craft to *p*.
11. 27. they shall speak lies, but it shall not *p*. 36.
3 *John* 2. I wish above all that thou mayest *p*.

PROSPERED.

Gen. 24. 56. seeing the Lord hath *p*. my way
Judg. 4. 24. the hand of Israel *p*. against Jabin
1 *Sam*. 18. † 5. and David went out and *p*. † 14.
2 *Sam*. 11. 7. David demanded how the war *p*.
2 *Kings* 18. 7. Hezekiah *p*. 2 *Chron*. 31. 21. | 32. 30.
1 *Chron*. 29. 23. Solom. *p*. ‖ 2 *Chron*. 14. 7. Asa *p*.
Ezra 6. 14. *p*. through the prophesying of Haggai
Job 9. 4. who hardened himself ag. him, and hath *p*.?
Dan. 6. 28. so this Daniel *p*. in the reign of Darius
8. 12. it cast down truth to the ground, and it *p*.
1 *Cor*. 16. 2. every man lay by, as God hath *p*. him

PROSPERETH.

Ezra 5. 8. and this work *p*. in their hands
Psal. 37. 7. fret not bec. of him that *p*. in his way
Prov. 17. 8. a gift, whithersoever it turneth it *p*.
3 *John* 2. mayest be in health, even as thy soul *p*.

PROSPERITY.

Deut. 23. 6. thou shalt not seek their *p*. all thy days
1 *Sam*. 25. 6. thus shall say to him that liveth in *p*.
1 *Kings* 10. 7. thy wisdom and *p*. exceedeth fame
Job 15. 21. in *p*. the destroyer shall come on him
36. 11. if serve him, shall spend their days in *p*.
Psal. 30. 6. in my *p*. I said, I shall never be moved
35. 27. Lord hath pleasure in the *p*. of his servant
73. 3. when I saw the *p*. of the wicked
118. 25. O Lord, I beseech thee, send now *p*.
122. 7. peace be within thy walls, *p*. in palaces
Prov. 1. 32. the *p*. of fools shall destroy them
Eccl. 7. 14. in the day of *p*. be joyful
Jer. 22. 21. I spake to thee in thy *p*.
33. 9. for all the *p*. that I procure to it
Lam. 3. 17. removed far from peace, I forgat *p*.
Dan. 8. † 25. by *p*. shall he destroy many
Zech. 1. 17. my cities thro' *p*. shall yet be spread
7. 7. when Jerusalem was inhabited and in *p*.

PROSPEROUS.

Gen. 24. 21. whether the Lord made his journey *p*
39. 2. Lord was with Joseph, he was a *p*. man
Josh. 1. 8. then shalt thou make thy way *p*.
Judg. 18. 5. whether the way we go shall be *p*.
Job 8. 6. make the habitation of righteousness *p*.
Isa. 48. 15. and he shall make his way *p*.
Zech. 8. 12. for the seed shall be *p*. vine give fruit
Rom. 1. 10. if at length I might have a *p*. journey

PROSPEROUSLY.

2 *Chron*. 7. 11. Solomon *p*. effected all that came
Psal. 45. 4. and in thy majesty ride *p*. because

PROSTITUTE.

Lev. 19. 29. do not *p*. thy daughter to be a whore

PROTECTEST.

Psal. 5. † 11. shout for joy, because thou *p*. them

PROTECTION.

Deut. 32. 38. let them rise up and be your *p*.

PROTEST, ED.

Gen. 43. 3. the man did solemnly *p*. to us, saying
1 *Sam*. 8. 9. hearken, yet *p*. solemnly unto them
1 *Kings* 2. 42. and I *p*. unto thee, saying, know
Jer. 11. 7. I earnestly *p*. to your fathers
Zech. 3. 6. the angel of the Lord *p*. to Joshua
1 *Cor*. 15. 31. I *p*. by your rejoicing in Christ

PROTESTING.

Gen. 43. † 3. the man *p*. protested to us, saying
Jer. 11. 7. and *p*. saying, obey my voice

PROTRACT.

Neh. 9. † 30. many years didst thou *p*. over them

PROUD.

Job 9. 13. the *p*. helpers do stoop under him
26. 12. by understanding he smiteth through the *p*.
38. 11. and here shall thy *p*. waves be stayed
40. 11. behold every one that is *p*. and abase him
12. look on every one that is *p*. bring him low
Psal. 12. 3. the tongue that speaketh *p*. things
31. 23. and plentifully rewardeth the *p*. doer
40. 4. blessed is the man who respecteth not the *p*.
86. 14. O God, the *p*. are risen against me
94. 2. lift up thyself, render a reward to the *p*.
101. 5. him that hath a *p*. heart will I not suffer
119. 21. thou hast rebuked the *p*. that are cursed
51. the *p*. have had me greatly in derision
69. the *p*. have forged a lie against me
78. let *p*. be ashamed, for they dealt perversely
85. the *p*. digged pits for me, not after thy law
122. be surety for me, let not the *p*. oppress me
123. 4. our soul is filled with contempt of the *p*.
124. 5. the *p*. waters had gone over our soul
138. 6. but the *p*. he knoweth afar off
140. 5. the *p*. have hid a snare for me and cords
Prov. 6. 17. Lord hateth a *p*. look, a lying tongue
15. 25. the Lord will destroy the house of the *p*.
16. 5. every one *p*. in heart is abomination to Lord
19. than to divide the spoil with the *p*.
21. 4. an high look and a *p*. heart is sin
24. *p*. scorner is his name, who deals in *p*. wrath
28. 25. he that is of a *p*. heart stirreth up strife
Eccl. 7. 8. the patient better than the *p*. in spirit
Isa. 2. 12. day of the Lord on every one that is *p*.
13. 11. I will cause the arrogancy of the *p*. to cease
16. 6. we have heard of the *p*. wrath of Moab
Jer. 13. 15. be not *p*. for the Lord hath spoken
43. 2. all the *p*. men answered Jeremiah
48. 29. heard pride of Moab, he is exceeding *p*.
50. 29. she hath been *p*. ‖ 31. O thou most *p*.
32. most *p*. shall stumble and fall, none raise him
Hab. 2. 5. he is a *p*. man, neither keepeth at home
Mal. 3. 15. we call the *p*. happy ‖ 4. 1. *p*. as stubble
Luke 1. 51. he hath scattered the *p*. in imagination
Rom. 1. 30. filled with unrighteousness, *p*. boasters
1 *Tim*. 6. 4. he is *p*. knowing nothing, but doting
2 *Tim*. 3. 2. men shall be lovers of themselves, *p*.
Jam. 4. 6. God resisteth the *p*. 1 *Pet*. 5. 5.

PROUDLY.

Exod. 18. 11. wherein dealt *p*. he was above them
1 *Sam*. 2. 3. talk no more so exceeding *p*.
Neh. 9. 10. thou knewest that they dealt *p*. 16, 29.
Psal. 17. 10. with their mouth they speak *p*.
31. 18. which speak grievous things *p*. against right
Isa. 3. 5. child shall behave himself *p*. agst. ancient
Dan. 5. † 20. and his mind hardened to deal *p*.
Obad. 12. neither shouldest thou have spoken *p*.

PROVE

Signifies, [1] *To try and examine*, 2 Cor. 13. 5. [2] *To make manifest by argument*, Acts 9. 22. Rom. 3. 9. [3] *To make good*, Acts 24. 13. [4] *To try by some affliction, that men may know their own hearts*, Deut. 8. 2. [5] *To find true*, Eccl. 7. 23. [6] *To judge*, Job 9. 20. [7] *To discern, approve of, and conform to*, Rom. 12. 2.

Exod. 16. 4. that I may *p*. them, *Deut*. 8. 16.
20. 20. fear not, for God is come to *p*. you
Deut. 8. 2. to humble thee, and to *p*. thee, to know
33. 8. holy one, whom thou didst *p*. at Massah
Judg. 2. 22. that through them I may *p*. Isr. 3. 1, 4.
6. 39. let me *p*. thee but this once with fleece
1 *Kings* 10. 1. she came to *p*. Solomon, 2 *Chr*. 9. 1.
Job 9. 20. if I say perfect, it shall *p*. me perverse

Job 13. † 15. I will *p.* mine own ways before him
Psal. 26. 2. examine me, O Lord, and *p.* me
Eccl. 2. 1. go to now, I will *p.* thee with mirth
Dan. 1. 12. *p.* thy servants, I beseech thee, ten days
Mal. 3. 10. bring the tithes, *p.* me now herewith
Luke 14. 19. I have bought oxen, I go to *p.* them
John 6. 6. this he said to *p.* him, for he knew
Acts 24. 13. neither can they *p.* the things, 25. 7.
Rom. 12. 2. that ye may *p.* what is that good will
2 *Cor.* 8. 8. to *p.* the sincerity of your love
13. 5. *p.* your own selves, know ye not yourselves?
Gal. 6. 4. but let every man *p.* his own work
1 *Thess.* 5. 21. *p.* all things, hold fast what is good

PROVED.

Gen. 42. 15. hereby ye shall be *p.* by life of Pharaoh
16. send one of you, that your words may be *p.*
Exod. 15. 25. made a statute, and there he *p.* them
1 *Sam.* 17. 39. he had not *p.* his sword, David said to Saul, I cannot go with these, I have not *p.* them
Psal. 17. 3. thou hast *p.* my heart and visited me
66. 10. thou, O God, hast *p.* us, thou hast tried us
81. 7. I *p.* thee at the waters of Meribah
95. 9. when your fathers *p.* me and saw my works
Eccl. 7. 23. all this have I *p.* by wisdom
Dan. 1. 14. he consented, and *p.* them ten days
Rom. 3. 9. we before *p.* Jews and Gentiles under sin
2 *Cor.* 8. 22. whom we have often *p.* diligent
1 *Tim.* 3. 10. and let these also be first *p.*
Heb. 3. 9. your fathers *p.* me, and saw my works

PROVETH.

Deut. 13. 3. for Lord your God *p.* you, to know

PROVING.

Acts 9. 22. Saul *p.* that this is very Christ
Eph. 5. 10. *p.* what is acceptable to the Lord

PROVENDER.

Gen. 24. 25. we have both straw and *p.* enough
32. the man gave straw and *p.* for camels
42. 27. one opened sack to give his ass *p.* in the inn
43. 24. the man gave their asses *p.*
Judg. 19. 19. yet there is both straw and *p.*
21. he brought him and gave *p.* to the asses
Isa. 30. 24. the oxen and asses shall eat clean *p.*

PROVERB.

The Hebrews *give the name of* Proverbs, Parables, *or* Similitudes, *to moral sentences, maxims, comparisons, or enigmas, expressed in a style that is poetical, figurative, close, and sententious: they call this kind of* Proverbs, Mishle. Solomon *says, that in his time maxims of this sort were the chief study of the learned.* A wise man will endeavour, *says he,* to understand a proverb, and the interpretation, the words of the wise, and their dark sayings, *Prov.* 1. 6. *In the* Proverbs *of* Solomon *we find rules for the conduct of all conditions of life; for kings, courtiers, men engaged in the affairs of the world; for masters, servants, fathers, mothers, and children.*

Deut. 28. 37. and ye shall be a *p.* and a by-word
1 *Sam.* 10. 12. it became a *p.* is Saul among prophets?
24. 13. as saith the *p.* of the ancients
1 *Kings* 9. 7. Israel shall be a *p.* and a by-word
2 *Chron.* 7. 20. this house will I make to be a *p.*
Psal. 69. 11. and I became a *p.* to them
Prov. 1. 6. to understand a *p.* and words of the wise
Isa. 14. 4. take up this *p.* against the king of Babylon
Jer. 24. 9. I will deliver them to be a *p.* and curse
Ezek. 12. 22. what is that *p.* ye have in land of Isr.?
23. I will make this *p.* cease, and they shall no more use it as a *p* in Israel, 18. 2, 3.
14. 8. I will make him a sign, and a *p.* and cut off
Hab. 2. 6. all these take up a taunting *p.* against him
Luke 4. 23. will surely say this *p.* physician heal thy.
John 16. 29. now speakest thou plainly, and no *p.*
2 *Pet.* 2. 22. it is happened according to the *p.*

PROVERBS.

Num. 21. 27. wherefore they that speak in *p.* say
1 *Kings* 4. 32. Solomon spake three thousand *p.*
Prov. 1. 1. the *p.* of Solomon, 10. 1. | 25. 1.
Eccl. 12. 9. the preacher set in order many *p.*
Ezek. 16. 44. behold, every one that useth *p.* shall
John 16. 25. these spoken in *p.* no more speak in *p.*

PROVIDE.

Gen. 22. 8. God will *p.* himself a lamb for offering
† 14. Abraham called the place, the Lord will *p.*
30. 30. now when shall I *p.* for mine own house?
Exod. 18. 21. shalt *p.* out of the people able men
1 *Sam.* 16. 17. *p.* me a man that can play well
2 *Chron.* 2. 7. with cunning men whom David did *p.*
Psal. 78. 20. can he *p.* flesh for his people?
Mat. 10. 9. *p.* neither gold nor silver in your purses
Luke 12. 33. *p.* yourselves bags which wax not old
Acts 23. 24. and *p.* them beasts to set Paul on
Rom. 12. 17. *p.* things honest in sight of all men
1 *Tim.* 5. 8. but if any *p.* not for his own house

PROVIDED.

Deut. 33. 21. he *p.* the first part for himself
1 *Sam.* 16. 1. I have *p.* me a king among his sons
2 *Sam.* 19. 32. he had *p.* the king of sustenance
1 *Kings* 4. 7. which *p.* victuals for the king, 27.
2 *Chron.* 32. 29. Hezekiah *p.* possessions of flocks
Psal. 65. 9. preparest corn, when thou hast *p.* for it
Luke 12. 20. whose shall those things be thou hast *p.*?
Heb. 11. 40. God having *p.* better things for us

PROVIDENCE.

Acts 24. 2. are done to this nation by thy *p.*

PROVIDETH.

Job 38. 41. who *p.* for the raven his food
Prov. 6. 8. and *p.* her meat in the summer

PROVIDING.

2 *Cor.* 8. 21. *p.* for honest things, not only in sight

PROVINCE, S.

1 *Kings* 20. 14. by the princes of the *p.* 15, 17, 19.
Ezra 4. 15. this city is hurtful to kings and *p.*
6. 2. there was found in the *p.* of the Medes
7. 16. carry the gold thou canst find in the *p.*
Neh. 7. 6. these are the children of the *p.* went up
11. 3. now these are the chief of the *p.*
Esth. 1. 1. Ahasuerus reigned over 127 *p.*
16. hath done wrong to all people in all *p.* 22.
2. 3. let the king appoint officers in all the *p.*
18. then the king made a release to the *p.*

Esth. 3. 8. is a people scattered in all *p.* of thy king.
13. Haman sent by posts to all the king's *p.*
4. 11. all the people of the king's *p.* do know
8. 9. 127 *p.* and to every *p.* according to
12. upon one day in all *p.* of king Ahasuerus
9. 4. Mordecai's fame went through all the *p.*
12. what have they done in the rest of the *p.*
28. these days should be kept through every *p.*
Eccl. 2. 8. I gathered the treasure of the *p.*
5. 8. if thou seest oppression in a *p.* marvel not
Lam. 1. 1. she that was princess among the *p.*
Ezek. 19. 8. nations set against him from the *p.*
Dan. 2. 48. the king made Daniel ruler over the *p.*
3. 1. he set up an image in the *p.* of Babylon
30. promoted Shadrach in the *p.* of Babylon
8. 2. I was at Shushan in the *p.* of Elam
11. 24. shall enter on the fattest places of the *p.*
Acts 23. 34. he asked of what *p.* he was
25. 1. now when Festus was come into the *p.*

PROVISION.

Gen. 42. 25. and to give them *p.* for the way
45. 21. Joseph gave them *p.* for the way
Josh. 9. 5. all the bread of their *p.* was dry
12. this our bread we took hot for our *p.*
1 *Kings* 4. 7. each man his month in a year made *p.*
22. Solomon's *p.* for one day was 30 measures
2 *Kings* 6. 23. he prepared great *p.* for them
1 *Chron.* 29. 19. for the which I have made *p.*
Psal. 132. 15. I will abundantly bless her *p.*
Dan. 1. 5. the king appointed them a daily *p.*
Rom. 13. 14. and make not *p.* for the flesh

PROVOCATION.

1 *Kings* 15. 30. Jeroboam made Israel sin by his *p.*
21. 22. for the *p.* wherewith Ahab provoked
2 *Kings* 19. † 3. it is a day of trouble, rebuke, and *p.*
23. 26. because of the *p.* Manasseh provoked
Neh. 9. 18. and had wrought great *p.* 26.
Job 17. 2. doth not mine eye continue in their *p.*?
Psal. 95. 8. harden not your hearts as in *p.* as in day of temptation in the wildern. *Heb.* 3. 8, 15.
Jer. 32. 31. this city hath been to me as a *p.*
Ezek. 20. 28. there they presented *p.* of offering

PROVOKE.

Exod. 23. 21. obey his voice, and *p.* him not
Num. 14. 11. how long will this people *p.* me?
Deut. 31. 20. if ye *p.* and break my covenant
Job 12. 6. and they that *p.* God are secure
Psal. 78. 40. how oft did they *p.* him in wilderness?
Isa. 3. 8. doings against Lord to *p.* eyes of his glory
Jer. 7. 19. do they *p.* me to anger? saith the Lord
44. 8. in that ye *p.* me to wrath with works
Luke 11. 53. began to urge and *p.* him to speak
Rom. 10. 19. I will *p.* to jealousy by them no peo.
11. 11. for to *p.* them to jealousy, 14.
1 *Cor.* 10. 22. do we *p.* the Lord to jealousy?
Eph. 6. 4. ye fathers, *p.* not your children to wrath
Heb. 3. 16. some when they had heard, did *p.*
10. 24. to *p.* to love and to good works

PROVOKED.

Num. 14. 23. nor shall any of them that *p.* me see it
16. 30. ye shall know these men have *p.* the Lord
Deut. 9. 8. in Horeb ye *p.* the Lord to wrath
22. at Taberah and Massah ye *p.* Lord to wrath
1 *Sam.* 1. 6. and her adversary also *p.* her sore
7. so she *p.* her, theref. she wept and did not eat
1 *Kings* 14. 22. *Jud. p.* him to jealousy with their sins
2 *Kings* 23. 26. Manasseh had *p.* him withal
1 *Chron.* 21. 1. Satan *p.* David to number Israel
Ezra 5. 12. after that our fathers had *p.* God
Psal. 78. 56. tempted and *p.* the most high God
106. 7. but *p.* him at the sea, even the Red sea
29. they *p.* him with their own inventions
33. because they *p.* the spirit of Moses, 43.
Zech. 8. 14. when your fathers *p.* me to wrath
1 *Cor.* 13. 5. charity is not easily *p.* thinketh no evil
2 *Cor.* 9. 2. and your zeal *p.* very many

PROVOKEDST.

Deut. 9. 7. forget not how thou *p.* Lord thy God

See ANGER.

PROVOKETH.

Prov. 20. 2. whoso *p.* him to anger sinneth ag. soul
Isa. 65. 3. people that *p.* me to anger to my face
Ezek. 8. 3. where was image which *p.* to jealousy

PROVOKING.

Deut. 32. 19. because of *p.* his sons and daughters
1 *Kings* 14. 15. they made groves, *p.* Lord to anger
16. 7. against Baasha in *p.* the Lord to anger, 13.
Psal. 78. 17. by *p.* the Most High in the wilderness
Gal. 5. 26. not desirous of vain glory, *p.* one another

PRUDENCE.

2 *Chr.* 2. 12. son endued with *p.* and understanding
Prov. 8. 12. I wisdom dwell with *p.* find knowledge
19. † 11. the *p.* of a man deferreth his anger
Eph. 1. 8. he hath abounded in all wisdom and *p.*

PRUDENT.

1 *Sam.* 16. 18. Dav. *p.* in matters, and a comely per
Prov. 12. 16. but a *p.* man covereth shame
23. a *p.* man concealeth knowledge
13. 16. every *p.* man dealeth with knowledge
14. 8. wisdom of the *p.* is to understand his way
15. but the *p.* man looketh well to his going
18. but the *p.* are crowned with knowledge
15. 5. but he that regardeth reproof is *p.*
16. 21. the wise in heart shall be called *p.*
18. 15. the heart of the *p.* getteth knowledge
19. 14. and a *p.* wife is from the Lord
22. 3. a *p.* man foreseeth evil and hideth, 27. 12.
Isa. 3. 2. take away the *p.* and the ancient
5. 21. woe to them that are *p.* in their own sight
10. 13. by my wisdom I have done it, for I am *p.*
29. 14. understanding of their *p.* men should be hid
Jer. 49. 7. is counsel perished from the *p.*?
Hos. 14. 9. who is *p.* and he shall know them?
Amos 5. 13. the *p.* shall keep silence in that time
Mat. 11. 25. hid these things from *p. Luke* 10. 21.
Acts 13. 7. the deputy Sergius Paulus, a *p.* man
1 *Cor.* 1. 19. to nothing understanding of the *p.*

PRUDENTLY.

Isa. 52. 13. my serv. shall deal *p.* he shall be exalted

PRUNE.

Lev. 25. 3. six years shalt thou *p.* thy vineyard
4. seventh year not sow thy field nor *p.*

PRUNED.

Isa. 5. 6. I lay it waste, it shall not be *p.* nor digged

PRUNING.

Isa. 2. 4. they shall beat their spears into *p.* hooks
18. 5. he shall cut off their sprigs with *p.* hooks
Joel 3. 10. beat your *p.* hooks into spears
Mic. 4. 3. they shall beat their spears into *p.* hooks

PSALM.

1 *Chron.* 16. 7. then David delivered first this *p.*
Psal. 81. 2. take a *p.* || 98. 5. with the voice of a *p.*
Mat. 26. † 30. when they had sung a *p.* they went out into the mount of Olives, *Mark* 14. † 26.
Acts 13. 33. as it is also written in the second *p.*
35. wherefore he saith also in another *p.* thou shalt
1 *Cor.* 14. 26. how is it every one of you hath a *p.*?

PSALMIST.

2 *Sam.* 23. 1. last words of David, sweet *p.* of Israel

PSALMS.

1 *Chron.* 16. 9. sing *p.* to him, *Psal.* 105. 2.
Neh. 12. † 8. the Levites over the *p.* of thanksgiving
Psal. 95. 2. make a joyful noise to him with *p.*
Luke 20. 42. David himself saith in the book of *p.*
24. 44. which were written in *p.* concerning me
Acts 1. 20. for it is written in the book of *p.*
Eph. 5. 19. speaking to yourselves in *p.* and hymns
Col. 3. 16. admonishing one another in *p.* and hymns
Jam. 5. 13. is any merry? let him sing *p.*

PSALTERY.

1 *Sam.* 10. 5. meet a company of prophets with a *p.*
Psal. 33. 2. sing to him with the *p.* 144. 9.
57. 8. awake, my glory, awake *p.* and harp, 108. 2.
71. 22. I will also praise thee with the *p.* 92. 3.
81. 2. bring hither the pleasant harp with the *p.*
150. 3. praise him with trumpet the *p.* and harp
Dan. 3. 5. when ye hear sound of the *p.* 7, 10, 15.

PSALTERIES, *See* CYMBALS.

PUBLICAN,

In Greek, Τελωνες, *was a farmer, or receiver of public money, an officer of the revenue, a man employed in collecting such impositions as are hateful to the people. Among the* Romans *there were two sorts of Farmers: some were general* Farmers, *who in every province had their deputies, and under-farmers, who collected the revenues and other profits of the empire, of which they gave an account to the emperor. These principal Farmers were men of great consideration in the government; and* Cicero *says, that among these were to be found the flower of the* Roman *knights, the ornament of the city, and the strength of the commonwealth. But the deputies, the under-farmers, the commissioners, the* Publicans *of the lower order, were looked upon as so many thieves and pickpockets.* Theocritus *being once asked, which was the most cruel of all beasts, made answer, That among the beasts of the wilderness, they were the bear and the lion; among the beasts of the city, they were the* Publican *and the* Parasite.

Among the Jews, *the name and profession of a* Publican *was the most odious thing in the world. This nation, in a particular manner, valued themselves upon their freedom:* We be *Abraham's* seed, and were never in bondage to any man, *John* 8. 33. *They could not, without the utmost reluctancy, see* Publicans *in their country, rigorously exacting those tributes and impositions that were laid on them by the* Romans. *Especially the* Galileans *or* Herodians *submitted to this badge of servitude not without the greatest impatience, and thought it even unlawful to pay tribute to a foreign power; as they shewed by that question they put to our Saviour,* Luke 20. 22. Is it lawful for us to give tribute to Cæsar, or no? *Those of their own nation that undertook this employ, they looked upon as no better than heathen,* Let him be unto thee as an heathen man, and a Publican, *Mat.* 18. 17. *It is said, that they would not allow them to come into their temple, or their synagogues, nor admit them to partake of their public prayers, or of their offices of judicature, or allow them to give testimony in a court of justice; and for certain they would not accept of their presents at the temple, no more than they would of the price of prostitution or of blood, or of any thing else of the like nature.*

There were many Publicans *in* Judea, *in the time of our Saviour.* Zaccheus *probably was one of the principal Farmers, since he is called the* chief among the Publicans, *Luke* 19. 2. *but* Matthew *was only an inferior Publican. The* Jews *reproached our Saviour with being a* friend of Publicans and sinners, *and of eating with them,* Luke 7. 34. *And our Saviour told the* Jews, That harlots and Publicans went into the kingdom of heaven before them, *Mat.* 21. 31. *In the parable of the* Publican *and* Pharisee, *who made their prayers together in the temple, we see with what sentiments of humility the view of his condition inspired the* Publican; *he keeps afar off, and probably dares not so much as enter the court of the people; he is afraid to lift up his eyes to heaven; he smites his breast, and submissively asks pardon of God,* Luke 18. 10, &c. Zaccheus *says to our Saviour, that he was ready to give half of his goods to the poor, and to restore fourfold of whatever he had unjustly acquired,* Luke 19. 8. *And this, because at that time the* Roman *laws required that whenever any* Publican *was convicted of extortion, he should be obliged to render four times the value of what he had extorted.*

PUBLICAN, S.

Mat. 5. 46. do not even the *p.* the same? 47.
9. 10. many *p.* sat with him, *Mark* 2. 15. *Luke* 5. 29.
11. said to his disciples, why eateth your master with *p.* and sinners, *Mark* 2. 16. *Luke* 5. 30.
10. 3. Philip, Thomas, and Matthew the *p.*
11. 19. a friend of *p.* and sinners, *Luke* 7. 34.
18. 17. let him be to thee as an heathen and a *p.*
21. 31. *p.* go into the kingdom of God before you
32. but the *p.* and the harlots believed him
Luke 3. 12. then came also *p.* to be baptized
5. 27. he saw a *p.* named Levi sitting at receipt
7. 29. the *p.* justified God, being baptized with

Luke 15. 1. then drew near to him the *p.* to hear him
18. 10. the one a Pharisee, and the other a *p.*
11. God, I thank thee, I am not as this *p.*
13. *p.* standing afar off, said, G. be merciful to me
19. 2. Zaccheus was chief among the *p.* and rich

PUBLIC.

Mat. 1. 19. not willing to make her a *p.* example

PUBLICLY.

Acts 18. 28. for he *p.* convinced the Jews, shewing
20. 20. but have shewed you, have taught you *p.*

PUBLISH.

Deut. 32. 3. I will *p.* the name of the Lord
1 *Sam.* 31. 9. to *p.* it in the house of their idols
2 *Sam.* 1. 20. *p.* it not in the streets of Askelon
Neh. 8. 15. should *p.* that they bring pine-branches
Psal. 26. 7. may *p.* with the voice of thanksgiving
Jer. 4. 5. *p.* in Jerusalem ‖ 16. *p.* against Jerusalem
5. 20. declare this, *p.* it in Judah, saying
31. 7. *p.* ye and say, O Lord, save thy people
46. 14. declare in Egypt, *p.* in Migdol, *p.* in Noph
50. 2. *p.* and conceal not, Babylon is taken
Amos 3. 9. *p.* in the palaces of Ashdod and Egypt
4. 5. proclaim and *p.* the free offerings
Mark 1. 45. but he began to *p.* it much, 5. 20.

PUBLISHED.

Esth. 1. 20. king's decree be *p.* thro' all empire, 22.
3. 14. the copy of Haman's decree was *p.* 8. 13.
Psal. 68. 11. great was the company that *p.* it
Jonah 3. 7. he caused it to be *p.* through Nineveh
Mark 7. 36. so much more a great deal they *p.* it
13. 10. the gospel must first be *p.* among nations
Luke 8. 39. he went and *p.* through the whole city
Acts 10. 37. that word ye know, which was *p.*
13. 49. word of the Lord was *p.* through all region

PUBLISHETH.

Isa. 52. 7. that *p.* peace, that *p.* salvation
Jer. 4. 15. voice *p.* affliction from mount Ephraim
Nah. 1. 15. behold the feet of him that *p.* peace

PUFF.

Job 11. † 20. their hopes shall be a *p.* of breath

PUFFED *up.*

1 *Cor.* 4. 6. no one of you be *p. up* against another
18. some are *p. up*, as though I would not come
19. will know, not speech of them that are *p. up*
5. 2. ye are *p. up* and have not rather mourned
13. 4. charity vaunteth not itself, is not *p. up*
Col. 2. 18. vainly *p. up* by his fleshly mind

PUFFETH *at.*

Psal. 10. 5. as for all his enemies, he *p. at* them
12. 5. set him in safety from him that *p. at* him

PUFFETH *up.*

1 *Cor.* 8. 1. knowledge *p. up*, charity edifieth

PULL, ED.

Gen. 8. 9. Noah *p.* the dove to him into the ark
19. 10. but the men *p.* Lot into the house
Josh. 8. † 6. till we have *p.* them from the city
1 *Kings* 13. 4. Jeroboam could not *p.* it in again
Ezra 6. 11. let timber be *p.* down from his house
Psal. 31. 4. *p.* me out of net they have laid for me
Isa. 22. 19. and from thy state shall *p.* thee down
Jer. 1. 10. set thee to *p.* down and destroy, 18. 7.
12. 3. *p.* them out like sheep for the slaughter
24. 6. I will build them and not *p.* down, 42. 10.
Lam. 3. 11. *p.* me in pieces, hath made me desolate
Ezek. 17. 9. shall he not *p.* up the roots thereof?
Amos 9. 15. and they shall no more be *p.* up
Mic. 2. 8. ye *p.* off the robe with the garment
Zech. 7. 11. but they *p.* away the shoulder
Mat. 7. 4. *p.* out mote out of thine eye, *Luke* 6. 42.
Luke 12. 18. I will *p.* down my barns and build
14. 5. and will not *p.* him out on the sabbath?
Acts 23. 10. lest Paul should have been *p.* in pieces

PULLING.

2 *Cor.* 10. 4. mighty to the *p.* down of strong holds

PULLING.

Jude 23. others save with fear, *p.* them out of fire

PULPIT.

Neh. 8. 4. Ezra the scribe stood upon a *p.* of wood

PULSE.

2 *Sam.* 17. 28. Barzillai brought beans and parched *p.*
Dan. 1. 12. let them give *p.* to eat, and water, 16.

PUNISH.

Lev. 26. 18. *p.* you seven times more for your sins, 24.
Prov. 17. 26. also to *p.* the just is not good
Isa. 10. 12. *p.* the stout heart of the king of Assyria
13. 11. I will *p.* the world for their evil
24. 21. the Lord shall *p.* the host of the high ones
26. 21. Lord cometh to *p.* inhabitants of the earth
27. 1. Lord with strong sword shall *p.* Leviathan
Jer. 9. 25. I will *p.* all them that are circumcised
11. 22. behold I will *p.* the men of Anathoth
13. 21. what wilt thou say when he shall *p.* thee?
21. 14. will *p.* you accord. to the fruit of your doings
23. 34. *p.* man ‖ 25. 12. *p.* king of Babylon, 50. 18.
27. 8. will *p.* that nation ‖ 29. 32. *p.* Shemaiah
30. 20. I will *p.* all that oppress them
36. 31. I will *p.* Jehoiakim and his seed
44. 13. I will *p.* them in Egypt, as I *p.* Jerusalem
29. a sign that I will *p.* you in this place
46. 25. I will *p.* the multitude of No and Pharaoh
51. 44. and I will *p.* Bel in Babylon
Hos. 4. 9. I will *p.* them for their ways and reward
14. I will not *p.* your daughters when commit
12. 2. and *p.* Jacob according to his ways
Amos 3. 2. you known, I will *p.* you for your iniq.
† 14. in the day that I will *p.* Israel
Zeph. 1. 8. in the day I will *p.* the princes
9. I will *p.* all those that leap on the threshold
12. I will *p.* men that are settled on their lees
Zech. 8. 14. as I thought to *p.* when your fathers
Acts 4. 21. finding nothing how they might *p.* them

PUNISHED.

Exod. 21. 20. if smite, he shall be surely *p.* 22.
21. he shall not be *p.* for he is his money
Ezra 9. 13. thou hast *p.* less than iniquities deserved
Job 31. 11. it is an iniquity to be *p.* by judges, 28.
Prov. 21. 11. when scorner is *p.* simple made wise
22. 3. but the simple pass on and are *p.* 27. 12.
Jer. 44. 13. as I have *p.* Jerusalem with the sword
50. 18. will punish as I have *p.* the king of Assyria
Zeph. 3. 7. not be cut off, howsoever I *p.* them
Zech. 10. 3. anger ag. the shepherds, I *p.* the goats
Acts 22. 5. to bring them bound to Jerusal. to be *p.*
26. 11. I *p.* them oft in every synagogue
2 *Thess.* 1. 9. shall be *p.* with everlasting destruction
2 *Pet.* 2. 9. unjust to the day of judgment to be *p.*

PUNISHMENT.

There were several sorts of punishment *in use among the* Jews, *which are mentioned in the scripture, as*

[1] The punishment of the cross: *this was a servile punishment, which was inflicted on the vilest of slaves: to be crucified, was a great mark of infamy to officers and men of quality. The common way of crucifying was by fastening the criminal with nails, one at each hand, and one at both his feet, or one at each of them. They were likewise bound frequently with cords; and this penalty, which seems in one sense gentler, because it occasions less pain, in another was more cruel, because the condemned person by this means was made to languish for a longer time. Before they nailed the person to the cross, they generally scourged him with whips, or leathern lashes. Our Saviour was severely scourged during his passion;* Pilate, *having pronounced sentence against him, ordered him to be scourged, and delivered him up to be crucified. The law ordained, that the persons executed should not be left upon the cross after sun-set, because he that is hanged in this manner is cursed by God,* Deut. 21. 22, 23.

[2] Suspension, hanging, or the punishment of the rope. *The* Jews *maintain, that none but idolaters and blasphemers underwent this punishment.* Haman *and his sons were hung upon a high gallows,* Esth. 7. 10. Pharaoh's *chief baker was first beheaded and afterwards hanged upon a gibbet,* Gen. 40. 22. *We read in the Scripture, that sometimes they hung up men alive, and sometimes hung up their carcases after they were dead,* Josh. 8. 29. 2 Sam. 21. 12.

[3] Stoning, or putting to death by casting stones. *This punishment was very much in use among the* Hebrews: *it is said, that this penalty was inflicted upon all those criminals that the law condemns to death, without expressing the particular kind of death: for example, the incest of a son with his mother, or of the son with his mother-in-law, or of a father with his daughter, or with his daughter-in-law; or of a man that debauches a woman that is contracted; or of her that is contracted, and consents to another; those that are guilty of the crimes of sodomy or bestiality; idolaters, blasphemers, magicians, conjurors, breakers of the sabbath; those that offer their children to* Moloch; *those that entice others to idolatry; a son rebellious to his father, and condemned by the judges.*

[4] Fire. *This punishment was very common. When* Judah *was informed that his daughter-in-law* Tamar *was with child, he would have had her burnt as an adulteress,* Gen. 38. 24. *The law of* Moses *inflicts the* punishment *of the fire upon the daughters of the priests who were guilty of fornication,* Lev. 21. 9. Nebuchadnezzar *caused* Daniel *and his companions to be thrown into a burning fiery furnace, because they would not worship his golden image,* Dan. 3. 21. *And by the law he was ordered to be burnt alive, who should marry the mother and her daughter,* Lev. 20. 14.

[5] The punishment of the rack, or tympanum. *This is met with in the Greek of St.* Paul *to the* Hebrews, 11. 35. *Interpreters are divided about the sense of this word,* τυμπανιζειν. *Some have explained it of the* Tressel, *or* Chivalet, *a punishment very frequent in antiquity, but very much unknown at this day: others think that the apostle alludes to the death of* John *the Baptist, and to that of St.* James, *who were both beheaded. Some think it signifies to flay alive, others take it in a general sense, for all kinds of capital punishments, and violent deaths: but interpreters are generally of opinion, that the apostle here means the* Bastinado, *or the punishment of the whip, and that there is an allusion to the cruelties exercised upon old* Eleazar, *and the seven brethren the* Maccabees. *The second book of* Mac. 6. 19. *speaking of the martyrdom of* Eleazar, *says, that he came to the* Tympanum.

[6] Imprisonment. *This was not always considered as a punishment, but was to keep and secure a person accused or suspected.* Joseph *detained his brother* Simeon *in prison, till he should be assured of the truth of what his brethren had told him concerning his father and his brother* Benjamin, *Gen.* 42. 19. *The blasphemer that was brought to* Moses, *Lev.* 24. 12. *and the man that was found gathering sticks on the sabbath-day,* Num. 15. 34. *were put in ward till the Lord declared the kind of* punishment *they were to undergo.*

But often imprisonment was made a punishment *when it was attended with shame and severities.*

When Joseph *was unjustly accused by* Potiphar's *wife, he was put in prison, and loaded with fetters,* Gen. 39. 20. Samson *was taken by the* Philistines, *cast into a dungeon, had his eyes put out, and forced to grind at the mill,* Judg. 16. 21. *Bonds, fetters, shackles, manacles, and chains, which usually attended imprisonment, must be looked upon as* punishments.

[7] The sword, or beheading. *In Scripture there are several instances of Decapitations.* Pharaoh's *chief baker had his head cut off; after which his body was hung upon a gibbet,* Gen. 40. 19. Abimelech, *son of* Gideon, *cut off the heads of seventy sons of* Gideon, *his brethren, upon one stone,* Judg. 9. 5. *The people of* Samaria *cut off the heads of seventy of the sons of* Ahab, *and sent them in baskets to* Jehu, 2 *Kings* 10. 7. John *the Baptist was beheaded in prison, by the order of* Herod, *Mat.* 14. 10.

[8] The precipice, or throwing headlong from the top of a rock: *this was not a common punishment: if it has been sometimes used among the* Hebrews, *it was in singular cases.* Amaziah *king of* Judah, *overcame ten thousand* Idumeans, *and made them prisoners of war, and cast them down from the top of a high rock,* 2 Chron. 25. 12.

[9] To be torn in pieces by thorns, or under harrows or sledges of iron. *There are some examples of these* punishments *in Scripture. When* Gideon *returned from pursuing the* Midianites, *he tore with thorns or brambles of the desert the chief men of the city of* Succoth, *who had insulted him,* Judg. 8. 16. *And* David *made the* Ammonites *undergo a punishment more cruel and severe,* 2 Sam. 12. 31. He put them under harrows and axes of iron, and made them pass through the brick-kiln. *These harrows or sledges of iron were machines proper for threshing of corn, in order to get the grain out of the straw, which were loaded with iron or stones, for bruising the straw. By the* Brick-kiln, *is either meant the furnace in which the bricks were burnt, or the place where the earth was beat and macerated, in which these miserable wretches were executed.*

[10] The saw, to be cut through the middle. *This* punishment *was not known among the* Hebrews. *Some are of opinion, that it came originally from the* Persians *or* Chaldeans. *It is certain that it is still in use among the* Switzers, *and that they put it in practice not many years ago, upon one of their countrymen guilty of a great crime: they put him in a kind of coffin, and sawed him at length, beginning at his head, as a piece of wood is sawn. The apostle* Paul, *in his Epistle to the* Hebrews, 11. 37. *speaking of the calamities suffered by the prophets and saints of the Old Testament, says, that* they were sawn asunder. *Several of the ancients have explained this passage concerning the death of* Isaiah, *who is said to have been put to death by king* Manasseh *with a* saw.

[11] Cutting off the hair of the guilty person. *This seems to be a* punishment *rather shameful than painful; and yet it is thought that pain likewise was added to the disgrace; and that they were not contented to shave or cut the hair, but tore it off with violence, as if they had been plucking a bird alive. This much the* Hebrew *signifies in* Neh. 13. 25. I contended with them, and smote certain of them, and plucked off the hair.

[12] To pluck out the eyes. *This is a* punishment *not common; and though* Moses *had appointed* that an eye should be given for an eye, and a tooth for a tooth, *Exod.* 21. 24. *yet it is the opinion of Commentators that this law was very seldom put in practice according to the letter; and that the offender was generally punished by a pecuniary penalty, which was converted to the use of the injured party. When the* Philistines *had laid hold on* Samson, *and intended to prevent his doing them any more harm, they put him in prison, and bored out his eyes,* Judg. 16. 21. Nebuchadnezzar *took king* Zedekiah, *and had his children put to death in his presence, then caused his eyes to be put out, and afterwards had him carried to* Babylon *in chains,* 2 Kings 25. 7.

[13] To cut off the extremities of the feet and hands *was a piece of cruelty formerly exercised by* Adoni-bezek *king of* Bezek, *upon seventy kings who had been conquered by him, and who ate like dogs under his table. But God thought fit to have him tortured after the same manner that he had tortured others.* The Israelites *conquered him, took him, and cut off the extremities of his hands and feet,* Judg. 1. 5, 6, 7. David *treated the murderers of* Ish-bosheth *in the same manner, and had their bodies hung up over the pool of* Hebron, 2 *Sam.* 4. 12.

Gen. 4. 13. my *p.* is greater than I can bear
19. † 15. lest thou be consumed in the *p.* of the city
Lev. 26. 41. than accept the *p.* of their iniquity, 43.
1 *Sam.* 28. 10. Saul sware, no *p.* shall happen to thee
2 *Kings* 7. † 9. they said, if we tarry, we shall find *p.*
Job 21. † 19. God layeth *p.* of iniquity for children
31. 3. and a strange *p.* to the workers of iniquity
Prov. 19. 19. a man of great wrath shall suffer *p.*
Lam. 3. 39. a man for the *p.* of his sins
4. 6. *p.* of my people is greater than the *p.* of Sodom
22. the *p.* of thine iniquity is accomplished
Ezek. 14. 10. they shall bear the *p.* of their iniquity,
the *p.* of prophets as *p.* of him that seeketh to him
Hos. 12. † 8. he shall have *p.* in whom is sin
Amos 1. 3. and for four I will not turn away the *p.*
thereof, 6, 9, 11, 13. ‖ 2. 1, 4, 6.
Zech. 14. 19. this shall be the *p.* of Egypt
Mat. 25. 46. these shall go into everlasting *p.*
2 *Cor.* 2. 6. sufficient to such a man is this *p.*
Heb. 10. 29. of how much sorer *p.* suppose ye
1 *Pet.* 2. 14. sent by him for the *p.* of evil doers

PUNISHMENTS.

Job 19. 29. for wrath bringeth the *p.* of the sword
Psal. 149. 7. to execute *p.* upon the people
Jer. 44. † 9. have ye forgot the *p.* of your fathers?

PUR.

Esth. 3. 7. they cast *p.* that is, the lot, before Haman
9. 24. for Haman had cast *p.* for to consume them
26. called these days Purim, after the name of *p.*
See PURIM.

PURCHASE, *Substantive.*

Gen. 49. 32. *p.* of field and cave that was therein
Lev. 22. † 11. if the priest buy a soul with *p.*
Jer. 32. 11. so I took the evidence of the *p.*
12. I gave evidence of the *p.* to Baruch, 14, 16.

PURCHASE, ED.

Gen. 25. 10. field Abraham *p.* of the sons of Heth
Exod. 15. 16. till people pass over which thou hast *p*
Lev. 25. 33. if a man *p.* of the Levites, then house
Ruth 4. 10. Ruth have I *p.* to be my wife
Psal. 74. 2. remember thy congregation thou hast *p.*
78. 54. mountain which his right hand had *p.*
Acts 1. 18. this man *p.* a field with iniquity
8. 20. thought the gift of God may be *p.* by money
20. 28. which he hath *p.* with his own blood

Eph. 1. 14. until the redemption of the *p.* possession
1 *Tim.* 3. 13. have used the office of deacon well, *p.*
1 *Pet.* 2. † 9. ye are a *p.* people, that ye should shew

PURE

Signifies, [1] *Simple, unmixed, uncompounded, as wine without water, gold or silver without dross,* Exod. 25. 17, 31. Deut. 32. 14. [2] *Holy, free from spot, stain, or the least mixture of sin,* Psal. 19. 8. 1 John 3. 3. [3] *One who is single-hearted and sincere, free from any reigning sin,* Mat. 5. 8. [4] *Devout and religious,* Prov. 30. 12. [5] *Tried or refined,* Psal. 119. † 140. Thy word is pure; *that is, it is perfectly free from all falsehood and deceit, and contains pure precepts, pure examples, great helps, and strong encouragements to purity, and dissuasives from sin.* [6] *Clear and free,* Acts 20. 26. [7] *Lawful to be used,* Rom. 14. 20. [8] *Believers, whose hearts are purified by faith,* Tit. 1. 15. [9] *Free from error, idolatry, and hypocrisy,* James 1. 27.

Exod. 27. 20. that they bring the *p.* oil, *Lev.* 24. 2.
30. 23. take *p.* myrrh ‖ 34. with *p.* frankincense
31. 8. the *p.* candlestick, 39. 37. *Lev.* 24. 4.
Lev. 24. 6. set cakes on the *p.* table before the Lord
7. thou shalt put *p.* frankincense on each row
Deut. 32. 14. didst drink the *p.* blood of the grape
2 *Sam.* 22. 27. with the *p.* thou wilt shew thyself *p.* with froward, thyself froward, *Psal.* 18. 26.
1 *Kings* 5. 11. and twenty measures of *p.* oil
2 *Chron.* 13. 11. the shewbread set on the *p.* table
Ezra 6. 20. all were *p.* and killed the passover
Job 4. 17. shall a man be more *p.* than his Maker?
8. 6. if thou wert *p.* and upright, surely now
11. 4. for thou hast said, my doctrine is *p.*
16. 17. not for any injustice, also my prayer is *p.*
25. 5. yea, the stars are not *p.* in his sight
Psal. 12. 6. the words of the Lord are *p.* words
19. 8. the commandment of the Lord is *p.*
119. 140. thy word is very *p.* therefore I love it
Prov. 15. 26. the words of the *p.* are pleasant
20. 9. who can say, I am *p.* from my sin?
11. whether his work be *p.* whether it be right
21. 8. but as for the *p.* his work is right
30. 5. every word of God is *p.* he is shield to them
12. a generation that are *p.* in their own eyes
Jer. 51. † 11. make *p.* the arrows, gather shields
Dan. 7. 9. the hair of his head like the *p.* wool
Mic. 6. 11. shall I count them *p.* with wicked
Zeph. 3. 9. I will turn to the people a *p.* language
Mal. 1. 11. in every place a *p.* offering be offered
Mark 14. † 3. an alabaster box of *p.* nard, precious
Acts 20. 26. I am *p.* from the blood of all men
Rom. 14. 20. all things indeed are *p.* but it is evil
Phil. 4. 8. whatsoever things are *p.* what lovely
1 *Tim.* 3. 9. the mystery of faith in a *p.* conscience
5. 22. neither be partaker of sins, keep thyself *p.*
2 *Tim.* 1. 3. whom I serve with a *p.* conscience
Tit. 1. 15. to the *p.* all things are *p.* but to them that are defiled and unbelieving nothing is *p.*
Heb. 10. 22. and our bodies washed with *p.* water
Jam. 1. 27. *p.* religion and undefiled is this, to visit the fatherless
3. 17. but the wisdom from above is first *p.*
2 *Pet.* 3. 1. in both which I stir up your *p.* minds
1 *John* 3. 3. purifieth himself even as he is *p.*
Rev. 15. 6. the seven angels clothed in *p.* linen
22. 1. he shewed me a *p.* river of water of life
See Heart, Gold.

PURELY.

Isa. 1. 25. and I will *p.* purge away thy dross

PURENESS.

Job 22. 30. it is delivered by the *p.* of thine hands
Prov. 22. 11. he that lov. *p.* of heart, king his friend
2 *Cor.* 6. 6. approving ourselves by *p.* by knowledge

PURER.

Lam. 4. 7. her Nazarites were *p.* than snow
Hab. 1. 13. thou art of *p.* eyes than to behold evil

PURGE.

2 *Chr.* 34. 3. Josiah began to *p.* Judah and Jerus.
Psal. 51. 7. *p.* me with hyssop, and I shall be clean
65. 3. our transgressions thou shalt *p.* them
79. 9. and *p.* away our sins for thy name's sake
Isa. 1. 25. and purely *p.* away thy dross and tin
Ezek. 20. 38. I will *p.* from among you the rebels
43. 20. thus shalt thou cleanse and *p.* it
26. seven days shall they *p.* the altar and purify it
Dan. 11. 35. some of them shall fall to *p.* them
Mal. 3. 3. and *p.* them as gold and silver, to offer
Mat. 3. 12. he will thoroughly *p.* his floor, and gather his wheat into the garner, *Luke* 3. 17.
1 *Cor.* 5. 7. *p.* out therefore the old leaven
2 *Tim.* 2. 21. if a man therefore *p.* himself from these
Heb. 9. 14. *p.* your conscience from dead works

PURGED.

1 *Sam.* 3. 14. iniquity of Eli's house shall not be *p.*
2 *Chron.* 34. 8. when he had *p.* the land and house
Prov. 16. 6. by mercy and truth iniquity is *p.*
Isa. 4. 4. and shall have *p.* the blood of Jerusalem
6. 7. thy iniquity is taken away, and thy sin *p.*
22. 14. surely this iniquity shall not be *p.*
27. 9. by this shall the iniquity of Jacob be *p.*
Ezek. 24. 13. because I have *p.* thee, and thou wast not *p.* thou shalt not be *p.* from thy filthiness
Heb. 1. 3. when he had by himself *p.* our sins
9. 22. almost all things are by the law *p.* by blood
10. 2. because that the worshippers once *p.*
2 *Pet.* 1. 9. hath forgotten he was *p.* from his old sins

PURGETH.

John 15. 2. every branch that beareth, he *p.* it

PURGING.

Prov. 20. † 30. blueness of a wound is a *p.* medicine
Mark 7. 19. goeth out into the draught, *p.* meats

PURIFICATION, S.

Num. 19. 9. it shall be kept, it is a *p.* for sin
17. take of ashes of the burnt heifer of *p.* for sin
2 *Chron.* 30. 19. according to *p.* of the sanctuary
Neh. 12. 45. porters kept the ward of their *p.*
Esth. 2. 3. the things of their *p.* be given them
12. so were the days of their *p.* accomplished
Luke 2. 22. when days of her *p.* were accomplished
Acts 21. 26. the accomplishment of the days of *p.*

PURIFY.

Num. 19. 12. shall *p.* himself with it the third day, 19.
20. shall be unclean, and shall not *p.* himself
31. 19. *p.* yourselves and your captives on third day
20. *p.* all your raiment, and all made of skins
Job 41. 25. by reason of breakings they *p.* themselves
Isa. 66. 17. that *p.* themselves in the gardens
Ezek. 43. 26. seven days shall they *p.* the altar
Mal. 3. 3. and he shall *p.* the sons of Levi
John 11. 55. went to Jerusalem to *p.* themselves
Acts 21. 24. take and *p.* thyself with them
Tit. 2. 14. and *p.* to himself a peculiar people
Jam. 4. 8. *p.* your hearts, ye double-minded

PURIFIED.

Lev. 8. 15. and *p.* the altar, and poured the blood
Num. 8. 21. the Levites were *p.* *Ezra* 6. 20.
31. 23. shall be *p.* with the water of separation
2 *Sam.* 11. 4. Bathsheba was *p.* from uncleanness
Psal. 12. 6. are pure words, as silver *p.* seven times
Prov. 30. † 5. every word of God is *p.*
Dan. 12. 10. many shall be *p.* and made white
Acts 24. 18. certain Jews from Asia found me *p.*
Heb. 9. † 18. nor first testament *p.* without blood
23. the patterns of things in the heavens be *p.*
1 *Pet.* 1. 22. seeing ye have *p.* your souls in obeying

PURIFIER.

Mal. 3. 3. he shall sit as a refiner and *p.* of silver

PURIFIETH.

Num. 19. 13. toucheth a dead body and *p.* not
1 *John* 3. 3. that hath this hope *p.* himself

PURIFYING.

Lev. 12. 4. shall continue in the blood of her *p.*
6. when the days of her *p.* are fulfilled
Num. 8. 7. sprinkle water of *p.* on them
1 *Chron.* 23. 28. office was in *p.* all holy things
Esth. 2. 12. with other things for *p.* of women
John 2. 6. after the manner of the *p.* of the Jews
3. 25. then there arose a question about *p.*
Heb. 9. 13. sanctifieth to the *p.* of the flesh

PURIFYING.

Acts 15. 9. *p.* their hearts by faith
21. 26. and the next day *p.* himself with them

PURIM,

Or Pur, *or* Phur; *that is to say,* Lots. *This was a very solemn feast of the* Jews, *instituted in memory of the lots that were cast by* Haman *the enemy of the* Jews. *These* Lots *were cast in the first month of the year,* Esth. 3. 7. *and marked out the twelfth month of the same year, for the execution of* Haman's *design, which was to destroy all the* Jews *of the kingdom of* Persia. *Thus the superstition of* Haman, *in casting and pursuing the event of these* lots, *was the cause of his own ruin, and of the preservation of the* Jews; *who had now time to avert this blow, by means of* Esther *the spouse of* Ahasuerus, *and to remove those ill impressions he had conceived of the* Jews. *In memory of this so signal and miraculous deliverance, the* Jews *instituted a feast, to which they gave the name of* Pur, *or* Purim.

Esth. 9. 26. called these days *P.* after name of Pur
28. and that these days of *P.* should not fail
29. to confirm this second letter of *P.* 31.
32. and the decree of Esther confirmed these *P.*

PURITY.

1 *Tim.* 4. 12. be thou an example in faith, in *p.*
5. 2. rebuke the younger as sisters, with all *p.*

PURLOINING.

Tit. 2. 10. not *p.* but shewing all good fidelity

PURPLE.

Exod. 25. 4. this is the offering, blue, *p.* and scarlet
26. 1. thou shalt make curtains of fine linen and *p.*
39. 3. the gold cut into wires, to work in the *p.*
Num. 4. 13. take away ashes and spread a *p.* cloth
Judg. 8. 26. *p.* raiment was on the kings of Midian
2 *Chron.* 2. 7. send a man cunning to work in *p.* 14.
3. 14. he made the vail of blue, and *p.* and crimson
Esth. 1. 6. fastened with cords of fine linen and *p.*
8. 15. Mordec. went out with garm. of linen and *p.*
Prov. 31. 22. her clothing is silk and *p.*
Cant. 3. 10. he made the covering of it of *p.*
7. 5. and the hair of thine head like *p.*
Jer. 10. 9. blue and *p.* is their clothing
Ezek. 27. 7. *p.* was that which covered thee
16. Syria occupied in thy fairs with emeralds, *p.*
Mark 15. 17. and they clothed him with *p.*
20. mocked him, they took off the *p.* from him
Luke 16. 19. a certain rich man clothed in *p.*
John 19. 2. the soldiers put on him a *p.* robe
5. then came Jesus forth wearing the *p.* robe
Acts 16. 14. a woman named Lydia, a seller of *p.*
Heb. 9. † 19. Moses took *p.* and sprinkled the book
Rev. 17. 4. the woman was arrayed in *p.* and scarlet
18. 12. none buyeth the merchandise or *p.*
16. that great city, that was clothed in *p.* and scarl.

PURPOSE.

Num. 14. † 34. ye shall know my altering of my *p.*
Ruth 2. 16. and let fall some handfuls of *p.* for her
Ezra 4. 5. hired counsellors to frustrate their *p.*
Neh. 8. 4. a pulpit of wood they made for the *p.*
Job 33. 17. that he may withdraw man from his *p.*
Prov. 20. 18. every *p.* is established by counsel
Eccl. 3. 1. and a time to every *p.* 17. | 8. 6.
5. † 8. if thou seest oppression, marvel not at the *p.*
Isa. 1. 11. to what *p.* is multitude of your sacrifices
14. 26. this is the *p.* that is purposed upon the earth
30. 7. the Egyptians shall help in vain, and to no *p.*
Jer. 6. 20. to what *p.* cometh to me incense?
49. 30. Nebuchadnezzar conceived a *p.* ag. Hazor
51. 29. for every *p.* of the Lord shall stand
Ezek. 38. † 10. thou shalt conceive a mischievous *p.*
Dan. 6. 17. that *p.* be not changed concerning Dan.
Mat. 26. 8. saying, to what *p.* is this waste?
Acts 11. 23. with *p.* of heart, they would cleave
26. 16. for I have appeared to thee for this *p.*
27. 13. supposing that they had obtained their *p.*
43. the centurion kept them from their *p.*
Rom. 8. 28. who are the called according to his *p.*
9. 11. that the *p.* of God according to election stand
17. even for this same *p.* have I raised thee up
Eph. 1. 11. according to the *p.* of him who worketh
3. 11. according to the eternal *p.* in Christ

Eph. 6. 22. I sent to you for the same *p.* *Col.* 4. 8.
2 *Tim.* 1. 9. called us accord. to his own *p.* and grace
3. 10. but thou hast fully known my *p.* faith
1 *John* 3. 8. for this *p.* Son of God was manifested

PURPOSES.

Gen. 6. † 5. the *p.* of man's heart was only evil
Job 17. 11. my days are past, my *p.* are broken off
Prov. 15. 22. without counsel *p.* are disappointed
Isa. 19. 10. they shall be broken in the *p.* thereof
Jer. 49. 20. hear counsel of the Lord and *p.* 50. 45.

PURPOSE, ED.

1 *Kings* 5. 5. I *p.* to build an house to the Lord
2 *Chr.* 28. 10. *p.* to keep under Judah and Jerus.
32. 2. Sennacherib *p.* to fight against Jerusalem
Psal. 17. 3. I am *p.* my mouth shall not transgress
140. 4. who have *p.* to overthrow my goings
Isa. 14. 24. and as I have *p.* so shall it stand
26. this is the purpose *p.* upon the whole earth
27. the Lord hath *p.* who shall disannul it?
19. 12. what the Lord hath *p.* upon Egypt
23. 9. Lord hath *p.* to stain the pride of all glory
46. 11. I have *p.* it, and I will also do it
Jer. 4. 28. I have *p.* it, and will not repent
26. 3. repent me of the evil which I *p.* to do them
36. 3. will hear all evil which I *p.* to do to them
49. 20. his purposes that he hath *p.* 50. 45.
Lam. 2. 8. the Lord hath *p.* to destroy the wall
Dan. 1. 8. Dan. *p.* in his heart not to defile himself
Acts 19. 21. Paul *p.* in Spirit to go to Jerusalem
20. 3. Paul *p.* to return through Macedonia
Rom. 1. 13. that oftentimes I *p.* to come to you
2 *Cor.* 1. 17. things I *p.* do I *p.* accord. to the flesh?
Eph. 1. 9. his will which he hath *p.* in himself
3. 11. eternal purpose which he *p.* in Christ Jesus

PURPOSETH.

2 *Cor.* 9. 7. every man as he *p.* in his heart, so give

PURPOSING.

Gen. 27. 42. Esau doth comfort himself, *p.* to kill thee

PURSE.

Prov. 1. 14. cast in thy lot, let us have one *p.*
Luke 10. 4. carry neither *p.* nor scrip, nor shoes
22. 35. when I sent you without *p.* and scrip
36. but now he that hath a *p.* let him take it

PURSES.

Mat. 10. 9. provide neither silv. nor brass in your *p.*
Mark 6. 8. they should take no money in their *p.*

PURSUE.

Gen. 35. 5. they did not *p.* after the sons of Jacob
Exod. 15. 9. the enemy said, I will *p.* I will overtake
Deut. 19. 6. lest the avenger of blood *p.* *Josh.* 20. 5.
28. 22. they shall *p.* thee until thou perish. 45.
Josh. 2. 5. *p.* after them, ye shall overtake them
8. 16. the men of Ai were called together to *p.*
10. 19. stay not, but *p.* after your enemies
1 *Sam.* 24. 14. after whom dost thou *p.*?
25. 29. a man is risen to *p.* thee and seek thy soul
26. 18. wherefore doth my lord thus *p.* me?
30. 8. shall I *p.* after this troop? he answered, *p.*
2 *Sam.* 17. 1. I will arise and *p.* after David
20. 6. take thy lord's servants, *p.* after Sheba, 7.
24. 13. wilt thou flee while enemies *p.* thee?
Job 13. 25. and wilt thou *p.* the dry stubble?
30. 15. terrors *p.* my soul as the wind
Psal. 34. 14. do good, seek peace and *p.* it
Isa. 5. † 11. that continue till wine *p.* them
30. 16. therefore shall they that *p.* you be swift
Jer. 48. 2. O madmen, the sword shall *p.* thee
Ezek. 35. 6. and blood shall *p.* thee
Hos. 8. 3. Israel, the enemy shall *p.* him
Amos 1. 11. bec. Edom did *p.* his broth. with sword
Nah. 1. 8. and darkness shall *p.* his enemies

PURSUED.

Gen. 14. 14. Abram *p.* them to Dan and Hobah, 15.
31. 23. Laban and his brethren *p.* Jacob, 36.
Exod. 14. 8. Pharaoh and the Egyptians *p.* after Israel, 9, 23. *Deut.* 11. 4. *Josh.* 24. 6.
Josh. 2. 7. *p.* the spies ‖ 8. 16. they of Ai *p.* 17.
Judg. 1. 6. *p.* after Adoni-bezek, and caught him
4. 16. but Barak *p.* after the chariots, 22.
7. 23. Gideon *p.* after the Midianites, 25. | 8. 12.
20. 45. Israel *p.* Benjamin unto Gidom
1 *Sam.* 7. 11. Israel *p.* the Philistines, 17. 52.
23. 25. Saul *p.* David ‖ 30. 10. Dav. *p.* Amalekites
2 *Sam.* 2. 19. and Asahel *p.* after Abner
24. Joab *p.* Abner ‖ 28. Joab *p.* Israel no more
20. 10. so Joab and Abishai *p.* after Sheba
22. 38. I have *p.* mine enemies, *Psal.* 18. 37.
1 *Kings* 20. 20. Syrians fled, and Isr. *p.* after them
2 *Kings* 25. 5. and the army of Chaldees *p.* the king and overtook him, *Jer.* 39. 5. | 52. 8.
2 *Chron.* 13. 19. Abijah *p.* after Jeroboam
14. 13. Asa and people *p.* the Ethiopians to Gerar
Isa. 41. 3. he *p.* them, and passed safely
Lam. 4. 19. they *p.* us upon the mountains, laid wait

PURSUER, S.

Josh. 2. 16. get to the mountain lest *p.* meet you
22. until the *p.* returned, the *p.* sought them
8. 20. and the people turned back upon the *p.*
Lam. 1. 6. are gone without strength before the *p.*

PURSUETH, ING.

Lev. 26. 17. and ye shall flee when none *p.* you
36. and they shall fall when none *p.* 37.
Judg. 8. 4. Gideon with 300 men, faint, yet *p.* them
5. I am *p.* Zebah and Zalmunna, kings of Midian
1 *Sam.* 23. 28. Saul returned from *p.* after David
2 *Sam.* 3. 22. behold, Joab came from *p.* a troop
18. 16. the people returned from *p.* after Israel
1 *Kings* 18. 27. your god is *p.* or on a journey
22. 33. perceived it was not the king, they turned back from *p.* Jehoshaphat, 2 *Chron.* 18. 32.
Prov. 11. 19. he that *p.* evil *p.* it to his own death
13. 21. evil *p.* sinners, to the righteous good repaid
19. 7. he *p.* them with words, yet they are wanting
28. 1. the wicked flee when no man *p.*

PURSUIT.

1 *Kings* 18. † 27. he is a god, talking, or hath a *p.*

PURTENANCE.

Exod. 12. 9. roast with fire, his head, legs, and *p.*

PUSH.

Exod. 21. 29. but if the ox were wont to *p.* 36.
32. if the ox *p.* a man-servant or maid-servant
Deut 33. 17. with them he shall *p.* the people

1 *Kings* 22. 11. with these shalt thou *p.* the Syrians, until thou have consumed them, 2 *Chron.* 18. 10.
Job 30. 12. they *p.* away my feet, and raise up
Psal. 44. 5. thro' thee will we *p.* down our enemies
Dan. 11. 40. at the end shall king of south *p.* at him

PUSHED.

Ezek. 34. 21. *p.* all the diseased with your horns

PUSHING.

Dan. 8. 4. I saw the ram *p.* westward and northward

PUT.

Gen. 2. 8. there God *p.* the man he had formed, 15.
3. 15. I will *p.* enmity between thee and woman
24. 2. *p.* thy hand under my thigh, 9. | 47. 29.
47. and I *p.* the ear-ring upon her face
27. 15. *p.* them upon Jacob her younger son
16. she *p.* the skins of the kids upon his hands
28. 11. Jacob *p.* the stones for his pillows
29. 3. *p.* the stone again on the well's mouth
30. 40. he *p.* his own flocks by themselves
42. when cattle were feeble, he *p.* not the rods
31. 34. Rachel *p.* them in the camels' furniture
32. 16. *p.* space betwixt drove and drove
38. 14. Tamar *p.* off her widow's garments
39. 4. all he had he *p.* into Joseph's hand
40. 15. that they should *p.* me into the dungeon
42. 17. he *p.* them altogether in ward
46. 4. Joseph shall *p.* his hand on thine eyes
48. 18. *p.* thy right hand upon his head
Exod. 3. 5. draw not nigh hither, *p.* off thy shoes from off thy feet, *Isa.* 20. 2. *Acts* 7. 33.
22. ye shall *p.* them on your sons and daughters
4. 6. Lord said, *p.* now thy hand in thy bosom
15. speak to him, and *p.* words in his mouth
5. 21. to *p.* a sword in their hand to slay us
8. 23. I will *p.* a division between my people
11. 7. may know the Lord doth *p.* a difference
15. 26. I will *p.* none of these diseases on thee
16. 33. *p.* an homer full of manna therein
22. 5. and *p.* in his beast in another man's field
8. to see whether he have *p.* in his hand
11. an oath that he hath not *p.* his hand
23. 1. *p.* not thine hand with the wicked
29. 24. thou shalt *p.* all in the hands of Aaron
30. 36. *p.* of the perfume before the testimony
32. 27. *p.* every man his sword by his side
33. 5. now *p.* off thy ornaments from thee
22. I will *p.* thee in a cleft of the rock
Lev. 8. 27. he *p.* all on Aaron's and his sons' hands
19. 14. nor *p.* a stumbling-block before the blind
24. 12. and they *p.* the blasphemer in ward
26. 8. *p.* ten thousand to flight, *Deut.* 32. 30.
Num. 6. 27. shall *p.* my name on the children of Isr.
11. 17. of spirit which is on thee, and *p.* upon them
29. the Lord would *p.* his Spirit on them
21. 9. Moses made a serpent of brass, and *p.* it on a
23. 5. the Lord *p.* a word in Balaam's mouth, 16.
Deut. 10. 2. thou shalt *p.* them in the ark
5. I *p.* the tables in the ark which I had made
11. 29. thou shalt *p.* the blessing on mount Gerizim
12. 5. the place he shall choose to *p.* his name, 21.
7. ye shall rejoice in all ye *p.* your hand to
18. 18. and will *p.* my words in his mouth
23. 24. but thou shalt not *p.* any grapes in thy vessel
Josh. 7. 11. *p.* it even among their own stuff
Judg. 12. 3. I *p.* my life in my hands, and passed
1 *Sam.* 2. 36. *p.* me into one of the priest's offices
8. 16. your king, he will *p.* your asses to work
14. 26. but no man *p.* his hand to his mouth
17. 39. and David *p.* them off him
54. but he *p.* Goliath's armour in his tent
19. 5. for he did *p.* his life in his hand
28. 21. I have *p.* my life in my hand
1 *Kings* 5. 3. Lord *p.* them under the soles of his feet
9. 3. to *p.* my name there, 11. 36. | 14. 21.
12. 29. the other of the calves *p.* he in Dan
18. 23. lay it on wood, and *p.* no fire under
22. 27. saith the king, *p.* this fellow in prison
2 *Kings* 4. 34. he *p.* his mouth upon his mouth
11. 12. the king's son, they *p.* the crown on him
13. 16. *p.* thine hand upon the bow, he *p.* his hand
19. 28. I will *p.* hook in thy nose, *Isa.* 37. 29.
21. 7. in this house and Jerusalem will I *p.* my name for ever, 2 *Chron.* 6. 20. | 12. 13. | 33. 7.
1 *Chron.* 11. 19. that have *p.* their lives in jeopardy
13. 10. because he *p.* his hand to the ark
21. 27. and the angel *p.* up his sword again
2 *Chron.* 6. 11. and in the house have I *p.* the ark
36. 3. the king of Egypt *p.* him down at Jerusalem
22. Cyrus *p.* the decree in writing, *Ezra* 1. 1.
Ezra 6. 12. destroy kings that *p.* their hand to alter
7. 27. hath *p.* such a thing in the king's heart
Neh. 2. 12. what God had *p.* in my heart to do
3. 5. their nobles *p.* not their necks to the work
4. 23. that every one *p.* them off for washing
6. 14. Tobiah would have *p.* me in fear, 19.
Esth. 9. 1. his decree drew near to be *p.* in execution
Job 4. 18. behold, he *p.* no trust in his servants
13. 14. wherefore do I *p.* my life in mine hand?
17. 3. lay down, *p.* me in a surety with thee
19. 13. he hath *p.* my brethren far from me
23. 6. no, but he would *p.* strength in me
38. 36. who *p.* wisdom in the inward parts
41. 2. canst thou *p.* an hook into his nose?
Psal. 4. 7. thou hast *p.* gladness in my heart
8. 6. thou hast *p.* all things under his feet, 1 *Cor.* 15. 25, 27. *Eph.* 1. 22. *Heb.* 2. 8.
9. 20. *p.* in fear, O Lord, that nations may know
30. 11. thou hast *p.* off my sackcloth and girded me
31. 18. let the lying lips be *p.* to silence
40. 3. he hath *p.* a new song in my mouth
14. let them be driven backward, and *p.* to shame, that wish me evil, 44. 7. | 53. 5.
44. 9. but thou hast cast off and *p.* us to shame
56. 8. *p.* thou my tears into thy bottle
78. 66. he *p.* them to a perpetual reproach
88. 18. lover and friend hast thou *p.* far from me
118. 8. better to trust in L. than to *p.* confid. in man
9. better to trust in L. than to *p.* confid. in princes
119. 31. O Lord, *p.* me not to shame
Prov. 23. 2. and *p.* a knife to thy throat
25. 8. when thy neighbour hath *p.* thee to shame
10. lest he that heareth it *p.* thee to shame

Eccl. 10. 10. then must he *p.* to more strength
Cant. 5. 3. I have *p.* off my coat, how shall I *p.* it on?
4. my beloved *p.* in his hand by hole of the door
Isa. 5. 20. woe to them that *p.* darkness for light
10. 13. I have *p.* down the inhabitants
11. 8. weaned child *p.* his hand on cockatrice' den
37. † 7. I will *p.* a spirit into him
42. 1. I have *p.* my Spirit upon him, *Mat.* 12. 18.
43. 26. *p.* me in remembrance, let us plead
47. 11. thou shalt not be able to *p.* it off
51. 16. I have *p.* words in thy mouth, *Jer.* 1. 9.
23. *p.* it into the hand of them that afflict thee
53. 10. to bruise him, he hath *p.* him to grief
59. † 19. Spirit of the Lord shall *p.* him to flight
21. the words I *p.* in thy mouth shall not depart
63. 11. where is he that *p.* his H. Spirit within him?
Jer. 3. 19. how shall I *p.* thee among the children
8. 14. for the Lord our God hath *p.* us to silence
12. 13. they have *p.* themselv. to pain, but not profit
31. 33. I will *p.* my law in their inward parts
32. 40. I will *p.* my fear in their hearts
47. 6. O sword, *p.* up thyself into thy scabbard
Ezek. 8. 17. they *p.* the branch to their nose
11. 19. I will give them one heart, I will *p.* a new spirit within you, 36. 26, 27. | 37. 14.
16. 14. through my comeliness I had *p.* upon thee
22. 26. her priests have *p.* no difference
29. 4. I will *p.* hooks in thy jaws, 38. 4.
30. 13. I will *p.* a fear in the land of Egypt
37. 6. and *p.* breath in you, and ye shall live
Dan. 5. 19. and whom he would he *p.* down
Joel 3. 13. *p.* in the sickle, for the harvest is ripe
Mic. 2. 12. I will *p.* them togeth. as sheep of Bozrah
7. 5. trust not a friend, *p.* ye not confid. in a guide
Zeph. 3. 19. where they have been *p.* to shame
Hag. 1. 6. earneth wages to *p.* it in a bag with holes
Mat. 5. 15. nor light candle and *p.* it under a bushel
9. 17. nor do men *p.* new wine into old bottles
19. 6. let not man *p.* asunder, *Mark* 10. 9.
22. 34. that he had *p.* the Sadducees to silence
25. 27. oughtest to *p.* my money to exchangers
26. 52. *p.* up again thy sword, *John* 18. 11.
27. 6. not lawful to *p.* them into the treasury
Mark 10. 16. *p.* his hands on them, and blessed them
Luke 1. 52. hath *p.* down mighty from their seats
15. 22. bring best robe, *p.* it on him, and *p.* a ring
John 5. 7. I have none to *p.* me into the pool
9. 15. he *p.* clay upon mine eyes, and I do see
19. 29. *p.* it upon hyssop, and *p.* it to his mouth
20. 25. unless I *p.* my finger into the print of nails
Acts 1. 7. the father hath *p.* in his own power
4. 3. they *p.* the apostles in hold unto next day
5. 18. and *p.* them in the common prison
25. behold, the men whom ye *p.* in prison
13. 46. seeing ye *p.* the word of God from you
15. 9. and *p.* no difference between us and them
10. to *p.* a yoke upon the neck of the disciples
Rom. 14. 13. that no man *p.* a stumbling block
1 *Cor.* 15. 24. he shall have *p.* down authority
25. till he *p.* all his enemies under his feet
2 *Cor.* 5. † 19. *p.* in us the word of reconciliation
8. 16. God, which *p.* the same earnest care in Titus
Eph. 4. 22. that ye *p.* off the old man, *Col.* 3. 9.
Col. 3. 8. ye also *p.* off these, anger, wrath
1 *Tim.* 4. 6. if thou *p.* the brethren in remembrance, shalt be a good minister, 2 *Tim.* 2. 14.
2 *Tim.* 1. 6. wherefore I *p.* thee in remembrance
Tit. 3. 1. *p.* them in mind to be subject to powers
Philem. 18. if he oweth, *p.* that on my account
Heb. 2. 5. to angels, hath he not *p.* in subjection
6. 6. if fall away, to renew them, seeing they crucify Son of G. afresh, and *p.* him to an open shame
8. 10. I will *p.* my laws into their mind, and write
10. 16. I will *p.* my laws into their hearts
Jam. 3. 3. we *p.* bits in the horses' mouths
1 *Pet.* 2. 15. ye may *p.* to silence the ignorance
2 *Pet.* 1. 12. to *p.* you always in remembrance
14. knowing that I must *p.* off this tabernacle
Jude 5. I will *p.* you also in remembrance
Rev. 2. 24. I will *p.* on you none other burden
17. 17. God hath *p.* in their hearts to fulfil his will

PUT *away.*

Gen. 35. 2. *p. away* the strange gods among you
Exod. 12. 15. *p. away* the leaven out of your houses
Lev. 21. 7. nor take a woman *p. away* from her husb.
Deut. 19. 13. *p. away* guilt of innocent blood, 21. 9.
22. 19. he may not *p.* her *away* all his days, 29.
Josh. 24. 14. *p. away* the strange gods your fathers served, 23. *Judg.* 10. 16. 1 *Sam.* 7. 3.
1 *Sam.* 1. 14. Eli said, *p. away* thy wine from thee
28. 3. Saul had *p. away* wizards out of the land
2 *Sam.* 7. 15. Saul whom I *p. away* before thee
12. 13. Nathan said, the Lord hath *p. away* thy sin
2 *Kings* 3. 2. Jehoram *p. away* the image of Baal
23. 24. all the abominations did Josiah *p. away*
2 *Chron.* 15. 8. Asa *p. away* the abominable idols
Ezra 10. 3. make a covenant to *p. away* the wives
19. they gave their hands to *p. away* their wives
Job 11. 14. if iniquity be in thine hand, *p.* it *away*
22. 23. *p. away* iniquity from thy tabernacle
Psal. 18. 22. I did not *p. away* his statutes from me
27. 9. *p.* not thy servant *away* in anger
88. 8. thou hast *p. away* mine acquaintance
Prov. 4. 24. *p. away* from thee a froward mouth
Isa. 50. 1. whom I have *p. away* your mother, *p. a.*
Jer. 3. 1. if a man *p. away* his wife, will he return
8. I had *p.* her *away*, and given her a bill of divorce
4. 1. if thou wilt *p. away* thine abominations
Ezek. 43. 9. let them *p. away* their whoredom
44. 22. nor shall priest take her that is *p. away*
Hos. 2. 2. let her *p. away* her whoredoms
Amos 6. 3. ye that *p.* far *away* the evil day
Mal. 2. † 16. if he hate her, *p.* her *away*
Mat. 1. 19. Jos. was minded to *p.* her *away* privily
5. 31. it hath been said, whoso shall *p. away* his wife, 32. | 19. 9. *Mark* 10. 11. *Luke* 16. 18.
Mark 10. 2. is it lawful for man to *p. away* his wife?
12. if a woman shall *p. away* her husband
1 *Cor.* 5. 13. *p. away* from you that wicked person
7. 11. let not the husband *p. away* his wife, 12.
13. 11. when a man, I *p. away* childish things
Eph. 4. 31. let anger and evil speaking be *p. away*

1 *Tim.* 1. 19. which some having *p. away*
Heb. 9. 26. to *p. away* sin by the sacrifice of himself.

See DEATH, EVIL.

PUT *forth.*

Gen. 3. 22. lest he *p. forth* and take of tree of life
8. 9. Noah *p. forth* his hand and took the dove
19. 10. the men *p. forth* their hand and pulled Lot
Exod. 4. 4. *p. forth* thine hand and take it by the tail
Deut. 33. 14. precious things *p. forth* by the moon
Judg. 3. 21. and Ehud *p. forth* his left hand
6. 21. the angel *p. forth* the end of the staff
14. 12. I will now *p. forth* a riddle to you, 13.
15. 15. Samson *p. forth* and took the jaw-bone
1 *Sam.* 14. 27. Jonath. *p. forth* the rod and dipped it
22. 17. the servants not *p. forth* to slay the priests
24. 10. not *p. forth* mine hand ag. Lord's anointed
2 *Sam.* 6. 6. Uzzah *p. f.* his hand to ark, 1 *Chr.* 13. 9.
15. 5. to do Absalom obeisance, he *p. forth* his hand
18. 12. yet not *p. forth* my hand against king's son
1 *Kings* 13. 4. Jerob *p. forth* his hand, and he *p. f.*
Job 1. 11. *p. forth* thy hand and touch all, 2. 5.
12. only upon himself *p.* not *forth* thy hand
Psal. 55. 20. he *p. forth* hands against him at peace
125. 3. lest the righteous *p. forth* their hands
Prov. 8. 1. doth not Understand. *p. forth* her voice?
25. 6. *p.* not *forth* thyself in presence of the king
Jer. 1. 9. L. *p. forth* his hand and touched my mouth
Ezek. 8. 3. he *p. forth* form of an hand and took me
17. 2. son of man, *p. forth* a riddle and speak
Mat. 8. 3. Jesus *p. forth* his hand and touched him, I will, be thou clean, *Mark* 1. 41. *Luke* 5. 13.
9. 25. but when people were *p. forth*, he went in
13. 24. another parable *p.* he *forth*, 31. *Luke* 14. 7.
Acts 5. 34. commanded to *p.* the apostles *forth*
9. 40. but Peter *p.* them all *forth*, and kneeled

PUT *on.*

Gen. 28. 20. bread to eat, and raiment to *p. on*
38. 19. Tamar *p. on* garments of her widowhood
Exod. 29. 30. his son that is priest, shall *p.* them *on*
33. 4. no man did *p. on* him his ornaments
Lev. 6. 10. the priest shall *p. on* his linen garment
11. he shall *p. on* other garments, and carry forth
16. 4. he shall *p. on* the holy linen coat
24. he shall *p. on* his garments and come forth
21. 10. high priest consecrated to *p. on* the garm.
Num. 16. 46. *p. on* incense, and go quickly to cong.
Deut. 22. 5. nor a man *p. on* a woman's garment
2 *Sam.* 1. 24. weep for Saul, who *p. on* ornaments
14. 2. I pray *p. on* now mourning apparel
20. 8. Joab's garment he had *p. on* was girded
1 *Kings* 22. 30. but *p.* thou *on* thy robes, 2 *Chr.* 18. 29.
2 *Kings* 3. 21. all that were able to *p. on* armour
Esth. 4. 1. Mordecai *p. on* sackcloth with ashes
5. 1. Esther *p. on* her royal apparel and stood
Job 27. 17. may prepare it, but the just shall *p.* it *on*
29. 14. I *p. on* righteousness, and it clothed me
Cant. 5. 3. I put off my coat, how shall I *p.* it *on?*
Isa. 51. 9. awake, awake, *p. on* strength, 52. 1.
52. 1. *p. on* thy beautiful garments, O Jerusalem
59. 17. he *p. on* righteousness as a breastplate, he *p. on* garments of vengeance for clothing
Jer. 13. 1. take a girdle and *p.* it *on* thy loins, 2.
46. 4. furbish the spears, and *p. on* the brigandines
Ezek. 24. 17. and *p. on* thy shoes upon thy feet
42. 14. and shall *p. on* other garments, 44. 19.
Jonah 3. 5. the people of Nineveh *p. on* sackcloth
Mat. 6. 25. nor what ye shall *p. on*, *Luke* 12. 22.
21. 7. they *p. on* the ass and colt their clothes
27. 28. they stripped him and *p. on* him scarlet robe
29. when they had platted a crown of thorns, they *p.* it *on* his head, *John* 19. 2.
48. one of them *p.* a sponge *on* a reed, *Mark* 15. 36.
Mark 6. 9. be shod with sandals, not *p. on* two coats
Luke 15. 22. bring and *p. on* him the best robe
John 19. 19. Pilate wrote a title and *p.* it *on* cross
Rom. 13. 12. and let us *p. on* armour of light
14. but *p.* ye *on* the Lord Jesus Christ
1 *Cor.* 12. † 23. on these we *p. on* more honour
15. 53. this corruptible must *p. on* incorruption
54. this mortal shall have *p. on* immortality
Gal. 3. 27. baptized into Christ, have *p. on* Christ
Eph. 4. 24. that ye *p. on* the new man, *Col.* 3. 10.
6. 11. *p. on* the whole armour of God, ye may be able
Col. 3. 12. *p. on* therefore bowels of mercies and kind.
14. *p. on* charity, which is the bond of perfectness

PUT *out.*

Gen. 38. 28. when she travailed one *p. out* his hand
Exod. 17. 14. *p. out* the remembrance of Amalek
Lev. 6. 12. the fire on the altar shall not be *p. out*
Num. 5. 2. *p. out* of the camp every leper, 4.
3. both male and female shall ye *p. out*
16. 14. wilt thou *p. out* the eyes of these men?
Deut. 7. 22. the Lord will *p. out* those nations
25. 6. that his name be not *p. out* of Israel
Judg. 16. 21. the Philistines *p. out* Samson's eyes
2 *Sam.* 13. 17. *p.* now this woman *out* from me
2 *Kings* 6. 7. he *p. out* his hand and took the axe
25. 7. and they *p. out* the eyes of Zedekiah and bound him with fetters, *Jer.* 39. 7. | 52. 11.
2 *Chron.* 29. 7. also they have *p. out* the lamps
Job 18. 5. the light of the wicked shall be *p. out*
6. the light shall be dark, and his candle be *p. out*, 21. 17. *Prov.* 13. 9. | 20. 20. | 24. 20.
Psal. 9. 5. thou hast *p. out* their name for ever
Ezek. 32. 7. when I *p.* thee *out* I will cover heaven
Mark 5. 40. when he had *p.* them all *out*, *Luke* 8. 54.
Luke 16. 4. when I am *p. out* of the stewardship
John 9. 22. he should be *p. out* of the synagogue
12. 42. lest they should be *p. out* of the synagogue
16. 2. they shall *p.* you *out* of the synagogues

PUT *trust.*

Judg. 9. 15. come and *p.* your *trust* in my shadow
2 *Kings* 18. 24. *p.* thy *trust* on Egypt, *Isa.* 36. 9.
1 *Chron.* 5. 20. because they *p.* their *trust* in him
Psal. 4. 5. and *p.* your *trust* in the Lord
5. 11. let all that *p.* their *trust* in thee rejoice
7. 1. O Ld. G. in thee I *p. trust*, 16. 1. | 25. 20. | 71. 1.
9. 10. that know thy name, will *p. trust* in thee
11. 1. in the Lord *p.* I my *trust*, 31. 1. | 71. 1.
17. 7. that savest them which *p.* their *trust* in thee
36. 7. *p.* their *trust* under the shadow of thy wings
56. 4. in God I have *p.* my *trust*, I will not fear

Psal. 73. 28. I have p. my trust in the Lord God
146. 3. p. not your trust in princes, nor son of man
Prov. 30. 5. shield to them that p. their trust in him
Jer. 39. 18. because thou hast p. thy trust in me
1 Thess. 2. 4. to be p. in trust with the gospel
Heb. 2. 13. and again, I will p. my trust in him

PUT, *Participle.*

Gen. 50. 26. Joseph was p. in a coffin in Egypt
Lev. 11. 32. the vessel, it must be p. into water
38. but if any water be p. on seed, be unclean
15. 19. she shall be p. apart seven days
18. 19. shalt not approach as long as she p. apart
2 Sam. 3. 34. hands not bound, nor feet p. in fetters
1 Kings 22. 10. the kings having p. on their robes
2 Kings 14. 12. Judah was p. to worse before Israel
1 Chron. 19. 16. the Syrians p. to the worse, 19.
27. 24. neither was the number p. in the account
2 Chron. 2. 14. to find out every device shall be p.
6. 24. if thy people Israel be p. to the worse
25. 22. Judah was p. to the worse before Israel
Ezra 2. 62. were not found, therefore were they as polluted, p. from the priesthood, Neh. 7. 64.
Psal. 35. 4. let them be p. to shame that seek after my soul, let them be turned back, 83. 17.
70. 2. and p. to confusion, that desire my hurt
71. 1. in thee I trust, let me never be p. to confus.
Prov. 25. 7. than that thou shouldest be p. lower
Eccl. 3. 14. what God doeth, nothing can be p. to it
Isa. 54. 4. for thou shalt not be p. to shame
Jer. 50. 42. they shall ride, every one p. in array
Zeph. 3. 19. where they have been p. to shame
Mat. 9. 16. for that which is p. in to fill it up
Mark 1. 14. now after that John was p. in prison
2. 22. new wine p. into new bottles, Luke 5. 38.
Luke 9. 62. no man having p. his hand to plough
John 12. 6. Judas bare what was p. in the bag
13. 2. devil having now p. into the heart of Judas
Heb. 2. 8. he left nothing that is not p. under him, but now we see not yet all things p. under him
Rev. 11. 9. not suffer dead bodies to be p. in graves

PUTTEST.

Num. 24. 21. and thou p. thy nest in a rock
Deut. 12. 18. bless all thou p. thine hands to, 15. 10.
2 Kings 18. 14. that which thou p. on me will I bear
Job 13. 27. thou p. my feet in stocks and lookest
Psal. 119. 119. thou p. away the wicked like dross
Hab. 2. 15. that p. thy bottle to him, makest drunken

PUTTETH.

Exod. 30. 33. who p. any on a stranger, be cut off
Num. 22. 38. the word that God p. in my mouth
Deut. 25. 11. woman p. forth her hand and taketh
27. 15. graven image, and p. it in a secret place
1 Kings 20. 11. boast himself as he that p. off harness
Job 15. 15. he p. no trust in saints, heavens not clean
28. 9. he p. forth his hand upon the rock
33. 11. he p. my feet in the stocks, marketh my steps
Psal. 15. 5. he that p. not his money to usury
66. † 9. which p. our soul in life and suffereth not
75. 7. God p. down one and setteth up another
Prov. 26. † 8. that p. a precious stone among stones
28. 25. that p. his trust in Lord shall be made fat
29. 25. who p. his trust in the Lord shall be safe
Cant. 2. 13. the fig-tree p. forth her green figs
Isa. 57. 13. p. his trust in me shall possess the land
Jer. 43. 12. as a shepherd p. on garment go forth
Lam. 3. 29. he p. his mouth in the dust, if be hope
Ezek. 14. 4. p. the stumbling block of iniquity, 7.
Mic. 3. 5. and he that p. not into their mouths
Mat. 9. 16. no man p. new cloth, Luke 5. 36.
24. 32. when branch is yet tender and p. forth leaves ye know that summer is nigh, Mark 13. 28.
Mark 2. 22. no man p. new wine into old bottles, new wine must be p. into new bottles, Luke 5. 37.
4. 29. immediately he p. in sickle, harvest come
Luke 8. 16. no man p. a lighted candle under a bed
11. 33. a candle, no man p. a lighted candle in secret
16. 18. whoso p. away his wife and marries another
John 10. 4. when he p. forth his own sheep, he goeth
Rom. 14. † 23. that p. a difference between meats

PUTTING.

Gen. 21. 14. bottle of water p. it on Hagar's shoulder
Lev. 16. 21. p. them upon the head of the goat
Judg. 7. 6. p. their hand to their mouth and lapped
Isa. 58. 9. p. forth of the finger and speaking vanity
Mal. 2. 16. God saith that he hateth p. away
Acts 9. 12. Ananias p. his hand on him, 17.
19. 33. they drew Alexander, Jews p. him forward
Rom. 15. 15. in some sort, as p. you in mind
Eph. 4. 25. wherefore p. away lying, speak truth
Col. 2. 11. in p. off the body of the sins of the flesh
1 Thess. 5. 8. p. on the breast-plate of faith and love
1 Tim. 1. 12. me faithful p. me into the ministry
2 Tim. 1. 6. the gift in thee by p. on of my hands
1 Pet. 3. 3. whose adorning, not p. on of apparel, but hidden man of the heart
21. not the p. away the filth of the flesh
2 Pet. 1. 13. to stir you up by p. you in remembrance

PUTRIFYING.

Isa. 1. 6. but wounds, and bruises, and p. sores

Q.

QUAILS,

Birds somewhat less than pigeons. God gave Quails *to the* Israelites *upon two occasions:* First, *in the wilderness of* Sin, *or* Zin, *a few days after they had passed over the* Red sea, *Exod.* 16. 13. *The* second *time was at the encampment, called in* Hebrew, Kibroth-hattaavah, *or the* graves of lust, *Num.* 11. 32. *The number of them was miraculous; for it is said, that* God rained flesh upon them as dust, and feathered fowls like as the sand of the sea, *Psal.* 78. 27. *They are said to be birds larger than sparrows, and we are told that their flesh is very delicious and agreeable. When God fed the* Israelites *with these, it happened to be in the spring, when the* Quails *passed from* Asia *into* Europe. *Then they are to be found in great numbers upon the coasts of the* Red sea *and the* Mediterranean. *God caused a wind to arise, that drove them within and about the camp of the* Israelites; *and it is in this that the miracle consists, that they were brought so seasonably to this place, and in so great numbers, as to suffice above a million of persons above a month. Some authors affirm, that in those eastern and southern countries,* Quails *are innumerable, so that in one part of* Italy, *within the compass of five miles, there were taken about an hundred thousand of them every day for a month together; and that sometimes they fly so thick over the sea, that being weary they fall into ships, sometimes in such numbers, that they sink them with their weight.*

Exod. 16. 13. that at even q. came up and covered
Num. 11. 31. a wind from the Lord brought q.
32. the people stood and they gathered the q.
Psal. 105. 40. the people asked, and he brought q.

QUAKE.

Joel 2. 10. earth shall q. before them, heavens tremble
Nah. 1. 5. the mountains q. at him, the hills melt
Mat. 27. 51. at Christ's death the earth did q.
Heb. 12. 21. Moses said, I exceedingly fear and q.

QUAKED.

Exod. 19. 18. and the whole mount q. greatly
1 Sam. 14. 15. the host trembled, and the earth q.

QUAKING.

Ezek. 12. 18. son of man, eat thy bread with q.
Dan. 10. 7. but a great q. fell on them, that they fled

QUANTITY.

Isa. 22. 24. shall hang on him vessels of small q.

QUARREL.

1 Tim. 3. † 3. a bishop not ready to q. but patient

QUARREL.

Lev. 26. 25. a sword shall avenge q. of my covenant
2 Kings 5. 7. see how he seeketh a q. against me
Mark 6. 19. Herodias had a q. against John
Col. 3. 13. forgiving, if any man have a q. ag. any

QUARRIES.

Judg. 3. 19. Ehud turned again from the q.
26. Ehud escaped and passed beyond the q.

QUARTER.

Gen. 19. 4. all people from every q. to Lot's house
Josh. 18. 14. Kirjath-jearim, this was the west q.
Isa. 47. 15. thy merchants shall wander to his q.
56. 11. every one for his gain from his q.
Mark 1. 45. and they came to him from every q.
See SOUTH.

QUARTERS.

Exod. 13. 7. no leaven shall be seen in thy q.
Deut. 22. 12. shalt make thee fringes on the four q.
1 Chron. 9. 24. in four q. were the porters
Jer. 49. 36. four winds from the four q. of heaven
Acts 9. 32. as Peter pass. thro' all q. came to Lydda
16. 3. because of the Jews which were in those q.
28. 7. in same q. were possessions of Publius
Rev. 20. 8. shall receive nations in four q. of earth

QUATERNIONS.

Acts 12. 4. he delivered Peter to four q. of soldiers

QUEEN.

This name is given, [1] *To the wife or consort of a king,* Neh. 2. 6. [2] *To a sovereign princess, or chief ruler of a kingdom,* 1 Kings 10. 1. [3] *To the true catholic church, espoused to Christ the King of his people, as to an husband,* Psalm 45. 9. [4] *To the false antichristian church, which through pride, presumption, and security, boasts that she is the only infallible and impregnable church, against which the gates of hell shall not prevail,* Rev. 18. 7. [5] *To the sun, moon, and stars, which the* Hebrew *idolaters called by the name of the* queen of heaven, *Jer.* 44. 17, 25. *They set up altars to her upon the platforms or roofs of their houses, or the corners of the streets, near their doors, and in groves. They offered cakes to her kneaded up with oil and honey, and made libations to her with wine and other liquors; these were offerings which the Lord had commanded to be made to himself,* Lev. 23. 13. Num. 6. 17.

1 Kings 10. 1. the q. of Sheba heard of the fame of Sol. she came to him with questions, 2 Chr. 9. 1.
4. when the q. had seen all Solomon's wisdom
10. no such spices as the q. of Sheba gave Solom.
13. king Solomon gave the q. of Sheba all her desire, whatsoever she asked, 2 Chron. 9. 9, 12.
11. 19. Pharaoh gave Hadad the sister of the q.
15. 13. Asa removed mother Maachah from being q. she had made an idol, 2 Chr. 15. 16.
2 Kings 10. 13. we go to salute children of the q.
Neh. 2. 6. the king said, the q. sitting by him
Esth. 1. 9. Vashti the q. made a feast for the women
11. to bring the q. ‖ 12. the q. refused to come
15. what shall we do to the q. Vashti?
16. the q. hath not done wrong to the king only
17. this deed of q. shall come abroad to all women
18. which have heard the deed of the q.
2. 4. let the maiden that pleaseth the king be q.
17. he made Esther q. instead of Vashti
4. 4. q. grieved ‖ 5. 3. what wilt thou, q. Esther?
5. 12. q. let no man to the banquet but himself
7. 2. what is thy petition, q. Esther? shall be grant.
6. then Haman was afraid before king and q.
7. Haman make request to the q. for his life
8. will he force q. also before me in the house?
8. 1. king gave house of Haman to Esther the q.
9. 31. as Mordecai and Esther the q. enjoined them
Psal. 45. 9. did stand the q. in gold of Ophir
Jer. 13. 18. say to the king and q. humble yourselves
44. 17. to burn incense to the q. of heaven
25. vowed to burn incense to the q. of heaven
Dan. 5. 10. the q. came into the banquet-house
Mat. 12. 42. the q. of the south shall rise up in the judgment with this generation, Luke 11. 31.
Acts 8. 27. eunuch under Candace q. of Ethiopians
Rev. 18. 7. she saith, I sit a q. and am no widow

QUEENS.

Cant. 6. 8. there are threescore q. and virgins, 9.
Isa. 49. 23. and their q. thy nursing mothers

QUENCH

Signifies, [1] *To hinder or extinguish,* 2 Sam. 14. 7. Cant. 8. 7. [2] *To let or hinder the consuming force of,* Heb. 11. 34.

Quench not the Spirit, 1 *Thess.* 5. 19. *You that have received the Spirit, and have had experience of the workings and motions thereof in and upon your hearts, take heed of doing, or neglecting, any thing that may render them ineffectual to you, either in whole or in part; but cherish them by a ready compliance therewith. Not that the habits of grace may be totally extinguished in such as are truly regenerated, yet they may be abated as to degree and lively exercise: but those common illuminations and convictions of the Spirit, which persons unregenerated, especially such as live under the gospel, do often find, may be totally lost,* Heb. 6. 4, 5, 6.

2 Sam. 14. 7. so they shall q. my coal which is left
21. 17. that thou q. not the light of Israel
Psal. 104. 11. the wild asses q. their thirst
Cant. 8. 7. waters cannot q. love, nor floods drown
Isa. 1. 31. both shall burn, and none shall q. them
42. 3. smoking flax shall he not q. Mat. 12. 20.
Jer. 4. 4. lest fury burn, that none can q. it, 21. 12.
Amos 5. 6. and there be none to q. it in Beth-el
Eph. 6. 16. able to q. the fiery darts of the wicked
1 Thess. 5. 19. q. not Spirit, despise not prophesyings

QUENCHED.

Num. 11. 2. Moses prayed, fire was q. 2 Chr. 34. 25.
2 Kings 22. 17. my wrath shall not be q. ag. this place
Psal. 118. 12. they are q. as the fire of thorns
Isa. 34. 10. it shall not be q. night nor day
43. 17. they are extinct, they are q. as tow
66. 24. worm shall not die, nor shall their fire be q.
Jer. 7. 20. my fury burn, and shall not be q. 17. 27.
Ezek. 20. 47. the flaming flame shall not be q. 48.
Mark 9. 43. into the fire that never shall be q. 45.
44. and where the fire is not q. 46. 48.
Heb. 11. 34. q. the violence of fire, escaped sword

QUESTION

Signifies, [1] *A demand to which an answer is required,* Mat. 22. 35. [2] *Contentions, quarrels, or disputes,* 1 Tim. 1. 4. *The apostle* Paul *would have his disciples* Timothy *and* Titus *to avoid vain* questions, *or vain disputes, which are only concerning genealogies, and the sense of the law, because this kind of* question *is more apt to give offence than to edify,* 2 Tim. 2. 23. Tit. 3. 9.

Of Questions *there are several sorts,* [1] Religious, *as when one asks the import, sense, and meaning of the statutes and commandments of God,* Deut. 6. 20. [2] Blasphemous, *such was the* Jews' *question to our Saviour,* John 8. 48. Say we not well, that thou art a Samaritan, and hast a devil? [3] Curious, *Luke* 13. 23. Lord, are there few that be saved? [4] Foolish and unlearned, *such as questions about genealogies, that recounting of ancestors, which proceeds from a vain mind, and tends to vain-glory; and questions about the observance of the ceremonial law, or the sense of some little things therein,* 2 Tim. 2. 23. Tit. 3. 9. [5] Hard, 1 *Kings* 10. 1. The queen of Sheba came to prove Solomon with hard questions; *that is, with enigmatical, parabolical, intricate, and perplexing questions, which were much used among the eastern sages,* Judg. 14. 12. [6] Captious, *such as are proposed to entangle and perplex a person, that, from his answers an occasion and opportunity may be had for accusing and punishing him; of this sort was the question of the* Pharisees *and* Herodians *to our Saviour,* Mark 12. 14. Is it lawful to give tribute to Cæsar, or no? [7] Hypocritical, *such was* Herod's *to the wise men,* Mat. 2. 7. He asked them diligently, what time the star appeared; *but concealed his bloody design of murdering* Christ; *which in a short time after he in vain endeavoured to effectuate, by murdering all the children that were in* Bethlehem. [8] Accusatory, *Neh.* 2. 19. Will ye rebel against the king? [9] Reprehensive, 1 *Sam.* 1. 14. How long wilt thou be drunken? [10] Affirmative, *Num.* 12. 2. Hath not the Lord also spoken by us? *that is, He hath spoken by us.* [11] Negative, *Num.* 23. 8. How shall I curse whom God hath not cursed? *that is, I cannot curse them.* [12] *A question may be propounded through pride and ambition: the disciples came to* Christ, *and asked him,* Who is the greatest in the kingdom of heaven? *Mat.* 18. 1. *The kingdom of heaven of which our Saviour talked, though they expected it should be perfected in heaven, yet they made account that it should be begun on earth, and administered in a pompous manner, as other earthly kingdoms are.*

To put one to the question, *was a punishment among the* Romans. *They put criminals to the* question, *or endeavoured to extort confessions from them, by whipping them with whips or scourges. Some think that the offender was stripped to his waist, and that his hands were tied to a pillar, that his back might be stretched out to receive the blows. Others are of opinion, that his hands were fastened to a stake drove into the ground, of a foot and a half or two feet high, so that the criminal stooping with his face towards the ground, might present his naked back to such as were appointed to scourge him.*

There is an example of this in Acts 22. 24. *When the apostle* Paul *made an oration to the people at* Jerusalem, *and related to them the manner of his conversion, they listened to him very attentively till he came to that part of his discourse, where he told them that God had sent him to preach to the* Gentiles; *then they raised their voices, and cried out, that he was not fit to live, and were going to put him to death:* Lysias *the tribune gave command, that he should be examined by scourging, or* be put to the question, *as the French expression is, agreeable to the* Greek *word here used; but when they were binding him,* Paul *asked the centurion there present, Is it lawful for you to scourge a* Roman *citizen, and uncondemned? upon which* Lysias *caused him to be unbound.*

QUESTION, *Substantive.*
Mat. 22. 35. then a lawyer asked him a q.
Mark 11. 29. I will ask you one q. answer me
12. 34. no man durst ask him any q. Luke 20. 40.
John 3. 25. there arose a q. between the disciples
Acts 15. 2. came to the apostles about this q.
18. 15. if it be a q. of words and names
19. 40. we are in danger to be called in q.
23. 6. of resurrection I am called in q. 24. 21.
1 Cor. 10. 25. asking no q. for conscience, 27.
QUESTION, *Verb.*
Mark 8. 11. the Pharisees began to q. him
9. 16. he asked the scribes, what q. ye with them?
QUESTIONED, ING.
2 Chron. 31. 9. then Hezekiah q. with the priests
Mark 1. 27. that they q. among themselves
9. 10. q. what rising from the dead should mean
14. he saw a multitude, and scribes q. with them
Luke 23. 9. Pilate q. with him in many words
QUESTIONS.
1 Kings 10. 1. the queen came to prove him with q.
3. Solomon told her all her q. 2 Chron. 9. 1, 2.
Mat. 22. 46. neither durst any ask him more q.
Luke 2. 46. both hearing and asking them q.
Acts 23. 29. to be accused of q. of their law
25. 19. but had certain q. against him
20. because I doubted of such manner of q.
26. 3. because I know thee to be expert in q.
1 Tim. 1. 4. which minister q. rather than edifying
6. 4. but doting about q. and strifes of words
2 Tim. 2. 23. but unlearned q. avoid, Tit. 3. 9.
QUICK.
Lev. 13. 10. and there be q. raw flesh in the rising
24. the q. flesh that burneth have a white spot
Num. 16. 30. and they go down q. into the pit
Psal. 55. 15. let them go down q. into hell
124. 3. then they had swallowed us up q.
Isa. 11. 3. and shall make him of q. understanding
Acts 10. 42. ordained to be judge of the q. and dead
2 Tim. 4. 1. who shall judge the q. and the dead
Heb. 4. 12. the word of God is q. and powerful
1 Pet. 4. 5. that is ready to judge the q. and dead
QUICKEN
Signifies, [1] *To give life to the dead,* Rom. 4. 17. [2] *To raise and cheer up such as languish, by renewing their comforts, and exciting their graces,* Psal. 119. 25. [3] *To bring such as are dead in sin into a state of spiritual life, by enduing them with a principle of grace and spiritual life in sanctification, and delivering them from the guilt of sin by justification,* Eph. 2. 1, 5. The last Adam was made a quickening spirit, 1 Cor. 15. 45. Christ, *the second* Adam, *or public person, and head of the new covenant, is partaker of the divine nature, and endued with the Holy Spirit, whereby he becomes the fountain of heavenly life to all his members,* Rom. 8. 10, 11. *And as the soul dwelling in the first* Adam's *body, made him a living soul, so* Christ's *dwelling in true believers, quickens and enables them both here and hereafter,* John 17. 23.
Psal. 71. 20. thou shalt q. me again, and bring me
80. 18. q. us, and we will call on thy name
119. 25. q. me according to thy word, 107, 154.
37. turn me from vanity, q. me in thy way
40. q. me in thy righteousness
88. q. me after thy loving-kindness, 159.
149. q. me according to thy judgment, 156.
143. 11. q. me, O Lord, for thy name's sake
Rom. 8. 11. shall also q. your mortal bodies
QUICKENED.
Psal. 119. 50. for thy word hath q. me
93. for with thy precepts thou hast q. me
1 Cor. 15. 36. that which thou sowest is not q.
Eph. 2. 1. you hath he q. who were dead in sins
5. hath q. us together with Christ, Col. 2. 13.
1 Pet. 3. 18. put to death in flesh, but q. by Spirit
QUICKENETH.
John 5. 21. Father q. them, Son q. whom he will
6. 63. it is Spirit that q. flesh profiteth nothing
Rom. 4. 17. believed, even God who q. the dead
2 Cor. 3. † 6. the letter killeth, but the Spirit q.
1 Tim. 6. 13. in the sight of God, who q. all things
QUICKENING.
1 Cor. 15. 45. the last Adam was made a q. spirit
QUICKLY.
Gen. 18. 6. make ready q. three measures of fine meal
27. 20. how hast thou found it so q. my son?
Exod. 32. 8. they have turned aside q. out of the way, Deut. 9. 12, 16. Judg. 2. 17.
Num. 16. 46. put on incense and go q. to congreg.
Deut. 9. 3. so shalt thou destroy them q. as Ld. said
12. get thee down q. ‖ 11. 17. lest ye perish q.
28. 20. till thou perish q. because of thy doings
Josh. 2. 5. pursue q. for ye shall overtake them
8. 19. the ambush arose q. out of their place
10. 6. come up to us q. and save us, and help us
23. 16. ye shall perish q. from off the land
1 Sam. 20. 19. thou shalt go down q. and come
2 Sam. 17. 16. therefore send q. and tell David
18. but they went both of them away q.
21. said to David, arise and pass q. over the water
2 Kings 1. 11. thus hath the king said, come down q.
2 Chron. 18. 8. fetch q. Micaiah the son of Imla
Psal. 94. † 17. my soul had q. dwelt in silence
Eccl. 4. 12. a threefold cord is not q. broken
Mat. 5. 25. agree with thine adversary q.
28. 7. go q. and tell his disciples that he is risen
8. they departed q. with fear, Mark 16. 8.
Luke 14. 21. go q. into the streets and lanes
16. 6. take thy bill, sit down q. and write fifty
John 11. 29. Mary arose q. and came to Jesus
13. 27. then said Jesus, that thou doest, do q.
Acts 12. 7. the angel, saying, arise up q. Peter
22. 18. Paul, get thee q. out of Jerusalem
Rev. 2. 5. repent, else I will come to thee q. 16.
3. 11. behold, I come q. hold fast, 22. 7, 12.
11. 14. behold, the third woe cometh q.
22. 20. surely I come q. even so, come Lord Jesus
QUICKSANDS.
Acts 27. 17. lest they should fall into q.

QUIET.
Judg. 16. 2. the Philistines laid wait, and were q.
18. 7. after manner of the Zidonians, q. and secure
27. came to Laish, to a people that were at q.
2 Kings 11. 20. all the people rejoiced, and the city was in q. they slew Athaliah, 2 Chron. 23. 21.
1 Chron. 4. 40. and the land was wide and q.
2 Chron. 14. 1. in his days the land was q. ten years
5. the kingdom was q. before him, 20. 30.
Job 3. 13. for now should I have been q. and slept
26. neither was I q. yet trouble came
21. 23. one man dieth, being wholly at ease and q.
Psal. 35. 20. devise against them that are q. in land
107. 30. then are they glad, because they be q.
Prov. 1. 33. whoso hearkeneth to me shall be in q.
Eccl. 9. 17. the words of wise men are heard in q.
Isa. 7. 4. say to him, take heed and be q. fear not
14. 7. the whole earth is at rest, and is q.
32. 18. my people shall dwell in q. resting-places
33. 20. thy eyes shall see Jerusalem a q. habitation
Jer. 30. 10. Jacob shall return and be in rest and q.
47. 6. O sword, how long will it be ere thou be q.?
7. how be q. seeing the Lord hath given charge
49. 23. there is sorrow on the sea, it cannot be q.
51. 59. and this Seraiah was a q. prince
Ezek. 16. 42. I will be q. and will be no more angry
Amos 1. † 3. for four transgress. I will not let be q.
Nah. 1. 12. tho' they be q. they shall be cut down
Acts 19. 36. ye ought to be q. and do nothing rashly
1 Thess. 4. 11. and that ye study to be q. and to work
1 Tim. 2. 2. that we may lead a q. and peaceable life
1 Pet. 3. 4. the ornament of a meek and q. spirit
QUIETED.
Ps. 131. 2. I have behaved and q. myself as a child
Zech. 6. 8. these q. my spirit in the north country
QUIETETH.
Job 37. 17. when he q. the earth by the south wind
QUIETLY.
2 Sam. 3. 27. Joab took Abner to speak q. and smote
Lam. 3. 26. and q. wait for the salvation of Lord
QUIETNESS.
Judg. 8. 28. the country was in q. forty years
1 Chron. 22. 9. I will give q. to Israel in his days
Job 20. 20. surely he shall not feel q. in his belly
34. 29. when he giveth q. who can make trouble?
Psal. 23. † 2. leadeth me beside the waters of q.
Prov. 17. 1. better is a dry morsel and q.
Eccl. 4. 6. better is handful with q. than both hands
Isa. 30. 15. in q. and confid. shall be your strength
32. 17. effect of righteousness, q. and assurance
Ezek. 19. † 10. thy mother like a vine in q.
Acts 24. 2. seeing that by thee we enjoy great q.
2 Thess. 3. 12. we exhort that with q. they work.
QUIT.
Exod. 21. 19. then shall he that smote him be q.
28. but the owner of the ox shall be q.
Josh. 2. 20. then we will be q. of thine oath
QUIT.
1 Sam. 4. 9. q. yourselves like men, 1 Cor. 16. 13.
QUITE.
Gen. 31. 15. and q. devoured also our money
Exod. 23. 24. thou shalt q. break down their images
Lev. 25. † 23. the land shall not be q. cut off
Num. 17. 10. shalt q. take away their murmurings
33. 52. and q. pluck down all their high places
2 Sam. 3. 24. sent Abner away, and he is q. gone
Job 6. 13. and is wisdom driven q. from me?
Hab. 3. 9. thy bow was made q. naked
QUIVER.
Gen. 27. 3. therefore take thy q. and thy bow
Job 39. 23. the q. rattleth against him
Psal. 127. 5. happy the man that hath his q. full
Isa. 22. 6. Elam bare the q. with chariots of men
49. 2. polished shaft in his q. hath he hid me
Jer. 5. 16. their q. is as an open sepulchre
Lam. 3. 13. arrows of his q. to enter into my reins
QUIVERED.
Hab. 3. 16. when I heard, my lips q. at the voice

R.

RABBI.
Rab, Rabbin, Rabban, Rabbam; *a name of dignity among the* Hebrews, *signifying Doctor, or Master. The name of* Rab *was given to their masters and doctors, to the chief of a class, and to the principal officers of the court of a prince: for example,* Nebuzar-adan, *general of the army of king* Nebuchadnezzar, *is always called* Rab Tabachim, *the master of the butchers, cooks, or guards,* 2 Kings 25. 8, 20. Daniel *speaks of* Ashpenaz the Rab *of the eunuchs of the house of* Nebuchadnezzar, *Dan.* 1. 3. *and of the* Rab *of the* Saganim, *or chief of the governors, or peers,* Dan. 2. 48. *This prophet himself was preferred to be the chief of the interpreters of dreams, or the* Rab *of the* Chartumim, *Dan.* 5. 11. *It appears that this name came originally from the* Chaldees; *for before the captivity, when any mention was made of* Judea, *it is not found that it was used, but only when any mention was to be made of the officers of the king of* Babylon.
Rab, *or* Rabban, *properly signifies* Master, *or one that excels in any thing.* Rabbi, *or* Rabbani, *is* my Master; Rabbin *is the plural. Thus* Rab *is of greater dignity than* Rabbi; *and* Rabbin, *or* Rabbim, *is a word of greater dignity than either* Rab, *or* Rabbi.
There were several gradations before they could arrive at the dignity of Rabbin. *He that was master, or head of the school, was called* Cacham, *or* Wise; *and he had the name of* Bachar, *or* Elow, *who aspired to the doctorship, and for this purpose frequented the school of the* Cacham. *When he was further advanced, he had the title of* Cabar *of the* Rab, *or the master's companion. And then, when he was further skilled in the knowledge of the law and the traditions, he was called only* Rab, *or* Rabbin, *and* Morena, *our master.*
The Cacham Rab, *or master* Rabbin, *decided all sorts of differences, determined what things were allowed, or forbidden, and judged in all matters of religion. He celebrated marriages, and declared divorces: he preached, if he had a talent for it, and was head of the academies. He had the head seat of the assemblies, and in the synagogues. He reprimanded the disobedient, and could even excommunicate them, which procured him great respect and authority. In their schools they sat upon raised chairs, and their scholars were at their feet: hence it is that* Paul *is said to have studied at the feet of* Rabbi Gamaliel, *Acts* 22. 3.
Our Saviour reprehends the scribes and Pharisees for affecting to have honourable titles given them, and to be the lords and guides of the people's faith; and exhorts his disciples not ambitiously to affect such titles, or any vain applause, or precedency one above another; telling them, that himself was the only Lawgiver and Teacher, who only can teach powerfully and inwardly, and in matters of faith and worship is only to be followed, Mat. 23. 7, 8.
Mat. 23. 7. they love to be called of men, r. r.
8. be not ye called r. for one is your master
John 1. 38. they said, R. where dwellest thou?
49. Nathanael saith, R. thou art the Son of God
3. 2. R. we know thou art a teacher come from God
26. R. he that was with thee, the same baptizeth
6. 25. they said, R. when camest thou hither?
RABBONI.
John 20. 16. Mary turned herself and saith, R.
RACA,
Or Racha, *is a* Syriac *word, which properly signifies* empty, vain, beggarly, foolish, *and which includes in it a strong idea of contempt.* Lightfoot *says, that in the books of the* Jews, *the word* Raca *is a term of the utmost contempt, and is used to be pronounced with certain gestures of indignation, as spitting, turning away the head, &c. The* Pharisees *in their lectures upon this law,* Thou shalt not kill, *extended it no further, than that a man should not, without a warrant, actually take away the life of another. But our Saviour gave them another sense of this law, namely, that if a man doth but in his heart nourish wrath and anger against another without a just cause; and lets it grow up into malice, and thoughts, and desires, of private revenge, though he be not by it obnoxious to courts of justice, yet he is accountable to God, and liable to his judgment: but if men suffer their passions to break out into reviling and opprobrious language, such as* Raca, *or* Thou fool, *they are not only liable to the eternal vengeance of God, but ought to be subjected to the punishment of the civil magistrate; these scornful, disdainful, and vilifying speeches being the beginnings of murder, provocatives to it, and indications of murderous hearts.* Mat. 5. 22. Whosoever shall say to his brother, *Raca,* shall be in danger of the council.
RACE.
Psal. 19. 5. rejoiceth as a strong man to run a r.
Eccl. 9. 11. I saw that the r. is not to the swift
1 Cor. 9. 24. they which run in a r. run all
Heb. 12. 1. run with patience the r. set before us
RAFTERS.
Cant. 1. 17. the beams of cedar, and our r. of fir
RAGE, *Substantive.*
2 Kings 5. 12. Naaman turned away in a r.
19. 27. I know thy r. against me, Isa. 37. 28.
2 Chron. 16. 10. Asa was in a r. with the seer
28. 9. and ye have slain them in a r. that reach.
Job 39. 24. he swalloweth the ground with r.
40. 11. cast abroad the r. of thy wrath
Psal. 7. 6. lift up thyself because of r. of enemies
Prov. 6. 34. for jealousy is the r. of a man
Dan. 3. 13. Nebuchad. commanded in his r. to bring
Hos. 7. 16. they shall fall for the r. of their tongue
RAGE, *Verb.*
Psal. 2. 1. why do the heathen r.? Acts 4. 25.
Prov. 29. 9. whether he r. or laugh, no rest
Jer. 46. 9. come up, ye horses, r. ye chariots
Nah. 2. 4. chariots shall r. in the streets shall justle
RAGED.
Psal. 46. 6. heathen r. the kingdoms were moved
RAGETH.
Prov. 14. 16. but the fool r. and is confident
RAGGED.
Isa. 2. 21. to go into the tops of the r. rocks
RAGING.
Psal. 89. 9. thou rulest the r. of the sea
Prov. 20. 1. wine is a mocker, strong drink is r
Jonah 1. 15. and the sea ceased from her r.
Luke 8. 24. he rebuked the wind and r. of the water
Jude 13. r. waves of the sea foaming out their shame
RAGS.
Prov. 23. 21. drowsiness shall clothe a man with r.
Isa. 64. 6. all our righteousnesses are as filthy r.
Jer. 38. 11. Ebedmelech took old rotten r.
12. put r. under thine arm holes, under cords
RAIL.
2 Chron. 32. 17. Sennacherib wrote letters to r.
RAILED.
1 Sam. 25. 14. Nabal r. on David's messengers
Mark 15. 29. they that passed by r. on Jesus
Luke 23. 39. one of the malefactors r. on him
RAILER.
1 Cor. 5. 11. keep not company with r. or drunkard
RAILING.
2 Pet. 2. 11. angels bring not r. accusation ag. them
Jude 9. durst not bring against him a r. accusation
RAILING.
1 Tim. 5. † 14. give none occasion to adversary for r.
6. 4. whereof cometh envy, strife, r.
1 Pet. 3. 9. not rendering r. for r. but contrariwise
RAIMENT.
Gen. 24. 53. the servant gave r. to Rebekah
27. 15. Rebekah took goodly r. of her son Esau
27. Isaac smelled his r. and blessed him
28. 20. if the Lord will give me r. to put on
41. 14. Joseph shaved, and changed his r.

Gen. 45. 22. gave to each man changes of r. but to Benjamin 300 pieces of silver and five changes of r.
Exod. 3. 22. borrow of the Egyptians r. 12. 35.
21. 10. her food and r. shall he not diminish
22. 9. any manner of trespass for sheep, for r.
26. if thou take thy neighbour's r. to pledge, 27.
Lev. 11. 32. when unclean beast falls on r. wash
Num. 31. 20. purify all your r. all made of skins
Deut. 8. 4. thy r. waxed not old upon thee
10. 18. the Lord loveth the stranger, giving him r.
21. 13. she shall put r. of her captivity from her
22. 3. lost r. restore, and all lost thing of brother
24. 13. that he may sleep in his r. and bless thee
17. thou shalt not take a widow's r. to pledge
Josh. 22. 8. return to your tents with much r.
Judg. 3. 16. Ehud girded a dagger under his r.
8. 26. purple r. that was on the kings of Midian
Ruth 3. 3. wash thyself and put thy r. upon thee
1 Sam. 28. 8. Saul disguised himself and put on r.
2 Kings 5. 5. Naaman took with him ten chang. of r.
7. 8. the lepers carried thence r. and hid it
2 Chron. 9. 24. presents to Solomon, gold, and r.
Esth. 4. 4. the queen sent r. to clothe Mordecai
Job 27. 16. and though he prepare r. as the clay
Psal. 45. 14. he brought to king in r. of needle-work
Isa. 14. 19. cast out as the r. of those that are slain
63. 3. and I will stain all my r.
Ezek. 16. 13. thy r. was of fine linen and silk
Zech. 3. 4. I will clothe thee with change of r.
Mat. 3. 4. John had his r. of camels' hair
6. 25. and the body more than r. Luke 12. 23.
28. why take ye thought for r.? consider the lilies
11. 8. a man clothed in soft r. Luke 7. 25.
17. 2. his r. white as light, Mark 9. 3. Luke 9. 29.
27. 31. put his own r. on him, and led him away
28. 3. and his r. was white as snow
Luke 10. 30. among thieves who stripped him of r.
23. 34. they parted his r. and cast lots, John 19. 24.
Acts 18. 6. Paul shook his r. and said to them
22. 20. I kept the r. of them that slew Stephen
1 Tim. 6. 8. having food and r. let us be content
Jam. 2. 2. and there came a poor man in vile r.
Rev. 3. 5. the same shall be clothed in white r.
18. buy white r. that thou mayest be clothed
4. 4. I saw twenty-four elders clothed in white r.

RAIN

Is the vapours exhaled by the sun, which fall from the clouds to the earth in drops, Eccl. 11. 3. *There are some who think, by some expressions of the scripture, that the ancient* Hebrews *imagined the* Rain *to be derived from certain great reservatories, which they supposed to be above the heavens, and which* Moses *calls the waters above the firmament, by way of contradistinction from the inferior waters, which are those of the sea, rivers, &c. For example*, Moses *says, that at the time of the Deluge, the* rain *did not fall according to the ordinary course of nature, but that the cataracts, the flood-gates of heaven were set open*, Gen. 7. 11. All the fountains of the great deep were broken up, and the windows of heaven were opened. *And* Hosea *says, that in times of great drought the clouds cry to the Lord, beseeching him to permit the waters which he keeps in his treasuries and repositories, to fall into them and replenish them*, Hos. 2. 21. I will hear the heavens.

The sacred writers often speak of the rain *of the former season, and of the* rain *of the latter season.* Deut. 11. 14. I will give you the rain of your land in his due season, the first *rain*, and the latter *rain: Also in* Hos. 6. 3. *Twice in the year there fell plenty of rain in* Judea; *in the beginning of the civil year, about* September *or* October, *and half a year after in the month* Abib *or* March, *which was the first month in the ecclesiastical or holy year, whence it is called* the latter rain in the first month, *Joel* 2. 23.

The Hebrews *often compare speech and discourse to* rain. *Deut.* 32. 2. My doctrine shall drop as the rain; *that is, As rain falling upon herbs and grass makes them fresh, fragrant, and flourishing, the same effect I may justly expect and hope that my discourse will have upon your hearts, namely, to make them soft, pliable, and fruitful.* Job *says, that in the time of his prosperity he was attended to with great respect and eagerness, that his* discourse distilled like soft rain: That they expected it like rain, and opened their mouth to receive his words, and therewith to satisfy their thirst, as the parched earth opens its mouth to receive the *rain* of the latter season, *Job* 29. 22, 23.

The Psalmist says, that God maketh lightnings for the rain, *Psal.* 135. 7. *He bringeth water even out of the fire; he maketh thick clouds, which being broken produce lightnings, and so are dissolved into showers of rain: Or*, he maketh lightnings with rain, *Jer.* 10. 13. *He causeth both of them to come out of the same cloud. Or thus: Lightning goes before thunder and rain; and when we perceive lightning, and hear a fresh clap of thunder during a storm, we conclude that the shower will soon come. This is easily applied. Lightning and thunder are produced only by the shock of clouds one against another; and the same shock is the cause of rain also. The prophet therefore may observe here, that lightning is as it were the forerunner and the natural token of rain.*

Gen. 7. 12. the r. was upon the earth forty days
8. 2. and the r. from heaven was restrained
Exod. 9. 33. and the r. was not poured on the earth
34. Pharaoh saw the r. ceased, he sinned yet more
Lev. 26. 4. then I will give you r. in due season, and land shall yield increase, Deut. 11. 14. | 28. 12.
Deut. 11. 11. land drinks water of the r. of heaven
17. he shut up the heaven that there be no r. 1 Kings 8. 35. 2 Chron. 6. 26. | 7. 13.
28. 24. the Lord shall make r. of thy land powder
32. 2. my doctrine shall drop as the r. as the dew
1 Sam. 12. 17. I will call on the Lord to send r.
1 Sam. 12. 18. Lord sent thunder and r. that day
2 Sam. 1. 21. let there be no dew nor r. upon you
23. 4. as grass springing by clear shining after r.
1 Kings 8. 36. then hear thou and give r. upon thy land thou hast given thy people, 2 Chr. 6. 27.
17. 1. there shall not be dew nor r. these years
7. brook dried up, because there had been no r.
14. till day that the Lord send r. on the earth
18. 1. shew to Ahab, I will send r. upon the earth
41. for there is a sound of abundance of r.
44. that the r. stop thee not || 45. was a great r.
2 Kings 3. 17. ye shall not see wind, nor see r.
Ezra 10. 9. people sat trembling for the great r.
13. people are many, and it is a time of much r
Job 5. 10. who giveth r. upon the earth
28. 26. and when he made a decree for r. and way
29. 23. they waited for me as for the r.
36. 27. clouds pour down r. according to vapour
37. 6. to small r. and to great r. of his strength
38. 28. hath r. a father? or who hath begotten dew?
Psal. 65. † 10. causest r. descend into the furrows
68. 9. thou, O God, didst send a plentiful r.
72. 6. he shall come down like r. on mown grass
84. 6. the r. also filleth the pools
105. 32. he gave them hail for r. and flaming fire
135. 7. he maketh lightnings for the r.
147. 8. sing to the Lord, who prepareth r. for earth
Prov. 25. 14. is like clouds and wind without r.
23. the north wind driveth away r.
26. 1. as snow in summer, and r. in harvest
28. 3. that oppresseth poor is like a sweeping r.
Eccl. 11. 3. if clouds be full of r. they empty
12. 2. nor the clouds return after the r.
Cant. 2. 11. winter is past, the r. is over and gone
Isa. 4. 6. tabernacle for a covert from storm and r.
5. 6. I will command clouds they rain no r. on it
18. † 4. like clear heat after r. and cloud of dew
30. 23. then shall he give the r. of thy seed
44. 14. he planteth an ash, and r. doth nourish it
55. 10. as the r. cometh down from heaven
Jer. 5. 24. let us fear the Lord that giveth r.
10. 13. he maketh lightnings with r. 51. 16.
14. 4. ground is chapt, for there was no r.
22. are there any vanities of Gentiles can cause r.?
Ezek. 1. 28. as the bow in the cloud in day of r.
38. 22. I will r. an overflowing r. and brimstone
Hos. 6. 3. and he shall make us as the r.
Joel 2. 23. he will cause to come down for you r.
Amos 4. 7. I have withholden the r. from you
Zech. 14. 17. even upon them shall be no r.
18. if family of Egypt go not up, that have no r.
Mat. 5. 45. he sendeth r. on the just and unjust
7. 25. and the r. descended, and floods came, 27.
Acts 14. 17. in that he did good, and gave us r.
28. 2. and received us, because of the present r.
Heb. 6. 7. the earth which drinketh in the r.
Jam. 5. 18. he prayed, and the heaven gave r.

See LATTER.

RAIN, *Verb*.

Gen. 2. 5. Lord had not caused it to r. on the earth
7. 4. cause it to r. forty days and forty nights
Exod. 9. 18. to-morrow I will cause it to r.
16. 4. I will r. bread from heaven for you
Job 20. 23. God shall r. his fury on him
38. 26. to cause it to r. on the earth
Psal. 11. 6. on the wicked he shall r. snares
Isa. 5. 6. the clouds, that they r. no rain on it
Ezek. 38. 22. I will r. an overflowing rain
Hos. 10. 12. till he come and r. righteousness on you
Amos 4. 7. I caused it to r. on one city, not on another
Jam. 5. 17. Elias prayed earnestly it might not r.
Rev. 11. 6. that it r. not in days of their prophecy

RAINBOW.

Rev. 4. 3. there was a r. round about the throne
10. 1. I saw an angel, and a r. was upon his head

RAINED.

Gen. 19. 24. Lord r. upon Sodom and Gomorrah
Exod. 9. 23. the Lord r. hail on the land of Egypt
Psal. 78. 24. and had r. down manna, flesh, 27.
Ezek. 22. 24. thou art the land not r. upon
Amos 4. 7. I withheld rain, one piece was r. upon; and the piece whereupon it r. not, withered
Luke 17. 29. the same day it r. fire from heaven
Jam. 5. 17. it r. not for three years and six months

RAINY.

Prov. 27. 15. a continual dropping in a r. day

RAISE

Signifies, [1] *To lift up*, 1 Sam. 2. 8. Psal. 113. 7. [2] *To invent, or relate*, Exod. 23. 1. [3] *To ordain and appoint*, Exod. 9. 16. [4] *To beget*, Gen. 38. 8. [5] *To keep in remembrance*, Ruth 4. 5. [6] *To be restored to life*, Mat. 11. 5. John 2. 19. [7] *To call to, and fit persons for any work*, Judg. 2. 16. [8] *To build*, Isa. 23. 13. [9] *To make to stand*, Psal. 107. 25.

Gen. 38. 8. marry her, and r. up seed to thy brother
Exod. 23. 1. thou shalt not r. a false report
Deut. 18. 15. Lord thy God will r. up a prophet like to me, to him hearken, 18. Acts 3. 22. | 7. 37.
25. 7. refuseth to r. up to brother a name in Israel
Josh. 8. 29. and r. thereon a great heap of stones
Ruth 4. 5. to r. up the name of the dead, 10.
1 Sam. 2. 35. I will r. me up a faithful priest
2 Sam. 12. 11. I will r. up evil ag. thee out of house
17. elders went to him to r. him up from earth
1 Kings 14. 14. the Lord shall r. up a king in Israel
1 Chron. 17. 11. I will r. up thy seed after thee
Job 3. 8. who are ready to r. up their mourning
19. 12. his troops r. up their way against me
30. 12. they r. up against me ways of destruction
Ps. 41. 10. Lord, be merciful to me, and r. me up
48. † 13. mark her bulwarks, r. up her palaces
Isa. 15. 5. they shall r. up a cry of destruction
29. 3. and I will r. forts against thee
44. 26. I will r. up the decayed places thereof
49. 6. my servant to r. up the tribes of Jacob
† 8. will give thee for a covenant to r. up the earth
58. 12. shalt r. up foundations of many generations
61. 4. they shall r. up the former desolations
Jer. 23. 5. I will r. to David a righteous branch
30. 9. David their king, whom I will r. up
50. 9. I will r. against Babylon an assembly
Jer. 50. 32. none shall r. him || 51. 1. r. a destr. wind
Ezek. 23. 22. I will r. up thy lovers against thee
34. 29. I will r. up for them a plant of renown
Hos. 6. 2. in the third day he will r. us up
Joel 3. 7. I will r. them whither ye have driven
Amos 5. 2. virgin of Israel, there is none to r. her up
6. 14. but, behold, I will r. a nation against you
9. 11. I will r. up the tabernacle of David, and I will r. up his ruins, and I will build it
Mic. 5. 5. we shall r. against him seven shepherds
Hab. 1. 3. there are that r. up strife and contention
6. I will r. up the Chaldeans, that hasty nation
Zech. 11. 16. I will r. up a shepherd in the land
Mat. 3. 9. to r. up children to Abraham, Luke 3. 8.
10. 8. heal the sick, cleanse the lepers, r. the dead
22. 24. his brother marry his wife, and r. up seed to his brother, Mark 12. 19. Luke 20. 28.
John 2. 19. and in three days I will r. it up
6. 39. I will r. it up again at last day, 39. 40, 44, 54.
Acts 2. 30. he would r. up Christ to sit on his throne
26. 8. why incredible that God should r. the dead?
1 Cor. 6. 14. and will also r. up us by his power
2 Cor. 4. 14. that he shall r. up us also by Jesus
Heb. 11. 19. accounting God was able to r. him up
Jam. 5. 15. and the Lord shall r. him up

RAISED.

Exod. 9. 16. I r. thee up to shew my pow. Rom. 9. 17.
Josh. 5. 7. children whom he r. up in their stead
7. 26. they r. over him a great heap of stones
Judg. 2. 16. nevertheless the Lord r. up judges, 18.
3. 9. the Lord r. up a deliverer to Israel, 15.
2 Sam. 23. 1. the man who was r. up on high, said
1 Kings 5. 13. Solomon r. up a levy of Israel, 9. 15.
2 Chron. 32. 5. and r. it up to the towers, 33. 14.
Ezra 1. 5. all whose spirit God r. to go up to build
Job 14. 12. not awake, nor be r. out of their sleep
Prov. 15. † 19. the way of righteous r. like a causeway
Cant. 8. 5. I r. thee up under the apple-tree
Isa. 14. 9. it r. up from their thrones kings of nations
23. 13. the Assyrian r. up the palaces of Chaldea
41. 2. who r. up the righteous man from the east
25. I have r. up one from the north
45. 13. I have r. him up in righteousness
Jer. 6. 22. a great nation shall be r. from the earth
25. 32. a great whirlwind shall be r. up from earth
29. 15. Lord hath r. us up prophets in Babylon
50. 41. many kings shall be r. from the earth
51. 11. Lord r. up the spirit of the kings of Medes
Dan. 7. 5. a bear r. up itself on one side
Amos 2. 11. I r. up of your sons for prophets
Zech. 2. 13. is r. up out of his holy habitation
9. 13. when I have r. up thy sons, O Zion
Mat. 1. 24. then Joseph being r. from sleep did
11. 5. the deaf hear, the dead are r. up, Luke 7. 22.
16. 21. he must go and suffer, be killed, and r. up again the third day, 17. 23. Luke 9. 22.
Luke 1. 69. hath r. up an horn of salvation for us
20. 37. now that the dead are r. Moses shewed
John 12. 1. Lazarus whom he r. from the dead, 9, 17.
Acts 2. 24. whom God hath r. up, 32. | 3. 15, 26. | 4. 10. | 5. 30. | 10. 40. | 13. 30, 33, 34. | 17. 31. Rom. 10. 9. 1 Cor. 6. 14. 2 Cor. 4. 14. Gal. 1. 1. Eph. 1. 20.
12. 7. angel r. up Peter || 13. 22. he r. up David
13. 23. hath God r. to Israel a Saviour Jesus
50. the Jews r. persecution against Paul
Rom. 4. 24. if we believe on him that r. up Jesus
25. who was r. again for our justification
6. 4. like as Christ was r. from the dead by Father
9. Christ being r. from the dead, dieth no more
7. 4. married, even to him who is r. from the dead
8. 11. if the Spirit of him that r. up Jesus dwell in you, he that r. up Christ shall quicken
1 Cor. 15. 15. r. up Christ; whom he r. not up
16. if the dead rise not, then is not Christ r.
17. if Christ be not r. your faith is vain, yet in sins
35. some men will say, how are the dead r.?
42. it is sown in corruption, r. in incorruption, 52.
43. it is r. in glory, it is r. in power
44. it is sown a natural body, r. a spiritual body
Eph. 2. 6. and hath r. us up together in Christ Jesus
Col. 2. 12. through operation of God who r. him from
1 Thess. 1. 10. wait for his Son, whom he r. from dead
2 Tim. 2. 8. remember Jesus of seed of David was r.
Heb. 11. 35. women received their dead r. to life
1 Pet. 1. 21. believe in God that r. him up from dead

RAISER.

Dan. 11. 20. then shall stand up a r. of taxes
Hos. 7. † 4. the r. will cease after he hath kneaded

RAISETH.

1 Sam. 2. 8. he r. poor out of dust, Psal. 113. 7.
Job 41. 25. when he r. himself, mighty are afraid
Psal. 107. 25. for he commands and r. stormy wind
145. 14. he r. those that be bowed down, 146. 8.
John 5. 21. for as the Father r. up the dead
2 Cor. 1. 9. but trust in God which r. the dead

RAISING.

Hos. 7. 4. oven heated by baker who ceaseth from r.
Acts 24. 12. nor found they me r. up the people

RAISINS.

1 Sam. 25. 18. Abigail took an hundred clusters of r.
30. 12. they gave the Egyptians two clusters of r.
2 Sam. 16. 1. Ziba met David with 100 bunches of r.
1 Chr. 12. 40. they brought bunches of r. and wine

RAM.

Gen. 15. 9. take a r. of three years old, and she-goat
22. 13. behind him a r. caught in a thicket by horns
Exod. 29. 15. take one r. || 16. thou shalt slay the r.
18. thou shalt burn the whole r. Lev. 8. 21.
22. it is a r. of consecration, 27, 31. Lev. 8. 22.
32. Aaron and his sons shall eat the flesh of the r.
Lev. 9. 2. take a r. for a burnt-offering, and offer
4. r. for peace offerings || 19. 21. for trespass off.
Num. 5. 8. besides the r. of the atonement
15. 11. thus shall it be done for one r. or a lamb
Ezra 10. 19. being guilty, they offered a r. for tresp.
Ezek. 43. 23. shall offer a r. without blemish, 25.
45. 24. prepare an ephah for a r. 46. 5, 7, 11.
46. 4. the prince shall offer to the Lord a r.
6. in the day of the new moon six lambs and a r.
Dan. 8. 3. I saw a r. which had two horns
4. I saw the r. pushing westward and northward

Dan. 8. 6 the goat ran to the r. that had two horns
7. come close to the r. there was no power in the r. none to deliver the r. out of the hands
20. the r. having two horns are the kings

RAMS.

Gen. 31. 10. r. which leaped were ring-straked, 12.
38. the r. of thy flock have I not eaten
32. 14. Jacob sent Esau 200 ewes and 20 r.
Deut. 32. 14. with r. of breed of Bashan and goats
1 Sam. 15. 22. and to hearken than the fat of r.
2 Kings 3. 4. Moab rendered 100,000 r. with wool
1 Chron. 29. 21. they sacrificed to the Lord 1000 r.
2 Chron. 17. 11. the Arabians brought 7700 r.
Ezra 6. 9. r. for offerings of the God of heaven
17. offered at dedication of the house 200 r.
7. 17. thou mayest buy with this money r. lambs
8. 35. offered ninety-six r. for a sin offering
Psal. 66. 15. with the fat of r. Isa. 34. 6.
114. 4. the mountains skipped like r. 6.
Isa. 1. 11. I am full of the burnt offerings of r.
34. 6. the sword is filled with fat of kidneys of r.
60. 7. the r. of Nebaioth shall minister to thee
Jer. 51. 40. bring them to the slaughter like r.
Ezek. 27. 21. Kedar occupied with thee in r.
34. 17. I judge between the r. and the he-goats
39. 18. ye shall drink the blood of r. of lambs
Mic. 6. 7. will Lord be pleased with thousands of r.
See BATTERING, SEVEN.

RAMS'-*horns*.

Josh. 6. 4. seven priests shall bear before the ark seven trumpets of r.-horns, 6, 8, 13.
5. when they make a long blast with the r.-horns

RAMS'-*skins*.

Exod. 25. 5. r.-skins dyed red, and badgers'-skins, and shittim-wood, 26. 14. | 35. 7. | 36. 19. | 39. 34.

RAMPART.

Lam. 2. 8. he made the r. and the wall to lament
Nah. 3. 8. than populous No, whose r. was the sea

RAN.

Gen. 18. 2. Abraham r. to meet them from tent-door
7. r. to herd || 24. 17. servant r. to meet Rebekah
24. 20. Rebekah r. to the well to draw water
28. the damsel r. and told her mother's house
29. Laban r. out to the man to the well
29. 12. and Rachel r. and told her father
13. Laban r. to meet Jacob and embraced him
33. 4. Esau r. to meet him, and embraced him
Exod. 9. 23. the fire r. along upon the ground
Num. 11. 27. there r. a young man and told Moses
16. 47. Aaron r. into midst of the congregation
Josh. 7. 22. the messenger r. to Aaron's tent
8. 19. the ambush r. into Ai, and set it on fire
Judg. 7. 21. all the host of Midian r. and fled
9. 21. Jotham r. away, and fled, and went to Beer
13. 10. Manoah's wife r. and shewed her husband
1 Sam. 3. 5. Samuel r. to Eli, and said, here am I
4. 12. a man of Benjamin r. out of the army
10. 23. and they r. and fetched Saul thence
17. 22. David r. into the army and saluted brethr.
51. David r. and stood upon the Philistine
20. 36. as the lad r. he shot an arrow beyond him
2 Sam. 18. 21. Cushi bowed himself to Joab and r.
23. Ahimaaz r. by the plain and overran Cushi
1 Kings 2. 39. two servants of Shimei r. away
18. 35. the water r. round about the altar
46. Elijah r. before Ahab to Jezreel
19. 20. Elisha left the oxen and r. after Elijah
22. 35. the blood r. into the midst of the chariot
2 Kings 23. † 12. king beat down, and r. from thence
Psal. 77. 2. my sore r. in the night and ceased not
105. 41. the waters r. in the dry places like a river
133. 2. the ointment that r. down upon the beard
Jer. 23. 21. I have not sent them, yet they r.
Ezek. 1. 14. the living creatures r. and returned
47. 2. there r. out waters on the right side
Dan. 8. 6. the goat r. to the ram in fury of his power
Mat. 8. 32. the herd of swine r. violently down a steep place into the sea, Mark 5. 13. Luke 8. 33.
27. 48. one r. and filled a spunge, Mark 15. 36.
Mark 6. 33. many knew him, and r. afoot thither
55. and r. through that whole region round about
Luke 15. 20. his father r. and fell on his neck
19. 4. Zaccheus r. before and climbed up a tree
24. 12. then arose Peter and r. to the sepulchre
John 20. 4. so they r. both together, other outrun
Acts 3. 11. the people r. together unto them
7. 57. they r. upon Stephen with one accord
8. 30. Philip r. to the chariot and heard him
12. 14. when she knew Peter's voice, she r. in
14. 14. Paul and Barnabas r. in among the people
21. 30. the people r. together and took Paul
21. 32. chief captain took soldiers and r. down
27. 41. they r. the ship aground and stuck fast
Jude 11. they r. greedily after the error of Balaam

RANG.

1 Sam. 4. 5. shouted, so that the earth r. again
1 Kings 1. 45. Israel shouted, so that the city r. again

RANGE.

Job 39. 8. the r. of the mountains is his pasture

RANGED.

1 Sam. 17. † 2. Saul and Israel r. the battle

RANGERS.

1 Chron. 12. † 33. of Zebulun r. of battle 50,000

RANGES.

Lev. 11. 35. or r. for pots, they shall be broken
2 Kings 11. 8. that cometh within r. let him be slain
15. have her forth without the r. 2 Chr. 23. 14.

RANGING.

Prov. 28. 15. as a roaring lion, and a r. bear, so a ruler

RANK.

Gen. 41. 5. ears came up upon one stalk, r. and good
7. seven thin ears devoured the seven r. ears
Exod. 13. † 18. Israel went up by five in a r.
Num. 2. 16. they shall set forth in the second r.
24. they shall go forward in the third r.
Judg. 7. † 11. then went to outside of the r. by five
1 Chr. 12. 33. of Zebulun 50,000 could keep r.
† 36. of Asher keeping their r. 40,000
38. men of war that could keep r. came to Hebron
Psal. 55. † 13. thou a man according to my r.
Gal. 4. † 25. Agar is in the same r. with Jerusalem

RANKS.

1 Kings 7. 4. light was against light in three r. 5.
Joel 2. 7. and they shall not break their r.
Mark 6. 40. they sat down in r. by hund. and fifties

RANSOM

Is a signification made, or price paid, for the redeeming of a captive, or for procuring a pardon for some notorious offender. God, giving directions to his ministers how to behave towards penitent sinners, says, Deliver him from going down to the pit, I have found a ransom, Job 33. 24. *Declare to him, that I have pardoned and will heal him; for I have found out an expedient, and a way of ransoming and redeeming sinners from death, both spiritual and eternal, which they by their sins have deserved: which is by the death of my Son, the Redeemer and Saviour: hence* Christ is called a Ransom. 1 Tim. 2. 6. Who gave himself a ransom for all, to be testified in due time. *Man being in a lost and deplorable condition, and liable to eternal death on account of his sins; the eternal Son of God, moved by his divine love, undertook to restore fallen man to the favour of God, and voluntarily endured the punishment due to our sins, and gave his most precious life and blood as the price of our redemption: and therefore such as* Christ *redeems from the spiritual bondage of sin and Satan, are called* the ransomed of the Lord, Isa. 35. 10.

RANSOM, *Substantive*.

Exod. 21. 30. he shall give for the r. of his life
30. 12. they shall give every man a r. for his soul
1 Sam. 12. † 3. of whose hand I received any r.?
Job 33. 24. deliver him from pit, I have found a r.
36. 18. then a great r. cannot deliver thee
Psal. 49. 7. nor can they give to God a r. for him
Prov. 6. 35. he will not regard any r. neither rest
13. 8. the r. of a man's life are his riches
21. 18. the wicked shall be a r. for the righteous
Isa. 43. 3. I gave Egypt for thy r. Seba for thee
Amos 5. † 12. they afflict the just, they take a r.
Mat. 20. 28. even as the Son of man came to give his life a r. for many, Mark 10. 45.
1 Tim. 2. 6. who gave hims. r. for all, to be testified

RANSOM.

Hos. 13. 14. I will r. them from power of the grave

RANSOMED.

Isa. 35. 10. the r. of the Lord shall return and come
51. 10. made the sea a way for the r. to pass over
Jer. 31. 11. Lord hath redeemed Jacob and r. him

RARE.

Dan. 2. 11. it is a r. thing that the king requireth

RASE.

Psal. 137. 7. r. it, r. it even to the foundation

RASH.

Eccl. 5. 2. be not r. with thy mouth, heart not hasty
Isa. 32. † 4. the heart of the r. shall understand
1 Cor. 13. † 4. charity is not r. is not puffed up.

RASHLY.

Acts 19. 36. ye ought to be quiet, and do nothing r.

RASHNESS.

2 Sam. 6. † 7. God smote Uzzah for his r. and he died

RATE.

Exod. 16. 4. people shall gather certain r. every day
1 Kings 10. 25. brought mules at a r. 2 Chr. 9. 24.
2 Kings 25. 30. a daily r. for every day all his days
2 Chron. 8. 13. even after a certain r. every day

RATHER.

Josh. 22. 24. if we have not r. done it for fear
2 Kings 5. 13. how much r. when he saith to thee
Job 7. 15. chooseth death r. than life, Jer. 8. 3.
32. 2. because he justified himself r. than God
36. 21. this hast thou chosen r. than affliction
Ps. 52. 3. and lying r. than to speak righteousness
84. 10. had r. be a door-keeper in house of God
Prov. 8. 10. receive knowledge r. than choice gold
16. 16. to get understand. r. to be chosen than silver
17. 12. meet a man, r. than a fool in his folly
22. 1. good name is r. to be chosen than great riches, loving favour r. than silver and gold
Mat. 10. 6. go r. to the lost sheep of house of Israel
28. r. fear him that is able to destroy in hell
18. 8. r. than having two hands to be cast into fire
9. r. than having two eyes to be cast into hell
25. 9. but go ye r. to them that sell, and buy
27. 24. but that r. tumult was made, he took water
Mark 5. 26. nothing bettered, but r. grew worse
15. 11. that he should r. release Barabbas to them
Luke 10. 20. r. rej. your names are written in heaven
11. 28. r. blessed are they that hear and keep
41. but r. give alms of such things as ye have
12. 31. but r. seek ye kingdom of God, all things
51. come to give peace, I tell you nay, r. division
17. 8. and will not r. say unto him, make ready
18. 14. he went down justified r. than the other
John 3. 19. and men loved darkness r. than light
Acts 5. 29. we ought to obey God r. than men
Rom. 3. 8. not r. let us do evil that good may come
8. 34. Christ died, yea, r. that is risen again
11. 11. but r. through their fall salvation is come
12. 19. avenge not, but r. give place to wrath
14. 13. not judge one another, but judge this r.
1 Cor. 5. 2. are puffed up, and have not r. mourned
6. 7. why do ye not r. take wrong? why not suffer?
7. 21. but if thou mayest be made free, use it r.
9. 12. if oth. be partak. of this power, are not we r.?
14. 1. desire r. that ye may prophesy, 5.
19. had r. speak five words with my understand.
2 Cor. 2. 7. so that ye ought r. to forgive him
3. 8. how ministration of the Spirit be r. glorious?
5. 8. willing r. to be absent from the body
12. 9. therefore I will r. glory in my infirmities
Gal. 4. 9. ye have known God, or r. known of God
Eph. 4. 28. steal no more, but r. let him labour
5. 4. let it not be named, but r. giving of thanks
11. with works of darkness, but r. reprove them
Phil. 1. 12. r. to the furtherance of the gospel
1 Tim. 1. 4. which minister questions r. than edify.
4. 7. and exercise thyself r. to godliness
6. 2. but r. do them service, because faithful
Philem. 9. yet for love's sake I r. beseech thee
Heb. 11. 25. choosing r. to suffer affliction with
Heb. 12. 9. r. be in subjection to the Father of spirits
13. let lame be turned out, but let it r. be healed
13. 19. but I beseech you the r. to do this
2 Pet. 1. 10. r. give diligence to make calling sure

RATTLETH.

Job 39. 23. the quiver r. against him, spear and shield

RATTLING.

Nah. 3. 2. noise of the r. of the wheels and horses

RAVEN, S.

Gen. 8. 7. Noah sent forth a r. which went forth
Lev. 11. 15. every r. is unclean, Deut. 14. 14.
1 Kings 17. 4. I have commanded the r. to feed thee
6. and the r. brought Elijah bread and flesh
Job 38. 41. who provideth the r. food, Psal. 147. 9.
Prov. 30. 17. the r. of the valley shall pick it out
Cant. 5. 11. his locks bushy, and black as a r.
Isa. 34. 11. the owl and the r. shall dwell in it
Luke 12. 24. consider the r. they neither sow

RAVENING.

Psal. 22. 13. they gaped upon me as a r. lion
Ezek. 22. 25. like a roaring lion r. the prey
27. her princes are like wolves r. the prey
Mat. 7. 15. but inwardly they are r. wolves

RAVENING.

Luke 11. 39. your inward part is full of r.

RAVENOUS.

Isa. 35. 9. nor any r. beast shall go up thereon
46. 11. calling a r. bird from the east
Ezek. 39. 4. I will give thee to the r. birds

RAVIN, *Verb*.

Gen. 49. 27. Benjamin shall r. as a wolf
Psal. 17. † 12. as a lion that desireth to r.

RAVIN.

Nah. 2. 12. the lion filled his dens with r.

RAVISHED.

Cant. 4. 9. thou hast r. my heart, my sister
Isa. 13. 16. the wives of Babylon shall be r.
Lam. 5. 11. they r. the women in Zion
Zech. 14. 2. the women in Jerusalem shall be r.

RAVISHED.

Prov. 5. 19. and be thou r. always with her love
20. why wilt thou be r. with a strange woman?

RAW.

Exod. 12. 9. eat not of it r. nor sodden with water
Lev. 13. 10. if there be quick r. flesh in the rising
14. but when the r. flesh appeareth in him
15. the priest see r. flesh, for r. flesh is unclean
1 Sam. 2. 15. he will not have sodden flesh, but r.
Mat. 9. † 16. no man putteth r. cloth to an old garment, for the rent is made worse, Mark 2. † 21.

RAZOR.

This is an instrument well known. It is said, Psal 52. 2. Thy tongue is like a sharp razor, working deceitfully. *Wherein the Psalmist, speaking of* Doeg *the* Edomite, *insinuates, that as a man pretending only to shave off the hair with a sharp razor, doth suddenly and unexpectedly cut the throat; so* Doeg *pretended only to vindicate himself from the imputation of disloyalty,* 1 Sam. 22. 9. *but really intended to expose the priests, who were* David's *friends, to* Saul's *fury and cruelty. And in* Isa. 7. 20. *God threatens* to shave Judah with a razor that is hired, &c. *that is, utterly to spoil and destroy* Judah, *by the successive kings of the* Assyrian *empire, as* Sennacherib, 2 Kings 18. 13. Esarhaddon, 2 Kings 19. 37. *and especially by* Nebuchadnezzar, *who having subdued the* Assyrian *monarchy, from thenceforth was king of* Assyria *as well as of* Chaldea, *and who completed the calamity of* Judah, *which was begun by the kings of* Assyria.

Num. 6. 5. all the days there shall no r. come upon his head, Judg. 13. 5. | 16. 17. 1 Sam. 1. 11.
8. † 7. cause a r. to pass over the flesh of the Levites
Psal. 52. 2. thy tongue like a sharp r. working
Isa. 7. 20. the Lord shall shave with a r. hired
Ezek. 5. 1. son of man, take thee a barber's r.

REACH.

Gen. 11. 4. a tower whose top may r. to heaven
Exod. 28. 42. linen breeches shall r. to the thighs
Lev. 5. † 7. if his hand cannot r. to a lamb, 14. † 21.
26. 5. your threshing shall r. to the vintage, and your vintage shall r. to the sowing time
Num. 34. 11. the border shall r. to the sea
Job 20. 6. and though his head r. unto the clouds
Isa. 8. 8. he shall r. even to the neck, O Immanuel
30. 28. breath shall r. to the midst of the neck
Jer. 48. 32. thy plants r. to the sea of Jazer
Zech. 14. 5. valley of the mountains shall r. to Azal
John 20. 27. r. hither thy finger, and r. thy hand
2 Cor. 10. 13. a measure to r. even unto you

REACHED.

Gen. 28. 12. the ladder's top r. to heaven
Ruth 2. 14. he r. her parched corn, she did eat
Dan. 4. 11. tree, whose height r. to heaven, 20.
2 Cor. 10. 14. as though we r. not to you
Rev. 18. 5. Babylon's sins have r. to heaven

REACHETH.

2 Chron. 28. 9. slain in a rage that r. up to heaven
Psal. 36. 5. thy faithfulness r. to the clouds
108. 4. and thy truth r. to the clouds
Prov. 31. 20. yea, she r. her hands to the needy
Jer. 4. 10. whereas the sword r. to the soul
18. it is bitter, because it r. to thine heart
51. 9. Babylon's judgment r. to heaven
Dan. 4. 22. for thy greatness r. to heaven

REACHING.

Phil. 3. 13. r. forth to those things which are before

READ.

Exod. 24. 7. he r. in the audience of the people
Josh. 8. 34. he r. all the words of the law, 35.
2 Kings 5. 7. when king of Israel had r. the letter
19. 14. Hezekiah received and r. the letter
22. 8. Shaphan r. the book of the law, 10.
23. 2. king Josiah r. in their ears all the words of the book of the covenant, 2 Chron. 34. 30.
2 Chron. 34. 24. I will bring all the curses r.
Ezra 4. 18. the letter hath been plainly r.
23. the king's letter was r. they made them cease
Neh. 8. 3. he r. before all book of the law, 8. | 13. 1.
18. from first day to the last he r. the law

Neh. 9. 3. they stood up in their place and *r.* in law
Esth. 6. 1. book of the records was *r.* before king
Isa. 37. 14. he received the letter, and *r.* it
Jer. 29. 29. Zephaniah the priest *r.* this letter
36. 10. then *r.* Baruch the words of Jeremiah
21. Jehudi *r.* it in the ears of the king and princes
23. when he *r.* three or four leaves, the king cut it
Mat. 12. 3. have ye not *r.*? 19. 4. | 21. 16. | 22. 31.
Mark 2. 25. | 12. 10, 26. *Luke* 6. 3.
John 19. 20. this title *r.* many of the Jews
Acts 8. 28. the eunuch *r.* Esaias the prophet
32. the place of scripture which he *r.* was this
13. 27. prophets are *r.* every sabbath-day, 15. 21.
15. 31. which when they had *r.* they rejoiced
23. 34. when the governor had *r.* the letter
2 Cor. 3. 2. ye are our epistle known and *r.* of all men
15. when Moses is *r.* the vail is upon their heart
Col. 4. 16. when this epistle is *r.* among you
1 Thess. 5. 27. I charge you that this epistle be *r.*

READ.

Deut. 17. 19. the king shall *r.* therein all his life
31. 11. thou shalt *r.* this law before all Israel
Isa. 29. 11. saying, *r.* this, I pray thee, 12.
34. 16. seek out of the book of the Lord and *r.*
Jer. 36. 6. go and *r.* in the roll thou hast written
15. they said, sit down now and *r.* it in our ears
51. 61. when thou comest to Babylon and shalt *r.*
Dan. 5. 7. whosoever shall *r.* this writing and shew
8. king's wise men, they could not *r.* the writing
17. let thy gifts be to thyself, yet I will *r.*
Mat. 21. 42. did ye never *r.* in the scriptures?
Luke 4. 16. Jesus went in and stood up for to *r.*
Acts 8. 30. Philip ran and heard him *r.* Esaias
2 Cor. 1. 13. we write none other things than what ye *r.*
Eph. 3. 4. whereby when ye *r.* ye may understand
Col. 4. 16. likewise *r.* the epistle from Laodicea
Rev. 5. 4. wept, because none worthy to *r.* the book

READEST.

Luke 10. 26. what is written in law, how *r.* thou?
Acts 8. 30. understandest thou what thou *r.*?

READETH.

Hab. 2. 2. make it plain, that he may run that *r.* it
Mat. 24. 15. when ye shall see the abomination, whoso *r.* let him understand, *Mark* 13. 14.
Rev. 1. 3. blessed is he that *r.* and they that hear

READING.

Neh. 8. 8. they caused them to understand the *r.*
Eccl. 12. † 12. much *r.* is a weariness of the flesh
Acts 13. 15. after the *r.* of the law and the prophets
2 Cor. 3. 14. vail untaken away in *r.* the Old Test.
1 Tim. 4. 13. till I come, give attendance to *r.*

READING.

Jer. 36. 8. *r.* in the book of the words of the Lord
51. 63. when thou hast made an end of *r.* this book

READINESS.

Acts 17. 11. they received the word with *r.* of mind
2 Cor. 8. 11. that as there was a *r.* to will
10. 6. having a *r.* to revenge all disobedience

READY.

Exod. 17. 4. the people be almost *r.* to stone me
19. 11. and be *r.* against the third day, 15.
34. 2. be *r.* in the morning, and come up to Sinai
Num. 32. 17. we will go *r.* armed before Israel
Deut. 1. 41. ye were *r.* to go up into the hill
26. 5. a Syrian *r.* to perish was my father
Josh. 4. † 13. about 40,000 *r.* armed pass over
8. 4. go not far from the city, but be ye all *r.*
1 Sam. 25. 18. Abigail took five sheep *r.* dressed
2 Sam. 15. 15. thy servants are *r.* to do whatsoever
18. 22. why run, seeing thou hast no tidings *r.*?
Ezra 7. 6. Ezra was a *r.* scribe in the law of Moses
Neh. 9. 17. but thou art a God *r.* to pardon
Esth. 3. 14. they should be *r.* against that day, 8. 13.
Job 3. 8. who are *r.* to raise up their mourning
12. 5. he that is *r.* to slip with his feet
15. 23. knoweth the day of darkness is *r.* at hand
24. anguish shall prevail as a king *r.* to battle
28. in houses which are *r.* to become heaps
17. 1. my days are extinct, the graves are *r.* for me
18. 12. and destruction shall be *r.* at his side
29. 13. the blessing of him *r.* to perish came on me
32. 19. my belly is *r.* to burst like new bottles
Psal. 38. 17. for I am *r.* to halt, and my sorrow
45. 1. my tongue is the pen of a *r.* writer
86. 5. thou, Lord, art good, and *r.* to forgive
88. 15. I am afflicted, and *r.* to die from my youth
Prov. 24. 11. to deliver those that are *r.* to be slain
31. 6. give strong drink to him that is *r.* to perish
Eccl. 5. 1. be more *r.* to hear than to give sacrifice
Isa. 27. 13. they shall come who were *r.* to perish
30. 13. this iniquity shall be as a breach *r.* to fall
32. 4. the tongue of stammerers be *r.* to speak plain
38. 20. the Lord was *r.* to save me, we will sing
41. 7. saying, it is *r.* for the soldering, he fastened
51. 13. the oppressor, as if he were *r.* to destroy
Dan. 3. 15. now if ye be *r.* to fall down and worship
Mat. 22. 4. fatlings are killed, and all things are *r.*
8. then saith he, the wedding is *r.* *Luke* 14. 17.
24. 44. therefore be ye also *r.* *Luke* 12. 40.
25. 10. they that were *r.* went in with him
Mark 14. 38. the spirit is *r.* but the flesh is weak
Luke 7. 2. a centurion's servant sick, and *r.* to die
22. 33. Lord, I am *r.* to go with thee into prison
John 7. 6. my time not come, your time is alway *r.*
Acts 20. 7. Paul preached to them, *r.* to depart
21. 13. I am *r.* not to be bound only, but to die
23. 15. we, or ever he come near, are *r.* to kill him
21. now are *r.* looking for a promise from thee
Rom. 1. 15. I am *r.* to preach the gospel at Rome
2 Cor. 8. 19. and the declaration of your *r.* mind
9. 2. Achaia was *r.* a year ago, zeal hath provoked
3. I sent brethren, that, as I said, ye may be *r.*
5. that the same might be *r.* as a matter of bounty
12. 14. the third time I am *r.* to come to you
1 Tim. 3. † 3. must not be *r.* to quarrel, as one in wine
6. 18. that ye be rich in good works, *r.* to distribute
2 Tim. 4. 6. for I am now *r.* to be offered
Tit. 3. 1. put in mind to be *r.* to every good work
Heb. 8. 13. that waxeth old, is *r.* to vanish away
1 Pet. 1. 5. salvation, *r.* to be revealed in the last time
3. 15. be *r.* always to give an answer to every man
4. 5. to give account to him that is *r.* to judge quick

1 Pet. 5. 2. not for filthy lucre, but of a *r.* mind
Rev. 3. 2. strengthen the things that are *r.* to die
12. 4. the woman which was *r.* to be delivered
See MADE, MAKE.

REALM.

2 Chron. 20. 30. the *r.* of Jehoshaphat was quiet
Ezra 7. 13. they of my *r.* who are minded to go
23. why should there be wrath against the *r.*?
Dan. 1. 20. he found them better than all in his *r.*
6. 3. the king thought to set him over the *r.*
9. 1. Darius, king over the *r.* of the Chaldeans
11. 2. he shall stir up all against the *r.* of Grecia

REAP

Signifies, [1] *To cut down corn,* Jam. 5. 4. [2] *To receive the fruit or reward of our works, whether good or bad,* Gal. 6. 7, 8. [3] *To expect increase,* Mat. 25. 26. [4] *To execute judgment on antichrist and his adherents,* Rev. 14. 15.

Lev. 19. 9. and when ye *r.* the harvest, 23. 10, 22.
shall not wholly *r.* the corners of thy field
25. 5. what groweth of itself thou shalt not *r.*
11. in jubilee ye shall neither sow nor *r.*
Ruth 2. 9. let thine eyes be on the field they *r.*
1 Sam. 8. 12. set your servants to *r.* his harvest
2 Kings 19. 29. in third year sow and *r.* *Isa.* 37. 30.
Job 4. 8. they that sow wickedness *r.* the same
24. 6. they *r.* every one his corn in the field
Psal. 126. 5. they that sow in tears shall *r.* in joy
Prov. 22. 8. he that soweth iniquity shall *r.* vanity
Eccl. 11. 4. he that regardeth the clouds shall not *r.*
Jer. 12. 13. they have sown wheat but shall *r.* thorns
Hos. 8. 7. have sown wind, they shall *r.* the whirlwind
10. 12. sow in righteousness *r.* in mercy
Mic. 6. 15. thou shalt sow, but shalt not *r.*
Mat. 6. 26. the fowls of the air *r.* not, *Luke* 12. 24.
25. 26. thou knewest I *r.* where I sowed not
John 4. 38. to *r.* whereon ye bestowed no labour
1 Cor. 9. 11. if we shall *r.* your carnal things
2 Cor. 9. 6. he which soweth sparingly shall *r.* sparing. he which soweth bountifully shall *r.* bountifully
Gal. 6. 7. whatever a man soweth, that shall he *r.*
8. soweth to flesh, shall of the flesh *r.* corruption, to Spirit, shall of the Spirit *r.* life everlasting
9. in due season we shall *r.* if we faint not
Rev. 14. 15. thrust in thy sickle and *r.* for the time is come for thee to *r.* for the harvest is ripe

REAPED.

Hos. 10. 13. ye have plowed wickedn. ye *r.* iniquity
Jam. 5. 4. the hire of labourers, which *r.* down your fields, the cries of them which *r.* are entered
Rev. 14. 16. thrust in his sickle, the earth was *r.*

REAPER.

Amos 9. 13. the plowman shall overtake the *r.*

REAPERS.

Ruth 2. 3. Ruth gleaned in the field after the *r.*
4. Boaz said to the *r.* the Lord be with you
7. I pray you, let me glean after the *r.*
2 Kings 4. 18. he went out to his father to the *r.*
Mat. 13. 30. I will say to the *r.* gather the tares
39. the enemy is the devil, and *r.* are the angels

REAPEST.

Lev. 23. 22. not make clean riddance when thou *r.*
Luke 19. 21. and thou *r.* that thou didst not sow

REAPETH.

Isa. 17. 5. the harvest-man *r.* the ears with his arm
John 4. 36. he that *r.* receiveth wages, that both he that soweth and he that *r.* may rejoice together
37. that saying is true, one soweth and another *r.*

REAPING.

1 Sam. 6. 13. and they of Beth-shemesh were *r.*
Mat. 25. 24. Ld. I knew that thou art an hard man, *r.* where thou hast not sown, *Luke* 19. 22.

REASON

Signifies, [1] *That faculty of the soul whereby we judge of things,* Dan. 4. 36. [2] *Proof, ground, or argument,* 1 Pet. 3. 15. [3] *To confer, dispute, or argue,* Mat. 16. 8. Mark 8. 16.

Reasonable service, *Rom.* 12. 1. *The spiritual sacrifice of a Christian, offering not the bodies of unreasonable beasts, as they were wont to do under the law; but himself wholly being a reasonable creature, as a sacrifice unto God his Creator and Redeemer, which is a most reasonable thing, to do him service and obedience in all things, according to his revealed will, which is a very reasonable rule.*

Reasonable service, *in* Greek, λογικη λατρεια, *may be such as will be agreeable to the notion of* ὁ Λογος, *the* Word, *as it signifies* Christ, *and then it is the* Christian service. *It may be as* λογος *signifies the* word, *or* scripture, *and then it will be that worship which is prescribed us in the scripture. It may be as* λογος, word, *is opposed to* νομος, law, *and then it will be the* evangelical worship. *Or it may be such a worship of God as is most agreeable to* reason, *as is before observed.*

1 Kings 9. 15. and this is the *r.* of the levy, which
Prov. 26. 16. than seven men that can render a *r.*
Eccl. 7. 25. I applied to search the *r.* of things
† 27. weighing one by one to find out the *r.*
Dan. 4. 36. at the same time my *r.* returned to me
Acts 6. 2. it is not *r.* we should leave the word
18. 14. O ye Jews, *r.* would that I should bear
1 Pet. 3. 15. that asketh you a *r.* of the hope in you

By REASON.

Gen. 41. 31. plenty not known *by r.* of that famine
47. 13. land of Canaan fainted *by r.* of the famine
Exod. 2. 23. Israel sighed *by r.* of the bondage
3. 7. I heard their cry *by r.* of their task-masters
8. 24. the land was corrupted *by r.* of the flies
Num. 9. 10. if any be unclean *by r.* of a dead body
18. 8. the hallowed things given *by r.* of anointing
32. shall bear no sin *by r.* of it, when ye heaved
Deut. 5. 5. for ye were afraid *by r.* of the fire
Josh. 9. 13. our shoes are become old *by r.* of journey
† 14. they received the men *by r.* of their victuals
Judg. 2. 18. for it repented the L. for their groanings *by r.* of them that oppressed and vexed them
1 Kings 14. 4. Ahijah's eyes were set *by r.* of age
2 Chr. 5. 14. not able to minister *by r.* of the cloud

2 Chr. 20. 15. be not afraid *by r.* of this great multit.
21. 15. thy bowels fall out, *by r.* of the sickness, 19.
Job 6. 16. brooks are blackish, *by r.* of the ice
17. 7. mine eye also is dim *by r.* of sorrow
31. 23. *by r.* of his highness I could not endure
35. 9. *by r.* of oppressions they make the oppressed cry, they cry out *by r.* of the arm of the mighty
37. 19. we cannot order speech *by r.* of darkness
41. 25. *by r.* of breakings they purify themselves
Psal. 38. 8. roared *by r.* of disquietness of my heart
44. 16. that blasphemeth *by r.* of the enemy
78. 65. a mighty man that shouteth *by r.* of wine
88. 9. mine eye mourneth *by r.* of affliction
90. 10. if *by r.* of strength they be fourscore years
102. 5. *by r.* of my groan. my bones cleave to skin
Prov. 20. 4. the sluggard will not plow *by r.* of cold
Isa. 49. 19. too narrow, *by r.* of the inhabitants
Ezek. 19. 10. full of branches *by r.* of many waters
21. 12. terrors *by r.* of sword shall be on my people
26. 10. *by r.* of the abundance of his horses
28. 17. Tyrus corrupted *by r.* of thy brightness
Dan. 8. 12. an host given him *by r.* of transgression
Jonah 2. 2. I cried *by r.* of my affliction to the Ld.
Mic. 2. 12. shall make great noise *by r.* of multitude
John 6. 18. the sea arose *by r.* of a great wind
12. 11. *by r.* of him many believed on Jesus
Rom. 8. 20. *by r.* of him who subjected same in hope
2 Cor. 3. 10. *by r.* of the glory that excelleth
Heb. 5. 3. *by r.* hereof he ought to offer for the sins
14. who *by r.* of use have their senses exercised
7. 23. priests not suffered to continue *by r.* of death
2 Pet. 2. 2. *by r.* of whom way of truth evil spoken of
Rev. 8. 13. *by r.* of the other voices of the trumpet
9. 2. sun and air were darkened *by r.* of the smoke
18. 19. all made rich *by r.* of the costliness

REASON, *Verb.*

1 Sam. 12. 7. that I may *r.* with you before the Ld.
Job 9. 14. and choose out my words to *r.* with you
13. 3. surely I would speak and desire to *r.* with G.
15. 3. should he *r.* with unprofitable talk?
Isa. 1. 18. come now and let us *r.* together
Jer. 12. † 1. let me *r.* the case with thee
Mat. 16. 8. Jesus said, why *r.* ye among yourselves, because ye have no bread? *Mark* 2. 8. | 8. 17.
Luke 5. 21. the scribes and Pharisees began to *r.*
22. Jesus said to them, what *r.* ye in your hearts?

REASONABLE.

Rom. 12. 1. living sacrifice, which is your *r.* service

REASONABLY.

Heb. 5. † 2. who can *r.* bear with the ignorant

REASONED.

Mat. 16. 7. and they *r.* among themselves, 21. 15.
Mark 8. 16. | 11. 31. *Luke* 20. 5.
Mark 2. 8. when Jesus perceived that they so *r.*
Luke 20. 14. the husbandmen *r.* among themselves
24. 15. while they *r.* Jesus himself drew near
Acts 17. 2. three sabbaths Paul *r.* with them
18. 4. he *r.* in the synagogue every sabbath
19. Paul *r.* with the Jews at Ephesus
24. 25. and as he *r.* of righteousness and judgment

REASONING.

Job 13. 6. hear now my *r.* and hearken to pleadings
Luke 9. 46. then there arose a *r.* among them
Acts 28. 29. the Jews departed, and had great *r.*

REASONING.

Mark 2. 6. there were certain scribes *r.* in their hearts
12. 28. and having heard them *r.* together

REASONINGS.

2 Cor. 10. † 5. casting down *r.* and every high thing

REASONS.

Job 32. 11. behold I waited, and gave ear to your *r.*
Isa. 41. 21. bring forth your *r.* saith king of Jacob

REBEL.

To rebel *is to fight or make war against a lawful sovereign, as* Absalom *did against his father* David, 2 Sam. 15. 10, &c. *Or to cast off the yoke of a lawful governor, as* Korah *and* Abiram, *Num.* 16. 1, 2, &c. Rebellion *cometh of the* Hebrew *word* Marah, *which signifies* bitterness, *because* rebellion *is a thing distasteful unto God, and provokes him to anger. Men are said to rebel,* [1] *Against the Lord,* Num. 14. 9. [2] *Against his words,* Psalm 107. 11. [3] *Against his Spirit,* Isa. 63. 10. [4] *Against an earthly king,* 1 Kings 12. 19.

Num. 14. 9. only *r.* not against the Lord, nor fear
Josh. 1. 18. whosoever doth *r.* he shall die
22. 16. ye have builded an altar that ye might *r.*
18. seeing that ye *r.* to-day against the Lord
19. *r.* not against the Lord, nor *r.* against us
29. God forbid that we should *r.* against the Lord
1 Sam. 12. 14. if ye will obey and not *r.* ag. Lord
15. and if ye will not obey the Lord, but *r.*
Neh. 2. 19. what do ye? will ye *r.* against the king?
6. 6. saith it, that thou and the Jews think to *r.*
Job 24. 13. they are of those that *r.* against the light
Psal. 78. † 40. how oft did they *r.* against him?
Isa. 1. 20. if ye refuse and *r.* ye shall be devoured
Hos. 7. 14. they assemble for corn, and *r.* against me

REBELLED.

Gen. 14. 4. and in the thirteenth year they *r.*
Num. 20. 24. because ye *r.* ag. my words at waters of Meribah, 27. 14. *Deut.* 1. 26, 43. | 9. 23.
1 Kings 12. 19. Rehoboam fled, so Israel *r.* ag. the house of David unto this day, *2 Chron.* 10. 19
2 Kings 1. 1. Moab *r.* against Israel, 3, 5, 7.
18. 7. Hezekiah *r.* against the king of Assyria
24. 1. Jehoiakim *r.* against Nebuchadnezzar
20. Zedekiah *r.* *2 Chron.* 36. 13. *Jer.* 52. 3.
2 Chron. 13. 6. Jeroboam hath *r.* against his lord
Neh. 9. 26. they were disobedient, and *r.* agst. thee
Psal. 5. 10. for they have *r.* against thee
105. 28. and they *r.* not against his word
107. 11. because they *r.* against the words of God
Isa. 1. 2. I have nourished children, and they have *r.*
63. 10. but they *r.* and vexed his Holy Spirit
Lam. 1. 18. I have *r.* || 20. I have grievously *r.*
3. 42. we have *r.* thou hast not pardoned
Ezek. 2. 3. I send thee to a nation that hath *r.*
17. 15. he *r.* in sending his ambassadors to Egypt
20. 8. but they *r.* against me, 13, 21.
Dan. 9. 5. we have *r.* by departing from thee
9. to our God mercy, though we have *r.* ag. him

Hos. 13. 16. Samaria hath r. against her God
REBELLEST.
2 Kings 18. 20. Rab shakeh said to Hezekiah, on whom dost thou trust, that thou r.? Isa. 36. 5.
REBELLION.
Num. 17. † 10. as a token against the children of r.
Deut. 31. 27. for I know thy r. and thy stiff neck
Josh. 22. 22. Israel he shall know if it be in r.
1 Sam. 15. 23. r. is as the sin of witchcraft
20. † 30. thou son of perverse r. do not I know
Ezra 4. 19. and that r. hath been made therein
Neh. 9. 17. and in their r. appointed a captain
Job 34. 37. for he addeth r. unto his sin
Prov. 17. 11. an evil man seeketh only r.
Jer. 28. 16. because thou hast taught r. 29. 32.
Ezek. 2. † 7. whether hear or forbear, they are r.
REBELLIOUS.
Deut. 9. 7. ye have been r. ag. the Lord, 24. | 31. 27.
21. 18. if a man have a stubborn and r. son
20. they shall say, this our son is stubborn and r.
1 Sam. 20. 30. thou son of the perverse r. woman
Ezra 4. 12. building the r. and the bad city, 15.
Psal. 66. 7. let not the r. exalt themselves
68. 6. but the r. dwell in a dry land
18. yea, for the r. also || 78. 8. and a r. generation
Isa. 1. 23. thy princes are r. companions of thieves
30. 1. woe to the r. children, saith the Lord
9. this is a r. people || 50. 5. I was not r.
65. 2. I have spread out my hands to a r. people
Jer. 4. 17. she hath been r. against me, saith Lord
5. 23. but this people hath a revolting and r. heart
Ezek. 2. 3. son of man, I send thee to a r. nation
5. they are a r. house, 6, 7. | 3. 9, 26, 27. | 12. 2, 3.
8. be not thou r. like that r. house, open thy mouth
12. 2. thou dwellest in the midst of a r. house
17. 12. say now to the r. house, know ye, 44. 6.
24. 3. and utter a parable to the r. house
REBELS.
Num. 17. 10. Aaron's rod kept for a token ag. the r.
20. 10. Moses and Aaron said, hear now, ye r.
Jer. 50. † 21. go up against the land of r.
Ezek. 2. † 6. though r. and thorns be with thee
20. 38. I will purge out from among you the r.
REBUKE, Substantive.
Deut. 28. 20. the Lord shall send on thee r.
2 Kings 19. 3. this is a day of r. Isa. 37. 3.
Psal. 18. 15. at thy r. at the blast of thy nostrils
76. 6. at thy r. the horse cast into a dead sleep
80. 16. they perish at the r. of thy countenance
104. 7. at thy r. they fled, they hasted away
Prov. 13. 1. but a scorner heareth not r.
8. but the poor heareth not r.
27. 5. open r. is better than secret love
Eccl. 7. 5. it is better to hear the r. of the wise
Isa. 25. 8. the r. of his people shall he take away
30. 17. thousand shall flee at the r. of one, at the r. of five shall ye flee, till left as a beacon
50. 2. behold, at my r. I dry up the sea
51. 20. thy sons lie full of the r. of thy God
66. 15. to render his r. with flames of fire
Jer. 15. 15. know that for thy sake I suffered r.
Hos. 5. 9. Ephraim shall be desolate in the day of r.
Phil. 2. 15. without r. in midst of a perverse nation
REBUKE
Signifies, [1] To reprove or check, Lev. 19. 17. [2] To restrain, Zech. 3. 2. Jude 9. [3] To silence, or command persons to hold their peace, Luke 19. 39. [4] To convince of sin, and bring to repentance, Isa. 2. 4. [5] To cure, Luke 4. 39. [6] To chasten, afflict, or correct, Psal. 6. 1.
Lev. 19. 17. thou shalt in any wise r. thy neighbour
Ruth 2. 16. that she may glean them, and r. her not
1 Chron. 12. 17. God look thereon, and r. it
Psal. 6. 1. O Lord, r. me not in thine anger, 38. 1.
68. 30. r. the company of spear-men, the bulls
Prov. 9. 8. r. a wise man, and he will love thee
24. 25. to them that r. him shall be delight
Isa. 2. 4. he shall r. many nations, Mic. 4. 3.
17. 13. the nations rush, but God shall r. them
54. 9. I would not be wroth with, nor r. thee
Zech. 3. 2. Lord said to Satan, the Lord r. thee, even the Lord that hath chosen Jerusalem, r. thee
Mal. 3. 11. I will r. the devourer for your sakes
Mat. 16. 22. Peter began to r. him, Mark 8. 32.
Luke 17. 3. if thy brother trespass r. him
19. 39. some said, Master, r. thy disciples
1 Tim. 5. 1. r. not an elder, but entreat him
20. them that sin, r. before all, that others may fear
2 Tim. 4. 2. r. exhort, with all long-suffering
Tit. 1. 13. wherefore r. them sharply, 2. 15.
Jude 9. Michael said, the Lord r. thee
Rev. 3. 19. as many as I love, I r. and chasten
REBUKED.
Gen. 31. 42. God hath seen and r. thee yesternight
37. 10. his father r. him, and said to him
Neh. 5. 7. and I r. the nobles and the rulers
Psal. 9. 5. hast r. the heathen, thou hast destroyed
106. 9. he r. the Red sea also, and it was dried up
119. 21. thou hast r. the proud that are cursed
Mat. 8. 26. he r. the wind, Mark 4. 39. Luke 8. 24.
17. 18. Jesus r. devil, and he departed out of him
19. 13. disciples r. them, Mark 10. 13. Luke 18. 15.
20. 31. the multitude r. the blind men
Mark 1. 25. he r. the devil, 9. 25. Luke 4. 35. | 9. 42.
8. 33. Jesus r. Peter, saying, get thee behind me
Luke 4. 39. he stood over her and r. the fever
9. 55. but Jesus turned, and r. James and John
18. 39. they that went before r. the blind man
23. 40. but the other thief answering r. him
Heb. 12. 5. nor faint when thou art r. of him
2 Pet. 2. 16. but Balaam was r. for his iniquity
REBUKER.
Hos. 5. 2. though I have been a r. of them all
REBUKETH.
Prov. 9. 7. he that r. a wicked man getteth a blot
28. 23. he that r. a man, after shall find more favour
Amos 5. 10. they hate him that r. in the gate
Nah. 1. 4. he r. the sea, and maketh it dry
REBUKES.
Psal. 39. 11. when thou with r. dost correct man
Ezek. 5. 15. execute judgments in furious r. 25. 17.

REBUKING.
2 Sam. 22. 16. foundations discovered at r. of Lord
REBUKING, Participle.
Luke 4. 41. he r. them, suffered them not to speak
RECALL.
Lam. 3. 21. this I r. to mind, therefore I hope
RECEIPT.
Mat. 9. 9. as Jesus passed, he saw Matthew sitting at the r. of custom, Mark 2. 14. Luke 5. 27.
RECEIVE
Signifies, [1] To take what is given, paid, or put into one's hands, 2 Sam. 18. 12. 2 Kings 5. 26. [2] To contain, 1 Kings 8. 64. [3] To entertain, lodge, or harbour, Acts 28. 2, 7. [4] To bear with, or suffer, 2 Cor. 11. 16. [5] To hearken to, Prov. 2. 1. [6] To believe, Mat. 11. 14. John 1. 12. [7] To give, Rev. 13. † 16. [8] To attend and assent to, Mat. 13. 20. [9] To admit one to be a member of the church, Rom. 14. 1. [10] To be endued with, Acts 1. 8. [11] To enjoy and possess, Heb. 10. 36. [12] To bear patiently and thankfully, Job 2. 10. [13] To be rewarded, Mat. 10. 41. [14] To have, Hos. 10. 6.
Exod. 29. 25. thou shalt r. the wave offering
Num. 18. 28. shall offer all your tithes which you r.
Deut. 33. 3. every one shall r. of thy words
1 Sam. 10. 4. which thou shalt r. of their hands
2 Sam. 18. 12. though I should r. a thousand shekels
1 Kings 5. 9. and thou shalt r. the cedar and fir
Job 2. 10. shall we r. good at the hand of God
27. 13. which they shall r. of the Almighty
Psal. 6. 9. the Lord will r. my prayer
24. 5. he shall r. the blessing from the Lord
49. 15. God will redeem my soul, for he shall r. me
73. 24. guide me, and afterward r. me to glory
75. 2. when I shall r. the congregation I will judge
Prov. 2. 1. my son, if thou wilt r. my words
10. 8. the wise in heart will r. commandments
Isa. 57. 6. offering, should I r. comfort in these?
Ezek. 16. 61. be ashamed, when thou shalt r. sisters
Dan. 2. 6. ye shall r. of me gifts and rewards
Hos. 10. 6. Ephraim shall r. shame, and Israel
Mic. 1. 11. he shall r. of you his standing
Zeph. 3. 7. I said, thou wilt r. instruction
Mat. 10. 41. a prophet, he shall r. a prophet's reward, a righteous man shall r. a righteous man's reward
11. 5. the blind r. their sight, the lame walk
14. if ye will r. it, this is Elias which was to come
18. 5. whoso shall r. one such little child in my name, receiveth me, Mark 9. 37. Luke 9. 48.
19. 11. he said, all men cannot r. this saying
29. he shall r. an hundred fold, Mark 10. 30.
20. 7. and whatsoever is right, that shall ye r.
21. 22. whatsoever ye ask, believing, ye shall r.
34. that they might r. the fruits of it
23. 14. long prayers, therefore ye shall r. the greater damnation, Mark 12. 40. Luke 20. 47.
Mark 4. 16. r. the word with gladness, Luke 8. 13.
20. these are such as hear the word and r. it
10. 51. Lord, that I might r. my sight, Luke 18. 41.
11. 24. when ye pray, believe that ye r. them
12. 2. that he might r. from the husbandmen
Luke 10. 8. whatsoever city ye enter, and they r.
16. 4. that they may r. me into their houses
9. they may r. you into everlasting habitations
23. 41. for we r. the due reward of our deeds
John 5. 43. if in his own name, him ye will r.
44. how can believe, which r. honour one of anoth.
7. 23. if a man on the sabbath r. circumcision
39. this spake of the Spirit, which they that believe on him should r. Holy Ghost not given
14. 3. I will come again, and r. you to myself
16. 14. for he shall r. of mine, and shew it to you
24. ask ye shall r. that your joy may be full
Acts 1. 8. but ye shall r. power after that Holy Gh.
2. 38. and ye shall r. the gift of the Holy Ghost
3. 21. Jesus, whom heavens must r. till restitution
8. 15. prayed, that they might r. the Holy Ghost
19. on whoms. I lay hands, may r. the Holy Ghost
9. 12. hands on him, that he might r. his sight
17. Jesus sent me, that thou mightest r. thy sight
10. 43. whoso. believeth, shall r. remission of sins
26. 18. that they may r. forgiveness of sins
Rom. 5. 17. more they which r. abundance of grace
13. 2. that resist shall r. to themselves damnation
16. 2. that ye r. her in Lord, as becometh saints
1 Cor. 3. 8. every man shall r. his own reward
14. if his work abide, he shall r. a reward
4. 7. if thou didst r. it, why dost thou glory?
14. 5. that the church may r. edifying
2 Cor. 5. 10. that every one may r. the things done
6. 17. touch not unclean thing, and I will r. you
7. 9. that ye might r. damage by us in nothing
8. 4. praying us, that we would r. the gift
11. 4. or if ye r. another spirit ye have not received
Gal. 3. 14. that we might r. promise of the Spirit
4. 5. that we might r. the adoption of sons
Eph. 6. 8. the same shall he r. of the Lord
Col. 3. 24. ye shall r. the reward of the inheritance
25. he shall r. for the wrong he hath done
Philem. 15. that thou shouldest r. him for ever
Heb. 7. 5. sons of Levi, who r. office of priesthood
8. and here men that die r. tithes
9. 15. which are called might r. promise, 10. 36.
11. 8. he should after r. for an inheritance
Jam. 1. 7. that man think he shall r. any thing
12. when tried, he shall r. the crown of life
3. 1. knowing, we shall r. greater condemnation
5. 7. until he r. the early and latter rain
1 Pet. 5. 4. ye shall r. a crown of glory, fadeth not
2 Pet. 2. 13. shall r. the reward of unrighteousness
1 John 3. 22. whatsoever we ask, we r. of him
5. 9. if we r. the witness of men, God is greater
2 John 8. but that we r. a full reward
Rev. 14. 9. if any man r. his mark in his forehead
17. 12. but r. power as kings one hour with beast
RECEIVE, Imperatively.
Gen. 33. 10. then r. my present at my hand
Job 22. 22. r. I pray thee, the law from his mouth
Prov. 4. 10. hear, O my son, and r. my sayings
8. 10. r. my instruction, and not silver, 19. 20.

Jer. 9. 20. let your ear r. the word of his mouth
Ezek. 3. 10. r. all my words in thine heart
Hos. 14. 2. say to him, r. us graciously
Mat. 19. 12. he that is able, let him r. it
Luke 18. 42. Jesus saith, r. thy sight, Acts 22. 13.
John 20. 22. he saith, r. ye the Holy Ghost
Acts 7. 59. saying, Lord Jesus, r. my spirit
Rom. 14. 1. him that is weak in the faith, r. ye
15. 7. r. ye one another, as Christ also received us
2 Cor. 7. 2. r. us, we have wronged no man
11. 16. yet as a fool r. me, that I may boast
Phil. 2. 29. r. him in the Lord with gladness
Col. 4. 10. and Marcus, if he come unto you, r. him
Philem. 12. r. him that is mine own bowels
17. if thou count me a partner, r. him as myself
Jam. 1. 21. r. with meekness the ingrafted word
RECEIVE, Negatively.
2 Kings 5. 16. but Elisha said, I will r. none
12. 7. r. no more money of your acquaintance
Job 2. 10. shall we r. good, and shall we not r. evil?
Jer. 17. 23. that they might not r. instruction
35. 13. will ye not r. instruct. to hearken to words?
Ezek. 36. 30. ye shall r. no more reproach of famine
Mat. 10. 14. whosoever shall not r. you, nor hear your words, shake off dust, Mark 6. 11. Luke 9. 5.
Mark 10. 15. whosoever shall not r. the kingdom of God as a little child, not enter therein, Luke 18. 17.
Luke 9. 53. they did not r. him, because his face was
10. 10. and they r. you not, go into the streets
18. 30. who shall not r. manifold more in this time
John 3. 11. we testify, and ye r. not our witness
27. a man can r. nothing, except it be given him
5. 34. but I r. not testimony from man
41. I r. not honour from men
43. I am come in Father's name, and ye r. me not
14. 17. Spirit of truth, whom the world cannot r.
Acts 22. 18. for they will not r. thy testimony
1 Cor. 4. 7. what hast thou that thou didst not r.?
2 Cor. 6. 1. that ye r. not the grace of God in vain
1 Tim. 5. 19. against an elder r. not an accusation
Jam. 4. 3. ye ask and r. not, because ye ask amiss
2 John 10. r. him not into your house
3 John 10. neither doth he himself r. the brethren
Rev. 18. 4. and that ye r. not of her plagues
RECEIVE, Infinitively.
Gen 4. 11. earth opened mouth to r. brother's blood
38. 20. to r. his pledge from woman's hand
Exod. 27. 3. thou shalt make his pans to r. his ashes
Deut. 9. 9. when I was gone up to r. the tables
1 Kings 8. 64. because brazen altar before L. was too little to r. the burnt offerings, 2 Chron. 7. 7.
2 Kings 5. 26. is it time to r. money, to r. garments?
12. 8. the priest consented to r. no more money
Prov. 1. 3. to r. the instruction of wisdom
Jer. 5. 3. but they have refused to r. correction
32. 33. they have not hearkened to r. instruction
Mal. 3. 10. there shall not be room enough to r. it
Mat. 19. 12. he that is able to r. it, let him r. it
Mark 2. 2. that there was no room to r. them
Luke 6. 34. of whom ye hope to r. as much again
19. 12. nobleman went to r. for himself kingdom
Acts 16. 21. teach customs not lawful for us to r.
18. 27. brethren exhorting the disciples to r. him
20. 35. it is more blessed to give than to r.
3 John 8. we therefore ought to r. such
Rev. 4. 11. thou art worthy, O Lord, to r. glory
5. 12. worthy is the Lamb to r. power and riches
13. 16. causeth to r. a mark in their right hand
RECEIVED.
Gen. 26. 12. Isaac r. the same year an hundred-fold
Exod. 32. 4. and Aaron r. them at their hand
36. 3. and they r. of Moses all the offering
Num. 12. 14. after that let Miriam be r. in again
23. 20. behold, I have r. commandment to bless
34. 14. two tribes and half r. inheritance, 15.
36. 3. their inheritance shall be put to the inheritance of the tribe whereunto they are r. 4.
Josh 9. † 14. r. the men by reason of victuals
13. 8. the Gadites have r. their inheritance
18. 2. which had not r. their inheritance
Judg. 13. 23. he would not have r. burnt offering
1 Sam. 12. 3. of whose hand have I r. any bribe?
25. 35. David r. of Abigail that she brought
1 Kings 10. 28. had linen yarn from Egypt, king's merchants r. linen yarn at a price, 2 Chr. 1. 16.
2 Kings 19. 14. Hezekiah r. the letter, Isa. 37. 14.
1 Chron. 12. 18. thine are we; then David r. them
Esth. 4. 4. Esther sent raiment, Mordecai r. it not
Job 4. 12. and mine ear r. a little thereof
Psal. 68. 18. thou hast r. gifts for men
Prov. 24. 32. I looked upon it, and r. instruction
Isa. 40. 2. she hath r. of the Lord's hand double
Jer. 2. 30. your children, they r. no correction
Ezek. 18. 17. hath not r. usury nor increase
Zeph. 3. 2. she obeyed not, she r. not correction
Mat. 10. 8. cast out devils, freely ye r. freely give
13. 19. this is he which r. seed by the way side
20. r. into stony || 22. thorns || 23. good ground
17. 24. they that r. tribute money came to Peter
20. 9. when came, they r. every man a penny, 10.
11. and when they had r. it, they murmured
34. immediately their eyes r. sight, followed him
25. 16. r. five talents || 17. r. two || 18. had r. one
27. I should have r. mine own with usury
Mark 7. 4. many things which they r. to hold
10. 52. he r. his sight, Luke 18. 43. Acts 9. 18.
15. 23. gave him wine with myrrh, but r. it not
16. 19. he was r. up into heaven, Acts 1. 9.
Luke 6. 24. woe to rich, for ye have r. your consol.
8. 40. was returned, the people gladly r. him
9. 11. r. them, and spake to them of kingdom
51. when time was come that he should be r. up
10. 38. and Martha r. him into her house
15. 27. because he hath r. him safe and sound
19. 6. Zaccheus came down and r. him joyfully
15. when he was returned, having r. kingdom
John 1. 11. he came to his own, his own r. him not
12. to as many as r. him, to them gave he power
16. out of fulness have all we r. grace for grace
3. 33. he that hath r. testimony, hath set his seal
4. 45. when he was come, Galileans r. him
6. 21. then they willingly r. him into the ship

John 9. 11. I went and washed, and I *r.* sight
15. Pharisees asked him how he had *r.* his sight
18. Jews did not believe that he had *r.* his sight
called parents of him that had *r.* his sight
10. 18. this commandment I *r.* of my Father
13. 30. he then having *r.* the sop, went out
17. 8. have given them thy words, and they *r.* them
18. 3. Judas then having *r.* a band of men
19. 30. when Jesus had *r.* the vinegar, he said
Acts 1. 9. and a cloud *r.* him out of their sight
2. 33. and having *r.* of the Father the promise
41. they that gladly *r.* his word were baptized
3. 7. immediately feet and ancle-bones *r.* strength
7. 38. who *r.* the lively oracles to give unto us
53. who have *r.* law by angels, and have not kept
8. 14. heard that Samaria had *r.* the word of God
17. laid hands on them, they *r.* the Holy Ghost
9. 19. when he had *r.* meat he was strengthened
10. 16. the vessel was *r.* again up into heaven
47. which have *r.* the Holy Ghost as well as we
11. 1. heard that Gentiles had *r.* the word of God
15. 4. when come, they were *r.* of the church
16. 24. who having *r.* such charge, thrust them into
17. 7. whom Jason hath *r.* these all do contrary
11. the Bereans *r.* the word with all readiness
19. 2. have ye *r.* the Holy Ghost since ye believed?
20. 24. the ministry which I have *r.* of the Lord
21. 17. when we were come, brethren *r.* us gladly
22. 5. from whom I *r.* letters to the brethren
26. 10. having *r.* authority from the chief priests
28. 2. barbarians kindled a fire and *r.* us every one
7. Publius *r.* us ‖ 30. Paul *r.* all that came
21. we neither *r.* letters out of Judea, nor brethren
Rom. 1. 5. by whom we have *r.* grace, for obedience
4. 11. and he *r.* the sign of circumcision, a seal
5. 11. by whom we have now *r.* the atonement
8. 15. ye have not *r.* the Spirit of bondage again to
fear, but ye have *r.* the Spirit of adoption
14. 3. judge him that eateth, for God hath *r.* him
15. 7. receive ye one another, as Christ also *r.* us
1 *Cor.* 2. 12. we have *r.* not the spirit of the world
4. 7. why dost glory, as if thou hadst not *r.* it?
11. 23. I *r.* of the Lord, that which I delivered
15. 1. which also ye have *r.* ‖ 3. which I *r.*
2 *Cor.* 4. 1. as we have *r.* mercy we faint not
7. 15. how with fear and trembling ye *r.* him
11. 4. if receive anoth. spirit, which ye have not *r.*
of the Jews five times *r.* I forty stripes
Gal. 1. 9. preach another gospel than that ye have *r.*
12. I *r.* it not of man, neither was I taught it
3. 2. *r.* ye the Spirit by the works of the law?
4. 14. but *r.* me as an angel of God, even as Christ
Phil. 4. 9. the things ye have *r.* and seen in me, do
† 18. I have *r.* all, having *r.* of Epaphroditus
Col. 2. 6. as ye have *r.* Christ, so walk ye in him
4. 10. touching whom ye *r.* commandments
17. take heed to the ministry thou hast *r.* in Lord
1 *Thess.* 1. 6. having *r.* the word in much affliction
2. 13. when ye *r.* word, *r.* it not as the word of man
4. 1. as ye have *r.* of us how ye ought to walk
2 *Thess.* 2. 10. because they *r.* not the love of truth
3. 6. not after the tradition which he *r.* of us
1 *Tim.* 3. 16. believed on in world, *r.* up into glory
4. 3. meats which God hath created to be *r.*
4. creature is good, if it be *r.* with thanksgiving
Heb. 2. 2. transgression *r.* just recompence of reward
7. 6. *r.* tithes of Abrah. and blessed him that had
11. for under it the people *r.* the law
10. 26. if we sin wilfully after we have *r.* knowledge
11. 11. through faith Sarai *r.* strength to conceive
13. these all died, not having *r.* the promises
17. he that *r.* promises offered up his only son
19. from whence also he *r.* him in a figure
31. when Rahab had *r.* the spies, *Jam.* 2. 25.
35. women *r.* their dead raised to life again
39. these all having obtained a good report thro'
faith, *r.* not the promise, God having provided
1 *Pet.* 1. 18. from your vain conversat. *r.* by tradit.
4. 10. as every one hath *r.* the gift, so minister
2 *Pet.* 1. 17. for he *r.* from God the Father honour
1 *John* 2. 27. anointing ye have *r.* abideth in you
2 *John* 4. as we have *r.* a command from the Father
Rev. 2. 27. give power, even as I *r.* of my Father
3. 3. remember how thou hast *r.* and heard
17. 12. ten kings who have *r.* no kingdom as yet
19. 20. them that had *r.* the mark of the beast
20. 4. had not *r.* the mark, reigned with Christ

RECEIVEDST.

Luke 16. 25. thou in thy life-time *r.* thy good things

RECEIVER.

Isa. 33. 18. where is the scribe? where is the *r.*?

RECEIVETH.

Judg. 19. 18. there is no man that *r.* me to house
Job 35. 7. or what *r.* he of thine hand?
Psal. 15. † 3. nor *r.* reproach against his neighbour
Prov. 21. 11. when wise is instructed, he *r.* knowl.
29. 4. but he that *r.* gifts, overthroweth it
Jer. 7. 28. this is a nation that *r.* not correction
Mal. 2. 13. or *r.* offering with good-will at your hand
Mat. 7. 8. every one that asketh *r.* *Luke* 11. 10.
10. 40. he that *r.* you, *r.* me, and he that *r.* me
r. him that sent me, *John* 13. 20.
41. he that *r.* a prophet, that *r.* a righteous man
13. 20. heareth the word, and anon *r.* it with joy
18. 5. one such little child in my name, *r.* me
Mark 9. 37. whosoever shall receive me, *r.* not me,
but him that sent me, *Luke* 9. 48.
Luke 15. 2. this man *r.* sinners, eateth with them
John 3. 32. and no man *r.* his testimony
4. 36. he that reapeth *r.* wages, and gathereth
12. 48. he that rejecteth me, and *r.* not my words
1 *Cor.* 9. 24. they run all, but one *r.* the prize
Heb. 6. 7. for the earth *r.* blessing from God
7. 8. men that die receive tithes, but there he *r.*
them, of whom it is witnessed that he liveth
9. Levi who *r.* tithes, paid tithes in Abraham
12. 6. and scourgeth every son whom he *r.*
Rev. 2. 17. no man knoweth, saving he that *r.* it
14. 11. whosoever *r.* the mark of his name

RECEIVETH *not.*

1 *Cor.* 2. 14. natural man *r.* *not* the things of God
3 *John* 9. I wrote, but Diotrephes *r.* us *not*

RECEIVING.

2 *Kings* 5. 20. spared Naaman, in not *r.* at his hands
Acts 17. 15. and *r.* a commandment to Silas
Rom. 1. 27. *r.* in themselves that recompence
11. 15. what shall *r.* of them be but life from dead?
Phil. 4. 15. as concerning giving and *r.* but ye only
Heb. 12. 28. wheref. we *r.* a kingdom which cannot
1 *Pet.* 1. 9. *r.* the end of your faith, the salvation

RECKON

Signifies, [1] *To cast up an account,* Mat. 18. 24. [2] *To esteem, repute, and number,* Luke 22. 37. [3] *To propound to one's self, or think with one's self,* Isa. 38. 13. [4] *To conclude, collect, and gather, as by reason and argument,* Rom. 6. 11.

Gen. 40. † 13. within 3 days Pharaoh shall *r.* † 19.
Lev. 25. 50. he shall *r.* with him that bought him
27. 18. the priest shall *r.* to him the worth, 23.
Num. 4. 32. by name ye shall *r.* the instruments
Ezek. 44. 26. they shall *r.* to him seven days
Mat. 18. 24. when he began to *r.* one was brought
Rom. 6. 11. *r.* yourselves to be dead indeed to sin
8. 18. I *r.* the sufferings of this present time
2 *Cor.* 10. † 2. which *r.* of us as though we walked

RECKONED.

Gen. 40. † 20. he *r.* with the butler and baker
Num. 18. 27. your heave offering *r.* as corn of flour
23. 9. the people shall not be *r.* among the nations
2 *Sam.* 4. 2. for Beeroth also was *r.* to Benjamin
2 *Kings* 12. 15. moreover, they *r.* not with the men
1 *Chr.* 5. 1. genealogy is not to be *r.* by birth-right
7. when the genealogy of generations was *r.*
17. all these were *r.* by genealogies, 7. 5, 7.
‖ 9. 1, 22. 2 *Chron.* 31. 19. *Ezra* 2. 62. ‖
8. 3. *Neh.* 7. 5, 64.
Psal. 40. 5. thy thoughts to us cannot be *r.* up
Isa. 38. 13. I *r.* till morning, that as a lion so will
Luke 22. 37. he was *r.* amongst the transgressors
Rom. 4. 4. the reward is not *r.* of grace, but of debt
9. faith was *r.* to Abr. ‖ 10. how was it then *r.*?

RECKONETH.

Mat. 25. 19. lord of those servants *r.* with them

RECKONING.

2 *Kings* 22. 7. there was no *r.* made with them
1 *Chron.* 23. 11. therefore they were in one *r.*

RECOMMENDED.

Acts 14. 26. from whence they had been *r.*
15. 40. Paul departed, being *r.* to the grace of God

RECOMPENCE,

A requital, retaliation, or amends, Luke 14. 12. *In* Rom. 1. 27. *we read, that the* Gentiles received that recompence of their error which was meet; and in *chap.* 11. 9. *it is said,* Let their table be made a snare and a recompence unto them. *In both which places the apostle speaks of that judgment of God, by which sin is punished with sin;* [1] *In the* Gentiles, *who abused their natural knowledge; how meet was it that they who had forsaken the* Author *of nature, should be given up, not to keep the* order *of nature! that they who had changed the glory of God into the similitude of beasts, should be left to do those things which beasts themselves abhorred!* [2] *In the* Jews, *abusing their revealed knowledge, for which their understandings were darkened, and spiritual blindness increased, so that they could discern nothing of heavenly things; and what things were delectable to them, were turned into their ruin and destruction.* Recompence *is also taken for that free and gracious reward which the saints shall have in heaven.* Luke 14. 14. For thou shalt be recompenced at the resurrection of the just.

Deut. 32. 35. to me belongeth vengeance and *r.*
Job 15. 31. not trust in vanity, vanity shall be his *r.*
Prov. 12. 14. the *r.* of a man's hand shall be rendered
Isa. 35. 4. even God will come with a *r.*
40. † 10. reward and *r.* for his works, 62. † 11.
59. 18. repay *r.* to his enemies, to the islands *r.*
66. 6. voice of Ld. that rendereth *r.* to his enemies
Jer. 51. 6. time of veng. he will render to her a *r.*
Lam. 3. 64. render to them a *r.* O Lord
Hos. 9. 7. days of *r.* are come, Israel shall know
Joel 3. 4. will ye render me a *r.*? speedily will I
7. I will return your *r.* on your own head
Luke 14. 12. they bid thee, and a *r.* be made thee
Rom. 1. 27. receiving that *r.* of their error
11. 9. let their table be made a *r.* to them
2 *Cor.* 6. 13. now for a *r.* in the same, be ye enlarged
Heb. 2. 2. transgression received a just *r.* of reward
10. 35. your confid. which hath great *r.* of reward
11. 26. for he had respect to the *r.* of reward

RECOMPENCES.

Isa. 34. 8. it is year of *r.* for controversy of Zion
59. † 18. according to their *r.* he will repay
Jer. 51. 56. the Lord God of *r.* shall surely requite

RECOMPENSE, *Verb.*

Num. 5. 7. he shall *r.* his trespass, and add the fifth
8. if he have no kinsman to *r.* the trespass unto
Ruth 2. 12. the Lord *r.* thy work and reward thee
2 *Sam.* 19. 36. why should the king *r.* me?
Job 34. 33. he will *r.* it, whether thou refuse
Prov. 20. 22. say not thou, I will *r.* evil
Isa. 65. 6. I will *r.* I will *r.* into their bosom
Jer. 16. 18. and first I will *r.* their iniquity and sin
25. 14. will *r.* according to their deeds, *Hos.* 12. 2.
50. 29. *r.* work ‖ *Ezek.* 7. 3. *r.* abominations, 8.
Ezek. 7. 4. *r.* thy ways, 9. ‖ 9. 10. ‖ 11. 21. ‖ 16. 43.
17. 19. mine oath and my covenant I will *r.*
23. 49. they shall *r.* your lewdness upon you
Joel 3. 4. if ye *r.* me, speedily will I return it
Luke 14. 14. shalt be blessed, for they cannot *r.* thee
Rom. 12. 17. *r.* to no man evil for evil
2 *Thess.* 1. 6. to *r.* tribulat. to them that trouble you
Heb. 10. 30. we know him that hath said, I will *r.*

RECOMPENSED.

Num. 5. 8. let the trespass be *r.* to the Lord
2 *Sam.* 22. 21. according to the cleanness of my
hands hath he *r.* me, 25. *Psal.* 18. 20, 24.
Prov. 11. 31. behold, the righteous shall be *r.*
Jer. 18. 20. shall evil be *r.* for good?
Ezek. 22. 31. their own way have I *r.* on their heads
Luke 14. 14. thou shalt be *r.* at the resurrection

Rom. 11. 35. and it shall be *r.* to him again

RECOMPENSEST.

Jer. 32. 18. thou *r.* iniquity of fathers to children

RECOMPENSETH.

Psal. 137. † 8. happy shall he be that *r.* thee

RECOMPENSING,

2 *Chron.* 6. 23. by *r.* his way upon his own head

RECONCILE.

Reconciliation, *is a restoring to favour, or making those friends who before were at variance, as God and the elect were, through sin, till of enemies they became friends, through the atonement made in the blood of* Christ, *and received by faith,* Eph. 2. 16. That he might reconcile both to God by the cross. *Col.* 1. 21. Ye were enemies, yet now hath he reconciled you. *The ministry of the gospel is called,* the ministry of reconciliation, 2 *Cor.* 5. 18. *because reconciliation is thereby published and declared to such as are yet enemies to God.*

To the making of reconciliation three things are required in him who is Mediator of it, [1] *That he make intercession for the offender.* [2] *That he satisfy the offended party for the wrong done.* [3] *To provide that the offender shall offend no more. All which our Lord Jesus Christ doth.* Isa. 53. 12. John 17. 22. Eph. 2. 16.

Lev. 6. 30. the blood is brought to *r.* withal
1 *Sam.* 29. 4. for wherewith should he *r.* himself
Ezek. 45. 20. so shall ye *r.* the house
Eph. 2. 16. that he might *r.* both to God by cross
Col. 1. 20. by him to *r.* all things to himself

RECONCILED.

Mat. 5. 24. go thy way, first be *r.* to thy brother
Rom. 5. 10. if when enemies we were *r.* to God
1 *Cor.* 7. 11. or let her be *r.* to her husband
2 *Cor.* 5. 18. who hath *r.* us to himself by Jesus Chr.
20. we pray you in Christ's stead, be ye *r.* to God
Col. 1. 21. you that were enemies, yet now hath he *r.*

RECONCILIATION.

Lev. 8. 15. sanctified it, to make a *r.* upon it
2 *Chron.* 29. 24. they made *r.* with their blood
Ezek. 45. 15. one lamb to make *r.* for them, 17.
Dan. 9. 24. to make *r.* for iniquity, and bring in
2 *Cor.* 5. 18. who hath given to us the ministry of *r.*
19. and hath committed to us the word of *r.*
Heb. 2. 17. to make *r.* for the sins of the people

RECONCILING.

Lev. 16. 20. when he had made an end of *r.* holy place
Rom. 11. 15. if the casting away be the *r.* of world
2 *Cor.* 5. 19. God was in Christ, *r.* the world

RECORD.

Exod. 20. 24. in all places where I *r.* my name
Deut. 30. 19. I call heaven and earth to *r.* 31. 28.
1 *Chron.* 16. 4. he appointed Levites to *r.* and praise
Isa. 8. 2. I took unto me faithful witnesses to *r.*
Acts 20. 26. I take you to *r.* this day, that I am pure

RECORD, *Substantive.*

Ezra 6. 2. and therein was a *r.* thus written
Job 16. 19. also now, behold, my *r.* is on high
John 1. 19. and this is the *r.* of John, when
32. John bare *r.* saying, I saw the Spirit, 34.
8. 13. thou bearest *r.* of thyself, thy *r.* is not true
14. though I bear *r.* of myself, yet my *r.* is true
12. 17. the people that was with him, bare *r.*
19. 35. he that saw bare *r.* and his *r.* is true
Rom. 10. 2. I bare them *r.* that they have a zeal
2 *Cor.* 1. 23. I call God for a *r.* upon my soul
8. 3. to their power I bear *r.* yea, and beyond
Gal. 4. 15. I bear you *r.* if it had been possible
Phil. 1. 8. God is my *r.* how greatly I long after you
Col. 4. 13. I bear him *r.* that he hath a zeal for you
1 *John* 5. 7. there are three that bear *r.* in heaven
10. because he believeth not *r.* God gave of his Son
11. this is the *r.* that God hath given us
3 *John* 12. we bare *r.* and our *r.* is true
Rev. 1. 2. who bare *r.* of the Word of God

RECORDED.

Neh. 12. 22. Levites were *r.* chief of the fathers

RECORDER.

2 *Sam.* 8. 16. Jehoshaphat the son of Ahilud was *r.*
20. 24. 1 *Kings* 4. 3. 1 *Chron.* 18. 15.
2 *Kings* 18. 18. and Joah the son of Asaph the *r.*
Isa. 36. 3, 22.
2 *Chron.* 34. 8. Joah son of Joahaz *r.* to repair

RECORDS.

Ezra 4. 15. that search be made in the book of *r.*
Esth. 6. 1. he commanded to bring the book of *r.*

RECOVER.

Judg. 11. 26. why did ye not *r.* them in that time
1 *Sam.* 30. 8. for thou shalt without fail *r.* all
2 *Sam.* 8. 3. as he went to *r.* his border at Euphrates
2 *Kings* 1. 2. enquire of Baal-zebub whether I shall *r.*
5. 3. the prophet would *r.* him of his leprosy
6. I have sent Naaman, that thou mayest *r.* him
7. that this man doth send to me to *r.* a man
11. and strike his hand over place, and *r.* the leper
8. 8. enquire by him, shall I *r.* of this disease? 9.
10. thou mayest *r.* ‖ 14. that shouldest surely *r.*
2 *Chron.* 13. 20. nor did Jeroboam *r.* strength again
14. 13. that they could not *r.* themselves
Psal. 39. 13. spare me, that I may *r.* strength
Isa. 11. 11. to *r.* the remnant of his people
38. 16. so wilt thou *r.* me and make me to live
21. and lay it for a plaister, and he shall *r.*
Hos. 2. 9. and I will *r.* my wool and my flax
Mark 16. 18. lay hands on the sick, and they shall *r.*
2 *Tim.* 2. 26. that they may *r.* themselves out of

RECOVERED.

1 *Sam.* 30. 18. David *r.* all the Amalekites took, 19.
22. not give them aught of spoil we have *r.*
2 *Kings* 13. 25. Joash beat him, and *r.* cities of Israel
14. 28. how he warred, and *r.* Damascus
16. 6. Rezin king of Syria *r.* Elath to Syria
20. 7. and they laid it on the boil, and he *r.*
Isa. 38. 9. when Hezekiah was sick, and was *r.* 39. 1
Jer. 8. 22. why is not the health of my people *r.*?
41. 16. Johanan took the people he had *r.*

RECOVERING.

Luke 4. 18. to preach *r.* of sight to the blind

RECOUNT.

Nah. 2. 5. he shall *r.* his worthies, they shall stumb.

RECTIFY.
Prov. 11. † 5. righteousness of perfect shall *r.* way

RED.
Gen. 25. 25. first came out *r.* all over like an hairy
30. Esau said, feed me with that same *r.* pottage
49. 12. Judah, his eyes shall be *r.* with wine
Exod. 25. 5. rams' skins dyed *r.* and badgers' skins, and shittim wood, 26. 14. | 35. 7. | 36. 19. | 39. 34.
35. 23. with whom was found *r.* skins of rams
Num. 19. 2. bring thee a *r.* heifer without spot
2 *Kings* 3. 22. Moabites saw the water *r.* as blood
Esth. 1. 6. on a pavement of *r.* blue, and white
Psal. 68. † 23. foot may be *r.* in blood of thy enemies
75. 8. the wine is *r.* it is full of mixture
Prov. 23. 31. look not on the wine when it is *r.*
Isa. 1. 18. though your sins be *r.* like crimson
27. 2. sing ye to her, a vineyard of *r.* wine
63. 2. wherefore art thou *r.* in thine apparel?
Nah. 2. 3. the shield of his mighty men is made *r.*
Zech. 1. 8. I saw by night a man riding on a *r.* horse and behind him were there *r.* horses and white
6. 2. in first chariot were *r.* horses, in second black
Mat. 16. 2. it will be fair weather, for sky is *r.* 3.
Rev. 6. 4. then went out another horse that was *r.*
12. 3. a great *r.* dragon, seven heads and ten horns

RED *sea.*
Exod. 10. 19. and cast the locusts into the *r. sea*
13. 18. God led them by the way of the *r. sea*
15. 4. chosen captains are drowned in the *r. sea*
22. Moses brought Israel from the *r. sea*
23. 31. I will set thy bounds from the *r. sea*
Num. 14. 25. get into the wilderness by the *r. sea*
21. 14. it is said, what did he in the *r. sea?*
Deut. 1. 40. take your journey by the *r. sea*
11. 4. how he made the *r. sea* to overflow them
Josh. 2. 10. heard how the Lord dried up the *r. sea*
4. 23. as the Lord your God did to the *r. sea*
24. 6. the Egyptians pursued after to the *r. sea*
Neh. 9. 9. thou heardest their cry by the *r. sea*
Psal. 106. 7. but provoked him at the *r. sea*
9. he rebuked the *r. sea,* and it was dried up
22. he had done terrible things by the *r. sea*
136. 13. to him who divided the *r. sea* in parts
15. overthrew Pharaoh and his host in the *r. sea*
Jer. 49. 21. noise thereof was heard in the *r. sea*
Acts 7. 36. he shewed wonders in the *r. sea*
Heb. 11. 29. by faith they passed through the *r. sea*

REDDISH.
Lev. 13. 19. a bright spot somewhat *r.* 24, 43.
42. a white *r.* sore, it is a leprosy sprung up
49. if the plague be *r.* in the garment or skin
14. 37. if the plague be with hollow strakes, *r.*

REDEEM
Signifies, [1] *To buy again something that had been sold, by paying back the price unto him that bought it,* Lev. 25. 25. | 27. 20. [2] *To deliver and bring out of bondage with a strong hand, and without any ransom, such as were kept prisoners by their enemies,* Deut. 7. 5. | 32. 6. [3] *To deliver sinners from the tyranny of Satan, from sin, death, and hell, by the purchase of Christ's blood, and the power of his grace. Thus is Christ both the* Ransomer, *and* ransom, Luke 1. 68. 1 Tim. 2. 6. Tit. 2. 14.

Redemption *sometimes signifies deliverance both from the guilt and power of sin, by forgiveness and sanctification,* Eph. 1. 7. *Sometimes it is taken for the whole work of a sinner's salvation, comprehending all things that belong to it.* Heb. 9. 12. Having obtained eternal redemption for us. *Our whole redemption, from the first act to the last, both for merit and efficacy, is wholly from Christ, and not at all from ourselves.* Lastly, *the last act of our salvation is the resurrection of our bodies and the sentence of the last judgment, after which the saints shall be glorified as the sons of God by adoption, their souls and bodies being reunited; in this sense* redemption *is taken,* Luke 21. 28. Rom. 8. 23.

To redeem time, *Eph.* 5. 16. *To embrace and improve every opportunity of doing good. It is a metaphor taken from merchants that diligently observe the time of buying and selling, and easily part with their pleasures for gain; that is, deny yourselves in your ease, pleasure, &c. to gain an opportunity of doing good.*

Exod. 6. 6. I will *r.* you with a stretched-out arm
13. 13. firstling of ass shalt *r.* with a lamb, 34. 20.
15. the first-born of my children I *r.* 34. 20.
Lev. 25. 25. and if any of his kin come to *r.* it
26. if he have none to *r.* it ‖ 29. he may *r.* it
32. the cities may the Levites *r.* at any time
48. when sold, one of his brethren may *r.* him
49. his uncle's son, or any of kin may *r.* him
27. 13. but if he will at all *r.* it, then he shall add
15. that sanctified his house will *r.* it, 19, 20, 31.
Num. 18. 15. the first-born of man shalt thou *r.*
16. from a month old shalt thou *r.*
17. the firstling of a goat thou shalt not *r.*
Ruth 2. † 20. man is one that hath right to *r.* 3. † 9.
4. 4. if thou wilt *r.* it, if not I will *r.* it
6. I cannot *r.* it for myself, *r.* thou it
2 *Sam.* 7. 23. what nation in earth is like Isr. whom God went to *r.* to himself? 1 *Chron.* 17. 21.
Neh. 5. 5. nor is it in our power to *r.* them
Job 5. 20. in famine he shall *r.* thee from death
6. 23. to *r.* me from the hand of the mighty
Psal. 25. 22. *r.* Isr. O God, out of all his troubles
26. 11. *r.* me and be merciful unto me
44. 26. arise, and *r.* us for thy mercies' sake
49. 7. none of them can *r.* his brother, nor give
15. but God will *r.* my soul from the grave
69. 18. draw nigh to my soul, and *r.* it, deliver me
72. 14. he shall *r.* their soul from deceit
130. 8. he shall *r.* Israel from all his iniquities
Isa. 50. 2. is my hand shortened that it cannot *r.*?
Jer. 15. 21. I will *r.* thee out of hand of terrible
Hos. 13. 14. I will *r.* them from death
Mic. 4. 10. the Lord shall *r.* thee from Babylon
Gal. 4. 5. to *r.* them that were under the law
Tit. 2. 14. that he might *r.* us from all iniquity

REDEEMED.
Gen. 48. 16. the angel which *r.* me from all evil
Exod. 15. 13. led forth people whom thou hast *r.*
21. 8. if please not, then shall he let her be *r.*
Lev. 19. 20. who lieth with a bondmaid not *r.*
25. 30. if a house in a walled city be not *r.*
31. but the houses of the villages may be *r.*
48. brother sold to a stranger may be *r.* again
54. if he be not *r.* then go out in year of jubilee
27. 20. if he hath sold the field, it shall not be *r.*
27. an unclean beast not *r.* then shall it be sold
28. no devoted thing to the Lord shall be *r.* 29.
33. the tithe and the change shall not be *r.*
Num. 3. 46. those be *r.* that are more than Levites
18. 16. those that are to be *r.* from a month old
Deut. 7. 8. the Lord hath *r.* you out of the house of bondmen, from king of Egypt, 15. 15. | 24. 18.
9. 26. thy people thou hast *r.* through thy greatness
13. 5. Lord which *r.* you out of house of bondage
21. 8. be merciful to Israel, whom thou hast *r.*
2 *Sam.* 4. 9. Lord hath *r.* my soul, 1 *Kings* 1. 29.
1 *Chron.* 17. 21. whom thou hast *r.* out of Egypt by thy great power, *Neh.* 1. 10. *Psal.* 77. 15.
Neh. 5. 8. we after our ability have *r.* the Jews
Psal. 31. 5. thou hast *r.* me, O Lord God of truth
71. 23. my soul shall rejoice which thou hast *r.*
74. 2. remember thine inheritance thou hast *r.*
106. 10. he *r.* them from the hand of the enemy
107. 2. let the *r.* of Lord say so, whom he hath *r.*
136. 24. and hath *r.* us from our enemies
Isa. 1. 27. Zion shall be *r.* with judgment
29. 22. thus saith the Lord, who *r.* Abraham
35. 9. no lion there. but the *r.* shall walk there
43. 1. fear not, I have *r.* thee, thou art mine
44. 22. return unto me, for I have *r.* thee
23. the Lord hath *r.* Jacob, 48. 20. *Jer.* 31. 11.
51. 11. therefore the *r.* of the Lord shall return
52. 3. and ye shall be *r.* without money
9. *r.* Jerusalem ‖ 62. 12. holy people *r.* of Lord
63. 4. year of my *r.* is come ‖ 9. in pity he *r.* them
Lam. 3. 58. O Lord, thou hast *r.* my life
Hos. 7. 13. tho' I *r.* them, yet they have spoken lies
Mic. 6. 4. I *r.* thee out of the house of servants
Zech. 10. 8. I will hiss for them, I have *r.* them
Luke 1. 68. he hath visited and *r.* his people
24. 21. it had been he who should have *r.* Israel
Gal. 3. 13. Christ *r.* us from the curse of the law
1 *Pet.* 1. 18. ye were not *r.* with corruptible things
Rev. 5. 9. thou hast *r.* us to God by thy blood
14. 3. none learn, but the 144,000 which were *r.*
4. these were *r.* from among men, being first fruits

REDEEMEDST.
2 *Sam.* 7. 23. which thou *r.* to thee from Egypt

REDEEMER.
Ruth 4. † 14. who hath not left thee without a *r.*
Job 19. 25. for I know that my *R.* liveth
Psal. 19. 14. O Lord, my strength and my *R.*
78. 35. they remembered the high God was their *r.*
Prov. 23. 11. their *R.* is mighty, he shall plead cause
Isa. 41. 14. and thy *R.* the Holy One of Israel, 54. 5.
43. 14. thus saith the Lord your *R.* the Holy One
44. 6. thus saith the Lord, his *R.* the Lord of hosts
24. saith the Lord thy *R.* 48. 17. | 49. 7. | 54. 8.
47. 4. as for our *R.* the Lord of hosts is his name
49. 26. shall know that I the Lord am thy *R.* 60. 16.
59. 20. *R.* shall come to Zion, to them that turn
63. 16. thou, O Lord, art our Father, our *R.*
Jer. 50. 34. their *R.* is strong, the Lord of hosts

REDEEMETH.
Psal. 34. 22. the Lord *r.* the souls of his servants
103. 4. who *r.* life from destruction, who crowns

REDEEMING.
Ruth 4. 7. this was the manner in Israel concern. *r.*
Eph. 5. 16. *r.* time, because the days are evil, *Col.* 4. 5.

REDEMPTION.
Exod. 8. † 23. I will put a *r.* between my people
Lev. 25. 24. ye shall grant a *r.* for the land
† 31. houses of the villages, *r.* belongeth to it
51. he shall give again the price of his *r.* 52.
Num. 3. 49. Moses took the *r.* money of them
Psal. 49. 8. *r.* of their soul is precious, and ceaseth
111. 9. he sent *r.* to his people, holy is his name
130. 7. with the Lord there is plenteous *r.*
Jer. 32. 7. the right of *r.* is thine to buy it, 8.
Luke 2. 38. to them that looked for *r.* in Jerusalem
21. 28. then look up, for your *r.* draweth nigh
Rom. 3. 24. justified through the *r.* that is in Christ
8. 23. for adoption, to wit, the *r.* of our body
1 *Cor.* 1. 30. Christ is made to us sanctification and *r.*
Eph. 1. 7. in whom have *r.* through blood, *Col.* 1. 14.
14. until the *r.* of the purchased possession
4. 30. whereby ye are sealed unto the day of *r.*
Heb. 9. 12. having obtained eternal *r.* for us
15. for *r.* of the transgressions that were under

REDNESS.
Prov. 23. 29. who hath woe? who hath *r.* of eyes

REDOUND.
2 *Cor.* 4. 15. that grace might *r.* to the glory of God

REED
Signifies, [1] *A plant growing in fenny and watery places,* Job 40. 21. [2] *A staff or rod of a reed, which was put in our Saviour's hand at his passion, by way of derision, instead of a sceptre,* Mat. 27. 29. [3] *A* Jewish *measure of six cubits three inches, or three yards three inches,* Ezek. 40. 3.

Egypt *is called a* reed, 2 Kings 18. 21. *in allusion to the* reeds *that were numerous upon the banks of the* Nile; *and a broken reed, to denote the inability and weakness of the* Egyptians *to support and aid* Hezekiah *against the* Assyrians. A bruised reed, *Isa.* 42. 3. *A believer weak in grace, who is of a broken and contrite heart for sin. Our Saviour, speaking of* John *the Baptist, says that he was not a* reed shaken with the wind, *Mat.* 11. 7. *He was not one of an unsettled mind; but constant and fixed in the truth: his testimony of me was always the same.*

1 *Kings* 14. 15. the Lord shall smite Israel as a *r.*
2 *Kings* 18. 21. thou trustest upon the staff of this bruised *r.* *Isa.* 36. 6.
Isa. 42. 3. a bruised *r.* shall he not break, and the smoking flax shall he not quench, *Mat.* 12. 20.
Ezek. 29. 6. they have been a staff of *r.* to Israel
40. 3. a man with a measuring *r.* in his hand
42. 16. the east side with measuring *r.* 17, 18, 19.
Mat. 11. 7. what went ye to see? a *r.* *Luke* 7. 24.
27. 29. they put a *r.* in his right hand, and bowed
30. they smote him with a *r.* *Mark* 15. 19.
48. one of them ran and put the spunge on a *r.* and gave him to drink, *Mark* 15. 36.
Rev. 11. 1. there was given me a *r.* like a rod
21. 15. had a golden *r.* to measure the city
16. he measured with the *r.* 12,000 furlongs

REEDS.
Job 40. 21. he lieth in the covert of the *r.*
Isa. 19. 6. the *r.* and flags shall wither, 7.
35. 7. in the habitation of dragons shall be *r.*
Jer. 51. 32. the *r.* they have burnt with fire
Ezek. 42. 16. he measured the east side with the measuring reed five hundred *r.* 17, 18, 19.
45. 1. the length shall be the length of 25,000 *r.*

REEL.
Psal. 107. 27. they *r.* to and fro, and stagger
Isa. 24. 20. earth shall *r.* to and fro like a drunkard

REFINE.
Zech. 13. 9. and I will *r.* them as silver is refined

REFINED.
2 *Sam.* 22. † 31. his way is perfect, the word of the Lord is *r.* *Psal.* 18. † 30. | 119. † 140.
1 *Chron.* 28. 18. for the altar *r.* gold by weight
29. 4. seven thousand talents of *r.* silver to overlay
Isa. 25. 6. a feast of wines on the lees well *r.*
48. 10. behold, I have *r.* thee, but not with silver
Zech. 13. 9. I will refine them, as silver is *r.*

REFINER.
Mal. 3. 2. he is like a *r.* fire, and like fuller's soap
3. he shall sit as a *r.* and purifier of silver

REFORMATION.
Heb. 9. 10. imposed on them until the time of *r.*

REFORMED.
Lev. 26. 23. and if ye will not be *r.* by these things

REFRAIN.
Gen. 45. 1. then Joseph could not *r.* himself
Job 4. † 2. but who can *r.* from words?
7. 11. therefore I will not *r.* my mouth
Prov. 1. 15. my son, *r.* thy foot from their path
Eccl. 3. 5. there is a time to *r.* from embracing
Isa. 48. 9. and for my praise I will *r.* for thee
64. 12. wilt thou *r.* thyself for these things, O Ld.?
Jer. 31. 16. *r.* voice from weeping, eyes from tears
Acts 5. 38. I say to you, *r.* from these men
1 *Pet.* 3. 10. let him *r.* his tongue from evil

REFRAINED.
Gen. 43. 31. Joseph *r.* himself, and said, set on bread
Esth. 5. 10. nevertheless, Haman *r.* himself
Job 29. 9. princes *r.* talking, and laid their hand
Psal. 40. 9. I have not *r.* my lips, thou knowest
119. 101. I have *r.* my feet from every evil way
Isa. 42. 14. I have been still, and *r.* myself
Jer. 14. 10. they have not *r.* their feet

REFRAINETH.
Prov. 10. 19. but he that *r.* his lips is wise

REFRESH
Signifies, [1] *To revive,* 1 Cor. 16. 18. [2] *To take rest,* Exod. 23. 12. [3] *To strengthen oneself by food,* 1 Kings 13. 7. [4] *To breathe,* Job 32. † 20.

Times of refreshing, *Acts* 3. 19. or times of cooling. *As afflictions are called a fiery trial, deliverance from them is a season of refreshing or cooling: such a time of refreshing after troubles, frequently comes in this life; but when this life ends, a deliverance comes from all afflictions to them that truly fear and serve God. It is a figurative manner of speaking, taken from the custom of labourers, who in the heat of the day repose themselves in cool shades.*

1 *Kings* 13. 7. come home with me and *r.* thyself
Acts 27. 3. Julius suffered Paul to *r.* himself
Phil. 20. brother, *r.* my bowels in the Lord

REFRESHED.
Exod. 23. 12. and that the stranger may be *r.*
31. 17. on the seventh day he rested and was *r.*
1 *Sam.* 16. 23. Dav. played, so Saul was *r.* and well
2 *Sam.* 16. 14. David and people with him *r.* thems.
Job 32. 20. I will speak that I may be *r.*
Rom. 15. 32. and that I may with you be *r.*
1 *Cor.* 16. 18. for they *r.* my spirit and yours
2 *Cor.* 7. 13. Titus, his spirit was *r.* by you all
2 *Tim.* 1. 16. Onesiphorus, for he often *r.* me
Phil. 7. the bowels of the saints are *r.* by thee

REFRESHETH.
Prov. 25. 13. for he *r.* the soul of his masters

REFRESHING.
Isa. 28. 12. this is the *r.* yet they would not hear
Acts 3. 19. when times of *r.* shall come from Lord

REFUGE
Is a strong hold, or place of safety, to fly to in danger, where men may be protected, and escape the enemy, Num. 35. 13. *God is called the* refuge of his people, *Deut.* 33. 27. *He defends them against the assaults of all their enemies. Christ is a refuge in his righteousness and blood,* Isa. 25. 4.

Cities of refuge. *In order to provide for the security of those, who unawares and without any design should kill a man, the Lord commanded* Moses *to appoint six cities of* refuge, *that whoever suddenly and against his will should spill the blood of a man, might retire thither, and have time to prepare for his defence and justification before the judges, so that the kinsman of the deceased might not pursue him thither, and kill him. Of these cities there were three on each side* Jordan; *those on this side* Jordan *were* Kedesh *of* Naphtali, Hebron, *and* Shechem. *Those beyond* Jordan *were* Bezer, Golan, *and* Ramoth-gilead, *Josh.* 20. 7, 8. *These cities were to be easy of access, and to have smooth and good roads to them, and bridges where there should be occasion: when there were any cross-roads, they took care to set up posts with an inscription, directing the way to the* city of refuge. *This city was to be well supplied with water and all kind of provisions. It was not allowed there to make any weapons, that the relations of the deceased might not be furnished there with arms to gratify their revenge. Though the manslayer had fled to the* city of refuge, *yet he was not thereupon exempt from the pursuits of justice: an information was preferred against him, he was summoned before the judges, and before the people, to clear himself, and to prove the murder was merely casual and involuntary. If he was found innocent, he dwelt safely in the city to which he had retired; if otherwise, he was put to death, according to the severity of the law. Though he was found innocent, he was not therefore immediately set at liberty; but to inspire the greater horror, even of involuntary murder, it seems as if the law would punish it with a kind of banishment; for he was obliged to dwell in this city, without going out of it, till the death of the high priest: and if before this time he should any where go out of the city, the revenger of blood might safely kill him,* Num. 35. 25, 26, 27, &c.

Num. 35. 13. six cities shall ye have for r. 15.
Deut. 33. 27. the eternal God is thy r.
Josh. 20. 3. shall be your r. from avenger of blood
2 Sam. 22. 3. he is my high tower and my r.
Ps. 9. 9. Lord also will be a r. for the oppressed, a r. in times of trouble, they that know thy name
14. 6. counsel of the poor, because the Lord is his r.
46. 1. God is our r. 7. 11. || 48. 3. God is known for r.
57. 1. in shadow of thy wings will I make my r. until these calamities be overpast, 61. † 4.
59. 16. thou hast been my r. in the day of trouble
62. 7. my r. is in God || 8. God is a r. for us
71. 7. wonder to many, thou art my strong r. 142. 5.
91. 2. he is my r. 9. || 94. 22. God is rock of my r.
104. 18. the high hills a r. for wild goats
142. 4. r. failed me || 5. thou art my r. and portion
Prov. 14. 26. his children shall have a place of r.
Isa. 4. 6. a place of r. || 25. 4. to the needy a r.
28. 15. for we have made lies our r. and under
17. the hail shall sweep away the r. of lies
Jer. 16. 19. O Lord, my r. in the day of affliction
Heb. 6. 18. who have fled for r. to lay hold on hope

REFUSE.

1 Sam. 15. 9. every thing that was vile and r.
Jer. 6. † 30. r. silver shall men call them because L.
Lam. 3. 45. thou hast made us as r. midst of people
Amos 8. 6. that we may sell the r. of wheat

REFUSE, Verb.

Exod. 4. 23. if thou r. to let them go, 8. 2. | 9. 2. | 10. 4.
10. 3. how long wilt thou r. to humble thyself?
16. 28. r. ye to keep my commandments and laws?
22. 17. if her father utterly r. to give her to him
Job 34. 33. whether thou r. or choose, and not I
Prov. 8. 33. hear instruction, be wise, and r. it not
21. 7. because they r. to do judgment
25. the desire of slothful, his hands r. to labour
Isa. 1. 20. but if ye r. shall be devoured with sword
7. 15. that he may know to r. the evil, 16.
Jer. 8. 5. they r. to return || 9. 6. they r. to know me
13. 10. this evil people which r. to hear my words
25. 28. if they r. to take the cup at thine hand
38. 21. if thou r. to go forth, this is the word
Acts 25. 11. if I be an offender, I r. not to die
1 Tim. 4. 7. but r. profane and old wives' fables
5. 11. but the younger widows r.
Heb. 12. 25. see that ye r. not him that speaketh

REFUSED.

Gen. 37. 35. but Jacob r. to be comforted, and said
39. 8. Joseph r. to lie with his master's wife
48. 19. Jacob r. to remove his hand
Num. 20. 21. Edom r. to give Israel passage
1 Sam. 8. 19. people r. to obey the voice of Samuel
16. 7. look not on him for I have r. him
28. 23. but Saul r. and said, I will not eat
2 Sam. 2. 23. howbeit Asahel r. to turn aside
13. 9. she poured out, but Amnon r. to eat
1 Kings 20. 35. and the man r. to smite him
21. 15. the vineyard he r. to give thee for money
2 Kings 5. 16. Naaman urged him to take, but he r.
Neh. 9. 17. our fathers hardened, and r. to obey
Esth. 1. 12. but the queen Vashti r. to come
Job 6. 7. the things that my soul r. to touch are as
Psal. 77. 2. my soul r. to be comforted
78. 10. and they r. to walk in his law
67. he r. tabernacle of Joseph, and chose Ephraim
118. 22. the stone which the builders r. is become
Prov. 1. 24. because I have called and ye r.
Isa. 54. 6. when thou wast r. saith thy God
Jer. 5. 3. they r. to receive correction, they r. to ret.
11. 10. their fathers who r. to hear my words
31. 15. Rachel r. to be comforted for her children
50. 33. all that took them r. to let them go
Ezek. 5. 6. for they have r. my judgments
Hos. 11. 5. Assyrian his king, because they r. to ret.
Zech. 7. 11. but they r. to hearken, and pulled away
Acts 7. 35. this Moses whom they r. saying
1 Tim. 4. 4. and nothing to be r. if it be received
Heb. 11. 24. by faith Moses r. to be called the son of
12. 25. who r. him that spake on earth

REFUSEDST.

Jer. 3. 3. a whore's forehead, thou r. to be ashamed

REFUSETH.

Exod. 7. 14. Pharaoh r. to let the people go
Num. 22. 13. the Lord r. to give me leave to go
14. the princes said, Balaam r. to come with us
Deut. 25. 7. my husband's brother r. to raise up name
Prov. 10. 17. but he that r. reproof, erreth
13. 18. shame shall be to him that r. instruction
15. 32. he that r. instruction despiseth his own soul
Isa. 8. 6. this people r. the waters of Shiloah
Jer. 15. 18. my wound which r. to be healed

REGARD.

Eccl. 8. 2. and that in r. of the oath of God
Dan. 3. † 13. these men have set no r. on thee
Acts 8. 11. to him they had r. because he had bewitch.

REGARD

Signifies, [1] *To look upon with concern or compassion,* Deut. 28. 50. [2] *To think of, consider, or lay to heart,* Isa. 5. 12. [3] *To have respect for,* 2 Kings 3. 14. [4] *To hear and answer,* Psal. 102. 17. [5] *To observe,* Rom. 14. 6. [6] *To look to with an approving covetous eye,* Job 36. 21. Psal. 66. 18. [7] *To set the heart unto,* Exod. 9. † 21. [8] *To lay to heart,* 1 Sam. 25. 25.

REGARD, Verb.

Gen. 45. 20. r. not your stuff, for Egypt is yours
Exod. 5. 9. and let them not r. vain words
Lev. 19. 31. r. not them that have familiar spirits
Deut. 28. 50. which shall not r. person of the aged
1 Sam. 4. 20. she answered not, nor did she r. it
25. 5. let not my lord r. this man of Belial
2 Sam. 13. 20. r. not this, he is thy brother
2 Kings 3. 14. were it not that I r. Jehoshaphat
Job 3. 4. that day, let not God r. it from above
35. 13. nor will the Almighty r. it
36. 21. take heed, r. not iniquity
Psal. 28. 5. they r. not the works of the Lord
31. 6. I have hated them that r. lying vanities
66. 18. if I r. iniquity in my heart, Lord not hear
94. 7. neither shall the God of Jacob r. it
102. 17. he will r. the prayer of the destitute
Prov. 5. 2. that thou mayest r. discretion
6. 35. he will not r. any ransom, nor will rest content
Isa. 5. 12. they r. not the work of the Lord
13. 17. the Medes who will not r. silver
18. † 4. I will r. my set dwelling like a clear heat
Lam. 4. 16. the Lord, he will no more r. them
Dan. 11. 37. r. God of his fathers, nor r. any god
Amos 5. 22. nor will I r. the peace-offering
Hab. 1. 5. behold r. and wonder marvellously
Mal. 1. 9. will he r. your persons? saith the Lord
Luke 18. 4. though I fear not God, nor r. man
Rom. 14. 6. to the Lord he doth not r. it

REGARDED.

Exod. 9. 21. he that r. not the word of the Lord
1 Kings 18. 29. there was no voice, nor any that r.
1 Chron. 17. 17. thou hast r. me as of high degree
Psal. 106. 44. nevertheless, he r. their affliction
Prov. 1. 24. I stretched out my hand, and no man r.
Dan. 3. 12. these men, O king, have not r. thee
Luke 1. 48. he r. the low estate of his handmaid
18. 2. the judge feared not God, neither r. man
Heb. 8. 9. and I r. them not, saith the Lord

REGARDEST.

2 Sam. 19. 6. thou r. not princes nor servants
Job 30. 20. I stand up and thou r. me not
Mat. 22. 16. r. not the persons of men, Mark 12. 14.

REGARDETH.

Deut. 10. 17. mighty and terrible, that r. not persons
Job 34. 19. nor r. the rich more than the poor
39. 7. neither r. the crying of the driver
Prov. 12. 10. a righteous man r. the life of his beast
13. 18. he that r. reproof shall be honoured
15. 5. but he that r. reproof is prudent
29. 7. wicked r. not to know the cause of the poor
Eccl. 5. 8. he that is higher than the highest r.
11. 4. he that r. the clouds shall not reap
Isa. 33. 8. he hath despised cities, he r. no man
Dan. 6. 13. they said, Daniel r. not thee, O king
Mal. 2. 13. he r. not the offering any more
Rom. 14. 6. he that r. a day, r. it to the Lord

REGARDERS.

Judg. 9. † 37. come along by plain of the r. of times

REGARDING.

Job 4. 20. they perish for ever without any r. it
Phil. 2. 30. not r. his life to supply your lack

REGENERATION

Is *the change and renovation of the soul by the Spirit and grace of God,* John 3. 5, 6. *It is called the new birth, and consists in the infusion of spiritual life into the soul,* John 5. 25. *whereby it is enabled to perform spiritual actions, and live to God,* Rom. 14. 8. Tit. 3. 5. Not by works of righteousness which we have done, but according to his mercy he saved us by the washing of *regeneration,* and renewing of the Holy Ghost. Jam. 1. 18. Of his own will begat he us by the word of truth. *And our Saviour speaking to* Nicodemus, *says,* Verily I say unto thee, Except a man be born again, he cannot see the kingdom of God, *John* 3. 3, 4, 5. *And the apostle* Peter *says in like manner,* That God hath begotten us again unto a lively hope, by the resurrection of Christ from the dead, 1 *Pet.* 1. 3. that is, *he hath given us a new birth, he hath regenerated and renewed us, and thereby wrought in us such a hope or assurance of salvation, as puts life into our souls; which hope is built upon the resurrection of* Christ, *and the doctrines depending on it, as the foundation of our resurrection and future glory, since the members must partake of the same condition with the head,* John 14. 19. *It is said,* Mat. 19. 28. Ye which have followed me in the *regeneration,* when the Son of man shall sit in the throne of his glory, ye shall also sit upon thrones. Ye which have followed me in the *regeneration,* that is, *ye my apostles, who have been my attendants and assistants, while I have been by my doctrine reforming the world; while I have been* regenerating *my church, and putting it into a new state; Or, joining* regeneration *with the following words,* In the regeneration when the Son of man shall sit, &c. *that is, at the day of judgment, when there shall be new heavens and earth, and your bodies shall be raised up again in a glorious manner, and your souls made perfectly happy; then you shall not only partake of the heavenly treasure, but shall be in the highest degree of dignity there.*

Mat. 19. 28. that ye which followed me in the r.
Tit. 3. 5. he saved us by the washing of r.

REGION.

Deut. 3. 4. all the r. of Argob the kingdom of Og, 13.
1 Kings 4. 11. the son of Abinadab in all r. of Dor
24. Solomon had dominion over all the r.
Mat. 3. 5. then went to him all the r. round Jordan
4. 16. peo. saw great light, and to them which sat in the r. and shadow of death light is sprung up
Mark 1. 28. his fame spread about throughout all the r. round about Galilee, Luke 4. 14. | 7. 17.
6. 55. and ran through that whole r. round about
Luke 3. 1. Philip tetrarch of the r. of Trachonitis
Acts 13. 49. word of the Lord published thro' the r.
14. 6. they fled to the r. that lieth round about
16. 6. when they had gone thro' the r. of Galatia

REGIONS.

Acts 8. 1. they were scattered thro' the r. of Judea
2 Cor. 10. 16. to preach the gospel in r. beyond you
11. 10. no man shall stop me in the r. of Achaia
Gal. 1. 21. afterwards I came into the r. of Syria

REGISTER.

Ezra 2. 62. these sought their r. Neh. 7. 64.
Neh. 7. 5. I found a r. of the genealogy of them

REHEARSE.

Exod. 17. 14. and r. it in the ears of Joshua
Judg. 5. 11. r. the righteous acts of the Lord

REHEARSED.

1 Sam. 8. 21. he r. them in the ears of the Lord
17. 31. they r. David's words before Saul
Acts 11. 4. Peter r. the matter from the beginning
14. 27. they r. all that God had done with them

REJECT

Signifies, [1] *To slight, or despise,* Hos. 4. 6. [2] *To cast off, or forsake,* Jer. 7. 29. | 14. 19. [3] *To refuse, or deny the granting of one's suit,* Mark 6. 26. [4] *To frustrate,* Mark 7. † 9.

That which beareth thorns and briars is rejected, *Heb.* 6. 8. *As the earth, when it is painfully tilled, and plentifully watered with rain from heaven, is good for nothing but to be burnt, if instead of good fruit it bringeth forth thorns and thistles; so they that enjoy the means of grace, and yet bring forth nothing but cursed fruit, displeasing to God, deserve no further care nor culture, but must expect to be deprived of the means of grace, and exposed to utter ruin.*

Lam. 5. † 22. wilt thou utterly r. us, thou art wroth
Hos. 4. 6. I will r. thee, that thou be no priest
Mark 6. 26. for his oath's sake he would not r. her
7. 9. full well ye r. the commandment of God
Tit. 3. 10. after the first and second admonition, r.

REJECTED.

1 Sam. 8. 7. they have not r. thee, but they r. me
10. 19. ye have this day r. your G. who saved you
15. 23. because thou hast r. the word of the Lord, he hath also r. thee from being king, 26.
16. 1. seeing I have r. him from being king
2 Kings 17. 15. they r. his statutes and his covenant
20. Lord r. all the seed of Isr. and afflicted them
Isa. 53. 3. he is despised and r. of men, man of sorro.
Jer. 2. 37. for the Lord hath r. thy confidence
6. 19. r. my law || 30. because the Lord hath r. them
7. 29. Lord hath r. the generation of his wrath
8. 9. lo, they have r. the word of the Lord
14. 19. hast thou utterly r. Judah?
Lam. 5. 22. but thou hast utterly r. us, thou art wroth
Hos. 4. 6. because thou hast r. knowledge
Mat. 21. 42. stone which the builders r. is become head of the corner, Mark 12. 10. Luke 20. 17.
Mark 8. 31. he shall be r. of the elders, Luke 9. 22.
Luke 7. 30. the lawyers r. the counsel of God
17. 25. but he must first be r. of this generation
Gal. 4. 14. my temptation in my flesh ye r. not
Heb. 6. 8. that which beareth thorns and briars is r.
12. 17. when would have inherited blessing, was r.

REJECTETH.

John 12. 48. he that r. me receiveth not my words
1 Thess. 4. † 8. he that r. r. not man, but God

REIGN.

To reign, *is to rule or command as a sovereign prince,* 2 Sam. 5. 4, 5. *God is the absolute monarch of the world, he governs and disposes of all things in heaven and in earth.* Psal. 93. 1. The Lord reigneth. Sin is said to reign, *Rom.* 6. 12. *when the lusts and motions of sin are readily obeyed, as one would obey the law and command of a king: when it exercises an uncontrolled absolute power in the soul.* Grace is said to reign, *Rom.* 5. 21. *when the righteousness of* Christ *being freely imputed, his Spirit reigns in our hearts, and we are governed by the motions and impulses thereof; so that sin cannot condemn us to death, nor rule over us, as it did before grace was planted in the soul. And such* as receive abundance of grace, *are said* to reign in life by Jesus Christ, *Rom.* 5. 17. *that is, they partake of spiritual life here, whereby they conquer sin, and obtain eternal life hereafter, when they reign in glory.*

1 Kings 6. 1. in fourth year of Solomon's r. over Isr.
2 Kings 24. 12. took Jehoiachin in 8th year of his r.
1 Chron. 4. 31. their cities to the r. of David
29. 30. king David's acts with all his r. written
2 Chron. 36. 20. till the r. of the kingdom of Persia
Neh. 12. 22. the priests recorded to the r. of Darius
Esth. 2. 16. was taken to king in 7th year of his r.
Luke 3. 1. in the fifteenth year of the r. of Tiberius

REIGN, Verb.

Gen. 37. 8. breth. said, shalt thou indeed r. over us?
Exod. 15. 18. Lord shall r. for ever, Psal. 146. 10.
Lev. 26. 17. they that hate you shall r. over you
Deut. 15. 6. the L. blesseth thee, thou shalt r. over many nations, but they shall not r. over thee
Judg. 9. 2. that 70 r. over you, or that one r. over you
8. the trees said, r. thou over us, 10. 12, 14.
1 Sam. 8. 7. that I should not r. over them
9. shew the manner of the king that shall r. 11.
9. 17. Lord said, this same shall r. over my people
11. 12. who is he that said, shall Saul r. over us?
12. 12. nay, but a king shall r. over us
2 Sam. 3. 21. thou mayest r. over all that thy heart
1 Kings 1. † 5. then Adonijah said, I will r.
11. hast thou not heard that Adonijah doth r.?
1. 13. assuredly Solomon shall r. after me, 17. 30.
24. hast thou said, Adonijah shall r. after me?
2. 15. Israel set their faces on me, that I should r.
11. 37. and I will take thee, and thou shalt r.
16. 15. Zimri did r. seven days in Tirzah
2 Chr. 1. 8. and hast made me to r. in his stead
23. 3. he said, behold, the king's son shall r.
Job 34. 30. that the hypocrite r. not, lest people
Prov. 8. 15. by me kings r. and princes decree justice
Eccl. 4. 14. for out of prison he cometh to r.
Isa. 24. 23. when the Lord of hosts shall r. in Zion

Isa. 32. 1. behold, a king shall *r.* in righteousness
Jer. 22. 15. shalt thou *r.* because thou closest thyself
23. 5. a king shall *r.* prosper and execute judgment
33. 21. that David should not have a son to *r.*
Mic. 4. 7. the Lord shall *r.* over them in Zion
Mat. 2. 22. when he heard that Archelaus did *r.*
Luke 1. 33. he shall *r.* over the house of Jacob
19. 14. we will not have this man to *r.* over us
27. enemies that would not that I should *r.* over
Rom. 5. 17. shall *r.* in life by one, Jesus Christ
21. even so might grace *r.* to life by Jesus Christ
6. 12. let not sin *r.* in your mortal bodies
15. 12. he that shall rise to *r.* over the Gentiles
1 *Cor.* 4. 8. would to God ye did *r.* that we might *r.*
15. 25. for he must *r.* till he put all enemies under
2 *Tim.* 2. 12. if we suffer, we shall *r.* with him
Rev. 5. 10. and we also shall *r.* on the earth
11. 15. and he shall *r.* for ever and ever
20. 6. they shall *r.* with him a thousand years
22. 5. they shall *r.* for ever and ever
See BEGAN.

REIGNED.

Gen. 36. 31. the kings that *r.* in the land of Edom
before any king *r.* over Israel, 1 *Chron.* 1. 43.
Judg. 9. 22. when Abimelech had *r.* three years
1 *Sam.* 13. 1. Saul *r.* one year, and when he *r.* two
2 *Sam.* 2. 10. Ish-bosheth Saul's son *r.* two years
5. 4. David *r.* forty years over Judah and Israel
5. David *r.* seven years in Hebron, thirty-three in
Jerusalem, 1 *Kings* 2. 11. 1 *Chron.* 3. 4. | 29. 27.
8. 15. David *r.* over Israel, 1 *Chron.* 18. 14. | 29. 26.
10. 1. Hanun his son *r.* in his stead, 1 *Chron.* 19. 1.
16. 8. house of Saul, in whose stead thou hast *r.*
1 *Kings* 4. 21. and Solomon *r.* over all kingdoms, 11.
42. 1 *Chron.* 29. 28. 2 *Chron.* 9. 26, 30
11. 24. Rezon *r.* in Damascus ‖ 25. *r.* over Syria
43. Rehoboam *r.* 12. 17. 2 *Chron.* 9. 31. | 10. 17.
14. 31. Abijam his son *r.* 2 *Chron.* 12. 16. | 13. 2.
15. 8. and Asa *r.* in his stead, 9. 10. 2 *Chron.* 14. 1
24. Jehoshaphat his son *r.* 2 *Chron.* 17. 1. | 20. 31.
25. Nadab *r.* ‖ 28. Baasha *r.* 29. ‖ 16. 6. Elah *r.*
16. 10. Zimri *r.* in his stead ‖ 22. Omri *r.* 23.
28. Omri died, and Ahab his son *r.* in his stead
22. 40. Ahaziah, Ahab's son, *r.* in his stead, 51.
2 *Kings* 8. 24, 26. 2 *Chron.* 22. 1, 2.
22. 42. Jehoshaphat *r.* 25 years, 2 *Chron.* 20. 31.
50. Jehoram *r.* 2 *Kings* 3. 1. ‖ 8. 17. 2 *Chr.* 21. 5, 20.
2 *Kings* 3. 27. his eldest son that should have *r.*
8. 15. Hazael *r.* ‖ 10. 35. Jehoahaz *r.* ‖ 36. Jehu *r.*
12. 1. Jehoash *r.* forty years in Jerusalem
21. Amaziah *r.* 14. 1. 2 *Chron.* 24. 27. | 25. 1.
13. 24. Benhadad *r.* ‖ 14. 16. Jeroboam *r.* 23.
14. 29. Zachariah *r.* ‖ 15. 2. Azariah *r.* 2 *Chr.* 26. 3.
15. 7. and Jotham *r.* 33. 2 *Chr.* 26. 23. | 27. 1, 8.
10. Shallum *r.* 13. ‖ 14. Menahem son of Gadi *r.* 17.
22. Pekahiah his son *r.* 23. ‖ 25. Pekah *r.* 27.
30. Hoshea *r.* ‖ 38. Ahaz *r.* 16. 2. 2 *Chr.* 28. 1.
16. 20. Hezekiah *r.* 18. 2. 2 *Chr.* 28. 27. | 29. 1.
19. 37. Esarhaddon *r.* in his stead, *Isa.* 37. 38.
20. 21. Manasseh *r.* 21. 1. 2 *Chr.* 32. 33. | 33. 1.
21. 18. Amon *r.* in his stead, 19. 2 *Chr.* 33. 20, 21.
26. Josiah *r.* in his stead, 22. 1. 2 *Chron.* 34. 1.
23. 31. Jehoahaz *r.* three months, 2 *Chron.* 36. 2.
36. Jehoiakim *r.* eleven years, 2 *Chron.* 36. 5.
24. 6. Jehoiachin his son *r.* 8. 2 *Chron.* 36. 8, 9.
18. Zedekiah *r.* 2 *Chr.* 36. 11. *Jer.* 37. 1. | 52. 1.
2 *Chron.* 22. 12. and Athaliah *r.* over the land
Esth. 1. 1. Ahasuerus *r.* from India to Ethiopia
Jer. 22. 11. touch. Shallum which *r.* instead of Josiah
Rom. 5. 14. death *r.* from Adam to Moses
17. for if by one man's offence death *r.* by one
21. that as sin hath *r.* unto death, so might grace *r.*
1 *Cor.* 4. 8. ye have *r.* as kings without us
Rev. 11. 17. hast taken thy great power, and hast *r.*
20. 4. lived and *r.* with Christ a thousand years

REIGNEST.

1 *Chr.* 29. 12. thou *r.* over all, and in thy hand power

REIGNETH.

1 *Sam.* 12. 14. ye and the king that *r.* over you
2 *Sam.* 15. 10. shall say, Absalom *r.* in Hebron
1 *Kings* 1. 18. Adonijah *r.* ‖ 2 *Kings* 9. † 13. Jehu *r.*
1 *Chr.* 16. 31. the Lord *r.* *Ps.* 96. 10. | 97. 1. | 99. 1.
Ps. 47. 8. God *r.* over the heathen, God sitteth on
93. 1. Ld. *r.* he is clothed with majesty and strength
Prov. 30. 22. for a servant when he *r.* and a fool
Isa. 52. 7. that saith unto Zion, thy God *r.*
Rev. 17. 18. which *r.* over the kings of the earth
19. 6. for the Lord God omnipotent *r.*

REIGNING.

1 *Sam.* 16. 1. I have rejected him from *r.* over Isr.

REINS,

Or Kidneys. *The* Hebrews *ascribe to the* Reins *or* Kidneys, *knowledge, joy, pain, pleasure: hence it is that in Scripture it is so often said, that God searcheth the hearts and the* reins, *Psal.* 7. 9. *Jer.* 17. 10. | 20. 12. *God upbraids the* Jews *with having him in their mouths, but not in their reins.* Jer. 12. 2. Thou art near in their mouth, and far from their reins: *thou art far from their hearts and affections: they have neither fear of thee, nor love for thee, nor desire after thee, nor delight in thee: nor are they obedient to thee. The prophet being under temptation, by reason of the prosperity of wicked men, complains that his distemper had set fire to his heart, and caused a great inflammation in his reins.* Psal. 73. 21. I was pricked in my reins: *I was heartily and deeply wounded with disquieting thoughts and tormenting passions, envy, sorrow, and anger. The* Psalmist *says, that* his reins instructed him, *Psal.* 16. 7. *that is, his inward thoughts and affections, being moved by the secret influence of God's Spirit, directed him how to serve and please God, and put his whole trust and confidence in him. And* Jeremiah *says, that* the Lord had sent the daughters of his quiver into his reins, *Lam.* 3. 13. *that is, he has pierced me with his arrows, he hath exhausted his whole quiver upon me; for the* daughters of the quiver *is a poetical expression for* arrows.
Lev. 15. † 2. when any man hath a running of the
r. because of his issue he is unclean, 22. † 4.

Job 16. 13. he cleaveth my *r.* asunder, he poureth
19. 27. though my *r.* be consumed within me
Psal. 7. 9. for righteous God trieth the heart and *r.*
16. 7. my *r.* also instruct me in the night-seasons
26. 2. examine me, O Lord, try my *r.* and my heart
73. 21. and thus I was pricked in my *r.*
139. 13. for thou hast possessed my *r.*
Prov. 23. 16. yea, my *r.* shall rejoice when thy lips
Isa. 11. 5. and faithfulness the girdle of his *r.*
Jer. 11. 20. O Lord of hosts, that triest the *r.*
12. 2. thou art in their mouth, and far from their *r.*
17. 10. I try the *r.* ‖ 20. 12. that seest the *r.*
Lam. 3. 13. he caused his arrow to enter into my *r.*
Rev. 2. 23. know I am he which searcheth the *r.*

REJOICE.

Deut. 12. 7. ye shall *r.* in all that ye put your hand
unto, ye and your households, 14. 26.
16. 14. thou shalt *r.* in thy feast, thou and thy son
15. God shall bless thee, therefore thou shalt *r.*
26. 11. and thou shalt *r.* in every good thing
28. 63. so the Lord will *r.* over you, 30. 9.
32. 43. *r.* O ye nations, with his people
33. 18. he said, *r.* Zebulun, in thy going out
Judg. 9. 19. *r.* ye in Abimelech, and he in you
16. 23. the lords of the Philistines gathered to *r.*
1 *Sam.* 2. 1. because I *r.* in thy salvation
19. 5. thou sawest it, and didst *r.* why wilt thou
1 *Chr.* 16. 10. glory in his holy name, let the heart
of them *r.* that seek the Lord, *Psal.* 105. 3.
32. let the fields *r.* and all that is therein
2 *Chron.* 6. 41. and let thy saints *r.* in goodness
20. 27. Lord hath made them to *r.* *Neh.* 12. 43.
Job 3. † 6. let it not *r.* among the days of the year
20. 18. and he shall not *r.* therein
21. 12. they *r.* at the sound of the organ
Psal. 2. 11. serve the Lord with fear, *r.* with tremb.
5. 11. let all that put their trust in thee *r.*
9. 14. I will *r.* in thy salvation
13. 4. those that trouble me *r.* when I am moved
5. my heart shall *r.* in thy salvation
14. 7. Jacob shall *r.* and Israel shall be glad
20. 5. we will *r.* in thy salvation, and in the name
21. 1. and in thy salvation how greatly shall he *r.*
30. 1. and hast not made my foes to *r.* over me
33. 21. for our heart shall *r.* in him, because trusted
35. 9. my soul shall *r.* in his salvation
19. let not mine enemies wrongfully *r.* over me
24. judge me, O Lord, and let them not *r.* over me
26. let them be ashamed that *r.* at mine hurt
38. 16. hear me, lest they should *r.* over me
48. 11. let mount Zion *r.* let Judah be glad
51. 8. that the bones thou hast broken may *r.*
58. 10. the righteous shall *r.* when he seeth
60. 6. G. hath spoken in holiness, I will *r.* 108. 7.
63. 7. in the shadow of thy wings will I *r.*
11. but the king shall *r.* in God
65. 8. the outgoings of morning and evening to *r.*
12. the little hills *r.* ‖ 66. 6. there did we *r.*
68. 3. let the righteous *r.* yea, exceedingly *r.*
4. *r.* before him ‖ 71. 23. my lips shall greatly *r.*
85. 6. revive us, that thy people may *r.* in thee
86. 4. *r.* the soul of thy servant, unto thee do I lift
89. 12. Tabor and Hermon shall *r.* in thy name
16. in thy name shall they *r.* all the day
42. thou hast made all his enemies to *r.*
96. 11. let the heavens *r.* ‖ 12. trees of the wood *r.*
97. 1. Lord reigneth, let the earth *r.* isles be glad
98. 4. make a loud noise, *r.* and sing praise
104. 31. the Lord shall *r.* in his works
106. 5. that I may *r.* in the gladness of thy nation
107. 42. the righteous shall see it and *r.*
109. 28. let them be ashamed, let thy servant *r.*
119. 162. I *r.* at thy word, as one that findeth
149. 2. let Israel *r.* in him that made him
Prov. 2. 14. who *r.* to do evil, and delight in froward.
5. 18. and *r.* with the wife of thy youth
23. 15. if thine heart be wise, mine heart shall *r.*
16. yea, my reins shall *r.* when thy lips speak
24. the father of the righteous shall greatly *r.*
25. shall be glad, and she that bare thee shall *r.*
24. 17. *r.* not when thine enemy falleth
27. 9. ointment and perfume *r.* the heart
28. 12. when right. men do *r.* there is great glory
29. 2. when righteous are in authority, people *r.*
6. but the righteous doth sing and *r.*
31. 25. and she shall *r.* in time to come
Eccl. 3. 12. for a man to *r.* and do good in his life
22. than that a man should *r.* in his works, 5. 19.
4. 16. they also that come after shall not *r.* in him
11. 8. but if a man live many years, and *r.* in them
9. *r.* O young man, in thy youth, let thy heart
Isa. 8. 6. and *r.* in Rezin and Remaliah's son
9. 3. and as men *r.* when they divide the spoil
13. 3. even them that *r.* in my highness
14. 8. yea, the fir-trees *r.* at thee, and the cedars
29. *r.* not thou, whole Palestina, because the rod
23. 12. he said, thou shalt no more *r.* O virgin
24. 8. the noise of them that *r.* endeth, joy ceaseth
29. 19. poor among men shall *r.* in the Holy One
35. 1. the desert shall *r.* ‖ 2. shall blossom and *r.*
61. 7. for confusion they shall *r.* in their portion
62. 5. as a bridegroom, so shall God *r.* over thee
65. 13. my servants shall *r.* but ye shall be ashamed
19. I will *r.* in Jerusalem, and joy in my people
66. 10. *r.* ye with Jerusalem, and be glad with her
14. and when ye see this, your heart shall *r.*
Jer. 31. 13. then shall the virgin *r.* in the dance,
and I will make them *r.* from their sorrow
32. 41. I will *r.* over them to do them good
51. 39. that they may *r.* and sleep, and not awake
Lam. 2. 17. he hath caused thine enemy to *r.* over
Ezek. 7. 12. let not the buyer *r.* nor seller mourn
35. 15. as thou didst *r.* at the inheritance of Israel
Hos. 9. 1. *r.* not, O Israel, for joy, as other people
Amos 6. 13. ye which *r.* in a thing of nought
Mic. 7. 8. *r.* not against me, O mine enemy
Zeph. 3. 11. will take away them that *r.* in thy pride
17. the Lord will *r.* over thee with joy
Zech. 2. 10. sing and *r.* O daught. of Zion, lo, I come
4. † 10. with the seven eyes of the Lord shall *r.*
9. 9. *r.* greatly, O daughter of Zion, shout
10. 7. and their heart shall *r.* as through wine

Luke 1. 14. and many shall *r.* at his birth
6. 23. *r.* ye in that day, and leap for joy
10. 20. in this *r.* not, rather *r.* because your names
15. 6. *r.* with me, for I have found my sheep
9. *r.* with me, for I have found the piece I lost
19. 37. whole multitude of the disciples began to *r.*
John 4. 36. he that soweth and that reapeth may *r.*
5. 35. ye were willing for a season to *r.* in his light
14. 28. if ye loved me, ye would *r.* because I said
16. 20. ye shall weep, but the world shall *r.*
22. but I will see you, and your heart shall *r.*
Acts 2. 26. therefore did my heart *r.* my tongue glad
Rom. 5. 2. and *r.* in hope of the glory of God
12. 15. *r.* with them that do *r.* and weep with them
15. 10. he saith, *r.* ye Gentiles, with his people
1 *Cor.* 7. 30. they that *r.* as tho' they rejoiced not
12. 26. is one honoured, all the members *r.* with it
2 *Cor.* 2. 3. lest I have sorrow of whom I ought to *r.*
7. 9. now I *r.* not that ye were made sorry
16. I *r.* that I have confidence in you in all things
Gal. 4. 27. *r.* thou barren that bearest not, break forth
Phil. 1. 18. and I therein do *r.* yea, and will *r.*
2. 16. that I may *r.* in the day of Christ
17. yea, if I be offered, I joy and *r.* with you all
18. for the same cause do ye joy and *r.* with me
28. that when ye see him again, ye may *r.*
3. 3. we worship God, and *r.* in Christ Jesus
Col. 1. 24. who now *r.* in my sufferings for you
1 *Thess.* 5. 16. *r.* evermore, pray without ceasing
Jam. 1. 9. let the brother of low degree *r.*
4. 16. but now ye *r.* in your boastings
1 *Pet.* 1. 6. wherein ye greatly *r.* though now ye are
8. *r.* with joy unspeakable and full of glory
4. 13. but *r.* in as much as ye are partakers
Rev. 11. 10. they that dwell on earth sh. *r.* over them
12. 12. therefore *r.* ye heavens, and ye that dwell
18. 20. *r.* over her, thou heaven, and ye apostles
See GLAD.

REJOICE *before the Lord.*

Lev. 23. 40. ye shall *r.* *before the Lord* seven days
Deut. 12. 12. ye shall *r.* *before the Lord* your God
18. shalt *r.* *bef. the Lord* thy God, 16. 11. | 27. 7.

REJOICE *in the Lord.*

Psal. 33. 1. *r. in the Lord,* O ye righteous, 97. 12.
Isa. 41. 16. *r. in the Lord,* glory in the Holy One
61. 10. I will greatly *r. in the Lord,* and be joyful
Joel 2. 23. ye children of Zion, *r. in the Lord*
Hab. 3. 18. yet I will *r. in the Lord,* I will joy
Zech. 10. 7. their heart shall *r. in the Lord*
Phil. 3. 1. finally, my brethren, *r. in the Lord*
4. 4. *r. in the Lord* alway, and again, I say, rejoice

REJOICED.

Exod. 18. 9. Jethro *r.* for all goodness done to Isr.
Deut. 28. 63. as the L. *r.* over you to do you good
30. 9. rejoice for good, as he *r.* over thy fathers
Judg. 19. 3. the father of the damsel saw him, he *r.*
1 *Sam.* 6. 13. the men of Beth-shemesh *r.* to see it
11. 15. Saul and all the men of Israel *r.* greatly
1 *Kings* 1. 40. the people *r.* so that the earth rent
5. 7. Hiram *r.* greatly at Solomon's words
2 *Kings* 11. 14. the people *r.* and blew with trumpets
when Joash was made king, 20. 2 *Chr.* 23. 13, 21.
1 *Chron.* 29. 9. the people *r.* and David also *r.*
2 *Chron.* 15. 15. and all Judah *r.* at the oath
24. 10. all the princes and all the people *r.*
29. 36. and Hezekiah *r.* and all the people
30. 25. the strangers out of Israel and Judah *r.*
Neh. 12. 43. all that day they offered great sacrifices and *r.* the wives also, and the children *r.*
44. for Judah *r.* for the priests and Levites
Esth. 8. 15. the city of Shushan *r.* and was glad
Job 31. 25. if I *r.* because my wealth was great
29. if I *r.* at the destruction of him that hated me
Psal. 35. 15. but in mine adversity they *r.*
97. 8. Sion was glad, and the daughters of Judah *r.*
119. 14. I have *r.* in the way of thy testimonies
Eccl. 2. 10. for my heart *r.* in all my labour
Jer. 15. 17. I *r.* not in the assembly of mockers
50. 11. ye *r.* O destroyers of mine heritage
Ezek. 25. 6. the Ammonites *r.* against Israel
Hos. 10. 5. the priests that *r.* on it shall mourn
Obad. 12. nor shouldest thou have *r.* over Judah
Jonah 4. † 6. Jonah *r.* with great joy for the gourd
Mat. 2. 10. when they saw the star, they *r.* with joy
Luke 1. 47. my spirit hath *r.* in God my Saviour
58. Elisabeth's friends and cousins *r.* with her
10. 21. in that hour Jesus *r.* in spirit, and said
13. 17. the people *r.* for the things that were done
John 8. 56. your father Abraham *r.* to see my day
Acts 7. 41. *r.* in the works of their own hands
15. 31. when had read, they *r.* for the consolation
16. 34. the jailer *r.* believing in God with his house
1 *Cor.* 7. 30. they that rejoice, as though they *r.* not
2 *Cor.* 7. 7. when he told us, so that I *r.* the more
Phil. 4. 10. but I *r.* in the Lord greatly
2 *John* 4. I *r.* greatly that I found, 3 *John* 3.

REJOICETH.

1 *Sam.* 2. 1. Hannah said, my heart *r.* in the Lord
Job 39. 21. the horse *r.* in his strength
41. † 22. and sorrow *r.* before leviathan
Psal. 16. 9. my heart is glad, and my glory *r.*
19. 5. which *r.* as a strong man to run a race
28. 7. therefore my heart greatly *r.* I will praise
Prov. 11. 10. when goeth well with righteous, city *r.*
13. 9. the light of the righteous *r.* but the lamp
15. 30. the light of the eyes *r.* the heart
29. 3. whoso loveth wisdom *r.* his father
Isa. 5. 14. and he that *r.* shall descend into it
62. 5. as the bridegroom *r.* over the bride
64. 5. thou meetest him that *r.* and worketh right
Ezek. 35. 14. when the whole earth *r.* I will make
Mat. 18. 13. I say to you, he *r.* more of that sheep
John 3. 29. the friend of the bridegroom *r.* greatly
1 *Cor.* 13. 6. *r.* not in iniquity, but *r.* in truth
Jam. 2. 13. and mercy *r.* against judgment

REJOICEST.

Jer. 11. 15. when thou doest evil, then thou *r.*

REJOICING.

1 *Kings* 1. 45. and they are come up from thence
2 *Chron.* 23. 18. to offer burnt-offerings with *r.*
Job 8. 21. till he fill thy lips with *r.*
Psal. 19. 8. his statutes are right, *r.* the heart

Ps. 45. 15. with *r.* shall be brought to king's palace
107. 22. let them declare his works with *r.*
118.15.the voice of *r.* is in the tabernacle of righteous
119. 111. for they are the *r.* of my heart
126. 6. he shall doubtless come again with *r.*
Prov. 8. 30. I was his delight, *r.* always before him
31. *r.* in the habitable part of his earth
Isa. 65. 18. for, behold, I create Jerusalem a *r.*
Jer. 15. 16. thy word was to me the *r.* of my heart
Hab. 3. 14. their *r.* was to devour the poor secretly
Zeph. 2. 15. this is the *r.* city that said, I am
Luke 15. 5. he layeth it on his shoulders *r.*
Acts 5. 41.*r.* that they were counted worthy to suffer
8. 39. and the eunuch went on his way *r.*
Rom. 12. 12. *r.* in hope, patient in tribulation
1 *Cor.* 15. 31. I protest by your *r.* which I have
2 *Cor.* 1. 12. for our *r.* is this, testimony of conscience
14. that we are your *r.* even as ye also are ours
6.10.as sorrowful, yet always *r.* as poor, yet making
Gal. 6. 4. then shall he have *r.* in himself
Phil. 1. 26. that your *r.* may be more abundant
1 *Thess.* 2. 19. for what is our crown of *r.* are not ye
Heb. 3. 6. the *r.* of the hope firm unto the end
Jam. 4. 16. in your boastings, all such *r.* is evil

RELEASE

Signifies, *a* remission, *or* discharge: *It is called in Hebrew,* Shemittah, *in Greek,* αφεσις; *that is,* forgiveness, *or* remission; *being the same word which in the New Testament is used for the pardon of sin,* Mat. 26. 28. Mark 1. 4. *of which this release of debts was a shadow.* Deut. 15. 2. This is the manner of the release: Every creditor that lendeth aught shall release it; *that is, not absolutely and finally forgive it, but forbear it for that year.*

Deut. 15. 1. at the end of seven years make a *r.*
2. this is the manner of the *r.* it is the Lord's *r.*
9. the seventh year, the year of *r.* is at hand
31. 10. in the solemnity of the year of *r.* in feast
Esth. 2. 18. he made a *r.* to provinces and gave gifts

RELEASE, *Verb.*

Deut. 15. 2. every creditor that lendeth shall *r.* it
3. what is thine with thy brother, hand shall *r.*
Mat. 27. 15. at that feast governor was wont to *r.* a prisoner whom they would, *Luke* 23. 17. *John* 18. 39.
17. Pilate said unto them, whom will ye that I *r.* unto you? 21. *Mark* 15. 9. *John* 18. 39.
Mark 15. 11. the chief priests moved the people, that he should rather *r.* Barabbas, *Luke* 23. 18.
Luke 23.16.I will therefore chastise him, and *r.* him
20. Pilate therefore, willing to *r.* Jesus, spake again
John 19. 10. and that I have power to *r.* thee?
12. from thenceforth Pilate sought to *r.* him

RELEASED.

Mat. 27. 26. then *r.* he Barabbas to them, and scourged Jesus, *Mark* 15. 15. *Luke* 23. 25.
Mark 15. 6. now at the feast he *r.* one prisoner

RELY.

2 *Chron.* 16. 8. because thou didst *r.* on the Lord

RELIED.

2 *Chr.* 13. 18. because they *r.* on the Lord God
16. 7. thou hast *r.* on Syria, and hast not *r.* on Lord

RELIEF.

Acts 11. 29.disciples determined to send *r.* to breth.

RELIEVE.

Lev. 25. 35. if brother poor, then thou shalt *r.* him
Isa. 1. 17. *r.* the oppressed, † righten the oppressed
Lam. 1. 11. given pleasant things for meat to *r.* soul
16. the comforter that should *r.* is far from me
19. while they sought meat to *r.* their souls
1 *Tim.* 5. 16. if any have widows, let them *r.* them, that it may *r.* them that are widows indeed

RELIEVED.

1 *Tim.* 5. 10. if she have *r.* the afflicted, if followed

RELIEVETH.

Psal. 146. 9. he *r.* the fatherless and the widow

RELIGION

Is taken, [1] *For a profession, or the external and ceremonial worship of the Jews, as it was corrupted by the traditions of the Pharisees,* Acts 26. 5. [2] *For true godliness, or real religion, even that inward piety of the heart, whereby God is truly acknowledged, feared, and loved, and which inclines persons to perform all duties of love or charity towards those that are in distress, especially for religion,* Jam. 1. 27. [3] *For superstition.* Col. 2. 18. Let no man beguile you of your reward, in worshipping of angels; *in the* Greek *it is,* εν θρησκεια των αγγελων, in the religion of angels. *Do not imitate those who affect to humble themselves before the angels, and to pay them a superstitious worship.*

Acts 26. 5. after the straitest sect of our *r.* I lived
Gal. 1. 13. ye heard my conversation in the Jews' *r.*
14. profited in the Jews' *r.* above many my equals
Jam. 1. 26. deceiveth his heart, this man's *r.* is vain
27. pure *r.* and undefiled before God, is this

RELIGIOUS.

Acts 13. 43. and *r.* proselytes followed Paul
Jam. 1. 26. if any among you seem to be *r.*

REMAIN.

Gen. 38. 11. *r.* a widow at thy father's house till
Exod. 8. 9. that the frogs *r.* in the river only, 11.
12. 10. let nothing of it *r.* until the morning
23. 18. nor fat of my sacrifice *r.* till morning
29. 34. if the flesh of consecrations *r.* burn it
Lev. 19. 6. if aught *r.* till third day, shall be burnt
25. 28. then that which is sold shall *r.* in the hand
27. 18. reckon, according to the years that *r.*
Num. 33. 55. those which ye let *r.* shall be pricks
Deut. 2. 34. we destroyed all, we left none to *r.*
16. 4. nor shall any of the flesh *r.* till morning
19. 20. those which *r.* shall hear and fear
21. 13. she shall *r.* in thine house, and bewail
23. his body shall not *r.* all night on the tree
Josh. 1. 14. your little ones and cattle shall *r.*
2. 11. neither did there *r.* any more courage
8. 22. so that they let none of them *r.* 10. 28, 30.
23. 4. I divided to you by lot these nations that *r.*
7. that ye come not among these nations that *r.*
12. else if ye cleave to these nations that *r.*

Judg. 5. 17. and why did Dan *r.* in ships?
21. 7. how shall do for wives for them that *r.* 16.
1 *Sam.* 20. 19. and thou shalt *r.* by the stone Ezel
1 *Kings* 11. 16. six months did Joab *r.* in Edom
18. 22. I, even I, only *r.* a prophet of the Lord
2 *Kings* 7. 13. let some take five of the horses that *r.*
Ezra 9. 15. for we *r.* yet escaped, as it is this day
Job 21. 32. yet shall he *r.* in the tomb
27. 15. those that *r.* of him shall be buried in death
37. 8. the beasts go to dens and *r.* in their places
Psal. 55. 7. then would I *r.* in the wilderness
Prov. 2. 21. and the perfect shall *r.* in the land
21. 16. shall *r.* in the congregation of the dead
Isa. 10. 32. as yet shall he *r.* at Nob that day
32. 16. righteousness shall *r.* in the fruitful field
65. 4. which *r.* among the graves, and lodge in
66. 22. as the new heavens and new earth shall *r.* before me, so shall your seed and your name *r.*
Jer. 8. 3. residue of them that *r.* of this evil family
17. 25. and this city shall *r.* for ever
24. 8. I will give the residue of Jerusalem that *r.*
27. 11. those will I let *r.* still in their own land
19. saith Lord, concerning the vessels that *r.* 21.
30. 18. the palace shall *r.* after the manner thereof
38. 4. he weakeneth the hands of the men that *r.*
42. 17. none of them shall *r.* 44. 14. | 51. 62.
44. 7. why commit ye evil, to leave you none to *r.*
Ezek. 7. 11. violence is risen up, none of them shall *r.*
17. 21. and they that *r.* shall be scattered
31. 13. on his ruin shall the fowls of heaven *r.*
32. 4. I will cause the fowls to *r.* upon Pharaoh
39. 14. shall sever out men to bury those that *r.* of
Amos 6. 9. if there *r.* ten men in one house
Obad. 14. nor delivered those that *r.* in distress
Zech. 5. 4. flying roll shall *r.* in midst of his house
12. 14. all the families that *r.* shall mourn apart
Luke 10. 7. in the same house *r.* eating such things
John 6. 12. he said, gather up the fragments that *r.*
15. 11. I have spoken, that my joy might *r.* in you
16. I have chosen you, that your fruit should *r.*
19. 31. that the bodies should not *r.* on the cross
1 *Cor.* 7. 11. if she depart, let her *r.* unmarried
15. 6. of whom the greater part *r.* to this present
1 *Thess.* 4. 15. we alive *r.* till coming of the Lord
17. we which are alive and *r.* shall be caught up
Heb. 12. 27. those things that cannot be shaken may *r.*
1 *John* 2. 24. if that which ye have heard *r.* in you
Rev. 3. 2. strengthen the things which *r.* ready to die

REMAINDER.

Exod. 26. † 13. a cubit on the other side in the *r.*
29. 34. then thou shalt burn the *r.* with fire
Lev. 6. 16. the *r.* shall Aaron and his sons eat
7. 16. on the morrow also the *r.* shall be eaten
17. but the *r.* on the third day shall be burnt
18. † 6. none approach to any that is *r.* of his flesh
2 *Sam.* 14. 7. shall not leave neither name nor *r.*
2 *Chron.* 36. † 20. *r.* from sword carried to Babylon
Psal. 76. 10. the *r.* of wrath shalt thou restrain
Jer. 51. † 35. the violence done to me and my *r.*

REMAINED.

Gen. 7. 23. Noah only *r.* alive, and they in the ark
14. 10. and they that *r.* fled to the mountain
Exod. 8. 31. he removed the flies, there *r.* not one
10. 15. there *r.* not any green thing in the trees
19. there *r.* not one locust in all coasts of Egypt
14. 28. there *r.* not so much as one chariot
Num. 11. 26. but there *r.* two of the men in camp
35. 28. because he should have *r.* in city of refuge
36. 12. their inheritance *r.* in house of their father
Deut. 3. 11. Og, king of Bashan, *r.* of the giants
4. 25. when thou shalt have *r.* long in the land
Josh. 10. 20. the rest who *r.* entered into fenced cities
11. 22. in Gath and Ashdod there *r.* Anakims
13. 12. who *r.* of the remnant of the giants
18. 2. and there *r.* of Israel seven tribes
21. 20. the Levites which *r.* of the Kohathites, 26.
Judg. 7. 3. there *r.* with Gideon but 10,000 men
1 *Sam.* 11. 11. they which *r.* were scattered so that
23. 14. David *r.* in a mountain in the wilderness
24. 3. David and his men *r.* in the sides of the cave
2 *Sam.* 13. 20. Tamar *r.* desolate in Absalom's house
1 *Kings* 22. 46. the Sodomites which *r.* he took out of
2 *Kings* 10. 11. Jehu slew all that *r.* of Ahab's, 17.
13. 6. and there *r.* the grove also in Samaria
25. 22. people that *r.* he set Gedaliah over them
1 *Chron.* 13. 14. the ark *r.* in the family of Obed-edom
Eccl. 2. 9. also my wisdom *r.* with me
Jer. 34. 7. for these defenced cities *r.* of Judah
37. 10. there *r.* but wounded men among them
16. Jeremiah had *r.* many days in the dungeon
21. he *r.* in the court of the prison, 38. 13.
39. 9. Nebuzar-adan carried away captive the remnant of the people that *r.* in the city, 52. 15.
41. 10. Ishmael carried away captive them that *r.*
48. 11. therefore his taste *r.* in him, his scent
51. 30. the mighty men have *r.* in their holds
Lam. 2. 22. in the day of the Lord's anger none *r.*
Ezek. 3. 15. I *r.* there astonished seven days
Dan. 10. 8. there *r.* no strength in me, 17.
13. and I *r.* there with the kings of Persia
Mat. 11. 23. had been done in Sod. it would have *r.*
14. 20. they took up the fragments that *r.* twelve baskets full, *Luke* 9. 17. *John* 6. 13.
Luke 1. 22. he beckoned to them, and *r.* speechless
Acts 5. 4. while it *r.* was it not thine own?
27. 41. the forepart stuck fast, and *r.* immoveable

REMAINEST.

Lam. 5. 19. thou, O Lord, *r.* for ever, *Heb.* 1. 11.

REMAINETH.

Gen. 8. 22. while earth *r.* seed-time shall not cease
Exod. 10. 5. that which *r.* to you from the hail
12. 10. that which *r.* until morning ye shall burn
16. 23. that which *r.* over lay it up for you
Lev. 8. 32. that *r.* of the flesh and bread shall burn
10. 12. take the meat offering that *r.* and eat it
16. 16. so shall he do for the tabernacle that *r.*
Num. 24. 19. and he shall destroy him that *r.*
Josh. 8. 29. a great heap of stones that *r.* to this day
13. 1. there *r.* yet much land to be possessed
2. this is the land that yet *r.* all Geshuri
Judg. 5. 13. he made him that *r.* have dominion
1 *Sam.* 6. 18. Abel, which stone *r.* unto this day

1 *Sam.* 16. 11. Jesse said, there *r.* yet the youngest
2 *Kings* 19. † 30. the escaping of Judah that *r.* shall again take root downward, *Isa.* 37. † 31.
1 *Chron.* 17. 1. the ark of the Ld. *r.* under curtains
Job 19. 4. and be it, my error *r.* with myself
21. 34. in your answers there *r.* falsehood
41. 22. in his neck *r.* strength, sorrow turned to joy
Isa. 4. 3. he that *r.* in Jerusalem shall be called holy
Jer. 38. 2. he that *r.* in this city shall die by sword
47. 4. to cut off from Tyrus every helper that *r.*
Ezek. 6. 12. he that *r.* and is besieged shall die
Hag. 2. 5. so my Spirit *r.* among you, fear ye not
Zech. 9. 7. he that *r.* even he shall be for our God
John 9. 41. ye say, we see; therefore your sin *r.*
1 *Cor.* 7. 29. it *r.* that they that have wives be as
2 *Cor.* 3. 11. much more that which *r.* is glorious
14. to this day *r.* the same veil untaken away
9. 9. it is written, his righteousness *r.* for ever
Heb. 4. 6. seeing it *r.* that some must enter therein
9. there *r.* therefore a rest to the people of God
10. 26. there *r.* no more sacrifice for sins
1 *John* 3. 9. doth not sin, for his seed *r.* in him

REMAINING.

Num. 9. 22. the cloud tarried, *r.* on the tabernacle
Deut. 3. 3. smote him, till none was left *r.* to Og
Josh. 10. 33. he left none *r.* 37, 39, 40. | 11. 8.
21. 40. which were *r.* of the families of the Levites
2 *Sam.* 21. 5. we should be destroyed from *r.* in coasts
2 *Kings* 10. 11. Jehu slew all, he left Ahab none *r.*
1 *Chron.* 9. 33. who *r.* in the chambers were free
Job 18. 19. nor shall have any *r.* in his dwelling
Jer. 30. † 23. a *r.* whirlwind shall fall on the wicked
Obad. 18. shall not be any *r.* of the house of Esau
John 1. 33. on whom thou shalt see the Spirit *r.*

REMEDY.

2 *Chron.* 36. 16. till wrath arose, till there was no *r.*
Prov. 6. 15. suddenly shall he be broken without *r.*
29. 1. shall suddenly be destroyed, and without *r.*

REMEMBER,

When referred to God, signifies, *To care for one, to pity, succour, and save him; or, when, after some delays and suspensions of his favour, he returns and shews kindness to him:* God remembered Noah; *he shewed himself careful of* Noah, *and the creatures that were with him in the ark, by providing for their deliverance from the deluge, according to his promise. He remembered* Abraham, Gen. 19. 29. *God remembered and heard* Abraham's *prayer in behalf of* Lot, *and sent him out of the overthrow.* God says, I will remember their sins no more, *Jer.* 31. 34. *that is, I will pardon them; I will blot them out of the book of my remembrance. When applied to men, it* signifies, [1] *Either to call to mind something past, or to keep in mind something for the time to come,* Exod. 20. 8. Luke 17. 32. [2] *To muse, or meditate upon,* Psal. 63. 6. [3] *To put trust and confidence in,* Psal. 20. 7. [4] *To consider,* Mat. 16. 9. [5] *To celebrate and extol,* 1 Chron. 16. 12. [6] *To make a collection or contribution for,* Gal. 2. 10. [7] *To call one to an account, to censure, or punish,* 3 John 10. [8] *To esteem,* Eccl. 9. 15.

Gen. 40. 23. yet did not the butler *r.* Joseph
Exod. 13. 3. Moses said to the people, *r.* this day
20. 8. *r.* the sabbath-day to keep it holy
32. 13. *r.* Abraham, Isaac, and Israel, *Deut.* 9. 27.
Num. 11. 5. we *r.* the fish which we did eat in Egypt
15. 39. *r.* all the commandments of the Lord
40. that ye may *r.* and do my commandments
Deut. 5. 15. and *r.* that thou wast a servant in the land of Egypt, 15. 15. | 16. 12. | 24. 18, 22.
7. 18. thou shalt *r.* what the Lord did to Pharaoh
8. 2. thou shalt *r.* all the way the Lord led thee
18. *r.* the Lord giveth thee power to get wealth
9. 7. *r.* how thou provokedst the Lord thy God
15. 15. *r.* that thou wast a bond-man in Egypt, and the Lord redeemed thee, 16. 12. | 24. 18, 22.
16. 3. *r.* the day when thou camest out of Egypt
24. 9. *r.* what the Lord thy God did to Miriam
25. 17. *r.* what Amalek did to thee by the way
32. 7. *r.* the days of old, consid. the years of many
Josh. 1. 13. *r.* word which Moses commanded you
Judg. 9. 2. *r.* also that I am your bone and flesh
1 *Sam.* 25. 31. Abigail said, then *r.* thine handmaid
2 *Sam.* 14. 11. let the king *r.* the Lord thy God
19. 19. neither do thou *r.* what thy servant did
2 *Kings* 9. 25. *r.* when I and thou rode after Ahab
20. 3. *r.* how I have walked before thee, *Isa.* 38. 3.
1 *Chr.* 16. 12. *r.* his marvellous works, *Psal.* 105. 5.
2 *Chron.* 6. 42. *r.* the mercies of David thy servant
Neh. 1. 8. *r.* the word thou commandedst Moses
4. 14. *r.* the Lord, which is great and terrible
13. 29. *r.* them that have defiled the priesthood
Job 4. 7. *r.* who ever perished, being innocent?
7. 7. O *r.* my life is wind, eye shall no more see good
10. 9. *r.* that thou hast made me as the clay
11. 16. and *r.* it as waters that pass away
36. 24. *r.* that thou magnify his work
41. 8. lay thine hand upon him, *r.* the battle
Psal. 20. 3. *r.* all thy offerings and accept sacrifice
7. but we will *r.* the name of the Lord our God
22. 27. all ends of world shall *r.* and turn to Lord
25. 6. *r.* thy mercies, they have been ever of old
7. *r.* not the sins of my youth, *r.* thou me
74. 2. *r.* thy congregat. which thou hast purchased
18. *r.* this, that the enemy hath reproached
22. *r.* how the foolish man reproacheth thee daily
79. 8. O *r.* not against us former iniquities
89. 47. *r.* how short my time is, why hast thou made
50. *r.* Lord the reproach of thy servants
103. 18. and to those that *r.* his commandments
119. 49. *r.* the word unto thy servant, upon which
132. 1. Lord, *r.* David, and all his afflictions
137. 7. *r.* O Lord, the children of Edom, who said
Prov. 31. 7. let him drink, and *r.* his misery no more
Eccl. 5. 20. he shall not much *r.* the days of his life
11. 8. yet let him *r.* the days of darkness
12. 1. *r.* now thy Creator in the days of thy youth
Cant. 1. 4. we will *r.* thy love more than wine
Isa. 43. 18. *r.* ye not the former things? 46. 9.
25. for mine own sake I will not *r.* thy sins

Isa. 44. 21. *r.* these, O Jacob and Isr. thou my serv
46. 8. *r.* this, and shew yourselves men
47. 7. neither didst *r.* the latter end of it
54. 4. shalt not *r.* the reproach of thy widowhood
64. 5. thou meetest those that *r.* thee in thy ways
9. be not wroth, neither *r.* iniquity for ever
Jer. 3. 16. neither shall they *r.* it, neither visit it
14. 10. he will now *r.* their iniquity, and visit
21. *r.* break not thy covenant with us
17. 2. whilst their children *r.* their altars and groves
18. 20. *r.* that I stood before thee to speak good
31. 20. since I spake I do earnestly *r.* him still
44. 21. and the people, did not the Lord *r.* them?
51. 50. ye that have escaped, *r.* the Lord afar off
Lam. 3. † 19. *r.* mine affliction and my misery
5. 1. *r.* O Lord, what is come upon us, consider
Ezek. 16. 61. then shalt *r.* thy ways, 20. 43. | 36. 31.
63. that thou mayest *r.* and be confounded
23. 27. so that thou shalt not *r.* Egypt any more
Hos. 8. 13. now will he *r.* their iniquity, and visit
9. 9. therefore he will *r.* iniquity, and visit their sins
Mic. 6. 5. O my people, *r.* now what Balak consult.
Hab. 3. 2. O Ld. revive thy work, in wrath *r.* mercy
Mal. 4. 4. *r.* the law of Moses my servant
Mat. 16. 9. neither *r.* the five loaves, *Mark* 8. 18.
27. 63. sir, we *r.* that deceiver said, I will rise again
Luke 1. 72. the mercy, and to *r.* his holy covenant
16. 25. *r.* that thou in thy lifetime receivedst
17. 32. *r.* Lot's wife || 24. 6. *r.* how he spake to you
John 15. 20. *r.* the word that I said unto you
16. 4. that when the time shall come, ye may *r.*
Acts 20. 31. *r.* that by the space of three years
35. *r.* the words of the Lord Jesus, how he said
Gal. 2. 10. they would that we should *r.* the poor
Eph. 2. 11. *r.* that ye being in time past Gentiles
Col. 4. 18. *r.* my bonds, grace be with you, amen
1 *Thess.* 2. 9. for ye *r.* brethr. our labour and travail
2 *Thess.* 2. 5. *r.* ye not that I told you these things?
2 *Tim.* 2. 8. *r.* that Jes. Christ was raised from dead
Heb. 13. 3. *r.* them that are in bonds, as bound
7. *r.* them which have the rule over you
Jude 17. *r.* the words spoken of the apostles of Jes.
Rev. 2. 5. *r.* from whence thou art fallen, and rep.
3. 3. *r.* how thou hast received, and hold fast

I REMEMBER.

Gen. 41. 9. saying, I do *r.* my faults this day
1 *Sam.* 15. 2. *I r.* that which Amalek did to Israel
Job 21. 6. even when *I r.* I am afraid, and trembling
Psal. 42. 4. when *I r.* these, I pour out my soul
63. 6. when *I r.* thee upon my bed, and meditate
137. 6. if *I* do not *r.* thee, let my tongue cleave
143. 5. *I r.* the days of old, I muse on thy works.
Jer. 2. 2. *I r.* thee the kindness of thy youth
Hos. 7. 2. consider not that I *r.* all their wickedness

I will REMEMBER.

Gen. 9. 15. *I will r.* my covenant between me, 16.
Lev. 26. 42. *I will r.* my covenant with Abraham
45. *I will* for their sakes *r.* the covenant
Psal. 42. 6. therefore *will I r.* thee from Jordan
77. 10. but *I will r.* the years of the right hand
11. *I will r.* the works, *I w. r.* thy wonders of old
Jer. 31. 34. and *I will r.* their sin no more, I will
forgive their iniquity, *Heb.* 8. 12. | 10. 17.
Ezek. 16. 60. *I will r.* my covenant with thee
3 *John* 10. *I will r.* his deeds which he doeth

REMEMBER *me.*

Gen. 40. † 14. *r. me* with thee, and shew kindness
Judg. 16. 28. *r. me*, that I may be at once avenged
1 *Sam.* 1. 11. look on thine handmaid, and *r. me*
Neh. 13. 14. *r. me*, O God, concerning this, 22, 31.
Job 14. 13. appoint me a set time, and *r. me*
Psal. 25. 7. *r. me*, for thy goodness' sake, O Lord
106. 4. *r. me* with the favour that thou bearest
Jer. 15. 15. O Lord, thou knowest, *r. me*, and visit
Ezek. 6. 9. and they that escape of you shall *r. me*
Zech. 10. 9. and they shall *r. me* in far countries
Luke 23. 42. L. *r. me* when thou comest to thy kingd.
1 *Cor.* 11. 2. that ye *r. me* in all things, and keep

REMEMBRANCE.

Exod. 17. 14. I will put out the *r.* of Amalek
Num. 5. 15. an offering, bringing iniquity to *r.*
Deut. 25. 19. thou shalt blot out the *r.* of Amalek
32. 26. I said, I would make the *r.* of them to cease
2 *Sam.* 18. 18. I have no son to keep my name in *r.*
1 *Kings* 17. 18. art thou come to call my sin to *r.*?
Job 18. 17. his *r.* shall perish from the earth
Psal. 6. 5. for in death there is no *r.* of thee
30. 4. give thanks at *r.* of his holiness, 97. 12.
34. 16. to cut off the *r.* of them from the earth
38. 1. a psalm of David, to bring to *r.* 70. 1.
77. 6. I call to *r.* my song in the night
83. 4. that the name of Israel be no more in *r.*
102. 12. and thy *r.* unto all generations
112. 6. the righteous shall be in everlasting *r.*
Eccl. 1. 11. there is no *r.* of former things
2. 16. there is no *r.* of the wise more than the fool
Isa. 26. 8. the desire of our soul is to the *r.* of thee
43. 26. put me in *r.* let us plead together
57. 8. behind the doors hast thou set up thy *r.*
Lam. 3. 20. my soul hath them still in *r.* is humbled
Ezek. 21. 23. but he will call to *r.* the iniquity
24. because, I say, that ye are come to *r.*
23. 19. calling to *r.* the days of her youth, 21.
29. 16. which bringeth their iniquity to *r.*
Mal. 3. 16. a book of *r.* was written before him
Mark 11. 21. Peter calling to *r.* saith to him
Luke 1. 54. he hath holpen Israel in *r.* of his mercy
22. 19. this do in *r.* of me, 1 *Cor.* 11. 24.
John 14. 26. he shall bring all things to your *r.*
Acts 10. 31. thine alms are had in *r.* before God
1 *Cor.* 4. 17. Timothy, who shall bring you into *r.*
11. 25. this do ye, as oft as ye drink it, in *r.* of me
Phil. 1. 3. I thank my God upon every *r.* of you
1 *Thess.* 3. 6. that ye have good *r.* of us always
1 *Tim.* 4. 6. if thou put the brethren in *r.*
2 *Tim.* 1. 3. that I have *r.* of thee in my prayers
5. when I call to *r.* the unfeigned faith in thee
6. wherefore I put thee in *r.* that thou stir up
2. 14. of these things put them in *r.* charging
Heb. 10. 3. in those sacrifices there is a *r.* of sins
32. but call to *r.* the former days in which
2 *Pet.* 1. 12. to put you always in *r.* *Jude* 5.
2 *Pet.* 1. 13. I think it meet to stir you up put. you in *r.*
15. be able to have these things always in *r.*
3. 1. I stir up your pure minds by way of *r.*
Rev. 16. 19. great Babylon came in *r.* before God

REMEMBRANCER.

2 *Sam.* 8. † 16. Jehoshaphat the son of Ahilud was
r. 20. † 24. 1 *Kings* 4. † 3. 1 *Chron.* 18. † 15.

REMEMBRANCES.

Job 13. 12. your *r.* are like to ashes, bodies to bodies

REMEMBERED.

Gen. 8. 1. God *r.* Noah || 19. 29. God *r.* Abraham
30. 22. God *r.* Rachel || 42. 9. Joseph *r.* dreams
Exod. 2. 24. God *r.* his covenant with Abraham, 6. 5.
Num. 10. 9. ye shall be *r.* before the Lord your God
Judg. 8. 34. children of Israel *r.* not the Lord
1 *Sam.* 1. 19. and the Lord *r.* Hannah
2 *Chr.* 24. 22. thus Joash *r.* not the kindness
Esth. 2. 1. Ahasuerus *r.* Vashti, what she had done
9. 28. that these days of Purim should be *r.*
Job 24. 20. the sinner shall be no more *r.*
Ps. 45. 17. I will make thy name to be *r.* in all gen.
77. 3. I *r.* God and was troubled, I complained
78. 35. they *r.* that God was their Saviour
39. for he *r.* that they were but flesh, a wind
42. they *r.* not his hand, when he delivered them
98. 3. he *r.* his mercy toward the house of Israel
105. 8. he hath *r.* his covenant for ever
42. for he *r.* his holy promise, and Abraham
106. 7. they *r.* not the multitude of thy mercies
45. he *r.* for them his covenant, and repented
109. 14. let the iniquity of his fathers be *r.*
16. because that he *r.* not to shew mercy
111. 4. hath made his wonderful works to be *r.*
119. 52. I *r.* thy judgments of old, O Lord
55. I have *r.* thy name, O Lord, in the night
136. 23. who *r.* us in our low estate, his mercy
137. 1. we sat down, yea, we wept, when we *r.* Zion
Eccl. 9. 15. yet no man *r.* that same poor man
Isa. 23. 16. sing many songs, that thou mayest be *r.*
57. 11. thou hast not *r.* me, nor laid to thy heart
63. 11. then he *r.* the days of old, Moses, and peo.
65. 17. and the former heavens shall not be *r.*
Jer. 11. 19. that his name may be no more *r.*
Lam. 1. 7. Jerusalem *r.* in the days of her afflictions
2. 1. *r.* not his footstool in the day of his anger
Ezek. 3. 20. his righteousness shall not be *r.* 33. 13.
16. 22. thou hast not *r.* the days of thy youth, 43.
21. 24. because ye made your iniquity to be *r.*
32. thou shalt be for fuel, thou shalt be no more *r.*
25. 10. that the Ammonites may not be *r.*
Hos. 2. 17. they shall no more be *r.* *Zech.* 13. 2.
Amos 1. 9. and *r.* not the brotherly covenant
Jonah 2. 7. when my soul fainted, I *r.* the Lord
Mat. 26. 75. Peter *r.* the words of Jes. *Luke* 22. 61.
Luke 24. 8. they *r.* his words, and told these things
John 2. 17. his disciples *r.* that it was written
22. when he was risen, they *r.* that he had said
12. 16. when Jesus was glorified then they *r.*
Acts 11. 16. then *r.* I the word of the Lord
Heb. 11. † 22. by faith Joseph *r.* the departing
Rev. 18. 5. and God hath *r.* her iniquities

REMEMBEREST.

Psal. 88. 5. like the slain whom thou *r.* no more
Mat. 5. 23. there *r.* that thy brother hath aught

REMEMBERETH.

Psal. 9. 12. when he maketh inquisition, he *r.*
103. 14. he knoweth our frame, he *r.* we are but dust
Eccl. 5. † 20. yet he *r.* the days of his life
Lam. 1. 9. she *r.* not her last end, she came down
John 16. 21. she *r.* no more the anguish, for joy
2 *Cor.* 7. 15. whilst he *r.* the obedience of you all

REMEMBERING.

Lam. 3. 19. *r.* mine affliction and my misery
1 *Thess.* 1. 3. *r.* without ceasing your work of faith

REMISSION.

Mat. 26. 28. blood shed for many, for the *r.* of sins
Mark 1. 4. baptism of repentance for *r.* *Luke* 3. 3.
Luke 1. 77. knowledge of salvation by *r.* of sins
24. 47. that *r.* should be preached in his name
Acts 2. 38. repent, and be baptized for *r.* of sins
10. 43. whosoever believeth shall receive *r.* of sins
Rom. 3. 25. for the *r.* of sins that are past
Heb. 9. 22. without shedding of blood is no *r.*
10. 18. where *r.* is, there is no more offering for sin

REMIT, TED.

John 20. 23. whose soever sins ye *r.* they are *r.*

REMNANT.

Gen. 45. † 7. God sent me before, to put for you a *r.*
Lev. 2. 3. the *r.* of meat offering shall be Aaron's
5. 13. *r.* shall be the priest's as a meat offering
14. 18. the *r.* of the oil that is in the priest's hand
Deut. 3. 11. for only Og king of Bashan remained
of the *r.* of giants, *Josh.* 12. 4. | 13. 12.
28. 54. his eye evil toward the *r.* of his children
Josh. 23. 12. if ye cleave to the *r.* of these nations
2 *Sam.* 21. 2. the Gibeonites were of *r.* of Amorites
1 *Kings* 12. 23. speak to the *r.* of the people, saying
14. 10. I will take away the *r.* of Jeroboam
22. 46. *r.* of the Sodomites Jehoshaphat took away
2 *Kings* 19. 4. lift up thy prayer for the *r.* *Isa.* 37. 4.
30. the *r.* escaped shall take root, *Isa.* 37. 31.
31. out of Jerusalem shall go forth a *r.* *Isa.* 37. 32.
21. 14. I will forsake the *r.* of mine inheritance
25. 11. the *r.* did Nebuzar-adan carry away
2 *Chron.* 30. 6. he will return to the *r.* of you
Ezra 3. 8. the *r.* of their brethren the priests
9. 8. grace shewed from L. to leave us a *r.* to escape
14. so that there should be no *r.* nor escaping
Neh. 1. 3. the *r.* that are left of the captivity
Job 22. 20. but the *r.* of them the fire consumed
Isa. 1. 9. unless the Ld. had left us a very small *r.*
7. † 3. the *r.* shall return, even the *r.* 10. 21.
11. 11. set his hand, to recover the *r.* of his people
16. there shall be an high-way for the *r.* of his
14. 22. I will cut off from Babylon the *r.*
30. I will kill thy root, and he shall slay thy *r.*
15. 9. I will bring lions on the *r.* of the land
16. 14. the *r.* shall be very small and feeble
17. 3. the kingdom shall cease from *r.* of Syria
46. 3. hearken all the *r.* of the house of Israel
Jer. 6. 9. they shall glean the *r.* of Israel as a vine
11. 23. and there shall be no *r.* of them
Jer. 15. 11. verily it shall be well with thy *r.*
23. 3. and I will gather the *r.* of my flock
25. 20. the *r.* of Ashdod did drink of the cup
31. 7. O Lord, save thy people, the *r.* of Israel
39. 9. Nebuzar-adan carried away the *r.* of people
40. 11. the king of Babylon had left a *r.* of Judah
15. Jews be scattered, and *r.* of Judah perish
41. 16. Johanan took the *r.* of the people, 43. 5.
42. 2. pray for us to the Lord, even for all this *r.*
15. hear the word of the Lord, ye *r.* of Judah
19. O ye *r.* of Judah, go ye not into Egypt
44. 12. I will take the *r.* of Judah, that have set
14. so that none of the *r.* of Judah shall escape
28. the *r.* shall know whose words shall stand
47. 4. Lord will spoil *r.* of the country of Caphtor
5. Ashkelon is cut off, with the *r.* of their valley
Ezek. 5. 10. the whole *r.* of thee will I scatter
6. 8. yet will I leave a *r.* that ye may have some
11. 13. Lord, wilt thou make an end of the *r.*?
14. 22. yet behold, therein shall be left a *r.*
23. 25. and thy *r.* shall fall by the sword
25. 16. I will destroy the *r.* of the sea coast
Joel 2. 32. in the *r.* whom the Lord shall call
Amos 1. 8. the *r.* of the Philistines shall perish
5. 15. God will be gracious to the *r.* of Joseph
9. 12. that they may possess the *r.* of Edom
Mic. 2. 12. I will surely gather the *r.* of Israel
4. 7. and I will make her that halted, a *r.*
5. 3. the *r.* of his brethren shall return to Israel
7. the *r.* of Jacob, in the midst of many people
8. the *r.* of Jacob shall be among the Gentiles
7. 18. the transgression of the *r.* of his heritage
Hab. 2. 8. all the *r.* of the people shall spoil thee
Zeph. 1. 4. and I will cut off the *r.* of Baal
2. 7. the coast shall be for the *r.* of house of Judah
9. the *r.* of my people shall possess them
3. 13. the *r.* of Israel shall not do iniquity
Hag. 1. 12. all the *r.* of the people obeyed the Lord
14. the Lord stirred up the spirit of the *r.*
Zech. 8. 6. if it be marvellous in the eyes of the *r.*
12. I will cause the *r.* of this people to possess
Mat. 22. 6. the *r.* took his servants, and slew them
Rom. 9. 27. Esaias also crieth, a *r.* shall be saved
11. 5. at this present time also there is a *r.*
Rev. 11. 13. the *r.* were affrighted, and gave glory
12. 17. the dragon went to make war with the *r.*
19. 21. the *r.* were slain with the sword of him that

REMORSE.

Rom. 11. † 8. God hath given them the spirit of *r.*

REMOVE.

Gen. 48. 17. he held up his father's hand to *r.* it
Num. 36. 7. so shall not the inheritance of Israel *r.*
from tribe to tribe, but keep to his tribe, 9.
Deut. 19. 14. shalt not *r.* thy neighbour's land-mark
Josh. 3. 3. then ye shall *r.* from your place and go
Judg. 9. 29. then would I *r.* Abimelech
2 *Sam.* 6. 10. so David would not *r.* the ark
2 *Kings* 23. 27. the Lord said, I will *r.* Judah also
24. 3. came on Judah, to *r.* them out of his sight
2 *Chron.* 33. 8. neither will I any more *r.* Israel
Job 24. 2. some *r.* the land-marks, they take away
27. 5. I will not *r.* mine integrity from me
Psal. 36. 11. let not the hand of the wicked *r.* me
39. 10. *r.* thy stroke away from me, I am consumed
119. 22. *r.* from me reproach and contempt
29. *r.* from me the way of lying, and grant me
Prov. 4. 27. turn not, *r.* thy foot from evil
5. 8. *r.* thy way far from her, and come not nigh
22. 28. *r.* not the ancient land-mark, 23. 10.
30. 8. *r.* from me vanity and lies
Eccl. 11. 10. therefore *r.* sorrow from thy heart
Isa. 10. † 27. his burden shall *r.* from thy shoulder
13. 13. the earth shall *r.* out of her place
31. † 2. yet he is wise, and will not *r.* his words
46. 7. he standeth, from his place shall he not *r.*
Jer. 4. 1. return unto me, then shalt thou not *r.*
27. 10. prophesy a lie, to *r.* you far from your land
32. 31. that I should *r.* it from before my face
50. 3. they shall *r.* they shall depart man and beast
8. *r.* out of the midst of Babylon, and go forth
Ezek. 12. 3. *r.* by day, thou shalt *r.* from thy place
21. 26. thus saith the Lord, *r.* the diadem
45. 9. O princes, *r.* violence and spoil
Hos. 5. 10. they were like them that *r.* the bound
Joel 2. 20. but I will *r.* the northern army
3. 6. that ye might *r.* them from their border
Mic. 2. 3. from which ye shall not *r.* your necks
Zech. 3. 9. I will *r.* the iniquity of that land
14. 4. half the mountain shall *r.* toward north
Mat. 17. 20. ye shall say, *r.* hence, and it shall *r.*
Luke 22. 42. if thou be willing, *r.* this cup from me
1 *Cor.* 13. 2. all faith, so that I could *r.* mountains
Rev. 2. 5. or else I will *r.* thy candlestick out of place

REMOVED.

Gen. 8. 13. Noah *r.* the covering of the ark
12. 8. Abram *r.* 13, 18. || 26. 22. Isaac *r.* from thence
30. 35. Jacob *r.* the he-goats that were spotted
47. 21. and Joseph *r.* the people to cities
Exod. 8. 31. the Lord *r.* the swarms of flies
14. 19. the angel of God *r.* and went behind them
20. 18. the people saw it and *r.* and stood afar off
Num. 12. 16. the people *r.* from Hazeroth to Paran
21. 12. they *r.* and pitched in the valley of Zared
13. *r.* and pitched on the other side of Arnon
33. 5. the children of Israel *r.* from Rameses
7. they *r.* from Etham || 9. Marah || 10. Elim
11. they *r.* from the Red sea || 14. *r.* from Alush
16. *r.* from the desert of Sinai || 21. from Libnah
24. *r.* from mount Shapher || 25. from Haradah
33. 26. *r.* from Makheloth || 28. from Terah
32. *r.* from Bene-jaakan || 34. from Jotbathah
36. they *r.* from Ezion-gaber || 37. from Kadesh
46. *r.* from Dibon-gad || from Almon-diblathaim
Deut. 28. 25. and shall be *r.* into all kingdoms
Josh. 3. 1. they *r.* from Shittim, and came to Jordan
14. when the people *r.* to pass over Jordan
11. † 15. Joshua *r.* nothing of all Lord commanded
1 *Sam.* 6. 3. known why his hand is not *r.* from you
18. 13. therefore Saul *r.* David from him
2 *Sam.* 20. 12. he *r.* Amasa out of the high-way
1 *Kings* 15. 12. Asa *r.* the idols his fathers ma'

1 *Kin.* 15. 13. Maachah his moth. even her he *r.* from being queen, for making an idol, 2 *Chron.* 15. 16.
14. the high places were not *r.* 2 *Kings* 15. 4, 35.
2 *Kings* 16. 17. Ahaz *r.* the laver from off the bases
17. 18. Lord *r.* Israel out of his sight, 23. | 23. 27.
26. the nations which thou hast *r.* know not
18. 4. Hezek. *r.* the high places, and brake images
1 *Chron.* 13. † 13. so David *r.* not the ark home
2 *Chron.* 35. 12. and they *r.* the burnt offerings
36. † 3. the king of Egypt *r.* Jehoahaz at Jerusal.
Job 14. 18. and the rock is *r.* out of his place
18. 4. shall the rock be *r.* out of his place?
19. 10. and my hope hath he *r.* like a tree
32. † 15. they *r.* speeches from themselves
36. 16. so would he have *r.* thee out of the strait
Psal. 46. 2. we will not fear though the earth be *r.*
81. 6. I *r.* his shoulder from the burden
103. 12. so far hath he *r.* our transgressions
104. 5. the earth, that it should not be *r.* for ever
125. 1. shall be as mount Zion, which cannot be *r.*
Prov. 10. 30. the righteous shall never be *r.*
Isa. 6. 12. till the Lord have *r.* men far away
10. 13. I have *r.* the bounds of the people
31. Madmenah is *r.* the inhabitants gather
17. † 11. harvest shall be *r.* in day of inheritance
22. 25. the nail fasten. in the sure place shall be *r.*
24. 20. the earth shall be *r.* like a cottage
26. 15. thou hast *r.* it far to all ends of the earth
29. 13. but have *r.* their heart far from me
30. 20. yet shall not thy teachers be *r.* to a corner
33. 20. not one of the stakes shall be *r.* any more
38. 12. mine age is *r.* from me as a shepherd's tent
54. 10. the hills shall be *r.* my kindness and the covenant of my peace shall not be *r.* saith Lord
Jer. 15. 4. I will cause them to be *r.* into kingdoms
24. 9. I will deliver them to be *r.* 29. 18. | 34. 17.
Lam. 1. 8. Jerusalem sinned, therefore she is *r.*
3. 17. and thou hast *r.* my soul far from peace
Ezek. 7. 19. their gold shall be *r.* gold not able
23. 46. I will give them to be *r.* and spoiled
36. 17. their way as the uncleanness of a *r.* woman
Amos 6. 7. and the banquet of them shall be *r.*
Mic. 2. 4. how hath he *r.* it from me, turning away
7. 11. in that day shall the decree be far *r.*
Mat. 21. 21. if ye shall say, be thou *r.* *Mark* 11. 23.
Acts 7. 4. he *r.* Abraham into this land, wherein
13. 22. when he had *r.* Saul, he raised up David
Gal. 1. 6. I marvel that ye are so soon *r.* from him

REMOVETH.

Deut. 27. 17. curs. that *r.* his neighbour's land-mark
Job 9. 5. which *r.* the mountains, and they know not
12. 20. he *r.* away the speech of the trusty
Eccl. 10. 9. whoso *r.* stones shall be hurt therewith
Isa. 27. † 8. when he *r.* his rough wind in day of east
Dan. 2. 21. he changeth the seasons, he *r.* kings

REMOVING.

Gen. 30. 32. *r.* from thy flock all the speckled
Isa. 14. † 6. who smote people in wrath without *r.*
49. 21. seeing I am a captive *r.* to and fro
Jer. 15. † 4. I will give them for a *r.* 24. † 9. | 34. † 17.
Lam. 1. † 8. therefore Jerusalem is become a *r.*
Ezek. 12. 3. therefore prepare the stuff for *r.* 4.
23. † 46. and I will give them for a *r.* and spoil
Heb. 12. 27. signifieth the *r.* of those things shaken

REND.

Exod. 39. 23. a band round, that ephod should not *r.*
Lev. 10. 6. neither *r.* your clothes, lest ye die
13. 56. priest shall *r.* the plague out of the garment
1 *Kings* 11. 11. I will surely *r.* the kingdom, 12, 31.
13. howbeit I will not *r.* away all the kingdom
31. behold, I will *r.* the kingdom, 14. 8.
2 *Chr.* 34. 27. didst *r.* thy clothes, and weep before
Eccl. 3. 7. a time to *r.* and a time to sew
Isa. 64. 1. oh that thou wouldest *r.* the heavens
Ezek. 13. 11. and a stormy wind shall *r.* it, 13.
29. 7. thou didst break and *r.* all their shoulder
Hos. 13. 8. and I will *r.* the caul of their heart
Joel 2. 13. *r.* your heart, and not your garments
Mat. 7. 6. lest they turn again and *r.* you
John 19. 24. let us not *r.* it, but cast lots for it

RENDER.

Num. 18. 9. every offer. they *r.* to me be most holy
Deut. 32. 41. I will *r.* vengeance to mine enemies
43. he will *r.* vengeance to his adversaries
Judg. 9. 57. evil of the men of Shechem did God *r.*
1 *Sam.* 26. 23. Ld. *r.* to every man his faithfulness
2 *Chr.* 6. 30. *r.* to every man according to his ways
Job 33. 26. for he will *r.* unto man his righteousness
34. 11. for the work of a man shall he *r.* to him
Psal. 28. 4. *r.* to them their desert, they regard not
38. 20. they that *r.* evil for good are adversaries
56. 12. O God, I will *r.* praises unto thee
79. 12. and *r.* to our neighbour seven-fold
94. 2. lift up thyself, *r.* a reward to the proud
116. 12. what shall I *r.* to the Ld. for all benefits?
Prov. 24. 12. doth not he know it, and shall not he *r.* to every man according to his works? *Rom.* 2. 6.
29. say not, I will *r.* to man accord. to his work
26. 16. than seven men that can *r.* a reason
Isa. 66. 15. Ld. will come, to *r.* his anger with fury
Jer. 51. 6. he will *r.* to Babylon a recompence, 24.
Lam. 3. 64. *r.* to them a recompence, O Lord
Hos. 14. 2. so will we *r.* the calves of our lips
Joel 3. 4. will ye *r.* me a recompence? if recompense
Zech. 9. 12. I declare, that I will *r.* double to thee
Mat. 21. 41. which shall *r.* him the fruits in season
22. 21. *r.* unto Cæsar, *Mark* 12. 17. *Luke* 20. 25.
Rom. 13. 7. *r.* therefore to all their dues, tribute
1 *Cor.* 7. 3. let husband *r.* to wife due benevolence
1 *Thess.* 3. 9. what thanks can we *r.* to God for you?
5. 15. see that none *r.* evil for evil to any man

RENDERED.

Judg. 9. 56. thus God *r.* wickedness of Abimelech
2 *Kings* 3. 4. the king of Moab *r.* to the king of Isr.
17. † 3. Hoshea *r.* Shalmaneser tribute
2 *Chr.* 32. 25. Hezekiah *r.* not according to benefit
Prov. 12. 14. recompence of man's hands be *r.* to him

RENDEREST.

Psal. 62. 12. *r.* to every man according to his work

RENDERETH.

Isa. 66. 6. a voice of the Lord that *r.* recompence

RENDERING.

1 *Pet.* 3. 9. not *r.* evil for evil, or railing for railing

RENDEST.

Jer. 4. 30. though thou *r.* thy face with painting

RENDING.

Psal. 7. 2. lest he tear my soul, *r.* it in pieces

RENEW.

To renew *sometimes signifies to establish, or confirm.* 1 Sam. 11. 14. Let us go to *Gilgal,* and renew the kingdom there: *let us ratify the covenant between* Saul *and the people concerning the kingdom, and instal him publicly and solemnly into it.* *Asa* renewed the altar of the Lord, 2 *Chron.* 15. 8. *He repaired, or rebuilt it, after it had been decayed through long use, or broken down by idolaters: or,* he consecrated and dedicated the altar, *which had been polluted by idolaters, and needed purification.* Job *says,* that God renewed his witnesses against him, *Job* 10. 17. *that is, He brought fresh plagues and judgments upon him, which were the witnesses and evidences both of his sin, and God's displeasure against him. In another place he says,* that his bow was renewed in his hand, *Job* 29. 20. *Or, as it is in the* Hebrew, *it* changed *itself, grew as it were a new bow, when other bows by much use grow weak and useless: or, it* changed *its strength, and got new force, as the word is used in* Isa. 40. 31. They that wait upon the Lord shall renew their strength; *they shall grow stronger and stronger in faith and patience.* *God* renews the face of the earth, *Psal.* 104. 30. *By his providence he preserves the succession of living creatures upon the earth, which otherwise would be desolate, and without inhabitants.* Renew our days as of old, *says* Jeremiah, *Lam.* 5. 21. *that is, Bring us out of our captivity, and restore us to our former flourishing condition.*

Renewing *is taken either,* [1] *For that work of the Spirit, whereby the elect, of enemies to God, and children of wrath, become the children of God, citizens with the saints, heirs and co-heirs with Christ, being by faith made partakers of his righteousness and sufferings, and having the image of God, which consists in righteousness and holiness, restored in their souls; and this is the same with regeneration, or being born again,* Tit. 3. 5. *Or,* [2] *For reviving, strengthening, and repairing of that which is decayed and blemished by sin,* Psal. 51. 10.

1 *Sam.* 11. 14. let us go to Gilgal and *r.* kingd. there
2 *Chron.* 24. † 4. Joash minded to *r.* house of Lord
Psal. 51. 10. and *r.* a right spirit within me
Isa. 40. 31. they that wait on L. shall *r.* strength
41. 1. let the people *r.* their strength, come near
Lam. 5. 21. turn us, O Lord, *r.* our days as of old
Heb. 6. 6. if they fall away, to *r.* them again to repentance

RENEWED.

2 *Chron.* 15. 8. Asa *r.* the altar of the Lord
Job 29. 20. and my bow was *r.* in my hand
Psal. 103. 5. so that thy youth is *r.* like the eagle's
2 *Cor.* 4. 16. yet the inward man is *r.* day by day
Eph. 4. 23. and be *r.* in the spirit of your mind
Col. 3. 10. the new man which is *r.* in knowledge

RENEWEST.

Job 10. 17. thou *r.* thy witnesses against me
Psal. 104. 30. and thou *r.* the face of the earth

RENEWING.

Rom. 12. 2. be transformed by the *r.* of your mind
Tit. 3. 5. he saved us by the *r.* of the Holy Ghost

RENOUNCED.

2 *Cor.* 4. 2. but have *r.* the hidden things of dishon.

RENOWN.

Gen. 6. 4. the giants, which were of old, men of *r.*
Num. 16. 2. famous in the congregation, men of *r.*
Ezek. 16. 14. thy *r.* went forth among the heathen
15. and playedst the harlot because of thy *r.*
34. 29. I will raise up for them a plant of *r.*
39. 13. it shall be to them a *r.* saith the Lord
Dan. 9. 15. and hast gotten thee *r.* as at this day

RENOWNED.

Num. 1. 16. these were the *r.* of the congregation
Isa. 14. 20. the seed of evil-doers shall never be *r.*
Ezek. 23. 23. captains, and great lords, and *r.*
26. 17. the *r.* city which was strong in the sea

RENT, *Substantive.*

Isa. 3. 24. and instead of a girdle there shall be a *r.*
Mat. 9. 16. and the *r.* is made worse, *Mark* 2. 21.
Luke 5. 36. then both the new maketh a *r.*

RENT, *Participle.*

Gen. 37. 33. Joseph is without doubt *r.* in pieces
Exod. 28. 32. an hole in the ephod, that it be not *r.*
Josh. 9. 4. they took wine bottles, old and *r.* 13.
2 *Sam.* 15. 32. Hushai came with his coat *r.*
1 *Kings* 13. 3. the altar shall be *r.* || 5. altar was *r.*
Ezra 9. 5. having *r.* my garment and my mantle
Mat. 27. 51. behold, the vail of the temple was *r.* in twain, *Mark* 15. 38. *Luke* 23. 45.
Mark 1. † 10. John saw the heavens *r.* and Spirit

See CLOTHES.

RENT, *Verb.*

Judg. 14. 6. Samson *r.* the lion as he would have *r.* a kid, and he had nothing in his hand
1 *Sam.* 15. 27. Saul *r.* the skirt of Samuel's mantle
28. Lord hath *r.* the kingdom from thee, 28. 17.
2 *Sam.* 13. 19. Tamar *r.* her garment that was on her
1 *Kings* 1. 40. the earth *r.* with the sound of them
11. 30. Ahijah *r.* Jeroboam's new garment
19. 11. and a strong wind *r.* the mountains
2 *Kings* 17. 21. he *r.* Isr. from the house of David
Ezra 9. 3. when I heard this, I *r.* my garment
Job 1. 20. then Job arose, and *r.* his mantle
2. 12. Job's friends *r.* every one his mantle
26. 8. and the cloud is not *r.* under them
Jer. 36. 24. they were not afraid, nor *r.* their garments
Ezek. 30. 16. Sin shall have pain, and No shall be *r.*
Mat. 27. 51. vail of the temple was *r.* and rocks *r.*
Mark 9. 26. the spirit cried, and *r.* him sore

REPAID.

Prov. 13. 21. but to the righteous good shall be *r.*

REPAIR.

2 *Kings* 12. 5. let the priests *r.* the breaches of the house of God, 22. 5, 6. 2 *Chr.* 24. 4. | 34. 8, 10.
7. why *r.* ye not the breaches of the house?
8. neither to *r.* the breaches of the house?
12. and hewed stone to *r.* the breaches, 22. 5, 6.
2 *Chron.* 24. 5. go and gather money to *r.* the house
12. and hired carpenters to *r.* the house of Lord
Ezra 9. 9. to give us a reviving to *r.* the house
Isa. 61. 4. and they shall *r.* the waste cities

REPAIRED.

Judg. 21. 23. Benjamin *r.* cities, and dwelt in them
1 *Kings* 11. 27. Solomon *r.* the breaches of the city
18. 30. Elijah *r.* the altar of the Lord broken down
2 *Kings* 12. 6. the priests had not *r.* the breaches
14. and *r.* therewith the house of the Lord
1 *Chron.* 11. 8. and Joab *r.* the rest of the city
2 *Chron.* 26. † 9. Uzziah *r.* the towers in Jerusalem
29. 3. Hezekiah *r.* the doors of the house
32. 5. Hezekiah *r.* Millo in the city of David
33. 16. Manasseh *r.* the altar of the Lord
Neh. 3. 4. next to them *r.* 5, 7, 8, 10, 12, 19.
6. after him *r.* 17, 18, 20, 22, 23, 24.

REPAIRER.

Isa. 58. 12. thou shalt be called the *r.* of the breach

REPAIRING.

2 *Chron.* 24. 27. concerning the *r.* of the house

REPAY.

Deut. 7. 10. not be slack, he will *r.* him to his face
Job 21. 31. who shall *r.* him what he hath done?
41. 11. who hath prevented me, that I should *r.* him?
Isa. 59. 18. according to their deeds he will *r.* fury, and to the islands he will *r.* recompence
Luke 10. 35. when I come again, I will *r.* thee
Rom. 12. 19. vengeance is mine, I will *r.* saith Lord
Philem. 19. I Paul have written it, I will *r.* it

REPAYETH.

Deut. 7. 10. and *r.* them that hate him to their face

REPEATETH.

Prov. 17. 9. he that *r.* matter, separateth very friends

REPENT.

Repentance *is taken* [1] *For that regret and reluctance that arise in a person, after having done something that he ought not to have done: when* Judas *saw that* Christ *was condemned, it is said of him, that he* repented *of what he had done,* Mat. 27. 3. *He was mightily afflicted in his mind about it, and wished it had not been done. But this* repentance *arises from a fear of the punishment denounced against sin, and is not accompanied with hatred of sin: as when a malefactor suffers for his crimes, he reflects upon his actions with sorrow; but this not being a sacred act, but proceeding from a violent principle, is consistent with as great a love to sin as he had before, and may be entirely terminated on himself; he may be sorry for his crimes, as they have exposed him to punishment, and yet not be grieved that thereby he has offended God.* This *is* legal repentance. [2] *For that saving grace wrought in the soul by the Spirit of God, whereby a sinner is made to see and be sensible of his sin, is grieved and humbled before God on account of it, not so much for the punishment to which sin has made him liable, as that thereby God is dishonoured and offended, his laws violated, and his own soul polluted and defiled; and this grief arises from love to God, and is accompanied with a hatred of sin, a love to holiness, and a fixed resolution to forsake sin, and an expectation of favour and forgiveness, through the merits of Christ. This is* evangelical or gospel repentance, *Mat.* 3. 2, 8. *Acts* 3. 19. 2 *Cor.* 7. 10.

The sacred writers often represent God as moved with regret, or repentance, or relenting, for having suffered or resolved upon certain things. It is said, that God repented that he had made man, *seeing that his wickedness had proceeded to such an extremity,* Gen. 6. 6. *It is elsewhere said, that* he repented of having made *Saul* king over his people, 1 *Sam.* 15. 11. *This is not to be understood as if God had conceived any regret at any thing that he had done wrong, or that he repents of a false step that he had made, as a man does when he perceives he has committed an error. God is not capable of* repentance *in this sense. But sometimes he changes his conduct towards those that are unfaithful to him, and after having treated them with mercy, he corrects them with severity, as if he had repented of what he had before done in their favour. Also God is said to repent of the evil he was about to inflict; when moved with compassion towards the miserable, or entreated by their prayers, he remits the punishment of their sins, or does not execute the threatenings he had made against them: Thus it is said in the* Psalms, that he repented according to the multitude of his mercies, *Psal.* 106. 45. *See Jer.* 18. 8.

Exod. 13. 17. lest peradventure the people *r.*
32. 12. turn from thy fierce wrath, and *r.* of this
Num. 23. 19. neither son of man, that he should *r.*
Deut. 32. 36. the Lord shall *r.* for his servants
1 *Sam.* 15. 29. and also the Strength of Israel will not *r.* for he is not a man that he should *r.*
1 *Kings* 8. 47. if they *r.* in the land of their captivity
Job 42. 6. I abhor myself, and *r.* in dust and ashes
Psal. 90. 13. let it *r.* thee concerning thy servants
110. 4. Lord hath sworn, and will not *r.* *Heb.* 7. 21.
135. 14. he will *r.* himself concerning his servants
Jer. 4. 28. I have purposed it, and will not *r.*
18. 8. if nation turn, I will *r.* of the evil, 26. 13.
10. if it do evil, then I will *r.* of the good
26. 3. that I may *r.* || 42. 10. for I *r.* of the evil
Ezek. 14. 6. *r.* and turn yourselv. from idols, 18. 30.
24. 14. neither will I spare, neither will I *r.*
Joel 2. 14. who knoweth if he will return and *r.* and leave a blessing behind him? *Jonah* 3. 9.
Mat. 3. 2. John the Baptist preached, saying, *r.* for the kingdom of heaven is at hand, 4. 17.
Mark 1. 15. Jesus preached, *r.* ye, and believe gospel
6. 12. they went and preached that men should *r.*
Luke 13. 3. except ye *r.* ye shall all likewise perish, 5.

Luke 16. 30. if one went from the dead, they will *r.*
17. 3. and if thy brother *r.* forgive him, 4.
Acts 2. 38. *r.* and be baptized every one of you
3. 19. *r.* ye theref. and be converted, that your sins
8. 22. *r.* of this thy wickedness, and pray God
17. 30. but commandeth all men every where to *r.*
26. 20. that they should *r.* and turn to God
2 *Cor.* 7. 8. made you sorry, I do not *r.* tho' I did *r.*
Rev. 2. 5. remember therefore and *r.* except thou *r.*
16. *r.* or else I will come unto thee quickly
21. I gave her space to *r.* of her fornication
22. except they *r.* of their deeds
3. 3. remember how thou hast received, and *r.*
19. I chasten, be zealous therefore and *r.*

REPENTANCE.

Hos. 13. 14. *r.* shall be hid from mine eyes
Mat. 3. 8. bring forth fruits meet for *r.* *Luke* 3. 8.
11. I indeed baptize you with water unto *r.*
9. 13. to call sinners to *r.* *Mark* 2. 17. *Luke* 5. 32.
Mark 1. 4. John did preach the baptism of *r.* for remission of sins, *Luke* 3. 3. *Acts* 13. 24. | 19. 4.
Luke 15. 7. than over ninety-nine which need no *r.*
24. 47. that *r.* and remission of sins be preached
Acts 5. 31. him hath God exalted for to give *r.* to Is.
11. 18. God also to the Gentiles granted *r.* to life
20. 21. testifying to the Greeks *r.* towards God
26. 20. should turn to God, and do works meet for *r.*
Rom. 2. 4. the goodness of God leadeth thee to *r.*
11. 29. the gifts and calling of God are without *r.*
2 *Cor.* 7. 9. but I rejoice that ye sorrowed to *r.*
10. godly sorrow worketh *r.* to salvation
2 *Tim.* 2. 25. if God peradventure will give them *r.*
Heb. 6. 1. not laying again the foundation of *r.*
6. if they fall away, to renew them again to *r.*
12. 17. he found no place of *r.* though he sought it
2 *Pet.* 3. 9. any perish, but that all should come to *r.*

REPENTED.

Gen. 6. 6. it *r.* the Lord, that he had made man
Exod. 32. 14. the Lord *r.* of the evil he thought to do, 2 *Sam.* 24. 16. 1 *Chr.* 21. 15. *Jer.* 26. 19.
Judg. 2. 18. it *r.* the Ld. because of their groanings
21. 6. the children of Israel *r.* for Benjamin, 15.
1 *Sam.* 15. 35. the Lord *r.* that he made Saul king
Psal. 106. 45. the Lord *r.* according to his mercies
Jer. 8. 6. no man *r.* him of his wickedness, saying
20. 16. as cities the Lord overthrew, and *r.* not
31. 19. surely after that I was turned, I *r.*
Amos 7. 3. the Lord *r.* for this, it shall not be, 6.
Jonah 3. 10. God *r.* of the evil that he had said
Zech. 8. 14. as I thought to punish you, and I *r.* not
Mat. 11. 20. to upbraid cities, because they *r.* not
21. they would have *r.* long ago, *Luke* 10. 13.
12. 41. the men of Nineveh shall rise, because they *r.* at the preaching of Jonas, *Luke* 11. 32.
21. 29. I will not, but afterward he *r.* and went
32. and ye, when ye had seen it, *r.* not afterward
27. 3. Judas *r.* himself, and brought the silver
2 *Cor.* 7. 10. worketh repentance not to be *r.* of
12. 21. many that have not *r.* of the uncleanness
Rev. 2. 21. I gave space to repent, and she *r.* not
9. 20. who were not killed by these plagues, yet *r.* not
21. neither *r.* of their murders nor their thefts
16. 9. blasphemed name of God, and *r.* not, 11.

REPENTEST.

Jonah 4. 2. art a gracious God, and *r.* thee of the evil

REPENTETH.

Gen. 6. 7. for it *r.* me that I have made them
1 *Sam.* 15. 11. it *r.* me that I have set up Saul king
Joel 2. 13. he is slow to anger, and *r.* him of the evil
Luke 15. 7. joy shall be over one sinner that *r.* 10.

REPENTING.

Jer. 15. 6. I will destroy thee, I am weary with *r.*

REPENTINGS.

Hos. 11. 8. my heart is turned, *r.* are kindled togeth.

REPETITIONS.

Mat. 6. 7. use not vain *r.* as the heathen do

REPLENISH.

Gen. 1. 28. be fruitful, multiply, and *r.* the earth, 9. 1.

REPLENISHED.

Isa. 2. 6. because they be *r.* from the east
23. 2. the merchants of Zidon have *r.* Tyre
Jer. 31. 25. and I have *r.* every sorrowful soul
Ezek. 26. 2. I shall be *r.* now she is laid waste
27. 25. thou wast *r.* and made very glorious

REPLIEST.

Rom. 9. 20. O man, who art thou that *r.* ag. God?

REPORT.

Gen. 37. 2. Joseph brought to his father their evil *r.*
Exod. 23. 1. thou shalt not raise a false *r.*
Num. 13. 32. they brought up an evil *r.* of the land
14. 37. men that did bring up the evil *r.* died
Deut. 2. 25. the nations who shall hear *r.* of thee
1 *Sam.* 2. 24. nay, my sons, it is no good *r.* I hear
1 *Kings* 10. 6. it was a true *r.* I heard, 2 *Chron.* 9. 5.
Neh. 6. 13. they might have matter for an evil *r.*
Prov. 15. 30. and a good *r.* maketh the bones fat
Isa. 23. 5. as at the *r.* concerning Egypt, so shall they be sorely pained at the *r.* of Tyre
28. 19. it shall be a vexation only to understand *r.*
53. 1. who hath believed our *r.*? to whom is the arm of the Lord revealed? *John* 12. 38. *Rom.* 10. 16.
Jer. 50. 43. the king of Babylon hath heard the *r.*
Hab. 3. † 3. I have heard thy *r.* and was afraid
Acts 6. 3. look out seven men of honest *r.* full of the Holy Ghost
10. 22. Cornelius was of good *r.* among the Jews
22. 12. Ananias having a good *r.* of the Jews
2 *Cor.* 6. 8. by evil *r.* and good *r.* as deceiv. yet true
Phil. 4. 8. whatever things are of good *r.* and pure
1 *Tim.* 3. 7. a bishop must have a good *r.* of them
Heb. 11. 2. by faith the elders obtained a good *r.*
39. these all having obtained a good *r.* thro' faith
3 *John* 12. Demetrius hath a good *r.* of all men

REPORT, *Verb.*

Jer. 20. 10. *r.* say they, and we will *r.* it
1 *Cor.* 14. 25. he will *r.* that God is in you of a truth

REPORTED.

Neh. 6. 6. it is *r.* among heathen, Gashmu saith it
7. shall it be *r.* to king according to these words
19. also they *r.* his good deeds before me
Esth. 1. 17. despise their husbands, when it shall be *r.*
Ezek. 9. 11. the man which had the inkhorn *r.*
Mat. 28. 15. this saying is commonly *r.* among Jews
Acts 4. 23. they *r.* all that the chief priests had said
16. 2. Timotheus was well *r.* of by the brethren
Rom. 3. 8. and not rather as we be slanderously *r.*
1 *Cor.* 5. 1. it is *r.* that there is fornication among you
1 *Tim.* 5. 10. a widow, well *r.* of for good works
1 *Pet.* 1. 12. minister things that are now *r.* to you

REPOSSESS.

Exod. 15. † 9. will draw sword, mine hand shall *r.* them

REPROACH

Signifies, [1] *Scorn, or derision*, Neh. 2. 17. | 5. 9. [2] *Shame, infamy, or disgrace*, Prov. 6. 33. [3] *Censures and reflections*, Isa. 51. 7. [4] *Injury, or contumely either in word, or deed*, 2 Cor. 12. 10. [5] *The sins of men, which cast dishonour or reproach upon God*, Rom. 15. 3. [6] *Sterility, or barrenness in women*, Gen. 30. 23. *This among the* Hebrews *was reckoned a* reproach, *because such did seem to be excluded from the promise made to* Abraham *concerning the multiplication of his seed; and because they were not in a capacity of having the* promised Seed *to be one of their posterity.* [7] *Uncircumcision, which the* Jews *counted a* reproach. *Josh.* 5. 9. This day have I rolled away the reproach of *Egypt* from off you. *I have freed you from that shame and dishonour which did lie upon you whilst you were bond slaves in the land of* Egypt, *by receiving you into covenant with me, acknowledging you for my peculiar people, and admitting you to have this privilege sealed unto you by circumcision. It is called* the reproach of Egypt, *either,* [1] *Because the* Egyptians *were not in covenant with God, neither did they partake of the seals of it, as may be gathered from* Exod. 2. 6. *where the child* Moses *was known to be an* Hebrew *by his mark; and therefore the* Egyptians, *as other nations, were aliens and strangers from God, and had in abomination by the church and people of God*, Eph. 2. 12. *Or,* [2] *Because the* Israelites *came out of* Egypt, *and were esteemed to be a sort of* Egyptians, *Num.* 22. 5. *which they justly thought a great* reproach; *but by their circumcision they were distinguished from them, and manifested to be another kind of people. Or,* [3] *Because many of them lay under this reproach in* Egypt, *having wickedly neglected this duty there for worldly reasons; and others of them continued in the same shameful condition for many years in the wilderness.*

Josh. 5. 9. I have rolled away the *r.* of Egypt
Judg. 5. † 18. Zebulun and Naphtali exposed to *r.*
1 *Sam.* 17. 26. and taketh away the *r.* from Israel
Neh. 1. 3. the remnant are in great affliction and *r.*
4. 4. and turn their *r.* upon their own head
5. 9. because of the *r.* of the heathen our enemies
Psal. 57. 3. he shall save me from the *r.* of him
69. 7. because for thy sake I have borne *r.*
20. *r.* hath broken my heart, I am full of heaviness
71. 13. let them be covered with *r.* that seek
78. 66. he put them to a perpetual *r.*
79. 12. their *r.* wherewith they reproached thee
89. 50. remember the *r.* of thy servants, how I bear in my bosom the *r.* of the mighty people
119. 22. remove from me *r.* and contempt
Prov. 6. 33. and his *r.* shall not be wiped away
18. 3. and with ignominy cometh *r.*
19. 26. is a son that causeth shame and *r.*
22. 10. cast out the scorner, strife and *r.* shall cease
Isa. 4. 1. called by thy name to take away our *r.*
51. 7. fear ye not the *r.* of men, nor be afraid
54. 4. not remember the *r.* of thy widowhood
Jer. 23. 40. I will bring an everlasting *r.* on you
31. 19. because I did bear the *r.* of my youth
51. 51. we are confounded, bec. we have heard *r.*
Lam. 3. 30. he is filled full with *r.*
61. thou hast heard their *r.* O Lord, against me
5. 1. remember, O Lord, consider and behold our *r.*
Ezek. 16. 57. discovered, as at the time of thy *r.*
21. 28. concerning the *r.* of Ammonites, say thou
36. 15. nor shalt thou bear *r.* of the people any more
30. that ye shall receive no more *r.* of famine
Dan. 11. 18. a prince for his own behalf shall cause the *r.* offered by him to cease, without his own *r.*
Hos. 12. 14. and his *r.* shall his Lord return to him
Joel 2. 17. and give not thine heritage to *r.*
Mic. 6. 16. therefore ye shall bear *r.* of my people
Zeph. 2. 8. I have heard the *r.* of Moab and Ammon
3. 18. to whom the *r.* of it was a burden
2 *Cor.* 11. 21. I speak as concerning *r.* as though weak
1 *Tim.* 3. 7. must have a good report lest fall into *r.*
4. 10. therefore we both labour and suffer *r.*
Heb. 11. 26. esteeming *r.* of Christ greater riches
13. 13. let us go without the camp, bearing his *r.*

A REPROACH.

Gen. 34. 14. we cannot do this, that were *a r.* to us
1 *Sam.* 11. 2. and lay it for *a r.* upon all Israel
Neh. 2. 17. let us build, that we be no more *a r.*
Psal. 15. 3. he that taketh not up *a r.* ag. neighbour
22. 6. *a r.* of men, and despised of the people
31. 11. I was *a r.* among all mine enemies
39. 8. make me not the *r.* of the foolish
44. 13. thou makest us *a r.* to our neighbours
79. 4. we are become *a r.* to our neighbours
89. 41. all spoil him: he is *a r.* to his neighbours
109. 25. I became also *a r.* to them, they shaked
Prov. 14. 34. but sin is *a r.* to any people
Isa. 30. 5. all ashamed of a people that were *a r.*
Jer. 6. 10. the word of the Lord is to them *a r.*
20. 8. the word of the Lord was made *a r.*
24. 9. I will deliver them for their hurt to be *a r.* and a proverb, 29. 18. | 42. 18. | 44. 8, 12.
49. 13. Bozrah shall become *a r.* and a curse
Ezek. 5. 14. I will make thee *a r.* among the nations
15. Jerusalem shall be *a r.* and a taunt
22. 4. I have made *a r.* unto the heathen
Dan. 9. 16. because thy people are become *a r.*
Joel 2. 19. and I will no more make you *a r.*

My REPROACH.

Gen. 30. 23. she said, God hath taken away *my r.*
1 *Sam.* 25. 39. that hath pleaded the cause of *my r.*
Job 19. 5. if indeed ye plead against me *my r.*
20. 3. I have heard the check of *my r.*
Psal. 69. 10. when I wept, that was *my r.*
19. thou hast known *my r.* and my shame
119. 39. turn away *my r.* which I fear
Luke 1. 25. to take away *my r.* among men

REPROACH.

Ruth 2. 15. saying, let her glean, and *r.* her not
2 *Kings* 19. 4. whom king of Assyria his master hath sent to *r.* the living God, 16. *Isa.* 37. 4, 17.
Neh. 6. 13. have matter that they might *r.* me
Job 27. 6. my heart shall not *r.* me so long as I live
Psal. 42. 10. as with a sword, mine enemies *r.* me
74. 10. how long shall the adversary *r.* me?
102. 8. mine enemies *r.* me all the day
Luke 6. 22. when men shall *r.* you for my sake

REPROACHED.

Lev. 19. † 20. who. lieth with a bond maid, *r.* by man
2 *Sam.* 21. † 21. when he *r.* Israel, Jonathan slew
2 *Kings* 19. 22. whom hast thou *r.*? *Isa.* 37. 23.
23. by thy messengers thou hast *r.* the Lord, and said, I am come to Lebanon, *Isa.* 37. 24.
Job 19. 3. these ten times have ye *r.* me
Psal. 55. 12. it was not an enemy that *r.* me
69. 9. that *r.* thee, are fallen upon me, *Rom.* 15. 3.
74. 18. remember this, that the enemy hath *r.*
79. 12. wherewith they have *r.* thee, O Lord
89. 51. wherewith thine enemies have *r.* O Lord they have *r.* the footsteps of thine anointed
Zeph. 2. 8. whereby they have *r.* my people
10. because they have *r.* and magnified themselv.
1 *Pet.* 4. 14. if ye be *r.* for Christ, happy are ye

REPROACHES.

Psal. 69. 9. and the *r.* of them that reproached thee are fallen upon me, *Rom.* 15. 3.
Isa. 43. 28. therefore I have given Israel to *r.*
2 *Cor.* 12. 10. I take pleasure in *r.* for Christ's sake
Heb. 10. 33. whilst ye were made a gazingstock by *r.*

REPROACHEST.

Luke 11. 45. Master, thus saying, thou *r.* us also

REPROACHETH.

Num. 15. 30. doth aught presumptuously, *r.* Lord
Psal. 44. 16. voice of him that *r.* and blasphemeth
57. † 3. he *r.* him that would swallow me up
74. 22. remember how the foolish man *r.* thee
119. 42. to answer him that *r.* me, *Prov.* 27. 11.
Prov. 14. 31. oppresseth poor, *r.* his Maker, 17. 5.

REPROACHFULLY.

Job 16. 10. they have smitten me on the cheek *r.*
1 *Tim.* 5. 14. give none occasion to speak *r.*

REPROBATE.

In Greek, αδοκιμος. *This word among* Metallists *is used to signify any metal that will not endure the* trial, *or when tried, that betrays itself to be* adulterate, *or* reprobate, *and of a coarse alloy: thus* Jeremiah *says of* Judah, *Jer.* 6. 30. Reprobate silver shall men call them, because the Lord hath rejected them. *They are not purged, nor refined, neither will they pass for current before God, or good men. The* Agones *take the word in another sense. As he that strives as he ought, and conquers, is* δοκιμος, approved; 2 *Tim.* 2. 15. *so he that loses the game and prize, that doth not run or strive according to the laws of the game, and so overcome, is said to be* αδοκιμος, *to* miscarry *in the race, and so to lose the reward: thus, at the close of an agonistical discourse of running and striving, the apostle* Paul *says,* I bring under my body, *I subdue my sensitive powers, and mortify my carnal affections,* lest when I have preached to others, I myself should be a cast-way, or reprobate, 1 *Cor.* 9. 27. *Lest I should be a counterfeit, a mere pretender, being void of true grace; and consequently such as God would reject as unfit, and unworthy to be rewarded by him.* A reprobate mind, *that is, a mind hardened in wickedness, and so stupid as not to discern between good and evil*, Rom. 1. 28.

Reprobation *is generally understood of the decree and purpose of God, to abandon the wicked to the greatest of evils, by not delivering them out of that mass of corruption, in which all mankind are involved by nature; and in not affording them the graces necessary to their arriving at eternal happiness: God does not reprobate men by making them wicked, but by not granting them the benefits of his gratuitous mercy.*

Jer. 6. 30. *r.* silver shall men call them, because
Rom. 1. 28. God gave them over to a *r.* mind
2 *Tim.* 3. 8. men *r.* concerning the faith
Tit. 1. 16. and being to every good work *r.*

REPROBATES.

2 *Cor.* 13. 5. that Christ is in you, except ye be *r.*
6. I trust ye shall know that we are not *r.*
7. should do that which is honest, tho' we be as *r.*

REPROOF.

Job 26. 11. and they are astonished at his *r.*
Prov. 1. 23. turn you at my *r.* I will pour out my Sp.
25. ye would none of my *r.* || 30. despised my *r.*
5. 12. have hated instruction, my heart despised *r.*
10. 17. but he that refuseth *r.* erreth
12. 1. but he that hateth *r.* is brutish
13. 18. he that regardeth *r.* shall be honoured
15. 5. but he that regardeth *r.* is prudent
10. and he that hateth *r.* shall die
31. heareth the *r.* of life, abideth among the wise
32. he that heareth *r.* getteth understanding
17. 10. a *r.* entereth more into a wise man than
29. 15. the rod and *r.* give wisdom, but a child
2 *Tim.* 3. 16. all scripture is profitable for *r.*

REPROOFS.

Psal. 38. 14. as a man in whose mouth are no *r.*
Prov. 6. 23. *r.* of instruction are the way of life
29. † 1. a man of *r.* that hardeneth his neck

REPROVE.

2 *Kings* 19. 4. *r.* the words of Rab-shakeh, *Isa.* 37. 4.
Job 6. 25. but what doth your arguing *r.*?
26. do ye imagine to *r.* words and speeches of one
13. 10. he will surely *r.* you if ye accept persons
22. 4. will he *r.* thee for fear of thee?
Psal. 50. 8. I will not *r.* thee for burnt offerings
21. but I will *r.* thee, and set them in order
141. 5. let him *r.* me, it shall be an excellent oil
Prov. 9. 8. *r.* not a scorner, lest he hate thee

Prov. 19. 25. and *r.* one that hath understanding
30. 6. lest he *r.* thee, and thou be found a liar
Isa. 11. 3. neither *r.* after the hearing of his ears
4. and *r.* with equity for the meek of the earth
37. 4. will *r.* the words which the Lord hath heard
Jer. 2. 19. and thy backslidings shall *r.* thee
Hos. 4. 4. let no man strive nor *r.* another
Mal. 2. † 3. behold I will *r.* your seed, and spread
John 16. 8. when come, he will *r.* the world of sin
Eph. 5. 11. have no fellowship, but rather *r.* them
2 *Tim.* 4. 2. *r.* rebuke, exhort, with all long suffering

REPROVED.

Gen. 20. 16. she was *r.* ‖ 21. 25. Abraham *r.* Abimel.
1 *Chr.* 16. 21. he suffered no man to do them wrong, yea he *r.* kings for their sakes, *Psal.* 105. 14.
Prov. 29. 1. he that being often *r.* hardeneth neck
Jer. 29. 27. why hast thou not *r.* Jeremiah?
Hab. 2. 1. and what I shall answer when I am *r.*
Luke 3. 19. Herod the tetrarch being *r.* by John
John 3. 20. nor cometh to light lest deeds should be *r.*
Eph. 5. 13. all things that are *r.* are made manifest

REPROVETH.

Job 40. 2. he that *r.* God, let him answer it
Psal. 119. † 42. so shall I answer him that *r.* me
Prov. 9. 7. he that *r.* a scorner getteth shame
15. 12. a scorner loveth not one that *r.* him
Isa. 29. 21. and lay a snare for him that *r.* in gate

REPROVER.

Prov. 25. 12. so is a wise *r.* upon an obedient ear
Ezek. 3. 26. thou shalt not be to them a *r.*

REPUTATION.

Eccl. 10. 1. so a little folly him that is in *r.* for wisd.
Acts 5. 34. Gamaliel had in *r.* among the people
Gal. 2. 2. privately to them which were of *r.*
Phil. 2. 7. but made himself of no *r.* and took on him
29. receive him therefore, hold such in *r.*

REPUTED.

Job 18. 3. wherefore are we *r.* vile in your sight?
Dan. 4. 35. all the inhabitants are *r.* as nothing

REQUEST, S.

Judg. 8. 24. Gideon said, I would desire a *r.* of you
2 *Sam.* 14. 15. that the king shall perform the *r.*
22. the king hath fulfilled the *r.* of his servant
Ezra 7. 6. the king granted him all his *r.*
Neh. 2. 4. king said, for what dost thou make *r.*?
Esth. 4. 8. go to the king, to make *r.* before him
5. 3. what is thy *r.* queen Esther? 6. | 7. 2. | 9. 12.
7. 3. my life be given me, my people at my *r.*
7. and Haman stood up to make *r.* for his life
Job 6. 8. O that I might have my *r.*?
Psal. 21. 2. and hast not withholden *r.* of his lips
106. 15. he gave them their *r.* but sent leanness
Rom. 1. 10. making *r.* for a prosperous journey
Phil. 1. 4. in every prayer making *r.* with joy
4. 6. let your *r.* be made known to God
1 *Thess.* 4. † 1. we *r.* you, that as ye have received

REQUESTED.

Judg. 8. 26. weight of the ear-rings that he *r.*
1 *Kings* 19. 4. and Elijah *r.* that he might die
1 *Chron.* 4. 10. and God granted Jabez what he *r.*
Neh. 13. † 6. Nehemiah earnestly *r.* of the king
Dan. 1. 8. he *r.* of the prince of the eunuchs
2. 49. Daniel *r.* of the king, and he set Shadrach

REQUIRE.

Gen. 9. 5. your blood will I *r.* of every beast, and at the hand of man will I *r.* the life of man
31. 39. I bare the loss, of my hand didst thou *r.* it
43. 9. I will be surety, of my hand shalt thou *r.* him
Deut. 10. 12. what doth the Lord *r.*? *Mic.* 6. 8.
18. 19. whoso will not hearken, I will *r.* it of him
23. 21. for the Lord will surely *r.* it of thee
Josh. 22. 23. let Lord himself *r.* it, 1 *Sam.* 20. 16.
2 *Sam.* 3. 13. but one thing I *r.* of thee, that is
4. 11. shall I not *r.* his blood at your hand?
19. 38. whatsoever thou shalt *r.* that will I do
1 *Kings* 8. † 31. if trespass, and he *r.* an oath of him
59. maintain the cause as the matter shall *r.*
1 *Chron.* 21. 3. why doth my lord *r.* this thing?
2 *Chron.* 24. 22. he said, Lord, look on it, and *r.* it
Ezra 7. 21. whatsoever Ezra shall *r.* of you
8. 22. I was ashamed to *r.* of the king a band
Neh. 5. 12. we will restore, and *r.* nothing of them
Psal. 10. 13. he hath said, thou wilt not *r.* it
Ezek. 3. 18. wicked man shall die in his iniquity, but his blood will I *r.* at thine hand, 20. | 33. 6, 8.
20. 40. and there will I *r.* your offerings
34. 10. and I will *r.* my flock at their hand
Luke 12. † 20. this night do they *r.* thy soul
1 *Cor.* 1. 22. for the Jews *r.* a sign, and the Greeks
7. 36. and need so *r.* let him do what he will

REQUIRED.

Gen. 42. 22. therefore behold, his blood is *r.*
Exod. 12. 36. they lent to them such things as they *r.*
1 *Sam.* 21. 8. because the king's business *r.* haste
2 *Sam.* 12. 20. when he *r.* they set bread before him
1 *Chr.* 15. 37. to minister, as every day's work *r.*
2 *Chron.* 8. 14. as duty of every day *r.* *Ezra* 3. 4.
24. 6. why hast thou not *r.* of the Levites to bring
Neh. 5. 18. yet *r.* not I the bread of the governor
Esth. 2. 15. she *r.* nothing but what Hegai appointed
Psal. 40. 6. and sin offering hast thou not *r.*
137. 3. and they that wasted us, *r.* of us mirth
Prov. 30. 7. two things have I *r.* of thee, deny not
Isa. 1. 12. who hath *r.* this at your hand, to tread
Luke 11. 50. may be *r.* of this generation, 51.
12. 20. this night thy soul shall be *r.* of thee
48. much is given, of him shall be much *r.*
19. 23. I might have *r.* mine own with usury
23. 24. gave sentence that it should be as they *r.*
1 *Cor.* 4. 2. it is *r.* of stewards to be faithful

REQUIREST.

Ruth 3. 11. fear not, I will do to thee all that thou *r.*

REQUIRETH.

Eccl. 3. 15. and God *r.* that which is past
Dan. 2. 11. it is a rare thing that the king *r.*

REQUIRING.

Luke 23. 23. were instant, *r.* he might be crucified

REQUITE.

Gen. 50. 15. Joseph will certainly *r.* us the evil
Deut. 32. 6. do ye thus *r.* Lord, O foolish people?
2 *Sam.* 2. 6. and I also will *r.* you this kindness
16. 12. it may be the Lord will *r.* me good for this

2 *Kings* 9. 26. I will *r.* thee in this plat, saith Lord
Psal. 10. 14. beholdest to *r.* it with thy hand
41. 10. O Lord, raise me up, that I may *r.* them
Jer. 51. 56. the God of recompences shall surely *r.*
1 *Tim.* 5. 4. let them learn to *r.* their parents

REQUITED.

Judg. 1. 7. as I have done, so God hath *r.* me
1 *Sam.* 25. 21. and he hath *r.* me evil for good

REQUITING.

2 *Chron.* 6. 23. judge thy servants by *r.* the wicked

REREWARD.

Num. 10. 25. the standard of Dan was the *r.*
Josh. 6. 9. and the *r.* came after the ark
13. but the *r.* came after the ark of the Lord
1 *Sam.* 29. 2. David and his men passed on in the *r.*
Isa. 52. 12. the God of Israel will be your *r.*
58. 8. the glory of the Lord shall be thy *r.*

RESCUE.

Deut. 28. 31. and thou shalt have none to *r.* them
Psal. 35. 17. *r.* my soul from their destructions
Hos. 5. 14. I will take away, and none shall *r.* him

RESCUED.

1 *Sam.* 14. 45. the people *r.* Jonathan, he died not
30. 18. and David *r.* his two wives
Acts 23. 27. then came I with an army, and *r.* him

RESCUETH.

Dan. 6. 27. he delivereth and *r.* and he worketh

RESEMBLANCE.

Zech. 5. 6. this is their *r.* through all the earth

RESEMBLE.

Luke 13. 18. whereunto shall I *r.* kingdom of God

RESEMBLED.

Judg. 8. 18. each one *r.* the children of a king

RESERVE.

Psal. 79. † 11. *r.* the children of death
Jer. 3. 5. will he *r.* his anger for ever? will he keep it
50. 20. for I will pardon them whom I *r.*
2 *Pet.* 2. 9. to *r.* the unjust to the day of judgment

RESERVED.

Gen. 27. 36. hast thou not *r.* a blessing for me?
Num. 18. 9. shall be thine of the most holy things *r.*
Judg. 21. 22. because we *r.* not to each his wife
Ruth 2. 18. she gave her mother that she had *r.*
2 *Sam.* 8. 4. but *r.* for 100 chariots, 1 *Chron.* 18. 4.
Job 21. 30. wicked is *r.* to the day of destruction
38. 23. which I have *r.* against time of trouble
Acts 25. 21. but when Paul had appealed to be *r.*
Rom. 11. 4. I have *r.* to myself 7000 men
1 *Pet.* 1. 4. an inheritance *r.* in heaven for you
2 *Pet.* 2. 4. delivered them to be *r.* to judgment
17. to whom the mist of darkness is *r.* for ever
3. 7. the heavens and earth are *r.* unto fire
Jude 6. angels he hath *r.* in everlasting chains
13. to whom *r.* the blackness of darkness

RESERVETH.

Jer. 5. 24. he *r.* to us the weeks of the harvest
Nah. 1. 2. the Lord *r.* wrath for his enemies

RESIDUE.

Exod. 10. 5. and the locusts shall eat the *r.*
1 *Chron.* 6. 66. *r.* of the sons of Kohath had cities
Neh. 11. 20. the *r.* of Israel were in all the cities
Isa. 21. 17. the *r.* of archers shall be diminished
28. 5. Lord shall be a diadem to *r.* of his people
38. 10. I am deprived of the *r.* of my years
44. 17. and the *r.* thereof he maketh a god
19. shall I make the *r.* thereof an abomination
Jer. 8. 3. chosen, by all the *r.* of them that remain
15. 9. the *r.* of them will I deliver to the sword
24. 8. and the *r.* of Jerusalem that remain
27. 19. saith, concerning the *r.* of the vessels
29. 1. that Jeremiah sent to the *r.* of the elders
39. 3. with all the *r.* of the princes of Babylon
41. 10. Ishmael carried captive the *r.* of the people
52. 15. and the *r.* of the people that remained
Ezek. 9. 8. wilt thou destroy all the *r.* of Israel
23. 25. and thy *r.* shall be devoured by the fire
34. 18. but ye must tread the *r.* of your pastures
36. 3. might be a possession of the *r.* to heathen
4. became a derision to the *r.* of the heathen
5. in the fire of my jealousy have I spoken against the *r.* of the heathen
48. 18. the *r.* in length over against the oblation
21. the *r.* shall be for the prince on one side
Dan. 7. 7. and stamped the *r.* with the feet, 19.
Joel 1. † 4. *r.* of palmer-worm locusts hath eaten
Zeph. 2. 9. the *r.* of my people shall spoil them
Hag. 2. 2. speak to Joshua and the *r.* of the people
Zech. 8. 11. I will not be to the *r.* as in former days
14. 2. the *r.* of the people shall not be cut off
Mal. 2. 15. yet had he the *r.* of the Spirit
Mark 16. 13. they went and told it to the *r.*
Acts 15. 17. that the *r.* might seek the Lord

RESIST.

Zech. 3. 1. Satan standing at his right hand to *r.*
Mat. 5. 39. but I say unto you, that ye *r.* not evil
Luke 21. 15. all your adversar. shall not be able to *r.*
Acts 6. 10. they were not able to *r.* the spirit
7. 51. ye do always *r.* the Holy Ghost as fathers
Rom. 13. 2. they that *r.* shall receive damnation
2 *Tim.* 3. 8. so do these also *r.* the truth
Jam. 4. 7. *r.* the devil and he will flee from you
5. 6. ye killed the just, and he doth not *r.* you
1 *Pet.* 5. 9. whom *r.* stedfast in the faith, knowing

RESISTED.

Rom. 9. 19. thou wilt say, who hath *r.* his will?
Heb. 12. 4. ye have not yet *r.* unto blood, striving

RESISTETH.

Rom. 13. 2. whoso *r.* the power, *r.* ordinance of God
Jam. 4. 6. God *r.* the proud, 1 *Pet.* 5. 5.

RESOLVED.

Luke 16. 4. I am *r.* what to do, when I am put out

RESORT.

Neh. 4. 20. *r.* ye thither to us, God will fight for us
Psal. 71. 3. whereunto I may continually *r.*
Mark 10. 1. and the people *r.* to him again
John 18. 20. in the temple, whither Jews always *r.*

RESORTED.

2 *Chron.* 11. 13. the priests and Levites *r.* to him
Mark 2. 13. multitude *r.* to him he taught them
John 10. 41. and many *r.* to him and said
18. 2. Jesus ofttimes *r.* thither with his disciples
Acts 16. 13. we spake to the women who *r.* thither

RESPECT.

God had respect to *Abel*, and to his offering, *Gen* 4. 4. *He looked to him with a favourable and gracious eye, he kindly accepted and owned him and his sacrifice, and testified this to* Cain *and all there present, either by an audible voice, or by some visible sign, by consuming his sacrifice by fire from heaven, as is generally conjectured; by which token God did afterwards frequently signify his acceptance of sacrifices*, Lev. 9. 24. Judg. 6. 21. 1 Kings 18. 38.

Respect of persons. *God appointed, that the Judges should pronounce their sentences without any* respect of persons, *Lev.* 19. 15. *Deut.* 1. 17. *That they should consider neither the poor, nor the rich, nor the weak, nor the powerful, but only attend to truth and justice, and give sentence according to the merits of the cause. God hath no respect of persons,* Deut. 10. 17. 2 Chron. 19. 7. *He deals justly and equally with all sorts of men, and as every one that truly fears and obeys him shall be accepted, so all incorrigible transgressors shall be severely punished, whether* Jews *or* Gentiles, *of whatsoever nation, family, name, or quality, they be.*

Gen. 4. 4. the Lord had *r.* to Abel and his offering
5. to Cain, and to his offering, he had not *r.*
Exod. 2. 25. God looked, and had *r.* unto them
Lev. 26. 9. for I will have *r.* unto you
1 *Kings* 8. 28. yet have thou *r.* unto the prayer of thy servant and his supplication, 2 *Chr.* 6. 19.
2 *Kings* 13. 23. and the Lord had *r.* unto them
2 *Chr.* 19. 7. there is no iniquity nor *r.* of persons with God. *Rom.* 2. 11. *Eph.* 6. 9. *Col.* 3. 25.
Psal. 74. 20. have *r.* unto covenant, for dark places
119. 6. when I have *r.* to all thy commandments
15. and I will have *r.* unto thy ways
117. I will have *r.* unto thy statutes continually
138. 6. yet hath he *r.* unto the lowly
Prov. 24. 23. it is not good to have *r.* of persons in judgment, nations shall abhor him, 28. 21.
Isa. 17. 7. his eyes shall have *r.* to the Holy One
22. 11. nor had *r.* to him that fashioned it long ago
2 *Cor.* 3. 10. for even that had no glory in this *r.*
Phil. 4. 11. not that I speak in *r.* of want
Col. 2. 16. let none judge you in *r.* of an holy day
Heb. 11. 26. Moses had *r.* to recompence of reward
Jam. 2. 1. have not the faith with *r.* of persons
3. ye have *r.* to him that weareth gay clothing
9. if ye have *r.* to persons, ye commit sin
1 *Pet.* 1. 17. who without *r.* of persons, judgeth

RESPECT, *Verb.*

Lev. 19. 15. thou shalt not *r.* the person of poor
Num. 16. 15. Moses said, *r.* not thou their offering
Deut. 1. 17. ye shall not *r.* persons in judgment, 16. 19.
2 *Sam.* 14. 14. neither doth God *r.* any person
Isa. 17. 8. nor shall *r.* that which his fingers made

RESPECTED.

Lam. 4. 16. they *r.* not the persons of the priest

RESPECTEDST.

Isa. 57. † 9. thou *r.* the king and didst increase

RESPECTER.

Acts 10. 34. I perceive God is no *r.* of persons

RESPECTETH.

Job 37. 24. he *r.* not any that are wise of heart
Psal. 40. 4. blessed is the man that *r.* not the proud

RESPITE.

Exod. 8. 15. when Pharaoh saw that there was *r.*
1 *Sam.* 11. 3. the elders said, give us seven days' *r.*

REST

Signifies, [1] *A ceasing from labour or works*, Exod. 5. 5. | 35. 2. [2] *A respite, or breathing-time, from open wars and hostilities*, Josh. 14. 15. [3] *A calmness, composure, and tranquillity of spirit, and a cheerful confidence in the promises and providence of God*, Psal. 116. 7. [4] *A quiet, fixed, and secure habitation, such was* Canaan *to the* Israelites, *Deut.* 3. 20. *and the temple on* Moriah *to the ark, which before had no fixed place, or settlement*, Psal. 132. 8. *And* Naomi *says to* Ruth, The Lord grant you may find rest, *that is, a comfortable settlement*, Ruth 1. 9. [5] *The church and house of God, wherein Christ rested by his love and grace*, Isa. 11. 10. [6] *A ceasing from tillage and husbandry*, Lev. 25. 5. [7] *That peace with God and their own consciences, which believers enjoy in this world, having the love of God shed abroad in their hearts by the Holy Ghost, witnessing their reconciliation, justification, renovation, and adoption, so that they rejoice in hope of the glory of God*, Mat. 11. 29. Heb. 4. 3. For we which have believed do enter into rest. [8] *God's sacred rest from the works of creation*, Heb. 4. 4. And God did rest the seventh day from all his works; *that is, after God had perfected the invisible and visible world, on the review of all his works, finding them very good, he was satisfied in all those discoveries of his own perfections in the works of his hands. God always enjoyed his own glory and blessedness even from eternity; but this rest hath respect to the precedent work of creation, and that joyful reflection that God made upon his own works; because they were according to the model of his infinite wisdom, he was infinitely pleased in them. This sacred rest, and that which was promised to the* Israelites *in the land of* Canaan, *are mentioned by the apostles as illustrations of that rest which the saints shall enjoy in heaven after all their works done for the glory of God on earth.* Heb. 4. 9. There remaineth therefore a rest to the people of God. *The* Israelites *were at first harassed in* Egypt *with cruel oppression, and they were to pass through a waste and wild wilderness, wherein they were to have many hard and difficult journeys: to those that did believe and obey,* Canaan *was promised as a land of rest; but this temporal* Canaan *was only a type of the heavenly* Canaan, *the land above, that flows with milk and honey; that is, where holiness and joy and pleasure are for ever in perfection.*

REST, *Substantive.*
Gen. 8. † 21. the Lord smelled a savour of *r.*
49. 15. Issachar saw that *r.* was good
Exod. 16. 23. to-morrow the *r.* of the holy sabbath
31. 15. but in the seventh is the sabbath of *r.* 35. 2. *Lev.* 16. 31. | 23. 3, 32. | 25. 4.
33. 14. my presence shall go, and I will give thee *r.*
Lev. 25. 5. for it is a year of *r.* to the land
Num. 28. † 2. offering for a savour of *r.* shall observe
Deut. 3. 20. until the Lord have given *r. Josh.* 1. 13.
12. 9. for ye are not as yet come to the *r.*
10. when he giveth you *r.* from your enemies
25. 19. when the Lord thy God hath given thee *r.*
28. 65. neither shall the sole of thy foot have *r.*
Josh. 1. 15. the Lord hath given your brethren *r.*
14. 15. Hebron the inheritance of Caleb, and the land had *r.* from war, *Judg.* 3. 11. | 5. 31.
21. 44. the Lord gave them *r.* round about
22. 4. God hath given *r.* ‖ 23. 1. Lord had given *r.*
Judg. 3. 30. and the land had *r.* eighty years
Ruth 1. 9. the Lord grant you may find *r.* each
3. 1. daughter, shall I not seek *r.* for thee
18. for the man will not be in *r.* till have finished
2 *Sam.* 7. 1. the Lord had given him *r.* from his enemies, 1 *Kings* 5. 4. | 8. 56. 2 *Chron.* 14. 6, 7.
14. † 17. word of my lord king shall now be for *r.*
1 *Chron.* 6. 31. after that the ark had *r.*
22. 9. who shall be a man of *r.* and I will give him *r.*
18. hath he not given you *r.* on every side?
23. 25. God of Israel hath given *r.* to his people
28. 2. I had in mine heart to build a house of *r.*
2 *Chron.* 15. 15. the Lord gave them *r.* round about
20. 30. for his God gave him *r.* round about
Ezra 6. † 10. they may offer sacrifices of *r.* to God
Neh. 9. 28. but after they had *r.* they did evil again
Esth 2. † 18. he made a *r.* to the provinces
9. 16. the Jews had *r.* from their enemies
Job 3. 13. I should have slept, then had I been at *r.*
17. and there the weary be at *r.*
26. I was not in safety, neither had I *r.*
11. 18. thou shalt take thy *r.* in safety
17. 16. when our *r.* together is in the dust
36. † 16. *r.* of thy table should be full of fatness
Psal. 38. 3. neither is there any *r.* in my bones
55. 6. then would I fly away and be at *r.*
94. 13. that thou mayest give him *r.* from adversity
95. 11. that they should not enter into my *r.*
116. 7. return to thy *r.* O my soul, for the Lord
132. 8. arise, O Lord, into thy *r.* thou and ark
14. this is my *r.* for ever, here will I dwell
Prov. 29. 17. correct thy son, he shall give thee *r.*
Eccl. 2. 23. his heart taketh not *r.* in the night
6. 5. this hath more *r.* than the other
Isa. 11. 10. Gentiles seek, and his *r.* shall be glor.
14. 3. the Lord shall give thee *r.* from thy sorrow
7. whole earth is at *r.* and quiet, *Zech.* 1. 11.
18. 4. Lord said, I will take my *r.* and consider
28. 12. this is *r.* wherewith ye cause weary to rest
30. 15. in returning and *r.* shall ye be saved
34. 14. and find for herself a place of *r.*
66. 1. and where is the place of my *r.?*
Jer. 6. 16. and ye shall find *r.* for your souls
30. 10. Jacob shall return and be in *r.* 46. 27.
50. 34. that he may give *r.* to the land
Ezek. 16. † 19. hast set it before them for savour of *r.*
20. † 41. I will accept with your savour of *r.*
38. 11. I will go to them that are at *r.*
Dan. 4. 4. I Nebuchadnez. was at *r.* in mine house
Mic. 2. 10. arise and depart, for this is not your *r.*
Zech. 9. 1. and Damascus shall be the *r.* thereof
Mat. 11. 28. come unto me and I will give you *r.*
29. and ye shall find *r.* to your souls
12. 43. seeking *r.* and findeth none, *Luke* 11. 24.
26. 45. sleep on now, and take your *r. Mark* 14. 41.
John 11. 13. that he had spoken of taking *r.* in sleep
Acts 7. 49. or what is the place of my *r.?*
9. 31. then had the churches *r.* through all Judea
2 *Thess.* 1. 7. to you who are troubled *r.* with us
Heb. 3. 11. they shall not enter into my *r.* 18.
4. 1. lest a promise being left us of enter. into *r.*
3. for we which have believed do enter into *r.*
5. and again, if they shall enter into my *r.*
8. for if Jesus had given them *r.* then not spoken
9. there remaineth a *r.* to the people of God
10. he that is entered into his *r.* hath ceased
11. let us labour therefore to enter into that *r.*
See No.

REST, *Adjective.*
Gen. 30. 36. Jacob fed the *r.* of Laban's flock
Exod. 28. 10. the names of the *r.* on the other stone
Lev. 5. 9. the *r.* of the blood shall be wrung out
14. 17. the *r.* of the oil that is in his hand, 29.
Num. 31. 8. beside the *r.* of them that were slain
32. and the booty, being the *r.* of the prey
Deut. 3. 13. the *r.* of Gilead gave I to the half tribe
Josh. 10. 20. the *r.* entered into fenced cities
Judg. 7. 6. but the *r.* bowed down to drink water
1 *Sam.* 15. 15. and the *r.* have we utterly destroyed
2 *Sam.* 10. 10. the *r.* of the people he delivered to Abishai his brother, 1 *Chron.* 19. 11.
1 *Kings* 20. 30. the *r.* fled to Aphek to the city
2 *Kings* 4. 7. live thou and thy children of the *r.*
1 *Chron.* 11. 8. Joab repaired the *r.* of the city
16. 41. Jeduthun and the *r.* chosen to give thanks
2 *Chr.* 24. 14. they brought the *r.* of the money
Neh. 2. 16. nor told it to the *r.* that did the work
6. 1. *r.* of our enemies heard I had built the wall
11. 1. the *r.* of the people also cast lots
Esth. 9. 12. what have done in the *r.* of provinces?
Psal. 17. 14. and leave the *r.* to their babes
Isa. 10. 19. the *r.* of the trees of his forest be few
Ezek. 45. 8. the *r.* of the land shall give to Israel
Dan. 2. 18. that Daniel should not perish with the *r.*
Zech. 11. 9. let the *r.* eat the flesh of another
Mat. 27. 49. *r.* said, let us see if Elias will come
Luke 12. 26. why take ye thought for the *r.?*
24. 9. and told to the eleven and to all the *r.*
Acts 2. 37. they said to Peter and the *r.* of apostles
5. 13. of *r.* durst no man join himself to them
27. 44. and the *r.* they escaped all safe to land
Rom. 11. 7. election obtained, and *r.* were blinded
1 *Cor.* 7. 12. to the *r.* speak I, not the Lord
1 *Cor.* 11. 34. the *r.* will I set in order when I come
1 *Pet.* 4. 2. not live *r.* of his time to lusts of men
Rev. 2. 24. to you I say, and to the *r.* in Thyatira
9. 20. the *r.* that were not killed repented not
20. 5. *r.* of the dead lived not again till 1000 years
See Acts.

REST, *Verb.*
Gen. 18. 4. wash your feet, and *r.* under the tree
Exod. 5. 5. ye make them *r.* from their burdens
23. 11. in the seventh year thou shalt let it *r.*
12. on the seventh day thou shalt *r.* 34. 21.
34. 21. in earing time and in harvest thou shalt *r.*
Lev. 23. † 32. from even to even shall ye *r.*
25. † 2. then shall the land *r.* to the Lord, 26. 34.
26. 35. because it did not *r.* in your sabbaths
Deut. 5. 14. thy maid-servant may *r.* as well as thou
Josh. 3. 13. as soon as the feet of the priests shall *r.*
2 *Sam.* 3. 29. let it *r.* on the head of Joab
7. 11. have caused thee to *r.* from thine enemies
21. 10. neither the birds to *r.* on them by day
2 *Kings* 2. 15. the spirit of Elijah doth *r.* on Elisha
2 *Chron.* 14. 11. we *r.* on thee, in thy name we go
Job 3. 18. there the prisoners *r.* together, hear not
14. 6. that he may *r.* till he shall accomplish
Psal. 16. 9. my flesh shall *r.* in hope, *Acts* 2. 26.
37. 7. *r.* in the Lord, and wait patiently for him
125. 3. rod of wicked shall not *r.* on the righteous
Prov. 6. 35. nor will he *r.* content, tho' thou g. gifts
Cant. 1. 7. where thou makest thy flock to *r.* at noon
Isa. 7. 19. all of them shall *r.* in the desolate valleys
11. 2. the Spirit of the Lord shall *r.* upon him
25. 10. in this mountain shall the hand of Lord *r.*
28. 12. wherewith ye may cause the weary to *r.*
30. † 32. the grounded staff shall *r.* upon him
34. 14. the screech-owl also shall *r.* there
51. 4. I will make my judgment to *r.* for a light
57. 2. enter into peace, they shall *r.* in their beds
20. are like the troubled sea, when it cannot *r.*
62. 1. for Jerusalem's sake I will not *r.*
63. 14. the Spirit of the Lord caused him to *r.*
Jer. 31. 2. when I went to cause him to *r.*
47. 6. put up into thy scabbard, *r.* and be still
Ezek. 5. 13. I will cause my fury to *r.* upon them, and will be comforted, 16. 42. | 21. 17. | 24. 13.
44. 30. that he may cause the blessing to *r.*
Dan. 12. 13. for thou shalt *r.* and stand in the lot
Hab. 3. 16. that I might *r.* in the day of trouble
Zeph. 3. 17. he will *r.* in love, he will joy over thee
Mark 6. 31. come into a desert place, and *r.* a while
Luke 10. 6. if son of peace there, your peace shall *r.*
2 *Cor.* 12. 9. that the power of Christ may *r.* on me
Heb. 4. 4. God did *r.* seventh day from his works
Rev. 4. 8. they *r.* not day and night saying, Holy
6. 11. that they should *r.* yet for a little season
14. 13. that they may *r.* from their labours

RESTED.
Gen. 2. 2. he *r.* on seventh day, 3. *Ex.* 20. 11. | 31. 17.
8. 4. the ark *r.* ‖ *Exod.* 10. 14. locusts *r.* in Egypt
Exod. 16. 30. the people *r.* on the seventh day
Num. 9. 18. as long as the cloud abode they *r.* 23.
10. 12. the cloud *r.* in the wilderness of Paran
36. when it *r.* he said, return, O Lord, to thous.
11. 25. when the Spirit *r.* upon them, 26.
Josh. 11. 23. and the land *r.* from war
1 *Sam.* 25. † 9. they spake in David's name, and *r.*
1 *Kings* 6. 10. the chambers *r.* on the house
2 *Chron.* 32. 8. people *r.* on the words of Hezekiah
Esth. 9. 17. on the 14th day of the same *r.* they, 18.
22. wherein the Jews *r.* from their enemies
Job 30. 27. my bowels boiled and *r.* not
Luke 23. 56. they *r.* sabbath-day, according to com.

RESTEST.
Rom. 2. 17. thou art a Jew, and *r.* in the law

RESTETH.
Job 24. 23. it be given him in safety, whereon he *r.*
Prov. 14. 33. wisdom *r.* in heart of him that hath
Eccl. 7. 9. for anger *r.* in the bosom of fools
Isa. 7. † 2. saying, Syria *r.* on Ephraim
1 *Pet.* 4. 14. for the Spirit of God *r.* upon you

RESTING.
Num. 10. 33. to search out a *r.* place for them
2 *Chron.* 6. 41. arise, O Lord, into thy *r.* place
Prov. 24. 15. spoil not his *r.* place
Isa. 32. 18. my people shall dwell in *r.* places
Jer. 50. 6. they have forgotten their *r.* place

RESTITUTION.
Exod. 22. 3. he should make full *r.* 5, 6, 12.
Job 20. 18. according to his substance shall *r.* be
Acts 3. 21. until the times of *r.* of all things

RESTORE
Signifies, [1] *To give back again,* Gen. 20. 14. Judg. 11. 13. [2] *To set again in the first state or condition,* Gen. 40. 13. Isa. 1. 26. Acts 1. 6. [3] *To recover, or get again,* 2 Kings 14. 25. [4] *To make restitution or satisfaction for pretended wrongs out of one's proper right or substance,* Psal. 69. 4. [5] *To heal or cure,* Mat. 12. 13. [6] *To reform the corrupt state of the church, both in doctrine, worship, and life,* Mat. 17. 11. [7] *To endeavour to bring a person, that has fallen into sin, to a sight of his sin, to a sense of God's pardoning mercy, and to amendment of life,* Gal. 6. 1.
Gen. 20. 7. now therefore *r.* the man his wife, and if thou *r.* her not, thou shalt surely die
40. 13. Pharaoh will *r.* thee to thy place
42. 25. to *r.* every man's money into his sack
Exod. 22. 1. he shall *r.* five oxen for an ox
4. if theft be certainly found, he shall *r.* double
Lev. 6. 4. he shall *r.* that which he took away
5. he shall even *r.* it in the principal
24. 21. he that killeth a beast, he shall *r.* it
25. 27. and *r.* the overplus to whom he sold it
28. but if he be not able to *r.* it to him
Num. 35. 25. congregation shall *r.* him to the city
Deut. 22. 2. things strayed thou shalt *r.* again
Judg. 11. 13. therefore *r.* those lands again peaceably
17. 3. I will *r.* it, 1 *Sam.* 12. 3. 1 *Kings* 20. 34.
2 *Sam.* 9. 7. I will *r.* thee all the land of Saul
12. 6. he shall *r.* the lamb fourfold
16. 3. to-day shall the house of Israel *r.* me
2 *Kings* 8. 6. *r.* all that was hers, and fruits of field
Neh. 5. 11. *r.* I pray you, to them ‖ 12. we will *r.*
Job 20. 10. and his hands shall *r.* their goods
18. that which he laboureth for, shall he *r.*
Psal. 51. 12. *r.* to me the joy of thy salvation
Prov. 6. 31. if he be found, he shall *r.* sevenfold
Isa. 1. 26. I will *r.* thy judges as at the first
42. 22. they are for spoil, and none saith *r.*
49. 6. and to *r.* the preserved of Israel
57. 18. I will lead and *r.* comforts unto him
Jer. 27. 22. I will *r.* them to this place
30. 17. I will *r.* health to thee, and heal thee
Ezek. 33. 15. if the wicked *r.* pledge, shall live
Dan. 9. 25. command to *r.* and to build Jerusalem
Joel 2. 25. I will *r.* you the years locust hath eaten
Mat. 17. 11. Elias shall come and *r.* all things
Luke 19. 8. have taken any thing, I *r.* him fourfold
Acts 1. 6. Lord, wilt thou *r.* kingdom to Israel?
Gal. 6. 1. *r.* such an one in the spirit of meekness

RESTORED.
Gen. 20. 14. Abimelech *r.* him Sarah his wife
40. 21. he *r.* the chief butler to his butlership
41. 13. me he *r.* to mine office, him he hanged
42. 28. my money is *r.* and it is in my sack
Deut. 28. 31. thine ass shall not be *r.* to thee
Judg. 17. 3. when he had *r.* the 1100 shekels, 4.
1 *Sam.* 7. 14. the cities taken from Israel were *r.*
1 *Kings* 13. 6. pray for me, that my hand may be *r.* to me: the king's hand was *r.* him again
2 *Kings* 8. 1. woman, whose son he had *r.* to life, 5.
14. 22. he built and *r.* Elath to Judah, 2 *Chron.* 26. 2.
25. he *r.* coast of Israel from Hamath to the sea
2 *Chron.* 8. 2. the cities Huram had *r.* to Solomon
Ezra 6. 5. the vessels brought to Babylon be *r.*
Psal. 69. 4. I *r.* that which I took not away
Ezek. 18. 7. but hath *r.* to the debtor his pledge
12. hath spoiled by violence, hath not *r.* pledge
Mat. 12. 13. he stretched his hand forth and it was *r.* whole like as the other, *Mark* 3. 5. *Luke* 6. 10.
Mark 8. 25. his sight was *r.* and he saw clearly
Heb. 13. 19. that I may be *r.* to you the sooner

RESTORER.
Ruth 4. 15. he shall be to thee a *r.* of thy life
Isa. 58. 12. shall be called *r.* of paths to dwell in

RESTORETH.
Psal. 23. 3. he *r.* my soul, he leadeth me in paths
Mark 9. 12. Elias cometh first and *r.* all things

RESTORING.
Psal. 19. † 7. law of the Lord is perfect, *r.* the soul
Mic. 2. † 4. instead of *r.* he hath divided our fields

RESTRAIN.
1 *Sam.* 9. † 17. this same shall *r.* my people
2 *Kings* 4. † 24. *r.* not for me to ride except I bid thee
Job 15. 8. and dost thou *r.* wisdom to thyself?
Psal. 76. 10. the remainder of wrath shalt thou *r.*
Dan. 9. † 24. seventy weeks determined to *r.* transg.

RESTRAINED.
Gen. 8. 2. and the rain from heaven was *r.*
11. 6. and now nothing will be *r.* from them
16. 2. Sarai said, Lord hath *r.* me from bearing
Exod. 36. 6. the people were *r.* from bringing
1 *Sam.* 3. 13. Eli's sons vile, and he *r.* them not
Isa. 63. 15. thy mercies toward me, are they *r.?*
Ezek. 30. † 18. at Tehaphnehes the day shall be *r.*
31. 15. I *r.* the floods thereof, and great waters
Acts 14. 18. with these sayings scarce *r.* they people

RESTRAINEST.
Job 15. 4. yea, thou *r.* prayer before God

RESTRAINT.
Lev. 23. † 36. it is a day of *r. Deut.* 16. † 8. 2 *Chr.* 7. † 9. *Neh.* 8. † 18. *Joel* 1. † 14.
Judg. 18. † 7. there was no heir of *r.* to put to shame
1 *Sam.* 14. 6. for there is no *r.* to the Lord to save
Jer. 17. † 8. shall not be careful in the year of *r.*

RESTRAINTS.
Jer. 14. † 1. the word of the Lord concerning *r.*

RESTS.
1 *Kings* 6. 6. he made narrowed *r.* round about

RESURRECTION.
The belief of a general resurrection *of the dead, which will come to pass at the end of the world, and which will be followed with an immortality either of happiness or misery, is a principal article of religion in common to the* Jew *and the* Christian: *it is very expressly taught both in the* Old *and* New Testament. *Job* 19. 25, 26, 27. And though after my skin worms destroy this body, yet in my flesh shall I see God, &c. *John* 5. 28, 29. Marvel not at this, for the hour is coming, in which all that are in the graves shall hear his voice, and shall come forth, they that have done good, unto the resurrection of life; and they that have done evil, unto the resurrection of damnation.

The resurrection *is a doctrine unknown to the wisest heathens, and peculiar to the gospel: some glimmerings they had of the soul's immortality, but no knowledge of the reviving of the body. But reason assists faith in this point, both as to the will of God, and his power for the performing it. The divine laws are the rule of duty to the entire man, and not to the soul only; and they are obeyed or violated by the soul and body in conjunction. The soul designs, the body executes. The senses are the open ports to admit temptations. Carnal affections deprave the soul, corrupt the mind, and mislead it. The heart is the fountain of profaneness, and the tongue expresses it:* Thus the members are instruments of iniquity. *And the body is obedient to the holy soul in doing or suffering for God; and denies its sensual appetites and satisfactions in compliance with reason and grace;* the members are instruments of righteousness. *Hence it follows, that there will be an universal* resurrection, *that the rewarding goodness of God may appear in making the bodies of his servants gloriously happy with their souls, and their souls completely happy in union with their bodies, to which they have a natural inclination; and his revenging justice may be manifest, in punishing the bodies of the wicked with eternal torments answerable to their guilt. And as to the possibility of the resurrection, the continual production of things in the world, is a clear demonstration of the power of God for that effect. There is an instance that our Saviour and the apostle* Paul *made use of, as an image of the resurrection:* A grain of corn sowed in the earth, corrupts and dies, and after springs up entire; *its death is a disposition to life,* John 12. 24. 1 Cor. 15. 36. *The essays of God's power in the works of returning nature, flowers and fruits in their season, instruct us how easily he can make those that are in the dust to awake to life.*

But more especially the resurrection of Christ *is the argument, the claim, and assurance of the resurrection of believers to glory. For God chose and appointed him to be the example and principle, from whom all divine blessings should be derived to them; accordingly he tells his disciples,* Because I live, ye shall live also, *John* 14. 19. *He is called* the first-fruits *of them that slept,* 1 Cor. 15. 20. *because as the first fruits were a pledge and assurance of the following harvest; and as from the condition of the first-fruits being offered to God, the whole harvest was entitled to a consecration, so our Saviour's resurrection to the life of glory is the earnest and assurance of ours. He is the* Head, *believers are his* members; *and therefore shall have communion with him in his life. It is recorded, to confirm the hope of believers, how early his power was displayed in forcing the grave to release its captives.* Mat. 27. 52, 53. And many bodies of saints which slept, arose, and came out of the graves after his resurrection, and went into the holy city, and appeared unto many. *From what he has done, to what he can do, the consequence is clear.*

THE RESURRECTION OF CHRIST *is the most important article of the gospel, and the demonstration of all the rest; hence St.* Paul *says,* 1 Cor. 15. 14. If Christ be not risen, then is our preaching vain, and your faith is also vain: *And* verse 17, If Christ be not raised, your faith is vain, ye are yet in your sins. *The apostles, being sent to convert the world, were to lay this down as the foundation of their preaching,* That Jesus Christ was raised from the dead, *that all might yield faith and obedience to him.* Acts 1. 21, 22. Wherefore of these men which have companied with us, all the time that the Lord Jesus went in and out among us, beginning from the baptism of John, unto the same day that he was taken up from us, must one be ordained to be a witness with us of his resurrection. *The* resurrection of Christ *confirms the faith of* Christians *in his person, as he is thereby declared to be the* Son of God with power, *Rom.* 1. 4. *He was the Son of God from eternity, as the* WORD; *and from the first moment of his incarnation as* GOD-MAN: *yet the honour of this relation was much eclipsed in his poor life and ignominious death; but in his resurrection God did publicly own him in the face of the world: therefore he is represented testifying from heaven,* Thou art my Son, this day have I begotten thee, *Acts* 13. 33. *His resurrection was likewise a most pregnant proof of the all-sufficiency of his satisfaction. The curse of the law accompanied his death, and seemed like an infinite weight to lie on his grave; but in rising again, the value and virtue of his sufferings was fully declared.* Rom. 4. 25. He was delivered for our offences, and was raised again for our justification: *Having as our surety paid our debt, and given full satisfaction to divine justice, he was released from the grave, and the discharge was most solemnly published to the world. On this doctrine of his resurrection, as was said, is also built our faith in his promises, to give life and glory to his servants. For how could we believe him to be the Author of life, who remained under the power of death? If he had been confined to the grave, all our hopes had been buried with him. But his resurrection is the cause, pattern, and argument of ours; and* Christ *may be said, not only to have raised his body from the grave, but also his church with him.*

Mat. 22. 23. came to him the Sadducees, who say there is no *r. Mark* 12. 18. *Acts* 23. 8. 1 *Cor.* 15. 12.
28. therefore in the *r.* whose wife shall she be of the seven? *Mark* 12. 23. *Luke* 20. 33.
30. in the *r.* they neither marry, nor are given
31. but as touching the *r.* have ye not read that
27. 53. and came out of the graves after his *r.*
Luke 14. 14. thou shalt be recompensed at the *r.*
20. 27. deny any *r.* ‖ 36. the children of the *r.*
John 5. 29. they that have done good to the *r.* of life, that have done evil, to the *r.* of damnation
11. 24. I know that my brother shall rise in the *r.*
25. Jesus said to her, I am the *r.* and the life
Acts 1. 22. to be a witness with us of his *r.*
2. 31. David spake of the *r.* of Christ
4. 2. they preached through Jesus *r.* from the dead
33. gave witness of the *r.* of the Lord Jesus
17. 18. because he preached Jesus and the *r.*
32. when they heard of the *r.* some mocked
23. 6. of the hope and *r.* I am called in question
24. 15. that there shall be a *r.* of the dead
21. I cried among them, touching *r.* of the dead
Rom. 1. 4. declared by the *r.* from the dead
6. 5. we shall be also in the likeness of his *r.*
1 *Cor.* 15. 13. but if there be no *r.* of the dead
21. by man came the *r.* ‖ 42. so is *r.* of the dead
Phil. 3. 10. that I may know the power of his *r.*
11. if I might attain to the *r.* of the dead
2 *Tim.* 2. 18. saying, that the *r.* is past already
Heb. 6. 2. of *r.* from the dead, and eternal judgment
11. 35. that they might obtain a better *r.*
1 *Pet.* 1. 3. a lively hope, by *r.* of Jesus from dead
3. 21. baptism doth save us, by *r.* of Jesus Christ
Rev. 20. 5. this is the first *r.*
Rev. 20. 6. blessed and holy is he hath part in first *r.*

RETAIN.

1 *Chr.* 29. † 14. my people that we should *r.* strength
Job 2. 9. dost thou still *r.* thine integrity?
Prov. 4. 4. he said, let thine heart *r.* my words
11. 16. gracious woman honour, strong men *r.* riches
Eccl. 8. 8. no man hath power to *r.* the spirit
Dan. 11. 6. she shall not *r.* the power of the arm
John 20. 23. whose soever sins ye *r.* they are retain.
Rom. 1. 28. did not like to *r.* God in their knowl.

RETAINED.

Judg. 7. 8. Gideon *r.* those three hundred men
19. 4. the damsel's father *r.* him, and he abode
Dan. 10. 8. left alone, and I *r.* no strength, 16.
John 20. 23. whose sins ye retain, they are *r.*
Philem. 13. whom I would have *r.* with me

RETAINETH.

Prov. 3. 18. and happy is every one that *r.* her
11. 16. grac. woman *r.* honour, strong men riches
Mic. 7. 18. he *r.* not his anger for ever

RETIRE.

2 *Sam.* 11. 15. set him in the hottest battle, and *r.*
Jer. 4. 6. set up standard toward Zion, *r.* stay not

RETIRED.

Judg. 20. 39. when the men of Israel *r.* in battle
2 *Sam.* 20. 22. they *r.* from the city every man

RETURN, *Substantive.*

Gen. 14. 17. went out to meet Abram after his *r.*
1 *Sam.* 7. 17. Samuel's *r.* was to Ramah, his house
2 *Sam.* 11 † 1. at *r.* of year Dav. sent, 1 *Chr.* 20. † 1.
1 *Kings* 20. 22. for at the *r.* of the year the king of Syria will come up against thee, 26.

RETURN

Signifies, [1] *To go back again,* Exod. 13. 17. [2] *To come again,* 2 Chron. 18. 26. [3] *To requite or recompense,* 1 Kings 2. 44. [4] *To repent, as when a sinner, who has erred from the ways of God's commandments, doth return to God by unfeigned repentance,* Isa. 10. 21. Ezek. 18. 32. [5] *To comply with sinners in their sinful courses, or to soothe them up therein,* Jer. 15. 19. [6] *To shew fresh signs of favour and mercy, after some afflictions for sins,* Psal. 6. 4. Joel 2. 14. [7] *To relate,* Exod. 19. 8. [8] *To depart or get away,* 1 Sam. 29. 4. [9] *To iterate,* Prov. 26. † 11.

Gen. 3. 19. in sweat eat bread, till thou *r.* to the ground, for dust thou art, to dust shalt thou *r.*
16. 9. *r.* to thy mistress and submit thyself
18. 10. he said, I will certainly *r.* to thee, 14.
31. 3. and *r.* to the land of thy kindred, 13.
32. 9. O God, the Lord, which saidst to me, *r.*
Exod. 4. 18. let me *r.* to my brethren in Egypt
19. the Lord said unto Moses, go *r.* into Egypt
13. 17. lest the people repent, and *r.* to Egypt
Lev. 25. 10. shall *r.* to his possession, 13, 27, 28.
41. and he shall *r.* unto his own family
27. 24. in year of jubilee, the field shall *r.* to him
Num. 8. † 25. from the age of fifty *r.* from warfare
10. 36. *r.* Lord, to the many thousands of Israel
14. 4. let us make a captain, and *r.* into Egypt
23. 5. the Lord said, *r.* unto Balak, and speak
32. 22. then afterward ye shall *r.* and be guiltless
35. 28. after the death of high priest, the slayer shall *r.* to the land of his possession, *Josh.* 20. 6.
Deut. 3. 20. then shall ye *r.* every man to his possession which I have given to you, *Josh.* 1. 15.
17. 16. nor shall he cause people to *r.* to Egypt
20. 5. let him go and *r.* to his house, 6, 7, 8.
30. 3. the Lord thy God will *r.* and gather thee
8. thou shalt *r.* and obey the voice of the Lord
Josh. 22. 4. now *r.* ye, and get you unto your tents
8. saying, *r.* with much riches to your tents
Judg. 7. 3. whosoever is fearful and afraid, let him *r.*
11. 31. when I *r.* from the children of Ammon
Ruth 1. 6. arose, that she might *r.* from Moab
8. Naomi said, go *r.* to her mother's house
10. surely we will *r.* with thee to thy people
15. *r.* thou after thy sister-in-law
1 *Sam.* 6. 3. but in any wise *r.* him trespass-offering
8. and put the jewels of gold which ye *r.* him
9. 5. Saul said to his servant, come, let us *r.*
26. 21. then said Saul, I have sinned *r.* my son Da.
29. 4. the princes said, make this fellow *r.* 7.
2 *Sam.* 2. 26. how long ere thou bid the people *r.*?
3. 16. then said Abner to him, go, *r.* he returned
10. 5. till beards be grown, then *r.* 1 *Chron.* 19. 5.
15. 19. wherefore goest thou also with us? *r.*
20. seeing I go whither I may, *r.* thou, and take
34. if thou *r.* to the city and say unto Absalom
19. 14. they said, *r.* thou and all thy servants
24. 13. advise and see what answer I shall *r.*
1 *Kings* 2. 32. the Lord shall *r.* his blood, 33.
44. Lord shall *r.* thy wickedness upon thine head
8. 48. so *r.* to thee with all their heart and soul
12. 24. ye shall not go, *r.* every man to his house
26. now shall the kingdom *r.* to house of David
19. 15. go, *r.* on thy way to the wilderness
22. 17. these have no master, let them *r.* every man to his house in peace, 2 *Chr.* 11. 4. | 18. 16.
28. if thou *r.* at all in peace, 2 *Chron.* 18. 27.
2 *Kings* 18. 14. saying, I have offended, *r.* from me
19. 7. the king of Assyria shall hear a rumour and shall *r.* to his own land, 33. *Isa.* 37. 7, 34.
20. 10. nay, but let the shadow *r.* backward
2 *Chron.* 6. 24. and shall *r.* and confess thy name
38. if they *r.* to thee with all their heart
10. 9. that we may *r.* answer to this people
18. 26. put this fellow in the prison until I *r.*
30. 6. he will *r.* to you ‖ 9. if ye *r.* unto him
Neh. 2. 6. the king said to me, when wilt thou *r.*?
4. 12. from all places, whence ye shall *r.* to us
Esth. 4. 15. Esther bade them *r.* Mordecai this answ.
9. 25. devise of Haman should *r.* upon his own head
Job 1. 21. and naked shall I *r.* thither
6. 29. *r.* yea, *r.* again, my righteousness is in it
7. 10. he shall *r.* no more to his house, nor place
15. 22. he believeth not that he shall *r.* out of dark.
17. 10. but as for you all, do ye *r.* and come now
22. 23. if thou *r.* to the Almighty, be built up
33. 25. he shall *r.* to the days of his youth
Job 35. † 4. I will *r.* words to thee, and companions
36. 10. commandeth that they *r.* from iniquity
Psal. 6. 4. *r.* O Lord, deliver my soul, O save me
10. let mine enemies *r.* and be ashamed
7. 7. for their sakes therefore *r.* thou on high
16. his mischief shall *r.* upon his own head
59. 6. they *r.* at evening ‖ 14. and let them *r.*
73. 10. therefore his people *r.* hither, and waters
74. 21. let not the oppressed *r.* ashamed, let poor
80. 14. *r.* we beseech thee, O God of hosts
90. 3. thou sayest, *r.* ye children of men
13. *r.* O Lord? how long? and let it repent thee
94. 15. judgment shall *r.* unto righteousness
104. 29. they die, and *r.* to their dust
116. 7. *r.* to thy rest, O my soul, Lord hath dealt
Prov. 2. 19. none that go unto her *r.* again, neither
26. 27. he that rolleth a stone, it will *r.* on him
Eccl. 1. 7. from whence rivers come, thither they *r.*
5. 15. naked shall he *r.* to go as he came
12. 2. nor the clouds *r.* after the rain
7. dust shall *r.* to the earth, and spirit *r.* to God
Cant. 6. 13. *r. r.* O Shulamite, *r. r.* that we may
Isa. 1. † 27. they that *r.* of her shall be redeemed
6. 13. yet in it a tenth shall *r.* and shall be eaten
10. 21. the remnant of Jacob shall *r.* to God, 22.
21. 12. if ye will inquire, inquire ye, *r.* come
35. 10. the ransomed of the Lord shall *r.* 51. 11.
41. † 28. that when I asked them could *r.* a word
44. 22. *r.* unto me, for I have redeemed thee
63. 17. *r.* for thy servant's sake, the tribes
Jer. 3. 1. shall he *r.* to her again? yet *r.* again to me
12. proclaim these words, *r.* backsliding Israel
22. *r.* ye backsliding children, and I will heal
4. 1. if thou wilt *r.* saith the Lord, *r.* unto me
12. 15. I will *r.* and have compassion on them
15. 19. thus saith the Lord, if thou *r.* let them *r.* unto thee, but *r.* not thou unto them
18. 11. *r.* ye every one from his evil way, 35. 15.
22. 10. for he shall *r.* no more his country
23. 14. that none doth *r.* from his wickedness
24. 7. for they shall *r.* with their whole heart
30. 10. and Jacob shall *r.* and be in rest, 46. 27.
31. 8. a great company shall *r.* thither
36. 3. that ye may *r.* every man from his evil way
7. it may be they will *r.* every one fr. his evil way
37. 7. behold, Pharaoh's army shall *r.* to Egypt
44. 14. that they should *r.* into the land of Judah, for none shall *r.* but such as escape, 28.
50. 9. their arrows none shall *r.* in vain
Ezek. 16. 55. when Sodom and Samaria shall *r.* they desire to *r.* then thou and thy daughters shall *r.*
18. 23. that wicked should *r.* from ways and live
46. 17. after it shall *r.* to the prince
Dan. 9. † 25. after sixty-two weeks shall street *r.*
10. 20. and now will I *r.* to fight with Persia
11. 9. and shall *r.* into his own land, 10, 28.
13. the king of the north shall *r.* and set forth
29. and the time apointed he shall *r.* and come
30. therefore he shall be grieved and *r.*
Hos. 2. 7. I will go and *r.* to my first husband
9. I will *r.* and take away my corn and my wine
3. 5. afterward shall the children of Israel *r.*
5. 15. I will go and *r.* to my place, till they
7. 16. they *r.* but not to the Most High
8. 13. visit their sins they shall *r.* to Egypt, 9. 3.
12. 14. his reproach shall his Lord *r.* unto him
14. 7. they that dwell under the shadow shall *r.*
Joel 2. 14. who knoweth if he will *r.* and repent
3. 4. speedily will I *r.* recompence on your head, 7.
Obad. 15. thy reward shall *r.* upon thine own head
Mic. 1. 7. they shall *r.* to the hire of an harlot
5. 3. then the remnant of his brethren shall *r.*
Mal. 1. 4. whereas Edom saith, we will *r.* and build
3. 7. *r.* to me, and I will *r.* to you, saith the Lord of hosts, but ye said, wherein shall we *r.*?
18. then shall ye *r.* and discern between righteous
Mat. 10. 13. if it be not worthy, let your peace *r.*
12. 44. he saith, I will *r.* into my house, *Luke* 11. 24.
24. 18. nor let him which is in the field, *r.* back
Luke 8. 39. *r.* to thine own house, shew how great
12. 36. when he will *r.* from the wedding
Acts 15. 16. after this I will *r.* and build again
18. 21. but I will again *r.* to you, if God will

To RETURN.

Exod. 4. 21. when thou goest *to r.* into Egypt
Num. 14. 3. were it not better for us *to r.* to Egypt
Deut. 17. 16. nor cause the people *to r.* into Egypt
Ruth 1. 7. they went *to r.* unto the land of Judah
16. entreat me not to leave thee, or *to r.*
1 *Sam.* 29. 11. so David and his men rose early *to r.*
2 *Chr.* 10. 6. what counsel give ye *to r.* answer, 9.
Neh. 9. 17. appointed a captain *to r.* to bondage
Jer. 5. 3. they have refused *to r.* 8. 5. *Hos.* 11. 5.
22. 27. to the land where they desire *to r.* 44. 14.
29. 10. in causing you *to r.* to this place, 30. 3. | 32. 44. | 33. 7, 11, 26. | 34. 22. | 42. 12.
34. 11. but they caused the servants *to r.* 16.
37. 20. cause me not *to r.* to the house, 38. 26.
Lam. 3. † 21. this I make *to r.* to my heart
Ezek. 21. 30. shall I cause it *to r.* into his sheath?
29. 14. cause them *to r.* to the land of Pathros
47. 6. caused me *to r.* to the brink of the river
Hos. 4. † 9. I will cause *to r.* their doings
11. 5. Assyrian be his king, bec. they refused *to r.*
Luke 19. 12. went to receive a kingdom and *to r.*
Acts 13. 34. now no more *to r.* to corruption
20. 3. he purposed *to r.* through Macedonia

RETURN *to,* or *unto the Lord.*

Deut. 30. 2. and shalt *r. unto the Lord,* and obey
1 *Sam.* 7. 3. if ye *r. unto the L.* with all your hearts
Isa. 19. 22. they shall *r. unto Ld.* he shall heal them
55. 7. let him *r. unto L.* he will have mercy on him
Hos. 6. 1. let us *r. unto the Lord,* for he hath torn
7. 10. they do not *r. to Lord* nor seek him for this
14. 1. O Israel, *r. unto L.* thy G. for thou hast fallen

Not RETURN.

Num. 32. 18. we will *not r.* to our houses till Israel
Deut. 28. † 31. thy ass taken, and shall *not r.* to thee
1 *Sam.* 15. 26. Samuel said, I will *not r.* with thee
2 *Sam.* 12. 23. go to him, but he shall *not r.* to me
1 *Kings* 13. 16. he said, I may *not r.* with thee
Job 7. † 7. mine eyes shall *not r.* to see good

Job 10. 21. before I go whence I shall not r. 16. 22.
39. 4. they go forth, and r. not unto them
Isa. 45. 23. the word is gone out, and shall not r.
55. 11. it shall not r. to me void, but accomplish
Jer. 8. 4. shall he turn away, and not r.?
15. 7. destroy, since they r. not from their ways
22. 11. he shall not r. thither any more, 27.
23. 20. the anger of the Lord shall not r. 30. 24.
Ezek. 7. 13. for seller shall not r. to what is sold, the whole multitude thereof which shall not r.
13. 22. that he should not r. from his wicked way
21. 5. my sword not r. any more into his sheath
35. 9. thy cities shall not r. and ye shall know
46. 9. he shall not r. by the way he came in
Hos. 7. 10. they do not r. to the Lord, nor seek him
11. 5. he shall not r. into the land of Egypt
9. I will not r. to destroy Ephraim, I am God
Mat. 2. 12. being warned they should not r. to Herod
Luke 17. 31. he in field, let him likewise not r. back

RETURNED.

Gen. 8. 3. waters r. from off the earth continually
9. the dove r. to him || 12. the dove r. not again
18. 33. and Abraham r. unto his place
22. 19. so Abraham r. to his young men
42. 24. Joseph r. again, and communed with them
43. 10. surely now we had r. this second time
18. because of the money that was r. in our sacks
Exod. 5. 22. Moses r. to the Lord and said, 32. 31.
14. 27. and the sea r. to his strength, 28.
19. 8. Moses r. the words of the people to Lord
Lev. 22. 13. if she is r. to her father's house
Num. 11. † 4. the children of Israel r. and wept, and said, who shall give us flesh to eat? Deut. 1. 45.
24. 25. Balaam rose up, and r. to his place
Josh. 2. 16. hide yourselves till pursuers be r. 22.
4. 18. that the waters of Jordan r. to their place
22. 9. the children of Reuben and of Gad r.
32. Phinehas and the princes r. from Reuben
Judg. 2. 19. when the judge was dead they r.
5. 29. yea, she r. answer to herself
7. 3. there r. of the people 22,000 from Gideon
8. 13. Gideon r. from battle before sun was up
11. 39. Gideon's daughter r. to her father
21. 23. the Benjamites r. to their inheritance
Ruth 1. 22. so Naomi and Ruth her daughter r.
1 Sam. 1. † 27. whom I obtained by petition shall be r.
6. 16. they r. to Ekron the same day
17. 57. David r. from the slaughter of Goliath
25. 39. the Lord hath r. the wickedness of Nabal
2 Sam. 1. 22. the sword of Saul r. not empty
3. 16. then said Abner, go, return, and he r.
6. 20. then David r. to bless his household
16. 8. Lord r. on thee all blood of house of Saul
17. 3. the man whom thou seekest, is as if all r.
19. 15. so the king r. and came to Jordan
23. 10. and the people r. after him only to spoil
1 Kings 13. 10. and r. not by the way that he came
33. after this thing Jeroboam r. not from evil
2 Kings 4. 35. Elisha r. and walked to and fro
5. 15. he r. to man of God, he and his company
2 Chron. 25. 10. and they r. home in great anger
32. 21. Sennacherib r. with shame of face to land
Ezra 5. 11. thus they r. us answer, saying
Neh. 4. 15. we r. all of us to the wall to work
9. 28. yet when they r. and cried unto thee
Psal. 35. 13. my prayer r. into mine own bosom
78. 34. they r. and enquired early after God
126. † 1. when the Lord r. the returning of Zion
Isa. 38. 8. so sun r. ten degrees, by which degrees
Jer. 3. 7. I said, turn thou unto me, but she r. not
14. 3. they r. with their vessels empty, were ashamed
18. † 4. so he r. and made it another vessel
40. 12. even all the Jews r. out of all places
Ezek. 1. 14. and the living creatures ran, and r.
17. and they r. not when they went
8. 17. and have r. to provoke me to anger
9. † 11. the man with the inkhorn r. the word
47. 7. when I had r. lo, at the bank of the river
Dan. 4. 34. mine understanding r. unto me
36. at the same time my reason r. unto me
Hos. 6. 11. when I r. the captivity of my people
Amos 4. 6. yet have ye not r. to me, 8. 9, 10, 11.
Zech. 1. 6. they r. and said, as the Lord thought
16. thus saith L. I am r. to Jerusal. with mercies
7. 14. land desolate, that no man passed thro' nor r.
8. 3. I am r. to Zion, and will dwell in midst
Mat. 21. 18. in the morning as he r. into the city
Mark 14. 40. when he r. he found them asleep
Luke 1. 56. and Mary r. to her own house
2. 20. shepherds r. glorifying God for all things
4. 1. Jesus full of the Holy Ghost r. from Jordan
14. Jesus r. in power of the Spirit into Galilee
8. 37. he went up into the ship and r. back again
40. when Jesus r. the people gladly received him
9. 10. the apostles when r. again told him all
10. 17. the seventy r. again with joy, saying
17. 18. are not found that r. to give glory to God
19. 15. when he was r. having received kingdom
23. 48. all the people smote their breasts and r.
56. they r. and prepared spices and rested sabbath
24. 9. r. from sepulchre and told all these things
33. they rose same hour, and r. to Jerusalem
52. they worshipped him, and r. to Jerusalem
Acts 1. 12. then r. they to Jerusalem from Olivet
5. 22. when the officers found them not, they r.
8. 25. the apostles r. to Jerusalem, and preached
12. 25. Barnabas and Saul r. from Jerusalem
13. 13. and John departing from them, r. to Jerusalem
14. 21. they r. again to Lystra and Iconium
21. 6. we took ship, and they r. home again
23. 32. they left the horsemen and r. to the castle
Gal. 1. 17. and I r. again unto Damascus
Heb. 11. 15. might have had opportunity to have r.
1 Pet. 2. 25. now r. to the Shepherd of your souls

RETURNETH.

Psal. 146. 4. his breath goeth, he r. to his earth
Prov. 26. 11. as a dog r. to his vomit, so a fool r.
Eccl. 1. 6. the wind r. according to his circuits
Isa. 55. 10. rain r. not thither, but watereth earth
Ezek. 35. 7. him that r. I will cut off from Seir
Zech. 9. 8. I will encamp because of him that r.

RETURNING.

Gen. 8. † 3. the waters returned in going and r.
† 7. the raven went forth in going and r.
Psal. 126. † 1. when the Lord returned r. of Zion
Isa. 30. 15. in r. and rest shall ye be saved
Luke 7. 10. and they r. found the servant whole
Acts 8. 28. was r. and sitting chariot, read Esaias
Heb. 7. 1. met Abraham r. from slaughter of kings

REVEAL.

To reveal *signifies, To discover that which was before concealed, as* to reveal *a secret,* Prov. 11. 13. *Also to make a person understand any part of divine truth which he knew not, or was in a mistake about before.* If in any thing ye be otherwise minded, God shall reveal even this unto you, *Phil.* 3. 15. *The apostle* Paul, *speaking of the gospel, says,* That therein is the righteousness of God revealed, *Rom.* 1. 17. that is, *That way, or method of becoming righteous, which is of God's institution, ordination, appointment, and establishment, and which alone he will accept of to life, namely by faith in Christ, is fully and plainly discovered in the gospel; which was wholly unknown to the* Gentiles, *and but obscurely made known to the* Jews. *And in verse* 18. *he says,* That the wrath of God is revealed from heaven against all ungodliness of men: *His displeasure was made known by those judgments which he inflicts upon sinners, and by their remorse and the challenges of their consciences.*

Revelation, *in Greek* Αποκαλυψις, *is the name given in particular to that part of the holy Scriptures which was revealed to* John *the Divine, in the isle of* Patmos, *whither he had been banished by* Domitian, *and which chiefly contains prophecies, or predictions concerning the state of the church in future ages. It is also called* Revelation, *when God makes manifest any thing to man in an extraordinary and supernatural manner, whether by dream, vision, ecstasy, or otherwise. St.* Paul *says, That he had not received the gospel by the ministry of men, but by a particular* Revelation *from God, who had immediately conveyed the knowledge of divine things unto him,* Gal. 1. 12. *And elsewhere, That he did not go up to* Jerusalem *after his conversion by the mere motion of his own mind, but in consequence of a* revelation *that he had for that purpose,* Gal. 2. 2. *The word* Apocalypsis *is used likewise to express the manifestation of* Christ *to the* Jews *and* Gentiles, *Luke* 2. 32. *The manifestation of the glory with which God will glorify his elect and his faithful servants at the last judgment,* Rom. 8. 18. *And the declaration of his just judgments, in his conduct both towards the godly and towards the wicked,* Rom. 2. 5.

Ruth 4. † 4. and I said, I will r. in thine ear
Job 20. 27. the heaven shall r. his iniquity
Psal. 119. † 18. r. mine eyes that I may behold
Jer. 33. 6. I will r. them abundance of peace
Dan. 2. 47. seeing thou couldest r. this secret
Mat. 11. 27. the Father, but the Son, and he to whomsoever the Son will r. him, Luke 10. 22.
Gal. 1. 16. called me by his grace, to r. his Son in me
Phil. 3. 15. God shall r. even this unto you

REVEALED.

Deut 29. 29. but things r. to us and our children
1 Sam. 3. 7. nor was the word of the Lord r. to him
21. the Lord r. himself to Samuel in Shiloh
9. † 15. now the Lord had r. the ear of Samuel
2 Sam. 7. 27. thou hast r. to thy servant, saying
1 Chron. 17. † 25. hast r. the ear of thy servant
Esth. 8. † 13. the copy of the writing r. to people
Psal. 98. † 2. his righteousness hath he r.
Isa. 22. 14. it was r. in mine ears by the Lord
23. 1. from the land of Chittim it is r. to them
40. 5. and the glory of the Lord shall be r.
53. 1. to whom is arm of Lord r.? John 12. 38.
56. 1. and my righteousness is near to be r.
Jer. 11. 20. for unto thee have I r. my cause
Dan. 2. 19. then was the secret r. to Daniel
30. this secret is not r. to me for any wisdom
10. 1. a thing was r. to Daniel, and was true
Mat. 10. 26. for there is nothing covered that shall not be r. nor hid that sh. not be known, Luke 12. 2.
11. 25. and hast r. them to babes, Luke 10. 21.
16. 17. flesh and blood hath not r. it unto thee
Luke 2. 26. it was r. to Simeon by the Holy Ghost
35. that the thoughts of many hearts may be r.
17. 30. shall be in day when the Son of man r.
Rom. 1. 17. therein is the righteousness of God r.
18. for the wrath of God is r. from heaven
8. 18. with the glory which shall be r. in us
1 Cor. 2. 10. God hath r. them to us by his Spirit
3. 13. day declare it, because it shall be r. by fire
14. 30. if any thing be r. to another that sitteth
Gal. 3. 23. the faith which should afterwards be r.
Eph. 3. 5. as it is now r. to his holy apostles
2 Thess. 1. 7. when the Lord Jesus shall be r.
2. 3. a falling away first, and that man of sin be r.
6. withholdeth, that he might be r. in his time
8. that wicked one be r. whom L. shall consume
1 Pet. 1. 5. to salvation, ready to be r. in last time
12. unto whom it was r. that not to themselves
4. 13. that when his glory shall be r. ye may be
5. 1. and also a partaker of glory that shall be r.

REVEALER.

Dan. 2. 47. your God a God of gods, a r. secrets

REVEALETH.

Job 33. † 16. then he r. the ears of men, and sealeth
Prov. 11. 13. a tale-bearer r. secrets, 20. 19.
Dan. 2. 22. he r. the deep and secret things
28. but there is a God in heaven that r. secrets
29. he that r. secrets maketh known to thee
Amos 3. 7. he r. his secrets to his servants prophets

REVELATION.

Rom. 2. 5. and r. of the righteous judgment of God
16. 25. according to r. of mystery kept secret
1 Cor. 1. † 7. waiting for the r. of our Lord Jesus
14. 6. except I shall speak to you either by r.
26. every one hath a r. hath an interpretation
Gal. 1. 12. but by the r. of Jesus Christ
Gal. 2. 2. and I went up by r. and communicated
Eph. 1. 17. may give you the Spirit of wisdom and r.
3. 3. how that by r. he made known to me
1 Pet. 1. 13. grace brought at the r. of Jesus Christ
Rev. 1. 1. the r. of Jesus Christ, which God gave

REVELATIONS.

2 Cor. 12. 1. I will come to visions and r. of the L.
7. lest I should be exalted thro' abundance of r.

REVELLINGS.

Gal. 5. 21. works of the flesh are r. and such like
1 Pet. 4. 3. when ye walked in lusts, r. banquetings

REVENGE.

Revenge, *as it includes a sense of sorrow and trouble for the injuries that are done to us, cannot by any means belong to God. None of his creatures can disturb his peace, or cause to him any trouble or resentment. Man has recourse to* revenge, *only because he is galled and sensible of injuries. When therefore it is said in scripture, that God revenges himself, it speaks after a popular and improper manner. He vindicates the injuries done to his justice and his majesty, and to the order he has established in the world, yet without any emotion of pleasure or displeasure. He revenges the injuries done to his servants because he is just, and because order and justice must be preserved. Men revenge themselves out of weakness, because they are offended, because they are too much influenced by self-love. A great soul overlooks and despises injuries; a soul enlightened by grace and faith, leaves the judgment and revenge of them to God, who has sufficiently declared himself, to make it understood by good men, that vengeance belongeth only to him;* To me belongeth vengeance and recompence, *Deut.* 32. 35. *He forbids malice and* revenge, *in express terms; he will not allow us to keep any resentment in our hearts against our brethren:* Thou shalt not hate thy brother in thine heart; thou shalt in any wise rebuke thy neighbour, and not suffer sin upon him: Thou shalt not avenge, nor bear any grudge against the children of thy people, *Lev.* 19. 17, 18. *And when God established the* Lex Talionis, *he does not thereby allow of* revenge, *but sets limits to it.* Non fomes, sed limes furoris est, *says* Austin. *He does not intend to provoke to anger, but to stop the progress and consequences of it.* Non ut id quod sopitum erat, hinc accenderetur: sed ne id quod ardebat, ultra extenderetur.

Jer. 15. 15. O Lord, r. me of my persecutors.
2 Cor. 10. 6. in readiness to r. all disobedience

REVENGE, *Substantive.*

Jer. 20. 10. and we shall take our r. on him
Ezek. 25. 15. because the Philistines have dealt by r.
2 Cor. 7. 11. yea, what r. it wrought in you

REVENGED.

Ezek. 25. 12. because Edom r. himself upon them

REVENGER.

Num. 35. 19. the r. shall slay the murderer, 21.
24. congregation shall judge between slayer and r.
25. deliver the slayer out of the hand of the r.
27. if r. find him without, and r. kill the slayer
Nah. 1. † 2. the Lord is a jealous God, and a r.
Rom. 13. 4. for he is minister of G. a r. to execute

REVENGERS.

2 Sam. 14. 11. that thou wouldest not suffer the r.

REVENGES.

Deut. 32. 42. from the beginning of r. on enemy
Psal. 94. † 1. O God of r. shew thyself, lift up thyself

REVENGETH.

Nah. 1. 2. the Lord r. the Lord r. and is furious

REVENGING.

Psal. 79. 10. by the r. of the blood of thy servants
Ezek. 25. † 12. Edom dealt by r. revengement

REVENUE.

Ezra 4. 13. so thou shalt endamage the r. of kings
Prov. 8. 19. my r. is better than choice silver
Isa. 23. 3. the harvest of the river is her r.

REVENUES.

Prov. 15. 6. but in the r. of the wicked is trouble
16. 8. a little is better than great r. without right
Jer. 12. 13. they shall be ashamed of your r.

REVERENCE.

Reverence *when it is said to be given to man, is a submissive humble carriage and respect, which inferiors owe to their superiors; thus,* Mephibosheth *did* reverence *to* David, *and acknowledged him for his sovereign,* 2 Sam. 9. 6. *And wives are commanded to* reverence their husbands, *Eph.* 5. 33. *that is, to esteem them, to fear them, not with a servile, but ingenuous fear, and such as proceeds from love, and to manifest their esteem by the whole of their carriage towards them. But when God is the object of our* reverence, *it signifies, That holy, humble, and filial fear of his displeasure, and that submissive, lowly, and self-abasing temper of spirit, with which we should approach to him in the duties of his worship, and with which we should demean ourselves under his chastenings; this temper being absolutely necessary and most congruous with respect to God, upon the account of his sovereignty, justice, and goodness, declared in his chastenings; and with respect to our frailty, our dependence upon him, our obnoxiousness to his law, and our obligations to him, that he will please to afflict us for our good. To this purpose the apostle speaks;* Heb. 12. 9. We have had fathers of our flesh who corrected us, and we gave them reverence; shall we not much rather be in subjection unto the Father of spirits, and live? *We have had our natural parents, who were our instructors and correctors, who made use of the rod, as well as the word, for our nurture, yet our bowels turned towards them; we have been covered with shame and blushing for our faults, and have submitted to their correction, so as to reform and turn from the faults for which they chastised us: and shall we not much rather submissively receive correction from God, reform under it, and resign our souls to him who is the Creator of them, and the sovereign, guardian, protector, and disposer of them? Likewise in the duties of prayer, hearing the word, and the like, an humble conception of God, as the supreme, eternal, and infinitely perfect Being; as the omnipresent, omniscient, and an incomprehensibly glorious Majesty, whose throne is in heaven, whose Name alone is excellent, whose glory is above the earth and heaven, would engage us to approach him with deep reverence and holy fear.* Heb. 12. 28, 29. Let us have grace, whereby we may serve God acceptably, with reverence and godly fear; for our God is a consuming fire.

Lev. 19. 30. shall *r.* my sanctuary, I am Lord, 26. 2.
Esth. 3. 2. all the king's servants in gate *r.* Haman
Mat. 21. 37. but last of all he sent to them his son, they will *r.* my son, *Mark* 12. 6. *Luke* 20. 13.
Eph. 5. 33. the wife see that she *r.* her husband

REVERENCE.

2 *Sam.* 9. 6. Mephibosheth did *r.* to David
1 *Kings* 1. 31. Bathsheba bowed, and did *r.* to king
Esth. 3. 2. Mordecai bowed not, nor did him *r.* 5.
Psal. 89. 7. to be had in *r.* of all that are about him
Heb. 12. 9. we gave them *r.* || 28. serve God with *r.*
1 *Pet.* 3. † 15. to give an answer of your hope with *r.*

REVEREND.

Psal. 111. 9. he sent redemp. holy and *r.* is his name

REVERSE.

Num. 23. 20. and he hath blessed, and I cannot *r.*
Esth. 8. 5. let it be written, to *r.* the letters devis.
8. and sealed with king's ring, may no man *r.*
Jer. 2. † 24. in her occasion who can *r.* it?

REVILE.

Exod. 22. 28. thou shalt not *r.* the gods, nor curse
Mat. 5. 11. blessed are ye when men shall *r.* you

REVILED.

Neh. 13. † 25. I contended with them, and *r.* them
Mat. 27. 39. that passed by *r.* him, wagg. their heads
Mark 15. 32. they that were crucified *r.* him
John 9. 28. they *r.* him, and said, thou art disciple
1 *Cor.* 4. 12. being *r.* we bless, being persecuted
1 *Pet.* 2. 23. who when he was *r.* *r.* not again

REVILERS.

1 *Cor.* 6. 10. nor *r.* shall inherit kingdom of God

REVILEST.

Acts 23. 4. they said, *r.* thou God's high priest

REVILETH.

Exod. 21. † 17. that *r.* his father shall be put to death

REVILINGS.

Isa. 51. 7. fear not, neither be ye afraid of their *r.*
Zeph. 2. 8. and the *r.* of the children of Ammon

REVIVE.

Neh. 4. 2. will they *r.* the stones out of the heaps?
Psal. 85. 6. wilt thou not *r.* us again, that thy people
138. 7. thou wilt *r.* me, thou shalt stretch forth
Isa. 57. 15. with a contrite spirit, to *r.* spirit of the humble, and to *r.* the heart of the contrite ones
Hos. 6. 2. after two days will he *r.* us, we shall live
14. 7. they shall *r.* as corn, and grow as the vine
Hab. 3. 2. O Lord, *r.* thy work in midst of the years

REVIVED.

Gen. 45. 27. the spirit of Jacob their father *r.*
Judg. 15. 19. his spirit came again, and he *r.*
1 *Kings* 17. 22. soul of the child came, and he *r.*
2 *Kings* 13. 21. and touched bones of Elisha, he *r.*
Rom. 7. 9. when the commandment came, sin *r.*
14. 9. to this end Christ both died, rose, and *r.*
Phil. 4. † 10. that now your care of me is *r.*

REVIVING.

Ezra 9. 8. to give us a little *r.* in our bondage, 9.

REVOLT.

Deut. 13. † 5. prophet spoken *r.* against the Lord
Isa. 59. 13. speaking oppress. and *r.* uttering false.
Jer. 28. † 16. because thou hast taught *r.* 29. † 32.

REVOLT.

2 *Chron.* 21. 10. the same time also did Libnah *r.*
Isa. 1. 5. be stricken, ye will *r.* more and more

REVOLTED.

2 *Kings* 8. 20. in his days Edom *r.* 22. 2 *Chr.* 21. 8, 10.
22. then Libnah *r.* at the same time
Isa. 31. 6. to him from whom Israel have deeply *r.*
Jer. 5. 23. but this people, they are *r.* and gone

REVOLTERS.

Jer. 6. 28. are all grievous *r.* walking with slanders
Hos. 5. 2. the *r.* are profound to make slaughter
9. 15. I will love them no more, princes are *r.*

REVOLTING.

Jer. 5. 23. this people hath a *r.* and rebellious heart

REVOLUTION.

Exod. 34. † 22. observe feast at the *r.* of the year
1 *Sam.* 1. † 20. when the *r.* of days was come about
2 *Chron.* 24. † 23. in the *r.* of the year Syria came

REWARD

Signifies, [1] *A recompence, requital, or amends, upon account of some service done, or good action performed, such as is due to labourers for their work,* 1 Tim. 5. 18. [2] *That free and unmerited recompence which shall be given to the godly by the goodness, bounty, and mercy of God, after all their labours in his service. This is a reward wholly of grace, in respect of us, or our deserving, but of justice on account of the purchase of it by the sacred treasure of* Christ's *blood, and the unchangeable tenor of the gospel, wherein God promises heaven to all obedient and true believers,* Mat. 5. 12. | 6. 6. [3] *That extreme and fearful punishment and recompence from the terrible majesty and revenging justice of God, which will be inflicted upon impenitent sinners,* Psal. 91. 8. [4] *A gift or bribe,* Deut. 27. 25. [5] *The fruit or benefit of labour in this world,* Eccl. 9. 5. [6] *Human applause,* Mat. 6. 2, 5. [7] *Comfort and joy,* Psal. 19. 11.

Gen. 15. 1. Abram, I am thy exceeding great *r.*
Num. 18. 31. for it is your *r.* for your service
Deut. 10. 17. a terrible God, who taketh not *r.*
27. 25. cursed that taketh *r.* to slay the innocent
Ruth 2. 12. a full *r.* be given thee of the Lord
2 *Sam.* 4. 10. who thought I would have given him *r.*
19. 36. the king recompense it me with such a *r.*
1 *Kings* 13. 7. go home, and I will give thee a *r.*
Job 6. 22. did I say, bring to me, or give a *r.*
7. 2. as an hireling looketh for *r.* of his work

Psal. 15. 5. nor taketh *r.* against the innocent
19. 11. and in keeping of them there is great *r.*
40. 15. let them be desolate for a *r.* of their shame
58. 11. verily, there is a *r.* for the righteous
70. 3. let them be turned back for *r.* of their shame
91. 8. only thou shalt see the *r.* of the wicked
94. 2. lift up thyself, render a *r.* to the proud
109. 20. let this be the *r.* of mine adversaries
127. 3. and the fruit of the womb is his *r.*
Prov. 11. 18. that soweth righteousness, a sure *r.*
21. 14. a *r.* in the bosom strong wrath
22. † 4. the *r.* of humility is riches and honour
23. † 18. surely there is a *r.* and thine expectation
24. 14. hast found wisdom, then there shall be a *r.*
20. for there shall be no *r.* to the evil man
Eccl. 4. 9. bec. they have a good *r.* for their labour
9. 5. neither have they any more a *r.*
Isa. 3. 11. the *r.* of his hands shall be given him
5. 23. which justify the wicked for *r.*
40. 10. his *r.* is with him, and his work, 62. 11.
45. 13. he shall let go my captives, not for *r.*
49. † 4. and my *r.* is with my God
Jer. 40. 5. the captain gave Jeremiah a *r.*
Ezek. 16. 34. thou givest *r.* and no *r.* is given thee
Hos. 9. 1. thou hast loved a *r.* upon every corn-floor
Obad. 15. thy *r.* shall return upon thine own head
Mic. 3. 11. heads thereof judge for *r.* priests teach
7. 3. the prince asketh, and judge asketh for a *r.*
Mat. 5. 12. great is your *r.* in heaven, *Luke* 6. 23.
46. if love them which love you, what *r.* have ye?
6. 1. otherwise ye have no *r.* of your Father in heav.
2. verily, I say to you, they have their *r.* 5, 16.
10. 41. he that receiveth a prophet, shall receive a prophet's *r.* shall receive a righteous man's *r.*
42. he shall in no wise lose his *r.* *Mark* 9. 41.
Luke 6. 35. but do good, and your *r.* shall be great
23. 41. for we receive the due *r.* of our deeds
Acts 1. 18. man purchased a field with *r.* of iniquity
Rom. 4. 4. him that worketh is the *r.* not reckoned
1 *Cor.* 3. 8. every man shall receive his own *r.*
14. if any man's work abide, he shall receive a *r.*
9. 17. if I do this thing willingly, I have a *r.*
18. what is my *r.* then? verily, that when I preach
Col. 2. 18. let no man beguile you of your *r.*
3. 24. ye shall receive the *r.* of the inheritance
1 *Tim.* 5. 18. the labourer is worthy of his *r.*
Heb. 2. 2. every transg. received a just recomp. of *r.*
10. 35. confidence, which hath great recomp. of *r.*
11. 26. he had respect to the recompence of the *r.*
2 *Pet.* 2. 13. shall receive the *r.* of unrighteousness
2 *John* 8. but that we receive a full *r.*
Jude 11. ran greedily after error of Balaam for *r.*
Rev. 11. 18. the time is come thou shouldest give *r.*
22. 12. I come quickly, and my *r.* is with me

REWARD.

Deut. 32. 41. and I will *r.* them that hate me
1 *Sam.* 24. 19. wherefore the Lord *r.* thee good
2 *Sam.* 3. 39. the Lord shall *r.* the doer of evil
2 *Chron.* 20. 11. behold, I say, how they *r.* us
Psal. 54. 5. he shall *r.* evil to mine enemies
Prov. 25. 22. heap coals, and the Lord shall *r.* thee
Hos. 4. 9. and I will *r.* them their doings
Mat. 6. 4. Father himself shall *r.* thee openly, 6, 18.
16. 27. he shall *r.* every man according to his works
2 *Tim.* 4. 14. Lord *r.* him according to his works
Rev. 18. 6. *r.* her, even as she rewarded you

REWARDED.

Gen. 44. 4. wherefore have ye *r.* evil for good?
1 *Sam.* 24. 17. for thou hast *r.* me good, whereas thou art more righteous than I, I have *r.* thee evil
2 *Sam.* 22. 21. the Ld. *r.* me according to my righteousness and cleanness of my hands, *Ps.* 18. 20.
2 *Chron.* 15. 7. be strong, your work shall be *r.*
Psal. 7. 4. if I have *r.* evil to him that was at peace
35. 12. they *r.* me evil for good, 109. 5.
103. 10. nor *r.* us according to our iniquities
Prov. 13. 13. that feareth the commandment be *r.*
Isa. 3. 9. for they have *r.* evil to themselves
Jer. 31. 16. thy work shall be *r.* saith the Lord
Rev. 18. 6. reward her, even as she *r.* you, double

REWARDER.

Heb. 11. 6. a *r.* of them that diligently seek him

REWARDETH.

Job 21. 19. he *r.* him, and he shall know it
Psal. 31. 23. and plentifully *r.* the proud doer
137. 8. happy he that *r.* thee, as thou hast served
Prov. 17. 13. whoso *r.* evil for good, evil not depart
26. 10. both *r.* the fool, and *r.* transgressors

REWARDS.

Num. 22. 7. with the *r.* of divination in their hand
Isa. 1. 23. every one loveth gifts, followeth after *r.*
Dan. 2. 6. ye shall receive of me gifts, and *r.* honour
5. 17. Daniel said, give thy *r.* to another
Hos. 2. 12. these are my *r.* my lovers have given me

RIB, S.

Gen. 2. 21. Adam slept, and God took one of his *r.*
22. the *r.* which God had taken from man
Exod. 30. † 4. make two rings by two *r.* of altar
2 *Sam.* 2. 23. Abner smote Asahel under the fifth *r.*
3. 27. Joab smote Abner || 20. 10. Joab smote Amasa
4. 6. Rechab and Baanah smote Ish-bosheth under the fifth *r.*
1 *Kings* 6. † 5. and he made *r.* round about
7. † 3. it was covered with cedar upon the *r.*
Dan. 7. 5. beast had three *r.* in the mouth of it

RIBBAND.

Num. 15. 38. on fringe of the borders a *r.* of blue

RICH

Signifies, [1] *One that has great incomes, or plenty of worldly good things,* 1 Tim. 6. 17. [2] *One that aboundeth in spiritual good things, being furnished with the graces of God's Spirit,* Jam. 2. 5. Rev. 2. 9. [3] *Such as in their own opinion are spiritually rich, when in reality they are not,* Rev. 3. 17. [4] *Such as place all their happiness and confidence in their outward prosperity,* Mat. 19. 24. Luke 6. 24. [5] *Wise and worthy men, who are richly furnished with excellent endowments of the mind,* Eccl. 10. 6.

Gen. 13. 2. Abram was very *r.* in cattle, in silver
14. 23. lest thou shouldest say, I have made Abr. *r.*
Exod. 30. 15. *r.* shall not give more, nor poor less

Lev. 25. 47. and if a stranger wax *r.* by thee
Ruth 3. 10. followedst not young men poor or *r.*
1 *Sam.* 2. 7. the Lord maketh poor and maketh *r.*
2 *Sam.* 12. 1. there were two men in one city, one *r.*
Job 15. 29. he shall not be *r.* neither shall his subst.
34. 19. nor regardeth the *r.* more than the poor
Psal. 45. 12. the *r.* shall entreat thy favour
49. 2. hear this, both *r.* and poor together
16. be not thou afraid when one is made *r.*
Prov. 10. 4. the hand of the diligent maketh *r.*
22. the blessing of the Lord, it maketh *r.*
13. 7. there is that maketh himself *r.* yet hath
14. 20. poor is hated, but the *r.* hath many friends
18. 23. but the *r.* answereth roughly
21. 17. he that loveth wine and oil shall not be *r.*
22. 2. *r.* and poor meet together, Lord is maker
7. the *r.* ruleth over the poor, and the borrower
16. he that giveth to the *r.* shall come to want
23. 4. labour not to be *r.* cease from thy wisdom
28. 6. than he that is perverse, though he be *r.*
20. but he that maketh haste to be *r.* 22.
Eccl. 5. 12. abund. of *r.* will not suffer him to sleep
10. 6. folly is set, and the *r.* sit in low place
20. and curse not the *r.* in thy bed-chamber
Isa. 53. 9. and with the *r.* in his death, because
Jer. 5. 27. therefore they are great, and waxen *r.*
Ezek. 27. 24. in chests of *r.* apparel, bound with
Hos. 12. 8. Ephraim said, yet I am become *r.*
Zech. 11. 5. say, blessed be the Lord, for I am *r.*
Mark 12. 41. many that were *r.* cast in much
Luke 1. 53. and the *r.* he hath sent empty away
6. 24. but woe unto you that are *r.* for ye received
12. 21. so is he that is not *r.* toward God
14. 12. call not thy *r.* neighbours, lest they bid thee
18. 23. he was very sorrowful, for he was very *r.*
19. 2. Zaccheus chief among publicans, was *r.*
Rom. 10. 12. same Lord is *r.* to all that call on him
1 *Cor.* 4. 8. now ye are full, now ye are *r.*
2 *Cor.* 6. 10. as poor, yet making many *r.*
8. 9. though he was *r.* yet for your sakes he became poor, that ye through his poverty might be *r.*
Eph. 2. 4. but God who is *r.* in mercy
1 *Tim.* 6. 9. they that will be *r.* fall into temptation
17. charge them that are *r.* in this world
18. that they do good, and be *r.* in good works
Jam. 1. 10. let the *r.* rejoice in that he is made low
2. 5. hath not God chosen the poor, *r.* in faith?
Rev. 2. 9. I know thy poverty, but thou art *r.*
3. 17. because thou sayest, I am *r.* and increased
18. I counsel to buy of me gold, thou mayest be *r.*
13. 16. he causeth the *r.* and poor to receive a mark
18. 3. the merchants of earth are waxed *r.* 15.
19. wherein were made *r.* all that had ships

RICH *man* or *men.*

2 *Sam.* 12. 2. the *r. man* had exceeding many flocks
4. there came a traveller to the *r. man*
Job 27. 19. *r. man* shall lie down but shall not be
Prov. 10. 15. the *r. man's* wealth is his strong city, the destruction of the poor is poverty, 18. 11
28. 11. the *r. man* is wise in his own conceit
Jer. 9. 23. let not the *r. man* glory in his riches
Mic. 6. 12. the *r. men* thereof are full of violence
Mat. 19. 23. a *r. man* shall hardly enter the kingdom
24. it is easier than for a *r. man* to enter into the kingdom of God, *Mark* 10. 25. *Luke* 18. 25.
27. 57. there came a *r. man* of Arimathea, Joseph
Luke 12. 16. the ground of a *r. man* brought forth
16. 1. there was a certain *r. man* had a steward
19. a *r. man* was clothed in purple and fine linen
21. the crumbs which fell from the *r. man's* table
22. the *r. man* also died and was buried
21. 1. and saw the *r. men* casting into the treasury
Jam. 1. 11. so also shall the *r. man* fade away
2. 6. do not *r. men* oppress you and draw you
5. 1. go to now, ye *r. men,* weep and howl
Rev. 6. 15. great men, and *r. men* hid themselves

RICHER.

Dan. 11. 2. the fourth shall be far *r.* than they all

RICHES.

Gen. 31. 16. the *r.* God hath taken that is ours
36. 7. *r.* were more than they might dwell together
Josh. 22. 8. return with much *r.* to your tents
Ruth 4. † 11. get thee *r.* in Ephratah, and be famous
1 *Sam.* 17. 25. the king will enrich with great *r.*
1 *Kings* 3. 11. neither hast asked *r.* 2 *Chron.* 1. 11.
13. I have given thee both *r.* and honour
10. 23. king Solomon exceeded all the kings of the earth for *r.* and wisdom, 2 *Chron.* 9. 22.
1 *Chron.* 29. 12. both *r.* and honour come of thee
28. David died full of days, *r.* and honour
2 *Chron.* 17. 5. brought presents to Jehoshaphat, he had *r.* and honour in abundance, 18. 1.
20. 25. they found *r.* with dead bodies and jewels
32. 27. Hezek. had exceeding much *r.* and honour
Esth. 1. 4. he shewed the *r.* of his glorious kingdom
5. 11. Haman told them of the glory of his *r.*
Job 20. 15. he swallowed down *r.* vomit them up
36. 19. will he esteem thy *r.*? no, not gold
Psal. 37. 16. is better than the *r.* of many wicked
39. 6. he heapeth up *r.* and knoweth not who shall
44. † 12. thou sellest thy people without *r.*
49. 6. they that boast themselves in their *r.*
52. 7. but trusted in the abundance of his *r.*
62. 10. if *r.* increase, set not your heart on them
73. 12. the ungodly prosper, they increase in *r.*
104. 24. O Lord, the earth is full of thy *r.*
112. 3. wealth and *r.* shall be in his house
119. 14. I have rejoiced as much as in all *r.*
Prov. 3. 16. and in her left hand *r.* and honour
8. 18. *r.* and honour are with me, yea durable
11. 4. *r.* profit not in the day of wrath
16. a woman retains honour, and strong men *r*
28. he that trusteth in his *r.* shall fall
13. 7. that maketh himself poor, yet hath great *r*
8. the ransom of a man's life are his *r.*
14. 24. the crown of the wise is their *r.*
19. 14. and *r.* are the inheritance of fathers
22. 1. a good name is rather to be chosen than *r.*
4. by the fear of the Lord are *r.* and honour
16. he that oppresseth the poor to increase his *r.*
23. 5. for *r.* certainly make themselves wings

Prov. 24. 4. chambers be filled with all pleasant r.
27. 24. for r. are not for ever, and doth crown
30. 8. give me neither poverty nor r. feed me
31. † 29. many daughters have gotten r.
Eccl. 4. 8. nor is his eye satisfied with r.
5. 13. even r. kept for the owners to their hurt
14. but those r. perish by evil travail
19. every man to whom God hath given r. 6. 2.
9. 11. nor yet r. to men of understanding
Isa. 8. 4. the r. of Damascus shall be taken away
10. 14. my hand found as a nest the r. of people
30. 6. they will carry their r. on young asses
45. 3. I will give thee hidden r. of secret places
61. 6. ye shall eat the r. of the Gentiles
Jer. 9. 23. let not the rich man glory in his r.
17. 11. so he that getteth r. and not by right
48. 36. because r. that he hath gotten is perished
Ezek. 26. 12. they shall make a spoil of thy r.
27. 12. Tarshish was thy merchant by reason of
the multitude of all kind of r. 18. 27, 33.
28. 4. with thy understanding thou hast gotten r.
5. by thy traffic hast thou increased thy r. and
thine heart is lifted up because of thy r.
Dan. 11. 2. thro' his r. shall stir up all against Grecia
13. the king of the north shall come with much r.
24. shall scatter among them the prey, spoil and r.
28. then shall he return into his land with great r.
Mat. 13. 22. care of this world and the deceitfulness
of r. choke the word, *Mark* 4. 19. *Luke* 8. 14.
Mark 10. 23. how hardly they that have r. enter
24. them that trust in r. to enter, *Luke* 18. 24.
Luke 16. † 9. make friends of r. of unrighteousness
11. who will commit to your trust the true r.?
Rom. 2. 4. or despisest thou the r. of his goodness?
9. 23. he might make known the r. of his glory
11. 12. if the fall of them be the r. of the world,
and the diminishing of them r. of the Gentiles
33. O the depth of the r. of the wisdom of God
2 Cor. 8. 2. abounded to the r. of their liberality
Eph. 1. 7. redemption according to r. of his grace
18. what the r. of the glory of his inheritance
2. 7. that he might shew exceeding r. of his grace
3. 8. that I should preach unsearchable r. of Christ
16. grant you according to the r. of his glory
Phil. 4. 19. according to his r. in glory by Christ Jes.
Col. 1. 27. what the r. of the glory of this mystery
2. 2. knit in love, to all the r. of the full assurance
1 Tim. 6. 17. nor trust in uncertain r. but in living G.
Heb. 11. 26. the reproach of Christ greater r. than
Jam. 5. 2. your r. are corrupted, your garments
Rev. 5. 12. worthy is Lamb to receive power and r.
18. 17. in one hour so great r. are come to nought

RICHLY.

Col. 3. 16. let the word of Christ dwell in you r.
1 Tim. 6. 17. but trust in living God, who giveth r.
Tit. 3. † 6. which he shed on us r. thro' Jesus Chr.

RID.

Gen. 37. 22. that he might r. him out of their hands
Exod. 6. 6. I will r. you out of their bondage
Lev. 26. 6. I will r. evil beasts out of the land
Psal. 82. 4. r. them out of the hand of the wicked
144. 7. send thine hand, r. me, and deliver me, 11.

RIDDANCE.

Lev. 23. 22. thou shalt not make clean r. of thy field
Zeph. 1. 18 he shall make even speedy r. of all them

RIDDEN.

Num. 22. 30. am not I thine ass, which thou hast r.?

RIDDETH.

2 Sam. 22. † 33. God is my strength, he r. my way

RIDDLE.

Judg. 14. 12. Samson said to them, I will now put
forth a r. to you, 13, 14, 15, 16, 17, 18, 19.
Ezek. 17. 2. son of man, put forth a r. and speak
1 Cor. 13. † 12. now we see in a r. then face to face

RIDE.

Gen. 41. 43. he made him to r. in the second chariot
Deut. 32. 13. he made him r. on high places of earth
Judg. 5. 10. speak, ye that r. on white asses
2 Sam. 6. † 3. they made to r. the ark, *1 Chron.* 13. † 7.
16. 2. the asses are for the king's household to r. on
19. 26. I said I will saddle an ass that I may r.
1 Kings 1. 33. cause Sol. r. upon my mule, 38. 44.
2 Kings 4. † 24. restrain not for me to r. except I bid
10. 16. so they made him to r. in his chariot
13. † 16. make thine hand to r. upon the bow
Esth. 6. † 9. and cause him to r. through the city
Job 30. 22. thou causest me to r. upon the wind
Psal. 45. 4. and in thy majesty r. prosperously
66. 12. thou hast caused men to r. over our heads
Isa. 30. 16. but ye said, we will r. upon the swift
58. 14. I will cause thee to r. on high places
Jer. 6. 23. they r. on horses set in array, 50. 42.
Hos. 10. 11. I will make Ephraim to r. Judah plow
14. 3. we will not r. upon horses
Hab. 3. 8. that thou didst r. upon thine horses
Hag. 2. 22. overthrow chariots, and those that r.

RIDER.

Gen. 49. 17. so that his r. shall fall backward
Exod. 15. 1. horse and r. thrown into the sea, 21.
Job 39. 18. she scorneth the horse and his r.
Jer. 51. 21. with thee will I break in pieces the horse
and his r. break in pieces the chariot and his r.
Zech. 12. 4. I will smite his r. with madness

RIDERS.

2 Kings 18. 23. if thou be able to set r. on, *Isa.* 36. 8.
Esth. 8. 10. and he sent letters by r. on mules
Hag. 2. 22. the horses and their r. shall come down
Zech. 10. 5. the r. on horses shall be confounded

RIDETH.

Lev. 15. 9. what saddle he r. on shall be unclean
Deut. 33. 26. who r. upon the heaven in thy help
Esth. 6. 8. and the horse that the king r. upon
Psal. 68. 4. extol him that r. on the heavens, 33.
Isa. 19. 1. behold, the Lord r. on a swift cloud
Amos. 2. 15. neither shall he that r. the horse deliver

RIDING.

Num. 22. 22. now Balaam was r. on his ass
2 Kings 4. 24. slack not thy r. for me, except I bid
Jer. 17. 25. kings shall enter r. in chariots, 22. 4.
Ezek. 23. 6. young men, horsemen r. on horses, 12.
23. great lords, all of them r. upon horses
38. 15. thou and many people with thee r. on horses
Zech. 1. 8. and behold, a man r. on a red horse
9. 9. thy king cometh unto thee r. upon an ass

RIDICULOUS.

Isa. 33. † 19. thou shalt not see a people of a r. tongue

RIDGES.

Ps. 65. 10. thou waterest the r. thereof abundantly

RIE, or RYE.

Exod. 9. 32. the wheat and r. were not smitten
Isa. 28. 25. cast in wheat, barley and r. in their place

RIFLED.

Zech. 14. 2. the houses r. and women ravished

RIGHT, *Substantive.*

Gen. 18. 25. shall not the Judge of all the earth do r?
Num. 27. 7. the daughters of Zelophehad speak r.
Deut. 21. 17. the r. of the first-born is his
Ruth 2. † 20. is one that hath r. to redeem, 3. † 9.
4. 6. redeem thou my r. to thyself, for I cannot
2 Sam. 19. 28. what r. have I to cry to the king?
43. we have also more r. in David than ye
1 Kings 8. † 45. hear thou in heaven their prayer,
and maintain their r. † 49. *2 Chr.* 6. † 35. † 39.
Neh. 2. 20. but ye have no portion nor r. in Jerus.
9. 33. for thou hast done r. we have done wickedly
Job 34. 6. should I lie against my r.? my wound
17. shall even he that hateth r. govern?
36. 6. but he giveth r. to the poor
Psal. 9. 4. thou hast maintained my r. judging r.
17. 1. hear the r. O L. attend to my cry, give ear
140. 12. the Lord will maintain the r. of the poor
Prov. 16. 8. than great revenues without r.
13. and they love him that speaketh r.
Isa. 10. 2. to take away the r. from poor of my peo.
32. 7. to destroy when the needy speaketh r.
59. † 8. there is no r. in their goings
Jer. 5. 28. the r. of the needy do they not judge
17. 11. he that getteth riches, and not by r.
32. 7. the r. of redemption is thine to buy it, 8.
48. † 30. those on whom he stayeth do not r.
Lam. 3. 35. to turn aside r. of a man bef. Most High
Ezek. 21. 27. be no more, till he come whose r. it is
22. † 29. they have oppressed the stranger without r.
Amos 5. 12. they turn aside the poor from their r.
Mal. 3. 5. that turn aside the stranger from his r.
John 1. † 12. to them gave he r. to be sons of God
Heb. 13. 10. an altar, whereof they have no r. to eat

RIGHT, *Adjective.*

Gen. 24. 48. the Lord who had led me in the r. way
Deut. 32. 4. a God of truth, just and r. is he
Josh. 9. 25. do as seemeth good and r. unto thee
Judg. 12. 6. he could not frame to pronounce it r.
1 Sam. 12. 23. I will teach you the good and r. way
2 Sam. 15. 3. see, thy matters are good and r.
1 Kings 9. † 12. the cities were not r. in his eyes
2 Kings 10. 15. is thy heart r. as my heart with thine
17. 9. Israel did secretly things that were not r.
Ezra 8. 21. to seek of him a r. way for us
Neh. 9. 13. thou gavest them r. judgments
Esth. 8. 5. and the thing seem r. before the king
Job 6. 25. how forcible are r. words! but what doth
34. 23. he will not lay on man more than r.
35. 2. thinkest thou this to be r. that thou saidst?
Psal. 19. 8. the statutes of the Lord are r.
45. 6. the sceptre of thy kingdom is a r. sceptre
51. 10. O God, renew a r. spirit within me
107. 7. he led them forth by the r. way
119. 75. thy judgments are r. ‖ 128. thy precepts r.
Prov. 4. 11. I have led thee in r. paths
8. 6. and the opening of my lips shall be r. things
9. they are all r. to them that find knowledge
12. 5. the thoughts of the righteous are r.
14. 12. there is a way which seemeth r. 16. 25.
20. 11. whether his work be pure, and whether r.
23. 16. when thy lips shall speak r. things
24. 26. shall kiss his lips that giveth a r. answer
Eccl. 4. 4. again I considered every r. work
11. † 6. thou knowest not whether shall be r.
Isa. 30. 10. which say, prophesy not to us r. things
45. 19. I the Lord declare things that are r.
Jer. 2. 21. I had planted thee wholly a r. seed
23. 10. their course is evil, and their force is not r.
34. 15. ye turned, and had done r. in my sight
Hos. 14. 9. for the ways of the Lord are r.
Amos 3. 10. for they know not to do r. saith Lord
Mark 5. 15. clothed, and in his r. mind, *Luke* 8. 35.
Luke 10. 28. thou hast answered r. this do and live
Acts 4. 19. whether it be r. in the sight of God
8. 21. thy heart is not r. in the sight of God
13. 10. not cease to pervert the r. ways of the L.
2 Pet. 2. 15. which have forsak. r. way, gone astray
Rev. 22. 14. that they may have r. to the tree of life

Is RIGHT.

Exod. 15. 26. if thou wilt diligently hearken and do
that which *is* r. in his sight, *1 Kings* 11. 38.
Deut. 6. 18. thou shalt do that *is* r. 12. 25. | 21. 9.
12. 8. every man doeth whatsoever *is* r. in own eyes
28. when thou doest that which *is* r. 13. 18.
Judg. 14. † 3. get her for me, she *is* r. in mine eyes
1 Kings 11. 33. hast not walked to do that *is* r.
2 Kings 10. 30. in execut. that which *is* r. in my eyes
Job 42. 7. have not spoken of me the thing that *is* r. 8.
Psal. 33. 4. for the word of the Lord *is* r.
Prov. 12. 15. the way of a fool *is* r. in his own eyes
21. 2. every way of man *is* r. in his own eyes
8. but as for the pure, his work *is* r.
Jer. 26. † 14. do with me as *is* r. in your eyes
Ezek. 18. 5. but if a man do that which *is* r.
19. he hath done that which *is* lawful and r. and
kept my statutes, 21. 27. | 33. 14, 16, 19.
Mat. 20. 4. whatsoever *is* r. I will give you
7. whatsoever *is* r. that shall ye receive
Luke 12. 57. and why judge ye not what *is* r.?
Eph. 6. 1. obey your parents in the Lord, this *is* r.

Was RIGHT.

Judg. 17. 6. there was no king in Israel, but every
man did that which *was* r. in his own eyes, 21. 25.
1 Sam. 18. † 20. the thing *was* r. in Saul's eyes
2 Sam. 17. † 4. the saying *was* r. in eyes of Absalom
1 Kings 14. 8. David do that which *was* r. 15. 5.
15. 11. Asa did that which *was* r. *2 Chron.* 14. 2.
22. 43. Jehoshaphat did that *was* r. *2 Chron.* 20. 32.
2 Kings 12. 2. Jehoash did that *was* r. *2 Chron.* 24. 2.
14. 3. Amaziah did that which *was* r. *2 Chr.* 25. 2.
15. 3. Azariah did which *was* r. *2 Chr.* 26. 4
34. Jotham did that which *was* r. *2 Chron.* 27. 2.
16. 2. Ahaz did not that which *was* r. in sight of L.
18. 3. Hezekiah did that *was* r. *2 Chron.* 29. 2.
22. 2. Josiah did that which *was* r. *2 Chron.* 34. 2.
1 Chron. 13. 4. the thing *was* r. in eyes of the people
2 Chron. 30. † 4. thing *was* r. in eyes of Hezekiah
Job 33. 27. I have perverted that which *was* r.
Psal. 78. 37. their heart *was* not r. with him
Jer. 17. 16. that which came out of my lips *was* r.

RIGHT.

Josh. 3. 16. the people passed over r. against Jericho

RIGHT *cheek.*

Mat. 5. 39. whoso shall smite thee on the r. *cheek*

RIGHT *corner.*

2 Kings 11. 11. guard stood round from the r. *corner*
See FOOT, HAND.

RIGHT *early.*

Psal. 46. 5. God shall help her, and that r. *early*

RIGHT *forth.*

Jer. 49. 5. ye shall be driven every man r. *forth*

RIGHT *on.*

Prov. 4. 25. let thine eyes look r. *on* and eye-lids
9. 15. to call passengers who go r. *on* their ways

RIGHT *pillar.*

1 Kings 7. 21. he set up the r. *pillar* called Jachin

RIGHT *well.*

Psal. 139. 14. and that my soul knoweth r. *well*

RIGHTEOUS.

See the *signification of* JUST.

Gen. 7. 1. for thee have I seen r. before me
18. 23. wilt thou destroy the r. with the wicked?
24. if there be fifty r. wilt thou destroy, and not
spare the place for the fifty r. that are therein?
25. that be far from thee to slay r. with wicked
26. if I find fifty r. in the city, I will spare
28. peradventure there shall lack five of fifty r.
20. 4. Lord, wilt thou slay also a r. nation
38. 26. Judah said, she hath been more r. than I
Exod. 23. 7. the innocent and r. slay thou not
8. gift perverteth the words of the r. *Deut.* 16. 19.
Num. 23. 10. let me die the death of the r.
Deut. 4. 8. what nation that hath judgments so r.
25. 1. they shall justify the r. *2 Chron.* 6. 23.
Judg. 5. 11. the r. acts of the Lord, *1 Sam.* 12. 7.
1 Sam. 24. 17. he said, thou art more r. than I
2 Sam. 4. 11. wicked men have slain a r. person
1 Kings 2. 32. who fell on two men more r. than he
8. 32. justifying the r. to give him according to his
2 Kings 10. 9. Jehu said to all the people, ye be r.
Ezra 9. 15. Lord God of Isr. thou art r. *Neh.* 9. 8
Job 4. 7. or where were the r. cut off?
9. 15. whom, tho' I were r. yet would I not answer
10. 15. if I be r. yet will I not lift up my head
15. 14. what is man, that he should be r.?
17. 9. r. also shall hold on his way, grow stronger
22. 3. is it any pleas. to Almighty that thou art r.?
19. the r. see it, and are glad, *Psal.* 107. 42.
23. 7. there the r. might dispute with him
32. 1. because he was r. in his own eyes
34. 5. Job hath said, I am r. ‖ 35. 7. if thou be r.
36. 7. he withdraweth not his eyes from the r. but
with kings are they on the throne, *Psal.* 34. 15.
40. 8. wilt thou condemn me that thou mayest be r.
Psal. 1. 5. nor sinners in the congregation of the r.
6. for the Lord knoweth the way of the r.
5. 12. for thou wilt bless the r. with favour, compass
7. 9. for the r. God trieth the hearts and reins
11. God judgeth the r. God is angry with wicked
11. 3. what can the r. do? ‖ 5. Lord trieth the r.
14. 5. for God is in the generation of the r.
19. 9. the judgments of the Lord are true and r.
altogether, 119. 7, 62, 106, 160, 164.
31. 18. lips speak contemptuously against the r.
32. 11. be glad in the Lord, and rejoice, ye r.
33. 1. rejoice in the Lord, O ye r. 97. 12.
34. 17. the r. cry, and the Lord heareth them
19. many are the afflictions of the r. Lord deliver.
21. they that hate the r. shall be desolate
35. 27. let them be glad that favour my r. cause
37. 17. but the Lord upholdeth the r.
21. but the r. sheweth mercy, and giveth
25. yet have I not seen r. forsaken, nor his seed
29. the r. shall inherit the land, and dwell therein
30. the mouth of the r. speaketh wisdom
32. the wicked watcheth the r. to slay him
39. but the salvation of the r. is of the Lord
52. 6. the r. also shall see, and fear, and laugh
55. 22. he shall never suffer the r. to be moved
58. 10. the r. shall rejoice when he seeth vengeance
11. verily there is a reward for the r.
64. 10. the r. shall be glad in the Lord, and trust
68. 3. but let the r. be glad, let them rejoice
69. 28. let them not be written with the r.
72. 7. in his days shall the r. flourish, and peace
75. 10. but the horns of the r. shall be exalted
92. 12. the r. shall flourish like the palm-tree
94. 21. they gather against the soul of the r.
97. 11. light is sown for r. and gladness for upright
112. 4. the Ld. is full of compassion and r. 116. 5.
6. the r. shall be in everlasting remembrance
118. 15. rejoicing is in the tabernacles of the r.
20. this gate, into which the r. shall enter
119. 106. sworn that I will keep thy r. judgments
137. r. art thou, O Lord, *Jer.* 12. 1.
138. thy testimonies are r. and very faithful
125. 3. the rod of the wicked shall not rest upon the
lot of the r. lest the r. put forth their hands
140. 13. the r. shall give thanks to thy name
141. 5. let the r. smite me, it shall be a kindness
142. 7. the r. shall compass me about, thou shalt
145. 17. the Lord is r. in all his ways, and holy
146. 8. Lord loveth the r. he preserveth strangers
Prov. 2. 7. he layeth up sound wisdom for the r.
20. that thou mayest keep the paths of the r.
3. 32. froward is abominat. but his secret is with r.
10. 3. the Lord will not suffer the r. to famish
16. labour of the r. tendeth to life, wicked to sin
21. the lips of the r. feed many, but fools die
24. but the desire of the r. shall be granted
25. but the r. is an everlasting foundation
28. the hope of the r. shall be gladness

Prov. 10.30. the r. shall never be removed, but wick.
32. the lips of the r. know what is acceptable
11. 8. the r. is delivered out of trouble
10. when it goeth well with the r. city rejoiceth
21. but the seed of the r. shall be delivered
23. the desire of the r. is only good
28. but the r. shall flourish as a branch
30. the fruit of the r. is a tree of life
31. behold, r. shall be recompensed in the earth
12. 3. but the root of the r. shall not be moved
5. thoughts of the r. are right, but the counsels
7. but the house of the r. shall stand
12. but the root of the r. yieldeth fruit
26. the r. is more excellent than his neighbour
13. 9. the light of the r. rejoiceth, but the lamp
21. but to the r. good shall be repaid
25. the r. eateth to the satisfying of his soul
14. 9. but among the r. there is favour
19. and the wicked bow at the gates of the r.
32. but the r. hath hope in his death
15. 6. in the house of the r. is much treasure
19. but the way of the r. is made plain
28. the heart of the r. studieth to answer
29. but he heareth the prayer of the r.
16. 13. r. lips are the delight of kings
18. 5. it is not good to overthrow the r. in judgm.
10. the r. runneth into it, and is safe
21. 18. the wicked shall be a ransom for the r.
26. but the r. giveth, and spareth not
23. 24. the father of the r. shall greatly rejoice
24. 15. lay not wait against the dwelling of the r.
24. he that saith to the wicked, thou art r.
28. 1. the wicked flee, but the r. are bold as a lion
10. whoso causeth the r. to go astray, shall fall
28. but when the wicked perish, the r. increase
29. 2. when the r. are in authority, people rejoice
6. but the r. doth sing and rejoice
7. the r. considereth the cause of the poor
16. but the r. shall see their fall
Eccl. 3. 17. God shall judge the r. and the wicked
7. 16. be not r. over-much, neither over-wise
8. 14. happeneth according to the work of the r.
9. 1. the r. and the wise are in the hand of God
2. there is one event to the r. and to the wicked
Isa. 3. 10. say ye to the r. it shall be well with him
5. 23. and take away the righteousness of the r.
24. 16. we have heard songs, even glory to the r.
26. 2. open ye, that the r. nation may enter in
41. 26. who hath declared, that we may say, he is r.
53. 11. my r. servant shall justify many
57. 1. r. perisheth, and no man layeth it to heart,
none considering that the r. is taken from the evil
60. 21. thy people also shall be all r. shall inherit
Jer. 12. 1. r. art thou, O Ld. when I plead with thee
20. 12. O Lord of hosts, that triest the r.
23. 5. that I will raise to David a r. branch
Ezek. 13. 22. with lies ye have made the r. sad
16. 52. thy sisters, they are more r. than thou
18. 20. the righteousness of the r. shall be on him
24. but when the r. turneth away from, 33. 18.
21. 3. I will cut off from thee the r. and wicked, 4.
33. 12. the righteousness of the r. shall not deliver
him in the day, nor shall the r. be able to live
13. when I shall say to the r. he shall live
Amos 2. 6. because they sold r. for silver, and poor
Hab. 1. 4. the wicked doth compass about the r.
13. wicked devoureth him that is more r. than he
Mal. 3. 18. discern betwen the r. and the wicked
Mat. 9. 13. I am not come to call the r. but sinners to repentance, *Mark* 2. 17. *Luke* 5. 32.
13. 43. then shall the r. shine forth as the sun
23. 28. ye outwardly appear r. to men, but within
29. because ye garnish the sepulchres of r.
35. that on you may come all r. blood shed on the earth, from blood of r. Abel to Zacharias
25. 37. then shall the r. answer, saying, Lord
46. but the r. shall go into life eternal
Luke 1. 6. and they were both r. before God
18. 9. who trusted they were r. and despised others
John 7. 24. judge not by appearance, but judge r.
17. 25. O r. Father, the world hath not known thee
Rom. 2. 5. and revelation of the r. judgment of G.
3. 10. it is written, there is none r. no not one
5. 19. so by obedience of one, many be made r.
2 *Thess.* 1. 5. a manifest token of r. judgment of G.
6. it is a r. thing with God to recompense tribulat.
2 *Tim.* 4. 8. the Lord, the r. Judge, shall give me
Heb. 11. 4. he obtained witness that he was r.
1 *Pet.* 3. 12. the eyes of the Lord are over the r.
4. 18. if r. scarcely be saved, where shall sinner
2 *Pet.* 2. 8. Lot vexed his r. soul from day to day
1 *John* 2. 1. we have an advocate, Jesus Christ the r.
29. if ye know that he is r. ye know every one
3. 7. he that doeth righteousness is r. as he is r.
12. his own works were evil, and his brother's r.
Rev. 16. 5. I heard the angel say, thou art r. O Ld.
7. O Lord, true and r. are thy judgments, 19. 2.
22. 11. and he that is r. let him be r. still

See LORD *is.*

RIGHTEOUS *man*, or *men*.

Psal. 37. 16. a little that a r. *man* hath is better
Prov. 10. 11. the mouth of a r. *man* is a well of life
12. 10. a r. *man* regardeth the life of his beast
13. 5. a r. *m.* hateth lying, but wicked is loathsome
21. 12. a r. *man* wisely considereth the house
25. 26. a r. *man* falling down before the wicked
28. 12. when r. *men* do rejoice, there is glory
Isa. 41. 2. who raised up the r. *man* from the east
Ezek. 3. 20. again, when a r. *man* doth turn, 18. 26.
21. nevertheless, if thou warn the r. *man*
23. 45. and the r. *men*, they shall judge them
Mat. 10. 41. he that receiveth a r. *man* in the name of a r. *man*, shall receive a r. *man's* reward
13. 17. many r. *men* have desired to see those things
Luke 23. 47. saying, certainly this was a r. *man*
Rom. 5. 7. scarcely for a r. *man* will one die
1 *Tim.* 1. 9. that the law is not made for a r. *man*
Jam. 5. 16. the fervent prayer of a r. *man* availeth
2 *Pet.* 2. 8. for that r. *man* dwelling among them

RIGHTEOUSLY.

Deut. 1. 16. hear causes, and judge r. *Prov.* 31. 9.
Psal. 67. 4. thou shalt judge the people r. 96. 10.
Isa. 33. 15. he that walketh r. shall dwell on high
Jer. 11. 20. O Lord of hosts, that judgest r.
Tit. 2. 12. that we should live soberly, r. and godly
1 *Pet.* 2. 23. committed to him that judgeth r.

RIGHTEOUSNESS

Signifies, [1] *That perfection of the divine nature, whereby God is most just, and most holy in himself, and in all his dealings with his creatures, and observes the strictest rules of rectitude and equity*, Job 36. 3. John 17. 25. [2] *The clemency, mercy, and goodness of God*, Deut. 6. 25. Psal. 51. 14. [3] *His truth and faithfulness in fulfilling and making good his promises*, Psal. 31. 1. Isa. 42. 6. | 45. 19. [4] *The blessed and gracious fruit and reward of righteousness*, Psal. 24. 5. Isa. 58. 8. [5] *The active and passive obedience of Christ, whereby he perfectly fulfilled the law, and propitiated the justice of God: which obedience being imputed to the elect, and received by faith, their sins are pardoned, their persons accepted, and they are brought to eternal glory*, Dan. 9. 24. *This* righteousness, *whereby a sinner is justified, is called* the righteousness of God, *Rom.* 1. 17. *because it is of God's institution, ordination, and appointment, and which alone he will accept of to life:* Or, *because it was performed by him who is God as well as man, and is therefore of infinite value and merit:* Or, *because it is opposed to the righteousness of works*, Rom. 10. 3. *It is called* the righteousness of faith, *Rom.* 4. 13. *because it is apprehended and applied by faith. And it is called* the law of righteousness, Rom. 9. 31. *in opposition to that law of righteousness, by which the unbelieving* Jews *sought to be justified. And* Christ *is called*, The Lord our Righteousness, *Jer.* 23. 6. *that is, The procurer and bestower of all that righteousness and holiness that are in believers.* [6] *That uprightness, equity, and justice in dealing, which ought to be between man and man*, Luke 1. 75. Eph. 4. 24. [7] *An eminent act of justice and piety, proceeding from a sincere zeal for God's honour, and the good of his people*, Psal. 106. 31. [8] *Holiness of life and conversation*, 1 Cor. 15. 34.

The doctrine of the gospel is called the word of righteousness, Heb. 5. 13. *because therein the righteousness of God is revealed to us, and it alone declares the way of becoming righteous.*

Deut. 6. 25. and it shall be our r. if we observe to do
24. 13. it shall be r. to thee before Lord thy God
33. 19. there they shall offer sacrifices of r.
Job 29. 14. I put on r. and it clothed me
36. 3. and I will ascribe r. to my Maker
Psal. 4. 5. offer the sacrifices of r. and trust in the L.
11. 7. for the righteous Lord loveth r. 33. 5.
15. 2. he that worketh r. shall never be moved
23. 3. he leadeth me in paths of r. for name's sake
24. 5. and r. from the God of his salvation
40. 9. I have preached r. in the great congregation
45. 4. because of truth, and meekness, and r.
7. thou lovest r. and hatest wickedness, *Heb.* 1. 9.
48. 10. thy right hand, O God, is full of r.
51. 19. then shalt be pleased with sacrifices of r.
52. 3. thou lovest lying, rather than to speak r.
58. 1. do ye indeed speak r. O congregation?
72. 2. he shall judge thy people with r. and poor
3. mountains shall bring peace, and little hills by r.
85. 10. r. and peace have kissed each other
11. and r. shall look down from heaven
13. r. shall go before him, and set us in the way
94. 15. but judgment shall return unto r.
96. 13. he shall judge the world with r. 98. 9.
97. 2. r. is the habitation of his throne
99. 4. thou executest r. in Jacob, 103. 6.
106. 3. blessed is he that doeth r. at all times
118. 19. open to me the gates of r. I will go into
119. 144. the r. of thy testimonies is everlasting
172. for all thy commandments are r.
132. 9. let thy priests be clothed with r. thy saints
Prov. 2. 9. then shalt thou underst. r. and judgment
8. 18. yea, durable riches and r. are with me
20. I lead in the way of r. in midst of the paths
10. 2. but r. delivereth from death, 11. 4.
11. 5. the r. of the perfect shall direct his way
6. the r. of the upright shall deliver them
18. to him that soweth r. shall be a sure reward
19. as r. tendeth to life so he that pursueth evil
12. 17. he that speaketh truth, sheweth forth r.
28. in the way of r. is life, and in the pathway
13. 6. r. keepeth him that is upright in the way
14. 34. r. exalteth a nation, sin is a reproach to
15. 9. he loveth him that followeth after r.
16. 8. better is a little with r. than great revenues
12. for the throne is established by r.
31. is a crown of glory, if found in the way of r.
21. 21. he that followeth after r. and mercy findeth life, r. and honour
Eccl. 3. 16. and the place of r. that iniquity was there
Isa. 1. 21. r. lodged in it, but now murderers
26. the city of r. ‖ 27. and her converts with r.
5. 23. which take away the r. of the righteous
10. 22. consumption decreed shall overflow with r.
11. 4. but with r. shall he judge the poor
5. and r. shall be the girdle of his loins
16. 5. judging and seeking judgment, and hasting r.
26. 9. the inhabitants of the world will learn r.
10. let favour be shewed, yet will he not learn r.
28. 17. and r. will I lay to the plummet
32. 16. and r. shall remain in the fruitful field
17. and the work of r. shall be peace, and the effect of r. quietness and assurance for ever
33. 5. Lord hath filled Zion with judgment and r.
41. † 2. who raised up r. from the east
45. 8. drop down, ye heavens, from above, and let skies pour down r. and let r. spring up together
19. I the Lord speak r. I declare right things
24. in the Lord have I r. † in the Lord is all r.
46. 12. hearken unto me, ye that are far from r.
51. 1. ye that follow after r. ‖ 7. ye that know r.
54. 17. their r. is of me, saith the Lord
58. 2. yet they seek me as a nation that did r.
Isa. 59. 17. for he put on r. as a breastplate
60. 17. will make thy officers peace, thine exact r
61. 3. that they might be called trees of r.
10. he hath covered me with the robe of r.
11. so Lord will cause r. and praise to spring forth
62. 1. until the r. thereof go forth as brightness
64. 5. thou meetest him that rejoiceth and work. r.
Jer. 9. 24. that I am the Lord which exercise r.
22. 3. execute ye judgment and r. and deliver
23. 6. this is his name, the Lord our r. 33. 16.
33. 15. at that time will I cause the branch of r. to grow up to David, and he shall execute r.
51. 10. the Lord hath brought forth our r.
Ezek. 14. 14. deliver their own souls by their r. 20.
18. 20. the r. of the righteous shall be upon him
33. 12. the r. of the righteous shall not deliver him
Dan. 4. 27. and break off thy sins by r.
9. 7. O Lord, r. belongeth unto thee, but to us
24. to bring in everlasting r. and to seal up vision
12. 3. they that turn many to r. shall shine as stars
Hos. 10. 12. till he come and rain r. upon you
Amos 5. 7. and who leave off r. in the earth
24. and let r. run down as a mighty stream
6. 12. ye have turned the fruit of r. into hemlock
Mic. 6. 5. that ye may know the r. of the Lord
Zeph. 2. 3. all ye meek of earth, seek r. seek meekn.
Mal. 4. 2. to you that fear shall the Sun of r. arise
Mat. 3. 15. thus it becometh us to fulfil all r.
5. 6. blessed are they that hunger and thirst after r.
20. except your r. exceed the r. of the Scribes
21. 32. for John came to you in the way of r.
Luke 1. 75. in r. before him all the days of our life
John 16. 8. he will reprove the world of sin and of r.
10. of r. bec. I go to my Father, ye see me no more
Acts 10. 35. he that worketh r. is accepted with him
13. 10. thou enemy of all r. wilt thou not cease
24. 25. as he reasoned of r. and judgm. Felix trem.
Rom. 1. 17. for therein is the r. of God revealed
2. 26. if uncircumcision keep the r. of the law
3. 5. if our unrighteousness commend the r. of God
21. the r. of God without the law is manifested
22. even the r. of God which is by faith of Christ
4. 6. to whom God imputeth r. without works
11. received sign of circumcision, a seal of the r. of the faith, that r. might be imputed to them also
13. for the promise was through the r. of faith
5. 17. they which receive gift of r. shall reign by Jes.
18. so by the r. of one the free gift came on all
21. so might grace reign through r. to eternal life
6. 13. yield your members instruments of r. to God
16. whether of sin to death, or of obedience unto r.
18. free from sin, ye became the servants of r.
19. so now yield your members servants to r.
20. when ye were serv. of sin, ye were free from r.
8. 4. that the r. of the law might be fulfilled in us
10. but the spirit is life because of r.
9. 30. that the Gentiles who followed not after r. have attained to r. even the r. which is of faith
31. but Israel which followed after the law of r. hath not attained to the law of r.
10. 3. they being ignorant, going about to establish their own r. have not submitted to the r. of God
5. Moses describeth the r. which is of the law
6. the r. which is of faith speaketh on this wise
10. for with the heart man believeth unto r.
14. 17. kingdom of God not meat and drink, but r.
1 *Cor.* 1. 30. in Christ, who of God is made unto us r.
15. 34. awake to r. and sin not, for some have not
2 *Cor.* 3. 9. much more doth the ministration of r.
5. 21. that we might be made the r. of God in him
6. 7. by the armour of r. on the right hand and left
14. what fellowship hath r. with unrighteousness
9. 10. your seed and increase the fruits of your r.
11. 15. be transformed as the ministers of r.
Gal. 2. 21. if r. come by law, Christ is dead in vain
3. 21. verily, r. should have been by the law
5. 5. we through the Spirit wait for the hope of r.
Eph. 5. 9. fruit of the Spirit is in all r. and truth
6. 14. and having on the breastplate of r.
Phil. 1. 11. being filled with the fruits of r. by Jesus
3. 6. touching r. which is in the law, blameless
9. but the r. which is of God by faith
1 *Tim.* 6. 11. and follow after r. 2 *Tim.* 2. 22.
2 *Tim.* 4. 8. there is laid up for me a crown of r.
Tit. 3. 5. not by works of r. which we have done
Heb. 1. 8. a sceptre of r. is sceptre of thy kingdom
5. 13. is unskilful in the word of r. he is a babe
7. 2. first being by interpretation king of r.
11. 7. and became heir of the r. which is by faith
33. through faith subdued kingdoms, wrought r.
12. 11. afterward it yieldeth peaceable fruit of r.
Jam. 1. 20. wrath of man worketh not r. of God
3. 18. the fruit of r. is sown in peace of them
1 *Pet.* 2. 24. we being dead to sin should live unto r.
2 *Pet.* 1. 1. obtained like faith through the r. of God
2. 5. spared not, but saved Noe a preacher of r.
21. been better not to have known the way of r.
3. 13. we look for a new earth, wherein dwelleth r.
1 *John* 2. 29. every one that doeth r. is born of God
3. 7. he that doeth r. is righteous, as he is righteous
10. whosoever doth not r. is not of God
Rev. 19. 8. for the fine linen is the r. of the saints

For RIGHTEOUSNESS.

Gen. 15. 6. Abram believed in the Lord, and he counted it to him *for* r. *Psal.* 106. 31. *Rom.* 4. 3.
Psal. 143. 11. *for* thy r. sake bring my soul out of
Isa. 5. 7. he looked *for* r. but behold a cry
Mat. 5. 10. blessed are they which are persec. *for* r.
Rom. 4. 5. his faith is counted *for* r. *Gal.* 3. 6.
9. reckoned ‖ 22. imputed to him *for* r. *Jam.* 2. 23.
10. 4. for Christ is the end of the law *for* r.
1 *Pet.* 3. 14. if ye suffer *for* r. sake, happy are ye

His RIGHTEOUSNESS.

1 *Sam.* 26. 23. the Lord render to every man *his* r.
1 *Kings* 8. 32. to give according to *his* r. 2 *Chr.* 6. 23.
Job 33. 26. for he will render unto man *his* r.
Psal. 7. 17. I will praise the Lord according to *his* r.
22. 31. they shall declare *his* r. to a people be borne
50. 6. the heavens shall declare *his* r. 97. 6.
98. 2. *his* r. hath he openly shewed in the sight
103. 17. and *his* r. unto children's children
111. 3. and *his* r. endureth for ever, 112. 3, 9.

Eccl. 7. 15. there is a just man that perisheth in his r.
Isa. 42. 21. the Lord is well pleased for his r. sake
59. 16. brought salvation, and his r. sustained him
Ezek. 3. 20. again, when a righteous man doth turn
from his r. and commit iniquity, 18. 24, 26.
18. 22. in his r. that he hath done he shall live
33. 12. not be able to live for his r. in the day
13. if he trust to his own r. and commit iniquity,
his r. he hath done shall not be remembered
Mic. 7. 9. will bring to light, and I shall behold his r.
Mat. 6. 33. but seek the kingdom of God, and his r.
Rom. 3. 25. to declare his r. for remiss. of sins, 26.
2 Cor. 9. 9. given to the poor, his r. remain. for ever

In RIGHTEOUSNESS.

Lev. 19. 15. in r. shalt thou judge thy neighbour
1 Kings 3. 6. as he walked bef. thee in truth and in r.
Ps. 9. † 4. thou sattest in the throne, judging in r.
8. and he shall judge the world in r.
17. 15. as for me, I will behold thy face in r.
65. 5. by terrible things in r. wilt thou answer us
Prov. 8. 8. all the words of my mouth are in r.
25. 5. his throne shall be established in r.
Isa. 5. 16. God that is holy shall be sanctified in r.
32. 1. behold, a king shall reign in r. and princes
42. 6. I the Lord have called thee in r.
45. 13. I have raised him in r. and will direct
23. the word is gone out of my mouth in r.
48. 1. mention the God of Israel, but not in r.
54. 14. in r. shalt thou be established
63. 1. I that speak in r. mighty to save
Jer. 4. 2. thou shalt swear, the Lord liveth, in r.
Hos. 2. 19. I will betroth thee unto me in r.
10. 12. sow to yourselves in r. reap in mercy
Zech. 8. 8. I will be their God in truth and in r.
Mal. 3. 3. that they may offer an offering in r.
Acts 17. 31. he will judge the world in r.
Rom. 9. 28. he will finish and cut it short in r.
Eph. 4. 24. which after God is created in r.
2 Tim. 3. 16. scripture is for instruction in r.
Rev. 19. 11. and in r. he doth judge and make war

My RIGHTEOUSNESS.

Gen. 30. 33. so my r. answer for me in time to come
Deut. 9. 4. saying, for my r. Lord hath brought me
2 Sam. 22. 21. the Lord rewarded me according to
my r. and cleanness of hands, 25. Ps. 18. 20, 24.
Job 6. 29. yea, return again, my r. is in it
27. 6. my r. I hold fast, and will not let it go
35. 2. that thou saidst, my r. is more than God's
Psal. 4. 1. hear me when I call, O God of my r.
7. 8. judge me, O Lord, according to my r.
35. † 27. let them be glad that favour my r.
Isa. 41. 10. uphold thee with the right hand of my r.
46. 13. I bring near my r. ‖ 51. 5. my r. is near
51. 6. and my r. shall not be abolished
8. but my r. shall be for ever, and my salvation
56. 1. salvat. is near to come, my r. to be revealed
Phil. 3. 9. may be found, not having mine own r.

Thy RIGHTEOUSNESS.

Deut. 9. 5. nor for thy r. or uprightness, 6.
Job 8. 6. make the habitation of thy r. prosperous
35. 8. and thy r. may profit the son of man
Psal. 5. 8. lead me, O Lord, in thy r. because
31. 1. in thee I trust, deliver me in thy r. 71. 2.
35. 24. judge me, O Lord, according to thy r.
28. and my tongue shall speak of thy r. 71. 24.
36. 6. thy r. is like the great mountains
10. O continue thy r. to the upright in heart
37. 6. he shall bring forth thy r. as the light
40. 10. I have not hid thy r. within my heart
51. 14. and my tongue shall sing aloud of thy r.
69. 27. and let them not come into thy r.
71. 15. my mouth shall shew forth thy r. all day
16. I will make mention of thy r. of thine only
19. thy r. O God, is very high, who is like to thee
72. 1. and give thy r. unto the king's son
88. 12. thy r. be known in land of forgetfulness
89. 16. and in thy r. shall they be exalted
119. † 7. when I have learned judgments of thy r.
40. quicken me in thy r. ‖ 123. for word of thy r.
142. thy r. is an everlast. right. thy law is the truth
143. 1. in faithfulness answer me, and in thy r.
11. for thy r. sake bring my soul out of trouble
145. 7. and they shall sing of thy r.
Isa. 48. 18. then had thy r. been as waves of the sea
57. 12. I will declare thy r. and thy works
58. 8. thy r. shall go before thee, glory of Lord
62. 2. and the Gentiles shall see thy r. and kings
Dan. 9. 16. O Lord, according to all thy r.

RIGHTEOUSNESS.

Judg. 5. † 11. they shall rehearse r. of the Lord
1 Sam. 12. † 7. that I may reason of the r. of Lord
Isa. 33. † 15. he that walketh in r. and speaketh
45. † 24. in the Lord is all r. and strength
64. 6. and all our r. is as filthy rags
Ezek. 3. † 20. when righteous turneth from his r.
33. 13. all his r. shall not be remembered
Dan. 9. 18. not for our r. but for thy great mercies

RIGHTLY.

Gen. 27. 36. Esau said, is not he r. named Jacob?
Luke 7. 43. he said to him, thou hast r. judged
20. 21. master, we know that thou teachest r.
2 Tim. 2. 15. r. dividing the word of truth

RIGOUR.

Exod. 1. 13. made Israel to serve with r. 14.
Lev. 25. 43. thou shalt not rule with r. 46, 53.

RING.

The antiquity of rings *is known from Scripture:* Abraham's *servant gave an* ear-ring *to* Rebekah, Gen. 24. 22. *After the victory that the* Israelites *obtained over the* Midianites, *they offered to the Lord the* rings *and* bracelets *that they had taken from the enemy*, Num. 31. 50. *It was a mark of government and authority, and was used chiefly to seal patents or public orders; thus when* Pharaoh *committed the government of all* Egypt *to* Joseph, *he took his ring from his finger, and gave it to* Joseph, *as a token of that authority with which he invested him, and which he intended he should exercise over all his people. In like manner did* Ahasuerus *to his favourite* Haman, *and to* Mordecai, *who succeeded* Haman *in his dignity*, Esth. 3. 10. | 8. 2. *When* Jacob *arrived at the land of* Canaan, *at his return from* Mesopotamia, *he gave orders to his people to put into his custody* all the strange gods which were in their hand, and all their ear-rings which were in their ears, Gen. 35. 4. *This seems to insinuate, and other writers expressly affirm, that those* strange gods *were superstitious or magical figures, engraven upon their* rings, *their bracelets, and the pendants in their ears. Or else, according to others, that these rings and pendants were upon the hands, and in the ears of these false gods.*

Gen. 41. 42. Pharaoh took off his r. from his hand
Exod. 26. 24. boards be coupled unto one r. 36. 29.
Esth. 3. 10. king Ahasuerus took his r. from his hand
12. and sealed with the king's r. 8. 8, 10.
8. 2. the king took off his r. gave it to Mordecai
Luke 15. 22. the father said, put a r. on his hand
Jam. 2. 2. if there come in a man with a gold r.

RINGLEADER.

Acts 24. 5. and a r. of the sect of the Nazarenes

RINGS.

Exod. 25. 12. thou shalt cast four r. of gold for it
14. put staves into the r. 15. | 27. 7. | 37. 5. | 38. 7.
26. 29. and make their r. of gold, 28. 23, 26, 27. | 30. 4. | 36. 34. | 37. 3, 13. | 39. 16, 19, 20.
27. 4. thou shalt make upon net four brazen r.
28. 28. they shall bind the breastplate by the r.
Num. 31. 50. prey gotten of jewels, bracelets, and r.
Esth. 1. 6. were hangings fastened to silver r. pillars
Cant. 5. 14. his hands are as gold r. set with beryl
Isa. 3. 21. will take away the r. and nose jewels
Ezek. 1. 18. their r. so high that they were dreadful,
their r. were full of eyes round about them four

RING-STRAKED.

Gen. 30. 35. removed he goats that were r.-straked
31. 8. if he said, the r.-straked shall be thy hire
10. rams were r.-straked, speckled, and grisled, 12.

RINSED.

Lev. 6. 28. the brasen pot be both scoured and r.
15. 11. and hath not r. his hands in water
12. every vessel of wood shall be r. in water

RIOT, *Substantive.*

Isa. 29. † 9. stay yourselves, wonder, take your r.
Tit. 1. 6. children not accused of r. or unruly
1 Pet. 4. 4. that you run not to the same excess of r.

RIOT.

2 Pet. 2. 13. as they that count it pleasure to r.

RIOTING.

Rom. 13. 13. walk not in r. and drunkenness

RIOTOUS.

Prov. 23. 20. be not amongst r. eaters of flesh
28. 7. he that is a companion of r. men shameth
Luke 15. 13. there wasted his substance with r. living

RIP.

2 Kings 8. 12. thou wilt r. up their women with child

RIPE.

Gen. 40. 10. the clusters brought forth r. grapes
Exod. 22. 29. to offer the first of thy r. fruits
Num. 13. 20. was the time of the first r. grapes
18. 13. whatsoever is first r. in the land be thine
Jer. 24. 2. one basket had good figs, even like the figs
that are first r. Hos. 9. 10. Nah. 3. 12.
Joel 3. 13. put in sickle, for the harvest is r.
Mic. 7. 1. my soul desired the first r. fruit
Mark 4. † 29. when the fruit is r. he puts in sickle
1 Cor. 14. † 20. but in understanding be of r. age
Rev. 14. 15. time to reap, for harvest of earth is r.
18. gather the clusters, for grapes are fully r.

RIPENING.

Isa. 18. 5. and the sour grape is r. in the flower

RIPPED.

2 Kings 15. 16. all the women with child he r. up
Hos. 13. 16. their women with child shall be r. up
Amos 1. 13. because they have r. up the women

RISE

Signifies, [1] *To get up from one's seat, or from bed*, Gen. 19. 2. Mark 10. 49. [2] *To proceed or come from*, Num. 24. 17. [3] *To be advanced to honour or authority*, Prov. 28. 12. [4] *To be moved or kindled*, Eccl. 10. 4. [5] *To shine*, Mat. 5. 45. [6] *To rebel*, 2 Sam. 18. 32. [7] *To stir or awake out of a spiritual sloth and security to a more lively frame*, Cant. 3. 2. [8] *To go forth*, Gen. 19. † 23.

Exod. 21. 19. if he r. again and walk abroad on staff
Num. 24. 17. and a sceptre shall r. out of Israel
Deut. 33. 11. smite them that r. that they r. not again
Josh. 18. 4. they shall r. and go through the land
Judg. 8. 21. then they said, r. thou, and fall on us
9. 33. thou shalt r. early, and set upon the city
1 Sam. 22. 13. that he should r. to lie in wait
24. 7. and suffered them not to r. against Saul
2 Sam. 12. 21. when child was dead, thou didst r.
18. 32. all that r. against thee be as Absalom is
Job 30. 12. upon my right hand r. the youth
Psal. 18. 38. wounded them, they were not able to r.
27. 3. tho' war should r. ag. me, will be confident
36. 12. they are cast down, shall not be able to r.
119. 62. at midnight I will r. to give thanks to thee
140. 10. into deep pits, that they r. not up again
Prov. 24. 22. for their calamity shall r. suddenly
28. 12. when the wicked r. a man is hidden, 28.
Cant. 3. 2. I will r. now and go about the city
Isa. 14. 21. prepare slaughter, that they do not r.
24. 20. the earth shall fall and not r. again
26. 14. they are deceased, they shall not r.
33. 10. now will I r. saith the Lord
43. 17. they shall lie down togeth. they shall not r.
54. 17. every tongue that shall r. thou shalt cond.
58. 10. then shall thy light r. in obscurity
Jer. 25. 27. drink ye, spue, fall and r. no more
51. 64. Babylon shall not r. from evil, I will bring
Amos 5. 2. the virgin of Israel shall no more r.
7. 9. I will r. against the house of Jeroboam
Mat. 5. 45. he maketh sun to r. on evil and good
20. 19. crucify him, and third day he shall r. again
Mark 9. 31. | 10. 34. Luke 18. 33. | 24. 7.
24. 7. for nation shall r. against nation, and kingdom against kingdom, Mark 13. 8. Luke 21. 10.
11. many false prophets shall r. Mark 13. 22.
Mat. 26. 46. r. let us be going, behold, he is at hand
27. 63. after three days I will r. again, Mark 8. 31.
Mark 4. 27. and should sleep, and r. night and day
10. 49. be of good comfort, r. he calleth thee
12. 23. in the resurrection, when they shall r. 25.
26. and as touching the dead, that they r.
Luke 11. 7. trouble me not, I cannot r. and give
8. though he will not r. because he is his friend
12. 54. when ye see a cloud r. out of the west
22. 46. he said to them, why sleep ye? r. and pray
24. 46. it behoved Christ to suffer and to r. from
John 5. 8. Jesus saith, r. take up thy bed and walk
11. 23. Jesus saith, thy brother shall r. again
24. I know he shall r. ‖ 20. 9. that he must r. again
Acts 10. 13. came a voice, r. Peter, kill and eat
26. 16. but r. and stand upon thy feet
23. should be the first that should r. from the dead
Rom. 15. 12. he that shall r. to reign over Gentiles
1 Cor. 15. 15. if so be the dead r. not, 16, 29, 32.
1 Thess. 4. 16. the dead in Christ shall r. first
Heb. 7. 11. what need that another priest should r.
Rev. 11. 1. r. and measure the temple of God

RISE *up.*

Gen. 19. 2. ye shall r. up early and go on your ways
31. 35. let it not displease, that I cannot r. up
Exod. 8. 20. r. up and stand before Pharaoh, 9. 13.
12. 31. r. up and get you forth from my people
Lev. 19. 32. thou shalt r. up before the hoary head
Num. 10. 35. r. up, Lord, let enemies be scattered
22. 20. if men come to call thee up, r. up and go
23. 18. r. up, Balak, and hear, thou son of Zippor
24. behold, the people shall r. up as a lion
Deut. 2. 13. now, r. up, said I, and get over brook
24. r. ye up, and pass over the river Arnon
19. 11. if a man r. up against his neighbour
15. one witness shall not r. up against a man
16. if a false witness r. up against any man
28. 7. the Lord will cause thine enemies that r. up
29. 22. the generation that shall r. up after you
31. 16. this people will r. up, and go a whoring
32. 38. their gods, let them r. up and help you
Josh. 8. 7. then ye shall r. up from the ambush
Judg. 20. 38. should make a great flame r. up, 40.
1 Sam. 29. 10. wherefore r. up early in morning
Neh. 2. 18. and they said, let us r. up and build
Job 20. 27. and the earth shall r. up against him
Psal. 3. 1. many are they that r. up against me
17. 7. save them from those that r. up against them
18. 48. liftest me above those that r. up against me
35. 11. false witn. did r. up, they laid to my charge
41. 8. now that he lieth, he shall r. up no more
44. 5. we will tread them under that r. up ag. us
59. 1. defend me from them that r. up against me
74. 23. the tumult of those that r. up against thee
92. 11. desire of the wicked that r. up against me
94. 16. who will r. up for me ag. the evil-doers?
127. 2. it is vain for you to r. up early, to sit up late
139. 21. grieved with those that r. up against thee?
Prov. 31. 28. her children r. up, and call her blessed
Eccl. 10. 4. if the spirit of the ruler r. up ag. thee
12. 4. he shall r. up at the voice of the bird
Cant. 2. 10. my beloved said to me, r. up, my love
Isa. 5. 11. woe unto them that r. up in the morning
14. 22. I will r. up against them, saith the Lord
28. 21. the Lord shall r. up as in mount Perazim
32. 9. r. up, ye women at ease, hear my voice
Jer. 37. 10. should r. up every man in his tent
47. 2. behold, waters r. up out of the north
49. 14. gather against her, and r. up to battle
51. 1. against them that r. up against me, a wind
Lam. 1. 14. from whom I am not able to r. up
Amos 8. 8. it shall r. up wholly as a flood, 9. 5.
14. even they shall fall, and never r. up again
Obad. 1. let us r. up against Edom in battle
Nah. 1. 9. affliction shall not r. up the second time
Hab. 2. 7. shall they not r. up suddenly that bite
Zeph. 3. 8. until the day that I r. up to the prey
Zech. 14. 13. his hand r. up against his neighbour
Mat. 10. 21. children shall r. up against their parents, and cause them to be put to death,
Mark 13. 12.
12. 41. the men of Nineveh shall r. up, Luke 11. 32.
42. queen of the south shall r. up, Luke 11. 31.
Mark 3. 26. and if Satan r. up against himself
14. 42. r. up, lo, he that betrayeth me is at hand
Luke 5. 23. whether is easier to say, r. up and walk
6. 8. he said, r. up and stand forth in the midst
Acts 3. 6. in the name of Jesus r. up and walk
Rev. 13. 1. I saw a beast r. up out of the sea

RISEN.

Gen. 19. 23. the sun was r. when Lot entered Zoar
Exod. 22. 3. if sun be r. on him, blood shall be shed
Num. 32. 14. ye are r. up in your fathers' stead
Judg. 9. 18. ye are r. up against my father's house
Ruth 2. 15. and when she was r. up to glean
1 Sam. 25. 29. yet a man is r. to pursue thee
2 Sam. 14. 7. behold, the whole family is r. up
1 Kings 8. 20. I am r. up in room of David, 2 Chr. 6. 10.
2 Kings 6. 15. the servant of the man of God was r.
2 Chron. 13. 6. the servant of Solomon is r. up
21. 4. when Jehoram was r. up to the kingdom
Psal. 20. 8. but we are r. and stand upright
27. 12. for false witnesses are r. up against me
54. 3. for strangers are r. up against me
86. 14. O God, the proud are r. against me
Isa. 60. 1. the glory of the Lord is r. upon thee
Ezek. 7. 11. violence is r. into a rod of wickedness
47. 5. for the waters were r. waters to swim in
Mic. 2. 8. even of late my people is r. up as enemy
Mat. 11. 11. there hath not r. a greater than John
14. 2. Herod said, this is John the Baptist, he is r.
from the dead, Mark 6. 14, 16. Luke 9. 7.
17. 9. until the Son of man be r. again, Mark 9. 9.
26. 32. after I am r. I will go before, Mark 14. 28.
27. 64. his disciples steal him away and say he is r.
28. 6. he is not here, he is r. as he said, Mark 16. 6.
Mark 16. 9. now when Jesus was r. early the first day
14. which had seen him after he was r. John 21. 14.
Luke 7. 16. that a great prophet is r. among us
9. 8. that one of the old prophets was r. 19.

Luke 13.25. when once the master of the house is *r.* up
24. 34. the Lord is *r.* indeed, and hath appeared
John 2. 22. when therefore he was *r.* from the dead
Acts 17. 3. that Christ must needs have *r.* again
Rom. 8. 34. Christ that died, yea rather that is *r.* again
1 *Cor.* 15. 13. if no resurrection, then is Christ not *r.*
14. if Christ be not *r.* ‖ 20. but now is Christ *r.*
Col. 2. 12. in baptism ye are also *r.* with him
3. 1. if ye be *r.* with Christ, seek those things above
Jam. 1. 11. for the sun is no sooner *r.* with heat

RISEST.

Deut. 6. 7. thou shalt talk of them when thou *r.* 11.19.

RISETH.

Deut. 22. 26. as when a man *r.* against his neighbour
Josh. 6. 26. cursed that *r.* up and buildeth Jericho
2 *Sam.* 23. 4. shall be as the light when the sun *r.*
Job 9. 7. which commandeth the sun and it *r.* not
14. 12. so man lieth down, and *r.* not
24. 22. he *r.* up and no man is sure of life
27. 7. he that *r.* up against me, as the unrighteous
31. 14. what then shall I do when God *r.* up?
Prov. 24. 16. a just man falleth. and *r.* up again
31. 15. she *r.* also while it is yet night, giveth meat
Isa. 47. 11. thou shalt not know from whence it *r.*
Jer. 46. 8. Egypt *r.* up like a flood and his waters
Mic. 7. 6. the daughter *r.* up against her mother
John 13. 4. Jesus *r.* from supper, and girded himself

RISING, *Substantive.*

Lev. 13. 2. if in skin of his flesh a *r.* or bright spot
10. the priest shall see if the *r.* be white, 19, 43.
28. if the spot stay, it is a *r.* of the burning
14. 56. this is the law for a *r.* and for a scab
Neh. 4. 21. held spears from the *r.* of the morning
Prov. 30. 31. a king, against whom there is no *r.*
Isa. 60. 3. and kings to the brightness of thy *r.*
Mark 9. 10. what the *r.* from the dead should mean
Luke 2. 34. this child is set for the fall and *r.* of many

Sun-RISING.

Num. 2. 3. on the east-side toward the *r.* of the *sun*
21. 11. before Moab, toward *sun-r.* 34. 15. *Deut.* 4. 41, 47. *Josh.* 12. 1. | 13. 5. | 19. 12, 27, 34.
Psal. 50. 1. called the earth from the *r.* of the *sun*
113. 3. from *r.* of *sun*, Lord's name is to be praised
Isa. 41. 25. from *r.* of *sun* shall he call on my name
45. 6. that they may know from the *r.* of the *sun*
59. 19. and fear his glory from the *r.* of the *sun*
Mal. 1. 11. from *r.* of *sun* my name shall be great
Mark 16. 2. came to the sepulchre at *r.* of the *sun*
Luke 1. † 78. the *sun-r.* from on high visited us

RISING.

2 *Chron.* 36. 15. sent by his messengers *r.* betimes
Job 16. 8. my leanness *r.* in me beareth witness
24. 5. as wild asses go forth, *r.* betimes for a prey
14. murderer *r.* with the light killeth the poor
Prov. 27. 14. he that blesseth his friend, *r.* early
Jer. 7. 13. I spake unto you, *r.* up early, and speaking, but ye heard not, 25. 3. | 35. 14.
25. I sent my servants the prophets to you *r.* up early, 25. 4. | 26. 5. | 29. 19. | 35. 15. | 44. 4.
11. 7. *r.* early, and protesting, say, obey my voice
32. 33. though I taught them, *r.* up early, teaching
Lam. 3. 63. sitting down and *r.* up, I am their music
Mark 1. 35. in the morning, *r.* before day, he prayed

RITES.

Num. 9. 3. keep it according to all the *r.* of it
Acts 6. † 14. this Jesus shall change the *r.*
Heb. 9. † 10. which stood in washings and carnal *r.*

RIVER

Is *a great stream of fresh water flowing in a channel from a source or spring into the sea,* Exod. 2. 5. *It is used to denote great plenty of any thing.* Job 29. 6. The rock poured me out rivers of oil, *that is, great plenty and abundance of oil.* Psal. 36. 8. Thou shalt make them drink of the river of thy pleasures. *Thou shalt make them partake of that abundant pleasure, delight, and satisfaction, which thou not only enjoyest thyself, but bestowest on thy people: And* river *may note the constancy and perpetuity of these pleasures, as well as their plenty. And in* John 7. 38. He that believeth on me, out of his belly shall flow rivers of living water; *that is, He shall be endued with the gifts and graces of the Spirit in a plentiful measure, which shall not only refresh himself, but shall break forth, and be communicated to others also for their refreshing. And of* Behemoth *it is said,* Job 40. 23. *that* he drinketh up a river, *that is, a great quantity of water, by an* hyperbole. Thou waterest the earth with the river of God, *says the Psalmist, that is, with plentiful showers of rain from the clouds,* Psal. 65. 9. *And in* Psal. 46. 4. There is a river, the streams whereof shall make glad the city of God; *that is, The gracious presence of God, and the blessings flowing from thence, shall make* Zion, *or the church of God, glad.*

Gen. 31. 21. Jacob rose up, and passed over the *r.*
36. 37. Saul of Rehoboth by the *r.* 1 *Chron.* 1. 48.
41. 1. Pharaoh dreamed, behold, he stood by the *r.*
Exod. 1. 22. every son ye shall cast into the *r.*
2. 5. daughter of Pharaoh came to wash at the *r.*
4. 9. the water of the *r.* shall become blood
7. 18. the fish in the *r.* shall die, and *r.* stink
8. 3. the *r.* shall bring forth frogs abundantly
9. that they may remain in the *r.* only, 11.
Deut. 2. 24. take your journey, pass over the *r.*
3. 16. I gave from Gilead even to the *r.* Arnon
Josh. 13. 9. the city in the midst of *r.* 2 *Sam.* 24. 5.
Judg. 4. 7. I will draw to the *r.* Kishon, Sisera
5. 21. *r.* Kishon that ancient *r.* swept them away
2 *Sam.* 17. 13. we will draw that city into the *r.*
1 *Kings* 4. 21. Solomon reigned over from the *r.*
Ezra 4. 10. the rest that are on this side the *r.*
16. thou shalt have no portion on this side the *r.*
5. 3. came Tatnai, governor on this side the *r.*
8. 15. I gathered them to *r.* that runneth to Ahava
Job 40. 23. behold he drinketh up *r.* and hasteth not
Psal. 36. 8. make them drink of *r.* of thy pleasures
46. 4. a *r.* the streams shall make glad city of God
65. 9. thou enrichest it with the *r.* of God
72. 8. have dominion from the *r.* to ends of earth
80. 11. she sent out her branches unto the *r.*

Psal. 105. 41. the waters ran in dry places like a *r.*
Isa. 8. 7. bringeth upon them the waters of the *r.*
11. 15. he shall shake his hand over the *r.*
19. 5. and the *r.* shall be wasted and dried up
23. 3. the harvest of the *r.* is her revenue
10. pass through thy land as a *r.* O daughter
27. 12. Lord shall beat off from channel of the *r.*
48. 18. then had thy peace been as a *r.* O daughter
66. 12. I will extend peace to her like a *r.*
Jer. 2. 18. to drink the waters of the *r.*
17. 8. and that spreadeth out her roots by the *r.*
Lam. 2. 18. let tears run down like *r.* day and night
Ezek. 29. 3. which hath said, my *r.* is my own, 9.
47. 5. it was *r.* that I could not pass over
9. every thing shall live whither the *r.* cometh
Amos 6. 14. afflict you to the *r.* of the wilderness
Mic. 7. 12. he shall come from the fortress to the *r.*
Zech. 9. 10. his dominion from *r.* to ends of earth
10. 11. all the deeps of the *r.* shall dry up
Mark 1. 5. and were baptized in the *r.* of Jordan
Acts 16. 13. on the sabbath we went by a *r.* side
Rev. 22. 1. he shewed me a pure *r.* of water of life
2. on either side of the *r.* was the tree of life
See BANK, BRINK, BEYOND, CHEBAR, EUPHRATES.

RIVERS.

Exod. 7. 19. stretch out thine hand on the *r.* 8. 5.
Lev. 11. 9. whatsoever hath fins in the *r.* ye may eat
10. all that have not fins in the *r.* ye may not eat
Deut. 10. 7. to Jotbath, a land of *r.* of waters
2 *Kings* 5. 12. are not the *r.* of Damascus better
19. 24. I have dried up all the *r.* *Isa.* 37. 25.
Job 20. 17. ye shall not see the *r.* of honey
28. 10. he cutteth out the *r.* among the rocks
29. 6. when the rock poured me out *r.* of oil
Psal. 1. 3. like a tree planted by the *r.* of water
74. 15. thou driedst up mighty *r.*
78. 16. he caused waters to run down like *r.*
44. had turned their *r.* into blood, and their floods
89. 25. I will set his right hand in the *r.*
107. 33. he turneth *r.* into a wilderness
119. 136. *r.* of waters run down mine eyes
137. 1. by the *r.* of Babylon there we sat and wept
Prov. 5. 16. and *r.* of waters in the streets
21. 1. in the hand of the Lord, as *r.* of waters
Eccl. 1. 7. all *r.* run into the sea, yet it is not full
Cant. 5. 12. as the eyes of doves by the *r.* of waters
Isa. 7. 18. the Lord shall hiss for the fly in the *r.*
18. 2. a nation, whose land *r.* have spoiled, 7.
19. 6. and they shall turn the *r.* far away
30. 25. and on every high hill *r.* and streams
32. 2. a man shall be as *r.* of water in a dry place
33. 21. the Lord will be to us a place of broad *r.*
41. 18. I will open *r.* in high places and fountains
42. 15. I will make the *r.* islands and dry up
43. 2. passest thro' the *r.* they shall not overfl. thee
19. and I will make *r.* in the desert, 20.
44. 27. to the deep, be dry, and will dry up thy *r.*
47. 2. uncover the thigh, pass over the *r.*
50. 2. I make *r.* a wilderness, their fish stinketh
Jer. 31. 9. I will cause them to walk by the *r.*
46. 7. whose waters are moved as the *r.* 8.
Lam. 3. 48. mine eye runneth down with *r.* of waters
Ezek. 6. 3. thus saith the Lord to the hills and *r.*
29. 3. the great dragon that lieth in midst of his *r.*
4. I will cause fish of thy *r.* to stick to thy scales, I will bring thee up out of midst of thy *r.*
5. I will leave thee, and all the fish of thy *r.*
10. behold, I am against thee, and against thy *r.*
30. 12. I will make the *r.* dry, and sell the land
31. 4. the deep set him up on high with her *r.*
12. his boughs are broken by the *r.* of the land
32. 2. thou camest forth with thy *r.* and troubledst
6. and the *r.* shall be full of thee
14. then will I cause their *r.* to run like oil
34. 13. I will feed them on mountains by the *r.*
35. 8. in all thy *r.* shall they fall that are slain
36. 6. say to the hills, to the *r.* and the valleys
47. 9. whithersoever the *r.* shall come, shall live
Joel 1. 20. for the *r.* of waters are dried up
3. 18. all the *r.* of Judah shall flow with waters
Mic. 6. 7. be pleased with ten thousands of *r.* of oil
Nah. 1. 4. rebuketh the sea, and drieth up the *r.*
2. 6. the gates of the *r.* shall be opened
3. 8. populous No, that was situate among the *r.*
Hab. 3. 8. was the Lord displeased against the *r.*?
9. thou didst cleave the earth with *r.*
John 7. 38. out of his belly shall flow *r.* of living water
Rev. 8. 10. the star fell on the third part of the *r.*
16. 4. the third angel poured out his vial on the *r.*

ROAD.

1 *Sam.* 27. 10. whither have ye made a *r.* to-day

ROAR.

1 *Chron.* 16. 32. let the sea *r.* *Psal.* 96. 11. | 98. 7.
Psal. 46. 3. we will not fear, tho' waters thereof *r.*
74. 4. thine enemies *r.* in thy congregations
104. 21. the young lions *r.* after their prey
Isa. 5. 29. they shall *r.* like young lions
30. in that day they shall *r.* against them
42. 13. L. shall *r.* he shall prevail against enemies
59. 11. we *r.* all like bears, and mourn sore
Jer. 5. 22. tho' they *r.* yet can they not pass over
25. 30. the Lord shall *r.* from on high, and utter
31. 35. divideth the sea, when the waves thereof *r.*
50. 42. their voice shall *r.* like the sea, shall ride
51. 38. they shall *r.* together like lions, and yell
55. when her waves do *r.* like great waters
Hos. 11. 10. he shall *r.* like a lion, when he shall *r.*
Joel 3. 16. the Lord shall *r.* out of Zion, *Amos* 1. 2.
Amos 3. 4. will a lion *r.* if he hath taken no prey?

ROARED.

Judg. 14. 5. a young lion *r.* against Samson
Psal. 38. 8. I have *r.* by reason of the disquietness
Isa. 51. 15. that divided the sea, whose waves *r.*
Jer. 2. 15. the young lions *r.* upon him, and yelled
Amos 3. 8. the lion hath *r.* who will not fear

ROARETH.

Job 37. 4. after it a voice *r.* he thundereth with voice
Jer. 6. 23. their voice *r.* like the sea, they ride
Rev. 10. 3. the angel cried, as when a lion *r.*

ROARING, *Substantive.*

Job 4. 10. the *r.* the teeth of the lion are broken

Psal. 22. 1. why so far from the words of my *r.*?
32. 3. my bones waxed old thro' my *r.* all the day
Prov. 19. 12. the king's wrath is as the *r.* of a lion
20. 2. the fear of a king is as the *r.* of a lion
Isa. 5. 29. their *r.* shall be like a lion, they shall roar
30. they shall roar like the *r.* of the sea
Ezek. 19. 7. land was desolate by the noise of his *r.*
Zech. 11. 3. a voice of the *r.* of young lions

ROARING, *Adjective.*

Psal. 22. 13. they gaped upon me as a *r.* lion
Prov. 28. 15. as a *r.* lion, so is a wicked ruler
Isa. 31. 4. as the young lion *r.* on his prey
Ezek. 22. 25. there is a conspiracy like a *r.* lion
Zeph. 3. 3. her princes within her are *r.* lions
Luke 21. 25. distress, the sea and the waves *r.*
1 *Pet.* 5. 8. the devil, as a *r.* lion, walketh about

ROARINGS.

Job 3. 24. my *r.* are poured out like the waters

ROAST, ED.

Exod. 12. 8. shall eat in that night flesh *r.* with fire
9. eat not of it raw, but *r.* with fire, *Deut.* 16. 7.
1 *Sam.* 2. 15. give flesh to *r.* for the priest
2 *Chron.* 35. 13. they *r.* the passover with fire
Isa. 44. 16. he roasteth *r.* is satisfied, he warmeth
19. yea, also, I have *r.* flesh, and eaten it
Jer. 29. 22. whom the king of Babylon *r.* in fire

ROASTETH.

Prov. 12. 27. the slothful man *r.* not that he took

ROB.

Lev. 19. 13. thou shalt not *r.* thy neighbour
26. 22. beasts, which shall *r.* you of your children
1 *Sam.* 23. 1. and they *r.* the threshing floors
Prov. 22. 22. *r.* not the poor, because he is poor
Isa. 10. 2. and that they may *r.* the fatherless
17. 14. and this is the lot of them that *r.* us
Ezek. 39. 10. spoil and *r.* those that robbed them
Mal. 3. 8. will a man *r.* God? yet ye have robbed me

ROBBED.

Judg. 9. 25. and they *r.* all that came by them
2 *Sam.* 17. 8. they be chafed in minds, as a bear *r.*
Psal. 119. 61. the bands of the wicked have *r.* me
Prov. 17. 12. let a bear *r.* of her whelps meet a man
Isa. 10. 13. and I have *r.* their treasures
42. 22. but this is a people *r.* and spoiled
Jer. 50. 37. a sword on her treasures, they shall be *r.*
Ezek. 33. 15. if the wicked give again that he had *r.*
39. 10. and they shall rob those that *r.* them
Mal. 3. 8. ye have *r.* me, wherein have we *r.* thee?
9. ye are cursed with a curse, for ye have *r.* me
2 *Cor.* 11. 8. I *r.* other churches, taking wages

ROBBER.

Job. 5. 5. and the *r.* swalloweth up their substance
18. 9. and the *r.* shall prevail against him
Prov. 23. † 28. she also lieth in wait as a *r.*
Ezek. 18. 10. if he beget a son that is a *r.*
John 10. 1. the same is a thief and a *r.*
18. 40. they cried, not this man, now Barabbas [was a *r.*

ROBBERS.

Job 12. 6. the tabernacles of *r.* prosper
Isa. 42. 24. and who gave Israel to the *r.*
Jer. 7. 11. is this house become a den of *r.*?
Ezek. 7. 22. for the *r.* shall enter into it, and defile it
Dan. 11. 14. the *r.* of thy people shall exalt thems.
Hos. 6. 9. as troops of *r.* wait for a man, so priests
7. 1. and the troop of *r.* spoileth without
Obad. 5. if *r.* by night, would they not have stolen
John 10. 8. all that came before me are *r.*
Acts 19. 37. these men are not *r.* of churches
2 *Cor.* 11. 26. in perils of waters, in perils of *r.*

ROBBERY.

Psal. 62. 10. and become not vain in *r.*
Prov. 21. 7. the *r.* of the wicked shall destroy them
Isa. 61. 8. I hate *r.* for burnt offering
Ezek. 22. 29. have exercised *r.* and vexed the poor
Amos 3. 10. who store up *r.* in their palaces
Nah. 3. 1. the bloody city is full of lies and *r.*
Phil. 2. 6. who thought it no *r.* to be equal with G.

ROBBETH.

Prov. 28. 24. whoso *r.* his father or his mother

ROBE.

God gives orders to Moses *to make* the robe of the ephod, *Exod.* 28. 31. *In Hebrew it is called* Meguil: *it was a long garment worn next under the ephod, which was girded about the high priest's body with the curious girdle of the ephod. Our Saviour says,* Beware of the Scribes, who desire to walk in long robes, *Luke* 20. 46. *The Scribes wore those garments in token of greater gravity than others:* Christ *condemns not the garb, but their affectation, ambition, vain glory, and seeming holiness, whereby they deceived the people.* The best robe *is the righteousness of* Christ *imputed to believers for their justification,* Luke 15. 22. *Heavenly glory is likewise set forth by* white robes, *Rev.* 6. 11. White robes were given them, *speaking of the martyrs: their innocency was cleared, and they made perfectly happy.*

Exod. 28. 4. they shall make an ephod and a *r.*
31. thou shalt make the *r.* of the ephod of blue
34. a golden bell on the hem of the *r.* 39. 25, 26.
29. 5. put upon Aaron the coat and *r.* *Lev.* 8. 7.
1 *Sam.* 18. 4. Jonathan stripped himself of his *r.*
24. 4. David cut off the skirt of Saul's *r.*
11. see the skirt of thy *r.* in my hand, for in that I cut off the skirt of thy *r.* and killed thee not
1 *Chron.* 15. 27. David was clothed with a *r.*
Job 1. † 20. then Job arose, and rent his *r.*
29. 14. my judgment was as a *r.* and a diadem
Isa. 22. 21. I will clothe him with thy *r.*
61. 10. hath covered me with *r.* of righteousness
Jonah 3. 6. the king arose and laid his *r.* from him
Mic. 2. 8. ye pull off the *r.* with the garment
Mat. 27. 28. they put on Jesus a scarlet *r.*
31. after that, they took the *r.* off from him
Luke 15. 22. bring forth the best *r.* and put it on
23. 11. his men of war arrayed him in a gorgeous *r.*
John 19. 2. they put on Jesus a purple *r.*
5. Jesus came forth, wearing the purple *r.*

ROBES.

2 *Sam.* 13. 18. with such *r.* were virgins apparelled
1 *Kings* 22. 10. the kings having put on their *r.*
30. but put thou on thy *r.* 2 *Chron.* 18. 9, 29

Ezek. 26. 16. the princes shall lay away their r.
Luke 20. 46. the Scribes desire to walk in long r.
Rev. 6. 11. and white r. were given unto them
7. 9. stood before the Lamb, clothed with white r.
13. what are these which are arrayed in white r.
14. these are they which have washed their r.

ROCK.

Palestine being a mountainous country, had also many rocks, which made part of the strength of the country; for in times of danger they retired to them, where they found a refuge against any sudden irruptions of the enemy. When the Benjamites were overcome, and almost exterminated by the Israelites of the other tribes, they secured themselves in the rock Rimmon, Judg. 20. 47. Samson kept garrison in the rock Etam, Judg. 15. 8. When David was persecuted by Saul, he often hid himself in caverns made in a rock: as at Maon, at Adullam, at En-gedi, where there was a cave of a vast extent, in which David and his people concealed themselves, and Saul entered into it, and continued for some time without discovering them, 1 Sam. 22. 1. | 23. 25. | 24. 2, 4, 5.

Mention is made in Scripture of several rocks, as, the rocks Bozez and Seneh, which were between Michmash and Gibeah, and which Jonathan, the son of Saul, climbed up, when he went to attack the Philistines, 1 Sam. 14. 4.

Sela-hamma-lekoth, or the rock of divisions: This was in the deserts of Maon, and had this name given it, because Saul was here obliged to quit his pursuit after David, and to return to the assistance of his country, which was then invaded by the Philistines, 1 Sam. 23. 28.

The rock of Horeb. From this rock Moses caused the waters to gush out, to supply the necessities of the people, when they were encamped at Rephidim, Exod. 17. 6.

The rock Adullam was in the neighbourhood of the city of the same name, in the tribe of Judah, 1 Sam. 22. 1.

The rock of the waters of Meribah, or Strife. This is the rock where the faith of Moses failed, and where the Scripture makes mention of his having hesitated in mind, and that he did not honour God as he ought before the children of Israel, Num. 20. 10, 11.

The name of rock is also given to God, by way of metaphor, because God is the strength, the refuge, and the asylum of his people, as the rocks were in those places, whither the people retired in case of an unforeseen attack or irruption of the enemy. The Lord is my rock and my fortress; who is a rock, save our God? Psal. 18. 2, 31. Then he forsook God which made him, and lightly esteemed the rock of his salvation, Deut. 32. 15.

It is said in Deut. 32. 13. That the Lord had settled his people in a high country, and made them to suck honey out of the rock, and oil out of the flinty rock. That is, he brought them out of Egypt, which was a flat country, and subject to inundations, and placed them in the land of Canaan, which was a mountainous country of great fertility; the hills of which were loaded with vines and olive-trees, and of which the very rocks were filled with swarms of bees, by which means the inhabitants had abundance of honey.

Rock is also used for a quarry, and, in a figurative sense, for the patriarch of a nation, or the first father, who is, as it were, the quarry from whom the men of that nation have proceeded, Isa. 51. 1. Look unto the rock whence ye are hewn; look unto Abraham and Sarah whose descendants you are.

The rock from which the Israelites were supplied with water, was a figure and type of Christ, as the apostle observes, 1 Cor. 10. 4. They drank of that spiritual rock that followed them, and that rock was Christ. Believers have their spiritual refreshing from Christ, as the thirsty Israelites were refreshed with the waters that gushed out of the rock in the wilderness. Christ likewise sustains and bears up his church, built upon him by faith, as a house upon a rock. Mat. 16. 18. And upon this rock will I build my church.

Rock also signifies unfruitful and stony-hearted hearers of the word, Luke 8. 6. A firm, solid, and immovable foundation, Mat. 7. 25. A safe or secure place of retreat, Num. 24. 21. Job 24. 8. Barren and rocky places, Job 29. 6.

Exod. 17. 6. I will stand before thee upon the r.
33. 21. the Lord said, thou shalt stand upon a r.
22. that I will put thee in a cleft of the r.
Num. 20. 8. speak to the r. before their eyes
10. must we fetch you water out of this r.?
11. Moses with his rod smote the r. twice
24. 21. and thou puttest thy nest in a r.
Deut. 8. 15. who brought thee water out of the r.
32. 4. he is the r. his work is perfect, a God of truth
13. he made him suck honey and oil out of the r.
15. he lightly esteemed the r. of his salvation
18. of the r. that begat thee thou art unmindful
30. except the r. had sold them, and L. had shut
31. their r. is not as our r. our enem. being judges
37. where is their r. in whom they trusted?
Judg. 6. 20. take and lay them on this r. he did so
21. rose fire out of the r. and consumed flesh
26. and build an altar to the Lord on this r.
7. 25. slew Oreb on the r. Oreb and Zeeb they slew
13. 19. Manoah offered it on a r. to the Lord
15. 8. Samson dwelt in the top of the r. Etam
20. 45. the Benjamites turned to the r. of Rimmon
1 Sam. 2. 2. neither is there any r. like our God
14. 4. a sharp r. on one side, sharp r. on other side
23. 25. David came down into a r. and abode
† 28. they called it the r. of divisions
2 Sam. 21. 10. Rizpah spread sackcloth on the r.
22. 2. he said, Lord is my r. Psal. 18. 2. | 92. 15.
3. the God of my r. in him will I trust, my shield
32. and who is a r. save our God? Psal. 18. 31.
47. the Lord liveth, blessed be my r. Psal. 18. 46.
and exalted be the God of the r. of my salvation

2 Sam. 23. 3. the God of Isr. said, the r. of Isr. spake
2 Kings 14. † 7. Amaziah took the r. by war
1 Chron. 11. 15. captains went to the r. to David
2 Chron. 25. 12. cast them down from the top of the r.
Neh. 9. 15. thou broughtest water for them out of the r. for their thirst, Psal. 78. 16. | 105. 41.
Job 14. 18. the r. is removed out of his place
18. 4. and shall the r. be removed out of his place?
19. 24. that they were graven in the r. for ever
24. 8. they embrace the r. for want of a shelter
28. 9. he putteth forth his hand upon the r.
29. 6. and the r. poured out rivers of oil
39. 1. time when wild goats of the r. bring forth?
28. she dwelleth on the r. on the crag of the r.
Psal. 19. † 14. O Lord, my r. and my Redeemer
27. 5. he shall set me up upon a r. 40. 2.
28. 1. unto thee will I cry, O Lord, my r.
31. 2. be thou my strong r. for an house of defence
3. for thou art my r. and my fortress, 71. 3.
42. 9. I will say to G. my r. why hast forgotten me
61. 2. lead me to the r. that is higher than I
62. 2. God only is my r. 6. ‖ 7. r. of my strength
71. † 3. be thou to me for a r. of habitation
73. † 26. God is the r. of my heart, and my portion
78. 20. behold, he smote the r. the waters gushed
35. they remembered that God was their r.
81. 16. with honey out of the r. have I satisfied thee
89. 26. r. of my salvation ‖ 94. 22. r. of my refuge
95. 1. make a joyful noise to the r. of our salvation
114. 8. which turned the r. into a standing water
Prov. 30. 19. the way of a serpent upon a r.
Cant. 2. 14. my dove, that art in the clefts of the r.
Isa. 2. 10. enter into the r. and hide thee in the dust
8. 14. for a r. of offence to both houses of Israel
10. 26. according to the slaughter at the r. of Oreb
17. 10. not mindful of the r. of thy strength
22. 16. that graveth an habitation for himself in a r.
26. † 4. in the Lord Jehovah is the r. of ages
30. † 29. when one goeth to come to the r. of Israel
31. † 9. and his r. shall pass away for fear
32. 2. a man shall be as the shadow of a great r.
42. 11. let the inhabitants of the r. sing
44. † 8. yea, there is no r. I know not any
48. 21. he caused waters to flow out of r. for them
51. 1. look unto the r. whence ye are hewn
Jer. 5. 3. they made their faces harder than a r.
13. 4. go, hide the girdle in a hole of the r.
18. 14. leave the snow which cometh from the r.
21. 13. I am against thee, O inhabitant of the r.
23. 29. a hammer that breaketh the r. in pieces
48. 28. leave cities, and dwell in the r. like the dove
49. 16. thou that dwellest in the clefts of the r.
Ezek. 24. 7. she set it upon the top of a r.
8. I have set her blood upon the top of a r.
26. 4. I will make her like the top of a r. 14.
Amos 6. 12. shall horses run upon the r.?
Obad. 3. thou that dwellest in the clefts of the r.
Hab. 1. † 12. O r. thou hast established them
Mat. 7. 24. a man which built his house upon a r.
25. for it was founded upon a r. Luke 6. 48.
16. 18. and upon this r. I will build my church
27. 60. and Joseph laid it in his own new tomb which he had hewn out in the r. Mark 15. 46.
Luke 8. 6. some fell upon a r. ‖ 13. they on the r.
Rom. 9. 33. as it is written, behold, I lay in Sion a stumbling stone, and r. of offence, 1 Pet. 2. 8.
1 Cor. 10. 4. for they drank of that spiritual r. that followed them, and that r. was Christ

ROCKS.

Num. 23. 9. for from the top of the r. I see him
1 Sam. 13. 6. then the people hid themselves in r.
24. 2. Saul went to seek David upon the r.
1 Kings 19. 11. a strong wind brake in pieces the r.
Job 28. 10. he cutteth out rivers among the r.
30. 6. to dwell in the caves of the earth, and in r.
Psal. 78. 15. he clave the r. in the wilderness
104. 18. and the r. are a refuge for the conies
Prov. 30. 26. yet make they their houses in the r.
Isa. 2. 19. they shall go into the holes of the r.
21. into clefts of the r. and tops of the ragged r.
7. 19. they shall rest in the holes of the r.
33. 16. his defence shall be the munitions of r.
57. 5. slaying the children under the clefts of the r.
Jer. 4. 29. the whole city shall climb on the r.
16. 16. shall hunt them out of the holes of the r.
51. 25. I will roll thee down from the r.
Nah. 1. 6. the r. are thrown down by him
Mat. 27. 51. the earth did quake, and the r. rent
Acts 27. 29. lest they should have fallen upon the r.
Rev. 6. 15. hid themselves in the dens and in the r.
16. and said to the r. fall on us, and hide us from

ROD

Is used sometimes for the branches of a tree, Gen. 30. 37. Jacob took him rods of green poplar, and of the hazel and chesnut-tree. Sometimes for a staff or wand, 1 Sam. 14. 27. Jonathan put forth the end of the rod that was in his hand, and dipped it in an honey-comb. Or for a shepherd's crook. Lev. 27. 32. And concerning the tithe of the herd, or of the flock, even of whatsoever passeth under the rod. Or for those rods and chastisements which God makes use of to correct men. 2 Sam. 7. 14. If he commit iniquity, I will chasten him with the rod of men. Job 9. 34. Let him take his rod away from me. The mighty power of the Messiah is sometimes represented by a rod of iron. Psal. 2. 9. Thou shalt break them with a rod of iron. Rev. 2. 27. He shall rule them with a rod of iron. Rod is put for a young sprout or branch, and to point out the miraculous birth of the Messiah, who was to proceed from a virgin mother. Isa. 11. 1. There shall come forth a rod out of the stem of Jesse, and a branch shall grow out of his roots. It signifies sometimes a tribe, or people. Psal. 74. 2. Remember the rod of thine inheritance which thou hast redeemed.

The gospel published by Christ himself, or by his apostles and ministers, being accompanied by his Spirit, is called the rod of his strength, or his strong and powerful rod, whereby he did his great exploits, and established his church in the world, Psal. 110. 2. It is also taken for the rod of discipline, or ecclesiastical censures, 1 Cor. 4. 21. Shall I come unto you with a rod? And for those means and instruments which God makes use of in his pastoral care over his people, Psal. 23. 4. Thy rod and thy staff, they comfort me. The rod of the wicked is their power and authority, Psal. 125. 3. Moab is called a strong staff, and a beautiful rod, Jer. 48. 17. They were a people that had been a rod against others, or had ruled over so many others; the rod and staff being the ensigns of power and government, as well as instruments for punishing offenders.

Exod. 4. 4. he caught it, and it bec. a r. in his hand
17. thou shalt take this r. in thine hand
20. Moses took the r. of God in his hand, 17. 9.
7. 9. thou shalt say to Aaron, take thy r. 19.
12. for they cast down every man his r.
20. he lifted up the r. and smote the waters, 14. 16.
21. 20. if a man smite his servant with a r.
Lev. 27. 32. whatsoever passeth under the r.
Num. 17. 2. write thou every man's name on his r.
8. the r. of Aaron for the house of Levi budded
20. 11. with his r. he smote the rock twice
1 Sam. 14. 27. Jonathan put forth the end of the r.
2 Sam. 7. 14. I will chasten him with the r. of men
Job 9. 34. let him take his r. away from me
21. 9. neither is the r. of God upon them
Psal. 2. 9. thou shalt break them with a r. of iron
23. 4. thy r. and thy staff they comfort me
74. 2. remember the r. of thine inheritance
89. 32. I will visit their transgression with a r.
110. 2. the Lord shall send the r. of thy strength
125. 3. r. of wicked shall not rest on the righteous
Prov. 10. 13. a r. is for the back of fools, 26. 3.
13. 24. he that spareth his r. hateth his son
14. 3. in the mouth of the foolish is a r. of pride
22. 8. and the r. of his anger shall fail
15. the r. of correction shall drive it away
23. 13. thou shalt beat him with the r. 14.
29. 15. the r. and reproof give wisdom
Isa. 9. 4. thou hast broken the r. of his oppressor
10. 5. O Assyrian, the r. of mine anger
15. as if the r. should shake itself against them
24. he shall smite with a r. and lift his staff
26. as his r. was on the sea, so shall he lift it up
11. 1. shall come forth a r. out of the stem of Jesse
4. shall smite the earth with the r. of his mouth
14. 29. the r. of him that smote thee is broken
28. 27. and the cummin is beaten out with a r.
30. 31. the Assyrian be beat. which smote with a r.
Jer. 1. 11. and said, I see a r. of an almond-tree
10. 16. Israel the r. of his inheritance, 51. 19.
48. 17. how is the beautiful r. broken!
Lam. 3. 1. have seen affliction by the r. of his wrath
Ezek. 7. 10. the r. hath blossomed, pride hath budd.
11. violence is risen up into a r. of wickedness
19. 14. fire is gone out of a r. of her branches, so that she hath no strong r. to be a sceptre to rule
20. 37. will cause you to pass under the r. and bring
21. 10. it contemneth the r. of my son, 13.
Mic. 5. 1. they shall smite Judge of Israel with a r
6. 9. hear ye the r. and who hath appointed it
7. 14. feed thy people with thy r. the flock
John 18. † 22. an officer struck Jesus with a r.
1 Cor. 4. 21. shall I come to you with a r. or in love?
Heb. 9. 4. wherein was Aaron's r. that budded
Rev. 2. 27. shall rule them with a r. of iron, 19. 15.
11. 1. there was given me a reed like to a r.
12. 5. who was to rule all nations with a r. of iron

RODE.

Gen. 24. 61. Rebekah and her damsels r. on camels
Judg. 10. 4. he had thirty sons that r. on thirty colts
12. 14. he had thirty nephews that r. on ass-colts
1 Sam. 25. 20. it was so Abigail r. on the ass, 42.
30. 17. none escaped, save 400 which r. on camels
2 Sam. 13. † 29. every man r. on his mule and fled
18. 9. Absalom r. upon a mule, went under the oak
22. 11. he r. on a cherub, and did fly, Psal. 18. 10.
1 Kings 13. 13. the old prophet r. on the ass
18. 45. and Ahab r. and went to Jezreel
2 Kings 9. 16. Jehu r. in a chariot and went to Jezreel
25. remember when I and thou r. together
Neh. 2. 12. nor any beast, save beast that I r. upon
Esth. 8. 14. the posts that r. on the mules went out

RODS.

Gen. 30. 37. Jacob took r. of green poplar
41. that they might conceive among the r.
Exod. 7. 12. Aaron's rod swallowed up their r.
Num. 17. 6. the princes gave him twelve r.
7. and Moses laid up the r. before the Lord
Ezek. 19. 11. she had strong r. for the sceptres
12. her strong r. were broken and withered
Mat. 26. † 67. and others smote him with r.
2 Cor. 11. 25. thrice was I beaten with r.

ROE, S.

1 Chron. 12. 8. as swift as the r. on the mountains
Prov. 5. 19. let her be as the hind and pleasant r.
6. 5. deliver thyself as a r. from the hunter
Cant. 2. 7. I charge you by the r. and hinds, 3. 5.
9. my beloved is like a r. or a young hart
17. turn, my beloved, be thou like r. or hart, 8. 14.
Isa. 13. 14. it shall be as the chased r. as a sheep

See Young.

Wild ROE.

2 Sam. 2. 18. Asahel was as light of foot as a wild r.

ROE-BUCK, S.

Deut. 12. 15. ye may eat of the r. 22. | 14. 5. | 15. 22.
1 Kings 4. 23. an hundred sheep, besides harts and r.

ROLL, Verb.

Gen. 29. 8. we cannot, till they r. away the stone
43. † 18. brought, that he may r. himself on us
Josh. 10. 18. and Joshua said, r. great stones
1 Sam. 14. 33. r. a great stone unto me this day
Ps. 37. † 5. r. thy way upon the Lord, trust in him, and he shall bring to pass, Prov. 16. † 3.
Jer. 51. 25. and I will r. thee down from the rocks
Amos 5. † 24. let judgment r. down as waters
Mic. 1. 10. in Aphrah, r. thyself in the dust
Mark 16. 3. who shall r. us away stone from sepu.

ROLL, Substantive.

Ezra 6. 2. and there was found at Achmetha a r.
Isa. 8. 1. take thee a great r. and write in it

Jer. 36. 2. take thee a *r.* of a book, write therein
6. go and read in the *r.* ‖ 28. take another *r.*
23. till all the *r.* was consumed in the fire
29. thus saith the Lord, thou hast burnt this *r.*
Ezek. 2. 9. an hand was sent unto me, and lo, a *r.*
3. 1. eat this *r.* ‖ 2. he caused me to eat that *r.*
3. fill thy bowels with this *r.* that I give thee
Zech. 5. 1. then I looked, and behold, a flying *r.* 2.

ROLLS.

Ezra 6. 1. search was made in the house of the *r.*

ROLLED.

Gen. 29. 3. they *r.* the stone from the well's mouth
10. that Jacob went near, and *r.* the stone
Josh. 5. 9. I have *r.* away the reproach of Egypt
Job 30. 14. in desolation they *r.* themselves on me
Psal. 22. † 8. he *r.* himself on the Lord to deliver him
Isa. 9. 5. with noise, and garments *r.* in blood
34. 4. the heavens shall be *r.* together, *Rev.* 6. 14.
Lam. 3. † 16. he hath *r.* me in ashes
Mat. 27. 60. he laid it in his own new tomb, he *r.* a great stone to door of the sepulchre, *Mark* 15. 46.
28. 2. the angel came and *r.* back the stone
Mark 16. 4. they saw that the stone was *r.* away
Luke 24. 2. and they found the stone *r.* away

ROLLER.

Ezek. 30. 21. not be bound up, to put a *r.* to bind it

ROLLETH.

Prov. 26. 27. he that *r.* a stone it will return on him

ROLLING.

Ezra 5. † 8. the house of God built with stones of *r.*

ROLLING.

Isa. 17. 13. the nations shall flee like a *r.* thing

ROOF.

Gen. 19. 8. they came under the shadow of my *r.*
Exod. 30. † 3. thou shalt overlay the *r.* with gold
Deut. 22. 8. thou shalt make a battlement for thy *r.*
Josh. 2. 6. but she brought them up to the *r.* and hid with flax which she had laid in order on the *r.*
Judg. 16. 27. on the *r.* were 3000 men and women
2 *Sam.* 11. 2. David walked on the *r.* of the house, and from the *r.* he saw a woman washing herself
18. 24. watchman went up to the *r.* over the gate
Neh. 8. 16. people made booths on the *r.* of his house
Ezek. 40. 13. he measured the gate from the *r.* of one
Mat. 8. 8. I am not worthy that thou shouldest come under my *r.* but speak the word only, *Luke* 7. 6.
Mark 2. 4. they uncovered the *r.* where he was

ROOF with *mouth.*

Job 29. 10. their tongue cleaved to *r.* of their *mouth*
Psal. 137. 6. let my tongue cleave to *r.* of my *mouth*
Cant. 7. 9. the *r.* of thy *mouth* like the best wine
Lam. 4. 4. tongue of child cleaveth to *r.* of his *mouth*
Ezek. 3. 26. I will make thy tongue cleave to *r.* of *m.*
Hos. 8. † 1. set the trumpet to the *r.* of thy *mouth*

ROOFS.

Jer. 19. 13. on whose *r.* they burnt incense, 32. 29.

ROOM.

Gen. 24. 23. is there *r.* in thy father's house for us?
25. we have *r.* to lodge in ‖ 31. *r.* for the camels
26. 22. for now the Lord hath made *r.* for us
Deut. 2. † 12. the children of Esau dwelt in their *r.*
2 *Sam.* 19. 13. if thou be not captain in the *r.* of Joab
1 *Kings* 2. 35. the king put Benaiah in Joab's *r.* and he put Zadok the priest in the *r.* of Abiathar
5. 1. had anointed him king in the *r.* of his father
5. thy son whom I will set in thy *r.* shall build
8. 20. I am risen in the *r.* of David, 2 *Chr.* 6. 10.
19. 16. and Elisha shalt thou anoint in thy *r.*
Psal. 31. 8. thou hast set my feet in a large *r.*
80. 9. thou preparedst *r.* before it, it filled the land
Prov. 18. 16. a man's gift maketh *r.* for him
Isa. 57. † 8. thou lovedst their bed, thou providedst *r.*
Mal. 3. 10. there shall not be *r.* enough to receive
Mat. 2. 22. Archelaus reigned in the *r.* of Herod
Mark 2. 2. that there was no *r.* to receive them
14. 15. he will shew you a large upper *r.* *Luke* 22. 12.
Luke 2. 7. because there was no *r.* for them in the inn
12. 17. I have no *r.* where to bestow my goods
14. 8. bidden to a wedding, sit not down in highest *r.*
9. thou begin with shame to take the lowest *r.*
10. when bidden, go and sit down in the lowest *r.*
22. Lord, it is done, and yet there is *r.*
Acts 1. 13. went up to an upper *r.* where was Peter
24. 27. Porcius Festus came into Felix' *r.*
1 *Cor.* 14. 16. how shall he that occupieth the *r.*

ROOMS.

Gen. 6. 14. *r.* shalt thou make in the ark, and pitch
1 *Kings* 20. 24. and put captains in their *r.*
1 *Chron.* 4. 41. destroyed them, and dwelt in their *r.*
Mat. 23. 6. they love the uppermost *r.* at feasts and chief seats in synag. *Mark* 12. 39. *Luke* 20. 46.
Luke 14. 7. how they chose out the chief *r.*

ROOT

Is *that part of a plant which extends itself downward, and which fastens the plant to the earth,* Job 14. 8. *It is said of such as received the seed into stony places,* that they had no root in themselves, *Mat.* 13. 21. *They had not the soil of a sincere heart, solid affections, firm and fixed resolutions, and habitual dispositions of grace. It is taken for the fountain, the cause, or occasion of any thing.* 1 Tim. 6. 10. The love of money is the root of all evil. Lest there be among you a root that beareth gall and wormwood, *Deut.* 29. 18. *Lest there should be among you some close idolaters, who concealing themselves from the public view, might secretly infect and poison others, and so draw down upon you the effects of God's anger. It is also taken for parents or progenitors.* Isa. 14. 29. Out of the serpent's root shall come forth a cockatrice; *meaning* Hezekiah, *who should be born of the royal family of* David. *And the apostle* Paul, *speaking of the conversion of the* Jews, *says,* Rom. 11. 16. If the root be holy, so are the branches; *that is, If* Abraham *and the patriarchs, from whom the* Jews *descended, were in covenant with God, the body of the nation is also in covenant with him, and consecrated to him, and therefore God will not cast them off for ever.* Christ Jesus *is by a metonomy called the* root of Jesse, *Isa.* 11. 10. *And the root of* David, *Rev.* 5. 5. *instead of a* Branch *growing out of the root: He is David's son, as he is man, yet David's* Root, *and* Lord, *as he is God, and gave a being to him and his family.* Psal. 110. 1. Their root shall be rottenness, and their blossom shall go up as dust, *Isa.* 5. 24. *that is, They shall be utterly destroyed, both root and branch, parents and children, old and young, as a tree that is rotten at the root cannot grow any more.*

ROOT, *Substantive.*

Deut. 29. 18. among you a *r.* that beareth gall
Judg. 5. 14. out of Ephraim was a *r.* against Amalek
2 *Kings* 19. 30. Judah shall again take *r.* downward
Job 5. 3. I have seen the foolish taking *r.*
14. 8. though the *r.* thereof wax old in the earth
19. 28. seeing the *r.* of the matter is found in me
29. 19. my *r.* was spread out by the waters
Psal. 80. 9. thou didst cause the vine to take deep *r.*
Prov. 12. 3. *r.* of the righteous shall not be moved
12. the *r.* of the righteous yieldeth fruit
Isa. 5. 24. so their *r.* shall be rottenness, and blossom
11. 10. there shall be a *r.* of Jesse, *Rom.* 15. 12.
14. 29. for out of the serpent's *r.* a cockatrice
30. and I will kill thy *r.* with famine
27. 6. them that come of Jacob to take *r.* 37. 31.
40. 24. yea, their stock shall not take *r.*
53. 2. he shall grow up as a *r.* out of a dry ground
Jer. 12. 2. yea, they have taken *r.* they grow
Ezek. 31. 7. for his *r.* was by great waters
Dan. 11. 7. out of a branch of her *r.* shall one stand
Hos. 9. 16. Ephraim is smitten, their *r.* is dried
Mal. 4. 1. it shall leave neither *r.* nor branch
Mat. 3. 10. and now also the axe is laid unto the *r.* of the trees, *Luke* 3. 9.
13. 6. because they had not *r.* they withered away, 21. *Mark* 4. 6, 17. *Luke* 8. 13.
Luke 17. 6. might say, be thou plucked up by the *r.*
Rom. 11. 16. if the *r.* be holy, so are the branches
17. with them partakers of the *r.* and fatness
18. thou bearest not the *r.* but the *r.* thee
1 *Tim.* 6. 10. the love of money is the *r.* of all evil
Heb. 12. 15. lest any *r.* of bitterness trouble you
Rev. 5. 5. *r.* of Dav. hath prevailed to open the book
22. 16. I am the *r.* and offspring of David

ROOT.

1 *Kings* 14. 15. he shall *r.* up Israel out of his land
Job 31. 12. and would *r.* out all mine increase
Psal. 52. 5. and *r.* thee out of the land of the living
Jer. 1. 10. this day I have set thee to *r.* out
Mat. 13. 29. lest ye *r.* up the wheat with them

ROOTED.

Deut. 29. 28. the Lord *r.* them out of their land
Job 18. 14. confidence shall be *r.* out of tabernacle
31. 8. yea, let my offspring be *r.* out
Prov. 2. 22. the transgressors shall be *r.* out of it
Zeph. 2. 4. and Ekron shall be *r.* up
Mat. 15. 13. my Father hath not planted, shall be *r.*
Eph. 3. 17. that ye being *r.* and grounded in love
Col. 2. 7. *r.* and built up in him, and stablished

ROOTING.

Ezra 7. † 26. whether it be to death, or to *r.* out

ROOTS.

2 *Chron.* 7. 20. I will pluck them up by the *r.*
Job 8. 17. his *r.* are wrapped about the heap
13. † 27. thou settest a print on the *r.* of my feet
18. 16. his *r.* shall be dried up beneath
28. 9. he overturneth the mountains by the *r.*
30. 4. who cut up juniper *r.* for their meat
36. † 30. behold, God covereth the *r.* of the sea
Isa. 11. 1. and a branch shall grow out of his *r.*
Jer. 17. 8. that spreadeth out her *r.* by the river
Ezek. 17. 6. and the *r.* thereof were under him
7. this vine did bend her *r.* toward him
9. shall he not pull up the *r.* thereof?
Dan. 4. 15. leave the stump of his *r.* 23, 26.
7. 8. three of the first horns plucked up by the *r.*
Hos. 14. 5. he shall cast forth his *r.* as Lebanon
Amos 2. 9. I destroyed his *r.* from beneath
Mark 11. 20. they saw fig-tree dried up from the *r.*
Jude 12. trees twice dead, plucked up by the *r.*

ROPES.

Judg. 16. 11. if they bind me with new *r.* 12.
2 *Sam.* 17. 13. then shall all Isr. bring *r.* to that city
1 *Kings* 20. 31. let us put *r.* on our heads, 32.
Acts 27. 32. the soldiers cut off the *r.* of the boat

RORE, *see* ROAR.

ROSE, *Substantive.*

Cant. 2. 1. I am *r.* of Sharon, and the lily of valleys
Isa. 35. 1. the desert shall blossom as the *r.*

ROSE, *Verb.*

Gen. 4. 8. Cain *r.* up against Abel, and slew him
19. 1. Lot *r.* up to meet them, and bowed himself
22. 3. Abraham *r.* early, and went to the place
25. 34. Esau did eat, and *r.* up, and went his way
32. 31. the sun *r.* upon him as he passed Penuel
37. 35. his sons and daughters *r.* to comfort him
Exod. 10. 23. nor *r.* any from his place for three days
12. 30. Pharaoh *r.* up in the night, and servants
15. 7. overthrown them that *r.* up against thee
33. 10. and all the people *r.* up and worshipped
Num. 25. 7. Phinehas *r.* up from the congregation
Deut. 33. 2. the Lord *r.* up from Seir unto them
Josh. 3. 16. the waters stood and *r.* up on an heap
Judg. 6. 21. there *r.* up fire out of the rock
20. 5. the men of Gibeah *r.* up against me
Ruth 3. 14. she *r.* up before one could know another
2 *Sam.* 22. 40. them that *r.* up against me, hast thou subdued under me, *Psal.* 18. 39.
1 *Kings* 2. 19. and the king *r.* up to meet her
2 *Kings* 7. 5. the lepers *r.* in the twilight to go
2 *Chron.* 26. 19. the leprosy *r.* up in his forehead
28. 15. the men which were expressed by name *r.* up
Psal. 124. 2. L. who was on our side when men *r.* up
Cant. 5. 5. I *r.* up to open to my beloved
Jer. 26. 17. then *r.* up certain of the elders
Lam. 3. 62. the lips of those that *r.* up against me
Dan. 3. 24. then Nebuchadnezzar *r.* up in haste
8. 27. I *r.* up and did the king's business
Jonah 1. 3. but Jonah *r.* up to flee to Tarshish
Zeph. 3. 7. they *r.* early and corrupted their doings
Luke 4. 29. *r.* up, and thrust him out of the city
5. 28. and he left all, *r.* up, and followed him
16. 31. not be persuaded tho' one *r.* from the dead
Luke 22. 45. when he *r.* from prayer and was come
24. 33. they *r.* up the same hour, and returned
John 11. 31. when they saw Mary that she *r.* up
Acts 5. 17. then high priest *r.* up, and all with him
36. for before these days *r.* up Theudas
10. 41. who did eat and drink with him after he *r.*
26. 30. king *r.* up, and the governor, and Bernice
Rom. 14. 9. to this end Christ both died and *r.*
1 *Cor.* 10. 7. the people did eat, and *r.* up to play
15. 4. he was buried and *r.* again the third day
12. now if Chr. be preached that he *r.* from dead
2 *Cor.* 5. 15. but live to him who died and *r.* again
1 *Thess.* 4. 14. if we believe that Jes. died and *r.* ag.
Rev. 19. 3. her smoke *r.* up for ever and ever

See MORNING.

ROSIN.

Ezek. 27. † 17. Judah traded in thy market oil and *r.*

ROT.

Num. 5. 21. when L. make thy thigh to *r.* 22. 27.
Prov. 10. 7. but the name of the wicked shall *r.*
Isa. 40. 20. he chooseth a tree that will not *r.*

ROTTEN.

Job 13. 28. and he, as a *r.* thing, consumeth
41. 27. he esteemed brass as *r.* wood
Jer. 38. 11. so Ebed-melech took old *r.* rags
12. put now these *r.* rags under thine arm-holes
Joel 1. 17. the seed is *r.* under their clods

ROTTENNESS.

Prov. 12. 4. but she that maketh ashamed, is as *r*
14. 30. but envy is the *r.* of the bones
Isa. 5. 24. so their root shall be as *r.* blossom as dust
Hos. 5. 12. I will be to the house of Judah as *r.*
Hab. 3. 16. when I heard *r.* entered into my bones

ROVERS.

1 *Chron.* 12. 21. they helped David against the *r.*

ROUGH.

Deut. 21. 4. bring the heifer to a *r.* valley
Isa. 27. 8. he stayeth his *r.* wind in the day of east
40. 4. and the *r.* places shall be made plain
Jer. 51. 27. cause horses to come as *r.* caterpillars
Dan. 8. 21. the *r.* goat is the king of Grecia
Zech. 13. 4. neither shall they wear a *r.* garment
Luke 3. 5. and the *r.* ways shall be made smooth

ROUGHLY.

Gen. 42. 7. Joseph spake *r.* unto them, 30.
1 *Sam.* 20. 10. what if thy father answer thee *r.*?
1 *Kings* 12. 13. and the king answered the people *r.* and forsook old men's counsel, 2 *Chr.* 10. 13.
Prov. 18. 23. but the rich answereth *r.*

ROUND.

Lev. 19. 27. ye shall not *r.* corners of your heads

ROUND.

Gen. 19. 4. compassed the house *r.* old and young
Exod. 16. 14. there lay a small *r.* thing on ground
Josh. 7. 9. the inhabitants shall environ us *r.*
1 *Kings* 7. 23. the molten sea was *r.* all about
35. a *r.* compass ‖ 10. 19. top of the throne was *r.*
Psal. 22. 12. strong bulls of Bashan have beset me *r.*
Cant. 7. 2. thy navel is like a *r.* goblet
Isa. 3. 18. the Lord will take away their *r.* tires
Ezek. 41. † 7. it was made broader and went *r.*
Luke 19. 43. thine enemies shall compass thee *r.*

ROUND *about.*

Gen. 35. 5. the terror of God was on cities *r. about*
Exod. 7. 24. digged *r. about* the river for water
16. 13. in the morning dew lay *r. about* the host
19. 12. thou shalt set bounds to the people *r. about*
Lev. 14. 41. cause the house to be scraped *r. about*
Num. 1. 50. the Levites encamp *r. about* tabernacle
11. 24. Moses set the elders *r. about* the tabernacle
16. 34. all Israel, that were *r. about* them fled
22. 4. company shall lick up all that are *r. about* us
Deut. 6. 14. gods of the people *r. about* you, 13. 7.
12. 10. when he giveth rest from all your enemies *r. about,* 25. 19. *Josh.* 21. 44. 2 *Chron.* 15. 15.
21. 2. measure the cities *r. about* him that is slain
Josh. 6. 3. and ye shall go *r. about* the city once
Judg. 19. 22. men beset the house *r. about,* 20. 5.
1 *Sam.* 23. 26. for Saul compassed David *r. about*
31. 9. they cut off Saul's head, and sent into the land of the Philistines *r. about,* 1 *Chron.* 10. 9.
2 *Sam.* 22. 12. and he made darkness pavilions *r. about* him, and thick clouds of the skies, *Psal.* 18. 11.
1 *Kings* 4. 24. Solomon had peace on all sides *r. about*
31. and his fame was in all nations *r. about*
18. 35. and the water ran *r. about* the altar
2 *Kings* 6. 17. and chariots of fire *r. about* Elisha
1 *Chr.* 9. 27. they lodged *r. about* the house of God
Job 10. 8. thine hands have fashioned me *r. about*
16. 13. his archers compass me *r. about*
19. 12. his troops encamp *r. about* my tabernacle
22. 10. therefore snares are *r. about* thee
37. 12. it is turned *r. about* by his counsels
41. 14. his teeth are terrible *r. about*
Psal. 3. 6. that set themselves against me *r. about*
27. 6. head be lifted above mine enemies *r. about*
34. 7. angel encampeth *r. about* them that fear him
44. 13. a derision to them that are *r. about,* 79. 4.
48. 12. walk about Zion, and go *r. about* her
59. 6. make a noise, and go *r. about* the city, 14.
76. 11. let all *r. about* him bring presents to him
88. 17. they came *r. about* me daily like water
89. 8. or like to thy faithfulness *r. about* thee
97. 3. he burneth up his enemies *r. about* him
125. 2. as the mountains are *r. about* Jerusalem
128. 3. children like olive plants *r. about* thy table
Isa. 29. 3. I will camp against thee *r. about*
42. 25. and it hath set him on fire *r. about*
49. 18. lift up thine eyes *r. about* and behold, 60. 4
Jer. 20. † 3. Lord hath called thy name, fear *r. about*
21. 14. a fire, it shall devour all things *r. about* it
46. 5. for fear was *r. about,* saith the Lord
50. 29. camp against Babylon *r. about*
51. 2. in trouble they shall be against her *r. about*
Ezek. 10. 12. the wheels were full of eyes *r. about*
34. 26. will make places *r. about* my hill a blessing
Joel 3. 11. gather yourselves together *r. about*
12. there will sit to judge all the heathen *r. about*
Amos 3. 11. an adversary even *r. about* the land
Jonah 2. 5. the depth closed me *r. about,* the weeds
Zech. 2. 5. I will be to her a wall of fire *r. about*
Mat. 21. 33. he hedged the vineyard *r. about.*

Luke 1. 65. fear came on all that dwelt *r. about*
2. 9. the glory of the Lord shone *r. about* them
Acts 9. 3. shined *r. about* him a light from heaven
Rom. 15. 19. *r. about* to Illyricum, I have preached
Rev. 4. 3. there was a rainbow *r. about* the throne
4. *r. about* the throne were four and twenty seats
6. four beasts ‖ 5. 11. angels *r. about* the throne
See CAMP.

ROUSE.

Gen. 49. 9. and as an old lion who shall *r.* him up

ROW, S.

Exod. 28. 17. set it in four *r.* of stones, 39. 10.
17. the first *r.* 39. 10. ‖ 18. the second *r.* 39. 11.
19. the third *r.* 39. 12. ‖ 20. the fourth *r.* 39. 13.
Lev. 24. 6. cakes, six on a *r.* on the pure table
7. thou shalt put pure frankincense on each *r.*
1 *Kings* 6. 36. he built the inner court with three *r.*
7. 2. four *r.* of cedar pillars ‖ 3. fifteen in a *r.*
4. there were windows in three *r.* and light
12. the great court round about was with three *r.*
18. two *r.* pomegranates, 42. 2 *Chron.* 4. 13.
2 *Chron.* 4. 3. two *r.* of oxen cast when it was cast
Ezra 6. 4. a *r.* of new timber, three *r.* of stones
Cant. 1. 10. thy cheeks comely with *r.* of jewels
Ezek. 46. 23. with boiling places under the *r.*

ROWED.

Jonah 1. 13. the men *r.* hard to bring it to land
John 6. 19. when they had *r.* 25 or 30 furlongs

ROWERS.

Ezek. 27. 26. thy *r.* brought thee into great waters

ROWING.

Mark 6. 48. he saw them toiling in *r.* wind contrary

ROYAL.

Gen. 49. 20. Asher shall yield *r.* dainties
Josh. 10. 2. Gibeon was as one of the *r.* cities
1 *Sam.* 27. 5. for why should I dwell in the *r.* city?
2 *Sam.* 12. 26. Joab fought, and took the *r.* city
1 *Kings* 10. 13. Solomon gave her of his *r.* bounty
2 *Kings* 11. 1. Athaliah the mother of Ahaziah destroyed all the seed *r.* 2 *Chron.* 22. 10.
1 *Chr.* 29. 25. Ld. bestowed on Solomon *r.* majesty
Esth. 1. 7. they gave them *r.* wine in abundance
11. to bring Vashti the queen with the crown *r.*
19. give her *r.* estate to another that is better
2. 16. so Esther was taken into his house *r.*
17. so that he set the crown *r.* on her head
5. 1. Esther put on her *r.* apparel, and the king sat on his *r.* throne in his *r.* house near the gate
6. 8. let *r.* apparel be brought, and the crown *r.*
8. 15. Mordecai went in *r.* apparel of blue and white
Isa. 62. 3. a *r.* diadem in the hand of thy God
Jer. 43. 10. he shall spread his *r.* pavilion over them
Dan. 6. 7. to establish a *r.* statute and make a decree
Acts 12. 21. Herod arrayed in *r.* apparel, sat on
Jam. 2. 8. if ye fulfil the *r.* law, ye do well
1 *Pet.* 2. 9. ye are a *r.* priesthood, an holy nation

RUBBING.

Luke 6. 1. and did eat, *r.* them in their hands

RUBBISH.

Neh. 4. 2. will they revive the stones out of the *r.*
10. strength is decayed and there is much *r.*

RUBY, RUBIES.

Exod. 28. † 17. the first row a *r.* 39. † 10.
Job 28. 18. price of wisdom is above *r.* *Prov.* 8. 11.
Prov. 3. 15. wisdom is more precious than *r.*
20. 15. there is gold, and a multitude of *r.*
31. 10. for her price is far above *r.*
Lam. 4. 7. Nazarites were more ruddy than *r.*
Ezek. 28. † 13. the *r.* was thy covering

RUDDER-*bands.*

Acts 27. 40. and loosed the *r.-bands*, and hoised up

RUDDY.

1 *Sam.* 16. 12. David was *r.* and beautiful, 17. 42.
Cant. 5. 10. my beloved is white and *r.* chiefest
Lam. 4. 7. her Nazarites were more *r.* than rubies

RUDE.

2 *Cor.* 11. 6. but though I be *r.* in speech

RUDIMENTS.

Gal. 4. † 3. in bondage under the *r.* of the world
† 9. how turn ye again to the beggarly *r.*
Col. 2. 8. lest any spoil you after the *r.* of the world
20. if dead with Christ from the *r.* of the world

RUE.

Luke 11. 42. for ye tithe mint, and *r.* and herbs

RUG.

Judg. 4. † 18. turned in, Jael covered him with a *r.*

RUIN.

2 *Chron.* 28. 23. but they were the *r.* of him
Psal. 89. 40. thou hast brought his holds to *r.*
Prov. 24. 22. who knoweth the *r.* of them both?
26. 28. and a flattering mouth worketh *r.*
Isa. 3. 6. and let this *r.* be under thy hand
23. 13. he brought the land of the Chaldeans to *r.*
25. 2. thou hast made of a defenced city, a *r.*
Ezek. 18. 30. so iniquity shall not be your *r.*
27. 27. thy company shall fall in the day of thy *r.*
31. 13. on his *r.* shall all the fowls remain
Luke 6. 49. it fell, the *r.* of that house was great

RUINS.

Ezek. 21. 15. that their *r.* may be multiplied
Amos 9. 11. in that day will I raise up his *r.*
Acts 15. 16. I will build again the *r.* thereof

RUINED.

Isa. 3. 8. for Jerusalem is *r.* and Judah is fallen
Ezek. 36. 35. and the *r.* cities are become fenced
36. shall know that I the Lord build the *r.* places

RUINOUS.

2 *Kings* 19. 25. that thou shouldest be to lay waste fenced cities into *r.* heaps, *Isa.* 37. 26.
Isa. 17. 1. Damascus not a city, it shall be a *r.* heap

RULE.

Gen. 1. † 16. the greater light for the *r.* of the day
1 *Kings* 22. 31. that had *r.* over Ahab's chariots
Esth. 9. 1. Jews had *r.* over them that hated them
Psal. 19. † 4. their *r.* is gone through all the earth
Prov. 17. 2. a wise servant shall have *r.* over a son
19. 10. for a servant to have *r.* over princes
25. 28. he that hath no *r.* over his own spirit
Eccl. 2. 19. yet shall he have *r.* over all my labour
Isa. 44. 13. the carpenter stretcheth out his *r.*
63. 19. we are thine, thou never barest *r.* over them
1 *Cor.* 15. 24. when he shall have put down all *r.*
2 *Cor.* 10. 13. according to the measure of the *r.*
15. be enlarged according to our *r.* abundantly
† 16. and not to boast in another man's *r.*
Gal. 6. 16. as many as walk according to this *r.*
Phil. 3. 16. let us walk by the same *r.* let us mind
Heb. 13. 7. remember them that have *r.* over you
17. obey them that have the *r.* over you
24. salute all them that have the *r.* over you
See BARE, BEAR.

RULE.

Gen. 1. 16. God made two great lights, the greater light to *r.* the day, and lesser light to *r.* night
18. to *r.* over the day, and over the night
3. 16. and thy husband shall *r.* over thee
4. 7. to thee be his desire, thou shalt *r.* over him
Lev. 25. 43. not *r.* over him with rigour, 46. 53.
Judg. 8. 22. *r.* thou over us, thou and thy son
23. I will not *r.* over you, nor shall my son *r.*
Psal. 28. † 9. *r.* them, and lift them up for ever
110. 2. *r.* thou in the midst of thine enemies
136. 8. sun to *r.* by day, for his mercy endur. ever
9. moon and stars to *r.* by night, for his mercy
Prov. 8. 16. by me princes *r.* and nobles, all judges
Isa. 3. 4. and babes shall *r.* over them
12. as for my people, women *r.* over them
14. 2. they shall *r.* over their oppressors
19. 4. a fierce king shall *r.* over them
28. 14. that *r.* this people that is in Jerusalem
32. 1. and princes shall *r.* in judgment
40. 10. and his arm shall *r.* for him
41. 2. who made the righteous man *r.* over kings
52. 5. they that *r.* over them make them to howl
Ezek. 19. 14. she hath no strong rod to be a scep. to *r.*
20. 33. with fury poured out will I *r.* over you
29. 15. they shall no more *r.* over the nations
Dan. 4. 26. shalt have known that the heavens *r.*
11. 3. mighty kings shall stand up, that shall *r.*
39. and he shall cause them to *r.* over many
Joel 2. 17. that the heathen should *r.* over them
Mic. 5. † 4. he shall *r.* in the strength of the Lord
7. † 14. *r.* thy people with thy rod, the flock
Zech. 6. 13. he shall sit and *r.* on his throne
Mat. 2. 6. a governor that shall *r.* my people Israel
Mark 10. 42. who are accounted to *r.* over Gentiles
Col. 3. 15. let the peace of God *r.* in your hearts
1 *Tim.* 3. 5. if a man know not how to *r.* his house
5. 17. elders that *r.* well, worthy of double honour
Rev. 2. 27. *r.* with a rod of iron, 12. 5. | 19. 15.

RULED.

Gen. 24. 2. his eldest servant that *r.* over all he had
41. 40. at thy word shall all my people be *r.*
1 *Kings* 5. 16. three thousand *r.* over the people
Ezra 4. 20. who have *r.* over all countries
Psal. 106. 41. they that hated them *r.* over them
Isa. 14. 6. he that *r.* nations in anger is persecuted
Lam. 5. 8. servants have *r.* over us, none delivereth
Ezek. 34. 4. with cruelty have ye *r.* over them
Dan. 5. 21. till he knew that God *r.* in kingdom

RULER.

Gen. 41. 43. Pharaoh made Joseph *r.* over all the land of Egypt, 45. 8. *Psal.* 105. 21.
43. 16. Joseph said to the *r.* of his house, bring
Exod. 22. 28. thou shalt not curse *r.* of thy people
Lev. 4. 22. when a *r.* hath sinned through ignorance
Num. 13. 2. every one a *r.* among them
1 *Sam.* 25. 30. appointed thee *r.* over my people Isr. 2 *Sam.* 6. 21. | 7. 8. 1 *Chron.* 11. 2. | 17. 7.
2 *Sam.* 7. 8. I took thee from following sheep to be *r.* over my people, over Israel, 1 *Chron.* 17. 7.
23. † 3. thou *r.* over men, ruling in fear of God
1 *Kings* 1. 35. I have appointed Solomon to be *r.*
1 *Chron.* 5. 2. for of Judah came the chief *r.*
9. 11. Azariah *r.* of house of God, 2 *Chron.* 31. 13.
2 *Chr.* 7. 18. there shall not fail thee a man to be *r.*
11. 22. he made Abijah *r.* among his brethren
Neh. 7. 2. and Hananiah the *r.* of the palace
11. 11. Seraiah was *r.* of the house of God
Psal. 68. 27. there is little Benjamin with their *r.*
105. 20. even the *r.* of the people, let him go free
Prov. 6. 7. the ant having no guide, overseer, or *r.*
23. 1. when thou sittest to eat with a *r.* consider
28. 15. so is a wicked *r.* over the poor people
29. 12. if a *r.* hearken to lies, his servants wicked
26. many seek *r.* favour, but judgment cometh
Eccl. 10. 4. if the spirit of the *r.* rise against thee
5. as an error which proceedeth from the *r.*
Isa. 3. 6. be thou our *r.* ‖ 7. make me not a *r.*
16. 1. send ye the lamb to the *r.* of the land
Jer. 51. 46. and violence in the land, *r.* against *r.*
Dan. 2. 10. no king nor *r.* asked such things
38. and hath made thee *r.* over them all, 48.
5. 7. shall be third *r.* in the kingdom, 16. 29.
Mic. 5. 2. out of thee shall he come that is to be *r.*
Hab. 1. 14 as creeping things that have no *r.*
Mat. 9. 18. behold, there came a certain *r.*
24. 45. whom his Lord hath made *r.* *Luke* 12. 42.
47. he shall make him *r.* over all his goods
25. 21. I will make thee *r.* over many things, 23.
Mark 5. 35. while he yet spake, there came from the *r.* of the synagogue's house, *Luke* 8. 49.
Luke 13. 14. the *r.* of the synagogue answered
John 2. 9. when the *r.* of the feast had tasted water
3. 1. a man named Nicodemus, a *r.* of the Jews
Acts 4. † 1. the *r.* of the temple came upon them
7. 27. who made thee a *r.* and a judge over us? 35.
35. the same did God send to be a *r.* and deliverer
18. 17. the Greeks beat Sosthenes the chief *r.*
23. 5. shalt not speak evil of the *r.* of thy people

RULERS.

Gen. 47. 6. then make them *r.* over my cattle
Exod. 18. 21. *r.* of thousands, *r.* of hundreds, 25.
34. 31. Moses called the *r.* of the congregation
35. 27. the *r.* brought onyx-stones to be set
Deut. 1. 13. and I will make them *r.* over you
Judg. 15. 11. knowest thou not the Philistines are *r.*
2 *Sam.* 8. 18. and David's sons were chief *r.*
1 *Kings* 9. 22. were *r.* of his chariots and horsemen
2 *Kings* 10. 1. Jehu wrote to the *r.* of Jezreel
11. 4. Jehoiada set *r.* over hundreds, 19.
1 *Chron.* 27. 31. all these were *r.* of the substance
2 *Chron.* 35. 8. *r.* of the house of God gave to priests
Ezra 9. 2. the hand of the *r.* chief in this trespass
Neh. 4. 16. the *r.* were behind the house of Judah
5. 7. I rebuked the *r.* and said, ye exact usury
11. 1. the *r.* of the people that dwelt at Jerusalem
12. 40. so stood I, and half of the *r.* with me
13. 11. then contended I with the *r.* and said
Esth. 9. 3. the *r.* of the provinces helped the Jews
Psal. 2. 2. the *r.* take counsel against the Lord
Isa. 1. 10. hear word of the Lord, ye *r.* of Sodom
14. 5. the Lord hath broken the sceptre of the *r.*
22. 3. all thy *r.* are fled together, they are bound
29. 10. and your *r.* the seers hath he covered
49. 7. to a servant of *r.* kings shall see and arise
Jer. 33. 26. I will not take any of his seed to be *r.*
51. 23. thee will I break in pieces captains and *r.*
28. prepare against her *r.* ‖ 57. make drunk her *r.*
Ezek. 23. 6. her lovers, which were captains and *r.*
23. I will raise up those *r.* against thee
Dan. 3. 3. all the *r.* were gathered together
7. † 27. and all *r.* shall serve and obey him
Hos. 4. 18. her *r.* with shame do love, give ye
Mark 5. 22. cometh one of the *r.* of the synagogue
13. 9. ye shall be brought before *r.* *Luke* 21. 12.
Luke 23. 13. when he had called together the *r.*
35. and *r.* also with the people derided him
24. 20. how our priests and *r.* delivered him
John 7. 26. do the *r.* know that this is the Christ?
48. have any of the *r.* believed on him?
12. 42. many among the chief *r.* believed on him
Acts 3. 17. through ignorance ye did it, as also did *r.*
4. 26. the *r.* were gathered against the Lord
13. 15. the *r.* of the synagogue sent to Paul
27. and their *r.* because they knew him not
14. 5. an assault made of the Jews, with their *r.*
16. 19. the damsel's masters drew them to the *r.*
17. 8. they troubled the people and *r.* of the city
Rom. 13. 3. *r.* not a terror to good works, but evil
Eph. 6. 12. we wrestle against the *r.* of the darkness

RULEST.

2 *Chron.* 20. 6. and *r.* not thou over all kingdoms
Psal. 89. 9. thou *r.* the raging of the sea

RULETH.

2 *Sam.* 23. 3. he that *r.* over men must be just
Psal. 59. 13. let them know that God *r.* in Jacob
66. 7. he *r.* by his power for ever, his eyes behold
103. 19. and his kingdom *r.* over all
Prov. 16. 32. that *r.* his spirit is better than he that
22. 7. rich *r.* over the poor, and the borrower
Eccl. 8. 9. wherein one man *r.* over another to hurt
9. 17. more than cry of him that *r.* among fools
Dan. 4. 17. the Most High *r.* among men, 25. 32.
Hos. 11. 12. but Judah yet *r.* with God, is faithful
Rom. 12. 8. he that *r.* with diligence
1 *Tim.* 3. 4. one that *r.* well his own house

RULING.

2 *Sam.* 23. 3. must be just, *r.* in the fear of God
Jer. 22. 30. sit on throne, and *r.* any more in Judah
1 *Tim.* 3. 12. *r.* their children and houses well

RUMBLING.

Jer 47. 3. at *r.* of his wheels, fathers not look back

RUMOUR, S.

2 *Kings* 19. 7. and he shall hear a *r.* *Isa.* 37. 7.
Jer. 49. 14. I have heard a *r.* from the Lord
51. 46. lest ye fear for the *r.* in the land, a *r.* shall come one year, in another year shall come a *r.*
Ezek. 7. 26. mischief on mischief, *r.* shall be upon *r.*
Obad. 1. we have heard a *r.* from the Lord
Mat. 24. 6. ye shall hear of wars and *r.* of wars
Mark 13. 7. when ye shall hear of wars and *r.* of wars
Luke 7. 17. this *r.* of him went forth thro' all Judea

RUMP.

Exod. 29. 22. thou shalt take of the ram and the fat and the *r.* *Lev.* 3. 9. | 7. 3. | 8. 25. | 9. 19.

RUN.

To run *is to move with a swift pace*, 2 Sam. 18. 19. *The Christian conversation is called a* race or running, 1 *Cor.* 9. 24. So run that you may obtain: *that is, Use such diligence, care, and constancy in your Christian course, that ye may obtain the prize of eternal glory set before you. It is spoken in allusion to the custom in their races, of hanging up a crown or garland at the goal, and such as first laid hold on it and took it down, had it as a reward. St.* Paul *says to the* Galatians, Ye did run well, who did hinder you? *Gal.* 5. 7. *that is, Ye were forward formerly in adhering to the true doctrine of justification by faith in* Christ, *and to Christian liberty, and you practised accordingly; who has turned you out of your way, or hindered you in your race, that you now expect to be justified by the works of the law, and submit yourselves to the yoke of ceremonies? The same apostle compares his labour and diligence in the work of his ministry to a* race. *Phil.* 2. 16. Holding forth the word of life, that I may rejoice in the day of Christ, that I have not run in vain. *And an eager pursuit of sinful courses is also by the apostle* Peter *compared to a* race. 1 *Pet.* 4. 4. That ye run not with them to the same excess of riot.

Gen. 41. † 14. they made Joseph *r.* out of dungeon
49. 22. whose branches *r.* over the wall
Lev. 15. 3. whether his flesh *r.* with his issue
25. if a woman's issue *r.* beyond the time
Judg. 18. 25. lest angry fellows *r.* upon thee
1 *Sam.* 8. 11. some shall *r.* before his chariots
17. 17. and *r.* to the camp to thy brethren
20. 6. asked me, that he might *r.* to Beth-lehem
36. *r.* find out now the arrows which I shoot
2 *Sam.* 15. 1. Absalom prepared chariots, horses, and fifty men to *r.* before him, 1 *Kings* 1. 5.
18. 19. let me now *r.* and bear tidings, 22. 23.
22. 30. by thee I have *r.* thro' a troop, *Psal.* 18. 29.
2 *Kings* 4. 22. that I may *r.* to the man of God
26. *r.* now, I pray thee, to meet her, and say
5. 20. as the Lord liveth, I will *r.* after Naaman
2 *Chron.* 16. 9. eyes of Lord *r.* to and fro thro' earth
Job 5. † 14. they *r.* into darkness in the day-time
Psal. 19. 5. and rejoiceth as strong man to *r.* a race
58. 7. let them melt as waters, which *r.* continually
59. 4. they *r.* and prepare thems. without my fault
78. 16. he caused waters to *r.* down like rivers
104. 10. the springs, which *r.* among the hills

Psal. 119. 32. I will r. the way of thy commandm.
136. rivers of waters r. down mine eyes, because
Prov. 1. 16. for their feet r. to evil, Isa. 59. 7.
Eccl. 1. 7. all the rivers r. into the sea, sea not full
Cant. 1. 4. draw me, we will r. after thee
Isa. 33. 4. as running of locusts shall he r. on them
40. 31. they shall r. and not be weary, shall walk
55. 5. nations that knew not thee shall r. to thee
Jer. 5. 1. r. ye to and fro thro' streets of Jerusalem
9. 18. that your eyes may r. down with tears
12. 5. if thou hast r. with the footmen
13. 17. mine eyes shall r. down with tears, because the Lord's flock is carried away captive, 14. 17.
49. 3. lament, and r. to and fro by the hedges
19. I will make him r. away from her, 50. 44.
51. 31. one post shall r. to meet another
Lam. 2. 18. let tears r. down like river day and night
Ezek. 24. 16. neither shall thy tears r. down
32. 14. cause their rivers to r. like oil, saith Lord
Dan. 12. 4. many shall r. to and fro, and knowledge
Joel 2. 4. and as horsemen, so shall they r.
7. they shall r. like mighty men, they shall climb
9. they shall r. in the city, shall r. on the wall
Amos 3. † 6. shall trumpet be blown, people not r.?
5. 24. but let judgment r. down as waters
6. 12. shall horses r. upon the rock? will one plow
8. 12. shall r. to and fro to seek word of the Lord
Nah. 2. 4. they shall r. like the lightnings
Hab. 2. 2. write vision, that he may r. that readeth it
Hag. 1. 9. and ye r. every man to his own house
Zech. 2. 4. r. speak to this young man, saying
4. 10. eyes of the Lord r. to and fro thro' the earth
Mat. 28. 8. they did r. to bring his disciples word
1 Cor. 9. 24. that they which r. in a race r. all, but one receiveth the prize, so r. that ye may obtain
26. I therefore so r. not as uncertainly, so fight I
Gal. 2. 2. lest by any means I should r. or had r. in
5. 7. ye did r. well, who did hinder you?
Phil. 2. 16. that I may rejoice, I have not r. in vain
2 Thess. 3. † 1. that the word of the Lord may r.
Heb. 2. † 1. lest at any time we should r. out
12. 1. let us r. with patience the race before us
1 Pet. 4. 4. that ye r. not to the same excess of riot

RUNNEST.

Prov. 4. 12. when thou r. thou shalt not stumble

RUNNETH.

Job 15. 26. he r. upon him, even on his neck
16. 14. he breaketh me, he r. upon me like a giant
Psal. 23. 5. thou anointest my head, my cup r. over
147. 15. his word r. very swiftly
Prov. 18. 10. the righteous r. into it, and is safe
Lam. 1. 16. mine eyes r. down with water, 3. 48.
Mat. 9. 17. the bottles break, and the wine r. out
John 20. 2. then she r. and cometh to Simon Peter
Rom. 9. 16. not of him that willeth, nor of him that r.

RUNNERS.

1 Sam. 22. † 17. the king said to the r. turn and slay
1 Kings 14. † 27. committed shields to the chief of r.

RUNNING.

Lev. 14. 5. one bird be killed over r. water, 6. 50.
51. dip them in r. water, and sprinkle the house
52. he shall cleanse the house with the r. water
15. 2. when any man hath a r. issue, 22. 4.
13. shall bathe his flesh in r. water, and be clean
Num. 19. 17. for an unclean person take r. water
2 Sam. 18. 24. and behold, a man r. alone, 26.
27. the r. of the foremost is like r. of Ahimaaz
2 Kings 5. 21. when Naaman saw him r. after him
2 Chron. 23. 12. Athaliah heard the people r.
Prov. 5. 15. and r. waters out of thine own well
6. 18. feet that be swift in r. to mischief
Isa. 33. 4. as the r. to and fro of locusts shall he run
Jer. 18. † 14. shall the r. waters be forsaken?
Ezek. 31. 4. with her rivers r. about his plants
Mark 9. 15. the people r. to him saluted him
25. when Jesus saw the people r. together
10. 17. there came one r. and kneeled to him
Luke 6. 38. good meas. and r. over shall men give
Acts 27. 16. and r. under a certain island, Clauda
Rev. 9. 9. as the sound of chariots r. to battle

RUSH.

Job 8. 11. can the r. grow up without mire?
Isa. 9. 14. L. will cut off branch and r. in one day
19. 15. nor any work which branch or r. may do

RUSH.

Isa. 17. 13. nations shall r. like rushing many waters

RUSHED.

Judg. 9. 44. Abimelech and company r. forward
20. 37. the liers in wait hasted and r. upon Gibeah
Job 1. † 17. the Chaldeans r. upon the camels
Mark 3. † 10. they r. upon Jesus to touch him
Acts 19. 29. they r. with one accord into theatre

RUSHES.

Isa. 35. 7. where dragons lay shall be reeds and r.

RUSHETH.

Jer. 8. 6. every one turned, as horse r. into battle

RUSHING.

Isa. 17. 12. woe to multitude and to r. of nations, that make a r. like the r. of many waters
13. nations shall rush like the r. of many waters
Jer. 47. 3. at r. of chariots fathers shall not look
Ezek. 3. 12. I heard a voice of a great r. 13.
Acts 2. 2. there came a sound as of r. mighty wind

RUST.

Mat. 6. 19. where moth and r. doth corrupt, 20.
Jam. 5. 3. r. of them shall be a witness against you

S.

SABAOTH,

Or rather Zabaoth, *an* Hebrew *word, that signifies* Hosts *or* Armies. Jehovah Sabaoth, The Lord of Hosts, *Rom.* 9. 29. *Whose host all creatures are, whether the host of heaven, or the angels and ministers of the Lord; or the stars and planets, which are as an army ranged in battle array, and performing the will of God: or the people of the Lord, both of the Old and New Testament, which is truly the army of the Lord, of which God is the General and Commander.* The Hebrew *word* Zaba *is also used to signify the service that his ministers perform for him in the tabernacle; because they are there, as it were, soldiers or guards attending at the court of their Prince,* Num. 4. 3, 23, 30.

Rom. 9. 29. except the Lord of s. had left us a seed
Jam. 5. 4. are entered into the ears of the Lord of s.

SABBATH.

This word in Hebrew שבת *signifies* Rest, *God having created the world in six days,* rested on the seventh, *Gen.* 2. 2. *that is, after God had perfected the invisible and visible world, on the review of all his works, finding them very good, he took pleasure, he was satisfied in all those discoveries of his own perfections in the works of his hands. He* blessed *this day, and* sanctified *it, because he had rested upon it. From that time he set it apart, and appointed it in a peculiar manner for his worship. And the* Hebrews *afterwards, in consequence of this designation, and to preserve the memory of the creation, sanctified, by his order, the* Sabbath-day, *or the seventh day, by abstaining from all work, labour, and servile employments, and by applying themselves to the service of the Lord, to the study of his law, and to prayer. And at mount* Sinai *by a positive, moral, and perpetual commandment God hath appointed one day in the seven to be kept holy to himself; which in the* New Testament *is called the* Lord's day, *and is to be continued to the end of the world as the* Christian Sabbath.

Sabbath *is also taken for the whole week.* Luke 18. 12. I fast twice in the week; *in the Greek it is,* I fast twice *in the* Sabbath. *Sometimes for the* sabbatical year, *which was celebrated among the* Jews *every seventh year, when the land was to rest, and to be left without culture,* Lev. 25. 2, 4. *God appointed the observation of the* sabbatical year *to enforce the acknowledgment of his sovereign authority over all things, and particularly over the land of* Canaan, *which he had given to the* Hebrews, *and in which they were but tenants at his will. Likewise for the trial and exercise of their obedience, and the demonstration of his providence, as well in the general towards men, as more especially towards his own people; and to wean them from inordinate love, and pursuit of, or trust to, worldly advantages; and to inure them to depend upon God alone, and upon God's blessing for their subsistence; and to put them in mind of that blessed and eternal rest provided for all the godly, wherein they shall be perfectly freed from all worldly labours and troubles.*

Sabbath *is likewise taken for all the* Jewish *festivals, indifferently,* Lev. 19. 3, 30. Keep my sabbaths; *that is, my feasts, as the* Passover, the feast of Tabernacles, &c. Ezekiel *says, that the* Sabbaths are signs that God has given to his people to distinguish them from other nations, *Ezek.* 20. 12, 20. *And* Moses, *in* Deut. 5. 15. The Lord hath brought thee out of Egypt, therefore the Lord thy God hath commanded thee to keep the Sabbath-day.

Sabbath *is also taken for the eternal rest and felicity in heaven, where* the spirits of just men *are* made perfect; *and the saints are delivered from sin and sorrow, from the guilt and power of sin, and even from the very being of sin, for* Jesus saves his people from their sins. *They will be blessed in heaven with* complete conformity to God, and uninterrupted communion with him; *and their happiness will be* eternal, for they will be ever with the Lord, *and will enjoy an* eternal Sabbath, *Heb.* 4. 9. There remaineth therefore a rest to the people of God: *In the Greek it is* σαββατισμος, a keeping of a sabbath.

A Sabbath-day's journey. *Long journeys were forbidden the* Jews *on* Sabbath-days. Pray that your flight be not in the winter, neither on the Sabbath-day, *says our Saviour,* Mat. 24. 20. *However it is evident they were allowed to go a certain space on that day, at least to the temple or tabernacle, from the remote parts of the city or camp. And St.* Luke *says, that the mount of* Olives *was distant from* Jerusalem *the space of a* sabbath-day's *journey,* Acts 1. 12. *The Rabbins generally fix this space at two thousand cubits, that is, about a mile.*

The second Sabbath after the first, *Luke* 6. 1. *Some have taken it for the second, others for the last, day of unleavened bread; and some for the day of Pentecost: the Passover was the first* Sabbath *according to them, and Pentecost the second. Others have thought, that the first grand* Sabbath *was the first sabbath of the civil year in the month* Tizri; *and that the second was the first of the holy year, or of the month* Nisan. *The opinion most generally followed, is of those who think that to have been the first* Sabbath, *which followed the second day of unleavened bread. The Jews thus reckoned their sabbaths from the passover to pentecost; the first was called* secundo-primum, *or second after the first; that is, the first after the second day of unleavened bread: The second was called* secundo-secundum, *or the second day of the sabbath after the second day of unleavened bread: The third was called* secundo-tertium, *or the third day of the* Sabbath *after the second day of unleavened bread: And so of all the rest, as far as* secundo septimum, *that is, the seventh day of the* Sabbath *after the second day of unleavened bread. This seventh* Sabbath *immediately preceded* Pentecost, *which was celebrated the fiftieth day after the second day of unleavened bread.*

The preparation of the sabbath, *in Greek* Παρασκευη. *The* Jews *gave the name of* Parasceue *to the sixth day of the week, because being not allowed on the sabbath to prepare their food, they provided the day before what was necessary for their subsistence on the sabbath. The evangelist* John *says, that* Friday, *on which our Saviour suffered, was the* preparation of the passover, John 19. 14. *because the passover was to be celebrated the day following. St.* Matthew *marks out the day by these words,* The day that followed the Parasceue, Mat. 27. 62. *All the Evangelists observe, that they delayed not to take down* Christ *from the cross, and to put him in the nearest tomb, because it was the evening of the* Parasceue, *and that the sabbath was to begin immediately after the setting of the sun, or the rising of the stars.*

Exod. 16. 23. to-morrow is the rest of the holy s.
25. eat that to-day, for to-day is to s. to the Lord
29. see, for that the Lord hath given you the s.
20. 10. the seventh day is the s. of the Lord thy God, 31. 15. | 35. 2. Lev. 23. 3. Deut. 5. 14
31. 14. ye shall keep the s. therefore, 16.
Lev. 16. 31. on that day the priest shall make an atonement, it shall be a s. of rest to you, 23. 3, 32.
23. 11. morrow after the s. priest shall wave it
15. count to you from the morrow after the s.
16. after seventh s. shall ye number fifty days
24. on first day of the month shall ye have a s.
32. from even to even shall ye celebrate your s.
39. on the first day shall be a s. on the eighth a s.
24. 8. every s. he shall set in order before Lord
25. 2. then shall the land keep a s. 4, 6.
Num. 28. 10. this is the burnt offering of every s.
2 Kings 4. 23. he said, it is neither new moon nor s.
11. 5. a third part of you that enter in on the s.
7. two parts of all you that go forth on the s. even they shall keep the watch, 9. 2 Chron. 23. 8.
16. 18. the covert for the s. turned Ahaz
1 Chron. 9. 32. to prepare the shew-bread every s.
2 Chron. 36. 21. as long as desolate she kept the s.
Neh. 9. 14. and madest known to them thy holy s.
10. 31. we would not buy it of them on the s.
13. 15. I saw some treading wine-presses on the s.
16. men of Tyre brought ware, and sold on the s.
18. ye bring wrath on Israel, by profaning the s.
19. the gates began to be dark before the s.
21. from that time came they no more on the s.
Isa. 56. 2. blessed is the man that keepeth the s. 6.
58. 13. turn thy foot from the s. call s. a delight
66. 23. from one s. to another shall all worship
Ezek. 46. 1. but on the s. it shall be opened
Amos 8. 5. saying, when will the s. be gone?
Mat. 28. 1. in the end of the s. came Mary
Mark 2. 27. the s. was made for man, not man for s.
28. the Son of man is Lord of the s. Luke 6. 5.
16. 1. when the s. was past, Mary Magdalene
Luke 6. 1. on the second s. after the first, he went
13. 10. teaching in the synagogue on the s.
15. doth not each on the s. loose his ox or his ass?
23. 54. it was the preparation, and the s. drew on
John 5. 18. because he not only had broken the s.
Acts 13. 42. these words he preached to them next s.
16. 13. on the s. we went out of city by river side
18. 4. he reasoned in the synagogue every s.
Heb. 4. † 9. there remaineth a keeping of a s.

See DAY, DAYS.

SABBATHS.

Exod. 31. 13. speak to the children of Israel, saying, my s. ye shall keep, Lev. 19. 3, 30. | 26. 2.
Lev. 23. 15. seven s. shall be complete
38. beside the s. of the Lord, and beside your gifts
25. 8. and thou shalt number seven s. of years
26. 34. land enjoy her s. even then shall the land rest and enjoy her s. 43. 2 Chron. 36. 21.
35. it shall rest, because it did not rest in your s.
1 Chron. 23. 31. to offer the burnt sacrifices in the s. 2 Chron. 2. 4. | 8. 13. | 31. 3. Neh. 10. 33.
Isa. 1. 13. new moons and s. I cannot away with
56. 4. saith Lord to the eunuchs that keep my s.
Lam. 1. 7. the adversaries did mock at her s.
2. 6. Lord caused the s. to be forgotten in Zion
Ezek. 20. 12. also I gave them my s. to be a sign
13. and my s. they greatly polluted, 16. 24.
22. 8. and thou hast profaned my s. 23. 38.
26. the priests have hid their eyes from my s.
44. 24. they shall keep my laws and hallow my s.
45. 17. it shall be prince's part to give offerings for s.
46. 3. the people shall worship at this gate in the s.
Hos. 2. 11. I will also make to cease her s.

SACK.

Gen. 42. 25. then Joseph commanded to restore every man's money into his s. 35. | 43. 21. | 44. 1.
44. 2. put my silver cup in s. mouth of youngest
11. they took down every man his s. to ground
12. and the cup was found in Benjamin's s.
Lev. 11. 32. or s. of unclean must be put in water

SACKBUT.

Dan. 3. 5. ye hear the sound of the s. 7, 10, 15.

SACKCLOTH.

This is a pure Hebrew *word, and has spread into many languages. Besides the common signification, which is very well known, it stands also for a suit of mourning, which was worn at the death of a friend or relation. In great calamities and troubles, they wore sackcloth about their bodies;* Gird you with sackcloth and mourn before Abner, *2 Sam.* 3. 31. Let us put sackcloth on our loins, and go out and implore the clemency of the king of Israel, 1 *Kings* 20. 31. Ahab tore his clothes, put on a shirt of *hair-cloth* next to his skin, fasted, and lay upon *sackcloth,* 1 Kings 21. 27. *And when* Mordecai *was informed of the ruin that threatened his nation, he put on sackcloth and covered his head with ashes,* Esth. 4. 1. *And* Job *says,* I have sewed sackcloth upon my skin, *Job* 16. 15.

On the contrary, in the time of joy, and upon the hearing of any good news, those that were clad in sackcloth, tore it from their bodies, and cast it from them, Psal. 30. 11. Thou hast put off my sackcloth, and girded me with gladness. *The prophets were commonly clothed in* sackcloth. *The Lord bids* Isaiah *to put off the sackcloth that was about his body, and to go naked,* Isa. 20. 2. Zechariah *says, that the false prophets should no longer prophesy in* sackcloth *to deceive the simple,* Zech. 13. 4. They shall prophesy 1260 days clothed in sackcloth, *Rev.* 11. 3.

Gen. 37. 34. and Jacob put s. upon his loins
2 Sam. 3. 31. he said, gird you with s. and mourn

2 *Sam.*21.10. Rizpah took *s.* and spread it on the rock
1 *Kings* 20. 31. the kings of Israel are merciful kings, let us put *s.* on our loins, and ropes, 32.
21. 27. Ahab put *s.* on his flesh, and lay in *s.*
2 *Kings* 6. 30. people looked, and he had *s.* within
19. 1. Hezekiah covered himself with *s. Isa.* 37. 1.
2. elders of the priests covered with *s. Isa.* 37. 2.
1 *Chr.* 21. 16. David and elders were clothed with *s.*
Esth. 4. 1. Mordecai rent his clothes, and put on *s.*
2. for none might enter the gate clothed with *s.*
Job 16. 15. I have sewed *s.* upon my skin
Psal. 30. 11. hast put off my *s.* and girded with glad.
35. 13. when they were sick, my clothing was *s.*
69. 11. I made *s.* also my garment, and a proverb
Isa. 3. 24. instead of a stomacher, a girding of *s.*
15. 3. in streets they shall gird themselves with *s.*
20. 2. go, and loose the *s.* from off thy loins
22. 12. in that day did Lord call to girding with *s.*
32. 11. strip you, and make you bare, and gird *s.* on your loins, *Jer.* 4. 8. | 6. 26. | 48. 37. | 49. 3.
50. 3. I make *s.* the covering of the heavens
Lam. 2. 10. they have girded themselves with *s.* virgins hang down their heads, *Ezek.* 7. 18. | 27. 31.
Dan. 9. 3. to seek the Lord with fasting and *s.*
Joel 1. 8. lament like a virgin girded with *s.* for
13. come, lie all night in *s.* ye ministers of God
Amos 8. 10. and I will bring up *s.* upon all loins
Jonah 3. 5. the people of Nineveh put on *s.*
6. the king covered him with *s.* and sat in ashes
8. but let man and beast be covered with *s.*
Rev. 6. 12. the sun became black as *s.* of hair
11. 3. they shall prophesy 1260 days, clothed in *s.*

SACKCLOTHES.

Neh. 9. 1. Israel were assembled with *s.* on them

SACKS.

Gen. 42. 25. to fill their *s.* with corn, 44. 1.
43. 12. the money was brought again in your *s.*
22. we cannot tell who put our money in our *s.*
23. your God hath given you treasure in your *s.*
Josh. 9. 4. the Gibeonites took old *s.* on their asses

SACRIFICE

Is *an offering made to God upon his altars by the hand of a lawful minister, to acknowledge his power, to own entire dependence on him, or to conciliate his favour.* A sacrifice *differs from a mere* oblation *in this, that in a* sacrifice *there must be a real change or destruction of the thing offered: whereas an* oblation *is but a simple offering of a gift. As men have always been under an obligation of acknowledging the supreme dominion of God over them, and whatever belongs to them; and as there have always been found persons that have conscientiously acquitted themselves of this duty, it is probable, that there have been always* sacrifices *in the world.*

Adam *and his sons,* Noah *and his descendants,* Abraham *and his posterity,* Job *and* Melchizedek, *before the law, have offered to God real* sacrifices *The law did only ascertain the quality, the number, and other circumstances of* sacrifices: *Before that, all was arbitrary. They offered the fruits of the earth, the fat of the milk of animals, the fleeces of sheep, or the blood and the flesh of the victims: Every one pursued his own humour, his acknowledgment, his zeal, or his devotion: But among the* Jews, *the law appointed what they were to offer, and in what quantities. Before the law was given, every one was the priest and minister of his own* sacrifices; *at least he was at liberty to choose what priest he pleased to offer his victims: This honour was generally conferred upon the most ancient, or head of a family, on princes, or men of the greatest virtue and integrity. But after* Moses *this was wholly confined to the family of* Aaron.

Of these sacrifices some were eucharistical, *and are called* peace-offerings, *by which the sacrificer acknowledged the bounty of God, and his own unworthiness, and rendered praise for a favour received, and desired the divine blessing. Others were* expiatory, *the* sin-offerings, *for averting of God's wrath: These offerings signified, That man is a sinner, and therefore obnoxious to the just indignation and extreme displeasure of the holy and righteous God; and that God was to be propitiated, and that he might pardon him: That God would not forgive sin without the atonement of justice, which required the death of the offender; but it being tempered with mercy, accepted a sacrifice in his stead. There was a double guilt contracted by those that were under the* Mosaical *dispensation.* [1] Typical, *from the breach of a ceremonial constitution which had no relation to morality; such were accidental diseases, the touching of a dead body, &c. which were esteemed vicious according to the law, and the defiled were excluded from sacred and civil society: but as those pollutions were penal, merely by the positive will of God, so the exercise of his supreme right being tempered with wisdom and equity, he ordained that the guilt should be abolished by a sacrifice, and that they should be fully restored to their former privileges: Thus the apostle says,* Heb. 9. 13. *That the blood of those sacrifices* sanctifieth to the purifying of the flesh; *that is, communicated a legal purity to the offerers, and consequently a right to approach the holy place. The reason of these institutions was, that the legal impurity might represent the true defilement of sin, and the expiatory sacrifices prefigure that great and admirable* Oblation *which should purge away all sin.* [2] *They had contracted a real guilt which respects the conscience, from the breach of the moral law, and which subjected the offender to death temporal and eternal. This could not be purged away by those sacrifices: For how is it possible, that the blood of a beast should cleanse the soul of man, or satisfy the justice of an offended God? On the contrary, they revived the guilt of sin, and reinforced the rigour of the law, and were a public profession of the misery of men. As the moral contained a declaration of our guilt, and God's right to punish, so all the parts of the ceremonial were either arguments and convictions of sin, or images of the punishment due for them. But as they had a relation to* Christ, *the great gospel sacrifice, who was their complement, so they signified the expiation of moral guilt by his sacrifice, and freed the sinner from that temporal death to which he was liable, as a representative of our freedom from eternal death by the blood of the cross. Hence in the New Testament Christ is called a* Lamb, *in the notion of a* sacrifice, The Lamb of God which taketh away the sin of the world, *John* 1. 29. The Lamb slain from the foundation of the world, *Rev.* 13. 8. *He was represented by the red heifer, whose ashes were the chief ingredient in the waters of purification,* Heb. 9. 13, 14. For if the blood of bulls and of goats, and the ashes of an heifer sprinkling the unclean, sanctifieth to the purifying of the flesh, how much more shall the blood of *Christ* purge the conscience? *Especially the anniversary sacrifice, which was the abridgment and recapitulation of the rest, hath an eminent respect to* Christ, *Heb.* 9. 7, 8.

As to the beasts sacrificed by the Jews, *and their manner of sacrificing them, See the* Signification *of* OFFERING.

Gen. 31. 54. then Jacob offered *s.* upon the mount
Exod. 5. 17. let us go and do *s.* to the Lord, 8. 8.
12. 27. say, it is the *s.* of the Lord's passover
23. 18. not offer blood of *s.* with leavened, 34. 25.
34. 15. and one call thee, and thou eat of his *s.*
25. nor shall *s.* of passover be left to morning
Lev. 7. 12. then he shall offer with *s.* of thanksgiving
13. leavened bread with *s.* of thanksgiving, 22. 29.
16. if *s.* be a vow, it shall be eaten the same day
17. 8. whoso offereth a *s.* and bringeth not to door
27. 11. any beast of which they do not offer a *s.*
Num. 15. 3. or make a *s.* in performing a vow, 8.
28. 6. it is for a sweet savour, a *s.* made by fire unto the Lord, 8, 13, 19, 24. | 29. 6, 13, 36.
Deut. 18. 3. the priests' due from them that offer *s.*
Josh. 22. 26. let us now build an altar, not for *s.*
Judg. 16. 23. for to offer a great *s.* to Dagon
1 *Sam.* 1. 21. went up to offer the yearly *s.* 2. 19.
2. 29. wherefore kick ye at my *s.* and offering?
3. 14. iniquity of Eli's house not purged with *s.*
9. 12. for there is a *s.* of people to-day in high place
13. because he doth bless the *s.* then they eat
15. 22. behold, to obey is better than *s.*
16. 3. call Jesse to the *s.* and I will shew thee, 5.
20. 6. there is a yearly *s.* for all the family, 29.
1 *Kings* 12. 27. if this people do *s.* at Jerusalem
18. 29. they prophesied till time of the evening *s.*
36. at the time of evening *s.* Elijah drew near
2 *Kings* 5. 17. not offer *s.* to other gods, but the Lord
10. 19. for I have a great *s.* to do to Baal
17. 36. him shall ye fear, and to him shall ye do *s.*
2 *Chron.* 2. 6. save only to burn *s.* before him
7. 5. king Solomon offered a *s.* of 22,000 oxen
12. chosen this place to myself for an house of *s.*
29. † 11. the Lord hath chosen you to offer *s.*
Ezra 9. 4. I sat astonied until the evening *s.*
5. at the evening *s.* I arose up from my heaviness
Psal. 40. 6. *s.* thou didst not desire, 51. 16.
50. 5. that have made a covenant with me by *s.*
116. 17. I will offer to thee the *s.* of thanksgiving
118. 27. bind the *s.* with cords to horns of altar
141. 2. and lifting up of my hands as evening *s.*
Prov. 15. 8. *s.* of the wicked is abomination
21. 3. to do justice is more acceptable than *s.*
Eccl. 5. 1. to hear than to give the *s.* of fools
Isa. 19. 21. the Egyptians shall do *s.* and oblation
34. 6. for the Lord hath a *s.* in Bozrah and Idumea
57. 7. even thither wentest thou to offer *s.*
Jer. 33. 11. the voice of them that bring *s.* of praise
18. nor want a man to do *s.* continually
46. 10. for God hath a *s.* in the north country
Ezek. 39. 17. gather together to my *s.* even a great *s.*
19. and drink blood till ye be drunken of my *s.*
44. 11. they shall slay the *s.* for the people
46. 24. where ministers boil the *s.* of the people
Dan. 8. 11. daily *s.* was taken away, 9. 27. | 11. 31.
12. an host was given him against the daily *s.*
13. how long shall be the vision of the daily *s.*?
12. 11. from the time daily *s.* shall be taken away
Hos. 3. 4. Israel shall abide many days without a *s.*
6. 6. I desired mercy, and not *s. Mat.* 9. 13. | 12. 7.
Amos 4. 5. offer a *s.* of thanksgiving with leaven
Jonah 1. 16. then the men offered a *s.* to the Lord
Zeph. 1. 7. for the Lord hath prepared a *s.* 8.
Mal. 1. 8. if ye offer the blind for *s.* is it not evil?
Mark 9. 49. every *s.* shall be salted with salt
Luke 2. 24. and to offer a *s.* according to the law
Acts 7. 41. in those days they offered *s.* to the idol
14. 13. and would have done *s.* with the people
18. that they had not done *s.* unto them
Rom. 8. † 3. by a *s.* for sin condemned sin in the flesh
12. 1. that ye present your bodies a living *s.*
1 *Cor.* 8. 4. are offered in *s.* to idols, 10. 19, 28.
Eph. 5. 2. a *s.* to God for a sweet smelling savour
Phil. 2. 17. if I be offered on the *s.* of your faith
4. 18. a *s.* acceptable, well pleasing to God
Heb. 7. 27. needeth not daily as those to offer up *s.*
9. 26. to put away sin by the *s.* of himself
10. 5. he saith, *s.* and offering thou wouldest not, 8.
12. after he had offered one *s.* for sins, for ever
26. there remaineth no more *s.* for sins
11. 4. Abel offered to God a more excellent *s.*
13. 15. by him let us offer the *s.* of praise

See BURNT, PEACE-OFFERING.

SACRIFICE, *Verb.*

Exod. 3. 18. let us go and *s.* to the Lord our God, 5. 3, 8. | 8. 27. | 10. 25. || 8. 25. go ye *s.*
8. 26. shall we *s.* abomination of the Egyptians?
29. in not letting the people go to *s.* to the Lord
13. 15. I *s.* to Lord all that openeth the matrix
20. 24. thou shalt *s.* thereon thy burnt offerings
Deut. 15. 21. any blemish, thou shalt not *s.* it, 17. 1.
16. 2. thou shalt therefore *s.* the passover, 6.
5. not *s.* the passover within any of thy gates
1 *Sam.* 1. 3. Elkanah went up yearly to *s.* to Lord
15. 15. the people spared the best to *s.* to the Lord
1 *Sam.* 15. 21. should have been destroyed to *s.* to L.
16. 2. and say, I am come to *s.* to the Lord, 5.
1 *Kings* 3. 4. Solomon went to Gibeon to *s.* there
12. † 32. Jeroboam offered to *s.* to calves he made
2 *Kings* 14. 4. as yet the people did *s.* and burnt incense on the high places, 2 *Chron.* 33. 17.
17. 35. nor shall *s.* to other gods, nor serve them
2 *Chron.* 11. 16. came to Jerusalem to *s.* to the Ld.
Ezra 4. 2. we seek your God, and do *s.* to him
Neh. 4. 2. will they *s.*? will they make end in a day?
Psal. 54. 6. I will freely *s.* to thee, I will praise
107. 22. let them *s.* sacrifices of thanksgiving
Ezek. 39. 17. gather to my *s.* that I do *s.* for you
Hos. 4. 13. they *s.* on the tops of the mountains
14. and they *s.* with harlots, therefore the people
8. 13. they *s.* but the Lord accepteth them not
12. 11. they are vanity, they *s.* bullocks in Gilgal
13. 2. they say, let the men that *s.* kiss the calves
Jonah 2. 9. I will *s.* to thee with thanksgiving
Hab. 1. 16. therefore they *s.* unto their net
Zech. 14. 21. they that *s.* shall seethe therein
Mal. 1. † 8. if ye offer the blind to *s.* is it not evil?
1 *Cor.* 10. 20. things Gentiles *s.* they *s.* to devils

SACRIFICED.

Exod. 32. 8. they made them a calf and *s.* thereunto
Deut. 32. 17. they *s.* unto devils, not to God
Josh. 8. 31. they *s.* thereon peace offerings
Judg. 2. 5. and they *s.* there unto the Lord
1 *Sam.* 2. 15. the servant said to the man that *s.*
6. 15. and *s.* sacrifices the same day to the Lord
11. 15. all the people went to Gilgal and *s.*
2 *Sam.* 6. 13. David *s.* oxen and fatlings
1 *Kings* 3. 2. only the people *s.* in the high places, 3. 2 *Kings* 12. 3. | 15. 4, 35. | 16. 4. 2 *Chron.* 28. 4.
11. 8. for his strange wives, and *s.* to their gods
2 *Kings* 17. 32. made of the lowest priests which *s.*
23. † 20. he *s.* all the priests of the high places
1 *Chron.* 21. 28. Lord answered him, then he *s.* there
2 *Chron.* 5. 6. all that assembled before ark *s.* sheep
28. 23. Ahaz *s.* to the gods of Damasc. which smote
33. 16. Manasseh *s.* on the altar of the Lord
22. for Amon *s.* to all the carved images
34. 4. and strowed it on graves of them that had *s.*
Psal. 106. 37. yea, they *s.* their sons unto devils
38. daughters, they *s.* to the idols of Canaan
Ezek. 16. 20. these thou *s.* to them to be devoured
39. 19. of my sacrifice which I have *s.* for you
Hos. 11. 2. they *s.* to Baalim, and burnt incense
Jonah 1. † 16. then the men *s.* a sacrifice to Lord
Mark 14. † 12. when they *s.* the passover
1 *Cor.* 5. 7. for even Christ our Passover is *s.* for us
Rev. 2. 14. to eat things *s.* to idols, 20.

SACRIFICEDST.

Deut. 16. 4. nor shall flesh thou *s.* remain all night

SACRIFICES.

Gen. 46. 1. Israel at Beer-sheba offered *s.* to God
Exod. 10. 25. Moses said, thou must give us also *s.*
18. 12. Jethro, Moses' father-in-law, took *s.* for G.
Lev. 10. 13. of the *s.* of the Lord made by fire
17. 5. the *s.* which they offer in the open field
7. they shall no more offer their *s.* to devils
Num. 25. 2. they called people to the *s.* of their gods
28. 2. my *s.* shall ye observe to offer in season
Deut. 12. 6. thither ye shall bring your *s.* and tithes
32. 38. which did eat the fat of their *s.*
33. 19. there they shall offer the *s.* of righteousness
Josh. 13. 14. *s.* of the Lord are their inheritance
22. 28. the altar not for *s.* but it is a witness, 29.
1 *Sam.* 6. 15. and sacrificed *s.* same day to the Lord
15. 22. hath Lord as great delight in *s.* as obeying
1 *Chron.* 29. 21. they sacrificed *s.* in abundance
2 *Chron.* 7. 1. fire came down and consumed the *s.*
29. 31. come near and bring *s.* they brought in *s.*
Ezra 6. 3. let the place where he offered *s.* be laid
10. that they may offer *s.* to God of heaven
Neh. 12. 43. also that day they offered great *s.*
Psal. 4. 5. offer *s.* of righteousness, put your trust
27. 6. therefore will I offer *s.* of joy, I will sing
50. 8. I will not reprove thee for thy *s.* offerings
51. 17. the *s.* of God are a broken spirit, a broken
19. then shalt be pleased with *s.* of righteousness
106. 28. joined to Baal peor, and eat *s.* of dead
107. 22. let them sacrifice the *s.* of thanksgiving
Prov. 17. 1. than a house full of *s.* with strife
Isa. 1. 11. to what purpose is the multitude of *s.*?
29. 1. add ye year to year, let them kill *s.*
43. 23. nor hast thou honoured me with thy *s.*
24. nor hast thou filled me with the fat of thy *s.*
56. 7. their *s.* shall be accepted on mine altar
Jer. 6. 20. nor are your *s.* sweet unto me
7. 21. put your burnt offerings to your *s.* and eat
22. nor commanded them concerning *s.*
17. 26. bringing *s.* of praise to house of the Lord
Ezek. 20. 28. they saw every high hill and offered *s.*
Hos. 4. 19. they shall be ashamed, because of their *s.*
9. 4. their *s.* shall be as the bread of mourners
13. † 2. they say, let *s.* of men kiss the calves
Amos 4. 4. and bring your *s.* every morning
5. 25. have ye offered unto me *s.* and offerings
Mark 12. 33. to love the Lord is more than all *s.*
Luke 13. 1. whose blood Pilate mingled with their *s.*
Acts 7. 42. have ye offered *s.* for forty years?
1 *Cor.* 10. 18. that eat the *s.* partakers of the altar
Heb. 5. 1. that he may offer gifts and *s.* for sins
8. 3. every high priest is ordained to offer *s.*
9. 9. in which were offered both gifts and *s.*
23. but the heavenly things with better *s.*
10. 1. can never with those *s.* make comers perfect
3. but in those *s.* there is a remembrance made
6. in *s.* for sin thou hast had no pleasure
11. offering oftentimes the same *s.* that never can
13. 16. for with such *s.* God is well pleased
1 *Pet.* 2. 5. an holy priesthood, to offer up spiritual *s.*

See BURNT.

SACRIFICETH.

Exod. 22. 20. he that *s.* to any god, save to Lord only
Eccl. 9. 2. to him that *s.* and to him that *s.* not
Isa. 65. 3. people that *s.* in gardens, and burn incense
66. 3. he that *s.* a lamb as if he cut off a dog's neck
Mal. 1. 14. which hath a male, and *s.* a corrupt thing

SACRIFICING.
1 *Kings* 8. 5. Israel were with him *s.* sheep and oxen
12. 32. *s.* to the calves that he had made
Rom. 15. † 16. that the *s.* up of Gentiles might be
SACRILEGE.
Rom. 2. 22. that abhorrest idols, dost thou commit *s.?*
SAD.
Gen. 40. 6. Joseph looked on them, beh. they were *s.*
1 *Sam.* 1. 18. her countenance was no more *s.*
1 *Kings* 21. 5. Jezebel said, why is thy spirit so *s.?*
Neh. 2. 1. I had not been before *s.* in his presence
2. the king said, why is thy countenance *s.?*
3. I said, why should not my countenance be *s.?*
Ezek. 13. 22. because with lies ye have made the heart of righteous *s.* whom I have not made *s.*
Mat. 6. 16. be not as hypocrites, of a *s.* countenan.
Mark 10. 22. he was *s.* at that saying, and went away
Luke 24. 17. communications as ye walk, and are *s.*
SADDER.
Dan. 1. † 10. why should he see your faces *s.?*
SADDLE.
Lev. 15. 9. what *s.* he rideth upon shall be unclean
SADDLE.
2 *Sam.* 19. 26. thy servant said, I will *s.* me an ass
1 *Kings* 13. 13. old prophet said, *s.* me the ass, 27.
SADDLED.
Gen. 22. 3. Abraham rose up early and *s.* his ass
Num. 22. 21. Bala. *s.* his ass, and went with princes
Judg. 19. 10. were with the Levite two asses *s.*
2 *Sam.* 16. 1. Ziba met David with couple of asses *s.*
17. 23. Ahithophel *s.* his ass, and gat him home
1 *Kings* 2. 40. Shimei *s.* and went after his servants
13. 13. so they *s.* him the ass, and he rode, 23, 27.
2 *Kings* 4. 24. the woman of Shunam *s.* an ass
SADDUCEES.
The disciples of Sadoc. *They constituted one of the four principal Sects of the* Jews. *What chiefly distinguished them from the other* Jews *was, the opinion they maintained concerning the existence of angels, and the immortality of the soul. They did not deny but that we had reasonable souls; but they maintained this soul was mortal; and by a necessary consequence they denied the rewards and punishments of another life. They pretended also, that what is said of the existence of angels, and of a future resurrection, are nothing but illusions.* Epiphanius, *and after him* Austin, *have advanced that the* Sadducees *denied the* Holy Ghost. *But neither the Evangelists nor* Josephus *accuse them of any error like this.*
They are likewise accused of rejecting all the books of scripture, except those of Moses; *and to support this opinion it is observed, that our Saviour makes use of no scripture against them, but passages taken out of the Pentateuch. But it is said, to vindicate them from this reproach, that they did not appear in* Israel *till after the number of the holy books were fixed, and that if they had been to choose out of the canonical Scriptures, the Pentateuch was less favourable to them than any other book, since it so often makes mention of angels. Besides, the* Sadducees *were present in the temple, and at other religious assemblies, where the books of the prophets were read indifferently, as well as those of* Moses. *They were in the chief employs of the nation, many of them were even priests. Would the* Jews *have suffered in these employments persons that rejected the greatest part of their Scriptures?*
As the Sadducees *acknowledged neither punishments nor recompences in another life, so they were inexorable in their chastising transgressors. They observed the law themselves, and caused it to be observed by others, with the utmost rigour. They admitted of none of the traditions, explications, or modifications of the* Pharisees; *they kept only to the text of the law; and maintained, that only what was written was to be observed.*
As to Sadoc *the founder of their Sect, it is said, that he succeeded one* Antigonus Socchœus, *as a disciple succeeds his master, in the tradition of his doctrine; which* Antigonus *had in the same manner succeeded* Simon the Just, *the high priest of the* Jews. *This* Simon the Just *died in the year of the world* 3711, *before the vulgar æra* 293. *So that* Sadoc *may have lived about the year of the world* 3740.
Mat. 3. 7. when he saw the *s.* come to his baptism
16. 1. the *s.* came tempting Jesus, and desired him
6. Jesus said, beware of the leaven of the *s.* 11.
12. but beware of the doctrine of the *s.*
22. 23. the same day came to him the *s.* which say
34. had heard that he had put the *s.* to silence
Acts 4. 1. the priests and the *s.* came upon them
5. 17. the *s.* laid their hands on the apostles
23. 6. Paul perceived that the one part were *s.*
7. arose a dissension between the Pharisees and *s.*
8. for the *s.* say, that there is no resurrection
SADLY.
Gen. 40. 7. he asked, say. why look ye so *s.* to day?
SADNESS.
Eccl. 7. 3. by *s.* of countenance heart is made better
SAFE.
1 *Sam.* 12. 11. Lord delivered you, and ye dwelled *s.*
2 *Sam.* 18. 29. is the young man Absalom *s.?* 32.
Job 21. 9. their houses are *s.* from fear, nor is rod
Psal. 119. 117. hold thou me up, and I shall be *s.*
Prov. 18. 10. the righteous run into it, and are *s.*
29. 25. whoso trusteth in the Lord shall be *s.*
Isa. 5. 29. they shall carry the prey away *s.*
Ezek. 34. 27. and they shall be *s.* in their land
Luke 15. 27. because he had received him *s.*
Acts 23. 24. that they may bring him *s.* to Felix
27. 44. and so they escaped all *s.* to land
Phil. 3. 1. to write the same things, for you it is *s.*
SAFEGUARD.
1 *Sam.* 22. 23. but with me thou shalt be in *s.*
SAFELY.
Psal. 78. 53. he led them on *s.* they feared not
Prov. 1. 33. whoso hearkeneth to me shall dwell *s.*
3. 23. then shalt thou walk in thy way *s.*
31. 11. heart of her husband doth *s.* trust in her
Isa. 41. 3. he pursued them, and passed *s.*

Hos. 2. 18. I will make them to lie down *s.*
Zech. 14. 11. Jerusalem shall be *s.* inhabited
Mark 14. 44. that is he, take and lead him away *s.*
Acts 16. 23. charging the jailor to keep them *s.*
See DWELL.
SAFETY.
Job 3. 26. I was not in *s.* nor had I rest, trouble came
5. 4. his children are far from *s.* and are crushed
11. that those which mourn may be exalted to *s.*
11. 18. and thou shalt take thy rest in *s.*
24. 23. though it be given him to be in *s.*
Psal. 12. 5. I will set him in *s.* from him that puffeth
22. † 9. keepest me in *s.* when on my mother's breasts
33. 17. an horse is a vain thing for *s.*
Prov. 11. 14. in multitude of counsellors is *s.* 24. 6.
21. 31. horse is for battle, but *s.* is of the Lord
Isa. 14. 30. the needy shall lie down in *s.*
Acts 5. 23. the prison found we shut with all *s.*
1 *Thess.* 5. 3. for when they shall say, peace and *s.*
See DWELL.
SAFFRON.
Cant. 4. 14. spikenard and *s.* calamus and cinnamon
SAID.
Gen. 2. 23. Adam *s.* this is bone of my bone
3. 1. the serpent *s.* hath God *s.* ye shall not eat?
9. 26. Noah *s.* blessed be the Lord God of Shem
21. 12. in all that Sarah hath *s.* hearken to her
24. 65. the servant had *s.* it is my master
41. 54. the dearth began to come, as Joseph *s.*
Exod. 5. 22. Moses returned to the Lord and *s.*
12. 31. rise up, go, serve the Lord as ye have *s.*
32. also take your flocks and herds, as ye have *s.*
17. 10. so Joshua did as Moses had *s.* to him
Lev. 10. 5. they carried them out, as Moses had *s.*
Num. 11. 21. thou hast *s.* I will give them flesh to eat
14. 31. little ones, ye *s.* should be a prey, *Deut.* 1. 39.
23. 30. Balak did as Balaam had *s.* and offered
36. 5. the tribe of the sons of Joseph hath *s.* well
Deut. 1. 21. as the God of thy fathers hath *s.*
Judg. 1. 20. they gave Hebron to Caleb as Moses *s.*
6. 36. if thou wilt save Israel, as thou hast *s.* 37.
1 *Sam.* 10. 15. tell me, I pray thee, what Samuel *s.*
11. 12. who is he that *s.* shall Saul reign over us?
12. 1. I have hearkened to you in all ye *s.* to me
27. 1. David *s.* I shall now perish by hand of Saul
2 *Sam.* 7. 25. and now, O Lord, do as thou hast *s.*
13. 35. behold, as thy servant *s.* so it is
23. 1. David, son of Jesse, *s.* the anointed of God of Jacob, and the sweet psalmist of Israel *s.*
1 *Kings* 2. 38. as my lord king hath *s.* so will I do
8. 29. thy eyes open toward place of which thou hast *s.* my name shall be there, 2 *Chron.* 6. 20.
12. 26. Jeroboam *s.* now shall the kingdom return
17. 13. Elijah *s.* to her, go, do as thou hast *s.*
22. 20. one *s.* on this manner, another *s.* on that
2 *Kings* 7. 17. and he died, as the man of God had *s.*
1 *Chron.* 17. 23. therefore, Lord, do as thou hast *s.*
Ezra 10. 12. as thou hast *s.* so must we do
Neh. 5. 2. there were that *s.* we are many, 3.
Esth. 5. 5. that he may do as Esther hath *s.*
8. I will do to-morrow as the king hath *s.*
Job 11. 4. for thou hast *s.* my doctrine is pure
31. 31. if the men of my tabernacle *s.* not
38. 11. when I *s.* hitherto shalt thou come
Psal. 12. 4. who *s.* with our tongue will we prevail
14. 1. fool *s.* in his heart, there is no God, 53. 1.
27. 8. my heart *s.* to thee, thy face will I seek
Prov. 7. 13. and with an impudent face, *s.* to him
Isa. 14. 13. thou hast *s.* I will ascend into heaven
28. 15. ye *s.* we have made a covenant with death
30. 16. ye *s.* no, for we will flee upon horses
47. 10. for thou hast *s.* none seeth me
Jer. 2. 8. the priests *s.* not, where is the Lord?
23. 25. I have heard what the prophets *s.*
28. 6. even the prophet Jeremiah *s.* amen
29. 15. because ye *s.* Lord hath raised up prophets
38. 25. declare unto us what thou hast *s.* to the king, also what the king *s.* unto thee
Lam. 4. 20. of whom we *s.* under his shadow shall live
Ezek. 9. 8. and I *s.* ah, Lord God, wilt thou destroy
12. 9. hath not the rebellious house *s.* to thee
26. 2. Tyrus hath *s.* against Jerusalem, 36. 2.
27. 3. O Tyrus, thou hast *s.* I am of perfect beauty
28. 2. because thou hast *s.* I am a god, I sit
29. 3. the great dragon who hath *s.* my river is mine own, and I have made it for myself
Dan. 3. 28. Nebuch. *s.* blessed be God of Shadrach
8. 13. and another saint *s.* to that saint who spake
Jonah 4. 8. Jonah *s.* it is better for me to die
Mic. 7. 10. her who *s.* to me, where is the Lord?
Zeph. 2. 15. the city that *s.* in her heart, I am
Mal. 3. 14. ye have *s.* it is vain to serve God
Mat. 17. 5. behold, a voice which *s.* this is my beloved Son, in whom I am well pleased, *Luke* 3. 22.
26. 35. likewise also *s.* all the disciples
64. Jesus saith unto him, thou hast *s.*
27. 63. sir, we remember that that deceiver *s.*
Mark 2. 14. as he passed by, he *s.* to Levi, follow me
Luke 1. 13. the angel *s.* to him, fear not, 30.
20. 39. the scribes *s.* Master, thou hast well *s.*
24. 23. had seen angels, who *s.* that he was alive
24. and found it even so as the women had *s.*
John 1. 23. make straight the way, as *s.* Esaias
5. 18. but *s.* also, that God was his Father
7. 38. as the scripture hath *s.* out of his belly flow
12. 41. these things *s.* Esaias, when he saw his glory
50. even as the Father *s.* unto me, so I speak
Acts 2. 38. then Peter *s.* repent, and be baptized
4. 23. reported all the chief priests had *s.* to them
7. 37. this is that Moses who *s.* unto Israel
17. 28. as certain of your own poets have *s.*
Rom. 7. 7. except law had *s.* thou shalt not covet
Gal. 1. 9. as we *s.* before, so say I now again
Heb. 7. 21. by him that *s.* to him, the Lord sware
10. 30. we know him that hath *s.* vengeance
Rev. 5. 14. and the four beasts *s.* amen.
Answered and SAID.
Exod. 24. 3. and all the people *answered and s.*
1 *Sam.* 10. 12. one of the same place *answered and s.*
Job 2. 4. Satan *answered and s.* skin for skin
40. 1. moreover the Lord *answered* Job *and s.*
Mat. 20. 13. he *answered* one of them *and s.* friend

Luke 9. 49. John *answ. and s.* Master, we saw one
See ANSWERED.
God SAID.
Gen. 3. 1. yea, hath *God s.* ye shall not eat? 3.
17. 23. circumcised the same day, as *God* had *s.*
31. 16. whatsoever *God* hath *s.* unto thee, do
2 *Chr.* 33. 7. set an idol in the house of which *G. s.*
Acts 7. 7. and the nation will I judge, *s. God*
2 *Cor.* 6. 16. temple of the living God, as *G.* hath *s.*
He SAID.
Gen. 19. 17. *he s.* escape for thy life, look not
20. 5. *s. he* not unto me, she is my sister?
31. 8. if *he s.* thus, speckled shall be thy wages
12. *he s.* lift up thine eyes and see the rams
32. 26. *he s.* let me go, for the day breaketh
27. *he s.* what is thy name? and *he s.* Jacob
41. 51. God, *s. he.* hath made me forget my toil
Exod. 18. 24. so Moses did all that *he* had *s.*
Deut. 11. 25. no man shall be able to stand before you, as *he* hath *s.* 18. 2. | 29. 13. *Josh.* 13. 14, 33.
Josh. 14. 10. the Lord hath kept me alive, as *he s.*
Judg. 8. 3. their ang. was abated when *he* had *s.* that
1 *Sam.* 3. 17. if thou hide any thing *he s.* to thee
1 *Kings* 2. 4. not fail thee, *s. he,* a man on throne
31. do as *he* hath *s.* fall upon him, and bury him
2 *Kings* 17. 23. as *he s.* by all his servants, prophets
1 *Chron.* 22. 11. build the house, as *he s.* of thee
2 *Chr.* 24. 22. *he s.* Lord, look on it, and require it
Job 28. 28. to man *he s.* behold, fear of the Lord
Psal. 10. 6. *he* hath *s.* in his heart, 11. 13.
106. 23. *he s.* that he would destroy them
Isa. 28. 12. to whom *he s.* this is rest wherewith
40. 6. the voice said, cry, *he s.* what shall I cry?
63. 8. for *he s.* surely they are my people
Jer. 40. 3. now the Lord hath done as *he* hath
Ezek. 9. 5. to the others *he s.* in mine hearing
29. 9. because *he* hath *s.* the river is mine
Jonah 3. 10. God repented of the evil *he* had *s.*
Mat. 27. 43. for *he s.* I am the Son of God
28. 6. he is not here, for he is risen, as *he s.*
Mark 14. 16. came and found as *he s. Luke* 22. 13.
16. 7. there shall ye see him, as *he s.* unto you
Luke 9. 33. Peter said, not knowing what *he s.*
13. 17. when *he s.* these, his advers. were ashamed
John 2. 22. the disciples remembered that *he s.* this
6. 6. this *he s.* to prove him, for he knew
9. 17. what sayest thou? *he s.* he is a prophet
12. 6. this *he s.* not that he cared for the poor
33. this *he s.* signifying what death he should die
18. 6. as soon as *he s.* to them, I am he, they fell
19. 30. *he s.* it is finished, and bowed his head
20. 20. when *he* had so *s.* he shewed his hands
22. when *he* had *s.* this, he breathed on them
Acts 7. 60. when *he* had *s.* this, he fell asleep
9. 5. *he s.* who art thou, Lord? I am Jesus
20. 35. how *he s.* it is more blessed to give than to
23. 7. when *he* had so *s.* there arose a dissension
2 *Cor.* 12. 9. *he s.* my grace is sufficient for thee
Heb. 1. 5. to which of the angels *s. he,* 13.
10. 9. then *s. he,* lo, I come, to do thy will, O Go
13. 5. for *he* hath *s.* I will never leave thee
Jam. 2. 11. *he* that *s.* do not commit adultery
Rev. 22. 6. *he s.* these things are faithful and true
I SAID.
Gen. 26. 9. because *I s.* lest I die for her
Exod. 3. 17. *I* have *s.* I will bring you up out of Egy.
23. 13. in all things that *I.* have *s.* be circumspect
Deut. 32. 26. *I s.* I would scatter them into corners
Josh. 1. 3. that have I given, as *I s.* to Moses
Judg. 6. 10. *I s.* unto you, I am the Lord your G.
1 *Sam.* 2. 30. *I s.* indeed, that thy house should walk
9. 23. bring the portion of which *I s.* set it by
2 *Sam.* 19. 29. *I s.* thou and Ziba divide the land
2 *Kings* 23. 27. house of which *I s.* my name shal.
Job 9. 22. this is one thing, therefore *I s.* it
29. 18. then *I s.* I shall die in my nest, multiply
32. 7. *I s.* days should speak, and years teach
Ps. 30. 6. in prosperity *I s.* I shall never be moved
39. 1. *I s.* I will take heed to my ways, not to sin
40. 7. then *s. I,* lo, I come, *Heb.* 10. 7.
41. 4. *I s.* Lord, be merciful to me, heal my soul
82. 6. *I* have *s.* ye are gods, and are children
94. 18. when *I s.* foot slippeth, mercy held me up
102. 24. *I s.* O my God, take me not away
142. 5. *I s.* thou art my refuge and portion
Eccl. 2. 1. *I s.* in my heart, go to now, 15. ‖ 3. 17, 18.
Isa. 6. 11. then *s. I,* Lord, how long? he answered
45. 19. *I s.* not to seed of Jacob, seek ye me in vain
65. 1. *I s.* behold me, behold me, to a nation
Ezek. 16. 6. *I s.* when thou wast in thy blood, live
John 1. 30. this is he of whom *I s.* after me cometh
3. 7. marvel not that *I s.* ye must be born again
8. 25. the same that *I s.* from the beginning
10. 36. because *I s.* I am the Son of God
11. 40. *s. I* not to thee, if thou wouldest believe
42. *I s.* it, that they may believe thou hast sent me
14. 28. ye have heard how *I s.* to you, I go away
16. 4. these things *I. s.* not at the beginning
18. 20. and in secret have *I s.* nothing
21. ask them which heard me, what I have *s.*
Acts 11. 8. *I s.* not so, Lord, for nothing common
2 *Cor.* 7. 3. *I* have *s.* that ye are in our hearts
9. 3. yet have I sent, that as *I s.* ye may be ready
See JESUS.
She SAID.
Gen. 4. 25. God, *s. she,* hath appointed me another
20. 5. even *she* herself *s.* he is my brother
24. 58. wilt thou go with this man? *she s.* I will
Exod. 4. 26. then *she s.* a bloody husband thou art
1 *Kings* 2. 14. I have somewhat to say, *she s.* say on
Mat. 15. 27. *she s.* truth, Lord, yet dogs eat crumbs
John 8. 11 *she s.* no man, Lord; Jesus said to her
11. 28. when *she* had so *s.* she went her way
20. 14. when *she* had thus *s.* she turned herself
Acts 5. 8. and *she s.* yea, for so much
They SAID.
Exod. 24. 7. and *they s.* all that the Lord hath said will we do, and be obedient
Deut. 5. 28. *they* have well *s.* all they have spoken
2 *Chron.* 22. 9. *s. they,* he is the son of Jehoshaphat
26. 23. they buried in field, for *they s.* he is a leper
Psal. 83. 4. *they* have *s.* come, let us cut them off

Jer. 2. 6. neither s. they, where is the Lord?
Mat. 9. 28. believe ye? they s. unto him, yea, Lord
27. 22. they all s. let him be crucified
Mark 3. 21. for they s. he is beside himself
30. because they s. he hath an unclean spirit
16. 8. amazed, nor s. they any thing to any man
Luke 19. 34. they s. the Lord hath need of him
Acts 12. 15. then s. they, it is his angel

SAID, Passively.

Gen. 10. 9. wherefore it is s. even as Nimrod
22. 14. as it is s. to this day, in mount of the Lord
Exod. 5. 19. after it was s. ye shall not minish
1 Kings 13. 17. it was s. by the word of the Lord
Job 3. 3. let the night perish, in which it was s.
34. 31. surely it is meet to be s. to God
Psal. 87. 5. of Zion it shall be s. this and that man
Prov. 25. 7. better it be s. to thee, come up hither
Eccl. 1. 10. is there any thing whereof it may be s.?
Isa. 25. 9. it shall be s. in that day, this is our God
Jer. 16. 14. it shall no more be s. the Lord liveth
Ezek. 13. 12. shall it not be s. where is the daubing
Hos. 1. 10. where it was s. to them, ye are not
Mat. 5. 21. it was s. by them of old time, 27, 33.
31. ye have heard it hath been s. 38, 43.
Luke 2. 24. according to that which is s. in law of L.
23. 46. having s. thus, he gave up the ghost
Rom. 9. 12. it was s. the elder shall serve younger
26. that where it was s. ye are not my people
Heb. 3. 15. whilst it is s. to day, if ye will hear, 4. 7.
11. 18. of whom it was s. in Isaac shall thy seed
Rev. 6. 11. and it was s. to them, they should rest

SAIDST.

Gen. 12. 19. why s. thou, she is my sister?
26. 9. and how s. thou, she is my sister?
32. 9. O God the Lord, which s. to me, return
12. thou s. I will surely do thee good, make seed
Exod. 32. 13. s. to them, I will multiply your seed
Judg. 9. 38. where is thy mouth wherewith thou s.
1 Kings 2. 42. thou s. word I have heard is good
Job 35. 2. thou s. my righteous. is more than God's
Psal. 27. 8. when thou s. seek ye my face
Isa. 47. 7. and thou s. I shall be a lady for ever
Jer. 2. 20. and thou s. I will not transgress
25. but thou s. there is no hope, I loved strangers
22. 21. I spake, but thou s. I will not hear
Lam. 3. 57. thou drewest near, thou s. for me
Ezek. 25. 3. because thou s. aha, ag. my sanctuary
Hos. 13. 10. of whom thou s. give me a king and prin.
John 4. 18. he is not thy husb. in that s. thou truly

SAIL, Substantive.

Isa. 33. 23. they could not spread the s.
Ezek. 27. 7. which thou spreadedst forth to be thy s.
Acts 27. 17. they strake s. and so were driven
40. and hoised up the main s. to the wind

SAIL.

Acts 20. 3. as he was about to s. into Syria
16. Paul had determined to s. by Ephesus
27. 1. when it was determ. we should s. into Italy
24. God hath given thee all them that s. with thee

SAILED.

Luke 8. 23. as they s. he fell asleep, came a storm
Acts 27. 4. when we launched, we s. under Cyprus
7. and when we had s. slowly many days

SAILING.

Acts 27. 9. and when s. was now dangerous

SAILING.

Acts 21. 2. and finding a ship s. over to Phenicia
27. 6. the centurion found a ship s. into Italy

SAILORS.

Rev. 18. 17. all company in ships, and s. stood afar off

SAINT

Signifies, [1] A holy or godly person, one that is so by profession, covenant, and conversation, Psal. 16. 3. Heb. 6. 10. [2] Those blessed spirits which are graciously admitted by God to partake of everlasting glory and blessedness, Rev. 18. 24. [3] The holy angels, Deut. 33. 2. Jude 14.

For the perfecting of the saints, Eph. 4. 12. To strengthen and confirm them more and more in their union to Christ their Head, and in their love to one another, and in faith and every grace, till they come to a perfect man in heaven, when grace shall be turned into glory.

Psal. 106. 16. they envied Aaron, the s. of the Lord
Dan. 8. 13. then I heard one s. speak. another s. said to that s. which spake how long shall vis. be trod.
Phil. 4. 21. salute every s. in Christ Jesus

SAINTS.

Deut. 33. 2. he came with ten thousands of s.
3. he loved the people; all his s. are in thy hand
1 Sam. 2. 9. he will keep the feet of his s.
2 Chron. 6. 41. let thy s. rejoice in goodness
Job 5. 1. and to which of the s. wilt thou turn?
15. 15. behold, he putteth no trust in his s.
Psal. 16. 3. but to the s. that are in the earth
30. 4. sing to the Lord, O ye s. of his, give thanks
31. 23. O love Lord, all ye his s. Lord preserveth
34. 9. fear the Lord, ye his s. there is no want
37. 28. for the Lord forsaketh not his s.
50. 5. gather my s. together to me, those made
52. 9. wait on thy name, for it is good before thy s.
79. 2. the flesh of thy s. to the beasts of the earth
89. 5. thy faithfulness in the congregation of the s.
7. God is to be feared in the assembly of the s.
97. 10. he preserveth the souls of his s.
116. 15. precious to the Lord is death of his s.
132. 9. and let thy s. shout for joy
16. and her s. shall shout aloud for joy
145. 10. all thy works praise, and s. shall bless thee
148. 14. he exalteth the praise of all his s.
149. 1. and his praise in the congregation of s.
5. let s. be joyful in glory, let them sing aloud
9. this honour have all his s. praise ye the Lord
Prov. 2. 8. he preserveth the way of his s.
Dan. 7. 18. but s. shall take the kingdom, 22, 27.
21. the same horn made war with the s.
25. and shall wear out the s. of the Most High
Hos. 11. 12. but Judah is faithful with the s.
Zech. 14. 5. God shall come and all s. with thee
Mat. 27. 52. many bodies of s. that slept arose
Acts 9. 13. how much evil he hath done to thy s.
32. Peter came down also to the s. at Lydda

Acts 9. 41. when he had called the s. and widows
26. 10. many of the s. did I shut up in prison
Rom. 1. 7. beloved of God, called to be s.
8. 27. because he maketh intercession for the s.
12. 13. distributing to the necessity of the s.
15. 25. but now I go to Jerusalem to minister to s.
26. to make a certain contribution for the poor s.
31. that my service may be accepted of the s.
16. 2. that ye receive her in Lord as becometh s.
15. salute all the s. with them, Heb. 13. 24.
1 Cor. 1. 2. to them that are sanctified, called to be s.
6. 1. dare any go to law, and not before the s.?
2. do ye not know that the s. shall judge world?
14. 33. of peace, as in all the churches of the s.
16. 1. now concerning the collection for the s.
15. have addicted themselves to the ministry of s.
2 Cor. 1. 1. with all the s. which are in Achaia
8. 4. and take upon us the ministering to the s.
9. 1. for as touching the ministering to the s.
12. not only supplieth the want of the s.
13. 13. all the s. salute you, Phil. 4. 22.
Eph. 1. 1. to the s. at Ephesus, and faithful in Christ
15. after I heard of your love to all the s.
18. riches of the glory of his inheritance in s.
2. 19. ye are fellow citizens with the s.
3. 8. to me who am less than the least of all s.
18. that ye may be able to comprehend with all s.
4. 12. for the perfecting of the s. for the ministry
5. 3. let it not be once named, as becometh s.
6. 18. praying with prayer and supplicat. for all s.
Phil. 1. 1. to all the s. in Christ Jesus at Philippi
Col. 1. 2. to all the s. and faithful at Colosse
4. since we heard of the love ye have to all the s.
12. partakers of the inheritance of the s. in light
26. the mystery now made manifest to his s.
1 Thess. 3. 13. at coming of our Lord with all his s.
2 Thess. 1. 10. he shall come to be glorified in his s.
1 Tim. 5. 10. if she have washed the s. feet
Philem. 5. love and faith, which thou hast to all s.
7. the bowels of the s. are refreshed by thee
Heb. 6. 10. in that ye have ministered to the s.
Jude 3. for the faith once delivered to the s.
14. the Lord cometh with 10,000 of his s.
Rev. 5. 8. which are the prayers of s. 8. 3, 4.
11. 18. that thou shouldest give reward to thy s.
13. 7. it was given him, to make war with the s.
10. here is the patience and faith of the s.
14. 12. here is the patience of the s.
15. 3. just and true are thy ways, thou King of s.
16. 6. for they have shed the blood of the s.
17. 6. the woman drunken with the blood of the s.
18. 24. in her was found the blood of the s.
19. 8. the fine linen is the righteousness of the s.
20. 9. and compassed the camp of the s. about

SAITH.

1 Kings 3. 23. the one s. this is my son that liveth, and the other s. nay, but thy son is dead
20. 2. thus s. Benhadad, thy silver and gold is mine
32. servant Benhadad s. I pray thee let me live
22. 27. s. king, put this fellow in pris. 2 Chr. 18. 26.
2 Kings 9. 18. thus s. the king, is it peace? 19.
18. 19. thus s. the great king, the king of Assyria
29. thus s. king, let not Hezekiah deceive, not able to deliver you, 31. 2 Chr. 32. 10. Isa. 36. 14.
19. 3. thus s. Hezek. this a day of trouble, Isa. 37. 3.
2 Chr. 36. 23. thus s. Cyrus, king of Pers. Ezra 1. 2.
Job 28. 14. the depth s. the sea s. it is not in me
33. 24. he is gracious to him, and s. deliver him
35. 10. but none s. where is God my maker?
Psal. 36. 1. the transgression of the wicked s.
Prov. 9. 4. that want understanding, she s. to him, 16.
20. 14. it is naught, it is naught, s. the buyer
22. 13. the slothful man s. there is a lion, 26. 13.
26. 19. that deceiveth, and s. am not I in sport?
Lam. 3. 37. who is he that s. and it cometh to pass?
Mat. 7. 21. not every one that s. to me, Lord, Lord
26. 18. say to him, Master s. my time is at hand
Mark 8. 29. Peter s. to him, thou art the Christ
15. 28. scripture was fulfilled which s. Jam. 2. 23.
Luke 18. 6. L. said, hear what the unjust judge s.
John 4. 10. if thou knewest who it is that s. give
19. 28. the scripture might be fulfilled, s. I thirst
Acts 7. 48. in temples made with hands, as s. proph.
21. 11. thus s. the Holy Ghost, so the Jews do
Rom. 3. 19. the law s. it s. to them that are under
4. 3. for what s. the scripture, 10. 8.
9. 17. for scripture s. to Pharaoh, for this purpose
10. 11. for scripture s. whoso. believeth on him
16. for Esaias s. 20. || 19. first Moses s.
11. 2. wot ye not what the scripture s. of Elias?
4. but what s. the answer of God to him?
1 Cor. 3. 4. for while one s. I am of Paul, another
9. 8. or s. not the law the same also?
14. 34. woman to be under obedience, as also s. law
Gal. 4. 30. what s. the scripture? 1 Tim. 5. 18.
Heb. 3. 7. as the Holy Ghost s. if ye will hear
Jam. 4. 5. do ye think the scripture s. in vain
Rev. 2. 7. let him hear what the Spirit s. to the churches, 11, 17, 29. | 3. 6, 13, 22.
8. s. the First and the Last || 18. s. Son of God
3. 14. s. the Amen || 14. 13. yea, s. the Spirit
18. 7. she s. I sit a queen, and am no widow
22. 20. he s. surely I come quickly, amen

God SAITH.

2 Chron. 18. 13. what my God s. that I will speak
24. 20. thus s. God, why transgress ye commands
Psal. 50. 16. to wicked God s. what hast thou to do
Isa. 42. 5. thus s. God the Lord, that created heavens
54. 6. when thou wast refused, s. thy God
57. 21. there is no peace, s. my God, to wicked
66. 9. bring forth and shut the womb, s. thy God
Acts 2. 17. shall come to pass in the last days, s. G.

He SAITH.

Gen. 41. 55. go to Joseph, what he s. to you, do
1 Sam. 9. 6. all that he s. cometh surely to pass
2 Sam. 17. 5. let us hear likewise what he s.
2 Kings 5. 13. when he s. to thee, wash and be clean
Job 37. 6. for he s. to the snow, be thou on earth
Prov. 23. 7. eat and drink, s. he to thee, his heart
24. 24. he that s. to wicked, thou art righteous
Eccl. 4. 8. nor s. he, for whom do I labour?
10. 3. and he s. to every one that he is a fool

Mark 11. 23. shall believe those things he s. shal come to pass, he shall have whatsoever he s.
John 2. 5. whatsoever he s. to you, do it
16. 18. what is this he s.? we cannot tell what he s.
19. 35. and he knoweth that he s. true
21. 15. he s. to Peter, feed my lambs, 16.
Acts 1. 4. which, s. he, ye have heard of me
22. 2. they kept the more silence, and he s.
Rom. 10. 21. to Israel he s. || 15. 10. again he s.
1 Cor. 6. 16. for two, s. he, shall be one flesh
9. 10. or, s. he it altogether for our sakes?
2 Cor. 6. 2. he s. I have heard thee in a time
Gal. 3. 16. he s. not, and to seeds, as of many
Heb. 8. 5. see, s. he, that thou make all things
13. in that he s. a new covenant, he made first old
See Jesus, Lord.

SAKE.

Gen. 8. 21. I will not curse the ground for man's s.
12. 16. he entreated Abram well for her s.
18. 29. he said, I will not do it for forty's s.
31. not for twenty's s. || 32. not for ten's s.
20. 11. they will slay me for my wife's s.
26. 24. I will multiply thy seed for Abraham's s.
39. 5. blessed the Egyptian's house for Joseph's s.
Exod. 18. 8. Lord had done to Egypt for Israel's s.
21. 26. let him go free for eye's s. || 27. for tooth's s.
Num. 11. 29. Moses said, enviest thou for my s.?
25. 11. while he was zealous for my s. among them
18. was slain in day of the plague for Peor's s.
1 Sam. 12. 22. not forsake his people for name's s
23. 10. Saul seeketh to destroy the city for my s.
2 Sam. 5. 12. Lord exalted kingdom for Israel's s.
7. 21. for thy word's s. hast done all, 1 Chr. 17. 19.
9. 1. I may shew him kindness for Jonathan's s. 7.
18. 5. deal gently for my s. with young man Absal.
1 Kings 8. 41. a stranger that cometh out of a far country for thy name's s. 2 Chron. 6. 32.
11. 12. for David thy father's s. 13. 32, 34. | 15. 4.
2 Kings 8. 19. | 19. 34. | 20. 6. Psal. 132. 10.
13. for Jerusalem's s. which I have chosen
Neh. 9. 31. not consume them for great mercies' s.
Job 19. 17. entreated for children's s. of my body
Psal. 6. 4. save me for thy mercies' s. 31. 16.
23. 3. he leadeth me for his name's s. 31. 3.
25. 7. remember thou me for thy goodness' s.
11. for thy name's s. pardon mine iniquity
44. 26. arise, redeem us for thy mercies' s.
69. 6. not be confounded for my s. O God
79. 9. purge away our sins for thy name's s.
106. 8. he saved them for his name's s.
109. 21. but do thou for me, for thy name's s.
115. 1. give glory, for thy mercy and truth's s.
143. 11. quicken me, for thy name's s. for thy righteousness' s. bring my soul out of trouble
Isa. 37. 35. for mine own s. and David's s.
42. 21. Ld. is well pleased for his righteousness' s.
43. 14. for your s. I have sent to Babylon
25. blotteth out thy transgressions for my own s.
45. 4. for Jacob's s. I have even called thee
48. 9. for my name's s. will I defer mine anger
11. even for mine own s. will I do it
62. 1. for Zion's s. for Jerusalem's s. I will not rest
63. 17. return for thy servant's s. the tribes
66. 5. that cast you out for my name's s. said
Jer. 14. 7. O Lord, do thou it for thy name's s.
21. do not abhor us for thy name's s.
Ezek. 20. 9. but I wrought for my name's s. that it should not be polluted, 14. 22, 44. | 36. 22.
Dan. 9. 17. shine on thy sanctuary, for the Lord's s.
19. defer not for thine own s. O my God
Jonah 1. 12. for my s. this great tempest is on you
Mic. 3. 12. shall Zion for your s. be plowed as a field
Mat. 5. 10. who are persecuted for righteousness' s.
11. shall say evil against you falsely for my s.
10. 18. ye shall be brought before governors and kings, for my s. Mark 13. 9. Luke 21. 12.
22. and ye shall be hated of all men, for my name's s. 24. 9. Mark 13. 13. Luke 21. 17.
39. he that loseth his life for my s. shall find it, 16. 25. Mark 8. 35. Luke 9. 24.
14. 3. Herod bound John for Herod. s. Mark 6. 17.
9. nevertheless, for the oath's s. Mark 6. 26.
19. 12. eunuchs for the kingdom of heaven's s.
29. that hath left lands for my name's s. shall receive hundred fold, Mark 10. 29. Luke 18. 29.
24. 22. there shall no flesh be saved, but for elect's s. those days shall be shortened, Mark 13. 20.
Mark 4. 17. persecution ariseth for the word's s.
Luke 6. 22. cast out your name for Son of man's s.
John 12. 9. the people came not for Jesus' s. only
13. 38. wilt thou lay down thy life for my s.?
14. 11. else believe me for the very works' s.
15. 21. these things shall do to you for my name's s.
Acts 9. 16. things he must suffer for my name's s.
26. 7. for which hope's s. I am accused of Jews
Rom. 4. 23. it was not written for his s. alone
11. 28. for gospel, they are enemies for your s.
13. 5. ye must needs be subject for conscience' s.
15. 30. for Lord's s. strive with me in your prayers
1 Cor. 4. 10. we are fools for Christ's s. ye are wise
9. 23. and this I do for the gospel's s.
10. 25. asking no question for conscience' s. 27.
28. this is offered in sacrifice to idols, eat not, for his s. that shewed it, and for conscience' s.
2 Cor. 4. 5. ourselves your servants for Jesus' s.
11. we are alway delivered to death for Jesus' s.
12. 10. I take pleasure in distresses for Christ's s.
Eph. 4. 32. as God for Christ's s. forgave you
Phil. 1. 29. but it is given also to suffer for his s.
Col. 1. 24. for his body's s. which is the church
3. 6. for which things' s. wrath of God cometh
1 Thess. 1. 5. what manner of men we were for your s.
5. 13. to esteem them highly for their work's s.
1 Tim. 5. 23. use a little wine, for thy stomach's s.
Tit. 1. 11. teaching things for filthy lucre's s.
Philem. 9. yet for love's s. I rather beseech thee
1 Pet. 2. 13. submit to every ordinance for Lord's s.
3. 14. but and if ye suffer for righteousness' s.
1 John 2. 12. your sins are forgiven for name's s.
2 John 2. for the truth's s. that dwelleth in us
3 John 7. because for his name's s. they went forth
Rev. 2. 3. and for my name's s. hast laboured

Thy SAKE.

Gen. 3. 17. cursed is the ground for *thy s.*
12. 13. that it may be well with me for *thy s.*
30. 27. that the Lord hath blessed me for *thy s.*
Psal. 44. 22. for *thy s.* are we killed all day long, we are as sheep for the slaughter, *Rom.* 8. 36.
69. 7. because for *thy s.* I have borne reproach
Isa. 54. 15. who. gather ag. thee, shall fall for *thy s.*
Jer. 2. † 2. I remember for *thy s.* the kindness
15. 15. know that for *thy s.* I have suffered rebuke
John 13. 37. I will lay down my life for *thy s.*

SAKES.

Gen. 18. 26. I will spare the place for their *s.*
Lev. 26. 45. I will for their *s.* rememb. the covenant
Deut. 1. 37. also the Lord was angry with me for your *s.* saying, thou shalt not go, 3. 26. | 4. 21.
Judg. 21. 22. be favourable to them for our *s.*
Ruth 1. 13. it grieveth me much for your *s.*
1 *Chr.* 16. 21. yea, he reproved kings for their *s.* he suffered no man to do them wrong, *Ps.* 105. 14.
Psal. 7. 7. for their *s.* therefore return thou on high
106. 32. it went ill with Moses for their *s.*
122. 8. for my brethren and companions' *s*
Isa. 65. 8. so will I do for my servant's *s.*
Ezek. 36. 22. I do not this for your *s.* O Israel, 32.
Dan. 2. 30. but for their *s.* that shall make known
Mal. 3. 11. and I will rebuke the devourer for your *s.* he shall not destroy the fruits of your ground
Mark 6. 26. and for their *s.* which sat with him
John 11. 15. I am glad for your *s.* I was not there
12. 30. this voice came not for me, but for your *s.*
17. 19. and for their *s.* I sanctify myself
Rom. 11. 28. they are beloved for the father's *s.*
1 *Cor.* 4. 6. I have transferred for your *s.*
9. 10. or saith he it for our *s.?* for our *s.* no doubt
2 *Cor.* 4. 15. for all things are for your *s.*
8. 9. though rich, yet for your *s.* became poor
1 *Thess.* 3. 9. we joy for your *s.* before God
2 *Tim.* 2. 10. I endure all things for the elect's *s.*

SALE.

Lev. 25. 27. let him count the years of the *s.* thereof
50. price of his *s.* shall be according to the years
Deut. 18. 8. besides that which cometh of the *s.*

SALT,

In Greek, ʻαλς; *in* Hebrew, Melach. *God appointed that* Salt *should be used in all the sacrifices that were offered to him:* Every oblation of thy meat offering shalt thou season with salt; neither shalt thou suffer the salt of the covenant of thy God to be lacking from thy meat offering: With all thine offerings thou shalt offer *salt*, Lev. 2. 13. *This signified that incorruption of mind, and sincerity of grace, which are necessary in all them that would offer an acceptable offering unto God; or it denoted that communion which they had with God in these exercises of his worship,* salt *being a symbol both of friendship and incorruption. It appears from* Ezek. 16. 4. *that heretofore they rubbed new-born children with* salt; in the day thou wast born thou wast not salted at all, nor swaddled at all. *Some think they did this, to dry up the humidity that abounds in children, and to close up the pores which are then too open. Others say, that salt hardens the skins of children, and makes them more firm. Others think, it was to hinder any corruptions that might proceed from cutting off the navel-string. Whatever was their end in it, the prophet here, in a continued allegory, describes the worthless, helpless, and despicable condition of the Jews at first, till God pitied and helped them, and bestowed all manner of precious blessings upon them.*

In 2 Kings 2. 21, *the prophet* Elisha *being desired to sweeten the waters of the fountain of* Jericho, *and make them fit to drink, required a new vessel to be brought to him, and some salt to be put therein. They followed his orders: He threw this* salt *into the spring, and said;* Thus saith the Lord, I have healed these waters; and for the future they shall not be the occasion either of death or barrenness: *So the waters became good for drinking, and lost all their former bad qualities. Naturally the* salt *must only have served to increase the brackishness or bitterness of this fountain; but the prophet is directed to make use of a remedy that seemed contrary to the effect which was produced, that the miracle might become the more evident.*

Our Saviour, in his sermon on the mount, tells his disciples, Ye are the salt of the earth, *Mat.* 5. 13. *Ye are persons, who being endued with grace yourselves, ought to season others, and preserve them from corruption; and the doctrine which ye profess is as opposite as can be to the putrefaction of the world, both in respect to corrupt doctrine and corrupt manners.* Salt *has an acrimony by which it pierceth the lump; so the word is piercing,* Heb. 4. 12. *By the* salt of the earth, *some understand marl, with which they manure their land in some countries, instead of dung.*

Salt *is the symbol of wisdom,* Col. 4. 6. Let your speech be always with grace, seasoned with *salt*. *It is the symbol of perpetuity and incorruption: Thus they said of a covenant,* It is a covenant of salt for ever, before the Lord, *Num.* 18. 19. *And in* 2 Chron. 13. 5. The Lord God of *Israel* gave the kingdom over *Israel* to *David* for ever, even to him, and to his sons, by a covenant of salt. Salt *is the symbol also of barrenness and sterility. When* Abimelech took the city of Shechem, *he destroyed it, and sowed the place with* salt, *that it might always remain desert and unfruitful,* Judg. 9. 45. Zephaniah *threatens the* Ammonites *and* Moabites, *from the Lord; Moab* shall be as *Sodom*, and the children of *Ammon* as *Gomorrah*, even the breeding of nettles, and *salt-pits*, and a perpetual desolation, *Zeph.* 2. 9. Salt *is likewise the symbol of hospitality, and of that fidelity that is due from servants, friends, guests, and domestics, to those that entertain them, and receive them at their tables. The governors of the provinces beyond the* Euphrates, *writing to king* Artaxerxes, *tell him,* Because we have maintenance from the king's palace, &c. *Ezra* 4. 14. *which in the* Chaldee *is,* Because we are salted with the salt of the palace.

Mineral salt; *or salt that is dug out of mines, in form of a hard stone. It is thought that* Lot's *wife was changed into a statue of such* mineral salt, *that she became as a rock or stone of* salt, Gen. 19. 26.

The Salt sea, Gen. 14. 3. *is the* Dead sea, *or the lake of* Sodom, *called likewise the lake* Asphaltites, *because of the great quantity of bitumen in it, so that no fish can live in its waters, and a man cannot without difficulty sink in them, by reason of the weight and density of them. The crimes of the inhabitants of* Sodom, Gomorrah, Zeboim, *and* Admah, *were come to such an height, that God destroyed these cities, together with their inhabitants, by fire from heaven. The plain wherein they stood, which before was pleasant and fruitful, like an earthly Paradise, was first inflamed by lightning, which put fire to the bitumen, with which it was replete, and was afterwards overflowed by the waters of the* Jordan, *which diffused themselves there, and formed the* Dead sea, *or* Salt sea. *This lake receives all the water of* Jordan, *of the brooks* Arnon *and* Jabbok, *and other waters which descend from all the neighbouring mountains; and notwithstanding it has no visible issue, it does not overflow. It is believed that it discharges itself by some subterraneous channels into the* Red sea, *or into the* Mediterranean. *According to* Josephus' *account, the lake of* Sodom *is* 580 *furlongs in length, from the mouth of the river* Jordan *to* Zoar, *that is, about two and twenty leagues, at three miles to a league; and* 150 *furlongs wide; that is to say, about five leagues of the same measure.*

Gen. 19. 26. Lot's wife became a pillar of *s.*
Lev. 2. 13. with all thy offerings thou shalt offer *s.*
Deut. 29. 23. and that the whole land thereof is *s.*
Josh. 11. † 8. Israel chased them to *s.* pits
15. 62. the children of Judah had the city of *s.*
Judg. 9. 45. beat down the city, and sowed it with *s.*
2 *Sam.* 8. 13. smiting the Syrians in the valley of *s.*
2 *Kings* 2. 20. bring me a new cruse, put *s.* therein
21. he went to the spring, and cast the *s.* in there
14. 7. Amaziah slew of Edom in the valley of *s.* 10,000, 1 *Chron.* 18. 12. 2 *Chron.* 25. 11.
Ezra 4. † 14. we are salted with the *s.* of the palace
6. 9. that which they have need of, wheat, *s.* wine
7. 22. and *s.* without prescribing how much
Job 6. 6. can what is unsavoury be eaten without *s.?*
Jer. 17. 6. but he shall inhabit places in a *s.* land
Ezek. 43. 24. the priest shall cast *s.* upon them
47. 11. the marishes thereof shall be given to *s.*
Zeph. 2. 9 surely Moab shall be as *s.* pits
Mat. 5. 13. ye are the *s.* of the earth, but if the *s.*
Mark 9. 49. every sacrifice shall be salted with *s.*
50. *s.* is good, but if *s.* have lost his saltness, wherewith will ye season it? have *s.* in yourselves
Luke 14. 34. *s.* is good, but if *s.* have lost savour
Col. 4. 6. let your speech be seasoned with *s.*
Jam. 3. 12. no fountain can yield *s.* water and fresh
See COVENANT.

SALT *sea.*

Gen. 14. 3. in the vale of Siddim, which is the *s. sea*
Num. 34. 12. goings out of it shall be at the *s. sea*
Deut. 3. 17. coast even to the *s. sea* under Ashdoth
Josh. 3. 16. the waters that came toward the *s. sea*
12. 3. sea of plain, even to *s. sea*, 15. 2, 5. | 18. 19.

SALTED.

Exod. 30. † 35. make it a perfume *s.* together
Ezra 4. † 14. we are *s.* with the salt of the palace
Ezek. 16. 4. thou wast not *s.* at all, nor swaddled
Mat. 5. 13. if salt lost savour wherewith shall it be *s.?*
Mark 9. 49. for every one shall be *s.* with fire, and every sacrifice shall be *s.* with salt; salt is good

SALTNESS.

Psal. 107. † 34. he turneth a fruitful land into *s.*
Mark 9. 50. but if the salt have lost his *s.*

SALVATION

Is *taken,* 1. *for deliverance from, or victory over, outward dangers and enemies.* Exod. 14. 13. Stand still, and see the salvation of the Lord; *See how he will deliver you from the* Egyptians *your enemies: and in* 1 Sam. 14. 45. Shall *Jonathan* die, who hath wrought this great salvation in *Israel? who by God's assistance hath obtained this signal victory over the* Philistines.

2. *For remission of sins, true faith, repentance, obedience, and other saving graces of the Spirit, which are the way to salvation.* Luke 19. 9. This day is *salvation* come to this house.

3. *For eternal happiness hereafter, which is the object of our hopes and desires: thus it is said,* To give knowledge of salvation to his people, *Luke* 1. 77. Godly sorrow worketh repentance unto salvation, 2 *Cor.* 7. 10. *And the gospel is called,* The gospel of salvation, *Eph.* 1. 13. *because it brings the good news that salvation is to be had; it offers salvation to lost sinners: it shews the way to attain it: it also fits for salvation, and at last brings to it.*

4. *For the Author of salvation.* Psal. 27. 1. The Lord is my light and my salvation: *He is my counsellor in all my difficulties, and my Comforter and Deliverer in all my distresses.*

5. *For the blessed Jesus, who is the Saviour of sinners. Luke* 2. 30. Mine eyes have seen thy salvation, *says* Simeon; *I have seen him whom thou hast sent into the world to be the Author and Procurer of salvation to lost sinners.*

6. *For the praise and benediction that is given to God. Rev.* 19. 1. Alleluia, *salvation*, and glory, and honour, and power, unto the Lord our God.

The Hebrews *but rarely make use of concrete terms, as they are called, but often of abstracted. Thus, instead of saying that God saves them, and protects them; they say, that God is their salvation. Thus,* the word of salvation, the joy of salvation, the rock of salvation, the shield of salvation, the horn of salvation, the tower of salvation, &c. *is as much as to say, The word that declares deliverance; the joy that attends the escaping a great danger; a rock where any one takes refuge, and where he may be in safety from his enemy; a buckler that secures from the arm of the enemy; a horn or ray of glory, of happiness, and salvation, &c.*

Exod. 14. 13. see the *s.* of the Lord, 2 *Chr.* 20. 17.
Deut. 32. 15. lightly esteemed the rock of his *s.*
1 *Sam.* 11. 13. the Lord wrought *s.* in Israel to day
14. 45. Jonathan, who hath wrought this great *s.*
19. 5. the Lord wrought a great *s.* for all Israel
2 *Sam.* 19. † 2. the *s.* was turned into mourning
22. 51. he is the tower of *s.* for his king
1 *Chron.* 11. † 14. the Lord saved them by a great *s.*
16. 23. shew forth from day to day his *s.*
35. save us, O God of our *s.* and gather us
2 *Chron.* 6. 41. let thy priests be clothed with *s.*
Psal. 3. 8. *s.* belongeth to the Lord, thy blessing is
14. 7. O that the *s.* of Israel were come, 53. 6.
20. † 6. by the strength of the *s.* of his right hand
24. 5. and righteousness from the God of his *s.*
35. 9. my soul shall rejoice in his *s.*
37. 39. the *s.* of the righteous is of the Lord
42. † 5. I shall praise him, his presence is *s.*
50. 23. to him will I shew the *s.* of God
60. † 11. for vain is the *s.* of man, 146. † 3.
65. 5. wilt thou answer us, O God of our *s.?*
68. 19. blessed be the Lord, even the God of our *s.*
20. he that is our God, is the God of *s.*
74. 12. working *s.* in the midst of the earth
78. 22. because they trusted not in his *s.*
79. 9. help us, O God of our *s.* for the glory
85. 4. turn us, O God of our *s.* cause anger to cease
9. surely his *s.* is nigh them that fear him
95. 1. make a joyful noise to the rock of our *s.*
96. 2. shew forth his *s.* from day to day
98. 2. the Lord hath made known his *s.*
3. ends of the earth have seen the *s.* of our God
116. 13. I will take the cup of *s.* and call on name
118. 15. the voice of *s.* is in tabernacles of righteous
119. 155. *s.* is far from wicked, they seek not thy
132. 16. I will clothe her priests with *s.*
144. 10. it is he that giveth *s.* unto kings
149. 4. he will beautify the meek with *s.*
Isa. 12. 3. shall ye draw water out of the wells of *s.*
25. 9. we will be glad and rejoice in his *s.*
26. 1. *s.* will God appoint for walls and bulwarks
33. 2. be thou our *s.* in the time of trouble
6. wisdom and knowledge, and strength of *s.*
45. 8. let the earth open, and let them bring forth *s.*
17. Israel shall be saved with an everlasting *s.*
46. 13. I will place *s.* in Zion for Israel my glory
49. 8. in a day of *s.* have I helped thee
52. 7. the feet of him that publisheth *s.*
10. ends of the earth shall see the *s.* of our God
59. 11. we look for *s.* but it is far from us
16. therefore his arm brought *s.* unto him
17. he put on an helmet of *s.* upon his head
60. 18. but shalt call thy walls *s.* thy gates praise
61. 10. he hath clothed me with the garments of *s.*
62. 1. and the *s.* thereof as a lamp that burneth
63. 5. therefore mine own arm brought *s.* to me
Jer. 3. 23. truly in vain is *s.* hoped for from the hills and mountains, truly in the Lord is the *s.* of Isr.
Lam. 3. 26. quietly wait for the *s.* of the Lord
Jonah 2. 9. I will pay that I vowed, *s.* is of the Ld.
Hab. 3. 8. thou didst ride on thy chariots of *s.*
13. thou wentest forth for *s.* of thy people, even for *s.* with thine anointed, woundedst the wicked
Zech. 9. 9. behold, thy King, he is just and having *s.*
Luke 1. 69. who hath raised up an horn of *s.* for us
77. to give knowledge of *s.* to his people
3. 6. all flesh shall see the *s.* of God
19. 9. Jesus said, this day is *s.* come to this house
John 4. 22. we know what we worship, for *s.* is of Jews
Acts 4. 12. neither is there *s.* in any other
13. 26. to you is the word of this *s.* sent
47. thou shouldest be for *s.* to ends of the earth
16. 17. these men shew to us the way of *s.*
28. 28. the *s.* of God is sent to the Gentiles
Rom. 1. 16. the gospel is the power of God to *s.*
10. 10. with the mouth confession is made to *s.*
11. 11. through their fall *s.* is come to the Gentiles
13. 11. now is our *s.* nearer than when we believed
2 *Cor.* 1. 6. whether we be comforted, it is for your *s.*
6. 2. in the day of *s.* have I succoured thee; now is the accepted time, behold now is the day of *s.*
7. 10. godly sorrow worketh repentance to *s.*
Eph. 1. 13. after ye heard the gospel of your *s.*
6. 17. take the helmet of *s.* and the sword of Spirit
Phil. 1. 28. which is to you an evident token of *s.*
2. 12. work out your own *s.* with fear and trembling
1 *Thess.* 5. 8. and for an helmet the hope of *s.*
9. hath appointed us to obtain *s.* by our Lord Je.
2 *Thess.* 2. 13. for God hath chosen you to *s.*
2 *Tim.* 2. 10. that they may obtain the *s.* in Christ
3. 15. scriptures are able to make thee wise to *s.*
Tit. 2. 11. the grace of God that bringeth *s.*
Heb. 1. 14. for them who shall be heirs of *s.*
2. 3. how shall we escape, if we neglect so great *s.?*
10. to make the Captain of their *s.* perfect through
5. 9. he became the Author of eternal *s.* to all that
6. 9. better things, and things that accompany *s.*
9. 28. shall appear the second time without sin to *s.*
1 *Pet.* 1. 5. who are kept through faith unto *s.*
9. receiving the end of your faith, *s.* of your souls
10. of which *s.* the prophets have inquired
2 *Pet.* 3. 15. the long-suffering of the Lord is *s.*
Jude 3. to write to you of the common *s.*
Rev. 7. 10. saying, *s.* to our God ‖ 19. 1. *s.* to Lord
12. 10. now is come *s.* and strength, and kingdom

My SALVATION.

Exod. 15. 2. the L. is my song, he is become *my s.*
2 *Sam.* 22. 3. he is my shield, the horn of *my s.*
47. exalted be the rock of *my s. Psal.* 18. 46.
23. 5. for this is all *my s.* and all my desire
Job 13. 16. he also shall be *my s.* for an hypocrite
Psal. 25. 5. for thou art the God of *my s.*

Psal. 27. 1 L. is my light and *my s.* 62. 6. *Isa.* 12. 2.
9. leave me not, O God of *my s.* 51. 14. | 88. 1.
38. 22. O Lord *my s.* || 62. 2. he only is *my s.* 6.
62. 1. my soul waits on G. from him cometh *my s.*
7. in God is *my s.* || 89. 26. my God, rock of *my s.*
91. 16. I will satisfy him, and shew him *my s.*
118. 14. the Lord is become *my s.* 21. *Isa.* 12. 2.
140. 7. O God, the Lord, the strength of *my s.*
Isa. 12. 2. behold, God is *my s.* he is become *my s.*
46. 13. my righteousn. not far, *my s.* shall not tarry
49. 6. thou mayest be *my s.* to the end of the earth
51. 5. *my s.* is gone forth || 6. *my s.* shall be for ever
8. and *my s.* from generation to generation
56. 1. *my s.* is near to come, and my righteousness
Mic. 7. 7. I will wait for the God of *my s.* my God
Hab. 3. 18. I will joy in the God of *my s.*
Phil. 1. 19. for I know that this shall turn to *my s.*

Thy SALVATION.

Gen. 49. 18. I have waited for *thy s.* O Lord
1 *Sam.* 2. 1. mouth enlarged, because I rejoice in *t. s.*
2 *Sam.* 22. 36. thou hast also given me the shield of *thy s.* thy gentleness made me great, *Psal.* 18. 35.
Psal. 9. 14. I will rejoice in *thy s.*
13. 5. my heart shall rejoice in *thy s.*
20. 5. we will rejoice in *thy s.* and set up banners
21. 1. and in *thy s.* how greatly shall he rejoice!
5. his glory is great in *thy s.* honour and majesty
35. 3. say unto my soul, I am *thy s.*
40. 10. I have declared thy faithfulness and *thy s.*
16. let such as love *thy s.* say, Lord be magnified
51. 12. restore unto me the joy of *thy s.* 70. 4.
69. 13. O God, hear me in the truth of *thy s.*
29. I am poor, let *thy s.* set me up on high
71. 15. my mouth shall shew forth *thy s.*
85. 7. shew us thy mercy, O Lord, grant us *thy s.*
106. 4. remember me, O visit me with *thy s.*
119. 41. let *thy s.* come according to thy word
81. my soul fainteth for *thy s.* but I hope in word
123. mine eyes fail for *thy s.* and for the word
166. Lord, I have hoped for *thy s.* and done
174. I have longed for *thy s.* O Lord
Isa. 17. 10. thou hast forgotten the God of *thy s.*
62. 11. say to Zion, behold, *thy s.* cometh
Luke 2. 30. for mine eyes have seen *thy s.*

SALUTATION.

Luke 1. 29. what manner of *s.* this should be
41. at *s.* of Mary babe leaped in her womb, 44.
Cor. 16. 21. brethren greet you, the *s.* of me, Paul, with mine own hand, *Col.* 4. 18. 2 *Thess.* 3. 17.

SALUTATIONS.

Mark 12. 38. scribes who love *s.* in the market-places

SALUTE.

1 *Sam.* 10. 4. they will *s.* thee and give thee two loav.
13. 10. Saul went to meet Samuel, that might *s.* him
25. 14. behold, David sent to *s.* our master
2 *Sam.* 8. 10. Toi sent Joram his son to *s.* David
2 *Kings* 4. 29. *s.* him not, if any *s.* thee, answer not
10. 13. we go to *s.* the children of the king
Mat. 5. 47. and if ye *s.* your brethren only
10. 12. when ye come into an house, *s.* it
Mark 15. 18. and began to *s.* him, hail, king of Jews
Luke 10. 4. nor shoes, and *s.* no man by the way
Acts 25. 13. Agrippa and Bernice came to *s.* Festus
Rom. 16. 5. *s.* my well-beloved Epenetus
7. *s.* Andronicus || 9. *s.* Urbane our helper
10. *s.* Apelles, *s.* Aristobulus' household
11. *s.* Herodian || 12. *s.* the beloved Persis
13. *s.* Rufus chosen in the Lord, and his mother
16. *s.* with an holy kiss, the churches *s.* you
22. I Tertius, who wrote this, *s.* you in the Lord
1 *Cor.* 16. 19. churches of Asia *s.* you, Aquila and Priscilla *s.* you much, with church in their house
2 *Cor.* 13. 13. all the saints *s.* you, *Phil.* 4. 22.
Phil. 4. 21. *s.* every saint in Christ Jesus
Col. 4. 15. *s.* the brethren in Laodicea and Nymphas
2 *Tim.* 4. 19. *s.* the household of Onesiphorus
Tit. 3. 15. all that are with me *s.* thee, greet thee
Philem. 23. there *s.* thee Epaphras and Marcus
Heb. 13. 24. *s.* them that have the rule over you; they of Italy *s.* you, grace be with you all
3 *John* 14. our friends *s.* thee, greet the friends

SALUTED.

Judg. 18. 15. the Danites came and *s.* Micah
1 *Sam.* 17. 22. David came and *s.* his brethren
30. 21. David came near to the people, and *s.* them
2 *Kings* 10. 15. Jehu *s.* Jehonadab, and said to him
Mark 9. 15. the people running to Jesus, *s.* him
Luke 1. 40. Mary entered, and *s.* Elisabeth
Acts 18. 22. Paul, when he had *s.* the church, went
21. 7. we came to Ptolemais, and *s.* the brethren
19. when Paul had *s.* James and the elders

SALUTETH.

Rom. 16. 23. Gaius mine host, and Erastus, *s.* you
Col. 4. 10. Aristarchus my fellow-prisoner, *s.* you
12. Epaphras, a servant of Christ, *s.* you
1 *Pet.* 5. 13. the church that is at Babylon, *s.* you

SAMARITAN.

Luke 10. 33. but a certain *S.* came where he was
17. 16. fell down giving him thanks, and he was a *S.*
John 8. 48. that thou art a *S.* and hast a devil

SAMARITANS.

2 *Kings* 17. 29. houses of high places the *S.* had made
Mat. 10. 5. into any city of the *S.* enter ye not
Luke 9. 52. they entered into a village of the *S.*
John 4. 9. the Jews have no dealings with the *S.*
39. many of the *S.* of that city believed on him
40. the *S.* besought him to tarry with them
Acts 8. 25. preached in many villages of the *S.*

SAME.

Gen. 5. 29. saying, this *s.* shall comf. us in our work
6. 4. the *s.* became mighty men, men of renown
10. 12. and Resen, the *s.* is a great city
14. 8. the *s.* is Zoar || 23. 2. the *s.* is Hebron, 19.
24. 14. let the *s.* be she thou hast appointed, 44.
26. 24. the Lord appeared to Isaac the *s.* night
44. 6. he overtook and spake to them these *s.* words
48. 7. in the way of Ephrath, the *s.* is Beth-lehem
Exod. 25. 31. his flowers shall be of the *s.* 37. 17.
36. knops and branches shall be of the *s.* 37. 22.
27. 2. his horns shall be of the *s.* 37. 25. | 38. 2.
28. 8. curious girdle of ephod shall be of *s.* 39. 5.
Num. 10. 32. the *s.* goodness will we do unto thee
Num. 15. 30. presumptuously, the *s.* reproacheth L.
Josh. 15. 8. the Jebusite, the *s.* is Jerusalem
Judg. 7. 4. the *s.* shall go, the *s.* shall not go
1 *Sam.* 9. 17. the *s.* shall reign over my people
2 *Sam.* 5. 7. Zion the *s.* is the city of David
1 *Kings* 13. 9. nor turn by the *s.* way thou camest
2 *Kings* 19. 29. and in the second year ye shall eat that which springeth of the *s.* *Isa.* 37. 30.
1 *Chron.* 1. 27. Abram, the *s.* is Abraham
16. 17. hath confirmed the *s.* to Jacob, *Ps.* 105. 10.
2 *Chr.* 13. 9. the *s.* may be a priest of them, no gods
18. 7. the *s.* is Micaiah the son of Imla
32. 12. hath not the *s.* Hezekiah taken away
Ezra 10. 23. Shimei, and Kelaiah, the *s.* is Kelita
Esth. 9. 1. month Adar, on thirteenth day of the *s.*
17. on the fourteenth || 18. on the fifteenth, 21.
Job 4. 8. they that sow wickedness reap the *s.*
13. 2. what ye know, the *s.* do I know also
Psal. 68. 23. and the tongue of thy dogs in the *s.*
75. 8. full of mixture, he poureth out of the *s.*
102. 27. but thou art the *s.* thy years have no end
113. 3. to the going down of the *s.* *Mal.* 1. 11.
Prov. 28. 24. the *s.* is the companion of a destroyer
Eccl. 9. 15. no man remembered that *s.* poor man
Jer. 28. 17. so Hananiah the prophet died the *s.* year
Ezek. 3. 18. *s.* wicked man shall die in his iniquity
21. 26. this shall not be the *s.* exalt him that is low
44. 3. the prince shall go out by the way of the *s.*
Dan. 7. 21. the *s.* horn made war with the saints
Amos 2. 7. a man and his father go in to the *s.* maid
Mat. 5. 19. the *s.* shall be called great in the kingd.
46. if love them, do not even the publicans the *s.*?
12. 50. the *s.* is my brother and sister, *Mark* 3. 35.
21. 42. the stone builders rejected, the *s.* is become the head of the corner, *Luke* 20. 17. 1 *Pet.* 2. 7.
24. 13. shall endure, *s.* shall be saved, *Mark* 13. 13.
26. 23. that dippeth his hand the *s.* shall betray me
48. that *s.* is he, hold him fast, *Mark* 14. 44.
27. 44. the thieves also cast the *s.* in his teeth
Mark 8. 35. lose life, the *s.* shall save it, *Luke* 9. 24.
9. 35. desire to be first, the *s.* shall be last of all
Luke 6. 33. for sinners also do even the *s.*
38. for with the *s.* measure that ye mete withal
7. 47. to whom little is forgiven the *s.* loveth little
9. 48. that is least among you, the *s.* shall be great
16. 1. the *s.* was accused that he wasted his goods
20. 47. the *s.* shall receive greater damnation
23. 51. the *s.* had not consented to the counsel
John 1. 2. the *s.* was in the beginning with God
7. the *s.* came for a witness of the light
33. the *s.* is he which baptizeth with the Holy Gh.
7. 18. the *s.* is true || 10. 1. the *s.* is a thief
8. 25. the *s.* I said to you from the beginning
11. 6. he abode two days still in the *s.* place
49. being high priest that *s.* year, 18. 13.
12. 48. the *s.* shall judge him in the last day
15. 5. abideth in me, the *s.* bringeth forth much fruit
Acts 1. 11. this *s.* Jesus shall so come in like manner
2. 36. God made that *s.* Jesus both Lord and Christ
7. 19. the *s.* dealt subtilly with our kindred
35. the *s.* did God send to be a ruler and deliverer
8. 35. began at the *s.* scripture and preached Jesus
13. 33. God hath fulfilled the *s.* to us their children
14. 9. the *s.* heard Paul speak, who beholding him
16. 17. the *s.* followed Paul and us, and cried
24. 20. or else let these *s.* here say, if they found
Rom. 1. 32. who knowing not only do the *s.*
2. 3. that judgest them which do, and doest the *s.*
8. 20. who hath subjected the *s.* in hope
10. 12. the *s.* Lord over all is rich to all that call
12. 4. all the members have not the *s.* office
16. be of the *s.* mind one toward another, mind not high things, 1 *Cor.* 1. 10. *Phil.* 4. 2. 1 *Pet.* 4. 1.
13. 3. do good, and thou shalt have praise of the *s.*
1 *Cor.* 1. 10. I beseech that ye all speak the *s.* thing
9. 8. or saith not the law the *s.* also?
10. 3. did all eat the *s.* spirit. meat || 4. the *s.* drink
12. 4. but the *s.* Spirit, 2 *Cor.* 4. 13. | 12. 18.
5. but the *s.* Lord || 6. but it is the *s.* God
15. 39. all flesh is not the *s.* flesh, one kind of men
2 *Cor.* 2. 2. but the *s.* which is made sorry by me
3. I wrote this *s.* unto you lest, when I came
8. 19. administered by us to the glory of the *s.* Lord
9. 5. that *s.* might be ready as a matter of bounty
Gal. 2. 8. the *s.* was mighty in me to the Gentiles
3. 7. the *s.* are the children of Abraham
Eph. 4. 10. he that descended is the *s.* that ascended
6. 8. the *s.* shall he receive of the Lord, bond or free
Phil. 1. 30. having the *s.* conflict which ye saw in me
2. 2. having *s.* love, being of one accord and mind
3. 16. let us walk by the *s.* rule, mind the *s.* things
Col. 4. 2. and watch in the *s.* with thanksgiving
2 *Tim.* 2. 2. the *s.* commit thou to faithful men
Heb. 1. 12. thou art the *s.* thy years shall not fail
2. 14. he also himself likewise took part of the *s.*
11. 9. the heirs with him of the *s.* promise
13. 8. Jesus Christ, *s.* yesterday, to-day, and for ever
Jam. 3. 2. if any offend not, the *s.* is a perfect man
1 *Pet.* 4. 10. even so minister the *s.* one to another
2 *Pet.* 2. 19. of the *s.* is he brought in bondage
3. 7. by the *s.* word are kept in store, reserved
1 *John* 2. 23. denies the Son, *s.* hath not the Father
27. as the *s.* anointing teacheth you all things
Rev. 3. 5. overcometh the *s.* shall be clothed in white
See DAY, HOUR.

SANCTIFICATION.

1 *Cor.* 1. 30. in Christ, who of God is made to us *s.*
1 *Thess.* 4. 3. this is the will of God, even your *s.*
4. should know how to possess his vessel in *s.*
2 *Thess.* 2. 13. through *s.* of the Spirit, 1 *Pet.* 1. 2.

SANCTIFY,

When referred to God, signifies,

1. *To separate and appoint any thing to an holy and religious use.* God sanctified the seventh day, *Gen.* 2. 3. The first-born were sanctified, *Exod.* 13. 2. *And thus the tabernacle, the temple, the priests, the altars, the sacrifices, &c. were sanctified under the law.*
2. *To cleanse a sinner from the pollution and filth of sin, to free him from the power and dominion of sin, and endue him with a principle of holiness; thus God by his Spirit sanctifies the elect, or true believers.* 1 Cor. 6. 11. And such were some of you, but ye are washed, but ye are sanctified.
3. *To manifest his glory and vindicate his honour from the blasphemies of the wicked,* Ezek. 36. 23. I will sanctify my great name. *I will clear up, and remove the objections, that the sufferings and sins of the* Jews *have raised among the* Babylonians: *they gave the heathen occasion to think meanly and contemptibly of me, but I will shew that I am infinite in greatness and goodness. And in* Num. 20. 13. This is the water of Meribah, because the children of Israel strove with the Lord, and he was sanctified in them. *He was sanctified among them by the demonstration of his omnipotence, veracity, and clemency towards the* Israelites, *and of his impartial holiness and severity against sin, even in his greatest friends and favourites, as* Moses *was. Thus God is said to sanctify himself.*
4. *To free the creature from the curse that sin has brought upon it, and make it fit for a free and holy use.* 1 Tim. 4. 5. The creature is sanctified by the word of God, and prayer.
5. *To separate, ordain, and appoint the* Messiah *to be the King and Head of his church.* John 10. 36. Say ye of him whom the Father hath sanctified, thou blasphemest, because I said, I am the Son of God? *that is, If the title of* Gods *be given to those to whom God has given some part of his dominion, then surely it does much more properly and truly belong to me, whom my Father has appointed to rule over all with himself, and whom he has separated and ordained for Mediator and King of his church; which office cannot be assumed or executed by any mere creature, but only by the eternal Son of God.*

To sanctify *is also spoken of man, and* signifies,

1. *To purify, and to be in a proper condition to appear before the Lord, and to partake of holy things.* Exod. 19. 10, 11, 22. And the Lord said unto Moses, Go unto the people, and sanctify them to-day and to-morrow, and let them wash their clothes; and be ready against the third day *to receive the law.* And let the priests also which come near to the Lord, sanctify themselves, lest the Lord break forth upon them.
2. *To prepare.* Num. 11. 18. Sanctify yourselves against to-morrow, and ye shall eat flesh. *Josh.* 3. 5. Sanctify yourselves, for to-morrow the Lord will do wonders among you. *That is, Prepare yourselves, endeavour to bring your hearts to a holy frame, that with faith, reverence, and admiration, you may behold the great work that God will do for you.*
3. *To praise God, to acknowledge his majesty, to worship him, to endeavour to make him known, adored, praised, and beloved by all those that are capable of it: thus men hallow or sanctify the name of God.* Isa. 8. 13. Sanctify the Lord of hosts himself, and let him be your fear. *And* Mat. 6. 9. Hallowed be thy name. *When we desire of God, that his name may be sanctified or hallowed, it is, that he may be honoured, praised, and glorified through the whole world, and especially by those who have the happiness of knowing him. Let them sanctify it by their holy lives, their fidelity, their submission to his orders: And they that know him not, that they may come to the knowledge of him, may hear his word, may become tractable to the instructions of his ministers. What is meant by* sanctifying the name of God, *may be yet better apprehended, by what is opposite to it; that is, profaning the name of God by vain swearing, blasphemy, and ascribing his name to idols; by furnishing wicked men and infidels with an occasion of blaspheming it by a bad life and scandalous conversation. It is said,* Lev. 10. 3. I will be sanctified in them that come nigh me; *in his priests, when by the terrible and exemplary punishment of* Nadab *and* Abihu, *the Lord shewed what purity he required in his servants, what punctual exactness he expected in his service. In* Num. 20. 12. *the Lord complains that* Moses *and* Aaron *did not sanctify him before the people of Israel: and how did they not sanctify him? By shewing some distrust to his words.* Because ye believed me not.

Saint, holy, holiness, *are epithets, which in a sovereign manner are ascribed to God, the author of all sanctity and holiness. So the* Cherubims *and* Seraphims *cry to him without ceasing,* Holy, Holy, Holy, *Isa.* 6. 3. *He is named by way of excellence, the* Saint, the Holy One of Israel, *Isa.* 10. 20. *All our holiness before him is nothing but pollution; his name is* Holy, *or rather* Holiness *itself.*

To sanctify *may be reduced to the four following significations:*

1. It signifies, *To confess and celebrate that to be holy, which in itself was so before,* Mat. 6. 9. *And thus it is to be understood wheresoever God is said to be sanctified.*
2. *To make persons holy, who were impure and defiled before,* 1 Cor. 6. 11. *And this is the sense of the word in those passages of Scripture where the elect are said to be sanctified.*
3. *To separate and set apart some things, or persons, from a common unto an holy use, as the tabernacle, temple, priests, &c.*
4. *To employ a thing in holy and religious exercises, in the worship of God in public and in private, and the celebration of his works; in this and the former sense the seventh day is sanctified,* Exod. 20. 8.

Sanctification *differs from* Justification, *thus:*

1. Justification, *is the absolution of a sinner from the guilt of sin and death; whereas* sanctification *is an alteration of qualities from evil to good.*
2. Justification *consists of remission of sins through the imputation of Christ's righteousness;* sancti-

fication *is the renovation of nature by the Holy Spirit.*
3. Justification *is perfect in this life; so is not* sanctification.
4. Justification *is in nature before* sanctification, *but not in order of time; for God only sanctifies those that are justified.*
Exod. 13. 2. *s.* unto me all the first-born, it is mine
19. 10. go and *s.* them to-day and to-morrow
22. and let the priests also *s.* themselves
23. set bounds about the mount, and *s.* it
28. 41. thou shalt anoint and *s.* Aaron and his sons, 29. 33. | 40. 13. *Lev.* 8. 12. | 21. 8.
29. 27. thou shalt *s.* the breast of the wave offering
36. and thou shalt *s.* the altar, 37. | 40. 10.
44. I will *s.* the tabernacle and the altar
30. 29. and thou shalt *s.* the tabernacle and all his vessels, 40. 10, 11. *Lev.* 8. 11.
31. 13. ye may know that I am the Lord that doth *s.* you, *Lev.* 20. 8. | 21. 8. *Ezek.* 20. 12.
Lev. 11. 44. ye shall *s.* yourselves, 20. 7. *Num.* 11. 18. *Josh.* 3. 5. | 7. 13. 1 *Sam.* 16. 5.
21. 15. nor profane his seed, I the Lord do *s.* him
23. for I the Lord do *s.* them, 22. 9, 16.
27. 14. when a man shall *s.* his house to be holy
16. if a man shall *s.* his field, 17, 18, 22.
26. only the Lord's firstling, no man shall *s.* it
Num. 20. 12. ye believed me not, to *s.* me, 27. 14.
Deut. 5. 12. keep the sab.-day, to *s.* it, *Neh.* 13. 22.
15. 19. all the firstling males thou shalt *s.*
Josh. 7. 13. up, *s.* the people, *s.* yourselves
2 *Kings* 10. † 20. Jehu said, *s.* an assembly for Baal
1 *Chron.* 15. 12. *s.* yourselves, 2 *Chr.* 29. 5. | 35. 6.
23. 13. that he should *s.* the most holy things
2 *Chron.* 29. 34. Levites more upright in heart, to *s.*
30. 17. for every one that was not clean to *s.*
Isa. 8. 13. *s.* the L. of hosts himself, him your fear
29. 23. they shall *s.* the Holy One of Jacob
66. 17. they that *s.* themselves in gardens
Ezek. 36. 23. I will *s.* my gr. name which was profa.
37. 28. heathen know, that I the Lord do *s.* Israel
38. 23. thus will I magnify myself, and *s.* myself
44. 19. they shall not *s.* people with garments, 46. 20.
Joel 1. 14. *s.* ye a fast, 2. 15. || 3. † 9. *s.* war
2. 16. *s.* the congregation, assemble the elders
John 17. 17. *s.* them through thy truth, word is truth
19. and for their sakes I *s.* myself, that they may
Eph. 5. 26. that he might *s.* and cleanse the church
1 *Thess.* 5. 23. the very God of peace *s.* you wholly
Heb. 13. 12. that he might *s.* people with his blood
1 *Pet.* 3. 15. but *s.* the Lord God in your hearts

SANCTIFIED.

Gen. 2. 3. God blessed the seventh day and *s.* it
Exod. 19. 14. Moses *s.* the people, and they washed
29. 43. the tabernacle shall be *s.* by my glory
Lev. 8. 10. *s.* the tabernacle, and all that was therein
15. *s.* the altar || 30. *s.* Aaron and his garments
10. 3. I will be *s.* in them that come nigh me
27. 15. if he that *s.* it will redeem his house
19. and if he that *s.* the field will redeem it
Num. 7. 1. *s.* the tabernac. instruments, and vessels
8. 17. I *s.* the first-born of Israel for myself
Deut. 32. 51. because ye *s.* me not in the midst of Isr.
Josh. 20. † 7. and they *s.* the cities of refuge
1 *Sam.* 7. 1. *s.* Eleazar his son to keep the ark of L.
16. 5. he *s.* Jesse and his sons to the sacrifice
21. 5. though it were *s.* this day in the vessel
1 *Chr.* 15. 14. the priests and Levites *s.* themselves
2 *Chron.* 5. 11. all the priests present were *s.*
7. 16. I have chosen and *s.* this house, 20.
29. 15. gathered their brethren, and *s.* themselves
17. they *s.* the house of the Lord in 8 days
19. all the vessels have we prepared and *s.*
34. till the other priests had *s.* themselves
30. 3. the priests had not *s.* themselves sufficiently
8. enter into his sanctu. which he hath *s.* for ever
15. the Levites were ashamed, and *s.* themselves
17. many in the congregation were not *s.*
24. a great number of the priests *s.* themselves
31. 18. in their set office they *s.* themselves
Neh. 3. 1. they built and *s.* the sheep gate
12. 47. they *s.* holy things to the Levites, and the Levites *s.* them to the children of Aaron
Job 1. 5. Job sent and *s.* his sons and his daughters
Isa. 5. 16. holy God shall be *s.* in righteousness
13. 3. I have commanded my *s.* ones
Jer. 1. 5. I *s.* thee, and ordained thee a prophet
Ezek. 20. 41. I will be *s.* in you, 36. 23.
28. 22. when I shall be *s.* in her || 38. 16. shall *s.* thee
25. be *s.* in them in sight of the heathen, 39. 27.
48. 11. it shall be for the priests that are *s.*
Zeph. 1. † 7. for the Lord hath *s.* his guests
John 10. 36. say ye of him, whom the Father *s.*
17. 19. that they also might be *s.* thro' thy truth
Acts 20. 32. an inheritance among them *s.* 26. 18.
Rom. 15. 16. being *s.* by the Holy Ghost
1 *Cor.* 1. 2. to them that are *s.* in Christ Jesus
6. 11. but now ye are *s.* in the name of the Lord
7. 14. the unbelieving husband is *s.* wife is *s.*
1 *Tim.* 4. 5. it is *s.* by the word of God and prayer
2 *Tim.* 2. 21. shall be a vessel *s.* for the Master's use
Heb. 2. 11. and they who are *s.* are all of one
10. 10. by the which will we are *s.* through Jesus
14. he hath perfected for ever them that are *s.*
29. blood of the covenant wherewith he was *s.*
Jude 1. to them that are *s.* by God the Father

SANCTIFIETH.

Mat. 23. 17. or the temple that *s.* the gold?
19. greater the gift, or the altar that *s.* the gift?
Heb. 2. 11. both he that *s.* and they that are sanctified
9. 13. if blood of bulls *s.* to the purifying of the flesh

SANCTUARY

Signifies, *A holy or sanctified place, a dwelling-place of the Most High. They called by this name that part of the temple of* Jerusalem, *which was the most secret, and most retired of all the rest, in which was the ark of the covenant, and wherein none but the high priest might enter, and he but once in a year, which was upon the day of solemn expiation. The same name was also given to the most sacred part of the tabernacle, which was set up in the wilderness, and which remained still some time after the building of the temple: each of these were called* Sanctuary, *or the* Holy of Holies, *or the* Most Holy Place, *Lev.* 4. 6. 1 *Kings* 6. 16. *It was a square of twenty cubits, and divided from the* holy place *by a curtain or veil of rich cloth.* Solomon *had embellished the inside of it with palm-trees in* relievo, *and cherubims of wood covered with plates of gold; and in general, the whole* Sanctuary *was adorned, and, as it were, overlaid, with plates of gold. From between the cherubims which covered the mercy-seat, God gave answers to his people, when they consulted him about momentous and important matters; hence, says the* Psalmist, *The* Lord send thee help from the sanctuary, *Psal.* 20. 2. *It was a type of Heaven, which is also called by the name of* Sanctuary, *Psal.* 102. 19. For he hath looked down from the height of his Sanctuary; from heaven did the Lord behold the earth. Sometimes the word Sanctuary *is used in general for the temple, taking its denomination from its principal part.* 2 *Chron.* 20. 8. They have built thee a Sanctuary therein, for thy name. *Sometimes for the holy place, for the place appointed for the public worship of the Lord.* Psal. 73. 17. Until I went into the Sanctuary of God. *It is taken likewise for the holy land, the land of* Canaan. *Exod.* 15. 17. Thou shalt bring them in, and plant them in the Sanctuary which thy hands have established. *Or, by* Sanctuary *here may be understood the temple on mount* Moriah, *which God would certainly cause to be built and established: the past tense being put for the future, to note the certainty of it, according to the style of the prophets. It is said,* Psal. 114. 2. Judah is God's Sanctuary: *that is, The children of* Israel *are the people of God's holiness, as they are called,* Isa. 63. 18. *or his holy people, sanctified and set apart from all the nations of the world, to be his peculiar people and possession. Lastly,* Sanctuary *is taken for a refuge, defence, or protection,* Isa. 8. 14. He shall be your sanctuary. *Ezek.* 11. 16. I will be to them as a little Sanctuary.
Exod. 15. 17. thou shalt plant them in the *s.*
25. 8. let them make me a *s.* that I may dwell
30. 13. give every one after the shekel of the *s.*
24. of cassia 500 shekels after the shekel of the *s.*
36. 1. to work all manner of work for the *s.* 3. 4.
6. not make any more work for offering of the *s.*
38. 24. shekels, after the shekel of the *s.* 25, 26. *Lev.* 5. 15. | 27. 3, 25. *Num.* 3. 47, 50. | 7. 13, 19, 25, 31, 37. | 18. 16.
27. of 100 talents were cast the sockets of the *s.*
Lev. 4. 6. sprinkle the blood before the vail of the *s.*
10. 4. carry your brethren from before the *s.*
12. 4. nor come into the *s.* till her purifying fulfilled
16. 33. he shall make an atonement for the holy *s.*
19. 30. ye shall reverence my *s.* I am the Lord, 26. 2.
21. 12. neither shall he go out of the *s.* nor profane the *s.* of his God; I am the Lord
Num. 3. 28. males 8600, keeping charge of the *s.*
38. Aaron and his sons keeping charge of the *s.*
4. 12. wherewith they minister in the *s.*
15. when they have made an end of covering the *s.*
7. 9. the service of *s.* belonging unto them
8. 19. when children of Israel come nigh to the *s.*
10. 21. Kohathites set forward, bearing the *s.*
18. 1. with thee shall bear the iniquity of the *s.*
3. they shall not come nigh the vessels of the *s.*
5. and ye shall keep the charge of the *s.*
19. 20. because he hath defiled the *s.* of the Lord
Josh. 24. 26. he set up a great stone by the *s.*
1 *Chron.* 9. 29. to oversee the instruments of the *s.*
22. 19. arise, and build ye the *s.* of the Lord
24. 5. divided by lot, for the governors of the *s.*
28. 10. hath chosen to build an house for the *s.*
2 *Chron.* 20. 8. they have built thee a *s.* therein
26. 18. go out of the *s.* for thou hast trespassed
29. 21. for a sin offering for the *s.* and Judah
30. 8. but yield yourselves to Lord, enter into his *s.*
19. according to the purification of the *s.*
36. 17. the king of Babylon slew men in the *s.*
Neh. 10. 39. where are the vessels of the *s.*
Psal. 20. 2. the Lord send thee help from the *s.*
28. † 2. towards the oracle of thy holy *s.*
29. † 2. worship the Lord in his glorious *s.*
63. 2. to see thee, as I have seen thee in the *s.*
68. 24. they have seen thy goings in the *s.*
73. 17. till I went into the *s.* of God, I understood
74. 3. all that the enemy hath done wickedly in *s.*
7. they have cast fire into thy *s.* they have defiled
77. 13. thy way, O God, is in the *s.* who so great
78. 54. he brought them to the border of his *s.*
69. and he built his *s.* like high palaces
96. 6. strength and beauty are in his *s.*
102. 19. he hath looked from the height of his *s.*
114. 2. Judah was his *s.* Israel his dominion
134. 2. lift up your hands in the *s.* bless the Lord
150. 1. praise the Lord, praise God in his *s.*
Isa. 8. 14. the Lord of hosts, he shall be for a *s.*
16. 12. that he shall come to his *s.* to pray
43. 28. I have profaned the princes of the *s.*
60. 13. to beautify the place of my *s.*
63. 18. our adversaries have trodden down thy *s.*
Jer. 17. 12. from the beginning is the place of our *s.*
Lam. 1. 10. hath seen the heathen entered into her *s.*
2. 7. the Lord hath abhorred his *s.*
20. shall the priest and prophet be slain in the *s.*?
4. 1. stones of the *s.* are poured out in the street
Ezek. 5. 11. because thou hast defiled my *s.*
11. 16. yet will I be to them as a little *s.*
23. 38. they defiled my *s.* in the same day
39. they came the same day into my *s.* to profane it
42. 20. between the *s.* and the profane place
44. 5. with every going forth of the *s.*
27. and in the day that he goeth into the *s.*
45. 3. in it shall be the *s.* and most holy place
47. 12. because their waters they issued out of the *s.*
48. 8. the *s.* shall be in the midst of it, 10, 21.
Dan. 8. 11. and the place of his *s.* was cast down
13. to give the *s.* to be trodden under foot
14. he said to me, then shall the *s.* be cleansed
Dan. 9. 17. and cause thy face to shine upon thy *s.*
26. the people shall destroy the city and the *s.*
11. 31. they shall pollute the *s.* of strength
Amos 7. † 13. Bethel is the king's *s.* and court
Zeph. 3. 4. her priests have polluted the *s.*
Heb. 8. 2. a minister of the *s.* and the true tabernacle
9. 1. verily the first covenant had a worldly *s.*
2. there was a tabernacle, which is called the *s.*
13. 11. whose blood is brought into the *s.*

SANCTUARIES.

Lev. 21. 23. shalt not go in, that he profane not my *s.*
26. 31. and I will bring your *s.* to desolation
Jer. 51. 51. strangers are come into *s.* of Lord's house
Ezek. 28. 18. hast defiled thy *s.* by thine iniquities
Amos 7. 9. the *s.* of Israel shall be laid waste

SAND.

A similitude taken from the sand *of the sea, is often made use of, to express a very great multitude, or a very great weight, or something very grievous and intolerable. God promises* Abraham *and* Jacob, *to multiply their posterity as the stars of heaven, and as the* sand of the sea, Gen. 22. 17. | 32. 12. Job *compares the weight of his afflictions and troubles to that of the sand of the sea.* Job 6. 3. Oh that my grief were weighed, for now it would be heavier than the sand of the sea. *And* Solomon *says,* that the sand and gravel are very heavy things, yet the anger of a fool is much heavier, *Prov.* 27. 3. *A fool's anger is more insupportable, more intolerable, as being without cause, without measure, without end.* Sand *is likewise of a slippery nature; hence it is said, that a house built upon it cannot stand,* Mat. 7. 26.
The prophet Jeremiah *magnifies the omnipotence of God, who has fixed the sand of the shore for the boundaries of the sea, and has said to it,* Hitherto thou shalt come, and here thou shalt break thy foaming waves, and shalt pass no further, *Jer.* 5. 22.
Gen. 22. 17. multiply thy seed as the *s.* 32. 12.
41. 49. Joseph gathered corn as the *s.* of the sea
Exod. 2. 12. he slew and hid the Egyptian in the *s.*
Deut. 33. 19. they shall suck of treasures hid in *s.*
Josh. 11. 4. there went out much people as the *s.*
Judg. 7. 12. their camels were as the *s.* by the sea
1 *Sam.* 13. 5. the Philist. gathered to fight as the *s.*
2 *Sam.* 17. 11. that all Israel be gathered as the *s.*
1 *Kings* 4. 20. Judah and Israel are many, as the *s.*
29. God gave Solomon largeness of heart as the *s.*
Job 6. 3. for now it would be heavier than the *s.*
29. 18. and I shall multiply my days as the *s.*
Psal. 78. 27. and feathered fowls like as the *s.*
139. 18. they are more in number than the *s.*
Prov. 27. 3. a stone is heavy, and the *s.* weighty
Isa. 10. 22. tho' thy people Isr. be as *s.* of the sea
48. 19. thy seed also had been as *s.* and offspring
Jer. 5. 22. which placed the *s.* for the bound of the sea
15. 8. that widows are increased to me above the *s.*
33. 22. as the *s.* of the sea, cannot be measured
Hos. 1. 10. Israel shall be as *s.* of sea, *Rom.* 9. 27.
Hab. 1. 9. they shall gather the captivity as the *s.*
Mat. 7. 26. a foolish man who built his house on *s.*
Heb. 11. 12. there sprang of one so many as the *s.*
Rev. 13. 1. I stood upon the *s.* of the sea and saw
20. 8. the number of whom is as the *s.* of the sea

SANDALS

At first were only soles tied to the feet with strings or thongs; afterwards they were covered; and at last they called even shoes sandals.
Mark 6. 9. but be shod with *s.* put not on two coats
Acts 12. 8. angel said, gird thyself, and bind thy *s.*

SANG.

Exod. 15. 1. then *s.* Moses and Israel this song
Num. 21. 17. Israel *s.* this song, spring, O well
Judg. 5. 1. then *s.* Deborah and Barak, saying
1 *Sam.* 29. 5. is not this David of whom they *s.*?
2 *Chr.* 29. 28. the singers *s.* the trumpeters sounded
30. *s.* praises with gladness, and bowed their heads
Neh. 12. 42. the singers *s.* aloud, with Jezrahiah
Job 38. 7. when the morning stars *s.* together
Psal. 106. 12. they believed his words, *s.* his praise
Acts 16. 25. Paul and Silas *s.* praises to God

SANK.

Exod. 15. 5. they *s.* into the bottom as a stone
10. they *s.* as lead in the mighty waters

SAP.

Psal. 104. 16. the trees of the Lord are full of *s.*

SAPPHIRE,

Is a precious stone, second only to the diamond in lustre, hardness, and price: there is frequent mention made of it in Scripture: Job *says,* there are places whose stones are sapphires, *Job* 28. 6. *that is, that* sapphires, *and other precious stones, are very common in some countries; they are mixed with the stones, and cut out of them and polished.* Pliny *says, that the best came out of* Media; *perhaps, out of the country of the* Sapires, *or from mount* Sephar, *mentioned by* Moses, *Gen.* 10. 30. *The oriental* sapphire *is of a blue sky-colour, or a fine azure; whence it is, that the prophets describe the throne of God, as it were of the colour of a* sapphire; *that is, of a celestial blue, or azure,* Exod. 24. 10.
Exod. 24. 10. as it were a paved work of *s.* stone
28. 18. the second row a *s.* a diamond, 39. 11.
Job 28. 16. wisdom cannot be valued with onyx or *s.*
Lam. 4. 7. her Nazarites, their polishing was of *s.*
Ezek. 1. 26. likeness of a throne, as appearance of *s.*
10. 1. there appeared over them as it were a *s.*
28. 13. the *s.* and the emerald were thy covering
Rev. 21. 19. the second foundation of the wall was *s.*

SAPPHIRES.

Job 28. 6. the stones of it are the place of *s.*
Cant. 5. 14. his belly as bright ivory, overlaid with *s.*
Isa. 54. 11. I will lay thy foundations with *s.*

SARDINE.

Rev. 4. 3. he was to look upon like a *s.* stone

SARDIUS,

Or Ruby, in Hebrew, Odem: *A gem found about Sardis, of a bloody colour; some translate it by* ruby, *or by* pyropus. *It was the first in* Aaron's *breast-plate.*

Exod. 28. 17. the first row shall be a s. 39. 10.
Ezek. 28. 13. the s. and diamond were thy covering
Rev. 21. 20. the sixth foundation of the wall was a s.

SARDONYX,

As if it were a Sardius united to an Onyx, as partaking of both their colours. The Onyx is a precious stone, commonly called Cornelian. The basis of the Cornelian is white, as the nail growing under the flesh. The Hebrew word Shohem has been translated by Sardonychus Lapis, which rather signifies an Emerald.
Rev. 21. 20. fifth foundation of wall of city was a s.

SAT.

Gen. 31. 34. Rach. had taken and s. upon the images
38. 14. Tamar covered with a vail, s. in open place
Exod. 12. 29. first-born of Pharaoh that s. on throne
16. 3. when we s. by the flesh-pots, and did eat
18. 13. on the morrow Moses s. to judge the people
Judg. 20. 26. they wept and s. before the Lord
1 Sam. 1. 9. how Eli s. on a seat by post of temple
4. 13. Eli s. on a seat by the wayside, watching
1 Kings 16. 11. as soon as he s. on his throne, he slew
21. 13. the children of Belial s. before Naboth
22. 10. the two kings s. each on his throne
2 Kings 6. 32. but Elisha s. in his house, and elders s. with him, and the king sent a messenger
1 Chron. 17. 1. as David s. in his house, he said
16. David s. before the Ld. and said, who am I?
Neh. 8. 17. they made booths, and s. under them
Job 29. 25. I chose out their way, and s. chief
Psal. 26. 4. I have not s. with vain persons
Jer. 3. 2. in the ways hast thou s. for them
15. 17. I s. not in the assembly of the mockers, nor rejoiced, I s. alone because of thy hand
36. 22. now the king s. in the winter-house
Ezek. 3. 15. I s. where they s. and remained there
8. 1. as I s. in my house, the elders s. before me
14. behold, there s. women weeping for Tammuz
20. 1. the elders came to inquire of the Ld. and s.
Dan. 2. 49. but Daniel s. in the gate of the king
Mat. 4. 16. people who s. in darkness saw great light; to them that s. in shadow of death light is sprung up
14. 9. for them which s. with him, Mark 6. 26.
26. 55. I s. daily with you teaching in the temple
58. Peter s. with the servants to see the end
Mark 10. 46. blind Bartimeus s. by the wayside begging, Luke 18. 35. John 9. 8.
16. 19. and he s. on the right hand of God
Luke 7. 15. he that was dead s. up, and beg. to speak
10. 39. Mary s. at Jesus' feet, and heard his words
19. 30. a colt whereon never man s. Mark 11. 2.
John 4. 6. Jesus wearied, s. thus on the well
Acts 2. 3. cloven tongues s. upon each of them
3. 10. he who s. for alms at the beautiful gate
Rev. 4. 3. he that s. on the throne was like a jasper
14. 14. on the cloud one s. like the Son of man
19. 11. he that s. upon him was called Faithful
19. to make war against him that s. on the horse

SAT down.

Exod. 32. 6. the people s. down to eat and to drink
Deut. 33. 3. and they s. down at thy feet
Ezra 9. 3. plucked off hair, and s. down astonied
10. 16. they s. down to examine the matter
Neh. 1. 4. I s. down and mourned certain days
Esth. 3. 15. the king and Haman s. down to drink
Job 2. 8. Job s. down among the ashes
Psal. 137. 1. there we s. down, yea, we wept
Cant. 2. 3. I s. down under his shadow with delight
Mat. 9. 10. many sinners came and s. down with him
26. 20. he s. down with the twelve, Luke 22. 14.
Luke 4. 20. gave book to the minister, and s. down
5. 3. s. down and taught the people out of the ship
John 8. 2. people came, he s. down and taught them
Acts 13. 14. they went into the synag. and s. down
16. 13. we s. down and spake to the women
Heb. 1. 3. s. down on the right hand of God, 10. 12.

SATAN,

Or Sathan, or Sathanas: this is a mere Hebrew word, and signifies an adversary, an enemy, an accuser. Satan, in Scripture, is sometimes taken in the sense of an adversary; for example, Christ says to Peter, Get thee behind me, Satan, thou art an offence unto me, Mat. 16. 23. That is, Begone, O mine adversary, thou that withstandest what I most desire, and what I came into the world about, namely, to lay down my life for the elect; in that thou dissuadest me from this, thou art an enemy to the redemption and salvation of mankind, which is a work fit for none but a devil. But most commonly Satan is taken for the Devil, Mat. 12. 26. If Satan cast out Satan, he is divided against himself. Rev. 20. 2. He laid hold on the dragon, that old serpent, which is the Devil and Satan, and bound him a thousand years. He is said to stand at Joshua's right hand, and to accuse him and the Jews before God, and to oppose them in building the temple, Zech. 3. 1.

The kingdom of Satan, Mat. 12. 26. Our Saviour represents Satan as a monarch, who has other subordinate devils obedient to him. Beelzebub is, as it were, their king. If Beelzebub, says he, cast out devils, his kingdom is divided against itself, he labours for his own ruin, which is by no means credible; it is therefore false, that I drive out devils in the name of Beelzebub. The apostle Paul declares in Acts 26. 18. that all those who believe not in Christ are under the empire and power of Satan.

The synagogue of Satan, of which the evangelist John makes mention, Rev. 2. 9. are probably the unbelieving Jews, the false zealots for the law of Moses, who at the beginning were the most eager persecutors of the Christians. They were very numerous at Smyrna, to the angel of which church St. John speaks in this passage.

The depths of Satan. St. John, writing to the Christians of the church of Thyatira, says to them, You know not the depths of Satan; which have not known the depths of Sathan, τα βαθεα τȣ σατανȣ, Rev. 2. 24. That is, the mysteries of the Nicolaitans, and of the Simonians, who concealed their errors under a mysterious abstruseness: they spoke of certain intelligences that had created the world, and that were in opposition to the Creator. They taught a profound knowledge concerning the nature of the angels, and their different degrees. They had secret books written in an abstruse and mysterious manner; and these are called the depths of Satan.

When Christ sent forth his disciples to preach in the cities and villages of Judea, they returned back with great joy, and told him, saying, Lord, even the devils are subject to us through thy name. Jesus tells them, I beheld Satan as lightning fall from heaven, Luke 10. 17, 18. He seems to allude to that passage of Isaiah; How art thou fallen from heaven, O Lucifer, son of the morning! Isa. 14. 12. By which he insinuated, that the kingdom of the devil was coming to a period; that Satan should soon lose his power and dominion in the world, by the preaching and miracles of the apostles. And in Luke 22. 31. he says, Simon, Simon, behold, Satan hath desired to have you, that he may sift you as wheat; but I have prayed for thee that thy faith fail not; shewing thereby what vain efforts the devil would make to destroy the infant church.

By collecting the passages where Satan or the Devil is mentioned, it may be observed: that he fell from heaven, with all his company; that God cast him down from thence for the punishment of his pride; that by his envy and malice, sin, death, and all other evils, came into the world; that by the permission of God he exercises a sort of government in the world over his subordinates, over apostate angels like himself: that God makes use of him to prove good men, and chastise bad ones; that he is a lying spirit in the mouth of false prophets, seducers, and heretics; that it is he, or some of his, that torment or possess men, that inspire them with evil designs, as he did David when he suggested to him to number his people, and to Judas to betray his Lord and Master, and to Ananias and Sapphira, to conceal the price of their field. That he roves full of rage, like a roaring lion, to tempt, to betray, to destroy us, and to involve us in guilt and wickedness. That his power and malice are restrained within certain limits, and controlled by the will of God. In a word, that he is an enemy to God and man, and uses his utmost endeavours to rob God of his glory, and men of their souls. See DEVIL.

1 Chron. 21. 1. s. provoked David to number Israel
Job 1. 6. and s. came also among them, 2. 1.
12. s. went out from the presence of the Lord
Psal. 109. 6. and let s. stand at his right hand
Zech. 3. 1. s. standing at his right hand to resist him
2. the Lord said to s. the Lord rebuke thee, O s.
Mat. 4. 10. Jesus saith to him, get thee hence, s.
12. 26. if s. cast out s. Mark 3. 23, 26. Luke 11. 18.
16. 23. get thee behind me, s. Mark 8. 33. Luke 4. 8.
Mark 4. 15. s. cometh and taketh away the word
Luke 10. 18. I beheld s. as lightning fall from heaven
13. 16. whom s. hath bound these eighteen years
22. 3. then entered s. into Judas Iscariot, of twelve
31. Simon, Simon, s. hath desired to have you
John 13. 27. and after the sop, s. entered into him
Acts 5. 3. why hath s. filled thine heart to lie?
26. 18. to turn them from the power of s. to God
Rom. 16. 20. God shall bruise s. under your feet
1 Cor. 5. 5. to deliver such an one to s. that spirit
7. 5. that s. tempt you not for your incontinency
2 Cor. 2. 11. lest s. should get an advantage of us
11. 14. s. himself is transformed into angel of light
12. 7. was given me the messenger of s. to buffet me
1 Thess. 2. 18. we would have come, but s. hind. us
2 Thess. 2. 9. whose coming is after the working of s.
1 Tim. 1. 20. whom I have delivered unto s.
5. 15. for some are already turned aside after s.
Rev. 2. 9. are not Jews, but the synagogue of s.
13. where Satan's seat is, where s. dwelleth
24. and who have not known the depths of s.
3. 9. I will make them of the synagogue of s.
12. 9. the great dragon was cast out, called s.
20. 2. he laid hold on the dragon, which is s.
7. s. shall be loosed out of his prison

SATIATE.

Jer. 31. 14. I will s. soul of the priests with fatness
46. 10. the sword shall be s. with their blood

SATIATED.

Jer. 31. 25. I have s. the weary soul, and replenished

SATISFACTION.

Num. 35. 31. shall take no s. for life of a murderer
32. shall take no s. for him that is fled for refuge

SATISFY.

Job 38. 27. to s. the desolate and waste ground
Psal. 90. 14. O s. us early with thy mercy
91. 16. with long life will I s. him, and shew salvat.
132. 15. I will s. her poor with bread
Prov. 5. 19. let her breasts s. thee at all times
6. 30. if he steal to s. his soul when he is hungry
Isa. 58. 10. if thou s. the afflicted soul, then thy light
11. Lord shall guide and s. thy soul in drought
Ezek. 7. 19. they shall not s. their souls, nor fill
Mark 8. 4. whence can a man s. these with bread

SATISFIED.

Exod. 15. 9. my lust shall be s. upon them
Lev. 26. 26. and ye shall eat and not be s.
Deut. 14. 29. the fatherless shall eat and be s.
33. 23. O Naphtali, s. with favour, and full
Job 19. 22. and why are ye not s. with my flesh?
27. 14. his offspring shall not be s. with bread
31. 31. oh that we had of his flesh! we cannot be s.
Psal. 17. 15. I shall be s. when awake with thy liken.
22. 26. the meek shall eat and be s. they shall praise
36. 8. they shall be s. with the fatness of thy house
37. 19. in the days of famine they shall be s.
59. 15. and let them grudge if they be not s.
63. 5. my soul shall be s. as with mar. and fatness
65. 4. we shall be s. with the goodness of thy house
81. 16. with honey out of rock should I have s. thee
Ps. 104. 13. the earth is s. with the fruit of thy works
105. 40. he s. them with the bread of heaven
Prov. 12. 11. he that tilleth his land shall be s.
14. a man be s. with good by the fruit of his mouth
14. 14. and a good man shall be s. from himself
18. 20. a man's belly be s. with fruit of his mouth
19. 23. and he that hath it shall abide s.
20. 13. open thine eyes, and thou shalt be s.
30. 15. there are three things that are never s.
Eccl. 1. 8. the eye is not s. with seeing, nor the ear
4. 8. neither is his eye s. with riches
5. 10. that loveth silver, shall not be s. with silver
Isa. 9. 20. shall eat and not be s. Mic. 6. 14.
44. 16. he roasteth roast and is s. he warms himself
53. 11. he shall see of travail of his soul, and be s.
66. 11. be s. with the breasts of her consolations
Jer. 31. 14. my people shall be s. with goodness
50. 10. all that spoil Chaldea shall be s. saith Lord
19. and his soul shall be s. on mount Ephraim
Lam. 5. 6. have given the hand to Egyptians to be s.
Ezek. 16. 28. and yet thou couldest not be s. 29.
Amos 4. 8. wandered to drink water, but were not s.
Hab. 2. 5. he is as death, and cannot be s.

SATISFIEST.

Psal. 145. 16. and thou s. the desire of every thing

SATISFIETH.

Psal. 103. 5. who s. thy mouth with good things
107. 9. for he s. the longing soul, and filleth hungry
Isa. 55. 2. and your labour for that which s. not

SATISFYING.

Prov. 13. 25. the righteous eateth to s. of his soul
Col. 2. 23. not in any honour to the s. of the flesh

SATTEST.

Psal. 9. 4. thou s. in the throne judging right
Ezek. 23. 41. thou s. upon a stately bed and a table

SATYR.

Isa. 34. 14. and the s. shall cry to his fellow

SATYRS.

Isa. 13. 21. owls shall dwell there, and s. dance there

SAVE

Signifies, 1. To deliver from temporal dangers, and protect and defend any one in them, Mat. 14. 30. Peter cried, saying, Lord, save me.
2. To deliver from the guilt, to free from the power and pollution of sin, Mat. 1. 21. For he shall save his people from their sins. Thus only Christ saves his people: they are justified by the imputation of his righteousness: and by the operation of his Spirit they are sanctified, the power and dominion of sin are subdued and weakened, and at last sin is utterly destroyed.
3. To obtain eternal life, Mat. 10. 22. But he that endureth to the end shall be saved.

Salvation is attributed,
1. To God, Jer. 17. 14. Save me, O Lord, and I shall be saved. God is often called by the name of Saviour, 2 Sam. 22. 3. The Lord is my refuge and my Saviour, Hos. 13. 4. There is no Saviour besides me, Isa. 45. 15. Verily thou art a God that hidest thyself, O God of Israel, the Saviour. God is the Saviour of saviours, and the God of gods: without him there is neither salvation, nor deliverance, nor succour to be hoped for. It is he that raises up Saviours to his people. He raised them up a Saviour in the person of Othniel, the son of Kenez, against the king of Mesopotamia, who oppressed them, Judg. 3. 9. He raised them up another in Ehud son of Gerah, against Eglon, king of the Moabites, Judg. 3. 15. And Obadiah promises, that the Lord will send Saviours upon the mountain of Zion, to judge the mountain of Esau, Obad. 21.
2. To Christ. The name Saviour is appropriated to the Messiah, who was prefigured by all those to whom the scriptures of the Old Testament give the name of Saviour, as Joshua, the judge of Israel, the kings, David, Solomon, Josiah, and the great men raised up in an extraordinary manner to deliver the people of God. The prophets had marked out Christ under the name of Saviour, Isa. 19. 20. The Lord shall send them a Saviour, and a great One, and he shall deliver them. And the apostles and sacred writers of the New Testament generally give to Christ the name of Saviour by way of eminence. When the angel proclaimed his birth, he said that he should be called Jesus, that is, a Saviour, for he shall save his people from their sins, Mat. 1. 21. And in John 4. 42. he is called the Saviour of the world. See Acts 13. 23. Phil. 3. 20.

This name is properly given to Christ. He saves his people from sin, from hell, and destruction: he hath not only merited salvation for them by his death; but he applies the purchased redemption by shedding abroad the Holy Ghost into their hearts, and by maintaining and constantly preserving the graces that are implanted in them, as the natural head doth distil and derive sense, motion, and life, into the natural body. He is a Saviour by merit, and a Saviour by efficacy: Hence he is said to be the Author of eternal salvation to all them that obey him, Heb. 5. 9. And to have obtained eternal redemption for us, Heb. 9. 12.
3. Salvation is attributed to faith, to the word of God, to baptism, and to men: These are only instruments and means which God makes use of either for beginning or furthering this work, Luke 7. 50. Jesus said to the woman, thy faith hath saved thee, go in peace. Jam. 1. 21. Receive with meekness the ingrafted word, which is able to save your souls. 1 Pet. 3. 21. The like figure whereunto, even baptism, doth also now save us. Rom. 11. 14. If by any means I may provoke to emulation them which are my flesh, and might save, that is, be an instrument of saving, some of them. And in 1 Cor. 7. 16. For what knowest thou, O wife, whether thou shalt save thy husband? or how knowest thou, O man, whether thou shalt save thy wife? The word directs and points out where salvation may be had; faith is the hand or instrument that receives Christ the author of salvation; baptism becomes an

effectual means of salvation, not from any virtue that is in the outward administration of it, but only by the blessing of Christ, *and the working of his Spirit in them that receive it, inclining and enabling them to believe and heartily to acquiesce in the covenant, which they make with God at baptism, whereof it is the seal. Good men likewise, by their admonitions and good example, are made instrumental in converting others to the faith,* Jam. 5. 20.

In Eph. 2. 5, 8. *it is said*, By grace ye are saved. [1] *In respect of God's eternal purpose, looking to nothing in the creature, but decreeing and purposing all benefits to them out of his free love and favour.* [2] *Because all the parts of this salvation are from this grace : as,* Conversion. *Gal.* 1. 15. When it pleased God, who separated me from my mother's womb, and called me by his grace. *Justification. Tit.* 3. 7. That being justified by his grace, we should be made heirs, according to the hope of eternal life. *All our qualifications and endowments, yea, and all the good we do, are of grace.* 1 *Cor.* 15. 10. By the grace of God I am what I am. *The outward means of salvation are of grace. Rom.* 10. 15. How shall they preach, except they be sent? *Eph.* 4. 8. He gave gifts unto men. *The price of our redemption was freely paid. John* 10. 17, 18. Therefore doth my Father love me, because I lay down my life, that I might take it again. No man taketh it from me, but I lay it down of myself. *The kingdom of heaven is freely prepared for us. John* 14. 2. I go to prepare a place for you. *And eternal life is freely bestowed. Rom.* 6. 23. But the gift of God is eternal life, through Jesus Christ our Lord.

Gen. 45. 7. God sent me before you to *s.* your lives
Deut. 20. 4. the Lord goeth with you to *s.* you
22. 27. she cried, and there was none to *s.* her
28. 29. shall be spoiled, and no man shall *s.* thee
Judg. 6. 14. go in this thy might, thou shalt *s.* Israel
15. O my Lord, wherewith shall I *s.* Israel?
31. will ye plead for Baal? will ye *s.* him?
36. if thou wilt *s.* Israel by mine hand, as hast said
37. then shall I know that thou wilt *s.* Israel
7. 7. by the 300 men that lapped will I *s.* you
1 *Sam.* 9. 16. anoint him, that he may *s.* my people
10. 24. the people shouted and said, God *s.* the king
2 *Sam.* 16. 16. 2 *Kings* 11. 12. 2 *Chron.* 23. 11.
14. 6. there is no restraint, to *s.* by many, or by few
19. 11. if thou *s.* not thyself this night, shall be slain
23. 2. the Lord said to David, go and *s.* Keilah
2 *Sam.* 3. 18. by the hand of David I will *s.* Israel
22. 28. the afflicted people thou wilt *s.* *Psal.* 18. 27.
42. but there was none to *s.* them, *Psal.* 18. 41.
1 *Kings* 1. 12. that thou mayest *s.* thine own life
25. behold, they say, God *s.* king Adonijah
34. blow trumpet, say, God *s.* king Solomon, 39.
20. 31. go to king, peradventure he will *s.* thy life
2 *Kings* 19. 34. for I will defend this city to *s.* it, for my own sake and servant David's sake, *Isa.* 37. 35.
Neh. 6. 11. would go into the temple to *s.* his life
Job 2. 6. behold, he is in thine hand, but *s.* his life
20. 20. he shall not *s.* of that which he desired
22. 29. and he shall *s.* the humble person
40. 14. that thine own right hand can *s.* thee
Psal. 12. † 1. *s.* Lord, for the godly man ceaseth
20. 9. *s.* Lord, let the king hear us when we call
28. 9. *s.* thy people, feed them also, *Jer.* 31. 7.
37. 40. he shall *s.* them, because they trust in him
44. 3. neither did their own arm *s.* them
60. 5. *s.* with thy right hand, and hear me, 108. 6.
69. 35. for God will *s.* Zion, and will build Judah
72. 4. he shall *s.* the children of the needy
13. and he shall *s.* the souls of the needy
76. 9. when God arose to *s.* the meek of the earth
86. 2. O my God, *s.* thy servant that trusteth in thee
16. and *s.* the son of thine handmaid
109. 31. *s.* him from those that condemn his soul
118. 25. *s.* I beseech thee, O Lord, send prosperity
145. 19. he also will hear their cry, and *s.* them
Prov. 20. 22. wait on the Lord, and he shall *s.* thee
Isa. 35. 4. behold, your God will come and *s.* you
45. 20. and pray unto a god that cannot *s.*
46. 7. he cannot answer, nor *s.* him out of trouble
47. 13. let now the astrologers stand up and *s.* thee
15. they shall wander, none shall *s.* thee
49. 25. thus saith the Lord, I will *s.* thy children
59. 1. Lord's hand is not shortened, that it cannot *s.*
63. 1. I that speak in righteousness, mighty to *s.*
Jer. 2. 28. let them arise, if they can *s.* thee
11. 12. but they shall not *s.* them at all in trouble
14. 9. shouldest be as a mighty man that cannot *s.*
15. 20. for I am with thee to *s.* thee, and to deliver thee, saith the Lord, 30. 11. | 42. 11. | 46. 27.
30. 10. O Isr. I will *s.* thee from afar, and thy seed
48. 6. flee, *s.* your lives, be like the heath in wilder.
Ezek. 3. 18. to warn the wicked, to *s.* his life
13. † 22. should not return, that I should *s.* his life
34. 22. therefore will I *s.* my flock, and will judge
36. 29. I will *s.* you ‖ 37. 23. I will *s.* them
Hos. 1. 7. but I will *s.* them by the Lord their God, and will not *s.* them by bow nor by sword
13. 10. where is there any other that may *s.* thee?
Hab. 1. 2. cry to thee of violence, and thou wilt not *s.*
Zeph. 3. 17. he will *s.*, he will rejoice over thee
19. I will *s.* her that halteth, and gather her
Zech. 8. 7. I will *s.* my people from the east country
9. 16. the Lord their God shall *s.* them in the day
10. 6. and I will *s.* the house of Joseph
12. 7. the Lord also shall *s.* the tents of Judah first
Mat. 1. 21. Jesus, shall *s.* his people from their sins
16. 25. for whosoever will *s.* his life shall lose it, *Mark* 8. 35. *Luke* 9. 24. | 17. 33.
18. 11. for the Son of man is come to *s.* that which was lost, *Luke* 19. 10.
27. 40. saying, thou that destroyest the temple, and buildest it in three days, *s.* thyself, *Mark* 15. 30.
42. saved others, himself he cannot *s.* *Mark* 15. 31.
49. let us see whether Elias will come to *s.* him
Mark 3. 4. is it lawful to *s.* life, or to kill? *Luke* 6. 9.
Luke 9. 56. is not come to destr. men's lives, but to *s.*
Luke 23. 35. let him *s.* himself, if he be Christ
37. *s.* thyself ‖ 39. if Christ, *s.* thyself and us
John 12. 47. I came not to judge, but to *s.* the world
Acts 2. 40. *s.* yourselves from this generation
27. 43. but the centurion, willing to *s.* Paul
Rom. 11. 14. if I might *s.* some of them, 1 *Cor.* 9. 22.
1 *Cor.* 1. 21. by the foolishness of preach. to *s.* them
7. 16. shalt *s.* thy husband, shalt *s.* thy wife
1 *Tim.* 1. 15. Christ came into the world to *s.* sinners
4. 16. in doing this thou shalt *s.* thyself and them
Heb. 5. 7. to him that was able to *s.* him from death
7. 25. he is able also to *s.* them to the uttermost
Jam. 1. 21. the word, which is able to *s.* your souls
2. 14. and have not works, can faith *s.* him
4. 12. one lawgiver, who is able to *s.* and to destroy
5. 15. the prayer of faith shall *s.* the sick
20. shall *s.* a soul from death, and hide sins
Jude 23. others *s.* with fear, pulling them out of fire

See ALIVE.

SAVE *me*.

2 *Kings* 16. 7. *s. me* out of hand of the king of Syria
Psal. 3. 7. arise, O Lord, *s. me*, O my God
6. 4. *s. me* for thy mercies' sake, 31. 16. | 109. 26.
7. 1. *s. me* from all them that persecute me
22. 21. *s. me* from the lion's mouth, thou hast heard
31. 2. be thou for an house of defence to *s. me*
44. 6. not trust in bow, nor shall my sword *s. me*
54. 1. *s. me*, O God, by thy name, and judge me
55. 16. I will call on God, and the Lord shall *s. me*
57. 3. he shall send from heaven and *s. me*
59. 2. deliver me, and *s. me* from bloody men
69. 1. *s. me*, for waters are come in unto my soul
71. 2. incline thine ear unto me, and *s. me*
3. thou hast given commandment to *s. me*
119. 94. *s. me*, for I have sought thy precepts
146. I cried unto thee, *s. me*, and I shall keep
138. 7. and thy right hand shall *s. me*
Isa. 38. 20. the Lord was ready to *s. me*, we will sing
Jer. 17. 14. O Lord, *s. me*, and I shall be saved
Mat. 14. 30. Peter cried, saying, Lord, *s. me*
John 12. 27. Father, *s. me* from this hour

SAVE *us*.

Josh. 10. 6. come up to us quickly, and *s. us*
22. 22. if it be in rebellion, *s. us* not this day
1 *Sam.* 4. 3. the ark may *s. us* from our enemies
7. 8. cease not to cry to the Lord, that he will *s. us*
10. 27. men of Belial said, how shall this man *s. us?*
11. 3. if there be no man to *s. us*, we will come
2 *Kings* 19. 19. *s.* thou *us* out of his hand, *Isa.* 37. 20.
1 *Chron.* 16. 35. *s. us*, O God of our salvation
Ps. 80. 2. stir up thy strength, and come and *s. us*
106. 47. *s. us*, O Lord our God, and gather us
Isa. 25. 9. we have waited for him, he will *s. us*
33. 22. the Lord is our king, he will *s.* us
Jer. 2. 27. in their trouble they will say, *s. us*
Lam. 4. 17. watched for a nation that could not *s. us*
Hos. 14. 3. Asshur shall not *s. us*, we will not ride
Mat. 8. 25. they awoke him, saying, Lord, *s. us*
1 *Pet.* 3. 21. even baptism, doth also now *s. us*

SAVE, for *Besides*.

Gen. 14. 24. *s.* what the young men have eaten
39. 6. he knew not aught, *s.* the bread he did eat
Exod. 12. 16. *s.* that which every man must eat
22. 20. he that sacrificeth to any god, *s.* to the Lord
Num. 14. 30. *s.* Caleb, 26. 65. | 32. 12. *Deut.* 1. 36.
Deut. 15. 4. *s.* when there shall be no poor among you
Josh. 11. 13. Israel burned none, *s.* Hazor only
19. that made peace with Israel, *s.* the Hivites
14. 4. they gave no part to the Levites, *s.* cities
Judg. 7. 14. is nothing else, *s.* the sword of Gideon
1 *Sam.* 21. 9. there is none other, *s.* that here
30. 17. there escaped none, *s.* 400 young men
22. *s.* to every man his wife and his children
2 *Sam.* 12. 3. poor man had nothing, *s.* one ewe lamb
22. 32. who is God, *s.* the Lord? *Psal.* 18. 31.
1 *Kings* 3. 18. was no stranger in the house, *s.* we two
8. 9. there was nothing in the ark *s.* the two tables
15. 5. *s.* in the matter of Uriah the Hittite
22. 31. fight not, *s.* with the king of Israel
2 *Kings* 4. 2. hath not any thing, *s.* a pot of oil
15. 4. *s.* that the high places were not removed
2 *Chron.* 2. 6. *s.* only to burn sacrifice before him
21. 17. no son left, *s.* Jehoahaz the youngest
Neh. 2. 12. nor any with me, *s.* the beast I rode on
Dan. 6. 7. ask a petition, *s.* of thee, O king, 12.
Mat. 11. 27. nor knoweth any the Father, *s.* Son
13. 57. not without honour, *s.* in his own country
17. 8. they saw no man, *s.* Jesus only, *Mark* 9. 8.
19. 11. cannot receive, *s.* they to whom it is given
Mark 5. 37. and he suffered no man to follow him, *s.* Peter, James, and John, *Luke* 8. 51.
6. 5. *s.* that he laid his hands upon a few sick folk
8. that they should take nothing, *s.* a staff only
Luke 4. 26. sent, *s.* unto Sarepta, a city of Sidon
17. 18. none found that returned, *s.* this stranger
18. 19. none is good, *s.* one, that is God
John 6. 22. there was no other boat, *s.* that one
46. hath seen the Father, *s.* he which is of God
13. 10. he needeth not, *s.* to wash his feet
Acts 20. 23. *s.* that the Holy Ghost witnesseth
21. 25. *s.* to keep themselves from fornication
1 *Cor.* 2. 2. not to know any thing, *s.* Jesus Christ
11. *s.* the spirit of man which is in man
2 *Cor.* 11. 24. five times receiv. forty stripes, *s.* one
Gal. 1. 19. I saw none, *s.* James, the Lord's brother
6. 14. God forbid that I should glory, *s.* in the cross
Rev. 13. 17. buy or sell, *s.* he that had the mark

SAVED.

Gen. 47. 25. they said, thou hast *s.* our lives
Exod. 1. 17. midwives *s.* the men children alive, 18.
Num. 22. 33. I had slain thee, and *s.* her alive
31. 15. Moses said, have ye *s.* all the women alive?
Josh. 6. 25. Joshua *s.* Rahab the harlot alive
Judg. 7. 2. lest Israel say, mine own hand hath *s.* me
8. 19. if he had *s.* them alive, I would not slay you
21. 14. they gave them wives which they had *s.*
1 *Sam.* 23. 5. David *s.* the inhabitants of Keilah
27. 11. David *s.* neither man nor woman alive
2 *Sam.* 19. 5. servants who this day have *s.* thy life
9. the king *s.* us, and now he is fled for Absalom
2 *Kings* 6. 10. *s.* himself there, not once nor twice
Neh. 9. 27. thou gavest them saviours, who *s.* them
Psal. 33. 16. no king is *s.* by multitude of an host
44. 7. but thou hast *s.* us from our enemies
106. 8. nevertheless, he *s.* them for his name's sake
10. he *s.* them from him that hated them
Isa. 43. 12. I have declared, and have *s.* and shewed
45. 22. look to me, and be ye *s.* all the ends of earth
Jer. 4. 14. wash thy heart, that thou mayest be *s.*
8. 20. the summer is ended, and we are not *s.*
Mat. 19. 25. when his disciples heard it, saying, who then can be *s.?* *Mark* 10. 26. *Luke* 18. 26.
24. 22. no flesh should be *s.* *Mark* 13. 20.
27. 42. he *s.* others, *Mark* 15. 31. *Luke* 23. 35.
Luke 1. 71. that we should be *s.* from our enemies
7. 50. he said, thy faith hath *s.* thee, 18. 42.
8. 12. takes away, lest they should believe and be *s.*
13. 23. Lord, are there few that be *s.?*
John 3. 17. that the world, through him, might be *s.*
5. 34. these things I say, that ye might be *s.*
Acts 2. 47. the Lord added such as should be *s.*
4. 12. there is no other name whereby we must be *s.*
15. 1. except ye be circumcised, ye cannot be *s.*
16. 30. he said, sirs, what must I do to be *s.?*
27. 20. all hope we should be *s.* was taken away
31. except these abide in the ship, ye cannot be *s.*
Rom. 8. 24. we are *s.* by hope, hope seen is not hope
10. 1. my prayer for Israel is, that they may be *s.*
1 *Cor.* 1. 18. to us who are *s.* it is the power of God
5. 5. that the spirit may be *s.* in day of the Lord
10. 33. but the profit of many, that they may be *s.*
15. 2. by which also ye are *s.* if ye keep in memory
2 *Cor.* 2. 15. we are sweet savour in them that are *s.*
Eph. 2. 5. hath quickened us with Chr. by gr. are *s.*
8. for by grace are ye *s.* through faith
1 *Thess.* 2. 16. to the Gentiles that they might be *s.*
2 *Thess.* 2. 10. because they received not the love of the truth, that they might be *s.*
1 *Tim.* 2. 4. who will have all men to be *s.* and come
Tit. 3. 5. but according to his mercy he *s.* us
1 *Pet.* 3. 20. wherein eight souls were *s.* by water
4. 18. if the righteous scarcely be *s.* where shall
2 *Pet.* 2. 5. but *s.* Noah, eighth person, a preacher
Rev. 21. 24. nations *s.* shall walk in the light of it

God or *Lord* SAVED.

Exod. 14. 30. *Lord s.* Israel that day, 1 *Sam.* 14. 23.
Deut. 33. 29. who is like thee, O people, *s.* by *Lord?*
1 *Sam.* 10. 19. ye have rejected your *God*, who *s.* you
2 *Kings* 14. 27. *Lord s.* them by hand of Jeroboam
1 *Chr.* 11. 14. *Lord s.* them by a great deliverance
2 *Chron.* 32. 22. thus *Lord s.* Hezekiah from Senn.
Psal. 34. 6. *Lord s.* him out of all his troubles
107. 13. the *Lord s.* them out of their distresses
Isa. 63. 9. angel of his presence, *s.* them in his love
2 *Tim.* 1. 9. *God* who hath *s.* us and called us
Jude 5. how that the *Lord*, having *s.* the people

Shall or *shalt be* SAVED.

Num. 10. 9. ye *shall be s.* from your enemies
2 *Sam.* 22. 4. I *shall be s.* from mine enem. *Ps.* 18. 3.
Psal. 80. 3. cause thy face to shine, we *s. be s.* 7. 19.
Prov. 28. 18. whoso walketh uprightly *shall be s.*
Isa. 30. 15. in returning and rest *shall* ye *be s.*
45. 17. but Israel *shall be s.* in Lord with salvation
64. 5. in those is continuance, and we *shall be s.*
Jer. 17. 14. O Lord, save me, and I *shall be s.*
23. 6. in his days Judah *shall be s.* 33. 16.
30. 7. Jacob's trouble, but he *shall be s.* out of it
Mat. 10. 22. be hated for my name's sake, but he that endureth to end *shall be s.* 24. 13. *Mark* 13. 13.
Mark 16. 16. he that believeth *shall be s.*
John 10. 9. by me, if any man enter, he *shall be s.*
Acts 2. 21. come to pass, that whosoever shall call on the name of the Lord, *shall be s.* *Rom.* 10. 13.
11. 14. whereby thou and thy house *shall be s.*
15. 11. we believe that through grace we *shall be s.*
16. 31. believe on Lord Jesus, and thou *shalt be s.*
Rom. 5. 9. we *shall be s.* from wrath through him
10. being reconciled, we *shall be s.* by his life
9. 27. tho' Israel be as sand, a remnant *shall be s.*
10. 9. shalt believe God raised him, thou *shalt be s.*
11. 26. so all Israel *shall be s.* as it is written
1 *Cor.* 3. 15. but he hims. *shall be s.* yet so as by fire
1 *Tim.* 2. 15. *shall be s.* in child-bearing, if continue

SAVEST.

2 *Sam* 22. 3. my Saviour, thou *s.* me from violence
Job 26. 2. how *s.* thou arm that hath no strength?
Psal. 17. 7. O thou that *s.* by thy right hand

SAVETH.

1 *Sam.* 14. 39. as the Lord liveth, who *s.* Israel
17. 47. the Lord *s.* not with sword and spear
Job 5. 15. but he *s.* the poor from the sword
Psal. 7. 10. my defence is of God, who *s.* the upright
20. 6. now know I that the Lord *s.* his anointed
34. 18. he *s.* such as be of a contrite spirit
107. 19. they cry, he *s.* them out of their distresses

SAVING.

Gen. 19. 19. mercy thou hast shewed me in *s.* my life
1 *Sam.* 25. † 26. withholden thee from *s.* thyself
Neh. 4. 23. *s.* that every one put them off for wash.
Psal. 20. 6. with the *s.* strength of his right hand
28. 8. he is the *s.* strength of his anointed
67. 2. thy *s.* health among all nations
Eccl. 5. 11. *s.* the beholding of them with their eyes
Amos 9. 8. *s.* that I will not utterly destroy Jacob
Mat. 5. 32. *s.* for the cause of fornication, causeth her
Luke 4. 27. and none was cleansed, *s.* Naaman
Heb. 10. 39. but of them that believe to the *s.* of the soul
11. 7. Noah prepared an ark to the *s.* of his house
Rev. 2. 17. no man knoweth, *s.* he that receiveth it

SAVIOUR.

See Signification of SAVE.

Judg. 3. † 9. the Lord raised up a *s.* to Israel
2 *Sam.* 22. 3. my high tower, my refuge, my *s.*
2 *Kings* 13. 5. and the Lord gave Israel a *s.*
Psal. 106. 21. they forgat God their *s.* who had done
Isa. 19. 20. he shall send them a *s.* a great one
43. 3. for I am the Holy One of Israel thy *s.*
Isa. 43. 11. I am the Lord, beside me there is no *s.*
45. 15. that hidest thyself, O God of Israel, the *s.*
21. a just God and a *s.* there is none beside me
49. 26. all flesh shall know that I am thy *s.*
60. 16. thou shalt know that I the Lord am thy *s*
63. 8. they are my people, so he was their *s.*
Jer. 14. 8. the *s.* of Israel in time of trouble

Hos. 13. 4. for there is no *s.* beside me
Luke 1. 47. my spirit hath rejoiced in God my *s.*
2. 11. is born this day in the city of David a *s.*
John 4. 42. this is Christ the *s.* of the world
Acts 5. 31. him hath G. exalted to be a prince and *s.*
13. 23. hath God raised to Israel a *s.* Jesus
Eph. 5. 23. and Christ is the *s.* of the body
Phil. 3. 20. from whence we look for the *s.*
1 *Tim.* 1. 1. by the commandment of God our *s.*
2. 3. is acceptable in the sight of God our *s.*
4. 10. we trust in living God, who is *s.* of all men
2 *Tim.* 1. 10. manifest by the appearing of our *s.*
Tit. 1. 3. according to the commandm. of God our *s.*
4. peace from the Lord Jesus Christ our *s.*
2. 10. they may adorn the doctrine of God our *s.*
13. looking for the glorious appearing of our *s.*
3. 4. after the kindness of God our *s.* appeared
6. he shed on us abundantly through Christ our *s.*
2 *Pet.* 1. 1. through righteousness of God and our *s.*
11. into everlasting kingdom of our Lord and *s.*
2. 20. through knowledge of the Lord and *s.* Jesus
3. 2. of us the apostles of the Lord and *s.*
18. but grow in the knowledge of our *s.* Christ
1 *John* 4. 14. the Father sent the Son to be the *s.*
Jude 25. to the only wise God our *s.* be glory

SAVIOURS.

Neh. 9. 27. thou gavest them *s.* who saved them
Obad. 21. and *s.* shall come up on mount Zion

SAVOUR.

Savour *properly signifies a scent or smell.* Eccl. 10. 1. Dead flies cause the ointment of the apothecary to send forth a stinking savour, *or* smell. *It also signifies acidity, sharpness, tartness, or that quality in bodies by which they give a relish to other bodies, and make them palatable, or by which they corrode other bodies.* Mat. 5. 13. But if the salt have lost its savour; *that is, its* acrimony *or* acidity. *It is likewise put for name, reputation, or character.* Exod. 5. 21. You have made our savour to be abhorred in the eyes of Pharaoh.

It is often said of sacrifices or offerings, that they were of a sweet savour unto the Lord. *When* Noah *had built an altar, and offered burnt-offerings upon it, the Lord is said to* have smelled a sweet savour, *or* a savour of rest, *Gen.* 8. 21. *that is, God graciously accepted of his sacrifice, it was pleasing and delightful to him, being a fruit of* Noah's *faith and thankfulness: These sacrifices God was graciously pleased to accept of, as they represented Christ the great gospel sacrifice, and as they were offered up by faith in him. The sacrifice of himself, which* Christ *offered to God for man is by the apostle* Paul *called* a sacrifice *of a sweet-smelling savour,* Eph. 5. 2. *God is satisfied and appeased thereby. The same apostle says,* 2 Cor. 2. 15. We are unto God a sweet savour of Christ in them that are saved, and in them that perish; that is, *We are careful to discharge our duty to all men by preaching the way of salvation to them, and by warning them of the danger of a sinful course; and our labours are acceptable to God, whatever effects they have upon souls. For God, whom we serve, will not judge of us, nor reward us, according to our success, but according to our faithfulness and diligence in his work. God accepteth of our labours as to good men, to whom we are instruments of eternal life and salvation: and though others despise the gospel, and refuse to hear the sweet and joyful sound of it, yet as to them also we are a sweet savour to God: For it is not for any neglect in us, as to our duty, if any perish, but from their own wilfulness and perverseness.*

Exod. 5. 21. ye have made our *s.* to be abhorred
Lev. 26. 31. will not smell *s.* of your sweet odours
Eccl. 10. 1. the ointment to send forth a stinking *s.*
Cant. 1. 3. because of the *s.* of thy good ointment
Joel 2. 20. his stink and his ill *s.* shall come up
Mat. 5. 13. if the salt has lost his *s. Luke* 14. 34.
2 *Cor.* 2. 14. maketh manifest the *s.* of his knowledge
16. the *s.* of death unto death, *s.* of life unto life

Sweet SAVOUR.

Gen. 8. 21. and the Lord smelled a *sweet s.*
Exod. 29. 18. it is a *sweet s.* an offering to the Lord,
Lev. 1. 9, 13, 17. | 2. 9. | 3. 5. | 8. 21.
Num. 15. 14. | 18. 17. | 28. 8.
25. for a *sweet s.* an offering to the Lord, 41. *Lev.*
2. 12. | 3. 16. | 4. 31. | 6. 15, 21. | 8. 28.
| 17. 6. | 23. 13. *Num.* 15. 7, 24. | 28. 2, 6,
13, 27. | 29. 2, 6, 8. *Ezek.* 16. 19.
Lev. 23. 18. of a *sweet s. Num.* 28. 24. | 29. 13, 36.
Num. 15. 3. to make a *sweet s.* unto the Lord
28. 13. for a burnt offering of a *sweet s.* to Lord
Ezek. 6. 13. where they did offer *sweet s.* to their idols
20. 28. there also they made their *sweet s.*
41. I will accept you with your *sweet s.*
2 *Cor.* 2. 15. for we are to God a *sweet s.* of Christ
Eph. 5. 2. a sacrifice to God for a *sweet*-smelling *s.*

Sweet SAVOURS.

Ezra 6. 10. may offer sacrifices of *sweet s.* to God

SAVOUREST.

Mat. 16. 23. thou *s.* not things of God, *Mark* 8. 33.

SAVOURY

Gen. 27. 4. make me *s.* meat, such as I love, 7, 14.
31. Esau had made *s.* meat, and brought it

SAW.

Gen. 3. 6. the woman *s.* the tree was good for food
6. 2. the sons of God *s.* the daughters of men
9. 22. Ham *s.* the nakedness of his father
23. they *s.* not ‖ 22. 4. Abraham *s.* the place afar
26. 28. they said, we *s.* the Lord was with thee
32. 25. when he *s.* that he prevailed not against him
38. 14. for she *s.* that Shelah was grown, not given
39. 3. his master *s.* that the Lord was with him
42. 21. in that we *s.* the anguish of his soul
43. 16. when Joseph *s.* Benjamin with them
45. 27. when he *s.* the wagons which Joseph sent
49. 15. Issachar *s.* that rest was good, and land
50. 15. his brethren *s.* that their father was dead
23. Joseph *s.* Ephraim's children of third gener.
Exod. 2. 2. when she *s.* that he was a goodly child
12. when he *s.* that there was no man, he slew
10. 23. they *s.* not one another for three days
14. 31. Israel *s.* that great work the Lord did
24. 10. and they *s.* the God of Israel, 11.
33. 10. all the people *s.* the cloudy pillar stand
Num. 13. 28. we *s.* the children of Anak there
22. 23. ass *s.* the angel of the Lord in the way, 27.
25. 7. and when Phinehas *s.* it he rose up
32. 9. when they *s.* the land, they discouraged Isr.
Deut. 4. 12. ye heard a voice, but *s.* no similitude, 15.
7. 19. the great temptations which thine eyes *s.*
Judg. 19. 30. all that *s.* it said, no such deed was done
Ruth 1. 18. when she *s.* she was stedfastly minded
1 *Sam.* 6. 13. they *s.* the ark, and rejoiced to see it
10. 14. when he *s.* that they were no where
17. 24. Israel, when they *s.* the man, fled from him
18. 28. Saul *s.* that the Lord was with David
2 *Sam.* 11. 2. David *s.* a woman washing herself
1 *Kings* 3. 28. *s.* that the wisdom of God was in him
16. 18. when Zimri *s.* that the city was taken
18. 17. when Ahab *s.* Elijah he said to him
19. 3. when he *s.* that, he arose and went for his life
2 *Kings* 2. 12. Elisha *s.* it, and he *s.* him no more
3. 22. *s.* the water on the other side as red as blood
4. 25. when the man of God *s.* her afar off
6. 17. L. opened eyes of the young man and he *s.*
13. 4. for he *s.* the oppression of Israel
16. 10. Ahaz *s.* an altar that was at Damascus, 12.
2 *Chron.* 15. 9. they *s.* that the Lord was with him
25. 21. and they *s.* one another in the face
31. 8. when princes *s.* heaps, they blessed the Lord
Neh. 6. 16. when *s.* these things they were cast down
Esth. 1. 14. the princes which *s.* the king's face
7. 7. he *s.* that there was evil determined ag. him
Job 2. 13. they *s.* that his grief was very great
3. 16. had not been, as infants which never *s.* light
20. 9. eye which *s.* him, shall see him no more
29. 8. the young men *s.* me, and hid themselves
11. when the eye *s.* me, it gave witness to me
Psal. 48. 5. they *s.* it, and so they marvelled
77. 16. waters *s.* thee, O God, the waters *s.* thee
95. 9. your fathers proved me, and *s.* my work
97. 4. the earth *s.* his lightnings and trembled
114. 3. sea *s.* it and fled, Jordan was driven back
Cant. 3. 3. *s.* ye him whom my soul loveth?
Isa. 41. 5. isles *s.* it, and feared, ends of the earth
Jer. 3. 7. and her treacherous sister Judah *s.* it
39. 4. when Zedekiah *s.* them, and men of war
44. 17. for then we were well, and *s.* no evil
Lam. 1. 7. adversaries *s.* her and did mock at her
Ezek. 8. 10. so I went in, and *s.* behold, every form
20. 28. then they *s.* every high hill, offered there
23. 16. as soon as she *s.* them, she doted on them
Dan. 3. 27. *s.* these men on whom fire had no power
4. 23. whereas the king *s.* a watcher coming down
5. 5. the king *s.* part of the hand that wrote
Hos. 5. 13. when Ephraim *s.* his sickness and Judah
s. his wound, then went Ephraim to the Assyrian
Hag. 2. 3. who among you *s.* this house in first glory?
Mat. 2. 9. the star which they *s.* went before them
3. 16. *s.* the Spirit of God descending, *Mark* 1. 10.
12. 22. the blind and dumb both spake and *s.*
17. 8. they *s.* no man, save Jesus only
21. 38. but when the husbandmen *s.* the son
22. 11. *s.* a man who had not on wedding garment
25. 37. Lord, when *s.* we thee an hungered, 44.
38. when *s.* we thee stranger ‖ 39. when *s.* thee sick
26. 71. another maid *s.* him, and said, this was with
Jesus of Nazareth, *Mark* 14. 69. *Luke* 22. 58.
27. 3. Judas, when he *s.* he was condemned, repented
28. 17. when they *s.* him they worshipped him
Mark 2. 5. when Jesus *s.* their faith he said to sick
8. 23. spit on his eyes, he asked him, if he *s.* aught
9. 38. saying, Master, we *s.* one casting out devils,
in thy name, and he follows not us, *Luke* 9. 49.
Luke 8. 34. when they *s.* what was done, they fled
47. when the woman *s.* that she was not hid
9. 32. when they were awake, they *s.* his glory
15. 20. his father *s.* him, had compassion on him
17. 15. one of them, when he *s.* he was healed
24. 24. they found it even so, but him they *s.* not
John 6. 26. ye seek me, not because ye *s.* miracles
8. 56. Abraham *s.* my day, and was glad
12. 41. these things said Esaias, when he *s.* his glory
19. 35. he that *s.* it, bare record, his record is true
20. 20. disciples were glad when they *s.* the Lord
Acts 4. 13. when they *s.* the boldness of Peter
6. 15. *s.* his face as it had been face of an angel
7. 55. Stephen *s.* glory of God and Jesus standing
8. 18. when Simon *s.* that Holy Ghost was given
39. caught Philip, that eunuch *s.* him no more
9. 8. when his eyes were opened, he *s.* no man
35. all at Lydda *s.* him, and turned to the Lord
40. and when Tabitha *s.* Peter, she sat up
10. 3. Cornelius *s.* a vision ‖ 11. *s.* heaven opened
12. 3. and because he *s.* it pleased the Jews
13. 36. David *s.* corruption ‖ 37. *s.* no corruption
16. 19. masters *s.* the hope of their gain was gone
17. 16. he *s.* the city wholly given to idolatry
22. 9. they *s.* indeed the light and were afraid
28. 6. had looked, and *s.* no harm come to him
Gal. 2. 7. but when they *s.* that the gospel of the
uncircumcision was committed to me
Phil. 1. 30. having the same conflict which ye *s.*
Heb. 3. 9. your fathers *s.* my works forty years
11. 23. because they *s.* he was a proper child
Rev. 1. 2. who bare record of all things he *s.*
11. 11. great fear fell on them who *s.* them
12. 13. when the dragon *s.* that he was cast out
18. 18. cried, when they *s.* smoke of her burning

SAW *joined with Lord or God.*

Gen. 1. 4. and *God s.* the light that it was good
10. God called the dry land earth, and *God s.*
that it was good, 12, 18, 21, 25, 31.
6. 5. *God s.* that the wickedness of man was great
29. 31. when the *Lord s.* that Leah was hated
Exod. 3. 4. when the *Lord s.* that he turned aside
Deut. 32. 19. when the *Lord s.* it, he abhorred
2 *Kings* 14. 26. the *Lord s.* the affliction of Israel
2 *Chron.* 12. 7. when *L. s.* they humbled themselves
Isa. 59. 15. the *Lord s.* it, and it displeased him
Isa. 59. 16. *L. s.* that there was no man, and wonder.
Jonah 3. 10. *God s.* their works, that they turned
Luke 7. 13. *Lord s.* her, he had compassion on her

I SAW.

Gen. 41. 19. such as *I* never *s.* in Egypt for badness
44. 28. one went out, and *I s.* him not since
Josh. 7. 21. when *I s.* among the spoils a garment
Judg. 12. 3. when *I s.* that he delivered me not
1 *Sam.* 22. 9. *I s.* the son of Jesse coming to Nob
28. 13. *I s.* gods ascending out of the earth
2 *Sam.* 18. 10. *I s.* Absalom hanged in an oak
29. *I s.* great tumult, but knew not what it was
1 *Kings* 22. 17. *I s.* all Israel scattered on the hills
19. *I s.* the Lord on his throne, 2 *Chron.* 18. 18.
Neh. 13. 15. in those days *s. I* in Judah some trading
Job 31. 21. when *I s.* my help in the gate
Psal. 73. 3. when *I s.* the prosperity of the wicked
Prov. 24. 32. then *I s.* and considered it well
Eccl. 2. 24. this also *I s.* from the hand of God
8. 10. so *I s.* the wicked buried, who had gone
Ezek. 11. 1. among whom *I s.* Jaazaniah son of Azur
16. 50. therefore I took them away as *I s.* good
23. 13. then *I s.* that she was defiled, took one way
Hos. 9. 10. *I s.* your fathers as first-ripe in fig-tree
13. Ephraim, as *I s.* Tyrus, is planted in pleasant
John 1. 32. *I s.* the Spirit descending upon him
48. when thou wast under the fig-tree, *I s.* thee
Acts 26. 13. *I s.* in the way a light from heaven
Gal. 1. 19. but other of the apostles *s. I* none
2. 14. when *I s.* that they walked not uprightly
Rev. 1. 17. when *I s.* him, I fell at his feet as dead

SAW.

The punishment of the SAW. *See* PUNISHMENT.
Isa. 10. 15. shall *s.* magnify ag. him that shaketh it?

SAWS.

2 *Sam.* 12. 31. he put Ammonites under *s.* 1 *Chr.* 20. 3.

SAWED.

1 *Kings* 7. 9. these were of costly stones *s.* with saws

SAWEST.

Gen. 20. 10. what *s.* thou that hast done this thing?
1 *Sam.* 19. 5. thou *s.* it and didst rejoice
28. 13. king said, be not afraid, for what *s.* thou
2 *Sam.* 18. 11. Joab said, and behold, thou *s.* him
Psal. 50. 18. when thou *s.* a thief, thou consentedst
Dan. 2. 31. thou, O king, *s.* a great image
34. thou *s.* till that a stone was cut out, 45.
4. 20. the tree thou *s.* which grew and was strong
8. 20. the ram which thou *s.* having two horns
Rev. 1. 20. seven stars thou *s.* seven candlesticks *s.*
17. 8. the beast that thou *s.* was, and is not
12. the ten horns which thou *s.* are ten kings, 16.
15. waters thou *s.* where whore sitteth are peoples
18. the woman which thou *s.* is that great city

SAWN.

Heb. 11. 37. they were stoned, they were *s.* asunder

SAY

Signifies, [1] *To speak, to tell, or relate,* Gen. 37. 20. | 44. 16. [2] *To utter, or pronounce,* Judg. 12. 6. [3] *To will and command with efficacy,* Gen. 1. 3, 6, 9. Luke 7. 7. [4] *To promise,* Luke 23. 43. [5] *To think, muse, or meditate,* Deut. 7. 17. Isa. 49. 21. Mat. 3. 9. [6] *To ask,* Mark 11. 31. [7] *To answer,* Exod. 3. 13, 14. [8] *To affirm and teach,* Mat. 17. 10. [9] *To expound,* Heb. 5. 11. [10] *To admonish,* Col. 4. 17. [11] *To confess, or acknowledge,* Luke 17. 10. [12] *To bear witness,* Acts 24. 20. [13] *To reason, or argue,* Jam. 2. 18.

Gen. 14. 23. lest thou shouldest *s.* I have made Abra.
34. 11. what ye shall *s.* to me I will give, 12.
37. 17. for I heard them *s.* let us go to Dothan
20. we will *s.* some evil beast hath devoured him
41. 15. I have heard *s.* that thou canst interpret it
44. 16. Judah said, what shall we *s.* to my Lord
50. 17. so shall ye *s.* to Joseph, forgive, I pray
Exod. 3. 14. thus shall ye *s.* to the children of Israel,
I AM hath sent me to you, 15. | 19. 3. | 20. 22.
4. 12. I will teach you what thou shalt *s.*
12. 26. when your children shall *s.* unto you
14. 3. Pharaoh will *s.* of the children of Israel
21. 5. if the servant shall *s.* I love my master
Num. 5. 22. and the woman shall *s.* amen, amen
11. 12. that thou shouldest *s.* to me, carry them
22. 19. that I may know what the Lord will *s.*
38. have I now any power at all to *s.* any thing?
Deut. 5. 27. hear all that the Lord our God shall *s.*
6. 21. then thou shalt *s.* to thy son, we were
9. 2. a people great, of whom thou hast heard *s.*
28. 67. in the morning thou shalt *s.* and at even *s.*
31. 17. so that they will *s.* in that day, are not
32. 27. lest they should *s.* our hand is high
Josh. 22. 27. your children may not *s.* our children
28. when they should *s.* to us in time to come
Judg. 7. 11. and thou shalt hear what they *s.*
16. 15. she said, how canst thou *s.* I love thee?
18. 24. what is this ye *s.* to me, what aileth thee?
1 *Sam.* 8. 7. in all they *s.* unto thee, hearken to voice
14. 10. if they *s.* thus, come up to us, we will go
20. 7. if he *s.* thus, thy servant shall have peace
2 *Sam.* 7. 8. therefore thou shalt *s.* to my servant
David, I took thee from sheep cote, 1 *Chr.* 7. 21.
15. 26. if he *s.* I have no delight in thee
21. 4. what you shall *s.* that will I do for you
1 *Kings* 1. 36. the Lord God of my lord *s.* so too
2. 17. speak I pray thee, for he will not *s.* thee nay
9. 8. they shall *s.* why hath the Lord done thus to
this land and to this house, 2 *Chron.* 7. 21.
13. 22. of which the Lord did *s.* eat no bread
22. 8. let not the king *s.* so, 2 *Chron.* 18. 7.
2 *Kings* 7. 4. if we *s.* we will enter into the city
9. 37. so that they shall not *s.* this is Jezebel
2 *Chron.* 18. 15. that thou *s.* nothing but truth to me
Ezra 8. 17. I told them what they should *s.* to Iddo
9. 10. O our God, what shall we *s.* after this?
Job 9. 12. he takes away, who can hinder him? who
will *s.* to him, what dost thou? *Eccl.* 8. 4.
21. 14. they *s.* unto God, depart from us
22. 29. then shalt thou *s.* there is lifting up
23. 5. I would understand what he would *s.* to me
28. 22. destruction and death *s.* we have heard
32. 11. whilst you searched out what to *s.*
33. 27. if any *s.* I have sinned, and perverted right

Job 37. 19. teach us what we shall s. unto him
Ps. 3. 2. many s. of my soul, there is no help in G.
4. 6. there be that s. who will shew us any good?
35. 25. let them not s. we have swallowed him up
58. 11. so that a man shall s. there is a reward
59. 7. they belch out, for who, s. they, doth hear?
94. 7. yet they s. Lord shall not see, nor G. of Jacob
129. 8. nor do they who go by s. blessing of the L.
Prov. 1. 11. if they s. come, let us lay wait for blood
20. 9. who can s. I have made my heart clean?
Eccl. 12. 1. when thou shalt s. I have no pleasure
Isa. 2. 3. many people shall go and s. come ye
29. 15. they s. who seeth us, and who knoweth us?
16. shall the work s. of him that made it? or the thing framed s. of him that framed it?
30. 10. who s. to the seers, see not, and to prophets
33. 24. and the inhabitant shall not s. I am sick
44. 5. one shall s. I am the Lord's, and another
45. 24. surely shall one s. in L. have I righteousness
48. 5. lest thou shouldest s. my idol hath done them
7. lest thou shouldest s. behold, I knew them
58. 3. why have we fast. s. they, and thou seest not?
9. thou shalt cry, and he shall s. here I am
Jer. 2. 27. in trouble they will s. arise and save us
5. 15. neither understandest what they s.
10. 11. thus shall ye s. them, the gods shall perish
14. 17. therefore thou shalt s. this word to them
20. 10. report, s. they, and we will report it
23. 7. they shall no more s. the Lord liveth
31. 29. they shall s. no more fathers have eaten
39. 12. do to him even as he shall s. unto thee
42. 20. according to all that the Lord shall s.
Ezek. 13. 7. whereas ye s. the Lord saith it
28. 9. wilt thou yet s. before him that slayeth thee?
Hos. 14. 3. nor will we s. to the work of our hands
8. Ephraim shall s. what have I to do with idols?
Mic. 2. 6. prophesy ye not, s. they to them that pro.
3. 11. they will s. is not the Lord among us?
Hab. 2. 1. I will watch to see what he will s. to me
Zech. 11. 5. they that sell them, s. I am rich
Mal. 1. 2. yet ye s. wherein loved us? 2. 14, 17. | 3. 13.
Mat. 3. 9. think not to s. in yourselves, Luke 3. 8.
5. 11. shall s. all manner of evil against you falsely
7. 22. many will s. to me in that day, Lord, Lord
13. 51. have ye understood? they s. yea, Lord
16. 13. Jesus said, whom do men s. that I the Son of man am? Mark 8. 27. Luke 9. 18.
15. whom s. ye that I am? Mark 8. 29. Luke 9. 20.
21. 3. if any man s. ought to you, ye shall s.
16. and s. to him, hearest thou what these s.?
25. if we should s. from heaven, he will s. to us, why not believe him? Mark 11. 31. Luke 20. 5.
26. if we shall s. of men, Mark 11. 32. Luke 20. 6.
23. 3. do not their works, for they s. and do not
Mark 1. 44. and saith, see thou s. nothing to any man
9. 6. he wist not what to s. for they were afraid
Luke 4. 23. ye will surely s. this proverb, heal thys.
7. 40. Simon, I have somewhat to s. to thee
12. 11. take ye no thought what ye shall s.
12. the Holy G. shall teach what ye ought to s.
John 4. 20. ye s. that Jerusalem is the place where
7. 26. he speaketh, and they s. nothing to him
8. 26. I have many things to s. of you, 16. 12.
48. s. we not well, that thou hast a devil?
54. of whom ye s. that he is your God
13. 13. ye call me master, ye s. well, for so I am
Acts 3. 22. him shall ye hear in all things he shall s.
4. 14. they could s. nothing against it
6. 14. we heard him s. that Jesus shall destroy
21. 23. do therefore this that we s. to thee
23. 18. who hath something to s. unto thee
24. 20. or else let these same here s. if found evil
26. 22. none other things but what Moses did s.
Rom. 3. 5. what shall we s. is God unrighteous?
8. as some affirm that we s. let us do evil
4. 1. what shall we s. then, shall we continue in sin? 6. 1. | 7. 7. | 8. 31. | 9. 14, 30.
9. 20. shall thing formed s. to him that formed it?
1 Cor. 12. 3. no man can s. that Jesus is the Lord
14. 16. how shall he s. amen at thy giving thanks?
23. will they not s. that ye are mad?
15. 12. how s. some that there is no resurrection?
2 Cor. 9. 4. we, that we s. not you, should be asham.
10. 10. for his letters, s. they, are weighty
1 Thess. 4. 15. this we s. to you by word of the L.
1 Tim. 4. 7. understanding neither what they s.
Tit. 2. 8. having no evil thing to s. of you
Philem. 19. albeit I do not s. how thou owest me
Heb. 5. 11. of whom we have many things to s.
7. 9. as I may so s. Levi paid tithes in Abraham
9. 11. that is to s. not of this building
10. 20. for us thro' the vail, that is to s. his flesh
11. 14. they that s. such things declare plainly
13. 6. so that we may boldly s. Lord is my helper
Jam. 1. 13. let no man s. when he is tempted
4. 13. go to, now, ye that s. to-day or to-morrow
15. for that ye ought to s. if the Lord will
1 John 1. 6. if we s. we have fellowship with him
8. if we s. we have no sin, we deceive ourselv. 10.
4. 20. if man s. I love God, and hateth his brother
5. 16. I do not s. that he shall pray for it
Rev. 2. 2. which s. they are apostles, and are not
9. which s. they are Jews, and are not, 3. 9.
22. 17. and the spirit and the bride s. come
See Began.

SAY, Imperatively.

Gen. 12. 13. s. I pray thee, thou art my sister
20. 13. at every place, s. of me, he is my brother
Deut. 1. 42. s. unto them, go not up, neither fight
Judg. 7. 18. s. the sword of the Lord and of Gideon
12. 6. they said to him, s. now Shibboleth
1 Sam. 15. 16. and he said to him, s. on, 2 Sam. 14. 12. 1 Kings 2. 14, 16. Luke 7. 40. Acts 13. 15.
Prov. 3. 28. s. not to thy neigh. go and come again
24. 29. s. not, I will do so to him as he hath done
30. 9. lest I deny thee, and s. who is the Lord?
Eccl. 7. 10. s. not thou, what is cause former days
Isa. 3. 10. s. ye to righteous, shall be well with him
35. 4. s. to them that are of fearful heart, fear not
40. 9. s. to the cities of Judah, behold your God
43. 9. or let them hear, and s. it is truth
56. 3. neither let the eunuch s. I am a dry tree

Isa. 62. 11. s. ye to daughter of Zion, behold thy
Jer. 1. 7. s. not, I am a child, for thou shalt go
46. 14. s. ye, stand fast, and prepare thee
48. 19. ask her that escapeth, and s. what is done
50. 2. s. Babylon is taken, Bel is confounded
Ezek. 6. 11. and stamp with thy foot, and s. alas
12. 11. s. I am your sign, like as I have done
19. 2. and s. what is thy mother? a lioness
21. 9. s. a sword, a sword is sharpened
28. s. the sword is drawn for the slaughter
Hos. 14. 2. s. unto him, take away all iniquity
Joel 2. 17. let them s. spare thy people, O Lord
3. 10. let the weak s. I am strong
Zech. 1. 3. s. unto them, turn ye unto me
Mat. 21. 3. s. Lord hath need of them, Mark 11. 3.
Luke 7. 7. s. in a word, and my serv. shall be heal.
10. 10. go out into the streets of the same, and s.
John 4. 35. s. not ye, there are yet four months
10. 36. s. ye of him the Father hath sanctified
Col. 4. 17. s. to Archippus, take heed to the ministry

I SAY.

Exod. 3. 13. his name, what shall I s. to them?
4. 23. I s. unto thee, let my son go to serve me
6. 29. speak all that I s. unto thee, Ezek. 44. 5.
Josh. 7. 8. what shall I s. when Isr. turneth backs
Judg. 7. 4. of whom I s. this shall go with thee
1 Sam. 20. 21. if I s. expressly to the lad, behold
2 Kings 4. 28. did not I s. do not deceive me?
7. 13. behold, I s. they are as all the multitude
2 Chron. 20. 11. behold, I. s. how they reward us
Job 6. 22. did I s. bring unto me, or give reward?
7. 13. when I s. my bed shall comfort me
9. 20. if I s. I am perfect, it shall prove me perverse
27. if I s. I will forget my complaint, leave off
10. 2. I will s. to God, do not condemn me
Psal. 27. 14. be of courage, wait, I s. on the Lord
73. 15. if I s. I will speak thus, I should offend
91. 2. I will s. of the Lord, he is my refuge
130. 6. I s. more than they that watch for morning
139. 11. if I s. the darkness shall cover me
Eccl. 6. 3. I s. an untimely birth is better than he
Isa. 36. 5. I s. sayest thou, but they are but vain words
38. 15. what shall I s.? he hath both spoken to me
43. 6. I will s. to the north, give up, and the south
Ezek. 2. 8. son of man, hear what I s. unto thee
3. 18. when I s. to the wicked, 33. 8, 14.
12. 25. I will s. the word, and will perform it
21. 24. because I. s. ye are come to remembrance
33. 13. when I s. to the righteous, he shall live
Mat. 8. 9. I s. unto this man, go, Luke 7. 8.
18. 22. I s. not unto thee, until seven times, but
Mark 2. 11. I s. to thee, arise, 5. 41. Luke 5. 24. | 7. 14.
Luke 6. 46. and do not the things which I s.
John 5. 34. these things I s. that ye might be saved
8. 46. if I s. the truth, why do ye not believe me?
55. if I should s. I know him not, shall be a liar
12. 27. what shall I s. Fa. save me from this hour
49. he gave me commandment, what I should s.
Rom. 3. 26. to declare, I s. his righteousness
9. 1. I s. the truth in Christ, I lie not
1 Cor. 1. 12. this I s. that every one of you saith
7. 29. but this I s. brethren, the time is short
9. 8. s. I these things as a man? or saith not the law
10. 15. I speak as to wise men, judge ye what I s.
19. what s. I then? that the idol is any thing
29. conscience, I s. not thy own, but of others
11. 22. what shall I s. to you? shall I praise you?
15. 50. now this I s. brethren, 2 Cor. 9. 6. Gal. 3. 17. | 5. 16. Eph. 4. 17. Col. 2. 4.
Gal. 1. 9. as we said before, so s. I now again
2 Tim. 2. 7. consider what I s. L. give thee unders.
Philem. 21. knowing thou wilt do more than I s.
Heb. 11. 32. what shall I more s.? time would fail me

I SAY unto you.

2 Sam. 13. 28. when I s. unto you, smite Amnon
2 Kings 2. 18. he said, did I not s. unto you, go not?
Mat. 6. 29. I s. unto you, that Solomon in all his glory
21. 31. I s. unto you, that publicans go before you
Mark 13. 37. what I s. unto you, I say unto all, watch
John 16. 26. I s. not unto you, I will pray the Fath.
Gal. 5. 2. I Paul s. unto you, if ye be circumcised
Rev. 2. 24. unto you I s. and to the rest in Thyatira

SAYEST.

Exod. 33. 12. see, thou s. to me, bring up this people
Num. 22. 17. I will do whatsoever thou s. unto me
Ruth 3. 5. all that thou s. unto me, I will do
1 Kings 18. 11. and now thou s. go tell thy lord, 14.
2 Kings 18. 20. thou s. but they are but vain words, I have counsel and strength for war, Isa. 36. 5.
2 Chron. 25. 19. thou s. lo, thou hast smitten Edom
Neh. 5. 12. we will restore, so will we do as thou s.
6. 8. there are no such things done as thou s.
Job 22. 13. and thou s. how doth God know?
Psal. 90. 3. and s. return, ye children of men
Prov. 24. 12. if thou s. behold, we knew it not
Isa. 40. 27. why s. thou, O Jacob, and speak. O Is.
47. 8. that s. in thine heart, I am, and none else
Jer. 2. 35. yet thou s. because I am innocent, I will plead with thee, because thou s. I have not sinned
Amos 7. 16. thou s. prophesy not against Israel
Mat. 26. 70. saying, I know not what thou s.
27. 11. art thou king of the Jews? Jesus said unto him, thou s. Mark 15. 2. Luke 23. 3. John 18. 37.
Mark 14. 68. Peter denied, saying, I know not, neither understand I what thou s. Luke 22. 60.
Luke 20. 21. Master, we know that thou s. rightly
John 1. 22. who art thou? what s. thou of thyself?
8. 5. that such should be stoned, but what s. thou?
33. s. thou, ye shall be made free? 12. 34. | 14. 9.
9. 17. they say to blind man, what s. thou of him?
18. 34. s. thou this of thyself or did others tell?
Rom. 2. 22. thou that s. a man should not steal
1 Cor. 14. 16. he understandeth not what thou s.
Rev. 3. 17. because thou s. I am rich, and increased

SAYING.

Gen. 37. 11. breth. envied, but his father observed s.
Deut. 1. 23. and the s. pleased me well
1 Sam. 18. 8. the s. displeased Saul, and he said
2 Sam. 17. 4. and the s. pleased Absalom well
6. shall we do after his s.? if not, speak thou
24. 19. David, according to the s. of God, went up
1 Kings 2. 38. and Shimei said, the s. is good

1 Kin. 12. 15. that he might perform his s. by Ahijah
13. 4. when Jeroboam heard s. of the man of God
32. the s. which he cried by the Lord shall come
15. 29. according to the s. of the L. 2 Kings 10. 17.
17. 15. accord. to the s. of Elijah, 2 Kings 2. 22.
2 Kings 5. 14. according to the s. of man of God, 8. 2.
Esth. 1. 21. the s. pleased the king and the princes
Psal. 49. 4. I will open my dark s. upon the harp
Jonah 4. 2. was not this my s. when in my country
Mat. 15. 12. were offended after they heard this s.
19. 11. all men cannot receive this s. save they
22. but when the young man heard this s.
28. 15. this s. is commonly reported among Jews
Mark 7. 29. for this s. go thy way, the devil is gone
8. 32. and he spake that s. openly
9. 10. and they kept that s. with themselves
32. they understood not that s. Luke 2. 50. | 9. 45.
10. 22. he was sad at that s. and went away
Luke 1. 29. she was troub. at his s. and cast in mind
2. 17. they made known abroad s. that was told
9. 45. and they feared to ask him of that s.
18. 34. this s. was hid from them, nor knew they
John 4. 37. herein is that s. true, one soweth
39. many believed, for the s. of the woman
42. now we believe, not because of thy s.
6. 60. this is an hard s. who can hear it
7. 36. what manner of s. is this that he said?
40. many, when they heard this s. said
8. 51. I say to you, if a man keep my s. 52.
55. but I know him and keep his s.
12. 38. that the s. of Esaias might be fulfilled
15. 20. if they have kept my s. they will keep yours
18. 9. that the s. of Jesus might be fulfilled, 32.
19. 8. when Pilate heard that s. he was afraid
21. 23. then went this s. abroad among brethren
Acts 6. 5. the s. pleased the whole multitude
7. 29. then fled Moses at this s. into Midian
16. 36. the keeper of the prison told this s. to Paul
Rom. 13. 9. it is briefly comprehended in this s.
1 Cor. 15. 54. then shall be brought to pass the s.
1 Tim. 1. 15. this is faithful s. that Christ Jesus came to save sinners, 4. 9. 2 Tim. 2. 11. Tit. 3. 8.
3. 1. this is a true s. if a man desire the office

SAYING, Participle.

1 Kings 1. 6. displeased in s. why hast thou done so?
Mat. 26. 44. he prayed third time, s. the same words
Mark 13. 6. s. I am Christ, and shall deceive many
Luke 11. 45. Master, thus s. thou reproachest us also
Acts 11. 7. a voice, s. arise, Peter, slay and eat
26. 22. s. none other things than those which

SAYINGS.

Num. 14. 39. Moses told these s. to the people
Judg. 13. 17. that when thy s. come to pass, may do
1 Sam. 25. 12. so David's young men told all those s.
2 Chron. 13. 22. Ahijah's s. are written in the story
33. 19. that are written among the s. of the seers
Psal. 49. 13. yet their posterity approve their s.
78. 2. open in parables, I will utter dark s. of old
Prov. 1. 6. to understand the dark s. of the wise
4. 10. hear, O my son, and receive my s.
20. my son attend, incline thine ear to my s.
Mat. 7. 24. whoso heareth these s. 26. Luke 6. 47.
28. when Jesus had ended these s. the people were astonished at his doctrine, 19. 1. | 26. 1. Luke 7. 1.
Luke 1. 65. all these s. were noised abroad in Judea
2. 51. his mother kept all these s. in her heart
9. 44. let these s. sink down into your ears
John 10. 19. there was a division again for these s.
14. 24. he that loveth me not, keepeth not my s.
Acts 14. 18. with these s. scarce restrained they peo.
19. 28. when heard these s. they were full of wrath
Rom. 3. 4. that thou mightest be justified in thy s.
Rev. 19. 9. he saith to me, these are true s. of God
22. 6. he said to me, these s. are faithful and true
7. blessed is he that keepeth the s. of this book
9. and of them who keep the s. of this book
10. seal not the s. of the prophecy of this book

SCAB.

Lev. 13. 2. when shall have in skin of his flesh a s.
6. it is but a s. ‖ 7. if s. spread much in skin, 8.
14. 56. this is the law for a s. and for a bright spot
Deut. 28. 27. the Lord will smite thee with a s.
Isa. 3. 17. therefore the Lord will smite with a s.

SCABBARD.

Jer. 47. 6. O sword, put up thyself into thy s.

SCABBED.

Lev. 21. 20. he that is scurvy or s. shall not approach
22. 22. or scurvy, or s. ye shall not offer to the L.

SCAFFOLD.

2 Chron. 6. 13. Solomon had made a brasen s.

SCALES.

Lev. 11. 9. these that have s. eat ye, Deut. 14. 9.
10. that have no s. ye shall not eat, 12. Deut. 14. 10.
Job 41. 15. his s. are his pride, shut up together
Isa. 40. 12. who weighed the mountains in s. and hills
Ezek. 29. 4. I will cause the fish to stick to thy s.
Acts 9. 18. there fell from his eyes as it had been s.

SCALETH.

Prov. 21. 22. a wise man s. the city o the mighty

SCALL.

Lev. 13. 30. it is a dry s. even a leprosy on the head
31. plague of the s. be not deeper than the skin, shall shut up him that hath the s. seven days, 33.
32. and behold, if the s. spread not, 34.
33. he shall be shaven, but the s. shall he not shave
35. but if the s. spread much, he is unclean, 36.
37. if the s. be at a stay, the s. is healed
14. 54. this is the law of all manner of leprosy and s

SCALP.

Psal. 68. 21. God shall wound the hairy s. of such

SCANDAL.

1 John 2. † 10. there is none occasion of s. in him

SCANDALS.

Mat. 13. † 41. gather out of his kingdom all s.

SCANT.

2 Kings 4. † 3. borrow the vessels abroad, s. not

SCANT.

Mic. 6. 10. and the s. measure that is abominable

SCAPE-GOAT. See Goat.

SCARCE.

Gen. 27. 30. Jacob was s. gone out from his father
Acts 14. 18. with these sayings s. restrained people

SCARCELY.
Rom. 5. 7. for s. for a righteous man will one die
1 Pet 4. 18. if the righteous s. be saved, where sinner

SCARCENESS.
Deut. 8. 9. where thou shalt eat bread without s.

SCAREST.
Job 7. 14. then thou s. me with dreams and terrifiest

SCARLET.
Gen. 38. 28. the midwife bound a s. thread, 30.
Exod. 25. 4. blue, and purple, and s. 26. 1, 31, 36. | 27. 16. | 28. 5, 6, 8, 15. | 35. 6, 23, 25. | 38. 18, 23.
39. 3. they did cut gold into wires, to work it in s.
Lev. 14. 4. to take two birds alive, and clean, cedar-wood, s. and hyssop, 6, 49, 51, 52. Num. 19. 6.
Num. 4. 8. they shall spread on them a cloth of s.
Josh. 2. 18. shalt bind this line of s. thread in window
21. and she bound the s. line in the window
2 Sam. 1. 24. weep over Saul, who clothed you in s.
Prov. 31. 21. her household are clothed with s.
Cant. 4. 3. thy lips are like a thread of s. thy speech
Isa. 1. 18. come now, though your sins be as s.
Lam. 4. 5. that were brought up in s. embrace dung.
Dan. 5. 7. shall be clothed with s. 16. 29.
Nah. 2. 3. the valiant men are in s. fir-trees shaken
Mat. 27. 28. they put on Jesus a s. robe
Heb. 9. 19. he took water, and s. wool, and hyssop
Rev. 17. 3. a woman sit on a s. coloured beast
4. the woman was arrayed in purple and s. colour
18. 12. no man buyeth the merchandise of s.
16. that great city that was clothed with s.

SCATTER.
Gen. 11. 9. from thence did Lord s. them on earth
49. 7. I will divide them in Jacob, s. them in Isr.
Lev. 26. 33. and I will s. you among the heathen
Num. 16. 37. take up the censers, and s. the fire
Deut. 4. 27. and the Lord shall s. you among the heathen, 28. 64. Jer. 9. 16. Ezek. 22. 15.
32. 26. I said, I would s. them into corners
1 Kings 14. 15. he shall s. them beyond the river
Neh. 1. 8. if ye transgress, I will s. you abroad
Job 18. † 11. terrors make afraid, and shall s. him
Psal. 59. 11. s. them by thy power, O Ld. our shield
68. 30. s. thou the people that delight in war
106. 27. he lifted up his hand to s. them in lands
144. 6. cast forth lightning, and s. them, shoot out
Isa. 28. 25. cast abroad fitches, and s. the cummin
30. † 22. thou shalt s. them as a menstruous cloth
41. 16. whirlwind shall s. them, and shall rejoice
Jer. 13. 24. therefore I will s. them as stubble
18. 17. I will s. them as with an east wind
23. 1. woe to the pastors that s. the sheep
49. 32. I will s. into all winds them that are in the utmost corners, 36. Ezek. 5. 10, 12.
Ezek. 5. 2. a third part thou shalt s. in the wind
6. 5. I will s. your bones round about your altars
10. 2. fill thine hand, and s. the coals over the city
12. 14. I will s. toward every wind all that help him
15. when I shall s. them among the nations
20. 23. that I would s. them among the heathen
29. 12. I will s. the Egyptians, 30. 23, 26.
Dan. 4. 14. hew down the tree, and s. his fruit
11. 24. he shall s. among them the prey and spoil
12. 7. to s. the power of the holy people
Hab. 3. 14. they came out as a whirlwind to s. me
Zech. 1. 21. lift up their horn over Judah to s. it
Mal. 2. † 3. I will s. dung on your faces, dung of fea.

SCATTERED.
Gen. 11. 4. lest we be s. abroad upon the earth
8. so the Lord s. them abroad from thence
Exod. 5. 12. the people were s. to gather stubble
Num. 10. 35. let thine enemies be s. Psal. 68. 1.
Deut. 30. 3. whither the Lord thy God hath s. thee
1 Sam. 11. 11. the Ammonites that remained were s.
13. 8. and the people were s. from Saul
11. because I saw the people were s. from me
2 Sam. 18. 8. the battle was s. over the country
20. † 22. and they were s. from the city
22. 15. he sent out arrows and s. them, Psal. 18. 14.
1 Kings 22. 17. I saw all Israel s. 2 Chron. 18. 16.
2 Kings 25. 5. his army were s. from him, Jer. 52. 8.
Esth. 3. 8. there is a certain people s. abroad
Job 4. 11. the stout lions' whelps are s. abroad
18. 15. brimstone shall be s. on his habitation
Psal. 44. 11. thou hast s. us among heathen, 60. 1.
53. 5. God hath s. the bones of him that encampeth
68. 14. when the Almighty s. kings in it
89. 10. thou hast s. thine enemies with thy arm
92. 9. all the workers of iniquity shall be s.
141. 7. our bones are s. at the grave's mouth
Isa. 18. 2. go ye messengers to a nation s. and peeled
7. the present shall be brought of a people s.
33. 3. at lifting up of thyself the nations were s.
Jer. 3. 13. and hast s. thy ways to the strangers
10. 21. and all their flocks shall be s.
23. 2. ye have s. my flock, and driven them away
30. 11. an end of all nations whither I have s. thee
31. 10. he that s. Isr. will gather him and keep him
40. 15. that all Jews should be s. and Judah perish?
50. 17. Israel is a s. sheep, lions have driven
Ezek. 6. 8. when ye shall be s. through the countries
11. 16. though I s. them, I will be a little sanctuary
17. I will gather and assemble you out of countries where ye have been s. 20. 34, 41. | 28. 25.
17. 21. they that remain shall be s. to all winds
29. 13. Egyptians gathered whither they were s.
34. 5. flock s. because there is no shepherd, they became meat to beasts of field when they were s.
6. my flock was s. on the face of the earth
12. in the day that he is among his sheep that are s. where they have been s. in the cloudy day
21. pushed the diseased till ye have s. them
36. 19. and I s. them among the heathen
46. 18. that my people be not s. every man
Joel 3. 2. plead for my people whom they have s.
Nah. 3. 18. thy people is s. on the mountains
Hab. 3. 6. the everlasting mountains were s.
Zech. 1. 19. these are the horns which have s. 21.
7. 14. I s. them with whirlwind among nations
13. 7. awake, O sword, smite the shepherd, and the sheep shall be s. Mat. 26. 31. Mark 14. 27.
Mat. 9. 36. they were s. as sheep having no shep.
Luke 1. 51. he hath s. the proud in the imagination
John 11. 52. gather in one the children that were s.
16. 32. hour cometh, is now, that ye shall be s.
Acts 5. 36. as many as obeyed Theudas were s.
8. 1. were s. abroad through the regions of Judea
4. were s. went every where preaching, 11. 19.
Jam. 1. 1. to the twelve tribes that are s. abroad
1 Pet. 1. 1. Peter to the strangers s. through Pontus

SCATTERETH.
Job 37. 11. the thick cloud he s. his bright cloud
38. 24. which s. the east-wind upon the earth
Psal. 147. 16. he s. the hoar-frost like ashes
Prov. 11. 24. there is that s. and yet increaseth
20. 8. a king s. away all evil with his eyes
26. a wise king s. the wicked, and bringeth wheel
Isa. 24. 1. the Lord s. the inhabitants of the earth
Mat. 12. 30. he not with me is ag. me, and he that gathereth not with me, s. abroad, Luke 11. 23.
John 10. 12. the wolf catcheth and s. the sheep

SCATTERING.
Job 37. † 9. and cold cometh out of the s. winds
Isa. 30. 30. the Lord shall shew his anger with s.

SCENT.
Job 14. 9. yet through the s. of water it will bud
Jer. 48. 11. therefore his s. is not changed
Hos. 14. 7. the s. thereof be the wine of Lebanon

SCEPTRE.

In Greek, σκηπτρον; *in* Hebrew, Shebet. *This word signifies,* I. *A rod of command, a staff of authority, which is supposed to be in the hand of kings, of sovereigns of a province, of the chief of the people.* Ahasuerus *carried in his hand a golden* sceptre, *Esth.* 8. 4. *The* sceptre *is a sign of power and authority; hence says* Isaiah, The Lord hath broken the *sceptre, or the power* of the rulers, *Isa.* 14. 5. *And* Amos *represents the sovereign power by* him that holds the sceptre, *Amos* 1. 5, 8.

II. *The* sceptre, *or the word* Shebet, *is put for the rod of correction, for the sovereign authority that punishes and humbles.* Thou shalt break them with a rod of iron, *or with an iron* sceptre, *Psal.* 2. 9. Solomon *uses the word* Shebet, *to express the rod with which the disobedient son is disciplined,* Prov. 22. 15.

III. *The* sceptre *is often taken for a tribe, probably, because the princes of each tribe carried a* sceptre, *as a wand of command, to shew their dignity; thus the word* shebet *is rendered in* 1 Sam. 9. 21. | 10. 19, 20, 21. | 15. 17. 1 Kings 11. 32.

IV. *The* sceptre, *or the* Hebrew *word* shebet, *signifies a shepherd's wand,* Lev. 27. 32. *The truncheon of a warrior, or any common staff,* 2 Sam. 23. 21. *And the rod or flail with which they thresh the smaller grain,* Isa. 28. 27.

Jacob *foretold to* Judah, *that the sceptre* should not depart from *Judah*, nor a lawgiver from between his feet, till *Shiloh* come, *Gen.* 49. 10. *By the* sceptre *and* lawgiver, *are meant divers forms of government: the first being the mark of regal power or sovereignty; the other title respects those whose power succeeded that of their kings, in the person of* Zerubbabel *and his successors: and this is that which should not depart from* Judah *till* Shiloh, *or the* Messiah, *should come. This prophesy doth not precisely respect the person of* Judah, *for he never ascended the throne, nor possessed the empire over his brethren; neither doth it respect his posterity as a tribe distinguished from the rest, although it had special advantages from that time: for the banner of* Judah *led the camp in their march through the wilderness,* Num. 2. 3. *That tribe had the first possession of the land of* Canaan, Josh. 15. 1. *And these were the beginnings of its future glory. And from* David *to the captivity, that tribe possessed the kingdom, but the glory of his sceptre was lost in the person of* Zedekiah. *Therefore the full meaning of the prophecy regards the people of* Israel, *in the relation they had to the tribe of* Judah: *for that tribe alone returned entire from the captivity, with some relics of* Levi *and* Benjamin; *so that the nation from that time was distinguished by the title of the* Jews, *in relation to it: and the right to dispose of the* sceptre *was always in the tribe of* Judah: *for the* Levites *that ruled after that time received their power from them: so that the intent of the prophesy is, that after the establishment of the supreme power in the family of* Judah, *it should not pass into the hands of strangers, but as a certain presage, and immediate forerunner of the coming of* Shiloh. *And this was fully accomplished: for in the captivity there was an interruption, rather than an extinction, of their government; their return was promised at the time they were carried captives to* Babylon: *but at the coming of Christ,* Judea *was a province of the* Roman *empire:* Herod, *an* Edomite, *sat on the throne; and as the tribe of* Judah *in general, so the family of* David *in particular, was in such a low state, that* Joseph *and* Mary, *who were descended from him, were constrained to lodge in a stable at* Bethlehem. *And since our blessed Saviour hath appeared on the earth, the* Jews *have lost all authority, their civil and ecclesiastical state is utterly ruined, and they bear the visible signs and marks of infamous servitude. For though great numbers of this people swarm all over the world, since the destruction of their temple and city by* Titus, *yet they have never been able to embody again into a nation, either in their own, or any other land; nor have they to this day ever found a place where they could re-establish their old constitution of law, or have a prince of their own to govern them by it.*

The Jews *seek in vain to put forced meanings upon this prophecy of* Jacob, *saying, that the* sceptre *intimates the dominion of strangers, to which they have been in subjection, or the hope of seeing, one day, the sceptre, or supreme power, settled again among themselves. In vain likewise they take refuge in their* Æchmalotarcha; *that is,* The Head of the captivity. *Such an officer the* Babylonish Jews had, *to whom they paid a voluntary submission, and who was always chosen by them out of the house of* David. *If such an officer be still there in being, he is no more than what their* Alabarcha *was at* Alexandria, *their* Ethnarcha, *at* Antioch, *or their* Episcopus Judæorum, *in* England; *that is, the head of that sect in that place, without sword or sceptre, or any power of coercion, or authority of jurisdiction, but what he hath by the voluntary submission of the* Jews *of that country, which was the case with their* Babylonian Æchmalotarcha. *Nothing therefore can be more vain than what the* Jews *urge as to this matter; that is, that in this* Æchmalotarcha *is still preserved both the* Sceptre *and the* Lawgiver *in the tribe of* Judah, *and that therefore the prophecy of* Jacob *is not yet fulfilled, nor the* Messiah *as yet come.*

Gen. 49. 10. the s. shall not depart from Judah
Num. 24. 17. and a s. shall rise out of Israel
Esth. 4. 11. the king shall hold out the golden s.
5. 2. king held out to Esther the golden s. 8. 4.
Psal. 45. 6. the s. of thy kingdom is a right s.
Isa. 14. 5. Lord hath broken the s. of the rulers
Ezek. 19. 11. she had strong rods for the s. of them
14. so that she hath no strong rod to be a s. to rule
Amos 1. 5. I will cut off him that holdeth the s.
8. will cut off him that holdeth s. from Ashkelon
Zech. 10. 11. and the s. of Egypt shall depart away
Heb. 1. 8. s. of righteousness is the s. of thy kingdom

SCHISM

Is *a word formed from the* Greek *word* Σχισμα, *which signifies rupture, or division. The apostle* Paul *exhorts the* Corinthians *to live in union together*, that there may be no divisions, or *schisms*, among them, 1 *Cor.* 1. 10, 11, 12. *As* heresy *is a departing from the communion of the church, in respect of doctrine, or some fundamental article of religion, so* schism *is taken for a separation from the society of the church for external things. Thus the divisions among the* Corinthians *were not about matters of faith, but occasioned from their having men's persons in admiration;* every one of you saith, I am of *Paul*, and I of *Apollos*, and I of *Cephas*, and I of *Christ*.

1 Cor. 12. 25. that there should be no s. in the body

SCHOLAR.
1 Chron. 25. 8. they cast lots, the teacher as the s.
Mal. 2. 12. Lord will cut off the master and the s.

SCHOOL.

Though it cannot be doubted, but that religious and devout men, from the first beginning of mankind, did take care to instruct their children and families in the fear of God, yet, for many ages, there is no mention made of academies, *or* schools *erected for this purpose. The* schools *or* colleges *of the prophets are the first of which we have any accounts in Scripture; where the children of the prophets, that is, their disciples, lived in the exercise of a retired and austere life, in study, and meditation, and reading of the law of God. It is said,* 1 Sam. 19. 18. David fled, and escaped, and came to *Samuel* to *Ramah*, and told him all that *Saul* had done to him: And he and *Samuel* went and dwelt at *Naioth*. *This* Naioth, *which was in the suburbs of* Ramah, *was the* academy *of the prophets. And it is probable, that among them* Samuel *chose to spend all the leisure time he could get from the necessary avocations of his public duty. We find more also under the prophets* Elijah *and* Elisha, *at* Beth-el, *and in the plain of* Jericho, 2 *Kings* 2. 3, 5. *These prophets were consulted upon affairs of importance; people went to hear their lessons, as appears from the woman of* Shunem, *with whom* Elisha *had lodged. Her husband asked her,* Why she went to see the prophet, seeing that day was neither the Sabbath, nor the new-moon, 2 *Kings* 4. 23. *which insinuates that these were the chief and usual times in which they resorted to the prophets for instruction. These* Schools *continued down to the captivity of* Babylon, *and it should seem, that even the captives went still to hear the prophets, when there were any in the places where they resided.* Ezekiel *relates several conversations that he had with the elders of* Israel, *who came to see him, and to consult him several times,* Ezek. 14. 1, 2. | 20. 1, 2, 3. *These* Schools, *or Societies, of the prophets, were succeeded by the synagogues. See* SYNAGOGUE.

Some make it a doubt whether there were any synagogues before the captivity of Babylon. *Yet we read in* Psal. 74. 8. They have burnt up all the synagogues of God in the land. *It is affirmed, however, that they were become so numerous in* Judea, *after the return from the captivity, that in the city of* Jerusalem *only, there were upwards of four hundred, according to some; or three hundred and ninety-four, according to others.*

The method of teaching in the Synagogues *and in the* Schools, *is observable in the Gospels and in the* Acts. *When* Jesus *was of the age of twelve years,* he was found in the temple in the midst of the doctors, hearing them, and asking them questions, *Luke* 2. 46. *By which it should seem, that the doctors of the law gave a general liberty to any person to propound questions to them about the law of God, to which they gave answers. Our Saviour entering another day into the synagogue of* Nazareth, *his own country, they presented to him the volume of the prophet* Isaiah: *He unfolded and opened it, and having read a passage out of the prophet, he rolled it up again, and sat down to speak,* Luke 4. 16, 17, *&c. As to the posture of the disciples in the schools, the apostle* Paul *speaks of it in* Acts 22. 3. I was brought up in this city, at the feet of *Gamaliel*. *The* Rabbin *sat upon a chair that was raised aloft; the scholars that were the greatest proficients, were upon benches just below their master; and the younger sort sat upon the ground on hassocks.*

Acts 19. 9. disputing in the s. of one Tyrannus

SCHOOL-MASTER.

Gal. 3. 24. the law was our s. to bring us to Christ
25. after faith we are no longer under a s.

SCIENCE.

Dan. 1. 4. children skilful in wisdom, understan. s.
1 Tim. 6. 20. avoiding babblings and oppositions of s.

SCOFF.

Hab. 1. 10. they shall s. at the kings and princes

SCOFFERS.

2 Pet. 3. 3. there shall come in last days s. walking

SCORCH.

Rev. 16. 8. power was given him to s. men with fire

SCORCHED.

Mat. 13. 6. when sun was up they were s. Mark 4. 6.
Rev. 16. 9. and men were s. with great heat

SCORN, Verb.

Job 16. 20. my friends s. me, mine eye poureth tears

SCORN.

Esth. 3. 6. he thought s. to lay hands on Mordecai
Ps. 44. 13. thou makest us a reproach and s. 79. 4.
Hab. 1. 10. and the princes shall be a s. to them
See LAUGHED.

SCORNER.

A scorner *is one who makes a mock of sin, and of God's threatenings and judgments against sinners; one who derides all wholesome reproofs and counsels, scoffs at religion, and contemns the word and faithful ministers of* God; *he is a monster of iniquity, having obtained the highest degree of sinning.* Psal. 1. 1. Blessed is the man that sitteth not in the seat of the scornful. Prov. 1. 22. How long will the scorners delight in their scorning? Solomon *describes the* Scorner *in a variety of expressions; he is one that takes* pleasure in scorning, Prov. 1. 22. *He is ready to hate such as rebuke him, and to entertain malicious and revengeful thoughts against them.* Prov. 9. 8. Reprove not a scorner, lest he hate thee. *He stoppeth his ears against reproofs.* Prov. 13. 1. A scorner heareth not rebuke. *He is proud, arrogant, and haughty,* Prov. 21. 24. *He causes strifes, contentions, and divisions in a society.* Prov. 22. 10. Cast out the scorner, and contention shall go out. *He brings others likewise into a snare, and that by his wicked counsels and courses, whereby he seduces and infects them, so that they are exposed to God's wrath.* Prov. 29. 8. Scornful men bring a city into a snare. *God's dreadful judgments are threatened against them in a remarkable manner.* Prov. 3. 34. | 9. 12. | 19. 29. Surely he scorneth the scorners. If thou scornest, thou alone shalt bear it. Judgments are prepared for scorners. *And it is said,* that he seeketh wisdom, and findeth it not, *Prov.* 14. 6. *He finds it not, because he doth not seek it aright, to wit, sincerely, earnestly, and seasonably, and in a constant and diligent use of all the means which God hath appointed to that end, and with an honest intention of employing his knowledge to the service of God, and the furtherance of his practice of religion.*

Prov. 9. 7. he that reproveth a s. getteth shame
8. reprove not a s. lest he hate thee, rebuke a wise
13. 1. but a s. heareth not rebuke
14. 6. a s. seeketh wisdom, and findeth it not
15. 12. a s. loveth not one that reproveth him
19. 25. smite a s. ‖ 22. 10. cast out the s.
21. 11. when s. is punished, simple is made wise
24. s. is his name, who dealeth in proud wrath
24. 9. and the s. is an abomination to men
Isa. 29. 20. the s. is consumed, and all that watch

SCORNERS.

Prov. 1. 22. how long will s. delight in their scorning
3. 34. surely he scorneth the s. but he giveth grace
19. 29. judgments are prepared for s. and stripes
Hos. 7. 5. he stretched out his hands with s.

SCORNEST.

Prov. 9. 12. if thou s. thou alone shalt bear it
Ezek. 16. 31. not been as harlot, in that thou s. hire

SCORNETH.

Job 39. 7. he s. the multitude of the city
18. the ostrich, she s. the horse and his rider
Prov. 3. 34. surely he s. the scorner, but giveth grace
19. 28. an ungodly witness s. judgment, and mouth

SCORNFUL.

Psal. 1. 1. nor sitteth in the seat of the s.
Prov. 29. 8. s. men bring a city into a snare
Isa. 28. 14. hear the word of the Lord, ye s. men

SCORNING.

Job 34. 7. who is like Job, who drinks up s. like [water?
Ps. 123. 4. is filled with s. of those that are at ease
Prov. 1. 22. how long will scorners delight in their s.

SCORPION.

A *venomous reptile, somewhat like a small lobster, that has a bladder full of dangerous poison: its head appears to be joined and continued to the breast: it has two eyes in the middle of its head, and two towards its extremity, between which come out, as it were two arms, which are divided into two like the claws of a lobster. It has eight legs, proceeding from its breast, every one of which is divided into six parts, covered with hair, at the end of which are six talons or claws. The belly is divided into seven rings, from the last of which the tail proceeds, which is divided into seven little heads, of which the last is armed with a sting. In some are observed six eyes, and in others eight may be visibly perceived. The tail is long, and made after the manner of a string of beads tied end to end, one to another: the last bigger than the others, and something longer; at the end of which are sometimes two stings, which are hollow, and filled with a cold poison, which it squirts into the part which it stings.*

The Scorpion *is of a blackish colour, like soot; it waddles as it goes, and fixes violently with its snout, and by its feet, on such persons as it seizes upon, so that it cannot be plucked off but with difficulty. They say, that the dam brings forth eleven young ones, which are small round worms; that after she has sat upon them, and hatched them, then they kill the mother. They are more mischievous to women than men, and more to girls than women. It is said, that the best and surest remedy against the bite of a* Scorpion *is, to squeeze it to pieces upon the wound.* Moses *says, that the* Israelites *passed through a great and terrible wilderness, wherein were fiery serpents, and* Scorpions, *Deut.* 8. 15. *The* Hebrew *reads* Hakarab, *or* Akrab; *from whence is* Akrabbim; *the ascent of* Akrabbim, *or* Scorpions, *Num.* 34. 4.

In scripture, Scorpions *are used in a figurative sense, for wicked, malicious, and crafty men, who, scorpion-like, wound, torment, and kill good men.* Ezek. 2. 6. Thou dwellest among Scorpions. *Our Saviour says to his disciples,* Luke 10. 19. Behold I give unto you power to tread on serpents and scorpions; *by which may be signified whatsoever the devil may make use of to hurt them. The disciples of Antichrist, who by their poisonous doctrines wound the souls of men, are likewise compared to* Scorpions, *Rev.* 9. 3.

Scorpions *were also a kind of whip armed with points, or pointed thorns, like the tail of a* Scorpion. *When the Israelites complained to* Rehoboam *of the weight of the yoke wherewith* Solomon *had loaded them,* Thy father made our yoke grievous, make it lighter, *he returned them this answer;* Whereas my father did lade with an heavy yoke, I will add to your yoke: my father hath chastised you with whips, but I will chastise you with scorpions, 1 *Kings* 12. 4, 11, 14.

Luke 11. 12. if he ask an egg, will he offer him a s.?
Rev. 9. 5. their torment was as the torment of a s.

SCORPIONS.

Deut. 8. 15. through that wilderness wherein were s.
1 Kings 12. 11. my father chastised you with whips, but I will chastise you with s. 14. 2 Chr. 10. 11, 14.
Ezek. 2. 6. tho' thou dost dwell among s. be not afraid
Luke 10. 19. I give you power to tread on ser. and s.
Rev. 9. 3. to them was given power, as s. have power
10. they had tails like to s. and stings in them

SCOURED.

Lev. 6. 28. if it be sodden in a brasen pot, it shall be s.

SCOURGE.

The punishment of the scourge, *or* whip, *was very common among the* Jews. *The law ordains, that* if the wicked man be worthy to be beaten, the judge shall cause him to lie down, and to be beaten before his face, according to his fault, by a certain number: Forty stripes he may give him, and not exceed: lest, if he should exceed, and beat him above these with many stripes, then thy brother should seem vile unto thee, *Deut.* 25. 1, 2, 3. *There were two ways of giving the lash; one with thongs or whips, made of ropes' ends, or straps of leather; the other, with rods, twigs, or branches of some tree.*

The Rabbins *think, that ordinary faults committed against the law, and submitted to the penalty of the* scourge, *were punished, not with blows with a rod, but with a whip. They hold, that all punishable faults, to which the law has not annexed the kind or degree of punishment, are to be punished by the* scourge. *The offender was stript from his shoulders to his middle, and was tied by his arms to a pretty low pillar, that he might lean forward, and the executioner might the more easily come at his back. The law directed that they should not exceed the number of forty stripes: and the* Jews, *that they might not transgress this law, seem to have made thirty-nine blows a fixed number, which they never went beyond, as may be gathered from* 2 Cor. 11. 24. *where the apostle says,* Of the Jews five times received I forty stripes save one. *But it is said, that in greater faults they struck with greater violence.*

The Rabbins *further say, that the penalty of the scourge was not at all ignominious among them, and that it could not be objected as a disgrace to those that had suffered it. They pretend, that no* Israelite, *not so much as the king, or high-priest, was exempted from this law, when he had committed any fault that deserved this punishment. But this must be understood of the punishment of whipping that was inflicted in their synagogues, and which was rather a legal and particular penalty, than a public and shameful correction.* Philo, *speaking of the manner in which* Flaccus *treated the* Jews *of* Alexandria, *says, he made them undergo the punishment of the whip, which,* says he, *is not less insupportable to a free man, than death itself. Our Saviour, speaking of the pains and ignominy of his passion, commonly puts his* scourging *in the first place,* Mat. 20. 19. Mark 10. 34. Luke 18. 33.

The punishment of scourging *inflicted on our Saviour, which is mentioned in* Mat. 27. 26. *has given occasion for several conjectures: Some say, that this punishment among the* Romans *was a solemn preparative to crucifixion, but this would make scourging a part of the sentence of death pronounced upon our Saviour, which it was not, as appears from* John 19. 1, 4, 6, &c. *where it is said, that* Pilate *again and again sought to release him, even after he was scourged, and that he told the* Jews *that he found no fault in him; but being pressed upon by the* Jews, *he at last gave sentence against him, that he should be crucified, which was not till some time after he had been scourged.* Grotius *explains this of the punishment of* putting one to the question, *which was common among the* Romans, *an example of which we have in* Acts 22. 24. *Concerning which, see* QUESTION. *But the gospels give no ground for this conjecture. The reason generally assigned for our Saviour's being scourged is, that* Pilate, *willing to deliver him from a capital sentence, appointed this of* scourging *to be inflicted on him: He proposed to the* Jews *the* scourging *of him, as a lighter punishment, proportionable to the crimes they laid against him, intending afterwards to release him. So that the notion of his scourging was that of a* lighter punishment, *to release him from a* greater; *though when that was inflicted, he was prevailed upon to gratify the* Jews, *by delivering* Jesus *up to be crucified.*

The scourge of the tongue. *Job* 5. 21. Thou shalt be hid from the scourge of the tongue, *or,* when the tongue scourgeth; *that is, from false accusations, and virulent slanders and reproaches.* Scourge, *figuratively, is taken for any instrument which God makes use of for executing his judgments: thus he used a destroying angel to scourge the* Assyrians, *Isa.* 10. 26. | 37. 36.

Job 5. 21. thou shalt be hid from s. of the tongue
9. 23. if the s. slay suddenly, he will laugh at trial
Isa. 10. 26. Lord of hosts shall stir up a s. for him
28. 15. when the overflowing s. shall pass, 18.
John 2. 15. when he had made a s. of small cords

SCOURGE.

Mat. 10. 17. they will s. you in their synagogues
20. 19. they shall s. him, Mark 10. 34. Luke 18. 33.
23. 34. some of them ye shall s. and persecute
Acts 22. 25. is it lawful for you to s. a Roman?

SCOURGED.

Lev. 19. 20. lie with a bond-maid, she shall be s.
Mat. 27. 26. and when they had s. Jes. he delivered him to be crucified, Mark 15. 15. John 19. 1.

SCOURGES.

Josh. 23. 13. s. in your sides, and thorns in your eyes

SCOURGETH.

Heb. 12. 6. the Ld. s. every son whom he receiveth

SCOURGING.

Acts 22. 24. that he should be examined by s.

SCOURGINGS.

Heb. 11. 36. others had trial of s. yea of bonds

SCRABBLED.

1 Sam. 21. 13. David feigned himself mad, and s.

SCRAPE.

Lev. 14. 41. shall pour out the dust that they s. off
Job 2. 8. Job took a potsherd to s. himself withal
Ezek. 26. 4. I will also s. her dust from her

SCRAPED.

Lev. 14. 41. he shall cause the house to be s. within
43. if plague come again, after he hath s. house

SCRIBE.

In Hebrew, Sopher; *in* Greek, γραμματευς. *This word is taken,* I. *For a clerk, writer, or secretary. This was a very considerable employment in the court of the kings of* Judah, *in which the scripture often mentions the secretaries, as the first officers of the crown.* Seraiah *was* Scribe, *or secretary, to king* David, 2 Sam. 8. 17. Sheva *is said to have filled that post,* 2 Sam. 20. 25. Elihoreph *and* Ahiah, *were secretaries to king* Solomon, 1 *Kings* 4. 3. Shebna *under* Hezekiah, 2 *Kings* 19. 2. and Shaphan *under* Josiah, 2 Kings 22. 8. *As there were but few in those times that could write well, the employment of a* Scribe *or writer was very considerable.*

II. *A* Scribe *is put for a Commissary or Mustermaster of an army, who makes the review of the troops, keeps the list or roll, and calls them over: Under the reign of* Uzziah *king of* Judah, *there is found* Jeil the Scribe, *who had under his hand the king's armies,* 2 Chron. 26. 11. *And at the time of the captivity, it is said,* The captain of the guard, *among other considerable persons,* took the principal Scribe of the host, *or Secretary of war,* who mustered the people of the land, 2 *Kings* 25. 19.

III. Scribe *is put for an able and skilful man, a doctor of the law, a man of learning, that understands affairs.* Jonathan, *David's uncle by the father's side, was* a counsellor, a wise man and a Scribe, 1 *Chron.* 27. 32. Baruch, *the disciple and secretary of* Jeremiah, *is called a* Scribe, *Jer.* 36. 26. *And* Ezra *is celebrated as a skilful* Scribe *in the law of his God,* Ezra 7. 6. *The* Scribes *of the people, who are frequently mentioned in the gospel, were public writers, and professed doctors of the law, which they read and explained to the people.*

Some place the original of Scribes *under* Moses; *but their name does not appear till under the* Judges. *It is said, that in the war of* Barak *against* Sisera, out of *Machir* came down governors, and out of *Zebulun* they that handle the pen of the writer, *Judg.* 5. 14. *Others think that* David *first instituted them, when he established the several classes of the priests and Levites.* The Scribes *were of the tribe of* Levi; *and at the time that* David *is said to have made the regulation of that tribe, we read that six thousand of them were constituted* Officers and Judges, 1 *Chron.* 23. 4. *among whom it is reasonable to believe the* Scribes *were included: For in* 1 Chron. 24. 6. *we read of* Shemaiah, the Scribe, one of the Levites; *and in* 2 Chron. 34. 13. *we find it written,* Of the Levites, there were Scribes and Officers.

It is not unlikely that they might have had their education among the colleges of the prophets; since we do not read of any other schools of learning than among them. Their very name implies some degree of scholarship, and that no inconsiderable one; since we find our Lord joining prophets and wise men, *and* Scribes *together,* Mat. 23. 34. *And the prophet* Isaiah, *and after him the apostle* Paul, *instancing them as such: Where is the wise? where is the Scribe? where is the disputer of this world?* Isa. 33. 18. 1 Cor. 1. 20.

The Scribes, *and doctors of the law, in scripture-phrase, mean the same thing: And he that in* Mat. 22. 35. *is called a doctor of the law,* or a lawyer, *in* Mark 12. 28. *is named a* Scribe, *or one of the* Scribes. *They seem to have had the sole expounding of the Scriptures; and therefore the disciples ask our Saviour,* Mat. 17. 10. Why then say the Scribes that *Elias* must first come? *And in* Mark 12. 35. How say the Scribes that Christ is the Son of *David*? *And* in Luke 20. 1, 2. while Christ was preaching the gospel, the chief priests and Scribes came upon him, with the elders, saying, tell us by what authority doest thou these things? or who is he that gave thee this authority? which they thought no one had a right to but themselves.

Though they were employed to be the judges, interpreters, and preachers of the law to the people, we find that they came, in length of time, greatly to abuse their trust; by delivering traditions, instead of Scripture, and thereby setting aside even the law itself. Thus they very pertly demanded of Christ, Mat. 15. 2, 3, &c. Why do thy disciples transgress the tradition of the elders? which our Lord fully answers by another question; Why do you transgress the commandment of God by your tradition? For God commanded, saying, Honour thy father, &c.

Their departure from the true faith in doctrine, was accompanied, as is generally the case, with a depravity of morals in their lives; for all their outward zeal and profession, they had little or no true religion at bottom. Therefore our Saviour says to his audience upon the mount, Except your righteousness shall exceed the righteousness of the Scribes and Pharisees, ye shall in no case enter into the kingdom of heaven, Mat. 5. 20. And he gives various instances of their irregular and unjust doings, in Mat. 23. 2, 3, 4, &c. And because they, the least of all men, could bear a reformation, we find them taking all occasions to oppose the preaching and spreading of the gospel: They murmur at our Lord, whenever they see him to do an act of charity or public good. They upbraid him for eating with publicans and sinners. They charge him with holding a correspondence with Beelzebub. They watch him; seek to lay hands on him; vehemently accuse him before the Roman governor; and at last suborn false witnesses to procure him to be crucified.

2 Sam. 8. 17. Seraiah was s. ‖ 20. 25. Sheva was s.
2 Kings 18. 18. there came out Eliakim, and Shebna
the s. 37. | 19. 2. Isa. 36. 3, 22. | 37. 2.
22. 3. the king sent Shaphan, the s. 8, 9, 10, 12.
2 Chron. 34. 15, 18, 20. Jer. 36. 10.
25. 19. he took principal s. of the host, Jer. 52. 25.
1 Chron. 24. 6. and Shemaiah the s. wrote them
27. 32. also Jonathan was a wise man and a s.
Ezra 4. 8. Shimshai the s. wrote a letter, 9, 17, 23.
7. 6. Ezra went from Babylon, was a ready s. in
the law, 11, 12. Neh. 8. 4, 9, 13. | 12. 26, 36.
Neh. 8. 4. Ezra the s. stood upon a pulpit of wood
13. 13. Shelemiah the priest, Zadok the s.
Isa. 33. 18. where is the s.? where is the receiver?
Jer. 36. 12. princes sat, even Elishama the s. 20, 21.
26. Baruch the s. 32. | 37. 15. Jonathan the s. 20.
Mat. 8. 19. a s. said, Master, I will follow thee
13. 52. s. instructed unto the kingdom of heaven
Mark 12. 32. the s. said unto him, well, Master
1 Cor. 1. 20. where is the s.? where is the disputer?

SCRIBES.

1 Kings 4. 3. Elihoreph and Ahiah, sons of Shisha, s.
1 Chron 2. 55. the families of the s. at Jabez
2 Chron. 34. 13. of Levites there were s. and officers
Esth. 3. 12. then were the king's s. called, 8. 9.
Jer. 8. 8. the pen of the s. is in vain
Mat. 5. 20. except exceed the righteousness of the s.
7. 29. for he taught them as one having authority,
and not as the s. Mark 1. 22.
16. 21. he must suffer many things of the s.
17. 10. why say s. Elias must come, Mark 9. 11.
20. 18. Son of man be betrayed to s. Mark 10. 33.
21. 15. when the s. saw, they were sore displeased
23. 2. the s. and Pharisees sit in Moses' seat
13. woe to you s. 14, 15, 23, 25, 27, 29. Luke 11. 44.
26. 3. then assembled the chief priests and s. and
elders of the people, Mark 14. 53. Luke 22. 66.
Mark 2. 6. went certain s. reasoning in their hearts
16. when the s. saw him eat with publicans
3. 22. the s. said, he hath Beelzebub, by prince
8. 31. Son of man must be rejected of s. Luke 9. 22.
9. 14. the s. questioning with the disciples
11. 18. the s. and chief priests heard it, and sought
how they might destroy him, Luke 19. 47.
27. s. say, by what authority doest thou these things?
12. 28. one of s. asked what is the first command?
35. how say s. that Christ is the Son of David?
38. he said to them, beware of s. Luke 20. 46.
14. 1. the s. sought how to take him by craft
Luke 5. 30. the s. and Pharisees murmured, 15. 2.
6. 7. s. watched him ‖ 20. 1. the s. came upon him
11. 53. the s. began to urge him vehemently
20. 19. priests and s. sought to lay hands on him
22. 2. the chief priests and s. sought to kill him
23. 10. the s. stood and vehemently accused him
John 8. 3. the s. brought a woman taken in adultery
Acts 4. 5. the s. gathered against the apostles
6. 12. the s. brought Stephen to the council
23. 9. the s. of the Pharisees part arose and strove

SCRIP.

1 Sam. 17. 40. David put smooth stones in a s.
Mat. 10. 10. provide no silv. nor s. for your journey,
nor two coats, Mark 6. 8. Luke 9. 3. | 10. 4.
Luke 22. 35. when I sent you without s. lacked ye
36. but now let him take his purse and his s.

SCRIPTURE,

Or Writing. There is great dispute concerning the first inventor of letters and writing. Some maintain that there was writing before the deluge, and that Adam was the inventor of letters. Others think, that Moses is the first author of whom we have any writings, and that before him there were no written monuments. Through the whole lives of the patriarchs, there are found no footsteps of any writing; neither does Moses quote any writing, that was extant before his own; for the book of the wars of the Lord, mentioned, Num. 21. 14. some think that it is a passage added to the text of Moses, or that it was a writing composed in his time. Others take it as a prophecy of what should afterwards be recorded in the books of Joshua and Judges; and instead of reading the text, It is said in the book of the wars of the Lord, they say the Hebrew will bear to be read in the future tense, It shall be said in the book of the wars.

All agree that it is an admirable invention: To paint speech, and speak to the eyes, and by tracing out characters in different forms to give colour and body to thoughts. It is also agreed by all, that there is nothing extant this day in the world, either more ancient, or more authentic, than the books of Moses; but it does not follow from thence, that there was no writing before him. It appears, on the contrary, that writing was known and common enough at that time both among the Egyptians and Hebrews. This people seemed already prepared and accustomed to express their thoughts and sentiments after this manner. And it is to be supposed, that the chief of the nation read the tables of the law. Moses had been instructed in all the knowledge of the Egyptians, and, doubtless, had learned their manner of writing.

The word Scripture generally stands for the sacred books of the Old and New Testament, written by holy men, as they were inspired, instructed, and enabled by the Holy Ghost. 2 Tim. 3. 16. All Scripture is given by inspiration of God, and is profitable for doctrine, to declare and confirm the truth: for reproof, to convince of sin, and confute errors; for correction, to reform the life; and for instruction in righteousness, that is, to teach us to make a further progress in the way to heaven; or to instruct us in the true righteousness revealed by the gospel of Jesus Christ, in which we may appear with comfort before God. Scripture is sometimes taken for some one sentence or passage of the sacred writings. Mark 15. 28. The scripture was fulfilled, which saith, And he was numbered with the transgressors. The passage referred to is recorded in Isa. 53. 12. Scripture is also taken for the Holy Ghost speaking in the Scripture, by whose inspiration the Scripture was written. Gal. 3. 8. The Scripture, foreseeing that God would justify the heathen through faith, preached before the gospel unto Abraham, saying, In thee shall all nations be blessed. And in John 5. 39, our Saviour says, Search the Scriptures, for in them ye think ye have eternal life, and they are they which testify of me: that is, Diligently examine the books of the Old Testament, which yourselves acknowledge do set forth the true way to eternal life: and upon due trial you will find, that all those prophecies and types are fulfilled in me; and that all the promises of life there made, have respect to me, and point me out as the true Messiah.

The inspired writings of the Old and New Testaments are called, the Scriptures, the Bible, or the Book, by way of eminency and distinction; because they far excel all other books: for, (1) They contain the whole will of God necessary to be known for our salvation. (2) They contain that wisdom which is far above all the wisdom of the world, 1 Cor. 2. 7. (3) They were inspired by the Holy Ghost, 2 Tim. 3. 16. 2 Pet. 1. 21. (4) They were penned by the most excellent of men, for wisdom and holiness, as Moses, David, Solomon, the prophets, apostles, and evangelists. (5) They are most perfect, pure, deep, and immutable, and contain all things necessary for faith and practice, Psal. 19. 7. 2 Tim. 3. 16, 17. 1 Pet. 1. 23. (6) No writings or scriptures but these bring such glory to God, or have such an efficacy in converting a soul, Psal. 19. 7, 8. Heb. 4. 12. (7) Though these books were written by divers men in divers ages, yet there is as great harmony in them, as if they had been written by one man.

Dan. 10. 21. shew what is noted in the s. of truth
Mark 12. 10. have ye not read this s. stone which
15. 28. the s. was fulfilled which saith, he was
Luke 4. 21. he said, this day is this s. fulfilled
John 2. 22. they believed the s. and the word Jesus
7. 38. he that believeth on me, as the s. saith
42. hath not the s. said, Christ cometh of David?
10. 35. word came, and the s. cannot be broken
19. 37. ag. another s. saith, they shall look on him
Acts 1. 16. this s. must needs have been fulfilled
8. 32. the place of the s. which he read was this
35. Philip began at the same s. and preached Jes.
Rom. 4. 3. what saith the s.? 11. 2. Gal. 4. 30.
9. 17. for the s. saith, 10. 11. 1 Tim. 5. 18.
Gal. 3. 8. the s. foreseeing that God would justify
22. but the s. hath concluded all under sin
2 Tim. 3. 16. all s. is given by inspiration of God
Jam. 4. 5. do you think the s. saith in vain
1 Pet. 2. 6. also it is contained in the s. I lay in Sion
2 Pet. 1. 20. no prophecy of s. is of private interpr.

SCRIPTURES.

Mat. 21. 42. have ye never read in the s. the stone
22. 29. ye do err, not knowing the s. Mark 12. 24.
26. 54. but how then shall the s. be fulfilled?
Mark 14. 49. but the s. must be fulfilled
Luke 24. 27. he expounded to them in all the s.
32. did not our heart burn, while he opened to us s.
45. opened underst. that they might understand s.
John 5. 39. search s. for in them ye think ye have
Acts 17. 2. he reasoned with them out of the s.
11. were more noble, and searched the s. daily
18. 24. a Jew named Apollos, mighty in the s.
28. shewing by the s. that Jesus was Christ
Rom. 1. 2. promised afore by prophets in the holy s.
15. 4. that we thro' comfort of s. might have hope
16. 26. and by the s. made known to all nations
1 Cor. 15. 3. Christ died ‖ 4. rose according to the s.
2 Tim. 3. 15. from a child thou hast known holy s.
2 Pet. 3. 16. unstable wrest, as they do also other s.

SCROLL.

Isa. 34. 4. heavens shall be rolled together as a s.
Rev. 6. 14. and the heaven departed as a s. rolled

SCUM.

Ezek. 24. 6 woe to the pot whose s. is therein
11. that the s. of it may be consumed
Ezek. 24. 12. she wearied hers. with lies, her s. went
not forth out of her, her s. shall be in the fire

SCURVY.

Lev. 21. 20. none shall appr. that is s. or scabbed
22. 22. the s. or scabbed ye shall not offer to Lord

SEA.

1 Kings 7. 23. he made a molten s. 2 Chron. 4. 2.
24. there were knops compassing s. round about
25. the s. was set above upon oxen, 2 Chron. 4. 4.
39. set the s. on right side of the house eastward
2 Kings 16. 17. Ahaz took down the s. from oxen
25. 13. the s. did Chaldees break in pieces, 16.
2 Chron. 4. 6. the s. was for the priests to wash in
15. one s. and twelve oxen under it
Jer. 27. 19. saith Lord, concerning the pillars and s.

SEA,

In Hebrew, Jum; in Greek, Θαλασσε. It is taken for that general collection of waters, which encompasses the earth, and has several names given it, according to the countries it washes, Gen. 1. 10. Exod. 20. 11. Psal. 95. 5. The Hebrews gave the name of Sea to all great collections of water, to great lakes or pools. Thus the Sea of Galilee, or of Tiberias, or of Cinnereth, is no other than the lake of Tiberias or Gennesareth in Galilee, Mat. 4. 18. | 8. 32. John 6. 1, 18. The Dead Sea, or Salt Sea, See SALT. The Sea of Jazer is the lake that was near the city Jazer, beyond Jordan, Jer. 48. 32. The Great Sea is the Mediterranean. They gave also the name of Sea to a very great brazen basin, that Solomon caused to be made for the temple, for the convenience of the priests, out of which they drew water for washing their hands or feet, or other things as occasion required, 1 Kings 7. 23.

The Arabians, and Orientals in general, sometimes give the name of Sea to great rivers, as the Nile, the Euphrates, the Tigris, and others, which by their magnitude, and by the extent of their overflowing, seem as little Seas or great lakes. Hence the country of Babylon which was watered by the Euphrates is called the Desert of the Sea, Isa. 21. 1. Jeremiah speaks of it in the same manner, Jer. 51. 36. I will dry up her sea, and make her springs dry. By which some understand, that God would deprive her of all necessaries for her succour; though others refer it to the particular stratagem by which Cyrus took Babylon, namely, by drying up in some measure the river Euphrates, that is, turning it into other channels. And Ezekiel describing the king of Egypt says, Ezek. 32. 2. Thou art as a whale of the seas; because his habitation was upon the banks of the Nile.

Sea is taken for a multitude, a deluge of enemies. Jer. 51. 42. The sea is come up upon Babylon. Also for the inhabitants of the islands of the sea. Isa. 60. 5. The abundance of the sea shall be converted unto thee. The islands or nations that formerly hated thee, shall love thee, and join with thee in religious worship; and shall bring their wealth, which they get by their merchandise, unto thee. Job says, Am I a sea or a whale, that thou settest a watch over me? Job 7. 12. Am I so unruly, and so ungovernable a creature, that thou needest to use extraordinary power to rule and subdue me? Am I as fierce and unruly as the sea, which would overwhelm the earth, and destroy its inhabitants, if thou didst not appoint boundaries to it? Or is my strength so great as that of the sea, which can endure so many violent storms one after another, and yet can subsist under them, and after them? No, Lord; thou knowest that I am but a weak, feeble creature, whom thou canst crush in a moment, without putting these chains upon me; without these insupportable pains and miseries. The prophet Micah says, Thou wilt cast all their sins into the depth of the sea, Mic. 7. 19. What is cast into the depth of the sea, is ordinarily accounted as lost, we have no expectation of finding it any more; so to cast sins into the depth of the sea, imports the full and free pardon of them.

By the sea of glass, mentioned Rev. 4. 6. most probably is signified the blood of Christ, whereby our persons and services are made acceptable to God. It is called a sea in allusion to that large vessel in the temple, out of which the priests drew water to wash themselves, and the sacrifices, and the instruments which they made use of for sacrificing, 1 Kings 7. 23. Its being represented as a sea of glass like unto crystal, may denote the spotless innocence of our Lord Jesus Christ, in his sufferings; that it was not the blood of a malefactor, but of an innocent person.

Exod. 14. 16. stretch thine hand over the s. 27.
21. Lord caused the s. to go back, made the s. dry
15. 10. thou didst blow, the s. covered them
20. 11. Lord made the s. and all that is therein,
Psal. 95. 5. Jonah 1. 9. Acts 4. 24. | 14. 15.
Num. 11. 31. a wind brought quails from the s.
Deut. 30. 13. nor is it beyond s. that thou shouldest
say, who shall go over the s. for us and bring it
Josh. 24. 6. you came unto the s. Egyptians pursued
7. he brought the s. upon them and covered them
1 Kings 10. 22. the king had at s. a navy of Tarshish
18. 43. he said, go up now, look toward the s.
2 Kings 14. 25. he restored the coast to the s. of plain
1 Chr. 16. 32. let the s. roar, Psal. 96. 11. | 98. 7.
2 Chr. 20. 2. cometh a multitude ag. thee beyond s.
Neh. 9. 11. thou didst divide the s. went tho' the s.
Job 26. 12. Psal. 74. 13. | 78. 13. Jer. 31. 35.
Job 7. 12. am I a s.? ‖ 38. 8. or who shut up the s.?
11. 9. the measure thereof is broader than the s.
14. 11. as the waters fail from s. and flood decays
28. 14. and the s. saith, it is not with me
41. 31. he maketh the s. like a pot of ointment
Psal. 66. 6. he turned the s. into dry land
72. 8. he shall have dominion from s. to s.
78. 53. but the s. overwhelmed their enemies
80. 11. she sent our her boughs to s. and branches
104. 25. so is this great wide s. wherein are things

Psal. 107. 23. they that go down to the s. in ships
114. 3. the s. saw it and fled ‖ 5. O thou s.
Prov. 8. 29. when he gave to the s. his decree
Isa. 11. 9. as the waters cover the s. Hab. 2. 14.
16. 8. her branches are stretched and gone over s.
19. 5. the waters shall fail from the s. and rivers
23. 2. the merchants of Zidon that pass over s.
4. be ashamed, O Zion, for the s. hath spoken
11. he stretched out his hand over the s. he shook
24. 14. they shall cry aloud from the s.
42. 10. sing to the Lord, ye that go down to the s.
50. 2. behold, at my rebuke I dry up the s.
51. 10. art thou not it which hath dried the s.?
57. 20. but the wicked are like the troubled s.
Jer. 6. 23. their voice roareth like s. and they ride
48. 32. O vine of Sibmah, thy plants are gone over s.
50. 42. their voice shall roar like the s. shall ride
51. 36. I will dry up her s. and make her springs dry
42. the s. is come up upon Babylon, she is covered
Lam. 2. 13. for thy breach is great like the s.
Ezek. 26. 3. as the s. causeth his waves to come
Dan. 7. 3. four great beasts came up from the s.
Amos 8. 12. they shall wander from s. to s.
Jonah 1. 11. what shall we do, that s. may be calm?
Mic. 7. 12. in that day he shall come from s. to s.
Nah. 1. 4. he rebuketh the s. and maketh it dry
3. 8. populous No, whose rampart was the s.
Hab. 3. 8. was thy wrath against s. that didst ride
15. thou didst walk through the s. with thy horses
Hag. 2. 6. I will shake the heavens, earth, and s.
Zech. 9. 10. his dominion shall be from s. to s.
10. 11. he shall pass through the s. with affliction
Mat. 8. 26. then he arose and rebuked the s.
27. even winds and s. obey him, Mark 4. 39, 41.
17. 27. go thou to the s. and cast an hook
23. 15. woe to hypocrites, for ye compass s. and land
Luke 21. 25. distress, the s. and the waves roaring
Acts 27. 40. they committed themselves to the s.
28. 4. this man, though he hath escaped the s.
1 Cor. 10. 1. all our fathers passed through the s.
Rev. 4. 6. and before the throne was a s. of glass
7. 2. to whom it was given to hurt the earth and s.
3. saying, hurt not the earth nor the s.
10. 6. who created the s. and the things therein
14. 7. fear God, and worship him that made the s.
15. 2. I saw a s. of glass, mingled with fire
20. 13. and the s. gave up the dead that were in it
21. 1. first earth passed, and there was no more s.

By the SEA.

Exod. 14. 2. before it shall ye encamp by the s.
9. Egyptians overtook them encamping by the s.
2 Sam. 17. 11. all Israel be gathered as sand by the s.
1 Kings 4. 20. Judah and Israel as sand by the s.
5. 9. I will convey them by the s. 2 Chron. 2. 16.
Isa. 18. 2. woe to that land sendeth ambassadors by s.
Jer. 46. 18. as Carmel by the s. so shall he come
Mark 4. 1. the multitude was by the s. on the land
Rev. 18. 17. as many as trade by the s. stood afar off

See COAST, GREAT.

In and into the SEA.

Exod. 14. 28. host of Pharaoh that came into the s.
15. 1. horse and rider hath he thrown into the s. 21.
4. Pharaoh's host hath he cast into the s.
19. his horse with horsemen went into the s.
Psal. 77. 19. thy way is in the s. thy path in great
89. 25. I will set his hand also in the s.
Eccl. 1. 7. all rivers run into the s. yet sea not full
Isa. 27. 1. he shall slay the dragon that is in the s.
43. 16. saith Lord, which maketh a way in the s.
Ezek. 26. 17. renowned city that was strong in the s.
18. the isles that are in the s. shall be troubled
47. 8. these waters go into the s. which being brought forth into the s. the waters shall be healed
Jonah 1. 4. there was a mighty tempest in the s.
5. mariners cast forth the wares into the s.
12. take me up, and cast me into the s. 15.
Zech. 9. 4. he will smite her power into the s.
10. 11. he shall smite the waves into the s.
Mat. 4. 18. casting a net into the s. Mark 1. 16.
8. 24. there arose a great tempest in the s.
32. whole herd of swine ran into the s. Mark 5. 13.
13. 47. kingdom of heaven like a net cast into the s.
21. 21. be thou cast into the s. Mark 11. 23.
Mark 9. 42. and he were cast into the s. Luke 17. 2.
Luke 17. 6. ye might say, be thou planted in the s.
John 21. 7. Peter did cast himself into the s.
Acts 27. 38. and cast out the wheat into the s.
43. they should cast themselves first into the s.
1 Cor. 10. 2. all baptized in the cloud, and in the s.
2 Cor. 11. 26. in perils in the s. among false brethren
Jam. 3. 7. beasts and things in the s. is tamed
Rev. 5. 13. every creature in the s. saying, blessing
8. 8. great mountain burning was cast into the s.
16. 3. and every living soul died in the s.
18. 19. were made rich all that had ships in the s.
21. a mighty angel cast a millstone into the s.

Of the SEA.

Gen. 1. 26. let us make man in our image, let them have dominion over fish of the s. 28. Psal. 8. 8.
9. 2. the fear of you upon all fishes of the s.
32. 12. and make thy seed as the sand of the s.
41. 49. Joseph gathered corn as the sand of the s.
49. 13. Zebulun shall dwell at the haven of the s.
Exod. 15. 8. depths congealed in the heart of the s.
19. brought again the waters of the s. upon them
Num. 11. 22. shall all the fish of the s. be gathered
2 Sam. 22. 16. and the channels of the s. appeared
1 Kings 18. 44. there ariseth a cloud out of the s.
Job 6. 3. it would be heavier than the sand of the s.
9. 8. which treadeth upon the waves of the s.
12. 8. the fishes of the s. shall declare to thee
36. 30. behold he covereth the bottom of the s.
38. 16. hast thou entered into the springs of the s.
Ps. 33. 7. he gathereth the waters of the s. together
68. 22. I will bring my people from depths of the s.
78. 27. feathered fowls like as the sand of the s.
89. 9. thou rulest the raging of the s. when waves
93. 4. the Lord is mightier than the waves of the s.
139. 9. and dwell in the uttermost parts of the s.
Isa. 5. 30. against them, like the roaring of the s.
9. 1. and afterwards afflict her by the way of the s.
10. 22. for tho' Isr. be as the sand of the s. yet a remnant shall return, Hos. 1. 10. Rom. 9. 27.
23. 4. even the strength of the s. hath spoken
48. 18. thy righteousness as the waves of the s.
51. 10. that hath made the depths of the s.
60. 5. abund. of the s. shall be converted unto thee
63. 11. he that brought them up out of the s.
Jer. 5. 22. placed the sand for the bound of the s.
33. 22. neither the sand of the s. be measured
Ezek. 26. 16. the princes of the s. shall come down
27. 3. Tyrus, O thou situate at the entry of the s.
9. the ships of the s. were in thee to occupy
29. all the pilots of the s. shall come down
38. 20. the fishes of the s. shall shake at my presence
Hos. 4. 3. the fishes of the s. shall be taken away
Amos 5. 8. that calleth for the waters of the s. 9. 6.
9. 3. hid from my sight in the bottom of the s.
Mic. 7. 19. thou wilt cast their sins into depths of s.
Hab. 1. 14. and makest men as the fishes of the s.
Zeph. 1. 3. I will consume the fishes of the s.
Mat. 4. 15. by the way of the s. beyond Jordan
18. 6. better he were drowned in the depth of the s.
Jam. 1. 6. he that wavereth is like a wave of the s.
Jude 13. raging waves of the s. foaming out their
Rev. 8. 8. the third part of the s. became blood
12. 12. woe to the inhabiters of earth and of the s.
13. 1. I stood and saw a beast rise up out of the s.
20. 8. the number of whom is as the sand of the s.

See MIDST.

On or upon the SEA.

Psal. 65. 5. of them that are afar off upon the s.
Jer. 49. 23. faint-hearted, there is sorrow on the s.
Mat. 14. 25. walking on s. Mark 6. 48. John 6. 19.
26. disciples saw him walking on the s. Mark 6. 49.
Rev. 7. 1. that the wind should not blow on the s.
10. 2. and he set his right foot upon the s.
5. the angel which I saw stand upon the s. 8.
15. 2. and I saw them stand on the s. of glass
16. 3. the second angel poured out his vial upon t. s.

SEA-faring men.

Ezek. 26. 17. that was inhabited of s.-faring men

SEA-monsters.

Lam. 4. 3. even the s.-monsters draw out the breast

See RED, SALT, SAND.

SEA-shore.

Gen. 22. 17. thy seed as sand which is upon the s.-s.
Exod. 14. 30. saw the Egyptians dead upon s.-s.
Josh. 11. 4. came together as the sand upon s.-shore
Judg. 5. 17. Asher continued on the s.-shore
1 Sam. 13. 5. the Philistines as sand on the s.-shore
1 Kings 4. 29. largeness of heart as sand on s.-shore
Jer. 47. 7. given it a charge against the s.-shore
Heb. 11. 12. of one sprang many, as sand by s.-s.

SEA-side.

Deut. 1. 7. turn you, and go by the way of the s.-s.
Judg. 7. 12. the Midianites lay as sand by the s.-side
2 Chron. 8. 17. Solomon went to Eloth at the s.-s.
Mat. 13. 1. the same day Jesus sat by the s.-side
Mark 2. 13. and he went forth again by the s.-side
4. 1. and he began again to teach by the s.-side
Acts 10. 6. Simon, whose house is by the s.-side, 32.

SEAS.

Gen. 1. 10. the gathering of the waters called he s.
22. multiply, and fill the waters in the s.
Lev. 11. 9. what hath fins and scales in the s. eat
10. that have not fins in the s. be an abomination
Deut. 33. 19. they shall suck of abundance of the s.
Neh. 9. 6. thou hast made the s. and all therein
Psal. 8. 8. whatsoever passeth thro' paths of the s.
24. 2. for he hath founded it upon the s.
65. 7. which stilleth the noise of the s. their waves
69. 34. let the s. praise him, and every thing
135. 6. what the L. pleased, that did he in the s.
Isa. 17. 12. which make a noise like noise of the s.
Jer. 15. 8. widows are increased above sand of s.
Ezek. 26. † 17. thou that wast inhabited of the s.
27. 4. thy borders are in the midst of the s.
25. thou wast made glorious in midst of the s.
26. hath broken thee in the midst of the s. 27. 34.
33. when thy wares went forth out of the s.
28. 2. I sit in seat of God, in midst of the s.
8. of them that are slain in the midst of the s.
32. 2. Pharaoh, thou art as a whale in the s.
Dan. 11. 45. tabernacle of his palace between the s.
Jonah 2. 3. thou hadst cast me into midst of the s.
Acts 27. 41. and falling into place where two s. met

SEAL

Is an instrument well known, wherewith letters and other writings are sealed and ratified. The ancient Hebrews *wore their seals or* signets *in rings on their fingers, or in bracelets on their arms.* Jezebel *wrote letters to the elders of* Israel, *to condemn* Naboth, *and sealed them with king* Ahab's seal, 1 Kings 21. 8. Haman *the* Agagite *sealed the decree of king* Ahasuerus *against the* Jews *with the king's seal,* Esth. 3. 12.

Pliny *observes,* lib. 33. cap. 1. *that the use of* seals *or* signets *was yet rare at the time of the* Trojan *war, and that they were obliged to shut up their letters with several knots: but among the* Hebrews *they are much more ancient.* Judah *the son of* Jacob *left his seal, his bracelet, and his staff, as a pledge with* Tamar, *whom he did not know,* Gen. 38. 18, 25. *And it is said in* Deut. 32. 34. Is not this laid up in store with me, and sealed up among my treasures? Job *says that God keeps the stars as under his seal, that he is governor and master of them, and allows them to appear when he thinks proper,* Job 9. 7. He sealeth up the stars. *And in* chap. 14. 17. My transgression is sealed up in a bag.

In civil contracts they generally made two originals: one continued open, and was kept by him for whose interest the contract was made; the other was sealed up, and deposited in some public office. It was sealed up to prevent any fraud or falsification. Jeremiah *bought a field in his country of* Anathoth, *of one named* Hanameel: *he wrote the contract, called witnesses, and sealed it up; and then put it into the hands of his disciple* Baruch, *and said to him;* Take these evidences, this evidence of the purchase, both which is sealed, and this evidence which is open, and put them in an earthen vessel, that they may continue many days, Jer. 32. 10, 11, 12, 14.

The apostle Paul *calls circumcision a seal of the righteousness of faith.* Rom. 4. 11. Abraham received the sign of circumcision, a seal of the righteousness of the faith which he had, yet being uncircumcised. *Circumcision was a seal, and an assurance, on God's part, both to* Abraham *and his spiritual seed, that he would give them* Christ *the promised seed out of the loins of* Abraham, *and in him accept of them as his peculiar people, pardon their sins, and cleanse them from their natural corruption, signified by their cutting off of their foreskins. It was a confirmation of the covenant of grace, and of the righteousness therein promised upon believing in* Christ. *And the same apostle, writing to the believing* Ephesians, *says,* In whom also, after that ye believed, ye were sealed with that Holy Spirit of promise, Eph. 1. 13. *In* Christ *as your head and representative* ye were sealed, *that is, assured and ascertained of your interest in the heavenly inheritance, which assurance was wrought in your souls by the immediate testimony of the Holy Spirit.*

It is said in 2 Tim. 2. 19. The foundation of God standeth sure, having this seal, the Lord knoweth them that are his; *that is, God's decree of election is unchangeable, upon which, as a firm foundation, the salvation of the elect depends; and also the work of grace, or principle of holiness, which God has laid in the hearts of the elect, to be as a foundation, root, or seed, for eternal life, remains immovable, having this seal, confirmation, or security, that God discerns his people from others, and will take care of them, and preserve them to eternal life. The apostle in* 1 Cor. 9. 2. *calls the* Corinthians the seal of his apostleship; The seal of mine apostleship are ye in the Lord. *Ye are the certain evidence of my divine call; my apostolical office hath a confirmation in you by the effect, as the writing is confirmed by the* seal. *For how can you think that the blessing of God should so far accompany the gospel which I preach, as to turn you from Pagan idolatry, and your lewd courses of life, to the true Christian religion, and to an holy life and conversation, if God had not been with me and sent me?*

In Rev. 5. 1. *John* saw a book sealed with seven seals. *This was the book of God's decrees and purposes relating to his church, as to what remarkable things should happen to it to the end of the world; its* being sealed *denotes that the matter contained in it was locked up from, and unknown to, the creatures. Elsewhere* sealing *denotes secrecy, as in* Isa. 8. 16. Dan. 12. 4. *It also denotes security, as in* Rev. 20. 3. He cast him into the bottomless pit, and shut him up, and set a seal upon him. *He put a restraint upon him, and made him absolutely incapable of doing any considerable mischief to the church. And in* Mat. 27. 66. They went and made the sepulchre sure, sealing the stone, and setting a watch.

The grace of sanctification wrought in the soul by the Holy Ghost, is the seal and assurance of our redemption to come, of a joyful resurrection. Eph. 4. 30. And grieve not the Holy Spirit of God, whereby ye are sealed unto the day of redemption. *One observes, that in the comparison of our* sanctification *with* sealing, *there are the following circumstances of likeness;* [1] *The letter written, or cabinet filled with treasure, is every good Christian,* 2 Cor. 4. 7. Heb. 10. 16. [2] *The wax appointed to be sealed, is the relenting heart of man, apt to take any impression,* Psal. 22. 14. [3] *The sealer is the Holy Ghost,* Eph. 1. 13. | 4. 30. [4] *The seal itself is the word of God, which being applied to the heart, makes an impression upon it.* [5] *The sealing, or impression active, is the act of applying the word of God, whether precept, or promise, by the Holy Ghost within, and the minister without, to the hearer.* [6] *The print, or impression passive, or the image of the seal left in the wax, is the knowledge, faith, and love of that truth, holiness, and happiness which God originally hath in himself, and his word from him, and the new man hath the true image thereof in himself,* Eph. 4. 23. Col. 3. 10. [7] *The use and end of this sealing, is the secrecy and safety of the thing sealed from the eyes of curiosity, and hands of violence, wherewith strangers or enemies would abuse it. So the children of God are past the censure of the wicked world,* 1 Cor. 2. 15. | 4. 3. *They are preserved as precious things, for God's own use, to be with him in heaven,* 2 Tim. 2. 20, 21. *They are freed from the malice and violence of men and devils, and from the stroke of God's justice,* Ezek. 9. 4. Mat. 16. 18. *The spouse in the* Canticles *wishes to be set as a seal upon her beloved's heart, as a seal upon his arm,* Cant. 8. 6. *that is, that she might be engraven upon the tables of his heart, that his mind and heart may be constantly set upon her. There seems to be an allusion to the graven tablets which were frequently worn upon the breast; and to the signet on a man's arm or hand, which men prized at a more than ordinary rate; as appears from* Jer. 22. 24. Hag. 2. 23. *and which are continually in their sight.*

1 Kings 21. 8. Jezebel sealed letters with Ahab's s.
Job 38. 14. it is turned as clay to the s. they stand
41. 15. his scales are shut up as with a close s.
Cant. 8. 6. set me as a s. on thy heart, as a s. on arm
John 3. 33. hath set to his s. that God is true
Rom. 4. 11. circumcis. a s. of righteousness of faith
1 Cor. 9. 2. the s. of mine apostleship are ye in Ld.
2 Tim. 2. 19. having this s. the Lord knoweth his
Rev. 6. 3. the sec. s. ‖ 5. the third s. ‖ 7. the fourth s.
9. the fifth s. ‖ 12. when he had opened the sixth s
7. 2. another angel, having the s. of the living G
8. 1. and when he had opened the seventh s

Rev. 9. 4. hurt only those that have not the *s.* of God
20. 3. and shut him up, and set a *s.* upon him

SEALS.

Rev. 5. 1. and I saw a book sealed with seven *s.*
2. who is worthy to loose the *s.* thereof?
5. Lion of tribe of Juda prevailed to loose the *s.*
9. thou art worthy to take and open the *s.*
6. 1. I saw when the Lamb opened one of the *s.*

SEAL.

Neh. 9. 38. our princes and priests *s.* unto it, 10. 1.
Isa. 8. 16. *s.* the law among my disciples
Jer. 32. 44. men shall subscribe evidences, and *s.* th.
Dan. 9. 24. seventy weeks to *s.* up the vision
12. 4. O Daniel, shut up the words, *s.* the book
Rev. 10. 4. *s.* those things the seven thunders uttered
22. 10. *s.* not the sayings of the prophecy of this book

SEALED.

Deut. 32. 34. is not this *s.* up among my treasures?
1 *Kings* 21. 8. the letters were *s.* with Ahab's seal
Esth. 3. 12. written and *s.* with the king's ring, 8. 8.
Job 14. 17. my transgression is *s.* up in a bag
Cant. 4. 12. my spouse is a fountain *s.*
Isa. 29. 11. the vision is as the words of a book *s.*
Jer. 32. 10. I subscribed and *s.* the evidence
11. so I took both that which was *s.* and open, 14.
Dan. 6. 17. the king *s.* it with his own signet
12. 9. for the words are closed up, and *s.* till the time
John 6. 27. for him hath God the Father *s.*
Rom. 15. 28. when I have *s.* to them this fruit
2 *Cor.* 1. 22. who hath *s.* us and given the earnest
Eph. 1. 13. ye were *s.* with that Holy Spirit of prom.
4. 30. grieve not the Spirit, whereby ye are *s.* to-day
Rev. 5. 1. I saw a book *s.* with seven seals
7. 3. hurt not earth nor sea, till we have *s.* servants
4. I heard the number of them which were *s.* there were *s.* 144,000 of all the tribes of Israel
5. of Judah were *s.* 12,000; of Reuben; of Gad *s.*
6. of Aser; of Nephthalim; of Manasses *s.*
7. of Simeon; of Levi; of Issachar were *s.* 12,000
8. of Zabulon; of Joseph; of Benjamin were *s.*

SEALEST.

Ezek. 28. 12. thou *s.* up the sum full of wisdom

SEALETH.

Job 9. 7. commandeth the sun, and *s.* up the stars
33. 16. he openeth their ears, and *s.* their instruction
37. 7. he *s.* up hand of every man, all may know

SEALING.

Neh. 9. † 38. princes and priests are at the *s.* 10. † 1.
Mat. 27. 66. *s.* the stone and setting a watch

SEAM.

John 19. 23. now the coat was without *s.* woven

SEARCH.

Deut. 13. 14. then shalt thou enquire and make *s.*
Ezra 4. 15. that *s.* may be made in the records, 5. 17.
19. *s.* hath been made, and it is found, 6. 1.
Job 8. 8. prepare thyself to the *s.* of their fathers
38. 16. hast thou walked in the *s.* of the depth?
Psal. 64. 6. they search and accomplish a diligent *s.*
77. 6. I commune, and my spirit made diligent *s.*
Jer. 2. 34. I have not found it by secret *s.*

SEARCH, *Verb.*

Lev. 27. 33. he shall not *s.* whether it be good
Num. 10. 33. to *s.* out a resting-place for them
13. 2. send thou men, that they may *s.* the land
32. the land through which we have gone to *s.* it
14. 7. the land we passed through to *s.* it is good
38. Joshua and Caleb of the men that went to *s.*
Deut. 1. 22. we will send men, and they shall *s.*
33. who went before to *s.* you out a place
Josh. 2. 2. there came men to *s.* the country, 3.
Judg. 18. 2. the Danites sent men to *s.* the land
1 *Sam.* 23. 23. if he be in the land, I will *s.* him out
2 *Sam.* 10. 3. hath not David rather sent his servants unto thee to *s.* the city, to spy it out? 1 *Chr.* 19. 3.
1 *Kings* 20. 6. will send my servants, and they shall *s.*
2 *Kings* 10. 23. *s.* that none of the servants of the Lord
Job 13. 9. is it good that he should *s.* you out?
Psal. 44. 21. shall not God *s.* this out, he knoweth
139. 23. *s.* me, O God, and know my heart
Prov. 25. 2. but the honour of kings to *s.* out a matter
27. for men to *s.* their own glory, is not glory
Eccl. 1. 13. I gave my heart to *s.* by wisdom, 7. 25.
Jer. 17. 10. I the Lord *s.* the heart, I try the reins
29. 13. when ye shall *s.* for me with all your heart
Lam. 3. 40. let us *s.* our ways, and turn to the Lord
Ezek. 34. 6. and none did *s.* or seek after them
8. neither did my shepherds *s.* for my flock
11. I will both *s.* my sheep, and seek them out
39. 14. after the end of seven months shall they *s.*
Amos 9. 3. I will *s.* and take them out thence
Zeph. 1. 12. I will *s.* Jerusalem with candles
Mat. 2. 8. and *s.* diligently for the young child
John 5. 39. *s.* the scriptures, they testify of me
7. 52. *s.* for out of Galilee ariseth no prophet

SEARCHED.

Gen. 31. 34. Laban *s.* the tent, but found them not, 35.
37. whereas thou hast *s.* all my stuff, thou found
44. 12. the steward *s.* for the cup, and began at eldest
Num. 13. 21. so they went up, and *s.* the land
32. brought up an evil report of the land, and *s.*
14. 6. Joshua and Caleb *s.* the land, 38.
34. after the number of days ye *s.* the land
Deut. 1. 24. came unto the valley of Eshcol, and *s.* it
Job 5. 27. we have *s.* it, know it for thy good
28. 27. he prepared it, yea, and *s.* it out
29. 16. the cause which I knew not, I *s.* out
32. 11. I waited, whilst ye *s.* out what to say
36. 26. can the number of his years be *s.* out
Psal. 139. 1. O Lord, thou hast *s.* me, and known me
Jer. 31. 37. and the foundations of the earth *s.* out
46. 23. cut down her forest, tho' it cannot be *s.*
Obad. 6. how are the things of Esau *s.* out
Acts 17. 11. the Bereans *s.* the scriptures daily
1 *Pet.* 1. 10. which salvation the prophets *s.* dilig.

SEARCHEST.

Job 10. 6. that thou *s.* after my sin and enquirest
Prov. 2. 4. if thou *s.* for her as for hid treasures

SEARCHETH.

1 *Chr.* 28. 9. for the Lord *s.* all hearts and underst.
Job 28. 3. and he *s.* out all perfection, the stones
39. 8. and he *s.* after every green thing
Prov. 18. 17. but his neighbour cometh, and *s.* him
Prov. 28. 11. the poor that hath underst. *s.* him out
Rom. 8. 27. that *s.* hearts, knows the mind of Spirit
1 *Cor.* 2. 10. for the Spirit *s.* all things, things of G.
Rev. 2. 23. know that I am he which *s.* the reins

SEARCHING.

Num. 13. 25. they returned from *s.* of the land
Job 11. 7. canst thou by *s.* find out God?
Prov. 20. 27. *s.* all the inward parts of the belly
Isa. 40. 28. there is no *s.* of his understanding
1 *Pet.* 1. 11. *s.* what time the Spirit of Christ did sig.

SEARCHINGS.

Judg. 5. 16. for the divisions of Reuben were great *s.*

SEARED.

1 *Tim.* 4. 2. having their conscience *s.* with a hot iron

SEASON.

Gen. 40. 4. and they continued a *s.* in ward
Exod. 13. 10. thou shalt keep this ordinance in his *s.*
Deut. 16. 6. at the *s.* thou camest forth out of Egypt
28. 12. to give the rain unto thy land in his *s.*
Josh. 24. 7. ye dwelt in the wilderness a long *s.*
2 *Kings* 4. 16. about this *s.* thou shalt embrace a son
17. and the woman bare a son at that *s.*
1 *Chron.* 21. 29. the altar was at that *s.* at Gibeon
2 *Chr.* 15. 3. for long *s.* been without the true God
Job 5. 26. to grave, as a shock of corn cometh in his *s.*
30. 17. my bones are pierced in the night *s.*
38. 32. canst thou bring forth Mazzaroth in his *s.*
Psal. 1. 3. a tree that bringeth forth fruit in his *s.*
22. 2. I cry in the night *s.* and am not silent
Prov. 15. 23. a word spoken in due *s.* how good is it?
Eccl. 3. 1. to every thing there is a *s.* and a time
Isa. 50. 4. I should know how to speak a word in *s.*
Jer. 5. 24. God giveth former and latter rain in his *s.*
33. 20. there should not be day and night in their *s.*
Ezek. 34. 26. cause the shower come down in *s.*
Dan. 7. 12. their lives were prolonged for a *s.*
Hos. 2. 9. take away my wine in the *s.* thereof
Mark 12. 2. at the *s.* he sent to the husbandmen
Luke 1. 20. my words shall be fulfilled in their *s.*
4. 13. the devil departed from him for a *s.*
13. 1. were present at that *s.* some that told him
20. 10. at the *s.* he sent a servant to husbandmen
23. 8. he was desirous to see him of a long *s.*
John 5. 4. for an angel went down at a certain *s.*
35. ye were willing for a *s.* to rejoice in his light
Acts 13. 11. be blind, not seeing the sun for a *s.*
19. 22. but he himself stayed in Asia for a *s.*
24. 25. when I have a convenient *s.* I will call
2 *Cor.* 7. 8. made you sorry, tho' it were but for a *s.*
2 *Tim.* 4. 2. be instant in *s.* out of *s.* rebuke, exhort
Philem. 15. perhaps he therefore departed for a *s.*
Heb. 11. 25. than enjoy the pleasures of sin for a *s.*
1 *Pet.* 1. 6. tho' for a *s.* if need be, ye are in heaviness
Rev. 6. 11. that they should rest yet for a little *s.*
20. 3. and after that he must be loosed a little *s.*

See Appointed, Due.

SEASONS.

Gen. 1. 14. lights shall be for signs, and *s.* and days
Exod. 18. 22. let them judge the people at all *s.* 26.
Lev. 23. 4. the feasts ye shall proclaim in their *s.*
Psal. 16. 7. my reins also instruct me in the night *s.*
104. 19. he appointeth the moon for *s.* the sun
Dan. 2. 21. he changeth the times and the *s.*
Mat. 21. 41. who shall render the fruits in their *s.*
Acts 1. 7. it is not for you to know the times and *s.*
14. 17. in that he gave us rain and fruitful *s.*
20. 18. how I have been with you at all *s.*
1 *Thess.* 5. 1. of the *s.* ye have no need that I write

SEASON.

Lev. 2. 13. every meat offer. shalt thou *s.* with salt
Mark 9. 50. wherewith will ye *s.* it? have salt

SEASONED.

Luke 14. 34. if lost savour wherewith shall it be *s.*?
Col. 4. 6. let your speech be always with grace, *s.*

SEAT.

The seat of Moses, *upon which the* Scribes *and* Pharisees *sat, is to express the authority of the doctors of the law, and the office of teaching which was granted to them, or which they took upon themselves. Our Lord commanded that they should be heard and respected; but he forbad that their actions should be made precedents and examples,* Mat. 23. 2, 3.

The seat of the Scorners, *of which there is mention in* Psal. 1. 1. *denotes an association or incorporation with libertines, and such as make a mock of religion, who corrupt as much by their scandalous example and conduct, as by their loose principles, all those that hear them and keep them company.* The seat of God *is his throne or judgment-seat,* Job 23. 3. O that I knew where I might find him! that I might come even to his seat! *To his judgment-seat to plead my cause before him; not upon terms of strict justice, but of grace and mercy. There is also* the seat of justice, *a bench or chair whereon magistrates sat when they administered justice,* Job 29. 7. When I prepared my seat in the street.

Judg. 3. 20. Eglon rose out of his *s.*
1 *Sam.* 1. 9. Eli sat upon a *s.* by a post, 4. 13.
4. 18. he fell from off the *s.* backward near the gate
20. 18. be missed, because thy *s.* will be empty
25. the king sat on his *s.* on a *s.* by the wall
2 *Sam.* 23. 8. the Tachmonite that sat in the *s.*
1 *Kings* 2. 19. caused a *s.* to be set for king's mother
Esth. 3. 1. set Haman's *s.* above all the princes
Job 23. 3. O that I might come even to his *s.*!
29. 7. when I prepared my *s.* in the street
Psal. 1. 1. nor sitteth in the *s.* of the scornful
Prov. 9. 14. a foolish woman sitteth on a *s.* in city
Ezek. 8. 3. where was the *s.* of the image of jealousy
28. 2. I sit in the *s.* of God in midst of the seas
Dan. 11. † 38. the Almighty in his *s.* he shall honour
Amos 6. 3. and cause the *s.* of violence to come near
Mat. 23. 2. the scribes and Pharisees sit in Moses' *s.*
Rev. 2. 13. thou dwellest where Satan's *s.* is

See Judgment, Mercy.

SEATED.

Deut. 33. 21. in a portion of the lawgiver was he *s.*

SEATS.

Jer. 18. † 3. behold, he wrought a work on the *s.*
Mat. 21. 12. he overthrew tables of money-changers and the *s.* of them that sold doves, *Mark* 11. 15.
23. 6. love chief *s.* in the synagogues, *Mark* 12. 39.
Luke 1. 52. hath put down the mighty from their *s.*
11. 43. for ye love the uppermost *s.* 20. 46.
Rev. 4. 4. four-and-twenty *s.* upon the *s.* 24 elders
11. 16. the elders which sat before God on their *s.*

SECOND.

Gen. 6. 16. with *s.* and third stories make the ark
32. 19. and so commanded he the *s.* and third
41. 43. he made him to ride in the *s.* chariot
Exod. 26. 4. the coupling of the *s.* 5. 10. | 36. 11, 12, 17.
28. 18. the *s.* row shall be an emerald, 39. 11.
Lev. 5. 10. he shall offer the *s.* for a burnt offering
Num. 2. 16. they shall set forth in the *s.* rank
Josh. 19. 1. the *s.* lot came forth to Simeon
Judg. 6. 25. the *s.* bullock of seven years old
26. take *s.* bullock, and offer ‖ 28. the *s.* was offered
1 *Sam.* 15. † 9. Saul spared of the best and *s.* sort
2 *Kings* 9. 19. then he sent out a *s.* on horseback
22. † 14. Huldah dwelt in Jerusalem in the *s.* part
1 *Chron.* 15. 18. with them brethren of the *s.* degree
2 *Chron.* 35. 24. his servants put him in the *s.* chariot
Ezra 1. 10. silver basons of a *s.* sort 410, vessels
Esth. 9. 29. to confirm this *s.* letter of Purim
Eccl. 4. 8. there is one alone, there is not a *s.*
15. with the *s.* child that shall stand up in his stead
Ezek. 10. 14. the *s.* face was the face of a man
Dan. 7. 5. behold, another beast, a *s.* like to a bear
8. † 3. but one horn was higher than the *s.*
Zeph. 1. 10. noise of a cry, an howling from the *s.*
Zech. 6. 2. in the *s.* chariot were black horses
Mat. 21. 30. he came to the *s.* and said likewise
22. 26. likewise the *s.* had her, and the third, unto the seventh, *Mark* 12. 21. *Luke* 20. 30.
39. *s.* commandment is like unto it, *Mark* 12. 31.
Luke 6. 1. and it came to pass on the *s.* sabbath
12. 38. if he shall come in *s.* watch or the third
19. 18. the *s.* came saying, L. thy pound gained
John 4. 54. this is the *s.* miracle that Jesus did
Acts 12. 10. when they were past the *s.* ward
13. 33. as it is written in *s.* psalm, thou art my son
1 *Cor.* 15. 47. the *s.* man is the Lord from heaven
2 *Cor.* 1. 15. that ye might have a *s.* benefit
Tit. 3. 10. after the first and *s.* admonition, reject
Heb. 8. 7. no place should have been sought for *s.*
9. 3. and after the *s.* vail, the tabernacle
7. into the *s.* went the high priest once a year
10. 9. taketh away first, that he may establish *s.*
2 *Pet.* 3. 1. this *s.* epistle I now write unto you
Rev. 2. 11. shall not be hurt of the *s.* death, 20. 6.
4. 7. the *s.* beast like a calf, the third had a face
6. 3. I heard the *s.* beast say, come and see
8. 8. *s.* angel sounded, and as it were a mountain
11. 14. the *s.* woe is past, the third woe cometh
16. 3. the *s.* angel poured out his vial on the sea
20. 14. death and hell, this is the *s.* death, 21. 8.
21. 19. the *s.* foundation of the wall was sapphire

See Day, Month.

SECOND *time.*

Gen. 22. 15. the angel called to Abraham the *s. t.*
41. 5. Pharaoh slept, and dreamed the *s. time*
43. 10. surely now we had returned this *s. time*
Lev. 13. 58. then it shall be washed the *s. time*
Num. 10. 6. when you blow an alarm the *s. time*
Josh. 5. 2. and circumcise Israel the *s. time*
1 *Sam.* 26. 8. I will not smite him the *s. time*
2 *Sam.* 14. 29. Absalom sent to Joab the *s. time*
1 *Kings* 9. 2. the L. appeared to Solomon the *s. time*
18. 34. do it the *s. time,* they did it the *s. time*
19. 7. the angel came again to Elijah the *s. time*
2 *Kings* 10. 6. Jehu wrote a letter the *s. time*
1 *Chr.* 29. 22. they made Solomon king the *s. time*
Esth. 2. 19. when virgins were gathered the *s. time*
Isa. 11. 11. Lord set his hand the *s. time* to recover
Jer. 1. 13. the word of Lord came to me the *s. time* saying, what seest thou? 13. 3. | 33. 1.
Jonah 3. 1. the word came to Jonah the *s. time*
Nah. 1. 9. affliction shall not rise up the *s. time*
Mat. 26. 42. he went again the *s. time* and prayed
Mark 14. 72. and the *s. time* the cock crew
John 3. 4. can he enter the *s. time* into the womb?
21. 16. Jesus saith to Peter the *s. time,* Simon
Acts 7. 13. at the *s. time* Joseph was made known
10. 15. the voice spake to Peter again the *s. time*
2 *Cor.* 13. 2. as if I were present the *s. time*
Heb. 9. 28. he shall appear the *s. time* without sin

SECOND *Year.*

Gen. 47. 18. they came the *s. year* to Joseph, and said
Exod. 40. 17. in the *s. year,* the first day of the month
Num. 1. 1. in the *s. year* after they were come
9. 1. in first month of *s. year,* the Lord spake to Mos.
10. 11. in the *s. year* the cloud was taken up
2 *Kings* 19. 29. this a sign, ye shall eat in the *s. year* that which springeth of the same, *Isa.* 37. 30.
2 *Chron.* 27. 5. Ammon paid Jotham the *s. year*
Ezra 3. 8. in the *s. year* of their coming to Jerusalem
4. 24. it ceased the *s. year* of Darius king of Persia
Dan. 2. 1. in the *s. year* of reign of Nebuchadnezz.
Hag. 1. 1. in *s. year* of Darius, 15. | 2. 10. *Zech.* 1. 7.

SECONDARILY.

1 *Cor.* 12. 28. God set *s.* prophets, thirdly teachers

SECRET

Is taken, [1] *For an affair which few people know, and that ought to be kept private,* Prov. 20. 19. He that goeth about as a talebearer, revealeth secrets. [2] *For that which is hid from the understanding of all men, and known only to God,* Deut. 29. 29. The secret things belong unto the Lord our God. *The counsels and purposes of God concerning persons or nations, and the reasons of his dispensations towards them, together with the time and manner of inflicting judgments, or shewing mercy, are hidden in his own bosom, and not to be pried into by us. And in* Amos 3. 7. The Lord will do nothing, but he revealeth his secret unto his servants the prophets. [3] *For the secret favour and blessing of God, protecting, directing, and succeeding persons in all their affairs.* Job 29. 4. When the secret of God was upon my tabernacle. *And in* Psal. 25. 14. The secret of the Lord is with them that fear him; and he will shew them his covenant. *His gracious and fatherly providence is towards them, taking care of them, and working for them, even then when God seems to frown upon them: his word is with them, to direct and guide them in the right way, to shew them their duty in all conditions, and the way to their eternal salvation: and this, though revealed, yet may be called a secret, because of the many and deep mysteries in it; because it is said to be hid from many of those, to whom it was revealed,* Mat. 11. 25. 2 Cor. 3. 13, 14, 15. *And because it is not to be understood to any purpose unless the mind be illuminated by the Spirit of God,* Psal. 119. 18, 19. [4] *For the hidden meaning and import of a dream or vision,* Dan. 4. 9. [5] *For that which is kept close from the knowledge of all other men, and whereof ourselves only are conscious.* Psal. 90. 8. Thou hast set our secret sins in the light of thy countenance. *Eccl.* 12. 14. For God shall bring every work into judgment, with every secret thing, whether it be good, or whether it be evil. *Rom.* 2. 16. In the day when God shall judge the secrets of men by Jesus Christ. *When God shall judge not only the outward actions of men, which are manifest to all, but their most hidden sins, and secret duties, their inward purposes, designs, and aims.* The numberer of secrets, *or the* wonderful numberer, *Dan.* 8. † 13. *By this is meant* Christ Jesus, *who is wonderful,* Isa. 9. 6. *and who hath all the hidden things of God numbered before him, and knows them perfectly, and revealeth to angels and men those secrets of the Father.*

Gen. 49. 6. O my soul, come not thou into their *s.*
Job 15. 8. hast thou heard the *s.* of God?
19. † 19. all the men of my *s.* abhorred me
24. † 15. the adulterer setteth his face in *s.*
29. 4. when the *s.* of God was upon my tabernacle
40. 13. hide them, and bind their faces in *s.*
Psal. 25. 14. the *s.* of Ld. is with them that fear him
27. 5. in *s.* of his tabern. shall he hide me, 31. 20.
64. 4. that they may shoot in *s.* at the perfect
139. 15. not hid from thee when I was made in *s.*
Prov. 3. 32. but his *s.* is with the righteous
9. 17. stolen waters, bread eaten in *s.* is pleasant
21. 14. a gift in *s.* pacifieth anger, a reward wrath
25. 9. and discover not a *s.* to another
26. † 26. whose hatred is covered in *s.*
Isa. 24. † 16. but I said, my *s.* to me, woe unto me
45. 19. I have not spoken in *s.* 48. 16.
Jer. 23. † 18. who hath stood in the *s.* of the Lord
Ezek. 28. 3. no *s.* that they can hide from thee
Dan. 2. 18. desire mercies of God concerning this *s.*
19. then was the *s.* revealed to Daniel in vision
27. the *s.* which the king hath demanded
30. this *s.* not revealed to me for any wisdom I have
47. seeing thou couldst reveal this *s.*
4. 9. because I know that no *s.* troubleth thee
Amos 3. 7. he revealeth his *s.* to his servants
Mat. 6. 4. that thine alms may be in *s.* and thy Father who seeth in *s.* shall reward thee openly, 6. 18.
6. pray to thy Father who is in *s.* and thy Father
18. thou appear to fast to thy Father who is in *s.*
John 7. 4. there is no man doth any thing in *s.*
10. he went up to the feast as it were in *s.*
18. 20. I spake openly, in *s.* have I said nothing
Eph. 5. 12. things which are done of them in *s.*

SECRET, *Adjective.*

Deut. 27. 15. cursed that putteth an idol in a *s.* place
29. 29. *s.* things belong unto the Lord our God
Judg. 3. 19. I have a *s.* errand unto thee, O king
13. 18. why askest thou my name, seeing it is *s.*?
1 *Sam.* 5. 9. they had emerods in their *s.* parts
19. 2. take heed, abide in a *s.* place, hide thyself
2 *Kings* 5. † 24. when Gehazi came to the *s.* place
Job 14. 13. O that thou wouldest keep me in *s.*
15. 11. is there any *s.* thing with thee?
20. 26. all darkness shall be hid in his *s.* places
Psal. 10. 8. in *s.* places doth he murder the innocent
17. 12. as a young lion lurking in *s.* places
18. 11. he made darkness his *s.* place
19. 12. cleanse thou me from *s.* faults
64. 2. hide me from the *s.* counsel of the wicked
81. 7. I answered thee in the *s.* place of thunder
90. 8. our *s.* sins in the light of thy countenance
91. 1. that dwelleth in the *s.* place of the Most H.
Prov. 27. 5. open rebuke is better than *s.* love
Eccl. 12. 14. shall bring into judgm. every *s.* thing
Cant. 2. 14. O my dove, that art in the *s.* places
Isa. 3. 17. the Lord will discover their *s.* parts
26. † 16. they have poured out a *s.* speech
45. 3. I will give thee hidden riches of *s.* places
Jer. 2. 34. I have not found it by *s.* search
13. 17. my soul shall weep in *s.* places for your pride
23. 24. can any hide himself in *s.* places, saith Lord
49. 10. Esau bare, I have uncovered his *s.* places
Lam. 3. 10. he was to me as a lion in *s.* places
Ezek. 7. 22. and they shall pollute my *s.* place
Dan. 2. 22. he revealeth the deep and *s.* things
Mat. 13. 35. I will utter things which have been kept *s.* from found. of the world, *Rom.* 16. 25.
24. 26. behold, he is in *s.* chambers, believe it not
Mark 4. 22. nothing hid, nor was any thing kept *s.* but that it should come abroad, *Luke* 8. 17.
Luke 11. 33. no man putteth a candle in a *s.* place

SECRETS.

Job 11. 6. that he would shew thee the *s.* of wisdom
Psal. 44. 21. for he knoweth the *s.* of the heart
Prov. 11. 13. a tale-bearer revealeth *s.* but he that
20. 19. that goeth as a tale-bearer, revealeth *s.*
Dan. 2. 28. but there is a God that revealeth *s.*
29. he that revealeth *s.* maketh known to thee
47. of a truth it is, your God is a revealer of *s.*
Rom. 2. 16. when God shall judge the *s.* of men
1 *Cor.* 14. 25. thus are the *s.* of his heart manifest

SECRETS.

Deut. 25. 11. and the wife taketh him by the *s.*

SECRETLY.

Gen. 31. 27. wherefore didst thou flee away *s.*?
Deut. 13. 6. if thy brother entice thee *s.* saying
27. 24. cursed be he that smiteth his neighbour *s.*
Lev. 28. 57. she shall eat them for want of all things *s.*
Josh. 2. 1. Joshua son of Nun, sent two men to spy *s.*
1 *Sam.* 18. 22. commune with David *s.* and say
23. 9. David knew that Saul *s.* practised mischief
2 *Sam.* 12. 12. for thou didst it *s.* but I will do this
2 *Kings* 17. 9. did *s.* those things that were not right
Job 4. 12. now a thing was *s.* brought to me
13. 10. will reprove you, if you *s.* accept persons
31. 27. and my heart hath been *s.* enticed
Psal. 10. 9. he lieth in wait *s.* as a lion in his den
31. 20. keep them *s.* in a pavilion from strife of tong.
Jer. 37. 17. Zedekiah asked *s.* is there any word?
38. 16. Zedekiah the king sware *s.* unto Jeremiah
40. 15. Johanan spake to Gedaliah in Mizpah *s.*
Hab. 3. 14. their rejoicing was to devour the poor *s.*
John 11. 28. she went and called Mary her sister *s.*
19. 38. Joseph was a disciple, but *s.* for fear of Jews

SECT.

This word is the same in the Greek *with the word* heresy, *though the sound be not so odious. Among the* Jews *were known four several* Sects, *which were distinguished by the singularity of their practices and opinions, and yet continuing united in communion with each other, and with the body of their nation. These* Sects *are those of the* Pharisees, *the* Sadducees, *the* Essenians, *and the* Herodians. *As to the first two* Sects; *see the* Significations *on* PHARISEES, *and* SADDUCEES.

The Essenians, *or* Essenes, *are not mentioned in Scripture, but they are described by* Josephus *and other historians:* Joseph de Bello, lib. 2. cap. 12. *He says, that they live in perfect union among themselves, and abhor voluptuousness, as poison of the most dangerous consequence. They do not marry, but they bring up other men's children with as much care as if they were their own, and infuse into them very early their own spirit and maxims. These children are all treated and clothed in the same manner, and do not change their dress till the clothes they have are entirely worn out.*

Some employ themselves in husbandry, others in trades, and manufactures of such things only as are of use in time of peace, their designs being to do good only, to themselves and other men. Before they admit any who desire it, to be of their Sect, *they put them to a year's probation, and during this time inure them to the practice of their most uneasy exercises. After this term, they permit them to come into the common refectory, which is as it were a sacred temple, where they all continue in profound silence. There they are served with bread, and every one has his particular mess. The priest says grace, after which they may eat; they finish their meal also with a prayer. After having proved such as desire to be of their* Sect *for a year, they permit them then to come into the place where they bathe when they come from their work; but they do not admit them into the inner part of the house, till they have gone through another trial of two years. When these two years are expired, they are allowed to make a kind of profession, whereby they engage themselves by the most awful oaths to observe the laws of piety, justice, and modesty; fidelity to God and their prince; never to discover the secrets of the* Sect *to strangers, and to preserve the books of their masters and the names of angels with great care. If any one violates these promises, and incurs the guilt of any notorious fault, he is expelled the society, and generally dies of want, because he can receive no food from any stranger, being tied to the contrary by these oaths.*

The Essenes *generally live long, and many reach the age of an hundred years; which is said to be owing to the simplicity of their diet, and the great regularity of their lives. They shew an incredible firmness under torments, whereof there were some eminent examples during the war between the* Romans *and the* Jews. *They hold the souls of men to be immortal, and believe that they descend from the most elevated part of the air into the bodies, which are animated by them, whither they are drawn by some natural attraction, which they are not able to resist. After death, they return with rapidity to the place from whence they came, being as it were freed from a long and melancholy captivity. As to the state of men's souls after death, they have the same sentiments almost as the heathens, who place the souls of good men in the* Elysian *fields, and those of wicked men in the kingdom of* Pluto, *where they are tormented according to the quality of their faults.*

Although the Essenes *were the most religious of their nation, they nevertheless did not go to the temple of* Jerusalem, *nor offered any bloody sacrifices. They were afraid of being polluted by the conversation of other men, whose lives were not so pure as theirs. They sent their offerings thither, and themselves offered up to God the sacrifice of a clean heart, free from the guilt of any great offences. They lived at a distance from the sea shore, for fear of being corrupted by the conversation of strangers. They chose rather to dwell in the fields, than in cities; and applied themselves to agriculture and other laborious exercises, which did not take them out of that solitude whereof they made profession.*

Their studies were neither logic, nor natural philosophy, but morality and the laws of Moses. *To these they applied themselves principally upon sabbath days, when they assembled in their synagogues, where every one was seated according to his rank; the elder above, the younger part of them below. One of the company read, and another of the most learned of them expounded. They made use of symbols very much, of allegories and parables, after the manner of the ancients. This is a summary of the description which* Josephus *gives of the* Essenes. *Some are of opinion that* John the Baptist *lived among them, till the time when he began to baptize and preach repentance.*

The Herodians, *so named from* Herod, *were another* Sect, *which was among the* Jews *in our Saviour's time, who had a* leaven, *or particular doctrines, distinct from those of the* Pharisees *and* Sadducees, *against whom our Saviour requires his followers to guard themselves,* Mark 8. 15. *People are much divided about this* Sect. *Some believe that the* Herodians *took* Herod *for the* Messiah; *but as there were several* Herods, *who were known to have reigned over the* Jews, *they are still divided to know which of them was acknowledged for the* Messiah. *The generality are for* Herod *the Great, the son of* Antipater, *who died in a short time after the birth of* Christ. *They say, that the* Herodians *grounded their opinion of* Herod's *being the* Messiah *upon the celebrated prophecy of* Jacob, *Gen.* 49. 10. The sceptre shall not depart from *Judah*, nor a lawgiver from between his feet, until *Shiloh* come; and unto him shall the gathering of the people be. *These marks they, mistaking the nature of* Christ's *kingdom, thought suited exactly with* Herod; *because he was a stranger, and withal a powerful, brave, and warlike prince, and appeared at a time when all the world were in expectation of the* Messiah. *And* Herod *is said to have procured the genealogical memoirs of the house of* David *to be burnt, that so no one might be able to prove that he was not of a family, from which it was well known that the* Messiah *was to spring.*

Others are of opinion, that Herod II. *surnamed* Antipas, *and Tetrarch of* Galilee, *was the head of the* Herodians. *He was a very ambitious and very politic prince, for our Saviour calls him,* Fox, *Luke* 13. 32. *He might be very well thought to be ambitious of passing for the* Messiah.

Some others believed Herod Agrippa, *who was appointed king of* Judea *by* Caligula, *to have given name to the* Herodians. *But how is this opinion maintainable, since the* Herodians *were already known some years before this prince ascended the throne?*

Many of the Fathers, and several Commentators, have asserted, that the Herodians *were people of* Herod's *retinue, who, to satisfy their curiosity, or make their court to their master, came with the* Pharisees *to tempt* Christ *upon paying tribute: but by the recital of the Evangelists it appears, that the* Herodians *were a* Sect *subsisting in* Judea *without any dependence on king* Herod, *and his power at* Jerusalem.

Some will have it, that the Herodians *were politicians who favoured the dominion of* Herod *and the* Romans *against the* Jews, *who were zealous for the liberty of their nation: the former maintained, that it was their duty to pay tribute to the kings established by the* Romans: *but the other* Jews *were of the contrary opinion.*

Dr. Prideaux *says, that the* Herodians *were a* Sect *formed amongst the* Jews, *and had particular doctrines distinct from those of the* Pharisees *and* Sadducees, *and that these doctrines were reducible to two heads:* [1] *In their belief that the dominion of the* Romans *over the* Jews *was just and lawful, and that it was their duty to submit to it.* [2] *That in the present circumstances they might with a good conscience follow many of the heathen modes and usages. It is certain, says he, that these were* Herod's *principles; since he excuses himself on the score of the necessity of the times, for acting in many things against the maxims of the* Jewish *religion.*

Their hypocritical loose way of professing and practising the law, or true religion, among other bad effects which it produced, made these strange factions and divisions, even among the vain professors themselves. Others think, that the Jews *divided themselves into several sects, in imitation of the* Greeks, *whose philosophers were divided into different factions; such as, the* Academics, *the* Stoics, *the* Peripatetics, *the* Epicureans, &c. *It seems as if the* Corinthians *had a mind to introduce something like this into* Christianity, *when they boasted,* I am a disciple of Paul, I of Apollos, I of Peter; *which abuse the apostle* Paul, *with great vehemence, corrects,* 1 Cor. 1. 12, 13. | 3. 22.

Acts 5. 17. which is the *s.* of the Sadducees
15. 5. the *s.* of the Pharisees which believed
24. 5. a ringleader of the *s.* of the Nazarenes
26. 5. after the straitest *s.* of our religion I lived
28. 22. this *s.* is every where spoken against

SECTS.

1 *Cor.* 11. † 19. there must be also *s.* amongst you

SECURE.

Judg. 8. 11. Gideon smote the host, for it was *s.*
18. 7. after the manner of the Zidonians, *s.*
10. when ye go ye shall come to a people *s.* 27.
Job 11. 18. thou shalt be *s.* because there is hope
12. 6. and they that provoke God are *s.*
Mat. 28. 14. we will persuade him, and *s.* you

SECURELY.

Prov. 3. 29. devise not evil against thy neighbour, seeing he dwelleth *s.* by thee
Mic. 2. 8. pull garment from them that pass by *s.*

SECURITY.

Acts 17. 9. and when they had taken *s.* of Jason

SEDITION.

Ezra 4. 15. that they moved *s.* in the city, 19.
Luke 23. 19. for a certain *s.* cast into prison, 25.
Acts 24. 5. we have found this man a mover of *s.*

SEDITIONS.

Gal. 5. 20. the works of the flesh are *s.* heresies

SEDUCE.

Mark 13. 22. shall shew signs and wonders to *s.*
1 *John* 2. 26. written concerning them that *s.* you
Rev. 2. 20. thou sufferest Jezebel to *s.* my servants

SEDUCED.

2 *Kings* 21. 9. Manasseh *s.* them to do more evil
Isa. 19. 13. they have also *s.* Egypt, even they
Ezek. 13. 10. they have also *s.* my people, saying

SEDUCERS.

2 *Tim.* 3. 13. but *s.* shall wax worse and worse

SEDUCETH.

Prov. 12. 26. but the way of the wicked *s.* them

SEDUCING.

1 *Tim.* 4.1.depart from faith, giving heed to *s.* spirits

SEE

Signifies, [1] *To behold, or perceive with the eyes,* Exod. 23. 5. [2] *To observe with approbation,* Gen. 1. 4. [3] *To look upon with consideration and observation,* Mat. 22. 11. [4] *To visit,* 1 Sam. 15. 35. 1 Cor. 16. 7. [5] *To suffer, or bear with,* Ezra 4. 14. [6] *To hear,* Exod. 20. 18. All the people saw the thunderings and the noise of the trumpet. *And in Rev.* 1. 12. I turned to see the voice that spake with me. [7] *To feel,* Psal. 90. 15. [8] *To taste of,* Luke 2. 26. John 8. 51. [9] *To know or learn,* Gen. 37. 14. [10] *To have abundance of knowledge, so as not to stand in need of instruction from others,* John 9. 41. [11] *To perceive and understand experimentally,* Exod. 5. 19. Rom. 7. 23. [12] *To beware, or take care,* Rev. 19. 10. | 22. 9. [13] *To know by divine revelation,* Isa. 2. 1. | 13. 1. [14] *To believe in, and rely upon,* Heb. 11. 27. [15] *To have the perfect and immediate fruition of the glorious presence of God in heaven.* Job 19. 26. Mat. 5. 8. Blessed are the pure in heart; for they shall see God.

Thus seeing, or to see, *is not only said of the sense of vision, by which we perceive external objects, but also of inward perception, of the knowledge of spiritual things, and even of that supernatural sight of hidden things, of prophecy, of visions, of ecstacies. Whence it is, that formerly they were called* Seers, *who afterwards were called* Nabi, *or prophets,* 1 Sam. 9. 9. *and that prophecies were called* visions, *Obad.* 1.

To see the goodness of the Lord, *Psal.* 27. 13. *is to enjoy the mercy or blessing which God hath promised.* Job *says,* O remember that my life is wind, mine eyes shall no more see good, *Job* 7. 7. *I shall die, and see no more: I shall no longer enjoy the good things of this world. And in Mat.* 5. 8. The pure in heart shall see God. *They shall* understand *the mysteries of salvation, they shall* perceive *the loving-kindness of God towards them in this life, and shall at length perfectly* enjoy *him in heaven.*

It is said, Exod. 24. 10. That the elders saw the God of Israel. *They did not see any resemblance of the divine nature, which is expressly denied,* Deut. 4. 15. *but some glorious appearance or token of God's special presence; or rather the Second Person of the Trinity, who then shewed himself to them in a human shape, as a testimony of his future incarnation.*

To see the face of the king, *Esth.* 1. 14. *is to be of his household, to approach near him, or to have familiar converse with him. The kings of* Persia, *under the pretence of maintaining that respect and majesty that was due to them, seldom permitted their subjects to see them, and hardly ever shewed themselves in public: none but their most intimate friends, or their familiar domestics, had the advantage of beholding their faces.*

*Gen.*2.19. brought to Adam, to *s.* what he would call
8. 8. he sent a dove to *s.* if the waters were abated
11. 5. and the Lord came down to *s.* the city
19. 21. he said unto him, *s.* I have accepted thee
22. † 14. the name of that place, the Lord will *s.*
27. 27. *s.* the smell of my son is as the smell of a field
29. † 32. and Leah called his name, *s.* a son
31. 5. he said, I *s.* your father's countenance
34. 1. Dinah went out to *s.* the daughters of land
42. 9. but to *s.* the nakedness of the land, 12.
44. 23. thou saidst, you shall *s.* my face no more
45. 12. your eyes *s.* and the eyes of my brother
24. he said, *s.* that ye fall not out by the way
28. I will go and *s.* Joseph before I die
48. 11. I had not thought to *s.* thy face, and lo
Exod. 1. 16. and when ye *s.* them upon the stools
3. 3. I will turn aside, and *s.* this great sight, 4.
4. 18. *s.* whether my brethren be yet alive
21. *s.* that thou do those wonders before Pharaoh
5. 19. the officers did *s.* they were in evil case
6. 1. now shalt thou *s.* what I will do to Pharaoh
10. 5. that one cannot be able to *s.* the earth
28. take heed to thyself, *s.* my face no more
29. hast spoken well, I will *s.* thy face no more
12. 13. when I *s.* the blood, I will pass over you
13. 17. lest the people repent when they *s.* war
14. 13. stand still and *s.* the salvation of the Lord
16. 29. *s.* for the Lord hath given you the sabbath
32. they may *s.* the bread wherewith I fed you
33. 20. for there shall no man *s.* me and live
23. and thou shalt *s.* my back parts
34. 10. the people shall *s.* the work of the Lord
Lev. 13. 10. and the priest shall *s.* him, 17.
20.17. if a man shall *s.* her nakedness, and she *s.* his
Num. 4. 20. shall not go in to *s.* holy things covered
11. 23. shalt *s.* whether my word come to pass
13. 18. *s.* the land what it is, and people that dwell
14. 23. nor shall any that provoked me *s.* it
22. 41. that thence he might *s.* the utmost part
23. 9. for from the top of the rocks I *s.* him
13. come to another place, whence thou mayest *s.* them, thou shalt *s.* but the utmost part of them
24. 17. I shall *s.* him, but not now, I shall behold
27. 12. and *s.* the land, which I have given to Isr.
32. 8. I sent your fathers from Kadesh to *s.* land
32. 11. surely none of the men that came up out of Egypt shall *s.* the land, *Deut.* 1. 35.
Deut. 1. 36. save Caleb, he shall *s.* land, will give
3. 25. I pray thee, let me *s.* the good land
28. cause to inherit the land which thou shalt *s.*
23. 14. that he *s.* no unclean thing in thee
28. 10. all people shall *s.* that thou art called by
34. sight of thine eyes which thou shalt *s.* 67.
68. thou shalt *s.* it no more again, and be sold
29. 4. the Lord hath not given you eyes to *s.*

Deut. 29. 22. when they *s.* the plagues of that land
30. 15. *s.* I have set before thee life and good
32. 20. he said, I will *s.* what their end will be
39. *s.* now, I, even I, am he, there is no G. with me
52. yet thou shalt *s.* land before thee, but not go
34. 4. I have caused thee to *s.* it with thine eyes
Josh. 22. 10. they built there a great altar to *s.* to
Judg. 14. 8. Samson turned aside to *s.* the carcase
16. 5. and *s.* wherein his great strength lieth
1 *Sam.* 2. 32. shall *s.* an enemy in my habitation
6. 13. they saw the ark, and rejoiced to *s.* it
12. 16. now *s.* this great thing the Lord will do
17. ye may *s.* that your wickedness is great
14. 17. number now, and *s.* who is gone from us
38. and *s.* wherein this sin hath been this day
15. 35. Samuel came no more to *s.* Saul, mourned
17. 28. art come, that thou mightest *s.* the battle
19. 3. and what I *s.* that I will tell thee
15. Saul sent messengers again to *s.* David
20. 29. let me get away, I pray, and *s.* my brethren
21. 14. then said Achish, you *s.* the man is mad
23. 22. know and *s.* his place, where his haunt is
24. 11. my father *s.* yea, *s.* the skirt of thy robe
26. 16. *s.* where king's spear is, and cruse of water
2 *Sam.* 13. 5. when thy father cometh to *s.* thee, let Tamar come, that I may *s.* it, and eat it at her
14. 32. now therefore, let me *s.* the king's face
15. 3. *s.* thy matters are good and right, Absal. said
24. 3. that the eyes of my Lord the king may *s.* it
13. *s.* what ans. I shall return him that sent me
1 *Kings* 12. 16. *s.* to thy house, David, 2 *Chr.* 10. 16.
17. 23. and Elijah said, *s.* thy son liveth
20. 7. and *s.* how this man seeketh mischief
22. the prophet said, mark and *s.* what thou dost
22. 25. thou shalt *s.* in that day, 2 *Chron.* 18. 24.
2 *Kings* 2. 10. if thou *s.* when I am taken from thee
5. 7. *s.* how he seeketh a quarrel against me
6. 17. Lord, I pray, open his eyes that he may *s.*
20. open the eyes of these men that they may *s.*
32. *s.* how this son of a murderer hath sent to
7. 2. thou shalt *s.* it with thine eyes, but not eat, 19.
13. let us send and *s.* || 14. saying, go and *s.*
8. 29. went down to *s.* Joram, 9. 16. 2 *Chr.* 22. 6.
9. 17. the watchman said, I *s.* a company
34. go *s.* now this cursed woman, and bury her
10. 16. come with me, and *s.* my zeal for the Ld.
19. 16. open, Lord, thine eyes, and *s.* *Isa.* 37. 17.
23. 17. then he said, what title is that that I *s.*
2 *Chr.* 18. 16. he said, I did *s.* all Israel scattered
20. 17. *s.* the salvation of the Lord with you
24. 5. go, and *s.* that ye hasten the matter
25. 17. come, let us *s.* one another in the face
Ezra 4. 14. was not meet to *s.* the king's dishonour
Neh. 9. 9. didst *s.* affliction of our fathers in Egypt
Esth. 3. 4. to *s.* if Mordecai's matters would stand
5. 13. so long as I *s.* Mordecai the Jew sitting
8. 6. Esther said, how can I endure to *s.* the evil that shall come on my people? to *s.* the destruct.
Job 3. 9. neither let it *s.* the dawning of the day
7. 7. mine eye shall no more *s.* good; my life wind
8. the eye that hath seen me shall *s.* me no more
9. 25. now my days flee away, they *s.* no good
10. 15. therefore *s.* thou mine affliction
17. 15. as for my hope, who shall *s.* it?
19. 26. worms destroy, yet in my flesh shall I *s.* G.
27. whom I shall *s.* for myself, and not another
20. 9. the eye which saw him shall *s.* him no more
21. 20. his eyes shall *s.* his destruction, shall drink
22. 19. the righteous *s.* it, and are glad
24. 1. why do they that know him not *s.* his days?
15. the adulterer saith, no eye shall *s.* me
28. 27. then did he *s.* it, and declare it, he prepar. it
31. 4. doth not he *s.* my ways, and count my steps?
33. 26. shall pray, and he will *s.* his face with joy
28. his soul, and his life shall *s.* the light
35. 5. look unto the heavens, and *s.* the clouds
36. 25. every man may *s.* it, man may behold it
Psal. 10. 11. he hath said, God will never *s.* it
14. 2. God looked to *s.* if any did understand, 53. 2.
16. 10. neither wilt thou suffer thine Holy One to *s.* corruption, *Acts* 2. 27, 31. | 13. 35.
22. 7. all they that *s.* me laugh me to scorn
27. 13. had believed to *s.* the goodness of the Lord
31. 11. they that did *s.* me without, fled from me
34. 8. O taste and *s.* that the Lord is good
12. that loveth many days, that he may *s.* good
37. 34. when the wicked are cut off, thou shalt *s.* it
40. 3. many shall *s.* it and trust in the Lord
41. 6. if he come to *s.* me, he speaketh vanity
49. 19. he shall go, they shall never *s.* light
52. 6. the righteous also shall *s.* and fear and laugh
59. 10. God shall let me *s.* my desire on my enem. God of mercy shall prevent me, 92. 11. | 118. 7.
63. 2. to *s.* thy power and glory, as I have seen
64. 5. they commune, they say, who shall *s.* them?
8. all that *s.* them shall flee away
66. 5. come and *s.* the works of God, he is terrible
69. 32. the humble shall *s.* this, and be glad
86. 17. that they which hate me may *s.* it
91. 8. thou shalt *s.* the reward of the wicked
97. 6. and all the people *s.* his glory
106. 5. that I may *s.* the good of thy chosen
107. 24. these *s.* the works of the Lord in the deep
42. righteous shall *s.* it and rejoice, all iniquity
112. 8. till he *s.* his desire upon his enemies
10. the wicked shall *s.* it and be grieved
119. 74. they will be glad when they *s.* me
128. 5. thou shalt *s.* the good of Jerusalem all days
6. thou shalt *s.* thy children's children, and peace
139. 16. thy eyes did *s.* my substance yet imperf.
24. search, *s.* if there be any wicked way in me
Prov. 24. 18. lest the Lord *s.* and it displease him
29. 16. but the righteous shall *s.* their fall
Eccl. 1. 10. whereof it may be said, *s.* this is new
2. 3. till I might *s.* what was good for sons of men
3. 18. that men might *s.* that themselves are beasts
22. bring him to *s.* what shall be after him
7. 11. by it there is profit to them that *s.* the sun
8. 16. to *s.* the business that is done upon earth
Cant. 2. 14. O my dove, let me *s.* thy countenance
6. 11. I went into the garden of nuts to *s.* the fruits, and to *s.* whether the vine flourished, 7. 12.

Isa. 5. 19. let him hasten his work, that we may *s.*
6. 10. lest they *s.* with their eyes, hear with ears
14. 16. they that *s.* thee shall narrowly look on thee
26. 11. they shall *s.* and be ashamed for their envy
29. 18. eyes of the blind shall *s.* out of obscurity
30. 20. but thine eyes shall *s.* thy teachers
32. 3. the eyes of them that *s.* shall not be dim
33. 17. thine eyes shall *s.* the king in his beauty
20. thine eyes shall *s.* Jerusalem a quiet habitation
35. 2. they shall *s.* the glory of the L. and excellency
40. 5. glory revealed, and all flesh shall *s.* it together
41. 20. that they may *s.* and know, and consider
48. 6. *s.* all this || 49. 7. kings shall *s.* and arise
52. 8. for they shall *s.* eye to eye, when the Lord
10. the earth shall *s.* salvation of our God
15. what had not been told them shall they *s.*
53. 2. when we shall *s.* him, there is no beauty
10. he shall *s.* his seed, he shall prolong his days
11. he shall *s.* of travail of his soul, and be satisfied
60. 5. then thou shalt *s.* and flow together
61. 9. all that *s.* them shall acknowledge them
62. 2. the Gentiles shall *s.* thy righteousness
64. 9. behold, *s.* we beseech, we are all thy people
66. 18. and they shall come and *s.* my glory
Jer. 1. 11. I *s.* a rod || 13. I *s.* a seething pot
2. 10. send to Kedar, *s.* if there be such a thing
19. know and *s.* that it is an evil thing and bitter
23. *s.* thy way in the valley what thou hast done
3. 2. and *s.* where thou hast not been lien with
4. 21. how long shall I *s.* the standard, and hear
5. 1. *s.* now and know, and seek in the broad places
6. 16. stand ye in the ways and *s.* and ask for paths
7. 12. go to my place, and *s.* what I did to it
11. 20. let me *s.* thy vengeance on them, 20. 12.
20. 18. out of the womb to *s.* labour and sorrow
22. 12. he shall die and *s.* this land no more
30. 6. *s.* whether man doth travail with child? why do I *s.* every man with his hands on his loins?
51. 61. and shalt *s.* and shalt read all these words
Lam. 1. 11. *s.* O Lord, consider, for I become vile
12. *s.* if there be any sorrow like my sorrow
Ezek. 8. 6. thou shalt *s.* greater abominations, 13. 15.
13. 9. that *s.* vanity || 16. *s.* visions of peace for her
16. 37. that they may *s.* all thy nakedness
20. 48. all flesh shall *s.* that I the L. have kindled it
21. 29. whiles they *s.* vanity unto thee, and divine
32. 31. Pharaoh shall *s.* them, and shall be comfort.
33. 6. but if the watchman *s.* the sword come
39. 21. all the heathen shall *s.* my judgment
Dan. 1. 10. why should he *s.* your faces worse liking
3. 25. lo, I *s.* four men loose, walking in the fire
Joel 2. 28. your old men shall dream dreams, your young men shall *s.* visions, *Acts* 2. 17.
Amos 6. 2. pass ye to Calneh and *s.* go ye to Hamath
Jonah 4. 5. might *s.* what would become of the city
Mic. 6. 9. the man of wisdom shall *s.* thy name
7. 10. then she that is mine enemy shall *s.* it
16. the nations shall *s.* and be confounded
Hab. 2. 1. I will watch to *s.* what he will say to me
Zech. 2. 2. to *s.* what is the breadth thereof
4. 10. shall *s.* the plummet in hand of Zerubbabel
5. 2. what seest thou? I answered, I *s.* a flying roll
5. lift your eyes *s.* what is this that goeth forth
9. 5. Ashkelon shall *s.* it, and fear, Gaza shall *s.* it
10. 7. yea, their children shall *s.* it, and be glad
Mal. 1. 5. and your eyes shall *s.* and ye shall say
Mat. 5. 8. blessed pure in heart, for they shall *s.* G.
16. they may *s.* your good works, and glorify
7. 5. and then shalt thou *s.* clearly to cast out the mote out of thy brother's eye, *Luke* 6. 42.
8. 4. *s.* thou tell no man, shew thyself to the priest, 9. 30. *Mark* 1. 44. *Acts* 23. 22.
11. 4. tell John those things ye do hear and *s.*
7. what went you out into wilderness to *s.*? a reed shaken with the wind, 8, 9. *Luke* 7. 24, 25, 26.
12. 38. Master, we would *s.* a sign from thee
13. 14. seeing, ye shall *s.* *Mark* 4. 12. *Acts* 28. 26.
15. heart gross, lest at any time they should *s.* with their eyes, hear with their ears, *Acts* 28. 27.
16. but blessed are your eyes, for they *s.*
17. many desired to *s.* those things which ye *s.*
15. 31. when they saw the blind to *s.* *Luke* 7. 22.
16. 28. till they *s.* the Son of man coming
22. 11. when the king came in to *s.* the guests
24. 6. shall hear of wars, *s.* that ye be not troubled
30. they shall *s.* the Son of man coming in the clouds of heaven, *Mark* 13. 26. *Luke* 21. 27.
26. 58. Peter sat with servants to *s.* the end
27. 4. they said, *s.* thou to that || 24. *s.* ye to it
49. let us *s.* whether Elias will come to save him
28. 6. come *s.* the place where the Lord lay
10. that they go into Galilee, there shall they *s.* me
Mark 5. 14. they went out to *s.* what was done
32. he looked to *s.* her that had done this thing
6. 38. go and *s.* || 8. 24. I *s.* men as trees walking
15. 32. let Christ descend that we may *s.* and believe
Luke 2. 15. let us go to Bethlehem and *s.* this
3. 6. and all flesh shall *s.* the salvation of God
8. 16. they who enter in may *s.* light, 11. 33.
20. thy brethren stand without, desiring to *s.* thee
9. 9. who is this? and he desired to *s.* him, 23. 8.
27. not taste of death till they *s.* kingdom of God
14. 18. I have bought ground, I must go and *s.* it
17. 22. when ye shall desire to *s.* one of the days
23. *s.* here, or *s.* there, go not after them
19. 3. Zaccheus sought to *s.* Jesus, who he was
4. he climbed into a sycamore-tree to *s.* him
20. 13. they will reverence him when they *s.* him
24. 39. behold, it is I myself, handle me and *s.*
John 1. 33. on whom thou shalt *s.* Spirit descending
39. come and *s.* 46. | 11. 34. *Rev.* 6. 1, 3, 5, 7.
50. thou shalt *s.* greater things than these
4. 29. *s.* a man who told me all things ever I did
8. 51. if man keep my sayings, shall never *s.* death
56. your father Abraham rejoiced to *s.* my day
9. 15. I washed, and do *s.* || 25. I was blind, now I *s.*
19. they asked them, how then doth he now *s.*?
39. I came into this world, that they who *s.* not might *s.* and that they who *s.* might be made blind
11. 40. if believe, thou shouldest *s.* the glory of God
12. 9. but that they might *s.* Lazarus also
21. the Greeks, saying, Sir, we would *s.* Jesus

John 16. 22. ye have sorrow, but I will s. you again
20. 25. except I s. in his hands the print of nails
Acts 15. 36. and visit our breth. and s. how they do
19. 21. after I have been there, I must also s. Rome
20. 25. ye all shall s. my face no more, 38.
22. 14. shouldst know his will, and s. that just One
28. 20. for this cause I called you, to s. you
Rom. 1. 11. for I long to s. you, that I may impart
7. 23. I s. another law in my members, warring
15. 21. whom he was not spoken of, they shall s.
24. for I trust to s. you in my journey
1 Cor. 8. 10. if any man s. thee that hast knowledge
16. 10. s. that he may be with you without fear
2 Cor. 8. 7. s. that ye abound in this grace also
Gal. 1. 18. I went up to Jerusalem to s. Peter
Eph. 3. 9. to make all men s. what is fellowship
5. 15. s. that ye walk circumspectly, not as fools
33. the wife s. that she reverence her husband
Phil. 1. 27. whether I come and s. you or be absent
2. 23. so soon as I s. how it will go with me
1 Thess. 2. 17. to s. your face with great desire
3. 6. desiring greatly to s. us, as we also to s. you
5. 15. s. that none render evil for evil to any man
1 Tim. 6. 16. whom no man hath seen, nor can s.
2 Tim. 1. 4. greatly desiring to s. thee, being mindf.
Heb. 8. 5. s. thou make all according to the pattern
12. 14. holiness, without which no man s. the Lord
25. s. that ye refuse not him that speaketh
13. 23. with whom, if he come shortly, I will s. you
1 Pet. 1. 22. s. that ye love one another fervently
3. 10. he that will s. good days, let him refrain
1 John 5. 16. if any man s. his brother sin a sin not
3 John 14. but I trust I shall shortly s. thee
Rev. 1. 7. he cometh, and every eye shall s. him
12. I turned to s. the voice that spake with me
3. 18. anoint with eye-salve, that thou mayest s.
6. 6. and s. thou hurt not the oil and the wine
11. 9. shall s. their dead bodies three days and half
16. 15. lest he walk naked, and they s. his shame
18. 7. for she saith, I sit a queen, shall s. no sorrow
9. when they shall s. the smoke of her burning
19. 10. he said to me, s. thou do it not, 22. 9.
22. 4. and they shall s. his face, name in foreheads

SEE *not*, or *not* SEE.

Gen. 21. 16. let me not s. the death of the child
27. 1. when Isaac was old, that he could not s.
43. 3. the man did protest, ye shall not s. my face, 5.
44. 26. for we may not s. the man's face except
48. 10. eyes of Israel were dim, he could not s.
Exod. 33. 20. thou canst not s. my face and live
Num. 11. 15. let me not s. my wretchedness
14. 23. surely they shall not s. the land I sware
23. 13. utmost part, and shall not s. them all
Deut. 22. 1. thou shalt not s. thy brother's ox go astray
4. thou shalt not s. thy brother's ass fall down
1 Sam. 3. 2. Eli, his eyes dim, he could not s. 4. 15.
2 Sam. 3. 13. not s. my face, except thou first bring
14. 24. the king said, let not Absalom s. my face
1 Kings 14. 4. Ahijah could not s. his eyes set
2 Kings 3. 17. ye shall not s. wind, nor shall ye s. rain
22. 20. thine eyes shall not s. all evil I will bring
Job 9. 11. lo, he goeth by me, and I s. him not
20. 17. he shall not s. the rivers of honey and butter
22. 11. or darkness that thou canst not s.
23. 9. he hideth himself that I cannot s. him
34. 32. that which I s. not teach thou me
35. 14. though thou sayest, thou shalt not s. him
37. 21. men s. not the bright light in the clouds
Psal. 49. 9. should still live, and not s. corruption
58. 8. pass away, that they may not s. the sun
69. 23. let their eyes be darkened, that they s. not
74. 9. we s. not our signs, there is no more prophet
89. 48. what man liveth, and shall not s. death
94. 7. yet they say, the Lord shall not s.
9. he that formed the eye, shall he not s.?
115. 5. eyes have they, but they s. not, 135. 16.
Isa. 26. 11. when thy hand is lifted up, they will n. s.
30. 10. children, which say to the seers, s. not
33. 19. thou shalt not s. a fierce people, a people
38. 11. I shall not s. the Lord, even the Lord
44. 9. they s. not, that they may be ashamed
18. he hath shut their eyes, that they cannot s.
Jer. 5. 21. which have eyes, and s. not, Ezek. 12. 12.
12. 4. they said, he shall not s. our last end
14. 13. the prophets say, ye shall not s. the sword
17. 6. like heath, he shall not s. when good cometh
8. he shall not s. when heat cometh
23. 24. can any hide, that I shall not s. him?
Ezek. 12. 6. that thou s. not the ground, 12.
13. yet shall he not s. it, though he shall die there
Dan. 5. 23. hast praised gods of gold, which s. not
Zeph. 3. 15. thou shalt not s. evil any more
Mat. 13. 13. because they seeing s. not and hear not
23. 39. ye shall not s. me henceforth, Luke 13. 35.
24. 2. Jesus said, s. ye not all these things?
Mark 8. 18. having eyes s. ye not? and ears, hear not
Luke 2. 26. not s. death, before he had seen Christ
8. 10. that seeing, they might not s. and hearing
17. 22. shall desire to s. and ye shall not s. it
John 3. 3. he cannot s. the kingdom of God
36. shall not s. life, but wrath abideth on him
9. 39. I am come, that they who s. not might s.
12. 40. that they should not s. with their eyes
16. 16. a little while, and ye shall not s. me, 17. 19.
18. 26. did I not s. thee in the garden with him?
Acts 22. 11. when I could not s. for the glory
Rom. 11. 8. hath given eyes, that they should not s.
10. let their eyes be darkened that they may not s.
1 Cor. 16. 7. for I will not s. you now by the way
Heb. 2. 8. but we s. not yet all things put under him
11. 5. was translated, that he should not s. death
1 Pet. 1. 8. though now ye s. him not, yet believing
2 Pet. 1. 9. he is blind, and cannot s. afar off

We SEE.

Gen. 37. 20. we shall s. what will become of dreams
Psal. 36. 9. in thy light shall we s. light
Jer. 5. 12. neither shall we s. sword or famine
42. 14. go into Egypt, where we shall s. no war
Mark 15. 32. that we may s. and believe, John 6. 30.
John 9. 41. now ye say, we s. your sin remaineth
Rom. 8. 25. but if we hope for that we s. not
1 Cor. 13. 12. now we s. through a glass darkly

1 Thess. 3. 10. praying that we might s. your face
Heb. 2. 9. but we s. Jes. who was made a little lower
3. 19. so we s. that they could not enter in because
1 John 3. 2. be like him, for we shall s. him as he is

Ye SEE, or SEE *ye*.

Exod. 14. 13. ye shall s. them again no more
16. 7. then ye shall s. the glory of the Lord
Josh. 3. 3. when ye s. the ark of the covenant
1 Sam. 10. 24. s. ye him whom Lord hath chosen?
2 Chron. 29. 8. to hissing, as ye s. with your eyes
30. 7. who gave them up to desolation, as ye s.
Neh. 2. 17. I said, ye s. the distress that we are in
Job 6. 21. ye s. my casting down, and are afraid
Cant. 6. 13. what will ye s. in the Shulamite
Isa. 6. 9. and s. ye indeed, but perceive not
18. 3. s. ye, when he lifteth up an ensign
42. 18. hear, ye deaf, look, ye blind, that ye may s.
66. 14. when ye s. your hearts shall rejoice
Jer. 2. 31. O generation, s. ye the word of the Lord
42. 18. and ye shall s. this place no more
Ezek. 13. 23. therefore ye shall s. no more vanity
14. 22. ye shall s. their way and their doings
23. they shall comfort you when ye s. their ways
Dan. 2. 8. because ye s. the thing is gone from me
Mat. 13. 17. many have desired to see those things
which ye s. and have not, Luke 10. 23.
24. 2. Jesus said, s. ye not all these things?
33. when ye shall s. all these things, know that it
is near, Mark 13. 29. Luke 21. 31.
26. 64. hereafter shall ye s. the Son of man sitting
on the right hand of power, Mark 14. 62.
27. 24. I am innocent, s. ye to it, Mark 15. 36.
28. 7. in Galilee there shall ye s. him, Mark 16. 7.
Luke 12. 54. when ye s. a cloud rise out of the west
55. and when ye s. the south wind blow, ye say
13. 28. when ye shall s. Abraham and the prophets
21. 20. when ye shall s. Jerusalem compassed
30. ye s. and know of yourselves, summer is nigh
24. 39. hath not flesh and bones, as ye s. me have
John 1. 51. hereafter ye shall s. heaven open
4. 48. except ye s. signs, ye will not believe
6. 62. what if ye shall s. the Son of man ascend
14. 19. but ye s. me || 16. 10. and ye s. me no more
16. 16. a little while ye shall s. me, 17, 19.
Acts 2. 33. shed this which ye now s. and hear
3. 16. made this man strong, whom ye s. and know
19. 26. ye s. and hear, that not alone at Ephesus
25. 24. ye s. this man, about whom Jews dealt
1 Cor. 1. 26. for ye s. your calling, brethren
Gal. 6. 11. ye s. how large a letter I have written
Phil. 2. 28. when ye s. him again, ye may rejoice
Heb. 10. 25. much more, as ye s. day approaching
Jam. 2. 24. ye s. how that by works man is justified
1 Pet. 1. 8. though now ye s. him not, yet ye rejoice

SEED.

Seed *in Scripture is taken,* [1] Properly, *for that thin, hot, spirituous humour in man's body, which is fitted by nature for the generation of mankind,* Gen. 38. 9. *Likewise for that matter which in all plants and fruits is disposed for the propagation of the kind,* Gen. 1. 11. | 47. 19. [2] Figuratively, *for that which is begotten; and this is spoken either,* (1) Collectively, *of many, of children, or posterity in general, as in* Gen. 17. 7, 8. *God says to* Abraham, I will establish my covenant between me and thee, and thy seed after thee in their generations. I will give unto thee, and to thy seed after thee, the land wherein thou art a stranger. *Or,* (2) Individually, *of one alone, as of* Seth, *Gen.* 4. 25. God hath appointed me another seed: *He hath given me another son. Also of Jesus Christ,* Gen. 3. 15. I will put enmity between thy seed and the woman's seed. *Gal.* 3. 16. He saith not, And to seeds, as of many, but as of one; and to thy *Seed,* which is *Christ.* (3) *For works of mercy,* Eccl. 11. 6.

The seed of Abraham *signifies,* [1] *The whole posterity of* Abraham, *according to the flesh, including both the bad and good.* Rom. 9. 7. Neither because they are the *seed of Abraham,* are they all children. [2] *The faithful only, whether* Jews or Gentiles, *who are endued with such a faith as* Abraham *had.* Rom. 4. 16. To the end the promise might be sure to all the seed, not to that only which is of the law, but to that also which is of the faith of *Abraham.* [3] Christ, *who came of* Abraham *according to the flesh.* Gal. 3. 16. To thy seed, which is *Christ. Or thus, Persons are called* Abraham's *seed, either carnally only, as they who valued themselves on account of their descent from* Abraham *after the flesh,* John 8. 33, 37. *Or carnally and spiritually too, as the believing* Jews: *or spiritually only, as the* Gentiles, *who had the same faith with* Abraham, *though they did not come out of his loins.*

The word of God is compared to seed, *Luke* 8. 5, 11. *which is sown in the heart, as the husbandman casts his seed into the ground. The word is called* an incorruptible seed, 1 *Pet.* 1. 23. *because continuing still the same, and being immutable in itself, it changes and renews the hearts of those that by faith receive it. Or, it may be understood of its being incorruptible effectively, because it leads and tends to an immortal life; it begets in the soul an abiding life, which shall continue for ever. Hence it is said,* 1 John 3. 9. Whosoever is born of God, doth not commit sin; for his *seed* remaineth in him: *the new or divine nature, the principle or habit of grace or holiness in the heart, remaineth or abideth in him.*

The apostle Paul, *writing to the* Romans, *quotes a passage out of* Isaiah, Except the Lord of sabaoth had left us a seed, we had been as *Sodoma,* and been made like unto *Gomorrah,* Rom. 9. 29. *What the apostle calls* seed, *is by the prophet called a* remnant, *Isa.* 1. 9. *It is an allusion to the custom among husbandmen, who spend the greatest part of their corn in bread and other food, reserving a small quantity of the choicest and best for seed: so would God deal with the* Israelites; *though they were innumerable as the sand, or as the stars, yet a few of them only should be delivered out of* Babylon, *and he would afterwards bring but a few of them, comparatively, to believe in* Christ.

Gen. 1. 11. bring forth herbs yielding s. 12, 29.
47. 19. give us s. || 23. lo, here is s. for you
24. and four parts shall be your own for s.
Exod. 16. 31. the manna was like coriander s.
Lev. 11. 37. their carcase fall on any sowing s.
38. but if any water be put upon the s.
19. 19. thou shalt not sow thy field with mingled s.
26. 16. and ye shall sow your s. in vain
27. 16. thy estimation shall be according to the s. an
homer of barley s. valued at 50 shekels
30. all the tithe of the s. of the land is the Lord's
Num. 20. 5. it is no place of s. or of figs or vines
Deut. 11. 10. not as Egypt, where thou sowedst s.
14. 22. shalt surely tithe all the increase of thy s.
22. 9. lest the fruit of thy s. sown be defiled
28. 38. thou shalt carry much s. into the field
1 Sam. 8. 15. the king will take the tenth of s.
1 Kings 18. 32. a trench contain two measures of s.
Job 39. 12. will the unicorn bring home thy s.
Psal. 126. 6. he that goeth forth bearing precious s.
Eccl. 11. 6. in the morning sow thy s. and evening
Isa. 5. 10. the s. of an homer shall yield an ephah
17. 11. in the morning make thy s. to flourish
23. 3. and by great waters the s. of Sihor
55. 10. that it may give s. to the sower and bread
Jer. 35. 7. nor shall sow s. nor plant vineyard
9. neither have we vineyard, field, nor s.
Ezek. 17. 5. he took also of the s. of the land
Joel 1. 17. the s. is rotten under their clods
Amos 9. 13. the treader overtake him that soweth s.
Hag. 2. 19. is the s. yet in the barn? yea, as yet
Zech. 8. 12. for the s. shall be prosperous, the vine
Mal. 2. 3. behold, I will corrupt your s. and spread
Mat. 13. 19. which receive s. by the way-side
20. s. into stony places || 22. s. among the thorns
23. but he that received s. into good ground
24. a man which sowed good s. in his field
27. sir, didst not thou sow good s. in thy field?
37. he that soweth the good s. is the Son of man
38. the good s. are the children of the kingdom
Mark 4. 26. if a man should cast s. into the ground
27. and the s. should spring and grow up
Luke 8. 5. a sower went out to sow his s. some fell
11. the parable is this; the s. is word of God
1 Cor. 15. 38. and to every s. his own body
2 Cor. 9. 10. he that ministereth s. to the sower
1 Pet. 1. 23. being born again, not of corruptible s.
1 John 3. 9. for his s. remaineth in him, cannot sin

See COPULATION.

SEED for *Posterity.*

Gen. 4. 25. God hath appointed me another s.
7. 3. to keep s. alive upon the face of the earth
15. 3. Abram said, to me thou hast given no s.
19. 32. that we may preserve s. of our father, 34.
38. 8. marry her, and raise up s. to thy brother,
Mat. 22. 24. Mark 12. 19. Luke 20. 28.
9. Onan knew that the s. should not be his
Lev. 12. 2. if a woman have conceived s. and born
21. 21. that hath a blemish of the s. of Aaron
22. 4. what man of the s. of Aaron is a leper
Num. 5. 28. then the woman shall conceive s.
16. 40. which is not of s. of Aaron come near
Deut. 1. 8. to give it to their s. after them, 11. 9.
4. 37. he chose their s. after them, 10. 15.
31. 21. forgotten out of the mouths of their s.
Ruth 4. 12. s. the Lord shall give of this woman
1 Sam. 2. 20. the Lord give thee s. of this woman
24. 21. that thou wilt not cut off my s. after me
1 Kings 11. 14. he was of the king's s. in Edom
39. I will for this afflict the s. of David
2 Kings 11. 1. Athaliah, mother of Ahaziah, arose
and destroyed all the s. royal, 2 Chr. 22. 10.
17. 20. the Lord rejected all the s. of Israel
25. 25. Ishmael of the s. royal came, Jer. 41. 1.
1 Chron. 16. 13. O ye s. of Israel his servant
Ezra 2. 59. they could not shew their s. Neh. 7. 61.
9. 2. the holy s. have mingled themselves
Neh. 9. 2. the s. of Israel separated themselves
Esth. 6. 13. if Mordecai be of the s. of the Jews
9. 27. the Jews took upon them and their s. 31.
28. nor memorial of them perish from their s.
Job 21. 8. their s. is established in their sight
Psal. 21. 10. their s. shalt thou destroy from earth
22. 23. praise him, all ye the s. of Jacob, glorify
him; and fear him, all ye the s. of Israel
30. a s. shall serve him, it shall be counted to Lord
37. 28. but the s. of the wicked shall be cut off
69. 36. the s. also of his servants shall inherit it
102. 28. their s. shall be established before thee
106. 27. to overthrow their s. among the nations
Prov. 11. 21. the s. of righteous shall be delivered
Isa. 1. 4. ah, sinful nation, a s. of evil-doers
6. 13. the holy s. shall be the substance thereof
14. 20. the s. of evil-doers shall never be renowned
45. 19. I said not unto s. of Jacob, seek ye me in vain
25. in the Lord shall all s. of Israel be justified
57. 3. the s. of the adulterer and the whore
4. ye not children of transgression, a s. of falseh.
61. 9. their s. shall be known among the Gentiles;
that they are the s. which the Lord hath blessed
65. 9. I will bring forth a s. out of Jacob
23. they are the s. of the blessed of the Lord
Jer. 2. 21. I had planted thee wholly a right s.
7. 15. I will cast out the whole s. of Ephraim
23. 8. which led the s. of the house of Israel
31. 27. I will sow with s. of man and s. of beast
36. then s. of Israel also shall cease as a nation
37. I will cast off all the s. of Israel, 33. 26.
33. 22. so will I multiply the s. of David my servant
Ezek. 17. 13. and hath taken of the king's s.
20. 5. I lifted up my hand to the s. of Jacob
43. 19. give to priests that be of the s. of Zadok
44. 22. they shall take maidens of the s. of Israel
Dan. 1. 3. bring of the children of the king's s.
2. 43. shall mingle themselves with the s. of men
9. 1. Darius of the s. of the Medes was made king
Mal. 2. 15. that he might seek a godly s.
Mark 12. 20. the first dying left no s. 21, 22.
John 7. 42. that Christ cometh of the s. of David

Acts 13. 23. of this man's s. hath God raised Jesus
Rom. 1. 3. was made of the s. of David, 2 Tim. 2. 8.
4. 16. that the promise might be sure to all his s.
9. 8. the children of the promise counted for the s.
29. except the Lord of sabaoth had left us a s.
Gal. 3. 19. it was added, till the s. should come
Heb. 11. 11. Sarah received strength to conceive s.
Rev. 12. 17. to make war with the remnant of her s.
See ABRAHAM.

His SEED.

Gen. 17. 19. my covenant with Isaac and his s.
46. 6. Jacob came, and all his s. with him, 7.
48. 19. and his s. shall become a multitude of nations
Exod. 28. 43. a statute of his s. after him, 30. 21.
Lev. 20. 2. that giveth any of his s. to Molech, 3, 4.
21. 15. nor shall ye profane his s. among people
Num. 14. 24. servant Caleb and his s. shall possess it
24. 7. and his s. shall be in many waters
25. 13. he shall have it, and his s. after him
Josh. 24. 3. I multiplied his s. and gave Isaac
2 Sam. 4. 8. hath avenged thee of Saul and his s.
22. 51. he shewed mercy to his anointed, to David
and his s. for evermore, Psal. 18. 50.
1 Kings 2. 33. on head of Joab, and his s. for ever,
upon David and his s. shall be peace for ever
Neh. 9. 8. thou madest a covenant to give it to his s.
Esth. 10. 3. and speaking peace to all his s.
Psal. 25. 13. his s. shall inherit the earth
37. 25. nor have I seen his s. begging bread
26. he is merciful, and his s. is blessed
89. 29. his s. also will I make to endure, 36.
112. 2. his s. shall be mighty upon earth
Isa. 53. 10. he shall see his s. shall prolong his days
Jer. 22. 28. why are they cast out, he and his s.?
30. for no man of his s. shall prosper
29. 32. and I will punish Shemaiah and his s.
33. 26. I will not take any of his s. to be rulers
36. 31. I will punish Jehoiachim and his s.
49. 10. Esau, his s. is spoiled, and he is not
Acts 7. 5. would give it to him and his s. after him
6. that his s. should sojourn in a strange land

Thy SEED.

Gen. 3. 15. will put enmity bet. thy s. and her seed
12. 7. to thy s. will I give this land, 13, 15. | 15. 18.
| 17. 8. | 24. 7. | 26. 3. | 28. 4, 13. | 35. 12. |
48. 4. Exod. 33. 1. Deut. 34. 4.
13. 16. I will make thy s. as dust, 16. 10. | 28. 14.
15. 5. he said to him, so shall thy s. be, Rom. 4. 18.
13. that thy s. shall be a stranger in a land
17. 7. my covenant between me and thy s. after
thee; to be a God to thee and thy s. 10.
9. thou and thy s. after thee in their generations
12. a stranger not of thy s. shall be circumcised
21. 12. in Isaac shall thy s. be called, Heb. 11. 18.
13. make Ishmael a nation, because he is thy s.
22. 17. thy s. possess the gate of enemies, 24. 60.
18. in thy s. shall all the nations of the earth be
blessed, 26. 4. | 28. 14. Acts 3. 25.
26. 24. and multiply thy s. for Abraham's sake
32. 12. thou saidst, I will make thy s. as the sand
48. 11. and lo, God hath shewed me also thy s.
Lev. 18. 21. not any of thy s. pass through the fire
21. 17. whosoever of thy s. hath any blemish
Num. 18. 19. the heave offerings I gave thee and thy s.
Deut. 28. 46. curses for a sign on thy s. for ever
59. Lord will make plagues of thy s. wonderful
30. 6. the Lord will circumcise the heart of thy s.
19. choose life, that thou and thy s. may live
1 Sam. 20. 42. the Lord be bet. my seed and thy s.
2 Sam. 7. 12. I will set up thy s. 1 Chron. 17. 11.
2 Kings 5. 27. leprosy shall cleave to thee and thy s.
Job 5. 25. thou shalt know that thy s. shall be great
Psal. 89. 4. thy s. will I establish for ever, and build
Isa. 43. 5. I will bring thy s. from the east and gather
44. 3. I will pour my Spirit upon thy s. and blessing
48. 19. thy s. also had been as the sand and offsp.
54. 3. and thy s. shall inherit the Gentiles
59. 21. my Spirit that is upon thee, shall not depart out of the mouth of thy s. nor thy seed's s.
Jer. 30. 10. thy s. from the land of captivity, 46. 27.
Gal. 3. 16. and to thy s. which is Christ

Your SEED.

Exod. 32. 13. all this land will I give to your s.
Lev. 22. 3. whosoever of your s. goeth to holy things
Isa. 66. 22. so shall your s. and your name remain

SEED-time.

Gen. 8. 22. s.-time and harvest shall not cease

SEEDS.

Gal. 3. 16. he saith not, and to s. as of many

SEEDS.

Deut. 22. 9. not sow thy vineyard with divers s.
Mat. 13. 4. when he sowed some s. fell by way-side
32. which is the least of all s. Mark 4. 31.

SEEING.

Exod. 4. 11. or who maketh the s. or the blind?

SEEING, Verb.

Exod. 22. 10. any beast be driven away, no man s.
Num. 35. 23. s. him not, cast it on him that he die
1 Kings 1. 48. given one to sit, mine eyes even s. it
Prov. 20. 12. the Lord maketh the s. eye
Eccl. 1. 8. the eye is not satisfied with s. nor ear
Isa. 21. 3. I was dismayed at the s. of it
33. 15. that shutteth his eyes from s. evil
42. 20. s. many things, but thou observest not
Ezek. 22. 28. s. vanity, and divining lies to them
Mat. 13. 13. in parables, because they s. see not
14. shall not understand, s. ye shall see and shall
not perceive, Mark 4. 12. Acts 28. 26.
John 9. 7. he went and washed and came s.
Acts 2. 31. he s. this, spake of the resurrection
3. 3. s. Peter and John about to go to the temple
7. 24. s. one of them suffer wrong, defended him
8. 6. the people s. the miracles that he did
9. 7. speechless, hearing a voice, but s. no man
13. 11. be blind, not s. the sun for a season
Heb. 11. 27. he endured as s. him who is invisible
2 Pet. 2. 8. in s. and hearing, vexed his right. soul

SEEING, Adverb.

Gen. 15. 2. what wilt thou give me, s. I go childless
22. 12. s. thou hast not withheld thine only son
24. 56. s. the Lord hath prospered my way
26. 27. wherefore come ye to me, s. ye hate me?
44. 30. s. his life is bound up in the lad's life
Num. 16. 3. s. all the congregation are holy
Judg. 13. 18. why askest thou my name, s. it is secret
17. 13. do me good, s. I have a Levite to my priest
21. 16. s. women are destroyed out of Benjamin
Ruth 1. 21. s. the Lord hath testified against me
1 Sam. 16. 1. s. I have rejected him from reigning
28. 16. s. the L. is departed from thee and become
1 Chron. 12. 17. s. there is no wrong in mine hands
Job 19. 28. s. the root of the matter is found in me
21. 22. s. he judgeth those that are high
24. 1. s. times are not hidden from the Almighty
Psal. 50. 17. s. thou hatest instruction, and castest
Prov. 3. 29. s. he dwelleth securely by thee
Isa. 49. 21. s. I have lost my children and am deso.
Jer. 47. 7. s. the Lord hath given it a charge
Dan. 2. 47. s. thou couldst reveal this secret
Luke 1. 34. how shall this be, s. I know not a man
23. 40. s. thou art in the same condemnation
Acts 17. 24. s. he is the Lord of heaven and earth
25. s. he giveth to all life and breath and all things
Rom. 3. 30. s. it is one God who shall justify
2 Cor. 3. 12. s. then that we have such hope
Col. 3. 9. s. that ye have put off the old man
Heb. 4. 6. s. it remaineth some must enter therein
14. s. then that we have a great high priest
5. 11. hard to be uttered, s. ye are dull of hearing
6. 6. s. they crucify the Son of God afresh
7. 25. s. he ever liveth to make intercession for them
12. 1. s. we are compassed about with witnesses
1 Pet. 1. 22. s. ye have purified your souls in obeying
2 Pet. 3. 14. s. ye look for such things, be diligent
17. s. ye know these things before, beware lest

SEEK.

Gen. 37. 16. Joseph said, I s. my brethren, tell me
43. 18. that he may s. occasion against us and fall
Num. 16. 10. and s. ye the priesthood also?
24. 1. Balaam went not to s. for enchantments
Deut. 4. 29. if thou s. him with all thy heart
12. 5. even to his habitation shall ye s. and come
22. 2. sheep be with thee till thy brother s. after it
1 Sam. 9. 3. Kish said to Saul his son, go s. the asses
10. 14. whither went ye? he said, to s. the asses
16. 16. to s. out a cunning player on an harp
23. 15. Saul come to s. his life, 25. | 24. 2. | 26. 2.
25. 26. they that s. evil to my Lord, be as Nabal
29. yet a man is risen to pursue and s. thy soul
26. 20. for king of Israel is come out to s. a flea
27. 1. Saul shall despair to s. me any more
28. 7. s. me a woman that hath a familiar spirit
2 Sam. 5. 17. the Philistines came up to s. David
1 Kings 2. 40. Shimei went to s. his servants
18. 10. whither my lord hath not sent to s. thee
19. 10. they s. my life to take it away, 14.
2 Kings 2. 16. let them go, and s. thy master
6. 19. and I will bring you to the man whom ye s.
1 Chron. 28. 8. s. the commandments of the Lord
9. if thou s. him, he will be found, 2 Chron. 15. 2.
2 Chron. 19. 3. hast prepared thine heart to s. God
30. 19. that prepareth his heart to s. God, Ld. God
31. 21. to s. his God, he did it with all his heart
34. 3. Josiah began to s. after the God of David
Ezra 4. 2. build, for we s. your God as ye do
7. 10. Ezra had prepared his heart to s. the law
8. 21. to s. him right way for us, and our little ones
22. name of God is on them for good that s. him
Neh. 2. 10. come a man to s. the welfare of Israel
Job 5. 8. I would s. unto God, and unto God commit
7. 21. shalt s. me in morning, but I shall not be
8. 5. if thou wouldst s. unto God betimes
20. 10. his children shall s. to please the poor
Psal. 4. 2. will ye love vanity, and s. after leasing
9. 10. thou hast not forsaken them that s. thee
10. 15. s. out his wickedness till thou find none
14. 2. to see if there were any that did s. God, 53. 2.
24. 6. this is the generation of them that s. him
27. 4. one thing have I desired, that will I s. after
8. s. ye my face, thy face, Lord, will I s.
34. 14. s. peace, and pursue it, 1 Pet. 3. 11.
35. 4. let them be put to shame that s. my soul
38. 12. they that s. my life, they that s. my hurt
40. 14. be confounded that s. after my soul, 70. 2.
54. 3. and oppressors s. after my soul
63. 1. thou art my God, early will I s. thee
9. those that s. my soul go into the lower parts
69. 6. let not those that s. thee be confounded
32. and your heart shall live that s. God
70. 4. let all those that s. thee rejoice and be glad
71. 13. be covered with dishonour that s. my hurt
24. they are brought unto shame that s. my hurt
83. 16. that they may s. thy name, O Lord
104. 21. the young lions s. their meat from God
109. 10. let his children s. their bread
119. 2. blessed, that s. him with their whole heart
45. I will walk at liberty, for I s. thy precepts
176. I have gone astray as a sheep, s. thy servant
122. 9. for the house of God, I will s. thy good
Prov. 1. 28. they shall s. me, but shall not find me
8. 17. and those that s. me early shall find me
21. 6. vanity tossed to and fro of them that s. death
23. 30. who hath woe? who hath sorrow? they that
tarry long at wine, they that go to s. mixt wine
35. when I shall awake, I will s. it yet again
29. 10. blood-thirsty hate upright, just s. his soul
26. many s. the ruler's favour, judgment from Ld.
Eccl. 1. 13. I gave my heart to s. out by wisdom
7. 25. I applied mine heart to s. out wisdom
8. 17. tho' a man labour to s. it, not able to find it
Cant. 3. 2. I will s. him whom my soul loveth
6. 1. thy beloved, that we may s. him with thee
Isa. 1. 17. learn to do well, s. judgment, relieve
8. 19. when shall say, s. unto them that have familiar
spirits; should not a people s. unto their God?
11. 10. be root of Jesse, to it shall the Gentiles s.
19. 3. they shall s. to the charmers and wizards
26. 9. with my spirit within me will I s. thee early
34. 16. s. ye out of the book of the Lord, and read
41. 12. thou shalt s. them, and not find them
17. when the needy s. water, and there is none
45. 19. I said not to Jacob, s. ye me in vain
58. 2. yet they s. me daily, and delight to know
Jer. 2. 24. that s. her, in her month shall find her
2. 33. why trimmest thou thy way to s. love?
4. 30. thy lovers despise thee, they will s. thy life
11. 21. the men of Anathoth, that s. thy life
19. 7. to fall by them that s. their lives, 21. 7.
9. they that s. their lives shall straiten them
22. 25. into hand of them that s. thy life, 38. 16.
29. 7. s. the peace of the city, whither carried
13. ye shall s. me, and find me, when ye search me
34. 20. into hand of them that s. their life, 21.
44. 30. I will give Pharaoh to them that s. his life
46. 26. Egyptians to those that s. their lives
49. 37. Elam dismayed before them that s. their life
Lam. 1. 11. all her people sigh, they s. bread
Ezek. 7. 25. they shall s. peace there shall be none
26. then shall they s. a vision of the prophet
34. 6. flock was scattered, none did s. after them
11. I will search my sheep, and s. them out
12. as a shepherd so will I s. out my sheep
16. I will s. that which was lost and bring again
Dan. 9. 3. I set my face unto God, to s. by prayer
Hos. 2. 7. he shall s. them, but not find them
Amos 5. 4. saith the Lord, s. me, and ye shall live
8. s. him that maketh the seven stars and Orion
14. s. good and not evil, that ye may live
8. 12. to s. the word of the Lord, and not find it
Nah. 3. 7. whence shall I s. comforters for thee?
11. thou shalt be hid, thou shalt s. strength
Zeph. 2. 3. s. ye the Lord, ye meek of the earth
Zech. 11. 16. a shepherd shall not s. the young one
12. 9. in that day I will s. to destroy all the nations
Mal. 2. 7. they should s. the law at his mouth
15. that he might s. a godly seed, take heed
Mat. 2. 13. Herod will s. young child to destroy him
6. 32. after all these things do the Gentiles s.
33. s. ye first the kingdom of God, Luke 12. 31.
7. 7. s. and ye shall find, knock, Luke 11. 9.
28. 5. for I know that ye s. Jesus, Mark 16. 6.
Mark 1. 37. they said to him, all men s. for thee
3. 32. thy mother and thy brethren s. for thee
8. 12. this generation s. after a sign, Luke 11. 29.
Luke 12. 30. these things do the nations s. after
13. 24. many, I say unto you, will s. to enter in
15. 8. doth she not s. diligently till she find it?
17. 33. whosoever shall s. to save his life, shall lose it
19. 10. the Son of man is come to s. and to save
24. 5. why s. ye the living among the dead?
John 1. 38. Jesus saith unto them, what s. ye?
6. 26. ye s. me, not because ye saw the miracles
7. 25. is not this he whom they s. to kill?
34. ye shall s. me, and shall not find me, 36.
8. 21. ye shall s. me, and shall die in your sins
37. are Abraham's seed, but ye s. to kill me, 40.
13. 33. ye shall s. me, and whither I go cannot come
18. 4. Jesus said unto them, whom s. ye? 7.
8. if ye s. me, let these go their way
Acts 10. 19. Spirit said, behold, three men s. thee
21. Peter said, behold, I am he whom ye s.
11. 25. Barnabas departed to Tarsus, to s. Saul
Rom. 2. 7. to them who s. for glory and honour
11. 3. I am left alone, and they s. my life
1 Cor. 1. 22. and the Greeks s. after wisdom
10. 24. let no man s. his own, but another's wealth
14. 12. s. that ye may excel to edifying of church
2 Cor. 13. 3. since ye s. a proof of Christ speaking
Gal. 1. 10. do I persuade, or s. to please men?
2. 17. if while we s. to be justified by Christ
Phil. 2. 21. for all s. their own things, not Christ's
Col. 3. 1. if risen, s. those things which are above
Heb. 11. 6. he is a rewarder of them that s. him
14. they declare plainly that they s. a country
13. 14. here we have no city, but we s. one to come
Rev. 9. 6. in those days shall men s. death, not find it
See FACE, LORD.

Not SEEK, or SEEK not.

Lev. 13. 36. the priest shall not s. for yellow hair
19. 31. neither s. after wizards to be defiled by them
Num. 15. 39. that ye s. not after your own heart
Deut. 23. 6. thou shalt not s. their peace, Ezra 9. 12.
Ruth 3. 1. daughter, shall I not s. rest for thee?
Psal. 10. 4. the wicked will not s. after God
119. 155. the wicked, they s. not thy statutes
Jer. 30. 14. all thy lovers, they s. thee not
45. 5. seekest thou great things? s. them not
Amos 5. 5. but s. not Beth-el, nor enter into Gilgal
Zech. 11. 16. a shepherd shall not s. the young one
Luke 12. 29. s. not what ye shall eat or drink
John 5. 30. because I s. not mine own will, but will
44. s. not the honour that cometh from God
8. 50. I s. not mine own glory, there is one seeketh
1 Cor. 7. 27. s. not to be loosed, s. not a wife
2 Cor. 12. 14. for I s. not yours, but you

SEEKEST.

Gen. 37. 15. the man asked him, what s. thou?
Judg. 4. 22. I will shew thee the man whom s.
2 Sam. 17. 3. the man thou s. is as if all returned
20. 19. thou s. to destroy a mother in Israel
1 Kings 11. 22. that thou s. to go to thy country
Prov. 2. 4. if thou s. her as silver, and searchest her
Jer. 45. 5. s. thou great things? seek them not
John 4. 27. yet no man said, what s. thou?
20. 15. Jesus saith unto her, woman whom s. thou?

SEEKETH.

1 Sam. 19. 2. Saul my father s. to kill thee
20. 1. what is my sin, that he s. my life?
22. 23. fear not, he that s. my life, s. thy life
23. 10. Saul s. to destroy the city for my sake
24. 9. why hearest thou, saying, David s. thy hurt?
2 Sam. 16. 11. who came forth of my bowels s. my life
1 Kings 20. 7. and see how this man s. mischief
2 Kings 5. 7. see how he s. a quarrel against me
Job 39. 29. from thence she s. the prey, her eyes
Psal. 37. 32. watcheth righteous, and s. to slay him
Prov. 11. 27. he that diligently s. good procureth favour, but he that s. mischief, it shall come unto
14. 6. a scorner s. wisdom and findeth it not
15. 14. he that hath understanding, s. knowledge
17. 9. he that covereth a transgression, s. love
11. an evil man s. only rebellion, a messenger
19. he that exalteth his gate, s. destruction
18. 1. having separated himself, s. all wisdom
15. and the ear of the wise s. knowledge
31. 13. the virtuous woman s. wool and flax

Eccl. 7. 28. which yet my soul s. but I find not
Isa. 40. 20. he s. unto him a cunning workman
Jer. 5. 1. any that s. the truth, I will pardon it
30. 17. this is Zion, whom no man s. after
38. 4. this man s. not the welfare of this people
Lam. 3. 25. the Lord is good to the soul that s. him
Ezek. 14. 10. as punishment of him that s. unto him
34. 12. as a shepherd s. out his flock in the day
Mat. 7. 8. and he that s. findeth, Luke 11. 10.
12. 39. an adulterous generation s. a sign, 16. 4.
18. 12. leaveth the 99, and s. that gone astray
John 4. 23. the Father s. such to worship him
7. 4. doeth in secret, and s. to be known openly
18. s. his own glory; s. his glory that sent him
8. 50. there is one that s. and judgeth
Rom. 3. 11. there is none that s. after God
11. 7. Israel hath not obtained that which he s.
1 Cor. 13. 5. charity s. not her own, thinketh no evil

SEEKING.

Esth. 10. 3. Mordecai s. the wealth of his people
Isa. 16. 5. s. judgment, and hasting righteousness
Mat. 12. 43. s. rest, and findeth none, Luke 11. 24.
13. 45. like to a merchantman s. goodly pearls
Mark 8. 11. s. of him a sign from heaven
Luke 2. 45. they turned back to Jerusalem, s. him
11. 54. s. to catch something out of his mouth
13. 7. behold, I come s. fruit, and find none
John 6. 24. and came to Capernaum, s. for Jesus
Acts 13. 8. s. to turn away the deputy from faith
11. went about s. some to lead him by the hand
1 Cor. 10. 33. not s. mine own profit, but of many
1 Pet. 5. 8. walketh about, s. whom he may devour

SEEM.

Gen. 27. 12. I shall s. to him as a deceiver
Deut. 15. 18. not s. hard, when thou sendest away
25. 3. then thy brother should s. vile unto thee
Josh. 24. 15. if it s. evil unto you to serve the Lord
Neh. 9. 32. let not all the trouble s. little before thee
Esth. 8. 5. if the thing s. right before the king
Nah. 2. 4. the chariot shall s. like torches
1 Cor. 11. 16. but if any man s. to be contentious
12. 22. those members which s. to be more feeble
2 Cor. 10. 9. I may not s. as if I would terrify you
Heb. 4. 1. lest any of you should s. to come short of it
Jam. 1. 26. if any among you s. to be religious
See GOOD.

SEEMED.

Gen. 19. 14. but he s. as one that mocked to his sons
29. 20. and they s. unto him but a few days
Eccl. 9. 13. this wisdom s. great unto me
Jer. 27. 5. given earth unto whom it s. meet unto me
Luke 24. 11. their words s. to them as idle tales
Gal. 2. 6. but these who s. to be somewhat
9. James, Cephas, and John, who s. to be pillars

SEEMETH.

Lev. 14. 35. it s. there is a plague in the house
Num. 16. 9. s. it but a small thing unto you?
1 Sam. 18. 23. s. it light to be a king's son-in-law?
Prov. 14. 12. there is a way which s. right, 16. 25.
18. 17. he that is first in his own cause s. just
Ezek. 34. 18. s. it a small thing to have eaten up
Luke 8. 18. from him be taken what he s. to have
Acts 17. 18. he s. a setter forth of strange gods
25. 27. it s. unreasonable to send a prisoner
1 Cor. 3. 18. if s. to be wise, let him become a fool
Heb. 12. 11. now no chastening s. to be joyous
See GOOD.

SEEMLY.

Prov. 19. 10. delight is not s. for a fool, much less
26. 1. rain in harvest, so honour is not s. for a fool

SEEN.

Gen. 31. 42. God hath s. mine affliction and labour
Exod. 10. 6. such locusts as fathers have not s.
Lev. 5. 1. whether he hath s. or known of swearing
Num. 14. 22. those men which have s. my glory
23. 21. nor hath he s. perverseness in Israel
27. 13. when thou hast s. it, thou shalt be gathered
Deut. 1. 28. we have s. the sons of the Anakims
31. thou hast s. how the Lord bare thee as a man
3. 21. thine eyes have s. all the Lord hath done
4. 3. s. what the Lord did because of Baal-peor
9. lest thou forget the things thine eyes have s.
5. 24. we have s. that God doth talk with man
10. 21. great and terrible things thine eyes have s.
11. 2. have not s. the chastisement of the Lord
7. but your eyes have s. all the great acts of Lord
21. 7. hands have not shed, nor have our eyes s. it
29. 3. the great temptations thine eyes have s.
33. 9. who said to his mother, I have not s. him
Josh. 24. 7. eyes have s. what I have done in Egypt
Judg. 2. 7. the elders who had s. the great works
13. 22. we shall die, because we have s. God
18. 9. we have s. land, behold, it is very good
1 Sam. 6. 16. five lords had s. it, they returned
23. 22. see his place, and who hath s. him there
24. 10. behold, this day thine eyes have s. how
2 Sam. 18. 21. go tell the king what thou hast s.
1 Kings 10. 4. queen of Sheba had s. Solomon's wis.
7. till I came and mine eyes had s. 2 Chr. 9. 3, 6.
13. 12. sons had s. what way man of God went
20. 13. hast thou s. all this great multitude?
2 Kings 20. 15. what have they s.? Hezekiah said, all things in mine house have they s. Isa. 39. 4.
23. 29. he slew Josiah, when he had s. him
Ezra 3. 12. many that had s. the first house, wept
Esth. 9. 26. of that which they had s. concerning
Job 7. 8. eye that hath s. me shall see me no more
8. 18. his place shall say, I have not s. thee
10. 18. oh that I had died, and no eye had s. me
13. 1. mine eye hath s. all this, mine ear heard
20. 7. they that have s. him shall say, where is he?
28. 7. a path which the vulture's eye hath not s.
38. 17. hast thou s. doors of the shadow of death?
22. or hast thou s. the treasures of hail?
Psal. 10. 14. thou hast s. it, for thou beholdest misch.
35. 21. our eye hath s. ‖ 22. this thou hast s.
48. 8. so have we s. in city of the Lord of hosts
54. 7. mine eye hath s. his desire on mine enemies
68. 24. they have s. thy goings, O God, of my God
90. 15. and the years wherein we have s. evil
98. 3. the ends of earth have s. salvation of God
Prov. 25. 7. the prince whom thine eyes have s.

Eccl. 4. 3. who hath not s. the evil work that is
6. 5. he hath not s. the sun, nor known any thing
6. yea, though I live, yet hath he s. no good
Isa. 6. 5. for mine eyes have s. the Lord of hosts
9. 2. that walked in darkness have s. a great light
64. 4. nor hath eye s. what he hath prepared for him
66. 8. who hath heard, who hath s. such things?
19. to the isles afar off that have not s. my glory
Jer. 1. 12. then said the Lord, thou hast well s.
3. 6. hast thou s. what backsliding Isr. hath done?
12. 3. thou hast s. me, and tried my heart
Lam. 1. 8. because they have s. her nakedness
10. she hath s. heathen entered into her sanctuary
2. 14. thy prophets have s. vain and foolish things for thee, they have s. false burdens and causes
16. thy enemies say, we have found, we have s. it
3. 59. O L. thou hast s. my wrong, judge my cause
60. thou hast s. all their vengeance against me
Ezek. 8. 12. thou hast s. what the ancients do
15. then said he, hast thou s. this? 17. | 47. 6.
13. 3. and have s. nothing ‖ 6. they have s. vanity
7. have ye not s. a vain vision, whereas ye say
Dan. 9. 21. Gabriel whom I had s. in the vision
Zech. 10. 2. and the diviners have s. a lie, and told
Mat. 2. 2. for we have s. his star in the east
13. 17. many prophets desired to see those things which ye see, and have not s. them, Luke 10. 24.
21. 32. and ye, when ye had s. it, repented not
Mark 9. 1. till they have s. the kingdom of God
9. they should tell no man what things they had s.
16. 14. they believed not them which had s. him
Luke 1. 22. they perceived that he had s. a vision
2. 20. praising God for all things they had s.
26. not see death before he had s. Lord's Christ
30. for mine eyes have s. thy salvation
5. 26. saying, we have s. strange things to-day
9. 36. told no man the things which they had s.
19. 37. for all the mighty works that they had s.
23. 8. he hoped to have s. some miracle done
24. 23. saying, that they had s. a vision of angels
37. and supposed that they had s. a spirit
John 1. 18. no man hath s. God at any time, the Son in bosom of Father declared him, 1 John 4. 12.
3. 11. verily we testify that we have s.
32. what he hath s. and heard that he testifieth
4. 45. the Galileans had s. all he did at Jerusalem
5. 37. ye have not at any time s. his shape
6. 14. those men, when they had s. the miracle
46. not that any man hath s. the Father
8. 57. not fifty years old, and hast thou s. Abraham?
9. 8. the neighbours which before had s. him
37. thou hast both s. and it is he that talketh
11. 45. had s. what Jesus did, believed on him
14. 9. he that hath s. me, hath s. the Father
15. 24. have s. and hated both me and my Father
20. 18. she had s. the Lord ‖ 25. have s. the Lord
29. Thomas, because thou hast s. hast believed
Acts 4. 20. we cannot but speak things we have s.
7. 44. according to the fashion that he had s.
9. 12. he hath s. in a vision a man named Ananias
27. declared to them how he had s. the Lord
10. 17. what this vision he had s. should mean
11. 13. he shewed us how he had s. an angel
23. when he had s. the grace of God was glad
16. 10. after he had s. vision we went to Maced.
40. they had s. the brethren, they comforted them
21. 29. they had s. before with him Trophimus
22. 15. be witness of what thou hast s. 26. 16.
1 Cor. 2. 9. eye hath not s. nor ear heard, nor entered
9. 1. have I not s. Jesus Christ our Lord?
Phil. 4. 9. things ye have heard and s. in me, do
Col. 2. 1. and for as many as have not s. my face
18. intruding into those things he hath not s.
1 Tim. 6. 16. whom no man hath s. or can see
1 John 1. 1. that which we have s. with our eyes
2. the life was manifested, and we have s. it
3. that which we have s. declare we unto you
3. 6. whosoever sinn. hath not s. him nor known
4. 14. we have s. and do testify, Father sent the Son
20. he that loveth not his brother whom he hath s. how can he love God whom he hath not s.?
3 John 11. he that doeth evil, hath not s. God
Rev. 1. 19. write the things which thou hast s.
22. 8. when I had heard and s. I fell down to worsh.

Have I SEEN.

Gen. 7. 1. thee have I s. righteous before me
1 Chron. 29. 17. now have I s. thy people to offer
Psal. 37. 25. yet have I not s. the righteous forsaken
Eccl. 7. 15. all things have I s. in days of my vanity
8. 9. all this have I s. and applied my heart
9. 13. this wisdom have I s. under the sun
Jer. 46. 5. wherefore have I s. them dismayed
Zech. 9. 8. for now have I s. with mine eyes

I have SEEN.

Gen. 31. 12. I have s. all that Laban doth to thee
32. 30. I have s. God face to face, and am preserved
33. 10. for therefore I have s. thy face, 46. 30.
Exod. 3. 7. I have s. the affliction of my people
9. I have also s. the oppression, 16.
32. 9. Lord said, I have s. this people, Deut. 9. 13.
Judg. 6. 22. alas, for because I have s. an angel
14. 2. I have s. a woman in Timnah, get her
1 Sam. 16. 18. I have s. a son of Jesse cunning
2 Kings 9. 26. I have s. yesterday blood of Naboth
20. 5. saith Lord, I have s. thy tears, Isa. 38. 5.
Job 4. 8. even as I have s. they that plow iniquity
5. 3. I have s. the foolish taking root, but I cursed
15. 17. hear me, that which I have s. I declare
31. 19. if I have s. any perish for want of clothing
Psal. 37. 35. I have s. the wicked in great power
55. 9. I have s. violence and strife in the city
63. 2. glory, so as I have s. thee in the sanctuary
119. 96. I have s. an end of all perfection
Eccl. 1. 14. I have s. all the works under the sun
3. 10. I have s. the travail which God hath given
5. 13. there is a sore evil which I have s. under sun
18. behold that which I have s. it is good to eat
6. 1. there is an evil which I have s. 10. 5.
10. 7. I h. s. servants upon horses, and princes walk
Isa. 44. 16. he saith, I am warm, I have s. the fire
57. 18. I have s. his ways, and will heal him
Jer. 7. 11. behold, I have s. it saith the Lord

Jer. 13. 27. I have s. thine adulteries and neighings
23. 13. I have s. folly in prophets of Samaria, 14.
Lam. 3. 1. I have s. affliction by rod of his wrath
Dan. 2. 26. make known unto me the dream I have s.
4. 9. the visions of my dream that I have s. 18.
Hos. 6. 10. I have s. an horrible thing in Israel
John 8. 38. I speak that I have s. with my Father
Acts 7. 34. I have s. the affliction of my people

Ye have SEEN.

Gen. 45. 13. tell my father of all that ye have s.
Exod. 14. 13. the Egyptians whom ye have s. to-day
19. 4. ye have s. what I did unto the Egyptians
20. 22. ye have s. that I have talked with you
Deut. 29. 2. ye have s. all that the Lord did in Egypt unto Pharaoh, his servants, and land, Josh. 23. 3.
17. ye have s. their abominations and idols
Judg. 9. 48. what ye have s. me do, do as I have done
1 Sam. 17. 25. have ye s. this man that is come up?
Job 27. 12. behold, all ye yourselves have s. it
Isa. 22. 9. ye have s. the breaches of the city
Jer. 44. 2. ye have s. all the evil I have brought
Ezek. 13. 8. ye have s. lies, therefore I am against you
Luke 7. 22. tell John what things ye have s.
John 6. 36. ye also have s. me, and believe not
8. 38. ye do that ye have s. with your Father
14. 7. henceforth ye know him, and have s. him
Acts 1. 11. Jesus shall so come, as ye have s. him go
Jam. 5. 11. and ye have s. the end of the Lord

SEEN, Passively.

Gen. 8. 5. were the tops of the mountains s.
9. 14. that the bow shall be s. in the cloud
22. 14. in the mount of the Lord it shall be s.
Exod. 13. 7. no leavened bread be s. Deut. 16. 4.
33. 23. back parts, but my face shall not be s.
34. 3. neither let any man be s. through the mount
Num. 14. 14. that thou, Lord, art s. face to face
Judg. 5. 8. was there a shield or spear s. amg. 40,000?
19. 30. there was no such deed done nor s.
2 Sam. 17. 17. for they might not be s. to come
22. 11. he was s. upon the wings of the wind
1 Kings 6. 18. all was cedar, there was no stone s.
8. 8. ends of the staves were not s. in holy place
10. 12. no such almug-trees were s. unto this day
Job 33. 21. his flesh is consumed, it cannot be s.
Psal. 18. 15. then the channels of water were s.
Isa. 1. † 12. when ye come to be s. before me
16. 12. when it is s. that Moab is weary
47. 3. thy nakedness covered, thy shame shall be s.
60. 2. and his glory shall be s. upon thee
Zech. 9. 14. and the Lord shall be s. over them
Mat. 6. 1. do not your alms to be s. of men, 5.
9. 33. saying, it was never so s. in Israel
23. 5. all their works they do to be s. of men
Mark 16. 11. they heard that he had been s. of her
Luke 24. † 31. and he ceased to be s. of them
Acts 1. 3. being s. of them forty days, 13. 31.
Rom. 1. 20. the invisible things of him are clearly s.
8. 24. but hope that is s. is not hope, for what a man
1 Cor. 15. 5. he was s. of Cephas, then of the twelve
6. after that he was s. of above 500 brethren
7. s. of James ‖ 8. last of all he was s. of me also
2 Cor. 4. 18. while we look not at things that are s. but at things which are not s. thgs. s. are temporal
1 Tim. 3. 16. God was manifest in flesh, s. of angels
Heb. 11. 1. faith is the evidence of things not s.
3. so that things which are s. were not made
7. Noah being warned of God of things not s.
13. having s. them afar off were persuaded
1 Pet. 1. 8. whom having not s. ye love, in whom
Rev. 11. 19. there was s. in his temple the ark

SEER.

See the Signification of PROPHET.

1 Sam. 9. 9. come, and let us go to the s. he that is now called a prophet was before-time called a s.
11. is the s. here? ‖ 18. where the s. house is
19. Samuel answered Saul, and said, I am the s.
2 Sam. 15. 27. the king said, art not thou a s.?
24. 11. word came to Gad, David's s. 1 Chr. 21. 9.
1 Chr. 9. 22. Samuel the s. did ordain in set office
25. 5. Heman the king's s. in words of God
26. 28. all that Samuel the s. had dedicated
29. 29. the acts of David are written in the book of Samuel the s. and in the book of Gad the s.
2 Chron. 9. 29. written in visions of Iddo the s.
12. 15. acts of Rehoboam in the book of Iddo the s.
16. 7. Hanani the s. came to Asa king of Judah
10. then Asa was wroth with the s. for this thing
19. 2. Jehu son of Hanani the s. went to meet
29. 25. the commandment of Gad the king's s.
30. with the words of David and Asaph the s.
35. 15. commandment of Jeduthun the king's s.
Amos 7. 12. said unto Amos, O thou s. flee away

SEERS.

2 Kings 17. 13. testified against Isr. and Judah by s.
2 Chron. 33. 18. words of the s. that spake to him
19. they are written among the sayings of the s.
Isa. 29. 10. your rulers, the s. hath he covered
30. 10. who say to the s. see not, and to prophets
Mic. 3. 7. then shall the s. be ashamed and diviners

SEEST.

Gen. 13. 15. the land thou s. to thee will I give it
16. 13. called the Lord that spake, thou God s. me
31. 43. Laban said, all that thou s. is mine
Exod. 10. 28. that day thou s. my face thou shalt die
Deut. 4. 19. lest when thou s. the sun thou worship
12. 13. offer not in every place that thou s.
20. 1. when thou goest to battle and s. horses
21. 11. and s. among captives a beautiful woman
Judg. 9. 36. thou s. the shadow of the mountains
1 Kings 21. 29. s. thou how Ahab humbleth himself
Job 10. 4. hast thou eyes, or s. thou as man seeth?
Prov. 22. 29. s. thou a man diligent in his business?
26. 12. s. thou a man wise in his own conceit?
29. 20. s. thou a man that is hasty in his words?
Eccl. 5. 8. if thou s. the oppression of the poor
Isa. 58. 3. wherefore have we fasted, and thou s. not?
7. when thou s. the naked, that thou cover him
Jer. 1. 11. the word came to Jeremiah, what s. thou?
13. | 24. 3. Amos 7. 8. | 8. 2. Zech. 4. 2. | 5. 2.
7. 17. s. thou not what they do in cities of Judah?
20. 12. O Lord, that s. the reins and the heart
32. 24. is come to pass, and behold thou s. it

Ezek. 8. 6. son of man, s. thou what they do?
40. 4. declare all thou s. to the house of Israel
Dan. 1. 13. and as thou s. deal with thy servants
Mark 5. 31. thou s. the multitude thronging thee
13. 2. Jesus said, s. thou these great buildings?
Luke 7. 44. he said to Simon, s. thou this woman?
Acts 21. 20. thou s. how many thousands believe
Jam. 2. 22. s. thou how faith wrought with works?
Rev. 1. 11. what thou s. write in a book and send it

SEETH.

Gen. 16. 13. have I also looked after him that s. me?
44. 31. when he s. lad is not with us, he will die
Exod. 4. 14. and when he s. thee he will be glad
12. 23. and when he s. the blood upon the lintel
Lev. 13. 20. when the priest s. the plague in sight
Deut. 32. 36. when he s. that their power is gone
1 Sam. 16. 7. Lord s. not as man s. looks on heart
2 Kings 2. 19. this city is pleasant, as my lord s.
Job 8. 17. and s. the place of stones
11. 11. s. wickedness, will he not then consider it?
22. 14. clouds are a covering to him that he s. not
28. 10. and his eye s. every precious thing
24. and he s. under the whole heaven
34. 21. his eyes are on man, he s. all his goings
42. 5. I have heard, but now mine eye s. thee
Psal. 37. 13. for he s. that his day is coming
49. 10. he s. that wise men die, likewise the fool
58. 10. righteous shall rejoice, when he s. vengean.
Eccl. 8. 16. nor day nor night, s. sleep with his eyes
Isa. 21. 6. let the watchmen declare what he s.
28. 4. when he that looketh upon it, s. it
29. 15. and they say who s. us? || 47. 10. none s. me
Ezek. 8. 12. they say, the Lord s. us not, 9. 9.
12. 27. the vision that he s. is for many days
18. 14. if he beget a son that s. his father's sins
33. 3. if when he s. the sword come, he blow
39. 15. when any s. a man's bone, then set up a sign
Mat. 6. 4. thy Father who s. in secret, 6, 18.
Mark 5. 38. he s. the tumult, and them that wept
Luke 16. 23. he s. Abraham afar off, and Lazarus
John 1. 29. the next day John s. Jesus coming
5. 19. do nothing but what he s. the Father do
6. 40. who s. the Son, and believeth on him
9. 21. by what means he now s. we know not
10. 12. but an hireling s. the wolf coming
11. 9. he stumbleth not, because he s. the light
12. 45. he that s. me, s. him that sent me
14. 17. because it s. him not, nor knoweth him
19. a little while, and the world s. me no more
20. 1. s. the stone taken away from the sepulchre
6. Peter went in and s. the linen clothes lie
12. and s. two angels in white, sitting, one at head
21. 20. s. the disciple whom Jesus loved, following
Rom. 8. 24. what a man s. why doth he yet hope for
2 Cor. 12. 6. think of me above what he s. me to be
1 John 3. 17. hath this world, and s. brother have need

SEETHE.

Exod. 16. 23. morrow is sabb. to-day s. that ye will s.
23. 19. the first-fruits bring, thou shalt not s. a kid
in his mother's milk, 34. 26. Deut. 14. 21.
29. 31. thou shalt s. his flesh in the holy place
2 Kings 4. 38. s. pottage for the sons of the prophets
Ezek. 24. 5. let them s. the bones therein
Zech. 14. 21. that sacrifice shall come and s. therein

SEETHING.

1 Sam. 2. 13. priest's servants came, while flesh was s.
Job 41. 20. goeth smoke as out of a s. pot or caldron
Jer. 1. 13. what seest thou? I said, I see a s. pot

SEIZE.

Josh. 8. 7. then ye shall rise up and s. upon the city
Job 3. 6. as for that night, let darkness s. upon it
Ps. 55. 15. let death s. upon them, let them go down
Mat. 21. 38. let us kill him, and s. on his inheritance

SEIZED.

Jer. 49. 24. Damascus is feeble, fear hath s. on her

SELAH.

This Hebrew word is found seventy-four times in the book of Psalms, and thrice in Habakkuk. The Septuagint, and other interpreters, translate Selah by Διαψαλμα Diapsalma, which signifies a rest or pause in singing; or a change of tone, according to others. Some will have it, that Selah marks the beginning of a new sense, or a new measure of verses. Others translate Selah by for ever, and say, that it joins what follows to that which goes before, and shews that what has been said deserves to be always remembered.

Some ancients have thought, that Selah shewed the intermission or cessation of the actual inspiration of the Psalmist, or of the internal motions of his devotions. There are who say that Selah has no signification, and that it is only a note of the ancient music, whose use is no longer known: for Selah may be taken away from all the places where it is found, without interrupting the sense of the Psalm. Others say, it was a note which shewed the elevation of the voice; and that in those places the reader should cry out, and make an exclamation.

But it is generally agreed and concluded, that the proper signification of Selah is, the end, or a pause: And though it be not always found at the end of the sense, nor at the end of a Psalm, yet the ancient musicians might sometimes put Selah in the margin of their Psalters, to shew where the pause was to be made, and where the tune ended. For if the ancient Hebrews sang with great pauses, ending all at once, and also beginning again all at once, which some think they did; then it was necessary to mark in the margin of the Psalm the place of the pause, and of the end, that the whole choir might rest at once, and begin again at the same time. But withal it is generally placed at some remarkable passage; which gives occasion to think that it served also to quicken the attention or observation of the singer and hearer.

Psal. 3. 2. many say, there is no help for him in G. s.
4. the Lord heard me out of his holy hill, s.
8. salvation, thy blessing is upon thy people, s.
32. 5. I will confess, forgavest iniquity of my sin, s.
See Psal. 4. 2, 4. | 7. 5. | 9. 16, 20. | 20. 3. | 21.
2. | 24. 6, 10. | 32. 4, 7. | 39. 5, 11. | 44.
8. | 46. 3, 7, 11. | 47. 4. | 48. 8. | 49. 13,
15. | 50. 6. | 52. 3, 5. | 54. 3. | 55. 7,
19. | 57. 3, 6. | 59. 5, 13. | 60. 4. | 61. 4. | 62.
4, 8. | 66. 4, 7, 15. | 67. 1, 4. | 68. 7, 19, 32.
| 75. 3. | 76. 3, 9. | 77. 3, 9, 15. | 81. 7. | 82.
2. | 83. 8. | 84. 4, 8. | 85. 2. | 87. 3, 6. | 88. 7,
10. | 89. 4, 37, 45, 48. | 140. 3, 5, 8. | 143. 6.
Hab. 3. 3, 9, 13.

SELDOM.

Prov. 25. † 17. let thy foot be s. in neighbour's house

Her SELF.

Lev. 15. 28. then shall she numb. to her s. seven days
21. 19. if she profane her s. by playing the whore
Num. 30. 3. if a woman bind her s. by a bond
Judg. 5. 29. yea, she returned answer to her s.
Ruth 1. † 18. that she strengthened her s. to go
1 Sam. 4. 19. she bowed her s. and travailed
25. 41. Abigail bowed her s. to the earth, and said
2 Sam. 11. 2. he saw a woman washing her s.
† 4. she had purified her s. from uncleanness
1 Kings 14. 5. she shall feign her s. another woman
Job 39. 18. what time she lifteth up her s. on high
Psal. 84. 3. the swallow found a nest for her s.
Prov. 31. 22. maketh her s. coverings of tapestry
Isa. 5. 14. therefore hell hath enlarged her s.
34. 14. screech-owl find for her s. a place of rest
61. 10. as a bride adorneth her s. with jewels
Jer. 3. 11. backsliding Israel hath justified her s.
4. 31. daughter of Zion that bewaileth her s.
49. 24. Damascus is feeble, and turn. her s. to flee
Ezek. 22. 3. the city maketh idols against her s.
23. 7. with all their idols she defiled her s.
24. 12. she hath wearied her s. with lies
Hos. 2. 13. she decked her s. with her ear-rings
Zech. 9. 3. Tyrus did build her s. a strong-hold
Mat. 9. 21. for she said within her s. if I touch
Mark 4. 28. the earth bringeth forth fruit of her s.
Luke 1. 24. Elisabeth hid her s. five months
13. 11. the woman could in no wise lift up her s.
Heb. 11. 11. thro' faith Sarah her s. received strength
Rev. 2. 20. Jezebel, who calleth her s. a prophetess
18. 7. how much she hath glorified her s. and lived
19. 7. and his wife hath made her s. ready
See HIMSELF.

It SELF.

Gen. 1. 11. the fruit-tree, whose seed is in it s. 12.
Lev. 7. 24. and the fat of the beast that dieth of it s.
not eat, 17. 15. | 22. 8. Deut. 14. 21.
18. 25. the land it s. vomiteth out inhabitants
25. 11. nor reap what groweth of it s. Isa. 37. 30.
1 Kings 7. 34. the undersetters were of the base it s.
Job 10. 22. a land of darkness, as darkness it s.
Psal. 41. 6. his heart gathereth iniquity to it s.
68. 8. even Sinai it s. was moved at the presence
Prov. 18. 2. that his heart may discover it s.
23. 31. the wine, when it moveth it s. aright
27. 16. the ointment which bewrayeth it s.
25. the tender grass sheweth it s. and herbs
Isa. 10. 15. shall axe boast it s. against him that
heweth? saw magnify it s.? rod shake it s.?
staff lift up it s.?
55. 2. let your soul delight it s. in fatness
60. 20. neither shall thy moon withdraw it s.
Jer. 31. 24. there shall dwell in Judah it s. husbandm.
Ezek. 1. 4. a fire unfolding it s. and bright. about it
4. 14. I have not eaten what dieth of it s. 44. 31.
17. 14. be base, that it might not lift it s. up
29. 15. nor exalt it s. any more above the nations
Dan. 7. 5. it raised up it s. on the one side
Mat. 6. 34. take thought for the things of it s.
12. 25. every kingdom divided agst. it s. is brought
to desolation, Mark 3. 24, 25. Luke 11. 17.
John 15. 4. as the branch cannot bear fruit of it s.
20. 7. but wrapped together in a place by it s.
21. 25. the world it s. could not contain the books
Rom. 8. 16. Spirit it s. bears witness with our spirit
21. the creature it s. also shall be delivered
26. the Spirit it s. maketh intercession for us
14. 14. that there is nothing unclean of it s.
1 Cor. 11. 14. doth not even nature it s. teach you?
13. 4. charity vaunteth not it s. is not puffed up
5. charity doth not behave it s. unseemly
2 Cor. 10. 5. casting down every thing that exalts it s.
Eph. 4. 16. unto the edifying of it s. in love
Heb. 9. 24. Chr. is entered into heaven it s. to appear
3 John 12. Demetrius hath good report of truth it s.

My SELF. [my s.

Gen. 3. 10. I was afraid, because naked, and hid
22. 16. by my s. have I sworn, in blessing I will
bless thee, Isa. 45. 23. Jer. 22. 5. | 49. 13.
Exod. 19. 4. I bare you, and brought you unto my s.
Num. 8. 17. I sanctified them for my s.
12. 6. I the Lord will make my s. known to him
Deut. 1. 9. I am not able to bear you my s. alone, 12.
Judg. 16. 20. I will go out and shake my s.
Ruth 4. 6. he said, I cannot redeem it for my s.
1 Sam. 13. 12. I forced my s. therefore, and offered
20. 5. let me go, that I may hide my s. in the field
25. 33. which hast kept me from avenging my s.
2 Sam. 18. 2. I will surely go forth with you my s.
22. 24. I have kept my s. from mine iniquity
1 Kings 18. 15. I will surely shew my s. unto him
22. 30. I will disguise my s. 2 Chron. 18. 29.
2 Kings 5. 18. I bow my s. in the house of Rimmon
2 Chron. 7. 12. I have chosen this place to my s.
Neh. 5. 7. I consulted with my s. and rebuked nobles
Esth. 5. 12. let no man come with the king but my s.
6. 6. delight to do honour more than to my s.
Job 6. 10. yea, I would harden my s. in sorrow
7. 20. why a mark, so that I am a burden to my s.
9. 20. if I justify my s. || 27. I will comfort my s.
30. if I wash my s. with snow water, and make
13. 20. then will I not hide my s. from thee
10. 1. I will leave my complaint upon my s.
19. 4. if I have erred, mine error remain. with my s.
27. whom I shall see for my s. and eyes behold
31. 17. or have eaten my morsel my s. alone
29. or if I lift up my s. when evil found him
42. 6. wherefore I abhor my s. and repent in dust
Ps. 35. 14. I behaved my s. as though he had been
my friend or brother, I bowed down heavily
57. 8. awake, my glory, I my s. awake early, 108. 2.
101. 2. I will behave my s. wisely in a perfect way
Psal. 109. 4. are my adver. but I give my s. to pray.
119. 16. I will delight my s. in thy statutes
47. I will delight my s. in thy commandments
52. I remembered thy judgm. and comforted my s.
131. 1. nor do I exercise my s. in great matters
2. surely I have behav. and quieted my s. as child
Eccl. 2. 3. I sought in my heart to give my s. to wine
19. my labour wherein I have shewed my s. wise
Isa. 33. 10. saith the Lord, now will I lift up my s.
43. 21. this people have I formed for my s.
44. 24. that spreadeth abroad the earth by my s.
Jer. 8. 18. I would comfort my s. against sorrow
21. 5. and I my s. will fight against you
Ezek. 14. 7. I the Lord will answer him by my s.
20. 5. in the day I made my s. known unto them, 9.
29. 3. my river is mine, I have made it for my s.
35. 11. I will make my s. known amongst them
38. 23. thus will I magnify my s. and sanctify my s.
Dan. 10. 3. neither did I anoint my s. at all
Mic. 6. 6. and bow my s. before the high God
Hab. 3. 16. when I heard, I trembled in my s.
Zech. 7. 3. separat. my s. as I have done many years
Luke 7. 7. neither thought I my s. worthy to come
24. 39. that it is I my s. handle me and see
John 5. 31. if I bear witness of my s. it is not true
7. 17. he shall know whether I speak of my s.
28. I am not come of my s. but he that sent me
8. 14. tho' I bear record of my s. my record is true
18. I am one that bear witness of my s.
28. when ye shall know that I do nothing of my s.
42. neither came I of my s. but he sent me
54. if I honour my s. my honour is nothing
10. 18. no man taketh, but I lay it down of my s.
12. 49. I have not spoken of my s. Father sent me
14. 3. I will come again, and receive you unto my s.
10. the words that I speak, I speak not of my s.
21. I will love him, and manifest my s. to him
17. 19. and for their sakes I sanctify my s.
Acts 7. † 37. a prophet of your brethren as I my s.
10. 26. saying, stand up, I my s. also am a man
20. 24. neither count I my life dear unto my s.
24. 10. I do more cheerfully answer for my s.
16. herein do I exercise my s. to have always
25. 22. Agrippa said, I would hear the man my s.
26. 9. I verily thought with my s. I ought to do
Rom. 9. 3. I could wish that my s. were accursed
11. 4. I have reserved to my s. 7000 men
15. 14. and I my s. also am persuaded of you
16. 2. a succourer of many, and of my s. also
1 Cor. 4. 4. for I know nothing by my s. yet am I
6. I have in a figure transfer. to my s. and Apollos
7. 7. I would that all men were even as I my s.
9. 19. yet have I made my s. servant unto all
27. lest that I my s. should be a castaway
2 Cor. 10. 1. now I Paul my s. beseech you
11. 7. have I commit. an offence in abasing my s.?
9. I have kept my s. from being burdens. to you
16. receive me, that I may boast my s. a little
12. 5. of my s. I will not glory but in infirmities
13. except that I my s. was not burdens. to you
Gal. 2. 18. I make my s. a transgressor
Phil. 2. 24. that I also my s. shall come shortly
3. 13. I count not my s. to have apprehended
Philem. 17. receive Onesimus as my s.

Own SELF.

Exod. 32. 13. to whom thou swarest by thine own s.
John 5. 30. I can of mine own s. do nothing
17. 5. Father, glorify thou me with thine own s.
1 Cor. 4. 3. yea, I judge not mine own s.
Philem. 19. how thou owest unto me even thine o. s.
1 Pet. 2. 24. who his own s. bare our sins in his body

SELF-same.

Mat. 8. 13. his servant was healed the s.-same hour
1 Cor. 12. 11. worketh that one and s.-same Spirit
2 Cor. 5. 5. he that wrought us for s.-same thing
7. 11. this s.-same thing that ye sorrowed after
See Same DAY.

Thy SELF.

Gen. 13. 9. separate thy s. I pray thee, from me
14. 21. give me the persons, take goods to thy s.
16. 9. return, and submit thy s. under her hands
33. 9. brother, keep that thou hast unto thy s.
Exod. 9. 17. as yet exaltest thy s. against my people
10. 3. how long wilt thou refuse to humble thy s.?
28. take heed to thy s. see my face no more, 34.
12. Deut. 4. 9. | 12. 13, 19, 30. 1 Sam. 19. 2.
18. 14. he said, why sittest thou thy s. alone?
22. so shall it be easier for thy s. and they bear
34. 2. come and present thy s. there before me
Lev. 9. 7. go and make an atonement for thy s.
18. 20. with thy neighbour's wife to defile thy s.
23. neither lie with any beast to defile thy s.
19. 18. thou shalt love thy neighbour as thy s. I am
the Lord, Mat. 19. 19. | 22. 39. Mark 12. 31.
34. the stranger, thou shalt love him as thy s.
Num. 11. 17. that thou bear it not thy s. alone
16. 13. except thou make thy s. a prince over us
Deut. 9. 1. to possess nations greater than thy s.
20. 14. even all the spoil shalt thou take to thy s.
22. 12. thy vesture wherewith thou coverest thy s.
Ruth 4. 6. redeem thou my right to thy s. I cannot
1 Sam. 20. 8. if iniquity be in me, slay me thy s.
25. 26. hath withholden thee from avenging thy s.
2 Sam. 5. 24. that then thou shalt bestir thy s.
7. 24. hast confirmed to thy s. thy people Israel
13. 5. lay down on thy bed and make thy s. sick
14. 2. feign thy s. a mourner, and put on apparel
18. 13. thy s. wouldst have set thy s. against me
22. 26. thou wilt shew thy s. merciful, Psal. 18. 25.
27. with pure thou wilt shew thy s. pure, Ps. 18. 26.
1 Kings 2. 2. be thou strong, and shew thy s. a man
3. 11. thou hast not asked for thy s. long life, nor
riches, but understanding, 2 Chron. 1. 11.
13. 7. come home with me, and refresh thy s.
14. 2. arise, I pray thee, and disguise thy s.
6. why feignest thou thy s. to be another?
18. 1. go shew thy s. to Ahab, and I will send rain
20. 22. strengthen thy s. and see what thou dost
40. so shall thy judgment be, thy s. hast decid. it
21. 20. because thou hast sold thy s. to work evil
2 Kings 22. 19. hast humbled thy s. 2 Chron. 34. 27
1 Chron. 21. 12. advise with thy s. what word

2 Chron. 20. 37. thou hast joined thy s. with Ahaziah
21. 13. hast slain thy brethren, better than thy s.
Esth. 4. 13. think not with thy s. thou shalt escape
Job 5. † 27. hear it, and know thou it for thy s.
15. 8. and dost thou restrain wisdom to thy s.
22. 21. acquaint thy s. with him, and be at peace
30. 21. with thy hand thou opposest thy s. agst. me
Psal. 7. 6. O Lord, in thine anger lift up thy s.
10. 1. why hidest thou thy s. in times of trouble?
35. 23. stir up thy s. and awake to my judgment
37. 4. delight thy s. also in the Lord, shall give
49. 18. praise thee, when thou dost well to thy s.
50. 21. that I was altogether such a one as thy s.
52. 1. why boastest thou thy s. in mischief?
60. 1. been displeased, O turn thy s. to us again
80. 15. branch thou madest strong for thy s. 17.
94. 1. shew thy s. ‖ 2. lift up thy s. thou judge
Prov. 6. 3. do this, my son, and deliver thy s. 5.
9. 12. if thou be wise, shalt be wise for thy s.
24. 19. fret not thy s. because of evil men
27. and make it fit for thy s. in the field
25. 6. put not forth thy s. in presence of the king
27. 1. boast not thy s. of to-morrow, knowest not
30. 32. thou hast done foolishly in lifting up thy s.
Eccl. 7. 16. be not righteous over much, nor make thy s. over wise; why shouldest thou destroy thy s.?
22. that thou thy s. also hast cursed others
Isa. 26. 20. hide thy s. as for a little moment
33. 3. lifting up thy s. the nations were scattered
45. 15. verily thou art a God that hidest thy s.
52. 2. shake thy s. from the dust, loose thy s.
57. 8. thou hast discovered thy s. to another
9. and thou didst debase thy s. even unto hell
58. 14. then shalt thou delight thy s. in the Lord
63. 14. to make thy s. a glorious name
64. 12. wilt thou refrain thy s. for these things?
65. 5. which say, stand by thy s. come not near
Jer. 2. 17. hast thou not procured this unto thy s.
4. 30. tho' thou clothest thy s. with crimson, in vain shalt thou make thy s. fair, lovers despise thee
6. 26. gird with sackcloth, wallow thy s. in ashes
17. 4. thy s. shall discontinue from thy heritage
20. 4. behold, I will make thee a terror to thy s.
22. 15. because thou closest thy s. in cedar
32. 8. the redemption is thine, buy it for thy s.
45. 5. and seekest thou great things for thy s.?
46. 19. furnish thy s. to go into captivity
47. 5. how long wilt thou cut thy s.?
6. O sword, put up thy s. into thy scabbard
Lam. 2. 18. give thy s. no rest, let not thy eye cease
3. 44. thou hast covered thy s. with a cloud
4. 21. thou shalt be drunken, make thy s. naked
Ezek. 3. 24. go shut thy s. within thine house
16. 17. thou madest to thy s. images of men
22. 4. and hast defiled thy s. in thine idols
23. 40. they came for whom thou didst wash thy s.
31. 10. because thou hast lifted up thy s. in height
38. 7. prepare for thy s. and all thy company
Dan. 5. 17. Daniel said, let thy gifts be to thy s.
23. but hast lifted up thy s. against the Lord
10. 12. and to chasten thy s. before thy God
Hos. 13. 9. O Israel, thou hast destroyed thy s.
Obad. 4. though thou exalt thy s. as the eagle
Mic. 1. 10. in house of Aphrah roll thy s. in dust
5. 1. now gather thy s. in troops, O daughter
Nah. 3. 15. make thy s. many as the canker-worm
Zech. 2. 7. deliver thy s. O Zion, that dwellest
Mat. 4. 6. if Son of God, cast thy s. down, Luke 4. 9.
5. 33. again, thou shalt not forswear thy s.
8. 4. shew thy s. to priest, Mark 1. 44. Luke 5. 14.
27. 40. save thy s. Mark 15. 30. Luke 23. 39.
Luke 4. 23. ye will say, physician, heal thy s.
6. 42. when thou thy s. beholdest not the beam
7. 6. Lord, trouble not thy s. for I am not worthy
10. 27. thou shalt love thy neighbour as thy s. Rom. 13. 9. Gal. 5. 14. Jam. 2. 8.
17. 8. will rather say, gird thy s. and serve me
John 1. 22. who art thou? what sayest thou of thy s.?
7. 4. if thou do these, shew thy s. to the world
8. 13. thou bearest record of thy s. it is not true
53. prophets are dead, whom makest thou thy s.
10. 33. thou, being a man, makest thy s. God
14. 22. Lord, how wilt thou manifest thy s. unto us
18. 34. sayest thou this of thy s.? or did others tell it?
21. 18. when thou wast young, thou girdedst thy s.
Acts 8. 29. go near, join thy s. to this chariot
12. 8. gird thy s. ‖ 16. 28. do thy s. no harm
21. 24. them take, purify thy s. with them, that all may know that thou thy s. walkest orderly
24. 8. thy s. mayest take knowledge of these things
26. 1. thou art permitted to speak for thy s.
24. Festus said, Paul, thou art beside thy s.
Rom. 2. 1. judgest another, thou condemnest thy s.
19. that thou thy s. art a guide of the blind
21. thou that teachest, teachest thou not thy s.
14. 22. hast thou faith? have it to thy s.
Gal. 6. 1. considering thy s. lest thou be tempted
1 Tim. 3. 15. how thou oughtest to behave thy s.
4. 7. and exercise thy s. rather unto godliness
15. these things, give thy s. wholly to them
16. take heed to thy s. and to thy doctrine; in doing this thou shalt save thy s. and them that hear thee
5. 22. nor partaker of others sins, keep thy s. pure
6. 5. men of corr. minds, from such withdraw thy s.
2 Tim. 2. 15. study to shew thy s. approved unto God
Tit. 2. 7. shewing thy s. a pattern of good works

SELF-will.

Gen. 49. 6. in their s.-will, they digged down a wall
See Fret, Hide.

SELF-willed.

Tit. 1. 7. for a bishop must not be s.-willed
2 Pet. 2. 10. presumptuous are they, s.-willed

SELL.

In case of extreme necessity the Hebrews *were allowed to sell their own liberty.* Lev. 25. 39. If thy brother that dwelleth by thee be waxen poor, and be sold unto thee, thou shalt not compel him to serve as a bond-servant. *Thou shalt not oppress him, nor sell him again as a slave; he shall abide with thee only as a workman for hire; and must be used kindly, as a brother, and as a member of the church of God as well as thyself. Fathers had a power of selling the liberty of their children.* Exod. 21. 7. If a man sell his daughter to be a maid servant, she shall not go out as the men-servants do. *Her master shall not dismiss her, as another slave is dismissed at the sabbatical year. He shall take her as his wife, or shall marry her to his son. If he cares to do neither of these, he shall set her at liberty.*

They sold also insolvent debtors, and even their children, as appears from 2 Kings 4. 1. *and* Mat. 18. 25. *Sometimes they sold free-men for slaves, as* Joseph *was sold by his brethren. This crime was called* Plagium, *and the law punished it with death.* Exod. 21. 16. He that stealeth a man, and selleth him, or if he be found in his hand, he shall surely be put to death. *The* Jews *confine this to the theft of a man of their own nation. The apostle* Paul, *writing to* Timothy, *places* plagiaries *amongst the greatest miscreants,* 1 Tim. 1. 10. Ἀνδραποδισταῖς, *in English,* Men-stealers. Esau *sold his birth-right,* Gen. 25. 33. *and is therefore called a* profane person, *Heb.* 12. 16. *for slighting that to which so many glorious privileges belonged. The* birth-right *was a special type of* Christ, *who was to be a* first-born: *and of the church called God's* first-born, *Exod.* 4. 22. *and of the great privileges of the church; particularly adoption, and eternal life.* Heb. 12. 23. *It is said, that the Lord had* sold *his people to their enemies, as a master parts with a vicious slave, to punish him for his infidelity and disobedience.* Deut. 32. 30. How should one chase a thousand, and two put ten thousand to flight, except their rock had sold them? *See* Judg. 2. 14. | 3. 8. | 10. 7.

The prophet Elijah *said to* Ahab, 1 *Kings* 21. 20. Thou hast sold thyself to work evil in the sight of the Lord. *Thou hast wilfully and wholly resigned up thyself to be a slave to thine own bad inclinations, to Satan, and his emissaries, to do whatsoever they persuade thee to do, as a slave is wholly in his master's power, and must employ all his time and strength for his service. The like is said of the idolatrous* Israelites, 2 *Kings* 17. 17. *The apostle* Paul *says, Rom.* 7. 14. But I am carnal, sold under sin. *He did not sell himself to sin, or to commit sin, as it is said of* Ahab; *but only he was overpowered sometimes by the tyranny of corruption, like a slave forced to be subject to a cruel master: he was not sin's servant or slave, but many times he was sin's captive against his will, as himself declares,* Rom. 7. 23.

Gen. 25. 31. Jacob said, s. me this day thy birth-right
37. 27. come, let us s. him to the Ishmaelites
Exod. 21. 7. if a man s. his daughter to be a servant
8. to s. her to strange nation, shall have no power
35. they shall s. the live ox and divide the money
22. 1. if a man steal an ox, and kill it, or s. it
Lev. 25. 14. if thou s. ought unto thy neighbour
29. if a man s. a dwelling-house in a walled city
47. if thy brother s. himself unto the stranger
Deut. 2. 28. thou shalt s. me meat for money
14. 21. s. that which dieth of itself unto an alien
21. 14. thou shalt not s. her at all for money
Judg. 4. 9. s. Sisera into the hand of a woman
1 Kings 21. 25. Ahab did s. himself to work wicked.
2 Kings 4. 7. go s. the oil, and pay thy debt, and live
Neh. 5. 8. and will ye even s. your brethren?
10. 31. bring victuals on the sabbath-day to s.
Prov. 23. 23. buy truth, and s. it not, also wisdom
Ezek. 30. 12. s. land into the hand of the wicked
48. 14. they shall not s. the first-fruits of the land
Joel 3. 8. I will s. your sons and daughters into hand of Judah, they shall s. them to the Sabeans
Amos 8. 5. new-moon be gone, that we may s. corn
6. yea, and s. the refuse of the wheat
Zech. 11. 5. and they that s. them say, I am rich
Mat. 19. 21. go and s. that thou hast, and come and follow me, Mark 10. 21. Luke 12. 33. | 18. 22.
25. 9. but go ye rather to them that s. and buy
Luke 22. 36. let him s. his garment, and buy a sword
Jam. 4. 13. we will buy and s. and get gain
Rev. 13. 17. that no man might buy or s. save he

SELLER.

Isa. 24. 2. as with the buyer, so with the s.
Ezek. 7. 12. let not buyer rejoice, nor the s. mourn
13. the s. shall not return to that which is sold
Acts 16. 14. a woman named Lydia, a s. of purple

SELLERS.

Neh. 13. 20. merchants and s. lodged without Jerus.

SELLEST.

Psal. 44. 12. thou s. thy people for nought, dost not

SELLETH.

Exod. 21. 16. he that stealeth a man and s. him, he shall surely be put to death, Deut. 24. 7.
Ruth 4. 3. he said, Naomi s. a part of land
Prov. 11. 26. blessing upon head of him that s. corn
31. 24. she maketh fine linen and s. it
Nah. 3. 4. that s. nations through her whoredoms
Mat. 13. 44. he s. all, and buyeth that field

SELVEDGE.

Exod. 26. 4. from the s. in the coupling, 36. 11.

Our SELVES.

Gen. 37. 10. shall we come and bow down our s.?
44. 16. Judah said, how shall we clear our s.?
Num. 32. 17. but we our s. will go ready armed
Deut. 2. 35. cattle we took for a prey unto our s. 3. 7.
1 Sam. 14. 8. we will discover our s. unto them
Ezra 4. 3. but we our s. together will build to Lord
8. 21. that we might afflict our s. before our God
Job 34. 4. let us know among our s. what is good
Psal. 83. 12. let us take to our s. the houses of God
100. 3. it is he that made us, and not we our s.
Prov. 7. 18. come, let us solace our s. with loves
Isa. 28. 15. and under falsehood have we hid our s.
56. 12. we will fill our s. with strong drink
Jer. 50. 5. come, let us join our s. to the Lord
Luke 22. 71. we our s. have heard, John 4. 42.
Acts 6. 4. but we will give our s. to prayer
23. 14. we have bound our s. under a curse
Rom. 8. 23. even we our s. groan within our s.
Rom. 15. 1. we ought to bear and not to please our s.
1 Cor. 11. 31. if we would judge our s. should not
2 Cor. 1. 4. wherewith we our s. are comforted of G.
9. that we should not trust in our s. but in God
3. 1. do we begin again to commend our s. to you?
5. not that we are sufficient of our s. to think any thing as of our s. but our sufficiency is of God
4. 2. commending our s. to every man's conscience
5. for we preach not our s. but Christ Jesus the Lord, and our s. your servants for Jesus' sake
5. 12. for we commend not our s. again unto you
13. whether we be besides our s. it is to God
6. 4. in all things approving our s. as ministers
7. 1. let us cleanse our s. from all filthiness of flesh
10. 12. or compare our s. with some that commend
14. we stretch not our s. beyond our measure
12. 19. again, think ye we excuse our s. unto you?
Gal. 2. 17. we our s. also are found sinners
1 Thess. 2. 10. how unblameably we behaved our s.
2 Thess. 1. 4. so that we our s. glory in you
3. 7. we behaved not our s. disorderly among you
9. but to make our s. an ensample unto you
Tit. 3. 3. for we our s. were sometimes foolish
Heb. 10. 25. not forsaking the assembling of our s.
1 John 1. 8. we deceive our s. the truth is not in us

Own SELVES.

Acts 20. 30. also of your own s. shall men rise
2 Cor. 8. 5. but first gave their own s. to the Lord
13. 5. prove your own s. know ye not your own s.
2 Tim. 3. 2. men shall be lovers of their own s.
Jam. 1. 22. not hearers, deceiving your own s.

Your SELVES.

Gen. 18. 4. wash, and rest your s. under the tree
45. 5. be not angry with your s. that ye sold me
49. 1. gather your s. together, 2. Jer. 6. 1. Ezek. 39. 17. Joel 3. 11. Zeph. 2. 1. Rev. 19. 17.
Exod. 19. 12. take heed to your s. Deut. 2. 4. | 4. 15, 23. | 11. 16. Josh. 23. 11. Jer. 17. 21.
30. 37. ye shall not make like perfume to your s.
32. 29. consecrate your s. to-day to the Lord
Lev. 11. 43. ye shall not make your s. abominable, neither shall ye make your s. unclean with them
11. 44. sanctify y. s. 20. 7. Num. 11. 18. Josh. 3. 5. | 7. 13. 1 Sam. 16. 5. 1 Chr. 15. 12. 2 Chr. 29. 5. | 35. 6.
44. nor shall ye defile your s. 18. 24, 30.
19. 4. nor make to your s. molten gods
Num. 16. 3. wherefore then lift you up your s.?
21. separate your s. from this congregation
31. 3. Moses said, arm some of your s. unto the war
18. the women-children keep alive for your s.
19. purify both your s. and your captives
Deut. 4. 16. take heed, lest ye corrupt your s. 25.
11. 23. shall possess mightier nations than your s.
14. 1. ye shall not cut your s. for the dead
31. 14. and present your s. in the tabernacle
29. I know that ye will utterly corrupt your s.
Josh. 2. 16. and hide your s. there three days
6. 18. and in any wise keep your s. from the accursed thing, lest ye make your s. accursed
8. 2. only the spoil take for a prey unto your s.
23. 7. nor serve them, nor bow your s. unto them
16. ye have served, and bowed your s. to them
24. 22. ye are witnesses against your s. have chosen
Judg. 15. 12. that ye will not fall upon me your s.
1 Sam. 4. 9. quit your s. like men, O ye Philistines
10. 19. present your s. before the Lord by tribes
14. 34. Saul said, disperse your s. among the people
1 Kings 18. 25. choose you one bullock for your s.
20. 12. set your s. in array, and they set themselves in array, 2 Chron. 20. 17. Jer. 50. 14.
2 Chron. 29. 31. now ye have consecrated your s.
30. 8. but yield your s. unto Lord, serve him
32. 11. to give over your s. to die by famine
35. 4. prepare your s. by the houses of your fathers
Ezra 10. 11. separate your s. from the people of
Neh. 13. 25. nor take their daughters for your s.
Job 19. 3. that you make your s. strange to me
5. if ye will indeed magnify your s. against me
27. 12. behold, all ye your s. have seen it
42. 8. and offer up for your s. a burnt offering
Isa. 8. 9. associate your s. gird your s. Joel 1. 13.
29. 9. stay your s. ‖ 46. 8. shew your s. men
49. 9. to them that are in darkness, shew your s.
50. 1. for your iniquities have ye sold your s.
11. that compass your s. about with sparks
52. 3. ye have sold your s. for nought
57. 4. against whom do ye sport your s.
5. by inflaming your s. with idols under every tree
61. 6. in their glory shall ye boast your s.
Jer. 4. 4. circumcise your s. to the Lord, take away
13. 18. humble your s. Jam. 4. 10. 1 Pet. 5. 6.
25. 34. wallow your s. in ashes, ye principal of flock
26. 15. ye shall bring innocent blood upon your s.
37. 9. thus saith the Lord, deceive not your s.
44. 8. that ye might cut your s. off and be a curse
Ezek. 14. 6. repent and turn your s. 18. 30, 32.
20. 7. defile not your s. with the idols of Egypt, 18.
31. ye pollute your s. ‖ 43. loathe your s. 36. 31.
44. 8. have set keepers of my charge for your s.
Hos. 10. 12. sow to your s. in righteousness
Amos 5. 26. the star of your God ye made to your s.
Zech. 7. 6. eat for your s. and drink for your s.
Mat. 3. 9. think not to say within your s. Luke 3. 8.
6. 19. lay not up for your s. ‖ 20. lay up for your s.
16. 8. Jesus said, why reason ye among your s.
23. 13. ye neither go in your s. Luke 11. 52.
15. two-fold more the child of hell than your s.
31. wherefore ye be witnesses unto your s.
25. 9. but go ye rather, and buy for your s.
Mark 6. 31. come ye your s. apart into a desert
9. 33. what was it that ye disputed among your s.
50. have salt in your s. and peace one with another
13. 9. but take heed to your s. they shall deliver you up, Luke 17. 3. | 21. 34. Acts 5. 35. | 20. 28.
Luke 11. 46. ye your s. touch not the burdens
12. 33. provide your s. bags which wax not old
36. ye your s. like men that wait for the Lord
57. why even of your s. judge ye not what is right
13. 28. prophets in the kingdom, ye your s. thrust ou
16. 9. make to your s. friends of the mammon
15. ye are they which justify your s. before men
17. 14. he said, go shew your s. unto the priest

Luke 21. 30. ye know of *your s.* that summer is nigh
22. 17. take this, and divide it among *your s.*
23. 28. but weep for *your s.* and for your children
John 3. 28. ye *your s.* bear me witness, that I said
6. 43. Jesus said, murmur not among *your s.*
16. 19. do ye inquire among *your s.* of that I said
Acts 2. 22. signs God did, as you *your s.* also know
40. save *your s.* from this untoward generation
13. 46. seeing ye judge *your s.* unworthy of life
15. 29. from which if ye keep *your s.* ye do well
20. 10. trouble not *your s.* for his life is in him
34. you *your s.* know that these hands ministered
Rom. 6. 11. reckon ye also *your s.* to be dead to sin
13. but yield *your s.* unto God, as those alive
16. to whom ye yield *your s.* servants to obey
12. 19. dearly beloved, revenge not *your s.* but
1 *Cor.* 5. 13. put from *your s.* that wicked person
6. 7. why do ye not rath. suffer *y. s.* to be defraud.?
7. 5. ye may give *your s.* to fasting and prayer
11. 13. judge in *your s.* is it comely that a woman pray unto God uncovered?
16. 16. I beseech, that ye submit *your s.* unto such
2 *Cor.* 7. 11. yea, what clearing of *your s.* in all things ye have approved *your s.* clear in this matter
11. 19. suffer fools gladly, seeing ye *your s.* are wise
13. 5. examine *your s.* whether ye be in the faith
Eph. 2. 8. through faith, and that not of *your s.*
5. 19. speaking to *your s.* in psalms and hymns
21. submitting *your s.* one to another in fear of G.
Col. 3. 18. wives, submit *your s.* unto your husbands
1 *Thess.* 2. 1. *y. s.* brethr. know our entrance to you
3. 3. *your s.* know that we are appointed thereunto
4. 9. ye *y. s.* are taught of G. to love one another
5. 2. *your s.* know that day of the Lord so cometh
11. wherefore comfort *your s.* together, and edify
13. and be at peace among *your s.* 15.
2 *Thess.* 3. 6. we command that ye withdraw *your s.*
7. *your s.* know how ye ought to follow us
Heb. 10. 34. knowing in *your s.* ye have in heaven
13. 3. remember, as being *your s.* also in the body
17. submit *your s.* ‖ *Jam.* 4. 7. submit *your s.* to G.
Jam. 2. 4. are ye not then partial in *your s.?*
1 *Pet.* 1. 14. not fashioning *your s.* to former lusts
2. 13. submit *your s.* to every ordinance of man
4. 1. arm *your s.* likewise with the same mind
8. above all things fervent charity among *your s.*
5. 5. ye younger, submit *your s.* unto the elder
1 *John* 5. 21. little children, keep *your s.* from idols
2 *John* 8. look to *y. s.* that we lose not those things
Jude 20. building up *your s.* on most holy faith
21. keep *your s.* in love of G. looking for mercy
See Assemble, ed.

SENATE.

Acts 5. 21. they called all the *s.* of Israel together

SENATORS.

Ps. 105. 22. to bind princes, and teach his *s.* wisdom

SEND.

Gen. 24. 7. God shall *s.* his angel before thee, 40.
12. I pray thee, *s.* me good speed this day
54. he said, *s.* me away unto my master, 56.
38. 17. wilt thou give me a pledge till thou *s.* it?
43. 4. if thou wilt *s.* our brother with us
45. 5. God did *s.* me before you, to preserve life
Exod. 4. 13. *s.* by hand of him whom thou wilt *s.*
7. 2. that he *s.* children of Israel out of his land
9. 19. *s.* therefore now, and gather thy cattle
12. 33. that they might *s.* them out in haste
33. 12. nor let me know whom thou wilt *s.* with me
Lev. 16. 21. *s.* him away by the hand of a fit man
Num. 13. 2. *s.* thou men to search land, of every tribe shall ye *s.* a man a ruler among them
31. 4. of every tribe *s.* a thousand to the war
Deut. 1. 22. we will *s.* men before us to search
7. 20. thy God will *s.* the hornet among them
19. 12. the elders shall *s.* and fetch him thence
24. 1. give her a bill of divorce, and *s.* her out
28. 20. Lord shall *s.* upon thee cursing and rebuke
48. shall serve enemies Lord shall *s.* against thee
Judg. 13. 8. let man of God thou didst *s.* come again
1 *Sam.* 5. 11. *s.* away the ark of God, 6. 8.
6. 2. tell us wherewith we shall *s.* it to his place
3. if ye *s.* away the ark of God, *s.* it not empty
9. 26. saying, up, that I may *s.* thee away
11. 3. give us respite, that we may *s.* messengers
12. 17. the Lord shall *s.* thunder and rain
16. 11. Samuel said to Jesse, *s.* and fetch David
19. Saul sent and said, *s.* me David thy son
25. 25. I saw not the young men thou didst *s.*
2 *Sam.* 11. 6. David saying, *s.* me Uriah the Hittite
14. 32. come hither, that I may *s.* thee to king
15. 36. by them ye shall *s.* unto me every thing
17. 16. now therefore *s.* quickly, and tell David
1 *Kings* 20. 9. all thou didst *s.* for thy serv. I will do
2 *Kings* 2. 16. he said, ye shall not *s.* ‖ 17. he said, *s.*
5. 7. doth *s.* to me to recover a man of his leprosy
6. 13. spy where he is, that I may *s.* and fetch him
7. 13. let us *s.* and see ‖ 9. 17. *s.* to meet Jehu
15. 37. the Lord began to *s.* against Judah Rezin
1 *Chron.* 13. 2. let us *s.* abroad unto our brethren
2 *Chr.* 2. 7. *s.* me therefore a man cunning to work
8. *s.* me also cedar-trees, fir-trees, algum-trees
6. 27. then hear thou, and *s.* rain upon thy land
28. 16. Ahaz did *s.* to king of Assyria to help him
32. 9. Sennacherib did *s.* servants to Hezekiah
Ezra 5. 17. let the king *s.* his pleasure to us
Neh. 2. 5. that thou wouldest *s.* me unto Judah
6. so it pleased the king to *s.* me, and I set a time
8. 10. eat, drink, and *s.* portions unto them, 12.
Job 21. 11. they *s.* forth their little ones as a flock
38. 35. canst thou *s.* lightnings, that they may go?
Psal. 20. 2. *s.* thee help from the sanctuary
43. 3. O *s.* out thy light and truth, let them lead
57. 3. he shall *s.* from heaven, and save me from reproach; God shall *s.* forth his mercy and truth
68. 9. thou, O God, didst *s.* a plentiful rain
33. he doth *s.* out his voice, a mighty voice
110. 2. shall *s.* rod of thy strength out of Zion
118. 25. O Lord, I beseech thee, *s.* now prosperity
144. 7. *s.* thine hand from above, rid me, deliver
Prov. 10. 26. so is the sluggard to them that *s.* him
22. 21. answ. words of truth to them that *s.* to thee
25. 13. so is faithful messenger to them that *s.* him

Eccl. 10. 1. ointment to *s.* forth a stinking savour
Isa. 6. 8. whom shall I *s.?* I said, here am I, *s.* me
10. 16. Lord shall *s.* among his fat ones leanness
16. 1. *s.* ye the lamb to the ruler of the land
19. 20. he shall *s.* them a Saviour, a great one
32. 20. that *s.* forth thither the feet of ox and ass
57. 9. didst *s.* thy messengers far off, and debase
Jer. 1. 7. thou shalt go to all that I shall *s.* thee
2. 10. *s.* unto Kedar ‖ 9. 17. *s.* for cunning women
27. 3. *s.* the yokes to king of Edom and Moab
29. 31. *s.* to all them of the captivity, saying
42. 5. for the which the Lord shall *s.* thee to us
6. we will obey the Lord, to whom we *s.* thee
Mat. 9. 38. pray ye therefore the Lord that he will *s.* forth labourers into his harvest, *Luke* 10. 2.
10. 34. think not that I am come to *s.* peace
12. 20. till he *s.* forth judgment unto victory
13. 41. Son of man shall *s.* forth his angels, and they shall gather them offend, 24. 31. *Mark* 13. 27.
15. 23. *s.* her away, for she crieth after us
21. 3. straightway he will *s.* them, *Mark* 11. 3.
Mark 3. 14. that he might *s.* them to preach, 6. 7.
5. 10. would not *s.* them away out of the country
12. besought him, saying, *s.* us into the swine
Luke 16. 24. *s.* Lazarus ‖ 27. *s.* to my father's house
John 14. 26. whom the Father will *s.* in my name
17. 8. they have believed that thou didst *s.* me
Acts 3. 20. he shall *s.* Jes. Christ who was preached
7. 35. same did God *s.* to be a ruler and deliverer
10. 5. and now *s.* men to Joppa, 32. ‖ 11. 13.
11. 29. disciples determined to *s.* relief to brethren
15. 22. to *s.* chosen men of their company, 25.
25. 3. that he would *s.* for him to Jerusalem
27. it seemeth unreasonable to *s.* a prisoner and
Phil. 2. 19. I trust in the Lord to *s.* Timotheus, 23.
25. I supposed it necessary to *s.* Epaphroditus
2 *Thess.* 2. 11. for this cause God shall *s.* delusions
Tit. 3. 12. when I shall *s.* Artemas unto thee
Jam. 3. 11. doth fountain *s.* sweet water and bitter?
Rev. 1. 11. write and *s.* it to seven churches in Asia
11. 10. and they shall *s.* gifts one to another

I SEND.

Exod. 23. 20. behold, *I s.* an angel before thee
Num. 22. 37. did *I* not earnestly *s.* unto thee?
1 *Sam.* 20. 12. if there be good, and *I s.* not to thee
21. 2. know the business whereabout *I s.* thee
2 *Chron.* 7. 13. if *I s.* pestilence, *Ezek.* 14. 19.
Isa. 6. 8. voice of the Lord, say. whom shall *I s.?*
Jer. 25. 15. cause all, to whom *I s.* thee to drink it
Ezek. 2. 3. *I s.* thee to the children of Israel, 4.
14. 21. when *I s.* my four sore judgments
Mat. 10. 16. behold, *I s.* you forth as sheep
11. 10. behold, *I s.* my messenger before thy face to prepare thy way, *Mark* 1. 2. *Luke* 7. 27.
23. 34. behold *I s.* you prophets and wise men
Mark 8. 3. if *I s.* them away fasting, they will faint
Luke 10. 3. *I s.* you forth as lambs among wolves
24. 49. *I s.* the promise of my Father upon you
John 13. 20. he that receiveth whom *I s.* receiv. me
20. 21. as my Father sent me, even so *s. I* you
Acts 25. 21. to be kept till *I s.* him to Cæsar
26. 17. from Gentiles, unto whom now *I s.* thee

I will SEND.

Gen. 27. 45. *I will s.* and fetch thee from thence
37. 13. come, and *I will s.* thee unto them
38. 17. he said, *I will s.* thee a kid from the flock
Exod. 3. 10. *I will s.* thee unto Pharaoh, *Acts* 7. 34.
8. 21. *I will s.* swarms of flies upon thee
9. 14. *I will s.* all my plagues upon thine heart
23. 27. *I will s.* my fear ‖ 28. *I will s.* hornets
33. 2. *I will s.* an angel before thee, and drive out
Lev. 26. 22. *I will s.* wild beasts among you
25. *I will s.* pestilence ‖ 36. *I will s.* faintness
Deut. 11. 15. *I will s.* grass in thy fields for cattle
32. 24. *I will s.* the teeth of beasts upon them
1 *Sam.* 9. 16. *I will s.* thee a man of Benjamin
16. 1. *I will s.* thee to Jesse the Bethlehemite
20. 13. then *I will s.* shew it thee, and *s.* thee away
1 *Kings* 18. 1. and *I will s.* rain upon the earth
20. 6. yet *I will s.* my servants unto thee to-morrow
34. *I will s.* thee away with this covenant
2 *Kings* 19. 7. *I will s.* a blast upon him, *Isa.* 37. 7.
Isa. 10. 6. *I will s.* him against hypocritical nation
66. 19. *I will s.* those that escape unto the nations
Jer. 8. 17. behold, *I will s.* serpents among you
9. 16. *I will s.* a sword after them till consumed, 24. 10. ‖ 25. 16, 27. ‖ 29. 17. ‖ 49. 37.
16. 16. *I will s.* for many fishers, many hunters
25. 9. *I will s.* and take the families of the north
43. 10. *I will s.* Nebuchadnezzar my servant
48. 12. behold, *I will s.* unto him wanderers
51. 2. and *I will s.* unto Babylon fanners
Ezek. 5. 16. *I will s.* famine, 17. ‖ 14. 13. *Amos* 8. 11.
7. 3. *I will s.* mine anger upon thee and judge
28. 23. *I will s.* unto her pestilence and blood
Joel 2. 19. *I will s.* you corn, and wine, and oil
Mal. 2. 2. *I will s.* a curse ‖ 4. 5. *I will s.* Elijah
3. 1. *I will s.* my messenger, and he shall prepare
Mat. 15. 32. *I will* not *s.* them away fasting
Luke 11. 49. *I will s.* them prophets and apostles
20. 13. what shall I do? *I will s.* my beloved son
John 15. 26. the Comforter whom *I will s.* 16. 7.
Acts 22. 21. *I will s.* thee far hence to the Gentiles
1 *Cor.* 16. 3. whom you shall approve, them *I will s.*
See Fire.

SENDEST.

Deut. 15. 13. when thou *s.* him out free, 18.
Josh. 1. 16. whithersoever thou *s.* us we will go
2 *Kings* 1. 6. that thou *s.* to enquire of Baal-zebub
Job 14. 20. changest countenance, and *s.* him away
Psal. 104. 30. thou *s.* thy Spirit, they are created

SENDETH.

Deut. 24. 3. and if the latter husband *s.* her out
1 *Kings* 17. 14. till the day that the Lord *s.* rain
Job 5. 10. and who *s.* waters upon the fields
12. 15. he *s.* them out, they overturn the earth
Psal. 104. 10. he *s.* the springs into the valleys
147. 15. he *s.* forth his commandment, 18.
Prov. 26. 6. that *s.* a message by the hand of a fool
Cant. 1. 12. my spikenard *s.* forth the smell thereof
Isa. 18. 2. that *s.* ambassadors by the sea in vessels
Mat. 5. 45. and *s.* rain on the just and on the unjust

Mark 11. 1. he *s.* forth two of his disciples, 14. 13.
Luke 14. 32. *s.* and desireth conditions of peace
Acts 23. 26. Claudius Lysias to Felix *s.* greeting

SENDING.

2 *Sam.* 13. 16. this evil in *s.* me away is greater
2 *Chron.* 36. 15. his *s.* messengers, *Jer.* 7. 25. ‖ 25. 4. ‖ 26. 5. ‖ 29. 19. ‖ 35. 15. ‖ 44. 4.
Esth. 9. 19. and of *s.* portions one to another, 22.
Psal. 78. 49. by *s.* evil angels among them
Isa. 7. 25. it shall be for the *s.* forth of lesser cattle
Ezek. 17. 15. rebelled in *s.* ambassadors unto Egypt
Rom. 8. 3. God *s.* his Son in likeness of sinful flesh

SENSE,

Or meaning of scripture. It is said, Neh. 8. 8. They read in the book, in the law of God distinctly, and gave the *sense,* and caused them to understand the reading. *A learned author says, that these five different* senses *may be distinguished in the Scripture.* The Grammatical Sense. The Historical or Literal Sense. The Allegorical or Figurative Sense. The Analogical Sense. The Tropological or Moral Sense.

I. The Grammatical Sense *is that which the words of the text present to the mind, according to the proper and usual signification of those words. Thus when it is said, that God repents, that he is in anger, that he ascends or descends, that he has eyes open, or ears attentive, &c. the grammatical* sense *of all these expressions might induce one to think that God is corporeal, and subject to the same weaknesses as ourselves. But as reason and sound faith do assure us, that he has none of our infirmities and imperfections; upon such occasions we are not to abide by, or confine ourselves to, the* Grammatical Sense.

II. The Literal and Historical Sense *is that which belongs to the history or fact, to the* sense *which the rehearsal and terms of the Scripture immediately present to the mind. Thus when it is said, that* Abraham *married* Hagar, *that he afterwards sent her away, that* Isaac *was born of* Sarah, *that he received circumcision: all these facts, taken in the historical and literal* sense, *mean nothing else than what is expressed in the history; that is, the marriage of* Abraham *with* Hagar, *the birth of* Isaac, &c.

III. The Allegorical and Figurative Sense *is that which examines what may be concealed under the terms, or under the event mentioned in the history. Thus the marriage of* Abraham *with* Hagar, *who was afterwards repudiated and driven away because of her insolence, and that of her son, is a figure or representation of the Synagogue, which was only as it were a slave, and which was divorced and rejected, because of its infidelity and ingratitude.* Sarah *is the figure of the* Christian Church, *and* Isaac *of the people chosen of God,* Gal. 4. 22, 23, 24, &c.

IV. The Analogical Sense, *or* Sense *of Analogy and Agreement, is that which refers some expressions of Scripture to eternal life and happiness; because of some conformity or similitude between the terms that are brought to express something coming to pass in this world, and what shall come to pass in heaven. For example, on occasion of the Sabbath, or of the seventh day's rest that was enjoined the people of God, a transition may be made to that repose or rest that the saints enjoy in heaven. On occasion of the* Israelites *entering into the land of promise, we naturally pass to treat of the entering of the Elect into heaven: these transitions the Apostle makes,* Heb. 3. 18, 19. ‖ 4. 1, 9.

V. The Moral or Tropological Sense *is that which deduces moral reflections for the conduct of life, and for the reformation of manners, from what is related historically or literally in Scripture. For example, on occasion of these words of* Deut. 25. 4. Thou shalt not muzzle the ox when he treadeth out the corn, St. Paul *says, that those that preach the gospel, and instruct us in the way to salvation, ought to be supplied with the necessaries of life,* 1 Cor. 9. 9, 10, 11, 14.

These five Senses *may be observed in this one word,* Jerusalem. *According to the Grammatical* Sense, *it signifies the* Vision of peace; *according to the literal and historical,* the capital city of *Judea; according to the allegorical,* the church militant; *according to the analogical,* the church triumphant; *according to the moral,* a faithful soul, *of which* Jerusalem *is a kind of figure.*

SENSES.

Heb. 5. 14. have their *s.* exercised to discern good

SENSUAL.

Jam. 3. 15. this wisdom is earthly, *s.* devilish
Jude 19. these be *s.* having not the Spirit

SENT.

Gen. 37. 32. they *s.* the coat of many colours
38. 20. Judah *s.* the kid by hand of his friend
25. Tamar *s.* to her father-in-law, saying, by
41. 14. then Pharaoh *s.* and called Joseph
42. 4. but Benjamin Jacob *s.* not with his brethren
45. 8. it was not you that *s.* me hither, but God
50. 16. they *s.* a messenger unto Joseph, saying
Exod. 3. 14. thou shalt say, I AM hath *s.* me to you
5. 22. Lord, why is it that thou hast *s.* me?
Num. 13. 16. the names of the men Moses *s.* 14. 36.
22. 10. Balak the king of Moab hath *s.* unto me
15. Balak *s.* yet again princes more honourable
Josh. 6. 17. because she hid the messengers we *s.*
14. 7. forty years old was I when Moses *s.* me
Judg. 20. 6. I cut her in pieces and *s.* her thro' Israel
1 *Sam.* 31. 9. *s.* into the land of the Philistines
2 *Sam.* 24. 13. what answer return him that *s.* me
1 *Kings* 18. 10. no nation whither my lord hath not *s.*
21. 11. the elders did as Jezebel had *s.* unto them
2 *Kings* 1. 6. return unto the king that *s.* you, and say
6. 10. and king of Israel *s.* to the place the man
14. 9. thistle *s.* to the cedar in Lebanon, saying
16. 11. Urijah built according as Ahaz had *s.*

2 Kings 18. 27. Rab-shakeh said to them, hath my master s. me to thy master to speak words? Isa. 36. 12.
19. 4. his master s. to reproach the living God
22. 15. she said, thus saith the Lord God of Israel, tell man that s. you unto me, 18. 2 Chron. 34. 23.
Ezra 4. 11. this is the copy of the letter they s.
Neh. 6. 4. they s. unto me four times after this sort
Psal. 105. 20. king s. and loosed him, the ruler
Isa. 48. 16. Lord God and his Spirit hath s. me
Jer. 14. 3. their nobles have s. their little ones
23. 21. I have not s. these prophets, yet they ran
29. 25. because thou hast s. letters in thy name
37. 7. thus shall ye say unto the king that s. you
42. 9. whom ye s. to present your supplication, 20.
Ezek. 23. 40. ye have s. for men to come from far
Dan. 3. 28. who had s. his angel and delivered
Hos. 5. 13. then Ephraim went and s. to king Jareb
Zech. 7. 2. when they had s. unto the house of God
Mat. 10. 40. he that receiveth me, receiveth him that s. me, Mark 9. 37. Luke 9. 48. John 13. 20.
21. 1. then s. Jesus two disciples, saying to them
27. 19. Pilate's wife s. unto him, saying, have
Mark 6. 27. immediately the king s. an executioner
Luke 7. 20. John Baptist hath s. us unto thee
10. 1. Jesus s. them two and two before his face
14. 17. he s. his servant at supper-time to say
19. 14. they s. a message after him, saying
23. 11. mocked him, and s. him again to Pilate
John 1. 22. we may give answer to them that s. us
4. 34. my meat is to do will of him that s. me
5. 23. honoureth not the Father who hath s. me
24. that believeth on him that s. me, 12. 44.
30. but will of him who s. me, 6. 38, 39, 40.
33. ye s. unto John, and he bare witness to truth
36. the same works I do bear witness that the Father hath s. me, 37. | 6. 57. | 8. 16, 18.
6. 44. except the Father which s. me draw him
7. 16. my doctrine is not mine, but his that s. me
18. but he that seeketh his glory that s. him
32. Pharisees and priests s. officers to take him
9. 4. I must work the works of him that s. me
10. 36. say ye of him whom the Father hath s.
11. 42. that they may believe thou hast s. me
12. 45. he that seeth me, seeth him that s. me
49. Father who s. me gave me a commandment
14. 24. word is not mine, but Father's who s. me
15. 21. because they know not him that s. me
16. 5. but now I go my way to him that s. me
17. 3. is life eternal, to know Jesus whom thou s.
18. as thou hast s. me into the world, so I s.
21. the world may believe that thou hast s. me
23. that the world may know thou hast s. me
25. and these have known that thou hast s. me
20. 21. as my Father hath s. me, even so send I you
Acts 5. 21. s. to the prison to have them brought
10. 29. I ask for what intent ye have s. for me
11. 30. s. it to the elders by Barnabas and Saul
13. 15. the rulers of the synagogue s. unto them
15. 27. we have therefore s. Judas and Silas
16. 36. the magistrates have s. to let you go
19. 31. Paul's friends s. unto him, desiring him
1 Cor. 1. 17. Christ s. me not to baptize, but to preach
2 Cor. 8. 18. we have s. with him the brother, 22.
Phil. 4. 16. in Thessalonica ye s. once and again
1 John 4. 14. testify that the Father s. the Son

SENT away.

Gen. 12. 20. Pharaoh s. away Abraham and his wife
21. 14. Abraham s. Ishmael and Hagar away
24. 59. they s. away Rebekah their sister
25. 6. Abraham s. Keturah's children away
26. 27. seeing ye hate me and have s. me away
29. as we have s. thee away in peace, thou art
28. 5. Isaac s. away Jacob to Padan-aram
6. Isaac had blessed Jacob and s. him away
31. 27. I might have s. thee away with mirth
42. surely thou hadst s. me away empty
45. 24. he s. his brethren away, they departed
Deut. 24. 4. s. her away, may not take her again
Josh. 2. 21. Rahab s. spies away, they departed
22. 6. Joshua s. Reubenites and Gadites away, 7.
Judg. 11. 38. Jephthah s. his daughter away
1 Sam. 10. 25. Samuel s. all the people away
19. 17. Saul said, why hast thou s. away my enemy?
2 Sam. 3. 21. David s. Abner away, and he went
24. why is it that thou hast s. him away?
10. 4. cut garments, and s. them away, 1 Chr. 19. 4.
1 Chron. 12. 19. lords of Philistines s. David away
Job 22. 9. thou hast s. widows away empty
Mark 12. 3. and they caught the servant and beat him and s. him away, 4. Luke 20. 10, 11.
Luke 1. 53. and the rich he hath s. empty away
8. 38. but Jesus s. him away, saying
Acts 13. 3. laid hands on them, they s. them away
17. 10. brethren immediately s. away Paul, 14.

God SENT.

Gen. 45. 7. God s. me before you to preserve life
Exod. 3. 13. the God of your fathers hath s. me
15. the God of Jacob hath s. me unto you
Judg. 9. 23. God s. evil spirit between Abimelech
1 Chron. 21. 15. God s. an angel unto Jerusalem
Neh. 6. 12. I perceived that God had not s. him
Jer. 43. 1. for which the Lord their God s. him
2. God hath not s. to thee to say, go not into Egypt
Dan. 6. 22. God hath s. his angel, and hath shut
John 3. 17. God s. not his Son to condemn world
34. he whom God hath s. speaketh words of God
Acts 3. 26. God hath raised his Son Jesus, s. him
10. 36. word God s. unto the children of Israel
Gal. 4. 4. God s. forth his Son made of a woman
6. God hath s. forth the Spirit of his Son
1 John 4. 9. God s. his only begotten Son into world
10. God s. his Son to be a propitiation for our sins
Rev. 22. 6. God s. his angel to shew his servants

He SENT.

Gen. 45. 23. to his father he s. after this manner
46. 28. he s. Judah before him unto Joseph
Exod. 18. 2. took Zipporah, after he had s. her back
Judg. 11. 28. Ammon hearkened not to words he s.
1 Sam. 17. 31. rehearsed words, and he s. for David
30. 26. he s. of the spoil unto the elders of Judah
2 Sam. 10. 5. he s. to meet them, 1 Chron. 19. 5.
14. 29. when he s. again, he would not come
22. 17. he s. from above, took me, Psal. 18. 16.
1 Kings 20. 7. for he s. unto me for my wives
2 Kings 17. 26. therefore he s. lions among them
2 Chron. 24. 19. yet he s. prophets to them to bring
25. 15. he s. unto Amaziah a prophet, which said
Esth. 5. 10. he s. and called for his friends
Psal. 78. 25. he s. them meat to the full
105. 17. he s. a man before them, even Joseph
26. he s. Moses his servant and Aaron
28. he s. darkness, and made it dark
106. 15. but he s. leanness into their soul
107. 20. he s. his word and healed them
111. 9. he s. redemption unto his people
Isa. 61. 1. he s. me to bind up the broken hearted, to proclaim liberty to the captives, Luke 4. 18.
Jer. 29. 28. he s. unto us in Babylon, saying
42. 21. for the which he hath s. me unto you
Lam. 1. 13. from above he s. fire into my bones
Zech. 2. 8. after the glory hath he s. me to nations
Mat. 21. 36. again he s. other serv. more than first
37. last of all he s. unto them his son, Mark 12. 4.
22. 7. he s. forth his armies, and destroyed those
John 1. 33. he that s. me to baptize with water
5. 38. for whom he hath s. him ye believe not
6. 29. that ye believe on him whom he hath s.
7. 28. he that s. me is true, ye know not, 8. 26.
29. but I know him, and he hath s. me
8. 29. and he that s. me is with me; the Father
42. neither came I of myself, but he s. me
Acts 24. 26. wherefore he s. for Paul the oftener
Rev. 1. 1. he s. and signified it by his angel to John

I SENT.

Gen. 32. 5. I have s. to tell my lord, to find grace
38. 23. I s. this kid, and thou hast not found her
Exod. 3. 12. this shall be a token that I have s. thee
Num. 32. 8. thus did your fathers when I s. them
Josh. 24. 5. I s. Moses also and Aaron, Mic. 6. 4.
Judg. 6. 14. thou shalt save Isr. have not I s. thee?
2 Kings 5. 6. I have s. Naaman my servant to thee
17. 13. the law which I s. to you by my servants
Isa. 42. 19. who is deaf, as my messenger that I s.?
43. 14. for your sake I have s. to Babylon
55. 11. it shall prosper in the thing whereto I s. it
Jer. 7. 25. I s. unto you all my servants the prophets, daily rising up early, 26. 5. | 35. 15. | 44. 4.
14. 14. I s. them not, nor commanded, nor spake to them, 15. | 23. 21, 32. | 27. 15. | 29. 9.
29. 31. I s. him not, he caused you to trust in a lie
Ezek. 3. 6. surely had I s. thee to them would hearken
Dan. 10. 11. O Daniel underst.; to thee am I now s.
Joel 2. 25. my great army which I s. among you
Amos 4. 10. I have s. among you the pestilence
Zech. 9. 11. I have s. forth thy prisoners out of pit
Mal. 2. 4. and ye shall know that I have s. this
Luke 4. 43. I must preach, for therefore am I s.
22. 35. when I s. you without purse and scrip
John 17. 18. so have I s. them into the world
Acts 10. 20. doubting nothing, for I have s. them
33. immediately theref. I s. thee, hast well done
1 Cor. 4. 17. for this cause have I s. to you Timotheus
2 Cor. 9. 3. yet have I s. brethren, lest our boasting
12. 17. did I make a gain of you by any whom I s.?
18. I desired Titus, and with him I s. a brother
Eph. 6. 22. whom I s. for same purpose, Col. 4. 8.
Phil. 2. 28. I s. him therefore the more carefully
1 Thess. 3. 5. for this I s. to know your faith
Phil. 12. whom I have s. again, receive him

See LORD.

SENT forth.

Gen. 8. 7. Noah s. forth a raven ‖ 10. s. forth dove
Prov. 9. 3. she hath s. forth her maidens, she crieth
Mat. 2. 16. Herod s. forth and slew all the males
10. 5. these twelve Jesus s. forth, and commanded
22. 3. and s. forth his servants to call them bidden
Mark 6. 17. Herod s. forth and laid hold upon John
Luke 20. 20. chief priests and scribes s. forth spies
Acts 9. 30. the brethren s. him forth to Tarsus
11. 22. they s. forth Barnabas as far as Antioch

SENT out.

Gen. 19. 29. God s. Lot out of midst of overthrow
1 Sam. 26. 4. David theref. s. out spies and unders.
2 Sam. 22. 15. and he s. out arrows, Psal. 18. 14.
Job 39. 5. who hath s. out the wild ass free?
Psal. 77. 17. clouds poured out, skies s. out a sound
80. 11. she s. out her boughs to sea, and branches
Jer. 24. 5. whom I have s. out of this place to Chald.
Ezek. 31. 4. she hath s. out her little rivers to trees
Acts 7. 12. Jacob s. out our fathers first
Jam. 2. 25. Rahab had s. them out another way

SENT, Passive.

Gen. 32. 18. it is a present s. to my lord Esau
1 Kings 14. 6. I am s. to thee with heavy tidings
Ezra 7. 14. forasmuch as thou art s. of the king
Prov. 17. 11. a cruel messenger shall be s. against him
Jer. 49. 14. an ambassador is s. unto the heathen
Ezek. 2. 9. behold, an hand was s. unto me, and lo
3. 5. art not s. to a people of a strange speech
23. 40. unto whom a messenger was s. and lo
Dan. 5. 24. then was part of the hand s. from him
Obad. 1. an ambassador is s. among the heathen
Mat. 15. 24. I am not s. but unto lost sheep of Israel
23. 37. and stonest them who are s. Luke 13. 34.
Luke 1. 19. I am Gabriel, and am s. to speak to thee
26. angel Gabriel was s. from God unto Nazar.
4. 26. but unto none of them was Elias s. save
John 1. 6. a man s. from God, whose name was Jo.
8. John was s. to bear witness of that light
24. they who were s. were of the Pharisees
3. 28. I said, I am not Christ, but s. before him
9. 7. wash in Siloam, which is by interpretation, s.
13. 16. nor he that is s. greater than he that s. him
Acts 10. 17. men that were s. had made inquiry
21. Peter went to the men who were s. 11. 11.
29. theref. came I to you as soon as I was s. for
13. 4. so they being s. forth by the Holy Ghost
26. to you is the word of this salvation s.
28. 28. the salvation of God is s. unto the Gentiles
Rom. 10. 15. how shall they preach, ex. they be s.?
Phil. 4. 18. received things which were s. from you
Heb. 1. 14. spirits s. forth to minister for them
1 Pet. 1. 12. with the Holy Ghost s. from heaven
1 Pet. 2. 14. or unto governors, as them that are s.
Rev. 5. 6. the seven spirits s. forth into the earth

SENTEST.

Exod. 15. 7. s. forth thy wrath, which consumed them
Num. 13. 27. we came to land whither thou s. us
24. 12. spake I not to the messengers thou s. us
1 Kings 5. 8. have considered things thou s. to me for

SENTENCE.

Deut. 17. 9. they shall shew thee the s. of judgment
10. thou shalt do according to the s. 11.
Psal. 17. 2. let my s. come forth from thy presence
Prov. 16. 10. a divine s. is in the lips of the king
Eccl. 8. 11. because s. is not executed speedily
Jer. 4. 12. now also will I give s. against them
Luke 23. 24. Pilate gave s. that it should be
Acts 15. 19. my s. is, that we trouble not them
2 Cor. 1. 9. we had the s. of death in ourselves

SENTENCES.

Dan. 5. 12. shewing of hard s. found in same Daniel
8. 23. a king understanding dark s. shall stand up

SEPARATE

Signifies, [1] *To part, divide, or put asunder*, Gen. 30. 40. [2] *To consecrate and set apart for some special ministry or service.* Acts 13. 2. Separate me Barnabas and Saul, for the work whereunto I have called them. [3] *To withdraw, or retire from worldly employments and enjoyments, and to devote oneself to the service of God; thus the* Nazarites *separated themselves*, Num. 6. 2. *some for life, others for a certain time only.* See NAZARITE. [4] *To forsake the communion of the church*, Jude 19. [5] *To excommunicate*, Luke 6. 22. [6] *To disperse, or scatter abroad into different parts of the world*, Deut. 32. 8. [7] *To be disowned, disregarded, and forsaken by a person*, Prov. 19. 4. The poor is separated from his neighbour; *that is, is forsaken by those who are most obliged to help him.* [8] *To distinguish persons from others, by conferring upon them many precious and valuable privileges and blessings; thus the Lord separated the* Israelites *from all other nations in the earth, and chose them for his peculiar people*, 1 Kings 8. 53.

Gen. 13. 9. Abram said, s. thys. I pray thee, from me
30. 40. Jacob did s. the lambs, and set the faces
Lev. 15. 31. thus shall ye s. the children of Israel
22. 2. speak to Aaron and his sons that they s.
Num. 6. 2. when man or woman shall s. themselves, to vow a vow, to s. themselves unto the Lord
3. the Nazarite shall s. himself from wine
8. 14. thus shalt thou s. the Levites from Israel
16. 21. s. yourselves from among this congregation
Deut. 19. 2. thou shalt s. three cities in thy land, 7.
29. 21. Lord shall s. him unto evil out of Israel
1 Kings 8. 53. didst s. them to be thine inheritance
Ezra 10. 11. s. yourselves from people of the land
Jer. 37. 12. Jeremiah went to s. himself thence
Mat. 25. 32. he shall s. them as a shepherd his sheep
Luke 6. 22. blessed are ye when men shall s. you
Acts 13. 2. s. me Barnabas and Saul for the work
Rom. 8. 35. who shall s. us from love of Christ?
39. nothing be able to s. us from love of God
Jude 19. these be they who s. themselves, sensual

SEPARATE.

Gen. 49. 26. shall be on the head of Joseph and of him that was s. from his brethren, Deut. 33. 16.
Josh. 16. 9. the s. cities of Ephraim were among
Ezek. 41. 12. building that was before the s. place
13. so he measured the house and the s. place
14. the breadth of the s. place toward the east
42. 1. chamber over against the s. place, 10, 13.
2 Cor. 6. 17. come out from among them, be ye s.
Heb. 7. 26. is holy, harmless, undefil. s. from sinners

SEPARATED.

Gen. 13. 11. then Abram and Lot s. themselves
14. Lord said, after that Lot was s. from him
25. 23. two manner of people be s. from thy bowels
Exod. 33. 16. so shall we be s. from people on earth
Lev. 20. 24. I am the Lord who have s. you from
25. which I have s. from you as unclean
Num. 16. 9. that the God of Israel hath s. you
Deut. 10. 8. the Lord s. the tribe of Levi to stand
32. 8. when he s. sons of Adam, he set bounds
1 Chron. 12. 8. of the Gadites there s. unto David
23. 13. Aaron was s. that he should sanctify
25. 1. David s. to the service of sons of Asaph
2 Chron. 25. 10. then Amaziah s. them, the army
Ezra 6. 21. all that had s. themselves unto them
8. 24. then I s. twelve of the chiefs of the priests
9. 1. priests and Levites have not s. themselves
10. 8. who would not come, be s. from congregation
16. all of them by their names were s. and sat
Neh. 4. 19. work is great, and we are s. upon wall
9. 2. Israel s. themselves from all strangers
10. 28. they that had s. clave to the brethren
13. 3. they s. from Israel the mixed multitude
Prov. 18. 1. through desire a man having s. himself
19. 4. but the poor is s. from his neighbour
Isa. 56. 3. the Lord hath s. me from his people
59. 2. iniquities have s. between you and your G.
Hos. 4. 14. for themselves are s. with whores
9. 10. they went and s. themselves unto that shame
Acts 19. 9. Paul departed, and s. the disciples
Rom. 1. 1. Paul an apostle, s. to the gospel of God
9. † 3. I could wish that I were s. from Christ
Gal. 1. 15. God who s. me from my mother's womb
2. 12. Peter withdrew and s. himself, fearing

SEPARATETH.

Num. 6. 5. till the days be fulfilled in which he s.
6. the days he s. he shall come at no dead body
Prov. 16. 28. and a whisperer s. chief friends
17. 9. he that repeateth a matter s. very friends
Ezek. 14. 7. or of the stranger which s. himself

SEPARATION.

Lev. 12. 2. the days of the s. for her infirmity
5. she shall be unclean two weeks, as in her s.
15. † 19. she shall be in her s. seven days
20. bed she lieth upon in her s. shall be unclean
25. an issue of blood out of the time of her s.
26. every bed shall be to her as the bed of her s.
16. † 22. goat shall bear iniquities to land of s
20. † 21. take his brother's wife, it is a s.

Num. 6. 4. days of *s.* shall eat nothing of vine-tree
5. all days of his *s.* no razor shall come on head
8. all the days of his *s.* he is holy unto the Lord
12. he shall consecrate to Lord the days of his *s.* and bring a lamb, because his *s.* was defiled
13. when the days of his *s.* are fulfilled
18. Nazarite shall shave the head of his *s.* and take the hair of his *s.* and put it in the fire
19. after the hair of the Nazarite's *s.* is shaven
21. his offering for his *s.* after the law of *s.*
19. 9. the ashes shall be kept for a water of *s.*
13. the water of *s.* hath not been sprinkled, 20.
21. he that sprinkleth water of *s.* shall wash his clothes, that toucheth water of *s.* shall be uncl.
31. 23. it shall be purified with the water of *s.*
Ezek. 42. 20. it had a wall round to make a *s.*
Zech. 13. † 1. fountain opened for *s.* for uncleanness

SEPARATING.

Zech. 7. 3. should I weep in the fifth month, *s.*

SEPULCHRE,

Or Grave. *The* Hebrews *have always taken great care about the burial of their dead. The greatest part of their* Sepulchres *were hollow places dug into rocks, as was that bought by* Abraham, *for the burying of* Sarah, *Gen.* 23. 6. *those of the kings of* Judah *and* Israel; *and that wherein our Saviour was laid in mount* Calvary. *Sometimes also their graves were dug in the ground, and commonly without their towns in burying-places, set apart on purpose. Generally they used to put some hewn stone, or other thing, over the grave, to shew it was a burying-place, that passengers might be warned not to come near it, that they might not be polluted.*

Our Saviour *in* Mat. 23. 27. *compares the hypocritical* Pharisees to whited sepulchres, *which appeared fine without, but inwardly were full of rottenness and corruption. It is said, that every year, on the fifteenth of* February, *the* Jews *took care to whiten their sepulchres anew. In* Luke 11. 44. *he compares them to* graves which appear not, and the men that walk over them are not aware of them, *or know not that the places are unclean, so that they contract an unknown and involuntary impurity. So they that conversed with these* Pharisees, *being deceived by their fair shews of religion and devotion, were easily insnared and drawn into sin by them.*

It is said, Mat. 23. 29, 30, 31. Wo unto you Scribes and Pharisees; because ye build the tombs of the prophets, and garnish the sepulchres of the righteous; And say, if we had been in the days of our fathers, we would not have been partakers with them in the blood of the prophets. Wherefore ye be witnesses unto yourselves, that ye are the children of them which killed the prophets. *As if our Saviour had said, Ye pretend a great deal of respect to the ancient prophets, and to disallow what your fathers did to them, by building and garnishing their tombs; yet this practice of yours seems rather to be an approbation of your fathers' wickedness, if one look upon it, either in the nature of the thing, for hereby you keep in memory what your fathers did against them: whereas, if you did detest it, you would rather do all you could that it might be utterly forgotten; or if one may judge of your affections to the dead prophets, by your usage of the living, namely, Myself and my Apostles.*

Gen. 23. 6. none shall withhold from thee his *s.*
Deut. 34. 6. no man knoweth of his *s.* unto this day
Judg. 8. 32. Gideon was buried in his father's *s.*
1 *Sam.* 10. 2. thou shalt find two men by Rachel's *s.*
2 *Sam.* 2. 32. they buried Asahel in his father's *s.*
4. 12 the head of Ishbosheth buried in Abner's *s.*
17. 23. Ahithophel buried in the *s.* of his father
21. 14. bones of Saul in the *s.* of Kish his father
1 *Kings* 13. 22. thy carcase shall not come to the *s.*
31. bury me in the *s.* wherein man of God is
2 *Kings* 9. 28. Ahaziah in the *s.* with his fathers
13. 21. they cast the man into the *s.* of Elisha
21. 26. Amon was buried in his *s.* in the garden
23. 17. they said, it is the *s.* of the man of God
30. Josiah buried in his own *s.* 2 *Chron.* 35. 24.
Psal. 5. 9. their throat is an open *s.* *Rom.* 3. 13.
Isa. 22. 16. that thou hast hewed thee out a *s.* here as he that heweth out a *s.* on high, and graveth
Mat. 27. 60. he rolled a great stone to the door of *s.*
61. the other Mary, sitting over against the *s.*
64. command that the *s.* be made sure, 66.
28. 1. and the other Mary came to see the *s.*
8. departed quickly from the *s.* with fear and joy
Mark 15. 46. Joseph wrapped him in the linen, and laid him in a *s.* and rolled a stone to the door of the *s.* *Luke* 23. 53. *Acts* 13. 29.
16. 2. they came to the *s.* at the rising of the sun
3. who shall roll the stone from the door of the *s.*
5. entering into the *s.* ‖ 8. they fled from the *s.*
Luke 23. 55. and the women also beheld the *s.*
24. 1. early in the morning they came to the *s.*
2. they found the stone rolled from *s.* *John* 20. 1.
9. returned from the *s.* ‖ 12. Peter ran to the *s.*
22. certain women which were early at the *s.*
24. certain of them with us went to the *s.*
John 19. 41. and in the garden there was a new *s.*
42. they laid Jesus, for the *s.* was nigh at hand
20. 1. cometh Mary when it was yet dark to *s.*
2. they have taken away the Lord out of the *s.*
3. that other disciple came to the *s.* 4, 8.
6. then cometh Peter, and went into the *s.*
11. Mary stood without at the *s.* weeping, as she wept, she stooped down and looked into the *s.*
Acts 2. 29. and his *s.* is with us unto this day
7. 16. Jacob laid in the *s.* that Abraham bought

SEPULCHRES.

Gen. 23. 6. in the choice of our *s.* bury thy dead
2 *Kings* 23. 16. Josiah spied the *s.* and took the bones out of the *s.* and burnt them upon the altar
2 *Chron.* 21. 20. Jehoram not buried in *s.* of kings
24. 25. Joash not ‖ 28. 27. Ahaz not buried in *s.* of kings
2 *Chron.* 32. 33. Hezekiah buried in chiefest of the *s.*
Neh. 2. 3. the place of my father's *s.* lieth waste
5. wouldst send me to the city of my father's *s.*
3. 16. Nehemiah repaired to place over-against *s.*
Mat. 23. 27. woe to you, for ye are like unto whited *s.*
29. because ye garnish the *s.* of the righteous
Luke 11. 47. ye build the *s.* of the prophets, 48.

SERAPHIMS.

Isa. 6. 2. above it stood the *s.* each had six wings
6. then flew one of the *s.* having a live coal

SERGEANTS.

Acts 16. 35. sent the *s.* saying, let these men go
38. the *s.* told these words unto the magistrates

SERPENT.

In Greek, οφις, *in* Hebrew, Nachash. *The craft, the wisdom, the subtilty of the* Serpent, *are things insisted on in Scripture, as qualities that distinguish them from other animals.* Moses *introduces the relation of* Eve's *temptation, by affirming,* Now the serpent was more subtil than any beast of the field which the Lord God had made, *Gen.* 3. 1. *And our Saviour recommends to his apostles to have the wisdom of the* Serpent, *Mat.* 10. 16. *They bring several proofs of this subtilty of the* Serpent. *They say, that the* Cerastes *hides himself in the sand, in order to bite the horse's foot, that he might throw his rider.* Jacob *makes an allusion to this in the blessing he gave to* Dan, *Gen.* 49. 17. Dan shall be a serpent by the way, an adder in the path; that biteth the horse heels, so that his rider shall fall backward. *It is likewise said of the* Serpent, *that when he is old, he has the secret of growing young again, and of stripping off his old skin or slough, by squeezing himself between two rocks. He assaults a man if he has his clothes on, but flees if he finds him naked. When he is assaulted, his chief care is to secure his head; because his heart being under his throat, and very near his head, the readiest way to kill him is to squeeze or cut off his head: hence in the curse that God gave the* Serpent, *he told him,* The seed of the woman shall bruise the serpent's head, *that is, the principal seat of his life,* Gen. 3. 15. *And many have supposed that his chief subtilty, or wisdom, as the gospel calls it, consists in this, that he chooses to expose his whole body to danger, that he may save his head. When he goes to drink at a fountain, he first vomits up all his poison, for fear of poisoning himself as he is drinking. Though this observation be not assented to by every body, it has nevertheless a great many defenders.*

It is said further of the Serpent's *subtilty, that it stops up its ears that it may not hear the voice of the charmer or enchanter. The* Psalmist *takes notice of this piece of subtilty of the Adder.* Psal. 58. 4. They are like the deaf adder, that stoppeth her ear; which will not hearken to the voice of charmers, charming never so wisely. *It is said, it applies one of its ears hard to the ground, and stops up the other with the end of its tail. Others say the subtilty of the* Serpent *consists in its agility and suppleness; or in a secret it has in recovering its sight by the juice of fennel. Every one proposes his own conjectures on this matter.*

Some place the venom of the Serpent *in its gall, others in its tongue, and others in its teeth. The Scripture in different passages expresses itself sometimes as supposing the gall of the* Serpent *to be its venom,* Job 20. 14. His meat in his bowels is turned, it is the gall of asps within him. David *seems to place it in the tongue.* Psal. 140. 3. They have sharpened their tongues like a serpent. *And* Solomon *in the teeth,* Prov. 23. 32. At the last it biteth like a serpent, and stingeth like an adder.

The Devil *is called a* Serpent, *Rev.* 12. 9. *both because he hid himself in the body of a real serpent when he seduced the first woman, and because of his serpentine disposition, being a subtil, crafty, and dangerous enemy to mankind.* See Devil. *Interpreters have much speculated concerning the nature of the first* Serpent, *that tempted* Eve. *Some have thought, that then the* Serpent, *or that kind of* Serpents, *there being several kinds of them, had two, four, or many feet, or moved upon the hinder part of its body, with head, breast, and belly upright. They ground their opinion on the curse that* God *gave the* Serpent, *Gen.* 3. 14. Upon thy belly shalt thou go. *Whereas formerly thou hadst a privilege above other kinds of* Serpents, *whereby thou didst go with erected breast, and didst feed upon the fruit of trees and other plants; now thou shalt be brought down to the same mean and vile estate with them. Others think that there is no probability that this animal was otherwise than what it is now; but what before the fall was natural to it, afterwards became painful, as nakedness was to man. It is put for wicked, malicious persons,* Mat. 23. 33.

Another curse that God gave the Serpent, *was,* That it should feed upon dust, *Gen.* 3. 14. Isaiah *says also,* Dust shall be the serpent's meat, *Isa.* 65. 25. *And in* Mic. 7. 17. They shall lick the dust like a serpent. *It is true, however, that they eat flesh, birds, frogs, fish, fruits, grass, &c. But as they continually creep upon the earth, it is impossible but that their food must be often defiled with dust and dirt. Some of them may really eat earth out of necessity, or at least earth-worms, which they cannot swallow without a good deal of dirt with them.*

Among other kinds of Serpents *mentioned in Scripture, are those fiery, flying serpents, that made so great a destruction among the* Israelites, *and were the death of so many people in the desert,* Num. 21. 6. *The Hebrew word here used for* Serpent, *is* Saraph, *which properly signifies* to burn; *and it is thought that this name was given to it, either because of its colour; or because of that heat and thirst it creates by its biting*

It was upon this occasion that the Lord commanded Moses *to make the* brasen serpent, *or the figure of the* Serpent Saraph, *and to raise it upon a pole, that the people who were bit by the* Serpents, *by looking upon this image, might be presently healed.* Moses *did so; and the event was answerable to this promise. By this account from Scripture we may understand something of greatest consequence was represented by it: For the only wise God ordains nothing without just reason. Why must a* Serpent *of brass be elevated on a pole? Could not the divine power recover them without it? Why must they look towards it? Could not a healing virtue be conveyed to their wounds, but through their eyes? All this had a direct reference to the mystery of* Christ, *and expressed the manner of his death, and the benefits derived from it. Therefore* Christ, *being the minister of the circumcision, chose this figure for the instruction of the Jews,* John 3. 14. As Moses lifted up the Serpent in the wilderness, even so must the Son of man be lifted up. *The biting of the* Israelites *by the fiery serpents doth naturally represent the effects of sin, that torment the conscience, and inflame the soul with the apprehension of future judgment. And the erecting of a* brasen serpent *upon a pole, that had the figure, not the poison of those serpents, doth in a lively manner set forth the lifting up of* Jesus Christ *on the cross, who only had the similitude of sinful flesh. The looking towards the* brasen serpent, *is a fit resemblance of believing in* Christ *crucified for salvation. The sight of the eye was the only means to derive virtue from it; and the faith of the heart is the means by which the sovereign efficacy of our Redeemer is conveyed.* John 6. 40. This is the will of him that sent me, that every one which seeth the Son and believeth on him, may have everlasting life.

This brasen serpent *was preserved among the* Israelites *down to the time of* Hezekiah, *who, being informed that the people paid a superstitious worship to it, had it broken in pieces, and by way of contempt gave it the name of* Nehushtan, *that is,* a brazen bauble or trifle, 2 *Kings* 18. 4.

Gen. 3. 1. the *s.* was more subtle than any beast
13. woman said, the *s.* beguiled me, 2 *Cor.* 11. 3.
49. 17. Dan shall be a *s.* by the way, an adder
Exod. 4. 3. the rod became a *s.* 7, 9, 10, 15.
Num. 21. 8. the Lord said, make thee a fiery *s.*
9. Moses made a *s.* of brass and put it on a pole; if a *s.* had bitten any man, he beheld the *s.* of brass
2 *Kings* 18. 4. Hezek. brake in pieces the brasen *s.*
Job 26. 13. his hand hath formed the crooked *s.*
Psal. 58. 4. their poison is like the poison of a *s.*
140. 3. they sharpened their tongues like a *s.*
Prov. 23. 32. at last it biteth like a *s.* and stingeth
30. 19. too wonderful, the way of a *s.* upon a rock
Eccl. 10. 8. whoso breaketh an hedge, *s.* shall bite him
11. surely the *s.* will bite without enchantment
Isa. 14. 29. out of the *s.* root shall come forth a cockatrice; his fruit shall be as a fiery flying *s.*
27. 1. the Lord shall punish the *s.* that crooked *s.*
30. 6. from whence come viper and fiery flying *s.*
65. 25. lion eat straw, and dust shall be the *s.* meat
Jer. 46. 22. the voice thereof shall go like a *s.*
Amos 5. 19. leaned hand on wall, and a *s.* bite him
9. 3. I will command the *s.* and he shall bite them
Mic. 7. 17. they shall lick the dust like a *s.*
Mat. 7. 10. will he give him a *s.*? *Luke* 11. 11.
John 3. 14. as Moses lifted up the *s.* so Son of man
Rev. 12. 9. that old *s.* called the devil, 20. 2.
14. where she is nourished from the face of the *s.*
15. the *s.* cast out of his mouth water as a flood

SERPENTS.

Exod. 7. 12. they cast down their rods, they became *s.*
Num. 21. 6. the Lord sent fiery *s.* among them
7. pray to Lord that he take away the *s.* from us
Deut. 8. 15. terrible wildern. wherein were fiery *s.*
32. 24. I will also send the poison of *s.* upon them
Jer. 8. 17. behold, I will send *s.* among you
Mat. 10. 16. be ye therefore wise as *s.* and harmless
23. 33. ye *s.* how can ye escape damnation of hell?
Mark 16. 18. they shall take up *s.* and if they drink
Luke 10. 19. I give unto you power to tread on *s.*
1 *Cor.* 10. 9. also tempted, and were destroyed of *s.*
Jam. 3. 7. for every kind of beasts and of *s.* is tamed
Rev. 9. 19. their tails were like unto *s.* and had heads

SERVANT

Is taken, I. *For a slave. The* Hebrews *had two sorts of* servants *or slaves. Some were strangers, either bought, or taken in the wars; and their masters kept them, exchanged them, sold them, or disposed of them as their own goods,* Lev. 25. 44, 45, &c. *The others were* Hebrew *slaves, who, being poor, sold themselves, or were sold to pay their debts: or were delivered up for* slaves *by their parents, in cases of necessity. This sort of* Hebrew *slaves continued in slavery but six years; then they might return to liberty again, and their masters could not retain them against their wills. If they would continue voluntarily with their masters, they were brought before the judges; there they made a declaration, that for this time they disclaimed the privilege of the law, had their ears bored with an awl, by applying them to the door-posts of their master; and after that they had no longer any power of recovering their liberty, except at the next year of jubilee,* Exod. 21. 2, 3, &c. Lev. 25. 40.

II. Servant *is also taken for a man that dedicates himself to the service of another, by the choice of his own will and inclination. Thus* Joshua *was the* servant *of* Moses, Elisha *of* Elijah, Gehazi *of* Elisha, *and the* Apostles *were servants of* Jesus Christ.

III. Servant *is put for the subjects of a prince. The* servants *of* Pharaoh, *the* servants *of* Saul, *and those of* David, *are their subjects in general, and their domestics in particular,* 2 Sam. 11. 11

| 12. 19. 1 Chron. 21. 3. In like manner also the Philistines, the Syrians, and several other nations, were servants of David; they obeyed him, they were his subjects, they paid him tribute, 2 Sam. 8. 6.

IV. Servants or slaves, as opposed to those that are free, and to the children of the promises, represent the Jews in contradistinction to the Christians; or those that were under the yoke of ceremonies, to those that are under the gospel dispensation. The Jews were the slaves represented by Hagar and Ishmael; the Christians are the children of liberty, represented by Sarah and by Isaac, Gal. 4. 3, 7, 22, 23, &c.

Servant, or servants of God. As all things are subject to the power and pleasure of God, and as none can resist his will or word; in this sense all creatures are God's servants, Psal. 119. 91. But more particularly by this name are called, [1] All faithful and godly persons, who being bought and redeemed from the bondage of sin and Satan, do serve and obey God in righteousness and holiness, Rom. 6. 22. [2] One that serveth and obeyeth God not only in a common profession of religion, but also in some particular function and calling: Thus the apostle Paul calls himself the servant of God, Rom. 1. 1. And in this sense, Christ Jesus is termed the Father's servant to execute his will as Mediator, in working man's redemption, Isa. 53. 11. My righteous servant. [3] One whom God makes use of as an instrument to effect and perform his will in the work of some particular mercy or judgment: Thus may Cyrus be called the servant of God, his shepherd and anointed, Isa. 44. 28. | 45. 1. And Nebuchadnezzar, Jer. 25. 9.

Moses is often, by way of eminence, called the servant of the Lord, Deut. 34. 5. Moses the servant of the Lord died, Josh. 1. 2. Moses my servant is dead. This title is often given him, not only to reflect honour upon him, but also to give authority to his laws and writings, in publishing of which he only acted as God's servant, in his name and stead: And likewise that the Israelites might not think of Moses above what was meet, remembering that he was not the Lord himself, but only his servant; and therefore not to be worshipped, nor yet too pertinaciously followed in all his institutions, when the Lord himself should come and abolish part of the Mosaical dispensation; it being but reasonable that the servant should give place to the Son and Heir, Heb. 3. 3, 5, 6.

Servant is also taken for a person of a servile ignoble condition and spirit, who is altogether unfit for places of dignity, Eccl. 10. 7. I have seen servants upon horses. The apostle Paul says, 1 Cor. 9. 19. I have made myself servant unto all, that I might gain the more. I have complied with their weaknesses and infirmities, so far as they were not sinful: I have denied myself in my liberty, and determined myself to that part in my actions, which I saw would most oblige, profit, and engage them to me so as to bring them in love with the gospel. The servant of sin, John 8. 34. is one who is in spiritual bondage, and under the power of sin and corruption.

Gen. 9. 25. Canaan, a s. of servants shall he be
24. 34. and he said, I am Abraham's s.
49. 15. Issachar bowed and became a s. to tribute
Exod. 21. 5. if the s. plainly say, I love my master
Deut. 5. 15. remember that thou wast a s. in Egypt
23. 15. thou shalt not deliver the s. that is escaped
1 Sam. 2. 13. priest's s. came and said, 15.
9. 27. Samuel said, bid the s. pass on before us
25. 41. let thy handmaid be a s. to wash the feet
29. 3. is not this David the s. of Saul the king?
30. 13. I am a young man s. to an Amalekite
2 Sam. 9. 2. of house of Saul, s. named Ziba, 19. 17.
16. 1. Ziba the s. of Mephibosheth met David
18. 29. when Joab sent the king's s. and me thy s.
1 Kings 11. 26. Jeroboam Solom. s. lift up his hand
12. 7. if thou wilt be a s. to this people this day
2 Kings 4. 24. she said to her s. drive and go forward
6. 15. when the s. of the man of God was risen
Neh. 2. 10. Tobiah the s. the Ammonite heard, 19.
Job 3. 19. and the s. is there free from his master
7. 2. as a s. earnestly desireth the shadow
41. 4. wilt thou take Leviathan for a s. for ever?
Psal. 105. 17. even Joseph, who was sold for a s.
Prov. 11. 29. the fool shall be s. to the wise of heart
12. 9. he that is despised and hath a s. is better
14. 35. the king's favour is toward a wise s.
17. 2. a wise s. shall have rule over a son that
19. 10. much less for a s. to rule over princes
22. 7. and the borrower is s. to the lender
29. 19. a s. will not be corrected with words
30. 10. accuse not s. to his master, lest he curse thee
22. the earth cannot bear a s. when he reigneth
Isa. 24. 2. as with the s. so with his master
49. 7. to a s. of rulers || Jer. 2. 14. is Israel a s.?
Dan. 6. 20. O Daniel, s. of the living God
10. 17. how can s. of my lord talk with my lord?
Mal. 1. 6. s. honoureth his master, if I be a master
Mat. 10. 24. nor the s. above his lord
25. it is enough for the s. to be as his lord
18. 26. the s. fell down and worshipped him
27. the lord of that s. was moved with compassion
32. O thou wicked s. I forgave thee all that debt
20. 27. and whosoever will be chief among you, let him be your s. 23. 11. Mark 10. 44.
24. 45. who then is a faithful and wise s. whom lord
46. blessed is that s. whom his lord, Luke 12. 43.
48. but if that evil s. shall say, Luke 12. 45.
50. the lord of that s. shall come, Luke 12. 46.
25. 21. well done, thou good and faithful s. enter thou into the joy of thy lord, 23. Luke 19. 17.
26. thou wicked and slothful s. Luke 19. 22.
30. cast the unprofitable s. into outer darkness
26. 51. Peter struck a s. of the high priest, and smote off his ear, Mark 14. 47. John 18. 10.
Mark 12. 2. and he sent to the husbandmen a s.
Luke 12. 47. that s. which knew his lord's will
14. 21. so that s. came and shewed his lord

Luke 17. 7. but which of you having a s. plowing
9. doth he thank that s.? I trow not
20. 10. and at the season he sent a s. 11.
John 8. 34. whoso committeth sin, is the s. of sin
35. the s. abideth not in the house for ever
13. 16. the s. is not greater than his lord, 15. 20.
15. 15. the s. knoweth not what his lord doeth
Rom. 1. 1. Paul a s. of Jesus Christ, an apostle
14. 4. who art thou that judgest another man's s.?
16. 1. I commend to you Phebe, a s. of the church
1 Cor. 7. 21. art thou called being a s.? care not for it
22. is called, being a s. is the Lord's free-man
9. 19. yet have I made myself a s. unto all
Gal. 1. 10. I should not be the s. of Christ
4. 1. as a child differeth nothing from a s.
7. wherefore thou art no more a s. but a son
Phil. 2. 7. he took upon him the form of a s.
Col. 4. 12. Epaphras, a s. of Christ, saluteth you
2 Tim. 2. 24. s. of Lord must not strive, but be gentle
Philem. 16. not now as a s. but above a s. a brother
Heb. 3. 5. Moses was faithful in his house as a s.
2 Pet. 1. 1. Simon Peter, a s. of Jesus Christ
Jude 1. Jude the s. of Jesus Christ to them sanctified
See David.

SERVANT, and SERVANTS of God.

Gen. 50. 17. forgive the s. of the God of thy father
1 Chr. 6. 49. as Moses the s. of God commanded
2 Chron. 24. 9. the collection, Moses the s. of G. said
Neh. 10. 29. to walk in God's law, which was given by Moses the s. of God to observe all commands
Dan. 6. 20. he said, O Daniel, s. of the living God
9. 11. written in the law of Moses the s. of God
Tit. 1. 1. a s. of God || Jam. 1. 1. James a s. of God
1 Pet. 2. 16. not using liberty, but as a s. of God
Rev. 7. 3. till we have sealed the s. of our God
15. 3. they sing the song of Moses the s. of God
See Hired.

His SERVANT.

Gen. 9. 26. and Canaan shall be his s. 27.
Exod. 14. 31. people believed Lord and his s. Moses
21. 20. if a man smite his s. and die under his hand
26. if he smite the eye of his s. that it perish
33. 11. but his s. Joshua departed not out of tabern.
Josh. 5. 14. Joshua said, what saith my L. to his s.?
9. 24. God commanded his s. Moses to give you
Judg. 7. 11. Gideon went down with Phurah his s.
19. 3. the Levite went, having his s. with him
9. when the man rose to depart, he and his s.
1 Sam. 19. 4. let not the king sin against his s.
22. 15. let not the king impute any thing to his s.
25. 39. the Lord hath kept his s. from evil
26. 18. why doth my Lord thus pursue after his s.?
19. let my lord the king hear the words of his s.
2 Sam. 9. 11. as my lord hath commanded his s.
14. 22. the king hath fulfilled the request of his s.
24. 21. wherefore is my lord come to his s.?
1 Kings 1. 51. swear, that he will not slay his s.
8. 56. which he promised by hand of Moses his s.
59. that he maintain the cause of his s. and Israel
14. 18. he spake by hand of his s. Ahijah, 15. 29.
19. 3. Elijah came and left his s. at Beer-sheba
2 Kings 9. 36. word which he spake by his s. Elijah
14. 25. the word which he spake by his s. Jonah
17. 3. Hoshea became his s. and gave him presents
24. 1. and Jehoiakim became his s. three years
1 Chron. 16. 13. O ye seed of Israel his s.
2 Chron. 32. 16. spake against his s. Hezekiah
Neh. 4. 22. let every one with his s. lodge within
Psal. 35. 27. Ld. hath pleasure in prosperity of his s.
105. 6. O ye seed of Abraham his s. he is our God
26. he sent Moses his s. and Aaron his chosen
42. for he remembered Abraham his s.
136. 22. gave even an heritage unto Israel his s.
Prov. 29. 21. that delicately bringeth up his s.
Isa. 44. 26. that confirmeth the word of his s.
48. 20. the Lord hath redeemed his s. Jacob
49. 5. Lord formed me from the womb to be his s.
50. 10. who that obeyeth the voice of his s.?
Jer. 34. 16. ye caused every man his s. to return
Mat. 8. 13. his s. was healed in the same hour
Luke 1. 54. he hath holpen his s. Israel in mercy
7. 3. beseeching that he would come and heal his s.
14. 17. and sent his s. at supper time to say
Rev. 1. 1. signified it by his angel unto his s. John
See Lord, Maid.

Man-SERVANT.

Exod. 20. 10. do no work, thou nor man-s. Deut. 5. 14.
17. not covet thy neighbour's man-s. Deut. 5. 21.
21. 27. and if he smite out his man-s. tooth
32. if the ox shall push a man-s. or maid-servant
Deut. 12. 18. must eat them, thou, and thy man-s.
16. 11. rejoice before Lord, thou and thy man-s.
14. rejoice in thy feast, thou and thy man-s.
Job 31. 13. if I did despise the cause of my man-s.
Jer. 34. 9. should let his man-s. go free, 10.

My SERVANT.

Gen. 26. 24. I will multiply thy seed for my s. sake
44. 10. he with whom it is found shall be my s. 17.
Num. 12. 7. my s. Moses is not so, who is faithful
8. why were ye not afraid to speak against my s.?
14. 24. but my s. Caleb had another spirit
Josh. 1. 2. Moses my s. is dead, therefore arise
1 Sam. 22. 8. that my son had stirred up my s.
27. 12. therefore he shall be my s. for ever
2 Sam. 19. 26. my lord, O king, my s. deceived me
2 Kings 5. 6. I have therewith sent Naaman my s.
21. 8. according to the law my s. Moses commanded
Job 1. 8. hast thou considered my s. Job? 2. 3.
19. 16. I called my s. and he gave me no answer
42. 7. ye have not spoken right, as my s. Job hath
8. go to my s. Job, he shall pray for you
Isa. 20. 3. like as my s. Isaiah hath walked naked
22. 20. in that day I will call my s. Eliakim
41. 8. but thou, Israel, art my s. fear not, 9.
42. 1. behold my s. whom I uphold, mine elect
19. who is blind but my s. that I sent?
43. 10. ye are witnesses and my s. I have chosen
44. 1. hear, O Jacob, my s. || 2. fear not, O Jac. my s.
21. remember those, for thou art my s. 49. 3.
45. 4. for Jacob my s. sake, and Israel mine elect
49. 6. it is a light thing thou shouldest be my s.
52. 13. behold my s. shall deal prudently, be very

Isa. 65. 8. so will I do for my s. sake not destr. them
Jer. 25. 9. Nebuchadnezzar my s. 27. 6. | 43. 10.
30. 10. fear thou not, O my s. Jacob, 46. 27, 28.
Ezek. 28. 25. land I have given my s. Jacob, 37. 25.
Hag. 2. 23. I will take thee, O Zerubbabel my s.
Zech. 3. 8. I will bring forth my s. the BRANCH
Mal. 4. 4. remember the law of Moses my s.
Mat. 8. 6. my s. lieth at home sick of the palsy
8. speak, and my s. shall be healed, Luke 7. 7.
9. and to my s. do this, and he doeth it, Luke 7. 8
12. 18. behold my s. whom I have chosen
John 12. 26. where I am, there shall also my s. be

Thy SERVANT.

Gen. 18. 3. pass not away, I pray thee, from thy s.
19. 19. behold, thy s. hath found grace, Neh. 2. 5.
24. 14. be she that thou hast appointed for thy s.
32. 10. not worthy of the mercies shewed to thy s.
18. then thou shalt say, they be thy s. Jacob's
33. 5. the children which God hath given thy s.
44. 31. grey hairs of thy s. our father to the grave
32. thy s. became surety for the lad to my father
Exod. 4. 10. nor since thou hast spoken unto thy s.
Lev. 25. 6. be meat for you, for thee, and for thy s.
Num. 11. 11. wherefore hast thou afflicted thy s.?
Deut. 3. 24. hast begun to shew thy s. thy greatness
15. 17. thro' his ear, and he shall be thy s. for ever
Judg. 7. 10. go thou down with Phurah thy s.
15. 18. this great deliverance into hand of thy s.
1 Sam. 3. 9. speak, Lord, for thy s. heareth, 10.
17. 36. thy s. slew both the lion and the bear
20. 7. if he say thus, thy s. shall have peace
22. 15. for thy s. knew nothing of all this
23. 11. O Lord God, I beseech thee, tell thy s.
28. 2. surely thou shalt know what thy s. can do
2 Sam. 7. 19. but thou hast spoken of thy s. house
20. for thou, Lord God, knowest thy s.
29. let it please thee to bless the house of thy s.
9. 6. Mephibosheth answered, behold thy s.
13. 35. the king's sons came, as thy s. said, so it is
15. 21. in death or life, even there will thy s. be
19. 27. he hath slandered thy s. unto my lord
24. 10. O Lord, take away the iniquity of thy s.
1 Kings 1. 26. but me, even me thy s. and Zadok the priest, and thy s. Solomon hath he not called
2. 38. as my lord the king said, so will thy s. do
3. 8. and thy s. is in the midst of thy people
9. give thy s. an understanding heart, to judge
8. 28. have thou respect to the prayer of thy s.
18. 12. but I thy s. fear the Lord from my youth
36. let it be known this day that I am thy s.
20. 32. thy s. Benhadad saith, I pray let me live
40. as thy s. was busy here and there, he was gone
2 Kings 4. 1. thy s. my husband is dead, and thou knowest thy s. did fear Lord, the creditor is come
5. 18. the Lord pardon thy s. in this thing
25. Gehazi said, thy s. went no whither
8. 13. but what, is thy s. a dog? || 16. 7. I am thy s.
Neh. 1. 11. prosper, I pray thee, thy s. this day
Psal. 19. 11. moreover, by them is thy s. warned
13. keep back thy s. from presumptuous sins
27. 9. put not thy s. away in anger, leave me not
31. 16. make thy face to shine upon thy s. save me
69. 17. hide not thy face from thy s. in trouble
86. 2. O my God, save thy s. that trusteth in thee
16. give thy strength unto thy s. and save me
89. 39. thou hast made void the covenant of thy s.
116. 16. truly I am thy s. 119. 125. | 143. 12.
Eccl. 7. 21. lest thou hear thy s. curse thee
Isa. 63. 17. return, for thy s. sake, the tribes
Dan. 9. 17. O God, hear the prayer of thy s.
Luke 2. 29. Lord, lettest thou thy s. depart in peace

SERVANTS.

Gen. 9. 25. Canaan, a servant of s. shall he be
27. 37. all his brethren have I given him for s.
Lev. 25. 55. to me the children of Israel are s.
Josh. 9. 11. go meet them, and say, we are your s.
1 Sam. 4. 9. that ye be not s. unto the Hebrews
17. 8. am not I a Philistine, and you s. to Saul?
9. if he kill me, then will we be your s. but if I kill him, then shall ye be our s. and serve us
22. 17. but the s. of the king would not put forth
25. 10. many s. break away from their masters
41. to wash the feet of the s. of my lord
2 Sam. 8. 2. so the Moabites became David's s.
6. the Syrians || 14. they of Edom bec. David's s.
9. 10. now Ziba had fifteen sons and twenty s.
12. all in the house of Ziba s. to Mephibosheth
10. 4. Hanun took David's s. and shaved the half of their beards, and cut garments, 1 Chr. 19. 4.
11. 11. the s. of my Lord are encamped in fields
1 Kings 2. 39. two of the s. of Shimei ran away
2 Kings 21. 23. the s. of Amon conspired against him
1 Chron. 21. 3. but are they not all my lord's s.?
2 Chr. 8. 9. of the children of Isr. Sol. made no s.
36. 20. carried to Babylon, where they were s.
Ezra 5. 11. we are the s. of the God of heaven
Neh. 5. 15. their s. bare rule over the people
9. 36. behold, we are s. this day, s. in the land
Job 1. 15. they have slain the s. with the sword, 17.
Psal. 123. 2. as the eyes of s. look to their masters
Eccl. 2. 7. I got me s. and had s. born in my house
10. 7. I have seen s. upon horses, and princes walking as s. upon the earth
Isa. 14. 2. Israel shall possess them for s. and handm.
Jer. 34. 11. caused the s. whom they had let go free to return, and brought them into subjection for s.
Lam. 5. 8. s. have ruled over us, none deliver
Dan. 3. 26. ye s. of the most high God, come forth
Joel 2. 29. upon the s. will I pour out my Spirit
Zech. 2. 9. behold, they shall be a spoil to their s.
Mat. 22. 13. then said the king to the s. bind him
25. 19. the lord of those s. cometh and reckoneth
Mark 14. 65. the s. did strike Jesus with their hands
Luke 12. 37. blessed are those s. found watching, 38.
17. 10. say, are unprofitable s. have done our duty
John 15. 15. henceforth I call you not s. for servant
Acts 16. 17. these men are s. of the most high God
Rom. 6. 16. to whom ye yield yourselves s. to obey
17. God be thanked, that ye were the s. of sin
18. made free, ye became the s. of righteousness
19. as ye have yielded your members s. to sin
20. s. of sin, ye were free from righteousness

Rom. 6. 22. being free from sin, and become s. to G.
1 Cor. 7. 23. ye are bought, be not ye the s. of men
2 Cor. 4. 5. and ourselves your s. for Jesus' sake
Eph. 6. 5. s. be obedient to your masters according
to the flesh, Col. 3. 22. Tit. 2. 9. 1 Pet. 2. 18.
6. not with eye-service, but as the s. of Christ
Phil. 1. 1. Paul and Timotheus the s. of Christ
Col. 4. 1. masters, give your s. what is just
1 Tim. 6. 1. let as many s. as are under the yoke
1 Pet. 2. 16. not using liberty, but as the s. of God
2 Pet. 2. 19. they themselves are the s. of corruption
Rev. 7. 3. till we have sealed the s. of our God
See Hired.

His SERVANTS.

Gen. 40. 20. Pharaoh made a feast unto all his s.
Exod. 9. 20. Pharaoh made his s. flee into houses
12. 30. Pharaoh rose in the night, he and his s.
Num. 22. 22. Balaam riding, and his two s. with him
Deut. 32. 36. Lord shall repent himself for his s.
43. for he will avenge the blood of his s.
1 Sam. 8. 14. take the best, and give to his s. 15.
17. ye will take the tenth, ye shall be his s.
19. 1. Saul spake to all his s. to kill David
22. 6. and all his s. were standing about him
2 Kings 5. 13. his s. came near, and spake unto him
1 Chron. 19. 3. are not his s. come to thee to search?
2 Chron. 12. 8. nevertheless, they shall be his s.
32. 16. his s. spake yet more against the Lord G.
Neh. 2. 20. therefore we his s. will arise and build
Job 4. 18. behold, he put no trust in his s. and angels
Psal. 69. 36. the seed also of his s. shall inherit it
105. 25. turned their heart, to deal subt. with his s.
135. 14. he will repent himself concerning his s.
Prov. 22. 12 if hearken to lies, all his s. are wicked
Isa. 56. 6. to love the name of the Lord, to be his s.
65. 15. the Lord shall call his s. by another name
66. 14. hand of the Lord be known toward his s.
Jer. 22. 4. riding in chariots, on horses, he and his s.
36. 31. punish him, his seed and his s. for iniquity
Ezek. 46. 17. if the prince give a gift to his s.
Dan. 3. 28. and delivered his s. that trusted in him
Mat. 18. 23. king who would take account of his s.
21. 34. he sent his s. to the husbandmen to receive
Luke 19. 13. he called his ten s. and delivered them
Rom. 6. 16. his s. ye are to whom ye obey
Rev. 1. 1. to shew his s. things that must come, 22. 6.
19. 2. hath avenged blood of his s. at her hand
5. praise God, all ye his s. and ye that fear him
22. 3. throne shall be in it, and his s. shall serve him
See Lord, Maid, Men.

My SERVANTS.

Lev. 25. 42. they are my s. whom I brought out, 55.
1 Sam. 21. 2. I have appointed my s. such a place
1 Kings 5. 6. my s. shall be with thy serv. 2 Chr. 2. 8.
20. 6. yet I will send my s. unto thee to-morrow
22. 49. let my s. go with thy serv. in the ships, but
2 Kings 9. 7. that I may avenge the blood of my s.
Neh. 4. 16. the half of my s. wrought in the work
23. neither I nor my s. put off our clothes
5. 10. I and my s. might exact of them money, corn
16. all my s. were gathered thither to the work
13. 19. and some of my s. set I at the gates
Isa. 65. 9. mine elect and my s. shall dwell there
13. my s. shall eat || 14. my s. shall sing for joy
Jer. 7. 25. I have even sent to you all my s. 44. 4.
John 18. 36. if kingd. of world, then would my s. fight
Acts 2. 18. on my s. I will pour out of my Spirit
Rev. 2. 20 calls herself a prophetess, to seduce my s.
See Prophets.

Thy SERVANTS.

Gen. 42. 11. we are true men, thy s. are no spies
44. 16. God hath found out the iniquity of thy s.
47. 3. thy s. are shepherds, both we and our fathers
50. 18. his brethren said, behold, we be thy s.
Exod. 5. 15. wheref. dealest thou thus with thy s.?
11. 8. these thy s. shall bow down themsel. to me
32. 13. remember Abr. and Israel thy s. Deut. 9. 27.
Num. 32. 25. thy s. will do as my lord command, 31.
Josh. 9. 8. Gibeonites said to Joshua, we are thy s.
10. 6. saying, slack not thy hand from thy s.
1 Sam. 12. 19. pray for thy s. to the Lord thy God
22. 14. who is so faithful among all thy s. as David?
2 Sam. 19. 7. and speak comfortably to thy s.
14. they sent this word, return thou and all thy s.
1 Kings 2. 39. they told Shimei, thy s. be in Gath
5. 6. my servants shall be with thy s. 2 Chr. 2. 8.
8. 23. who keepest covenant and mercy with thy s.
32. hear thou and judge thy s. 2 Chron. 6. 23.
10. 8. happy are these thy s. 2 Chron. 9. 7.
12. 7. they will be thy s. for ever, 2 Chron. 10. 7
2 Kings 6. 3. one said, be content, and go with thy s.
Neh. 1. 10. now these are thy s. and thy people
11. let thine ear be attentive to prayer of thy s.
Psal. 79. 2. the bodies of thy s. have they given
10. by the revenging of the blood of thy s. shed
89. 50. remember, Lord, the reproach of thy s.
90. 13. let it repent thee concerning thy s.
16. let thy work appear to thy s. and thy glory
102. 14. for thy s. take pleasure in her stones
28. children of thy s. shall continue, their seed
119. 91. they continue this day, for all are thy s.
Isa. 37. 24. by thy s. hast thou reproached the Ld.
Dan. 1. 12. prove thy s. I beseech thee, ten days
13. and as thou seest, deal with thy s.
Acts 4. 29. grant unto thy s. that with all boldness
See Women.

SERVE.

Gen. 15. 13. thy seed shall s. them 400 years
14. that nation whom they shall s. will I judge
25. 23. and the elder shall s. the younger
27. 29. let people s. thee, nations bow down to thee
40. by thy sword shalt thou live, and s. brother
29. 15. shouldst thou therefore s. me for nought?
18. I will s. thee seven years for Rachel
27. thou shalt s. with me seven other years
Exod. 1. 13. they made Israel to s. with rigour
3. 12. ye shall s. God upon this mountain
4. 23. I say, let my son go, that he may s. me
7. 16. let my people go, that they may s. me in
the wilderness, 8. 1, 20. | 9. 1, 13. | 10. 3.
14. 12. saying, let us alone, that we may s. Egyptians, for it had been better for us to s. them
Exod. 20. 5. not bow down to them, nor s. Deut. 5. 9.
21. 2. an Hebrew servant, six years he shall s.
6. shall bore his ear, and he shall s. him for ever
Lev. 25. 39. shalt not compel him to s. as bond-serv.
40. he shall s. thee unto the year of Jubilee
Num. 4. 24. the family of the Gershonites to s.
26. shall bear all made for them, so shall they s.
8. 25. from the age of fifty they shall s. no more
18. 21. the tenth to Levi, for their service they s.
Deut. 4. 19. thou shouldest be driven to s. them
6. 13. thou shalt fear the Lord thy G. and s. him,
10. 12, 20. | 11. 13. | 13. 4. Josh. 22. 5. | 24.
14, 15. 1 Sam. 7. 3. | 12. 14, 20, 24.
15. 12. if brother be sold to thee, and s. six years
20. 11. shall be tributaries to thee, and shall s. thee
28. 48. therefore shalt thou s. thine enemies
Josh. 24. 15. choose you this day whom you will s.
Judg. 9. 28. should s. Shechem, should s. Hamor
38. who is Abimelech, that we should s. him?
1 Sam. 10. 7. do thou as occasion shall s. thee
11. 1. make covenant with us, and we will s. thee
12. 10. but now deliver us, and we will s. thee
17. 9. then shall ye be our servants, and s. us
2 Sam. 16. 19. whom should I s.? should I not s.
22. 44. a people I knew not shall s. me, Ps. 18. 43.
1 Kings 12. 4. now therefore make thou this heavy
yoke lighter, and we will s. thee, 2 Chron. 10. 4.
2 Kings 10. 18. but Jehu shall s. Baal much
25. 24. dwell in the land, and s. the king of Baby-
lon, Jer. 27. 11, 12, 17. | 28. 14. | 40. 9.
1 Chron. 28. 9. and s. him with a perfect heart
2 Chron. 29. 11. the Lord hath chosen you to s. him
34. 33. Josiah made all present to s. the Ld. God
Job 21. 15. what Almighty, that we should s. him?
36. 11. if they obey and s. him, they shall spend
39. 9. will the unicorn be willing to s. thee?
Psal. 22. 30. a seed shall s. him, and be accounted
72. 11. yea, all kings, all nations shall s. him
97. 7. confounded be all they that s. graven images
101. 6. walketh in a perfect way, he shall s. me
Isa. 14. 3. bondage wherein thou wast made to s.
19. 23. the Egyptians shall s. with the Assyrians
43. 23. I have not caused thee to s. with offering
24. but thou hast made me to s. with thy sins
56. 6. join themselves to the Lord to s. him
60. 12. the nation that will not s. thee shall perish
Jer. 5. 19. so shall ye s. strangers in land not yours
17. 4. I will cause thee to s. thine enemies
25. 11. these nations shall s. the king of Babylon
14. many nations shall s. themselves, 27. 7.
27. 6. beasts of the field have I given to s. him
8. the nation that will not s. king of Babylon, 13.
9. the prophets that say ye shall not s. 14.
30. 8. strangers shall no more s. themselves of him
34. 9. that none should s. himself of them, 10.
40. 9. saying, fear not to s. the Chaldeans; dwell
10. as for me, behold, I will s. the Chaldeans
Ezek. 20. 32. families of the countries to s. wood
39. O house of Isr. go s. ye every one his idols
40. Israel all of them in the land shall s. me
29. 18. his army s. a great service against Tyrus
48. 18. increase for food to them that s. the city
19. that s. the city, shall s. it out of all tribes
Dan. 3. 17. our God whom we s. is able to deliver
28. they might not s. any, except their own God
7. 14. people, nations, and languages, should s. him
27. and all dominions shall s. and obey him
Zeph. 3. 9. call on Lord, to s. him with one consent
Mal. 3. 14. ye have said it is in vain to s. God
Mat. 4. 10. him only shalt thou s. Luke 4. 8.
6. 24. no man can s. two masters; ye cannot s. God
and mammon, Luke 16. 13.
Luke 1. 74. that we being delivered, might s. him
10. 40. that my sister hath left me to s. alone
12. 37. I say, he will come forth and s. them
15. 29. lo, these many years do I s. thee
17. 8. will not rather say, gird thyself and s. me
22. 26. and he that is chief, as he that doth s.
John 12. 26. if any man s. me, let him follow me
Acts 6. 2. that we leave word of God, and s. tables
7. 7. shall they come forth and s. me in this place
27. 23. stood by me the angel of God whom I s.
Rom. 1. 9. for God is my witness, whom I s. with
my spirit in gospel of his Son, without ceasing
6. 6. that henceforth we should not s. sin
7. 6. that we should s. in newness of spirit, not in
25. so then, with the mind I s. the law of God
9. 12. it was said, the elder shall s. the younger
16. 18. for they that are such s. not our Lord
Gal. 5. 13. but by love s. one another
Col. 3. 24. receive reward, for ye s. the Lord Christ
1 Thess. 1. 9. ye turned from idols to s. living God
2 Tim. 1. 3. I thank G. whom I s. from my fathers
Heb. 8. 5. who s. to the example of heavenly things
9. 14. purge from dead works to s. the living God
12. 28. grace, whereby we may s. God acceptably
13. 10. no right to eat, which s. the tabernacle
Rev. 7. 15. they s. him day and night in his temple
22. 3. of the Lamb, and his servants shall s. him

SERVE, joined with gods.

Exod. 23. 24. shalt not s. their gods, Deut. 6. 14. | 28.
14. Josh. 23. 7. 2 Kings 17. 35. Jer. 25. 6. | 35. 15.
33. if thou s. their gods, it will be a snare to thee
Deut. 4. 28. there ye shall s. gods, the work of men's
hands, wood, 28. 36, 64. Jer. 16. 13.
7. 4. will turn, that they may s. other gods, 31. 20.
8. 19. if thou s. other gods, and worship them, 11.
16 | 30. 17. Josh. 24. 20. 2 Chron. 7. 19.
12. 30. how do these nations s. their gods?
13. 2. let us go after and s. other gods, 6. 13.
29. 18. turneth away from God to s. other gods
Josh. 24. 16. God forbid we should s. other gods
Judg. 2. 19. they corrupted themselves more than
their fathers to s. other gods, Jer. 11. 10. | 13. 10.
1 Sam. 26. 19. driven me, saying, go s. other gods
Jer. 44. 3. provoke me to anger, to s. other gods
Dan. 3. 12. they s. not thy gods, nor worship image
14. do ye not s. my gods? || 18. we will not s. thy g.
See Lord.

SERVED.

Gen. 14. 4. twelve years they s. Chedorlaomer
29. 20. Jacob s. seven years for Rachel, 30.
Gen. 30. 26. give me my children for whom I s. thee
29. he said, thou knowest how I have s. thee
31. 6. with all my power I have s. your father
41. I s. thee 14 years for thy two daughters
Deut. 12. 2. wherein the nations s. their gods
17. 3. hath gone and s. other gods, and worshipped
them, the sun or moon, 29. 26. Josh. 23. 16.
Josh. 24. 2. your fathers s. other gods, 15.
14. put away the gods which your fathers s.
31. and Israel s. Lord all the days of Joshua, and
of the elders that overlived Joshua, Judg. 2. 7.
Judg. 2. 11. Israel s. Baalim, 13. | 3. 7. | 10. 6, 10.
3. 6. they gave daughters to sons, and s. their gods
8. Israel s. Chushan-rishathaim eight years
14. so Israel s. Eglon king of Moab 18 years
8. 1. men of Ephr. said, why hast thou s. us thus?
10. 13. ye have forsaken me, and s. other gods
16. they put away gods, s. Lord 1 Sam. 7. 4.
2 Sam. 10. 19. the Syrians made peace and s. Israel
16. 19. as I have s. in thy father's presence
1 Kings 4. 21. they brought presents and s. Solomon
9. 9. because they s. other gods, 2 Chron. 7. 22.
16. 31. Ahab s. Baal || 22. 53. Ahaziah s. Baal
2 Kings 10. 18. Jehu said, Ahab s. Baal a little
18. 7. Hezekiah s. not the king of Assyria
21. 3. Manasseh s. host of heaven, 2 Chron. 33. 3.
21. Amon s. idols his father s. 2 Chron. 33. 22.
2 Chron. 24. 18. princes of Judah s. groves and idols
Neh. 9. 35. they have not s. thee in their kingdom
Psal. 106. 36. and they s. their idols, which were
137. 8. that rewardeth thee as thou hast s. us
Eccl. 5. 9. the king himself is s. by the field
Jer. 5. 19. as ye have s. strange gods in your land
8. 2. before the sun and moon, whom they have s.
16. 11. have walked after other gods and s. them
22. 9. they worshipped other gods and s. them
34. 14. when he hath s. thee six years, let him go
Ezek. 29. 18. for the service which he had s. 20.
34. 27. delivered out of the hand of those that s.
Hos. 12. 12. Israel s. for a wife, he kept sheep
Luke 2. 37. Anna s. God night and day in the temple
John 12. 2. they made him a supper, and Martha s.
Acts 13. 36. after David had s. his generation
Rom. 1. 25. who worshipped and s. the creature
Phil. 2. 22. he hath s. with me in the gospel

SERVEDST.

Deut. 28. 47. thou s. not the Lord with gladness

SERVEST.

Dan. 6. 16. thy God whom thou s. will deliver
20. is thy God whom thou s. able to deliver thee

SERVETH.

Num. 3. 36. under the charge of Merari all that s.
Mal. 3. 17. as a man spareth his son that s. him
18. between him that s. God, and him that s. not
Luke 22. 27. whether greater, he that sitteth at meat
or he that s.? but I am among you as one that s.
Rom. 14. 18. he that in these things s. Christ is
1 Cor. 14. 22. prophecy s. not them that believe not
Gal. 3. 19. wherefore then s. the law? it was added

SERVICE.

Gen. 29. 27. for the s. that thou shalt serve with me
30. 26. thou knowest the s. which I have done
Exod. 1. 14. in all manner of s. in field; all their s.
wherein they made them serve was with rigour
12. 25. come to land, ye shall keep this s. 13. 5.
26. children shall say, what mean you by this s.?
27. 19. all vessels in all the s. thereof be of brass
31. 10. may make the clothes of the s. 35. 19.
36. 5. people bring more than enough for the s.
Num. 3. 7. tribe of Levi to do s. of tabernacle, 8.
26. the charge of the Gershonites for the s.
31. s. of sanctuary the charge of Kohathites, 4. 4.
4. 19. Aaron and sons shall appoint them to the s.
23. all that enter in to perform the s. to do work
24. this is the s. of the Gershonites, 27. 28.
30. the s. of the sons of Merari, 33. 43.
7. 5. that they may do the s. of the tabernacle
8. 11. the Levites may execute the s. of the Lord
24. they shall go in to wait upon s. of tabernacle
25. from 50 years shall cease waiting on the s.
16. 9. a small thing to bring you to do the s.
18. 4. the Levites be joined to thee for all the s.
6. the Levites are given as a gift to do the s.
21. have given all tenth in Israel for their s. 31.
Josh. 22. 27. be a witness, that we might do the s.
1 Kings 12. 4. make thou the grievous s. lighter
1 Chron. 6. 31. whom David set over the s.
9. 13. very able men for the work of the s. 26. 8.
24. 3. David distributed them in their s.
28. 13. the Levites for all the work of the s.
21. the priests shall be with thee for all the s.
29. 5. who is willing to consecrate his s. to Lord?
7. and gave for the s. of house of God, gold, silver
2 Chron. 8. 14. the courses of the priests to their s.
12. 8. they may know my s. and s. of the kingdoms
24. 12. and gave the money to such as did the s.
29. 35. so the s. of the house was set in order
31. 2. appointed every man according to his s.
21. in every work that he began in the s.
35. 2. encouraged them to the s. of the Lord
10. so the s. of the Lord was prepared, 16.
Ezra 6. 18. in their courses, for the s. of God, 7. 19.
Neh. 10. 32. with the third part of a shekel for s.
Psal. 104. 14. causeth herb to grow for the s. of man
Jer. 22. 13. that useth neighbour's s. without wages
Ezek. 29. 18. caused his army to serve a great s.
44. 14. keepers of the charge of house for all the s.
John 16. 2. who killeth you will think he doth God s.
Rom. 9. 4. to whom pertaineth the s. of God
12. 1. sacrifice to God, which is your reasonable s.
15. 31. that my s. may be accepted of the saints
2 Cor. 9. 12. for the administration of this s. not only
11. 8. taking wages of them to do you s.
Gal. 4. 8. did s. to them who by nature are no gods
Eph. 6. 7. with good-will doing s. as to the Lord
Phil. 2. 17. if I be offered upon the s. of your faith
30. to supply your lack of s. toward me
1 Tim. 6. 2. rather do s. because they are beloved
Heb. 9. 1. first covenant had ordinances of divine s.
6. the priests accomplishing the s. of God
9. that could not make him that did the s. perfect
Rev. 2. 19. I know thy works, and charity, and s.

Bond-SERVICE.

1 *Kings* 9. 21. Solomon did levy a tribute of *bond-s.*

Eye-SERVICE.

Eph. 6. 6. not with *eye-s.* as men-pleasers, but as ser.

SERVILE.

Lev. 23. 7. ye shall do no *s.* work, 8. 21, 25, 35, 36.
Num. 28. 18, 25, 26. | 29. 1, 12, 35.

SERVING.

Exod. 14. 5. that we have let Israel go from *s.* us
Deut. 15. 18. worth a double hired servant in *s.* thee
Luke 10. 40. Martha was cumbered about much *s.*
Acts 20. 19. *s.* the Lord with all humility of mind
26. 7. our twelve tribes instantly *s.* G. day and night
Rom. 12. 11. not slothful, fervent in spirit, *s.* Lord
Tit. 3. 3. were sometimes foolish, *s.* divers lusts

SERVITOR.

2 *Kings* 4. 43. *s.* said, shall I set this before 100 men?

SERVITUDE.

2 *Chr.* 10. 4. ease somewhat grievous *s.* of thy father
Lam. 1. 3. Judah is gone because of great *s.*

SET.

Gen. 1. 17. God *s.* the stars in firmament of heaven
4. 15. and the Lord *s.* a mark upon Cain
6. 16. door of the ark shalt *s.* in the side thereof
9. 13. I do *s.* my bow in the cloud for a token
18. 8. Abraham *s.* calf before them, they did eat
19. 16. the angels *s.* Lot without the city Sodom
31. 37. *s.* it before my brethren and thy brethren
41. 33. let Pharaoh *s.* him over the land of Egypt
41. I have *s.* thee over all the land of Egypt
43. 9. if I bring him not, and *s.* him before thee
48. 20. Jacob *s.* Ephraim before Manasseh
Exod. 7. 23. nor did he *s.* his heart to this also
9. † 21. he that *s.* not his heart to the word of Lord
13. 12. *s.* apart to Lord all that open the matrix
19. 12. *s.* bounds, 23. || 26. 35. *s.* the table without
21. 1. judgments which thou shalt *s.* before them
23. 31. I will *s.* thy bounds from the Red sea
25. 30. thou shalt *s.* on table shew bread before me
40. 4. *s.* in order things that are to be *s.* in order
5. *s.* altar of gold || 6. *s.* altar of burnt offering
7. *s.* the laver || 20. he *s.* the staves || 23. the bread
Lev. 24. 8. every sabb. he shall *s.* it in order before L.
26. 11. I will *s.* my tabernacle among you
Num. 2. 9. camp of Judah, these shall first *s.* forth
4. 15. as the camp is to *s.* forward
5. 16. the priest shall *s.* her before the Lord
8. 13. thou shalt *s.* the Levites before Aaron
10. 17. *s.* forward, bearing the tabernacle
21. 8. Lord said, *s.* the fiery serpent upon a pole
27. 16. let the Lord *s.* a man over the congregation
Deut. 1. 8. I have *s.* the land before you, 21.
4. 8. as all this law which I *s.* before you, 44.
7. 7. Ld. did not *s.* his love on you, because more
11. 26. I *s.* before you a blessing and a curse
32. to do all the judgments which I *s.* before you
14. 24. choose to *s.* his name there, *Neh.* 1. 9.
17. 14. and shalt say, I will *s.* a king over me
15. in any wise shalt *s.* him the Lord shall choose
19. 14. land-mark, which they of old time have *s.*
26. 4. *s.* down the basket before the altar, 10.
28. 1. the Lord thy God will *s.* thee on high
56. would not *s.* sole of her foot on the ground
30. 15. I have *s.* before you life and death, 19.
32. 8. he *s.* bounds of the people by the numbers
46. *s.* your hearts unto all the words I testify
Josh. 24. 25. he *s.* them a statute in Shechem
Judg. 6. 18. till I bring and *s.* my present before thee
7. 5. that lappeth, him shalt thou *s.* by himself
19. and they had but newly *s.* the watch
22. Lord *s.* every man's sword against his fellow
1 *Sam.* 2. 8. he raiseth up poor out of the dust, to *s.*
them among princes; he hath *s.* world on them
4. † 20. she answered not, nor *s.* her heart
5. 2. the Philistines *s.* the ark of God by Dagon
9. 20. as for thine asses, *s.* not thy mind on them
10. 19. ye have said, nay, but *s.* a king over us
12. 13. the Lord hath *s.* a king over you
13. † 21. yet they had a file to *s.* the goads
17. 2. Saul and Israel *s.* the battle in array, 8.
2 *Sam.* 10. 17. 1 *Kings* 20. 12. 1 *Chron.* 19. 17.
2 *Sam.* 6. 3. they *s.* the ark of God on a new cart
11. 15. *s.* Uriah in forefront of the hottest battle
19. 28. yet didst thou *s.* thy servant at thy table
1 *Kings* 2. 15. that all Israel *s.* their faces on me
5. 5. son, whom I will *s.* on throne shall build
12. 29. he *s.* the one in Beth-el, the other in Dan
21. 9. and *s.* Naboth on high among the people, 12.
2 *Kings* 4. 4. thou shalt *s.* aside that which is full
10. let us *s.* for him there a bed and a table
38. *s.* on the great pot, and seethe pottage
43. what, should I *s.* this before an hundred men?
6. 22. *s.* bread and water before them to eat and dr.
20. 1. *s.* thine house in order, for shalt die, *Isa.* 38. 1.
1 *Chron.* 16. 1. they *s.* the ark in midst of the tent
22. 19. *s.* your heart to seek the Lord your God
29. 3. because I *s.* my affection to house of God
2 *Chron.* 11. 16. *s.* their hearts to seek the Lord
20. 3. he feared, and *s.* himself to seek the Lord
24. 13. they *s.* the house of God in his state
35. 2. Josiah *s.* the priests in their charges
Ezra 6. 18. they *s.* the priests in their divisions
Neh. 2. 6. it pleased the king, and I *s.* him a time
4. 9. we *s.* a watch against them day and night
9. 37. it yieldeth much increase to kings *s.* over us
12. † 47. they *s.* apart holy things to the Levites
13. 11. I gathered and *s.* them in their place
Job 1. † 8. hast thou *s.* thy heart on my servant?
6. 4. the terrors of God *s.* themselves against me
7. 17. that thou shouldst *s.* thine heart upon him
20. why hast thou *s.* me as a mark against thee?
9. 19. who shall *s.* me a time to plead?
19. 8. and he hath *s.* darkness in my paths
30. 1. have disdained to *s.* with the dogs of my flock
13. they *s.* forward my calamity, have no helper
33. 5. *s.* thy words in order before me, stand up
34. 14. if he *s.* his heart upon man, if he gather
24. break mighty men and *s.* others in their stead
38. 33. canst thou *s.* dominion thereof in earth?
Psal. 2. 2. the kings of the earth *s.* themselves
6. yet have I *s.* my king on my holy hill of Zion
3. 6. I will not be afraid if 10,000 *s.* themselves

Psal. 4. 3. the Lord hath *s.* apart him that is godly
8. 1. who hast *s.* thy glory above the heavens
12. 5. I will *s.* him in safety from him that puffeth
16. 8. I have *s.* the Lord always before me
19. 4. in them hath he *s.* a tabernacle for the sun
21. † 6. for thou hast *s.* him to be blessings for ever
† 12. therefore thou shalt *s.* him as a butt
31. 8. thou hast *s.* my feet in a large room
40. 2. brought me up, and *s.* my feet upon a rock
48. † 13. *s.* your heart to her bulwarks
50. 21. I will *s.* them in order before thine eyes
54. 3. they have not *s.* God before them
59. † 1. *s.* me on high from such as rise against me
62. 10. if riches, *s.* not your heart upon them
73. 18. surely thou didst *s.* them in slippery places
74. 17. thou hast *s.* all the borders of the earth
78. 7. that they might *s.* their hope in God
8. a generation that *s.* not their heart aright
† 43. how he had *s.* his signs in Egypt
85. 13. and shall *s.* us in the way of his steps
86. 14. violent men have not *s.* thee before them
90. 8. thou hast *s.* our iniquities before thee
91. 14. because he hath *s.* his love upon me, therefore I will deliver him and *s.* him on high
101. 3. I will *s.* no wicked thing before my eyes
104. 9. hast *s.* bound that they may not pass over
109. 6. *s.* thou a wicked man over him, let Satan
113. 8. that he may *s.* him with princes, even with
118. 5. Lord answered, and *s.* me in a large place
132. 11. fruit of the body will I *s.* upon thy throne
140. 5. the proud have *s.* gins for me
141. 3. *s.* a watch, O Lord, before my mouth
Prov. 1. 25. ye have *s.* at nought all my counsel
22. 28. the land-mark which thy fathers have *s.*
23. 5. wilt thou *s.* thine eyes on that which is not?
24. † 32. then I saw, and *s.* mine heart upon it
25. † 6. *s.* not out thy glory in presence of the king
27. † 23. and *s.* thy heart to thy herds
29. † 8. scornful men *s.* a city on fire
Eccl. 3. 11. also he hath *s.* the world in their heart
7. 14. God hath *s.* the one against the other
12. 9. he sought out, and *s.* in order many proverbs
Cant. 8. 6. *s.* me as a seal upon thine heart
Isa. 7. 6. let us *s.* a king in midst of it, son of Tabeal
14. 1. the Lord will *s.* them in their own land
17. 10. and thou shalt *s.* it with strange slips
19. 2. I will *s.* Egyptians against Egyptians
21. 6. go *s.* a watchman, let him declare what
22. 7. shall *s.* themselves in array at the gate
27. 4. who would *s.* briers and thorns against me
41. 19. I will *s.* in the desert, the fir-tree and pine
42. 4. till he have *s.* judgment in the earth
44. 7. who as I, shall *s.* it in order for me?
46. 7. they carry him, and *s.* him in his place
57. 7. on a high mountain hast thou *s.* thy bed
62. 6. I have *s.* watchmen on thy walls, *Jer.* 6. 17.
66. 19. and I will *s.* a sign among them, and send
Jer. 1. 10. see, I have *s.* thee over the nations
5. 26. lay wait, they *s.* a trap, they catch men
6. 27. I have *s.* thee for a tower and a fortress
7. 12. the place where I *s.* my name at the first
30. they *s.* their abominations in the house
9. 13. have forsaken my law which I *s.* before them
21. 8. I *s.* before you the way of life and death
24. 6. for I will *s.* mine eyes on them for good
26. 4. to walk in my law, which I *s.* before you
34. 16. his servant, whom he had *s.* at liberty
35. 5. I *s.* pots of wine before sons of Rechabites
38. 22. women said, thy friends have *s.* thee on
39. † 12. *s.* thine eyes on him, and do him no harm
40. † 4. come, and I will *s.* mine eyes upon thee
44. 10. nor walked in statutes which I *s.* before you
Lam. 3. 6. hath *s.* me in dark places, as dead of old
12. he hath *s.* me as a mark for the arrow
Ezek. 5. 5. I have *s.* it in the midst of the nations
7. 20. therefore have I *s.* it far from them
9. 4. *s.* a mark on the foreheads of men that sigh
12. 6. for I have *s.* thee for a sign unto Israel
16. 18. thou hast *s.* my oil before thy images, 19.
17. 22. I will take off highest branch, I will *s.* it
19. 8. then nations *s.* against him on every side
22. 7. in thee have they *s.* light by father and moth.
24. 2. king of Babylon *s.* himself against Jerusal.
3. *s.* on a pot, *s.* it on, and also pour water
7. her blood, she *s.* it upon the top of a rock, 8.
25. when I take them whereon they *s.* their minds
26. 20. I shall *s.* glory in the land of the living
27. 10. they of Persia *s.* forth thy comeliness
28. 2. tho' thou *s.* thy heart as the heart of God
14. art anointed cherub, and I have *s.* thee so
32. 25. they *s.* her a bed in the midst of her slain
37. 26. I will *s.* my sanctuary in midst of them
39. 21. I will *s.* my glory among the heathen
40. 4. *s.* thy heart upon all that I shall shew thee
44. 8. have *s.* keepers of my charge in my sanctuary
Dan. 6. 3. king thought to *s.* him over the realm
14. he *s.* his heart on Daniel to deliver him
9. 10. to walk in his laws which he *s.* before us
10. 12. thou didst *s.* thine heart to understand
Hos. 2. 3. lest I *s.* her as in day that she was born
4. 8. and they *s.* their heart on their iniquity
6. 11. O Judah, he hath *s.* an harvest for thee
11. 8. how shall I *s.* thee as Zeboim?
Amos 8. 5. sabb. be gone, that we may *s.* forth wheat
9. 4. I will *s.* mine eyes upon them for evil, not for
Obad. 4. though thou *s.* thy nest among the stars
Hab. 2. 9. that he may *s.* his nest on high, be deliv.
Zeph. 3. † 19. and I will *s.* them for a praise
Hag. 1. † 5. *s.* your heart on your ways, saith Lord
Zech. 3. 5. I said, let them *s.* a fair mitre on his head
5. 11. it shall be *s.* there upon her own base
6. 11. make crowns, and *s.* them on head of Josh.
8. 10. I *s.* all men, every one against his neighbour
Mat. 10. 35. I am come to *s.* a man at variance
25. 33. he shall *s.* the sheep on his right hand
Mark 12. 1. and *s.* an hedge about it, and digged
Luke 4. 18. to *s.* at liberty them that are bruised
10. 34. and *s.* him on his own beast and brought
11. 6. friend come, I have nothing to *s.* before
23. 11. Herod with men of war, *s.* him at nought
John 2. 10. every man doth *s.* forth good wine
3. 33. he hath *s.* to his seal, that God is true

Acts 7. 5. no not so much as to *s.* his foot on
13. 9. then Paul *s.* his eyes on him and said
47. I have *s.* thee to be a light to the Gentiles
18. 10. no man shall *s.* on thee to hurt thee
Rom. 3. 25. whom God *s.* forth to be a propitiation
14. 10. why dost thou *s.* at nought thy brother?
1 *Cor.* 4. 9. God hath *s.* forth us the apostles last
6. 4. *s.* them to judge who are least esteemed in ch.
12. 18. now God hath *s.* the members in the body
28. God hath *s.* some in the church, first apostles
Eph. 1. 20. when he *s.* him at his own right hand
Col. 3. 2. *s.* your affect. on things above, not on earth
Heb. 2. 7. thou didst *s.* him over work of thy hands
Rev. 3. 8. I have *s.* before thee an open door
20. 3. and he shut him up, and *s.* a seal upon him

SET *up.*

Gen. 28. 18. Jacob took the stone and *s.* it *up* for a
pillar, and poured oil on it, 22. | 31. 45. | 35. 14.
Exod. 40. 2. shalt *s. up* the tabernacle of the tent
8. thou shalt *s. up* the court || 18. boards || 21. vail
28. he *s. up* hanging at door of tabernacle, 33.
Lev. 26. 1. nor shall ye *s. up* any image of stone
Num. 1. 51. the tabernacle, Levites shall *s.* it *up*
7. 1. that Moses had fully *s. up* the tabernacle
10. 21. and other did *s.* it *up* against they came
Deut. 27. 2. that thou shalt *s. up* these stones, 4.
Josh. 4. 9. Joshua *s. up* twelve stones in Jordan
6. 26. shall he *s. up* gates of it, 1 *Kings* 16. 34.
Judg. 18. 30. children of Dan *s. up* graven image
31. they *s.* them *up* Micah's graven image
1 *Sam.* 15. 11. it repenteth me I have *s. up* Saul
12. behold, Saul hath *s.* him *up* a place, and gone
2 *Sam.* 3. 10. to *s. up* throne of David over Israel
7. 12. I will *s. up* thy seed after thee, which shall
1 *Kings* 15. 4. to *s. up* his son after him and establish
2 *Kings* 17. 10. they *s.* them *up* images and groves
1 *Chr.* 21. 18. *s.* them *up* an altar in threshing-floor
2 *Chron.* 25. 14. Amaziah *s.* them *up* to be his gods
33. 19. Manasseh *s. up* groves and graven images
Ezra 2. 68. offered freely to *s. up* God's house
4. 12. Jews have *s. up* the walls thereof, 13. 16.
5. 11. build the house a great king of Israel, *s. up*
6. 11. being *s. up*, let him be hanged thereon
9. 9. to give us a reviving to *s. up* house of God
Neh. 3. 1. they built sheep-gate, they sanctified it,
and *s. up* the doors of it, 3. 6, 13, 14, 15. | 7. 1.
6. 1. tho' at that time I had not *s. up* the doors
Job 5. 11. to *s. up* on high those that be low
16. 12. hath shaken me and *s.* me *up* for his mark
Psal. 20. 5. the name of G. we will *s. up* our banners
27. 5. he shall hide me, and *s.* me *up* upon a rock
69. 29. let thy salvation, O God, *s.* me *up* on high
74. 4. they *s. up* their ensigns for signs
89. 42. thou hast *s. up* right hand of adversaries
Prov. 8. 23. I was *s. up* from everlast. from begin.
Isa. 9. 11. Lord shall *s. up* the adversaries of Rezin
11. 12. he shall *s. up* an ensign for the nations
23. 13. they *s. up* towers thereof, raised palaces
45. 20. that *s. up* wood of their graven image
49. 22. behold I will *s. up* my standard to people
57. 8. thou hast *s. up* thy remembrance
Jer. 4. 6. *s. up* the standard toward Zion, retire
10. 20. there is none to *s. up* my curtains
11. 13. have ye *s. up* altars to that shameful thing?
23. 4. and I will *s. up* shepherds over them
31. 21. *s.* thee *up* way-marks, make high heaps
50. 2. *s. up* a standard, publish, 51. 12, 27.
51. 12. *s. up* the watchmen, prepare ambushes
Lam. 2. 17. he hath *s. up* horn of thy adversaries
Ezek. 14. 3. these men have *s. up* their idols
31. 4. the deep *s.* him *up* on high with her rivers
34. 23. I will *s. up* one shepherd over them
Dan. 2. 44. God of heaven shall *s. up* a kingdom
3. 14. nor worship the golden image I have *s. up*
5. 19. whom he would he *s. up* and put down
12. 11. abomination that maketh desolate *s. up*
Hos. 8. 4. they have *s. up* kings but not by me
Mal. 3. 15. they that work wickedness are *s. up*
Mat. 27. 37. and *s. up* over his head this accusation
Acts 6. 13. and *s. up* false witnesses, who said
15. 16. I will build again the ruins, and *s.* it *up*

SET, *Passive.*

Gen. 24. 33. there was *s.* meat before him to eat
28. 11. sun was *s.* || 12. a ladder was *s.* upon earth
Exod. 25. 7. stones *s.* in ephod, 28. 11. | 35. 9, 27.
26. 17. two tenons *s.* in order against another
32. 22. knowest people, they are *s.* on mischief
37. 3. the rings *s.* || 39. 37. the lamps *s.* in order
1 *Sam.* 18. 30. so that his name was much *s.* by
26. 24. behold, as thy life was much *s.* by this day
2 *Sam.* 12. 30. crown *s.* on Dav. head, 1 *Chr.* 20. 2.
1 *Kings* 2. 19. a seat to be *s.* for the king's mother
14. 4. Ahijah could not see, for his eyes were *s.*
2 *Kings* 12. 4. the money that every man is *s.* at
1 *Chron.* 9. 22. porters appointed in their *s.* office
19. 10. Joab saw the battle was *s.* against him
29. 2. David gave onyx-stones and stones to be *s.*
2 *Chron.* 6. 10. and I am *s.* on the throne of Israel
29. 35. service of the house of L. was *s.* in order
31. 15. in their *s.* office to give their brethren
18. in their *s.* office they sanctified themselves
Job 36. 16. and what should be *s.* on thy table
Psal. 10. 8. his eyes are privily *s.* against the poor
122. 5. there are *s.* thrones of judgment, of David
141. 2. let my prayer be *s.* forth before thee
Prov. 18. † 10. righteous run into it, and is *s.* aloft
29. † 25. puts trust in the Lord, shall be *s.* on high
Eccl. 8. 11. the heart is fully *s.* in them to do evil
10. 6. folly *s.* in great dignity; rich sit in low place
Cant. 5. 12. his eyes are as the eyes of doves fitly *s.*
14. his hands are as gold rings *s.* with the beryl
15. his legs are *s.* upon sockets of fine gold
7. 2. thy belly as a heap of wheat *s.* with lilies
Isa. 3. 24. and instead of well *s.* hair, baldness
21. 8. I am *s.* in my ward whole nights
Jer. 6. 23. *s.* in array, as men for war, *Joel* 2. 5.
31. 29. children's teeth are *s.* on edge, *Ezek.* 18. 2.
30. man that eateth, his teeth shall be *s.* on edge
Ezek. 22. 10. they humbled her that was *s.* apart
Dan. 7. 10. judgment was *s.* books were opened
Nah. 3. 13. the gates of thy land shall be *s.* open
Mat. 5. 14. a city *s.* on a hill cannot be hid

Mat. 27. 19. when he was *s.* on judgment-seat, wife
Mark 1. 32. when sun did *s.* they brought diseased
4. 21. a candle, and not to be *s.* on a candlestick
9. 12. must suffer many things, and be *s.* at nought
Luke 2. 34. this child is *s.* for the fall and rising
7. 8. for I also am a man *s.* under authority
10. 8. eat such things as are *s.* before you
John 2. 6. there were *s.* six water-pots of stone
Acts 4. 11. the stone *s.* at nought of you builders
19. 27. our craft is in danger to be *s.* at nought
26. 32. this man might have been *s.* at liberty
1 *Cor.* 10. 27. whatsoever is *s.* before you eat
Gal. 3. 1. Chr. had been evidently *s.* forth crucified
Phil. 1. 17. I am *s.* for the defence of the gospel
Heb. 6. 18. to lay hold on the hope *s.* before us
8. 1. who is *s.* on right hand of the throne, 12. 2.
12. 1. let us run the race that is *s.* before us
2. who for joy that was *s.* before him, endured
13. 23. our brother Timothy is *s.* at liberty
Jude 7. the cities are *s.* forth for an example
Rev. 3. 21. am *s.* down with my Father in throne
4. 2. a throne was *s.* in heaven, one sat on throne

SET *day.*

Acts 12. 21. on a *s. day,* Herod arrayed in royal ap.
See FACE, FACES, FEASTS.

SET *time.*

Gen. 17. 21. Sarah shall bear to thee at this *s. time*
21. 2. at the *s. time* of which God had spoken
Exod. 9. 5. the Lord appointed a *s. time,* saying
1 *Sam.* 13. 8. according to *s. time* Sam. appointed
2 *Sam.* 20. 5. Amasa tarried longer than the *s. time*
Job 14. 13. that thou wouldst appoint me a *s. time*
Psal. 102. 13. the *s. time* to favour her is come

SETTER.

Acts 17. 18. seems to be a *s.* forth of strange gods

SETTEST.

Deut. 23. 20. in all thou *s.* thy hand to, 28. 8, 20.
Job 7. 12. am I a sea, that thou *s.* a watch over me?
13. 27. thou *s.* a print on the heels of my feet
Psal. 21. 3. thou *s.* a crown of gold on his head
41. 12. thou *s.* me before thy face for ever

SETTETH.

Exod. 30. † 8. when Aaron *s.* up the lamps
Num. 1. 51. when the tabernacle *s.* forward
4. 5. when camp *s.* forward, Aaron shall come
Deut. 24. 15. he is poor, and *s.* his heart upon it
27. 16. cursed be he that *s.* light by his father
2 *Sam.* 22. 34. *s.* me on high places, *Psal.* 18. 33.
Job 24. † 15. the adulterer *s.* his face in secret
28. 3. he *s.* an end to darkness, and searcheth
40. † 17. he *s.* up his tail like a cedar
Psal. 36. 4. he *s.* himself in a way that is not good
65. 6. which by his strength *s.* fast mountains
68. 6. God *s.* solitary in families, he brings out
75. 7. he putteth down one, and *s.* up another
83. 14. as the flame *s.* the mountains on fire
107. 41. yet *s.* poor on high from affliction
Isa. 44. † 19. none *s.* to his heart, nor is there know.
Jer. 5. 26. they lay wait as he that *s.* snares
43. 3. but Baruch *s.* thee on against us
Ezek. 14. 4. that *s.* up his idols in his heart, 7.
Dan. 2. 21. he removeth kings and *s.* up kings
4. 17. he *s.* up over it the basest of men
Mat. 4. 5. and *s.* him on a pinnacle of the temple
Luke 8. 16. but *s.* it on a candlestick that they see
Jam. 3. 6. tongue *s.* on fire the course of nature

SETTING.

Ezek. 43. 8. in their *s.* of their threshold by mine
Mat. 27. 66. sealing the stone, and *s.* a watch
Luke 4. 40. when sun was *s.* they brought the sick

SETTINGS.

Exod. 28. 17. thou shalt set in it *s.* of stones

SETTLE.

Ezek. 43. 14. from the ground even to the lower *s.*
17. and the *s.* shall be fourteen cubits long
20. put blood on four corners of the *s.* 45. 19.

SETTLE.

1 *Chron.* 17. 14. but I will *s.* him in mine house
Ezek. 36. 11. I will *s.* you after your old estates
Luke 21. 14. *s.* it in your hearts, not to meditate
1 *Pet.* 5. 10. but God stablish, strengthen, *s.* you

SETTLED.

1 *Kings* 8. 13. built a *s.* place for thee to abide in
2 *Kings* 8. 11. he *s.* his countenance stedfastly
Psal. 30. † 7. thou hast *s.* strength for my mountain
39. † 5. every man *s.* is altogether vanity
119. 89. for ever, O Lord, thy word is *s.* in heaven
Prov. 8. 25. before mountains were *s.* before hills
Jer. 48. 11. Moab been at ease, he hath *s.* on his lees
Zeph. 1. 12. punish men that are *s.* on their lees
Col. 1. 23. if ye continue in faith grounded and *s.*

SETTLEST.

Psal. 65. 10. thou *s.* furrows thereof, makest soft

SEVEN.

Besides the known signification of this word, it is also used in scripture as a number of perfection. In the sacred books, and in the religion of the Jews, *a great number of events and mysterious circumstances are set forth by the number of* seven. *God consecrated the* seventh day, *on which he ceased from his works of creation, as a day of rest and repose. This rest of the* seventh day, *according to the apostle, intimates eternal rest,* Heb. 4. 4, 9. *And not only the* seventh *day is honoured among the* Jews, *by the rest of the* sabbath, *but every* seventh year *is also consecrated to the rest of the earth, by the name of a* sabbatical year; *as also the* seven *times* seventh *year, or forty-nine years, is the year of* Jubilee. *In the prophetic style, a week often stands for* seven *years,* Dan. 9. 24, 25. Jacob *served his father-in-law* Laban seven *years for each of his daughters.* Pharaoh's *mysterious dream represented to his imagination* seven *fat oxen, and* seven *lean ones;* seven *full ears of corn, and as many that were blasted: these stood for* seven *years of plenty, and* seven *of scarcity. The golden candlestick had* seven *branches:* seven *trumpets,* seven *priests that sounded them;* seven *days to surround the walls of* Jericho, *Josh.* 6. 4, 6, 8, 15. *In the* Revelation *are the* seven *churches,* seven *candlesticks,* seven *spirits,* seven *stars,* seven *lamps,* seven *seals,* seven *angels,* seven *vials,* seven *plagues, &c.*

In certain passages the number seven *is put for a great number:* Isaiah *says, that* seven *women should lay hold of one man, to ask him to marry them,* Isa. 4. 1. Hannah *the mother of* Samuel *says, that she who was barren should have* seven *children, that is, several children,* 1 Sam. 2. 5. *God threatens his people, to smite them* seven times *for their transgression, that is, several times,* Lev. 26. 24. *The* Psalmist, *speaking of very pure silver, says, it is* purified seven times, *Psal.* 12. 6. *And in* Psal. 79. 12. Render unto our neighbours sevenfold into their bosom. *Punish them severely, and as often as they deserve it. The slothful man thinks himself wiser than seven men that can give a reason for their actions,* Prov. 26. 16. *In these and many other passages, the certain number* seven *is placed for an uncertain and indefinite number.*

Gen. 7. † 2. of every clean beast take to thee *s.*
41. 2. there came up *s.* well-favoured kine
3. *s.* other kine came up, 4. 18, 19, 20, 26, 27.
5. *s.* ears of corn came up, rank and good
6. *s.* thin ears, and blasted, 7, 22, 23, 24, 26, 27.
46. 25. the sons of Bilhah, all the souls were *s.*
Exod. 2. 16. the priest of Midian had *s.* daughters
Lev. 23. 15. *s.* sabbaths shall be complete
25. 8. shalt number *s.* sabbaths of years to thee
Num. 23. 1. Balaam said to Balak, build me here
s. altars, and prepare *s.* oxen and *s.* rams, 29.
4. and he said, I have prepared *s.* altars, 14.
Deut. 7. 1. *s.* nations greater and might. than thou
16. 9. *s.* weeks thou shalt number to thee, begin
28. 7. Ld. cause enemies to flee before thee *s.* ways
25. thou shalt flee *s.* ways before them
Josh. 6. 4. *s.* priests bearing *s.* trumpets, 6, 8, 13.
18. 2. there remained of Isr. *s.* tribes not received
5. and they shall divide it into *s.* parts, 6.
9. described it by cities into *s.* parts in a book
Judg. 16. 7. if they bind me with *s.* green withs
13. if thou weavest *s.* locks ‖ 19. shave off *s.* locks
1 *Sam.* 2. 5. so that the barren hath born *s.*
6. 1. the ark was with the Philistines *s.* months
16. 10. Jesse made *s.* of his sons to pass before Sam.
2 *Sam.* 21. 9. they fell all *s.* together and put to death
1 *Chron.* 3. 24. and the sons of Elioenai were *s.*
5. 13. their breth. of house of their fathers were *s.*
2 *Chron.* 29. 21. they brought *s.* bullocks, *s.* rams
Ezra 7. 14. sent of king and of his *s.* counsellors
Esth. 1. 10. *s.* chamberlains that served in presence
14. the *s.* princes which saw the king's face
2. 9. he gave her *s.* maidens meet to be given her
Job 5. 19. in *s.* troubles no evil shall touch thee
Prov. 6. 16. yea *s.* are an abomination unto him
9. 1. wisdom hath hewn out her *s.* pillars
26. 25. for there are *s.* abominations in his heart
Eccl. 11. 2. give a portion to *s.* also to eight
Isa. 4. 1. in that day *s.* women take hold of one man
11. 15. the Lord shall smite it in the *s.* streams
Jer. 15. 9. she that hath born *s.* languisheth
Ezek. 39. 12. *s.* months shall they be burying them
14. after the end of *s.* months shall they search
40. 22. they went up unto it by *s.* steps, 26.
41. 3. and the breadth of the door *s.* cubits
Dan. 9. 25. unto the Messiah, shall be *s.* weeks
Mic. 5. 5. we shall raise against him *s.* shepherds
Zech. 3. 9. behold, upon one stone shall be *s.* eyes
4. 2. his *s.* lamps thereon, and *s.* pipes to *s.* lamps
10. plummet in hand of Zerubbabel with those *s.*
Mat. 15. 34. they said, *s.* loaves, 36. *Mark* 8. 5.
37. they took up *s.* baskets full, *Mark* 8. 8.
16. 10. nor the *s.* loaves among four thousand
22. 25. now there were with us *s.* brethren, and the
first deceased, *Mark* 12. 20. *Luke* 20. 29.
28. in resurrection whose wife shall she be of *s.*
Mark 12. 22. and *s.* had her, 23. *Luke* 20. 31, 33.
16. 9. out of whom he cast *s.* devils, *Luke* 8. 2.
Acts 13. 19. when he destroyed *s.* nations in Canaan
21. 8. Philip who was one of the *s.* deacons
Rev. 1. 4. John to *s.* churches in Asia, grace to you
11. write, and send it to the *s.* churches in Asia
12. being turned, I saw *s.* golden candlesticks
13. in midst of *s.* candlesticks one like Son of man
20. *s.* stars are the angels of the churches, the *s.*
candlesticks thou sawest are the *s.* churches
2. 1. who walketh in midst of *s.* golden candlesticks
5. 6. I beheld Lamb as slain, having *s.* horns, and
s. eyes, which are the *s.* spirits of God sent forth
8. 2. I saw the *s.* angels which stood before God
6. the *s.* angels prepared themselves to sound
10. 3. when he cried, *s.* thunders uttered voices
4. seal up what the *s.* thunders have uttered
12. 3. behold, a great dragon, having *s.* heads, and
s. crowns upon his heads, 13. 1. | 17. 3, 7.
15. 1. I saw *s.* angels having the *s.* last plagues, 6.
7. gave to *s.* angels *s.* golden vials full of wrath
8. no man was able to enter into the temple, till
the *s.* plagues of the *s.* angels were fulfilled
16. 1. I heard a voice, saying to the *s.* angels
17. 1. and there came one of the *s.* angels which
had the *s.* vials, and talked with me, 21. 9.
17. 9. the *s.* heads are *s.* mountains on which
10. there are *s.* kings, five are fallen, one is, other
11. the beast is of the *s.* and goeth into perdition
See DAYS, HUNDRED.

SEVEN *bullocks.*

Num. 23. 29. prepare me here *s. bullocks, s.* rams
29. 32. on the seventh day *s. bullocks,* two rams
1 *Chron.* 15. 26. Levites offered *s. bullocks, s.* rams
2 *Chron.* 29. 21. they brought *s. bullocks, s.* rams
Job 42. 8. take to you now, *s. bullocks, s.* rams
Ezek. 45. 23. prepare a burnt-offering, *s. bullocks*

SEVEN-FOLD.

Gen. 4. 15. vengeance shall be taken on him *s.*
24. if Cain shall be avenged *s.* Lamech 70 and *s.*
Psal. 79. 12. render *s.* into their bosom reproach
Prov. 6. 31. but if he be found he shall restore *s.*
Isa. 30. 26. and the light of the sun shall be *s.*
See LAMBS, LAMPS.

SEVEN *men.*

2 *Sam.* 21. 6. let *s. men* of his sons be delivered
Prov. 26. 16. than *s. men* that can render a reason
Jer. 52. 25. took *s. men* that were near the king
Acts 6. 3. look out *s. m.* of honest rep. full of Holy G.

SEVEN *rams,* See SEVEN *bullocks.*
See SEALS.

SEVEN *sons.*

Ruth 4. 15. thy daughter is better than *s. sons*
Job 1. 2. and there were born unto him *s. sons*
42. 13. he had also *s. sons,* and three daughters
Acts 19. 14. there were *s. sons* of one Sceva a Jew

SEVEN *spirits.*

Mat. 12. 45. then goeth he, and taketh with himself
s. other *spirits* more wicked, *Luke* 11. 26.
Rev. 1. 4. from *s. spirits* before the throne of God
3. 1. these saith he that hath the *s. spirits* of God
4. 5. seven lamps, which are the *s. spirits* of God
5. 6. seven eyes, which are the *s. spirits* of God

SEVEN *stars.*

Amos 5. 8. seek him that maketh the *s. stars*
Rev. 1. 16. had in his right hand *s. stars,* 2. 1. | 3. 1.
20. mystery of *s. stars,* thou sawest in my right
hand; *s. stars* are the angels of the *s.* churches

SEVEN and *thirty,* See THIRTY.
See THOUSAND.

SEVEN *times.*

Gen. 33. 3. Jacob bowed before Esau *s. times*
Lev. 4. 6. priest shall sprinkle of the blood *s. times*
17. | 8. 11. | 14. 7. | 16. 14, 19. *Num.* 19. 4.
14. 16. shall sprinkle oil with his fingers *s. times,* 27.
51. dip in blood, and sprinkle the house *s. times*
25. 8. thou shalt number *s. times* seven years
26. 18. I will punish you *s. times* more, 21, 24, 28.
Josh. 6. 4. he shall compass the city *s. times,* 15.
1 *Kings* 18. 43. said to his servant, go again, *s. times*
2 *Kings* 4. 35. child neesed *s. times,* and opened eyes
5. 10. Elisha sent, go wash in Jordan *s. times,* 14.
Psal. 12. 6. words are as silver purified *s. times*
119. 164. *s. times* a day do I praise thee, because
Prov. 24. 16. a just man falleth *s. times,* and riseth
Dan. 3. 19. heat the furnace one *s. times* more than
4. 16. let *s. times* pass over him, 23, 25, 32.
Mat. 18. 21. how oft shall I forgive? till *s. times*
22. I say not, till *s. times,* but until 70 *times s.*
Luke 17. 4. if thy brother trespass agst. thee *s. times*
a day, and *s. times* a day turn again to thee

SEVEN *and twenty,* See TWENTY.

SEVEN YEARS.

Gen. 29. 18. I will serve thee *s. years* for Rachel
20. served *s. years* ‖ 27. serve *s.* other *years,* 30.
41. 26. the seven good kine are *s. years,* and the
seven good ears are *s. years,* the dream is one
27. seven thin and ill-favoured kine are *s. years*
seven empty ears shall be *s. years* of famine
29. there come *s. years* of plenty, 34, 47, 48.
30. there shall arise *s. years* of famine, 36. 54.
53. the *s. years* of plenteousness were ended
Lev. 25. 8. thou shalt number seven times *s. years*
Num. 13. 22. Hebron was built *s. years* before Zoan
Deut. 15. 1. at end of every *s. years* a release, 31. 10.
Judg. 6. 1. Lord delivered Israel to Midian *s. years*
25. take the second bullock of *s. years* old
12. 9. Ibzan of Bethlehem judged Israel *s. years*
2 *Sam.* 2. 11. David was king in Hebron *s. years*
six months, 5. 5. 1 *Kings* 2. 11. 1 *Chron.* 29. 27.
24. 13. shall *s. years* of famine come to thee?
1 *Kings* 6. 38. Sol. was *s. years* in building temple
2 *Kings* 8. 1. famine shall come upon land *s. years*
2. she sojourned with the Philistines *s. years*
11. 21. Athaliah was slain, and *s. years* old was
Jehoash when he began to reign, 2 *Chron.* 24. 1.
Jer. 34. 14. at end of *s. years* let ye go every man
Ezek. 39. 9. shall burn weapons with fire *s. years*
Luke 2. 36. Anna lived with an husband *s. years*

SEVENS.

Gen. 7. 2. of every clean beast shalt thou take by *s.*
3. of fowls of the air by *s.* the male and female

SEVENTEEN.

Gen. 37. 2. Jos. being *s.* years old was feeding flock
47. 28. Jacob lived in the land of Egypt *s.* years
1 *Kings* 14. 21. Rehoboam reigned *s.* years in Jerus.
2 *Kings* 13. 1. Jehoahaz son of Jehu reigned *s.* years
Jer. 32. 9. Jerem. bought field, weighed *s.* shekels

SEVENTEENTH.

Gen. 7. 11. on *s.* day the fountains were broken up
8. 4. ark rested on the *s.* day in seventh month
1 *Kings* 22. 51. Ahaziah began to reign the *s.* year
2 *Kings* 16. 1. in *s.* year of Pekah son of Remaliah
1 *Chron.* 24. 15. the *s.* lot came to Hezir
25. 24. the *s.* lot came to Joshbekashah

SEVENTH.

Exod. 21. 2. in *s.* he shall go out free for nothing
31. 15. but in the *s.* is the sabbath of rest to Lord
Lev. 23. 16. unto the morrow after the *s.* sabbath
Josh. 6. 16. at the *s.* time when the priests blew
19. 40. and *s.* lot came out for the tribe of Dan
1 *Kings* 18. 44. at the *s.* time there arose a cloud
1 *Chron.* 2. 15. David was the *s.* son of Jesse
24. 10. the *s.* lot came forth to Hakkoz
26. 3. Elioenai the *s.* son of Meshelemiah
5. Issachar was the *s.* son of Obed-edom
27. 10. the *s.* captain for the *s.* month was Helez
Mat. 22. 26. second also, and the third, to the *s.*
John 4. 52. yesterday at *s.* hour the fever left him
Jude 14. Enoch the *s.* from Adam prophesied
Lev. 8. 1. and when he had opened the *s.* seal
10. 7. in the days of the voice of the *s.* angel
11. 15. the *s.* angel sounded, there were voices
16. 17. *s.* angel poured out his vial into the air
21. 20. the *s.* foundation was a chrysolite
See DAY.

SEVENTH *month.*

Gen. 8. 4. ark rested in *s. month* on the mountains
Lev. 16. 29. in *s. m.* afflict your souls, 23. 27. | 25. 9.
23. 24. in the *s. month* shall ye have a sabbath
Num. 29. 1. in *s. month* an holy convocation, 12.
1 *Kings* 8. 2. Israel assembled at feast of the *s. m.*
2 *Kings* 25. 25. in *s. m.* Ishmael killed Gedaliah,
the Jews and Chaldees with him, *Jer.* 41. 1.
2 *Chr.* 7. 10. in *s. month* Solomon sent them away
31. 7. they finished the heaps in the *s. month*
Ezra 3. 1. when *s. month* was come, and the children
of Israel were in the cities, *Neh.* 7. 73

Ezra 3. 6. from first day of s. m. began they to offer
Neh. 8. 2. on the first day of the s. month Ezra read
14. in feasts of s. month Isr. shall dwell in booths
Jer. 28. 17. so Hananiah died in the s. month
Ezek. 45. 25. in the s. month shall he do the like
Hag. 2. 1. in the s. month the word came to Haggai
Zech. 7. 5. when ye mourned in fifth and s. month
8. 19. the fast of the s. month shall be to Judah joy

SEVENTH year.

Exod. 23. 11. but the s. year thou shalt let it rest
Lev. 25. 4. in the s. year shall be a sabbath of rest
20. if ye say, what shall we eat in the s. year?
Deut. 15. 9. saying, the s. year, year of release, is at hand, thine eye be evil against thy brother
12. in the s. year thou shalt let him go free
2 Kings 11. 4. in the s. year Jehoiada sent and set the rulers with the captains, 2 Chron. 23. 1.
12. 1. in s. year of Jehu Jehoash began to reign
18. 9. in s. year of Hoshea king of Assyria came
Ezra 7. 7. went to Jerus. in s. year of Artaxerxes, 8.
Neh. 10. 31. leave s. year exaction of every debt
Esth. 2. 16. Esther was taken to king in s. year
Jer. 52. 28. people carried away captive in s. year
Ezek. 20. 1. in the s. year elders came to inquire

SEVENTY.

Gen. 4. 24. if Cain, truly Lamech s. and seven-fold
5. 12. and Cainan lived s. years, and begat
11. 26. Terah lived s. years, and begat Abram
12. 4. Abram was s. five years old, when he depart.
Exod. 1. 5. of the loins of Jacob were s. souls
24. 1. come up, thou, and s. elders of Israel, 9.
38. 29. the brass of the offering was s. talents
Num. 7. 13. his offering was one silver bowl of s. shekels, 19, 25, 31, 37, 43. 49, 55, 61, 67, 73, 79.
85. each bowl weighing s. shekels of silver
11. 16. gather unto me s. men of the elders, 24.
25. he gave of the spirit unto the s. elders
Judg. 9. 56. wickedness, in slaying his s. brethren
2 Kings 10. 1. Ahab had s. sons in Samaria, 6.
7. they took king's sons, and slew s. persons
Ezra 2. 40. children of Hodaviah s. four, Neh. 7. 43.
8. 7. of sons of Elam, with Jeshaiah s. males
14. of the sons of Zabbud, with them s. males
Psal. 90. † 10. as for our days, they are s. years
Isa. 23. 15. that Tyre shall be forgotten s. years
17. after end of s. years, the Lord will visit Tyre
Jer. 25. 11. shall serve the king of Babylon s. years
12. when s. years are accomplished, 29. 10.
Ezek. 8. 11. there stood before them s. men
Dan. 9. 2. accomplish s. years in desolat. of Jerus.
24. s. weeks are determined upon thy people
Zech. 7. 5. even those s. years did ye fast to me
Mat. 18. 22. not till seven times, but until s. times
Luke 10. 1. Lord appointed other s. also, and sent
17. the s. returned again with joy, saying, Lord

SEVER.

Exod. 8. 22. I will s. in that day the land of Goshen
9. 4. Ld. shall s. between cattle of Israel and Egy.
Ezek. 39. 14. shall s. out men of continual employ
Mat. 13. 49. and s. the wicked from among the just

SEVERED.

Lev. 20. 26. I have s. you from other people
Deut. 4. 41. Moses s. three cities on this side Jordan
Judg. 4. 11. Heber had s. himself from Kenites

SEVERAL.

Num. 28. 13. and a s. tenth deal of flour mingled with oil for a meat offering, 21, 29. | 29. 10, 15.
2 Kings 15. 5. Azariah was leper to the day of his death, and dwelt in a s. house, 2 Chron. 26. 21.
2 Chr. 11. 12. in every s. city put shields and spears
28. 25. in every s. city of Judah made high places
31. 19. also of the sons of Aaron in every s. city
Mat. 25. 15. every man according to his s. ability
Rev. 21. 21. every s. gate was of one pearl, street

SEVERALLY.

1 Cor. 12. 11. dividing to every man s. as he will

SEVERITY.

Rom. 11. 22. behold therefore the goodness and s. of God, on them who fell s. but to thee goodness

SEW.

Eccl. 3. 7. a time to rend, and a time to s. a time
Ezek. 13. 18. woe to women s. pillows to arm holes

SEWED.

Gen. 3. 7. they s. fig-leaves together, made aprons
Ezra 4. † 12. they s. together the foundations
Job 16. 15. I have s. sackcloth upon my skin

SEWEST.

Job 14. 17. in a bag, and thou s. up mine iniquity

SEWETH.

Mark 2. 21. no man s. piece of new cloth on an old

SHADE.

Ps. 121. 5. the Lord is thy s. upon thy right hand

SHADOW

Is the representation which any thing makes of itself, being interposed between the sun or a light, and any solid body, Isa. 38. 8. Acts 5. 15. *Also a place sheltered from the sun,* Job 7. 2. As a servant desireth the shadow. *The law is called a shadow of good things to come,* Heb. 10. 1. *that is, the* Mosaical economy *was only a dark obscure representation of* Christ, *who was the substance of the legal types and shadows. Some are of opinion that the apostle here alludes to the custom of* Painters, *who first make a rude draught, and from it draw a perfect and lively picture; then the sense of the words is this, The old covenant did contain only dark resemblances and types of heavenly things, no lively representations of them; this being reserved unto the time of the gospel, wherein* Christ *and all spiritual blessings in him are clearly and plainly manifested. Others think that the apostle alludes to* the shadow *of a body, and makes this the sense; That the old covenant had only types, wherein* Christ *and heavenly things through him were darkly represented, not the substance and truth of the things themselves.*

A Shadow *being made by the sun, follows its motions, and is in perpetual variation, until at last it quite vanish and disappear; in this sense the life of man is compared to a shadow,* 1 Chr. 29. 15. Our days on earth are as a shadow, and there is none abiding. Job *says,* 17. 7. All my members are as a shadow: *that is, I am shrunk to nothing, and become a mere anatomy or ghost.*

The shadow of death. *Job says,* Let the shadow of death stain the day wherein I was born, Job 3. 3. *that is, such a dismal darkness as is in the place of the dead; or, so gross and palpable darkness, that by its horrors and damps may take away men's spirits and lives.* The morning is to murderers and adulterers as the shadow of death; *that is, terrible and hateful. because it both discovers them and their works of darkness, and hinders their practices.* Job 24. 17. The valley of the shadow of death; *that is, the depth of the most terrible and affrighting dangers,* Psal. 23. 4.

Gen. 19. 8. they came under the s. of my roof
Judg. 9. 15. then come and put your trust in my s.
36. thou seest the s. of the mountains as if men
2 Kings 20. 9. shall the s. go forward ten degrees?
10. it is a light thing for the s. to go down ten
11. and he brought the s. ten degrees backward
1 Chron. 29. 15. our days on earth are as a s. Job 8. 9.
Job 7. 2. as a servant earnestly desireth the s.
14. 2. he fleeth also as a s. and continueth not
17. 7. and all my members are as a s
40. 22. the shady trees cover him with their s.
Psal. 17. 8. hide me under the s. of thy wings
36. 7. put their trust under the s. of thy wings, 57. 1.
63. 7. in the s. of thy wings will I rejoice
80. 10. the hills were covered with the s. of it
91. 1. shall abide under the s. of the Almighty
102. 11. my days are like a s. that declineth
109. 23. I am gone like a s. when it declineth
144. 4. man is vanity, his days are as s. Eccl. 8. 13.
Eccl. 6. 12. his vain life which he spendeth as a s.
Cant. 2. 3. I sat under his s. with great delight
Isa. 4. 6. a tabernacle for a s. in day-time from heat
16. 3. make thy s. as the night in the noon-day
25. 4. O Lord, thou hast been a s. from the heat
5. bring down the heat with s. of a cloud
30. 2. to strengthen, and trust in the s. of Egypt
3. and the trust in s. of Egypt your confusion
32. 2. as the s. of a great rock in a weary land
34. 15. owl lay and hatch, and gather under her s.
38. 8. I will bring again the s. of the degrees
49. 2. in s. of his hand hath he hid me, 51. 16.
Jer. 48. 45. they stood under the s. of Heshbon
Lam. 4. 20. we said, under his s. we shall live
Ezek. 17. 23. in the s. thereof shall they dwell
31. 6. and under his s. dwelt all great nations
12. all the people are gone down from his s.
17. that dwelt under his s. in midst of heathen
Dan. 4. 12. the beasts of the field had s. under it
Hos. 4. 13. under elms, because s. thereof is good
14. 7. they that dwell under his s. shall return
Jonah 4. 5. made a booth, and sat under it in s.
6. over Jonah, that it might be s. over his head
Mark 4. 32. that fowls may lodge under the s. of it
Acts 5. 15. that s. of Peter might overshadow some
Col. 2. 17. which are a s. of things to come, but
Heb. 8. 5. who serve unto the s. of heavenly things
10. 1. the law having a s. of good things to come
Jam. 1. 17. with whom is no s. of turning
See Death.

SHADOWS.

Cant. 2. 17. till the day break, and s. flee away, 4. 6.
Jer. 6. 4. for s. of the evening are stretched out

SHADOWING.

Isa. 18. 1. woe to the land s. with wings, which is
Ezek. 31. 3. Assyrian was a cedar with a s. shroud
Heb. 9. 5. over cherubims of glory s. the mercy-seat

SHADY.

Job 40. 21. he lieth under the s. trees in the covert
22. the s. trees cover him with their shadow

SHAFT.

Exod. 25. 31. his s. and branches, his bowls and flowers, shall be of the same, 37. 17. Num. 8. 4.
Isa. 49. 2. and he hath made me a polished s.

SHAKE.

Exod. 29. † 24. s. them to and fro for wave offering
Judg. 16. 20. Samson said, I will go out and s. mys.
Neh. 5. 13. also I shook my lap, and said, so God s.
Job 4. 14. fear came, which made my bones to s.
15. 33. he shall s. off his unripe grape as the vine
16. 4. I could heap up words, and s. my head at you
Psal. 22. 7. they shoot out the lip, they s. head
46. 3. tho' the mountains s. with swelling thereof
68. † 9. thou didst s. out a plentiful rain
69. 23. and make their loins continually to s.
72. 16. the fruit thereof shall s. like Lebanon
Isa. 2. 19. when he ariseth to s. the earth, 21.
10. 15. as if the rod should s. itself against them
32. he shall s. his hand against the mount
11. 15. the Lord shall s. his hand over the river
13. 2. exalt the voice unto them, s. the hand
13. I will s. heavens, Joel 3. 16. Hag. 2. 6, 21.
24. 18. the foundations of the earth do s.
33. 9. Bashan and Carmel s. off their fruits
52. 2. s. thyself from the dust, O Jerusalem
Jer. 23. 9. mine heart is broken, all my bones s.
Ezek. 26. 10. thy walls shall s. at noise of horsemen
15. shall not the isles s. at the sound of thy fall?
27. 28. the suburbs shall s. at the sound of the cry
31. 16. I made nations s. at the sound of his fall
38. 20. all men of the earth shall s. at my presence
Dan. 4. 14. s. off his leaves, and scatter his fruit
Amos 9. 1. smite the lintel, that the posts may s.
Hag. 2. 7. I will s. all nations, desire of all nations
Zech. 2. 9. behold, I will s. my hand on them
Mat. 10. 14. when ye depart out of that house, or city, s. off the dust of your feet, Mark 6. 11. Luke 9. 5.
28. 4. and for fear of him the keepers did s.
Luke 6. 48. stream beat that house, and could not s. it
Heb. 12. 26. once more I s. not the earth only

SHAKED.

Psal. 109. 25. they looked on me, they s. their heads

SHAKEN.

Lev. 26. 36. the sound of a s. leaf shall chase them
1 Kings 14. 15. shall smite Isr. as a reed is s. in water
2 Kings 19. 21. hath despised thee, the daughter of Jerusalem hath s. her head at thee, Isa. 37. 22.
Neh. 5. 13. even thus be he s. out and emptied
Job 16. 12. taken me by my neck, s. me to pieces
38. 13. that the wicked might be s. out of it
Psal. 18. 7. the foundations of the hills were s.
Nah. 2. 3. and the fir-trees shall be terribly s.
3. 12. if s. they fall into the mouth of the eater
Mat. 11. 7. a reed s. with the wind, Luke 7. 24.
24. 29. stars shall fall from heaven, and powers of heaven shall be s. Mark 13. 25. Luke 21. 26.
Luke 6. 38. give good measure, pressed, s. together
Acts 4. 31. when they had prayed, the place was s.
16. 26. so that the foundations of the prison were s.
2 Thess. 2. 2. ye be not soon s. in mind, or troubled
Heb. 12. 27. removing of those things that are s. that those things which cannot be s. may remain
Rev. 6. 13. as a fig-tree when s. of a mighty wind

SHAKETH.

Job 9. 6. which s. the earth out of her place
Psal. 29. 8. the voice of the Lord s. the wilderness
60. 2. heal the breaches thereof, for it is s.
Isa. 10. 15. shall saw magnify against him that s. it?
19. 16. the hand of the Lord which he s. over it
33. 15. he that s. his hand from holding of bribes

SHAKING.

Job 41. 29. he laugheth at the s. of a spear
Psal. 44. 14. the s. of the head among the people
Isa. 17. 6. as the s. of an olive tree, 24. 13.
19. 16. shall fear, because of the s. of the hand
30. 32. and in battles of s. shall he fight with it
Ezek. 37. 7. behold a s. and bones came together
38. 19. in that day there shall be a great s. in Israel

SHAMBLES.

1 Cor. 10. 25. whatsoever is sold in the s. that eat

SHAME

Is taken, (1) *For that affection which ariseth by reason of some civil dishonesty or filthiness, and appears in the countenance by blushing.* Gen. 2. 25. They were naked, and were not ashamed. *There was neither deformity in their bodies, nor guilt in their souls, the cause of shame.* (2) *For trouble and perturbation of mind and conscience, being grieved and cast down at the remembrance of sin against God;* Rom. 6. 21. What fruit had ye in those things whereof ye are now ashamed? *And in* Ezra 9. 6. I am ashamed and blush to lift up my face to thee, my God, for our iniquities are increased over our head. *This is shame of conscience, which in wicked men is an evil affection, and part of the torment of hell; but in the godly it is a good affection, a sign and fruit of their repentance.* Jer. 31. 19. Ephraim smote upon his thigh, and was ashamed. (3) *For a shameful idol, which would bring the worshippers of it to shame at last,* Hos. 9. 10. They went to Baal-peor, and separated themselves unto that shame. (4) *For scorn, derision, and contempt,* Ezek. 36. 6. Ye have borne the shame of the heathen.

To uncover the shame, *or nakedness, of a person, are synonymous terms.* Isaiah *threatens the* Egyptians, *that they should be led away captive stark naked, without any thing to cover their shame or their nakedness,* Isa. 20. 4. *And the same prophet says,* Thy nakedness shall be uncovered, yea, thy shame shall be seen, *Isa.* 47. 3. *It is said,* Prov. 3. 35. Shame shall be the promotion of fools; *Their promotion shall be their own shame, and the disgrace of those that promote them. And in* Prov. 9. 7. He that reproveth a scorner, getteth to himself shame: *He loseth his labour, and shall only get discredit by it. The apostle says,* Rom. 5. 5. Hope maketh not ashamed. *Such hope, which is the fruit of faith, patience, and experience, shall not be disappointed, but shall certainly obtain the good things hoped for, and so bring matter of rejoicing, and not of shame.*

Exod. 32. 25. Aaron made them naked unto their s.
Judg. 18. 7. was none to put them to s. in any thing
1 Sam. 20. 34. because his father had done him s.
2 Sam. 13. 13. whither shall I cause my s. to go?
2 Chron. 32. 21. returned with s. of face to his land
Job 8. 22. that hate thee shall be clothed with s.
Psal. 4. 2. how long will ye turn my glory into s.?
35. 4. put them to s. that seek after my soul
26. let them be clothed with s. and dishonour
40. 14. let them be put to s. wish me evil, 83. 17.
15. let them be desolate for a reward of their s.
44. 7. thou hast put them to s. that hated us, 53. 5.
9. but thou hast cast off and put us to s.
15. the s. of my face hath covered me, 69. 7.
69. 19. thou hast known my reproach and s.
70. 3. let them be turned back for reward of their s.
71. 24. let them be brought unto s. that seek hurt
83. 16. fill their faces with s. O Lord
89. 45. thou hast covered him with s.
109. 29. let mine adversaries be clothed with s.
119. 31. stuck to thy testimon. O L. put not to s.
132. 18. his enemies will I clothe with s.
Prov. 3. 35. but s. shall be the promotion of fools
9. 7. he that reproveth a scorner, getteth s.
10. 5. that sleeps in harvest, is a son that causeth s.
11. 2. when pride cometh, then cometh s.
12. 16. but a prudent man covereth s.
13. 5. a wicked man is loathsome and cometh to s.
18. s. shall be to him that refuseth instruction
14. 35. but his wrath is against him that causeth s.
17. 2. shall have rule over a son that causeth s.
18. 13. answereth before he heareth, it is s. to him
19. 26. that chaseth his mother, is a son causeth s.
25. 8. when thy neighbour hath put thee to s.
10. lest he that heareth it put thee to s.
29. 15. child left to himself brings his mother to s.
Isa. 20. 4. their buttocks uncovered, to s. of Egypt
22. 18. chariots shall be the s. of thy lord's house
30. 3. the strength of Pharaoh shall be your s. 5.
47. 3. be uncovered, yea, thy s. shall be seen
50. 6. I hid not my face from s. and spitting
54. 4. fear not, thou shalt not be put to s. nor confounded, for thou shalt forget s. of thy youth
61. 7. for your s. you shall have double
Jer. 3. 24. s. devoured the labour of our fathers
25. we lie down in s. and our confusion covers us

Jer. 13. 26. I will discover, that thy s. may appear
20. 18. that my days may be consumed with s.
23. 40. and a perpetual s. not be forgotten
46. 12. the nations have heard of thy s. thy cry
48. 39. how hath Moab turned back with s.
51. 51. s. hath covered our faces, for strangers
Ezek. 7. 18. s. shall be on all faces, and baldness
16. 52. bear thine own s. for thy sins, 54.
63. never open thy mouth because of thy s.
32. 24. yet have they born their s. with them, 25.
30. bear their s. with them that go down to pit
34. 29. nor bear the s. of the heathen any more
36. 6. because ye have borne the s. of the heathen
7. the heathen, they shall bear their s. 44. 13.
15. nor cause to hear in thee s. of the heathen
39. 26. after that they have borne their s.
Dan. 12. 2. many of them shall awake, some to s.
Hos. 4. 7. therefore I will change their glory into s.
18. her rulers with s. do love, give ye
9. 10. they separated themselves unto that s.
10. 6. Ephraim shall receive s. Israel be ashamed
Obad. 10. for thy violence s. shall cover thee
Mic. 1. 11. pass ye away, having thy s. naked
2. 6. shall not prophesy, they shall not take s.
7. 10. s. shall cover her which said, where is Lord ?
Nah. 3. 5. I will shew the kingdoms thy s.
Hab. 2. 10. thou hast consulted s. to thy house
16. thou art filled with s. for glory, drink thou
Zeph. 3. 5. but the unjust knoweth no s.
19. get praise, where they have been put to s.
Luke 14. 9. thou begin with s. to take lowest room
Acts 5. 41. they were counted worthy to suffer s.
1 Cor. 6. 5. I speak to your s. 15. 34.
11. 6. if it be a s. for a woman to be shorn
14. if a man have long hair, it is a s. unto him
14. 35. it is a s. for a woman to speak in church
2 Cor. 4. † 2. but renounced the hidden things of s.
Eph. 5. 12. a s. to speak of things done of them
Phil. 3. 19. whose glory is in their s. who mind
Heb. 6. 6. crucify afresh, and put him to an open s.
12. 2. he endured the cross, despising the s.
Jude 13. raging waves, foaming out their own s.
Rev. 3. 18. that s. of thy nakedness do not appear
16. 15. lest he walk naked, and they see his s.

SHAME.

Ruth 2. † 15. let her glean among sheaves, s. her not
1 Cor. 4. 14. I write not these things to s. you
11. 22. despise ye church of God, and s. them ?

SHAMED.

1 Sam. 25. † 7. thy shepherds with us, we s. them not
† 15. men were good unto us, and we were not s.
2 Sam. 19. 5. thou hast s. the faces of all thy servants
Psal. 14. 6. you have s. the counsels of the poor

SHAMETH.

Prov. 28. 7. companion of riotous men s. his father

SHAMEFACEDNESS.

1 Tim. 2. 9. that women adorn themselves with s.

SHAMEFUL.

Jer. 11. 13. ye have set up altars to that s. thing
Hab. 2. 16. and s. spueing be on thy glory

SHAMEFULLY.

Hos. 2. 5. she that conceived them, hath done s.
Mark 12. 4. sent him away s. handled, Luke 20. 11.
1 Thess. 2. 2. and were s. entreated, as ye know

SHAMELESSLY.

2 Sam. 6. 20. as one of vain fellows s. uncovereth

SHAPE.

Luke 3. 22. descended in bodily s. like dove on him
John 5. 37. not heard his voice, nor seen his s.

SHAPEN.

Psal. 51. 5. behold, I was s. in iniquity, and in sin

SHAPES.

Rev. 9. 7. the s. of the locusts were like horses

SHARE.

1 Sam. 13. 20. went down to sharpen every man his s.

SHARP.

Exod. 4. 25. Zipporah took a s. stone and cut off
Josh. 5. 2. make thee s. knives, and circumcise again
3. Joshua made s. knives and circumcised Israel
1 Sam. 14. 4. between the passages there was s. rock
Job 41. 30. s. stones are under him, he spreadeth
s. pointed things upon the mire
Psal. 45. 5. arrows s. in the heart of king's enemies
52. 2. thy tongue like a s. razor working deceitfully
57. 4. whose teeth are spears, their tongue s. sword
120. 4. s. arrows of mighty with coals of juniper
Prov. 5. 4. but her end is s. as a two-edged sword
25. 18. a man that bears false witness is s. arrow
Isa. 5. 28. they shall come, whose arrows are s.
41. 15. I will make thee a s. threshing instrument
49. 2. he hath made my mouth like a s. sword
Ezek. 5. 1. take thee a s. knife and cause it to pass
Acts 15. 39. the contention was so s. between Paul
Rev. 1. 16. out of his mouth went a s. two-edged
sword, his countenance was as the sun, 19. 15.
2. 12. these things saith he that hath the s. sword
14. 14. Son of man in his hand a s. sickle, 17.
18. the angel cried to him that had the s. sickle

SHARPEN.

Deut. 6. † 7. thou shalt s. them to thy children
1 Sam. 13. 20. went down to s. every man his share
21. yet they had a file for axes, and to s. goads

SHARPENED.

Psal. 140. 3. they s. their tongues like a serpent
Ezek. 21. 9. a sword is s. and furbished, 10, 11.

SHARPENETH.

Job 16. 9. mine enemy s. his eyes upon me
Prov. 27. 17. iron s. iron, so a man s. his friend

SHARPER.

Mic. 7. 4. the most upright is s. than a thorn hedge
Heb. 4. 12. the word of God is s. than any sword

SHARPLY.

Judg. 8. 1. and they did chide with Gideon s.
Tit. 1. 13. rebuke them s. that they may be sound

SHARPNESS.

2 Cor. 13. 10. lest being present I should use s.

SHAVE.

Lev. 13. 33. shall be shaven, but scall shall he not s.
14. 8. the unclean person shall s. off his hair, 9.
21. 5. nor shall they s. the corner of their beard
Num. 6. 9. then he shall s. his head in the day of
his cleansing, on the seventh day shall he s. it
Num. 6. 18. Nazarite shall s. head of his separation
8. 7. let them s. their flesh, and wash their clothes
Deut. 21. 12. captive shall s. her head, pare her nails
Judg. 16. 19. she caused him to s. off seven locks
Isa. 7. 20. Lord shall s. with a razor that is hired
Ezek. 44. 20. neither shall they s. their heads
Acts 21. 24. be at charges, that they s. their heads

SHAVED.

Gen. 41. 14. Joseph s. and changed his raiment
2 Sam. 10. 4. s. off half their beards, 1 Chron. 19. 4.
Job 1. 20. Job rent his mantle and s. his head

SHAVEN.

Lev. 13. 33. be s. but the scall shall he not shave
Num. 6. 19. after the hair of his separation is s.
Judg. 16. 17. if I be s. my strength will go from me
22. the hair began to grow again after he was s.
Jer. 41. 5. fourscore men having their beards s.
1 Cor. 11. 5. that is even all one as if she were s.
6. if it be a shame to be s. let her be covered

SHEAF.

Gen. 37. 7. behold, my s. arose, and also stood upright;
behold, your sheaves made obeisance to my s.
Lev. 23. 10. ye shall bring a s. of the first-fruits
11. ye shall wave the s. before the Lord, 12.
Deut. 24. 19. hast forgot a s. shalt not go to fetch it
Job 24. 10. they take away the s. from the hungry
Zech. 12. 6. governors of Judah like a torch in a s.

SHEAVES.

Gen. 37. 7. behold, we were binding s. in the field
Ruth 2. 7. let me glean and gather among the s. 15.
Neh. 13. 15. some on the sabbath bringing in s.
Psal. 126. 6. he shall come bringing s. with him
129. 7. nor he that bindeth s. his bosom
Amos 2. 13. I am pressed under you, as cart full of s.
Mic. 4. 12. the Lord shall gather them as the s.

SHEAR.

Gen. 31. 19. and Laban went to s. his sheep
38. 13. Judah goeth to Timnah to s. his sheep
Deut. 15. 19. nor shalt s. the firstling of thy sheep
1 Sam. 25. 4. David heard that Nabal did s. his sheep

SHEARER.

Acts 8. 32. and like a lamb dumb before his s.

SHEARERS.

Gen. 38. 12. and Judah went up unto his sheep s.
1 Sam. 25. 7. now I have heard that thou hast s.
11. shall I take my flesh I have killed for my s.
2 Sam. 13. 23. Absalom had s. in Baal hazor, 24.
Isa. 53. 7. as a sheep before her s. is dumb, opens not

SHEARING.

1 Sam. 25. 2. and Nabal was s. sheep in Carmel

SHEARING-HOUSE.

2 Kings 10. 12. Jehu met brethren of Ahaziah at s.-h.
14. he slew them at the pit of the s.-h.

SHEATH.

1 Sam. 17. 51. David drew the sword out of his s.
2 Sam. 20. 8. with a sword fastened in the s. thereof
1 Chron. 21. 27. the angel put the sword into his s.
Ezek. 21. 3. I will draw his sword out of the s. 4, 5.
30. shall I cause it to return into his s. ? will judge
John 18. 11. Jesus said, put up thy sword into s.

SHED.

2 Sam. 20. 10. Joab s. Amasa's bowels to the ground
Mat. 26. 28. is s. for many for the remission of sins
Acts 2. 33. received the promise of Holy Ghost, he
hath s. forth this which ye now see and hear
Rom. 5. 5. love of G. is s. in our hearts by Holy Ghost
Tit. 3. 6. which he s. on us abundantly thro' Jes. Ch.
See BLOOD.

SHEDDER.

Ezek. 18. 10. if he beget a son that is a s. of blood

SHEDDETH.

Gen. 9. 6. whoso s. man's blood, his blood shall be sh.
Ezek. 22. 3. the city s. blood in the midst of it

SHEDDING.

Heb. 9. 22. and without s. of blood is no remission

SHE-GOATS, See GOATS.

SHEEP.

Gen. 4. 2. Abel a keeper of s. Cain tiller of ground
29. 6. Rachel his daughter cometh with the s. 9.
Exod. 9. 3. the hand of the Lord is upon the s.
12. 5. ye shall take it out from the s. or the goats
20. 24. thou shalt sacrifice thereon thy s. and oxen
22. 1. if a man steal a s. and kill it or sell it, 4, 9.
10. if a man give to his neighbour a s. to keep
30. likewise do with the firstling of s. 34. 19.
Lev. 1. 10. if his offering be of the s. or goats
7. 23. shall eat no manner of fat of s. or of goats
22. 19. ye shall offer a male of the s. or goats, 21.
27. 26. no man shall sanctify the firstling of a s.
Num. 18. 17. the firstling of s. thou shalt not redeem
32. 24. build ye cities and folds for your s. 36.
Deut. 7. 13. he will bless the flocks of thy s.
17. 1. thou shalt not sacrifice s. wherein is blemish
18. 3. the priest's due from them that offer s. 4.
22. 1. thou shalt not see thy brother's s. go astray
28. 4. blessed shall be the flocks of thy s.
18. cursed shall be the flocks of thy s. 31, 51.
32. 14. that he might eat butter of kine, milk of s.
Josh. 6. 21. they destroyed at Jericho ox and s.
7. 24. Joshua took Achan's s. and tent, and all he had
Judg. 6. 4. the Midianites left neither s. nor oxen
1 Sam. 8. 17. the king will take the tenth of your s.
14. 32. the people flew upon the spoil and took s.
34. bring hither every man his ox and his s.
15. 3. slay both ox and s. ‖ 9. Saul spread the s.
14. what meaneth this bleating of s. in my ears ?
21. the people took of the spoil s. and oxen
16. 11. the youngest, behold, he keepeth the s.
19. send me David thy son, who is with the s.
17. 15. David returned to feed his father's s.
20. he rose early and left the s. with a keeper
34. David said, thy servant kept his father's s.
25. 2. Nabal had 3000 s. he was shearing his s.
18. Abigail hasted, and took five s. ready dressed
27. 9. David took away the s. the oxen, and asses
2 Sam. 7. 8. I took thee from following the s.
17. 29. Barzillai brought David butter and s.
24. 17. David said, lo, I have sinned, but these s.
what have they done ? 1 Chron. 21. 17.
1 Kings 1. 19. Adonij. slain s. oxen and fat cattle, 25.
4. 23. Solomon's provision for one day hundred s.
8. 5. all the congregation sacrificing s. and oxen
1 Kings 8. 63. Solomon offered s. 2 Chr. 5. 6. | 7. 5.
2 Kings 5. 26. is it a time to receive s. and oxen ?
1 Chron. 5. 21. they took from Hagarites 250,000 s.
12. 40. they brought oxen and s. abundantly
2 Chron. 14. 15. Asa carried from the Ethiopians s.
15. 11. and they offered of the spoil 7000 s.
18. 2. Ahab killed s. and oxen for Jehoshaphat
29. 33. the consecrated things were 3000 s.
30. 24. Hezekiah the king did give 7000 s. and the
princes gave to the congregation 10,000 s.
31. 6. they brought in the tithes of oxen and s.
Neh. 5. 18. for Nehemiah daily one ox, six choice s.
Job 1. 3. his substance also was 7000 s. 3000 camels
16. the fire is fallen, and hath burnt up the s.
31. 20. if he were not warmed with fleece of my s.
42. 12. for he had 14,000 s. and 6000 camels
Psal. 8. 7. for thou hast given him all s. and oxen
44. 11. thou hast given us like s. for meat
49. 14. like s. are laid in the grave, death feed
74. 1. why doth thine anger smoke against thy s. ?
78. 52. but made his own people go forth like s.
79. 13. so we thy people and s. of thy pasture
95. 7. and we are the s. of his hand, 100. 3.
119. 176. I have gone astray like a lost s.
144. 13. that our s. may bring forth thousands
Cant. 4. 2. thy teeth are like a flock of s. 6. 6.
Isa. 7. 21. in that day a man shall nourish two s.
22. 13. behold, joy and gladness, and killing of s
53. 6. all we like s. are gone astray ; we have
Jer. 12. 3. pull them out like s. for the slaughter
23. 1. woe be unto the pastors that scatter the s.
50. 6. my people hath been lost s. their shepherds
17. Israel is as scattered s. lions have driven him
Ezek. 34. 6. my s. wander through the mountains
11. I will search my s. and seek them out, 12.
Hos. 12. 12. Israel served, and for a wife he kept s
Joel 1. 18. the flocks of s. are made desolate
Mic. 5. 8. as a young lion among the flocks of s.
Zech. 13. 7. awake, O sword, smite the shepherd and
s. shall be scattered, Mat. 26. 31. Mark 14. 27.
Mat. 7. 15. beware of false prophets in s. clothing
10. 6. go rather to the lost s. of the house of Israel
12. 11. if one s. fall into a pit on the sabbath
12. how much then is a man better than a s. ?
15. 24. I am not sent but unto the lost s. of Israel
18. 12. if a man have 100 s. and one be gone
13. he rejoiceth more of that s. Luke 15. 4, 6.
25. 32. as a shepherd divideth his s. from goats
33. he shall set s. on his right hand, but goats
John 2. 14. he found in the temple those that sold s
15. he drove them out of the temple, and the s.
10. 2. that entereth by door is shepherd of the s.
3. the s. hear his voice, 27. ‖ 4. the s. follow him
7. then said Jesus, verily I am the door of the s.
8. were robbers, but the s. did not hear them
11. the good Shepherd giveth his life for his s.
12. an hireling leaveth the s. and fleeth, 13.
14. good Shepherd, I know my s. ‖ 16. other s. I h.
15. the Father, and I lay down my life for the s.
26. because ye are not of my s. as I said unto you
21. 16. he saith unto Peter, feed my s. 17.
Heb. 13. 20. Lord Jesus, that great Shepherd of s.
Rev. 18. 13. none buyeth s. horses, slaves, and souls

As SHEEP.

Num. 27. 17. be not as s. which have no shepherd
1 Kings 22. 17. I saw all Israel scattered on the hills,
as s. that have no shepherd, 2 Chron. 18. 16.
Psal. 44. 22. we are killed all the day long, we are
counted as s. for the slaughter, Rom. 8. 36.
Isa. 13. 14. it shall be as s. that no man taketh up
53. 7. and as s. before his shearers is dumb
Mic. 2. 12. I will put them together as s. of Bozra
Mat. 9. 36. compassion, because fainted and were
scattered as s. having no shepherd, Mark 6. 34.
10. 16. I send you forth as s. in midst of wolves
Acts 8. 32. he was led as a s. to the slaughter
1 Pet. 2. 25. ye were as s. going astray, but returned

SHEEP-COTE.

2 Sam. 7. 8. I took thee from the s. 1 Chron. 17. 7.

SHEEP-COTES.

1 Sam. 24. 3. Saul came to the s. after David

SHEEP-FOLD.

John 10. 1. he that entereth not the s. by the door

SHEEP-FOLDS.

Num. 32. 16. we will build s. for our cattle
Judg. 5. 16. why abodest thou among the s. ?
Psal. 78. 70. he chose David, took him from the s.

SHEEP-gate.

Neh. 3. 1. Eliashib and brethren built the s.-gate
32. between going up of the corner to the s.-g.
12. 39. they went on to the s.-gate, and they stood

SHEEP-market.

John 5. 2. there is at Jerusalem by the s.-market a
pool, called in the Hebrew tongue, Bethesda

SHEEP-master.

2 Kings 3. 4. Mesha king of Moab was a s.-master
See SHEARERS.

SHEEP-skins.

Heb. 11. 37. they wandered in s.-s. and goat-skins

SHEET.

Acts 10. 11. a vessel descending as a great s. 11. 5.

SHEETS.

Judg. 14. 12. then I will give you thirty s. and thirty
13. then shall give me thirty s. and thirty changes

SHEKEL.

Gen. 24. 22. the man took an ear-ring of half a s.
Exod. 30. 13. a s. after the s. of the sanctuary, a s. is
20 gerahs, Num. 3. 47. Ezek. 45. 12.
15. the poor shall not give less than half a s.
1 Sam. 9. 8. I have here the fourth part of a s.
2 Kings 7. 1. measure of fine flour for a s. 16. 18.
Neh. 10. 32. charged yearly with the third of a s.
Amos 8. 5. making the ephah small, and the s. great

SHEKELS.

Gen. 23. 15. my lord, the land is worth 400 s. 16.
24. 22. two bracelets for her hands of ten s. weight
Exod. 21. 32. he shall give her master thirty s.
30. 23. of pure myrrh 500 s. of sweet cinnamon
250 s. of sweet calamus 250 s.
Lev. 5. 15. the estimation by s. 27. 3, 4, 5, 6, 7, 16.
Num. 7. 14. one spoon of ten s. of gold full of incense, 20, 26, 32, 38, 44, 50, 56, 62, 68, 74, 80.

Deut. 22. 19. they shall amerce him in 100 *s.*
29. man shall give to the damsel's father fifty *s.*
Josh. 7. 21. when I saw in the spoils 200 *s.* of silver
Judg. 8. 26. weight of golden ear-rings was 1700 *s.*
17. 2. the 1100 *s.* I took it ‖ 3. had restored the *s.*
10. I will give thee ten *s.* of silver by the year
2 *Sam.* 14. 26. Absalom weighed his hair, 200 *s.*
18. 11. I would have given thee ten *s.* and a girdle
24. 24. David bought oxen for fifty *s.* of Araunah
1 *Kings* 10. 16. six hundred *s.* of gold to one target
2 *Kings* 15. 20. exacted of each man 50 *s.* of silver
1 *Chron.* 21. 25. so David gave to Ornan 600 *s.*
Neh. 5. 15. former govern. had taken 40 *s.* by year
Jer. 32. 9. I bought the field for 17 *s.* of silver
Ezek. 4. 10. meat shall be by weight twenty *s.* a day
See SANCTUARY.

SHELTER.

Job 24. 8. they embrace the rock for want of a *s.*
Ps. 61. 3. for thou hast been *s.* for me and a tower

SHEPHERD.

See Signification on PASTOR.

Gen. 46. 34. every *s.* is abomination to the Egypt.
49. 24. from thence is the *s.* the stone of Israel
1 *Sam.* 17. 40. he put the stones into a *s.* bag he had
Psal. 23. 1. the Lord is my *s.* I shall not want
80. 1. give ear, O *s.* of Israel, thou that leadest
Eccl. 12. 11. the words which are given from one *s.*
Isa. 38. 12. mine age is departed from me as *s.* tent
40. 11. he shall feed his flock like a *s.* gather lambs
44. 28. the Lord that saith of Cyrus, he is my *s.*
63. 11. that brought them up with *s.* of his flock
Jer. 31. 10. and keep him as a *s.* doth his flock
43. 12. array himself as a *s.* putteth on his garment
49. 19. who is that *s.* that will stand, 50. 44.
51. 23. I will also break in pieces *s.* and his flock
Ezek. 34. 5. they were scatter. because there is no *s.*
8. my flock became prey, because there was no *s.*
12. as a *s.* seeketh out his flock among the sheep
23. I will set up one *s.* over them, my servant
David shall feed them, and be their *s.* 37. 24.
Amos 3. 12. as the *s.* takes out of mouth of the lion
Zech. 10. 2. they were troubled, bec. there was no *s.*
11. 15. take to thee the instruments of a foolish *s.*
11. 16. lo, I will raise up a *s.* in the land
17. woe to the idle *s.* that leaveth the flock, sword
13. 7. awake, O sword, ag. my *s.* and my fellow
John 10. 12. but he that is an hireling, and not *s.*
14. I am good *s.* know my sheep, and am known
16. and there shall be one fold and one *s.*
Heb. 13. 20. our Ld. Jesus that great *s.* of the sheep
1 *Pet.* 2. 25. but ye are now returned unto the *s.*
5. 4. when chief *s.* shall appear, ye shall receive
See SHEEP.

SHEPHERDS.

Gen. 46. 32. men are *s.* ‖ 47. 3. thy servants are *s.*
Exod. 2. 17. and the *s.* came and drove them away
19. an Egyptian delivered us out of hand of *s.*
1 *Sam.* 25. 7. now thy *s.* with us, we hurt them not
Cant. 1. 8. and feed thy kids beside the *s.* tents
Isa. 13. 20. nor shall the *s.* make their folds there
31. 4. when multitude of *s.* is called forth ag. him
56. 11. and they are *s.* that cannot understand
Jer. 6. 3. the *s.* with their flocks shall come unto her
23. 4. I will set up *s.* over them, who shall feed
25. 34. howl, ye *s.* ‖ 35. the *s.* have no way to flee
36. a voice of the cry of the *s.* and an howling
33. 12. in all the cities shall be an habitation of *s.*
50. 6. their *s.* have caused them to go astray
Ezek. 34. 2. prophesy against the *s.* of Israel, woe
to the *s.* of Israel, should not *s.* feed the flocks?
8. my flock a prey, nor did my *s.* search for my
flock, but *s.* fed themselves, and fed not my flock
10. thus saith the Lord, behold, I am against the
s. neither shall the *s.* feed themselves any more
Amos 1. 2. and the habitations of the *s.* shall mourn
Mic. 5. 5. then shall we raise against him seven *s.*
Nah. 3. 18. thy *s.* slumber, O king of Assyria, nobles
Zeph. 2. 6. the sea coasts shall be cottages for *s.*
Zech. 10. 3. mine anger was kindled against the *s.*
11. 3. there is a voice of the howling of the *s.*
5. and their own *s.* pity them not
8. three *s.* also I cut off in one month
Luke 2. 8. there were in the same country *s.* in field
18. those things which were told them by the *s.*
20. the *s.* returned, glorifying and praising God

SHERD.

Isa. 30. 14. there shall not be found a *s.* to take fire

SHERDS.

Ezek. 23. 34. thou shalt break the *s.* thereof

SHERIFFS.

Dan. 3. 2. Nebuchadnezzar sent to gather the *s.*
3. then the *s.* and rulers were gathered together

SHEW, *Substantive.*

Psal. 39. 6. surely every man walketh in a vain *s.*
Isa. 3. 9. the *s.* of their countenance doth witness
Luke 20. 47. and for a *s.* make long prayers
Gal. 6. 12. as many as desire to make a fair *s.* in flesh
Col. 2. 15. spoiled powers, made *s.* of them openly
23. which things have *s.* of wisdom in will worship

SHEW-*bread.*

See *Signification* on BREAD.

Exod. 25. 30. shalt set upon a table *s. bread* before me
35. 13. make the table, and the *s. bread*, 39. 36.
Num. 4. 7. on table of *s. bread* shall spread a cloth
1 *Sam.* 21. 6. there was no bread but the *s. bread*
1 *Kings* 7. 48. table of gold whereon the *s. bread* was
1 *Chr.* 9. 32. sons of Kohathites to prepare *s. bread*
23. 29. service both for the *s. bread* and fine flour
28. 16. David gave gold for the tables of *s. bread*
2 *Chron.* 2. 4. an house for the continual *s. bread*
4. 19. made tables whereon the *s. bread* was set
13. 11. the *s. bread* also set they in order
29. 18. have cleansed *s. bread* table with vessels
Neh. 10. 33. to charge ourselves for the *s. bread*
Mat. 12. 4. how he entered into the house of God,
and did eat the *s. bread*, *Mark* 2. 26. *Luke* 6. 4.
Heb. 9. 2. a tabernacle, wherein was the *s. bread*

SHEW.

Exod. 7. 9. Pharaoh shall speak, saying, *s.* miracle
9. 16. I raised thee up for to *s.* in thee my power
10. 1. that I might *s.* my signs before him
13. 8. and thou shalt *s.* thy son in that day

Exod. 14. 13. see the salvation L. will *s.* to you to day
18. 20. shalt *s.* way they must walk, *Deut.* 1. 33.
25. 9. made it according to all that I *s.* thee
33. 13. *s.* me now thy way ‖ 18. *s.* me thy glory
Deut. 5. 5. I stood to *s.* you the word of the Lord
7. 2. make no covenant, nor *s.* mercy unto them
13. 17. that the Lord may *s.* thee mercy
17. 9. they shall *s.* thee the sentence of judgment
10. thou shalt do as they shall *s.* thee, 11.
28. 50. not regard old, nor *s.* favour to young
32. 7. ask thy father, and he will *s.* thee
Josh. 5. 6. the Lord sware he would not *s.* the land
Judg. 1. 24. the spies said, *s.* us we pray thee, the
entrance into the city, and we will *s.* thee mercy
6. 17. then *s.* me a sign that thou talkest with me
1 *Sam.* 3. 15. Samuel feared to *s.* Eli the vision
8. 9. *s.* them the manner of the king that shall reign
9. 6. man of God peradventure can *s.* us our way
27. stand, that I may *s.* thee the word of God
10. 8. I will come and *s.* thee what thou shalt do
14. 12. come up to us, and we will *s.* you a thing
20. 2. my father will do nothing, he will *s.* it me
12. if I then send not unto thee, and *s.* it thee
22. 17. they knew when he fled, and did not *s.* it
25. 8. ask thy young men, and they will *s.* thee
2 *Sam.* 15. 25. he will *s.* me, both it and his habitat.
1 *Kings* 1. 52. if he will *s.* himself a worthy man
2. 2. be thou strong therefore, and *s.* thyself a man
18. 1. came to Elijah, go *s.* thyself to Ahab, 2.
2 *Kings* 6. 11. will ye not *s.* me which of us is for king
2 *Chr.* 16. 9. to *s.* himself strong in behalf of them
Ezra 2. 59. they could not *s.* their fathers' house,
whether they were of Israel, *Neh.* 7. 61.
Neh. 9. 19. the pillar of fire to *s.* them light
Esth. 1. 11. to *s.* the people and princes her beauty
2. 10. Mordecai charged her not to *s.* her kindred
4. 8. gave him a copy of the writing to *s.* Esther
Job 10. 2. *s.* me wherefore thou contendest with me
11. 6. he would *s.* thee the secrets of wisdom
32. 6. I was afraid, durst not *s.* you my opinion
33. 23. if a messenger to *s.* to man his uprightness
Psal. 4. 6. many will say, who will *s.* us any good?
9. 14. that I may *s.* forth all thy praise in gates
16. 11. wilt *s.* me the path of life, in thy presence
25. 4. *s.* me thy ways, O Lord, teach me thy paths
14. the Lord will *s.* them his covenant
51. 15. and my mouth shall *s.* forth thy praise
71. 15. my mouth shall *s.* forth thy righteousness
79. 13. we thy people will *s.* forth thy praise
85. 7. *s.* us mercy, O Lord, grant us thy salvation
86. 17. *s.* me a token of good, that they may see it
88. 10. wilt thou *s.* wonders to the dead
92. 15. to *s.* that Lord is upright, he is my rock
94. 1. O G. whom vengeance belongeth, *s.* thyself
106. 2. who can *s.* forth all his praise?
Prov. 18. 24. a man must *s.* himself friendly
Isa. 27. 11. he that formed them will *s.* no favour
30. 30. the Lord shall *s.* lighting down of his arm
41. 22. let them bring them forth and *s.* us what
shall happen, let them *s.* the former things
23. *s.* the things that are to come hereafter
43. 9. who among them can *s.* us former things?
21. people have I formed, shall *s.* forth my praise
44. 7. things that are coming, let them *s.* to them
46. 8. remember this, and *s.* yourselves men
49. 9. say to them in darkness, *s.* yourselves
58. 1. *s.* my people their transgression and sins
60. 6. they shall *s.* forth the praises of the Lord
Jer. 16. 10. thou shalt *s.* them all these words
13. into a land, where I will not *s.* you favour
42. 3. thy God may *s.* us the way we may walk
51. 31. to *s.* the king of Babylon his city is taken
Ezek. 22. 2. thou shalt *s.* her all her abominations
33. 31. for with their mouth they *s.* much love
37. 18. wilt thou not *s.* us what thou meanest?
40. 4. set thine heart upon all that I shall *s.* thee
43. 10. son of man, *s.* the house to house of Israel
11. *s.* them the form of the house and fashion
Dan. 2. 2. the sorcerers for to *s.* king his dreams
4. and we will *s.* the interpretation, 7.
6. if ye *s.* the dream and interpretation, therefore
s. the dream and interpretation thereof
10. not a man that can *s.* the king's matter
16. he would *s.* the king the interpretation
27. the secret cannot the wise men *s.* to the king
4. 2. I thought it good to *s.* the signs and wonders
5. 7. whosoever shall *s.* me the interpretation
9. 23. command came, and I am come to *s.* thee
Hab. 1. 3. why dost thou *s.* me iniquity?
Mat. 8. 4. go thy way, *s.* thyself to the priest, and
offer the gift, *Mark* 1. 44. *Luke* 5. 14. ‖ 17. 14.
11. 4. go and *s.* John these things ye do hear
12. 18. he shall *s.* judgment to the Gentiles
14. 2. he is risen, therefore mighty works do *s.*
forth themselves in him, *Mark* 6. 14.
16. 1. the Pharisees desired he would *s.* a sign
22. 19. *s.* me the tribute money, *Luke* 20. 24.
24. 1. came to *s.* him the buildings of the temple
24. for there shall arise false Christs, and shall *s.*
great signs and wonders, *Mark* 13. 22.
Mark 14. 15. he will *s.* you a large upper room furnished, there make ready for us, *Luke* 22. 12.
Luke 1. 19. I am sent to *s.* thee these glad tidings
8. 39. *s.* how great things God hath done to thee
John 5. 20. he will *s.* him greater works than these
7. 4. if thou do these things *s.* thyself to the world
11. 57. if any knew where he was they should *s.* it
14. 8. *s.* us the Father and it sufficeth us, 9.
16. 13. and he will *s.* you things to come
14. he shall receive of mine, and *s.* it to you, 15.
25. but I shall *s.* you plainly of the Father
Acts 1. 24. Lord *s.* whether of these thou hast chosen
7. 3. and come into the land which I shall *s.* thee
12. 17. and he said, go, *s.* these things to James
16. 17. the men who *s.* to us the way of salvation
24. 27. Felix willing to *s.* the Jews a pleasure
26. 23. that he should *s.* light to the people
Rom. 2. 15. who *s.* the work of the law written
9. 17. I have raised thee, that I might *s.* my power
22. what if God, willing to *s.* his wrath, endured
1 *Cor.* 11. 26. ye do *s.* the Lord's death till he come
12. 31. yet *s.* I to you a more excellent way

1 *Cor.* 15. 51. I *s.* you mystery, we shall not all sleep
2 *Cor.* 8. 24. *s.* ye to them the proof of your love
Eph. 2. 7. that he might *s.* the exceeding riches
1 *Thess.* 1. 9. for they themselves *s.* of us what mann.
1 *Tim.* 1. 16. that Christ might *s.* all long-suffering
5. 4. let them learn first to *s.* piety at home
6. 15. which in his times he shall *s.* who is the
2 *Tim.* 2. 15. study to *s.* thyself approved to God
Heb. 6. 11. that every one of you *s.* the same dilig.
17. God willing to *s.* to the heirs of promise
Jam. 2. 18. *s.* me thy faith without thy works
3. 13. let him *s.* his works out of good conversation
1 *Pet.* 2. 9. ye should *s.* forth the praises of him
1 *John* 1. 2. and *s.* unto you that eternal life
Rev. 1. 1. he sent his angel to *s.* his servants, 22. 6.

I will SHEW.

Gen. 12. 1. get thee unto a land that *I will s.* thee
Exod. 33. 19. I will be gracious to whom I will be
gracious, *I will s.* mercy on whom *I will s.* mercy
Judg. 4. 22. *I will s.* thee man whom thou seekest
1 *Sam.* 16. 3. *I will s.* thee what thou shalt do
20. 13. to do thee evil, then *I will s.* it thee
1 *Kings* 18. 15. *I will* surely *s.* myself to Ahab
2 *Kings* 7. 12. *I will s.* you what Syrians have done
Job 15. 17. *I will s.* thee that which I have seen
32. 10. I also *will s.* mine opinion, 17. ‖ 36. 2.
Psal. 9. 1. *I will s.* forth all thy marvellous works
50. 23. *I will s.* the salvation of God, 91. 16.
Jer. 18. 17. *I will s.* them the back, and not face
33. 3. *I will s.* thee great and mighty things
42. 12. *I will s.* mercies unto you, cause to return
Dan. 2. 24. *I will s.* the king the interpretation
10. 21. but *I will s.* thee what is noted in script.
11. 2. and now *I will s.* thee the truth. Behold
Joel 2. 30. *I will s.* wonders in heaven, *Acts* 2. 19.
Mic. 7. 15. *I will s.* to him marvellous things
Nah. 3. 5. *I will s.* the nations thy nakedness
Zech. 1. 9. angel said, *I will s.* thee what these be
Luke 6. 47. *I will s.* to whom he is like
Acts 9. 16. *I will s.* him how great things he must suf.
Jam. 2. 18. *I will s.* thee my faith by my works
Rev. 4. 1. *I will s.* thee things which must be
17. 1. *I will s.* thee the judgment of the whore
21. 9. *I will s.* thee the bride the Lamb's wife
See KINDNESS.

SHEWED.

Lev. 13. 19. a white spot, and it be *s.* to priest, 49.
Num. 13. 26. and *s.* them the fruit of the land
Deut. 34. 12. which Moses *s.* in the sight of Israel
Judg. 1. 25. and when he *s.* them the entrance
4. 12. *s.* Sisera, that Barak was gone up to Tabor
13. 10. the woman made haste, and *s.* her husband
16. 18. come up, for he hath *s.* me all his heart
Ruth 2. 11. it hath been *s.* me all that thou hast done
1 *Sam.* 11. 9. came and *s.* it to the men of Jabesh
19. 7. Jonathan *s.* him all those things
22. 21. Abiathar *s.* Dav. that Saul had slain priests
24. 18. Saul said to David, thou hast *s.* this day
how thou hast dealt well with me
2 *Sam.* 11. 22. messenger *s.* David all Joab had sent
1 *Kings* 1. 27. thou hast not *s.* it to thy servant
16. 27. Omri, and his might that he *s.* 22. 45.
2 *Kings* 6. 6. where fell it? he *s.* him the place
11. 4. took an oath, and *s.* them the king's son
20. 13. Hezekiah hearkened to them, and *s.* them
all the house of his precious things, *Isa.* 39. 2.
15. there is nothing I have not *s.* them, *Isa.* 39. 4.
Esth. 1. 4. when he *s.* riches of his glorious kingdom
2. 10. Esther had not *s.* her people nor kindred, 20.
3. 6. for they had *s.* him the people of Mordecai
Job 6. 14. to afflicted pity should be *s.* from his friend
Psal. 71. 18. until I have *s.* thy strength to this gen.
105. 27. they *s.* his signs among them, *Acts* 7. 36.
142. 2. poured my complaint, I *s.* before him my
Prov. 26. 26. his wickedness shall be *s.* before cong.
Eccl. 2. 19. labour, wherein I have *s.* myself wise
Isa. 40. 14. who *s.* to him the way of understanding
Ezek. 22. 26. they *s.* no difference between clean
Mat. 28. 11. and *s.* to chief priests all things done
Luke 4. 5. devil *s.* him all kingdoms of the world
7. 18. the disciples of John *s.* him these things
10. 37. and he said, he that *s.* mercy on him
14. 21. that serv. came and *s.* his lord these things
20. 37. that the dead are raised, Moses *s.* at bush
John 10. 32. many good works have I *s.* you
20. 20. he *s.* unto them his hands and his side
21. 1. Jesus *s.* hims. again to disciples, 14. *Acts* 1. 3.
Acts 4. 22. on whom this miracle of healing was *s.*
7. 26. Moses *s.* himself to them as they strove
36. after he had *s.* wonders and signs
52. which *s.* before of the coming of the just One
11. 13. he *s.* how he had seen an angel in his house
19. 18. many that believed confessed, *s.* their deeds
20. 20. but have *s.* and have taught you publicly
35. I have *s.* you all things, how so labouring
23. 22. tell no man thou hast *s.* these things to me
26. 20. but first Paul *s.* to them of Damascus
28. 2. the barbarous people *s.* no little kindness
21. none of brethren *s.* or spake any harm of thee
1 *Cor.* 10. 28. eat not, for his sake that *s.* it
Heb. 6. 10. love which ye have *s.* toward his name
Jam. 2. 13. shall have judgment that *s.* no mercy
Rev. 21. 10. angel *s.* me the great city Jerusalem
22. 1. he *s.* me a pure river of water of life
8. I fell down to worship the angel who *s.* me
God, or *Lord* SHEWED, *expressly, or implicitly.*
Gen. 19. 19. thy mercy *s.* to me in saving my life
24. 14. that thou hast *s.* kindness to my master
32. 10. not worthy of the least of the mercies *s.*
39. 21. the *Lord s.* Joseph mercy, and gave favour
41. 25. *God s.* Pharaoh what he is about to do
39. forasmuch as *God* hath *s.* thee all this
48. 11. and lo, *God* hath *s.* me also thy seed
Exod. 15. 25. he cried, and the *Lord s.* him a tree
25. 40. look thou make them after the pattern *s.*
thee in the mount, 26. 30. ‖ 27. 8. *Heb.* 8. 5.
Lev. 24. 12. that the mind of the *Lord* might be *s.*
Num. 8. 4. to the pattern the *Lord* had *s.* Moses
14. 11. all signs I have *s.* among them, *Deut.* 6. 22.
Deut. 4. 36. and upon earth he *s.* thee his great fire
5. 24. behold, the *Lord* our *God s.* us his glory
34. 1. the *Lord s.* him all the land of Gilead

Judg. 13. 23. nor would he have *s.* all these things
1 *Kings* 3. 6. Solomon said, thou hast *s.* to thy servant David my father great mercy, 2 *Chron.* 1. 8.
2 *Kings* 8. 10. *Lord* hath *s.* me, he shall surely die
13. the *Lord* hath *s.* me that thou shalt be king
2 *Chron.* 7. 10. for goodness the *Lord* had *s.* David
Ezra 9. 8. grace hath been *s.* from *Lord* our *God*
Psal. 31. 21. he hath *s.* me his marvellous kindness
60. 3. thou hast *s.* thy people hard things
71. 20. thou hast *s.* me great and sore troubles
78. 11. they forgat his wonders he had *s.* them
98. 2. his righteousness hath *s.* in sight of heathen
111. 6. he *s.* his people the power of his works
118. 27. *God* is the *Lord* who hath *s.* us light
Isa. 26. 10. let favour be *s.* to wicked, yet not learn
43. 12. I have *s.* when there was no strange god
48. 3. I *s.* them, I did them suddenly, came to pass
5. before it came to pass I *s.* it thee
Jer. 24. 1. the *Lord s.* me two baskets of figs
38. 21. this is the word that the *Lord* hath *s.* me
Ezek. 11. 25. all things that the *Lord* hath *s.* me
20. 11. gave statutes and *s.* them my judgments
Amos 7. 1. thus hath the *Lord s.* me, 4. 7. | 8. 1.
Mic. 6. 8. he hath *s.* thee, O man, what is good
Zech. 1. 20. and the *Lord s.* me four carpenters
3. 1. he *s.* me Joshua standing before angel of *Lord*
Luke 1. 51. he hath *s.* strength with his arm
58. heard how *Lord* had *s.* great mercy on her
Acts 3. 18. but those things which *God* before had *s.*
10. 28. *God s.* I should not call any man common
40. *God* raised him the third day and *s.* him
Rom. 1. 19. is manifest, for *God* hath *s.* it to them
2 *Pet.* 1. 14. even as our *Lord* Jesus hath *s.* me

SHEWEDST.

Neh. 9. 10. and *s.* signs and wonders upon Pharaoh
Jer. 11. 18. I know it, then thou *s.* me their doings

SHEWEST.

Job 10. 16. thou *s.* thyself marvellous upon me
Jer. 32. 18. thou *s.* loving-kindness to thousands
John 2. 18. Jews said, what sign *s.* thou to us? 6. 30.

SHEWETH.

Gen. 41. 28. what God is about to do, he *s.* to Pharaoh
Num. 23. 3. whatsoever he *s.* me, I will tell thee
1 *Sam.* 22. 8. none *s.* me that my son made a league
2 *Sam.* 22. 51. he *s.* mercy to his anointed, to David, and to his seed for evermore, *Psal.* 18. 50.
Job 36. 9. he *s.* them their work and transgressions
33. noise thereof *s.* concerning it, the cattle also
Psal. 19. 1. and the firmament *s.* his handy work
2. and night unto night *s.* knowledge
112. 5. good man *s.* favour, and lendeth, will guide
147. 19. he *s.* his word unto Jacob, his statutes
Prov. 12. 17. he that speaks truth, *s.* forth right
27. 25. the hay appears, the tender grass *s.* itself
Isa. 41. 26. yea, there is none that *s.* your words
Mat. 4. 8. and *s.* him all kingdoms of the world
John 5. 20. Father loveth, and *s.* the Son all things

SHEWING.

Exod. 20. 6. and *s.* mercy unto thousands, *Deut.* 5. 10.
Psal. 78. 4. *s.* to generation to come praises of Lord
Cant. 2. 9. my beloved *s.* himself thro' the lattice
Dan. 4. 27. break off thine iniquities by *s.* mercy
5. 12. *s.* of hard sentences found in the same Daniel
Luke 8. 1. *s.* glad tidings of the kingdom of God
Acts 9. 39. and *s.* the coats which Dorcas made
18. 28. *s.* by scripture that Jesus was Christ
2 *Thess.* 2. 4. as God, *s.* himself that he is God
Tit. 2. 7. in all things *s.* thyself pattern of good works
10. not purloining, but *s.* all good fidelity
3. 2. but be gentle, *s.* all meekness to all men

SHEWING.

Luke 1. 80. was in deserts till day of his *s.* to Israel

SHIELD

Is *a piece of defensive armour. The common materials of a shield were wood: it was covered with leather, with plates of gold, or brass. Sometimes they were made all of gold, or brass. Those that* Solomon *made were of massy gold,* 1 Kings 10. 17. Shishak *king of* Egypt *took these away, and* Rehoboam *made others of brass to serve in their stead,* 1 Kings 14. 26, 27.

In Scripture *God is often called the* shield *of his people:* I am thy shield, *says God to* Abraham, Gen. 15. 1. *I will protect and defend thee. The* Psalmist *says,* Thou, Lord, wilt bless the righteous; with favour wilt thou compass him as with a shield, *Psal.* 5. 12. *With thy love and gracious providence thou wilt keep him safe on every side. Princes and great men are also called the* shield *of the people, because by their office they are, or should be, the common parents and protectors of their people, to defend them from all oppressions and injuries.* Psal. 47. 9. The shields of the earth belong unto God, *are dependent upon him. Faith in Scripture is likewise called a shield,* Eph. 6. 16. *because it derives strength from* Christ *for overcoming the temptations of Satan.*

They hung up their shields *upon towers for ornaments, or as trophies of victory, to make use of them upon occasion. The tower of* David *was adorned with a thousand* shields. Cant. 4. 4. Thy neck is like the tower of *David,* builded for an armoury, whereon there hang a thousand bucklers, all shields of mighty men. *By* neck, *Commentators understand the grace of faith, which, as is said, is called a* shield; *and this shews that by faith the church is strong and victorious over all her enemies.*

Gen. 15. 1. I am thy *s.* and exceeding great reward
Deut. 33. 29. saved by the Lord, the *s.* of thy help
Judg. 5. 8. I Deborah arose a mother in Israel, was there a *s.* or spear seen among 40,000 in Israel?
1 *Sam.* 17. 7. one bearing a *s.* went before him, 41.
45. thou comest to me with a spear and a *s.*
2 *Sam.* 1. 21. there the *s.* of the mighty is vilely cast away, *s.* of Saul as tho' not anointed with oil
22. 3. he is my *s.* *Ps.* 3. 3. | 28. 7. | 119. 114. | 144. 2.
36. given me the *s.* of thy salvation, *Psal.* 18. 35.
1 *Kings* 10. 17. three pound of gold went to one *s.*
2 *Kings* 19. 32. he shall not come before it with a *s.* nor cast a bank against it, *Isa.* 37. 33.
1 *Chron.* 12. 8. the Gadites that could handle *s.*
24. the children of Judah that bare *s.* and spear
34. of Naphtali with *s.* and spear 37,000
2 *Chr.* 25. 5. choice men that could handle sp. and *s.*
Job 39. 23. glittering spear and *s.* rattleth ag. him
Psal. 5. 12. with favour wilt compass him as with *s.*
33. 20. the Lord is our *s.* 59. 11. | 84. 9. | 89. † 18.
35. 2. take hold of the *s.* and buckler, and stand
76. 3. there brake he the arrows of bow, the *s.*
84. 11. L. G. is sun and *s.* will give grace and glory
91. 4. his truth shall be thy *s.* and buckler
115. 9. he is their help and their *s.* 10. 11.
Prov. 30. 5. he is a *s.* to them that put trust in him
Isa. 21. 5. arise, ye princes, and anoint the *s.*
22. 6. Elam bare quiver, Kir uncovered the *s.*
Jer. 46. 3. order buckler and *s.* draw near to battle
9. come forth, Libyans, that handle the *s.*
Ezek. 23. 24. they shall set ag. thee buckler and *s.*
27. 10. they hanged the *s.* and helmet in thee, 11.
Nah. 2. 3. the *s.* of his mighty men is made red
Eph. 6. 16. above all taking the *s.* of faith

SHIELDS.

2 *Sam.* 8. 7. David took the *s.* of gold that were on the servants of Hadadezer, 1 *Chr.* 18. 7.
1 *Kings* 10. 17. Solomon made 300 *s.* of beaten gold, the king put them in Lebanon, 2 *Chron.* 9. 16.
14. 26. Shishak took away all, even all *s.* of gold which Solomon had made, 2 *Chron.* 12. 9.
27. Rehoboam made in their stead brazen *s.* and committed them to chief of guards, 2 *Chr.* 12. 10.
2 *Kings* 11. 10. priest gave king Dav. *s.* 2 *Chr.* 23. 9.
2 *Chr.* 11. 12. in every several city put *s.* and spears
14. 8. out of Benjamin that bare *s.* 17. 17.
26. 14. Uzziah prepared for them *s.* and spears
32. 5. Hezek. made darts and *s.* in abundance, 27.
Neh. 4. 16. the other half of them held spears and *s.*
Job 41. † 15. strong pieces of *s.* are his pride
Psal. 47. 9. the *s.* of the earth belong to God
Cant. 4. 4. whereon hang buckl. all *s.* of mighty men
Jer. 51. 11. make bright the arrows, gather the *s.*
Ezek. 38. 4. even great company with buckl. and *s.* 5.
39. 9. they shall burn the *s.* and the weapons

SHIGGAION.

This word is found in the title of Psal. 7. *It cometh from another* Hebrew *word which signifies to* stray or wander; *whence some do conjecture, that it was a various song, running from one kind of tune into another; and that it was used in great anguishes of heart, when as the thoughts and stirrings of the heart, through the greatness of trouble, do vary and fall from one strain to another in a straying and scattering manner.*

Some think it is an instrument of Music; others translate it, The error of David; *others,* The secret of David; *others,* The delight of David; *and others again,* The disquiet of David. *Some think it ought to be translated,* A song of trouble, *or* A song of consolation of David: *The* Arabic *word* Schaga *signifies,* to be in trouble; *and the* Hebrew *word* Schagah, *or* Shagah, to rejoice, to be comforted.

SHILOH,

One of the glorious names of the Messias, *denoting him to be the only procurer of our happiness; and our alone peace maker with God: for it importeth a Saviour, or happy, blessed, peaceable, or a peace-maker, &c. from the root* Shalah, *he was quiet, and in peace; he was safe and happy. It is found,* Gen. 49. 10. The sceptre shall not depart from *Judah,* nor a lawgiver from between his feet, until SHILOH come, and unto him shall the gathering of the people be. *All* Christian *commentators agree, that this word ought to be understood of the* Messiah; *of* Jesus Christ. Jerom *translates it by* Qui mittendus est, He who is to be sent, *and manifestly reads* Shiloach, sent, *instead of* Shiloh. *The* Septuagint *translate it,* Until the coming of him to whom it is reserved; *or,* till we see arrive that which is reserved for him.

Some translate, The sceptre shall not depart from Judah, till he comes to whom it belongs: *others,* till the coming of the Peace-maker, *or the* Pacific; *or of prosperity: others,* till the birth of him who shall be born of a woman, who shall conceive without the knowledge of a man. *Otherwise, the sceptre shall not depart from* Judah, till its end, till its ruin, till the downfall of the kingdom of the *Jews. A certain author derives* Shiloh *from* shalah, *which sometimes signifies* to be weary, to suffer; *till his labours, his sufferings, his passion, should come to pass.*

SHINE.

Num. 6. 25. the Lord make his face *s.* upon thee
Job 3. 4. that day be dark; neither let light *s.* on it
10. 3. thou shouldest *s.* on counsel of the wicked
11. 17. thou shalt *s.* forth, thou shalt be as morning
18. 5. and the spark of his fire shall not *s.*
22. 28. and the light shall *s.* upon thy ways
36. 32. the light he commandeth it not to *s.*
37. 15. when he caused the light of his cloud to *s.*
41. 18. by his neesings a light doth *s.* and his eyes
32. he maketh a path to *s.* after him
Psal. 31. 16. make thy face to *s.* upon thy servant
67. 1. cause his face to *s.* upon us, 80. 3, 7, 19.
80. 1. that dwellest between cherubims, *s.* forth
104. 15. and oil to make his face to *s.* and bread
119. 135. make thy face to *s.* upon thy servant
Eccl. 8. 1. a man's wisdom maketh his face to *s.*
Isa. 13. 10. the moon shall not cause her light to *s.*
60. 1. arise, *s.* for thy light is come, glory of Lord
Jer. 5. 28. they are waxen fat, they *s.* they overpass
Dan. 9. 17. cause thy face to *s.* upon thy sanctuary
12. 3. that be wise, shall *s.* as stars for ever and ever
Mat. 5. 16. let your light so *s.* before men to see your
13. 43. then shall the righteous *s.* forth as the sun
17. 2. his face did *s.* as sun, and his raiment white
2 *Cor.* 4. 4. lest light of gospel of Christ should *s.*
6. God who commanded light to *s.* out of darkn.
Phil. 2. 15. among whom ye *s.* as lights in world
Rev. 18. 23. light of a candle shall *s.* no more at all
21. 23. city had no need of sun nor moon to *s.* in it

SHINED.

Deut. 33. 2. the Lord *s.* forth from mount Paran
Job 29. 3. when his candle *s.* upon my head
31. 26. if I beheld the sun when it *s.* or the moon
Psal. 50. 2. out of Zion perfect. of beauty God hath *s.*
Isa. 9. 2. upon them hath the light *s.*
Ezek. 43. 2. and the earth *s.* with his glory
Acts 9. 3. suddenly there *s.* about him a light
12. 7. the angel came, and a light *s.* in the prison
2 *Cor.* 4. 6. for God hath *s.* in our hearts to give light

SHINETH.

Job 25. 5. behold even to the moon, and it *s.* not
Psal. 139. 12. but the night *s.* as the day
Prov. 4. 18. as shining light that *s.* more and more
Mat. 24. 27. as lightning *s.* even to the west
Luke 17. 24. and *s.* to other part under heaven
John 1. 5. the light *s.* in darkness, and the darkness
2 *Pet.* 1. 19. as to a light that *s.* in a dark place
1 *John* 2. 8. darkness is past, the true light now *s.*
Rev. 1. 16. his countenance was as the sun *s.*

SHINING.

2 *Sam.* 23. 4. as grass springing by clear *s.* after rain
Ezra 8. † 27. and two vessels of *s.* brass precious
Prov. 4. 18. the path of the just is as the *s.* light
Isa. 4. 5. will create the *s.* of a flaming fire by night
Joel 2. 10. the stars shall withdraw their *s.* 3. 15.
Hab. 3. 11. they went at the *s.* of thy glittering spear
Mark 9. 3. his raiment became *s.* white as snow
Luke 11. 36. when the *s.* of a candle giveth light
24. 4. two men stood by them in *s.* garments
John 5. 35. he was a burning and a *s.* light
Acts 26. 13. a light above the brightness of sun *s.*

SHIP.

Prov. 30. 19. the way of a *s.* in the midst of the sea
Isa. 33. 21. no gallant *s.* shall pass thereby
Jonah 1. 3. Jonah found a *s.* going to Tarshish
4. a tempest, so that the *s.* was like to be broken
5. mariners cast forth the wares into the *s.*
Mat. 4. 21. in a *s.* with Zebedee their father
22. and they left the *s.* and followed him
8. 24. that the *s.* was covered with the waves
14. 24. the *s.* was tossed with waves, *Mark* 4. 37.
Mark 1. 19. who were in the *s.* mending their nets
20. they left their father Zebedee in the *s.*
4. 38. he was in the hinder part of the *s.* asleep
8. 14. neither had they in the *s.* but one loaf
John 6. 21. and immediately the *s.* was at the land
21. 6. he said, cast the net on right side of the *s.*
Acts 20. 38. and they accompanied him to the *s.*
21. 2. finding a *s.* sailing over unto Phenicia
27. 2. and entering into a *s.* of Adramyttium

SHIPS.

Gen. 49. 13. Zebulun shall be an haven for *s.*
Num. 24. 24. and *s.* shall come from Chittim
Deut. 28. 68. L. shall bring thee into Egypt with *s.*
Judg. 5. 17. and why did Dan remain in *s.*?
1 *Kings* 9. 26. king Solomon made a navy of *s.*
22. 48. Jehoshaphat made *s.* of Tarshish to go to Ophir, the *s.* were broken, 2 *Chron.* 20. 37.
49. let my servants go with thine in the *s.*
2 *Chron.* 8. 18. Huram sent him by his servants, *s.*
9. 21. king's *s.* went to Tarshish every three years
Job 9. 26. they are passed away as the swift *s.*
Psal. 48. 7. thou breakest the *s.* of Tarshish
104. 26. there go the *s.* there is that Leviathan
107. 23. they that go down to the sea in *s.* that do
Prov. 31. 14. she is like the merchant *s.* she brings
Isa. 2. 16. the day of Lord on the *s.* of Tarshish
23. 1. howl, ye *s.* of Tarshish, no entering in, 14.
43. 14. the Chaldeans, whose cry is in the *s.*
60. 9. the *s.* of Tarshish first, to bring thy sons
Ezek. 27. 9. all *s.* of the sea with their mariners
25. *s.* of Tarshish did sing of thee in thy market
29. the pilots shall come down from their *s.*
30. 9. the messengers go forth from me in *s.*
Dan. 11. 30. for *s.* of Chittim shall come ag. him
40. king of the north shall come with many *s.*
Luke 5. 7. they filled both the *s.* they began to sink
Jam. 3. 4. behold also the *s.* though they be great
Rev. 8. 9. the third part of the *s.* were destroyed
18. 17. the company in *s.* stood afar off and cried
19. wherein were made rich all that had *s.*

SHIP-*boards.*

Ezek. 27. 5. have made all thy *s.-boards* of fir-trees

SHIP-MASTER.

Jonah 1. 6. *s.* said, what meanest thou, O sleeper?
Rev. 18. 17. every *s.* and sailors afar off, cried

SHIP-MEN.

1 *Kings* 9. 27. Hiram sent *s.* that had knowl. of sea
Acts 27. 30. the *s.* were about to flee out of the ship

SHIPPING.

John 6. 24. they took *s.* and came to Capernaum

SHIPWRECK.

2 *Cor.* 11. 25. once was I stoned, thrice I suffered *s.*
1 *Tim.* 1. 19. some concerning faith have made *s.*

SHITTAH-*tree.*

Isa. 41. 19. I will plant in the wilderness the *s.-tree*

SHITTIM-*wood.*

Exod. 25. 5. and badgers' skins and *s.-wood,* 35. 7.
10. shall make an ark of *s.-w.* 37. 1. *Deut.* 10. 3.
13. thou shalt make staves of *s.-wood,* 28. | 27. 6. | 37. 4, 15, 28. | 38. 6.
23. thou shalt make a table of *s.-wood,* 37. 10.
26. 15. make boards for tabernacle of *s.-wood,* 36. 20.
26. thou shalt make bars of *s.-wood,* 36. 31.
32. upon four pillars of *s.-wood,* 37. | 36. 36.
27. 1. thou shalt make an altar of *s.-wood,* 30. 1.
35. 24. every man with whom was found *s.-wood*

SHIVERS.

Rev. 2. 27. as vessels of a potter shall be broken to *s.*

SHOCK.

Job 5. 26. like as *s.* of corn cometh in his season

SHOCKS.

Judg. 15. 5. Samson burnt up the *s.* and standing corn

SHOD.

2 *Chron.* 28. 15. took the captives and *s.* them
Ezek. 16. 10. I *s.* thee with badgers' skin and girded
Mark 6. 9. be *s.* with sandals, put not on two coats
Eph. 6. 15. *s.* with the preparation of the gospel

SHOE

Is *put for,* [1] *The ground under feet,* Deut. 33. 25. [2] *The weakest means,* Psal. 60. 8. | 108. 9

[3] *Freedom from danger*, Cant. 7. 1. [4] *A contemptible price*, Amos 2. 6. | 8. 6. *To cast the shoe over a country, is to subdue that country, &c.* Psal. 60. 8. *To loose the shoe was*, [1] *A sign of reverence*, Exod. 3. 5. [2] *Of disgrace*, Deut. 25. 10. [3] *Of a contract*, Ruth 4. 7. [4] *Of mourning*, Ezek. 24. 17.

The apostle exhorts the Ephesians *to have* their feet shod with the preparation of the gospel of peace, *Eph.* 6. 15. *that is, to have a prepared and resolved frame of heart, which the gospel teaches and works; and which, like leg or foot harness, would enable them to walk with a steady pace in the ways of religion, notwithstanding the hardships, dangers, and difficulties that attend it.*

To go barefoot *was a sign of mourning and humiliation:* David went up by the ascent of mount Olivet barefoot, 2 *Sam.* 15. 30. *See* Isa. 20. 2, 4. Ezek. 24. 17. *The man that refused to raise up seed unto his brother deceased, had his shoe taken off by his brother's wife in presence of the elders,* Deut. 25. 9. *This was done, partly as a sign of his resignation of his right to the woman, and her husband's inheritance, as the* plucking off the shoe *signifies in* Ruth 4. 7. *and partly, as a note of infamy; to signify that he deserved to be treated like a servant or captive, who in token of submission and obedience went barefoot*, Isa. 20. 4. *It is said*, Psal. 60. 8. Over Edom will I cast my shoe. *I will take possession of them, I will trample upon them, and use them like slaves.* A pair of shoes, in Amos 2. 6. *denotes a small inconsiderable bribe.* To bear one's shoes, or untie the latchet of one's shoes, *is to perform the meanest services for him. See* Mat. 3. 11. Mark 1. 7. Luke 3. 16.

Deut. 25. 9. his brother's wife shall loose his *s.*
10. the house of him that hath his *s.* loosed
29. 5. thy *s.* is not waxen old upon thy foot
Josh. 5. 15. thy *s.* from off thy foot, for the place
Ruth 4. 7. man plucked off his *s.* and gave it to him
8. buy it for thee, so he drew off his *s.*
Ps. 60. 8. over Edom will I cast out my *s.* 108. 9.
Isa. 20. 2. and put off thy *s.* from thy foot, he did so

SHOE-*latchet*.
Gen. 14. 23. I will not take from thread to *s.-latchet*
John 1. 27. whose *s.-latchet* I am not worthy to loose

SHOES.
Exod. 3. 5. put off thy *s.* from thy feet, *Acts* 7. 33.
12. 11. thus shall ye eat it, with your *s.* on your feet
Deut. 33. 25. *s.* shall be iron and brass, as thy days
Josh. 9. 5. old *s.* and clouted upon their feet, old gar.
13. our *s.* are become old with a long journey
1 *Kings* 2. 5. put the blood in his *s.* on his feet
Cant. 7. 1. how beautiful are thy feet with *s.!*
Isa. 5. 27. nor the latchet of their *s.* be broken
Ezek. 24. 17. put on thy *s.* upon thy feet, 23.
Amos 2. 6. because they sold the poor for pair of *s.*
8. 6. that we may buy the needy for a pair of *s.*
Mat. 3. 11. whose *s.* I am not worthy to bear
10. 10. carry neither *s.* nor staves, *Luke* 10. 4.
Mark 1. 7. the latchet of whose *s.* I am not worthy to stoop down and unloose, *Luke* 3. 16. *Acts* 13. 25.
Luke 15. 22. put ring on his hand, and *s.* on his feet
22. 35. when I sent you without purse and *s.*

SHONE.
Exod. 34. 29. wist not that the skin of his face *s.*
30. the skin of his face *s.* they were afraid, 35.
2 *Kings* 3. 22. rose up early, sun *s.* upon the water
Luke 2. 9. glory of the Lord *s.* round about them
Acts 22. 6. suddenly there *s.* from heaven great light
Rev. 8. 12. the day *s.* not for a third part of it

SHOOK.
2 *Sam.* 6. 6. Uzzah took hold, for oxen *s.* the ark
22. 8. the earth *s.* *Psal.* 18. 7. | 68. 8. | 77. 18.
Neh. 5. 13. I *s.* my lap, and said, so God shake
Isa. 23. 11. he stretched out and *s.* the kingdoms
Acts 13. 51. but they *s.* off the dust of their feet
18. 6. he *s.* his raiment, and said unto them
28. 5. he *s.* off beast into the fire, and felt no harm
Heb. 12. 26. whose voice then *s.* the earth

SHOOT.
Exod. 36. 33. he made the middle bar to *s.* through
1 *Sam.* 20. 20. I will *s.* three arrows on the side
36. run, find out the arrows which I *s.*
2 *Sam.* 11. 20. knew ye not they would *s.?*
2 *Kings* 13. 17. then Elisha said, *s.* and he shot
19. 32. he shall not *s.* an arrow there, *Isa.* 37. 33.
1 *Chron.* 5. 18. valiant men able to *s.* with bow
2 *Chron.* 26. 15. he made engines to *s.* arrows
Psal. 11. 2. they may privily *s.* at upright in heart
22. 7. they *s.* out the lip, they shake the head
58. 7. when he bendeth his bow to *s.* his arrows
64. 3. to *s.* their arrows, even bitter words
4. that they may *s.* in secret at the perfect
7. but God shall *s.* at them with an arrow
144. 6. *s.* out thine arrows, and destroy them
Jer. 50. 14. all ye that bend the bow, *s.* at her
Ezek. 31. 14. nor *s.* up their top among boughs
36. 8. ye shall *s.* forth your branches, and yield
Luke 21. 30. when they now *s.* forth, ye know

SHOOTERS.
2 *Sam.* 11. 24. *s.* shot from off the wall on thy servant

SHOOTETH.
Job 8. 16. and his branch *s.* forth in his garden
Isa. 27. 8. in meas. when it *s.* forth, thou wilt debate
Mark 4. 32. mustard seed *s.* out great branches

SHOOTING.
1 *Chron.* 12. 2. could use right hand and left in *s.*
Amos 7. 1. in the *s.* up of the latter growth

SHORE.
Mat. 13. 2. the whole multitude stood on the *s.*
48. which when it was full, they drew to *s.*
John 21. 4. when morning, Jesus stood on the *s.*
Acts 21. 5. we kneeled down on the *s.* and prayed
27. 39. they discovered a certain creek with a *s.*
40. hoised up the main-sail, and made toward *s.*
See SEA.

SHORN.
Cant. 4. 2. teeth like a flock of sheep that are even *s.*
Acts 18. 18. having *s.* his head in Cenchrea, had vow

1 *Cor.* 11. 6. if woman be not covered, let her be *s.* if it be a shame to be *s.* or shaven, let her be cover.

SHORT.
Num. 11. 23. Mos. said, is the Lord's hand waxen *s.?*
Job 17. 12. the light is *s.* because of darkness
20. 5. the triumphing of the wicked is *s.*
Psal. 89. 47. remember how *s.* my time is
Rom. 3. 23. all have sinned and come *s.* of glory of G.
9. 28. because a *s.* work will Lord make on earth
1 *Cor.* 7. 29. this I say, brethren, the time is *s.*
1 *Thess.* 2. 17. being taken from you for a *s.* time
Rev. 12. 12. he knoweth that he hath but a *s.* time
17. 10. when he cometh, ye must continue *s.* space
See COME, CUT.

SHORTENED.
Psal. 89. 45. the days of his youth hast thou *s.*
102. 23. he weakened my strength, he *s.* my days
Prov. 10. 27. the years of the wicked shall be *s.*
Isa. 50. 2. is my hand *s.* at all, that it cannot redeem?
59. 1. behold, the Lord's hand is not *s.* not to save
Mat. 24. 22. except those days should be *s.* no flesh be saved, but for the elect's sake *s.* *Mark* 13. 20.

SHORTER.
Isa. 28. 20. the bed is *s.* than that a man can stretch

SHORTLY.
Gen. 41. 32. is established, G. will *s.* bring it to pass
Jer. 27. 16. vessels shall *s.* be brought ag. from Bab.
Ezek. 7. 8. now will I *s.* pour out my fury upon thee
Acts 25. 4. that he himself would depart *s.* thither
Rom. 16. 20. God of peace bruise Sat. under feet *s.*
1 *Cor.* 4. 19. I will come to you *s.* if the Lord will
Phil. 2. 19. I trust to send Timotheus *s.* unto you
24. I trust that I also myself shall come *s.*
1 *Tim.* 3. 14. I write, hoping to come unto thee *s.*
2 *Tim.* 4. 9. do thy diligence to come *s.* unto me
Heb. 13. 23. with whom if he come *s.* I will see you
2 *Pet.* 1. 14. *s.* I must put off this my tabernacle
3 *John* 14. but I trust I shall *s.* see thee and speak
Rev. 1. 1. things that must *s.* come to pass, 22. 6.

SHORTNESS.
Exod. 6. † 9. but they hearkened not for *s.* of spirit

SHOT.
Gen. 40. 10. it budded, and her blossoms *s.* forth
49. 23. the archers *s.* at him, and hated him
Exod. 19. 13. he shall surely be stoned, or *s.* thro'
Num. 21. 30. we have *s.* at them, Heshbon is perish.
1 *Sam.* 20. 37. the arrow which Jonathan had *s.*
2 *Sam.* 11. 24. the shooters *s.* from off the wall
2 *Kings* 13. 17. then Elisha said, shoot, and he *s.*
2 *Chron.* 35. 23. the archers *s.* at king Josiah
Psal. 18. 14. *s.* out lightnings, and discomfited them
Jer. 9. 8. their tongue is an arrow *s.* out, speaks deceit
Ezek. 17. 6. it became a vine, and *s.* forth sprigs
7. this vine *s.* forth her branches toward him
31. 5. the multitude of waters when he *s.* forth
10. he hath *s.* up his top among the thick boughs

SHOT, *Substantive*.
Gen. 21. 16. Hagar sat down as it were a bow *s.*
Jer. 6. † 6. hew down trees, pour out the engine of *s.*
32. † 24. behold, the engines of *s.* come into the city
Ezek. 26. † 8. he shall pour out the engine of *s.*

SHOVEL.
Isa. 30. 24. that hath been winnowed with the *s.*

SHOVELS.
Exod. 27. 3. thou shalt make his pans and his *s.*
38. 3. he made the pots, and the *s.* and the basons
Num. 4. 14. they shall put on the purple cloth *s.*
1 *Kings* 7. 40. Hiram made the lavers, the *s.* and the basons of brass, 45. 2 *Chron.* 4. 11, 16.
2 *Kings* 25. 14. pots and *s.* he took away, *Jer.* 52. 18.

SHOULDER
Is *a part of the body well known.* To give or lend his shoulder, *for bearing of a burden, signifies to submit to servitude.* Issachar bowed his shoulder to bear, and became a servant unto tribute, *Gen.* 49. 15. *The* Messiah *has delivered his people from the rod, or from the yoke, to which they were subject.* Isa. 9. 4. Thou hast broken the staff of his shoulder. *And in* Isa. 10. 27. *the prophet comforting* Israel *with the promise of deliverance from* Assyria, *says,* His burden shall be taken away from off thy shoulder. *The Scripture calls that* a rebellious shoulder, a withdrawing shoulder, *that will not submit to the yoke,* Neh. 9. † 29. *and those that bear it together with joint consent,* serving with one shoulder, *Zeph.* 3. † 9.

Heretofore they wore the marks of honour and command upon their shoulders. Job *desires of God to decide his cause;* Surely I would take it upon my shoulder, *as a trophy or badge of honour,* and bind it as a crown to me, *Job* 31. 36. Isaiah *says that the* Messiah *shall bear the mark of his government upon his* shoulder. *Isa.* 9. 6. The government shall be upon his shoulder. *God promises* Eliakim *the son of* Hilkiah, *to give him the* key of the house of David, and to lay it upon his shoulder; so he shall open, and none shall shut; and he shall shut, and none shall open.

To be borne upon shoulders, *sometimes stands for a kind of honour and distinction. God says* that he would lift up his hand to the Gentiles, and set up his standard to the people; and they shall bring thy sons in their arms, and thy daughters shall be carried upon their shoulders, *Isa.* 49. 22. *Sometimes this denotes great wickedness, or some great disgrace. God commanded* Ezekiel *to make a breach in the wall, and carry out thereby on his* shoulders *in the night time, to represent the taking of* Jerusalem, *and the captivity of the king and his people.* Ezek. 12. 6, 7. In their sight bear upon thy shoulders, &c.

It is said, Deut. 33. 12. That the Lord shall dwell between Benjamin's shoulders; *that is, God's temple, wherein he dwelt, shall be built upon mount* Moriah, *which is in the tribe of* Benjamin; shoulder *being elsewhere put for* border, *or* side, *as in* Num. 34. † 11. To fly upon the shoulders, *Isa.* 11. 14. *is to rise up against one, to attack him, to offer violence to him.*

Gen. 21. 14. putting the bread on Hagar's *s.*
24. 15. Rebekah with her pitcher upon her *s.* 45.

Gen. 49. 15. Issachar bowed his *s.* to bear, became ser.
Exod. 28. 7. the ephod shall have two *s.* pieces
25. put the ends of the chains on the *s.* pieces
29. 27. sanctify the *s.* of the heave-offering
39. 4. they made *s.* pieces for it to couple it
Num. 6. 19. priest shall take sodden *s.* of the ram, to put in the hands of the Nazarite, *Deut* 18. 3.
Josh. 4. 5. take ye every man a stone upon his *s.*
Judg. 9. 48. Abimelech laid a bow on his *s.*
1 *Sam.* 9. 24. and the cook took up the *s.*
10. † 9. when Saul had turned his *s.* to go
1 *Kings* 7. † 39. he put bases on right *s.* of the house
2 *Kings* 11. † 11. guard stood about the king with his weapons from the right *s.* 2 *Chron.* 23. † 10.
Neh. 9. 29. withdrew the *s.* and hardened their neck
Job 31. 36. surely I would take it on my *s.* bind it
Psal. 81. 6. I removed his *s.* from the burden
Isa. 9. 4. thou hast broken the staff of his *s.*
6. and the government shall be upon his *s.*
10. 27. his burden shall be taken from off thy *s.*
22. 22. the key of David will I lay upon his *s.*
46. 7. they bear him upon the *s.* they carry him
Ezek. 12. 7. I bare it on my *s.* in their sight
12. prince shall bear upon his *s.* in the twilight
24. 4. gather the pieces, even the thigh and *s.*
25. † 9. therefore I will open the *s.* of Moab
29. 7. thou didst break and rent all their *s.* 18.
34. 21. ye have thrust with side and with *s.*
Hos. 6. † 9. priests murder in the way with one *s.*
Zeph. 3. † 9. to serve the Lord with one *s.*
Zech. 7. 11. but they refused and pulled away the *s.*
Luke 15. 5. when found it lays it on his *s.* rejoicing

SHOULDER-BLADE.
Job 31. 22. then let mine arm fall from my *s.*

Heave-SHOULDER.
Lev. 7. 34. the *heave-s.* have I taken, *Num.* 6. 20.
10. 14. the *heave s.* shall ye eat in a clean place
15. the *heave-s.* and wave breast shall they bring

Right SHOULDER.
Exod. 29. 22. thou shalt take of the ram the *right s.*
Lev. 7. 32. the *right s.* shall ye give unto the priest
33. offereth, shall have the *right s.* for his part
8. 25. Moses took the fat and the *right s.*
26. put them on the fat, and upon the *right s.*
9. 21. the *right s.* waved is thine. *Num.* 18. 18.

SHOULDERS.
Gen. 9. 23. they laid the garment upon both their *s.*
Exod. 12. 34. their troughs bound upon their *s.*
28. 12. shalt put two stones on *s.* of ephod, 39. 7.
Num. 7. 9. sons of Kohath should bear on their *s.*
Deut. 33. 12. and he shall dwell between his *s.*
Judg. 16. 3. Samson took bar and all put upon his *s.*
1 *Sam.* 9. 2. from his *s.* and upward higher, 10. 23.
17. 6. he had a target of brass between his *s.*
1 *Chron.* 15. 15. the Levites bare the ark on their *s.*
2 *Chron.* 35. 3. it shall not be a burden upon your *s.*
Isa. 11. 14. but they shall fly on the *s.* of Philistines
14. 25. and his burden depart from off their *s.*
30. 6. will carry riches upon the *s.* of young asses
49. 22. thy daughters shall be carried upon their *s.*
Ezek. 12. 6. in their sight shall bear it upon thy *s.*
Mat. 23. 4. they bind burdens, lay them on men's *s*

SHOUT, *Substantive*.
Num. 23. 21. and the *s.* of a king is among them
Josh. 6. 5. the people shouted with a great *s.* 20.
1 *Sam.* 4. 5. with a great *s.* so that the earth rang
6. what meaneth the noise of this great *s.?*
2 *Chron.* 13. 15. then the men of Judah gave a *s.*
Ezra 3. 11. with a great *s.* when they praised Lord
13. could not discern the *s.* of joy from weeping
Psal. 47. 5. God is gone up with *s.* Lord with sound
Jer. 25. 30. Lord shall give a *s.* as they tread grapes
51. 14. they shall lift a *s.* against Babylon
Acts 12. 22. the people gave *s.* saying voice of a God
1 *Thess.* 4. 16. L. shall descend from heaven with a *s.*

SHOUT.
Exod. 32. 18. is not voice of them that *s.* for mastery
Josh. 6. 5. when ye hear trumpet, all people shall *s.*
10. shall not *s.* till I bid you *s.* then shall ye *s.*
16. *s.* for the Lord hath given you the city
Psal. 47. 1. *s.* unto God with the voice of triumph
Isa. 12. 6. cry out and *s.* thou inhabitant of Zion
42. 11. let them *s.* from the top of the mountains
44. 23. *s.* ye lower parts of the earth, break forth
Jer. 31. 7. sing and *s.* among chief of the nations
50. 15. Babylon had sinned, *s.* ag. her round abou
Lam. 3. 8. when I *s.* he shutteth out my prayer
Zeph. 3. 14. *s.* O Israel, be glad with all the heart
Zech. 9. 9. *s.* O daughter of Jerusalem, king cometh

SHOUTED.
Exod. 32. 17. as they *s.* he said, there is a noise
Lev. 9. 24. when the fire consumed, they *s.* and fell
Josh. 6. 20. so the people *s.* when the priests blew
Judg. 15. 14. the Philistines *s.* against Samson
1 *Sam.* 4. 5. all Isr. *s.* with great shout because of ark
10. 24. the people *s.* and said, God save the king
17. 20. as the host was going forth and *s.* for battle
52. the men of Israel and Judah *s.* and pursued
2 *Chron.* 13. 15. as Judah *s.* God smote Jeroboam
Ezra 3. 11. when they praised the Lord, they *s.*
12. many of the people *s.* aloud for joy, 13.
See JOY.

SHOUTETH.
Psal. 78. 65. like a mighty man that *s.* by reason of wine

SHOUTING.
2 *Sam.* 6. 15. brought up ark with *s.* 1 *Chron.* 15. 28.
2 *Chron.* 15. 14. they sware to the Lord with *s.*
Job 39. 25. he smelleth the battle and *s.* afar off
Prov. 11. 10. when the wicked perish, there is *s.*
Isa. 16. 9. the *s.* for summer-fruits is fallen, 10.
Jer. 20. 16. let them hear the *s.* at noon-tide
48. 33. none shall tread with *s.* their *s.* shall be no *s.*
Ezek. 21. 22. to lift up the voice with *s.* to appoint
Amos 1. 14. a fire shall devour Rabbah with *s.*
2. 2. Moab shall die with tumult, *s.* and trumpet

SHOUTINGS.
Zech. 4. 7. he shall bring forth head-stone with *s.*

SHOWER.
Ezek. 13. 11. there shall be an overflowing *s.* 13.
34. 26. I will cause *s.* to come down in his season
Luke 12. 54. straightway ye say there cometh a *s.*

SHOWERS.

Deut. 32. 2. my speech shall distil as *s.* on the grass
Job 24. 8. the poor are wet with *s.* of the mountains
Psal. 65. 10. thou makest the earth soft with *s.*
72. 6. king shall come like *s.* that water the earth
Jer. 3. 3. therefore the *s.* have been withholden
14. 22. can cause rain, or can the heavens give *s.?*
Ezek. 34. 26. in his season shall be *s.* of blessing
Mic. 5. 7. remnant of Jacob shall be as *s.* on grass
Zech. 10. 1. the Lord shall give them *s.* of rain

SHRANK.

Gen. 32. 32. therefore Israel eat not of sinew that *s.*

SHRED.

2 *Kings* 4. 39. came and *s.* wild gourds into pottage

SCREECH-OWL.

Isa. 34. 14. *s.* also shall rest there and find for herself

SHRINES.

Acts 19. 24. Demetrius who made silver *s.* for Diana

SHROUD.

Ezek. 31. 3. Assyrian was a cedar with shadowing *s.*

SHRUBS.

Gen. 21. 15. Hagar cast the child under one of the *s.*

SHUN.

2 *Tim.* 2. 16. but *s.* profane and vain babblings

SHUNNED.

Acts 20. 27. I have not *s.* the whole counsel of God

SHUT, *Actively, Passively.*

Gen. 7. 16. went in of all flesh, the Lord *s.* him in
Exod. 14. 3. the wilderness hath *s.* them in
Num. 12. 14. let her be *s.* out from camp seven days
15. Miriam was *s.* out from the camp seven days
24. † 3. the man who had his eyes *s.* but now open
Deut. 15. 7. nor *s.* thy hand from thy poor brother
Josh. 2. 7. they *s.* the gate of Jericho
Judg. 3. † 15. Ehud was *s.* of his right hand
9. 51. they *s.* the tower to them, and gat them up
1 *Sam.* 23. 7. for he is *s.* in, by entering into a town
Neh. 13. 19. I commanded gates to be *s.* till after sab.
Psal. 69. 15. let not the pit *s.* her mouth upon me
Isa. 6. 10. *s.* their eyes, lest they see with their eyes
22. 22. key of Dav. on his shoulder, so he shall open and none shall *s.* he shall *s.* and none shall open
44. 18. for he hath *s.* their eyes, they cannot see
45. 1. to open before him, and gates shall not be *s.*
52. 15. the kings shall *s.* their mouths at him
60. 11. thy gates shall not be *s.* day nor night
66. 9. shall I *s.* the womb, saith thy God?
Ezek. 3. 24. Spirit said, go *s.* thys. within thine house
44. 1. gate which looketh toward the east was *s.*
2. this gate shall be *s.* it shall not be opened, God hath entered in by it, therefore it shall be *s.*
46. 1. the gate shall be *s.* the six working-days
2. the gate shall not be *s.* till the evening
12. after his going forth, one shall *s.* the gate
Dan. 6. 22. my God hath *s.* the lions' mouths
Acts 5. 23. the prison truly found we *s.* in safety
Rev. 11. 6. these have power to *s.* heav. that it rain not
21. 25. gates shall not be *s.* by day, no night there

See Door.

SHUT *up.*

Lev. 13. 4. then the priest shall *s.* him *up* that hath plague seven days, 5, 21, 26, 31, 33, 50, 54.
11. the priest shall not *s.* him *up*, he is unclean
14. 38. the priest shall *s. up* the house seven days
46. he that goeth in while the house is *s. up*
Deut. 11. 17. wrath be kindled, and he *s. up* heaven
32. 30. except their rock the Lord had *s.* them *up*
36. when he seeth there is none *s. up* nor left
Josh. 6. 1. now when Jericho was straitly *s. up*
1 *Sam.* 1. 5. the Lord had *s. up* Hannah's womb
6. because the Lord had *s. up* her womb
6. 10. hid them and *s. up* their calves at home
17. † 46. this day will the Lord *s.* thee *up*
23. † 12. will the men of Keilah *s.* me *up?*
24. † 18. when Lord had *s.* me *up* into thy hand
26. † 8. God hath *s. up* thine enemy into thy hand
2 *Sam.* 18. † 28. blessed be the Lord who hath *s. up*
20. 3. concubines were *s.* up to day of their death
1 *Kings* 8. 35. when heav. is *s. up*, 2 *Chr.* 6. 26. | 7. 13.
14. 10. I will cut off from Jeroboam him that is *s. up* and left in Israel, 21. 21. 2 *Kings* 9. 8.
2 *Kings* 14. 26. there was not any *s. up* nor left
17. 4. therefore the king of Assyria *s.* him *up*
2 *Chron.* 28. 24. Ahaz *s. up* doors of house, 29. 7.
Neh. 6. 10. the house of Shemaiah who was *s. up*
Job 3. 10. because it *s.* not *up* my mother's womb
11. 10. if he cut off, and *s. up*, who can hinder him?
16. † 11. God hath *s.* me *up* to the ungodly
38. 8. or who hath *s. up* the sea with doors?
41. 15. his scales are *s. up* together as a seal
Psal. 31. 8. hast not *s.* me *up* into hand of the enemy
77. 9. hath he in anger *s. up* his tender mercies?
78. † 48. he *s. up* also their cattle to the hail
88. 8. I am *s. up*, and I cannot come forth
Cant. 4. 12. a spring *s. up*, a fountain sealed
Isa. 19. † 4. *s. up* into the hand of a cruel lord
24. 10. every house is *s. up*, no man can come in
22. they shall be *s. up* in the prison, and be visited
Jer. 13. 19. the cities of the south shall be *s. up*
20. 9. his word was as fire *s. up* in my bones
32. 2. the prophet was *s. up* by Zedekiah, 3.
33. 1. word of Lord came, while he was *s. up*, 39. 15.
36. 5. I am *s. up*, I cannot go to the Lord's house
Dan. 8. 26. *s. up* the vision || 12. 4. *s. up* the words
Obad. † 14. nor should have *s. up* those that remain
Mat. 23. 13. ye *s. up* kingdom of heaven against men
Luke 3. 20. added this, that he *s. up* John in prison
4. 25. when the heaven was *s. up* three years
Acts 26. 10. many saints did I *s. up* in prison
Rom. 11. † 32. God hath *s.* them *up* in unbelief
Gal. 3. 23. *s. up* to the faith that should be revealed
Rev. 20. 3. *s. up* the devil, and set a seal upon him

SHUTTETH.

Job 12. 14. he *s.* up a man, there can be no opening
Prov. 16. 30. he *s.* his eyes to devise froward things
17. 28. he that *s.* his lips is a man of understanding
Isa. 33. 15. and *s.* his eyes from seeing evil
Lam. 3. 8. also when I cry, he *s.* out my prayer
1 *John* 3. 17. and *s.* up his bowels of compassion
Rev. 3. 7. openeth, no man *s.* and *s.* no man openeth

SHUTTING.

Josh. 2. 5. about time of *s.* the gate, men went out

SHUTTLE.

Job 7. 6. my days are swifter than a weaver's *s.*

SICK

Is taken *not only for one that is under some bodily indisposition, as in* 1 Sam. 30. 13. Luke 7. 10. *but also for such as are sensible of the burden of their sins, and earnestly desire to be delivered from them by* Christ *the great Physician.* Mat. 9. 12. They that be whole need not a physician, but they that are sick. *The spouse says, Cant.* 2. 5. Stay me with flagons, comfort me with apples: for I am sick of love: *that is, You that are members of the church, whether ministers, or others, afford me what help you can, for the supporting, strengthening, and comforting of my soul, by applying the promises of the gospel, and such other means as may conduce to my relief; for I am greatly troubled, and in a languishing estate, for want of all that full enjoyment and sense of* Christ's *love which I so earnestly desire.*

The efficient cause of sickness *is God,* Lev. 26. 16. Deut. 28. 27, 35, 59, 60, 61. *The meritorious cause is sin, as appears from the forecited places, where* sickness *and disease are threatened as a punishment for sin. The instrumental cause is either Satan, who sometimes is permitted by God to inflict diseases upon persons, as he did on* Job, *chap.* 2. 6. 7. *Or intemperance, as drunkenness, incontinency, and the like. The end of* sickness *is to punish the wicked,* 1 Sam. 5. 6. *To try the patience and constancy of the godly, as in* Job *and* Hezekiah. *Or to manifest the glory of God,* John 9. 3. | 11. 4.

Gen. 48. 1. one told Joseph, behold thy father is *s.*
Lev. 15. 33. the law of her that is *s.* of her flowers
Deut. 29. † 22. wherewith the Lord hath made it *s.*
1 *Sam.* 19. 14. when Saul sent, she said, he is *s.*
30. 13. master left me, because 3 days ago I fell *s.*
2 *Sam.* 12. 15. the Lord struck the child, it was *s.*
13. 2. Amnon was so vexed, he fell *s.* for Tamar
5. make thyself *s.* || 6. Amnon made himself *s.*
1 *Kings* 14. 1. Abijah the son of Jeroboam fell *s.*
5. wife of Jerob. cometh to ask for son, for he is *s.*
17. 17. after this the son of the woman fell *s.*
22. † 34. Ahab said unto driver, carry me out, for I am made *s.* 2 *Chron.* 18. † 33. | 35. † 23.
2 *Kings* 1. 2. Ahaziah fell down in Samaria, was *s.*
8. 7. Benhadad the king of Syria was *s.*
29. Ahaziah king of Judah went to see Joram son of Ahab, because he was *s.* 2 *Chron.* 22. 6.
13. 14. Elisha was fallen *s.* of sick. whereof he died
20. 1. in those days was Hezekiah *s.* unto death, 2 *Chron.* 32. 24. *Isa.* 38. 1.
12. had heard that Hezek. had been *s.* *Isa.* 39. 1.
Neh. 2. 2. king said, why sad, seeing thou art not *s.*
Ps. 35. 13. when they were *s.* my clothing sackcloth
41. † 1. blessed is he that considereth the *s.*
Prov. 13. 12. hope deferred maketh the heart *s.*
23. 35. they have stricken me, and I was not *s.*
Cant. 2. 5. comfort me with apples, I am *s.* of love
5. 8. I charge you, tell him that I am *s.* of love
Isa. 1. 5. whole head is *s.* and the whole heart faint
33. 24. the inhabitant shall not say, I am *s.*
38. 9. when Hezek. had been *s.* and was recovered
Jer. 14. 18. behold them that are *s.* with famine
Ezek. 34. 4. nor have ye healed that which was *s.*
16. and will strengthen that which was *s.*
Dan. 8. 27. I Daniel fainted, and was *s.* certain days
Hos. 7. 5. princes made him *s.* with bottles of wine
Mic. 6. 13. will I make thee *s.* in smiting thee
Mal. 1. 8. if ye offer the lame and *s.* is it not evil?
13. and ye brought that torn, the lame, and the *s.*
Mat. 4. 24. and they brought to him all *s.* people
8. 14. his wife's mother *s.* of a fever, *Mark* 1. 30.
16. and healed all that were *s.* 14. 14.
9. 12. they that be whole need not a physician, but they that are *s.* *Mark* 2. 17. *Luke* 5. 31.
10. 8. heal the *s.* cleanse the lepers, *Luke* 9. 2. | 10. 9.
25. 36. I was *s.* and ye visited me, I was in prison
39. saw we thee *s.* in prison and came to thee? 44.
Mark 6. 5. that he laid his hands on a few *s.* folk
56. they laid the *s.* in the streets, *Acts* 5. 15.
16. 18. lay hands on the *s.* and they shall recover
Luke 7. 2. centurion's servant was *s.* and ready to die
10. found the servant whole that had been *s.*
John 4. 46. a certain nobleman's son was *s.* at Caper.
11. 1. a man, named Lazarus of Bethany, was *s.* 2.
3. Lord, behold, he whom thou lovest, is *s.*
6. he had heard he was *s.* he abode 2 days
Acts 9. 37. in those days Dorcas was *s.* and died
19. 12. were brought unto the *s.* handkerchiefs
28. 8. the father of Publius lay *s.* of a fever
Phil. 2. 26. because ye had heard that he had been *s.*
27. for indeed he was *s.* nigh unto death
2 *Tim.* 4. 20. but Trophimus have I left at Miletum *s.*
Jam. 5. 14. is any *s.* let him call elders of the church
15. prayer of faith shall save the *s.* Lord raise up

See Palsy.

SICKLY.

1 *Cor.* 11. 30. for this cause many are *s.* among you

SICKNESS.

Exod. 23. 25. I will take *s.* away from the midst of thee
Lev. 20. 18. if a man lie with a woman having her *s.*
Deut. 7. 15. the Lord will take from thee all *s.*
28. 61. every *s.* that is not written in this law
1 *Kings* 8. 37. whatsoever *s.* there be, 2 *Chron.* 6. 28.
17. 17. his *s.* was so sore, there was no breath left
2 *Kings* 13. 14. Elisha sick of the *s.* whereof he died
2 *Chron.* 21. 15. thou shalt have great *s.* by disease of thy bowels, by reason of the *s.* day by day
19. his bowels fell out by reason of his *s.* so he died
Psal. 41. 3. thou wilt make all his bed in his *s.*
Eccl. 5. 17. hath much sorrow and wrath with his *s.*
Isa. 38. 9. when Hezekiah was recovered of his *s.*
12. will cut me off with pining *s.* from day to night
Hos. 5. 13. when Ephraim saw his *s.* Judah his wound
Mat. 4. 23. Jesus went about healing all manner of *s.*
9. 35. Jesus went about preaching and heal. every *s.*
10. 1. power to heal all manner of *s.* *Mark* 3. 15.
John 11. 4. he said, this *s.* is not unto death

SICKNESSES.

Deut. 28. 59. and sore *s.* and of long continuance
29. 22. they shall say, when they see the *s.* L. laid
Mat. 8. 17. spoken, saying, himself bare our *s.*

SICKLE.

Deut. 16. 9. as thou beginnest to put *s.* to the corn
23. 25. not move a *s.* unto thy neighbour's corn
Jer. 50. 16. cut off him that handleth *s.* in harvest
Joel 3. 13. put ye in the *s.* for the harvest is ripe
Mark 4. 29. immediately he putteth in the *s.*
Rev. 14. 14. having crown, and in his hand sharp
15. an angel crying, thrust in thy *s.* 16, 18, 19.
17. another angel came, he also having a sharp *s.*

SIDE.

Gen. 6. 16. door of the ark shall set in the *s.* thereof
Exod. 2. 5. her maidens walked along by river *s.*
12. 7. shalt strike blood on the two *s.* posts, 22.
23. when he seeth blood on the lintel and *s.* posts
17. 12. Aaron and Hur stayed up Moses' hands, the one on the one *s.* and the other on the other *s.*
32. 26. who is on the Lord's *s.* let him come to me
27. put every man his sword by his *s.* go in and out
Lev. 1. 11. he shall kill it on *s.* of altar northward
5. blood shall be wrung out at the *s.* of the altar
5. 9. blood of sin offering sprinkled on *s.* of altar
Num. 22. 24. a wall on this *s.* and a wall on that *s.*
24. 6. they are spread as gardens by the river's *s.*
32. 19. we will not inherit on yonder *s.* Jordan
Deut. 4. 32. ask from one *s.* of heaven to the other
31. 26. put the book of the law in *s.* of the ark
Judg. 19. 1. a Levite sojourned on *s.* of Ephraim, 18.
1 *Sam.* 4. 18. fell backward by the *s.* of the gate
6. 8. put the mice in a coffer by the *s.* of the ark
20. 20. I will shoot three arrows on the *s.* thereof
25. the king sat, and Abner sat by Saul's *s.*
2 *Sam.* 2. 16. and thrust his sword into his fellow's *s.*
13. 34. the king's sons came by way of the hill *s.*
16. 13. Shimei went along on the hill's *s.* against
2 *Kings* 9. 32. Jehu said, who is on my *s.* who?
1 *Chron.* 12. 18. thine are we, David, and on thy *s.*
2 *Chron.* 11. 12. having Judah and Benjamin on his *s.*
Neh. 4. 18. every one had his sword girded by his *s.*
Job 18. 12. and destruction shall be ready at his *s.*
Psal. 91. 7. thousand shall fall at thy *s.* ten thous.
118. 6. the Lord is on my *s.* I will not fear
124. 1. if it had not been the Lord on our *s.* 2.
Eccl. 4. 1. on the *s.* of their oppressors was power
Isa. 60. 4. thy daughters shall be nursed at thy *s.*
Ezek. 4. 8. thou shalt not turn from one *s.* to another
9. the number of days thou shalt lie upon thy *s.*
9. 2. with a writer's inkhorn by his *s.* 3. 11.
25. 9. I will open the *s.* of Moab from the cities
34. 21. because ye have thrust with *s.* and shoulder
Dan. 7. 5. and it raised up itself on one *s.* three ribs
11. 17. she shall not stand on his *s.* nor be for him
John 19. 18. the two thieves, on either *s.* one
34. but one of soldiers with a spear pierced his *s.*
20. 20. he shewed unto them his hands and his *s.*
25. except I thrust my hand into *s.* will not believe
27. reach thy hand, and thrust it into my *s.*
Acts 12. 7. angel smote Peter on the *s.* raised him up
16. 13. on the sabbath we went out by a river *s.*
Rev. 22. 2. on either *s.* of river was the tree of life

See Chambers.

Every SIDE.

Num. 16. 27. from tabernacle of Abiram on *every s.*
Judg. 7. 18. blow ye the trumpets on *every s.*
8. 34. remembered not the Lord, who had delivered them from their enemies on *every s.* 1 *Sam.* 12. 11.
1 *Sam.* 14. 47. Saul fought ag. enemies on *every s.*
1 *Kings* 5. 3. wars which were about him on *every s.*
4. the Lord hath given me rest on *every s.*
1 *Chr.* 22. 18. hath he not given you rest on *every s.*
2 *Chron.* 14. 7. he hath given us rest on *every s.*
32. 22. thus the Lord guided them on *every s.*
Job 1. 10. put an hedge about all he hath on *every s.*
18. 11. terror shall make him afraid on *every s.*
19. 10. he hath destroyed me on *every s.* I am gone
Psal. 12. 8. the wicked walk on *every s.* while
31. 13. fear was on *every s.* while they took counsel
65. 12. and the little hills rejoice on *every s.*
71. 21. thou shalt comfort me on *every s.*
Jer. 6. 25. fear is on *every s.* 20. 10. | 49. 29.
Ezek. 16. 33. that they may come to thee on *every s.*
19. 8. the nations set against him on *every s.*
23. 22. I will bring them against thee on *every s.*
28. 23. judged by the sword upon her on *every s.*
36. 3. they have swallowed you up on *every s.*
37. 21. saith Lord, I will gather them on *every s.*
39. 17. gather yourselves to my sacrifice on *every s.*
Luke 19. 43. enemies shall keep thee in on *every s.*
2 *Cor.* 4. 8. we are troubled on *every s.* 7. 5.

Farther SIDE.

Mark 10. 1. Jesus came by the *farther s.* of Jordan

See Left.

On this SIDE.

Exod. 37. 8. one cherub *on this s.* other on that *s.*
Num. 11. 31. brought quails a day's journey *on this s.*
22. 24. a wall being *on this s.* and on that side
32. 19. inheritance *on this s.* Jordan, 32. | 34. 15.
35. 14. three cities of refuge *on this s.* Jordan
Josh. 8. 22. some *on this s.* of Ai, and some on that
33. Israel and judges stood *on this s.* the ark
1 *Sam.* 20. 21. if I say, the arrows are *on this s.*
23. 26. Saul went *on this s.* of the mountain
Ezra 4. 16. shalt have no portion *on this s.* the river
5. 3. governor *on this s.* the river, 6. | 6. 13. | 8. 36.
Neh. 3. 7. to throne of the governor *on this s.* river
Ezek. 1. 23. every one had two wings, *on this s.*
40. 39. were two tables *on this s.* and two on that
41. four tables *on this s.* four tables on that side
47. 12. on bank of river *on this s.* shall grow trees
Dan. 12. 5. there stood other two, the one *on this s.*
Zech. 5. 3. every one that stealeth shall be cut off as *on this s.* every one that sweareth, on that side

On other SIDE.

Josh. 24. 2. your fathers dwelt *on other s.* the flood
1 *Sam.* 14. 40. I and Jonathan will be *on the other s.*
2 *Kings* 3. 22. saw water *on other s.* as red as blood
2 *Chron.* 9. 19. twelve lions stood *on* one and *other s*
Obad. 11. on the day thou stoodest *on the other s.*
John 6. 25. had found him *on the other s.* of the sea

Right SIDE.
1 *Kings* 6. 8. door for middle chamber was on *r. s.*
7. 39. put five bases on the *right s.* the house; set
the sea on the *right s.* the house, 2 *Chron.* 4. 10.
49. five candlesticks on the *right s.* 2 *Chron.* 4. 8.
Ezek. 1. 10. had the face of a lion on the *right s.*
4. 6. lie again on thy *right s.* and shalt bear
47. 1. from under *right s.* of house ran waters, 2.
Zech. 4. 3. olive-trees, one on *right s.* the bowl, 11.
Mark 16. 5. saw young man on *right s.* of sepulchre
Luke 1. 11. angel standing on *right s.* of the altar
John 21. 6. cast the net on the *right s.* of the ship
See Sea, South, Way, West.

SIDES.
Exod. 32. 15. the tables were written on both *s.*
Num. 33. 55. shall be thorns in your *s. Judg.* 2. 3.
Josh. 23. 13. they shall be scourges in your *s.*
Judg. 5. 30. a prey of needle-work on both *s.*
1 *Sam.* 24. 3. David and his men in *s.* of the cave
1 *Kings* 4. 24. Solom. had peace on all *s.* round him
Psal. 48. 2. beautiful is Zion on the *s.* of the north
128. 3. thy wife as a fruitful vine by *s.* of thy house
Isa. 14. 13. I will sit also in the *s.* of the north
15. thou shalt be brought down to *s.* of the pit
66. 12. ye shall be borne upon her *s.* and dandled
Jer. 6. 22. a great nation raised from *s.* of the earth
48. 28. maketh her nest in the *s.* of the holes
49. 32. I will bring their calamity from all *s.*
Ezek. 1. 17. they went upon their four *s.* 10. 11.
32. 23. whose graves are set in the *s.* of the pit
48. 1. for these are his *s.* east and west
Dan. 2. † 32. his belly and his *s.* were of brass
Amos 6. 10. say unto him that is by *s.* of the house
Jonah 1. 5. Jonah was gone down to *s.* of the ship
Hab. 3. † 4. he had bright beams out of his *s.*

SIEGE.
Deut. 20. 19. shalt not cut to employ them in the *s.*
28. 53. thou shalt eat thy children in the *s.*
55. because nothing left him in the *s.* 57.
2 *Chr.* 32. 10. whereon do ye trust, that ye abide in *s.*?
Isa. 29. 3. I will lay *s.* against thee with a mount
Jer. 19. 9. shall eat the flesh of his friend in the *s.*
Ezek. 4. 2. lay *s.* against it, and build a fort, 3.
5. 2. when the days of the *s.* are fulfilled
Mic. 5. 1. he hath laid *s.* ag. us, they shall smite
Nah. 3. 14. draw thee waters for the *s.* fortify
Zech. 12. 2. a cup of trembling, when in the *s.*

SIEVE.
Isa. 30. 28. to sift the nations with the *s.* of vanity
Amos 9. 9. I will sift, like as corn is sifted in a *s.*

SIFT.
Isa. 30. 28. to *s.* the nations with the sieve of vanity
Amos 9. 9. I will *s.* Israel as corn is sifted in a sieve
Luke 22. 31. Simon, Satan hath desired to *s.* you

SIGH.
Isa. 24. 7. wine mourneth, all merry-hearted do *s.*
Lam. 1. 4. her priests *s.* || 11. all her people *s.*
21. they have heard that I *s.* none to comfort me
Ezek. 9. 4. set a mark on foreheads of men that *s.*
21. 6. *s.* therefore with the breaking of thy loins,
and with bitterness *s.* before their eyes

SIGHED.
Exod. 2. 23. Israel *s.* by reason of the bondage
Mark 7. 34. and looking up to heaven, he *s.*
8. 12. *s.* deeply in his spirit, and saith, why doth

SIGHEST.
Ezek. 21. 7. when they say to thee, wheref. *s.* thou?

SIGHETH.
Lam. 1. 8. yea, she *s.* and turneth backward

SIGHING.
Job 3. 24. my *s.* cometh before I eat, roarings poured
Psal. 12. 5. for the *s.* of the needy will I arise
31. 10. my life is spent with grief, my years with *s.*
79. 11. let the *s.* of the prisoner come before thee
Isa. 21. 2. all the *s.* thereof have I made to cease
35. 10. obtain joy, and sorrow and *s.* shall flee away
Jer. 45. 3. I fainted in my *s.* and I find no rest

SIGHS.
Lam. 1. 22. for my *s.* are many, my heart is faint

SIGHT.
Gen. 2. 9. every tree that is pleasant to the *s.*
Exod. 3. 3. I will now turn and see this great *s.*
24. 17. *s.* of glory of Lord was like devouring fire
Lev. 13. 3. the plague in *s.* be deeper, 20, 25, 30.
4. in *s.* be not deeper than the skin, 31, 32, 34.
14. 37. if the plague in *s.* be lower than the wall
Num. 13. 33. we saw the giants, and we were in our
own *s.* as grasshoppers, and so we were in their *s.*
27. 19. before congr. and give him charge in their *s.*
Deut. 28. 34. shalt be mad for *s.* of thine eyes, 67.
Josh. 23. 5. God shall drive them from out of your *s.*
24. 17. which did those great signs in our *s.*
2 *Sam.* 23. † 21. he slew an Egyptian, a man of *s.*
1 *Kings* 7. † 4. and *s.* was against *s.* in three ranks
2 *Kings* 2. † 7. fifty of sons of prophets stood in *s.*
Job 18. 3. why are we reputed vile in your *s.*?
19. 15. me for a stranger, I am an alien in their *s.*
21. 8. their seed is established in their *s.* with them
34. 26. he striketh them in the open *s.* of others
41. 9. shall not one be cast down at the *s.* of him?
Psal. 79. 10. be known among the heathen in our *s.*
Eccl. 6. 9. better is *s.* of the eyes than wandering
Isa. 5. 21. them that are prudent in their own *s.*
11. 3. he shall not judge after the *s.* of his eyes
Jer. 51. 24. I will render evil done in Zion in your *s.*
Ezek. 4. 12. thou shalt bake it with dung in their *s.*
12. 3. prepare, and remove by day in their *s.*
5. dig thou thro' the wall in their *s.* and carry out
20. 9. in whose *s.* I made myself known to them
14. heathen in whose *s.* I brought them out, 22.
43. shall loathe yourselves in your own *s.* 36. 31.
21. 23. shall be as a false divination in their *s.*
23. † 16. at the *s.* of her eyes she doted on them
43. 11. shew the forms thereof, and write in their *s.*
Dan. 4. 11. *s.* thereof to end of all the earth, 20.
8. † 5. the goat had a horn of *s.* between his eyes
Hos. 2. 2. put away her whoredoms out of her *s.*
Mat. 11. 5. the blind receive their *s.* the lame walk,
the lepers are cleansed, 20. 34. *Luke* 7. 21.
Luke 4. 18. preach the recovering of *s.* to the blind
23. 48. that came to that *s.* smote their breasts
24. 31. they knew him, he vanished out of their *s.*
John 9. 11. I went and washed, and I received *s.*
Acts 1. 9. and a cloud received him out of their *s.*
7. 31. when Moses saw it, he wondered at the *s.*
9. 9. was three days without *s.* nor eat nor drink
18. he received *s.* forthwith, arose, was baptized
2 *Cor.* 5. 7. for we walk by faith, not by *s.*
Heb. 12. 21. so terrible was the *s.* that Moses said

SIGHT *of God.*
Prov. 3. 4. find good understanding in the *s. of God*
Luke 16. 15. is abomination in the *s. of God*
Acts 4. 19. whether right in *s. of God* to hearken
8. 21. thy heart is not right in the *s. of God*
10. 31. thy alms had in remembrance in *s. of God*
2 *Cor.* 2. 17. in the *s. of God* speak we in Christ
4. 2. to every man's conscience in the *s. of God*
7. 12. our care for you in *s. of God* might appear
Gal. 3. 11. no man justified by the law in *s. of God*
1 *Thess.* 1. 3. remembering work of faith in *s. of God*
1 *Tim.* 2. 3. this is good and acceptable in *s. of God*
6. 13. I give thee charge in the *s. of God*
1 *Pet.* 3. 4. which is in the *s. of God* of great price

***His* SIGHT.**
Exod. 15. 26. if wilt do that which is right in *his s.*
Lev. 13. 5. behold, if the plague in *his s.* be at a stay
37. but if the scall be in *his s.* at a stay
Num. 19. 5. and one shall burn the heifer in *his s.*
Deut. 4. 37. he brought thee out in *his s.* out of Egypt
Judg. 6. 21. the angel of Lord departed out of *his s.*
2 *Sam.* 12. 9. why despised Lord, to do evil in *his s.*
13. 8. so Tamar went and made cakes in *his s.*
2 *Kings* 17. 18. remove them out of *h. s.* 20, 23. | 24. 3.
1 *Chron.* 19. 13. the Lord do what is good in *his s.*
Job 15. 15. the heavens are not clean in *his s.*
25. 5. yea, the stars are not pure in *his s.*
40. † 24. will any take him in *his s.*?
Psal. 10. 5. thy judgments are far above out of *h. s.*
72. 14. precious shall their blood be in *his s.*
Eccl. 2. 26. God giveth to a man that is good in *his s.*
8. 3. be not hasty to go out of *his s.* stand not in evil
Hos. 6. 2. he will raise us, and we shall live in *his s.*
Mark 10. 52. Bartimeus immediately received *his s.*
and followed Jesus in the way, *Luke* 18. 43.
John 9. 15. asked how he had received *his s.* 18.
Acts 9. 12. a vision that he might receive *his s.*
Rom. 3. 20. by law shall no flesh be justi. in *his s.*
Col. 1. 22. thro' death to present you holy in *his s.*
Heb. 4. 13. every creature is manifest in *his s.*
13. 21. working what is well pleasing in *his s.*
1 *John* 3. 22. do those things that are pleas. in *his s.*

***In the* SIGHT.**
Gen. 21. 11. the thing was grievous in Abraham's *s.*
47. 18. there is not ought left *in the s.* of my lord
Exod. 4. 30. and did the signs *in the s.* of the people
7. 20. he smote the waters *in the s.* of Pharaoh
9. 8. Moses sprinkled the ashes *in the s.* of Phar.
11. 3. Moses great *in the s.* of Pharaoh's servants
17. 6. Moses did so *in the s.* of the elders of Israel
19. 11. the L. will come down *in the s.* of people
40. 38. fire by night *in the s.* of Israel all journeys
Lev. 20. 17. shall be cut off *in the s.* of their people
26. 45. out of Egypt *in the s.* of the heathen
Num. 3. 4. Ithamar ministered *in the s.* of Aaron
20. 27. Aaron and Eleazar went *in the s.* of cong.
25. 6. brought Midianitish woman *in the s.* of Mo.
33. 3. went with high hand *in the s.* of Egyptians
Deut. 4. 6. for this is your wisdom *in the s.* of nations
31. 7. Moses said to Joshua *in the s.* of all Israel
34. 12. terror Moses shewed *in the s.* of all Israel
Josh. 3. 7. to magnify thee *in the s.* of Israel, 4. 14.
10. 12. he said, *in the s.* of Israel, sun, stand still
1 *Sam.* 18. 5. David accepted *in the s.* of the peop.
2 *Sam.* 12. 11. lie with thy wives *in the s.* of this sun
1 *Chr.* 28. 8. *in the s.* of all Israel keep command.
29. 25. Lord magnified Solomon *in the s.* of Israel
2 *Chr.* 32. 23. Hezekiah magnified *in s.* of nations
Ezra 9. 9. shewed mercy *in the s.* of kings of Persia
Neh. 1. 11. grant him mercy *in the s.* of this man
8. 5. opened the book *in the s.* of all the people
Ps. 78. 12. marvellous things did he *in s.* of fathers
98. 2. he openly shewed *in the s.* of the heathen
Prov. 1. 17. in vain net is spread *in the s.* of any bird
4. 3. tender and beloved *in the s.* of my mother
Eccl. 11. 9. and walk *in the s.* of thine eyes
Jer. 19. 10. break the bottle *in the s.* of the men
32. 12. I gave the evidence *in the s.* of Hanameel
43. 9. hid stones *in the s.* of the men of Judah
Ezek. 5. 8. execute judgments *in the s.* of the nations
14. Jerus. a reproach *in the s.* of all that pass by
16. 41. judgment on thee *in the s.* of many women
20. 22. name not be polluted *in s.* of the heathen
28. 18. I will bring thee to ashes *in the s.* of all
25. be sanctified in them *in s.* of heathen, 39. 27.
36. 34. lay desolate *in the s.* of all them that pass
Hos. 2. 10. I will discover lewd. *in s.* of her lovers
Acts 7. 10. gave him wisdom *in the s.* of Pharaoh
Rom. 12. 17. provide things honest *in s.* of all men
2 *Cor.* 2. † 10. I forgave it *in the s.* of Christ
Rev. 13. 13. maketh fire come down *in s.* of men
14. miracles he had power to do *in s.* of the beast
See Lord.

***My* SIGHT.**
Gen. 23. 4. that I may bury my dead out of *my s.* 8.
Exod. 33. 12. thou hast found grace in *my s.* 17.
1 *Sam.* 29. 6. thy coming in is good in *my s.*
9. I know that thou art good in *my s.* as an angel
2 *Sam.* 6. 22. and I will be base in *mine* own *s.*
13. 5. let Tamar come, and dress the meat in *my s.*
6. come, and make me a couple of cakes in *my s.*
1 *Kings* 8. 25. not fail thee a man in *my s.* 2 *Chr.* 6. 16.
9. 7. this house which I have hallowed for my
name will I cast out of *my s.* 2 *Chron.* 7. 20.
11. 38. if thou wilt do that is right in *my s.*
2 *Kings* 21. 15. have done that which was evil in *my s.*
23. 27. I will remove Judah also out of *my s.*
1 *Chr.* 22. 8. thou hast shed much blood in *my s.*
Psal. 101. 7. that tell. lies, shall not tarry in *my s.*
Isa. 43. 4. since thou wast precious in *my s.*
Jer. 4. 1. will put away abominations out of *my s.*
7. 15. I will cast you out of *my s.* as your brethren
30. the children of Judah have done evil in *my s.*
15. 1. cast them out of *my s.* and let them go
18. 10. if it do evil in *my s.* that it obey not
Jer. 34. 15. ye turned, and had done right in *my s.*
Ezek. 10. 2. he went in *my s.* to fill his hand
19. mounted up from the earth in *my s.*
Amos 9. 3. be hid from *my s.* in the bottom of the sea
Mark 10. 51. what wilt thou I should do to thee?
Lord, that I might receive *my s. Luke* 18. 41.

***Thy* SIGHT.**
Gen. 19. 19. thy servant hath found grace in *thy s.*
21. 12. God said, let it not be grievous in *thy s.*
33. 10. Jacob said, if I have found grace in *thy s.*
47. 29. *Exod.* 33. 13, 16. | 34. 9. *Judg.* 6. 17.
Lev. 25. 53. shall not rule with rigour in *thy s.*
1 *Sam.* 15. 17. when thou wast little in *thine* own *s.*
2 *Sam.* 7. 9. have cut off thine enemies out of *thy s.*
19. this was yet a small thing in *thy s.*
14. 22. knoweth I have found grace in *thy s.*
2 *Kings* 1. 13. let my life be precious in *thy s.* 14.
20. 3. done what was good in *thy s. Isa.* 38. 3.
Psal. 5. 5. the foolish shall not stand in *thy s.*
9. 19. arise, Lord, let heathen be judged in *thy s.*
19. 14. meditat. of my heart be acceptable in *thy s.*
51. 4. I have sinned, and done this evil in *thy s.*
76. 7. who may stand in *thy s.* when thou art angry?
90. 4. thousand years in *thy s.* are but as yesterday
143. 2. for in *thy s.* shall no man be justified
Isa. 26. 17. so have we been in *thy s.* O Lord
Jer. 18. 23. neither blot out their sin from *thy s.*
Jonah 2. 4. then I said, I am cast out of *thy s.*
Mat. 11. 26. so it seemed good in *thy s. Luke* 10. 21.
Luke 15. 21. have sinned against heaven and in *thy s.*
18. 42. Jesus said unto him, receive *thy s.*
Acts 9. 17. sent me that thou mightest receive *thy s.*
22. 13. stood and said, brother Saul, receive *thy s.*
See Favour, Find.

SIGHTS.
Luke 21. 11. shall be fearful *s.* signs from heaven

SIGN,
Or token, *is taken,* I. *for any thing that serves to express or represent another thing: as, when the Lord gave to* Noah *the rainbow, as a sign or token of his covenant,* Gen. 9. 12, 13. *and when he appointed* Abraham *the use of circumcision, as the sign and seal of the covenant he made with him and his posterity,* Gen. 17. 11. Rom. 4. 11. *Circumcision was a sign, evidence, or assurance, both of the blessings promised by God, and of man's obligation to the duties required. The sun and moon are appointed by God for signs and seasons,* Gen. 1. 14. *They represent the quality of the weather by the manner of their rising or setting, by their eclipses, conjunctions, &c.* Mat. 16. 2, 3. *Sometimes they are forerunners of great calamities, and remarkable events in the course of human affairs, by their strange appearances, unusual conjunctions, &c.* Luke 21. 25, 26. Acts 2. 19, 20.

II. Sign *is put for a miracle:* Thou shalt take this rod in thine hand, wherewith thou shalt do signs, *says the Lord to Moses,* Exod. 4. 17. *and if the* Egyptians *do not believe the first sign, they will believe the second,* Exod. 4. 8. *The word* sign *is frequent in this sense in scripture.*

III. *A sign or token is often put for the proof or evidence of a thing: for example,* This shall be a token, *or sign,* unto thee, that I have sent thee, *Exod.* 3. 12. Shew me a sign that thou talkest with me, *that is, a proof,* Judg. 6. 17. What shall be the sign, *or* evidence, that the Lord will heal me? 2 *Kings* 20. 8. *This acceptation agrees with the first above mentioned.*

IV. The signs of heaven; the signs of the magicians; *are the* phenomena *of the heavens, the motions of the stars and planets, the appearances of meteors, and the like; and the impostures of magicians, which they make use of to deceive the weak.* The Lord frustrateth the tokens, *or* signs, of the liars, and maketh diviners mad, *Isa.* 44. 25. *And in* Jer. 10. 2. Be not dismayed at the signs of heaven, for the heathen are dismayed at them.

To be a sign to the house of Israel, *that is, to be a prophecy, type, or prediction of what should happen to the house of* Israel. *Thus the prophet* Ezekiel *by the type of a siege shews what should happen to* Jerusalem *some time after,* Ezek. 4. 3. *And in chap.* 14. 8. *the Lord pours down his vengeance upon sinners, and makes them as a* sign, *as a public and sensible proof, of his wrath. The prophet* Isaiah *says,* Behold, I and the children whom the Lord hath given me, are for signs and for wonders in *Israel,* Isa. 8. 18. *We are a gazing-stock to them, and wondered at for our folly in believing the promises of God.*

Exod. 4. 8. if they believe not nor hearken to voice
of first *s.* they will believe the voice of the latter *s.*
8. 23. I will put division, to-morrow shall this *s.* be
13. 9. it shall be a *s.* to thee upon thine hand
31. 13. my sabbaths ye shall keep, for it is a *s.* between me and you, 17. *Ezek.* 20. 12, 20.
Num. 16. 38. and they shall be a *s.* unto Israel
26. 10. fire devoured them, and they became a *s.*
Deut. 6. 8. bind them for a *s.* on thy hand, 11. 18.
13. 1. if there arise a prophet, and giveth thee a *s.*
2. and *s.* come to pass whereof he spake to thee
28. 46. they shall be on thee for a *s.* and a wonder
Josh. 4. 6. that this may be a *s.* among you
Judg. 6. 17. then shew me a *s.* thou talkest with me
20. 38. was an appointed *s.* between Israel and liers
1 *Sam.* 2. 34. this shall be a *s.* to thee, in one day
they shall die both of them, 2 *Kings* 19. 29.
14. 10. we will go up, this shall be a *s.* unto us
1 *Kings* 13. 3. gave a *s.* the same day, saying, this
is the *s.* the Lord hath spoken, altar shall be rent
5. according to the *s.* the man of God hath given
2 *Kings* 20. 8. what shall be the *s.* Lord will heal
9. this *s.* shalt have of L. *Isa.* 37. 30. | 38. 7, 22.
2 *Chr.* 32. 24. he spake to him, he gave him a *s.*
Isa. 7. 11. ask thee a *s.* of Lord thy God, ask
14. L. himself shall give you a *s.* behold a virgin
19. 20. it shall be for a *s.* unto the Lord of hosts
20. 3. as Isaiah hath walked bare-foot for a *s.*
55. 13. it shall be for a name, for an everlasting *s.*

Isa. 66. 19. I will set a *s.* among them and will send
Jer. 6. 1. set up a *s.* of fire in Beth-haccerem
44. 29. and this shall be a *s.* to you, *Luke* 2. 12.
Ezek. 4. 3. this shall be a *s.* to the house of Israel
12. 6. I have set thee for a *s.* to Israel, 11.
14. 8. I will make him a *s.* a proverb, and cut off
24. 24. thus Ezekiel is a *s.* ‖ 27. thou shalt be a *s.*
39. 15. then shall he set up a *s.* by it till buriers
Mat. 12. 38. saying, Master we would see a *s.* from thee, 16. 1. *Mark* 8. 11. *Luke* 11. 16.
39. an evil and adulterous generation seeketh after a *s.* 16. 4. *Mark* 8. 12. *Luke* 11. 29.
there shall no *s.* be given but the *s.* of the prophet Jonas, *Mark* 8. 12. *Luke* 11. 29, 30.
24. 3. and what shall be the *s.* of thy coming?
30. then shall appear the *s.* of the Son of man
26. 48. now he that betrayed him gave them a *s.*
Mark 13. 4. what *s.* when all these things shall be
Luke 2. 34. for a *s.* which shall be spoken against
John 2. 18. what *s.* shewest thou unto us? 6. 30.
Acts 28. 11. a ship, whose *s.* was Castor and Pollux
Rom. 4. 11. he received *s.* of circumcision, a seal
1 *Cor.* 1. 22. for Jews require *s.* Greeks seek wisdom
14. 22. wherefore tongues are *s.* not to them that
Rev. 15. 1. I saw another *s.* in heaven, seven angels

SIGN.

Dan. 6. 8. O king, establish decree, *s.* the writing

SIGNED.

Dan. 6. 9. wherefore king Darius *s.* the writing
10. when Daniel knew that the writing was *s.*
12. they spake, hast thou not *s.* a decree

SIGNS.

Gen. 1. 14. let them be for *s.* and for seasons, for days
Exod. 4. 9. if they will not believe these two *s.*
17. with this rod in thy hand thou shalt do *s.*
28. Moses told Aaron all words of Lord and all *s.* which he had commanded, 30. *Josh.* 24. 17
7. 3. I will multiply my *s.* in the land of Egypt
10. 2. mayest tell thy son my *s.* which I have done
Num. 14. 11. for all the *s.* which I have shewed
Deut. 4. 34. to take him a nation by *s.* 26. 8.
6. 22. Lord shewed *s.* on Egypt, on Pharaoh and on all his household, *Neh.* 9. 10. *Psal.* 78. 43.
7. 19. the great *s.* which thine eyes saw, 29. 3.
34. 11. in all *s.* which the Lord sent him to do
1 *Sam.* 10. 7. when these *s.* are come unto thee
9. and all those *s.* came to pass that day
2 *Kings* 23. † 5. put down them that burn to twelve *s.*
Job 38. † 32. canst thou bring forth the twelve *s.*?
Psal. 74. 4. they set up their ensigns for *s.*
9. we see not our *s.* there is no more any prophet
105. 27. shewed his *s.* among them, and wonders
Isa. 8. 18. behold, I and the children are for *s.*
Jer. 10. 2. be not dismayed at the *s.* of heaven
32. 20. which hast set *s.* and wonders in Egypt
21. hast brought forth Israel out of Egypt with *s.*
Dan. 4. 2. I thought it good to shew *s.* and wonders
3. how great are his *s.*? how mighty his wonders
6. 27. he worketh *s.* in heaven and in earth
Mat. 16. 3. can ye not discern the *s.* of the times?
24. 24. there shall arise false Christs and false prophets, and shall shew great *s.* *Mark* 13. 22.
Mark 16. 17. these *s.* follow them that believe
20. confirming the word with *s.* following
Luke 1. 62. they made *s.* to his father Zachariah
21. 11. and great *s.* shall there be from heaven
25. there shall be *s.* in the sun, moon, and stars
John 4. 48. except ye see *s.* ye will not believe
20. 30. and many other *s.* truly did Jesus
Acts 2. 19. I will shew *s.* in the earth beneath
22. a man approved of God by *s.* which God did
43. many *s.* were done by the apostles, 5. 12.
4. 30. that *s.* may be done by the name of Jesus
7. 36. after he had shewed *s.* and wonders in Egypt
8. 13. then Simon wondered, beholding the *s.* done
14. 3. granted *s.* and wonders to be done by hands
Rom. 15. 19. things Christ hath not wrought by me through mighty *s.* and wonders, 2 *Cor.* 12. 12.
2 *Thess.* 2. 9. after the working of Satan, with *s.*
Heb. 2. 4. G. bear. them witness with *s.* and wond.

SIGNET.

Gen. 38. 18. give me thy *s.* and thy staff, 25.
Exod. 28. 11. with work of an engraver on stone, like the engravings of a *s.* 21, 36. | 39. 14, 30.
Jer. 22. 24. tho' Coniah were *s.* on my right hand
Dan. 6. 17. the king sealed it with his own *s.*
Hag. 2. 23. I will take thee and make thee as a *s.*

SIGNETS.

Exod. 39. 6. onyx-stones graven as *s.* are graven

SIGNIFICANT.

1 *Cor.* 14. † 9. so you, except you utter words *s.*

SIGNIFICATION.

1 *Cor.* 14. 10. and none of them without *s.*

SIGNIFY.

Acts 21. 26. to *s.* the accomplishment of the days
23. 15. *s.* thee to chief captain that he bring Paul
25. 27. and not to *s.* the crimes laid against him
1 *Pet.* 1. 11. signifying what Spirit in them did *s.*

SIGNIFIED.

Acts 11. 28. Agabus *s.* there should be dearth
Rev. 1. 1. *s.* it by his angel to his servant John

SIGNIFIETH.

Heb. 12. 27. *s.* removing of those things shaken

SIGNIFYING.

John 12. 33. this he said, *s.* by what death he should glorify God, 18. 32. | 21. 19.
Heb. 9. 8. the Holy Ghost this *s.* that the way

SILENCE.

This word does not only signify the ordinary silence, *or refraining from speaking; but also, in the style of the* Hebrews, *it is taken for* to be quiet, to remain immovable. *Josh.* 10. 12, 13. Sun, stand thou still upon *Gibeon:* Hebrew, *be silent.* And the sun stood still, and the moon stayed, *or* were silent, *at the commandment of* Joshua. *And in Prov.* 26. 20. Where there is no tale-bearer, the strife ceaseth, *or* is silent. Silence *is taken for an entire ruin or destruction, for a total subjection,* Isa. 15. 1. *Ar of Moab* is laid waste, and brought to silence, *or, is utterly destroyed. Also in Jer.* 8. 14. The Lord our God hath put us to silence, *or, has brought great calamities upon us.* Silence *is also taken for death and the grave.* Psal. 94. 17. Unless the Lord had been my help, my soul had almost dwelt in silence. *And in* Psal. 115. 17. The dead praise not the Lord, neither any that go down into silence. *The prophet* Jeremiah *says,* Let us enter into the defenced cities, and let us be silent there, *Jer.* 8. 14. *Let us hasten to some places of strength to secure ourselves, and let us sit still, and not say a word to provoke so potent an enemy as the* Chaldeans are.

Job 4. 16. an image was before me, there was *s.*
29. 21. men gave ear, and kept *s.* at my counsel
Psal. 31. 18. let the lying lips be put to *s.*
39. 2. I was dumb with *s.* I held my peace
94. 17. my soul had almost dwelt in *s.*
115. 17. neither any that go down into *s.*
Isa. 15. 1. Moab brought to *s.* Kir brought to *s.*
Jer. 8. 14. the Lord our God hath put us to *s.*
Lam. 3. 28. he sitteth alone and keepeth *s.* because
Amos 8. 3. they shall cast them forth with *s.*
Mat. 22. 34. had heard he had put Sadducees to *s.*
Acts 21. 40. there was made a great *s.* he spake
22. 2. that he spake in Hebrew, they kept more *s.*
1 *Tim.* 2. 11. let woman learn in *s.* with subjection
12. I suffer not a woman to teach, nor to usurp authority over the man, but to be in *s.*
1 *Pet.* 2. 15. may put to *s.* ignorance of foolish men
Rev. 8. 1. there was *s.* in heaven half an hour
See KEEP, KEPT.

SILENT.

Josh. 10. † 12. he said, sun, be *s.* upon Gibeon
Judg. 16. † 2. they were *s.* all the night, saying
1 *Sam.* 2. 9. the wicked shall be *s.* in darkness
7. † 8. be not *s.* from us from crying to the Lord
2 *Sam.* 19. † 10. why are ye *s.* in bringing king back?
1 *Kings* 22. † 3. Ramoth is ours, be *s.* from taking it
Job 13. † 13. be *s.* from me, that I may speak
Psal. 22. 2. I cry in the night-season, and am not *s.*
28. 1. be not *s.* to me, lest if thou be *s.* to me
30. 12. my glory may sing praise to thee, not be *s.*
31. 17. let the wicked be *s.* in the grave
37. † 7. be *s.* to the Lord, and wait patiently
62. † 1. truly my soul is *s.* upon God
65. † 1. praise is *s.* for thee, O God, in Zion
Prov. 26. † 20. where no tale-bearer, strife is *s.*
Isa. 23. † 2. be *s.* still, ye inhabitants of the isle
47. 5. sit thou *s.* and get thee into darkness
Jer. 8. 14. enter defenced cities, let us be *s.* there
38. † 27. so they were *s.* from him
Exod. 24. † 17. be *s.* make no mourning for dead
Amos 8. † 3. they shall cast forth dead bodies, be *s.*
Jonah 1. † 11. that the sea may be *s.* from us
4. † 8. that God prepared a *s.* east wind
Hab. 2. † 20. be *s.* all the earth before him
Zeph. 3. † 17. he will be *s.* in his love, he will joy
Zech. 2. 13. be *s.* O all flesh, before the Lord

SILK.

Gen. 41. † 42. Pharaoh arrayed Joseph in vest. of *s.*
Prov. 31. 22. her clothing is *s.* and purple
Ezek. 16. 10. I girded thee, I covered thee with *s.*
13. thy raiment was of *s.* and broidered work
Rev. 18. 12. no man buyeth her merchandise of *s.*

SILLY.

Job 5. 2. and envy slayeth the *s.* one
Hos. 7. 11. Ephr. also is like a *s.* dove without heart
2 *Tim.* 3. 6. they who lead captive *s.* women laden

SILVER.

This metal does not appear to have been in use before the deluge; at least, Moses *says nothing of it before that time, he speaks only of the metals of brass and iron,* Gen. 4. 22. *But in* Abraham's *time it was become common, and traffic was carried on with this metal.* Gen. 13. 2. *Abraham* was very rich in silver and in gold: *And* he bought a sepulchre for his wife *Sarah* for four hundred shekels of silver, *Gen.* 23. 15. *This* silver *was not coined, according to all appearance, but was only in bars, or ingots, and in commerce it was always weighed.*

The silver cord, *Eccl.* 12. 6. *By this Commentators generally understand the pith, or marrow of the back-bone, which comes from the brain, and thence goeth down to the very lowest end of the back-bone, together with the nerves and sinews, which, as anatomists observe, are nothing else but the production and continuation of the marrow. And this is aptly compared to a* cord, *both for its figure, which is very long and round, and for its use, which is to draw and move the parts of the body; and it is compared to* silver, *both for its excellency and colour, which is white and bright, even in a dead, and much more in a living body.*

Gen. 23. 15. the land is worth 400 shekels of *s.*
16. and Abraham weighed 400 shekels of *s.*
Exod. 20. 23. ye shall not make gods of *s.* or gold
26. 19. sockets of *s.* 21, 25, 32. | 36. 24, 26, 30, 36.
27. 17. their hooks shall be of *s.* 38. 19.
35. 24. they did offer an offering of *s.* and of brass
38. 25. *s.* of them that were numbered of congreg.
Lev. 5. 15. ram with thy estimation by shekels of *s.*
27. 3. thy estimation of male 50 shekels of *s.*
27. 6. of male five, of female three shekels of *s.*
16. an homer of barley seed at fifty shekels of *s.*
Num. 7. 13. his offering was one *s.* charger, 19, 25, 31, 37, 43, 49, 55, 61, 67, 73, 79. one *s.* bowl of 70 shekels, 19, 25, 31, 37, 43, &c.
84. twelve chargers of *s.* twelve *s.* bowls
85. each charger of *s.* weighing 130 shekels
10. 2. make thee two trumpets of *s.* for the calling of the assembly, and journeying of the camps
Deut. 22. 19. shall amerce him in 100 shekels of *s.*
29. shall give to damsel's father 50 shekels of *s.*
Josh. 7. 21. I saw 200 shekels of *s.* then I coveted
22. was hid in his tent, and the *s.* under it, 24.
Judg. 17. 2. 1100 shekels of *s.* that were taken from thee, behold, the *s.* is with me, I took it
3. when he had restored the *s.* ‖ 4. took the *s.*
10. I will give thee ten shekels of *s.* by the year
1 *Sam.* 9. 8. at hand fourth part of a shekel of *s.*
2 *Sam.* 18. 11. I would have given 10 shekels of
2 *Sam.* 18. 12. tho' I should receive 1000 shekels of *s.*
24. 24. bought flour and oxen for 50 shekels of *s.*
1 *Kings* 10. 21. none were of *s.* 2 *Chron.* 9. 20.
27. king made *s.* to be in Jerusalem as stones
20. 39. else thou shalt pay a talent of *s.*
2 *Kings* 5. 22. give them, I pray thee, a talent of *s.*
15. 20. exacted of each man fifty shekels of *s.*
18. 15. Hezekiah gave him all *s.* that was found
22. 4. that Hilkiah may sum the *s.* brought
1 *Chron.* 28. 14. *s.* of all instruments of *s.* 29. 2, 5.
15. for candlesticks of *s.* ‖ 17. for basins of *s.*
2 *Chron.* 17. 11. brought Jehoshaphat presents of *s.*
Neh. 5. 15. former gover. had taken 40 shekels of *s.*
Job 3. 15. with princes who filled houses with *s.*
22. 25. thy defence, thou shalt have plenty of *s.*
27. 16. tho' he heap up *s.* as the dust, and raiment
17. and the innocent shall divide the *s.*
28. 15. nor shall *s.* be weighed for price of wisdom
Psal. 12. 6. words of the Lord are pure, as *s.* tried
66. 10. for thou, O God, hast tried us, as *s.* is tried
Prov. 2. 4. if seekest her as *s.* and searchest for her
3. 14. merchandise of wisdom is better than of *s.*
8. 10. receive my instruction, and not *s.*
19. and my revenue than choice *s.*
10. 20. the tongue of the just is as choice *s.*
16. 16. to get understanding chosen rather than *s.*
17. 3. fining-pot is for *s.* and the furnace for gold
25. 4. take away the dross from the *s.*
Eccl. 5. 10. loveth *s.* shall not be satisfied with *s.*
Cant. 8. 9. we will build on her a palace of *s.*
Isa. 1. 22. thy *s.* is become dross, thy wine mixed
30. 22. shall defile covering of thy images of *s.*
48. 10. behold I have refined thee, but not with *s.*
60. 17. for iron I will bring *s.* and for wood brass
Jer. 6. 30. reprobate *s.* shall men call them
10. 9. *s.* spread into plates is brought from Tarshish
32. 9. I weighed him even seventeen shekels of *s.*
Ezek. 22. 18. Israel they are even the dross of *s.*
20. as they gather *s.* brass, and iron, and lead
22. as *s.* is melted in the midst of the furnace
27. 12. with *s.* Tarshish traded in thy fairs
Dan. 2. 32. this image's breast and arms were of *s.*
Hos. 9. 6. pleasant places for *s.* nettles shall possess
13. 2. they made them molten images of their *s.*
Amos 2. 6. because they sold the righteous for *s.*
8. 6. that we may buy poor for *s.* and the needy
Zeph. 1. 11. howl, all they that bear *s.* are cut off
Zech. 9. 3. Tyrus heaped up *s.* as dust and fine gold
13. 9. and I will refine them as *s.* is refined
Mal. 3. 3. he shall sit as a refiner and purifier of *s.*
See FILLETS, GOLD, PIECES.

SILVERLINGS.

Isa. 7. 23. there were thousand vines at thousand *s.*

SILVER *smith.*

Acts 19. 24. Demetrius a *s. smith* made shrines

Talents of SILVER.

1 *Kings* 16. 24. bought hill Samaria for two *tal. of s.*
2 *Kings* 5. 5. Naaman took with him ten *tal. of s.*
23. and bound two *talents of s.* into two bags
15. 19. Menahem gave Pul 1000 *talents of s.*
1 *Chron.* 19. 6. Hanun sent 1000 *talents of s.*
22. 14. I prepared a thousand thousand *talents of s.*
29. 4. and seven thousand *talents of* refined *s.*
2 *Chr.* 25. 6. hired mighty men for 100 *talents of s.*
27. 5. Ammon gave Jotham 100 *talents of s.*
36. 3. condemned land in 100 *talents of s.*
Ezra 7. 22. I decree it be done to 100 *talents of s.*
8. 26. I weighed to their hand 650 *talents of s.*
Esth. 3. 9. I will pay ten thousand *talents of s.*

Vessels of SILVER.

Num. 7. 85. all the *s. vessels* weighed 2400 shekels
2 *Sam.* 8. 10. Joram brought with him *vessels of s.*
1 *Kings* 10. 25. every man his present, *vessels of s.*
2 *Kings* 12. 13. there were not made *vessels of s.*
1 *Chron.* 18. 10. and with him all manner of *vessels of s.* gold and brass, 2 *Chron.* 24. 14.
Ezra 1. 6. strengthened their hands with *ves. of s.* 11.
5. 14. *vessels* of gold and *s.* of the house of God, which Nebuchadnezzar took
6. 5. let the golden and *s. vessels* be restored
8. 26. I weighed *s. vessels* an hundred talents
Dan. 5. 2. commanded to bring golden and *s. vess.*
11. 8. carry with their precious *ves. of s.* and gold

SILVER.

Gen. 44. 2. put my *s.* cup in sack's mouth of youngest
Prov. 26. 23. like a potsherd covered with *s.* dross
Eccl. 12. 6. or ever *s.* cord be loosed or bowl broken
Isa. 40. 19. the goldsmith casteth *s.* chains
Mat. 27. 6. the chief priests took the *s.* pieces
Acts 19. 24. Demetrius made *s.* shrines for Diana
See VESSELS *just before.*

SIMILITUDE.

Num. 12. 8. the *s.* of the Lord shall he behold
Deut. 4. 12. ye heard voice of words, but saw no *s.* 15.
16. lest ye make you the *s.* of any figure
2 *Chron.* 4. 3. under it was *s.* of oxen round about
Psal. 106. 20. changed their glory into *s.* of an ox
144. 12. corner stones polished after *s.* of a palace
Dan. 10. 16. one like the *s.* of the sons of men
Rom. 5. 14. after the *s.* of Adam's transgression
Heb. 7. 15. after *s.* of Melchisedec ariseth a priest
Jam. 3. 9. men who are made after the *s.* of God

SIMILITUDES.

Hos. 12. 10. I have used *s.* by ministry of prophets

SIMPLE

Is taken, [1] *For one who is harmless, innocent, and free from deceit,* Rom. 16. 19. *St.* Paul *would have the* Romans *be* wise unto that which is good, and simple concerning evil; *that is, discerning in the choice of good, to distinguish the good from the bad doctrine; but they must avoid whatever has the appearance of evil as children who, without much reasoning, fly from every thing that does but seem hurtful to them: he would have them so innocent as not to deceive, and yet so prudent as not to be deceived.* [2] *For such as are ignorant, weak, and subject to delusion, yet sincere and willing to be taught: such simple ones are invited to* Wisdom's *feast; and are opposed to such as are proud and self-conceited,* Prov. 9. 4. Whoso is simple, let him turn in hither. [3] Simple *is taken for a silly, foolish,* credulous man, who is easily deceived with the smooth words and fair pretences of false and deceitful men, Prov. 14. 15. The simple believeth every word; and this simple man is opposed to the prudent man, who looketh well to his goings; who not only orders his conversation and dealings in the world with due circumspection, but also judges of the words and professions of others by their conversations. [4] It is taken for ignorant, easy, and credulous persons, who are soon cheated by the world and the devil, and who do not understand their own interest, but persist in their sinful courses. Prov. 22. 3. But the simple pass on, and are punished. Simple here is opposed to the wise and prudent man, who foreseeing the calamity or judgment of God threatened, does by prayer and repentance put himself under the protection of the Almighty. [5] Simplicity is sometimes taken for fidelity and liberality. Rom. 12. 8. He that giveth, let him do it with simplicity. He that distributes the church's stock to the poor, let him do it faithfully, without fraud; impartially, not for favour or affection; gently, without fierceness; and liberally, according to every one's necessity.

Psal. 19. 7. the law of the Lord making wise the s.
116. 6. Lord preserveth the s. I was brought low
119. 130. it giveth understanding to the s.
Prov. 1. 4. to give subtilty to s. to young knowledge
22. how long, ye s. ones, will ye love simplicity
32. the turning away of the s. shall slay them
7. 7. I beheld among the s. ones a young man
8. 5. O ye s. understand wisdom, and ye fools
9. 4. whoso is s. let him turn in hither, 16.
13. a foolish woman is s. and knoweth nothing
14. 15. s. believeth every word, but prudent man
18. s. inherit folly ‖ 19. 25. the s. will beware
21. 11. the scorner is punished, the s. made wise
22. 3. the s. pass on and are punished, 27. 12.
Ezek. 45. 20. so thou shalt do for him that is s.
Rom. 16. 18. by fair speeches deceive hearts of s.
19. have you wise to good, and s. concerning evil

SIMPLICITY.

2 Sam. 15. 11. they went in their s. and knew not
Prov. 1. 22. how long, simple ones, will ye love s.?
Rom. 12. 8. he that giveth, let him do it with s.
2 Cor. 1. 12. in s. we had our conversation in world
11. 3. be corrupted from the s. that is in Christ

SIN

Is any thought, word, action, omission, or desire, contrary to the law of God. Sin is any want of conformity to, or transgression of the law, 1 John 3. 4. It is taken, [1] For original corruption, or the depravity and naughtiness of our corrupt nature, which is prone to all evil. Psal. 51. 5. Behold, I was shapen in iniquity, and in sin did my mother conceive me. Rom. 7. 8. Sin taking occasion by the commandment, wrought in me all manner of concupiscence. [2] For actual sin, which flows from the corruption of nature. Jam. 1. 15. When lust hath conceived, it bringeth forth sin. [3] It is taken for the guilt and defilement of sin. Psal. 51. 2. Wash me throughly from mine iniquity, and cleanse me from my sin. And in Heb. 10. 2. The worshippers, once purged, should have had no more conscience of sins. [4] For the punishment of sin, Gen. 4. 7. And if thou doest not well, sin lieth at the door; be sure thy sin will find thee out; thou shalt not long enjoy the fruits of thy wickedness, but a dreadful judgment shall tread upon the heels of thy sin. And in Gen. 19. 15. Lest thou be consumed in the iniquity or punishment of the city. [5] Sin is taken both for the guilt and punishment of sin. Psal. 32. 1. Blessed is he whose sin is covered. And in Mat. 9. 2. Son, thy sins be forgiven thee: the guilt of them is pardoned, and so the punishment shall be removed. [6] The name of sin is often given to the sacrifice of expiation, or to the sacrifice for sin, Lev. 4. 3, 25, 29. What is there rendered sin offering, is in Hebrew, sin. St. Paul says, that God was pleased that Jesus Christ, who knew no sin, should be our victim of expiation, 2 Cor. 5. 21. For he hath made him to be sin for us, who knew no sin, that we might be made the righteousness of God in him. [7] Sin is taken for any fault, either in doctrine or life. John 8. 46. Which of you convinceth me of sin? [8] For infidelity and unbelief. John 16. 9. The Spirit will convince the world of sin, because they believe not on me. [9] For a sinful course of life. Jam. 1. 15. Sin, when it is finished, bringeth forth death. [10] For the remainders of sin in such as are renewed and regenerated. Rom. 6. 12. Let not sin therefore reign in your mortal body: since you are regenerated, and spiritually alive, let not the remainders of corruption exercise an uncontrolled absolute power in you. [11] It is taken for sin greatly aggravated. John 15. 22, 24. If I had not come and spoken to them, they had not had sin: they had not been guilty of this particular sin of infidelity in rejecting me; or, their sin had not been so heinous as now it is; or, they had had more to say in excuse for their sin. [12] For the idols or calves at Dan and Beth-el, which were the occasion of the sin of Samaria. Amos 8. 14. They that swear by the sin of Samaria.

God was not the author of sin or of death; it is inconsistent with the divine holiness and purity to incline the creature to sin: As God cannot be tempted to evil, neither tempts he any man, Jam. 1. 13. But sin and death entered into the world by the malice of the devil; and Adam, by his disobedience, and yielding to the temptation of Satan, has made us all guilty in the eyes of God. See DEVIL, FALL. Jesus Christ, by his death, hath restored life to us; by his obedience he has reconciled us to God the Father; instead of children of wrath, as we were, he has merited for us the character of children of God. The apostle Paul, in several places, speaks of the misery which the first Adam brought on himself and his posterity, and of the blessings which Christ the second Adam has purchased for his children. See Rom. 3. 23. | 5. 12. | 6. 23. 1 Cor. 15. 21, 22. Though sin be permitted of God, he can no more be the author of it, than light is the author of darkness, 1 John 1. 5. Sin is not a creature, or a being, but rather the privation of a being; as light is the privation of darkness, so is sin a privation of holiness.

Presumptuous sins. David prays that God would keep him back from presumptuous sins, Psal. 19. 13. From known and evident sins, such as proceed from the choice of the perverse will against the enlightened mind, which are committed with deliberation, with design, resolution, and eagerness, against the checks of conscience, and the motions of God's Spirit: such sins are direct rebellion against God, a despising of his command, and provoke his pure eyes.

Original sin was the rebellion of the first man Adam against his Creator, which was a sin of universal efficacy, which derives a guilt and stain to mankind in all ages of the world. The account the scripture gives of it, is grounded on the relation which all men have to Adam as their natural and moral principal or head.

I. Their natural. God created one man in the beginning, from whom all others derive their beings: And that the unity might be the more entire, he formed him that aid which was necessary for communicating his kind to the world. He hath made of one blood all nations of men, for to dwell on all the face of the earth, Acts 17. 26. And as the whole race of mankind was virtually in Adam's loins, so it was presumed to give virtual consent to what he did; when he broke, all suffered shipwreck that were contained in him as their natural original.

II. He was the moral principal of mankind. In the first treaty between God and man, Adam was considered, not as a single person, but as the representative of a nation, and contracted for all his descendants by ordinary generation: his person was the fountain of theirs, and his will the representative of theirs. From hence his vast progeny became a party in the covenant, and had a title to the benefits contained in it upon his obedience, and was liable to the curse upon his violation of it. Upon this ground the apostle institutes a parallel between Adam and Christ. Rom. 5. 19. That as by one man's disobedience many were made sinners; so by the obedience of one shall many be made righteous. As Christ in his death on the cross did not suffer as a private person, but as a surety and sponsor representing the whole church, as it is said, 2 Cor. 5. 14. If one died for all, then were all dead: So the first Adam, who was the figure of him that was to come, Rom. 5. 14. in his disobedience was esteemed a public person representing the whole race of mankind; and by a just law it was not restrained to himself.

The Scripture proves in many places that the sin of Adam was communicated to all his posterity, and that it has infected and corrupted it. Eph. 2. 3. We were by nature the children of wrath; that is, liable to punishment, and that hath relation to guilt. And in Rom. 5. 12. By one man sin entered into the world, and death by sin; and so death passed upon all men, as a just sentence upon the guilty, for that all have sinned. Job describes this sin, Who can bring a clean thing out of an unclean? not one, Job 14. 4. It is the universal law of nature, that every thing produces its like, not only in regard of the same nature, that is propagated from one individual to another, without a change of the species, but in respect of the qualities with which that nature is eminently affected. The Psalmist David likewise speaks of this sin, Psal. 51. 5. Behold, I was shapen in iniquity, and in sin did my mother conceive me.

The sin against the Holy Ghost. Our Saviour says in Mat. 12. 31, 32. Wherefore I say unto you, All manner of sin and blasphemy shall be forgiven unto men, but the blasphemy against the Holy Ghost shall not be forgiven unto men. And whoever shall speak a word against the Son of man, it shall be forgiven him: but whosoever speaketh against the Holy Ghost, it shall not be forgiven him, neither in this world, neither in the world to come. Interpreters have differently explained the sin against the Holy Ghost. St. Ambrose in one place makes it to consist in denying the deity of the Son. In another place he says, it consists in denying the divinity of the Holy Ghost, and in imputing his works to the power of the devil: And in his book of Repentance he extends it to heresy and schism. Hermas says, that the sin against the Holy Ghost is the blaspheming of God; and another author says, that it is the renouncing of God: Others think the irremissible sin, to be that of a hardened, impenitent, and insolent sinner: Grotius espouses this opinion, and gives for examples of this crime, the sin of Korah, Pharaoh, Simon Magus, Ananias, and Sapphira.

The generality of interpreters place the sin against the Holy Ghost, mentioned by our Saviour, in the wilful malice of those that withstand the evidence of truth, and who will not acknowledge the miracles of Christ to be wrought by the finger of God, but maliciously, and against the conviction of their own consciences, impute them to the prince of darkness. This was certainly the crime of the Pharisees, to whom Christ applied his discourse; and those also become guilty of the same crime, who oppose or persecute the doctrine, ways, and servants of Christ, because they are spiritual, or have any thing of the Spirit appearing in them, and that contrary to their own convictions. Such as are guilty of this sin, are excepted from pardon, because the death of Christ was not appointed for the expiation of it: And there being no sacrifice, there can be no satisfaction, and consequently no pardon. For if we sin wilfully after we have received the knowledge of the truth, there remaineth no more sacrifice for sins, Heb. 10. 26, 27, &c. The wisdom and justice of God require this severity against such sinners: For if he that despised Moses' law, died without mercy, of how much sorer punishment shall he be thought worthy, who hath trodden under foot the Son of God, and hath counted the blood of the covenant, wherewith he was sanctified, an unholy thing, and hath done despite to the Spirit of grace! that is, They renounce their Redeemer as if he were not the Son of God, and virtually consent to the cruel sentence passed against him, as if he had blasphemed when he declared himself to be so: and thereby out-sin his sufferings. How reasonable is it therefore that they should be for ever deprived of the benefits, who obstinately reject the means that purchased them. The same apostle speaks also of this sin in Heb. 6, 4, 5, 6. For it is impossible for those who were once enlightened, and have tasted of the heavenly gift, and were made partakers of the Holy Ghost: and have tasted the good word of God, and the powers of the world to come, if they shall fall away, to renew them again unto repentance: seeing they crucify to themselves the Son of God afresh, and put him to an open shame: that is, Such as have attained to some acquaintance with the doctrine of the gospel, and have had some experience of the power and efficacy of the Holy Ghost from heaven in gospel administrations and worship; yea, even some of the extraordinary gifts of the Spirit; who have likewise relished comfort and sweetness in the doctrine and promises of the gospel; and particularly having heard that the Redeemer saves them from wrath, and instates them in happiness beyond what is attainable here on earth; their self-love has externally closed with the revelation, and made application of it to itself: Now, says the apostle, if such shall turn apostates, it is impossible, in regard of any law, rule, or constitution of God, to bring them to repentance whereby they should be restored to their former condition; and this because they despise the means of salvation, they shew themselves to be of the same opinion with those that did crucify Christ, and they would do it again, were it in their power; and actually do it as much as they can by persecuting his members. The great unpardonable sin against the Holy Ghost, appears to be a presumptuous sin against some more than ordinary illuminations, convictions, and taste of gospel grace, whereby a man doth knowingly and studiously rebel against the truth, and maliciously persecute it in himself and others from an universal hatred of it for itself, Mat. 12. 31, 32. Heb. 6. 4, 5. Job 24. 13. Heb. 10. 29. Acts 13. 41. 1 John 5. 16.

From the above-mentioned passage, in Heb. 6. it appears, [1] That it cannot be any sin that is committed ignorantly. St. Paul was a blasphemer, but was forgiven, because he did it ignorantly. [2] It must be a sin knowingly committed against the operations of the Holy Ghost, and the convictions of conscience; it is a sinning wilfully after having received the knowledge of the truth, and having been made partakers of the Holy Ghost. [3] Apostasy seems to be an ingredient in it, If they fall away, says the apostle. [4] It takes in malice and persecution; the Pharisees did not only impute the miracles of our Saviour to the devil, but they spake it out of malice, designing to destroy him. [5] Though impenitency cannot be called that sin, yet it comes into the number of its ingredients; and therefore the Apostle says of such sinners, It is impossible to renew them again to repentance.

Gen. 4. 7. if thou doest not well, s. lieth at the door
Exod. 34. 7. forgiving iniquity, transgression, and s.
Lev. 4. 3. if priest s. according to the s. of people
14. when s. is known, congregation shall offer
6. 26. the priest that offereth it for s. 9. 15.
19. 17. and not suffer s. upon thy neighbour
22. the s. which he hath done shall be forgiven
Num. 5. 6. when a man or woman shall commit s.
12. 11. I beseech thee lay not the s. upon us
19. 9. it is a purification for s. 17.
27. 3. our father died in his own s. had no sons
Deut. 15. 9. cry to Lord and it be s. to thee, 24. 15.
19. 15. one witness shall not rise up for any s.
21. 22. if man have committed s. worthy of death
22. 26. there is in damsel no s. worthy of death
23. 21. L. shall require it, and it would s. in thee
22. if thou forbear to vow, it shall be no s.
24. 16. every man shall be put to death for his own s. 2 Kings 14. 6. 2 Chron. 25. 4.
1 Sam. 15. 23. for rebellion is as s. of witchcraft
1 Kings 8. 34. forgive the s. of thy people Israel
36. forgive s. of thy servants, 2 Chron. 6. 25, 27.
12. 30. and this thing became a s. 13. 34.
2 Kings 12. 16. the s. money was the priest's
Job 20. 11. his bones are full of s. of his youth
Psal. 32. 1. blessed is he whose s. is covered
51. 5. and in s. did my mother conceive me
59. 12. for s. of their mouth let them be taken
109. 7. and let his prayer become s.
14. let not the s. of his mother be blotted out
Prov. 10. 16. the fruit of the wicked tendeth to s.
19. in multitude of words there wanteth not s.
13. † 6. but wickedness overthroweth s.
14. 9. fools make a mock at s. but among righteous
34. but s. is a reproach to any people
21. 4. and the plowing of the wicked is s.
24. 9. the thought of foolishness is s.
Isa. 5. 18. wo to them draw s. as it were with cart-rope
30. 1. and cover, that they may add s. to s.
31. 7. his idols which your hands have made for s.
53. 10. thou shalt make his soul an offering for s.
12. he bare the s. of many, and made intercession
Jer. 17. 1. s. of Judah written with a pen of iron

Jer. 17. 3. I will give high plac. for a s. in thy bord.
51. 5. though their land was filled with s.
Lam. 4. 6. than the punishment of the s. of Sodom
Hos. 4. 8. they eat up s. of my people, set their heart
10. 8. the s. of Israel shall be destroyed
12. 8. they shall find no iniquity in me that were s.
Amos 8. 14. they that swear by the s. of Samaria
Mic. 1. 13. she is the beginning of s. to Zion
6. 7. shall I give fruit of my body for s. of my soul
Zech. 13. 1. there shall be a fountain opened for s.
14. † 19. this shall be the s. of Egypt
Mat. 12. 31. all manner of s. shall be forgiven to men
John 1. 29. which taketh away the s. of the world
8. 7. he that is without s. among you, let him cast
34. whoso committeth s. is the servant of s.
9. 41. if ye were blind, he should have no s.
15. 22. if I had not come, they had not had s. 24.
16. 8. Comforter, he will reprove the world of s.
9. of s. because they believe not on me
19. 11. he that delivered me hath the greater s.
Acts 7. 60. Lord, lay not this s. to their charge
Rom. 3. 9. proved Jews and Gentiles are all under s.
20. for by the law is the knowledge of s.
4. 7. blessed are they whose s. is covered
5. 12. s. entered into the world, and death by s.
13. for till the law s. was in the world
20. where s. abounded, grace much more abound
21. that as s. reigned unto death, even so grace
6. 1. what shall we say? shall we continue in s.?
2. how shall we that are dead to s. live therein?
6. with him, that the body of s. might be destroyed that henceforth we should not serve s.
7. for he that is dead is freed from s.
10. for in that he died, he died to s. once
11. reckon ye yourselves to be dead indeed unto s.
12. let not s. therefore reign in your mortal body
13. nor yield your members as instruments to s.
14. for s. shall not have dominion over you
16. his servants ye are, whether of s. unto death
17. God be thanked, ye were the servants of s.
18. being then made free from s. 22.
20. for when ye were the servants of s. ye were
23. for wages of s. is death, but the gift of God
7. 7. is law s.? God forbid, I had not known s.
8. s. taking occasion wrought in me all manner of concupiscence: for without the law s. was dead
9. commandment came, s. revived, and I died
11. for s. by the commandment slew me
13. but s. that it might appear, s. that s. by the commandment might become exceeding sinful
14. law is spiritual, but I am carnal, sold under s.
17. no more I, but s. that dwelleth in me, 20.
23. and bringing me into captivity to law of s.
25. but with the flesh, the law of s.
8. 3. and for s. condemned s. in the flesh
10. if Christ be in you, body is dead because of s.
14. 23. for whatsoever is not of faith, is s.
1 Cor. 6. 18. every s. a man doth is without body
15. 56. O death, where is thy sting? the sting of death is s. and the strength of s. is the law
2 Cor. 5. 21. made him to be s. for us, who knew no s.
Gal. 2. 17. is therefore Christ the minister of s.?
3. 22. the scripture hath concluded all under s.
2 Thess. 2. 3. and that man of s. be revealed
Heb. 3. 13. be hardened thro' the deceitfulness of s.
4. 15. was tempted like as we are, yet without s.
9. 26. but once hath he appeared to put away s.
28. he shall appear without s. to salvation
10. 6. in sacrifices for s. thou hast had no pleasure
8. offering for s. thou wouldst not, nor pleasure
18. where remission, is no more offering for s.
11. 25. than to enjoy pleasures of s. for a season
12. 1. let us lay aside s. that doth easily beset us
4. ye have not yet resisted, striving against s.
13. 11. the bodies of those beasts for s. are burnt
Jam. 1. 15. when lust hath conceived, it bringeth forth s. and s. when finished, bringeth forth death
2. 9. if ye have respect to persons, ye commit s.
4. 17. knoweth, and doth not good, to him it is s.
1 Pet. 2. 22. who did no s. nor was guile found
4. 1. that suffered in flesh hath ceased from s.
2 Pet. 2. 14. having eyes that cannot cease from s.
1 John 1. 7. blood of Christ cleanseth us from all s.
8. if we say we have no s. we deceive ourselves
3. 4. whoso committeth s. transgresseth also the law, for s. is the transgression of the law
5. he was manifested, and in him is no s.
8. he that committeth s. is of the devil
9. whosoever is born of God doth not commit s.
5. 16. if any man see his brother s. a s. which is not to death, there is a s. unto death
17. all unrighteousness is s. and there is a s. not unto death, whosoever is born of G. sinneth not
See Fear.

Great SIN.

Gen. 20. 9. brought on me and my kingdom great s.
Exod. 32. 21. that hast brought this great s. on them
30. Moses said, ye have sinned a great s.
31. and said, oh, this people have sinned a great s.
1 Sam. 2. 17. s. of the young men was very great
2 Kings 17. 21. Jeroboam made them sin a great s.

His SIN.

Lev. 4. 3. bring for his s. he sinned a young bullock
23. or if his s. come to his knowledge, 28.
26. the priest shall make an atonement for his s. and it shall be forgiven, 35. | 5. 6, 10, 13.
28. he shall bring a kid of the goats for his s.
5. 6. he shall bring his trespass offering for his s.
1 Kings 15. 26. Nadab walked in the way of his s.
34. Baasha walked in way of Jeroboam and his s.
16. 19. Zimri walked in his s. || Omri in his s.
2 Kings 21. 16. beside his s. wherewith made Judah
17. acts of Manasseh, and his s. that he sinned
2 Chron. 33. 19. all his s. before he was humbled
Job 34. 37. for he addeth rebellion to his s.
Isa. 27. 9. this is all the fruit to take away his s.
Ezek. 3. 20. he shall die in his s. 18. 24.
33. 14. if he turn from his s. and do right
Hos. 13. 12. iniquity is bound up, his s. is hid
Mic. 3. 8. truly I am full to declare to Israel his s.

My SIN.

Gen. 31. 36. what is my s. that thou hast pursued me?
Exod. 10. 17. therefore forgive my s. only this once
1 Sam. 15. 25. I pray thee, pardon my s. turn with me
20. 1. what is my s. before thy father to seek my life
1 Kings 17. 18. come to call my s. to remembrance
Job 10. 6. that thou searchest after my s.
13. 23. make me to know transgression and my s.
14. 16. dost thou not watch over my s.
35. 3. what profit if I be cleansed from my s.
Psal. 32. 5. I acknowledged my s. and iniquity to thee, and thou forgavest the iniquity of my s.
38. 3. nor rest in my bones because of my s.
18. mine iniquity, for I will be sorry for my s.
51. 2. wash me throughly, cleanse me from my s.
3. my s. is ever before me || 59. 3. not for my s. O L.
Prov. 20. 9. who can say, I am pure from my s.?
Dan. 9. 20. and whilst I was confessing my s.
See Offering.

Our SIN.

Exod. 34. 9. Lord, pardon our iniquity and our s.
Jer. 16. 10. what is our s. we have committed

Their SIN.

Gen. 18. 20. L. said, because their s. is very grievous
50. 17. forgive, I pray thee, their s. 2 Chron. 7. 14.
Exod. 32. 32. yet now, if thou wilt forgive their s.
34. in the day when I visit, I will visit their s.
Num. 5. 7. they shall confess their s. they have done
Deut. 9. 27. look not unto stubbornness, nor their s.
1 Kings 8. 35. if they turn from their s. 2 Chr. 6. 26.
Neh. 4. 5. let not their s. be blotted out from thee
Psal. 85. 2. forgiven, thou hast covered all their s.
Isa. 3. 9. they declare their s. as Sodom, hide it not
Jer. 16. 18. I will recompense their s. double
18. 23. neither blot out their s. from thy sight
31. 34. and I will remember their s. no more
36. 3. that I may forgive their iniquity and their s.
John 15. 22. now they have no cloak for their s.

Thy SIN.

2 Sam. 12. 13. the Lord also hath put away thy s.
Isa. 6. 7. thine iniq. is taken away, thy s. is purged

Your SIN.

Exod. 32. 30. I shall make atonement for your s.
Num. 32. 23. be sure your s. will find you out
Deut. 9. 21. I took your s. the calf which ye had made
John 9. 41. ye say we see, therefore your s. remaineth

SIN, Verb.

Gen. 39. 9. how can I do this wickedn. and s. ag. God?
42. 22. Reuben said, do not s. against the child
Exod. 20. 20. his fear may be before you, that s. not
23. 33. not dwell, lest they make thee s. ag. me
Lev. 4. 2. if a soul shall s. thro' ignorance ag. com.
3. if the priest s. || 13. if congregation s.
27. if any one of the common people s. thro' ignor.
5. 1. if a soul s. and hear the voice of swearing
15. if a soul commit a trespass and s. thro' ignor. in the holy things of the Lord, 17. Num. 15. 27.
6. 2. if a soul s. and lie unto his neighbour
Num. 16. 22. shall one s. wilt thou be wroth with all?
Deut. 20. 18. so should you s. against L. your God
24. 4. thou shalt not cause the land to s. Lord give
1 Sam. 2. 25. if one man s. against another; if a man s. against the Lord, who shall entreat for him?
12. 23. God forbid I should s. in ceasing to pray
14. 33. behold, the people s. against the Lord
34. slay them, and s. not in eating with the blood
19. 4. let not the king s. against his servant
5. why wilt thou s. against innocent blood?
1 Kings 8. 46. if they s. against thee, 2 Chron. 6. 36.
2 Kings 21. 11. Manasseh made Judah to s. with idols
2 Chron. 6. 22. if a man s. against his neighbour
Neh. 6. 13. that I should be afraid, and do so, and s.
13. 26. did not Solomon s. by these things?
Job 2. 10. in all this did not Job s. with his lips
5. 24. thou shalt visit thy habitation and not s.
10. 14. if I s. thou markest me, not acquit
31. 30. neither have I suffered my mouth to s.
Psal. 4. 4. stand in awe, and s. not, commune
39. 1. I will take heed that I s. not with my tongue
119. 11. that I might not s. against thee
Eccl. 5. 6. suffer not thy mouth to cause thy flesh to s.
Jer. 32. 35. do this abomination to cause Judah to s.
Ezek. 3. 21. that righteous s. not, and he doth not s.
Hos. 8. 11. because Ephraim hath made many altars to s. altars shall be unto him to s.
13. 2. and now they s. more and more and made
Mat. 18. 21. Lord, how oft shall my brother s.?
John 5. 14. s. no more, lest worse thing come to thee
8. 11. neither do I condemn thee, s. no more
9. 2. who did s. this man or his parents?
Rom. 6. 15. shall we s. because we are not under law?
1 Cor. 8. 12. when ye s. so against the brethren and wound their conscience, ye s. against Christ
15. 34. awake to righteousness, and s. not
Eph. 4. 26. be ye angry, and s. not, let not the sun
1 Tim. 5. 20. them that s. rebuke before all
Heb. 10. 26. if we s. wilfully after knowl. of truth
1 John 2. 1. these things I write unto you that ye s. not, and if any man s. we have an advocate
3. 9. he cannot s. because he is born of God
5. 16. if any man see his brother s. not to death, he shall give him life for them that s. not to death
See Israel.

SINCE.

Gen. 30. 30. the Lord hath blessed thee s. my com.
44. 28. the one went out, and I saw him not s.
46. 30. let me die, s. I have seen thy face
Exod. 5. 23. for s. I came to Pharaoh to speak
9. 18. hail not in Egypt, s. the foundation thereof
24. in the land of Egypt, s. it became a nation
Num. 22. 30. thou hast ridden on ever s. I was thine
Deut. 34. 10. there arose not a prophet s. in Israel
Josh. 2. 12. swear, s. I have shewed you kindness
3. † 4. ye have not passed this way s. yesterday
14. 10. Lord kept me alive, even s. the Lord spake
Ruth 2. 11. all thou hast done s. death of thy husbd.
1 Sam. 9. 24. s. I said, I have invited the people
21. 5. about these three days s. I came out
29. 3. I found no fault in him s. he fell to me
2 Sam. 7. 6. s. the time that I brought up Israel
11. and s. I commanded judges, 1 Chron. 17. 10.
13. † 28. will you not s. I have commanded you
2 Chron. 30. 26. s. Solomon not like passover
31. 10. s. the people began to bring the offerings
Ezra 4. 2. s. the days of Esar-haddon king of Assur
5. 16. s. that time till now hath it been in building
9. 7. s. days of our fathers have we been in trespass
Job 20. 4. s. man was placed upon earth
38. 12. hast thou commanded morning s. thy days?
Isa. 14. 8. s. thou art laid down, no feller is come
16. 13. hath spoken concerning Moab s. that time
43. 4. s. thou wast precious in my sight, hast been
44. 7. s. I appointed the ancient people
64. 4. s. the beginning men have not heard
Jer. 15. 7. s. they return not from their ways
20. 8. for s. I spake, I cried out, I cried violence
23. 38. but s. ye say, the burden of the Lord
31. 20. s. I spake against him, I remember him still
44. 18. s. we left off to burn incense to the queen
48. 27. s. thou spakest of him, thou skippedst
Dan. 12. 1. as never was s. there was a nation
Hag. 2. 16. s. those days when one came
Mat. 24. 21. such as was not s. the beginning
Mark 9. 21. how long is it ago s. this came to him?
Luke 1. 70. been s. the world began, John 9. 32.
7. 45. s. the time I came in, she hath not ceased
16. 16. s. then the kingdom of God is preached
24. 21. is the third day s. these things were done
Acts 3. 21. s. the world began, Rom. 16. 25.
19. 2. ye received the Holy Ghost s. ye believed?
24. 11. but twelve days s. I went to Jerusalem
1 Cor. 15. 21. for s. by man came death, by man came
2 Cor. 13. 3. s. ye seek a proof of Christ in me
Col. 1. 4. s. we heard of your faith in Christ Jesus
Heb. 7. 28. but word of oath which was s. the law
2 Pet. 3. 4. for s. the fathers fell asleep, all things
Rev. 16. 18. as was not s. men were upon the earth
See Day.

SINCERE,

Or Sincerity. *This word properly signifies truth and uprightness, when the heart and tongue agree together.* Sincerity *is opposed to double-mindedness or deceit, when the sentiments of the heart are contrary to the language of the mouth. The* Latin word, sincerus, *is derived from* sine and cera, *without wax, honey separated from the wax, or pure honey. In the Scripture* sincere *signifies pure, or without mixture,* 1 Pet. 2. 1. Desire the sincere milk of the word; *that is, unmixed with errors, traditions, and heresies, free from deceits. St.* Paul *would have the* Philippians *to be pure, impartial, and unbiassed in their choice; that their behaviour may be innocent, and give no offence to any body,* Phil. 1. 10. that ye may be sincere and without offence till the day of *Christ. The same Apostle speaks of* sincerity *and truth, or of purity and truth, which he sets in opposition to the leavened bread of impurity and filthiness,* 1 Cor. 5. 8. Let us keep the feast, not with old leaven, neither with the leaven of malice and wickedness; but with the unleavened bread of sincerity and truth. *That is, Let the whole of our lives be like the* Jewish *feast of the* Passover *and unleavened bread; let us not spend them with the leaven of malice and wickedness, allowing ourselves in any way of sin, either by corrupt affections, sinful actions, or tolerating among us any scandalous offence; but let us practise all Christian purity, and hold fast the truth that has been delivered to us. And he reproaches the false apostles with not preaching* Christ, *sincerely, purely, with upright and disinterested sentiments of the heart,* Phil. 1. 16. The one preach Christ of contention, not sincerely.

Gen. 17. † 1. walk before me, and be thou s.
Deut. 18. † 13. thou shalt be s. with Lord thy God
Psal. 119. † 1. blessed are the s. in the way
Eph. 4. † 15. being s. in love may grow up into him
Phil. 1. 10. ye may be s. till day of Christ, 2. † 15.
1 Pet. 2. 2. as new-born babes desire s. milk of word

SINCERELY.

Judg. 9. 16. now if ye have done truly and s. 19.
Phil. 1. 16. the one preach Christ, not s.

SINCERITY.

Gen. 20. † 5 in the s. of my heart have I done this
Josh. 24. 14. fear and serve the Lord in s. and truth
1 Cor. 5. 8. with unleavened bread of s. and truth
2 Cor. 1. 12. in godly s. we have had our conversation
2. 17. but as of s. in the sight of God speak we
8. 8. and to prove the s. of your love
Eph. 6. 24. grace with them that love our L. J. in s.
Tit. 2. 7. in doctrine shewing gravity, s.

SINEW.

Gen. 32. 32. Israel eat not of the s. that shrank, because he touched Jacob in the s. that shrank
Isa. 48. 4. because thy neck is an iron s. brow brass

SINEWS.

Job 10. 11. thou hast fenced me with bones and s.
30. 17. my bones are pierced, and my s. take no rest
40. 17. the s. of his stones are wrapped together
Ezek. 37. 6. I will lay s. upon you and bring flesh
8. the s. and the flesh came up upon them

SINFUL.

Num. 32. 14. ye are risen an increase of s. men
Isa. 1. 4. ah s. nation, a people laden with iniquity
Amos 9. 8. eyes of the Lord are on the s. kingdom
Mark 8. 38. shall be ashamed in this s. generation
Luke 5. 8. depart from me, for I am s. man, O Lord
24. 7. must be delivered into the hands of s. men
Rom. 7. 13. that sin might become exceeding s.
8. 3. God sending his Son in the likeness of s. flesh

SING.

Exod. 15. 21. s. to the Lord, 1 Chron. 16. 23. Psal. 30. 4. | 95. 1. | 96. 1, 2. | 98. 1. | 147. 7. | 149. 1. Isa. 12. 5.
32. 18. but the noise of them that s. do I hear
Num. 21. 17. spring up, O well, s. ye unto it
1 Sam. 21. 11. did they not s. one to another?
1 Chron. 16. 9. s. unto him, s. psalms unto him
33. then shall the trees of the wood s. out
2 Chron. 20. 22. when they began to s. and praise
29. 30. Hezekiah commanded the Levites to s.
Job 29. 13. I caused the widow's heart to s. for joy
Psal. 21. 13. so will we s. and praise thy power
33. 2. praise the Lord, s. to him with the psaltery
3. s. unto him a new song, Isa. 42. 10.

Psal. 51. 14. my tongue *s.* of thy righteousn. 145. 7.
65. 13. the valleys shout for joy, they also *s.*
66. 2. *s.* forth the honour of his name, make praise
4. the earth *s.* to thee, they shall *s.* to thy name
67. 4. let the nations be glad and *s.* for joy
68. 32. *s.* to God, ye kingdoms of the earth
71. 22. to thee will I *s.* with the harp, 98. 5.
81. 1. *s.* aloud unto God our strength, make noise
104. 12. the fowls which *s.* among the branches
105. 2. *s.* to him, *s.* psalms unto him, talk ye
137. 3. saying, *s.* us one of the songs of Zion
4. how shall we *s.* Lord's song in a strange land!
138. 5. yea, they shall *s.* in the ways of the Lord
149. 5. let the saints *s.* aloud upon their beds
Prov. 29. 6. but the righteous doth *s.* and rejoice
Isa. 23. 15. after seventy years shall Tyre *s.* as harlot
24. 14. they shall *s.* for the majesty of the Lord
26. 19. awake and *s.* ye that dwell in dust
27. 2. in that day *s.* ye to her, vineyard of red wine
35. 6. then shall the tongue of the dumb *s.*
38. 20. therefore we will *s.* my songs all days
42. 11. let the inhabitants of the rock *s.*
44. 23. *s.* O ye heavens, for L. hath done it, 49. 13.
52. 8. with the voice together shall they *s.*
9. *s.* to the Lord, ye waste places of Jerusalem
54. 1. *s.* O barren, thou that didst not bear
65. 14. behold, my servants shall *s.* for joy of heart
Jer. 31. 7. *s.* with gladness for Jacob, and shout
12. they shall come and *s.* in the height of Zion
51. 48. all that is therein shall *s.* for Babylon
Ezek. 27. 25. the ships of Tarshish did *s.* of thee
Hos. 2. 15. she shall *s.* as in the days of youth
Zeph. 2. 14. their voice shall *s.* in the windows
3. 14. *s.* O daughter of Zion, *Zech.* 2. 10.
Jam. 5. 13. is any merry? let him *s.* psalms
Rev. 15. 3. they *s.* song of Moses and of the Lamb

I will SING.

Exod. 15. 1. *I will s.* to the L. *Judg.* 5. 3. *Psal.* 13. 6.
Psal. 57. 7. my heart is fixed, O God, *I will s.*
9. *I will s.* unto thee among the nations
59. 16. *I will s.* of thy power, of thy mercy, 89. 1.
17. unto thee, O my strength, *will I s.* for God is
101. 1. *I will s.* of mercy and judgment, O Lord
104. 33. *I will s.* to the Lord as long as I live
144. 9. *I will s.* a new song unto thee, O God
Isa. 5. 1. now *will I s.* to my well-beloved a song
Rom. 15. 9. for this cause *will I s.* to thy name
1 *Cor.* 14. 15. I will pray with spirit, *I will s.* with
the spirit, and *I will s.* with the understanding

See PRAISE, PRAISES.

SINGED.

Dan. 3. 27. nor was an hair of their head *s.*

SINGER.

1 *Chron.* 6. 33. Heman a *s.* the son of Joel
Heb. 3. 19. to chief *s.* on my stringed instruments

SINGERS.

1 *Kings* 10. 12. king made psalteries for *s.* 2 *Chr.* 9. 11.
1 *Chron.* 9. 33. these are the *s.* chief, 15. 16.
15. 19. so *s.* were appointed to sound with cymbals
27. the Levites and the *s.* had fine linen
2 *Chr.* 5. 13. the trumpeters and *s.* were as one
20. 21. Jehoshaphat appointed *s.* unto the Lord
23. 13. the people rejoiced and also the *s.* 29. 28.
35. 15. the *s.* the sons of Asaph were in their place
Ezra 2. 41. the *s.* an hundred twenty and eight
70. so the *s.* dwelt in their cities, *Neh.* 7. 73.
7. 7. some of the *s.* went up unto Jerusalem
24. it shall not be lawful to impose toll upon *s.*
10. 24. the *s.* gave their hands to put away wives
Neh. 7. 1. the porters and the *s.* were appointed
10. 29. the *s.* clave to their brethren, their nobles
11. 22. the *s.* were over the business of the house
23. a portion shall be for the *s.* 12. 47. | 13. 5.
12. 28. sons of *s.* gathered themselves together
29. the *s.* had builded them villages round about
42. *s.* sang aloud || 45. *s.* kept ward of their God
46. in the days of David, there were chief of *s.*
13. 10. for the Levites and the *s.* were fled
Psal. 68. 25. *s.* went before, players followed after
87. 7. as well the *s.* as the players shall be there
Ezek. 40. 44. the chambers of the *s.* in inner court

Men-SINGERS, *Women*-SINGERS.

Eccl. 2. 8. I gat me *men-s.* and *women-s.*

SINGETH.

Prov. 25. 20. so is he that *s.* songs to a heavy heart

SINGING.

1 *Sam.* 18. 6. women came out of cities of Israel *s.*
1 *Chron.* 6. 32. and they ministered with *s.*
13. 8. David and all Isr. played before God with *s.*
2 *Chron.* 23. 18. to offer the burnt offerings with *s.*
30. 21. *s.* with loud instruments unto the Lord
Neh. 12. 27. kept the dedication of the wall with *s.*
Psal. 30. † 5. but *s.* cometh in the morning
100. 2. come before his presence with *s.*
105. † 43. he brought forth his chosen with *s.*
107. † 22. and declare his works with *s.*
126. 2. then was our tongue filled with *s.*
† 5. they that sow in tears shall reap in *s.*
Cant. 2. 12. the time of the *s.* of birds is come
Isa. 14. 7. earth is at rest, they break forth into *s.*
16. 10. in the vineyards there shall be no *s.*
35. 2. it shall blossom and rejoice with joy and *s.*
44. 23. break forth into *s.* ye mountains, O forest
48. 20. flee from the Chaldeans with a voice of *s.*
49. 13. be joyful, O earth, and break forth into *s.*
51. 11. the redeemed shall come with *s.* to Zion
54. 1. break forth into *s.* O barren, and cry aloud
55. 12. the mountains shall break forth into *s.*
Zeph. 3. 17. rest in his love, will joy over thee with *s.*
Eph. 5. 19. *s.* in your heart to the Lord, *Col.* 3. 16.

SINGING-*men*, SINGING-*women*.

2 *Sam.* 19. 35. can I hear voice of *s.-men, s.-women*
2 *Chron.* 35. 25. all the *s.-men* spake of Josiah
Ezra 2. 65. two hundred *s.-men*, 200 *s.-women*
Neh. 7. 67. they had 245 *s.-men* and *s.-women*

SINGLE.

Ezek. 23. † 47. the company shall *s.* them out

SINGLE.

Mat. 6. 22. if therefore thine eye be *s.* thy whole
body shall be full of light, *Luke* 11. 34.

SINGLENESS.

Acts 2. 46. did eat meat with gladness and *s.* of heart

Eph. 6. 5. serv. obey in *s.* of your heart, *Col.* 3. 22.

SINGULAR.

Lev. 27. 2. when a man shall make a *s.* vow

SINK.

Job 38 † 6. whereon are the foundations made to *s.*
Psal. 69. 2. I *s.* in deep mire where is no standing
14. deliver me out of the mire, and let me not *s.*
Jer. 51. 64. thus shall Babylon *s.* and shall not rise
Mat. 14. 30. beginning to *s.* he cried, Lord, save me
Luke 5. 7. filled both ships, so that they began to *s.*
9. 44. let these sayings *s.* down into your ears

SINNED.

Exod. 9. 34. Pharaoh *s.* yet more, hardened his heart
32. 30. Moses said, ye have *s.* a great sin, 31.
33. whosoever hath *s.* him will I blot out
Lev. 4. 3. bring for the sin he hath *s.* a bullock
14. when the sin the congregation have *s.*
22. when ruler *s.* 23. || 28. one of common people *s.*
5. 5. he shall confess he hath *s.* in that thing
6. for sin which he hath *s.* shall bring a female
10. priest shall make atonement for the sin he hath
s. and shall be forgiven, 11. 13. *Num.* 6. 11.
6. 4. because he hath *s.* shall restore what he took
Num. 12. 11. lay not sin on us wherein we have *s.*
32. 23. behold, ye have *s.* against the Lord
Deut. 9. 16. I looked, and behold ye had *s.* ag. Lord
18. your sins which ye *s.* in doing wickedly
Josh. 7. 11. Isr. hath *s.* and transgressed my covenant
Judg. 11. 27. wherefore I have not *s.* agains thee
1 *Sam.* 19. 4. because he hath not *s.* against thee
24. 11. know that I have not *s.* against thee
1 *Kings* 8. 33. because they have *s.* against thee, and
shall turn again to thee, 35. 2 *Chr.* 6. 24, 26.
50. forgive thy people that *s.* 2 *Chron.* 6. 39.
15. 30. sins of Jeroboam which he *s.* 16. 13, 19.
18. 9. what have I *s.* that thou wouldst deliver
2 *Kings* 17. 7. Israel had *s.* against Lord their God
21. 17. the sin that Manasseh had *s.* is written
Neh. 9. 29. but *s.* against thy judgments
Job 1. 5. Job said, it may be that my sons have *s.*
22. in all this Job *s.* not, nor charged G. foolishly
8. 4. if children have *s.* against him and have cast
24. 19. so doth the grave those who have *s.*
Psal. 78. 17. they *s.* yet more against him, 32.
Isa. 43. 27. thy first father hath *s.* and thy teachers
Jer. 2. 35. because thou sayest, I have not *s.*
33. 8. their iniquity, whereby they have *s.* ag. me
40. 3. because ye have *s.* and not obeyed, 44. 23.
50. 7. because they have *s.* ag. the L. *Zeph.* 1. 17.
14. for Babylon hath *s.* against the Lord
Lam. 1. 8. Jerusalem hath grievously *s.* is removed
5. 7. our fathers have *s.* and are not, we have borne
Ezek. 18. 24. in his sin he hath *s.* in them shall he
28. 16. have filled with violence, and thou hast *s.*
37. 23. of their dwelling places wherein they *s.*
Hos. 4. 7. as they increased so they *s.* against me
10. 9. O Israel thou hast *s.* from days of Gibeah
Hab. 2. 10. and thou hast *s.* against thy soul
John 9. 3. neither this man *s.* nor his parents
Rom. 2. 12. for as many as have *s.* without law; as
have *s.* in the law, shall be judged by the law
3. 23. for all have *s.* and come short, 5. 12.
5. 14. death reigned even over them that had not *s.*
16. not as it was by one that *s.* so is the gift
1 *Cor.* 7. 28. but and if thou marry, thou hast not *s.*
and if a virgin marry she hath not *s.*
2 *Cor.* 12. 21. I shall bewail many that have *s.*
13. 2. I write to them which heretofore have *s.*
Heb. 3. 17. was it not with them that had *s.?*
2 *Pet.* 2. 4. for if God spared not the angels that *s.*
1 *John* 1. 10. if we say we have not *s.* we deceive ours.

I have SINNED.

Exod. 9. 27. Pharaoh said, *I have s.* this time, 10. 16.
Num. 22. 34. Balaam said to angel of Lord, *I have s.*
Josh. 7. 20. indeed *I have s.* ag. Lord God of Israel
1 *Sam.* 15. 24. Saul said, *I have s.* 30. | 26. 21.
2 *Sam.* 12. 13. David said to Nathan, *I have s.*
against the Lord, 24. 10, 17. 1 *Chr.* 21. 8, 17.
19. 20. thy servant doth know that *I have s.*
Job 7. 20. *I have s.* || 33. 27. if any say *I have s.*
Psal. 41. 4. heal my soul, for *I have s.* against thee
51. 4. against thee, thee only *h. I s.* done this evil
Mic. 7. 9. *I have s.* against him, till he plead my cause
Mat. 27. 4. Judas said, *I have s.* in betraying inno.
Luke 15. 18. the prodigal said, father, *I have s.* 21.

We have SINNED.

Num. 12. 11. lay not sin on us, wherein *we have s.*
14. 40. we will go up, for *we have s. Deut.* 1. 41.
21. 7. *we have s.* we have spoken against the Lord
Judg. 10. 10. *we have s.* because we have forsaken
our God and served Baalim, 1 *Sam.* 12. 10.
15. *we have s.* do to us what seemeth good to thee
1 *Sam.* 7. 6. they fasted that day, and said, *we have s.*
1 *Kings* 8. 47. *we have s.* and have done perversely
2 *Chr.* 6. 37. saying, *we have s.* we have done amiss
Neh. 1. 6. and confess the sins which *we have s.*
Psal. 106. 6. *we have s.* with our fathers, we have
Isa. 42. 24. the Lord, he against whom *we have s.*
64. 5. behold thou art wroth, for *we have s.*
Jer. 3. 25. we lie down in our shame, for *we have s.*
8. 14. hath given us water of gall, for *we have s.*
14. 7. for our backslidings are many, *we have s.*
20. acknowledge our wickedness, for *we have s.*
Lam. 5. 16. crown is fallen, woe to us that *we have s.*
Dan. 9. 5. *we have s.* and have committed iniquity
8. to us belongeth confusion, because *we have s.*
11. the curse is poured on us, because *we have s.*
15. O Lord, *we have s.* we have done wickedly

SINNER.

Prov. 11. 31. much more the wicked and the *s.*
13. 6. but wickedness overthroweth the *s.*
22. the wealth of the *s.* is laid up for the just
Eccl. 2. 26. but to the *s.* he giveth travail, to gather
7. 26. but the *s.* shall be taken by her
8. 12. tho' *s.* do evil an hundred times, yet I know
9. 2. as is the good, so is the *s.* and he that sweareth
18. but one *s.* destroyeth much good
Isa. 65. 20. *s.* being 100 years old shall be accursed
Luke 7. 37. behold woman in the city who was a *s.*
39. would have known this woman she is a *s.*
15. 7. joy in heaven over one *s.* that repenteth, 10.
18. 13. saying, God be merciful to me a *s.*

Luke 19. 7. was gone to be guest with man that is a *s.*
John 9. 16. how can a man a *s.* do such miracles?
24. give God praise, we know this man is a *s.*
25. he said, whether he be a *s.* I know not
Rom. 3. 7. why yet am I also judged as a *s.?*
Jam. 5. 20. he that converteth a *s.* shall save a soul
1 *Pet.* 4. 18. where shall the ungodly and *s.* appear

SINNERS.

Gen. 13. 13. the men of Sodom were *s.* exceedingly
Num. 16. 38. Eleazar, take the censers of these *s.*
1 *Sam.* 15. 18. utterly destroy the *s.* the Amalekites
Ps. 1. 1. blessed that standeth not in the way of *s.*
5. nor *s.* in the congregation of the righteous
25. 8. therefore will he teach *s.* in the way
26. 9. gather not my soul with *s.* nor my life
51. 13. and *s.* shall be converted unto thee
104. 35. let the *s.* be consumed out of the earth
Prov. 1. 10. if *s.* entice thee, consent thou not
13. 21. evil pursueth *s.* but to the righteous good
23. 17. let not thine heart envy *s.* be in fear of Ld.
Isa. 1. 28. the destruction of the *s.* shall be together
13. 9. he shall destroy the *s.* thereof out of it
33. 14. the *s.* in Zion are afraid, fearfulness
Amos 9. 10. all *s.* of my people shall die by sword
Mat. 9. 10. many *s.* sat at meat with Jes. *Mark* 2. 15.
11. they said, why eateth your master with pub-
licans and *s.? Mark* 2. 16. *Luke* 5. 30. | 15. 2.
13. for I am not come to call the righteous, but *s.*
to repentance, *Mark* 2. 17. *Luke* 5. 32.
11. 19. a friend of publicans and *s. Luke* 7. 34.
26. 45. the hour is at hand, and the Son of man is
betrayed into the hands of *s. Mark* 14. 41.
Luke 6. 32. for *s.* also love those that love them
33. what thank have ye? for *s.* also do even same
34. for *s.* also lend to *s.* to receive again
13. 2. suppose ye that these were *s.* above all, 4.
15. 1. the publicans and *s.* for to hear him
John 9. 31. we know that God heareth not *s.*
Rom. 5. 8. while we were yet *s.* Christ died for us
19. by one man's disobedience many were made *s.*
Gal. 2. 15. we Jews by nature, not *s.* of Gentiles
17. but if we ourselves also are found *s.*
1 *Tim.* 1. 9. the law is made for *s.* for unholy
15. that Christ Jesus came to save *s.* I am chief
Heb. 7. 26. an high-priest, holy, separate from *s.*
12. 3. him that endured such contradiction of *s.*
Jam. 4. 8. cleanse your hands, ye *s.* purify hearts
Jude 15. speeches which ungodly *s.* have spoken

SINNEST.

Job 35. 6. if thou *s.* what dost thou against him?

SINNETH.

Num. 15. 28. make aton. for soul that *s.* ignorantly
29. have one law for him that *s.* thro' ignorance
Deut. 19. 15. one witn. shall not rise in any sin he *s.*
1 *Kings* 8. 46. for there is no man that *s.* not, if they
sin against God, 2 *Chron.* 6. 36. *Eccl.* 7. 20.
Prov. 8. 36. he that *s.* against me wrongeth his soul
14. 21. he that despiseth his neighbour *s.*
19. 2. he that hasteth with his feet *s.*
20. 2. whoso provoketh a king, *s.* ag. his own soul
Ezek. 14. 13. when the land *s.* then will I stretch out
18. 4. the soul that *s.* it shall die, 20.
33. 12. for his righteousness in the day he *s.*
1 *Cor.* 6. 18. but fornicator *s.* against his own body
7. 36. let him do what he will *s.* not, let them marry
Tit. 3. 11. he that is such is subverted and *s.*
1 *John* 3. 6. whosoever abideth in him *s.* not, whosoever *s.* hath not seen him nor known him
8. is of the devil, for devil *s.* from the beginning
5. 18. we know whosoever is born of God *s.* not

SINNING.

Gen. 20. 6. for I withheld thee from *s.* against me
Lev. 6. 3. in any of these that man does, *s.* therein

SINS.

1 *Kings* 14. 16. shall give Israel up, because of *s.* of
15. 3. Abijam walked in the *s.* of Rehoboam
30. smote Nadab because of the *s.* of Jeroboam
16. 13. for all the *s.* of Baasha, and the *s.* of Elah
19. for his *s.* which Zimri sinned in doing evil
31. a light thing to walk in the *s.* of Jeroboam
2 *Kings* 3. 3. Jehoram cleaved to the *s.* of Jeroboam
10. 29. from the *s.* of Jeroboam Jehu departed not
13. 6. Israel departed not from the *s.* of Jeroboam
11. Joash || 14. 24. Jeroboam departed not from *s.*
15. 9. Zachariah || 18. Menahem dep. not from *s.*
24. Pekahiah || 28. Pekah departed not from *s.*
17. 22. Israel walked in all the *s.* of Jeroboam
24. 3. to remove Judah for the *s.* of Manasseh
2 *Chron.* 28. 10. are there not even with you *s.?*
Neh. 1. 6. and confess the *s.* of the children of Isr.
Job 13. 23. how many are mine iniquities and *s.?*
Ps. 19. 13. keep thy servant from presumptuous *s.*
25. 7. remember not the *s.* of my youth
Prov. 5. 22. shall be holden with the cords of his *s.*
10. 12. hatred stirreth up strifes, love cover. all *s.*
28. 13. he that covereth his *s.* shall not prosper
Isa. 40. 2. she hath received double for all her *s.*
43. 24. but thou hast made me to serve with thy *s*
25. I blot out and will not remember thy *s*
44. 22. I have blotted out as a cloud thy *s.*
Jer. 15. 13. substance will I give to spoil for all thy *s.*
30. 14. because thy *s.* were increased, 15.
50. 20. *s.* of Judah sought for, and not be found
Lam. 3. 39. a man for the punishment of his *s.*
4. 13. for the *s.* of her prophets and her priests
22. O daughter of Edom, he will discover thy *s.*
Ezek. 16. 51. nor hath Samaria committ. half thy *s.*
52. bear thou thine own shame for thy *s.*
18. 14. if he beget son that seeth all his father's *s.*
21. if the wicked will turn from all his *s.*
23. 49. and he shall bear the *s.* of your idols
33. 16. none of his *s.* shall be mentioned to him
Dan. 4. 27. break off thy *s.* by righteousness
9. 24. 70 weeks are determ. to make an end of *s.*
Mic. 1. 5. for the *s.* of the house of Israel is all this
6. 13. in making thee desolate because of thy *s.*
Mat. 26. 28. shed for many for the remission of *s.*
Mark 1. 4. John did baptize and preach the baptism
of repentance for the remission of *s. Luke* 3. 3.
Luke 24. 47. that remission of *s.* should be preached
John 9. 34. they said, thou wast altogether born in *s.*
20. 23. whosesoever *s.* ye remit, whose *s.* ye retain

Acts 2. 38. repent and be baptized for remission of s.
5. 31. to give repentance and remission of s.
10. 43. whoso believeth, shall receive remission of s.
22. 16. wash away thy s. calling on name of Lord
Rom. 3. 25. for the remission of s. that are past
7. 5. the motions of s. did work in our members
Eph. 2. 1. you hath quickened, who were dead in s. 5.
Col. 2. 11. in putting off the body of s. of the flesh
1 Tim. 5. 22. nor be partakers of other men's s.
24. some men's s. open beforehand, going before
2 Tim. 3. 6. who lead capt. silly women laden with s.
Heb. 2. 17. to make reconciliation for s. of people
5. 1. that he may offer gifts and sacrifices for s.
3. for people, so also for himself, to offer for s.
7. 27. first for his own s. then for the people's
9. 28. Christ was once offered to bear s. of many
10. 2. should have had no more conscience of s.
3. there is a remembrance again made of s.
4. not possi. blood of bulls and goats take away s.
11. the same sacrifices can never take away s.
12. after he had offered one sacrifice for s. for ever
26. there remaineth no more sacrifice for s.
Jam. 5. 20. save soul, and shall hide multitude of s.
1 Pet. 2. 24. we being dead to s. should live to right.
3. 18. for Christ also hath once suffered for s.
4. 8. for charity shall cover the multitude of s.
2 Pet. 1. 9. forgotten he was purged from his old s.
1 John 2. 2. but also for the s. of the whole world
Rev. 18. 4. that ye be not partakers of her s.
5. for her s. have reached unto heaven
See Forgive, Forgiven.

My SINS.

Psal. 51. 9. hide thy face from my s. and blot out
69. 5. O God, my s. are not hid from thee
Isa. 38. 17. thou hast cast my s. behind thy back

Our SINS.

1 Sam. 12. 19. for we have added to all our s. this evil
2 Chron. 28. 13. ye intend to add more to our s.
Neh. 9. 37. the kings set over us because of our s.
Psal. 79. 9. purge away our s. for thy name's sake
90. 8. our secret s. in the light of thy countenance
103. 10. hath not dealt with us according to our s.
Isa. 59. 12. for our s. testify against us
Ezek. 33. 10. if our s. be upon us, we pine away
Dan. 9. 16. because of our s. thy people are become
1 Cor. 15. 3. how that Christ died for our s. accord.
Gal. 1. 4. who gave himself for our s. to deliver us
Heb. 1. 3. when had himself purged our s. sat down
1 Pet. 2. 24. who his own self bare our s. in his body
1 John 1. 9. if we confess our s. he is faithful and just to forgive us our s. and to cleanse us
2. 2. he is the propitiation for our s. 4. 10.
3. 5. he was manifested to take away our s.
Rev. 1. 5. washed us from our s. in his own blood

Their SINS.

Lev. 16. 16. because of their transgress. in their s.
21. shall confess over the live goat all their s.
34. to make atonement for their s. once a year
Num. 16. 26. lest ye be consumed in all their s.
1 Kings 14. 22. they provoked him with their s.
16. 2. to provoke me to anger with their s.
Neh. 9. 2. Israel stood and confessed their s.
Isa. 58. 1. shew the house of Jacob their s.
Jer. 14. 10. and visit their s. Hos. 8. 13. | 9. 9.
Mic. 7. 19. cast all their s. into the depth of the sea
Mat. 1. 21. he shall save his people from their s.
3. 6. were baptized, confessing their s. Mark 1. 5.
Mark 4. 12. and their s. should be forgiven them
Luke 1. 77. of salvation by the remission of their s.
Rom. 11. 27. when I shall take away their s.
1 Thess. 2. 16. to fill up their s. alway
Heb. 8. 12. for I will be merciful to their s.
10. 17. their s. and iniquities I will remem. no more

Your SINS.

Lev. 16. 30. that ye may be clean from all your s.
26. 18. punish you yet seven times for your s. 24, 28.
21. I will bring plagues on you accord. to your s.
Deut. 9. 18. nor drink water, because of your s.
Josh. 24. 19. is an holy God, will not forgive your s.
Isa. 1. 18. tho' your s. be as scarlet, shall be as snow
59. 2. and your s. have hid his face from you
Jer. 5. 25. your s. have withholden good things
Ezek. 21. 24. so that in all your doings your s. appear
Amos 5. 12. for I know your transgr. and mighty s.
John 8. 21. ye shall seek me, and die in your s. 24.
Acts 3. 19. repent, that your s. may be blotted out
1 Cor. 15. 17. if Christ be not raised, ye are in your s.
Col. 2. 13. you being dead in your s. hath he quick.
1 John 2. 12. because your s. are forgiven you

SIR.

Gen. 43. 20. s. we came at first time to buy food
Mat. 13. 27. s. didst not thou sow good seed in field?
21. 30. he said, I go s. and went not
27. 63. s. we remember that that deceiver said
John 4. 11. s. thou hast nothing to draw with
15. s. give me this water that I thirst not
19. s. I perceive that thou art a prophet
49. the nobleman saith, s. come ere my child die
5. 7. s. I have no man to put me into the pool
12. 21. certain Greeks saying, s. we would see Je.
20. 15. s. if thou have borne him hence, tell me
Rev. 7. 14. I said unto him, s. thou knowest

SIRS.

Acts 7. 26. s. ye are brethren, why do ye wrong
14. 15. crying out, s. why do ye these things?
16. 30. he said, s. what must I do to be saved?
19. 25. s. ye know that by this craft we have
27. 10. s. I perceive this voyage will be with hurt
21. Paul said, s. ye should have hearkened to me
25. wherefore, s. be of good cheer, I believe God

SIRNAME.

Isa. 44. 5. and s. himself by the name of Israel

SIRNAME.

Mat. 10. 3. Lebbeus, whose s. was Thaddeus
Acts 10. 5. Simon, whose s. is Peter, 32. | 11. 13.
12. 12. John, whose s. was Mark, 25. | 15. 37.

SIRNAMED.

Isa. 45. 4. I have s. thee, tho' thou hast not known me
Mark 3. 16. and Simon he s. Peter, Acts 10. 18.
17. he s. them Boanerges, the sons of thunder
Luke 22. 3. Satan entered into Judas, s. Iscariot
Acts 1. 23. Joseph called Barsabas, who was s. Jus.
Acts 4. 36. Joses, who by the apostles was s. Barnabas
15. 22. to send Judas, s. Barsabas, and Silas

SISTER.

This name has much the same latitude as that of brother. It is used, not only for sister *by father and mother, but also for her who is only a near relation. Thus Sarah is called* sister to Abraham, *though she was only his niece according to some, or his* sister *by the father's side only, according to others,* Gen. 12. 13. | 20. 12. *In the gospel, the brothers and* sisters of Jesus Christ *are no other than his cousins, the sons and daughters of the* sisters *of the Virgin* Mary, *Mat.* 13. 56. *Mark* 6. 3. *In* Lev. 18. 18. *it is forbidden* to take a wife to her sister; *that is, according to some, to marry two* sisters, *or, according to the generality of interpreters, to marry a second wife when one has one before; so that this passage forbids polygamy. Sometimes the word* sister *shows a resemblance of conditions and inclinations. The prophets call* Jerusalem *the* sister *of* Sodom *and* Samaria, *because it delighted in the imitation of their idolatry and iniquity,* Jer. 3. 8, 10. Ezek. 16. 46.

In the Song of Solomon, *the name of* sister, *given to the spouse, is a name of tenderness, love, and affection, and shews the great affection which* Christ *has for his church, which cannot be sufficiently expressed by any one relation, but must borrow the perfections and affections of all, to describe it: this name may likewise shew that* Christ *and his church have but one Father, to wit, God, so that the church is every way royal; the* daughter *of a king, the* sister *of a king,* Cant. 4. 9, 10, 12. *In* Cant. 8. 8. *the spouse speaking to her beloved, says,* We have a little sister, and she hath no breasts, what shall we do for our sister in the day when she shall be spoken for? *The believers of the* Jewish *church, who here consult with* Christ, *as it were, tell him that they had a little* sister, *meaning the Gentile church, which as yet was not ripe for marriage with* Christ: *how shall we promote their conversion, say they, when the tenders of reconciliation are made to them?*

Our Lord Jesus Christ *says,* Mat. 12. 50. Whosoever shall do the will of my Father who is in heaven, the same is my brother, and sister, and mother: *that is, Whosoever shall give real evidence of true faith by sincere obedience, shall be as dear to me as my nearest natural relations; or, as the nearest relations are to any person.* Job, *in his afflictions, exclaims,* I have said to the worm, thou art my mother, and my sister; *thou art near akin to me, we are of the same original, and thou art continually with me,* Job 17. 14. *The wise man advises his pupil to say to Wisdom,* thou art my sister; *that is, acquaint and delight thyself with her, and let her have the command of thy heart, and the conduct of thy life,* Prov. 7. 4. *As* Christians *were used to salute one another by the name of brothers or brethren, so they called* Christian *women, who professed the same faith in* Chist, *by the name of* sisters, *Jam.* 2. 15, 16, If a brother or sister be naked, and destitute of daily food, &c.

Gen. 24. 59. they sent away Rebekah their s.
60. thou art our s. be thou mother of thousands
29. 13. when Laban heard of Jacob his s. son
30. 1. Rachel envied her s. and said unto Jacob
34. 13. because he had defiled Dinah their s. 27.
14. we cannot give our s. to one uncircumcised
31. should he deal with our s. as with an harlot?
Exod. 2. 4. his s. stood afar off to wit what would
6. 20. Amram took Jochebed his father's s. to wife
15. 20. Miriam s. of Aaron took a timbrel in hand
Lev. 18. 9. shalt not uncover the nakedness of thy s.
11. she is thy s. || 18. not take a wife to her s.
12. not nakedness of father's s. || 13. mother's s.
20. 17. if a man take his s. and see her nakedness
19. nor nakedness of thy father's s. mother's s.
21. 3. for his s. a virgin, for her may he be defiled
Num. 6. 7. a Nazarite shall not be defiled for his s.
Deut. 27. 22. cursed be he that lieth with his s.
Judg. 15. 2. is not her younger s. fairer than she?
2 Sam. 13. 1. Absalom had a fair s. named Tamar
2. Amnon so vexed that he fell sick for his s. Tamar
4. I love Tamar, my brother Absalom's s.
22. because he had forced his s. Tamar, 32.
21. †8. the king took the five son's of Michal's s.
2 Kings 11. 2. but Jehosheba s. of Ahaziah took Joash, they hid him and his nurse, 2 Chron. 22. 11.
Cant. 8. 8. we have a little s. and she hath no breasts, what shall we do for our s. in the day?
Jer. 3. 7. and her treacherous s. Judah saw it
8. her s. feared not || 10. her s. hath not turned
22. 18. shalt not lament for him, saying, ah, my s.
Ezek. 16. 45. thou art the s. of thy sisters who loath.
46. thy elder s. is Samaria, thy younger s. Sodom
48. Sodom thy s. hath not done as thou hast done
49. this was the iniquity of thy s. Sodom, pride
56. for thy s. Sod. was not mentioned in the day
22. 11. another in thee hath humbled his s.
23. 4. Aholah the elder, and Aholibah her s.
11. and when her s. Aholibah saw this
18. like as my mind was alienated from her s.
31. thou hast walked in the way of thy s.
32. shalt drink of thy s. cup deep and large, 33.
44. 25. for s. that hath no husband they may defile
Mat. 12. 50. the same is my brother, s. and mother
Luke 10. 39. she had a s. called Mary, John 11. 1, 5.
John 11. 3. therefore his s. sent unto him, saying, L.
19. 25. there stood by the cross his mother's s.
Acts 23. 16. Paul's s. son heard of their lying in wait
Rom. 16. 1. I commend to you Phebe our s. a serv.
1 Cor. 7. 15. a brother or a s. is not under bondage
9. 5. have we not power to lead about a s. a wife?
Col. 4. 10. Marcus s. son to Barnabas saluteth you
Jam. 2. 15. if a brother or s. be naked and destitute
2 John 13. the children of thy elect s. greet thee

SISTER-*in-law*.

Ruth 1. 15. behold, thy s.-in-law is gone back to her people and gods, return thou after thy s.-in-law

My SISTER.

Gen. 12. 13. say, I pray thee, thou art my s.
19. why saidst, she is my s.? 20. 2, 5, 12. | 26. 7, 9
30. 8. I have wrestled with my s. and prevailed
2 Sam. 13. 5. say to him, let my s. Tamar come, 6.
11. Amnon said to her, come lie with me, my s.
20. Absalom said, hold now thy peace, my s.
Job 17. 14. I have said to the worm, thou art my s.
Prov. 7. 4. say to wisdom, thou art my s. and call
Cant. 4. 9. hast ravished my heart, my s. my spouse
10. how fair is thy love, my s. my spouse
12. a garden inclosed is my s. my spouse, a spring
5. 1. I am come into my garden my s. my spouse
2. open to me, my s. my love, my undefiled
Mark 3. 35. same is my brother, my s. and mother
Luke 10. 40. dost thou not care that my s. left me?

SISTERS.

Josh. 2. 13. swear ye will save alive my fath. my s.
1 Chron. 2. 16. whose s. were Zeruiah and Abigail
Job 1. 4. they called for their three s. to eat and drink
42. 11. then came all his brethren and all his s.
Ezek. 16. 45. and thou art the sister of thy s.
51. thou hast justified thy s. in all thy abom. 52.
55. when thy s. and daughters shall return
61. shalt be ashamed when thou receive thy s.
Hos. 2. 1. say ye unto your s. Ruhamah
Mat. 13. 56. are not his s. with us? Mark 6. 3.
19. 29. that hath forsaken s. or father, or mother, or wife, for my sake, Mark 10. 29. Luke 14. 26.
Mark 10. 30. shall receive 100 fold, houses, breth. s.
1 Tim. 5. 2. intreat younger women, as s. with purity

SIT.

Num. 32. 6. shall brethren go to war and ye s. here?
Judg. 5. 10. speak ye that s. in judgment and walk
Ruth 3. 18. s. still, my daughter, till thou know
4. 1. ho, such a one turn aside, s. down here, 2.
1 Sam. 9. 22. and made them s. in the chiefest place
16. 11. we will not s. down till he come hither
20. 5. I should not fail to s. with the king
2 Sam. 19. 8. behold, the king doth s. in the gate
1 Kings 1. 13. Solomon shall s. on my throne, 17.
48. who hath given one to s. on my throne, 3. 6.
8. 25. there shall not fail thee a man to s. on the throne of Israel, 2 Chron. 6. 16. Jer. 33. 17.
2 Kings 7. 3. why s. we here till we die? 4.
10. 30. thy sons shall s. on the throne, 15. 12.
18. 27. sent me to men who s. on wall, Isa. 36. 12.
Psal. 26. 5. and will not s. with the wicked
69. 12. they that s. in the gate speak against me
107. 10. such as s. in darkn. and shadow of death
110. 1. said to my Lord, s. thou at my right hand
119. 23. princes also did s. and speak against me
127. 2. it is vain for you to rise early and s. up late
132. 12. their children shall s. upon thy throne
Eccl. 10. 6. folly in dignity, and rich s. in low place
Isa. 3. 26. being desolate, shall s. on the ground
14. 13. I will s. upon mount of the congregation
16. 5. he shall s. upon the throne in truth
30. 7. I have cried, their strength is to s. still
42. 7. bring them that s. in darkness out of prison
47. 1. s. in the dust, s. on the ground, 52. 2.
5. s. thou silent, get thee into darkness, O daughter
8. thou that sayest, I shall not s. as a widow
14. there shall not be a fire to s. before it
Jer. 8. 14. why do we s. still? assemble yourselves
13. 13. I will fill them that s. on David's throne
18. s. down now, 36. 15. || 48. 18. and s. in thirst
36. 30. he shall have none to s. upon the throne
Lam. 1. 1. how doth city s. solitary was full of peo
2. 10. elders of Zion s. on ground and keep silence
Ezek. 26. 16. they shall s. upon the ground
28. 2. because thou hast said, I s. in seat of God
33. 31. and they s. before thee as my people
44. 3. prince shall s. in it to eat bread before Lord
Dan. 7. 9. I beheld till the ancient of days did s.
26. but the judgment shall s. they shall take away
Joel 3. 12. there will I s. to judge the heathen
Mic. 4. 4. they shall s. every man under his vine
7. 8. when I s. in darkness, Lord shall be a light
Zech. 3. 8. thou and thy fellows that s. before me
6. 13. he shall s. and rule upon his throne
Mal. 3. 3. he shall s. as a refiner and purifier of silver
Mat. 8. 11. many shall s. down with Abraham
19. 28. when Son of man shall s. on throne of his glory, ye shall s. on twelve thrones, 25. 31. Luke 22. 30.
20. 21. my two sons may s. one on thy right hand
23. but to s. on my right hand, Mark 10. 37, 40.
22. 44. s. thou on my right hand till I make thy enemies thy footstool, Mark 12. 36. Luke 20. 42. Heb. 1. 13.
23. 2. the scribes and Pharisees s. in Moses' seat
26. 36. s. ye here while I pray yonder, Mark 14. 32.
Luke 9. 14. make them s. by fifties in a company
12. 37. make them to s. down, and will serve them
13. 29. and shall s. down in the kingdom of God
14. 8. when bidden s. not down in highest room
16. 6. take thy bill, s. down quickly, and write fifty
17. 7. will say to him, go, and s. down to meat
John 6. 10. Jesus said, make the men s. down
Acts 2. 30. would raise up Christ to s. on his throne
8. 31. that he would come up and s. with him
1 Cor. 8. 10. to see thee s. at meat in the idol's temple
Eph. 2. 6. hath made us s. in heavenly places
Jam. 2. 3. and say, s. thou here in a good place
Rev. 3. 21. will I grant to s. with me in my throne
17. 3. I saw a woman s. on scarlet-coloured beast
18. 7. for she saith in her heart, I s. a queen

SITH.

Ezek. 35. 6. s. thou hast not hated blood, even blood shall pursue thee

SITTEST.

Exod. 18. 14. why s. thou thyself alone?
Deut. 6. 7. thou shalt talk of them when thou s. in thine house, and walkest, 11. 19.
Psal. 50. 20. thou s. and speakest against thy broth.
Prov. 23. 1. when thou s. to eat with a ruler
Jer. 22. 2. hear, O king of Judah, that s. on the throne
Acts 23. 3. s. thou to judge me after the law?

SITTETH.
Exod. 11. 5. from the first-born that *s.* on his throne
Lev. 15.4. every thing whereon he *s.* shall be unclean
6. whereon he or she *s.* be unclean, 20, 23, 26.
Deut. 17. 18. when he *s.* on the throne he shall write
1 *Kings* 1. 46. Solomon *s.* on throne of the kingdom
Esth. 6. 10. do so to Mordecai that *s.* at the gate
Psal. 1. 1. nor *s.* in the seat of the scornful
2. 4. he that *s.* in the heavens shall laugh
10. 8. he *s.* in the lurking places of the villages
29. 10. Lord *s.* on the flood; yea, the Lord *s.* king
for ever, the L. will give strength to his people
47. 8. God *s.* on the throne of his holiness
99. 1. Lord reigneth, he *s.* between the cherubims
Prov. 9. 14. for she *s.* at the door of her house
20. 8. a king that *s.* in the throne of judgment
31. 23. when he *s.* among the elders of the land
Cant. 1. 12. while king *s.* at his table my spikenard
Isa. 28. 6. spirit of judgm. to him that *s.* in judgm.
40. 22. it is he that *s.* on the circle of the heavens
Jer. 17. 11. as the partridge *s.* on eggs
29. 16. saith of the king that *s.* upon the throne
Lam. 3. 28. he *s.* alone and keepeth silence
Zech. 1. 11. behold, all the earth *s.* still, and is at rest
5. 7. a woman that *s.* in the midst of the ephah
Mat. 23. 22. sweareth by him that *s.* thereon
Luke 14. 28. *s.* not down first and counteth, 31.
22. 27. whether is greater, he that *s.* at meat or he
that serveth? is not he that *s.* at meat?
1 *Cor.* 14.30. if any thing be reveal. to anoth. that *s.* by
Col. 3. 1. where Christ *s.* on the right hand of God
2 *Thess.* 2. 4. he, as God, *s.* in the temple of God
Rev. 5. 13. power to him that *s.* upon the throne
6. 16. from the face of him that *s.* on the throne
7. 10. salvation to our God which *s.* on the throne
15. he that *s.* on throne shall dwell among them
17. 1. the whore that *s.* upon many waters, 15.
9. are seven mountains, on which the woman *s.*

SITTING.
Deut. 22. 6. and the dam *s.* on the young or eggs
Judg. 3. 20. Eglon was *s.* in a summer-parlour
1 *Kings* 10. 5. she saw *s.* of his servants, 2 *Chr.* 9. 4.
13. 14. found the man of God *s.* under an oak
22. 19. I saw the Lord *s.* on his throne, and all the
host of heaven standing, 2 *Chr.* 18. 18. *Isa.* 6. 1.
2 *Kings* 4. 38. sons of the prophets were *s.* before him
9. 5. behold, the captains of the host were *s.*
Neh. 2. 6. the king said, the queen also *s.* by him
Esth. 5. 13. so long as I see Mordecai the Jew *s.*
Psal. 139. 2. thou knowest my down-*s.* and up-rising
Jer. 17. 25. kings *s.* on throne of David, 22. 4, 30.
38. 7. the king then *s.* in the gate of Benjamin
Lam. 3. 63. behold their *s.* down and rising up
Mat. 9. 9. *s.* at receipt of, *Mark* 2. 14. *Luke* 5. 27.
11. 16. like children *s.* in the markets, *Luke* 7. 32.
20. 30. behold, two blind men *s.* by the way side
21. 5. thy king cometh, *s.* on an ass, *John* 12. 15.
26. 64. ye shall see the Son of man *s.* on the right
hand of God, coming in the clouds, *Mark* 14. 62.
27. 36. and *s.* down, they watched him there
61. the other Mary *s.* over against the sepulchre
Mark 5. 15. they see him that was possessed *s.*
16. 5. they saw a young man *s.* on the right side
Luke 2. 46. they found him *s.* in midst of doctors
5. 17. the Pharisees and doctors of the law *s.* by
8. 35. found him *s.* clothed, and in his right mind
10. 13. had repented, *s.* in sackcloth and ashes
John 2. 14. he found the changers of money *s.*
20. 12. Mary seeth two angels in white *s.*
Acts 2. 2. it filled the house where they were *s.*
8. 28. eunuch was returning, and *s.* in his chariot
Rev. 4. 4. upon the seats I saw twenty-four elders *s.*

SITTING-PLACE.
2 *Chron.* 9. 18. and stays on each side of *s.-place*

SITUATE.
Ezek. 27. 3. Tyrus, O thou that art *s.* at entry of sea
Nah. 3. 8. populous No that was *s.* among rivers

SITUATION.
2 *Kings* 2. 19. behold, the *s.* of the city is pleasant
Psal. 48. 2. beautiful for *s.* joy of earth is mount Zion

SIX.
Lev. 24. 6. *s.* cakes on a row on the pure table
Num. 7. 3. *s.* covered waggons, and twelve oxen
2 *Sam.* 21. 20. man of great stature that had on every
hand *s.* fingers, every foot *s.* toes, 1 *Chr.* 20. 6.
1 *Chr.* 4. 27. Shimei had sixteen sons and *s.* daught.
26. 17. eastward were *s.* Levites, northward four
Ezek. 46. 4. the burnt offering that the prince shall
offer to the Lord, shall be *s.* lambs without blemish
6. in the day of the new moon shall be *s.* lambs

SIX *boards.*
Exod. 26. 22. westward thou shalt make *s. boards*
36. 27. for the sides of tabernacle he made *s. b.*
See BRANCHES.

SIX *brethren.*
Acts 11. 12. moreover these *s. brethren* accompanied

SIX *cities.*
Num. 35. 6. there shall be *s. cities* for refuge, 13, 15.

SIX *cubits.*
1 *Sam.* 17. 4. Goliath's height was *s. cubits* and a span
1 *Kings* 6. 6. the middle chamber was *s. cubits* broad
Ezek. 40. 5. a measuring-reed of *s. cubits* long
12. the little chambers were *s. cubits* on this side
41. 1. he measured posts *s. cubits* broad on one side
3. door *s. cubits* ‖ 5. wall of the house *s. cubits*
8. foundations were a full reed of *s.* great *cubits*
Dan. 3. 1. the breadth of the image of gold *s. c.*

SIX *curtains.*
Exod. 26. 9. couple *s. curtains* by themselves, 36. 16.
See DAYS, HUNDREDS.

SIX *measures.*
Ruth 3. 15. Boaz gave Ruth of barley *s. measures*
17. she said, these *s. m.* of barley gave he me

SIX *men.*
Ezek. 9. 2. *s. men* came from way of the higher gate

SIX *months.*
2 *Sam.* 2. 11. the time David was king in Hebron,
was seven years, *s. months*, 5. 5. 1 *Chron.* 3. 4.
1 *Kings* 11. 16. *s. months* Joab remained in Edom
2 *Kings* 15. 8. Zachariah reigned *s. m.* over Israel
Esth. 2. 12. purifying *s. months* with oil of myrrh,
and *s. months* with sweet odours and other things
Luke 4. 25. when heaven was shut up three years
and *s. months*, and great famine, *Jam.* 5. 17.
Acts 18. 11. Paul continued at Corinth a year *s. m.*

SIX *names.*
Exod. 28. 10. *s.* of their *names* on one stone, and
the other *s. names* of the rest on the other stone

SIX *paces.*
2 *Sam.* 6. 13. when Levites gone *s. p.* he sacrificed

SIXSCORE.
1 *Kings* 9. 14. Hiram sent Solomon *s.* talents of gold

SIX *sheep.*
Neh. 5. 18. prepared for me daily *s.* choice *sheep*

SIX *sons.*
Gen. 30. 20. will dwell with me, I have born *s. sons*
1 *Chron.* 3. 22. and the *sons* of Shechaniah *s.*
8. 38. and Azel had *s. sons*, whose names are, 9. 44.

SIX *steps.*
1 *Kings* 10. 19. the throne had *s. steps*, top round
20. twelve lions on the *s. steps*, 2 *Chron.* 9. 18.

SIX *things.*
Prov. 6. 16. these *s. things* doth the Lord hate

SIX *times.*
2 *Kings* 13. 19. shouldst have smitten five or *s. times*

SIX *troubles.*
Job 5. 19. shall deliver thee in *s. troubles*, in seven

SIX *water-pots.*
John 2. 6. there were set there *s. water-pots* of stone

SIX *wings.*
Isa. 6. 2. stood the seraphims, each one had *s. wings*
Rev. 4. 8. four beasts had each *s. wings* about him

SIX *years.*
Gen. 31. 41. I served thee *s. years* for thy cattle
Exod. 21. 2. *s. years* he shall serve, and in seventh he
shall go out free, *Deut.* 15. 12. *Jer.* 34. 14.
23. 10. *s. years* thou shalt sow thy land and gather
Lev. 25. 3. *s. years* thou shalt prune thy vineyard
Deut. 15. 18. double hired servant in serving *s. years*
Judg. 12. 7. and Jephthah judged Israel *s. years*
1 *Kings* 16. 23. Omri reigned *s. years* in Tirzah
2 *Kings* 11. 3. Joash was hid with his nurse in the
house of the Lord *s. years*, 2 *Chron.* 22. 12.

SIXTH.
Gen. 30. 19. Leah conceived, bare Jacob the *s.* son
Exod. 26. 9. thou shalt double *s.* curtain in tabern.
Lev. 25. 21. will command my bless. on you *s.* year
Josh. 19. 32. the *s.* lot came out for Naphtali
2 *Sam.* 3. 5. Ithream, David's *s.* son, 1 *Chron.* 3. 3.
2 *Kings* 18. 10. in *s.* year of Hezek. Samaria taken
Ezra 6. 15. house was finished in *s.* year of Darius
Ezek. 4. 11. drink water by measure, *s.* part of him
8. 1. in the *s.* year the hand of Lord fell upon me
39. 2. I will leave but the *s.* part of thee
45. 13. the oblation the *s.* part of an ephah
46. 14. a meat offering the *s.* part of an ephah
Mat. 20. 5. again he went out about the *s.* hour
27. 45. there was darkness over all the land from
the *s.* to ninth hour, *Mark* 15. 33. *Luke* 23. 44.
John 4. 6. about the *s.* hour Jesus sat on the well
19. 14. and he was crucified about the *s.* hour
Acts 10. 9. Peter went to pray about the *s.* hour
Rev. 6. 12. when he opened *s.* seal, an earthquake
9. 13. the *s.* angel sounded, and I heard a voice
14. saying to the *s.* angel, loose the four angels
16. 12. *s.* angel poured out vial on river Euphrates
21. 20. the *s.* foundation of the wall was sardius
See DAY, MONTH.

SIXTEEN.
Gen. 46. 18. Zilpah bare to Jacob *s.* souls
Exod. 26. 25. sockets of silver, *s.* sockets, 36. 30.
2 *Kings* 13. 10. Jehoash reigned *s.* years in Samaria
14. 21. and made Azariah, when *s.* years old, king
15. 33. Jotham reigned over Judah *s.* years in Je-
rusalem, 2 *Chron.* 27. 1, 8. | 28. 1.
1 *Chr.* 4. 27. Shimei had *s.* sons and six daughters
24. 4. among sons of Eleazar were *s.* chief men
2 *Chr.* 13. 21. Abijah begat sons and *s.* daughters

SIXTEENTH.
1 *Chron.* 24. 14. the *s.* lot came forth to Immer
25. 23. the *s.* lot came forth to Hananiah

SIXTY. [Jared
Gen. 5. 15. Mahalaleel lived *s.* years, and begat
21. Enoch lived *s.* five years, and begat Methusel.
Lev. 27. 3. estimation of the male from twenty to *s.*
7. if it be from *s.* years old above thy estimation
Num. 7. 88. offer *s.* rams, *s.* he-goats, *s.* lambs
Mat. 13. 8. brought forth *s.* fold, 23. *Mark* 4. 8, 20.

SIZE.
Exod. 36. 9. the curtains were all of one *s.* 15.
1 *Kings* 6. 25. both cherubims of one measure and *s.*
7. 37. all the bases of one measure and of one *s.*
1 *Chr.* 23. 29. for all manner of *s.* David left charge

SKILL.
1 *Kings* 5. 6. thou knowest there is not any that can
s. to hew timber like the Sidonians, 2 *Chron.* 2. 8.
2 *Chron.* 2. 7. send me a man that can *s.* to grave
34. 12. all that could *s.* of instruments of music

SKILL.
Eccl. 9. 11. nor yet favour to men of *s.* but time
Dan. 1. 17. G. gave them knowledge and *s.* in wisd.
9. 22. I am now come to give thee *s.* and understan.

SKILFUL.
1 *Chr.* 5. 18. sons of Reuben and Gadites *s.* in war
15. 22. Chenaniah instructed, because he was *s.*
28. 21. there shall be with thee every willing *s.* man
2 *Chr.* 2. 14. I have sent a cunning man *s.* to work
Isa. 3. †3. the Lord taketh away the *s.* of speech
Ezek. 21. 31. give you into the hand of *s.* to destroy
Dan. 1. 4. children *s.* in all wisdom and cunning
Amos 5. 16. such are *s.* of lamentation to wailing

SKILFULLY.
Ps. 33. 3. sing a new song, play *s.* with loud noise

SKILFULNESS.
Psal. 78. 72. and guided them by *s.* of his hands

SKIN.
Exod. 22. 27. his covering, it is his raiment for *s.*
29. 14. bullock's flesh, *s.* and dung burn, *Lev.* 4. 11.
34. 29. Moses wist not that *s.* of face shone, 30, 35.
Lev. 7. 8. the priest that offereth shall have the *s.*
11. 32. if dead fall on *s.* or sack, it shall be unclean
13. 2. shall have in the *s.* a rising like the plague
3. the priest shall look on the plague in the *s.* of
the flesh, and if deeper than the *s.* of his flesh
Lev. 13. 4. if bright spot be white in *s.* of his flesh
5. if the plague spread not in the *s.* 6, 22, 28.
7. if scab spread abroad in the *s.* 8, 27, 35, 36.
10. if the rising be white in the *s.* it is a leprosy
11. it is an old leprosy in the *s.* of his flesh
56. then he shall rend it out of garment or *s.*
15. 17. every *s.* whereon is seed washed with water
Num. 19. 5. burn heifer, her *s.* and flesh and blood
Job 2. 4. *s.* for *s.* all a man hath will he give for life
7. 5. my *s.* is broken, and become loathsome
10. 11. thou hast clothed me with *s.* and flesh
16. 15. I sewed sackcloth on my *s.* and defiled
18. 13. it shall devour the strength of his *s.*
19. 20. bone cleaveth to my *s.* and to my flesh,
and I am escaped with the *s.* of my teeth
26. though after my *s.* worms destroy this body
30. 30. my *s.* is black upon me, bones are burnt
41. 7. canst thou fill his *s.* with barbed irons?
Psal. 102. 5. my groaning my bones cleave to my *s.*
Jer. 13. 23. can the Ethiopian change his *s.*?
Lam. 3. 4. my flesh and *s.* hath he made old
4. 8. their *s.* cleaveth to their bones, is withered
5. 10. our *s.* was black like an oven for famine
Ezek. 37. 6. I will cover you with *s.* put breath, 8.
Mic. 3. 2. who pluck off their *s.* and their flesh
3. who eat flesh, and flay their *s.* from off them
Mark 1. 6. John had a girdle of *s.* about his loins

SKINS.
Gen. 3. 21. Lord made coats of *s.* and clothed them
27. 16. she put *s.* of kids of goats upon his hands
Exod. 35. 23. every man with whom were found red
s. of rams and badgers' *s.* brought them
Lev. 13. 59. this is the law of the plague of *s.*
16. 27. they shall burn in fire their *s.* and flesh
Num. 31. 20. purify your raiment, all made of *s.*
Heb. 11. 37. wandered about in sheep *s.* and goat *s*

SKIP.
Psal. 29. 6. he maketh them also to *s.* like a calf

SKIPPED.
Psal. 114. 4. the mountains *s.* like rams, 6.

SKIPPEDST.
Jer. 48. 27. since thou spakest of him, thou *s.* for joy

SKIPPING.
Cant. 2. 8. behold, he cometh *s.* upon the hills

SKIRT
Is the part of a garment below the waist. Ruth
says to Boaz, Cast thy skirt over me, *Ruth* 3.
9. *that is, Take me into thy protection, by taking*
me to be thy wife. It is spoken in allusion to
the ancient custom or ceremony of the bridegroom's
spreading the skirt of his garment over the bride;
to signify his right to her, his authority over her,
and his obligation to protect her. So also in Ezek.
16. 8. I spread my skirt over thee: *I betrothed*
thee, and engaged by covenant to love, cherish,
protect, and guard thee. The prophet Jeremiah
says, that the filthiness of *Jerusalem* is in her
skirts, *Lam.* 1. 9. *Her wickedness is evident, she*
is not ashamed to expose it to the view of all. The
Lord threatens to discover the skirts of Israel *and*
Judah *upon their faces, Jer.* 13. 26. I will discover thy skirts upon thy face; *I will throw thy*
skirts upon thy face; and so discover thy naked-
ness; that is, I will bring thee into a most dis-
graceful, contemptible condition, by those judg-
ments which I will inflict upon thee. It is said
in Deut. 22. 30. A man shall not discover his
father's skirt; *the skirt of the mother's garment,*
that is, her nakedness; which is called his father's skirt; *because his father and mother were*
one flesh, or because his father alone had the right
to uncover it.
Deut. 22. 30. man shall not uncover his father's *s.*
27. 20. because he uncovereth his father's *s.*
Ruth 3. 9. spread therefore thy *s.* over thine handm.
1 *Sam.* 15. 27. he laid hold on the *s.* of his mantle
24. 4. David cut off the *s.* of Saul's robe privily
5. heart smote him, because he cut off Saul's *s.*
11. father, see the *s.* of thy robe in my hand
Ezek. 16. 8. behold, I spread my *s.* over thee
Hag. 2. 12. if one bear holy flesh in the *s.* and
with his *s.* do touch bread, pottage, wine,
or oil
Zech. 8. 23. shall take hold of *s.* of him that is a Jew

SKIRTS.
Psal. 133. 2. that went down to *s.* of his garments
Jer. 2. 34. in *s.* is found blood of poor innocents
13. 22. for thy iniquity are thy *s.* discovered
26. therefore will I discover thy *s.* *Nah.* 3. 5.
Lam. 1. 9. her filthiness is in her *s.* remembered not
Ezek. 5. 3. shalt take and bind a few hairs in thy *s.*

SKULL.
Judg. 9. 53. cast a piece of millstone to break his *s.*
2 *Kings* 9. 35. they found no more of Jezebel than *s.*
Mat. 27. 33. when come to Golgotha, that is to say,
the place of a *s.* *Mark* 15. 22. *John* 19. 17

SKY.
Deut. 33. 26. who rideth in his excellency on *s.*
Job 37. 18. hast thou with him spread out the *s.*?
Mat. 16. 2. it will be fair weather, for *s.* is red, 3.
Luke 12. 56. ye can discern face of the *s.* and earth
Heb. 11. 12. so many as the stars of *s.* in multitude

SKIES.
2 *Sam.* 22. 12. he made thick clouds of the *s.* his
pavilions round about him, *Psal.* 18. 11.
Psal. 77. 17. clouds poured out *s.* sent out a sound
Isa. 45. 8. and let the *s.* pour down righteousness
Jer. 51. 9. for her judgment is lifted up even to *s.*

SLACK.
Deut. 7. 10. he will not be *s.* to him that hateth him
Josh. 18. 3. how long are ye *s.* to go to possess land!
Prov. 10. 4. become poor that dealeth with a *s.* hand
Zeph. 3. 16. shall be said to Zion, let not hands be *s*
2 *Pet.* 3. 9. Lord is not *s.* concerning his promise

SLACK.
Deut. 23. 21. when vow a vow thou shalt not *s.* to pay
Josh. 10. 6. saying, *s.* not thy hand from servants
2 *Kings* 4. 24. *s.* not riding for me except I bid thee

SLACKED.
Hab. 1. 4. law is *s.* judgment doth never go forth

SLACKNESS.
2 *Pet.* 3. 9. Lord is not slack, as some men count *s*

SLAIN, *Active.*

Gen. 4. 23. for I have s. a man to my wounding
Num. 14. 16. therefore he hath s. them in wildern.
22. 33. surely now I had s. thee, saved her alive
Deut. 1. 4. after he had s. Sihon king of Amorites
21. 1. and it be not known who hath s. him
Judg. 9. 18. and have s. his sons upon one stone
15. 16. jaw-bone of an ass have I s. 1000 men
20. 5. the men of Gibeah thought to have s. me
1 Sam. 18. 7. Saul hath s. his thousands, 21. 11.
22. 21. shewed Dav. that Saul had s. Lord's priests
2 Sam. 1. 16. saying, I have s. the Lord's anointed
3. 30. Abner, because he had s. their broth. Asahel
4. 11. when wicked men have s. righteous person
12. 9. hast s. Uriah with the sword of Ammon
13. 30. Absalom hath s. all king's sons, none left
32. they have not s. all, for Amnon only is dead
21. 12. when the Philistines had s. Saul in Gilboa
16. Ishbi-benob thought to have s. David
1 Kings 1. 19. Adonijah hath s. oxen and sheep, 25.
9. 16. Pharaoh had gone up and s. the Canaanites
13. 26. therefore the lion hath torn and s. him
16. 16. people heard say, Zimri hath s. the king
19. 1. Ahab told how he had s. all the prophets
10. for Israel have s. thy prophets, 14.
2 Kings 14. 5. he slew his servants who had s. king
2 Chron. 21. 13. hast s. thy breth. better than thyself
22. 1. for the band of men had s. all the eldest
9. when they had s. Ahaziah, they buried him
23. 21. city was quiet after they had s. Athaliah
28. 9. have s. them in rage that reacheth to heaven
Esth. 9. 12. the Jews have s. 500 men in Shushan
Job 1. 15. the Sabeans have s. the servants, 17.
Prov. 7. 26. many strong men have been s. by her
Isa. 14. 20. because thou hast destroyed and s. people
Jer. 33. 5. bodies of men whom I have s. in my anger
41. 4. day after he had s. Gedaliah, 9, 16, 18.
Lam. 2. 21. hast s. them in day of thy anger, 3. 43.
Ezek. 16. 21. that thou hast s. my children
23. 39. when they had s. their children to idols
Hos. 6. 5. I have s. them by words of my mouth
Amos 4. 10. your young men have I s. with sword
Acts 2. 23. ye have taken, by wicked hands have s.
7. 52. have s. them that shewed coming of just One
23. 14. we will eat nothing till we have s. Paul

SLAIN, *Passive.*

Gen 34. 27. the sons of Jacob came upon the s.
Lev. 14. 51. dip them in the blood of the s. bird
26. 17. and ye shall be s. before your enemies
Num. 11. 22. shall the flocks, and the herds be s.?
19. 16. whosoever toucheth any s. 18. | 31. 19.
23. 24. eat of prey, and drink the blood of the s.
25. 14. name of the Israelite that was s. was Zimri
15. name of woman that was s. was Cozbi, 18.
31. 8. besides the rest of them that were s.
Deut. 21. 1. if one be found s. in land giveth thee
3. the elders of the city next to the s. man
28. 31. thine ox shall be s. before thine eyes
32. 42. make mine arrows drunk with blood of s.
Josh. 11. 6. will I deliver them up all s. before Israel
13. 22. Balaam also among them that were s.
Judg. 16. † 24. the destroyer who multiplied our s.
20. 4. the husband of the woman that was s.
1 Sam. 4. 11. ark taken, Hophni and Phinehas were s.
19. 6. as the Lord liveth, he shall not be s.
11. if thou save not, to-morrow thou shalt be s.
20. 32. wherefore shall he be s. what hath he done
31. 1. men of Israel fled before the Philistines, and fell down s. in mount Gilboa, 1 Chron. 10. 1.
8. when the Philistines came to strip the s.
2 Sam. 1. 19. beauty of Israel is s. on high places
22. from the blood of s. from fat of the mighty
25. O Jonathan, thou wast s. in thy high places
18. 7. when Israel were s. before David's servants
1 Kings 11. 15. when Joab was gone to bury the s.
2 Kings 3. 23. this is blood, the kings are surely s.
11. 2. stole Joash from among them that were s.
8. he that cometh within ranges let him be s.
16. they laid hands on her, and there was she s.
1 Chr. 5. 22. there fell down many s. war was of G.
2 Chr. 13. 17. fell s. of Israel 500,000 chosen men
Esth. 7. 4. for we are sold, I and my people, to be s.
9. 11. number of the s. in Shushan the palace
Job 39. 30. and where the s. are, there is she
Psal. 62. 3. ye shall be s. all of you, as bowing wall
88. 5. like the s. that lie in the grave
89. 10. thou hast broken Rahab in pieces as one s.
Prov. 22. 13. the slothful man saith, I shall be s.
24. 11. to deliver those that are ready to be s.
Isa. 10. 4. and they shall fall under the s.
14. 19. and as the raiment of those that are s.
22. 2. thy s. men were not s. with sword or dead
26. 21. the earth also shall no more cover her s.
27. 7. is he s. according to slaughter of s. by him
34. 3. their s. also shall be cast out, stink come up
66. 16. and the s. of the Lord shall be many
Jer. 9. 1. that I might weep for s. of my people
14. 18. if I go into the field, behold s. with sword
18. 21. let their young men be s. by sword in battle
25. 33. s. of the Lord be from one end of earth
41. 9. and Ishmael filled the pit with the s.
51. 4. thus the s. shall fall in land of Chaldeans
47. and all her s. shall fall in the midst of her
49. as Babylon hath caused s. of Israel to fall, so at Babylon shall fall the s. of all the earth
Lam. 2. 20. shall priest and prophet be s. in sanct.
4. 9. they that be s. with sword, are better than they that be s. with hunger, for these pine away
Ezek. 6. 7. and the s. shall fall in the midst of you
13. when the s. men shall be among their idols
9. 7. defile the house and fill the courts with s.
11. 6. ye have multiplied your s. in the city, ye have filled the streets with the s.
7. your s. are the flesh, and this city the caldron
21. 14. sword of s. it is the sword of great men s.
29. to bring thee upon necks of them that are s.
26. 6. her daughters in field shall be s. by sword
28. 8. thou shalt die deaths of them that are s.
30. 4. great pain when the s. shall fall in Egypt
11. they shall fill the land with the s.
31. 17. went into hell with him unto them that be s.
18. shalt lie with them s. with sword, 32. 29.
Ezek. 32. 20. they shall fall in the midst of the s. 25.
21. they lie s. by the sword, 22, 23, 24.
25. all of them uncircumcised s. by sword, 26, 30.
31. even Phar. and all his army s. by sword, 32.
35. 8. I will fill his mountains with his s. men
37. 9. come, O breath, breathe upon these s.
Dan. 2. 13. decree went forth that wise men should be s. they sought Daniel and his fellows to be s.
5. 30. in that night was Belshazzar the king s.
7. 11. I beheld, even till beast was s. and destroyed
11. 26. army overflow, and many shall fall down s.
Nah. 3. 3. there is multitude of s. number of carcases
Zeph. 2. 12. ye Ethiopians shall be s. by my sword
Luke 9. 22. Son of man must be s. and be raised
Acts 5. 36. Theudas was s. as many as obeyed him
7. 42. O Israel, have ye offered to me s. beasts?
13. 28. yet desired they Pilate that he should be s.
Eph. 2. 16. by the cross, having s. enmity thereby
Heb. 11. 37. they were stoned, were s. with sword
Rev. 2. 13. Antipas, who was s. among you
5. 6. in the midst stood a Lamb, as it had been s.
9. thou wast s. || 12. the Lamb that was s. 13. 8.
6. 9. souls of them that were s. for word of God
11. 13. in the earthquake were s. of men 7000
18. 24. in her found the blood of all that were s.
19. 21. remnant s. with sword of him that sat

SLANDER.

Num. 14. 36. to murmur by bringing up a s. on land
Psal. 31. 13. for I have heard the s. of many
Prov. 10. 18. he that uttereth a s. is a fool

SLANDERED.

2 Sam. 19. 27. he hath s. thy servant to my Lord

SLANDEREST.

Psal. 50. 20. thou s. thine own mother's son

SLANDERETH.

Psal. 101. 5. whoso s. his neigh. him will I cut off

SLANDERERS.

1 Tim. 3. 11. their wives must be grave, not s.

SLANDEROUSLY.

Rom. 3. 8. and not rather, as we be s. reported

SLANDERS.

Jer. 6. 28. they are all revolters walking with s.
9. 4. and every neighbour will walk with s.

SLANG.

1 Sam. 17. 49. Dav. took from his bag a stone and s. it

SLAVE, S.

Jer. 2. 14. is Israel a servant? is he home-born s.?
Rev. 18. 13. no man buyeth the merchandise of s.

SLAUGHTER.

1 Sam. 14. 14. the first s. which Jonathan made
30. for had there not been now much greater s.
17. 57. as David returned from s. of Philistine, Abner brought him before Saul, 18. 6. 2 Sam. 1. 1.
2 Sam. 17. 9. is s. among people who follow Absalom
2 Chron. 25. 14. Amaziah was come from the s.
Psal. 44. 22. we are counted as sheep for the s.
Prov. 7. 22. he goeth after her, as an ox to the s.
Isa. 10. 26. according to the s. of Midian at Oreb
14. 21. prepare s. for his child. for iniquity of fath.
27. 7. according to s. of them that are slain by him
34. 2. he hath destroyed, and delivered them to s.
53. 7. he is brought as a lamb to s. Jer. 11. 19.
65. 12. and ye shall all bow down to the s.
Jer. 7. 32. no more Tophet, but valley of s. 19. 6.
12. 3. thou hast seen and tried my heart, pull them out like sheep for s. prepare them for day of s.
25. 34. for the days of your s. are accomplished
48. 15. his chosen young men are gone down to s.
50. 27. let them go down to the s. woe to them
51. 40. I will bring them down like lambs to the s.
Ezek. 9. 2. and every man a s. weapon in his hand
21. 10. it is sharpened to make sore s. it is furbished
15. it is made bright, it is wrapped up for the s.
22. was divination to open the mouth in the s.
28. the sword is drawn, for the s. it is furbished
26. 15. when the s. is made in the midst of thee
Hos. 5. 2. and revolters are profound to make s.
Obad. 9. of the mount of Esau may be cut off by s.
Zech. 11. 4. thus saith Lord, feed the flock of s.
7. I will feed flock of s. O poor flock
Acts 8. 32. eunuch read, he was led as a sheep to s.
9. 1. Saul yet breathing out s. against the disciples
Rom. 8. 36. we are counted as sheep to the s.
Heb. 7. 1. Melch. met Abra. returning from s. of kings
Jam. 5. 5. have nourished your hearts, as in day of s.

See GREAT.

SLAY.

Gen. 4. 14. that every one that findeth me shall s. me
20. 4. Lord, wilt thou s. also a righteous nation?
11. and they will s. me for my wife's sake
27. 41. then will I s. my brother Jacob
34. 30. they shall gather together ag. me and s. me
37. 20. come now therefore and let us s. him
26. Judah said, what profit is it if we s. brother?
42. 37. s. my two sons if I bring him not to thee
43. 16. bring these men home, s. and make ready
Exod. 4. 23. behold, I will s. thy son, even first-born
23. 7. the innocent and righteous s. thou not
29. 16. thou shalt s. ram and sprinkle his blood
32. 12. for mischief did he bring them out to s. them
27. s. every man his brother and companion
Lev. 4. 29. s. sin-offering, 33. || 14. 13. s. the lamb
20. 15. if a man lie with a beast, ye shall s. beast
Num. 19. 3. one shall s. red heifer before his face
25. 5. s. ye every one his men joined to Baal-peor
35. 19. revenger of blood shall s. the murderer, 21.
Deut. 19. 6. lest avenger of blood pursue and s. him
Josh. 13. 22. Israel did s. Balaam the son of Beor
Judg. 8. 19. had saved them alive, would not s. you
20. he said to Jether his first-born, up and s. them
9. 54. s. me, that men say not, a woman slew him
1 Sam. 2. 25. because the Lord would s. them
5. 11. send away the ark of God that it s. us not
14. 34. bring any man his ox, and s. here, sin not
15. 3. spare them not, but s. both man and woman
19. 15. bring him up to me, that I may s. him
20. 8. if there be in me iniquity, s. me thyself
22. 17. king said, turn and s. the priests of the L.
2 Sam. 1. 9. Saul said to me, stand upon me and s.
1 Kings 1. 51. let king swear to me he will not s.
3. 26. give her living child, in no wise s. it, 27.
15. 28. Nadad did Baasha s. and reigned in stead
1 Kings 18. 12. when he cannot find thee, he shall s. me
19. 17. escapeth sword of Hazael shall Jehu s. that escapeth sword of Jehu shall Elisha s.
20. 36. as soon as thou art departed, lion shall s. thee
2 Kings 8. 12. and their young men wilt thou s.
10. 25. go in and s. them, let none come forth
17. 26. God hath sent lions, and they s. them
2 Chron. 23. 14. s. her not in the house of the Lord
29. 34. priests too few to s. all the burnt offerings
Neh. 4. 11. we will s. them and cause work cease
Job 9. 23. if the scourge s. suddenly, he will laugh
13. 15. though he s. me, yet will I trust in him
20. 16. shall suck poison, viper's tongue shall s. him
Psal. 34. 21. evil shall s. wicked that hate righteous
59. 11. s. them not, lest my people forget, scatter
94. 6. they s. the widow and the stranger
109. 16. that he might s. the broken in heart
139. 19. surely thou wilt s. the wicked, O God
Prov. 1. 32. turning away of the simple shall s. them
Isa. 11. 4. with breath of his lips shall he s. wicked
14. 30. with famine, and he shall s. thy remnant
27. 1. Lord shall s. the dragon that is in the sea
65. 15. for Lord God shall s. thee, call his serv.
Jer. 5. 6. a lion out of the forest shall s. them
20. 4. he shall carry Judah captive and s. them
29. 21. shall s. Ahab and Zedekiah before your eyes
40. 15. let me go, I pray thee, and I will s. Ishmael, son of Nethaniah; wherefore should he s. thee?
41. 8. ten men were found that said, s. us not
50. 27. s. all her bullocks, woe to them, day is come
Ezek. 9. 6. s. utterly old and young, both maids and
23. 47. they shall s. their sons and daughters
26. 8. he shall s. with sword thy daughters in field
11. he shall s. thy people by the sword
44. 11. they shall s. the burnt-offering and sacrifice
Hos. 2. 3. set like a dry land and s. her with thirst
9. 16. tho' they bring forth, yet will I s. the fruit
Amos 2. 3. I will s. all princes thereof with him
9. 1. I will s. the last of them with the sword
4. will I command sword, and it shall s. them
Zech. 11. 5. whose possessors s. them and hold
Luke 11. 49. some of them they shall s. and persec.
19. 27. bring hither, and s. them before me

To SLAY.

Gen. 18. 25. that be far from thee to s. the righteous
22. 10. Abraham stretched his hand to s. his son
37. 18. they conspired against him to s. him
Exod. 2. 15. Pharaoh sought to s. Moses, but he fled
5. 21. to put a sword in their hand to s. us
21. 14. if a man come on neighbour to s. with guile
Deut. 9. 28. brought them out to s. them in wilderness
27. 25. cursed that taketh reward to s. innocent
1 Sam. 5. 10. they have brought the ark to s. us
19. 5. why then sin, to s. David without a cause?
11. Saul went to watch him and s. him in morning
20. 33. it was determined of his father to s. David
2 Sam. 3. 37. it was not of the king to s. Abner
21. 2. Saul sought to s. them in his zeal to Israel
1 Kings 17. 18. O man, art thou come to s. my son?
18. 9. delivered me into the hand of Ahab to s. me
2 Chron. 20. 23. utterly to s. and destroy them
Neh. 6. 10. they will come to s. thee, in night to s. th.
Esth. 8. 11. to s. the power that would assault them
Psal. 37. 14. to s. such as be of upright conversation
32. watcheth righteous, and seeketh to s. him
Jer. 15. 3. will appoint the sword to s. dogs, to tear
18. 23. thou knowest all their counsel to s. me
40. 14. that Baalis hath sent Ishmael to s. thee
Ezek. 13. 19. to s. the souls that should not die
40. 39. two tables to s. thereon the burnt offering
Dan. 2. 14. Arioch was gone forth to s. wise men
Hab. 1. 17. and not spare continually to s. nations
John 5. 16. Jews persecute Jesus, and sought to s. him
Acts 5. 33. they took counsel to s. the apostles
9. 29. but they went about to s. him
Rev. 9. 15. angels prepared to s. the third part of men

SLAYER.

Num. 35. 11. shall appoint cities of refuge that the s. may flee thither, Deut. 4. 42. | 19. 3, 4. Josh. 20. 3.
24. shall judge between s. and revenger of blood
25. congregation shall deliver s. from revenger
26. if the s. shall at any time come without city
27. and the revenger of blood find and kill the s.
28. but after the death of high-priest, the s. shall return into the land of his possession, Josh. 20. 6.
Deut. 19. 6. lest the avenger of blood pursue the s.
Josh. 20. 5. then they shall not deliver the s. up
21. 13. gave Hebron to be a city of refuge for s.
21. gave Shechem || 27. Golan || 32. Kedesh for the s.
38. Ramoth in Gilead to be a city of refuge for s.
Ezek. 21. 11. the sword is furbished to be given to s.

SLAYETH.

Gen. 4. 15. the Lord said to him, whosoever s. Cain
Deut. 22. 26. riseth against his neighbour and s. him
Job 5. 2. wrath killeth and envy s. the silly one
Ezek. 28. 9. wilt thou say before him that s. thee, I am God? shalt be a man in hand of him that s. thee

SLAYING.

Josh. 8. 24. when Israel made an end of s. 10. 20.
Judg. 9. 56. God rendered wickedness in s. his breth.
1 Kings 17. 20. brought evil on widow by s. her son
Isa. 22. 13. behold, s. oxen, killing sheep, eating flesh
57. 5. s. the children in the valleys under the rocks
Ezek. 9. 8. while they were s. them, and I was left

SLEEP.

Sleeping, slumbering, *is taken either for the* sleep, *or repose of the body, or for the* sleep *of the soul, which is supineness, indolence, stupidity; or for the* sleep *of death.*

Ahasuerus *could not sleep,* Esth. 6. 1. I will both lay me down in peace, and sleep, *says* David, Psal. 4. 8. Awake, thou that sleepest, and arise from the dead, and *Christ* shall give thee light. *He speaks to those that were dead in sin and infidelity, who were going on securely in sin, without sense of danger.* I sleep, but my heart waketh, *says the spouse,* Cant. 5. 2. *that is, The flesh, the unrenewed part, prevails to make me slothful and secure, and to lay aside the exercise of grace at present; but the renewed part is sensible of, and strives against, this distemper. This is a sleep of sloth, ease, and security, which even the godly may fall into. There is also the* sleep *of death.* You shall sleep with your fathers, *you shall die as they are dead,* 1 *Kings* 1. 21. That they may sleep a perpetual sleep, *Jer.* 51. 39. Many that sleep in the dust of the earth shall awake, *Dan.* 12. 2. *And in* John 11. 11. *Lazarus* sleepeth, but I go that I may awake him out of sleep: *He is dead, but I will go and raise him up. St.* Peter *says of the wicked,* their damnation slumbereth not, 2 *Pet.* 2. 3. *God is not asleep, he will not forget to punish them in his own due time. And* Solomon *says,* *Prov.* 23. 21. Drowsiness shall clothe a man with rags: *The slumberer, the slothful, shall come to poverty.*

Isaiah *speaks of a superstitious practice among the* Pagans, *who went to* sleep *in the temples of their idols, to obtain prophetic dreams.* Isa. 65. 4. Which remain among the graves, and lodge in the monuments. *The word* monuments *signifies* places kept, *or* observed. *Some interpret it of idol temples; some of caves and dens, in which the heathens used to worship their idols, and some of tombs, or monuments for dead persons. The prophet speaks of the superstitious and idolatrous* Jews, *who, in contempt of the prophets of the temple of the Lord, and in imitation of the heathen, went into the tombs and temples of idols, to sleep there, and to have dreams that might discover future events to them.*

Gen. 2. 21. God caused a deep *s.* to fall upon Adam
15. 12. sun going down, a deep *s.* fell on Abram
28. 16. Jacob awaked out of his *s.* and he said
31. 40. thus I was, my *s.* departed from mine eyes
Judg. 16. 14. Samson awaked out of his *s.* 20.
1 *Sam.* 26. 12. a deep *s.* from God fallen on them
Job 4. 13. when deep *s.* falleth on men, 33. 15.
14. 12. shall not awake, nor raised out of their *s.*
Psal. 13. 3. lighten my eyes, lest I *s.* the *s.* of death
76. 5. the stout-hearted have slept their *s.*
6. both chariot and horse are cast into a deep *s.*
78. 65. then the Lord awakened as one out of *s.*
90. 5. thou carriest them away, they are as a *s.*
127. 2. for so he giveth to his beloved *s.*
132. 4. I will not give *s.* to mine eyes or slumber
Prov. 3. 24. shalt lie down, and thy *s.* shall be sweet
4. 16. their *s.* is taken away, unless they cause some to fall
6. 4. give not *s.* to thine eyes, nor slumb. to eyelids
9. O sluggard, when wilt thou arise out of thy *s.?*
10. yet a little *s.* a little slumber, 24. 33.
19. 15. slothfulness casteth into a deep *s.*
20. 13. love not *s.* lest thou come to poverty
Eccl. 5. 12. the *s.* of a labouring man is sweet
8. 16. there is that neither day nor night seeth *s.*
Isa. 29. 10. Lord poured out on you spirit of deep *s.*
Jer. 31. 26. I awaked, and my *s.* was sweet to me
51. 39. that they may sleep a perpetual *s.* 57.
Dan. 2. 1. spirit troubled, and his *s.* brake from him
6. 18. passed the night and his *s.* went from him
8. 18. I was in a deep *s.* on my face, 10. 9.
Zech. 4. 1. as a man that is wakened out of *s.*
Mat. 1. 24. then Joseph being raised from *s.* did
Luke 9. 32. they with him were heavy with *s.*
John 11. 11. I go that I may awake him out of *s.*
13. that he had spoken of taking of rest in *s.*
Acts 16. 27. the keeper awaking out of his *s.*
20. 9. there sat Eutychus being fallen into a deep *s.*
Rom. 13. 11. it is high time to awake out of *s.*

SLEEP, *Verb.*

Gen. 28. 11. Jacob lay down in that place to *s.*
Exod. 22. 27. it is his raiment, wherein shall he *s.?*
Deut. 24. 12. thou shalt not *s.* with his pledge
13. he may *s.* in his own raiment and bless thee
31. 16. thou shalt *s.* with thy fathers, 2 *Sam.* 7. 12.
Judg. 16. 19. and she made him *s.* upon her knees
1 *Sam.* 3. 3. and Samuel was laid down to *s.*
1 *Kings* 1. 21. lord the king shall *s.* with his fathers
Esth. 6. 1. on that night could not the king *s.*
Job 7. 21. for now shall I *s.* in the dust
Psal. 4. 8. I will lay me down in peace and *s.*
13. 3. lighten my eyes, lest I *s.* the sleep of death
121. 4. that keep Israel shall neither slumber nor *s.*
Prov. 4. 16. they *s.* not except have done mischief
6. 9. how long wilt thou *s.* O sluggard?
10. a little folding of the hands to *s.* 24. 33.
Eccl. 5. 12. the *s.* of a labouring man is sweet, but abundance of the rich will not suffer him to *s.*
Cant. 5. 2. I *s.* but my heart waketh, it is the voice
Isa. 5. 27. none shall stumble, none shall slumb. nor *s.*
Jer. 51. 39. they may *s.* a perpetual sleep, 57.
Ezek. 34. 25. and they shall *s.* in the woods
Dan. 12. 2. many that *s.* in the dust shall awake
Mat. 26. 45. *s.* on now, and take rest, *Mark* 14. 41.
Mark 4. 27. and should *s.* and the seed should spring
Luke 22. 46. he said, why *s.* ye? rise and pray
John 11. 12. Lord, if he *s.* he shall do well
1 *Cor.* 11. 30. for this cause many among you *s.*
15. 51. we shall not all *s.* but we shall all be changed
1 *Thess.* 4. 14. them who *s.* in Jesus, will God bring
5. 6. therefore let us not *s.* as do others, but watch
7. for they that *s. s.* in the night
10. who died for us, that whether we wake or *s.*

SLEEPER.

Jon. 1. 6. what meanest thou, O *s.* arise, call on thy G.

SLEEPEST.

Psal. 44. 23. awake, why *s.* thou, O Lord? arise
Prov. 6. 22. when thou *s.* it shall keep thee
Mark 14. 37. Simon, *s.* thou? couldst not watch one
Eph. 5. 14. he saith, awake, thou that *s.* and arise

SLEEPETH.

1 *Kings* 18. 27. Elijah said, peradventure he *s.*
Prov. 10. 5. he that *s.* in harvest is son causeth shame
Hos. 7. 6. their baker *s.* all night, in morning burns
Mat. 9. 24. he said to them, give place, for the maid is not dead but *s. Mark* 5. 39. *Luke* 8. 52.
John. 11. 11. he saith, our friend Lazarus *s*

SLEEPING.

1 *Sam.* 26. 7. behold, Saul lay *s.* within the trench
Isa. 56. 10. watchmen blind, *s.* loving to slumber
Mark 13. 36. lest coming suddenly he find you *s.*
14. 37. he cometh and findeth them *s.* and saith
Acts 12. 6. Peter was *s.* between two soldiers

SLEIGHT.

Eph. 4. 14. and carried about by the *s.* of men

SLENDER.

Lev. 21. † 20. a man too *s.* not come nigh to offer

SLEPT.

Gen. 2. 21. Adam *s.* ‖ 41. 5. Pharaoh *s.* and dreamed
2 *Sam.* 11. 9. Uriah *s.* at door of the king's house
1 *Kings* 3. 20. took my son while thine handmaid *s.*
19. 5. as he lay and *s.* an angel touched him
Job 3. 13. now should I have been quiet and have *s.*
Psal. 3. 5. I laid me down and *s.* I awaked, for L.
76. 5. the stout-hearted have *s.* their sleep
Mat. 13. 25. while men *s.* his enemy sowed tares
25. 5. while bridegroom tarried, they slumb. and *s.*
27. 52. many bodies of saints which *s.* arose
28. 13. his disciples stole him away while we *s.*
1 *Cor.* 15. 20. become the first-fruits of them that *s.*
See FATHERS.

SLEW.

Gen. 4. 25. another seed inst. of Abel, whom Cain *s.*
34. 25. they *s.* all the males ‖ 26. they *s.* Hamor
49. 6. for in their anger they *s.* a man and digged
Exod. 2. 12. Moses *s.* the Egyptian, and hid him
13. 15. the Lord *s.* all the first-born in Egypt
Lev. 8. 15. he *s.* bullock and took the blood, 23.
9. 8. Aaron *s.* the calf of the sin offering, 15.
12. he *s.* the burnt offering, presented the blood
Num. 31. 7. they *s.* all the males of Midian
8. they *s.* kings of Midian, Balaam also they *s.*
Josh. 8. 21. they turned and *s.* the men of Ai
9. 26. delivered the Gibeonites, they *s.* them not
10. 26. Joshua *s.* the five kings and hanged them
Judg. 1. 4. they *s.* of them in Bezek 10,000 men
10. they *s.* Sheshai ‖ 17. they *s.* the Canaanites
3. 29. they *s.* of Moab 10,000 men, all lusty
31. Shamgar *s.* of the Philistines 600 men
7. 25. they *s.* Oreb and Zeeb the two princes
8. 17. he *s.* men of Penuel ‖ 21. *s.* Zebah, Zalmunna
18. what manner of men were they whom ye *s.?*
9. 5. Abimel. *s.* his breth. 70 persons on one stone
14. 19. Samson *s.* thirty men of Ashkelon
15. 15. with the jaw-bone Samson *s.* 1000 men
16. 24. hath delivered our enemy, who *s.* many of us
30. the dead which he *s.* at his death were more
1 *Sam.* 1. 25. Elkanah and Hannah *s.* a bullock
4. 2. the Philistines *s.* of Israel 4000 men
11. 11. Israel *s.* the Ammonites until heat of day
14. 13. and his armour-bearer *s.* after him
32. the people *s.* oxen and calves on the ground
34. every man brought his ox and *s.* them there
17. 36. thy servant *s.* both the lion and the bear
19. 5. put his life in his hand, and *s.* the Philistine
22. 18. Doeg *s.* 85 persons that did wear an ephod
29. 5. of whom they sang, Saul *s.* thousands
30. 2. the Amalekites *s.* not any great or small
31. 2. the Philistines *s.* Jonathan and Abinadab
2 *Sam.* 3. 30. Joab and Abishai his brother *s.* Abner
4. 12. David *s.* them and cut off their hands
8. 5. David *s.* of the Syrians 22,000 men
10. 18. David *s.* the men of 700 chariots of Syrians
21. 1. for Saul, because he *s.* the Gibeonites
23. 20. he *s.* two lion-like men of Moab, he *s.* lion in midst of a pit in time of snow, 1 *Chr.* 11. 22.
21. he *s.* an Egyptian, a goodly man, 1 *Chr.* 11. 23.
1 *Kings* 2. 5. did to Abner and Amasa, whom he *s.*
16. 11. Zimri on the throne *s.* all house of Baasha
18. 13. what I did when Jezebel *s.* prophets of L.
40. they took them, and Elijah *s.* proph. of Baal
2 *Kings* 9. 31. had Zimri peace, who *s.* his master?
10. 9. behold, I *s.* him, but who *s.* all these?
17. he *s.* all that remained to Ahab in Samaria
11. 18. the people *s.* Mattan the priest of Baal
20. they *s.* Athaliah, 2 *Chron.* 23. 15, 17.
14. 5. when kingdom was confirmed Amaziah *s.* servants that had slain his father, 2 *Chron.* 25. 3.
6. but their children he *s.* not, 2 *Chron.* 25. 4.
7. he *s.* of Edom in valley of salt, 1 *Chron.* 18. 12.
16. 9. king of Assyria took Damascus and *s.* Rezin
17. 25. the Lord sent lions which *s.* some of them
21. 23. the servants of Amon conspired and *s.* him
24. people of the land *s.* them, 2 *Chron.* 33. 25.
23. 20. Josiah *s.* all the priests of the high places
25. 7. Nebuchadnezzar *s.* sons of Zedekiah before his eyes, and bound Zedekiah, *Jer.* 39. 6. ‖ 52. 10.
1 *Chron.* 7. 21. whom men of Gath in that land *s.*
2 *Chron.* 21. 4. Jehoram *s.* all his breth. with sword
22. 8. Jehu found, and *s.* the princes of Judah
28. 6. Pekah *s.* in Judah in one day 120,000
Neh. 9. 26. they *s.* thy prophets which testified
Esth. 9. 16. the Jews *s.* of their foes 75,000
Psal. 78. 31. wrath of God *s.* the fattest of them
34. when he *s.* them, then they sought him
105. 29. turned waters into blood, and *s.* their fish
135. 10. who *s.* great kings ‖ 136. 18. *s.* famous kings
Isa. 66. 3. he that killeth an ox is as if he *s.* a man
Jer. 20. 17. because he *s.* me not from the womb
41. 3. Ishmael *s.* all the Jews that were with him
8. he forbare, and *s.* them not among their breth.
Lam. 2. 4. and *s.* all that were pleasant to the eye
Dan. 3. 22. fire *s.* the men that took up Shadrach
5. 19. whom he would he *s.* he kept alive
Mat. 2. 16. Herod sent, and *s.* all the children
22. 6. the remnant took his servants and *s.* them
23. 35. whom ye *s.* between the temple and altar
Luke 13. 4. on whom tower in Siloam fell and *s.*
Acts 5. 30. raised Jesus, whom *s.* and hanged on tree
10. 39. Jesus whom they *s.* and hanged on a tree
Rom. 7. 11. for sin by the commandment *s.* me
1 *John* 3. 12. not as Cain who *s.* his brother

SLEW *him.*

Gen. 4. 8. Cain rose up against Abel and *s. him*
38. 7. Er was wicked, and the Lord *s. him*
10. the thing displeased the Lord, and he *s. him*
Judg. 9. 54. that men say not of me, a woman *s. him*
12. 6. they took and *s. him* at passages of Jordan
1 *Sam.* 17. 35. I caught him by beard and *s. him*
50. David smote the Philistine and *s. him*
2 *Sam.* 1. 10. so I stood upon him and *s. him*
4. 7. they smote Ish-bosheth and *s. him*
10. I took hold of him, and *s. him* in Ziklag
18. 15. ten young men compassed Absal. and *s. him*
21. 21. Jonathan the son of Shimeah *s. him*
2 *Sam.* 23. 21. went down and *s. him* with own spear
1 *Kings* 2. 34. Benaiah fell upon Joab and *s. him*
13. 24. lion met him by th way, and *s. him,* 20. 36.
2 *Kings* 10. 9. I consp. against my master and *s. him*
14. 19. Amaziah fled, but they sent after him to Lachish, and *s. him* there, 2 *Chron.* 25. 27.
15. 10. Shallum conspired against him, and *s. him*
14. Menahim smote Shallum, and *s. him*
30. Hoshea conspired against Pekah and *s. him*
23. 29. Pharaoh-necho *s. him* at Megiddo
1 *Chr.* 10. 14. enquired not of L. therefore *s.* he *him*
2 *Chr.* 22. 11. hid Joash, so that Athaliah *s. him* not
24. 25. his own servants *s. him* on his bed
32. 21. they that came forth of his own bowels *s. h.*
33. 24. his servants *s. him* in his own house
Jer. 26. 23. fetched Urijah to Jehoiakim who *s. him*
41. 2. Ishmael *s. him* whom king made governor
Mat. 21. 39. they cast him out of vineyard and *s. him*
Acts 22. 20. I kept the raiment of them that *s. him*

SLEWEST.

1 *Sam.* 21. 9. the sword of Goliath whom thou *s.*

SLIDE.

Deut. 32. 35. their foot shall *s.* in due time
Psal. 26. 1. I have trusted in the Ld. I shall not *s.*
37. 31. law of God in his heart, none of his steps [shall *s.*

SLIDDEN.

Jer. 8. 5. why then is this people of Jerus. *s.* back?

SLIDETH.

Hos. 4. 16. Israel *s.* back as a backsliding heifer

SLIGHTLY.

Jer. 6. 14. have healed hurt of my people *s.* 8. 11.

SLIME.

Gen. 11. 3. they had brick for stone, *s.* for mortar
Exod. 2. 3. she daubed the ark with *s.* and pitch

SLIME-*pits.*

Gen. 14. 10. the vale of Siddim was full of *s.-pits*

SLING, *Verb.*

Judg. 20. 16. every one could *s.* stones at an hair
1 *Sam.* 25. 29. thine enemies, them shall he *s.* out
Jer. 10. 18. I will *s.* out the inhabitants at once

SLING

Is an instrument of cords, made use of to throw stones with the greater violence. The Hebrews *heretofore made great use of them. Those of the tribe of* Benjamin *had so much skill and dexterity in managing the* sling, *that they could hit their mark to a hair, without the least error. This must be owned to be an hyperbolical expression; however, it proves their great abilities in the management of the* sling, *Judg.* 20. 16. *It is known what glory* David *obtained, when he knocked down by a stroke of his sling the giant* Goliath, *who was the terror of all* Israel, 1 *Sam.* 17. 49. *The Scripture takes notice, that when* David *was at* Ziklag, *there came to him a company of able* slingers, *who could use their left hands with the same facility as their right,* 1 Chron. 12. 2. Uzziah *king of* Judah *made great collections of arms in his magazines, and particularly there were bows and* slings *for casting of stones,* 2 Chron. 26. 14.

1 *Sam.* 17. 40. David had *s.* in his hand, he drew near
50. David prevailed over the Philistine with a *s.*
25. 29. sling enemies as out of the middle of a *s.*
Prov. 26. 8. as he that bindeth stone in a *s.* so is he

SLINGS.

2 *Chron.* 26. 14. Uzziah prepared *s.* to cast stones

SLINGERS.

2 *Kings* 3. 25. the *s.* went about it and smote it

SLING-STONES.

Job 41. 28. *s.* are turned with him into stubble

SLIP.

2 *Sam.* 22. 37. that my feet did not *s. Psal.* 18. 36.
Job 12. 5. he that is ready to *s.* with his feet
Psal. 17. 5. hold up, that my footsteps *s.* not
Jer. 37. † 12. Jeremy went to *s.* away from thence
Heb. 2. 1. lest at any time we should let them *s.*

SLIPPERY.

Psal. 35. 6. let their way be dark and *s.* let angel
73. 18. surely thou didst set them in *s.* places
Jer. 23. 12. their way shall be to them as *s.* ways

SLIPPETH.

Deut. 19. 5. and the head *s.* from the helve
Psal. 38. 16. when my foot *s.* they magnify them
94. 18. when I said, my foot *s.* thy mercy held me

SLIPS.

Isa. 17. 10. therefore thou shalt set it with strange *s.* [up

SLIPT.

1 *Sam.* 19. 10. David *s.* out of Saul's presence
Psal. 73. 2. as for me, my steps had well nigh *s.*

SLOTHFUL.

Judg. 18. 9. be not *s.* to go to possess the land
Prov. 12. 24. but the *s.* shall be under tribute
27. *s.* roasteth not that he took in hunting
15. 19. the way of the *s.* is as a hedge of thorns
18. 9. the *s.* is brother to him that is a great waster
19. 24. the *s.* hideth his hand in his bosom, 26. 15.
21. 25. the desire of *s.* killeth him, refuse to labour
22. 13. the *s.* man saith, there is a lion, 26. 13.
24. 30. I went by field of the *s.* and the vineyard
Mat. 25. 26. his lord said, thou wicked and *s.* serv.
Rom. 12. 11. not *s.* in business, fervent in spirit
Heb. 6. 12. that ye be not *s.* but followers of them

SLOTHFULNESS.

Prov. 19. 15. *s.* casteth into deep sleep, an idle soul
Eccl. 10. 18. by much *s.* the building decayeth

SLOW.

Exod. 4. 10. I am *s.* of speech, and of a *s.* tongue
Neh. 9. 17. but thou art a God *s.* to anger
Prov. 14. 29. is *s.* to wrath, is of great understanding
Luke 24. 25. O fools and *s.* of heart to believe
Tit. 1. 12. the Cretians are liars, *s.* bellies
Jam. 1. 19. every man *s.* to speak, *s.* to wrath
See ANGER.

SLOWLY.

Acts 27. 7. when we had sailed *s.* many days

SLUGGARD.

Prov. 6. 6. go to the ant, thou *s.* consider her ways
9. how long wilt thou sleep, O *s.* when wilt arise
10. 26. as smoke to the eyes, so is the *s.* to them
13. 4. the soul of the *s.* desireth, and hath nothing
20. 4. *s.* will not plow, theref. shall he beg in harv.
26. 16. *s.* is wiser in his own conceit than seven men

SLUICES.
Isa. 19. 10. all that make s. and ponds for fish
SLUMBER, *Substantive.*
Psal. 132. 4. I will not give s. to mine eye-lids
Prov. 6. 4. give not sl. to thine eyes, nor s. to eye-lids
10. yet a little sleep, little s. little folding, 24. 33.
Rom. 11. 8. God hath given them the spirit of s.
SLUMBER.
Psal. 121. 3. he that keepeth thee will not s.
4. he that keepeth Israel, shall neither s. nor sleep
Isa. 5. 27. none shall s. nor sleep among them
56. 10. his watchmen lying down, loving to s.
Nah. 3. 18. thy shepherds s. O king of Assyria
SLUMBERED.
Mat. 25. 5. while the bridegroom tarried they all s.
SLUMBERETH.
2 Pet. 2. 3. lingereth not, and their damnation s. not
SLUMBERINGS.
Job 33. 15. God speaketh in s. upon the bed
SMALL.
Gen. 30. 15. is it a s. matter thou hast taken my hus.
41. † 23. behold, seven ears s. and blasted
Exod. 9. 9. it shall become s. dust in all land of Egypt
16. 14. a s. round thing, as s. as the hoar frost
18. 22. every s. matter they shall judge, 26.
30. 36. thou shalt beat the spices very s.
Lev. 16. 12. his hands full of sweet incense beaten s.
Num. 16. 9. a s. thing that God hath separated you
13. is it a s. thing that thou hast brought us up?
32. 41. Jair went and took the s. towns thereof
Deut. 9. 21. I ground the calf s. even as s. as dust
32. 2. my doctrine shall distil as s. rain, speech as
2 Sam. 7. 19. and this was yet a s. thing in thy sight,
is this the manner of man, O Lord, 1 Chr. 17. 17.
17. 13. till there be not one s. stone found there
22. 43. I beat them as s. as the dust, Psal. 18. 42.
1 Kings 2. 20. I desire one s. petition of thee, say not
19. 12. and after the fire, a still s. voice
2 Kings 19. 26. therefore their inhabitants were of
s. power, they were dismayed, Isa. 37. 27.
23. 6. grove and high place he stampt s. to powd. 15.
2 Chr. 24. 24. the Syrians came with a s. company
35. 8. gave for passover offerings 2600 s. cattle
9. to chief of Levites gave 5000 s. cattle
Job 8. 7. though thy beginning was s. yet thy end
15. 11. are the consolations of God s. with thee?
36. 27. for he maketh s. the drops of water
Psal. 119. 141. I am s. yet do not I forget precepts
Prov. 24. 10. if thou faint in adversity, strength is s.
Isa. 1. 9. except the Lord had left to us a s. remnant
7. 13. is it a s. thing for you to weary men?
16. 14. the remnant shall be very s. and feeble
22. 24. shall hang upon him all vessels of s. quantity
29. 5. moreover, thy strangers shall be like s. dust
40. 15. the nations are counted as the s. dust
41. 15. shalt thresh the mountains, and beat them s.
43. 23. thou hast not brought me the s. cattle
54. 7. for a s. moment have I forsaken thee
60. 22. a s. one shall become a strong nation
Jer. 30. 19. will glorify them, and they shall not be s.
44. 28. yet a s. number shall return out of Egypt
49. 15. I will make thee s. among the heathen
Ezek. 16. 20. is this of thy whoredoms a s. matter?
† 47. but that was lothed as a s. thing
34. 18. seem. it s. to have eaten the good pasture?
Dan. 11. 23. and shall become strong with a s. people
Amos 7. 2. by whom shall Jacob arise? for he is s. 5.
Obad. 2. I have made thee s. among the heathen
Zech. 4. 10. for who hath despised day of s. things?
Mark 8. 7. they had a few s. fishes, and he blessed
John 2. 15. when he had made a scourge of s. cords
6. 9. who hath five barley-loaves and two s. fishes
Acts 12. 18. there was no s. stir among the soldiers
15. 2. Paul and Barnabas had no s. dissension
19. 23. there arose no s. stir about that way
24. Demetrius brought no s. gain to the craftsmen
27. 20. and no s. tempest lay on us
1 Cor. 4. 3. very s. thing that I should be judged of you
Jam. 3. 4. the ships are turned with a very s. helm
See Great.
SMALLEST.
1 Sam. 9. 21. am not I a Benjamite, of s. of tribes?
1 Cor. 6. 2. are ye unworthy to judge the s. matters?
SMART.
Prov. 11. 15. he that is surety for stran. shall s. for it
SMELL.
See *Signification* on Savour.
Gen. 27. 27. Isaac smelled the s. of his raiment, see,
the s. of my son is as s. of a field Lord hath blessed
Cant. 1. 12. my spikenard sendeth forth the s. thereof
2. 13. the vines with the tender grape give a good s.
4. 10. the s. of thy ointment better than all spices
11. the s. of thy garments is like the s. of Lebanon
7. 8. and the s. of thy nose like apples
13. mandrakes give a s. and at our gates all fruits
Isa. 3. 24. instead of sweet s. there shall be stink
Dan. 3. 27. nor the s. of the fire had passed on them
Hos. 14. 6. his beauty as the olive, his s. as Lebanon
Phil. 4. 18. the things sent an odour of sweet s.
SMELL, *Verb.*
Exod. 30. 38. who. shall make like to that to s. thereto
Lev. 26. 31. I will not s. the savour of your odours
Deut. 4. 28. shall serve gods, which neither see nor s.
1 Sam. 26. † 19. if the Lord stirred thee, let him s.
Ps. 45. 8. all thy garm. s. of myrrh, aloes and cassia
115. 6. ears, hear not, noses have they, they s. not
Amos 5. 21. I will not s. in your solemn assemblies
SMELLED.
Gen. 8. 21. L. s. a sweet savour and said in his heart
27. 27. Isaac s. smell of his raiment and blessed him
SMELLETH.
Job 39. 25. he s. the battle afar off and the shouting
SMELLING.
Cant. 5. 5. my fingers with sweet s. myrrh on handles
13. his lips like lilies dropping sweet s. myrrh
Eph. 5. 2. himself sacrifice to God for sweet s. savour
SMELLING.
1 Cor. 12. 17. if whole hearing, where were the s.?
SMITE.
To smite *signifies, to strike or beat,* Mat. 26. 67. Others smote him with the palms of their hands. *Acts* 23. 2. The high-priest commanded to smite Paul on the mouth. *It is often used for* to put to death. David *smote the* Philistine; *he put* Goliath *to death,* 1 Sam. 17. 49. *The Lord smote* Nabal; *he smote* Uzzah; *that is, he put them to death,* 1 Sam. 25. 38. 2 Sam. 6. 7. *And in* Exod. 12. 12. I will smite all the first-born in Egypt. To smite, *is also put for to* afflict; *to strike with fear, with the pestilence, with poverty, with ulcers, with distempers, with wounds,* Num. 14. 12. Deut. 28. 22, 27, 28, 35. To smite an army, *is to beat it, to rout it entirely.* Deut. 29. 7. Sihon and Og came out against us unto battle, and we smote them, *we obtained a victory over them.* God smote the Philistines in the hinder parts, *Psal.* 78. 66. *He sent them the piles, or hemorrhoids, or other diseases of the fundament.* To smite with the tongue, *Jer.* 18. 18. Come, let us smite him with the tongue. *Let us overwhelm him with injuries and reproaches; let us load him with all sorts of scandalous reproaches.*
To smite the thigh, *denotes indignation, trouble, astonishment.* Jer. 31. 19. After I was instructed, I smote upon my thigh. *Being made sensible of my sins, I was brought to a sorrow for them, and detestation of them.* To strike hand against hand, *may either be a token of amazement, sorrow, and trouble; or it may be a token of joy and pleasure in seeing justice executed on obstinate sinners.* Ezek. 21. 14. Prophesy, and smite thine hands together. He shall smite the earth with the rod of his mouth, *Isa.* 11. 4. *He shall destroy ungodly, earthly-minded men, who are enemies to his church and people, by the word of his mouth.* David's heart smote him for having cut off the lappet of Saul's garment; *he had a remorse, his conscience being tender, checked him for it,* 1 Sam. 24. 5.
Gen. 32. 8. if Esau come to one company and s. it
11. I fear him, lest he will come and s. me
Exod. 7. 17. I will s. upon the waters in the river
8. 16. say to Aaron, s. the dust of the land
12. 23. he will not suffer the destroyer to s. you
17. 6. behold, thou shalt s. the rock in Horeb
21. 18. if men strive together, and one s. another
20. if a man s. his serv. and he die under his hand
26. if a man s. the eye of his servant or his maid
27. if he s. out his man servants's or maid's tooth
Num. 22. 6. I shall prevail, that we may s. them
24. 17. a sceptre out of Isr. shall s. corners of Moab
25. 17. vex the Midianites and s. them
35. 16. if he s. him with an instrument of iron
17. and if he s. him with throwing a stone
18. or if he s. him with a hand-weapon of wood
21. or in enmity s. him with his hand that he die
Deut. 7. 2. thou shalt s. Canaanites and destroy them
13. 15. thou shalt surely s. inhabitants of that city
19. 11. if any s. his neighbour mortally that he die
20. 13. thou shalt s. every male thereof with sword
Josh. 7. 3. but let two or three thousand s. Ai
10. 4. come and help me that we may s. Gibeon
19. pursue after, and s. the hindmost of them
12. 6. then did Moses and Israel s. 13. 12.
Judg. 6. 16. thou shalt s. the Midianites as one man
20. 31. then Benj. began to s. as at other times, 39.
21. 10. go and s. the inhabitants of Jabesh-gilead
1 Sam. 15. 3. go and s. Amalek, and spare them not
17. 46. I will s. thee, and take thine head
18. 11. Saul said, I will s. David to the wall
19. 10. Saul sought to s. David to the wall
20. 33. Saul cast a javelin at him to s. him
23. 2. shall I go and s. Philistines? Go s. Philist.
26. 8. therefore let me s. him to the earth at once,
I pray thee, I will not s. the second time
2 Sam. 2. 22. why should I s. thee to the ground?
13. 28. when I say, s. Amnon, then kill him
15. 14. lest he s. city with the edge of the sword
17. 2. people shall flee, and I will s. the king only
18. 11. Joab said, why didst thou not s. him there?
1 Kings 20. 35. he said in the word of the L. s. me,
I pray thee, and the man refused to s. him, 37.
2 Kings 3. 19. shall s. every fenced city, choice city
6. 21. my father, shall I s. them? shall I s. them?
22. thou shalt not s. them, wouldest thou s. those
9. 7. thou shalt s. the house of Ahab thy master
27. Jehu said, s. him also in the chariot
13. 17. shall s. Syrians, till thou have consumed them
18. he said to the king, s. upon the ground
19. whereas now thou shalt s. Syria but thrice
Psal. 121. 6. sun shall not s. thee by day nor moon
141. 5. let righteous s. me, it shall be a kindness
Prov. 19. 25. s. a scorner, the simple will beware
Isa. 10. 24. he shall s. thee with a rod and lift up
49. 10. neither shall the heat nor sun s. them
58. 4. ye fast to s. with the fist of wickedness
Jer. 18. 18. come, let us s. him with the tongue
21. 7. Nebuchadrezzar king of Babyl. shall s. Judah
43. 11. he shall s. the land of Egypt, 46. 13.
49. 28. Kedar, Hazor, Nebuchadrezzar, shall s.
Ezek. 5. 2. take a third part of hair, and s. about it
6. 11. s. with thy hand, and stamp with thy foot
9. 5. go ye after him through the city and s.
21. 12. son of man s. therefore upon thy thigh
14. prophesy, and s. thine hands together
Amos 9. 1. he said s. the lintel of the door
Mic. 5. 1. they shall s. judge of Israel on the cheek
Nah. 2. 10. the heart melteth, the knees s. together
Zech. 10. 11. and shall s. the waves in the sea
11. 6. deliver the men, and they shall s. the land
Mat. 5. 39. whoso shall s. thee on thy right cheek
24. 49. shall begin to s. his fellow-servants to eat
Luke 22. 49. Lord, shall we s. with the sword?
Acts 23. 2. commanded to s. Paul on the mouth
2 Cor. 11. 20. ye suffer, if a man s. you on the face
Rev. 11. 6. two witnesses have power to s. the earth
SMITE, *referred to* God, *expressly or implicitly.*
Gen. 8. 21. nor will I s. any more every living thing
Exod. 3. 20. I will stretch out my hand and s. Egypt
8. 2. behold, I will s. all thy borders with frogs
9. 15. that I may s. thee and thy people with pestil.
12. 12. I will s. all the first-born in land of Egypt
13. will pass over you, when I s. land of Egypt 23.
Num. 14. 12. I will s. them with the pestilence
Deut. 28. 22. L. shall s. with consumption and fever
27. L. shall s. with the botch || 28. s. with madness
35. Lord shall s. thee in the knees and the legs
33. 11. s. thro' the loins of them that rise ag. him
1 Sam. 26. 10. David said, the Lord shall s. him
2 Sam. 5. 24. then bestir thyself, for then shall the
L. go out to s. the Philistines, 1 Chron. 14. 15.
1 Kings 14. 15. L. shall s. Israel as a reed is shaken
2 Kings 6. 18. Elisha said, s. this people with blind.
2 Chr. 21. 14. with a great plague will the Lord s.
Isa. 3. 17. L. will s. with a scab daughters of Zion
11. 4. he shall s. the earth with rod of his mouth
15. and shall s. Egypt in the seven streams, 19. 22.
Jer. 21. 6. I will s. the inhabitants of this city
Ezek. 21. 17. I will also s. mine hands together
32. 15. when I shall s. them that dwell in Egypt
39. 3. I will s. thy bow out of thy left hand
Amos 3. 15. I will s. the winter-house with the summer-house, and the houses of ivory shall perish
6. 11. Lord will s. the great house with breaches
Zech. 9. 4. the Lord will s. her power in the sea
12. 4. in that day I will s. every horse and his rider
13. 7. awake, O sword, s. the shepherd, and sheep
shall be scattered, Mat. 26. 31. Mark 14. 27.
14. 12. plague wherewith L. will s. the people, 18.
Mal. 4. 6. lest I come and s. the earth with a curse
Rev. 19. 15. that with it he should s. the nations
SMITERS.
Isa. 50. 6. I gave my back to the s. and my cheeks
SMITEST.
Exod. 2. 13. he said, wherefore s. thou thy fellow?
John 18. 23. if I have spoken well, why s. thou me?
SMITETH.
Exod. 21. 12. he that s. man so he die, be put to death
15. he s. father and mother, surely put to death
Deut. 25. 11. and wife of one draweth near to deliver
her husband out of hand of him that s. him
27. 24. cursed be he that s. his neighbour secretly
Josh. 15. 16. he that s. Kirjath-sepher, Judg. 1. 12.
2 Sam. 5. 8. that s. the Jebusites, 1 Chron. 11. 6.
Job 26. 12. by understanding he s. thro' the proud
Isa. 9. 13. the people turn not to him that s. them
Lam. 3. 30. he giveth his cheek to him that s. him
Ezek. 7. 9. ye shall know that I am the Lord that s.
Luke 6. 29. that s. thee on one cheek, turn the other
SMITH.
1 Sam. 13. 19. there was no s. found in land of Isr.
Isa. 44. 12. the s. with tongs worketh in the coals
54. 16. I have created the s. that bloweth the coals
Acts 19. 24. certain man named Demetrius, silver s.
2 Tim. 4. 14. Alexander copper s. did me much evil
SMITHS.
2 Kings 24. 14. Nebuchadnezzar carried away all
the princes, the craftsmen and s. 16. Jer. 24. 1.
Jer. 29. 2. after the s. were departed from Jerusal.
SMITING.
Exod. 2. 11. Moses spied an Egyptian s. an Hebrew
2 Sam. 8. 13. when he returned from s. the Syrians
1 Kings 20. 37. smote him, so that in s. wounded him
2 Kings 3. 24. they went forward s. the Moabites
Mic. 6. 13. therefore I will make thee sick in s. thee
SMITTEN.
Exod. 7. 25. seven days after the L. had s. the river
9. 31. and the flax and the barley was s.
32. but the wheat and the rye were not s.
22. 2. if a thief be found, and be s. that he die
Num. 14. 42. go not up, that ye be not s. Deut. 1. 42.
22. 28. what have I done to thee that thou hast s. me?
32. wheref. hast thou s. thine ass these three times?
33. 4. Egyptians buried their first-born Lord had s.
Deut. 28. 7. Lord shall cause thine enemies to be s.
25. L. shall cause thee be s. before thine enemies
Judg. 1. 8. Judah had s. Jerusal. and set it on fire
20. 32. Benjam. said, they are s. bef. us as at first
36. saw they were s. || 39. surely they are s. down
1 Sam. 4. 2. Isr. was s. before the Philistines? 10.
3. why hath Lord s. us to-day before Philistines?
5. 12. the men that died not, were s. with emerods
6. 19. people lamented because Lord had s. many
7. 10. the Philistines were s. before Israel
13. 4. Saul had s. a garrison of the Philistines
30. 1. Amalek had s. Ziklag, and burnt it with fire
2 Sam. 2. 31. David's serv. had s. of Abner's men
8. 9. when Toi heard that David had s. the host of
Hadadezer, he sent to Dav. 10. 1 Chr. 18. 9, 10.
10. 15. when the Syrians saw that they were s. 19.
11. 15. retire ye from him, that he may be s. and die
1 Kings 8. 33. when thy people Israel be s. down
11. 15. after he had s. every male in Edom
2 Kings 2. 14. and when he also had s. the waters
3. 23. the kings have surely s. one another
13. 19. thou shouldest have s. five or six times, then
hadst thou s. Syria till thou hadst consumed it
14. 10. thou hast indeed s. Edom, 2 Chron. 25. 19.
2 Chron. 20. 22. Moab and mount Seir were s.
25. 16. forbear, why shouldest thou be s.?
26. 20. Uzziah hasted, because the L. hath s. him
28. 17. the Edomites had come and s. Judah
Job 16. 10. they have s. me upon the cheek
Ps. 3. 7. save me, for thou hast s. all mine enemies
69. 26. they persecute him whom thou hast s.
102. 4. my heart is s. and withered like grass
143. 3. he hath s. my life down to the ground
Isa. 5. 25. therefore the Lord hath s. his people
24. 12. and the gate is s. with destruction
27. 7. hath he s. him, as he smote those smote him?
53. 4. yet we did esteem him stricken, s. of God
Jer. 2. 30. in vain have I s. your children
14. 19. why hast thou s. us, and there is no healing
37. 10. for tho' ye had s. whole army of Chaldeans
Ezek. 22. 13. I have s. my hand at thy dishonest gain
33. 21. one came to me, saying, the city is s.
40. 1. in the fourteenth year after the city was s.
Hos. 6. 1. he hath s. and he will bind us up
9. 16. Ephraim is s. their root is dried up
Amos 4. 9. I have s. you, yet have not returned to me
Acts 23. 3. and commanded me to be s. against law?
Rev. 8. 12. and the third part of the sun was s.
SMOKE
Is *the black exhalation which ascends from fire*
Gen. 19. 28. The smoke of the city went up as

the smoke of a furnace. Solomon *observes, that as smoke is hurtful and offensive to the eyes, so is a sluggish messenger unserviceable and vexatious to them that send him,* Prov. 10. 26. *The anger and wrath of God are signified by* smoke. *Psal.* 18. 8. There went up a smoke out of his nostrils; *God manifested his great displeasure against my adversaries. It is spoken after the manner of men; it being usual for persons transported with great anger to show their rage by their breathing.* Smoke *denotes a grievous judgment or calamity; either because smoke is generally accompanied with fire, or because it causeth a great darkness in the air. Isa.* 14. 31. There shall come from the north a smoke. To create a cloud and smoke upon Mount Zion, *denotes that God would not only direct his people, as he did the* Israelites *by a pillar of cloud, but that he would also be their protector and their glory,* Isa. 4. 5.

The smoking flax shall he not quench, *Isa.* 42. 3. *Mat.* 12. 20. *Christ will not deal roughly and rigorously with those that come to him, but will use all gentleness and kindness to them, passing by their greatest sins, bearing with their present infirmities, cherishing and encouraging the smallest beginnings of grace; and comforting and healing wounded consciences. In the* Revelation, *the perpetuity and eternity of the torments of the damned, is thus expressed,* The smoke of their torment ascendeth up for ever and ever, *Rev.* 14. 11.

Gen. 19. 28. Abraham looked toward Sodom, and lo, the smoke of the country went up as *s.* of a furnace
Exod. 19. 18. Mount Sinai was altogether on a *s.*
Josh. 8. 20. the *s.* of Ai ascended up to heaven, 21.
Judg. 20. 38. they should make *s.* rise out of city
40. when pillar of *s.* began to rise out of the city
2 *Sam.* 22. 9. there went up a *s.* out of his nostrils, and fire out of his mouth devoured, *Psal.* 18. 8.
Job 41. 20. out of his nostrils goeth *s.* as caldron
Psal. 37. 20. the wicked shall consume into *s.*
68. 2. as *s.* is driven away, so drive them away
102. 3. my days are consumed like *s.* and bones
119. 83. for I am become like a bottle in the *s.*
Prov. 10. 26. as *s.* to eyes, so is a sluggard to them
Cant. 3. 6. that cometh out of wild. like pillars of *s.*
Isa. 4. 5. L. will create on her assemblies *s.* by day
6. 4. the posts moved, the house was filled with *s.*
9. 18. they shall mount up like the lifting up of *s.*
14. 31. for there shall come from the north a *s.*
34. 10. the *s.* thereof shall go up for ever
51. 6. for the heavens shall vanish away like *s.*
65. 5. these are a *s.* in my nose, a fire that burneth
Hos. 13. 3. they shall be as the *s.* out of chimney
Joel 2. 30. in earth blood, and fire, and pillars of *s.*
Nah. 2. 13. I will burn her chariots in the *s.*
Acts 2. 19. blood, fire, and vapour of *s.* shew wond.
Rev. 8. 4. *s.* of the incense ascended up before God
9. 2. there arose a *s.* out of the bottomless pit
3. there came out of the *s.* locusts on earth
17. out of their mouths issued fire and *s.*
18. the third part of men killed by the fire and *s.*
14. 11. the *s.* of their torment ascended up for ever
15. 8. temple was filled with *s.* from glory of God
18. 9. kings shall lament for her when they see *s.*
18. cried when they saw the *s.* of her burning
19. 3. and her *s.* rose up for ever and ever

SMOKE.

Deut. 29. 20. anger of Ld. shall *s.* against that man
Psal. 74. 1. O God, why doth thine anger *s.?*
104. 32. he toucheth the hills, and they *s.*
144. 5. touch the mountains, and they shall *s.*

SMOKING.

Gen. 15. 17. when it was dark, behold, a *s.* furnace
Exod. 20. 18. all the people saw the mountain *s.*
Isa. 7. 4. for the two tails of these *s.* firebrands
42. 3. the *s.* flax shall he not quench, *Mat.* 12. 20.

SMOOTH.

Gen. 27. 11. Esau is a hairy man, and I am *s.* man
16. she put the skins of kids on the *s.* of his neck
1 *Sam.* 17. 40. David chose him five *s.* stones
Isa. 30. 10. who say, speak unto us *s.* things
57. 6. among *s.* stones of the stream is thy portion
Luke 3. 5. and the rough ways shall be made *s.*

SMOOTH.

Jer. 23. † 31. I am ag. prophets that *s.* their tongues

SMOOTHER.

Psal. 55. 21. words of his mouth were *s.* than butter
Prov. 5. 3. and her mouth is *s.* than oil

SMOOTHETH.

Isa. 41. 7. he that *s.* with hammer him that smote

SMOTE.

Gen. 19. 11. they *s.* the men at door with blindness
36. 35. *s.* Midian in field of Moab, 1 *Chron.* 1. 46.
Exod. 7. 20. he lift up the rod, and *s.* the waters
8. 17. he *s.* the dust ‖ 9. 25. the hail *s.* every herb
12. 27. who passed over when he *s.* the Egyptians
29. the Ld. *s.* all the first born in land of Egypt
Num. 3. 13. | 8. 17. *Ps.* 78. 51. | 105. 36. | 135. 8.
Num. 11. 33. Ld. *s.* the people with a great plague
14. 45. the Amalekites came down and *s.* them
20. 11. Moses *s.* the rock twice, *Psal.* 78. 20.
22. 23. Balaam *s.* the ass to turn her, 25. 27.
24. 10. Balak *s.* his hands together, and said
32. 4. the country the Lord *s.* is a land for cattle
Deut. 25. 18. Amalek *s.* the hindmost of thee
29. 7. Sihon and Og came ag. us, and we *s.* them
Josh. 7. 5. the men of Ai *s.* of them about 36 men
9. 18. *s.* them not, because the princes had sworn
11. 11. they *s.* all the souls that were therein
12. and *s.* all the kings with the sword, 17.
20. 5. because he *s.* his neighbour unwittingly
Judg. 4. 21. Jael *s.* the nail into Sisera's temples
5. 26. with hammer she *s.* Sisera, she *s.* off his head
7. 13. came unto a tent, and *s.* it that it fell
15. 8. Samson *s.* them hip and thigh with slaughter
20. 35. the Lord *s.* Benjamin before Israel
1 *Sam.* 4. 8. these are the gods that *s.* the Egyptians
6. 9. we shall know it is not his hand that *s.* us
19. he *s.* the men of Beth shemesh, *s.* the people
17. 49. David *s.* the Philistine in his forehead
19. 10. Saul *s.* the javelin into the wall: Dav. fled
25. 38. that the Lord *s.* Nabal that he died

1 *Sam.* 30. 17. Da. *s.* them from twilight to next day
2 *Sam.* 14. 7. deliver him that *s.* his brother
1 *Kings* 22. 24. Zedekiah *s.* Micaiah, 2 *Chr.* 18. 23.
2 *Kings* 2. 8. Elijah *s.* waters ‖ 14. Elisha *s.* waters
6. 18. and he *s.* them with blindness
15. 5. the Lord *s.* the king, so that he was a leper
16. opened not to Menahem, therefore he *s.* it
19. 35. angel of the Lord *s.* 185,000, *Isa.* 37. 36.
2 *Chron.* 13. 15. God *s.* Jeroboam and all Israel
14. 12. the Lord *s.* the Ethiopians before Asa
Neh. 13. 25. and cursed them, and *s.* certain of them
Psal. 78. 31. and *s.* down the chosen men of Israel
66. he *s.* his enemies in the hinder parts
Cant. 5. 7. the watchmen found me, they *s.* me
Isa. 10. 20. shall no more stay on him that *s.* them
14. 6. he who *s.* the people is persecuted
29. because the rod of him that *s.* thee is broken
30. 31. the Assyrian shall be beaten down which *s.*
41. 7. encouraged him that *s.* the anvil
60. 10. in my wrath I *s.* thee, but in my favour
Jer. 20. 2. then Pashur *s.* Jeremiah the prophet
31. 19. after I was instructed I *s.* upon my thigh
41. 2. then arose Ishmael and *s.* Gedaliah
46. 2. Pharaoh necho, which Nebuchadrezzar *s.*
Dan. 2. 34. a stone cut out, which *s.* the image, 35.
5. 6. Belshazzar's knees *s.* one against another
8. 7. the he-goat moved with choler *s.* the ram
Jonah 4. 7. a worm *s.* the gourd, that it withered
Hag. 2. 17. I *s.* you with blasting and mildew
Mat. 26. 51. Peter drew his sword, *s.* off his ear
68. prophesy, who is he that *s.* thee, *Luke* 22. 64.
Luke 18. 13. but the publican *s.* upon his breast
23. 48. many beholding Jesus, *s.* their breasts
Acts 12. 7. angel *s.* Peter on side and raised him up

SMOTE *him.*

Exod. 21. 19. then shall he that *s. him* be quit
Num. 35. 21. he that *s. him* shall surely die
1 *Sam.* 24. 5. afterwards David's heart *s. him*
2 *Sam.* 2. 23. *s. him* under the fifth rib, 3. 27. | 4. 6.
6. 7. God *s. him* there for his error, 1 *Chr.* 13. 10.
1 *Kings* 20. 37. man *s. him,* so that he wounded him
2 *Kings* 19. 37. his sons *s. him* with sword, *Isa.* 37. 38.
2 *Chron.* 28. 5. Syria *s. him,* king of Israel *s. him*
Isa. 27. 7. hath he smitt. as he smote those that *s. him*
57. 17. for the iniquity of his covetousness I *s. him*
Jer. 37. 15. princes were wroth with Jer. and *s. him*
Mat. 26. 67. others *s. him* with palms of their hands
27. 30. they took the reed and *s. him* on the head,
Mark 15. 19. *Luke* 22. 63. *John* 19. 3.
Acts 12. 23. immediately angel of the Lord *s. him*

SMOTEST.

Exod. 17. 5. take rod wherewith thou *s.* the river

SNAIL.

Lev. 11. 30. the lizard, the *s.* and mole are unclean
Psal. 58. 8. as a *s.* let every one of them pass away

SNARE.

Exod. 10. 7. how long shall this man be *s.* unto us?
23. 33. for if thou serve their gods, it will surely be a *s.* unto thee, *Deut.* 7. 16. *Judg.* 2. 3.
34. 12. make no covenant with the inhabitants of the land, lest it be a *s.* in midst of thee
Judg. 8. 27. which thing became a *s.* unto Gideon
1 *Sam.* 18. 21. will give him her, that she may be a *s.*
28. 9. wherefore then layest thou a *s.* for my life?
Job 18. 8. he is cast into a net, he walketh on a *s.*
10. the *s.* is laid for him in the ground and a trap
Psal. 69. 22. let their table become a *s.* unto them, and that for their welfare a trap, *Rom.* 11. 9.
91. 3. he shall deliver thee from *s.* of the fowler
106. 36. served their idols, which were *s.* to them
119. 110. wicked have laid *s.* for me, yet erred not
124. 7. our soul is escaped as a bird out of the *s.* of the fowler; the *s.* is broken and we are escaped
140. 5. proud have hid a *s.* for me, spread a net
141. 9. keep me from the *s.* which they have laid
142. 3. in the way have they privily laid *s.* for me
Prov. 7. 23. as a bird hasteth to *s.* and knoweth not
18. 7. a fool's lips are the *s.* of his soul
20. 25. *s.* to man who devoureth that which is holy
22. 25. lest learn his ways, and get a *s.* to thy soul
29. 6. in the transgression of an evil man is a *s.*
8. scornful men bring a city into *s.* but wise men
25. the fear of man bringeth a *s.* whoso put. trust
Eccl. 9. 12. as the birds that are caught in the *s.*
Isa. 8. 14. for a *s.* to the inhabitants of Jerusalem
24. 17. fear, and the pit, and the *s.* are upon thee, O inhabitant of the earth, 18. *Jer.* 48. 43, 44.
29. 21. that lay a *s.* for him that reproveth in gate
Jer. 50. 24. I have laid a *s.* for thee, O Babylon
Lam. 3. 47. fear and a *s.* is come upon us
Ezek. 12. 13. he shall be taken in my *s.* 17. 20.
Hos. 5. 1. because ye have been a *s.* on Mizpah
9. 8. but the prophet is a *s.* of a fowler in his ways
Amos 3. 5. can a bird fall in a *s.* upon the earth where no gin is for him? shall one take up a *s.?*
Luke 21. 35. for as a *s.* shall it come on all that dwell
1 *Cor.* 7. 35. not that I may cast a *s.* upon you
1 *Tim.* 3. 7. lest he fall into the *s.* of the devil
6. 9. they that will be rich, fall into a *s.* and lusts
2 *Tim.* 2. 26. they may recover out of *s.* of the devil

SNARED.

Deut. 7. 25. not take the silver of idols, lest *s.* therein
12. 30. take heed that thou be not *s.* by them
Psal. 9. 16. wicked is *s.* in work of his own hands
Prov. 6. 2. art *s.* with words of thy mouth, 12. 13.
Eccl. 9. 12. so are the sons of men *s.* in an evil time
Isa. 8. 15. many shall stumble and fall and be *s.*
28. 13. that they might fall, and be *s.* and taken
42. 22. they are all of them *s.* in holes, hid in prison

SNARES.

Josh. 23. 13. they shall be *s.* and traps unto you
2 *Sam.* 22. 6. *s.* of death prevented me, *Psal.* 18. 5.
Job 22. 10. therefore *s.* are round about thee
40. 24. behemoth's nose pierceth thro' *s.*
Psal. 11. 6. on wicked he shall rain *s.* and brims.
38. 12. they that seek after my life lay *s.* for me
64. 5. they commune of laying *s.* privily
Prov. 13. 14. to depart from the *s.* of death, 14. 27.
22. 5. thorns and *s.* are in the way of the froward
Eccl. 7. 26. the woman whose heart is *s.* and nets
Jer. 5. 26. they lay wait as he that setteth *s.*
18. 22. for they have digged and hid *s.* for my feet

SNATCH.

Isa. 9. 20. he shall *s.* on right hand and be hungry

SNORTING.

Jer. 8. 16. the *s.* of his horses was heard from Dan

SNOUT.

Prov. 11. 22. as a jewel of gold in a swine's *s.* so fair

SNOW.

Exod. 4. 6. behold his hand was leprous as *s.*
Num. 12. 10. Miriam became leprous, white as *s.*
2 *Sam.* 23. 20. slew lion in midst of a pit, in time of *s.*
2 *Kings* 5. 27. Gehazi went out a leper white as *s.*
Job 6. 16. are blackish, and wherein the *s.* is hid
9. 30. if I wash mys. in *s.* wat. and make hands clean
24. 19. heat consumeth *s.* waters, so grave sinned
37. 6. he saith to the *s.* be thou on the earth
38. 22. hast thou entered into treasures of the *s.*
Psal. 51. 7. wash me, and I shall be whiter than *s.*
68. 14. it was white as *s.* in Salmon
147. 16. he giv. *s.* like wool, scattereth hoar frost
148. 8. fire, hail, *s.* and vapour fulfilling his word
Prov. 25. 13. as the cold of *s.* in time of harvest
26. 1. as *s.* in summer, so honour is not seemly
31. 21. she is not afraid of the *s.* for her household
Isa. 1. 18. tho' sins be as scarlet shall be white as *s.*
55. 10. as the *s.* from heaven returneth not thither
Jer. 18. 14. will a man leave the *s.* of Lebanon
Lam. 4. 7. her Nazar. purer than *s.* whiter than milk
Dan. 7. 9. garment was white as *s.* hair like wool
Mat. 28. 3. his raiment white as *s.* *Mark* 9. 3.
Rev. 1. 14. his head and his hairs as white as *s.*

SNOWY.

1 *Chron.* 11. 22. he slew a lion in a pit in a *s.* day

SNUFFED.

Jer. 14. 6. the wild asses *s.* up the wind like dragons
Mal. 1. 13. ye have *s.* at it, saith the Lord of hosts

SNUFF-*dishes.*

Exod. 25. 38. *s.-dishes* shall be of pure gold, 37. 23.
Num. 4. 9. take a cloth, and cover his *s.-dishes*

SNUFFERS.

Exod. 37. 23. *s.* of pure gold, 1 *Kings* 7. 50. 2 *Chr.* 4. 22.
2 *Kings* 12. 13. *s.* made of money that was brought
25. 14. pots and *s.* took they away, *Jer.* 52. 18.

SNUFFETH.

Jer. 2. 24. a wild ass that *s.* up the wind at pleasure

SO.

Gen. 12. 4. *so* Abraham departed, as L. had spoken
15. 5. as the stars, *so* shall thy seed be, *Rom.* 4. 18.
25. 22. Rebekah said, if it be *so,* why am I thus
31. 28. thou hast now done foolishly in *so* doing
43. 11. if it must be *so* now do this, take fruits
Exod. 6. 9. Moses spake *so* to the children of Israel
10. 10. let Lord be *so* with you, as I will let you go
25. 9. after the pattern, even *so* shall ye make it
39. 43. as the L. commanded, *so* had they done it
Lev. 7. 7. as the sin offering, *so* is trespass offering
8. 35. for *so* I am commanded, 10. 13.
24. 19. as he hath done, *so* shall be done to him, 20.
Num. 4. 26. bear all that is made, *so* shall they serve
15. 15. as ye are, *so* shall the stranger be before L.
25. 8. *so* the plague was stayed, *Psal.* 106. 30.
Deut. 7. 19. *so* shall the Lord do to all the nations
8. 20. as nations Lord destroyeth, *so* shall ye perish
17. 7. *so* thou shalt put the evil away from among you, 19. 19. | 21. 21. | 22. 21, 22, 24.
22. 26. for as when man riseth, even *so* is this matt.
33. 25. and as thy days, *so* shall thy strength be
Josh. 14. 11. as strength then, even *so* is strength now
Judg. 1. 7. as I have done, *so* God hath requited me
5. 31. *so* let all thine enemies perish, O Lord
8. 18. they answered, as thou art, *so* were they
21. for as the man is, *so* is his strength
15. 11. as they did to me, *so* have I done to them
1 *Sam.* 9. 21. wherefore then speakest thou *so* to me?
11. 7. *so* shall it be done unto his oxen
15. 33. *so* shall thy mother be childl. among women
19. 17. Saul said, why hast thou deceived me *so*
25. 25. as his name is, *so* is he, Nabal is his name
30. 24. *so* shall his part be that tarrieth by the stuff
2 *Sam.* 7. 8. *so* shalt thou say to my servant David
13. 35. king's sons come, as thy servants said, *so* it is
16. 10. *so* let him curse. Who shall then say, wherefore hast thou done *so?* 1 *Kings* 1. 6.
22. 4. *so* shall I be saved from my enemies, *Ps.* 18. 3.
24. 25. *so* the Lord was entreated for the land
1 *Kings* 1. 30. even *so* will I certainly do this day
36. the Lord God of my lord the king say *so* too
20. 40. the king said, *so* shall thy judgment be
22. 8. he said, let not king say *so,* 2 *Chron.* 18. 7.
2 *Kings* 7. 20. *so* it fell out to him, peo. trode on him
2 *Chr.* 20. 20. *so* be established, *so* shall ye prosper
35. 6. *so* kill the passover and sanctify yourselves
Ezra 4. 24. *so* it ceased to the second year of Darius
Neh. 2. 4. *so* I prayed ‖ 5. 13. *so* God shake out
8. 17. to that day had not children of Israel done *so*
9. 10. *so* didst thou get thee a name, as it is this day
Esth. 4. 16. and so will I go in unto the king
Job 5. 27. *so* it is, hear it ‖ 21. 4. and if it were *so*
9. 2. I know it is *so* of truth, but how should man be
23. 7. *so* should I be deliv. for ever from my judge
32. 22. in *so* doing, my maker would take me away
Psal. 21. 13. *so* will we sing and praise thy power
35. 25. let them not say, *so* would we have it
37. 3. do good, *so* shalt thou dwell in the land
42. 1. *so* panteth my soul after thee, O God
45. 11. *so* shall the King desire thy beauty
48. 8. as we have heard, *so* have we seen in the city
10. *so* is thy praise to the ends of the earth
63. 2. to see thy glory, *so* as seen thee in sanctuary
73. 22. *so* foolish was I, and ignorant, as a beast
78. 72. *so* he fed them ‖ 79. 13. *so* we thy people
80. 18. *so* will not we go back from thee, quicken
81. 12. *so* I gave them up ‖ 90. 11. *so* is thy wrath
103. 13. *so* the Lord pitieth them that fear him
109. 17. *so* let it come, so let it be far from him
115. 8. *so* is every one that trusteth in them, 135. 18.
147. 20. he hath not dealt *so* with any nation
Prov. 3. 4. *so* shall find favour and good understand.
22. *so* shall they be life to thy soul, grace to neck
6. 11. *so* shall thy poverty come, 24. 34.
10. 25. as the whirlwind, *so* is the wicked no more
23. 7. as he thinketh in his heart, *so* is he
Eccl. 3. 19. as the one dieth, *so* dieth the other

Eccl. 5. 16. that in all points as he came, *so* sh. he go
9. 2. as is the good, *so* is sinner, he that sweareth
Isa. 14. 24. *so* shall it come to pass, *so* shall it stand
18. 4. for *so* Lord said to me, I will take my rest
24. 2. as with the people, *so* with the priest
26. 17. *so* have we been in thy sight, O Lord
36. 6. *so* is Phar. king of Egypt to all trust in him
47. 12. wherein thou hast laboured, if *so* be thou shalt be able to profit; if *so* thou mayest prevail
53. 7. as a lamb, *so* he openeth not his mouth
62. 5. *so* shall thy sons; *so* shall G. rejoice over thee
63. 8. they are my people, *so* he was their Saviour
66. 13. *so* will I comfort you, ye shall be comforted
22. saith L. *so* shall your seed and name remain
Jer. 5. 31. and my people love to have it *so*
10. 18. will distress them, that they may find it *so*
11. 4. *so* shall be my people, I your G. *Ezek.* 37. 23.
19. 11. saith L. *so* will I break this people and city
35. 11. come, let us go, *so* we dwell at Jerusalem
38. 20. obey the Lord, *so* shall it be well unto thee
39. 14. *so* he dwelt among the people
42. 17. *so* shall be with all men that set their faces
Lam. 3. 29. mouth in dust, if *so* be there may be hope
Ezek. 12. 11. as I have done, *so* shall be done to them
16. 44. saying, as is the mother, *so* is the daughter
18. 30. repent, *so* iniquity shall not be your ruin
28. 14. cherub that covereth, I have set thee *so*
45. 20. *so* thou shalt do, *so* shall ye reconcile house
Dan. 3. 17. if it be *so*, our God is able to deliver us
Hos. 3. 3. shalt abide for me, *so* will I be for thee
13. 6. *so* were they filled || *Joel* 2. 4. *so* shall they run
Amos 5. 14. *so* the Lord of hosts shall be with you
Zeph. 3. 7. *so* their dwelling should not be cut off
Hag. 2. 5. *so* my Sp. remaineth among you, fear not
14. *so* is this people, *so* is this nation before me
Zech. 1. 6. to our doings, *so* hath he dealt with us
8. 13. *so* will I save you, and ye shall be a blessing
14. 15. *so* shall be plague of horse, as this plague
Mat. 3. 15. Jes. said, Suffer it to be *so* now, it becom.
5. 12. for *so* persecuted they prophets before you
16. let your light *so* shine || 19. shall teach men *so*
6. 30. if God *so* clothe the grass of the field
8. 13. as thou hast believed, *so* be it done unto thee
9. 33. marvelled, saying it was never *so* seen in Isr.
11. 26. even *so*, Fath. for *so* it seemed, *Luke* 10. 21.
12. 40. *so* shall Son of man be, *Luke* 11. 30. | 17. 24.
19. 10. if the case of the man be *so* with his wife
24. 46. when cometh shall find *so* doing, *Luke* 12. 43.
Mark 7. 18. are ye *so* without understanding also?
10. 43. but *so* shall it not be among you
Luke 12. 38. if he come in watch and find them *so*
54. and *so* it is || 24. 24. found it *so* as women said
John 3. 16. God *so* loved the world that he gave his
12. 50. even as the Father said to me, *so* I speak
13. 13. ye say well, for *so* I am || 14. 31. *so* I do
15. 8. ye bear much fruit, *so* shall be my disciples
9. as Father hath loved me, *so* have I loved you
17. 18. *so* have I also sent them into world, 20. 21.
18. 22. saying, Answerest thou the high priest *so?*
Acts 1. 11. this Jesus shall *so* come in like manner
3. 18. he hath *so* fulfilled || 7. 1. are these things *so?*
8. 32. as a lamb dumb, *so* opened he not his mouth
13. 47. for *so* hath the Lord commanded us
14. 1. they *so* spake, that a great multitude believed
16. 5. *so* were the churches established in the faith
19. 20. *so* mightily grew word of God and prevailed
20. 13. for *so* had appointed, minding to go a-foot
24. 14. *so* worship I the God of my fathers
27. 44. *so* came to pass they escaped all safe to land
Rom. 5. 15. but not as the offence, *so* also is free gift
8. 8. *so* they that are in the flesh cannot please God
9. 16. *so* then it is not of him that willeth nor run.
11. 26. *so* all Israel shall be saved, as it is written
12. 20. *so* doing shalt heap coals of fire on his head
14. 12. *so* every one shall give account to God
1 *Cor.* 3. 15. he hims. shall be saved, yet *so* as by fire
4. 1. let man *so* account of us, as ministers of Chr.
5. 3. concerning him that hath *so* done this deed
6. 5. is it *so* that there is not wise man among you?
7. 17. *so* let him walk, *so* ordain I in all churches
26. I say that it is good for a man *so* to be
40. but she is happier if she *so* abide, my judgm.
8. 12. when ye sin *so* against the brethren
9. 14. even *so* hath Lord ordained to live by gospel
24. *so* run, 26. || 11. 28. *so* let him eat that bread
12. 12. all members are one body, *so* also is Christ
15. 11. *so* we preach, and *so* ye believed
2 *Cor.* 10. 7. as he is Christ's, *so* are we Christ's
11. 9. *so* will I keep mys. from being burdensome
22. are they Hebrews? *so* am I; Israelites? *so* am I
12. 16. but be it *so*, I did not burden you
Gal. 4. 29. but as then persecuted, even *so* it is now
6. 2. bear burdens, and *so* fulfil the law of Christ
Eph. 2. 15. of twain, one new man, *so* making peace
Phil. 3. 17. brethren, mark them which walk *so*
4. 1. my brethren, *so* stand fast in the Lord
Col. 2. 6. as ye receive Christ Jes. *so* walk ye in him
1 *Thess.* 2. 4. even *so* we speak, not as pleasing men
4. 17. and *so* shall we ever be with the Lord
Heb. 3. 11. *so* I sware in my wrath, shall not enter
7. 9. as I may *so* say, Levi paid tithes in Abraham
1 *Pet.* 1. 15. *so* be ye holy || 2. 15. *so* is the will of G.
3. 17. it is better, if the will of God be *so*, to suffer
1 *John* 2. 6. he ought hims. *so* to walk as he walked
4. 11. G. *so* loved us, we ought to love one another
17. because as he is, *so* are we in this world
Rev. 1. 7. even *so* amen || 22. 20. even *so* come, L. Jes.

SO *be it.*

Josh. 2. 21. Rahab said, accor. to your words, *so be it*
Jer. 11. 5. I answered and said, *so be it*, O Lord
See DID, DIED, DO, GREAT, LONG, MUCH.

Not SO.

Gen. 19. 7. do *not so* wickedly || 18. oh *not so*, my L.
29. 26. it must *not* be *so* done in our country
48. 18. *not so* my father, this is the first-born
Exod. 10. 11. *not so*, go ye that are men and serve L.
Num. 12. 7. servant Moses is *not so*, who is faithful
Judg. 2. 17. obeying the Lord, but they did *not so*
14. 15. is it *not so?* || 1 *Sam.* 20. 2. it is *not so*
2 *Sam.* 20. 21. the matter is *n. so*, but a man lift. up
23. 5. altho' my house be *not so* with God, yet hath
Job 9. 35. and not fear him, but it is *not so* with me
Job 24. 25. if it be *not so*, who will make me a liar
35. 15. but now because it is *not so* he hath visited
Psal. 1. 4. ungodly are *not so*, but are like the chaff
Prov. 15. 7. the heart of the foolish doeth *not so*
Isa. 10. 7. howbeit meaneth *not so*, nor heart think so
16. 6. the pride of Moab, but his lies shall *not* be *so*
Jer. 48. 30. *not* be *so*, his lies shall *not so* effect it
Mat. 19. 8. but from the beginning it was *not so*
20. 26. but it shall *not* be *so* am. you, who will be
25. 9. *not so*, lest there be not enough for us
Luke 1. 60. *not so*, but he shall be called John
22. 26. exerc. lordship over them, but shall *n.* be *so*
John 14. 2. if it were *not so*, I would have told you
Acts 10. 14. but Peter said, *not so*, Lord, 11. 8.
Rom. 5. 3. *not* only *so*, but we glory in tribulations
11. *not* only *so*, but we also joy in God thro' Jesus
Eph. 4. 20. but ye have *not so* learned Christ
Jam. 3. 10. these things ought *not so* to be

SO *that.*

Gen. 21. 6. *so that* all that hear will laugh with me
28. 21. *so that* I come again to my father's house
47. 13. *so that* land of Egypt and Canaan fainted
Exod. 10. 20. *so that* he would not let Isr. go, 11. 10.
21. 12. he that smiteth a man, *so that* he die
Deut. 28. 34. *s. t.* thou shalt be mad for sight of eyes
Judg. 2. 14. *so that* they could not longer stand
1 *Sam.* 4. 5. shouted, *so that* the earth rang again
18. 30. *so that* his name was much set by
1 *Kings* 8. 25. *s. t.* thy child. take heed, 2 *Chron.* 6. 16.
2 *Kings* 8. 15. spread it on his face, *so that* he died
9. 37. *so that* they shall not say, this is Jezebel
18. 5. *so that* after him was none like him of kings
Ezra 9. 14. *so that* there should be no remnant
Job 1. 3. *so that* this man was greatest in the east
7. 20. set as a mark, *so that* I am a burden to myself
Psal. 40. 12. *so that* I am not able to look up
58. 11. *so that* a man shall say, there is a reward
78. 53. he led them safely, *so that* they feared not
106. 32. *s. t.* it went ill with Moses for their sakes
Eccl. 6. 2. *so that* he wanteth nothing for his soul
Isa. 47. 7. *s. t.* thou didst not lay these things to heart
60. 15. been forsaken, *s. t.* no man went thro' thee
Jer. 33. 26. *so that* I will not take any of his seed
44. 22. *so that* the Lord could no longer bear
Ezek. 21. 24. *so that* in all your doings sins appear
31. 9. *so that* all the trees in Eden envied him
Dan. 8. 4. *so that* no beast might stand before him
Zech. 1. 21. *so that* no man did lift up his head
Mark 15. 5. Jes. answered not, *so t.* Pilate marvelled
Luke 16. 26. *so that* they which would pass to you
Rom. 1. 20. *so that* they are without excuse
15. 19. *so that* from Jerus. I have preached gospel
2 *Cor.* 2. 7. *so that* contrariwise ye should forgive
7. 7. *so that* I rejoiced the more
Gal. 5. 17. *so that* ye cannot do the things ye would
1 *Thess.* 1. 7. *so t.* ye were ensamples to all that bel.
Heb. 13. 6. *so t.* we may boldly say, L. is my helper

Was SO, or SO *was.*

Gen. 1. 7. and it *was so*, 9, 11, 15, 24, 30.
41. 13. as he interpreted to us, *so* it *was*
Num. 9. 16. *so* it *was* always, cloud covered it by nig.
20. *so* it *was* when cloud was on tabernacle
21. *so* it *was* when cloud abode from even
Judg. 6. 38. dew be on the fleece only, and it *was so*
19. 30. it *w. so* that all who saw it said, no such deed
1 *Sam.* 5. 7. when men of Ashdod saw that it *was so*
10. 9. it *was so* that when he turned from Samuel
30. 25. it *was so* from that day forward made a stat.
2 *Sam.* 15. 2. it *was so* when any came to the king
5. it *was so* that when any man came nigh to him
16. 23. *so was* all the counsel of Ahithophel
1 *Kings* 13. 9. *so was* it charged me by word of Lord
2 *Kings* 17. 7. *so* it *was* that Israel had sinned ag. L.
23. *so was* Isr. carried away to Assyria to this day
2 *Chron.* 29. 25. *so was* the commandment of Lord
Luke 2. 6. and *so* it *was* that while they were there
21. Jesus, who *was so* named of the angel
5. 10. and *so was* also James and John astonished
Acts 12. 15. Rhoda constantly affirmed it *was* even *so*

SOBER.

2 *Cor* 5. 13. whether we be *s.* it is for your cause
1 *Thess.* 5. 6. let us not sleep, but let us watch and be *s.*
8. but let us who are of the day be *s.* putting on
1 *Tim.* 3. 2. a bishop then must be *s.* *Tit.* 1. 8.
11. deacons' wives must be *s.* faithful in all things
Tit. 2. 2. that aged men be *s.* grave, temperate
4. they may teach the young women to be *s.*
1 *Pet.* 1. 13. gird up the loins of your mind, be *s*
4. 7. be ye therefore *s.* and watch unto prayer
5. 8. be *s.* be vigilant, because your adversary devil

SOBERLY.

Rom. 12. 3. but to think *s.* accord. to measure of faith
Tit. 2. 12. teaching us that we should live *s.* right.

SOBER-*minded.*

Tit. 2. 6. likewise exhort young men to be *s.-minded*

SOBERNESS.

Acts 26. 25. but speak forth the words of *s.*

SOBRIETY.

Rom. 12. † 3. every man ought to think to *s.*
1 *Tim.* 2. 9. that women adorn themselves with *s.*
15. if they continue in faith and holiness with *s.*

SOCKET.

Exod. 38. 27. an hundred talents, a talent for a *s.*

SOCKETS.

Exod. 26. 19. make forty *s.* of silver, 21. | 36. 24, 26.
two *s.* under one board for two tenons, two *s.* under another board, 21, 25. | 36. 24, 26.
25. and their *s.* of silver, sixteen *s.* 36. 30, 36.
37. thou shalt cast five *s.* of brass for them, 36. 38.
27. 10. their twenty *s.* shall be of brass, 38. 10, 11.
12. on west side pillars ten, their *s.* ten, 38. 12.
14. the hangings on one side, their *s.* three
15. on the other side shall be three *s.* 38. 14, 15.
16. their pillars shall be four, their *s.* four
17. hooks shall be of silver and their *s.* brass, 18.
35. 11. make bars, pillars, *s.* of the tabernacle
17. hangings of the court, pillars, and their *s.*
38. 27. *s.* of the sanctuary, *s.* of the veil, hundred *s.*
30. of the brass of the offerings he made *s.*
31. *s.* of the court, and the *s.* of the court gate
40. 18. reared the tabernacle and fastened his *s.*
Num. 3. 36. under the custody and charge of the sons of Merari shall be the *s.* 37. | 4. 31, 32.
Cant. 5. 15. as pillars of marble set on *s.* of gold

SOD.

Gen. 25. 29. Jacob *s.* pottage, Esau came from field
2 *Chron.* 35. 13. other holy offerings *s.* they in pots

SODDEN.

Exod. 12. 9. eat not of it raw, nor *s.* with water
Lev. 6. 28. earthen vessel wherein it is *s.* shall be broken, if it be *s.* in brasen pot, it shall be scoured
Num. 6. 19. the priest shall take the *s.* shoulder
1 *Sam.* 2. 15. will not have *s.* flesh of thee, but raw
Lam. 4. 10. the women have *s.* their own children

SODERING.

Isa. 41. 7. it is ready for *s.* he fastened it with nails

SOFT.

Job 23. 16. for G. maketh my heart *s.* and troubleth
41. 3. will he speak *s.* words unto thee?
Psal. 65. 10. thou makest it *s.* with showers
Prov. 15. 1. a *s.* answer turneth away wrath
25. 15. and a *s.* tongue breaketh the bone
Mat. 11. 8. a man clothed in *s.* raiment; they that wear *s.* clothing are in king's houses, *Luke* 7. 25.

SOFTER.

Ps. 55. 21. words were *s.* than oil, yet drawn swords

SOFTLY.

Gen. 33. 14. I will lead *s.* as cattle, children be able
Judg. 4. 21. Jael went *s.* to him, and smote the nail
Ruth 3. 7. she came *s.* and uncovered his feet
1 *Kings* 21. 27. Ahab fast. lay in sackcloth, went *s.*
Isa. 8. 6. refuseth the waters of Shiloah that go *s.*
38. 15. I shall go *s.* all my years in bittern. of soul
Acts 27. 13. when south wind blew *s.* they sailed

SOIL.

Psal. 37. † 35. like a tree growing in his own *s.*
Ezek. 17. 8. it was planted in a good *s.* by great [waters

SOJOURN.

Gen. 12. 10. Abraham went down into Egypt to *s.*
19. 9. they said, this one fellow came in to *s.*
26. 3. *s.* in this land, and I will be with thee
47. 4. they said, for to *s.* in the land are we come
Exod. 12. 48. when a stranger will *s.* with thee, and keep passover, *Lev.* 19. 33. *Num.* 9. 14. | 15. 14.
Lev. 17. 8. of strangers who *s.* that offereth sacrifice
10. of strangers that *s.* that eateth any blood
13. who *s.* among you that hunteth any beast
20. 2. of strangers that *s.* that giv. seed to Molech
25. 45. of strangers that *s.* of them shall ye buy
Judg. 17. 8. a Levite went to *s.* where he could
9. said to Micah, I go to *s.* where I may find place
Ruth 1. 1. Elimelech went to *s.* in country of Moab
1 *Kings* 17. 20. evil on the widow with whom I *s.*
2 *Kings* 8. 1. arise, *s.* wheresoever thou canst *s.*
Psal. 15. † 1. who shall *s.* in thy tabernacle?
120. 5. woe is me, that I *s.* in Mesech, dwell in tents
Isa. 23. 7. her own feet shall carry her afar off to *s.*
52. 4. my people went down into Egypt to *s.* there
Jer. 42. 15. if ye wholly set your faces to enter into Egypt, and go to *s.* there, 17. | 44, 12, 14, 28.
22. ye shall die in place whither ye desire to *s.*
Lam. 4. 15. they said, they shall no more *s.* there
Ezek. 20. 38. I will bring them from where they *s*
47. 22. divide it to you and strangers who *s.* among
Acts 7. 6. that his seed should *s.* in a strange land

SOJOURNED.

Gen. 20. 1. from thence Abraham *s.* in Gerar
21. 34. and *s.* in the Philistines' land many days
32. 4. I *s.* with Laban, and stayed there until now
35. 27. Hebron, where Abraham and Isaac *s.*
Deut. 18. 6. if a Levite come from where he *s.*
26. 5. *s.* in Egypt with a few, and became a nation
Judg. 17. 7. a Levite *s.* in Bethlehem-Judah
19. 16. an old man of Ephraim *s.* in Gibeah
2 *Kings* 8. 2. she *s.* in the land of the Philistines
Psal. 105. 23. and Jacob *s.* in the land of Ham
Heb. 11. 9. by faith he *s.* in the land of promise

SOJOURNER.

Gen. 23. 4. I am *s.* with you, give me burying-place
Lev. 22. 10. *s.* of priest shall not eat of holy thing
25. 35. a *s.* fallen in decay thou shalt relieve
40. thy brother shall be as a *s.* with thee
47. *s.* was rich by thee, and brother sell hims. to *s.*
Num. 35. 15. these six cities a refuge for Isr. and *s.*
Ps. 39. 12. I am a stranger, *s.* as all my fathers were

SOJOURNERS.

Lev. 25. 23. for ye are strangers and *s.* with me
2 *Sam.* 4. 3. the Beerothites were *s.* in Gittaim
1 *Chron.* 29. 15. we are *s.* as were all our fathers

SOJOURNETH.

Exod. 3. 22. every woman shall borrow of her that *s.*
12. 49. one law shall be to him that is home-born, and to stranger that *s.* among you, *Lev.* 16. 29.
Lev 17. 12. nor shall any stranger that *s.* eat blood
18. 26. that *s.* among you shall keep my statutes
25. 6. sabbath of the land meat for stranger that *s.*
Num. 15. 15. one ordinance shall be for you and for the stranger that *s.* with you, 16. 29. | 19. 10.
26. and it shall be forgiven the stranger that *s.*
Josh. 20. 9. these cities of refuge for stranger that *s.*
Ezra 1. 4. whoso remaineth in any place where he *s*
Ezek. 14. 7. every one that *s.* in Isr. who separateth
47. 23. that in what tribe stranger *s.* there give

SOJOURNING.

Exod. 12. 40. the *s.* of Isr. in Egypt was 430 years
Judg. 19. 1. a certain Levite *s.* on mount Ephraim
1 *Pet.* 1. 17. pass the time of your *s.* here in fear

SOAKED.

Isa. 34. 7. their land shall be *s.* with blood, their

SOLACE.

Prov. 7. 18. come, let us *s.* ourselves with loves

SOLD, *Actively, Passively.*

Gen. 25. 33. Esau *s.* his birthright unto Jacob
31. 15. our father hath *s.* us, devoured our money
37. 28. they *s.* Joseph to the Ishmaelites for sil ver
36. the Midianites *s.* him into Egypt to Potiphar
41. 56. Joseph *s.* corn unto the Egyptians
42. 6. he it was that *s.* to all the people of land
45. 4. I am Jos. your broth. whom ye *s.* into Egypt
5. be not angry with yours. that ye *s.* me hither
47. 20. for the Egyptians *s.* every man his field
22. wherefore the priests *s.* not their lands
Exod. 22. 3. if he have noth. then shall be *s.* for theft

Lev. 25. 23. the land shall not be s. for ever
25. then shall he redeem that which his brother s.
33. house that was s. shall go out in year of jubilee
34. but the field of the suburbs may not be s.
42. brethren shall not be s. as bond-men
27. 28. no devoted thing shall be s. or redeemed
Deut. 15. 12. and if thy brother be s. unto thee
28. 68. there shall ye be s. unto your enemies
32. 30. except their Rock had s. them and shut them
Judg. 2. 14. he s. them into hands of their enemies
3. 8. s. them to Chushan-rishathaim || 4. 2. to Jabin
10. 7. s. them into the hands of the Philistines
1 *Sam.* 12. 9. he s. them into the hand of Sisera
1 *Kings* 21. 20. thou hast s. thyself to work evil
2 *Kings* 6. 25. ass's head was s. for 80 pieces of silver
7. 1. a measure of fine flour s. for a shekel, 16.
17. 17. Israel s. themselves to do evil in sight of Ld.
Neh. 5. 8. have redeemed our brethren who were s. to the heathen, or shall they be s. unto us?
13. 15. I testified in day wherein they s. victuals
16. who brought ware and s. on the sabbath
Esth. 7. 4. for we are s. I and my people to be slain and perish; but if we had been s. for bond-men
Psal. 105. 17. Joseph who was s. for a servant
Isa. 50. 1. which of my creditors is it to whom I s. you? for your iniquities have ye s. yourselves
52. 3. ye have s. yourselves for nought, be redeemed
Jer. 34. 14. let go his brother who hath been s.
Lam. 5. 4. water for money, our wood is s. unto us
Ezek. 7. 13. seller shall not return to that which is s.
Joel 3. 3. and they have s. a girl for wine to drink
6. children of Judah have ye s. to the Grecians
7. I will raise them out of place whither ye s. them
Amos 2. 6. they s. the righteous for silver and poor
Mat. 10. 29. are not two sparrows s. for a farthing?
13. 46. went and s. all that he had and bought it
18. 25. his lord commanded him to be s.
21. 12. cast out them that s. and bought, overthrew seats of them that s. *Mark* 11. 15. *Luke* 19. 45.
26. 9. for this ointment might have been s. for much and given to the poor, *Mark* 14. 5. *John* 12. 5.
Luke 12. 6. are not five sparrows s. for two farthings
17. 28. they bought, they s. they planted, they built
John 2. 14. found in the temple those that s. oxen
16. said to them that s. doves, take these hence
Acts 2. 45. and s. their possessions and goods, 4. 34.
4. 37. Joses having land s. it, and brought money
5. 1. Ananias s. || 8. ye s. the land for so much?
4. after it was s. was it not in thine own power?
Rom. 7. 14. law is spirit. but I am carnal, s. under sin
1 *Cor.* 10. 25. whatsoever is s. in shambles, that eat
Heb. 12. 16. for one morsel of meat s. his birth-right

SOLDIER.

John 19. 23. and made four parts, to every s. a part
Acts 10. 7. Cornelius called a devout s. that waited on
28. 16. suffered Paul to dwell by himself, with a s.
2 *Tim.* 2. 3. endure hardness as a good s. of Christ
4. may please him who hath chosen him to be a s.

SOLDIERS.

2 *Chron.* 25. 13. the s. fell upon the cities of Judah
Ezra 8. 22. I was ashamed to require of the king s.
Isa. 15. 4. the armed s. of Moab shall cry out
Mat. 8. 9. having s. under me, *Luke* 7. 8.
27. 27. the s. took Jesus and gathered to him s.
28. 12. they gave large money unto the s.
Luke 3. 14. s. demanded, saying, what shall we do?
23. 36. the s. mocked him, offered him vinegar
John 19. 2. s. platted a crown of thorns, put it on
23. the s. took his garments, and also his coat
24. these things the s. did || 32. s. brake the legs
34. but one of the s. with a spear pierced his side
Acts 12. 4. delivered Peter to four quaternions of s.
6. same night Peter was sleeping between two s.
18. there was no small stir among the s.
21. 32. when they saw the chief captain and s.
35. so it was, that he was borne of the s.
23. 23. make ready 200 s. to go to Cesarea
27. 31. Paul said to the s. except these abide
32. then the s. cut off the ropes of the boat
42. the s. counsel was to kill the prisoners

SOLE.

Gen. 8. 9. dove found no rest for the s. of her foot
Deut. 28. 35. with a sore botch from s. of thy foot
56. would not set the s. of her foot upon ground
65. neither shall the s. of thy foot have rest
Josh. 1. 3. every place s. of your foot shall tread on
2 *Sam.* 14. 25. from s. of foot to crown was no blemish
Job 2. 7. Satan smote Job from the s. of his foot
Isa. 1. 6. from s. of foot to head there is no soundness
Ezek. 1. 7. s. of their feet like the s. of a calf's foot
See FEET.

SOLEMN.

Num. 10. 10. in your s. days ye shall blow trumpets
Psal. 92. 3. to sing praise with a s. sound
Isa. 1. 13. it is iniquity, even the s. meeting
Lam. 2. 22. thou hast called as in a s. day, my terr.
Hos. 9. 5. what will ye do in s. day, in day of feast?
Zech. 8. †19. the fast shall be joy and s. times
See ASSEMBLY, FEAST, FEASTS.

SOLEMNITY.

Deut. 31. 10. in the s. of the year of release
Isa. 30. 29. shall have song, as when a holy s. is kept

SOLEMNITIES.

Isa. 33. 20. look upon Zion, the city of our s.
Ezek. 45. 17. prince give burnt offerings in s. of Isr.
46. 11. in the s. meat offering shall be an ephah

SOLEMNLY.

Gen. 43. 3. the man did s. protest unto us, saying
1 *Sam.* 8. 9. yet protest s. to them, and shew them

SOLITARY.

Num. 23. †3. Balaam went s. and God met him
Job 3. 7. let that night be s. let no joyful voice come
30. 3. for want and famine they were s.
Psal. 68. 6. God setteth the s. in families
107. 4. they wandered in the wilderness in a s. way
Isa. 35. 1. wildern. and s. place shall be glad for them
Lam. 1. 1. how doth city sit s. that was full of peop.
Mark 1. 35. Jesus depart. into a s. place, and prayed

SOLITARILY.

Mic. 7. 14. feed thy people which dwell s. in wood

SOME.

Gen. 19. 19. Lot said, lest s. evil take me, and I die
33. 15. let me now leave with thee s. of folk
37. 20. come, let us slay him, and cast him into s. pit, and we will say, s. evil beast hath devoured him
47. 2. took s. of his brethren and presented to Pha.
Exod. 16. 17. and they gathered s. more, s. less
20. but s. of them left of it till the morning
27. s. went out on seventh day to gather, found
Lev. 4. 7. shall put s. of blood on horns of altar, 18.
17. the priest shall dip his finger in s. of the blood
Num. 21. 1. Arad took s. of them prisoners
27. 20. thou shalt put s. of thine honour upon him
Deut. 24. 1. bec. he hath found s. uncleanness in her
Ruth 2. 16. let fall s. of handfuls of purpose for her
1 *Sam.* 24. 10. s. bade me kill thee, but spared thee
2 *Sam.* 17. 9. he is hid in s. pit, or in s. other place
1 *Kings* 14. 13. in him there is found s. good thing
2 *Kings* 7. 9. s. mischief will come upon us
2 *Chron.* 12. 7. but I will grant s. deliverance
16. 10. Asa oppressed s. of people the same time
Ezra 10. 44. s. had wives by whom they had childr.
Neh. 5. 3. s. said, we have mortgaged our lands
13. 15. saw I s. treading wine-presses on Sabbath
19. and s. of my servants set I at the gates
Job 24. 2. s. remove land-marks, take away flocks
Psal. 20. 7. s. trust in chariots, s. in horses
69. 20. I looked for s. to take pity, there was none
Prov. 4. 16. sleep taken away, unless they cause s. fall
Jer. 49. 9. would they not leave s. gleaning-grapes?
Dan. 8. 10. and it cast down s. of the host and stars
11. 35. s. of them of understanding shall fall
12. 2. s. to everlasting life, and s. to shame
Amos 4. 11. overthrown s. as God overthrew Sodom
Obad. 5. would they not leave s. grapes?
Mat. 13. 4. s. fell by way side, *Mark* 4. 4. *Luke* 8. 5.
5. s. fell on stony places, not much earth, *Mark* 4. 5.
7. and s. fell among thorns, *Mark* 4. 7. *Luke* 8. 7.
16. 14. s. say thou art John the Baptist, s. Elias, others Jeremias, *Mark* 8. 28. *Luke* 9. 19.
28. there be s. standing here, who shall not taste of death till Son of man, *Mark* 9. 1. *Luke* 9. 19.
19. 12. s. eunuchs which were so born, s. made
23. 34. ye shall kill and crucify, s. ye shall scourge
28. 17. they worshipped him, but s. doubted
Luke 8. 6. s. fell upon a rock, and withered away
21. 16. and s. of you shall cause to be put to death
John 6. 64. there are s. of you that believe not
Acts 5. 15. shadow of Peter overshadow s. of them
8. 9. giving out that himself was s. great one
31. how can I except s. man should guide me?
13. 11. seeking s. to lead him by the hand
17. 4. s. of them believed || 21. hear s. new thing
32. s. mocked || 27. 34. I pray you take s. meat
19. 32. s. cried one thing, s. another, 21. 34.
27. 44. s. on boards, s. on broken pieces of the ship
28. 24. s. believed and s. believed not
Rom. 1. 11. that I may impart to you s. spirit. gift
13. that I might have s. fruit among you also
3. 3. for what if s. did not believe?
8. as s. affirm that we say, let us do evil that good
5. 7. for a good man s. would even dare to die
11. 14. if by any means I might save s. of them
17. and if s. of the branches be broken off
1 *Cor.* 4. 18. now s. are puffed up as though not come
6. 11. such were s. of you, but ye are washed
8. 7. for s. with conscience of the idol eat it
9. 22. that I might by all means save s.
10. 7. neither be idolaters as were s. of them
8. commit fornication, as s. of them committed
9. as s. tempted Christ and were destroyed
10. nor murmur ye as s. of them murmured
12. 28. and God hath set s. in the church
15. 6. greater part remain, but s. are fallen asleep
12. how say s. that there is no resurrection?
34. for s. have not the knowledge of God
2 *Cor.* 10. 2. I think to be bold ag. s. who think of us
12. for we dare not compare ourselves with s.
Gal. 1. 7. but there be s. that trouble you
Eph. 4. 11. he gave s. prophets, s. evangelists
Phil. 1. 15. s. indeed preach Christ even of envy
2 *Thess.* 3. 11. there are s. among you walk disorderly
1 *Tim.* 1. 3. charge s. that they teach no other doct.
6. from which s. having swerved, have turned
19. s. having put away, have made shipwreck
4. 1. that in latter times s. shall depart from faith
5. 15. s. are already turned aside after Satan
24. s. men's sins open before-hand, s. men follow
25. the good works of s. are manifest before-hand
6. 10. which while s. coveted after, they have erred
2 *Tim.* 2. 18. and overthrew the faith of s.
20. s. vessels to honour and s. to dishonour
Heb. 3. 4. for every house is builded by s. man
16. for s. when they heard, did provoke
4. 6. it remaineth, that s. must enter therein
10. 25. not forsaking as the manner of s. is
11. 40. having provided s. better thing for us
13. 2. for thereby s. entertained angels unawares
2 *Pet.* 3. 9. Lord is not slack, as s. count slackness
16. in which are s. things hard to be understood
Jude 22. of s. have compassion, making a difference
Rev. 2. 10. the devil shall cast s. of you into prison

SOMEBODY.

Luke 8. 46. Jesus said, s. hath touched me
Acts 5. 36. rose up Theudas, boasting hims. to be s.

SOMETHING.

1 *Sam.* 20. 26. for he thought, s. hath befallen him
Mark 5. 43. that s. should be given her to eat
Luke 11. 54. and seek. to catch s. out of his mouth
John 13. 29. or that he should give s. to the poor
Acts 3. 5. he gave heed expect. to receive s. of them
23. 15. as though ye would inquire s. more perf.
18. this young man who hath s. to say to thee
Gal. 6. 3. for if a man think himself to be s.

SOMETIMES.

Eph. 2. 13. ye who were s. afar off are made nigh
5. 8. for ye were s. darkness, but now light in L.
Col. 1. 21. you that were s. alienated and enemies
3. 7. in which ye walked s. when ye lived in them
Tit. 3. 3. we ourselves also were s. foolish, deceiv.
1 *Pet.* 3. 20. who s. were disobedient in days of Noe

SOMEWHAT.

Lev. 4. 13. have done s. against commandments, 27.
22. when a ruler hath done s. through ignorance
13. 6. if the plague be s. dark, 21, 26, 28, 56.
19. there be a bright spot, and s. reddish, 24.
1 *Sam.* 2. †36. put me s. about the priesthood
1 *Kings* 2. 14. he said, I have s. to say unto thee
2 *Kings* 5. 20. I will run after him, and take s. of him
2 *Chron.* 10. 4. ease s. grievous servitude of thy father
9. ease s. the yoke || 10. make it s. lighter for us
Luke 7. 40. Simon, I have s. to say unto thee
Acts 23. 20. as to inquire s. of him more perfectly
25. 26. O king, that I might have s. to write
Rom. 15. 24. if first I be s. filled with your company
2 *Cor.* 5. 12. that you may have s. to answer them
10. 8. tho' I should boast s. more of our authority
Gal. 2. 6. but of those who seemed to be s.
Heb. 8. 3. of necessity this man have s. also to offer
Rev. 2. 4. nevertheless, I have s. against thee

SON.

This name is given to a male child considered in the relation he bears to his parents. Seth *was the* son *of* Adam, *and* Enos *was son to* Seth, Gen. 4. 25, 26. *It is given also to a grandson;* Mephibosheth *is called the* son *of* Saul, 2 Sam. 19. 24. *though he was the son of* Jonathan, *who was* Saul's *son,* 2 Sam. 9. 6. *It is put for a successor, or the descendant of a man,* I am the son of the wise, the son of ancient kings, *Isa.* 19. 11. *Thus the posterity of* Jacob *are called frequently the* children of Israel. Son *is a name given by masters and teachers to their scholars;* Eli *called* Samuel *his son,* 1 Sam. 3. 6. *And* Solomon *frequently calls his pupil* son, Prov. 1. 8. *And this name they gave them to shew their paternal authority and affection, and to make them more attentive and obedient.* St. Paul *calls* Timothy *his own son,* 1 Tim. 1. 2. To Timothy my own son in the faith; *who truly resembles me, and has been confirmed in the faith by my means.* Obed *is called the son of* Naomi. Ruth 4. 17. There is a son born to Naomi; *one who will nourish, comfort, and assist her, as a dutiful son succours his parents.* Hazael *calls* Benhadad Elisha's *son, one that honoured him as a son does his father,* 2 Kings 8. 9. *God calls the posterity of* Jacob *his son.* Exod. 4. 22. Israel is my son, even my first-born. *They are the first and only nation that I have chosen for my peculiar people.* Ezekiel *is called* Son of man *about eighty-nine times: And* Christ *about eighty times in the Evangelists.*

SONS *of God. See on* CHILD.

Gen. 17. †12. he that is s. of eight days be circumc.
16. I will give thee a s. of Sarah, 19. | 18. 10, 14.
21. 2. Sarah bare Abraham a s. in his old age, 7.
10. cast out this bond woman and her s.
24. 36. Sarah my master's wife bare a s.
44. the Lord hath appointed for my master's s.
51. and let her be thy master's s. wife
29. 33. he hath therefore given me this s. also
30. 6. God hath heard me, and given me a s.
24. the Lord shall add to me another s.
35. 17. fear not, thou shalt have this s. also
†18. the s. of my sorrow; s. of the right hand
37. 3. because he was the s. of his old age
Exod. 1. 16. if it be a s. then ye shall kill him
22. every s. that is born ye shall cast into river
2. 10. the child grew, and he became her s.
4. 25. Zipporah cut off the foreskin of her s.
12. †5. your lamb shall be s. of a year, *Lev.* 12. †6.
21. 31. whether he have gored a s. or a daughter
23. 12. the s. of thy handmaid may be refreshed
29. 30. that s. that is priest in stead put them on
Lev. 12. 6. the days of her purifying for a s.
24. 10. the s. of an Israelitish woman strove in
11. the Israelitish woman's s. blasphemed
25. 49. his uncle, or his uncle's s. may redeem him
Num. 23. 18. hearken unto me thou s. of Zippor
27. 4. because he hath no s. || 8. if die and have no s.
Deut. 13. 6. if s. of thy mother entice thee secretly
21. 16. that he may not make the s. of the beloved, first-born, before the s. of the hated, 17.
18. if a man have a stubborn and rebellious s.
20. this our s. is stubborn and rebellious, not obey
28. 56. eye shall be evil towards her s. and daught.
Josh. 6. 26. in his youngest s. set up the gates of it
15. 8. border went by the valley of s. of Hinnom
Judg. 5. 12. arise, lead captive, thou s. of Abinoam
9. 18. have made the s. of his maid-servant king
28. Gaal said, is not he the s. of Jerubbaal?
11. 2. for thou art the s. of a strange woman
34. besides her he had neither s. nor daughter
13. 3. but thou shalt conceive and bear a s. 5, 7.
24. the woman bare a s. and called him Samson
Ruth 4. 13. Ruth bare a s. || 17. a s. born to Naomi
1 *Sam.* 1. 23. Hannah gave her s. suck until weaned
4. 20. women said, fear not, for thou hast born a s.
9. 2. Kish had s. whose name was Saul a young m.
10. 11. what is this that is come to s. of Kish?
13. †1. Saul the s. of one year in his reigning
16. 18. I have seen the s. of Jesse that is cunning
17. 55. whose s. is this? || 58. whose s. art thou?
18. †17. only be thou s. of valour for me and fight
20. 27. wherefore cometh not the s. of Jesse?
30. thou s. of the perverse rebellious woman
31. for as long as the s. of Jesse liveth on ground
22. 7. will s. of Jesse give you fields and vineyards
9. Doeg said, I saw the s. of Jesse coming to Nob
12. Saul said, hear now, thou s. of Ahitub
25. 10. who is s. of Jesse? || 17. he is such a s. of Bel.
2 *Sam.* 1. 13. he said, I am the s. of a stranger
9. 3. Jonathan hath yet s. who is lame on his feet
9. given thy master's s. all that pertained to Saul
10. that master's s. may have food to eat; Mephibosheth thy master's s. shall eat at my table
10. 2. I will shew kindness to the s. of Nahash
16. 3. king said, and where is thy master's s.?
18. 12. not put forth my hand against the king's s.
18. I have no s. to keep my name in remembrance
20. shall bear no tidings, because king's s. is dead
20. 1. nor have we inheritance in the s. of Jesse
1 *Kings* 3. 6. thou hast given him a s. to sit on throne
26. for her bowels yearned upon her s.

Kings 5.7. hath given Dav. a wise s. over this people
7. 14. Hiram was a widow's s. of tribe of Naphtali
12. 16. no inheritance in s. of Jesse, 2 Chron. 10. 16.
14. 1. Abijah the s. of Jeroboam fell sick
5. she cometh to ask a thing of thee for her s.
17. 17. the s. of the mistress of the house fell sick
20. brought evil on the widow, by slaying her s.
22. 26. carry him to Joash king's s. 2 Chr. 18. 25.
2 Kings 1. 17. Jehoram reigned, because he had no s.
4. 6. she said to her, s. bring me yet a vessel
16. about this season thou shalt embrace a s.
17. and the woman bare a s. at that season
28. did I desire a s. of my lord? ‖ 37. took up her s.
6. 29. give s. to eat him, and she hath hid her s.
32. see ye how this s. of a murderer hath sent
8. 1. the woman whose s. he had restored to life
5. this is her s. whom Elisha restored to life
11. 1. Athaliah saw her s. was dead, 2 Chr. 22. 10.
4. Jehoiada shewed them the king's s.
12. he brought forth the king's s. and put crown
1 Chron. 12. 18. and on thy side, thou s. of Jesse
20. 6. and he also was the s. of the giant
22. 9. behold, a s. shall be born to thee, a man of rest
2 Chron. 21. 17. so that there was never a s. left him
22. 9. buried him, because he is s. of Jehoshaphat
23. 3. he said, behold, the king's s. shall reign
Neh. 11. 14. Zabdiel their overseer, s. of great men
Job 18. 19. he shall neither have s. nor nephew
Psal. 2. 12. kiss the s. lest he be angry, and ye perish
50. 20. thou slanderest thine own mother's s.
72. 1. and thy righteousness unto the king's s.
† 17. as a s. to continue his father's name
86. 16. and save the s. of thine handmaid
89. 22. nor shall the s. of wickedness afflict him
116. 16. I am the s. of thine handmaid
Prov. 3. 12. as a father s. in whom he delighteth
4. 3. I was my father's s. only beloved of my mother
10. 1. a wise s. maketh a glad father, 15. 20.
5. he that gathereth in summer is a wise s. sleepeth in harvest, s. causeth shame, 17. 2. | 19. 26.
13. 1. a wise s. heareth his father's instruction
17. 25. foolish s. is a grief to his father, and bittern.
19. 13. a foolish s. is the calamity of his father
28. 7. whoso keepeth the law, is a wise s.
31. 2. and what, the s. of my womb, s. of my vows?
Eccl. 5. 14. he begetteth a s. nothing in his hand
10. 17. blessed land, when king is the s. of nobles
Isa. 5. † 1. a vineyard in the horn of the s. of oil
7. 4. not afraid of the anger of the s. of Remaliah
6. let us set a king in it, even the s. of Tabeal
9. the head of Samaria is Remaliah's s.
14. behold, a virgin shall conceive and bear a s.
9. 6. unto us a child is born, unto us a s. is given
14. 12. how art thou fallen, O Lucifer, s. of morning
22. I will cut off from Babylon s. and nephew
19. 11. I am s. of the wise, the s. of ancient kings
21. † 10. O my threshing, and the s. of my floor
49. 15. not have compassion on the s. of her womb
56. 3. neither let the s. of the stranger speak
Jer. 6. 26. make thee mourning, as for an only s.
33. 21. should not have a s. to reign on his throne
Ezek. 14. 20. they shall deliver neither s. nor daught.
18. 4. soul of the s. is mine, soul that sins shall die
10. if he beget s. that is a robber, shedder of blood
14. a s. that seeth his father's sins and doeth not
19. why doth not s. bear iniquity of the father?
when the s. hath done what is lawful and right
20. s. not bear iniquity of father, nor father of s.
44. 25. for s. or daughter they may defile thems.
Hos. 1. 3. he took Gomer, which bare him a s. 8.
13. 13. he is an unwise s. for he should not stay long
Amos 7. 14. I was no prophet, nor was I a prophet's s.
8. 10. I will make it as mourning of an only s.
Mic. 7. 6. for the s. dishonoureth the father
Mal. 1. 6. s. honoureth his father, a servant his master
Mat. 1. 21. she shall bring forth a s. Luke 1. 31.
9. 2. Jesus said, s. be of good cheer, Mark 2. 5.
10. 37. he that loveth s. or daughter more than me
11. 27. no man knoweth s. but Father, nor any the Father, save s. and he to whom s. Luke 10. 22.
13. 55. the carpenter's s. Mark 6. 3. Luke 4. 22.
16. 16. thou art Christ the s. of the living God
21. 28. and said, s. go work to-day in my vineyard
38. but when husbandmen saw the s. they said
22. 42. what think ye of Christ? whose s. is he?
Mark 12. 6. having yet one s. his well-beloved
13. 12. father shall betray the s. children rise up
32. that hour knoweth not the s. but Father
14. 61. art thou the Christ, the s. of the blessed?
Luke 1. 13. Elisabeth shall bear thee s. name John
32. he shall be called the s. of the Highest
36. Elisabeth conceived a s. ‖ 57. brought forth s.
2. 48. mother said, s. why hast thou dealt with us?
3. 23. Jesus about 30 years, being, as was supposed, the s. of Joseph, who was the s. of Heli
7. 12. dead man carried out, only s. of his mother
10. 6. if s. of peace be there, your peace shall rest
11. 11. if a s. shall ask bread of any of you
12. 53. the father shall be divided against the s.
15. 13. the younger s. gathered all together
31. s. thou art ever with me, all is thine
16. 25. s. remember, that thou in thy life-time
19. 9. forasmuch as he also is the s. of Abraham
John 1. 18. only begotten s. who is in bosom of Father
45. we have found Jesus of Nazareth s. of Joseph
3. 35. the Father loveth the s. given, 5. 20.
36. that believeth on the s. that believeth not s.
4. 46. a certain nobleman whose s. was sick
5. 19. s. can do nothing of himself, what things seeth Father do, these things doth the s. likewise
21. even so the s. quickeneth whom he will
22. but hath committed all judgment to the s.
23. that all men should honour the s. he that honoureth not the s. honoureth not the Father
26. so hath he given to s. to have life in himself
6. 40. every one who seeth s. and believeth on him
42. they said, is not this Jesus the s. of Joseph?
8. 35. but s. abideth for ever ‖ 9. 19. is this your s.?
36. if s. theref. shall make you free, shall be free
9. 20. his parents said, we know that this is our s.
14. 13. that the Father may be glorified in the s.
17. 12. none of them is lost but the s. of perdition

John 21. 15. Simon s. of Jonas, lov. thou me more th.
Acts 4. 36. Barnabas, s. of consolation, a Levite
7. 21. took him up, and nourished for her own s.
13. 22. I have found David the s. of Jesse, a man
23. 6. I am Pharisee, the s. of a Pharisee
16. Paul's sister's s. heard of their lying in wait
Rom. 9. 9. at this time Sarah shall have a s.
1 Cor. 15. 28. then shall s. also himself be subject
Gal. 4. 7. no more a serv. but s. and if s. then an heir
30. cast out the bond-woman and her s. for the s. of the bond-woman shall not be heir with the s.
Phil 2. 22. as a s. with father, he served in gospel
Col. 4. 10. and Marcus sister's s to Barnabas
2 Thess. 2. 3. that man of sin the s. of perdition
1 Tim. 1. 18. this charge I commit to thee s. Timothy
Heb. 1. 5. I will be a fath. and he shall be to me a s.
8. but to the s. he saith, thy throne is for ever
3. 6. but Christ as a s. over his own house
5. 8. tho' he were a s. yet learned he obedience
7. 28. but the word of the oath maketh the s.
11. 24. refused to be called s. of Pharaoh's daughter
12. 6. and scourgeth every s. whom he receiveth
7. for what s. is he whom father chasteneth not?
2 Pet. 2. 15. following the way of Balaam, s. of Bozor
1 John 2. 22. is antichrist that denieth Father and s.
23. whosoever denieth the s. the same hath not the Father, but he that acknowledgeth the s.
24. ye also shall continue in the s. and in Father
4. 14. Father sent the s. to be the Saviour of world
5. 12. he that hath the s. hath life; and he that hath not the s. of God hath not life
2 John 3. from Lord Jesus Christ s. of the Father
9. he that abideth hath both the Father and the s.
See David.

SON of God.

Dan. 3. 25. form of the fourth is like the s. of God
Mat. 4. 3. if thou be the s. of God, command that these stones be made bread, 27. 40. Luke 4. 3, 9.
8. 29. to do with thee, Jesus thou s. of G.? art thou come to torment us before the time? Luke 8. 28.
14. 33. saying, of a truth thou art the s. of God
26. 63. tell us whether thou be Christ the s. of God
27. 43. for he said, I am the s. of God
54. truly this was the s. of God, Mark 15. 39.
Mark 1. 1. the gospel of Jesus Christ the s. of God
3. 11. saying, thou art the s. of God, John 1. 49.
Luke 1. 35. that holy thing shall be called s. of God
3. 38. was the s. of Adam, which was the s. of God
4. 41. devils came out of many, crying out, thou art Christ the s. of God, John 6. 69. | 11. 27.
22. 70. they said, art thou then the s. of God?
John 1. 34. I bare record, that this is the s. of God
3. 18. not believed in the only begotten s. of God
5. 25. dead shall hear the voice of the s. of God
9. 35. he said, dost thou believe on the s. of God?
10. 36. because I said, I am the s. of God
11. 4. that the s. of God might be glorified thereby
19. 7. because he made himself the s. of God
20. 31. believe that Jesus is Christ, the s. of God
Acts 8. 37. I believe that Jesus Christ is s. of God
9. 20. he preached Christ, that he is the s. of God
Rom. 1. 4. declared to be the s. of God with power
2 Cor. 1. 19. for the s. of God was not yea and nay
Gal. 2. 20. I live by the faith of the s. of God
Eph. 4. 13. come in unity of knowledge of s. of God
Heb. 4. 14. a great high priest, Jesus the s. of God
6. 6. they crucify to themselves s. of God afresh
7. 3. but made like to the s. of God abideth a priest
10. 29. who hath trodden under foot the s. of God
1 John 3. 8. for this purpose s. of God was manifested
4. 15. whoso shall confess Jesus is the s. of God
5. 5. he that believeth Jesus is the s. of God
10. he that believeth on the s. of God hath witness
13. that ye may believe on the name of s. of God
20. and we know that the s. of God is come
Rev. 2. 18. write these things, saith the s. of God

His SON.

Gen. 4. 17. called the city after name of his s. Enoch
9. 24. Noah knew what his younger s. had done
21. 11. thing was very grievous because of his s.
22. 10. Abraham took the knife to slay his s.
13. offered him for burnt offering instead of his s.
24. 48. take my master's brother's daughter to his s.
25. 6. sent from Isaac his s. while he yet lived
11. after the death of Abram, God blessed his s.
34. 20. Shechem his s. came to gate of their city
26. they slew Hamor and Shechem his s.
37. 34. Jacob mourned for his s. many days
Exod. 21. 9. if he hath betrothed her to his s.
32. 29. consecrate, even every man upon his s.
Lev. 21. 2. but for his s. he may be defiled
Num. 20. 26. and put them on Eleazar his s. 28.
Deut. 1. 31. God bare thee, as a man doth bear his s.
7. 3. thy daughter thou shalt not give to his s.
8. 5. as a man chasteneth his s. so the L. chasteneth
18. 10. not any maketh his s. to pass thro' the fire
2 Sam. 13. 37. David mourned for his s. every day
16. 19. should I not serve in presence of his s.?
19. 2. how the king was grieved for his s.
1 Kings 11. 35. take kingdom out of his s. hand
36. and to his s. will I give one tribe, that David
15. 4. give him a lamp, to set up his s. after him
16. 13. for all the sins of Elah his s. they sinned
2 Kings 3. 27. took his eldest s. should have reigned
16. 3. Ahaz made his s. to pass thro' the fire
21. 6. Manasseh made his s. pass through the fire
7. of which Lord said to David and to Solomon his s. will I put my name, 2 Chron. 33. 7.
23. 10. no man might make his s. pass through fire
2 Chron. 24. 22. thus Joash the king slew his s.
Prov. 13. 24. he that spareth his rod, hateth his s.
29. 21. shall have him become his s. at length
30. 4. what is his s. name, if thou canst tell
Jer. 27. 7. all nations shall serve his s. and his son's s.
Dan. 5. 22. thou his s. O Belshaz. hast not humbled
Mal. 3. 17. spare them, as a man spareth his s.
Mat. 7. 9. what man, whom if his s. ask bread
21. 37. last of all he sent unto them his s.
22. 2. a king who made a marriage for his s.
45. how is he then his s.? Mark 12. 37. Luke 20. 44.
John 3. 16. that he gave his only begotten s.
17. God sent not his s. to condemn the world

John 4. 5. ground that Jacob gave to his s. Joseph
47. that he would come down and heal his s.
Acts 3. 13. God hath glorified his s. Jesus
26. God having raised up his s. Jesus, sent him
Rom. 1. 9. whom I serve in the gospel of his s.
5. 10. were reconciled to God by death of his s.
8. 3. God sending his own s. in likeness of flesh
29. to be conformed to the image of his s.
32. he that spared not his own s. but delivered
1 Cor. 1. 9. called to the fellowship of his s. Jesus
Gal. 1. 16. it pleased God to reveal his s. in me
4. 4. God sent forth his s. made of a woman
6. God sent the spirit of his s. into your hearts
Col. 1. 13. translated us into kingdom of his dear s.
1 Thess. 1. 10. and to wait for his s. from heaven
Heb. 1. 2. G. in last days hath spoken to us by his s.
11. 17. Abraham offered up his only begotten s.
Jam. 2. 21. when had offered Isaac his s. on altar
1 John 1. 3. our fellowsh. is with Fath. and his s. Jes.
7. blood of Jes. C. his s. cleanseth us from all sin
3. 23. that we believe on the name of his s. Jesus
4. 9. God sent his only begotten s. into the world
10. and sent his s. to be propitiation for our sins
5. 9. the witness, which he hath testified of his s.
10. that believeth not God, made him a liar, he believeth not record God gave of his s.
11. this life is in his s. ‖ 20. we are in his s. Jesus

SON-in-law.

Gen. 19. 12. hast thou here any besides s.-in-law?
Judg. 15. 6. Samson the s.-in-law of the Timnite
19. 5. the damsel's father said unto his s.-in-law
1 Sam. 18. 18. I should be s.-in-law to the king, 23.
21. Saul said, thou shalt this day be my s.-in law
22. now therefore be the king's s.-in law
26. it pleased David well to be king's s.-in-law
27. that he might be the king's s.-in-law
22. 14. who is so faithful as the king's s.-in-law?
2 Kings 8. 27. Jehoram was s.-in-l. of house of Ahab
Neh. 6. 18. Tobiah was s.-in-law to Shechaniah
13. 28. was s.-in-law to Sanballat the Horonite
See Beloved.

My SON.

Gen. 21. 10. Ishmael shall not be heir with my s.
23. swear that thou wilt not deal falsely with my s.
22. 7. my father, and he said, here am I, my s.
8. my s. God will provide himself a lamb
24. 3. shalt not take wife to my s. of Canaanites, 37.
4. go to my kindred, and take wife to my s. 7, 38.
6. that thou bring not my s. thither again, 8.
27. 8. now therefore, my s. obey my voice, 43.
13. his mother said, upon me be thy curse, my s.
18. he said, here am I, who art thou, my s.?
21. whether thou be my very s. Esau, or not, 24.
27. see, the smell of my s. is as smell of a field
37. and what shall I do now unto thee, my s.?
34. 8. the soul of my s. longeth for your daughter
37. 33. and he knew it, and said, it is my s. coat
35. I will go into the grave to my s. mourning
38. 11. remain, till Shelah my s. be grown
26. because that I gave her not to Shelah my s.
42. 38. he said, my s. shall not go down with you
43. 29. he said, God be gracious to thee, my s.
45. 28. it is enough, Joseph my s. is yet alive
48. 19. Jacob said, I know it, my s. I know it
49. 9. from the prey, my s. thou art gone up
Exod. 4. 22. Israel is my s. even my first-born
23. let my s. go, that he may serve me
Josh. 7. 19. my s. give glory to the God of Israel
Judg. 8. 23. neither shall my s. rule over you
17. 2. mother said, blessed be thou of the L. my s.
3. dedicated for my s. to make a graven image
1 Sam. 3. 6. I called not my s. lie down again
4. 16. and he said, what is there done, my s.?
10. 2. sorroweth, saying, what shall I do for my s.?
14. 39. though it be in Jonathan my s. he shall die
40. I and Jonathan my s. will be on the other side
42. cast lots between me and Jonathan my s.
22. 8. that my s. hath made a league with son of Jesse, or that my s. hath stirred up my servant
24. 16. is this thy voice, my s. David? 26. 17.
26. 21. I have sinned, return, my s. David
25. Saul said, blessed be thou, my s. David
2 Sam. 7. 14. I will be his father, he shall be my s.
13. 25. king said, nay, my s. let us not all now go
14. 11. not suffer revengers, lest they destroy my s.
16. destroy me and my s. out of the inheritance
16. 11. behold my s. who came forth of my bowels
18. 22. Joab said, wherefore wilt thou run, my s.?
33. the king was moved, and wept, thus he said, O my s. Absalom, my s. my s. Absalom, 19. 4.
1 Kings 1. 21. I and my s. be counted offenders
3. 20. she arose and took my s. from beside me
21. behold, it was not my s. which I did bear
22. the woman said, nay, but the living is my s.
23. thy son is the dead, and my s. is the living
17. 12. that I may dress it for me and my s.
18. she said, art thou come to me to slay my s.?
2 Kings 6. 28. and we will eat my s. to-morrow
29. so we boiled my s. and did eat him, give thy s.
14. 9. give thy daughter to my s. 2 Chron. 25. 18.
1 Chron. 17. 13. and he shall be my s. 22. 10.
22. 11. now, my s. L. will be with thee, and prosper
28. 6. I have chosen him to be my s. will be his fath.
9. thou, Solomon, my s. know God of thy fath.
29. 1. Solomon my s. whom God alone hath chosen
19. give to Solomon my s. a perfect heart to keep
Ps. 2. 7. L. said to me, thou art my s. this day have I begotten thee, Acts 13. 33. Heb. 1. 5. | 5. 5.
Prov. 3. 11. my s. despise not the chastening of the Lord, nor be weary of his correction, Heb. 12. 5.
6. 3. do this now, my s. and deliver thyself
23. 26. my s. give me thine heart, observe my ways
24. 21. my s. fear thou the Lord and the king
27. 11. my s. be wise, and make my heart glad
31. 2. what, my s. and what, the son of my vows
Eccl. 12. 12. further, by these my s. be admonished
Jer. 31. 20. is Ephraim my dear s.? is pleasant child?
Ezek. 21. 10. it contemneth rod of my s. as every tree
Hos. 11. 1. I called my s. out of Egypt, Mat. 2. 15.
Mat. 3. 17. voice saying, this is my beloved s. 17. 5.
17. 15. Lord, have mercy on my s. he is lunatic
21. 37. they will reverence my s. Mark 12. 6.

Mark 9. 17. Master, I have brought to thee *my s.*
Luke 9. 38. Master, I beseech thee, look upon *my s.*
15. 24. for this *my s.* was dead and is alive again
1 *Tim.* 1. 2. to Timothy *my* own *s.* in the faith
2 *Tim.* 2. 1. *my s.* be strong in grace that is in Chr.
Tit. 1. 4. to Titus *mine* own *s.* after common faith
Philem. 10. I beseech thee for *my s.* Onesimus
Rev. 21. 7. I will be his God, he shall be *my s.*

Thy SON.

Gen. 22. 2. take now *thy s.* thine only *s.* Isaac
12. thou hast not withheld *thy s.* thine only *s.* 16.
24. 5. must I needs bring *thy s.* again to the land?
27. 32. he said, I am *thy s.* thy first-born Esau
37. 32. know now whether it be *thy s.* coat or no
48. 2. behold, *thy s.* Joseph cometh unto thee
Exod. 4. 23. I will slay *thy s.* even thy first-born
10. 2. tell in the ears of *thy s.* and son's *s.*
13. 8. thou shalt shew *thy s.* in that day, saying
14. when *thy s.* asketh thee, what is this? shalt say, by strength brought from Egypt, *Deut.* 6. 20.
20. 10. not do any work, thou, nor *thy s.* seventh day is the sabbath, thou shalt not do, *Deut.* 5. 14.
Deut. 6. 21. then thou shalt say unto *thy s.*
7. 3. nor his daughter shalt thou take unto *thy s.*
4. they will turn away *thy s.* from following me
12. 18. eat them before Ld. thou and *thy s.* 16. 11, 14.
13. 6. if *thy s.* entice thee secretly, saying
Judg. 6. 30. bring out *thy s.* that he may die
8. 22. rule over us, thou, *thy s.* and thy son's *s.*
1 *Sam.* 16. 19. Saul said, send me David *thy s.*
25. 8. give to thy servants, and to *thy s.* David
2 *Sam.* 14. 11. there shall not one hair of *thy s.* fall
1 *Kings* 1. 12. save thy life and life of *thy s.* Solom.
13. *thy s.* Solomon shall reign after me, 17, 30.
3. 22. the dead is *thy s.* ‖ 23. and *thy s.* is the dead
5. 5. *thy s.* whom I will set upon thy throne
11. 12. I will rend it out of the hand of *thy s.*
13. I will give one tribe to *thy s.* for David's sake
17. 13. and after make for thee and for *thy s.*
19. give me *thy s.* ‖ 23. Elisha said, see, *thy s.* liveth
2 *Kings* 4. 36. when she came, he said, take up *thy s.*
6. 28. give *thy s.* that we may eat him to-day, 29.
16. 7. saying, I am thy servant, and *thy s.*
1 *Chr.* 28. 6. Solomon *thy s.* shall build me my house, I have chosen him to be my *s.* 2 *Chr.* 6. 9.
Prov. 19. 18. chasten *thy s.* while there is hope
29. 17. correct *thy s.* and he shall give thee rest
Luke 9. 41. Jesus said, bring *thy s.* hither
15. 19. am no more worthy to be called *thy s.* 21.
30. as soon as this *thy s.* was come who devoured
John 4. 50. go thy way, *thy s.* liveth, 51, 53.
17. 1. glorify *thy s.* that *thy s.* also may glorify thee
19. 26. he saith to his mother, woman, behold *thy s.*

SON *of man*.

Ezek. 2. 1. he said, *s. of man*, stand upon thy feet
3. *s. of man*, I send thee to the children of Israel
6. and thou, *s. of man*, be not afraid of them
8. thou *s. of man*, hear what I say unto thee
3. 1. *s. of man*, eat that thou findest, eat this roll
3. *s. of man*, cause thy belly to eat, fill thy bowels
4. *s. of man*, go get thee to the house of Israel
10. *s. of man*, all the words that I speak receive
17. *s. of man*, I have made thee a watchman
25. O *s. of man*, they shall put bands upon thee
4. 1. thou also, *s. of man*, take thee a tile before thee
16. *s. of man*, I will break staff of bread in Jerus.
5. 1. thou *s. of man*, take thee a sharp knife
6. 2. *s. of man*, set thy face towards mountains
7. 2. thou *s. of man*, thus saith the Lord God
8. 5. *s. of man*, lift up thine eyes toward north
6. he said, *s. of man*, seest thou what they do?
8. he said, *s. of man*, dig now in the wall
12. *s. of man*, hast thou seen what ancients do?
15. he said, hast thou seen this, O *s. of man?* 17.
11. 2. *s. of man*, these are the men that devise
4. prophesy against them, prophesy, O *s. of man*
15. *s. of man*, thy brethren are they unto whom
12. 2. *s. of man*, thou dwellest in a rebellious house
3. therefore thou *s. of man*, prepare thee stuff
9. *s. of man*, hath not the house of Israel said
18. *s. of man*, eat thy bread with quaking
22. *s. of man*, what is that proverb that ye have
27. *s. of man*, behold, they of house of Israel say
13. 2. *s. of man*, prophesy against the prophets
17. thou *s. of man*, set thy face against thy people
14. 3. *s. of man*, these men have set up their idols
13. *s. of man*, when the land sinneth against me
15. 2. *s. of man*, what is the vine-tree more than any tree
16. 2. *s. of man*, cause Jerus. know her abominat.
17. 2. *s. of man*, put forth a riddle and speak
20. 3. *s. of man*, speak to the elders of Israel
4. *s. of man*, wilt thou judge them? cause to know
27. therefore *s. of man*, speak to house of Israel
46. *s. of man*, set thy face toward the south
21. 2. *s. of man*, set thy face toward Jerusalem
6. sigh therefore, thou *s. of man*, with bitterness
9. *s. of m.* prophesy and say, a sword, a sword, 28.
12. cry and howl, *s. of m.* for it shall be on people
14. *s. of man*, prophesy and smite thine hands
19. also thou *s. of man*, appoint thee two ways
22. 2. thou *s. of man*, wilt thou judge the city?
18. *s. of man*, house of Isr. is to me become dross
24. *s. of man*, say to her, thou art the land that
23. 2. *s. of m.* there were two women of one mother
36. *s. of m.* wilt thou judge Aholah and Aholibah?
24. 2. *s. of man*, write thee the name of the day
16. *s. of man*, I take away the desire of thine eyes
25. *s. of man*, shall it not be in the day when
25. 2. *s. of man*, set thy face against Ammonites
26. 2. *s. of man*, because that Tyrus hath said
27. 2. *s. of man*, take up a lamentation, 28. 12.
28. 2. *s. of man*, say unto the prince of Tyrus
21. *s. of man*, set thy face against Zidon
29. 2. *s. of man*, set thy face against Pharaoh
18. *s. of man*, Nebuchadrezzar caused his army
30. 2. *s. of man*, prophesy, and say, thus saith L.
21. *s. of man*, I have broken the arm of Pharaoh
31. 2. *s. of man*, speak to Pharaoh king of Egypt
32. 2. *s. of man*, take up a lamentation for Pharaoh
18. *s. of man*, wail for the multitude of Egypt
33. 2. *s. of man*, speak to children of thy people
7. thou, O *s. of man*, I have set thee a watchman

Ezek. 33. 10. O *s. of man*, speak to the house of Isr.
12. thou *s. of man*, say to the children of Israel
24. *s. of man*, they that inhabit those wastes of Isr.
30. *s. of man*, thy people still are talking ag. thee
34. 2. *s. of man*, prophesy against the shepherds
35. 2. *s. of man*, set thy face against mount Seir
36. 1. thou *s. of man*, prophesy to the mountains
17. *s. of man*, when the house of Israel dwelt
37. 3. he said, *s. of man*, can these bones live?
9. prophesy, *s. of man*, and say to wind, come
11. *s. of man*, these bones are the house of Israel
16. *s. of man*, take thee one stick, and write on it
38. 2. *s. of man*, set thy face against Gog
14. theref. *s. of man*, prophesy and say unto Gog
39. 1. thou *s. of man*, prophesy ag. Gog and say
17. thou *s. of man*, thus saith the Lord, 43. 18.
40. 4. *s. of man*, behold with thine eyes, and hear
43. 7. he said, *s. of man*, the place of my throne
10. *s. of man*, shew the house to house of Israel
44. 5. *s. of man*, mark well, behold with thine eyes
47. 6. he said, *s. of man*, hast thou seen this?

See MAN.

SONG.

We find in Scripture several songs *composed upon important occasions; for example,* Moses *made one after the passage through the Red sea, to thank God for the deliverance of his people, and celebrate the greatness of this miracle,* Exod. 15. 1, 2, &c. David *composed a mournful* song *upon the death of* Saul *and* Jonathan, *and another upon the death of* Abner, 2 *Sam.* 1. 18, 19. | 3. 33. Jeremiah *wrote his* Lamentations, *which are a* song, *wherein he deplores the calamities and ruin of* Jerusalem; *and he made another upon the death of* Josiah *king of* Judah, 2 Chron. 35. 25. Deborah *and* Barak *made a triumphant hymn after the defeat of* Sisera, *Judg.* 5. 1, 2, 3, &c. *The* Canticles, *or* Solomon's Song, *and the* 45th Psalm, *are songs to celebrate a spiritual and divine wedding, such sort of pieces as the* Greeks *call* Epithalamia. Hannah *the mother of* Samuel, *and king* Hezekiah, *returned thanks to God for the favours they had received, in solemn and spiritual* songs, 1 Sam. 2. 1, 2, &c. Isa. 38. 10, 11, &c. *The* songs *composed by the Virgin* Mary, *by* Zacharias *the father of* John the Baptist, *and old* Simeon, *are of the same nature; they are thanksgivings to God for blessings received from him,* Luke 1. 46, 68. | 2. 29, 30.

THE SONG OF SONGS, *in* Hebrew, Schir Haschirim, *the most excellent of all songs. The* Christian *church, as well as the synagogue, has always received this book of* Canticles *among the Scriptures as generally owned to be canonical. The form of it is dramatical, wherein several parts of it are uttered by, or in the name of, several persons; which are chiefly four, the bridegroom and bride, and the friends or companions of the one, and of the other. The design of the book in general, is to describe the passionate loves and happy marriage of two persons, their mutual satisfaction therein, and the blessed fruits and effects thereof. But then it is not to be understood carnally, concerning* Solomon *and* Pharaoh's *daughter, although the inspired author may allude to that; but they who would penetrate the meaning, and comprehend the whole mystery of it, must raise their conceptions above things relating to flesh and blood, and contemplate in it the espousals of* Christ *with the church, and with every believer. So that this book is a continued allegory, wherein, under the terms of a common wedding, a divine and supernatural marriage is expressed.*

The Hebrews, *apprehending it might be understood in a gross and carnal manner, forbade the reading of it before the age of thirty; and indeed nothing is more dangerous than to read it with carnal thoughts and dispositions; people not only being liable to the hazard of losing thereby all the esteem which they ought to have for this book, but of even wounding the soul instead of edifying it.*

Such as deny this spiritual book to be canonical, say, that neither Christ, nor his Apostles, have ever cited it, and that the name of God is not once to be found in it. To this it is replied, that there are several other sacred books, which our Saviour has not expressly quoted; and that in an allegory, wherein the Son of God is concealed under the figure of an Husband, it is not necessary that he should be expressed by his proper name. If he were by name mentioned, it would cease to be an allegory.

Exod. 15. 1. then sang Moses and the children of Israel this *s.* unto the Lord, *Num.* 21. 17.
2. the Lord is my strength and *s.* and he is become my salvation, *Psal.* 118. 14. *Isa.* 12. 2.
Deut. 31. 19. write this *s.* that this *s.* may be witness
21. this *s.* shall testify ‖ 22. Moses wrote this *s.*
30. Moses spake the words of this *s.* 32. 44.
Judg. 5. 12. awake, awake, Deborah, utter a *s.*
2 *Sam.* 22. 1. David spake to Lord words of this *s.*
1 *Chr.* 6. 31. they whom David set over service of *s.*
15. 22. Chenaniah chief of Levites was for a *s.* 27.
25. 6. these were under their father for *s.* in house
2 *Chron.* 29. 27. *s.* of the Lord began with trumpets
Job 30. 9. now I am their *s.* I am their by-word
Psal. 28. 7. and with my *s.* will I praise him
33. 3. sing unto him a new *s.* *Isa.* 42. 10.
40. 3. and he hath put a new *s.* in my mouth
42. 8. and in the night his *s.* shall be with me
69. 12. and I was the *s.* of the drunkards
30. I will praise the name of God with a *s.*
77. 6. I call to remembrance my *s.* in night
96. 1. O sing to the Lord a new *s.* 98. 1. | 149. 1.
137. 3. for there they required of us a *s.* and mirth
4. how shall we sing Lord's *s.* in a strange land?
144. 9. I will sing a new *s.* unto thee, O God
Eccl. 7. 5. than for a man to hear the *s.* of fools
Cant. 1. 1. the *s.* of songs which is Solomon's
Isa. 5. 1. now will I sing a *s.* of my beloved

Isa. 24. 9. they shall not drink wine with a *s.*
26. 1. in that day shall this *s.* be sung in Judah
30. 29. ye shall have a *s.* as in the night
Lam. 3. 14. I was a derision and their *s.* all the day
Ezek. 33. 32. thou art to them as a very lovely *s.*
Rev. 5. 9. they sung a new *s.* thou art worthy, 14. 3.
14. 3. no man could learn that *s.* but the 144,000
15. 3. they sing the *s.* of Moses and *s.* of the Lamb

SONGS.

Gen. 31. 27. I might have sent thee away with *s.*
Judg. 9. † 27. they trod the grapes and made *s.*
1 *Kings* 4. 32. his *s.* were a thousand and five
1 *Chron.* 13. † 8. David prayed before God with *s.*
25. 7. that were instructed in the *s.* of the Lord
Neh. 12. 46. in the days of David there were *s.*
Job 35. 10. God my maker, who giveth *s.* in night
Ps. 32. 7. shall compass about with *s.* of deliverance
119. 54. have been my *s.* in house of pilgrimage
137. 3. saying, sing us one of the *s.* of Zion
Prov. 25. 20. so is he that singeth *s.* to heavy heart
Cant. 1. 1. the song of *s.* which is Solomon's
Isa. 23. 16. make sweet melody, sing many *s.*
24. 16. from utter. part of earth have we heard *s.*
35. 10. the ransomed shall come to Zion with *s.*
38. 20. will sing my *s.* to the stringed instruments
Ezek. 26. 13. I will cause the noise of thy *s.* to cease
Amos 5. 23. take away from me the noise of thy *s.*
8. 3. *s.* of the temple shall be howlings in that day
10. I will turn all your *s.* into lamentation
Hab. 3. † 1. a prayer according to variable *s.*
Eph. 5. 19. speak. to yours. in psalms and spirit. *s.*
Col. 3. 16. admonish. one anoth. in hymns, spirit. *s.*

SONS.

Gen. 7. 13. the *s.* of Noah entered into the ark
9. 18. the *s.* of Noah that went forth of the ark
19. these are the three *s.* of Noah, and of them
10. 1. and to them were *s.* born after the flood
19. 14. Lot went out and spake to his *s.*-in-law
23. 11. in the presence of the *s.* of my people
27. 29. and let thy mother's *s.* bow down to thee
34. 27. *s.* of Jacob came upon slain and spoiled
37. 2. and the lad was with the *s.* of Bilhah
42. 5. and the *s.* of Israel came to buy corn
11. we are all one man's *s.* we are no spies, 32.
46. 5. the *s.* of Israel carried Jacob in waggons
Exod. 29. † 30. he of his *s.* that is priest in his stead
32. 2. break off ear-rings in the ears of your *s.*
Lev. 26. 29. ye shall eat the flesh of your *s.*
Num. 16. 7. ye take too much on you, ye *s.* of Levi
27. stood in door of their tents their wives and *s.*
27. 3. our father died in his own sin, and had no *s.*
36. 3. if they be married to *s.* of other tribes
Deut. 23. 17. nor a sodomite of the *s.* of Israel
32. 8. when he separated the *s.* of Adam
Josh. 15. 14. Caleb drove 3 *s.* of Anak, *Judg.* 1. 20.
Judg. 8. 19. there were even the *s.* of my mother
30. Gideon had 70 *s.* ‖ 10. 4. Jair had thirty *s.*
12. 14. Abdon had forty *s.* and thirty nephews
19. 22. certain *s.* of Belial beset house round about
Ruth 1. 11. are there yet any more *s.* in my womb?
1 *Sam.* 1. 8. am not I better to thee than ten *s.?*
2. 12. *s.* of Eli were *s.* of Belial, knew not Lord
8. 11. will take your *s.* and appoint them for hims.
26. † 16. as the Lord liveth, ye are the *s.* of death
2 *Sam.* 2. 18. there were three *s.* of Zeruiah there
3. 39. these men *s.* of Zeruiah be too hard for me
9. 11. Mephibosheth eat as one of the king's *s.*
13. 23. and Absalom invited all the king's *s.*
30. saying, Absalom hath slain all the king's *s.*
16. 10. what to do with you, ye *s.* of Zeruiah? 19. 22.
23. 6. but *s.* of Belial shall be as thorns thrust away
1 *Kings* 1. 9. he called all the king's *s.* 19. 25.
2. 7. but shew kindness to *s.* of Barzillai Gileadite
4. 31. for he was wiser than the *s.* of Mahol
20. 35. a certain man of the *s.* of the prophets
21. 10. set two men, *s.* of Belial, before him
2 *Kings* 4. 5. she shut door upon her and upon her *s.*
10. 3. look out the meetest of your master's *s.*
8. they have brought the heads of the king's *s.*
11. 2. stole him from the king's *s.* 2 *Chron.* 22. 11.
25. 7. they slew *s.* of Zedekiah before his eyes, and put out eyes of Zedekiah, *Jer.* 39. 6. | 52. 10.
1 *Chr.* 5. 1. his birth-right was given to *s.* of Joseph
21. 20. Ornan and his four *s.* with him hid thems.
24. 28. of Mahli came Eleazar, who had no *s.*
28. 4. among the *s.* of my fathers, he liked me
2 *Chron.* 23. 3. the Lord said of the *s.* of David
24. 25. for blood of the *s.* of Jehoiada the priest
25. † 13. *s.* of the band fell on the cities of Judah
28. † 6. Pekah slew in one day 120,000 *s.* of valour
Neh. 13. 28. one of the *s.* of Joiada was son-in-law
Esth. 9. 10. the ten *s.* of Haman slew they
13. let Haman's ten *s.* be hanged on gallows, 14.
Job 5. † 7. the *s.* of the burning coal lift up to fly
Psal. 18. † 44. *s.* of stranger shall yield obedience
29. † 1. O ye *s.* of mighty give to the Lord glory
89. 6. who among *s.* of mighty can be likened?
144. 12. that our *s.* may be as plants grown up
Prov. 31. † 5. pervert judgment of all *s.* of affliction
† 8. in the cause of such as are *s.* of destruction
Eccl. 2. † 7. I got maidens, and had *s.* of my house
Cant. 2. 3. as apple-tree so is my beloved among *s.*
Isa. 51. 18. there is none to guide her among all *s.*
56. 6. *s.* of stranger that join themselves to Lord
57. 3. draw near hither, ye *s.* of the sorceress
60. 10. the *s.* of the stranger shall build thy walls
14. the *s.* of them that afflicted thee shall come
61. 5. the *s.* of the alien shall be your plowmen
62. 8. *s.* of the stranger shall not drink thy wine
Jer. 6. 21. the fathers and *s.* shall fall upon them
13. 14. even fathers and *s.* together will I dash
19. 5. they built the high-places to burn their *s.*
29. 6. take wives, beget *s.* take wives for your *s.*
35. 5. I set before *s.* of Rechabites pots full of wine
6. ye shall drink no wine, ye, nor your *s.* for ever
49. 1. hath Israel no *s.?* hath he no heir?
Lam. 3. † 13. caused *s.* of his quiver to enter my reins
4. 2. precious *s.* of Zion, comparable to fine gold
Ezek. 5. 10. fathers shall eat their *s.* *s.* their fathers
20. 31. when ye make your *s.* pass through the fire
23. 37. they caused their *s.* to pass through the fire
Hos. 1. 10. ye are the *s.* of the living God

Amos 2. 11. I raised up of your *s.* for prophets
Mic. 6. † 6. shall I come with calves, *s.* of a year old
Zech. 4. † 14. he said, these are the two *s.* of oil
Mal. 3. 3. he shall purify *s.* of Levi, and purge them
6. therefore ye *s.* of Jacob are not consumed
Mark 3. 17. Boanerges, which is, the *s.* of thunder
Luke 11. 19. by whom do your *s.* cast them out
1 *Cor.* 4. 14. but as my beloved *s.* I warn you
Gal. 4. 5. that we might receive the adoption of *s.*
6. because ye are *s.* God hath sent forth Spirit
Heb. 2. 10. bring many *s.* to glory to make captain
11. 21. Jacob blessed both *s.* of Joseph and worship.
12. 7. if chastened, God dealeth with you as with *s.*
8. if not chastened, then are ye bastards, and not *s.*
See AARON. DAUGHTER.

SONS *of God.*

Gen. 6. 2. the *s. of God* saw the daughters of men
4. the *s. of God* came in to the daughters of men
Job 1. 6. *s. of God* came to present themselves, 2. 1.
38. 7. when all the *s. of God* shouted for joy
Hos. 1. 10. shall be said, ye are *s. of* the living *God*
John 1. 12. he gave them power to become *s. of God*
Rom. 8. 14. as are led by spirit of God, are *s. of God*
19. waiteth for the manifestation of *s. of God*
Phil 2. 15. that ye may be harmless, the *s. of God*
1 *John* 3. 1. that we should be called the *s. of God*
2. beloved, now are we *s. of God,* not appear

His SONS.

Gen. 7. 7. Noah went into ark and *his s.* and his wife
8. 18. Noah went forth, and *his s.* and his wife
9. 1. God blessed Noah and *his s.* and said to them
25. 9. *his s.* Isaac and Ishmael buried him in cave
35. 35. he gave them into the hands of *his s.*
35. 29. *his s.* Esau and Jacob buried him
49. 33. had made an end of commanding *his s.*
50. 12. *his s.* did unto him as he commanded
13. *his s.* carried him into the land of Canaan
Exod. 18. 5. Jethro came with *his s.* and wife to Moses
28. 1. take Aaron and *his s.* to minister to me
41. thou shalt put the garments on *his s.* 29. 8.
29. 20. put blood on the tip of the right ear of *his s.*
21. thou shalt sprinkle the blood upon *his s.*
27. sanctify that which is for *his s.* *Lev.* 8. 30.
Lev. 6. 22. priest of *his s.* that is anointed shall offer
Num. 21. 35. they smote Og and *his s.* and people
Deut. 2. 33. we smote Sihon, *his s.* and his people
18. 5. Lord hath chosen him and *his s.* to minister
21. 16. when he maketh *his s.* to inherit what hath
Judg. 9. 18. have slain *his s.* 70 persons on one stone
17. 5. Micah consecrated one of *his s.* became priest
11. the Levite was to him as one of *his s.*
18. 30. he and *his s.* were priests to tribe of Dan
1 *Sam.* 2. 22. now Eli heard all that *his s.* did
3. 13. because *his s.* made themselves vile
8. 1. Sam. when old made *his s.* judges over Israel
3. *his s.* walked not in his ways, but turned aside
16. 1. I have provided me a king among *his s.*
30. 6. all people was grieved, every man for *his s.*
31. 2. the Philistines followed hard upon Saul and upon *his s.* and slew Jonathan, 1 *Chron.* 10. 2.
2 *Sam.* 21. 6. let seven men of *his s.* be delivered to us
1 *Kings* 13. 11. *his s.* came and told him all works
12. *his s.* had seen what way the man of G. went
21. 29. but in *his s.* days will I bring the evil
2 *Kings* 9. 26. I have seen blood of Naboth and *his s.*
19. 37. *his s.* smote him with sword, *Isa.* 37. 38.
2 *Chr.* 11. 14. Jeroboam and *his s.* had cast them off
13. 5. even to him and *his s.* by a covenant of salt
21. 7. to give a light to him, and to *his s.* for ever
17. carried away *his s.* save the youngest of *his s.*
36. 20. where they were servants to him and *his s.*
Ezra 6. 10. and pray for life of the king and *his s.*
Esth. 9. 25. that he and *his s.* be hanged on gallows
Job 1. 4. and *his s.* went and feasted in their houses
14. 21. *his s.* come to honour, he knoweth it not
38. 32. or canst thou guide Arcturus with *his s.?*
42. 16. after this, Job saw *his s.* and *his s.* sons
Jer. 35. 14. Jonadab comm. *his s.* not to drink wine
Ezek. 46. 16. if prince give a gift to any of *his s.*
Dan. 11. 10. *his s.* shall be stirred up and assemble
See MAN.

My SONS.

Gen. 48. 9. Joseph said to his father, they are *my s.*
1 *Sam.* 2. 24. nay, *my s.* for it is no good report I hear
12. 2. Samuel said, behold, *my s.* are with you
1 *Chron.* 28. 5. of all *my s.* he hath chosen Solomon
2 *Chr.* 29. 11. Hezekiah said, *my s.* be not negligent
Job 1. 5. Job said, it may be that *my s.* have sinned
Isa. 45. 11. ask me of things to come concern. *my s.*
1 *Cor.* 4. 14. but as *my* beloved *s.* I warn you
See SEVEN.

Thy SONS.

Gen. 6. 18. thou shalt come into ark, thou and *t. s.*
8. 16. go forth of ark, thou, thy wife, and *thy s.*
Exod. 12. 24. ordinan. to thee and *thy s.* *Num.* 18. 8.
22. 29. first-born of *thy s.* shalt thou give to me
34. 16. make *thy s.* go a whoring after their gods
20. all the first-born of *thy s.* thou shalt redeem
Lev. 10. 9. do not drink wine, nor *thy s.* with thee
14. because it is thy due, and *thy s.* due
Num. 18. 1. thou and *thy s.* shall bear the iniquity
2. but thou and *thy s.* with thee shall minister
7. thou and *thy s.* shall keep your priests' office
9. shall be most holy for thee and for *thy s.*
11. I have given them to thee and to *thy s.*
Deut. 4. 9. but teach them *thy s.* and *thy s.* sons
1 *Sam.* 2. 29. and honourest *thy s.* above me
8. 5. thou art old, and *thy s.* walk not in thy ways
28. 19. to-morrow shalt thou and *thy s.* be with me
2 *Sam.* 9. 10. thou and *thy s.* shall till land for him
2 *Kings* 4. 4. shalt shut door upon thee and *thy s.*
15. 12. L. said to Jehu, *thy s.* shall sit on throne of Israel to fourth generation, 1 *Chron.* 17. 11.
20. 18. *thy s.* shall be eunuchs in Babyl. *Isa.* 39. 7.
Isa. 49. 22. and they shall bring *thy s.* in their arms
51. 20. *t. s.* have fainted, they lie at head of streets
60. 4. they come to thee, *t. s.* shall come from far, 9.
62. 5. as young man marrieth virgin, so shall *thy s.*
Jer. 48. 46. *thy s.* and daughters are taken captives
Zech. 9. 13. and raised up *thy s.* O Zion, ag. *thy s.*

Two SONS.

Gen. 10. 25. to Eber were born *two s.* 1 *Chr.* 1. 19.
Gen. 34. 25. *two* of the *s.* of Jacob slew the males
41. 50. to Joseph were born *two s.* before famine
42. 37. slay my *two s.* if I bring him not to thee
44. 27. ye know that my wife bare me *two s.*
48. 1. and he took with him his *two s.* 5.
Exod. 18. 3. Jethro took Zipporah and her *two s.*
Lev. 16. 1. after the death of the *two s.* of Aaron
Ruth 1. 1. he, his wife, *two s.* Mahlon and Chilion, 2.
3. she was left and her *two s.* ‖ 5. left of her *two s.*
1 *Sam.* 2. 34. that shall come upon thy *two s.*
4. 4. the *two s.* of Eli were there with the ark
17. thy *two s.* Hophni and Phinehas are dead
2 *Sam.* 14. 6. thy handmaid had *two s.* they strove
15. 36. they had there with them their *two s.*
21. 8. but the king took the *two s.* of Rizpah
2 *Kings* 4. 1. creditor to take *two s.* to be bond-men
Mat. 20. 21. grant that these my *two s.* may sit
21. 28. a certain man had *two s.* *Luke* 15. 11.
26. 37. took with him Peter and *two s.* of Zebed.
Acts 7. 29. stranger in Midian, where he begat *two s.*
Gal. 4. 22. it is written that Abraham had *two s.*

SOON.

Exod. 2. 18. how is it that ye are come so *s.* to-day?
Deut. 4. 26. that ye shall *s.* utterly perish from land
Job 32. 22. in so doing my Maker *s.* take me away
Psal. 37. 2. they shall *s.* be cut down like the grass
68. 31. shall *s.* stretch out her hands unto God
81. 14. I should *s.* have subdued their enemies
90. 10. for it is *s.* cut off, and we fly away
106. 13. they *s.* forgat his works, they waited not
Prov. 14. 17. he that is *s.* angry dealeth foolishly
Mat. 21. 20. how *s.* is the fig-tree withered away
Gal. 1. 6. I marvel that ye are so *s.* removed from
2 *Thess.* 2. 2. ye be not *s.* shaken in mind or troubled
Tit. 1. 7. not self-will. not *s.* angry, not given to wine

As SOON *as.*

Exod. 32. 19. *as s. as* he came nigh unto the camp
Josh. 8. 19. ran *as s. as* he had stretched his hand
2 *Sam.* 22. 45. *as s. as* they hear they shall be obedient to me, strangers shall submit, *Psal.* 18. 44.
Psal. 58. 3. they go astray *as s. as* they be born
Luke 1. 23. *as s. as* his ministration were accompl.
Phil. 2. 23. *as s. as* I see how it will go with me

SOONER.

Heb. 13. 19. that I may be restored to you the *s.*
Jam. 1. 11. sun is no *s.* risen, but it withereth grass

SOOTHSAYER,

Diviner, *or* Magician. *Some derive this word from* Haanan, *which signifies a cloud; because this kind of diviners raised their conjectures from the various figures and motions of the clouds and sky; or from the flight and chattering of birds and fowls in the air. Others derive the word from* Haajin, *an eye, to signify astrologers, who foretell future contingent things, by the superstitious observation of the stars and planets. Others think, that the word signifies such magicians, who, by playing hocus-pocus tricks, endeavour thereby to impose upon the eyes and understanding of the spectators: making things, by their magical skill, appear otherwise than in truth they are. Others again understand by it such as give answers to those that repair to them for advice and direction in their affairs, deriving it from a word that signifies* to answer. *Lastly, some suppose it may be derived from a word which signifies* a set-time, *and by it understand such as observe days and times, as good or bad, lucky or unlucky; such as those that did cast lots before* Haman, *Esth.* 3. 7.

In Exod. 7. 11. *there is mention made of* Pharaoh's *sorcerers or magicians, who acted by the power of the devil, whom by certain rites and ceremonies they engaged to their assistance, resisted* Moses, *and by their enchantments counterfeited his true miracles before* Pharaoh. *Of these the two chief were* Jannes *and* Jambres, 2 *Tim.* 3. 8. *These names are not to be found in the story of the Old Testament, but are taken out of other records of the* Jews, *or were known in* St. Paul's *time by tradition. The Paraphrast* Jonathan *says, that they were the two sons of* Balaam, *who accompanied him, when he went to* Balak *king of* Moab.

These magicians wrought no true miracle, but only in shew and appearance, which, by the permission of God, was not difficult for the devil to do, either by altering the air and the spectator's sight, and by causing their rods both to look and move like serpents; or by a sudden and secret conveyance of real serpents thither, and removing the rods. Moses *however expresses himself throughout in such a manner as might persuade one, that* Pharaoh's *magicians really operated the same effects as he himself produced: so that* Pharaoh *and his whole court were persuaded, that the power of their magicians was equal to that of* Moses, *till the* Egyptians, *not being able to produce lice, as* Moses *had done, were constrained to own,* that the finger of God was concerned in it, *Exod.* 8. 18, 19. *Till then they had acknowledged nothing divine or supernatural in any thing he did. And it is agreed, that magic and juggling tricks, evil angels and sorcerers, may sometimes imitate very nearly true miracles and the operations of the Almighty.* Moses's *manner of expressing himself is a great evidence of the truth of scripture story, and that it was not written by fiction and design. For if* Moses *had written these books to deceive the world, and to advance his own reputation, as some take the liberty to say, it is ridiculous to think that he would have put in this and many other passages, which might seem so much to eclipse his honour, and the glory of his works.*

Daniel *also speaks of* magicians, *and the* diviners *that were in* Chaldea *under king* Nebuchadnezzar. *He names four sorts of them,* Dan. 2. 2. I. Chartumim, *which, according to* Theodotion, *signifies enchanters; according to the Septuagint, sophists: according to St.* Jerom, Ariolos, *diviners, fortune-tellers, casters of nativities.* II. Asaphim. *This word has a great resemblance to the* Greek *word* σοφοι, *wise men.* Grotius *thinks it is derived from the* Greek. Theodotion *and* Jerom *have rendered it by* magicians, *and the Septuagint by* philosophers. III. Mecasphim, *which by St.* Jerom *and the* Greeks *is translated* malifici, *enchanters; such people as make use of noxious herbs and drugs, the blood of victims, and the bones of the dead, for their superstitious operations.* IV. Casdim, *or* Chaldeans. *This word has two different significations. The first intimates the* Chaldean *people, who had then* Nebuchadnezzar *for their monarch. The second expresses a sort of philosophers called also* Chaldeans, *who dwelt in a separate part of the city, and were exempt from all public offices and employments. Their study was physic, astrology, divination, the foretelling of future events by the observation of the stars, the interpretation of dreams, the science of auguries, the worship of the gods, &c.*

All these inquisitive and superstitious arts are strictly forbidden by the law of God, all wherein any conjurations or invocations of the devil are used; in a word, all the black art, and all superstitious ceremonies made use of by magicians, sorcerers, enchanters, witches, wizards, necromancers, exorcists, astrologers, soothsayers, interpreters of dreams, fortune-tellers, casters of nativities, &c. *in practising their diabolical arts, whether it be to hurt mankind, or to procure them health, or any other advantages. God hath forbidden to consult such persons upon pain of death,* Lev. 20. 6. Saul *did what he could to drive them out of the country of* Israel, 1 *Sam.* 28. 3. *But, for all this, many were still to be found; and the* Israelites *were always much addicted to these sorts of superstitions. And the same prince who had been so eager in driving them out of his dominions, at last went to consult one himself,* 1 Sam. 28. 7, 8, &c. *See* DIVINATION, EXORCISTS.

Josh. 13. 22. Balaam son of Beor *s.* did Israel slay

SOOTHSAYERS.

Isa. 2. 6. hast forsaken thy people, because they are *s.*
Dan. 2. 27. the secret cannot the *s.* shew to the king
5. 7. king cried aloud to bring Chaldeans and *s.*
11. whom the king made master of the *s.*
Mic. 5. 12. and thou shalt have no more *s.*

SOOTHSAYING.

Acts 16. 16. who brought her masters much gain by *s.*

SOP.

John 13. 26. he it is to whom I shall give a *s.* when he had dipped the *s.* he gave it to Judas Iscariot
27. after the *s.* Satan entered into him, 30.

SOAP.

Jer 2. 22. for tho' thou wash and take thee much *s.*
Mal. 3. 2. who may abide his com.? is like fuller's *s.*

SORCERER.

Acts 13. 6. found a certain *s.* a false prophet, a Jew
8. but Elymas the *s.* withstood them, seeking

SORCERERS.

Exod. 7. 11. then Phar. also called wise men and *s.*
Jer. 27. 9. therefore hearken not to your *s.*
Dan. 2. 2. Nebuchadnezzar commanded to call *s.*
Mal. 3. 5. I will be a swift witness against the *s.*
Rev. 21. 8. and *s.* shall have their part in the lake
22. 15. for without are dogs and *s.* murderers

SORCERESS.

Isa. 57. 3. but draw near hither, ye sons of the *s.*

SORCERY.

Acts 8. 9. a man Simon, who before-time used *s.*

SORCERIES.

Isa. 47. 9. they shall come on thee for thy *s.*
12. stand now with the multitude of thy *s.*
Acts 8. 11. that of long time bewitched them with *s.*
Rev. 9. 21. neither repented they of their *s.*
18. 23. for by thy *s.* were all nations deceived

SORE.

Gen. 19. 9. they pressed *s.* upon the man, even Lot
31. 30. because thou *s.* longest after father's house
41. 56. the famine waxed *s.* in the land of Egypt
57. *s.* in all lands ‖ 43. 1. *s.* in Canaan, 47. 4, 13.
50. 10. they mourned with a *s.* lamentation
Deut. 6. 22. L. shewed signs great and *s.* on Egypt
28. 35. the Lord shall smite thee with a *s.* botch
59. *s.* sicknesses, and of long continuance
Judg. 10. 9. so that Israel was *s.* distressed
14. 17. he told her, because she lay *s.* upon him
15. 18. Samson was *s.* athirst, and called on Lord
20. 34. ten thousand came ag. Gibeah, battle was *s.* 1 *Sam.* 31. 3. 2 *Sam.* 2. 17. 2 *Kings* 3. 26.
21. 2. the people lifted up their voices, and wept *s.*
1 *Sam.* 1. 6. her adversary also provoked her *s.*
10. Hannah prayed to the Lord, and wept *s.*
5. 7. his hand is *s.* on us, and on Dagon our God
14. 52. there was *s.* war against the Philistines
28. 15. Saul answered, I am *s.* distressed, 21.
2 *Sam.* 13. 36. the king and his servants wept *s.*
1 *Kings* 17. 17. sickn. so *s.* no breath was left in him
18. 2. and there was a *s.* famine in Samaria
2 *Kings* 6. 11. the king of Syria was *s.* troubled
20. 3. and Hezekiah wept *s.* *Isa.* 38. 3.
2 *Chron.* 21. 19. so Jehoram died of *s.* diseases
28. 19. Ahaz transgressed *s.* against Lord
35. 23. have me away, for I am *s.* wounded
Ezra 10. 1. for the people wept very *s.*
Neh. 13. 8. it grieved me *s.* therefore I cast forth
Job 2. 7. Satan smote Job with *s.* boils
Psal. 2. 5. and vex them in his *s.* displeasure
6. 3. my soul is *s.* vexed, but thou, O L. how long
10. let mine enemies be ashamed, and *s.* vexed
38. 2. arrows stick fast, thine hand presseth me *s.*
8. I am feeble and *s.* broken, I roared by disquiet
44. 19. tho' hast *s.* broken us in place of dragons
55. 4. my heart is *s.* pained within me, and terrors
71. 20. thou hast shewed me great and *s.* troubles
118. 13. thou hast thrust *s.* at me, that I might fall
18. L. hath chastened me *s.* but not given me over
Prov. 11. † 15. he that is surety shall be *s.* broken
Eccl. 1. 13. this *s.* travail hath God given, 4. 8.
5. 13. there is *s.* evil I have seen under sun, 16.
Isa. 27. 1. with *s.* and great sword punish leviathan
59. 11. we roar like bears, mourn *s.* like doves
64. 9. be not wroth very *s.* O Lord, nor remember
12. wilt thou hold thy peace, afflict us very *s.?*

Jer. 13. 17. mine eye shalt weep *s.* and run down
22. 10. but weep *s.* for him that goeth away
52. 6. famine was *s.* in city, there was no bread
Lam. 1. 2. she weepeth *s.* in the night and her tears
3. 52. mine enemies chased me *s.* like a bird
Ezek. 14. 21. when I send my four *s.* judgments
21. 10. it is sharpened to make a *s.* slaughter
Dan. 6. 14. the king was *s.* displeased with himself
Mic. 2. 10. it shall destroy you even with *s.* destruct.
Zech. 1. 2. the Lord hath been *s.* displeased, 15.
Mat. 17. 15. for he is lunatic, and *s.* vexed
21. 15. saying, Hosanna, they were *s.* displeased
Mark 6. 51. they were *s.* amazed in themselves
9. 26. spirit cried, rent him *s.* and came out of him
14. 33. Jesus began to be *s.* amazed and heavy
Acts 20. 37. they all wept *s.* and kissed Paul
See AFRAID.

SORE.

Gen. 34. 25. on the third day, when they were *s.*
Job 5. 18. he maketh *s.* and bindeth up, woundeth

SORE.

Lev. 13. 42. if a white reddish *s.* it is a leprosy
43. if rising of *s.* be white reddish in his head
2 *Chron.* 6. 28. whatsoever *s.* or sickness there be
29. when every one shall know his own *s.* grief
Psal. 38. 11. my friends stand aloof from my *s.*
77. 2. my *s.* ran in the night and ceased not
Rev. 16. 2. there fell a grievous *s.* upon the men

SORES.

Isa. 1. 6. but wounds, and bruises, and putrifying *s.*
Ezek. 47. † 12. leaf thereof shall be for bruises and *s.*
Luke 16. 20. beggar Lazarus at his gate full of *s.* 21.
Rev. 16. 11. blasphemed G. bec. of their pains and *s.*

SORELY.

Gen. 49. 23. archers *s.* grieved him and shot at him
Isa. 23. 5. so shall be *s.* pained at the report of Tyre

SORER.

Heb. 10. 29. of how much *s.* punishment suppose ye

SORROW

Is a passion that contracts the heart, sinks the spirits, and spoils the health of the body. St. Paul *advises the* Thessalonians, *not to suffer themselves to be overcome with sorrow for the godly that are dead, not to sorrow after a heathenish manner, as those that had no hope of a future resurrection,* 1 Thess. 4. 13. *The apostle here does not condemn their* sorrow, *but only the excess of it. Grace destroys not nature, but regulates it; nor takes it away the affections, but moderates them. For to mourn for the dead, especially those that die in the Lord, is a duty that both nature, grace, and the practice of godly men, teach, and which God requireth.* Abraham *mourned and wept for* Sarah *his wife,* Gen. 23. 2. Jacob *for his son* Joseph, *supposing he had been torn by wild beasts,* Gen. 37. 34. *And* Joseph *and his brethren for their father* Jacob, *Gen.* 50. 10. *The contrary is reproved by God himself. Isa.* 57. 1. The righteous perisheth, and no man layeth it to heart; and merciful men are taken away, none considering that the righteous is taken away from the evil to come: *and to die unlamented is reckoned as a curse.* Jer. 22. 18. They shall not lament for *Jehoiakim,* saying, ah my brother, or ah my sister, &c. *It is only then* immoderate sorrow *the apostle here means; which is likewise forbidden in the Old Testament,* Lev. 19. 28. Deut. 14. 1. Ye shall not make any cuttings in your flesh for the dead; *which was a practice among the heathen, both in the worship of their idols, and in their solemn mournings.*

The apostle in 2 Cor. 7. 10. *distinguishes two sorts of* sorrow, *one a godly, and the other a worldly,* sorrow. Godly sorrow *is that which is wrought in the soul by the Spirit of God, which arises from a sense of sin; the root of it is a love to God, and the manner of it such as was agreeable to the will of God. The apostle in the following verse makes it appear that this* sorrow *of the* Corinthians *was* godly, *by the excellent fruits and effects of it. Behold, says he, what* carefulness *it wrought in you to amend what had been amiss!* What clearing of yourselves. *You shewed that you did not approve of the fault of other members of your church.* Yea, what indignation! *namely, against the offender, and yourselves for your neglect.* Yea, what fear! *namely, of divine vengeance, if you should persist in that neglect, or of transgressing again.* Yea, what vehement desire! *To take away the scandal, and to give every good man satisfaction.* Yea, what zeal! *For the glory of God, and to perform what I had commanded in my former epistle concerning the incestuous person. He adds,* yea, what revenge *it wrought in you against the offender, by punishing of him!*

Worldly sorrow *is a sorrow occasioned by worldly troubles, and carnal considerations, which, the apostle says,* worketh death; *while men bow down under their burdens, and through impatience destroy themselves, as* Ahithophel, Judas, &c. *Or when men fix their thoughts upon sad objects, and so afflict themselves with them, that they bring themselves into diseases which issue in death.*

Gen. 3. 16. I will greatly multiply thy *s.* and conception, in *s.* thou shalt bring forth children
17. in *s.* shalt thou eat of it all days of thy life
35. † 18. she called his name, the son of my *s.*
42. 38. if mischief befall him, then shall ye bring down my gray hairs with *s.* to grave, 44. 29, 31.
Exod. 15. 14. *s.* take hold of inhabitants of Palestina
Lev. 26. 16. terror shall cause *s.* of heart
Deut. 28. 65. the Lord shall give thee *s.* of mind
1 *Chron.* 4. 9. saying, because I bare him with *s.*
Neh. 2. 2. this is nothing else but *s.* of heart
Esth. 9. 22. the month was turned from *s.* to joy
Job 3. 10. because it hid not *s.* from mine eyes
6. 10. yea, I would harden myself in *s.*
17. 7. mine eye is dim by reason of *s.* my members
41. 22. and *s.* is turned into joy before him
Psal. 13. 2. having *s.* in my heart daily
38. 17. and my *s.* is continually before me
39. 2. I held my peace, and my *s.* was stirred

Psal. 55. 10. mischief also and *s.* are in midst of it
90. 10. yet is their strength labour and *s.*
107. 39. again they are brought low through *s.*
116. 3. I found trouble and *s.* called I on the Lord
Prov. 10. 10. he that winketh with eye, causeth *s.*
22. Lord maketh rich, he addeth no *s.* with it
15. 13. but by *s.* of heart the spirit is broken
17. 21. he that begetteth a fool, doth it to his *s.*
23. 29. who hath woe? who hath *s.*? contentions
Eccl. 1. 18. he that increaseth knowl. increaseth *s.*
5. 17. he hath much *s.* and wrath with sickness
7. 3. *s.* is better than laughter, heart made better
11. 10. therefore remove *s.* from thy heart
Isa. 5. 30. if one look unto the land, behold *s.*
14. 3. the Lord shall give thee rest from thy *s.*
17. 11. shall be an heap in the day of desperate *s.*
29. 2. I will distress Ariel, and there shall be *s.*
35. 10. and *s.* and sighing shall flee away
50. 11. this shall ye have, ye shall lie down in *s.*
51. 11. and *s.* and mourning shall flee away
65. 14. my servts. shall sing, but ye shall cry for *s.*
Jer. 8. 18. when I would comfort myself against *s.*
20. 18. out of womb, to see labour and *s.*?
30. 15. why criest thou? thy *s.* is incurable
31. 13. I will make them rejoice from their *s.*
45. 3. for the Lord hath added grief to my *s.*
49. 23. there is *s.* on the sea, it cannot be quiet
Lam. 1. 12. see if there be any *s.* like unto my *s.*
18. behold my *s.* ‖ 3. 65. give them *s.* of heart
Ezek. 23. 33. thou shalt be filled with drunk. and *s.*
Luke 22. 45. he found them sleeping for *s.*
John 16. 6. said these things, *s.* filled your heart
20. sorrowful, but your *s.* shall be turned to joy
21. a woman when she is in travail, hath *s.*
22. and ye now therefore have *s.* but I will see you again, and your heart shall rejoice
Rom. 9. 2. that I have continual *s.* in my heart
2 *Cor.* 2. 3. when I came, I should have *s.* from them
7. lest be swallowed up with overmuch *s.*
7. 10. for godly *s.* worketh repentance to salvation, but the *s.* of the world worketh death
Phil. 2. 27. but on me also, lest I have *s.* upon *s.*
Rev. 18. 7. so much *s.* give her, and shall see no *s.*
21. 4. there shall be no more death, neither *s.*

SORROW, *Verb.*

Jer. 31. 12. and they shall not *s.* any more at all
51. 29. and the land shall tremble and *s.*
Hos. 8. 10. they shall *s.* a little for the burden
1 *Thess.* 4. 13. that ye *s.* not as others have no hope

SORROWS.

Exod. 3. 7. I have heard their cry, for I know their *s.*
2 *Sam.* 22. 6. *s.* of hell compassed me about, snares of death prevented me, *Psal.* 18. 4, 5. | 116. 3.
Job 9. 28. I am afr. of all my *s.* not hold me innoc.
21. 17. God distributeth *s.* in his anger
39. 3. they bow themselves, they cast out their *s.*
Psal. 16. 4. *s.* shall be multiplied that hasten after
32. 10. many *s.* shall be to wicked but he that trust.
127. 2. it is vain to rise up, to eat the bread of *s.*
Eccl. 2. 23. for all his days are *s.* and his travel grief
Isa. 13. 8. pangs and *s.* shall take hold of them
53. 3. a man of *s.* and acquainted with grief
4. surely he hath borne griefs and carried our *s.*
Jer. 13. 21. shall not *s.* take as a woman in travail
49. 24. *s.* have taken her as a woman in travail
Dan. 10. 16. by vision my *s.* are turned upon me
Hos. 13. 13. the *s.* of travail. woman shall come on him
Mat. 24. 8. these are beginning of *s.* *Mark* 13. 8.
1 *Tim.* 6. 10. pierced themselves thro' with many *s.*

SORROWED.

2 *Cor.* 7. 9. now I rejoice that ye *s.* to repentance
11. self-same thing that ye *s.* after a godly sort

SORROWETH.

1 *Sam.* 10. 2. and lo, thy father *s.* for you

SORROWFUL.

1 *Sam.* 1. 15. my lord, I am a woman of a *s.* spirit
Job 6. 7. things my soul refused are as my *s.* meat
Psal. 69. 29. I am poor and *s.* let salvat. set me up
Prov. 14. 13. even in laughter the heart is *s.*
Jer. 31. 25. I have replenished every *s.* soul
Zeph. 3. 18. I will gather them that are *s.*
Zech. 9. 5. Gaza also shall see it, and be very *s.*
Mat. 19. 22. he went away *s.* *Luke* 18. 23, 24.
26. 22. and they were exceeding *s.* *Mark* 14. 19.
37. and he began to be *s.* and very heavy
38. my soul is exceed. *s.* unto death, *Mark* 14. 34.
John 16. 20. ye shall be *s.* but sorrow shall be turned
2 *Cor.* 6. 10. as *s.* yet always rejoicing, as poor yet
Phil. 2. 28. may rejoice and I may be the less *s.*

SORROWING.

Luke 2. 48. behold, thy father and I sought thee *s.*
Acts 20. 38. *s.* they should see his face no more

SORRY.

1 *Sam.* 22. 8. there is none of you that is *s.* for me
Neh. 8. 10. this day is holy to Lord, neither be ye *s.*
Psal. 38. 18. declare iniquity, I will be *s.* for my sin
Isa. 51. 19. two things come, who shall be *s.* for thee
Mat. 14. 9. and the king was *s.* *Mark* 6. 26.
17. 23. and they were exceeding *s.*
2 *Cor.* 2. 2. if I make you *s.* same which is made *s.*
7. 8. tho' I made you *s.* same epistle made you *s.*
9. I rej. not that ye were made *s.* for ye were *s.*

SORT.

Gen. 6. 19. two of every *s.* shalt bring into ark, 20.
7. 14. every bird of every *s.* into the ark
1 *Sam.* 15. † 9. they spared of second *s.* and lambs
1 *Chron.* 24. 5. they divided one *s.* with another
29. 14. that we should be able to offer after this *s.*
Ezra 1. 10. basons of gold, silver basons of second *s.*
4. 8. they wrote to Artaxerxes king after this *s.*
Neh. 6. 4. yet sent to me four times after this *s.*
Ezek. 23. 42. with men of the common *s.* Sabeans
39. 4. I will give thee to ravenous birds of every *s.*
44. 30. the first of every oblation of every *s.*
Dan. 1. 10. worse liking than children of your *s.*
3. 29. there is no other G. can deliver after this *s.*
Acts 17. 5. but took lewd fellows of the baser *s.*
Rom. 15. 15. I have written more boldly in some *s.*
1 *Cor.* 3. 13. try every man's work, of what *s.* it is
2 *Cor.* 7. 11. that ye sorrowed after a godly *s.*
2 *Tim.* 3. 6. of this *s.* are they who creep into houses
3 *John* 6. bring on their journey after a godly *s.*

SORTS.

Deut. 22. 11. shalt not wear a garment of divers *s.*
Neh. 5. 18. once in ten days store of all *s.* of wine
Psal. 78. 45. he sent divers *s.* of flies. 105. 31.
Eccl. 2. 8. I gat musical instrum. and that of all *s.*
Ezek. 27. 24. were thy merchants in all *s.* of things
38. 4. all of them clothed with all *s.* of armour

SOTTISH.

Jer. 4. 22. my people is foolish, they are *s.* children

SOUGHT.

Gen. 43. 30. he *s.* where to weep, entered his cham.
Exod. 2. 15. when Pharaoh heard, he *s.* to slay Mo.
4. 19. for all the men are dead which *s.* thy life
24. that the Lord met him and *s.* to kill him
33. 7. every one that *s.* Lord went out to tabern.
Lev. 10. 16. Moses diligently *s.* goat of sin offering
Num. 35. 23. was not his enemy, nor *s.* his harm
Deut. 13. 10. beca. he *s.* to thrust thee away fr. L.
Josh. 2. 22. pursuers *s.* the spies, but found them not
Judg. 14. 4. Samson *s.* occasion against Philistines
18. 1. Danites *s.* them an inheritance to dwell in
1 *Sam.* 19. 10. Saul *s.* to smite David to the wall
27. 4. Saul *s.* no more again for him
2 *Sam.* 3. 17. ye *s.* for David in times past to be king
4. 8. the head of thine enemy that *s.* thy life
21. † 1. and David *s.* the face of the Lord
2. Saul *s.* to slay them in his zeal to Israel
1 *Kings* 1. 3. they *s.* for a fair damsel thro' Israel
10. 24. all the earth *s.* to Solomon to hear
11. 40. Solomon *s.* therefore to kill Jeroboam
2 *Kings* 2. 17. *s.* three days for Elijah, found him not
1 *Chron.* 26. 31. among the Hebronites were *s.* for
2 *Chron.* 14. 7. because we have *s.* the Lord our G
16. 12. yet in his disease he *s.* not to the Lord
17. 3. Jehoshaphat *s.* not unto Baalim
4. but *s.* to the Lord God of his father
22. 9. he *s.* Ahaziah, and they caught him; because Jehoshaphat *s.* the Lord with all his heart
25. 15. why hast thou *s.* after gods of Edom? 20.
26. 5. he *s.* God in the days of Zechariah; as long as he *s.* the Lord God made him to prosper
Ezra 2. 62. these *s.* their register, *Neh.* 7. 64.
Neh. 12. 27. they *s.* the Levites out of all places
Esth. 2. 21. they *s.* to lay hand on the king, 6. 2.
3. 6. wherefore Haman *s.* to destroy all the Jews
9. 2. to lay hand on such as *s.* their hurt
Psal. 34. 4. I *s.* the Lord, and he heard me, 77. 2.
86. 14. assemblies of violent men *s.* after my soul
111. 2. *s.* out of all that have pleasure therein
119. 10. with my whole heart have I *s.* thee
94. save me, for I have *s.* thy precepts
Prov. 28. † 12. but when wicked rise, man is *s.* for
Eccl. 7. 29. they have *s.* out many inventions
12. 9. preacher *s.* out and set in order many prov.
10. the preacher *s.* to find acceptable words
Isa. 62. 12. shalt be called, *s.* out, city not forsaken
65. 1. I am *s.* of them that asked not for me; I am found of them that *s.* me not, *Rom.* 10. 20.
10. shall be a place for my people that have *s.* me
Jer. 8. 2. before sun and moon, whom they have *s.*
10. 21. for the pastors have not *s.* the Lord
26. 21. the king *s.* to put him to death
44. 30. I gave Zedekiah to Nebu. that *s.* his life
50. 20. iniquity of Israel shall be *s.* for, be none
Lam. 1. 19. while they *s.* meat to relieve their souls
Ezek. 22. 30. and I *s.* for a man among them
26. 21. tho' *s.* yet shalt thou never be found again
34. 4. neither have ye *s.* that which was lost
Dan. 2. 13. they *s.* Daniel and his fellows to be slain
4. 36. my counsellors and my lords *s.* unto me
6. 4. the princes *s.* occasion against Daniel
8. 15. when I, even I, had *s.* for the meaning
Obad. 6. how are Esau's hidden things *s.* up
Zeph. 1. 6. and those that have not *s.* the Lord
Zech. 6. 7. and the bay went forth and *s.* to go
Mat. 2. 20. they are dead which *s.* the child's life
21. 46. *s.* to lay hands, *Mark* 12. 12. *Luke* 20. 19.
26. 16. covenanted with him, and from that time he *s.* opportunity to betray him, *Luke* 22. 6.
59. they *s.* false witness against Jesus to put him to death, but found none, *Mark* 14. 55.
Mark 11. 18. the scribes heard it, and *s.* how they might destroy him, 14. 1. *Luke* 19. 47. | 22. 2.
Luke 2. 48. thy father and I *s.* thee sorrowing
49. how is it that ye *s.* me? wist ye not that I must
5. 18. and they *s.* means to bring him in
6. 19. the whole multitude *s.* to touch him
11. 16. others *s.* of him a sign from heaven
13. 6. he *s.* fruit thereon, and found none
19. 3. Zaccheus *s.* to see Jesus who he was
John 5. 16. the Jews *s.* to slay him, 18. | 7. 1.
7. 11. then the Jews *s.* him at the feast, 11. 56.
30. then they *s.* to take him, 10. 39.
11. 8. Master, the Jews of late *s.* to stone thee
19. 12. from thenceforth Pilate *s.* to release him
Acts 12. 19. and when Herod had *s.* for Peter
17. 5. they *s.* to bring them out to the people
Rom. 9. 32. because *s.* it not by faith but by works
1 *Thess.* 2. 6. nor of men *s.* we glory, neither of you
2 *Tim.* 1. 17. in Rome he *s.* me out very diligently
Heb. 8. 7. no place should have been *s.* for second
12. 17. though he *s.* it carefully with tears

SOUGHT *him.*

1 *Sam.* 10. 21. when *s. him* he could not be found
13. 14. the Lord hath *s. him* a man to be captain
23. 14. Saul *s. him* every day, God delivered him
1 *Chron.* 15. 13. we *s. him* not after the due order
2 *Chron.* 14. 7. have *s. him,* he hath given us rest
15. 4. when they *s. him,* he was found of them
15. for they *s. him* with their whole desire
Psal. 37. 36. I *s. him,* but he could not be found
78. 34. when he slew them, then they *s. him*
Cant. 3. 1. by night on my bed I *s. him* whom my soul loveth; I *s. him* but I found him not, 2. | 5. 6.
Luke 2. 44. and they *s. him* among their kinsfolk
4. 42. and the people *s. him,* and came unto him

SOULDIER, *See* SOLDIER.

SOUL.

This word in Scripture, especially in the style of the Hebrews, *is very equivocal. It is taken,* 1. *For that spiritual, reasonable, and immortal substance in man, which is the origin of our thoughts, of our desires, of our reasonings; which distinguishes us from the brute creation, and which bears some resemblance to its divine Maker.* Mat. 10. 28. Fear him which is able to destroy both soul and body. *This substance must be spiritual because it thinks; it must be immortal, because it is spiritual. The Scripture indeed ascribes to beasts a soul, a spirit, life, and respiration, which may be a second acceptation of the word, as in* Gen. 1. 24. Let the earth bring forth the living creature, *in* Hebrew, *the* living soul. *So in* Lev. 17. 11. The life, *in* Hebrew, the soul of the flesh is in the blood. *And in* Eccl. 3. 21. Who knoweth the spirit of the beast that goeth downward? *This soul is the spirit, the breath, which is the principle of animal life, and which is common to men and brutes. But the Scripture allows to man alone the privileges of understanding, the knowledge of God, wisdom, immortality, the hope of future happiness, and of eternal life. It only threatens men with the punishment of another life and the pains of hell.*

II. Soul *is taken for the whole person, both soul and body;* Give me the persons, *in* Hebrew, souls, and take the goods to thyself, *says the king of* Sodom to Abraham, *Gen.* 14. 21. *And in* Gen. 12. 5. Abram took Sarai his wife, and Lot his brother's son, and all their substance that they had gathered, and the souls that they had gotten in Haran; *that is, the servants they had purchased, or the children that had been born to them.*

III. *It is taken for the life of man.* Psal. 33. 19. To deliver the soul from death; *to save them alive. And in* Psal. 7. 5. Let the enemy persecute my soul, and take it, *let him take away my life. And often in the* Psalms.

IV. *It is taken sometimes for death, or a dead body.* Num. 9. 6. Some were defiled by the dead body of a man, *in* Hebrew, by the soul of a man. *And in* Num. 6. 6. he shall come at no dead body, *in* Hebrew, dead soul. *Also in* Psal. 16. 10. Thou wilt not leave my soul in hell; *that is, thou wilt not suffer my body to continue long in the grave, or in a state of death. Sometimes it is taken for a living body.* Psal. 105. 18. He was laid in iron, *in* Hebrew, his soul came into iron.

V. *It is used for desire, love, inclination,* Gen. 23. 8. If it be your mind; *in* Hebrew, if it please or be agreeable to your soul. 1 *Sam.* 18. 1. The soul of Jonathan was knit with the soul of David; *he had a great love and affection for him. So in* Prov. 27. 7. The full soul, *That is, a man whose desire or appetite is fully satisfied.*

Gen. 1. † 20. the moving creature that hath *s.*
† 30. to every thing wherein there is a living *s.*
2. 7. God breathed and man became a living *s.*
34. 8. the *s.* of my son longeth for your daughter
35. 18. as her *s.* was in departing, for she died
Exod. 12. † 16. save that which every *s.* must eat
23. † 9. for ye know the *s.* of a stranger
Lev. 4. 2. if a *s.* shall sin through ignorance
† 27. and if any *s.* of the common people sin
5. 1. if a *s.* sin, and hear the voice of swearing
2. or if *s.* touch any unclean thing, shall be unclean
4. if a *s.* swear ‖ 15. if a *s.* commit a trespass
17. if a *s.* sin and commit any of these things
6. 2. if a *s.* lie ‖ 17. 12. no *s.* of you shall eat blood
17. 11. it is blood maketh an atonement for the *s.*
22. 11. if the priest buy any *s.* with his money
23. 30. whatsoever *s.* doth any work in that day
26. 15. or if your *s.* abhor my judgments
43. because their *s.* abhorred my statutes
Num. 9. 13. even the same *s.* shall be cut off
21. 4. the *s.* of the people was much discouraged
30. 4. every bond wherewith she hath bound her *s.* shall stand, 5, 6, 7, 8, 9, 10, 11, 12, 13.
31. 28. one *s.* of five hundred for the Lord
Deut. 11. 13. and to serve him with all your *s.*
18. ye shall lay up these my words in your *s.*
13. 3. proveth you know whether you love the Ld. your G. with all your *s. Josh.* 22. 5. 1 *Kings* 2. 4.
Judg. 18. † 25. lest fellows bitter of *s.* run on thee
1 *Sam.* 18. 1. *s.* of Jonathan was knit to *s.* of David
22. † 2. every one bitter of *s.* came to David
25. 29. *s.* of my lord bound up in bundle of life
30. 6. because the *s.* of all the people was grieved
2 *Sam.* 5. 8. the blind that are hated of David's *s.*
13. 39. the *s.* of David longed to go to Absalom
17. † 8. thy father and his men be bitter of *s.*
1 *Kings* 8. 48. and so return to thee with all their *s.*
17. 21. let this child's *s.* come into him again
2 *Kings* 4. 27. let her alone for her *s.* is vexed
23. 3. to keep his commandments with all their *s.*
1 *Chron.* 22. 19. now set your *s.* to seek the Lord
2 *Chr.* 6. 38. if they return to thee with all their *s.*
15. 12. to seek the Lord God with all their *s.*
Job 3. 20. why is life given to the bitter in *s.?*
12. 10. in whose hand is the *s.* of every living thing
16. 4. if your *s.* were in my soul's stead
24. 12. and the *s.* of the wounded crieth out
31. † 39. if I caused the *s.* of the owners to expire
36. † 14. their *s.* dieth in youth, and their life is
Psal. 17. † 9. hide from my enemies against the *s.*
19. 7. the law of Lord is perfect converting the *s.*
33. 19. to deliver their *s.* from death and keep alive
34. 22. the Lord redeemeth the *s.* of his servants
49. 8. the redemption of their *s.* is precious
72. 14. he shall redeem their *s.* from deceit and viol.
74. 19. O deliver not the *s.* of thy turtle-dove
78. 50. he spared not their *s.* from death
86. 4. rejoice the *s.* of thy servant, O Lord
94. 21. they gather against the *s.* of the righteous
106. 15. but he sent leanness into their *s.*
107. 5. hungry and thirsty their *s.* fainted in them
9. he satisfieth longing *s.* and filleth hungry *s.*
18. their *s.* abhorreth all manner of meat
26. their *s.* is melted because of trouble
Prov. 10. 3. not suffer the *s.* of righteous to famish
11. 25. liberal *s.* shall be made fat that watereth
Prov. 13. 2. but *s.* of transgressors shall eat violence
4. the *s.* of the sluggard desireth and hath not
19. the desire accomplished is sweet to the *s.*
16. 24. pleasant words are sweet to the *s.*
19. 2. the *s.* be without knowledge it is not good
15. and an idle *s.* shall suffer hunger
21. 10. the *s.* of the wicked desireth evil
22. 23. Lord will spoil *s.* of those that spoiled them
25. 13. for he refresheth the *s.* of his masters
25. as cold waters to a thirsty *s.* so is good news
27. 7. the full *s.* loatheth an honey-comb; but to the hungry *s.* every bitter thing is sweet
† 9. so a man's friend by the counsel of the *s.*
31. † 6. give wine to them that are bitter of *s.*
Isa. 3. 9. woe to their *s.* they have rewarded evil
† 20. I will take away the houses of the *s.*
10. † 18. it shall consume from the *s.* to the flesh
32. 6. to make empty the *s.* of the hungry
46. † 2. but their *s.* is gone into captivity
49. † 7. thus saith Ld. to him that is despised in *s.*
55. 2. let your *s.* delight itself in fatness
3. come unto me, hear, and your *s.* shall live
58. 10. and if thou satisfy the afflicted *s.*
66. 3. their *s.* delighteth in their abominations
Jer. 4. 10. whereas the sword reacheth to the *s.*
20. 13. he hath delivered the *s.* of the poor
31. 12. their *s.* shall be as a watered garden
14. and I will satiate the *s.* of the priests
25. thus saith the Lord, I have satiated the weary *s.* and I have replenished every sorrowful *s.*
38. 16. as the Lord liveth, that made us this *s.*
40. † 14. hath sent Ishmael to strike thee in *s.*
44. † 14. they have lift up their *s.* to return
Lam. 1. 11. hath given for meat to relieve the *s.*
2. 12. when their *s.* was poured out into bosom
3. 25. the Lord is good to the *s.* that seeketh him
Ezek. 18. 4. all souls are mine, as *s.* of father, so *s.* of son is mine, the *s.* that sinneth, it shall die, 20.
24. 21. what your *s.* pitieth shall fall by sword
† 25. I take from them the lifting up of the *s.*
25. † 6. thou hast rejoiced in *s.* with all thy despite
Hos. 9. 4. their *s.* shall not come into house of Lord
Jonah 2. 5. waters compassed me about even to the *s.*
Mat. 10. 28. but are not able to kill the *s.* fear him that can destroy both *s.* and body in hell
Mark 12. 33. to love him with all the heart and *s.*
Acts 2. 43. fear came on every *s.* many wonders done
3. 23. every *s.* which will not hear that prophet
4. 32. multitude that believed of one heart and *s.*
Rom. 2. 9. anguish on every *s.* of man that doeth evil
13. 1. let every *s.* be subject to the higher powers
1 *Thess.* 5. 23. that your *s.* and body be preserved
Heb. 4. 12. word of God piercing to dividing of *s.*
6. 19. which hope we have as an anchor of the *s.*
10. 39. but of them that believe to saving of the *s.*
Jam. 5. 20. he shall save a *s.* from death and hide
1 *Pet.* 2. 11. from fleshly lusts which war ag. the *s.*
2 *Pet.* 2. 8. Lot vexed his right. *s.* from day to day
Rev. 16. 3. and every living *s.* died in the sea
See AFFLICTED, BITTERNESS.

His SOUL.

Gen. 34. 3. *his s.* clave to Dinah Jacob's daughter
42. 21. are guilty, when we saw anguish of *his s.*
Exod. 30. 12. shall give a ransom for *his s.* to Lord
Num. 30. 2. or swear an oath to bind *his s.* to Lord
Deut. 24. † 15. he is poor, and lifteth *his s.* to it
Judg. 10. 16. *his s.* was grieved for misery of Israel
16. 16. she urged him, so that *his s.* was vexed
2 *Kings* 23. 25. there was no king like Josiah who turned to the Lord with all *his s.* 2 *Chron.* 34. 31.
Job 14. 22. and *his s.* within him shall mourn
18. † 4. he teareth *his s.* in his anger
21. 25. another dieth in the bitterness of *his s.*
23. 13. what *his s.* desireth, even that he doeth
27. 8. the hypocrite, when God taketh away *his s.*
31. 30. neither to sin, by wishing a curse to *his s.*
32. † 2. he justified *his s.* rather than God
33. 18. he keepeth back *his s.* from the pit
20. and *his s.* abhorreth dainty meat
22. yea, *his s.* draweth near unto the grave
28. he will deliver *his s.* from the pit, 30.
Psal. 10. † 3. the wicked boasteth of *his s.* desire
11. 5. but the wicked loveth violence, *his s.* hateth
24. 4. who hath not lifted up *his s.* to vanity
25. 13. *his s.* shall dwell at ease, and seed shall inherit the earth
49. 18. though while he lived he blessed *his s.*
89. 48. shall he deliver *his s.* from the grave?
105. † 18. feet hurt with fetters, *his s.* came into iron
109. 31. to save from those that condemn *his s.*
Prov. 6. † 16. seven are an abomination to *his s.*
30. if he steal to satisfy *his s.* when he is hungry
13. 25. the righteous eateth to satisfying of *his s.*
16. 17. he that keepeth his way, preserveth *his s.*
18. 7. a fool's lips are the snare of *his s.*
21. 23. whoso keepeth his mouth, keepeth *his s.*
22. 5. that doth keep *his s.* shall be far from them
23. 14. and shalt deliver *his s.* from hell
29. 10. hate the upright, but the just seek *his s.*
Eccl. 2. 24. that he should make *his s.* enjoy good
6. 2. so that he wanteth nothing for *his s.*
3. and *his s.* be not filled with good
Isa. 29. 8. but he awaketh and *his s.* is empty; behold he is faint and *his s.* hath appetite
44. 20. that he cannot deliver *his s.* nor say
53. 10. when shalt make *his s.* an offering for sin
11. he shall see of travail of *his s.* and be satisfied
12. because he poured out *his s.* unto death
Jer. 50. 19. *his s.* shall be satisfied on mount Ephr.
51. 6. flee and deliver every man *his s.* 45.
Ezek. 18. 27. doeth what is right, he shall save *his s.*
33. 5. he that taketh warning, shall deliver *his s.*
Amos 2. † 14. neither shall the mighty deliver *his s.*
Mic. 7. † 3. the great man uttereth mischief of *his s.*
Hab. 2. 4. *his s.* that is lifted up, is not upright in him
Mat. 16. 26. if gain whole world, and lose *his* own *s.* what can man give in exchange for *s.*? *Mark* 8. 37.
Acts 2. 31. *his s.* was not left in hell nor flesh did see

My SOUL.

Gen. 12. 13. and *my s.* shall live because of thee
19. 20. O let me escape thither, and *my s.* shall live
27. 4. that *my s.* may bless thee before I die, 25.
Gen. 49. 6. O *my s.* come not thou into their secret
Lev. 26. 11. and *my s.* shall not abhor you, 30.
Num. 23. † 10. let *my s.* die death of the righteous
Judg. 5. 21. O *my s.* thou hast trodden down strength
16. † 30. let *my s.* die with the Philistines
1 *Sam.* 1. 15. but have poured out *my s.* before Ld.
24. 11. yet thou huntest *my s.* to take it
26. 21. because *my s.* was precious in thine eyes
2 *Sam.* 4. 9. David answered Rechab, as the Lord liveth, who hath redeemed *my s.* 1 *Kings* 1. 29.
Job 6. 7. the things *my s.* refused, are as my meat
7. 15. so that *my s.* chooseth strangling and death
9. 21. though perfect, yet would I not know *my s.*
10. 1. *my s.* is weary of life, speak bitterness of *my s.*
19. 2. how long will ye vex *my s.* with words?
27. 2. and the Almighty, who hath vexed *my s.*
30. 15. they pursue *my s.* as the wind
16. and now *my s.* is poured out upon me
25. was not *my s.* grieved for the poor?
Ps. 3. 2. who say of *my s.* there is no help in God
6. 3. *my s.* is sore vexed, but, O Lord, how long?
4. deliver *my s.* 17. 13. | 22. 20. | 116. 4. | 120. 2.
7. 2. lest he tear *my s.* like a lion, rending it
5. let the enemy persecute *my s.* and take it
11. 1. how say ye to *my s.* flee as a bird to mountain
13. 2. how long shall I take counsel in *my s.?*
16. 10. thou wilt not leave *my s.* in hell, *Acts* 2. 27.
23. 3. he restoreth *my s.* ‖ 25. 1. to thee I lift *my s.*
25. 20. O keep *my s.* and deliver me, I trust in thee
26. 9. gather not *my s.* with sinners, nor my life
30. 3. thou hast brought up *my s.* from the grave
† 12. that *my s.* may sing praise to thee
31. 7. thou hast known *my s.* in adversities
9. yea, *my s.* and my belly are consumed
34. 2. *my s.* shall make her boast in the Lord
35. 3. say unto *my s.* I am thy salvation
4. let them be put to shame that seek after *my s.*
7. without cause they have digged a pit for *my s.*
9. and *my s.* shall be joyful in the Lord
12. they rewarded me to the spoiling of *my s.*
13. as for me, I humbled *my s.* with fasting
17. rescue *my s.* from their destructions
40. 14. let them be confounded that seek after *my s.*
41. 4. heal *my s.* for I have sinned against thee
42. 1. as the hart, so panteth *my s.* after thee, O G.
2. *my s.* thirsteth for the living God, 143. 6.
4. when I remember, I pour out *my s.* in me
5. why art thou cast down, O *my s.?* 11. | 43. 5
6. O my God, *my s.* is cast down within me
49. 15. God will redeem *my s.* from the grave
54. 3. and oppressors seek after *my s.*
4. the Lord is with them that uphold *my s.*
55. 18. he hath delivered *my s.* in peace from bat.
56. 6. they mark my steps, when they wait for *my s*
13. for thou hast delivered *my s.* from death
57. 1. be merciful, O G. for *my s.* trusteth in thee
4. *my s.* is among lions ‖ 6. *my s.* is bowed down
59. 3. for lo, they lie in wait for *my s.*
62. 1. truly *my s.* waiteth upon God, my salvation
5. *my s.* wait thou only upon God, my expectation
63. 1. O God, *my s.* thirsteth for thee in a dry land
5. *my s.* shall be satisfied as with marrow and fat
8. *my s.* followeth hard after thee, thy right hand
9. but those that seek *my s.* to destroy it shall go
66. 16. I will declare what God hath done for *my s.*
69. 1. for the waters are come in unto *my s.*
10. when I wept and chastened *my s.* with fasting
18. draw nigh to *my s.* and redeem it, deliver me
70. 2. confounded that seek after *my s.* 71. 13.
71. 23. *my s.* shall rejoice which thou hast redeemed
77. 2. my sore ran, *my s.* refused to be comforted
84. 2. *my s.* longeth for the courts of the Lord
86. 2. preserve *my s.* ‖ 13. thou hast delivered *my s.*
4. for to thee, O Lord, do I lift up *my s.* 143. 8.
14. assemblies of violent men sought after *my s.*
88. 3. *my s.* is full of troubles, my life draweth nigh
14. L. why castest thou off *my s.?* why hidest thou
94. 17. *my s.* had almost dwelt in silence
19. in thoughts within thy comforts delight *my s.*
103. 1. bless the Lord, O *my s.* 2, 22. | 104. 1, 35.
109. 20. reward of them that speak against *my s.*
116. 7. return unto thy rest, O *my s.*
8. for thou hast delivered *my s.* from death
119. 20. *my s.* breaketh for the longing it hath
25. *my s.* cleaveth to the dust, quicken thou me
28. *my s.* melteth for heaviness, strengthen me
81. *my s.* fainteth for salvation, but I hope
109. *my s.* is continually in my hand, yet not forget
129. therefore doth *my s.* keep them
167. *my s.* hath kept thy testimonies
175. let *my s.* live, and it shall praise thee
120. 2. deliver *my s.* O Lord, from lying lips
6. *my s.* hath dwelt with him that hateth peace
130. 5. I wait for the Lord, *my s.* doth wait, 6.
131. 2. *my s.* is even as a weaned child
138. 3. and strengthen me with strength in *my s.*
139. 14. and that *my s.* knoweth right well
141. 8. in thee is my trust, leave not *my s.* destitute
142. 4. refuge failed me, no man cared for *my s.*
7. bring *my s.* out of prison, that I may praise thy
143. 3. for the enemy hath persecuted *my s.*
11. O Lord, bring *my s.* out of trouble
146. 1. praise the Lord, praise the Lord, O *my s.*
Eccl. 4. 8. for whom do I bereave *my s.* of good?
7. 28. which yet *my s.* seeketh, but I find not
Cant. 1. 7. O thou whom *my s.* loveth, 3. 1, 2, 3, 4.
5. 6. *my s.* failed when he spake, I sought him
6. 12. *my s.* made me like chariots of Ammi-nadib
Isa. 1. 14. your new moons and feasts *my s.* hateth
26. 9. with *my s.* have I desired thee in the night
38. 17. thou hast in love to *my s.* delivered it
42. 1. behold mine elect, in whom *my s.* delighteth
61. 10. *my s.* shall be joyful in my God
Jer. 4. 19. hast heard, O *my s.* sound of the trumpet
31. *my s.* is wearied because of murderers
5. 9. shall not *my s.* be avenged? 29. | 9. 9.
6. 8. be instructed, O Jer. lest *my s.* depart from thee
12. 7. beloved of *my s.* into the hand of her enemies
13. 17. *my s.* sh. weep in secret places for your pride
18. 20. for they have digged a pit for *my s.*
32. 41. I will rejoice over them with *my* whole *s.*
Lam. 1. 16. the comforter that should relieve *my s.*

Lam. 3. 17 thou hast removed my s. far off from pe.
20. my s. hath them still in remembrance
24. Lord is my portion, saith my s. will I hope
58. O Lord, thou hast pleaded the causes of my s.
Ezek. 4. 14. behold, my s. hath not been polluted
Jonah 2. 7. when my s. fainted within me, I remem.
Mic. 6. 7. the fruit of my body for the sin of my s.
7. 1. my s. desired the first ripe fruit
Zech. 11. 8. three shepherds I cut off, my s. loathed
Mat. 12. 18. my beloved, in whom my s. is well pleas.
26. 38. my s. is exceeding sorrowful, Mark 14. 34.
Luke 1. 46. my s. doth magnify the Lord
12. 19. I will say to my s. soul, eat, drink
John 12. 27. is my s. troubled, and what shall I say?
2 Cor. 1. 23. I call God for a record upon my s.
Heb. 10. 38. my s. shall have no pleasure in him

Our SOUL.

Num. 11. 6. our s. is dried away, nothing but manna
21. 5. no bread, our s. loatheth this light bread
Psal. 33. 20. our s. waiteth for Lord, he is our help
35. † 25. let them not say, ah, our s. would have it
44. 25. for our s. is bowed down to the dust
66. 9. bless our God, who holdeth our s. in life
123. 4. our s. is exceedingly filled with scorning
124. 4. the stream had gone over our s. 5.
7. our s. is escaped as a bird out of the snare
Isa. 26. 8. the desire of our s. is to thy name

Own SOUL.

Deut. 13. 6. if a friend is as thine own s. entice thee
1 Sam. 18. 1. the soul of Jonathan was knit to David, and he loved him as his own s. 3. | 20. 17.
Psal. 22. 29. and none can keep alive his own s.
Prov. 6. 32. he that doeth it, destroyeth his own s.
8. 36. but he that sinneth, wrongeth his own s.
11. 17. the merciful man doeth good to his own s.
15. 32. he that refuseth instruction despis. his own s.
19. 8. he that getteth wisdom, loveth his own s.
16. he that keep. commandments keep. his own s.
20. 2. that provoketh king, sinneth against his own s.
29. 24. whoso is partner with thief, hateth own s.
Mat. 16. 26. what is a man profited, if he shall gain whole world and lose his own s.? Mark 8. 36.
Luke 2. 35. sword shall pierce thro' thy own s. also

That SOUL.

Gen. 17. 14. not circumcised, that s. shall be cut off from his people, Exod. 31. 14. Lev. 7. 20, 21, 25, 27. | 19. 8. Num. 15. 30.
Exod. 12. 15. whoso eateth leavened bread, that s. shall be cut off from Israel, Num. 19. 13.
19. whoso eateth leavened bread, that s. shall be cut off from congregation of Israel, Num. 19. 20.
Lev. 17. 10. I will set my face against that s. 20. 6.
22. 3. that s. shall be cut off from my presence
23. 30. that s. will I destroy from his people
Num. 15. 31. that s. shall utterly be cut off

Thy SOUL.

Gen. 27. 19. eat, that thy s. may bless me, 31.
Deut. 4. 9. take heed, and keep thy s. diligently
29. shalt find him, if seek him with all thy s.
6. 5. love the Lord thy God with all thy s. 30. 6.
10. 12. to serve the Lord thy God with all thy s.
12. 15. whatsoever thy s. lusteth after, 14. 26.
26. 16. do with all thy s. || 30. 2. obey with all thy s.
30. 2. obey his voice with all thy heart and thy s.
10. if thou turn unto the Lord with all thy s.
1 Sam. 2. 16. then take as much as thy s. desireth
20. 4. whatsoever thy s. desireth, I will do for thee
23. 20. come according to all the desire of thy s.
25. 29. yet a man is risen to pursue and seek thy s.
1 Kings 11. 37. shalt reign according all thy s. desir.
Psal. 121. 7. the Lord shall preserve thy s.
Prov. 2. 10. when knowledge is pleasant to thy s.
3. 22. so shall be life to thy s. and grace to thy neck
19. 18. and let not thy s. spare for his crying
22. 25. learn his ways, and get a snare to thy s.
24. 12. he that keepeth thy s. doth not he know it?
14. so shall the knowledge of wisdom be to thy s.
29. 17. yea, he shall give delight to thy s.
Isa. 51. 23. which have said to thy s. bow down
58. 10. if thou draw out thy s. to the hungry
11. the Lord shall satisfy thy s. in drought
Jer. 14. 19. hath thy s. loathed Zion? why smitten us?
38. 17. go forth then, thy s. shall live, 20.
Ezek. 3. 19. thou hast delivered thy s. 21. | 33. 9.
Hab. 2. 10. and thou hast sinned against thy s.
Mat. 22. 37. thou shalt love Lord with all thy heart and with all thy s. Mark 12. 30. Luke 10. 27.
Luke 12. 20. this night thy s. shall be required of thee
3 John 2. thou mayest prosper, even as thy s. prosp.
Rev. 18. 14. the fruits thy s. lusted after are departed
See LIVETH.

SOULS.

Gen. 12. 5. Abraham took s. they had got in Haran
14. † 21. give me the s. and take goods to thyself
36. † 6. Esau took all the s. of his house
46. 15. the s. by Leah were thirty and three
18. by Zilpah sixteen s. || 22. by Rachel fourteen s.
25. all the s. Jacob had by Bilhah were seven
26. all the s. that came into Egypt, sixty and six
27. the sons of Joseph in Egypt were two s. all the s. of house of Jacob were seventy s. Exod. 1. 5.
Exod. 12. 4. take a lamb according to number of s.
16. † 16. an homer according to the number of s.
30. 15. an offering to Lord, to make an atonement for your s. 16. Lev. 17. 11. Num. 31. 50.
Lev. 18. 29. even s. that commit them shall be cut off
20. 25. ye shall not make your s. abominable
Num. 16. 38. of these sinners against their own s.
30. 9. every vow wherewith have bound their s.
Josh. 10. 28. he utterly destroyed them and all the s. that were therein, 30, 32. | 11. 11.
23. † 11. take good heed therefore unto your s.
14. ye know in all your hearts and in all your s.
1 Sam. 25. 29. s. of thine enemies shall he sling out
1 Chron. 5. † 21. they took of s. of men 100,000
Esth. 9. † 31. these days they had decreed for their s.
Psal. 72. 13. and shall save the s. of the needy
97. 10. he preserveth the s. of his saints
Prov. 11. 30. and he that winneth s. is wise
14. 25. a true witness delivereth s.
Isa. 47. † 14. they shall not deliver their s.
57. 16. spirit should fail, and s. which I made

Jer. 2. 34. in thy skirts is found the blood of s.
6. 16. ye shall find rest for your s. Mat. 11. 29.
26. 19. thus might we procure great evil ag. our s.
37. † 9. thus saith the Lord, deceive not your s.
42. † 20. ye have used deceit against your s.
44. 7. why commit this great evil against your s.?
Lam. 1. 19. they sought meat to relieve their s.
Ezek. 7. 19. they shall not satisfy their s.
13. 18. to hunt s. will ye hunt s. of my people, 20. will ye save the s. alive that come unto you?
19. to slay the s. that should not die
14. 14. they should deliver but their own s.
18. 4. all s. are mine || 22. 25. they have devoured s.
22. 27. her princes are like wolves to destroy s.
Luke 21. 19. in your patience possess your s.
Acts 2. 41. there were added to them 3000 s.
7. 14. he called Jacob and his kindred 75 s.
14. 22. confirming the s. of the disciples, exhorting
15. 24. have troubled you, subverting your s.
27. 37. we were in all in the ship 276 s.
2 Cor. 12. † 15. I would be spent for your s.
1 Thess. 2. 8. to have imparted our own s. to you
Heb. 13. 17. obey them, for they watch for your s.
Jam. 1. 21. the word which is able to save your s.
1 Pet. 1. 9. end of your faith the salvation of your s.
22. seeing have purified your s. in obeying truth
2. 25. are returned to the Shepherd of your s.
3. 20. wherein few, that is, eight s. were saved
4. 19. commit the keeping of their s. to him
2 Pet. 2. 14. cannot cease from sin beguil. unstable s.
Rev. 6. 9. I saw under the altar the s. of them slain
18. 13. no man buyeth slaves and s. of men
20. 4. I saw the s. of them that were beheaded
See AFFLICT.

SOUND, Substantive.

Exod. 28. 35. his s. shall be heard when he goeth in
Lev. 25. † 9. cause the trumpet loud of s. to sound
26. 36. the s. of a shaken leaf shall chase them
Josh. 6. 5. when ye hear the s. of the trumpet, 20.
2 Sam. 5. 24. when thou hearest the s. of a going in the tops of the mulberry-trees, 1 Chron. 14. 15.
6. 15. they brought up the ark with shouting and the s. of the trumpet, 1 Chron. 15. 28.
15. 10. when ye hear the s. say Absalom reigns
1 Kings 1. 40. the earth rent with the s. of them
41. when Joab heard the s. of the trumpet
14. 6. when Ahijah heard the s. of her feet
18. 41. for there is a s. of abundance of rain
2 Kings 6. 32. is not s. of his master's feet behind him?
1 Chron. 16. 5. but Asaph made a s. with cymbals
42. with trumpets and those that should make a s.
2 Chron. 5. 13. as one, to make one s. to be heard
Neh. 4. 20. in what place ye hear s. of the trumpet
Job 15. 21. a dreadful s. in his ears, in prosperity
21. 12. and rejoice at the s. of the organ
37. 2. hear the s. that goeth out of his mouth
39. 24. nor believeth he it is the s. of the trumpet
Psal. 47. 5. the L. gone up with the s. of a trumpet
77. 17. cloud poured out water, skies sent out a s.
89. 15. blessed are people that know the joyful s.
92. 3. sing upon the harp with a solemn s.
98. 6. sing with trumpets and s. of cornet
150. 3. praise him with the s. of the trumpet
Eccl. 7. † 6. as the s. of thorns under a pot
12. 4. when the s. of the grinding is low
Jer. 4. 19. hast heard, O my soul, the s. of trumpet
21. how long shall I hear the s. of the trumpet?
6. 17. saying, hearken to the s. of the trumpet?
8. 16. the land trembled at the s. of the neighing
25. 10. I will take from them s. of the millstones
42. 14. where we shall hear no s. of the trumpet
50. 22. a s. of battle is in the land, and of destruction
51. 54. a s. of a cry cometh from Babylon
Ezek. 10. 5. the s. of the cherubim's wings was heard
26. 13. the s. of thy harps shall be no more heard
15. shall not the isles shake at the s. of thy fall?
27. 28. suburbs shall shake at s. of cry of thy pilots
31. 16. I made nations to shake at s. of his fall
33. 4. heareth the s. and taketh no warning
5. he heard s. of trumpet and took not warning
Dan. 3. 5. at what time ye hear the s. 7, 10, 15.
Amos 2. 2. Moab shall die with s. of trumpet
6. 5. that chaunt to the s. of the viol, and invent
Mat. 24. 31. he shall send his angels with a great s.
John 3. 8. hearest the s. but canst not tell whence
Acts 2. 2. suddenly there came a s. from heaven
Rom. 10. 18. verily their s. went into all the earth
1 Cor. 14. 7. even things without life giving s.
8. for if the trumpet give an uncertain s.
Heb. 12. 19. ye are not come to the s. of a trumpet
Rev. 1. 15. and his voice as the s. of many waters
9. 9. the s. of their wings was as the s. of chariots
18. 22. the s. of a millstone shall be heard no more

SOUND, Adjective.

Psal. 119. 80. let my heart be s. in thy statutes
Prov. 2. 7. he layeth up s. wisdom for the righteous
3. 21. my son, keep s. wisdom and discretion
8. 14. counsel is mine and s. wisdom, I am unders.
14. 30. a s. heart is the life of the flesh, but envy
Luke 15. 27. because hath received him safe and s.
1 Tim. 1. 10. if any other thing contrary to s. doct.
2 Tim. 1. 7. for God hath given us spirit of s. mind
13. hold fast the form of s. words thou hast heard
4. 3. when they will not endure s. doctrine
Tit. 1. 9. he may be able by s. doctrine to exhort
13. rebuke them, that they may be s. in the faith
2. 1. speak the things which become s. doctrine
2. that the aged men be s. in faith, in charity
8. s. speech that cannot be condemned

SOUND, Verb.

Lev. 25. 9. trumpet of jubilee to s. in day of atonement make the trumpet s. through all the land
Num. 10. 7. shall blow, but you shall not s. an alarm
1 Chr. 15. 19. Heman and Asaph were appoint. to s.
Isa. 16. 11. wherefore my bowels shall s. for Moab
Jer. 48. 36. my heart shall s. for Moab like pipes
Joel 2. 1. and s. an alarm in my holy mountain
Mat. 6. 2. therefore do not s. a trumpet before thee
1 Cor. 15. 52. for the trumpet shall s. dead be raised
Rev. 8. 6. the seven angels prepared themselves to s.
13. trumpet of the three angels who are yet to s.
10. 7. when the seventh angel shall begin to s.

SOUNDED.

Exod. 19. 19. when the voice of the trumpet s. long
1 Sam. 20. 12. Jonathan said, when I have s. father
2 Chron. 7. 6. the priests s. trumpets, 13. 14.
23. 13. the people rejoiced, and s. with trumpets
29. 28. the singers sang, and the trumpeters s.
Neh. 4. 18. he that s. the trumpet was by me
Luke 1. 44. as soon as voice of salutat. s. in my ears
1 Thess. 1. 8. from you s. out the word of the Lord
Rev. 8. 7. the first angel s. and there followed hail
8. the second s. || 10. third s. || 12. fourth angel s.
9. 1. the fifth s. || 13. sixth s. || 11. 15. seventh s.

SOUNDED.

Acts 27. 28. they s. and found it twenty fathoms; they s. again and found it fifteen fathoms

SOUNDETH.

Exod. 19. 13. when the trumpet s. long, come up

SOUNDING.

1 Chr. 15. 16. singers with instruments of music s.
2 Chron. 5. 12. and with them 120 priests s.
13. 12. his priests with s. trumpets to cry alarm
Psal. 150. 5. praise him upon the high s. cymbals
Isa. 63. 15. where is thy zeal and s. of thy bowels?
Ezek. 7. 7. and not the s. again of mountains
1 Cor. 13. 1. and have not charity, I am as s. brass

SOUNDNESS.

Ps. 38. 3. there is no s. in my flesh for thy anger, 7.
Isa. 1. 6. there is no s. in it, but wounds and bruises
Acts 3. 16. hath given him this perfect s. before you

SOUNDS.

1 Cor. 14. 7. except they give a distinction in the s.

SOUR.

Isa. 18. 5. when the s. grape is ripening in the flower
Jer. 31. 29. the fathers have eaten a s. grape, and the children's teeth are set on edge, Ezek. 18. 2.
30. every man that eateth the s. grape, teeth be
Hos. 4. 18. their drink is s. they have committed

SOUTH.

Gen. 12. 9. and Abram journeyed towards the s.
13. 1. Abram went up into the s. || 3. went from s.
28. 14. thou shalt spread abroad to north and s.
Exod. 26. 35. on side of the tabernacle toward the s.
Num. 13. 29. Amalekites dwell in the land of the s.
Deut. 33. 23. O Naphtali, possess thou west and s.
Josh. 10. 40. Joshua smote the country of the s.
18. 5. Judah shall abide in their coast on the s.
Judg. 1. 9. to fight against the Canaanites in the s.
1 Sam. 20. 41. David arose out of a place toward s
27. 10. against the s. of Judah, s. of Jerahmeelites
30. 1. the Amalekites had invaded the s. 14.
2 Sam. 24. 7. they went out to the s. of Judah
1 Kings 7. 25. three looking towards s. 2 Chr. 4. 4.
1 Chron. 9. 24. the porters were toward the s.
2 Chron. 28. 18. Philistines invaded the s. of Judah
Job 9. 9. which maketh the chambers of the s.
37. 9. out of the s. cometh the whirlwind
39. 26. and stretch her wings toward the s.
Psal. 75. 6. promotion cometh not from east nor s.
89. 12. the north and s. thou hast created them
107. 3. and gathered them from the north and s.
126. 4. turn our captivity as the streams in the s.
Eccl. 1. 6. the wind goeth toward the s.
11. 3. if the tree falleth toward the s. or the north
Isa. 21. 1. as whirlwinds in the s. pass through
30. 6. the burden of the beasts of the s.
43. 6. and I will say to the s. keep not back
Jer. 13. 19. the cities of the s. shall be shut up
17. 26. from the s. bringing burnt offerings
32. 44. men shall buy fields in the cities of the s.
33. 13. in the cities of the s. shall the flocks pass
Ezek. 20. 46. set thy face toward the s. and drop thy word toward the s. prophesy against the s. field
47. say to forest of s. faces from s. to nor. be burnt
21. 4. my sword against all flesh from s. to north
40. 2. by which was as the frame of a city on s.
24. after that he brought me toward the s.
44. and their prospect was toward the s.
41. 11. and another door was toward the s.
46. 9. shall go out by way of the s. gate; and he that entereth by the way of s. go forth by north
Dan. 8. 9. a little horn waxed great toward the s.
11. 5. and the king of the s. shall be strong
6. king's daughter of the s. shall come to north
9. king of the s. shall come into his kingdom
11. king of the s. shall be moved with choler
15. and the arms of the s. shall not withstand
25. and the king of the s. shall be stirred up
29. he shall return, and come toward the s.
40. the king of the s. shall push at him
Obad. 19. they of s. shall possess the mount of Esau
20. the captivity shall possess the cities of the s.
Hab. 3. † 3. God came from s. from mount Paran
Zech. 7. 7. when men inhabited the s. and the plain
9. 14. God shall go with whirlwinds of the s.
14. 4. half of the mountain remove toward the s.
Mat. 12. 42. queen of the s. shall rise in judgment
Luke 13. 29. come from s. to sit down with Abraham
Acts 8. 26. saying, arise, and go toward the s.
Rev. 21. 13. on the s. the gates, on the west three

SOUTH-border.

Num. 34. 3. s.-border the outmost coast of salt-sea
Josh. 15. 2. the s.-border of Judah from the shore

SOUTH-country.

Gen. 20. 1. Abraham sojourned toward the s.-coun.
24. 62. for Isaac dwelt in the s.-country
Josh. 11. 16. Joshua took all the s.-country, 12. 8.
Zech. 6. 6. the grisled go forth toward the s.-country

SOUTH-field.

Ezek. 20. 46. prophesy ag. the forest of the s.-field

SOUTH-land.

Josh. 15. 19. thou hast given me s.-land, Judg. 1. 15.

SOUTH-quarter.

Num. 34. 3. s.-quarter from Zin by coast of Edom
Josh. 18. 15. s.-quarter from end of Kirjath-jearim

SOUTH-Ramoth.

1 Sam. 30. 27. to them which were in s.-Ramoth

SOUTH-side.

Exod. 26. 18. twenty boards on the s.-side, 36. 23.
Num. 2. 10. on s.-side shall be standard of Reuben
10. 6. camps which lie on the s.-side go forward
Ezek. 42. 18. he measured the s.-side 500 reeds
47. 1. the waters came at the s.-side of the altar

Ezek. 48. 16. and the s.-side 4500 measures, 33.

SOUTH-ward.

Gen. 13. 14. Lord said to Abraham look s.-ward
Num. 3. 29. Kohath pitch on side of tabern. s.-w.
13. 17. Moses said, get ye up this way s.-ward
Dan. 8. 4. I saw the ram pushing s.-ward

SOUTH-west.

Acts 27. 12. Phenice lying towards the s.-west

SOUTH-wind.

Job 37. 17. he quieteth the earth by the s.-wind
Ps. 78. 26. by his power he brought in the s.-wind
Cant. 4. 16. come, thou s.-wind, blow on my garden
Luke 12. 55. when see s.-w. blow there will be heat
Acts 27. 13. and when the s.-wind blew softly

SOW.

2 Pet. 2. 22. the s. washed, to her wallowing in mire

SOW

Signifies, [1] *To scatter seeds on the earth*, Gen. 26. 12. Lev. 25. 3. [2] *To preach the gospel*, Mat. 13. 19. 1 Cor. 9. 11. [3] *To disperse worldly goods among the poor*, 2 Cor. 9. 6. [4] *To be buried, and laid like seed in the earth, subject to rottenness and putrefaction*, 1 Cor. 15. 42, 43.

He that soweth to the flesh, Gal. 6. 8. *One that leads such a course of life as is agreeable to his corrupt nature, that layeth out his estate, and bestows all his time and pains in the service of the flesh, and so makes provision only for this present life.*

He that soweth to the spirit, Gal. 6. 8. *He that layeth out his estate, or spendeth his time, strength, and talents for the glory of God, in obedience to the commands, motions, and dictates of the Spirit; and particularly that useth his estate for the maintenance of the gospel, and upholding the ministry of it.*

He that soweth and he that reapeth, John 4. 36. *the prophets and John the Baptist, who have sowed the seeds of instruction among the people formerly, and taught them the principles of saving truth; and you, my disciples, that succeed them, whose ministry I will use in bringing people to embrace me and my doctrine, thereby to perfect those truths which were formerly taught them concerning me.*

Gen. 47. 23. here is seed for you and ye sh. s. the land
Exod. 23. 10. six years s. the land, Lev. 25. 3.
Lev. 19. 19. shall not s. with mingled seed, Deut. 22. 9.
25. 4. in the seventh year thou shalt not s. 11.
20. we shall not s. nor gather in our increase
22. ye shall s. the eighth year
26. 16. ye shall s. your seed in vain, for enemies
2 Kings 19. 29. in the third year s. ye, Isa. 37. 30.
Job 4. 8. they that s. wickedness reap the same
31. 8. then let me s. and let another eat
Psal. 107. 37. s. fields and plant vineyards
126. 5. they that s. in tears shall reap in joy
Eccl. 11. 4. he that observeth the wind, shall not s.
6. in the morning s. thy seed, and in the evening
Isa. 28. 24. doth the plowman plow all day to s.?
30. 23. give rain of seed thou shalt s. ground withal
32. 20. blessed are ye that s. beside all waters
Jer. 4. 3. break fallow-ground, s. not among thorns
31. 27. I will s. the house of Israel with seed
35. 7. neither shall ye build house nor s. seed
Hos. 2. 23. and I will s. her unto me in the earth
10. 12. s. to yourselves in righteousn. reap in mercy
Mic. 6. 15. thou shalt s. but thou shalt not reap
Zech. 10. 9. I will s. them among the people
Mat. 6. 26. the fowls of the air s. not, nor reap
13. 3. a sower went forth to s. when he sowed some seeds fell by the way-side, Mark 4. 3. Luke 8. 5.
27. didst not thou s. good seed in thy field?
Luke 12. 24. consider ravens they neither s. nor reap
19. 21. reapest that thou didst not s. 22.

SOWED.

Gen. 26. 12. Isaac s. in that land same year received
Judg. 9. 45. Abimelech s. Shechem with salt
Mat. 13. 4. when he s. some fell by the way-side, and the fowls devoured them, Mark 4. 4. Luke 8. 5.
24. which s. good seed || 25. the enemy s. tares, 39.

SOW. See SEW.

SOWEDST.

Deut. 11. 10. not as Egypt, where thou s. thy seed

SOWN.

Lev. 11. 37. if a carcase fall on sowing seed to be s.
Deut. 21. 4. to a rough valley neither eared nor s.
22. 9. lest the fruit of thy seed s. be defiled
29. 23. generation see that land is not s. nor bear.
Judg. 6. 3. when Israel had s. the Midianites came
Psal. 97. 11. light is s. for the righteous, and gladness
Isa. 19. 7. every thing s. by the brooks shall wither
40. 24. shall not be planted, yea, shall not be s.
61. 11. as the garden causeth the things s. to spring
Jer. 2. 2. thou wentest after me in a land not s.
12. 13. they have s. wheat, but shall reap thorns
Ezek. 36. 9. I am for you, and ye shall be tilled and s.
Hos. 8. 7. they have s. the wind, shall reap whirlwind
Nah. 1. 14. that no more of thy name be s.
Hag. 1. 6. ye have s. much, and bring in little
Mat. 13. 19. catcheth away that was s. Mark 4. 15.
25. 24. an hard man, reaping where thou hast not s.
Mark 4. 16. these are they which s. on stony ground
18. s. among thorns || 20. are s. in good ground
31. which when it is s. is less than all the seeds
1 Cor. 9. 11. if we have s. to you spiritual things
15. 42. it is s. in corruption || 43. is s. in dishonour
44. it is s. a natural body, raised a spiritual body
2 Cor. 9. 10. multiply your seed s. and increase fruits
Jam. 3. 18. the fruit of righteousness is s. in peace

SOWER.

Isa. 55. 10. that it may give seed to the s. and bread
Jer. 50. 16. cut off s. from Babylon, and him that
Mat. 13. 3. behold, a s. went forth to sow, when he sowed some seeds by way-side, Mark 4. 3. Luke 8. 5.
18. hear ye therefore the parable of the s.
Mark 4. 14. s. soweth the word, these by way-side
2 Cor. 9. 10. now he that ministereth seed to the s.

SOWEST.

1 Cor. 15. 36. that which thou s. is not quickened
37. thou s. not that body that shall be, but bare grain

SOWETH.

Prov. 6. 14. he s. discord || 19. he that s. discord
11. 18. to him that s. righteousness be a sure reward
16. 28. a froward man s. strife, and a whisperer
22. 8. he that s. iniquity shall reap vanity
Amos 9. 13. treader shall overtake him that s. seed
Mat. 13. 37. he that s. good seed, is the Son of man
Mark 4. 14. sower s. the word, these by way-side
John 4. 36. both he that s. and reapeth may rejoice
37. that saying true, one s. and another reapeth
2 Cor. 9. 6. he who s. sparingly, he who s. bountifully
Gal. 6. 7. for whatsoever a man s. that shall he reap
8. that s. to his flesh, shall reap corruption; but he that s. to the Spirit, shall reap life everlasting.

SOWING.

Lev. 11. 37. if their carcase fall on any s. to be sown
26. 5. and the vintage shall reach to the s. time

SPACE.

Gen. 29. 14. Jacob abode with him the s. of a month
32. 16. and put a s. between drove and drove
Lev. 25. 8. the s. of seven sabbaths of years shall be
30. if it be not redeemed in the s. of a full year
Josh. 3. 4. there shall be a s. between you and it
1 Sam. 26. 13. s. between Dav. company and Saul's
Ezra 9. 8. for a little s. grace hath been shewed
Jer. 28. 11. within the s. of two full years
Luke 22. 59. about the s. of one hour after
Acts 5. 7. about s. of three hours his wife came in
34. commanded to put the apostles forth a little s.
7. 42. offered slain beasts by the s. of forty years
13. 20. gave judges about the s. of 450 years
21. God gave them Saul for the s. of 40 years
19. 8. he spake boldly the s. of three months
10. and this continued by the s. of two years
34. all with one voice about s. of two hours cried
20. 31. by the s. of three years I ceased not
Jam. 5. 17. it rained not by the s. of three years
Rev. 2. 21. I gave her s. to repent of her fornication
8. 1. there was silence about the s. of half an hour
14. 20. and blood came by the s. of 1600 furlongs
17. 10. when come, he must continue a short s.

SPACES.

1 Kings 7. † 5. s. and pillars were square in prospect
Neh. 7. † 4. now the city was broad in s.
Isa. 22. † 18. he shall toss thee into country large of s.
33. † 21. the Lord will be to us a place broad of s.

SPAKE.

Gen. 19. 14. Lot went out, and s. to his sons-in-law
24. 30. saying, thus s. the man unto me
29. 9. while he yet s. with them, Rachel came
39. 10. it came to pass as she s. to Joseph day by day
42. 14. that is it that I s. to you, saying, ye are spies
23. for he s. unto them by an interpreter
43. 27. the old man of whom ye s. is he yet alive?
29. is this your younger brother of whom ye s.?
50. 17. and Joseph wept when they s. unto him
Num. 12. 1. Miriam and Aaron s. against Moses
21. 5. and the people s. against God and Moses
Deut. 1. 43. so I s. to you, and ye would not hear
28. 68. Lord shall bring thee by way whereof I s.
Judg. 19. 22. they s. to the master of the house
Ruth 4. 1. behold, the kinsman of whom Boaz s.
1 Sam. 1. 13. now Hannah s. in her heart, lips moved
18. 24. told him, saying, on this manner s. David
20. 26. nevertheless Saul s. not any thing that day
30. 6. for the people s. of stoning him
2 Sam. 12. 18. while child was alive, we s. to him
1 Kings 1. 42. while he yet s. behold, Jonathan
3. 22. thus they s. before king Solomon
2 Kings 2. 22. according to saying which Elisha s.
9. 12. and he said, thus and thus s. he to me
1 Chr. 21. 19. David went up at saying which Gad s.
2 Chron. 18. 19. one s. saying after this manner
30. 22. Hezekiah s. comfortably to them, 32. 6.
32. 16. his servants s. yet more ag. the Lord God
19. they s. against the God of Jerusalem
33. 18. that s. to Manasseh in the name of Lord
Neh. 13. 24. their childr. s. half in speech of Ashdod
Esth. 3. 4. it came to pass, when they s. daily to him
Job 2. 13. they sat down, and none s. a word to him
19. 18. I arose, and they s. against me
29. 22. after my words they s. not again
32. 16. for they s. not, but stood still, answered not
Psal. 39. 3. fire burned, then s. I with my tongue
78. 19. yea, they s. against God, they said, can G.
106. 33. so that he s. unadvisedly with his lips
Prov. 30. 1. the man s. to Ithiel and Ucal
Cant. 2. 10. my beloved s. and said, rise up, my love
5. 6. my soul failed when he s. I sought him
Jer. 8. 6. I hearkened and heard, they s. not aright
20. 8. for since I s. I cried out, I cried violence
Ezek. 24. 18. so I s. to the people in the morning
Dan. 7. 11. voice of great words which the horn s.
Hos. 13. 1. when Ephraim s. trembling, exalted him.
Mal. 3. 16. that feared Lord s. often one to another
Mat. 9. 18. while he s. these to them, 17. 5. | 26. 47. Mark 5. 35. | 14. 43. Luke 8. 49. | 22. 47, 60.
33. dev. was cast out, dumb s. 12. 22. Luke 11. 14.
21. 45. they perceived that he s. of them
Luke 1. 55. as he s. to our fathers, to Abraham
2. 50. they understood not the saying which he s.
9. 11. he s. unto them of the kingdom of God
31. who s. of his decease to be at Jerusalem
22. 65. other things blasphemously s. they ag. him
24. 6. remember how he s. to you in Galilee
36. as they thus s. Jesus stood in midst of them
John 1. 15. John said, this was he of whom I s.
7. 13. no man s. openly of him for fear of Jews
46. the officers said, never man s. like this man
8. 27. they understood not that he s. of the Father
10. 6. what things they were which he s. to them
41. all things that John s. of this man were true
11. 13. howbeit Jesus s. of his death
51. this s. he not of hims. he prophesied that Jes.
12. 29. others said, an angel s. to him
38. saying might be fulfilled which he s. 18. 9, 32.
41. when he saw his glory, and s. of him
13. 22. disciples looked, doubting of whom he s.
24. he should ask who it should be of whom he s.
13. 28. no man knew for what intent he s. this
21. 19. this s. he, signifying by what death he
Acts 6. 10. not able to resist spirit by which he s.
8. 6. gave heed to those things which Philip s.
10. 44. while Peter yet s. these words, H. Ghost fell
13. 45. Jews s. ag. those things that were spoken
14. 1. and so s. that a great multitude believed
19. 9. but s. evil of that way before the multitude
20. 38. sorrowing most for the words which he s.
22. 9. they heard not voice of him that s. to me
26. 24. as he thus s. for himself, Festus said
28. 25. well s. the Holy Ghost by Esaias the proph.
1 Cor. 13. 11. when I was a child, I s. as a child
14. 5. I would that ye all s. with tongues
Gal. 4. 15. where is then the blessedness ye s. of?
Heb. 7. 14. of which tribe Moses s. nothing of priest
12. 25. who refused him that s. on earth
2 Pet. 1. 21. holy men of God s. as they were moved
Rev. 1. 12. I turned to see the voice that s. with me
13. 11. I beheld another beast s. as a dragon

God SPAKE.

Gen. 35. 15. Jacob called place where God s. Beth-el
Exod. 20. 1. God s. all these words saying, I am Ld.
Deut. 1. 6. the Lord our God s. to us in Horeb
Josh. 23. 14. not one thing failed of good things G. s.
Mark 12. 26. how in the bush God s. to him
John 9. 29. we know that God s. unto Moses
Acts 7. 6. and God s. on this wise, that his seed
Heb. 1. 1. God who s. in time past to the fathers
See LORD, *expressly*.

Lord or *God* SPAKE, *implicitly*.

Gen. 24. 7. G. who s. to me, and sware to me, saying
1 Sam. 9. 17. behold the man whom I s. to thee of
28. 17. and the L. hath done to him as he s. by me
2 Sam. 7. 7. s. I a word with any of tribes of Israel?
23. 3. God said, the rock of Israel s. to me
1 Kings 6. 12. word which I s. unto David thy father
2 Chron. 6. 4. who hath fulfilled that which he s.
32. 24. he s. to him, and gave him a sign
Psal. 33. 9. he s. and it was done, he commanded
99. 7. he s. unto them in the cloudy pillar
105. 31. he s. and there came flies and lice
34. he s. and the locusts came, and caterpillars
Isa. 65. 12. when I s. ye did not hear, 66. 4.
Jer. 7. 13. I s. to you, rising up early and speaking
22. I s. not to your fathers, I brought them
14. 14. I sent them not, neither s. unto them
19. 5. which I commanded not, nor s. it
22. 21. I s. unto thee in thy prosperity, but saidst
31. 20. for since I s. against him, I remember him
Ezek. 1. 28. I heard a voice of one that s. 2. 2.
10. 2. he s. unto the man clothed with linen
Dan. 9. 12. he confirmed his words which he s.
Hos. 12. 4. found him in Beth-el, there he s. with us
Luke 1. 70. as he s. by mouth of his holy prophets
24. 44. these are the words which I s. to you
Heb. 4. 4. he s. in a certain place on this wise

SPAKEST.

Judg. 13. 11. art thou the man s. to the woman?
17. 2. the silver thou s. of also in mine ears
1 Sam. 28. 21. hearkened to words which thou s.
1 Kings 8. 24. thou s. also with thy mouth, and hast fulfilled it with thine hand, 2 Chron. 6. 15.
26. let thy word be verified which thou s. to Dav.
53. didst separate them, as thou s. by Moses
Neh. 9. 13. and s. with them from heaven
Psal. 89. 19. then thou s. in vision to thy Holy One
Jer. 48. 27. since thou s. of him, skippedst for joy

SPAN.

Exod. 28. 16. a s. shall be the length, and a s. the breadth of the breast-plate of judgment, 39. 9.
1 Sam. 17. 4. Goliath's height six cubits and a s.
Isa. 40. 12. who hath meted out heaven with the s.?
Lam. 2. 20. shall women eat their childr. of a s. long
Ezek. 43. 13. the border of the altar shall be a s.

SPANNED.

Isa. 48. 13. my right hand hath s. the heavens

SPANGLED.

Isa. 3. † 19. I will take away the s. ornaments

SPARE.

Gen. 18. 24. not s. the place for the fifty righteous
26. then I will s. all the place for their sakes
45. † 20. let not your eye s. your stuff
Deut. 13. 8. thou shalt not s. nor conceal him
29. 20. Lord will not s. him, but anger of Lord
1 Sam. 15. 3. now go, destroy Amalek, s. them not
Neh. 13. 22. and s. me according to thy mercy
Job 6. 10. let him not s. I have not concealed words
16. 13. he cleaveth my reins asunder, doth not s.
20. 13. though he s. it and forsake it not
27. 22. for God shall cast upon him, and not s.
30. 10. they s. not to spit in my face
Psal. 39. 13. O s. me that I may recover strength
72. 13. he shall s. the poor and needy, and save
Prov. 6. 34. he will not s. in the day of vengeance
19. 18. let not thy soul s. for his crying
Isa. 9. 19. people as fuel, no man shall s. brother
13. 18. their eye shall not s. children
30. 14. and he shall break it, he shall not s.
54. 2. s. not, lengthen cords, strengthen stakes
58. 1. cry aloud, s. not, lift up voice like a trumpet
Jer. 13. 14. I will not s. them, Ezek. 24. 14.
21. 7. he shall not s. them || 50. 14. s. no arrows
51. 3. s. ye not her young men, destroy her host
Ezek. 5. 11. I will dimin. thee, nor shall mine eye s. nor will I have any pity, 7. 4, 9. | 8. 18. | 9. 10.
9. 5. let not your eye s. neither have ye pity
Joel 2. 17. let them say, s. thy people, O Lord
Jonah 4. 11. should not I s. Nineveh that great city?
Hab. 1. 17. and not s. continually to slay the nations
Mal. 3. 17. I will s. them as a man spareth his son
Luke 15. 17. hired servants have bread enough to s.
Rom. 11. 21. take heed, lest he also s. not thee
1 Cor. 7. 28. such shall have trouble, but I s. you
2 Cor. 1. 23. that to s. you I came not as yet to Corinth
13. 2. that if I come again, I will not s.

SPARED.

1 Sam. 15. 9. but Saul and the people s. Agag
15. for the people s. the best of the sheep
24. 10. some bade me kill thee, but mine eye s.
2 Sam. 12. 4. s. to take of his own flock and herd
21. 7. the king s. Mephibosheth son of Jonathan
2 Kings 5. 20. master hath s. Naaman this Syrian
Psal. 78. 50. he s. not their soul from death

Ezek. 20. 17. mine eye s. them from destroying
Jonah 4. † 10. Lord said, thou hast s. the gourd
Rom. 8. 32. he that s. not his own Son but delivered
11. 21. if God s. not the natural branches
2 Pet. 2. 4. if God s. not the angels that sinned
5. and s. not the old world, but saved Noah

SPARETH.

Prov. 13. 24. he that s. his rod, hateth his son
17. 27. he that hath knowledge s. his words
21. 26. but the righteous giveth, and s. not
Mal. 3. 17. I will spare them, as a man s. his son

SPARING.

Acts 20. 29. wolves shall enter in, not s. the flock

SPARINGLY.

2 Cor. 9. 6. this I say, he who soweth s. shall reap s.

SPARK.

Job 18. 5. and the s. of his fire shall not shine
Isa. 1. 31. and the maker of it shall be as a s.

SPARKS.

Job 5. 7. man is born to trouble, as s. fly upward
41. 19. out of mouth go burning lamps, s. of fire
Prov. 26. † 18. as madmen who casteth s. and death
Isa. 50. 11. that compass yourselves about with s.
Dan. 3. † 22. the s. of the fire slew those men

SPARKLED.

Ezek. 1. 7. s. like the colour of burnished brass

SPARROW.

Psal. 84. 3. yea, the s. hath found an house
102. 7. I am as a s. alone upon the house-top

SPARROWS.

Lev. 14. † 4. take for him two s. alive and clean
Mat. 10. 29. are not two s. sold for a farthing?
31. are of more value than many s. Luke 12. 7.
Luke 12. 6. are not five s. sold for two farthings?

SPAT.

John 9. 6. when he had thus spoken, he s. on ground

SPEAK.

Gen. 18. 27. I have taken on me to s. to God, 31.
24. 50. we cannot s. unto thee bad or good
31. 24. take heed thou s. not to Jacob good or bad
32. 4. thus shall ye s. to my lord Esau, 19.
44. 16. what shall we say? what shall we s.?
Exod. 4. 14. Aaron, I know that he can s. well
5. 23. since I came to s. to Pharaoh in thy name
7. 2. thou shalt s. all that I command thee
23. 2. shalt not s. in a cause to decline after many
29. 42. where I will meet you, to s. there to thee
32. 12. wherefore should Egyptians s. and say?
34. 35. until he went in to s. with the Lord
Num. 12. 8. were ye not afraid to s. against Moses
14. 15. who have heard the fame of thee will s.
21. 27. why they that s. in proverbs say, come
22. 8. I will bring word, as the Lord shall s. to me
35. the word I s. to thee, that thou shalt s.
23. 5. return to Balak, and thus thou shalt s.
12. must I not take heed to s. that which the Lord
27. 7. the daughters of Zelophehad s. right
Deut. 18. 19. words which he shall s. in my name
20. who shall presume to s. a word in my name
26. 5. and thou shalt s. and say before the Lord
Josh. 22. 24. your children might s. to our children
1 Sam. 25. 17. a son of Belial that a man cannot s. to
2 Sam. 3. 19. and Abner went also to s. to David
27. Joab took him aside to s. with him quietly
7. 17. accord. to this vision so did Nathan s. to Dav.
19. 10. why s. ye not one word of bringing back
20. 16. come near hither that I may s. with thee
18. they were wont to s. in old time, saying
1 Kings 2. 19. she went to s. to him for Adonijah
12. 7. wilt s. good words to them, 2 Chron. 10. 7.
10. saying, thus shalt thou s. to this people
22. 24. spirit from me to s. to thee, 2 Chr. 18. 23.
2 Kings 18. 27. hath my master sent me to thy master
and to thee to s. these words? Isa. 36. 12.
1 Chron. 17. 18. what can David s. more to thee?
2 Chron. 32. 17. wrote letters to rail and s. ag. God
Neh. 13. 24. and could not s. in the Jews' language
Esth. 6. 4. to s. to the king to hang Mordecai
Job 8. 2. how long wilt thou s. these things?
11. 5. but, oh that God would s. against thee
13. 7. will ye s. wickedly for G. and talk for him?
18. 2. mark, and afterwards we will s.
27. 4. my lips shall not s. wickedness nor deceit
32. 7. I said, days should s. and teach wisdom
36. 2. shew that I have yet to s. on God's behalf
37. 20. if a man s. he shall be swallowed up
41. 3. will he s. soft words unto thee?
Psal. 2. 5. then shall he s. to them in his wrath
5. 6. thou shalt destroy them that s. leasing
12. 2. they s. vanity, they s. with a double heart
17. 10. with their mouth they s. proudly
28. 3. which s. peace to their neighbours
29. 9. in his temple doth every one s. of his glory
31. 18. which s. grievous things proudly ag. right.
35. 20. for they s. not peace, but devise deceitful
28. my tongue shall s. of thy righteousness
38. 12. they s. mischievous things all day long
40. 5. if I would declare and s. of them
41. 5. enemies s. evil of me, when shall he die?
49. 3. my mouth shall s. of wisdom and meditation
52. 3. lovest lying rather than to s. righteousness
59. 12. and for cursing and lying which they s.
63. 11. mouth of them that s. lies shall be stopped
69. 12. they that sit in the gate s. against me
71. 10. for mine enemies s. against me
73. 8. they are corrupt, they s. wickedly, s. loftily
85. 8. I will hear what the Lord will s. he will s.
peace to his people, but let them not turn to folly
94. 4. how long shall they utter and s. hard things?
109. 20. let this be the reward of them that s. evil
115. 5. they have mouths, but they s. not, 135. 16.
119. 23. princes also did sit and s. against me
172. my tongue shall s. of thy word
127. 5. they shall s. with the enemies in the gate
139. 20. for they s. against thee wickedly
145. 6. men shall s. of might of thy terrible acts
11. they shall s. of the glory of thy kingdom
21. my mouth shall s. the praise of the Lord
Prov. 8. 7. my mouth shall s. truth, and wickedness
23. 16. my reins rejoice, when lips s. right things
Eccl. 3. 7. a time to be silent, and a time to s.
Cant. 7. 9. causing lips of those that are asleep to s.

Isa. 8. 20. if they s. not according to this word
14. 10. all they shall s. and say unto thee
19. 18. five cities in Egypt shall s. lang. of Canaan
28. 11. with another tongue shall he s. to this peop.
29. 4. and thou shalt s. out of the ground
32. 4. tongue of the stammerers shall s. plainly
32. 6. for the vile person will s. villany
50. 4. that I should know how to s. in season
52. 6. they shall know that I am he that doth s.
59. 4. trust in vanity, and s. lies, conceive misch.
Jer. 1. 7. whatsoever I command thee, thou shalt s.
5. 14. saith the Lord, because ye s. this word
7. 27. thou shalt s. all these words to them
9. 5. they will not s. the truth, taught to s. lies
10. 5. idols are upright as palm-trees, they s. not
12. 6. believe not, tho' they s. fair words unto thee
13. 12. therefore thou shalt s. this word to them
18. 7. at what instant I shall s. about a nation, 9.
20. I stood before thee to s. good for them
20. 9. I said, I will not s. any more in his name
23. 16. they s. a vision of their own heart
26. 2. s. all the words I commanded thee to s. 8.
15. the Lord hath sent me to s. these words
29. 24. thus shalt thou also s. to Shemaiah
32. 4. and shall s. with him mouth to mouth
34. 3. he shall s. with thee mouth to mouth
Ezek. 2. 7. and thou shalt s. my words to them
3. 10. all my words that I shall s. receive in heart
20. 49. they say of me, doth he not s. parables?
24. 27. and thou shalt s. and be no more dumb
32. 21. strong among the mighty shall s. to him
33. 8. if dost not s. to warn wicked from his way
10. thus ye s. ‖ 30. and s. one to another
37. 18. when the children of thy people shall s.
Dan. 2. 9. ye have prepared corrupt words to s.
3. 29. s. any thing amiss ag. the God of Shadrach
7. 25. he shall s. great words agst. the Most High
11. 27. shall s. lies at one table, but not prosper
Hab. 2. 3. but at the end it shall s. and not lie
Zech. 9. † 17. corn shall make the young men s.
Mat. 10. 19. how or what ye shall s. Mark 13. 11.
20. for it is not ye that s. Mark 13. 11.
12. 34. how can ye being evil s. good things?
36. every idle word that men shall s. give account
46. his mother stood without, desiring to s. with
Mark 2. 7. why doth this man thus s. blasphemies?
9. 39. shall do a miracle, that lightly s. evil of me
14. 71. saying, I know not this man of whom ye s.
16. 17. in my name they shall s. with new tongues
Luke 1. 19. I am sent to s. to thee and to shew thee
20. not able to s. till these shall be performed
22. when he came out he could not s. to them
4. 41. he rebuking them, suffered them not to s.
6. 26. woe to you, when all men shall s. well of you
11. 53. and to provoke him to s. of many things
12. 10. whosoever shall s. a word ag. Son of man
John 3. 11. verily we s. that we do know, and testify
9. 21. he is of age, ask him, he shall s. for himself
16. 13. he shall not s. of himself, that shall he s.
25. when I shall no more s. to you in proverbs
Acts 2. 7. are not all these which s. Galileans?
11. we do hear them s. in tongues works of God
4. 17. that they s. to no man in this name
18. not to s. at all, 5. 40. ‖ 20. we cannot but s.
29. that with all boldness they may s. thy word
6. 11. we have heard him s. blasphemous words
13. this man ceaseth not to s. blasphemous words
10. 32. when he cometh shall s. unto thee
11. 15. as I began to s. ‖ 14. 9. same heard Paul s.
21. 39. I beseech thee suffer me to s. to people
23. 5. thou shalt not s. evil of ruler of thy people
26. 1. Paul, thou art permitted to s. for thyself
25. I s. forth the words of truth and soberness
Rom. 15. 18. I will not dare to s. of any of those th.
1 Cor. 1. 10. that ye all s. same thing and no divisions
2. 13. which things also we s. not in man's wisdom
3. 1. I could not s. to you as to spiritual but carnal
12. 30. do all s. with tongues? ‖ 14. 23. if all s.
14. 35. it is a shame for women to s. in church
39. and forbid not to s. with tongues
2 Cor. 2. 17. in the sight of God s. we in Christ
4. 13. we also believe and therefore s.
12. 19. we s. before God in Christ, but for edifying
Eph. 5. 12. it is a shame to s. of those things done
Col. 4. 4. that I may make manifest, as I ought to s.
1 Thess. 1. 8. so that we need not to s. any thing
2. 4. even so we s. not as pleasing men but God
16. forbidding us to s. to the Gentiles
Tit. 3. 2. put them in mind to s. evil of no man
Heb. 2. 5. the world to come, whereof we s.
6. 9. tho' we thus s. ‖ 9. 5. of which we cannot s.
Jam. 1. 19. brethren, let every man be slow to s.
1 Pet. 2. 12. whereas they s. against you as evil-doers
3. 10. let him refrain his lips that they s. no guile
16. whereas they s. evil of you, as of evil-doers
2 Pet. 2. 10. they are not afraid to s. evil of dignities
12. s. evil of the things that they understand not
18. for when they s. great swell. words of vanity
1 John 4. 5. are of world, therefore s. they of world
Jude 8. these filthy dreamers s. evil of dignities
10. but these s. evil of those things they know not
Rev. 2. 24. not known depths of Satan, as they s.
13. 15. that the image of the beast should both s.

SPEAK, *Imperatively.*

Exod. 20. 19. s. thou with us, and we will hear
Num. 20. 8. s. ye to the rock before their eyes
Deut. 3. 26. L. said, s. no more to me of this matter
5. 27. s. thou to us all that Lord shall s. to thee
Judg. 5. 10. s. ye that ride on white asses
19. 30. consider, take advice, and s. your minds
1 Sam. 3. 9. s. Lord, for thy servant heareth, 10.
2 Sam. 17. 6. shall we do after his say, if not s. thou
1 Kings 22. 13. s. that which is good, 2 Chron. 18. 12.
2 Kings 18. 26. s. in Syrian language, Isa. 36. 11.
Esth. 5. 14. and to-morrow s. thou to the king
Job 12. 8. or s. to the earth, and it shall teach thee
13. 22. or let me s. and answer thou me
33. 32. s. for I desire to justify thee
34. 33. therefore s. what thou knowest
Ps. 75. 5. lift not your horn, s. not with a stiff neck
Prov. 23. 9. s. not in the ears of a fool
Isa. 8. 10. s. word, it shall not stand, God is with us

Isa. 30. 10. who say, s. unto us smooth things
40. 2. s. ye comfortably to Jerusal. and cry to her
41. 1. let them come near, then let them s.
56. 3. neither let the son of a stranger s. saying
Jer. 1. 17. s. to them all that I command thee
23. 28. hath my word, let him s. word faithfully
Dan. 10. 19. and I said, let my lord s.
Zech. 8. 16. s. every man the truth, Eph. 4. 25.
Mat. 8. 8. only s. word, my servant shall be healed
10. 27. what I tell in darkness, that s. ye in light
Mark 13. 11. what shall be given in that hour, s. ye
Luke 12. 13. s. to my brother, that he divide inherit.
Acts 2. 29. let me freely s. to you of patriarch David
5. 20. go, stand and s. in the temple to the people
18. 9. be not afraid, but s. hold not thy peace
1 Cor. 14. 28. let him s. to himself and to God
29. let prophets s. two or three, the other judge
Tit. 2. 1. s. the things that become sound doctrine
15. these things s. and exhort, and rebuke
Jam. 2. 12. so s. ye and do, as they that shall be judg.
4. 11. s. not evil one of another, brethren
1 Pet. 4. 11. let him s. as the oracles of God

I SPEAK.

Exod. 19. 9. that the people may hear when I s.
23. 22. but if thou shalt obey and do all that I s.
Num. 22. 38. G. putteth in my mouth that shall I s.
Deut. 5. 1. hear judgments which I s. in your ears
11. 2. I s. not with your childr. who have not known
1 Kings 22. 14. what the Lord saith, that will I s.
Job 9. 19. if I s. of strength, lo, he is strong
35. then would I s. and not fear him
13. 3. surely I would s. to the Almighty
13. hold your peace, let me alone, that I may s.
16. 4. I also could s. as ye do, I could heap words
6. though I s. my grief is not assuaged
37. 20. shall it be told him that I s.? if a man sp.
Psal. 45. 1. I s. of things which I have made
77. 4. I am so troubled that I cannot s.
120. 7. but when I s. they are for war
Isa. 45. 19. I the Lord s. righteousness, I declare
63. 1. I that s. in righteousness, mighty to save
Jer. 1. 6. ah, Lord, I cannot s. for I am a child
6. 10. to whom shall I s. and give warning?
28. 7. hear this word that I s. in thine ears
38. 20. obey the voice of the Lord which I s.
Ezek. 3. 27. when I s. with thee, I will open mouth
Dan. 10. 11. O Daniel, understand words that I s.
Mat. 13. 13. therefore s. I to them in parables
John 4. 26. Jesus saith, I that s. to thee am he
6. 63. the words that I s. to you, they are spirit
7. 17. whether it be of G. or whether I s. of mys.
8. 26. I s. to the world those things I heard of him
28. as my Father taught me, I s. these things
38. I s. that which I have seen with my Father
12. 49. he gave commandment, what I should s.
50. what I s. as the Father said to me, so I s.
13. 18. I s. not of all, I know whom I have chosen
14. 10. the words that I s. I s. not of myself
17. 13. and these things I s. in the world
Acts 21. 37. may I s. to thee? ‖ 26. 26. I also s. freely
Rom. 3. 5. is God unrighteous? I s. as a man
6. 19. I s. after the manner of men, Gal. 3. 15.
7. 1. for I s. to them that know the law
11. 13. I s. to you Gentiles, I am apostle of Gent.
1 Cor. 6. 5. I s. to your shame, 15. 34.
7. 6. I s. this by permission, not of commandment
12. but to the rest s. I, not the Lord
35. and this I s. for your own profit
10. 15. I s. as to wise men, judge ye what I say
13. 1. though I s. with tongues of men and angels
14. 6. except I shall s. to you by revelation
18. I s. with tongues more than you all
19. I had rather s. five words with understanding
2 Cor. 6. 13. I s. as to my children, be ye enlarged
7. 3. I s. not this to condemn you, for I have said
11. 17. that which I s. I s. it not after the Lord
21. I s. as concerning reproach. I s. foolishly
23. are they ministers? I s. as a fool, I am more
Eph. 5. 32. but I s. concerning Christ and church
6. 20. that therein I may s. boldly, as I ought to s.
Phil. 4. 11. not that I s. in respect of want
1 Tim. 2. 7. I s. the truth in Christ, I lie not

I will SPEAK, or will I SPEAK.

Gen. 18. 30. let not Lord be angry, and I will s. 32.
Num. 12. 6. and I will s. to him in a dream
8. with him will I s. mouth to mouth apparently
24. 13. but what L. saith that will I s. cannot go
beyond command, 1 Kings 22. 14. 2 Chr. 18. 13.
Deut. 32. 1. give ear, O ye heavens, and I will s.
Judg. 6. 39. Gideon said, I will s. but this once
2 Sam. 14. 15. thy handmaid said, I will s. to king
1 Kings 2. 18. well, I will s. for thee to the king
Job 7. 11. I will s. in the anguish of my spirit
10. 1. I will s. in the bitterness of my soul
32. 20. I will s. that I may be refreshed
33. 31. mark well, hold thy peace, and I will s.
42. 4. hear, I beseech thee, and I will s.
Psal. 50. 7. hear, O my people, and I will s.
73. 15. if I say, I will s. thus, I should offend
119. 46. I will s. of thy testimonies before kings
145. 5. I will s. of the honour of thy majesty
Prov. 8. 6. hear, for I will s. of excellent things
Jer. 5. 5. I will get me to great men, and I will s.
Ezek. 2. 1. stand on thy feet, and I will s. to thee
12. 25. I will s. and word I s. shall come to pass
Hos. 2. 14. I w. allure her, and s. comfortably to her
1 Cor. 14. 21. with other lips will I s. to this people

SPEAKER.

Ps. 140. 11. let not an evil s. be established in earth
Acts 14. 12. because he was the chief s.

SPEAKEST.

1 Sam. 9. 21. wherefore then s. thou so to me?
2 Sam. 19. 29. why s. thou any more of thy matters?
2 Kings 6. 12. the words thou s. in thy bed-chamber
Job 2. 10. thou s. as one of the foolish women
Psal. 50. 20. thou sittest and s. against thy brother
51. 4. that thou mightest be justified when thou s.
Isa. 40. 27. why s. thou, O Israel, my way is hid
Jer. 40. 16. for thou s. falsely of Ishmael
43. 2. thou s. falsely, the Lord hath not sent thee
Ezek. 3. 18. thou givest him not warning, nor s.
Zech. 13. 3. for thou s. lies in the name of the Lord

Mat. 13. 10. why *s.* thou to them in parables?
Luke 12. 41. L. *s.* thou this parable to us or to all?
John 16. 29. now *s.* thou plainly, and *s.* no proverb
19. 10. Pilate saith to him, *s.* thou not unto me?
Acts 17. 19. may we know this whereof thou *s.*?

SPEAKETH.

Gen. 45. 12. that it is my mouth that *s.* to you
Exod. 33. 11. spake to Moses as a man *s.* to friend
Num. 23. 26. all that the Lord *s.* that must I do
Deut. 18. 22. when a prophet *s.* in the name of Ld.
Job 17. 5. he that *s.* flattery to his friends
33. 14. for God *s.* once, yea, twice, yet man
Psal. 12. 3. shall cut off tongue that *s.* proud things
15. 2. and he that *s.* the truth in his heart
37. 30. the mouth of the righteous *s.* wisdom
41. 6. and if he come to see me, he *s.* vanity
144. 8. whose mouth *s.* vanity, 11.
Prov. 2. 12. from the man that *s.* froward things
6. 13. he *s.* with his feet, he teacheth with fingers
19. a false witness that *s.* lies and soweth discord
10. 32. the mouth of the wicked *s.* frowardness
12. 17. he that *s.* truth, sheweth forth righteousn.
18. there is that *s.* like the piercings of a sword
14. 25. but a deceitful witness *s.* lies
16. 13. and they love him that *s.* right
19. 5. that *s.* lies not escape ‖ 9. *s.* lies shall perish
21. 28. but the man that heareth, *s.* constantly
26. 25. when he *s.* fair, believe him not
Isa. 9. 17. an evil-doer, and every mouth *s.* folly
32. 7. to destroy, even when the needy *s.* right
33. 15. he that *s.* uprightly shall dwell on high
Jer. 9. 8. their tongue *s.* deceit; one *s.* peaceably
10. 1. hear the word which the Lord *s.* to you
28. 2. thus *s.* the Lord the God of Israel, 29. 25. | 30. 2. *Hag.* 1. 2. *Zech.* 6. 12. | 7. 9.
Ezek. 10. 5. as voice of Almighty God when he *s.*
Amos 5. 10. they abhor him that *s.* uprightly
Mat. 10. 20. but Spirit of your Father who *s.* in you
12. 32. whoso *s.* a word against the Son of man; but whosoever *s.* against the Holy Ghost
34. how can ye being evil speak good? for out of abundance of the heart mouth *s.* *Luke* 6. 45.
John 3. 31. he that is of the earth, *s.* of the earth
34. he whom God sent, *s.* the words of God
7. 18. he that *s.* of himself, seeketh his own glory
26. but lo, he *s.* boldly, they say nothing to him
8. 44. when he *s.* a lie, he *s.* of his own
19. 12. who maketh himself a king, *s.* ag. Cesar
Acts 8. 34. I pray, of whom *s.* the prophet this?
Rom. 10. 6. righteousness of faith *s.* on this wise
1 *Cor.* 14. 2. he that *s.* in an unknown tongue; howbeit in the Spirit he *s.* mysteries
3. he that prophesieth, *s.* unto men to edification
4. that *s.* in an unknown tongue edifieth himself
5. greater is he that prophesieth, than he that *s.*
11. I shall be to him that *s.* a barbarian
13. let him that *s.* in an unknown tongue
1 *Tim.* 4. 1. now Spirit *s.* expressly in latter times
Heb. 11. 4. and by it he being dead, yet *s.*
12. 5. forgotten the exhortation which *s.* to you
24. that *s.* better things than that of Abel
25. see that ye refuse not him that *s.* much more if we turn away from him that *s.* from heaven
Jam. 4. 11. he that *s.* evil of his brother and judgeth his brother, *s.* evil of the law and judgeth the law
Jude 16. and their mouth *s.* great swelling words

SPEAKING.

Gen. 24. 15. before he had done *s.* Rebekah came
45. and before I had done *s.* in mine heart
Deut. 5. 26. God *s.* out of the midst of the fire
11. 19. *s.* of them when thou sittest in thine house
Ruth 1. 18. then she left *s.* unto her
Esth. 10. 3. and *s.* peace to all his seed
Job 1. 16. while he was yet *s.* another came, 17, 18.
4. 2. but who can withhold himself from *s.*?
32. 15. they answered no more, they left off *s.*
Psal. 34. 13. and thy lips from *s.* guile
58. 3. go astray as soon as they be born, *s.* lies
Isa. 58. 9. if thou take away from thee *s.* vanity
13. nor *s.* thine own words on my holy day
59. 13. in lying, and *s.* oppression and revolt
65. 24. and while they are yet *s.* I will hear
Jer. 7. 13. rising up early, and *s.* 25. 3. | 35. 14.
38. 4. he weakeneth the hands in *s.* such words
27. they left off *s.* the matter was not perceived
Dan. 7. 8. and a mouth *s.* great things, *Rev.* 13. 5.
8. 13. I heard one saint *s.* and another said
9. 20. whiles I was *s.* praying and confessing, 21.
Acts 14. 3. they abode, *s.* boldly in the Lord
20. 30. *s.* perverse things, to draw away disciples
1 *Cor.* 12. 3. no man *s.* by Spirit calleth Jesus accur.
2 *Cor.* 13. 3. since ye seek a proof of Christ *s.* in me
Eph. 4. 15. but *s.* the truth in love may grow up
5. 19. *s.* to yourselves in psalms, hymns, and songs
1 *Tim.* 4. 2. shall depart from faith, *s.* lies in hypocrisy
5. 13. busy-bodies *s.* things which they ought not
1 *Pet.* 4. 4. to the same excess of riot, *s.* evil of you
See End.

SPEAKING.

Mat. 6. 7. think they shall be heard for much *s.*
Eph. 4. 31. let all evil *s.* be put away from you

SPEAKINGS.

1 *Pet.* 2. 1. laying aside all guile, envies, and evil *s.*

SPEAR.

Josh. 8. 18. the Lord said, stretch out thy *s.* 26.
Judg. 5. 8. was there a *s.* seen among 40,000 in Isr.
1 *Sam.* 13. 22. *s.* with any, but with Saul and Jona.
17. 7. and the staff of his *s.* was like a weaver's beam, 2 *Sam.* 21. 19. 1 *Chron.* 20. 5.
45. thou comest with a sword, and with a *s.*
47. the Lord saveth not with sword and *s.*
21. 8. is there not here under thy hand *s.* or sword
26. 7. and Saul's *s.* stuck at his bolster, 11.
8. let me smite him, I pray thee, with the *s.*
16. now see where the king's *s.* is, and the cruse
2 *Sam.* 1. 6. behold, Saul leaned upon his *s.*
2. 23. Abner with the end of the *s.* smote Asahel
23. 7. must be fenced with iron and staff of a *s.*
8. he lifted up his *s.* against 800, whom he slew
18. he lifted up *s.* against 300, 1 *Chron.* 11. 11, 20.
21. he slew Egyptian with his own *s.* 1 *Chr.* 11. 23.
Job 39. 23. quiver rattleth, glittering *s.* and shield
Job 41. 26. *s.* of him that layeth at him cannot hold
29. Leviathan laugheth at the shaking of a *s.*
Psal. 35. 3. draw also out the *s.* stop the way
46. 9. he breaketh bow and cutteth *s.* in sunder
Jer. 6. 23. they shall lay hold on bow and *s.*
Nah. 3. 3. the horseman lifteth up the sword and *s.*
Hab. 3. 11. at the shining of the glittering *s.*
John 19. 34. a soldier with a *s.* pierced his side

SPEARS.

1 *Sam.* 13. 19. lest Hebrews make them swords or *s.*
2 *Kings* 11. 10. to captains did priest give king David's *s.* that were in the temple, 2 *Chr.* 23. 9.
2 *Chr.* 11. 12. in ev. several city he put shields and *s.*
26. 14. Uzziah prepared for them shields and *s.*
Neh. 4. 13. I set the people with their *s.* and bows
16. the other half of them held the *s.* 21.
Psal. 57. 4. whose teeth are *s.* and arrows
Isa. 2. 4. shall beat *s.* into pruning hooks, *Mic.* 4. 3.
Jer. 46. 4. furbish the *s.* and put on the brigandines
Ezek. 39. 9. they shall burn *s.* with fire seven years
Joel 3. 10. beat your pruning-hooks into *s.*

SPEARMEN.

Psal. 68. 30. rebuke the company of *s.* the bulls
Acts 23. 23. saying, make ready two hundred *s.*

SPECIAL.

Deut. 7. 6. Lord hath chosen thee to be a *s.* people
Mal. 3. † 17. when I make up my *s.* treasure
Acts 19. 11. *s.* miracles done by the hand of Paul
See Especially.

SPECKLED.

Gen. 30. 32. removing from thence the *s.* cattle
31. 8. the *s.* shall be thy wages, the cattle bare *s.*
Jer. 12. 9. mine heritage is to me as a *s.* bird
Zech. 1. 8. behind were red horses, *s.* and white

SPECTACLE.

1 *Cor.* 4. 9. for we are made a *s.* to the world

SPED.

Judg. 5. 30. have they not *s.*? have they not divided

SPEECH.

Gen. 4. 23. heark. to my *s.* ‖ 11. 1. earth was of one *s.*
Exod. 4. 10. Moses said, O my Lord, I am slow of *s.*
Deut. 22. 14. and give occasions of *s.* against her
32. 2. my *s.* shall distil as dew, as the small rain
1 *Sam.* 16. † 18. a son of Jesse, and prudent in *s.*
2 *Sam.* 14. 20. to fetch about this form of *s.*
19. 11. seeing the *s.* of all Israel is come to king
1 *Kings* 3. 10. and Solomon's *s.* pleased the Lord
Neh. 13. 24. their childr. spake half in *s.* of Ashdod
Job 12. 20. he removeth away the *s.* of the trusty
13. 17. hear diligently my *s.* and my declaration, 21. 2. *Psal.* 17. 6. *Isa.* 28. 23. | 32. 9.
15. † 4. and thou restrainest *s.* before God
24. 25. who will make my *s.* nothing worth?
29. 22. and my *s.* dropped upon them
37. 19. we cannot order our *s.* by reason of darkn.
Psal. 19. 2. day unto day uttereth *s.* night unto night
3. there is no *s.* where their voice is not heard
64. † 5. they encourage themselves in an evil *s.*
Prov. 1. † 6. to understand an eloquent *s.*
7. 21. with her fair *s.* she caused him to yield
17. 7. excellent *s.* becometh not a fool
Cant. 4. 3. thy lips are like scarlet, thy *s.* is comely
Isa. 3. † 3. I will take away the skilful of *s.*
26. † 16. they have poured out a secret *s.*
29. 4. shalt be brought down, thy *s.* shall be low out of the dust; thy *s.* shall whisper out of the dust
33. 19. of a deeper *s.* than thou canst perceive
Jer. 31. 23. as yet they shall use this *s.* in Judah
Ezek. 1. 24. the voice of *s.* as the noise of an host
3. 5. thou art not sent to a people of a strange *s.* 6.
Hab. 3. 2. O Ld. I have heard thy *s.* and was afraid
Mat. 26. 73. art one of them, thy *s.* bewray. thee
Mark 7. 32. one that had an impediment in his *s.*
14. 70. art a Galilean, and thy *s.* agreeth thereto
John 8. 43. why do ye not understand my *s.*?
Acts 14. 11. their voice, saying in the *s.* of Lycaonia
20. 7. preached and continued his *s.* till midnight
1 *Cor.* 2. 1. I came not with excellency of *s.* or wisd.
4. *s.* was not with enticing words of man's wisdom
4. 19. I will know, not the *s.* but the power
2 *Cor.* 3. 12. we use great plainness of *s.*
7. 4. great is my boldness of *s.* toward you
10. 10. bodily presence weak, his *s.* is contemptible
11. 6. though I be rude in *s.* yet not in knowledge
Col. 4. 6. let your *s.* be always with grace, seasoned
Tit. 2. 8. sound *s.* that cannot be condemned

SPEECHES.

Num. 12. 8. I will speak with him not in dark *s.*
Job 6. 26. and the *s.* of one that is desperate
15. 3. or with *s.* wherewith he can do no good?
32. 14. neither will I answer him with your *s.*
† 15. they removed *s.* from themselves
Rom. 16. 18. by fair *s.* deceive the hearts of simple
Jude 15. to convince them of all their hard *s.*

SPEECHLESS.

Mat. 22. 12. not a wedding garment, and he was *s.*
Luke 1. 22. Zacharias beckoned them and remained *s.*
Acts 9. 7. men which journeyed with him stood *s.*

SPEED.

Gen. 24. 12. O Lord, I pray thee, send me good *s.*
Ezra 6. 12. have made a decree, let it be done with *s.*
Isa. 5. 26. behold, they shall come with *s.* swiftly
Acts 17. 15. for to come to him with all *s.*
2 *John* 10. receive him not, nor bid him God *s.*
11. that biddeth him God *s.* is partaker of evil
See Make, Made.

SPEEDY.

Zeph. 1. 18. shall make even a *s.* riddance of all them

SPEEDILY.

1 *Sam.* 27. 1. than that I should *s.* escape to Philist.
2 *Sam.* 17. 16. lodge not in plains, but *s.* pass over
2 *Chron.* 35. 13. other holy offerings divided they *s.*
Ezra 6. 13. as the king had sent, so they did *s.*
7. 17. that thou mayest buy *s.* with this money
21. that what Ezra shall require, it be done *s.*
26. let judgment be executed *s.* upon him
Esth. 2. 9. he *s.* gave her her things for purification
Psal. 31. 2. deliver me *s.* ‖ 69. 17. hear me *s.* 143. 7.
79. 8. let thy tender mercies *s.* prevent us
102. 2. in the day when I call, answer me *s.*
Eccl. 8. 11. because sentence is not executed *s.*
Isa. 58. 8. and thy health shall spring forth *s.*
Joel 3. 4. and if ye recompense me, *s.* will I return
Zech. 8. 21. let us go *s.* and pray before the Lord
Luke 18. 8. I tell you, that he will avenge them *s.*

SPEND.

Deut. 32. 23. I will *s.* mine arrows upon them
Job 21. 13. they *s.* their days in wealth, and go down
36. 11. they *s.* their days in prosperity, and years
Psal. 90. 9. we *s.* our years as a tale that is told
Isa. 55. 2. why *s.* money for that which is not bread?
Acts 20. 16. because he would not *s.* time in Asia
2 *Cor.* 12. 15. I will very gladly *s.* and be spent for you

SPENDEST.

Luke 10. 35. whatsoever thou *s.* more, I will repay

SPENDETH.

Prov. 21. 20. but a foolish man *s.* it up
29. 3. that keepeth com. with harlots, *s.* substance
Eccl. 6. 12. days of vain life, which he *s.* as a shadow

SPENT.

Gen. 21. 15. and the water was *s.* in the bottle
47. 18. we will not hide it how that our money is *s.*
Lev. 26. 20. and your strength shall be *s.* in vain
Judg. 19. 11. when they were by Jebus, day was far *s.*
1 *Sam.* 9. 7. for the bread is *s.* in our vessels
Job 7. 6. my days are *s.* without hope
17. † 1. my spirit is *s.* my days are extinct
Psal. 31. 10. for my life is *s.* with grief
Isa. 49. 4. I have *s.* my strength for nought
Jer. 37. 21. till all the bread in the city was *s.*
Mark 5. 26. and had *s.* all that she had, *Luke* 8. 43.
6. 35. when the day was far *s.* *Luke* 24. 29.
Luke 15. 14. when the prodigal had *s.* all
Acts 17. 21. *s.* their time to tell some new thing
Rom. 13. 12. the night is far *s.* the day is at hand
2 *Cor.* 12. 15. I will gladly spend and be *s.* for you

SPEW, *See* Spue.

SPICE.

Exod. 35. 28. rulers brought *s.* and oil for the light
Cant. 5. 1. I have gathered my myrrh with my *s.*

SPICES.

Gen. 43. 11. carry down man a present, balm and *s.*
Exod. 25. 6. and *s.* for anointing oil, 35. 8.
30. † 7. Aaron shall burn thereon incense of *s.*
23. take thou unto thee principal *s.* of myrrh, 34.
37. 29. he made the pure incense of sweet *s.*
39. † 38. they brought incense of sweet *s.*
1 *Kings* 10. 2. camels that bare *s.* 10. 2 *Chron.* 9. 1.
25. they brought to Solomon *s.* 2 *Chron.* 9. 24.
2 *Kings* 20. 13. Hezekiah shewed them *s.* ointment and all that was found in his treasures, *Isa.* 39. 2.
1 *Chron.* 9. 29. some were appointed to oversee *s.*
30. sons of the priests made the ointment of *s.*
2 *Chron.* 9. 9. the queen of Sheba gave Solomon *s.*
16. 14. divers *s.* prepared for the burial of Asa
32. 27. Hezekiah made treasures for *s.* and gold
Cant. 4. 10. the smell of thine ointments than all *s.*
14. myrrh and aloes, with all the chief *s.*
16. blow upon my garden, that *s.* may flow out
5. 13. his cheeks are as a bed of *s.* as sweet flowers
6. 2. my beloved is gone down to the beds of *s.*
8. 14. to a young hart upon the mountains of *s.*
Ezek. 27. 22. occupied in fairs with chief of all *s.*
Mark 16. 1. Mary had bought sweet *s.* *Luke* 24. 1.
Luke 23. 56. returned and prepared *s.* and ointments
John 19. 40. they wound it in linen with the *s.*

SPICE.

Ezek. 24. 10. consume the flesh and *s.* it well

SPICE-*merchants.*

1 *Kings* 10. 15. of the traffic of the *s.-merchants*

SPICED.

Cant. 8. 2. I would cause thee to drink of *s.* wine

SPICERY.

Gen. 37. 25. Ishmaelites bearing *s.* balm and myrrh
2 *Kings* 20. † 13. shewed house of his *s.* *Isa.* 39. 2.

SPIDER.

Job 8. 14. and whose trust shall be a *s.* web
Prov. 30. 28. the *s.* taketh hold with her hands
Isa. 59. 5. hatch cockatrice' eggs and weave *s.* web

SPIE, *See* Spy.

SPIKENARD.

Cant. 1. 12. my *s.* sendeth forth the smell thereof
4. 13. with pleasant fruits, camphire with *s.* 14.
Mark 14. 3. there came a woman having an alabaster box of ointment of *s.* very precious, *John* 12. 3.

SPILLED.

Gen. 38. 9. Onan *s.* his seed on the ground
Mark 2. 22. bottles burst, and wine is *s.* *Luke* 5. 37.

SPILT.

2 *Sam.* 14. 14. we are as water *s.* on the ground

SPIN.

Exod. 35. 25. women that were wise-hearted, did *s.*
Mat. 6. 28. they toil not, neither *s.* *Luke* 12. 27.

SPINDLE.

Prov. 31. 19. she layeth her hands to the *s.*

SPIRIT.

In Hebrew, Ruach; *in* Greek, Πνευμα. *In Scripture the word* Spirit *is taken,* [1] *For the Holy Ghost, the third person of the holy Trinity, who inspired the prophets, animates good men, pours his grace into our hearts, imparts to us light and comfort, in whose* Name *we are baptized, as well as in those of the* Father *and* Son; *that enlivening* Spirit *who proceeds from the Father and Son,* Mat. 3. 16. John 3. 8. | 15. 26. *The* Holy Ghost *is called* Spirit, *being, as it were, breathed, and proceeding from the* Father *and* Son, *who inspire and move our hearts by him; or, because he breatheth where he listeth; stirring up spiritual motions in the hearts of believers, purifying and quickening them; or because he is a spiritual, invisible, and incorporeal essence. He is called* holy, *both because he is most holy in himself, and the Sanctifier, the Worker of holiness in the creature. He is called a* person, *because whatsoever belongs to a person, as to understand, to will, to give, to call, to do, to subsist of himself, doth agree to the* Spirit; *who appeared in a visible shape,* Luke 3. 22. Acts 2. 3. *gave the Apostles sundry tongues,* Acts 2. 4, 8. *hath power to confer and bestow on the church the gift of tongues, of miracles, of faith, of healing, of prophecy, &c.* 1 Cor. 12. 8, 9, 10, 11, 12. *which cannot be attributed to any quality or motion cre-*

ated. Lastly, he is called the third person, *not in order of time, or dignity of nature, but in order and manner of subsisting.*
[2] Spirit *is taken for the immediate inspiration, and extraordinary help, of the Spirit of God.* Mat. 22. 43. How then doth David in Spirit call him Lord, *that is, by the inspiration of the Holy Ghost.* 1 Cor. 14. 15. I will pray with the Spirit, *that is, by the immediate gift and extraordinary help of the Spirit.* [3] *For the extraordinary gifts and graces of the Spirit,* Gal. 3. 2. [4] *For the counsels, motions, and directions of the Spirit.* Rom. 8. 1. Who walk not after the flesh, but after the Spirit. [5] Spirit *is taken for the renewed nature, or spiritual part in man.* Mat. 26. 41. The Spirit is willing, but the flesh is weak. [6] *For spiritual zeal.* 1 Tim. 4. 12. Be thou an example of believers in spirit. [7] *For judgment, authority, and consent,* 1 Cor. 5. 4. [8] *It signifies pure, holy, and spiritual.* John 3. 6. That which is born of the Spirit, is spirit; *that is, that which is wrought by the Spirit of God is of a spiritual nature, and so, suitable to the kingdom of God.* [9] *It is taken for the gospel, which is the ministration of the Spirit, and by whose influence it becomes effectual to change the hearts of sinners, to turn them from the power of Satan unto God, and to make them truly spiritual and holy.* 2 Cor. 3. 6, 8. Who hath made us able ministers of the new testament, not of the letter, but of the spirit. [10] *For the thoughts, affection, and care.* Col. 2. 5. Though I be absent in the flesh, yet I am with you in the spirit. [11] *For a temper, frame, or disposition of soul or spirit.* Psal. 51. 10. Renew a right spirit within me.
[12] Spirit *signifies the reasonable soul, which continues in being even after the death of the body; that spiritual, reasoning, and choosing substance, capable of eternal happiness.* Acts 7. 59. Lord Jesus, receive my spirit, *or,* my soul. [13] *Good angels are called spirits, immaterial and intelligent, but created and dependent beings.* Heb. 1. 14. Are they not all ministering spirits? [14] *The devils are often called* unclean spirits, evil spirits, *Mark* 5. 13. *Luke* 7. 21. *So in* 1 *Sam.* 18. 10. The evil spirit from God came upon Saul. [15] Spirit *signifies an apparition or ghost.* Mat. 14. 26. When the disciples saw Jesus walking on the sea, they were troubled, saying, it is a spirit. *And our Saviour, after his resurrection, appearing to his disciples,* they were affrighted, and supposed they had seen a spirit, *or* ghost; *but he said to them,* handle me, and see, for a spirit hath not flesh and bones as ye see me have, *Luke* 24. 37, 39. [16] *It is taken for a person that pretended to be inspired, or for a doctrine offered as the immediate revelation of the Spirit.* 1 John 4. 1. Believe not every spirit. [17] *For passion, wrath, or anger.* Eccl. 10. 4. If the spirit of the ruler rise up against thee. [18] *For the breath, the respiration, the animal life that is in beasts.* Eccl. 3. 21. The spirit of the beast that goeth downward. [19] Spirit *is also taken for the wind.* Amos 4. 13. He that createth the wind, *or* spirit. These are the four spirits of the heavens, *in* Hebrew, winds, *Zech.* 6. 5. *And in* John 3. 8. The wind bloweth where it listeth, *in* Greek, πνευμα, *the spirit.*
The spirit of a sound mind; the spirit of wisdom and understanding; the spirit of knowledge; the spirit of grace and prayer; the spirit of prophecy, *and the like, signify several effects, works, and gifts, together with the author and cause, which is the Holy Spirit infusing them. On the contrary, the* spirit of pride, covetousness, fury, uncleanness, *do signify these vices, and the devil, that wicked spirit, the author of them.*
Grieve not the Holy Spirit, *Eph.* 4. 30. *Men may be said to grieve the Spirit of God, by withstanding his holy inspirations, the motions of his grace, or by living in a lukewarm and negligent manner. Also by despising his gifts, or neglecting them; by abusing his favours, either out of vanity, curiosity, or negligence. And in a contrary sense, we stir up the Spirit of God which is in us (as* St. Paul *advises* Timothy, 2 *Tim.* 1. 6.) *by the practice of godliness, by our exactness in complying with his motions, by fervour in his service, by renewing our gratitude, &c.* See the *Significations* on DISCERN, EARNEST, PRISON, QUENCH, SOW.

Gen. 7. † 22. in whom was breath of the *s.* of life
26. † 35. which were a bitterness of *s.* to Isaac
41. 8. Pharaoh's *s.* was troubled in the morning
45. 27. the *s.* of Jacob their father revived
Exod. 6. 9. hearkened not to Moses for anguish of *s.*
35. 21. every one whom his *s.* made willing
Num. 11. 17. I will take of *s.* that is on thee, 25.
26. the *s.* rested upon them and they prophesied
29. that the Lord would put his *s.* upon them
14. 24. Caleb, because he had another *s.* with him
27. 18. take Joshua, a man in whom is the *s.*
Deut. 2. 30. for the Lord thy God hardened his *s.*
Josh. 5. 1. nor was there *s.* in them any more
Judg. 8. † 3. then their *s.* was abated toward him
15. 19. when he had drunk his *s.* came again
1 *Sam.* 30. 12. when he had eaten his *s.* came to him
1 *Kings* 10. 5. there was no *s.* in her, 2 *Chron.* 9. 4.
21. 5. Jezebel his wife said, why is thy *s.* so sad?
22. 21. there came forth a *s.* 2 *Chron.* 18. 20.
2 *Kings* 2. 9. let a double portion of thy *s.* be on me
15. they said, *s.* of Elijah doth rest on Elisha
1 *Chron.* 5. 26. the Lord stirred up the *s.* of Pul
12. 18. then the *s.* came upon Amasai, and said
28. 12. the pattern of all that he had by the *s.*
2 *Chron.* 21. 16. against Jehoram *s.* of Philistines
Ezra 1. 5. with them whose *s.* God raised to go up
Neh. 9. 30. testifiedst by the *s.* in thy prophets
Job 4. 15. then a *s.* passed before my face
15. 13. that thou turnest thy *s.* against God
20. 3. *s.* of my understanding causeth me to answer
Job 26. 4. and whose *s.* came from thee?
13. by his *s.* he garnished the heavens, his hand
32. 8. there is a *s.* in man, inspiration of Almighty
18. the *s.* within me constraineth me
34. 14. if he gather to him his *s.* and his breath
Psal. 32. 2. and in whose *s.* there is no guile
51. 10. a clean heart, renew a right *s.* within me
12. and uphold me with thy free *s.*
76. 12. he shall cut off the *s.* of princes
78. 8. and whose *s.* was not stedfast with God
104. 30. thou sendest forth thy *s.* they are created
106. 33. so they provoked his *s.* so that he spake unadvisedly with his lips
139. 7. whither shall I go from thy *s.?*
143. 10. *s.* is good, lead me to land of uprightness
Prov. 14. 29. he that is hasty of *s.* exalteth folly
15. 4. but perverseness therein is a breach in the *s.*
16. 18. and an haughty *s.* goeth before a fall
32. that ruleth *s.* better than he that taketh city
18. 14. the *s.* of a man will sustain his infirmity
20. 27. the *s.* of man is the candle of the Lord
25. 28. that hath no rule over his *s.* is like a city
Eccl. 3. 21. who knoweth the *s.* of man, *s.* of beast
7. 9. be not hasty in thy *s.* to be angry
8. 8. no man hath power over *s.* to retain the *s.*
10. 4. if the *s.* of the ruler rise against thee
11. 5. thou knowest not what is the way of the *s.*
12. 7. and the *s.* shall return to God who gave it
Isa. 19. 3. the *s.* of Egypt shall fail in midst thereof
29. 10. L. hath poured on you the *s.* of deep sleep
24. they that erred in *s.* shall come to understand.
31. 3. and their horses flesh and not *s.*
32. 15. till the *s.* be poured upon us from on high
34. 16. and his *s.* it hath gathered them
37. † 7. behold, I will put a *s.* into him
42. 5. he that giveth *s.* to them that walk therein
48. 16. the Lord God and his *s.* hath sent me
54. 6. as a woman forsaken and grieved in *s.*
57. 16. *s.* shall fail before me and souls I have made
61. 1. the *s.* of Lord God is on me, *Luke* 4. 18.
3. the garment of praise for the *s.* of heaviness
Jer. 51. 11. Lord raised the *s.* of king of Medes
Ezek. 1. 12. whither *s.* was to go, they went, 20.
21. for the *s.* was in the wheels, 10. 17.
2. 2. *s.* entered into me when he spake to me, 3. 24.
3. 12. then the *s.* took me up and I heard, 11. 24.
14. so *s.* lifted me up, and took me away, and I went in the heat of my *s.* 8. 3. | 11. 1.
13. 3. woe to prophets that follow their own *s.*
21. 7. ev. *s.* shall faint, all knees be weak as water
Dan. 2. 1. Nebuchadnezzar's *s.* was troubled
4. 8. and in whom is the *s.* of the holy gods, before him I told the dream, 9. 18. | 5. 11, 14.
5. 12. an excellent *s.* were found in Daniel, 6. 3.
Hos. 9. † 7. prophet is a fool, man of the *s.* is mad
Amos 4. † 13. for lo, he that createth the *s.*
Mic. 2. 11. if man walking in *s.* and falsehood do lie
Hag. 1. 14. the Lord stirred up the *s.* of Zerubbabel
Zech. 7. 12. hath sent in his *s.* by former prophets
12. 1. and formeth *s.* of man within him
Mal. 2. 15. yet had he the residue of the *s.* therefore take heed to your *s.* that ye deal not treacherously, 16.
Mat. 4. 1. Jesus was led up of the *s.* *Luke* 4. 1.
14. 26. were troubled; saying it is a *s.* *Mark* 6. 49.
22. 43. how then doth David in *s.* call him Lord?
26. 41. the *s.* indeed is willing, *Mark* 14. 38.
Mark 1. 10. the *s.* descending on him, *John* 1. 32.
12. the *s.* driveth him into the wilderness
8. 12. and he sighed deeply in his *s.* and saith
9. 20. *s.* tare him || 26. the *s.* cried and rent him
Luke 1. 17. he shall go before him in the *s.* of Elias
80. and the child waxed strong in *s.* 2. 40.
2. 27. and he came by the *s.* into the temple
4. 14. Jesus returned in power of *s.* into Galilee
8. 55. her *s.* came again, and she arose straightway
9. 55. ye know not what manner of *s.* ye are of
10. 21. in that hour Jesus rejoiced in *s.* and said
13. 11. a woman who had a *s.* of infirmity
24. 37. they supposed that they had seen a *s.*
39. for a *s.* hath not flesh and bones as I have
John 1. 33. on whom thou shalt see *s.* descending
3. 34. God giveth not the *s.* by measure to him
4. 23. worship the Father in *s.* and in truth
24. G. is a *s.* they must worship him in *s.* and truth
6. 63. it is the *s.* that quickeneth; words that I speak unto you, they are *s.* and they are life
7. 39. this spake he of *s.* || 11. 33. he groaned in *s.*
13. 21. he was troubled in *s.* and testified and said
Acts 2. 4. they spake as *s.* gave them utterance
6. 10. and they were not able to resist the *s.*
8. 29. then the *s.* said to Philip, go near and join
10. 19. the *s.* said unto Peter, 11. 12.
11. 28. Agabus signif. by *s.* there should be dearth
16. 7. they assayed, but the *s.* suffered them not
17. 16. his *s.* was stirred within him when he saw
18. 5. Paul was pressed in *s.* || 25. being fervent in *s.*
20. 22. now I go bound in the *s.* to Jerusalem
21. 4. the disciples said to Saul through the *s.*
23. 8. Sadducees say that there is no angel nor *s.*
9. but if a *s.* or an angel hath spoken to him
Rom. 1. 4. Son of God according to the *s.* of holiness
2. 29. circumcision is that of heart in the *s.*
8. 1. who walk not after the flesh, but after *s.* 4.
2. the law of the *s.* of life hath made me free
5. they that are after the *s.* the things of the *s.*
9. ye are not in the flesh but *s.* if so be that *s.*
10. but the *s.* is life because of righteousness
11. if *s.* of him that raised up Jesus from the dead, shall quicken your mortal bodies by his *s.*
13. but if ye thro' the *s.* mortify deeds of body
16. the *s.* itself beareth witness with our *s.*
23. but ourselves who have first-fruits of the *s.*
26. the *s.* also helpeth our infirmities; but the *s.* maketh intercession for us with groanings
27. he knoweth what is the mind of the *s.*
12. 11. fervent in *s.* || 15. 30. for the love of the *s.*
1 *Cor.* 2. 4. but in demonstration of *s.* and of power
10. but God hath revealed them unto us by his *s.* for the *s.* searcheth all things, the deep things of God
11. save the *s.* of a man which is in him
1 *Cor.* 2. 12. not *s.* of world, but *s.* who is of God
5. 3. I verily as absent in body, but present in *s.*
5. that *s.* may be saved in day of the Lord Jesus
6. 17. he that is joined to the Lord is one *s.*
20. glorify God in your body and in your *s.*
7. 34. that she may be holy both in body and *s.*
12. 4. are diversities of gifts, but same *s.* 8, 9, 11.
8. to one is given by the *s.* the word of wisdom
13. for by one *s.* are we all baptized into one body; have been all made to drink into one *s.*
14. 2. howbeit in the *s.* he speaketh mysteries
15. I will sing with *s.* || 16. shalt bless with the *s.*
15. 45. the last Adam was made a quickening *s.*
2 *Cor.* 3. 6. ministers of new testament, not of letter but of the *s.* letter killeth, but the *s.* giveth life
8. how shall not ministrat. of *s.* be rather glorious
17. the Lord is that *s.* where the *s.* of Lord is
4. 13. we having the same *s.* of faith, we believe
7. 1. cleanse from all filthiness of the flesh and *s.*
13. because his *s.* was refreshed by you all
11. 4. another *s.* which ye have not received
12. 18. walked we not in the same *s.* and same steps
Gal. 3. 2. received ye the *s.* by the works of the law
3. are ye so foolish, having begun in the *s.?*
5. he therefore that ministereth to you the *s.*
14. might receive the promise of the *s.* thro' faith
4. 6. God hath sent forth the *s.* of his son
5. 5. for we thro' *s.* wait for hope of righteousness
16. walk in the *s.* || 18. but if ye be led by the *s.*
17. for the flesh lusteth against the *s.* and the *s.* against the flesh, and these are contrary
25. if we live in the *s.* let us walk in the *s.*
6. 8. soweth to *s.* shall of the *s.* reap life everlasting
18. grace of our Lord be with your *s.* *Philem.* 25.
Eph. 2. 2. the *s.* that now worketh in the children
18. we have access by one *s.* to the Father
22. for an habitation of God through the *s.*
3. 5. as it is now revealed to his apostles by the *s.*
16. strengthened with might by his *s.* in inner man
4. 3. to keep unity of the *s.* in the bond of peace
4. there is one body, and one *s.* as ye are called
23. and be renewed in the *s.* of your mind
5. 18. be not drunk with wine, but be filled with *s.*
6. 17. take sword of the *s.* which is word of God
18. praying always with all prayer in the *s.*
Phil. 1. 19. and the supply of the *s.* of Jesus Christ
27. that ye stand fast in one *s.* with one mind
2. 1. if there be any fellowship of the *s.* if bowels
3. 3. the circumcision, which worship G. in the *s.*
Col. 1. 8. who declared to us your love in the *s.*
2. 5. tho' absent in flesh, yet am I with you in *s.*
1 *Thess.* 5. 19. quench not *s.* despise not prophesyin.
23. pray your *s.* soul, and body, be preser. blamel.
2 *Thess.* 2. 2. or be troubled, neither by *s.* nor word
8. Lord shall consume with the *s.* of his mouth
13. chosen you thro' sanctification of *s.* and belief
1 *Tim.* 3. 16. God manifest, justified in *s.* seen of angels
4. 1. now the *s.* speaketh expressly in latter times
12. be thou an example in *s.* in faith, in purity
2 *Tim.* 4. 22. the Lord Jesus Christ be with thy *s.*
Heb. 4. 12. to the dividing asunder of soul and *s.*
9. 14. who thro' the eternal *s.* offered himself to Gd.
Jam. 2. 26 for as the body without the *s.* is dead
4. 5. the *s.* that dwelleth in us lusteth to envy
1 *Pet.* 1. 2. thro' sanctification of the *s.* to obedience
22. ye have purified in obeying truth thro' the *s.*
3. 4. even the ornament of a meek and quiet *s.*
18. being put to death in flesh, but quickened by *s.*
4. 6. but live according to God in the *s.*
1 *John* 3. 24. by the *s.* which he hath given us
4. 1. beloved, believe not every *s.* but try the spirits
2. every *s.* that confesseth Jesus Christ is come
3. every *s.* that confesseth not that Jesus is come
13. dwell in him, because hath given us of his *s.*
5. 6. it is the *s.* that beareth witness, *s.* is truth
8. witness in earth, the *s.* the water, and the blood
Jude 19. these be sensual, not having the *s.*
Rev. 1. 10. I was in the *s.* on the Lord's day
2. 7. hear what *s.* saith to churches, he that hath an ear, let him hear, 11, 17, 29. | 3. 6, 13, 22.
4. 2. and immediately I was in the *s.* and behold
11. 11. the *s.* of life from God entered into them
14. 13. blessed are the dead, yea, saith the *s.*
17. 3. so he carried me away in the *s.* 21. 10.
22. 17. and the *s.* and the bride say, come

SPIRIT *of adoption.*
Rom. 8. 15. but ye have received the *s. of adoption*

SPIRIT *of antichrist.*
1 *John* 4. 3. and this is that *s. of antichrist* ye heard

SPIRIT *of bondage.*
Rom. 8. 15. ye have not received the *s. of bondage*

Born of the SPIRIT.
John 3. 5. except man be *born of the s.* he cannot enter
6. that which is *born of the s.* is spirit
8. so is every one that is *born of the s.*
Gal. 4. 29. persecuted him that was *born* after *the s.*

Broken SPIRIT.
Psal. 51. 17. the sacrifices of God are a *broken s.*
Prov. 15. 13. by sorrow of the heart the *s.* is *broken*
17. 22. but a *broken s.* drieth the bones
See CONTRITE.

SPIRIT *of burning.*
Isa. 4. 4. the blood of Jerusal. by the *s. of burning*

SPIRIT *of Christ.*
Rom. 8. 9. if any man have not the *s. of Christ*
1 *Pet.* 1. 11. what the *s. of Christ* in them did signify

SPIRIT *of counsel.*
Isa. 11. 2. the *s. of counsel* shall rest upon him

SPIRIT *of divination.*
Acts 16. 16. a damsel possessed with *s. of divination*

Dumb SPIRIT.
Mark 9. 17. I brought my son, who hath a *dumb s.*
25. thou *dumb s.* I charge thee, come out of him

Earnest of the SPIRIT.
2 *Cor.* 1. 22. who hath given us the *earn. of the s.* 5. 5.

SPIRIT *of error.*
1 *John* 4. 6. hereby know we the *s.* of truth and error
See EVIL.

Faithful SPIRIT.
Prov. 11. 13. he that is of *faithful s.* concealeth mat
See FAMILIAR.

SPIRIT *of fear.*
2 Tim. 1. 7. God hath not given us the s. of fear
Foul SPIRIT.
Mark 9. 25. he rebuked the foul s. saying to him
Rev. 18. 2. Babyl. is become the hold of every foul s.
Fruit of the SPIRIT.
Gal. 5. 22. the fruit of the s. is love, joy, peace
Eph. 5. 9. for the fruit of the s. is in all goodness
Good SPIRIT.
Neh. 9. 20. thou gavest thy good s. to instruct them
Psal. 143. 10. thy s. is good, lead me into the land
SPIRIT *of God.*
Gen. 1. 2. s. of God moved on the face of the waters
41. 38. as this is, a man in whom the s. of God is
Exod. 31. 3. have filled Bezaleel with s. of God, 35. 31.
Num. 24. 2. and the s. of God came on Balaam
1 Sam. 10. 10. the s. of God came on Saul, and he prophesied among them, 11. 6. | 19. 23.
19. 20. s. of God came on the messengers of Saul
2 Chron. 15. 1. the s. of God came upon Azariah
Job 27. 3. and the s. of God is in my nostrils
33. 4. s. of God hath made me, breath of Almighty
Ezek. 11. 24. in vision by the s. of God into Chaldea
Mat. 3. 16. he saw s. of God descending like a dove
12. 28. but if I cast out devils by the s. of God
Rom. 8. 9. if so be that the s. of God dwell in you
14. for as many as are led by the s. of God
15. 19. mighty signs by the power of the s. of God
1 Cor. 2. 11. knoweth no man, but the s. of God
14. receiveth not the things of the s. of God
3. 16. and that the s. of God dwelleth in you
6. 11. ye are sanctified by the s. of our God
7. 40. I think also that I have the s. of God
12. 3. no man speaking by the s. of God, calleth
2 Cor. 3. 3. written with the s. of the living God
Eph. 4. 30. and grieve not the holy s. of God
1 Pet. 4. 14. for the s. of God resteth on you
1 John 4. 2. hereby know ye the s. of God
SPIRIT *of glory.*
1 Pet. 4. 14. for the s. of glory resteth on you
SPIRIT *of grace.*
Zech. 12. 10. I will pour on house of David s. of grace
Heb. 10. 29. and hath done despite to the s. of grace
See HOLY.
Humble SPIRIT.
Prov. 16. 19. better it is to be of an humble s.
29. 23. but honour shall uphold the humble in s.
Isa. 57. 15. with him also that is of an humble s.
SPIRIT *of jealousy.*
Num. 5. 14. and s. of jealousy come upon him, 30.
SPIRIT *of judgment.*
Isa. 4. 4. purged blood of Jerusalem by s. of judgm.
28. 6. the Lord shall be for a s. of judgment to him
SPIRIT *of knowledge.*
Isa. 11. 2. the s. of knowledge shall rest upon him
See LORD, LYING.
SPIRIT *of meekness.*
1 Cor. 4. 21. shall I come to you in the s. of meekness?
Gal. 6. 1. restore such an one in the s. of meekness
My SPIRIT.
Gen. 6. 3. my s. shall not always strive with man
Job 6. 4. the poison whereof drinketh up my s.
7. 11. I will speak in the anguish of my s.
10. 12. and thy visitation hath preserved my s.
21. 4. if so, why should not my s. be troubled
Psal. 31. 5. into thine hand I commit my s.
77. 3. I complained, and my s. was overwhelmed
6. and my s. made diligent search
142. 3. when my s. was overwhelmed in me
143. 4. therefore is my s. overwhelmed in me
7. hear me speedily, O Lord, my s. faileth
Prov. 1. 23. behold, I will pour out my s. unto you
Isa. 26. 9. yea, with my s. will I seek thee early
30. 1. that cover with a covering, but not of my s.
38. 16. in all these things is the life of my s.
42. 1. I have put my s. upon him, shall bring forth
44. 3. I will pour my s. upon thy seed
59. 21. my s. that is upon thee shall not depart
Ezek. 3. 14. and I went in the heat of my s.
36. 27. and I will put my s. within you, 37. 14.
39. 29. for I have poured out my s. on house of Isr.
Dan. 2. 3. my s. was troubled || 7. 15. grieved in my s.
Joel 2. 28. I will pour out my s. upon all flesh, your sons and daughters shall prophesy, 29. Acts 2. 17, 18.
Hag. 2. 5. so my s. remaineth among you, fear ye not
Zech. 4. 6. not by might, nor by power, but by my s.
6. 8. these have quieted my s. in the north country
Mat. 12. 18. I will put my s. upon him, shall shew
Luke 1. 47. my s. hath rejoiced in God my Saviour
23. 46. Father, into thy hands I commend my s.
Acts 7. 59. Stephen said, Lord Jesus, receive my s.
Rom. 1. 9. whom I serve with my s. in the gospel
1 Cor. 5. 4. when ye are gathered together and my s.
14. 14. my s. prayeth, but my understanding is
16. 18. for they have refreshed my s. and yours
2 Cor. 2. 13. I had no rest in my s. bec. I found not
New SPIRIT.
Ezek. 11. 19. I will put a new s. within you, 36. 26.
18. 31. and make you a new heart and a new s.
Newness of SPIRIT.
Rom. 7. 6. that we should serve in newness of the s.
Patient SPIRIT.
Eccl. 7. 8. patient in s. is better than proud in spirit
Perverse SPIRIT.
Isa. 19. 14 the Lord hath mingled a perverse s.
Poor SPIRIT.
Mat. 5. 3. blessed are the poor in s. theirs the kingd.
SPIRIT *of promise.*
Eph. 1. 13. were sealed with that holy s. of promise
SPIRIT *of prophecy.*
Rev. 19. 10. testimony of Jesus is the s. of prophecy
SPIRIT *of slumber.*
Rom. 11. 8. God hath given them the s. of slumber
Sorrowful SPIRIT.
1 Sam. 1. 15. my lord, I am a woman of a sorrowf. s.
SPIRIT *of truth.*
John 14. 17. s. of truth whom world cannot receive
15. 26. even the s. of truth which proceedeth
16. 13. when s. of truth is come, will guide you
1 John 4. 6. hereby know we s. of truth and error
See VEXATION.

Unclean SPIRIT.
Zech. 13. 2. I will cause uncl. s. to pass out of land
Mat. 12. 43. when the unclean s. is gone out of a man, he walketh thro' dry places, Luke 11. 24.
Mark 1. 23. in their synagogue a man with an un. s.
26. and when the unclean s. had torn him
3. 30. because they said, he hath an unclean s.
5. 2. there met him a man with an unclean s.
8. come out of the man, thou unclean s. Luke 8. 29.
7. 25. whose young daughter had an unclean s.
Luke 9. 42. Jesus rebuked unclean s. and healed him
SPIRIT *of understanding.*
Isa. 11. 2. the s. of understand. shall rest upon him
SPIRIT *of whoredoms.*
Hos. 4. 12. for the s. of whoredoms caused them to err
5. 4. for s. of whoredoms is in the midst of them
SPIRIT *of wisdom.*
Exod. 28. 3. whom I have filled with s. of wisdom
Deut. 34. 9. Joshua was full of the s. of wisdom
Isa. 11. 2. the s. of wisdom shall rest upon him
Eph. 1. 17. that God may give to you s. of wisdom
Wounded SPIRIT.
Prov. 18. 14. but a wounded s. who can bear?
SPIRITS.
Num. 16. 22. O God, the G. of s. of all flesh, 27. 16.
Psal. 104. 4. who maketh his angels s. Heb. 1. 7.
Prov. 16. 2. but the Lord weigheth the s.
Zech. 6. 5. these are the four s. of the heavens
Mat. 8. 16. and he cast out the s. with his word
10. 1. he gave them power ag. unclean s. Mark 6. 7.
Mark 1. 27. for with authority commandeth he the unclean s. and they obey him, Luke 4. 36.
3. 11. unclean s. fell down before him, and cried
5. 13. the unclean s. entered into the swine
Luke 10. 20. rejoice not that s. are subject to you
Acts 5. 16. were vexed with unclean s. were healed
8. 7. for unclean s. crying, came out of many
1 Cor. 12. 10. to another discerning of s.
14. 32. s. of the prophets are subject to the proph.
Eph. 6. † 12. for we wrestle against wicked s.
1 Tim. 4. 1. depart from faith, giving heed to seduc. s.
Heb. 1. 14. are they not all ministering s.
12. 9. be in subjection to Father of s. sent to minister
23. and to the s. of just men made perfect
1 Pet. 3. 19. he went and preached to the s. in prison
1 John 4. 1. try the s. whether they are of God
Rev. 16. 13. I saw three uncl. s. like frogs come out
14. they are the s. of devils, working miracles
See EVIL, FAMILIAR, SEVEN.
SPIRITUAL.
Hos. 9. 7. the prophet is a fool, the s. man is mad
Rom. 1. 11. that I may impart to you some s. gift
7. 14. we know that the law is s. but I am carnal
15. 27. have been made partakers of their s. things
1 Cor. 2. 13. we speak, comparing s. things with s.
15. but he that is s. judgeth all things
3. 1. I could not speak to you as unto s. but as carnal
9. 11. if we have sown unto you s. things
10. 3. and did all eat the same s. meat
4. drink of the same s. drink, drank of that s. rock
12. 1. now concerning s. gifts, brethren
14. 1. desire s. gifts || 12. ye are zealous of s. gifts
37. if any man think himself a prophet or s.
15. 44. it is raised a s. body, there is a s. body
46. that was not first which is s. but that which is natural; and afterwards that which is s.
Gal. 6. 1. ye which are s. restore such an one in meek.
Eph. 1. 3. who hath blessed us with all s. blessings
5. 19. speaking to yourselves in psalms and s. songs
6. 12. wrestle against s. wickedness in high places
Col. 1. 9. that ye might be filled with all s. understanding
3. 16. admonish. one another in psalms and s. songs
1 Pet. 2. 5. are built up a s. house, to offer s. sacrifices
SPIRITUALLY.
Rom. 8. 6. but to be s. minded is life and peace
1 Cor. 2. 14. nor know them, because are s. discerned
Rev. 11. 8. which s. is called Sodom and Egypt
SPIT.
Lev. 15. 8. that hath the issue, s. on him that is clean
Num. 12. 14. if her father had but s. in her face
Deut. 25. 9. she shall s. in his face and shall say
Job 30. 10. and they spare not to s. in my face
Mat. 26. 67. they did s. in his face, and buffeted him
27. 30. and they s. upon him and smote him
Mark 7. 33. and he s. and touched his tongue
8. 23. when he had s. on his eyes, he asked him
10. 34. they shall s. upon him and shall kill him
14. 65. and some began to s. on him, 15. 19.
SPITE.
Psal. 10. 14. for thou beholdest s. to requite it
SPITEFULLY.
Mat. 22. 6. they entreated them s. and slew them
Luke 18. 32. he shall be s. entreated and spitted on
SPITTED.
Luke 18. 32. he shall be spitefully entreated and s. on
SPITTING.
Isa. 50. 6. I hid not my face from shame and s.
SPITTLE.
1 Sam. 21. 13. he let his s. fall down on his beard
Job 7. 19. let alone, till I swallow down my s.
30. † 10. they withhold not s. from my face
John 9. 6. he made clay of s. and anointed the eyes
SPOIL, *Substantive.*
Gen. 49. 27. and at night he shall divide the s.
Exod. 15. 9. the enemy said, I will divide the s.
Num. 31. 9. Israel took the s. of their cattle, 11.
12. and they brought the prey and s. to Moses
Deut. 2. 35. cattle we took for prey and the s. of the cities which we took, 3. 7. Josh. 8. 27. | 11. 14.
13. 16. thou shalt gather all the s. and burn it
20. 14. the s. thou shalt take to thyself, Josh. 8. 2.
Judg. 5. 30. meet for the necks of them that take s.
14. 19. Samson slew thirty men and took their s.
1 Sam. 14. 30. if had eaten freely to-day of the s.
32. the people flew upon the s. and took sheep
15. 19. but didst fly upon the s. and didst evil
21. but the people took of the s. sheep and oxen
30. 16. because the great s. that they had taken
19. neither s. nor any thing was lacking
20. took the flocks and said, this is David's s.
22. we will not give them ought of the s.

1 Sam. 30. 26. he sent of s. to elders of Jud. and his friends; behold a present of the s. of enemies
2 Sam. 3. 22. Joab brought in a great s. with them
12. 30. he brought forth of the s. of Rabbah
2 Kings 3. 23. now, therefore, Moab, to the s.
21. 14. they shall become a s. to their enemies
1 Chron. 20. 2. from Rabbah he brought much s.
2 Chr. 14. 13. they carried away s. from Ethiop. 14.
15. 11. they offered to Lord at same time of the s.
20. 25. when Jehoshaphat came to take the s. they were three days in gathering the s. it was so much
24. 23. the Syrians sent s. to the king of Damascus
25. 13. smote 3000 of them, and took much s.
28. 8. they took much s. and brought s. to Samaria
14. so the armed men left the captives and the s.
15. with the s. they clothed all that were naked
Ezra 9. 7. our kings have been delivered to a s.
Esth. 3. 13. to take the s. of them for a prey, 8. 11.
9. 10. but on the s. laid they not their hand
Job 29. 17. I plucked the s. out of his teeth
Ps. 68. 12. she that tarried at home divided the s.
119. 162. rejoice at thy word, as one findeth great s.
Prov. 1. 13. we shall fill our houses with s.
16. 19. than to divide the s. with the proud
31. 11. so that he shall have no need of s.
Isa. 3. 14. the s. of the poor is in your houses
8. 4. the s. of Samaria shall be taken away
9. 3. and as men rejoice when they divide the s.
10. 6. I will give him a charge to take the s.
33. 4. your s. shall be gathered, like the gathering
23. then is the prey of a great s. divided
42. 22. they are for a s. and none saith, restore
24. who gave Jacob for a s.? did not the Lord
53. 12. he shall divide the s. with the strong
Jer. 2. † 14. is Isr. a servant? why is Isr. become s.?
6. 7. violence and s. is heard in her, before me grief
15. 13. thy substance and treasures will I give to s.
17. 3 I will give thy substance and treasures to s.
20. 8. since I spake, I cried violence and s.
30. 16. and they that s. thee shall be a s.
49. 32. the multitude of their cattle shall be a s.
50. 10. and Chaldea shall be a s. saith the Lord
Ezek. 7. 21. I will give it to the wicked for a s.
25. 7. Ammonite for a s. || 26. 5. Tyrus a s. 12.
29. 19. Nebuchadrezzar shall take s. of Egypt
38. 12. I will go up to take a s. and to take a prey
13. shall say to thee, art thou come to take a s.
45. 9. O princes of Israel, remove violence and s.
Dan. 11. 24. he shall scatter among them the s.
33. yet they shall fall by s. many days
Hos. 9. † 6. for lo, they are gone, because of s.
Amos 3. † 10. who store up s. in their palaces
5. † 9. that strengtheneth s. against the strong
Nah. 2. 9. take the s. of silver, take the s. of gold
Hab. 2. 17. the s. of beasts shall cover thee
Zech. 2. 9. they shall be a s. to their servants
14. 1. thy s. shall be divided in the midst of thee
SPOIL, *Verb.*
Exod. 3. 22. and ye shall s. the Egyptians
1 Sam. 14. 36. and s. them until morning light
2 Sam. 23. 10. people returned after him only to s.
Psal. 44. 10. and they who hate us s. for themselves
89. 41. all that pass by the way s. him
109. 11. and let the stranger s. his labour
Prov. 22. 23. will s. soul of those that spoiled them
24. 15. O wicked man, s. not his resting-place
Cant. 2. 15. take us the foxes that s. the vines
Isa. 11. 14. they shall s. them of the east together
17. 14. this is the portion of them that s. us
33. 1. when shalt cease to s. thou shalt be spoiled
Jer. 5. 6. a wolf of the evening shall s. them
20. 5. I will give Jerusalem to them that shall s. it
30. 16. and they that s. thee shall be a s.
47. 4. the day that cometh to s. the Philistines
49. 28. go up to Kedar, and s. the men of the east
50. 10. all that s. her, shall be satisfied, saith Lord
Ezek. 14. 15. and they s. it, so that it be desolate
32. 12. and they shall s. the pomp of Egypt
39. 10. they shall s. those that spoiled them
Hos. 10. 2. shall break their altars, s. their images
13. 15. he shall s. the treas. of all pleasant vessels
Hab. 2. 8. all the remnant of the people shall s. thee
Zeph. 2. 9. the residue of my people shall s. them
Mat. 12. 29. or else how can one enter into a strong man's house, and s. his goods? Mark 3. 27.
Col. 2. 8. beware lest any man s. you thro' philosop.
SPOILED.
Gen. 34. 27. the sons of Jacob came and s. the city
29. they s. all that was in Hamor's house
Exod. 12. 36. and they s. the Egyptians
Deut. 28. 29. thou shalt be only oppressed and s.
Judg. 2. 14. into the hand of spoilers that s. them
16. out of the hand of those that s. them
1 Sam. 14. 48. delivered Isr. from them that s. them
17. 53. and they s. the Philistines' tents
2 Kings 7. 16. Israel s. the tents of the Syrians
2 Chron. 14. 14. Asa s. all the cities of Gerar
Job 12. 17. he leadeth counsellors away s.
19. leads princes away s. overthrows mighty
Psal. 76. 5. the stout-hearted are s. they have slept
Prov. 22. 23. and spoil the soul of those that s. them
Isa. 13. 16. their houses shall be s. their wives ravis.
18. 2. a nation whose land the rivers have s. 7.
24. 3. the land shall be utterly emptied and s.
33. 1. woe to thee that spoilest, and wast not s.
42. 22. but this is a people robbed and s.
Jer. 2. 14. is Israel a servant? why is he s.?
4. 13. woe unto us, for we are s.
20. for whole land is s. suddenly my tents are s.
30. and when thou art s. what wilt thou do?
9. 19. how are we s.! || 10. 20. my tabernacle is s.
21. 12. and deliver him that is s. 22. 3.
25. 36. for the Lord hath s. their pasture
48. 1. Nebo is s. || 15. Moab is s. and gone, 20.
49. 3. howl, for Ai is s. 10. Esau, his seed is s.
51. 55. because the Lord hath s. Babylon
Ezek. 18. 7. and hath s. none by violence, 16.
12. hath oppressed, hath s. by violence, 18.
23. 46. I will give them to be removed and s.
39. 10. they shall spoil those that s. them
Hos. 10. 14. and all thy fortresses shall be s.
Amos 3. 11. and thy palaces shall be s.

Amos 5. 9. that strengtheneth the s. agst. the strong
Mic. 2. 4. shall lament, and say, we be utterly s.
Hab. 2. 8. because thou hast s. many nations
Zech. 2. 8. he sent me to the nations which s. you
11. 2. howl, because the mighty are s.
3. their glory is s. for the pride of Jordan is s.
Col. 2. 15. and having s. principalities and powers

SPOILER.

Isa. 16. 4. be thou a covert from face of s. the s. cease.
21. 2. the s. spoileth, go up, O Elam; besiege
Jer. 6. 26. for the s. shall suddenly come on us
15. 8. I have brought upon them a s. at noon-day
48. 8. the s. shall come upon every city
18. for the s. of Moab shall come upon thee
32. the s. is fallen upon thy summer fruits
51. 56. because the s. is come upon Babylon

SPOILERS.

Judg. 2. 14. anger of the Lord was hot, and he delivered them into the hand of the s. 2 Kings 17. 20.
1 Sam. 13. 17. the s. came out of camp of Philistines
14. 15. the garrison and the s. they also trembled
Jer. 12. 12. the s. are come upon all high places
51. 48. for the s. shall come to her from the north
53. yet from me shall s. come to her, saith Lord

SPOILEST.

Isa. 33. 1. woe to thee that s. and thou wast not spoil.

SPOILETH.

Psal. 35. 10. who deliverest needy from him that s.
Isa. 21. 2. the spoiler s. || Hos. 7. 1. troop of robbers s.
Nah. 3. 16. the canker-worm s. and flieth away

SPOILING.

Psal. 35. 12. me evil for good, to the s. of my soul
Isa. 22. 4. because of the s. of the daughter of people
Jer. 48. 3. a voice from Horonaim s. and destruction
Hab. 1. 3. for s. and violence are before me
Heb. 10. 34. for ye took joyfully the s. of your goods

SPOILS.

Josh. 7. 21. I saw among the s. a goodly garment
1 Chron. 26. 27. out of s. in battle did they dedicate
Isa. 25. 11. shall bring down their pride with the s.
Luke 11. 22. he taketh his armour and divideth his s.
Heb. 7. 4. Abraham gave the tenth of the s.

SPOKEN.

Gen. 18. 19. Lord may bring what he hath s. of him
Num. 14. 28. as ye have s. in mine ears, so will I do
21. 7. for we have s. against the Lord and thee
23. 19. hath he s. and shall he not make it good?
Deut. 5. 28. I have heard the words they have s. to thee, they have well said all that they have s.
13. 5. because he hath s. to turn you away from L.
18. 17. they have well s. that which they have s.
1 Sam. 25. 30. the Lord hath done all he hath s.
2 Sam. 2. 27. unless thou hadst s. people had gone up
14. 19. turn from ought my lord the king hath s.
17. 6. Ahithophel hath s. after this manner
1 Kings 2. 23. if Adonijah have not s. this word
12. 9. what counsel give ye, that we may answer this people who have s. to me? 2 Chron. 10. 9.
18. 24. and all the people said, it is well s.
2 Kings 4. 13. wouldst thou be s. for to the king?
Job 33. 2. behold, my tongue hath s. in my mouth
34. 35. Job hath s. without knowledge and wisdom
42. 7. ye have not s. of me as my servant Job, 8.
Psal. 66. 14. my mouth hath s. when in trouble
87. 3. glorious things are s. of thee, O city of God
109. 2. they have s. against me with a lying tongue
Prov. 15. 23. a word s. in due season, how good is it!
25. 11. a word fitly s. is like apples of gold
Eccl. 7. 21. take no heed to all words that are s.
Cant. 8. 8. in the day when she shall be s. for
Isa. 23. 4. for the sea hath s. || 38. 15. he hath s.
59. 3. your hands are defiled, your lips have s. lies
Jer. 26. 16. he hath s. to us in the name of the Lord
29. 23. and have s. lying words in my name
33. 24. considerest thou not what this people have s.
44. 25. ye and your wives have s. with your mouths
Ezek. 13. 7. have ye not s. a lying divination
8. because ye have s. vanity, and seen lies
Dan. 4. 31. O king Nebuchadnezzar, to thee it is s.
Hos. 7. 13. yet they have s. lies against me
10. 4. they have s. words, swearing falsely
Amos 5. 14. Lord shall be with you, as ye have s.
Obad. 12. nor shouldst thou have s. proudly in distr.
Mic. 6. 12. the inhabitants thereof have s. lies
Zech. 10. 2. for the idols have s. vanity and diviners
Mal. 3. 13. what have we s. so much against thee?
Mat. 26. 65. high priest saying, he hath s. blasphemy
Mark 14. 9. shall be s. of for a memorial of her
Luke 2. 33. marvelled at things which were s. of him
34. and for a sign which shall be s. against
12. 3. what ye have s. in darkness, what s. in ear
18. 34. nor knew they the things which were s.
John 15. 22. if I had not come and s. to them
Acts 3. 24. as many as have s. foretold of these days
8. 24. none of these things ye have s. come on me
13. 40. lest that come on you s. of in the prophets
46. the word should first have been s. to you
16. 14. Lydia attended to the things that were s.
19. 36. seeing that these things cannot be s. against
23. 9. but if a spirit or angel hath s. to him
27. 11. more than those things that were s. by Paul
35. when had thus s. took bread and gave thanks
28. 22. we know that every where it is s. against
Rom. 1. 8. your faith is s. of thro' the whole world
4. 18. according to that which was s. so thy seed be
14. 16. let not then your good be evil s. of
15. 21. to whom he was not s. of they shall see
1 Cor. 10. 30. why am I evil s. of for that for which
14. 9. how shall it be known what is s.?
Heb. 1. 2. hath in these last days s. to us by his Son
2. 2. for if the word s. by angels was stedfast
3. 5. for a testimony of those things to be s. after
4. 8. he would not afterward have s. of another day
7. 13. for he of whom these things are s. pertaineth
8. 1. of things which we have s. this is the sum
12. 19. intreated the word should not be s. any more
13. 7. who have s. unto you the word of God
1 Pet. 4. 14. on their part he is evil s. of
2 Pet. 2. 2. the way of truth shall be evil s. of
3. 2. ye may be mindful of words which were s. be.
Jude 15. which ungodly sinners have s. against him
17. remember the words which were s. before

SPOKEN with God, expressly.

Gen. 21. 2. at set time of which God had s. to him
Deut. 26. 19. an holy people to thy G. as he hath s.
Psal. 60. 6. God hath s. in his holiness, 108. 7.
62. 11. God hath s. once, twice have I heard
Mat. 22. 31. that which was s. to you by God
Acts 3. 21. which God hath s. by his holy prophets
See LORD.

I have, or have I SPOKEN.

Gen. 28. 15. I have done which I have s. to thee
41. 28. this is the thing I have s. to Pharaoh
Exod. 32. 13. all this land I have s. of will I give
34. lead people to the place of which I have s.
1 Sam. 1. 16. out of my grief have I s. hitherto
3. 12. perform ag. Eli all things which I have s.
20. 23. as touching the matter which I have s.
Job 21. 3. and after that I have s. mock on
40. 5. once have I s. but I will not answer
Psal. 116. 10. I will walk before L. in land of living, I believed, therefore have I s. 2 Cor. 4. 13.
Isa. 45. 19. I have not s. in secret, 48. 16.
46. 11. I have s. it, I will also bring it to pass
48. 15. I, even I, have s. yea I have called him
Jer. 4. 28. I h. s. it, I have proposed it, will not rep.
23. 21. I have not s. to them yet they prophesied
25. 3. I h. s. to you rising early, and speak. 35. 14.
30. 2. write thee all words I have s. to thee, 36. 2.
35. 17. because I have s. but they have not heard
Ezek. 12. 28. but word which I have s. shall be done
13. 7. ye say, Lord saith it, albeit I have not s.
26. 5. for I have s. it, saith the Lord, 28. 10.
36. 5. surely in the fire of my jealousy have I s. 6.
38. 17. art thou he of whom I have s. in old time
19. for in jealousy and fire of my wrath have I s.
39. 8. it is come, this is the day whereof I have s.
Hos. 12. 10. I have also s. by the prophets
John 12. 48. the word that I have s. shall judge him
49. for I have not s. of myself but the Father
14. 25. these things have I s. 15. 11. | 16. 1, 25, 33.
15. 3. ye are clean thro' the word I have s. to you
18. 23. if I have s. evil, bear witness of the evil

Had SPOKEN.

Gen. 44. 2. according to the word Joseph had s.
Num. 23. 2. and Balak did as Balaam had s.
1 Kings 13. 11. told father words he had s. to king
21. 4. which Naboth the Jezreelite had s. to him
2 Kings 1. 17. according to word which Elijah had s.
7. 18. it came to pass as the man of God had s.
Ezra 8. 22. because we had s. unto the king
Neh. 2. 18. I told also king's words that he had s.
Esth. 7. 9. Mordecai, who had s. good for the king
Job 32. 4. now Elihu had waited till Job had s.
Jer. 36. 4. Baruch wrote words L. had s. by Jerem.
Dan. 10. 11. and when he had s. this word to me
15. when he had s. such words, I became dumb
19. when he had s. unto me, I was strengthened
Mark 1. 42. as soon as he had s. the leprosy departed
12. 12. for they knew that he had s. the parable against them, and they left him, Luke 20. 19.
Luke 19. 28. when he had thus s. 24. 40. John 9. 6. | 11. 43. | 18. 22. Acts 19. 41. | 20. 36. | 26. 30.
John 4. 50. the man believed word that Jesus had s.
11. 13. they thought he had s. of taking rest
21. 19. when he had s. this, he saith, follow me
Acts 9. 27. Barnabas declared that he had s. unto him
28. 25. departed, after Paul had s. one word
Heb. 9. 19. when Moses had s. every precept to peo.

SPOKEN with prophet.

Deut. 18. 22. but prophet hath s. it presumptuously
Ezek. 14. 9. if prophet be deceived when he hath s.
Mat. 2. 17. what was s. by Jeremy the prophet, 27. 9.
23. that it might be fulfilled which was s. by the prophet, be called a Nazarene, 13. 35. | 27. 35.
3. 3. this is he that was s. of by the prophet Esaias
4. 14. that it might be fulfilled which was s. by Esaias the prophet, 8. 17. | 12. 17. | 21. 4.
24. 15. when ye shall see the abomination of desolation s. of by Daniel the prophet, Mark 13. 14.
Luke 24. 25. to believe all that the prophets have s.
Acts 2. 16. this was s. of by the prophet Joel
Jam. 5. 10. take, my brethren, prophets who have s.

Thou hast SPOKEN.

Gen. 19. 21. this city for the which thou hast s.
Exod. 4. 10. nor since thou hast s. to thy servant
10. 29. Moses said, thou hast s. well, not see
33. 17. I will do this thing that thou hast s.
Num. 14. 17. power of Lord be great, as thou hast s.
Deut. 1. 14. the thing which thou hast s. is good
Ruth 2. 13. thou hast s. friendly to thine handmaid
2 Sam. 6. 22. the maid-servants which thou hast s. of
7. 19. but thou hast s. also of thy servant's house for a great while to come, 25. 1 Chron. 17. 17, 23.
2 Kings 20. 19. then said Hezekiah to Isaiah, good is the word of Lord which thou hast s. Isa. 39. 8.
Esth. 6. 10. let nothing fail of all that thou hast s.
Job 33. 8. surely thou hast s. in my hearing
Jer. 3. 5. behold, thou hast s. and done evil things
32. 24. and that which thou hast s. is come to pass
44. 16. as for the word that thou hast s. unto us
51. 62. O Lord, thou hast s. against this place
Ezek. 35. 12. I have heard blasphemies thou hast s.

SPOKES.

1 Kings 7. 33. their felloes and s. were all molten

SPOKESMAN.

Exod. 4. 16. he shall be thy s. unto the people

SPOON.

Num. 7. 14. one s. of ten shekels of gold, full of incense, 20, 26, 32, 38, 44, 50, 56, 62.

SPOONS.

Exod. 25. 29. make the dishes thereof and s.
37. 16. he made his dishes and his s. and bowls
Num. 4. 7. and put thereon the dishes and the s.
7. 84. twelve silver bowls, twelve s. of gold, 86.
1 Kings 7. 50. the s. were of pure gold, 2 Chr. 4. 22.
2 Kings 25. 14. the s. took he away, Jer. 52. 18, 19.
2 Chron 24. 14. of rest of the money s. were made

SPORT, Substantive.

Judg. 16. 25. that Samson may make s. and he made s.
27. thousand that beheld while Samson made s.
Prov. 10. 23. it is as s. to a fool to do mischief
21. † 17. he that loveth s. shall be a poor man
26. 19. that deceiveth and saith, am not I in s.?

SPORT.

Isa. 57. 4. against whom do ye s. yourselves?

SPORTING.

Gen. 26. 8. Isaac was s. with Rebekah his wife
2 Pet. 2. 13. s. themselves with their own deceivings

SPOT.

Num. 19. 2. bring thee a red heifer without s.
28. 3. two lambs without s. 9. 11. | 29. 17, 26.
Deut. 32. 5. their s. is not the s. of his children
Job 11. 15. thou shalt lift up thy face without s.
Cant. 4. 7. thou art all fair, there is no s. in thee
Eph. 5. 27. a glorious church, not having s.
1 Tim. 6. 14. keep this commandment without s.
Heb. 9. 14. who offered himself without s. to God
1 Pet. 1. 19. as of a lamb without s. or blemish
2 Pet. 3. 14. that ye may be found without s.
See BRIGHT.

SPOTTED.

Gen. 30. 32. removing from thence all the s. cattle
33. every one that is not s. shall be counted stolen
39. the flocks brought forth cattle speckled and s.
Jude 23. hating even the garment s. by the flesh

SPOTS.

Jer. 13. 23. or can the leopard change his s.?
2 Pet. 2. 13. s. they are and blemishes, sporting
Jude 12. these are s. in your feasts of charity

SPOUSE.

Cant. 4. 8. come with me from Lebanon, my s.
9. thou hast ravished my heart, my sister, my s.
10. how fair is thy love, my sister, my s.
11. thy lips, O my s. drop as the honey-comb
12. a garden inclosed is my sister, my s.
5. 1. I am come into my garden, my sister, my s.

SPOUSES.

Hos. 4. 13. and your s. shall commit adultery
14. I will not punish your s. when they commit

SPOUTS. See WATER-SPOUTS.

SPRANG.

Mark 4. 8. and did yield fruit that s. up, Luke 8. 8.
Acts 16. 29. then he called for a light and s. in
Heb. 7. 14. for it is evident our Lord s. out of Juda
11. 12. therefore there s. of one so many as the stars
See SPRUNG.

SPREAD.

Gen. 33. 19. field where Jacob had s. his tent, 35. 21.
Lev. 13. 5. and the plague s. not in the skin, 6, 23, 28
32. and behold, if the scall s. not, 34.
35. but if the scall s. much in the skin, 36.
51. if the plague be s. in a garment, 14. 39, 44.
53. and if the plague be not s. 55. | 14. 48.
Num. 4. 7. on the table they shall s. cloth of blue, 11.
8. they shall s. a scarlet cloth || 13. s. a purple cloth
14. they shall s. on it a covering of badgers' skins
Deut. 22. 17. s. the cloth before the elders of city
Judg. 8. 25. they s. a garment, and cast in ear-rings
15. 9. then the Philistines s. themselves in Lehi
1 Sam. 4. † 2. and when the battle was s.
2 Sam. 5. 18. the Philistines also came and s. themselves in valley of Rephaim, 22. 1 Chr. 14. 9, 13.
16. 22. they s. Absalom a tent on top of the house
17. 19. woman s. a covering on the well's mouth
21. 10. Rizpah s. sackcloth for her on the rock
1 Kings 6. 32. carved upon them carvings of cherubims, and s. gold upon cherubims and palm-trees
8. 54. he arose, with his hands s. up to heaven
2 Kings 8. 15. Hazael s. a thick cloth on his face
19. 14. s. the letter before the Lord, Isa. 37. 14.
Psal. 105. 39. he s. a cloud for a covering
140. 5. they have s. a net by the way-side
Prov. 1. 17. surely in vain net is s. in sight of fowler
Isa. 14. 11. worm is s. under thee, worms cover thee
19. 8. they that s. nets on the waters shall languish
33. 23. they could not s. the sail, lame take the prey
58. 5. and to s. sackcloth and ashes under him
Jer. 8. 2. and they shall s. them before the sun
10. 9. silver s. into plates is brought from Tarshish
Lam. 1. 13. he hath s. net for my feet, turned me back
Ezek. 2. 10. and he s. the roll before me
12. 13. my net also will I s. upon him, 17. 20.
26. 14. thou shalt be a place to s. nets upon
Hos. 5. 1. because ye have been a net s. upon Tabor
7. 12. when they shall go, I will s. my net on them
14. 6. his branches shall s. his beauty as olive-tree
Joel 2. 2. as the morning s. upon the mountains
Hab. 1. 8. their horsemen shall s. themselves
Mal. 2. 3. behold, I will s. dung upon your faces
Mat. 21. 8. and a very great multitude s. their garments in the way, Mark 11. 8. Luke 19. 36.
Acts 4. 17. but that it s. no further among the people

SPREAD abroad.

Gen. 10. 18. families of the Canaanites were s. abroad
28. 14. thou shalt s. abroad to the west and east
Exod. 9. 29. I will s. abroad my hands to the Lord
33. Moses s. abroad his hands to the Lord
40. 19. he s. abroad the tent over the tabernacle
Lev. 13. 7. but if the scab s. much abroad, 22. 27.
Num. 11. 32. they s. abr. the quails round the camp
1 Sam. 30. 16. they were s. abroad on the earth
2 Sam. 22. 43. I did stamp and s. abroad mine enemies
1 Chron. 14. 13. the Philistines s. themselves abroad
2 Chron. 26. 8. Uzziah's name s. abroad, 15.
Zech. 1. 17. my cities thro' prosperity be s. abroad
2. 6. I have s. you abroad as the four winds
Mat. 9. 31. but they when departed s. abroad his fame in all that country, Mark 1. 28. | 6. 14.
1 Thess. 1. 8. your faith to God-ward is s. abroad

SPREAD forth.

Num. 24. 6. as valleys are they s. forth as gardens
1 Kings 8. 7. the cherubims s. forth their two wings
22. Solomon s. forth his hands, 2 Chron. 6. 12, 13.
38. know the plague of his own heart, and s. forth his hands towards this house, 2 Chr. 6. 29.
Isa. 1. 15. when ye s. forth your hands, I will hide
25. 11. he shall s. forth hands, as he that swimmeth
42. 5. thus saith God, he that s. forth the earth
Ezek. 47. 10. they shall be a place to s. forth nets

SPREAD over.

Num. 4. 6. they shall s. over it a cloth wholly of blue
Ruth 3. 9. s. therefore thy skirt over thine handmaid
Isa. 25. 7. and the vail that is s. over all nations
Jer. 43. 10. he shall s. his royal pavilion over them
48. 40. and he shall s. his wings over Moab

Jer. 49. 22. and he shall s. his wings over Bozrah
Ezek. 16. 8. I s. my skirt over thee and covered thee
19. 8. then the nations s. their net over him

SPREAD out.

Exod. 37. 9. cherubims s. out wings, 1 Chr. 28. 18.
Ezra 9. 5. I s. out my hands to the Lord my God
Job 29. 19. my root was s. out by the waters
37. 18. hast thou with him s. out the sky?
Isa. 48. † 13. palm of my hand hath s. out heavens
65. 2. have s. out my hands to a rebellious people
Lam. 1. 10. the adversary hath s. out his hand
Ezek. 32. 3. I will therefore s. out my net over thee

SPREADEST.

Ezek. 27. 7. fine linen which thou s. forth for thy sail

SPREADETH.

Lev. 13. 8. if the priest see that scab s. in the skin
Deut. 32. 11. as an eagle s. abroad her wings
Job 9. 8. God who alone s. out the heavens
26. 9. and he s. his cloud upon it
36. 30. behold, he s. his light upon it, and covereth
41. 30. he s. sharp pointed things on the mire
Prov. 29. 5. a man that flattereth his neighb. s. a net
Isa. 25. 11. as he that swimmeth s. forth his hands
40. 19. and the goldsmith s. it over with gold
22. that s. the heavens as a tent to dwell in
44. 24. I the Ld. that s. abroad the earth by myself
Jer. 4. 31. the daughter of Zion s. her hands
17. 8. a tree that s. out her roots by the river
Lam. 1. 17. Zion s. forth her hands, none comfort her

SPREADING.

Lev. 13. 57. and if it appears, it is a s. plague
Psal. 37. 35. I have seen the wicked s. himself
Ezek. 17. 6. and it grew, and became a s. vine

SPREADING.

Ezek. 26. 5. it shall be a place for the s. of nets

SPREADINGS.

Job 36. 29. can any understand the s. of the clouds?

SPRIGS.

Isa. 18. 5. for afore harvest he shall cut off the s.
Ezek. 17. 6. it became a vine, and shot forth s.

SPRING.

2 Kings 2. 21. he went forth to the s. of the waters
Prov. 25. 26. is as a troubled fountain and corrupt s.
Cant. 4. 12. my sister, my spouse, is a s. shut up
Isa. 58. 11. shalt be like s. of water, whose waters fail
Hos. 13. 15. his s. shall become dry and fountain dried

SPRINGS.

Deut. 4. 49. to the plain under the s. of Pisgah
Josh. 10. 40. Joshua smote all the country of the s.
12. 8. the kings in the plains and in the s.
15. 19. give me s. of water, gave upper s. Judg. 1. 15.
Job 38. 16. hast thou entered into the s. of the sea?
Psal. 87. 7. all my s. are in thee
104. 10. he sendeth the s. into the valleys
107. 33. he turneth the water s. into dry ground
35. he turneth dry ground into water s.
Isa. 35. 7. and the thirsty land become s. of water
41. 18. I will make the dry land s. of water
49. 10. even by the s. of water shall he guide them
Jer. 51. 36. I will dry up her sea and make her s. dry

SPRING.

1 Sam. 9. 26. about s. of the day Samuel called Saul
See DAY spring.

SPRING.

Ezek. 17. 9. it shall wither in all the leaves of her s.

SPRING.

Num. 21. 17. Israel sang, s. up, O well, sing ye to it
Deut. 8. 7. and depths that s. out of valleys and hills
Judg. 19. 25. when the day began to s. they let her go
Job 5. 6. neither doth trouble s. out of the ground
38. 27. to cause bud of the tender herb to s. forth
Psal. 85. 11. truth shall s. out of the earth
92. 7. when the wicked s. as the grass
Isa. 42. 9. before they s. forth, I tell you of them
43. 19. I will do a new thing, now it shall s. forth
44. 4. they shall s. up as among the grass, as willows
45. 8. and let righteousness s. up together
58. 8. and thine health shall s. forth speedily
61. 11. as garden causeth things that are sown to s.
Lord will cause praise to s. forth before nations
Joel 2. 22. be not afraid, for the pastures do s.
Mark 4. 27. the seed should s. he knoweth not how

SPRINGETH.

1 Kings 4. 33. even to hyssop that s. out of the wall
2 Kings 19. 29. ye shall eat in the second year that
which s. of same, and in third sow, Isa. 37. 30.
Hos. 10. 4. thus judgment s. up as hemlock in field

SPRINGING.

Psal. 65. 10. thou blessedst the s. thereof

SPRINGING.

Gen. 26. 19. they found there a well of s. water
2 Sam. 23. 4. as the tender grass s. out of the earth
John 4. 14. shall be in him a well of water s. up
Heb. 12. 15. lest any root of bitterness s. up trouble you

SPRINKLE.

Exod. 9. 8. let Moses s. the ashes toward the heaven
Lev. 14. 7. he shall s. on him that is to be cleansed
16. the priest shall s. of the oil with his finger
27. priest shall s. of the oil with his right finger
51. and shall s. the house seven times
16. 14. he shall s. on the mercy-seat eastward, 15.
Num. 8. 7. s. water of purifying upon them
19. 18. shall s. it upon the tent, and all the vessels
19. the clean person shall s. it on the unclean
Isa. 52. 15. so shall he s. many nations, kings shall
Ezek. 36. 25. then will I s. clean water upon you

SPRINKLED.

Exod. 9. 10. Moses s. the ashes up toward heaven
Num. 19. 13. because water was not s. on him, 20.
Job 2. 12. and s. dust on their heads toward heaven
Isa. 59. † 5. that which is s. as if there brake out a
viper, their webs shall not become garments
Hos. 7. † 9. grey hairs are s. here and there
Heb. 9. 19. he s. both the book and all the people
10. 22. having our hearts s. from an evil conscience
See BLOOD.

SPRINKLETH.

Lev. 7. 14. it shall be the priest's that s. the blood
Num. 19. 21. he that s. the water of separation

SPRINKLING.

Heb. 9. 13. the ashes of an heifer s. the unclean
11. 28. through faith he kept the s. of the blood
Heb. 12. 24. we are come to blood of s. that speak.
1 Pet. 1. 2. and the s. of the blood of Jesus Christ

SPROUT.

Job 14. 7. there is hope of a tree that it will s. again

SPRUNG.

Gen. 41. 6. seven thin ears s. up after them, 23.
Lev. 13. 42. it is a leprosy s. up in his bald head
Mat. 4. 16. them who sat in shad. of death, light s. up
13. 5. and forthwith they s. up, Mark 4. 5.
7. the thorns s. up and choked them, Luke 8. 7.
26. but when blade was s. up and brought forth
Luke 8. 6. as soon as it was s. up, it withered away

SPUE.

Lev. 18. 28. that the land s. you not out also, 20. 22.
Jer. 25. 27. drink, s. and fall, and rise no more
Rev. 3. 16. so then I will s. thee out of my mouth

SPUED.

Lev. 18. 28. as it s. out nations that were before you

SPEWING.

Hab. 2. 16. and shameful s. shall be on thy glory

SPUN.

Exod. 35. 25. women brought that which they had s.
26. and all the women s. goats' hair

SPUNGE.

Mat. 27. 48. one of them took a s. and filled it with
vinegar, gave him to drink, Mark 15. 36. John 19. 29.

SPY.

Num. 13. 16. men which Moses sent to s. land, 17.
21. 32. and Moses sent to s. out Jaazer
Josh. 2. 1. Josh. sent two men to s. secretly, 6. 23, 25.
Judg. 18. 2. the Danites sent to s. the land, 14, 17.
2 Sam. 10. 3. David hath sent his servants to s. out
the city, and overthrow it, 1 Chron. 19. 3.
2 Kings 6. 13. he said, go and s. where he is
Gal. 2. 4. who came in privily to s. out our liberty

SPIED.

Exod. 2. 11. he s. an Egyptian smiting an Hebrew
2 Kings 9. 17. a watchman s. the company of Jehu
13. 21. behold, they s. a band of men
23. 16. he s. sepulchres that were there in mount
See ESPY, ESPIED.

SPIES.

Gen. 42. 9. Joseph said to them, ye are s. 14. 16.
11. we are no s. 31. ‖ 30. the man took us for s.
34. then shall I know ye are no s. but true men
Num. 21. 1. Israel came by the way of the s.
Josh. 6. 23. the young men that were s. went in
Judg. 1. 24. the s. saw a man come out of the city
1 Sam. 26. 4. David theref. sent out s. and understood
2 Sam. 15. 10. Absalom sent s. thro' tribes of Israel
Luke 20. 20. they watched him and sent forth s.
Heb. 11. 31. when Rahab had receiv. s. with peace

SQUARE.

1 Kings 7. 5. all doors and posts were s. with window
Ezek. 45. 2. s. round about, and 50 cubits round ab.
See FOUR-SQUARE.

SQUARED.

Ezek. 41. 21. the posts of the temple were s.

SQUARES.

Ezek. 43. 16. twelve broad, square in four s. thereof
17. and fourteen broad in the four s. thereof

STABILITY.

Isa. 33. 6. knowledge shall be the s. of thy times

STABLE, Substantive.

Ezek. 25. 5. I will make Rabbah a s. for camels

STABLE.

1 Chr. 16. 30. world also shall be s. not to be moved

STABLENESS.

Psal. 37. † 3. in truth and s. thou shalt be fed
See ESTABLISH, ED, ETH.

STACKS.

Exod. 22. 6. so that the s. of corn be consumed

STACTE.

This Greek *word signifies the gum that distils from the myrrh-trees.* Moses *speaks of* stacte *in the enumeration of the drugs that were to enter into the composition of the perfume, which was to be offered in the holy place upon the golden altar.* The Hebrew *reads* Neteph, *which signifies liquid myrrh, or the purest and most valuable part of the myrrh, which, as some think, was brought from it by contusion. Some take it for balm.*
Exod. 30. 34. take to thee sweet spices, s. and onycha

STAFF.

Gen. 32. 10. with my s. I passed over this Jordan
38. 18. she said, give me thy signet and s. 25.
Exod. 12. 11. eat it, with your s. in your hand
21. 19. if he rise again, and walk abroad on his s.
Num. 13. 23. they bare grapes between two on a s.
22. 27. Baalam smote the ass with a s.
Judg. 6. 21. the angel put forth the end of his s.
1 Sam. 17. 7. the s. of his spear was like a weaver's
beam, one bare a shield before him, 2 Sam. 21. 19.
40. David took his s. in his hand, and his sling
2 Sam. 3. 29. let there not fail one that leaneth on a s.
23. 7. he must be fenced with the s. of a spear
21. he went down to him with a s. 1 Chron. 11. 23.
2 Kings 4. 29. take my s. lay my s. on child's face
31. Gehazi laid the s. on the face of the child
18. 21. thou trustest on s. of this reed, Isa. 36. 6.
Psal. 23. 4. thy rod and thy s. they comfort me
Isa. 3. 1. the Lord will take from Judah the s.
9. 4. for thou hast broken the s. of his shoulder
10. 5. and the s. in their hand is mine indignation
15. or as if the s. should lift up itself as no wood
24. and shall lift up his s. against thee
14. 5. the Lord hath broken the s. of the wicked
28. 27. but the fitches are beaten out with a s.
30. 32. in every place where grounded s. shall pass
Jer. 48. 17. say, how is the strong s. broken
Ezek. 29. 6. have been a s. of reed to house of Israel
Hos. 4. 12. and their s. declareth unto them
Zech. 8. 4. every man with his s. in his hand for age
11. 10. and I took my s. even beauty, and cut it
14. then I cut asunder my other s. even bands
Mark 6. 8. take nothing for journey, save a s. only
Heb. 11. 21. worshipped, leaning on the top of his s.
See BREAD.

STAGGER.

Job 12. 25. to s. like a drunken man, Psal. 107. 27.
Psal. 99. † 1. the Lord reigneth, let the earth s.
Isa. 29. 9. they s. but not with strong drink

STAGGERED.

Rom. 4. 20. he s. not at the promise of God

STAGGERETH.

Isa. 19. 14. as a drunken man s. in his vomit

STAGGERING.

1 Sam. 25. † 31. that this shall be no s. unto thee

STAIN.

Job 3. 5. let darkness and the shadow of death s. it
Isa. 23. 9. Lord purposed to s. the pride of all glory
63. 3. their blood sprinkled, I will s. my raiment

STAIRS.

1 Kings 6. 8. and they went up with winding s.
2 Kings 9. 13. and put it under him on top of the s.
Neh. 9. 4. then stood on the s. Jeshua and Bani
Cant. 2. 14. that art in the secret places of the s.
Ezek. 43. 17. and his s. shall look towards the east
Acts 21. 40. Paul stood on the s. and beckoned

STAKES.

Isa. 33. 20. not one of the s. shall ever be removed
54. 2. lengthen thy cords and strengthen thy s.

STALK.

Gen. 41. 5. seven rank ears came up on one s. 22.
Jer. 11. † 19. let us destroy the s. with his bread
Hos. 8. 7. it hath no s. the bud shall yield no meal

STALKS.

Josh. 2. 6. and she hid them with the s. of flax

STALL.

Jer. 46. † 21. her hired men like bullocks of s.
Amos 6. 4. eat the calves out of the midst of the s.
Mal. 4. 2. ye shall grow up as calves of the s.
Luke 13. 15. on sabbath loose his ox from the s.

STALLS.

1 Kings 4. 26. Solomon had forty thousand s. of
horses, and 12,000 horsemen, 2 Chron. 9. 25.
2 Chron. 32. 28. Hezekiah had s. for all manner of
beasts, and cotes for flocks
Hab. 3. 17. although there shall be no herd in the s.

STALLED.

Prov. 15. 17. than a s. ox and hatred therewith

STAMMERERS.

Isa. 32. 4. the tongue of the s. shall speak plainly

STAMMERING.

Isa. 28. 11. with s. lips and another tongue will speak
33. 19. thou shalt not see a people of a s. tongue

STAMP.

2 Sam. 22. 43. I did s. them as the mire of the street
Ezek. 6. 11. smite with thy hand, s. with thy foot

STAMPED.

Deut. 9. 21. I s. the calf and ground it very small
2 Kings 23. 6. Josiah s. the grove small to powder
15. s. high places small to powder and burnt grove
2 Chron. 15. 16. Asa cut down her idol and s. it
Ezek. 25. 6. because thou hast s. with the feet
Dan. 7. 7. a fourth beast s. residue with the feet, 19.
8. 7. the he-goat cast down and s. upon the ram
10. it cast down some of stars, and s. upon them

STAMPING.

Jer. 47. 3. at noise of the s. of the hoofs of the horses

STANCHED.

Luke 8. 44. immediately woman's issue of blood s.

STAND.

Ezek. 29. 7. thou madest their loins to be at a s.

STAND, Verb.

Exod. 33. 10. people saw cloudy pillar s. at door
Lev. 27. 14. as priest shall estimate it, so shall it s. 17.
Num. 30. 4. then all her vows shall s. 5, 7, 11.
12. then her vows or bond shall not s. her husband
Deut. 18. 5. God hath chosen him to s. to minister
25. 8. if he s. to it and say, I like not to take her
Josh. 20. 4. when he shall s. at entering gate of city
1 Sam. 12. 16. now s. and see this great thing Ld. will
19. 3. I will go out and s. before my father in field
1 Kings 8. 11. cloud filled the house, priests could
not s. to minister, because of cloud, 2 Chr. 5. 14.
17. 1. Elijah said to Ahab, as the Lord liveth, be-
fore whom I s. 18. 15. 2 Kings 3. 14. | 5. 16.
2 Kings 5. 11. I thought he will come out and s.
10. 4. two kings stood not, how then shall we s.?
1 Chr. 21. 16. David saw the angel of the Lord s.
23. 30. to s. every morning to thank and praise Ld.
2 Chron. 34. 32. he caused all present to s. to it
Ezra 10. 14. let all the rulers of congregation s.
Esth. 3. 4. to see if Mordecai's matters would s.
8. 11. to gather themselves, and to s. for their life
Job 8. 15. he shall lean on his house, it shall not s.
19. 25. and that he shall s. at the latter day on earth
38. 14. it is turned, and they s. as a garment
Psal. 38. 11. and my kinsman s. afar off
45. 9. on right hand did s. queen in gold of Ophir
78. 13. and he made the waters to s. as an heap
102. † 26. they shall perish, but thou shalt s.
107. † 25. he maketh to s. the stormy wind
109. 6. and let Satan s. at his right hand
31. he shall s. at the right hand of the poor
122. 2. our feet shall s. within thy gates, O Jerus.
130. 3. if mark iniquities, O Lord, who shall s.?
Prov. 12. 7. but the house of the righteous shall s.
19. 21. nevertheless counsel of the Lord shall s.
25. 6. and s. not in place of great men
Eccl. 8. 3. s. not in an evil thing, he doeth what
pleaseth
Isa. 7. 7. thus saith Lord God, it shall not s. 8. 10.
11. 10. shall be a root of Jesse, shall s. for an ensign
14. 24. and as I have purposed, so it shall s.
21. 8. my lord, I s. continually on watch-tower
28. 18. and your agreement with hell shall not s.
32. 8. and by liberal things shall he s.
40. 8. but the word of our God shall s. for ever
46. 10. counsel shall s. and I will do all my pleas.
47. 12. s. now with thine inchantm. and sorceries
61. 5. and strangers shall s. and feed your flocks
Jer. 6. 16. s. ye in the ways and see, ask for old paths
44. 28. know whose word shall s. mine or theirs
46. 21. did not s. because day was come on them
Ezek. 17. 14. but by keeping of his cov. it might s.
Dan. 2. 44. and the kingdom shall s. for ever
11. 6. king of the north shall not s. nor his arm
25. but the king of the south shall not s.
Amos 2. 15. nor shall he s. that handleth the bow
Mic. 5. 4. he shall s. and feed in strength of the Ld.
Nah. 2. 8. s. s. shall they cry, none shall look back
Mal. 3. 2. and who shall s. when he appeareth

Mat. 12. 25. a house or kingdom divided ag. itself shall not s. 26. Mark 3. 24, 25. Luke 11. 18.
Mark 11. 25. and when ye s. praying, forgive
Acts 1. 11. why s. ye gazing up into heaven?
5. 20. go, s. and speak in the temple to the people
25. 10. Paul said, I s. at Cesar's judgment-seat
26. 6. now I s. and am judged for hope of promise
Rom. 5. 2. have access into this grace wherein we s.
9. 11. purposed of G. according to election might s.
14. 4. for God is able to make him s.
1 Cor. 15. 1. I declare the gospel wherein ye s.
30. and why s. we in jeopardy every hour
2 Cor. 1. 24. are helpers of your joy, for by faith ye s.
Eph. 6. 13. to withstand and having done all to s.
14. s. having your loins girt about with truth
1 Pet. 5. 12. this is true grace of God wherein ye s.
Rev. 3. 20. behold, I s. at the door and knock
6. 17. great day is come, who shall be able to s.?
18. 15. merchants s. afar off for fear of her torm.

STAND *abroad*.

Deut. 24. 11. s. abroad, man shall bring the pledge

STAND *against*.

Lev. 19. 16. nor shall s. ag. blood of thy neighbour
Num. 30. 9. every vow of a widow shall s. ag. her
Jer. 44. 29. that my words shall s. ag. you for evil
Eph. 6. 11. that may be able to s. ag. wiles of devil

STAND *aloof*.

Psal. 38. 11. my lovers and my friends s. aloof

STAND *back*.

Gen. 19. 9. said, s. back, this fellow came in to sojo.

STAND *before*.

Exod. 8. 20. rise up early, s. before Pharaoh, 9. 13.
9. 11. the magicians could not s. before Moses
17. 6. I will s. before thee on the rock in Horeb
Lev. 18. 23. nor shall any woman s. before a beast
26. 37. and ye shall have no power to s. before your enemies, Josh. 7. 12, 13. Judg. 2. 14.
Num. 16. 9. to s. before the congregation to minister
27. 21. and he shall s. before Eleazar the priest
35. 12. till he s. before congregation, Josh. 20. 6.
Deut. 7. 24. there shall no man be able to s. before thee, 11. 25. Josh. 1. 5. | 10. 8. | 23. 9.
9. 2. who can s. before the children of Anak?
10. 8. tribe of Levi to s. before the Lord to minister to him, 2 Chron. 29. 11. Ezek. 44. 11, 15.
19. 17. both the men shall s. before the Lord
29. 10. ye s. this day all of you before the Lord
1 Sam. 6. 20. who is able to s. before holy Lord G.?
16. 22. let David, I pray thee, s. before me
1 Kings 1. 2. let a young virgin s. before the king
10. 8. happy are these thy servants who s. before thee and hear thy wisdom, 2 Chron. 9. 7.
19. 11. go, and s. on the mount before the Lord
2 Chron. 20. 9. we s. before this house in thy presence
Ezra 9. 15. we cannot s. before thee because of this
Job 41. 10. who then is able to s. before me?
Psal. 5. + 5. the foolish shall not s. before thine eyes
147. 17. cast forth ice, who can s. before his cold?
Prov. 22. 29. a man diligent in business, he shall s. before kings, he shall not s. before mean men
27. 4. but who is able to s. before envy?
Jer. 7. 10. come and s. before me in this house
15. 19. if thou return, thou shalt s. before me
35. 19. Jonadab shall not want a man to s. before me
40. + 10. I will dwell at Mizpah to s. before Chald.
49. 19. who is like me? who will appoint? who is that shepherd that will s. before me? 50. 44.
Dan. 1. 5. that at the end they might s. before king
8. 4. so that no beast might s. before him
7. there was no power in the ram, to s. before him
11. 16. none shall s. before him, he shall stand
Nah. 1. 6. who can s. before his indignation?
Luke 21. 36. and worthy to s. before the Son of man
Rom. 14. 10. all shall s. before judgment-seat of Ch.
Rev. 20. 12. I saw dead small and great s. before G.

STAND *by*.

Gen. 24. 43. behold I s. by the well of water
Exod. 7. 15. and thou shalt s. by the river's brink
18. 14. and all the people s. by thee unto even
Num. 23. 3. s. by thy burnt-offering, and I will go
Neh. 7. 3. while they s. by let them shut the doors
Isa. 65. 5. who say, s. by thyself, I am holier than th.
Jer. 48. 19. s. by the way and ask, what is done
Ezek. 46. 2. prince shall s. by the post of the gate
Zech. 3. 7. give places to walk among these that s. by
4. 14. are two anointed ones that s. by the Lord
John 11. 42. but because of the people which s. by

STAND *fast*.

Psal. 89. 28. and my covenant shall s. fast with him
111. 8. all his command. s. fast for ever and ever
Jer. 46. 14. say ye, s. fast, and prepare thee
1 Cor. 16. 13. watch ye, s. fast in faith, be strong
Gal. 5. 1. s. fast therefore in liberty Christ made us
Phil. 1. 27. s. fast in one spirit || 4. 1. s. fast in Lord
1 Thess. 3. 8. for now we live, if ye s. fast in Lord
2 Thess. 2. 15. s. fast, and hold traditions taught

STAND *forth*.

Jer. 46. 4. get up, and s. forth with your helmets
Mark 3. 3. he saith to the man, s. forth, Luke 6. 8.

STAND *here*.

Gen. 24. 13. behold, I s. here by the well of water
Num. 23. 15. he said, s. here by thy burnt-offering
Deut. 5. 31. but as for thee, s. thou here by me
2 Sam. 18. 30. the king said, turn aside, and s. here
Mat. 20. 6. saith to them, why s. ye here all day idle?
Mark 9. 1. some s. here who shall not taste of death
Acts 4. 10. even by him doth this man s. here whole

STAND *in*.

Judg. 4. 20. s. in the door of the tent, and say
2 Chr. 35. 5. s. in holy place according to divisions
Psal. 1. 5. the ungodly shall not s. in the judgment
4. 4. s. in awe, sin not, commune with your heart
5. 5. foolish shall not s. in thy sight, thou hatest
24. 3. and who shall s. in his holy place?
33. 8. let all inhabitants of the world s. in awe
76. 7. who may s. in thy sight when once angry?
89. 43. and hast not made him to s. in the battle
134. 1. who by night s. in house of Lord, 135. 2.
Jer. 7. 2. s. in gate of Lord's house and proclaim
14. 6. the wild asses did s. in the high places
17. 19. s. in the gate of the children of the people
26. 2. s. in the court of the Lord's house and speak

Ezek. 13. 5. ye have not gone up to s. in the battle
22. 30. that should s. in gap before me for the land
44. 24. in controversy they shall s. in judgment
Dan. 1. 4. as had ability in them to s. in king's pal.
11. 16. and he shall s. in the glorious land
12. 13. and shall s. in thy lot at the end of the days
Zech. 14. 4. feet s. in that day on Mount of Olives
Mat. 24. 15. when ye see abom. s. in holy place
Luke 1. 19. I am Gabriel, that s. in presence of God
1 Cor. 2. 5. your faith should not s. in wisdom of men
Gal. 4. 20. to change my voice, for I s. in doubt of you

STAND *on*.

Exod. 17. 9. to-morrow I will s. on top of the hill
2 Kings 6. 31. if the head of Elisha shall s. on him
Dan. 11. 17. she shall not s. on his side nor be for him
31. arms shall s. on his part, pollute the sanctuary
Rev. 15. 2. s. on sea of glass, having the harps of G.

STAND *out*.

Psal. 73. 7. their eyes s. out with fatness, have more

STAND *perfect*.

Col. 4. 12. may s. perfect and complete in will of G.

STAND *still*.

Exod. 14. 13. Moses said, fear ye not, s. still and see the salvation of God, 2 Chron. 20. 17.
Num. 9. 8. s. still, I will hear what L. will comm.
Josh. 3. 8. that bear ark, ye shall s. still in Jordan
10. 12. sun s. still upon Gibeon, and moon in Ajalon
1 Sam. 9. 27. s. thou still a while, that I may shew
12. 7. now s. still that I may reason with you
14. 9. then we will s. still in our place and not go
Job 37. 14. s. still and consider the works of God
Jer. 51. 50. ye that have escaped sword s. not still
Acts 8. 38. eunuch commanded the chariot to s. still

STAND *strong*.

Psal. 30. 7. thou hast made mountain to s. strong

STAND *there*.

Num. 11. 16. that they may s. there with thee
Deut. 18. 7. as Levites who s. there before the Lord
Jam. 2. 3. and say to the poor s. thou there

STAND *together*.

Isa. 50. 8. let us s. together, who is mine adversary

STAND *up*.

Exod. 9. + 16. for this cause I made thee to s. up
Neh. 9. 5. s. up and bless Lord your God for ever
Job 30. 20. I s. up, and thou regardest me not
33. 5. set thy words in order before me, s. up
Psal. 35. 2. take hold of shield, s. up for my help
94. 16. who will s. up for me against the workers
Eccl. 4. 15. with child that shall s. up in his stead
Isa. 27. 9. the groves and images shall not s. up
44. 11. let them s. up yet they shall fear
47. 13. let the monthly prognosticators s. up
48. 13. when I call to them, they s. up together
51. 17. awake, awake, s. up, O Jerusalem
Ezek. 31. 14. nor their trees s. up in their height
Dan. 8. 22. four kingdoms shall s. up out of nation
23. a king of fierce countenance shall s. up
25. he shall also s. up against prince of princes
11. 2. behold, there shall s. up three kings in Persia
3. and a mighty king shall s. up and shall rule, 4.
7. out of a branch of her roots shall one s. up
14. many shall s. up against king of the south
20. then shall s. up in his estate a raiser of taxes
21. and in his estate shall s. up a vile person
12. 1. and at that time shall Michael s. up
Nah. 1. + 6. who s. up in the fierceness of his anger
Acts 10. 26. Peter said, s. up, I myself also am a man

STAND *upon*.

Exod. 33. 21. Lord said, thou shall s. upon a rock
Deut. 27. 12. these shall s. upon mount Gerizim
13. these shall s. upon mount Ebal to curse
Josh. 3. 13. and they shall s. upon an heap
2 Sam. 1. 9. Saul said, s. upon me, pray thee slay me
1 Kings 19. 11. s. upon the mount before the Lord
Ezek. 2. 1. son of man, s. upon thy feet, Acts 26. 16.
27. 29. the pilots of the sea shall s. upon the land
33. 26. ye s. upon sword, ye work abominations
47. 10. fishes shall s. up. it from En-gedi to Eneglaim
Dan. 7. 4. and made s. upon the feet as a man
8. + 18. and he made me s. upon my standing
Hab. 2. 1. I will s. upon my watch, set me on tower
Zech. 14. 12. flesh consume, while they s. upon feet
Rev. 10. 5. angel I saw s. upon sea, lift. up his hand

STAND *upright*.

Psal. 20. 8. but we are risen and s. upright
Dan. 10. 11. O Daniel, understand words, s. upright
Acts 14. 10. he said to the cripple, s. upright on feet

STAND *with*.

Num. 1. 5. names of the men that shall s. with you

STAND *without*.

Ezra 10. 13. and we are not able to s. without
Mat. 12. 47. s. without, desiring to speak, Luke 8. 20.
Luke 13. 25. ye begin to s. without, and to knock

STANDARD.

Num. 1. 52. and every man by his own s. 2. 2, 17.
2. 3. on the east-side shall the s. of Judah pitch
10. on the south-side shall be the s. of Reuben
18. on the west-side shall be the s. of Ephraim
25. on the north-side shall be the s. of Dan
10. 14. in the first place went the s. of Judah
Isa. 49. 22. behold, I will set up my s. to people
59. 19. the Lord shall lift up a s. against him
62. 10. go through, lift up a s. for the people
Jer. 4. 6. set up s. toward Zion, retire, stay not
21. how long shall I see the s. and hear trumpet
50. 2. set ye up a s. in the land, 51. 12, 27.

STANDARD-*bearer*.

Isa. 10. 18. they shall be as when a s.-bearer fainteth

STANDARDS.

Num. 2. 31. Dan shall go hindmost with their s.
34. so they pitched by their s. and set forward

STANDEST.

Gen. 24. 31. come in, wherefore s. thou without?
Exod. 3. 5. put off thy shoes, the place whereon thou s. is holy ground, Josh. 5. 15. Acts 7. 33.
Psal. 10. 1. why s. thou afar off, O Lord?
Rom. 11. 20. they were broken off, thou s. by faith

STANDETH.

Num. 14. 14. and that thy cloud s. over them
Deut. 1. 38. but Josh. son of Nun, who s. bef. thee
17. 12. that will not hearken to the priest that s.
29. 15. but with him that s. here with us this day

Judg. 16. 26. to feel pillars whereon the house s.
Esth. 6. 5. behold Haman s. in the court
7. 9. behold also the gallows s. in Haman's house
Psal. 1. 1. nor s. in the way of sinners, nor sitteth
26. 12. my foot s. in an even place, in cong. bless L.
33. 11. the counsel of the Lord s. for ever
82. 1. God s. in the congregation of the mighty
119. + 90. thou hast established the earth, and it s.
161. but my heart s. in awe of thy word
Prov. 8. 2. wisdom s. in the top of high places
Cant. 2. 9. behold, he s. behind wall, he look. forth
Isa. 3. 13. Lord s. up to plead, s. to judge people
46. 7. they set him in his place, and he s.
59. 14. justice s. afar off, truth is fallen in street
Dan. 12. 1. the great prince who s. for thy people
Zech. 11. 16. nor shall he feed that that s. still
John 1. 26. s. one among you, whom ye know not
3. 29. the friend of the bridegroom s. and heareth
Rom. 14. 4. to his own master he s. or falleth
1 Cor. 7. 37. nevertheless he that s. stedfast in heart
8. 13. I will eat no flesh while the world s.
10. 12. let him that thinketh he s. take heed
2 Tim. 2. 19. the foundation of God s. sure
Heb. 10. 11. ev. priest s. daily minister. and offering
Jam. 5. 9. behold, the judge s. before the door
Rev. 10. 8. angel who s. on the sea and the earth

STANDING, *Substantive*.

1 Kings 10. + 5. queen saw the s. of his ministers
2 Chr. 30. + 16. they stood in s. according to law
Neh. 13. + 11. I gather. them, and set them in their s.
Psal. 69. 2. I sink in deep mire where there is no s.
Dan. 8. + 18. but he made me stand upon my s.
10. + 11. O Dan. understand and stand upon thy s.
Mic. 1. 11. he shall receive of you his s.

STANDING.

Lev. 26. 1. make no idols, nor rear ye up a s. image
Num. 22. 23. angel of the Lord s. in the way, 31.
1 Sam. 19. 20. and Samuel s. as appointed over them
22. 6. all his servants were s. about him
1 Kings 13. 25. and the lion s. by the carcase, 28.
14. + 23. they also built them s. images and groves
22. 19. host of heaven s. by him, 2 Chron. 18. 18.
2 Chron. 9. 18. and two lions s. by the stays
Esth. 5. 2. when king saw Esther queen s. in court
Psal. 107. 35. he turneth wilderness into a s. water
114. 8. which turned the rock into a s. water
Amos 9. 1. I saw the Lord s. upon the altar
Mic. 5. 13. I will cut off thy s. images from thee
Zech. 3. 1. Satan s. at his right hand to resist him
6. 5. which go forth from s. before Lord of earth
Mat. 6. 5. they love to pray s. in the synagogues
16. 28. I say to you, there be some s. here, Luke 9. 27.
20. 3. he saw others s. idle in the market, 6.
Mark 3. 31. his brethren and his mother s. without
13. 14. the abomination s. where it ought not
Luke 1. 11. an angel s. on the right side of the altar
18. 13. the publican s. afar off smote on his breast
John 8. 9. Jesus was alone, and woman s. in midst
20. 14. she saw Jesus s. knew not that it was Jesus
Acts 2. 14. but Peter s. up with eleven, said to them
4. 14. and beholding the man healed s. with them
5. 23. saying, we found the keepers s. without
25. men are s. in the temple teaching the people
7. 55. and Jesus s. on the right hand of God, 56.
22. 20. I was s. by and consenting to his death
Heb. 9. 8. while the first tabernacle was yet s.
2 Pet. 3. 5. earth s. out of the water and in water
Rev. 7. 1. four angels s. on four corners of the earth
11. 4. two candlesticks s. before the God of earth
18. 10. s. afar off for the fear of her torment
19. 17. I saw an angel s. in the sun, and he cried

See CORN.

STANK.

Exod. 7. 21. fish in the river died, and the river s.
8. 14. they gathered frogs on heaps, and land s.
16. 20. left of it, the manna bred worms and s.
2 Sam. 10. 6. Ammon saw they s. before David

STARE.

Psal. 22. 17. may tell my bones, look and s. on me

STAR.

In Hebrew כּכב, Cochab. *Under the name of* stars, *the ancient* Hebrews *comprehended all the heavenly bodies, constellations, planets, and all the luminaries, except the sun and moon. The idolatrous* Israelites *called the sun and moon, the king and queen of heaven; and the stars were, as it were, their army or militia,* Deut. 4. 19. | 17. 3. Jer. 7. 18. *The beauty and splendour that men have observed in the stars, and the great advantages that they derive from thence; the wonderful order that they have discovered in their courses; the influence that has been ascribed to them in the production and preservation of animals, of fruit, plants, and minerals, have prevailed with a great number of people in the world to impute to them life, knowledge, power, and to pay them a sovereign worship and adoration.*

To give the Hebrews *a caution against the idolatry that prevailed through almost all the East, of worshipping the sun, moon, and stars,* Moses *informs them, that God gave them their being, and that he separated them from that mass of matter which he had produced out of nothing,* Gen. 1. 14, 15, 16. *And in* Deut. 4. 19. *he tells them that they were not made for the worship, but for the use, of men, even of the meanest and most barbarous people under heaven;* which the Lord hath divided to all nations under the whole heaven.

The number of the stars was looked upon as infinite: and the Psalmist, *to exalt the power, magnificence, and infinite knowledge of God, says, that he numbers the stars, and calls them by their names. He is described as a king, taking a review of his army, and gives every one of his soldiers such a name as he thinks fit. When the Scripture would express a very extraordinary increase and multiplication, it uses the similitude of the stars of heaven, or of the sand of the sea;* I will multiply thy seed as the stars of heaven, and as the sand which is upon the sea shore, Gen. 15. 5. | 22. 17. | 26. 4. Bildad, Job's *friend, says, that in the eyes of God the stars themselves* are impure; that he can discern many spots and blemishes in them which we cannot see, Job 25. 5. And in chap. 9. ver. 7. it is said, that God locks them up as with a key, and hinders them from appearing, but when he pleases. When the Scripture describes a time of public calamity, of sorrows, fears, troubles, and perplexities, it is said, the stars withhold their light, and are covered with darkness, that they fall from heaven and disappear, Ezek. 32. 7. Mat. 24. 29.

The sacred books sometimes seem to ascribe knowledge to the sun, moon, and stars: they are excited to praise the Lord, Psal. 148. 3. The moon is said to withdraw her light, Ezek. 32. 7. to obey the voice of Joshua, Josh. 10. 12. That the sun stopped its course, at the command of this general of God's people: that the sun rises as a bridegroom, that comes out of his nuptial chamber, Psal. 19. 5. Moses seems to favour their opinion, who impute influences to the sun and moon, when he promises to Joseph the precious fruits brought forth by the sun, and the precious things put forth by the moon, Deut. 33. 14. The Psalmist says, that the sun knows the time and place of his sitting, Psal. 104. 19. And Solomon, that the sun also riseth, and the sun goeth down, and hasteth to his place where he arose, Eccl. 1. 5. But these expressions, which are merely popular, are not to be understood literally; for then it must be said, that the earth, the trees, and the waters are animated, there being expressions in Scripture that would insinuate as much. All the creatures glorify God, bless the Lord, and obey him, each in its way. If any thing more be allowed to the sun, the moon, or the stars, it is because they are creatures of greater perfection, and by which the glory and majesty of God shine forth in a more eminent and conspicuous manner.

Amos, speaking of the idolatry of the Israelites in the wilderness, informs us, that they carried along with them the star of their God, Amos 5. 26. St. Stephen, in Acts 7. 43. quoting this passage of Amos according to the Septuagint, says, Ye took up the tabernacle of Moloch, and the star of your god Remphan. This last word has given occasion to a great number of conjectures. Grotius thinks it to have been the same deity as Rimmon, an idol of the people of Damascus. Rimmon signifies high, which Grotius takes for Saturn, because this planet is the most elevated of all; but others take it for the sun. Some derive Remphan from the Hebrew word Rapha, to be negligent, soft, or slothful; because Saturn is the slowest or most slothful of all the planets. The Arabic word Reph, signifies voracity, a quality very well agreeing to Saturn, who, according to the fable, devoured his own children. Vossius believes Rephan, or, as Amos has it, Chium, was the moon. Others think Remphan to be the name of a king of Egypt, who was placed by his people in the rank of the gods. Diodorus Siculus, lib. 1. page 39. says that king Remphis succeeded Proteus. But this author does not say that he ever had been deified, and speaks of him as a prince very unworthy of having divine honour paid to him. The opinion that is most common is, that it was a representation of the planet Saturn.

The star foretold by Balaam in Num. 24. 17. There shall come a star out of Jacob, and a sceptre shall arise out of Israel, and shall smite the corners of Moab, and destroy all the children of Sheth. By this star is meant a ruler, a conqueror, a great prince, which according to some was king David, who conquered the Moabites; but it primarily and chiefly points at Jesus Christ, the Messiah, who is of the seed and posterity of Jacob, who is the true star which fills the world with its brightness, and who is called the bright and morning star, Rev. 22. 16. Some have thought, that in this place Balaam foretold the appearance of that real star, which arose at the time of our Saviour's birth, and which guided the Magi into Judea, to see the person whose birth was declared by that star. But this star did not come out of Jacob; and that cannot be applied to this star, which is said there; which plainly points at a ruler, a king, a conqueror.

The star that appeared to the Magi, or wise men, and conducted them to Beth lehem, where our Saviour was born, has furnished matter for many conjectures. Some ancient authors have asserted, that it was a new star purposely created to declare to men the birth of the Messiah. Others take it for a kind of comet, which appeared preternaturally in the air. Lightfoot thinks, that the same light which appeared to the shepherds near Beth-lehem, might also be visible afar off to the Magi, hanging over Judea, and so be their guide to find our Saviour. Others have pretended that it was an angel clothed with a luminous body in form of a star, which taking his course towards Judea, determined the Magi to follow him: they found their opinion upon this; that this star appeared to be rational and intelligent, appearing and disappearing, stopping, and going forward, in such manner as was necessary for the conduct of the Magi, to the proper place. It is said, that some writers believed this star was the Holy Ghost, which appeared to the Magi under the form of a star, as he appeared at the baptism of Christ under the form of a dove. Lastly, Calmet says, that this star was an inflamed meteor, in the middle region of the air, which having been observed by the Magi with miraculous and extraordinary circumstances, was taken by them for the star so long foretold by Balaam; and that afterwards they resolved to follow it, and to seek the new-born king, whose coming it declared. It was therefore, says he, a light that moved in the air before them, something like the pillar of cloud in the desert. Inward inspiration, the light of the Holy Ghost, the solicitation of grace, were the motives which engaged them to follow this phenomenon.

The time which the Magi took up in their journey to Judea, is a point that has much exercised the chronologers. Those who suppose they came from the remotest part of Persia, allow them two years for their journey; supposing that the star appeared to them two years before the birth of our Saviour. In this the text of the gospel seems something favourable to them, saying that Herod put to death the children of Beth-lehem, from two years old and under, according to the time that the Magi had shewed him, Mat. 2. 16. Others will have it, that the star did not arise till the moment of our Saviour's birth; and these are yet divided; for some think that the Magi did not arrive at Beth-lehem till two years after the birth of our Saviour. Others make them arrive there thirteen days after his birth; and that they might make the greater haste, they assign them dromedaries to ride upon. There are those that think that the star appeared from the moment of Christ's incarnation, or even from the conception of John the Baptist. But the exact time of their departure is not fixed; though most have agreed that the day of their arrival at Beth-lehem should be on the thirteenth day from our Lord's birth.

There are still some difficulties started, whether this star was seen by every body, or only by the Magi. Some think that every body saw it, that all the people were witnesses of this phenomenon; that some, not knowing the mystery of it, contented themselves to wonder at it; and that it was to the Magi only that God revealed the signification of it, and gave them an inclination to follow it. Others, on the contrary, believe that few people saw it; that the Magi themselves only saw it by fits, and from time to time, when it was necessary to them as a guide, and to encourage them to persevere in their resolution. Lastly, the generality will have it, that the Magi saw it for the greatest part of their journey, and that it disappeared to them only when they arrived at Jerusalem; then they found themselves under a necessity of inquiring, where they might find the new-born King of the Jews.

By stars are sometimes meant the princes and nobles of a kingdom. Dan. 8. 10. Pastors or ministers of the gospel, who ought to shine like stars in respect of the brightness and purity of their lives and doctrine, are also called stars, Rev. 1. 20. In Job 38. 7. the angels are called stars, who joined together in extolling and praising God for his wonderful work of creation.

By day-star, 2 Pet. 1. 19. is meant either a more full, clear, and explicit knowledge of Christ, and the mysteries of the gospel, which in comparison of the dark shadows and prophetical writings, was a morning-star, bringing a fuller manifestation of the truths of God, than the prophets did, whose predictions are now accomplished. Or, by day-star may be understood that full and perfect knowledge which believers shall have, when in heaven they shall see God face to face; and this day is opposed to the whole time of this life, which, notwithstanding all endeavours after knowledge, may be called a night of error and ignorance.

Num. 24. 17. there shall come a *s.* out of Jacob
Amos 5. 26. but ye have borne the *s.* of your god
Mat. 2. 2. for we have seen his *s.* in the east
7. Herod enquired of them what time *s.* appeared
9. lo, *s.* which they saw in east, went before them
10. when they saw *s.* they rejoiced with great joy
Acts 7. 43. ye took up the *s.* of your god Remphan
1 Cor. 15. 41. one *s.* differeth from another *s.* in glory
Rev. 8. 10. there fell a great *s.* from heaven, 11.
9. 1. a *s.* fell from heaven unto the earth

Day-STAR.

2 Pet. 1. 19. till the *day-s.* arise in your hearts

Morning STAR.

Rev. 2. 28. and I will give him the *morning s.*
22. 16. I am the bright and *morning s.*

STAR-*gazers*.

Isa. 47. 13. let the *s.-gazers* stand up and save thee

STARS.

Gen. 1. 16. God made two lights, he made *s.* also
15. 5. tell the *s.* if thou be able to number them
37. 9. sun, moon, and eleven *s.* made obeisance
Deut. 4. 19. when seest *s.* should be driven to worship
Judg. 5. 20. the *s.* in their courses fought ag. Sisera
Neh. 4. 21. from the morning till the *s.* appeared
Job 3. 9. let the *s.* of the twilight thereof be dark
9. 7. who commandeth sun, and sealeth up the *s.*
22. 12. behold height of the *s.* how high they are
25. 5. yea, the *s.* are not pure in his sight
38. 7. when the morning *s.* sang together
Psal. 8. 3. moon and *s.* which thou hast ordained
136. 9. the moon and *s.* to rule by night
147. 4. he telleth number of the *s.* he calleth them
148. 3. praise him, sun, moon, all ye *s.* of light
Eccl. 12. 2. while the sun or *s.* be not darkened
Isa. 14. 13. I will exalt my throne above *s.* of God
Jer. 31. 35. giveth the *s.* for a light by night
Ezek. 32. 7. I will make the *s.* thereof dark
Dan. 8. 10. it cast down some of the *s.* to ground
12. 3. they shall shine as the *s.* for ever and ever
Joel 2. 10. *s.* shall withdraw their shining, 3. 15.
Obad. 4. though thou set thy nest among the *s.*
Luke 21. 25. there shall be signs in sun, moon, and *s.*
Acts 27. 20. when neither sun nor *s.* appeared
1 Cor. 15. 41. and another glory of *s.* for one star
Heb. 11. 12. so many as *s.* of the sky in multitude
Jude 13. those are raging waves, wandering *s.* whom
Rev. 8. 12. the third part of the *s.* was smitten
12. 1. and upon her head a crown of twelve *s.*
See HEAVEN, SEVEN.

STATE.

Psal. 39. 5. ev. man at his best *s.* is altogether vanity
Mat. 12. 45. seven spirits more wicked, the last *s.* of that man is worse than the first, Luke 11. 26.
See ESTATE.

STATELY.

Ezek. 23. 41. sattest upon a *s.* bed and table prepared

STATION.

2 Chron. 35. † 15. sons of Asaph were in their *s.*
Isa. 22. 19. I will drive thee from thy *s.* and state

STATURE.

Num. 13. 32. the people we saw are men of great *s.*
1 Sam. 16. 7. look not on the height of his *s.*
28. † 20. Saul fell with the fulness of his *s.*
2 Sam. 21. 20. a man of great *s.* with six fingers and with six toes, 1 Chron. 11. 23. | 20. 6.
Cant. 7. 7. this thy *s.* is like a palm-tree and breasts
Isa. 10. 33. the high ones of *s.* shall be hewn down
45. 14. men of *s.* shall come over unto thee
Ezek. 13. 18. make kerchiefs on head of every *s.*
17. 6. it grew and became a spreading vine of low *s.*
19. 11. her *s.* was exalted among thick branches
31. 3. the Assyrian was a cedar of an high *s.*
Mat. 6. 27. not add one cubit to his *s.* Luke 12. 25.
Luke 2. 52. Jes. increased in wisdom and *s.* in fav.
19. 3. Zaccheus little of *s.* climbed up to see Jesus
Eph. 4. 13. measure of the *s.* of fulness of Christ

STATUTE.

Exod. 15. 25. there he made a *s.* and ordinance
29. 9. priests' office shall be theirs for perpetual *s.*
Lev. 3. 17. a perpetual *s.* 16. 34. | 24. 9. Num. 19. 21.
Num. 27. 11. it shall be for a *s.* of judgment, 35. 29.
Josh. 24. 25. and he set them a *s.* in Shechem
1 Sam. 30. 25. David made it a *s.* for Isr. to this day
Psal. 81. 4. for this was a *s.* for Israel and a law
Dan. 6. 7. captains consulted to establish a royal *s.*
15. that no *s.* king establisheth may be changed

STATUTES.

Exod. 18. 16. I do make them know the *s.* of God
Lev. 10. 11. that ye may teach Israel all the *s.*
Num. 30. 16. these are the *s.* the Lord commanded
Deut. 4. 6. which shall hear all these *s.* and sayings
6. 24. the Lord commanded us to do all these *s.*
16. 12. and thou shalt observe and do these *s.*
17. 19. that he may learn to keep these *s.* to do them
1 Kings 3. 3. walking in the *s.* of David his father
2 Kings 17. 8. and walked in *s.* of the heathen, 19.
34. neither do they after their *s.* or ordinances
37. the *s.* he wrote, ye shall observe to do
2 Chron. 33. 8. that they take heed to do the *s.*
Neh. 9. 14. thou commandest them *s.* and laws
Psal. 19. 8. *s.* of Lord are right, rejoicing the heart
Ezek. 20. 25. I gave them *s.* that were not good
33. 15. if the wicked walk in the *s.* of life
Mic. 6. 16. for *s.* of Omri are kept and works of Ahab
See *Statute for* EVER.

His STATUTES.

Exod. 15. 26. if thou wilt give ear to his commandm. and keep all *his s.* Deut. 6. 17. | 10. 13. | 11. 1.
Deut. 27. 10. shalt do *his s.* which I command thee
28. 15. if thou wilt not observe to do *his s.*
2 Sam. 22. 23. *his s.* I did not depart from them
1 Kings 8. 61. let your hearts be perf. to walk in *his s.*
2 Kings 17. 15. they rejected *his s.* and his covenant
23. 3. made a covenant to keep *his s.* 2 Chr. 34. 31.
Ezra 7. 11. to Ezra even a scribe of *his s.* to Israel
Psal. 18. 22. I did not put away *his s.* from me
105. 45. that they might observe *his s.* and laws
Jer. 44. 23. nor walked in his law, nor in *his s.*
See JUDGMENTS.

My STATUTES.

Gen. 26. 5. because Abraham kept *my s.* and laws
Lev. 18. 5. ye shall theref. keep *my s.* 26. | 19. 19.
25. 18. ye shall do *my s.* || 26. 3. if ye walk in *my s.*
26. 15. if ye despise *my s.* || 43. they abhorred *my s.*
1 Kings 3. 14. if thou wilt keep *my s.* as David did
9. 6. will not keep *my s.* || 11. 11. hast not kept *my s.*
11. 34. he kept *my s.* || 2 Kings 17. 13. keep *my s.*
2 Chron. 7. 19. if ye turn away, and forsake *my s.*
Psal. 50. 16. what hast thou to do to declare *my s.*
89. 31. if they break *my s.* keep not commandments
Jer. 44. 10. neither have they walked in *my s.*
Ezek. 5. 6. hath changed *my s.* more than nations
7. Ld. saith, because ye have not walked in *my s.*
11. 20. they may walk in *my s.* and do them
18. 19. when the sun hath kept all *my s.*
36. 27. and I will cause you to walk in *my s.*
Zech. 1. 6. *my s.* did take hold of your fathers

Thy STATUTES.

1 Chr. 29. 19. give him a perfect heart to keep *thy s.*
Psal. 119. 12. blessed art thou, O Lord, teach me *thy s.* 26, 33, 64, 68, 124, 135.
16. I will delight myself in *thy s.* not forget word
23. but thy servant did meditate in *thy s.*
48. and I will meditate in *thy s.*
54. *thy s.* have been my songs in my pilgrimage
71. I have been afflicted, that I might learn *thy s.*
80. let my heart be sound in *thy s.* be not ashamed
83. I am like a bottle, yet do I not forget *thy s.*
112. I inclined my heart to perform *thy s.* alway
117. I will have respect to *thy s.* continually
118. hast trodden down them that err from *thy s.*
155. for the wicked seek not *thy s.*
171. my lips praise, when thou hast taught *thy s.*

STAVES.

Exod. 25. 13. thou shalt make *s.* of shittim-wood and overlay with gold, 28. | 27. 6. | 30. 5. | 37. 4.
14. put *s.* into rings, 15. | 27. 7. | 37. 5. | 38. 7.
37. 15. he made *s.* of shittim-wood, 28. | 38. 5.
40. 20. he set *s.* on the ark and put mercy-seat
Num. 4. 6. they shall put in *s.* thereof, 8, 11, 14.
21. 18. nobles of the people digged with their *s.*
1 Sam. 17. 43. am I a dog, that comest to me with *s.*?
1 Chron. 15. 15. the Levites carried the ark with *s.*
Hab. 3. 14. thou didst strike through with his *s.*
Zech. 11. 7. I took unto me two *s.* I fed the flock
Mat. 10. 10. nor take two coats nor *s.* Luke 9. 3.
26. 47. Judas came and with him a great multitude with *s.* from chief priests, Mark 14. 43
55. are ye come as against thief with swords and *s.* for to take me? Mark 14. 48. Luke 22. 52.

STAY.

Lev. 13. 5. behold, if plague in his sight be at a *s.*
37. but if the scall in his sight be at a *s.*
2 Sam. 22. 19. but the Lord was my *s.* Psal. 18. 18.
Isa. 3. 1. the Lord doth take away the *s.* and staff, the whole *s.* of bread, and the whole *s.* of water

Isa. 19. 13. even they that are the *s.* of tribes thereof
1 *Tim.* 3. † 15. church of God, pillar and *s.* of truth

STAYS.

1 *Kings* 10. 19. there were *s.* on either side throne; two lions stood beside the *s.* 2 *Chr.* 9. 18.
Jer. 50. † 36. a sword is upon the chief s.

STAY.

Gen. 19. 17. neither *s.* thou in all the plain, escape
Exod. 9. 28. I will let you go, ye shall *s.* no longer
Lev. 13. 23. if bright spot *s.* in his place, 28.
Josh. 10. 19. *s.* not, but pursue after your enemies
Ruth 1. 13. would ye *s.* for them from hav. husbands
1 *Sam.* 15. 16. *s.* and I will tell thee what Lord said
20. 38. Jonathan cried, make speed, haste, *s.* not
2 *Sam.* 24. 16. *s.* now thine hand, 1 *Chr.* 21. 15.
Job 37. 4. he will not *s.* them when his voice is heard
38. 37. or who can *s.* the bottles of heaven
Psal. 59. † 15. let them wander for meat if they be not satisfied, then they will *s.* all night
Prov. 28. 17. shall flee to pit, let no man *s.* him
Cant. 2. 5. *s.* me with flagons, I am sick of love
Isa. 10. 20. shall no more *s.* on him that smote him
29. 9. *s.* yourselves and wonder, cry ye out and cry
30. 12. because ye trust, and *s.* on oppression
31. 1. woe to them *s.* on horses, trust in chariots
48. 2. for they *s.* themselves on the God of Israel
50. 10. let him trust in Lord, and *s.* on his God
Jer. 4. 6. *s.* not, for I will bring evil from north
20. 9. I was weary with forbearing, I could not *s.*
Dan. 4. 35. none can *s.* his hand, or say unto him
Hos. 13. 13. not *s.* in the place of breaking forth

STAYED.

Gen. 8. 10. and Noah *s.* yet other seven days, 12.
32. 4. with Laban, and I have *s.* there until now
Exod. 10. 24. only let your flocks and herds be *s.*
17. 12. and Aaron and Hur *s.* up Moses' hands
Num. 16. 48. stood between dead and living, plague was *s.* 50. | 25. 8. 2 *Sam.* 24. 25. *Psal.* 106. 30.
Deut. 10. 10. I *s.* in mount forty days and nights
Josh. 10. 13. and sun stood still, and the moon *s.*
1 *Sam.* 20. 19. and when thou hast *s.* three days
24. 7. David *s.* his servants with these words
30. 9. where those that were left behind *s.*
2 *Sam.* 17. 17. now Jonathan *s.* by En-rogel
24. 21. that the plague may be *s.* 1 *Chron.* 21. 22.
1 *Kings* 22. 35. the king was *s.* up in his chariot, and died, and blood ran into the chariot, 2 *Chr.* 18. 34.
2 *Kings* 4. 6. there is not a vessel more, and oil *s.*
13. 18. smite on ground, and he smote thrice, and *s.*
15. 20. the king of Assyria *s.* not in the land
Job 38. 11. and here shall thy proud waves be *s.*
Isa. 26. 3. wilt keep him whose mind is *s.* on thee
Lam. 4. 6. that was overthrown, no hands *s.* on her
Ezek. 31. 15. and the great waters were *s.*
Hag. 1. 10. heaven is *s.* the earth is *s.* from her fruit
Luke 4. 42. the people came to him and *s.* him
Acts 19. 22. but he himself *s.* in Asia for a season

STAYETH.

Isa. 27. 8. he *s.* his rough wind in day of east-wind
Jer. 48. † 30. those on whom he *s.* do not right

STEAD.

Gen. 2. 21. he closed up the flesh in *s.* thereof
4. 25. God appointed me another seed in *s.* of Abel
22. 13. Abraham offered the ram in *s.* of his son
30. 2. am I in God's *s.* ‖ 44. 33. abide in *s.* of the lad
Exod. 4. 16. he shall be thy spokesman, he shall be to thee in *s.* of a mouth? shall be to him in *s.* of God
5. 12. people scattered to gather stub. in *s.* of straw
29. 30. that son that is priest in his *s.* *Lev.* 16. 32.
Num. 3. 12. I have taken the Levites in *s.* of all first-born, the Levites shall be mine, 41. 45. | 8. 16.
41. cattle of the Levites in *s.* of cattle of Isr. 45.
5. 19. with another in *s.* of thy husband, 20. 29.
10. 31. and thou mayest be to us in *s.* of eyes
32. 14. behold, ye are risen up in your father's *s.*
Deut. 2. 12. the children of Esau dwelt in their *s.*
21. the Ammonites dwelt in their *s.* 22. 23.
10. 6. Eleazar Aaron's son ministered in his *s.*
Josh. 5. 7. their children whom he raised in their *s.*
Judg. 15. 2. take, I pray, her sister in *s.* of her
2 *Sam.* 16. 8. Saul, in whose *s.* thou hast reigned
17. 25. he made Amasa captain in *s.* of Joab
1 *Kings* 1. 30. Solom. shall sit on my throne in my *s.*
35. sit on my throne, for he shall be king in my *s.*
3. 7. Lord, thou hast made me king in *s.* of David
14. 27. Rehoboam made in their *s.* brasen shields
2 *Kings* 17. 24. placed in cities of Samaria in *s.* of Isr.
Esth. 2. 4. let her be queen in *s.* of Vashti, 17.
Job 16. 4. if your soul were in my soul's *s.*
31. 40. if my land cry against me, let thistles grow in *s.* of wheat, and cockle in *s.* of barley
33. 6. behold, I am accord. to thy wish in God's *s.*
34. 24. and he shall set others in their *s.*
Psal. 45. 16. in *s.* of thy fathers shall be thy children
Prov. 11. 8. and the wicked cometh in his *s.*
Eccl. 4. 15. with the child that shall stand up in his *s.*
Isa. 3. 24. it shall come to pass that in *s.* of sweet smell there shall be stink, in *s.* of a girdle a rent
55. 13. in *s.* of the thorn shall come up fir-tree, and in *s.* of the brier shall come up myrtle-tree
Ezek. 16. 32. who taketh strangers in *s.* of her husb.
Hos. 1. † 10. in *s.* of that where it was said to them
2 *Cor.* 5. 20. we pray you in Christ's *s.* be ye reconc.
Philem. 13. that in thy *s.* might have ministered to me
See REIGNED.

STEADS.

1 *Chr.* 5. 22. they dwelt in their *s.* till the captivity

STEADY.

Exod. 17. 12. Moses' hands were *s.* going down of sun
2 *Tim.* 2. † 19. the foundation of God standeth *s.*

STEAL.

Among the Hebrews *theft was not punished with death.* Prov. 6. 30, 31. Men do not despise a thief, if he steal to satisfy his soul when he is hungry. But if he be found, he shall restore seven-fold; he shall give all the substance of his house. *The law allowed the killing of a night robber,* Exod. 22. 2. *because it was supposed his intention was to murder as well as to rob: it condemned a common thief to make double restitution, if the beast he stole were found in his hand alive,* Exod. 22. 4. *If he stole an ox and killed it, he was to restore it five-fold, if a sheep, only four-fold,* Exod. 22. 1. *It is thought that the theft of an ox, or of any of that kind, was punished the more severely, because this animal is of more use than others, and likewise because it argued a greater boldness and customariness in the thief to steal that which more easily might be discovered. If the thief did not make restitution, they seized what was in his house, put it up to sale, and even sold himself, if he had not wherewithal to make satisfaction,* Exod. 22. 3. *In the passage just now quoted,* Prov. 6. 3. *the wise man says, that the thief was to restore* seven-fold *the value of the thing stolen. But* seven-fold *may be here put for many-fold, he shall make abundant satisfaction.*

Though there was no penalty annexed to the law forbidding theft, except restitution; yet to steal away a freeman, or an Hebrew, *and to reduce him to the state of servitude, was punished with death,* Exod. 21. 16. He that stealeth a man and selleth him, or if he be found in his hand, he shall surely be put to death. *The* Jews *do not think that the stealing of a man of any other nation deserves death, but only the theft of a free* Hebrew. *If it be a stranger that is stole, they were only condemned to restitution. They found this distinction upon a law in* Deut. 24. 7. *which limits this law concerning man-stealing:* If a man be found stealing any of his brethren of the children of Israel; *which exception the* Septuagint *and* Onkelos *have inserted in the text of* Exod. 21. 16. *This crime is called* Plagium. *See* SELL.

Some have thought that mere theft among the Hebrews *had no particular mark of infamy annexed to it in some cases.* Solomon *says,* Prov. 6. 30. Men do not despise a thief, if he steal to satisfy his soul when he is hungry. *The law inflicts no peculiar punishment on him, and he is not made to undergo any shameful or ignominious penalty:* If he is found, he shall restore seven-fold, he shall give all the substance of his house. *This is all the danger he is exposed to in stealing, except he had not wherewithal to make restitution, in which case he was reduced to bondage. Many people inhabiting round about* Judea, *seem to have made robbery a kind of profession.* Isaac *foretold to* Esau, *that he should live by his sword, that is, that he should maintain himself by plundering,* Gen. 27. 40. Ishmael, *the son of* Abraham, *had no other trade than war and rapine; he was a* wild man *and an* archer, *he was always at war with his neighbours.* His hand will be against every man, and every man's hand against him, *Gen.* 16. 12. | 21. 20. *His posterity the* Ishmaelites *followed the example of their father, and, as some affirm, made no scruple to rob upon the high-way.*

When the Israelites *were just upon the point of departing out of* Egypt, *they borrowed of their* Egyptian *neighbours, valuable garments, vessels of gold and silver, and carried them along with them into the wilderness.* Exod. 11. 2, 3. Speak now in the ears of the people, and let every man borrow of his neighbour, and every woman of her neighbour, jewels of silver, and jewels of gold. And the Lord gave the people favour in the sight of the Egyptians. *It is inquired, whether the* Hebrews *could lawfully borrow these things of the* Egyptians, *which they had no intention to restore to them again? and whether this was not to commit a manifest theft and injustice? Commentators give several answers to this question. Some say, that upon this occasion, God plainly dispensed with that law; by which he had obliged the* Hebrews *not to commit any theft; or rather, that being the absolute Master of every thing, he transferred to the* Hebrews *that right that the* Egyptians *had to these things. Others insinuate another reason, which is, that God would recompense the* Hebrews *for the labours that they had suffered in* Egypt, *and allowed them to pay themselves by their own hands, by detaining what they borrowed of the* Egyptians. *This way of paying oneself cannot be allowed regularly; but in these circumstances, having no other way of doing themselves justice, and being authorized by the express command of God, they might have recourse to this expedient.*

Others look upon this, not as a theft, but as a fair booty got in a just war. The Egyptians *were enemies to the* Hebrews; *they had unjustly persecuted them for a long time, and took from them the means of defending themselves, and of recovering their liberty. They might therefore lawfully deprive them of their goods by a wile, and a kind of stratagem, by pretending to borrow of them what they never intended to return.*

Some here distinguish between such Israelites *who acted in the simplicity of their hearts, and sincerely obeyed the commands of God, and those that followed the motions of their own covetous desires. The first are excused from sin by the uprightness of their intentions, but not the second, who were ready enough to rob the* Egyptians, *if they could do it with impunity, even though God had not allowed them to borrow any thing from them.*

Others observe, that the Egyptians *were indebted to the* Hebrews, *not only for their goods, but for their lives also, because of the benefits they had received from the Patriarch* Joseph, *when they were under the greatest necessity. The* Israelites *were unjustly oppressed by a cruel slavery in* Egypt: *the* Egyptians *exercised all kinds of violences against them, and overwhelmed them with calamities, even to the rendering their lives uneasy to them. The* Hebrews *had built them cities, and had very much improved the riches of these inhuman masters: who, instead of acknowledging these services, intended even to take away their lives from them. What injustice therefore could there be, if the* Israelites *should take again a small part of that which they had procured for the* Egyptians? *And if they should receive a small recompence for so many services they had done them? They came poor out of* Egypt, *whereas they ought to have got much riches together, if they had not been reduced into an unjust servitude: and, just as a freeman, who had been stolen away and sold for a slave, might, without injustice, set himself at liberty, and pay himself for his labour, by taking from his master a small reward for his service: so the* Israelites, *at their departure out of* Egypt, *might receive something as a recompence, since a great deal was due to them.*

Gen. 31. 27. wherefore didst thou *s.* away from me
44. 8. how then should we *s.* silver or gold?
Exod. 20. 15. thou shalt not *s.* *Lev.* 19. 11. *Deut.* 5. 19. *Mat.* 19. 18. *Rom.* 13. 9.
22. 1. if a man *s.* an ox, he shall restore five
2 *Sam.* 19. 3. as people *s.* away when flee in battle
Prov. 6. 30. if he *s.* to satisfy his soul when hungry
30. 9. or lest I be poor and *s.* and take name of G.
Jer. 7. 9. will ye *s.* murder, and commit adultery
23. 30. I am against the prophets that *s.* my words
Mat. 6. 19. and where thieves break through and *s.*
20. where thieves do not break through nor *s.*
27. 64. lest his disciples come and *s.* him away
Mark 10. 19. do not kill, do not *s.* *Luke* 18. 20.
John 10. 10. the thief cometh not, but for to *s.*
Rom. 2. 21. that preach. man sho. not *s.* dost thou *s.*
Eph. 4. 28. let him that stole *s.* no more, but labour

STEALERS.

1 *Tim.* 1. 10. but the law was made for men-*s.*

STEALETH.

Exod. 21. 16. he that *s.* a man, and selleth him
Job 21. † 18. and as chaff that the storm *s.* away
27. 20. a tempest *s.* him away in the night
Zech. 5. 3. for every one that *s.* shall be cut off

STEALING.

Deut. 24. 7. if a man be found *s.* any of his brethr.
Hos. 4. 2. by swearing and *s.* they break out

STEALTH.

2 *Sam.* 19. 3. the people gat them by *s.* into the city
Job 4. † 12. now a thing was by *s.* brought to me

STEDFAST.

Job 11. 15. yea, thou shalt be *s.* and shalt not fear
Psal. 78. 8. whose spirit was not *s.* with God
37. neither were they *s.* in his covenant
Dan. 6. 26. he is the living God, and *s.* for ever
1 *Cor.* 7. 37. he that stand. in his heart *s.* doeth well
15. 58. therefore, my beloved brethren, be ye *s.*
2 *Cor.* 1. 7. and our hope of you is a *s.* knowing
Heb. 2. 2. for if the word spoken by angels was *s.*
3. 14. if we hold our confidence *s.* to the end
6. 19. which hope we have as an anchor sure and *s.*
1 *Pet.* 5. 9. whom resist *s.* in the faith, knowing

STEDFASTLY.

Ruth 1. 18. when she saw that she was *s.* minded
2 *Kings* 8. 11. and he settled his countenance *s.*
Luke 9. 51. he *s.* set his face to go to Jerusalem
Acts 1. 10. while they looked *s.* behold, two men
2. 42. they continued *s.* in the apostles' doctrine
6. 15. they all looking *s.* on him, saw his face as if
7. 55. Stephen looked up *s.* into heaven, saw glory
14. 9. who *s.* beholding him, and perceiving he had
2 *Cor.* 3. 7. Israel could not *s.* behold face of Moses
13. could not *s.* look to the end of that abolished

STEDFASTNESS.

Psal. 5. † 9. for there is no *s.* in their mouth
Col. 2. 5. beholding the *s.* of your faith in Christ
2 *Pet.* 3. 17. beware lest ye fall from your own *s.*

STEEL.

2 *Sam.* 22. 35. a bow of *s.* is broken, *Psal.* 18. 34.
Job 20. 24. the bow of *s.* shall strike him through
Jer. 15. 12. shall iron break northern iron and *s.*?

STEEP.

Ezek. 38. 20. the *s.* places shall fall, and every wall
Mic. 1. 4. as waters that are poured down *s.* place
Mat. 8. 32. the swine ran violently down a *s.* place, and perished in waters, *Mark* 5. 13. *Luke* 8. 33.

STEM.

Isa. 6. † 13. as teil-tree and oak whose *s.* is in them
11. 1. there shall come a rod out of the *s.* of Jesse

STEP.

1 *Sam.* 20. 3. there is but *s.* between me and death
Job 31. 7. if my *s.* hath turned out of the way

STEPPED.

John 5. 4. whosoever first *s.* in was made whole

STEPPETH.

John 5. 7. while I am coming, another *s.* down before me

STEPS.

Exod. 20. 26. neither go up by *s.* to mine altar
2 *Sam.* 22. 37. thou hast enlarged my *s.* *Ps.* 18. 36.
1 *Kings* 10. 19. the throne had six *s.* 2 *Chron.* 9. 18.
20. twelve lions stood on the *s.* 2 *Chron.* 9. 19.
Job 14. 16. for now thou numberest my *s.*
18. 7. the *s.* of his strength shall be straitened
23. 11. my foot hath held his *s.* his way have I kept
29. 6. when I washed my *s.* with butter, and rock
31. 4. doth not he see my ways and count my *s.*
37. I would declare to him the number of my *s.*
Psal. 17. 11. they have now compassed us in our *s.*
37. 23. *s.* of a good man are ordered by the Lord
31. the law in his heart, none of his *s.* shall slide
44. 18. nor have our *s.* declined from thy way
56. 6. they mark my *s.* when they wait for my soul
57. 6. they have prepared a net for my *s.*
73. 2. but as for me, my *s.* had well nigh slipped
85. 13. and shall set us in the way of his *s.*
119. 133. order my *s.* in thy way, let not iniquity
Prov. 4. 12. when goest thy *s.* shall not be straitened
5. 5. her feet go down to death, *s.* take hold on hell
16. 9. but the Lord directeth his *s.*
Isa. 26. 6. the *s.* of the needy shall tread it down
Jer. 10. 23. it is not in man that walk. to direct his *s.*
Lam. 4. 18. they hunt our *s.* we cannot go in streets
Ezek. 40. 22. they went up to it by seven *s.* 26.
31. and the going up to it had eight *s.* 34. 37.
49. he brought me by *s.* whereby they went up to it
Dan. 11. 43. the Ethiopians shall be at his *s.*
Rom. 4. 12. but walk in *s.* of that faith of Abraham
2 *Cor.* 12. 18. walked we not in the same *s.*?

1 *Pet.* 2. 21. an example that ye should follow his *s.*

STERN.

Acts 27. 29. they cast four anchors out of the *s.*

STEWARD.

Gen. 15. 2. and the *s.* of my house is this Eliezer
43. 19. they came near to the *s.* of Joseph's house
1 *Kings* 16. 9. drinking drunk in the house of his *s.*
Dan. 1. + 11. then said Daniel to the *s.*
Mat. 20. 8. the Lord of the vineyard saith to his *s.*
Luke 8. 3. Joanna the wife of Chuza, Herod's *s.*
12. 42. who then is that faithful and wise *s.*
16. 1. there was a certain rich man who had a *s.*
2. give account, for thou mayest be no longer *s.*
8. and the Lord commended the unjust *s.*
Tit. 1. 7. a bishop must be blameless as the *s.* of G.

STEWARDS.

1 *Chr.* 28. 1. and David assembled captains and *s.*
1 *Cor.* 4. 1. as ministers and *s.* of mysteries of God
2. it is required in *s.* that a man be found faithful
1 *Pet.* 4. 10. as good *s.* of manifold grace of God

STEWARDSHIP.

Luke 16. 2. he said to him, give an account of thy *s.*
3. for my lord taketh away from me the *s.* 4.

STICK.

Job 33. 21. his bones that were not seen, *s.* out
41. 17. his scales are joined, they *s.* together
Psal. 38. 2. for thine arrows *s.* fast in me
Ezek. 29. 4. I will cause the fish to *s.* to thy scales

STICKETH.

Prov. 18. 24. there is a friend *s.* closer than a brother

STICK.

2 *Kings* 6. 6. cut down a *s.* and cast it in thither
Lam. 4. 8. their skin is withered and become like a *s.*
Ezek. 37. 16. take one *s.* write on it, take another *s.*
17. and join them one to another into one *s.* 19.

STICKS.

Num. 15. 32. a man that gathered *s.* on the sabbath
33. they that found him gathering *s.* brought him
1 *Kings* 17. 10. the widow woman was gathering *s.*
12. behold, I am gathering two *s.* to go in
Ezek. 37. 20. and the *s.* whereon thou writest
Acts 28. 3. when Paul had gathered a bundle of *s.*

STIFF.

Jer. 17. 23. they obeyed not, but made their neck *s.*

STIFF-*hearted.*

Ezek. 2. 4. they are impudent children and *s.-hearted*

STIFF *neck.*

Deut. 31. 27. I know thy rebellion and thy *s. neck*
Psal. 75. 5. lift your horn, speak not with a *s. neck*

STIFF-*necked.*

Exod. 32. 9. behold, this people is a *s.-necked* people
33. 3. thou art a *s.-necked* people, *Deut.* 9. 6.
5. say to Israel, ye are a *s.-necked* people
34. 9. for it is a *s.-necked* people, *Deut.* 9. 13.
Deut. 10. 16. circumc. your heart, be no more *s.-nec.*
2 *Chron.* 30. 8. be not *s.-necked* as your fathers were
Acts 7. 51. ye *s.-necked*, ye always resist Holy Gh.

STIFFENED.

2 *Chron.* 36. 13. he *s.* his neck and harden. his heart

STILL.

Gen. 41. 21. but they were *s.* ill-favoured as at first
Exod. 9. 2. if thou refuse, and wilt hold them *s.*
Lev 13. 57. and if it appear *s.* in the garment
Num. 14. 38. but Joshua and Caleb lived *s.*
Josh. 24. 10. therefore Balaam blessed you *s.*
1 *Sam.* 12. 25. but if ye shall *s.* do wickedly
26. 25. Saul said, thou also shalt *s.* prevail
2 *Sam.* 14. 32. it had been good to have been there *s.*
16. 5. Shimei came forth, and cursed *s.* as he came
2 *Kings* 7. 4. and if we sit *s.* here, we die also
12. 3. the people sacrificed *s.* and burnt incense in the high places, 15. 4, 35. 2 *Chron.* 33. 17.
2 *Chron.* 22. 9. had no power to keep *s.* the kingdom
Job 2. 3. and *s.* he holdeth fast his integrity
9. his wife said, dost thou *s.* retain thine integrity?
3. 13. for now should I have lain *s.* and been quiet
20. 13. though he keep it *s.* within his mouth
Psal. 49. 9. that he should *s.* live for ever and not see
68. 21. such a one as goeth on *s.* in his trespasses
78. 32. for all this they sinned *s.* and believed not
84. 4. in thy house they will be *s.* praising thee
92. 14. they shall *s.* bring forth fruit in old age
139. 18. when I awake, I am *s.* with thee
Eccl. 12. 9. he *s.* taught the people knowledge
Isa. 5. 25. his anger is not turned away, but his hand is stretched out *s.* 9. 12, 17, 21. | 10. 4.
Jer. 8. 14. why do we sit *s.*? assemble yourselves
23. 17. they say *s.* unto them that despise me
27. 11. those will I let remain *s.* in their own land
31. 20. I do earnestly remember him *s.* my bowels
42. 10. If ye will *s.* abide in this land, will build you
Lam. 3. 20. my soul hath them *s.* in remembrance
Ezek. 33. 30. thy people *s.* are talking against thee
41. 7. there was a winding about *s.* upward
Zech. 11. 16. nor feed that that standeth *s.*
John 7. 9. when had said these words, abode *s.* 11. 6.
Acts 15. 34. it pleased Silas to abide *s.* 17. 14.
Rom. 11. 23. if they abide not *s.* in unbelief, be graff.
1 *Tim.* 1. 3. I besought thee to abide *s.* at Ephesus
Rev. 22. 11. let him be unjust *s.* filthy *s.* holy *s.*

See STAND, STOOD.

STILL, *

Exod. 15. 16. they shall be as *s.* as a stone, till people
Judg. 18. 9. the land is very good, and are ye *s.*?
1 *Kings* 19. 12. and after the fire a *s.* small voice
22. 3. Ramoth in Gilead is ours, and we be *s.*
Job 4. + 16. there was silence, I heard *s.* voice, say.
Psal. 4. 4. commune with your heart and be *s.*
8. 2. that thou mightest *s.* the enemy and avenger
23. 2. he leadeth me beside the *s.* waters
46. 10. be *s.* and know that I am God
76. 8. the earth feared, and was *s.*
83. 1. hold not thy peace, and be not *s.* O God
107. 29. storm a calm, so that waves thereof are *s.*
Isa. 23. 2. be *s.* ye inhabitants of the isle
30. 7. I have cried, their strength is to sit *s.*
42. 14. I have been *s.* and refrained myself
Jer. 47. 6. O thou sword of the Lord, rest and be *s.*
Mark 4. 39. he arose and said to the sea, peace, be *s.*

STILLED.

Num. 13. 30. Caleb *s.* the people before Moses
Neh. 8. 11. so the Levites *s.* all the people

STILLEST.

Psal. 89. 9. when the waves arise thou *s.* them

STILLETH.

Psal. 65. 7. who *s.* the noise of the seas, of waves

STING.

1 *Cor.* 15. 55. where is thy *s.*? || 56. *s.* of death is sin

STINGS.

Rev. 9. 10. were *s.* in their tails, power to hurt men

STINGETH.

Prov. 23. 32. at the last it *s.* like an adder

STINK, *Substantive.*

Isa. 3. 24. instead of sweet smell, there shall be *s.*
34. 3. their *s.* shall come out of their carcases
Joel 2. 20. his *s.* shall come up, and ill sav. come up
Amos 4. 10. have made *s.* of your camps to come up

STINK.

Gen. 34. 30. ye have made me to *s.* of the land
Exod. 5. + 21. have made our savour to *s.* in the eyes
7. 18. the fish shall die, and the river shall *s.*
16. 24. the manna that was laid up did not *s.*
1 *Sam.* 13. + 4. Israel did *s.* with the Philistines
27. + 12. he hath made his people Israel to *s.*
1 *Chr.* 19. + 6. Ammon saw they made them to *s.*
Psal. 38. 5. my wounds *s.* and are corrupt

STINKETH.

Isa. 50. 2. their fish *s.* because there is no water
John 11. 39. Martha said, Lord, by this time he *s.*

STINKING.

Psal. 14. + 3. they are become *s.* all together
Eccl. 10. 1. cause ointment to send forth a *s.* savour

STIR.

Num. 24. 9. he lay as a lion, who shall *s.* him up?
Job 17. 8. innocent *s.* up himself ag. the hypocrite
41. 10. none is so fierce that dare *s.* him up
Psal. 35. 23. *s.* up thyself, and awake to judgment
78. 38. and he did not *s.* up all his wrath
80. 2. *s.* up thy strength, and come and save us
Prov. 15. 1. but grievous words *s.* up anger
Cant. 2. 7. that ye *s.* not up my love, 3. 5. | 8. 4.
Isa. 10. 26. the Lord shall *s.* up a scourge for him
13. 17. behold, I will *s.* up the Medes against them
42. 13. he shall *s.* up jealousy like a man of war
Dan. 11. 2. he shall *s.* up all against realm of Grecia
25. he shall *s.* up his power against the king
2 *Tim.* 1. 6. that thou *s.* up the gift of God in thee
2 *Pet.* 1. 13. I think it meet to *s.* you up, 3. 1.

STIR.

Acts 12. 18. there was no small *s.* among the soldiers
19. 23. there arose no small *s.* about that way

STIRS.

Isa. 22. 2. thou that art full of *s.* a tumultuous city

STIRRED.

Exod. 35. 21. whose heart *s.* him up, 26. | 36. 2.
1 *Sam.* 22. 8. that my son hath *s.* up my serv. ag. me
26. 19. if the Lord have *s.* thee up against me
1 *Kings* 11. 14. Lord *s.* up an adversary to Solomon
23. God *s.* him up another adversary, Rezon
21. 25. none like Ahab, whom Jezebel his wife *s.* up
1 *Chron.* 5. 26. and God *s.* up the spirit of Pul
2 *Chron.* 21. 16. L. *s.* up ag. Jehoram the Philistines
36. 22. Lord *s.* up the spirit of Cyrus, *Ezra* 1. 1.
Psal. 39. 2. I was dumb, and my sorrow was *s.*
Dan. 11. 10. but his sons shall be *s.* up and assemble
25. the king of the south shall be *s.* up to battle
Hag. 1. 14. the Lord *s.* up the spirit of Zerubbabel
Acts 6. 12. they *s.* up the people, 17. 13. | 21. 27.
13. 50. but the Jews *s.* up the devout women
14. 2. the unbelieving Jews *s.* up the Gentiles
17. 16. at Athens, Paul his spirit was *s.* in him

STIRRETH.

Deut. 32. 11. as an eagle *s.* up her nest, fluttereth over
Prov. 10. 12. hatred *s.* up strifes, but love covereth
15. 18. a wrathful man *s.* up strife, 29. 22.
28. 25. he that is of a proud heart *s.* up strife
Isa. 14. 9. hell from beneath *s.* up the dead for thee
64. 7. none *s.* up himself to take hold on thee
Luke 23. 5. he *s.* up people teaching thro' all Jewry

STOCK.

Lev. 25. 47. or to the *s.* of the stranger's family
Job 14. 8. though the *s.* thereof die in the ground
Isa. 40. 24. yea, their *s.* shall not take root in earth
44. 19. shall I fall down to the *s.* of a tree?
Jer. 2. 27. saying to a *s.* thou art my father
10. 8. are brutish, the *s.* is a doctrine of vanities
Acts 13. 26. children of the *s.* of Abraham
Phil. 3. 5. of the *s.* of Israel, an Hebrew of Hebrews

STOCKS.

Job 13. 27. thou puttest my feet also in the *s.*
33. 11. he putteth my feet in *s.* marketh my paths
Prov. 7. 22. or as a fool to the correction of the *s.*
Jer. 3. 9. she committed adultery with stones and *s.*
20. 2. then Pashur put Jeremiah in the *s.* 3.
29. 26. that thou shouldst put him in prison and *s.*
Hos. 4. 12. my people ask counsel at their *s.*
Acts 16. 24. who made their feet fast in the *s.*

Gazing-STOCK.

Nah. 3. 6. and I will set thee as a *gazing-s.*
Heb. 10. 33. ye were made a *gazing-s.* by reproaches

STOICS

Were a sort of heathen philosophers, who took their name from the Greek *word* Στοα, *signifying a porch or entry, because* Zeno, *the head of the* Stoics, *kept his school in a porch of the city of* Athens. *They held, that a wise man ought to be free from all passions, never to be moved either with joy or grief, esteeming all things to be ordered by an inevitable necessity and fate.* Josephus *says, that the* Pharisees *approach very near to the sentiments of the* Stoics. *They affected the same stiffness, patience, apathy, austerity, and insensibility. The sect of the* Stoics *was still considerable at* Athens, *when* St. Paul *came thither, since he had conferences with them,* Acts 17. 18.

STOLE.

Gen. 31. 20. Jacob *s.* away unawares to Laban
2 *Sam.* 15. 6. so Absalom *s.* the hearts of Israel
2 *Kings* 11. 2. Jehosheba *s.* Joash from among king's sons, they hid him from Athaliah, 2 *Chron.* 22. 11.
Mat. 28. 13. his disciples *s.* him while we slept
Eph. 4. 28. let him that *s.* steal no more, but labour

STOLEN.

Gen. 30. 33. that shall be counted *s.* with me
Gen. 31. 19. and Rachel had *s.* her father's imag. 32.
26. that thou hast *s.* away unawares to me
30. yet wherefore hast thou *s.* my gods?
39. didst require it, wheth. *s.* by day, or *s.* by night
40. 15. indeed I was *s.* away out of the land
Exod. 22. 7. if the stuff be *s.* out of the house
12. if it be *s.* from him, he shall make restitution
Josh. 7. 11. they have *s.* and dissembled also
2 *Sam.* 19. 41. why have men of Judah *s.* thee away
21. 12. the men of Jabesh had *s.* the bones of Saul
Prov. 9. 17. *s.* waters are sweet, bread eaten in sec.
Obad. 5. would they not have *s.* till they had enough?

STOMACH.

1 *Tim.* 5. 23. but use a little wine for thy *s.* sake

STOMACHER.

Isa. 3. 24. instead of a *s.* a girding of sackcloth

STONE

Is *a mineral well known, of which there are divers kinds. As to the precious stones, or gems, of which mention is made in Scripture, all that can be found concerning them in the Commentators, is not much to be relied on, since neither the* Jews, *nor even the ancient* Greek *interpreters, seem to have had a sufficient knowledge of the proper signification of the original terms.*

The corner-stone, or the head-stone of the corner, *Psal.* 118. 22. *This is that which is put as the angle of a building, whether at the foundation, or at the top of the wall.* Jesus Christ *is that* corner-stone *which was rejected by the* Jews, *but is become the* corner-stone of the *church, and the* stone *that binds and unites the* Jews *and* Gentiles *in the union of the same faith,* Mat. 21. 42. Eph. 2. 15, 20. *And as* corner-stones *and* foundation-stones *in buildings use to be chosen with care, and to be thoroughly examined by the builder; so* Christ *is called a* tried stone, a sure foundation. *Isa.* 28. 16. I lay in Zion a tried stone, a sure foundation. *I have tried, I have approved of him as every way sufficient to be the foundation and head of the church. And because this* stone *is not set up by man, but sent by God, therefore he is said to be* cut out of the mountain without hands, *Dan.* 2. 45. *And because unbelievers refuse to be laid upon this stone and so perish, therefore it is called* a stone of stumbling, a rock of offence, *that is, an occasion of sin and ruin, at whom they will take offence and stumble, so as to fall and be broken,* Isa. 8. 14, 15. 1 Pet. 2. 8. *This was accomplished at the coming of the* Messiah, *whom the* Jews *rejected to their own destruction, as not answering their carnal expectations, not suiting with their way of building: that is, not to be made use of for promoting and carrying on their worldly projects and interest.* Christ *is likewise called* a precious stone, *because of his excellency, glory, and beauty; he is called* a chosen, an elect stone, *because he was chosen and appointed by the Father to the work of redemption before the foundation of the world,* 1 Pet. 1. 20. | 2. 4, 6. *He is likewise termed a* living stone, 1 Pet. 2. 4. *He communicates spiritual life to those that close with him, and are built upon him. Lastly, this* stone *is said to* have seven eyes, *Zech.* 3. 9. *to note that the* Messiah *should be endued with perfect wisdom and knowledge, to order all things in the church, to watch over it, and to take care of all the concerns thereof.*

As Christ *the* Head *is called a* stone, *so also his members, true believers, who are built upon, and derive spiritual life from the foundation,* Christ, *are called* stones. 1 *Pet.* 2. 5. Ye also as lively stones are built up a spiritual house. *As the law was engraven on two tables of stones, so believers have the law written in their hearts. They are* stones *for their constancy, strength, and unmoveableness in all the storms of life. They are* stones *for continuance and durableness. As* stones *are dug out of a quarry, so believers are selected and chosen from the rest of mankind. They are united with* Christ *and true Christians in one body; like the* stones *of a house, compact among themselves, and upon the foundation.*

A heart of stone. Job, *speaking of the Leviathan, says, that* his heart is as firm as a stone, yea, as hard as a piece of the nether millstone, *Job* 41. 24. *That is, he is of a very extraordinary strength, boldness, and courage. It is said,* 1 Sam. 25. 37. *that* Nabal's *heart died within him, and he became as a* stone, *when he was told of the danger he had incurred by his imprudence. His heart became immovable like a* stone, *it was contracted, or convulsed, and this convulsion was the occasion of his death.* Ezekiel *says, that* the Lord will *take away* from his people their heart of stone, and give them a heart of flesh, *Ezek.* 36. 26. *that he will take away the stubborn, senseless, and untractable disposition of the heart, that receives no kindly impressions from the word, providence, or Spirit of God in his ordinary operations and influences, that hardens itself in a day of provocation, that is hardened by the deceitfulness of sin, he will take this away, and give a tender, tractable temper and disposition. Much to the same sense is that which* John *the* Baptist *said,* Mat. 3. 9. that God is able to raise up children unto Abraham even of stones; *that is, from among the heathen; or even of the* stones *of the desert, God was able to raise up a spiritual seed to* Abraham.

A stone *is sometimes put for an idol of* stone, *Hab.* 2. 19. Woe unto him that saith to the wood, awake, and to the dumb stone, arise, it shall teach. Hezekiah *in his prayer says,* The kings of Assyria have cast the gods of the nations into the fire; for they were no gods, but the work of men's hands, wood and stone, *Isa.* 37. 19. *And in* Jer. 2. 27. Saying to a stock, thou art my father, and to a stone, thou hast brought me forth. To be reduced to an heap of stones, *is said of a city or house which is entirely ruined and demolished.* Mic. 1. 6. I will make Samaria as an heap of the field, and as the plantings of a vineyard. *So in* Isa. 17. 1. Damascus is taken away from being a city, and it shall be a ruinous heap. *Thus also our Saviour, speaking of the destruction of* Jerusalem, *says, that one* stone *shall not remain upon another*, Mat. 24. 2.

The white stone, *Rev.* 2. 17. I will give him a white stone; *I will give him a full and public pardon and absolution. It is spoken in allusion to an ancient custom of delivering a* white stone *to such as they acquitted in judgment. They used likewise to give a* white stone *as a reward to such as conquered in their games; such as allude to this, make this the sense; I will give him a full and ample reward.*

Solomon *says in* Proverbs 26. 8. As he that bindeth a stone in a sling, so is he that giveth honour to a fool. *When a stone is fastened to the sling, the slinger hinders his own design of throwing it, he loses his labour; so does the man who gives honour to a fool. But the words may be otherwise rendered*, as he that putteth a precious stone in an heap of stones, *where it is obscured and lost: and as this little* stone *does not augment the heap, nor is so much as seen upon it; so honour heaped upon a fool does not render him wore worthy of consideration. Others translate it*, to tie a stone in a piece of purple, is to give honour to a fool. *As nothing can be so ill placed as a stone in a piece of fine cloth; so are honours ill placed upon a fool.*

Great heaps of stones, *raised up for a witness of any memorable event, and to preserve the remembrance of some matter of great importance, are the most ancient monuments among the* Hebrews. *In those elder ages, before the use of writing, these monuments were instead of inscriptions, medals, or histories.* Jacob *and* Laban *raised such a monument upon mount* Gilead, *in memory of their covenant*, Gen. 31. 46. Joshua *erected one at* Gilgal, *made of stones taken out of the* Jordan, *to preserve the memorial of his miraculous passage over this river*, Josh. 4. 5, 6, 7. *The* Israelites *that dwelt beyond* Jordan *also raised one upon the banks of the river, as a testimony that they constituted but one nation with their brethren on the other side*, Josh. 22. 10.

The Hebrews *also give the name of* stones *to the weights they use in commerce*, Lev. 19. 36. Just weights shall ye have: *the* Hebrew *says*, just stones. *And in* Deut. 25. 13. Thou shalt not have in thy bag divers weights, a great and a small: *the* Hebrews *say*, A stone and a stone. *Also* Prov. 11. 1. A just weight is his delight; *in* Hebrew, a perfect stone. *See also* Prov. 16. 11. | 20. 10. Stones *are likewise taken for a violent shower of hail.* Josh. 10. 11. The Lord cast down great stones from heaven upon them. *The punishment of stoning; See* PUNISHMENT.

Gen. 11. 3. they had brick for *s.* and slime for mortar
28. 18. Jacob set up a *s.* for a pillar, 22. | 31. 45.
29. 3. they rolled *s.* from the well's mouth, 8, 10.
35. 14. Jacob set up a pillar of *s.* in the place
49. 24. from thence is the shepherd, the *s.* of Isr.
Exod. 4. 25. Zipporah took a sharp *s.* and cut off
15. 5. they sank into the bottom as a *s.*
16. by great. of thine arm they shall be as still as *s.*
17. 12. and they took a *s.* and put it under him
20. 25. if thou wilt make me an altar of *s.*
21. 18. and if one smite another with a *s.*
28. 10. six of their names on one *s.* 10. on other *s.*
11. with the work of an engraver in *s.*
Lev. 26. 1. nor shall ye set up any image of *s.* in land
Num. 35. 17. if he smite him with throwing a *s.* 23.
Deut. 25. † 13. shalt not have in thy bag a *s.* and a *s.*
Josh. 4. 5. take ye up every man of you *s.* on shoul.
15. 6. the border went up to the *s.* of Bohan
18. 17. the border descended to the *s.* of Bohan
24. 27. behold, this *s.* shall be a witness unto us
Judg. 9. 5. he slew seventy persons on one *s.* 18.
1 *Sam.* 6. 18. which *s.* remaineth unto this day
7. 12. Samuel set up a *s.* and called it Eben-ezer
17. 49. David took from his bag a *s.* and slang it, the *s.* sunk into the Philistine's forehead
50. David prevailed over the Philistine with a *s.*
20. 19. and thou shalt remain by the *s.* Ezel
25. 37. Nabal's heart died in him, he became as a *s.*
2 *Sam.* 5. † 11. Hiram sent hewers of *s.* of the wall
17. 13. till there be not one small *s.* found there
1 *Kings* 6. 7. house was built of *s.* made ready before
18. all was cedar, there was no *s.* seen
2 *Kings* 3. 25. on good land cast every man his *s.*
1 *Chron.* 22. 15. there are with thee hewers of *s.*
2 *Chron.* 2. 14. skilful to work in gold, silver, and *s.*
Neh. 9. 11. thou threwest as a *s.* into mighty waters
Job 28. 2. and brass is molten out of the *s.*
38. 30. waters are hid as with a *s.* deep is frozen
41. 24. his heart is as firm as a *s.* yea, as hard as
Psal. 91. 12. angels shall bear thee up, lest thou dash thy foot against a *s. Mat.* 4. 6. *Luke* 4. 11.
118. 22. *s.* which the builders refused, is become head *s.* of the corner, *Mat.* 21. 42. *Mark* 12. 10.
Prov. 11. † 1. but a perfect *s.* is his delight
20. † 10. a *s.* and a *s.* are alike abomination to L.
26. 8. as he that bindeth a *s.* in a sling, so is he
27. as he that rolleth a *s.* it will return upon him
27. 3. a *s.* is heavy, a fool's wrath is heavier
Jer. 2. 27. and to a *s.* thou hast brought me forth
51. 26. they shall not take of thee a *s.* for a corner, nor a *s.* for foundations, but shalt be desolate
Lam. 3. 53. they have cast a *s.* upon me
Dan. 2. 34. a *s.* was cut out of the mountain, 45.
6. 17. and a *s.* was laid upon the mouth of the den
Amos 9. † 9. yet shall not the least *s.* fall on earth
Hab. 2. 11. for the *s.* shall cry out of the wall
19. woe to him that saith to the dumb *s.* arise
Hag. 2. 15. from before *s.* was laid upon a *s.* in tem.
Zech. 3. 9. for behold, the *s.* that I have laid before Joshua, upon one *s.* shall be seven eyes
4. 7. he shall bring forth the head *s.* thereof
7. 12. they made their hearts as adamant *s.*
Mat. 7. 9. if ask bread, will he give *s.? Luke* 11. 11.
21. 44. whosoever shall fall on this *s.* shall be broken, but on whom. it shall fall, *Luke* 20. 18.
Mat. 24. 2. verily I say, there shall not be left one *s.* upon another, *Mark* 13. 2. *Luke* 19. 44. | 21. 6.
27. 66. sealing the *s.* || 28. 2. angel rolled back *s.*
Luke 4. 3. command this *s.* that it be made bread
20. 17. *s.* which the builders rejected, is become the head of the corner, *Acts* 4. 11. 1 *Pet.* 2. 7.
22. 41. he was withdrawn from them a *s.* cast
24. 2. found *s* rolled away, *Mark* 16. 4. *John* 20. 1.
John 1. 42. Cephas, which is by interpretation a *s.*
2. 6. and there were set there six water-pots of *s.*
8. 7. that is without sin, let him first cast *s.* at her
11. 38. it was a cave, and a *s.* lay upon it
39. take ye away *s.* || 41. they took away the *s.*
Acts 17. 29. that the Godhead is like to *s.* graven
Rev. 16. 21. hail fell every *s.* the weight of a talent
18. 21. an angel took up a *s.* like a great millstone

Burdensome STONE.

Zech. 12. 3. I will make Jerusalem a *burdensome s.*
See CORNER, GREAT, HEWED.

Hewn STONE.

Exod. 20. 25. thou shalt not build altar of *hewn s.*
2 *Kings* 22. 6. to builders and masons, to buy timber and *hewn s.* to repair the house, 2 *Chron.* 34. 11.
Lam. 3. 9. he hath enclosed my ways with *hewn s.*
Ezek. 40. 42. the four tables were of *hewn s.*
Amos 5. 11. ye have built houses of *hewn s.* but not
Luke 23. 53. laid it in sepulchre that was *hewn* in *s.*

Living STONE.

1 *Pet.* 2. 4. to whom coming as to *liv. s.* chosen of G.

Precious STONE.

Prov. 17. 8. a gift is a *precious s.* to him that hath it
26. † 8. putteth a *precious s.* in an heap of stones
Cant. 5. † 12. his eyes are set as a *p. s.* in a ring
Isa. 28. 16. I lay in Zion a *p.* corner *s.* 1 *Pet.* 2. 6.
Ezek. 28. 13. every *precious s.* was thy covering
Rev. 17. 4. she was decked with gold and *p. s.*
21. 11. her light was like to a *s.* most *precious*
See STUMBLING.

STONE-*squarers.*

1 *Kings* 5. 18. builders and *s.-s.* did hew them

Tables of STONE.

Exod. 24. 12. I will give thee *tables of s.* 31. 18.
34. 1. L. said, hew thee two *tables of s. Deut.* 10. 1.
4. and he hewed two *tables of s. Deut.* 10. 3.
Deut. 4. 13. he wrote on the two *tables of s.* 5. 22.
9. 9. when I was gone up to receive the *tables of s.*
10. the Lord delivered to me two *tables of s.*
11. the Lord gave me the two *tables of s.*
1 *Kings* 8. 9. was nothing in ark save two *tables of s.*
2 *Cor.* 3. 3. not in *t. of s.* but in fleshly tables of heart

Tried STONE.

Isa. 28. 16. behold, I lay in Zion a stone, a *tried s.*

White STONE.

Rev. 2. 17. I will give him a *white s.* and new name

STONE, joined with *wood.*

Exod. 7. 19. may be blood in vessels of *wood* and *s.*
Deut. 4. 28. there serve gods the work of men's hands, *wood* and *s.* 28. 36, 64. | 29. 17. 2 *Kings* 19. 18. *Isa.* 37. 19. *Ezek.* 20. 32.
Dan. 5. 4. praised the gods of gold, *wood* a *s.* 23.
Rev. 9. 20. should not worship idols of *wood* and *s.*

STONE *of Zoheleth.*

1 *Kings* 1. 9. Adonijah slew sheep by *s. of Zoheleth*
See WALL.

STONE, *Verb.*

Exod. 8. 26. shall we sacrifice, and will they not *s.* us?
17. 4. what shall I do? they be almost ready to *s.* me
Lev. 20. 2. people of land shall *s.* him with stones
27. they shall *s.* the wizards with stones
24. 14. let congregation *s.* him that cursed, 16, 23.
Num. 14. 10. congregation bade *s.* them with stones
15. 35. they shall *s.* the sabbath-breaker, 36.
Deut. 13. 10. shalt *s.* with stones enticers to idolat.
17. 5. shalt *s.* idolaters || 21. 21. *s.* rebellious son
22. 21. they shall *s.* her that playeth the whore
24. ye shall *s.* adulterers with stones, that they die
1 *Kings* 21. 10. carry Naboth out, *s.* him that he die
Ezek. 16. 40. and they shall *s.* thee with stones
23. 47. the company shall *s.* them with stones
Luke 20. 6. if we say, of men, the people will *s.* us
John 10. 31. the Jews took up stones again to *s.* him
32. for which of those good works do ye *s.* me?
33. saying, for a good work we *s.* thee not
11. 8. Master, the Jews of late sought to *s.* thee
Acts 14. 5. there was an assault made to *s.* them

STONED.

Exod. 19. 13. he shall surely be *s.* or shot through
21. 28. then the ox shall be surely *s.* 29, 32.
Josh. 7. 25. all Israel *s.* Achan with stones
1 *Kings* 12. 18. all Israel *s.* Adoram, 2 *Chr.* 10. 18.
21. 13. they *s.* Naboth with stones, 14, 15.
2 *Chron.* 24. 21. they *s.* Zechariah in the court
Mat. 21. 35. the husbandmen beat one, *s.* another
John 8. 5. Moses commanded that such should be *s.*
Acts 5. 26. they feared lest they should have been *s.*
7. 58. they *s.* Stephen, calling upon God, 59.
14. 19. having *s.* Paul, drew him out of the city
2 *Cor.* 11. 25. thrice was I beaten, once was I *s.*
Heb. 11. 37. they were *s.* they were sawn asunder
12. 20. if a beast touch the mount it shall be *s.*

STONES.

Gen. 31. 46. Jacob said to his brethren, gather *s.*
Exod. 28. 11. thou shalt engrave the two *s.* 12.
17. set in it settings of *s.* even four rows of *s.*
21. the *s.* shall be with the names of Israel
39. 7. that they should be *s.* for a memorial to Israel
Lev. 14. 40. command that they take away the *s.*
42. shall put other *s.* in the place of those *s.*
45. he shall break down the house, the *s.* of it
19. † 36. just *s.* a just ephah, and hin shall ye have
21. 20. or hath his *s.* broken, shall not offer
Deut. 8. 9. a land whose *s.* are iron, and out of hills
23. 1. that is wounded in the *s.* shall not enter
27. 4. ye shall set up these *s.* in mount Ebal
5. build an altar of *s.* || 8. write on the *s.* words
Josh. 4. 3. and take you hence twelve *s.* 9.
6. saying, what mean you by these *s.?* 21.
8. and took twelve *s.* out of the midst of Jordan
20. those twelve *s.* did Joshua pitch in Gilgal
8. 32. he wrote on the *s.* a copy of the law
Judg. 20. 16. every one could sling *s.* at an hair-brea.
1 *Sam.* 17. 40. David chose him five smooth *s.*
2 *Sam.* 16. 6. Shimei cast *s.* at David and serv. 13.
1 *Kings* 5. 18 so they prepared timber and *s.* to build
7. 10. *s.* of eight cubits, and *s.* of ten cubits
10. 27. king made silver to be in Jerusalem as *s.* and cedars as sycamore trees, 2 *Chr.* 1. 15. | 9. 27.
15. 22. took away the *s.* of Ramah, 2 *Chr.* 16. 6.
18. 31. Elijah took twelve *s.* according to number
32. with the *s.* he built an altar in name of Lord
2 *Kings* 3. 19. mar every good piece of land with *s.*
25. only Kir-haraseth left they the *s.* thereof
16. 17. and put it upon a pavement of *s.*
1 *Chron.* 12. 2. in hurling of *s.* and shooting arrows
2 *Chron.* 26. 14. Uzziah prepared slings to cast *s.*
Neh. 4. 2. will they revive the *s.* out of the heaps?
Job 5. 23. thou shalt be in league with *s.* of field
6. 12. is my strength the strength of *s.?*
8. 17. his roots are wrapped, and seeth place of *s.*
14. 19. the waters wear the *s.* thou washest away
22. 24. the gold of Ophir as the *s.* of the brooks
28. 6. the *s.* of it are the place of sapphires
40. 17. the sinews of his *s.* are wrapped together
Psal. 102. 14. thy servants take pleasure in her *s.*
137. 9. that dasheth thy little ones against the *s.*
Prov. 16. † 11. all the *s.* of the bag are his work
Eccl. 3. 5. a time to cast away *s.* a time to gather *s.*
10. 9. whoso removeth *s.* shall be hurt therewith
Isa. 5. 2. he fenced it and gathered out the *s.* thereof
14. 19. that go down to the *s.* of the pit
27. 9. he maketh the *s.* of the altar as chalk *s.*
54. 11. behold, I will lay thy *s.* with fair colours
12. I will make the borders of pleasant *s.*
57. 6. among the smooth *s.* of the stream
60. 17. bring for *s.* iron || 62. 10. gather out the *s.*
Jer. 3. 9. she committed adultery with *s.* and stocks
43. 10. and I will set his throne on these *s.*
Lam. 4. 1. the *s.* of the sanctuary are poured out
Ezek. 26. 12. they shall lay thy *s.* in the water
28. 14. thou hast walked in midst of the *s.* of fire
16. I will destroy thee from midst of the *s.* of fire
Mic. 1. 6. I will pour down the *s.* into the valley
Zech. 5. 4. shall consume it with the *s.* thereof
9. 16. for they shall be as a *s.* of a crown lifted up
Mat. 3. 9. of these *s.* to raise up children, *Luke* 3. 8.
4. 3. command that these *s.* be made bread
Mark 5. 5. crying, and cutting himself with *s.*
12. 4. and at him they cast *s.* and wounded him
13. 1. Master, see what manner of *s.* are here
Luke 19. 40. the *s.* would immediately cry out
John 8. 59. they took up *s.* to cast at him, 10. 31.
2 *Cor.* 3. 7. if ministration engraven in *s.* was glori.
1 *Pet.* 2. 5. ye as lively *s.* are built up spiritual house
See STONE, *Verb.*

Corner-STONES.

Psal. 144. 12. that our daughters may be as *corner-s.*
See COSTLY.

STONES *of darkness.*

Job 28. 3. he searcheth out the *s. of darkness*

STONES *of emptiness.*

Isa. 34. 11. he shall stretch out upon it *s. of emptin.*

Glistering STONES.

1 *Chr.* 29. 2. I have prepared *glistering s.* for house

Gravel STONES.

Lam. 3. 16. he hath broken my teeth with *gravel s.*
See GREAT.

Heap of STONES.

Josh. 7. 26. they raised a great *heap of s.* on Achan
8. 29. and raise a great *heap of s.* on the king of Ai
2 *Sam.* 18. 17. they laid a *heap of s.* on Absalom

Hewed STONES.

1 *Kings* 5. 17. they brought *hewed s.* to lay foundat.
7. 9. according to the measures of *hewed s.* 11.

Hewn STONES.

Isa. 9. 10. bricks fallen, but we will build with *h. s.*

Marble STONES.

1 *Chron.* 29. 2. I have prepared *m. s.* in abundance

Precious STONES.

2 *Sam.* 12. 30. was a talent of gold with *precious s.*
1 *Kings* 10. 2. queen of Sheba came with *precious s.*
11. navy of Hiram brought *prec. s.* 2 *Chr.* 9. 10.
1 *Chron.* 29. 2. I prepared all manner of *precious s.*
8. with whom *precious s.* were found, gave them
2 *Chr.* 3. 6. he garnished the house with *precious s.*
32. 27. he made himself treasuries for *precious s.*
Ezek. 27. 22. they occupied in thy fairs with *prec. s.*
Dan. 11. 38. a god shall he honour with *precious s.*
1 *Cor.* 3. 12. if any man build on this foundation *p. s.*
Rev. 18. 12. for no man buyeth *prec. s.* any more
16. that great city decked with gold and *prec. s.*
21. 19. foundations garnished with *precious s.*

Whole STONES.

Deut. 27. 6. shalt build the altar of *w. s. Josh.* 8. 31.

Wrought STONES.

1 *Chron.* 22. 2. he set masons to hew *wrought s.*

STONEST.

Mat. 23. 37. *s.* them that are sent to thee, *Luke* 13. 34.

STONY.

Ps. 141. 6. when judges are overthrown in *s.* places
Ezek. 11. 19. I will take the *s.* heart, 36. 26.
Mat. 13. 5. some fell on *s.* places, 20. *Mark* 4. 5, 16.

STONING.

1 *Sam.* 30. 6. for the people spake of *s.* David

STOOD.

Gen. 18. 22. but Abraham *s.* yet before the Lord
29. † 35. his name Judah, and Leah *s.* from bearing
Exod. 14. 19. the pillar of cloud *s.* behind them
Num. 16. 48. he *s.* between the dead and the living
Deut. 4. 11. ye came near and *s.* under the mount.
5. 5. I *s.* between the Lord and you, to shew you
Josh. 3. 16. the waters *s.* and rose up on an heap
4. 3. take twelve stones where the priests' feet *s.* 9.
Judg. 6. 31. Joash said to all that *s.* against him
16. 29. two middle pillars on which the house *s.*
1 *Sam.* 3. 10. the L. *s.* and called Samuel, Samuel
4. † 15. Eli's eyes *s.* that he could not see
10. 23. when he *s.* among the people, he was higher
17. 8. Goliath *s.* and cried to the armies of Israel
22. 7. Saul said to the servants that *s.* about him
17. the king said to footmen that *s.* about him
1 *Kings* 8. 14. the king blessed all the congregation, and all congregat. of Israel, *s.* 2 *Chr.* 6. 3. | 7. 6.
55. Solomon *s.* and blessed all the congregation
14. † 4. Abijah, his eyes *s.* for hoariness

2 Kings 2. 7. sons of the prophets *s.* to view afar off
23. 3. and all the people *s.* to the covenant
2 Chr. 6. 13. and on the brasen scaffold Solomon *s.*
Neh. 9. 2. they *s.* and confessed their sins and their
Esth. 9. 16. the other Jews *s.* for their lives
Psal. 33. 9. he commanded and it *s.* fast
Isa. 6. 2. above it *s.* the seraphims each had six win.
Jer. 46. 15. they *s.* not because Lord did drive them
48. 45. they *s.* under the shadow of Heshbon
Ezek. 1. 21. and when those *s.* these *s.* 10. 17.
24. when they *s.* they let down their wings
25. and there was a voice when they *s.*
Dan. 8. 17. Gabriel came near where I *s.*
10. 11. when he had spoken this, I *s.* trembling
11. 1. I *s.* to confirm and to strengthen him
12. 5. I looked, and behold, there *s.* other two
Jonah 1.† 15. and the sea *s.* from her raging
Hab. 3. 6. he *s.* and measured the earth, he beheld
Zech. 1. 8. he *s.* among the myrtle-trees, 10, 11.
Mat. 12. 46. his mother and brethren *s.* without
Luke 6. 8. he that had the withered hand *s.* forth
18. 11. the Pharisee *s.* and prayed thus with hims.
John 18. 25. Simon Peter *s.* and warmed himself
20. 11. but Mary *s.* without at sepulchre weeping
Acts 3. 8. the lame man leaping up *s.* and walked
9. 7. the men which journ. with him *s.* speechless
16. 9. there *s.* a man of Macedonia and prayed
27. 21. but Paul *s.* forth in the midst of them
Heb. 9. 10. *s.* only in meats, and drinks, and washin.

STOOD *above.*

Gen. 28. 13. behold, the Lord *s. above* the ladder
2 Chron. 24. 20. Zechariah *s. above* the people
Psal. 104. 6. the waters *s. above* the mountains

STOOD *afar.*

Exod. 2. 4. his sister *s. afar* off, to wit what be done
20. 18. the people removed and *s. afar* off, 21.
Luke 17. 12. ten that were lepers, who *s. afar* off
23. 49. all his acquaintance *s. afar* off beholding
Rev. 18. 17. as many as trade by sea *s. afar* off

STOOD *at.*

Exod. 19. 17. they *s. at* the nether part of the mount
33. 8. they *s.* every man *at* his tent-door
9. the cloudy pillar *s. at* the door of the tabernac.
2 Kings 5. 9. Naaman *s. at* door of house of Elisha
2 Chron. 5. 12. singers *s. at* the east end of the altar
23. 13. the king *s. at* his pillar, at the entering in
Ezek. 10. 19. cherubims *s. at* door of the east gate
21. 21. the king *s. at* the parting of the way
Luke 7. 38. woman *s. at* his feet behind him, weep.
John 18. 16. but Peter *s. at* the door without
Rev. 8. 3. another angel came and *s. at* the altar

STOOD *before.*

Gen. 19. 27. to the place where he *s. before* the Lord
43. 15. went down to Egypt, and *s. before* Joseph
Exod. 9. 10. they took ashes and *s. before* Pharaoh
Lev. 9. 5. the congregation *s. before* the Lord
Num. 27. 2. daughters of Zelophehad *s. before* Mos.
Josh. 20. 9. until he *s. before* the congregation
Judg. 20. 28. Phinehas *s. before* ark in those days
1 Sam. 16. 21. David came and *s. before* Saul
1 Kings 1. 28. Bath-sheba *s. before* king David
3. 15. Solomon *s. before* the ark of the covenant
16. two women that were harlots *s. before* him
8. 22. Solomon *s. before* the altar, *2 Chron.* 6. 12.
12. 6. old men that *s. before* Solomon, *2 Chr.* 10. 6.
8. young men that *s. before* him, *2 Chron.* 10. 8.
22. 21. spirit *s. before* the Lord, *2 Chron.* 18. 20.
2 Kings 4. 12. the Shunammite *s. before* Elisha
5. 15. Naaman returned and *s. before* Elisha
25. Gehazi went in and *s. before* his master
8. 9. Hazael came and *s. before* Elisha
10. 4. behold, two kings *s.* not *before* him
Esth. 8. 4. so Esther arose, and *s. before* the king
Psal. 106. 23. had not Moses his chosen *s. before* him
Jer. 15. 1. though Moses and Samuel *s. before* me
18. 20. I *s. before* thee to speak good for them
52. † 12. captain which *s. before* king of Babylon
Ezek. 8. 11. there *s. before* them seventy men
Dan. 1. 19. therefore they *s. before* the king, 2. 2.
2. 31. O king, this great image, *s. before* thee
3. 3. they *s. before* the image Nebuchadnez. set up
7. 10. ten thousand times ten thousand *s. before* him
8. 3. behold, there *s. before* the river a ram
15. there *s. before* me as the appearance of a man
Zech. 3. 3. now Joshua *s. before* the angel
4. and he spake to those that *s. before* him
Mat. 27. 11. and Jesus *s. before* the governor
Acts 10. 17. behold, three men *s. before* the gate
30. a man *s. before* me in bright clothing
12. 14. she told how Peter *s. before* the gate
24. 20. let these say, while I *s. before* the council
Rev. 7. 9. I saw great multitude *s. before* the throne
8. 2. I saw the seven angels which *s. before* God
12. 4. and the dragon *s. before* the woman

STOOD *beside.*

2 Sam. 15. 2. Absalom *s. beside* the way of the gate
1 Kings 10. 19. and two lions *s. beside* the stays
Jer. 36. 21. the princes which *s. beside* the king
Ezek. 9. 2. the six men *s. beside* the brasen altar
10. 6. then he went in and *s. beside* the wheels

STOOD *by.*

Gen. 18. 2. he looked, and lo, three men *s. by* him
24. 30. behold, he *s. by* the camels at the well
41. 1. Pharaoh dreamed, and lo, he *s. by* the river
45. 1. not refrain himself before all that *s. by* him
Exod. 18. 13. Moses sat, and the people *s. by* Moses
Num. 23. 6. Balak *s. by* his burnt-sacrifice, 17.
Judg. 3. 19. all that *s. by* him went out from him
18. 16. the men *s. by* the entering of the gate
1 Sam. 1. 26. the woman that *s. by* thee, praying
2 Sam. 13. 31. servants *s. by* with clothes rent
1 Kings 13. 1. and Jeroboam *s. by* the altar to burn
24. ass *s. by* it, the lion also *s. by* the carcase
2 Kings 2. 7. and they two *s. by* Jordan, 13.
11. 14. behold, the king *s. by* a pillar, 23. 3.
18. 17. they *s. by* conduit of upper pool, *Isa.* 36. 2.
1 Chron. 21. 15. the angel *s. by* the threshing floor
Jer. 44. 15. then the women that *s. by* answered
Ezek. 43. 6. and the man *s. by* me and said
Dan. 7. 16. I came near to one of them that *s. by*
Zech. 3. 5. and the angel of the Lord *s. by*
Mark 14. 47. one of them that *s. by* drew a sword
Mark 15. 35. some of them that *s. by* when they heard
Luke 5. 1. he *s. by* the lake of Gennesareth
19. 24. he said to them that *s. by*, take from him
24. 4. two men *s. by* them in shining garments
John 18. 22. an officer that *s. by* struck Jesus
19. 25. there *s. by* the cross of Jesus his mother
Acts 1. 10. two men *s. by* them in white apparel
9. 39. and all the widows *s. by* him weeping
22. 25. Paul said to the centurion that *s. by*
23. 2. commanded them that *s. by* to smite him
4. they that *s. by* said, revilest thou the high priest?
11. the night following the Lord *s. by* him
27. 23. there *s. by* me this night the angel of God

STOOD *in.*

Exod. 5. 20. met Moses and Aaron, who *s. in* the way
32. 26. then Moses *s. in* the gate of the camp
Num. 12. 5. Lord *s. in* the door of the tabernacle
16. 18. they laid incense thereon, and *s. in* the door
27. Dathan and Abiram *s. in* door of their tents
22. 22. the angel of the Lord *s. in* the way, 24.
26. angel went further and *s. in* a narrow place
Josh. 3. 17. the priests *s. in* midst of Jordan, 4. 10.
Judg. 9. 7. Jotham *s. in* the top of mount Gerizim
35. Gaal *s. in* the entering of the gate of the city
44. Abimelech || 18. 17. the priests *s. in* the entering
2 Sam. 23. 12. he *s. in* the midst of the ground
1 Kings 19. 13. and he *s. in* entering in of the cave
2 Kings 3. 21. they gathered, and *s. in* the border
4. 15. the Shunammite *s. in* the door, and he said
2 Chron. 30. 16. and they *s. in* their place, 35. 10.
34. 31. king *s. in* his place, and made a covenant
Neh. 8. 7. and all the people *s. in* their place
Esth. 5. 1. Esther *s. in* the inner-court of the house
Jer. 19. 14. Jeremiah *s. in* court of the Lord's house
23. 18. for who hath *s. in* counsel of the Lord
22. but if they had *s. in* my counsel and caused
Ezek. 8. 11. Jaazaniah *s. in* the midst of them
Obad. 14. nor shouldest *s. in* cross-way to cut off those
Luke 24. 36. Jesus himself *s. in* the midst of them, and
saith to them, peace be to you, *John* 20. 19, 26.
Acts 17. 22. then Paul *s. in* the midst of Mars-hill
Rev. 5. 6. *in* the midst of the elders *s.* a lamb

STOOD *on.*

1 Sam. 17. 3. Philistines *s. on* a mountain on the one
side, Israel *s. on* a mountain on the other side
26. 13. then David *s. on* the top of an hill
2 Sam. 2. 25. Benjamin *s. on* the top of an hill
1 Chron. 6. 39. Asaph, who *s. on* his right hand
44. the sons of Merari *s. on* the left hand
2 Chron. 3. 13. the cherubims *s. on* their feet
Ezek. 10. 3. the cherubims *s. on* the right side
Mat. 13. 2. the whole multitude *s. on* the shore
John 21. 4. when morning, Jesus *s. on* the shore
Acts 21. 40. Paul *s. on* stairs and beckoned to people
Rev. 14. 1. and lo, a lamb *s. on* the mount Sion

STOOD *over.*

Num. 7. † 2. who *s. over* them that were numbered
Deut. 31. 15. the pillar of cloud *s. over* the door
Josh. 5. 13. behold, a man *s. over*-against him
Ezek. 10. 4. glory of the Lord *s. over* the threshold
18. glory of the Lord *s. over* cherubims
Mat. 2. 9. the star *s. over* where the young child was
Luke 4. 39. he *s. over* her and rebuked the fever

STOOD *round.*

Gen. 37. 7. behold, your sheaves *s. round* about
Acts 14. 20. as the disciples *s. round* about him
25. 7. Jews *s. round* about Paul, and laid complaints
Rev. 7. 11. all the angels *s. round* about the throne

STOOD *still.*

Josh. 10. 13. the sun *s. still*, and the moon stayed
11. 13. as for cities that *s. still* in their strength
2 Sam. 2. 23. as many as came to the place *s. still*
28. Joab blew a trumpet and all the people *s. still*
20. 12. when the man saw that all people *s. still*
Neh. 12. 39. and they *s. still* in the prison-gate
Job 4. 16. a spirit *s. still* but I could not discern
32. 16. for they spake not, but *s. still*
Hab. 3. 11. sun and moon *s. still* in their habitation
Mat. 20. 32. and Jesus *s. still* and called them
Mark 10. 49. Jesus *s. still* and commanded him
Luke 7. 14. and they that bare him *s. still*

STOOD *there.*

Exod. 34. 5. the L. descended and *s.* with him *there*
1 Sam. 6. 14. the ark came into the field and *s. there*
1 Kings 10. 20. twelve lions *s. there*, *2 Chron.* 9. 19.
Ezek. 3. 23. behold, the glory of the Lord *s. there*
Hos. 10. 9. from the days of Gibeah *there* they *s.*
Mat. 27. 47. some of them that *s. there*, *Mark* 11. 5.
John 18. 18. the servants and officers *s. there*

STOOD *up.*

Gen. 23. 3. Abraham *s. up* from before his dead
7. Abraham *s. up* and bowed himself to people
Exod. 2. 17. but Moses *s. up* and helped them
Num. 11. 32. the people *s. up* all that day and night
1 Chron. 21. 1. Satan *s. up* ag. Israel and provoked
28. 2. then David the king *s. up* upon his feet
2 Chron. 13. 4. Abijah *s. up* and said, hear me
20. 19. the Levites *s. up* to praise the Lord God
23. Ammon and Moab *s. up* against mount Seir
28. 12. *s. up* against them that came from the war
Ezra 2. 63. not eat of holy things till there *s. up* a
priest with Urim and Thummim, *Neh.* 7. 65.
Neh. 8. 5. when he opened the book people *s. up*
9. 3. they *s. up* in their place and read the law
4. then *s. up* upon the stairs, of the Levites
Esth. 5. 9. Haman saw that Mordecai *s.* not *up*
7. 7. Haman *s. up* to make request for his life
Job 4. 15. a spirit passed, the hair of my flesh *s. up*
29. 8. young men saw me, and aged arose and *s. up*
30. 28. I *s. up* and cried in the congregation
Ps. 106. 30. then *s. up* Phinehas and executed judg.
Ezek. 37. 10. they lived, and *s. up* upon their feet
Dan. 8. 22. that being broken, whereas four *s. up* for it
Luke 4. 16. Jesus *s. up* to read in the synagogue
10. 25. a certain lawyer *s. up* and tempted him
Acts 1. 15. in those days Peter *s. up* and said
4. 26. the kings of the earth *s. up* against the Lord
5. 34. then *s. up* one Gamaliel, a doctor of law
11. 28. Agabus *s. up*, and signified by the spirit
13. 16. Paul *s. up*, and beckoning with his hand
25. 18. against whom when the accusers *s. up*

STOOD *upon.*

Gen. 41. 17. behold, I *s. upon* the bank of the river
1 Sam. 17. 51. David ran and *s. upon* the Philistine
2 Sam. 1. 10. so I *s. upon* Saul, and slew him
1 Kings 7. 25. sea *s. upon* twelve oxen, *2 Chron.* 4. 4.
2 Kings 13. 21. he revived, and *s. upon* his feet
Neh. 8. 4. Ezra the scribe *s. upon* a pulpit of wood
Ezek. 11. 23. glory of the Lord *s. upon* the mount
Amos 7. 7. the Lord *s. upon* a wall made by a line
Rev. 11. 11. the two prophets *s. upon* their feet
13. 1. and I *s. upon* the sand of the sea, and saw

STOOD *with.*

Gen. 45. 1. there *s. with* him no man, while Joseph
2 Kings 11. 11. every man *s. w.* his weapons in hand
2 Chron. 29. 26. the Levites *s. with* instruments
Ezra 3. 9. then Joshua *s. with* his sons and brethren
Lam. 2. 4. he *s. with* his right hand as an adversary
Luke 9. 32. they saw the two men that *s. with* him
John 18. 5. Judas who also betrayed *s. with* them
18. Peter *s. with* them, and warmed himself
2 Tim. 4. 16. no man *s. with* me || 17. Lord *s. with* me

STOODEST.

Num. 22. 34. I knew not that thou *s.* in the way
Deut. 4. 10. the day that thou *s.* before the Lord
Obad. 11. in the day that thou *s.* on the other side

STOOL.

2 Kings 4. 10. let us set for him a bed, table, and *s.*

STOOLS.

Exod. 1. 16. he said, when ye see them upon the *s.*

STOOP.

Job 9. 13. the proud helpers do *s.* under him
Prov. 12. 25. heaviness maketh the heart of man *s.*
Isa. 46. 2. they *s.* they bow down together
Mark 1. 7. I am not worthy to *s.* down and unloose

STOOPED.

Gen. 49. 9. Judah *s.* down, he couched as a lion
1 Sam. 24. 8. David *s.* || 28. 14. Saul *s.* to the ground
2 Chron. 36. 17. had no compassion on him that *s.*
John 8. 6. Jes. *s.* down and wrote with his finger, 8.
20. 11. and as she wept, she *s.* down, and looked

STOOPETH.

Isa. 46. 1. Bel boweth down, Nebo *s.* their idols

STOOPING.

Luke 24. 12. *s.* down saw linen clothes, *John* 20. 5.

STOP.

1 Kings 18. 44. get down, that the rain *s.* thee not
2 Kings 3. 19. ye shall *s.* all wells of water, 25.
2 Chron. 32. 3. he took counsel to *s.* the waters
Psal. 35. 3. *s.* the way ag. them that persecute me
107. 42. and all iniquity shall *s.* her mouth
Ezek. 39. 11. it shall *s.* the noses of the passengers
2 Cor. 11. 10. no man shall *s.* me of this boasting

STOPPED.

Gen. 8. 2. and the windows of heaven were *s.*
26. 15. the Philistines had *s.* the wells, 18.
Lev. 15. 3. or his flesh be *s.* from his issue
2 Chr. 32. 4. who *s.* all the fountains and the brook
30. Hezekiah *s.* the water-course
Neh. 4. 7. and that the breaches began to be *s.*
Ps. 63. 11. the mouth that speaketh lies shall be *s.*
Jer. 51. 32. and that the passages are *s.* and reeds
Zech. 7. 11. but they refused, and *s.* their ears
Acts 7. 57. they *s.* their ears, and ran upon him
Rom. 3. 19. that every mouth may be *s.* and be guil.
Tit. 1. 11. whose mouths must be *s.* who subvert
Heb. 11. 33. who thro' faith *s.* the mouths of lions

STOPPERS.

Ezek. 27. † 9. the wise men were thy *s.* of chinks

STOPPETH.

Job 5. 16. poor hath hope, and iniquity *s.* her mouth
Psal. 58. 4. like the deaf adder that *s.* her ear
Prov. 21. 13. whoso *s.* his ears at the cry of the poor
Isa. 33. 15. and *s.* his ears from hearing of blood

STORE.

Amos 3. 10. saith the Lord, who *s.* up violence and
robbery in their palaces

STORE.

Gen. 26. 14. Isaac had flocks and great *s.* of servants
41. 36. that food shall be for *s.* to land in famine
Lev. 25. 22. ye shall eat of the old *s.* 26. 10.
Deut. 28. 5. blessed shall be thy basket and thy *s.*
17. cursed shall be thy basket and thy *s.*
32. 34. is not this laid up in *s.* with me and sealed
1 Kings 10. 10. she gave king of spices very great *s.*
2 Kings 20. 17. fathers have laid up in *s.* to this day
1 Chron. 29. 16. all this *s.* cometh of thine hand
2 Chron. 11. 11. he put *s.* of victuals, wine in them
31. 10. and that which is left is this great *s.*
Neh. 5. 18. *s.* of all sorts of wine was prepared
Ps. 144. 13. our garners affording all manner of *s.*
Isa. 39. 6. that which thy fathers have laid up in *s.*
Nah. 2. 9. for there is none end of the *s.* and glory
1 Cor. 16. 2. let every one of you lay by him in *s.*
1 Tim. 6. 19. laying up in *s.* a good foundation
2 Pet. 3. 7. which by the same word are kept in *s.*

STORE-*cities.*

1 Kings 9. 19. *cities* of *s.* Solomon had, *2 Chr.* 8. 6.
2 Chron. 8. 4. and all the *s.-cities* which he built
16. 4. they smote all the *s.-cities* of Naphtali
17. 12. Jehoshaphat built *s.-cities* in Judah

STORE-*house.*

Mal. 3. 10. bring all the tithes into the *s.-house*
Luke 12. 24. the ravens have no *s.-house* nor barn

STORE-*houses.*

Gen. 41. 56. Joseph opened all the *s.-h.* and sold
Deut. 28. 8. command blessing on thee in thy *s.-h.*
1 Chron. 27. 25. over the *s.-house* was Jehonathan
2 Chron. 32. 28. Hezekiah made *s.-houses* also
Psal. 33. 7. he layeth up the depth in *s.-houses*
Jer. 50. 26. open her *s.-houses*, cast her up as heaps

STORK,

A kind of bird; the Hebrews *call it* Chaseda, *or* Chasidah, *which signifies pity or mercy, probably because of the tenderness it shows to its dam, whom it never forsakes, but feeds and defends, even to death. The* stork *is a bird of passage, which in winter goes into the hot countries,* Jer. 8. 7. The stork in the heaven knoweth her appointed time, and the turtle, and the crane, and the swallow, observe the time of their coming. Jerom *and the* Septuagint *sometimes render the* Hebrew *word* Chasidah *by* Herodius *the heron.*

and sometimes by pelican or kite; but interpreters are pretty well agreed, that it signifies a stork. Moses *places it among unclean birds,* Lev. 11. 19. *The* Psalmist *says,* As for the stork, the fir-trees are her house, *Psal.* 101. 17. *They for ordinary make their nests upon some high tower, or the top of an house; but in* Palestine, *where the coverings of their houses were flat, they built in the highest trees.*

The stork *has its beak and its legs long and red; it feeds upon serpents, frogs, and insects. Its plumage would be quite white, if it was not that the extremity of its wings are black, and also some small part of its head and thighs. It sits for the space of thirty days, and lays but four eggs. Formerly they would not eat the* stork, *but at present it is much esteemed for the deliciousness of its flesh. They go away in the midst of* August, *and return at* Spring. Bellonius *says, that when they go away, the* stork *that comes last to the place of rendezvous is killed upon the spot. They go away in the night to the southern countries.*

Lev. 11. 19. the *s.* thou shalt not eat, *Deut.* 14. 18.
Job 39. † 13. gavest thou feathers to the *s.?*
Psal. 104. 17. as for the *s.* the fir-trees are her house
Jer. 8. 7. the *s.* knoweth her appointed times
Zech. 5. 9. they had wings like the wings of a *s.*

STORM.

Job 21. 18. and as chaff that the *s.* carrieth away
27. 21. and as *s.* hurleth him out of his place
Psal. 55. 8. I would hasten my escape from windy *s.*
83. 15. and make them afraid with thy *s.*
107. 29. he maketh the *s.* a calm, waves are still
Isa. 4. 6. and for a covert from *s.* and from rain
25. 4. for thou hast been a refuge from the *s.*
28. 2. which as destroying *s.* shall cast down to earth
29. 6. thou shalt be visited with *s.* and tempest
Ezek. 38. 9. thou shalt ascend and come like a *s.*
Nah. 1. 3. Lord hath his way in the whirlwind and *s.*
Mark 4. 37. and there arose a great *s.* of wind
Luke 8. 23. there came down a *s.* of wind on the lake

STORMY.

Psal. 107. 25. he commandeth and raiseth the *s.* wind
148. 8. snow and vapour, *s.* wind fulfilling his word
Ezek. 13. 11. hail-stones shall fall, *s.* wind shall rend
13. I will even rend it with a *s.* wind in my fury

STORY.

2 *Chron.* 13. 22. the acts of Abijah in the *s.* of Iddo
24. 27. written in the *s.* of the book of the kings

STORIES.

Gen. 6. 16. with second and third *s.* make the ark
Ezek. 41. 16. galleries three *s.* over-against the door
42. 3. was gallery against gallery in three *s.* 6.
Amos 9. 6. it is he that buildeth his *s.* in the heaven

STOUP, *See* STOOP.

STOUT.

Job 4. 11. the *s.* lion's whelps are scattered abroad
Isa. 10. 12. I will punish the fruit of the *s.* heart
Dan. 7. 20. whose look was more *s.* than his fellows
Mal. 3. 13. your words have been *s.* against me

STOUT-*hearted.*

Psal. 76. 5. *s.-h.* are spoiled, they slept their sleep
Isa. 46. 12. hearken unto me, ye *s.-hearted*

STOUTNESS.

Isa. 9. 9. that say in the pride and *s.* of heart

STRAIGHT.

Josh. 6. 5. shall ascend every man *s.* before him, 20.
1 *Sam.* 6. 12. the kine took *s.* way to Beth-shemesh
Psal. 5. 8. make thy way *s.* before my face
Prov. 4. 25. let thine eye-lids look *s.* before thee
Eccl. 1. 15. that which is crooked cannot be made *s.*
7. 13. for who can make that *s.* he made crooked?
Isa. 40. 3. make *s.* in desert a highway for our God
4. the crooked shall be made *s.* and the rough places plain, 42. 16. | 45. 2. *Luke* 3. 5.
Jer. 31. 9. I will cause them to walk in a *s.* way
Ezek. 1. 7. and their feet were *s.* feet, they sparkled
9. they went every one *s.* forward, 12. | 10. 22.
23. under the firmament were their wings *s.*
Mat. 3. 3. prepare ye the way of the Lord, make his paths *s.* *Mark* 1. 3. *Luke* 3. 4. *John* 1. 23.
Luke 13. 13. she was made *s.* and glorified God
Acts 9. 11. arise and go into street which is called *s.*
Heb. 12. 13. and make *s.* paths for your feet

STRAIGHTWAY.

1 *Sam.* 9. 13. ye shall *s.* find him before he go up
28. 20. then Saul fell *s.* all along on the earth
Prov. 7. 22. he goeth after her *s.* as an ox goeth
Dan. 10. 17. *s.* there remained no strength in me
Mat. 3. 16. Jesus went *s.* out of water, *Mark* 1. 10.
4. 20. and they *s.* left their nets, *Mark* 1. 18.
21. 3. ye shall say, the Lord hath need of them, and *s.* he will send them hither, *Mark* 11. 3.
27. 48. *s.* one of them ran and took a spunge
Mark 5. 29. *s.* the fountain of her blood was dried up
6. 54. *s.* they knew him || *Luke* 5. 39. *s.* desireth new
Luke 14. 5. will not *s.* pull him out on sabbath-day?
John 13. 32. and God shall *s.* glorify him
Acts 5. 10. then fell she down *s.* at his feet and yielded
9. 20. and *s.* he preached Christ in the synagogues
16. 33. the jailer was baptized, he and all his *s.*
22. 29. then *s.* they departed from him
23. 30. when it was told me, I sent *s.* to thee
Jam. 1. 24. *s.* forgetteth what manner of man he was

STRAIN.

Mat. 23. 24. guides *s.* at a gnat and swallow a camel

STRAIT.

1 *Sam.* 13. 6. when Israel saw that they were in a *s.*
2 *Sam.* 24. 14. I am in a great *s.* 1 *Chron.* 21. 13.
Job 36. 16. would have removed thee out of the *s.*
Dan. 9. † 25. the street and wall built in *s.* of times
Phil. 1. 23. for I am in a *s.* betwixt two, desire

STRAITS.

Job 20. 22. in fuln. of his sufficiency he shall be in *s.*
Lam. 1. 3. persecutors overtook her between the *s.*

STRAIT.

2 *Kings* 6. 1. behold, place we dwell is too *s.* for us
Isa. 49. 20. the place is too *s.* for me, give place to me
Mat. 7. 13. enter ye in at *s.* gate, for wide is the gate
14. because *s.* is gate and way narrow, *Luke* 13. 24.

STRAITEN.

Jer. 19. 9. they that seek their lives, shall *s.* them

STRAITENED.

Job 18. 7. the steps of his strength shall be *s.*
37. 10. and the breadth of the waters is *s.*
Prov. 4. 12. when thou goest, thy steps shall not be *s.*
Ezek. 42. 6. therefore the building was *s.* more than
Mic. 2. 7. is spirit of Lord *s.?* these his doings
Luke 12. 50. how am I *s.* till it be accomplished!
2 *Cor.* 6. 12. ye are not *s.* in us, are *s.* in your bowels

STRAITENETH.

Job 12. 23. he enlargeth nations and *s.* them again

STRAITEST.

Acts 26. 5. after the most *s.* sect of our religion

STRAITLY.

Gen. 43. 7. man asked us *s.* of our state and kindred
Exod. 13. 19. for Joseph had *s.* sworn Israel
Josh. 6. 1. Jericho was *s.* shut up, none went out, and
1 *Sam.* 14. 28. thy father *s.* charged people with oath
Mat. 9. 30. he *s.* charged them, saying, see that no man know it, *Mark* 3. 12. | 5. 43. *Luke* 9. 21.
Mark 1. 43. he *s.* charged him and sent him away
Acts 4. 17. but let us *s.* threaten them not to speak
5. 28. did not we *s.* command you not to teach?

STRAITNESS.

Exod. 6. † 9. they hearkened not to Moses for *s.* of spi.
Deut. 28. 53. shalt eat flesh of thy childr. in *s.* 55. 57.
Job 36. 16. into a broad place where there is no *s.*
Isa. 42. † 16. I will make crooked things into *s.*
Jer. 19. 9. they shall eat flesh of his friend in the *s.*
Heb. 1. † 8. a sceptre of *s.* is sceptre of thy kingdom

STRAKE.

Acts 27. 17. they fearing *s.* sail, and so were driven
See STRUCK.

STRAKES.

Gen. 30. 37. Jacob pilled white *s.* in rods of hasel
Lev. 14. 37. if plague be in the walls with hollow *s.*

STRANGE.

Gen. 42. 7. but Joseph made himself *s.* unto them
Job 19. 3. not ashamed that ye make yours. *s.* to me
17. my breath is *s.* to my wife, tho' I entreated
Prov. 21. 8. the way of man is froward and *s.*
Jer. 18. † 14. will man leave snow of Lebanon? shall running waters be forsaken for the *s.* cold water?
1 *Pet.* 4. 4. wherein they think it *s.* ye run not with th.
12. think it not *s.* concerning trial, as tho' *s.* thing

STRANGE *act.*

Isa. 28. 21. that ye may bring to pass his act, his *s.* act

STRANGE *apparel.*

Zeph. 1. 8. punish such are clothed with *s. apparel*
See CHILDREN.

STRANGE *cities.*

Acts 26. 11. I persecuted them even to *s. cities*

STRANGE *country.*

Heb. 11. 9. he sojourned as in a *s. country*

STRANGE *doctrines.*

Heb. 13. 9. be not carried about with *s. doctrines*

STRANGE *fire.*

Lev. 10. 1. Nadab and Abihu offered *s. fire* before the Lord, and they died, *Num.* 3. 4. | 26. 61.

STRANGE *flesh.*

Jude 7. as Sodom and Gomorrah, going after *s. flesh*
See GOD, GODS.

STRANGE *incense.*

Exod. 30. 9. ye shall offer no *s. incense* thereon

STRANGE *land.*

Exod. 2. 22. have been a stranger in a *s. land*, 18. 3.
Psal. 137. 4. how shall we sing Lord's song in a *s. l.*
Acts 7. 6. that his seed should sojourn in a *s. land*

STRANGE *language.*

Psal. 114. 1. Israel went from a people of *s. l.*

STRANGE *nation.*

Exod. 21. 8. to sell her to a *s. n.* he hath no power

STRANGE *punishment.*

Job 31. 3. a *s. punishm.* to the workers of iniquity

STRANGE *lips.*

Isa. 17. 10. and thou shalt set it with *s. lips*

STRANGE *speech.*

Ezek. 3. 5. thou art not sent to a people of *s. s.* 6.

STRANGE *thing.*

Hos. 8. 12. but they were counted as a *s. thing*
1 *Pet.* 4. 12. as tho' some *s. thing* happened to you

STRANGE *things.*

Luke 5. 26. saying, we have seen *s. things* to-day
Acts 17. 20. thou bringest certain *s. things* to our ears

STRANGE *vanities.*

Jer. 8. 19. why provoked me to anger with *s. v.?*

STRANGE *vine.*

Jer. 2. 21. how turned into degener. plant of a *s. vine*

STRANGE *waters.*

2 *Kings* 19. 24. I have digged and drunk *s. waters*

STRANGE *wives.*

1 *Kings* 11. 8. and likewise did he for all his *s. wives*
Ezra 10. 2. we have taken *s. wives*, 10, 14, 17, 44.
11. and separate yourselves from the *s. wives*
18. sons of priests were found to have taken *s. w.*
Neh. 13. 27. to transgress ag. God, in marrying *s. w.*

STRANGE *woman.*

Judg. 11. 2. for thou art the son of a *s. woman*
Prov. 2. 16. to deliver thee from the *s. woman*
5. 3. the lips of a *s. woman* drop as an honey-comb
20. why wilt thou be ravished with a *s. woman*
6. 24. to keep thee from flattery of *s. woman*, 7. 5.
20. 16. take a pledge of him for a *s. woman*, 27. 13.
23. 27. and a *s. woman* is a narrow pit

STRANGE *women.*

1 *Kings* 11. 1. king Solomon loved many *s. women*
Prov. 22. 14. the mouth of *s. women* is a deep pit
23. 33. thine eyes shall behold *s. women*, heart utter

STRANGE *work.*

Isa. 28. 21. that he may do his work, his *s. work*

STRANGER.

[1] *One that is in a strange land, being at a distance from the place of his nativity.* Gen. 23. 4. I am a stranger with you. [2] *One that is not a Jew, but of some other nation,* Isa. 14. 1. The strangers shall be joined with them; *that is, many of the Gentiles.* [3] *Any one that was not of* Aaron's *seed, notwithstanding he were an* Israelite. *Num.* 3. 10. The stranger that cometh nigh shall be put to death. *See* Num. 16. 40. | 18. 4. [4] *One that uses this world as if he used it not, who does not think himself at home while in this world, but has his mind and eye fixed on his country which is above.* Psal. 39. 12. I am a stranger with thee, and a sojourner, as all my fathers were. *Heb.* 11. 13. They confessed that they were strangers and pilgrims on earth. [5] *Such as were without all title to, or interest in, either the outward privileges, or saving blessings, of the covenant of grace.* Eph. 2. 12. At that time ye were strangers from the covenant of promise, *namely, during your heathenism.* [6] *One who is not of the king's stock and family.* Mat. 17. 25, 26. Of whom do the kings of the earth take custom or tribute? of their own children, or of strangers? [7] *One who being made a captive, has lost his former liberty and dignity, which he enjoyed in his own country.* Obad. 12. Thou shouldest not have looked on the day of thy brother, in the day that he became a stranger. [8] *A woman that is not a man's own wife.* Prov. 5. 20. Why wilt thou embrace the bosom of a stranger? [9] *Profane or unclean persons.* Joel 3. 17. There shall no strangers pass through her any more. *None of the enemies of the church shall invade and subdue it any more, nor profane persons mingle themselves with it, so as to corrupt her doctrine or worship.* [10] *Persons of a perfidious and barbarous disposition, who, though of the same nation, yet carry themselves as if they were void of all piety and humanity. Thus* David *calls the* Ziphites, *though* Israelites, *strangers,* Psal. 54. 3. [11] *Persecuted, or banished Christians.* Heb. 13. 2. Be not forgetful to entertain strangers. [12] *False teachers, such as are strangers to sound doctrine.* John 10. 5. And a stranger will they not follow. *As to the two sorts of* strangers *among the* Jews, *namely,* Advena justitiæ, *and* Advena portæ, *See* PROSELYTE.

Gen. 15. 13. know that thy seed shall be a *s.* in a land
17. 8. give land wherein thou art a *s.* 28. 4. | 37. 1.
12. or that is bought with money of any *s.*
27. bought with money of the *s.* were circumcised
23. 4. I am a *s.* with you, *Psal.* 39. 12. | 119. 19.
Exod. 2. 22. I have been a *s.* in a strange land
12. 19. shall be cut off, whether a *s.* or born in the land, *Lev.* 16. 29. | 17. 15. *Num.* 15. 30.
43. there shall no *s.* eat thereof, 29. 33.
48. when a *s.* will keep the passover, *Num.* 9. 14.
49. one law shall be to him that is home-born and the *s.* *Lev.* 24. 22. *Num.* 9. 14. | 15. 15, 16, 29.
18. † 3. the name of the one was a *s.* there
20. 10. nor *s.* that is within thy gates, *Deut.* 5. 14.
22. 21. thou shalt not vex or oppress a *s.*
23. 9. ye know heart of a *s.* seeing ye were strangers
12. shalt rest, that the *s.* may be refreshed
30. 33. whosoever putteth any of it upon a *s.*
Lev. 17. 12. neither shall any *s.* among you eat blood
19. 10. thou shalt leave them for *s.* 23. 22. | 25. 6.
33. if a *s.* sojourn in the land ye shall not vex him
34. the *s.* be as one born among you, *Num.* 15. 15
22. 10. there shall no *s.* eat of the holy thing, 13.
12. if she be married to a *s.* she may not eat
25. neither from a *s.* hand shall ye offer the bread
24. 16. as well *s.* when blasphemeth put to death
25. 35. yea, tho' he be a *s.* thou shalt relieve him
47. if a *s.* wax rich by thee, and thy poor brother sell himself to the *s.* or his family
Num. 1. 51. Levites set up tabernacle, the *s.* that cometh nigh shall be put to death, 3. 10, 38.
15. 14. and if a *s.* sojourn and will offer an offering
16. 40. that no *s.* come near to offer incense bef. L.
18. 4. and a *s.* shall not come nigh unto you
7. the *s.* that cometh nigh shall be put to death
19. 10. it shall be to Israel and *s.* a statute for ever
35. 15. six cities of refuge for *s.* *Josh.* 20. 9.
Deut. 1. 16. hear and judge righteously betw. the *s.*
10. 18. the Lord loveth the *s.* in giving him food
19. love the *s.* for ye were strangers in Egypt
14. 21. shalt give that which dieth of itself to *s.*
17. 15. not set a *s.* over thee who is not thy brother
23. 7. because thou wast a *s.* in his land
20. unto a *s.* thou mayest lend upon usury
25. 5. the wife shall not marry without to a *s.*
26. 11. thou shalt rejoice, thou, and the *s.* among you
28. 43. the *s.* shall get up above thee very high
29. 11. and thy *s.* to enter into covenant with God
22. *s.* shall say, why hath the Lord done thus
31. 12. gather thy *s.* that he may hear and learn
Josh. 8. 33. the *s.* stood to hear words of law read
Judg. 19. 12. we will not turn aside to city of a *s.*
Ruth 2. 10. why have I found grace, seeing I am a *s.?*
2 *Sam.* 1. 13. I am the son of a *s.* an Amalekite
15. 19. for thou art a *s.* and also an exile
1 *Kings* 3. 18. there was no *s.* with us in the house
8. 41. moreover concerning a *s.* 2 *Chron.* 6. 32.
43. do according to all the *s.* calleth, 2 *Chr.* 6. 33.
Job 15. 19. and no *s.* passed among them
19. 15. and my maids count me for a *s.*
† 27. whom mine eyes shall behold, and not a *s.*
31. 32. the *s.* did not lodge in street, but I opened
Psal. 69. 8. I am become a *s.* to my brethren
94. 6. they slay the widow and the *s.* and murder
109. 11. and let the *s.* spoil his labour
137. † 4. how shall sing Lord's song in land of *s.?*
Prov. 2. 16. to deliver thee even from the *s.*
5. 10. and thy labours be in the house of a *s.*
20. why wilt thou embrace the bosom of a *s.?*
6. 1. if thou hast stricken thine hand with a *s.*
7. 5. they may keep thee from the *s.* who flatters
11. 15. he that is surety for a *s.* shall smart for it
14. 10. and a *s.* doth not intermeddle with his joy
20. 16. take his garm. that is surety for a *s.* 27. 13.
27. 2. let a *s.* praise thee, and not thine own lips
Eccl. 6. 2. not power to eat thereof, but a *s.* eateth it
Isa. 56. 3. neither let the son of a *s.* speak, saying
6. the sons of the *s.* that join themselves to Lord
62. 8. the sons of the *s.* shall not drink thy wine
Jer. 14. 8. why shouldest thou be as a *s.* in the land
Ezek. 14. 7. every *s.* that setteth up his idols
22. 7. they dealt by oppression with the *s.* 29.
44. † 7. brought into my sanctuary children of a *s.*

Ezek. 44. 9. no *s.* uncircumc. shall enter my sanct
47. 23. that in what tribe the *s.* sojourneth
Obad. 12. in the day that he became a *s.*
Mal. 3. 5. and that turn aside the *s.* from his right
Mat. 25. 35. I was a *s.* and ye took me in, 43.
38. when saw we thee a *s.* and took thee in? 44.
Luke 17. 18. not found that returned, save this *s.*
24. 18. art thou only a *s.* in Jerus. and not known
John 10. 5. *s.* will they not follow, but flee from him
Acts 7. 29. Moses was a *s.* in the land of Midian
See FATHERLESS.

STRANGERS.

Gen. 31. 15. are we not counted of him *s.?*
36. 7. the land wherein they were *s.* *Exod.* 6. 4.
Exod. 22. 21. for ye were *s.* in the land of Egypt,
23. 9. *Lev.* 19. 34. | 25. 23. *Deut.* 10. 19.
Lev. 17. 8. *s.* that offer an oblation, 22. 18.
10. whatsoever of the *s.* that eateth any blood
13. the *s.* that hunteth shall pour out the blood
20. 2. of the *s.* that give his seed to Molech
25. 45. of the children of the *s.* shall ye buy
Deut. 24. 14. thou shalt not oppress a serv. tho' of *s.*
31. 16. will go a whoring after gods of the *s.* of land
Josh. 8. 35. the *s.* that were conversant among them
Judg. 10. † 16. they put away the gods of *s.*
2 *Sam.* 22. 45. *s.* shall submit themselves unto me
46. *s.* shall fade away and be afraid, *Ps.* 18. 44,45.
1 *Chr.* 16. 19. when ye were *s.* in it, *Psal.* 105. 12.
22. 2. David commanded to gather the *s.* in Israel
29. 15. for we are *s.* as were all our fathers
2 *Chron.* 2. 17. and Solomon numbered all the *s.*
15. 9. and Asa gathered all Judah and the *s.*
30. 25. the *s.* of Israel and all Judah rejoiced
Neh. 9. 2. seed of Isr. separated thems. from all *s.*
13. 30. thus cleansed I them from all *s.* and appoin.
Ps. 54. 3. for *s.* are risen up ag. me, and oppressors
146. 9. the Lord preserveth the *s.* he relieveth
Prov. 5. 10. lest *s.* be filled with thy wealth
17. let them be only thine own, not *s.* with thee
Isa. 1. 7. your cities burnt, your land *s.* devour it in
your presence, it is desolate, as overthrown by *s.*
2. 6. they please themselves in the children of *s.*
5. 17. the waste places of the fat ones shall *s.* eat
14. 1. and the *s.* shall be joined with them
25. 2. thou hast made a palace of *s.* to be no city
5. thou shalt bring down the noise of *s.*
29. 5. multitude of thy *s.* shall be like small dust
60. 10. the sons of *s.* shall build up thy walls
61. 5. and *s.* shall stand and feed your flocks
Jer. 2. 25. I have loved *s.* and after them will I go
3. 13. thou hast scattered thy ways to the *s.*
5. 19. so shall ye serve *s.* in a land that is not yours
30. 8. *s.* shall no more serve themselves of him
35. 7. that ye may live in the land where ye be *s.*
51. 51. for *s.* are come into the sanctuaries of Lord
Lam. 5. 2. our inherit. is turned to *s.* houses to aliens
Ezek. 7. 21. I will give it into hand of *s.* for a prey
11. 9. I will deliver you into the hands of *s.*
16. 32. a wife who taketh *s.* instead of her husband
28. 7. behold therefore I will bring *s.* upon thee
10. thou shalt die the deaths by the hand of *s.*
30. 12. I will make the land waste by the hand of *s.*
31. 12. *s.* have cut him off, and have left him
44. 7. in that ye have brought into my sanctuary *s.*
47. 22. for an inheritance to you and to the *s.*
Hos. 7. 9. *s.* have devoured his strength, know. it not
8. 7. if so be it yield, the *s.* shall swallow it up
Joel 3. 17. there shall no *s.* pass thro' her any more
Obad. 11. in the day that *s.* carried away captive
Mat. 17. 25. of whom take tribute? of childr. or of *s.*
26. Peter saith to him, of *s.* || 27. 7. to bury *s.* in
John 10. 5. for they know not the voice of *s.*
Acts 2. 10. and *s.* of Rome, Jews and proselytes
13. 17. when they dwelt as *s.* in the land of Egypt
Eph. 2. 12. were *s.* from the covenants of promise
19. therefore ye are no more *s.* but fellow-citizens
1 *Tim.* 5. 10. if she have lodged *s.* if she have washed
Heb. 11. 13. confessed they were *s.* and pil. on earth
13. 2. be not forgetful to entertain *s.* for some
1 *Pet.* 1. 1. to the *s.* scattered thro' Pontus, Galatia
2. 11. I beseech you as *s.* pilgrims, abst. from lusts
3 *John* 5. dost faithfully, whatsoever thou dost to *s.*

STRANGELY.

Deut. 32. 27. lest adversaries should behave them. *s.*

STRANGLED.

Nah. 2. 12. the lion did tear and *s.* for his lionesses
Acts 15. 20. that they abstain from things *s.* 29. | [21. 25.

STRANGLING.

Job 7. 15. so that my soul chooseth *s.* and death

STRAW.

Gen. 24. 25. we have both *s.* and provender enough
32. he gave *s.* and provender for the camels
Exod. 5. 7. ye shall no more give *s.* 10, 16, 18.
11. go ye, get you *s.* where you can find it
Judg. 19. 19. yet there is both *s.* and provender
1 *Kings* 4. 28. brought barley also, and *s.* for horses
Job 41. 27. esteemeth iron as *s.* brass as rotten wood
Isa. 11. 7. and the lion shall eat *s.* like the ox, 65. 25.
25. 10. Moab shall be trodden down, even as *s.*

STRAWED.

Exod. 32. 20. he ground the calf, *s.* it on the water
2 *Chron.* 34. 4. he *s.* upon the graves of them that
Mat. 21. 8. cut down branches and *s.* th. *Mark* 11. 8.
25. 24. and gathering where thou hast not *s.*
26. and gather where I have not *s.*

STREAM.

Num. 21. 15. what he did at the *s.* of the brooks
Job 6. 15. and as the *s.* of brooks they pass away
Psal. 124. 4. then the *s.* had gone over our soul
Isa. 27. 12. the Ld. shall beat off to the *s.* of Egypt
30. 28. his breath as an overflowing *s.* shall reach
33. like a *s.* of brimstone, doth kindle it
57. 6. among smooth stones of the *s.* is thy portion
66. 12. the glory of the Gentiles like a flowing *s.*
Dan. 7. 10. fiery *s.* issued and came forth before him
Amos 5. 24. and righteousness as a mighty *s.*
Luke 6. 48. the *s.* beat vehemently on that house, 49.

STREAMS.

Exod. 7. 19. stretch out thine hand on their *s.* 8. 5.
Psal. 46. 4. *s.* whereof shall make glad city of G.
78. 16. he brought *s.* also out of rock, and waters
20. the waters gushed out, the *s.* overflowed

Psal. 126. 4. turn ag. our captiv. as *s.* in the south
Cant. 4. 15. well of living waters, *s.* from Lebanon
Isa. 11. 15. the Lord shall smite it in the seven *s.*
30. 25. on every high hill shall be *s.* of waters
33. 21. will be to us a place of broad rivers and *s.*
34. 9. the *s.* thereof shall be turned into pitch
35. 6. waters break out and *s.* in the desert

STREET.

Gen. 19. 2. but we will abide in the *s.* all night
Deut. 13. 16. thou shalt gather all the spoil into *s.*
Josh. 2. 19. any go out of thy house into the *s.*
Judg. 19. 15. he sat down in a *s.* of the city, 17.
20. the old man said, only lodge not in the *s.*
2 *Sam.* 21. 12. had stolen from the *s.* of Beth-shan
22. 43. I did stamp them as the mire of the *s.*
2 *Chr.* 29. 4. and gathered them in the east *s.* 32. 6.
Ezra 10. 9. all the people sat in *s.* of house of God
Neh. 8. 1. the people gathered as one man into the *s.*
3. he read therein before the *s.* that was before
16. so people made booths in the *s.* of water-gate
Esth. 6. 9. bring him on horseback thro' the *s.* 11.
Job 18. 17. and he shall have no name in the *s.*
29. 7. when I prepared my seat in the *s.*
31. 32. stranger did not lodge in the *s.* but I open.
Prov. 7. 8. passing thro' the *s.* near her corner
Isa. 42. 2. his voice not heard in *s.* *Mat.* 12. 19.
51. 23. and thou hast laid thy body as the *s.*
59. 14. for truth is fallen in the *s.* and equity
Jer. 37. 21. give him daily bread out of bakers' *s.*
Lam. 2. 19. that faint for hunger in top of every *s.*
4. 1. stones are poured out in the top of every *s.*
Ezek. 16. 24. made thee an high place in every *s.* 31.
Dan. 9. 25. the *s.* shall be built again and the wall
Acts 9. 11. and go into the *s.* called Straight
12. 10. Peter went on, and passed through one *s.*
Rev. 11. 8. their dead bodies shall lie in the *s.* of city
21. 21. and the *s.* of the city was pure gold
22. 2. in the midst of the *s.* was the tree of life

STREETS.

Num. 22. † 39. and they came to a city of *s.*
2 *Sam.* 1. 20. publish it not in the *s.* of Askelon
1 *Kings* 20. 34. thou shalt make *s.* in Damascus
Psal. 18. 42. I did cast them out as dirt in the *s.*
55. 11. deceit and guile depart not from her *s.*
144. 13. sheep may bring forth ten thous. in our *s.*
14. that there be no complaining in our *s.*
Prov. 1. 20. wisdom uttereth her voice in the *s.*
5. 16. and rivers of waters in the *s.*
7. 12. now is she without, now in the *s.* and lieth
22. 13. there is a lion without, I shall be slain in *s.*
26. 13. the slothful man saith, a lion is in the *s.*
Eccl. 12. 4. and the doors shall be shut in the *s.*
5. and the mourners go about the *s.*
Cant. 3. 2. I will go about the city in the *s.*
Isa. 5. 25. and their carcases were torn in midst of *s.*
10. 6. to tread them down like the mire of the *s.*
15. 3. in their *s.* they shall gird themselves
24. 11. there is a crying for wine in the *s.*
51. 20. thy sons lie at the head of all the *s.*
Jer. 5. 1. run ye to and fro thro' the *s.* of Jerusalem
7. 17. seest thou not what they do in *s.* of Jerusalem
34. cause to cease from the *s.* of Jerusalem mirth
9. 21. death come, cut off young men from the *s.*
11. 6. proclaim these words in the *s.* of Jerusalem
13. according to the number of the *s.* of Jerusalem
14. 16. people shall be cast out in the *s.* of Jerusalem
33. 10. mirth shall be heard in the *s.* of Jerusalem
44. 6. my anger was kindled in the *s.* of Jerusalem
9. wickedness they have committed in *s.* of Jerus.
21. the incense that ye burn in *s.* of Jerusalem
48. 38. there shall be lamentation in the *s.* of Moab
49. 26. her young men shall fall in her *s.* 50. 30.
51. 4. and they that are thrust through in her *s.*
Lam. 2. 11. sucklings swoon in the *s.* of the city, 12.
21. the young and the old lie on ground in the *s.*
4. 5. they that did feed delicately, are desolate in *s.*
8. her Nazarites are not known in the *s.*
14. they have wandered as blind men in the *s.*
18. they hunt our steps that we cannot go in our *s.*
Ezek. 7. 19. they shall cast their silver in the *s.*
11. 6. ye have filled the *s.* thereof with the slain
26. 11. with the hoofs of his horses tread down thy *s.*
28. 23. I will send pestilence and blood into her *s.*
Amos 5. 16. wailing be in all *s.* and say, alas, alas!
Mic. 7. 10. shall be trodden down as mire of the *s.*
Nah. 2. 4. chariots shall rage in the *s.* shall justle
3. 10. were dashed in pieces at the top of the *s.*
Zeph. 3. 6. I made their *s.* waste and none passeth
Zech. 8. 4. old men and old women shall dwell in *s.*
5. the *s.* of the city shall be full of boys and girls
9. 3. Tyrus heaped up fine gold as mire in the *s.*
10. 5. who tread down their enemies in the *s.*
Mat. 6. 2. do not sound a trumpet before thee in *s.*
5. for they love to pray standing in corners of *s.*
Mark 6. 56. they laid the sick in the *s.* *Acts* 5. 15.
Luke 10. 10. go out into the *s.* of the same, and say
13. 26. shall begin to say, thou hast taught in our *s.*
14. 21. go out quickly into *s.* and lanes of the city

STRENGTH.

Gen. 4. 12. ground shall not henceforth yield her *s.*
Exod. 13. 3. by *s.* the Lord brought you out, 14. 16.
Num. 23. 22. he hath the *s.* of an unicorn, 24. 8.
Judg. 5. 21. O my soul, thou hast trodden down *s.*
1 *Sam.* 2. 4. they that stumbled are girt with *s.*
9. wicked be silent, for by *s.* shall no man prevail
10. he shall give *s.* unto his king, and exalt horn
15. 29. the *s.* of Israel will not lie, nor repent
28. 22. and eat, that thou mayest have *s.* in going on
2 *Sam.* 22. 40. thou hast girded me with *s.* to battle,
hast subdued them under me, *Psal.* 18. 32, 39.
1 *Kings* 7. † 21. he set up pillars in the temple, he
called the left pillar, in it is *s.* 2 *Chron.* 3. † 17.
2 *Kings* 2. † 16. there be with us fifty sons of *s.*
18. 20. I have counsel and *s.* for war, *Isa.* 36. 5.
19. 3. and there is no *s.* to bring forth, *Isa.* 37. 3.
1 *Chron.* 16. 27. *s.* and gladness are in his place
28. give to Lord glory and *s.* *Psal.* 29. 1. | 96. 7.
26. 8. they, their sons, and brethren, able men for *s.*
29. 12. in thine hand it is to give *s.* unto all
† 14. that we should obtain *s.* to offer willingly
2 *Chr.* 2. † 6. hath obtained *s.* to build him an house
13. 20. neither did Jeroboam recover *s.* again

2 *Chr.* 30. † 21. singing with instruments of *s.* to Lord
Ezra 4. † 13. thou shalt endamage the *s.* of kings
Neh. 4. 10. *s.* of the bearers of burdens is decayed
Job 9. † 13. the helpers of *s.* do stoop under him
19. if I speak of *s.* lo, he is strong, if of judgment
12. 13. with him is wisdom and *s.* hath counsel, 16.
21. and he weakeneth the *s.* of the mighty
17. † 9. he that hath clean hands, shall add *s.*
18. 13. it shall devour the *s.* of his skin
22. † 25. and thou shalt have silver of *s.*
23. 6. no, but he would put *s.* in me
30. 2. whereto might *s.* of their hands profit me
† 21. with *s.* of thy hand thou opposest ag. me
31. † 39. if eaten the *s.* thereof without money
36. 19. he will not esteem all the forces of *s.*
39. 19. hast thou given the horse *s.?*
41. 22. in his neck remaineth *s.* sorrow turned to joy
Psal. 8. 2. out of mouth of babes hast ordained *s.*
20. 6. with the saving *s.* of his right hand
27. 1. Lord is the *s.* of my life, of whom be afraid
28. 8. and he is the saving *s.* of his anointed
29. 11. the Lord will give *s.* to his people
30. † 7. thou hast settled *s.* for my mountain
31. † 2. be thou to me for a rock of *s.* a defence
33. 16. the mighty is not delivered by much *s.*
39. 13. O spare me, that I may recover *s.* before I go
46. 1. God is our refuge and *s.* a help, 81. 1.
60. 7. Ephraim is the *s.* of mine head, 108. 8.
† 9. who will bring me into the city of *s.?*
62. † 11. I heard this that *s.* belongeth unto God
68. 34. ascribe ye *s.* unto God, his *s.* is in clouds
35. God of Israel is he that giveth *s.* and power
73. 26. but God is the *s.* of my heart and portion
74. † 15. thou driedst up rivers of *s.*
81. 1. sing aloud unto God our *s.* make a noise
84. 5. blessed is the man whose *s.* is in thee
7. they go from *s.* to *s.* every one of them in Zion
90. 10. and if by reason of *s.* they be fourscore
93. 1. the Lord is clothed with majesty and *s.*
95. 4. the *s.* of the hills is his also
96. 6. *s.* and beauty are in his sanctuary
99. 4. the king's *s.* also loveth judgment
138. 3. thou strengthenedst me with *s.* in my soul
140. 7. O God the Lord, the *s.* of my salvation
Prov. 8. 14. I have *s.* || 10. 29. way of Lord is *s.*
14. 4. but much increase is by the *s.* of ox
21. 22. a wise man casteth down the *s.* thereof
24. 5. yea, a man of knowledge increaseth *s.*
31. 17. she girdeth her loins with *s.* strengtheneth
25. *s.* and honour are her clothing, she shall rej.
Eccl. 9. 16. then I said, wisdom is better than *s.*
10. 10. if iron be blunt, then must put to more *s.*
17. princes eat for *s.* and not for drunkenness
Isa. 5. 22. and men of *s.* to mingle strong drink
10. 13. by the *s.* of my hand I have done it
23. 4. the sea hath spoken, even the *s.* of the sea
25. 4. thou hast been a *s.* to the poor, a *s.* to the
needy in his distress, a refuge from the storm
26. 4. in the Lord JEHOVAH is everlasting *s.*
28. 6. for *s.* to them that turn the battle to gate
30. 3. the *s.* of Pharaoh shall be your shame
33. 6. wisdom shall be stability and *s.* of salvation
40. 9. O Jerusalem, lift up thy voice with *s.*
29. to them that have no might, he increaseth *s.*
42. 25. he hath poured on him the *s.* of battle
44. 12. he worketh it with the *s.* of his arms
45. 24. in the Lord have I righteousness and *s.*
51. 9. awake, awake, put on *s.* O arm of Lord
Jer. 20. 5. moreover I will deliver all *s.* of this city
51. 53. tho' she should fortify the height of her *s.*
Lam. 1. 6. they are gone without *s.* before pursuer
Ezek. 30. 15. will pour my fury on sin, *s.* of Egypt
18. the pomp of her *s.* shall cease in her, 33. 28.
Dan. 2. 37. God hath given thee power, *s.* glory
41. but there shall be in it of the *s.* of the iron
3. † 20. he commanded the mighty of *s.* to bind
11. 15. neither shall there be any *s.* to withstand
17. to enter with the *s.* of his whole kingdom
31. they shall pollute the sanctuary of *s.*
Joel 3. 16. the Lord the *s.* of the children of Israel
Amos 6. 13. have we not taken horns by our own *s.?*
Nah. 1. † 7. the Lord is *s.* in the day of trouble
3. 9. Ethiopia and Egypt were her *s.* Put and Lubim
11. thou also shalt seek *s.* because of the enemy
Hag. 2. 22. I will destroy *s.* of kingdoms of heathen
Luke 1. 51. he hath shewed *s.* with his arm
Acts 3. 7. his feet and ancle bones received *s.*
Rom. 5. 6. when yet without *s.* Christ died
1 *Cor.* 15. 56. sting is sin, the *s.* of sin is the law
2 *Cor.* 1. 8. we were pressed out of measure, above *s.*
Heb. 11. 11. Sara herself received *s.* to conceive seed
Rev. 3. 8. for thou hast a little *s.* hast kept my word
5. 12. worthy is Lamb to receive *s.* and honour
12. 10. a voice saying, now is come salvation and *s.*
17. 13. these shall give their power and *s.* to beast

His STRENGTH.

Exod. 14. 27. and the sea returned to *his s.*
Deut. 21. 17. he is the beginning of *his s.*
Judg. 8. 21. rise thou, for as the man is, so is *his s.*
16. 5. entice him, see wherein *his* great *s.* lieth
9. *his s.* was not known || 19. *his s.* went from him
2 *Kings* 9. 24. Jehu drew a bow with *his* full *s.*
1 *Chr.* 16. 11. seek the Lord and *his s.* *Psal.* 105. 4.
Job 18. 7. the steps of *his s.* shall be straitened
12. *h. s.* shall be hunger-bitten, destruction ready
13. even first-born of death shall devour *his s.*
21. 23. one dieth in *his* full *s.* being wholly at ease
37. 6. he saith to the great rain of *his s.*
39. 11. wilt thou trust him because *his s.* is great?
21. rejoiceth in *his s.* || 40. 16. *his s.* is in his loins
Psal. 33. 17. nor shall he deliver any by *his* great *s.*
52. 7. this is the man that made not God *his s.*
59. 9. because of *his s.* will I wait upon thee
65. 6. who by *his s.* setteth fast the mountains
68. 34. ascribe *s.* to God, *his s.* is in the clouds
78. 4. shewing to the generation to come *his s.*
61. delivered *his s.* into captivity and his glory
Isa. 31. † 9. he shall pass over to *his s.* for fear
44. 12. he is hungry, and *his s.* faileth
62. 8. the Lord hath sworn by the arm of *his s*
63. 1. travelling in the greatness of *his s.?*
Dan. 11. 2. by *his s.* shall stir up all against Grecia

Hos. 7. 9. strangers devoured his s. he knoweth not
12. 3. and by his s. he had power with God
Rev. 1. 16. his countenance was as the sun in his s.

In STRENGTH.

Gen. 49. 24. but his bow abode in s. and the arms
1 Kings 19. 8. went in the s. of that meat forty days
Job 3. † 17. and there the wearied in s. be at rest
9. 4. he is wise in heart, and mighty in s. 36. 5.
Psal. 71. 16. I will go in the s. of the Lord God
103. 20. bless Lord, ye his angels that excel in s.
147. 10. he delighteth not in the s. of an horse
Prov. 24. † 5. a wise man is in s. yea increaseth st.
Isa. 8. † 11. Lord spake thus to me in s. of hand
30. 2. to strengthen themselves in s. of Pharaoh
Mic. 5. 4. and he shall feed in the s. of the Lord
Acts 9. 22. but Saul increased the more in s.

My STRENGTH.

Gen. 49. 3. Reuben, thou art the beginning of my s.
Exod. 15. 2. Lord is my s. and song, 2 Sam. 22. 33.
Psal. 18. 2. | 28. 7. | 118. 14. Isa. 12. 2.
Josh. 14. 11. as my s. was then, even so is my s. now
Judg. 16. 17. if I be shaven, my s. will go from me
Job 6. 11. what is my s. that I should hope?
12. is my s. of stones? or is my flesh of brass?
Psal. 18. 1. I will love thee, O Lord, my s.
19. 14. O Ld. my s. 22. 19. || 22. 15. my s. is dried up
31. 4. pull me out of the net, for thou art my s.
10. my s. fails bec. of my iniquity, 38. 10. | 71. 9.
43. 2. thou art the God of my s. why go I mourning?
59. 17. to thee, O my s. will I sing; God is defence
62. 7. art rock of my s. || 102. 23. he weakened my s.
139. † 15. my s. was not hid from thee, when I was
144. 1. blessed be L. my s. who teacheth my hands
Isa. 27. 5. let him take hold of my s. to make peace
49. 4. I have spent my s. for nought, and in vain
5. yet I shall be glorious, my God shall be my s.
Jer. 16. 19. O Lord my s. || Hab. 3. 19. God is my s.
Lam. 1. 14. they are wreathed, he made my s. to fall
3. 18. I said my s. and hope is perished from Lord
Zech. 12. 5. shall be my s. in Lord of hosts their God
2 Cor. 12. 9. for my s. is made perfect in weakness
See No.

Their STRENGTH.

Josh. 11. 13. as for cities that stood still in their s.
Psal. 37. 39. he is their s. in the time of trouble
73. 4. are no bands in their death, their s. is firm
78. 51. he smote the chief of their s. 105. 36.
89. 17. for thou art the glory of their s.
90. 10. yet is their s. labour and sorrow
Prov. 20. 29. the glory of young men is their s.
Isa. 30. 7. I have cried, their s. is to sit still
40. 31. they that wait on Lord shall renew their s.
41. 1. and let the people renew their s.
63. 6. I will bring down their s. to the earth
Ezek. 24. 25. when I take from them their s.
Joel. 2. 22. the fig-tree and vine do yield their s.

Thy STRENGTH.

Exod. 15. 13. thou hast guided them in thy s.
Deut. 33. 25. and as thy days, so shall thy s. be
Judg. 16. 6. tell me wherein thy s. lieth, 15.
2 Chron. 6. 41. thou and ark of thy s. Psal. 132. 8.
Psal. 21. 1. the king shall joy in thy s. O Lord
13. be thou exalted, O Lord, in thine own s.
54. 1. save me by thy name, judge me by thy s.
68. 28. thy God hath commanded thy s.
71. 18. until I have shewed thy s. to this generation
74. 13. thou didst divide the sea by thy s.
77. 14. thou hast declared thy s. among the people
80. 2. stir up thy s. and come and save us
86. 16. O turn to me, give thy s. to thy servant
110. 2. Lord shall send rod of thy s. out of Zion
Prov. 5. † 10. lest strangers be filled with thy s.
24. 10. if faint in day of adversity, thy s. is small
31. 3. give not thy s. unto women, nor thy ways
Isa. 17. 10. hast not been mindful of rock of thy s.
52. 1. awake, awake, put on thy s. O Zion
63. 15. where is thy zeal and thy s. the sounding
Amos 3. 11. he shall bring down thy s. from thee
Mark 12. 30. thou shalt love the Lord thy God with
all thy heart and with all thy s. 33. Luke 10. 27.

Your STRENGTH.

Lev. 26. 20. and your s. shall be spent in vain
Neh. 8. 10. for the joy of the Lord is your s.
Isa. 23. 14. howl, ye ships, your s. is laid waste
30. 15. in quietness and confidence will be your s.
Ezek. 24. 21. my sanctuary, excellency of your s.

STRENGTHEN.

Lev. 25. † 35. if thy brother be poor s. him
Deut. 3. 28. but charge Joshua, encourage and s. him
Judg. 16. 28. s. me, I pray thee, only this once
19. † 5. s. thine heart with a morsel of bread
1 Kings 20. 22. go s. thys. mark and see what dost
Ezra 6. 22. to s. their hands in the work of house
Neh. 6. 9. now therefore, O God, s. my hands
Job 16. 5. but I would s. you with my mouth
Psal. 20. 2. Lord send thee help, s. thee out of Zion
27. 14. wait on Lord, he shall s. thy heart, 31. 24.
41. 3. Lord will s. him on the bed of languishing
68. 28. s. that which thou hast wrought for us
89. 21. be established, mine arm also shall s. him
119. 28. s. thou me according to thy word
Isa. 22. 21. and I will s. him with thy girdle
30. 2. to s. themselves in the strength of Pharaoh
33. 23. they could not well s. their mast
35. 3. s. ye the weak hands || 41. 10. I will s. thee
54. 2. lengthen thy cords, and s. thy stakes
Jer. 4. † 6. set up the standard, s. stay not
23. 14. they s. also the hands of evil doers
Ezek. 7. 13. nor shall any s. himself in iniquity
16. 49. neither did she s. hand of poor and needy
30. 24. I will s. arms of the king of Babylon, 25.
34. 16. and I will s. that which was sick
Dan. 11. 1. even I stood to confirm and to s. him
Amos 2. 14. and the strong shall not s. his force
Zech. 10. 6. and I will s. the house of Judah
12. I will s. them in the Lord, they shall walk
Luke 22. 32. when thou art converted, s. brethren
1 Pet. 5. 10. God make you perfect, stablish, s. you
Rev. 3. 2. be watchful and s. things which remain

STRENGTHENED, Actively, Passively.

Gen. 48. 2. Israel s. himself, and sat upon the bed
Judg. 3. 12. the Lord s. Eglon against Israel
Judg. 7. 11. and afterwards shall thine hands be s
9. † 24. which s. his hands to kill his brethren
1 Sam. 23. 16. Jonathan went and s. hand in God
2 Sam. 2. 7. therefore now let your hands be s.
1 Chron. 11. 10. who s. themselves with David
2 Chron. 1. 1. and Solomon was s. in his kingdom
11. 17. so they s. the kingdom of Judah
12. 1. when Rehob. had s. himself, he forsook law
13. 7. and have s. themselves against Rehoboam
17. 1. Jehoshaphat s. himself against Israel
21. 4. Jehoram s. himself and slew all his brethren
23. 1. Jehoiada s. himself and took the captains
24. 13. they set house of God in his state, and s. it
25. 11. Amaziah s. himself, and led forth people
26. 8. for Uzziah s. himself exceedingly
28. 20. came and distressed Ahaz, but s. him not
32. 5. Hezekiah s. himself, and built the wall
Ezra 1. 6. all that were about them s. their hands
7. 28. I was s. as hand of my God was upon me
Neh. 2. 18. they s. their hands for this good work
Job 4. 3. and thou hast s. the weak hands
4. and thou hast s. the feeble knees
Psal. 52. 7. and s. himself in his wickedness
147. 13. for he hath s. the bars of thy gates
Prov. 7. † 13. she s. her face and said to him
8. 28. when he s. the fountains of the deep
Isa. 45. † 1. saith to Cyrus, whose rig. hand I have s.
Ezek. 13. 22. ye have s. the hands of the wicked
34. 4. the diseased have ye not s. nor healed sick
Dan. 10. 18. one touched me, and s. me, 19.
11. 6. he that begat her and s. her in these times
12. shall cast down many, but he shall not be s. by
Hos. 7. 15. tho' I have bound and s. their arms
Acts 9. 19. Saul was s. || Eph. 3. 16. to be s. with might
Col. 1. 11. s. with all might according to his power
2 Tim. 4. 17. the Lord stood with me and s. me

STRENGTHENEDST.

Psal. 138. 3. and s. me with strength in my soul

STRENGTHENETH.

Job 15. 25. he s. himself against the Almighty
Psal. 104. 15. and bread which s. man's heart
Prov. 24. † 5. yea, a man of knowledge s. might
31. 17. she girdeth her loins, and s. her arms
Eccl. 7. 19. wisdom s. the wise more than ten men
Isa. 44. 14. the cypress and oak he s. for himself
Amos 5. 9. that s. the spoiled against the strong
Phil. 4. 13. I can do all things thro' Christ who s. me

STRENGTHENING.

Luke 22. 43. there appeared an angel s. him
Acts 18. 23. Paul went to Galatia, s. all the disciples

STRETCH.

Exod. 7. 19. s. out thy hand upon waters of Egypt
8. 5. s. forth thine hand over streams and rivers
16. s. out thy rod and smite dust of land
25. 20. cherub. shall s. forth their wings on high
Josh. 8. 18. s. out spear that is in thy hand to Ai
2 Kings 21. 13. I will s. over Jerus. line of Samaria
1 Chron. 21. † 10. I s. out three things, choose one
Job 11. 13. if thou s. out thine hands toward him
39. 26. doth the hawk s. her wings toward south?
Psal. 68. 31. shall soon s. out her hands to God
Isa. 28. 20. shorter than that a man can s. himself
34. 11. he shall s. upon it the line of confusion
54. 2. s. forth the curtains of thy habitat. let them
Jer. 10. 20. there is none to s. forth my tent
Ezek. 30. 25. king of Babyl. shall s. out my sword
Amos 6. 4. and s. themselves upon their couches
Mat. 12. 13. Jesus said to man, s. forth thy hand
John 21. 18. thou shalt s. forth thy hands
2 Cor. 10. 14. for we s. not ourselves beyond meas.

STRETCHED, Actively, Passively.

Gen. 22. 10. Abraham s. forth hand to slay his son
48. 14. Israel s. out right hand, laid it on Ephraim
Exod. 8. 6. Aaron s. out his hand over waters, 17.
9. 23. Moses s. forth his rod toward heaven, 10. 13.
10. 22. Moses s. forth hand to heaven, 14. 21, 27.
Josh. 8. 18. and Joshua s. out the spear, 26.
19. they ran as soon as he had s. out his hand
2 Sam. 6. † 17. set ark in tabernacle David had s.
1 Kings 6. 27. cherubims s. forth their wings
17. 21. he s. himself on child, 2 Kings 4. 34, 35.
1 Chron. 21. 16. angel with a sword s. over Jerusalem
Job 38. 5. who hath s. the line upon it?
Psal. 44. 20. or s. our hands to a strange god
88. 9. I have s. out my hands unto thee
136. 6. to him that s. out the earth above waters
Prov. 1. 24. because I have s. out my hand
Isa. 3. 16. because they walk with s. forth necks
5. 25. he hath s. forth his hand against them; his hand is s. out still, 9. 12, 17, 21. | 10. 4.
14. 26. this is the hand that is s. out on all nations
27. hand is s. out, and who shall turn it back?
16. 8. her branches are s. out, are gone over sea
23. 11. he s. out his hand over sea, shook kingdom
42. 5. that s. out the heavens, 45. 12. | 51. 13.
Jer. 6. 4. the shadows of the evening are s. out
10. 12. he s. out the heavens by his discretion
51. 15. he s. out heaven by his understanding
Lam. 2. 8. the Lord hath s. out a line
Ezek. 1. 11. and their wings were s. upward
10. 7. one cherub s. forth his hand to the fire
16. 27. behold, I have s. out my hand over thee
Hos. 7. 5. he s. out his hand with scorners
Amos 6. 7. that s. themselves shall be removed
Zech. 1. 16. a line shall be s. forth upon Jerusalem
Mat. 12. 13. and he s. forth his hand, Mark 3. 5.
Luke 22. 53. ye s. forth no hands against me
Acts 12. 1. Herod s. his hands to vex the church
Rom. 10. 21. all day long I have s. forth my hands
See Arm.

STRETCHEDST.

Exod. 15. 12. thou s. out thy right hand, earth swal.

STRETCHEST.

Psal. 104. 2. who s. out the heavens like a curtain

STRETCHETH.

Job 15. 25. for he s. out his hand against God
26. 7. he s. out the north over the empty place
Prov. 31. 20. she s. out her hand to the poor
Isa. 40. 22. that s. out the heavens as a curtain
44. 13. the carpenter s. out his rule, marketh
24. that s. forth the heavens alone, Zech. 12. 1.

STRETCHING.

Isa. 8. 8. s. of his wings shall fill thy land, O Im.
Acts 4. 30. by s. forth thy hand to heal

STRIFE.

Gen. 13. 7. there was a s. between the herdmen
8. Abram said, let there be no s. between me
Exod. 17. † 7. he called the name of the place s.
Num. 20. † 13. this is the water of s. because Israel
27. 14. ye rebelled in the s. of the congregation
Deut. 1. 12. how can I myself alone bear your s.!
Judg. 12. 2. I and people were at great s. with Amm.
2 Sam. 19. 9. all the people were at s. thro' Israel
Psal. 31. 20. shalt keep them from s. of tongues
55. 9. for I have seen violence and s. in the city
80. 6. thou makest us a s. to our neighbours
106. 32. they angered him at the waters of s.
Prov. 15. 18. a wrathful man stirreth up s. 29. 22.
but he that is slow to anger appeaseth s.
16. 28. a froward man soweth s. and a whisperer
17. 1. than a house full of sacrifices, with s.
14. beginning of s. is as when one letteth out
19. he loveth transgression, that loveth s.
20. 3. it is an honour for a man to cease from s.
22. 10. cast out the scorner, and s. shall cease
26. 17. he that meddleth with s. belong. not to him
20. where there is no tale-bearer, the s. ceaseth
21. so is a contentious man to kindle s.
28. 25. he that is of a proud heart stirreth up s.
30. 33. the forcing of wrath bringeth forth s.
Isa. 41. † 11. the men of thy s. shall perish
58. 4. behold, ye fast for s. and debate, to smite
Jer. 15. 10. that thou hast born me a man of s.
Ezek. 47. 19. even to the waters of s. 48. 28.
Hab. 1. 3. there are that raise up s. and contention
Luke 22. 24. there was a s. among the disciples
Rom. 13. 13. walk honestly, not in s. and envying
1 Cor. 3. 3. there is among you s. and envying
Gal. 5. 20. the works of the flesh are s. wrath
Phil. 1. 15. some indeed preach Christ even of s.
2. 3. let nothing be done thro' s. or vain glory
1 Tim. 6. 4. whereof cometh envy, s. railings
Heb. 6. 16. and an oath is to them an end of all s.
Jam. 3. 14. but if ye have bitter envying and s.
16. where s. is, there is confusion and evil work

STRIFES.

Prov. 10. 12. hatred stirreth up s. love covers sins
2 Cor. 12. 20. lest there be envyings, wraths, s.
1 Tim. 6. 4. doting about questions and s. of words
2 Tim. 2. 23. knowing that they do gender s.

STRIKE.

Exod. 12. 7. and s. blood on the two side-posts, 22.
Deut. 21. 4. and shall s. off the heifer's neck there
2 Kings 5. 11. will come and s. his hand over the place
Job 17. 3. who is he that will s. hands with me?
20. 24. and the bow of steel shall s. him through
Psal. 110. 5. shall s. thro' kings in day of his wrath
Prov. 7. 23. till a dart s. through his liver
11. † 15. that hateth those that s. hands is sure
17. 26. it is not good to s. princes for equity
22. 26. be not thou one of them that s. hands
Jer. 40. † 14. hath sent Ishmael to s. thee in soul
Ezek. 39. † 2. I will s. thee with six plagues
Hos. 14. † 5. he shall s. forth his roots as Lebanon
Hab. 3. 14. thou didst s. through with his staves
Mark 14. 65. did s. Jesus with palms of their hands

STRICKEN, Actively, Passively.

Gen. 18. 11. Abram and Sarah well s. in age, 24. 1.
Josh. 13. 1. now Joshua was s. in years, 23. 1, 2.
Judg. 5. 26. when Jael had s. through his temples
1 Kings 1. 1. king David was old and s. in years
Prov. 6. 1. if thou hast s. thy hand with a stranger
23. 35. they have s. me, and I was not sick
Isa. 1. 5. why should ye be s. any more? revolt more
16. 7. surely they are s. || 53. 4. did esteem him s.
53. 8. for the transgression of my people was he s.
Jer. 5. 3. thou hast s. them, they have not grieved
Lam. 4. 9. s. through for want of the fruits of field
Luke 1. 7. Zach. and Elisabeth well s. in years, 18.

STRIKER.

1 Tim. 3. 3. a bishop must be sober, no s. Tit. 1. 7.

STRIKETH.

Job 34. 26. he s. them as wicked men in sight
Prov. 17. 18. a man void of understanding s. hands
Rev. 9. 5. as torment of scorpion, when he s. a man

STRING.

Psal. 11. 2. they make ready their arrow upon s.
Mark 7. 35. s. of his tongue was loosed, he spake

STRINGS.

Psal. 21. 12. shalt make ready their arrows upon s.
92. 3. sing to him with the psaltery, with an instrument of ten s. 33. 2. | 144. 9.

STRINGED.

1 Sam. 18. † 6. women came with three s. instrum.
Ps. 150. 4. praise him with s. instruments and org.
Isa. 38. 20. we will sing my songs to s. instruments
Hab. 3. 19. to chief singer on my s. instruments

STRIPE.

Exod. 21. 25. shalt give wound for wound, s. for s.

STRIPES.

See the Signification of Scourge.

Deut. 25. 3. forty s. he may give him, and not exceed; if he beat him above these with many s.
2 Sam. 7. 14. and with s. of the children of men
Psal. 89. 32. then will I visit their iniquity with s.
Prov. 17. 10. than an hundred s. into a fool
19. 29. and s. are prepared for the back of fools
20. 30. so do s. the inward parts of the belly
Isa. 53. 5. with his s. we are healed, 1 Pet. 2. 24.
Luke 12. 47. he who knew, be beaten with many s.
48. he who knew not shall be beaten with few s.
Acts 16. 23. when they had laid many s. upon them
33. took them same hour, and washed their s.
2 Cor. 6. 5. in s. in imprisonments, in tumults
11. 23. in s. above measure, in prisons, in deaths
24. of Jews five times received I forty s. save one

STRIP

Num. 20. 26. and s. Aaron of his garments
1 Sam. 31. 8. Philist. came to s. slain, 1 Chr. 10. 8.
Isa. 32. 11. s. ye, make ye bare, gird sackcl. on loins
Ezek. 16. 39. they shall s. thee of thy clothes, 23. 26.
Hos. 2. 3. lest I s. her naked, and set her as in day

STRIPPED.

Gen. 37. 23. that they *s.* Joseph out of his coat
Exod. 33. 6. Israel *s.* themselves of their ornaments
Num. 20. 28. Moses *s.* Aaron of his garments
1 *Sam.* 18. 4. Jonathan *s.* himself of the robe on him
19. 24. Saul *s.* off his clothes also, and prophesied
31. 9. the Philistines *s.* Saul of his armour
2 *Chron.* 20. 25. precious jewels which they *s.* off
Job 19. 9. he *s.* me of my glory, and taken crown
22. 6. for thou hast *s.* naked of their clothing
Mic. 1. 8. therefore I will go *s.* and naked
Mat. 27. 28. they *s.* Jesus, put on him s arlet robe
Luke 10. 30. thieves, which *s.* him of his raiment

STRIPLING.

1 *Sam.* 17. 56. king said, inquire whose son the *s.* is

STRIVE.

Gen. 6. 3. my spirit shall not always *s.* with man
26. 20. the herdmen of Gerar did *s.* with Isaac's
Exod. 21. 18. if men *s.* together, and one smite an.
22. if man *s.* and hurt a woman with child, he shall be surely punished, *Deut.* 25. 11.
Deut. 33. 8. with whom thou didst *s.* at Meribah
Judg. 11. 25. did he ever *s.* ag. Isr. or fight ag. them
Job 33. 13. why dost thou *s.* against him?
Ps. 35. 1. plead my cause with them that *s.* with me
Prov. 3. 30. *s.* not with a man without cause
25. 8. go not forth hastily to *s.* lest thou know not
Isa. 41. 11. and they that *s.* with thee shall perish
45. 9. let the potsherd *s.* with potsherds of earth
Hos. 4. 4. let no man *s.* thy people are as they that *s.*
Mat. 12. 19. he shall not *s.* nor shall any hear voice
Luke 13. 24. *s.* to enter in at the strait gate
Rom. 15. 30. *s.* with me in your prayers to G. for me
2 *Tim.* 2. 5. and if a man also *s.* for masteries
14. that they *s.* not about words to no profit
24. and the servant of the Lord must not *s.*

STRIVED.

Rom. 15. 20. so have I *s.* to preach the gospel

STRIVEN.

Jer. 50. 24. because thou hast *s.* against the Lord

STRIVETH.

Isa. 45. 9. woe to him that *s.* with his Maker
1 *Cor.* 9. 25. ev. man that *s.* for mastery is temperate

STRIVING.

Phil. 1. 27. with one mind *s.* for faith of the gospel
Col. 1. 29. *s.* accord. to his working, which worketh
4. † 12. always *s.* fervently for you in prayers
Heb. 12. 4. ye have not resisted to blood, *s.* ag. sin

STRIVINGS.

2 *Sam.* 22. 44. hast delivered me from the *s.* of the people, and made head of heathen, *Psal.* 18. 43.
Tit. 3. 9. avoid contentions and *s.* about the law

STROKE.

Deut. 17. 8. if a matter too hard between *s.* and *s.*
19. 5. and his hand fetcheth a *s.* with the axe to cut
21. 5. by their word shall every *s.* be tried
2 *Sam.* 20. † 10. Joab doubled not his *s.* Amasa died
2 *Chr.* 21. † 14. with a great *s.* will the Lord smite
Esth. 9. 5. Jews smote their enemies with the *s.*
Job 23. 2. my *s.* is heavier than my groaning
36. 18. beware lest he take thee away with his *s.*
Psal. 38. † 11. my friends stand aloof from my *s.*
39. 10. remove thy *s.* away from me
Isa. 14. 6. he smote the people with a continual *s.*
30. 26. the Lord healeth the *s.* of their wound
53. † 8. for he was cut off out of the land, for the transgression of my people was the *s.* upon him
Ezek. 24. 16. I take desire of thine eyes with a *s.*

STROKES.

Prov. 18. 6. a fool's mouth calleth for *s.*

STRONG.

Gen. 49. 14. Issachar is a *s.* ass, couching down
24. and the arms of his hands were made *s.*
Exod. 6. 1. with a *s.* hand shall let them go, 13. 9.
10. 19. the Lord turned a mighty *s.* west wind
14. 21. L. caused sea to go back by a *s.* east wind
Num. 20. 20. Edom came against him with a *s.* hand
21. 24. border of the children of Ammon was *s.*
24. 21. Balaam said, *s.* is thy dwelling-place
28. 7. the *s.* wine to be poured out to the Lord
Deut. 2. 36. there was not one city too *s.* for us
22. † 25. if man take *s.* hold of her, and lie with her
28. 50. a nation *s.* of face, which shall not regard
Josh. 14. 11. as yet I am as *s.* this day, as I was day
17. 13. when Israel were waxen *s.* *Judg.* 1. 28.
23. 9. Lord hath driven out great nations and *s.*
Judg. 6. † 2. the hand of Midian was *s.* ag. Israel
† 26. build an altar on the top of this *s.* place
9. 51. but there was a *s.* tower within the city
14. 14. out of the *s.* came forth sweetness
18. 26. Micah saw that they were too *s.* for him
1 *Sam.* 14. 52. when Saul saw any *s.* man, he took him
2 *Sam.* 2. † 16. that place was called field of *s.* men
3. 6. Abner made himself *s.* for the house of Saul
10. 11. if the Syrians be too *s.* for me, if Ammon be too *s.* for thee, I will help, 1 *Chron.* 19. 12.
11. 25. make thy battle more *s.* against the city
15. 12. the conspiracy was *s.* the people increased
22. 18. he deliv. me from my *s.* enemy, that hated me, for they were too *s.* for me, *Psal.* 18. 17.
1 *Kings* 2. † 8. Shimei, who cursed me with *s.* curse
8. 42. for they shall hear of thy name and *s.* hand
19. 11. a great and *s.* wind rent the mountains
2 *Chron.* 11. 12. he made the cities exceeding *s.*
17. so they made Rehoboam *s.* three years
16. 9. eyes run to shew himself *s.* in behalf of them
26. 16. when Uzziah was *s.* he was lifted up
Neh. 1. 10. thou hast redeemed by thy *s.* hand
9. 25. and they took *s.* cities and a fat land
Job 8. 2. words of thy mouth be like a *s.* wind
9. 19. if I speak of strength, lo, he is *s.*
30. 21. with thy *s.* hand thou opposest thyself
37. 18. hast thou spread out the sky that is *s.*
40. 18. bones are as *s.* pieces of brass, like bars
Psal. 19. 5. and rejoiceth as a *s.* man to run a race
24. 8. Lord *s.* and mighty, Lord mighty in battle
30. 7. thou hast made my mountain to stand *s.*
31. 2. be thou my *s.* rock, and house to save me
21. he hath shewed me his kindness in a *s.* city
35. 10. the poor from him that is too *s.* for him
† 18. I will praise thee among *s.* people
38. 19. mine enemies are lively and they are *s.*
Psal. 60. 9. who will bring me into *s.* city? 108. 10.
61. 3. thou hast been a *s.* tower from the enemy
71. 3. be my *s.* habitation ‖ 7. thou art my *s.* refuge
80. 15. the branch thou madest *s.* for thyself, 17.
89. 8. O Lord, who is a *s.* Lord like unto thee?
13. *s.* is thy hand, and high is thy right hand
136. 12. with a *s.* hand and a stretched out arm thou broughtest them out, *Jer.* 32. 21.
Prov. 7. 26. yea, many *s.* men have been slain by her
10. 15. rich man's wealth is his *s.* city, 18. 11.
11. 16. woman retains honour, and *s.* men retain
14. 26. in the fear of the Lord is a *s.* tower
18. 10. the name of the Lord is a *s.* tower
19. a brother is harder to be won than a *s.* city
21. 14. a reward in the bosom pacifieth *s.* wrath
24. 5. wise man is *s.* ‖ 30. 25. ants are a people not *s.*
Eccl. 9. 11. I saw that the battle is not to the *s.*
12. 3. when the *s.* men shall bow themselves
Cant. 8. 6. set me as a seal, for love is *s.* as death
Isa. 1. 31. the *s.* shall be as tow, maker as a spark
8. 7. Lord bringeth on them waters, *s.* and many
11. the Lord spake thus to me with a *s.* hand
17. 9. his *s.* cities shall be as a forsaken bough
25. 3. therefore shall the *s.* people glorify thee
26. 1. shall this song be sung, we have a *s.* city
27. 1. with his *s.* sword shall punish Leviathan
28. 2. behold the Lord hath a mighty and *s.* one
22. be ye not mockers, lest your bands be made *s.*
31. 1. that trust in horsemen, because they are *s.*
40. 10. behold, the Lord will come with a *s.* hand
26. for that he is *s.* in power, not one faileth
41. 21. bring forth your *s.* reasons, saith King of Jac.
53. 12. and he shall divide the spoil with the *s.*
56. † 11. yea they are *s.* of appetite
60. 22. a small one shall become a *s.* nation
Jer. 5. † 6. because their backslidings are *s.*
21. 5. I will fight against you with a *s.* arm
48. 14. how say ye, we are mighty, *s.* men for war
17. all about him say, how is the *s.* staff broken!
49. 19. he shall come up against habitation of the *s.*
50. 34. their Redeemer is *s.* the Lord of hosts
44. he shall come up unto the habitation of the *s.*
51. 12. make the watch *s.* set up the watchmen
Ezek. 3. 8. I have made thy face *s.* thy forehead *s.*
14. but the hand of the Lord was *s.* upon me
7. 24. I will make the pomp of the *s.* to cease
19. 11. had *s.* rods for sceptres of them that rule
12. her *s.* rods were broken and withered
14. so she hath no *s.* rod to be a sceptre to rule
26. 11. thy *s.* garrisons shall go down to ground
17. the renowned city which wast *s.* in the sea
30. 21. to bind it, to make it *s.* to hold the sword
22. and I will break the *s.* arms of Pharaoh
32. 21. *s.* shall speak to him out of midst of hell
34. 16. but I will destroy the fat and the *s.*
Dan. 4. 11. the tree grew and was *s.* 20.
22. it is thou, O king, art grown and become *s.*
7. 7. the fourth beast terrible, *s.* exceedingly
8. 8. when he was *s.* the great horn was broken
11. 23. he shall become *s.* with a small people
Joel 1. 6. for nation is come up on my land, *s.* 2. 2.
2. 5. as the noise of a *s.* people set in battle-array
11. for he is *s.* that executeth his word
3. 10. let the weak say, I am *s.*
Amos 2. 9. the Amorite was *s.* as the oaks
14. and the *s.* shall not strengthen his force
† 16. he that is *s.* of heart shall flee away
5. 9. that strengtheneth the spoiled ag. the *s.*
Mic. 4. 3. he shall rebuke *s.* nations afar off
7. I will make her that was cast far off, *s.* nations
6. 2. hear, ye *s.* foundations of the earth
Nah. 2. 1. make thy loins *s.* fortify thy power
Zech. 6. † 3. in fourth chariot grisled and *s.* horses
8. 22. *s.* nations shall come to seek the Lord
Mat. 12. 29. how can one enter into a *s.* man's house except he first bind the *s.* man? *Mark* 3. 27.
14. † 30. but when he saw wind *s.* he was afraid
Luke 1. 80. the child grew and waxed *s.* 2. 40.
11. 21. when a *s.* man armed keepeth his palace
Acts 3. 16. thro' faith hath made this man *s.*
Rom. 4. 20. was *s.* in faith, giving glory to God
15. 1. we that are *s.* ought to bear infirm. of weak
1 *Cor.* 4. 10. we are weak, but ye are *s.*
2 *Cor.* 12. 10. for when I am weak, then am I *s.*
13. 9. we are glad when we are weak, and ye are *s.*
2 *Thess.* 2. 11. God shall send them *s.* delusion
Heb. 5. 7. when had offered up prayers with *s.* crying
12. such as have need of milk, and not of *s.* meat
14. *s.* meat belongs to them that are of full age
6. 18. we might have a *s.* consolat. who have fled
11. 34. who out of weakness were made *s.*
1 *John* 2. 14. ye are *s.* word of God abideth in you
Rev. 5. 2. I saw a *s.* angel proclaim with loud voice
18. 2. he cried with a *s.* voice, Babylon is fallen
8. for *s.* is the Lord God who judgeth her

Be STRONG.

Num. 13. 18. see whether they *be s.* or weak
28. the people *be s.* that dwell in the land
Deut. 11. 8. keep commandments, that ye may *be s.*
12. † 23. only *be s.* that thou eat not the blood
Josh. 17. 18. drive out Canaanites, though they *be s.*
1 *Sam.* 4. 9. *be s.* and quit yourselves like men
2 *Sam.* 16. 21. the hands of all with thee shall *be s.*
1 *Kings* 2. 2. *be* thou *s.* and shew thyself a man
1 *Chron.* 19. 12. if the Syrians *be* too *s.* for me, if Ammon *be* too *s.* for thee I will help thee
28. † 7. if he *be s.* to do my commandments
10. the Lord hath chosen thee, *be s.* and do it
2 *Chron.* 15. 7. *be s.* your work shall be rewarded
25. 8. if thou wilt go, do it, *be s.* for the battle
Ezra 9. 12. that ye may *be s.* and eat good of land
Psal. 144. 14. that our oxen may *be s.* to labour
Isa. 35. 4. say to them of a fearful heart, *be s.*
Ezek. 22. 14. can thy hands *be s.* in the days I deal
Dan. 2. 40. the fourth kingdom shall *be s.* as iron
42. the kingdom shall *be* partly *s.* partly broken
10. 19. he said, peace be to thee, *be s.* yea, *be s.*
11. 5. the king of the south shall *be s.* and he shall *be s.* above him and have dominion
32. but people that know their God shall *be s.*
Hag. 2. 4. *be s.* O Zerubbabel, *be s.* O Joshua, *be s.* all ye people of land, saith the Lord, and work
Zech. 8. 9. let hands *be s.* ye that hear in these days
13. fear not but let your hands *be s.* [*be s.*
1 *Cor.* 16. 13. stand fast in faith, quit you like men,
Eph. 6. 10. finally, brethren, *be s.* in the Lord
2 *Tim.* 2. 1. my son, *be s.* in grace that is in Christ

See COURAGE, DRINK.

STRONG *hold* and *holds.*

Num. 13. 19. whether in tents or in *s. holds*
Judg. 6. 2. Israel made them caves and *s. holds*
1 *Sam.* 23. 14. David abode in wilderness in *s. holds*
19. doth not Dav. hide himself with us in *s. holds?*
29. and David dwelt in *s. holds* at En-gedi
2 *Sam.* 5. 7. David took the *s. hold* of Zion
24. 7. and came to the *s. hold* of Tyre
2 *Kings* 8. 12. their *s. holds* wilt thou set on fire
2 *Chron.* 11. 11. Rehoboam fortified the *s. holds*
Psal. 89. 40. thou hast brought his *s. holds* to ruin
Isa. 23. 11. to destroy the *s. holds* thereof
31. 9. and he shall pass over to his *s. holds* for fear
Jer. 48. 18. the spoiler shall destroy thy *s. holds*
41. Kerioth is taken, the *s. holds* are surprised
Lam. 2. 2. he hath thrown down *s. holds* of Judah
5. the Lord hath destroyed his *s. holds*
Dan. 11. 24. forecast his devices against the *s. holds*
39. thus shall he do in the most *s. holds*
Mic. 4. 8. the *s. hold* of the daughter of Zion
Nah. 1. 7. Lord is a *s. hold* in the day of trouble
3. 12. all thy *s. holds* shall be like fig-trees
14. draw thee waters for siege, fortify thy *s. hold*
Hab. 1. 10. they shall deride every *s. hold*
Zech. 9. 3. and Tyrus did build herself a *s. hold*
12. turn ye to the *s. hold,* ye prisoners of hope
2 *Cor.* 10. 4. but mighty to pulling down of *s. holds*

STRONG *ones.*

Psal. 10. 10. that the poor may fall by his *s. ones*
Jer. 8. 16. at sound of the neighing of his *s. ones*

STRONGER.

Gen. 25. 23. one people shall be *s.* than the other
30. 41. whensoever the *s.* cattle did conceive
42. so the feebler were Laban's, and *s.* Jacob's
Num. 13. 31. we be not able, they are *s.* than we
Judg. 14. 18. the men said, what is *s.* than a lion?
2 *Sam.* 1. 23. Saul and Jonathan were *s.* than lions
3. 1. but David waxed *s.* and *s.* and Saul weaker
13. 14. but Amnon being *s.* than she, forced her
1 *Kings* 20. 23. their gods are gods of hills, therefore *s.* surely we shall be *s.* than they, 25.
Job 17. 9. he that hath clean hands shall be *s.* and *s.*
Psal. 105. 24. he made them *s.* than their enemies
142. 6. deliver me, for they are *s.* than I
Jer. 20. 7. thou art *s.* than I, and hast prevailed
31. 11. ransomed from him that was *s.* than he
Luke 11. 22. when a *s.* than he shall come upon him
1 *Cor.* 1. 25. the weakness of God is *s.* than men
10. 22. do we provoke Lord? are we *s.* than he?

STRONGEST.

Prov. 30. 30. a lion which is *s.* among beasts

STRONGLY.

Judg. 8. † 1. Ephraimites did chide Gideon *s.*
1 *Chron.* 11. † 10. these men held *s.* with David
Ezra 6. 3. let the foundation thereof be *s.* laid

STROVE.

Gen. 26. 20. called Ezek. bec. they *s.* with him, 21.
22. digged another well, and for that they *s.* not
Exod. 2. 13. two men of the Hebrews *s.* together
Lev. 24. 10. and a man of Israel *s.* in the camp
Num. 20. 13. the children of Israel *s.* with the Lord
26. 9. this is that Dathan, who *s.* against Moses
2 *Sam.* 14. 6. they two *s.* together in the field
Dan. 7. 2. the four winds *s.* upon the great sea
John 6. 52. the Jews *s.* among themselves, saying
Acts 7. 26. Moses shewed himself to them as they *s.*
23. 9. and *s.* saying, we find no evil in this man

STRUCK.

1 *Sam.* 2. 14. he *s.* it into the pan or kettle or pot
2 *Sam.* 12. 15. the Lord *s.* the child, and it was sick
20. 10. Joab *s.* him not again, and Amasa died
2 *Chron.* 13. 20. the Lord *s.* Jeroboam, and he died
Mat. 26. 51. one of them *s.* a servant of high-priest's
Luke 22. 64. they *s.* Jesus on the face, *John* 18. 22.

STRUGGLED.

Gen. 25. 22. the children *s.* together within her

STUBBLE.

Exod. 5. 12. scattered to gather *s.* instead of straw
15. 7. sentest thy wrath which consumed them as *s.*
Job 13. 25. and wilt thou pursue the dry *s.?*
21. 18. they are as *s.* before the wind, and as chaff
41. 28. sling stones are turned with him into *s.*
29. darts are counted as *s.* he laugheth at a spear
Psal. 83. 13. make them as *s.* before the wind
Isa. 5. 24. as fire devoureth the *s.* so their root be
33. 11. she shall conceive chaff and bring forth *s.*
40. 24. whirlwind shall take them away as *s.*
41. 2. he gave them as driven *s.* to his bow
47. 14. they shall be as *s.* the fire shall burn them
Jer. 13. 24. therefore will I scatter them as *s.*
Joel 2. 5. like noise of a flame, that devoureth the *s.*
Obad. 18. and the house of Esau shall be for *s.*
Nah. 1. 10. they shall be devoured as *s.* fully dry
Mal. 4. 1. all that do wickedly and proud be *s.*
1 *Cor.* 3. 12. on this foundation gold, wood, hay, *s.*

STUBBORN.

Deut. 21. 18. if a man have a *s.* and rebellious son
20. and they shall say to elders, this our son is *s.*
Judg. 2. 19. they ceased not from their *s.* way
Psal. 78. 8. and might not be as their fathers, a *s.* generation
Prov. 7. 11. she is loud and *s.* her feet abide not

STUBBORNNESS.

Deut. 9. 27. look not to *s.* of this people nor sin
29. † 19. peace, tho' I walk in *s.* of mine heart
1 *Sam.* 15. 23. and *s.* is as iniquity and idolatry
Jer. 3. † 17. nor walk after the *s.* of their heart
7. † 24. but they walked in *s.* of their evil heart, 9. † 14. | 11. † 8. | 13. † 10. | 16. † 12.
23. † 17. say to them that walk in *s.* no evil come

STUCK.

1 *Sam.* 26. 7. his spear *s.* in the ground at his bolster
Psal. 119. 31. I have *s.* unto thy testimonies
Acts 27. 41. for part of the ship *s.* fast and remained

STUDS.

Cant. 1. 11. will make borders of gold with *s.* of silv.

STUDY.

The chief study of the Hebrews was always the law of the Lord. The practice of this is recommended throughout the whole Old Testament. Moses commanded, that the law of the Lord should always be in their mouths day and night; that it should be as a memorial before their eyes, and a signal in their hands: he would have them engrave it on their hearts; that they should teach it their children: that they should always meditate upon it, whether sitting in their houses, walking in the fields, in the night time, while they slept, and when they awoke in the morning; that they should wear it as a bracelet to their arm, and write it upon their door-posts. This was the study of the prophets, the patriarchs, and all good Israelites, Exod. 13. 9. Deut. 6. 7.

But their study was not confined only to their laws and ceremonies prescribed by Moses: they studied their histories, and even their genealogies; so that the children of the Jews, according to Jerom, knew at their finger-ends all the genealogies that are found in the Chronicles. From their tenderest infancy, as Josephus relates, they were accustomed to study the laws of God, to learn them by heart, to practise them, and they were so addicted to them, that they were ready to lay down their lives for their observation. After they had the writings of the prophets, they applied themselves very earnestly to know the sense of the prophecies, and to study the hidden meaning of them. We see it by Daniel, who applied himself with so much care to unfold the meaning of his own revelations, and of those of the prophet Jeremiah, who fixed the time for the completing the captivity of the people of God, Dan. 7. 28. | 9. 2, 3, 22, 23, 24. And the apostle Peter informs us, what was the study of the prophets. They searched what times and what other circumstances the Spirit of Christ, who spoke in them, had marked out, when they predicted the sufferings of our Saviour, and the glory that was to follow, 1 Pet. 1. 11.

After the conquests of Alexander the Great, the Jews, who were mingled with the Grecians, in the greatest part of the provinces of the East, began to have a taste for their language and their studies. In imitation of the Grecian philosophers, they divided themselves into different sects. Some of them, as the Pharisees, espoused some of the opinions of the Stoics and Platonicians; others, as the Sadducees, embraced some of the notions of the Epicureans; others, as the Essenians, says Philo, had a contempt for logic, physics, and metaphysics; which they thought useless, and matter of mere curiosity. They only applied themselves to morality and the laws of God, which they explained after a sublime and allegorical manner.

In our Saviour's time it appears, that the main study of the Jewish doctors was chiefly the traditions of their fathers. Christ upbraids them frequently with having forsaken the law of God and its true meaning, to ascribe meanings and applications to it, contrary to the sense of the law and the intention of the lawgiver. St. Paul, who had been bred up in these principles, shows also the absurdity of them, in his Epistles, always calling back the laws to their original and to their true sense. But all this was not able to cure the spirit of the Jews upon this article; at this day they are more bigoted to their traditions than ever, and they make them the greatest part of their study.

Eccl. 12. 12. and much s. is a weariness of the flesh
1 Thess. 4. 11. that ye s. to be quiet and to work
2 Tim. 2. 15. s. to shew thyself approved unto God

STUDIETH.

Prov. 15. 28. heart of the righteous s. to answer
24. 2. for their heart s. destruction, their lips talk

STUFF.

Gen. 31. 37. whereas thou hast searched all my s.
45. 20. regard not your s. good of Egypt is yours
Exod. 22. 7. if a man deliver money or s. to keep
36. 7. the s. they had was sufficient for the work
Josh. 7. 11. they have put it even am. their own s.
1 Sam. 10. 22. he hath hid himself among the s.
25. 13. and two hundred abode by the s.
30. 24. so shall his part be that tarrieth by s.
Ezek. 12. 3. prepare thee s. for removing and remove
4. then shalt thou bring forth thy s. by day, 7.
Luke 17. 31. be on house-top, and his s. in house

STUMBLE.

Prov. 3. 23. shalt walk, and thy foot not s. 4. 12.
4. 19. the wicked know not at what they s.
Isa. 5. 27. none shall be weary, nor s. among them
8. 15. and many among them shall s. and fall
28. 7. they err in vision, they s. in judgment
59. 10. we grope, we s. at noon-day as in night
63. 13. that led them that they should not s.
Jer. 13. 16. before your feet s. on dark mountains
18. 15. they have caused them to s. in their ways
20. 11. theref. my persecutors shall s. not prevail
31. 9. to walk in a way wherein they shall not s.
46. 6. they shall s. and fall toward the north
50. 32. and the most proud shall s. and fall
Dan. 11. 19. but he shall s. and fall, not be found
Nah. 2. 5. they shall s. in their walk
3. 3. multitude of slain, they s. upon their corpses
Mal. 2. 8. ye have caused many to s. at the law
1 Pet. 2. 8. a rock of offence to them that s. at word

STUMBLED.

1 Sam. 2. 4. and they that s. are girt with strength
1 Chron. 13. 9. to hold the ark, for the oxen s.
Ps. 27. 2. when they came to eat up my flesh, they s.
Jer. 46. 12. for the mighty man hath s. ag. mighty
Rom. 9. 32. for they s. at that stumbling-stone
11. 11. I say then, have they s. that th. should fall?

STUMBLETH.

Prov. 24. 17. and let not thy heart be glad when he s.
John 11. 9. if any man walk in the day, he s. not
10. but if a man walk in the night, he s.
Rom. 14. 21. nor to eat any thing whereby thy broth. s.

STUMBLING.

1 John 2. 10. and there is none occasion of s. in him

STUMBLING-BLOCK.

See Signification on OFFENCE.

Lev. 19. 14. thou shalt not put a s. before the blind
Ps. 119. † 165. that love thy law they shall have no s.
Isa. 57. 14. take up the s. out of the way of my people
Ezek. 3. 20. and I lay a s. before him, he shall die
7. 19. because it is the s. of their iniquity
14. 3. they put the s. of their iniquity, 4, 7.
44. † 12. they were a s. of iniquity to Israel
Rom. 11. 9. let their table be made a trap, a s.
14. 13. that no man put a s. in his brother's way
1 Cor. 1. 23. we preach Christ crucified, to Jews a s.
8. 9. take heed lest this liberty of yours become a s.
Rev. 2. 14. who taught Balak to cast a s. before Israel

STUMBLING-BLOCKS.

Jer. 6. 21. behold, I will lay s. before this people
Zeph. 1. 3. I will consume the s. with the wicked

STUMBLING-stone.

Isa. 8. 14. he shall be for a stone of s. to Israel
Rom. 9. 32. for they stumbled at that s.-stone
33. behold, I lay in Sion a s.-st. and rock of offence
1 Pet. 2. 8. a stone of s. to them that stumble at word

STUMP.

1 Sam. 5. 4. only the s. of Dagon was left to him
Dan. 4. 15. yet leave the s. in the earth, 23, 26.

SUBDUE.

Gen. 1. 28. God said, replenish the earth and s. it
1 Chr. 17. 10. moreover I will s. all thine enemies
Psal. 47. 3. he shall s. the people under us
127. † 5. they shall s. their enemies in the gate
Isa. 45. 1. I have holden, to s. nations before him
Dan. 7. 24. another rise, and he shall s. three kings
Mic. 7. 19. he will turn again, he will s. our iniquit.
Zech. 9. 15. they shall devour and s. with sling stones
Phil. 3. 21. he is able to s. all things to himself

SUBDUED.

Num. 32. 22. and the land be s. before the Lord
29. and the land shall be s. before you
Deut. 20. 20. thou shalt build bulwarks, until be s.
33. † 29. and thine enemies shall be s. unto thee
Josh. 18. 1. and the land was s. before them
Judg. 3. 30. so Moab was s. || 4. 23. God s. Jabin
8. 28. thus Midian was s. || 11. 33. Ammon was s.
1 Sam. 7. 13. the Philistines were s. hand of Lord was
against them, 2 Sam. 8. 1. 1 Chr. 18. 1. | 20. 4.
2 Sam. 8. 11. silver and gold of all nations which he s.
22. 40. girded me with strength, them that rose up
against me hast thou s. under me, Psal. 18. 39.
1 Chron. 22. 18. and the land is s. before the Lord
Psal. 81. 14. I should soon have s. their enemies
1 Cor. 15. 28. and when all things shall be s. unto him
Heb. 11. 33. who through faith s. kingdoms

SUBDUEDST.

Neh. 9. 24. thou s. the inhabitants of the land

SUBDUETH.

Ps. 18. 47. it is G. that s. the people under me, 144. 2.
Dan. 2. 40. forasmuch as iron breaks and s. all things

SUBJECT.

Gen. 3. † 16. thy desire shall be s. to thy husband
4. † 7. his desire shall be s. to thee, thou shalt rule
Luke 2. 51. Jesus went down, and was s. to them
10. 17. saying, Lord, even the devils are s. to us
20. rejoice not that the spirits are s. to you
Rom. 3. † 19. world may be s. to the judgment of G.
8. 7. for it is not s. to the law of God, nor can be
20. for the creature was made s. to vanity
13. 1. let every soul be s. to the higher powers
5. wherefore ye must needs be s. not only for wrath
1 Cor. 14. 32. the spirits of prophets are s. to prophets
15. 28. then shall the Son also himself be s. to him
Eph. 5. 24. as the church is s. to Christ, so let the wives
Col. 2. 20. why, as tho' living, are ye s. to ordinances
Tit. 3. 1. put them in mind to be s. to powers
Heb. 2. 15. who were all their life-time s. to bondage
Jam. 5. 17. Elias was s. to like passions as we are
1 Pet. 2. 18. servants be s. to your mast. with all fear
3. 22. angels and powers being made s. to him
5. 5. yea, all of you be s. one to another

SUBJECTED.

Rom. 8. 20. of him who hath s. the same in hope

SUBJECTION.

Psal. 106. 42. their enemies were brought into s.
Jer. 34. 11. and they brought them into s. 16.
1 Cor. 9. 27. I keep under and bring my body into s.
2 Cor. 9. 13. they glorify God for your professed s.
Gal. 2. 5. to whom we gave place by s. not for an hour
1 Tim. 2. 11. let the woman learn in silence with all s.
3. 4. having his children in s. with all gravity
Heb. 2. 5. hath he not put in s. the world to come
8. thou hast put all things in s. under his feet
12. 9. rather be in s. to the Father of spirits and live
1 Pet. 3. 1. wives, be in s. to your husbands, 5.

SUBMIT.

Gen. 16. 9. return, and s. thyself under her hands
2 Sam. 22. 45. strangers shall s. themselves to me, as
soon as they hear, shall be obed. to me, Ps. 18. 44.
Ps. 66. 3. thine enemies shall s. themselves to thee
68. 30. till every one s. himself with pieces of silv.
1 Cor. 16. 16. that ye s. yourselves unto such
Eph. 5. 22. wives, s. yourselves to your own husbands, as unto the Lord, Col. 3. 18.
Heb. 13. 17. s. yourselves for they watch for souls
Jam. 4. 7. s. yourselves therefore to G. resist devil
1 Pet. 2. 13. s. yourselves to every ordinance of man
5. 5. likewise, ye younger, s. yourselves to the elder

SUBMITTED.

1 Chron. 29. 24. the sons of David s. to Solomon
Ps. 81. 15. the haters of the L. should have s. to him
Rom. 10. 3. have not s. to the righteousness of God

SUBMITTING.

Eph. 5. 21. s. yourselves one to anoth. in fear of G.

SUBORNED.

Acts 6. 11. then they s. men who said, we have heard

SUBSCRIBE.

Isa. 44. 5. another shall with his hand s. unto the Ld.
Jer. 32. 44. men shall s. evidences, and seal them

SUBSCRIBED.

Jer. 32. 10. I s. the evidence, and sealed it
12. in presence of the witnesses that s. the book

SUBSTANCE.

Gen. 7. 4. I will destr. every living s. from off earth
23. every living s. was destroyed, man and cattle
12. 5. Abram took all the s. they had gathered
13. 6. their s. was great, so that they could not dwell
15. 14. afterward they shall come out with great s.
34. 23. shall not their cattle and their s. be ours?
36. 6. and Esau took his cattle and all his s.
Deut. 11. 6. the earth swallowed them up, all then s.
33. 11. bless, Lord, his s. and accept the work
Josh. 14. 4. they gave to the Levites cities for their s.
1 Sam. 9. † 1. his name was Kish, a mighty man of s
1 Chron. 27. 31. all these were the rulers of the s.
28. 1. the stewards over all the s. of the king
2 Chr. 21. 17. they carr. away all s. in king's house
31. 3. he appointed also the king's portion of his s.
32. 29. God had given Hezekiah s. very much
35. 7. Josiah gave bullocks, these were of king's s.
Ezra 8. 21. to seek of him a right way for our s.
10. 8. would not come, all his s. should be forfeited
Job 1. 3. Job's s. also was seven thousand sheep
10. and his s. is increased in the land
5. 5. and the robber swalloweth up their s.
6. 22. did I say, give a reward for me of your s.?
15. 29. he shall not be rich, nor shall his s. continue
20. 18. according to his s. shall the restitution be
22. 20. whereas our s. is not cut down, but remnant
30. 22. thou liftest me up, and dissolvest my s.
Psal. 17. 14. they leave their s. to their babes
105. 21. he made Joseph ruler over all his s.
139. 15. my s. was not hid from thee, when made
16. thine eyes did see my s. yet being unperfect
Prov. 1. 13. we shall find all precious s. we shall fill
3. 9. honour the L. with thy s. and the first-fruits
6. 31. he shall give all the s. of his house
8. 21. that I may cause those that love me inherit s.
10. 3. but he casteth away the s. of the wicked
12. 27. but the s. of a diligent man is precious
28. 8. he that by usury increaseth his s.
29. 3. keeps company with harlots, spendeth his s.
Cant. 8. 7. if a man would give all his s. for love
Isa. 6. 13. as a teil-tree and as an oak whose s. is
in them, so the holy seed shall be s. thereof
Jer. 15. 13. thy s. will I give to the spoil, 17. 3.
Hos. 12. 8. I am become rich, I have found me out s.
Obad. 13. nor laid hands on their s. in their calamity
Mic. 4. 13. I will consecrate their s. to L. of earth
Luke 8. 3. which ministered to him of their s.
15. 13. the prodigal wasted his s. with riotous liv.
Heb. 10. 34. knowing that ye have in heav. better s.
11. 1. now faith is the s. of things hoped for

SUBTIL.

Gen. 3. 1. now serpent was more s. than any beast
2 Sam. 13. 3. and Jonadab was a very s. man
Prov. 7. 10. with attire of an harlot, and s. of heart

SUBTILLY.

1 Sam. 23. 22. for it is told me that he dealeth very s.
Psal. 105. 25. to deal s. with his servants
Acts 7. 19. the same dealt s. with our kindred

SUBTILTY.

Gen. 27. 35. he said, thy brother came with s.
2 Kings 10. 19. Jehu did it in s. that he might destr.
Prov. 1. 4. to give s. to the simple, to the young man
8. † 12. I wisdom dwell with s. and find out
Mat. 26. 4. they might take Jesus by s. and kill him
Acts 13. 10. Paul said, O full of all s. and mischiet
2 Cor. 11. 3. the serpent beguiled Eve thro' his s.

SUBVERT.

Lam. 3. 36. to s. a man the Lord approveth not
Tit. 1. 11. who s. whole houses, teaching things

SUBVERTED.

Tit. 3. 11. he that is such is s. and sinneth

SUBVERTING.

Acts 15. 24. have troubled you with words, s. souls
2 Tim. 2. 14. words to no profit, but to s. of hearers

SUBURBS.

Lev. 25. 34. but the field of the s. may not be sold
Num. 35. 3. the s. of them shall be for their cattle
7. forty-eight cities shall ye give with their s.
Josh. 14. 4. save cities with s. for their cattle, 21. 2.
2 Kings 23. 11. he took away horses by chamber in s.
2 Chr. 11. 14. Levites left their s. and came to Jud.
Ezek. 27. 28. the s. shall shake at the sound of pilots
45. 2. fifty cubits round about for the s. thereof
48. 15. be a profane place for dwelling and for s.
17. the s. of the city shall be toward the north

See CITIES.

SUCCEED.

Deut. 25. 6. the first-born shall s. his brother dead

SUCCEEDED.

Deut. 2. 12. but the children of Esau s. them, 22.
21. Ammonites s. them, and dwelt in their stead

SUCCEEDEST.

Deut. 12. 29. when thou s. them in their land, 19. 1.

SUCCESS.

Josh. 1. 8. for then thou shalt pros. and have good s.
Job 22. † 2. not be profitable to God, if he may be
profitable, doth his good s. depend thereon?
Ps. 111. † 10. good s. have they that do his comman.
Prov. 3. † 4. so shalt thou find favour and good s.

SUCCOUR.

2 Sam. 8. 5. when Syrians came to s. Hadadezer
18. 3. it is better that thou s. us out of the city
Heb. 2. 18. he is able to s. them that are tempted

SUCCOURED.

2 Sam. 21. 17. Abishai s. him, and smote Philistines
2 Cor. 6. 2. and in the day of salvation have I s. thee

SUCCOURER.

Rom. 16. 2. she hath been a s. of many and of myself

SUCH.

Gen. 4. 20. Jabal was father of s. as dwell in tents
21. Jubal was the father of s. as handle the harp
27. 4. make me savoury meat, s. as I love, 9. 14.
46. Jacob take wife of daugh. of Heth, s. as these
30. 32. speckled and spotted, of s. shall be my hire
41. 19. s. as I never saw in Egypt for badness
44. 15. wot ye not that s. a man as I can divine?
Exod. 9. 18. s. hail as hath not been in Egypt, 24.
10. 14. were no s. locusts as they, nor shall be s.
11. 6. shall be great cry, s. as there was none like it
18. 21. thou shalt provide able men, s. as fear G.
34. 10. s. as have not been done in all the earth

Lev. 11. 34. meat on which s. water cometh be unclean, all drink that be drunk in every s. vessel
14. 22. two pigeons s. as he is able to get, 30, 31.
20. 6. the soul that turneth after s. I will cut off
22. 6. soul that hath touched any s. shall be unclean
27. 9. giveth of s. to the Lord, shall be holy
Num. 8. 16. instead of s. as open every womb
Deut. 4. 32. whether there hath been any s. thing
5. 29. O that there were s. an heart in them to fear me
13. 11. shall do no more any s. wickedness, 19. 20.
14. that s. abomination is wrought am. you, 17. 4.
16. 9. s. time as thou beginnest to put the sickle
Judg. 3. 2. at least s. as before knew nothing thereof
19. 30. there was no s. deed done or seen to this day
1 Sam. 4. 7. hath not been s. a thing heretofore
25. 17. he is s. a son of Belial, a man cannot speak
2 Sam. 9. 8. thou shouldest look on s. a dead dog as I
11. † 25. for the sword devoureth so and s.
13. 18. for with s. robes were virgins apparelled
14. 13. wherefore then hast thou thought s. a thing
16. 2. that s. as be faint in wilderness may drink
19. 36. why should recompense me with s. reward?
1 Kings 10. 10. there came no more s. abund. of spices
12. there came no s. almug-trees, 2 Chron. 9. 11.
2 Kings 6. 9. beware that thou pass not s. a place
7. 19. if Lord make windows, might s. a thing be?
21. 12. am bringing s. evil on Jerusalem and Judah
23. 22. surely there was not holden s. a passover
1 Chron. 12. 33. s. as went forth to battle, 36.
29. 25. the Lord bestowed on him s. royal majesty
2 Chron. 1. 12. s. as none of the kings have had
9. 9. nor was any s. spice as the queen gave Solomon
11. 16. s. as set their hearts to seek the Lord God
23. 13. people rejoiced, and s. taught to sing praise
24. 12. gave it to s. as did the work of the house
30. 5. they had not done it of a long time in s. sort
Ezra 4. 10. peace, and at s. a time, 11, 17. | 7. 12.
6. 21. all s. as had separated themselves to them
7. 25. all s. as know the laws of thy God
27. which hath put s. a thing in the king's heart
8. 31. and of s. as lay in wait by the way
9. 13. and hast given us s. deliverance as this
10. 3. put away the wives, and s. are born of them
Neh. 6. 11. I said, should s. a man as I flee?
Esth. 4. 11. except s. to whom the king shall hold out
14. thou art come to the kingdom for s. a time
9. 2. to lay hand on s. as sought their hurt
27. and upon all s. as joined themselves to them
Job 15. 13. and lettest s. words go out of thy mouth
18. 21. surely s. are the dwellings of the wicked
Psal. 25. 10. to s. as keep his covenant, 103. 18.
27. 12. s. as breathe out cruelty risen up ag. me
37. 14. to slay s. as be of upright conversation
22. s. as be blessed of him shall inherit earth
40. 4. respecteth not proud nor s. turn aside to lies
16. let s. as love thy salvation say, 70. 4.
55. 20. his hands against s. as be at peace with him
73. 1. God is good to s. as are of a clean heart
107. 10. s. as sit in darkness, and shadow of death
125. 5. as for s. as turn aside to crooked ways
139. 6. s. knowledge is too wonderful for me
144. 15. happy is that people that is in s. a case
Prov. 11. 20. but s. as are upright are his delight
28. 4. but s. as keep the law contend with them
31. 8. in cause of s. as are appointed to destruction
Eccl. 4. 1. behold, the tears of s. as were oppressed
Isa. 9. 1. dimness shall not be s. as was in her vexat.
10. 20. and s. as are escaped of the house of Jacob
20. 6. behold, s. is our expectation, whither we flee
37. 30. ye shall eat this year s. as groweth of itself
58. 5. is it s. a fast that I have chosen?
66. 8. who hath heard s. a thing? who hath seen s.
Jer. 2. 10. consider, and see if there be s. a thing
5. 9. my soul be avenged on s. a nation, 29. | 9. 9.
15. 2. s. as are for death to death, s. as are for sword, s. as are for famine, s. as are for captivity, 43. 11.
21. 7. I will deliver s. as are left in this city for pest.
38. 4. in speaking s. words unto them
44. 14. for none shall return, but s. as shall escape
Dan. 1. 4. s. as had ability in them to stand in palace
10. 15. and when he had spoken s. words to me
11. 32. s. as do wickedly shall he corrupt
12. 1. there shall be a time of trouble, s. as nev. was
Amos 5. 16. they shall call s. as are skilful to wailing
Mic. 5. 15. in anger and fury s. they have not heard
Zeph. 1. 8. s. as are clothed with strange apparel
Mat. 9. 8. glorified G. who had given s. power to men
18. 5. whoso shall receive one s. little child in my name, receiveth me, Mark 9. 37.
19. 14. suffer little children to come to me, for of s. is the kingdom of God, Mark 10. 14. Luke 18. 16.
24. 21. then shall be great tribulation, s. as was not since beginning of the world, Mark 13. 19.
44. in s. an hour as ye think not, the Son cometh
26. 18. he said, go into the city to s. a man and say
Mark 4. 18. sown among thorns, s. as hear the word
20. sown in good ground, are s. as hear the word
33. with many s. parables spake he to them
John 4. 23. for the Father seeketh s. to worship him
8. 5. Moses commanded that s. should be stoned
9. 16. can a man that is a sinner do s. miracles?
Acts 2. 47. the L. added daily s. as should be saved
3. 6. s. as I have, give I thee, rise up and walk
15. 24. to whom we gave no s. commandment
16. 24. who having received s. a charge thrust them
18. 15. for I will be no judge of s. matters
21. 25. have concluded, that they observe no s. thing
22. 22. said, away with s. a fellow from the earth
25. 20. because I doubted of s. manner of questions
26. 29. were almost and altogether s. as I am
Rom. 16. 18. they that are s. serve not our L. Jesus
1 Cor. 5. 1. s. fornication as is not so much as named
6. 11. and s. were some of you, but ye are washed
7. 15. brother or sister is not under bond. in s. cases
28. s. shall have trouble in flesh, but I spare you
10. 13. no temptation, but s. as is common to man
11. 16. seem to be contentious, we have no s. cust.
15. 48. s. are they that are earthy, s. are they that
16. 16. that ye submit yourselves to s. and every one
18. therefore acknowledge ye them that are s.
2 Cor. 2. 6. sufficient to s. a man is this punishment
3. 4. s. trust have we through Christ to God-ward
2 Cor. 3. 12. seeing then that we have s. hope, we use
10. 11. let s. an one think, s. as we are in word by letters, s. will we be indeed when we are present
11. 13. for s. are false apostles, deceitful workers
12. 20. I fear, I shall not find you s. as I would; and that I shall be found to you s. as ye would not
Gal. 5. 23. meekness against s. there is no law
Eph. 5. 27. not having spot or wrinkle, or any s. thing
Phil. 2. 29. receive him, and hold s. in reputation
1 Thess. 4. 6. because the Ld. is the avenger of all s.
2 Thess. 3. 12. now them that are s. we command
1 Tim. 6. 5. corrupt men, from s. withdraw thyself
2 Tim. 3. 5. traitors, heady, from s. turn away
Tit. 3. 11. that he that is s. is subverted and sinneth
Heb. 5. 12. ye are become s. as have need of milk
7. 26. s. an high priest became us, who is holy
8. 1. have s. an high priest, who is set on right hand
12. 3. him that endured s. contradiction of sinners
13. 16. for with s. sacrifices God is well pleased
Jam. 4. 13. to morrow we will go into s. a city
16. in your boastings, all s. rejoicing is evil
2 Pet. 1. 17. when there came s. a voice to him
3 John 8. we therefore ought to receive s. to be
Rev. 5. 13. and s. as are in the sea heard I, saying
16. 18. s. as was not since men were on the earth
20. 6. on s. the second death hath no power

SUCH *like.*

Ezek. 18. 14. and considereth, and doeth not s. like
Gal. 5. 21. drunkenness, revellings, and s. like

SUCH *an one.*

Gen. 41. 38. he said, can we find s. an one as this is?
Ruth 4. 1. ho, s. an one, turn aside, sit down here
Job 14. 3. dost thou open thine eyes on s. an one?
Psal. 50. 21. thoughtest that I was s. a one as thyself
68. 21. hairy scalp of s. a one as goeth on in trespass.
1 Cor. 5. 5. to deliver s. an one unto Satan
11. if a drunkard, with s. an one no not to eat
2 Cor. 2. 7. s. a one should be swallowed up with sorr.
10. 11. let s. an one think this, that such as we are
12. 2. s. an one caught up to the third heaven
5. of s. an one will I glory, yet not of myself
Gal. 6. 1. restore s. an one in the spirit of meekness
Philem. 9. I beseech, being s. a one as Paul the aged

SUCH *and* SUCH.

1 Sam. 21. 2. appointed my servants to s. and s. place
2 Sam. 12. 8. I would have given s. and s. things
2 Kings 6. 8. in s. and s. a place shall be my camp

SUCH *things.*

Exod. 12. 36. they lent s. things as they required
Lev. 10. 19. and s. things have befallen me
Deut. 25. 16. they that do s. things are an abominat.
Judg. 13. 23. nor have told us s. things as these
1 Sam. 2. 23. Eli said to them, why do ye s. things?
2 Kings 19. 29. shall eat s. things as grow of themsel.
25. 15. the captain took s. things as were of gold
Neh. 6. 8. there are no s. things done as thou sayest
Esth. 2. 9. with s. things as belonged to her
Job 12. 3. yea, who knoweth not s. things as these?
16. 2. Job said, I have heard many s. things
23. 14. and many s. things are with him
Jer. 18. 13. ask ye now who hath heard s. things
Ezek. 17. 15. shall he escape that doth s. things?
Dan. 2. 10. there is no king that asked s. things
Mark 7. 8. many other s. like things ye do, 13.
13. 7. be not troubled, s. things must needs be
Luke 9. 9. but who is this of whom I hear s. things
10. 7. remain, eating s. things as they give, 8.
11. 41. but give alms of s. things as ye have.
13. 2. were sinners, because they suffered s. things
John 7. 32. that the people murmured s. things
Acts 25. 18. they brought no accusation of s. things
28. 10. they laded us with s. things as were necessary
Rom. 1. 32. who commit s. things are worthy of death
2. 2. judgment against them who commit s. things
3. O man, that judgest them which do s. things
Gal. 5. 21. that do s. things shall not inherit kingdom
Heb. 11. 14. they that say s. things declare plainly
13. 5. be content with s. things as ye have
2 Pet. 3. 14. beloved, seeing that ye look for s. things

SUCK, *Substantive.*

Gen. 21. 7. that Sarah should have given children s.
1 Sam. 1. 23. so Hannah abode and gave her son s.
1 Kings 3. 21. when I rose to give my child s.
Isa. 40. † 11. he shall gently lead those that give s.
Lam. 4. 3. the sea-monsters give s. to their young
Mat. 24. 19. woe to them with child, and to them that give s. in those days, Mark 13. 17. Luke 21. 23.
Luke 23. 29. blessed are the paps that never gave s.

SUCK.

Deut. 32. 13. he made him to s. honey out of the rock
33. 19. they shall s. of the abundance of the seas
Job 3. 12. or why the breast that I should s.?
20. 16. he shall s. the poison of asps
39. 30. her young ones also s. up blood
Isa. 60. 16. thou shalt s. the milk of the Gentiles, and shalt s. the breast of kings and know the Lord
66. 11. that ye may s. and be satisfied with breasts
12. then shall ye s. ye shall be borne on her sides
Ezek. 23. 34. thou shalt even drink it and s. it out
Joel 2. 16. gather children and those that s. breasts

SUCKED.

Cant. 8. 1. that s. the breasts of my mother
Luke 11. 27. blessed are the paps that thou hast s.

SUCKING.

Num. 11. 12. as a nursing father beareth the s. child
1 Sam. 7. 9. Samuel took a s. lamb and offered it
Isa. 11. 8. s. child shall play on the hole of the asp
49. 15. can a woman forget her s. child?
Lam. 4. 4. tongue of the s. child cleaveth to mouth

SUCKLING.

Deut. 32. 25. the s. also with the man of grey hairs
1 Sam. 15. 3. slay both man and woman, infant and s.
Jer. 44. 7. to cut off from you child and s.

SUCKLINGS.

1 Sam. 22. 19. Doeg smote children and s. of Nob
Psal. 8. 2. out of mouth of babes and s. Mat. 21. 16.
Lam. 2. 11. the s. swoon in the streets of the city

SUDDEN.

Job 22. 10. therefore s. fear troubleth thee
Prov. 3. 25. be not afraid of s. fear nor of desolation
1 Thess. 5. 3. then s. destruction cometh upon them

SUDDENLY.

Num. 6. 9. and if any man die very s. by him
12. 4. the Lord spake s. unto Moses and Aaron
35. 22. but if he thrust him s. without enmity
Deut. 7. 4. the anger of the L. will destroy you s.
Josh. 10. 9. Joshua came unto them s. 11. 7.
2 Sam. 15. 14. lest he overtake us s. and smite the city
2 Chron. 29. 36. rejoiced, for the thing was done s.
Job 5. 3. taking root, but s. I cursed his habitation
9. 23. if the scourge slay s. he will laugh at trial
Psal. 6. 10. let them return and be ashamed s.
64. 4. s. do they shoot at him and fear not
7. with an arrow s. shall they be wounded
Prov. 6. 15. therefore his calamity shall come s. he shall be broken s. without remedy
7. † 22. he goeth after her s. an ox to the slaughter
24. 22. for their calamity shall rise s.
29. 1. shall s. be destroyed, and that without remedy
Eccl. 9. 12. when it falleth s. upon them
Isa. 29. 5. yea, it shall be at an instant s.
30. 13. as a breach, whose breaking cometh s.
47. 11. and desolation shall come upon thee s.
48. 3. I did them s. and they came to pass
Jer. 4. 20. s. are my tents spoiled and my curtains
6. 26. for the spoiler shall s. come upon us
15. 8. I have caused him to fall upon it s.
18. 22. when thou shalt bring a troop s. on them
49. 19. but I will s. make him run away, 50. 44.
51. 8. Bab. is s. fallen and destroyed, howl for her
Hab. 2. 7. shall they not rise up s. that shall bite thee
Mal. 3. 1. the Lord shall s. come to his temple
Mark 9. 8. s. saw no man any more, save Jesus only
13. 36. lest coming s. he find you sleeping
Luke 2. 13. s. there was with the angel a multitude
9. 39. a spirit taketh him, and he s. crieth out
Acts 2. 2. and s. there came a sound from heaven
9. 3. s. there shined a light from heaven, 22. 6.
16. 26. and s. there was a great earthquake
28. 6. when he should have fallen down dead s.
1 Tim. 5. 22. lay hands s. on no man, keep thys. pure

SUE.

Mat. 5. 40. and if any man will s. thee at the law

SUFFER.

Exod. 12. 23. the Ld. will not s. the destroyer to come
22. 18. thou shalt not s. a witch to live
Lev. 2. 13. nor shalt s. salt of the cov. to be lacking
19. 17. thou shalt rebuke him, and not s. sin upon him
22. 16. or s. them to bear the iniquity of trespass
Num. 21. 23. Sihon would not s. Israel to pass
Deut. 21. † 12. and she shall s. her nails to grow
Josh. 10. 19. s. them not to enter their cities
Judg. 1. 34. not s. them to come down to the valley
15. 1. but her father would not s. him to go in
16. 26. Samson said, s. me that I may feel the pillars
2 Sam. 14. 11. not s. the revengers of blood any more
1 Kings 15. 17. that he might not s. any to go out
Esth. 3. 8. it is not for the king's profit to s. them
6. † 10. s. not a whit to fail of all thou hast spoken
Job 9. 18. he will not s. me to take my breath
21. 3. s. me that I may speak, after that mock on
24. 11. tread their wine-presses, and s. thirst
36. 2. s. me a little, and I will shew thee
Psal. 9. 13. consider my trouble which I s. of them
16. 10. thou wilt not leave my soul, nor wilt thou s. thine holy One to see corruption, Acts 2. 27. | 13. 35.
34. 10. the young lions do lack and s. hunger
55. 22. he will never s. the righteous to be moved
88. 15. while I s. thy terrors, I am distracted
89. 33. nor will I s. my faithfulness to fail
101. 5. an high look and a proud heart, will not I s.
121. 3. he will not s. thy foot to be moved
Prov. 10. 3. L. will not s. soul of righteous to famish
19. 15. and an idle soul shall s. hunger
19. a man of great wrath shall s. punishment
Eccl. 5. 6. s. not thy mouth to cause thy flesh to sin
12. the abundance of the rich not s. him to sleep
Ezek. 44. 20. nor s. their locks to grow long
Hos. 5. † 4. their doings will not s. them to turn to G.
Mat. 3. 15. Jesus said to him, s. it to be so now
8. 21. s. me first to bury my father, Luke 9. 59.
31. s. us to go away into the swine, Luke 8. 32.
16. 21. that he must s. many things of the elders, 17. 12. Mark 8. 31. | 9. 12. Luke 9. 22. | 17. 25.
17. 17. how long shall I s. you? bring him hither to me, Mark 9. 19. Luke 9. 41.
19. 14. s. little children, Mark 10. 14. Luke 18. 16.
23. 13. neither s. ye them that are entering to go in
Mark 7. 12. ye s. him no more to do ought for his fat.
11. 16. Jes. would not s. any man to carry a vessel
Luke 22. 15. desired to eat this passover before I s.
51. s. ye thus far, he touch. his ear and healed him
24. 46. it behoved Christ to s. Acts 3. 18. | 26. 23.
Acts 3. 18. God before shewed that Christ should s.
5. 41. they were counted worthy to s. shame
7. 24. seeing one of them s. wrong he defended him
9. 16. how gr. things he must s. for my name's sake
21. 39. I besech thee, s. me to speak to the people
Rom. 8. 17. if so be that we s. with him th. we may be
1 Cor. 3. 15. if any man's work be burnt, he sh. s. loss
4. 12. being reviled, we bless; being persecut. we s.
6. 7. why not rather s. yourselves to be defrauded?
9. 12. we have not used this power but s. all things
10. 13. God will not s. you to be tempted above that
12. 26. if one member s. all members s. with it
2 Cor. 1. 6. the same sufferings which we also s.
11. 19. for ye s. fools gladly, seeing ye are wise
20. for ye s. if a man bring you into bondage?
Gal. 5. 11. if I preach, why do I yet s. persecution
6. 12. lest they should s. persecution for cross of Ch.
Phil. 1. 29. given you to believe and to s. for his sake
4. 12. I am instructed to abound and to s. need
1 Thess. 3. 4. we told you before, that we should s.
2 Thess. 1. 5. the kingdom of God for which ye also s.
1 Tim. 2. 12. I s. not a woman to teach nor to usurp
4. 10. for therefore we both labour and s. reproach
2 Tim. 1. 12. for the which cause I also s. these things
2. 9. wherein I s. trouble as an evil doer to bonds
12. if we s. we shall also reign with him
3. 12. all that live godly shall s. persecution
Heb. 11. 25. choosing rather to s. affliction with peo.
13. 3. remember them who s. adversity
22. brethren, s. the word of exhortation

Jam. 5.†7. *s.* therefore with long patience, brethren
1 *Pet.* 2. 20. but if when ye do well, and *s.* for it
3. 14. but if ye *s.* for righteousn. sake, happy are ye
17. it is better that ye *s.* for well doing than evil
4. 15. but let none of you *s.* as a murderer or thief
16. yet if any man *s.* as a Christian, not be asham.
19. let them that *s.* according to the will of God
Rev. 2. 10. fear none of those things that thou shalt *s.*
11. 9. not *s.* dead bodies to be put in their graves

SUFFERED.

Gen. 20. 6. therefore *s.* I thee not to touch her
31. 7. but God *s.* him not to hurt me
28. and hast not *s.* me to kiss my sons and daught.
Deut. 8. 3. he humbled thee, and *s.* thee to hunger
18. 14. the Lord thy God hath not *s.* thee so to do
Judg. 3. 28. and they *s.* not a man to pass over
1 *Sam.* 24. 7. David *s.* them not to rise against Saul
2 *Sam.* 21. 10. and *s.* not the birds to rest on them
1 *Chron.* 16. 21. he *s.* no man to do them wrong, he reproved kings for their sakes, *Psal.* 105. 14.
Job 31. 30. neither have I *s.* my mouth to sin
Jer. 15. 15. know that for thy sake I *s.* rebuke
Mat. 3. 15. Jes. said, suff. it to be so; then he *s.* him
19. 8. Moses *s.* you to put away your wives
24. 43. nor *s.* his house to be broken, *Luke* 12. 39.
27. 19. I have *s.* many things this day in a dream
Mark 1. 34. he *s.* not the devils to speak, *Luke* 4. 41.
5. 19. howbeit, Jesus *s.* him not, but said to him
26. and had *s.* many things of many physicians
37. and he *s.* no man to follow him, save Peter
10. 4. Moses *s.* to write a bill of divorcement
Luke 8. 32. he *s.* them to enter into the swine
51. he *s.* no man to go in, save Peter, James, John
13. 2. were sinners, because they *s.* such things
24. 26. O fools, ought not Chr. have *s.* these things?
Acts 13. 18. about forty years *s.* he their manners
14. 16. who *s.* all nations to walk in their own ways
16. 7. they essayed, but the Spirit *s.* them not
17. 3. alleging that Christ must needs have *s.*
19. 30. disciples *s.* him not to enter in unto people
28. 16. but Paul was *s.* to dwell by himself
2 *Cor.* 7. 12. I did it not for his cause that *s.* wrong
11. 25. once was I stoned, thrice I *s.* shipwreck
Gal. 3. 4. have ye *s.* so many things in vain?
Phil. 3. 8. for whom I have *s.* the loss of all things
1 *Thess.* 2. 2. but even after that we had *s.* before
14. ye have *s.* like things of your own countrymen
Heb. 2. 18. for in that he hims. hath *s.* being tempted
5. 8. he learned obedience by things which he *s.*
7. 23. they were not *s.* continue by reason of death
9. 26. for then must he often have *s.* since foundat.
13. 12. wherefore Jesus also *s.* without the gate
1 *Pet.* 2. 21. Chr. *s.* for us, leaving us an example
23. when he *s.* he threatened not, but committed
3. 18. for Chr. hath once *s.* for sins, just for unjust
4. 1. as Christ hath *s.* for us in the flesh, he that hath *s.* in the flesh hath ceased from sin
5. 10. after ye have *s.* a while, make you perfect

SUFFEREST.

Rev. 2. 20. because thou *s.* that woman Jezebel

SUFFERETH.

Psal. 66. 9. bless G. who *s.* not our feet to be moved
107. 38. blesseth, and *s.* not their cattle to decrease
Mat. 11. 12. the kingdom of heaven *s.* violence
Acts 28. 4. yet vengeance *s.* him not to live
1 *Cor.* 13. 4. charity *s.* long and is kind, envieth not

SUFFERING.

Acts 27. 7. the wind not *s.* us, we sailed under Crete
Jam. 5. 10. for an example of *s.* affliction, and patie.
1 *Pet.* 2. 19. if a man endure grief, *s.* wrongfully
Jude 7. an example, *s.* the vengeance of eternal fire

SUFFERING.

Heb. 2. 9. for the *s.* of death, crowned with glory

SUFFERINGS.

Rom. 8. 18. I reckon that the *s.* of this present time
2 *Cor.* 1. 5. for as the *s.* of Christ abound in us
6. enduring the same *s.* which we also suffer
7. ye are partakers of the *s.* so of the consolation
Phil. 3. 10. that I may know the fellowship of his *s.*
Col. 1. 24. who now rejoice in my *s.* for you
Heb. 2. 10. make captain of salvation perfect thro' *s.*
1 *Pet.* 1. 11. it testified before-hand the *s.* of Christ
4. 13. in as much as ye are partakers of Christ's *s.*
5. 1. I am a witness of the *s.* of Christ, and partaker

SUFFICE.

Num. 11. 22. shall herds be slain to *s.* them? or shall the fish of the sea be gathered together to *s.* them?
Deut. 3. 26. let it *s.* thee, speak no more to me of this
1 *Kings* 20. 10. if dust of Samaria shall *s.* for people
Ezek. 44. 6. let it *s.* you of all your abomin. 45. 9.
Hos. 12.†8. Ephraim said, all my labours *s.* me not
1 *Pet.* 4. 3. for the time past may *s.* to have wrought

SUFFICED.

Judg. 21. 14. gave them wives, yet so they *s.* them not
Ruth 2. 14. she did eat, and was *s.* and left
18. gave her that she had reserved, after she was *s.*

SUFFICETH.

John 14. 8. Lord, shew us the Father and it *s.* us

SUFFICIENCY.

Lev. 5. †7. if his hand cannot reach to the *s.* of a lamb, then two turtle-doves or pigeons, 12. †8.
25. †26. if his hand hath found *s.* to redeem it
Job 20. 22. in fulness of his *s.* he shall be in straits
2 *Cor.* 3. 5. we are not sufficient, but our *s.* is of God
9. 8. *s.* in all things, ye may abound in good work

SUFFICIENT.

Exod. 36. 7. for the stuff they had was *s.* for work
Deut. 15. 8. thou shalt lend him *s.* for his need
33. 7. let his hand be *s.* for him, thou an help to him
Prov. 25. 16. eat so much honey as is *s.* for thee
Isa. 40. 16. and Lebanon is not *s.* to burn, nor the beasts thereof *s.* for a burnt offering
Mat. 6. 34. *s.* to the day is the evil thereof
Luke 14. 28. whether he have *s.* to finish it
John 6. 7. two hundred penny-worth of bread is not *s.*
2 *Cor.* 2. 6. *s.* to such a man is this punishment
16. we are a savour, and who is *s.* for these things?
3. 5. not that we are *s.* of ourselves to think
12. 9. he said to me, my grace is *s.* for thee

SUFFICIENTLY.

2 *Chron.* 30. 3. priests had not sanctified themselves *s.*
Isa. 23. 18. that dwell before the Lord to eat *s.*

SUIT.

Judg. 17. 10. I will give thee a *s.* of apparel
2 *Sam.* 15. 4. that ev. man who hath any *s.* or cause
Job 11. 19. yea, many shall make *s.* unto thee

SUITS.

Isa. 3. 22. will take away changeable *s.* of apparel

SUM, *Substantive.*

Exod. 21. 30. if there be laid on him a *s.* of money
30. 12. when thou takest the *s.* of children of Isr.
38. 21. this is the *s.* of the tabernacle of testimony
Num. 1. 2. take the *s.* of all the congregation, 26. 2.
49. thou shalt not take the *s.* of the Levites
4. 2. take the *s.* of the sons of Kohath
22. take also the *s.* of the sons of Gershon
26. 4. take the *s.* of people from twenty years old
31. 26. take the *s.* of the prey that was taken
49. have taken the *s.* of the men of war
2 *Sam.* 24. 9. Joab gave up *s.* to king, 1 *Chr.* 21. 5
Esth. 4. 7. the *s.* of money that Haman promised
Psal. 139. 17. how great is the *s.* of them!
Ezek. 28. 12. thou sealest up the *s.* full of wisdom
Dan. 7. 1. Daniel told the *s.* of the dream
Acts 7. 16. Abraham bought for a *s.* of money
22. 28. with a great *s.* obtained I this freedom
Heb. 8. 1. of the things we have spoken this is the *s.*

SUM.

2 *Kings* 22. 4. that he may *s.* the silver brought

SUMMER.

Gen. 8. 22. *s.* and winter, day and night, shall not cease
Psal. 32. 4. my moisture is turned into drought of *s.*
74. 17. thou hast made *s.* and winter
Prov. 6. 8. which provideth her meat in *s.* 30. 25.
10. 5. he that gathereth in *s.* is a wise son
26. 1. as snow in *s.* and as rain in harvest
Isa. 28. 4. and as the hasty fruit before the *s.*
Jer. 8. 20. the harvest is past, the *s.* is ended
Dan. 2. 35. as the chaff of the *s.* threshing-floors
Zech. 14. 8. in *s.* and in winter shall it be
Mat. 24. 32. when fig-tree puts forth leaves, ye know that *s.* is nigh, *Mark* 13. 28. *Luke* 21. 30.

SUMMER *chamber.*

Judg. 3. 24. surely he covers his feet in his *s. chamber*

SUMMER-*fruit.*

2 *Sam.* 16. 2. bread and *s.-fruit* for young men to eat
Amos 8. 1. behold, a basket of *s.-fruit.* 2.

SUMMER-*fruits.*

2 *Sam.* 16. 1. Ziba brought 100 bunches of *s.-fruits*
Isa. 16. 9. for the shouting for thy *s.-fruits* is fallen
Jer. 40. 10. but ye, gather ye wine and *s.-fruits*, 12.
48. 32. the spoiler is fallen on *s.-fruits* and vintage
Mic. 7. 1. I am as when they have gathered *s.-fruits*

SUMMER-*house.*

Amos 3. 15. I will smite winter-house with *s.-house*

SUMMER-*parlour.*

Judg. 3. 20. Eglon was sitting in a *s.-parlour*

SUMMER.

Isa. 18. 6. and the fowls shall *s.* upon them

SUMPTUOUSLY.

Luke 16. 19. the rich man fared *s.* every day

SUN.

This is the great luminary that God created at the beginning, to preside over the day, as also he created the moon to rule over the night, Gen. 1. 16. *The sun has been the object of worship and adoration to the greatest part of the people of the East. It is thought to be the* sun *that the Phenicians worshipped under the name of* Baal, *the Moabites under the name of* Chemosh, *the Ammonites by that of* Moloch, *and the Israelites by the name of* Baal, *and by the* king of the host of heaven. *They did not separate his worship from that of the moon, whom they called* Astarta, *and the* queen of heaven. *They paid this worship upon high places, in groves, and upon the roofs of their houses. The Israelites had a caution against this worship.* Deut. 4. 15, 19. Take ye therefore good heed unto yourselves,—lest thou lift up thine eyes unto heaven, and when thou seest the *sun*, and the moon, and the stars, even all the host of heaven, shouldest be driven to worship them, and serve them, which the Lord thy God hath divided unto all nations under the whole heaven. *And in* Deut. 17. 3, 4, 5. *such are condemned to death, as shall be perverted to the worship of strange gods, of the* sun, *or of the moon. Josiah king of Judah took away out of the temple of the Lord, the horses, and burnt the chariots, that the kings his predecessors had consecrated to the* sun, 2 Kings 23. 11. *Job says, that he looked upon it as a very great crime, and as renouncing the God that is above, to kiss his hand as a token of adoration, when he saw the* sun *in all its glory and splendour,* Job 31. 26, 27, 28. *Ezekiel saw in the Spirit, in the temple of the Lord, five and twenty men of Judah, who turned their backs upon the sanctuary, and had their faces towards the east, worshipping the* sun *at his rising,* Ezek. 8. 16.

The sun is frequently alluded to in a great part of the noble similitudes that the sacred authors make use of. To represent a very great calamity, they say, the sun was obscured, and the moon withdrew her light, *Isa.* 13. 10. | 24. 23. *Jer.* 15. 9. *Ezek.* 32. 7. *Amos* 8. 9. *To express a long continuance of any thing that is glorious and illustrious, in Scripture style it is said,* It shall continue as long as the *sun* endures, *Psal.* 72. 5, 17. *The compass of the whole earth is marked out by those words,* from the rising of the *sun* to the going down of the same, *Psal.* 50. 1. | 113. 3. *To be hung upon a gibbet in the face of the* sun, *to be exposed in the fields to the birds of the air, and to the heat of the* sun, *expresses a particular degree of ignominy,* Num. 25. 4. Jer. 8. 2. Under the *sun; that is to say, in the world,* Eccl. 1. 9, 14, &c. Jesus Christ *is called the* sun of righteousness, *Mal.* 4. 2. *he enlightens, quickens, and comforts his people.* A woman clothed with the *sun*, and the moon under her feet, *signifies the church clothed with the righteousness of Christ, purity of doctrine, and a holy conversation; contemning and undervaluing worldly things, and the Mosaical worship,* Rev. 12. 1.

The Scripture acquaints us with three very extraordinary and miraculous things relating to the sun. *The first was, when it stood still at the command of Joshua,* Josh. 10. 12. 13. *The second, when it returned back in the time of king Hezekiah,* 2 Kings 20. 11. *And the third, when it was involved in darkness, though the moon was then at the full, at the time of our Saviour's crucifixion,* Mat. 27. 45.

Gen. 15. 17. it came to pass when the *s.* went down
19. 23. the *s.* was risen when Lot entered Zoar
28. 11. Jacob tarried all night, bec. the *s.* was set
32. 31. as he passed over Penuel, the *s.* rose on him
37. 9. the *s.* moon, and stars made obeisance to me
Exod. 16. 21. and when the *s.* waxed hot it melted
22. 3. if *s.* be risen, blood shall be shed for him
Lev. 22. 7. and when the *s.* is down, he shall be clean and afterwards eat holy things, *Deut.* 23. 11.
Num. 25. 4. hang them up before the Lord, ag. the *s.*
Deut. 4. 19. lest when thou seest the *s.* and moon
17. 3. and hath worshipped either the *s.* or moon
24. 15. nor shall the *s.* go down upon it, he is poor
33. 14. for the precious fruits brought forth by *s.*
Josh. 1. 4. to sea, toward the going down of the *s.*
8. 29. as soon as the *s.* was down, Joshua commanded
10. 12. *s.* stand thou still upon Gibeon, and moon
13. and the *s.* stood still, and the moon stayed
Judg. 5. 31. let them that love him be as *s.* his might
8. 13. Gideon returned before the *s.* was up
9. 33. as soon as the *s.* is up, thou shalt rise early
14. 18. they said to him before the *s.* went down
19. 14. *s.* went down when they were by Gibeah
1 *Sam.* 11. 9. by the *s.* be hot, ye shall have help
2 *Sam.* 2. 24. the *s.* went down, they were at Ammah
3. 35. if taste bread or ought till the *s.* be down
12. 11. shall lie with thy wives in sight of this *s.*
12. but I will do this thing before Israel and the *s.*
23. 4. as the light of morning when the *s.* riseth
2 *Kings* 3. 22. they rose, and *s.* shone upon the water
23. 5. them also that burn incense to *s.* and moon
11. and burnt the chariots of the *s.* with fire
2 *Chron.* 14. †5. Asa took high places and *s.* images
34. †4. Josiah brake down the *s.* images on high
Neh. 7. 3. let not gates be opened till the *s.* be hot
Job 8. 16. the hypocrite is green before the *s.*
9. 7. which commandeth the *s.* and it riseth not
30. 28. I went mourning without the *s.* I stood
31. 26. if I beheld *s.* when it shined or the moon
Psal. 19. 4. in them hath he set a tabernacle for *s.*
58. 8. pass away that they may not see the *s.*
72. 5. shall fear thee as long as *s.* and moon endure
17. his name shall be continued as long as the *s.*
74. 16. thou hast prepared the light and the *s.*
84. 11. for the Lord God is a *s.* and shield
89. 36. his throne shall endure as the *s.* before me
104. 22. the *s.* ariseth, they gather themselves
121. 6. the *s.* shall not smite thee by day
136. 8. to him that made the *s.* to rule by day
148. 3. praise ye him, *s.* and moon, and stars of light
Eccl. 1. 5. the *s.* also ariseth, and the *s.* goeth down
6. 5. moreover, he hath not seen the *s.* nor known
7. 11. by it there is profit to them that see the *s.*
11. 7. a pleasant thing for the eyes to behold the *s.*
12. 2. while the *s.* or the stars be not darkened
Cant. 1. 6. because the *s.* hath looked upon me
6. 10. that looketh forth, fair as moon, clear as the *s.*
Isa. 19. †18. one shall be called the city of the *s.*
24. 23. then the *s.* shall be ashamed, Ld. shall reign
30. 26. the light of the moon shall be as the light of the *s.* and the light of the *s.* shall be sevenfold
38. 8. is gone down in *s.* dial, so the *s.* returned
49. 10. nor shall the heat nor *s.* smite them
60. 19. the *s.* shall be no more thy light by day
20. *s.* shall no more go down, nor moon withdraw
Jer. 8. 2. they shall spread the bones before the *s.*
15. 9. her *s.* is gone down while it was yet day
19. †2. which is by the entry of the *s.* gate
31. 35. which giveth the *s.* for a light by day
43. †13. he shall break the house of the *s.*
Ezek. 8. 16. they worshipped the *s.* toward the east
32. 7. I will cover the *s.* with a cloud
Joel 2. 10. the *s.* and the moon shall be darkened, 3. 15. *Mat.* 24. 29. *Mark* 13. 24. *Luke* 23. 45.
31. *s.* shall be turned into darkness, moon into
Amos 8. 9. I will cause the *s.* to go down at noon
Jonah 4. 8. when the *s.* did arise, and the *s.* beat on the head of Jonah that he wished to die
Mic. 3. 6. the *s.* shall go down over the prophets
Nah. 3. 17. but when the *s.* ariseth, they flee away
Hab. 3. 11. *s.* and moon stood still in their habitation
Mal. 4. 2. to you shall the *s.* of righteousness arise
Mat. 5. 45. he maketh his *s.* to rise on evil and good
13. 6. when *s.* was up they were scorched, *Mark* 4. 6.
43. then shall the righteous shine as the *s.*
17. 2. his face did shine as the *s.* *Rev.* 1. 16. | 10. 1.
Mark 1. 32. when the *s.* did set they brought the sick
Luke 4. 40. now when the *s.* was setting, brought sick
21. 25. there shall be signs in the *s.* and the moon
Acts 2. 20. the *s.* into darkness, the moon into blood
13. 11. shalt be blind, not seeing the *s.* for a season
26. 13. I saw a light above the brightness of the *s.*
27. 20. when neither *s.* nor stars appeared
1 *Cor.* 15. 41. there is one glory of the *s.* and another
Eph. 4. 26. let not the *s.* go down upon your wrath
Jam. 1. 11. *s.* is no sooner risen with a burning heat
Rev. 6. 12. the *s.* became black as sackcloth of hair
7. 16. nor shall the *s.* light on them nor any heat
8. 12. and a third part of the *s.* was smitten
9. 2. the *s.* and the air were darkened by smoke
12. 1. there appeared a woman clothed with the *s.*
16. 8. the fourth angel poured out his vial on the *s.*
19. 17. I saw an angel standing in the *s.* he cried
21. 23. and the city had no need of the *s.* 22. 5.

See GOETH, GOING, RISING.

Under the SUN.

Eccl. 1. 3. what profit of all labour which he taketh *under the s.?* 2. 18, 19, 20, 22. | 5. 18. | 9. 9.
9. and there is no new thing *under the s.*
14. I have seen all the works done *under s.* all is vanity and vexation, 2. 17. | 4. 3. | 8. 17. | 9. 3.
2. 11. and there was no profit *under the s.*
3. 16. I saw *under the s.* the place of judgment

Eccl. 4. 1. all the oppressions that are done *un. the s.*
7. then I returned, and I saw vanity *under the s.*
5. 13. an evil I have seen *under the s.* 6. 1. ‖ 10. 5.
6. 12. tell what shall be after him *under the s.*
8. 9. I applied my heart to every work *under the s.*
15. mirth, a man hath no better thing *under the s.*
9. 6. nor any portion in any thing *under the s.*
9. all days which he hath given thee *under the s.*
11. I saw *under the s.* that race is not to the swift
13. this wisdom have I seen also *under the s.*

SUNDER.

Psal. 46. 9. he breaks the bow, cutteth the spear in *s.*
107. 14. and he brake their bands in *s.*
16. and he hath cut the bars of iron in *s.*
Isa. 27. 9. as chalk stones that are beaten in *s.*
45. 2. I will cut in *s.* the bars of iron
Nah. 1. 13. for now I will burst thy bonds in *s.*
Luke 12. 46. he will come and cut him in *s.*

SUNDERED.

Job 41. 17. his scales stick together, they cannot be *s.*
Ps. 22. † 14. all my bones are *s.* my heart is like wax

SUNDRY.

Heb. 1. 1. God who at *s.* times spake to the fathers

SUNG.

Ezra 3. 11. they *s.* together by course in praising L.
Isa. 26. 1. in that day shall this song be *s.* in Judah
Mat. 26. 30. when they had *s.* an hymn, they went out into the mount of Olives, *Mark* 14. 26.
Rev. 5. 9. they *s.* a new song, saying, thou art worthy
14. 3. they *s.* as it were a new song bef. the throne

SUNK, *Actively, Passively.*

Num. 11. † 2. when Moses prayed to the L. the fire *s.*
1 *Sam.* 17. 49. that the stone *s.* into his forehead
2 *Kings* 9. 24. and Jehoram *s.* down in his chariot
Psal. 9. 15. heathen are *s.* down in the pit they made
Jer. 38. 6. they let him down, so Jer. *s.* in the mire
22. thy feet are *s.* in the mire, they are turned back
Lam. 2. 9. her gates are *s.* into the ground
Acts 20. 9. Eutychus *s.* down with sl. and fell down

SUP.

Isa. 42. † 14. I will destroy and *s.* up at once
Obad. † 16. yea, all the heathen shall drink and *s.* up
Hab. 1. 9. their faces shall *s.* up as the east-wind
Luke 17. 8. say, make ready wherewith I may *s.*
Rev. 3. 20. I will *s.* with him, and he with me

SUPPED.

1 *Cor.* 11. 25. he took the cup, when he had *s.*

SUPERFLUITY.

Jam. 1. 21. lay apart all filthiness, *s.* of naughtiness

SUPERFLUITIES.

Amos 6. † 4. lie on beds of ivory and abound with *s.*

SUPERFLUOUS.

Lev. 21. 18. whatsoever man hath any thing *s.*
22. 23. a bullock, or lamb, that hath any thing *s.*
2 *Cor.* 9. 1. as to ministering it is *s.* for to write to you

SUPERSCRIPTION.

It was a custom among the Romans to write the crime for which any man suffered death, in a table, and carry it before him to execution; and as of other kinds of death, so in particular of those that were crucified. Whence appears the propriety of all these expressions in the Evangelists, ἐπιγραφη της αἰτιας; the superscription of the cause of his crimes. *Mark* 15. 26. ἡ αἰτια ἐπανω της κεφαλης γεγραμμενη, *the charge,* or cause written over his head, *Mat.* 27. 37. *And simply* ἐπιγραφη, superscription, *Luke* 23. 38. *And* τιτλος, title, *John* 19. 19.

Mat. 22. 20. Jesus saith unto them, whose is this image and *s.? Mark* 12. 16. *Luke* 20. 24.
Mark 15. 26. the *s.* of his accusation, *Luke* 23. 38.

SUPERSTITION.

Acts 25. 19. but had questions ag. him of their own *s.*

SUPERSTITIOUS.

Acts 17. 22. I perceive that in all things ye are too *s.*

SUPPER.

Mark 6. 21. Herod on his birth-d. made a *s.* to lords
Luke 14. 12. when thou makest a dinner or *s.*
16. a certain man made a great *s.* and bade many
17. and sent his servant at *s.* time to say to them
24. none of those were bidden shall taste of my *s.*
22. 20. likewise also the cup after *s.* saying, this cup
John 12. 2. there they made Jesus a *s.* Martha served
13. 2. and *s.* being ended ‖ 4. Jesus riseth from *s.*
21. 20. disciple who also leaned on his breast at *s.*
1 *Cor.* 11. 20. this is not to eat the Lord's *s.*
21. for every one taketh before other his own *s.*
Rev. 19. 9. blessed that are called to the marriage *s.*
17. he cried, come to the *s.* of the great God

SUPPING.

Hab. 1. † 9. the *s.* up of their faces as the east-wind

SUPPLANT.

Jer. 9. 4. for every brother will utterly *s.*

SUPPLANTED.

Gen. 27. 36. for he hath *s.* me these two times

SUPPLANTER.

Gen. 27. † 36. he said, is not he rightly named a *s.*

SUPPLE.

Ezek. 16. 4. neither wast washed in water to *s.* thee

SUPPLIANTS.

Zeph. 3. 10. my *s.* shall bring mine offering

SUPPLICATION.

1 *Sam.* 13. 12. and I have not made *s.* to the Lord
1 *Kings* 8. 28. have respect to his *s.* 2 *Chron.* 6. 19.
30. hearken thou to the *s.* 45. 49. 2 *Chron.* 6. 35.
33. and make *s.* to thee, 47. 2 *Chron.* 6. 24.
52. that thine eyes may be open to *s.* of thy servant
54. had made end of praying all this prayer and *s.*
59. these my words wherewith I have made *s.*
9. 3. I have heard thy *s.* that thou hast made
2 *Chron.* 6. 29. what *s.* shall be made of any man
33. 13. Lord heard Manasseh's *s.* then knew the L.
Esth. 4. 8. and should make *s.* to him for her people
Job 8. 5. and wouldest make thy *s.* to the Almighty
9. 15. but I would make my *s.* to my judge
Ps. 6. 9. the L. hath heard my *s.* receive my prayer
30. 8. and unto the Lord I made my *s.* 142. 1.
55. 1. give ear, and hide not thyself from my *s.*
119. 170. let my *s.* come before thee, deliver me
Isa. 45. 14. they shall make *s.* to thee, saying
Jer. 36. 7. it may be they will present their *s.* to Ld.
Jer. 37. 20. O king, let my *s.* be accepted before thee
38. 26. I presented my *s.* bef. the king not to return
42. 2. let our *s.* be accepted bef. thee and pray for us
9. to whom ye sent me to present your *s.* bef. him
Dan. 6. 11. then these men and Daniel making *s.*
9. 20. while I was presenting my *s.* before my God
Hos. 12. 4. he wept and made *s.* unto him, found him
Acts 1. 14. continued with one accord in pray. and *s.*
Eph. 6. 18. with all prayer and *s.* in spir. for all saints
Phil. 4. 6. but in every thing by prayer and *s.*

SUPPLICATIONS.

2 *Chr.* 6. 21. hearken to *s.* of thy servant and people
39. then hear thou their prayer and their *s.*
Job 41. 3. will Leviathan make many *s.* unto thee?
Psal. 28. 2. hear voice of my *s.* when I cry, 140. 6.
6. he hath heard voice of my *s.* 31. 22. ‖ 116. 1.
86. 6. give ear and attend to the voice of my *s.*
130. 2. let thy ears be attentive to my *s.* 143. 1.
Jer. 3. 21. weeping and *s.* of Israel were heard
31. 9. come with weep. and with *s.* will I lead them
Dan. 9. 3. I set my face to seek by prayer and *s.*
17. hear the prayer of thy servant and his *s.*
18. we do not present our *s.* for our righteousness
23. at the beginning of thy *s.* the command came
Zech. 12. 10. and I will pour the Spirit of gr. and *s.*
1 *Tim.* 2. 1. the first of all *s.* be made for all men
5. 5. she continueth in *s.* and prayers night and day
Heb. 5. 7. when he had offered up prayers and *s.*

SUPPLY, *Substantive.*

2 *Cor.* 8. 14. that your abundance may be a *s.* for their want, that their abundance a *s.* for your want
Phil. 1. 19. thro' prayer and the *s.* of the Spir. of Jes.

SUPPLY, *Verb.*

Phil. 2. 30. not regarding his life to *s.* lack of serv.
4. 19. but my G shall *s.* all your need by Chr. Jes.

SUPPLIED.

1 *Cor.* 16. 17. what lacking on your part, they have *s.*
2 *Cor.* 11. 9. what was lacking to me, the brethren *s.*

SUPPLIETH.

2 *Cor.* 9. 12. not only *s.* the want of the saints
Eph. 4. 16. compelled by that which every joint *s.*

SUPPORT, ED.

Gen. 27. † 37. with corn and wine have I *s.* him
Psal. 20. † 2. the Lord *s.* thee out of Zion
Acts 20. 35. ye ought to *s.* the weak, 1 *Thess.* 5. 14.

SUPPOSE.

2 *Sam.* 13. 32. let not my lord *s.* that they have slain
Luke 7. 43. I *s.* that he to whom he forgave most
12. 51. *s.* ye that I am come to give peace on earth
13. 2. *s.* ye that these Galileans were sinners
John 21. 25. I *s.* the world could not contain books
Acts 2. 15. for these are not drunken, as ye *s.*
1 *Cor.* 7. 26. I *s.* that this is good for the present
2 *Cor.* 11. 5. I *s.* I was not behind the chiefest apost.
Heb. 10. 29. of how much sorer punishment *s.* ye
1 *Pet.* 5. 12. by Silvanus, a faithful brother, as I *s.*

SUPPOSED.

Mat. 20. 10. they *s.* they should have received more
Mark 6. 49. they *s.* it had been a spirit, and cried out
Luke 3. 23. Jesus being, as was *s.* the son of Joseph
24. 37. terrified and *s.* that they had seen a spirit
Acts 7. 25. for he *s.* his brethren would have underst.
21. 29. whom they *s.* that Paul had brought to temp.
25. 18. brought none accusat. of such things as I *s.*
Phil. 2. 25. I *s.* it necess. to send to you Epaphrodit.

SUPPOSING.

Luke 2. 44. they *s.* him to have been in the company
John 20. 15. she *s.* him to be gardener, saith to him
Acts 14. 19. who drew Paul out, *s.* he had been dead
16. 27. jailer *s.* that the prisoners had been fled
27. 13. *s.* that they had obtained their purpose
Phil 1. 16. *s.* to add affliction to my bonds
1 *Tim* 6. 5. men of corrupt minds, *s.* gain is godlin.

SUPREME.

1 *Pet.* 2. 13. submit, whether it be to the king as *s.*

SURE.

Gen. 23. 17. borders, field, and cave were made *s.* 20.
Exod. 3. 19. I am *s.* the king will not let you go
Num. 32. 23. and be *s.* your sin will find you out
Deut. 12. 23. only be *s.* that thou eat not the blood
1 *Sam.* 2. 35. and I will build him a *s.* house
20. 7. then be *s.* that evil is determined by him
25. 28. for the Lord will make my Lord a *s.* house
2 *Sam.* 1. 10. because I was *s.* that he could not live
23. 5. with me covenant ordered in all things and *s.*
1 *Kings* 11. 38. that I will build thee a *s.* house
Ezra 9. † 8. and to give us a constant and *s.* abode
Neh. 9. 38. we make a *s.* covenant, and write it
11. † 23. that a *s.* ordinance should be for the singers
Job 24. 22. he riseth up and no man is *s.* of life
Psal. 19. 7. the testimony of the L. is *s.* making wise
93. 5. thy testimonies are very *s.* O Lord
111. 7. all his commandments are *s.*
Prov. 6. 3. humble thyself and make *s.* thy friend
11. 15. and he that hateth suretiship, is *s.*
18. to him soweth righteousness shall be *s.* reward
Isa. 22. 23. I will fasten him as a nail in a *s.* place, 25.
28. 16. behold, I lay in Zion for a *s.* foundation
32. 18. my people shall dwell in *s.* dwellings
33. 16. bread shall be given him, waters shall be *s.*
55. 3. even the *s.* mercies of David, *Acts* 13. 34.
Jer. 15. † 18. thou be to me as waters that be not *s.?*
Dan. 2. 45. and the interpretation thereof is *s.*
4. 26. thy kingdom shall be *s.* unto thee
Mat. 27. 64. that the sepulchre be made *s.* 66.
65. he said, go your way, make it as *s.* as you can
Luke 10. 11. be *s.* of this the kingdom of God is come
John 6. 69. we believe are *s.* and that thou art Christ
16. 30. now are we *s.* that thou knowest all things
Rom. 2. 2. we are *s.* that the judgment of God is true
4. 16. to end the promise might be *s.* to all the seed
15. 29. I am *s.* that when I come unto you
2 *Tim.* 2. 19. the foundation of God standeth *s.*
Heb. 6. 19. hope we have as anchor *s.* and stedfast
2 *Pet.* 1. 10. give all diligence to make your call. *s.*
19. we have also a more *s.* word of prophecy

SURELY.

Gen. 2. 17. in day thou eatest thereof, thou shalt *s.* die
3. 4. serpent said to the woman, ye shall not *s.* die
9. 5. and your blood of your lives will I require
18. 18. Abraham shall *s.* become a great nation
20. 7. if thou restore her not, thou shalt *s.* die
Gen. 20. 11. *s.* the fear of God is not in this place
28. 16. Jac. said, *s.* Ld. is in this place, I knew it not
22. I will *s.* give the tenth unto thee
29. 14. Laban said, *s.* thou art my bone and my flesh
32. *s.* the Lord hath looked upon my affliction
30. 16. come in unto me, for *s.* I have hired thee
31. 42. *s.* thou hadst sent me away now empty
32. 12. and thou saidst, I will *s.* do thee good
42. 16. *s.* ye are spies ‖ 44. 28. *s.* he is torn in pieces
43. 10. *s.* now we had returned this second time
46. 4. and I will also *s.* bring thee up again
50. 24. I die, G. will *s.* visit you, 25. *Exod.* 13. 19.
Exod. 2. 14. Moses said, *s.* this thing is known
3. 7. I have *s.* seen the affliction of Israel, 16.
4. 25. she said, *s.* a bloody husband art thou to me
11. 1. he shall *s.* thrust you out hence all together
18. 18. thou wilt *s.* wear away, thou and this people
19. 13. but he shall *s.* be stoned, or shot through
21. 20. if he die, he shall be *s.* punished, 22.
28. if an ox gore, then the ox shall be *s.* stoned
36. he shall *s.* pay ox for ox, dead shall be his own
22. 6. he that kindleth fire shall *s.* make restitution
14. if it be hurt or die, he shall *s.* make it good
16. if lie with her, shall *s.* endow her to be his wife
23. if they cry at all to me, I will *s.* hear their cry
23. 4. thou shalt *s.* bring it back to him again
5. if thou see, thou shalt *s.* help him
33. if serve their gods, will *s.* be snare, 1 *Kings* 11. 2.
40. 15. anointing shall *s.* be an everlasting priesthood
Num. 13. 27. and *s.* it floweth with milk and honey
14. 23. *s.* they shall not see the land which I sware
35. I will *s.* do it to all this evil congregation
18. 15. the first-born of man shalt thou *s.* redeem
22. 33. *s.* now I had slain thee, and saved her alive
23. 23. *s.* there is no enchantment against Jacob
26. 65. L. had said, they shall *s.* die in the wildern.
27. 7. thou shalt *s.* give them a possession of inherit.
32. 11. *s.* none from twenty years old and upward, shall see the land I sware to Abraham, *Deut.* 1. 35.
Deut. 4. 6. *s.* this great nation is a wise people
8. 19. I testify this day that ye shall *s.* perish, 30. 18.
13. 9. but thou shalt *s.* kill the idolater
15. thou shalt *s.* smite the inhabitants of that city
15. 8. thou shalt *s.* lend him sufficient for his need
10. shalt *s.* give thy poor brother not to be grieved
16. 15. thou shalt *s.* rejoice in the feast of taberna.
22. 4. thou shalt *s.* help him to lift them up again
23. 21. the Lord will *s.* require thy vow of thee
31. 18. and I will *s.* hide my face in that day
Josh. 14. 9. *s.* the land shall be thine inheritance
Judg. 3. 24. they said, *s.* he covereth his feet
4. 9. and Deborah said, I will *s.* go with thee
6. 16. the L. said to Gideon, *s.* I will be with thee
11. 31. cometh forth to meet me, shall *s.* be the L.'s
15. 13. we will bind, but *s.* we will not kill thee
20. 39. *s.* they are smitten down before us as in first
1 *Sam.* 9. 6. all that he saith cometh *s.* to pass
15. 32. Agag said, *s.* the bitterness of death is past
17. 25. they said, to defy Israel is he come up
20. 26. for Saul thought, *s.* he is not clean
22. 22. I knew it that Doeg would *s.* tell Saul
24. 20. I know well that thou shalt *s.* be king
25. 21. *s.* in vain have I kept all this fellow hath
34. *s.* there had not been left to Nabal any
28. 2. *s.* thou shalt know what thy servant can do
29. 6. *s.* as the Lord liveth, thou hast been upright
30. 8. pursue, for thou shalt *s.* overtake them
2 *Sam.* 2. 27. *s.* the people had gone up every one
9. 7. I will *s.* shew thee kindn. for Jonathan's sake
11. 23. he said, *s.* the men prevailed against us
15. 21. *s.* where the king shall be, there will I be
18. 2. I will *s.* go forth with you myself also
20. 18. she spake, they shall *s.* ask counsel at Abel
24. 24. nay, but I will *s.* buy it of thee at a price
1 *Kings* 8. 13. I have *s.* built thee house to dwell in
11. 11. I will *s.* rend the kingdom from thee
13. 32. saying against the altar shall *s.* come to pass
18. 15. I will *s.* shew myself unto him to-day
20. 23. and *s.* we shall be stronger than they, 25.
22. 32. they said, *s.* it is the king of Israel
2 *Kings* 3. 14. *s.* were it not I regard Jehoshaphat
23. they said, this is blood, the kings are *s.* slain
5. 11. behold, I thought, he will *s.* come out to me
8. 14. he told me that thou shouldest *s.* recover
9. 26. *s.* I have seen yesterday the blood of Naboth
18. 30. the Lord will *s.* deliver us, *Isa.* 36. 15.
23. 22. *s.* there was not holden such a passover
24. 3. *s.* at command of the Ld. came this on Judah
Esth. 6. 13. not prevail, but shalt *s.* fall before him
Job 8. 6. if pure and upright, *s.* would awake for thee
13. 3. *s.* I would speak to the Almighty
10. he will *s.* reprove you, if ye accept persons
14. 18. *s.* the mountain falling cometh to nought
18. 21. *s.* such are the dwellings of the wicked
20. 20. *s.* he shall not feel quietness in his belly
28. 1. *s.* there is a vein for the silver, place for gold
31. 36. *s.* take it upon my shoulder, and bind it
33. 8. *s.* thou hast spoken in mine hearing
34. 12. yea, *s.* G. will not do wickedly, nor Almighty
35. 13. *s.* God will not hear vanity nor regard it
Psal. 32. 6. *s.* in the floods they shall not come nigh
39. 6. *s.* every man walketh in vain shew
11. his beauty consumes, *s.* every man is vanity
73. 18. *s.* thou didst set them in slippery places
76. 10. *s.* the wrath of man shall praise thee
77. 11. *s.* I will remember thy wonders of old
85. 9. *s.* his salvation is nigh them that fear him
91. 3. *s.* he shall deliver thee from snare of fowler
112. 6. *s.* he shall not be moved for ever
131. 2. *s.* have behaved and quieted myself as a child
132. 3. *s.* I will not come into my house
139. 19. *s.* thou wilt slay the wicked, O God
140. 13. *s.* righteous shall give thanks to thy name
Prov. 1. 17. *s.* in vain the net is spread in sight of bird
3. 34. *s.* scorneth the scorners, but giveth grace to
10. 9. he that walketh uprightly, walketh *s.*
22. 16. that giveth to the rich, shall *s.* come to want
23. 18. *s.* there is an end ‖ 30. 2. *s.* I am more brutish
30. 33. *s.* the churn. of milk bringeth forth butter
Eccl. 4. 16. *s.* this is also vanity and vexation of spirit
7. 7. *s.* oppression maketh a wise man mad

Eccl. 8. 12. *s.* it shall be well with them that fear God
10. 11. *s.* the serpent will bite without enchantment
Isa. 7. 9. will not believe, *s.* ye shall not be establish.
14. 24. *s.* as I have thought so shall it come to pass
16. 7. for Kir-hareseth ye shall mourn, *s.* are stricken
19. 11. *s.* the princes of Zoan are fools
22. 14. *s.* this iniquity shall not be purged from you
17. behold, the Lord will *s.* cover thee
18. he will *s.* violently turn and toss thee like ball
29. 16. *s.* your turning of things upside down
40. 7. the grass withereth, *s.* the people is grass
45. 14. *s.* God is in thee, and there is none else
24. *s.* in the L. have I righteousness and strength
49. 4. yet *s.* my judgment is with the Lord
53. 4. *s.* he hath borne our griefs, and carried our sor.
54. 15. they shall *s.* gather together, but not by me
60. 9. *s.* the isles shall wait for me, ships of Tarshish
62. 8. *s.* I will no more give thy corn to thy enemies
63. 8. he said, *s.* they are my people, childr. not lie
Jer. 2. 35. thou sayest, *s.* his anger shall turn from me
3. 20. *s.* as a wife treacherously depart. from husb.
4. 10. *s.* thou hast greatly deceived this people
5. 2. *s.* they swear falsely ‖ 4. I said, *s.* these are poor
8. 13. I will *s.* consume them, saith the Lord
16. 19. *s.* our fathers have inherited lies, vanity
22. 6. yet *s.* I will make thee a wilderness
22. *s.* thou shalt be ashamed for thy wickedness
24. 8. *s.* saith the Lord, so will I give Zedekiah
26. 15. ye shall *s.* bring innocent blood on yourselves
31. 18. have *s.* heard Ephraim bemoaning himself
19. *s.* after that I was turned, I repented
20. therefore I will *s.* have mercy on him, saith L.
34. 3. but thou shalt *s.* be taken and delivered
36. 16. we will *s.* tell the king of all these words
37. 9. the Chaldeans shall *s.* depart from us
38. 3. this city shall *s.* be given to the king of Bab.
39. 18. I will *s.* deliver thee, thou shalt not fall
44. 25. we will *s.* perform our vows that we vowed
29. that my words shall *s.* stand ag. you for evil
46. 18. *s.* as Carmel by the sea, so shall he come
49. 12. thou shalt not go unpunished, but *s.* drink it
20. *s.* the least of the flock shall draw them, 50. 45.
51. 14. saying, *s.* I will fill thee with men
56. for the L. G. of recompences, shall *s.* requite
Ezek. 3. 21. he shall *s.* live, because he is warned,
18. 9, 17, 19, 21, 28. | 33. 13, 15, 16.
5. 11. *s.* because thou hast defiled my sanctuary
17. 16. *s.* in the place where the king dwelleth
20. 33. *s.* with a mighty hand will I rule over you
31. 11. he shall *s.* deal with him, I have driven him
33. 27. *s.* they in the wastes shall fall by the sword
34. 8. as I live, *s.* because my flock became a prey
36. 5. *s.* in the fire of my jealousy have I spoken
7. *s.* the heathen, they shall bear their shame
38. 19. *s.* in that day there shall be a great shaking
Hos. 5. 9. I have made known that which shall *s.* be
12. 11. *s.* they are vanity, they sacrifice bullocks
Amos 3. 7. *s.* the L. will do nothing, but he reveals
5. 5. for Gilgal shall *s.* go into captivity, and Bethel
7. 11. Israel shall *s.* be led away captive, 17.
8. 7. *s.* I will never forget any of their works
Mic. 2. 12. I will *s.* assemble, O Jacob, all of thee, I
will *s.* gather remnant of Isr. as sheep of Bozrah
Hab. 2. 3. because it will *s.* come, it will not tarry
Zeph. 2. 9. as I live *s.* Moab shall be as Sodom
3. 7. *s.* thou wilt fear me, and receive instruction
Mat. 26. 73. *s.* thou art one of them, *Mark* 14. 70.
Luke 1. 1. things which are most *s.* believed among us
4. 23. ye will *s.* say unto me this proverb, physician
John 17. 8. have known *s.* that I came out from thee
Heb. 6. 14. saying, *s.* blessing, I will bless thee
Rev. 22. 20. saith, *s.* I come quickly, even so come L. J.
See Die.

SURELY *be put to death.*

Gen. 26. 11. toucheth this man, shall *s. be put to d.*
Exod. 19. 12. toucheth mount, shall *s. be put to d.*
21. 12. he that killeth a man, shall *s. be put to d.*
15. he that smiteth his father, shall *s. be put to d.*
16. he that stealeth a man shall *s. be put to death*
17. that curseth his father shall *s. p. to d. Lev.* 20. 9.
22. 19. whosoever lieth with a beast, shall *s. be put
to death, Lev.* 20. 15, 16.
31. 14. that defileth the sabbath *s. be put to d.* 15.
Lev. 20. 2. giveth his seed to Molech, *s. be put to d.*
10. adulterer and adulteress shall *s. be put to d.*
11. lieth with father's wife, both shall *s. be p. to d.*
12. lie with his daught.-in law, both *s. be put to d.*
13. if a man lie with mankind, both *s. be put to d.*
24. 16. he that blasphemeth, shall *s. be put to d.*
17. and he that killeth any man, shall *s. be put
to death, Num.* 35. 16, 17, 18, 21, 31.
27. 29. not be redeemed, but shall *s. be put to d.*
Judg. 21. 5. who came not up, shall *s. be put to d.*
Jer. 38. 15. wilt thou not *s. put* me *to death*

SURETY

Is one who undertakes to pay another man's debt, in case the principal debtor, either through unfaithfulness or poverty should prove insolvent. It was an ancient custom in suretiship for the surety *to give his hand to, or strike hands with the creditor, thereby obliging himself to the payment of the debt, in case of the insolvency of the principal debtor. Thus it is said in* Job 17. 3. Who is he that will strike hands with me? *And in* Prov. 6. 1, 2. My son, if thou be *surety* for thy friend; if thou hast stricken thy hand with a stranger; thou art snared with the words of thy mouth. *Solomon in this passage does not condemn suretiship, which in some cases is not only lawful, but even an act of justice, of prudence, and charity; thus Judah became* surety *to his father for his brother Benjamin,* Gen. 42. 37. | 44. 32. *and Paul to Philemon for Onesimus,* Philem. 18, 19. *Solomon only forbids his disciple to become* surety *rashly, without considering for whom, or how far he does oblige himself, or how he could discharge the debt, if occasion should require it.*

In Heb. 7. 22. *Jesus Christ is called the surety* of a better testament. *Sins are by analogy called* debts: *for as a debt obliges the debtor to payment, so sin doth the sinner to punishment. Christ, according to the covenant of redemption, or agreement between the Father and him, interposed as our* surety; *and entering into this relation, he sustained the persons of sinners, (for in the estimate of the law, the* surety *and debtor are but one person,) and being judicially one with them, according to the order of justice, he was liable to their punishment. For though the displeasure of God was primarily and directly against the sinner, yet the effects of it fell upon Christ, who undertook for him. And according to this undertaking, Christ as our* surety, *fulfilled the preceptive part of the moral law, by the innocency and holiness of his life; and he underwent the penalty of the law when he offered up himself a sacrifice to satisfy divine justice, and reconcile us to God. And in consequence of the atonement made by this sacrifice, the Holy Spirit is given, to enable man to perform what is required of him in the gospel; namely, to repent, to believe, and obey the Redeemer, and wholly to rely upon his sacrifice for obtaining the favour of God; and Christ, by his intercession, secures to believers all the blessings of God's covenant for time and eternity. To which the Psalmist alludes,* Psal. 119. 122. Be *surety* for thy servant for good: *do thou undertake and plead my cause against all mine enemies, as a surety rescues the poor persecuted debtor from the hands of a severe and merciless creditor.*

Gen. 43. 9. I will be *s.* for him, shalt require him of
44. 32. for thy servant became *s.* for the lad
Job 17. 3. lay down now, put me in a *s.* with thee
Psal. 119. 122. be *s.* for thy servant for good
Prov. 6. 1. my son, if thou be *s.* for thy friend
11. 15. he that is *s.* for a stranger shall smart for it
17. 18. and becometh *s.* in presence of his friend
20. 16. his garment that is *s.* for a stranger, 27. 13.
Heb. 7. 22. was Jesus made *s.* of a better testament

SURETIES.

Prov. 22. 26. be not one of them that are *s.* for debts

Of a SURETY.

Gen. 15. 13. know *of a s.* thy seed shall be a stranger
18. 13. shall I *of a s.* bear a child, who am old?
26. 9. Abimelech said, behold, *of a s.* she is thy wife
Acts 12. 11. I know *of a s.* the L. hath sent his angel

SURETISHIP.

Prov. 11. 15. and he that hateth *s.* is sure

SURFEITING.

Luke 21. 34. lest your hearts be overcharged with *s.*

SURMISINGS.

1 *Tim.* 6. 4. whereof cometh envy, strife, evil *s.*

SURNAME. *See* Sirname.

SURPLUSAGE.

Exod. 26. † 13. a cubit on the other side in the *s.*

SURPRISED.

Isa. 33. 14. sinners afraid, fearfulness *s.* hypocrites
Jer. 48. 41. Kerioth is taken, the strong holds are *s.*
51. 41. how is the praise of the whole earth *s.!*

SUSPENSE.

Luke 3. † 15. as people were in *s.* and all men mused
12. † 29. seek not what shall eat, live not in caref. *s.*

SUSTAIN.

1 *Kings* 17. 9. commanded a widow woman to *s.* thee
Neh. 9. 21. yea, forty years didst thou *s.* them
Ps. 55. 22. cast thy burden on Lord, he shall *s.* thee
Prov. 18. 14. the spirit of a man will *s.* his infirmity

SUSTAINED.

Gen. 27. 37. and with corn and wine have I *s.* him
Psal. 3. 5. I awaked, for the Lord *s.* me
Isa. 59. 16. and his righteousness, it *s.* him

SUSTENANCE.

Judg. 6. 4. Midianites left no *s.* for Israel, nor sheep
2 *Sam.* 19. 32. Barzillai had provided the king of *s.*
Acts 7. 11. dearth in Canaan, our fathers found no *s.*

SWADDLED.

Lam. 2. † 20. women eat children *s.* with their hands
2. 22. those that I have *s.* hath my enemy consumed
Ezek. 16. 4. thou wast not salted at all, nor *s.* at all

SWADDLING.

Job 38. 9. I made thick darkness a *s.* band for it
Luke 2. 7. and she wrapped him in *s.* clothes, 12.

SWALLOW,

In Hebrew, Sis, *is a plaintive bird, and a bird of passage. Mention is made of the* swallow *in* Isa. 38. 14. Like a crane or a *swallow,* so did I chatter. *My complaint and cry were like to the noise of a* swallow, *quick and frequent; and like that of a crane, loud and frightful. And in* Jer. 8. 7. The stork in the heaven knoweth her appointed times, and the turtle, and the crane, and the *swallow,* observe the time of their coming.

The swallow *is of a black colour, with some spots of a dirty black under her belly; its flight is very unequal, and its sight is very quick. It appears in spring and summer, and goes away in autumn. It is thought that it passes the sea, and withdraws into hotter climates, where it either hides itself in holes in the earth, or even in marshes, and under the water, wherein sometimes great lumps of* swallows *have been fished up, fixed one to another by the claws and beak: and when they are laid in a warm place, they move and recover, though before they seemed to be dead. It is called* χελιδών *in Greek, whence comes the name of the herb* Chelidone, *in English* Celandine, *or* swallow-wort, *because it is pretended, that with this herb the* swallow *opens the eyes of her young ones, though they should even be blinded on purpose. It is said that the flesh of these birds, burnt to ashes, is excellent for distempers of the eyes. The* swallow *is said to breed twice a year, once in the climate to which she transports herself while our winter lasts; and again in those six months she continues in this country. Their chief food are the flies that they catch as they fly. They commonly make their nest in chimneys, and every year return to the same place. Their nests are made of clay, mingled with bits of straw or chaff: and it is said, that when they want clay or mud, they plunge themselves in water, then rolling in the dust, make clay for themselves.*

Psal. 84. 3. the *s.* hath found a nest for herself
Prov. 26. 2. as the *s.* by flying, so the curse causeless
Isa. 38. 14. like a crane or a *s.* so did I chatter
Jer. 8. 7. crane and *s.* observe time of their coming

SWALLOW, *Verb.*

Num. 16. 30. if the earth open and *s.* them up
31. for they said, lest the earth *s.* us up also
2 *Sam.* 20. 19. why wilt thou *s.* up inheritance of L.
20. far be it from me, that I should *s.* up or destroy
Job 2. † 3. thou movedst me to *s.* him up without cause
7. 19. nor let me alone till I *s.* down my spittle
20. 18. he shall restore, and not *s.* it down
Psal. 21. 9. the Lord shall *s.* them up in his wrath
56. 1. be merciful to me, O G. man would *s.* me up
2. mine enemies would daily *s.* me up
57. 3. from the reproach of him that would *s.* me up
69. 15. neither let the deep *s.* me up
Prov. 1. 12. let us *s.* them up alive as the grave
Eccl. 10. 12. but the lips of a fool will *s.* up himself
Isa. 3. † 12. they lead me, *s.* up the way of thy paths
19. † 3. and I will *s.* up the counsel thereof
25. † 7. he will *s.* up the face of the covering
8. will *s.* up death in victory, Ld. will wipe away
42. † 14. I will destroy and *s.* up at once
Hos. 8. 7. if so be it yield, the strangers shall *s.* it up
Amos 8. 4. hear this, O ye that *s.* up the needy
Obad. 16. they shall drink, and they shall *s.* down
Jonah 1. 17. the Lord prepared a fish to *s.* up Jonah
Mat. 23. 24. guides who strain at a gnat, and *s.* camel

SWALLOWED.

Exod. 7. 12. but Aaron's rod *s.* up their rods
15. 12. stretchedst thy right hand, the earth *s.* them
Num. 16. 32. earth opened and *s.* 26. 10. *Deut.* 11. 6.
2 *Sam.* 17. 16. but pass over, lest the king be *s.* up
Job 6. 3. heav. than sand, theref. my words are *s.* up
20. 15. he hath *s.* down riches, he shall vomit them
37. 20. if a man speak, surely he shall be *s.* up
Psal. 35. 25. let them not say, we have *s.* him up
106. 17. the earth opened and *s.* up Dathan
107. † 27. stagger, and all their wisdom is *s.* up
124. 3. then they had *s.* us up quick
Isa. 9. † 16. they that are led of them are *s.* up
28. 7. the priest and the prophet are *s.* up of wine
49. 19. they that *s.* thee up, shall be far away
Jer. 51. 34. he hath *s.* me up like a dragon
44. will bring out of his mouth that which hath *s.*
Lam. 2. 2. Lord hath *s.* up all the habitat. of Jacob
5. he hath *s.* up Israel, he hath *s.* up all her palaces
16. they hiss and say, we have *s.* her up
Ezek. 36. 3. because they have *s.* you up on ev. side
Hos. 8. 8. Israel is *s.* up among the Gentiles
1 *Cor.* 15. 54. death is *s.* up in victory
2 *Cor.* 2. 7. lest such one should be *s.* up with sorrow
5. 4. that mortality might be *s.* up of life
Rev. 12. 16. the earth opened and *s.* up the flood

SWALLOWETH.

Job 5. 5. and the robber *s.* up their substance
39. 24. he *s.* the ground with fierceness and rage

SWAN.

Lev. 11. 18. the *s.* the pelican, unclean, *Deut.* 14. 16.

SWARE.

Gen. 21. 31. Beersheba, because they *s.* both of them
24. 7. the Lord God of heaven that *s.* to me
9. the servant *s.* to him concerning that matter
25. 33. Jacob said, swear to me, and he *s.* to him
26. 3. I will perform the oath which I *s.* to Abraham
31. Abimelech and Isaac *s.* to one another
31. 53. and Jacob *s.* by the fear of his father Isaac
47. 31. Joseph *s.* to Jacob his father
50. 24. God will bring you to land he *s.* to Abrah.
Exod. 13. 5. the land which the Lord *s.* to thy fathers
to give thee, 11. | 33. 1. *Num.* 14. 16, 30. | 32.
11. *Deut.* 1. 8, 35. | 6. 10, 18, 23. | 7. 13. | 8. 1.
| 11. 9, 21. | 26. 3. | 28. 11. | 30. 20. | 31. 21, 23. |
34. 4. *Josh.* 1. 6. | 5. 6. | 21. 43.
Num. 32. 10. the Lord's anger was kindled, and he *s.*
saying, none of the men shall enter, *Deut.* 1. 34.
Deut. 2. 14. till men of war were wasted, as Ld. *s.*
4. 21. Lord *s.* that I should not go over Jordan
31. he will not forget the covenant which he *s.*
7. 12. keep mercy which he *s.* to thy salvation
8. 18. may establish his covenant which he *s.* 9. 5.
Josh. 6. 22. bring out Rahab, as ye *s.* unto her
9. 15. princes of congregation *s.* to the Gibeonites
20. because of the oath which we *s.* to them
14. 9. Moses *s.* on that day, saying, surely the land
21. 44. Ld. gave them rest according to all that he *s.*
Judg. 2. 1. brought to land which I *s.* to your fathers
1 *Sam.* 19. 6. Saul *s.* that David shall not be slain
20. 3. David *s.* moreover to Jonathan, and said
24. 22. David *s.* to Saul, and Saul went home
28. 10. Saul *s.* by the Lord to the witch at En-dor
2 *Sam.* 3. 35. Dav. *s.* he would not eat till sun be down
19. 23. king David *s.* to Shimei, 1 *Kings* 2. 8.
1 *Kings* 1. 29. king David *s.* to Bath-sheba, 30.
2. 23. Solomon *s.* that Adonijah should die
2 *Kings* 25. 24. Gedaliah *s.* to them, *Jer.* 40. 9.
2 *Chr.* 15. 14. they *s.* to the Lord with a loud voice
Ezra 10. 5. they *s.* to put away the strange wives
Psal. 95. 11. to whom I *s.* in my wrath, *Heb.* 3. 11
132. 2. how he *s.* to Ld. and vowed to G. of Jacob
Jer. 38. 16. so the king *s.* secretly to Jeremiah
Ezek. 16. 8. I *s.* and entered into covenant with thee
20. † 5. when I *s.* to the seed of Jacob, 47. † 14.
Dan. 12. 7. *s.* by him that liveth for ever, *Rev.* 10. 6.
Mark 6. 23. Herod *s.* to the daughter of Herodias
Luke 1. 73. to remember oath which he *s.* to Abrah.
Heb. 3. 18. to whom *s.* he that they should not enter
6. 13. he could swear by no greater, he *s.* by himself
7. 21. that said, the Lord *s.* and will not repent
See Their Fathers.

SWAREST.

Exod. 32. 13. to whom thou *s.* by thine own self
Num. 11. 12. carry them to land thou *s.* to fathers
Deut. 26. 15. land given us, as thou *s.* to our fathers
1 *Kings* 1. 17. thou *s.* that Solomon shall reign
Psal. 89. 49. kindnesses thou *s.* to David in truth

SWARM.

Exod. 8. 24. there came a grievous *s.* of flies
Judg. 14. 8. a *s.* of bees and honey in carcase of lion

SWARMS.

Exod. 8. 21. I will send *s.* of flies upon thee, houses
of the Egyptians shall be full of *s.* of flies

Exod. 8. 22. that no s. of flies shall be in Goshen
29. that the s. of flies may depart from Pharaoh
31. he removed the s. of flies from Pharaoh

SWEAR.

God hath prohibited all false oaths, and all useless and customary swearing; but when necessity and the importance of the matter require it, he allows us to swear by his name, but not in the name of any false gods, or in the name of inanimate things, whether on earth, or in heaven, or by the stars, or by the life of any man whatever, Lev. 19. 12. Exod. 20. 7. ‖ 23. 13. Deut. 6. 13. Jer. 4. 2. Our Saviour, who came into the world not to destroy the law, but to fulfil it, forbids all kinds of oaths, Mat. 5. 34. And the primitive Christians understood and observed this command in a literal sense, as may be seen from Tertullian, Eusebius, Chrysostom, Basil, Jerom, &c. However, it is acknowledged, that neither the apostles nor fathers have absolutely condemned swearing, or the use of oaths upon every occasion, and all subjects. There are circumstances wherein we cannot morally be excused from it: but we never ought to swear but upon urgent necessity, and to do some considerable good by it.

That a person swear lawfully, he must have a regard, [1] To the object; that he swear by the Lord alone; for seeing we deify and make that our God which we swear by, therefore we forsake the true God if we swear by that which is no God, Jer. 5. 7. [2] To the manner; that he swear in truth, in judgment, and in righteousness, Jer. 4. 2. that he swear not falsely, or deceitfully, but that which is agreeable to truth; that he swear not rashly, but upon due consideration of all circumstances: and that he swear nothing but what is agreeable to justice and equity. [3] He must have a regard to the end; that God may be glorified, our duty discharged, controversies appeased, our brethren satisfied, or our own or others' innocency cleared.

Gen. 21. 23. Abimelech said to Abraham s. to me
24. and Abraham said, I will s.
24. 3. and I will make thee s. by the Lord God
37. my master made me s. saying, not take a wife
25. 33. Jacob said, s. to me, and he sware to him
47. 31. Jacob said unto Joseph, s. unto me
50. 5. father made me s. ‖ Lev. 5. 4. if a soul s.
Exod. 6. 8. bring to land concerning which I did s.
Lev. 19. 12. and ye shall not s. by my name falsely
Num. 30. 2. if a man s. an oath to bind his soul
Deut. 6. 13. and thou shalt s. by his name, 10. 20.
Josh. 2. 12. Rahab said to spies, s. to me by the Lord
17. this thy oath which thou hast made us s. 20.
23. 7. nor cause to s. by their gods nor serve them
Judg. 15. 12. s. to me that ye will not fall upon me
1 Sam. 20. 17. Jonathan caused David to s. again
24. 21. s. that thou wilt not cut off my seed after me
30. 15. s. by God that thou wilt neither kill me
2 Sam. 19. 7. I s. by the Lord, if thou go not out
1 Kings 1. 13. didst not thou s. Solomon shall reign
51. saying, let king Solomon s. unto me to day
2. 42. did I not make thee to s. by the Lord?
8. 31. if any man trespass, and an oath be laid on him to cause him to s. 2 Chron. 6. 22.
2 Chron. 36. 13. Nebuchadnezzar made him s. by G.
Ezra 10. 5. then Ezra made Levites and all Isr. to s.
Neh. 13. 25. and I made them s. by God, saying
Isa. 3. 7. in that day sh. he s. I will not be an healer
19. 18. five cities in Egypt shall s. to the Lord
45. 23. word gone that to me every tongue shall s.
48. 1. which s. by the Lord, but not in truth
65. 16. that sweareth, shall s. by the God of truth
Jer. 4. 2. thou shalt s. the Lord liveth in truth
5. 2. tho' they say, the Lord liveth, they s. falsely
7. 9. will ye steal, murder, commit adultery, and s.
12. 16. if they will learn the ways of my people, to s. by my name, as they taught people to s. by Baal
22. 5. I s. by myself, saith Ld. this house become
32. 22. hast given them this land thou didst s.
Hos. 4. 15. neither go ye up to Beth-aven nor s.
Amos 8. 14. they that s. by the sin of Samaria
Zeph. 1. 5. that s. by the Lord, that s. by Malcham
Mat. 5. 34. s. not at all ‖ 36. s. not by thy head
23. 16. shall s. by the temple, s. by gold of temple
18. whoso shall s. by the altar, it is nothing
20. whoso therefore shall s. by the altar, sweareth
21. shall s. by the temple ‖ 22. shall s. by heaven
26. 74. then began he to curse and s. Mark 14. 71.
Heb. 6. 13. he could s. by no greater, he s. by himself
16. for men verily s. by the greater, and an oath
Jam. 5. 12. above all things, my brethren, s. not

SWEARERS.

Mal. 3. 5. I will be a swift witness against false s.

SWEARETH.

Lev. 6. 3. or have found what was lost, and s. falsely
Psal. 15. 4. that s. to his hurt, and changeth not
63. 11. every one that s. by him shall glory
Eccl. 9. 2. and he that s. as he that feareth an oath
Isa. 65. 16. he that s. shall swear by God of truth
Zech. 5. 3. and every one that s. shall be cut off
4. it shall enter into the house of him s. falsely
Mat. 23. 18. whosoever s. by the gift, he is guilty
20. s. by the altar ‖ 21. s. by temple, and by him
22. s. by throne of God, and by him that sitteth

SWEARING.

Lev. 5. 1. if a soul sin, and hear the voice of s.
Jer. 23. 10. for because of s. the land mourneth
Hos. 4. 2. by s. and lying, and steal, they break out
10. 4. spoken words, s. falsely in making a covenant
Heb. 7. †21. those priests were made without s. an oath

SWEAT.

Gen. 3. 19. in the s. of thy face shalt thou eat bread
Ezek. 44. 18. shall gird with any thing that causeth s.
Luke 22. 44. his s. was as it were great drops of blood

SWEEP.

Isa. 14. 23. I will s. it with the besom of destruction
28. 17. the hail shall s. away the refuge of lies
Luke 15. 8. doth not s. the house and seek diligently

SWEEPING.

Prov. 28. 3. is like a s. rain which leaveth no food

SWEET.

Exod. 15. 25. tree cast into waters, waters made s.
30. 23. take of myrrh and s. cinnamon half so much
2 Sam. 1. † 23. Saul and Jonathan were s. in their lives
23. 1. David the s. psalmist of Israel said
Neh. 8. 10. go your way, eat the fat, and drink the s.
Job 20. 12. though wickedness be s. in his mouth
21. 33. the clods of the valley shall be s. to him
38. 31. canst thou bind the s. influences of Pleiades?
Psal. 55. 14. we took s. counsel together and walked
104. 34. my meditation of him shall be s.
119. 103. how s. are thy words unto my taste!
141. 6. they shall hear my words, for they are s.
Prov. 3. 24. shall lie down, and thy sleep shall be s.
9. 17. stolen waters are s. bread in secret is pleasant
13. 19. the desire accomplished is s. to the soul
16. 24. pleasant words are s. to the soul and health
20. 17. bread of deceit is s. to a man, but afterwards
23. 8. thou shalt vomit up, and lose thy s. words
24. 13. eat the honey-comb, which is s. to thy taste
27. 7. to the hungry soul every bitter thing is s.
Eccl. 5. 12. the sleep of a labouring man is s.
11. 7. truly the light is a s. and a pleasant thing
Cant. 2. 3. his fruit was s. ‖ 14. for s. is thy voice
5. 5. my fingers dropped with s. smelling myrrh
13. his cheeks are as a bed of spices, as s. flowers, his lips like lilies, dropping s. smelling myrrh
16. his mouth is most s. yea, he is altogether lovely
Isa. 3. † 19. the Lord will take away the s. balls
24. instead of s. smell, there shall be stink
5. 20. woe to them that put bitter for s. and s. for bit.
23. 16. make s. melody, sing songs to be remember.
Jer. 6. 20. nor your sacrifices s. unto me
31. 26. I awaked, and my sleep was s. unto me
Jam. 3. 11. send at same place s. water and bitter?
Rev. 10. 9. it shall be in thy mouth s. as honey, 10.
18. † 12. no man buyeth their s. wood any more

SWEET calamus.

Exod. 30. 23. take of s. calamus 250 shekels

SWEET cane.

Isa. 43. 24. thou hast brought me no s. c. with money
Jer. 6. 20. the s. cane came from a far country

See Incense, Odours, Savour.

SWEET spices.

Exod. 30. 34. take to thee s. spices with frankincense
37. 29. he made the pure incense of s. spices
Mark 16. 1. bought s. s. that they might anoint him

SWEET wine.

Isa. 49. 26. be drunken with blood as with s. wine
Amos 9. 13. the mount shall drop s. wine, hills melt
Mic. 6. 15. and s. wine, but shalt not drink wine

SWEETER.

Judg. 14. 18. men of city said, what is s. than honey?
Psal. 19. 10. thy word is s. than the honey-comb
119. 103. thy words are s. than honey to my mouth

SWEETLY.

Job 24. 20. worm shall feed s. on him, not rememb.
Cant. 7. 9. like the best wine, that goeth down s.

SWEETENED.

Psal. 55. † 14. we s. counsel together and walked

SWEETNESS.

Judg. 9. 11. should I forsake my s. and good fruit?
14. 14. and out of the strong came forth s.
Prov. 16. 21. the s. of the lips increaseth learning
27. 9. so doth s. of a man's friend by hearty counsel
Ezek. 3. 3. the roll was in my mouth as honey for s.

SWELL.

Num. 5. 21. thy thigh to rot, and thy belly to s. 22.
27. her belly shall s. and her thigh shall rot
Deut. 8. 4. nor did thy foot s. these forty years

SWELLED.

Neh. 9. 21. yea, forty years their feet s. not

SWELLING.

Psal. 46. 3. though mountains shake with s. thereof
Isa. 30. 13. as a breach s. out in a high wall
Jer. 12. 5. then how wilt thou do in the s. of Jordan?
49. 19. like a lion from the s. of Jordan, 50. 44.
2 Pet. 2. 18. speak great s. words of vanity
Jude 16. and their mouth speaketh great s. words

SWELLINGS.

2 Cor. 12. 20. I fear lest there be s. tumults among you

SWEPT.

Judg. 5. 21. the river of Kishon s. them away
Jer. 46. 15. why are thy valiant men s. away?
Mat. 12. 44. I will return to my house, when come, he findeth it empty, s. and garnished, Luke 11. 25.

SWERVED.

1 Tim. 1. 6. which some having s. have turned aside

SWIFT.

Deut. 28. 49. shall bring a nation as s. as the eagle
1 Kings 4. † 28. straw for the horses and s. beasts
1 Chr. 12. 8. were as s. as roes on the mountains
Job 9. 26. they are passed away as the s. ships
24. 18. he is s. as the waters, he beholdeth not
Prov. 6. 18. feet that be s. in running to mischief
Eccl. 9. 11. I saw that the race is not to the s.
Isa. 18. 2. go, ye s. messengers, to a nation peeled
19. 1. behold the Lord rideth upon a s. cloud
30. 16. but ye said, no, for we will ride on the s. therefore shall they that pursue you be s.
66. 20. they shall bring your brethren on s. beasts
Jer. 2. 23. thou art a s. dromedary travers. her ways
46. 6. let not s. flee away, nor mighty men escape
Amos 2. 14. therefore the flight shall perish from s.
15. he that is s. of foot shall not deliver himself
Mic. 1. 13. O Lachish, bind the chariot to s. beast
Mal. 3. 5. I will be s. witness against the sorcerers
Rom. 3. 15. their feet are s. to shed blood
Jam. 1. 19. let every man be s. to hear, slow to speak
2 Pet. 2. 1. shall bring on themselves s. destruction

SWIFTER.

2 Sam. 1. 23. were s. than eagles, stronger than lions
Job 7. 6. my days are s. than a weaver's shuttle
9. 25. now my days are s. than a post, they flee away
Jer. 4. 13. his horses are s. than eagles, woe unto us
Lam. 4. 19. our persecutors are s. than the eagles
Hab. 1. 8. their horses are s. than the leopards

SWIFTLY.

Psal. 147. 15. his word runneth very s.
Isa. 5. 26. behold, they shall come with speed s.
Dan. 9. 21. Gabriel being caused to fly s. touched me
Joel 3. 4. if ye recompense me s. and speedily

SWIM.

2 Kings 6. 6. he cast in the stick, and the iron did s.
Psal. 6. 6. all the night make I my bed to s.
Isa. 25. 11. that swimmeth spread forth hands to s.
Ezek. 47. 5. for the waters were risen, waters to s. in
Acts 27. 42. lest any of them should s. out and escape
43. and commanded that they which could s.

SWIMMEST.

Ezek. 32. 6. I will water the land wherein thou s.

SWIMMETH.

Isa. 25. 11. as he that s. spreadeth forth his hands

SWINE

Is an animal well known, the use of which was forbid to the Hebrews, Lev. 11. 7. It is said, they had the flesh of this animal in such detestation, that they would not so much as pronounce its name, but instead of it said, That beast, That thing. In 2 Macc. 6. 18, &c. when old Eleazar was taken by the servants of Antiochus Epiphanes, he was vehemently urged to taste swine's flesh, or at least to pretend to taste it. They opened his mouth by force, to compel him to eat of it; but he chose rather to suffer death than to break the law of God, and to give offence to the weaker people of his nation.

Porphyry affirms, that the Hebrews and Phenicians abstained from pork, because there was none in their country. He might rather have said, there was none, or but very little, because they bred no hogs, by reason of that abhorrence they had conceived for them: for it is certain they might have had them if they had pleased; and that there were herds of swine in our Saviour's time, is evident from Mat. 8. 30, 31. Mark 5. 11.

Our Saviour in Mat. 7. 6. forbids his disciples to cast their pearls before swine, lest they trample them under their feet, and turn again and rend you. He would have them to use discretion in dispensing holy things, especially by way of admonition, or reproof. Preach not the gospel to those that persecute you for your message, neither apply the promises to the profane. The prodigal son, in Luke 15. 15. when he had spent all, was reduced to such distress as to be glad to feed swine; this denotes the base work and drudgery that sinners employ themselves about. It is said in Prov. 11. 22. As a jewel of gold in a swine's snout, so is a fair woman who is without discretion. Both the Jewish and Arabian women sometimes used to wear rings in their nostrils to adorn themselves. But nothing can be more ridiculous than to put a gold ring or a jewel in a swine's snout. St. Peter compares those sinners that frequently relapse into their former sins, to a sow that, as soon as she is washed, goes again to wallow in the mire, 2 Pet. 2. 22.

Lev. 11. 7. the s. is unclean to you, Deut. 14. 8.
Prov. 11. 22. as a jewel of gold in a s. snout, so is
Isa. 65. 4. which eat s. flesh and broth of abominable
66. 3. an oblation, as if he offered s. blood
17. eating s. flesh, and abomination, and the mouse
Mat. 7. 6. neither cast ye your pearls before s.
8. 30. an herd of s. feeding, Mark 5. 11. Luke 8. 32.
31. suffer us to go into the herd of s. Mark 5. 12.
32. they went into the s. Mark 5. 13. Luke 8. 33. the whole herd of s. ran violently down
Mark 5. 14. and they that fed the s. fled and told
16. they told them also concerning the s.
Luke 15. 15. he sent him into his fields to feed s.
16. have filled his belly with husks the s. did eat

SWOLLEN.

Acts 28. 6. they looked when he should have s.

SWOON.

Lam. 2. 11. because the children s. in the streets

SWOONED.

Lam. 2. 12. when they s. as the wounded in streets

SWORD.

The sword in Scripture is often used for war. Lev. 26. 25. I will bring a sword upon you; I will cause war to come. By the sword shalt thou live, Gen. 27. 40. Thou shalt support thyself by war and rapine. By sword is understood the vengeance and judgments which God inflicts upon sinners. Deut. 32. 41, 42. If I whet my glittering sword. My sword shall devour flesh. Also the instrument which God uses to employ for executing his judgments, Psal. 17. 13. Deliver my soul from the wicked, which is thy sword. Sword is figuratively put for power and authority, Rom. 13. 4. He beareth not the sword in vain. The magistrate hath not received his power to no purpose; but that he may punish offenders, and defend the good. The apostle alludes to the custom of princes, who had certain officers going before them, bearing the ensigns of their authority. All they that take the sword shall perish with the sword, Mat. 26. 52. They that take up the sword by their own authority, and would do justice to themselves, deserve to be put to death by the sword of authority. Or, those that take the sword to smite another, generally suffer by it themselves. The word of God is called the sword of the Spirit, Eph. 6. 17. It is a spiritual sword, or a means provided by the Spirit of God, and made effectual by him to cut the sinews of the strongest temptations, to kill or mortify the inward lusts and corruptions of the heart, to subdue the most fixed obstinacy of the mind, and the most resolute purposes of the will, Heb. 4. 12. Moses calls God the sword of Israel's excellency, Deut. 33. 29. He is their strength, the author of all their past or approaching victories, by whose assistance they did excel, and gloriously conquer, and triumph over their enemies. Our Saviour says, Mat. 10. 34. I came not to send peace, but a sword. My coming and preaching the gospel will prove in the event, through the devil's malice, the corruptions of men's hearts, and their madness on their idolatry and superstition, an occasion of much variance and division, even between nearest relations, yea, and of bodily death, and many calamities and persecutions

Gen. 3. 24. he placed cherubims, and a flaming *s.*
34. 25. took each man his *s.* and came on the city
Exod. 5. 21. to put a *s.* in their hands to slay us
32. 27. he said, put every man his *s.* by his side
Lev. 26. 6. nor shall the *s.* go through your land
25. I will bring a *s.* upon you, *Ezek.* 5. 17. | 6. 3. | 14. 17. | 29. 8. | 33. 2.
33. and I will draw out a *s.* after you
37. they shall fall as it were before a *s.*
Num. 22. 23. the angel's *s.* drawn in his hand, 31.
29. I would there were a *s.* in mine hand
Deut. 32. 25. the *s.* without, and terror within
33. 29. and who is the *s.* of thy excellency
Josh. 5. 13. stood with his *s.* drawn in his hand
24. 12. but not with thy *s.* nor with thy bow
Judg. 7. 14. this is nothing save the *s.* of Gideon
18. say, the *s.* of the Lord, and of Gideon, 20.
22. and the Lord set every man's *s.* against his fellow through all the host, 1 *Sam.* 14. 20.
8. 10. for there fell 120,000 men that drew *s.*
20. the youth drew not his *s.* for he feared
9. 54. he said unto him, draw thy *s.* and slay me
20. 2. four hundred thousand that drew *s.* 17.
15. twenty and six thousand men that drew *s.*
25. eighteen thousand men; all these drew the *s.*
35. Israel destroyed 25,100 men that drew the *s.*
46. all that fell were 25,000 that drew the *s.*
1 *Sam.* 13. 22. neither *s.* nor spear was found
15. 33. as thy *s.* hath made women childless, so
17. 39. David girded his *s.* on his armour, 25. 13.
50. but there was no *s.* in the hand of David
51. David ran and took his *s.* and slew him
18. 4. even to his *s.* and to his bow and girdle
21. 8. is there not here under thy hand a spear or *s.*
9. the *s.* of Goliath is here wrapt in a cloth
22. 10. and he gave him the *s.* of Goliath
13. in that thou hast given him bread, and a *s.*
25. 13. David said, gird ye on every man his *s.* and they girded on every man his *s.*
31. 4. draw thy *s.* and thrust me through therewith, therefore Saul took a *s.* and fell upon it
5. his armour bearer fell also upon his *s.* and died
2 *Sam.* 1. 22. the *s.* of Saul returned not empty
2. 16. and thrust his *s.* in his fellow's side
26. Abner said, shall the *s.* devour for ever?
3. 29. not fail one that falleth on the *s.*
11. 25. the *s.* devoureth one as well as another
12. 10. the *s.* shall never depart from thy house
18. 8. and the wood devoured more than the *s.*
20. 10. Amasa took no heed to the *s.* in his hand
23. 10. and his hand clave unto the *s.*
24. 9. in Israel 800,000 men that drew the *s.*
1 *Kings* 3. 24. bring me a *s.* and they brought a *s.*
19. 17. him that escapeth the *s.* of Hazael
1 *Chron.* 5. 18. men able to bear buckler and *s.*
10. 4. draw thy *s.* and thrust me through therewith, so Saul took a *s.* and fell upon it
5. his armour-bearer fell likewise on the *s.*
21. 5. an hundred thousand men that drew *s.* and Judah was 470,000 that drew *s.*
12. while that the *s.* of thine enemies overtake, or else three days the *s.* of the Lord
16. the angel having a *s.* drawn in his hand
27. and he put up his *s.* again into the sheath
30. he was afraid, because of the *s.* of the angel
2 *Chron.* 20. 9. as when the *s.* or judgment cometh
Ezra 9. 7. we and our kings are delivered to the *s.*
Neh. 4. 18. every one had his *s.* girded by his side
Esth. 9. 5. Jews smote all their enemies with the *s.*
Job 5. 20. in war to deliver from power of the *s.*
15. 22. and he is waited for of the *s.*
19. 29. be ye afraid of the *s.* for wrath bringeth the punishment of the *s.*
20. 25. the glittering *s.* cometh out of his gall
27. 14. if children be multiplied, it is for the *s.*
40. 19. can make his *s.* to approach unto him
41. 26. the *s.* of him that layeth at him cannot hold
Psal. 7. 12. if he turn not he will whet his *s.*
17. 13. deliver from the wicked, which is thy *s.*
37. 14. the wicked have drawn out the *s.*
15. their *s.* shall enter into their own heart
45. 3. gird thy *s.* on thy thigh, with thy glory
57. 4. and their tongue a sharp *s.*
64. 3. who whet their tongue like a *s.* and bend
76. 3. there brake he the shield and the *s.*
78. 62. he gave his people over unto the *s.*
149. 6. and a two-edged *s.* in their hand
Prov. 5. 4. but her end is sharp as a two edged *s.*
12. 18. that speaketh like the piercings of a *s.*
25. 18. a man that beareth false witness is a *s.*
Cant. 3. 8. every man hath his *s.* upon his thigh
Isa. 2. 4. nation shall not lift up *s.* against nation
31. 8. the *s.* not of a mean man shall devour him
34. 6. the *s.* of the Lord is filled with blood
41. 2. he gave them as the dust to his *s.*
49. 2. he hath made my mouth like a sharp *s.*
51. 19. the famine and the *s.* are come to thee
65. 12. therefore will I number you to the *s.*
66. 16. by his *s.* will the Lord plead with all flesh
Jer. 2. 30. your own *s.* devoured your prophets
4. 10. whereas the *s.* reacheth unto the soul
5. 12. neither shall we see *s.* nor famine, 14. 13.
6. 25. for the *s.* of the enemy is on every side
9. 16. I will send a *s.* after them till I have consumed them, 24. 10. | 25. 27. | 29. 17. | 49. 37.
12. 12. for the *s.* of the Lord shall devour
14. 13. the prophets say, ye shall not see the *s.*
15. say *s.* and famine shall not be in this land
16. shall be cast in the streets because of the *s.*
15. 2. such as are for the *s.* to the *s.* 43. 11.
3. I will appoint the *s.* to slay, and dogs to tear
9. the residue of them will I deliver to the *s.*
18. 21. pour out their blood by the force of the *s.*
25. 16. and they shall be mad because of the *s.*
29. for I will call for a *s.* *Ezek.* 38. 21.
31. he will give them that are wicked to the *s.*
31. 2. the people left of the *s.* found grace
32. 24. the city is given because of the *s.*
34. 17. I proclaim a liberty for you to the *s.*
42. 16. the *s.* ye feared shall overtake you then
44. 28. yet a small number which escape the *s.*
46. 10. the *s.* shall devour and be satiate, 14.

Jer. 47. 6. O thou *s.* of the Lord, how long ere quiet
48. 2. O madmen, the *s.* shall pursue thee
10. cursed that keepeth back his *s.* from blood
50. 16. for fear of the oppressing *s.* they shall turn
35. a *s.* is on the Chaldeans, saith the Lord
36. a *s.* is on the liars, a *s.* is on her mighty men
37. a *s.* is on their horses, a *s.* on her treasures
51. 50. ye that have escaped the *s.* go away
Lam. 5. 9. we gat bread by peril because of the *s.*
Ezek. 5. 2. I will draw out a *s.* after them, 12.
17. and I will bring the *s.* upon thee, 6. 3.
6. 8. ye may have some that shall escape the *s.*
7. 15. the *s.* is without, the pestilence within
11. 8. ye have feared the *s.* and I will bring a *s.*
14. 17. if I bring a *s.* and say, *s.* go through
21. when I send my four sore judgments, the *s.*
21. 9. prophesy and say, a *s.* a *s.* is sharpened, 11
12. terrors, by reason of the *s.* on my people
13. and what if the *s.* contemn even the rod?
14. let their *s.* be doubled, the *s.* of the great men slain, it is the *s.* of great men that are slain
15. set the point of the *s.* against the gates
19. appoint two ways, that the *s.* may come
20. appoint a way, that *s.* may come to Rabbath
28. the *s.* the *s.* is drawn for the slaughter
30. 4. and the *s.* shall come upon Egypt
21. to bind it, to make it strong to hold the *s.*
22. I will cause the *s.* to fall out of his hand
32. 11. the *s.* of the king of Babylon shall come
33. 3. if when he seeth the *s.* come on the land
4. if the *s.* come and take him away, 6.
6. but if the watchmen see the *s.* come, if the *s.* come and take any person from among them
26. ye stand upon your *s.* and ye defile
35. 5. thou hast shed blood by the force of the *s.*
Hos. 2. 18. and I will break the bow and the *s.*
11. 6. and the *s.* shall abide on his cities
Amos 9. 4. thence will I command the *s.*
Mic. 4. 3. nation shall not lift up *s.* against nation
6. 14. thou deliverest, will I give up to the *s.*
Nah. 2. 13. the *s.* shall devour the young lions
3. 3. the horsemen lifteth up both the bright *s.*
15. there the *s.* shall cut thee off
Zech. 9. 13. made thee as the *s.* of a mighty man
11. 17. the *s.* shall be upon his arm, and his eye
13. 7. awake, O *s.* against my shepherd
Mat. 10. 34. I came not to send peace, but a *s.*
26. 51. one of them drew his *s.* and struck a servant, *Mark* 14. 47. *John* 18. 10.
52. put up again thy *s.* *John* 18. 11.
Luke 2. 35. a *s.* shall pierce through thy own soul
22. 36. he that hath no *s.* let him buy one
Acts 16. 27. he drew his *s.* and would have killed
Rom. 8. 35. shall *s.* separate us from love of Christ
13. 4. for he beareth not the *s.* in vain
Eph. 6. 17. *s.* of spirit which is the word of God
Heb. 4. 12. and sharper than any two-edged *s.*
Rev. 1. 16. out of his mouth went a two-edged *s.*
2. 12. which hath the sharp *s.* with two edges
6. 4. and there was given to him a great *s.*
19. 15. out of his mouth goeth a sharp *s.* 21.

By the SWORD.

Gen. 27. 40. *by the s.* thou shalt live and serve
Lev. 26. 7. they shall fall before you *by the s.* 8.
2 *Sam.* 1. 12. because they were fallen *by the s.*
2 *Chron.* 29. 9. our fathers have fallen *by the s.*
Job 33. 18. and his life from perishing *by the s.*
36. 12. they obey not, they shall perish *by the s.*
Psal. 44. 3. they got not the land *by their s.*
78. 64. their priests fell *by the s.* their widows
Jer. 11. 22. thus saith the Lord, their young men shall die *by the s.* 18. 21. *Lam.* 2. 21.
14. 12. but I will consume them *by the s.*
15. *by s.* and fam. shall those prophets be consumed
16. 4. shall be consumed *by the s.* 44. 12, 18, 27.
19. 7. and I will cause them to fall *by the s.*
21. 9. abideth, shall die *by the s.* 38. 2. | 42. 17, 22.
27. 13. why will ye die *by the s.* by the famine?
32. 36. this city shall be delivered *by the s.*
33. 4. houses which are thrown down *by the s.*
34. 4. O Zedekiah, thou shalt not die *by the s.*
44. 13. as I have punished Jerusalem *by the s.*
Ezek. 26. 6. her daughters shall be slain *by the s.*
11. he shall slay thy people *by the s.*
28. 23. the wounded shall be judged in her *by the s.*
31. 18. lie with them that be slain *by the s.* 32. 20, 21, 22, 25, 30. | 33. 27.
39. 23. they trespassed, so they fell all *by the s.*
Hos. 1. 7. I will not save them by bow nor *by s.*
Amos 7. 11. Jeroboam shall die *by the s.*
9. 10. the sinners of my people shall die *by the s.*
Hag. 2. 22. every one *by the s.* of his brother
Rev. 13. 14. had the wound *by a s.* and did live

See EDGE, FALL.

From the SWORD.

Exod. 18. 4. delivered me *from the s.* of Pharaoh
Lev. 26. 36. they shall flee as fleeing *from a s.*
1 *Kings* 19. 17. him that escapeth *from the s.* of Jehu
2 *Chron.* 36. 20. that escaped *from the s.* carried he
Job 5. 15. but he saveth the poor *from the s.*
39. 22. neither turneth he back *from the s.*
Psal. 22. 20. deliver my soul *from the s.* my darling
144. 10. who delivereth David *from the* hurtful *s.*
Isa. 21. 15. for they fled *from the* drawn *s.*
31. 8. but he shall flee *from the s.*
Jer. 21. 7. such as are left *from the s.* from famine
46. 16. arise, let us go *from the* oppressing *s.*
Ezek. 12. 16. I'll leave a few men of them *from s.*
38. 8. the land that is brought back *from the s.*

My SWORD.

Gen. 48. 22. which I took from Amorite with *my s.*
Exod. 15. 9. I will draw *my s.* my hand shall destroy
Deut. 32. 41. and if I whet *my* glittering *s.*
42. and *my s.* shall devour flesh
1 *Sam.* 21. 8. neither brought *my s.* nor my weapons
Psal. 44. 6. neither shall *my s.* save me
Isa. 34. 5. *my s.* shall be bathed in heaven
Ezek. 21. 3. I will draw *my s.* out of his sheath
4. therefore *my s.* shall go out of his sheath
5. I the Lord have drawn *my s.* out of his sheath
30. 24. I have put *my s.* in his hand, 25.
32. 10. be afraid, when I shall brandish *my s.*

Zeph. 2. 12. Ethiopians, ye shall be slain by *my s.*

With the SWORD.

Gen. 31. 26. daughters as captives taken *with the s.*
Exod. 5. 3. lest he fall on us *with the s.* or pestilence
22. 24. and I will kill you *with the s.*
Num. 19. 16. whoso toucheth one slain *with the s.*
20. 18. lest I come out against thee *with the s.*
31. 8. Balaam also they slew *with the s.*
Deut. 28. 22. the Lord shall smite thee *with the s.*
Josh. 10. 11. whom Israel slew *with the s.* 13. 22.
11. 10. he smote the king of Hazor *with the s.*
1 *Sam.* 17. 45. thou comest to me *with a s.* and spear
47. the Lord saveth not *with s.* and spear
2 *Sam.* 12. 9. thou hast killed Uriah *with the s.*
20. 8. a girdle *with a s.* fastened upon his loins
21. 16. Ishbi-benob being girded *with a s.*
1 *Kings* 1. 51. will not slay his servant *with the s.*
2. 8. I will not put thee to death *with the s.*
32. better than he, and slew them *with the s.*
19. 1. how he had slain all the prophets *with the s.*
10. and slain thy prophets *with the s.* 14.
2 *Kings* 8. 12. young men wilt thou slay *with the s.*
11. 15. have Athaliah forth, and him that followeth her, kill *with the s.* 2 *Chron.* 23. 14.
20. they slew Athaliah *with the s.* 2 *Chron.* 23. 21.
19. 37. his son smote Sennacherib king of Assyria *with the s.* 2 *Chron.* 32. 21. *Isa.* 37. 38.
2 *Chron.* 21. 4. and slew all his brethren *with the s.*
36. 17. who slew their young men *with the s.*
Ps. 42. 10. as *with a s.* in my bones enemies reproach
Isa. 1. 20. rebel, ye shall be devoured *with the s.*
14. 19. that are slain, thrust through *with a s.*
22. 2. thy slain men are not slain *with the s.*
27. 1. the Lord *with his* strong *s.* shall punish
Jer. 5. 17. shall impoverish thy cities *with the s.*
14. 18. then behold the slain *with the s.*
20. 4. and he shall slay Judah *with the s.*
26. 23. who slew Urijah *with the s.* and cast
27. 8. that nation will I punish *with the s.*
29. 18. I will persecute them *with the s.*
41. 2. smote Gedaliah *with the s.* and slew him
Lam. 4. 9. they that be slain *with the s.* are better
Ezek. 7. 15. he that is in the field shall die *with the s.*
23. 10. the Assyrians slew her *with the s.*
26. 8. shall slay the daughters of Tyrus *with the s.*
31. 17. they also went down to hell with them that be slain *with the s.* 32. 28, 32. | 35. 8.
Amos 1. 11. he did pursue his brother *with the s.*
4. 10. your young men have I slain *with the s.*
7. 9. rise against house of Jeroboam *with the s.*
9. 1. I will slay the last of them *with the s.*
Mic. 5. 6. shall waste the land of Assyria *with the s.*
Mat. 26. 52. that take the *s.* shall perish *with the s.*
Luke 22. 49. Lord, shall we smite *with the s.?*
Acts 12. 2. Herod killed James *with the s.*
Heb. 11. 37. were tempted, were slain *with the s.*
Rev. 2. 16. I will fight against them *with the s.*
6. 8. and power to kill *with s.* and with hunger
13. 10. that killeth *with s.* must be killed *with s.*
19. 21. the remnant were slain *with the s.*

SWORDS.

1 *Sam.* 13. 19. lest the Hebrews make them *s.*
2 *Kings* 3. 26. took with him 700 men that drew *s.*
Neh. 4. 13. I even set the people with their *s.*
Psal. 55. 21. yet his words were drawn *s.*
59. 7. behold, they belch out, *s.* are in their lips
Prov. 30. 14. a generation, whose teeth are as *s.*
Cant. 3. 8. they all hold *s.* being expert in war
Isa. 2. 4. and they shall beat their *s.* into plough shares, their spears into pruning-hooks, *Mic.* 4. 3.
21. 15. they fled from the *s.* and from the bow
Ezek. 16. 40. shall thrust thee through with their *s.*
23. 47. and shall despatch them with their *s.*
28. 7. strangers shall draw their *s.* and defile
30. 11. they shall draw their *s.* against Egypt
32. 12. by the *s.* of the mighty will I cause to fall
27. they have laid their *s.* under their heads
Joel 3. 10. beat your plough-shares into *s.*
Mat. 26. 47. with Judas was a great multitude with *s.* from the chief priests, *Mark* 14. 43.
55. are ye come out as against a thief with *s.* and staves to take me? *Mark* 14. 48. *Luke* 22. 52.
Luke 22. 38. Lord, behold here are two *s.*

SWORN.

Gen. 22. 16. by myself have I *s.* saith the Lord, *Isa.* 45. 23. *Jer.* 49. 13. | 51. 14. *Amos* 6. 8.
Exod. 13. 19. Joseph had straitly *s.* Israel
17. 16. the Lord hath *s.* that he will have war
Lev. 6. 5. that about which he hath *s.* falsely
Deut. 7. 8. would keep the oath he had *s.* *Jer.* 11. 5.
13. 17. multiply thee, as he hath *s.* to thy fathers
19. 8. if he enlarge thy coast, as he hath *s.*
28. 9. shall establish thee, as he hath *s.* 29. 13.
31. 7. bring thee to land Lord hath *s.* *Neh.* 9. 15.
Josh. 9. 18. because the princes had *s.* to them
19. we have *s.* to them by the Lord, 2 *Sam.* 21. 2.
Judg. 2. 15. against them for evil, as Lord had *s.*
21. 1. now the men of Israel had *s.* in Mizpeh
7. we have *s.* not to give them wives, 18.
1 *Sam.* 3. 14. I have *s.* unto the house of Eli
20. 42. go in peace, forasmuch as we have *s.*
2 *Sam.* 3. 9. except as the Lord hath *s.* to David
21. 2. children of Israel had *s.* to Gibeonites
2 *Chron.* 15. 15. they had *s.* with all their hearts
Neh. 6. 18. there were many in Judah *s.* to him
9. 15. the land which thou hadst *s.* to give them
Psal. 24. 4. who hath not *s.* deceitfully
89. 3. I have *s.* unto David my servant
35. once have I *s.* by my holiness, *Amos* 4. 2.
102. 8. that are mad against me, are *s.* against me
110. 4. the Lord hath *s.* and will not repent
119. 106. I have *s.* and I will perform it
132. 11. the Lord hath *s.* in truth to David
Isa. 14. 24. the Lord of hosts hath *s.* saying
45. 23. I have *s.* by myself, the word is gone out
54. 9. I have *s.* that waters of Noah no more go over the earth, so have I *s.* I would not be wrath
62. 8. the Lord hath *s.* by his right hand
Jer. 5. 7. they have *s.* by them that are no gods
44. 26. behold, I have *s.* by my great name
Ezek. 21. 23. to them that have *s.* oaths
Amos 8. 7. Lord hath *s.* by the excellency of Jacob

Mic. 7. 20. wilt perform the mercy thou hast s.
Acts 2. 30. knowing God hath s. by an oath to him
7. 17. time of promise drew nigh which God had s.
Heb. 4. 3. I have s. in my wrath, if they enter

SYCAMINE.

Luke 17. 6. say to this s. tree, be thou plucked up

SYCAMORE

Is a tree called the Egyptian fig-tree; its name is composed of συκος, a fig tree, and μωρος, a mulberry-tree. It partakes of the nature of each of these trees; of the mulberry-tree in its leaves, and of the fig-tree in its fruit, which is pretty like a fig in its shape and bigness. This fruit grows neither in clusters, nor at the ends of the branches, but sticking to the trunk of the tree. Its taste is pretty much like a wild fig. Amos says, I was no prophet, neither was I a prophet's son, but I was an herdman, and a gatherer of sycamore-fruit, or wild figs, Amos 7. 14. Pliny and other naturalists observe, that this fruit does not grow ripe till it is rubbed with iron combs, after which rubbing it ripens in four days. And Jerom upon Amos says, that without this management the figs cannot be eaten, because of their intolerable bitterness.

To make this tree fruitful, they made chinks and clefts in the bark, through which a kind of milky liquor continually distils. This, they say, causes a little bough to be formed, sometimes having six or seven figs upon it. They are hollow, without grains, and there is found a little yellow matter which is generally a nest of grubs. These figs are sweet, but not good for the stomach: they weaken it, and create a loathing, but at the same time moisten and refresh. A great many of these sycamores grow in Egypt; and some of them are said to be of such substance, that three men can hardly grasp them. There were also some in Judea, as appears from Luke 19. 4. where Zaccheus is said to have climbed up into a sycamore tree to see Jesus pass by, being of so low a stature that he could not otherwise see him because of the multitude.

SYCAMORE fruit.

Amos 7. 14. an herdman and a gatherer of s.-fruit

SYCAMORE-tree.

Luke 19. 4. Zaccheus climbed up into a s.-tree

SYCAMORE-trees.

1 Kings 10. 27. Solomon made cedars to be as s.-trees for abundance, 2 Chron. 1. 15. | 9. 27.
1 Chron. 27. 28. over the s.-trees was Baal-hanan
Psal. 78. 47. he destroyed their s. trees with frost

SYCAMORES.

Isa. 9. 10. the s. are cut down, but we will change

SYMPHONY.

This word is taken for the agreement of several voices, and a concert of several instruments, or for a particular sort of instrument. St. Luke takes it in the first sense, when he says, that the brother of the prodigal son, returning out of the field, heard in his father's house a concert of instruments, and the rejoicing of those that danced, or the voices of those that sung, ηκυσε συμφωνιας και χορων, Luke 15. 25. Daniel takes it in the second sense, for an instrument of music, Dan. 3. 5. which some think was a viol, or some instrument approaching thereto.—In our English translation it is called a dulcimer.

Dan. 3. † 5. at what time ye hear sound of the cornet, flute, harp, s.

SYNAGOGUE.

In Greek συναγωγη, of συναγειν, to gather together, signifies an assembly, as in Rev. 2. 9. | 3. 9. where St. John calls the false and hypocritical professors in Smyrna and Philadelphia, the synagogue of Satan, a congregation or assembly of men, who worship and serve the devil by errors and profaneness, and yet pretend they are the only true church of God. But most commonly the word synagogue is used to denote the place where the Jews assembled to pray, to read, and to hear the reading of the holy books, and other instructions. It is often mentioned in the Gospels and the Acts, because Christ and his apostles generally went to preach in the synagogues.

Authors are not agreed about the time when the Jews first began to have synagogues. Some will have it that they are as ancient as the ceremonial law. It cannot be denied, say they, that the Jews did worship God publicly every sabbath, and on other holy occasions, even then when they neither did nor could go up to Jerusalem; it is therefore very presumable that both conscience and prudence did direct them to appoint convenient places for that purpose. Some footsteps of them were to be seen so early as in the time of Elisha. Devout persons, in the time of this prophet, assembled themselves to him on the sabbath-day, to hear the law read to them, 2 Kings 4. 23. And the author of Psal. 74th, describing the havoc that the army of Nebuchadnezzar had made in Jerusalem, says, they have burned up all the synagogues of God in the land, Psal. 74. 8.

On the contrary, many learned men have thought them of but a late institution. Dr. Prideaux affirms, that they had no synagogues before the Babylonish captivity, for the main service of the synagogue, says he, being the reading of the law unto the people, where there was no book of the law to be read, there certainly could be no synagogue. But how rare the book of the law was through all Judea before the Babylonish captivity, many texts of Scripture tell us. When Jehoshaphat sent teachers through all Judea, to instruct the people in the law of God, they carried a book of the law with them, 2 Chron. 17. 9. which they needed not have done, if there had been any copies of the law in those cities to which they went; which certainly there would have been, had there been any synagogues in them. And when Hilkiah found the law in the temple, 2 Kings 22. 8. neither he nor king Josiah needed to have been so surprised at it, had books of the law been common in those times. Their behaviour on that occasion sufficiently proves they had never seen it before, which could not be the case, had there then been any other copies of it to be found among the people. And if there were no copies of the law at that time among them, there could then be most certainly no synagogues for them to resort to, for the hearing of it read unto them. From whence he concludes, there could be no synagogues among the Jews, till after the Babylonish captivity.

This learned author says, that if it be examined into, how it came to pass that the Jews were so prone to idolatry before the Babylonish captivity, and so strongly and cautiously, even to superstition, fixed against it after that captivity, the true reason hereof will appear to be, that they had the law and the prophets every week constantly read unto them after that captivity, which they had not before. For before that captivity, they having no synagogues for public worship, or public instruction, nor any places to resort to for either, unless the temple at Jerusalem, or the cities of the Levites, or to the prophets, when God was pleased to send such among them, for want hereof great ignorance grew among the people: God was little known among them, and his laws in a manner wholly forgotten. And therefore as occasions offered, they were easily drawn into all the superstitious and idolatrous usages of the neighbouring nations; till at length, for the punishment hereof, God gave them up to a dismal destruction in the Babylonish captivity: but after that captivity, and the return of the Jews from it, synagogues being erected among them in every city, to which they constantly resorted for public worship, and where every week they had the law from the first, and after that from the time of Antiochus's persecution, the prophets also read unto them, and were by sermons and exhortations there delivered, at least every sabbath, instructed in their duty, and excited to the obedience of it: this kept them in a thorough knowledge of God and his laws. And the threats they found in the prophets against the breakers of them, after these also came to be read among them, deterred them from transgressing against them. So that the law of Moses was never more strictly observed by them than from the time of Ezra (when synagogues first came into use among them) to the time of our Saviour; and they would have been unblamable herein, had they not overdone it, by adding corrupt traditions of their own devising, whereby, at length, they made the law itself of none effect, as our Saviour chargeth them, Mat. 15. 6.

As to Psal. 74. 8. They have burned up all the synagogues of God in the land: in the original, Col moadhe El, that is, all the assemblies of God; by which, says Dr. Prideaux, I acknowledge must be understood the places where the people did assemble to worship God. But this doth not infer that those places were synagogues; and there are none of the ancient versions, excepting that of Aquila, that so render this passage. The chief place where the Israelites assembled for the worship of God, was the temple at Jerusalem, and before that was built, the tabernacle; and the open court before the altar was that part, in both of them, where the people assembled to offer up their prayers unto God. But those that lived at a distance from the tabernacle, while that was in being, and afterwards from the temple, when that was built, not being able at all times to resort thither, they built courts, like those in which they prayed at the tabernacle and at the temple, therein to offer up their prayers unto God, which in aftertimes we find called by the name of proseuchæ. Into one of them our Saviour is said to have gone to pray, and to have continued therein a whole night, Luke 6. 12. What our English translation there renders, and continued all night in prayer to God, is in the original και ην διανυκτερευων ἐν τη Προσευχη του Θεου, that is, And he continued all night in a proseucha of God. In another of them, St. Paul taught the people of Philippi, Acts 16. 13, 16. In these two verses, what we render in our English version by the word prayer, is in the original a proseucha, or place of prayer.

The proseuchæ differed from the synagogues in several particulars. [1] In synagogues the prayers were offered up in public forms in common for the whole congregation; but in the proseuchæ they prayed, as in the temple, every one apart for himself; and so our Saviour prayed in the proseuchæ he went into. [2] The synagogues were covered houses; but the proseuchæ were open courts; they had no covering, except perhaps the shade of some trees, or some covered galleries. [3] The synagogues were all built on elevated places, within the cities to which they did belong; but the proseuchæ were without the cities, in the fields, especially near rivers. So this author concludes, that when the Psalmist says, that they burned up the synagogues of God, he may be understood of the proseuchæ, or of the schools of the prophets, or the places where the Levites taught the people in their cities.

After the time of the Maccabees, synagogues became frequent in Israel. It is affirmed, that in the city of Jerusalem alone, were no less than four hundred and sixty, or even four hundred and eighty; but herein they are supposed to have spoken hyperbolically, and to have expressed an uncertain large number by a certain one. Every trading fraternity had a synagogue of their own, and even strangers built some for those of their own nation. Hence it is, that in Acts 6. 9. mention is made of the synagogues of the Libertines, Cyrenians, Alexandrians, Cilicians, and Asiatics; which were appointed for the use of such of the inhabitants of these cities, or of these nations, as should at any time be at Jerusalem.

The Jewish authors give this general rule for the construction of synagogues. Wherever there are ten batelnim, a synagogue ought to be built. The signification of the word batelnim has been much controverted. Buxtorf thinks them to be persons receiving a stipend for duly assisting at divine service, that there may be always ten persons, at least, to assemble together. Lightfoot imagines them to have been ministers and officers of the synagogue. Others think this the most probable opinion, namely, that they were persons of a mature age, free, and in a condition to assist constantly at the service, on all days of assembling, which were, at least, two days a week, beside the sabbath: so that always upon these days there were present that number of assistants, without which the service could not be performed. When there were ten such persons in a town or city, they called it a great city, and here they might build a synagogue.

As the synagogue-service was to be on three days every week, for the sake of hearing the law; so it was to be thrice on those days, for the sake of their prayers. For it was a constant rule among them, that all were to pray unto God three times every day, that is, in the morning, at the time of the morning sacrifice; and in the evening, at the time of the evening sacrifice; and at the beginning of the night, because till then the evening sacrifice was still left burning upon the altar. It was anciently among God's people the steady practice of good and religious persons, to offer up their prayers to God thrice every day. This we find David did. Psal. 55. 17. Evening, morning, and at noon, will I pray. And Daniel, notwithstanding the king's decree to the contrary, says, that he kneeled upon his knees three times a day, and prayed, and gave thanks unto his God, Dan. 6. 10. By which it is implied, that he did not only at that time thus pray, but that it was always his constant custom so to do.

When synagogues were erected among the Jews, the hours of public devotion in them on their synagogue days, were, as to morning and evening prayers, the same hours in which the morning and evening sacrifices were offered up at the temple. And the same hours were also observed in their private prayers wherever performed. For the offering of incense on the golden altar in the holy place, at every morning and evening sacrifice in the temple, was instituted on purpose to offer up unto God the prayers of the people, who were then without, praying unto him. Hence it was, that St. Luke tells us, that while Zacharias went into the temple to burn incense, the whole multitude of the people were praying without at the time of incense, Luke 1. 9, 10. And for the same reason it is that David prayed, Let my prayer be set forth before thee as incense, and the lifting up of my hands as the evening sacrifice, Psal. 141. 2. And according to this usage is to be explained what we find in Rev. 8. 3, 4, 5. where it is said, that an angel came and stood at the altar, having a golden censer, and there was given unto him much incense, that he should offer it up with the prayers of all saints, upon the golden altar, which was before the throne: and the smoke of the incense, which came with the prayers of the saints, ascended up before God out of the angel's hand. The angel here mentioned, is the angel of the covenant, Christ our Lord, who intercedes for us with God, and, as our Mediator, constantly offers up our prayers unto him. And the manner of his doing this is set forth by the manner of the typical representation of it in the temple.

For as there, at every morning and evening sacrifice, the priest, in virtue of that sacrifice, entering into the holy place, and presenting himself at the golden altar, which stood directly before the mercy-seat, (the throne of God's visible presence among them during the tabernacle and the first temple,) did burn incense thereon, while the people were at their prayers without, thereby, as an intercessor to God for them, to offer up their prayers to him for his gracious acceptance, and to make them ascend up before him from out of his hands as a sweet-smelling savour in his presence; so Christ, our true priest, and most powerful intercessor, by virtue of that one sacrifice of himself once offered up, being entered into the holy place, the heaven above, is there continually present before the throne of mercy, to be a constant intercessor for us unto God; and while we are here in the outer court of his church in this world, offering up our prayers unto God; he there presents them unto him for us, and through his hands they are accepted as a sweet-smelling savour in his presence.

And it being well understood among the Jews that the offering up of the daily sacrifices, and the burning of incense upon the altar of incense, at the time of those sacrifices, was for the rendering of God propitious to them, and making their prayers to be acceptable in his presence, they were very careful to make the times of these offerings, and the times of their prayers, both at the temple, and every where else, to be exactly the same.

The most pious and devout persons that were at Jerusalem, chose on those times to go up into the temple, and there to offer up their prayers unto God; thus Peter and John are said to go up into the temple at the hour of prayer, being the ninth hour of the day, which was at three in the afternoon, the time of the offering up the evening sacrifice, Acts 3. 1. Those who were in other places, or being at Jerusalem, had not leisure to go up to the temple, performed their devotions elsewhere. If it were a synagogue-day, they went into the synagogue, *and there prayed with the congregation: and if it were not a* synagogue-day *they then prayed in private by themselves; and if they had leisure to go to the* synagogue, *they chose that for the place to do it in, thinking such a holy place the properest for such a holy exercise, though performed there in their private persons only; but if they had not leisure to go to such a holy place, then they prayed wherever they were at the hour of prayer, though it were in the street or market-place. And for this it was that our Saviour found fault with them, when he told them,* Mat. 6. 5. *that* they loved to pray standing in the *synagogues*, and in the corners of the streets, *thereby affecting more* to be seen of men, *than to be accepted of by God. But many of them had upper rooms in their houses, which were as chapels, particularly set apart, and consecrated for this purpose. In such a one Cornelius was* praying at the ninth hour of the day, *that is, at the time of the evening sacrifice, when the angel appeared unto him,* Acts 10. 30. *And such a one Peter went up into to pray* about the sixth hour of the day, *Acts* 10. 9. *when he had the vision of the great sheet, that is, at half an hour past twelve or thereabout; for then the evening sacrifice did begin on great and solemn days, and such a one it seems hereby that was. And in such* an upper room where the apostles assembled together in prayer, *when the Holy Ghost descended upon them,* Acts 1. 13.

In the synagogue *was the* ark or chest, *wherein lay the book of the law, that is, the* Pentateuch, *or* five books *of Moses. This chest, they say, was made after the model of the ark of the covenant, and always placed in that part of the* synagogue *which looked towards the* Holy Land, *if the* synagogue *was out of it; but if it was within it, then the chest was placed towards Jerusalem; and if the* synagogue *stood in this city, the chest was set towards the* holy of holies. *Out of this ark it was they took, with a great deal of ceremony, and before the whole congregation, the book of the law, when they were to read it. In the midst of the* synagogue *was a* desk or pulpit, *upon which the book or roll of the law was read very solemnly. There likewise he stood who intended to harangue the people.*

As to the seats or pews *whereon the people sat to hear the law read and expounded; of these some were more honourable than others. The former were for those who were called* Elders, *not so much upon the account of their age as of their gravity, prudence, and authority. These* Elders *sat with their backs towards the forementioned chest, and their faces towards the congregation, who looked towards the ark. These* seats of the Elders *are those which are called in* Mat. 23. 6. the chief seats, *and which our Saviour ordered his disciples not to contend for, or affect, as the Pharisees did. The women were therein distinct from the men, and seated in a gallery enclosed with lattices, so that they might see and hear, but not be seen.*

To regulate and take care of all things belonging to the synagogue *service, there was appointed a council, or assembly of grave and wise persons, well versed in the law, over whom was set a president, who is called the* ruler of the synagogue, *Luke* 8. 41. *He presided in the assemblies, and in judicial affairs that were sometimes decided there, against those who had given any scandal, and transgressed the law in any important matter. As for* scourging, *some are of opinion, that it was a punishment not falling under the jurisdiction of the rulers of the* synagogues, *but belonging to the civil courts, which they take to be meant by the* synagogues, *where our Saviour tells his disciples they should be scourged,* Mat. 10. 17. *Others, on the contrary, maintain, that by the word* synagogues *in the place here quoted, we are to understand* synagogues *properly so called. As to the manner of* scourging, *see* SCOURGE.

The same presidents invited those to speak in the synagogue, *whom they thought capable of it, and offered that honour to strangers, if there were any that seemed to have the gift of speaking. St. Paul being at Antioch of Pisidia, was invited by the rulers of the* synagogue *to make a discourse to them for their edification,* Acts 13. 14, 15. *And it is very probable, that whenever our Saviour preached in the* synagogues *it was not without the permission of the president, or chief ruler, though it be not expressly said so in the gospel, because it was a known custom.*

The rulers of the synagogue *were likewise bound to take care of the poor. There were in every* synagogue *two treasury chests, one for poor strangers, and the other for their own poor. Those who were charitably inclined, put their alms into these chests at their coming into the* synagogue *to pray. Upon extraordinary occasions they sometimes made public collections; in which cases, the rulers of the* synagogue *ordered the person whose business it was to collect the alms, to ask every body for their charity. Every one promised according as he was disposed, and afterwards they gathered from house to house what had been promised, for the Jews meddled not with money on their sabbath-day.*

These rulers likewise taught the people. This they did sometimes by way of dispute and conference, by questions and answers, or else by continued discourses like sermons. All these different ways of teaching they called by the general name of searching; *the discourse they styled a* search, *or* inquisition, *and him that made it, a* searcher. *The Hebrew word* darafch, *signifies, to* dive into the sublime, profound, mystical, allegorical, and prophetical senses *of holy Scripture.*

The synagogue *of the* Libertines, or freed men, *Acts* 6. 9. *was, according to many interpreters, that of those Jews, who having been led away captive by Pompey and by Sosias, had afterwards recovered their liberty, and were retired to Jerusalem, when Tiberias drove away the Jews out of Italy. Others will have it, that St. Luke wrote* Libystinorum, *and not* Libertinorum; *and that the* Libystini *were people of Libya, joining to Egypt. Others by these* Libertines *understood the sons of such Jews as were free denizens of Rome.*

Mat. 12. 9. when departed, he went into their *s.*
13. 54. he taught them in their *s. Mark* 6. 2.
Mark 1. 23. and there was in their *s.* a man with an unclean spirit, *Luke* 4. 33.
29. when they were come out of *s. Luke* 4. 38.
5. 22. Jairus by name, one of the rulers of the *s.* besought Jesus, 36. 38. *Luke* 8. 41, 49.
Luke 4. 16. as his custom was, he went into the *s.* on the sabbath-day
20. the eyes of all in the *s.* were fastened on him
7. 5. he loveth our nation and hath built us a *s.*
John 6. 59. these things said he in the *s.*
9. 22. that he should be put out of the *s.*
12. 42. lest they should be put out of the *s.*
18. 20 I ever taught in the *s.* and temple
Acts 6. 9. then arose certain of the *s.* which is called the *s.* of Libertines, disputing with Stephen
13. 14. they went into the *s.* on the sabbath-day, and sat down
15. the rulers of the *s.* sent to them, saying
42. and when the Jews were gone out of the *s.*
14. 1. Paul and Barnabas went both into the *s.*
17. 1. to Thessalonica where was a *s.* of the Jews
17. therefore he disputed in the *s.* with the Jews and with devout persons
18. 4. and he reasoned in the *s.* every sabbath
7. Justus, whose house joined hard to the *s.*
8. Crispus the chief ruler of the *s.* believed
17. Greeks took Sosthenes chief ruler of the *s.*
26. Apollos began to speak boldly in the *s.*
22. 19. beat in every *s.* such as believed, 26. 11.
Jam. 2. † 2. if there come into your *s.* a man
Rev. 2. 9. but are the *s.* of Satan
3. 9. I will make them of the *s.* of Satan

SYNAGOGUES.

Psal. 74. 8. they have burned up all the *s.* of G.
Mat. 4. 23. Jes. went teaching in their *s.* and preaching the gospel, 9. 35. *Mark* 1. 39. *Luke* 13. 10.
6. 2. as the hypocrites do in the *s.*
5. for they love to pray standing in the *s.*
10. 17. they will scourge you in their *s.* 23. 34.
23. 6. and love the chief seats in the *s. Mark* 12. 39. *Luke* 11. 43. | 20. 46.
Mark 13. 9. and in the *s.* ye shall be beaten
Luke 4. 15. he taught in the *s.* being glorified
44. and he preached in the *s.* of Galilee
12. 11. and when they bring you unto the *s.*
21. 12. delivering you up to the *s.* and prisons
John 16. 2. they shall put you out of the *s.*
Acts 9. 2. Saul desired of him letters to the *s.*
20. straightway he preached Christ in the *s.*
13. 5. Paul and Barnabas preached in the *s.*
15. 21. being read in the *s.* every sabbath-day
24. 12. neither raising up the people in the *s.*

T.

TABERNACLE

Signifies, [1] *A tent or pavilion raised on posts to lodge under,* Num. 24. 5. Mat. 17. 4. [2] *A house or dwelling,* Job 11. 14. | 22. 23. [3] *A kind of tent to take up and down, as occasion required; which was as it were the palace of the Most High, the dwelling of the God of Israel; wherein the Israelites, during their journeyings in the wilderness, performed the chief of their religious exercises, offered their sacrifices, and worshipped God. It was thirty cubits in length, and ten in breadth and in height. It was divided into two partitions: the first was called,* The Holy Place, *which was twenty cubits long, and ten wide: here were placed the table of shew-bread, the golden candlestick, and the golden altar of incense. The second was called,* The most Holy Place, *whose length was ten cubits, and breadth ten cubits, wherein, before the building of the temple, the* ark of the covenant *was kept, which was a symbol of God's gracious presence with the Jewish church. The* most Holy *was divided from the* Holy Place *by a curtain, or veil of very rich cloth, which hung upon four pillars of shittim-wood, that were covered with plates of gold,* Exod. 26. 1. Heb. 9. 2, 3. [4] *Christ's human nature, of which the Jewish tabernacle was a type, wherein God dwells really, substantially, and personally,* Heb. 8. 2. | 9. 11. [5] *The true church militant,* Psal. 15. 1. [6] *Our natural body, in which the soul lodges as in a tabernacle,* 2 Cor. 5. 1. 2 Pet. 1. 13. [7] *The tokens of God's gracious presence,* Rev. 21. 3.

The feast of tabernacles, *Lev.* 23. 34. *was so called, because the Israelites kept it under green tents or arbours, in memory of their dwelling in tents in their passage through the wilderness. It was one of the three great solemnities, wherein all the males were obliged to present themselves before the Lord. It was celebrated after harvest, on the* 15*th day of the month Tisri, which answers to our month of September. The feast continued eight days; but the first day and the last were the most solemn. Herein they returned thanks to God for the fruits of the earth they had then gathered in, and were also put in mind that they were but pilgrims and travellers in this world.*

Exod. 25. 9. make it after the pattern of the *t.*
26. 1. thou shalt make the *t.* with ten curtains
6. couple the curtains, and it shall be one *t.* 36. 13.
7. thou shalt make curtains of goats' hair to be a covering upon the *t.* 35. 11. | 36. 14.
15. shalt make boards for the *t.* of shittim wood, 17, 20, 26. | 36. 20, 22, 23, 28, 31, 32.
26. make bars for the *t.* 27. | 30. rear up the *t.*
27. 9. and thou shalt make the court of the *t.*
Exod. 27. 19. all the vessels of the *t.* of brass, 39. 40.
29. 43. the *t.* shall be sanctified by my glory
31. 7. they may make all the furniture of the *t.*
33. 7. Moses pitched the *t.* without the camp
11. but Joshua departed not out of the *t.*
35. 18. the pins of the *t.* 38. 20, 31.
36. 8. them that wrought the work of the *t.*
39. 32. thus was the work of the *t.* finished
33. and they brought the *t.* to Moses, the tent
40. 2. thou shalt set up the *t.* ‖ 9. anoint the *t.*
17. on the first month, on the first day, the *t.* was reared up, 18. *Num.* 7. 1.
19. he spread abroad the tent over the *t.*
21. he brought the ark into the *t.* and set up
33. he reared up the court round about the *t.*
34. the glory of the Lord filled the *t.* 35.
36. the cloud was taken up from over the *t. Num.* 9. 17. | 10. 11. | 12. 10.
38. for the cloud of the Lord was on the *t.* by day, and fire by night, *Num.* 9. 18, 19, 22.
Lev. 8. 10. Moses anointed the *t.* and all therein
15. 31. that they die not when they defile my *t.*
17. 4. bringeth not an offering before the *t.*
26. 11. I will set my *t.* among you, not abhor you
Num. 1. 50. appoint Levites over the *t.* shall bear the *t.* shall encamp round about the *t.* 53.
51. and when the *t.* setteth forward, and when the *t.* is to be pitched, Levites set it up
53. the Levites shall keep the charge of the *t.* of testimony, 3. 7, 25. | 18. 3. | 31. 30, 47.
3. 7. before the *t.* to do the service of the *t.*
23. the Gershonites shall pitch behind the *t.*
35. the Merarites shall pitch northward of the *t.*
38. those that encamp before the *t.* eastward
4. 16. the oversight of the *t.* pertaineth to Eleazar
25. they shall bear the curtains of the *t.*
31. shall bear the boards of the *t.* and bars thereof
5. 17. the priest shall take of the dust of the *t.*
7. 3. they brought their offering before the *t.*
9. 15. on the day that the *t.* was reared up, the cloud covered the *t.* namely the tent of testimony
10. 21. the Kohathites did set up the t.
11. 24. Moses set seventy elders round about the *t.*
26. but they went not out unto the *t.*
16. 9. seemeth it small to do the service of the *t.*
24. get you up from about the *t.* of Korah, 27.
17. 13. whoso cometh near to the *t.* shall die
Deut. 31. 15. L. appeared in *t.* in a pillar of cloud
Josh. 22. 19. wherein the Lord's *t.* dwelleth
1 *Sam.* 2. † 32. see the affliction of the *t.*
2 *Sam.* 6. 17. they set the ark in the midst of the *t.*
7. 6. but I have walked in a tent and in a *t.*
1 *Kings* 1. 39. Zadok took a horn of oil out of the *t.*
2. 28. Joab fled to the *t.* of the Lord and altar
8. 4. vessels in the *t.* were brought up, 2 *Chr.* 5. 5.
1 *Chron.* 6. 48. the Levites for the service of the *t.*
9. 19. Korahites were keepers of the gates of the *t.*
23. they had the oversight of the house of the *t.*
16. 39. the priests before the *t.* of the Lord
17. 5. but have gone from one *t.* to another
21. 29. for the *t.* which Moses made in wilderness
23. 26. they shall no more carry the *t.*
2 *Chron.* 1. 5. he put the brazen altar before the *t.*
Job 5. 24. shalt know that thy *t.* shall be in peace
18. 6. the light shall be dark in his *t.* and his candle
14. his confidence shall be rooted out of his *t.*
15. destruction shall dwell in his *t.* because not his
19. 12. his troops encamp round about my *t.*
20. 26. it shall go ill with him that is left in his *t.*
29. 4. when the secret of God was upon my *t.*
31. 31. If the men of my *t.* said not, oh that
36. 29. can any understand the noise of his *t.*?
Psal. 15. 1. Lord, who shall abide in thy *t.*?
19. 4. in them hath he set a *t.* for the sun
26. † 8. I have loved the *t.* of thy honour
27. 5. in the secret of his *t.* shall he hide m
6. I will offer in his *t.* sacrifices of joy
61. 4. I will abide in thy *t.* for ever
76. 2. in Salem is his *t.* his dwelling-place in Zion
78. 60. so that he forsook the *t.* of Shiloh
67. moreover he refused the *t.* of Joseph
132. 3. I will not come into the *t.* of my house, 7.
Prov. 14. 11. the *t.* of the upright shall flourish
Isa. 4. 6. there shall be a *t.* for a shadow from heat
16. 5. he shall sit upon it in the *t.* of David
33. 20. a *t.* that shall not be taken down
Jer. 10. 20. my *t.* is spoiled, all my cords broken
Lam. 2. 4. he slew all that were pleasant in the *t.*
6. he hath violently taken away his *t.*
Ezek. 37. 27. my *t.* also shall be with them
41. 1. which was the breadth of the *t.*
Amos 5. 26. but ye have borne the *t.* of Moloch
9. 11. in that day will I raise up the *t.* of David
Acts 7. 43. ye took up the *t.* of Moloch
46. who desired to find a *t.* for the God of Jacob
15. 16. and will build again the *t.* of David
2 *Cor.* 5. 1. if our house of this *t.* be dissolved
4. we that are in this *t.* do groan, being burdened
Heb. 8. 2. the true *t.* which the Lord pitched
5. when Moses was about to make the *t.*
9. 2. there was a *t.* made, called the sanctuary
3. the *t.* which is called the holiest of all
6. the priests went always into the first *t.*
8. while as the first *t.* was yet standing
11. an high priest by a greater and more perfect *t.*
21. he sprinkled with blood the *t.* and vessels
13. 10. they have no right to eat which serve *t.*
2 *Pet.* 1. 13. think it meet, as long as I am in this *t.*
14. knowing that shortly I must put off my *t.*
Rev. 13. 6. to blaspheme his name and his *t.*
15. 5. behold the temple of the *t.* was opened
See CONGREGATION, DOOR.

TABERNACLE *of witness.*

Num. 17. 7. Moses laid up the rods in the *t. of w.*
8. on the morrow Moses went into the *t. of w.*
18. 2. shall minister before the *t. of witness*
2 *Chron.* 24. 6. to bring the collection for *t. of w.*
Acts 7. 44. our fathers had the *t. of witness*

TABERNACLES.

Num. 24. 5. how goodly are thy *t.* O Israel
Job 11. 14. let not wickedness dwell in thy *t.*
12. 6. the *t.* of robbers prosper, and they that

Job 15. 34. and fire shall consume the t. of bribery
22. 23. thou shalt put away iniquity far from thy t.
Psal. 43. 3. let them bring me unto thy t.
46. 4. make glad the holy place of t. of Most High
78. 51. smote chief of their strength in t. of Ham
83. 6. the t. of Edom have consulted together
84. 1. how amiable are thy t. O Lord of Hosts
118. 15. salvation is in the t. of the righteous
132. 7. we will go into his t. and worship
Dan. 11. 45. he shalt plant the t. of his palaces
Hos. 9. 6. thorns shall be in their t.
12. 9. will yet make thee to dwell in t.
Mal. 2. 12. Lord will cut off the man out of the t.
Mat. 17. 4. Lord, if thou wilt, let us make here three t. Mark 9. 5. Luke 9. 33.
Heb. 11. 9. Abraham dwelling in t. with Isaac
See FEAST.

TABLE

Signifies, [1] *A frame of wood made for several uses*, 1 Kings 2. 7. [2] *The altar of God*, Mal. 1. 7, 12. [3] *Provision for food, either for body or soul*, Psal. 69. 22. [4] *The two tables of stone whereon the law was written*, Exod. 32. 15.
That ye may eat and drink at my *table*, Luke 22. 30. *That ye may partake of the highest delights which I have prepared for you, and enjoy the nearest communion with me in glory.*
To serve tables, *Acts* 6. 2. *To provide for the poor, that they may have whereof to eat at their tables.*
Exod. 25. 23. shalt also make a t. of shittim wood
27. places of staves to bear the t. 28. | 37. 14.
26. 35. thou shalt set the t. without the veil
30. 27. thou shalt anoint the t. and all his vessels
31. 8. Bezaleel shall make the t. and the altar
37. 10. he made the t. || 16. the vessels on the t.
39. 33. they brought the t. unto Moses, the tent
40. 4. thou shalt bring in the t. and set in order
22. put the t. in the tent of the congregation
Lev. 24. 6. shalt set six on a row on the pure t.
Num. 3. 31. the Kohathites' charge shall be the t.
Judg. 1. 7. kings gathered their meat under my t.
1 Sam. 20. 29. he cometh not to the king's t.
34. Jonathan arose from the t. in fierce anger
2 Sam. 9. 7. Dav. said, Mephibosheth shall eat bread at my t. continually. 10. 11, 13. | 19. 28.
1 Kings 2. 7. let them be of those that eat at thy t.
4. 27. for all that came to king Solomon's t.
10. 5. when the queen of Sheba saw the meat of his t. and the attendance, 2 Chron. 9. 4.
13. 20. as they sat at t. the word of the Lord came
18. 19. the prophets which eat at Jezebel's t.
2 Kings 4. 10. let us set for him a t. and a stool
Neh. 5. 17. there were at my t. 150 Jews
Job 36. 16. that which should be set on thy t.
Psal. 23. 5. thou preparest a t. before me
69. 22. let their t. become a snare before them
78. 19. can God furnish a t. in the wilderness
128. 3. thy children like olive plants about thy t.
Prov. 3. 3. write them on the t. of thy heart, 7. 3.
9. 2. wisdom hath also furnished her t.
Cant. 1. 12. while the king sitteth at his t.
Isa. 21. 5. prepare the t. eat, watch, drink, arise
30. 8. now go write it before them in a t.
65. 11. that prepare a t. for that troop
Jer. 17. 1. it is graven on the t. of their heart
Ezek. 23. 41. and a t. prepared before it
39. 20. thus ye shall be filled at my t. with horses
41. 22. this is the t. that is before the Lord
44. 16. and they shall come near to my t.
Dan. 11. 27. they shall speak lies at one t.
Mal. 1. 7. the t. of the Lord is contemptible
12. ye say, the t. of the Lord is polluted
Mat. 15. 27. she said, yet the dogs eat the crumbs which fall from their master's t. Mark 7. 28.
Luke 16. 21. crumbs which fell from rich man's t.
22. 21. that betrayeth me, is with me on the t.
30. that ye may eat and drink at my t.
John 12. 2. Lazarus was one of them that sat at t.
13. 28. no man at the t. knew for what intent
Rom. 11. 9. let their t. be made a snare and a trap
1 Cor. 10. 21. cup of Lord and devils, ye cannot be partakers of the Lord's t. and of the t. of devils
See SHEW-BREAD.

Writing TABLE.

Luke 1. 63. Zacharias asked for a w. t. and wrote

TABLES.

Exod. 32. 15. the t. were written on both sides
16. t. were the work of God, graven on the t.
19. he cast the t. out of his hands, and brake them
34. 1. I will write on these t. the words in first t.
Deut. 10. 4. he wrote on the t. according to first
5. and put the t. in the ark, Heb. 9. 4.
1 Chr. 28. 16. David gave gold for t. of shew-bread
2 Chr. 4. 8. Solomon also made ten t. and placed
19. the t. whereon the shew-bread was set
Isa. 28. 8. all t. are full of vomit and filthiness
Ezek. 40. 41. eight t. whereupon they slew sacrifices
42. four t. were of hewn stone for burnt offering
Hab. 2. 2. write the vision, and make it plain on t.
Mat. 21. 12. he overthrew the t. of the money-changers, and sellers of doves, Mark 11. 15.
Mark 7. 4. as the washing of cups, pots, and of t.
John 2. 15. drove them out and overthrew the t.
Acts 6. 2. leave the word of God and serve t.
2 Cor. 3. 3. not in t. of stone, but fleshly t. of heart
See STONE, TWO.

TABLETS.

Exod. 35. 22. they brought t. all jewels of gold
Num. 31. 50. we brought t. to make an atonement
Isa. 3. 20. I will take away the t. and ear-rings

TABRET.

Gen. 31. 27. have sent thee away with t. and harp
1 Sam. 10. 5. coming from the high place with a t.
Job 17. 6. a by-word, and aforetime I was as a t.
Isa. 5. 12. the t. pipe, and wine are in their feasts

TABRETS.

1 Sam. 18. 6. women came to meet Saul with t.
Isa. 24. 8. the mirth of t. ceaseth, joy ceaseth
30. 32. it shall be with t. and harps
Jer. 31. 4. thou shalt again be adorned with thy t.
Ezek. 28. 13. the workmanship of thy t. and pipes

TABERING.

Nah. 2. 7. the voice of doves t. on their breasts

TACHES.

Exod. 26. 6. thou shalt make fifty t. of gold
11. thou shalt make fifty t. of brass, 35. 11.
33. thou shalt hang up the vail under the t.
36. 13. he made fifty t. of gold and brass, 18.
39. 33. they brought his t. his boards, and bars

TACKLING.

Acts 27. 19. third day we cast out the t. of the ship

TACKLINGS.

Isa. 33. 23. thy t. are loosed, could not strengthen

TAIL

Signifies, [1] *The train of a beast, fowl, or fish*, Exod. 4. 4. [2] *Low, base, or contemptible*, Deut. 28. 13. [3] *The power, policy, and flatteries, by which the devil and his instruments corrupt and allure ministers of the church from the simplicity and purity of their doctrine, to error, superstition, and profaneness*, Rev. 12. 4. [4] *An army*, Isa. 7. 4.
Exod. 4. 4. put out thine hand, take it by the t.
Deut. 28. 13. make thee the head, not the t. 44.
Josh. 10. † 19. pursue, cut off the t. of them
Judg. 15. 4. Samson caught foxes, and turned t. to t.
Job 40. 17. behemoth moveth his t. like a cedar
Isa. 9. 14. Lord will cut off from Isr. head and t.
15. the prophet that teacheth lies, he is the t.
19. 15. no work which the head or t. may do
Rev. 12. 4. his t. drew the third part of the stars

TAILS.

Judg. 15. 4. and put a firebrand between two t.
Isa. 7. 4. for the two t. of these smoking firebrands
Rev. 9. 10. t. like to scorpions, stings in their t.
19. power in their t. their t. were like serpents

TAKE

Signifies, [1] *To lay hold on, or seize*, 1 Kings 18. 40. [2] *To receive from another*, 2 Kings 5. 15. [3] *To yield*, 2 Thess. 1. † 8. [4] *To bear*, John 1. † 29. [5] *To give*, Deut. 1. † 13. [6] *To spoil*, Deut. 20. † 14. [7] *To possess or impoverish*, Judg. 14. † 15. [8] *To be chosen*, 1 Tim. 5. † 9. [9] *To remove*, John 2. 16.
Gen. 13. 9. if thou wilt t. the left hand I will go
14. 21. give me the persons, t. the goods to thyself
19. 15. arise, t. thy wife and thy two daughters
22. 2. t. now thy son, thine only son Isaac
24. 3. thou shalt not t. a wife to my son of, 37.
48. to t. my master's brother's daughter to his son
31. 32. discern what is thine with me, t. it to thee
50. if thou t. other wives besides my daughters
34. 9. and t. our daughters unto you
16. and we will t. your daughters to us
38. 23. let her t. it to her, lest we be shamed
Exod. 6. 7. I will t. you to me for a people
10. 26. for thereof must we t. to serve the Lord
17. 5. and thy rod t. in thine hand, and go
20. 7. thou shalt not t. the name of the Lord thy God in vain, not hold guiltless, Deut. 5. 11.
21. 14. t. him from mine altar, that he may die
23. 8. and thou shalt t. no gift, Deut. 16. 19.
34. 9. pardon and t. us for thine inheritance
16. lest thou t. of their daughters, Deut. 7. 3.
Lev. 18. 17. neither shalt thou t. her son's daughter
18. neither shalt thou t. a wife to her sister
20. 14. and if a man t. a wife, and her mother
21. 7. the priests shall not t. a wife that is a whore, nor t. a woman put away, Ezek. 44. 22.
13. he shall t. a wife in her virginity
25. 36. t. thou no usury of him, or increase
46. ye shall t. them as an inheritance for children
Num. 8. 6. t. the Levites from among Israel
11. 17. I will t. of the spirit that is on thee
16. 3. Korah said, ye t. too much upon you, 7.
35. 31. ye shall t. no satisfaction for the life, 32.
Deut. 1. 13. t. ye wise men and understanding
4. 34. and t. him a nation, from the midst of nation
15. 17. then thou shalt t. an awl, and thrust
22. 18. the elders of that city shall t. that man
30. a man shall not t. his father's wife
24. 4. may not t. her again to be his wife
6. no man shall t. a millstone to pledge
17. nor t. a widow's raiment to pledge
25. 8. if he say, I like not to t. her
Josh. 6. 18. when ye t. of the accursed thing
7. 14. the family which the Ld. shall t. the household which the Lord shall t. shall come
8. 29. they should t. his carcase down from the tree
10. 42. their land did Joshua t. at one time
20. 4. they shall t. him into the city to them
22. 19. then t. ye possession among us, rebel not
Judg. 5. 30. for the necks of them that t. spoil
14. 3. that thou goest to t. a wife of uncircumcised
15. have ye called us to t. that we have?
19. 30. consider, t. advice, and speak your minds
Ruth 2. 10. thou shouldest t. knowledge of me
1 Sam. 2. 16. then t. as much as thy soul desireth, and if not I will t. it by force
8. 11. he will t. your sons for himself, his chariots
13. he will t. your daughters, || 14. t. your fields
15. t. the tenth of your seed || 16. t. men-servants
17. 18. how thy brethren fare, and t. their pledge
46. and t. thine head from thee
19. 14. Saul sent messengers to t. David, 20.
21. 9. if thou wilt t. that, t. it, there is no other
24. 11. yet thou huntest my soul to t. it
25. 11. shall I then t. my bread and my water
26. 11. t. now the spear that is at his bolster
2 Sam. 12. 4. he spared to t. of his own flock
11. I will t. thy wives before thine eyes
28. t. it, lest I t. the city, and it be called
16. 9. let me go over, and t. off his head
19. 19. the king should t. it to his heart, 13. 33.
30. Mephibosheth said, yea, let him t. all
1 Kings 11. 31. he said to Jeroboam, t. ten pieces
34. I will not t. the whole kingdom
14. 3. t. ten loaves || 18. 40. t. prophets of Baal
20. 18. come for war or peace, t. them alive
21. 15. arise, t. possession of the vineyard, 16.
22. 26. t. Micaiah, carry him back, 2 Chr. 18. 25.
2 Kings 4. 1. the creditor is come to t. my sons
29. t. my staff and go || 5. 15. t. a blessing
5. 16. urged him to t. it || 20. I will t. somewhat
2 Kings 5. 23. t. two talents || 8. 8. t. a present and go
9. 1. t. this box of oil in thine hand, 3.
10. 6. t. ye the heads of your master's sons
14. t. them alive || 12. 5. let the priests t. it
13. 15. Elisha said, t. bow and arrows, 18.
19. 30. shall yet t. root downward, Isa. 37. 31.
1 Chron. 21. 24. I will not t. that which is thine
Ezra 5. 14. those did Cyrus t. || 15. t. vessels
9. 12. not t. their daughters, Neh. 10. 30. | 13. 25.
Esth. 6. 10. t. the apparel, and do so to Mordecai
Job 23. 10. he knoweth the way that I t.
24. 3. they t. the widow's ox for a pledge
9. and they t. a pledge of the poor
30. 17. and my sinews t. no rest
31. 36. surely I would t. it upon my shoulder
41. 4. wilt thou t. him for a servant for ever?
42. 8. therefore t. to you now seven bullocks
Psal. 2. 2. the rulers t. counsel against the Lord
7. 5. let the enemy persecute my soul, and t. it
50. 9. I will t. no bullock out of thy house
16. shouldest t. my covenant in thy mouth
51. 11. and t. not thy Holy Spirit from me
71. 11. t. him, for there is none to deliver him
75. † 2. when I shall t. a set time, I will judge
81. 2. t. a psalm || 83. 12. t. the houses of God
89. 33. my kindness will I not utterly t. from him
109. 8. and let another t. his office
116. 13. I will t. the cup of salvation and call
119. 43. t. not the word of truth utterly out
139. 9. if I t. the wings of the morning
20. and thine enemies t. thy name in vain
Prov. 5. 22. his own iniquities shall t. the wicked
6. 25. neither let her t. thee with her eyelids
27. can a man t. fire in his bosom, not be burned
7. 18. let us t. our fill of love till the morning
20. 16. t. his garment that is surety for stranger, t. a pledge of him for a strange woman, 27. 13.
30. 9. and t. the name of my God in vain
Eccl. 5. 15. and shall t. nothing of his labour
19. and to t. his portion and rejoice in his labour
Cant. 2. 15. t. us the foxes, the little foxes
Isa. 27. 6. he shall cause them of Jacob to t. root
28. 19. from the time it goeth, it shall t. you
30. 14. not a sherd to t. fire from the hearth
33. 23. the prey is divided, the lame t. the prey
40. 24. their stock shall not t. root in the earth
44. 15. he will t. thereof and warm himself
47. 2. t. the millstones, and grind meal
3. I will t. vengeance, I will not meet as a man
57. 13. vanity shall t. them, wind carry them
58. 2. they t. delight in approaching to God
66. 21. I will also t. of them for priests and Levites
Jer. 2. 22. t. thee much soap || 3. 14. t. one of a city
13. 4. t. the girdle that thou hast got, 6.
21. shall not sorrows t. thee as a woman in travail
15. 19. if thou t. forth the precious from the vile
16. 2. thou shalt not t. thee a wife in this place
18. 22. for they have digged a pit to t. me
19. 1. t. of the ancients of the people of the priests
20. 10. and we shall t. our revenge on him
25. 9. I will t. all the families of the north
10. I will t. from them the voice of mirth
28. if they refuse to t. the cup at thine hand
29. 6. t. ye wives, and beget sons and daughters
32. 24. they are come to the city to t. it
25. buy the field for money, and t. witnesses, 44.
28. Nebuchadrezzar king of Babylon shall t. it
39. 12. t. Jeremiah, and look well to him
46. 11. go up into Gilead, and t. balm, 51. 8.
50. 15. t. vengeance upon her; as she hath done, do
51. 26. they shall not t. of thee a stone for a corner
36. behold I will t. vengeance for thee
Lam. 2. 13. what thing shall I t. to witness for thee?
Ezek. 4. 1. t. thee a tile || 3. t. an iron pan
9. t. unto thee wheat, barley, and beans
5. 1. t. a sharp knife, t. a rasor, t. balances
10. 6. t. fire from between the wheels
11. 19. I will t. the stony heart out of their flesh
14. 5. that I may t. the house of Israel
15. 3. will men t. a pin of it to hang any vessel
21. 26. remove the diadem, t. off the crown
22. 16. thou shalt t. thine inheritance in thyself
24. 5. t. the choice of the flock, and burn bones
8. it might cause fury to come up to t. vengeance
25. when I t. from them their strength
29. 19. t. a multitude, t. her spoil, t. her prey
33. 2. if people of the land t. a man of their coasts
36. 24. I will t. you from among the heathen
37. 16. t. thee one stick, t. another stick, write
19. I will t. the stick of Joseph, and will put
38. 12. to t. a spoil and to t. a prey
13. art thou come to t. prey, to t. a great spoil
46. 18. the prince not t. the people's inheritance
Dan. 7. 18. but the saints shall t. the kingdom
11. 15. the king shall t. the most fenced cities
18. he shall turn to the isles, and shall t. many
Hos. 1. 2. go t. unto thee a wife of whoredoms
11. 4. I was as they that t. off the yoke on jaws
14. 2. t. with you words, and turn to the Lord
Amos 5. 11. ye t. from him burdens of wheat
12. they afflict the just, they t. a bribe
9. 2. thence shall mine hand t. them, 3.
Jonah 4. 3. t. I beseech thee, my life from me
Mic. 2. 2. they covet fields and t. them by violence
6. shall not prophesy, that they shall not t. shame
Nah. 1. 2. the Lord will t. vengeance on adversaries
2. 9. t. ye the spoil of silver, t. the spoil of gold
Hab. 1. 10. for they shall heap dust and t. it
Hag. 1. 8. build the house, I will t. pleasure in it
2. 23. will I t. thee, O Zerubbabel my servant
Zech. 6. 10. t. of them of the captivity, of Heldai
11. 15. t. yet instruments of a foolish shepherd
Mat. 1. 20. fear not to t. unto thee Mary thy wife
2. 13. and t. the young child and its mother
6. 25. t. no thought for your life, 28, 31, 34. | 10. 19. Mark 13. 11. Luke 12. 11, 22, 26.
11. 12. and the violent t. the kingdom by force
29. t. my yoke upon you, and learn of me
15. 26. not meet to t. children's bread, Mark 7. 27.
16. 5. they had forgotten to t. bread, Mark 8. 14.
17. 25. of whom the kings of the earth t. custom
18. 16. then t. with thee one or two more

Mat. 20. 14. *t.* that thine is and go thy way
24. 17. let him on house-top not come down to *t.* any thing out of his house, *Mark* 13. 15.
25. 28. *t.* therefore the talent from him, give it
26. 4. that they might *t.* Jesus, *Mark* 14. 1, 44.
26. Jesus took bread and said, *t.* eat, this is my body, *Mark* 14. 22. 1 *Cor.* 11. 24.
45. sleep on now, and *t.* your rest, *Mark* 14. 41.
52. they that *t.* the sword shall perish by sword
55. with swords and staves to *t.* me, *Mark* 14. 48.
Mark 6. 8. *t.* nothing for their journey, *Luke* 9. 3.
12. 19. his brother should *t.* his wife, *Luke* 20. 28.
15. 24. casting lots what every man should *t.*
36. whether Elias will come to *t.* him down
Luke 6. 4. David did *t.* and eat shew-bread
29. forbid him not to *t.* thy coat also
10. 35. *t.* care of him ‖ 12. 19. soul, *t.* thine ease
14. 9. then begin with shame to *t.* the lowest room
16. 6. *t.* thy bill, 7. ‖ 22. 17. *t.* this and divide it
19. 24. *t.* from him the pound, and give it to him
22. 36. he that hath a purse, let him *t.* it
John 2. 16. Jesus said to them, *t.* these things hence
6. 7. that every one of them may *t.* a little
15. that they would come and *t.* him by force
7. 30. they sought to *t.* him, 32. | 10. 39. | 11. 57.
10. 17. therefore my father loveth me, because I lay down my life, that I might *t.* it again, 18.
16. 15. he shall *t.* of mine, and shew it unto you
17. 15. thou shouldest *t.* them out of the world
18. 31. *t.* ye him, and judge him according to your
19. 6. Pilate saith, *t.* ye him, and crucify him
Acts 1. 20. and his bishoprick let another *t.*
12. 3. Herod proceeded further to *t.* Peter also
15. 14. to *t.* out of them a people for his name
37. Barnabas determined to *t.* with them John
38. Paul thought not good to *t.* him with them
20. 13. sailed to Assos, there intending to *t.* in Paul
26. wherefore I *t.* you to record this day
21. 24. them *t.* and purify thyself with them
27. 33. Paul besought them to *t.* meat, 34.
1 *Cor.* 6. 7. why do you not rather *t.* wrong?
15. shall I then *t.* the members of Christ
9. 9. doth God *t.* care for oxen?
2 *Cor.* 8. 4. and *t.* upon us the ministering to saints
11. 20. for ye suffer, if a man *t.* of you
12. 10. therefore I *t.* pleasure in infirmities
Eph. 6. 13. *t.* to you the whole armour of God
17. and *t.* the helmet of salvation, and sword
1 *Tim.* 3. 5. how shall he *t.* care of the church
2 *Tim.* 4. 11. *t.* Mark, and bring him with thee
Heb. 7. 5. a commandment to *t.* tithes of people
Jam. 5. 10. *t.* my brethren, the prophets an example
1 *Pet.* 2. 20. if ye *t.* it patiently, it is acceptable
Rev. 3. 11. hold fast, that no man *t.* thy crown
5. 9. thou art worthy to *t.* the book, and to open
6. 4. power given him to *t.* peace from the earth
10. 8. *t.* the little book ‖ 9. *t.* it and eat it
22. 17. let him *t.* the water of life freely

TAKE *away.*

Gen. 30. 15. wouldest thou *t. aw.* my son's mandrakes
42. 36. and ye will *t.* Benjamin *away*
Exod. 2. 9. *t.* this child *away*, and nurse it for me
8. 8. that he may *t. away* the frogs from me
10. 17. that he may *t. aw.* from me this death only
23. 25. and I will *t.* sickness *away*, *Deut.* 7. 15.
33. 23. I will *t. aw.* mine hand, and thou shalt see
Lev. 3. 4. it shall be *t. away*, 10, 15. | 4. 9. | 7. 4.
4. 31. he shall *t. away* all the fat thereof, 35.
14. 40. command that they *t. away* the stones
Num. 4. 13. shalt *t. away* the ashes from the altar
17. 10. thou shalt quite *t. away* their murmurings
21. 7. pray that he may *t. aw.* the serpents from us
Josh. 7. 13. until ye *t. away* the accursed thing
2 *Sam.* 4. 11. shall I not *t.* you *away* from the earth
5. 6. except thou *t. away* the blind and the lame
24. 10. *t. away* the iniquity of thy servant
1 *Kings* 2. 31. mayest *t. away* the innocent blood
14. 10. *t. aw.* the remnant of the house of Jeroboam
16. 3. *t. aw.* the posterity of Baasha ‖ 21. 21. of Ahab
19. 4. it is enough now, O Lord, *t. away* my life
10. and they seek my life, to *t.* it *away*, 14.
20. 6. what is pleasant, shall my servants *t. away*
24. *t.* the kings *a.* and put captains in their rooms
2 *Kings* 2. 3. the Lord will *t. away* thy master, 5.
6. 32. see how he hath sent to *t. away* mine head
18. 32. till I come and *t.* you *away*, *Isa.* 36. 17.
1 *Chr.* 17. 13. I will not *t.* my mercy *away* from him
Esth. 4. 4. sent to *t. away* his sackcloth from him
Job 7. 21. why dost thou not *t. away* mine iniquity
9. 34. let him *t.* his rod *away* from me
24. 2. they violently *t. away* flocks
10. they *t. away* the sheaf from the hungry
32. 22. in so doing, my Maker would soon *t.* me *a.*
36. 18. beware, lest he *t.* thee *away* with his stroke
Psal. 26. † 9. *t.* not *away* my soul with sinners
31. 13. they devised to *t. away* my life
52. 5. he shall *t.* thee *away* and pluck thee out
58. 9. he shall *t.* them *away* as with a whirlwind
102. 24. *t.* me not *away* in the midst of my days
Prov. 22. 27. why should he *t. aw.* thy bed from thee
25. 4. *t. away* the dross from the silver
5. *t. away* the wicked from before the king
Isa. 1. 25. and I will *t. away* all thy tin
3. 1. *t. away* the stay and staff ‖ 18. *t. away* bravery
4. 1. to *t. aw.* our reproach ‖ 5. 5. I will *t. aw.* hedge
5. 23. *t. away* the righteousness of the righteous
10. 2. to *t. away* the right from the poor
25. 8. the rebuke of his people shall he *t. away*
27. 9. this is all the fruit, to *t. away* his sin
39. 7. and of thy sons shall they *t. away*
40. 24. the whirlwind shall *t.* them *away*
58. 9. if thou *t. away* from the midst of thee
Jer. 4. 4. *t. away* the foreskins of your heart
5. 10. destroy and *t. away* her battlements
15. 15. *t.* me not *away* in thy long-suffering
Ezek. 11. 18. shall *t. away* the detestable things
23. 25. they shall *t. away* thy nose and thine ears
26. *t. away* thy fair jewels ‖ 29. *t. away* thy labour
24. 16. behold, I *t. away* the desire of thine eyes
33. 4. if the sword come and *t.* him *away*, 6.
36. 26. and I will *t. away* the stony heart out of
45. 9. *t. away* your exactions from my people

Dan. 7. 26. and they shall *t. away* his dominion
11. 31. they shall *t. away* the daily sacrifice
Hos. 1. 6. but I will utterly *t.* them *away*
2. 9. and *t. away* my corn in the time thereof
17. for I will *t. away* the names of Baalim
4. 11. whoredom, wine, and new wine *t. a.* the heart
5. 14. I will *t. away* and none shall rescue
14. 2. say unto him *t. a.* all iniquity, receive us
Amos 4. 2. that he will *t.* you *away* with hooks
5. 23. *t. away* from me the noise of thy viols
Mic. 2. 2. they covet houses, and *t.* them *away*
Zeph. 3. 11. I will *t. away* out of the midst of thee
Zech. 3. 4. *t. away* the filthy garments from him
9. 7. I will *t. away* his blood out of his mouth
Mal. 2. 3. and one shall *t.* you *away* with dung
Mat. 5. 40. and *t. away* thy coat, let him have thy
22. 13. *t. away* and cast him into outer darkness
Mark 14. 36. Father, *t. away* this cup from me
Luke 1. 25. to *t. away* my reproach among men
17. 31. let him not come down to *t.* it *away*
John 11. 39. Jesus said, *t. away* the stone
48. the Romans shall *t. a.* our place and nation
Rom. 11. 27. when I shall *t. away* their sins
Heb. 10. 4. that blood of bulls should *t. away* sins
1 *John* 3. 5. he was manifested to *t. away* our sins
Rev. 22. 19. if any man *t. away* from the words of the book, God shall *t. a.* his part out of book
See COUNSEL.

TAKE *heed.*

Gen. 31. 24. *t. heed* that thou speak not to Jacob, 29.
Exod. 10. 28. *t. heed* to thyself, 34. 12. *Deut.* 4. 9. 12. 13, 19, 30. 1 *Sam.* 19. 2. 1 *Tim.* 4. 16.
19. 12. *t. heed* to yourselves, *Deut.* 2. 4. | 4. 15, 23. | 11. 16. *Josh.* 23. 11. *Jer.* 17. 21.
Num. 23. 12. must I not *t. heed* to speak that which
Deut. 24. 8. *t. heed* in the plague of leprosy
27. 9. *t. heed* and hearken, O Israel, this day
Josh. 22. 5. *t.* diligent *heed* to do the commandment
1 *Kings* 2. 4. if thy children *t. heed* to their way, 8. 25. 2 *Chron.* 6. 16.
1 *Chr.* 28. 10. *t. heed* for the Lord hath chosen thee
2 *Chr.* 19. 6. *t. heed* what ye do, ye judge not for men
7. let the fear of the Lord be on you, *t. heed*
33. 8. so that they will *t. heed* to do, *Ezra* 4. 22
Job 36. 21. *t. heed*, regard not iniquity
Psal. 39. 1. I said, I will *t. heed* to my ways
Eccl. 7. 21. *t.* no *heed* to all words that are spoken
Isa. 7. 4. say unto him, *t. heed* and be quiet, fear not
Jer. 9. 4. *t.* ye *heed* every one of his neighbour
Hos. 4. 10. they have left off to *t. heed* to the Lord
Mal. 2. 15. therefore *t. heed* to your spirit, 16.
Mat. 6. 1. *t. heed* that you do not alms before men
16. 6. *t. h.* of the leaven of Pharisees, *Mark* 8. 15.
18. 10. *t. heed* that ye despise not one of these
24. 4. *t. heed* that no man deceive you, *Mark* 13. 5.
Mark 4. 24. he said to them, *t. heed* what you hear
13. 9. *t. heed* to yourselves, *Luke* 17. 3. | 21. 34. *Acts* 5. 35. | 20. 28.
23. *t. h.* I have foretold you ‖ 33. *t. h.* watch, pray
Luke 8. 18. *t. heed* therefore how ye hear
11. 35. *t. heed* that the light in thee be not darkness
12. 15. *t. heed* and beware of covetousness
21. 8. he said, *t. heed* that ye be not deceived
Acts 22. 26. saying, *t. heed* what thou doest
Rom. 11. 21. *t. heed* lest he also spare not thee
1 *Cor.* 3. 10. let every man *t. heed* how he buildeth
8. 9. *t. heed* lest this liberty of yours become
10. 12. let him that standeth *t. heed* lest he fall
Gal. 5. 15. *t. heed* ye be not consumed one of another
Col. 4. 17. *t. heed* to the ministry thou hast received
Heb. 3. 12. *t. heed* of an evil heart of unbelief
2 *Pet.* 1. 19. whereunto ye do well to *t. heed*

TAKE *hold.*

Exod. 15. 14. sorrow shall *t. hold* on the inhabitants
15. trembling shall *t. hold* upon them
26. 5. that the loops may *t. hold* one of another
Deut. 32. 41. and if mine hand *t. hold* of judgment
Job 27. 20. terrors *t. hold* on him as waters
36. 17. judgment and justice *t. hold* on thee
38. 13. it might *t. hold* on the ends of the earth
Psal. 35. 2. *t. hold* of shield and buckler, and help
69. 24. let thy wrathful anger *t. hold* of them
Prov. 2. 19. nor *t.* thee *hold* of the paths of life
4. 13. *t.* fast *hold* of instruction, let her not go
5. 5. her feet go down, her steps *t. hold* on hell
Eccl. 7. 18. it is good that thou *t. hold* of this
Cant. 7. 8. I will *t. hold* of the boughs thereof
Isa. 3. 6. when a man shall *t. hold* of his brother
4. 1. seven women shall *t. hold* of one man, saying
13. 8. pangs and sorrows shall *t. hold* of them
27. 5. or let him *t. hold* of my strength, and make
56. 4. to the eunuchs that *t. hold* of my covenant
64. 7. that stirreth up himself to *t. hold* of thee
Mic. 6. 14. thou shalt *t. hold* but shalt not deliver
Zech. 1. 6. did they not *t. hold* of your fathers?
8. 23. ten men shall *t. hold* of him that is a Jew
Luke 20. 20. that they might *t. hold* of his words
26. and they could not *t. hold* of his words

TAKE *up.*

Gen. 41. 34. *t. up* the fifth part of the land of Egypt
Lev. 6. 10. and the priest shall *t. up* the ashes
Num. 16. 37. *t. up* the censers out of the burning
Josh. 3. 6. *t. up* the ark of the covenant, 6. 6.
4. 5. *t. up* every man a stone out of Jordan
2 *Kings* 2. 1. when the Lord would *t. up* Elijah
4. 36. he said *t. up* thy son ‖ 6. 7. *t. up* the iron
9. 25. *t. up* and cast him into the portion of field
Neh. 5. 2. we *t. up* corn for them that we may eat
Psal. 16. 4. nor *t. up* their names into my lips
27. 10. then the Lord will *t.* me *up*
Isa. 14. 4. that thou shalt *t. up* this proverb
57. 14. *t. up* the stumbling-block out of the way
Jer. 7. 29. *t. up* a lamentation on the high places
9. 10. for the mountains will *t. up* weeping
18. *t. up* wailing for us ‖ 38. 10. *t. up* Jeremiah
Ezek. 19. 1. *t. up* a lamentation for the princes
26. 17. *t. up* a lamentation for Tyrus, 27. 2, 32.
28. 12. *t. up* a lamentation upon king of Tyrus
32. 2. *t. up* a lamentation for Pharaoh
Amos 3. 5. shall one *t. up* a snare from the earth
5. 1. hear this word which I *t. up* against you
6. 10. and a man's uncle shall *t.* him *up*

Jonah 1. 12. *t.* me *up* and cast me forth into the sea
Mic. 2. 4. in that day shall one *t. up* a parable
Hab. 1. 15. they *t. up* all of them with the angle
2. 6. shall not all these *t. up* a parable against him
Mat. 9. 6. Jesus saith, arise, *t. up* thy bed, *Mark* 2. 9, 11. *Luke* 5. 24. *John* 5. 8, 11, 12.
16. 24. let him *t. up* his cross and follow me, *Mark* 8. 34. | 10. 21. *Luke* 9. 23.
17. 27. and *t. up* the fish that first cometh up
Mark 16. 18. they shall *t. up* serpents

TAKEN.

Gen. 2. 22. rib which Lord God had *t.* from man
23. called woman, because she was *t.* out of man
3. 19. for out of the ground wast thou *t.* 23.
4. 15. vengeance shall be *t.* on him seven fold
12. 15. the woman was *t.* into Pharaoh's house
19. so I might have *t.* her to me to wife
14. 14. Abram heard that his brother was *t.*
18. 27. I have *t.* upon me to speak to the Lord
20. 3. for the woman which thou hast *t.* is a wife
27. 33. who, where is he that hath *t.* venison
31. 16. the riches God hath *t.* from our father
34. now Rachel had *t.* the images, and put them
Exod. 25. 15. staves shall not be *t.* from the rings
Lev. 7. 34. the heave shoulder have I *t.* of Israel
Num. 3. 12. behold, I have *t.* the Levites for the first-born of Israel, 8. 16, 18. | 18. 6.
5. 13. neither she be *t.* with the manner
10. 17. and the tabernacle was *t.* down
16. 15. I have not *t.* one ass from them, nor hurt
31. 49. we have *t.* the sum of the men of war
36. 3. their inheritance be *t.* from the lot
Deut. 4. 20. Lord hath *t.* you out of the iron furnace
20. 7. hath betrothed a wife, and hath not *t.* her
24. 1. when a man hath *t.* a wife, and married
5. when a man hath *t.* a new wife, he shall be free at home, and cheer up his wife which he hath *t.*
Josh. 7. 11. they have *t.* of the accursed thing
15. he that is *t.* shall be burnt with fire
16. and the tribe of Judah was *t.*
17. Zabdi was *t.* ‖ 18. and Achan was *t.*
Judg. 11. 36. as the Lord hath *t.* vengeance
14. 9. he told not them that he had *t.* the honey
15. 6. because he had *t.* his wife, and given her
17. 2. the 1100 shekels that were *t.* from thee
1 *Sam.* 4. 11. the ark of God was *t.* 17, 19, 21, 22.
7. 14. the cities which the Philistines had *t.*
10. 21. Saul was *t.* ‖ 12. 3. whose ox have I *t.*?
12. 4. nor hast thou *t.* ought of any man's hand
14. 41. and Saul and Jonathan were *t.*
42. Saul said, cast lots, and Jonathan was *t.*
30. 5. and David's two wives were *t.* captives
19. was nothing lacking that they had *t.* to them
2 *Sam.* 12. 9. hast *t.* his wife to be thy wife, 10.
27. and I have *t.* the city of waters
16. 8. behold, thou art *t.* in thy mischief
23. 6. because they cannot be *t.* with hands
1 *Kings* 16. 18. when Zimri saw that the city was *t.*
21. 19. hast thou killed and also *t.* possession?
2 *Kings* 2. 10. if thou see me when I am *t.* from thee
18. 10. the ninth year of Hosea, Samaria was *t.*
1 *Chron.* 24. 6. one principal household being *t.* for Eleazar, and one *t.* for Ithamar
2 *Chron.* 28. 11. deliver the captives you have *t.*
30. 2. king had *t.* counsel to keep the passover
Ezra 9. 2. for they have *t.* of their daughters
10. 2. and we have *t.* strange wives, 14, 17, 18.
44. all these had *t.* strange wives
Neh. 5. 15. and had *t.* of them bread and wine
Esth. 2. 15. who had *t.* Esther for his daughter
16. so Esther was *t.* to king Ahasuerus
8. 2. king took off his ring he had *t.* from Haman
Job 16. 12. he hath also *t.* me by my neck
19. 9. he hath *t.* the crown from mine head
22. 6. thou hast *t.* a pledge from thy brother
24. 24. they are *t.* out of the way, as all other
28. 2. iron is *t.* out of the earth, brass is molten
Psal. 9. 15. in the net they hid is their own foot *t.*
10. 2. let them be *t.* in the devices that they have
59. 12. let them even be *t.* in their pride
83. 3. have *t.* crafty counsel against thy people
119. 111. thy test. have I *t.* as an heritage for ever
Prov. 3. 26. the L. shall keep thy foot from being *t.*
6. 2. thou art *t.* with the words of thy mouth
7. 20. he hath *t.* a bag of money with him
11. 6. transgressors shall be *t.* in their own naught.
Eccl. 2. 18. I hated my labour which I had *t.*
3. 14. nothing put to it, nor any thing *t.* from it
7. 26. but the sinner shall be *t.* by her
9. 12. as the fishes that are *t.* in an evil net
Isa. 7. 5. have *t.* evil counsel against thee
8. 15. many shall be broken, and snared, and *t.*
23. 8. who hath *t.* this counsel against Tyre
24. 18. shall be *t.* in the snare, *Jer.* 48. 44.
28. 13. that they might be broken, snared, and *t.*
33. 20. a tabernacle that shall not be *t.* down
41. 9. thou whom I have *t.* from ends of the earth
49. 24. shall the prey be *t.* from the mighty
51. 22. behold, I have *t.* the cup of trembling
53. 8. he was *t.* from prison and from judgment
Jer. 6. 11. the husband with the wife shall be *t.*
8. 9. the wise men are ashamed, dismayed, and *t.*
12. 2. thou hast planted, they have *t.* root
34. 3. but thou shalt surely be *t.* 38. 23.
38. 28. till the day that Jerusalem was *t.*
39. 5. when they had *t.* him, they brought him
40. 1. when he had *t.* him, being bound in chains
10. and dwell in your cities, that ye have *t.*
48. 1. Kiriathaim is *t.* ‖ 7. thou shalt be *t.*
33. joy and gladness is *t.* from the plentiful field
41. Kirioth is *t.* ‖ 46. thy sons are *t.* captives
49. 20. hear the counsel he hath *t.* against Edom
24. anguish and sorrows have *t.* Damascus
30. Nebuchadnezzar hath *t.* counsel against you
50. 2. publish and say, Babylon is *t.* 24. | 51. 31, 41
Lam. 4. 20. the anointed of the Lord was *t.*
Ezek. 12. 13. the prince of Israel be *t.* in my snare
15. 3. shall wood be *t.* thereof to do any work?
16. 17. thou hast also *t.* thy fair jewels of gold
20. thou hast *t.* thy sons and thy daughters
17. 12. is come, and hath *t.* the king thereof
13. *t.* of the king's seed, hath *t.* an oath of him

Ezek. 17. 20. and he shall be t. in my snare
18. 8. not upon usury, neither hath t. any increase
13. hath given upon usury, and hath t. increase
17. that hath t. off his hand from the poor
19. 4. heard of him, he was t. in their pit, 8.
21. 23. call to remembrance, that they may be t.
22. 12. in thee have they t. gifts, hast t. usury
25. 15. have t. vengeance with a despiteful heart
Dan. 5. 2. vessels, which his father had t. out, 3.
Joel 3. 5. because ye have t. my silver and gold
Amos 3. 4. will ye cry out, if ye have t. nothing, 5.
12. so shall Israel be t. that dwell in Samaria
6. 13. have we not t. to us horns by our strength
Zech. 14. 2. the city shall be t. and houses rifled
Mat. 9. 15. the bridegroom shall be t. from them
16. 7. it is because we have t. no bread
21. 43. the kingdom of God shall be t. from you
24. 40. one shall be t. Luke 17. 34, 35, 36.
28. 12. and had t. counsel, they gave large money
Mark 4. 25. from him t. even that which he hath
6. 41. when he had t. the five loaves he looked up
9. 36. when he had t. him in his arms, he said
Luke 5. 5. we toiled all night, and have t. nothing
9. at the draught of fishes which they had t.
19. 8. if I have t. any thing from any man
John 7. 44. and some of them would have t. him
8. 3. brought to him a woman t. in adultery, 4.
Acts 2. 23. ye have t. and by wicked hands crucified
8. 33. for his life is t. from the earth
23. 27. this man was t. of the Jews
27. 33. and continued fasting having t. nothing
Rom. 9. 6. not as tho' the word hath t. none effect
1 Cor. 10. 13. there hath no temptation t. you
1 Thess. 2. 17. being t. from you for a short time
2 Thess. 2. 7. will let, until he be t. out of the way
1 Tim. 5. 9. let not a widow be t. into the number
2 Tim. 2. 26. who are t. captive by him at his will
Heb. 5. 1. every high priest t. from among men
2 Pet. 2. 12. made to be t. and destroyed, speak evil
Rev. 5. 8. and when he had t. the book, the beasts
11. 17. thou hast t. to thee thy great power
19. 20. and the beast was t. and with him

TAKEN *away*.

Gen. 21. 25. a well Abimelech's servants had t. a.
27. 35. Jacob came and hath t. *away* thy blessing
36. behold now he hath t. *away* my blessing
30. 23. Rachel said, God hath t. *away* my reproach
31. 1. Jacob hath t. *away* all that is our father's
9. thus God hath t. *away* the cattle of your father
Exod. 14. 11. hast thou t. us a. to died in wilderness
Lev. 4. 31. as the fat is t. a. from the sacrifice, 35.
6. 2. trespass in a thing t. *away* by violence
14. 43. after that he hath t. *away* the stones
Deut. 26. 14. nor t. *away* ought for any unclean use
28. 31. thine ass shall be violently t. *away* from
Judg. 18. 24. ye have t. a. my gods which I made
1 Sam. 21. 6. in the day when it was t. *away*
1 Kings 22. 43. the high places were not t. *away*, 2 Kings 12. 3. | 14. 4. 2 Chr. 15. 17. | 20. 33.
2 Kings 2. 9. ask, before I be t. *away* from thee
18. 22. and whose altars Hezekiah hath t. *away*, 2 Chron. 32. 12. Isa. 36. 7.
2 Chron. 19. 3. in that thou hast t. *away* the groves
Job 1. 21. the Lord gave, and the Lord hath t. *away*
20. 19. hath violently t. a. an house he built not
27. 2. as God liveth who hath t. a. my judgment
34. 5. and God hath t. *away* my judgment
20. and the mighty shall be t. *away* without hand
Psal. 85. 3. thou hast t. *away* all thy wrath
Prov. 4. 16. their sleep is t. *away* unless they cause
Isa. 6. 7. thine iniquity is t. *away*, thy sin purged
8. 4. the spoil of Samaria shall be t. *away*
10. 27. the burden shall be t. a. from the shoulder
16. 10. gladness is t. a. || 17. 1. Damascus is t. *away*
49. 25. the captives of the mighty shall be t. *away*
52. 5. that my people is t. *away* for nought
57. 1. merciful men are t. *away*, righteous is t. a.
64. 6. our iniquities like wind have t. us *away*
Jer. 16. 5. I have t. *away* my peace from this people
Lam. 2. 6. hath violently t. *away* his tabernacle
Ezek. 33. 6. he is t. *away* in his iniquity
Dan. 7. 12. they had their dominion t. *away*
8. 11. by him the daily sacrifice was t. a. 12. 11.
Hos. 4. 3. the fishes of the sea also shall be t. *away*
Amos 4. 10. and I have t. *away* your horses
Mic. 2. 9. ye have t. *away* my glory for ever
Zeph. 3. 15. the Lord hath t. *away* thy judgments
Mat. 13. 12. from him shall be t. *away* even that he hath, 25. 29, Luke 8. 18. | 19. 26.
Mark 2. 20. the bridegroom shall be t. a. Luke 5. 35.
Luke 10. 42. that good part which shall not be t. a.
11. 52. ye have t. *away* the key of knowledge
John 19. 31. and that they might be t. *away*
20. 1. seeth the stone t. *away* from the sepulchre
2. they have t. *away* the Lord || 13. t. a. my Lord
Acts 8. 33. in his humiliation his judgment was t. a.
27. 20. all hope that we should be saved was t. a.
1 Cor. 5. 2. he that hath done this, might be t. *away*
2 Cor. 3. 16. nevertheless the veil shall be t. *away*

TAKEN *hold*.

1 Kings 9. 9. and have t. *hold* upon other gods
Job 30. 16. days of affliction have t. *hold* upon me
Psal. 40. 12. mine iniquities have t. *hold* upon me
119. 143. trouble and anguish have t. *hold* on me
Isa. 21. 3. pangs have t. *hold* on me, as of a woman
Jer. 6. 24. anguish hath t. *hold* on us, and pain

TAKEN *up*.

Exod. 40. 36. cloud was t. *up* from over tabernacle
37. if the cloud were not t. *up* till it was t. *up*
Num. 9. 17. when the cloud was t. *up*, 21.
22. but when it was t. *up* they journeyed, 10. 11.
2 Sam. 18. 9. Absalom was t. *up* between heaven
Isa. 10. 29. they have t. *up* their lodging at Geba
Jer. 29. 22. of them shall be t. *up* a curse by Judah
Ezek. 36. 3. ye are t. *up* in the lips of talkers
Dan. 6. 23. so Daniel was t. *up* out of the den
Luke 9. 17. there was t. *up* of the fragments
Acts 1. 2. till the day in which he was t. *up*
9. while they beheld, he was t. *up*, and a cloud
11. this same Jesus which is t. *up* from you
22. unto that same day he was t. *up* from us
20. 9. Eutychus fell down, and was t. *up* dead
Acts 27. 17. had t. *up* the boat || 40. t. *up* the anchors

TAKEST.

Exod. 4. 9. the water thou t. out of the river
30. 12. when thou t. the sum of children of Israel
Judg. 4. 9. journey thou t. not be for thy honour
Ps. 104. 29. thou t. away their breath, they die
144. 3. what is man, that thou t. knowledge of him?
Isa. 58. 3. afflicted our soul, and thou t. no knowl.
Luke 19. 21. thou t. up that thou layedst not down

TAKEST *heed*.

1 Chr. 22. 13. if thou t. *heed* to fulfil the statutes

TAKETH.

Exod. 20. 7. that t. his name in vain, Deut. 5. 11.
Deut. 10. 17. regardeth not persons, nor t. reward
24. 6. for he t. a man's life to pledge
25. 11. putteth her hand and t. him by the secrets
27. 25. cursed be he that t. reward to slay innocent
32. 11. as an eagle t. them, beareth them on her
Josh. 7. 14. the tribe which the Lord t. shall come
15. 16. smiteth Kirjath sepher, and t. it, Judg. 1. 12.
1 Sam. 17. 26. and t. away reproach from Israel
1 Kings 14. 10. as man t. away dung, till all be gone
Job 5. 5. and t. it even out of the thorns
13. he t. the wise in their craftiness. 1 Cor. 3. 19.
9. 12. behold, he t. away, who can hinder him?
12. 20. and t. away the understanding of the aged
24. he t. away the heart of the chief of the people
27. 8. what is the hope when God t. away his soul?
40. 24. he t. it with his eyes, his nose pierceth
Psal. 15. 3. nor t. up reproach against his neighb.
5. nor t. reward against the innocent
118. 7. Lord, t. my part with them that help me
137. 9. happy shall he be that t. and dasheth little
147. 10. he t. not pleasure in the legs of a man
11. the Lord t. pleasure in them that fear him
149. 4. for the Lord t. pleasure in his people
Prov. 1. 19. which t. away the life of the owners
16. 32. rules his spirit, is better than he that t. city
17. 23. a wicked man t. gift out of the bosom
25. 20. as he that t. away a garment in cold weather
26. 17. is like one that t. a dog by the ears
Eccl. 1. 3. of all his labour which he t. under the sun
2. 23. his heart t. not rest in the night
Isa. 13. 14. and as a sheep that no man t. up
40. 15. he t. up the isles as a very little thing
44. 14. the carpenter t. the cypress and the oak
51. 18. nor is there any that t. her by the hand
Ezek. 16. 32. who t. strangers instead of her husband
33. 4. and t. not warning || 5. he that t. warning
Amos 3. 12. as the shepherd t. out of mouth of lion
Mat. 4. 5. the devil t. him up into the holy city
8. t. him up into an exceeding high mountain
9. 16. t. from garment, and rent worse, Mark 2. 21.
10. 38. that t. not his cross, and followeth after me
12. 45. he goeth, t. seven other spirits, Luke 11. 26.
17. 1. Jes. t. Peter, James, and John, and bringeth into an high mountain, Mark 9. 2. | 14. 33.
Mark 4. 15. Satan cometh, and t. away the word that was sown in their hearts, Luke 8. 12.
5. 40. he t. the father and mother of the damsel
9. 18. wheresoever he t. him, he teareth him
Luke 6. 29. him that t. away thy cloak, forbid not
30. and of him that t. thy goods, ask them not
9. 39. a spirit t. him, and he suddenly crieth out
11. 22. a stronger t. from him all his armour
16. 3. my lord t. away from me the stewardship
John 1. 29. Lamb of God, who t. away sin of world
10. 18. no man t. it from me, I lay it down of mys.
15. 2. branch that beareth not fruit, he t. away
16. 22. and your joy no man t. from you
21. 13. Jes. then cometh, t. bread, and giveth them
Rom. 3. 5. is God unrighteous, who t. vengeance?
1 Cor. 11. 21. in eating, every one t. before another
Heb. 5. 4. no man t. this honour to himself but he
10. 9. he t. away the first that he may establish

Taketh HOLD.

Job 21. 6. afraid, and trembling t. *hold* on my flesh
Prov. 30. 28. the spider t. *hold* with her hands
Isa. 56. 6. every one that t. *hold* of my covenant

TAKING.

2 Chron. 19. 7. with God there is no t. of gifts
Job 5. 3. I have seen the foolish t. root, but cursed
Psal. 119. 9. by t. heed thereto, according to thy
Jer. 50. 46. at noise of t. of Babylon earth moved
Ezek. 25. 12. dealt against Judah by t. vengeance
Hos. 11. 3. I taught Ephraim also to go, t. them by their arms, but they knew not that I healed them
Mat. 6. 27. which of you by t. thought, Luke 12. 25.
Mark 13. 34. Son of man is as a man t. a far journey
Luke 4. 5. the devil t. him up into a high mountain
19. 22. t. up that I laid not down, and reaping that
John 11. 13. he had spoken of t. rest in sleep
Rom. 7. 8. sin t. occasion by the commandment, 11.
2 Cor. 2. 13. t. my leave of them, I went to Maced.
11. 8. t. wages of them to do you service
Eph. 6. 16. above all, t. the shield of faith
2 Thess. 1. 8. in flaming fire t. vengeance on them
1 Pet. 5. 2. t. the oversight thereof willingly
3 John 7. they went forth t. nothing of the Gentiles

TALE.

Psal. 90. 9. we spend our years as a t. that is told

TALE-*bearer*.

Lev. 19. 16. shalt not go up and down as a t.-*bearer*
Prov. 11. 13. a t.-*bearer* revealeth secrets, 20. 19.
18. 8. the words of a t.-b. are as wounds. 26. 22.
26. 20. where there is no t.-*bearer* strife ceaseth

TALES.

Ezek. 22. 9. are men that carry t. to shed blood
Luke 24. 11. their words seemed to them as idle t.

TALE.

Exod. 5. 8. the t. of bricks which they did make
18. no straw, yet shall he deliver the t. of bricks
1 Sam. 18. 27. gave the foreskins in full t. to king
1 Chron. 9. 28. should bring vessels in and out by t.

TALENT

Signifies, [1] *A weight among the Jews, containing 3000 shekels; which, computing the shekel at 3 shillings sterling, amounts to 450 pounds for a talent of silver: and allowing the proportion of gold to silver to be as sixteen to one, a talent of gold will amount to 7200 pounds. Others, making the shekel of less value, compute a talent of silver to be in English money, 342 pounds, 3 shillings, and 9 pence. The talent of gold 5,475 pounds,* Exod. 25. 39. | 38. 25. [2] *The gifts of God bestowed on men,* Mat. 25. 15.

Exod. 25. 39. of a t. of pure gold make it, 37. 24.
38. 27. an hundred sockets, a t. for a socket
2 Sam. 12. 30. the weight of the crown was a t.
1 Kings 20. 39. else thou shalt pay a t. of silver
2 Kings 5. 22. give them a t. of silver and changes
23. 33. a tribute of a t. of gold, 2 Chron. 36. 3.
Zech. 5. 7. behold, there was lifted a t. of lead
Mat. 25. 25. I went and hid thy t. in the earth
28. take therefore the t. from him and give it
Rev. 16. 21. every stone about the weight of a t.

TALENTS.

Exod. 38. 24. the gold of the offering was 29 t.
27. of 100 t. of silver were cast the sockets
1 Kings 16. 24. bought the hill Samaria for two t.
2 Kings 5. 5. Naaman took ten t. || 23. take two t.
15. 19. Menahem gave Pul 1000 t. of silver
18. 14. appointed to Hezekiah 300 t. and 30 of gold
23. 33. land to a tribute of 100 t. 2 Chron. 36. 3.
1 Chron. 19. 6. Ammonites sent 1000 t. of silver
29. 4. David gave 3000 t. of gold to the house
7. gave of gold 5000 t. and of silver 10,000 t.
2 Chron. 25. 9. what shall we do for the 100 t.?
27. 5. the children of Ammon gave him 100 t.
Mat. 18. 24. one which owed him 10,000 t.
25. 15. to one he gave five t. to another two

See GOLD, SILVER.

TALK.

Job 11. 2. should a man full of t. be justified?
15. 3. should he reason with unprofitable t.?
Prov. 14. 23. the t. of the lips tendeth to penury
Eccl. 10. 13. end of his t. is mischievous madness
Mat. 22. 15. they might entangle him in his t.

TALK.

Num. 11. 17. I will come down and t. with thee
Deut. 5. 24. have seen that God doth t. with man
6. 7. shalt t. of them when thou sittest in thy house
1 Sam. 2. 3. t. no more so exceeding proudly
2 Kings 18. 26. t. not with us in the Jews' language
1 Chron. 16. 9. sing unto him, sing psalms, t. ye of all his wondrous works, Psal. 105. 2.
Job 13. 7. and will ye t. deceitfully for him?
Psal. 69. 26. they t. to the grief of them whom
71. 24. my tongue shall t. of thy righteousness
77. 12. I will meditate and t. of thy doings
119. 27. so shall I t. of thy wondrous works
145. 11. speak of thy kingdom and t. of thy power
Prov. 6. 22. when thou awakest it shall t. with thee
24. 2. heart studieth, and their lips t. of mischief
Jer. 12. 1. let me t. with thee of thy judgments
Ezek. 3. 22. arise and I will there t. with thee
Dan. 10. 17. how can thy servant t. with my lord
John 14. 30. I will not t. much with you, for prince

TALKED.

Gen. 45. 15. after that his brethren t. with him
Exod. 20. 22. seen that I have t. with you, Deut. 5. 4.
33. 9. and the Lord t. with Moses
34. 29. the skin of his face shone while he t.
1 Sam. 14. 19. while Saul t. unto the priest
2 Chron. 25. 16. it came to pass as he t. with him
Jer. 38. 25. if the princes hear that I have t.
Luke 9. 30. t. with him two men, Moses and Elias
24. 32. heart burn while he t. with us by the way
John 4. 27. marvelled that he t. with the woman
Acts 10. 27. as Peter t. with Cornelius he went in
20. 11. and t. long, even till break of day
26. 31. they t. between themselves, saying
Rev. 21. 15. he that t. with me had a golden reed

TALKERS.

Ezek. 36. 3. ye are taken up in the lips of t.
Tit. 1. 10. there are many unruly and vain t.

TALKEST.

Judg. 6. 17. shew me a sign that thou t. with me
1 Kings 1. 14. while thou yet t. with the king
John 4. 27. no man said, why t. thou with her?

TALKETH.

Psal. 37. 30. and his tongue t. of judgment
John 9. 37. seen him, and it is he that t. with thee

TALKING.

Gen. 17. 22. and he left off t. with him
1 Kings 18. 27. he is a god, he is t. or pursuing
Esth. 6. 14. while they were t. with him
Ezek. 33. 30. thy people are still t. against thee
Mat. 17. 3. Moses and Elias t. with him, Mark 9. 4.
Rev. 4. 1. as the voice of a trumpet t. with me

TALKING.

Job 29. 9. the princes refrained t. and laid their hand
Eph. 5. 4. neither filthiness, nor foolish t.

TALL.

Deut. 2. 10. a people t. as the Anakims, 21. | 9. 2.
2 Kings 19. 23. and will cut down the t. cedar trees and the choice fir trees thereof, Isa. 37. 24.

TALLER.

Deut. 1. 28. the people is greater and t. than we

TAME.

Mark 5. 4. often bound, neither could any man t. him
Jam. 3. 8. but the tongue can no man t. is unruly

TAMED.

Jam. 3. 7. things of the sea is t. and hath been t.

TANNER.

Acts 9. 43. Peter tarried with one Simon a t.
10. 6. he lodged with one Simon a t. 32.

TAPESTRY, *See* COVERINGS.

TARE.

2 Sam. 13. 31. the king arose and t. his garments
2 Kings 2. 24. two she-bears t. forty-two children
Mark 9. 20. straightway the spirit t. him, Luke 9. 42.

TARES

Signify, *A kind of pulse noxious and hurtful to corn,* Mat. 13. 29. To which are compared, *The wicked in the world, but especially hypocrites,* Mat. 13. 38.

Mat. 13. 25. his enemy sowed t. among the wheat
26. the blade sprung up, then appeared the t. also
27. sow good seed, from whence then hath it t.?
29. lest while you gather up the t. you root up
36. declare to us the parable of the t. of the field

TARGET.

1 Sam. 17. 6. Goliath had a t. of brass

1 Kings 10. 16. beaten gold, six hundred shekels of gold went to one t. 2 Chron. 9. 15.

TARGETS.

1 Kings 10. 16. Solomon made two hundred t.
2 Chr. 14. 8. Asa had an army that bare t. and spears

TARRY

Signifies, [1] *To abide and continue*, Gen. 27. 44. [2] *To stay behind*, Exod. 12. 39. [3] *To wait or stay for*, Exod. 24. 14. [4] *To delay, defer, or put off*, Gen. 45. 9. [5] *To be established*, Psal. 101. † 7. [6] *To guard*, 1 Sam. 30. 24. [7] *To lodge*, Gen. 19. 2.

Gen. 19. 2. and t. all night, and wash your feet
27. 44. and t. with Laban a few days till fury
30. 27. if I have found favour in thine eyes t.
45. 9. thus saith thy son, come down to me, t. not
Exod. 12. 39. they were thrust out, and could not t.
24. 14. t. ye here for us till we come again to you
Lev. 14. 8. the leper shall t. out of his tent seven days
Num. 22. 19. I pray you t. here also this night
Judg. 5. 28. why t. the wheels of his chariots?
6. 18. he said, I will t. until thou come again
19. 6. t. all night, 9. || 10. the man would not t.
Ruth 1. 13. would ye t. for them till they were grown
3. 13. t. this night, and it shall be in the morning
1 Sam. 1. 23. t. until thou have weaned him
10. 8. seven days shalt thou t. till I come to thee
14. 9. if they say, t. till we come to you
2 Sam. 10. 5. t. at Jericho till your beards be grown, and then return, 1 Chron. 19. 5.
11. 12. t. here to-day || 15. 28. I will t. in the plain
18. 14. Joab said, I may not t. thus with thee
19. 7. there will not t. one with thee this night
2 Kings 2. 2. t. here the Lord sent me, 4. 6.
7. 9. the lepers said, if we t. till the morning light
9. 3. then open the door and flee, and t. not
14. 10. smitten Edom, glory of this, and t. at home
Psal. 101. 7. a liar shall not t. in my sight
Prov. 23. 30. they that t. long at the wine
Isa. 46. 13. not far off, and my salvation shall not t.
Jer. 14. 8. that turneth aside to t. for a night
Hab. 2. 3. though it t. wait for it, for it will not t.
Mat. 26. 38. t. ye here and watch, Mark 14. 34.
Luke 24. 29. and he went in to t. with them
49. but t. ye in the city of Jerusalem, till endued
John 4. 40. besought that he would t. with them
21. 22. if I will that he t. till I come, 23.
Acts 10. 48. they prayed Peter to t. certain days
18. 20. they desired Paul to t. longer time with them
28. 14. were desired to t. with them seven days
1 Cor. 11. 33. wherefore t. one for another
16. 7. I trust to t. a while with you, if Lord permit
8. but I will t. at Ephesus until Pentecost
1 Tim. 3. 15. but if I t. long that thou mayest
Heb. 10. 37. he that shall come, will come, and not t.

TARRIED.

Gen. 24. 54. Abraham's servant t. all night
28. 11. Jacob t. there all night and took stones
31. 54. Jacob and Laban t. all night in the mount
Num. 9. 19. when the cloud t. long, 22.
Judg. 3. 25. they t. till they were ashamed
26. Ehud escaped while they t. and passed
19. 8. they t. till afternoon and did eat both of them
Ruth 2. 7. save that she t. a little in the house
1 Sam. 13. 8. he t. seven days according to set time
2 Sam. 11. 1. but David t. still at Jerusalem
15. 17. the king t. in a place that was far off
29. Zadok and Abiathar t. at Jerusalem
20. 5. but he t. longer than the set time
2 Kings 2. 18. when they came, for he t. at Jericho
Psal. 68. 12. and she that t. at home divided the spoil
Mat. 25. 5. while the bridegroom t. they all slept
Luke 1. 21. the people marvelled that he t. so long
2. 43. the child Jesus t. behind in Jerusalem
John 3. 22. then he t. with them, and baptized
Acts 9. 43. Peter t. many days in Joppa with Simon
15. 33. Judas and Silas exhorted and t. at Antioch
18. 18. Paul t. a good while at Corinth and sailed
20. 5. these going before t. for us at Troas
21. 4. and finding the disciples, we t. seven days
10. as we t. many days at Cesarea came Agabus
25. 6. Festus t. at Jerusalem more than ten days
27. 33. this is the fourteenth day ye have t. fasting
28. 12. landing at Syracuse, we t. three days

TARRIEST.

Acts 22. 16. and now why t. thou? arise, be baptized

TARRIETH.

1 Sam. 30. 24. so shall his part be that t. by stuff
Mic. 5. 7. that t. not for a man, nor waiteth for

TARRYING.

Psal. 40. 17. make no t. O my God, 70. 5.

TASK.

Exod. 5. 19. ye shall not minish from your daily t.

TASKS.

Exod. 5. 13. saying, fulfil your works, your daily t.
14. why not fulfilled your t. in making brick

TASK-masters.

Exod. 1. 11. set over them t.-masters to afflict them
3. 7. heard their cry by reason of their t.-masters
5. 6. and Pharaoh commanded t.-masters, saying
10. t.-masters told them || 13. t.-masters hastened them
14. officers which the t.-masters had set over them

TASTE

Signifies, [1] *To prove, or try the relish of any thing by the palate, or tongue*, Job 34. 3. [2] *To have an inward experimental knowledge of a thing*, Psal. 34. 8. [3] *To eat a little*, 1 Sam. 14. 29, 43. [4] *To drink*, Dan. 5. 2.

Have *tasted* of the heavenly gift, Heb. 6. 4. *Have had some transient experience of the power and efficacy of the Holy Ghost from heaven, in gospel administration and worship, so as to relish comfort and sweetness in the doctrine and promises of the gospel.*

To *taste* death, Heb. 2. 9. *To feel the bitterness of death, yet not to be long detained under it.*

TASTE, *Substantive.*

Exod. 16. 31. the t. of manna was like wafers
Num. 11. 8. the t. of it was as the t. of fresh oil
Job 6. 6. is there any t. in the white of an egg?
30. cannot my t. discern perverse things?
Psal. 119. 103. how sweet are thy words to my t.!
Prov. 24. 13. the honey-comb is sweet to the t.
Cant. 2. 3. and his fruit was sweet to my t.
Jer. 48. 11. therefore his t. remained in him

TASTE, *Verb.*

1 Sam. 14. 43. I did but t. a little honey, and lo
2 Sam. 3. 35. if I t. bread or ought else till sun be down
19. 35. can thy servant t. what I eat or drink?
Job 12. 11. doth not the mouth t. his meat
Psal. 34. 8. O t. and see that the Lord is good
Jonah 3. 7. neither herd nor flock t. any thing
Mat. 16. 28. there be some standing here which shall not t. of death, Mark 9. 1. Luke 9. 27.
Luke 14. 24. none bidden shall t. of my supper
John 8. 52. keep my saying, he shall never t. death
Col. 2. 21. touch not, t. not, handle not
Heb. 2. 9. that he should t. death for every man

TASTED.

1 Sam. 14. 24. so none t. any food || 29. I t. honey
Dan. 5. 2. Belshazzar whilst he t. wine, commanded
Mat. 27. 34. when he had t. thereof, he would
John 2. 9. the ruler had t. the water made wine
Heb. 6. 4. and have t. of the heavenly gift
5. have t. the good word of God and powers of
1 Pet. 2. 3. if ye have t. that the Lord is gracious

TASTETH.

Job 34. 3. ear trieth words as the mouth t. meat
Prov. 31. † 18. t. that her merchandise is good

TATLERS.

1 Tim. 5. 13. not only idle but t. and busy bodies

TAVERNS.

Acts 28. 15. came to meet us as far as the three t.

TAUGHT.

Deut. 4. 5. I have t. you statutes and judgments
31. 22. Moses t. the children of Israel this song
Judg. 8. 16. with them he t. the men of Succoth
2 Kings 17. 28. and t. them how to fear the Lord
2 Chron. 6. 27. thou hast t. them the good way
17. 9. the Levites t. the people in Judah
23. 13. people rejoiced, such as t. to sing praise
30. 22. that t. the good knowledge of the Lord
35. 3. Josiah said to the Levites that t. all Israel
Neh. 8. 9. the Levites that t. the people said
Psal. 71. 17. O God, thou hast t. me, 119. 102.
119. 171. when thou hast t. me thy statutes
Prov. 4. 4. he t. me also, and said, let thine heart
11. I have t. thee in the way of wisdom
31. 1. the prophecy that his mother t. him
Eccl. 12. 9. he still t. the people knowledge
Isa. 29. 13. their fear is t. by the precepts of men
40. 13. or being his counsellor hath t. him, 14.
54. 13. all thy children shall be t. of God
Jer. 2. 33. therefore hast thou t. the wicked
9. 5. they have t. their tongues to speak lies
14. after Baalim, which their fathers t. them
12. 16. as they t. my people to swear by Baal
13. 21. for thou hast t. them to be captains
28. 16. thou hast t. rebellion against the Lord
29. 32. he hath t. rebellion against the Lord
32. 33. though I have t. them, rising up early
Ezek. 23. 48. women t. not to do after lewdness
Hos. 10. 11. Ephraim is as a heifer that is t.
11. 3. I t. Ephraim to go, taking them by their arms
Zech. 13. 5. for man t. me to keep cattle from youth
Mat. 7. 29. he t. them as one having authority, and not as the scribes, Mark 1. 22.
28. 15. they took money, and did as they were t.
Mark 6. 30. told him all things they had done and t.
10. 1. as he was wont he t. them again
Luke 11. 1. teach us to pray, as John t. his disciples
13. 26. and thou hast t. in our streets
John 6. 45. and they shall be all t. of God
7. 14. Jesus went up into the temple, and t. 28. Mark 12. 35. Luke 19. 47. | 20. 1.
8. 2. all the people came, he sat down and t. them
28. as my father hath t. me, I speak these
18. 20. I ever t. in the synagogue and temple
Acts 4. 2. being grieved that they t. the people
5. 21. they entered into the temple early and t.
11. 26. Paul and Barnabas t. much people, 14. 21.
15. 1. certain men t. the brethren, and said, except
18. 25. Apollos t. diligently the things of the Lord
20. 20. I have shewed you, and t. you publicly
22. 3. t. according to the perfect manner of the law
Gal. 1. 12. nor was I t. it but by revelation
6. 6. let him that is t. in the word communicate
Eph. 4. 21. if so be ye have been t. by him as truth
Col. 2. 7. stablished in the faith, as ye have been t.
1 Thess. 4. 9. ye are t. of God to love one another
2 Thess. 2. 15. hold the traditions ye have been t.
Tit. 1. 9. holding the word, as he hath been t.
1 John 2. 27. even as the anointing hath t. you
Rev. 2. 14. who t. Balak to cast a stumbling-block

TAUNT.

Jer. 24. 9. I will deliver them to be a t. and a curse
Ezek. 5. 15. so it shall be a reproach and a t.

TAUNTING.

Isa. 14. † 4. thou shalt take up this t. speech
Hab. 2. 6. all these take up a t. proverb against him

TAXATION.

2 Kings 23. 35. exacted of every one according to t.

TAXED, *Active, Passive.*

2 Kings 23. 35. but Jehoiakim t. the land to give
Luke 2. 1. a decree that all the world should be t.
3. all went to be t. || 5. Joseph went to be t.

TAXES.

Dan. 11. 20. then shall stand up a raiser of t.

TAXING.

Luke 2. 2. and this t. was first made when Cyrenius
Acts 5. 37. rose up Judas in the days of the t.

TEACH

Signifies, [1] *To instruct or cause to learn*, Psal. 119. 25. Mat. 28. 19. [2] *To accustom to*, Jer. 9. 5. [3] *To admonish*, Mark 8. 31. | 9. 31. [4] *To suggest or put into one's mind*, Luke 12. 12. [5] *To signify and give notice*, Prov. 6. 13. [6] *To counsel and direct*, Hab. 2. 19.

Exod. 4. 15. and I will t. you what ye shall do
35. 34. God hath put in his heart that he may t.
Lev. 10. 11. that ye may t. Israel all the statutes
14. 57. to t. when it is unclean and when clean
Deut. 4. 1. hearken to the judgments which I t. you
10. and that they may t. their children
Deut. 4. 14. the Lord commanded me to t. you, 6. 1.
20. 18. they t. you not to do after their abominations
24. 8. to all that the priests the Levites shall t. you
31. 19. write and t. the children of Israel this song
33. 10. they shall t. Jacob thy judgments
Judg. 13. 8. t. us what we shall do to the child
1 Sam. 12. 23. I will t. you the good and right way
2 Sam. 1. 18. bade them t. the use of the bow
2 Chron. 17. 7. to t. in the cities of Judah
Ezra 7. 10. and to t. in Israel statutes and judgments
Job 21. 22. shall any t. God knowledge
27. 11. I will t. you by the hand of God
32. 7. and multitude of years should t. wisdom
37. 19. t. us what we shall say unto him, for we
Psal. 25. 8. therefore he will t. sinners in the way
9. the meek will he guide and t. his way
12. him that feareth Lord shall he t. in the way
34. 11. I will t. you the fear of the Lord
51. 13. then will I t. transgressors thy ways
90. 12. so t. us to number our days that we may
105. 22. to bind princes, and t. his senators wisdom
Prov. 9. 9. t. a just man, and he will increase in
Isa. 2. 3. and he will t. us of his ways, Mic. 4. 2.
28. 9. whom shall he t. knowledge, and to unders.
26. for his G. doth instruct and t. him discretion
Jer. 9. 20. and t. your daughters wailing and lam.
31. 34. they shall t. no more every man his neighbour, for all shall know the Lord, Heb. 8. 11.
Ezek. 44. 23. t. my people the difference between
Dan. 1. 4. whom they might t. learn. of Chaldeans
Mic. 3. 11. priests thereof t. for hire and prophets
Hab. 2. 19. saith to the dumb stone, arise, it shall t.
Mat. 5. 19. shall t. men so || 28. 19. t. all nations
Luke 11. 1. Lord, t. us to pray, as John taught his
12. 12. the Holy Ghost shall t. you what to say
John 7. 35. t. the Gentiles || 9. 34. dost thou t. us?
14. 26. the Holy Ghost shall t. you all things
Acts 1. 1. treatise of all that Jes. began to do and t.
4. 18. to speak nor t. in the name of Jesus, 5. 28.
5. 42. they ceased not to t. and preach Jesus Chr.
16. 21. t. customs which are not lawful for us
1 Cor. 4. 17. as I t. every where in every church
11. 14. doth not even nature itself t. you
14. 19. that by my voice I might t. others
1 Tim. 1. 3. charge some they t. no other doctrine
2. 12. but I suffer not a woman to t. nor usurp
3. 2. a bishop must be apt to t. 2 Tim. 2. 24.
4. 11. these things command and t.
6. 2. these things t. and exhort
3. if any man t. otherwise, he is proud
2 Tim. 2. 2. faithful men who shall be able to t. oth.
Tit. 2. 4. that they t. young women to be sober
Heb. 5. 12. ye have need that one t. you again
1 John 2. 27. and need not that any man t. you
Rev. 2. 20. thou sufferest that woman Jezebel to t.

See BEGAN.

TEACH *me.*

Job 6. 24. t. me and I will hold my tongue
34. 32. that which I see not, t. thou me
Psal. 25. 4. t. me thy paths || 5. lead me and t. me
27. 11. t. me thy way, O L. and lead me, 86. 11.
119. 12. t. me thy statutes, 26, 33, 64, 68, 124, 135.
66. t. me good judgments || 108. t. me thy judgm.
143. 10. t. me to do thy will, for thou art my God

TEACH *thee.*

Exod. 4. 12. I will t. thee what thou shalt say
Deut. 17. 11. the sentence which they shall t. thee
Job 8. 10. thy fathers, shall not they t. thee?
12. 7. but ask the beasts, and they shall t. thee
8. or speak to the earth, and it shall t. thee
33. 33. hold thy peace, I shall t. thee wisdom
Psal. 32. 8. I will t. thee in the way thou shalt go
45. 4. thy right hand shall t. thee terrible things

TEACH *them.*

Exod. 18. 20. thou shalt t. them ordinances and laws
24. 12. I have written that thou mayest t. them
Deut. 4. 9. t. them thy sons, and thy sons' sons
5. 31. the judgments which thou shalt t. them
6. 7. t. them diligently to thy children, 11. 19.
Judg. 3. 2. that Israel might know to t. them war
1 Kings 8. 36. that thou t. them the good way where.
2 Kings 17. 27. let him t. them the manner of the G.
Ezra 7. 25. and t. ye them that know them not
Psal. 132. 12. keep my testimony that I shall t. them
Mat. 5. 19. whosoever shall do and t. them shall be
Mark 6. 34. he began to t. them many things
8. 31. to t. them that the son of man must suffer

TEACHER

Signifies, [1] *A tutor, master, or instructor*, 1 Chron. 25. 8. [2] *A public minister, who by wholesome doctrine instructeth the church*, Eph. 4. 11. [3] *Such as privately instruct others in the knowledge of spiritual things*, Tit. 2. 3.

1 Chron. 25. 8. cast lots, as well the t. as the scholar
Joel 2. † 23. hath given you a t. of righteousness
Hab. 2. 18. what profiteth the image, a t. of lies
John 3. 2. we know thou art a t. come from God
Rom. 2. 20. confident that thou art a t. of babes
1 Tim. 2. 7. I am a t. of the Gentiles, 2 Tim. 1. 11.

TEACHERS.

Psal. 119. 99. more understanding than all my t.
Prov. 5. 13. and have not obeyed the voice of my t.
Isa. 30. 20. yet shall not thy t. be removed into a corner any more, but thine eyes shall see thy t.
43. 27. thy t. have transgressed against me
Dan. 12. † 3. they that be t. shall shine
Acts 13. 1. at Antioch were certain prophets and t.
1 Cor. 12. 28. hath set prophets, t. || 29. are all t.?
Eph. 4. 11. he gave some evangelists, pastors, and t.
1 Tim. 1. 7. desiring to be t. of law, understanding
2 Tim. 4. 3. they shall heap to themselves t. having
Tit. 2. 3. that the aged women be t. of good things
Heb. 5. 12. when for the time ye ought to be t.
2 Pet. 2. 1. as there shall be false t. among you

TEACHEST.

Psal. 94. 12. blessed is the man whom thou t.
Mat. 22. 16. we know that thou art true, and t. the way of God in truth, Mark 12. 14. Luke 20. 21.
Acts 21. 21. thou t. the Jews to forsake Moses
Rom. 2. 21. thou that t. another, t. thou not thyself?

TEACHETH.

2 Sam. 22. 35. he t. my hands to war, Psal. 18. 34.

Job 15. † 5. thy mouth t. thine iniquity
35. 11. who t. us more than the beasts of the earth
36. 22. behold, God exalteth, who t. like him?
Psal. 94. 10. he that t. man knowledge, not know
144. 1. which t. my hands to war, and fingers
Prov. 6. 13. a wicked man t. with his fingers
16. 23. the heart of the wise t. his mouth
Isa. 9. 15. the prophet that t. lies, he is the tail
48. 17. I am thy God which t. thee to profit
Acts 21. 28. the man that t. all men every where
Rom. 12. 7. or he that t. on teaching
1 Cor. 2. 13. we speak not in the words which man's wisdom t. but which the Holy Ghost t.
Gal. 6. 6. let him communicate to him that t.
1 John 2. 27. as the same anointing t. you all things

TEACHING.

2 Chron. 15. 3. Israel hath been without a t. priest
Jer. 32. 33. I taught them rising up early and t. them
Mat. 4. 23. Jesus went about Galilee, t. in their synagogues, preaching gospel, 9. 35. Luke 13. 10.
15. 9. in vain they do worship me, t. for doctrines the commandments of men, Mark 7. 7.
21. 23. the elders came unto him as he was t.
26. 55. I sat daily with you, t. in the temple
28. 20. t. them to observe all things whatsoever
Luke 23. 5. t. throughout all Jewry from Galilee
Acts 5. 25. the apostles t. the people in the temple
15. 35. Paul and Barnabas in Antioch t. preaching
18. 11. Paul t. the word of God at Corinth
28. 31. Paul t. at Rome with all confidence
Rom. 12. 7. or he that teacheth on t.
Col. 1. 28. warning and t. every man in all wisdom
3. 16. t. and admonishing one another in psalms
Tit. 1. 11. t. things which they ought not
2. 12. t. us, that denying ungodliness and lusts

TEAR

Signifies, [1] To rend, or pull in pieces, Hos. 13. 8. [2] To destroy, Psal. 7. 2. Amos 1. 11. [3] To slander or reproach, Psal. 35. 15. [4] To thresh, Judg. 8. † 7.
Judg. 8. 7. then will I t. your flesh with thorns
Psal. 7. 2. lest he t. my soul like a lion, rending it
35. 15. they did t. me, and ceased not
50. 22. consider this, lest I t. you in pieces
Jer. 15. 3. I will appoint over them the dogs to t.
16. 7. nor shall men t. themselves for them
Ezek. 13. 20. your pillows I will t. from your arms
21. your kerchiefs will I t. and deliver my people
Hos. 5. 14. I, even I, will t. and go away
13. 8. I will devour, the wild beast shall t. them
Amos 1. 11. cast off pity, his anger did t. perpetual.
Nah. 2. 12. the lion did t. enough for his whelps
Zech. 11. 16. the shepherd shall t. their claws

TEARETH.

Deut. 33. 20. Gad dwelleth as a lion, and t. the arm
Job 16. 9. he t. me in his wrath, who hateth me
18. 4. he t. himself in his anger, shall the earth be
Mic. 5. 8. as a young lion t. in pieces, none deliver
Mark 9. 18. wheresoever he taketh him, he t. him, and he foameth and pineth away, Luke 9. 39.

TEARS

Signify, [1] Drops of water issuing out of the eyes, Psal. 6. 6. | 42. 3. [2] Sorrow and affliction, Psal. 126. 5. Isa. 25. 8.
2 Sam. 16. † 12. may be the Lord will look on my t.
2 Kings 20. 5. I have seen thy t. Isa. 38. 5.
Job 16. 20. but mine eye poureth out t. unto God
Psal. 6. 6. I water my couch with my t. all night
39. 12. O Lord, hold not thy peace at my t.
42. 3. my t. have been my meat day and night
56. 8. put thou my t. in thy bottle, are in thy book
80. 5. thou feedest them with the bread of t. and givest them t. to drink in great measure
116. 8. thou hast delivered mine eyes from t.
126. 5. they that sow in t. shall reap in joy
Eccl. 4. 1. behold the t. of such as were oppressed
Isa. 16. 9. I will water thee with t. O Heshbon
25. 8. the Lord will wipe away t. from all faces
Jer. 9. 1. O that mine eyes were a fountain of t.!
18. our eyes may run down with t. and eye-lids
13. 17. and mine eyes shall run down with t.
14. 17. let mine eyes run with t. night and day
31. 16. refrain from weeping, thine eyes from t.
Lam. 1. 2. she weeps, and her t. are on her cheeks
2. 11. mine eyes do fail with t. my bowels
18. let t. run down like a river day and night
Ezek. 24. 16. neither shall thy t. run down
Mal. 2. 13. covering the altar of the Lord with t.
Mark. 9. 24. the father said with t. Lord, I believe
Luke 7. 38. and she began to wash his feet with her t.
44. but she hath washed my feet with t.
Acts 20. 19. serving the Lord with many t.
31. I ceased not to warn every one with t.
2 Cor. 2. 4. I wrote to you with many t.
2 Tim. 1. 4. to see thee, being mindful of thy t.
Heb. 5. 7. when he offered up supplications with t.
12. 17. though he sought it carefully with t.
Rev. 7. 17. God shall wipe away all t. 21. 4.

TEATS.

Isa. 32. 12. they shall lament for the t.
Ezek. 23. 3. there they bruised the t. 21.

TEDIOUS.

Acts 24. 4. that I be not further t. to thee

TEETH

Signifies, [1] That wherewith a creature chews its food, Num. 11. 33. [2] Slanderous speeches and pernicious calumnies, Psal. 57. 4. Prov. 30. 14. Break their teeth, Psal. 58. 6. Take away their power and instruments of doing mischief, and disable them from hurting me.
Gen. 49. 12. and his t. shall be white with milk
Num. 11. 33. while the flesh was yet between their t.
Deut. 32. 24. I will send the t. of beasts upon them
1 Sam. 2. 13. came with a flesh-hook of three t.
1 Kings 10. † 22. bringing elephants' t. 2 Chr. 9. † 21.
Job 4. 10. the t. of the young lions are broken
13. 14. wherefore do I take my flesh in my t.?
19. 20. I am escaped with the skin of my t.
29. 17. and plucked the spoil out of t. of wicked
41. 14. Leviathan's t. are terrible round about
Psal. 3. 7. thou hast broken the t. of the ungodly
57. 4. whose t. are spears and arrows, and tongue

Psal. 58. 6. break their t. O God, in their mouth
124. 6. hath not given us as a prey to their t.
Prov. 10. 26. as vinegar to the t. so the sluggard
30. 14. whose t. are swords, jaw-t. as knives
Cant. 4. 2. thy t. are like a flock of sheep, 6. 6.
Isa. 41. 15. make thee an instrument having t.
Jer. 31. 29. children's t. are set on edge, Ezek. 18. 2.
30. eateth sour grapes, his t. shall be set on edge
Lam. 3. 16. hath broken my t. with gravel-stones
Dan. 7. 5. it had three ribs between the t. of it
7. a fourth beast had great iron t. 19.
Joel 1. 6. he hath the cheek t. of a great lion
Amos 4. 6. I have given you cleanness of t.
Mic. 3. 5. that bite with their t. and cry peace
Zech. 9. 7. his abominations from between his t.
Mat. 27. 44. was crucified, cast the same in his t.
Rev. 9. 8. their t. were as the t. of lions

See Gnash.

TELL

Signifies, [1] To count, number, or reckon, Gen. 15. 5. [2] To declare or make known, Gen. 12. 18. | 21. 26. [3] To teach, Exod. 10. 2. Deut. 17. 11. [4] To confess, Josh. 7. 19. [5] To publish, 2 Sam. 1. 20. [6] To explain and unfold, Ezek. 24. 19. Dan. 2. 36.
Gen. 15. 5. t. the stars if thou be able to number
32. 5. and I have sent to t. my Lord to find grace
43. 6. as to t. the man whether ye had a brother
22. we cannot t. who put our money in our sacks
45. 13. t. my father of all my glory in Egypt
Exod. 10. 2. mayest t. in the ears of thy son
Lev. 14. 35. t. the priest, saying, it seemeth to me
Num. 14. 14. they will t. it to the inhabitants
1 Sam. 6. 2. t. us wherewith we shall send it to his
9. 8. give to the man of God, to t. us our way
17. 55. as the soul liveth, O king, I cannot t.
22. 22. I knew that he would surely t. Saul
23. 11. O God of Israel, I beseech thee t. thy serv.
27. 11. lest they should t. on us, saying, so did Dav.
2 Sam. 1. 20. t. it not in Gath, publish it not in
7. 5. go t. my servant David, 1 Chron. 17. 4.
12. 18. feared to t. him that the child was dead
22. while the child was alive, I said, who can t.
15. 35. thou shalt t. to Zadok and Abiathar
18. 21. go t. the king what thou hast seen
1 Kings 1. 20. that thou shouldest t. who shall reign
18. 8. go, t. thy lord, Elijah is here, 11. 14.
12. when I come and t. Ahab, he will slay me
20. 9. t. my lord the king, all thou didst send
11. t. him, let not him that girdeth on his harness
2 Kings 7. 9. that we may t. the king's household
9. 12. and they said, it is false; t. us now
15. let none escape to go to t. it in Jezreel
22. 15. t. the man that sent you, 2 Chron. 34. 23.
Psal. 22. 17. I may t. all my bones, they stare on me
26. 7. publish and t. of all thy wondrous works
48. 12. go round about her, t. the towers thereof
13. that ye may t. the generation following
Prov. 30. 4. what his son's name, if thou canst t.
Eccl. 6. 12. who can t. what shall be after, 10. 14.
8. 7. for who can t. him when it shall be?
10. 20. that which hath wings shall t. the matter
Cant. 5. 8. t. him that I am sick of love
Isa. 6. 9. go and t. this people || 48. 20. t. this
Jer. 15. 2. t. such as are for death, to death
23. 27. by their dreams which they t. 28. 32.
36. 16. we will t. the king of all these words
17. t. us now how thou didst write these words
48. 20. t. in Arnon, that Moab is spoiled
Ezek. 24. 19. wilt thou not t. us what things are?
Dan. 2. 4. O king, t. thy servants the dream, 7, 9.
36. we will t. the king the interpretation thereof
Joel 1. 3. t. ye your children, let your children t.
Jonah 3. 9. who can t. if God will turn and repent
Mat. 8. 4. see thou t. no man, Mark 8. 26, 30. | 9. 9. Luke 5. 14. | 8. 56. Acts 23. 22.
16. 20. he charged his disciples that they should t. no man, Mark 7. 36. Luke 9. 21.
17. 9. t. the vision to no man, until the Son of man
18. 15. t. him his fault || 17. t. it unto the church
21. 5. t. ye the daughter of Sion, behold thy king
24. 3. t. us when shall these things be, Mark 13. 4.
26. 63. that thou t. us, whether thou be the Christ the Son of God, Luke 22. 67. John 10. 24.
28. 7. go and t. his disciples that he is risen
9. as they went to t. his disciples, Mark 16. 7.
Mark 1. 30. and anon they t. him of her
5. 19. t. them how great things the Lord hath done
11. 33. we cannot t. Mat. 21. 27. Luke 20. 7.
Luke 7. 22. t. John what things ye have seen
13. 32. go ye, t. that fox, I cast out devils
John 3. 8. but canst not t. whence it cometh
4. 25. when he is come, he will t. us all things
8. 14. ye cannot t. whence I come, and whither I go
16. 18. a little while? we cannot t. what he saith
18. 34. or did others t. it thee of me?
Acts 15. 27. who shall t. you the same things
17. 21. but either to t. or hear some new thing
23. 17. he hath a certain thing to t. him
2 Cor. 12. 2. whether out of the body I cannot t. 3.
Heb. 11. 32. for the time would fail to t. of Gideon

TELL me.

Gen. 12. 18. why didst not t. me she was thy wife?
21. 26. nor didst thou t. me, nor heard I of it
24. 23. t. me whose daughter art thou?
49. t. me, and if not, t. me that I may turn
29. 15. t. me what shall thy wages be?
31. 27. steal away from me, and didst not t. me
32. 29. t. me thy name || 37. 16. t. me where they feed
Josh. 7. 19. t. me now what thou hast done, hide it not
Judg. 16. 6. t. me wherein thy great strength lieth
Ruth 4. 4. if thou wilt not redeem it, t. me
1 Sam. 9. 18. t. me where the seer's house is
10. 15. t. me I pray thee what Samuel said to you
14. 43. Saul said, t. me what thou hast done
20. 10. David said to Jonathan, who shall t. me?
2 Sam. 1. 4. how went the matter, t. me, I pray thee
13. 4. why art thou lean, wilt thou not t. me?
1 Kings 22. 16. that thou t. me nothing but the truth
2 Kings 4. 2. what shall I do for thee, t. me
8. 4. t. me the great things that Elisha hath done
Job 34. 34. let men of understanding t. me

Cant. 1. 7. t. me, O thou whom my soul loveth
Mat. 21. 24. ask you one thing, which if you t. me
Luke 7. 42. t. me which of them will love most
John 20. 15. t. me where thou hast laid him
Acts 5. 8. t. me, whether ye sold the land for so much
22. 27. t. me art thou a Roman? he said, yea
23. 19. asked him what is that thou hast to t. me?
Gal. 4. 21. t. me, ye that desire to be under the law

TELL thee.

Gen. 22. 2. on one of the mountains I will t. thee of
26. 2. dwell in the land which I will t. thee of
Exod. 14. 12. this is the word we did t. thee in Egypt
Num. 23. 3. whatsoever he sheweth me, I will t. thee
Deut. 17. 11. the judgment which they shall t. thee
32. 7. ask thy elders, and they will t. thee
Judg. 14. 16. I have not told it and shall I t. it thee?
Ruth 3. 4. he will t. thee what thou shalt do
1 Sam. 9. 19. I will t. thee all that is in thine heart
15. 16. I will t. thee what the Lord hath said to me
19. 3. and what I see, that I will t. thee
20. 9. if I knew, then would not I t. it thee?
1 Kings 14. 3. t. thee what shall become of the child
22. 18. did I not t. thee that he would prophesy no good thing of me, but evil, 2 Chr. 18. 17.
1 Chr. 17. 10. I t. thee that Lord will build thee
Job 1. 15. I am escaped alone to t. thee, 16, 17, 19.
8. 10. shall not thy fathers teach thee and t. thee
12. 7. ask fowls of the air, and they shall t. thee
Psal. 50. 12. if I were hungry I would not t. thee
Isa. 19. 12. let thy wise men t. thee now and know
Jer. 19. 2. proclaim the words that I shall t. thee
Luke 12. 59. I t. thee, thou shalt not depart thence
22. 34. I t. thee, the cock shall not crow twice till
Acts 10. 6. t. thee what thou oughtest to do, 11. 14.
Rev. 17. 7. I will t. thee the mystery of the woman

I TELL you, or TELL I you.

Gen. 49. 1. that I may t. you what shall befall you
Isa. 5. 5. I will t. you what I will do to my viney.
42. 9. before they spring forth, I t. you of them
Mat. 10. 27. what I t. you in darkness, that speak
21. 27. neither t. I you by what authority I do these things, Mark 11. 33. Luke 20. 8.
Mark 11. 29. I will t. you by what authority I do
Luke 4. 25. but I t. you of a truth, 9. 27.
10. 24. I t. you that many prophets and kings
12. 51. I t. you nay, but rather division
13. 3. I t. you nay, but except ye repent, 5.
27. I t. you I know you not whence you are
17. 34. I t. you there shall be two in one bed
18. 8. I t. you that he will avenge them speedily
14. I t. you this man went to his house justified
19. 40. I t. you that if these should hold their peace
22. 67. he said, if I t. you ye will not believe
John 3. 12. how shall ye believe if I t. y. of heavenly
8. 45. because I t. you the truth, Gal. 4. 16.
13. 19. now I t. you before it come, that when it is
16. 7. I t. you the truth, it is expedient for you
Gal. 5. 21. of which I t. you before, as I have told
Phil. 3. 18. of whom I now t. you even weeping

TELLEST.

Psal. 56. 8. thou t. my wanderings, put my tears
Isa. 40. † 9. O thou that t. good tidings

TELLETH.

2 Sam. 7. 11. the Lord t. thee that he will build
2 Kings 6. 12. Elisha t. the king of Israel the words
Psal. 41. 6. when he goeth abroad he t. it
101. 7. he that t. lies shall not tarry in my sight
147. 4. he t. the number of the stars, calleth them
Jer. 33. 13. under the hands of him that t. them
John 12. 22. Philip cometh and t. Andrew

TELLING, Substantively.

Judg. 7. 15. when Gideon heard the t. of the dream

TELLING.

2 Sam. 11. 19. hast made an end of t. the matters
2 Kings 8. 5. as he was t. the king how he restored

TEMPERANCE.

Acts 24. 25. as he reasoned of t. and judgment
Gal. 5. 23. meekness, t. against such there is no law
2 Pet. 1. 6. add to knowledge t. and to t. patience

TEMPERATE.

1 Cor. 9. 25. that striveth for the mastery, is t.
Tit. 1. 8. a bishop must be t. || 2. 2. aged men t.

TEMPER.

Ezek. 46. 14. an hin of oil to t. with fine flour

TEMPERED.

Exod. 29. 2. take cakes and unleavened t. with oil
30. 35. a perfume t. together, pure and holy
1 Cor. 12. 24. but God hath t. the body together

TEMPEST

Signifies, [1] A most violent commotion of the air, either with or without rain, hail, or snow, Acts 27. 18, 20. [2] Grievous and unexpected afflictions, Job 9. 17. [3] God's terrible judgments on the wicked, Psal. 11. 6. | 83. 15.
Job 9. 17. for he breaketh me with a t.
27. 20. a t. stealeth him away in the night
Psal. 11. 6. on the wicked shall he rain a t.
55. 8. I would hasten from the windy storm and t.
83. 15. so persecute them with thy t. and make
Isa. 28. 2. hath a strong one, which as a t. of hail
29. 6. thou shalt be visited with storm and t.
30. 30. the Assyrian shall be beaten with a t.
32. 2. and a man shall be a covert from the t.
54. 11. O thou afflicted, tossed with t. behold
Amos 1. 14. with a t. in the day of the whirlwind
Jonah 1. 4. there was a mighty t. in the sea
12. for my sake this great t. is come upon you
Mat. 8. 24. there arose a great t. in the sea
Acts 27. 18. being exceedingly tossed with a t.
20. no small t. lay on us, hope was taken away
Heb. 12. 18. ye are not come to darkness and t.
2 Pet. 2. 17. clouds that are carried with a t.

TEMPESTUOUS.

Psal. 50. 3. it shall be very t. round about him
Jonah 1. 11. the sea wrought and was t. 13.
Hab. 3. † 14. they were t. to scatter me
Acts 27. 14. there arose against it a t. wind

TEMPLE

Signifies, A house or dwelling of God, a building erected and set apart for the worship of the true God. It is spoken, First, Of that magnificent building erected by Solomon at Jerusalem, *the foundations whereof were laid in the year of the world* 2992, *before Christ* 1008, *before the vulgar æra* 1012; *and it was finished in the year of the world* 3000, *and dedicated in* 3001; *before Christ*, 999, *before the vulgar æra*, 1003. *The glory of this* temple *was not in the bigness of it; for that alone was but a small pile of building, as containing no more than an hundred and fifty feet in length, and an hundred and five in breadth, taking the sanctuary, the sanctum, and the porch or entrance, from out to out. The main grandeur and excellency of it consisted,* [1] *In its* ornaments; *its workmanship being every where exceeding curious, and its overlayings rich and costly.* [2] *In its* materials; *being built of new large stones, hewn out in the most curious and artful manner.* [3] *In its* out-buildings; *which were large, beautiful, and sumptuous. But what still was the main glory of this* temple, *were those extraordinary marks of the divine favour with which it was honoured, namely,* [1] *The* ark of the covenant, *in which were put the tables of the law, and the mercy-seat which was upon it, from whence the divine oracles were given out by an audible voice, as often as God was consulted in behalf of his people.* [2] *The Shechinah, or the divine presence, manifested by a visible cloud resting over the mercy-seat.* [3] *The* Urim *and* Thummim, *by which the high priest consulted God in difficult and momentous cases relating to the public interest of the nation, and,* [4] *The holy fire which came down from heaven upon the altar at the consecrating of the* temple, 1 Kings 18. 38. 2 Chron. 7. 1. It is spoken, Secondly, *Of the tabernacle, which was of the same use and significancy as the* temple *was*, 1 Sam. 1. 9. | 3. 3. Thirdly, *Of Christ's body or human nature, in which the fulness of the Godhead dwells bodily, as the glory of God did visibly in the* temple, John 2. 19, 21. Col. 2. 9. Fourthly, *Of heaven, which is God's throne*, Psal. 11. 4. Rev. 7. 15. Fifthly, *Of the church of God*, [1] *Distributively, considered in the particular members thereof, who are set apart from profane uses, and dedicated to the service of God; and to whom he manifests his gracious presence by his Spirit*, 1 Cor. 3. 16. [2] *Collectively, in respect of the whole*, Eph. 2. 21.

1 Sam. 1. 9. Eli sat on a seat by a post of the *t.*
2 Sam. 22. 7. he did hear my voice out of his *t.* and my cry did enter into his ears, *Psal.* 18. 6.
1 Kings 6. 17. the *t.* before it was 40 cubits long
2 Chron. 35. 20. when Josiah had prepared the *t.*
36. 7. and put the vessels in his *t.* at Babylon
Ezra 4. 1. that they builded the *t.* unto the Lord
5. 14. vessels took out of the *t.* brought to *t.* 6. 5.
Neh. 6. 10. hid ourselves in the *t.* shut doors of the *t.*
Psal. 27. 4. beauty of L. and to inquire in his *t.*
29. 9. in his *t.* doth every one speak of his glory
48. 9. we have thought of thy loving kindness, O God, in the midst of thy *t.*
68. 29. because of thy *t.* at Jerusalem shall kings
Isa. 6. 1. and lifted up, and his train filled the *t.*
44. 28. and to the *t.* thy foundation shall be laid
66. 6. a voice from the *t.* a voice of the Lord
Jer. 50. 28. declare the vengeance of his *t.* 51. 11.
Ezek. 41. 1. afterward he brought me to the *t.*
Dan. 5. 2. the golden vessels taken out of the *t.* 3.
Amos 8. 3. songs of the *t.* shall be howlings that day
Zech. 8. 9. let your hands be strong, that the *t.* might be built
Mal. 3. 1. the Lord shall come suddenly to his *t.*
Mat. 4. 5. set him on a pinnacle of the *t.* *Luke* 4. 9.
12. 6. that in this place is one greater than the *t.*
23. 16. blind guides, who say, whosoever shall swear by the *t.* or by the gold of the *t.* 17. 21.
35. whom ye slew between the *t.* and the altar
24. 1. to shew him the buildings of the *t.* *Luke* 21. 5.
26. 61. I am able to destroy the *t.* of God
27. 40. thou that destroyest the *t.* *Mark* 15. 29.
51. behold the vail of the *t.* was rent in twain, *Mark* 15. 38. *Luke* 23. 45.
Mark 11. 16. should carry any vessel thro' the *t.*
14. 58. I will destroy this *t.* made with hands
Luke 2. 37. Anna a widow departed not from the *t.*
John 2. 15. he drove them all out of the *t.* and sheep
19. destroy this *t.* || 21. he spake of *t.* of his body
20. forty and six years was this *t.* in building
Acts 3. 2. whom they laid daily at the gate of the *t.* to ask alms of them that entered the *t.* 10.
19. 27. the *t.* of goddess Diana should be despised
21. 30. they took Paul and drew him out of the *t.*
24. 6. who also hath gone about to profane the *t.*
25. 8. neither against the *t.* nor against Cesar
1 Cor. 3. 16. know ye not that ye are the *t.* of God
17. if any man defile the *t.* of God, him shall G. destroy, for the *t.* of G. is holy, which *t.* ye are
6. 19. your body is the *t.* of the Holy Ghost
8. 10. see these sit at meat in an idol's *t.*
9. 13. they who minister live of the things of the *t.*
2 Cor. 6. 16. what agreement hath the *t.* of God with idols? for ye are the *t.* of the living God
Rev. 7. 15. and serve him day and night in his *t.*
11. 1. saying, rise and measure the *t.* of God
19. the *t.* of God was opened in heaven, and the ark of the testament was seen in his *t.*
14. 15. another angel came out of the *t.* 17.
15. 5. the *t.* of the tabernacle was opened
6. and the seven angels came out of the *t.*
8. *t.* was filled with smoke from the glory of God
16. 1. and I heard a great voice out of the *t.* 17.
21. 22. and I saw no *t.* therein, for the Lord God Almighty and the Lamb are the *t.* of it
See HOLY, LORD.

In or *into the* TEMPLE.

2 Kings 11. 10. king David's spears that were *in t.*
1 Chron. 6. 10. executed the priest's office *in the t.*
10. 10. and fastened his head *in the t.* of Dagon
2 Chron. 4. 7. he set ten candlesticks *in the t.* 8.
Ezra 5. 15. go carry these vessels *into the t.*
Neh. 6. 11. would go *into the t.* to save his life
Mat. 12. 5. the priests *in the t.* profane the sabbath
21. 12. went *into the t.* cast out all them that sold and bought *in the t.* *Mark* 11. 15. *Luke* 19. 45.
Mat. 21. 14. the blind and lame came to him *in the t.*
15. children crying *in the t.* and saying, Hosanna
26. 55. I sat daily teaching *in the t.* *Luke* 21. 37.
27. 5. he cast down the pieces of silver *in the t.*
Mark 14. 49. I was daily teach. *in the t.* *Luke* 22. 53.
Luke 1. 21. marvelled that he tar. so long *in the t.*
22. they perceived that he had seen a vision *in t.*
2. 27. and he came by the spirit *into the t.*
46. they found him *in the t.* sitting in the midst
18. 10. two men went up *into the t.* to pray
24. 53. and were continually *in the t.* praising God
Acts 2. 46. continuing with one accord *in the t.*
3. 1. Peter and John went up together *into the t.*
3. about to go *into t.* || 5. 20. stand and speak *in t.*
5. 25. the men are standing *in the t.* and teaching
21. 26. Paul entered *into t.* || 27. saw him *in the t.*
28. and further, brought Greeks also *into the t.* 29.
22. 17. even while I prayed *in t.* I was in a trance
24. 12. they neither found me *in the t.* disputing
18. certain Jews found me purified *in the t.*
26. 21. for these causes the Jews caught me *in t.*
2 Thess. 2. 4. so that he as God sitteth *in the t.* of God
Rev. 3. 12. him will I make a pillar *in the t.* of my G.
15. 8. and no man was able to enter *into the t.*

TEMPLES.

Judg. 4. 21. Jael smote the nail into his *t.* 22.
5. 26. when she had stricken through his *t.*
Cant. 4. 3. thy *t.* like a piece of pomegranate, 6. 7.

TEMPLES.

Hos. 8. 14. for Isr. forgot his Maker, and buildeth *t.*
Joel 3. 5. ye carried into your *t.* my goodly things
Acts 7. 48. howbeit the Most High dwelleth not in *t.* made with hands, 17. 24.

TEMPORAL.

2 Cor. 4. 18. for the things which are seen are *t.*

TEMPT

Is spoken, [I] *Of God*, Gen. 22. 1. *who does not* tempt *or try men in order to know their tempers and dispositions, as if he were ignorant of them; but to exercise their graces, to prove their faith, love, and obedience; to confirm and strengthen them by such trials, and to give succeeding ages patterns of obedience, to shew them his satisfaction with such as obey, and his displeasure at such as do not.* [II] *Of men, who are said to* tempt the Lord, [1] *When they unseasonably require of him sensible proofs of his divine presence, of his power, or of his goodness. Thus the Israelites in the desert often* tempted the Lord, Exod. 17. 2, 7. *as if they had had reason to have doubted of his presence among them, of his goodness or power, after all he had done in their favour.* [2] *When men expose themselves to such dangers, from which they cannot escape but by the miraculous interposition of his providence; for God requires of men the performance only of such actions as are within the ordinary measures of their strength, being under no obligation to work miracles in their favour*, Mat. 4. 7. [3] *When men set themselves to commit sin so impudently, as if they did it on purpose to try whether God was just or powerful enough to punish them for it*, Mal. 3. 15. [III] *Of Satan, who* tempts *us to bring us to evil, to sin, to distrust, to a contempt of God and his laws, to pride, vanity, &c. He lays snares for us, even in our best actions, to make us lose the benefit of them, by imputing the merit of them to ourselves only, and not to God. He* tempted *David, and prevailed with him to number the people out of confidence and vain curiosity*, 1 Chron. 21. 1. *He* tempted *our Saviour in the wilderness, and in vain endeavoured to infuse into him sentiments of pride and ambition*, Luke 4. 2, 3, 4. *He* tempted *Ananias and Sapphira, to make them* lie to the Holy Ghost, *Acts* 5. 3.

Gen. 22. 1. God did *t.* Abraham and said unto him
Exod. 17. 2. Moses said, wherefore do ye *t.* the L.?
Deut. 6. 16. ye shall not *t.* the Lord your God
Isa. 7. 12. I will not ask, nor will I *t.* the Lord
Mal. 3. 15. yea, they that *t.* God are delivered
Mat. 4. 7. Jesus said, it is written again, thou shalt not *t.* the Lord thy God, *Luke* 4. 12.
22. 18. why *t.* ye me? *Mark* 12. 15. *Luke* 20. 23.
Acts 5. 9. ye have agreed together to *t.* the Spirit
15. 10. now therefore why *t.* ye God to put a yoke
1 Cor. 7. 5. that Satan *t.* you not for your incontin.
10. 9. neither let us *t.* Chr. as some of them tempted

TEMPTATION

Signifies, [1] *Those means and enticements which the devil makes use of to ensnare and allure mankind*, Mat. 6. 13. | 26. 41. [2] *Those afflictions and troubles, whereby God tries his people*, Jam. 1. 2, 12. [3] *Persecution for religion*, Luke 8. 13.

Exod. 17. † 7. called the name of the place *t.*
Psal. 95. 8. hear his voice, harden not your hearts, as in the day of *t.* in the wilderness, *Heb.* 3. 8.
Mat. 6. 13. and lead us not into *t.* *Luke* 11. 4.
26. 41. watch and pray, that ye enter not into *t.* *Mark* 14. 38. *Luke* 22. 40, 46.
Luke 4. 13. when the devil had ended all his *t.*
8. 13. have no root, and in a time of *t.* fall away
1 Cor. 10. 13. no *t.* hath taken you; will with *t.*
Gal. 4. 14. and my *t.* in my flesh ye despised not
1 Tim. 6. 9. they that will be rich fall into *t.*
Jam. 1. 12. blessed is the man that endureth *t.*
Rev. 3. 10. I will keep thee also from the hour of *t.*

TEMPTATIONS.

Deut. 4. 34. take a nation out of a nation by *t.*
7. 19. the great *t.* thine eyes saw, and signs, 29. 3.
Luke 22. 28. ye have continued with me in my *t.*
Acts 20. 19. serving God with many tears and *t.*
Jam. 1. 2. count it joy when ye fall into divers *t.*
1 Pet. 1. 6. ye are in heaviness thro' manifold *t.*
2 Pet. 2. 9. L. knows how to deliver the godly out of *t.*

TEMPTED.

Exod. 17. 7. and because they *t.* the Lord, saying
Num. 14. 22. and have *t.* me now these ten times
Deut. 6. 16. not tempt God as ye *t.* him in Massah
Psal. 78. 18. and they *t.* God in their heart, 41.
56. yet they *t.* and provoked the most high God
Ps. 95. 9. when fathers *t.* me, proved me, *Heb.* 3. 9.
106. 14. but lusted, and *t.* God in the desert
Mat. 4. 1. to be *t.* of the devil, *Mark* 1. 13. *Luke* 4. 2.
Luke 10. 25. a lawyer *t.* him, saying, Master
1 Cor. 10. 9. as some of them *t.* and were destroyed
13. who will not suffer you to be *t.* above that
Gal. 6. 1. considering thyself, lest thou also be *t.*
1 Thess. 3. 5. lest by some means the tempter *t.* you
Heb. 2. 18. he himself hath suffered, being *t.*
4. 15. but was in all points *t.* like as we are, yet
11. 37. they were sawn asunder, were *t.* were slain
Jam. 1. 13. let no man say when he is *t.* I am *t.* of God, for God cannot be *t.* with evil, nor tempteth
14. but every man is *t.* when he is drawn of lust

TEMPTER.

Mat. 4. 3. when the *t.* came to him, he said
1 Thess. 3. 5. lest by some means the *t.* have tempt.

TEMPTETH.

Jam. 1. 13. cannot be tempted, neither *t.* any man

TEMPTING.

Mat. 16. 1. the Pharisees *t.* Christ, and seeking a sign, *Mark* 8. 11. *Luke* 11. 16.
19. 3. the Pharisees also came to him, *t.* him
22. 35. the lawyer asked him a question, *t.* him
Mark 10. 2. a man to put away his wife, *t.* him
John 8. 6. this they said, *t.* him, that they might

TEN.

Gen. 16. 3. Abraham dwelt *t.* years in Canaan
18. 32. peradventure *t.* shall be found there, and he said, I will not destroy it for *t.* sake
24. 10. the servant took *t.* camels of his masters
22. took bracelets for her hands of *t.* shekels
32. 15. Jacob took *t.* bulls and *t.* foals for Esau
42. 3. Joseph's *t.* brethren went to buy corn
45. 23. Joseph sent *t.* asses and *t.* she-asses
Exod. 26. 1. make a tabernacle with *t.* curtains
27. 12. their pillars *t.* and their sockets *t.*
34. 28. wrote *t.* commandments, *Deut.* 4. 13. | 10. 4.
Lev. 26. 26. *t.* women shall bake your bread
27. 5. and for the female *t.* shekels, 7.
Num. 7. 14. one spoon of *t.* shekels, 20. 26.
11. 32. he that gathered least gathered *t.* homers
29. 23. and on the fourth day *t.* bullocks
Josh. 17. 5. there fell *t.* portions to Manasseh
21. 5. Kohath had by lot out of Ephraim, Manasseh, and Dan, *t.* cities, 1 *Chron.* 6. 61.
22. 14. Israel sent with Phinehas *t.* princes
Judg. 6. 27. Gideon took *t.* men of his servants
12. 11. Elon a Zebulonite judged Israel *t.* years
17. 10. I will give thee *t.* shekels of silver
20. 10. we will take *t.* men of an hundred
Ruth 1. 4. they dwelt in Moab about *t.* years
4. 2. Boaz took *t.* men of the elders of the city
1 Sam. 1. 8. am not I better to thee than *t.* sons?
17. 17. take these *t.* loaves, and run to the camp
18. carry these *t.* cheeses to the captain
25. 5. David sent out *t.* young men to Nabal
2 Sam. 15. 16. David left *t.* concubines to keep house
18. 11. and I would have given thee *t.* shekels
15. *t.* young men smote Absalom, and slew him
19. 43. they said, we have *t.* parts in the king
20. 3. the king took his *t.* concubines, and put them
1 Kings 4. 23. *t.* fat oxen in one day for Solomon
7. 24. *t.* knots in a cubit compassing the sea round
27. and he made *t.* bases of brass, 37.
38. he made *t.* lavers of brass, 43. 2 *Chron.* 4. 6.
11. 31. take thee *t.* pieces; I will give *t.* tribes, 35.
14. 3. take with thee *t.* loaves to Ahijah
2 Kings 5. 5. Naaman took *t.* talents, *t.* changes
13. 7. leave but fifty horsemen and *t.* chariots
15. 17. Menahem reigned *t.* years in Samaria
25. 25. Ishmael came, and *t.* men with him, and smote Gedaliah, *Jer.* 41. 1, 2.
2 Chron. 4. 7. he made *t.* candlesticks || 8. *t.* tables
Ezra 8. 24. and *t.* of their brethren with them
Neh. 11. 1. bring one of *t.* to dwell at Jerusalem
Esth. 9. 10. the *t.* sons of Haman slew they, 12.
13. and let Haman's *t.* sons be hanged, 14.
Psal. 33. 2. instrument of *t.* strings, 92. 3. | 144. 9.
Eccl. 7. 19. more than *t.* mighty men in the city
Isa. 5. 10. *t.* acres of vineyard shall yield one bath
Ezek. 45. 14. an homer of *t.* baths, *t.* baths an homer
Dan. 7. 7. the fourth beast had *t.* horns, 20, 24.
Amos 5. 3. shall leave *t.* to the house of Israel
6. 9. if *t.* men remain in one house, they shall die
Hag. 2. 16. since those days when one came to an heap of twenty measures, there were but *t.*
Zech. 5. 2. the breadth of the roll is *t.* cubits
8. 23. *t.* men shall take hold of him that is a Jew
Mat. 20. 24. and when the *t.* heard it, *Mark* 10. 41.
25. 1. the kingdom shall be likened to *t.* virgins
28. and give it to him that hath *t.* talents
Luke 15. 8. what woman having *t.* pieces of silver
17. 12. there met him *t.* men that were lepers
17. Jesus said, were there not *t.* cleansed?
19. 13. and delivered them *t.* pounds, and said
16. Lord, thy pound hath gained *t.* pounds
17. well, have thou authority over *t.* cities
24. and give it to him that hath *t.* pounds
25. they said, Lord, he hath *t.* pounds
Rev. 12. 3. a dragon having *t.* horns, 13. 1. | 17. 3.
17. 7. woman and beast of seven heads and *t.* horns
12. and the *t.* horns thou sawest are the *t.* kings
16. the *t.* horns thou sawest shall hate the whore
See CUBITS, DAYS, DEGREES, THOUSAND, THOUSANDS.

TEN *times.*

Gen. 31. 7. and hath changed my wages *t. times*, 41.
Num. 14. 22. and have tempted me now these *t. tim.*
Neh. 4. 12. when Jews came, they said unto us, *t. t.*
Job 19. 3. these *t. times* have ye reproached me
Dan. 1. 20. he found them *t. times* better than all

TENS.

Exod. 18. 21. place such over them to be rul. of *t.* 25.
Deut. 1. 15. I made them heads, captains over *t.*

TENTH.

Gen. 28. 22. I will surely give the *t.* to thee
Lev. 27. 32. the *t.* shall be holy to the Lord
Num. 18. 21. I have given children of Levi the *t.*
Deut. 23. 2. a bastard not enter to *t.* generation, 3.
1 Sam. 8. 15. king will take the *t.* of your seed
17. he will take the *t.* of your sheep and vineyards

1 Chr. 12. 13. t. captain of sons of Gad, Jeremiah
24. 11. the t. lot came forth to Shecaniah
25. 17. the t. lot came forth to Shimei
27. 13. the t. captain for the t. month, Meharai
Isa. 6. 13. but yet in it shall be a t. and return
Jer. 32. 1. in the t. year of Zedekiah king of Judah
John 1. 39. for it was about the t. hour
Rev. 21. 20. the t. foundation a chrysoprasus
See DAY, DEAL, MONTH, PART.

TEND.

Prov. 21. 5. thoughts of diligent t. to plenteousness

TENDETH.

Prov. 10. 16. the labour of the righteous t. to life
11. 19. as righteousn. t. to life, so he that pursues
24. there is that withholdeth, but it t. to poverty
14. 23. the talk of the lips t. only to penury
19. 23. the fear of the Lord t. to life

TENDER

Signifies, [1] *Weak and feeble*, Gen. 33. 13. [2] *Nice and delicate*, Deut. 28. 56. [3] *Young and carefully educated*, Prov. 4. 3. [4] *Pitiful, or of a compassionate and forgiving temper*, Eph. 4. 32.

Gen. 1. † 11. let the earth bring forth t. grass
18. 7. Abraham ran and fetched a calf t. and good
33. 13. my Lord knoweth that the children are t.
41. † 43. they cried before him, t. father
Deut. 28. 54. so the man that is t. among you
56. the t. and delicate woman among you
32. 2. shall distil as the small rain on the t. herb
2 Sam. 3. † 39. I am this day t. tho' anointed king
23. 4. as the t. grass springing out of the earth
2 Kings 22. 19. because thy heart was t. 2 Chr. 34. 27.
1 Chron. 22. 5. Solomon is young and t. 29. 1.
Job 14. 7. that the t. branch will not cease
38. 27. to cause the bud of the t. herb to spring
Psal. 23. † 2. to lie down in pastures of t. grass
Prov. 4. 3. t. and beloved in sight of my mother
27. 25. hay appears, and the t. grass sheweth itself
Cant. 2. 13. the vines with t. grape give a good smell
15. foxes spoil vines, for our vines have t. grapes
7. 12. let us see whether the t. grape appear
Isa. 7. † 4. fear not, neither let thy heart be t.
47. 1. thou shalt no more be called t. and delicate
53. 2. he shall grow up before him as a t. plant
Ezek. 17. 22. I will crop off a t. one and plant it
Dan. 1. 9. now God brought Daniel into t. love
4. 15. leave the stump in earth, in the t. grass, 23.
Mat. 24. 32. when his branch is t. Mark 13. 28.
Luke 1. 78. through the t. mercy of our God
Jam. 5. 11. the Lord is pitiful, and of t. mercy

TENDER-*hearted*.

2 Chr. 13. 7. when Rehoboam was young and t.-h.
Eph. 4. 32. be kind and t.-hearted one to another
See MERCIES.

TENDERNESS.

Deut. 28. 56. to set her foot on the ground for t.

TENONS.

Exod. 26. 17. two t. in one board, 19. | 36. 22, 24.

TENOR.

Gen. 43. 7. according to the t. of these words
Exod. 34. 27. after t. of these words I made a coven.

TENT

Signifies, [1] *An apartment, or lodging-place made of canvass or other cloth on poles*, Gen. 4. 20. Num. 1. 52. [2] *The covering of the tabernacle*, Exod. 26. 11. [3] *The church*, Cant. 1. 8.

Gen. 9. 21. and Noah was uncovered in his t.
12. 8. Abram removed and pitched his t. 13. 3.
13. 12. Lot pitched his t. towards Sodom
18. Abram removed his t. and dwelt in the plain
18. 1. he sat in t. door || 6. he hastened into the t.
9. where is Sarah thy wife? he said, in the t.
24. 67. he brought her into his mother Sarah's t.
26. 17. and Isaac pitched his t. in the valley
25. built an altar, and pitched his t. at Beer-sheba
31. 25. Jacob had pitched his t. in the mount
33. Laban went into Jacob's t. Leah's t. Rachel's t.
33. 18. Jacob pitched his t. before Shalem, 19.
35. 21. Israel spread his t. beyond the tower
Exod. 18. 7. Moses and Jethro came into the t.
26. 11. couple the t. together that it may be one
33. 8. stood every man at his t. door, and looked
10. they worshipped every man in his t. door
35. 11. make the tabernacle his t. and covering
36. 18. he made taches to couple the t. together
19. he made a covering for the t. of rams' skins
39. 33. and they brought the t. to Moses
40. 19. he spread abroad the t. over the tabernacle, and put the covering of the t. above upon it
Lev. 14. 8. leper shall tarry out of his t. seven days
Num. 3. 25. the charge of Gershon shall be the t.
9. 15. the cloud covered the t. of the testimony
11. 10. heard the people weep every man in his t.
19. 14. the law when a man dieth in a t. all that come into the t. and is in the t. shall be unclean
18. and a clean person shall sprinkle the t.
25. 8. he went after the man of Israel into the t.
Josh. 7. 21. hid in the earth in the midst of my t.
22. they ran into the t. and it was hid in his t.
23. they took them out of the midst of the t.
24. all Israel burnt his t. and all that he had
Judg. 4. 17. Sisera fled on his feet to the t. of Jael
20. he said to her, stand in the door of the t.
21. Jael took a nail of the t. and an hammer
5. 24. blessed shall she be above women in the t.
7. 8. he sent the rest of Israel every man to his t.
7. 13. a cake of barley-bread came unto a t.
19. † 9. that to-morrow thou mayest go to thy t.
20. 8. saying, we will not any of us go to his t.
1 Sam. 4. 10. and they fled every man into his t. 2 Sam. 18. 17. | 19. 8.
13. 2. rest of the people he sent every man to his t.
17. 54. David put Goliath's armour into his t.
2 Sam. 7. 6. but I have walked in a t. 1 Chr. 17. 5.
16. 22. they spread Absalom a t. on the top of house
20. 22. and they retired every man to his t.
2 Kings 7. 8. these lepers went into one t. another t.
1 Chron. 15. 1. David pitched a t. for the ark of God
16. 1. they set it in the midst of the t. 2 Chron. 1. 4.
2 Chron. 25. 22. and they fled every man to his t.
Job 21. † 28. where is the t. of the tabernacle of

Psal. 78. 60. the t. which he placed among men
Isa. 13. 20. nor shall the Arabian pitch t. there
38. 12. mine age is removed as a shepherd's t.
40. 22. spreadeth them out as a t. to dwell in
54. 2. enlarge the place of thy t. let them stretch
Jer. 10. 20. there is none to stretch forth my t.
37. 10. they should rise up every man in his t.

TENT-*makers*.

Acts 18. 3. by their occupation they were t.-makers

TENTS.

Gen. 4. 20. Adah was the father of such as dwell in t.
9. 27. Japheth shall dwell in the t. of Shem
13. 5. Lot also had flocks, and herds, and t.
25. 27. Jacob was a plain man, dwelling in t.
31. 33. Laban went into the maid-servants' t.
Exod. 16. 16. gather ye for them that are in t.
Num. 1. 52. children of Israel shall pitch their t.
9. 17. where the cloud abode, they pitched t.
18. cloud abode, they rested in their t. 20, 22, 23.
13. 19. whether they dwell in t. or strong holds
16. 26. depart from the t. of these wicked men
27. came out, and stood in the door of their t.
24. 2. and Balaam saw Israel abiding in his t.
5. how goodly are thy t. O Jacob, and thy tabern.
Deut. 1. 27. and ye murmured in your t. and said
33. to search you out a place to pitch your t. in
5. 30. go say to them, get ye into your t. again
11. 6. the earth swallowed them up and their t.
16. 7. and thou shalt turn and go unto thy t.
33. 18. he said, rejoice Issachar, in thy t.
Josh. 22. 4. return ye, and get you into your t. 6.
8. return with much riches unto your t.
Judg. 6. 5. the Midianites came with their t.
8. 11. went by the way of them that dwelt in t.
1 Sam. 17. 53. they spoiled the Philistines' t.
2 Sam. 11. 11. ark, Israel and Judah abide in t.
20. 1. every man to his t. 1 Kin. 12. 16. 2 Chr. 10. 16.
1 Kings 8. 66. Israel went to their t. 2 Chron. 7. 10.
20. † 12. was drinking, he and the kings, in t.
2 Kings 7. 7. and the Syrians left their t. 10.
16. Israel spoiled the t. of the Syrians
8. 21. and the people fled into their t. 14. 12.
13. 5. the children of Israel dwelt in their t.
1 Chron. 4. 41. they came and smote the t. of Ham
5. 10. and they dwelt in the Hagarites' t.
2 Chron. 14. 15. they smote also the t. of cattle
31. 2. to praise in the gates of the t. of the Lord
Ezra 8. 15. at Ahava we abode in t. three days
Psal. 69. 25. and let none dwell in their t.
78. 55. made tribes of Israel to dwell in their t.
84. 10. than to dwell in the t. of wickedness
106. 25. murmured in their t. and hearkened not
120. 5. woe is me, that I dwell in the t. of Kedar
Cant. 1. 5. I am black, but comely, as the t. of Kedar
8. and feed thy kids beside the shepherds' t.
Jer. 4. 20. suddenly are my t. spoiled, and curtains
6. 3. they shall pitch their t. against her round about
30. 18. will bring again the captivity of Jacob's t.
35. 7. but all your days ye shall dwell in t.
10. but we have dwelt in t. and have obeyed
49. 29. their t. and flocks shall they take away
Hab. 3. 7. I saw the t. of Cushan in affliction
Zech. 12. 7. the Lord shall save the t. of Judah first
14. 15. so shall be the plague of all in these t.

TERMED.

Isa. 62. 4. thou shalt no more be t. forsaken, neither shall thy land any more be t. desolate

TERRESTRIAL.

1 Cor. 15. 40. there are bodies t. the glory of the t.

TERRIBLE.

Exod. 34. 10. for it is a t. thing that I will do
Deut. 1. 19. went thro' that t. wilderness, 8. 15.
7. 21. the Lord thy God is a mighty God and t. 10. 17. Neh. 1. 5. | 4. 14. | 9. 32.
10. 21. hath done for thee t. things, 2 Sam. 7. 23.
Judg. 13. 6. was like an angel of God, very t.
Job 37. 22. with God is t. majesty
39. 20. the glory of his nostrils is t.
41. 14. his teeth are t. round about
Psal. 45. 4. thy right hand shall teach thee t. things
47. 2. for the Lord Most High is t. he is king over
65. 5. by t. things in righteousness wilt answer us
66. 3. say unto God, how t. art thou in thy works!
5. t. in his doing towards the children of men
68. 35. thou art t. out of thy holy places
76. 12. he is t. to the kings of the earth
86. † 14. assemblies of t. men sought my soul
99. 3. let them praise thy great and t. name
106. 22. who had done t. things by the Red sea
145. 6. men shall speak of the might of thy t. acts
Cant. 6. 4. thou art t. as an army with banners
Isa. 13. 11. I will lay low the haughtiness of the t.
18. 2. go to a people t. || 7. from a people t.
21. 1. it cometh from the desert, from a t. land
25. 3. the city of the t. nations shall fear thee
4. when the blast of the t. ones is as a storm
5. the branch of the t. ones shall be brought low
29. 5. the multitude of the t. ones shall be as chaff
20. for the t. one is brought to nought
49. 25. and the prey of the t. shall be delivered
64. 3. when thou didst t. things, which we
Jer. 15. 21. redeem thee out of the hand of the t.
20. 11. the Lord is with me as a mighty t. of one
Lam. 5. 10. skin was black, because of t. famine
Ezek. 1. 22. was as the colour of the t. crystal
28. 7. behold therefore I will bring the t. of the nations upon thee, 30. 11. | 31. 12.
32. 12. I will cause to fall the t. of the nations
Dan. 2. 31. the form of the image was t.
7. 7. I saw a fourth beast dreadful and t. and strong
Joel 2. 11. the day of the Lord is great and very t.
31. before the great and t. day of the Lord come
Hab. 1. 7. the Chaldeans are t. and dreadful
Zeph. 2. 11. the Lord will be t. unto Moab
Heb. 12. 21. so t. was the sight that Moses said

TERRIBLENESS.

Deut. 26. 8. the Lord brought us out with great t.
1 Chr. 17. 21. to make thee a name of greatness and t.
Jer. 49. 16. thy t. hath deceived thee and the pride

TERRIBLY.

Isa. 2. 19. he ariseth to shake t. the earth, 21.
Nah. 2. 3. and the fir-trees shall be t. shaken

TERRIFY.

Job 3. 5. let the blackness of the day t. it
9. 34. let him take his rod, and let not his fear t.
31. 34. or did the contempt of families t. me?
Psal. 10. † 18. man of the earth may no more t.
2 Cor. 10. 9. seem as if I would t. you by letters

TERRIFIED.

Gen. 45. † 3. for they were t. at his presence
Deut. 20. 3. fear not nor be t. because of them
1 Sam. 16. † 14. an evil spirit from the Lord t. him
Luke 21. 9. when ye shall hear of wars, be not t.
24. 37. but they were t. and affrighted
Phil. 1. 28. and in nothing t. by your adversaries

TERRIFIEST.

Job 7. 14. then thou t. me through visions

TERRACES.

2 Chron. 9. 11. made of algum-trees t. to the house

TERROR

Signifies, [1] *Great fear or dread*, Gen. 35. 5. [2] *Dreadful and unexpected judgments*, Psal. 73. 19. [3] *An example striking* terror *into others*, Ezek. 27. 36. [4] *Those threatenings, whereby the wicked endeavour to affect good men with fear*, 1 Pet. 3. 14. [5] *The great and terrible day of judgment*, 2 Cor. 5. 11.

Gen. 35. 5. and the t. of God was upon the cities
Lev. 26. 16. I will even appoint over you t.
Deut. 32. 25. the sword without and t. within
34. 12. in all the great t. which Moses shewed
Josh. 2. 9. and that your t. is fallen upon us
Job 31. 23. destruction from God was a t. to me
33. 7. behold, my t. shall not make thee afraid
Psal. 91. 5. shalt not be afraid for the t. by night
Isa. 10. 33. the Lord will lop the bough with t.
19. 17. the land of Judah shall be a t. to Egypt
33. 18. thine heart shall meditate t. where is
54. 14. thou shalt be far from t. it shall not
Jer. 17. 17. be not a t. to me || 20. 4. a t. to thyself
32. 21. and hast brought forth Israel with great t.
Ezek. 26. 17. cause t. to be on all that haunt it
21. I will make thee a t. 27. 36. | 28. 19.
32. 23. which caused t. in the land, 24, 25, 26, 27
30. with their t. they are ashamed of their might
32. I have caused my t. in the land of the living
Rom. 13. 3. for rulers are not a t. to good works
2 Cor. 5. 11. knowing therefore the t. of the Lord
1 Pet. 3. 14. be not afraid of their t. nor troubled

TERRORS.

Deut. 4. 34. assayed to take a nation by great t.
Job 6. 4. the t. of God do set themselves in array
18. 11. t. shall make him afraid on every side
14. and it shall bring him to the king of t.
20. 25. the sword cometh, t. are upon him
24. 17. they are in the t. of the shadow of death
27. 20. t. take hold on him as waters, a tempest
30. 15. t. are turned upon me, they pursue me
39. † 20. the glory of his nostrils are t.
Psal. 55. 4. the t. of death are fallen upon me
73. 19. they are utterly consumed with t.
88. 15. while I suffer thy t. I am distracted
16. wrath goeth over me, thy t. have cut me off
Jer. 15. 8. I caused t. to fall upon the city
Lam. 2. 22. thou hast called my t. round about
5. † 10. our skin black as an oven, because of t.
Ezek. 21. 12. t. by reason of the sword shall be on

TESTAMENT

Signifies, [I] *An act of the last will of a person who hath death in his view, and disposes of his estate, and gives orders as to what he would have done after his decease*, Heb. 9. 17. [II] *The covenant which God was graciously pleased to make known after the fall of Adam, which contains the method in which sinners may be saved; namely, by the blood of Christ only. This covenant is called* old, Heb. 8. 13. *not because it differed in substance from the new; for it did not bind such as were under it to obtain justification by works: for its being delivered with blood*, Exod. 24. 8. *taught them that justification was to be had only by faith in Christ's blood; but it is called* old *in regard of the manner of its dispensation, because it was administered to the Jews in many figures, shadows, rites, and sacrifices, with other obscure and dark revelations and prophecies: and also in regard it was to be abrogated, and the* New Testament or Covenant *to come in its stead, which is so called*, [1] *Because it is ratified by the blood and actual sufferings of Christ, which were typified by the sacrifices and sprinkling of blood, under the old dispensation.* [2] *It contains a more full and clear revelation of the mysteries of religion, and is attended with a larger measure of the gifts and graces of the Holy Spirit*, Joel 2. 28. 2 Tim. 1. 10. [3] *It is propounded and extended to all, and not confined to one nation only, as it was to the Jews under the legal dispensation*, Mat. 28. 19. [4] *It is never to wax old or be abolished.* [III] *The books or inspired writings of Moses and the prophets, which contain the substance of God's covenant with the Jews under the legal dispensation*, 2 Cor. 3. 14.

Mat. 26. 28. this is my blood in new t. Mark 14. 24.
Luke 22. 20. this cup is the new t. 1 Cor. 11. 25.
2 Cor. 3. 6. who made us able ministers of the new t.
14. remains the same vail, in reading the old t.
Gal. 3. † 15. tho' it be but a man's t. yet if confirmed
Heb. 7. 22. was Jesus made a surety of a better t.
9. 15. he is the mediator of the new t. for the redemption of the transgressions under the first t.
16. where a t. is there must also be the death
17. for a t. is of force after men are dead
20. this is the blood of the t. God enjoined
12. † 24. to Jesus the Mediator of the new t.
13. † 20. through the blood of the everlasting t.
Rev. 11. 19. seen in his temple, the ark of his t.

TESTATOR.

Heb. 9. 16. must of necessity be the death of the t.
17. it is of no strength at all while the t. liveth

TESTIFY

Signifies, [1] *To bear witness*, Acts 20. 24. | 26. 5 [2] *To avouch, or affirm*, John 3. 11. [3] *To publish and declare freely and boldly*, Acts 20.

21. [4] *To declare a charge, or indictment against one,* Psal. 50. 7. [5] *To protest, or speak against,* Neh. 13. 15.
Num. 35. 30. one witness not *t.* against any person
Deut. 8. 19. I *t.* against you that ye shall perish
19. 16. if a false witness *t.* against any man
31. 21. this song shall *t.* against them as witness
32. 46. set your hearts to the words which I *t.*
Neh. 9. 34. wherewith thou didst *t.* against them
Job 15. 6. yea, thine own lips *t.* against thee
Psal. 50. 7. O Israel, I will *t.* against thee, 81. 8.
Isa. 59. 12. before thee, and our sins *t.* against us
Jer. 14. 7. though our iniquities *t.* against us
Hos. 5. 5. the pride of Israel doth *t.* to his face
Amos 3. 13 hear ye, and *t.* in the house of Jacob
Mic. 6. 3. O people, what have I done? *t.* against me
Luke 16. 28. send Lazarus, that he may *t.* to them
John 2. 25. needed not that any should *t.* of man
3. 11. and *t* that we have seen ‖ 5. 39. they *t.* of me
7. 7. because I *t.* of it ‖ 15. 26. he shall *t.* of me
Acts 2. 40. with many other words did he *t.*
10. 42. to *t.* that it is he who was ordained of God
20. 24. to *t.* the gospel of the grace of God
26. 5. my manner of life know they, if they would *t.*
Gal. 5. 3. I *t.* to every man that is circumcised
Eph. 4. 17. this I say, and *t.* in the Lord, that ye
1 John 4. 14. and we have seen and do *t.* that
Rev. 22. 16. I Jesus have sent my angel to *t.*
18. I *t.* to every man that heareth the words

TESTIFIED.

Exod. 21. 29. and it hath been *t.* to his owner
Deut. 19. 18. hath *t.* falsely against his brother
Ruth 1. 21. seeing the Lord hath *t.* against me
2 Sam. 1. 16. thy mouth hath *t.* against thee
2 Kings 17. 13. yet the Lord *t.* against Israel
15. his testimonies which he *t.* against them
2 Chr. 24. 19. prophets *t.* against them, Neh. 9. 26.
Neh. 13. 15. I *t.* against them when they sold, 21.
Jer. 42. † 19. know certainly I have *t.* against you
John 4. 39. for the saying which the woman *t.*
44. Jesus himself *t.* that a prophet, 13. 21.
Acts 8. 25. when they had *t.* and preached the word
18. 5. Paul *t.* to the Jews, that Jesus was Christ
23. 11. for as thou hast *t.* of me at Jerusalem
28. 23. to whom he *t.* the kingdom of God
1 Cor. 15. 15. are false, because we have *t.* of God
1 Thess. 4. 6. as we have forewarned you and *t.*
1 Tim. 2. 6. who gave himself, to be *t.* in due time
Heb. 2. 6. but one in a certain place *t.* saying
1 Pet. 1. 11. when it *t.* beforehand the sufferings
1 John 5. 9. the witness which God hath *t.* of his Son
3 John 3. and *t.* of the truth that is in thee

TESTIFIEDST.

Neh. 9. 29. and *t.* against them by thy Spirit, 30.

TESTIFIETH.

Hos. 7. 10. the pride of Israel *t.* to his face
John 3. 32. what he hath seen and heard that he *t.*
21. 24. the disciple which *t.* of these things
Heb. 7. 17. for he *t.* thou art a priest for ever
Rev. 22. 20. he which *t.* these things, saith

TESTIFYING.

Acts 20. 21. *t.* both to the Jews and to the Greeks
Heb. 11. 4. obtained witness, God *t.* of his gifts
1 Pet. 5. 12. *t.* that this is the true grace of God

TESTIMONY

Signifies, [1] *A witnessing evidence, or proof,* Acts 14. 3. [2] *The whole scripture, or word of God, which declares what is to be believed, practised, and expected by us,* Psal. 19. 7. [3] *The two tables of stone, whereon the law or ten commandments were written, which were witnesses of that covenant made between God and his people,* Exod. 25. 16, 21. | 31. 18. [4] *The book of the law which testifies of God's will and man's duty,* 2 Kings 11. 12. [5] *The gospel, which testifies of Christ, and declares the will of God concerning the way of saving sinners,* 1 Cor. 1. 6. | 2. 1. 2 Tim. 1. 8. [6] *The ark, in which the law was deposited,* Exod. 16. 34.
Exod. 16. 34. laid the pot of manna before the *t.*
25. 16. thou shalt put into the ark the *t.* 21.
27. 21. without the vail which is before the *t.*
30. 6. mercy-seat that is over the *t.* Lev. 16. 13.
36. beat it small, and put it before the *t.*
31. 18. and he gave unto Moses two tables of *t.*
32. 15. the two tables of *t.* were in his hand, 34. 29.
38. 21. this is the sum of the tabernacle of *t.*
Num. 1. 50. the Levites over the tabernacle of *t.*
53. Levites shall pitch about the tabernacle of *t.*
9. 15. the cloud covered the tent of the *t.*
10. 11. the cloud was taken off the tabernacle of *t.*
17. 4. thou shalt lay up the rods before the *t.*
10. bring Aaron's rod again before the *t.*
Ruth 4. 7. gave his shoe, and this was a *t.* in Israel
2 Kings 11. 12. gave the king the *t.* 2 Chr. 23. 11.
Psal. 78. 5. for he established a *t.* in Jacob
81. 5. thus he ordained in Joseph for a *t.*
119. 88. so shall I keep the *t.* of thy mouth
122. 4. the tribes go up to the *t.* of Israel
132. 12. if thy children will keep my *t.*
Isa. 8. 16. bind up the *t.* ‖ 20. to the law and to the *t.*
Mat. 8. 4. offer the gift Moses commanded for a *t.* Mark 1. 44. Luke 5. 14.
10. 18. for a *t.* against them, Mark 13. 9.
Mark 6. 11. shake off the dust for a *t.* Luke 9. 5.
Luke 21. 13. and it shall turn to you for a *t.*
John 3. 32. and no man receiveth his *t.*
33. he that received his *t.* hath set to his seal
8. 17. it is written, the *t.* of two men is true
21. 24. and we know that his *t.* is true
Acts 13. 22. to whom also he gave *t.* and said
14. 3. who gave *t.* to the word of his grace
22. 18. for they will not receive thy *t.* of me
1 Cor. 1. 6. as the *t.* of Christ was confirmed in you
2. 1. I came, declaring unto you the *t.* of God
2 Cor. 1. 12. the *t.* of our conscience, in simplicity
2 Thess. 1. 10. because our *t.* among you was believed
1 Tim. 2. † 6. gave himself to be a *t.* in due time
2 Tim. 1. 8. be not ashamed of the *t.* of our Lord
Heb. 3. 5. for a *t.* of those things which were
11. 5. Enoch had this *t.* that he pleased God
Rev. 1. 2. who bare record of the *t.* of Jesus Christ
Rev. 1. 9. I was in the isle of Patmos for *t.* of Jesus
6. 9. the souls of them that were slain for the *t.*
11. 7. when they shall have finished their *t.*
12. 11. they overcame by the word of their *t.*
17. make war with them which have *t.* of Jesus
15. 5. tabernacle of the *t.* in heaven was opened
19. 10. of thy brethren that have the *t.* of Jesus for the *t.* of Jesus is the Spirit of prophecy

See ARK.

TESTIMONIES.

Deut. 4. 45. these are the *t.* which Moses spake
6. 17. you shall diligently keep the *t.* of your God
20. what mean the *t.* which God commanded you
1 Kings 2. 3. to keep his statutes and his *t.* 2 Kings 23. 3. 1 Chron. 29. 19. 2 Chron. 34. 31.
2 Kings 17. 15. rejected his *t.* and followed vanity
Neh. 9. 34. nor have our kings hearkened to thy *t.*
Psal. 25. 10. to such as keep his covenant and his *t.*
78. 56. and kept not his *t.* ‖ 93. 5. thy *t.* are sure
99. 7. they kept his *t.* and the ordinance he gave
119. 2. blessed are they that keep his *t.* and seek him
14. I have rejoiced in the way of thy *t.* as much
22. for I have kept thy *t.* 167, 168.
24. thy *t.* are my delight ‖ 31. I stuck to thy *t.*
36. incline my heart to thy *t.* not to covetousness
46. I will speak of thy *t.* also before kings
59. and I turned my feet to thy *t.*
79. let those that have known thy *t.* turn to me
95. the wicked waited, but I will consider thy *t.*
99. I have underst. for thy *t.* are my meditation
111. thy *t.* have I taken as an heritage for ever
119. I love thy *t.* ‖ 125. that I may know thy *t.*
129. thy *t.* are wonderful, therefore doth my soul
138. thy *t.* are righteous and very faithful
144. the righteousness of thy *t.* is everlasting
146. I cried, save me, and I shall keep thy *t.*
152. concerning thy *t.* I have known of old
157. yet do I not decline from thy *t.*
Jer. 44. 23. because ye have not walked in his *t.*

TEIL-*tree.*

Isa. 6. 13. as a *t.-tree* and as an oak whose substance

THANK.

Luke 6. 32. that love you, what *t.* have you? 33, 34.

THANK.

1 Chron. 16. 4. he appointed Levites to *t.* the Lord
7. David delivered this psalm to *t.* the Lord
23. 30. to stand every morning to *t.* the Lord
29. 13. we *t.* thee and praise thy glorious name
Dan. 2. 23. I *t.* thee and praise thee, O God
Mat. 11. 25. at that time, Jesus said, I *t.* thee, O Father, Lord of heaven and earth, Luke 10. 21.
Luke 17. 9. doth he *t.* that servant? I trow not
18. 11. God, I *t.* thee, that I am not as other men
John 11. 41. Father, I *t.* thee, that thou heardest me
Rom. 1. 8. I *t.* my God through Jesus Christ, 7. 25.
1 Cor. 1. 4. I *t.* my God always on your behalf
14. I *t.* God that I baptized none of you, but
14. 18. I *t.* my God I speak with tongues more
Phil. 1. 3. I *t.* God on every remembrance of you
1 Thess. 2. 13. for this cause also *t.* we God
2 Thess. 1. 3. we are bound to *t.* God always for you
1 Tim. 1. 12. I *t.* Jesus Christ who hath enabled me
2 Tim. 1. 3. I *t.* God, whom I serve with pure consc.
Philem. 4. I *t.* my God, making mention of thee

See OFFERING.

THANKED.

2 Sam. 14. 22. Joab bowed himself and *t.* the king
1 Kings 8. † 66. and the people *t.* the king, and went
Acts 28. 15. Paul *t.* God and took courage
Rom. 6. 17. but God be *t.* that ye were the servants

THANKFUL.

Psal. 100. 4. be *t.* to him, bless his name, Col. 3. 15.
Rom. 1. 21. they glorified him not, neither were *t.*

THANKFULNESS.

Acts 24. 3. we accept it, most noble Felix, with all *t.*

THANKING.

2 Chron. 5. 13. the singers were as one in *t.* the Lord

THANK-*worthy.*

1 Pet. 2. 19. for this is *t.-w.* if a man endure grief

THANKS.

Neh. 12. 31. I appointed companies that gave *t.*
40. so stood the two companies that gave *t.*
Dan. 6. 10. he prayed and gave *t.* before his God
Mat. 26. 27. he took the cup and gave *t.* Luke 22. 17.
Mark 8. 6. he took the seven loaves and gave *t.*
14. 23. when he had given *t.* he gave it to them
Luke 2. 38. Anna gave *t.* to the Lord, and spake
22. 19. he took bread, and gave *t.* and brake it
John 6. 11. when he had given *t.* he distributed
23. they did eat bread, after the L. had given *t.*
Acts 27. 35. Paul took bread, and gave *t.* to God
Rom. 14. 6. he that eateth, eateth to the Lord, for he giveth God *t.* he eateth not, and giveth God *t.*
1 Cor. 11. 24. when he had given *t.* he brake it
14. 17. for thou verily givest *t.* well, but the other
15. 57. *t.* be to God, who giveth us the victory
2 Cor. 1. 11. *t.* may be given to many on our behalf
2. 14. *t.* be to God who causeth us to triumph
8. 16. *t.* to God, who put the same care in Titus
9. 15. *t.* be to God for his unspeakable gift
Eph. 5. 20. giving *t.* always for all things to God
1 Thess. 3. 9. what *t.* can we render to God again
Heb. 13. 15. offer sacrifices of praise, giving *t.*
Rev. 4. 9. give *t.* to him that sat on the throne

See GIVE, GIVING.

THANKSGIVING

Signifies, [1] *An acknowledging and confessing, with gladness, the benefits and mercies, which God bestows either upon ourselves or others,* Phil. 4. 6. 1 Tim. 2. 1. [2] *The sacrifice of* thanksgiving, Lev. 7. 12, 15. [3] *Psalms of* thanksgiving, Neh. 12. † 8. We are to give thanks to God, [1] *For spiritual blessings, such as willing hearts to do works of piety and charity,* 1 Chron. 29. 13, 14. [2] *For moral blessings, as wisdom and knowledge,* Dan. 2. 23. [3] *For saving graces,* Rom. 1. 8. 1 Cor. 1. 4. [4] *For the judgments of God upon the wicked,* Psal. 9. 1, 2, 3. [5] *For the enlarging of Christ's kingdom,* Rev. 11. 17. [6] *For deliverance from the body of death,* Rom. 7. 25. 1 Cor. 15. 57. [7] *For temporal deliverances,* Exod. 15. 1, 2. [8] *For Christ, the unspeakable gift of God,* Luke 2. 38. [9] *For the deliverance of God's ministers,* 2 Cor. 1. 11.
Lev. 7. 12. if he offer it for a *t.* 13, 15. | 22. 29.
Neh. 11. 17. the principal to begin the *t.* in prayer
12. 8. which was over the *t.* he and his brethren
46. there were songs of praise and *t.* to God
Psal. 26. 7. that I may publish with the voice of *t.*
50. 14. offer unto God *t.* and pay thy vows to most
69. 30. and I will magnify him with *t.*
95. 2. let us come before his face with *t.*
100. 4. enter into his gates with *t.* and praise
107. 22. let them sacrifice sacrifices of *t.*
116. 17. I will offer to thee sacrifices of *t.*
147. 7. sing to the Lord with *t.* sing praise
Isa. 51. 3. *t.* and melody shall be found therein
Jer. 30. 19. and out of them shall proceed *t.*
Amos 4. 5. offer a sacrifice of *t.* with leaven
Jonah 2. 9. I will sacrifice to thee with voice of *t.*
2 Cor. 4. 15. thro' *t.* of many grace might redound
9. 11. which causeth through us *t.* to God
Phil. 4. 6. with *t.* let your requests be made known
Col. 2. 7. in the faith, abounding therein with *t.*
4. 2. continue and watch in the same with *t.*
1 Tim. 4. 3. God created to be received with *t.*
4. every creature is good if it be received with *t.*
Rev. 7. 12. *t.* and honour be to our God for ever

THANKSGIVINGS.

Neh. 12. 27. to keep the dedication with *t.*
2 Cor. 9. 12. but is abundant by many *t.* to God

THANK *offerings.*

Ezek. 43. † 27. the priests shall make your *t. offer.*
45. † 15. and for *t. offerings* to make reconciliation
† 17. shall prepare the sin offering and *t. offerings*
Amos 5. † 22. neither will I regard the *t. offerings*

THAT.

Gen. 2. 11. *t.* is it which compasseth the land
19. what Adam called, *t.* was the name thereof
18. 25. *t.* be far from thee, to slay the righteous
30. 33. *t.* shalt be accounted stolen with me
Exod. 30. 38. whosoever shall make like to *t.*
Lev. 10. 20. when Moses heard *t.* he was content
26. 44. yet for all *t.* I will not cast them away
Num. 6. 21. besides *t.* his hands shall get
22. 20. the word which I say, *t.* shalt thou do
24. 13. Lord saith *t.* will I speak, 1 Kings 22. 14.
Judg. 8. 3. anger was abated, when he had said *t.*
11. 36. do according to *t.* which proceeded
1 Sam. 9. 24. behold, *t.* which is left, set it before
21. 9. Goliath's sword, if thou wilt take *t.* take it
24. 19. for *t.* thou hast done to me this day
30. 23. with *t.* which the Lord hath given us
2 Sam. 12. 8. if *t.* had been too little, I would
19. 6. in *t.* thou lovest thine enemies and hatest
24. 24. offer of *t.* which doth cost me nothing
2 Kings 14. 6. according to *t.* which was written in the law of Moses, 2 Chron. 35. 26.
19. 20. *t.* which thou hast prayed to me against
2 Chron. 6. 15. *t.* which thou hast promised, 16.
Ezra 6. 9. *t.* which they have need of be given
7. 18. *t.* do after the will of your God
Job 3. 25. *t.* which I was afraid of is come to me
15. 17. *t.* which I have seen I will declare
20. 20. he shall not save of *t.* which he desired
23. 13. what his soul desireth even *t.* he doeth
34. 32. *t.* which I see not, teach thou me
Psal. 27. 4. *t.* will I seek after, that I may dwell
69. 4. then I restored *t.* which I took not away
10. when I wept, *t.* was to my reproach
Eccl. 1. 9. the thing *t.* hath been, it is *t.* which shall be; *t.* which is done, is *t.* which shall be done
15. *t.* which is wanting cannot be numbered
2. 3. see what was *t.* good for the sons of men
3. 9. what profit in *t.* wherein he laboureth?
15. and God requireth *t.* which is past
5. 4. when thou vowest, pay *t.* thou hast vowed
11. 6. thou knowest not whether this or *t.* prosper
Isa. 21. 10. *t.* which I have heard of the Lord
52. 15. for *t.* which had not been told them shall they see, *t.* they had not heard shall consider
Jer. 15. 4. for *t.* which Manasseh did in Jerusalem
45. 4. *t.* which I have built, *t.* which I planted
Dan. 6. 13. *t.* Daniel regardeth not thee, O king
11. 36. for *t.* is determined shall be done
Zech. 11. 9. *t. t.* dieth, let it die, *t. t.* is to be cut off
Mat. 1. 20. for *t.* which is conceived in her is of
9. 22. woman was made whole from *t.* hour, 15. 28.
10. 15. for Sodom than for *t.* city, Mark 6. 11.
13. 12. taken away *t.* he hath, 25. 29. Mark 4. 25.
20. 7. *t.* shall ye receive ‖ 23. 3. *t.* observe and do
27. 4. they said, what is *t.* to us? see thou to *t.*
Mark 7. 20. *t.* which cometh out, *t.* defileth man
13. 11. what shall be given in *t.* hour, *t.* speak
Luke 4. 6. all will I give, for *t.* is delivered to me
8. 18. shall be taken, even *t.* he seemeth to have
11. 40. did not he *t.* made *t.* which is without make *t.* which is within also?
16. 12. not faithful in *t.* which is another man's
16. 15. *t.* which is highly esteemed among men
17. 10. we have done *t.* which was our duty to do
24. 12. wondering at *t.* which was come to pass
John 1. 8. he was not *t.* light ‖ 9. *t.* was the light
3. 6. *t.* which is born of flesh, *t.* born of the Spirit
11. we speak *t.* we know, testify *t.* we have seen
4. 18. is not thy husband, in *t.* saidst thou truly
37. herein is *t.* saying true, one soweth another
5. 12. what man is *t.* which said to thee, take up
6. 27. labour for *t.* meat which endureth
32. Moses gave you not *t.* bread from heaven
48. I am *t.* bread of life ‖ 58. this is *t.* bread
8. 38. I speak *t.* I have seen with my father; ye do *t.* which ye have seen with your father
13. 27. *t.* thou doest, do quickly ‖ 14. 13. *t.* will I do
16. 13. what he shall hear, *t.* shall he speak
21. 22. what is *t.* to thee, follow thou me, 24.
23. went abroad, *t. t.* disciple should not die
Acts 2. 16. this is *t.* which was spoken by prophet Joel
4. 21. all glorified God for *t.* which was done
24. when they heard *t.* they lifted up, 5. 21. 33.
7. 37. this is *t.* Moses which said unto Israel
10. 37. *t.* word you know, which was published
Rom. 1. 19. because *t.* which may be known of God
4. 18. according to *t.* which was spoken, so shall

Rom. 6. 10. in t. he died, in t. he liveth, liveth to God
7. 6. t. being dead wherein we were held, t. we
13. was then t. which is good made death to me?
15. t. I do, I allow not || 19. t. I would not, t. do I
1 Cor. 5. 13. put away from you t. wicked person
6. 8. nay, you defraud, and t. your brethren
10. 4. t. spiritual rock, and t. rock was Christ
30. spoken of, for t. for which I give thanks
11. 23. t. which also I delivered unto you
28. let him eat of t. bread, and drink of t. cup
13. 10. t. which is perfect, t. which is in part
14. 21. and yet for all t. they will not hear me
15. 37. and t. which thou sowest thou sowest not
t. body that shall be, but bare grain
46. t. was not first which is spiritual, but t. which
2 Cor. 3. 11. if t. which is done away was glorious
8. 12. it is accepted according to t. a man hath
11. 12. what I do, t. I will do, that I may cut off
Gal. 6. 7. what a man soweth, t. shall he reap
Phil. 3. 12. that I may apprehend t. for which I am
1 Thess. 3. 10. might perfect t. which is lacking
5. 21. prove all things, hold fast t. which is good
1 Tim. 4. 8. life t. now is, and of t. which is to come
6. 20. keep t. which is committed to thy trust
Philem. 18. if he oweth put t. on mine account
Heb. 5. 7. and was heard in t. he feared
6. 19. which entereth into t. within the veil
12. 20. could not endure t. which was commanded
13. 17. for t. is unprofitable for you
Jam. 4. 15. if L. will, we shall live, and do this or t.
1 Pet. 3. 13. who is he t. will harm you, if ye be
followers of t. which is good? 3 John 11.
1 John 1. 1. t. which was from the beginning
3. t. which we have seen and heard, 2. 24.
2. 24. let t. abide in you which ye have heard
Rev. 2. 25. t. which ye have, hold fast till I come
See AFTER, DAY, MAN, PLACE, SO, SOUL, THING, TIME.

THEATRE.

Acts 19. 29. they rushed with one accord into the t.
31. that he would not adventure himself into t.

THEE.

Gen. 7. 1. t. have I seen righteous before me
17. 2. and I will multiply t. exceedingly
22. 17. that in blessing I will bless t.
23. 11. the field gave I t. and the cave gave I t.
39. 9. neither kept back any thing from me but t.
Deut. 28. 43. the stranger shall get above t.
1 Sam. 8. 7. they have not rejected t. but me
20. 22. behold the arrows are beyond t. 37.
2 Sam. 18. 12. the king charged t. and Abishai
Psal. 86. 14. they have not set t. before them
Jer. 15. 11. I will cause enemy to entreat t. well
Ezek. 7. 9. I will recompense t. according to thy
29. 5. I will leave t. and all the fish of thy rivers
Mat. 25. 37. when saw we t. an hungred, and fed t.
38. when saw we t. a stranger || 39. saw t. sick
Luke 14. 9. he that bade t. and him come and say
Rom. 11. 18. but the root t. || 21. lest he spare not t.

About THEE.

Job 11. 18. thou shalt dig about t. and take thy rest
Isa. 26. 20. shut thy doors about t. hide thyself
Jer. 46. 14. sword devour round about t. Ezek. 5. 12.
49. 5. bring fear from all those that be about t.
Ezek. 5. 14. among nations that are round about t.
15. an astonishment to the nations round about t.
Luke 19. 43. thy enemies shall cast a trench about t.
Acts 12. 8. cast thy garment about t. and follow me

After THEE.

Gen. 17. 7. to thy seed a. t. 8, 9, 10. | 35. 12. | 48. 4.
Deut. 4. 40. with thy children after t. 12. 25, 28.
Judg. 5. 14. after t. Benjamin among thy people
2 Sam. 7. 12. and I will set up thy seed after t.
1 Kings 1. 14. I also will come in after t. and confirm
3. 12. nor a. t. shall any arise like thee, 2 Chr. 1. 12.
Psal. 42. 1. so panteth my soul after t. O God
63. 8. my soul followeth hard after t. thy right hand
143. 6. my soul thirsteth after t. as a thirsty land
Cant. 1. 4. draw me, we will run after t.
Isa. 45. 14. they shall come after t. in chains
Jer. 12. 6. they have called a multitude after t.
Dan. 2. 39. after t. shall rise another kingdom
Hos. 5. 8. cry at Beth-aven, after t. O Benjamin

Against THEE.

Exod. 15. 7. overthrown them that rose against t.
23. 29. lest the beast of the field multiply against t.
Num. 21. 7. we have sinned, for we have spoken ag. t.
Deut. 6. 15. the anger of the Lord be kindled ag. t.
15. 9. and he cry to the Lord against t. 24. 15.
23. 4. because they hired Balaam against t. to curse
28. 7. they shall come out ag. t. one way, and flee
48. enemies which the Lord shall send ag. t. 49.
31. 26. that it may be there for a witness against t.
Judg. 9. 31. behold they fortify the city against t.
10. 10. we have sinned ag. t. Neh. 1. 6. Jer. 14. 7, 20.
11. 27. I have not sinned against t. 1 Sam. 24. 11.
1 Sam. 19. 4. because he hath not sinned against t.
2 Sam. 1. 16. for thy mouth hath testified against t.
12. 11. behold, I will raise up evil against t.
18. 31. avenged thee of all that rose up ag. t. 32.
1 Kings 8. 33. because they have sinned against t.
35. 2 Chron. 6. 24, 26.
46. if they sin against t. and repent, 2 Chr. 6. 36.
50. forgive thy people that have sinned against t.
and all their transgressions, 2 Chron. 6. 39.
20. 22. the king of Syria will come up against t.
2 Kings 19. 9. he is come out to fight against t.
2 Chron. 14. 11. O Lord, let not man prevail ag. t.
18. 22. and the Lord hath spoken evil against t.
20. 2. there cometh a great multitude against t.
35. 21. I come not against t. this day, but against
Neh. 1. 7. we have dealt very corruptly against t.
9. 26. nevertheless they rebelled against t.
Job 7. 20. why hast thou set me as a mark against t.
11. 5. but, oh that God would open his lips ag. t.
15. 6. yea, thine own lips testify against t.
42. 7. my wrath is kindled against t. and thy friends
Psal. 5. 10. cast them out, they have rebelled ag. t.
21. 11. for they intended evil ag. t. they imagine
41. 4. Lord, heal my soul, for I have sinned ag. t.
50. 7. hear, O Israel, and I will testify against t.
51. 4. against t. have I sinned, and done this evil

Ps. 74. 23. that rise up against t. 139. 21. Eccl. 10. 4.
119. 11. thy word I hid, that I might not sin ag. t.
139. 20. for they speak against t. wickedly
Isa. 7. 5. have taken evil counsel against t. saying
10. 24. the Assyrian shall lift up his staff against t.
Jer. 1. 19. they shall fight against t. but they shall
not prevail against t. for I am with thee, 15. 20.
21. 13. behold, I am against t. 50. 31. | 51. 25.
Ezek. 5. 8. | 21. 3. | 26. 3. | 28. 22. | 29. 3, 10.
| 35. 3. | 38. 3. | 39. 1. Nah. 2. 13. | 3. 5.
Lam. 2. 16. thy enemies opened their mouth ag. t.
Ezek. 33. 30. thy people still are talking against t.
Amos 7. 10. saying, Amos hath conspired against t.
Mal. 3. 13. what have we spoken so much against t.
Mat. 5. 23. that thy brother hath aught against t.
18. 15. if thy brother trespass ag. t. Luke 17. 3, 4.
26. 62. which these witn. ag. t. Mark 14. 60. | 15. 4.
Rev. 2. 4. nevertheless, I have somewhat against t.
14. but I have a few things against t. 20.

At THEE.

2 Kings 19. 21. hath shaken her head at t. Isa. 37. 22.
Isa. 14. 8. yea, the fir-trees rejoice at t. and cedars
52. 14. astonish. at t. Ezek. 26. 16. | 27. 35. | 28. 19.
Lam. 2. 15. all that pass by clap their hands at t.
Ezek. 27. 36. the merchants shall hiss at t.
32. 10. I will make many people amazed at t.

Before THEE.

Gen. 13. 9. is not the whole land before t. separate
17. 18. said, O that Ishmael might live before t.
20. 15. behold my land is bef. t. dwell where, 47. 6.
24. 7. the Lord God of heaven shall send his angel
before t. Exod. 23. 20, 23. | 32. 34. | 33. 2.
51. behold, Rebekah is before t. take her and go
31. 35. let it not displease, I cannot rise up before t.
33. 12. I will go b. t. Isa. 45. 2. | 43. 9. set him bef. t.
Exod. 17. 6. behold, I will stand before t. there
23. 27. I will send my fear before t. and destroy
28. I will send hornets before t. which shall drive
out the Canaanite before t. 29, 30, 31. |
34. 11. Deut. 4. 38. | 9. 4, 5. | 18. 12.
33. 19. I will make all my goodness pass before t.
and I will proclaim the name of the Ld. before t.
34. 24. I will cast out b. t. Deut. 6. 19. | 7. 1. | 9. 4.
Num. 10. 35. let them that hate thee flee before t.
Deut. 7. 24. no man able to st. b. t. Josh. 1. 5. | 10. 8.
28. 7. they shall flee before t. seven ways
30. 15. I have set before t. this day life and good
31. 3. and Joshua, he shall go over before t. 8.
32. 52. yet thou shalt see the land before t.
33. 10. shall teach, they shall put incense before t.
Judg. 4. 14. is not the Lord gone out before t.?
6. 18. bring forth, and set it before t. 1 Sam. 9. 24.
1 Sam. 28. 22. let me set a morsel of bread before t.
2 Sam. 5. 24. then shall the Lord go out before t.
7. 15. as I took it from Saul, whom I put away b. t.
16. be established for ever bef. t. 26. 1 Chr. 17. 24.
1 Kings 3. 6. as he walk. b. t. || 12. none like thee b. t.
8. 23. thy servants that walk before t. 2 Chr. 6. 14.
10. 8. which stand continually before t. 2 Chr. 9. 7.
14. 9. hast done evil above all that were before t.
2 Kings 20. 3. how I have walked before t. Isa. 38. 3.
1 Chr. 14. 15. go out, for God is gone forth before t.
17. 13. as I took it from him that was before t.
Ezra 9. 15. behold, we are before t. in our trespasses, we cannot stand before t. because of this
Neh. 4. 5. let not their sin be blotted out before t.
9. 8. and foundest his heart faithful before t.
32. let not all the trouble seem little before t.
Ps. 38. 9. L. all my desire is before t. and groaning
39. 5. and mine age is as nothing before t.
69. 19. mine adversaries are all before t.
73. 22. so foolish was I, I was as a beast before t.
79. 11. let the sighing of the prisoner come before t.
88. 2. let my prayer come before t. incline, 141. 2.
90. 8. thou hast set our iniquities before t.
119. 168. my ways are b. t. || 169. let cry come b. t.
Prov. 23. 1. consider diligently what is before t.
Isa. 9. 3. they joy before t. as men when they divide
58. 8. and thy righteousness shall go before t.
Jer. 17. 16. came out of my lips, was right before t.
18. 20. I stood before t. to turn away thy wrath
28. 8. the prophets that have been before t. of old
40. 4. all the land is before t. go whither it seemeth
Lam. 1. 22. let all their wickedness come before t.
Ezek. 33. 31. and they sit before t. as my people
Dan. 6. 22. also before t. O king, have I done no hurt
Mic. 6. 4. I sent before t. Moses, Aaron, and Miriam
Zech. 3. 8. thou and thy fellows that sit before t.
Mat. 6. 2. do not sound a trumpet before t.
11. 10. behold, I send my messenger, which shall
prepare thy way before t. Mark 1. 2. Luke 7. 27.
Luke 15. 18. I will say, father, I have sinned bef. t.
Acts 23. 30. to say before t. what they had ag. him
24. 19. who ought to have been here bef. t. to object
25. 26. and especially before t. O king Agrippa
Rev. 3. 8. behold, I have set before t. an open door

Behind THEE.

Gen. 19. 17. escape for thy life, look not behind t.
Deut. 25. 18. Amalek smote the feeble behind t.
Ps. 50. 17. seeing thou castest my words behind t.
Isa. 30. 21. thine ears shall hear a word behind t.

Beside THEE.

Ruth 4. 4. for there is none to redeem it beside t.
1 Sam. 2. 2. for there is none beside t. 2 Sam. 7. 22.
1 Chron. 17. 20.
Psal. 73. 25. none on earth that I desire beside t.
Isa. 26. 13. other lords beside t. have had dominion
64. 4. neither hath the eye seen, O God, beside t.

Between THEE.

Gen. 3. 15. I will put enmity bet. t. and the woman
17. 2. I will make my covenant betw. me and t. 7.
31. 44. let it be for a witness bet. me and t. 48. 50.
49. Lord watch b. me and t. when we are absent
1 Sam. 20. 23. the Lord be b. t. and me for ever, 42.
Ezek. 4. 3. set it for a wall of iron b. t. and the city
Mal. 2. 14. the Lord hath been witness bet. t. and
Mat. 18. 15. tell him his fault bet. t. and him alone

By THEE.

Exod. 18. 14. the people stand by t. from morning
1 Sam. 1. 26. I am woman that stood by t. praying
9. 23. portion of which I said to thee, set it by t.
2 Sam. 22. 30. by t. I ran thro' a troop, Psal. 18. 29.

Psal. 71. 6. by t. have I been holpen from the womb
Prov. 3. 28. when hast it by t. || 29. dwell securely by t.
Isa. 26. 13. by t. we will make mention of thy name
Ezek. 16. 6. when I passed by t. and saw thee, 8.
Acts 24. 2. seeing that by t. we enjoy quietness
Philem. 7. the bowels of the saints are refreshed by t.

Concerning THEE.

Josh. 14. 6. the thing the L. said concern. t. and me
1 Sam. 25. 30. the good that he hath spoken con. t.
2 Sam. 14. 8. the king said, I will give charge con. t.
1 Kings 22. 23. the Lord hath spoken evil concern. t.
Nah. 1. 14. the L. hath given commandment con. t.
Mat. 4. 6. shall give his angels charge concern. t.
Acts 28. 21. neither received we letters concern. t.

For THEE.

Gen. 6. 21. food for t. and them || 20. 7. shall pray for t.
Exod. 9. 30. but as for t. and thy servants, I know
Lev. 25. 6. sabbath shall be meat for t. and them
Num. 18. 9. shall be most holy for t. and thy sons
Deut. 5. 31. as for t. stand by me, 18. 14. 2 Sam. 13. 13.
Judg. 7. 4. and I will try them for t. there
13. 15. till we shall have made ready a kid for t.
18. 19. better for t. to be a priest to house of one man
Ruth 3. 1. shall I not seek rest for t. || 4. 8. buy it for t.
1 Sam. 9. 24. to this time hath it been kept for t.
20. 4. what thy soul desireth, I will do it for t.
2 Sam. 1. 26. I am distressed for t. brother Jonathan
10. 11. if the Syrians be too strong for t. help me
18. 33. would God I had died for t. O Absalom
19. 38. what thou requirest, that I will do for t.
1 Kings 2. 18. I will speak for t. unto the king
17. 13. and after make for t. and for thy son
20. 34. thou shalt make streets for t. in Damascus
2 Kings 2. 9. Elijah said, ask what I shall do for t. 4.
4. 13. say now unto her, what is to be done for t. 2.
2 Chron. 7. 17. and as for t. Dan. 2. 29. Zech. 9. 11.
Job 8. 6. if upright, surely now he would awake for t.
18. 4. shall the earth be forsaken for t.?
Psal. 63. 1. O God, my soul thirsteth for t. my flesh
65. 1. praise waiteth for t. O God, in Sion
119. 126. it is time for t. O Lord, to work
Cant. 7. 13. fruits I have laid up for t. O my beloved
Isa. 14. 9. hell from beneath is moved for t. to meet
26. 8. O Lord, we have waited for t. 33. 2.
43. 3. I gave Ethiopia and Seba for t.
4. I loved thee, therefore will I give men for t.
48. 9. and for my praise will I refrain for t.
51. 19. these are come, who shall be sorry for t.
Jer. 32. 17. behold, there is nothing too hard for t.
34. 5. so shall they burn odours for t. and lament
48. 32. I will weep for t. || 50. 24. I laid a snare for t.
51. 36. therefore will I take vengeance for t.
Lam. 2. 13. what thing shall I take to witness for t.
14. thy prophets have seen for t. false burdens
Ezek. 7. 6. it watcheth for t. behold, it is come
32. 10. their king shall be horribly afraid for t.
Hos. 3. 3. shalt not be for another, so will I be for t.
6. 11. also, O Judah, he hath set a harvest for t.
Nah. 3. 7. whence shall I seek comfort for t.
Mat. 5. 29. for it is profitable for t. 30.
11. 24. be more tolerable for Sodom than for t.
14. 4. it is not lawful for t. to have her, Mark 6. 18.
17. 4. one for t. one for Moses, Mark 9. 5. Luke 9. 33.
18. 8. better for t. to enter into life, 9. Mark 9. 43, 45.
Mark 1. 37. they said unto him, all men seek for t.
3. 32. thy mother and thy brethren seek for t.
5. 19. how great things the Lord hath done for t.
Luke 22. 32. but I have prayed for t. that thy faith
John 11. 28. the master is come, and calleth for t.
Acts 9. 5. hard for t. to kick against pricks, 26. 14.
10. 22. to send for t. into his house and to hear
24. 25. have a convenient season, I will call for t.
2 Cor. 12. 9. he said, my grace is sufficient for t.

From THEE.

Gen. 18. 25. that be far from t. to slay the righteous
27. 45. until thy brother's anger turn away from t.
30. 2. hath withheld from t. the fruit of the womb
Exod. 8. 29. and Moses said, behold, I go out from t.
33. 5. therefore now put off thy ornaments from t.
Deut. 12. 21. if the place be too far from t. 14. 24.
15. 12. thou shalt let him go free from t. 13, 18.
16. I will not go away from t. || 20. 15. cities far
from t.
30. 11. it is not hidden from t. neither is it far off
Judg. 17. 2. the shekels that were taken from t.
1 Sam. 1. 14. Eli said to her, put away thy wine f. t.
15. 28. hath rent the kingdom from t. 1 Kings 11. 11.
17. 46. smite thee, I will take thine head from t.
20. 9. far be it from t. Mat. 16. 22.
2 Sam. 13. 13. for he will not withhold me from t.
2 Kings 2. 9. what I shall do, before I be taken fr. t.
20. 18. of thy sons that shall issue from t. Isa. 39. 7.
Ezra 4. 12. the Jews which came up from t. to us
Job 42. 2. no thought can be withholden from t.
Psal. 38. 9. and my groaning is not hid from t.
69. 5. O God, my sins are not hid from t.
73. 27. they that are far from t. shall perish
80. 18. so will not we go back from t. quicken us
139. 12. yea, the darkness hideth not from t.
15. my substance was not hid from t. when I was
Isa. 54. 8. in a little wrath I hid my face from t.
10. but my kindness shall not depart from t.
Jer. 6. 8. be instructed, lest my soul depart from t.
Ezek. 21. 3. I will cut off from t. the righteous, 4.
22. 5. those that be far from t. shall mock thee
24. 16. I take away from t. the desire of thine eyes
28. 3. there is no secret that they can hide from t.
Mic. 1. 16. for they are gone into captivity from t.
Zech. 3. 4. I have caused thine iniquity to pass fr. t.
Mat. 5. 29. pluck it out and cast it fr. t. 30. | 18. 8, 9.
John 17. 8. known surely that I came out from t.
Acts 23. 21. ready, looking for a promise from t.
See DEPART, ED.

In THEE.

Gen. 12. 3. in t. shall all families be blessed, 28. 14.
48. 20. in t. shall Israel bless, saying, God make
Exod. 9. 16. I raised thee up, to shew in t. my power
Deut. 23. 14. that he see no unclean thing in t.
21. it would be sin in t. || 22. shall be no sin in t.
1 Sam. 18. 22. behold the king hath delight in t.
25. 28. evil hath not been found in t. 29. 6.
2 Sam. 15. 26. but if he say, I have no delight in t.

2 Chron. 19. 3. there are good things found in t.
Psal. 5. 11. put trust in t. 7. 1. | 9. 10. | 16. 1. | 17. 7. | 25. 2, 20. | 31. 1, 19. | 55. 23. let them that love thy name be joyful in t.
9. 2. rejoice in t. 40. 16. | 70. 4. | 85. 6. Cant. 1. 4.
22. 4. our fathers trusted in t. they trusted, 5.
31.14. I trusted in t. || 33. 22. hope in t. 38.15. | 39.7.
56.3. trust in t. 57. 1. | 84.12. | 86.2. | 141. 8. | 143.8.
81. 9. there shall no strange god be in t.
84. 5. blessed is the man whose strength is in t.
87. 7. all my springs are in t.
Cant. 4. 7. thou art all fair, there is no spot in t.
Isa. 26. 3. keep him because he trusteth in t.
45. 14. surely God is in t. and there is none else
62. 4. Hephzibah, for the Lord delighteth in t.
Jer. 2. 19. an evil thing, that my fear is not in t.
Ezek. 5. 9. I will do in t. what I have not done
10. and I will execute judgments in t. 15.
16. 31. the contrary is in t. from other women
20. 47. I will kindle a fire in t. it shall devour
22. 6. were in t. to their power to shed blood
7. in t. have they set light by father or mother
9. in t. are men that carry tales to shed blood
12. in t. have they taken gifts to shed blood
25.4. they shall set their palaces in t. dwellings in t.
27. 8. thy wise men, O Tyrus, that were in t. 9.
28. 15. was perfect, till iniquity was found in t.
38. 16. when I shall be sanctified in t. O Gog
Dan. 4. 9. spirit of the holy gods is in t. 18. | 5. 14.
Hos. 14. 3. for in t. the fatherless findeth mercy
Mic. 1. 13. for transgressions of Isr. were found in t.
4. 9. why dost thou cry? is there no king in t.?
Mat. 6. 23. if the light that is in t. be darkness
11. 23. mighty works which have been done in t.
Luke 3. 22. my beloved Son, in t. I am well pleased
11. 35. the light which is in t. be not darkness
19. 44. not leave in t. one stone upon another
John 17. 21. as thou, Father, art in me, and I in t.
Rom. 9. 17. that I might shew my power in t.
Gal. 3. 8. in t. shall all nations be blessed
1 Tim. 4. 14. neglect not the gift that is in t.
2 Tim. 1. 5. the unfeigned faith that is in t. first in Lois and Eunice, and I am persuaded in t. also
6. that thou stir up the gift of God which is in t.
3 John 3. brethren testified of the truth that is in t.
Rev. 18. 22. shall be heard no more at all in t.
23. a candle shall shine no more at all in t.

Into THEE.

Isa. 52. 1. no more come into t. the uncircumcised

Of THEE.

Gen. 12. 2. I will make of t. a great nation, 17. 6. | 35. 11. | 46. 3. | 48. 4. Exod. 32. 10.
13. and my soul shall live because of t.
41. 15. I have heard say of t. that thou canst
Num. 14. 15. which have heard the fame of t.
Deut. 2. 25. begin to put the dread of t. and the fear of t. tremble and be in anguish because of t.
10. 12. what doth the L. require of t. Mic. 6. 8.
Ruth 2. 19. he that did take knowledge of t.
1 Sam. 19. 3. I will commune with my father of t.
24. 12. Lord judge, and the Lord avenge me of t.
2 Sam. 3. 13. but one thing I will require of t.
24. 24. but I will surely buy it of t. at a price
1 Kings 2. 16. and now I ask one petition of t. 20.
11. 11. Lord said, forasmuch as this is done of t.
1 Chron. 22. 11. build the house as he said of t.
29. 12. both riches and honour come of t.
14. all things come of t. of thine have we given
Job 11. 6. that God exacteth of t. less than thine
38. 3. for I will demand of t. 40. 7. | 42. 4.
42. 5. I have heard of t. by the hearing of the ear
Psal. 22. 25. my praise shall be of t. 71. 6.
87. 3. glorious things are spoken of t. O city of G.
Prov. 25. 17. lest he be weary of t. and hate thee
30. 7. two things have I required of t. deny me not
Isa. 58. 12. they that shall be of t. shall build places
64. 7. none stirreth up himself to take hold of t.
Jer. 30. 11. I will not make a full end of t. 46. 28.
34. 4. thus saith the Lord of t. thou shalt not die
51. 26. they shall not take of t. a stone for a corner
Ezek. 29. 8. I will cut off man and beast out of t.
32. 6. and the rivers shall be full of t.
Dan. 2. 23. hast made known what we desired of t.
6. 7. shall ask a petition, save of t. O king, 12.
Mic. 2. 12. I will surely assemble all of t.
5. 2. yet out of t. shall come forth the ruler
7. 17. and they shall fear because of t.
Nah. 1. 11. one is come out of t. a wicked counsellor
Zeph. 3. 18. who are of t. to whom the reproach
Mat. 2. 6. for out of t. shall come a governor
3. 14. saying, I have need to be baptized of t.
5. 42. and from him that would borrow of t.
Mark 11. 14. no man eat fruit of t. hereafter
Luke 1. 35. holy thing which shall be born of t.
6. 30. give to every man that asketh of t.
12. 20. this night thy soul shall be required of t.
16. 2. he said, how is it that I hear this of t.?
John 17. 7. whatsoever thou hast given me are of t.
Acts 10. 22. send for thee, and to hear words of t.
28. 21. neither shewed nor spake any harm of t.
22. we desire to hear of t. what thou thinkest
1 Cor. 12. 21. say to the hand, I have no need of t.
Philem. 20. let me have joy of t. in the Lord

See, In the MIDST.

Off THEE.

Gen. 40. 19. Pharaoh shall lift up thy head from off t. and the birds shall eat thy flesh from off t.
Nah. 1. 13. now will I break his yoke from off t.

On or upon THEE.

Gen. 16.5. my wrong be u. t. || 38. 29. this breach u. t.
Exod. 15. 26. I will put none of these diseases upon t.
Lev. 19. 19. nor linen nor woollen come upon t.
Num. 6. 25. the Lord make his face shine upon t.
26. the Lord lift up his countenance upon t.
11. 17. I will take of the spirit which is upon t.
Deut. 4. 30. all these things are come upon t. 30. 1.
13. 17. the Lord may have compassion upon t. 30. 3.
19.10. so blood be upon t. || 28. 2. blessings come on t.
28. 15. all these curses shall come upon t. 20. 45.
Judg. 16. 9. the Philistines be upon t. 12, 14, 20.
1 Sam. 9. 20. is it not upon t. and thy father's house
24. 12. but mine hand shall not be upon t. 13.

1 Kings 1. 20. the eyes of all Israel are upon t.
13. 2. O altar, upon t. shall he offer the priests, and men's bones shall be burnt upon t.
21. 21. behold, I will bring evil upon t. and take
2 Kings 4. 4. thou shalt shut door upon t. and pour
2 Chron. 14. 11. help us, O Lord, for we rest upon t.
19. 2. therefore is wrath upon t. from the Lord
20. 12. we know not what to do, but our eyes upon t.
Job 4. 5. but now it is come upon t. and thou faintest
Psal. 17. 6. I have called upon t. 31. 17. | 86. 5, 7. | 88. 9. Lam. 3. 57.
22.10. I was cast up. t. || 25. 3. wait up. t. 5, 21. | 59.9.
63. 6. meditate on t. || 104. 27. these wait u. t. 145.15.
Cant. 6. 13. return, return, that we may look upon t.
Isa. 1. 25. and I will turn my hand upon t. and purge
24. 17. fear, and the pit, and the snare are upon t.
26. 3. wilt keep him, whose mind is stayed upon t.
47. 9. they shall come upon t. in their perfection
11. evil and desolation shall come upon t. 13.
49. 18. and bind them on t. as a bride doth
54. 8. with kindness will I have mercy on t. 10.
59. 21. my spirit that is upon t. shall not depart
60. 1. and the glory of the Lord is risen upon t. 2.
Jer. 14. 22. therefore we will wait upon t. for thou
15. 5. for who shall have pity upon t. O Jerusalem?
30. 16. all that prey upon t. will I give for a prey
Ezek. 3. 25. behold, they shall put bands upon t. 4.8.
5. 17. and I will bring the sword upon t. 29. 8.
29. 7. when they leaned upon t. thou brakest
Mat. 18. 33. had compassion, even as I had pity up. t.
21. 19. let no fruit grow on t. henceforward
Luke 1. 35. the Holy Ghost shall come upon t.
19. 43. for the days shall come upon t. that thine
Acts 13. 11. behold, the hand of the Lord is upon t.
18. 10. no man shall set on t. to hurt thee
22. 19. they know that I beat them that believ. on t.
1 Tim. 1. 18. prophecies which went before on t.
Rev. 3. 3. I will come on t. as a thief, and thou shalt not know what hour I will come upon t.

Over THEE.

Gen. 3. 16. thy husband, and he shall rule over t.
Deut. 15. 6. but they shall not reign over t.
17. 15. thou shalt in any wise set him king over t. thou mayest not set a stranger over t. 28. 36.
30. 9. the Lord will again rejoice over t. for good
Psal. 91. 11. give his angels charge over t. Luke 4.10.
Isa. 62. 5. so shall thy God rejoice over t.
Jer. 13. 21. hast taught them to be chief over t.
Lam. 2. 17. caused thine enemy to rejoice over t.
Ezek. 16. 8. I spread my skirt over t. and covered
32. 3. I will therefore spread out my net over t.
Dan. 4. 25. and seven times shall pass over t. 32.
Nah. 3. 19. all that hear shall clap the hands over t.
Zeph. 3. 17. he will rejoice over t. he will joy over t.

Through THEE.

Psal. 44. 5. thr. t. will we push down our enemies

To or unto THEE.

Gen. 4. 7. unto t. shall be his desire, thou shalt rule
13. 15. to t. will I give it, 17. | 17. 8. | 26. 3. | 28. 4, 13. | 35. 12.
18. 10. he said, I will certainly return unto t. 14.
20. 16. behold, he is to t. a covering of the eyes
27. 29. let people and nations bow down to t.
28. 15. done that which I have spoken to t. of
22. I will surely give the tenth of all unto t.
29. 19. better I give her to t. than to another
31. 12. I have seen all that Laban doth unto t.
16. now then whatsoever God hath said unto t. do
32. discern what is thine with me, and take to t.
39. that which was torn I brought not unto t.
52. that I will not pass over this heap to t.
38. 16. go to, I pray thee, let me come in unto t.
42. 37. if I bring him not to t. 43. 9. | 44. 32.
44. 8. behold, the money we brought again unto t.
50. 17. forgive, I pray thee, for they did unto t. evil
Exod. 3. 12. and this shall be a token unto t.
4. 16. he shall be to t. instead of a mouth
13. 9. it shall be unto t. for a sign, 2 Kings 19. 29. Isa. 38. 7.
18. 22. a great matter they shall bring unto t.
28. 1. take unto t. Aaron thy brother and his sons
30. 23. take thou also unto t. principal spices
33. 5. that I may know what to do unto t.
Lev. 21. 8. he shall be holy unto t. for I am holy
24. 2. that they bring unto t. pure oil olive
Num. 6. 25. the Lord be gracious unto t.
11. 23. whether my word shall come to pass unto t.
18. 2. that the tribe of Levi may be joined unto t. 4.
19. it is a covenant of salt unto t. and to thy seed
22. 38. Balaam said to Balak, lo, I am come unto t.
Deut. 4. 35. unto t. it was shewed that thou mightest
7. 25. shalt not take the gold of their gods unto t.
15. 9. he cry to Lord and it be sin unto t. 24. 15.
18. 15. the Lord will raise up unto t. a prophet
18. I will raise them up a prophet like unto t.
22. 7. let the dam go, and take the young to t.
23. 15. servant escaped from his master unto t.
33. 29. who is like unto t. 1 Sam. 26. 15. Psal. 35. 10. | 71. 19.
Josh. 1. 17. as to Moses, so will we hearken unto t.
2. 18. bring all thy father's household home unto t.
Judg. 7. 4. of whom I say unto t. this shall not go
17. 3. now therefore I will restore it unto t.
Ruth 3. 13. if he will perform unto t. the part of
4. 15. he shall be unto t. a restorer of thy life, daughter-in-law who is better to t. than seven sons
1 Sam. 1. 8. am not I better to t. than ten sons?
8.7. in all that they say unto t. || 8. so do they unto t.
9. 17. behold the man I speak to t. of shall reign
11. 3. and then we will come out to t.
16. 3. thou shalt anoint him whom I name unto t.
17. 45. but I come to t. in the name of the Lord
20. 21. for there is peace to t. || 25. 6. peace be to t.
28. 8. bring me him up whom I shall name unto t.
10. there shall no punishment happen to t.
2 Sam. 3. 12. to bring about all Israel unto t.
12. 14. the child that is born unto t. shall surely die
17. 3. and I will bring back all the people unto t.
19. 7. that will be worse unto t. than all the evil
20. 21. his head shall be thrown to t. over the wall
22. 50. I will give thanks unto t. Psal. 18. 49. | 30. 12. | 75. 1. | 119. 62.

2 Sam. 24. 12. choose thee one that I may do it u. t.
1 Kings 3. 12. neither shall any arise like unto t.
8. 52. hearken in all that they call for unto t.
11. 31. and I will give ten tribes unto t.
38. I will be with thee, and will give Israel unto t.
14. 6. for I am sent to t. with heavy tidings
19. 20. go back again, for what have I done to t.
20. 6. I will send my servants unto t. to-morrow
21. 3. give the inheritance of my fathers unto t.
22. 24. went the spirit from me to speak unto t.?
2 Kings 2. 10. if thou see me, it shall be so unto t.
5. 6. now when this letter is come unto t. behold
27. the leprosy of Naaman shall cleave unto t.
6. 7. take it up to t. || 8. 14. what said Elisha to t.
9. 5. he said, I have an errand to t. O captain
11. wherefore came this mad fellow to t.?
20. 14. from whence came they unto t.? Isa. 39. 3.
1 Chr. 12. 18. peace be unto t. and thine helpers
16. 18. unto t. will I give the land, Psal. 105. 11.
2 Chr. 26. 18. it appertaineth not unto t. Uzziah
Ezra 10. 4. arise, for this matter belongeth unto t.
Neh. 9. 26. testified against them to turn them to t.
Esth. 3. 11. the silver is given to t. the people also
Job 7. 20. I have sinned, what shall I do unto t.?
Ps. 5. 2. hearken unto me, for unto t. will I pray, 3.
10. 14. the poor committeth himself unto t.
16. 2. my Lord, my goodness extendeth not to t.
22. 5. they cried unto t. and were delivered
25. 1. unto t. O L. do I lift up my soul, 86. 4. | 143. 8.
27. 8. my heart said unto t. thy face will I seek
28. 1. unto t. will I cry, 2. | 30. 8. | 31. 22. | 56. 9. | 61. 2. | 86. 3. | 88. 13. | 130. 1. | 141. 1.
30. 12. may sing praise to t. 56. 12. | 59. 17. | 66. 4. | 71. 22, 23
32. 5. I acknowledged my sin unto t. and iniquity
62. 12. also unto t. O Lord, belongeth mercy
65. 1. and unto t. shall the vow be performed
2. thou hearest prayer, unto t. shall all flesh come
69. 13. my prayer is unto t. in an acceptable time
86. 8. among the gods there is none like unto t.
89. 8. O Lord G. who is a strong Lord like unto t.?
101. 1. unto t. O Lord, will I sing, 108. 3. | 138. 1. | 144. 9. Heb. 2. 12.
102. 1. hear my prayer, and let my cry come unto t.
120. 3. what shall be given unto t. thou false tongue
123. 1. unto t. will I lift up mine eyes, 141. 8.
139. 12. darkness and light are both alike to t.
Prov. 22. 19. made known to t. this day, even to t.
23. 7. eat and drink, saith he to t. but his heart
25. 7. better it be said unto t. come up hither
Isa. 14. 10. all they shall speak and say unto t.
30. 19. he will be very gracious unto t. at thy cry
36. 12. hath my master sent me to t. to speak
47. 9. but these two things shall come to t.
15. thus shall they be unto t. with whom thou
49. 18. all these gather together and come to t.
51. 19. these two things are come unto t.
55. 5. nations that knew not thee shall run unto t.
60. 19. neither shall the moon give light unto t. the Lord shall be unto t. an everlasting light
Jer. 2. 31. we are lords, we will come no more unto t.
3. 22. behold, we come unto t. for thou art our God
10. 6. forasmuch as there is none like unto t.
7. who would not fear, for to t. doth it appertain?
11. 20. for unto t. have I revealed my cause, 20. 12.
15. 19. let them return unto t. but return not thou
20. 15. man-child is born unto t. making him glad
22. 21. I spake unto t. in thy prosperity, but thou
30. 15. I have done these things unto t.
38. 20. which I speak un. t. so it shall be well un. t.
40. 4. if thou come with me, I will look well un. t.
44. 16. as for the word, we will not hearken unto t
45. 5. but thy life will I give unto t. for a prey
48. 27. for was not Israel a derision unto t.?
Lam. 2. 13. what thing shall I liken to t. O Jerus. what shall I equal to t. that I may comfort thee?
4. 21. the cup also shall pass through unto t.
5. 21. turn thou us unto t. and we shall be turned
Ezek. 3. 6. they would have hearkened unto t.
7. the house of Israel would not hearken unto t.
16. 5. no eye pitied thee, to do any of these unto t
6. I said unto t. when thou wast in thy blood, live
34. givest a reward, and no reward is given unto t
60. I will establish unto t. an everlasting covenan
61. and I will give them unto t. for daughters
Dan. 4. 26. thy kingdom shall be sure unto t.
31. to t. it is spoken, the kingdom is departed
9. 7. O Lord, righteousness belongeth unto t.
Hos. 6. 4. O Ephraim, what shall I do unto t.?
Joel 1. 19. to t. will I cry || 20. the beasts cry unto t.
Amos 4. 12. thus will I do unto t. I will do this unto t.
Jonah 1. 11. they said, what shall we do unto t.?
2. 7. my prayer came in unto t. into thy temple
Mic. 2. 11. saying, I will prophesy unto t. of wine
4. 8. un. t. shall it come || 6. 3. what have I done u. t.
7. 12. he shall come to t. even from Assyria
Hab. 1. 2. I even cry out unto t. of violence
2. 16. cup of the Lord's right hand be turned unto t.
Zech. 2. 11. the Lord of hosts hath sent me unto t.
9. 9. behold, thy king cometh unto t. Mat. 21. 5.
Mat. 8. 13. as thou hast believed, so be it done unto t.
16. 17. flesh and blood hath not revealed it unto t.
18. and I say also unto t. that thou art Peter
19. I will give unto t. the keys of the kingdom
22. be it far from thee, this shall not be unto t.
18. 17. let him be unto t. as an heathen and publican
22. Jesus saith, I say not unto t. till seven times
20. 14. I will give unto this last even as unto t.
23. 37. thou stonest them sent unto t. Luke 13. 34.
25. 44. or in prison, and did not minister unto t.
Mark 5. 41. I say unto t. arise, Luke 5. 24. | 7. 14.
10. 51. what wilt thou that I do unto t. Luke 18. 41.
Luke 1. 19. I am sent to speak un. t. and shew thee
7. 7. I thought not myself worthy to come unto t.
40. I have somewhat to say u. t. he saith, say on
8. 39. how great things God hath done unto t.
John 4. 26. Jesus saith, I that speak unto t. am he
5. 14. sin no more, lest a worse thing come unto t.
9. 26. what did he to t. || 11. 40. said I not unto t.
17. 11. these are in world, and I am come to t. 13.
18. 30. we would not have delivered him unto t.
19. 11. he that delivered me u. t. hath the great. sin

John 21. 22. what is that to t. follow thou me, 23.
Acts 9. 17. Jesus that appeared unto t. sent me
10. 32. who when he cometh, shall speak unto t.
33. immediately therefore I sent to t.
21. 37. he said to the captain, may I speak unto t.?
26. 16. for I have appeared unto t. for this purpose
Rom. 15. 9. for this cause will I confess to t.
2 Tim. 1. 14. that good thing committed unto t. keep
Philem. 11. but now profitable to t. and me
16. a brother to me, but how much more to t.
Rev. 11. 17. thou hast taken to t. thy great power

Towards THEE.

1 Sam. 19.4. his works have been very good towards t.
2 Kings 3. 14. I would not look towards t. nor see thee
Jer. 12. 3. thou hast tried mine heart towards t.
Ezek. 16. 42. so will I make my fury towards t. to rest
63. because of shame, when I am pacified t. t.
Rom. 11. 22. but towards t. goodness, if thou continue

Under THEE.

Deut. 28. 23. the earth that is under t. shall be iron
Psal. 45. 5. arrows whereby the people fall under t.
Prov. 22. 27. why should he take thy bed from und. t.
Isa. 14. 11. worm is spread und. t. worms cover thee
Obad. 7. that eat thy bread have laid a wound un. t.

With THEE.

Gen. 6. 18. with t. will I establish my covenant
17. 4. my covenant is with t. Ex. 34. 27. Deut. 29. 12.
19. 9. now will we deal worse with t. than with them
21. 22. saying, God is with t. in all that thou doest
24. 40. the Lord will send his angel with t.
26. 3. I will be with t. ‖ 24. I am with t. 28. 15. | 31. 3. | 46. 4. Exod. 3. 12. Deut. 31. 23. Josh. 1. 5. | 3. 7. 1 Kings 11. 38. Isa. 43. 2.
28. we saw certainly that the Lord was with t.
Exod. 18. 19. hearken, and God shall be with t.
25. 22. and there I will meet with t. 30. 6, 36.
33. 14. my presence shall go with t. Deut. 31. 6. 8. Judg. 6. 16.
Lev. 19. 13. wages shall not abide with t. all night
Num. 5. 19. if no man hath lien with t. be thou free
20. some man hath lien with t. beside thy husband
22. 9. G. said to Balaam, what men are these with t.?
Deut. 2. 7. the Lord thy God hath been with t.
4. 40. that it may go well with t. 5. 16. | 6. 3, 18. | 12. 25, 28. | 19. 13. | 22. 7.
15. 16. if he will not go because he is well with t.
20. 1. the Lord thy God is with t. Josh. 1. 9. Judg. 6. 12. 2 Sam. 7. 3.
20. against the city that maketh war with t.
23. 16. he shall dwell with t. even among you
Judg. 4. 9. and she said, I will surely go with t.
7. 2. the people that are with t. are too many
4. this shall go with t. ‖ 19. 20. peace be with t.
Ruth 3. 1. rest for thee, that it may be well with t.
1 Sam. 10. 7. for God is with t. Luke 1. 28.
14. 7. behold, I am with t. according to thine heart
17. 37. the Lord be with t. 20. 13. 1 Chr. 22. 11. 16.
21. 1. why art thou alone, and no man with t.
28. 19. I will deliver Israel with t. to Philistines
29. 8. hast thou found, so long as I have been with t.
2 Sam. 3. 12. and behold my hand shall be with t.
7. 9. I was w. t. 1 Chr. 17. 8. ‖ 13. 20. Amnon been w. t.
13. 26. king said to him, why should he go with t.
14. 17. Lord thy God will be with t. 1 Chr. 28. 20.
15. 20. return thou, mercy and truth be with t.
18. 14. then said Joab, I may not tarry thus with t.
19. 7. there will not tarry one with t. this night
1 Kings 2. 8. thou hast with t. Shimei who cursed me
3. 6. as he walked in uprightness of heart with t.
6. 12. then will I perform my word with t.
13. 8. I will not go in with t. nor eat bread, 16.
17. 18. what have I to do with t. 2 Kings 3. 13. 2 Chron. 35. 21. Mark 5. 7. Luke 8. 28. John 2. 4.
2 Kings 4. 26. is it well w. t. ‖ 5. 26. went not heart w. t.
14. 10. even thou and Judah with t. 2 Chron. 25. 19.
2 Chron. 14. 11. Lord, it is nothing with t. to help
18. 3. and we will be with t. Ezra 10. 4.
25. 7. O king, let not the army of Israel go with t.
Job 5. 23. the beasts shall be at peace with t.
10. 13. I know that this is with t.
14. 3. and bringest me into judgment with t.
5. seeing the number of his months are with t.
15. 11. are the consolations of God small with t.? is there any secret thing with t.
36. 4. he that is perfect in knowledge with t.
40. 15. behold now behemoth, which I made with t.
Psal. 5. 4. neither shall evil dwell with t.
36. 9. for with t. is the fountain of life
39. 12. I am a stranger with t. and a sojourner
73. 23. nevertheless I am continually with t.
94. 20. shall iniquity have fellowship with t.
116. 7. the Lord hath dealt bountifully with t.
128. 2. happy shalt thou be, it shall be well with t.
130. 4. but there is forgiveness with t.
139. 18. when I awake, I am still with t.
Prov. 2. 1. and hide my commandments with t.
5. 17. be only thine own and not strangers with t.
6. 22. it shall talk with t. ‖ 23. 7. his heart is not w. t.
Cant. 6. 1. that we may seek him with t.
Isa. 16. 4. let mine outcasts dwell with t. Moab
41. 10. I am with t. 43. 5. Jer. 1. 8, 19. | 15. 20. | 30. 11. | 46. 28. Acts 18. 10.
11. they that strive with t. shall perish, 12.
49. 25. contend with him that contendeth with t.
54. 9. I have sworn that I would not be wroth w. t.
Jer. 2. 35. I will plead with t. ‖ 12. 1. when I plead w. t.
34. 3. and he shall speak with t. mouth to mouth
51. 20. with t. will I break in pieces the nations
21. with t. will I break in pieces horse and rider
22. with t. will I break in pieces old and young
23. with t. will I break shepherd and husbandman
Ezek. 2. 6. though briars and thorns be with t.
3. 22. go into the plain, I will there talk with t.
16. 8. and I entered into a covenant with t.
59. I will even deal with t. as thou hast done
62. and I will establish my covenant with t.
22. 14. in the days that I shall deal with t.
27. 21. they occupied with t. in lambs and rams
32. 4. I will fill the beasts of the earth with t.
38. 6. his bands and many people w. t. 9. 15. | 39. 4.
Hos. 4. 5. the prophet shall fall with t. in the night
Amos 6. 10. and shall say, is there yet any with t.

Obad. 7. the men that were at peace with t.
Zech. 14. 5. shall come, and all the saints with t.
Mal. 1. 8. will he be pleased with t. or accept persons?
Mat. 8. 29. behold, they cried out, what have we to do with t. Mark 1. 24. Luke 4. 34.
12. 47. stand without, desiring to speak with t.
18. 16. then take with t. one or two more
26. 35. Peter said, tho' I sh. die with t. Mark 14. 31.
Luke 22. 33. I am ready to go w. t. both into prison
John 3. 26. he that was with t. beyond Jordan
9. 37. seen him, and it is he that talketh with t.
17. 5. with the glory which I had with t. before
21. 3. they say unto him, we also go with t.
Acts 8. 20. Peter said, thy money perish with t.
Eph. 6. 3. hon. thy father that it may be well with t.
1 Tim. 6. 21. grace be w. t ‖ 2 Tim. 4. 11. bring w. t. 13.

Within THEE.

Deut. 28. 43. the stranger within t. shall get above
Psal. 122. 8. I will now say, peace be within t.
147. 13. he hath blessed thy children within t.
Prov. 22. 18. is pleasant, if thou keep them within t.
Jer. 4. 14. shall thy vain thoughts lodge within t.
Luke 19. 44. and they shall lay thy children within t.

Without THEE.

Gen. 41. 44. without t. shall no man lift up his hand

See TEACH, TELL.

THEFT, S.

Exod. 22. 3. then he shall be sold for his t.
4. if the t. be certainly found in his hand alive
Mat. 15. 19. out of the heart proceed t. Mark 7. 22.
Rev. 9. 21. neither repented they of their t.

THEIRS.

Gen. 15. 13. shall be a stranger in a land that is not t.
34. 23. shall not every beast of t. be ours?
43. 34. mess was five times as much as any of t.
Exod. 29. 9. and the priests' office shall be t.
Lev. 18. 10. for t. is thine own nakedness
Num. 16. 26. depart and touch nothing of t.
18. 9. every oblation of t. every meat offering of t.
Josh. 21. 10. for t. was the first lot, 1 Chron. 6. 54.
2 Chron. 18. 12. let thy word be like one of t.
Jer. 44. 28. whose words shall stand, mine or t.
Ezek. 7. 11. none shall remain, nor any of t.
44. 29. every delicate thing in Israel shall be t.
Hab. 1. 6. to possess dwelling places that are not t.
Mat. 5. 3. for t. is the kingdom of heaven, 10.
1 Cor. 1. 2. call on our Lord, both t. and ours
2 Tim. 3. 9. folly shall be manifest, as t. was

THEM.

Gen. 1. 27. male and female created he t.
Num. 14. 31. your little ones, t. will I bring in
Deut. 28. 61. t. will the Lord bring upon thee
1 Sam. 2. 30. t. that honour me, I will honour
25. 29. t. shall he sling out, as out of a sling
1 Kings 13. 11. t. they told also to their father
2 Kings 23. 5. t. that burned incense unto Baal
1 Chron. 15. 2. t. hath the Lord chosen to carry
2 Chron. 8. 8. t. did Solomon make to pay tribute
Psal. 5. 11. let t. shout for joy, let t. that love
35. 19. nor let t. wink with eye that hate me
68. 1. let t. also that hate him flee before him
Isa. 41. 12. even t. that contended with thee
56. 7. even t. will I bring to my holy mountain
Dan. 6. 24. they cast t. into the den of lions
Zeph. 1. 5. t. that worship the host of heaven
3. 11. take away t. that rejoice in thy pride
Mat. 13. 41. shall gather out t. which do iniquity
24. 16. then let t. which be in Judea flee into the mountains, Mark 13. 14. Luke 21. 21.
Mark 16. 13. they told it, neither believed they t.
Luke 4. 18. to set at liberty t. that are bruised
11. 52. and t. that were entering in ye hindered
19. 45. cast out t. that sold and t. that bought
24. 33. found the eleven, and t. that were with t.
John 10. 16. other sheep I have, t. also must I bring
Acts 15. 19. my sentence is, that we trouble not t.
21. 24. t. take and purify thyself with t.
22. 19. that I beat t. that believed on thee
Rom. 8. 30. moreover, t. he also called, t. he also justified, and t. he also glorified
11. 14. provoke to emulation t. which are my flesh
1 Cor. 5. 12. to judge t. also that are without
13. but t. that are without God judgeth
16. 18. therefore acknowledge ye t. that are such
1 Thess. 4. 14. even so t. also that sleep in Jesus
2 Thess. 3. 12. now t. that are such, we command
1 Tim. 4. 16. shalt save thyself and t. that hear thee
5. 20. t. that sin rebuke before all, that others
Heb. 10. 14. hath perfected t. that are sanctified
13. 3. remember t. that are in bonds, as bound
1 Pet. 4. 19. let t. that suffer according to will of G.
Rev. 9. 17. thus I saw horses and t. that sat on t.
11. 1. and measure t. that worship therein
13. 6. to blaspheme t. that dwell in heaven
19. 20. beast was taken, and t. that worshipped

Above THEM.

Exod. 18. 11. they dealt proudly, he was above t.
Num. 3. 49. of them that were over and above t.
2 Sam. 22. 49. lifted above t. that rose against me
2 Chr. 34. 4. images that were above t. he cut down

About THEM.

Gen. 35. 5. terror was on the cities round about t.
Ruth 1. 19. that all the city was moved about t.
2 Kings 17. 15. after the heathen that were about t.
2 Chron. 14. 7. and make about t. walls and towers
Ezra 1. 6. all about t. strengthened their hands
Ezek. 1. 18. were full of eyes round about t. four
28. 26. all those that despise them round about t.
Mark 9. 14. he saw a great multitude about t.
Luke 1. 65. fear came on all that dwelt round about t.
2. 9. the glory of the Lord shone round about t.
Jude 7. and the cities about t. in like manner

After THEM.

Gen. 41. 3. seven other kine came up after t. 19. 27.
23. and seven ears withered sprung up after t.
30. shall arise after t. seven years of famine
48. 6. thy issue which thou begettest after t.
Exod. 10. 14. neither after t. shall be such locusts
14. 4. he shall follow after t. and I will be honoured
Lev. 20. 6. that turneth to go a whoring after t.
Deut. 1. 8. to give it to them and their seed after t.
4. 37. therefore he chose their seed after t. 10. 15.

Deut. 12. † 30. take heed, that thou be not snared a. t.
Josh. 2. 5. pursue after t. quickly ye shall overtake
7. the men pursued af. t. 8. 16. Judg. 8. 12. | 20. 45.
Judg. 2. 10. there arose another generation after t.
Ruth 2. 9. the field that they reap, go thou after t.
1 Sam. 6. 12. the lords of the Philistines went a. t.
14. 22. they followed hard after t. in the battle
1 Kings 9. 21. upon the children that were left after t. did Solomon levy tribute, 2 Chron. 8. 8.
2 Kings 7. 15. they went after t. to Jordan, and lo
10. 29. Jehu departed not from after t. to wit
1 Chr. 14. 14. go not up a. t. ‖ Neh. 12. 38. and I a. t.
Job 30. 5. they cried after t. as after a thief
Jer. 2. 25. I loved strangers, and after t. will I go
9. 16. I will send a sword after t. 49. 37. Ezek. 5. 2, 12. | 12. 14.
25. 26. the king of Sheshach shall drink after t.
32. 18. thou recompensest the iniquity of the fathers into the bosom of their children after t.
39. fear me, for the good of their children after t.
39. 5. but the Chaldeans' army pursued after t.
50. 21. waste and utterly destroy after t.
Ezek. 29. 16. when they shall look after t.
34. 6. was scattered, none did search or seek after t.
Dan. 7. 24. and another king shall rise after t.
Zech. 6. 6. and the white horses go forth after t.
7. 14. thus the land was desolate after t.
Luke 17. 23. see here, or see there, go not a. t. 21. 8.
Acts 20. 30. to draw away disciples after t.

Against THEM.

Gen. 14. 15. he divided himself against t. by night
Exod. 32. 10. that my wrath may wax hot against t.
Num. 12. 9. Deut. 2. 15. | 31. 17. Judg. 2. 15.
Num. 16. 19. Korah gathered the congregation ag. t.
21. 33. Og king of Bashan went out against t.
Deut. 20. 19. destroy trees by forcing an axe ag. t.
28. 25. thou shalt go out one way ag. t. and flee
31. 21. this song shall testify ag. t. as a witness
28. and call heaven and earth to record ag. t.
Josh. 8. 22. the other issued out of the city ag. t.
22. 33. did not intend to go up ag. t. in battle
Judg. 11. 25. did he ever strive or fight against t.
2 Sam. 24. 1. he moved Dav. ag. t. to say, go number
2 Kings 17. 15. testimonies which he testified ag. t.
1 Chron. 5. 11. children of Gad dwelt over ag. t.
20. they were helped ag. t. for they cried to God
2 Chron. 20. 16. to-morrow go ye down ag. t. 17.
24. 19. prophets testified ag. t. Neh. 9. 26, 29, 30, 34.
28. 12. stood up ag. t. that came from the war
Ezra 4. 5. hired counsellors against t. to frustrate
8. 22. but his wrath is against t. that forsake him
Neh. 4. 9. we set a watch against t. day and night
5. 7. and I set a great assembly against t.
9. 10. knewest that they dealt proudly against t.
12. 9. brethren were over ag. t. in the watches
13. 2. hired Balaam ag. t. ‖ 15. I testified ag. t. 21.
Psal. 17. 7. savest from those that rise up ag. t.
34. 16. the face of the Lord is against t. that do evil, 1 Pet. 3. 12.
Isa. 3. 9. their countenance doth witness against t.
5. 25. he hath stretched forth his hand against t.
13. 17. behold, I will stir up the Medes against t.
14. 22. I will rise up ag. t. ‖ 63. 10. he fought ag. t.
Jer. 1. 16. and I will utter my judgments ag. t.
4. 12. I will give sentence a. t. ‖ 23. 32. I am a. t.
25. 30. prophesy a. t. Ezek. 6. 2. | 13. 17. | 25. 2.
26. 19. evil he pronounced ag. t. 35. 17. | 36. 31.
Lam. 1. 13. he sent fire, and it prevaileth ag. t.
Ezek. 15. 7. and I will set my face against t.
20. 8. to accomplish my anger ag. t. in Egypt
35. 11. thou hast used out of thy hatred ag. t.
38. 17. that I would bring thee against t.
Dan. 7. 21. and the same horn prevailed against t.
Hos. 8. 5. mine anger is kindled against t.
10. 10. the people shall be gathered against t.
Mat. 10. 18. for a testimony against t. Mark 6. 11. | 13. 9. Luke 9. 5.
Mark 12. 12. spoken that parable ag. t. Luke 20. 19.
Acts 13. 51. shook off the dust of their feet against t.
16. 22. the multitude rose up together against t.
19. 16. in whom evil spirit was, prevailed ag. t.
26. 10. I gave my voice a. t. ‖ 11. being mad a. t.
Rom. 2. 2. judgment of God is ag. t. that commit
Col. 3. 19. love your wives, and be not bitter ag. t.
2 Pet. 2. 11. bring not railing accusation against t.
Rev. 11. 7. the beast shall make war against t.

See FIGHT, OVER.

Among or *amongst* THEM.

Gen. 47. 6. knowest any man of activity among t.
Exod. 7. 5. bring children of Israel from among t.
10. 2. tell my signs which I have done amongst t.
25. 8. that I may dwell a. t. 29. 46. Psal. 68. 18.
30. 12. that there be no plague a. t. when numbered
Lev. 15. 31. defile my tabernacle that is among t.
Num. 1. 47. the Levites were not numbered am. t.
11. 1. and the fire of the Lord burnt among t. 3.
4. the mixt multitude among t. fell a lusting
16. 3. and the Lord is among t. Psal. 68. 17.
18. 20. Aaron shall have no part a. t. Josh. 14. 3.
23. 21. and the shout of a king is among t.
Deut. 7. 20. the Lord will send the hornet among t.
Josh. 8. 33. the stranger, as he that was born a. t.
35. the strangers that were conversant among t.
9. 16. they understood that they dwelt among t.
20. 4. give him a place that he may dwell am. t.
24. 5. according to that which I did amongst t.
Judg. 1. 30. but the Canaanites dwelt among t.
10. 16. put away the strange gods from among t.
1 Sam. 6. 6. when he wrought among t. Neh. 9. 17
9. 22. made them sit in the chiefest place among t.
10. 10. prophets met him, and he prophesied a. t.
2 Sam. 19. 28. set thy servant am. t. that did eat
2 Kings 17. 25. therefore the Lord sent lions a. t.
1 Chr. 21. 6. Levi and Benjamin not counted a. t.
26. 31. there were found mighty men among t.
2 Chron. 20. 25. found am. t. abundance of spoil
28. 15. and clothed all that were naked among t.
Ezra 2. 65. there were among t. 200 singing men
Neh. 4. 11. till we come in the midst a. t. and slay
Esth. 9. 21. wrote to establish the Purim among t.
Job 1. 6. and Satan came also among t. 2. 1.
15. 19. and no stranger passed among t.

Psal. 22. 18. they part my garments *among t.* and cast lots on my vesture, *Mat.* 27. 35. *John* 19. 24.
55. 15. let death seize them, wickedness is *a. t.*
57. 4. and I lie even *among t.* that are set on fire
68. 25. *a. t.* were damsels playing with timbrels
78. 45. he sent divers sorts of flies *among t.*
49. trouble, by sending evil angels *among t.*
99. 6. and Samuel *a. t.* that call upon his name
105. 27. they shewed his signs *a. t.* and wonders
136. 11. and brought out Israel from *among t.*
Cant. 4. 2. and none is barren *among t.* 6. 6.
Isa. 5. 27. none shall be weary or stumble *among t.*
8. 15. and many *among t.* shall stumble and fall
41. 28. for I beheld, and there was no man *a. t.*
43. 9. who *a. t.* can declare this, and shew things
48. 14. which *among t.* hath declared these things
66. 19. I will set a sign *among t.* and will send
Jer. 6. 15. they shall fall *among t.* that fall, 8. 12.
18. and know, O congregation, what is *among t.*
12. 14. pluck out the house of Judah from *a. t.*
24. 10. I will send famine and pestilence *among t.*
25. 16. because of the sword that I will send *a. t.*
37. 10. there remained but wounded men *among t.*
41. 8. ten men found *among t.* that said, slay us not
Lam. 1. 17. Jerusalem as a menstruous woman *a. t.*
Ezek. 2. 5. there hath been a prophet *a. t.* 33. 33.
3. 15. and remained there *among t.* seven days
25. and thou shalt not go out *among t.*
9. 2. and one man *among t.* had a writer's inkhorn
12. 10. concerneth all Israel that are *among t.*
12. and the prince that is *among t.* shall bear
22. 26. I am profan. *a. t.* ‖ 30. I sought a man *a. t.*
33. 33. they shall know that a prophet been *a. t.*
34. 24. and my servant David a prince *among t.*
35. 11. I will make myself known *among t.*
Dan. 1. 19. *among t.* was found none like Daniel
7. 8. there came up *among t.* another little horn
11. 24. he shall scatter *among t.* the prey and spoil
Hos. 7. 7. there is none *among t.* that calleth to me
Zech. 12. 8. that is feeble *a. t.* shall be as David
14. 13. tumult from the Lord shall be *among t.*
Mat. 11. 11. I say, *a. t.* that are born of women
Mark 6. 41. and the two fishes divided he *a. t.*
Luke 9. 46. then there arose a reasoning *among t.*
22. 24. and there was also a strife *among t.*
55. Peter sat down *among t.* in the hall
John 9. 16. and there was a division *among t.*
15. 24. if I had not done *among t.* the works which
Acts 4. 34. nor was there any *among t.* that lacked
17. 33. so Paul departed from *among t.*
18. 11. continued, teaching the word of God *a. t.*
20. 32. inheritance *a. t.* that are sanctified, 26. 18.
Rom. 11. 17. a wild olive tree, were grafted in *a. t.*
1 *Cor.* 2. 6. we speak wisdom *a. t.* that are perfect
2 *Cor.* 6. 17. come out from *a. t.* and be ye separate
2 *Pet.* 2. 8. that righteous man dwelling *among t.*
3 *John* 9. who loveth the pre-eminence *among t.*
Jude 15. to convince all that are ungodly *among t.*
Rev. 7. 15. sitteth on the throne shall dwell *a. t.*

At THEM.

Num. 21. 30. we have shot *at t.* Heshbon is perished
Deut. 7. 21. thou shalt not be affrighted *at t.*
Psal. 10. 5. as for all his enemies, he puffeth *at t.*
59. 8. but thou, O Lord, shalt laugh *at t.*
64. 7. but God shall shoot *at t.* with an arrow
Jer. 10. 2. for the heathen are dismayed *at t.*

Before THEM.

Gen. 18. 8. and set it *b. t.* ‖ 33. 3. he passed over *b. t.*
Exod. 10. 14. *before t.* there were no such locusts
13. 21. the Lord went *before t.* by day, *Num.* 14. 14.
21. 1. judgments which thou shalt set *before t.*
Num. 10. 33. and the ark of the Lord went *before t.*
27. 17. to go out and in *before t.* 1 *Sam.* 18. 16.
Deut. 2. 12. destroyed them from *before t.* 21, 22.
1 *Chron.* 5. 25. *Neh.* 9. 24.
28. 25. and thou shalt flee seven ways *before t.*
Josh. 6. 13. armed men went *before t.* rereward after
18. 1. and the land was subdued *before t.*
21. 44. stood not a man of their enemies *before t.*
Judg. 3. 27. Ehud *before t.* ‖ 7. 24. take *b. t.* waters
1 *Sam.* 10. 5. with a tabret, a pipe and harp, *before t.*
2 *Sam.* 10. 16. and Shobach went *b. t.* 1 *Chr.* 19. 16.
20. 8. when they were in Gibeon, Amasa went *b. t.*
1 *Kings* 8. 50. give them compassion *b. t.* 2 *Chr.* 30. 9.
22. 10. prophets prophesied *before t.* 2 *Chr.* 18. 9.
2 *Kings* 3. 24. so that the Moabites fled *before t.*
4. 31. Gehazi passed on *b. t.* ‖ 44. so he set it *b. t.*
6. 22. set bread and water *bef. t.* that they may eat
17. 11. whom the Lord carried away *before t.*
2 *Chron.* 7. 6. the priest sounded trumpets *before t.*
Neh. 12. 36. and Ezra the scribe *before t.*
Psal. 22. 25. I'll pay my vows *before t.* that fear him
54. 3. they have not set God *before t.* 86. 14.
78. 55. he cast out the heathen also *before t.*
105. 17. he sent a man *before t.* even Joseph
Eccl. 4. 16. no end of all that have been *before t.*
9. 1. either love or hatred by all that is *before t.*
Isa. 30. 8. now go write it *before t.* in a table
42. 16. I will make darkness light *before t.*
63. 12. that led them, dividing the water *before t.*
Jer. 1. 17. not dismayed, lest I confound thee *bef. t.*
9. 13. have forsaken my law which I set *before t.*
32. 13. and I charged Baruch *before t.* saying
33. 24. they should no more be a nation *before t.*
49. 37. to be dismayed *before t.* that seek their life
Ezek. 8. 11. and there stood *before t.* seventy men
16. 18. hast set mine oil and incense *before t.* 19.
23. 24. I will set judgment *before t.* they shall judge
32. 10. when I shall brandish my sword *before t.*
44. 11. shall stand *before t.* to minister to them
Joel 2. 3. a fire devoureth *bef. t.* and behind them,
the land is as the garden of Eden *before t.*
10. the earth shall quake *before t.* the sun be dark
Amos 2. 9. yet I destroyed the Amorite *before t.*
Mic. 2. 13. the breaker is come up *bef. t.* and their
king shall pass *b. t.* and Lord on head of them
Zech. 12. 8. David as the angel of the Lord *before t.*
Mat. 2. 9. lo, the star which they saw went *before t.*
14. 6. she danced *b. t.* ‖ 26. 70. but he denied *b. t.*
17. 2. and was transfigured *before t.* *Mark* 9. 2.
Mark 6. 41. gave to his disciples to set *b. t.* 8. 6, 7.
10. 32. Jesus went *before t.* and they were amazed
Luke 22. 47. Judas went *b. t.* ‖ 24. 43. he did eat *b. t.*
19. 28. ascending up to Jerus. Jesus went *before t.*
John 10. 4. shepherd goeth *before t.* sheep follow
12. 37. tho' he had done so many miracles *before t.*
Acts 16. 34. he set meat *b. t.* ‖ 22. 30. set Paul *b. t.*
Gal. 2. 14. I said to Peter *bef. t.* all, if thou being

Behind THEM.

Exod. 14. 19. the pillar removed and stood *behind t.*
Josh. 8. 20. when the men of Ai looked *behind t.*
Judg. 20. 40. the Benjamites looked *behind t.*
2 *Sam.* 5. 23. but fetch a compass behind *t.*
2 *Chron.* 13. 13. an ambushment to come about *b. t.*
Joel 2. 3. *b. t.* a flame burneth, *b t.* a wilderness

Besides THEM

Job 1. 14. and the asses were feeding *beside t.*
Ezek. 10. 16. wheels turned not from *b. t.* 19. | 11. 22.
Mat. 25. 20. I have gained *besides t.* five talents, 22.

Between THEM.

Exod. 22. 11. an oath of the Ld. shall be *between t.*
28. 33. and bells of gold *between t.* round about
Josh. 8. 11. now there was a valley *betw. t.* and Ai
1 *Sam.* 17. 3. a valley *between t.* and the Philistines
26. 13. David stood, a great space being *between t.*
2 *Sam.* 14. † 6. and there was no deliverer *betw. t.*
21. 7. because of the Lord's oath *between t.*
1 *Kings* 18. 6. so they divided the land *between t.*
Job 41. 16. that no air can come *between t.*
Zech. 6. 13. counsel of peace shall be *betw. t.* both
Acts 15. 39. the contention was so sharp *between t.*

By THEM.

Lev. 19. 31. nor after wizards to be defiled *by t.*
Josh. 23. 7. nor cause to swear *by t.* nor serve
Judg. 3. 1. the Lord left, to prove Israel *by t.* 4.
2 *Sam.* 15. 36. *by t.* ye shall send to me every thing
2 *Chron.* 24. 13. and the work was perfected *by t.*
Job 36. 31. for *by t.* judgeth he the people
Psal. 19. 11. moreover *by t.* is thy servant warned
Isa. 7. 20. namely *by t.* beyond the river
Jer. 5. 7. and have sworn *by t.* that are no gods
Ezek. 1. 19. creatures went, the wheels went *by t.*
14. 3. should I be enquired at of all *by t.?*
Hab. 1. 16. because *by t.* their portion is fat
Mat. 5. 21. that it was said *by t.* of old, 27. 33.
Mark 6. 48. he cometh, and would have passed *by t.*
Luke 24. 4. two men stood *by t.* in white, *Acts* 1. 10.
Acts 4. 16. a notable miracle has been done *by t.*
15. 12. what wonders God had wrought *by t.*
Rom. 10. 5. who doeth those things shall live *by t.*
19. I will provoke you to jealousy *by t.*
1 *Cor.* 1. 11. *by t.* which are of the house of Chloe
1 *Tim.* 1. 18. thou *by t.* mightest war a good warfare
Heb. 2. 3. confirmed to us *by t.* which heard him
1 *Pet.* 1. 12. which are now reported to you *by t.*

Concerning THEM.

Num. 32. 28. so *con. t.* Moses commanded Eleazar
Judg. 15. 3. Samson said, *con. t.* I shall be blameless
Neh. 11. 23. it was the king's commandment *con. t.*
1 *Thess.* 4. 13. to be ignorant *con. t.* which are asleep
1 *John* 2. 26. have I written *con. t.* that seduce you

For THEM.

Gen. 6. 21. it shall be for food for thee and *for t.*
34. 21. the land, behold, it is large enough *for t.*
43. 32. and they set on bread *for t.* by themselves
Exod. 14. 25. let us flee, the Lord fighteth *for t.*
Lev. 4. 20. and the priest shall make an atonement
for t. 9. 7. | 10. 17. *Num.* 8. 21. | 16. 46.
7. 7. there is one law *for t.* the priest shall have it
Num. 10. 33. to search out a resting-place *for t.*
11. 22. shall herds be slain *for t.* fishes gather. *for t.*
Deut. 28. 32. fail with longing *for t.* all the day
33. 2. from his right hand went a fiery law *for t.*
Josh. 18. 10. Joshua cast lots *for t.* in Shiloh
19. 9. the part of Judah was too much *for t.*
47. the coast of Dan went out too little *for t.*
Judg. 21. 16. how shall we do for wives *for t.?*
17. there must be an inheritance *for t.* escaped
Ruth 1. 13. would ye tarry *for t.* till they were gro.
2 *Chron.* 30. 18. but Hezekiah prayed *for t.* saying
34. 21. go enquire of the Lord for me and *for t.*
Neh. 1. 5. God keepeth mercy *for t.* that love him
5. 2. we take up corn *for t.* that we may eat and live
9. 15. broughtest forth water *for t.* out of the rock
Esth. 5. 8. come to the banquet I shall prepare *for t.*
Job 6. 19. the companies of Sheba waited *for t.*
22. 17. and what can the Almighty do *for t.?*
24. 5. wilderness yieldeth food *for t.* and children
Psal. 31. 19. which thou hast laid up *for t.* that
fear thee, *for t.* that trust in thee
104. 8. to the place which thou hast founded *for t.*
106. 45. and he remembered *for t.* his covenant
126. 2. the Lord hath done great things *for t.*
Isa. 23. 13. till the Assyrian founded it *for t.*
18. for her merchandise shall be *for t.* that dwell
34. 17. he hath cast the lot *for t.* he divided to them
35. 1. the solitary places shall be glad *for t.*
Jer. 3. 2. in the ways hast thou sat *for t.* as Arabian
7. 16. neither lift up cry nor prayer *for t.*
16. 6. nor shall men lament *for t.* nor cut themselv.
7. neither shall men tear themselves *for t.*
18. 20. I stood before thee to speak good *for t.*
28. 13. but thou shalt make *for t.* yokes of iron
Ezek. 7. 11. neither shall there be wailing *for t.*
11. 21. but as *for t.* whose heart walketh after
16. 21. to cause them to pass thro' the fire *for t.*
20. 6. to bring into a land I had espied *for t.*
34. 10. that my flock may not be meat *for t.*
29. and I will raise up *for t.* a plant of renown
36. 37. I will yet be enquired of to do it *for t.*
45. 15. one lamb to make reconciliation *for t.*
46. 17. but his inheritance shall be his son's *for t.*
48. 10. *for t.* even for the priests shall be oblation
Dan. 2. 35. no place was found *for t.* *Rev.* 20. 11.
Hos. 2. 18. make a covenant *for t.* with the beasts
Zech. 10. 8. I will hiss *for t.* and gather them, for
10. into Lebanon place shall not be found *for t.*
Mat. 5. 44. pray *for t.* which despitefully use you,
and persecute you, *Luke* 6. 28.
12. 4. nor lawful *for t.* that were with him
18. 19. it shall be done *for t.* of my Father
Mark 10. 24. how hard *for t.* that trust in riches
Luke 2. 7. there was no room *for t.* in the inn
John 6. 7. is not sufficient *for t.* that every one
John 17. 9. I pray *for t.* I pray not for the world, 20
Acts 8. 15. Peter and John prayed *for t.* that they
10. 24. Cornelius waited *f. t.* and had called friends
17. 16. now while Paul waited *for t.* at Athens
1 *Cor.* 2. 9. things which God hath prepared *for t.*
7. 8. it is good *for t.* if they abide even as I
14. 22. but prophesying serveth *for t.* that believe
2 *Cor.* 5. 15. should live unto him which died *for t.*
Col. 2. 1. I knew what great conflict I have *for t.*
4. 13. hath a great zeal *for t.* that are in Laodicea
Heb. 1. 14. spirits sent forth to minister *for t.* heirs
7. 25. he ever liveth to make intercession *for t.*
11. 16. for he hath prepared *for t.* a city
2 *Pet.* 2. 21. it had been better *for t.* not to known
1 *John* 5. 16. give life *for t.* that sin not to death

From THEM.

Gen. 11. 6. now nothing will be restrained *from t.*
42. 24. he took *from t.* Simeon and bound him
Num. 16. 15. I have not taken one ass *from t.*
18. 26. the tithes which I have given you *from t.*
35. 8. *from t.* that have many ye shall give many;
but *from t.* that have few ye shall give few
Deut. 22. 1. sheep go astray, and hide thyself *f. t.* 4.
31. 17. hide my face *f. t.* 32. 20. *Ezek.* 7. 22. *Mic.* 3. 4.
1 *Sam.* 6. 7. and bring their calves home *from t.*
1 *Chron.* 14. 14. go not after them, turn away *from t.*
2 *Chron.* 20. 10. but they turned *f. t.* and destroyed
Psal. 31. 15. deliver me *from t.* that persecute me
59. 1. defend me *from t.* that rise up against me
84. 11. no good thing will he withhold *from t.*
Prov. 3. 27. withhold not good *from t.* to whom
22. 5. that doth keep his soul shall be far *from t.*
Eccl. 2. 10. what mine eyes desired I kept not *from t.*
Cant. 3. 4. it was but a little that I passed *from t.*
Jer. 8. 13. things I have given shall pass *from t.*
9. 2. that I might leave my people and go *from t.*
18. 20. I stood to turn away thy wrath *from t.*
25. 10. I will take *from t.* the voice of mirth
32. 40. I will not turn away *fr. t.* to do them good
Ezek. 7. 20. therefore I have set it far *from t.*
23. 17. and her mind was alienated *from t.*
24. 25. the day when I take *from t.* their strength
39. 23. therefore hid I my face *from t.* 24.
29. neither will I hide my face any more *from t.*
Hos. 5. 6. he hath withdrawn himself *from t.*
11. 2. as they called them, so they went *from t.*
Mic. 2. 8. pull off the robe with the garment *from t.*
Mat. 9. 15. the bridegroom shall be taken *from t.*
Mark 2. 20. *Luke* 5. 35.
Mark 14. 52. he left the cloth, and fled *fr. t.* naked
Luke 9. 45. understood not, it was hid *from t.* 18. 34.
24. 51. he was parted *from t.* and carried to heaven
John 12. 36. departed, and did hide himself *from t.*
Acts 7. 39. would not obey, but thrust him *from t.*
Rom. 15. 31. that I may be delivered *from t.* that
2 *Cor.* 2. 3. I should have sorrow *from t.* of whom
11. 12. I may cut off occasion *from t.* which desire
Heb. 7. 6. whose descent is not counted *from t.*
2 *Pet.* 2. 18. clean escaped *from t.* who live in error
Rev. 9. 6. desire to die, and death shall flee *from t.*
See Depart, ed.

In THEM.

Exod. 20. 11. for the Lord made heaven and earth,
the sea, and all that *in t.* is, *Acts* 4. 24.
29. 29. to be anointed and be consecrated *in t.*
Lev. 10. 3. I will be sanctified *in t.* that come nigh
18. 5. he shall live *in t.* *Neh.* 9. 29. *Ezek.* 20. 11,
13, 21. *Gal.* 3. 12.
Num. 20. 13. strove, and he was sanctified *in t.*
Deut. 5. 29. O that there were such an heart *in t.*
32. 28. nor is there any understanding *in t.*
Josh. 5. 1. nor was there spirit *in t.* any more
24. 13. cities which ye built not, and ye dwell *in t.*
2 *Kings* 5. 12. may I not wash *in t.* and be clean?
Job 4. 21. doth not their excellency *in t.* go away
Psal. 19. 4. *in t.* he set a tabernacle for the sun
107. 5. hungry, thirsty, their soul fainted *in t.*
115. 8. so is every one that trusts *in t.* 135. 18.
147. 11. Lord taketh pleasure *in t.* that fear him
Prov. 8. 8. there is nothing froward or perverse *in t.*
Eccl. 3. 12. I know there is no good *in t.*
8. 11. their heart is fully set *in t.* to do evil
12. 1. thou shalt say I have no pleasure *in t.*
Isa. 6. 13. teil-tree and oak, whose substance is *in t.*
8. 20. it is because there is no light *in t.*
Jer. 2. 37. and thou shalt not prosper *in t.*
5. 13. the word is not *in t.* ‖ 8. 9. what wisdom is *in t.*
10. 5. cannot do evil, nor is it *in t.* to do good
14. and there is no breath *in t.* 51. 17.
29. 5. build ye houses, and dwell *in t.* 28.
Ezek. 5. 6. my statutes they have not walked *in t.*
13. when I have accomplished my fury *in t.*
10. 17. the spirit of the living creature was *in t.*
18. 24. in trespass and sin, *in t.* shall he die, 26.
28. 25. and when I shall be sanctified *in t.* in sight
33. 10. pine away *in t.* ‖ 37. 8. was no breath *in t.*
Dan. 5. 3. his wives and concubines drank *in t.* 23.
Hos. 14. 9. are right and the just shall walk *in t.*
Amos 5. 11. built houses, but ye shall not dwell *in t.*
Obad. 18. they shall kindle *in t.* and devour them
Mal. 2. 17. that doeth evil, he delighteth *in t.*
Mat. 13. 14. *in t.* is fulfilled the prophecy of Esaias
Luke 13. 14. *in t.* therefore come and be healed
John 5. 39. *in t.* ye think ye have eternal life
17. 10. thine are mine, and I am glorified *in t.*
23. I *in t.* thou in me ‖ 26. may be *in t.* and I *in t.*
Rom. 1. 19. may be known of God, is manifest *in t.*
32. but have pleasure *in t.* that do them
2 *Cor.* 2. 15. *in t.* that are saved, *in t.* that perish
6. 16. God said, I will dwell *in t.* and walk *in t.*
Eph. 2. 10. God ordained that we should walk *in t.*
4. 18. alienated through the ignorance that is *in t.*
Col. 3. 7. in which ye walked, when ye lived *in t.*
2 *Thess.* 2. 10. all deceivableness *in t.* that perish
1 *Tim.* 4. 16. continue *in t.* for in doing this
Heb. 4. 2. not being mixed with faith *in t.* that
1 *Pet.* 1. 11. the spirit of Christ which was *in t.*
2 *Pet.* 3. 16. speaking *in t.* of these things
Rev. 5. 13. and all that are *in t.* heard I, saying
12. 12. rejoice, ye heavens, and ye that dwell *in t.*
15. 1. for *in t.* is filled up the wrath of God
20. 13. delivered up the dead which were *in t.*

Rev. 21. 14. *in t.* the names of the twelve apostles

Into THEM.

Ezek. 37. 10. the breath came *into t.* and they lived
Mark 5. 12. send that we may enter *into t.* *Luke* 8. 32.
Rev. 11. 11. the spirit of life from God entered *into t.*

Of THEM.

Gen. 3. 7. the eyes *of t.* both were opened and knew
19. 13. the cry *of t.* is waxen great before God
Exod. 20. 5. generation *of t.* that hate me, *Deut.* 5. 9.
6. to thousands *of t.* that love me, *Deut.* 5. 10.
35. 35. *of t.* that do any work and that devise
Lev. 4. 2. if a soul shall do against any *of t.*
11. 4. *of t.* ye shall not eat || 22. *of t.* eat, *Deut.* 20. 19.
22. 22. nor make an offering by fire *of t.* on altar
25. 44. *of t.* buy bondmen and bondmaids, 45.
26. 43. the land also shall be left *of t.* and enjoy
Num. 1. 21. those that were numbered *of t.* 23. 25.
| 2. 4, 13. | 3. 22, 34.
3. 49. took money *of t.* that were over and above
7. 5. take it *of t.* || 11. 26. were *of t.* that were written
14. 23. nor shall any *of t.* that provoked me see
16. 34. fled at the cry *of t.* || 26. 64. not a man *of t.*
33. 55. that those which ye let remain *of t.*
Deut. 1. 29. neither be afraid *of t.* 7. 18. | 20. 1, 3.
Josh. 11. 6. *Neh.* 4. 14.
2. 6. ye sh. buy meat *of t.* buy water *of t.* for money
33. 11. loins *of t.* that rise, and *of t.* that hate him
Josh. 10. 8. there shall not a man *of t.* stand before
2 *Sam.* 6. 22. and *of t.* shall I be had in honour
2 *Kings* 10. 14. and slew them, nor left he any *of t.*
1 *Chron.* 5. 20. they cried, he was intreated *of t.*
Ezra 8. 20. all *of t.* were expressed by name
Neh. 10. 31. would not buy it *of t.* on the sabbath
Job 14. 21. are low, but he perceiveth it not *of t.*
Psal. 19. 11. in keeping *of t.* there is great reward
21. 12. make ready arrows against the face *of t.*
24. 6. this is the generation *of t.* that seek him
34. 19. but the Lord delivered him out *of t.* all
22. none *of t.* that trust in him shall be desolate
40. 5. if I would speak *of t.* they are more than
65. 5. and *of t.* that are afar off upon the sea
84. 5. in whose heart are the ways *of t.*
102. 26. all *of t.* shall wax old like a garment
Prov. 21. 6. tossed to and fro *of t.* that seek death
Eccl. 7. 18. that feareth God shall come forth *of t.*
Isa. 9. 16. they that are led *of t.* are destroyed
17. 14. this is the portion *of t.* that spoil us
19. 22. he shall be intreated *of t.* and heal them
39. 2. Hezekiah was glad *of t.* and shewed them
41. 28. that when I asked *of t.* could answer
42. 9. before they spring forth I tell you *of t.*
22. spoiled, they are all *of t.* snared in holes
44. 9. that make an image, are all *of t.* vanity
65. 1. I am sought *of t.* that asked not for me, I am
found *of t.* that sought me not, *Rom.* 10. 20.
66. 19. and I will send those that escape *of t.*
21. I will take *of t.* for priests and Levites
Jer. 8. 19. because *of t.* that dwell in far country
10. 5. be not afraid *of t.* *Ezek.* 2. 6. *Luke* 12. 4.
23. 14. they are all *of t.* unto me as Sodom
25. 14. great kings shall serve themselves *of t.*
29. 22. and *of t.* shall be taken up a curse by all
30. 19. and out *of t.* shall proceed thanksgiving
34. 9. that none should serve himself *of t.* 10.
42. 17. and none *of t.* shall remain, *Ezek.* 7. 11.
Ezek. 7. 16. all *of t.* mourning every one for iniquity
20. 40. all *of t.* in the land shall serve me
23. 6. all *of t.* desirable young men, 12. 23.
15. in dyed attire, all *of t.* princes to look to
38. 4. all *of t.* clothed with all sorts of armour
11. and gates all *of t.* dwelling without walls
Hos. 13. 2. they say *of t.* let the men kiss the calves
Amos 9. 1. cut in the head all *of t.* he that fleeth *of t.*
Mic. 3. 2. who pluck off their skin from *off t.* 3.
7. 13. land desolate because *of t.* that dwell therein
Zech. 11. 13. goodly price that I was prized at *of t.*
Mat. 21. 31. whether *of t.* twain did the will of his
45. they perceived that he spake *of t.*
Mark 12. 23. whose wife shall she be *of t.* *Luke* 20. 33.
Luke 6. 13. *of t.* he chose twelve named apostles
7. 42. tell me, which *of t.* will love him most?
9. 46. which *of t.* should be greatest? 22. 24.
22. 23. which *of t.* it was that should do this thing?
58. another saw him and said, thou art also *of t.*
John 4. 52. then inquired he *of t.* the hour when
16. 4. ye may remember that I told you *of t.*
18. 9. *of t.* which thou gavest me, have I lost none
Acts 15. 14. to take out *of t.* a people for his name
23. 21. there lie in wait *of t.* more than forty men
Rom. 11. 12. if the fall *of t.* be the riches of world,
and diminishing *of t.* the riches of the Gentiles
15. if the casting away *of t.* be the reconciling
2 *Tim.* 3. 11. out *of t.* all the Lord delivered me
Heb. 10. 39. we are not *of t.* who draw back, but *of t.*
Jam. 3. 18. is sown in peace *of t.* that make peace
Rev. 22. 9. *of t.* which keep the sayings of this

See Both, One, Some.

On or *upon* THEM.

Gen. 31. 34. Rachel had taken images and sat *u. t.*
48. 16. Jacob said, let my name be named *on t.*
Exod. 15. 9. my lust shall be satisfied *upon t.*
19. 22. lest the Lord break forth *upon t.* 24.
32. 21. that thou hast brought so great a sin *upon t.*
34. nevertheless I will visit their sin *upon t.*
Lev. 20. 11. their blood shall be *upon t.* 12, 13, 16, 27.
26. 36. *upon t.* that are left will I send a faintness
Num. 11. 17. and I will put of the spirit *upon t.* 29.
16. 33. the earth closed *upon t.* and they perished
Deut. 7. 16. thine eye shall have no pity *upon t.*
25. shalt not desire the silver or gold that is *on t.*
9. 10. *on t.* was written according to all Lord spake
27. 5. thou shalt not lift up any iron tool *upon t.*
32. 23. I will heap mischiefs *upon t.* I will spend
35. the things that shall come *upon t.* make haste
Josh. 10. 11. the Lord cast down great stones *u. t.*
Judg. 9. 57. and *upon t.* came the curse of Jotham
1 *Kings* 18. 28. till the blood gushed out *upon t.*
2 *Kings* 18. 23. if able to set riders *u. t.* *Isa.* 36. 8.
23. 20. he burnt men's bones *upon t.* and returned
1 *Chron.* 9. 27. because the charge was *upon t.*
2 *Chron.* 29. 23. and they laid their hands *on t.*
Acts 6. 6. | 8. 17. | 13. 3.
2 *Chron.* 32. 26. so that wrath of Lord came not *u. t.*
33. 11. Lord brought *upon t.* king of Assyria
36. 17. he brought *upon t.* the king of the Chaldees
Ezra 3. 3. for fear was *up. t.* because of the people
Esth. 8. 17. for the fear of the Jews fell *upon t.*
9. 3. because the fear of Mordecai fell *upon t.*
27. Jews took *upon t.* to keep the days of Purim
Job 4. 19. how much less *on t.* that dwell in houses
21. 9. neither is the rod of God *upon t.*
Psal. 33. 18. eye of the Lord is *up. t.* that fear him
48. 6. fear took hold *upon t.* there, and pain as of
62. 10. if riches increase, set not your heart *upon t.*
69. 24. pour out thine indignation *upon t.*
78. 24. and had rained down manna *upon t.* to eat
27. he rained flesh also *up. t.* as dust and fowls
49. he cast *upon t.* the fierceness of his anger
94. 23. he shall bring *upon t.* their own iniquity
103. 17. mercy to everlasting *upon t.* that fear him
106. 29. and the plague brake in *upon t.*
118. 7. therefore shall I see my desire *upon t.* that
Isa. 9. 2. *upon t.* hath the light shined
26. 16. a prayer, when thy chastening was *upon t.*
27. 11. that made them will not have mercy *on t.*
49. 10. he that hath mercy *on t.* shall lead them
Jer. 2. 3. evil shall come *upon t.* saith the Lord
11. 8. I will bring *u. t.* 11. | 23. 12. | 36. 31. | 49. 37.
12. 15. I will return, and have compassion *on t.*
24. 6. I will set mine eyes *up. t.* for good, 32. 42.
33. 26. to return, for I will have mercy *upon t.*
46. 21. the day of their calamity was come *up. t.*
Ezek. 23. 16. she doted *up. t.* || 37. 8. flesh came *u. t.*
44. 17. no wool shall come *u. t.* while they minister
Dan. 3. 27. nor the smell of fire had passed *on t.*
Hos. 5. 10. I will pour out my wrath *u. t.* like water
7. 12. they shall go, I will spread my net *upon t.*
Amos 9. 4. I will set mine eyes *u. t.* for evil and not
Hab. 1. 13. wherefore lookest thou *up. t.* that deal
Zech. 10. 6. bring them again, for I have mercy *u. t.*
14. 17. who will not come up *upon t.* shall be no
Mat. 19. 13. should put his hands *u. t.* *Mark* 10. 16.
Luke 1. 50. and his mercy is *on t.* that fear him
2. 9. and lo, the angel of the Lord came *upon t.*
John 20. 22. when he said this, he breathed *on t.*
Acts 4. 1. as they spake, the Sadducees came *u. t.*
3. they laid hands *on t.* || 33. great grace was *up. t.*
5. 5. great fear came *on* all *t.* that heard these things
11. 15. the Holy Ghost fell *on t.* as on us, 19. 6.
19. 13. took *upon t.* to call over them which had
16. and the man leapt *on t.* and overcame them
21. 23. we have four men which have a vow *on t.*
Rom. 11. 22. *on t.* which fell, severity; but to thee
Gal. 6. 16. peace be *on t.* and mercy, and on Israel
1 *Thess.* 2. 16. wrath is come *u. t.* to the uttermost
5. 3. then sudden destruction cometh *upon t.*
2 *Thess.* 1. 8. taking vengeance *on t.* that know not
Heb. 5. 2. and *on t.* that are out of the way
Rev. 6. 10. avenge our blood *on t.* that dwell on
7. 16. nor shall the sun light *on t.* nor any heat
11. 11. and great fear fell *upon t.* which saw them
16. 2. and *upon t.* which worshipped his image

Over THEM.

Exod. 1. 11. they did set *over t.* task-masters
5. 14. which Pharaoh's task-masters had set *over t.*
18. 21. place such *over t.* to be rulers of thousands
Num. 7. 2. and were *over t.* that were numbered
14. 14. have heard that thy cloud standeth *over t.*
Judg. 9. 8. the trees went to anoint a king *over t.*
11. 11. the people made Jephthah captain *over t.*
1 *Sam.* 8. 7. rejected me that I sh. not reign *over t.*
9. the manner of the king that shall reign *over t.*
19. 20. and Samuel standing as appointed *over t.*
22. 2. and David became a captain *over t.*
2 *Sam.* 2. 7. Judah have anointed me king *over t.*
1 *Chron.* 9. 20. Phinehas was the ruler *over t.*
27. 26. and *over t.* that did the work was Ezri
2 *Chron.* 2. 11. he hath made thee king *over t.* 9. 8.
Neh. 9. 28. so that they had the dominion *over t.*
Esth. 9. 1. the enemies hoped to have power *over t.*
Psal. 49. 14. the upright shall have dominion *over t.*
106. 41. and they that hated them ruled *over t.*
Prov. 20. 26. a wise king bringeth the wheel *over t.*
Isa. 3. 4. babes shall rule *o. t.* || 12. women rule *o. t.*
19. 4. a fierce king shall rule *over t.* saith the Lord
52. 5. they that rule *over t.* make them to howl
Jer. 15. 3. and I will appoint *over t.* four kinds
23. 4. I will set shepherds *over t.* which shall feed
31. 28. like as I have watched *over t.* to pluck up,
so will I watch *over t.* to build and to plant
32. 41. yea, I will rejoice *over t.* to do them good
44. 27. I will watch *over t.* for evil, not for good
Ezek. 10. 1. appeared *over t.* as a sapphire stone
19. glory of the God of Israel was *over t.* 11. 22.
34. 23. and I will set up one shepherd *over t.*
37. 24. David my servant shall be king *over t.*
Dan. 2. 38. and hath made thee ruler *over t.* all
Joel 2. 17. that the heathen should rule *over t.*
Mic. 3. 6. and the day shall be dark *over t.*
4. 7. the Lord shall reign *over t.* in mount Zion
Hab. 1. 14. creeping things that have no ruler *over t.*
Zech. 9. 14. and the Lord shall be seen *over t.*
Mat. 20. 25. the princes of the Gentiles exercise
dominion *over t.* *Mark* 10. 42. *Luke* 22. 25.
Luke 11. 44. the men that walk *over t.* are not aware
19. 27. who would not that I should reign *over t.*
Acts 19. 13. to call *over t.* that had evil spirits
Rom. 5. 14. even *over t.* that had not sinned after
Col. 2. 15. a shew of them, triumphing *over t.* in it
Rev. 9. 11. they had a king *over t.* whose name is
11. 10. earth shall rejoice *over t.* and make merry

Through THEM.

Judg. 2. 22. that *thro' t.* I may prove Israel whether
Jer. 9. 10. are burnt up, so that none can pass *thro' t.*

To or *unto* THEM.

Gen. 37. 13. come, and I will send thee *unto t.*
42. 7. strange *unto t.* and spake roughly *unto t.*
25. give them provision, thus did Joseph *unto t.*
50. 21. Joseph comforted them, spoke kindly *un. t.*
Exod. 2. 25. and G. had respect *un. t.* 2 *Kings* 13. 23.
3. 13. what shall I say *unto t.* || 14. 20. darkness *to t.*
14. 22. the waters were a wall *to t.* on the right
20. 5. thou shalt not bow down thyself *to t.* nor
serve them, *Josh.* 23. 7. 2 *Kings* 17. 35.
Exod. 30. 21. shall be a statute for ever *to t.* *Lev.* 17. 7.
Lev. 6. 17. I have given it *unto t.* for their portion
Num. 4. 19. but thus do *un. t.* || 8. 22. so did they *un. t.*
16. 30. swallow up, with all that appertain *unto t.*
33. 56. I shall do to you, as I thought to do *unto t.*
35. 6. and *to t.* ye shall add forty and two cities
Deut. 1. 8. which the L. sware to give *unto t.* 31. 23.
4. 7. what nation who hath God so nigh *unto t.*?
Josh. 9. 20. this we will do *un. t.* || 26. so did he *un. t.*
Judg. 2. 17. and they bowed themselves *unto t.*
9. 33. mayest do *to t.* as thou shalt find occasion
15. 11. as they did unto me, so have I done *unto t.*
1 *Sam.* 30. 19. there was nothing lacking *to t.*
27. sent spoil *to t.* which were in, 28, 29, 30, 31.
2 *Sam.* 20. 3. and fed them, but went not in *unto t.*
1 *Kings* 12. 7. if thou wilt speak good words *to t.*
2 *Kings* 9. 18. saying, the messenger came *to t.* 20.
12. 5. let the priests take it *to t.* every man
1 *Chron.* 9. 27. the opening thereof pertained *to t.*
2 *Chron.* 32. 6. and spake comfortably *to t.*
Ezra 4. 20. tribute and custom was paid *unto t.*
6. 21. such as had separated themselves *unto t.*
Neh. 5. 11. restore *to t.* this day their lands, houses
Esth. 9. 22. month was turned *unto t.* from sorrow
Job 24. 12. yet God layeth not folly *to t.*
17. morning is *to t.* even as the shadow of death
Psal. 28. 4. give them, render *to t.* their desert
34. 9. for there is no want *to t.* that fear him
44. 3. because thou hadst a favour *unto t.*
83. 9. do *unto t.* as to the Midianites, as to Sisera
115. 8. they that make them are like *un. t.* 135. 18.
125. 4. do good *to t.* that are upright in heart
Prov. 2. 7. a buckler *to t.* that walk uprightly
3. 18. a tree of life *to t.* that lay hold on her
8. 9. they are right *to t.* that find knowledge
10. 26. so is the sluggard *to t.* that send him
14. 22. mercy and truth be *to t.* that devise good
25. 13. so is a faithful messenger *to t.* that send
30. 5. a shield *unto t.* that put their trust in him
Eccl. 7. 12. wisdom gives life *to t.* that have it
Isa. 19. 3. seek *to t.* that have familiar spirits
28. 13. the word was *unto t.* precept upon precept
40. 29. *to t.* that have no might he increaseth
42. 5. hath given spirit *to t.* that walk therein
16. these things will I do *unto t.* and not forsake
49. 9. *to t.* that are in darkness, *Mat.* 4. 16. *Luke* 1. 79.
56. 5. *to t.* will I give in my house a place and name
57. 6. *to t.* hast thou poured a drink-offering
59. 20. *to t.* that turn from transgression in Jacob
61. 7. everlasting joy shall be *unto t.*
Jer. 5. 13. thus shall it be done *unto t.*
6. 10. the word of the Lord is *unto t.* a reproach
15. 19. let them return, but return not thou *unto t.*
18. 8. repent of the evil I thought to do *unto t.*
31. 32. brake covenant, tho' I was husband *unto t.*
Lam. 1. 22. and do *unto t.* as thou hast done to me
3. 25. the Lord is good *unto t.* that wait for him
65. give them sorrow of heart, thy curse *unto t.*
Ezek. 2. 4. I do send thee *unto t.* and thou shalt say
3. 6. had I sent thee *unto t.* they had hearkened
26. and thou shalt not be *to t.* a reprover
11. 16. yet will I be *to t.* as a little sanctuary
12. 11. as I have done, so shall it be done *unto t.*
20. 9. in whose sight I made myself known *unto t.*
33. 32. lo, thou art *unto t.* as a very lovely song
39. 13. and it shall be *to t.* a renown
44. 12. because they ministered *unto t.* before idols
48. 12. oblation shall be *unto t.* a thing most holy
18. shall be for food *unto t.* that serve the city
Dan. 4. 19. the dream be *to t.* that hate thee
6. 2. that the princes might give account *unto t.*
9. 4. and keeping mercy *to t.* that love him
11. 34. but many shall cleave *to t.* with flatteries
Hos. 4. 12. and their staff declareth *unto t.*
7. 13. destruction *unto t.* because they transgressed
11. 4. I was *to t.* as they that take off the yoke
Jonah 3. 10. evil that he said, he would do *unto t.*
Mic. 2. 6. prophesy ye not, say they *to t.* that
prophesy, they shall not prophesy *to t.*
Mat. 6. 8. be ye not like *unto t.* || 7. 12. do ye so *to t.*
17. 13. that he spake *unto t.* of John the Baptist
21. 36. other servants, they did *unto t.* likewise
25. 9. but go ye rather *to t.* that sell, and buy
Mark 4. 11. but *to t.* that are without in parables
10. 40. shall be given *to t.* for whom it is prepared
Luke 2. 51. he went down, and was subject *unto t.*
6. 31. that men do to you, do ye also *to t.* likewise
33. if ye do good *to t.* that do good to you
34. if ye lend *to t.* of whom ye hope to receive
11. 13. give the Holy Spirit *to t.* that ask him
16. 28. that he may testify *unto t.* lest they come
20. 15. what shall Lord of the vineyard do *unto t.*?
23. 28. Jesus turning *unto t.* said, weep not for me
24. 11. their words seemed *unto t.* as idle tales
27. he expounded *unto t.* in all the scriptures
John 1. 12. *to t.* gave he power to become the sons
of God, even *to t.* that believe on his name
22. we may give an answer *to t.* that sent us
2. 24. but Jesus did not commit himself *unto t.*
8. 27. that he spake *to t.* of the Father
20. 23. sins ye remit, they are remitted *unto t.*
Acts 1. 16. who was guide *to t.* that took Jesus
2. 3. there appeared *unto t.* cloven tongues, as of fire
41. there were added *unto t.* about 3,000 souls
5. 13. of the rest durst no man join himself *to t.*
32. whom God hath given *to t.* that obey him
14. 18. that they had not done sacrifice *unto t.*
16. 10. had called us to preach the gospel *unto t.*
20. 34. my necessities, and *to t.* that were with me
25. 11. no man may deliver me *unto t.* I appeal
Rom. 1. 19. is manifest, for G. hath shewed it *u. t.*
2. 7. *to t.* who by patient continuance in well-doing
8. 28. work together for good *to t.* that love God
10. 20. made manifest *unto t.* that asked not after me
1 *Cor.* 1. 2. *unto t.* that are sanctified in Christ Jesus
24. *unto t.* that are called, both Jews and Greeks
9. 3. my answer *to t.* that do examine me, is this
14. 34. for it is not permitted *unto t.* to speak
2 *Cor.* 4. 3. if gospel hid, it is hid *to t.* that are lost
Gal. 1. 17. *to t.* which were apostles before me
6. 10. *unto t.* who are of the household of faith
Eph. 2. 17. and preached peace *to t.* that were nigh

Phil. 1. 28. is to t. an evident token of perdition
2 Thess. 1. 6. tribulation to t. that trouble you
1 Tim. 4. 15. meditate, give thyself wholly to t.
2 Tim. 4. 8. but unto all t. that love his appearing
Tit. 3. 13. that nothing be wanting unto t.
Heb. 3. 18. not enter, but to t. that believed not
4. 2. to us was the gospel preached as well as unto t.
8. 10. I will be to t. a God, they to me a people
12. 11. yieldeth unto t. that are exercised thereby
19. word should not be spoken to t. any more
Jam. 1. 12. Lord promised to t. that love him, 2. 5.
1 Pet. 4. 6. gospel preached also to t. that are dead
2 Pet. 1. 1. to t. that obtained like precious faith
2. 22. happened unto t. according to the proverb
Rev. 9. 3. unto t. was given power as the scorpions
5. to t. it was given that they should not kill them
20. 4. they sat, and judgment was given unto t.
See Say, Wo.

Toward THEM.

Psal. 103. 11. so great his mercy toward t. that fear
Mat. 14. 14. Jesus was moved with compassion toward t. and healed their sick, Mark 6. 34.
Col. 4. 5. walk in wisdom toward t. that are without
1 Thess. 4. 12. honestly toward t. that are without

Under THEM.

Num. 16. 31. ground clave asunder that was under t.
Job 26. 8. and the cloud is not rent under t.

With THEM.

Gen. 19. 9. we will deal worse with thee than with t.
34. 8. Hamor communed with t. saying, my son
43. 16. when Joseph saw Benjamin with t. he said
Exod. 6. 4. I have established my covenant with t.
23. 32. shall make no covenant with t. Deut. 7. 2.
Lev. 26. 39. that are left shall pine away with t.
44. and to break my covenant with t.
Num. 22. 12. thou shalt not go w. t. || 20. arise, go w. t.
32. 19. we will not inherit with t. on yonder side
Deut. 2. 5. take good heed, meddle not with t. 19.
5. 29. would fear me, that it might be well with t.
7. 3. neither make marriages with t. Josh. 23. 12.
5. thus shall ye deal with t. destroy their altars
9. who keepeth covenant with t. that love him
Josh. 9. 15. and Joshua made peace with t. 16.
Judg. 1. 22. they also went, and the Lord was with t.
19. 24. and do with t. what seemeth good unto you
1 Sam. 10. 6. and thou shalt prophesy with t.
15. 6. go, get you down, lest I destroy you with t.
2 Sam. 12. 17. he would not, nor did he eat with t.
15. 36. they have there with t. their two sons
1 Kings 8. 46. and thou be angry with t. 2 Chr. 6. 36.
2 Kings 6. 16. are more than they that be with t.
11. 9. with t. that should go out on the sabbath, and came to Jehoiada, 2 Chron. 23. 8.
22. 7. there was no reckoning made with t.
1 Chron. 9. 25. their brethren were to come with t.
2 Chron. 5. 12. and with t. 120 priests sounding
14. 11. with many, or with t. that have no power
17. 8. with t. he sent Levites, and with t. Elishama
9. had the book of the law of the Lord with t.
22. 12. and he was with t. hid in the house of God
Ezra 5. 2. with t. were the prophets of God helping
Neh. 9. 13. thou spakest with t. from heaven
24. that they might do with t. as they would
13. 25. and I contended with t. and cursed them
Esth. 3. 11. to do with t. as it seemeth good to thee
Job 21. 8. their seed is established in their sight w. t.
Psal. 9. 6. their memorial is perished with t.
25. 14. secret of the Lord is with t. that fear him
35. 1. plead my cause with t. that strive with me
42. 4. I went with t. to the house of God
54. 4. the Lord is with t. that uphold my soul, 118. 7.
88. 4. I am counted with t. that go down into pit
119. 93. for with t. thou hast quickened me
Prov. 1. 15. my son, walk not thou in the way with t.
24. 1. evil men, neither desire to be with t.
28. 4. but such as keep the law contend with t.
Eccl. 8. 12. it shall be well with t. that fear God
Isa. 14. 1. and the stranger shall be joined with t.
20. thou shalt not be joined with t. in burial
34. 7. and the unicorns shall come down with t.
57. 8. enlarged thy bed and made a covenant w. t.
59. 21. this is my covenant with t. saith the Lord
60. 9. to bring their silver and their gold with t.
61. 8. I will make an everlasting covenant with t.
65. 23. blessed of Lord, and their offspring with t.
Jer. 18. 23. deal thus with t. in time of thine anger
27. 18. and if the word of the Lord be with t.
31. 8. I will gather with t. the blind and the lame
32. 40. I will make an everlasting covenant with t.
Ezek. 16. 17. thou madest images of men, and didst commit whoredoms with t. 28. | 23. 7, 43.
26. 20. bring thee down with t. that go down to pit
31. 14. w. t. that go down to pit, 32. 18, 24, 25, 29.
34. 25. I will make w. t. covenant of peace, 37. 26.
30. I the Lord their God am with t. Zech. 10. 5.
37. 27. my tabernacle shall be with t. I their God
Hos. 5. 5. Judah also shall fall with t.
Mat. 9. 15. can the children fast as long as the bridegroom is with t.? Mark 2. 19. Luke 5. 34.
13. 29. lest ye root up also the wheat with t.
23. 30. we would not have been partakers with t.
25. 3. took their lamps, and took no oil with t.
Mark 16. 20. they preached, the L. working with t.
Luke 15. 2. he eateth w. t. || 18. 7. tho' he bear w. t.
24. 33. found the eleven and them that were w. t.
John 17. 12. while I was with t. in the world, I kept
18. 5. Judas which betrayed him stood with t.
20. 24. but Thomas was not w. t. when Jesus came
Acts 9. 28. he was with t. coming in and going out
39. which Dorcas made while she was with t.
10. 20. arise, and go with t. || 11. 3. didst eat with t.
11. 12. spirit bade me go with t. nothing doubting
21. and the hand of the Lord was with t.
12. 25. they took with t. John surnamed Mark
14. 27. rehearsed all that God had done w. t. 15. 4.
15. 38. Paul thought not good to take him with t.
20. 36. he kneeled down and prayed with t. all
21. 24. be at charges with t. that they may shave
Rom. 11. 17. and with t. partakest of the root
12. 15. bless and curse not, rejoice with t. that do rejoice, and weep with t. that weep
Eph. 5. 7. be not ye therefore partakers with t.

Eph. 6. 24. grace be with t. that love our L. Jes. Chr.
1 Thess. 4. 17. shall be caught up together with t.
2 Tim. 2. 22. peace be with t. that call on the Lord
Heb. 3. 17. was it not with t. that had sinned?
8. 8. for finding fault with t. he saith, behold
10. 16. this is the covenant I will make with t.
11. 31. the harlot Rahab perished not with t.
13. 3. them that are in bonds, as bound with t.
1 Pet. 3. 7. ye husbands, dwell with t. according
4. 4. that ye run not with t. to the same excess
2 Pet. 2. 20. latter end is worse w. t. than beginning
Rev. 9. 19. had heads, and with t. they do hurt
21. 3. tabernacle with men will dwell with t.

Without THEM.

Lev. 26. 43. while she lieth desolate without t.
See Teach.

THEMSELVES.

Gen. 19. 11. they wearied t. to find the door
43. 32. for them by t. for the Egyptians by t.
Exod. 5. 7. let them go and gather straw for t.
12. 39. nor had they prepared for t. victual
32. 7. for thy people have corrupted t. Deut. 9. 12. | 32. 5. Judg. 2. 19. Hos. 9. 9.
Num. 8. 7. let them wash, and so make t. clean
Deut. 32. 31. even our enemies t. being judges
1 Sam. 3. 13. because his sons make t. vile, and he
14. 11. both of them discovered t. to the garrison
1 Kings 8. 47. if they shall bethink t. 2 Chr. 6. 37.
18. 23. let them choose one bullock for t.
2 Kings 8. 20. Edom made king over t. 2 Chr. 21. 8.
17. 17. sold t. to do evil in the sight of the Lord
32. made to t. of the lowest of them priests
19. 29. ye shall eat such things as grow of t.
1 Chron. 19. 6. they had made t. odious to David
2 Chron. 7. 14. if my people shall humble t.
12. 6. the princes and the king humbled t. 7.
20. 25. precious jewels which they stript off for t.
35. 14. afterwar. they made ready for t. and priests
Ezra 9. 2. they have taken of their daughters for t.
Esth. 9. 31. and as they had decreed for t. and seed
Job 24. 16. houses which they had marked for t.
30. 14. in the desolation they rolled t. upon me
41. 23. they are firm in t. they cannot be moved
Psal. 2. 2. the kings of the earth set t. against God
9. 20. the nations may know t. to be but men
44. 10. and they which hate us spoil for t.
57. 6. into the midst whereof they are fallen t.
106. 28. they joined t. also to Baal-peor, and ate
140. 8. grant not their desires, lest they exalt t.
Prov. 23. 5. riches make t. wings, they fly away
Eccl. 3. 18. they might see that they t. are beasts
Isa. 2. 6. and they please t. in children of strangers
3. 9. for they have rewarded evil to t.
46. 2. but t. are gone into captivity
47. 14. they shall not deliver t. from the flame
48. 2. for they call t. of the holy city, and stay
56. 6. sons of the stranger that join t. to the Lord
Jer. 2. 24. all they that seek her will not weary t.
4. 2. and the nations shall bless t. in him
7. 19. do they not provoke t. || 9. 5. they weary t.
11. 17. for the evil they have done against t.
12. 13. have put t. to pain, but shall not profit
16. 6. nor cut t. nor make t. bald for them
27. 7. and great kings shall serve t. of him
30. 21. and their nobles shall be of t.
34. 10. that none should serve t. of them any more
Ezek. 10. 17. they were lifted up, these lift up t.
22. was the same, their appearances and t.
14. 18. but they only shall be delivered t.
34. 2. woe to shepherds of Israel that do feed t.
10. nor shall the shepherds feed t. any more
45. 5. shall also the Levites of the house have for t.
Hos. 4. 14. for t. are separated with whores
7. 14. they assembled t. for corn and wine
9. 10. but they separated t. to that shame
Hab. 1. 7. their judgments shall proceed of t.
2. 13. the people shall weary t. for very vanity
Zech. 4. 12. which empty the golden oil out of t.
11. 5. who slay them, and hold t. not guilty
Mat. 14. 2. John Baptist is risen, therefore mighty works do shew forth t. in him, Mark 6. 14.
16. 7. reasoned among t. Mark 8. 16. Luke 20. 14.
19. 12. there be eunuchs, who made t. eunuchs
21. 25. reasoned with t. Mark 11. 31. Luke 20. 5.
23. 4. but they t. will not move them with one
Mark 4. 17. receive it, and have no root in t.
9. 10. and they kept that saying with t.
Luke 7. 30. rejected the counsel of God against t.
18. 9. he spake to certain who trusted in t.
20. 20. sent spies which should feign t. just men
23. 12. for before they were at enmity between t.
John 17. 13. they might have my joy fulfilled in t.
18. 28. they t. went not into the judgment hall
Acts 15. 32. Judas and Silas being prophets also t.
16. 37. but let them come t. and fetch us out
18. 6. and when they opposed t. and blasphemed
21. 25. that they keep t. from things offered to idols
23. 12. certain Jews bound t. under a curse, 21.
24. 15. a resurrection which they t. also allow
28. 25. and when they agreed not among t.
29. the Jews had great reasoning among t.
Rom. 1. 22. professing t. to be wise, they beca. fools
24. to dishonour their own bodies between t.
27. receiving in t. that recompence of their error
2. 14. these having not the law, are a law to t.
10. 3. have not submitted t. to righteousness of God
13. 2. they that resist shall receive to t. damnation
1 Cor. 6. 9. nor abusers of t. with mankind
2 Cor. 5. 15. should not henceforth live to t. but to
8. 3. beyond their power they were willing of t.
10. 12. measuring t. by t. comparing t. with t.
11. 13. transforming t. into the apostles of Christ
Gal. 6. 13. for neither do they t. keep the law
Eph. 4. 19. who have given t. over to lasciviousness
Phil. 2. 3. let each esteem other better than t.
1 Thess. 1. 9. for they t. shew of us what manner
1 Tim. 1. 10. them that defile t. with mankind
2. 9. women adorn t. in modest apparel, 1 Pet. 3. 5.
3. 13. they purchased to t. good degree and boldn.
6. 19. laying up in store for t. a good foundation
2 Tim. 2. 25. instructing those that oppose t.
26. may recover t. out of the snare of the devil

2 Tim. 4. 3. but they shall heap to t. teachers, having
Tit. 1. 12. one of t. even a prophet of their own
Heb. 6. 6. seeing they crucify to t. the Son of God
1 Pet. 1. 12. that not to t. but as they did minister
2 Pet. 2. 1. and bring upon t. swift destruction
13. sporting t. with their own deceivings while
19. they t. are the servants of corruption
Jude 7. giving t. over to fornication, going after
10. they corrupt t. || 12. feeding t. without fear
19. who separate t. sensual, having not the Spirit
See Gather, Hide, Spread.

THEN.

Gen. 4. 26. t. began men to call upon the Lord
13. 7. the Canaanite dwelt t. in the land
16. t. shall thy seed also be numbered
27. 41. t. will I slay my brother Jacob
28. 21. t. shall the Lord be my God
44. 26. if our brother be with us t. will we go down
49. 4. t. defilest thou it; he went up to my couch
Lev. 26. 41. if t. their hearts be humbled, and they t. accept of the punishment of their iniquity
42. t. I will remember my covenant with Jacob
Josh. 14. 11. as my strength was t. so is it now
12. if the Lord be with me, t. I shall be able
Judg. 5. 8. they choose new gods, t. was war in gates
1 Sam. 15. 14. what meaneth t. this bleating of sheep
25. 31. t. remember thine handmaid
1 Kings 8. 32. t. hear thou in heaven, 34, 36, 39, 45, 49.
22. 47. there was t. no king in Edom, a deputy
2 Kings 1. 10. t. let fire come down from heaven
8. 16. Jehoshaphat being t. king of Israel
9. 3. t. open the door and flee and tarry not
1 Chron. 11. 16. and David was t. in the hold
2 Chron. 33. 13. t. Manasses knew the Lord was God
Ezra 5. 1. t. the prophets prophesied to the Jews
2. t. rose Zerubbabel to build the house of God
Esth. 5. 9. t. went Haman forth that day joyful
14. t. said Zeresh his wife, and his friends to him
7. 10. t. was the king's wrath pacified
Job 3. 13. should have slept, t. had I been at rest
11. 11. he seeth also, will he not t. consider it?
22. 26. t. shalt thou have delight in the Almighty
29. t. thou shalt say there is lifting up
38. 21. knowest thou it, because thou wast t. born
Psal. 27. 10. t. the Lord will take me up
51. 13. t. will I teach transgressors thy ways
55. 12. was not an enemy, t. I could have borne it
69. 4. t. I restored that which I took not away
106. 12. t. believed they his words, they sang
119. 6. t. shall I not be ashamed, when I have
Prov. 2. 5. t. shalt thou understand the fear of Lord
9. t. shalt thou understand righteousness
24. 14. t. there shall be a reward, thy expectation
Isa. 32. 16. t. judgment shall dwell in the wilderness
58. 8. t. shall thy light break forth as the morning
9. t. shalt thou call, and the Lord shall answer
Jer. 4. 1. t. shalt thou not remove
11. 15. when thou dost evil, t. thou rejoicest
18. t. thou shewedst me their doings
23. 22. t. they should have turned them from
33. 26. t. will I cast away the seed of Jacob
Ezek. 39. 28. t. shall they know that I am the Lord
Dan. 5. 24. t. was part of the hand sent from him
Mal. 3. 16. t. they that feared the Lord spake often
Mat. 5. 24. and t. come and offer thy gift
9. 15. t. shall they fast, Mark 2. 20. Luke 5. 35.
12. 29. t. will he spoil his house, Mark 3. 27.
16. 27. and t. he shall reward every man according
17. 26. Jesus saith, t. are the children free
19. 25. were amazed, saying, who t. can be saved? Mark 10. 26. Luke 18. 26.
24. 14. for a witness to all, t. shall the end come
21. for t. shall be great tribulation, such not since
26. 56. t. all the disciples forsook him and fled
Mark 12. 37. and whence is he t. his son?
13. 14. t. let them that be in Judea flee to the mountains, Luke 21. 21.
Luke 6. 42. t. shalt thou see clearly to pull out
John 1. 21. asked they what t. art thou Elias?
25. they asked him, why baptizest thou t.?
7. 33. and t. I go unto him that sent me
8. 28. t. shall ye know that I am he, and that I do
Acts 2. 38. t. Peter said to them, repent and be bapt.
41. t. they that gladly received his word were bapt.
11. 18. t. hath God to the Gentiles granted, 26. 20.
Rom. 6. 21. what fruit had ye t. in those things?
7. 7. what shall we say t. is the law sin? 9. 14.
8. 17. if children, t. heirs, heirs of God, joint heirs
11. 5. so t. at this present there is a remnant
1 Cor. 4. 5. t. shall every man have praise of God
10. 19. what say I t. that the idol is any thing
13. 12. but t. face to face, now I know in part, t. shall I know even as also I am known
14. 15. what is it t.? || 2 Cor. 12. 10. t. am I strong
Gal. 2. 21. come by the law, t. Christ is dead in vain
3. 29. if ye be Christ's, t. are ye Abraham's seed
4. 29. but as t. he that was born after the flesh
6. 4. t. shall he have rejoicing in himself
1 Thess. 5. 3. t. sudden destruction cometh upon them
2 Thess. 2. 8. t. shall that wicked one be revealed
Heb. 7. 27. first for his own sins, t. for the people's
12. 8. t. are ye bastards, and not sons
1 John 3. 21. t. have we confidence towards God

THENCE.

Gen. 24. 7. thou shalt take a wife to my son from t.
27. 45. then I will send and fetch thee from t.
49. 24. from t. is the shepherd, the stone of Israel
Num. 13. 23. they cut down from t. a branch, 24.
23. 13. Balak said, curse me them from t. 27.
Deut. 4. 29. if from t. thou shalt seek the Lord
5. 15. the Lord brought thee out t. 6. 23. | 24. 18.
19. 12. the elders shall send and fetch him t.
30. 4. from t. will the Lord gather thee, and from t. will he fetch thee. Neh. 1. 9.
Judg. 19. 18. to mount Ephraim, from t. am I
1 Sam. 4. 4. might bring from t. the ark of the covenant of the L. of hosts, 2 Sam. 6. 2. 1 Chr. 13. 6.
1 Kings 2. 36. go not forth from t. any whither
2 Kings 2. 21. shall not be from t. any more death
23. and he went up from t. to Beth-el
25. from t. to Carmel, and from t. to Samaria
7. 8. the lepers carried t. silver and gold and hid it

2 Chron. 26. 20. they thrust out Uzziah from t.
Ezra 6. 6. now therefore, be ye far from t.
Isa. 52. 11. depart ye, depart, go ye out from t.
65. 20. there shall be no more t. an infant of days
Jer. 5. 6. every one that goes t. shall be torn
22. 24. were the signet yet would I pluck thee t.
36. 29. cause to cease from t. man and beast
37. 12. went forth to separate himself t.
43. 12. and he shall go forth from t. in peace
49. 16. as the eagle I will bring thee down from t.
Ezek. 11. 18. shall take all abominations from t.
Hos. 2. 15. I will give her her vineyards from t.
Amos 6. 2. from t. go ye to Hamath the great
9. 2. dig into hell, t. shall my hand take them, 3.
4. t. will I command the sword, it shall slay
Obad. 4. among stars, t. will I bring thee down
Mat. 5. 26. thou shalt by no means come out t.
10. 11. who worthy, and there abide, till ye go t.
Mark 6. 11. when ye depart t. shake off the dust
Luke 16. 26. that would come from t. to us cannot

THENCEFORTH.

Lev. 22. 27. t. it shall be accepted for you
2 Chron. 32. 23. Hezekiah was magnified from t.
Mat. 5. 13. is t. good for nothing, but to be cast out
John 19. 12. from t. Pilate sought to release him

THERE.

Gen. 2. 8. t. he put the man whom he had formed
18. 28. if I find forty-five t. I will not destroy it
32. 29. he blessed him t. || 35. 7. t. God appeared
49. 31. t. they buried Abraham and Sarah, t. they buried Isaac and Rebekah his wife
Exod. 8. 22. Goshen, no swarms of flies shall be t.
15. 25. t. he made a statute, t. he proved them
17. 6. behold I will stand before thee t. in Horeb
24. 12. come up into the mount, and be t. 34. 2.
34. 28. and he was t. with the Lord forty days
Lev. 8. 31. t. eat it || 16. 23. shall leave them t.
Num. 11. 17. I will come and talk with thee t.
13. 28. moreover we saw the children of Anak t. 33. Deut. 1. 28. Josh. 14. 12.
20. 1. and Miriam died t. and was buried t.
26. and Aaron shall die t. 28. Deut. 10. 6.
Deut. 4. 28. t. ye shall serve gods, work of men's hands, wood and stone, 28. 36, 64. Jer. 16. 13.
10. 5. and t. they be unto this day, Josh. 4. 9.
12. 5. your God shall choose to put his name t. 14. 23. | 16. 2, 11. 1 Kings 8. 29. | 9. 3.
31. 26. it may be t. for a witness against thee
Judg. 5. 27. where he bowed, t. he fell down dead
7. 4. bring them down, I'll try them for thee t.
21. 9. none of the inhabitants of Jabesh-gilead t.
Ruth 1. 17. where thou diest, t. will I be buried
1 Sam. 1. 3. the priests of the Lord were t. 4. 4.
28. and Hannah worshipped the Lord t.
11. 14. go to Gilgal, and renew the kingdom t.
15. t. they made Saul king before the Lord, t. they sacrificed, and t. they rejoiced
21. 7. a certain man of the servants of Saul t.
22. 22. I knew when Doeg the Edomite was t.
2 Sam. 3. 27. Joab smote Abner t. under the fifth rib
6. 7. God smote Uzzah t. and t. he died by ark of G.
15. 21. even t. also will thy servant be
35. hast thou not t. Zadok and Abiathar
1 Kings 8. 8. staves, and t. they are to this day
11. 36. I have chosen to put my name t. 2 Kings 23. 27. 2 Chron. 6. 5, 6. | 7. 16. Neh. 1. 9.
17. 4. I commanded the ravens to feed thee t.
18. 10. when they said he is not t. he took an oath
19. 3. came to Beer-sheba, and left his servant t.
2 Kings 2. 21. Elisha went, and cast the salt in t.
4. 11. he came and lay t. || 7. 4. and we shall die t.
7. 5. when they were come, t. was no man t. 10.
1 Chron. 14. 12. when they left their gods, t.
2 Chron. 28. 9. but a prophet of the Lord was t.
32. 21. they slew Sennacherib t. with the sword
Ezra 6. 12. God hath caused his name to dwell t.
Job 3. 17. t. the wicked cease from troubling, and t. the weary be at rest
18. t. the prisoners rest together, and hear not
19. small and great are t. the servant is free from
23. 7. t. the righteous might dispute with him
35. 12. t. they cry, but none giveth answer
39. 30. and where the slain are, t. is she
Psal. 14. 5. t. were they in great fear, 53. 5.
45. 12. the daughter of Tyre shall be t. with a gift
48. 6. fear took hold upon them t. and pain
66. 6. went through flood, t. did we rejoice in him
69. 35. will build cities that they may dwell t.
87. 4. Philistia and Tyre, this man was born t. 6.
7. singers and players on instruments shall be t.
104. 26. t. go the ships, t. is that Leviathan
133. 3. t. the Lord commanded the blessing
139. 8. thou art t. || 10. t. shall thy hand lead me
Prov. 8. 27. I was t. || 9. 18. that the dead are t.
26. 20. where no wood is, t. the fire goeth out
Eccl. 3. 16. that wickedness was t. iniquity was t.
17. for there is a time t. for every purpose
11. 3. where the tree falleth, t. it shall be
Cant. 8. 5. t. thy mother, brought thee forth
Isa. 13. 20. nor shall shepherds make their fold t.
21. but wild beasts of the desert shall lie t.
22. 18. t. shalt thou die, and t. the chariots
23. 12. to Chittim, t. also shalt thou have no rest
28. 10. line upon line, here a little and t. a little
33. 21. t. glorious Lord will be a place of rivers
35. 8. and an highway shall be t. and a way
9. no lion, but the redeemed shall walk t.
48. 16. t. am I || 65. 9. my servant shall dwell t.
Jer. 8. 22. is t. no balm in Gilead, no physician t.?
18. 2. t. will I cause thee to hear my words
20. 6. t. thou shalt die, and shalt be buried t.
22. 26. another country t. shall ye die, 42. 16.
27. 22. and t. shall they be till I visit them
38. 28. he was t. when Jerusalem was taken
42. 14. will go into Egypt, and t. will we dwell
47. 7. against Ashkelon, t. hath he appointed it
Ezek. 3. 22. go to the plain, I will t. talk with thee
12. 13. he shall not see it, though he shall die t.
17. 20. I will plead with him t. for his trespass
20. 28. and they offered t. their sacrifices, t. they presented the provocation of their offering
35. and t. will I plead with you face to face
Ezek. 20. 40. t. will I accept them, t. requ. offerings
22. 20. and I will leave you t. and melt you
23. 3. t. were their breasts pressed, t. they bruised
29. 14. and they shall be t. a base kingdom
32. 22. Ashur is t. and all her company
35. 10. we will possess it, whereas the Lord was t.
48. 35. name of the city shall be, the Lord is t.
Hos. 2. 15. and she shall sing t. as in her youth
7. 9. yea, grey hairs are here and t. upon him
9. 15. t. I hated them || 12. 4. t. he spake with us
Joel 3. 2. I will plead with them t. for my people
Amos 6. 12. will one plow t. with oxen?
7. 12. into Judah, t. eat bread and prophesy t.
Mic. 4. 10. t. be delivered, t. Lord shall redeem thee
Zeph. 1. 14. the mighty man shall cry t. bitterly
Mat. 2. 13. be thou t. till I bring thee word
5. 23. t. rememberest that thy brother hath ought
24. leave t. thy gift before the altar
6. 21. where treasure is, t. will your heart be also
8. 12. t. shall be gnashing of teeth, 22. 13. | 24. 51.
12. 45. they enter in, and dwelt t. Luke 11. 26.
18. 20. in my name, t. I am in the midst of them
24. 23. lo here is Christ, or t. Mark 13. 21.
25. 25. I hid thy talent, t. thou hast that is thine
27. 36. and sitting down, they watched him t.
28. 7. in Galilee, t. shall ye see him, Mark 16. 7.
Mark 1. 38. let us go, that I may preach t. also
6. 5. and he could t. do no mighty work, save that
Luke 10. 6. and if the son of peace be t. your peace
12. 18. t. will I bestow all my fruits and goods
John 12. 26. where I am, t. shall my servant be
14. 3. that where I am, t. ye may be also
Acts 20. 22. the things that shall befall me t.
22. 10. t. it shall be told thee of all things which
Rom. 9. 26. t. be called the children of living God
Rev. 21. 25. for there shall be no night t. 22. 5.

THEREABOUT.

Luke 24. 4. as they were much perplexed t.
See Abode, Is, None, One, Strand, Stood, Was.

THEREAT.

Exod. 30. 19. wash their hands and feet t. 40. 31.
Mat. 7. 13. and many there be which go in t.

THEREBY.

Gen. 24. 14. t. shall I know thou hast shewed
Lev. 11. 43. that ye should be defiled t.
Job 22. 21. with God, t. good will come unto thee
Prov. 20. 1. whoso is deceived t. is not wise
Eccl. 10. 9. cleaveth wood, shall be endangered t.
Isa. 33. 21. nor shall gallant ships pass t.
Jer. 18. 16. passeth t. shall be astonished, 19. 8.
51. 43. neither doth any son of man pass t.
Ezek. 12. 5. dig through wall and carry out t. 12.
33. 12. he shall not fall t. || 18. he shall die t.
19. and do what is lawful, he shall live t.
Zech. 9. 2. and Hamath also shall border t.
John 11. 4. that Son of God might be glorified t.
Eph. 2. 16. by the cross, having slain the enmity t.
Heb. 12. 11. yields to them who are exercised t.
15. root springing up, and t. many be defiled
13. 2. for t. some have entertained angels
1 Pet. 2. 2. milk of the word that ye may grow t.

THEREFORE.

Gen. 2. 24. t. shall a man leave his father and mother
17. 9. God said, thou shalt keep my covenant t.
42. 21. guilty, t. is this distress come upon us
Exod. 1. 20. t. God dealt well with the midwives
4. 12. t. go || 5. 8. they be idle, t. they cry, 17.
12. 17. t. shall ye observe this day, 13. 10.
16. 29. t. he giveth you on the sixth day bread
31. 14. ye shall keep the sabbath t. for it is holy
Lev. 11. 44. ye shall t. be holy, I am holy, 45. | 21. 6.
18. 25. t. I do visit the iniquity thereof upon it
26. ye shall t. keep my statutes and judgments
30. t. keep my ordinances, 19. 37. | 20. 22. | 22. 9.
25. 17. ye shall not t. oppress one another, but fear
Num. 3. 12. t. the Levites shall be mine
Deut. 5. 15. t. the Lord thy God commanded thee to keep the sabbath day, 15. 11, 15. | 24. 18, 22.
28. 48. t. thou shalt serve thine enemies
Judg. 11. 8. t. we turn again to thee now
1 Sam. 1. 28. t. also I have lent him to the Lord
28. 18. t. hath the Lord done this thing to thee
2 Sam. 6. 23. t. Michal had no child to her death
1 Kings 2. 2. be strong t. and shew thyself a man
20. 42. t. thy life shall go for his life, and people
2 Kings 1. 6. t. thou shalt not come down, 16.
19. 18. t. they have destroyed them
1 Chron. 10. 14. t. he slew Saul, and turned kingdom
2 Chron. 7. 22. t. hath he brought all this evil
30. 7. t. gave them up to desolation, as ye see
Neh. 2. 20. t. we his servants will arise and build
13. 28. t. I chased him from me
Job 21. 14. t. they say to God, depart from us
35. 14. judgment is before him, t. trust in him
42. 8. t. take unto you seven bullocks, seven rams
Psal. 16. 9. t. my heart is glad || 31. 3. t. lead me
36. 7. t. the children of men put their trust in thee
45. 2. t. God hath blessed thee for ever
7. t. God hath anointed thee with oil of gladness
17. t. shall the people praise thee for ever
55. 19. have no changes, t. they fear not God
63. 7. t. in shadow of thy wings I will rejoice
73. 10. t. his people return hither
91. 14. set his love on me, t. will I deliver him
106. 23. t. he said, that he would destroy them
116. 10. I believed, t. have I spoken, 2 Cor. 4. 13.
119. 104. t. I hate every false way
129. are wonder, t. doth my soul keep them
139. 19. depart from me t. ye bloody men
Prov. 17. 14. t. leave off contention before it be
Eccl. 5. 2. God is in heaven, t. let thy words be few
8. 6. t. the misery of man is great upon him
11. t. the heart of men is set in them to do evil
Isa. 3. 17. t. the Lord will smite with a scab
10. 16. t. the Lord of hosts shall send leanness
24. 6. t. hath the curse devoured the earth
42. 25. t. he hath poured the fury of his anger
59. 16. t. his arm brought salvation unto him
Jer. 6. 15. t. they shall fall among them that fall
40. 3. ye obeyed not, t. this thing is come on you
Lam. 3. 24. Lord is my portion t. will I hope in him
Jonah 4. 2. t. I fled before unto Tarshish
Zech. 1. 16. t. I am returned to Jerus. with mercies
7. 12. t. came a great wrath from the Lord
Mal. 3. 6. t. ye sons of Jacob are not consumed
Mat. 5. 48. be ye t. perfect || 10. 31. fear ye not t.
19. 6. what t. God hath joined together let not
27. we have forsaken all, what shall we have t.
24. 42. watch t. 44. | 25. 13. Mark 13. 35.
28. 19. go ye t. teach all nations, baptizing them
Mark 1. 38. t. came I forth || 12. 27. ye t. do err
Luke 4. 43. for t. am I sent || 6. 36. be ye t. merciful
11. 19. by whom t. shall they be your judges
49. t. also said the wisdom of God, I will send
14. 20. I married a wife, and t. I cannot come
20. 15. what t. shall the Lord of the vineyard do unto them? Mark 12. 9.
33. t. in the resurrection whose wife of them is she
John 3. 29. this my joy t. is fulfilled
8. 47. ye t. hear them not, because not of God
9. 41. but ye say, we see, t. your sin remaineth
10. 17. t. doth my Father love me, because I lay
12. 50. what I speak t. as Father said, so I speak
15. 19. I have chosen you, t. the world hateth you
Acts 3. 19. repent ye t. and be converted, that your
Rom. 4. 22. t. it was imputed to him for righteous.
12. 20. t. if thine enemy hunger, feed him
1 Cor. 6. 20. t. glorify God in your body and spirit
12. 15. not the hand, is it t. not of the body, 16.
15. 58. t. be ye stedfast, unmovable, always
2 Cor. 8. 7. t. as ye abound in every thing, in faith
Eph. 5. 7. be not ye t. partakers with them
24. t. as the church is subject to Christ, so wives
2 Tim. 1. 8. be not t. ashamed of the testimony of L.
See Now.

THEREFROM.

Josh. 23. 6. that ye turn not aside t. to right or left
2 Kin. 3. 3. sins of Jeroboam, he departed not t. 13. 2.

THEREIN.

Gen. 9. 7. multiply t. || 18. 24. for fifty righteous t.
23. 11. the cave that is t. I give it to thee, 17, 20.
34. 10. the land before you, dwell and trade t. 21.
Exod. 16. 24. neither was there any worm t.
31. 14. doeth any work t. be cut off, 35. 2.
40. 3. shalt thou put t. the ark of the testimony
9. anoint the tabernacle and all t. Lev. 8. 10.
Lev. 6. 3. sinning t. || 7. done in trespassing t.
13. 21. no white hairs t. || 37. black hairs t.
18. 4. ordinances to walk t. Judg. 2. 22. Isa. 42. 5
22. 21. perfect, there shall be no blemish t.
23. 3. ye shall do no work t. it is the sabbath of the Lord, Deut. 16. 8. Num. 29. 7. Jer. 17. 24
7. ye shall do no servile work t. 8, 21, 25, 35, 36. Num. 28. 18. | 29. 35
25. 19. shall eat your fill and dwell t. in safety
Num. 13. 20. whether there be wood t. or not
16. 7. put fire t. and put incense in them, 46.
Deut. 7. 25. nor take it, lest thou be snared t.
13. 15. destroy all that is t. Josh. 10. 28, 39.
15. 21. if there be any blemish t. if it be lame
17. 19. he shall read t. all the days of his life
20. 11. people that is found t. shall be tributaries
29. 23. nor beareth, nor any grass groweth t.
Josh. 1. 8. thou shalt meditate t. day and night
6. 17. the city and all t. shall be accursed, 24.
1 Kings 8. 16. an house, that my name might be t.
2 Kings 2. 20. bring me a new cruse, and put salt t.
1 Chron. 16. 32. let the fields rejoice, and all that is t. Psal. 96. 12.
Ezra 4. 19. rebellion and sedition been made t.
Neh. 6. 1. wall, that there was no breach left t.
7. 4. city was large, but the people were few t.
5. found it written t. 13. 1. || 8. 3. he read t.
9. 6. made the earth, the seas, and all that is t. Psal. 24. 1. | 69. 34. | 98. 7.
Job 3. 7. night solitary, let no joyful voice come t.
20. 18. restitution, and he shall not rejoice t.
Psal. 37. 29. the righteous shall dwell t. for ever
69. 36. and they that love his name shall dwell t.
107. 34. a fruitful land into barrenness, for wickedness of them that dwell t. Jer. 12. 4.
111. 2. sought out of all that have pleasure t.
119. 35. thy commandments, t. do I delight
146. 6. God who made the sea and all that t. is, Acts 14. 15. | 17. 24. Rev. 10. 6.
Prov. 22. 14. shall fall t. 26. 27. Jer. 23. 12. Hos. 14. 9.
Isa. 7. 6. and let us make a breach t. for us
33. 24. the people that dwell t. shall be forgiven
35. 8. the wayfaring men, tho' fools, shall not err t.
51. 3. joy and gladness shall be found t.
6. they that dwell t. shall die in like manner
59. 8. whosoever goeth t. shall not know peace
Jer. 6. 16. good way and walk t. we will not walk t.
9. 13. have not obeyed my voice, neither walked t.
44. 2. and no man dwelleth t. 48. 9. | 50. 3, 40.
51. 48. and all that is t. shall sing for Babylon
Ezek. 14. 22. behold, t. shall be left a remnant
24. 6. woe to bloody city, to pot whose scum is t.
Hos. 4. 3. every one shall mourn, that dwelleth t. Amos 8. 8. | 9. 5.
Zech. 13. 8. Lord saith, two parts t. shall be cut off and die, but the third part shall be left t.
Mark 10. 15. he shall not enter t. Luke 18. 17.
Acts 1. 20. be desolate and let no man dwell t.
Rom. 1. 17. for t. is the righteousness of G. revealed
6. 2. how that are dead to sin, live any longer t.?
1 Cor. 7. 24. wherein he is called, t. abide with God
Eph. 6. 20. that t. I may speak boldly as I ought
Phil. 1. 18. and I t. do rejoice, and will rejoice
Col. 2. 7. taught, abounding t. with thanksgiving
Heb. 4. 6. it remaineth that some must enter t.
10. 8. offering wouldest not, nor hadst pleasure t.
Jam. 1. 25. whoso looketh into—and continueth t.
2 Pet. 3. 10. the earth and works t. shall be burnt up
Rev. 11. 1. rise and measure them that worship t.
13. 12. causeth them that dwell t. to worship beast
21. 22. and I saw no temple t. God is the temple
See Dwelt.

THEREINTO.

Luke 21. 21. let not them in the countries enter t.

THEREOF.

Gen. 2. 17. in the day thou eatest t. surely die, 3. 5.
Exod. 3. 20. all my wonders which I will do in midst t.

Exod. 10. 26. for *t.* must we take to serve the L. our G.
12. 43. no stranger shall eat *t.* 45. 48. 2 *Kings* 7. 2.
44. when circumcised, then shall he eat *t.*
Deut. 26. 14. I have not eaten *t.* in my mourning
2 *Kings* 4. 43. they shall eat and leave *t.* 44.
Job 24. 13. they know not the ways *t.* nor abide
Psal. 34. 2. the humble shall hear *t.* and be glad
Prov. 16. 33. the whole disposing *t.* is of the Lord
Eccl. 6. 2. God giveth him not power to eat *t.*

THEREON.

Exod. 20. 24. shalt sacrifice *t.* the burnt offerings
40. 35. because the cloud abode *t.* *Num.* 9. 22.
2 *Sam.* 17. 19. the woman spread ground corn *t.*
19. 26. I will saddle me an ass that I may ride *t.*
1 *Chron.* 12. 17. the God of our fathers look *t.*
Ezra 6. 11. and being set up, let him be hanged *t.*
Esth. 7. 9. then the king said, hang Haman *t.*
Isa. 30. 12. and trust in perverseness, and stay *t.*
Ezek. 15. 3. will take a pin of it to hang a vessel *t.*
Mat. 21. 7. they set him *t.* *Luke* 19. 35. *John* 12. 14.
19. and found nothing *t.* *Mark* 11. 13. *Luke* 13. 6.
Mark 14. 72. and when he thought *t.* he wept
1 *Cor.* 3. 10. laid the foundation, another buildeth *t.*
Rev. 5. 3. was not able to open book or look *t.* 4.
6. 4 and power was given to him that sat *t.*
21. 12. city had twelve gates, and names written *t.*

THEREOUT.

Lev. 2. 2. he shall take *t.* his handful of flour
Judg. 15. 19. in the jaw, and there came water *t.*

THERETO.

Exod. 30. 38. shall make like unto that to smell *t.*
Lev. 5. 16. add the fifth part *t.* 6. 5. | 27. 13, 31.
18. 23. neither stand before a beast to lie down *t.*
Num. 19. 17. running water shall be put *t.* in a vessel
Deut. 12. 32. thou shalt not add *t.* nor diminish
Judg. 11. 17. but king of Edom would not hearken *t.*
1 *Chron.* 22. 14. I prepared, and thou mayest add *t.*
2 *Chron.* 10. 14. your yoke heavy, but I will add *t.*
21. 11. Jehoram compelled Judah *t.*
Psal. 119. 9. by taking heed *t.* according to thy word
Isa. 44. 15. maketh an image, and falleth down *t.*
Mark 14. 70. a Galilean, thy speech agreeth *t.*
Gal. 3. 15. no man disannulleth or addeth *t.*

THEREUNTO.

Exod. 32. 8. they made a molten calf, and sacrificed *t.*
Deut. 1. 7. and go to all the places nigh *t.*
Eph. 6. 18. and watching *t.* with all perseverance
1 *Thess.* 3. 3. for you know that we are appointed *t.*
Heb. 10. 1. can never make the comers *t.* perfect
1 *Pet.* 3. 9. knowing that ye are *t.* called, that ye

THEREUPON.

Ezek. 16. 16. thou deckedst and playedst the harlot *t.*
Zeph. 2. 7. the remnant of Judah shall feed *t.*
1 *Cor.* 3. 10. take heed how he buildeth *t.*
14. any man's work abide which he hath built *t.*

THEREWITH.

1 *Sam.* 12. 3. any bribe to blind mine eyes *t.*
17. 51. drew his sword, and cut off his head *t.*
31. 4. and thrust me through *t.* 1 *Chron.* 10. 4.
2 *Kings* 5. 6. I have *t.* sent Naaman my servant
12. 14. and repaired *t.* the house of the Lord
Prov. 15. 16. than great treasure and trouble *t.*
17. an ox, and hatred *t.* || 17. 1. quietness *t.*
25. 16. lest thou be filled *t.* and vomit it
Eccl. 1. 13. hath given sore travel to be exercised *t.*
10. 9. whoso removeth stones shall be hurt *t.*
Ezek. 4. 15. and thou shalt prepare thy bread *t.*
Joel 2. 19. corn, oil, wine, ye shall be satisfied *t.*
Phil. 4. 11. state, I have learned *t.* to be content
1 *Tim.* 6. 8. food and raiment, let us be *t.* content
Jam. 3. 9. *t.* bless we God, and *t.* curse we men
3 *John* 10. prating against us, and not content *t.*

THESE.

Gen. 10. 5. by *t.* were the isles of Gentiles divided, 32.
27. 46. if Jacob take a wife of such as *t.* what good
31. 43. *t.* daughters, *t.* children, *t.* cattle is mine
32. 17. asketh, saying, whose are *t.* before thee
43. 16. Joseph said, bring *t.* men home, make ready, for *t.* men shall dine with me at noon
Exod. 14. 20. but the cloud gave light by night to *t.*
21. 11. and if he do not *t.* three unto her, then she
32. 4. *t.* be thy gods, O Israel, which brought, 8.
Lev. 5. 13. his sin that he hath sinned in one of *t.*
11. 4. *t.* ye shall not eat || 29. *t.* shall be unclean
9. *t.* shall ye eat, 21. 22. *Deut.* 14. 9.
24. and for *t.* ye shall be unclean, whoso toucheth
22. 22. ye shall not offer *t.* to the Lord, 25.
Num. 26. 53. unto *t.* the land shall be divided, for
64. but among *t.* there was not a man of them
Deut. 27. 12. *t.* stand on mount Gerizim to bless
13. and *t.* shall stand upon mount Ebal to curse
1 *Sam.* 16. 10. Samuel said, the L. hath not chosen *t.*
17. 39. David said to Saul, I cannot go with *t.*
2 *Sam.* 16. 2. the king said, what meanest thou by *t.*?
1 *Kings* 10. 10. as *t.* which the queen of Sheba gave
11. 2. Solomon clave to *t.* strange women in love
17. 1. there shall not be dew nor rain *t.* years, but
22. 11. thus saith the Lord, with *t.* shalt thou push the Syrians, 2 *Chron.* 18. 10.
17. Lord said, *t.* have no master, 2 *Chron.* 18. 16.
2 *Kings* 25. 20. Nebuzar-adan took *t.* and brought
2 *Chron.* 35. 7. *t.* were of the king's substance
Ezra 2. 62. *t.* sought their register among those
Neh. 7. 61. *t.* went and could not shew their house
10. 1. now *t.* that sealed the covenant were Nehem.
Job 12. 3. yea, who knoweth not such things as *t.*?
Psal. 104. 27. *t.* wait all on thee, that thou mayest
Eccl. 7. 10. that the former days were better than *t.*
12. 12. further, by *t.* my son, be admonished
Isa. 34. 16. no one of *t.* shall fail, none want her mate
39. 3. what said *t.* men || 44. 21. remember *t.* O Jacob
49. 12. *t.* shall come from far, *t.* from the north, and from the west, and *t.* from Sinim
21. who hath begotten me *t.* who brought up *t.*? I was left alone, *t.* where had they been
57. 6. should I receive comfort in *t.*?
Jer. 5. 5. but *t.* have altogether broken the yoke
38. 9. *t.* men have done evil in all they have done
16. nor will I give thee into hand of *t.* men that
52. 22. and the pomegranates were like to *t.*
Lam. 4. 9. for *t.* pine away, stricken thro' for want

Ezek. 1. 21. when those went, *t.* went, and when those stood, *t.* stood, 10. 17.
8. 15. thou shalt see greater abominations than *t.*
14. 3. *t.* men have set up their idols in their heart
16. 5. none eye pitied thee, to do any of *t.* to thee
20. and *t.* hast thou sacrificed unto them to be
23. 10. *t.* discovered her nakedness, they took her
27. 21. in *t.* were they thy merchants
37. 18. saying, shew us what thou meanest by *t.*
Dan. 3. 13. they brought *t.* men before the king
21. *t.* men were bound || 27. princes saw *t.* men
6. 2. over *t.* Darius set three presidents, Daniel first
11. then *t.* men assembled, and found Daniel, 15.
7. 17. *t.* great beasts, which are four, are four kings
Hag. 2. 13. if one unclean by a dead body touch *t.*
Zech. 1. 9. I will shew thee what *t.* be, 4. 5, 13.
19. I said to the angel, what be *t.*? 21. | 4. 12.
Mat. 5. 37. what is more than *t.* cometh of evil
6. 29. Solomon was not arrayed like one of *t.*
21. 16. they said, hearest thou what *t.* say?
22. 40. on *t.* commandments hang all the law
23. 23. *t.* ought ye to have done, and not leave other
25. 40. as you have not done it to the least of *t.*
45. as ye did it not to one of the least of *t.*
46. and *t.* shall go into everlasting punishment
26. 62. what is it which *t.* witness? *Mark* 14. 60.
Mark 12. 31. no other commandment greater than *t.*
40. *t.* shall receive greater damnation
13. 2. Jesus said, seest thou *t.* great buildings?
Luke 1. 19. and am sent to shew thee *t.* glad tidings
3. 8. that God is able of *t.* stones to raise up children
9. 44. let *t.* sayings sink down into your ears
John 1. 50. thou shalt see greater things than *t.*
5. 3. in *t.* lay a great multitude of impotent folk
19. what he doth, *t.* doth the Son likewise
20. he will shew him greater works than *t.*
6. 5. whence shall we buy bread that *t.* may eat?
7. 31. and said, will he do more miracles than *t.*?
17. 20. neither pray I for *t.* alone, but for them
25. and *t.* have known that thou hast sent me
18. 8. if therefore ye seek me, let *t.* go their way
21. 15. Simon, lovest thou me more than *t.*?
Acts 1. 21. of *t.* which companied with us
24. shew whether of *t.* two thou hast chosen
2. 13. others said, *t.* men are full of new wine
3. 24. all prophets have likewise foretold of *t.* days
4. 16. saying, what shall we do to *t.* men?
5. 36. before *t.* days rose up Theudas, boasting
38. refrain from *t.* men, and let them alone
10. 47. can any forbid that *t.* should not be baptized
17. 6. *t.* that have turned the world upside down
11. *t.* were more noble than those in Thessalonica
Rom. 2. 14. *t.* having not the law, are a law to thems.
11. 24. how much more shall *t.* be graffed
31. even so have *t.* also now not believed
1 *Cor.* 12. 23. upon *t.* we bestow more honour
13. 13. *t.* three, but the greatest of *t.* is charity
2 *Cor.* 7. 1. having *t.* promises, let us cleanse ourselves
Gal. 2. 6. but of *t.* who seemed to be somewhat
Col. 4. 11. *t.* only are my fellow-workers to kingdom
1 *Tim.* 3. 10. and let *t.* also first be proved, then
2 *Tim.* 2. 21. if a man purge himself from *t.* he shall
Heb. 9. 23. patterns should be purified with *t.* but heavenly things with better sacrifices than *t.*
10. 18. now where remission of *t.* is, there is no
2 *Pet.* 1. 4. by *t.* might be partakers of divine nature
2. 12. but *t.* as brute beasts made to be taken
Jude 14. Enoch also prophesied of *t.* saying, behold
19. *t.* be they who separate themselves, sensual
Rev. 11. 6. *t.* have power to shut heaven, that it
14. 4. *t.* were redeemed || 17. 13. *t.* have one mind
22. 6. he said, *t.* sayings are faithful and true

See ABOMINATIONS.

THESE *are*, or *are* THESE.

Gen. 38. 25. by the man whose *t. are* || 48. 8. whose *t. a.*
Exod. 6. 26. *t. are* that Aaron and Moses, to whom
21. 1. *t. are* the judgments, *Lev.* 26. 46. *Deut.* 6. 1.
Lev. 11. 31. *t. are* unclean || 23. 2. *t. are* my feasts, 4.
Num. 22. 9. and God said, what men *are t.* with thee
Deut. 22. 17. *t. are* the tokens of her virginity
1 *Kings* 9. 13. what cities *are t.* thou hast given me?
10. 8. happy *are t.* thy servants, which stand
1 *Chr.* 2. 18. her sons *are* || 4. 22. *t. are* ancient things
Neh. 1. 10. now *t. are* thy servants, and thy people
Job 26. 14. *t. are* part of his ways, but how little
Psal. 73. 12. behold, *t. are* the ungodly, who prosper
Isa. 60. 8. who *are t.* that flee as a cloud, as doves
65. 5. *t. are* a smoke in my nose, a fire that burneth
Jer. 5. 4. surely *t. are* poor, they are foolish
7. 4. saying, the temple of the Lord *are t.*
Ezek. 11. 2. *t. are* the men that devise mischief
36. 20. they said, *t. are* the people of the Lord
Dan. 2. 28. visions of thy head on thy bed *are t.*
Mic. 2. 7. is the spirit straitened? *are t.* his doings?
Zech. 1. 9. then said, I, O my Ld. what *are t.* 4. 4. | 6. 4.
Mark 4. 15. and *t. are* they by the way-side
16. on stony || 18. thorny || 20. good ground
13. 8. famines *t. are* the beginnings of sorrows
Luke 8. 21. my mother and brethren *are t.* which
John 10. 21. *t. are* not the words of him that hath
17. 11. but *t. are* in the world, and I come to thee
20. 31. but *t. are* written that ye might believe
Acts 2. 15. *t. are* not drunken, as ye suppose
Rom. 9. 8. *t. are* not the children of God
Gal. 5. 17. *t. are* contrary the one to the other
19. the works of the flesh are manifest, which *are t.*
2 *Pet.* 2. 17. *t. are* wells without water, clouds
Jude 16. *t. are* murmurers, walking after their lusts
Rev. 7. 13. what *are t.* which are arrayed in white?
14. *t. are* they which came out of great tribulat.
14. 4. *t. are* they which are not defiled with women
t. are they which follow the Lamb whithersoever
19. 9. *t. are* the true sayings of God, 22. 6.

See THINGS, WORDS.

THEY.

Num. 14. 12. of thee a nation mightier than *t.*
16. 33. *t.* and all theirs went down into the pit
18. 3. not come nigh that neither *t.* nor you also die
22. 15. sent more, and more honourable than *t.*
1 *Kings* 20. 23. surely we shall be stronger than *t.* 25.
2 *Kings* 6. 16. are more than *t.* that be with them
Psal. 69. 4. *t.* that hate me, *t.* that would destroy

Eccl. 5. 8. regardeth, and there be higher than *t.*
Isa. 9. 21. and *t.* together shall be against Judah
28. 7. but *t.* also have erred through wine
30. 16. therefore *t.* that pursue you be swift
57. 6. *t.* are thy lot, to them thou hast offered
58. 12. *t.* that shall be of thee shall build the old
Jer. 2. 26. so *t.* their kings and priests ashamed
9. 16. whom neither *t.* nor their fathers have known, 19. 4. | 44. 3.
49. 12. *t.* whose judgment was not to drink of cup
Ezek. 2. 3. *t.* and their fathers have transgressed
16. 47. thou wast corrupted more than *t.* in ways
51. multiplied abominations more than *t.* 52.
34. 30. they shall know that *t.* are my people
Mat. 12. 3. what David did when an hungred, and *t.* that were with him, *Mark* 2. 25. *Luke* 6. 3.
19. 11. receive this, save *t.* to whom it is given
20. 25. *t.* that are great exercise authority upon
Mark 2. 17. *t.* that are wh. have no need, *Luke* 5. 31.
8. 9. and *t.* that had eaten were about 4000
10. 23. how hardly shall *t.* which have riches
11. 9. *t.* that went before and *t.* that followed cried
Luke 7. 10. and *t.* that were sent, returning to house
8. 13. *t.* on the rock are *t.* which receive the word
22. 28. ye are *t.* which have continued with me
John 4. 45. for *t.* also went unto the feast
5. 25. dead shall hear, and *t.* that hear shall live
29. *t.* that have done good, *t.* that have done evil
39. scriptures, and *t.* are *t.* which testify of me
6. 9. two fishes, but what are *t.* amongst so many?
9. 39. I am come, that *t.* which see not might see, and that *t.* which see might be made blind
17. 16. *t.* are not of the world, even as I am not
21. that *t.* all may be one, as thou art in me
23. that *t.* may be made perfect in one
24. Father, I will that *t.* whom thou hast given me be with me, that *t.* may behold my glory
18. 28. *t.* went not in, lest *t.* should be defiled
Acts 11. 2. *t.* of circumcision contended with him
19. now *t.* that were scattered abroad on persec.
13. 27. *t.* that dwell at Jerusalem, because *t.* knew him not
15. 11. through grace we shall be saved, even as *t.*
21. 12. we and *t.* of that place besought him
Rom. 3. 9. are we better than *t.*? no, in no wise
4. 14. for if *t.* which are of the law be heirs
8. 8. *t.* that are in the flesh cannot please God
23. not only *t.* but ourselves also groan within
9. 8. *t.* which are the children of the flesh, are not
11. 23. *t.* also, if *t.* abide not still in unbelief
16. 18. for *t.* that are such serve not our Ld. Jesus
1 *Cor.* 7. 29. *t.* that have wives, as tho' *t.* had none
30. *t.* that weep, *t.* that rejoice, *t.* that buy
31. *t.* that use this world, as not abusing it
9. 24. that *t.* who run in a race run all, but one
11. 19. that *t.* which are approved may be made
15. 11. whether it were I or *t.* so we preach, and so
18. then *t.* also which are fallen asleep in Christ
23. afterwards *t.* that are Christ's, *Gal.* 5. 24.
48. as is earthy, such are *t.* that are earthy
Gal. 2. 6. *t.* who seemed somewhat added nothing
9. *t.* gave the right hand of fellowship to me
3. 7. know ye, that *t.* which are of faith, 9.
5. 12. I would *t.* were cut off that trouble you
21. *t.* who do such things shall not inherit kingd.
6. 13. nor *t.* who are circumcised keep the law
1 *Thess.* 1. 9. *t.* shew of us what entering in we had
5. 7. for *t.* that sleep, *t.* that be drunken
1 *Tim.* 3. 13. *t.* that used the office of a deacon
5. 17. *t.* who labour in the word and doctrine
25. and *t.* that are otherwise cannot be hid
6. 9. *t.* that will be rich fall into temptation
2 *Tim.* 3. 6. of this sort are *t.* which creep into
Tit. 3. 8. that *t.* which have believed in God might
Heb. 1. 4. hath obtain. more excellent name than *t.*
4. 6. seeing *t.* to whom it was first preached
11. 40. that *t.* without us should not be perfect
13. 17. they watch, as *t.* that must give account
24. salute all the saints, *t.* of Italy salute you
Jam. 2. 12. as *t.* that shall be judged by the law
1 *John* 2. 19. they went out that *t.* might be made manifest, that *t.* were not all of us
4. 5. *t.* are of the world, *t.* speak of the world
Jude 19. these be *t.* who separate themselv. sensual
Rev. 1. 7. *t.* who pierced him, kindreds shall wail
3. 4. for *t.* are worthy, 16. 6. || 7. 13. whence came *t.*
7. 14. these are *t.* who came out of great tribulat.
14. 4. for *t.* are virgins, these are *t.* which follow the Lamb whithersoever he goeth
12. here are *t.* that keep the commandments
21. 27. but *t.* that are written in Lamb's book

THICK.

Deut. 32. 15. thou art waxen fat, thou art grown *t.*
2 *Sam.* 18. 9. the mule went under the *t.* boughs
2 *Kings* 8. 15. he took a *t.* cloth, and dipt it in water
Neh. 8. 15. fetch branches of *t.* trees to make booths
Job 15. 26. runneth on the *t.* bosses of his bucklers
Psal. 74. 5. as he lifted up axes on the *t.* trees
Ezek. 6. 13. their slain shall be under every *t.* oak
19. 11. her stature was exalted among *t.* branches
31. 3. his top was among the *t.* boughs, 10, 14.
Hab. 2. 6. to him that ladeth himself with *t.* clay
Luke 11. 29. when people were gathered *t.* together

See CLOUDS, DARKNESS.

THICKER.

1 *Kings* 12. 10. say to them, my little finger shall be *t.* than my father's loins, 2 *Chron.* 10. 10.

THICKET.

Gen. 22. 13. a ram caught in a *t.* by his horns
Jer. 4. 7. the lion is come up from his *t.*

THICKETS.

1 *Sam.* 13. 6. Isr. did hide themselves in *t.* in rocks
Isa. 9. 18. wickedness shall kindle in the *t.* of forest
10. 34. he shall cut down the *t.* of the forest
Jer. 4. 29. the whole city shall flee and go into *t.*

THICKNESS.

1 *Kings* 7. † 46. cast them in the *t.* of the ground
2 *Chron.* 4. 5. the *t.* of the sea was an hand-breadth
Jer. 52. 21. the *t.* of the pillars was four fingers
Ezek. 41. 9. the *t.* of the wall was five cubits
42. 10. the chambers were in the *t.* of the wall
Zech. 14. † 6. the light shall not be clear, nor *t.*

THIEF

Signifies, [1] *One that takes away any thing unlawfully from another, whether privately or violently*, Job 30. 5. Luke 10. 30. [2] *A seducer who by false doctrines steals from the church of God the true meaning of the Scripture*, John 10. 10. [3] *Such as exercise fraudulent dealing and unlawful gain*, Mat. 21. 13.

Exod. 22. 2. if a t. be found breaking up, 7.
8. if the t. be not found, then the master of house
Deut. 24. 7. be found stealing, then that t. shall die
Job 24. 14. the murderer in the night is as a t.
30. 5. they cried after them as after a t.
Psal. 50. 18. when thou sawest a t. then thou
Prov. 6. 30. men do not despise t. if he steal to satisfy
29. 24. whoso is partner with a t. hateth his soul
Jer. 2. 26. as a t. is ashamed when he is found
Hos. 7. 1. the t. cometh in, and robbers without
Joel 2. 9. they shall enter at the windows like a t.
Zech. 5. 4. it shall enter into the house of the t.
Mat. 24. 43. what watch t. would come, Luke 12. 39.
26. 55. are ye come as against a t. with swords and staves to take me? Mark 14. 48. Luke 22. 52.
Luke 12. 33. in heaven, where no t. approacheth
John 10. 1. by the door, the same is a t. and a robber
10. the t. cometh not but to steal and to kill
12. 6. but because he was a t. and had the bag
1 Thess. 5. 2. day of Ld. cometh as a t. 2 Pet. 3. 10.
4. that that day should overtake you as a t.
1 Pet. 4. 15. but let none of you suffer as a t.
Rev. 3. 3. I will come on thee as a t. 16. 15.

THIEVES.

Isa. 1. 23. thy princes are companions of t.
Jer. 48. 27. was not Israel found among t.?
49. 9. if t. by night, they will destroy, Obad. 5.
Mat. 6. 19. and where t. break through and steal
20. and where t. do not break through nor steal
21. 13. made it a den of t. Mark 11. 17. Luke 19. 46.
27. 38. two t. crucified with him, Mark 15. 27.
44. the t. also cast the same in his teeth
Luke 10. 30. went down to Jericho and fell among t.
36. which was neighbour to him that fell among t.?
John 10. 8. all that ever came before me are t.
1 Cor. 6. 10. nor t. inherit the kingdom of God

THIGH.

Gen. 24. 2. put thy hand under my t. 9. | 47. 29.
32. 25. he touched the hollow of Jacob's t.
31. and as he passed he halted upon his t.
46. † 26. that came out of Jacob's t. Exod. 1. † 5.
Num. 5. 21. the Lord maketh thy t. to rot, 22, 27.
Judg. 3. 16. Ehud did gird a dagger on his right t.
21. Ehud took the dagger from his right t.
8. † 30. Gideon had seventy sons going out of his t.
15. 8. and Samson smote them hip and t.
Psal. 45. 3. gird thy sword on thy t. O most mighty
Cant. 3. 8. every man hath his sword on his t.
Isa. 47. 2. uncover the t. pass over the rivers
Jer. 31. 19. I was instructed, I smote upon my t.
Ezek. 21. 12. cry and howl, smite therefore upon t.
24. 4. gather the t. and shoulder into the pot
Rev. 19. 16. he hath on his t. a name written

THIGHS.

Exod. 28. 42. breeches shall reach from loins to the t.
Cant. 7. 1. the joints of thy t. are like jewels
Dan. 2. 32. his belly and his t. were of brass

THIN.

Gen. 41. 6. and behold seven t. ears, 7, 23, 24.
27. the seven t. kine are seven years
Exod. 39. 3. they beat the gold into t. plates
Lev. 13. 30. and there be in it a yellow t. hair
2 Sam. 13. † 4. why art thou t. from day to day?
1 Kings 7. 29. certain additions made of t. work
Isa. 17. 4. the glory of Jacob shall be made t.

THINE.

Gen. 14. 23. I will not take any thing that is t.
20. 7. thou shalt die, thou and all that are t.
31. 32. discern what is t. with me and take it
33. † 9. Esau said, be that to thee, that is t.
48. 6. and thy issue after them shall be t.
Lev. 10. 15. it shall be t. and thy sons with thee, Num. 18. 9, 11, 13, 14, 15, 18.
Num. 22. 30. hast ridden on ever since I was t.
Deut. 15. 3. what is t. with thy brother, release
28. † 41. shall beget sons, but they shall not be t.
30. 4. if any of t. be driven into outmost parts
Josh. 17. 18. but the mountains shall be t. and the out goings of it shall be t.
Judg. 15. † 2. her younger sister, let her be t.
1 Sam. 2. 33. the man of t. whom I shall not cut off
15. 28. and hath given it to a neighbour of t.
2 Sam. 16. 4. t. are all that pertained to Mephibosh.
1 Kings 3. 26. let it neither be mine nor t. but divide
20. 4. O king, I am t. and all that I have
21. 19. in the place dogs shall lick thy blood, even t.
1 Chron. 12. 18. t. are we, David, and on thy side
21. 24. for I will not take that which is t.
29. 11. t. O Lord, is the greatness, power, and the glory, the earth is t. t. is the kingdom
Psal. 71. 16. mention thy righteousness, even t. only
74. 16. the day is t. the night also is t.
89. 11. the heavens are t. the earth also is t.
119. 94. I am t. save me, I sought thy precepts
Isa. 45. 14. the labour of Egypt shall be t.
63. 19. we are t. thou never barest rule over them
Jer. 32. 8. for the right of inheritance is t.
Mat. 6. 13. t. is the kingdom || 20. 14. take that is t.
25. 25. hid thy talent, lo, there thou hast that is t.
Luke 4. 7. if thou wilt worship me, all shall be t.
5. 33. but t. eat and drink || 15. 31. all I have is t.
22. 42. nevertheless, not my will but t. be done
John 17. 6. t. they were || 9. for they are t.
10. and all mine are t. and t. mine

THING.

Gen. 21. 11. the t. was very grievous to Abraham
24. 50. the t. proceedeth from the Lord
34. 7. which t. ought not to be done, 2 Sam. 13. 12.
19. the young men deferred not to do the t.
38. 10. and the t. which he did displeased the Lord, 2 Sam. 11. 27.
41. 32. because the t. is established by God
Exod. 10. 15. remained not any green t. in the trees
18. 11. in the t. wherein they dealt proudly he was
Exod. 18. 17. Jethro said, t. that thou doest is not g.
22. 9. for any manner of lost t. which another
15. if it be an hired t. it came for his hire
34. 10. a terrible t. that I will do with thee
Lev. 2. 3. a t. most holy of your offerings, 10.
4. 13. and the t. be hid from the eyes of assembly
6. 2. trespass in a t. taken away by violence
4. the t. deceitfully gotten, or the lost t.
12. 4. she shall touch no hallowed t. nor come
20. 17. it is a wicked t. they shall be cut off
Num. 16. 30. but if Lord make a new t. earth open
Deut. 1. 14. the t. which thou hast spoken is good
12. 32. what t. soever I command you, observe
13. 14. if it be truth, and the t. certain, 17. 4.
18. 22. if the t. follow not, nor come to pass
32. 47. it is not a vain t. for you, it is your life
Josh. 6. 18. keep yourselves from the accursed t.
22. 33. the t. pleased the children of Israel
Judg. 8. 27. which t. became a snare to Gideon
19. 24. but unto this man do not so vile a t.
Ruth 3. 18. till he have finished the t. to day
1 Sam. 3. 11. behold, I will do a t. in Israel at which
17. what is the t. that the Lord hath said to thee?
4. 7. there hath not been such a t. heretofore
8. 6. the t. displeased Samuel, when they said
14. 12. come up to us, and we will shew you a t.
18. 20. they told Saul, and the t. pleased him
2 Sam. 13. 33. let not my lord take the t. to heart
14. 13. wherefore hast thou thought such a t.?
18. hide not the t. that I shall ask thee
15. 35. what t. thou shalt hear, tell to Zadok
17. 19. she spread corn, and the t. was not known
1 Kings 14. 5. the wife of Jeroboam cometh to ask t.
2 Kings 2. 10. Elijah said, thou hast asked a hard t.
7. 19. make windows in heaven, might such a t. be
20. 9. have this sign, that the Lord will do the t.
1 Chron. 13. 4. t. was right in the eyes of the people
17. 23. let the t. thou hast spoken be established
2 Chron. 29. 36. for the t. was done suddenly
30. 4. the t. pleased the king and congregation
Ezra 7. 27. hath put such a t. in the king's heart
Esth. 2. 4. the t. pleased the king, and he did so
22. the t. was known to Mordecai, who told it
5. 14. the t. pleased Haman, and he caused gallows
8. 5. and if the t. seem right before the king
Job 3. 25. the t. I greatly feared is come upon me
4. 12. now a t. was secretly brought to me
6. 8. O that God would grant me the t. I long for
13. 28. he as a rotten t. consumeth, as a garment
14. 4. who can bring a clean t. out of an unclean?
22. 28. thou shalt decree a t. it shall be established
23. 14. he peformeth the t. is appointed for me
26. 3. how hast plentifully declared the t. as it is?
42. 7. not spoken of me the t. that is right, 8.
Psal. 2. 1. why do the people imagine a vain t.?
33. 17. an horse is a vain t. for safety
38. 20. because I follow the t. that good is
89. 34. nor alter the t. that is gone out of my lips
101. 3. I will set no wicked t. before mine eyes
Prov. 4. 7. wisdom is the principal t. therefore get
22. 18. for it is a pleasant t. if thou keep them
25. 2. it is the glory of God to conceal a t.
Eccl. 1. 9. the t. that hath been, it is that which shall be, and there is no new t. under the sun
7. 8. better is the end of a t. than the beginning
8. 1. and who knoweth the interpretation of a t.?
15. a man hath no better t. than to eat and drink
11. 7. a pleasant t. it is for eyes to behold the sun
Isa. 7. 13. is it a small t. for you to weary men
15. 6. there is no green t. || 17. 13. a rolling t.
29. 16. shall the t. framed say of him that framed it
21. that turn aside the just for a t. of nought
40. 15. he taketh up the isles as a very little t.
41. 12. and they shall be as a t. of nought
43. 19. I will do a new t. it shall spring forth
55. 11. it shall prosper in the t. whereto I sent it
66. 8. who hath heard such a t. who hath seen
Jer. 2. 10. consider, and see if there be such a t.
5. 30. a horrible t. is committed in the land
11. 13. ye set up altars to that shameful t. to Baal
14. 14. they prophesy unto you a t. of nought
18. 13. the virgin of Israel hath done a horrible t.
23. 14. I have seen in the prophets a horrible t.
31. 22. Lord hath created a new t. in the earth
38. 14. I will ask thee a t. hide nothing from me
42. 3. that God may shew us the t. that we may do
4. that whatsoever t. the Lord shall answer you
44. 17. we will do what t. goeth out of our mouth
Lam. 2. 13. what t. shall I take to witness for thee? what t. shall I liken to thee?
Ezek. 14. 9. if deceived when he hath spoken a t.
16. 47. but as if it were a very little t.
Dan. 2. 5. the king said, the t. is gone from me, 8.
11. and it is a rare t. that the king requireth
15. Arioch made the t. known to Daniel
17. Daniel made the t. known to Hananiah
4. 33. the same hour was the t. fulfilled on Neb.
5. 15. could not shew the interpretation of the t.
26. this is the interpretation of the t. Mene
6. 12. the t. is true, according to the law
10. 1. a t. was revealed to Daniel, and the t. was true, and he understood the t. and the vision
Hos. 6. 10. I have seen an horrible t. in Israel
8. 12. but they were counted as a strange t.
Amos 6. 13. ye which rejoice in a t. of nought
Mal. 1. 14. and sacrificeth to the Lord a corrupt t.
Mark 1. 27. what t. is this? what new doctr. is this?
Luke 12. 11. how or what t. ye shall answer
John 5. 14. sin no more, lest a worse t. come to thee
9. 30. the man said, herein is a marvellous t.
Acts 10. 28. it is unlawful t. for man that is a Jew
17. 21. but either to tell or hear some new t.
21. 25. have written, that they observe no such t.
23. 17. for he hath a certain t. to tell him
25. 26. of whom I have no certain t. to write
26. 8. why should it be thought a t. incredible
10. which t. I also did in Jerusalem, and many
Rom. 9. 20. shall t. formed say to him that formed it
1 Cor. 1. 10. I beseech that ye all speak the same t.
4. 3. with me it is a very small t. that I be judged
8. 7. some eat it as a t. offered unto an idol
2 Cor. 5. 5. hath wrought us for the self-same t. is G.
2 Cor. 7. 11. this self-same t. that ye sorrowed after
Phil. 3. 16. nevertheless, let us mind the same t.
2 Thess. 1. 6. seeing it is a righteous t. with God
Heb. 10. 29. the blood of the covenant an unholy t.
31. a fearful t. to fall into the hands of living G
1 Pet. 4. 12. as though some strange t. happened
1 John 2. 8. which t. is true in him, and in you
Rev. 2. 15. doctrine of Nicolaitans, which t. I hate

See ACCURSED.

Any THING.

Gen. 14. 23. I will not take any t. that is thine
18. 14. is any t. too hard for the Lord
19. 22. cannot do any t. till thou be come thither
22. 12. neither do thou any t. unto the lad
30. 31. Jacob said, thou shalt not give me any t.
39. 9. neither hath he kept back any t. from me
23. he looked not to any t. under his hand
Exod. 20. 4. thou shalt not make unto thee any likeness of any t. Deut. 4. 18, 23, 25. | 5. 8.
17. nor any t. that is thy neighbour's, Deut. 5. 21.
Lev. 6. 7. forgiven him for any t. he hath done
13. 48. in any t. made of skin, 49, 52, 53, 57, 59.
15. 6. that sitteth on any t. whereon he sat, 23.
10. who toucheth any t. that was under him, 22.
19. 26. ye shall not eat any t. with the blood
21. 18. or that hath any t. superfluous, 22, 23.
Num. 20. 19. I will go thro' without doing any t. else
22. 38. have I now any power at all to say any t.?
35. 22. cast upon him any t. without laying wait
Deut. 4. 32. if there hath been any such t. as this
8. 9. thou shalt not lack any t. in the land
14. 3. thou shalt not eat any abominable t.
21. ye shall not eat any t. that dieth of itself
16. 4. nor shall there any t. of the flesh remain
23. 19. usury of any t. that is lent upon usury
24. 10. when thou dost lend thy brother any t.
31. 13. their children who have not known any t.
Josh. 21. 45. there failed not ought of any t. spoken
Judg. 11. 25. art thou any t. better than Balak?
18. 7. that might put them to shame in any t.
10. a place where there is no want of any t. 19. 19.
1 Sam. 3. 17. God do so to thee, if thou hide any t.
20. 26. but Saul spake not any t. that day
39. but the lad knew not any t. only Jonathan
21. 2. let no man know any t. of the business
22. 15. let not the king impute any t. to his servant
25. 15. we were not hurt, neither missed we any t.
30. 19. there was not lacking any t. had taken
2 Sam. 13. 2. he thought it hard to do any t. to her
15. 11. they went in simplicity, they knew not any t.
1 Kings 10. 3. there was not a. t. hid from the king
15. 5. turned not aside from any t. commanded
20. 33. whether any t. would come from him
2 Kings 4. 2. hath not any t. save a pot of oil
1 Chron. 26. 28. whosoever hath dedicated any t.
2 Chron. 9. 20. silver was not any t. accounted of
23. 19. that none unclean in any t. should enter in
Job 15. 11. is there any secret t. with thee?
33. 32. if thou hast any t. to say, answer me
Psal. 34. 10. that seek L. shall not want any good t.
141. 4. incline not my heart to any evil t.
Eccl. 1. 10. any t. whereof it may be said, this is new
3. 14. nothing be put to it, nor any t. taken from it
5. 2. heart not be hasty to utter any t. before God
9. 5. dead know not any t. nor have they a reward
Jer. 32. 27. is there any t. too hard for me?
38. 5. for the king is not he that can do any t.
42. 21. nor any t. for which he hath sent me to you
Dan. 3. 29. which speak any t. amiss against God
Jonah 3. 7. let neither man nor beast taste any t.
Mat. 18. 19. if two shall agree touching any t.
24. 17. to take any t. out of his house, Mark 13. 15.
Mark 4. 22. nor was any t. kept secret, Luke 8. 17.
9. 22. if thou canst do any t. have compassion on us
11. 13. if haply he might find any t. thereon
16. 8. neither said they any t. to any man
Luke 19. 8. if I have taken any t. from any man
22. 35. lacked ye any t.? and they said, nothing
John 1. 3. and without him was not any t. made
46. can there any good t. come out of Nazareth?
7. 4. there is no man that doeth any t. in secret
14. 14. if ye ask any t. in my name, I will do it
Acts 10. 14. I have never eaten any t. common
17. 25. as tho' he needed any t. seeing he giveth
25. 8. nor against Cæsar have I offended any t.
11. or if I committed any t. worthy of death
Rom. 8. 33. lay any t. to the charge of God's elect
13. 8. owe no man any t. but to love one another
14. 21. nor any t. whereby thy brother stumbleth
1 Cor. 2. 2. nor to know any t. save Jesus crucified
3. 7. neither is he that planteth any t. nor watereth
8. 2. if any man think that he knoweth any t.
10. 19. what say I then? that the idol is any t.
14. 35. if learn any t. let them ask their husbands
2 Cor. 2. 10. to whom ye forgive any t. I forgive, for if I forgave any t. I forgave in the person of Chr.
3. 5. not sufficient to think any t. as of ourselves
6. 3. giving no offence in any t. that the ministry
7. 14. for if I have boasted any t. to him of you
Gal. 5. 6. neither circumcision availeth any t. nor
Eph. 5. 27. not having wrinkle, or any such t.
Phil. 3. 15. if in any t. ye be otherwise minded
1 Thess. 1. 8. so that we need not to speak any t.
1 Tim. 1. 10. and if there be any other t. contrary
Jam. 1. 7. that he shall receive any t. of the Lord
1 John 5. 14. if we ask any t. according to his will
Rev. 9. 4. that they should not hurt any green t.
21. 27. in no wise enter any t. that defileth

Every THING.

Gen. 6. 17. every t. that is in the earth shall die
8. 1. God remembered Noah and every living t.
9. 3. every moving t. that liveth shall be meat
Lev. 15. 4. every t. whereon he sitteth, unclean
20. every t. she sitteth on shall be unclean
23. 37. ye shall offer every t. upon his day
27. 28. every devoted t. is most holy to the Lord
Num. 18. 14. every t. devoted in Israel shall be thine, Ezek. 44. 29.
15. every t. that openeth the matrix be thine
31. 23. every t. that may abide fire, make it go
Deut. 23. 9. then keep thee from every wicked t.
Josh. 4. 10. the priests stood till every t. was finished

1 *Sam.* 15. 9. *every t.* that was vile they destroyed
2 *Sam.* 15. 36. send unto me *every t.* ye can hear
Esth. 6. 13. told *every t.* that had befallen him
Job 28. 10. and his eyes seeth *every* precious *t.*
39. 8. and he searcheth after *every* green *t.*
42. 2. I know that thou canst do *every t.*
Psal. 150. 6. let *every t.* that hath breath praise Lord
Prov. 27. 7. to the hungry *every* bitter *t.* is sweet
Eccl. 3. 1. to *every t.* there is a season and a time
11. hath made *every t.* beautiful in his time
12. 14. work into judgment with *every* secret *t.*
Isa. 19. 7. *every t.* sown by the brook shall wither
Ezek. 47. 9. *every t.* shall live where rivers come
Mat. 8. 33. told *every t.* and what was befallen
1 *Cor.* 1. 5. in *every t.* ye are enriched, 2 *Cor.* 9. 11.
2*Cor.* 8.7. as ye are bound in every *t.* in faith, in love
10. 5. and *every* high *t.* that exalteth itself
Eph. 5. 24. be subject to their husbands in *every t.*
Phil. 4. 6. in *every t.* by prayer and supplication
1 *Thess.* 5. 18. in *every t.* give thanks, for this is
See CREEPETH, CREEPING, EVIL, GOOD, GREAT, HOLY, LIGHT, LIVING, ONE, SMALL.

That THING.

Gen. 18. 17. hide from Abraham *that t.* which I do
Exod. 9. 6. and the Lord did *that t.* on the morrow
Lev. 5. 5. shall confess that he hath sinned in *that t.*
Deut. 17. 5. which have committed *that* wicked *t.*
Luke 9. 21. he charged them to tell no man *that t.*
12. 26. if ye be not able to do *that t.* which is least
Rom. 14. 22. not himself in *that t.* which he alloweth

This THING.

Gen. 19. 21. I have accepted thee concerning *this t.*
20. 10. sawest thou that thou hast done *this t.*
21. 26. I wot not who hath done *this t.* neither
22. 16. done *this t.* and not withheld thy son
30. 31. if wilt do *this t.* I will again feed flock
34. 14. we cannot do *this t.* to give our sister
41. 28. *this* is the *t.* I have spoken to Pharaoh
44. 7. that we should do according to *this t.*
Exod. 1. 18. why have ye done *this t.* and saved
2. 14. and Moses said, surely *this t.* is known
15. Pharaoh heard *this t.* he sought to slay Moses
9. 5. to-morrow the Lord shall do *this t.* in land
12. 24. observe *this t.* for an ordinance to thee
16. 16. *this* is the *t.* which the Lord commanded, 32. | 35. 4. *Lev.* 8. 5. | 9. 6. | 17. 2. *Num.* 30. 1. | 36. 6. *Deut.* 15. 15. | 24. 18, 22.
18. 14. what is *this t.* thou doest to the people?
18. *this t.* is too heavy for thee, thou art not able
23. if thou shalt do *this t.* and God command thee
29. 1. *this* is the *t.* that thou shalt do to them
33. 17. I will do *this t.* that thou hast spoken
Num. 32. 20. if ye will do *this t.* if ye will go armed
36. 6. *this t.* Lord commands about daughters
Deut. 1. 32. yet in *this t.* ye did not believe God
15. 10. for *this t.* the Lord thy God shall bless thee
22. 20. if *this t.* be true, and tokens be not found
32. 47. thro' *this t.* ye shall prolong your days
Josh. 9. 24. we were afraid, and have done *this t.*
22. 24. have not rather done it for fear of *this t.*
Judg. 6. 29. they said one to another, who hath done *this t.?* Gideon hath done *this t.*
11. 37. let *this t.* be done for me, let me alone
20. 9. *this* shall be the *t.* which we will do
21. 11. and *this* is the *t.* that ye shall do
1*Sam.* 20. 2. why should my father hide *t. t.* from me
24. 6. the Lord forbid that I should do *this t.*
26. 16. *this t.* is not good that thou hast done
28. 10. no punishment happen to thee for *this t.*
18. Lord hath done *this t.* unto thee this day
2 *Sam.* 2. 6. requite, because ye have done *this t.*
11. 11. as thy soul liveth, I will not do *this t.*
25. say to Joab, let not *this t.* displease thee
12. 5. the man that hath done *this t.* shall die
6. because he did *this t.* and had no pity
12. but I will do *this t.* before all Isr. and the sun
13. 20. he is thy brother, regard not *this t.*
14. 13. the king doth speak *this t.* as one faulty
15. I am come to speak of *this t.* unto the king
20. my lord, thy servant Joab hath done *this t.*
24. 3. why doth my lord the king delight in *this t.?*
1 *Kings* 1. 27. is *this t.* done by my lord the king?
3. 10. pleased Lord that Solomon had asked *t. t.* 11.
11. 10. had commanded him concerning *this t.*
12. 24. return every man, for *this t.* is from me
30. made two calves, and *this t.* became a sin
13. 33. after *this t.* Jeroboam returned not
34. *this t.* became sin to the house of Jeroboam
20. 9. tell my lord the king *this t.* I may not do
24. do *this t.* take the kings away, every man
2 *Kings* 5. 18. in *this t.* the Lord pardon thy serv.
6. 11. the king of Syria was troubled for *this t.*
7. 2. Lord would make windows, might *this t.* be
11. 5. *this* is the *t.* that ye shall do, 2 *Chron.* 23. 4.
17. 12. the Lord had said, ye shall not do *this t.*
1 *Chron.* 11. 19. God forbid that I should do *this t.*
21. 3. why then doth my lord require *this t.?*
7. and God was displeased with *this t.*
8. I have sinned, because I have done *this t.*
2 *Chron.* 11. 4. return every man, *this t.* done of me
16. 10. was in rage with him, because of *this t.*
Ezra 9. 3. when I heard *this t.* I rent my garment
10. 2. there is hope in Israel concerning *this t.*
13. we are many that have transgressed in *this t.*
Neh. 2. 19. what is *this t.* that ye do? will ye rebel
Isa. 38. 7. Lord will do *this t.* that he hath spoken
Jer. 7. 23. but *this* is the *t.* that I command them
22. 4. if ye do *t. t.* indeed, then shall enter in kings
40. 3. therefore *this t.* is come upon you
16. Gedaliah said, thou shalt not do *this t.*
44. 4. oh do not *this* abominable *t.* that I hate
Mark 5. 32. he looked to see her that had done *this t.*
Luke 2. 15. and see *this t.* which is come to pass
22. 23. which of them it was that should do *this t.*
John 18. 34. sayest thou *this t.* of thyself?
Acts 5. 4. why hast thou conceived *this t.* in heart?
26. 26. for *this t.* was not done in a corner
Rom. 13. 6. attending continually upon *this* very *t.*
1 *Cor.* 9. 17. if I do *this t.* willingly, I have a reward
2 *Cor.* 12. 8. for *this t.* I besought the Lord thrice
Phil. 1. 6. being confident in *this* very *t.* that he who

Phil. 3. 13. but *this* one *t.* I do, I press toward mark

Unclean THING.

Lev. 5. 2. or if a soul touch any *unclean t.* 7. 21.
7. 19. flesh that toucheth *unclean t.* not be eaten
20. 21. take his brother's wife, it is an *unclean t.*
Deut. 23. 14. that he see no *unclean t.* in thee
Judg. 13. 4. and eat not any *unclean t.* 7, 14.
Isa. 52. 11. touch no *unclean t.* 2 *Cor.* 6. 17.
64. 6. we are all as an *unclean t.* we all do fade
Acts 10. 14. have never eaten any *t.* that is *unclean*

THINGS.

Gen. 45. 23. ten asses laden with the good *t.* of Egypt
Lev. 4. 2. if a soul sin thro' ignorance concerning *t.* which ought not to be done, 13, 22, 27.
Deut. 4. 9. lest thou forget *t.* thine eyes have seen
22. 3. and with all lost *t.* of thy brother's he hath lost
29. 29. the secret *t.* belong unto the Lord our God
32. 35. the *t.* that shall come on them make haste
33. 15. for the chief *t.* of the ancient mountains
Judg. 18. 27. took the *t.* which Micah had made
1 *Sam.* 12. 21. for then should ye go after vain *t.*
15. 21. but the people took the chief of the *t.*
2 *Sam.* 24. 12. I offer thee three *t.* 1 *Chron.* 21. 10.
1 *Kings* 7. 51. Solomon brought in the *t.* dedicated
15. 15. Asa brought in the *t.* 2 *Chron.* 15. 18.
2 *Kings* 17. 11. and Israel wrought wicked *t.* to prov.
1 *Chron.* 4. 22. and these are ancient *t.*
9. 31. the office over *t.* that were made in pans
29. 2. prepared gold for *t.* of gold, silver for *t.* of silver, brass for *t.* of brass, iron for *t.* of iron
2 *Chron.* 12. 12. and also in Judah *t.* went well
Esth. 2. 3. let *t.* for purification be given them, 12.
Job 5. 9. who doth marvellous *t.* without number
6. 7. the *t.* that my soul refuseth to touch
30. cannot my taste discern perverse *t.?*
12. 22. he discovereth deep *t.* out of darkness
13. 20. only do not two *t.* to me, then will I not hide
26. for thou writest bitter *t.* against me
41. 34. he beholdeth all high *t.* is king over pride
42. 3. I have uttered *t.* too wonderful for me
Psal. 12. 3. cut off tongue, that speaketh proud *t.*
17. 2. thine eyes behold the *t.* that are equal
31. 18. which speak grievous *t.* proudly
35. 11. they laid to my charge *t.* I knew not
38. 12. that seek my hurt, speak mischievous *t.*
45. 1. I speak of the *t.* which I have made
4. thy right hand shall teach thee terrible *t.*
60. 3. thou hast shewed thy people hard *t.*
65. 5. by terrible *t.* wilt thou answer us, O God
72. 18. the G. of Israel, who only doth wondrous *t.*
78. 12. marvellous *t.* did he in Egypt, 98. 1.
86. 10. thou art great, and dost wondrous *t.*
87. 3. glorious *t.* are spoken of thee, O city of God
94. 4. how long shall they utter and speak hard *t.?*
106. 22. who had done terrible *t.* by the Red sea
113. 6. himself to behold the *t.* that are in heaven
119. 18. I may behold wondrous *t.* out of thy law
131. 1. in great matters, or in *t.* too high for me
Prov. 2. 12. from the man that speaketh froward *t.*
8. 6. I will speak of excellent *t.* of right *t.*
16. 30. he shutteth his eyes to devise froward *t.*
22. 20. I have written to thee excellent *t.*
23. 16. shalt rejoice, when thy lips speak right *t.*
33. and thine heart shall utter perverse *t.*
30. 7. two *t.* have I required of thee, deny them not
15. there are three *t.* that are never satisfied
18. there be three *t.* that be too wonderful
21. for three *t.* the earth is disquieted
24. four *t.* which are little on the earth
29. there be three *t.* which go well, yea four
Eccl. 1. 11. nor any remembrance of *t.* to come
7. 25. to seek out wisdom and the reason of *t.*
Isa. 12. 5. sing to Lord, for he hath done excellent *t.*
25. 1. sing to Lord, for thou hast done wonderful *t.*
6. Ld. shall make unto all people a feast of fat *t.*
29. 16. surely your turning of *t.* upside down
30. 10. which say, prophesy not to us right *t.*
32. 8. but the liberal deviseth liberal *t.* and by liberal *t.* shall he stand
41. 23. shew the *t.* that are to come hereafter
42. 9. former *t.* come to pass, and new *t.* I declare
16. I will make crooked *t.* straight
44. 7. the *t.* that are coming and shall come
45. 11. ask me of *t.* to come concerning my sons
19. I the Lord speak, I declare *t.* that are right
48. 6. I have shewed thee new *t.* even hidden *t.*
56. 4. the eunuchs that choose the *t.* that please me
64. 3. thou didst terrible *t.* we looked not for
11. and all our pleasant *t.* are laid waste
65. 4. broth of abominable *t.* is in their vessels
Jer. 2. 8. walked after *t.* that do not profit, 16. 19.
8. 13. the *t.* I have given them shall pass away
31. 5. the planters shall eat them as common *t.*
Lam. 1. 7. Jerusalem remembered her pleasant *t.*
11. they have given her pleasant *t.* for meat
2. 14. thy prophets have seen foolish *t.* for thee
Ezek. 11. 5. I know the *t.* that come in your mind
16. 16. like *t.* shall not come, nor shall it be so
38. 10. at the same time shall *t.* come into thy mind
Dan. 2. 22. he revealeth the deep and secret *t.*
11. 36. shall speak marvellous *t.* against G. of gods
Joel 3. 5. carried into your temples my goodly *t.*
Obad. 6. how are the *t.* of Esau searched out! how are his hidden *t.* sought up!
Mic. 7. 15. I will shew unto him marvellous *t.*
Zech. 4. 10. for who hath despised the day of small *t.*
Mat. 6. 34. morrow take thought for *t.* of itself
13. 52. brings out of his treasure *t.* new and old
16. 23. savourest not *t.* that be of G. *Mark* 8. 33.
22. 21. render therefore to Cesar the *t.* that are Cesar's, and to God the *t.* that are God's, *Mark* 12. 17. *Luke* 20. 25.
Mark 4. 19. lusts of other *t.* entering in, choke word
7. 15. but the *t.* which come out of him defile
Luke 5. 26. saying, we have seen strange *t.* to-day
6. 46. call me Lord, and do not the *t.* which I say
10. 23. blessed the eyes which see the *t.* that ye see
12. 15. in the abundance of the *t.* he possesseth
48. and did commit *t.* worthy of stripes
18. 27. the *t.* which are impossible with men are
19. 42. hadst known the *t.* which belong to thy peace
22. 37. for the *t.* concerning me have an end

Luke 23. 48. all people behold. *t.* which were done
24. 18. hast not known the *t.* which are come to pass
27. he expounded the *t.* concerning himself
John 1. 50. thou shalt see greater *t.* than these
3. 12. if I have told you earthly *t.* heavenly *t.*
16. 13. the Spirit will shew you *t.* to come
Acts 1. 3. speaking of *t.* pertaining to the kingdom
4. 20. we cannot but speak the *t.* we have seen
25. and why did the people imagine vain *t.?*
32. that ought of the *t.* he possessed was his own
8. 12. preaching the *t.* concerning the kingd. of God
15. 20. that they abstain from *t.* strangled, 29.
16. 14. she attended to the *t.* spoken of Paul
18. 25. Apollos taught diligently the *t.* of the Ld.
19. 8. persuading *t.* concerning the kingdom of G.
20. 22. not knowing the *t.* that shall befall me
30. shall men arise, speaking perverse *t.* to draw
21. 25. that they keep from *t.* offered to idols
24. 13. neither can they prove the *t.* whereof
26. 22. saying none other *t.* than the prophets
28. 24. some believed the *t.* that were spoken
Rom. 1. 20. the invisible *t.* of him are clearly seen, being understood by the *t.* that are made
2. 1. for thou that judgest doest the same *t.*
14. Gentiles do by nature *t.* contained in the law
18. and approvest the *t.* that are more excellent
8. 5. mind the *t.* of the flesh, mind *t.* of the Spirit
38. nor *t.* present, nor *t.* to come, 1 *Cor.* 3. 22.
12. 16. mind not high *t.* ‖ 17. provide *t.* honest
14. 19. follow after *t.* that make for peace, and edify
15. 4. whatsoever *t.* were written aforetime
27. if Gentiles made partakers of spiritual *t.* their duty is to minister to them in carnal *t.*
1 *Cor.* 1. 27. God hath chosen the foolish *t.* of the world, weak *t.* to confound *t.* which are mighty
28. base *t.* and *t.* despised hath God chosen
2. 9. the *t.* which God hath prepared for them
10. the Spirit searcheth the deep *t.* of God
11. what man knoweth *t.* of man, so the *t.* of God knoweth no man, but the Spirit of God
12. we might know the *t.* that are freely given us
13. which *t.* we speak, comparing spiritual *t.*
14. man receiveth not the *t.* of the Spirit of God
4. 5. will bring to light the hidden *t.* of darkness
6. 3. much more *t.* that pertain to this life, 4.
7. 32. unmarried careth for the *t.* of the Lord, 34.
33. married careth for the *t.* that are of the world
8. 1. now as touching *t.* offered to idols, we know
9. 11. if we have sown spiritual *t.* if reap carnal *t.*
10. 20. that the *t.* which the Gentiles sacrifice
13. 11. when I became man, I put away childish *t.*
14. 7. and even *t.* without life giving sound
37. acknowledge that the *t.* that I write to you
16. 14. let all your *t.* be done with charity
2 *Cor.* 1. 13. for we write none other *t.* unto you
17. or the *t.* that I purpose, do I purpose according
4. 2. but have renounced the hidden *t.* of dishonesty
18. while we look not at the *t.* which are seen, *t.* seen are temporal, *t.* not seen are eternal
5. 10. every one may receive the *t.* done in his body
17. old *t.* are passed away, all *t.* are become new
8. 21. providing for honest *t.* in sight of L. and men
10. 7. do ye look on *t.* after the outward appearance
13. we will not boast of *t.* without our meas. 15.
16. and not to boast in another man's line of *t.*
11. 30. I will glory of the *t.* which concern mine
Gal. 2. 18. if I build again the *t.* which I destroyed
4. 24. which *t.* are an allegory, for these are two
5. 17. so that ye cannot do the *t.* that ye would
Eph. 6. 9. and ye, masters, do the same *t.* to them
Phil. 1. 10. that ye may approve *t.* that are excellent
12. *t.* which happened unto me have fallen out
2. 4. look not every man on his own *t.* but every man also on the *t.* of others
10. of *t.* in heaven, *t.* in earth, *t.* under earth
21. seek not the *t.* which are Jesus Christ's
3. 1. to write the same *t.* ‖ 19. who mind earthly *t.*
4. 8. whatsoev. *t.* are true, honest, just, pure, lovely
18. I am full, having received the *t.* sent from you
Col. 1. 20. whether *t.* in earth, or *t.* in heaven
2. 17. which are shadow of *t.* to come, *Heb.* 10. 1.
23. which *t.* have indeed a shew of wisdom
3. 2. set your affection on *t.* above, not on *t.* on earth
6. for which *t.* sake the wrath of God cometh
1 *Thess.* 2. 14. for ye also have suffered like *t.* of your
2 *Thess.* 3. 4. and will do the *t.* which we command
1 *Tim.* 5. 13. speaking *t.* which they ought not
2 *Tim.* 2. 2. the *t.* which thou hast heard of me
3. 14. continue in *t.* which thou hast learned
Tit. 1. 5. thou shouldest set in order the *t.* wanting
11. teaching *t.* they ought not for lucre's sake
2. 1. speak thou *t.* which become sound doctrine
Heb. 2. 1. give heed to the *t.* which we have heard
17. be faithful high priest in *t.* pertain. to G. 5. 1.
5. 8. yet learned he obedience by the *t.* he suffered
6. 9. but, beloved, we are persuaded better *t.* of you, and *t.* that accompany salvation
18. that by two immutable *t.* in which it was
8. 1. of the *t.* we have spoken this is the sum
5. to the example and shadow of heavenly *t.*
9. 23. that the patterns of *t.* in the heavens be purified, but heavenly *t.* with better sacrifices
11. 1. now faith is the substance of *t.* hoped for, the evidence of *t.* not seen
3. *t.* seen were not made of *t.* which do appear
7. Noah being warned of G. of *t.* not seen as yet
20. blessed Jacob and Esau concerning *t.* to come
12. 24. that speaketh better *t.* than that of Abel
Jam. 3. 7. and *t.* in the sea are tamed of mankind
1 *Pet.* 1. 12. they did minister *t.* which are now reported; which *t.* the angels desire to look into
18. ye were not redeemed with corruptible *t.*
2 *Pet.* 2. 12. speak evil of *t.* they understand not
1 *John* 2. 15. neither the *t.* that are in the world
Rev. 1. 1. the revelation of Jesus Christ to shew to his servants *t.* must shortly come to pass, 22. 6
19. write the *t.* which thou hast seen, the *t.* which are, and *t.* which shall be hereafter
2. 14. but I have a few *t.* against thee, to eat *t.* sacrificed to idols, and to commit fornication, 20
3. 2. strengthen the *t.* which remain, ready to die
4. 1. I will shew thee the *t.* must be hereafter

Rev. 10. 6. and sware by him who created heaven, earth, sea, and all t. that therein are
21. 4. for the former t. are passed away
22. 19. take his part from t. written in this book
See CREEPING, DEDICATE, DETESTABLE, FORMER, PRECIOUS.

All THINGS.

Gen. 9. 3. as the green herb have I given you all t.
24. 1. the Lord hath blessed Abraham in all t.
66. the servant told Isaac all t. that he had done
Exod. 23. 13. in all t. I have said, be circumspect
29. 35. do according to all t. I commanded thee
Lev. 8. 36. Aaron and his sons did all t. commanded
Num. 1. 50. the Levites over all t. that belong to it
31. 20. and purify all t. made of wood and skins
Deut. 1. 18. I commanded you all t. ye should do
4. 7. as the Lord our God is in all t. we call for
12. 8. ye shall not do after all t. that we do here
28. 47. servedst not for the abundance of all t.
48. shalt serve thine enemies in want of all t.
57. eat them for want of all t. secretly in siege
Josh. 1. 17. as we hearkened to Moses in all t.
2. 23. the spies told him all t. that befell them
Ruth 4. 7. this was the manner, to confirm all t.
1 Sam. 3. 12. perform all t. concerning Eli's house
17. if thou hide any of all t. he said to thee
19. 7. and Jonathan shewed David all those t.
2 Sam. 11. 18. Joab sent and told David all the t.
14. 20. to know all t. that are in the earth
23. 5. he made a covenant ordered in all t. and sure
1 Kings 21. 26. he did all t. as did the Amorites
2 Kings 11. 9. the captains did according to all t. that Jehoiada the priest commanded, 2 Chr. 23. 8.
14. 3. Amaziah, according to all t. that Joash did
20. 15. they have seen all t. that are in my house
1 Chron. 29. 14. all t. come of thee, and of thine
2 Chron. 5. 1. Solomon brought all t. dedicated
31. 5. tithe of all t. brought they in abundantly
Neh. 9. 6. the Lord made all t. Acts 14. 15. | 17. 24, 25. Col. 1. 16. Rev. 4. 11.
Job 41. 34. he beholdeth all high t. he is a king
Psal. 8. 6. thou hast put all t. under his feet, 1 Cor. 15. 27. Eph. 1. 22.
57. 2. cry to God that performeth all t. for me
119. 128. precepts concerning all t. to be right
Prov. 3. 15. wisdom is more precious than all t. 8. 11.
16. 4. the Lord hath made all t. for himself
26. 10. the great God that formed all t. rewardeth
28. 5. they that seek the Lord understand all t.
Eccl. 1. 8. all t. are full of labour, man cannot utter
7. 15. all t. have I seen in days of my vanity
9. 2. all t. come alike to all, there is one event
3. this is an evil among all t. done under the sun
10. 19. but money answereth all t.
Isa. 44. 24. I am the Lord that maketh all t. 66. 2.
Jer. 10. 16. for he is the former of all t. 51. 19.
17. 9. the heart is deceitful above all t. and wicked
42. 5. if we do not even according to all t. for which
44. 18. we wanted all t. and have been consumed
Ezek. 11. 25. I spake all t. the Lord hath shewed me
38. 20. all creeping t. shall shake at my presence
44. 30. the first of all t. shall be the priest's
Dan. 2. 40. forasmuch as iron subdueth all t.
Zeph. 1. 2. I will consume all t. from off the land
Mat. 7. 12. all t. ye would that men should do to you
11. 27. all t. are delivered to me, Luke 10. 22.
13. 41. they shall gather all t. that offend
17. 11. Elias shall restore all t. Mark 9. 12.
19. 26. with man this is impossible, but with God all t. are possible, Mark 10. 27. | 14. 36.
21. 22. all t. whatsoever ye shall ask in prayer
22. 4. tell them which are bidden, behold all t. are ready, come unto the marriage, Luke 14. 17.
23. 20. sweareth by it, and by all t. thereon
28. 20. teaching them to observe all t. I commanded
Mark 4. 34. he expounded all t. to his disciples
6. 30. they told him all t. what they had done
7. 37. astonished, saying, he hath done all t. well
9. 23. all t. are possible to him that believeth
13. 23. take heed, I have foretold you all t.
Luke 2. 20. praising God for all t. they had heard
39. performed all t. according to the law of God
9. 43. they wondered at all t. which Jesus did
11. 41. and behold, all t. are clean unto you
18. 31. all t. written concerning Son of man shall be accomplished, 21. 22. | 24. 44. John 19. 28.
John 1. 3. all t. were made by him
3. 35. and hath given all t. into his hand, 13. 3.
4. 25. when he is come, he will tell us all t.
29. see a man who told me all t. that ever I did
5. 20. the Father sheweth the Son all t. he doeth
10. 41. all t. that John spake of him were true
14. 26. the Comforter, the Holy Ghost, shall teach you all t. and bring all t. to your remembrance
15. 15. all t. I have heard, I have made known
16. 15. all t. that the Father hath, are mine
30. we now are sure that thou knowest all t.
17. 7. that all t. thou hast given me, are of thee
18. 4. Jesus therefore knowing all t. 19. 28.
21. 17. Peter said, Lord, thou knowest all t.
Acts 2. 44. that believed had all t. common, 4. 32.
3. 21. till the times of restitution of all t.
22. him shall ye hear in all t. he shall say to you
10. 33. to hear all t. commanded thee of God
39. we are witnesses of all t. which he did
13. 39. all that believe are justified from all t.
14. 15. G. who made heaven, earth, sea, and all t.
20. 35. I have shewed you all t. how ye ought
22. 10. and there it shall be told thee of all t.
24. 14. believing all t. which are written
26. 2. touching all the t. whereof I am accused
Rom. 8. 28. and we know that all t. work for good
32. how shall he not also freely give us all t.?
11. 36. of him, and thro' him, and to him, are all t.
14. 2. for one believeth that he may eat all t.
20. all t. indeed are pure, but it is evil for him
1 Cor. 2. 10. the Spirit searcheth all t. deep things
15. but he that is spiritual judgeth all t.
3. 21. let no man glory in men, for all t. are yours
4. 13. are the offscouring of all t. to this day
6. 12. all t. are lawful unto me, but all t. are not expedient, all t. are lawful for me, 10. 23.
1 Cor. 8. 6. one God the Father, of whom are all t. one Lord Jesus Christ, by whom are all t.
9. 12. suffer all t. || 22. I am made all t. to all men
25. every man that striveth is temperate in all t.
10. 33. even as I please all men in all t.
11. 2. I praise you that ye remember me in all t.
12. but all t. are of God, 2 Cor. 5. 18.
13. 7. charity beareth all t. believeth all t. hopeth all t. endureth all t.
14. 26. let all t. be done unto edifying
40. let all t. be done decently and in order
15. 28. when all t. shall be subdued, then shall the Son be subject to him that put all t. under him
2 Cor. 2. 9. know whether ye be obedient in all t.
4. 15. for all t. are for your sakes, that grace
5. 17. old things are passed away, a. t. become new
6. 4. in all t. approving ourselves as ministers
10. as having nothing, yet possessing all t.
7. 11. in all t. ye have approved yourselves
14. but as we spake all t. to you in truth, even so
16. that I have confidence in you in all t.
9. 8. that ye having all sufficiency in all t.
11. 6. we have been made manifest to you in all t.
9. in all t. I kept myself from being burdensome
12. 19. but we do all t. for your edifying
Gal. 3. 10. cursed that continueth not in all t.
Eph. 1. 10. gather together in one all t. in Christ
11. worketh all t. after the counsel of his will
22. gave him to be head over all t. to the church
3. 9. in God, who created all t. by Jesus Christ
4. 10. he ascended up, that he might fill all t.
15. grow up unto him in all t. which is the head
5. 13. all t. that are reproved are made manifest
20. giving thanks always for all t. unto God
6. 21. shall make known to you all t. Col. 4. 9.
Phil. 2. 14. do all t. without murmurings
3. 8. I count all t. but loss for know. of Christ my Lord, for whom I have suffered the loss of all t.
21. he is able even to subdue all t. to himself
4. 12. every where, and in all t. I am instructed
13. I can do all t. thro' Ch. who strengtheneth me
Col. 1. 17. he is before all t. by him all t. consist
18. in all t. he might have the pre-eminence
20. and by him to reconcile all t. to himself
3. 20. children, obey your parents in all t.
22. servants, obey in all t. your masters
1 Thess. 5. 21. prove all t. hold fast that which is good
1 Tim. 3. 11. their wives must be faithful in all t.
4. 8. but godliness is profitable unto all t.
6. 13. in the sight of God who quickeneth all t.
17. living God who giveth us richly all t. to enjoy
2 Tim. 2. 7. the Lord give thee understanding in all t.
10. therefore I endure all t. for the elect's sake
4. 5. but watch thou in all t. endure afflictions
Tit. 1. 15. unto the pure all t. are pure
2. 7. in all t. shewing thyself a pattern of good
9. to be obedient, and please them well in all t.
10. they may adorn the doctrine of God in all t.
Heb. 1. 2. whom he hath appointed heir of all t.
3. upholding all t. by the word of his power
2. 8. thou hast put all t. in subjection under his feet; but now we see not yet all t. put under him
10. for whom are all t. and by whom are all t.
17. in all t. it behoved him to be like his brethren
3. 4. he that built all t. is God
4. 13. all t. are naked and opened unto the eyes
8. 5. make all t. according to the pattern shewed
9. 22. almost all t. are by the law purged by blood
13. 18. in all t. willing to live honestly
Jam. 5. 12. above all t. my brethren, swear not
1 Pet. 4. 7. the end of all t. is at hand, be sober
8. above all t. have fervent charity among yours.
11. that God in all t. may be glorified thro' Jesus
2 Pet. 1. 3. hath given us all t. that pertain to life
3. 4. all t. continue as they were from beginning
1 John 2. 20. ye have an unction, and ye know all t.
27. as the same anointing teacheth you all t.
3. 20. God is greater than heart, and knoweth all t.
3 John 2. I wish above all t. that thou prosper
Rev. 1. 2. who bare record of all t. that he saw
4. 11. thou hast created all t. and for thy pleasure
21. 5. I make all t. new || 7. he shall inherit all t.
See EVIL, HOLY, MANY, SUCH.

These THINGS.

Gen. 24. 28. told them of her mother's house these t.
42. 36. Jacob said, all these t. are against me
Lev. 5. 5. when he shall be guilty in one of these t. 17.
18. 24. defile not yourselves in any of these t.
20. 23. for they committed all these t. therefore
26. 23. and if ye will not be reformed by these t.
Num. 4. 15. these t. the burden of sons of Kohath
15. 13. all born of the country shall do these t.
29. 39. these t. ye shall do to the Lord in feasts
35. 29. these t. shall be for a statute of judgment
Deut. 4. 30. when all these t. are come upon me
18. 12. all that do these t. are an abomination
30. 1. when all these t. are come upon thee, then
Josh. 2. 11. we heard these t. our hearts did melt
Judg. 13. 23. nor would he have shewed us these t.
1 Sam. 25. 37. when his wife had told him these t.
2 Sam. 23. 17. these t. did these three mighty men, 1 Chron. 11. 19.
22. these t. did Benaiah, 1 Chron. 11. 24.
24. 23. these t. did Araunah give to the king
1 Kings 18. 36. I have done all these t. at thy word
2 Kings 23. 17. proclaimed these t. thou hast done
2 Chron. 3. 3. in these t. was Solomon instructed
Neh. 13. 26. did not king Solomon sin by these t.?
Job 8. 2. how long wilt thou speak these t.?
10. 13. these t. hast thou hid in thine heart
33. 29. lo, all these t. worketh God with man
Psal. 15. 5. he that doeth these t. shall never be mov.
42. 4. I remember these t. I pour out my soul
50. 21. these t. hast thou done and I kept silence
Prov. 6. 16. these six t. doth the Lord hate, yea seven
24. 23. these t. also belong to the wise
Eccl. 11. 9. for these t. God will bring thee to judgm.
Isa. 38. 16. O Lord, by these t. men live, and in all these t. is the life of my spirit
40. 26. and behold, who hath created these t.?
42. 16. these t. will I do, and not forsake them
45. 7. I form the light, I the Lord do all these t.
Isa. 47. 7. so that thou didst not lay these t. to thy heart
9. these two t. shall come to thee in a moment
13. let the astrologers save thee from these t.
48. 14. which among them hath declared these t.
51. 19. these two t. are come unto thee, who shall
64. 12. wilt thou refrain thyself for these t. O Lord
Jer. 3. 7. I said, after she had done all these t.
4. 18. thy doings have procured these t. to thee
5. 9. shall I not visit for these t.? 29. | 9. 9.
25. your iniquities have turned away these t.
9. 24. for in these t. do I delight, saith the Lord
13. 22. if thou say, wherefore come these t. on me?
14. 22. wait on thee, thou hast made all these t.
30. 15. for thy sins I have done these t. to thee
Lam. 1. 16. for these t. I weep, mine eye runneth
5. 17. our heart is faint, for these t. our eyes are dim
Ezek. 16. 30. seeing thou dost all these t. 17. 18.
43. because thou hast fretted me in all these t.
17. 12. know ye not what these t. mean, tell them
18. 10. that doeth the like to any one of these t.
23. 30. I will do these t. unto thee, because thou
24. 19. wilt thou not tell what these t. are to us?
Dan. 10. 21. none that holdeth with me in these t.
12. 7. all these t. shall be finished
8. O my Lord, what shall be the end of these t.?
Hos. 14. 9. who is wise, he shall understand these t.
Zech. 8. 16. these are the t. which ye shall do
17. for all these are t. that I hate, saith the Lord
Mat. 1. 20. but while he thought on these t.
2. 3. when Herod heard these t. he was troubled
6. 32. after all these t. do the Gentiles seek, knows that ye have need of all these t. Luke 12. 30.
33. all these t. shall be added to you, Luke 12. 31.
11. 25. hast hid these t. from the wise, Luke 10. 21.
13. 51. Jesus saith, have ye understood these t.?
56. whence then hath this man these t. Mark 6. 2.
15. 20. these are the t. which defile a man
19. 20. all these t. have I kept from my youth
21. 23. by what authority dost thou these t. Mark 11. 28. Luke 20. 2.
24. I will tell you by what authority I do these t. 27. Mark 11. 29, 33. Luke 20. 8.
23. 36. all these t. shall come on this generation
24. 2. Jesus said to them, see ye not all these t.?
3. when shall these t. be? Mark 13. 4. Luke 21. 7.
6. all these t. must come to pass, Luke 21. 9, 28.
33. when ye shall see all these t. know that it is near, Mark 13. 29. Luke 21. 31.
34. till all these t. be fulfilled, Mark 13. 30.
Luke 1. 20. till the day that these t. be performed
2. 19. but Mary kept these t. and pondered them
14. 6. they could not answer him to these t.
15. 26. he called, and asked what these t. meant?
18. 34. and they understood none of these t.
21. 36. to escape all these t. that shall come
23. 31. for if they do these t. in a green tree
24. 21. to-day is third day since these t. were done
26. ought not Christ to have suffered these t.?
48. and ye are witnesses of these t.
John 2. 16. he said to them, take these t. hence
18. what sign, seeing that thou dost these t.
3. 9. Nicodemus said to him, how can these t. be?
10. a master of Israel, and knowest not these t.?
5. 16. he had done these t. on the sabbath-day
7. 4. if thou do these t. shew thyself to the world
12. 16. these t. understood not his disciples, they remembered that these t. were written of him
41. these t. said Esaias, when he saw his glory
13. 17. if ye know these t. happy are ye if ye do them
15. 21. all these t. will they do unto you, 16. 3.
19. 24. these t. therefore the soldiers did
36. these t. were done, that the scriptures should be
Acts 5. 32. and we are his witnesses of these t.
7. 1. these t. so? || 14. 15. sirs, why do ye these t.?
50. hath not my hand made all these t.?
51. when they heard these t. they were cut to heart
8. 24. pray for me, that none of these t. come on me
15. 17. saith the Lord, who doth all these t.
17. 20. we would know what these t. mean
19. 36. seeing these t. cannot be spoken against
20. 24. none of these t. move me, neither count I
24. 9. the Jews assented, saying, these t. were so
25. 9. and there be judged of these t. before me
26. 16. to make thee a witness of these t.
26. the king knoweth of these t. before whom
Rom. 8. 31. what shall we then say to these t.?
10. 5. the men that doth these t. shall live by them
14. 18. for he that in these t. serveth Christ
1 Cor. 9. 8. say I these t. as a man, or saith not law
15. I used none of these t. nor have I written
10. 6. these t. were our examples, to the intent
2 Cor. 2. 16. and who is sufficient for these t.?
Eph. 5. 6. because of these t. cometh wrath of God
Phil. 4. 8. if there be any praise, think on these t.
Col. 3. 14. and above all these t. put on charity
1 Tim. 4. 6. put brethren remembrance of these t.
11. these t. command || 15. meditate on these t.
5. 7. these t. give in charge || 21. observe these t.
6. 2. these t. exhort, Tit. 2. 15. || 11. flee these t.
2 Tim. 2. 14. of these t. put them in remembrance
Tit. 3. 8. these t. I will that thou affirm constantly, these t. are good and profitable to men
Heb. 7. 13. for he of whom these t. are spoken
Jam. 3. 10. brethren, these t. ought not to be so
2 Pet. 1. 8. for if these t. be in you and abound
9. but he that lacketh these t. is blind
10. for if ye do these t. ye shall never fall
12. I will put you in remembrance of these t.
15. to have these t. always in remembrance
3. 11. seeing all these t. shall be dissolved, what
16. in his epistles, speaking in them of these t.
17. seeing ye know these t. before, beware
Rev. 22. 8. the feet of angel who shewed me these t.
16. to testify to you these t. in the churches
20. he which testifieth these t. saith, I come

Those THINGS.

Exod. 29. 33. eat those t. wherewith atonement made
Lev. 22. 2. in those t. which they allow unto me
Deut. 29. 29. those t. which are revealed belong to us
2 Kings 17. 9. children of Israel did secretly those t.
Ps. 107. 43. whoso will observe those t. they shall

Isa. 66. 2. for all those t. hath mine hand made, and
all those t. have been, saith the Lord
Ezek. 42. 14. approach to those t. that are for people
Mat. 13. 17. desired to see those t. which ye see, and
hear those t. which ye hear, Luke 10. 24.
Mark 1. 44. offer those t. which Moses commanded
Luke 1.45. a performance of those t. which were told
2. 18. wondered at those t. told them by shepherds
12. 20. whose shall those t. be thou hast provided
John 8. 29. I do always those t. that please him
Acts 3. 18. but those t. he hath so fulfilled
8. 6. gave heed to those t. which Philip spake
13. 45. spake against those t. which were spoken
17. 11. they searched whether those t. were so
18. 17. and Gallio cared for none of those t.
26. 16. of those t. in which I will appear to thee
27. 11. more than those t. spoken by Paul
Rom. 1. 28. to do those t. which are not convenient
4. 17. calleth those t. which be not, as though were
6. 21. what fruit had you in those t. whereof ye are
now ashamed, for the end of those t. is death
15. 17. I may glory in those t. which pertain to God
18. I will not dare to speak of any of those t.
1 Cor. 8. 4. eating of those t. offered to idols, 10.
2 Cor. 11. 28. besides those t. which are without
Eph. 5. 12. it is a shame even to speak of those t.
Phil. 3. 13. forgetting those t. which are behind, and
reaching to those t. which are before
4. 9. those t. which ye have learned and seen do
Col. 2. 18. intruding into those t. he hath not seen
3. 1. seek those t. which are above, where Christ
Heb. 3. 5. was faithful for a testimony of those t.
12. 27. the removing of t. t. which are shaken, that
those t. which cannot be shaken may remain
Jam. 2. 16. ye give not those t. which are needful
1 John 3. 22. do those t. that are pleasing in his sight
2 John 8. we lose not those t. we have wrought
Jude 10. but speak evil of those t. they know not
Rev. 1. 3. blessed are they that keep those t.
2. 10. fear none of those t. which thou shalt suffer
10. 4. seal up those t. the seven thunders uttered
20. 12. the dead were judged out of those t. written

Unclean THINGS.

Hos. 9. 3. and they shall eat unclean t. in Assyria

What THINGS.

Exod. 10. 2. tell thy son what t. I have wrought
Mat. 6. 8. Father knows what t. ye have need of
Mark 9. 9. should tell no man what t. they had seen
10. 32. began to tell them what t. should happen
11. 24. what t. soever ye desire when ye pray
Luke 7. 22. go, tell John what t. ye have seen
24. 19. what t. they said to him concerning Jesus
35. and they told what t. were done in the way
John 5. 19. what t. he doth, these doth the Son
10. 6. they understood not what t. they were
11. 46. some told them what t. Jesus had done
Acts 21. 19. what t. God wrought among Gentiles
Phil. 3. 7. what t. were gain to me, I counted loss

THINK.

Gen. 40. 14. but t. on me, when it be well with thee
Num. 36. 6. let them marry to whom they t. best
2 Sam. 13. 33. to t. that all the king's sons are dead
2 Chron. 13. 8. ye t. to withstand kingdom of Lord
Neh. 5. 19. t. on me, my God, for good, according
6. 6. reported, that thou and the Jews t. to rebel
14. my God, t. thou on Tobiah and Sanballat
Esth. 4. 13. t. not thou shalt escape in king's house
Job 31. 1. why then should I t. upon a maid?
41. 32. one would t. the deep to be hoary
Eccl. 8. 17. further, though a wise man t. to know it
Isa. 10. 7. nor doth his heart t. so, but in his heart
Jer. 23. 27. t. to cause my people forget my name
29. 11. I know the thoughts that I t. toward you
Ezek. 38. 10. and thou shalt t. an evil thought
Dan. 7. 25. he shall t. to change times and laws
11. † 24. t. his thoughts against the strong holds
Jonah 1. 6. if so be that God will t. upon us
Zech. 11. 12. if ye t. good give me my price, if not
Mat. 3. 9. and t. not to say within yourselves
5. 17. t. not that I am come to destroy the law
6. 7. t. they shall be heard for much speaking
9. 4. why t. ye evil in your hearts || 18. 12. how t. ye
10. 34. t. not I am come to send peace on earth
21. 28. what t. you? a certain man had two sons
22. 42. what t. ye of Christ? 26. 66. Mark 14. 64.
24. 44. in such an hour as ye t. not, Luke 12. 40.
Luke 13. 4. t. ye that they were sinners above all
John 5. 39. in them ye t. ye have eternal life
45. do not t. I will accuse you to the Father
11. 56. what t. ye, that he will not come to feast?
16. 2. killeth you, will t. that he doth God service
Acts 13. 25. whom t. ye that I am? I am not he
17. 29. not to t. that the Godhead is like to gold
26. 2. I t. myself happy, king Agrippa, because
Rom. 12. 3. not to t. of himself more highly than he
ought to t. but to t. soberly as God hath dealt
1 Cor. 4. 6. ye might learn in us not to t. of men
9. I t. that God hath set forth us the apostles
7. 36. if any man t. that he behaveth uncomely
40. I t. also that I have the Spirit of God
8. 2. if any man t. that he knoweth any thing
12. 23. of body, which we t. to be less honourable
14. 37. if any man t. himself to be a prophet
2 Cor. 3. 5. of ourselves to t. any thing as of ourselves
10. 2. I t. to be bold against some which t. of us
7. that he is Christ, let him t. this again, 11.
11. 16. I say again, let no man t. me a fool
12. 6. lest any t. of me above what he seeth me to be
Gal. 6. 3. if a man t. himself to be something
Eph. 3. 20. is able to do above all that we ask or t.
Phil. 4. 8. if there be any praise, t. on these things
Jam. 1. 7. let not that man t. he shall receive
4. 5. do ye t. that the scripture saith in vain?
1 Pet. 4. 4. wherein they t. strange that ye run not
12. t. it not strange concerning the fiery trial
2 Pet. 1. 13. I t. it meet as long as I am in this tabern.

THINKEST.

2 Sam. 10. 3. t. thou that David doth honour thy
father, in sending comforters? 1 Chron. 19. 3.
Job 35. 2. t. thou this right, that thou saidst, my
Mat 17. 25. Jesus said, what t. thou? 22. 17.
26. 53. t. thou that I cannot pray to my Father

Luke 10. 36. which t. thou was neighbour to him?
Acts 28. 22. we desire to hear of thee what thou t.
Rom. 2. 3. t. thou this, O man, that judgest them

THINKETH.

1 Sam. 20. † 4. whatsoever thy soul t. I will do
2 Sam. 18. 27. me t. the running of the foremost is
Psal. 40. 17. I am poor, yet the Lord t. on me
Prov. 23. 7. for as he t. in his heart, so is he
Luke 8. † 18. be taken that which he t. he hath
1 Cor. 10. 12. let him that t. he standeth, take heed
13. 5. charity seeketh not her own, t. no evil
Phil. 3. 4. if any other man t. he hath whereof

THINKING.

2 Sam. 4. 10. t. to have brought good tidings
5. 6. t. David cannot come in hither

THIRD.

Gen. 32. 19. so commanded he the second and the t.
50. 23. saw Ephraim's children of t. generation
Exod. 20. 5. to the t. and fourth generation of them
that hate me, 34. 7. Num. 14. 18. Deut. 5. 9.
28. 19. and the t. row a ligure, an agate, 39. 12.
Num. 2. 24. the camp of Ephraim in the t. rank
Deut. 23. 8. an Edomite shall enter in t. generation
Josh. 19. 10. the t. lot came up for Zebulun
2 Kings 1. 13. he sent again a captain of the t. fifty
1 Chron. 24. 8. the t. lot came forth to Harim
25. 10. the t. lot came forth to Zaccur
27. 5. the t. captain of the host for the t. month
Isa. 19. 24. Israel shall be the t. with Egypt
Ezek. 10. 14. and the t. was the face of a lion
Dan. 2. 39. and another t. kingdom of brass
5. 7. and shall be the t. ruler in the kingdom, 16. 29.
Zech. 6. 3. and in the t. chariot white horses
Mat. 20. 3. and he went out about the t. hour
22. 26. likewise t. died, Mark 12. 21. Luke 20. 31.
Mark 15. 25. it was t. hour, and they crucified him
Luke 12. 38. come in the t. watch, and find them so
20. 12. he sent the t. and they wounded him
Acts 2. 15. seeing it is but the t. hour of the day
20. 9. Eutychus fell down from the t. loft
23. 23. be ready at the t. hour of the night
2 Cor. 12. 2. such an one caught up to the t. heaven
Rev. 4. 7. and the t. beast had a face as a man
6. 5. had opened the t. seal, I heard the t. beast
8. 10. the t. angel sounded, there fell a star
11. 14. and behold, the t. woe cometh quickly
14. 9. and the t. angel followed them, saying
16. 4. the t. angel poured out his vial on the rivers
21. 19. the t. foundation was a chalcedony

See DAY, MONTH, PART.

THIRD time.

1 Sam. 3. 8. the Lord called Samuel the t. time
19. 21. Saul sent messengers again the t. time
1 Kings 18. 34. do it the t. time, they did it the t. time
Ezek. 21. 14. let the sword be doubled the t. time
Mat. 26. 44. and he prayed the t. time, Mark 14. 41.
John 21. 14. the t. time Jesus shewed himself
17. saith unto him the t. time, lovest thou me?
Peter was grieved, bec. he said to him, t. time
2 Cor. 12. 14. the t. time I am ready to come, 13. 1.

THIRD year.

Deut. 26. 12. t. year, which is the year of tithing
1 Kings 15. 28. in t. year of Asa, did Baasha slay, 33.
18. 1. word of the Lord came to Elijah in t. year
22. 2. in t. year, Jehoshaphat came to king of Israel
2 Kings 18. 1. in the t. year of Hoshea son of Elah
19. 29. in the t. year sow ye and reap, Isa. 37. 30.
2 Chron. 17. 7. in t. year of Jehoshaphat's reign
27. 5. the Ammonites paid the second and t. year
Esth. 1. 3. in the t. year of the reign of Ahasuerus
Dan. 1. 1. in the t. year of the reign of Jehoiakim
8. 1. in the t. year of the reign of Belshazzar
10. 1. in the t. year of Cyrus king of Persia

THIRDLY.

1 Cor. 12. 28. t. teachers, after that miracles

THIRST, Substantive.

Exod. 17. 3. to kill us and our children with t.
Deut. 28. 48. thou shalt serve thine enemies in t.
29. 19. imagin. of heart, to add drunkenness to t.
Judg. 15. 18. and now I shall die for t. and fall
2 Chron. 32. 11. doth persuade you to die by t.
Neh. 9. 15. thou broughtest water for their t. 20.
Job 24. 11. tread their wine-presses and suffer t.
Psal. 69. 21. in my t. they gave me vinegar to drink
104. 11. the wild asses quench their t.
Isa. 5. 13. and their multitude dried up with t.
41. 17. and when their tongue faileth for t.
50. 2. their fish stinketh, and dieth for t.
Jer. 2. 25. and withhold thy throat from t.
48. 18. come down from thy glory and sit in t.
Lam. 4. 4. cleaveth to the roof of his mouth for t.
Hos. 2. 3. lest I strip her naked, and slay her with t.
Amos 8. 11. not a t. for water, but of hearing words
13. the virgins and young men shall faint for t.
2 Cor. 11. 27. in hunger and t. in fastings often

THIRST, Verb.

Isa. 49. 10. they shall not hunger, nor t. nor heat
Mat. 5. 6. which hunger and t. after righteousness
John 4. 13. drinketh of this water, shall t. again
14. whosoever drinketh, shall never t. 6. 35.
15. sir, give me this water, that I t. not
7. 37. if any t. let him come to me and drink
19. 28. after this Jesus saith, I t.
Rom. 12. 20. if thine enemy t. give him drink
1 Cor. 4. 11. even to this present hour we t.
Rev. 7. 16. and they shall not t. any more

THIRSTED.

Exod. 17. 3. people t. there for water and murmured
Isa. 48. 21. they t. not when he led them through

THIRSTETH.

Psal. 42. 2. my soul t. for God, 63. 1. | 143. 6.
Isa. 55. 1. ho, every one that t. come to the waters

THIRSTY.

Judg. 4. 19. give me a little water, for I am t.
2 Sam. 17. 29. the people is t. in the wilderness
Psal. 63. 1. my flesh longeth in a t. land, 143. 6.
107. 5. hungry and t. their soul fainted in them
Prov. 25. 21. if thine enemy be t. give him drink
25. as cold waters to a t. soul, so is good news
29. 10. the blood-t. hate the upright, but the just
Isa. 21. 14. brought water to him that was t.
29. 8. it shall be as when a t. man dreameth

Isa. 32. 6. he will cause the drink of the t. to fail
35. 7. the t. land shall become springs of water
44. 3. for I will pour water upon him that is t.
65. 13. my servants shall drink, but ye shall be t.
Ezek. 19. 13. she is planted in a dry and t. ground
Mat. 25. 35. for I was t. and ye gave me drink
37. when saw we thee t. and gave thee drink?
42. for I was t. and ye gave me no drink

THIRTEEN.

Gen. 17. 25. Ishmael his son was t. years old
Num. 29. 13. ye shall offer t. young bullocks, 14.
1 Kings 7. 1. was building his own house t. years
1 Chron. 26. 11. the sons and brethren of Hosah t.
Ezek. 40. 11. the length of the gate t. cubits

THIRTEENTH.

Gen. 14. 4. and in the t. year they rebelled
1 Chron. 24. 13. the t. lot came forth to Huppah
25. 20. the t. lot came forth to Shubael
Jer. 1. 2. in the t. year of the reign of Josiah
25. 3. from the t. year of Josiah the son of Amon

See DAY.

THIRTIETH.

2 Kings 15. 13. Shallum to reign in nine and t. year
17. in the nine and t. year of king Azariah
25. 27. in the seven and t. year of the captivity of
Jehoiachin king of Judah, Jer. 52. 31.
2 Chr. 15. 19. no war to the five and t. year of Asa
16. 1. in the six and t. year of the reign of Asa
Neh. 5. 14. the two and t. year of Artaxerxes, 13. 6.

THIRTY.

Gen. 6. 15. the height of the ark was t. cubits
11. 14. Salah lived t. years, and begat Eber
18. Peleg lived t. years, and begat Reu
22. Serug lived t. years, and begat Nahor
18. 30. peradventure there shall be t. found, he
said, I will not do it if I find t. there
32. 15. t. milch camels with their colts, forty kine
41. 46. Joseph was t. years old when he stood
Exod. 21. 32. shall give to their master t. shekels
26. 8. the length of one curtain t. cubits, 36. 15.
Lev. 27. 4. thy estimation shall be t. shekels
Num. 4. 3. from t. years old and upwards even to
fifty, 23, 30, 35, 39, 43, 47. 1 Chron. 23. 3.
Judg. 10. 4. Jair had t. sons, and they had t. cities
12. 9. Ibzan had t. sons and t. daughters he sent
abroad, took in t. daughters for his sons
14. Abdon had forty sons and t. nephews
14. 11. they brought t. companions to be with him
12. give you t. sheets, t. change of garments
13. ye shall give t. sheets, t. change of garments
19. Samson slew t. men, and took their spoil
20. 31. to smite about t. men of Israel, 39.
1 Sam. 9. 22. Saul sat among them, about t. persons
2 Sam. 5. 4. David was t. years old when he began
23. 13. and three of the t. chief went down
23. Benaiah was more honourable than the t. 1
Chron. 11. 15, 25. | 27. 6.
24. Asahel, brother of Joab, was one of the t.
1 Kings 4. 22. provision for one day was t. measures
6. 2. height of the house of the Lord was t. cubits
7. 2. height of the house of the forest was t. cubits
6. the breadth of the porch was t. cubits
23. a line of t. cubits did compass it about
2 Kings 18. 14. appointed to Hezekiah t. talents
1 Chron. 11. 42. Adina a captain, and t. with him
Ezra 1. 9. the number of them was t. chargers
10. t. basons of gold, silver basons 410
Jer. 38. 10. take from hence t. men with thee
Ezek. 40. 17. t. chambers were on the pavement
41. 6. and the side chambers were t. in order
46. 22. there were courts joined of t. cubits broad
Zech. 11. 12. they weighed for my price t. pieces
13. and I took the t. pieces of silver, Mat. 27. 9.
Mat. 13. 8. brought some t. fold, 23. Mark 4. 8, 20.
26. 15. they covenanted with him for t. pieces
27. 3. Judas brought again the t. pieces of silver
Luke 3. 23. Jesus began to be about t. years of age
John 6. 19. had rowed about 25 or t. furlongs

See DAYS.

THIRTY one.

Josh. 12. 24. the kings Joshua subdued t. and one
1 Kings 16. 23. in the t. and one year of king Asa
2 Kings 22. 1. Josiah eight years old, and reigned
t. and one years in Jerusalem, 2 Chron. 34. 1.

THIRTY two.

Gen. 11. 20. Reu lived t. two years, and begat Serug
Num. 31. 40. the Lord's tribute was t. two persons
1 Kings 20. 1. t. two kings were with Ben-hadad, 16.
22. 31. the king commanded his t. two captains
2 Kings 8. 17. Jehoram was t. two years old when
he began to reign, 2 Chron. 21. 5, 20.

THIRTY three.

Gen. 46. 15. all the souls of sons and daughters, t. t.
Lev. 12. 4. in blood of purifying t. three days
2 Sam. 5. 5. David reigned in Jerusal. t. and three
years. 1 Kings 2. 11. 1 Chron. 3. 4. | 29. 27.

THIRTY four.

Gen. 11. 16. Eber lived t. four years and begat Peleg

THIRTY five.

Gen. 11. 12. Arphaxad lived five and t. years
1 Kings 22. 42. Jehoshaphat was t. five years old
when he began to reign, 2 Chron. 20. 31.
2 Chron. 3. 15. made two pillars t. five cubits high

THIRTY six.

Josh. 7. 5. the men of Ai smote t. six men of Israel

THIRTY seven.

2 Sam. 23. 39. Uriah the Hittite t. seven in all
2 Kings 13. 10. in the t. and seventh year of Joash

THIRTY eight. [years

Deut. 2. 14. till come over brook Zered t. eight
1 Kings 16. 29. in the t. and eighth year of Asa
2 Kings 15. 8. in the t. and eighth year of Azariah
John 5. 5. which had an infirmity t. eight years

THIRTY nine.

2 Chron. 16. 12. Asa in the t. and n. year diseased

See THOUSAND.

THIS.

Gen. 5. 29. t. same shall comfort us concern. work
15. 4. saying, t. shall not be thine heir, but he shall
18. 32. and I will speak yet but t. once
19. 9. they said, t. one fellow came in to sojourn
29. 27. we will give thee t. also for the service

Gen. 31. 15. but in t. will we consent unto you
37. 32. sent the coat, and said, t. have we found
38. 28. bound a thread, saying, t. came out first
44. 5. is not t. it in which my Lord drinketh?
29. if ye take t. from me, and mischief befall him
Exod. 3. 12. t. shall be a token that I sent thee
7. 17. in t. thou shalt know that I am the Lord
23. neither did he set his heart to t. also
30. 13. t. they shall give, each half a shekel
Num. 18. 9. t. shall be thine of the most holy things from the fire, *Deut.* 18. 3.
24. 23. alas, who shall live when God doth t.?
Deut. 32. 29. O that they were wise and underst. t.
34. is not t. laid up in store with me and sealed
Judg. 7. 4. t. shall go with thee, t. shall not go
16. 18. come up t. once, for he hath shewed all
1 *Sam.* 16. 8. neither hath the Lord chosen t. 9.
20. 3. and he saith, let not Jonathan know t.
25. 31. that t. be no grief unto thee
2 *Sam.* 7. 19. t. was a small thing in thy sight
19. 21. shall not Shimei be put to death for t.?
23. 17. is not t. the blood of the men that went
1 *Kings* 3. 9. to judge t. thy so great a people
11. 27. and t. was the cause that he lift his hand
39. I will for t. afflict the seed of David, but not
17. 24. by t. I know that thou art a man of God
2 *Kings* 4. 43. should I set t. before an hundred men
14. 10. glory of t. and tarry at home
24. 3. at commandment of Lord came t. on Judah
2 *Chr.* 1. 11. because t. was in thine heart, not asked
25. 9. the Lord is able to give thee more than t.
Ezra 5. 17. let him send his pleasure concerning t.
6. 11. let his house be made a dunghill for t.
7. 27. put such a thing as t. in the king's heart
8. 23. so we fasted, and besought our God for t.
9. 13. and hast given us such deliverance as t.
15. we cannot stand before thee because of t.
Neh. 13. 14. remember me concerning t. 22.
Esth. 4. 14. art come to kingd. for such a time as t.
Job 5. 27. lo, t. we have searched it, so it is
12. 9. the hand of the Lord hath wrought t.
17. 8. upright men shall be astonied at t.
20. 2. for t. I make haste ‖ 4. knowest thou not t.
21. 2. hear and let t. be your consolation
33. 12. in t. thou art not just, I will answer
35. 2. thinkest thou t. to be right, that thou saidst
Psal. 11. 6. t. shall be the portion of their cup
27. 3. though war rise, in t. will I be confident
32. 6. for t. shall every one that is godly pray
35. 22. t. thou hast seen, keep not silence
41. 11. by t. I know that thou favourest me
44. 21. shall not God search t. out? he knoweth
48. 14. for t. God is our God for ever and ever
49. 13. t. their way is their folly, yet their
50. 22. now consider t. ye that forget God
56. 9. shall turn back, t. I know, for God is for me
62. 11. twice have I heard t. that power belongs
69. 31. t. also shall please the Lord better than ox
32. the humble shall see t. and be glad, your heart
73. 16. when I thought to know t. it was painful
78. 21. the Lord heard t. and was wroth, 59.
81. 4. for t. was a statute for Israel and a law
5. t. he ordained in Joseph for a testimony
92. 6. neither doth a fool understand t.
109. 20. let t. be the reward of mine adversaries
119. 56. t. I had, because I kept thy precepts
149. 9. t. honour have all his saints, praise Lord
Eccl. 4. 4. for t. a man is envied of his neighbour
6. 5. t. hath more rest than the other
7. 10. thou dost not inquire wisely concerning t.
18. it is good that thou shouldest take hold of t. yea also from t. withdraw not thine hand
27. t. have I found ‖ 29. lo, t. only have I found
11. 6. whether shall prosper, either t. or that
Isa. 1. 12. who hath required t. at your hand?
6. 7. and he said, lo, t. hath touched thy lips
9. 7. the zeal of the Lord of hosts will perform t.
22. 14. surely t. iniquity shall not be purged
27. 9. by t. shall the iniquity of Jacob be purged
28. 29. t. also cometh forth from the Lord
29. 11. saying, read t. I pray thee, 12.
30. 7. therefore have I cried concerning t.
43. 9. who among them can declare t.? 45. 21.
46. 8. remember t. ‖ 48. 20. declare ye, tell t.
47. 8. therefore hear now t. 48. 1, 16. | 51. 21.
50. 11. t. shall ye have of mine hand, ye shall
56. 2. blessed is the man that doeth t.
58. 5. wilt thou call t. a fast, an acceptable day?
6. is not t. the fast that I have chosen?
66. 14. when ye see t. your hearts shall rejoice
Jer. 2. 12. be astonished, O ye heavens, at t.
17. hast thou not procured t. unto thyself?
4. 8. for t. gird you with sackcloth, lament
28. for t. shall the earth mourn, and heavens
5. 7. how shall I pardon thee for t.?
9. be avenged on such a nation as t. 29. | 9. 9.
9. 24. but let him that glorieth, glory in t.
16. 21. I will t. once cause them to know my hand
22. 16. was not t. to know me, saith the Lord?
21. t. hath been thy manner from thy youth
23. 26. how long shall t. be in the heart of prophets
31. 33. t. shall be the covenant that I will make
32. 8. I knew that t. was the word of the Lord
Lam. 3. 21. t. I recall to mind, therefore I hope
5. 17. for t. our heart is faint, our eyes are dim
Ezek. 8. 15. he said, hast thou seen t.? 17. | 47. 6.
16. 49. t. was the iniquity of thy sister Sodom
20. 27. in t. your fathers have blasphemed me
21. 26. saith the Lord, t. shall not be the same
23. 11. and when her sister Aholibah saw t.
24. 24. t. cometh, ye shall know, 33. 33.
36. 37. I will yet for t. be inquired of by Israel
44. 2. t. gate shall be shut, no man shall enter
Dan. 6. 5. shall not find occasion against t. Daniel, 28.
Hos. 7. 16. t. shall be their derision in Egypt
Amos 4. 5. t. liketh you, O children of Israel
7. 3. the Lord repented for t. it shall not be, 6.
8. 8. shall not the land tremble for t.?
9. 12. saith the Lord that doth t.
Jonah 4. 2. was not t. my saying in my country?
Zeph. 2. 10. t. shall they have for their pride
Zech. 6. 15. t. shall come to pass if ye will obey Lord
Zech. 14. 12. t. shall be the plague wherewith, 15.
19. t. shall be the punishment of Egypt
Mal. 1. 9. t. hath been by your means
13. should I accept t. of your hands? saith Lord
2. 12. the L. will cut off the man that doth t.
Mat. 12. 7. but if ye had known what t. meaneth
13. 55. is not t. the carpenter's son? *Mark* 6. 3. *Luke* 4. 22. *John* 6. 42.
16. 22. saying, Lord, t. shall not be unto thee
24. 43. know t. that if the good man of the house had known in what watch, *Luke* 12. 39.
26. 13. shall also t. that t. woman hath done
27. 54. saying, truly t. was the Son of God
28. 14. and if t. come to the governor's ears
Mark 12. 31. and the second is like, namely, t.
Luke 1. 18. whereby shall I know t. for I am old
34. how shall t. be, seeing I know not a man?
66. saying, what manner of child shall t. be?
3. 20. added yet t. above all, that he shut up John
6. 3. have ye not read so much as t. what David
10. 11. be sure of t. ‖ 20. in t. rejoice not
15. 24. t. my son was dead and is alive again
22. 17. take t. and divide it among yourselves
37. that t. must yet be accomplished in me
23. 47. certainly t. was a righteous man
John 1. 15. saying, t. was he of whom I spake
2. 22. his disciples remembered he had said t.
4. 27. on t. came his disciples, and marvelled
29. is not t. the Christ? ‖ 5. 28. marvel not at t.
6. 6. t. he said to prove him, for he himself knew
7. 25. is not t. he whom they seek to kill?
8. 40. t. did not Abraham ‖ 11. 26. believest thou t.
11. 51. t. spake he not of himself, but prophesied
12. 6. t. he said, not that he cared for the poor
13. 28. for what intent he spake t. unto him
35. by t. shall all men know ye are my disciples
15. 13. greater love hath no man than t.
16. 30. by t. we believe that thou camest from God
Acts 1. 11. t. Jesus shall so come in like manner
2. 12. what meaneth t.? ‖ 31. he seeing t. before
32. t. Jesus hath God raised up, whereof we all
33. he hath shed forth t. which ye now see
37. when they heard t. they were pricked
3. 12. ye men of Israel, why marvel ye at t.?
5. 24. they doubted whereunto t. would grow
6. 14. that t. Jesus of Nazareth shall destroy t. place
7. 35. t. Moses whom they refused, did God send
40. as for t. Moses, we wot not what is become
8. 22. repent therefore of t. thy wickedness
32. the place of scripture which he read was t.
9. 21. is not t. he that destroyed them which
13. 48. when the Gentiles heard t. they were glad
15. 15. to t. agree the words of the prophets
16. 18. t. did she many days, but Paul turned
19. 5. when they heard t. they were baptized
24. 14. but t. I confess to thee, that after the way
Rom. 2. 3. thinkest thou t. O man, that judgest
6. 6. knowing t. that our old man is crucified
9. 10. not only t. but when Rebecca conceived
15. 28. when therefore I have performed t.
1 *Cor.* 1. 12. t. I say, every one saith, I am of Paul
9. 3. my answer to them that examine me is t.
11. 17. in t. that I declare to you, I praise not
22. shall I praise you in t.? I praise you not
15. 34. have not knowledge, I speak t. to shame
2 *Cor.* 5. 2. in t. we groan earnestly, desiring
7. 3. I speak not t. to condemn you, for I said
8. 5. t. they did, not as we hoped, but first gave
10. 7. let him of himself think t. again, 11.
13. 9. and t. also we wish, even your perfection
Gal. 3. 2. t. would I learn of you, received ye
5. 14. the law is fulfilled in one word, even in t.
Eph. 4. 17. t. I say therefore, and testify in the Lord
5. 5. for t. ye know, that no whoremonger
Phil. 1. 9. t. I pray, that your love may abound
19. I know that t. shall turn to my salvation
2 *Thess.* 3. 10. when with you, t. we commanded you
1 *Tim.* 1. 9. knowing t. *Jam.* 1. 3. 2 *Pet.* 1. 20. | 3. 3.
4. 16. in doing t. thou shalt both save thyself and
Heb. 7. 21. but t. with an oath ‖ 27. t. did he once
1 *John* 3. 10. in t. the children of God are manifest
4. 9. in t. was manifested the love of God
5. 2. by t. we know that we love children of God
Jude 5. put you in remembrance, tho' ye once kn. t.
Rev. 2. 6. t. thou hast, that thou hatest the deeds
See ALL, AFTER, BOOK, CAUSE, CHILD, CITY, DAY, DOCTRINE, DO, DONE, EVIL, HOUSE, LAND, LAW, LIFE, MAN, MONTH, PEOPLE, THING, WORD, WORLD.

Is THIS.

Gen. 3. 13. Lord said to the woman, what is t. that thou hast done? 12. 18. | 26. 10. | 29. 25.
24. 65. what man is t. that walketh in the field?
42. 28. what is t. that God hath done unto us?
43. 29. is t. your younger brother, of whom
44. 15. what deed is t. that ye have done?
Exod. 13. 14. saying, what is t.? *Judg.* 18. 24.
17. 3. wherefore is t. that thou hast brought us
Josh. 22. 16. what trespass is t. ye committed?
Judg. 15. 11. what is t. thou hast done? 2 *Sam.* 12. 21.
20. 12. what wickedness is t. done among you?
1 *Sam.* 10. 11. what is t. come to the son of Kish?
24. 16. Saul said, is t. thy voice, my son David?
2 *Sam.* 7. 19. is t. the manner of man, O Lord God?
16. 17. is t. thy kindness to thy friend?
2 *Kings* 18. 19. what confidence is t. wherein
Ezra 10. 13. nor is t. a work of one day or two
Job 38. 2. who is t. that darkeneth counsel?
Cant. 3. 6. who is t. cometh out of the wilderness?
8. 5. who is t. that cometh up from the wilderness?
Isa. 23. 7. is t. your joyous city, whose antiquity
63. 1. who is t. that cometh from Edom, with
Jer. 30. 21. for who is t. that engaged his heart?
46. 7. who is t. that cometh up as a flood?
Ezek. 16. 20. is t. of thy whoredoms a small matter
Zech. 3. 2. is not t. a brand plucked out of the fire?
5. 5. and see what is t. that goeth forth
Mat. 8. 27. saying, what manner of man is t. that the winds obey him? *Mark* 4. 41. *Luke* 8. 25.
12. 23. people said, is not t. the son of David?
21. 10. who is t.? ‖ *Mark* 1. 27. what thing is t.?
Luke 1. 43. whence is t. to me, that mother of my L.
Luke 4. 36. what a word is t. with auth. he comman.
5. 21. who is t. which speaketh blasphemies?
7. 49. who is t. that forgiveth sins also?
9. 9. but who is t. of whom I hear such things?
20. 17. he said, what is t. then that is written
John 7. 36. what manner of saying is t. he said
9. 19. is t. your son, who ye say was born blind?
16. 17. what is t. that he saith unto us? 18.
2 *Cor.* 1. 12. for our rejoicing is t. the testimony
Eph. 3. 8. to me is t. grace given, to preach to Gent.
Jam. 1. 27. pure religion and undefiled is t.

THIS *is*.

Gen. 2. 23. Adam said, t. is now bone of my bones
20. 13. t. is thy kindness which thou shalt shew me
28. 17. Jacob said, t. is none other but the house of God, and t. is the gate of heaven
32. 2. when Jacob saw them, he said, t. is God's host
41. 38. Pharaoh said, can we find such a one as t.
48. 18. not so, father, for t. is the first born
Exod. 3. 15. t. is my name for ever, and my memorial
8. 19. the magicians said, t. is the finger of God
16. 23. t. is that which the Lord hath said
Lev. 10. 3. t. is that the Lord spake, saying
Num. 8. 24. t. is it that belongeth to the Levites
18. 11. and t. is thine, the heave offering of gift
Deut. 13. 11. do no more such wickedness as t. is
15. 2. and t. is the manner of the release
1 *Sam.* 16. 12. arise, anoint him, for t. is he
1 *Kings* 11. 11. forasmuch as t. is done of thee
13. 3. t. is the sign which the Lord hath spoken
2 *Kings* 3. 18. t. is but a light thing in sight of L.
6. 19. t. is not the way, neither is this the city
8. 5. O king, t. is the woman, and t. is her son
9. 37. so that they shall not say, t. is Jezebel
2 *Chron.* 28. 22. t. is that king Ahaz
Neh. 2. 2. t. is nothing but sorrow of heart
9. 18. t. is thy God that brought thee out of Egypt
Job 8. 19. behold, t. is the joy of his way
10. 13. I know that t. is with thee
18. 21. t. is the place of him that knoweth not God
20. 29. t. is the portion of a wicked man, 27. 13.
Psal. 24. 6. t. is the generation of them that seek him
68. 16. t. is the hill God desireth to dwell in
77. 10. t. is my infirmity, but I will remember
109. 27. that they may know that t. is thy hand
118. 23. t. is the Lord's doing, *Mat.* 21. 42.
119. 50. t. is my comfort in mine affliction
132. 14. t. is my rest for ever, here will I dwell
Eccl. 1. 10. whereof it may be said, see, t. is new
5. 19. to rejoice in labour, t. is the gift of God
12. 13. for t. is the whole duty of man
Cant. 5. 16. t. is my beloved, and t. is my friend
Isa. 12. 5. sing to Lord, t. is known in all the earth
25. 9. lo, t. is our God, we have waited for him
27. 9. t. is all the fruit, to take away his sin
28. 12. t. is the rest, and t. is the refreshing
30. 21. saying, t. is the way, walk ye in it
54. 9. for t. is as the waters of Noah unto me
17. t. is the heritage of the servants of the Lord
59. 21. as for me, t. is my covenant with them
Jer. 4. 18. t. is thy wickedness, it is bitter
7. 28. t. is a nation that obeyeth not the Lord
10. 19. t. is a grief ‖ 13. 25. t. is thy lot
23. 6. t. is the name whereby he shall be called, THE LORD OUR RIGHTEOUSNESS, 33. 16.
30. 17. t. is Zion, whom no man seeketh after
Ezek. 5. 5. t. is Jerusalem, I set it in the midst of
19. 14. t. is a lamentation, and shall be for a lam.
31. 18. t. is Pharaoh and all his multitude
Dan. 5. 25. t. is the writing that was written
Mic. 2. 10. arise, depart, for t. is not your rest
Zeph. 2. 15. t. is the rejoicing city that dwelt
Zech. 5. 3. t. is the curse that goeth forth
6. he said, t. is an ephah ‖ 8. t. is wickedness
Mat. 3. 3. for t. is he that was spoken of by Esaias
17. t. is my beloved Son, 17. 5. *Mark* 9. 7. *Luke* 9. 35.
7. 12. for t. is the law and the prophets
11. 10. t. is he of whom it is written, *Luke* 7. 27.
14. t. is Elias which was for to come
13. 19. t. is he had received seed by the way
19. 26. Jesus said, with men t. is impossible
21. 38. t. is the heir, *Mark* 12. 7. *Luke* 20. 14.
22. 38. t. is the first commandment, *Mark* 12. 30.
26. 26. Jesus said, take, eat, t. is my body
28. t. is my blood, *Mark* 14. 22, 24. *Luke* 22. 19, 20. 1 *Cor.* 11. 24, 25.
Mark 14. 69. t. is one of them, and he denied again
Luke 7. 39. have known what manner of woman t. is
22. 53. t. is your hour and the power of darkness
John 1. 19. and t. is the record of John
30. t. is he of whom I said, after me cometh a man
34. I bare record that t. is the Son of God
3. 19. t. is the condemnation, that light is come
4. 42. that t. is indeed the Christ, 7. 26, 41.
6. 29. t. is the work of God, that ye believe
39. t. is the Father's will which sent me, 40.
50. t. is the bread which cometh from heaven
58. t. is that bread which came down from heaven
60. t. is an hard saying, who can hear it?
9. 9. some said, t. is he ‖ 20. we know t. is our son
15. 12. t. is my commandment, that ye love
17. 3. t. is life eternal, that they might know
Acts 2. 16. t. is that which was spoken by Joel
7. 37. t. is that Moses which said unto Israel
38. t. is he that was in the church in wilderness
9. 22. Saul increased, proving that t. is very Christ
Rom. 11. 27. t. is my covenant, *Heb.* 8. 10. | 10. 16.
1 *Cor.* 11. 20. t. is not to eat the Lord's supper
Eph. 6. 1. obey your parents, for t. is right
Phil. 1. 22. if I live, t. is the fruit of my labour
Col. 3. 20. for t. is well pleasing to the Lord
1 *Thess.* 4. 3. for t. is the will of God, 5. 18.
1 *Tim.* 1. 15. t. is a faithful saying, 3. 1. | 4. 9. *Tit.* 3. 8.
2. 3. for t. is acceptable in the sight of God
1 *Pet.* 2. 19. t. is thank-worthy, if a man endure
20. take patiently, t. is acceptable with God
1 *John* 1. 5. t. is the message we have, 3. 11.
2. 25. and t. is the promise, even eternal life
3. 23. t. is his commandment, that we should believe
4. 3. and t. is that spirit of antichrist
5. 3. t. is the love of God, that we keep his com.
4. and t. is the victory, even our faith

1 John 5. 6. t. is he that came by water and blood
9. t. is the witness of God which he testified
11. t. is the record, that God hath given life
14. t. is the confidence that we have in him
20. t. is the true God, and eternal life
2 John 6. t. is love that we walk after his command.
7. t. is a deceiver and an antichrist
Rev. 20. 5. years were finished, t. is the first resurr.
14. into lake of fire, t. is the second death

THISTLE.

2 Kings 14. 9. the t. that was in Lebanon, a wild beast trod down the t. 2 Chron. 25. 18.
Hos. 10. 8. thorn and t. shall come up on their altars

THISTLES.

Gen. 3. 18. thorns and t. shall it bring forth
Job 31. 40. let t. grow instead of wheat
Mat. 7. 16. do men gather figs of t.?

THITHER.

Gen. 19. 20. this city is near, oh let me escape t.
22. haste thee, escape t. till thou be come t.
24. 6. that thou bring not my son t. again, 8.
Exod. 26. 33. that thou mayest bring in t. the ark
Num. 35. 6. that the slayer may flee t. 11. 15. Deut. 4. 42. | 19. 3, 4. Josh. 20. 3, 9.
Deut. 1. 37. saying, thou shalt not go in t. 38, 39.
12. 5. unto his habitation, t. thou shalt come
6. t. ye shall bring your burnt-offerings, 11.
Judg. 8. 27. Israel went t. a whoring after it
9. 51. and t. fled all the men and women
1 Sam. 2. 14. so they did to Israelites that came t.
5. 8. and they carried the ark of God about t.
10. 22. they inquired if the man should come t.
1 Kings 6. 7. make ready before it was brought t.
2 Kings 2. 8. waters were divided hither and t. 14.
4. 8. Elisha turned in t. to eat bread, 11.
5. † 25. she said, thy servant went not hither and t.
6. 9. for t. the Syrians are come down
17. 27. saying, carry t. one of the priests whom
Neh. 4. 20. resort ye t. to us, God shall fight for us
13. 9. t. brought I again the vessels of the house
Job 6. 20. they came t. and were ashamed
Isa. 55. 10. the rain returneth not t. again
Jer. 22. 11. he shall not return t. any more
27. but to the land, t. shall they not return
Ezek. 1. 20. they went, t. was their spirit to go
11. 18. Israel shall come t. and shall take away
47. 9. because these waters shall come t.
Joel 3. 11. t. cause thy mighty ones to come down
Mat. 2. 22. he was afraid to go t. but being warned
Luke 17. 37. t. will the eagles be gathered together
John 7. 34. where I am, t. ye cannot come, 36.
11. 8. to stone thee, and goest thou t. again?
18. 2. Jesus oft-times resorted t. with his disciples
3. Judas cometh t. with lanterns and torches
Acts 8. 30. Philip ran t. to him, and heard him
16. 13. spake to the women which resorted t.

THITHERWARD.

Judg. 18. 15. turned t. and came to Micah's house
Jer. 50. 5. ask the way to Zion, with their faces t.

THONGS.

Acts 22. 25. as they bound him with t. Paul said

THORN

Is a prickly shrub well known. It was with thorns *that Gideon chastised the men of Succoth, who refused to relieve his army, when they were pursuing Zeba and Zalmunna, two kings of Midian,* Judg. 8. 7, 16. *Either he chastised or beat their naked bodies with thorny rods till they died; or he laid them down upon* thorns, *on the ground, and brought the cart-wheel upon them, which did both tear their flesh, and bruise them to death.* Thorns *are put for great difficulties and impediments.* Job 5. 5. Whose harvest the hungry eateth up, and taketh it even out of the thorns. *And in* Hos. 2. 6. I will hedge up thy way with thorns; *I will bring thee into straits and difficulties. It is likewise put for the heat of a fire kindled by* thorns. *Psal.* 58. 9. Before your pots can feel the thorns. *St. Paul says,* 2 Cor. 12. 7. *that lest he should have been exalted above measure, through the abundance of the revelations which he had,* there was given to him a thorn in the flesh, *that is, some racking pain in his body; or terrors of conscience, or some diabolical violent temptation.*
The Lord told the Israelites, that such of the inhabitants of Canaan, as they should let remain in the land, would be pricks in their eyes and *thorns* in their sides; *that is, they would be very hurtful and pernicious to them,* Num. 33. 55. *The wicked are compared to* thorns, *not only because of their barrenness, and unprofitableness in any thing that is good,* Mat. 7. 16, 19. Do men gather grapes of *thorns? But also because of their pernicious hurtful disposition towards the church and people of God,* Josh. 23. 13. Ezek. 28. 24. *To sow among thorns, is to preach the word to worldly and carnal hearts,* Mat. 13. 7, 22. *Many are deluded, and betrayed to a neglect of their souls, through an excessive care about getting, keeping, and managing their estates: so that prosperity is their snare. The soldiers, to insult our Saviour, and to despise his royalty,* platted a crown of *thorns,* and put it upon his head, *Mat.* 27. 29. Thorns *were the fruit of the curse for man's sin.* Gen. 3. 18. *Christ bears our curse, and takes it away from us.*
2 Chron. 25. † 18. t. in Lebanon, sent to the cedar
Job 41. 2. canst thou bore his jaw through with a t.?
Prov. 26. 9. as a t. goeth into the hand of a drunkard
Isa. 55. 13. instead of the t. shall come the fir-tree
Ezek. 28. 24. there shall be no more any grieving t.
Hos. 10. 8. the t. shall come up on their altars
Mic. 7. 4. the most upright is sharper than a t. hedge
2 Cor. 12. 7. there was given to me a t. in the flesh

THORNS.

Gen. 3. 18. t. and thistles shall it bring forth to thee
Exod. 22. 6. if fire break out and catch in t.
Num. 33. 55. they shall be t. in your sides, Judg. 2. 3.
Josh. 23. 13. but they shall be t. in your eyes
2 Sam. 23. 6. the sons of Belial shall be as t.
2 Chron. 33. 11. which took Manasseh among the t.

Ps. 58. 9. before your pots can feel the t. take them
118. 12. they are quenched as the fire of t.
Prov. 15. 19. way of slothful man is an hedge of t.
22. 5. t. and snares are in the way of the froward
24. 31. and lo it was all grown over with t.
Eccl. 7. 6. as the crackling of t. under a pot
Cant. 2. 2. as the lily among t. so is my love
Isa. 7. 19. they shall rest upon all t. and bushes
33. 12. as t. cut up shall they be burnt in fire
34. 13. and t. shall come up in her palaces
Jer. 4. 3. break your ground, and sow not among t.
12. 13. they have sown wheat, but shall reap t.
Hos. 2. 6. behold, I will hedge up thy way with t.
9. 6. t. shall be in their tabernacles
Nah. 1. 10. while they be folden together as t.
Mat. 7. 16. do men gather grapes of t.? Luke 6. 44.
13. 7. fell among t. 22. Mark 4. 7, 18. Luke 8. 7, 14.
27. 29. when they had platted a crown of t. they put it on his head, Mark 15. 17. John 19. 2.
See Briers.

THOROW, See Through.

THOSE.

Gen. 33. 5. Esau said, who are t. with thee?
1 Kings 2. 7. let them be of t. that eat at thy table
9. 21. upon t. did Solomon levy a tribute
Ezra 1. 8. t. did Cyrus king of Persia bring forth
Esth. 9. 5. did what they would to t. that hated them
Job 5. 11. to set up on high t. that be low
21. 22. seeing he judgeth t. that are high
24. 13. they are of t. that rebel against the light
19. so doth the grave t. which have sinned
27. 15. t. that remain of him shall be buried in death
Psal. 37. 9. t. that wait on the Lord shall inherit
50. 5. t. that have made a covenant with me
92. 13. t. planted in house of Lord shall flourish
119. 79. let t. that fear thee turn to me, and t. that have known thy testimonies
132. as thou usedst to do to t. that love thy name
139. 21. am not I grieved with t. that rise up
Prov. 8. 17. t. that seek me early shall find me
Eccl. 1. 11. with t. that shall come after
Isa. 35. 8. an high-way, but it shall be for t.
64. 5. t. that remember thee in thy ways, in those is continuance, we shall be saved
Jer. 27. 11. t. will I let remain in their land
Dan. 4. 37. t. that walk in pride he is able to abase
Zeph. 1. 6. and t. that have not sought the Lord
Mat. 16. 23. thou savourest t. things that be of men
Luke 7. 28. among t. that are born of woman
19. 27. but t. mine enemies bring hither and slay
John 8. 10. woman, where are t. thine accusers?
17. 11. keep thro' thy name t. thou hast given me
12. t. that thou gavest me I have kept, none lost
Acts 3. 24. from Samuel and t. that follow after
1 Cor. 14. 23. there come in t. that are unlearned
Phil. 3. 7. what things gain, t. I counted loss for Ch.
1 Tim. 4. 10. Saviour, especially of t. that believe
Heb. 5. 14. belongeth to t. who by reason of use
2 Pet. 2. 6. an ensample to t. that live ungodly
18. they allure t. that were clean escaped
See Days, Things.

THOU.

Gen. 3. 12. the woman whom t. gavest to be with [me
20. 7. if not restore, know thou, that t. shalt surely die, t. and all that are thine, 1 Sam. 22. 16.
24. 60. t. art our sister, be t. mother of thousands
26. 29. t. art now the blessed of the Lord
41. 39. there is none so discreet and wise as t. art
40. only in the throne will I be greater than t.
45. 10. t. shalt be near to me, t. and thy childr.
49. 8. t. art he whom thy brethren shall praise
Exod. 19. 24. t. shalt come up, t. and Aar. with thee
Num. 16. 11. t. and all the company are gathered
16. be t. and they, and Aaron before the Lord
Deut. 5. 14. that thy servant may rest as well as t.
7. 1. hath cast out nations mightier than t. 20. 1.
13. 6. t. hast not known, t. nor thy fathers, 28. 64.
30. 19. that both t. and thy seed may live
1 Sam. 15. 28. to a neighbour that is better than t.
24. 17. he said, t. art more righteous than I
25. 33. blessed be t. that kept me from coming
2 Sam. 12. 7. Nathan said to David, t. art the man
15. 2. then Absalom said, of what city art t.?
19. 29. I have said, t. and Ziba divide the land
1 Kings 8. 39. t. even t. knowest the hearts of all
18. 18. t. and thy father's house trouble Israel
20. 14. who shall order the battle? he said, t.
2 Kings 9. 25. that when I and t. rode after Ahab
14. 10. why meddle, that t. shouldest fall, even t. and Judah with thee? 2 Chron. 25. 19.
19. 15. t. art the God, even t. alone of all the kingdoms, 19. Neh. 9. 6. Isa. 37. 20.
Neh. 9. 17. but t. art a God ready to pardon
Esth. 4. 14. but t. and thy father's house shall be destroyed, who knoweth whether t. art come
Job 35. 5. the clouds which are higher than t.
Psal. 23. 4. I will fear no evil, for t. art with me
55. 13. but it was t. a man, mine equal, my guide
71. 6. t. art he that took me out my mother's bowels
76. 7. t. even t. art to be feared, and who may stand in thy sight when once t. art angry?
83. 18. t. whose name is Jehovah, art most high
102. 27. but t. art the same, thy years have no end
109. 27. they may know, that t. Ld. hast done it
118. 28. t. art my God, and I will praise thee
119. 114. t. art my hiding-place and my shield
132. 8. arise into thy rest, t. and ark of thy strength
139. 8. if I ascend up into heaven, t. art there
Cant. 1. 7. tell me, O t. whom my soul loveth
Isa. 41. 9. t. art my servant, I have chosen thee
44. 17. and saith, deliver me, for t. art my god
45. 15. verily t. art a god that hidest thyself
51. 12. who art t. that t. shouldest be afraid of man
63. 16. t. art our father, t. O Lord, art our father
65. 5. come not near to me, I am holier than t.
Jer. 17. 4. t. shalt discontinue from thy heritage
20. 6. there t. shalt die, t. and all thy friends
27. 13. why will ye die, t. and thy people, by sword
Lam. 5. 19. t. O L. remainest for ever, thy throne
Ezek. 7. 7. O t. that dwellest in the land, the time
16. 52. they are more righteous than t.
Dan. 4. 22. it is t. O king, that art become strong

Dan. 5. 22. t. his son, hast not humbled thine heart
Jonah 1. 8. whence comest t. of what people art t.?
Mic. 2. 7. O t. that art named the house of Jacob
4. 8. t. O tower of the flock, to thee shall it come
Hab. 1. 12. art t. not from everlasting, O Lord?
Zech. 4. 7. who art t. O great mountain, before Zerub
Mat. 6. 6. but t. when t. prayest, enter thy closet
17. but t. when t. fastest, anoint thine head
16. 16. t. art Christ, the Son of the living God, Mark 8. 29. Luke 4. 41. John 11. 27.
26. 39. nevertheless, not as I will, but as t. wilt
69. saying t. also wast with Jesus, Mark 14. 67.
Luke 1. 28. hail t. that art highly favoured
7. 19. saying, art t. he that should come? 20.
14. 8. lest a more honourable than t. be bidden
16. 5. he said, how much owest t. unto my lord? 7
25. t. in thy life-time receivedst thy good things but now he is comforted, and t. art tormented
19. 42. if t. hadst known, even t. in this thy day
John 1. 19. to ask him, who art t. 22. | 8. 25. | 21. 12
21. they asked, art t. Elias? art t. that prophet?
42. t. art Simon, thou shalt be called Cephas
3. 10. art t. a master of Israel, and knowest not
4. 9. that t. being a Jew, askest drink of me
7. 52. they said to him, art t. also of Galilee?
8. 5. but what sayest t.? || 9. 28. t. art his disciple
9. 37. t. hast seen him, and he talketh with thee
17. 23. I in them, and t. in me, that they may be perf.
18. 17. art not t. one of this man's disciples?
Acts 1. 24. t. Lord, who knowest the hearts of all
8. 23. that t. art in the gall of bitterness and bond
11. 14. whereby t. and thy house shall be saved
13. 10. t. child of the devil, t. enemy, wilt t. not cease to pervert the right ways of the Lord?
33. t. art my son, this day have I begotten thee
21. 38. art not t. that Egyptian which madest
22. 27. tell me, art t. a Roman? he said, yea
26. 29. I would, that not only t. but all that hear
Rom. 2. 21. t. therefore which teachest another
1 Tim. 4. 12. but be t. an example of the believers
6. 11. but t. O man of God, flee these things
2 Tim. 1. 8. be not t. ashamed of the testimony
2. 1. t. therefore, my son, be strong in grace
Philem. 12. t. therefore receive him that is mine
Heb. 1. 10. t. Lord, hast laid foundation of earth
12. they shall be changed, but t. art the same
Jam. 4. 12. who art t. that judgest another?
Rev. 4. 11. t. art worthy, O Lord, to receive glory
5. 9. t. art worthy to take the book, and to open
See Alone.

THOUGH.

Gen. 40. 10 and the vine was as t. it budded
Lev. 5. 17. t. he wist it not, yet is he guilty
25. 35. thou shalt relieve him, t. he be a stranger
Deut. 29. 19. t. I walk in the imagination of heart
Josh. 17. 18. for thou shalt drive out Canaanites, t. they have iron chariots and t. they be strong
Judg. 13. 16. t. thou detain me, I will not eat
15. 7. t. ye have done this, yet will I be avenged
Ruth 2. 13. t. not like one of thy handmaidens
1 Sam. 14. 39. t. it be in Jonathan, he shall die
20. 20. I will shoot arrows. as t. I shot at a mark
21. 5. t. it were sanctified this day in the vessel
2 Sam. 3. 39. I am this day weak, t. anointed king
18. 12. t. I should receive a thousand shekels
Neh. 1. 9. t. there were of you cast out to uttermost
Job 13. 15. t. he slay me, yet will I trust in him
20. 12. t. wickedness be sweet in his mouth
27. 8. what the hypocrite's hope, t. he hath gained
16. t. he heap up silver as the dust, and prepare
Psal. 35. 14. as t. he had been my friend or brother
37. 24. t. he fall, he shall not utterly be cast down
138. 6. t. the Lord be high, yet hath he respect
Prov. 11. 21. t. hand join in hand, 16. 5.
28. 6. than he that is perverse, t. he be rich
29. 19. t. he understand, he will not answer
Isa. 35. 8. the way-faring men t. fools, shall not err
45. 4. sirnamed thee, t. thou hast not known me, 5.
Lam. 3. 32. t. he cause grief, he will have compassion
Ezek. 2. 6. t. briers and thorns be with thee, t. they be a rebellious house, 3. 9. | 12. 3.
14. 14. t. these three men were in it, 16, 18, 20.
26. 21. t. thou be sought for, yet never be found
Dan. 5. 22. not humbled, t. thou knewest all this
Mic. 5. 2. t. thou be little among thousands of Judah
Nah. 1. 12. t. they be quiet, and likewise many
Hab. 1. 5. ye will not believe, t. it be told you
2. 3. t. it tarry, wait for it, it will surely come
Mat. 26. 35. t. I should die with thee, yet not deny
Luke 9. 53. face was as t. he would go to Jerusalem
18. 7. avenge his elect, t. he bear long with them
24. 28. he made as t. he would have gone further
John 8. 6. wrote on the ground, as t. he heard not
10. 38. t. ye believe not me, believe the works
11. 25. t. he were dead, yet shall he live
Acts 3. 12. as t. by our power we made him walk
13. 41. ye shall not believe, t. a man declare it
17. 25. as t. he needed any thing, seeing he gives
27. t. he be not far from every one of us
23. 15. as t. ye would inquire something, 20.
28. 4. whom t. he hath escaped the sea, yet veng.
Rom. 4. 17. things which be not, as t. they were
7. 3. she is no adulteress, t. she is married to another
1 Cor. 7. 29. that have wives, be as t. they had none
30. as t. they wept not, as t. they rejoiced not
2 Cor. 4. 16. but t. our outward man perish, yet
8. 9. t. he was rich, yet for us he became poor
10. 3. for t. we walk in the flesh, we do not war
12. 11. in nothing am I behind, t. I be nothing
13. 7. do what is honest, t. we be as reprobates
Gal. 1. 8. t. we or an angel preach another gospel
4. 1. heir differeth nothing t. he be lord of all
Phil. 3. 4. t. I might also have confidence in flesh
12. not as t. I had attained or were perfect
Col. 2. 5. for t. I be absent in the flesh, yet am I
20. why, as t. living, are ye subject to ordinances
Heb. 5. 8. t. he were a son, yet learned obedience
6. 9. are persuaded better things, t. we thus speak
12. 17. t. he sought it carefully with tears
Jam. 2. 14. t. a man say he hath faith, and not works
1 Pet. 4. 12. as t. some strange thing happened
2 Pet. 1. 12. put you in remembrance, t. ye know them

Jude 5. put you in remembrance, *t.* ye once knew th.

THOUGHT.

Gen. 20. 11. I *t.* the fear of God is not in this place
38. 15. Judah saw her, he *t.* her to be an harlot
48. 11. Israel said, I had not *t.* to see thy face
50. 20. but as for you, ye *t.* evil against me
Exod. 32. 14. Lord repented of the evil he *t.* to do
Num. 24. 11. I *t.* to promote thee to great honour
33. 56. I shall do unto you, as I *t.* to do to them
Deut. 19. 19. shall ye do to him, as he *t.* to have done
Judg. 15. 2. I verily *t.* that thou hadst hated her
20. 5. the men of Gibeah *t.* to have slain me
1 *Sam.* 1. 13. therefore Eli *t.* she had been drunken
18. 25. Saul *t.* to make David fall by Philistines
2 *Sam.* 4. 10. who *t.* I would have given him a rew.
13. 2. Amnon *t.* it hard to do any thing to her
21. 16. Ishbi-benob *t.* to have slain David
2 *Kings* 5. 11. I *t.* he will surely come out to me
2 *Chron.* 11. 22. Rehoboam *t.* to make Abijah king
32. 1. Sennacherib *t.* to win them for himself
Neh. 6. 2. but they *t.* to do me mischief
Esth. 3. 6. he *t.* scorn to lay hands on Mordecai alone
6. 6. Haman *t.* in his heart, to whom would the king
Psal. 48. 9. we have *t.* of thy loving kindness
73. 16. when I *t.* to know this, it was too painful
119. 59. I *t.* on my ways, and turned my feet to test.
Prov. 30. 32. if thou hast *t.* evil, lay thine hand
Isa. 14. 24. as I have *t.* so shall it come to pass
Jer. 18. 8. I will repent of the evil I *t.* to do
Jonah 1. † 4. so that the ship was *t.* to be broken
Zech. 1. 6. like as the Lord of hosts *t.* to do to us
8. 14. as I *t.* to punish you ‖ 15. I *t.* to do well
Mal. 3. 16. a book for them that *t.* on his name
Mat. 1. 20. but while he *t.* on these things
Mark 14. 72. and when he *t.* thereon he wept
Luke 7. 7. nor *t.* I myself worthy to come to thee
12. 17. he *t.* within himself, what shall I do
19. 11. they *t.* the kingdom of God should appear
John 11. 13. they *t.* he had spoken of taking rest
Acts 8. 20. *t.* the gift of God may be purchased
10. 19. while Peter *t.* on the vision, Spirit said
12. 9. wist not it was true, but *t.* he saw a vision
15. 38. Paul *t.* not good to take him with him
26. 8. why should it be *t.* a thing incredible?
9. I *t.* I ought to do many things contrary to Jesus
1 *Cor.* 13. 11. when I was a child, I *t.* as a child
Phil. 2. 6. *t.* it not robbery to be equal with God
Heb. 10. 29. much sorer punishment he be *t.* worthy

THOUGHTEST.

Psal. 50. 21. thou *t.* I was such a one as thyself

THOUGHT,

Or thinking, *is not always taken for the pure operation of the mind while it thinks, without passing a judgment, or taking any resolution. The* thought *often includes a formed design of doing something, as in* Psal. 56. 5. All their *thoughts* are against me for evil: *Their purposes and resolutions are to do me mischief. So in* Prov. 12. 5. The *thoughts* of the righteous are right: *His constant purpose is to deal justly and truly. And* Psal. 33. 11. The counsel of the Lord standeth for ever, the *thoughts* of his heart to all generations: *All his purposes, designs, and undertakings, are successful and irresistible. And* Psal. 146. 4. In that very day his *thoughts* perish: *All his designs and endeavours, either for himself or for others. St.* Paul *says,* Rom. 2. 15. Their *thoughts* the mean while accusing, or else excusing, one another; *when their conscience bears testimony to them, either for good or evil. Thought is put for inward reasoning.* Luke 9. 46, 47. There arose a reasoning among them: and Jesus perceiving the *thought* of their heart. *Also for immoderate or anxious care.* Mat. 10. 19. Take no *thought* what ye shall speak. *It is taken for the opinion.* Job 12. 5. He that is ready to slip with his feet, is as a lamp despised in the *thought* of him that is at ease; *or, in the opinion of such as are in a plentiful condition.*

Deut. 15. 9. that there be not a *t.* in thy wicked heart
1 *Sam.* 9. 5. return, lest my father take *t.* for us
Job 12. 5. is despised in the *t.* of him that is at ease
42. 2. that no *t.* can be withholden from thee
Psal. 49. 11. their *t.* is, their houses shall continue
64. 6. the inward *t.* of every one of them is deep
139. 2. thou understandest my *t.* afar off
Prov. 24. 9. the *t.* of foolishness is sin
Eccl. 10. 20. curse not the king, no not in thy *t.*
Isa. 26. † 3. keep him whose *t.* is stayed on thee
Ezek. 38. 10. and thou shalt think an evil *t.*
Amos 4. 13. he declareth to man what is his *t.*
Mat. 6. 25. I say to you, take no *t.* for your life, 31. 34. | 10. 19. *Mark* 13. 11. *Luke* 12. 11, 22.
27. which of you by taking *t.* can add one cubit to his stature? *Luke* 12. 25.
28. why take ye *t.* for raiment? *Luke* 12. 26.
Acts 8. 22. if the *t.* of thy heart may be forgiven
2 *Cor.* 10. 5. bring into captivity every *t.* to Christ

THOUGHTS.

Gen. 6. 5. the imagination of *t.* of his heart was evil
Judg. 5. 15. for Reuben there were great *t.* of heart
1 *Kings* 18. † 21. how long halt ye between two *t.*?
1 *Chron.* 28. 9. the Lord understandeth the *t.*
29. 18. keep this in the imagination of the *t.*
Job 4. 13. in *t.* from the visions of the night
17. † 7. mine eye is dim, all my *t.* are as a shadow
11. my purposes are broken off, even my *t.*
20. 2. therefore do my *t.* cause me to answer
21. 27. I know your *t.* and devices ye imagine
Psal. 10. 4. will not seek God, God is not in all his *t.*
33. 11. and the *t.* of his heart to all generations
40. 5. thy *t.* cannot be reckoned up in order
56. 5. all their *t.* are against me for evil
73. † 7. they pass the *t.* of the heart
92. 5. how great are thy works! thy *t.* very deep
94. 11. the Lord knoweth the *t.* of man, vanity
19. in the multitude of my *t.* within me thy
119. 113. I hate vain *t.* but thy law do I love
139. 17. how precious are thy *t.* to me, O God
23. search me, O God, try me, and know my *t.*
146. 4. in that very day his *t.* perish
Prov. 12. 5. the *t.* of the righteous are right
15. 26. the *t.* of the wicked are an abomination
16. 3. commit—and thy *t.* shall be established
21. 5. the *t.* of the diligent tend to plenteousness
Isa. 55. 7. let the unrighteous man forsake his *t.*
8. for my *t.* are not your *t.* saith the Lord
9. so are my *t.* higher than your *t.*
59. 7. their feet run to evil, their *t.* are *t.* of iniquity
65. 2. people walketh after their own *t.*
66. 18. for I know their works and their *t.*
Jer. 4. 14. how long shall vain *t.* lodge in thee?
6. 19. evil on people, even the fruit of their *t.*
23. 20. till he have performed the *t.* of his heart
29. 11. I know the *t.* that I think towards you, *t.* of peace and not evil, to give an expected end
Dan. 2. 30. thou mightest know the *t.* of thy heart
4. 5. Nebuchadnezzar's *t.* upon bed troubled him
19. Daniel was astonished, and his *t.* troubled him
5. 6. then king Belshazzar's *t.* troubled him
10. the queen said, let not thy *t.* trouble thee
11. † 24. think his *t.* against the strong holds
Mic. 4. 12. but they know not the *t.* of the Lord
Mat. 9. 4. Jesus, knowing their *t.* said, 12. 25. *Luke* 5. 22. | 6. 8. | 9. 47. | 11. 17.
15. 19. out of the heart proceed evil *t.* *Mark* 7. 21.
Luke 2. 35. the *t.* of many hearts may be revealed
24. 38. and why do *t.* arise in your hearts?
Rom. 2. 15. their *t.* accusing, or else excusing
14. † 1. but not to judge his doubtful *t.*
1 *Cor.* 3. 20. the Lord knoweth the *t.* of the wise
Heb. 4. 12. the word of God is a discerner of the *t.*
Jam. 2. 4. ye are become judges of evil *t.*

THOUSAND.

Gen. 20. 16. I have given thy brother a *t.* pieces
Num. 31. 4. of every tribe a *t.* send to war, 5. 6.
35. 4. suburbs of cities are *t.* cubits round about
Deut. 1. 11. the Lord make you a *t.* times so many
7. 9. God who keepeth covenant to a *t.* generations
32. 30. how should one chase a *t.*? *Josh.* 23. 10.
Judg. 6. † 15. my *t.* is the meanest in Manasseh
9. 49. the men of Shechem died, about a *t.* men
15. 15. Samson slew a *t.* men therewith, 16.
20. 10. an hundred of a *t.* a *t.* out of ten thousand
1 *Sam.* 17. 18. ten cheeses to the captain of their *t.*
18. 13. Saul made David his captain over a *t.*
25. 2. Nabal had three *t.* sheep and a *t.* goats
2 *Sam.* 8. 4. and David took from him a *t.* chariots and seven hundred horses, 1 *Chron.* 18. 4.
18. 12. though I should receive a *t.* shekels
19. 17. there were a *t.* men of Benjamin with him
1 *Kings* 3. 4. a *t.* burnt-offerings did Solomon offer upon that altar, 2 *Chron.* 1. 6.
2 *Kings* 15. 19. Menahem gave Pul a *t.* talents
24. 16. carried away craftsmen and smiths a *t.*
1 *Chron.* 12. 14. and the greatest was over a *t.*
34. of Naphtali a *t.* captains, and with them
16. 15. word he commanded to a *t.* generations
19. 6. the children of Ammon sent a *t.* talents
29. 21. they sacrificed sacrifices unto the Lord a *t.* bullocks, a *t.* rams, and a *t.* lambs
2 *Chron.* 30. 24. Hezekiah did give a *t.* bullocks
Ezra 1. 9. Cyrus did bring forth a *t.* chargers
10. thirty basons of gold, and other vessels a *t.*
Job 9. 3. he cannot answer him one of a *t.*
33. 23. if there be an interpreter, one of a *t.*
42. 12. Job had a *t.* yoke of oxen, a *t.* she-asses
Psal. 50. 10. the cattle on a *t.* hills are mine
84. 10. a day in thy courts is better than a *t.*
90. 4. a *t.* years in thy sight are but as yesterday
91. 7. a *t.* shall fall at thy side, and ten thousand
Eccl. 6. 6. yea, though he live a *t.* years twice told
7. 28. one man among a *t.* have I found, but a wom.
Cant. 4. 4. whereon there hang a *t.* bucklers
8. 11. for the fruit was to bring a *t.* pieces
12. thou, O Solomon, must have a *t.*
Isa. 7. 23. where were a *t.* vines, at a *t.* silverlings
30. 17. one *t.* shall flee at the rebuke of one
60. 22. a little one shall become a *t.* and a small one
Ezek. 47. 3. the man measured a *t.* cubits
4. again he measured a *t.* and brought me thro', 5.
Dan. 5. 1. Belshazzar made a great feast to a *t.* of his lords, and drank wine before the *t.*
Amos 5. 3. the city that went out by a *t.* shall leave
2 *Pet.* 3. 8. be not ignorant, one day is with the Lord as a *t.* years, and a *t.* years as one day
Rev. 20. 2. and he bound Satan a *t.* years
3. deceive nations no more, till *t.* years be fulfilled
4. and they reigned with Christ a *t.* years
7. and when the *t.* years are expired

One THOUSAND *two hundred sixty.*

Rev. 11. 3. they shall prophesy *one t.* 260 days
12. 6. they should feed her *one t.* 260 days

One THOUSAND *two hundred ninety.*

Dan. 12. 11. there shall be *one t.* 290 days

One THOUSAND *three hundred thirty-five.*

Dan. 12. 12. blessed that cometh to the *t.* 335 days

One THOUSAND *six hundred.*

Rev. 14. 20. by the space of *one t.* 600 furlongs

Two THOUSAND.

Num. 35. 5. ye shall measure on the east-side *two t.* cubits, on the west-side *two t.* south-side *two t.*
Josh. 3. 4. space between you and the ark *two t.*
1 *Kings* 7. 26. the molten sea contained *two t.* baths
2 *Kings* 18. 23. and I will deliver thee *two t.* horses if thou be able to set riders upon, *Isa.* 36. 8.
Neh. 7. 72. the people gave *two t.* pounds of silver
Mark 5. 13. about *two t.* swine were choked in sea

Two THOUSAND *two hundred.*

Neh. 7. 71. fathers gave *two t.* 200 pounds of silver

Two THOUSAND *three hundred.*

Dan. 8. 14. to *two t.* 300 days, sanctuary cleansed

Two hundred THOUSAND.

2 *Chron.* 28. 8. carried captive of brethren 200 *t.*

Two hundred eighty THOUSAND.

2 *Chr.* 14. 8. and out of Benjamin *two hun. eighty t.*

Two hundred THOUSAND THOUSAND.

Rev. 9. 16. the number of horsemen were *two hundred thousand thousand*

Three THOUSAND.

Exod. 32. 28. there fell of the people *three t.*
Josh. 7. 4. there went to Ai about *three t.* men
Judg. 15. 11. *three t.* went to bind Samson
16. 27. there were upon the roof *three t.* men
1 *Sam.* 13. 2. Saul chose *three t.* men of Israel
24. 2. then Saul took *three t.* chosen men, 26. 2.
25. 2. Naboth had *three t.* sheep and a *t.* goats
1 *Kings* 4. 32. Solomon spake *three t.* proverbs
2 *Chron.* 4. 5. the molten sea held *three t.* baths
Job 1. 3. his substance was *three t.* camels
Jer. 52. 28. carried away captive *three t.* Jews
Acts 2. 41. were added to them *three t.* souls

Four THOUSAND.

1 *Sam.* 4. 2. they slew of Israel about *four t.* men
1 *Chron.* 23. 5. *four t.* porters, *four t.* praised Lord
2 *Chron.* 9. 25. Solomon had *four t.* stalls for horses
Mat. 15. 38. they that eat were *four t.* *Mark* 8. 9.
16. 10. seven loaves among *four t.* *Mark* 8. 20.
Acts 21. 38. leddest into the wilderness *four t.* men

Four THOUSAND *five hundred.*

Ezek. 48. 16. on the north-side of the city *four t.* 500 measures, east-side, south-side, west-side *four t.* 500 measures, 30, 32, 33, 34.

Five THOUSAND.

Josh. 8. 12. and he took about *five t.* men
Judg. 20. 45. they gleaned of them *five t.* men
1 *Chron.* 29. 7. and gave of gold *five t.* talents
2 *Chron.* 35. 9. for offerings *five t.* small cattle
Ezra 2. 69. they gave *five t.* pounds of silver
Mat. 14. 21. they that had eaten were about *five t.*
16. 9. nor remember the five loaves of the *five t.* *Mark* 6. 44. | 8. 19. *Luke* 9. 14. *John* 6. 10.
Acts 4. 4. number that believed were about *five t.*

Five THOUSAND *four hundred.*

Ezra 1. 11. vessels of gold and silver *five t.* 400

Six THOUSAND.

1 *Sam.* 13. 5. against Israel with *six t.* horsemen
2 *Kings* 5. 5. Naaman took *six t.* pieces of gold
1 *Chron.* 23. 4. and *six t.* were officers and judges
Job 42. 12. for Job had *six t.* camels

Six THOUSAND *seven hundred and twenty.*

Ezra 2. 67. their asses, *six t. seven hundred and twenty*, *Neh.* 7. 69.

Seven THOUSAND.

1 *Kings* 19. 18. yet have I left me *seven t.* in Israel who have not bowed to Baal, *Rom.* 11. 4.
20. 15. children of Israel, being *seven t.*
2 *Kings* 24. 16. carried away men of might *sev. t.*
1 *Chron.* 12. 25. of Simeon, mighty men, *seven t.*
18. 4. David took from him *seven t.* horsemen
19. 18. David slew of the Syrians *seven t.* men
29. 4. I prepared *seven t.* talents of silver
2 *Chron.* 15. 11. they offered *seven t.* sheep
30. 24. Hezekiah gave congregation *seven t.* sheep
Job 1. 3. his substance also was *seven t.* sheep
Rev. 11. 13. in earthquake were slain *seven t.* men

Seven THOUSAND *seven hundred.*

2 *Chron.* 17. 11. Arabians brought Jehoshaphat *seven t.* 700 rams, *seven t.* 700 he-goats

Ten THOUSAND.

Lev. 26. 8. an hundred shall put *ten t.* to flight
Num. 10. † 36. return to the *ten t.* thousands of Isr
Deut. 32. 30. how should two put *ten t.* to flight?
33. 2. Lord came with *ten t.* of saints, *Jude* 14.
Judg. 1. 4. they slew of them in Bezek *ten t.* men
3. 29. they slew of Moab *ten t.* men, all lusty
4. 6. Barak, go, and take *ten t.* men of Naphtali
10. he went up with *ten t.* men at his feet, 14.
7. 3. and there remained to Gideon *ten t.*
20. 34. there came up against Gibeah *ten t.* men
2 *Sam.* 18. 3. but now thou art worth *ten t.* of us
1 *Kings* 5. 14. sent them to Lebanon, *ten t.* a month
2 *Kings* 13. 7. leave to Jehoahaz *ten t.* footmen
14. 7. Amaziah slew of Edom in the valley *ten t.*
24. 14. he carried away even *ten t.* captives
2 *Chron.* 25. 11. smote of the children of Seir *ten t.*
12. other *ten t.* left alive, did Judah carry away
27. 5. the Ammonites gave Jotham the same year *ten t.* measures of wheat, and *ten t.* of barley
30. 24. Hezekiah gave congregation *ten t.* sheep
Esth. 3. 9. I will pay *ten t.* talents of silver
Psal. 91. 7. *ten t.* shall fall at thy right hand
Cant. 5. 10. my beloved is the chiefest among *ten t.*
Ezek. 45. 1. the breadth of the land shall be *ten t.* 3. 5. | 48. 9, 10, 13, 18.
Dan. 7. 10. *ten t.* times *ten t.* stood before him
Mat. 18. 24. which owed him *ten t.* talents
Luke 14. 31. whether he be able with *ten t.* to meet
1 *Cor.* 4. 15. for though you have *ten t.* instructors
14. 19. than *ten t.* words in an unknown tongue
Rev. 5. 11. number of them was *ten t.* times *ten t.*

Ten THOUSANDS.

Deut. 33. 17. they are the *ten t.* of Ephraim
1 *Sam.* 18. 7. Dav. slain his *ten t.* 8. | 21. 11. | 29. 5.
Psal. 3. 6. I will not be afraid of *ten t.* of people
144. 13. that our sheep may bring forth *ten t.*
Dan. 11. 12. he shall cast down many *ten t.*
Mic. 6. 7. or be pleased with *ten t.* rivers of oil

Twelve THOUSAND.

Josh. 8. 25. all that fell of Ai were *twelve t.*
Judg. 21. 10. sent *twelve t.* men to Jabesh-gilead
1 *Kings* 4. 26. Solomon had *twelve t.* horsemen, 10. 26. 2 *Chron.* 1. 14. | 9. 25
Rev. 7. 5. of tribe of Juda, Reuben, Gad, sealed *t. t.*
6. of Aser, Naphthalim, Manasses, sealed *tw. t.*
7. of Simeon, Levi, Issachar, were sealed *tw. t.*
8. of Zabulon, Joseph, Benjamin, sealed *tw. t.*
21. 16. he measured the city *twelve t.* furlongs

Fourteen THOUSAND.

Job 42. 12. for Job had *fourteen t.* sheep

Fourteen THOUSAND *seven hundred.*

Num. 16. 49. that died in the plague *fourteen t.* 700

Sixteen THOUSAND.

Num. 31. 40. the persons were *sixteen t.* 46.

Sixteen THOUSAND *seven hundred fifty.*

Num. 31. 52. gold of offering *sixteen t. seven hundred* and *fifty* shekels

Seventeen THOUSAND *two hundred.*

1 *Chron.* 7. 11. sons of Jediel *seventeen t. two hund.*

Eighteen THOUSAND.

Judg. 20. 25. destroyed of Israel *eighteen t.* men
44. there fell of Benjamin *eighteen t.* men
1 *Chr.* 12. 31. of half-tribe of Manasseh *eighteen t.*
18. 12. Abishai slew of the Edomites *eighteen t.*
29. 7. they gave of brass *eighteen t.* talents

Twenty THOUSAND.

2 Sam. 8. 4. David took from Hadadezer king of Zobah, twenty t. footmen, 1 Chron. 18. 4.
10. 6. the children of Ammon hired Syrians, 20 t.
18. 7. slaughter of Absalom's company twenty t.
1 Kings 5. 11. Solomon gave Hiram twenty t. measures of wheat, 2 Chron. 2. 10.
Neh. 7. 71. fathers gave to work twen. t. drams, 72.
Psal. 68. 17. the chariots of God are twenty t.
Luke 14. 31. to meet him that cometh, with twenty t.

Twenty-two THOUSAND.

Num. 3. 39. the number of Levites twenty-two t.
43. the first-born males were twenty-two t.
26. 14. of families of Simeonites twenty-two t.
Judg. 7. 3. there returned of Gideon's army 22 t.
20. 21. Benjamin destroyed of Israel twenty-two t.
2 Sam. 8. 5. David slew of the Syrians twenty-two t. men, 1 Chron. 18. 5.
1 Kings 8. 63. Solomon offered twenty-two t. oxen, 2 Chron. 7. 5.
1 Chron. 7. 2. of Tola twen.-two t. ‖ 7. of Bela 22 t.

Twenty-three THOUSAND.

Num. 26. 62. numbered of Levites twenty-three t.
1 Cor. 10. 8. and fell in one day three and twenty t.

Twenty-four THOUSAND.

Num. 25. 9. died in the plague twenty-four t.
1 Chron. 23. 4. 24 t. Levites to forward the work
27. 1. the officers that served were twenty-four t.

Twenty-five THOUSAND.

Judg. 20. 35. destroyed of Benjamites tw.-five t. 46.
Ezek. 45. 1. holy portion of land twenty-five t. reeds in length, 3, 5, 6. | 48. 8, 9, 10, 13.

Twenty-six THOUSAND.

Judg. 20. 15. Benjamin numbered twenty-six t.
1 Chron. 7. 40. of Asher, apt to war, twenty-six t.

Twenty-seven THOUSAND.

1 Kings 20. 30. a wall fell on twenty-seven t. men

Twenty-eight THOUSAND.

1 Chron. 12. 35. Danites, expert in war, 28 t.

Thirty THOUSAND.

Num. 31. 39. and the asses were thirty t. 45.
Josh. 8. 3. Joshua chose thirty t. mighty men
1 Sam. 4. 10. there fell of Israel thirty t. footmen
11. 8. and the men of Judah were thirty t.
13. 5. Philistines gathered thirty t. chariots
2 Sam. 6. 1. David gathered thirty t. chosen men
1 Kings 5. 13. and the levy was thirty t. men

Thirty-two THOUSAND.

Num. 31. 35. thirty-two t. women taken captives
1 Chron. 19. 7. Ammon hired thirty-two t. chariots

Thirty-two THOUSAND two hundred.

Num. 1. 35. number of Manasseh 32 t. 200, 2. 21.

Thirty-two THOUSAND five hundred.

Num. 26. 37. of Ephraim were numbered 32 t. 500

Thirty-three THOUSAND.

2 Chron. 35. 7. gave thirty-three t. bullocks

Thirty-five THOUSAND.

Num. 1. 37. of Benjamin were thirty-five t.

Thirty-six THOUSAND.

Num. 31. 38. the beeves were thirty and six t.
44. pertained to congregation thirty-six t. beeves
1 Chron. 7. 4. the bands of soldiers were thirty-six t.

Thirty-seven THOUSAND.

1 Chron. 12. 34. of Naphtali thirty and seven t.

Thirty-eight THOUSAND.

1 Chron. 23. 3. Levites from thirty years, 38 t.

Forty THOUSAND.

Josh. 4. 13. about forty t. prepared for war
Judg. 5. 8. was there a shield seen among forty t.?
2 Sam. 10. 18. David slew forty t. horsemen
1 Kings 4. 26. Solomon had forty t. stalls of horses
1 Chron. 12. 36. of Asher, expert in war, forty t.
19. 18. David slew of Syrians, forty t. footmen

Forty THOUSAND five hundred.

Num. 1. 33. of Ephraim were forty t. 500, 2. 19.
26. 18. of Gad were numbered forty t. and 500

Forty-one THOUSAND five hundred.

Num. 1. 41. of Asher numbered 41 t. 500, 2. 28.

Forty-two THOUSAND.

Judg. 12. 6. fell of Ephraimites forty-two t.
Ezra 2. 64. whole congregation forty-two t. Neh. 7. 66.

Forty-three THOUSAND seven hundred thirty.

Num. 26. 7. of Reubenites forty-three t. 730

Forty-four THOUSAND seven hundred sixty.

1 Chron. 5. 18. of Reubenites to war 44 t. 760

Forty-five THOUSAND four hundred.

Num. 26. 50. of Naphtali were forty-five t. 400

Forty-five THOUSAND six hundred.

Num. 26. 41. numbered of Benjamin forty-five t. 600

Forty-five THOUSAND six hundred fifty.

Num. 1. 25. were numbered of Gad 45 t. 650, 2. 15.

Forty-six THOUSAND five hundred.

Num. 1. 21. of Reuben forty-six t. and 500, 2. 11.

Fifty THOUSAND.

1 Sam. 6. 19. the Lord smote fifty t. and seventy men
1 Chron. 5. 21. took of the Hagarites' sheep fifty t.
12. 33. of Zebulun fifty t. could keep rank
Acts 19. 19. the price of the book fifty t. pieces

Fifty-two THOUSAND seven hundred.

Num. 26. 34. of Manasseh fifty-two t. and seven h.

Fifty-three THOUSAND four hundred.

Num. 1. 43. of Naphtali fifty-three t. 400, 2. 30.

Fifty-four THOUSAND four hundred.

Num. 1. 29. of Issachar fifty-four t. four h. 2. 6.

Fifty-seven THOUSAND four hundred.

Num. 1. 31. of Zebulun fifty-seven t. four h. 2. 8.

Fifty-nine THOUSAND three hundred.

Num. 1. 23. of Simeon fifty-nine t. three h. 2. 13.

Sixty THOUSAND.

2 Chron. 12. 3. Shishak came with sixty t. horsemen

Sixty THOUSAND five hundred.

Num. 26. 27. of Zebulunites, sixty t. and five hun.

Sixty-one THOUSAND.

Num. 31. 34. the booty was sixty one t. asses
Ezra 2. 69. they gave sixty one t. drams of gold

Sixty two THOUSAND seven hundred.

Num. 1. 39. of tribe of Dan sixty-two t. 700, 2. 26.

Sixty-four THOUSAND three hundred.

Num. 26. 25. of Issachar sixty-four t. and three h.
43. of the Shuhamites sixty-four t. four hundred

Seventy THOUSAND.

2 Sam. 24. 15. there died of the people seventy t.
1 Kings 5. 15. Solomon had seventy t. that bare burdens, 2 Chron. 2. 2, 18.
1 Chron. 21. 14. there fell of Israel seventy t.

Seventy-two THOUSAND.

Num. 31. 33. booty of beeves was seventy-two t.

Seventy-four THOUSAND six hundred.

Num. 1. 27. number of Judah 74 t. and 600, 2. 4.

Seventy-five THOUSAND.

Num. 31. 32. the booty was seventy-five t. sheep
Esth. 9. 16. Jews slew of their foes seventy-five t.

Seventy six THOUSAND five hundred.

Num. 26. 22. numbered of Judah seventy-six t. 500

Eighty THOUSAND.

1 Kings 5. 15. Solomon had eighty t. hewers in the mountains, 2 Chron. 2. 2, 18.

Eighty-seven THOUSAND.

1 Chron. 7. 5. of Issachar, reckoned eighty-seven t.

THOUSAND THOUSAND.

1 Chron. 21. 5. all they of Israel were a t. t.
22. 14. I have prepared a t. t. talents of silver
2 Chron. 14. 9. the Ethiopian came with a t. t.

Two hundred THOUSAND THOUSAND.

Rev. 9. 16. army of horsemen two hundred t. t.

THOUSANDS.

Gen. 24. 60. be thou the mother of t. of millions
Exod. 18. 21. place such over them rulers of t. 25.
20. 6. shewing mercy to t. of them, Deut. 5. 10.
34. 7. keeping mercy for t. forgiving iniquity
Num. 1. 16. there were the princes of tribes, heads of t. in Israel, 10. 4. Josh. 22. 14, 21, 30.
10. 36. return, O Lord, to the many t. of Israel
31. 5. there were delivered out of the t. of Israel
Deut. 1. 15. so I made them captains over t.
33. 17. and they are the t. of Manasseh
1 Sam. 8. 12. he will appoint him captains over t.
10. 19. therefore present yourselves by your t.
18. 8. and to me they have ascribed but t.
22. 7. will the son of Jesse make you captains of t.?
23. 23. I'll search him throughout the t. of Judah
29. 2. the lords of the Philistines passed on by t.
2 Sam. 18. 4. and all the people came out by t.
Psal. 119. 72. thy law is better than t. of gold
Jer. 32. 18. thou shewest loving-kindness to t.
Dan. 7. 10. thousand t. ministered unto him
Mic. 5. 2. tho' thou be little among the t. of Judah
6. 7. will the Lord be pleased with t. of rams?
Acts 21. 20. how many t. of Jews which believe
Rev. 5. 11. the number of them was t. of t.

See CAPTAINS.

THREAD.

Gen. 14. 23. I will not take from a t. to a latchet
38. 28. she bound on his hand a scarlet t. 30.
Josh. 2. 18. shalt bind this scarlet t. in the window
Judg. 16. 9. he brake the withs as a t. of tow
12. he brake the ropes from his arms as a t.
Cant. 4. 3. thy lips are like a t. of scarlet

THREATEN, ED.

Acts 4. 17. but let us straitly t. them not to speak, 21.
1 Pet. 2. 23. when he suffered he t. not

THREATENING, INGS.

Acts 4. 29. Lord, behold their t. and grant thy serv.
9. 1. Saul yet breathing out t. and slaughter
Eph. 6. 9. do the same things to them, forbearing t.

THREE.

Gen. 18. 2. he looked, and lo, t. men stood by him
Exod. 21. 11. and if he do not these t. unto her
25. 32. t. branches of the candlestick, 37. 18.
33. t. bowls made like unto almonds, 37. 19.
27. 1. the height of the altar shall be t. cubits, 38. 1.
14. pillars t. their sockets t. 15. | 38. 14, 15.
Lev. 14. 10. shall take t. tenth deals of fine flour for a meat-offering, Num. 15. 9. | 28. 12.
27. 6. thy estimation for the female, t. shekels
Num. 12. 4. come out, ye t. and they t. came out
28. 20. t. tenth deals for a bullock, 28. | 29. 3, 9, 14.
35. 14. ye shall give t. cities on this side Jordan
Deut. 4. 41. Moses severed t. cities, 19. 2, 3, 7, 9.
17. 6. at the mouth of t. witnesses, 19. 15.
Josh 15. 14. and Caleb drove thence the t. sons of Anak, Judg. 1. 20.
18. 4. t. men of each tribe to describe the land
Judg. 7. 20. the t. companies blew the trumpets
9. 43. he divided the people into t. companies
1 Sam. 1. 24. Hannah took with her t. bullocks
2. 13. servant came with a flesh-hook of t. teeth
21. Hannah bare t. sons and two daughters
10. 3. there shall meet thee t. men, one carrying t. kids, another carrying t. loaves of bread
11. 11. Saul put the people in t. companies
17. 13. the t. eldest of Jesse's sons followed Saul, 14.
20. 20. I will shoot t. arrows on the side thereof
31. 6. Saul died, and his t. sons, 1 Chron. 10. 6.
8. they found Saul and his t. sons fallen
2 Sam. 14. 27. to Absalom there were born t. sons
18. 14. Joab thrust t. darts through Absalom
23. 9. Eleazar one of the t. mighty, 1 Chr. 11. 12.
13. t. of the thirty chief went down to David
16. t. mighty brake through the Philistines, 17.
18. Abishai brother of Joab chief among t. 19.
19. howbeit, he attained not to the first t. 23.
22. Benaiah had the name among t. mighty men
24. 12. I offer thee t. things, 1 Chron. 21. 10.
1 Kings 6. 36. he built the inner court with t. rows
7. 4. and there were windows in t. rows
25. it stood upon t. oxen looking toward the north, t. to the west, t. to the south, t. to the east
10. 17. t. pound of gold went to one shield
2 Kings 3. 10. Lord hath called these t. kings, 13.
1 Chron. 2. 16. the sons of Zeruiah were t.
3. 23. sons of Neariah t. ‖ 23. 23. sons of Mushi t.
25. 5. God gave Heman fourteen sons and t. daugh.
Ezra 6. 4. let the foundations be laid with t. rows
Job 1. 2. were born to Job t. daughters, 42. 13.
17. the Chaldeans made out t. bands and fell
2. 11. Job's t. friends heard of all this evil
Prov. 30. 15. t. things which are never satisfied
18. there be t. things too wonderful for me
21. for t. things the earth is disquieted
29. there be t. things which go well, yea four
Isa. 17. 6. two or t. berries in the top of the bough
Ezek. 14. 14. though these t. men were in it, 16, 18.
40. 10. the little chambers were t. on this side, 21.
Ezek. 41. 6. side chambers were t. one over another
48. 31. t. gates, after names of tribes, 32, 33, 34.
Dan. 3. 24. did not we cast t. men bound into fire?
6. 2. and Darius set over these t. presidents
7. 5. it had t. ribs in the mouth between the teeth
8. t. of the first horns were plucked up, 20, 24.
10. 2. I Daniel was mourning t. full weeks, 3.
11. 2. there shall stand up t. kings in Persia
Amos 1. 3. for t. transgressions of Damascus
6. of Gaza ‖ 9. Tyrus ‖ 11. Edom ‖ 13. Ammon
2. 1. t. transgressions of Moab ‖ 4. Judah ‖ 6. Israel
4. 8. so two or t. cities wandered to one city
Zech. 11. 8. t. shepherds I cut off in one month
Mat. 13. 33. hid in t. measures of meal, Luke 13. 21.
17. 4. if thou wilt, let us make here t. tabernacles, Mark 9. 5. Luke 9. 33.
18. 16. in mouth of two or t. witnesses, 2 Cor. 13. 1.
20. where two or t. are gathered in my name
Luke 10. 36. which of these t. was neighbour to him?
11. 5. shall say to him, friend, lend me t. loaves
12. 52. divided, t. against two, and two against t.
Acts 5. 7. t. hours after, when his wife came in
10. 19. behold, t. men seek thee, 11. 11.
28. 15. come to meet us as far as the t. taverns
1 Cor. 13. 13. now abideth these t. faith, hope, charity
14. 27. by two, or at most by t. and that by course
29. let the prophets speak two or t. and other
1 Tim. 5. 19. but before two or t. witnesses
Heb. 10. 28. died under two or t. witnesses
1 John 5. 7. there are t. that bear record in heaven
8. t. bear witness in earth, and these t. agree
Rev. 6. 6. and t. measures of barley for a penny
8. 13. trumpet of t. angels who are yet to sound
9. 18. by these t. was the third part of men killed
16. 13. I saw t. unclean spirits like frogs come
19. the great city was divided into t. parts
21. 13. on the east t. gates, on the north t. gates, on the south t. gates, and on the west t. gates

See DAYS.

THREE months.

Gen. 38. 24. about t. months after, it was told
Exod. 2. 2. was a goodly child, she hid him t. months
2 Sam. 6. 11. the ark of the Lord continued in the house of Obed-edom t. months, 1 Chron. 13. 14.
24. 13. wilt thou flee t. months before thine enemies, while they pursue thee? 1 Chron. 21. 12.
2 Kings 23. 31. Jehoahaz son of Josiah reigned t. months in Jerusalem, 2 Chron. 36. 2.
24. 8. Jehoiachin reigned t. months, 2 Chr. 36. 9.
Amos 4. 7. there were yet t. months to harvest
Acts 7. 20. Moses was nourished up t. months
19. 8. Paul spake boldly the space of t. months
20. 3. Paul abode in Greece t. months
Heb. 11. 23. Moses was hid t. months of his parents

THREE times.

Exod. 23. 14. t. times thou shalt keep a feast to me
17. t. times in the year all thy males shall appear before the Lord God, Deut. 16. 16.
Num. 22. 28. thou hast smitten me these t. times, 32.
33. the ass turned from me these t. times
24. 10. thou hast blessed them these t. times
Judg. 16. 15. thou hast mocked me these t. times
1 Sam. 20. 41. David arose and bowed t. times
1 Kings 9. 25. Solomon offered t. times a year
17. 21. Elijah stretched himself on the child t. times
2 Kings 13. 25. t. times did Joash beat Hazael
2 Chron. 8. 13. offering t. times in the year
Dan. 6. 10. he kneeled on his knees t. times a day
13. Daniel maketh his petition t. times a day
Acts 11. 10. this was done t. times, and drawn up

THREE years.

Gen. 15. 9. take an heifer of t. years old, a she-goat t. years old, and a ram t. years old
Lev. 19. 23. fruit as uncircumcised t. years
25. 21. it shall bring forth fruit for t. years
Deut. 14. 28. at the end of t. years bring the tithe
Judg. 9. 22. when Abimelech had reigned t. years
2 Sam. 13. 38. Absalom was in Geshur t. years
21. 1. was a famine in the days of David t. years
1 Kings 2. 39. at end of t. years Shimei's serv. ran
10. 22. once in t. years came the navy of Tharshish, bringing gold and silver, 2 Chron. 9. 21.
15. 2. Abijam reigned t. years in Jerus. 2 Chr. 13. 2.
22. 1. they continued t. years without war
2 Kings 17. 5. Assyrians besieged Samaria t. years
18. 10. and at the end of t. years they took it
24. 1. Jehoiakim became his servant t. years
1 Chron. 21. 12. choose thee either t. years' famine, or three months to be destroyed, &c.
2 Chron. 11. 17. made Rehoboam strong t. years, t. years they walked in way of David and Solomon
13. 2. Abijah reigned t. years in Jerusalem
31. 16. males, from t. years old and upward
Isa. 15. 5. unto Zoar, an heifer of t. years old
16. 14. within t. years as years of an hireling
20. 3. as Isaiah walked barefoot t. years
Jer. 48. 34. as an heifer of t. years old
Dan. 1. 5. so nourishing them t. years
Amos 4. 4. and bring your tithes after t. years
Luke 4. 25. heaven shut up t. years, Jam. 5. 17.
13. 7. these t. years I come seeking fruit, find none
Acts 20. 31. t. years I ceased not to warn every one
Gal. 1. 18. after t. years I went up to Jerusalem

See HUNDRED.

THREEFOLD.

Eccl. 4. 12. and a t. cord is not quickly broken

THREESCORE.

Gen. 25. 26. Isaac t. years old when she bare them
Deut. 3. 4. took from them t. cities, Josh. 13. 30.
2 Sam. 2. 31. so that three hundred and t. died
1 Kings 4. 13. to him pertained t. great cities
22. his provision was t. measures of meal
6. 2. the length of the Lord's house was t. cubits and breadth thereof twenty cubits, 2 Chr. 3. 3.
2 Kings 25. 19. and he took t. men of the people
1 Chron. 2. 21. Hezron married when t. years old
2 Chron. 11. 21. Rehoboam took t. concubines
Ezra 6. 3. height of temple t. cubits breadth t.
Cant. 3. 7. t. valiant men are about it
6. 8. there are t. queens fourscore concubine
Jer. 52. 25. put to death t. men of the people
Dan. 3. 1. an image, whose height was t. cubits

Luke 24. 13. from Jerusalem about t. furlongs
1 Tim. 5. 9. let not a widow be taken under t.
See SIXTY.
THREESCORE and one.
Num. 31. 39. Lord's tribute of asses, t. and one
THREESCORE and two.
1 Chron. 26. 8. able men t. and two of Obed-edom
Dan. 5. 31. Darius about t. and two years old
9. 25. in t. and two weeks the street shall be built
26. after t. and two weeks Messiah be cut off
THREESCORE and five.
Isa. 7. 8. within t. and five years Ephraim broken
THREESCORE and six.
Gen. 46. 26. the souls that came with Jacob t. and six
Lev. 12. 5. in blood of her purifying t. and six days
THREESCORE and seven.
Neh. 7. 72. peo. gave t. and seven priests garments
THREESCORE and eight.
1 Chr. 16. 38. Obed-edom with brethren t. and eight
THREESCORE and ten.
Gen. 46. 27. all the souls of the house of Jacob which came into Egypt, were t. and ten, Deut. 10. 22.
50. 3. they mourned for Israel t. and ten days
Exod. 15. 27. in Elim were twelve wells of water, and t. and ten palm-trees, Num. 33. 9.
Judg. 1. 7. t. and ten kings, their thumbs cut off
8. 30. and Gideon had t. and ten sons, 9. 2.
9. 4. they gave him t. and ten pieces of silver
5. he slew t. and ten persons on one stone, 18. 24.
12. 14. sons and nephews, that rode on t. a. t. ass-c.
2 Chron. 29. 32. brought t. and ten bullocks
36. 21. land kept sabbath, to fulfil t. and ten years
Psal. 90. 10. the days of our years are t. and ten
Zech. 1. 12. hast had indignation t. and ten years
Acts 23. 23. make ready t. and ten horsemen
See SEVENTY.
THREESCORE and twelve.
Num. 31. 38. Lord's tribute t. and twelve beeves
THREESCORE and fifteen.
Acts 7. 14. Joseph's kindred t. and fifteen souls
THREESCORE and seventeen.
Judg. 8. 14. the elders of Succoth t. and seventeen
THRESH.
Judg. 8. † 7. then I will t. your flesh with thorns
Isa. 41. 15. thou shalt t. the mountains and beat
Jer. 51. 33. is like a floor, it is time to t. her
Mic. 4. 13. arise, and t. O daughter of Zion
Hab. 3. 12. thou didst t. the heathen in anger
THRESHED.
Judg. 6. 11. Gideon t. wheat by the wine-press
Isa. 25. † 10. Moab shall be t. down under him
28. 27. fitches not t. with a threshing instrument
Amos 1. 3. because they t. Gilead with instruments
THRESHETH.
Deut. 25. † 4. not muzzle the ox when he t. corn
1 Cor. 9. 10. t. in hope, be partaker of his hope
THRESHING.
Lev. 26. 5. your t. shall reach unto the vintage
2 Sam. 24. 22. here be t. instruments, 1 Chron. 21. 23.
2 Kings 13. 7. had made them like the dust by t.
1 Chron. 21. 20. now Ornan was t. wheat
Isa. 21. 10. O my t. and the corn of my floor
28. 28. because he will not ever be t. it
41. 15. will make thee a new sharp t. instrument
Joel 3. † 14. multitudes in the valley of t.
See FLOOR, FLOORS.
THRESHOLD.
Judg. 19. 27. behold, her hands were upon the t.
1 Sam. 5. 4. the palms of his hands cut off on the t.
5. 5. tread not on the t. of Dagon unto this day
1 Kings 14. 17. when she came to t. the child died
2 Kings 12. † 9. keeper of t. 22. † 4. | 25. † 18. Esth. 2. † 21. | 6. † 2. Jer. 35. † 4. | 52. † 24.
Psal. 84. † 10. I would rather choose to sit at the t.
Isa. 6. † 4. the posts of the t. moved at the voice
Ezek. 9. 3. the glory of God was gone up to t. 10. 4.
10. 18. the glory of God departed from the t.
43. 8. in their setting of their t. by my thresholds
46. 2. the prince shall worship at the t. of the gate
47. 1. waters issued out from under the t. eastward
Zeph. 1. 9. I will punish all that leap on the t.
THRESHOLDS.
1 Chron. 9. † 19. keepers of the t. 2 Chron. 23. † 4.
Neh. 12. 25. keeping ward at the t. of the gates
Ezek. 43. 8. in setting of their threshold by my t.
Zeph. 2. 14. desolation shall be in the t. for he shall
THREW.
2 Sam. 16. 13. Shimei t. stones at David and cast
2 Kings 9. 33. they t. Jezebel down, and he trod her
2 Chron. 31. 1. and they t. down the high places
Mark 12. 42. there came a certain poor widow and she t. in two mites, which make a farthing
Luke 9. 42. the devil t. him down, and tare him
Acts 22. 23. as they cried, and t. dust in the air
THREWEST.
Neh. 9. 11. their persecutors thou t. into the deeps
THRICE.
Exod. 34. 23. t. in the year shall all appear, 24.
2 Kings 13. 18. and Joash smote t. and stayed
19. whereas now thou shalt smite Syria but t.
Job 33. † 29. these things worketh God twice and t.
Mat. 26. 34. thou shalt deny me t. 75. Mark 14. 30, 72. Luke 22. 34, 61. John 13. 38.
Acts 10. 16. this was done t. vessel was received up
2 Cor. 11. 25. t. was I beaten with rods, once was I stoned, t. I suffered shipwreck
12. 8. for this thing I besought the Lord t.
THROAT.
Psal. 5. 9. their t. is an open sepulchre, Rom. 3. 13.
69. 3. I am weary of my crying, my t. is dried
115. 7. neither speak they through their t.
149. † 6. let the high praises of God be in their t.
Prov. 23. 2. put a knife to thy t. if given to appetite
Isa. 58. † 1. cry with the t. lift up thy voice
Jer. 2. 25. and withhold thy t. from thirst
Mat. 18. 28. the servant took him by the t.
THRONE,
Is used for that magnificent seat whereon sovereign princes usually sit, to receive the homage of their subjects, or to give audience to ambassadors; where they appear with pomp and ceremony, and from whence they dispense justice. The Scripture describes the throne *of Solomon, as the finest and richest* throne *in the world,* 1 Kings 10. 20. There was not the like made in any kingdom. *It was all of ivory, and plated with pure gold. The ascent was by six steps; the back was round, and two arms supported the seat. Twelve golden lions, one on each side of every step, made a principal part of its ornament.* Throne *is also put for sovereign power and dignity, it being the symbol of royalty and regal authority; thus Pharaoh tells Joseph,* Gen. 41. 40. Only in the *throne* will I be greater than thou.
Heaven is the throne *of God,* Isa. 66. 1. *The highest heavens are the place where he most manifests his power and glory, and shews himself in his majesty.* Justice and judgment are the habitation of the *throne* of the Lord, *Psal.* 89. 14. *Just judgment, or justice in judging, is the basis or foundation of all his proceedings, and the stability of his* throne *and government.* Christ Jesus is set down at the right hand of the *throne* of God, *Heb.* 12. 2. *and from thence he discovers himself in his state and glory, as the great Ruler of the world, the King of kings, and Lord of lords. Our Saviour, to express the rest and satisfaction, the glory, honour, and dignity, which the saints of God shall be possessed of in heaven, tells his disciples,* Luke 22. 30. That ye may sit on *thrones*, judging the twelve tribes of Israel. *The cherubims that were upon the ark of the covenant, were also considered as a kind of* throne *of God; from whence it is said in many places, that* God dwelleth between the cherubims, 1 Sam. 4. 4. 2 Sam. 6. 2. 2 Kings 19. 15. *Angels are called* thrones, *Col.* 1. 16. *as having kingly power; and they are also called* chief princes. *Dan.* 10. 13.
Gen. 41. 40. only in the t. will I be greater
Deut. 17. 18. when he sitteth on t. of his kingdom
1 Sam. 2. 8. to make them inherit the t. of glory
2 Sam. 3. 10. to set up the t. of David over Israel
7. 13. I will stablish t. of his kingdom for ever, 16.
1 Kings 1. 13. Solom. shall sit on my t. 17, 24, 30, 35.
48. hath given one to sit on my t. this day
2. 4. there shall not fail thee a man on the t. of Israel, 8. 25. | 9. 5. 2 Chron. 6. 16. Jer. 33. 17.
12. Solomon sat on t. of David his father, 24. | 8. 20. | 10. 9. 1 Chron. 29. 23. 2 Chron. 6. 10.
10. 18. the king made a great t. 2 Chron. 9. 17.
2 Kings 10. 3. set him on his father's t. and fight
30. to fourth generation shall sit on the t. 15. 12.
11. 19. Joash sat on the t. 2 Chron. 23. 20.
Neh. 3. 7. repaired to the t. of the governor
Job 36. 7. but with kings are they on the t.
Psal. 9. 4. thou sattest in the t. judging right
11. 4. the Lord's t. is in heaven, his eyes behold
45. 6. thy t. O G. is for ever, Lam. 5. 19. Heb. 1. 8.
47. 8. God sitteth on the t. of his holiness
89. 4. I will build thy t. to all generations
14. justice and judgment are habitation of thy t.
94. 20. shall t. of iniq. have fellowship with thee?
132. 11. of fruit of thy body will I set on thy t.
12. their children shall sit on thy t. for ever
Prov. 20. 8. a king that sitteth in t. of judgment
Isa. 6. 1. I saw also the Lord sitting upon a t.
9. 7. on t. of David and his kingdom, to order it
14. 13. I will exalt my t. above the stars of God
22. 23. Eliakim shall be for a glorious t.
47. 1. there is no t. O daughter of Chaldeans
66. 1. the heaven is my t. and earth, Acts 7. 49.
Jer. 3. 17. shall call Jerusalem the t. of the Lord
13. 13. I will fill the kings that sit on David's t.
14. 21. do not disgrace the t. of thy glory
17. 12. a glorious high t. from the beginning
25. kings sitting on the t. of David, 22. 4, 30.
22. 2. O king, that sittest upon the t. 29. 16.
36. 30. he shall have none to sit on the t. of David
49. 38. I will set my t. in Elam, and will destroy
Ezek. 1. 26. was the likeness of a t. 10. 1.
43. 7. the place of my t. shall Isr. no more defile
Hag. 2. 22. I will overthrow the t. of kingdoms
Mat. 5. 34. by heaven, for it is God's t. 23. 22.
19. 28. the Son of man shall sit in the t. 25. 31.
Luke 1. 32. the Lord shall give him the t. of David
Heb. 4. 16. let us come boldly to the t. of grace
8. 1. on the right hand the t. of God, 12. 2.
Rev. 3. 21. to him will I grant to sit in my t.
4. 2. a t. was set in heaven, and one sat on the t.
3. there was a rainbow round about the t.
4. about the t. were four and twenty seats
5. and out of the t. proceeded lightnings and thunderings, there were seven lamps before t.
6. before the t. there was a sea of glass, in t. and round about the t. were four beasts full of eyes
9. beasts gave thanks to him that sat on the t.
10. fall before him that sat on the t. 7. 11.
5. 1. in the hand of him that sat on the t. a book
6. and lo, in the midst of the t. stood a Lamb
7. took the book out of hand of him that sat on t.
11. the voice of many angels about the t.
13. glory be to him that sitteth on the t.
6. 16. hide us from him that sitteth on the t.
7. 9. a great multitude stood before the t.
10. salvation to our God which sitteth on the t.
15. they are before the t. of God, and serve him, he that sitteth on the t. shall dwell among them
17. the Lamb in midst of the t. shall feed them
8. 3. the golden altar which was before the t.
14. 3. they sung as it were a new song before the t.
5. they are without fault before the t. of God
16. 17. there came a voice from the t. 19. 5.
19. 4. they worshipped God that sat on the t.
20. 11. I saw a great white t. and him that sat on it
21. 5. he that sat on t. said, behold, I make all new
22. 1. a pure river proceeding out of the t.
3. the t. of God and of the Lamb shall be in it
His THRONE.
Exod. 11. 5. from first-born that sits on his t. 12. 29.
2 Sam. 14. 9. and the king and his t. be guiltless
1 Kings 1. 37. the Lord make his t. greater, 47.
2. 19. he bowed himself, and sat down on his t.
33. upon his seed, and on his t. shall be peace
1 Kings 16. 11. as soon as Zimri sat on his t. he slew
22. 10. the king of Israel, and Jehoshaphat king of Judah, sat each on his t. 2 Chron. 18. 9.
19. I saw the Lord sitting on his t. 2 Chron. 18. 18.
2 Kings 13. 13. and Jeroboam sat upon his t.
25. 28. set his t. above t. of kings, Jer. 52. 32.
Job 26. 9. he holdeth back the face of his t.
Psal. 9. 7. he hath prepared his t. for judgment
89. 29. his t. to endure as the days of heaven
36. his t. shall endure as the sun before me
44. thou hast cast his t. down to the ground
97. 2. and judgment the habitation of his t.
103. 19. Lord hath prepared his t. in the heavens
Prov. 20. 28. and his t. is upholden by mercy
Jer. 1. 15. set each his t. at the gates of Jerusalem
33. 21. that David should not have a son on his t.
43. 10. and I will set his t. upon these stones
Dan. 5. 20. he was deposed from his kingly t.
7. 9. his t. was like the fiery flame, his wheels
Jonah 3. 6. the king of Nineveh rose from his t.
Zech. 6. 13. he shall sit and rule upon his t. and he shall be a priest on his t. and counsel of peace
Acts 2. 30. would raise up Christ to sit on his t.
Rev. 1. 4. from seven spirits which are before his t.
3. 21. as I am set down with my Father in his t.
12. 5. her child was caught up to God, to his t.
See ESTABLISH, ESTABLISHED.
THRONES.
Psal. 122. 5. for there are set t. of judgment
Isa. 14. 9. it hath raised up from their t. the kings
Ezek. 26. 16. princes shall come down from their t.
Dan. 7. 9. I beheld, till the t. were cast down
Mat. 19. 28. ye shall sit upon twelve t. judging the twelve tribes of Israel, Luke 22. 30.
Col. 1. 16. all created by him, whether they be t.
Rev. 20. 4. and I saw t. and they sat upon them
THRONG.
Mark 3. 9. the multitude, lest they should t. him
Luke 8. 45. the multitude t. thee and press thee
THRONGED.
Mark 5. 24. and much people t. him, Luke 8. 42.
THRONGING.
Mark 5. 31. thou seest the multitude t. thee
THROUGH.
Num. 25. 8. Phinehas thrust both of them t.
2 Kings 1. 2. Ahaziah fell t. lattice, and was sick
Job 14. 9. yet t. the scent of water it will bud
Psal. 73. 9. their tongue walketh t. the earth
Eccl. 10. 18. t. idleness the house droppeth t.
Cant. 2. 9. he looketh, shewing himself t. the lattice
Isa. 27. 4. I would go t. them, I would burn them
43. 2. when thou passest t. waters, t. the fire
62. 10. go t. go t. the gates, prepare the way
Ezek. 46. 19. after he brought me t. the entry
47. 4. he measured, and brought me t. waters
Zech. 13. 9. I will bring the third part t. fire
Mat. 12. 43. he walketh t. dry places, seeking rest
Luke 5. 19. they let him down t. the tiling
John 15. 3. ye are clean t. the word I have spoken
17. 11. keep t. thine own name those given me
17. sanctify them, t. thy truth, thy word is truth
20. 31. believing ye might have life t. his name
Rom. 5. 1. we have peace with God t. our Lord Jesus
6. 23. gift of God is eternal life t. Jesus Christ
8. 13. but if ye t. the spirit mortify the deeds
11. 36. of him, t. him, to him, are all things
16. 27. to God only wise be glory t. Jesus Christ
2 Cor. 4. 15. t. the thanksgiving of many redound
Gal. 2. 19. for I t. the law am dead to the law
Eph. 2. 7. in his kindness towards us t. Christ Jesus
22. for an habitation of God t. the Spirit
4. 6. one God, who is above all, and t. all, in all
18. t. the ignorance that is in them because of
1 Tim. 6. 10. pierced themselves t. with sorrows
Heb. 9. 14. who t. the eternal Spirit offered himself
10. 20. t. the vail, that is to say, his flesh
13. 20. t. the blood of the everlasting covenant
THROUGHLY.
Exod. 21. 19. and shall cause him to be t. healed
2 Kings 11. 18. his images brake they in pieces t.
Job 6. 2. oh that my grief were t. weighed
Psal. 51. 2. wash me t. from mine iniquity, cleanse
Jer. 6. 9. they shall t. glean the remnant of Israel
7. 5. if ye t. amend your ways and your doings, if ye t. execute judgment between man and man
50. 34. he shall t. plead their cause to give rest
Ezek. 16. 9. I t. washed away thy blood from thee
Mat. 3. 12. he will t. purge his floor, Luke 3. 17.
2 Cor. 11. 6. but we have been t. made manifest
2 Tim. 3. 17. man of G. t. furnished to all good works
THROUGHOUT.
Josh. 24. 3. I led Abraham t. the land of Canaan
1 Sam. 23. 23. search him t. thousands of Judah
2 Chron. 31. 20. thus did Hezekiah t. all Judah
Mark 14. 9. this gospel shall be preached t. the world
John 19. 23. without seam, woven from the top t.
Rom. 1. 8. your faith is spoken of t. the world
See GENERATIONS.
THROW.
Judg. 2. 2. ye shall t. down their altars, but have not
6. 25. t. down the altar of Baal thy father hath
2 Kings 9. 33. t. her down, so they threw her down
Jer. 1. 10. I set thee over the nations to t. down
31. 28. as I have watched over them, to t. down
Ezek. 16. 39. they shall t. down thine eminent place
Mic. 5. 11. I will t. down all thy strong holds
Mal. 1. 4. they shall build, but I will t. down
THROWING.
Num. 35. 17. if he smite him with t. a stone
THROWN.
Exod. 15. 1. the horse and his rider hath he t. 21.
Judg. 6. 32. because he hath t. down his altar
2 Sam. 20. 21. his head be t. to thee over the wall
1 Kings 19. 10. Israel have t. down thine altars, 14.
Jer. 31. 40. it shall not be t. down any more
50. 15. foundations fallen, her walls are t. down
Lam. 2. 2. the Lord hath t. down in his wrath
17. he hath t. down, and hath not pitied
Ezek. 29. 5. I will leave thee t. into the wilderness
38. 20. and the mountains shall be t. down
Nah. 1. 6. and the rocks are t. down by him

Mat. 24. 2. not one stone left upon another, that shall not be t. down, Mark 13. 2. Luke 21. 6.
Luke 4. 35. when the devil had t. him in the midst
Rev. 18. 21. the city of Babylon shall be t. down

THRUST.

Exod. 11. 1. he shall surely t. you out hence
12. 39. because they were t. out of Egypt
Num. 22. 25. Balaam's ass t. herself to the wall
25. 8. Phinehas t. both of them through
35. 20. but if he t. him of hatred, that he die
22. but if he t. him suddenly without enmity
Deut. 13. 5. hath spoken to t. thee out of the way
10. because he sought to t. thee from the Lord
15. 17. t. the awl through his ear to the door
33. † 14. precious things t. forth by the moon
27. he shall t. out the enemy from before thee
Judg. 3. 21. Ehud t. the dagger into his belly
6. 38. he t. fleece together, and wringed the dew
9. 41. and Zebul t. out Gaal and his brethren
54. his young men t. Abimelech through
11. 2. wives' sons grew up, and they t. out Jeph.
1 Sam. 11. 2. that I may t. out all your right eyes
31. 4. Saul said, t. me through therewith, lest these uncircumcised come and t. me, 1 Chron. 10. 4.
2 Sam. 2. 16. and t. his sword in his fellow's side
15. † 14. lest Absalom overtake us, and t. upon us
18. 14. Joab t. 3 darts through the heart of Absalom
23. 6. the sons of Belial shall be as thorns t. away
1 Kings 2. 27. Solomon t. out Abiathar from priesth.
2 Kings 4. 27. but Gehazi came near to t. her away
2 Chron. 26. 20. they t. Uzziah out from thence
Psal. 118. 13. thou hast t. at me, that I might fall
Isa. 13. 15. every one found shall be t. through
14. 19. as the raiment of those that are t. through
Jer. 51. 4. they that are t. through in her streets
Ezek. 16. 40. they shall t. thee through with swords
21. † 12. princes are t. down to the sword with
34. 21. because ye have t. with side and shoulder
46. 18. to t. them out of their possessions
Joel 2. 8. neither shall one t. another, shall walk
Zech. 13. 3. shall t. him through when he prophesieth
Mat. 11. † 12. they that t. men take it by force
Luke 4. 29. they rose and t. him out of the city
5. 3. and prayed him he would t. out a little
10. 15. thou Capernaum, shalt be t. down to hell
13. 28. Jacob in heaven, and you yourselves t. out
John 20. 25. and t. my hand into his side, 27.
Acts 7. 27. he that did the wrong t. him away
39. but our fathers t. him from them
16. 24. who t. them into the inner prison
37. and now do they t. us out privily?
27. 39. minded, if it were possible, to t. in the ship
Heb. 12. 20. it shall be stoned or t. through with
Rev. 14. 15. t. in thy sickle, for the harvest is ripe
16. he sat on the cloud, t. in his sickle on the earth
18. t. in thy sharp sickle and gather the clusters
19. the angel t. in his sickle into the earth

THRUSTETH.

Job 32. 13. God t. him down, not man

THUMB.

Exod. 29. 20. then shalt thou put it on the t. of their right hand, Lev. 8. 23, 24. | 14. 14, 17, 25, 28.

THUMBS.

Judg. 1. 6. they caught him and cut off his t.
7. seventy kings having their t. and toes cut off

THUMMIM.

Urim and Thummim; According to the Hebrew, Exod. 28. 30. the literal signification of these two words is, light and perfection, or the shining and the perfect. According to St. Jerome, doctrine and judgment. According to the LXX, declaration or manifestation, and truth. Some will have it, that the Urim and Thummim are only epithets or explanations of the stones of the breastplate of the high priest; as if it were said, Thou shalt put therein stones that are shining and perfect. Others, to prove that the Urim and Thummim were not the same thing with the twelve stones in the breastplate, give the following reasons. (1) Because the stones were set and engraven in the breastplate, Exod. 28. 17, 21. the Urim and Thummim only put into it, which is a word of quite different and more loose and large signification, and therefore probably does not design the same thing. (2) It is not likely, that in such a brief account of the sacred utensils, the same command would be repeated again; especially in more dark and general words than it was mentioned before. And how could Moses put it in, when the workmen had fastened it there before? Or, why should he be required to put it in the breastplate, when it was fastened to it already, and could not, without violence, be taken from it? (3) Because the stones were put in by the workmen, Exod. 39. 10. the Urim and Thummim by Moses himself, Lev. 8. 8. It is objected, that where the stones are mentioned, there is no mention of Urim and Thummim, as in Exod. 39. 10. And that where the Urim and Thummim are mentioned, there is no mention made of the stones, as in Lev. 8. 8. which seems to shew they were one and the same thing. To which they answer, that there is an evident reason for both these omissions; of the former in Exodus, because Moses mentions only those things which were made by the workmen, whereas the Urim and Thummim seems to have been made immediately by God, or by Moses with God's direction: of the latter in Leviticus, because the stones are implied in the breastplate as a part of it, and fastened to it, whereas there Moses only mentions what was put in by himself. Some say, that the Urim and Thummim were two little golden figures which gave responses, which were shut up in the breastplate as in a purse, and which answered, with an articulate voice, to all such questions as were put to them by the high priest. Others think, that the name JEHOVAH written upon a plate of gold, was that the Scripture calls Urim and Thummim. There are various other conjectures concerning the Urim and Thummim, but nothing certain, because the Scripture is silent in this matter. It may suffice us to know, that this was a singular piece of divine workmanship, which the high priest was obliged to wear upon solemn occasions, as one of the conditions upon which God engaged to give him answers.

There is a great diversity of opinions likewise concerning the manner in which God was consulted by Urim and Thummim. It is agreed, that this way of consultation was used only in affairs of very great importance: that the high priest was the only officiating minister in this ceremony; and that for this he was to be clothed in all his pontifical habits; particularly he was to have on his breastplate, to which the Urim and Thummim was affixed; and lastly, that he was not allowed to perform this solemn consultation for a private person, but only for the king, for the president of the Sanhedrim, for the general of the army of Israel, or for other public persons: and even then, not upon any affair of a private nature, but for things that relate to the public welfare of church or state.

When the Urim and Thummim was to be consulted, the high priest put on his robes, and presented himself not in the sanctuary, where he could not enter but once a year, but in the holy place, before the curtain that parted the most holy from the holy place. There standing upright, and turning his face toward the ark of the covenant, upon which the divine presence reposed, he proposed the matter for which he had been consulted. Behind him, at some distance out of the holy place, stood the person for whom God was consulted, expecting with humility and reverence, the answer that it should please the Lord to give him. The Rabbins, who are followed by Josephus, Philo, and several of the ancient fathers, are of opinion that the high priest having then his eyes fixed upon the stones of the breastplate, which was before him, he there read the answer of the Lord. The letters that raised themselves out of their places, and that shined with more than ordinary lustre, were formed into the answer desired. For example, when David inquired of God, whether he should go up to one of the cities of Judah, 2 Sam. 2. 1. it was answered him, Alah, go up. The three letters, Ain, Lamed, and He, came out of their places, as it were, and raised themselves above the rest, to compose that word which contained the answer.

But there are some difficulties in this opinion. All the letters of the Hebrew alphabet were not found in the breastplate: there were four wanting, Heth, Teth, Zade, and Koph. To supply these, the Rabbins pretend that the names of Abraham, Isaac, and Jacob, were also upon the breastplate: but for all that, Teth would be still wanting. Therefore they say, that this title also was read there, Col elle-schibte-Israel.—See here all the tribes of Israel. But all this is advanced without proof, and without the least probability. A second difficulty is this, that though one should admit all that the Hebrew doctors suggest in this affair, yet by what rules did the high priest make a combination of these letters, and how put he them together? For it is not said that they came out of their places, but that they only raised themselves above the rest. Suppose, for example, that any six of the letters should have swelled and shined with more than ordinary lustre; how must the high priest dispose them, which must be first or last? It is answered, that in this circumstance, he was always inspired and filled with the spirit of prophecy; but if it were so, then the Urim and Thummim would have been unnecessary: for why must miracles be multiplied without any occasion? The high priest needed only speak himself. And perhaps the whole use of the Urim and Thummim was this, to be a sign to the high priest that the Lord would replenish him with an internal and supernatural light, and make him know his will in what was inquired after.

Others think, with a great deal of probability, that God then gave his answers in articulate voices, which were heard within the sanctuary, and from between the cherubims, which covered the ark or the propitiatory. When the Israelites made peace with the Gibeonites, they were blamed for not having inquired at the mouth of the Lord, Josh. 9. 14. which insinuates that he had been used to make his voice heard when he was consulted.

If it be inquired how long the custom of consulting God by Urim and Thummim subsisted in Israel; the Rabbins think, that it continued no longer than under the tabernacle. It is a maxim among them, that the Holy Spirit spake to the children of Israel by Urim and Thummim while the tabernacle remained; and under the first temple, that is, the temple of Solomon, by the prophets; and under the second temple, or after the captivity of Babylon, by the Bath-kol, or the daughter of the voice. By this they mean a voice sent from heaven, as that which was heard at the baptism of Christ, and at his transfiguration, Mat. 3. 17. | 17. 5.

Spencer has adopted this opinion, and endeavours to support it by these two arguments. The first is, that the Urim and Thummim were a consequence of the divine government, or of the Theocracy of the Hebrews. While the Lord immediately governed his people, it was necessary that there should always be a means at hand to consult him, and to have recourse to him. Secondly, that this method was established to consult God upon affairs that concerned the common interest of the whole nation. But the Theocracy ceased, says he, when the kingdom became hereditary in the person and family of Solomon. The interests of the nation ceased to be common, after the division of Israel into two monarchies; one governed by Rehoboam and the other by Jeroboam. Lastly, what seems to be more convincing than any reasons drawn from a conformity of things, it does not appear from the sacred history, that there are any footsteps of consulting the Lord by Urim and Thummim, after the construction of the temple of Solomon to the time of its destruction; and after its destruction, all are agreed, that this was never restored to them again.

Exod. 28. 30. thou shalt put on the breastplate of judgment, the urim and the t. Lev. 8. 8.
Deut. 33. 8. let thy t. and urim be with thy holy one
Ezra 2. 63. stood up priest with urim and t. Neh. 7. 67.

THUNDER.

Exod. 9. 23. the Lord sent t. and hail, the fire ran
29. the t. shall cease, nor shall there be hail
1 Sam. 7. 10. the Lord thundered with great t.
12. 17. he shall send t. || 18. the Lord sent t.
Job 26. 14. the t. of his power who can understand?
28. 26. a way for the lightning of the t. 38. 25.
39. 19. hast thou clothed his neck with t.?
25. he smelleth the t. of the captains afar off
Psal. 77. 18. the voice of thy t. was in the heavens
81. 7. I answered thee in the secret place of t.
104. 7. at the voice of thy t. they hasted away
Isa. 29. 6. thou shalt be visited of the Lord with t.
Mark 3. 17. Boanerges, which is, the sons of t.
Rev. 6. 1. I heard, as it were, the noise of t.
14. 2. I heard a voice, as the voice of a great t.

THUNDER.

1 Sam. 2. 10. out of heaven shall he t. upon them
Job 40. 9. or canst thou t. with a voice like him?

THUNDERS.

Exod. 9. 33. and the t. and hail ceased, 34.
19. 16. there were t. and lightnings, Rev. 16. 18.
See Seven.

THUNDERBOLTS.

Psal. 78. 48. he gave their flocks to hot t.

THUNDERED.

1 Sam. 7. 10. the Lord t. with a great thunder
2 Sam. 22. 14. the Lord t. from heaven, Psal. 18. 13.
John 12. 29. they that heard it, said that it t.

THUNDERETH.

Job 37. 4. he t. with the voice of his excellency
5. God t. marvellously with his voice
Psal. 29. 3. the God of glory t. the Lord is on waters

THUNDERINGS.

Exod. 9. 28. that there be no more mighty t.
20. 18. and all the people saw the t.
Rev. 4. 5. out of the throne proceeded t. 19. 6.
8. 5. and there were voices and t. 11. 19.

THUS.

Gen. 6. 22. t. did Noah, according as G. commanded
20. 16. t. she was reproved || 25. 22. why am I t.?
Exod. 5. 15. wherefore dealest thou t. with us?
12. 11. t. shall ye eat it, with your loins girded
14. 11. wherefore hast thou dealt t. with us?
Lev. 15. 31. t. separate the children of Israel
16. 3. t. shall Aaron come into the holy place
Num. 8. 14. t. shalt thou separate the Levites
11. 15. if thou deal t. with me, kill me
Deut. 29. 24. wherefore hath the Lord done t.
Josh. 7. 10. wherefore liest thou t. on thy face?
Judg. 8. 1. men said, why hast thou served us t.?
13. 18. why askest thou t. after my name?
1 Sam. 14. 9. if they say t. to us, tarry till we come
10. but if they say t. come up to us, then we will
20. 7. if he say t. it is well, 2 Sam. 15. 26.
2 Sam. 6. 22. I will yet be more vile than t.
18. 14. Joab said, I may not tarry t. with thee
33. as he went t. he said, O my son Absalom
1 Kings 3. 22. t. they spake before the king
2 Chron. 32. 22. t. the Lord saved Hezekiah
Ezra 5. 11. and t. they returned us answer
6. 2. and therein was a record t. written
Neh. 5. 13. even t. be he shaken out and emptied
Esth. 6. 9. t. shall it be done to the man whom, 11.
Job 27. 12. why then are ye t. altogether vain?
Psal. 73. 15. if I say I will speak t. behold
21. t. my heart was grieved, and I was pricked
128. 4. t. shall the man be blessed that feareth Lord
Isa. 24. 13. when t. it shall be in the midst of land
47. 15. t. shall they be unto thee with whom
Jer. 4. 27. for t. hath the Lord said, 6. 6.
5. 13. t. shall it be done unto them
18. 23. deal t. with them in time of thine anger
22. 8. why hath the Lord done t. to this great city?
26. 19. t. might we procure evil against our souls
Ezek. 31. 18. to whom art thou t. like in glory?
Amos 2. 11. is it not even t. O children of Israel
Mal. 1. 13. t. ye brought an offering should I accept
Mat. 2. 5. t. it is written of the prophet, Luke 24. 46.
3. 15. t. it becomes us to fulfil all righteousness
26. 54. scriptures be fulfilled, that t. it must be
Luke 1. 25. t. hath Lord dealt with me in the days
2. 48. son, why hast thou t. dealt with us?
11. 45. master, t. saying, thou reproachest us also
17. 30. t. shall it be when Son of man is revealed
18. 11. Pharisee prayed t. God, I thank thee
22. 51. Jesus answered and said, suffer ye t. far
23. 46. Jesus having said t. he gave up the ghost
24. 36. as they t. spake, Jesus himself in the midst
40. when he had t. spoken, he shewed his hands
46. t. it is written, t. it behoved Christ to suffer
John 4. 6. Jesus wearied with journey, sat t. on well
11. 43. when had t. spoken, he cried, Lazarus come
48. if we let him t. alone, all will believe
Acts 21. 11. he said, t. saith the Holy Ghost
Rom. 9. 20. thing formed say, why hast made me t.?
1 Cor. 14. 25. t. are secrets of his heart made manifest
2 Cor. 5. 14. for the love of Christ constrains us, because we t. judge, that if one died for all, then all dead
Phil. 3. 15. let as many as be perfect, be t. minded
Heb. 6. 9. better things of you, though we t. speak
Rev. 9. 17. t. I saw horses in vision, them that sat
16. 5. art righteous, because thou hast judged t.
See Did, Do, Lord.

THUS and THUS.

Josh. 7. 20. Achan said t. and t. have I done
Judg. 18. 4. t. and t. dealeth Micah with me
2 Sam. 17. 15. t. and t. did Ahithophel counsel Absalom, and t. and t. have I counselled
1 Kings 14. 5. t. and t. shalt say to Jeroboam's wife
2 Kings 5. 4. t. and t. said the maid of Israel
9. 12. he said, t. and t. spake he to me, saying

THYINE.
Rev. 18. 12. none buy the merchandise of *t.* wood

TIDINGS.
Exod. 33. 4. when the people heard these evil *t.*
1 *Sam.* 4. 19. when Phinehas' wife heard the *t.*
11. 4. they told the *t.* of the men of Jabesh, 5.
27. 11. David saved none alive to bring *t.* to Gath
2 *Sam.* 4. 4. when *t.* came of Saul and Jonathan
13. 30. *t.* came, saying, Absalom hath slain the
18. 19. let me now run and bear the king *t.*
20. Joab said, thou shalt not bear *t.* this day
22. why wilt thou run? thou hast no *t.* ready
31. Cushi came, Cushi said, *t.* my lord the king
1 *Kings* 2. 28. then *t.* came to Joab and Joab fled
14. 6. for I am sent to thee with heavy *t.*
1 *Chron.* 10. 9. and sent to carry *t.* to their idols
Psal. 112. 7. he shall not be afraid of evil *t.*
Jer. 20. 15. cursed be the man that brought *t.*
49. 23. for they have heard evil *t.* faint-hearted
Ezek. 21. 7. that thou shalt answer for the *t.*
Dan. 11. 44. *t.* out of the east shall trouble him
Luke 1. 19. I am sent to shew thee these glad *t.* 2. 10.
8. 1. shewing the glad *t.* of the kingdom of God
Acts 11. 22. *t.* of these things came to the church
13. 32. and we declare unto you, glad *t.* the promise
21. 31. *t.* came to the chief captain of the band
Rom. 10. 15. that bring glad *t.* of good things

TIE. [*See* GOOD.
1 *Sam.* 6. 7. and *t.* the kine to the cart, 10.
1 *Kings* 18. † 44. *t.* thy chariot, and get thee down
20. † 14. who shall *t.* the battle? he said, Thou
Prov. 6. 21. bind on thy heart and *t.* about thy neck

TIED.
Exod. 39. 31. and they *t.* to it a lace of blue
2 *Kings* 7. 10. no man there, but horses *t.* asses *t.*
Mat. 21. 2. ye shall find an ass *t.* and a colt with her, bring them to me, *Mark* 11. 2. 4. *Luke* 19. 30.

TILE.
Ezek. 4. 1. thou also, son of man, take thee a *t.*

TILING.
Luke 5. 19. they let him down thro' the *t.* with couch

TILL.
Gen. 19. 22. do any thing *t.* thou be come thither
1 *Sam.* 22. 3. *t.* I know what God will do for me
2 *Sam.* 3. 35. if I taste bread *t.* the sun be down
2 *Chron.* 26. 15. he was helped *t.* he was strong
36. 16. *t.* the wrath arose, *t.* there was no remedy
Ezra 2. 63. *t.* there stood up a priest, *Neh.* 7. 65.
9. 14. be angry with us *t.* thou hadst consumed us
Job 14. 14. all days will I wait *t.* my change come
27. 5. *t.* I die || *Isa.* 22. 14. not purged, *t.* ye die
Psal. 10. 15. seek his wickedness *t.* thou find none
Prov. 29. 11. a wise man keepeth it in *t.* afterwards
Eccl. 2. 3. *t.* I might see what was that good
Cant. 2. 7. stir not up my love *t.* he please, 3. 5.
Isa. 5. 8. that lay field to field, *t.* there be no place
62. 7. and give him no rest, *t.* he establish, and *t.* he make Jerusalem a praise in the earth
Jer. 49. 9. destroy *t.* they have enough, *Obad.* 5.
52. 3. *t.* he had cast them out from his presence
Lam. 3. 50. *t.* the Lord look down from heaven
Ezek. 28. 15. was perfect *t.* iniquity was found in
Dan. 4. 23. *t.* sever. times pass over him
12. 13. but go thou thy way *t.* the end be
Hos. 5. 15. *t.* they acknowledge their offence
10. 12. *t.* he rain righteousness upon you
Mat. 1. 25. *t.* she had brought forth her first-born
5. 18. *t.* heaven and earth pass, one jot not pass
Luke 12. 50. I am straitened *t.* it be accomplished
15. 8. doth not seek diligently *t.* she find it
19. 13. he said unto them, occupy *t.* I come
John 21. 22. if I will that he tarry *t.* I come, 23.
Acts 7. 18. *t.* another king arose who knew not Joseph
23. 12. not eat, *t.* they had killed Paul, 14, 21.
Eph. 4. 13. *t.* we all come in the unity of faith
Phil. 1. 10. without offence, *t.* the day of Christ
1 *Tim.* 4. 13. *t.* I come, give attendance to reading
Rev. 2. 25. that which ye have, hold fast *t.* I come
7. 3. *t.* we have sealed the servants of our God
15. 8. *t.* the seven plagues were fulfilled
20. 3. *t.* the thousand years should be fulfilled
See CONSUMED, MORNING, UNTIL.

TILL, *Verb.*
Gen. 2. 5. was not a man to *t.* the ground, 3. 23.
2 *Sam.* 9. 10. and thy servants shall *t.* the land
Jer. 27. 11. they shall *t.* it, and dwell therein

TILLAGE.
1 *Chron.* 27. 26. Ezri was over them that were for *t.*
Neh. 10. 37. Levites might have the tithes of *t.*
Prov. 13. 23. much food is in the *t.* of the poor

TILLED.
Ezek. 36. 9. I am for you, ye shall be *t.* and sown
36. 34. and the desolate land shall be *t.*

TILLER.
Gen. 4. 2. but Cain was a *t.* of the ground

TILLEST.
Gen. 4. 12. when thou *t.* ground, it shall not yield

TILLETH.
Prov. 12. 11. he that *t.* land shall be satisfied
28. 19. he that *t.* his land shall have plenty

TIMBER.
Lev. 14. 45. he shall break down the *t.* thereof
1 *Kings* 5. 18. so they prepared *t.* and stones to build the house, 1 *Chron.* 22. 14. 2 *Chron.* 2. 9.
15. 22. and they took away the *t.* of Ramah
Ezra 5. 8. *t.* is laid in the walls, work prospereth
6. 11. let *t.* be pulled down from his house
Neh. 2. 8. that he may give me *t.* to make beams
Ezek. 26. 12. they shall lay thy *t.* in the water
Hab. 2. 11. the beam out of the *t.* shall answer
Zech. 5. 4. it shall consume it with the *t.* thereof

TIMBREL.
Exod. 15. 20. and Miriam took a *t.* in her hand
Job 21. 12. they take the *t.* and harp, and rejoice
Psal. 81. 2. take a psalm, bring hither the *t.*
149. 3. let them sing praises to him with the *t.*
150. 4. praise him with the *t.* and dance, praise

TIMBRELS.
Exod. 15. 20. all the women went out after her with *t.*
Judg. 11. 34. his daughter came out with *t.*
2 *Sam.* 6. 5. David and house of Israel played before the Lord on *t.* 1 *Chron.* 13. 8.
Psal. 68. 25. were the damsels playing with *t.*
Jer. 31. † 4. thou shalt be adorned with thy *t.*

TIME.
This term is commonly taken for the measure of motion, or for the duration of any thing. It is also taken for opportunity, or the favourable moment of doing or omitting any thing. Eccl. 8. 5. A wise man's heart discerneth both *time* and judgment: *he knows both what he ought to do, and what are the fittest seasons for doing it. Our Saviour says, in* John 7. 6, 8. My *time* is not yet come; *by which some understand, the* time *of his death; others, the season of his appearing publicly in the world; and others, the* time *of his going up to the feast of tabernacles: that is, I know my* time *to go, when it will be most safe and proper for me. I shall be there some* time *during the feast, but* my *time* is not yet come. *The* time *of the vengeance of God is sometimes called the* time of the Lord, the *time* of his visiting. *Jer.* 50. 27, 31. Woe unto them, for their day is come, the *time* of their visitation.

To gain the *time, is mentioned in* Dan. 2. 8. I know of certainty that ye would gain the *time. The magicians required a length of* time *from the king to explain his dream, hoping that his desire of knowing might have passed away, or that the dream might have come into his memory. St. Paul advises the faithful* to redeem the *time,* because the days are evil, *Eph.* 5. 16. *Time* is redeemed *when we carefully embrace and improve all the occasions and opportunities which the Lord presents unto us for his glory, and the good of ourselves and others; not suffering these seasons to be stolen from us, and lost by cares and thoughts about the world: and whereas we have lost and misimproved much* time, *we ought therefore to double our diligence, and do the more good in* time *to come.*

King Ahasuerus consulted with the wise men who knew the *times,* Esth. 1. 13. *That is, he advised with his counsellors that understood the history, the customs, and the laws of the Persians. The knowledge of history is one of the principal qualifications of a statesman. For how should he know the interest of his country, if he is ignorant of its* times, *revolutions, and remarkable occurrences? St. Jerom has it in his translation, he consulted the sages that were always near his person, according to the custom of kings. The Chaldee paraphrast will have it, that he consulted the children of Issachar, who were skilful in the knowledge of* times *and seasons. This tribe was noted for their knowledge of the* times. 1 Chron. 12. 32. Of the children of Issachar, which were men that had understanding of the *times,* to know what Israel ought to do. *Some by this understand their knowledge of the stars, and of the several seasons and changes of the air; which might be of good use in husbandry, to which this tribe was addicted. Others think, that by this is to be understood their political prudence in discerning and embracing the fit seasons for all their actions.*

Christ Jesus says to his apostles, who asked him if he was soon to restore the kingdom to Israel, It is not for you to know the *times* and seasons, which the Father hath put in his own power, *Acts* 1. 7. *They still thought that the kingdom of the* Messiah *was to be a temporal kingdom: but afterwards they were undeceived, and the Holy Ghost, which they received at the* time *of Pentecost, instructed them, that the complete kingdom of the* Messiah, *the renewing of all things, was not to take place before the end of the world,* Acts 3. 20, 21. *where St. Peter, speaking to the Jews, calls this* time, a *time* of refreshing, *and the* times of the restitution of all things. *St. Paul,* 1 Thess. 5. 1, 2. *makes use of almost the same terms, in which our Saviour expressed himself to his apostles, concerning his last coming.* But of the *times* and seasons ye have no need that I write unto you: for ye know that the day of the Lord cometh as a thief in the night.

Time *is put for a year.* Seven times, *that is, seven years,* Dan. 4. 16. Acceptable *time, is the* time *of the favour, of the goodness, and of the mercy, of God,* Psal. 69. 13. My prayer is unto thee in an acceptable *time. I pray in a* time *of grace. I seek thee when thou mayest be found in a good day, in the day of grace and mercy. The devils complained,* Mat. 8. 29. *that Christ was* come to torment them before the *time: that is, before the last judgment, at which the devils will be thrown for ever into the fire prepared for them.* The fulness of *time, is the* time *which God had appointed and predicted as the fittest season for the coming of the* Messiah, *Gal.* 4. 4. *The Psalmist says,* Psal. 31. 15. My *times* are in thy hand: *that is, the* time *of my life, how long I shall live; or all the affairs and events of my life are wholly in thy power, to dispose and order as thou seest fit.*

Gen. 18. 10. return according to the *t.* of life, 14.
24. 11. the *t.* that women go out to draw water
39. 5. from the *t.* he had made him overseer
47. 29. the *t.* drew nigh that Israel must die
Exod. 21. 19. only he shall pay for loss of his *t.*
Lev. 15. 25. if beyond the *t.* of her separation
18. 18. a wife besides the other in her life-*t.*
Num. 13. 20. the *t.* was the *t.* of first ripe grapes
26. 10. what *t.* the fire devoured 250 men
Deut. 16. 9. such *t.* thou put the sickle to the corn
Josh. 10. 27. at the *t.* of the going down of the sun Joshua commanded, 2 *Chron.* 18. 34.
42. and their land did Joshua take at one *t.*
Judg. 18. 31. all the *t.* the house of God was in Shiloh
2 *Sam.* 7. 11. since the *t.* I commanded judges
11. 1. at the *t.* when kings go forth to battle
23. 8. against eight hundred he slew at one *t.*
2 *Kings* 5. 26. is it *t.* to receive money and garments
1 *Chron.* 9. 25. were to come from *t.* to *t.* with them
Ezra 4. 10. peace, and at such a *t.* 17. | 7. 12.
10. 13. people are many, and it is a *t.* of rain
Neh. 2. 6. when wilt thou return? and I set him a *t.*
Job 6. 17. what *t.* they wax warm they vanish
9. 19. if of judgment, who shall set me a *t.* to plead
15. 32. it shall be accomplished before his *t.*
22. 16. wicked, which were cut down out of *t.*
38. 23. which I reserved against the *t.* of trouble
39. 1. knowest thou the *t.* they bring forth? 2.
Psal. 32. 6. in a *t.* when thou mayest be found
37. 19. they shall not be ashamed in the evil *t.*
41. 1. the Lord will deliver him in *t.* of trouble
56. 3. what *t.* I am afraid, I will trust in thee
69. 13. my prayer is to thee in an acceptable *t.*
81. 15. their *t.* should have endured for ever
89. 47. remember how short my *t.* is
105. 19. until the *t.* that his word came
Eccl. 3. 1. there is a *t.* to every purpose, 17. | 8. 6.
2. a *t.* to be born, and a *t.* to die; a *t.* to plant
7. 17. why shouldest thou die before thy *t.*?
8. 5. a wise man's heart discerneth *t.* and judgment
9. 11. but *t.* and chance happeneth to them all
12. so are the sons of men snared in an evil *t.*
Isa. 26. 17. that draweth near the *t.* of her delivery
28. 19. from the *t.* it goeth forth it shall take you
45. 21. who hath declared this from ancient *t.*
48. 16. from the *t.* that it was, there am I
49. 8. in an acceptable *t.* have I heard thee, and in a day of salvation helped thee, 2 *Cor.* 6. 2.
60. 22. I the Lord will hasten it in his *t.*
Jer. 6. 15. at the *t.* I visit they shall be cast down
8. 7. crane and swallow observe the *t.* of coming
15. looked for a *t.* of health, and behold trouble
14. 8. the Saviour thereof in *t.* of trouble
19. and for the *t.* of healing, and behold trouble
30. 7. it is even the *t.* of Jacob's trouble
46. 21. and the *t.* of their visitation, 50. 27.
49. 8. the *t.* that I will visit him, 50. 31.
19. and who will appoint me the *t.*? 50. 44.
51. 33. Babylon like a floor, it is *t.* to thresh her
Ezek. 4. 10. from *t.* to *t.* shalt thou eat it
16. 8. thy *t.* was the *t.* of love, I spread my skirt
57. as at the *t.* of thy reproach of daughters
30. 3. day is near, it shall be the *t.* of the heathen
Dan. 2. 8. I know that ye would gain the *t.*
9. to speak before one, till the *t.* be changed
16. Daniel desired that he would give him *t.*
3. 5. at what *t.* ye hear the sound of cornet, 15.
7. 12. yet their lives were prolonged for a *t.*
22. the *t.* came that the saints possessed kingdom
25. until a *t.* and the dividing of *t.* 12. 7.
8. 17. at the *t.* of the end shall be the vision
9. 21. touched me about the *t.* of evening oblation
11. 24. he shall forecast his devices for a *t.*
35. to make them white, to the *t.* of the end
40. at the *t.* of the end shall the king of the south
12. 1. and there shall be a *t.* of trouble
4. seal the book, even to the *t.* of the end, 9.
11. from the *t.* the daily sacrifice be taken away
Hos. 10. 12. it is *t.* to seek the Lord, till he come
Mic. 5. 3. till the *t.* that she which travaileth
Hag. 1. 4. is it *t.* to dwell in your ceiled houses?
Zech. 14. 7. that at evening *t.* it shall be light
Mal. 3. 11. nor vine cast her fruit before the *t.*
Mat. 1. 11. about the *t.* they were carried away
2. 7. Herod enquired what *t.* star appeared
8. 29. art thou come to torment us before the *t.*?
21. 34. and when the *t.* of the fruit drew near
26. 18. the master saith, my *t.* is at hand
Mark 1. 15. the *t.* is fulfilled, repent and believe
4. 17. have no root, and so endure but for a *t.*
6. 35. this is a desert, and now the *t.* is far passed
11. 13. for the *t.* of figs was not yet
13. 33. watch, for ye know not when the *t.* is
Luke 1. 57. Elisabeth's full *t.* came to be delivered
4. 5. shewed him all kingdoms in a moment of *t.*
7. 45. but this woman, since the *t.* I came in
8. 13. which in *t.* of temptation fall away
13. 35. ye shall not see me till the *t.* come when
19. 44. thou knewest not the *t.* of thy visitation
John 7. 6. my *t.* is not come, your *t.* is always ready
16. 2. the *t.* cometh, that whosoever killeth you
25. the *t.* cometh when I shall no more speak
Acts 1. 21. all the *t.* the Lord went in and out
7. 17. but when the *t.* of the promise drew nigh
20. in which *t.* Moses was born, and was fair
17. 21. spent their *t.* in nothing else, but to tell
Rom. 13. 11. it is high *t.* to awake out of sleep
1 *Cor.* 4. 5. therefore judge nothing before the *t.*
7. 5. defraud not, except with consent for a *t.*
29. but this I say, brethren, the *t.* is short
Eph. 5. 16. redeeming the *t.* *Col.* 4. 5.
1 *Thess.* 2. 17. being taken from you for a short *t.*
2 *Thess.* 2. 6. that he might be revealed in his *t.*
2 *Tim.* 4. 3. *t.* come, when they will not endure
6. and the *t.* of my departure is at hand
Heb. 4. 16. may find grace to help in *t.* of need
5. 12. when for the *t.* ye ought to be teachers
9. 9. which was a figure for the *t.* then present
10. imposed on them till the *t.* of reformation
11. 32. the *t.* would fail me to tell of Gideon
Jam. 4. 14. a vapour that appeareth a little *t.*
1 *Pet.* 1. 11. what manner of *t.* the spirit of Christ
17. pass the *t.* of your sojourning here in fear
4. 2. he should no longer live the rest of his *t.*
Rev. 1. 3. for the *t.* is at hand, 22. 10.
10. 6. sware, that there should be *t.* no longer
11. 18. *t.* of the dead, that they should be judged
12. 12. he knoweth that he hath but a short *t.*
14. she is nourished for a *t.* and times, and half a *t.*

Any TIME.
Lev. 25. 32. the Levites may redeem at *any t.*
Num. 35. 26. if the slayer at *any t.* come without
1 *Sam.* 20. 12. sounded my father to morrow *any t.*
1 *Kings* 1. 6. father had not displeased him at *any t.*
Mat. 4. 6. angels shall bear thee up, lest at *any t.* thou dash thy foot against a stone, *Luke* 4. 11.
5. 25. lest at *any t.* the adversary deliver thee
13. 15. lest at *any t.* they should see, *Mark* 4. 12.
Luke 15. 29. nor transgressed I at *any t.* thy com.
21. 34. lest at *any t.* your hearts be overcharged
John 1. 18. no man hath seen God at *any t.*
5. 37. nor have ye heard his voice at *any t.*
Acts 11. 8. nothing unclean hath at *any t.* entered

1 Cor. 9. 7. who goeth a warfare any t. at his charges
1 Thess. 2. 5. nor at any t. used we flattering words
Heb. 1. 5. to which of the angels said he at any t. 13.
2. 1. lest at any t. we should let them slip
1 John 4. 12. no man hath seen God at any t.
See APPOINTED, BEFORE, COME, DAY, DUE.

In the TIME.

Gen. 38. 27. came to pass in the t. of her travail
Exod. 34. 18. commanded in the t. of month Abib
Judg. 10. 14. let them deliver in the t. of tribulation
15. 1. in the t. of wheat harvest Samson visited
1 Kings 15. 23. in the t. of old age he was diseased
2 Chron. 28. 22. in the t. of distress did he trespass
Neh. 9. 27. in the t. of their trouble thou heardest
Psal. 4. 7. more than in the t. when corn increased
21. 9. as a fiery oven in the t. of thine anger
27. 5. in the t. of trouble he shall hide me
37. 39. he is their strength in the t. of trouble
71. 9. cast me not off in the t. of old age
Prov. 25. 13. as the cold of snow in the t. of harvest
19. confidence in unfaithful man in the t. of trouble
Isa. 33. 2. be thou our salvation in the t. of trouble
Jer. 2. 27. in the t. of trouble they will say
28. if they can save thee in the t. of trouble
8. 12. in the t. of visitation they shall be cast down
10. 15. in the t. of visitation they perish, 51. 18.
11. 12. shall not save them at all in the t. of trouble
14. I will not hear them in the t. that they cry
15. 11. verily I will cause enemy to entreat thee well in the t. of evil, and in the t. of affliction
18. 23. deal thus with them in the t. of thine anger
50. 16. handleth the sickle in the t. of harvest
Ezek. 27. 34. in the t. when thou shalt be broken
35. 5. had a perpetual hatred, in the t. of their calamity, in the t. that their iniquity had an end
Hos. 2. 9. I will take away my corn in the t. thereof
Zech. 10. 1. ask rain in the t. of the latter rain
Mat. 13. 30. in the t. of harvest I will say to reapers
Luke 4. 27. were many lepers in the t. of Eliseus
See LAST, LONG, MANY, OLD, PAST, PROCESS.

Same TIME.

Num. 32. 10. Lord's anger was kindled the same t.
Deut. 9. 20. I prayed for Aaron also the same t.
2 Kings 8. 22. yet Edom revolted, then Libnah revolted at the same t. 2 Chron. 21. 10.
2 Chron. 15. 11. they offered the same t. 700 oxen
16. 10. Asa oppressed the people at the same t.
Ezra 5. 3. at the same t. came to them Tatnai
Jer. 39. 10. gave them vineyards at the same t.
Ezek. 38. 10. at the same t. shalt thou think evil
Dan. 4. 36. at the same t. my reason returned
12. 1. trouble, such as never was to that same t.
Acts 19. 23. the same t. there arose no small stir
See SECOND, SET.

That TIME.

Judg. 11. 26. why did ye not recover in that t.
1 Sam. 11. 9. to-morrow by that t. the sun be hot
Ezra 5. 16. since that t. hath it been in building
Neh. 4. 16. to pass from that t. forth, 13. 21.
Isa. 16. 13. spoken concerning Moab since that t.
18. 7. in that t. shall the present be brought
44. 8. have I not told thee from that t. and declared
45. 21. who hath told it from that t.?
48. 8. from that t. that thine ear was not opened
Jer. 50. 4. that t. Israel shall come weeping
20. in that t. the iniquity of Israel not be found
Amos 5. 13. the prudent keep silence in that t.
Mat. 4. 17. from that t. Jesus began to preach
16. 21. from that t. began to shew his disciples
26. 16. from that t. Judas sought opportunity
Luke 16. 16. since that t. kingdom of G. is preached
John 6. 66. from that t. many disciples went back
Acts 12. 1. about that t. Herod stretched to vex

At that TIME.

Num. 22. 4. Balak was king of Moab at that t.
Deut. 1. 9. and I spake to you at that t. saying
16. I charged your judges at that t. saying
18. I commanded you at that t. 3. 18.
3. 21. I commanded Joshua at that t. saying
23. I besought the Lord at that t. saying
5. 5. I stood between the Lord and you at that t.
9. 19. the Lord hearkened to me at that t. 10. 10.
1 Sam. 14. 18. the ark was at that t. with Israel
2 Chron. 13. 18. Israel brought under at that t.
30. 3. they could not keep the passover at that t.
35. 17. Israel kept the passover at that t.
Jer. 3. 17. at that t. they shall call Jerusalem
8. 1. at that t. they shall bring out the bones
33. 15. at that t. cause the branch of righteousness
Dan. 12. 1. at that t. shall Michael stand up
Mic. 3. 4. will hide his face from them at that t.
Zeph. 1. 12. at that t. I will search Jerusalem
3. 19. at that t. I will undo all that afflict thee
20. at that t. will I bring you again, in time
Luke 23. 7. himself was at Jerusalem at that t.
Acts 8. 1. at that t. was a great persecution
Eph. 2. 12. at that t. ye were without Christ
See THIRD.

This TIME.

Gen. 29. 34. this t. will my husband be joined
Exod. 8. 32. Pharaoh hardened his heart at this t.
9. 14. I will at this t. send all my plagues
18. to-morrow about this t. I will cause it to rain
27. and Pharaoh said, I have sinned this t.
Num. 23. 23. according to this t. it shall be said
Judg. 13. 23. nor would as at this t. have told us
21. 22. for ye did not give unto them at this t.
1 Sam. 9. 13. for about this t. ye shall find him
2 Sam. 17. 7. the counsel is not good at this t.
1 Kings 2. 26. I will not at this t. put thee to death
19. 2. to-morrow this t. 20. 6. 2 Kings 7. 1, 18. | 10. 6.
Neh. 13. 6. in all this t. was not I at Jerusalem
Esth. 4. 14. for if thou holdest thy peace at this t. art come to the kingdom for such a t. as this
Psal. 113. 2. blessed be the Lord from this t. forth
115. 18. we will bless the Lord from this t. forth
121. 8. he will preserve thee from this t. forth
Isa. 48. 6. I have shewed new things from this t.
Jer. 3. 4. wilt thou not from this t. cry unto me?
51. 6. this is the t. of the Lord's vengeance
Mic. 2. 3. nor go haughtily, for this t. is evil
Mat. 24. 21. tribulation such as was not since the beginning of the world to this t. Mark 13. 19.
Mark 10. 30. but he shall receive an hundred-fold now in this t. and eternal life, Luke 18. 30.
Luke 12. 56. how is it ye do not discern this t.?
John 11. 39. Lord, by this t. he stinketh
Acts 1. 6. wilt thou at this t. restore the kingdom?
24. 25. Felix answered, go thy way for this t.
Rom. 3. 26. to declare at this t. his righteousness
8. 18. that the sufferings of this present t.
9. 9. at this t. will I come, Sara shall have a son
11. 5. so at this present t. there is a remnant
1 Cor. 16. 12. his will was not to come at this t.
2 Cor. 8. 14. that now at this t. your abundance

TIMES.

Gen. 27. 36. he hath supplanted me these two t.
Lev. 19. 26. ye shall not observe t. Deut. 18. 10, 14.
Deut. 4. 42. the slayer hated him not in t. past
Judg. 13. 25. the Spirit began to move him at t.
16. 20. I will go out as at other t. and shake
20. 30. put themselves in array as at other t.
31. the Benjamites began to kill as at other t.
1 Sam. 3. 10. the Lord called as at other t. Samuel
18. 10. David played with his hand as at other t.
20. 25. the king sat on his seat as at other t.
2 Kings 19. 25. hast thou not heard long ago how of ancient t. that I have formed it? Isa. 37. 26.
21. 6. Manasseh observed t. 2 Chron. 33. 6.
1 Chr. 12. 32. men that had understanding of the t.
29. 30. the t. that went over him and over Israel
2 Chron. 15. 5. in those t. there was no peace
Esth. 1. 13. the wise men which knew the t.
Job 24. 1. t. are not hidden from the Almighty
Psal. 9. 9. Lord will be a refuge in t. of trouble
10. 1. why hidest thou thyself in t. of trouble?
31. 15. my t. are in thy hand, deliver me from enem.
44. 1. what works thou didst in the t. of old
77. 5. I have considered the years of ancient t.
Isa. 33. 6. knowledge shall be the stability of thy t.
46. 10. from ancient t. things not yet done
Ezek. 12. 27. he prophesied of the t. far off
Dan. 2. 21. he changeth the t. and the seasons
7. 25. he shall think to change t. and laws
9. 25. the streets shall be built in troublous t.
11. 14. in those t. there shall many stand up
12. 7. for a time, t. and an half, Rev. 12. 14.
Mat. 16. 3. but can ye not discern the signs of the t.?
Luke 21. 24. till the t. of the Gentiles be fulfilled
Acts 1. 7. it is not for you to know the t. or seasons
3. 19. when the t. of refreshing shall come
21. till the t. of restitution of all things
14. 16. who in t. past suffered all nations to walk
17. 26. hath determined the t. before appointed
30. the t. of this ignorance God winked at
Rom. 11. 30. as ye in t. past have not believed God
2 Cor. 11. 24. of the Jews five t. received I forty stripes
Gal. 1. 23. that he which persecuted us in t. past
4. 10. ye observe days and months, t. and years
Eph. 1. 10. in the dispensation of the fulness of t.
1 Thess. 5. 1. of the t. ye have no need that I write
1 Tim. 4. 1. in latter t. some shall depart from faith
6. 15. which in his t. he shall shew who is king
2 Tim. 3. 1. in last days perilous t. shall come
Tit. 1. 3. hath in due t. manifested his word
Heb. 1. 1. God who at sundry t. spake to the fathers

All TIMES.

Lev. 16. 2. that he come not at all t. within the vail
1 Kings 8. 59. maintain cause of his people at all t.
Psal. 34. 1. I will bless the Lord at all t. his praise
62. 8. trust in him at all t. ye people pour out heart
106. 3. blessed is he that doth righteousness at all t.
119. 20. for longing it hath to thy judgments at all t.
Prov. 5. 19. let her breasts satisfy thee at all t.
17. 17. a friend loveth at all t. a brother is born for
See APPOINTED, MANY, SEVEN, TEN, THREE.

TINGLE.

1 Sam. 3. 11. at which the ears of every one that hears it shall t. 2 Kings 21. 12. Jer. 19. 3.

TINKLING.

Isa. 3. 16. mincing and making a t. with their feet
18. take away the bravery of their t. ornaments
1 Cor. 13. 1. I am become as a t. cymbal

TIN.

Num. 31. 22. t. that may abide fire, make go thro' fire
Isa. 1. 25. and I will take away all thy t.
Ezek. 22. 18. all they are brass, and t. and iron
20. as they gather lead and t. into the furnace
27. 12. Tarshish was thy merchant in t. and lead

TIP.

Luke 16. 24. may dip the t. of his finger in water
See Right EAR.

TIRE.

Ezek. 24. 17. bind the t. of thy head upon thee

TIRED.

2 Kings 9. 30. Jezebel t. her head and looked

TIRES.

Isa. 3. 18. the Lord will take away their t.
Ezek. 24. 23. and your t. shall be on your heads

TITHE.

The practice of paying tithes *is very ancient; for we find*, Gen. 14. 20. *that Abraham gave* tithes *to Melchizedek, king of Salem, at his return from his expedition against Chedorlaomer, and the four kings in confederacy with him. Abraham gave him the* tithe *of all the booty taken from the enemy. Jacob imitated this piety of his grandfather when he vowed to the Lord the* tithe *of all the substance he might acquire in Mesopotamia*. Gen. 28. 22. Of all that thou shalt give me, I will surely give the *tenth* unto thee; *for the maintenance of thy worship, and other pious uses. Under the law, Moses ordained*, Lev. 27. 30, 31, 32. All the *tithe* of the land, whether of the seed of the land, or of the fruit of the tree, is the Lord's; it is holy unto the Lord, &c.

There were three sorts of tithes *to be paid from the people, (besides those from the Levites to the priests,)* Num. 28. 26, 27, &c. (1) *To the Levites for their maintenance*, Num. 18. 21, 24. (2) *For the Lord's feasts and sacrifices, to be eaten in the place which the Lord should choose* to put his name there; *to wit, where the ark should be, the tabernacle or temple. This tenth part was either sent to Jerusalem in kind, or, if it was too far, they sent the value in money, which was to be laid out for oxen, sheep, wine, or what else they pleased*, Deut. 14. 22, 23, 24, &c. (3) *Besides these two, there was to be, every third year, a* tithe *for the poor, to be eaten at their own dwellings*, Deut. 14. 28, 29. *Some are of opinion that this third* tithe *was not different from the second before taken notice of, except that in the third year it was not brought to the temple, but was used upon the spot by every one in the city of his habitation. So that there were only, according to them, two sorts of tithes, that which was given to the Levites and priests, and that which was applied to making feasts of charity, either in the temple of Jerusalem, or in other cities.*

Tithes *were paid to God as a sign of homage and gratitude: thus Abraham's giving* tithes *of the spoil to Melchizedek, was a token that he owned his victory and success to be from God; and when* tithes *were kept back from the priests, the Lord complained that he was robbed*, Mal. 3. 8. *The paying of them was an honouring of God*, Prov. 3. 9. *Hence the apostle proves the superiority of Melchizedek and his priesthood above the patriarch Abraham, and the priesthood of Levi, because Abraham, and Levi in his loins, paid* tithes *unto him, as* the lesser unto the greater, *Heb.* 7. 4, 5, 6, &c.

In the New Testament, *neither our Saviour nor his apostles have commanded any thing in this affair of* tithes: *only when our Lord sent his apostles to preach in the cities of Israel, he forbad them to carry their purse or provisions along with them, but to enter into the houses of those that were willing to receive them, and to eat what should be set before them; for* the labourer, *says he*, is worthy of his hire, *and of his maintenance*, Mat. 10. 10. Luke 10. 7, 8. *St. Paul would have it, that he that receives instruction, should administer some of his* good things *to him that gives it him*, Gal. 6. 6. *It is agreeable to nature and reason, that* they which wait at the altar should live by the altar, 1 Cor. 9. 13. *And as God, under the law, ordained and appointed a living or maintenance for his ministers, so as they needed not, as other men, to labour with their hands to get bread to eat; so under the New Testament, God has ordained, that those who are taken off from worldly employments, and spend their time in the study and preaching of the gospel, should have a livelihood for their labour.* 1 Cor. 9. 14. Even so hath the Lord ordained, that they which preach the gospel should live of the gospel. *And in the 7th verse*, Who goeth a warfare at his own charges?

The most barbarous nations, and the heathen Greeks and Romans, out of a principle of religion common to all men, have often dedicated their tithes *to their gods. Some have made it a standing obligation, others have done it upon particular occasions, and by the impulse of a transient devotion. Laertius says, that when Pisistratus, tyrant at Athens, wrote to Solon, to persuade him to return to Athens, he tells him, "that every one there pays the tithe of his goods for the offering of sacrifices to the gods,"* Laert. Lib. 1. *Pliny says, that the Arabian merchants who traded in spices durst not sell any till they had paid the* tithe *to their god Sabis. And Plutarch, in more places than one, mentions a custom of the Romans, of offering to Hercules the* tithe *of what they took from their enemies.*

Lev. 27. 30. all the t. of the land is the Lord's
32. concerning the t. of the herd of the flock
Num. 18. 26. ye shall offer a tenth part of the t.
Deut. 12. 17. not eat within thy gates the t. of corn
14. 23. eat t. in the place the Lord shall choose
28. at the end of three years bring forth the t.
2 Chron. 31. 5. they brought in the first-fruits of corn and the t. of all things, 6, 12. Neh. 13. 12.
Neh. 10. 38. the Levites shall bring up t. of tithes
Mat. 23. 23. ye pay t. of mint, anise, and cummin

TITHE, *Verb.*

Deut. 14. 22. thou shalt surely t. increase of thy seed
Luke 11. 42. for ye t. mint, and rue, and all herbs

TITHES.

Gen. 14. 20. Abraham gave Melchizedek t. of all
Lev. 27. 31. if a man will redeem ought of his t.
Num. 18. 24. the t. I have given to the Levites
26. when ye take of the children of Israel t.
28. offer an heave offering to Lord of all your t.
Deut. 12. 6. thither ye shall bring your t. 11.
26. 12. thou hast made an end of tithing the t.
Neh. 10. 37. that the Levites might have the t.
12. 44. and some were appointed for the t.
13. 5. where aforetime they laid the t. of corn
Amos 4. 4. bring your t. after three years, Mal. 3. 10
Mal. 3. 8. ye have robbed me of t. and offerings
Luke 18. 12. I give t. of all that I possess
Heb. 7. 5. the priests have commandment to take t.
6. he received t. of Abraham, and blessed him
8. and here men that die receive t.
9. Levi who received t. paid t. in Abraham

TITHING.

Deut. 26. 12. made end of t. third year is year of t.

TITLE.

2 Kings 23. 17. he said, what t. is that that I see
John 19. 19. Pilate wrote a t. and put it on the cross
20. this t. then read many of the Jews

TITLES.

Job 32. 21. nor let me give flattering t. to man
22. for I know not to give flattering t.

TITTLE.

Mat. 5. 18. one t. shall in no wise pass from the law
Luke 16. 17. than for one t. of the law to fail

TO *and* FRO. *See* FRO.

TOE.

Exod. 29. 20. upon the great t. of their right foot
Lev. 8. 23, 24. | 14. 14, 17, 25, 28

TOES.
Judg. 1. 6. cut off his thumbs and his great *t.*
7. seventy kings having thumbs and *t.* cut off
1 *Chron.* 20. 6. whose fingers and *t.* were, 24.
Dan. 2. 41. thou sawest the *t.* part of iron, 42.

TOGETHER.
Deut. 22. 10. thou shalt not plow with ox and ass *t.*
Judg. 19. 29. he divided her, *t.* with her bones
1 *Sam.* 31. 6. all his men died that same day *t.*
1 *Kings* 3. 18. and we were *t.* there was no stranger
11. 1. women, *t.* with the daughter of Pharaoh
2 *Kings* 9. 25. when thou and I rode *t.* after Ahab
Ezra 4. 3. we ourselves *t.* will build to the Lord
Neh. 6. 7. let us take counsel *t.* ‖ 10. let us meet *t.*
Job 3. 18. there the prisoners rest *t.* they hear not
10. 8. have fashioned me *t.* round about
17. 16. shall go down, when our rest *t.* is in the dust
24. 4. the poor of the earth hide themselves *t.*
34. 15. all flesh shall perish *t.* man shall turn to dust
Psal. 2. 2. the rulers take counsel *t.* against the L.
14. 3. they are all *t.* become filthy, *Rom.* 3. 12.
34. 3. magnify the L. and let us exalt his name *t.*
37. 38. the transgressors be destroyed *t.* *Isa.* 1. 28.
Prov. 22. 2. the rich and poor meet *t.* Lord is maker
29. 13. the poor and the deceitful man meet *t.*
Eccl. 4. 11. if two lie *t.* then they have heat
Isa. 9. 21. and they *t.* shall be against Judah
26. 19. *t.* with my dead body shall they arise
41. 23. do good or evil, that we may behold it *t.*
52. 8. with the voice *t.* shall they sing, 9.
65 25. the wolf and the lamb shall feed *t.*
Ezek. 37. 7. the bones came *t.* bone to his bone
Amos 1. 15. go into captivity, he and his princes *t.*
3. 3. can two walk *t.* except they be agreed?
Mat. 18. 20. where two or three are gathered *t.*
19. 6. what God hath joined *t.* *Mark* 10. 9.
Luke 15. 6. he calleth *t.* his friends and neighbours
Acts 2. 44. and all that believed were *t.* and had
5. 9. that ye have agreed *t.* to tempt the Spirit
Rom. 8. 28. we know that all things work *t.* for good
Eph. 2. 5. hath quickened us *t.* ‖ 6. hath raised us *t.*
21. in whom all the building fitly framed *t.* 22.
Phil. 1. 27. striving *t.* for the faith of the gospel
3. 17. breth. be followers *t.* of me, and mark them
Col. 2. 2. be comforted, being knit *t.* in love, 19.
13. you being dead in sins, hath he quickened *t.*
1 *Thess.* 4. 17. shall be caught up *t.* ‖ 5. 10. live *t.*
2 *Thess.* 2. 1. we beseech you by our gathering *t.*
1 *Pet.* 3. 7. as being heirs *t.* of the grace of life
See DWELL.

TOIL.
Gen. 5. 29. comfort us concerning our work and *t.*
41. 51. God, said he, hath made me forget my *t.*

TOIL, *Verb.*
Mat. 6. 28. they *t.* not nor spin, *Luke* 12. 27.

TOILED.
Luke 5. 5. Simon said, Master, we have *t.* all night

TOILING.
Mark 6. 48. and he saw them *t.* in rowing

TOKEN.
Gen. 9. 12. this is the *t.* of the covenant, 13, 17.
17. 11. and it shall be a *t.* of the covenant
Exod. 3. 12. this shall be a *t.* that I sent thee
12. 13. the blood shall be for a *t.* on the houses
13. 16. it shall be for a *t.* upon thine hand
Num. 17. 10. to be kept for a *t.* against the rebels
Josh. 2. 12. swear unto me, and give me a true *t.*
Psal. 86. 17. shew me a *t.* for good, that they
Mark 14. 44. Judas had given them a *t.* saying
Phil. 1. 28. is to them an evident *t.* of perdition
2 *Thess.* 1. 5. a manifest *t.* of righteous judgment
3. 17. of Paul, which is the *t.* in every epistle

TOKENS.
Deut. 22. 15. being *t.* of damsel's virginity, 17, 20.
Job 21. 29. and do ye not know their *t.*?
Psal. 65. 8. they also are afraid at thy *t.*
135. 9. who sent *t.* in the midst of thee, O Egypt
Isa. 44. 25. that frustrateth the *t.* of the liars

TOLD.
Gen. 3. 11. who *t.* thee that thou wast naked
9. 22. and Ham *t.* his two brethren without
24. 33. I will not eat till I have *t.* mine errand
37. 5. Joseph *t.* his brethren the dream, 9.
10. he *t.* it to his father and his brethren
Num. 23. 26. *t.* not I thee, all that the Lord speaketh
Deut. 17. 4. it be *t.* thee, and behold it be true
Judg. 6. 13. his miracles which our fathers *t.* of
7. 13. there was a man that *t.* a dream to his fellow
13. 6. I asked not, neither *t.* he me his name
23. nor would at this time have *t.* such things
14. 2. he came up, and *t.* his father and mother
6. but he *t.* not his father, 9, 16. 1 *Sam.* 14. 1.
17. on the seventh day he *t.* her, she *t.* the riddle
16. 17. she urged him, he *t.* her all his heart, 18.
1 *Sam.* 10. 16. he *t.* us that the asses were found
25. 19. but Abigail *t.* not her husband Nabal
2 *Sam.* 11. 5. and the woman sent and *t.* David
17. 17. a wench went and *t.* them, they *t.* David
1 *Kings* 10. 3. Solomon *t.* her all her questions, not
any thing which he *t.* not, 2 *Chron.* 9. 2.
13. 11. the words they *t.* also to their father
25. *t.* in the city where old prophet dwelt
1 *Chron.* 17. 25. hast *t.* thou wilt build an house
Ezra 8. 17. I *t.* them what they should say to Iddo
Esth. 5. 11. Haman *t.* of the glory of his riches
8. 1. for Esther had *t.* what he was unto her
Job 15. 18. which wise men have *t.* from fathers
Psal. 44. 1. and our fathers have *t.* us, 78. 3.
Isa. 44. 8. have not I *t.* thee from that time?
45. 21. who hath *t.* it from that time? have not I?
52. 15. what had not been *t.* them, shall they see
Jonah 1. 10. the men knew, because he had *t.* them
Mat. 8. 33. they went into the city and *t.* every thing
14. 12. took up the body, and went and *t.* Jesus
Mark 16. 13. they went and *t.* it to the residue
John 5. 15. the man *t.* the Jews it was Jesus
Acts 9. 6. be *t.* thee what thou must do, 22. 10.
23. 16. he entered into the castle and *t.* Paul
2 *Cor.* 7. 7. when he *t.* us your earnest desire

TOLD *him.*
Gen. 22. 3. the place of which God had *t. him*, 9.
1 *Sam.* 3. 13. I have *t. him* I will judge his house
1 *Sam.* 3. 18. Samue. *t. him* every whit and hid noth.
10. 16. of the matter of the kingdom he *t. him* not
25. 36. she *t. him* nothing till morning light
2 *Kings* 6. 10. to the place the man of God *t. him*
Job 37. 20. shall it be *t. him* that I speak
Mark 5. 33. but the woman *t. him* all the truth

TOLD *me.*
Judg. 16. 10. thou hast mocked me and *t. me* lies, 13.
15. hast not *t. me* wherein thy strength lieth
1 *Sam.* 23. 22. it is *t. me* that he dealeth subtilly
2 *Sam.* 4. 10. when one *t. me*, saying Saul is dead
1 *Kings* 10. 7. the half was not *t. me*, 2 *Chron.* 9. 6.
14. 2. *t. me* I should be king over this people
2 *Kings* 4. 27. hid it from me and hath not *t. me*
8. 14. he *t. me* that thou shouldest surely recover
John 4. 29. see a man which *t. me* all things, 39.
Acts 27. 25. it shall be even as it was *t. me*

TOLD *you.*
Isa. 40. 21. hath it not been *t. you* from beginning?
Hab. 1. 5. ye will not believe though it be *t. you*
Mat. 24. 25. behold, I have *t. you* before
28. 7. there ye shall see him, lo, I have *t. you*
John 3. 12. if I have *t. you* earthly things
8. 40. seek to kill me, a man that hath *t. you* truth
9. 27. he said, I have *t. you* already, 10. 25.
14. 2. if it were not so, I would have *t. you*
29. now I have *t. you* before it come to pass
16. 4. these things have I *t. you*, that when time
shall come, ye may rememb. that I *t. you* of them
18. 8. Jesus said, I have *t. you* that I am he
2 *Cor.* 13. 2. I *t. you* before, and foretell you
Gal. 5. 21. as I have also *t. you* in time past
Phil. 3. 18. many walk of whom I have *t. you*
1 *Thess.* 3. 4. we *t. you* that we should suffer
2 *Thess.* 2. 5. when with you, I *t. you* these things
Jude 18. they *t. you* there should be mockers

TOLD, *Passive.*
Josh. 9. 24. it was certainly *t.* thy servants
1 *Kings* 8. 5. the sheep and oxen could not be *t.*
18. 13. was it not *t.* my lord, what I did when
2 *Kings* 12. 11. and they gave the money, being *t.*
Psal. 90. 9. we spend our years as a tale that is *t.*
Isa. 7. 2. it was *t.* the house of David, saying
Dan. 8. 26. and the vision which is *t.* is true
Mat. 26. 13. there shall this be *t.* for a memorial
Luke 1. 45. a performance of things which were *t.*
2. 18. wondered at those things *t.* by shepherds

TOLERABLE.
Mat. 10. 15. it shall be more *t.* for Sodom and Gomorrah, 11. 24. *Mark* 6. 11. *Luke* 10. 12.
11. 22. more *t.* for Tyre and Sidon, *Luke* 10. 11.

TOLL.
Ezra 4. 13. then will they not pay *t.* and custom
20. *t.* tribute and custom was paid to them
7. 24. it shall not be lawful to impose *t.* on them

TOMB.
Job 21. 32. and he shall remain in the *t.*
Mat. 27. 60. Joseph laid the body in his own new *t.*
Mark 6. 29. his disciples laid John's corpse in a *t.*

TOMBS.
Mat. 8. 28. met him two possessed with devils, coming out of the *t.* *Mark* 5. 2, 3, 5. *Luke* 8. 27.
23. 29. because ye build the *t.* of the prophets

TONGS.
Exod. 25. 38. shalt make thee *t.* thereof of pure gold
Num. 4. 9. they shall cover his *t.* with a cloth of blue
1 *Kings* 7. 49. lamps and *t.* of gold, 2 *Chron.* 4. 21.
Isa. 6. 6. a coal which he had taken with the *t.*
44. 12. the smith with the *t.* worketh in coals

TONGUE.
This word is taken in three different senses. (1) *For the material* tongue, *or organ of speech,* Jam. 3. 5. The *tongue* is a little member. (2) *For the* tongue *or language that is spoken in any country.* Deut. 28. 49. The Lord shall bring a nation against thee, whose *tongue* thou shalt not understand. (3) *For good or bad discourse.* Prov. 12. 18. But the *tongue* of the wise is health: *His discourse is sound and wholesome in itself, and tends to the comfort and benefit of others. On the contrary,* He that hath a perverse *tongue* falleth into mischief, *Prov.* 17. 20. *that is, He that speaks deceitfully or wickedly. Many questions are proposed about* tongues, *taken in the second sense, or for language. It is asked,* (1) *If God was the author of the first* tongue? *and if he gave it to Adam by infusion? or if Adam invented it, and acquired it by industry and labour?* (2) *If this language is still in being? And,* (3) *If so, then which is it?*

Profane authors, and such as had no knowledge of the Holy Scriptures, or of the history of the creation of the world, imagined that men were produced by chance in different parts of the world, and came out of the ground, as also all other animals besides; that at first they had no language, nor any notions of things; that first of all mere necessity, and afterwards conveniency, taught them to invent certain sounds, or words, by which to communicate their notions to one another: that hence languages were formed, which became different from each other, because they were invented separately, and their authors had no communication with one another.

But the knowledge we have now of the origin of mankind does not leave us any room to doubt, but as God created Adam perfect, so he endued him with language to express his thoughts and conceptions. Therefore we find, that the first man, presently after his creation, returns answers to God, speaks to his wife, and gives names to the brute creatures. His children and successors probably spake the same language as himself, down to the deluge; and after the deluge, till the confusion of tongues *that happened at Babel.*

Men are not agreed as to the manner in which this famous confusion was brought about. It is doubted whether all of a sudden God might not make all men forget their own language, and give them a new one, entirely different from the former: or, whether by confounding their ideas, and disturbing their imaginations, he put into their mouths different dialects of the first language: so that the primitive tongue *remaining uncorrupt in some families became at once a foreign* tongue *to those that spoke it before; as also that the dialects of the primitive language became barbarous and unknown to those who were the depositaries, as it were, of the ancient language. Or, whether God might not permit that men should be perplexed, and become unintelligible to each other, and therefore separate, and that their separation should give occasion to this change of language, by the necessary consequence of distance of place, and want of communication with each other. These several opinions have each had their patrons and maintainers.*

As to the first tongue *which God communicated to Adam at his creation, there have been but few nations in the world which have not had the ambition of having it for their own* tongue; *but the generality of critics have declared for the Hebrew* tongue, *and given it the preference before all others. The conciseness, simplicity, energy, and fertility of it, and the relation it has to the most ancient oriental languages, which seem to derive their origin from it, the etymology of the names whereby the first of mankind were called, which naturally occurs in this language: the names of animals which are all significant in the Hebrew* tongue, *and describe the nature and property of these very animals, particulars which are not to be observed in any other language: all these characters meeting together, raise a prejudice very much in favour of its primacy and excellency. It has further another privilege, namely, that the most ancient and venerable books in the world are written in Hebrew.*

Nevertheless several other very able critics are of opinion, that the Hebrew tongue, *such as we see it at present in the Bible, and as it was in the time of Moses, is not the primitive language, pure and uncorrupted; they observe many words in the Bible, the originals whereof are not to be found in Hebrew. Thus they are willing to allow, that there are more footsteps of Adam's language preserved in the Hebrew than in any other* tongue; *but this, they say, has undergone divers changes and alterations, and in the series of so many ages, from Adam down to Moses, many roots of this language were lost, and others of a foreign extraction received.*

To gnaw one's *tongue, is a token of fury, despair, and torment. The men that worship the beast are said to* gnaw their *tongues* for pain, *Rev.* 16. 10. A *tongue* of the sea, a *tongue* of land, *are terms used in Scripture for the extremity or point of the Dead sea; as in* Josh. 15. † 2. Their south border was from the shore of the salt sea, from the *tongue* that looketh southward. *Or, for a peninsula, a cape, a promontory of land, stretching out into the sea,* Josh. 18. † 19. The scourge of the *tongue,* Job 5. 21. *By this are to be understood, malicious discourses, scandal, calumny, insulting and offensive speeches.*

The gift of *tongues, which God granted to the apostles and disciples assembled at Jerusalem, on the day of Pentecost,* Acts 2. 3, 4, &c. *was communicated to the faithful, as may be seen by the epistles of St. Paul, which regulate the manner in which this great privilege was to be made use of in their assemblies,* 1 Cor. 12. 10. | 14. 2. &c. *It continued in the church as long as God thought it necessary, for the conversion of the heathen, and the confirming of believers. In* 1 Cor. 13. 1. *St Paul says,* Though I speak with the *tongues* of men and of angels, and have not charity, I am become as sounding brass, or a tinkling cymbal. *By which is not to be understood that the angels have any sensible tongue, either common or proper: the apostle intends to use a kind of hyperbole; that is, I would have every one set a due value upon the gift of* tongues; *but though a man should have all the eloquence that can be imagined, could he speak as well as angels themselves, this inestimable gift would be of little use to him as to salvation, if he is without charity, or a principle of true love to God and man in his heart.*

Exod. 11. 7. against Isr. shall not a dog move his *t.*
Josh. 10. 21. none moved his *t.* against Israel
Judg. 7. 5. that lappeth of the water with his *t.*
Job 5. 21. shall be hid from the scourge of the *t.*
15. 5. and thou choosest the *t.* of the crafty
20. 12. though he hide wickedness under his *t.*
16. poison of asps, the viper's *t.* shall slay him
29. 10. their *t.* cleaved to roof of their mouth
Psal. 5. 9. they flatter with their *t.*
10. 7. under his *t.* is mischief and vanity
12. 3. shall cut off *t.* that speaketh proud things
4. who have said, with our *t.* will we prevail
15. 3. he that backbiteth not with his *t.* nor doth
34. 13. keep thy *t.* from evil, 1 *Pet.* 3. 10.
37. 30. and his *t.* talketh of judgment
50. 19. and thy *t.* frameth deceit
52. 2. thy *t.* deviseth mischiefs like a razor
57. 4. and their *t.* is a sharp sword
64. 3. who whet their *t.* like a sword, and bend
8. shall make their *t.* to fall on themselves
68. 23. *t.* of thy dogs may be dipped in the same
73. 9. and their *t.* walketh through the earth
109. 2. they have spoken against me with lying *t.*
120. 3. what shall be done to thee, thou false *t.*?
126. 2. then was our *t.* filled with singing
Prov. 6. 17. God hateth a proud look, a lying *t.*
24. from the flattery of the *t.* of a strange woman
10. 20. the *t.* of the just is as choice silver
31. but the froward *t.* shall be cut out
12. 18. but the *t.* of the wise is health
19. but a lying *t.* is but for a moment
15. 2. the *t.* of the wise useth knowledge aright
4. a wholesome *t.* is a tree of life, but perverseness
16. 1. and the answer of the *t.* is from the Lord
17. 4. and a liar giveth ear to a naughty *t.*
20. he that hath a perverse *t.* falls into mischief
18. 21. death and life are in the power of the *t.*

Prov. 21. 6. getting of treasures by a lying *t.* is van.
23. whoso keepeth his *t.* keepeth his soul from
25. 15. and a soft *t.* breaketh the bone
23. so doth an angry countenance a backbiting *t.*
26. 28. a lying *t.* hateth those afflicted by it
28. 23. than he that flattereth with the *t.*
30. † 10. hurt not with thy *t.* a servant to master
31. 26. and in her *t.* is the law of kindness
Eccl. 10. † 11. the master of the *t.* is no better
Cant. 4. 11. honey and milk are under thy *t.*
Isa. 3. 8. because their *t.* is against the Lord
5. † 24. as the *t.* of fire devoureth the stubble
30. 27. and his *t.* is as a devouring fire
32. 4. the *t.* of the stammerers shall speak plainly
33. 19. thou shalt not see a people of stammering *t.*
35. 6. then shall the *t.* of the dumb sing
41. 17. and when their *t.* faileth for thirst
45. 23. that unto me every *t.* shall swear
50. 4. the Lord hath given me the *t.* of the learned
54. 17. every *t.* that shall rise against thee
57. 4. against whom draw ye out the *t.*?
59. 3. your *t.* hath muttered perverseness
Jer. 9. 3. they bend their *t.* like their bow for lies
5. they have taught their *t.* to speak lies
8. their *t.* is as an arrow shot out, it speaketh
18. 18. come, and let us smite him with the *t.*
Lam. 4. 4. the *t.* of the sucking child cleaveth
Ezek. 3. † 5. art not sent to a people heavy of *t.*
26. I will make thy *t.* cleave to roof of thy mouth
Hos. 7. 16. princes shall fall for the rage of their *t.*
Hab. 1. 13. holdest thy *t.* when wicked devoureth
Zech. 14. 12. their *t.* shall consume in their mouth
Mark 7. 33. and he spit, and touched his *t.*
35. and straightway his *t.* was loosed, *Luke* 1. 64.
Jam. 1. 26. seemeth religious, and bridleth not his *t.*
3. 5. so the *t.* is a little member, and boasteth
6. the *t.* is a fire ‖ 8. the *t.* can no man tame
1 *John* 3. 18. nor let us love in *t.* but in truth
See DECEITFUL, HOLD.

My TONGUE.

2 *Sam.* 23. 2. Spirit spoke, and his word was in *my t.*
Esth. 7. 4. if we had been sold, I had held *my t.*
Job 6. 30. is there iniquity in *my t.*
27. 4. nor speak wickedn. nor shall *my t.* utter deceit
33. 2. behold, *my t.* hath spoken in my mouth
Psal. 22. 15. and *my t.* cleaveth to my jaws
35. 28. and *my t.* shall speak of thy righteousness
and praise all day long, 51. 14. | 71. 24.
39. 1. I will take heed that I sin not with *my t.*
3. my heart was hot, then spake I with *my t.*
45. 1. *my t.* is the pen of a ready writer
66. 17. and God was extolled with *my t.*
119. 172. *my t.* shall speak of thy word
137. 6. let *my t.* cleave to the roof of my mouth
139. 4. not a word in *my t.* but thou knowest it
Luke 16. 24. may dip his finger, and cool *my t.*
Acts 2. 26. my heart did rejoice, *my t.* was glad

TONGUE.

Josh. 7. † 21. I saw a *t.* of gold, and coveted it

TONGUE.

Josh. 15. † 2. from the *t.* that looked southward
18. † 19. out-goings at the north *t.* of the salt-sea
Isa. 11. 15. Lord shall destroy the *t.* of Egyptian sea

TONGUE for *Language, Speech.*

Gen. 10. 5. isles were divided every one after his *t.*
Exod. 4. 10. I am slow of speech, and of a slow *t.*
Deut. 28. 49. a nation whose *t.* shall not understand
Ezra 4. 7. the writing of the letter was written in
the Syrian *t.* and interpreted in the Syrian *t.*
Isa. 28. 11. for with another *t.* will he speak
Dan. 1. 4. they might teach the *t.* of the Chaldeans
John 5. 2. a pool, called in the Hebrew *t.* Bethesda
Acts 1. 19. a field called in their proper *t.* Aceldama
2. 8. and how hear we every man in our own *t.*?
26. 14. a voice saying in the Hebrew *t.* Saul, Saul
Rom. 14. 11. and every *t.* shall confess to God
1 *Cor.* 14. 2. that speaks in unknown *t.* 4, 13, 14, 19, 27.
9. except ye utter by the *t.* words easy understood
26. every one of you hath a psalm, hath a *t.*
Phil. 2. 11. that every *t.* confess that Jesus is Lord
Rev. 5. 9. thou hast redeemed us out of every *t.*
9. 11. whose name in the Hebrew *t.* is Abaddon
14. 6. having the gospel to preach to every *t.*
16. 16. called in the Hebrew *t.* Armageddon

TONGUED.

1 *Tim.* 3. 8. deacons must be grave, not double-*t.*

TONGUES.

Gen. 10. 20. the sons of Ham, after their *t.*
31. these are the sons of Shem, after their *t.*
Ps. 31. 20. thou shalt keep them from the strife of *t.*
55. 9. destroy, O Lord, and divide their *t.*
78. 36. and they lied to him with their *t.*
140. 3. they sharpened their *t.* like a serpent
Isa. 66. 18. shall come, I will gather all nations and *t.*
Jer. 23. 31. that use their *t.* and say, he saith
Mark 16. 17. they shall speak with new *t.*
Acts 2. 3. there appeared to them cloven *t.*
4. and they began to speak with other *t.*
11. we hear in our *t.* the wonderful works of God
10. 46. for they heard them speak with *t.*
19. 6. and they spake with *t.* and prophesied
Rom. 3. 13. with their *t.* they have used deceit
1 *Cor.* 12. 10. to another divers kinds of *t.* 28.
30. do all speak with *t.*? do all interpret?
13. 1. though I speak with the *t.* of men and angels
8. whether there be *t.* they shall cease
14. 5. I would ye all spake with *t.* but rather
6. brethren, if I come to you speaking with *t.*
18. I thank God, I speak with *t.* more than you all
21. with men of other *t.* will I speak to people
22. *t.* are for a sign ‖ 23. if all speak with *t.*
39. brethren, forbid not to speak with *t.*
Rev. 7. 9. people and *t.* stood before the throne
10. 11. must prophesy again before nations and *t.*
11. 9. *t.* and nations shall see their dead bodies
13. 7. and power was given him over all *t.*
16. 10. and they gnawed their *t.* for pain
17. 15. the waters thou sowest are nations and *t.*

TOOK.

Gen. 5. 24. and Enoch was not, for God *t.* him
21. 21. his mother *t.* him a wife out of Egypt
24. 7. God, which *t.* me from my father's house
42. 30. the lord of the land *t.* us for spies
Num. 3. 49. Moses *t.* the redemption-money, 50.
11. 25. the Lord *t.* of the Spirit that was on him
21. 1. king Arad *t.* some of them prisoners
23. 11. I *t.* thee to curse mine enemies, and lo
Deut. 1. 15. so I *t.* the chief of your tribes
2. 35. only the cattle we *t.* for a prey to ourselves
3. 4. there was not a city we *t.* not from them
9. 21. I *t.* your sin, the calf which ye had made
22. 14. I *t.* this woman and found her not a maid
Josh. 7. 21. then I coveted them, and *t.* them
9. 14. the men *t.* of their victuals, and asked not
24. 3. I *t.* your father Abraham from other side
Judg. 16. 21. Philistines *t.* Samson, put out his eyes
17. 2. behold, the silver is with me, I *t.* it
19. 15. no man *t.* them into his house to lodging
25. the man *t.* his concubine, and brought her
20. 6. I *t.* my concubine, and cut her in pieces
1 *Sam.* 2. 14. brought up, the priest *t.* for himself
5. 1. and the Philistines *t.* the ark of God, 2.
10. 1. Samuel *t.* a vial of oil and poured on Saul
14. 47. so Saul *t.* the kingdom over Israel
15. 21. the people *t.* of the spoil, sheep and oxen
16. 13. Samuel *t.* horn of oil and anointed David
18. 2. Saul *t.* him, would not let him go home
26. 12. David *t.* the spear from Saul's bolster
2 *Sam.* 1. 10. I *t.* the crown and brought it hither
6. 6. Uzzah *t.* hold of it for the oxen shook it
7. 8. I *t.* thee from the sheep-cote, to be ruler
15. my mercy shall not depart, as I *t.* it from Saul
12. 4. but *t.* the poor man's lamb and dressed it
1 *Kings* 1. 39. Zadok the priest *t.* an horn of oil
3. 20. she arose and *t.* my son from beside me
20. 34. the cities my father *t.* I will restore
2 *Kings* 10. 31. but Jehu *t.* no heed to walk in the law
1 *Chron.* 11. 5. yet David *t.* the castle of Zion
2 *Chron.* 33. 11. which *t.* Manasseh among thorns
Ezra 5. 14. vessels which Nebuchadnezzar *t.* 6. 5.
Esth. 2. 7. whom Mordecai *t.* for his own daughter
6. 11. then *t.* Haman the apparel and the horse
9. 27. *t.* on them, that they would keep Purim
Job 10. † 8. thine hands *t.* pains upon me
Psal. 22. 9. he that *t.* me out of the womb, 71. 6.
48. 6. fear *t.* hold on them there, and pain
55. 14. we *t.* sweet counsel together, and walked
78. 70. he chose David, and *t.* from the sheep-folds
Isa. 8. 2. I *t.* me faithful witnesses to record
40. 14. with whom *t.* he counsel, who instructed
Jer. 25. 17. then *t.* I the cup at the Lord's hand
31. 32. in the day I *t.* them by the hand, *Heb.* 8. 9.
39. 14. even they *t.* Jeremiah out of prison
Ezek. 8. 3. and he *t.* me by a lock of mine head
10. 7. he *t.* fire from between the cherubims
33. 5. he heard the trumpet, and *t.* not warning
Amos 7. 15. the Lord *t.* me as I followed the flock
Zech. 11. 7. I *t.* me two staves, beauty and bands
13. I *t.* the thirty pieces and cast to the potter
Mat. 8. 17. himself *t.* our infirmities, and bare
13. 33. like leaven which a woman *t.* *Luke* 13. 21.
25. 3. the foolish virgins *t.* no oil ‖ 35. ye *t.* me in
43. I was a stranger and ye *t.* me not in
Mark 12. 20. the first *t.* a wife, and left no seed
21. the second *t.* her and died, *Luke* 20. 29, 30.
14. 49. in the temple teaching, and ye *t.* me not
John 19. 27. that disciple *t.* her to his own home
Acts 1. 16. who was guide to them who *t.* Jesus
9. 27. but Barnabas *t.* him, and declared to them
12. 25. *t.* with them John whose sirname was Mark
19. 13. *t.* on them to call over them which had
24. 6. whom we *t.* and would have judged by law
28. 15. Paul thanked God and *t.* courage
Gal. 2. 1. I went up and I *t.* Titus with me also
Phil. 2. 7. and *t.* upon him the form of a servant
Col. 2. 14. *t.* it out of the way, nailing it to his cross
Heb. 2. 14. he also himself *t.* part of the same
10. 34. ye *t.* joyfully the spoiling of your goods
Rev. 5. 7. he *t.* the book ‖ 8. 5. angel *t.* the censer
10. 10. I *t.* the little book out of the angel's hand

TOOK *away.*

Gen. 27. 36. he *t. away* my birth-right, behold
Exod. 10. 19. a west-wind *t. away* the locusts
13. 22. he *t.* not *away* the pillar of cloud by day
Lev. 6. 4. he shall restore that which ye *t. away*
Judg. 8. 21. Gideon *t. away* their ornaments
11. 13. Israel *t. away* my land when they came up
15. Israel *t.* not *away* the land of Moab
1 *Sam.* 27. 9. David *t. away* the sheep and oxen
1 *Kings* 14. 26. Shishak *t. away* the treasures
15. 12. Asa *t. away* the Sodomites out of the land
22. and they *t. away* the stones of Ramah
2 *Kings* 23. 11. Josiah *t. away* the horses of the sun
25. 14. all the vessels wherewith they ministered,
the Chaldeans *t. away,* 15. *Jer.* 52. 18, 19.
2 *Chron.* 14. 3. Asa *t. away* the altars ‖ 5. images
17. 6. Jehoshaphat *t. away* the high places
30. 14. Hezekiah *t. away* the altars in Jerusalem
33. 15. Manasseh *t. away* the strange gods
Psal. 69. 4. I restored that which I *t.* not *away*
Cant. 5. 7. the keepers *t. away* my vail from me
Ezek. 16. 50. I *t.* them *away* as I saw good
Hos. 13. 11. and I *t.* the king *away* in my wrath
Mat. 24. 39. the flood came and *t.* them all *away*
John 11. 41. then they *t. away* the stone from place

He TOOK.

Gen. 34. 2. Shechem saw her, *he t.* her, and lay with
Exod. 4. 6. when *he t.* it out, his hand was leprous
24. 7. *he t.* the book of the covenant and read
32. 20. and *he t.* the calf which they had made
34. 34. *he t.* the vail off, until he came out
Lev. 8. 16. *he t.* all the fat on the inwards, 25.
Judg. 8. 16. *he t.* the elders of the city and thorns
Ruth 4. 2. *he t.* ten men of the elders of the city
1 *Sam.* 11. 7. *he t.* a yoke of oxen and hewed them
14. 52. Saul saw any valiant man, *he t.* him to him
15. 8. *he t.* Agag king of the Amalekites alive
17. 40. *he t.* his staff in his hand and chose him
2 *Sam.* 13. 11. *he t.* hold of her, and said, lie with me
18. 14. *he t.* three darts, and thrust them through
22. 17. he sent from above, *he t.* me, *Psal.* 18. 16.
1 *Kings* 17. 19. *he t.* her son out of her bosom
2 *Kings* 2. 14. *he t.* the mantle of Elijah that fell
3. 27. *he t.* his eldest son and offered him for a
2 *Kings* 5. 24. *he t.* them from their hand and besto.
8. 15. *he t.* a thick cloth and dipped it in water
13. 15. and *he t.* unto him bow and arrows
Job 2. 8. *he t.* him a potsherd to scrape himself
Prov. 12. 27. slothful roasteth not that which *he t.*
Hos. 12. 3. *he t.* his brother by the heel in the womb
Mat. 15. 36. *he t.* the seven loaves, *Mark* 8. 6.
26. 27. *he t.* the cup, *Luke* 22. 17. 1 *Cor.* 11. 25.
37. *he t.* with him Peter, James, John, *Luke* 9. 28.
27. 24. *he t.* water and washed his hands, saying
Mark 8. 23. and *he t.* the blind man by the hand
9. 36. *he t.* a child and set him in the midst
Luke 9. 16. *he t.* the five loaves and two fishes
10. 35. *he t.* out two-pence and gave to the host
22. 19. and *he t.* bread, 24. 30. *Acts* 27. 35.
Acts 16. 33. *he t.* them the same hour and washed
21. 11. *he t.* Paul's girdle and bound his hands
Heb. 2. 16. *he t.* not on him the nature of angels
9. 19. *he t.* the blood of calves and of goats

They TOOK.

Gen. 6. 2. *they t.* them wives which they chose
14. 11. and *they t.* all the goods of Sodom
12. and *they t.* Lot, Abram's brother's son
Num. 16. 18. and *they t.* every man his censer
Deut. 1. 25. and *they t.* of the fruit of the land
Josh. 6. 20. the people went up and *they t.* the city
8. 23. the king of Ai, *they t.* alive and brought him
11. 19. save Hivites, all other *they t.* in battle
Judg. 3. 6. *they t.* their daughters to be wives
2 *Kings* 10. 14. *they t.* them alive and slew them
Lam. 5. 13. *they t.* the young men to grind
Ezek. 23. 13. I saw that *they t.* both one way
Dan. 5. 20. and *they t.* his glory from him
Mat. 21. 46. because *they t.* him for a prophet
28. 15. so *they t.* the money, and did as taught
Mark 12. 8. *they t.* him, and killed him, and cast him
Luke 22. 54. *they t.* him, and led him, *John* 19. 16.
Acts 4. 13. and *they t.* knowledge of them that
13. 29. *they t.* him down from the tree and laid
18. 26. *they t.* him, and expounded the way of God

TOOK *up.*

Num. 23. 7. Balaam *t. up* his parable and said,
18. | 24. 3, 15, 20, 21, 23.
Josh. 3. 6. the priests *t. up* the ark, 6. 12. 1 *Kings* 8. 3
Judg. 19. 28. then the man *t. up* his concubine
1 *Sam.* 9. 24. and the cook *t. up* the shoulder
2 *Sam.* 2. 32. they *t. up* Asahel and buried him
4. 4. Mephibosheth's nurse *t.* him *up* and fled
1 *Kings* 13. 29. and the prophet *t. up* the carcase
2 *Kings* 2. 13. he *t. up* also the mantle of Elijah
4. 37. the Shunammite *t. up* her son and went out
10. 15. and he *t.* him *up* to him into the chariot
Neh. 2. 1. I *t. up* the wine and gave it to the king
Jer. 38. 13. they *t.* Jeremiah *up* out of the dungeon
Ezek. 3. 12. then the Spirit *t.* me *up,* 11. 24. | 43. 5.
Dan. 3. 22. the flame slew men that *t. up* Shadrach
Jonah 1. 15. so they *t. up* Jonah, and cast him forth
Mat. 14. 12. they *t. up* the body of John, *Mark* 6. 29.
20. they *t. up* of the fragments that remained, 15.
37. *Mark* 6. 43. | 8. 8, 20.
16. 9. and how many baskets ye *t. up,* 10.
Mark 2. 12. and he *t. up* the bed and went forth
10. 16. he *t.* them *up* in his arms and blessed them
Luke 2. 28. *t.* him *up* in his arms and blessed God
John 8. 59. *t. up* stones to cast at him, 10. 31.
Acts 7. 21. Pharaoh's daughter *t.* Moses *up*
43. yea, ye *t. up* the tabernacle of Moloch
10. 26. but Peter *t.* him *up,* saying, stand up
21. 15. we *t. up* our carriages and went to Jerusalem
Rev. 18. 21. and a mighty angel *t. up* a stone

TOOKEST.

Psal. 99. 8. tho' thou *t.* vengeance of their inventions
Ezek. 16. 18. and *t.* thy broidered garments

TOOL.

Exod. 20. 25. if lift up thy *t.* thou hast polluted it
32. 4. and he fashioned it with a graving *t.*
Deut. 27. 5. thou shalt not lift up any iron *t.* on them
1 *Kings* 6. 7. nor any *t.* of iron heard in the house

TOOTH

Is a useful member of the body known by every body. The Hebrews call ivory, tooth, *or the* elephant's *tooth,* 1 Kings 10. † 22. *They sometimes also called the prominence of a rock by the name of* tooth, 1 *Sam.* 14. † 4. Between the passages there was a sharp rock; *in Hebrew,* the *tooth* of a rock. *And the rock from which God caused the water to gush out, for quenching Samson's thirst, is called* maktesh, *that is, the* jaw-tooth, *Judg.* 15. 19. *It was ordered by the law of retaliation, that they should give* tooth for tooth, Exod. 21. 24. *This law is, by most interpreters, reckoned only minatory; yet so as that it was literally to be inflicted, except the injuring party would give such satisfaction as the injured person accepted, or the judges determined.*

To gnash the *teeth is a token of sorrow, rage, despair, hatred, and passion. The Psalmist says,* Psal. 35. 16. That his enemies gnash upon him with their *teeth, out of rage and hatred. And the gospel in several places speaks of* the gnashing of the *teeth of the damned out of rage and despair.* God breaks the *teeth* of the wicked, *Psal.* 3. 7. *he puts it out of their power to injure good men. The wicked complain, that* the fathers have eaten sour grapes, and their children's *teeth* are set on edge, *Ezek.* 18. 2. *As if they had said, "Our fathers have sinned, and we are obliged to undergo the punishment thereof, though we are not guilty." Amos tells the idolatrous Jews, that God had sent them* cleanness of teeth, *that is, famine. They should not have wherewithal to defile their* teeth, *Amos* 4. 6.

Exod. 21. 24. thou shalt give *t.* for *t.* *Lev.* 24. 20.
Deut. 19. 21. *Mat.* 5. 38.
27. if he smite out his man-servant's or his maid
servant's *t.* he shall let him go free for his *t.* sake
Prov. 25. 19. is like a broken *t.* a foot out of joint

TOP.

Gen. 11. 4. tower whose *t.* may reach unto heaven
28. 12. the *t.* of the ladder reached to heaven
18. Jacob poured oil on the *t.* of the stone

Exod. 19. 20. Lord came down on t. of mount Sinai, and called Moses to t. of the mount, 34. 2.
24. 17. like devouring fire on the t. of the mount
28. 32. there shall be an hole in the t. of it
30. 3. shall overlay the t. with pure gold, 37. 26.
Num. 14. 40. they gat into the t. of the mountain
20. 28. Aaron died there in the t. of the mount
23. 9. for from the t. of the rocks I see him
Deut. 3. 27. get up into the t. of Pisgah, 34. 1.
28. 35. from sole of foot to the t. of thy head
33. 16. on t. of the head of him that was separated
Judg. 6. 26. build an altar on the t. of this rock
9. 51. the people gat up to the t. of the tower
15. 8. Samson dwelt in the t. of the rock Etam
1 Sam. 9. 25. communed on the t. of the house, 26.
2 Sam. 16. 22. spread a tent on the t. of the house
1 Kings 10. 19. the t. of the throne round behind
21. † 9. and set Naboth on the t. of the people
2 Kings 9. 13. put it under him on t. of the stairs
2 Chron. 25. 12. cast them from the t. of the rock
Esth. 5. 2. Esther touched the t. of the sceptre
Psal. 72. 16. handful of corn on t. of mountains
102. 7. I am as a sparrow alone on the house-t.
Prov. 8. 2. she standeth in the t. of high places
21. 9. better dwell in corner of house-t. 25. 24.
23. 34. or as he that lieth on the t. of a mast
Cant. 4. 8. look from the t. of Amana, from the t.
Isa. 2. 2. the Lord's house shall be established in the t. of the mountains, and be exalted, Mic. 4. 1.
17. 6. two or three berries in the t. of the bough
30. 17. left as a beacon on the t. of a mountain
42. 11. let them shout from the t. of the mountains
Lam. 2. 19. that faint for hunger in t. of every street
4. 1. the stones are poured out in t. of every street
Ezek. 17. 4. he cropt off the t. of his young twigs
22. I will crop off from the t. of his young twigs
24. 7. her blood, she set it on the t. of a rock
8. I have set her blood on the t. of a rock
26. 4. I will make her like the t. of a rock, 14.
31. 3. his t. was among the thick boughs, 10, 14.
43. 12. law of the house on the t. of the mountains
Nah. 3. 10. her children dashed at t. of all the streets
Mat. 24. 17. let him who is on the house-t. not come down, Mark 13. 15. Luke 17. 31.
27. 51. vail rent from t. to the bottom, Mark 15. 38.
Luke 5. 19. they went on the house-t. and let down
John 19. 23. was woven from the t. throughout
Heb. 11. 21. and worshipped, leaning on t. of his staff
See CARMEL, HILL.

TOPS.

Gen. 8. 5. the t. of the mountains were seen
2 Sam. 5. 24. when thou hearest the sound of a going in the t. of the mulberry-trees, 1 Chron. 14. 15.
2 Kings 19. 26. were as the green herb, as the grass upon the house-t. Psal. 129. 6. Isa. 37. 27.
Job 24. 24. and cut off as the t. of the ears of corn
Isa. 2. 21. to go into the t. of the ragged rocks
15. 3. on the t. of houses every one shall howl
22. 1. that thou art wholly gone up to the house-t.
Jer. 48. 38. there shall be lamentation on all house-t.
Ezek. 6. 13. their slain men shall be in t. of mountains
Hos. 4. 13. they sacrifice on the t. of the mountains
Zeph. 1. 5. worship the host of heaven on house-t.
Mat. 10. 27. that preach ye upon the house t.
Luke 12. 3. shall be proclaimed on the house-t.

TOPAZ.

In Hebrew, Pitdath. *The Seventy, St. Jerom, Junius, and the greatest part of the modern interpreters, translate* Pitdath *by* Topaz ; *the Paraphrasts, Onkelos, and Jonathan, by a green* stone ; *which agrees perfectly well with the* Topaz, *of which the finest are green, as Pliny observes,* lib. 37. cap. 8. *Yet others maintain, that the most beautiful* Topazes *are of the colour of gold. It is pretended this stone took its name of* Topaz *from an island in the Red sea, which has the same name. Pliny will have Juba, king of Mauritania, to have been the first that found them. But if it was known to Moses, it must be much more ancient than Juba. Job speaks of the* Pitdath *of Cush, or Ethiopia,* Job 28. 19. *which may confirm their opinion who make the* Topaz *to come from the Red sea ; because there was a country of Cush lying upon the eastern shore of this sea. This stone was the second of the first row in the breast plate, and had the name of* Simeon *upon it,* Exod. 28. 17.

Exod. 28. 17. the first row a sardius, a t. 39. 10.
Job 28. 19. the t. of Ethiopia shall not equal it
Ezek. 28. 13. the sardius, the t. was thy covering
Rev. 21. 20. the eighth, beryl, the ninth a t.

TOPHET.

It is thought that Tophet *was the butchery, or place of slaughter, at Jerusalem, lying to the south of the city, in the valley of the children of Hinnom. It is also said, that a constant fire used to be kept there, for burning the carcases, and other filthiness, that were brought thither from the city. It was in the same place that they cast away the ashes and remains of the images of false gods, when they demolished their altars, and broke down their statues. Isaiah seems to allude to this custom, of burning dead carcases in* Tophet, *when speaking of the defeat of the army of Sennacherib, he says ;* For *Tophet* is ordained of old ; yea, for the king it is prepared ; he hath made it deep and large. The pile thereof is fire and much wood ; the breath of the Lord, like a stream of brimstone, doth kindle it. *Though this may be figuratively understood of* hell.

Others think the name of Tophet *is given to the valley of Hinnom, because of the sacrifices that were offered there to the god Moloch, by beat of drum, which in Hebrew is called* Toph. *It was in this manner that these sacrifices were offered. The statue of Moloch was of brass, hollow within, with its arms extended, and stooping a little forward. They lighted a great fire within the statue, and another before it. They put upon its arms the child they intended to sacrifice, which soon fell into the fire at the foot of the statue, putting forth cries, as may easily be imagined. To stifle the noise of these cries and howlings, they made a great rattling of drums and other instruments, that the spectators might not be moved with compassion at the clamours of these miserable victims. And this, as they say, was the manner of sacrificing in* Tophet.

Jeremiah upbraids the Israelites with having built temples to Moloch, in the valley of Hinnom, in Tophet, *to burn their children there in the fire,* Jer. 7. 31. *The same prophet shews, that* Tophet *was a polluted and unclean place, where they used to throw the carcases to which they refused burial,* Jer. 7. 32. | 19. 11, 12, 13. *King Josiah defiled the place of* Tophet, *where the temple of Moloch stood, that nobody might go thither any more to sacrifice their children to that cruel heathenish deity,* 2 Kings 23. 10.

2 Kings 23. 10. Josiah defiled t. in the valley
Isa. 30. 33. for t. is ordained of old, for the king
Jer. 7. 31. they have built the high places of t.
32. that it shall no more be called t. 19. 6.
19. 11. they shall bury in t. till there be no place
12. saith the Lord, I will even make this city as t.
13. Jerusalem shall be defiled as t.
14. then came Jeremiah from t. whither sent

TORCH.

Zech. 12. 6. make the governors of Judah like a t.

TORCHES.

Judg. 7. † 16. he put t. within the pitchers
15. † 4. Samson caught 300 foxes and took t.
Nah. 2. 3. the chariots shall be with flaming t.
4. the chariots shall seem like t. they shall run
John 18. 3. Judas cometh with lanterns and t.

TORMENT.

Luke 16. 28. lest they come into this place of t.
1 John 4. 18. no fear in love, because fear hath t.
Rev. 9. 5. their t. was as the t. of a scorpion
14. 11. the smoke of their t. ascendeth for ever
18. 7. so much t. and sorrow give her, I sit a queen
10. standing afar off for the fear of her t. 15.

TORMENT, *Verb.*

Mat. 8. 29. art thou come to t. us before the time?
Mark 5. 7. that thou t. me not, Luke 8. 28.

TORMENTS.

Mat. 4. 24. that were taken with divers diseas. and t.
Luke 16. 23. in hell he lift up his eyes being in t.

TORMENTED.

Mat. 8. 6. Lord, my servant lieth grievously t.
Luke 16. 24. send Lazarus, for I am t. in this flame
25. but now he is comforted, and thou art t.
Heb. 11. 37. wandered, being destitute, afflicted, t.
Rev. 9. 5. but that they should be t. five months
11. 10. because these two prophets t. them that
14. 10. he shall be t. with fire and brimstone
20. 10. and shall be t. day and night for ever

TORMENTORS.

Mat. 18. 34. his lord delivered him to the t.

TORN.

Gen. 31. 39. that which was t. of beasts I brought not
44. 28. and I said, surely he is t. in pieces
Exod. 22. 13. if t. in pieces, let him bring it for witness, he shall not make good what was t.
31. be holy, nor shall eat any flesh t. of beasts
Lev. 7. 24. fat of that which is t. may be used
17. 15. if any eat that which was t. he shall wash
22. 8. dieth of itself, or t. of beasts, shall not eat
1 Kings 13. 26. to the lion, which hath t. him
28. the lion had not eaten carcase, nor t. the ass
Isa. 5. 25. carcases t. in the midst of the streets
Jer. 5. 6. every one that goeth out shall be t.
Ezek. 4. 14. I have not eaten of that which is t.
44. 31. the priests shall not eat any thing that is t.
Hos. 6. 1. for he hath t. and he will heal us
Mal. 1. 13. and ye brought that which was t.
Mark 1. 26. when the unclean spirit hath t. him

TORTOISE.

In Hebrew, Choled, *which the Septuagint translate by* land crocodile, *others by* green-frog. *It is numbered among the unclean animals,* Lev. 11. 29. *This* land crocodile *is a sort of lizard, which feeds upon the sweetest flowers it can find ; this makes its entrails to be very much valued for their agreeable smell. St. Jerome says, that the Syrians used to eat crocodiles of this kind, which live upon the land only.*

Lev. 11. 29. the t. shall be unclean unto you

TORTURED.

Acts 22. 29. departed, who should have t. him
Heb. 11. 35. others were t. not accepting deliverance

TOSS.

Isa. 22. 18. he will turn and t. thee like a ball
Jer. 5. 22. though the waves thereof t. themselves

TOSSED.

Psal. 109. 23. I am t. up and down as the locust
Prov. 21. 6. is a vanity, t. to and fro of them that
Isa. 54. 11. O thou afflicted, t. with tempest
Mat. 14. 24. but the ship was now t. with waves
Acts 27. 18. being exceedingly t. with a tempest
Eph. 4. 14. we be no more children t. to and fro
Jam. 1. 6. for he that wavereth is like a wave t.

TOSSINGS.

Job 7. 4. I am full of t. to the dawning of the day
2 Cor. 6. † 5. approving ourselves in t. in labours

TOTTERING.

Psal. 62. 3. ye shall be all of you as a t. fence

TOUCH.

Gen. 3. 3. not eat of it, nor shall ye t. it lest ye die
20. 6. therefore suffered I thee not to t. her
Exod. 19. 12. that ye t. not the border of it
13. there shall not an hand t. it, but shall die
Lev. 5. 2. or if a soul t. any unclean thing
3. or if he t. the uncleanness of man, 7. 21.
6. 27. whatsoever shall t. the flesh thereof
11. 8. their carcase ye shall not t. Deut. 14. 8.
31. whosoever doth t. them when dead, be unclean
12. 4. he shall t. no hallowed thing, nor come
Num. 4. 15. they shall not t. any holy thing
16. 26. depart and t. nothing of theirs
Josh. 9. 19. now therefore we may not t. them
Ruth 2. 9. I charged that they should not t. thee
2 Sam. 14. 10. and he shall not t. thee any more
18. 12. beware that none t. the young man Absalom
23. 7. man that shall t. them must be fenced
1 Chr. 16. 22. t. not mine anointed, Psal. 105. 15.
Job 1. 11. but t. all he hath, and he will curse thee
2. 5. t. his bone and his flesh, he will curse thee
5. 19. in seven there shall no evil t. thee
6. 7. the things that my soul refused to t.
Ps. 144. 5. t. the mountains, and they shall smoke
Isa. 6. † 7. he caused it to t. my mouth, and said
52. 11. t. no unclean thing, 2 Cor. 6. 17.
Jer. 12. 14. that t. the inheritance of my people
Lam. 2. † 2. strong holds he hath made to t. ground
4. 14. so that men could not t. their garments
15. they cried, it is unclean, depart, t. not
Hag. 2. 12. if one with his skirt do t. bread
13. if one that is unclean t. any of these
Mat. 9. 21. if I may but t. his garment, Mark 5. 28.
14. 36. besought him that they might t. the hem of his garment, Mark 5. 28. | 6. 56. | 8. 22.
Mark 3. 10. they press. on him to t. him, Luke 6. 19.
8. 22. they besought him to t. the blind man
Luke 11. 46. ye yourselves t. not the burdens
18. 15. brought infants, that he would t. them
John 20. 17. Jesus saith unto her, t. me not
1 Cor. 7. 1. it is good for a man not to t. a woman
Col. 2. 21. t. not, taste not, handle not
Heb. 11. 28. that destroy first-born, should t. them
12. 20. if so much as a beast t. the mountain

TOUCHED.

Gen. 26. 29. do us no hurt, as we have not t. thee
32. 25. he t. the hollow of Jacob's thigh, 32.
Lev. 22. 6. the soul which hath t. any such
Num. 31. 19. and whosoever hath t. any slain
Judg. 6. 21. the angel of the Lord t. the flesh
1 Sam. 10. 26. a band, whose hearts God had t.
1 Kings 6. 27. wings of the cherubims t. one anoth.
19. 5. an angel t. him, and said, arise, eat, 7.
2 Kings 13. 21. when the man t. the bones of Elisha
Esth. 5. 2. so Esther t. the top of the sceptre
Job 19. 21. pity me, for the hand of G. hath t. me
Isa. 6. 7. lo, this hath t. thy lips, thy sin is purged
Jer. 1. 9. then the Lord t. my mouth, and said
Dan. 8. 5. and the he-goat t. not the ground
18. but he t. me, 9. 21. | 10. 10, 16, 18.
Mat. 8. 3. and Jesus t. him, Mark 1. 41. Luke 5. 13.
15. and he t. her hand, and the fever left her
9. 20. a woman diseased with an issue of blood t. the hem of his garment, Mark 5. 27. Luke 8. 44.
29. then t. he their eyes, saying, 20. 34.
14. 36. as many as t him made whole, Mark 6. 56.
Mark 5. 30. who t. my clothes, 31. Luke 8. 45, 47.
7. 33. was deaf, and he spit, and t. his tongue
Luke 7. 14. he came and t. the bier, they stood still
8. 47. she declared for what cause she had t. him
22. 51. and Jesus t. his ear and healed him
Acts 27. 3. and the next day we t. at Sidon
Heb. 4. 15. not an high priest which cannot be t.
12. 18. not come to the mount that might be t.

TOUCHETH.

Gen. 26. 11. he that t. this man shall surely die
Exod. 19. 12. whosoever t. the mount, shall die
29. 37. whatsoever t. the altar shall be holy
30. 29. that t. them, shall be holy, Lev. 6. 18.
Lev. 7. 19. the flesh that t. any unclean thing
11. 24. whosoever t. their carcase, 27, 36, 39.
26. every one that t. them shall be unclean
15. 5. whoso t. his bed, shall wash his clothes
7. t. his flesh ‖ 10. t. any thing under him
11. whomsoever he t. that hath the issue
12. the vessel of earth that he t. shall be broken
19. whoso t. her ‖ 21. whosoever t. her bed
22. whosoever t. any thing that she sat upon
23. if on her bed, when he t. it, he shall be unclean till the even, 27. | 22. 4, 5. Num. 19. 22.
Num. 19. 11. he that t. the dead body, 13. 16.
18. t. a bone ‖ 21. t. the water of separation
Judg. 16. 9. as a thread is broken when it t. fire
Job 4. 5. now it t. thee, and thou art troubled
Psal. 104. 32. he t. the hills and they smoke
Prov. 6. 29. whosoever t. her, shall not be innocent
Ezek. 17. 10. shall wither, when the east wind t. it
Hos. 4. 2. they break out, and blood t. blood
Amos 9. 5. the Lord of hosts is he that t. the land
Zech. 2. 8. he that t. you t. the apple of his eye
Luke 7. 39. known what woman this is that t. him
1 John 5. 18. and that wicked one t. him not

TOUCHING.

Gen. 27. 42. Esau, as t. thee, doth comfort himself
Lev. 5. 13. for him, as t. his sin that he hath sinned
Num. 8. 26. thus do to the Levites t. their charge
1 Sam. 20. 23. t. matter thou and I have spoken of
2 Kings 22. 18. t. the words which thou hast heard
Job 37. 23. t. the Almighty, we cannot find him out
Psal. 45. 1. things which I have made t. the king
Isa. 5. 1. a song of my beloved, t. his vineyard
Jer. 1. 16. utter judgments t. all their wickedness
21. 11. t. the house of the king of Judah, say
22. 11. thus saith Lord t. Shallum king of Judah
Ezek. 7. 13. the vision is t. the whole multitude
Mat. 18. 19. as t. any thing that they shall ask
22. 31. but as t. the resurrection of the dead, have ye not read, Mark 12. 26. Acts 24. 21.
Luke 23. 14. t. those things whereof ye accuse him
Acts 5. 35. what ye intend to do as t. these men
21. 25. as t. the Gentiles who believe, have written
Rom. 11. 28. as t. the election, they are beloved
1 Cor. 8. 1. now as t. things offered unto idols
16. 12. t. our brother Apollos, I desired him
2 Cor. 9. 1. as t. the ministering to the saints
Phil. 3. 5. of the Hebrews, as t. the law, a Pharisee
6. t. the righteousness in the law, blameless
Col. 4. 10. t. whom ye received commandments
1 Thess. 4. 9. t. brotherly love, ye need not that
2 Thess. 3. 4. we have confidence in the Ld. t. you

TOW.

Judg. 16. 9. break withs, as a thread of t. is broken
Isa. 1. 31. and the strong shall be as t. and the maker
43. 17. they are extinct, they are quenched as t.

TOWARD, *or* TOWARDS.

Gen. 48. 13. Joseph took them both, Ephraim t. Israel's left hand, Manasseh t. Israel's right hand
Num. 24. 1. he set his face t. the wilderness
Deut. 28. 54. his eye shall be evil t. his brother

Deut. 28. 56. shall be evil t. her husband, son, daug.
Judg. 5. 9. my heart is t. the governors of Israel
1 Sam. 20. 12. behold, if there be good t. David
1 Kings 8. 29. mayest hearken to the prayer thy servant shall make t. this place, 30. 35. 2 Chr. 6. 21.
2 Chron. 24. 16. because Jehoiada had done good in Israel, both t. God, and t. his house
Ezra 3. 11. his mercy endureth for ever t. Israel
Psal. 5. 7. I will worship t. thy holy temple, 138. 2.
25. 15. mine eyes are ever t. the Lord, for he shall
28. 2. when I lift my hands t. thy holy oracle
Prov. 14. 35. the king's favour is t. a wise servant
Isa. 63. 7. the great goodness t. house of Israel
Jer. 15. 1. my mind could not be t. this people
Dan. 6. 10. his windows being open t. Jerusalem
8. 9. the litt e horn waxed great t. the south
Jonah 2. 4. yet I will look t. thy holy temple
Mat. 28. 1. as it began to dawn t. first day of week
Luke 2. 14. on earth peace, good will t. men
12. 21. that layeth up treasure, and not rich t. God
24. 29. saying, abide with us for it is t. evening
Acts 20. 21. testifying to Jews and Greeks repentance t. God, and faith t. our Lord Jesus Christ
24. 16. conscience void of offence t. God and t. men
Philem. 5. hearing of thy love and faith which thou hast t. the Lord Jesus Christ, and t. all saints
See HEAVEN, HIM, ME, THEE, THEM, US, YOU.

TOWEL.

John 13. 4. he riseth, and took a t. and girded hims.
5. he began to wash, and wipe their feet with the t.

TOWER,

In Hebrew, Migdal. [1] *It is put for proud lofty men*, Isa. 2. 15. | 30. 25. [2] *The Lord Jesus Christ*, Psal. 61. 3. Prov. 18. 10.

The Scripture mentions several towers. The *tower* of Siloam *mentioned in* Luke 13. 4. *was probably near the fountain of that name, to the east of Jerusalem: or, as others think, it was over the fountain, and fell upon the people who had come thither to wash themselves, or to receive benefit by the waters.*

The *tower* of the flock, Mic. 4. 8. *Some refer this to the* tower *of Edar, which was in the neighbourhood of Beth-lehem,* Gen. 35. 21. *They say likewise, that the shepherds, to whom the angel revealed the birth of our Saviour, were near to this* tower, Luke 2. 8, 15. *Many interpreters assert that the passage of Micah, wherein mention is made of the tower* of the flock, *stood for the city of Beth-lehem, out of which our Saviour was to come. Others maintain, that the prophet intended it for the city of Jerusalem, in which there was a tower of this name, through which the flocks of sheep were driven into the sheep-market.*

The *tower* of the watchman, 2 Kings 17. 9. From the *tower* of the watchman to the fenced city; *this form of speaking expresses in general all the places of the country, from the least to the greatest. The* towers *of the watchmen, or of the shepherds, stood alone in the midst of the plain, to lodge the shepherds and herdmen, who looked after the flocks, or to set watchmen in to keep the fruits of the earth, or to give notice of the approach of enemies. King Uzziah caused several* towers *to be built for the shepherds in the desert, and made many cisterns there, because he had a great number of flocks,* 2 Chron. 26. 10. *The* tower *Edar mentioned before, and that which Isaiah takes notice of, which was built in the midst of a vineyard,* Isa. 5. 2. *were of the same kind.*

The *tower* of Shechem, Judg. 9. 46, &c. *This* tower *was as a citadel or fortress, standing upon higher ground than the rest of the city, and capacious enough to receive above a thousand persons. After Abimelech had taken and rased the city of Shechem, he endeavoured to take possession of this* tower, *to which a great part of the inhabitants of the city had retired: but as he could not take it, because it was exceeding strong, he resolved to set it on fire. To this purpose he went up to mount Zalmon, cut down an arm of a tree, and laid it upon his shoulders, and commanded all his people to follow his example. They therefore brought with them a great quantity of fuel, filled the ditch with it, and set it on fire: so that all those who had taken refuge in the* tower *either perished by the flames, or were stifled by the smoke.*

The Scripture speaks of the tower *of Phanuel, of the* tower *of Succoth, of Babel, and of some others, which were also a kind of citadels and fortresses of these cities.* Let us build us a city and a *tower*, Gen. 11. 4, 5.

Gen. 11. 4. go to, let us build us a city and a t.
5. the Lord came down to see the city and t.
35. 21. Isr. spread his tent beyond the t. of Edar
Judg. 8. 9. when I come, I will break down this t.
17. he beat down the t. of Penuel and slew men
9. 46. men of the t. of Shechem entered an hold
51. but there was a strong t. within the city
2 Sam. 22. 51. he is the t. of salvation for his king
2 Kings 5. 24. when he came to the t. he took them
Psal. 61. 3. hast been a strong t. from the enemy
Prov. 18. 10. the name of the Lord is a strong t.
Cant. 4. 4. thy neck is like the t. of David
7. 4. thy neck is as a t. of ivory, thy nose is as the t. of Lebanon, looking towards Damascus
Isa. 5. 2. he built a t. in the midst of the vineyard
Jer. 6. 27. I have set thee for a t. and a fortress
31. 38. the city shall be built from t. of Hananeel
Ezek. 29. 10. Egypt desolate, from the t. of Syene
30. 6. from the t. of Syene shall they fall in it
Mic. 4. 8. thou, O t. of the flock, to thee shall it come
Hab. 2. 1. I will set me upon the t. and watch
Zech. 14. 10. shall be inhabited from t. of Hananeel
Mat. 21. 33. built a t. let it out to husb. Mark 12. 1.
Luke 13. 4. those 18 on whom the t. in Siloam fell
14. 28. which of you intending to build a t.

High TOWER.

2 Sam. 22. 3. God is my high t. Psal. 18. 2. | 144. 2.
Isa. 2. 15. the day of the Lord on every high t.

TOWERS.

2 Chron. 14. 7. let us build cities and make t.
26. 9. moreover Uzziah built t. in Jerus.
26. 10. he built t. in desert and dig. wells
27. 4. Jotham built castles and t. in the forests
32. 5. Hezekiah raised up the wall to the t.
Psal. 48. 12. go round about Zion and tell her t.
Cant. 8. 10. I am a wall, and my breasts like t.
Isa. 23. 13. the Assyrian set up the t. thereof
30. 25. on every high hill rivers, when the t. fall
32. 14. the forts and t. shall be for dens for ever
33. 18. where is he that counted the t.?
Ezek. 26. 4. they shall break down her t. 9.
27. 11. and the Gammadims were in thy t.
Zeph. 3. 6. their t. are desolate, streets waste

TO WIT.

Gen. 24. 21. to wit whether Lord made journey pr.
Exod. 2. 4. to wit what would be done to him
2 Cor. 5. 19. to wit, God was in Christ reconciling
8. 1. we do you to wit of the grace of God bestowed

TOWN.

Josh. 2. 15. Rahab's house was on the t. wall
1 Sam. 16. 4. and the elders of the t. trembled
23. 7. shut in, by entering into a t. that hath gates
27. 5. let them give me a place in some t.
Hab. 2. 12. woe to him that builds a t. with blood
Mat. 10. 11. into whatsoever t. ye shall enter
Mark 8. 23. he led the blind man out of the t.
26. nor go into the t. nor tell it to any in t.
John 7. 42. Christ cometh out of the t. of Bethlehem
11. 1. the t. of Mary and her sister Martha
30. now Jesus was not yet come into the t.

TOWNS.

Esth. 9. 19. the Jews that dwelt in unwalled t.
Jer. 19. 15. I will bring on all her t. the evil
Zech. 2. 4. Jerus. be inhabited as t. without walls
Luke 9. 6. they departed and went through the t.
12. that they may go into the t. and lodge

TOWN-CLERK.

Acts 19. 35. when the t. had appeased the people

TRADE.

Gen. 46. 32. their t. hath been about cattle, 34.

TRADES.

Tit. 3. † 14. let ours also learn to profess honest t.

TRADE, *Verb*.

Gen. 34. 10. dwell and t. you therein, 21.
Rev. 18. 17. as many as t. by sea, stood afar off

TRADED.

Ezek. 27. 12. Tarshish t. in thy fairs with tin
13. Javan, Tubal, Meshech, t. the persons of men
14. they of house of Togarmah t. with horses
17. Judah and Israel t. in thy market wheat
Mat. 25. 16. received five talents, went and t.

TRADING.

Luke 19. 15. how much every man had gained by t.

TRADITION,

[1] *Is put for a doctrine first delivered by speech from God, and afterwards writ in his book for the use of the church. This is an object of our faith,* 1 Cor. 11. † 2. 2 Thess. 2. 15. [2] *A human ordinance or ceremony, handed down from one to another, as the Jews' oral Law. These are good or bad, according as they agree with, or deviate from, the word of God, which is our only rule of faith and practice.*

Our Saviour in the gospel has often declared against the traditions *of the Pharisees,* Mat. 15. 2, 3. The Scribes and Pharisees said to Jesus, Why do thy disciples transgress the *tradition* of the elders? for they wash not their hands when they eat bread. *This washing was a ceremony not contrary to the law of God, but rather a matter of decency, which they might freely use, in a civil way, so long as they placed nothing of religion in it: but in this they were to be condemned, because they placed religion in it, and had no divine warrant for it. Our Saviour answers them by another question;* Why do ye also transgress the commandment of God by your *traditions? And though Christ does not say that this* tradition *of washing was contrary to the command, (though others were,) yet by an instance which he gives in the following verses, he shews that none of their* traditions *were binding; for otherwise his reply would be invalid. The law he instances in, is the fifth commandment,* Honour thy father and mother; *which includes maintenance and relief; but by your* traditions, *says he, ye warrant children to give this answer to their parents who are poor, and seek relief and support from them,* It is a gift by whatsoever thou mightest be profited by me; *that is, I have consecrated all the overplus of my estate, more than will serve for my own maintenance, as a religious offering or gift to God, and therefore you must excuse me; this you think frees them from any obligation to relieve their parents, and consequently from any transgression of the law; but I tell you, that thus ye have made the commandment of God of none effect by your* tradition.

The Jews call their traditions *the* Oral Law, *pretending that God delivered them to Moses by word of mouth upon Mount Sinai, at the same time that he gave him the written law: That this lawgiver taught them to the elders of the people, and committed them to them as a trust, which they were to convey down to their successors, and so on.*

The church of Rome is very near akin to the Jews in this matter. She holds, that, besides what we have in the New Testament, the apostles delivered many things to the primitive church only by word of mouth, *which have since that time been imparted to succeeding churches; to the observation of which, Christians are as much obliged as to the written word. The council of Trent says concerning* traditions, "*That the truth and discipline of the Catholic Church are comprehended both in the sacred books and in the* traditions, *which have been received from the mouth of Jesus Christ himself, or of his apostles, and which have been preserved and transmitted to us, by an uninterrupted chain and succession.*"

The doctrine of the reformed churches concerning traditions *is,* "*That the Holy Scripture containeth all things necessary to salvation; so that whatsoever is not read therein, nor may be proved thereby, is not to be required of any man, that it should be believed as an article of faith, or be thought requisite or necessary to salvation.*"

Mat. 15. 2. why do thy disciples transgress the t. of the elders, not wash their hands? Mark 7. 5.
3. Jesus said to them, why do you transgress the commandment of God by your t.? Mark 7. 9.
6. thus ye have made the commandment of God of none effect by your t. Mark 7. 13.
Mark 7. 3. holding the t. of the elders, 8, 9.
Col. 2. 8. lest any spoil you after the t. of men
2 Thess. 3. 6. not after the t. which he received of us
1 Pet. 1. 18. received by t. from your fathers

TRADITIONS.

1 Cor. 11. † 2. keep the t. as I delivered them
Gal. 1. 14. being zealous of the t. of my fathers
2 Thess. 2. 15. hold the t. ye have been taught

TRAFFICK.

Gen. 42. 34. your brother, and ye shall t. in the land

TRAFFICK, *Substantive*.

1 Kings 10. 15. besides that had of t. of merchants
Ezek. 17. 4. he carried it into a land of t.
28. 5. by thy t. hast thou increased thy riches
18. hast defiled thy sanctuaries by iniquity of t.

TRAFFICKERS.

Isa. 23. 8. whose t. are the honourable of the earth

TRAIN.

1 Kings 10. 2. she came to Jerusalem with a great t.
Isa. 6. 1. Lord lifted up, and his t. filled the temple

TRAIN.

Prov. 22. 6. t. up a child in the way he should go

TRAINED.

Gen. 14. 14. Abram armed his t. servants, 318.

TRAITOR.

Luke 6. 16. and Judas Iscariot which was the t.

TRAITORS.

2 Tim. 3. 4. in the last days shall men be t. heady

TRAMPLE.

Psal. 91. 13. the dragon shalt thou t. under feet
104. † 20. all the beasts do t. on the forest
Isa. 63. 3. for I will t. them in my fury
Mat. 7. 6. pearls, lest they t. them under their foot

TRAMPLINGS.

Judg. 5. † 22. the horse-hoofs broken by their t.

TRANCE.

Num. 24. 4. saw the vision falling into a t. 16.
Acts 10. 10. he fell into a t. and saw heaven opened
11. 5. I was praying, and in a t. I saw a vision
22. 17. while I prayed in the temple, I was in a t.

TRANQUILLITY.

Dan. 4. 27. if it may be a lengthening of thy t.

TRANSFERRED.

1 Cor. 4. 6. these things I have in figure t. to myself

TRANSFIGURED.

The history of Christ's transfiguration *is recorded by St. Matthew, Mark, and Luke. All three agree that this* transfiguration *was celebrated upon a mountain, which most interpreters think to be mount Tabor. Matthew,* chap. 17. 1. *says, but six days;* Luke, 9. 28. *mentions eight days after the promise our Saviour made, that* some of them should not taste of death, till they saw the Son of man coming in his kingdom. *Some think it probable, that St. Luke counted inclusively, reckoning the day of the promise, (taking the* Son of man's coming in his kingdom, *to mean his* transfiguration,) *and the day of the execution: whereas St. Matthew had regard only to the six intermediate days.*

It is thought that this transfiguration *happened in the night; and from thence proceeded the sleep, with which the apostles were oppressed. Moreover, St. Luke observes, that the* next day they came down from the mountain, *Luke* 9. 37. *therefore they had passed the preceding night there. The fathers say, that the design of this* transfiguration *was, to fulfil the promise which Christ had made some days before, that he would let some of his disciples see a glimpse of his glory before their death; and to fortify them against the scandal of the cross, and of the death he was to suffer, by giving them this convincing proof that he was the* Messiah. *It is observed, that the condition in which Jesus Christ appeared among men, humble, poor, despised, was a true and continual* transfiguration; *whereas the* transfiguration *itself, in which he shewed himself in the real splendour of his glory, was his true and natural condition.*

As to the appearing of Moses and Elias, it is asked how the apostles could know them? To which it is answered, that our Lord Jesus Christ might call them by their names, or that he might tell them afterwards, that they were those two great men; or they knew them by immediate revelation. It is observed in this apparition, that the law represented by Moses, and the prophets represented by Elias, give testimony to our Saviour.

Mat. 17. 2. and he was t. before them, Mark 9. 2.

TRANSFORMED.

Rom. 12. 2. but be ye t. by renewing of your mind
2 Cor. 11. 14. for Satan is t. into an angel of light
15. it is no great thing if his ministers also be t.

TRANSFORMING.

2 Cor. 11. 13. t. themselves into apostles of Christ

TRANSGRESS.

Num. 14. 41. wherefore now do ye t. the commandment of the Lord? not prosper, 2 Chron. 24. 20.
1 Sam. 2. 24. ye make the Lord's people to t.
Neh. 1. 8. if ye t. I will scatter you abroad
13. 27. shall we hearken to you to t. against God
Psal. 17. 3. I am purposed my mouth shall not t.
25. 3. let them be ashamed who t. without cause
Prov. 28. 21. for a piece of bread that man will t.
Jer. 2. 20. burst bands, and thou saidst I will not t.
Ezek. 20. 38. I will purge out them that t.
Amos 4. 4. come to Beth-el and t. bring your tithes
Mat. 15. 2. why do thy disciples t. the tradition?
3. why do ye also t. the commandment of God?
Rom. 2. 27. who by circumcision dost t. the law

TRANSGRESSED.

Deut. 26. 13. I have not t. thy commandments

Josh. 7. 11. Israel hath sinned, and they have also *t.* my covenant I commanded them, 15.
23. 16. when ye have *t.* covenant of Lord your G.
1 *Sam.* 14. 33. ye have *t.* roll a stone unto me
15. 24. I have *t.* the commandment of the Lord
1 *Kings* 8. 50. wherein they have *t.* against thee
1 *Chron.* 2. 7. Achar, who *t.* in the thing accursed
5. 25. they *t.* against the God of their fathers
10. † 13. Saul died for his transgression which he *t.*
2 *Chron.* 12. 2. because they *t.* against the Lord
26. 16. Uzziah *t.* against the Lord his God
28. 19. and Ahaz *t.* sore against the Lord
36. 14. the priests and the people *t.* very much
Ezra 10. 10. ye have *t.* and taken strange wives
13. we are many that have *t.* in this thing
Isa. 24. 5. because they have *t.* the laws
43. 27. and thy teachers have *t.* against me
66. 24. shall look on men's carcases that have *t.*
Jer. 2. 8. the pastors *t.* against me and prophets
29. why will ye plead? ye all have *t.* against me
3. 13. only acknowledge that thou hast *t.*
33. 8. I will pardon iniquities whereby they *t.*
34. 18. I will give the men that *t.* my covenant
Lam. 3. 42. we have *t.* and have rebelled
Ezek. 2. 3. they and their fathers have *t.* against me
18. 31. cast away your transgressions whereby ye *t.*
Dan. 9. 11. yea, all Israel have *t.* thy law
Hos. 7. 13. destruction to them, because they have *t.*
Zeph. 3. 11. not ashamed for doings wherein thou *t.*
Luke 15. 29. nor *t.* I at any time thy commandm.
See COVENANTS.

TRANSGRESSEST.
Esth. 3. 3. why *t.* thou the king's commandment?

TRANSGRESSETH.
Prov. 16. 10. his mouth *t.* not in judgment
Hab. 2. 5. because he *t.* by wine, he is a proud man
1 *John* 3. 4. whoso committeth sin, *t.* the law
2 *John* 9. whoso *t.* and abideth not in doctrine

TRANSGRESSING.
Deut. 17. 2. any that wrought wickedness in *t.* coven.
Isa. 59. 13. in *t.* and lying against the Lord

TRANSGRESSION.
Exod. 34. 7. forgiving *t.* and sin, *Num.* 14. 18.
Josh. 22. 22. or if it be in *t.* against the Lord
1 *Sam.* 24. 11. that there is no *t.* in my hand
1 *Chr.* 9. 1. who were carried to Babylon for their *t.*
10. 13. so Saul died for his *t.* he committed
2 *Chron.* 29. 19. vessels which Ahaz cast away in *t.*
Ezra 9. 4. because of *t.* of those carried away
10. 6. for he mourned because of their *t.*
Job 7. 21. and why dost thou not pardon my *t.*
8. 4. and he have cast them away for their *t.*
13. 23. make me to know my *t.* and my sin
14. 17. my *t.* is sealed up in a bag, thou sewest
33. 9. I am clean without *t.* I am innocent
34. 6. my wound is incurable without *t.*
Psal. 19. 13. I shall be innocent from the great *t.*
32. 1. blessed is he whose *t.* is forgiven, whose sin
36. 1. the *t.* of the wicked saith within my heart
59. 3. they lie in wait for my soul, not for my *t.*
89. 32. then will I visit their *t.* with a rod
107. 17. fools because of their *t.* are afflicted
Prov. 12. 13. the wicked is snared by *t.* of his lips
17. 9. he that covereth a *t.* seeketh love
19. he loveth *t.* that loveth strife
19. 11. and it is his glory to pass over a *t.*
28. 2. for the *t.* of a land many are the princes
24. whoso robbeth father, and saith, it is no *t.*
29. 6. in the *t.* of an evil man there is a snare
16. when the wicked are multiplied, *t.* increaseth
22. and a furious man aboundeth in *t.*
Isa. 24. 20. the *t.* thereof shall be heavy on it
53. 8. for the *t.* of my people was he stricken
57. 4. are ye not children of *t.* a seed of falsehood?
58. 1. cry aloud, and shew my people their *t.*
59. 20. and to them that turn from *t.* in Jacob
Ezek. 33. 12. shall not deliver him in the day of his *t.*
Dan. 8. 12. against the daily sacrifice by reason of *t.*
13. concerning sacrifice, and the *t.* of desolation
9. 24. seventy weeks are determined to finish the *t.*
Amos 4. 4. at Gilgal multiply *t.* bring your tithes
Mic. 1. 5. for the *t.* of Jacob is all this, and for the sins of Israel; what is the *t.* of Jacob?
3. 8. I am full of power to declare to Jacob his *t.*
6. 7. shall I give my first-born for my *t.* and sin?
7. 18. that passeth by the *t.* of the remnant of his
Acts 1. 25. ministry from which Judas by *t.* fell
Rom. 4. 15. for where no law is, there is no *t.*
5. 14. had not sinned after similitude of Adam's *t.*
1 *Tim.* 2. 14. the woman being deceived was in the *t.*
Heb. 2. 2. every *t.* received just recompence of rew.
1 *John* 3. 4. for sin is the *t.* of the law

TRANSGRESSIONS.
Exod. 23. 21. for he will not pardon your *t.* for my
Lev. 16. 16. shall make atonement because of their *t.*
21. Aaron shall confess over the goat all their *t.*
Josh. 24. 19. he will not forgive your *t.* nor sins
1 *Kings* 8. 50. forgive thy people all their *t.*
Job 31. 33. if I covered my *t.* as Adam, by hiding
35. 6. if thy *t.* be multiplied, what dost thou to him?
36. 9. then he sheweth them their work and *t.*
Psal. 5. 10. cast them out in multitude of their *t.*
25. 7. remember not the sins of my youth, nor my *t.*
32. 5. I said I will confess my *t.* unto the Lord
39. 8. deliver me from all my *t.* and make me not
51. 1. have mercy upon me, blot out all my *t.*
3. for I acknowledge my *t.* my sin is before me
65. 3. as for our *t.* thou shalt purge them away
103. 12. so far hath he removed our *t.* from us
Isa. 43. 25. I, even I, am he that blotteth out thy *t.*
44. 22. I have blotted out as a thick cloud thy *t.*
50. 1. and for your *t.* is your mother put away
53. 5. but he was wounded for our *t.* he was bruised
59. 12. our *t.* are multiplied before thee, and our sins testify against us, for our *t.* are with us
Jer. 5. 6. shall be torn because their *t.* are many
Lam. 1. 5. for the multitude of her *t.* gone into
14. the yoke of my *t.* is bound by his hand
22. do to them, as hast done to me for all my *t.*
Ezek. 14. 11. nor be polluted any more with their *t.*
18. 22. all his *t.* they shall not be mentioned
28. because he turneth away from all his *t.*
Ezek. 18. 30. repent, and turn yoursel. from your *t.*
31. cast away all your *t.* whereby ye transgressed
21. 24. in that your *t.* are discovered that your sins
33. 10. if our *t.* be upon us, and we pine away
37. 23. nor defile themselves any more with *t.*
39. 24. according to their *t.* have I done to them
Amos 1. 3. for three *t.* of Damascus, and for four
6. for three *t.* of Gaza ‖ 9. Tyrus ‖ 11. Edom
13. for three *t.* of Ammon ‖ 2. 1 Moab ‖ 4 Judah
2. 6. Israel ‖ 3. 14. I will visit the *t.* of Israel
5. 12. I know your manifold *t.* and your sins
Mic. 1. 13. for the *t.* of Israel were found in thee
Gal. 3. 19. the law was added because of *t.* till see
Heb. 9. 15. for the redemption of the *t.* that were

TRANSGRESSOR.
Prov. 21. 18. the *t.* shall be ransom for the upright
22. 12. he overthroweth the words of the *t.*
Isa. 48. 8. thou wast called a *t.* from the womb
Gal. 2. 18. if I build again, I make myself a *t.*
Jam. 2. 11. yet if thou kill, thou art become a *t.*

TRANSGRESSORS.
Psal. 37. 38. but the *t.* shall be destroyed together
51. 13. then will I teach *t.* thy ways, and sinners
59. 5. be not merciful to any wicked *t.*
Prov. 2. 22. and the *t.* shall be rooted out of it
11. 3. but the perverseness of *t.* shall destroy them
6. but *t.* shall be taken in their own naughtiness
13. 2. but the soul of the *t.* shall eat violence
15. giveth favour, but the way of *t.* is hard
23. 28. and she increaseth the *t.* among men
26. 10. the great God rewardeth the fool and the *t.*
Isa. 1. 28. the destruction of *t.* shall be together
46. 8. remember, bring it again to mind, O ye *t.*
53. 12. and he was numbered with the *t.* and he bare the sin of many, and made intercession for the *t.*
Dan. 8. 23. when the *t.* are come to the full, a king
Hos. 14. 9. but the *t.* shall fall therein, just walk
Mark 15. 28. he was numbered with *t.* *Luke* 22. 37.
Jam. 2. 9. ye are convinced of the law as *t.*

TRANSLATE.
2 *Sam.* 3. 10. to *t.* the kingdom from house of Saul

TRANSLATED.
Col. 1. 13. *t.* us into the kingdom of his dear Son
Heb. 11. 5. Enoch was *t.* that he should not see death

TRANSLATION.
Heb. 11. 5. before his *t.* he had this testimony

TRANSPARENT.
Rev. 21. 21. street of city was as it were *t.* glass

TRANSPORTATION.
Ezra 1. † 11. these did Sheshbazzar bring of the *t.*
4. † 1. the sons of the *t.* builded the temple
6. † 16. the sons of the *t.* kept the dedication

TRAP, S.
Josh. 23. 13. but they shall be *t.* and snares to you
Job 18. 10. and a *t.* is laid for him in the way
Ps. 69. 22. have been for welfare, let it become a *t.*
Jer. 5. 26. they lay wait, set a *t.* they catch men
Rom. 11. 9. let their table be made a snare, a *t.*

TRAVAIL.
Gen. 38. 27. in the time of her *t.* behold, twins
Psal. 48. 6. fear and pain took hold upon them as of a woman in *t.* *Jer.* 6. 24. | 13. 21. | 22. 23. | 49. 24. | 50. 43. *Mic.* 4. 9, 10.
Isa. 23. 4. I *t.* not ‖ 53. 11. see the *t.* of his soul
54. 1. sing, thou that didst not *t.* with child
Jer. 4. 31. I have heard a voice as of a woman in *t.*
30. 6. see whether a man doth *t.* why every man with his hands on his loins as of a woman in *t.*
John 16. 21. a woman when she is in *t.* hath sorrow
Gal. 4. 19. my children, of whom I *t.* in birth
1 *Thess.* 5. 3. destruction cometh, as *t.* on a woman

TRAVAILED.
Gen. 35. 16. Rachel *t.* ‖ 38. 28. Tamar *t.*
1 *Sam.* 4. 19. Phinehas' wife bowed herself, and *t.*
Isa. 66. 7. before she *t.* she brought forth
8. as soon as Zion *t.* she brought forth children

TRAVAILEST.
Gal. 4. 27. break forth and cry, thou that *t.* not

TRAVAILETH.
Psal. 7. 14. behold, he *t.* with iniquity, conceived
Isa. 13. 8. they shall be in pain as a woman that *t.*
21. 3. as the pangs of a woman that *t.*
Jer. 31. 8. and with them her that *t.* with child
Mic. 5. 3. till she who *t.* hath brought forth
Rom. 8. 22. the whole creation *t.* in pain until now

TRAVAILING.
Isa. 42. 14. now will I cry like a *t.* woman
Hos. 13. 13. the sorrows of a *t.* woman shall come
Rev. 12. 2. a woman cried, *t.* in birth and pained

TRAVEL.
Exod. 18. 8. Moses told Jethro, the *t.* by the way
Num. 20. 14. thou knowest the *t.* that hath befallen
Eccl. 1. 13. this sore *t.* hath God given to men
2. 23. for all his days are sorrows, his *t.* is grief
26. but to the sinner he giveth *t.* to gather
3. 10. I have seen the *t.* God hath given to men
4. 4. again I considered all *t.* and every work
6. than both the hands full with *t.* and vexation
8. this is also vanity, yea, it is a sore *t.*
5. 14. but those riches perish by evil *t.*
Lam. 3. 5. he hath compassed me with gall and *t.*
Acts 19. 29. Gaius, Paul's companion in *t.*
2 *Cor.* 8. 19. was chosen of churches to *t.* with us
1 *Thess.* 2. 9. for ye remember our labour and *t.*
2 *Thess.* 3. 8. but wrought with *t.* night and day

TRAVELLED.
Acts 11. 19. *t.* as far as Phenice and Cyprus

TRAVELLER.
2 *Sam.* 12. 4. there came a *t.* to the rich man
Job 31. 32. but I opened my doors to the *t.*

TRAVELLERS.
Judg. 5. 6. and the *t.* walked through by-ways

TRAVELLETH.
Josh. 15. 20. wicked man *t.* with pain all his days
Prov. 6. 11. poverty come as one that *t.* 24. 34.

TRAVELLING.
Isa. 21. 13. in Arabia lodge, O ye *t.* companies
63. 1. who is this *t.* in the greatn. of his strength?
Mat. 25. 14. the kingdom of heaven is as a man *t.*

TRAVERSING.
Jer. 2. 23. thou art a swift dromedary *t.* her ways

TREACHEROUS.
Isa. 21. 2. *t.* dealer dealeth treacherously, 24. 16.
Jer. 3. 7. turned not, and her *t.* sister Judah saw it
8. yet her *t.* sister Judah feared not, but played
10. her *t.* sister Judah hath not turned to me
11. Israel hath justified herself more than *t.* Judah
9. 2. for they be an assembly of *t.* men
Zeph. 3. 4. her prophets are light and *t.* persons

TREACHEROUSLY.
Judg. 9. 23. men of Shechem dealt *t.* with Abimelech
1 *Sam.* 14. † 33. ye have dealt *t.* roll a great stone
Isa. 33. 1. thou dealest *t.* they dealt not *t.* with thee
48. 8. for I knew that thou wouldest deal very *t.*
Jer. 3. 20. as a wife *t.* departeth from her husband
5. 11. the house of Judah hath dealt *t.* *Mal.* 2. 11.
12. 1. why are all they happy that deal very *t.*?
6. even they have dealt *t.* with thee
Lam. 1. 2. all her friends have dealt *t.* with her
Hos. 5. 7. they have dealt *t.* against the Lord
6. 7. there have they dealt *t.* against me
Mal. 2. 10. why do we deal *t.* every man against
14. thy wife against whom thou hast dealt *t.*
15. let none deal *t.* against the wife of his youth
16. take heed to your spirit, that ye deal not *t.*

TREACHERY.
2 *Kings* 9. 23. Joram said, there is *t.* O Ahaziah

TREAD.
Deut. 11. 24. whereon the soles of your feet *t.*
25. the dread of you on all the land that ye *t.*
33. 29. thou shalt *t.* upon their high places
1 *Sam.* 5. 5. none *t.* on the threshold of Dagon
Job 24. 11. *t.* their wine-presses, and suffer thirst
40. 12. and *t.* down the wicked in their place
Psal. 7. 5. let him *t.* down my life on the earth
44. 5. through thy name will we *t.* them under
60. 12. he shall *t.* down our enemies, 108. 13.
91. 13. thou shalt *t.* upon the lion and adder
Isa. 1. 12. who hath required this, to *t.* my courts?
10. 6. to *t.* them down, like the mire of the streets
14. 25. and upon my mountains *t.* him under foot
16. 10. treaders shall *t.* out no wine in presses
26. 6. the foot shall *t.* it down, feet of the poor
63. 3. for I will *t.* them in mine anger, 6.
Jer. 25. 30. a shout, as they that *t.* the grapes
48. 33. wine to fail, none shall *t.* with shouting
50. † 26. *t.* her as heaps, and destroy her utterly
Ezek. 26. 11. with hoofs of his horses shall he *t.*
34. 18. but ye must *t.* the residue with your feet
Dan. 7. 23. the fourth beast shall *t.* it down
Hos. 10. 11. Ephraim loveth to *t.* out the corn
Mic. 1. 3. the Lord will *t.* on the high places
5. 5. when the Assyrian shall *t.* in our palaces
6. 15. thou shalt *t.* olives, but not anoint thee
Nah. 3. 14. *t.* the mortar, make strong brick-kiln
Zech. 10. 5. as mighty men which *t.* their enemies
Mal. 4. 3. and ye shall *t.* down the wicked
Luke 10. 19. I will give you power to *t.* on scorpions
Rom. 16. † 20. God shall *t.* Satan under your feet
Rev. 11. 2. the holy city shall they *t.* under foot

TREADER, S.
Isa. 16. 10. the *t.* shall tread out no wine in presses
Amos 9. 13. the *t.* of grapes shall overtake the sower

TREADETH.
Deut. 25. 4. thou shalt not muzzle the ox when he *t.* out the corn, 1 *Cor.* 9. 9. 1 *Tim.* 5. 18.
Job 9. 8. which *t.* upon the waves of the sea
Prov. 27. † 7. full soul *t.* under foot an honey comb
Isa. 18. † 2. a nation that meteth out and *t.* down
41. 25. he shall come as the potter *t.* clay
63. 2. thy garments like him that *t.* in the wine-fat
Amos 4. 13. he that *t.* on the high places of the earth
Mic. 5. 6. and when he *t.* within our borders
8. if he go through, he both *t.* down and teareth
Rev. 19. 15. he *t.* the wine-press of the wrath of God

TREADING.
2 *Chr.* 22. † 7. the *t.* down of Ahaziah was of God
Neh. 13. 15. I saw some *t.* wine-presses on sabbath
Isa. 7. 25. it shall be for the *t.* of lesser cattle
22. 5. it is a day of trouble and of *t.* down
42. † 22. they are for a *t.* and none saith, restore
Amos 5. 11. forasmuch as your *t.* is on the poor

TREASON.
1 *Kings* 16. 20. the rest of acts of Zimri and his *t.*
2 *Kings* 11. 14. Athaliah cried *t.* *t.* 2 *Chr.* 23. 13.

TREASURE,
In Hebrew, Ozer. *The word* treasure, *among the Hebrews, signifies any thing collected together, provisions, magazines. So they say, a* treasure *of corn, of wine, of oil, of honey*, Jer. 41. 8. *So also* treasures *of gold, silver, brass*, Ezek. 28. 4. Dan. 11. 43. *Snow, winds, hail, rain, waters, are in the* treasuries *of God*, Job 38. 22. Psal 135. 7. *This denotes that God hath them as much at his disposal as any man hath that which he hath laid up in his stores. The wise men opened their* treasures, *that is, their packets or bundles, to offer presents to our Saviour*, Mat. 2. 11.

Lay up *treasures* in heaven, *Mat.* 6. 20. *Lay out your wealth upon the poor members of Christ, for* he that hath pity upon the poor, lendeth unto the Lord, and he will pay him again, *Prov.* 19. 17. *Or, let heavenly and spiritual things, such as the light of God's countenance, the graces of his Spirit, and those things which accompany salvation, be of greater account with you than all worldly things; make them the* treasure *on which ye set your hearts. The steward of Joseph's house acquainted his brethren, when they found their money returned in their sacks, that* God had given them *treasure* in their sacks; *by his power and providence secretly putting it there*, Gen. 43. 23. *Treasures* of wickedness *stand for all ill-got riches*, Prov. 10. 2. *Treasures* of wickedness *will bring no man profit.*

Treasure *is often used to express any thing whatever in great abundance; as in* Col. 2. 3. In Jesus Christ are hid all the *treasures* of wisdom and knowledge. *St. Paul says*, Rom. 2. 5. Thou *treasurest* up wrath against the day of wrath: *that is, Thou provokest more and more the wrath of God against thee; by heaping up sins, thou heapest up the judgment of God upon thyself:*

as men add to their treasure *of wealth, so dost thou add to thy* treasure *of punishment. It is put for the knowledge of the gospel, and the ministry thereof.* 2 Cor. 4. 7. We have this *treasure* in earthen vessels. The good *treasure* of the heart, *is a holy frame of heart, together with that stock and plenty of holy thoughts and affections that are there,* Mat. 12. 35. *The Lord tells the children of Israel,* Exod. 19. 5. If ye will obey my voice indeed, and keep my covenant, then ye shall be a peculiar *treasure* unto me. *Ye shall be highly prized and loved, and carefully kept by me, as men's* treasures *generally are.*

Gen. 43. 23. God hath given you *t.* in your sacks
Exod. 19. 5. ye shall be a peculiar *t.* to me, *Ps.* 135. 4.
Deut. 28. 12. the Lord shall open to thee his good *t.*
1 *Chron.* 29. 8. gave them to the *t.* of house of Lord
Ezra 2. 69. gave after their ability to *t.* of work
Neh. 7. 70. the Tirshatha gave to *t.* 1000 drams
7. 71. the fathers gave to the *t.* of the work
Psal. 17. 14. whose belly thou fillest with hid *t.*
135. 4. Lord hath chosen Israel for his peculiar *t.*
Prov. 15. 6. in house of the righteous is much *t.*
16. a little, than great *t.* and trouble therewith
21. 20. there is a *t.* to be desired, and oil in dwell.
Eccl. 2. 8. I gathered the peculiar *t.* of kings
Isa. 33. 6. the fear of the Lord is his *t.*
Ezek. 22. 25. have taken the *t.* and precious things
Hos. 13. 15. he shall spoil *t.* of all pleasant vessels
Mal. 3. † 17. be mine, when I make up my special *t.*
Mat. 6. 21. for where your *t.* is, there, *Luke* 12. 34.
12. 35. a good man out of the good *t.* of his heart,
an evil man out of the evil *t.* *Luke* 6. 45.
13. 44. the kingdom of heaven is like to a *t.* hid
52. who bringeth out of his *t.* things new and old
19. 21. go and sell that thou hast, and thou shalt
have *t.* in heaven, *Mark* 10. 21. *Luke* 18. 22.
Luke 12. 21. so is he that layeth up *t.* for himself
33. provide a *t.* in the heavens, which faileth not
Acts 8. 27. an eunuch, who had charge of all her *t.*
2 *Cor.* 4. 7. we have this *t.* in earthen vessels, that
Jam. 5. 3. ye have heaped *t.* for the last days

TREASURE-*cities.*

Exod. 1. 11. and they built for Pharaoh *t.-cities*

TREASURE-*house.*

Ezra 5. 17. let search be made in the king's *t.-house*
7. 20. bestow it out of the king's *t.-house*
Neh. 10. 38. the Levites bring the tithe into *t.-house*
Dan. 1. 2. brought vessels into *t.-house* of his god

TREASURED.

Isa. 23. 18. Tyre, it shall not be *t.* nor laid up

TREASURER.

Ezra 1. 8. Cyrus brought forth the vessels by the *t.*
Isa. 22. 15. get thee unto this *t.* even unto Shebna

TREASURERS.

Ezra 7. 21. I Artaxerxes make a decree to all *t.*
Neh. 13. 13. and I made *t.* over the treasuries
Dan. 3. 2. Nebuchadnezzar gathered the *t.* 3.

TREASURES.

Deut. 32. 34. is not this sealed up among my *t.*
33. 19. they shall suck of *t.* hid in the sand
1 *Kings* 7. 51. he put dedicated things among the *t.*
14. 26. Shishak took away the *t.* of the house
15. 18. Asa took gold left in the *t.* 2 *Chr.* 16. 2.
2 *Kings* 12. 18. Jehoash took gold found in *t.* 14. 14.
16. 8. Ahaz took gold that was found in the *t.*
18. 15. Hezekiah gave him silver found in the *t.*
20. 13. Hezekiah shewed them silver and gold and
all that was found in his *t.* 15. *Isa.* 39. 2, 4.
24. 13. Nebuchadnezzar carried out thence all the
t. of the house of the Lord, and the *t.* of the
king's house, 2 *Chron.* 36. 18.
1 *Chron.* 26. 20. Ahijah was over *t.* of the house
22. Joel || 24. Shebuel was ruler of the *t.*
26. Shelomith and his brethren were over the *t.*
27. 25. and over the king's *t.* was Azmaveth
2 *Chr.* 8. 15. king's commandment concerning the *t.*
Neh. 12. 44. some were appointed for the *t.*
Job 3. 21. which dig for it more than for hid *t.*
38. 22. hast thou entered into the *t.* of the snow?
or hast thou seen the *t.* of the hail?
Prov. 2. 4. if thou searchest for her as for hid *t.*
8. 21. I will fill the *t.* of those that love me
10. 2. *t.* of wickedness profit nothing
21. 6. the getting of *t.* by a lying tongue is vanity
Isa. 2. 7. neither is there any end of their *t.*
10. 13. for he saith, I have robbed their *t.*
30. 6. they will carry their *t.* on bunches of camels
45. 3. and I will give thee the *t.* of darkness
Jer. 10. 13. he bringeth wind out of his *t.* 51. 16.
15. 13. thy *t.* I will give to the spoil, 17. 3. | 20. 5.
41. 8. slay us not, for we have *t.* in the field
48. 7. because thou hast trusted in thy *t.*
49. 4. backsliding daughter, that trusted in her *t.*
50. 37. a sword is on her *t.* they shall be robbed
51. 13. that dwellest on many waters abundant in *t.*
Ezek. 28. 4. hast gotten silver and gold into thy *t.*
Dan. 11. 43. he shall have power over the *t.* of gold
Mic. 6. 10. are there yet the *t.* of wickedness in house?
Mat. 2. 11. and when they had opened their *t.*
6. 19. lay not up for yourselves *t.* on earth
20. but lay up for yourselves *t.* in heaven
Col. 2. 3. in whom are hid all the *t.* of wisdom
Heb. 11. 26. greater riches than the *t.* in Egypt

TREASUREST.

Rom. 2. 5. *t.* up wrath against the day of wrath

TREASURY.

Josh. 6. 19. gold and silver shall come into *t.* 24.
Jer. 38. 11. went into the house under the *t.*
Mat. 27. 6. it is not lawful to put them into the *t.*
Mark 12. 41. Jesus sat over-against the *t.* and be-
held how the people cast money into the *t.*
Luke 21. 1. Jesus saw rich men casting gifts into *t.*
John 8. 20. these words spake Jesus in the *t.*

TREASURIES.

1 *Chron.* 9. 26. these Levites were over the *t.*
28. 11. David gave Solomon pattern of the *t.* 12.
2 *Chron.* 32. 27. Hezekiah made *t.* for silver
Neh. 13. 12. Judah brought the tithe unto the *t.*
13. and I made treasurers over the *t.*
Esth. 3. 9. I will pay, to bring it into the king's *t.*
Esth. 4. 7. that Haman promised to pay to king's *t.*
Psal. 135. 7. he bringeth the wind out of his *t.*

TREATISE.

Acts 1. 1. the former *t.* have I made, O Theophilus

TREE.

Both good and wicked men are compared to trees. The godly, *says the Psalmist*, shall be like a tree planted by the rivers of water, that bringeth forth his fruit in his season, *Psal.* 1. 3. *His soul shall be plentifully fed from heaven with the never-failing influences of grace and consolation, whereby he shall be made fruitful in every good word and work. John the Baptist says,* Mat. 3. 10. The axe is laid to the root of the trees; therefore every tree which bringeth not forth good fruit, is hewn down and cast into the fire; that is, "*The judgment of God hangs over your heads, ready to seize upon you, if ye be either barren, or do not bring forth good fruit: Vengeance is as nigh unto you, as the tree is to falling, to whose root the axe is already applied.*" *Our Saviour speaks to the same purpose in the latter part of his sermon upon the mount,* Mat. 7. 19. *The godly are called* trees of righteousness, *that is, persons bringing forth the fruits of righteousness,* Isa. 61. 3. *The wicked are called* trees whose fruit withereth; *whose lives are full of all wickedness,* Jude 12. *The king of Assyria's army are called* trees. *Isa.* 10. 19. The rest of the trees of his forest shall be few, that a child may write them; *The remainder of his mighty host shall be so few, that the meanest accomptant may be their muster-master.*

There is mention made in Scripture of several kinds of trees *and plants, but there is hardly any thing less certain, than the Hebrew names of them. When the Jews had planted a vine or fruit-tree, they were not allowed to eat of the fruit for the first three years. They offered to God that of the fourth year, and afterwards might use whatever those trees produced at their discretion,* Lev. 19. 23. *See* FRUIT.

Tree of life, *Gen.* 2. 9. *so called, because it was a natural means of preserving man's life, and freeing him from all infirmities, diseases, and decays, during his abode on earth; and also a sacramental pledge of his continuance in that life, upon condition of his perfect obedience. But this* tree of life *was to him a* tree of death, *because of his infidelity and disobedience.*

The tree of knowledge of good and evil, *Gen.* 2. 9, 17. *so called, because by the eating of it man came to know experimentally the vast difference between good and evil; and the greatness of that good he formerly enjoyed, by the loss of it; and the greatness of that evil he had brought upon himself, by the feeling of it. And this was another sacramental pledge, which sealed death spiritual, temporal, and eternal, in case of disobedience.*

Jesus Christ is called the tree of life, *Rev.* 2. 7. | 22. 2. *He will be to all his members as a* tree *of eternal life, satisfying and refreshing them with fellowship and communion with himself.*

Gen. 1. 29. I have given you every *t.* for meat
2. 9. God made every *t.* to grow, the *t.* of life also,
and the *t.* of knowledge of good and evil
16. of every *t.* of the garden thou mayest eat
2. 17. but of the *t.* of knowledge shalt not eat, 3. 3.
3. 6. when the woman saw that the *t.* was good
11. and he said, hast thou eaten of the *t.*? 17.
12. the woman gave me of the *t.* and I did eat
22. and now lest he take also of the *t.* of life
24. cherubims, to keep the way of the *t.* of life
18. 4. wash your feet, rest yourselves under the *t.*
8. he stood by them under the *t.* and they did eat
21. † 33. and Abraham planted a *t.* in Beer-sheba
40. 19. in three days Pharaoh shall hang thee on a *t.*
Exod. 9. 25. the hail brake every *t.* of the field
10. 5. the locusts shall eat every *t.* which groweth
15. 25. he cried, and the Lord shewed him a *t.*
Lev. 27. 30. tithe of land, seed or fruit of *t.* is Lord's
Deut. 19. 5. fetcheth a stroke to cut down the *t.*
20. 19. for the *t.* of the field is man's life
21. 22. and if thou hang him on a *t.*
23. his body shall not remain all night on the *t.*
22. 6. if a bird's nest chance in the way in any *t.*
Josh. 8. 29. take the king of Ai down from the *t.*
1 *Sam.* 22. 6. now Saul abode under a *t.* in Ramah
31. 13. they buried them under a *t.* at Jabesh
2 *Kings* 3. 19. and shall fell every good *t.*
Esth. 2. 23. they were both hanged on a *t.*
5. † 14. let a *t.* be made of fifty cubits high
7. † 9. behold also the *t.* fifty cubits high
Job 14. 7. there is hope of a *t.* if it be cut down
19. 10. and mine hope hath he removed like a *t.*
24. 20. and wickedness shall be broken as a *t.*
Psal. 1. 3. like a *t.* planted by the rivers of water
Prov. 3. 18. she is a *t.* of life to them lay hold on her
11. 30. the fruit of the righteous is a *t.* of life
13. 12. but when the desire cometh, it is a *t.* of life
15. 4. a wholesome tongue is a *t.* of life
Eccl. 11. 3. if the *t.* fall toward the south or the
north; where the *t.* falleth, there shall it be
Isa. 30. † 17. ye be left as a *t.* bereft of branches
40. 20. he chooseth a *t.* that will not rot
44. 19. shall I fall down to the stock of a *t.*?
56. 3. neither let the eunuch say, I am a dry *t.*
65. 22. as days of a *t.* are the days of my people
66. 17. that purify themselves behind one *t.*
Jer. 10. 3. for one cutteth a *t.* out of the forest
11. 19. let us destroy the *t.* with the fruit
17. 8. he shall be as a *t.* planted by the waters
Ezek. 15. 2. what is the vine-*t.* more than any *t.*
17. 24. brought down the high *t.* exalted the low *t.*
dried up the green *t.* made dry *t.* to flourish
21. 10. it contemneth rod of my son, as every *t.*
31. 8. nor any *t.* in the garden of God was like him
34. 27. *t.* of the field shall yield her fruit
36. 30. I will multiply the fruit of the *t.*
Dan. 4. 10. and behold a *t.* || 11. the *t.* grew 20.
14. he cried, and said thus, hew down the *t.* 23.
Joel 2. 22. fear not for the *t.* beareth her fruit
Mat. 3. 10. every *t.* that bringeth not forth good
fruit is cast into the fire, 7. 19. *Luke* 3. 9.
7. 17. every good *t.* bringeth forth good fruit, but
a corrupt *t.* bringeth forth evil fruit, *Luke* 6. 43.
18. a good *t.* cannot bring forth evil fruit
12. 33. either make the *t.* good and his fruit good
for the *t.* is known by his fruit, *Luke* 6. 44
13. 32. mustard seed becometh a *t.* *Luke* 13. 19.
Luke 17. 6. ye might say to the sycamine *t.*
Acts 5. 30. Jesus whom ye slew and hanged on a *t.*
10. 39. Jesus, whom they slew, and hanged on a *t.*
13. 29. they took him down from the *t.* and laid
Gal. 3. 13. cursed is every one that hangeth on a *t.*
1 *Pet.* 2. 24. bare our sins in his own body on the *t.*
Rev. 2. 7. to him will I give to eat of the *t.* of life
7. 1. that the wind should not blow on any *t.*
9. 4. they should not hurt any green thing, nor *t.*
22. 2. in the midst was there the *t.* of life
14. that they may have right to the *t.* of life
See GREEN.

TREES.

Gen. 3. 8. hid themselves amongst the *t.* of garden
23. 17. all the *t.* were made sure to Abraham
Exod. 10. 15. the locusts did eat the fruit of the *t.*
Lev. 19. 23. ye shall have planted all manner of *t.*
23. 40. ye shall take the boughs of goodly *t.*
26. 4. and the *t.* of the field shall yield their fruit
20. neither shall the *t.* of the land yield fruits
Num. 24. 6. as *t.* of lign-aloes which the Lord hath
planted, and as cedar *t.* beside the waters
Deut. 16. 21. thou shalt not plant a grove of any *t.*
20. 19. thou shalt not destroy the *t.* thereof by axe
20. the *t.* thou knowest not to be *t.* for meat
28. 42. all thy *t.* and fruit shall the locust consume
Josh. 10. 26. Joshua hanged them on five *t.*
27. and they took them down off the *t.*
Judg. 9. 8. the *t.* went forth to anoint a king
9. and go to be promoted over the *t.* 11. 13.
10. the *t.* said to the fig-tree, reign over us
12. *t.* said to the vine || 14. *t.* said to the bramble
48. Abimelech cut down a bough from the *t.*
1 *Kings* 4. 33. he spake of *t.* from cedar in Lebanon
2 *Kings* 3. 25. and they felled all the good *t.*
1 *Chron.* 16. 33. then shall the *t.* of the wood sing
at the presence of the Lord, *Psal.* 96. 12.
Neh. 10. 35. to bring the first-fruits of all *t.* 37.
Job 40. 21. he lieth under the shady *t.* 22.
Psal. 74. 5. as he had lifted up axes on thick *t.*
78. 47. he destroyed their sycamore *t.* with frost
104. 16. the *t.* of the Lord are full of sap
105. 33. and brake the *t.* of their coasts
148. 9. fruitful *t.* and cedars praise the Lord
Eccl. 2. 5. I planted *t.* of all kinds of fruit
Cant. 2. 3. as the apple-tree among the *t.* of the wood
4. 14. with all *t.* of frankincense, myrrh, aloes
Isa. 7. 2. his heart was moved as the *t.* of the wood
† 19. they shall rest upon all commendable *t.*
10. 19. the rest of the *t.* of his forest shall be few
44. 14. which he strengtheneth among the *t.*
55. 12. all the *t.* of the fields shall clap their hands
61. 3. they might be called *t.* of righteousness
Jer. 6. 6. Lord said, hew down *t.* and cast a mount
7. 20. my fury shall be poured out upon the *t.*
Ezek. 17. 24. all the *t.* of the field shall know
20. 28. they saw all the thick *t.* and offered
31. 5. his height was exalted above all the *t.*
9. so that all the *t.* of Eden envied him
47. 7. many *t.* on the one side and on the other
12. by the rivers shall grow all *t.* for meat
Joel 1. 12. all the *t.* of the field are withered
19. the flame hath burnt all the *t.* of the field
Mat. 3. 10. the axe is laid to the root of *t.* *Luke* 3. 9.
21. 8. others cut down branches from the *t.* and
strewed them in the way, *Mark* 11. 8.
Mark 8. 24. he said, I see men as *t.* walking
Luke 21. 29. behold the fig-tree and all the *t.*
Jude 12. they are *t.* whose fruit withereth
Rev. 7. 3. hurt not the *t.* till we have sealed
8. 7. and the third part of the *t.* was burnt up
See PALM.

TREMBLE.

Deut. 2. 25. the nations shall *t.* because of thee
20. 3. fear not and do not *t.* because of them
Ezra 10. 3. of those that *t.* at the commandment
Job 9. 6. shaketh the earth, the pillars thereof *t.*
26. 11. the pillars of heaven *t.* and are astonished
Psal. 60. 2. thou hast made the earth to *t.*
99. 1. the Lord reigneth, let the people *t.*
114. 7. *t.* thou earth at the presence of the Lord
Eccl. 12. 3. when the keepers of the house shall *t.*
Isa. 5. 25. the hills did *t.* their carcases were torn
14. 16. is this the man that made the earth to *t.*
32. 11. *t.* ye women that are at ease, be troubled
64. 2. that the nations may *t.* at thy presence
66. 5. hear word of Lord, ye that *t.* at his word
Jer. 5. 22. will ye not *t.* at my presence who placed
10. 10. at his wrath the earth shall *t.* and nations
33. 9. and they shall *t.* for all the goodness
51. 29. the land of Babylon shall *t.* and sorrow
Ezek. 26. 16. they shall *t.* at every moment, 32. 10.
18. now shall the isles *t.* in the day of thy fall
Dan. 6. 26. that men *t.* before the God of Daniel
Hos. 11. 10. then the children shall *t.* from the west
11. they shall *t.* as a bird out of Egypt, as a dove
Joel 2. 1. let all the inhabitants of the land *t.*
10. the earth shall quake, the heavens shall *t.*
Amos 8. 8. shall not the land *t.* for this and mourn?
Hab. 3. 7. the captains of the land of Midian did *t.*
Jam. 2. 19. the devils also believe and *t.*

TREMBLED.

Gen. 27. 33. Isaac *t.* very exceedingly, and he said
Exod. 19. 16. the people that was in the camp *t.*
Judg. 5. 4. the earth *t.* and the heavens dropped,
2 *Sam.* 22. 8. *Psal.* 18. 7. | 77. 18. | 97. 4.
1 *Sam.* 4. 13. Eli's heart *t.* for the ark of God
14. 15. the spoilers *t.* || 16. 4. the elders of town *t.*
28. 5. Saul was afraid, and his heart greatly *t.*
Ezra 9. 4. were assembled to me every one that *t.*
Jer. 4. 24. and lo the mountains *t.* *Hab.* 3. 10.
8. 16. whole land *t.* at the sound of the neighing
of his strong ones
Dan. 5. 19. all people and nations *t.* before him

Hab. 3. 16. when I heard my belly t. and I t. in myself that I might rest in the day of trouble
Mark 16. 8. fled from the sepulchre, for they t.
Acts 7. 32. then Moses t. ‖ 24. 25. Felix t.

TREMBLETH.

Job 37. 1. at this also my heart t. and is moved
Psal. 104. 32. he looketh on earth and it t.
119. 120. my flesh t. for fear of thee and am afraid
Isa. 66. 2. I will look to him that t. at my word

TREMBLING.

Gen. 27. † 33. Isaac trembled with a great t.
Exod. 15. 15. t. take hold on the mighty men of Mo.
Deut. 28. 65. the Lord shall give thee a t. heart
1 Sam. 13. 7. and all the people followed him t.
14. 15. in the host there was a very great t.
Ezra 10. 9. all people sat t. because of this matter
Job 4. 14. fear came upon me and t. which made
21. 6. I am afraid and t. taketh hold on my flesh
Psal. 2. 11. serve Lord with fear and rejoice with t.
55. 5. fearfulness and t. are come upon me
Isa. 51. 17. hast drunken the dregs of the cup of t.
22. I have taken out of thy hand the cup of t.
Jer. 30. 5. we have heard a voice of t. of fear
Ezek. 12. 18. son of man, drink thy water with t.
26. 16. they shall clothe themselves with t.
Dan. 10. 11. when he had spoken this, I stood t.
Hos. 13. 1. when Ephraim spake t. he exalted
Zech. 12. 2. I will make Jerusalem a cup of t.
Mark 5. 33. the woman fearing and t. Luke 8. 47.
Acts 9. 6. Saul t. said, L. what wilt have me to do?
16. 29. gaoler came t. and fell down before Paul
1 Cor. 2. 3. I was with you in fear and much t.
2 Cor. 7. 15. how with fear and t. ye received him
Eph. 6. 5. servants, be obedient with fear and t.
Phil. 2. 12. work out your salvation with fear and t.

TRENCH.

1 Sam. 17. 20. David came to the t. and shouted
26. 5. Saul lay sleeping within the t. 7.
1 Kings 18. 32. Elijah made a t. about the altar
35. and he filled the t. also with water, 38.
Luke 19. 43. thy enemies shall cast a t. about thee

TRESPASS.

Gen. 31. 36. what is my t. that thou hast pursued
50. 17. we pray thee forgive the t. of thy servants
Exod. 22. 9. for all manner of t. whether for ox
Lev. 5. 15. he shall bring for his t. to the Lord a ram
26. 40. if they shall confess their t. trespassed
Num. 5. 6. when any do a t. against the Lord
7. he shall recompense his t. with the principal
8. if he have no kinsman to recompense the t.
27. if she have done t. against her husband
1 Sam. 25. 28. forgive the t. of thine handmaid
1 Chr. 21. 3. why will he be a cause of t. to Israel?
2 Chron. 24. 18. wrath came on Judah for their t.
28. 13. ye intend to add more to our sin and t.
33. 19. Manasseh's prayer and t. are written
Ezra 9. 2. the rulers have been chief in this t.
6. and our t. is grown up unto the heavens
7. we have been in a great t. to this day, 13.
10. 10. taken strange wives, to increase t. of Israel
19. they offered a ram of the flock for their t.
Ezek. 17. 20. I will plead with him there for his t.
18. 24. in his t. he hath trespassed, he shall die
Dan. 9. 7. because of their t. they trespassed

TRESPASSES.

Ezra 9. 15. behold, we are before thee in our t.
Psal. 68. 21. such a one as goeth on still in his t.
Ezek. 39. 26. they have borne their shame and t.
Mat. 6. 14. for if ye forgive men their t.
15. but if ye forgive not men their t. neither will your Father forgive your t. 18. 35.
Mark 11. 25 your Father may forgive you your t.
26. neither will your Father forgive your t.
2 Cor. 5. 19. not imputing their t. unto them
Eph. 2. 1. you quickened who were dead in t. and sins
Col. 2. 13. he quickened, having forgiven you all t.
See COMMIT, COMMITTED, OFFERING.

TRESPASS-*money*.

2 Kings 12. 16. the t.-money was not brought

TRESPASS.

1 Kings 8. 31. if any man t. against his neighbour
2 Chron. 19. 10. warn that they t. not against Lord
28. 22. Ahaz did t. yet more against the Lord
Mat. 18. 15. if brother t. tell him his fault
Luke 17. 3. if thy brother t. against thee, rebuke him
4. if he t. against thee seven times in a day

TRESPASSED.

Lev. 5. 19. he hath certainly t. against the Lord
26. 40. if they confess their trespass which they t.
Num. 5. 7. recompensed to him against whom he t.
Deut. 32. 51. because ye t. against me among Israel
2 Chron. 26. 18. go out of sanctuary, for thou hast t.
29. 6. for our fathers have t. and done evil in eyes
30. 7. be not like fathers who t. against Lord God
33. 23. but Amon t. more and more
Ezra 10. 2. we have t. against our G. strange wives
Ezek. 17. 20. his trespass that he t. against me
39. 23. because they t. against me, 26.
Dan. 9. 7. their trespass that they t. against thee
Hos. 8. 1. because they have t. against my law

TRESPASSING.

Lev. 6. 7. for any thing that he hath done in t.
Ezek. 14. 13. the land sinneth against me by t.

TRIAL.

Job 9. 23. he will laugh at the t. of the innocent
Ezek. 21. 13. because it is a t. what if the sword
2 Cor. 8. 2. how that in a great t. of affliction
Heb. 11. 36. others had t. of cruel mockings
1 Pet. 1. 7. that the t. of your faith might be found
4. 12. think it not strange concerning the fiery t.

TRIBE.

Jacob having twelve sons, who were the heads of so many great families, which altogether formed a great nation; every one of these families was called a tribe. *But Jacob on his death-bed adopted Ephraim and Manasseh, the sons of Joseph, and would have them also to constitute two* tribes *of Israel,* Gen. 48. 5. *Instead of twelve* tribes, *there were now thirteen, that of Joseph being divided into two. However, in the distribution of lands to the people made by Joshua, by the command of God, they counted but twelves* tribes, *and made but twelve lots. For the* tribe *of Levi, which was appointed to the service of the tabernacle of the Lord, had no share in the distribution of the land, but only some cities to dwell in, and the first-fruits, tithes, and oblations of the people, which was all their subsistence,* Num. 35. 2. Josh. 13. 7, 8, 14, 33.

The twelve tribes, *while they were in the desert, encamped round about the tabernacle of the covenant, every one according to its order. To the east were those of Judah, Zebulun, and Issachar. To the west were Ephraim, Manasseh, and Benjamin. To the south, Reuben, Simeon, and Gad. And to the north were Dan, Asher, and Naphtali. The Levites were distributed round about the tabernacle, nearer the holy place than the other* tribes, *Num.* 2. 2, 3, &c.

In the marches of the army of Israel, the twelve tribes *were divided into four great bodies, each composed of three* tribes. *The first body, which was the front of the army, was made up of the* tribes *of Judah, Issachar, and Zebulun. The second was composed of Reuben, Simeon, and Gad. Between the second and third body of troops, came the Levites and the priests, with the ark of the Lord, the curtain, the planks, the pillars, and all the other furniture of the tabernacle. The third body of the army was composed of the* tribes *of Ephraim, Manasseh, and Benjamin. The fourth and last, which brought up the rear, was made up of the* tribes *of Dan, Asher, and Naphtali,* Num. 10. 5, 6, 14, &c. *We have an account of the division of the land of Canaan among the twelve* tribes *in the book of Joshua.*

The twelve tribes *continued united under one head, making but one state, one people, and one monarchy, till after the death of Solomon. Then ten of the* tribes *of Israel revolted from the house of David, and received for their king Jeroboam, the son of Nebat; and only the* tribes *of Judah and Benjamin continued under the government of Rehoboam,* 1 Kings 12. 16, 20. *This separation may be looked upon as the chief cause of those great calamities that afterwards happened to those two kingdoms, and to the whole Hebrew nation. For it was the cause of the alteration and change of the old religion, and of the ancient worship of their forefathers. Jeroboam, the son of Nebat, substituted the worship of golden calves instead of the worship of the Lord; which was the occasion of the ten* tribes *forsaking the temple of the Lord,* 1 Kings 12. 26, 27, &c. *This schism likewise caused an irreconcileable hatred between the ten* tribes *and those of Judah and Benjamin, and created a great number of wars and disputes between them. The Lord being provoked, delivered them up to their enemies, Tiglath-pileser first carried away captives of the* tribes *of Reuben, Gad, Naphtali, and the half* tribe *of Manasseh, which were beyond Jordan, and carried them beyond the Euphrates,* 2 Kings 15. 29. 1 Chron. 5. 26.

Some years after, Shalmaneser, king of Assyria, took the city of Samaria, destroyed it, took away the rest of the inhabitants of Israel, carried them beyond the Euphrates, and sent other inhabitants into the country to cultivate and possess it, 2 Kings 17. 6, 24. | 18. 10, 11. *Thus ended the kingdom of the ten* tribes *of Israel. It has been a great question among the Fathers and Interpreters, whether these ten* tribes *still continued in their settlement beyond the Euphrates, or whether they returned again into their own country. The greatest part are of opinion, that they never did return. Others, on the contrary, think they did return; but at the same time acknowledge, that this return is not clearly made out by history, because it was performed by insensible degrees: and was not so complete and entire, but that a great number of Israelites still remained beyond the Euphrates.*

As to the tribes *of Judah and Benjamin, who remained under the government of the kings of the family of David, they continued a much longer time in their own country: but at last, after they had fulfilled the measure of their iniquity, God delivered them into the hands of their enemies. Nebuchadnezzar took the city of Jerusalem, entirely ruined it, and burnt the temple, and took away all the inhabitants of Judah and Benjamin to Babylon, and to the other provinces of his empire. This captivity continued for seventy years, as the prophet had foretold them,* Jer. 25. 11, 12. | 29. 10. *The return from this captivity is plainly assigned in* 2 Chron. 36. 20, 21, 22, 23. *and in the books of Ezra and Nehemiah.*

Chronologers fix the end of the kingdom of the ten tribes *in the year of the world* 3283, *before Christ* 717. *And the captivity of Judah and Benjamin in the year of the world* 3416, *before Christ* 584.

Num. 1. 4. and with you there shall be a man of every t. head of house of his fathers, 13. 2. | 34. 18.
4. 18. cut ye not off the t. of the Kohathites
18. 2. the t. of thy father bring thou with thee
31. 4. of every t. a thousand sent to war, 5, 6.
36. 5. the t. of the sons of Joseph hath said well
6. they shall marry only to the family of the t. 8.
9. neither shall the inheritance remove from one t. to another t. but keep to his own inheritance
Deut. 1. 23. I took one of a t. Josh. 3. 12. | 4. 2, 4.
29. 18. family or t. whose heart turneth away
Josh. 7. 14. t. which the Lord taketh shall come
18. 4. give out from you three men for each t.
Judg. 18. 19. or that thou be a priest to a t.
21. 3. there should be one t. lacking in Israel, 6.
1 Kings 11. 13. but will give one t. to thy son, 32. 36.
1 Chr. 6. 61. who were left of the family of that t.
Ezek. 47. 23. in what t. the stranger sojourneth
Heb. 7. 13. for he pertaineth to another t.
14. of Juda; of which t. Moses spake nothing
See REUBEN, SIMEON, *and the rest.*

TRIBES.

Exod. 28. 21. his name according to the 12 t. 39. 14.
Num. 24. 2. abiding in tents according to their t.
33. 54. according to t. of your fathers shall inherit
34. 13. to give to the nine t. Josh. 13. 7. | 14. 2.
15. the two t. and the half have received their inheritance on this side Jordan, Josh. 14. 3.
Deut. 1. 13. take ye wise men, known among your t.
12. 5. the place which the Lord shall choose out of all your t. to put his name there, 14
18. 5. thy God hath chosen him out of all thy t.
Josh. 7. 14. ye shall be brought according to your t.
1 Sam. 10. 19. present yoursel. before Ld. by your t.
1 Kings 11. 31. and I will give ten t. to thee
18. 31. twelve stones according to number of the t.
Psal. 105. 37. was not one feeble among their t.
122. 4. whither the t. go up, the t. of the Lord
Isa. 19. 13. they that are the stay of t. thereof
49. 6. be my servant to raise up the t. of Jacob
63. 17. return for the t. of thine inheritance
Ezek. 45. 8. give to Israel according to their t.
Hab. 3. 9. according to the oaths of the t.
Mat. 24. 30. then shall all the t. of the earth mourn
Acts 26. 7. unto which promise our 12 t. hope to come
Jam. 1. 1. to the twelve t. which are scattered
Rev. 7. 4. were sealed 144,000 of all the t.
See ISRAEL.

TRIBULATION.

Deut. 4. 30. when thou art in t. if thou turn to Ld.
Judg. 10. 14. let them deliver you in the time of t.
1 Sam. 26. 24. let him deliver me out of all t.
Mat. 13. 21. when t. ariseth, he is offended
24. 21. then shall be great t. such as was not
29. immediately after the t. Mark 13. 24.
John 16. 33. in the world ye shall have t. but be
Acts 14. 22. we must thro' much t. enter kingdom
Rom. 2. 9. t. and angu. on every soul that doth evil
5. 3. knowing that t. worketh patience
8. 35. shall t. separate us from the love of Christ?
12. 12. rejoicing in hope, patient in t.
2 Cor. 1. 4. who comforteth us in all our t.
7. 4. I am exceeding joyful in all our t.
1 Thess. 3. 4. we told you that we should suffer t.
2 Thess. 1. 6. recompense t. to them that trouble you
Rev. 1. 9. John who am your companion in t.
2. 9. I know thy works, and t. and poverty
10. behold, ye shall have t. ten days.
22. I will cast them into great t. except repent
7. 14. these are they which came out of great t.

TRIBULATIONS.

1 Sam. 10. 19. himself saved you out of all your t.
Rom. 5. 3. not only so, but we glory in t. also
Eph. 3. 13. I desire that ye faint not at my t.
2 Thess. 1. 4. for your faith in all t. that ye endure

TRIBUTARY.

Isa. 31. † 8. and his young men shall be t.
Lam. 1. 1. she that was great, how is she become t.!

TRIBUTARIES.

Deut. 20. 11. the people found therein shall be t.
Judg. 1. 30. the Canaanites became t. 33, 35.

TRIBUTE,

In Greek φορος' *in Hebrew,* Mass; *which is derived from the verb* Masas, *to* melt, *or* liquefy. *The Hebrews acknowledged none for sovereign over them but God alone: whence Josephus calls their government a* Theocracy, *or divine government. They acknowledged the sovereign dominion of God by a* tribute, *or capitation, of half a shekel a head, which every Israelite paid him yearly,* Exod. 30. 13. *Our Saviour, in* Mat. 17. 25. *thus reasons with Peter;* What thinkest thou, Simon? Of whom do the kings of the earth take custom or *tribute?* of their own children, or of strangers? *Meaning, that as he was the Son of God, he ought to be exempt from the capitation.*

Tribute *is a sum of money paid to princes, or rulers, in token of the duty and subjection which subjects owe unto them, and as a recompence for their care and protection, and in order to support them in their authority and dignity. After the Jews were conquered by the Romans, they still continued very tenacious of their liberty, and gloried much in the right they had to it; as appears from* John 8. 33. *They made it a question, whether it was agreeable to the law of God, to pay taxes to a pagan conqueror, and therefore they ask our Saviour,* Mat. 22. 17. What thinkest thou? Is it lawful to give *tribute* unto Cesar or not? *Christ in his answer plainly shews them, that religion did not exempt them from their civil duties, and obedience to princes in things wherein they have a power to command;* Render unto Cesar the things that are Cesar's. *And the apostle Paul recommends and inculcates to the faithful Christians submission and obedience to princes, and a conscientious discharge of their duty in paying them their* tributes. *Rom.* 13. 7. Render to all their dues; *tribute* to whom *tribute* is due, custom to whom custom.

Solomon, at the beginning of his reign, compelled the Canaanites, who were left in the country, to pay him tribute, *and to perform the drudgery of the public works he had undertaken: and as to the children of Israel, he would not suffer them to be employed therein, but made them his soldiers, his ministers, his chief officers, to command his armies, his chariots, and his horsemen,* 1 Kings 9. 21, 22, 23. 2 Chron. 8. 9. *Yet, however, towards the end of his reign, he imposed a* tribute *upon them, and made them work at the public buildings; which much alienated their minds from him, and sowed the seeds of that discontent which afterwards appeared in an open revolt, by the rebellion of Jeroboam the son of Nebat,* 1 Kings 5. 13, 14. | 9. 15. | 11. 27. *Jeroboam was at first obliged to take shelter in Egypt; but afterwards the defection became general, by the total revolt of the ten tribes. It was upon account of these taxes and levies, that the Israelites said to Rehoboam the son of Solomon,* Thy father made our yoke grievous; now therefore make thou the grievou.

service of thy father, and his heavy yoke which he put upon us, lighter, and we will serve thee, *1 Kings* 12. 4.
Gen. 49. 15. Issachar became a servant to *t.*
Num. 31. 28. levy a *t.* to the Lord of men of war
37. the Lord's *t.* of the sheep was 675
38. beeves, Lord's *t.* 72. || 39. asses, Lord's *t.* 61.
40. the persons 16,000, the Lord's *t.* 32 persons
Deut. 16. 10. with a *t.* of a free-will offering
Josh. 16. 10. Canaanites serve under *t.* 17. 13.
2 *Sam.* 20. 24. and Adoram was over the *t.* 1 *Kings* 4. 6. | 12. 18. 2 *Chron.* 10. 18.
1 *Kings* 9. 21. upon these did Solomon levy a *t.*
2 *Kings* 17. † 3. Hoshea became servant and gave *t.*
23. 33. Pharaoh-necho put the land to a *t.*
2 *Chron.* 8. 8. them did Solomon make to pay *t.*
17. 11. some of the Philistines brought *t.* silver
Ezra 4. 13. then will they not pay *t.* and custom
20. and toll, *t.* and custom was paid to them
6. 8. of the *t.* expenses be given to these men
7. 24. not lawful to impose *t.* on the Levites
Neh. 5. 4. we have borrowed money for king's *t.*
Prov. 12. 24. but the slothful shall be under *t.*
Isa. 31. † 8. and his young men shall be for *t.*
Mat. 17. 24. they that received *t.* money came to Peter and said, doth not your master pay *t.*?
25. of whom do the kings of the earth take *t.*?
22. 17. what thinkest thou? is it lawful to give *t.* to Cesar, or no? *Mark* 12. 14. *Luke* 20. 22.
19. shew me the *t.* money; they brought a penny
Luke 23. 2. and forbidding to give *t.* to Cesar
Rom. 13. 6. for this cause pay ye *t.* also
7. render therefore *t.* to whom *t.* is due, custom

TRICKLETH.
Lam. 3. 49. mine eye *t.* down, and ceaseth not

TRIE, *See* TRY.

TRIMMED.
2 *Sam.* 19. 24. Mephibosheth had not *t.* his beard
Mat. 25. 7. all those virgins arose and *t.* their lamps

TRIMMEST.
Jer. 2. 33. why *t.* thou thy way to seek love?

TRIPPING.
Isa. 3. † 16. walking and *t.* nicely as they go

TRIUMPH.
2 *Sam.* 1. 20. lest daughters of the uncircumcised *t.*
Psal. 25. 2. let not mine enemies *t.* over me
41. 11. because mine enemy doth not *t.* over me
60. 8. Philistia, *t.* thou because of me
92. 4. I will *t.* in the works of thy hands
94. 3. Lord, how long shall the wicked *t.*?
106. 47. gather us to give thanks and *t.* in thy praise
108. 9. Moab is my wash-pot, over Philistia will I *t.*
2 *Cor.* 2. 14. which always causeth us to *t.* in Christ

TRIUMPH.
Psal. 47. 1. shout unto God with the voice of *t.*

TRIUMPHED.
Exod. 15. 1. for he hath *t.* gloriously, 21.

TRIUMPHING, *Substantive.*
Job 20. 5. that the *t.* of the wicked is short

TRIUMPHING.
Col. 2. 15. made a show of them, *t.* over them in it

TRODE.
Judg. 9. 27. they *t.* the grapes and cursed Abimelech
20. 43. Israel *t.* the Benjamites down with ease
2 *Kings* 7. 17. the people *t.* upon him in the gate, 20.
9. 33. Jehu *t.* Jezebel under foot
14. 9. a beast *t.* down the thistle, 2 *Chron.* 25. 18.
Luke 12. 1. insomuch that they *t.* one on another

TRODDEN.
Deut. 1. 36. to Caleb will I give the land that he hath *t.* upon, because he followed Lord, *Josh.* 14. 9.
Judg. 5. 21. O my soul, thou hast *t.* down strength
Job 22. 15. the old way which wicked men have *t.*
28. 8. the lion's whelps have not *t.* it, nor fierce lion
Psal. 119. 118. thou hast *t.* down all that err
Isa. 5. 5. and the vineyard shall be *t.* down
14. 19. art cast out, as a carcase *t.* under feet
18. 2. go to a nation meted out and *t.* down, 7.
25. 10. Moab shall be *t.* under him as straw is *t.*
28. 3. the drunkards of Ephraim shall be *t.* under
18. scourge pass through then ye shall be *t.* down
63. 3. I have *t.* the wine-press alone, of people none
18. our adversaries have *t.* down thy sanctuary
Jer. 12. 10. they have *t.* my portion under foot
Lam. 1. 15. the Lord hath *t.* under foot the mighty men, he hath *t.* the virgin the daughter of Judah
Ezek. 16. † 6. when I saw thee *t.* under foot
27. † 6. they have made hatches of ivory well *t.*
34. 19. my flock eat what ye have *t.* under feet
Dan. 8. 13. give the sanctuary and host to be *t.*
Mic. 7. 10. now shall she be *t.* as mire of the streets
Mat. 5. 13. salt unsavoury to be *t.* under foot of men
Luke 8. 5. some fell by the way-side and was *t.* down
21. 24. Jerusalem shall be *t.* down of the Gentiles
Heb. 10. 29. who hath *t.* under foot the Son of God
Rev. 14. 20. the wine-press was *t.* without the city

TROOP.
Gen. 30. 11. a *t.* cometh; † she called his name a *t.*
49. 19. Gad, a *t.* shall overcome him, he at last
1 *Sam.* 30. 8. saying, shall I pursue after this *t.*?
2 *Sam.* 2. 25. children of Benjamin became one *t.*
3. 22. behold, Joab came from pursuing a *t.*
22. 30. by thee have I run thro' a *t.* *Psal.* 18. 29.
23. 11. the Philistines were gathered into a *t.*
13. the *t.* pitched in the valley of Rephaim
Isa. 65. 11. are they that prepare a table for that *t.*
Jer. 18. 22. when shalt bring a *t.* suddenly on them
Hos. 7. 1. the *t.* of robbers spoileth without
Amos 9. 6. he hath founded his *t.* in the earth

TROOPS.
Exod. 38. † 8. looking-glasses of women assemb. by *t.*
Job 6. 19. *t.* of Tema looked, companies of Sheba
19. 12. his *t.* come together and raise their way
Jer. 5. 7. they assembled by *t.* in the harlots' houses
Hos. 6. 9. and as *t.* of robbers wait for a man
Mic. 5. 1. gather thyself in *t.* O daughter of *t.*
Hab. 3. 16. he will invade them with his *t.*

TROUBLE.
1 *Chron.* 22. 14. in my *t.* I prepared for house of L.
2 *Chron.* 15. 4. when they in *t.* did turn and sought the Lord, he was found of them, *Neh.* 9. 27.
Neh. 9. 32. let not all the *t.* seem little before thee
Job 3. 26. neither was I quiet, yet *t.* came
5. 6. neither doth *t.* spring out of the ground
7. yet man is born to *t.* as the sparks fly upward
14. 1. man is of a few days and full of *t.*
15. 24. *t.* and anguish shall make him afraid
27. 9. will God hear his cry when *t.* cometh?
30. 25. did not I weep for him that was in *t.*?
34. 29. he giveth quietness, who can make *t.*?
38. 23. which I reserved against the time of *t.*
Psal. 9. 9. Lord will be a refuge in times of *t.*
13. O Lord, consider my *t.* which I suffer
10. 1. why hidest thou thyself in times of *t.*?
22. 11. be not far from me, for *t.* is near
27. 5. for in time of *t.* he shall hide me
31. 7. I will be glad, thou hast considered my *t.*
9. have mercy upon me, O Lord, for I am in *t.*
32. 7. thou shalt preserve me from *t.* and compass
37. 39. he is their strength in the time of *t.*
41. 1. the Lord will deliver him in time of *t.*
46. 1. God is our refuge, a present help in *t.*
54. 7. for he hath delivered me out of *t.*
60. 11. give us help from *t.* vain is the help of man
66. 14. my mouth hath spoken when I was in *t.*
69. 17. hide not thy face from me for I am in *t.*
73. 5. they are not in *t.* as other men
78. 33. and their years did he consume in *t.*
49. he cast upon them indignation and *t.*
81. 7. thou calledst in *t.* and I delivered thee
91. 15. I will be with him in *t.* I will deliver him
102. 2. hide not thy face from me when I am in *t.*
107. 6. they cried to the Lord in their *t.* 13. 19.
26. their soul is melted because of *t.*
28. then they cry unto the Lord in their *t.*
116. 3. the pains of hell gat hold on me, I found *t.*
119. 143. *t.* and anguish have taken hold on me
138. 7. tho' I walk in midst of *t.* thou wilt revive me
142. 2. I poured out my complaint before him, I shewed before him my *t.*
143. 11. O Lord, bring my soul out of *t.*
Prov. 11. 8. righteous is delivered out of *t.* 12. 13.
15. 6. but in the revenues of the wicked is *t.*
16. little, than great treasure and *t.* therewith
25. 19. confidence in an unfaithful man in *t.* is like
Isa. 1. 14. your new-moons, they are a *t.* to me
8. 22. they shall look to the earth and behold *t.*
17. 14. and behold, at evening tide *t.* and before
26. 16. L. in *t.* have they visited thee, poured out
30. 6. into the land of *t.* they will carry riches
33. 2. be thou our salvation also in time of *t.*
46. 7. yet can he not save him out of his *t.*
65. 23. they shall not bring forth for *t.* are seed
Jer. 2. 27. in time of *t.* they will say, save us
28. if they can save thee in the time of thy *t.*
8. 15. we looked for health, and behold *t.*
11. 12. but shall not save them at all in time of *t.*
14. in the time that they cry to me for their *t.*
14. 8. the Saviour of Israel in time of *t.*
19. we looked for time of healing, and behold *t.*
30. 7. that day is great, it is the time of Jacob's *t.*
Lam. 1. 21. all mine enemies have heard of my *t.*
Dan. 12. 1. and there shall be a time of *t.* such as
1 *Cor.* 7. 28. such shall have *t.* in the flesh
2 *Cor.* 1. 4. be able to comfort them which are in *t.*
8. we would not have you ignorant of our *t.*
2 *Tim.* 2. 9. wherein I suffer *t.* as an evil-doer
See DAY.

TROUBLES.
Deut. 31. 17. many evils and *t.* shall befal them, 21.
Job 5. 19. he shall deliver thee in six *t.* yea in seven
Psal. 25. 17. the *t.* of mine heart are enlarged
22. redeem Israel, O God, out of all his *t.*
34. 6. the Lord saved him out of all his *t.*
71. 20. thou which hast shewed me sore *t.* shall
88. 3. incline thine ear, for my soul is full of *t.*
Prov. 21. 23. his tongue, he keepeth his soul from *t.*
Isa. 65. 16. because former *t.* are forgotten and hid
Mark 13. 8. and there shall be famine and *t.*

TROUBLE.
Josh. 6. 18. lest ye *t.* the camp of Israel
7. 25. Joshua said, the Lord shall *t.* thee this day
Judg. 11. 35. thou art one of them that *t.* me
2 *Chr.* 32. 18. they cried in Jews' language to *t.* them
Psal. 2. † 5. and *t.* them in his sore displeasure
3. 1. Lord, how are they increased that *t.* me?
13. 4. those that *t.* me, rejoice when I am moved
Ezek. 32. 13. neither shall the foot of man *t.* them any more, nor the hoofs of beasts *t.* them
Dan. 4. 19. let not the interpretation *t.* thee
5. 10. O king, let not thy thoughts *t.* thee
11. 44. but tidings out of the north shall *t.* him
Mat. 26. 10. why *t.* ye the woman? *Mark* 14. 6.
Luke 7. 6. Lord, *t.* not thyself, for I am not worthy
11. 7. he shall say, *t.* me not, the door is shut
Acts 15. 19. that we *t.* not Gentiles turned to God
16. 20. these men do exceedingly *t.* our city
20. 10. *t.* not yourselves, for his life is in him
Gal. 1. 7. but there be some that *t.* you and pervert
5. 12. I would they were cut off who *t.* you
6. 17. from henceforth let no man *t.* me, for I bear
2 *Thess.* 1. 6. tribulation to them that *t.* you
Heb. 12. 15. lest any root of bitterness *t.* you

TROUBLED.
Gen. 34. 30. ye have *t.* me, to make me to stink
41. 8. in the morning Pharaoh's spirit was *t.*
45. 3. his brethren were *t.* at his presence
Exod. 14. 24. the Lord *t.* the host of Egyptians
Josh. 7. 25. Joshua said, why hast thou *t.* us?
1 *Sam.* 14. 29. Jonath. said, my father hath *t.* the land
16. 14. and an evil spirit from the Lord *t.* him
28. 21. the woman saw that Saul was sore *t.*
2 *Sam.* 4. 1. Abner dead, all the Israelites were *t.*
1 *Kings* 18. 18. I have not *t.* Israel, but thou and
2 *Kings* 6. 11. the king of Syria was sore *t.* for this
Ezra 4. 4. then the people *t.* them in building
Job 4. 5. now it toucheth thee and thou art *t.*
21. 4. if it were so, why should not my spirit be *t.*?
23. 15. therefore am I *t.* at his presence
34. 20. and the people shall be *t.* at midnight
Psal. 30. 7. thou didst hide thy face and I was *t.*
38. 6. I am *t.* || 77. 4. I am so *t.* that I cannot speak
39. † 2. I held my peace and my sorrow was *t.*
Psal. 46. 3. though the waters thereof roar and be *t.*
48. 5. for the kings were *t.* and hasted away
77. 3. I remembered God and was *t.* I complained
16. the waters were afraid, the depths also were *t.*
83. 17. let them be confounded and *t.* for ever
90. 7. consumed by anger, by thy wrath are we *t.*
104. 29. thou hidest thy face, they are *t.*
Prov. 25. 26. is as a *t.* fountain and corrupt spring
Isa. 32. 10. many days and years shall ye be *t.*
11. tremble, ye women, be *t.* ye careless ones
57. 20. but the wicked are like the *t.* sea
Jer. 31. 20. therefore my bowels are *t.* for him
Lam. 1. 20. I am in distress, my bowels are *t.* 2. 11.
Ezek. 7. 27. the hands of the people shall be *t.*
26. 18. the isles that are in the sea shall be *t.*
27. 35. their kings shall be *t.* in countenance
Dan. 2. 1. Nebuchadnezzar's spirit was *t.* 3.
4. 5. and the visions of my head *t.* me, 7. 15
19. Daniel astonished, his thoughts *t.* him
5. 6. Belshazzar's thoughts *t.* him, 9.
7. 28. as for me, my cogitations much *t.* me
Zech. 10. 2. were *t.* because there was no shepherd
Mat. 2. 3. Herod was *t.* and all Jerusalem with him
14. 26. saw him on sea, they were *t.* *Mark* 6. 50.
24. 6. see that ye be not *t.* for all these things must come to pass, *Mark* 13. 7. *John* 14. 1, 27
Luke 1. 12. Zacharias was *t.* || 29. Mary was *t.*
10. 41. Martha, thou art *t.* about many things
24. 38. why are ye *t.* and why do thoughts arise?
John 5. 4. an angel went down and *t.* the water
7. I have no man when water is *t.* to put me in
11. 33. Jesus groaned and was *t.* 12. 27. | 13. 21.
Acts 2. † 6. the multitude were *t.* in mind
15. 24. some that went from us have *t.* you
17. 8. and they *t.* the people and the rulers
2 *Cor.* 4. 8. we are *t.* on every side, 7. 5.
2 *Thess.* 1. 7. and to you that are *t.* rest with us
2. 2. that ye be not *t.* neither by spirit, by word
1 *Pet.* 3. 14. not afraid of their terror, nor be *t.*

TROUBLEDST.
Ezek. 32. 2. and thou *t.* the waters with thy feet

TROUBLER.
1 *Chr.* 2. 7. Achar, the *t.* of Israel, who transgressed

TROUBLESOME.
Job 16. † 2. I have heard *t.* comforters are ye all
20. † 22. every hand of the *t.* shall come on him

TROUBLEST.
Mark 5. 35. why *t.* thou the Master any further?

TROUBLETH.
1 *Sam.* 16. 15. an evil spirit from God *t.* thee
1 *Kings* 18. 17. Ahab said, art thou he that *t.* Israel?
Job 22. 10. therefore sudden fear *t.* thee, snares, and
23. 16. God maketh my heart soft, Almighty *t.* me
Prov. 11. 17. he that is cruel *t.* his own flesh
29. he that *t.* his own house shall inherit wind
15. 27. he that is greedy of gain *t.* his own house
Dan. 4. 9. I know that no secret *t.* thee, tell me
Luke 18. 5. because this widow *t.* me I will avenge
Gal. 5. 10. he that *t.* you shall bear his judgment

TROUBLING.
Job 3. 17. there the wicked cease from *t.* and weary
John 5. 4. who stepped in first after *t.* of the water

TROUBLOUS.
Dan. 9. 25. the wall shall be built again in *t.* times

TROUGH, S.
Gen. 24. 20. she emptied her pitcher into the *t.*
30. 38. Jacob set the rods in the watering *t.*
Exod. 2. 16. they filled the *t.* to water their flock
8. 3. the frogs shall go into thy kneading-*t.*
12. 34. their kneading-*t.* bound up in their clothes

TROW.
Luke 17. 9. doth he thank that servant? I *t.* not

TRUCE-*breakers.*
2 *Tim.* 3. 3. in the last days men shall be *t.-breakers*

TRUE.
See Signification on TRUTH.
Gen. 42. 11. we are *t.* men, 31. || 19. if ye be *t.* men
33. hereby shall I know that ye are *t.* men, 34.
Deut. 17. 4. if ye be *t.* and thing certain, 22. 20.
Josh. 2. 12. swear unto me, and give me a *t.* token
Ruth 3. 12. it is *t.* that I am thy near kinsman
2 *Sam.* 7. 28. thou art that God, and thy words be *t.*
1 *Kings* 10. 6. it was a *t.* report I heard, 2 *Chr.* 9. 5.
22. 16. tell me nothing but that which is *t.*
Neh. 9. 13. thou gavest them *t.* laws, good statutes
Psal. 19. 9. the judgments of the Lord are *t.*
119. 160. thy word is *t.* from the beginning
Prov. 14. 25. a *t.* witness delivereth souls
Jer. 42. 5. the Lord be a *t.* witness between us
Ezek. 18. 8. he that hath executed *t.* judgment
Dan. 3. 14. is it *t.* O Shadrach, do not ye serve
24. *t.* O king || 6. 12. king said, the thing is *t.*
8. 26. vision which is told is *t.* shut up vision
10. 1. a thing was revealed and the thing was *t.*
Zech. 7. 9. execute *t.* judgment and shew mercy
Mat. 22. 16. we know that thou art *t.* *Mark* 12. 14.
Luke 16. 11. will commit to your trust the *t.* riches
John 1. 9. that was the *t.* light which lighteth every
4. 23. when the *t.* worshippers shall worship Father
37. and herein is that saying *t.* one soweth
5. 31. if I witness of myself, my witness is not *t.*
32. the witness which he witnesseth of me is *t.*
6. 32. but my Father giveth you the *t.* bread
7. 18. the same is *t.* || 8. 13. thy record is not *t.*
28. he that sent me is *t.* whom ye know not, 8. 26.
8. 14. yet my record is *t.* || 16. my judgment is *t.*
17. it is written, the testimony of two men is *t.*
10. 41. all things that John spake of this man were *t.*
15. 1. I am the *t.* vine, my Father the husbandman
19. 35. he bare record, and his record is *t.* 21. 24.
Acts 12. 9. wist not that it was *t.* which was done
2 *Cor.* 1. 18. but as God is *t.* our word was not yea
6. 8. approving ourselves, as deceivers, and yet *t.*
Eph. 4. 24. new man after G. is created in *t.* holiness
Phil. 4. 3. I entreat thee also, *t.* yoke-fellow, help
8. whatsoever things are *t.* think on these
1 *Tim.* 3. 1. this is a *t.* saying, if a man desire
Tit. 1. 13. this witness is *t.* wherefore rebuke
Heb. 8. 2. *t.* tabernacle which the Lord pitched
9. 24. holy places which are the figures of the *t.*
10. 22. let us draw near with a *t.* heart in full
1 *Pet.* 5. 12. that this is the *t.* grace of God wherein

2 Pet. 2. 22. according to the *t.* proverb, the dog is
1 John 2. 8. which thing is *t.* in him and in you, because darkness past, the *t.* light now shineth
5. 20. that we may know him that is *t.* and we are in him that is *t.* even in his Son Jesus Christ
3 John 12. and we know that our record is *t.*
Rev. 3. 7. these things saith the holy, he that is *t.*
14. these things saith the faithful and *t.* witness
6. 10. they cried, how long, O Lord, holy and *t.*?
15. 3. just and *t.* are thy ways, thou king of saints
16. 7. *t.* and righteous are thy judgments, 19. 2.
19. 9. these are the *t.* sayings of God, 22. 6.
11. he that sat upon him was called Faithful and *T.*
21. 5. write, for these words are *t.* and faithful

TRUE *God.*

2 Chron. 15. 3. Israel hath been without the *t. God*
Jer. 10. 10. the Lord is the *t. God*, the living God
John 17. 3. this eternal life, to know the only *t. God*
1 Thess. 1. 9. turned from idols to serve the *t. God*
1 John 5. 20. this is the *t. God* and eternal life

TRULY.

Gen. 24. 49. and now if ye will deal *t.* 47. 29.
48. 19. *t.* his younger brother shall be greater
Num. 14. 21. as *t.* as I live, saith the Lord, 28.
Deut. 14. 22. thou shalt *t.* tithe the increase of seed
Josh. 2. 14. that we will deal *t.* and kindly with thee
24. *t.* the Lord hath delivered all the land
Judg. 9. 16. if ye have done *t.* and sincerely, 19.
1 Sam. 20. 3. *t.* there is but step between me and dea.
Job 36. 4. for *t.* my words shall not be false
Psal. 62. 1. *t.* my soul waiteth upon God, from him
73. 1. *t.* God is good to Israel, even to such as are
116. 16. *t.* I am thy servant, I am thy servant
Prov. 12. 22. they that deal *t.* are his delight
Eccl. 11. 7. *t.* the light is sweet, and pleasant thing
Jer. 3. 23. *t.* in vain is salvation hoped for from hills, *t.* in the Lord God is the salvation of Israel
10. 19. *t.* this is a grief and I must bear it
28. 9. be known that the Lord hath *t.* sent him
Ezek. 18. 9. hath kept my judgments to deal *t.*
Mic. 3. 8. but *t.* I am full of power to declare
Mat. 9. 37. the harvest *t.* is plenteous, *Luke* 10. 2.
17. 11. Elias *t.* shall first come and restore all things
27. 54. saying, *t.* this was the Son of God
Mark 14. 38. the spirit *t.* is ready, the flesh is weak
Luke 20. 21. but thou teachest the way of God *t.*
22. 22. *t.* Son of man goeth as it was determined
John 4. 18. I have no husband, in that saidst thou *t.*
17. †19. that they also might be *t.* sanctified
Acts 1. 5. for John *t.* baptized with water, ye shall
3. 22. for Moses *t.* said to the fathers, a prophet
5. 23. the prison *t.* found we shut with safety
2 Cor. 12. 12. *t.* signs of an apostle were wrought
Heb. 7. 23. and they *t.* were many priests, because
11. 15. *t.* if they had been mindful of that country
1 John 1. 3. *t.* our fellowship is with the Father

TRUMP.

1 Cor. 15. 52. at the last *t.* the dead shall be raised
1 Thess. 4. 16. Lord shall descend with the *t.* of God

TRUMPET.

See Signification on FEAST.

Exod. 19. 16. the voice of the *t.* exceeding loud
20. 18. the people heard the noise of the *t.*
Num. 10. 4. and if they blow but with one *t.*
Judg. 7. 16. and he put a *t.* in every man's hand
18. when I blow with a *t.* then blow ye also
Psal. 81. 3. blow up the *t.* in the new moon
Isa. 18. 3. and when he bloweth a *t.* hear ye
27. 13. that the great *t.* shall be blown and come
58. 1. cry aloud, lift up thy voice like a *t.*
Jer. 4. 5. blow ye the *t.* in the land, cry, gather
6. 1. blow the *t.* in Tekoah and set up a sign
51. 27. blow the *t.* among the nations, prepare
Ezek. 7. 14. they have blown the *t.* to make ready
33. 3. if he blow the *t.* and warn the people
6. but if the watchman blow not the *t.*
Hos. 5. 8. blow ye the *t.* in Ramah, cry aloud
8. 1. set the *t.* to thy mouth, he shall come
Joel 2. 1. blow the *t.* in Zion, sound alarm, 15.
Amos 3. 6. shall a *t.* be blown, and people not afraid?
Zeph. 1. 16. a day of the *t.* against fenced cities
Zech. 9. 14. and the Lord God shall blow the *t.*
Rev. 1. 10. I heard a great voice, as of a *t.* 4. 1.
8. 13. by reason of the other voices of the *t.*
9. 14. saying to the sixth angel which had the *t.*

See BLEW, SOUND, *Subst. Verb.*

TRUMPETS.

Lev. 23. 24. a memorial of blowing *t.* *Num.* 29. 1.
Num. 10. 2. make two *t.* of silver of a whole piece
8. the sons of Aaron shall blow with the *t.*
9. then ye shall blow an alarm with the *t.*
10. shall blow with *t.* over your burnt-offerings
31. 6. and with the *t.* to blow in his hand
Josh. 6. 4. the priests shall blow with the *t.*
8. priests bearing the seven *t.* of rams' horns
9. the priests that blew with the *t.* 13, 16, 20.
Judg. 7. 8. the two hundred men took *t.* 16.
18. when I blow, then blow ye the *t.* on every side
19. they blew the *t.* brake the pitchers, 20, 22.
2 Kings 9. 13. they blew with *t.* saying, Jehu is king
11. 14. and trumpeters blew with *t.* and cymbals
12. 13. were not made for house of the Lord *t.*
1 Chron. 13. 8. played with cymbals and with *t.*
15. 24. the priests did blow with *t.* before ark of God, 16. 6, 42. *2 Chr.* 5. 12. | 7. 6. | 13. 12, 14.
28. all Israel brought up the ark with *t.* and cymb.
2 Chron. 5. 13. when they lift up their voice with *t.*
29. 27. the song of the Lord began with the *t.*
Job 39. 25. the horse saith among the *t.* ha, ha
Psal. 98. 6. with *t.* make a joyful noise before Lord

See SEVEN.

TRUMPETERS.

2 Kings 11. 14. princes and *t.* stood by the king
2 Chron. 5. 13. as the *t.* and singers were as one
29. 28. the singers sang, and the *t.* sounded
Rev. 18. 22. the voice of *t.* shall be heard no more

TRUST.

1 Chron. 9. †22. whom David did ordain in their *t.*
†26. the four chief porters were in their *t.*
†31. Mattithiah had the *t.* over things in pans
Job 8. 14. and whose *t.* shall be a spider's web
15. 15. behold, he putteth no *t.* in his saints
Psal. 40. 4. blessed is he that maketh the Lord his *t.*
71. 5. O Lord God, thou art my *t.* from my youth
141. 8. in thee is my *t.* leave not my soul destitute
Prov. 22. 19. that thy *t.* may be in the Lord
28. 25. that puts his *t.* in the Lord shall be made fat
29. 25. who putteth his *t.* in the Lord shall be safe
Isa. 30. 3. the *t.* in Egypt shall be your confusion
57. 13. that putteth *t.* in me shall possess the land
Luke 16. 11. commit to your *t.* the true riches?
2 Cor. 3. 4. such *t.* have we thro' Christ to God-ward
1 Tim. 1. 11. gospel, which was committed to my *t.*
6. 20. keep that which is committed to thy *t.*

See PUT.

TRUST, *Verb.*

Ruth 2. 12. under whose wings thou art come to *t.*
2 Sam. 22. 3. in him will I *t.* *Psal.* 18. 2. | 91. 2.
31. a buckler to all that *t.* in him, *Psal.* 18. 30.
2 Kings 18. 20. now on whom dost thou *t.* that rebellest against me? *2 Chr.* 32. 10. *Isa.* 36. 5.
21. so is Pharaoh to all that *t.* in him, *Isa.* 36. 6.
22. if ye say, we *t.* in Lord our God, *Isa.* 36. 7.
30. neither let Hezekiah make you *t.* in the Lord, saying, Lord will deliver us, *Isa.* 36. 15.
Job 13. 15. though he slay me, yet will I *t.* in him
15. 31. let not him that is deceived *t.* in vanity
35. 14. judgment is before him, therefore *t.* in him
39. 11. wilt thou *t.* him because he is strong?
Psal. 20. 7. some *t.* in chariots, and some in horses
25. 2. I *t.* in thee, 31. 6. | 55. 23. | 56. 3. | 143. 8.
31. 19. thou hast wrought for them that *t.* in thee
34. 22. none that *t.* in him shall be desolate
37. 3. *t.* in the Lord, 5. | 40. 3. | 62. 8. | 115. 9, 10, 11. *Prov.* 3. 5. *Isa.* 26. 4.
40. he shall save them, because they *t.* in him
44. 6. I will not *t.* in my bow, nor shall sword save
49. 6. they that *t.* in their wealth, and boast
52. 8. I *t.* in the mercy of God for ever and ever
61. 4. I will *t.* in the covert of thy wings
62. 10. *t.* not in oppression, become not vain
64. 10. the righteous shall be glad, and *t.* in him
91. 4. and under his wings shalt thou *t.*
118. 8. it is better to *t.* in the Lord than to put, 9.
119. 42. I shall have to answer, for I *t.* in thy word
125. 1. that *t.* in the Lord shall be as mount Zion
144. 2. my fortress, my shield, and he in whom I *t.*
Prov. 31. 11. the heart of her husband doth *t.* in her
Isa. 12. 2. God my salvation, I will *t.* and not be afraid
14. 32. Zion, and the poor of his people shall *t.* in it
30. 2. and to *t.* in the shadow of Egypt
12. because ye *t.* in oppression and perverseness
31. 1. and *t.* in chariots, because they are many
42. 17. be ashamed that *t.* in graven images
50. 10. let him *t.* in the name of the Lord and stay
51. 5. wait on me, and on mine arm shall they *t.*
59. 4. they *t.* in vanity and speak lies, they conceive
Jer. 7. 4. *t.* ye not in lying words, saying, the temple
8. ye *t.* in lying words that cannot profit
14. which is called by my name, wherein ye *t.*
9. 4. take ye heed, and *t.* ye not in any brother
28. 15. makest this people to *t.* in a lie, 29. 31.
46. 25. I will punish Pharaoh and all that *t.* in him
49. 11. them alive, and let thy widows *t.* in me
Ezek. 16. 15. but thou didst *t.* in thy beauty
33. 13. if he *t.* to his own righteousness and commit
Hos. 10. 13. because thou didst *t.* in thy way
Amos 6. 1. them that *t.* in the mountain of Samaria
Mic. 7. 5. *t.* ye not in a friend, put not confidence
Nah. 1. 7. the Lord knoweth them that *t.* in him
Zeph. 3. 12. they shall *t.* in the name of the Lord
Mat. 12. 21. and in his name shall the Gentiles *t.* *Rom.* 15. 12.
Mark 10. 24. how hard for them that *t.* in riches
John 5. 45. one that accuseth Moses, in whom ye *t.*
Rom. 15. 24. for I *t.* to see you in my journey
1 Cor. 16. 7. but I *t.* to tarry a while with you
2 Cor. 1. 9. that we should not *t.* in ourselv. but in G.
10. in whom we *t.* that he will yet deliver us
13. I *t.* you shall acknowledge even to the end
5. 11. I *t.* are made manifest in your consciences
10. 7. if any man *t.* to himself, that he is Christ's
13. 6. I *t.* ye shall know we are not reprobates
Phil. 3. 4. if any thinketh he hath whereof to *t.*
1 Tim. 4. 10. because we *t.* in the living God
6. 17. that they *t.* not in uncertain riches, but in
Heb. 13. 18. for we *t.* we have a good conscience
2 John 12. but I *t.* to come unto you and speak
3 John 14. but I *t.* I shall shortly see thee and speak

TRUSTED.

Deut. 32. 37. where is their rock in whom they *t.*?
Judg. 11. 20. Sihon *t.* not Israel to pass through
20. 36. because they *t.* to the liers in wait
2 Kings 18. 5. he *t.* in the Lord God of Israel
Ps. 13. 5. but I have *t.* in thy mercy, my heart shall
22. 4. our fathers *t.* in thee; they have *t.* and thou didst deliver them, 5.
8. he *t.* on the Lord that he would deliver him
26. 1. I have *t.* also in the Lord, 28. 7. | 31. 14.
33. 21. because we have *t.* in his holy name
41. 9. mine own familiar friend in whom I *t.*
52. 7. but *t.* in the abundance of his riches
78. 22. because they *t.* not in his salvation
Isa. 47. 10. for thou hast *t.* in thy wickedness
Jer. 13. 25. because thou hast *t.* in falsehood
48. 7. for because thou hast *t.* in thy works
49. 4. O daughter that *t.* in her treasures, saying
Dan. 3. 28. G. delivereth his servants that *t.* in him
Zeph. 3. 2. she *t.* not in the Lord, she drew not near
Mat. 27. 43. he *t.* in God, let him deliver him now
Luke 11. 22. taketh all his armour wherein he *t.*
18. 9. he spake to certain which *t.* in themselves
24. 21. we *t.* it had been he that redeemed Israel
Eph. 1. 12. praise of his glory, who first *t.* in Christ
13. in whom ye also *t.* after ye heard the word
2 Tim. 1. †12. for I know whom I have *t.*
1 Pet. 3. 5. holy women who *t.* in God, adorned

TRUSTEDST.

Deut. 28. 52. thy walls come down wherein thou *t.*
Jer. 5. 17. shall impoverish thy cities wherein thou *t.*
12. 5. if in the land of peace wherein thou *t.*

TRUSTEST.

2 Kings 18. 19. thus saith the king of Assyria, what confidence is this wherein thou *t.*? *Isa.* 36. 4.
2 Kings 18. 21. *t.* on staff of bruised reed, *Isa.* 36. 6.
19. 10. let not thy God in whom thou *t.* *Isa.* 37. 10.

TRUSTETH.

Job 24. †22. he riseth up and *t.* not his own life
40. 23. he *t.* that he can draw up Jordan into his
Psal. 21. 7. for the king *t.* in the Lord thro' mercy
32. 10. that *t.* in the Lord mercy shall compass him
34. 8. Lord is good, blessed is the man that *t.* in him, 84. 12. *Prov.* 16. 20. *Jer.* 17. 7.
57. 1. be merciful unto me, for my soul *t.* in thee
86. 2. O my God, save thy servant that *t.* in thee
115. 8. so is every one that *t.* in them, 135. 18.
Prov. 11. 28. he that *t.* in his riches shall fall
28. 26. he that *t.* in his own heart is a fool
Isa. 26. 3. will keep him in peace bec. he *t.* in thee
Jer. 17. 5. cursed be the man that *t.* in man
Hab. 2. 18. the maker of his work *t.* therein
1 Tim. 5. 5. she that is a widow indeed, *t.* in God

TRUSTING.

Psal. 112. 7. his heart is fixed, *t.* in the Lord

TRUSTY.

Job 12. 20. he removeth away the speech of the *t.*

TRUTH

Is taken, (1) *For what is opposed to a falsehood, a lie, a deceit.* Prov. 12. 17. He that speaketh *truth,* showeth forth righteousness; but a false witness deceit. *And St. Paul says,* I speak the *truth* in Christ, I lie not. (2) *For fidelity, sincerity, and punctuality in keeping promises. Generally to* truth, *taken in this sense, is joined* mercy, *or* kindness, *as in* Gen. 24. 27. *Eliezer, the servant of Abraham, gives thanks to God, that* he had not left destitute his master of his mercy and his *truth: he hath showed him his* mercy *in giving him plenty of good things, and his* truth *in fulfilling and performing all his promises to him. Or, mercy and truth may express a stable, constant, and permanent mercy, or kindness; that is, "Blessed be the Lord, who has favoured my master Abraham in so constant and uniform a manner." The Psalmist in several places extols the* mercy *and* truth *of God. It is his* mercy *that prevents and promises, and it is his* truth *that executes and performs.* In Psal. 57. 10. *he says,* Thy mercy is great unto the heavens, and thy *truth* unto the clouds. *This expresses their greatness, immensity, and extent; and that all creatures partake of them.* (3) Truth *is put for the true doctrine of the gospel.* Gal. 3. 1. Who hath bewitched you, that you should not obey the *truth?* (4) Truth *is put for the substance of the types and ceremonies of the law.* John 1. 17. The law was given by Moses, but grace and *truth* came by Jesus Christ: *the fulfilling of all the types and prophecies in the law, was by and in Christ. So in* John 14. 6. I am the *truth.* "*I am the* truth *and substance of all the types and shadows of the law:" or, say others, "I am the great doctor of my church, who teach them what course to take to get to heaven."* (5) True *is put for reality, and is opposed to that which is not original and of itself.* Eph. 4. 21. John 1. 9. That was the true light: *Christ has light in himself, and from himself; he is the original fountain-light, from whence light is derived to all others.* (6) True *is opposed to hypocrisy, dissimulation, or formality.* Heb. 10. 22. Let us draw near with a *true* heart; *that is, with uprightness, integrity, and sincerity of heart.*

Gen. 24. 27. hath not left destitute master of his *t.*
32. 10. I am not worthy of the least of all the *t.*
42. 16. be proved, whether there be any *t.* in you
Exod. 18. 21. men of *t.* ‖ 34. 6. Lord abundant in *t.*
Deut. 13. 14. behold, if it be *t.* ‖ 32. 4. a God of *t.*
2 Sam. 2. 6. the Lord shew kindness and *t.* to you
15. 20. return thou, mercy and *t.* be with thee
1 Kings 17. 24. the word of the L. in thy mouth is *t.*
2 Kin. 20. 19. if peace & *t.* be in my days, *Isa.* 39. 8.
2 Chron. 18. 15. that thou say nothing but the *t.*
31. 20. Hezekiah wrought that which was *t.*
Neh. 9. †13. and thou gavest them laws of *t.*
Esth. 9. 30. sent letters with words of peace and *t.*
Psal. 15. 2. he that speaketh the *t.* in his heart
25. 10. the paths of the Lord are mercy and *t.*
31. 5. thou hast redeemed me, O Lord God of *t.*
45. 4. ride thou prosperously, because of *t.*
51. 6. thou desirest *t.* in the inward parts
57. 3. God shall send forth his mercy and his *t.*
60. 4. banner may be displayed because of the *t.*
61. 7. O prepare mercy and *t.* which may preserve
85. 10. mercy and *t.* are met together, righte. peace
11. *t.* shall spring out of the earth, and righteousn.
86. 15. thou art plenteous in mercy and *t.*
89. 14. mercy and *t.* shall go before thy face
91. 4. his *t.* shall be thy shield and buckler
96. 13. he shall judge the people with his *t.*
98. 3. he hath remembered his mercy and his *t.*
100. 5. his *t.* endureth to all generations, 117. 2.
119. 30. I have chosen the way of *t.* thy judgments
142. and thy law is the *t.* 151.
146. 6. the Lord is God who keepeth *t.* for ever
Prov. 3. 3. let not mercy and *t.* forsake thee
8. 7. for my mouth shall speak *t.* wickedness abom.
12. 17. he that speaks *t.* sheweth righteousness
19. the lip of *t.* shall be established for ever
14. 22. mercy and *t.* be to them that devise good
16. 6. by mercy and *t.* iniquity is purged, by fear
20. 28. mercy and *t.* preserve the king, his throne
22. 21. might make thee know the certainty of the words of *t.* thou mightest answer the words of *t.*
23. 23. buy the *t.* and sell it not, also wisdom
Eccl. 12. 10. what was written were words of *t.*
Isa. 25. 1. thy counsels are faithfulness and *t.*
26. 2. the nation which keepeth *t.* may enter in
42. 3. he shall bring forth judgment unto *t.*
43. 9. or let them hear, and say, it is *t.*
59. 4. nor any pleadeth for *t.* they speak lies
14. for *t.* is fallen in the street, and equity cannot
15. yea, *t.* faileth, and he that departeth from evil
Jer. 5. 1. if there be any that seeketh the *t.*
3. O Lord, are not thine eyes upon the *t.*?
7. 28. *t.* is perished and cut off from their mouth

Jer. 9. 3. they are not valiant for the t. on the earth
5. they will deceive and will not speak the t.
10. † 10. but the Lord is the God of t.
14. † 13. I will give you peace of t. in this place
33. 6. revealed to them abundance of peace and t.
Dan. 4.37. the king of heaven, all whose works are t.
7. 16. I asked him the t. of all this, 19.
8. 12. and it cast down the t. to the ground
10. 21. which is noted in the scripture of t.
11. 2. and now will I shew thee the t. behold
Hos. 4. 1. there is no t. nor mercy in the land
Mic. 7. 20. thou wilt perform the t. to Jacob
Zech. 7. † 9. saying, judge judgment of t. and shew
8. 3. Jerusalem shall be called a city of t.
16. speak ye every man the t. Eph. 4. 25. execute the judgment of t. and peace in your gates
19. therefore love the t. and peace
Mal. 2. 6. the law of t. was in his mouth
Mat.15.27. she said, t. Lord, yet dogs eat the crumbs
Mark 5. 33. the woman fearing told him all the t.
12.32. scribes said, well, Master, thou hast said the t.
John 1. 14. the only-begotten, full of grace and t.
17. but grace and t. came by Jesus Christ
5. 33. ye sent John, he bare witness unto the t.
8.32. ye shall know the t. the t. shall make you free
40. ye seek to kill me, a man that told you the t.
44. abode not in t. because there is no t. in him
45. because I tell you the t. ye believe me not
46. and if I say the t. why do ye not believe?
14. 6. I am the way, and the t. and the life
16. 7. I tell you t. it is expedient that I go away
13. the Spirit of t. will guide you into all t.
17. 19. they might be sanctified through the t.
18. 37. I came that I should bear witness to the t. every one that is of the t. heareth my voice
38. Pilate saith unto him, what is t.?
Acts 26. 25. but I speak forth the words of t.
Rom. 1. 18. who hold the t. in unrighteousness
25. who changed the t. of God into a lie
2. 2. the judgment of God is according to t.
8. but unto them that do not obey the t.
20. which hast the form of the t. in the law
3. 7. for if the t. of God hath more abounded
9. 1. I say the t. in Christ, I lie not, my conscience
15. 8. was a minister of circumcision for t. of God
1 Cor. 5. 8. but with the unleavened bread of t.
2Cor.4.2. but by manifestation of the t. commending
7. 14. even so our boasting I made is found a t.
11. 10. as the t. of Christ is in me none shall stop
12. 6. I shall not be a fool, for I will say the t.
13. 8. we can do nothing against t. but for the t.
Gal. 2. 5. the t. of the gospel might continue with
14. they walked not according to t. of the gospel
3. 1. that ye should not obey the t. 5. 7.
4. 16. your enemy, because I tell you the t.?
Eph. 4. 15. but speaking the t. in love, may grow
21. have been taught by him as the t. is in Jesus
† 24. after God is created in holiness of t.
5. 9. for the fruit of the Spirit is in all t.
6. 14. stand having your loins girt about with t.
2 Thess. 2. 10. they received not the love of the t.
12. might be damned, who believed not t.
13. hath chosen to salvation, thro' belief of the t.
1 Tim. 2. 4. to come to the knowledge of the t.
7. I speak the t. in Christ and lie not
3. 15. the church, the pillar and ground of t.
4. 3. to be received of them which know the t.
6. 5. men of corrupt minds, and destitute of the t.
2 Tim. 2. 18. who concerning the t. have erred
25. give repentance to acknowledging of the t.
3. 7. not able to come to the knowledge of the t.
8. as Jannes and Jambres, so do these resist the t.
4. 4. they shall turn away their ears from the t.
Tit. 1. 1. according to the acknowledging of t.
14. commandments of men that turn from the t.
Heb. 10. 26. after we received knowledge of the t.
Jam. 3. 14. glory not, and lie not against the t.
5. 19. brethren, if any of you err from the t.
1 Pet. 1. 22. have purified your souls in obeying t.
2 Pet. 2. 2. the way of t. shall be evil spoken of
1 John 1. 6. walk in darkness we lie and do not the t.
8. we deceive ourselves, the t. is not in us
2. 4. the t. is not in him ‖ 27. is t. and is no lie
21. I have not written, because ye know not the t. but because ye know it, and no lie is of the t.
3. 19. and hereby we know that we are of the t.
5. 6. beareth witness, because the Spirit is t.
2 John 1. but also all they that have known the t.
2. for the t. sake that dwelleth in us, and with us
3 John 3. came and testified of the t. that is in thee
8. that we might be fellow-helpers to the t.
12. hath good report of all men and of the t.

In TRUTH.

Josh. 24. 14. serve him *in t.* 1 Sam. 12. 24.
Judg. 9. 15. if *in t.* ye anoint me king over you
1 Kings 2. 4. walk *in t.* ‖ 3. 6. as he walked *in t.*
2 Kings 20. 3. remember how I have walked *in t.*
Psal. 33. 4. all his works are done *in t.* 111. 8.
37. † 3. shalt dwell, and *in t.* thou shalt be fed
132. 11. the Lord hath sworn *in t.* to David
145. 18. Lord is nigh to all that call upon him *in t.*
Isa. 10. 20. shall stay on the Holy One of Israel *in t.*
16. 5. he shall sit upon it *in t.* judging and seeking
48. 1. make mention of God of Israel, but not *in t.*
61. 8. I will direct their work *in t.* and make
Jer. 4. 2. thou shalt swear, the Lord liveth *in t.*
32. † 41. I will plant them in this land *in t.*
Zech. 8.8. I will be their God *in t.* and righteousness
Mat. 22.16. teachest the way of G. *in t.* Mark 12.14.
John 4. 23. shall worship him in spirit and *in t.* 24.
2 Cor. 7. 14. as we speak all things to you *in t.*
Phil. 1. 18. whether *in t.* Christ is preached
Col. 1. 6. since ye knew the grace of God *in t.*
1 Thess. 2. 13. but as it is *in t.* the word of God
1 John 3. 18. let us not love in tongue, but *in t.*
2 John 3. the Son of the Father, *in t.* and love
4. I rejoiced, that I found of thy children walking *in t.* as commanded from the Father, 3 John 4.

In the TRUTH.

Psal. 69. 13. hear me *in the t.* of thy salvation
John 8. 44. he was a murderer and abode not *in t.*
1 Cor. 13. 6. but charity rejoiceth *in the t.*

2 Pet. 1. 12. tho' ye be established *in the* present *t.*
2 John 1. elect lady, whom I love *in the t.* 3 John 1.
3 John 3. even as thou walkest *in the t.*

Of a TRUTH.

1 Sam. 21. 5. *of a t.* women have been kept from us
2 Kings 19. 17. *of a t.* Lord, the kings of Assyria have destroyed the nations, Isa. 37. 18.
Job 9. 2. I know it is so *of a t.* but how should man
Isa. 5. 9. *of a t.* many houses shall be desolate
Jer. 26. 15. for *of a t.* the Lord hath sent me to you
Dan. 2. 47. *of a t.* it is, your God is a God of gods
Mat. 14. 33. *of a t.* thou art the Son of God
Luke 4. 25. but I tell you *of a t.* 9. 27.
12. 44. *of a t.* I say unto you he will make, 21. 3.
22. 59. *of a t.* this fellow also was with him
John 6. 14. this is *of a t.* that prophet, 7. 40.
Acts 4. 27. *of a t.* against thy holy child Jesus
10. 34. *of a t.* I perceive that God is no respecter
1 Cor. 14. 25. will report that God is in you *of a. t.*

See SPIRIT.

Thy TRUTH.

Psal. 25. 5. lead me in *thy t.* and teach me
26. 3. before my eyes and I have walked in *thy t.*
30. 9. shall the dust praise and declare *thy t.*?
40. 10. and *thy t.* from the great congregation
11. let *thy t.* continually preserve me
43. 3. send out thy light and *thy t.* let them lead
54. 5. to mine enemies, cut them off in *thy t.*
57. 10. and *thy t.* unto the clouds, 108. 4.
71. 22. I will praise *thy t.* ‖ 86. 11. will walk in *thy t.*
89. 49. which thou swarest to David in *thy t.*
115. 1. to thy name give glory for *thy t.* sake, 138. 2.
Isa. 38. 18. that go into the pit cannot hope for *thy t.*
19. the father to children shall make known *thy t.*
Dan. 9. 13. that we might understand *thy t.*
John 17. 17. sanctify them through *thy t.* thy word

Word of TRUTH.

Psal. 119. 43. take not *word of t.* out of my mouth
2 Cor. 6. 7. approving ourselves by the *word of t.*
Eph. 1. 13. after him that ye heard the *word of t.*
Col. 1. 5. whereof ye heard before in the *word of t.*
2 Tim. 2. 15. rightly dividing the *word of t.*
Jam. 1. 18. of his own will begat he us by *word of t.*

TRY.

Judg. 7. 4. and I will t. them for thee there
2 Chron. 32. 31. howbeit God left him to t. him
Job 7. 18. that thou shouldest t. him every moment
12. 11. doth not the ear t. words and mouth taste?
Psal. 11. 4. his eye-lids t. the children of men
26. 2. t. my reins and my heart ‖ 139. 23. t. me
Jer. 6. 27. that thou mayest know and t. their way
9. 7. I will melt them and t. them, Zech. 13. 9.
17. 10. I the Lord search the heart, t. the reins
Lam. 3. 40. let us search and t. our ways, and turn
Dan. 11. 35. some of them shall fall to t. them
1 Cor. 3. 13. the fire shall t. every man's work
Phil. 1. † 10. ye may t. things that are excellent
1 Pet. 4. 12. the fiery trial which is to t. you
1 John 4. 1. t. the spirits whether they are of God
Rev. 3. 10. hour of temptation, to t. them on earth

TRIED.

Deut. 21. 5. by the Levites shall every stroke be t.
2 Sam. 22. 31. the word of the Lord is t. Psal. 18. 30.
Job 23. 10. when he hath t. me, I shall come as gold
34. 36. my desire is that Job may be t. to the end
Psal. 12. 6. as silver is t. in a furnace of earth
17. 3. thou hast t. me and shalt find nothing
66. 10. for thou, O God, hast t. us, as silver is t.
105. 19. the word of the Lord t. him
119. † 140. thy word is t. therefore I love it
Isa. 28. 16. behold, I lay in Zion a t. stone
Jer. 12. 3. thou hast t. mine heart towards thee
Dan. 12. 10. many shall be purified and t.
Zech. 13. 9. and I will try them as gold is t.
Heb. 11. 17. by faith Abraham when he was t.
Jam. 1. 12. when t. he shall receive the crown
1 Pet. 1. 7. than of gold, though it be t. with fire
Rev. 2. 2. hast t. them which say they are apostles
10. cast some of you into prison, that ye may be t.
3. 18. I counsel thee to buy of me gold t. in the fire

TRIEST.

1 Chron. 29. 17. I know that thou t. the heart
Jer. 11. 20. O Lord, that t. the reins and heart
20. 12. but, O Lord of hosts, that t. the righteous

TRIETH.

Job 34. 3. ear t. words, as the mouth tasteth meat
Psal. 7. 9. the righteous God t. the hearts and reins
11. 5. the Lord t. the righteous, hateth the wicked
Prov. 17. 3. furnace for gold, but Lord t. the hearts
1 Thess. 2. 4. not men, but God who t. our hearts

TRYING.

Jam. 1. 3. the t. of your faith worketh patience

TUMBLED.

Judg. 7. 13. a cake of barley bread t. into the host

TUMULT.

1 Sam. 4. 14. what meaneth the noise of this t.?
2 Sam. 18. 29. I saw a t. but knew not what it was
2 Kings 19. 28. because they rage against me and thy t. is come up into mine ears, Isa. 37. 29.
Psal. 65. 7. which stilleth the t. of the people
74. 23. the t. of those that rise up against thee
83. 2. for, lo, thine enemies make a t.
Isa. 33. 3. at the noise of the t. the people fled
Jer. 11. 16. with noise of a great t. he kindled fire
Hos. 10. 14. therefore shall t. rise among thy people
Amos 2. 2. and Moab shall die with t. with shouting
Zech. 14. 13. a great t. from the Lord among them
Mat. 27. 24. but rather a t. was made, he took water
Mark 5. 38. he seeth the t. and them that wept
Acts 21. 34. he could not know the certainty for t.
24. 18. neither with multitude, nor with t.

TUMULTS.

Amos 3. 9. behold the great t. in the midst thereof
2 Cor. 6. 5. approving ourselves as ministers in t.
12. 20. lest there be whisperings, swellings, t.

TUMULTUOUS.

Isa. 13. 4. a t. noise of the kingdoms gathered
22. 2. thou that art a t. city, a joyous city
Jer. 48. 45. shall devour the head of the t. ones

TURN.

Esth. 2. 12. when every maid's t. was come to go in
15. now when the t. of Esther was come to go in

TURN, *Verb.*

Gen. 24. 49. that I may t. to the right hand or left
Exod. 23. 27. make thine enemies t. their backs
32. 12. t. from thy fierce wrath and repent of evil
Lev. 19. 4. t. ye not unto idols, nor make gods
Num. 14. 25. to-morrow t. you, get to wilderness
20. 17. we will not t. to the right hand nor left
21. 22. we will not t. into the fields or vineyards
22. 23. he smote the ass to t. her into the way
26. where was no way to t. to the right or left
Deut. 1.7. t. you, and go to the mount of the Amorites
40. and t. ye, take you journey into the wilderness
13. 17. that Lord may t. from fierceness of his anger
14. 25. then shalt t. it into money and bind it up
30. 3. then the Lord will t. their captivity
31. 20. then will they t. to other gods and serve them
Josh. 1. 7. t. not from it to the right hand or left
22. 23. an altar to t. from following the Lord, 29.
24. 20. then he will t. and do you hurt and consume
Judg. 20. 8. nor will any of us t. into his house
1 Sam. 14. 7. t. thee, behold, I am with thee
22. 17. t. and slay the priests of the Lord, 18.
2 Sam. 14. 19. none can t. to the right or left hand
24. the king said, let him t. to his own house
15. 31. Lord, t. Ahithophel's counsel to foolishness
1 Kings 8.35. t. from their sin, 2 Chron. 6.26, 37. | 7.14.
9. 6. if you shall at all t. from following me
17. 3. get hence, t. thee eastward and hide thyself
22. 34. he said, t. thine hand, 2 Chron. 18. 33.
2 Kings 9. 18. and Jehu said, t. thee behind me, 19.
17. 13. t. ye from your evil ways and keep my commandments, Jer. 18. 8. | 26. 3. Zech. 1. 3. 4.
1 Chron. 12. 23. to t. the kingdom of Saul to him
2 Chron. 35. 22. but Josiah would not t. his face
Neh. 1. 9. if ye t. and keep my commandments, Ezek. 3. 20. | 18. 21. | 33. 11, 14, 19.
4. 4. and t. their reproach on their own head
9. 26. prophets which testified to t. them to thee
Job 5. 1. and to which of the saints wilt thou t.?
14. 6. t. from him that he may rest till he shall
23. 13. but he is in one mind, and who can t. him?
24. 4. they t. the needy out of the way, the poor
Psal. 4. 2. how long will ye t. my glory into shame?
7. 12. if he t. not, he will whet his sword
20. † 3. the Lord t. to ashes the burnt sacrifice
21. 12. thou shalt make them t. their back
25. 16. t. thee unto me, 69. 16. | 86. 16.
85. 4. t. us, O God of our salvation, and cause
119. 79. let those that fear thee t. unto me
132. 11. Lord hath sworn to David, he will not t.
Prov. 1. 23. t. you at my reproof, I will pour out
4. 15. pass not by it, t. from it and pass away
27. t. not to the right hand nor to the left
Eccl. 3. 20. all are of dust, and all t. to dust again
Cant. 2. 17. t. my beloved, and be thou like a roe
Isa. 1. 25. I will t. my hand on thee and purge
13. 14. they shall every man t. to his own people
19. 6. and they shall t. the rivers far away
22. 18. he will violently t. and toss thee like a ball
23. 17. she shall t. to her hire, and shall commit
28. 6. for strength to them that t. the battle
30. 21. when ye t. to the right hand and left
31. 6. t. ye to him from whom Israel hath revolted
59. 20. to them that t. from transgression in Jacob
Jer. 2. 35. surely his anger shall t. from me
3. 7. and I said, t. unto me, but returned not, 14.
13. 16. before he t. it into the shadow of death
31. 13. for I will t. their mourning into joy
18. t. thou me, and I shall be turned, thou art
44. 5. hearkened not to t. from their wickedness
50. 16. they shall t. every one to his people
Lam. 5. 21. t. us unto thee, O L. we shall be turned
Ezek. 3. 19. he t. not from his wickedness, 33. 9.
4. 8. shalt not t. thee from one side to another
7. 22. my face will I t. also from them
14. 6. repent and t. yourselves from your idols, 18. 30, 32. | 33. 9, 11. Hos. 12. 6. Joel 2. 12.
36. 9. I will t. unto you, and ye shall be tilled
38. 12. to t. thine hand upon the desolate places
Dan. 9. 13. that we might t. from our iniquities
11. 18. shall he t. his face unto the isles, and take many; shall cause reproach t. upon him
19. then he shall t. his face toward the fort
12. 3. and they that t. many to righteousness
Hos. 5. 4. they will not frame their doings to t.
12. 6. therefore t. thou to thy God, keep mercy
Amos 1. 8. and I will t. mine hand against Ekron
5. 7. ye who t. judgment to wormwood
8. 10. and I will t. your feasts into mourning
Jonah 3. 8. let them t. every one from his evil way
Zeph. 3. 9. then will I t. to people a pure language
Zech. 9. 12. t. ye to strong hold ye prisoners of hope
13. 7. I will t. mine hand upon the little ones
Mal. 4. 6. he shall t. the heart of fathers to children
Mat. 5. 39. on thy right cheek, t. to him the other
Luke 1. 17. to t. the hearts of the fathers to children
21. 13. and it shall t. to you for a testimony
Acts 13. 46. of life, lo we t. to the Gentiles
14. 15. that ye should t. from these vanities
26. 18. and to t. them from darkness to light
20. that they should repent and t. to God
Phil. 1. 19. I know this shall t. to my salvation
Tit. 1. 14. commandments of men that t. from truth
Jam. 3. 3. and we t. about their whole body
2 Pet. 2. 21. to t. from the holy commandment
Rev. 11. 6. and have power to t. waters to blood

TURN *again.*

Lev. 13. 16. if the raw flesh *t. again* and be changed
Judg. 11. 8. therefore we *t. again* to thee now
Ruth 1. 11. she said, *t. again,* my daughters, 12.
1 Sam. 15. 25. I pray thee, *t. again* with me, 30.
1 Kings 8. 33. when Israel shall *t. again* to thee
12. 27. heart of this people *t. again* to their lord
13. 9. eat not, nor *t. again* by the same way, 17.
2 Kings 1. 6. go *t. again* to the king that sent you
20. 5. *t. again* and tell Hezekiah the captain
2 Chron. 30. 6. *t. again* to the Lord ‖ 9. if ye *t. again*
Job 34. 15. and man shall *t. again* into dust
Psal. 18. 37. nor did I *t. ag.* till they were consumed
60. 1. hast been displeased, O *t.* thyself to us *again*
80. 3. *t.* us *again,* O Lord God of hosts, 7, 19.
85. 8. speak peace, but let them not *t. again* to folly

Psal. 104. 9. that they t. not again to cover the earth
126. 4. t. again our captivity, as streams in south
Jer. 25. 5. t. ye again every one from his evil way
31. 21. t. again, O virgin of Israel, t. again to cities
Lam. 3. 40. let us try our ways and t. again to the L.
Ezek. 8. 6. t. again and thou shalt see, 13. 15.
Mic. 7. 19. he will t. again, he will have compassion
Zech 10. 9. shall live with their children and t. ag.
Mat. 7. 6. lest they t. again and rend you
Luke 10. 6. if not, it shall t. to you again
17. 4. and seven times in a day t. again to thee
Gal. 4. 9. how t. ye again to the weak elements

TURN aside.

Exod. 3. 3. I will now t. aside and see this sight
Deut. 5. 32. shall not t. aside to the right hand
11. 16. and ye t. aside and serve other gods, 28.
17. 20. that he t. not aside from commandment
31. 29. after my death ye will t. aside from the way
Josh. 23. 6. that ye t. not aside therefrom to the right hand or the left, 1 Sam. 12. 20, 21.
Ruth 4. 1. ho, such a one, t. aside, sit down here
2 Sam. 2. 21. Asahel, t. aside and take his armour
23. howbeit he refused to t. aside
18. 30. the king said, t. aside, and stand here
Job 36. † 18. a great ransom cannot t. thee aside
Psal. 40. 4. respecteth not such as t. aside to lies
101. 3. I hate the work of them that t. aside
125. 5. as for such as t. aside to crooked ways
Isa. 10. 2. to t. aside the needy from judgment
29. 21. t. aside the just for a thing of nought
30. 11. get out of the way, t. aside out of the path
Lam. 3. 35. to t. aside the right of a man before thee
Amos 2. 7. and that t. aside the way of the meek
5. 12. and they t. aside the poor in the gate
Mal. 3. 5. and that t. aside the stranger from right

TURN away.

Gen. 27. 44. tarry till thy brother's fury t. away
45. till thy brother's anger t. away from thee
Num. 32. 15. for if ye t. away from after him, Deut. 30. 17. Josh. 22. 16. 2 Chron. 7. 19.
Deut. 7. 4. they will t. away thy son from following
13. 5. he hath spoken to t. you away from the Lord
17. 17. multiply wives, that his heart t. not away
23. 14. that he see no unclean thing and t. away
1 Kings 2. † 16. I ask one petition, t. not aw. my face
11. 2. surely they will t. away your heart
2 Kings 18. 24. how wilt thou t. away the face of one captain and put thy trust on Egypt? Isa. 36. 9.
1 Chron. 14. 14. go not up, t. away from them
2 Chron. 6. 42. O Lord God, t. not away the face of thine anointed, remember mercies, Psal. 132. 10.
25. 27. Amaziah did t. away from following Lord
29. 10. to make a covenant with God of Israel, that wrath may t. away, 30. 8. Ps. 106. 23. Prov. 24. 18.
30. 9. the Lord will not t. away his face from you
Job 9. † 12. who can t. him away? 11. † 10.
Ps. 119. 37. t. away mine eyes from beholding vanity
39. t. away my reproach which I fear
Prov. 25. 10. and lest thine infamy t. not away
29. 8. but wise men t. away wrath
Cant. 6. 5. t. away thine eyes from me, for they
Isa. 47. † 10. thy wisdom caused thee to t. away
58. 13. if thou t. away thy foot from the sabbath
Jer. 2. 24. in her occasion who can t. her away?
3. 19. and thou shalt not t. away from me
8. 4. saith L. shall he t. away and not return?
18. 20. I stood to t. away thy wrath from them
29. 14. I will t. away your captivity, Zeph. 2. 7.
32. 40. that I will not t. away from them
Lam. 2. 14. not discovered iniquity, to t. a. captivity
Ezek. 14. 6. t. away your faces from abominations
Amos 1. 3. and for four I will not t. away the punishment thereof, 6, 9, 11, 13. | 2. 1, 4, 6.
Jonah 3. 9. God will t. away from his fierce anger
Mal. 2. 6. and did t. many away from iniquity
Mat. 5. 42. would borrow of thee, t. not thou away
Acts 13. 8. seeking to t. away the deputy from faith
Rom. 11. 26. shall t. away ungodliness from Jacob
2 Tim. 3. 5. traitors, heady, from such t. away
4. 4. they shall t. away their ears from truth
Heb. 12. 25. how escape, if we t. away from him?

TURN back.

Deut. 23. 13. t. b. and cover that which comes fr. thee
2 Kings 19. 28. I will put a hook in thy nose and t. thee back by the way thou camest, Isa. 37. 29.
Psal. 44. 10. makest us to t. back from the enemy
56. 9. when I cry, then shall mine enemies t. back
Isa. 14. 27. his hand stretched, who shall t. it back?
Jer. 4. 28. neither will I t. back from it
6. 9. t. back thine hand as a grape-gatherer
21. 4. behold, I will t. back the weapons of war
49. 8. flee ye, t. back, dwell deep, O inhabitants
Ezek. 38. 4. and I will t. thee back, 39. 2.
Zeph. 3. 20. when I t. back your captivity
Mark 13. 16. not t. back to take up his garment
Gal. 4. † 9. how t. ye back to beggarly elements?

TURN in.

Gen. 19. 2. behold now, my lords, t. in, I pray you
Judg. 4. 18. t. in, my lord, t. in to me, fear not
19. 11. let us t. in to this city of the Jebusites
2 Kings 4. 10. that the man of God shall t. in thith.
Prov. 9. 4. whoso is simple, let him t. in hither, 16.

TURN to the Lord.

Deut. 4. 30. if thou t. to the Lord thy God, 30. 10.
2 Chron. 15. 4. in their trouble did t. to the Lord
Psal. 22. 27. ends of the world shall t. to the Lord
Lam. 3. 40. let us try our ways and t. to the Lord
Hos. 14. 2. take with you words and t. to the Lord
Joel 2. 13. rend your heart and t. to the Lord
Luke 1. 16. many of Israel shall he t. to the Lord
2 Cor. 3. 16. nevertheless when it shall t. to the Lord

TURNED.

Gen. 3. 24. a flaming sword which t. every way
42. 24. Joseph t. about from them and wept
Exod. 7. 15. the rod which was t. to a serpent
7. 17. the waters which are in the river shall be t. to blood, 20. Psal. 78. 44. | 105. 29.
14. 5. heart of Pharaoh was t. against the people
Lev. 13. 3. when the hair is t. white, 10. 17, 20, 25.
Num. 21. 33. they t. and went by way of Bashan
22. 33. the ass saw me and t. from me three times
Deut. 23. 5. t. the curse into a blessing, Neh. 13. 2.
Deut. 31. 18. in that they are t. unto other gods
Josh. 7. 26. Lord t. from the fierceness of his anger
Judg. 2. 17. they t. quickly out of the way
15. 4. Samson took fire-brands and t. tail to tail
20. 42. therefore they t. their backs before Israel
1 Sam. 4. † 19. travailed, for her pains were t on her
10. 6. and thou shalt be t. into another man
14. 21. even they also t. to be with the Israelites
47. whithersoever he t. himself he vexed them
15. 27. as Samuel t. about to go away, he laid
17. 30. and David t. from him towards another
2 Sam. 2. 19. Asahel t. not from following Abner
19. 2. the victory that day was t. into mourning
1 Kings 2. 15. howbeit the kingdom is t. about
28. Joab t. after Adonijah, tho' not after Absalom
8. 14. the king t. his face about, and blessed Israel
11. 9. because his heart was t. from the Lord
2 Kings 5. 12. so Naaman t. and went away in rage
16. 18. Ahaz t. the covert from the house of the Ld.
20. 2. t. his face to the wall, and prayed, Isa. 38. 2.
23. 16. as Josiah t. himself he spied sepulchres
25. was no king that t. to the Lord like him
26. Lord t. not from the fierceness of his wrath
1 Chron. 10. 14. he t. the kingdom unto David
2 Chron. 12. 12. the wrath of the Lord t. from him
20. 10. they t. from them and destroyed them not
29. 6. for our fathers have t. their backs
Ezra 6. 22. t. the heart of the king of Assyria
10. 14. until the wrath of our God be t. from us
Neh. 9. 35. neither t. they from their wicked works
Esth. 9. 1. though it was t. to the contrary that Jews
22. the month which was t. to them from sorrow
Job 16. 11. God t. me into the hands of the wicked
19. 19. and they whom I loved are t. against me
20. 14. yet his meat in his bowels is t. the gall
28. 5. and under it is t. up as it were fire
30. 15. terrors are t. upon me, they pursue my soul
31. my harp is t. to mourning, and my organ
31. 7. if my step hath t. out of the way, my heart
38. 14. it is t. as clay to the seal, they stand as
41. 22. and sorrow is t. into joy before him
42. 10. and the Lord t. the captivity of Job
Psal. 9. 17. the wicked shall be t. into hell
30. 11. thou hast t. my mourning into dancing
66. 6. he t. the sea into dry land, they went through
81. 14. and t. my hand against their adversaries
105. 25. he t. their heart to hate his people
114. 8. which t. the rock into a standing water
119. 59. I t. my feet unto thy testimonies
Eccl. 2. 12. and I t. myself to behold wisdom
Isa. 21. 4. night of my pleasure he t. into fear
29. 17. Lebanon shall be t. into a fruitful field
34. 9. the streams thereof shall be t. into pitch
53. 6. we have t. every one to his own way
63. 10. therefore he was t. to be their enemy
Jer. 2. 21. how art thou t. into a degenerate plant?
27. they have t. their back to me, not their face
3. 10. Judah hath not t. to me with her whole heart
6. 12. their houses shall be t. unto others
8. 6. no man repented, every one t. to his course
23. 22. they should have t. them from their evil way
31. 18. and I shall be t. || 19. after that I was t.
32. 33. they t. unto me the back, and not the face
34. 15. and ye were now t. and had done right
16. but ye t. and polluted my name and caused
48. 39. how hath Moab t. thee back with shame?
Lam. 1. 20. behold, Lord, mine heart is t. within me
3. 3. surely against me is he t. he turneth his hand
5. 2. our inheritance is t. to strangers, our houses
15. joy is ceased, our dance is t. into mourning
21. turn us unto thee, O Lord, and we shall be t.
Ezek. 1. 9. they t. not when they went, 12. | 10. 11.
17. 6. a vine, whose branches t. toward him
26. 2. she is t. unto me, I shall be replenished
Dan. 10. 8. my comeliness was t. into corruption
16. by the vision my sorrows are t. upon me
Hos. 7. 8. among the people Ephraim is a cake not t.
11. 8. Ephraim, mine heart is t. within me
Joel 2. 31. sun shall be t. into darkness, Acts 2. 20.
Amos 6. 12. for ye have t. judgment into gall
Jonah 3. 10. that they t. from their evil way
Hab. 2. 16. the cup of Lord's right hand be t. to thee
Zech. 14. 10. all the land shall be t. into a plain
Mark 5. 30. Jesus t. about in the press, and said
Luke 22. 61. the Lord t. and looked upon Peter
John 16. 20. but your sorrow shall be t. into joy
Acts 7. 42. God t. and gave them up to worship
9. 35. all at Lydda saw him and t. to the Lord
11. 21. a great number believed and t. to the Lord
15. 19. which from the Gentiles are t. to God
17. 6. these that have t. the world upside down
1 Thess. 1. 9. shew how ye t. to God from idols
2 Tim. 4. 4. and they shall be t. unto fables
Heb. 11. 34. t. to flight the armies of the aliens
12. 13. lest that which is lame be t. out of the way
Jam. 3. 4. yet are they t. with a very small helm
4. 9. let your laughter be t. to mourning
2 Pet. 2. 22. the dog is t. to his own vomit again

TURNED again.

Exod. 4. 7. behold it was t. again as his other flesh
Judg. 3. 19. Ehud t. again from the quarries
8. 33. Israel t. again, went a whoring after Baalim
20. 41. when Israel t. again, Benjamites amazed
1 Sam. 15. 31. so Samuel t. again after Saul, and S.
2 Sam. 22. 38. I t. not again till I had consumed
2 Kings 5. 26. when the man t. again from his chariot
Psal. 126. 1. when Lord t. again the captiv. of Zion

TURNED aside.

Exod. 3. 4. the Lord saw that he t. aside to see
32. 8. they have t. aside quickly, Deut. 9. 12, 16.
Judg. 14. 8. he t. aside to see the lion's carcase
1 Sam. 6. 12. the kine t. not aside to the right
8. 3. but t. aside after lucre, and took bribes
1 Kings 15. 5. David t. not aside from any thing
20. 39. a man t. aside and brought a man to me
2 Kings 22. 2. Josiah t. not aside to right hand or left
Job 6. 18. the paths of their way are t. aside
Psal. 78. 57. they were t. aside like a deceitful bow
Cant. 6. 1. whither is thy beloved t. aside?
Isa. 44. 20. a deceived heart hath t. him aside
Lam. 3. 11. he hath t. aside my ways and pulled
1 Tim. 1. 6. have t. aside unto vain jangling
1 Tim. 5. 15. for some are already t. aside after [Satan

TURNED away.

Num. 14. 43. because ye are t. away from the Lord
20. 21. wherefore Israel t. away from him
25. 4. that the anger of the Lord may be t. away
11. Phinehas hath t. my wrath away from Israel
1 Kings 11. 3. and his wives t. away his heart, 4.
21. 4. and Ahab t. away, and would eat no bread
2 Chron. 29. 6. our fathers t. away their faces
Psal. 66. 20. which hath not t. away my prayer
78. 38. yea, many a time t. he his anger away
Isa. 5. 25. for all this his anger is not t. away, but his hand is stretched out still, 9. 12, 17, 21. | 10. 4.
12. 1. thy anger is t. away || 50. 5. nor t. I away
59. 14. and judgment is t. away backward
Jer. 5. 25. your iniquities have t. away these things
38. 22. thy feet are sunk, they are t. away back
46. 5. wherefore have I seen them t. away back?
50. 6. shepherds have t. them away on mountains
Dan. 9. 16. let thy fury be t. away from Jerusalem
Hos. 14. 4. for mine anger is t. away from him
Nah. 2. 2. the L. hath t. away excellency of Jacob
Acts 19. 26. this Paul hath t. away much people
2 Tim. 1. 15. all they in Asia be t. away from me

TURNED back.

Josh. 8. 20. the people t. back upon the pursuers
11. 10. Joshua at that time t. back, and took
1 Sam. 15. 11. Saul is t. back from following me
2 Sam. 1. 22. the bow of Jonathan t. not back
1 Kings 18. 37. that thou hast t. their heart back
22. 33. saw it was not king of Israel, they t. back
2 Kings 1. 5. when messengers t. back, why t. back
2. 24. he t. back and looked on them, and cursed
15. 20. so the king of Assyria t. back and stayed
1 Chron. 21. 20. Ornan t. back and saw the angel
Job 34. 27. because they t. back from him
Psal. 9. 3. when mine enemies are t. back, shall fall
35. 4. let them be t. back that devise, 70. 2, 3.
44. 18. our heart is not t. back from thy way
78. 9. children of Ephraim t. back in day of battle
41. yea, they t. back and tempted God, 57.
129. 5. and let them be t. back that hate Zion
Isa. 42. 17. they shall be t. back that trust in images
Jer. 4. 8. the anger of the Lord is not t. back
11. 10. they are t. back to iniquities of fathers
46. 21. they also are t. back, and are fled away
Lam. 1. 13. he hath t. me back, and made me faint
Zeph. 1. 6. them that are t. back from the Lord
Luke 2. 45. t. back again to Jerusalem seeking him
17. 15. one of the lepers t. back and glorified God
John 20. 14. she t. herself back and saw Jesus
Acts 7. 39. in their hearts t. back again into Egypt

TURNED in.

Gen. 19. 3. the two angels t. in unto Lot
38. 1. Judah t. in to Hirah the Adullamite
Judg. 4. 18. when Sisera had t. in unto Jael
18. 3. the Danites t. in thither and said to him
2 Kings 4. 8. Elisha t. in thither to eat bread
11. he t. into the chamber and lay there

TURNEST.

1 Kings 2. 3. mayest prosper whithersoever thou t.
Job 15. 13. that thou t. thy Spirit against God
Psal. 90. 3. thou t. man to destruction, and sayest

TURNETH.

Lev. 20. 6. soul that t. after wizards to go after them
Deut. 29. 18. whose heart t. away this day from God
Josh. 7. 8. what shall I say, when Isr. t. their backs?
2 Kings 21. † 13. he wipeth and t. it upon the face
Job 39. 22. the horse t. not back from the sword
Psal. 107. 33. he t. rivers into a wilderness
35. he t. the wilderness into a standing water
146. 9. the way of the wicked he t. upside down
Prov. 15. 1. a soft answer t. away wrath, but words
17. 8. a gift, whithersoever it t. prospereth
21. 1. he t. the king's heart whithersoever he will
26. 14. as the door t. upon his hinges, so doth
28. 9. that t. away his ear from hearing the law
30. 30. a lion that t. not away for any
Eccl. 1. 6. the wind t. about unto the north
Cant. 1. 7. why should I be as one that t. aside?
Isa. 9. 13. the people t. not to him that smiteth
24. 1. the Lord t. the earth upside down
44. 25. that t. wise men backward, and maketh
Jer. 14. 8. that t. aside to tarry for a night
49. 24. Damascus is feeble, and t. herself to flee
Lam. 1. 8. yea, she sigheth and t. backward
3. 3. he t. his hand against me all the day
Ezek. 18. 24. when righteous t. away, 26. | 33. 18.
27. when the wicked man t. away, 28. | 33. 12
Amos 5. 8. t. the shadow of death into morning

TURNING.

2 Kings 21. 13. I will wipe Jerusalem as a dish, t. it
2 Chron. 36. 13. he hardened his heart from t. to L.
Prov. 1. 32. the t. away of simple shall slay them
Isa. 29. 16. your t. of things upside down as clay
57. † 17. I hid me and was wroth, went on t. away
Mic. 2. 4. t. away he hath divided our fields
Acts 3. 26. to bless you in t. you from your iniquit.
Jam. 1. 17. with whom is no shadow of t.
2 Pet. 2. 6. t. Sodom and Gomorrah into ashes
Jude 4. t. the grace of God into lasciviousness

TURTLE, S.

Gen. 15. 9. take a t. dove and a young pigeon
Lev. 1. 14. shall bring his offering of t. doves
5. 7. he shall bring for his trespass two t. doves or young pigeons, 12. 8. | 14. 22, 30. | 15. 14, 29.
11. if he be not able to bring two t. doves
12. 6. she shall bring a t.-dove for a sin-offering
Num. 6. 10. on eighth day he shall bring two t.
Psal. 74. 19. O deliver not the soul of thy t.-dove
Cant. 2. 12. the voice of the t. is heard in our land
Jer. 8. 7. t. and crane observe the time of coming
Luke 2. 24. to offer a sacrifice, a pair of t.-doves

TUTORS.

Gal. 4. 2. the heir while a child is under t. and gov.

TWAIN.

1 Sam. 18. 21. be my son-in-law in the one of the t.
2 Kings 4. 33. shut the door on them t. and prayed
Isa. 6. 2. the seraphims, with t. he covered his face, with t. he covered his feet, and with t. he did fly
Jer. 34. 18. when they cut the calf in t. and passed
Ezek. 21. 19. both t. shall come out of one land

Mat. 5. 41. compel thee to go a mile, go with him *t.*
19. 5. cleave to wife, and they *t.* shall be one flesh
6. wherefore they are no more *t.* *Mark* 10. 8.
21. 31. whether of *t.* did the will of his father?
27. 21. whether of the *t.* will ye that I release?
51. the vail of temple was rent in *t.* *Mark* 15. 38.
Eph. 2. 15. to make in himself of *t.* one new man

TWELFTH.

1 *Kings* 19. 19. twelve yoke of oxen, he with the *t.*
1 *Chron.* 24. 12. the *t.* lot came forth to Jakim
25. 19. the *t.* lot came forth to Hashabiah
27. 15. the *t.* captain for the *t.* month, Heldai
2 *Chron.* 34. 3. in the *t.* year of Josiah's reign
Esth. 3. 7. in the *t.* year of king Ahasuerus
Ezek. 32. 1. in the *t.* year, in the *t.* month
17. in the *t.* year and fifteenth day of the month
33. 21. in the *t.* year of our captivity, tenth month
Rev. 21. 20. the *t.* foundation was an amethyst
See DAY, MONTH.

TWELVE.

Gen. 14. 4. *t.* years they served Chedorlaomer
17. 20. *t.* princes shall Ishmael beget, 25. 16.
35. 22. now the sons of Jacob were *t.*
42. 13. they said, thy servants are *t.* brethren, 32.
49. 28. all these are the *t.* tribes of Israel
Exod. 15. 27. they came to Elim, where were *t.* wells
24. 4. *t.* pillars according to the *t.* tribes of Israel
28. 21. shall be *t.* precious stones, 39. 14.
Lev. 24. 5. and thou shalt bake *t.* cakes thereof
Num. 1. 44. *t.* princes ‖ 7. 3. they brought *t.* oxen
7. 84. *t.* chargers, *t.* silver bowls, *t.* spoons
87. *t.* bullocks, *t.* rams, *t.* lambs of the first year
17. 2. *t.* rods, according to house of fathers, 6.
29. 17. on second day offer *t.* young bullocks
Deut. 1. 23. I took *t.* men of you, one of a tribe
Josh. 3. 12. take ye *t.* men out of the tribes, 4. 2.
4. 3. take ye *t.* stones out of Jordan, 8, 9, 20.
2 *Sam.* 2. 15. there arose and went over by number *t.* of Benjamin, and *t.* of the servants of David
1 *Kings* 4. 7. Solomon had *t.* officers over all Israel
7. 25. the sea stood on *t.* oxen, 44. 2 *Chron.* 4. 15.
10. 20. *t.* lions on the one side, 2 *Chron.* 9. 19.
11. 30. Ahijah rent Jeroboam's garm. in *t.* pieces
18. 31. Elijah took *t.* stones and built an altar
19. 19. found Elisha plowing with *t.* yoke of oxen
1 *Chr.* 25. 9. with brethren and sons *t.* *So to the end.*
Ezra 6. 17. for a sin offering *t.* he-goats, 8. 35.
8. 24. there I separated *t.* of the chief of priests
Neh. 5. 14. *t.* years not eaten bread of the governor
Job 38. † 32. canst thou bring forth the *t.* signs?
Jer. 52. 20. *t.* brazen bulls, Nebuzar-adan took away
Ezek. 43. 16. the altar shall be *t.* cubits long, *t.* broad
47. 13. inherit the land according to the *t.* tribes
Dan. 4. 29. at end of *t.* months he walked in palace
Mat. 9. 20. a woman was diseased with an issue of blood *t.* years, *Mark* 5. 25. *Luke* 8. 43.
10. 2. the names of the *t.* apostles, *Luke* 6. 13.
14. 20. they took up of fragments *t.* baskets, *Mark* 6. 43. | 8. 19. *Luke* 9. 17. *John* 6. 13.
19. 28. ye also shall sit upon *t.* thrones, judging the *t.* tribes of Israel, *Luke* 22. 30.
26. 20. now when even was come, he sat down with the *t.* *Mark* 14. 17. *Luke* 22. 14.
47. while he yet spake, Judas one of the *t.* came, *Mark* 14. 10, 43. *Luke* 22. 47. *John* 6. 71.
53. shall give me more than *t.* legions of angels
Mark 5. 42. she was of the age of *t.* years, *Luke* 8. 42.
14. 20. it is one of the *t.* that dippeth with me
Luke 2. 42. and when Jesus was *t.* years old
John 6. 70. Jesus said, have I not chosen you *t.*?
11. 9. are there not *t.* hours in the day?
20. 24. Thomas one of the *t.* was not with them
Acts 7. 8. and Jacob begat the *t.* patriarchs
19. 7. prophesied, and all the men were about *t.*
24. 11. but *t.* days since I went up to Jerusalem
26. 7. to which promise our *t.* tribes hope to come
1 *Cor.* 15. 5. he was seen of Cephas, then of the *t.*
Jam. 1. 1. to the *t.* tribes which are scattered abroad
Rev. 12. 1. and upon her head a crown of *t.* stars
21. 12. the city had *t.* gates, at the gates *t.* angels
14. the wall of the city had *t.* foundations, and in them the names of the *t.* apostles of the Lamb
21. the *t.* gates were *t.* pearls, street pure gold
22. 2. the tree of life bare *t.* manner of fruits
See HUNDRED, THOUSAND.

TWENTY.

Gen. 18. 31. peradventure there shall be *t.* found there, he said, I will not destroy it for *t.* sake
31. 38. this *t.* years have I been with thee, 41.
32. 14. for a present for Esau, *t.* he-goats, *t.* rams
15. and ten bulls, *t.* she asses, and ten foals
37. 28. they sold Joseph for *t.* pieces of silver
Exod. 30. 13. a shekel is *t.* gerahs, *Lev.* 27. 25. *Num.* 3. 47. | 18. 16. *Ezek.* 45. 12.
14. from *t.* years old and above, 38. 26. *Num.* 1. 3, 18, 20. | 14. 29. | 26. 2. | 32. 11. 1 *Chron.* 23. 24, 27. 2 *Chron.* 25. 5. | 31. 17. *Ezra* 3. 8.
Lev. 27. 3. thy estimation of the male from *t.* years
5. from five years old to *t.* years, *t.* shekels
Num. 11. 19. shall not eat neither ten days, nor *t.* days
18. 16. the shekel of the sanctuary is *t.* gerahs
Judg. 4. 3. Jabin mightily oppressed Israel *t.* years
11. 33. Jephthah smote from Aroer even *t.* cities
15. 20. Samson judged Israel *t.* years, 16. 31.
1 *Sam.* 7. 2. the ark was in Kirjath-jearim *t.* years
14. 14. Jonathan and his armour-bearer slew *t.* men
2 *Sam.* 3. 20. Abner came to David with *t.* men
9. 10. Ziba had fifteen sons and *t.* servants, 19. 17.
1 *Kings* 4. 23. Solomon's provision daily, *t.* oxen
9. 10. came to pass at the end of *t.* years, when Solomon had built the two houses, 2 *Chron.* 8. 1.
11. Solomon gave Hiram *t.* cities in Galilee
2 *Kings* 4. 42. brought the man of God *t.* loaves
Ezra 8. 27. I even weighed *t.* basons of gold
Ezek. 4. 10. thy meat by weight, *t.* shekels a day
40. 49. the length of the porch was *t.* cubits
41. 2. the breadth of the door was *t.* cubits
Hag. 2. 16. when one came to an heap of *t.* measures, to draw out fifty vessels, there were but *t.*
Zech. 5. 2. the length of the flying roll *t.* cubits
Acts 27. 28. and sounded, and found it *t.* fathoms

TWENTY-*two.*

Judg. 10. 3. Jair judged Israel *t. two* years
1 *Kings* 14. 20. Jeroboam reigned *t.-two* years
16. 29. Ahab reigned over Israel *t.-two* years
2 *Kings* 8. 26. Ahaziah was *t.* and *two* years old
21. 19. Amon *t.-two* years old, when began to reign
1 *Chron.* 12. 28. of his father's house *t.-two* captains
2 *Chron.* 13. 21. but Abijah begat *t.* and *two* sons

TWENTY-*three.*

Judg. 10. 2. Tola judged Israel *t.-three* years
2 *Kings* 23. 31. Jehoahaz was *t.-three* years old
1 *Chron.* 2. 22. Jair had *t.-three* cities in Gilead
Jer. 25. 3. from 13th year of Josiah to *t.-third* year
52. 30. in the *t.-third* year of Nebuchadnezzar

TWENTY-*four.*

Num. 7. 88. the offerings were *t.* and *four* bullocks
2 *Sam.* 21. 20. fingers and toes *t.-four* in number
1 *Kings* 15. 33. Baasha reigned *t.* and *four* years
Hag. 2. 18. consider from *t.-fourth* day and ninth mon.
Rev 4. 4. round about the throne were *t.-four* seats, and on the seats I saw *t. four* elders sitting
5. 8. the *t.-four* elders fell down, 11. 16. | 19. 4.

TWENTY-*five.*

Num. 8. 24. from *t.-five* years old and upward
1 *Kings* 22. 42. Jehoshaphat reigned *t.* and *five* years in Jerusalem, 2 *Chron.* 20. 31.
2 *Kings* 14. 2. Amaziah was *t.-five* years old when he began to reign, 2 *Chron.* 25. 1.
15. 33. Jotham *t.-five* years old, 2 *Chron.* 27. 1, 8.
18. 2. Hezekiah *t.-five* years old, 2 *Chron.* 29. 1.
23. 36. Jehoiakim *t.-five* years, 2 *Chron.* 36. 5.
Neh. 6. 15. the wall finished in *t.-fifth* day of Elul
Jer. 52. 31. *t.-fifth* day Evil-merodach lifted up

TWENTY-*six.*

1 *Kings* 16. 8. in *t.-six* of Asa, Elah began to reign

TWENTY-*seven.*

Gen. 8. 14. *t.-sev.* day of second month, earth dried
1 *Kings* 16. 10. *t.-seventh* of Asa, Zimri reigned, 15.
2 *Kings* 25. 27. on *t.-seventh* day of twelfth month

TWENTY-*eight.*

Exod. 26. 2. length of curtain *t.-eight* cubits 36. 9.
2 *Kings* 10. 36. Jehu reigned *t.* and *eight* years
2 *Chron.* 11. 21. Rehoboam begat *t.-eight* sons

TWENTY-*nine.*

Gen. 11. 24. Nahor lived *t.-nine* years and begat
2 *Kings* 14. 2. Amaziah reigned *t.-nine* years
18. 2. Hezekiah *t.-nine* years, 2 *Chr.* 25. 1. | 29. 1.
See THOUSAND.

TWICE.

Gen. 41. 32. for that the dream was doubled *t.*
43. † 10. surely now we had returned *t.* by this
Exod. 16. 5. and it shall be *t.* as much, 22.
Num. 20. 11. with his rod he smote the rock *t.*
1 *Sam.* 18. 11. David avoided out of his presence *t.*
1 *Kings* 11. 9. which had appeared unto him *t.*
2 *Kings* 6. 10. saved himself there not once nor *t.*
Neh. 13. 20. lodged without Jerusalem once or *t.*
Job 33. 14. for God speaketh once, yea *t.* yet man
40. 5. yea *t.* but I will proceed no further
42. 10. Lord gave Job *t.* as much as he had before
Psal. 62. 11. *t.* have I heard, power belongeth to G.
Eccl. 6. 6. though he live a thousand years *t.* told
Mark 14. 30. cock crow *t.* thou shalt deny me, 72.
Luke 18. 12. I fast *t.* in the week, I give tithes
Jude 12. *t.* dead, plucked up by the roots

TWIGS.

Ezek. 17. 4. he cropped off the top of his young *t.*
22. I will crop off from the top of his young *t.*

TWILIGHT.

1 *Sam.* 30. 17. and David smote them from the *t.*
2 *Kings* 7. 5. the lepers rose in the *t.* to go to the camp
7. the Syrians arose and fled in the *t.* left tents
Job 3. 9. let the stars of the *t.* thereof be dark
24. 15. the eye of the adulterer waiteth for the *t.*
Prov. 7. 9. he went the way to her house in the *t.*
Ezek. 12. 6. in sight thou shalt carry it forth in the *t.*
7. I digged, and brought it forth in the *t.* and bare
12. the prince shall bear it in the *t.* and go forth

TWINED, *See* FINE.

TWINKLING.

1 *Cor.* 15. 52. be all changed, in the *t.* of an eye

TWINS.

Gen. 25. 24. Rebekah had *t.* ‖ 38. 27. Tamar had *t.*
Cant. 4. 2. whereof every one bear *t.* 6. 6.
5. thy breasts like two roes that are *t.* 7. 3.

TWO.

Gen. 4. 19. and Lamech took unto him *t.* wives
6. 19. *t.* of every sort shalt thou bring into the ark
7. 2. of beasts that are not clean by *t.* 9. 15.
25. 23. *t.* nations are in thy womb, and *t.* manner of people shall be separated from thy bowels
27. 36. he hath supplanted me these *t.* times
32. 10. over Jordan, and now I am become *t.* bands
49. 14. Issachar is an ass couching between *t.* burd.
Exod. 16. 22. they gathered *t.* omers for one man
21. 21. if he continue a day or *t.* not be punished
Lev. 5. 7. shall bring *t.* turtle-doves or *t.* pigeons, 12. 8. | 14. 22. | 15. 14, 29. *Num.* 6. 10.
11. if he be not able to bring *t.* turtle-doves
12. 5. if a maid, then she shall be unclean *t.* weeks
16. 7. Aaron shall take *t.* goats ‖ 8. cast lots upon *t.*
24. 6. shalt set the cakes in *t.* rows, six on a row
Num. 7. 3. brought a waggon for *t.* of the princes
17. *t.* oxen, 23, 29, 35, 41, 47, 53, 59, 65, 71.
10. 2. make thee *t.* trumpets of silver for calling
22. 22. his ass, Balaam's *t.* servants were with him
29. 14. the *t.* rams. 17, 20, 23, 26, 29, 32.
31. 27. and divide the prey into *t.* parts
Deut. 3. 8. *t.* kings, 21. | 4. 47. *Josh.* 2. 10. | 9. 10.
17. 6. at the mouth of *t.* or three witnesses be put to death, 19. 15. *Mat.* 18. 16. 2 *Cor.* 13. 1.
21. 15. if a man have *t.* wives, one beloved
32. 30. how should *t.* put ten thousand to flight?
Josh. 14. 3. *t.* tribes, 4. | 21. 16. ‖ 21. 25. *t.* cities
Judg. 5. 30. divided to every man a damsel or *t.*
11. 37. let me alone *t.* months, that I may bewail
16. 28. that I may be avenged for my *t.* eyes
Ruth 1. 19. they *t.* went till they came to Beth-lehem
4. 11. which *t.* did build the house of Israel
1 *Sam.* 1. 2. *t.* wives, 27. 3. | 30. 5, 18. 2 *Sam.* 2. 2.
2 *Sam.* 8. 2. even with *t.* lines measured he to put
1 *Kings* 2. 5. and what he did to the *t.* captains
1 *Kings* 3. 18. there was none save we *t.* in the house
5. 12. Hiram and Sol. *t.* made a league together
14. and *t.* months they were at home
11. 29. and they *t.* were alone in the field
12. 28. Jeroboam made *t.* calves, 2 *Kings* 17. 16.
17. 12. I am gathering *t.* sticks to dress it
18. 21. how long halt ye between *t.* opinions?
20. 27. Israel pitched like *t.* little flocks of kids
2 *Kings* 1. 14. fire burnt up the *t.* former captains
2. 6. they *t.* went on ‖ 24. came forth *t.* she-bears
5. 22. give, I pray, thee, *t.* changes of garments
23. be content, take *t.* talents, and he urged him
7. 1. *t.* measures of barley for a shekel, 16, 18.
10. 4. behold, *t.* kings stood not before him
1 *Chron.* 4. 5. Ashur, father of Tekoa, had *t.* wives
11. 21. of three, he was more honourable than the *t.*
2 *Chron.* 24. 3. Jehoiada took for Joash *t.* wives
Job 13. 20. only do not *t.* things unto me, then
42. 7. my wrath is kindled against thy *t.* friends
Prov. 30. 7. *t.* things have I required of thee
Eccl. 4. 9. *t.* are better than one, because they have
11. if *t.* lie together ‖ 12. *t.* shall withstand him
Cant. 4. 5. thy *t.* breasts are like *t.* young roes, 7. 3.
6. 13. Shulamite, as it were company of *t.* armies
Isa. 17. 6. *t.* or three berries in top of the bough
47. 9. but these *t.* things shall come to thee
51. 19. these *t.* things are come unto thee
Jer. 2. 13. my people have committed *t.* evils
3. 14. I will take one of a city, and *t.* of a family
Ezek. 21. 19. thou son of man appoint thee *t.* ways
23. 2. there were *t.* women, daughters of one mother
35. 10. hast said, these *t.* nations shall be mine
37. 22. and they shall be no more *t.* nations
47. 13. tribes of Isr. Joseph shall have *t.* portions
Dan. 12. 5. looked, and behold, there stood other *t.*
Amos 3. 3. can *t.* walk together, except they be agreed
4. 8. so *t.* or three cities wandered unto one city
Zech. 4. 3. *t.* olive trees by it, 11, 12.
14. these are the *t.* anointed ones that stand
5. 9. there came out *t.* women who had wings
6. 1. four chariots from between *t.* mountains
11. 7. I took unto me *t.* staves and fed the flock
13. 8. *t.* parts therein shall be cut off and die
Mat. 6. 24. no man can serve *t.* masters, *Luke* 16. 13.
18. 8. than having *t.* hands or *t.* feet, *Mark* 9. 43.
9. rather than having *t.* eyes, *Mark* 9. 47.
16. not hear, then take with thee one or *t.* more
19. that if *t.* of you shall agree on earth touching
20. where *t.* or three are gathered in my name
22. 40. on these *t.* hang all the law and prophets
24. 40. then shall *t.* be in the field, one taken
25. 17. he that had received *t.* he gained other *t.*
Mark 6. 7. he began to send them forth by *t.* and *t.*
11. 1. he sendeth *t.* disciples, 14. 13. *Luke* 19. 29.
12. 42. she threw in *t.* mites, which make a farthing
16. 12. after that Jesus appeared to *t.* of them
Luke 3. 11. he that hath *t.* coats, let him impart
7. 41. a certain creditor which had *t.* debtors
9. 3. neither take money, nor have *t.* coats apiece
10. 35. took out *t.* pence and gave them to the host
Acts 1. 24. shew whether of these *t.* thou hast chosen
1 *Cor.* 6. 16. for *t.* shall be one flesh, *Eph.* 5. 31.
14. 27. let it be by *t.* or at the most by three
29. let prophets speak *t.* or three, and let other
Gal. 4. 24. an allegory, for these are the *t.* covenants
Phil. 1. 23. for I am in a strait betwixt *t.* a desire
1 *Tim.* 5. 19. but before *t.* or three witnesses
Heb. 6. 18. that by *t.* immutable things we might
10. 28. died without mercy under *t.* or three witn.
Rev. 9. 12. there come *t.* woes more hereafter
11. 3. I will give power to my *t.* witnesses
4. these are *t.* olive trees and *t.* candlesticks
10. because these *t.* prophets tormented them
12. 14. and to the woman were given *t.* wings
13. 11. and he had *t.* horns like a lamb, spake as
See DAUGHTERS, DAYS, KIDNEYS, LAMBS, SONS.

TWO *men.*

Exod. 2. 13. *t. men* of the Hebrews strove together
Num. 11. 26. there remained *t. men* in the camp
Josh. 2. 1. he sent out *t. men* to spy secretly
4. Rahab hid the *t. men* ‖ 23. the *t. men* returned
1 *Sam.* 10. 2. find *t. men* by Rachel's sepulchre
2 *Sam.* 12. 1. there were *t. m.* in one city, one rich
1 *Kings* 2. 32. fell on *t. m.* more righteous than he
21. 10. set *t. m.* sons of Belial before Naboth, 13.
Mat. 9. 27. *t.* blind *men* followed him, crying
Luke 9. 30. behold, there talked with him *t. men*
17. 34. *t. men* in one bed ‖ 36. *t. men* in the field
18. 10. *t. men* went up to the temple to pray
24. 4. as they were perplexed, behold, *t. men* stood by them in shining garments, *Acts* 1. 10.
John 8. 17. that the testimony of *t. men* is true
Acts 9. 38. they sent *t. men* to Peter, desiring him

TWO *tables.*

Exod. 31. 18. gave to Moses *t. tables* of testimony
32. 15. the *t. tables* were in his hands, 34. 29.
34. 1. hew thee *t. tables* of stone, *Deut.* 10. 1.
4. he hewed *t. tables* of stone, *Deut.* 10. 3.
Deut. 4. 13. he wrote upon the *t. tables*, 5. 22.
9. 10. the Lord delivered unto me *t. tables*, 11.
1 *Kings* 8. 9. there was nothing in the ark save the *t. tables* of stone put at Horeb, 2 *Chron.* 5. 10.
Ezek. 40. 39. *t. tab.* on this side ‖ 40. *t. tab.* on that

TWO *years.*

Gen. 11. 10. begat Arphaxad *t. years* after the flood
45. 6. these *t. years* hath the famine been in land
1 *Sam.* 13. 1. when Saul had reigned *t. years*
2 *Sam.* 2. 10. Ish-bosheth Saul's son reigned *t. years*
13. 23. after *t. years*, Absalom had sheep shearers
14. 28. Absalom dwelt *t. years* in Jerusalem
1 *Kings* 15. 25. Nadab reigned over Israel *t. years*
16. 8. Elah ‖ 22. 51. Ahaziah reigned *t. years*
2 *Kings* 15. 23. Pekahiah ‖ 21. 19. Amon, 2 *Chr.* 33. 21.
2 *Chron.* 21. 19. after *t. years* his bowels fell out
Jer. 28. 3. within *t. y.* I'll bring again vessels, 11.
Amos 1. 1. words of Amos *t. y.* before earthquake
Mat. 2. 16. slew children from *t. years* and under
Acts 19. 10. *t. years* they in Asia heard the word
28. 30. Paul dwelt *t. years* in his hired house

TWO-FOLD.
Mat. 23. 15. ye make him *t.* more the child of hell
See TWENTY THIRTY, FORTY, FIFTY, HUNDRED, THOUSAND.

TYPES.
1 *Cor.* 10. † 11. these things happened to them for *t.*

U.

UMPIRE.
Job 9. † 33. neither is there any *u.* betwixt us

UNACCUSTOMED.
Jer. 31. 18. Ephraim, as a bullock *u.* to the yoke

UNADVISEDLY.
Psal. 106. 33. so that he spake *u.* with his lips

UNAWARES.
Gen. 31. 20. Jacob stole away *u.* to Laban, 26.
Num. 35. 11. slayer may flee thither, who killeth any person *u.* 15. *Deut.* 4. 42. *Josh.* 20. 3, 9.
Psal. 35. 8. let destruction come on him at *u.*
Luke 21. 34. and so that day come upon you *u.*
Gal. 2. 4. because of false brethren *u.* brought in
Heb. 13. 2. for some have entertained angels *u.*
Jude 4. for there are certain men crept in *u.*

UNBELIEVERS.
Luke 12. 46. will appoint him his portion with *u.*
1 *Cor.* 6. 6. but brother goeth to law before *u.*
14. 23. and there come in those that are *u.*
2 *Cor.* 6. 14. be ye not unequally yoked with *u.*

UNBELIEVING.
Acts 14. 2. the *u.* Jews stirred up the Gentiles
1 *Cor.* 7. 14. for the *u.* husband is sanctified by the wife, the *u.* wife is sanctified by the husband
15. but if the *u.* depart, let him depart, a brother
Tit. 1. 15. unto them that are *u.* is nothing pure
Rev. 21. 8. the *u.* shall have their part in the lake

UNBELIEF
Is taken sometimes for weak faith, as in Mark 9. 24. Lord, I believe, help thou mine *unbelief. It is a capital and fountain evil; and generally it is taken for a privation and utter want of faith, when the promises and threatenings in God's word are wholly distrusted. Those Jews who did not rely on God's word, but rejected the promises, rebelled against the precepts, and murmured against the providence of God, could not enter into the promised land, but were consumed in the wilderness,* Heb. 3. 19. *And this nation was afterwards rejected by God, because of their* unbelief; *they would not accept of* Christ; *nor acknowledge him for the* Messiah, *Rom.* 11. 20. *because of unbelief,* they were broken off. *And as the Israelites, by reason of* unbelief, *were not allowed to enter into Canaan,* so unbelievers *shall not enter into heaven. The law of faith is unalterable.* John 3. 36. He that believeth not the Son shall not see life.
Unbelief *renders the benefits of Christ fruitless and ineffectual; it is said,* Mark 6. 5, 6. *that Christ could do no mighty works in his own country,* because of their *unbelief; it made them unfit for receiving benefit from his miracles, and therefore he suspended his miraculous power.* Unbelief *often begets confusion, and disables men to do that which otherwise they would have been able to do, if they had believed; thus when the man brought his son, who was a lunatic, to the apostles, to be cured by them; they seeing his condition so bad, by reason of the devil that possessed him, and that for so long a time together, questioned whether the power they had received would enable them to cast him out and cure the man,* Mat. 17. 16. Unbelief *hath often corporal punishment attending it: Zacharias, because he believed not the words of the angel, was struck dumb for a season,* Luke 1. 20. Unbelievers have their part in the lake that burns with fire and brimstone, *Rev.* 21. 8. *Christ died not to expiate final infidelity. This sin charges all the guilt of sinners upon themselves. It renders the sufferings of Christ fruitless as to them: For it is not the preparation of a sovereign remedy that cures the disease, but the application of it. As our sins were imputed to Christ, upon account of his union with us in nature, and his consent to become our surety; so his righteousness is meritoriously imputed unto us, upon our union with him by a true and lively faith. It is not from any defect of mercy in God, or righteousness in Christ, but for the obstinate refusal of it, that men certainly perish in* unbelief.
Mat. 13. 58. he did not many works, because of *u.*
17. 20. could not cast him out, because of your *u.*
Mark 6. 6. and he marvelled because of their *u.*
9. 24. Lord, I believe, help thou mine *u.*
16. 14. and upbraided them with their *u.*
Rom. 3. 3. shall their *u.* make faith without effect?
4. 20. he staggered not at the promise through *u.*
11. 20. well, because of *u.* they were broken off
23. if they abide not still in *u.* shall be grafted
30. yet have now obtained mercy thro' their *u.*
32. for God hath concluded them all in *u.*
Eph. 5. † 6. the wrath of God on the children of *u.*
1 *Tim.* 1. 13. because I did it ignorantly in *u.*
Heb. 3. 12. lest be in any of you an evil heart of *u.*
19. they could not enter in because of *u.* 4. 6.
4. 11. lest any fall after the same example of *u.*

UNBLAMEABLE.
Col. 1. 22. to present you holy, *u.* in his sight
1 *Thess.* 3. 13. he may stablish your hearts *u.*

UNBLAMEABLY.
1 *Thess.* 2. 10. how *u.* we have behaved ourselves

UNCERTAIN.
1 *Cor.* 14. 8. if the trumpet give an *u.* sound
1 *Tim.* 6. 17. nor trust in *u.* riches, but in God

UNCERTAINLY.
1 *Cor.* 9. 26. I therefore so run, not as *u.* so fight I

UNCHANGEABLE.
Heb. 7. 24. but this man hath an *u.* priesthood

UNCIRCUMCISED.
Gen. 17. 14. the *u.* man-child shall be cut off
Gen. 34. 14. cannot give our sister to one that is *u.*
Exod. 6. 12. Pharaoh hear me who am of *u.* lips, 30.
12. 48. for no *u.* person shall eat of the passover
Lev. 19. 23. shall count the fruit *u.* three years
26. 41. if then their *u.* hearts be humbled
Josh. 5. 7. Joshua circumcised, for they were *u.*
Judg. 14. 3. that thou goest to take a wife of the *u.*
15. 18. now shall I fall into the hands of these *u.*
1 *Sam.* 14. 6. let us go to the garrison of the *u.*
17. 26. for who is this *u.* Philistine? 36.
31. 4. lest these *u.* come and abuse me, 1 *Chr.* 10. 4.
2 *Sam.* 1. 20. lest the daughters of the *u.* triumph
Isa. 52. 1. there shall no more come into thee the *u.*
Jer. 6. 10. their ear is *u.* they cannot hearken
9. 25. I will punish the circumcised with the *u.*
26. these nations are *u.* all house of Israel are *u.*
Ezek. 28. 10. thou shalt die the death of the *u.*
31. 18. thou shalt lie in the midst of the *u.* 32. 19, 21, 24, 25, 26, 27, 28, 29, 30, 32.
44. 7. ye have brought strangers *u.* in heart and *u.* in flesh into my sanctuary to pollute it, 9.
Acts 7. 51. ye stiff necked and *u.* in heart and ears
11. 3. thou wentest in to men *u.* and didst eat
Rom. 4. 11. faith which he had yet being *u.* 12.
1 *Cor.* 7. 18. circumcised, let him not become *u.*

UNCIRCUMCISION.
Rom. 2. 25. if a breaker, thy circumcision is made *u.*
26. if the *u.* keep the righteousness of the law, shall not his *u.* be counted for circumcision?
27. shall not *u.* which is by nature judge thee?
3. 30. which shall justify the *u.* through faith
4. 9. cometh this blessedness on circumcision or *u.*
10. how was it then reckoned? when he was in circumcision or in *u.* not in circumcision but *u.*
1 *Cor.* 7. 18. is any man called in *u.*? let him not be
19. circumcision is nothing, and *u.* is nothing
Gal. 2. 7. when saw the gospel of *u.* committed to me
5. 6. neither circumcision availeth nor *u.* 6. 15.
Eph. 2. 11. who are called *u.* by that called circum.
Col. 2. 13. and you being dead in the *u.* of your flesh
3. 11. neither circumcision nor *u.* but Christ is all

UNCLE.
Lev. 10. 4. the son of Uzziel, the *u.* of Aaron
20. 20. if a man lie with his *u.* wife, he hath uncovered his *u.* nakedness, they shall bear their sin
25. 49. either his *u.* or *u.* son may redeem him
1 *Sam.* 10. 14. and Saul's *u.* said unto him, 15.
14. 50. captain was Abner, son of Ner, Saul's *u.*
1 *Chron.* 27. 32. Jonathan David's *u.* a counsellor
Esth. 2. 7. Mordecai brought up his *u.* daughter, 15.
Jer. 32. 7. Hanameel the son of Shallum thine *u.*
8. so Hanameel my *u.* son came unto me, 9. 12.
Amos 6. 10. and a man's *u.* shall take him up

UNCLEAN.
Lev. 5. 2. if a soul touch any *u.* thing the carcase of *u.* cattle or *u.* things, he shall be *u.* 11. 26.
10. 10. put difference between *u.* and clean, 11. 47.
11. 4. it is *u.* to you, 5, 6, 7, 29, *Deut.* 14. 19.
8. they are *u.* unto you, 26, 27, 28, 31. *Deut.* 14. 7.
24. for these ye shall be *u.* until the evening, 25, 28, 31, 32, 33, 39, 40. | 14. 46. | 15. 5, 6, 7, 8, 10, 11, 16, 17, 18, 19, 21, 22, 23, 27. | 17. 15. | 22. 6. *Num.* 19. 7, 8, 10, 21, 22.
32. it shall be *u.* 33, 34, 35, 36, 38. | 15. 4, 9, 20, 24, 26.
12. 2. then she shall be *u.* seven days, 5. | 15. 25.
13. 3. priest shall look on him and pronounce him *u.* 8, 11, 15, 20, 22, 25, 27, 30, 44, 59.
11. for he is *u.* 14. 36, 44, 46. | 15. 2, 24.
45. the leper, in whom the plague is, shall cry, *u. u.*
14. 40. they shall cast them into an *u.* place, 41. 45.
57. to teach when it is *u.* and when it is clean
22. 5. whoso toucheth, whereby he may be made *u.*
Num. 6. 7. he shall not make himself *u.* for father
Deut. 12. 15. *u.* and clean eat thereof, 22. | 15. 22.
Josh. 22. 19. if the land of your possession be *u.*
Ezra 9. 11. the land ye go to possess is an *u.* land
Job 36. 14. the life of hypocrites is among the *u.*
Eccl. 9. 2. there is one event to the clean and *u.*
Isa. 6. 5. I am undone, I am a man of *u.* lips, I dwell in the midst of a people of *u.* lips
35. 8. be a way, the *u.* shall not pass over it
52. 1. there shall no more come into thee the *u.*
Lam. 4. 15. depart ye, it is *u.* depart, dep. touch not
Ezek. 22. 26. put no difference between clean and *u.*
44. 23. cause them discern between the clean and *u.*
Hos. 9. 3. they shall eat *u.* things in Assyria
Hag. 2. 13. if one that is *u.* touch it, shall it be *u.*
14. and that which they offer there is *u.*
Luke 4. 33. a man who had a spirit of an *u.* devil
Acts 10. 28. not call any man common or *u.* 11. 8.
Rom. 14. 14. nothing is *u.* of itself, but to him that esteemeth any thing to be *u.* to him it is *u.*
1 *Cor.* 7. 14. else were your children *u.* but now
2 *Cor.* 6. 17. touch not *u.* thing, I will receive you
Eph. 5. 5. that no *u.* person hath any inheritance
Heb. 9. 13. the ashes of an heifer sprinkling the *u.*
Rev. 18. 2. Babyl. is become a cage of every *u.* bird
See BEAST, SPIRIT, THING.

UNCLEAN *Spirits.*
Mat. 10. 1. he gave power against *u. spir. Mark* 6. 7.
Mark 1. 27. he commandeth *u. spirits, Luke* 4. 36.
3. 11. and *u. spirits,* when they saw him, cried
5. 13. the *u. spirits* went out and entered into swine
Acts 5. 16. them which were vexed with *u. spirits*
8. 7. for *u. spirits* came out of many possessed
Rev. 16. 13. I saw three *u. spirits* like frogs come

UNCLEANNESS.
Lev. 5. 3. if he touch the *u.* of man, whatsoever *u.* it be, a man shall be defiled, 7. 21. | 22. 5.
7. 20. that eateth, having his *u.* on him, 22. 3.
14. 19. for him that is to be cleansed from his *u.*
15. 31. thus ye shall separate Israel from their *u.*
18. 19. as long as she is put apart for her *u.*
Num. 5. 19. if thou hast not gone aside to *u.*
19. 13. he shall be unclean, his *u.* is yet upon him
Deut. 23. 10. by reason of *u.* that chanceth him
24. 1. because he hath found some *u.* in her
2 *Sam.* 11. 4. for she was purified from her *u.*
2 *Chron.* 29. 16. the priests brought out all the *u.*
Ezra 9. 11. they have filled the land with their *u.*
Ezek. 36. 17. way as the *u.* of a removed woman
Ezek. 39. 24. according to their *u.* have I done to them
Zech. 13. 1. shall be a fountain opened for sin and *u.*
Mat. 23. 27. but are within full of bones, and all *u.*
Rom. 1. 24. wherefore God also gave them up to *u.*
6. 19. ye have yielded your members servants to *u.*
2 *Cor.* 12. 21. and have not repented of the *u.*
Gal. 5. 19. the works of the flesh are these, *u.* strife
Eph. 4. 19. to work all *u.* with greediness
5. 3. all *u.* let not be once be named among you
Col. 3. 5. mortify therefore fornication, *u.* and covet.
1 *Thess.* 2. 3. for our exhortation was not of *u.*
4. 7. God hath not called us to *u.* but to holiness
2 *Pet.* 2. 10. them that walk in the lust of *u.*

UNCLEANNESSES.
Ezek. 36. 29. I will save you from all your *u.*

UNCLOTHED.
2 *Cor.* 5. 4. not for that we would be *u.* but clothed

UNCOMELY.
1 *Cor.* 7. 36. that he behaveth *u.* towards his virgin
12. 23. our *u.* parts have more abundant comeliness

UNCONDEMNED.
Acts 16. 37. they have beaten us openly *u.* Romans
22. 25. to scourge a man that is a Roman and *u.*

UNCORRUPTNESS.
Tit. 2. 7. in doctrine shewing *u.* gravity, sincerity

UNCOVER.
Lev. 10. 6. *u.* not your heads neither rend clothes
18. 6. not *u.* nakedness of one that is near of kin
7. the nakedness of thy father shalt thou not *u.*
8. nakedness of thy father's wife ‖ 9. of thy sister
10. nakedness of thy son's daughter shalt not *u.*
11. the nakedness of thy father's wife's daughter
12. father's sister ‖ 13. mother's sister, 20. 19.
14. not *u.* the nakedness of thy father's brother
15. thy daughter-in law ‖ 16. thy brother's wife
17. not *u.* the nakedness of a woman and her daugh.
18. shalt not *u.* the nakedness of thy wife's sister
19. not *u.* nakedness of a woman put apart, 20. 18.
21. 10. the high priest shall not *u.* his head
Num. 5. 18. the priest shall *u.* the woman's head
Ruth 3. 4. and thou shalt go in and *u.* his feet
1 *Sam.* 20. † 2. he will *u.* mine ear ‖ † 12. *u.* thine ear
Isa. 47. 2. *u.* thy locks, *u.* the thigh pass over

UNCOVERED.
Gen. 9. 21. and Noah was *u.* within his tent
Lev. 20. 11. he hath *u.* his father's nakedness
17. *u.* his sister's ‖ 20. *u.* his uncle's nakedness
18. she hath *u.* the fountain of her blood
Ruth 3. 7. she came softly and *u.* his feet and laid
2 *Sam.* 6. 20. who *u.* himself as the vain fellows
Isa. 20. 4. led away even with their buttocks *u.*
22. 6. Elam bare the quiver, and Kir *u.* the shield
47. 3. thy nakedness shall be *u.* thy shame seen
Jer. 49. 10. but I have *u.* his secret places
Ezek. 4. 7. and thine arm shall be *u.* shalt prophesy
Hab. 2. 16. drink, and let thy foreskin be *u.*
Mark 2. 4. they *u.* the roof where he was
1 *Cor.* 11. 5. that prophesieth with her head *u.*
13. is it comely that a woman pray unto God *u.*?

UNCOVERETH.
Lev. 20. 19. for he *u.* his near kin, bear their iniquity
Deut. 27. 20. because he *u.* his father's skirt
1 *Sam.* 22. † 8. there is none that *u.* mine ear
2 *Sam.* 6. 20. as one of the vain fellows *u.* himself
Job 33. † 16. he *u.* the ears of men and sealeth

UNCTION.
1 *John* 2. 20. but ye have an *u.* from the Holy One

UNDEFILED.
Psal. 119. 1. blessed are the *u.* in the way
Cant. 5. 2. open to me my love, my dove, my *u.*
6. 9. my dove, my *u.* is one; she is the only one
Heb. 7. 26. an high priest who is holy, harmless, *u.*
13. 4. marriage is honourable in all, and the bed *u.*
Jam. 1. 27. pure religion and *u.* before God
1 *Pet.* 1. 4. to an inheritance incorruptible, *u.*

UNDER.
Gen. 49. 25. blessings of the deep that lieth *u.*
Exod. 6. 6. I will bring you out from *u.* the burdens
Josh. 7. 21. in the midst of my tent and silver *u.* it
Ruth 2. 12. *u.* whose wings thou art come to trust
1 *Sam.* 21. 3. what is *u.* thy hand give me five loaves
1 *Kings* 18. 23. lay it on wood, and put no fire *u.*
2 *Kings* 8. 20. Edom revolted from *u.* hand of Judah
13. 5. Israel went out from *u.* the Syrians
2 *Chr.* 28. 10. ye purpose to keep *u.* Judah for bond.
Psal. 44. 5. through thy name will we tread them *u.*
Cant. 8. 3. his right hand should be *u.* my head
Isa. 57. 5. with idols *u.* every green tree, *Jer.* 2. 20.
Jer. 10. 11. the gods, they shall perish from the earth, and from *u.* these heavens, *Lam.* 3. 66.
Dan. 4. 14. let the beasts get away from *u.* it
9. 12. *u.* the whole heaven hath not been done
Hos. 4. 12. have gone a whoring from *u.* their God
Mat. 2. 16. slew children from two years old and *u.*
8. 9. I am *u.* authority, having soldiers *u.* me
Luke 7. 6. that thou shouldst enter *u.* my roof
John 1. 48. when thou wast *u.* the fig-tree, I saw thee
Rom. 3. 9. we have proved that they are all *u.* sin
6. 15. because we are not *u.* the law, but *u.* grace
7. 14. the law is spiritual, but I am carnal, sold *u.* sin
1 *Cor.* 6. 12. I will not be brought *u.* power of any
9. 20. to them that are *u.* the law, as *u.* the law
27. I keep *u.* my body and bring it into subjection
10. 1. how that all our fathers were *u.* the cloud
Gal. 3. 10. *u.* the curse ‖ 22. concluded all *u.* sin
23. before faith came, we were kept *u.* the law
25. faith is come, we are no longer *u.* a school. mas.
Phil. 2. 10. of things in earth and things *u.* the earth
1 *Tim.* 6. 1. as many servants as are *u.* the yoke
Heb. 7. 11. for *u.* it the people received the law
Jude 6. he hath reserved in chains *u.* darkness
See FEET, HIM, LAW, ME, SUN, THEE, THEM, US.

UNDERGIRDING.
Acts 27. 17. they used helps, *u.* the ship, fearing

UNDERNEATH.
Deut. 33. 27. and *u.* are the everlasting arms

UNDERSETTERS.
1 *Kings* 7. 30. the four corners thereof had *u.* 34.

UNDERSTAND.
Gen. 11. 7. they may not *u.* one another's speech
41. 15. I heard say that thou canst *u.* a dream

Num. 16. 30. ye shall u. that these have provoked
Deut. 28. 49. a nation whose tongue thou shalt not u.
2 Kings 18. 26. speak, I pray thee, to thy servants in the Syrian language, for we u. it, Isa. 36. 11.
1 Chron. 28. 19. the Lord made me u. in writing
Neh. 8. 3. he read before those that could u.
7. the Levites caused the people to u. the law, 8, 13.
Job 6. 24. cause me to u. wherein I have erred
23. 5. I would u. what he would say unto me
26. 14. the thunder of his power who can u.?
32. 9. neither do the aged u. judgment
36. 29. can any u. the spreadings of the clouds?
Psal. 14. 2. if there were any that did u. 53. 2.
19. 12. who can u. his errors? cleanse thou me
82. 5. they know not, neither will they u.
92. 6. knoweth not, neither doth a fool u. this
94. 8. u. ye brutish among the people, and, ye fools
107. 43. they shall u. the loving kindness of the L.
119. 27. make me u. the way of thy precepts
100. I u. more than the ancients, because I keep
Proc. 2. 5. then shalt thou u. the fear of the Lord
9. then shalt thou u. righteousness and equity
8. 5. O ye simple, u. wisdom, and, ye fools, be of
14. 8. the wisdom of the prudent is to u. his way
19. 25. reprove one, and he will u. knowledge
20. 24. how can a man then u. his own way?
28. 5. evil men u. not judgment, but they that seek the Lord u. all things
29. 19. for though he u. he will not answer
Isa. 6. 9. he said, hear ye indeed, but u. not
10. lest they u. with their heart, John 12. 40.
28. 9. whom shall he make to u. doctrine?
19. it shall be a vexation only to u. the report
32. 4. the heart of the rash shall u. knowledge
33. 19. a stammering tongue that thou canst not u.
40. † 14. and who made him u. and taught him?
41. 20. u. together that the Lord hath done this
43. 10. that ye may know and u. that I am he
44. 18. he hath shut their hearts, that they cannot u.
56. 11. and they are shepherds that cannot u.
Jer. 9. 12. who is the wise man that may u. this?
Ezek. 3. 6. to people whose words thou canst not u.
Dan. 8. 16. make this man to u. the vision
17. but he said unto me, u. O son of man
9. 13. and u. thy truth ‖ 23. u. the matter, 25.
10. 12. from the day thou didst set thy heart to u.
14. I am come to make thee u. what shall befall
11. 33. and they that u. shall instruct many
12. 10. the wicked shall not u. the wise shall u.
Hos. 4. 14. the people that doth not u. shall fall
14. 9. who is wise, and he shall u. these things?
Mic. 4. 12. neither u. they the counsel of the Lord
Mat. 13. 13. they hear not, neither do they u.
14. hear and not u. ‖ 15. 10. hear and u. Mark 7. 14.
15. 17. do not ye yet u.? 16. 9, 11. Mark 8. 17, 21.
24. 15. whoso readeth, let him u. Mark 13. 14.
Mark 4. 12. and not perceive, that hearing they may hear and not u. Luke 8. 10. Acts 28. 26.
14. 68. I know not nor u. I what thou sayest
Luke 24. 45. that they might u. the scriptures
John 8. 43. why do ye not u. my speech?
Rom. 15. 21. they that have not heard shall u.
1 Cor. 13. 2. and tho' I u. all mysteries am nothing
Heb. 11. 3. thro' faith we u. the worlds were framed
2 Pet. 2. 12. but these speak evil of things they u. not

UNDERSTANDEST.

Job 15. 9. what u. thou, which is not in us?
Psal. 139. 2. thou u. my thoughts afar off
Jer. 5. 15. neither u. thou what they say
Acts 8. 30. Philip said, u. thou what thou readest

UNDERSTANDETH.

1 Chron. 28. 9. Lord u. the imaginations of thoughts
Job 28. 23. God u. the way thereof and knoweth
Psal. 49. 20. man that is in honour and u. not
Prov. 8. 9. they are all plain to him that u.
14. 6. but knowledge is easy unto him that u.
Jer. 9. 24. let him glory in this, that he u. me
Mat. 13. 19. when any heareth the word and u. it not
23. is he that heareth the word and u. it
Rom. 3. 11. there is none that u. none seeketh God
1 Cor. 14. 2. speaketh not to men, for no man u.
16. say amen, seeing he u. not what thou sayest

UNDERSTANDING.

Exod. 31. 3. I have filled Bezaleel with wisdom and u. and in knowledge, 35. 31. | 36. 1.
Deut. 4. 6. for this is your wisdom and your u.
32. 28. neither is there any u. in them
1 Kings 3. 11. but hast asked for thyself u. to discern
4. 29. and God gave Solomon wisdom and u.
7. 14. Hiram was filled with wisdom and u.
1 Chron. 12. 32. were men that had u. of the times
22. 12. only the Lord give thee wisdom and u.
2 Chr. 2. 12. given David a wise son endued with u.
26. 5. Zechariah had u. in the visions of God
Ezra 8. 16. for Joiarib and Elnathan men of u.
Neh. 8. 2. before all that could hear with u.
10. 28. every one having knowledge and having u.
Job 12. 3. but I have u. as well as you
12. in length of days is u. ‖ 13. he hath u.
20. he taketh away the u. of the aged
17. 4. for thou hast hid their heart from u.
20. 3. the spirit of my u. causeth me to answer
26. 12. and by his u. he smiteth through the proud
28. 12. and where is the place of u.? 20.
28. to man he said, to depart from evil is u.
32. 8. the inspiration of Almighty giveth them u.
34. 10. therefore hearken to me, ye men of u.
16. if now thou hast u. hear this, hearken
34. let men of u. tell me, let a wise man hearken
38. 4. where wast thou? declare, if thou hast u.
36. or who hath given u. to the heart?
39. 17. neither hath he imparted to her u.
Psal. 32. 9. be ye not as the mule that hath no u.
47. 7. God is the King, sing ye praises with u.
49. 3. the meditation of my heart, shall be of u.
119. 34. give me u. 73, 125, 144, 169.
99. I have more u. ‖ 130. thy word giveth u.
104. thro' thy precepts I get u. therefore I hate
147. 5. great is our Lord, his u. is infinite
Prov. 1. 2. to know wisdom, to perceive words of u.
2. 2. so that thou apply thine heart to u.
3. and if thou liftest up thy voice for u.
6. out of his mouth cometh knowled. and u.
11. discretion preserve thee, u. shall keep thee
3. 5. trust in the Lord and lean not to thine own u.
13. happy is the man that getteth u.
19. by u. hath he established the heavens
4. 1. ye children, attend to know u. ‖ 5. get u. 7.
5. 1. my son, bow thine ear to my u.
6. 32. whoso committeth adultery, lacketh u.
7. 4. thou art my sister, and call u. thy kinswoman
8. 1. and doth not u. put forth her voice?
14. I am u. ‖ 9. 6. and go in the way of u.
9. 4. as for him that wanteth u. she saith, 16.
10. and the knowledge of the holy is u.
10. 13. in lips of him that hath u. wisdom is found
14. 29. he that is slow to wrath is of great u.
33. wisdom resteth in heart of him that hath u.
15. 14. heart of him that hath u. seeks knowledge
32. but he that heareth reproof getteth u.
16. 16. to get u. rather to be chosen than silver
22. u. is a well-spring of life to him that hath it
17. 24. wisdom is before him that hath u.
18. 2. a fool hath no delight in u. but that his heart
19. 8. he that keepeth u. shall find good
25. reprove one that hath u. he will understand
21. 16. a man that wandereth out of the way of u.
30. there is no u. nor counsel against the Lord
23. 23. buy also wisdom, and instruction, and u.
24. 3. and by u. an house is established
28. 11. the poor that hath u. searcheth him out
16. the prince that wanteth u. is an oppressor
30. 2. and have not the u. of a man
Eccl. 9. 11. bread to wise nor yet riches to men of u.
Isa. 11. 2. the spirit of u. shall rest upon him
3. make him of quick u. in the fear of the Lord
27. 11. for it is a people of no u. therefore he that
29. 14. the u. of their prudent men shall be hid
16. say of him that framed it, he had no u.?
24. they also that erred in spirit shall come to u.
40. 14. and who shewed to him the way of u.?
28. the Lord, there is no searching of his u.
44. 19. neither is there knowledge nor u. to say
Jer. 3. 15. give pastors which shall feed you with u.
4. 22. for my people is foolish, they have no u.
5. 21. hear, O foolish people, and without u.
51. 15. he hath stretched out the heaven by his u.
Ezek. 28. 4. with thy u. thou hast got riches
Dan. 1. 17. Daniel had u. in visions and dreams
20. in all matters of u. he found them better
2. 21. he giveth knowledge to them that know u.
4. 34. mine u. returned to me, I blessed Most High
5. 11. light and u. was found in him, 12, 14.
9. 22. I am now come forth to give thee u.
10. 1. and Daniel had u. of the vision
11. 35. some of them of u. shall fall, to try them
Hos. 13. 2. have made idols according to their own u.
Obad. 7. a wound under thee, there is no u. in him
8. shall I not destroy u. out of the mount of Esau?
Mat. 15. 16. are ye also yet without u.? Mark 7. 18.
Mark 12. 33. and to love him with all the u.
Luke 1. 3. to me, having had perfect u. of things
2. 47. all that heard were astonished at his u.
24. 45. then opened he their u. that they might
Rom. 1. 31. without u. covenant-breakers
1 Cor. 1. 19. bring to nothing the u. of the prudent
14. 14. my spirit prayeth, but my u. is unfruitful
15. I will pray with the u. sing with the u.
19. I had rather speak five words with my u.
20. be not children in u. but in u. be men
Eph. 1. 18. the eyes of your u. being enlightened
4. 18. having the u. darkened, being alienated
Phil. 4. 7. the peace of God which passeth all u.
Col. 1. 9. that ye might be filled with all spiritual u.
2. 2. to all riches of the full assurance of u.
2 Tim. 2. 7. the Lord give thee u. in all things
1 John 5. 20. the Son of God hath given us an u.
Rev. 13. 18. him that hath u. count number of beast

See GOOD.

Man of UNDERSTANDING.

Ezra 8. 18. and they brought us a *man of u.*
Prov. 1. 5. a *man of u.* shall attain unto wise counsels
10. 23. but a *man of u.* hath wisdom
11. 12. but a *man of u.* holdeth his peace
15. 21. but a *man of u.* walketh uprightly
17. 27. a *man of u.* is of an excellent spirit
28. that shutteth his lips, is esteemed a *man of u.*
20. 5. but a *man of u.* will draw out counsel
28. 2. by a *man of u.* the state shall be prolonged

Void of UNDERSTANDING.

Prov. 7. 7. I discerned a young man *void of u.*
10. 13. a rod for back of him that is *void of u.*
12. 11. that followeth vain persons is *void of u.*
17. 18. a man *void of u.* striketh hands, is surety
24. 30. by the vineyard of the man *void of u.*

UNDERSTANDINGS.

Job 32. † 11. behold, I gave ear to your u.
Isa. 40. † 14. and who shewed to him the way of u.

UNDERSTANDING, *Adjective.*

Deut. 1. 13. take ye wise men and u. and known
4. 6. surely this great nation is an u. people
1 Kings 3. 9. give thy servant an u. heart to judge
12. lo, I have given thee a wise and an u. heart
Prov. 8. 5. and, ye fools, be ye of an u. heart
Dan. 1. 4. u. science ‖ 8. 23. u. dark sentences
Eph. 5. 17. but u. what the will of the Lord is
1 Tim. 1. 7. teachers, u. neither what they say

UNDERSTOOD.

Gen. 42. 23. they knew not that Joseph u. them
Deut. 32. 29. O that they were wise, that they u.
1 Sam. 4. 6. they u. that the ark of Lord was come
26. 4. David u. that Saul was come in deed
2 Sam. 3. 37. peo. u. it was not of Dav. to slay Abn.
Neh. 8. † 2. the law before all that u. in hearing
12. they had u. the words that were declared
13. 7. I u. of the evil Eliashib did for Tobiah
Job 13. 1. lo, mine ear hath heard and u. it
42. 3. therefore have I uttered that I u. not
Psal. 73. 17. went to sanctuary, then u. I their end
81. 5. where I heard a language that I u. not
106. 7. our fathers u. not thy wonders in Egypt
Isa. 40. 21. have ye not u. from foundations of earth
44. 18. not known nor u. for he shut their eyes
Dan. 8. 27. was astonished at the vision, but none u.
Dan. 9. 2. I Dan. u. by books ‖ 10. 1. he u. vision
12. 8. I heard, but I u. not, then said I, O my L.
Mat. 13. 51. have ye u. all these things? yea, Lord
16. 12. then u. they how he bade them not beware
17. 13. they u. that he spake of John the Baptist
Mark 9. 32. but they u. not that saying, Luke 2. 50. | 9. 45. John 8. 27. | 10. 6.
Luke 18. 34. and they u. none of these things
John 12. 16. these things u. not his disciples
Acts 7. 25. he supposed they would have u. that G. by his hand would deliver them, but they u. not
23. 27. I rescued him, having u. he was a Roman
34. and when I u. that he was of Cilicia
Rom. 1. 20. being u. by the things that are made
1 Cor. 13. 11. when I was a child, I u. as a child
14. 9. except ye utter by tongue words easy to be u.
2 Pet. 3. 16. in which are some things hard to be u.

UNDERTAKE.

Isa. 38. 14. O Lord, I am oppressed, u. for me

UNDERTOOK.

Esth. 9. 23. the Jews u. to do as they had begun

UNDO.

Isa. 58. 6. is not this the fast? to u. heavy burdens
Zeph. 3. 19. at that time I will u. all that afflict thee

UNDONE.

Num. 21. 29. thou art u. O people of Chemosh
Josh. 11. 15. Josh. left nothing u. of all commanded
Isa. 6. 5. woe is me, for I am u. am of unclean lips
Mat. 23. 23. not to leave the other u. Luke 11. 42

UNDRESSED.

Lev. 25. 5. nor gather grapes of thy vine u. 11.

UNEQUAL.

Ezek. 18. 25. hear, now, are not your ways u.? 29.

UNEQUALLY.

2 Cor. 6. 14. be not u. yoked with unbelievers

UNFEIGNED.

2 Cor. 6. 6. by kindness, by Holy Ghost, by love u.
1 Tim. 1. 5. charity out of a pure heart, and faith u.
2 Tim. 1. 5. when I call to remembrance the u. faith
1 Pet. 1. 22. thro' Spirit unto u. love of the brethren

UNFAITHFUL.

Prov. 25. 19. confidence in an u. man in trouble

UNFAITHFULLY.

Psal. 78. 57. they dealt u. like their fathers
Mal. 2. † 14. let none deal u. against the wife

UNFRUITFUL.

Mat. 13. 22. the care of this world, and the deceitfulness of riches, choke the word, and he becometh u. Mark 4. 19.
1 Cor. 14. 14. spirit prays, but my understand. is u.
Eph. 5. 11. have no fellowship with the u. works
Tit. 3. 14. to maint. good works, that they be not u.
2 Pet. 1. 8. ye shall neither be barren nor u. in the

UNGIRDED.

Gen. 24. 32. the man u. the camels, and gave straw

UNGODLY.

2 Sam. 22. 5. when waves of death compassed me, the floods of u. men made me afraid, Psal. 18. 4.
2 Chr. 19. 2. Jehu said, shouldest thou help the u.
Job 16. 11. God hath delivered me to the u.
34. 18. is it fit to say to princes, ye are u.?
Psal. 1. 1. that walketh not in the counsel of the u.
4. the u. are not so ‖ 5. u. not stand in judgment
6. but the way of the u. shall perish
3. 7. thou hast broken the teeth of the u.
43. 1. and plead my cause against an u. nation
73. 12. these are the u. who prosper in the world
Prov. 16. 27. u. man diggeth up evil, and in his lips
19. 28. an u. witness scorneth judgment
Rom. 4. 5. but believeth on him that justifieth the u.
5. 6. in due time Christ died for the u.
1 Tim. 1. 9. the law is for the u. and for sinners
1 Pet. 4. 18. where shall the u. and sinner appear?
2 Pet. 2. 5. bringing in the flood on world of the u.
6. ensample to those who after should live u.
3. 7. to day of judgment and perdition of u. men
Jude 4. u. men turning the grace of our God into
15. to convince all that are u. of their u. deeds
18. who should walk after their own u. lusts

UNGODLINESS.

Rom. 1. 18. the wrath of G. revealed against all u.
11. 26. and he shall turn away u. from Jacob
2 Tim. 2. 16. they will increase unto more u.
Tit. 2. 12. that denying u. and worldly lusts

UNHOLY.

Lev. 10. 10. may put difference between holy and u.
1 Tim. 1. 9. the law was made for the u. and profane
2 Tim. 3. 2. for men shall be unthankful, u.
Heb. 10. 29. counted blood of covenant an u. thing

UNICORN,

In Greek, μονοκερος*; in Hebrew,* Reem. *It is much disputed among the learned, whether there be, or ever was, such a creature as we call the* unicorn; *or whether this* Reem *be the rhinoceros, as some would have it; or a certain kind of wild goat, called* Oryx, *which is very large and strong, and untractable; or one of that kind of wild oxen, or bulls called* Uri; *which some think the most probable opinion, as best agreeing with the Scripture accounts of it. It is said to have but one horn, growing out of its forehead between its eye-lids, but as hard as iron.* Job 39. 10. Canst thou bind the *unicorn* with his band in the furrow? *Moses, magnifying the strength of Joseph, says, that* his horns are like the horns of *unicorns; that is, his strength and power shall be very great,* Deut. 33. 17. *And the Psalmist says,* Thou hast heard me from the horns of the *unicorns; thou hast delivered me when I was in great danger of being destroyed by the power of mine enemies,* Psal. 22. 21.

Num. 23. 22. as it were the strength of an u. 24. 8.
Job 39. 9. will the u. be willing to serve thee?
10. canst thou bind the u. in the furrows?
Psal. 29. 6. Lebanon and Sirion like a young u.
92. 10. my horn shall exalt like horn of an u.

UNICORNS.

Deut. 33. 17. his horns are like the horns of u.
Psal. 22. 21. heard me from the horns of the u.
Isa. 34. 7. and the u. shall come down with them

UNITE.

Psal. 86. 11. u. my heart to fear thy name

UNITED.
Gen. 49. 6. to their assembly, mine honour, be not *u.*
UNITY.
Psal. 133. 1. for brethren to dwell together in *u.*
Eph. 4. 3. endeavouring to keep the *u.* of the Spirit
13. till we come in the *u.* of the faith
UNJUST.
Psal. 43. 1. O God, deliver me from the *u.* man
Prov. 11. 7. and the hope of *u.* men perisheth
28. 8. who by *u.* gain increaseth his substance
29. 27. an *u.* man is an abomination to the just
Zeph. 3. 5. but the *u.* knoweth no shame
Mat. 5. 45. he sendeth rain on the just and *u.*
Luke 16. 8. the Lord commended the *u.* steward
10. he that is *u.* in the least, is *u.* also in much
18. 6. the Lord said, hear what the *u.* judge saith
11. I thank thee, I am not as other men are, *u.*
Acts 24. 15. a resurrection both of the just and *u.*
1 *Cor.* 6. 1. dare any of you go to law before the *u.*?
1 *Pet.* 3. 18. Christ suffered, the just for the *u.*
2 *Pet.* 2. 9. reserve the *u.* to the day of judgment
Rev. 22. 11. he that is *u.* let him be *u.* still
UNJUSTLY.
Psal. 82. 2. how long will ye judge *u.* and accept
Isa. 26. 10. in land of uprightness will he deal *u.*
UNKNOWN.
Acts 17. 23. as I beheld your devotions, I found an altar with this inscription, to the *u.* God
1 *Cor.* 14. 2. that speaketh in an *u.* tongue, 4, 13, 27.
14. if I pray in an *u.* tongue, my spirit prayeth
19. than ten thousand words in an *u.* tongue
2 *Cor.* 6. 9. as *u.* and yet well known; as dying
Gal. 1. 22. I was *u.* by face unto the churches
UNLADE.
Acts 21. 3. there the ship was to *u.* her burden
UNLAWFUL.
Acts 10. 28. an *u.* thing for a man that is a Jew
2 *Pet.* 2. 8. vexed his soul with their *u.* deeds
UNLEARNED.
Acts 4. 13. they perceived that they were *u.*
1 *Cor.* 14. 16. he that occupieth the room of the *u.*
23. and there come in those that are *u.* 24.
2 *Tim.* 2. 23. but foolish and *u.* questions avoid
2 *Pet.* 3. 16. which they that are *u.* wrest to their
UNLEAVENED.
Exod. 12. 39. they baked *u.* cakes of the dough
Lev. 2. 4. it shall be an *u.* cake of fine flour mingled with oil, or *u.* wafers anointed with oil, 5.
7. 12. he shall offer *u.* cakes mingled with oil
8. 26. and Moses took one *u.* cake, and wafers
Num. 6. 19. the priest shall take one *u.* cake, one *u.* wafer, and put them on the hands of the Nazarite
Josh. 5. 11. they did eat of old corn of the land *u.*
Judg. 6. 19. Gideon made ready a kid and *u.* cakes
20. take the flesh and *u.* cakes, and lay them
21. the angel touched the flesh and *u.* cakes; fire out of the rock consumed the flesh and *u.* cakes
1 *Chron.* 23. 29. their office for flour and *u.* cakes
1 *Cor.* 5. 7. that ye may be a new lump, as ye are *u.*
See BREAD.
UNLESS.
Lev. 22. 6. be unclean *u.* he wash his flesh with water
Num. 22. 33. *u.* she had turned from me, I had slain
2 *Sam.* 2. 27. *u.* thou hadst spoken, people had gone
Psal. 27. 13. I had fainted, *u.* I had believed to see
94. 17. *u.* the Lord had been my help, my soul had
119. 92. *u.* thy law had been my delight, I should
Prov. 4. 16. sleep not, *u.* they cause some to fall
1 *Cor.* 15. 2. ye are saved, *u.* ye have believed in vain
UNLOOSE.
Mark 1. 7. the latchet of whose shoes I am not worthy to stoop down and *u.* *Luke* 3. 16. *John* 1. 27.
UNMARRIED.
1 *Cor.* 7. 8. I say to the *u.* ‖ 11. let her remain *u.*
32. he that is *u.* ‖ 34. the *u.* woman careth for
UNMERCIFUL.
Psal. 43. † 1. plead my cause against an *u.* nation
Rom. 1. 31. without natural affection, implacable, *u.*
UNMINDFUL.
Deut. 32. 18. of rock that begat thee thou art *u.*
UNMOVABLE.
Acts 27. 41. and the forepart of the ship remained *u.*
1 *Cor.* 15. 58. my brethren, be ye stedfast, *u.*
UNOCCUPIED.
Judg. 5. 6. in days of Shamgar, high-ways were *u.*
UNPERFECT.
Psal. 139. 16. did see my substance, yet being *u.*
UNPREPARED.
2 *Cor.* 9. 4. if they come with me, and find you *u.*
UNPROFITABLE.
Job 15. 3. should he reason with *u.* talk?
Mat. 25. 30. cast the *u.* servant into outer darkness
Luke 17. 10. likewise say ye, we are *u.* servants
Rom. 3. 12. they are altogether become *u.*
Tit. 3. 9. genealogies, for they are *u.* and vain
Philem. 11. which in time past was to thee *u.*
Heb. 13. 17. not with grief, for that is *u.* for you
UNPROFITABLENESS.
Heb. 7. 18. for the weakness and *u.* thereof
UNPUNISHED.
Prov. 11. 21. join in hand, the wicked shall not be *u.*
16. 5. hand join in hand, the proud shall not be *u.*
17. 5. that is glad at calamities, shall not be *u.*
19. 5. a false witness shall not be *u.* 9.
28. † 20. maketh haste to be rich shall not be *u.*
Jer. 25. 29. should ye be utterly *u.* shall not be *u.*
30. 11. I will not leave thee altogether *u.*
46. 28. yet will I not leave thee wholly *u.*
49. 12. shalt thou go *u.*? thou shalt not go *u.*
UNQUENCHABLE.
Mat. 3. 12. gather his wheat into the garner, but burn up the chaff with *u.* fire, *Luke* 3. 17.
UNREASONABLE.
Acts 25. 27. it seemeth to me *u.* to send a prisoner
2 *Thess.* 3. 2. that we may be delivered from *u.* men
UNREBUKABLE.
1 *Tim.* 6. 14. that thou keep this commandment *u.*
UNREPROVABLE.
Col. 1. 22. to present you holy, *u.* in his sight
UNRIGHTEOUS.
Exod. 23. 1. put not thy hand to be an *u.* witness
Job 27. 7. that riseth against me be as the *u.*
Psal. 71. 4. deliver me out of the hand of the *u.*
Isa. 10. 1. woe unto them that decree *u.* decrees
55. 7. let the *u.* man forsake his thoughts
Luke 16. 11. not been faithful in the *u.* mammon
Rom. 3. 5. is God *u.* who taketh vengeance?
1 *Cor.* 6. 9. the *u.* shall not inherit the kingdom
Heb. 6. 10. for God is not *u.* to forget your works
UNRIGHTEOUSLY.
Deut. 25. 16. all that do *u.* are an abomination
UNRIGHTEOUSNESS.
Lev. 19. 15. ye shall do no *u.* in judgment, 35.
Psal. 92. 15. he is my rock, there is no *u.* in him
Jer. 22. 13. to him that buildeth his house by *u.*
Luke 16. 9. make friends of the mammon of *u.*
John 7. 18. the same is true, and no *u.* is in him
Rom. 1. 18. all *u.* of men who hold the truth in *u.*
29. being filled with all *u.* fornication, envy
2. 8. but to them that obey *u.* indignation, wrath
3. 5. if our *u.* commend the righteousness of God
6. 13. now yield members as instruments of *u.*
9. 14. is there *u.* with God? God forbid
2 *Cor.* 6. 14. what fellowship righteousness with *u.*?
2 *Thess.* 2. 10. and with all deceivableness of *u.*
12. who believed not, but had pleasure in *u.*
Heb. 8. 12. for I will be merciful to their *u.*
2 *Pet.* 2. 13. and shall receive the reward of *u.*
15. the way of Balaam who loved the wages of *u.*
1 *John* 1. 9. is faithful to cleanse us from all *u.*
5. 17. all *u.* is sin; there is a sin not unto death
UNRIPE.
Job 15. 33. he shall shake off his *u.* grape as vine
UNRULY.
1 *Thess.* 5. 14. brethren, warn them that are *u.*
Tit. 1. 6. children, not accused of riot, or *u.*
10. for there are many *u.* and vain talkers
Jam. 3. 8. the tongue is an *u.* evil, full of poison
UNSATIABLE.
Ezek. 16. 28. with Assyrians, because thou wast *u.*
UNSAVOURY.
Job 6. 6. can what is *u.* be eaten without salt?
Jer. 23. † 13. I have seen an *u.* thing in prophets
UNSEARCHABLE.
Job 5. 9. God who doth great things and *u.*
Psal. 145. 3. great is the Lord, his greatness is *u.*
Prov. 25. 3. and the heart of kings is *u.*
Rom. 11. 33. how *u.* are his judgments, and his ways
Eph. 3. 8. I should preach the *u.* riches of Christ
UNSEEMLY.
Rom. 1. 27. men with men working that which is *u.*
1 *Cor.* 13. 5. charity doth not behave itself *u.*
UNSHOD.
Jer. 2. 25. withhold thy foot from being *u.*
UNSKILFUL.
Heb. 5. 13. babe is *u.* in the word of righteousness
UNSOCIABLE.
Rom. 1. † 31. covenant-breakers, *u.* implacable
UNSPEAKABLE.
2 *Cor.* 9. 15. thanks be to God for his *u.* gift
12. 4. caught up into paradise and heard *u.* words
1 *Pet.* 1. 8. in whom ye rejoice with joy *u.* full of
UNSPOTTED.
Jam. 1. 27. to keep himself *u.* from the world
UNSTABLE.
Gen. 49. 4. *u.* as water, thou shalt not excel
Jam. 1. 8. a double minded man is *u.* in all his ways
2 *Pet.* 2. 14. cannot cease from sin, beguiling *u.* souls
3. 16. which they that are unlearned and *u.* wrest
UNSTOPPED.
Isa. 35. 5. and the ears of the deaf shall be *u.*
UNTAKEN.
2 *Cor.* 3. 14. remaineth the same vail *u.* away
UNTEMPERED.
Ezek. 13. 10. one built up a wall, and lo others daubed it with *u.* mortar, 11, 14, 15. | 22. 28.
UNTHANKFUL.
Luke 6. 35. for he is kind to the *u.* and to the evil
2 *Tim.* 3. 2. men shall be blasphemers, *u.* unholy
UNTIL.
Gen. 28. 15. *u.* I have done that I have spoken
32. 4. I have sojourned and stayed there *u.* now
46. 34. our trade from our youth, even *u.* now
49. 10. nor a lawgiver depart, *u.* Shiloh come
Num. 14. 19. hast forgiven this people *u.* now
Judg. 18. 30. sons were priests to Dan *u.* the captivity
1 *Sam.* 9. 13. for the people will not eat *u.* he come
15. 35. Samuel came no more to see Saul *u.* his death
2 *Sam.* 19. 7. that befell thee from thy youth *u.* now
24. nor trimmed, *u.* the day he came in peace
1 *Kings* 22. 27. feed him with bread and water of affliction, *u.* I come in peace, 2 *Chron.* 18. 26.
2 *Kings* 8. 6. restore, since she left the land *u.* now
Ezra 4. 21. city be not built, *u.* another command
5. 16. since then *u.* now hath it been building
10. 14. *u.* the fierce wrath of God be turned
Job 14. 13. keep me secret *u.* thy wrath be past
Psal. 36. 2. *u.* his iniquity be found to be hateful
73. 17. *u.* I went into the sanctuary of God
132. 5. *u.* I find out a place for the Lord, an habit.
Cant. 2. 17. *u.* the daybreak and the shadows flee, 4. 6.
Isa. 32. 15. *u.* the spirit be poured upon us
36. 17. *u.* I come and take you away to a land
62. 1. *u.* the righteousness thereof go forth
Jer. 32. 5. and there shall he be *u.* I visit him
44. 27. be consumed *u.* there be an end of them
Ezek. 21. 27. overturn, *u.* he come whose right it is
Mic. 7. 9. bear indignation *u.* he plead my cause
Mat. 2. 13. be thou there *u.* I bring thee word
11. 13. for all the law and the prophets prophesied *u.* John, this is Elias, *Luke* 16. 16.
Luke 21. 24. Jerusalem be trodden down *u.* the times of the Gentiles be fulfilled, *Rom.* 11. 25.
24. 49. *u.* ye be endued with power from on high
Acts 1. 2. *u.* the day in which he was taken up
Rom. 5. 13. for *u.* the law sin was in the world
1 *Cor.* 4. 5. judge nothing *u.* the Lord come
Phil. 1. 6. will perform it *u.* the day of Jesus Christ
2 *Thess.* 2. 7. will let *u.* he be taken out of the way
1 *Tim.* 6. 14. *u.* the appearing of our Lord Jesus
Rev. 17. 17. *u.* the words of God shall be fulfilled
20. 5. lived not *u.* the 1000 years were finished
UNTIMELY.
Job 3. 16. or as an hidden *u.* birth I had not been
Psal. 58. 8. pass away like the *u.* birth of a woman
Eccl. 6. 3. I say that an *u.* birth is better than he
Rev. 6. 13. even as a fig-tree casteth her *u.* figs
UNTOWARD.
Acts 2. 40. save yourselves from this *u.* generation
UNWALLED.
Deut. 3. 5. we took sixty cities, beside *u.* towns
Esth. 9. 19. the Jews that dwelt in the *u.* towns
Ezek. 38. 11. I will go up to the land of *u.* villages
UNWASHEN.
Mat. 15. 20. these things defile a man, but to eat with *u.* hands defileth not a man, *Mark* 7. 2, 5.
UNWEIGHED.
1 *Kings* 7. 47. Solomon left all the vessels *u.*
UNWISE.
Deut. 32. 6. do ye thus requite the L. O *u.* people?
Hos. 13. 13. he is an *u.* son, he should not stay long
Rom. 1. 14. I am debtor to the wise and to the *u.*
Eph. 5. 17. wherefore be ye not *u.* but understanding
UNWITTINGLY.
Lev. 22. 14. if a man eat of the holy thing *u.*
Josh. 20. 3. the slayer that killeth any person *u.* 5.
UNWORTHY.
Acts 13. 46. seeing we judge ourselves *u.* of life
1 *Cor.* 6. 2. are ye *u.* to judge the smallest matter?
UNWORTHILY.
1 *Cor.* 11. 27. shall drink this cup of the Lord *u.*
29. for he that eateth and drinketh *u.* eateth
UP, *Verb.*
Gen. 19. 14. Lot said, *up*, get ye out of this place
44. 4. Joseph said, *up*, follow after the men
Exod. 32. 1. *up*, make us gods that shall go before us
Josh. 7. 13. *up*, sanctify the people, and say, sanctify
Judg. 4. 14. *up*, for this is the day in which the Lord
8. 20. he said to his first-born, *up* and slay them
9. 32. *up*, thou and the people that is with thee
19. 28. *up*, and let us be going, but none answered
1 *Sam.* 9. 25. saying, *up*, that I may send thee away
UP.
Num. 14. 40. they rose *up* early and gat them *up*, saying, we be here and will go *up*, for we have sinned
42. go not *up*, for the Lord is not among you
44. they presumed to go *up* unto the hill top
Judg. 8. 13. Gideon returned from battle before sun *up*
9. 33. as soon as sun is *up* thou shalt rise early
1 *Sam.* 29. 10. as soon as ye be *up* early, depart
2 *Sam.* 24. 11. when David was *up* the word came
Mat. 13. 6. and when the sun was *up* they were scorched, because they had not root, *Mark* 4. 6.
UP.
Psal. 88. 15. I am ready to die from my youth *up*
Ezek. 41. 16. from the ground *up* to the windows
Mat. 19. 20. these things I kept from my youth *up*
Luke 18. 21. all these I kept from my youth *up*
John 2. 7. and they filled them *up* to the brim
See DOWN.
UPBRAID.
Judg. 8. 15. Zebah and Zal. with whom ye did *u.* me
Mat. 11. 20. then began he to *u.* the cities wherein
UPBRAIDED.
Mark 16. 14. he *u.* them with their unbelief
UPBRAIDETH.
Jam. 1. 5. that giveth to all men liberally and *u.* not
UPHELD.
Isa. 63. 5. arm brought salvat. and my fury it *u.* me
UPHOLD.
Job 36. † 17. judgment and justice should *u.* thee
Psal. 51. 12. and *u.* me with thy free Spirit
54. 4. the Lord is with them that *u.* my soul
119. 116. *u.* me according to thy word
Prov. 29. 23. honour shall *u.* the humble in spirit
Isa. 41. 10. I will *u.* thee with the right hand of my
42. 1. behold my servant whom I *u.* mine elect
63. 5. and I wondered that there was none to *u.*
Ezek. 30. 6. they also that *u.* Egypt shall fall
UPHOLDEN.
Job 4. 4. thy words have *u.* him that was falling
Prov. 20. 28. the king's throne is *u.* by mercy
UPHOLDEST.
Psal. 41. 12. as for me, thou *u.* me in mine integrity
UPHOLDETH.
Psal. 37. 17. but the Lord *u.* the righteous
24. for the Lord *u.* him with his hand
63. 8. my soul followeth, thy right hand *u.* me
145. 14. the Lord *u.* all that fall, and raiseth up
UPHOLDING.
Heb. 1. 3. *u.* all things by the word of his power
UPPER.
Exod. 12. 7. shall strike blood on the *u.* door-posts
Lev. 13. 45. he shall put a covering on his *u.* lip
Deut. 24. 6. no man take the *u.* millstone to pledge
Josh. 15. 19. he gave her the *u.* springs, *Judg.* 1. 15.
2 *Kings* 18. 17. when they were come up, they stood by the conduit of the *u.* pool, *Isa.* 7. 3. | 36. 2.
Ezek. 24. † 17. and cover not thy *u.* lip
Zeph. 2. 14. cormorant shall lodge in the *u.* lintels
Mark 14. 15. he will shew you *u.* room, *Luke* 22. 12.
Acts 1. 13. they went up into an *u.* room
19. 1. Paul having passed through the *u.* coasts
See CHAMBER.
UPPERMOST.
Gen. 40. 17. in the *u.* basket were all bakemeats
Isa. 17. 6. two or three in the top of the *u.* bough
9. his strong cities shall be as an *u.* branch
Mat. 23. 6. they love the *u.* rooms at feasts and chief seats in synagogues, *Mark* 12. 39. *Luke* 11. 43.
UPRIGHT.
Gen. 6. † 9. Noah was an *u.* man in his generations
17. † 1. I am God, walk before me and be thou *u.*
37. 7. and lo, my sheaf arose and also stood *u.*
Lev. 26. 13. broken your yoke and made you go *u.*
Josh. 10. † 13. in the book of the *u.* 2 *Sam.* 1. † 18.
1 *Sam.* 29. 6. said to David, surely as Lord liveth, thou hast been *u.* with me, 2 *Chron.* 29. 34.
2 *Sam.* 22. 24. I was also *u.* before him, *Psal.* 18. 23.
26. with the merciful merciful, and with the *u.* man thou wilt shew thyself *u.* *Psal.* 18. 25.
2 *Chron.* 29. 34. for Levites were more *u.* in heart
Job 1. 1. Job was a perfect and *u.* man, 8. | 2. 3.
8. 6. if thou wert *u.* he would awake for thee
12. 4. the just *u.* man is laughed to scorn
17. 8. *u.* men shall be astonished at this

Psal. 11. 7. his countenance doth behold the *u.*
19. 13. then shall I be *u.* I shall be innocent
25. 8. the Lord is good and *u.* 92. 15.
33. 1. rejoice, for praise is comely for the *u.*
37. 14. to slay such as be of *u.* conversation
18. the Lord knoweth the days of the *u.*
37. mark the perfect man and behold the *u.*
49. 14. the *u.* shall have dominion over them
111. 1. I will praise the L. in the assembly of the *u.*
112. 2. the generation of the *u.* shall be blessed
4. unto the *u.* there ariseth light in darkness
119. 137. art righteous and *u.* are thy judgments
125. 4. do good to them that are *u.* in their hearts
140. 13. the *u.* shall dwell in thy presence
Prov. 2. 21. for the *u.* shall dwell in the land
10. 29. the way of the Lord is strength to the *u.*
11. 3. the integrity of the *u.* shall guide them
6. the righteousness of the *u.* shall deliver them
11. by the blessings of the *u.* the city is exalted
20. such as are *u.* in their way are his delight
12. 6. the mouth of the *u.* shall deliver them
13. 6. righteousness keepeth the *u.* in the way
14. 11. the tabernacle of the *u.* shall flourish
15. 8. but the prayer of the *u.* is his delight
16. 17. the highway of the *u.* is to depart from evil
21. 18. the transgressor shall be a ransom for the *u.*
29. but as for the *u.* he directeth his way
28. 10. the *u.* shall have good things in possession
29. 10. the bloodthirsty hate the *u.* but the just
27. he that is *u.* is an abomination to the wicked
Eccl. 7. 29. have found that God hath made man *u.*
12. 10. what was written was *u.* words of truth
Cant. 1. 4. remember thy love, the *u.* love thee
Isa. 26. 7. thou most *u.* dost weigh the path of just
Jer. 10. 5. they are *u.* as palm-tree, but speak not
Dan. 8. 18. but he touched me and set me *u.*
11. 17. set his face to enter and *u.* ones with him
Mic. 7. 2. is none *u.* among men, all lie in wait
4. the most *u.* is sharper than a thorn hedge
Hab. 2. 4. behold, his soul lifted up is not *u.* in him
See HEART, STAND, STOOD.

UPRIGHTLY.

Psal. 15. 2. walketh *u.* shall abide in thy tabernacle
58. 1. do ye judge *u.*? ‖ 75. 2. I will judge *u.*
84. 11. withhold no good from them that walk *u.*
Prov. 2. 7. he is a buckler to them that walk *u.*
10. 9. he that walketh *u.* walketh surely
15. 21. but a man of understanding walketh *u.*
28. 18. whoso walketh *u.* shall be saved, but perverse
Isa. 33. 15. he that speaketh *u.* shall dwell on high
Amos 5. 10. they abhor him that speaketh *u.*
Mic. 2. 7. my words do good to him that walketh *u.*
Gal. 2. 14. when I saw that they walked not *u.*

UPRIGHTNESS.

1 *Kings* 3. 6. as he walked before thee in *u.* of heart
1 *Chron.* 29. 17. I know that thou hast pleasure in *u.*
Job 4. 6. is not this thy hope and the *u.* of thy ways?
33. 23. an interpreter, to shew unto man his *u.*
Psal. 9. 8. he shall minister judgment unto people *u.*
25. 21. let integrity and *u.* preserve me, I wait
111. 8. they stand fast for ever and are done in *u.*
143. 10. thy spirit good, lead me into land of *u.*
Prov. 2. 13. who leave the paths of *u.* to walk
14. 2. he that walketh in *u.* feareth the Lord
28. 6. better is the poor that walketh in his *u.*
Isa. 26. 7. the way of the just is *u.* thou dost weigh
10. in the land of *u.* will he deal unjustly
57. 2. rest in their beds each one walking in his *u.*
Dan. 11. † 17. set his face to enter, and *u.* with him
See HEART.

UPRISING.

Psal. 139. 2. thou knowest my down-sitting and *u.*

UPROAR.

1 *Kings* 1. 41. this noise of the city being in an *u.*
Mat. 26. 5. lest there be an *u.* *Mark* 14. 2.
Acts 17. 5. the Jews set all the city on an *u.*
19. 40. to be called in question for this day's *u.*
20. 1. after the *u.* was ceased, Paul called to him
21. 31. tidings came that all Jerusalem was in an *u.*
38. art not thou the Egyptian who madest an *u.*?

UPSIDE *down.*

2 *Kings* 21. 13. wiping Jerusalem as a man wipeth a dish, turning it *u. down*
Psal. 146. 9. way of the wicked he turneth *u. down*
Isa. 24. 1. the Lord turneth the earth *u. down*
29. 16. surely your turning of things *u. down*
Acts 17. 6. that have turned the world *u. down*

UPWARD.

Exod. 38. 26. from twenty years old and *u.* *Num.* 1. 3, 20, 22, 24, 26, 28. | 11. 29. 1 *Chron.* 23. 24. 2 *Chron.* 31. 17. *Ezra* 3. 8.
Num. 3. 15. shalt number every male from a month old and *u.* 22, 28, 34, 39, 40, 43. | 26. 62.
4. 3. from thirty years old and *u.* even to fifty, 23, 30, 35, 39, 43, 47. 1 *Chron.* 23. 3.
8. 24. from twenty and five years old and *u.*
1 *Sam.* 9. 2. Saul was higher from shoulders *u.* 10. 23.
2 *Kings* 19. 30. remnant shall bear fruit *u.* *Isa.* 37. 31.
2 *Chron.* 31. 16. males from three years old and *u.*
Job 5. 7. man is born to trouble as sparks fly *u.*
Eccl. 3. 21. the spirit of man that goeth *u.*
Isa. 8. 21. curse their king and God, and look *u.*
38. 14. mine eyes fail with looking *u.* undertake
Ezek. 1. 27. from appearance of his loins *u.* 8. 2.
41. 7. and there was a winding about still *u.*
Hag. 2. 15. consider from this day and *u.* 18.

URGE.

Luke 11. 53. scribes and pharisees began to *u.* him

URGED.

Gen. 33. 11. Jacob *u.* Esau, and he took it
Judg. 16. 16. Delilah *u.* Samson, and he told all
19. 7. rose to depart, his father-in-law *u.* him
2 *Kings* 2. 17. when they *u.* him till he was ashamed
5. 16. Naaman *u.* Elisha ‖ 23. he *u.* Gehazi

URGENT.

Exod. 12. 33. the Egyptians were *u.* on the people
Dan. 3. 22. the king's commandment was *u.*

URIM.

See Signification on THUMMIM.

Exod. 28. 30. thou shalt put in the breast-plate of judgment, the *u.* and the thummim, *Lev.* 8. 8.
Num. 27. 21. ask counsel after the judgment of *u.*

Deut. 33. 8. let thy *u.* be with thy Holy One
1 *Sam.* 28. 6. neither by dreams, by *u.* nor prophets
Ezra 2. 63. not eat till there stood up a priest with *u.* and with thummim, *Neh.* 7. 65.

US.

Deut. 5. 3. with *us* even *us* who are all of *us* alive
Luke 23. 39. if thou be Christ, save thyself and *us*
Rom. 9. 24. even *us* whom he hath called, not only
1 *Cor.* 4. 9. God hath set forth *us* the apostles
6. 14. and will also raise up *us* by his own power
2 *Cor.* 1. 14. you have acknowledged *us* in part
21. he which establisheth *us* with you, is God
5. 18. who hath reconciled *us* to himself by Christ
Phil. 3. 17. brethren, as ye have *us* for an ensample
1 *Thess.* 5. 8. let *us* who are of the day be sober
9. for God hath not appointed *us* to wrath
Jam. 1. 18. of his own will begat he *us* by the word

About US.

Num. 22. 4. lick up all that are round *about us*
Neh. 5. 17. that came from heathen that are *about us*
6. 16. the heathen *about us* saw these things
Dan. 9. 16. thy people a reproach to all *about us*

After US.

Josh. 8. 6. for they will come out *after us*
22. 27. it may be witness to our generations *after us*
Mat. 15. 23. send her away, for she crieth *after us*

Against US.

Gen. 43. 18. that he may seek occasion *against us*
Exod. 1. 10. join our enemies and fight *against us*
16. 7. what are we that ye murmur *against us*?
8. your murmurings are not *against us* but God
Deut. 2. 32. Sihon came out *against us*, 29. 7. | 3. 1. Og
Josh. 8. 5. when the men of Ai came out *against us*
10. 6. the kings of the Amorites gathered *against us*
22. 19. rebel not against the Lord, nor *against us*
Judg. 15. 10. said, why are ye come up *against us*
1 *Sam.* 30. 23. delivered company that came *aga. us*
2 *Sam.* 11. 23. surely the men prevailed *against us*
21. 5. the man that devised *against us*
2 *Kings* 22. 13. great is the wrath of Lord *against us*
2 *Chron.* 20. 12. this great company that cometh *ag.us*
Psal. 44. 5. tread them under that rise *against us*
79. 8. remember not *against us* former iniquities
124. 2. Lord for us, when men rose up *against us*
3. when their wrath was kindled *against us*
Isa. 14. 8. no feller is come up *against us*
59. 12. and our sins testify *against us*, *Jer.* 14. 7.
Jer. 16. 10. Lord pronounced all this evil *against us*
21. 2. Nebuchadnezzar maketh war *against us*
13. which say, who shall come down *against us*?
43. 3. but Baruch setteth thee on *against us*
Lam. 3. 46. have opened their mouths *against us*
5. 22. rejected us, thou art very wroth *against us*
Dan. 9. 12. confirmed his words he spake *against us*
Mark 9. 40. Jesus said, forbid him not, he that is not *against us* is on our part, *Luke* 9. 50.
Rom. 8. 31. if God be for us, who can be *against us*?
Col. 2. 14. blotting out the hand-writing *against us*
3 *John* 10. prating *against us* with malicious words

Among or *Amongst* US.

Gen. 23. 6. thou art a mighty prince *among us*
Exod. 17. 7. saying, is the Lord *among us* or not?
34. 9. let my lord, I pray thee, go *among us*
Deut. 31. 17. because our God is not *among us*
Josh. 9. 7. peradventure ye dwell *among us*, 22.
22. 19. pass over and take possession *among us*
31. we perceive the Lord is *among us*
Judg. 18. 25. let not thy voice be heard *among us*
1 *Sam.* 4. 3. when it cometh *among us* it may save
1 *Kings* 5. 6. not *among us* any can skill to hew timb.
Job 34. 37. he clappeth his hands *amongst us*
Psal. 74. 9. not *among us* any that knoweth how long
Prov. 1. 14. cast in thy lot *among us* let us have
Isa. 33. 14. who *among us* shall dwell with the devouring fire? who with everlasting burnings?
Mic. 3. 11. they will say, is not the Lord *among us*?
Luke 7. 16. a great prophet is risen up *among us*
John 1. 14. Word was made flesh and dwelt *among us*
Acts 1. 21. Lord Jesus went in and out *among us*
15. 7. God made choice *among us* that Gentiles

At US.

1 *Pet.* 4. 17. if it first begin *at us* what the end be

Before US.

Exod. 32. 23. for they said unto me, make us gods which shall go *before us*, *Acts* 7. 40.
Deut. 1. 22. ye said, we will send men *before us*
2. 33. the Lord our God delivered him *before us*
Josh. 4. 23. which he dried up from *before us*
8. 6. they flee *before us* ‖ 24. 18. drave out *before us*
Judg. 11. 24. the Lord shall drive out *before us*
20. 32. smitten down *before us* as at the first, 39.
1 *Sam.* 8. 20. king may judge us and go out *before us*
9. 27. Samuel said, bid thy servant pass on *before us*
2 *Chron.* 14. 7. while the land is yet *before us*
Isa. 30. 11. cause Holy One of Israel cease *before us*
Dan. 9. 10. to walk in his laws which he set *before us*
Heb. 6. 18. to lay hold on the hope set *before us*
12. 1. let us run the race that is set *before us*

Behind US.

Gen. 32. 18. and, behold, also he is *behind us*, 20.

Between or *betwixt* US.

Gen. 26. 28. let there be now an oath *betwixt us*
31. 37. that they may judge *betwixt us* both
53. the God of Abraham judge *betwixt us*
Josh. 22. 25. Lord made Jordan a border *between us*
27. that it may be a witness *between us*, 28, 34.
Judg. 11. 10. Lord be witness *between us*, *Jer.* 42. 5.
Job 9. 33. neither is there any days-man *betwixt us*
Luke 16. 26. *between us* and you, is a great gulf
Acts 15. 9. put no difference *between us* and them
Eph. 2. 14. the middle wall of partition *between us*

By US.

Num. 12. 2. hath not the Lord spoken also *by us*?
2 *Kings* 4. 9. this is a man of G. which passeth *by us*
2 *Cor.* 1. 19. Jesus was preached among you *by us*
20. are in him amen, to the glory of God *by us*
2. 14. manifest the savour of his knowledge *by us*
3. 3. to be the epistle of Christ, ministered *by us*
5. 20. as tho' God did beseech you *by us* we pray
7. 9. ye might receive damage *by us* in nothing
8. 19. which is administered *by us* to glory of L. 20.

Concerning US.

2 *Kings* 22. 13. do according to all written *con. us*

For US.

Gen. 26. 22. now the Lord hath made room *for us*
31. 14. is there yet any inheritance *for us*?
Exod. 14. 12. better *for us* to serve the Egyptians
24. 14. tarry ye here *for us* until we come again
Num. 14. 3. better *for us* to return into Egypt
9. fear not the people, for they are bread *for us*
Deut. 2. 36. there was not one city too strong *for us*
30. 12. say, who shall go up *for us* to heaven?
13. shouldest say, who shall go over sea *for us*?
Josh. 5. 13. art thou *for us* or for our adversaries?
22. 17. is the iniquity of Peor too little *for us*?
Judg. 1. 1. who go up *for us* against the Canaanites?
1 *Sam.* 7. 8. cease not to cry unto the Lord *for us*
9. 5. come, lest my father take thought *for us*
14. 6. it may be the Lord will work *for us*
2 *Sam.* 18. 3. if we flee they will not care *for us*
21. 4. neither *for us* shalt thou kill any man
2 *Kings* 4. 13. behold, thou hast been careful *for us*
6. 1. the place where we dwell is too strait *for us*
2 *Chron.* 13. 10. as *for us*, the Lord is our God
Ezra 8. 21. to seek of him a right way *for us*
Neh. 4. 20. resort, our God shall fight *for us*
Psal. 47. 4. he shall choose our inheritance *for us*
62. 8. trust in him, God is a refuge *for us*
68. 28. strengthen that thou hast wrought *for us*
126. 3. the Lord hath done great things *for us*
Isa. 6. 8. whom shall I send, and who will go *f. us*
26. 12. Lord, thou wilt ordain peace *for us*
Jer. 9. 18. let them take up a wailing *for us*
14. 19. hast smitten, and there is no healing *for us*
21. 2. inquire, I pray thee, of the Lord *for us*
37. 3. pray to the Lord our God *for us*, 42. 2, 20.
Lam. 4. 17. as *for us*, our eyes as yet failed
Mat. 17. 4. Peter said to Jesus, Lord, it is good *for us* to be here, *Mark* 9. 5. *Luke* 9. 33.
25. 9. not so, lest there be not enough *for us*
Mark 14. 15. upper room, there make ready *for us*
Luke 1. 69. hast raised up horn of salvation *for us*
9. 50. for he that is not against us is *for us*
Rom. 4. 24. *for us* to whom it shall be imputed
5. 8. while we were sinners, Christ died *for us*
8. 26. the Spirit maketh intercession *for us*
31. if God be *for us*, who can be against us?
32. spared not, but delivered him up *for us* all
34. Christ also maketh intercession *for us*
1 *Cor.* 5. 7. even Christ is sacrificed *for us*
2 *Cor.* 1. 11. helping together by prayer *for us*
4. 17. our light affliction worketh *for us*
5. 21. he hath made him to be sin *for us*
Gal. 3. 13. Christ redeemed us, made a curse *for us*
Eph. 5. 2. hath loved us, and given himself *for us*
Col. 4. 3. withal, praying *for us*, that God would
1 *Thess.* 5. 10. who died *for us*, 1 *John* 3. 16.
25. pray *for us*, 2 *Thess.* 3. 1. *Heb.* 13. 18.
Tit. 2. 14. who gave himself *for us*, that he might
Heb. 6. 20. whither the forerunner is *for us* entered
9. 12. having obtained eternal redemption *for us*
24. now to appear in the presence of God *for us*
10. 20. living way, which he hath consecrat. *for us*
11. 40. G. having provided some better thing *for us*
1 *Pet.* 2. 21. because Chr. hath suffered *for us*, 4. 1.

From US.

Gen. 26. 16. Abimelech said to Isaac, go *from us*
1 *Sam.* 6. 20. and to whom shall he go up *from us*?
14. 17. number now, and see who is gone *from us*
2 *Chr.* 29. 10. his wrath turn *from us*, *Ezra* 10. 14.
Psal. 2. 3. let us cast away their cords *from us*
103. 12. hath removed our transgressions *from us*
Isa. 59. 9. therefore is judgment far *from us*
11. we look for salvation, but it is far *from us*
64. 7. for thou hast hid thy face *from us*
Jer. 4. 8. the anger of the Ld. is not turned *from us*
21. 2. that Nebuchadrezzar may go up *from us*
38. 25. hide it not *from us*, we will not kill thee
Acts 1. 22. to the day he was taken up *from us*
15. 24. heard that certain who went out *from us*
2 *Thess.* 2. 2. nor by word, nor by letter as *from us*
1 *John* 2. 19. they went out *from us*, but not of us
See DEPART.

In US.

Num. 14. 8. if the L. delight *in us*, he will bring us
Job 15. 9. what understand. thou, which is not *in us*
Isa. 26. 12. thou hast wrought all our works *in us*
John 17. 21. that they also may be one *in us*
Rom. 8. 4. that the law might be fulfilled *in us*
18. with the glory which shall be revealed *in us*
1 *Cor.* 4. 6. ye might learn *in us* not to think
2 *Cor.* 1. 5. as sufferings of Christ abound *in us*
4. 12. so death worketh *in us*, but life in you
6. 12. ye are not straitened *in us*, but in yourselv.
Eph. 3. 20. according to power that worketh *in us*
2 *Tim.* 1. 14. by Holy Ghost which dwelleth *in us*
Jam. 4. 5. the spirit that dwelleth *in us* lusteth
1 *John* 1. 8. truth is not *in us* ‖ 10. his word not *in us*
3. 24. hereby we know that he abideth *in us*
4. 12. if we love, God dwelleth *in us*, 13.
2 *John* 2. for the truth's sake which dwelleth *in us*

Of US.

Gen. 3. 22. behold, the man is become as one *of us*
Num. 31. 49. and there lacketh not a man *of us*
Josh. 2. 24. the inhabitants faint because *of us*
Judg. 16. 24. our enemy, which slew many *of us*
20. 18. which *of us* shall go up first to the battle?
2 *Kings* 6. 11. which *of us* is for the king of Israel?
Ezra 8. 23. we besought G. he was entreated *of us*
Psal. 115. 12. the Lord hath been mindful *of us*
Isa. 53. 6. he hath laid on him the iniqu. *of us* all
63. 16. our father, tho' Abraham be ignorant *of us*
Jer. 6. 24. anguish hath taken hold *of us*, and pain
14. 9. yet thou, O Lord, art in the midst *of us*
Acts 17. 27. tho' he be not far from every one *of us*
Rom. 4. 16. Abraham, who is the father *of us* all
1 *Cor.* 4. 1. so account *of us* as ministers of Christ
2 *Cor.* 2. 11. lest Satan get an advantage *of us*, for we
4. 7. that the power may be of God, and not *of us*
10. 2. some who think *of us*, as if we walked
Gal. 4. 26. Jerusalem, which is the mother *of us* all
Eph. 4. 7. but to every one *of us* is given grace
1 *Thess.* 1. 6. ye became followers *of us* and of Ld.

1 Thess. 1. 9. they thems. shew of us what entering in
2. 13. ye received the word which ye heard of us
3. 6. ye have good remembrance of us always
4. 1. that as ye have received of us how to walk
2 Thess. 3. 6. not after tradition he received of us
2 Pet. 3. 2. the commandment of us the apostles
1 John 2. 19. they were not of us, for if they had been of us they might shew they were not all of us

On US, or upon US.

Gen. 26. 10. shouldest have brought guilt. upon us
42. 21. therefore is this distress come upon us
43. 18. fall upon us and take us for bond-men
Exod. 5. 3. lest he fall upon us with pestilence
Num. 12. 11. I beseech thee, lay not the sin upon us
Deut. 31. 17. are not these evils come upon us?
Josh. 9. 20. let them live lest wrath be upon us
Judg. 8. 21. they said, rise thou and fall upon us
1 Sam. 5. 7. his hand is sore upon us and Dagon
1 Kings 12. 4. make thou this heavy yoke which he put upon us lighter, 9. 2 Chron. 10. 4, 9.
2 Kings 7. 9. some mischief will come upon us
1 Chr. 15. 13. Lord our God made a breach upon us
2 Chr. 20. 9. if when evil cometh upon us as sword
34. 21. for great is the wrath poured upon us
Ezra 8. 18. by the good hand of our God upon us, 31.
9. 13. after all that is come upon us for our evil
Neh. 9. 32. the trouble little that hath come upon us
33. thou art just in all that is brought upon us
13. 18. did not our God bring all this evil upon us?
Job 9. 33. that might lay his hand upon us both
Psal. 4. 6. lift up light of thy countenance upon us
33. 22. let thy mercy, O Lord, be upon us
44. 17. all this is come upon us yet have we not
67. 1. God bless us, cause his face to shine upon us
90. 17. the beauty of the Lord our God be upon us
123. 2. our eyes wait on L. till he have mercy up. us
3. have mercy upon us, O L. have mercy upon us Mat. 9. 27. | 20. 30, 31. Luke 17. 13.
Isa. 32. 15. until the Spirit be poured upon us
Lam. 3. 47. fear and a snare is come upon us
5. 1. remember, O Lord, what is come upon us
Ezek. 33. 10. if our transgressions and sins be upon us
Dan. 9. 11. therefore the curse is poured upon us
12. by bringing upon us a great evil, 13, 14.
Hos. 10. 8. they shall say to mountains, cover us, and to hills, fall on us. Luke 23. 30. Rev. 6. 16.
Jonah 1. 7. for whose cause this evil is on us, 8.
Mic. 3. 11. they will say, none evil can come upon us
7. 19. he will turn and have compassion upon us
Mat. 27. 25. his blood be on us and our children
Acts 3. 4. look on us || 5. 28. this man's blood up. us
12. or why look ye so earnestly on us as though
11. 15. Spirit fell on them, as on us at the beginning
Rom. 16. 6. Mary, who bestowed much labour on us
Tit. 3. 6. which he shed on us abundantly thro' Jes.
1 John 3. 1. love the Father hath bestowed on us

Over US.

Gen. 37. 8. said, shalt thou indeed reign over us?
Exod. 2. 14. who made thee judge over us, Acts 7. 27.
Num. 16. 13. thou make thyself a prince over us
Judg. 8. 22. Israel said to Gideon, rule over us
9. 8. the trees said to the olive-tree, reign over us
10. to the fig-tree || 12. to vine || 14. to bramble
1 Sam. 8. 19. but we will have a king over us, 10. 19.
11. 12. who said, shall Saul reign over us?
2 Sam. 5. 2. in time past, when Saul was king over us
19. 10. and Absalom whom we anointed over us
Neh. 9. 37. the kings whom thou hast set over us
Psal. 12. 4. lips are our own, who is Lord over us
Isa. 26. 13. other lords have had dominion over us
Lam. 5. 8. servants have ruled over us none to deliver
Luke 19. 14. will not have this man to reign over us

Through US.

2 Cor. 9. 11. causeth through us thanksgiving to God

To or unto US.

Gen. 19. 31. there is not a man to come in unto us
20. 9. said, what hast thou done unto us? 26. 10.
31. 21. let us take their daughters to us for wives
39. 14. brought an Hebrew unto us to mock us
42. 28. afraid, saying one to another, what is this that God hath done unto us? Jer. 5. 19.
Num. 10. 31. thou mayest be to us instead of eyes
32. what goodness Lord shall do unto us, the same
Deut. 5. 27. speak thou unto us and we will hear
29. 29. but the things revealed belong unto us
30. 12. go up to heaven and bring it unto us
13. shall go over the sea and bring it unto us
Josh. 9. 25. we are in thy hand, as it seemeth good and right to thee to do unto us do, Judg. 10. 15.
Judg. 13. 8. let the man of God come again unto us
15. 10. we come to do to him, as he hath done to us
18. 19. go with us, and be to us a father and a priest
1 Sam. 4. 8. woe unto us, Jer. 4. 13. | 6. 4. Lam. 5. 16.
14. 9. if they thus say unto us, tarry till we come
25. 15. but the men were very good unto us
16. they were a wall unto us by night and by day
1 Chron. 13. 3. bring again the ark of God to us
Ezra 4. 12. the Jews which came from thee to us
Neh. 5. 8. shall your brethren be sold unto us
Job 34. 4. let us choose to us judgment, let us know
Psal. 60. 1. hast scattered, O turn thyself to us ag.
115. 1. not unto us, O Lord, not unto us but thy name
Isa. 1. 9. except had left unto us a very small remn.
9. 6. unto us a child is born, unto us a son is given
14. 10. they shall say, art thou become like unto us?
28. 15. the scourge shall not come unto us
30. 10. prophesy not unto us right things, speak unto us smooth things, prophesy deceits
33. 21. Lord will be unto us a place of broad rivers
36. 11. speak not to us in the Jews' language
Jer. 5. 24. he reserveth to us the appointed weeks
26. 16. hath spoken to us in the name of the Lord
42. 5. for which the Lord shall send thee to us
44. 16. as for the word thou hast spoken unto us
Lam. 5. 4. water for money, our wood is sold un. us
Ezek. 11. 15. unto us is this land given in possession
24. 19. tell us what these things are to us?
Dan. 9. 7. but unto us confusion of faces, 8.
Hos. 6. 3. he shall come unto us as the rain
10. 3. what then should a king do to us?
Jonah 1. 11. that the sea may be calm unto us
Zech. 1. 6. like as the Lord thought to do unto us
Mat. 20. 12. thou hast made them equal unto us
25. 11. saying, Lord, Lord, open to us, Luke 13. 25.
27. 4. what is that to us? see thou to that
Luke 1. 2. even as they delivered them unto us
2. 15. which the Lord hath made known unto us
10. 17. even the devils are subject unto us
12. 41. speakest thou this parable unto us?
16. 26. neither can they pass to us that would
John 2. 18. what sign shewest thou unto us?
14. 22. that thou wilt manifest thyself unto us?
16. 17. what is this that he saith unto us?
Acts 7. 38. who received the oracles to give unto us?
10. 41. to us who did eat and drink with him
11. 17. God gave them the like gift as unto us
13. 33. God hath fulfilled the same unto us
Rom. 5. 5. by the Holy Ghost which is given unto us
1 Cor. 1. 18. but unto us it is the power of God
30. in Christ, who of God is made unto us wisdom
2. 10. God revealed them unto us by his Spirit
8. 6. but to us there is but one God, the Father
2 Cor. 5. 19. committed to us word of reconciliation
8. 5. gave themselves unto us by the will of God
7. therefore as ye abound in your love to us
Col. 1. 8. who declared unto us your love in Spirit
4. 3. that God would open unto us a door of utter.
Heb. 4. 2. for unto us was the gospel preached
1 Pet. 1. 12. but unto us they did minister the things

To US-WARD.

Psal. 40. 5. thy thoughts which are to us-ward
Eph. 1. 19. the greatness of his power to us-ward
2 Pet. 3. 9. but his long-suffering to us-w. not will.

Toward US.

Psal. 85. 4. cause thine anger toward us to cease
117. 2. his merciful kindness is great toward us
Rom. 5. 8. God commendeth his love toward us
Eph. 1. 8. wherein he hath abounded toward us
2. 7. in his kindness toward us through Christ
1 John 4. 9. was manifested the love of God toward us

Under US.

Psal. 47. 3. he shall subdue the people under us

With US.

Gen. 31. 50. no man is with us, see, God is witness
34. 9. and make ye marriages with us and give
10. ye shall dwell w. us || 23. they dwell with us
43. 4. if thou send our brother with us, 44. 26.
44. 30. seeth that the lad is not with us, 31.
Exod. 3. 18. the God of the Hebrews met with us, 5. 3.
14. 11. wherefore hast thou dealt thus with us?
20. 19. speak thou with us, let not God speak with us
33. 16. is it not in that thou goest with us?
Num. 10. 29. come thou with us, we will do thee good
32. it shall be, if thou go with us that goodness
11. 18. for it was well with us in Egypt
14. 9. and the Lord is with us, fear them not
22. 14. Balaam refuseth to come with us
Deut. 5. 2. the Lord made a covenant with us 3.
29. 15. but with him that standeth here with us, also with him that is not here with us this day
Josh. 9. 6. therefore make a league with us, 11.
Judg. 6. 13. O my lord, if the Lord be with us
11. 8. we turn again, that thou mayest go with us
18. 19. they said, hold thy peace and go with us
1 Sam. 5. 7. the ark of God shall not abide with us
2 Sam. 13. 26. let my brother Amnon go with us
21. 17. shall go no more out with us to battle
1 Kings 3. 18. there was no stranger with us in house
8. 57. the Lord our God be with us as he was
2 Kings 6. 16. fear not, they that be with us are more than they that be with them, 2 Chron. 32. 7.
2 Chron. 13. 12. behold, God is with us, 32. 8.
Ezra 4. 3. you have nothing to do with us to build
9. 14. wouldst not thou be angry with us till thou
Job 15. 10. with us are the grey-headed and aged
Psal. 46. 7. the Lord of hosts is with us, 11.
85. 5. wilt thou be angry with us for ever?
103. 10. he hath not dealt with us after our sins
Prov. 1. 11. come with us || Isa. 8. 10. God is with us
Isa. 59. 12. for our transgressions are with us
Jer. 8. 8. we are wise, the law of the Lord is with us
14. 21. remember, break not thy covenant with us
42. 6. that it may be well with us when we obey
Hos. 12. 4. found in Bethel, there he spake with us
Zech. 1. 6. as our doings, so hath he dealt with us
Mat. 1. 23. being interpreted, is, God with us
13. 56. his sisters are all with us, Mark 6. 3.
22. 25. now there were with us seven brethren
Luke 2. 48. son, why hast thou thus dealt with us?
9. 49. forbad him, because he followeth not with us
24. 29. abide with us || 32. while he talked with us
Acts 1. 17. for he was numbered with us and had
2. 29. his sepulchre is with us unto this day
1 Cor. 16. 16. to every one that helpeth with us
2 Cor. 8. 19. who was chosen to travel with us
2 Thess. 1. 7. to you who are troubled, rest with us
2 Pet. 1. 1. have obtained like precious faith with us
1 John 1. 3. that ye may have fellowship with us
2. 19. would no doubt have continued with us
2 John 2. the truth shall be with us for ever

Within US.

Luke 24. 32. did not our hearts burn within us while he opened to us the scriptures?

Without US.

1 Cor. 4. 8. ye have reigned as kings without us
Heb. 11. 40. that they without us not be made perfect

USE.

Lev. 7. 24. the fat may be used in any other u.
Deut. 26. 14. nor taken ought for any unclean u.
2 Sam. 1. 18. bade them teach Judah u. of the bow
1 Chron. 28. 15. according to the u. of candlestick
Rom. 1. 26. for women did change the natural u.
27. the men leaving the natural u. of the woman
Eph. 4. 29. which is good to the u. of edifying
2 Tim. 2. 21. shall be a vessel meet for master's u.
Heb. 5. 14. by u. have their senses exercised to

USES.

Tit. 3. 14. to maintain good works for necessary u.

USE, Passive.

Lev. 19. 26. neither shall ye u. enchantment
Num. 10. 2. u. trumpets for calling of the assembly
15. 39. after which ye u. to go a whoring
Deut. 2. †9. u. no hostility against Moab nor contend
1 Chron. 12. 2. could u. both right hand and left
Jer. 23. 31. that u. their tongues, and say, he saith
31. 23. as yet they shall u. this speech in Judah
46. 11. in vain shalt thou u. many medicines
Ezek. 12. 23. they shall no more u. it as a proverb
16. 44. shall u. this proverb against thee, saying
18. 2. what mean ye, that ye u. this proverb?
3. ye shall not have occasion to u. this proverb
21. 21. the king of Babylon stood to u. divination
Joel 2. †17. should u. a by-word against them
Mat. 5. 44. do good to them that hate you, pray for them that despitefully u. you, Luke 6. 28.
6. 7. when ye pray, u. not vain repetitions
Acts 14. 5. assault made to u. apostles despitefully
1 Cor. 7. 21. if thou mayest be made free, u. it rather
31. they that u. this world as not abusing it
2 Cor. 1. 17. when thus minded, did I u. lightness?
3. 12. have hope, we u. great plainness of speech
13. 10. lest being present, I should u. sharpness
Gal. 5. 13. u. not liberty for an occasion to the flesh
1 Tim. 1. 8. the law is good if a man u. it lawfully
3. 10. then let them u. the office of a deacon
5. 23. u. a little wine for thy stomach's sake
1 Pet. 4. 9. u. hospitality one to another without

USED.

Exod. 21. 36. if the ox hath u. to push in time past
Lev. 7. 24. the fat may be u. in any other use
Judg. 14. 10. for so u. the young men to do
20. whom Samson had u. as his friend
2 Kings 17. 17. u. enchantments, 21. 6. 2 Chron. 33. 6.
Jer. 2. 24. a wild ass u. to the wilderness that
Ezek. 22. 29. the people of land have u. oppression
35. 11. according to thy envy which thou hast u.
Hos. 12. 10. and u. similitudes by the prophets
Mark 2. 18. the disciples of John u. to fast
Acts 8. 9. Simon Magus before-time u. sorcery
19. 19. many also of them which u. curious arts
Rom. 3. 13. with their tongues they u. deceit
1 Cor. 9. 12. we have not u. this power, but suffer
15. but I have u. none of these things
1 Thess. 2. 5. nor at any time u. we flattering words
1 Tim. 3. 13. they that have u. the office of a deacon
Heb. 10. 33. companions of them that were so u.

USEST.

Psal. 119. 132. as thou u. to those that fear thy name

USETH.

Deut. 18. 10. not be found any that u. divination
Esth. 6. 8. apparel which the king u. to wear
Prov. 15. 2. the tongue of the wise u. knowledge
18. 23. the poor u. entreaties, but rich answereth
Jer. 22. 13. u. his neighbour's service without wages
Ezek. 16. 44. that u. proverbs, shall use this proverb
Heb. 5. 13. every one that u. milk is unskilful in

USING.

Col. 2. 22. which all are to perish with the u.
1 Pet. 2. 16. and not u. your liberty for a cloak of

USURP.

1 Tim. 2. 12. I suffer not a woman to u. authority

USURER.

Exod. 22. 25. thou shalt not be to him as an u.

USURY.

By usury *is generally understood the gain of any thing above the principal, or that which was lent, exacted only in consideration of the loan, whether it be in money, corn, wares, or the like.*

It is most commonly taken for an unlawful profit, which a person makes of his money or goods.

The Hebrew word for usury *signifies* biting. *The law of God prohibits rigorous imposing conditions of gain for the loan of money or goods, and exacting them without respect to the condition of the borrower, whether he gain or lose; whether poverty occasioned his borrowing, or a visible prospect of gain by employing the borrowed goods.*

It is said in Exod. 22. 25, 26. If thou lend money to any of my people that is poor by thee, thou shalt not be to him as an *usurer,* neither shalt thou lay upon him *usury,* &c. *And in* Lev. 25. 35, 36, 37. If thy brother be waxen poor, and fallen in decay with thee, then thou shalt relieve him, yea, though he be a stranger, or a sojourner, that he may live with thee: Take thou no *usury* of him, &c. *This law forbids the taking of usury from a brother that was poor, an Israelite reduced to poverty, or from a proselyte. But in* Deut. 23. 20. *God seems to tolerate* usury *towards strangers;* Unto a stranger thou mayest lend upon *usury. By strangers, in this passage, some understand the Gentiles in general, or all such as were not Jews, excepting proselytes. Others think that by strangers are meant the Canaanites, and the other people that were devoted to slavery and subjection; of these the Hebrews were permitted to exact usury, but not of such strangers with whom they had no quarrel, and against whom the Lord had not denounced his judgments.*

The Hebrews were plainly commanded in Exod. 22. 25, &c. *not to receive usury for money from any that borrowed for necessity, as in that case in* Neh. 5. 5, 7. *And such provision the law made for the preserving of estates to their families by the year of Jubilee; for a people that had little concern in trade, could not be supposed to borrow money but out of necessity; but they were allowed to lend upon usury to strangers, whom yet they must not oppress. This law therefore, in the strictness of it, seems to have been peculiar to the Jewish state; but in the equity of it, it obligeth us to shew mercy to those we have advantage against, and to be content to share with those we lend to in loss, as well as profit, if Providence cross them. And upon this condition, a valuable commentator says, "It seems as lawful for me to receive interest for money, which another takes pains with, improves, but runs the hazard of in trade, as it is to receive rent for my land which another takes pains with, improves, but runs the hazard of in husbandry."*

Exod. 22. 25. neither shalt thou lay upon him u.
Lev. 25. 36. take thou no u. of him or increase, 37.
Deut. 23. 19. shalt not lend on u. to thy brother
20. unto a stranger thou mayest lend upon u.

Neh. 5. 7. ye exact u. ‖ 10. let us leave off this u.
Psal. 15. 5. he that putteth not his money to u.
Prov. 28. 8. he that by u. increaseth substance
Isa. 24. 2. as with taker of u. so with giver of u.
Jer. 15. 10. I have neither lent on u. nor men have lent to me on u. yet every one doth curse me
Ezek. 18. 8. that hath not given forth on u. 17.
13. given forth on u. ‖ 22. 12. thou hast taken u.
Mat. 25. 27. received mine own with u. Luke 19. 23.

UTMOST, OUTMOST.

Gen. 49. 26. to the u. bound of the everlasting hills
Num. 22. 41. might see the u. of the people, 23. 13.
Deut. 30. 4. if any of you be driven out to o. parts
Jer. 9. 26. I will punish Egypt, Judah, Edom, and all that are in the u. corners, 25. 23. | 49. 32.
Luke 11. 31. she came from u. parts to hear Solomon

UTTER, *Verb.*

Lev. 5. 1. if he do not u. it then he shall bear iniquity
Josh. 2. 14. our life if ye u. it not this our business
20. if thou u. it, we will be quit of thine oath
Judg. 5. 12. awake, Deborah, u. song, arise, Barak
Job 8. 10. shall not they u. words out of their heart?
15. 2. should a wise man u. vain knowledge?
27. 4. nor shall my tongue u. deceit
33. 3. and my lips shall u. knowledge clearly
Psal. 78. 2. I will u. dark sayings of old
94. 4. how long shall they u. hard things
106. 2. who can u. the mighty acts of the Lord?
119. 171. my lips shall u. praise, when thou hast
145. 7. they shall u. the memory of thy goodness
Prov. 14. 5. but a false witness will u. lies
23. 33. thine heart shall u. perverse things
Eccl. 1. 8. all things full of labour, man cannot u. it
5. 2. let not thine heart be hasty to u. before God
Isa. 32. 6. a vile person will u. error against Lord
48. 20. tell this, u. it even to the end of the earth
Jer. 1. 16. I will u. my judgments against them
25. 30. u. his voice from his holy habitation
51. † 14. they shall u. a shout against Babylon
Ezek. 24. 3. u. a parable unto the rebellious house
Joel 2. 11. Lord shall u. his voice before his army
3. 16. u. his voice from Jerusalem, Amos 1. 2.
Mat. 13. 35. I will u. things have been kept secret
1 Cor. 14. 9. except u. words easy to be understood
2 Cor. 12. 4. which is not lawful for a man to u.

UTTER, *Adjective.*

Num. 21. † 3. he called the place, u. destruction
1 Kings 20. 42. a man I appointed to u. destruction
Nah. 1. 8. he will make an u. end of the place
Zech. 14. 11. there shall be no more u. destruction

UTTER, OUTER.

Ezek. 10. 5. the sound was heard to the o. court
42. 1. he brought me forth into the u. court

UTTERANCE.

Acts 2. 4. they spake, as the Spirit gave them u.
1 Cor. 1. 5. that ye are enriched by him in all u.
2 Cor. 8. 7. as ye abound in u. and knowledge
Eph. 6. 19. praying, that u. may be given to me
Col. 4. 3. that God would open to us a door of u.

UTTERED.

Num. 30. 6. if she had a husband when she u. 8.
Judg. 11. 11. Jephthah u. all his words before Lord
2 Sam. 22. 14. the Most High u. his voice, Psal. 46. 6.
Job 26. 4. to whom hast thou u. words?
42. 3. therefore have I u. that I understood not
Psal. 66. 14. which my lips u. when in trouble
Hab. 3. 10. deep u. his voice and lifted his hands
Rom. 8. 26. with groanings which cannot be u.
Heb. 5. 11. many things to say and hard to be u.
Rev. 10. 3. had cried, seven thunders u. their voices
4. when the seven thunders had u. their voices

UTTERETH.

Job 15. 5. for thy mouth u. thine iniquities
Psal. 19. 2. day unto day u. speech, night unto night
Prov. 1. 20. wisdom u. her voice in the streets
21. in the city she u. her words, saying, how long
10. 18. and he that u. a slander, is a fool
29. 11. a fool u. all his mind, but a wise man keeps
Jer. 10. 13. when he u. his voice, 51. 16.
Mic. 7. 3. the great man u. his mischievous desire

UTTERING.

Isa. 59. 13. u. from the heart words of falsehood

UTTERLY.

Exod. 17. 14. u. put out remembrance of Amalek
22. 17. if her father u. refuse to give her to him
23. 24. thou shalt u. overthrow their idols
Lev. 13. 44. priest shall pronounce him u. unclean
26. 44. in land of enemies I will not destroy u.
Num. 15. 31. that soul shall u. be cast off, his iniquity
21. 2. then I will u. destroy their cities
30. 12. if her husband hath u. made them void
Deut. 3. 6. u. destroying men, women, and children
4. 26. if ye corrupt yourselves, ye shall u. perish
7. 2. thou shalt u. destroy the Canaanites, 20. 17.
26. shalt u. detest the silver and gold of images
12. 2. ye shall u. destroy the high places
13. 15. destroying u. the city of idolaters with sword
31. 29. after my death ye will u. corrupt yourselves
Josh. 11. 20. that he might u. destroy them
17. 13. the children of Isr. put Canaanites to tribute, but did not u. drive them out, Judg. 1. 28.
Judg. 15. 2. I thought thou hadst u. hated her
21. 11. ye shall u. destroy every male and woman
1 Sam. 15. 3. smite, u. destroy the Amalekites, 18.
27. 12. he hath made Israel u. to abhor him
2 Sam. 17. 10. he that is valiant shall u. melt
23. 7. the sons of Belial as thorns shall be u. burnt
1 Kings 9. 21. the Canaanites Isr. could not u. destr.
2 Kings 19. 11. what the kings of Assyria have done to all lands, by destroying them u. Isa. 37. 11.
2 Chron. 20. 23. u. to slay them of mount Seir
Neh. 9. 31. thou didst not u. consume them
Psal. 37. 24. though he fall shall not u. be cast down
73. 19. the wicked are u. consumed with terrors
89. 33. my loving-kindness not u. take from him
119. 8. I will keep thy statutes, O forsake me not u.
43. take not the word of truth u. out of my mouth
Cant. 8. 7. substance for love, it would u. be contem.
Isa. 2. 18. and the idols he shall u. abolish
6. 11. he answered, until the land be u. desolate
11. 15. Lord u. destroy the tongue of Egyptian sea
24. 3. land be u. emptied ‖ 19. earth is u. broken
Isa. 37. 11. Assyria have done by destroy. them u.
40. 30. and the young men shall u. fall, but they
56. 3. Lord hath u. separated me from his people
60. 12. yea, those nations shall be u. wasted
Jer. 9. 4. for every brother will u. supplant
12. 17. if they will not obey, I will u. pluck up
14. 19. hast thou u. rejected Judah, loathed Zion
23. 39. behold, I, even I, will u. forget you
25. 9. I will u. destroy them, 50. 21, 26. | 51. 3, 58.
29. and should ye be u. unpunished?
Lam. 5. 22. but thou hast u. rejected us, art wroth
Ezek. 9. 6. slay u. old and young, maids, children
17. 10. being planted, shall it not u. wither?
27. 31. and they shall make themselves u. bald
29. 10. I will make the land of Egypt u. waste
Dan. 11. 44. shall go forth u. to make away many
Hos. 1. 6. but I will u. take them away
10. 15. shall the king of Israel be u. cut off
Amos 9. 8. I will u. destroy the house of Jacob
Mic. 2. 4. that day shall one say, we be u. spoiled
Nah. 1. 15. for the wicked he is u. cut off
Zeph. 1. 2. I will u. consume all things from land
Zech. 11. 17. his right eye shall be u. darkened
1 Cor. 6. 7. now there is u. a fault among you
2 Pet. 2. 12. shall u. perish in their own corruption
Rev. 18. 8. Babylon shall be u. burnt with fire
See DESTROYED.

UTTERMOST.

2 Kings 7. 5. when lepers came to u. part of camp, 8.
Neh. 1. 9. there were of you cast out to u. part
Psal. 2. 8. I will give u. parts for thy possession
Mat. 5. 26. till thou hast paid the u. farthing
12. 42. she came from the u. parts to hear Solomon
Mark 13. 27. shall gather his elect from the u. part
Acts 24. 22. I will know the u. of your matter
1 Thess. 2. 16. wrath is come on them to the u.
Heb. 7. 25. is able to save them to u. that come to G.
See UTMOST.

V.

VAGABOND.

Gen. 4. 12. a fugitive and v. shalt thou be in earth
14. I shall be a fugitive and v. in the earth
Acts 19. 13. then certain v. Jews took on them

VAGABONDS.

Psal. 109. 10. let his children be v. and beg

VAIL, or VEIL.

A curtain, or cover, which the Jewish women wore over their heads and faces, in token of modesty, of reverence, and subjection to their husbands, Gen. 24. 65. 1 Cor. 11. 3, 6, 7, 10. *The Lord commanded Moses to make a* vail *of blue, and purple, and scarlet, and therewith to divide the* holy *of* holies, *which represented the highest heaven, from the* holy place, *where the church militant, or its representatives, met and served God,* Exod. 26. 31, 32, 33. *This* vail *typified the human nature of Christ, adorned with excellent gifts and graces, by which he has opened for us a way into heaven,* Heb. 10. 19, 20. *It signified also the separation between the Jews and Gentiles, which is now removed by Christ,* Eph. 2. 14. *and therefore, at the death of Christ, this* vail *was* rent in twain, *Mat.* 27. 51. *which shewed that the partition wall betwixt Jews and Gentiles was pulled down; that God was leaving his temple, and abolishing all legal and ceremonial worship. The apostle speaks of the* vail *of ignorance, blindness, and hardness of heart, which keeps the Jews from understanding the scriptures of the Old Testament, the spiritual sense and meaning of the law, and from seeing that* Christ is the end of the law for righteousness; *this* vail *was cast over them, for their wilful and malicious rejecting the gospel-light,* John 9. 39. 2 Cor. 3. 13, 15.

Gen. 24. 65. Rebekah took a v. and covered herself
38. 14. Tamar covered herself with a v. wrapped
Exod. 26. 31. and thou shalt make a v. of blue
34. 33. Moses put a v. on his face, 35.
36. 35. and he made a v. of blue, 2 Chron. 3. 14.
40. 3. thou shalt cover the ark with the v.
Lev. 16. 2. come not into holy place within the v.
15. and bring his blood within the v.
21. 23. only he shall not go in unto the v. nor come
24. 3. without the v. shall Aaron order it
Ruth 3. 15. bring the v. that thou hast upon thee
Cant. 5. 7. keepers of the walls took away my v.
Isa. 25. 7. destroy the v. spread over all nations
Mat. 27. 51. the v. of the temple was rent in twain from top to bottom, Mark 15. 38. Luke 23. 45.
2 Cor. 3. 13. not as Moses which put a v. over face
14. for to this day remaineth the same v. untaken away, which v. is done away in Christ
15. but even to this day the v. is upon their heart
16. nevertheless, the v. shall be taken away
Heb. 6. 19. which entereth into that within the v.
9. 3. and after the second v. the tabernacle, called
10. 20. through the v. that is to say, his flesh

VAILS.

Isa. 3. 23. in that day the Lord will take away the v.

VAIN,

And vanity, *are taken in several senses in Scripture.* (1) *For that which is unprofitable without fruit.* Eccl. 1. 2. Vanity of vanities, all is vanity. *All worldly things, and all men's designs, and studies, and works about them, are absolutely* vain, *and insufficient to procure satisfaction and happiness.* (2) *It signifies* empty, *without any substance; as* emptiness *is opposed to that which is* full, *or* heavy, *or* true. 1. *To* fulness; *so promises not fulfilled are said to be* vain promises. *And Job calls the days of his affliction* months of vanity; *that is, empty of solid joy, peace, or comfort,* Job 7. 3. *And in* Psal. 2. 1. Why do the people imagine a *vain* thing? *that is, an empty thing, without reason or hope.* 2. *As it is opposed to* gravity; *as light and inconstant men are called* vain men; *in which sense idolaters are called* vain *persons, like the wind, and idols are called* vanity, *because of their nothingness and impotence.* 2 Kings 17. 15, They followed vanity and became *vain. So in* Isa. 41. 29. They are all vanity, their works are nothing; their molten images are wind and confusion. 3. *As it is opposed to* truth; *as deceitful men and liars are called* vain men, *and lies are called* vanity, *Psal.* 4. 2. How long will ye love vanity and seek after leasing? *And* in 2 Kings 18. 20. They are but *vain* words: *thy words come not from thy heart; thou speakest against thy knowledge.* Vain *is often put for false.* Exod. 20. 7. Thou shalt not take the name of the Lord thy God in *vain.* "*Thou shalt not swear to confirm a thing that is false; thou shalt not appeal to the Lord as a witness of thy lies; or, thou shalt not take uselessly, needlessly, and without very good and substantial reasons, the name of God to witness what thou affirmest." The Hebrew word* shave, *which is here translated by* vain, *is put for* false *in some places of Scripture; as* Exod. 20. 16. Hos. 10. 4. (3) Vanity *is taken for that which frustrates and disappoints a person of his end; in this sense the hope and confidence of every unregenerate man may justly be called* vain, *because it will deceive and disappoint him at the last, when he shall stand in most need of help and comfort. It is said,* Psal. 60. 11. *Vain* is the help of man; *that is, a deceitful safeguard, a disappointing help, only feeding the expectation with a fruitless hope.* (4) *It signifies that which is weak, and obnoxious to change and corruption. Thus all worldly things are but vanity,* Eccl. 1. 2. *And* the creature was made subject to vanity, *to disorders and destruction,* Rom. 8. 20. *Man also, as to his continuance in the world,* is like vanity, *he is like a vapour or breath, which is gone in an instant.* (5) *It signifies* iniquity. *Psal.* 119. 37, Turn away mine eyes from beholding vanity, *that is, iniquity, and the deceitfulness of sin, whereby I may be ensnared, and drawn away from the truth.* (6) *It signifies foolishness, joined with ignorance and blindness.* Job 11. 12. For *vain* man would be wise; *that foolish creature man, who since the fall is void of all true wisdom and solid knowledge, and judgment of the things of God.*

Vain man, *does not only signify men puffed up with pride, and full of vanity, but also worthless and insignificant persons, without religion, without rule or conduct, as in* 2 Chron. 13. 7. There are gathered to Jeroboam *vain* men, the children of Belial. *The Hebrew says, men void of sense, or beggars; miserable children, without a yoke, worthless children.*

Exod. 5. 9. and let them not regard v. words
Deut. 32. 47. for it is not a v. thing for you
Judg. 9. 4. wherewith Abimelech hired v. persons
11. 3. there were gathered v. men to Jephthah
1 Sam. 12. 21. for then should ye go after v. things, which cannot profit nor deliver, for they are but v.
2 Sam. 6. 20. as one of the v. fellows uncovereth
2 Kings 17. 15. became v. and went after heathen
18. 20. but they are but v. words, Isa. 36. 5.
2 Chron. 13. 7. are gathered to Jeroboam v. men
Job 11. 11. he knoweth v. men, he seeth wickedness
12. for v. man would be wise, tho' man be born
15. 2. should a wise man utter v. knowledge?
16. 3. Job said, shall v. words have an end?
27. 12. why then are ye thus altogether v.?
Psal. 2. 1. the people imagine a v. thing, Acts 4. 25
26. 4. I have not sat with v. persons
33. 17. an horse is a v. thing for safety
39. 6. surely every man walketh in a v. shew
60. 11. for v. is the help of man, 108. 12.
62. 10. become not v. in robbery, if riches increase
119. 113. I hate v. thoughts, but thy law do I love
127. 2. it is v. for you to rise up early, to sit up
Prov. 12. 11. followeth v. persons is void of unders.
28. 19. that followeth v. persons shall have poverty
31. 30. favour is deceitful and beauty is v.
Eccl. 6. 12. all days of his v. life which he spends
Isa. 1. 13. bring no more v. oblations, incense is
36. 5. they are but v. words, I have counsel
Jer. 2. 5. walked after vanity, and are become v.
4. 14. how long thy v. thoughts lodge within thee!
10. 3. for the customs of the people are v.
23. 16. the prophets make you v. they speak
Lam. 2. 14. thy prophets have seen v. things
4. 17. as for us, our eyes failed for our v. help
Ezek. 12. 24. there shall be no more any v. vision
13. 7. have ye not seen a v. vision and spoken
Mal. 3. 14. ye have said, it is v. to serve God
Mat. 6. 7. when ye pray, use not v. repetitions
Rom. 1. 21. but became v. in their imaginations
1 Cor. 3. 20. the thoughts of the wise are v.
15. 14. and if Christ be not risen, then is our preaching v. and your faith is also v. 17.
Eph. 5. 6. let no man deceive you with v. words
Col. 2. 8. lest any spoil you thro' philos. and v. deceit
1 Tim. 1. 6. have turned aside to v. jangling
6. 20. avoiding prof. and v. babblings, 2 Tim. 2. 16.
Tit. 1. 10. there are many unruly and v. talkers
3. 9. for they are unprofitable and v.
Jam. 1. 26. deceives his heart, this man's relig. is v.
2. 20. wilt thou know, O v. man, that saith
1 Pet. 1. 18. redeemed from your v. conversation

In VAIN.

Exod. 20. 7. thou shalt not take name of Lord in v. Deut. 5. 11.
Lev. 26. 16. and ye shall sow your seed in v.
20. and your strength shall be spent in v.
1 Sam. 25. 21. in v. have I kept all Nabal hath
Job 9. 29. if I be wicked, why then labour I in v.?
21. 34. how then comfort ye me in v. seeing
35. 16. therefore doth Job open his mouth in v.
39. 16. her labour is in v. without fear
41. 9. behold, the hope of him is in v.
Psal. 39. 6. surely they are disquieted in v.
73. 13. verily I have cleansed my heart in v.
89. 47. wherefore hast thou made all men in v.?
127. 1. they labour in v. watchmen waketh in v.
139. 20. and thine enemies take thy name in v.

Prov. 1. 17. surely *in v.* the net is spread in sight
30. 9. lest I take the name of my God *in v.*
Isa. 30. 7. for the Egyptians shall help *in v.*
45. 18. he created it not *in v.* he formed it
19. I said not to seed of Jacob, seek ye me *in v.*
49. 4. then I said, I have laboured *in v.* I have spent my strength for nought and *in v.*
65. 23. they shall not labour *in v.* nor bring forth
Jer. 2. 30. *in v.* have I smitten your children
3. 23. *in v.* is salvation hoped for from hills
4. 30. *in v.* shalt thou make thyself fair
6. 29. bellows burnt, the founder melteth *in v.*
8. 8. how do ye say we are wise, lo, certainly *in v.* made he it, the pen of the scribes is *in v.*
46. 11. *in v.* shalt thou use many medicines
50. 9. their arrows, none shall return *in v.*
51. 58. and the people shall labour *in v.*
Ezek. 6. 10. shall know that I have not said *in v.*
Heb. 2. + 13. people shall weary themselves *in v.*
Zech. 10. 2. and the diviners comfort *in v.*
Mat. 15. 9. but *in v.* they worship me, *Mark* 7. 7.
Rom. 13. 4. for he beareth not the sword *in v.*
1 *Cor.* 15. 2. unless ye have believed *in v.*
10. his grace bestowed upon me was not *in v.*
58. that your labour is not *in v.* in the Lord
2 *Cor.* 6. 1. ye receive not the grace of God *in v.*
9. 3. lest our boasting of you should be *in v.*
Gal. 2. 2. lest by any means I should run *in v.*
21. come by the law, then Christ is dead *in v.*
3. 4. are ye so foolish? have ye suffered so many things *in v.*? if it be yet *in v.*
4. 11. lest I have bestowed on you labour *in v.*
Phil. 2. 16. holding forth word of life, that I may rejoice that I have not run *in v.* nor laboured *in v.*
1 *Thess.* 2. 1. our entrance, that it was not *in v.*
3. 5. have tempted you, and our labour be *in v.*
Jam. 4. 5. do ye think the Scripture saith *in v.?*

VAIN *glory.*

Gal. 5. 26. let us not be desirous of *v. glory*
Phil. 2. 3. let nothing be done through *v. glory*

VAINLY.

Col. 2. 18. *v.* puffed up by his fleshly mind

VALE.

Gen. 14. 3. kings were joined in *v.* of Siddim, 8.
10. the *v.* of Siddim was full of slime pits
37. 14. he sent Joseph out of the *v.* of Hebron
Deut. 1. 7. go to all places in the hills and in the *v.*
Josh. 10. 40. Joshua smote the country of the *v.*
1 *Kings* 10. 27. Solom. made silver to be as stones, and cedars as sycamore-trees in *v.* 2 *Chr.* 1. 15.
Jer. 33. 13. in the cities of the *v.* shall flocks pass

VALIANT.

1 *Sam.* 14. 52. when Saul saw any *v.* man, he took
16. 18. I have seen a son of Jesse, a mighty *v.* man
18. 17. be *v.* for me, and fight the Lord's battles
26. 15. David said to Abner, art not thou a *v.* man?
31. 12. all the *v.* men took the body of Saul
2 *Sam.* 2. 7. be ye *v.* 13. 28. ‖ 17. 10. he that is *v.*
11. 16. to Uriah, where he knew that *v.* men were
23. 20. Benaiah the son of Jehoiada, the son of a *v.* man of Kabzeel, 1 *Chron.* 11. 22.
1 *Kings* 1. 42. come in, for thou art a *v.* man
1 *Chron* 7. 2. the sons of Tola were *v.* men
11. 26. the *v.* men of the armies were Asahel
2 *Chr.* 26. 17. and with him eighty priests, *v.* men
Cant. 3. 7. behold his bed which is Solomon's, threescore *v.* men are about it, of the *v.* of Israel
Isa. 10. 13. put down inhabitants like a *v.* man
33. 7. behold, their *v.* ones shall cry without
Jer. 9. 3. but they are not *v.* for the truth
46. 15. why are thy *v.* men swept away?
Nah. 2. 3. the *v.* men are in scarlet, the chariots
3. + 18. thy *v.* ones shall dwell in the dust
Heb. 11. 34. who through faith waxed *v.* in fight

VALIANTEST.

Judg. 21. 10. sent to Jabesh 12,000 men of the *v.*

VALIANTLY.

Num. 24. 18. Edom a possession, Israel shall do *v.*
1 *Chron.* 19. 13. and let us behave ourselves *v.*
Psal. 60. 12. through God we shall do *v.* 108. 13.
118. 15. the right hand of the Lord doeth *v.* 16.

VALLEY.

There are several valleys *mentioned in Scripture; as the valley of* Berachah, *or of blessing, in the tribe of Judah, to the west of the Dead sea,* 2 Chron. 20. 26.

The *vale* of Siddim, *Gen.* 14. 3. *In the Hebrew it is the valley of* Hashbedim, *which some translate the* vale *of the* fields, *others the* vale *of* chalk; *the* Septuagint, *the vale of salt. It was in this vale that the cities of Sodom and Gomorrah were built; and where afterwards the lake Asphaltites, or the Dead sea was formed.*

The *valley* of Shaveh, *or otherwise,* the king's dale, *Gen.* 14. 17. 2 *Sam.* 18. 18. Shaveh *is a city lying in the king's dale, over-against Jerusalem, according to Eusebius. It was in this* valley *that Melchizedek met Abraham, at his return from his victory over the five kings. But some think this interview was at the foot of mount Tabor.*

The *valley* of Eshcol, *or the* valley *of* grapes, *Num.* 32. 9. *This name was given to the* valley *of the land of promise, wherein the spies of the children of Israel gathered the bunch of grapes, which they brought to the camp of Kadesh, upon a pole between two men,* Num. 13. 23. 24. *This* valley *was to the south of the promised land.*

The *valley* of Jezreel, *Josh.* 19. 18. *This* valley *extends itself east and west from Scythopolis to the foot of mount Carmel; in it there was a celebrated city built, of the same name, which belonged to the tribe of Issachar. Ahab had a palace there,* 1 Kings 21. 1, 23. *and this city became famous on the score of Naboth's vineyard, and the vengeance which God executed on Jezebel at Jezreel,* 2 Kings 9. 33, *&c.*

The *valley* of Achor, *Josh.* 7. 24. *This* valley *was in the territory of Jericho, and in the tribe of Benjamin, where Achan, his sons and daughters, were stoned to death. God says, that* he will give the *valley* of Achor for a door of hope, *Hos.* 2. 15. *that is, some beginnings of mercy and blessings, as the earnest and pledges of future favours. As this valley was a door of hope to Israel of their enjoyment of the promised land, so would God deal with repenting Israel at the times there pointed out.*

The *valley* of Jehoshaphat, *Joel* 3. 2. *Some are of opinion that this* valley *is that where king Jehoshaphat obtained so signal a victory, and with so much ease, against the Moabites, Ammonites, and their confederates,* 2 Chron. 20. 1, 2, &c. *This* valley *lay towards the Dead sea, beyond the wilderness of Tekoah; and after this event it was called the* valley of blessing, 2 Chron. 20. 26. *because of the solemn blessings and praises that were given to God in it upon this occasion. Others think, that the* valley of Jehoshaphat *lies between the walls of Jerusalem and the mount of Olives, and that it is watered with the brook Kidron, which runs through the midst of this vale. There are likewise some who maintain, that the ancient Hebrews had no distinct knowledge of any particular place under the name of the valley of* Jehoshaphat; *and that Joel intended by it to shew in general the place where God was to execute his judgments against the nations, and will appear at the last judgment with all the brightness of his majesty.* Jehoshaphat, *in Hebrew, signifies* the judgment of God. *And it is very probable, that the* valley of Jehoshaphat, *or* God's judgment, *mentioned in Joel, is symbolical. From this passage the Jews, and many Christians, have been of opinion, that the last judgment will be solemnized in the* valley *of Jehoshaphat.*

The *valley* of Hinnom, *in Hebrew, it is* Gehennon, *whence comes the word* Gehenna. See TOPHET.

The *valley* of vision, *Isa.* 22. 1. *in the prophetical and figurative style, signifies Jerusalem. It is called a* valley *by antiphrasis, because it stood upon a mountain; or, according to others, it is called a* valley *comparatively to those higher mountains wherewith it was encompassed. And the additional name of* vision *was given to it, because of the many and clear visions and revelations of God's mind in that place above all other parts of the world; or, as others will have it, because the temple of Jerusalem was built upon mount Moriah, which is* the mountain of vision, *Gen.* 22. 14.

The fat *valleys,* Isa. 28. 1. *are those which lie below and about the city of Samaria. This country was very fat and fruitful. Samaria stood upon a rising ground that commanded these* valleys.

The *valley* of passengers, *Ezek.* 39. 11. *It is thought that this stands for the great road, which was at the foot of mount Carmel, to go from Judea, Egypt, and the country of the Philistines, into Phœnicia; and back from Phœnicia into those countries. This road was to the east of the Mediterranean sea.*

The *valley* of Succoth, *was beyond Jordan, and near the city of Succoth. The Psalmist puts the* valley of Succoth *for the whole country beyond Jordan,* Psal. 60. 6.

The *valley* of Elah, 1 *Sam.* 17. 2. *Saul was here encamped with the army of Israel, when the giant Goliath came to insult the troops of the Hebrews. This* valley *was to the south of Jerusalem, towards Sochoh and Azekah.*

Gen. 14. 17. king of Sodom met him at *v.* of Shaveh
Num. 32. 9. for when they went up to *v.* of Eshcol
Deut. 1. 24. they came to *v.* of Eshcol, searched it out
21. 4. elders shall bring the heifer to a rough *v.* and strike off the heifer's neck in the *v.*
34. 3. the plain of *v.* of Jericho, a city of palm-trees
6. he buried Moses in a *v.* in the land of Moab
Josh. 7. 24. they brought them to the *v.* of Achor
10. 12. and, thou moon, in the *v.* of Ajalon
15. 8. which is at the end of the *v.* of the giants
Judg. 1. 19. not drive out inhabitants of the *v.*
5. 15. Barak, he was sent on foot into the *v.*
7. 8. the host of Midian was beneath in the *v.* 12.
16. 4. Samson loved a woman in the *v.* of Sorek
1 *Sam.* 6. 13. reaping their wheat-harvest in the *v.*
21. 9. whom thou slewest in the *v.* of Elah
2 *Sam.* 5. 18. the Philistines also came and spread themselves in the *v.* of Rephaim, 22. | 23. 13.
8. 13. from smiting the Syrians in the *v.* of salt
2 *Kings* 2. 16. the Spirit hath cast him into some *v.*
3. 16. he said, make this *v.* full of ditches
14. 7. he slew of Edom in the *v.* of salt, 1 *Chr.* 18. 12.
2 *Chron.* 20. 26. they assembled in *v.* of Berachah
28. 3. Ahaz burnt incense in the *v.* of Hinnom
35. 22. Josiah came to fight in *v.* of Megiddo
Job 21. 33. the clods of the *v.* shall be sweet to him
39. 21. he paweth in the *v.* and rejoiceth in strength
Psal. 23. 4. yea, though I walk thro' the *v.* of death
60. 6. I will mete out the *v.* of Succoth, 108. 7.
84. 6. who passing thro' *v.* of Baca, make it a well
Prov. 30. 17. the ravens of the *v.* shall pick it out
Cant. 6. 11. I went down to see the fruits of the *v.*
Isa. 17. 5. that gathereth ears in the *v.* of Rephaim
22. 1. the burden of the *v.* of vision
5. for it is a day of trouble in the *v.* of vision
28. 4. beauty which is on the head of the fat *v.*
21. he shall be wroth as in the *v.* of Gibeon
40. 4. every *v.* shall be exalted, every hill made low
65. 10. *v.* of Achor a place for herds to lie down
Jer. 2. 23. see thy way in the *v.* know what thou
7. 32. *v.* of Hinnom, but *v.* of slaughter, 19. 6.
21. 13. I am against thee, O inhabitant of the *v.*
48. 8. the *v.* also shall perish, and plain destroyed
49. 4. why gloriest thou in thy flowing *v.?*
Ezek. 37. 1. in the *v.* which was full of bones
Hos. 1. 5. break the bow of Isr. in the *v.* of Jezreel
2. 15. give the *v.* of Achor for a door of hope
Joel 3. 2. bring them into the *v.* of Jehoshaphat
14. multitudes, multitudes in the *v.* of decision
18. a fountain shall water the *v.* of Shittim
Zech. 12. 11. as the mourning in the *v.* of Megiddon
14. 4. mount cleave, and there shall be a great *v.*
5. ye shall flee to the *v.* of the mountains
Luke 3. 5. every *v.* be filled, every hill brought low

See GATE.

VALLEYS.

Num. 24. 6. as the *v.* are they spread forth
Deut. 8. 7. depths that spring out of the *v.* and hills
11. 11. but the land is a land of hills and *v.*
1 *Kings* 20. 28. God of hills, but he is not God of *v*
Job 30. 6. to dwell in clifts of *v.* in caves of earth
39. 10. or will he harrow the *v.* after thee?
Psal. 65. 13. the *v.* are covered over with corn
104. 8. they go down by the *v.* unto the place
10. he sendeth the springs into the *v.* which run
Cant. 2. 1. I am the rose of Sharon, the lily of the *v.*
Isa. 22. 7. thy choicest *v.* shall be full of chariots
24. + 15. wherefore glorify the Lord in the *v.*
28. 1. which are on the head of the fat *v.*
41. 18. I will open fountains in midst of the *v.*
57. 5. slaying the children in the *v.* under rocks
Jer. 49. 4. wherefore gloriest thou in the *v.*
Ezek. 6. 3. thus saith the Lord to the *v.* 36. 4, 6.
7. 16. be on the mountains like doves of the *v.*

VALOUR.

Judg. 3. 29. they slew of Moab 10,000 men of *v.*
6. 12. Lord is with thee, thou mighty man of *v.*
11. 1. Jephthah the Gileadite, a mighty man of *v.*
1 *Sam.* 18. + 17. only be thou a son of *v.* for me
2 *Sam.* 2. + 7. and be ye the sons of *v.* 13. + 28.
1 *Kings* 11. 28. Jeroboam was a mighty man of *v.*
2 *Kings* 5. 1. Naaman ‖ 1 *Chr.* 12. 28. Zadok man of *v.*
2 *Chron.* 17. 17. Eliada a mighty man of *v.*

See Mighty MEN.

VALUE.

Job 13. 4. forgers of lies, ye are all physicians of no *v.*
Mat. 10. 31. fear ye not therefore, ye are of more *v.* than many sparrows, *Luke* 12. 7.

VALUE.

Lev. 27. 8. present himself, the priest shall *v.* him
12. priest shall *v.* it, whether it be good or bad
Mat. 27. 9. whom they of children of Israel did *v.*

VALUED.

Lev. 27. 16. homer of barley-seed *v.* at 50 shekels
Job 28. 16. wisdom cannot be *v.* with gold of Ophir
19. neither shall it be *v.* with pure gold
Mat. 27. 9. of silver, the price of him that was *v.*

VALUEST.

Lev. 27. 12. as thou *v.* it who art priest, so shall it be

VANISH.

Job 6. 17. what time they wax warm, they *v.*
Isa. 51. 6. the heavens shall *v.* away like smoke
1 *Cor.* 13. 8. whether knowledge, it shall *v.* away
Heb. 8. 13. which waxeth old, is ready to *v.* away

VANISHED.

Jer. 49. 7. saith the Ld. of hosts, is their wisdom *v.?*
Luke 24. 31. and he *v.* out of their sight

VANISHETH.

Job 7. 9. as the cloud is consumed and *v.* away
Jam. 4. 14. life is even a vapour that *v.* away

VANITY.

See *Signification* on VAIN.

2 *Kings* 17. 15. they followed *v.* and became vain
Job 7. 3. so am I made to possess months of *v.*
16. let me alone, for my days are *v.*
15. 31. let not him that is deceived trust in *v.* for *v.* shall be his recompense
35. they conceive mischief and bring forth *v.*
31. 5. if I have walked with *v.* or hasted to deceit
35. 13. surely God will not hear *v.* nor regard it
Psal. 4. 2. O sons of men, how long will ye love *v.*
10. 7. under his tongue is mischief and *v.*
12. 2. they speak *v.* every one to his neighbour
24. 4. who hath not lift up his soul unto *v.*
36. + 4. the wicked deviseth *v.* upon his bed
39. 5. every man at his best estate is altogether *v.*
11. every man is *v.* ‖ 94. 11. thoughts of man *v.*
41. 6. come to see me, he speaketh *v.* 144. 8, 11.
62. 9. men of low degree are *v.* lighter than *v.*
78. 33. therefore their days did he consume in *v.*
119. 37. turn away mine eyes from beholding *v.*
144. 4. man is like to *v.* his days are as a shadow
Prov. 13. 11. wealth gotten by *v.* shall be diminished
21. 6. getting of treasures by a lying tongue is *v.*
22. 8. he that soweth iniquity shall reap *v.*
30. 8. remove from me *v.* and lies, give not poverty
Eccl. 1. 2. *v.* of vanities, saith the preacher, all is *v.* 14. | 3. 19. | 11. 8. | 12. 8.
2. 1. this is also *v.* 15, 19, 21, 23. | 4. 8, 16. | 5. 10. | 6. 2, 9. | 7. 6. | 8. 10, 14.
11. behold, all was *v.* and vexation, 17, 26. | 4. 4.
4. 7. I saw *v.* ‖ 6. 4. for he cometh in with *v.*
6. 11. there be many things that increase *v.*
+ 12. the number of the days of the life of his *v.*
7. 15. all things have I seen in the days of my *v.*
8. 14. there is a *v.* that is done on the earth
9. 9. live joyfully with wife all the days of thy *v.*
11. 10. for childhood and youth are *v.*
Isa. 5. 18. wo to them that draw iniq. with cords of *v.*
30. 28. to sift the nations with the sieve of *v.*
40. 17. all nations to him are counted *v.*
23. he maketh the judges of the earth as *v.*
41. 29. behold, they are all *v.* 44. 9.
57. 13. wind shall carry them, *v.* shall take them
58. 9. if thou take away *v.* ‖ 59. 4. they trust in *v.*
Jer. 2. 5. they have walked after *v.* become vain
10. + 3. for the statutes of the people are *v.*
15. they are *v.* and the work of errors, 51. 18.
16. 19. surely our fathers have inherited *v.*
18. 15. my people have burnt incense to *v.*
Ezek. 13. 6. they have seen *v.* and divination, 22. 28.
8. because ye have spoken *v.* and seen lies
9. prophets see *v.* 21. 29. ‖ 23. shall see no more *v.*
Hos. 12. 11. surely they are *v.* they sacrifice bullocks
Hab. 2. 13. peo. shall weary themselves for very *v.*
3. + 7. I saw the tents of Cushan under *v.*
Zech. 10. 2. for the idols have spoken *v.*
Rom. 8. 20. the creature was made subject to *v.*
Eph. 4. 17. not as Gentiles walk in *v.* of their mind
2 *Pet.* 2. 18. they speak great swelling words of *v.*

VANITIES.
Deut. 32. 21. they have provoked me to anger with their *v.* 1 *Kings* 16. 13, 26. *Jer.* 8. 19.
Psal. 31. 6. I have hated them that regard lying *v.*
Eccl. 1. 2. vanity of *v.* saith the preacher, 12. 8.
5. 7. in the multitude of dreams there are *v.*
Jer. 10. 8. foolish, the stock is a doctrine of *v.*
14. 22. are any among the *v.* that can cause rain?
Jonah 2. 8. they that observe lying *v.* forsake their
Acts 14. 15. that ye should turn from these *v.*

VAPOUR.
Job 36. 27. they pour down rain according to the *v.*
33. the cattle also concerning the *v.*
Psal. 148. 8. hail, snow, and *v.* fulfilling his word
Acts 2. 19. will shew signs in the earth, *v.* of smoke
Jam. 4. 14. for what is your life? it is even a *v.*

VAPOURS.
Psal. 135. 7. he causeth the *v.* to ascend from the ends of the earth, *Jer.* 10. 13. | 51. 16.

VARIABLE.
Hab. 3 † 1. a prayer according to *v.* songs

VARIABLENESS.
Jam. 1. 17. Father of lights, with whom is no *v.*

VARIANCE.
Mat. 10. 35. I am come to set a man at *v.* ag. father
Gal. 5. 20. the works of the flesh are hatred, *v.*

VAUNT.
Judg. 7. 2. lest Israel *v.* themselves against me

VAUNTETH.
1 *Cor.* 13. 4. charity *v.* not itself, is not puffed up

VEHEMENT.
Cant. 8. 6. love is a fire that hath a *v.* flame
Jonah 4. 8. that God prepared a *v.* east wind
2 *Cor.* 7. 11. yea, what *v.* desire it wrought in you?

VEHEMENTLY.
Mark 14. 31. but Peter spake the more *v.* not deny
Luke 6. 48. the stream beat *v.* on that house, 49.
11. 53. the Pharisees began to urge him *v.*
23. 10. the scribes stood and *v.* accused him

VEIN.
Job 28. 1. surely there is a *v.* for the silver

VENERABLE.
Phil. 4. † 8. finally, whatsoever things are *v.*

VENGEANCE.
Gen. 4. 15. *v.* shall be taken on him seven-fold
Deut. 32. 35. to me belongeth *v.* and recompence, *Psal.* 94. 1. *Heb.* 10. 30.
41. I will render *v.* to mine enemies
43. for he will render *v.* to his adversaries
Judg. 11. 36. the Lord hath taken *v.* for thee
Psal. 58. 10. shall rejoice, when he seeth the *v.*
99. 8. thou tookest *v.* of their inventions
149. 7. to execute *v.* upon the heathen and punishm.
Prov. 6. 34. he will not spare in the day of *v.*
Isa. 34. 8. it is the day of the Lord's *v.* and the year of recompences for Zion, 61. 2. *Jer.* 51. 6.
35. 4. behold your God will come with *v.*
47. 3. I will take *v.* *Jer.* 51. 36.
59. 17. and he put on the garments of *v.* for clothing
63. 4. for the day of *v.* is in mine heart
Jer. 11. 20. let me see thy *v.* on them, 20. 12.
46. 10. a day of *v.* ‖ 50. 15. the *v.* of the Lord, 28.
50. 28. the *v.* of Lord, the *v.* of his temple, 51. 11.
Lam. 3. 60. thou hast seen all their *v.* against me
Ezek. 24. 8. might cause fury come up to take *v.*
25. 12. Edom by taking *v.* hath greatly offended
14. I will lay my *v.* on Edom by hand of Israel
15. because the Philistines have taken *v.*
17. when I shall lay my *v.* on the Philistines
Mic. 5. 15. I will execute great *v.* *Ezek.* 25. 17.
Nah. 1. 2. Lord will take *v.* on his adversaries
Luke 21. 22. for these be the days of *v.* that all
Acts 28. 4. whom *v.* suffereth not to live
Rom. 3. 5. is God unrighteous who taketh *v.*?
12. 19. *v.* is mine, I will repay, saith the Lord
2 *Thess.* 1. 8. Lord revealed in flaming fire, taking *v.*
Jude 7. an example, suffering the *v.* of eternal fire

VENISON.
Gen. 25. 28. Isaac loved Esau, because he eat of his *v.*
27. 3. go to the field and take me some *v.* 7.
19. arise, I pray thee, and eat of my *v.* 31.
25. bring it near, and I will eat of my son's *v.*
33. Isaac said, where is he that hath taken *v.*?

VENOM.
Deut. 32. 33. their wine is the cruel *v.* of asps

VENOMOUS.
Acts 28. 4. the barbarians saw the *v.* beast hang

VENT.
Job 32. 19. my belly is as wine which hath no *v.*

VENTURE.
1 *Kings* 22. 34. a certain man drew a bow at a *v.* and smote the king of Israel, 2 *Chron.* 18. 33.

VERIFIED.
Gen. 42. 20. so shall your words be *v.* and not die
1 *Kings* 8. 26. let thy word be *v.* 2 *Chron.* 6. 17.

VERILY.
Gen. 42. 21. we are *v.* guilty concerning our brother
Exod. 31. 13. saying, *v.* my sabbaths ye shall keep
Judg. 15. 2. I *v.* thought thou hadst hated her
1 *Kings* 1. 43. *v.* our Lord hath made Solomon king
2 *Kings* 4. 14. *v.* she hath no child, her husb. is old
1 *Chron.* 21. 24. I will *v.* bring it for the full price
Job 19. 13. my acquaint. are *v.* estranged from me
Psal. 37. 3. do good, and *v.* thou shalt be fed
39. 5. *v.* every man at his best state is vanity
58. 11. *v.* there is a reward for the righteous, *v.* he is a God that judgeth in the earth
66. 19. but *v.* God hath heard me, hath attended
73. 13. *v.* I have cleansed my heart in vain
Isa. 45. 15. *v.* thou art a God that hidest thyself
Jer. 15. 11. *v.* it shall be well with thy remnant, *v.* I will cause the enemy to entreat thee well
Mat. 5. 18. *v.* I say unto you, 6. 2, 5, 16. | 8. 10. | 10. 15, 23, 42. | 11. 11. | 13. 17. | 16. 28. | 17. 20. | 18. 3, 13, 18. | 19. 23, 28. | 21. 21, 31. | 23. 36. | 24. 2, 34, 47. | 25. 12, 40, 45. | 26. 13. *Mark* 3. 28. | 6. 11. | 8. 12. | 9. 1, 41. | 10. 15, 29. | 11. 23. | 12. 43. | 13. 30. | 14. 9, 18, 25. *Luke* 4. 24. | 11. 51. | 12. 37. | 13. 35. | 18. 17, 29. | 21. 32.
26. *v.* I say unto thee, 26. 34. *Mark* 14. 30. *Luke* 23. 43.

Mark 9. 12. Elias *v.* cometh first and restoreth all
Acts 16. 37. nay *v.* let them come and fetch us
19. 4. John *v.* baptized with baptism of repentance
22. 3. am *v.* a man which am a Jew, born in Tarsus
26. 9. I *v.* thought I ought to do many things
Rom. 2. 25. for circumcision *v.* profiteth if thou keep
10. 18. *v.* their sound went into all the earth
15. 27. it hath pleased them *v.* debtors they are
1 *Cor.* 5. 3. I *v.* as absent in body, present in spirit
Gal. 3. 21. *v.* righteousness had been by the law
Heb. 2. 16. *v.* he took not on him nature of angels
6. 16. for men *v.* swear by the greater, an oath
12. 10. for they *v.* for a few days chastened us
1 *Pet.* 1. 20. who *v.* was foreordained before foundat.
1 *John* 2. 5. in him *v.* is the love of God perfected

VERILY, VERILY.
John 1. 51. *v.* *v.* I say unto you, 5. 19, 24, 25. | 6. 26, 32, 47, 53. | 8. 34, 51, 58. | 10. 1, 7. | 12. 24. | 13. 16, 20, 21. | 14. 12. | 16. 20, 23.
3. 3. *v.* *v.* I say unto thee, 5. 11. | 13. 38. | 21. 18.

VERITY.
Psal. 111. 7. the works of his hands are *v.*
1 *Tim.* 2. 7. a teacher of the Gentiles in faith and *v.*

VERMILION.
Jer. 22. 14. ceiled with cedar and painted with *v.*
Ezek. 23. 14. images of Chaldeans pourtrayed with *v.*

VERTUE, *See* VIRTUE.

VERY.
Gen. 27. 21. whether thou be my *v.* son Esau
Exod. 9. 16. in *v.* deed for this I raised thee up
Num. 12. 3. now the man Moses was *v.* meek
Deut. 30. 14. but the word is *v.* nigh unto thee
1 *Sam.* 25. 34. in *v.* deed except thou hadst hasted
26. 4. understood that Saul was come in *v.* deed
2 *Sam.* 24. 10. for I have done *v.* foolishly
2 *Chron.* 20. 35. king Ahaziah did *v.* wickedly
Neh. 1. 7. we have dealt *v.* corruptly against thee
Psal. 5. 9. their inward part is *v.* wickedness
35. 8. into that *v.* destruction let him fall
71. 19. thy righteousness also, O God, is *v.* high
89. 2. thy faithfulness establish in the *v.* heavens
92. 5. O Lord, thy thoughts are *v.* deep
93. 5. thy testimonies are *v.* sure, holiness becomes
119. 138. thy testimonies are *v.* faithful
140. thy word is *v.* pure, therefore I love it
146. 4. in that *v.* day his thoughts perish
147. 15. his word runneth *v.* swiftly
Prov. 17. 9. repeats a matter, he separateth *v.* friends
Isa. 10. 25. for yet a *v.* little while, 29. 17.
33. 17. shall behold the land that is *v.* far off
40. 15. he taketh up the isles as a *v.* little thing
Jer. 2. 12. be ye *v.* desolate, saith the Lord
4. 19. my bowels, I am pained at my *v.* heart
Ezek. 2. 3. they have transgressed to this *v.* day
16. 47. but as if that were a *v.* little thing
Hab. 2. 13. the people shall labour in the *v.* fire, and the people weary themselves for *v.* vanity
Mat. 10. 30. the *v.* hairs of your head are numbered
24. 24. if it were possible, shall deceive the *v.* elect
John 7. 26. that this is the *v.* Christ, *Acts* 9. 22.
8. 4. this woman was taken in adultery, in *v.* act
14. 11. else believe me for the *v.* work's sake
1 *Thess.* 5. 23. the *v.* God of peace sanctify you
Heb. 10. 1. and not the *v.* image of the things
Jam. 5. 11. the Lord is *v.* pitiful, of tender mercy
See GREAT, MUCH.

VESSEL.
Deut. 23. 24. eat grapes, but not put any in thy *v.*
1 *Sam.* 21. 5. though sanctified this day in the *v.*
1 *Kings* 17. 10. fetch me a little water in a *v.*
2 *Kings* 4. 6. bring yet a *v.* there is not a *v.* more
Psal. 2. 9. dash them in pieces like a potter's *v.*
31. 12. I am forgotten, I am like a broken *v.*
Prov. 25. 4. there shall come forth a *v.* for the finer
Isa. 66. 20. Israel bring an offering in a clean *v.*
Jer. 18. 4. the *v.* was marred in hand of the potter
22. 28. is he a *v.* wherein is no pleasure?
25. 34. and ye shall fall like a pleasant *v.*
48. 11. Moab hath not been emptied from *v.* to *v.*
38. for I have broken Moab like a *v.*
51. 34. Nebuchadnezzar hath made me an empty *v.*
Ezek. 4. 9. put them in one *v.* and make bread
15. 3. or will men take a pin of it to hang any *v.*?
Hos. 8. 8. shall be as a *v.* wherein is no pleasure
Mark 11. 16. should carry any *v.* thro' the temple
Luke 8. 16. no man covereth a candle with a *v.*
Acts 9. 15. for he is a chosen *v.* unto me
10. 11. Peter saw a certain *v.* descending, 11. 5.
Rom. 9. 21. hath power to make one *v.* to honour
1 *Thess.* 4. 4. know to possess his *v.* in sanctification
2 *Tim.* 2. 21. he shall be a *v.* to honour, sanctified
1 *Pet.* 3. 7. dwell with them according to knowledge, giving honour to wife as to weaker *v.*

VESSELS.
Gen. 43. 11. take of the best fruits in your *v.*
Exod. 40. 10. anoint the altar and *v.* *Lev.* 8. 11.
Num. 18. 3. Levites not come nigh *v.* of sanctuary
1 *Sam.* 9. 7. for the bread is spent in our *v.*
21. 5. and the *v.* of the young men are holy
2 *Kings* 4. 3. go borrow thee *v.* abroad of all thy neighbours, even empty *v.* borrow not a few
2 *Chron.* 29. 19. the *v.* king Ahaz did cast away
Ezra 1. 7. Cyrus the king brought forth the *v.*
5. 15. take these *v.* ‖ 7. 19. *v.* are given to thee
8. 25. he weighed the silver and the *v.* 33.
Neh. 13. 9. thither brought I again the *v.* of house
Isa. 18. 2. even in *v.* of bulrushes on the waters
22. 24. all *v.* of small quantity, the *v.* of cups
52. 11. be ye clean that bear the *v.* of the Lord
65. 4. broth of abominable things is in their *v.*
Jer. 14. 3. they returned with their *v.* empty
27. 16. *v.* of the Lord's house brought again, 28. 3.
Dan. 5. 23. they have brought the *v.* of his house
Hos. 13. 15. he shall spoil treasure of all pleasant *v.*
Hag. 2. 16. to draw out fifty *v.* out of the press
Mat. 13. 48. they gathered the good into *v.*
25. 4. but the wise took oil in their *v.* with lamps
Rom. 9. 22. the *v.* of wrath ‖ 23. the *v.* of mercy
Rev. 2. 27. as *v.* of a potter shall they be broken
See BRASS, EARTHEN, GOLD, SILVER.

VESTMENTS.
2 *Kings* 10. 22. bring forth *v.* for the worshippers

VESTRY.
2 *Kings* 10. 22. Jehu said to him that was over the *v.*

VESTURE, S.
Gen. 41. 42. and arrayed Joseph in *v.* of fine linen
Deut. 22. 12. make fringes on the quarters of thy *v.*
Psal. 22. 18. they part my garments, they cast lots upon my *v.* *Mat.* 27. 35. *John* 19. 24.
102. 26. as a *v.* shalt thou change them
Heb. 1. 12. and as a *v.* shalt thou fold them up
Rev. 19. 13. he was clothed with a *v.* dipt in blood
16. on his *v.* and on his thigh a name written

VEX.
Exod. 22. 21. thou shalt not *v.* a stranger, *Lev.* 19. 33.
Lev. 18. 18. not take a wife to her sister to *v.* her
Num. 25. 17. *v.* the Midianites and smite them
18. for they *v.* you with their wiles and beguiled
33. 55. those which ye let remain shall *v.* you
2 *Sam.* 12. 18. how will he *v.* himself if we tell
2 *Chron.* 15. 6. God did *v.* them with adversity
Job 19. 2. how long will ye *v.* my soul and break
Psal. 2. 5. and *v.* them in his sore displeasure
Isa. 7. 6. let us go up against Judah and *v.* it
11. 13. and Judah shall not *v.* Ephraim
Ezek. 32. 9. I will *v.* the hearts of many people
Hab. 2. 7. shall they not awake that shall *v.* thee?
Acts 12. 1. Herod did *v.* certain of the church

VEXATION.
Deut. 28. 20. the Lord shall send on thee *v.*
Eccl. 1. 14. is vanity and *v.* of spirit, 2. 11, 17.
17. this also is *v.* of spirit, 2. 26. | 4. 4, 16. | 6. 9.
2. 22. what hath man of the *v.* of his heart?
4. 6. than both the hands full with *v.* of spirit
Isa. 9. 1. shall not be such as was in her *v.*
28. 19. be a *v.* only to understand the report
65. 14. but ye shall howl for *v.* of spirit

VEXATIONS.
2 *Chron.* 15. 5. great *v.* were on all the inhabitants

VEXED.
Num. 20. 15. the Egyptians *v.* us and our fathers
Judg. 2. 18. by reason of them that *v.* them
10. 8. that year the Ammonites *v.* Israel
16. 16. so that his soul was *v.* unto death
1 *Sam.* 14. 47. Saul *v.* his enemies on every side
2 *Sam.* 13. 2. Amnon was so *v.* that he fell sick
2 *Kings* 4. 27. let her alone, for her soul is *v.*
Neh. 9. 27. thou deliveredst to enemies who *v.* them
Job 27. 2. the Almighty, who hath *v.* my soul
Psal. 6. 2. my bones are *v.* ‖ 3. my soul is sore *v.*
10. let mine enemies be ashamed and sore *v.*
Isa. 63. 10. they rebelled and *v.* his Holy Spirit
Ezek. 22. 5. which art infamous and much *v.*
7. in thee they *v.* the fatherless ‖ 29. *v.* the poor
Mat. 15. 22. my daughter is grievously *v.* with devil
17. 15. L. have mercy, for he is lunatic and sore *v.*
Luke 6. 18. and they that were *v.* with unclean spirits, and they were healed, *Acts* 5. 16.
2 *Pet.* 2. 7. delivered just Lot *v.* with conversation
8. *v.* his righteous soul from day to day

VIAL.
1 *Sam.* 10. 1. Samuel took a *v.* of oil and poured it
Rev. 16. 2. the first angel poured his *v.* on the earth
3. second *v.* on the sea ‖ 4. third *v.* on the rivers
8. fourth *v.* on sun ‖ 10. fifth *v.* on seat of beast
12. sixth *v.* on Euphrates ‖ 17. seventh *v.* into air

VIALS.
Rev. 5. 8. having golden *v.* full of odours
15. 7. gave the seven angels seven golden *v.*
16. 1. go and pour out the *v.* of the wrath of God
17. 1. one of the angels which had seven *v.* 21. 9.

VICTORY.
1 *Sam.* 15. † 29. also the *v.* of Israel will not lie
2 *Sam.* 19. 2. *v.* that day was turned to mourning
23. 10. the Lord wrought a great *v.* that day, 12.
2 *Kings* 5. † 1. by him the Lord had given *v.* to Syria
1 *Chron.* 29. 11. thine, O Lord, is the *v.* and majesty
Psal. 98. 1. his holy arm hath gotten him the *v.*
Prov. 21. † 31. day of battle, but *v.* is of the Lord
Isa. 25. 8. he will swallow up death in *v.* and wipe away tears from all faces, 1 *Cor.* 15. 54.
Mat. 12. 20. till he send forth judgment unto *v.*
1 *Cor.* 15. 55. thy sting, O grave, where is thy *v.*?
57. but thanks be to God, who giveth us the *v.*
1 *John* 5. 4. and this is the *v.* even our faith
Rev. 15. 2. them had gotten the *v.* over the beast

VICTUAL, S.
Gen. 14. 11. they took the goods of Sodom, and *v.*
Exod. 12. 39. neither had they prepared any *v.*
Lev. 25. 37. nor lend him thy *v.* for increase
Deut. 23. 19. usury of money, usury of *v.* of any th.
Josh. 1. 11. prepare *v.* ‖ 9. 11. take *v.* with you
9. 14. the men took of their *v.* and asked not
Judg. 17. 10. I will give a suit of apparel and *v.*
1 *Sam.* 22. 10. he gave him *v.* and sword of Goliath
1 *Kings* 4. 7. which provided *v.* for the king, 27.
11. 18. Pharaoh appointed him *v.* and gave land
1 *Chron.* 12. † 40. they that were nigh brought *v.*
Neh. 10. 31. if the people bring *v.* on the sabbath
13. 15. I testified against them in day they sold *v.*
Jer. 40. 5. so captain gave Jeremiah *v.* and a reward
44. 17. for then had we plenty of *v.* and were well
Mat. 14. 15. went into villages to buy *v.* *Luke* 9. 12.

VICTUALLED.
1 *Kings* 20. † 27. the children of Israel were *v.*

VIEW.
Josh. 2. 7. go *v.* the land ‖ 7. 2. *v.* the country
2 *Kings* 2. 7. the sons of the prophets stood to *v.* 15.

VIEWED.
Josh. 7. 2. the men *v.* Ai ‖ *Ezra* 8. 15. I *v.* the people
Neh. 2. 13. and I *v.* the walls of Jerusalem, 15.

VIEWERS.
Isa. 47. † 13. let the *v.* of the heavens stand up

VIGILANT.
1 *Tim.* 3. 2. a bishop must be *v.* of good behaviour
1 *Pet.* 5. 8. be sober, be *v.* because your adversary

VIGOUR.
Dan. 10. † 8. my *v.* was turned into corruption

VILE.
Deut. 25. 3. lest thy brother should seem *v.* to thee
Judg. 19. 24. but to this man do not so *v.* a thing
1 *Sam.* 3. 13. because his sons made themselves *v.*
15. 9. every thing that was *v.* they destroyed
2 *Sam.* 6. 22. and I will yet be more *v.* than thus

Job 18. 3. why are we reputed v. in your sight?
40. 4. behold, I am v. what shall I answer thee?
Psal. 15. 4. in whose eyes a v. person is contemned
Isa. 32. 5. the v. person be no more called liberal
6. for the v. person will speak villany
Jer. 15. 19. take forth the precious from the v.
29. 17. and I will make them like v. figs
Lam. 1. 11. see, O Lord, for I am become v.
Dan. 11. 21. in his estate shall stand up a v. person
Nah. 1. 14. I will cut off the graven and molten image, and will make thy grave, for thou art v.
3. 6. I will cast filth on thee, and make thee v.
Rom. 1. 26. God gave them up to v. affections
Phil. 3. 21. who shall change our v. body that it may
Jam. 2. 2. there come in a poor man in v. raiment

VILELY.

2 Sam. 1. 21. shield of the mighty is v. cast away

VILER.

Job 30. 8. of base men, they were v. than the earth

VILEST.

Ps. 12. 8. the wicked when the v. men are exalted

VILLAGE.

Mat. 21. 2. go into the v. over-against you, and ye shall find an ass, Mark 11. 2. Luke 19. 30.
Luke 24. 13. two of them went that same day to a v.
28. they drew nigh unto the v. whither they went

VILLAGES.

Exod. 8. 13. and the frogs died out of the v.
Lev. 25. 31. the houses of the v. counted as fields
Judg. 5. 7. the inhabitants of the v. ceased
Neh. 6. 2. let us meet together in one of the v.
Esth. 9. 19. Jews of v. made the 14th day of Adar
Cant. 7. 11. come, my beloved, let us lodge in the v.
Ezek. 38. 11. I will go up to the land of unwalled v.
Hab. 3. 14. thou didst strike the head of his v.
Mat. 14. 15. multitude, that they may go into the v. and buy themselves victuals, Mark 6. 36.
See CITIES.

VILLANY.

Isa. 9. † 17. and every mouth speaketh v.
32. 6. for the vile person will speak v.
Jer. 29. 23. they have committed v. in Israel
Hos. 2. † 10. and now will I discover her v.

VINE.

Vineyards. *There were in Palestine many excellent vineyards. Jacob, in his blessing to Judah, says,* Binding his foal unto the *vine,* and his ass's colt unto the choice *vine;* he washed his garments in *wine,* and his clothes in the blood of grapes, Gen. 49. 11. *This was to show the abundance of vines that should fall to his lot. The spouse in* Cant. 1. 14. *compares her beloved to* a cluster of camphire, or cypress, that grows in the vineyards of En-gedi. *The cypress-tree is a shrub that grows as high as a pomegranate-tree; its leaves are like those of the olive-tree, its blossom is white and sweet, and its fruit hangs like clusters of grapes, and is of a very agreeable scent. Those grapes of the cypress that came from the vineyards of En-gedi were of great reputation.*

God compares his people to a vine, which he had brought out of Egypt, and planted in Palestine, as a good soil, but which, instead of bringing forth good fruit, brought forth only bitter fruit and wild grapes, Psal. 80. 8. Isa. 5. 1, *&c. He alludes to the custom of transplanting trees for their more advantageous growth. Our Saviour says, that "the householder having let his vineyard to tenants, who ought to have rendered him the fruit of it, instead of that they abused his servants, and killed his own Son, who went to require the payment of what was owing to him,"* Mat. 21. 33, *&c. In this parable, the householder is God the Father; his planting a vineyard, denotes his establishing a church among the Jews, and furnishing it with all needful helps and means to make it spiritually fruitful; his letting it out to husbandmen, denotes his committing the care of it to the public pastors, the priests, and Levites, and governors of the church: his servants are the prophets and apostles, sent to stir them up to faith and obedience, or holiness of life; his Son is Jesus Christ; and the scope of this parable is to show the Jews their obstinate impenitency under all means, and their incurableness, in their evil entreating God's messengers from time to time, and their crucifying of Christ; for which God will unchurch them, and set up a church among the Gentiles, and ruin the commonwealth of the Jews. In* John 15. 1. *Christ says,* I am the true *vine,* and my Father is the husbandman. "*I am the root, fountain, and head of influence, whence my people and members derive life, grace, fruitfulness, and all good; and my Father orders all things concerning my branches or members, by ingrafting them into me, by visiting, defending, supporting, pruning, and purging them continually, to make them fruitful.*"

The *vine* of Sodom, *Deut.* 32. 32. Their *vine* is the *vine* of Sodom: *that is,* a vine *of a plant from Sodom, which brings forth only bitter grapes, and of which no use can be made. It is affirmed, that the fruits which grow about the Dead sea are all rotten within: and when they are opened, are full only of dust. Moses by this would show, that the people of Israel were degenerated, that their principles and practices were all corrupt and abominable. To express a time of public tranquillity, of profound peace, it is said, that* every one lives in quiet under his own *vine,* and under his own fig-tree, 1 *Kings* 4. 25. *Mic.* 4. 4.

Noah planted the vine after the deluge, and was the first that cultivated it, Gen. 9. 20. *Many are of opinion, that wine was not unknown before the deluge, and that this patriarch only continued to cultivate the vine after this great catastrophe, as he had done before: but the fathers think that he knew not the force of* wine, *having never used it before, nor having ever seen any one use it. He is supposed to be the first that pressed out the juice of the grape, and to have reduced it to a potable liquor. Before him, men only ate the grapes, like other fruit.*

Gen. 40. 9. in my dream, behold, a v. was before me
10. and in the v. were three branches, it budded
49. 11. Judah is a lion's whelp, binding his foal to the v. and his ass's colt to the choice v.
Lev. 25. 5. nor gather grapes of thy v. undressed, 11.
Num. 6. 4. he shall eat nothing made of the v. tree
Deut. 32. 32. for their v. is of the v. of Sodom
Judg. 9. 12. the trees said to the v. reign over us
13. 14. not eat any thing that cometh of the v.
1 Kings 4. 25. dwelt safely every man under his v.
2 Kings 4. 39. found a wild v. and gathered gourds
18. 31. eat ye every man of his own v. Isa. 36. 16.
Job 15. 33. shall shake off his unripe grape as the v.
Psal. 80. 8. thou hast brought a v. out of Egypt
14. look down, and behold, and visit this v.
128. 3. thy wife shall be as a fruitful v. by sides
Cant. 6. 11. to see whether the v. flourished, 7. 12.
7. 8. thy breasts shall be as clusters of the v.
Isa. 5. 2. he planted it with the choicest v.
16. 8. for the v. of Sibmah languisheth
9. I will bewail the v. of Sibmah, Jer. 48. 32.
24. 7. the new wine mourneth, the v. languisheth
32. 12. they shall lament for the fruitful v.
34. 4. as the leaf falleth off from the v. as a fig
Jer. 2. 21. yet I had planted thee a noble v. how then turned into degenerate plant of strange v.?
6. 9. they shall glean the remnant of Israel as a v.
8. 13. there shall be no grapes on the v. nor figs
Ezek. 15. 2. what is the v. tree more than any tree?
6. as the v. tree which I have given for fuel
17. 6. it became a spreading v. of low stature
7. this v. did bend her roots towards him
19. 10. thy mother is like a v. in thy blood
Hos. 10. 1. Israel is an empty v. he bringeth fruit
14. 7. they shall revive as corn, grow as the v.
Joel 1. 7. he laid my v. waste, barked my fig-tree
12. the v. is dried up, the fig-tree languisheth
2. 22. the fig-tree and the v. yield their strength
Mic. 4. 4. they shall sit every man under his v.
Hag. 2. 19. as yet the v. hath not brought forth
Zech. 3. 10. shall ye call every man under the v.
8. 12. the v. shall give her fruit, the heavens dew
Mal. 3. 11. neither shall your v. cast her fruit
Mat. 26. 29. I will not drink of this fruit of v. till in my Father's kingdom, Mark 14. 25. Luke 22. 18.
John 15. 1. I am the true v. my Father is husbandman, 5.
4. branch cannot bear fruit, except it abide in v.
Jam. 3. 12. my brethren, can a v. bear figs?
Rev. 14. 18. gathers clusters of the v. of the earth
19. the angel gathered the v. of the earth

VINES.

Num. 20. 5. it is no place of v. or pomegranates
Deut. 8. 8. a land of wheat, barley, and v. honey
Psal. 78. 47. he destroyed their v. with hail
105. 33. he smote their v. also and fig trees
Cant. 2. 13. and the v. give a good smell
15. take us the foxes, the little foxes, that spoil the v. for our v. have tender grapes
Isa. 7. 23. where there were a thousand v.
Jer. 5. 17. they shall eat up thy v. and fig-trees
31. 5. thou shalt yet plant v. on the mountains
Hos. 2. 12. I will destroy her v. and her fig-trees
Hab. 3. 17. neither shall fruit be in the v.

VINE-*dressers.*

2 Kings 25. 12. the captain of the guard left the poor of the land to be v.-dressers, Jer. 52. 16.
2 Chr. 26. 10. Uzziah had husbandm. and v.-dressers
Isa. 61. 5. sons of alien shall be your v.-dressers
Joel 1. 11. be ashamed, howl, O ye v.-dressers

VINEGAR.

Is made of wine, beer, cider, and even of water. The ancients had several kinds of vinegar *which they made use of for drink. Boaz told Ruth, that she might come and dip her morsel in the* vinegar, *along with his people,* Ruth 2. 14. *Harvesters made use of this liquor for their refreshment: And this was a custom not only among the Jews, but also among the Romans. The emperor Pescennius Niger gave orders, that his soldiers should drink nothing but* vinegar *on their marches, and Constantine the Great allowed his soldiers* wine *and* vinegar *alternately every day.*

It is thought that the vinegar *which the Roman soldiers offered to our Saviour at his crucifixion, was the* vinegar *they made use of for their own drinking,* Mat. 27. 48. *This* vinegar *was not of that sort we make use of for salads and sauces, but a small wine called* pesca, *or* sera. *They make great use of it in Spain and Italy, in harvest-time. They use it likewise on shipboard, to correct the ill taste of water. The Scripture forbids the Nazarites to use* vinegar, *and all sorts of liquors that come from the vine, and which are capable of inebriating,* Num. 6. 3.

However, there was a kind of strong vinegar, *which was not proper for drinking, or which was not used till it was well diluted. Solomon says,* Prov. 10. 26. As vinegar to the teeth, so is the sluggard to them that send him. "*As vinegar by its cold and sharpness offends the teeth and the palate, so a sluggish messenger is unserviceable and vexatious to those who employ him." And in* Prov. 25. 20. As *vinegar* upon nitre, so is he that singeth songs to an heavy heart. *That is,* "as vinegar *being thrown upon nitre is a thing improper, for it renders it less useful and not so effectual to take out spots or blemishes, so he that singeth songs to an heavy heart, does that which is unseasonable and offensive, for his grief is thereby rather increased than diminished.*"

Num. 6. 3. a Nazarite shall drink no v. of wine
Ruth 2. 14. eat bread and dip thy morsel in the v.
Psal. 69. 21. they gave me gall for my meat, in my thirst they gave me v. to drink, Mat. 27. 34.
Prov. 10. 26. as v. to the teeth, so is the sluggard
25. 20. as v. upon nitre, so is he that singeth
Mat. 27. 48. they took a spunge and filled it with v. Mark 15. 36. Luke 23. 36. John 19. 29, 30.

VINEYARD.

Gen. 9. 20. Noah planted a v. and drank wine
Exod. 22. 5. if a man shall cause a v. to be eaten
23. 11. in like manner thou shalt deal with thy v.
Lev. 19. 10. and thou shalt not glean thy v.
25. 3. and six years thou shalt prune thy v.
4. neither sow thy field, nor prune thy v.
Deut. 20. 6. what man is he that hath planted a v.?
22. 9. thou shalt not sow thy v. with divers seeds, lest the fruit of thy seed and v. be defiled
23. 24. when thou comest into thy neighbour's v.
24. 21. when thou gatherest the grapes of thy v.
28. 30. thou shalt plant a v. and not gather grapes
1 Kings 21. 1. Naboth had a v. hard by the palace
2. give me thy v. I will give thee a better v. 6.
7. eat bread, I will give thee the v. of Naboth
Psal. 80. 15. the v. thy right hand hath planted
Prov. 24. 30. I went by v. of the man void of unders.
31. 16. with fruit of her hand she planteth a v.
Cant. 1. 6. but mine own v. have I not kept
8. 11. Solomon had a v. he let the v. to keepers
12. my v. which is mine, is before me, O Solomon
Isa. 1. 8. daughter of Zion is left as a cottage in a v.
3. 14. for ye have eaten up the v. spoil of the poor
5. 1. sing a song of my beloved touching his v.
7. for the v. of Lord of hosts is the house of Israel
10. yea, ten acres of v. shall yield one bath
27. 2. in that day sing ye to her, a v. of red wine
Jer. 12. 10. many pastors have destroyed my v.
35. 7. the Rechabites shall not plant v. 9.
Mic. 1. 6. I will make Samaria as plantings of a v.
Mat. 20. 1. went early to hire labourers into his v.
4. he said unto them, go ye also into the v. 7.
21. 28. he said, son, go work to-day in my v.
33. a certain householder planted a v. and let it out to husbandmen, Mark 12. 1. Luke 20. 9.
Luke 13. 6. a man had a fig-tree planted in his v.
7. then said he unto the dresser of his v. behold
1 Cor. 9. 7. who planteth a v. and eateth not fruit?

VINEYARDS.

Num. 16. 14. hast not given us inheritance of v.
20. 17. we will not pass through the v. 21. 22.
22. 24. angel of the Lord stood in a path of the v.
Deut. 6. 11. he swore to give thee v. and olive-trees which thou plantedst not, Josh. 24. 13. Neh. 9. 25.
28. 39. thou shalt plant v. and dress them
Judg. 15. 5. the foxes burnt up the v. and olives
21. 20. saying, go and lie in wait in the v.
1 Sam. 8. 14. he will take your fields and your v.
22. 7. will the son Jesse give every one of you v.?
2 Kings 5. 26. is it a time to receive v. and sheep?
18. 32. till I take you to a land of bread and v.
19. 29. in the third year sow, reap, and plant v.
1 Chron. 27. 27. over the v. was Shimei, over the increase of the v. for the wine-cellars was Zabdi
Neh. 5. 3. we have mortgaged our v. and houses
11. restore to them their v. and olive-yards
Job 24. 18. he beholdeth not the way of the v.
Psal. 107. 37. sow the fields and plant v. to yield
Eccl. 2. 4. I builded me houses, I planted me v.
Cant. 1. 6. they made me the keeper of the v.
14. as a cluster of camphire in the v. of En-gedi
7. 12. let us get up early to the v. let us see if vine
Isa. 16. 10. in the v. there shall be no singing
65. 21. they shall build houses and inhabit, shall plant v. and eat the fruit of them, Amos 9. 14.
Jer. 32. 15. houses and v. shall be possessed again
39. 10. Nebuzar-adan gave the poor v. and fields
Ezek. 28. 26. they shall build houses and plant v.
Hos. 2. 15. I will give her her v. from thence
Amos 4. 9. the palmer-worm devoured your v.
5. 11. ye have planted v. but ye shall not drink
17. and in all v. shall be wailing, I will pass
Zeph. 1. 13. they shall plant v. but not drink the wine

VINTAGE.

Lev. 26. 5. your threshing shall reach to the v. and the v. shall reach to the sowing time
Judg. 8. 2. is it not better than the v. of Abiezer?
Job 24. 6. they gather the v. of the wicked
Isa. 16. 10. I have made their v. shouting to cease
24. 13. as the gleaning grapes when v. is done
32. 10. the v. shall fail, gathering shall not come
Jer. 48. 32. the spoiler is fallen upon thy v.
Mic. 7. 1. I am as the grape-gleanings of the v.
Zech. 11. 2. the forest of the v. is come down

VIOL.

Isa. 5. 12. harp and v. and wine are in their feasts
Amos 6. 5. that chant to sound of the v. and invent

VIOLS.

Isa. 14. 11. the noise of thy v. is brought down
Amos 5. 23. I will not hear the melody of thy v.

VIOLATED.

Ezek. 22. 26. her priests have v. my law, profaned

VIOLENCE.

Gen. 6. 11. and the earth was filled with v. 12.
49. † 5. their swords are weapons of v.
Lev. 6. 2. if one lie in any thing taken away by v.
2 Sam. 22. 3. my Saviour, thou savest me from v.
1 Chron. 12. † 17. seeing there is no v. in my hands
Job 19. † 7. I cry out of v. but I am not heard
Psal. 11. 5. him that loveth v. his soul hateth
18. † 48. hast delivered me from the man of v.
25. † 19. and they hate me with hatred of v.
55. 9. I have seen v. and strife in the city
58. 2. you weigh the v. of your hands in earth
72. 14. he shall redeem their soul from v.
73. 6. therefore v. covereth them as a garment
Prov. 3. † 31. envy thou not a man of v.
4. 17. for they drink the wine of v.
10. 6. v. covereth the mouth of the wicked, 11.
13. 2. the soul of the transgressors shall eat v.
28. 17. a man that doeth v. to the blood of any
Isa. 53. 9. because he had done no v. nor was deceit
59. 6. and the act of v. is in their hands
60. 18. v. shall no more be heard in thy land
Jer. 6. 7. v. and spoil is heard in her, before me
20. 8. for since I spake, I cried v. and spoil
22. 3. and do no wrong, do no v. to the stranger
17. thine eyes, thy heart are for v to do it
23. † 10. their v. is evil, their force not right
51. 35. v. done to me and my flesh be upon Babylon
46. a rumour, v. in the land, ruler against ruler

Ezek. 7. 11. v. is risen up into a rod of wickedness
23. make a chain, for the city is full of v.
8. 17. they have filled the land with v. 28. 16.
12. 19. because of the v. of them that dwell
18. 7. if a man hath spoiled none by v. 16.
12. but if he hath spoiled and oppressed by v. 18.
22. † 26. her priests have offered v. to my law
45. 9. O princes of Israel, remove v. and spoil
Joel 3. 19. Edom shall be a wilderness for the v.
Amos 3. 10. who store up v. in their palaces
6. 3. ye that cause the seat of v. to come near
Obad. 10. for thy v. shame shall cover thee
Jonah 3. 8. let them turn every one from the v.
Mic. 2. 2. they covet fields, and take them by v.
6. 12. for the rich men thereof are full of v.
Hab. 1. 2. how long shall I cry out to thee of v.
3. v. is before me || 9. they shall come all for v.
2. 8. and for the v. of the land, of the city
17. v. of Lebanon cover thee, v. of the land
Zeph. 1. 9. fill their masters' hous. with v. and deceit
3. 4. her priests have done v. to the law
Mal. 2. 16. for one covereth v. with his garment
Mat. 11. 12. the kingdom of heaven suffereth v.
Luke 3. 14. do v. to no man, nor accuse any falsely
Acts 5. 26. the captain brought them without v.
21. 35. Paul borne of soldiers for v. of people
27. 41. the hinder part was broken for v. of waves
Heb. 11. 34. through faith quenched the v. of fire
Rev. 18. 21. with v. shall Babylon be thrown down

VIOLENT.

2 Sam. 22. 49. thou hast lifted me up on high, thou hast delivered me from the v. man, Psal. 18. 48.
Psal. 7. 16. his v. dealing come on his own pate
86. 14. the assemblies of v. men sought my soul
140. 1. preserve me from the v. man, 4.
11. evil shall hunt the v. man to overthrow him
Prov. 16. 29. a v. man enticeth his neighbour
Eccl. 5. 8. if thou seest v. perverting of judgment
Mat. 11. 12. the v. take it by force, heaven

VIOLENTLY.

Gen. 21. 25. Abimelech's servants had v. taken
Lev. 6. 4. he shall restore that which he took v.
Deut. 28. 31. thine ass shall be v. taken away
Job 20. 19. he hath v. taken away an house
24. 2. they v. take away flocks, and feed thereof
† 19. draught and heat v. take the snow waters
Isa. 22. 18. he will surely v. turn and toss thee
Lam. 2. 6. he hath v. taken away his tabernacle
Mat. 8. 32. whole herd of swine ran v. into the sea, and perished in waters, Mark 5. 13. Luke 8. 33.

VIOLET.

Esth. 1. † 6. where were green and v. hangings
8. † 15. Mordecai went out in apparel of v.

VIPER.

A serpent, about half a yard in length, but the most poisonous in its bite of all the European serpents. It is called vipera, *quasi* vivipara, *because it brings forth its young alive. Generally the* viper *is not very long, the largest being not above half an ell long, and its thickness not above an inch. It has a flat head, with a snout rising up, like that of a pig. The male has only two teeth, but the female has several; and the male is said to be commonly blacker than the female. It is said, that when the* viper *brings forth, the young ones kill the dam; but this is contradicted by experience. Though she brings forth her young alive, they are inclosed in little skins, that break open on the third day. The poison of the* viper *is very dangerous, but its flesh is good in many distempers.*

The viper *is mentioned in several places of Scripture.* Job 20. 16. The *viper's* tongue shall slay him. *The Hebrew word* Peten, *they say, rather signifies the* asp *than the* viper. *Isaiah speaks also of the* viper. *Isa.* 30. 6. *where the Hebrew has* Ephee; *which is thought to be the true name of the* viper, *John the Baptist, and afterwards our Saviour, called the Scribes and Pharisees a* generation of *vipers, a wicked brood of wicked parents, who by their poisonous doctrines ruined the souls of men,* Mat. 3. 7. | 12. 34.

Job 20. 16. of asps, the v. tongue shall slay him
Isa. 30. 6. from whence come the v. and serpent
41. † 24. your work is worse than of a v.
59. 5. that which is crushed breaks out into a v.
Acts 28. 3. there came v. and fasten. on Paul's hand

VIPERS.

Mat. 3. 7. O generation of v. 12. 34. | 23. 33. Luke [3. 7.

VIRGIN,

In Greek, παρθενος*; in Hebrew,* Almah. *These words properly signify an unmarried young woman, that has preserved the purity of her body. In this sense we meet with it in the famous passage of Isaiah,* Behold, a *virgin* shall conceive and bear a son, *Isa.* 7. 14. *meaning, she would be a* virgin *as well after as before her bringing forth. But sometimes* virgin *is made use of to express a young woman, whether she has kept her virginity or no.* Joel 1. 8. Lament like a *virgin* girded with sackcloth for the husband of her youth. *The more precisely to express the state of virginity, the Scripture often adds to the words* maid *or* virgin, *these or such like words,* neither had any man known her, *Gen.* 24. 16. *Num.* 31. 17.

The Hebrew word Almah, *signifies* a person concealed; *for young unmarried women lived in retired apartments, where the men did not use to go; and when young women were obliged to go out, they were always veiled, and never appeared uncovered but before their nearest relations. When Amnon, the son of David, had conceived a violent passion for his sister Tamar, he could not get private converse with her because she was a* virgin, *and kept up very close.* 2 Sam. 13. 2. For she was a *virgin*, and Amnon thought it hard for him to do any thing to her. *And in the book of Maccabees, it is said that when Heliodorus came to Jerusalem, to take away the treasures of the temple, the most recluse* virgins *came out of their retirements; some appeared in the streets, some at their windows, and others upon the walls,* 2 Macc. 3. 19. *And it is well known that young women in the East do not appear in public, but are shut up in their houses and in their mothers' apartments.*

Virgin *is often used in Scripture for a people, a city, a nation. The* virgin, *the daughter of Babylon, the* virgin, *the daughter of Zion, the* virgin, *the daughter of Israel, &c. These phrases signify the province, the land, the people of Babylon, Zion, Israel, &c. The professors of religion in general are called* virgins, *such as are not defiled with any scandalous sin, nor erroneous opinion.* Mat. 25. 1. The kingdom of heaven shall be likened unto ten *virgins*, which took their lamps. *They are all called* virgins, *because they made profession of holiness; yet only five deserved the name, they having not only a profession, but a true faith and love to feed their profession: the others made a profession, but had not the truth of grace in the heart. The character of* virgins *is principally given to those that adhere stedfastly to Christ, and abhor every thing that has any shew of violating their fidelity to him.* Rev. 14. 4. These are they which are not defiled with women, *that are not corrupted with the erroneous doctrine and idolatrous worship of the anti-christian church,* for they are *virgins: They keep close to Christ in all his ordinances, and are led by his word and Spirit. The apostle says,* I have espoused you to one husband, that I may present you as a chaste *virgin* to Christ, 2 *Cor.* 11. 2.

Gen. 24. 16. Rebekah was fair to look upon, a v.
43. when the v. cometh forth to draw water
Lev. 21. 3. for his sister, a v. he may be defiled
14. he shall take a v. of his own people to wife
Deut. 22. 19. he brought an evil name upon a v.
23. a v. betrothed || 28. a v. not betrothed
32. 25. destroy both the young man and the v.
2 Sam. 13. 2. Amnon fell sick for Tamar, she was a v.
2 Kings 19. 21. the v. the daughter of Zion hath despised thee and laughed thee to scorn, Isa. 37. 22.
Isa. 7. 14. behold a v. shall conceive, Mat. 1. 23.
23. 12. shalt no more rejoice, O thou oppressed v.
47. 1. come down and sit in the dust, O v. of Bab.
62. 5. for as a young man marrieth a v. so thy sons
Jer. 14. 17. the v. daughter of my people is broken
18. 13. v. of Israel hath done a horrible thing
31. 4. and thou shalt be built, O v. of Israel
13. then shall the v. rejoice in the dance
21. turn again, O v. of Israel, to these thy cities
46. 11. take balm, O v. the daughter of Egypt
Lam. 1. 15. Lord hath trodden v. daughter of Judah
2. 13. that I may comfort thee, O v. daughter of Zion
Joel 1. 8. lament like a v. girded with sackcloth
Amos 5. 2. the v. of Israel is fallen, no more rise
Luke 1. 27. the angel was sent from God to a v.
1 Cor. 7. 28. if a v. marry, she hath not sinned
34. there is difference between a wife and a v.
37. decreed that he will keep his v. doeth well
2 Cor. 11. 2. that I may present you as a chaste v.

VIRGINS.

Exod. 22. 17. shall pay according to the dowry of v.
2 Sam. 13. 18. were kings' daughters v. apparelled
Esth. 2. 17. Esther found favour above all the v.
Psal. 45. 14. the v. her companions that follow her
Cant. 1. 3. as ointment, therefore do the v. love thee
6. 8. threescore queens and v. without number
Isa. 23. 4. I travail not, nor do I bring up v.
Lam. 1. 4. her priests sigh, her v. are afflicted
18. my v. and young men are gone into captivity
2. 10. the v. of Jerusalem hang down their heads
21. v. and young men are fallen by the sword
Amos 8. 13. in that day shall the fair v. faint
Mat. 25. 1. kingdom of heaven is likened to ten v.
Acts 21. 9. Philip had four daughters, v. prophesied
1 Cor. 7. 25. concerning v. I have no commandment
Rev. 14. 4. which are not defiled, for they are v.

Young VIRGINS.

Judg. 21. 12. at Jabesh-gilead were four hundred young v.
1 Kings 1. 2. let there be sought for king a young v.
Esth. 2. 2. let there be fair young v. sought for king
3. they may gather together all the fair young v.

VIRGINITY.

Lev. 21. 13. he shall take a wife in her v.
Deut 22. 15. bring the tokens of her v. 17, 20.
Judg. 11. 37. that I may bewail my v. 38.
Ezek. 23. 3. they bruised the teats of their v. 8.
Luke 2. 36. Anna lived seven years from her v.

VIRTUE,

In Greek, αρετη, *or* δυναμις. *It is in opposition to vice, and is taken,* (1) *For moral* virtue, *probity of manners among men, as the generical word that contains all moral and christian* virtues *under it; in this sense it is used,* Phil. 4. 8. If there be any *virtue*, think on these things. *If there be any other commendable practice amongst any, diligently consider and practise it.* (2) *It is taken for the power, the wisdom, the goodness, and truth of God, which he manifests in bringing the elect out of a state of ignorance and unbelief into his marvellous light,* 1 Pet. 2. 9. That ye should shew forth the praises [*or* virtues] of him who hath called you out of darkness into his marvellous light. *Also in* Mark 5. 30. virtue *is put for power,* Jesus knowing that *virtue* had gone out of him. (3) *It is taken for christian courage and resolution in all dangers and troubles that persons may meet with.* 2 Pet. 1. 5. Add to your faith, *virtue.* (4) *It is put for miracles.* Mat. 7. 22. Have we not done many wonderful works in thy name. *In the original it is* δυναμεις πολλας, many *virtues.*

Mark 5. 30. v. had gone out of him, Luke 6. 19. | 8. 46.
Phil. 4. 8. if there be any v. think on these things
2 Pet. 1. 3. of him that hath called us to glory and v.
5. add to your faith v. and to v. knowledge

VIRTUES.

1 Pet. 2. † 9. that ye should shew forth the v. of him

VIRTUOUS.

Ruth 3. 11. all know that thou art a v. woman
Prov. 12. 4. a v. woman is a crown to her husband
31. 10. who can find v. woman? price above rubies

VIRTUOUSLY.

Prov. 31. 29. many daughters have done v. but thou

VISAGE.

Isa. 52. 14. his v. was marred more than any man
Lam. 4. 8. their v. is blacker than a coal
Dan. 3. 19. and the form of his v. was changed

VISIBLE.

Col. 1. 16. by him were all things created, v. and inv.

VISION.

See the Signification *on* PROPHET, ORACLE, THUMMIM, VISIT.

Num. 24. 4. which saw the v. of the Almighty, 16.
1 Sam. 3. 1. word was precious, there was no open v.
15. and Samuel feared to shew Eli the v.
2 Sam. 7. 17. according to all these words and this v. so did Nathan speak to David, 1 Chr. 17. 15.
2 Chron. 32. 32. they are written in the v. of Isaiah
Job 20. 8. be chased away as a v. of the night
Psal. 89. 19. thou spakest in v. to thy Holy One
Prov. 29. 18. where there is no v. the people perish
Isa. 1. 1. the v. of Isaiah || Obad. 1. v. of Obadiah
21. 2. a grievous v. is declared unto me
22. 1. the burden of the value of v. 5.
28. 7. they err in v. they stumble in judgment
29. 7. they shall be as a dream of a night v.
11. the v. is become as a book that is sealed
Jer. 14. 14. they prophesy unto you a false v.
23. 16. they speak a v. of their own heart
Lam. 2. 9. her prophets find no v. from the Lord
Ezek. 7. 13. v. is touching the whole multitude
26. then shall they seek a v. of the prophet
8. 4. according to the v. that I saw, 11. 24. | 43. 3.
12. 22. days are prolonged and every v. faileth
23. say to them, the effect of every v. is at hand
24. there shall be no more any vain v. nor divinat
27. the v. that he seeth is for many days to come
13. 7. have ye not seen a vain v. and spoken?
Dan. 2. 19. was revealed to Daniel in a night v.
7. 2. I saw in my v. by night, the four winds strove
8. 1. a v. appeared unto me, even unto me Daniel
13. how long shall be the v. concerning sacrifice?
16. Gabriel, make this man to understand the v.
17. for at the time of the end shall be the v.
26. shut up the v. || 27. I was astonished at the v.
9. 21. whom I had seen in the v. at the beginning
23. consider the v. || 24. and to seal up the v.
10. 1. and he had understanding of the v.
7. I alone saw the v. men with me, saw not v. 8.
14. for yet the v. is for many days
16. by the v. my sorrows are turned upon me
11. 14. shall exalt themselves to establish the v.
Mic. 3. 6. night to you that ye shall not have a v.
Nah. 1. 1. the book of the v. of Nahum
Hab. 2. 2. write the v. and make it plain on tables
3. for the v. is yet for an appointed time, at end
Zech. 13. 4. prophets be ashamed every one of his v.
Mat. 17. 9. charged, saying, tell the v. to no man
Luke 1. 22. they perceived that he had seen a v.
24. 23. saying, that they had seen a v. of angels
Acts 10. 17. while Peter doubted of the v. 19.
11. 5. in a trance I saw a v. a vessel descend
12. 9. wist not it was true, but thought he saw a v.
16. 9. a v. appeared to Paul in the night, 18. 9.
26. 19. I was not disobedient to the heavenly v.
Rev. 9. 17. and thus I saw the horses in the v.

In a VISION.

Gen. 15. 1. word of the Lord came to Abram in a v.
Num. 12. 6. I will make myself known to him in a v.
Ezek. 11. 24. brought me in a v. by the Spirit of G.
Dan. 8. 2. I saw in a v. and I was by the river Ulai
Acts 9. 10. to Ananias said the Lord in a v.
12. Saul hath seen in a v. a man named Ananias
10. 3. Cornelius saw in a v. an angel of God

VISIONS.

Gen. 46. 2. God spake to Israel in v. of the night
2 Chron. 9. 29. written in the v. of Iddo the seer
26. 5. Zechariah had understanding in v. of God
Job 4. 13. in thoughts from the v. of the night
7. 14. then thou terrifiest me through v.
Ezek. 1. 1. heavens opened, I saw the v. of God
8. 3. he brought me in the v. of God to Jerusalem
13. 16. prophets which see v. of peace for her
40. 2. in v. he brought me to the land of Israel
Dan. 1. 17. Daniel had understanding in all v.
2. 28. the v. of thy head on thy bed, are these
4. 5. and the v. of my head troubled me
7. 1. Daniel had v. of his head upon his bed
7. I saw in the night v. and behold, 13.
15. and the v. of my head troubled me
Hos. 12. 10. I have multiplied v. I used similitudes
Joel 2. 28. your young men shall see v. Acts 2. 17.
2 Cor. 12. 1. I will come to v. and revelations

VISIT.

God visits *men both in mercy and in wrath. He* visited *Sarah in his mercy, and gave her a son,* Gen. 21. 1. *He* visited *the Israelites in Egypt, and sent Moses to deliver them,* Exod. 3. 16. *He* visited *Hannah the mother of Samuel, and gave her sons and daughters,* 1 Sam. 2. 21. *And he* visited *and redeemed his people by the coming of the* Messiah, *Luke* 1. 68. *God* visits *also in his wrath and in his vengeance. He* visits the iniquity of the fathers upon the children, to the third and fourth generations, *Exod.* 20. 5. visiting, *that is, remembering, inquiring into, or punishing. He threatens to* visit *the iniquity of the worshippers of the golden calf in the day of his vengeance,* Exod. 32. 34. *Nothing is more frequent in the language of the prophets, than the verb* to visit, *taken in the sense of punishing, chastising, and revenging.* To visit *is also taken for paying* visits *of civility, friendship, or duty. Moses went* to visit *his brethren,* Acts 7. 23. *And Paul and Barnabas went* to visit *the churches they had planted,* Acts 15. 36.

Vision *is a revelation from God, which among the Jews were of four sorts:* [1] *By the Holy Spirit immediately,* Acts 9. 10. [2] *By Urim and Thummim.* [3] *By a voice from heaven spoken by an angel,* Acts 10. 3. [4] *By prophecy, which were twofold, either in dreams, or when awake, in a trance, or ecstasy,* Acts 10. 3, 17. | 12. 9. | 16. 9.

Gen. 50. 24. God will surely v. you, 25. *Exod.* 13. 19.
Exod. 32. 34. when I v. I will v. their sin on them
Lev. 18. 25. I do v. the iniquity thereof upon it
Job 5. 24. thou shalt v. thy habitation and not sin
7. 18. that thou shouldest v. him every morning
Psal. 59. 5. O Lord, awake to v. all the heathen
80. 14. look down from heaven and v. this vine
89. 32. then will I v. their transgression with rods
106. 4. remember me, O v. me with thy salvation
Isa. 10. † 12. I will v. upon the stout heart of king
23. 17. the Lord will v. Tyre, she shall turn
24. † 21. Lord shall v. upon the host of high ones
Jer. 3. 16. neither shall they v. the ark of the Lord
5. 9. shall I not v. for these things? 29. | 9. 9.
6. 15. at time I v. them, they shall be cast down
9. † 25. I will v. upon all that are circumcised
11. † 22. I will v. upon the men of Anathoth
13. † 21. wilt thou say when he shall v. on thee
14. 10. will remember iniquity and v. their sins
15. 15. O Lord, thou knowest, remember and v.
23. 2. I will v. on you the evil of your doings
† 34. I will v. upon that man and his house
25. † 12. that I will v. upon the king of Babylon
27. 22. and there shall they be till I v. them
29. 10. I will v. you and perform my good word
32. 5. and there shall he be till I v. him
49. 8. the time I will v. Esau || 50. 31. v. Babylon
Lam. 4. 22. he will v. thine iniquity, O Edom
Hos. 2. 13. I will v. on her the days of Baalim
8. 13. remember, now will he v. their sins, 9. 9.
Amos 3. 14. I will also v. the altars of Beth-el
Zeph. 2. 7. Lord shall v. and turn their captivity
Zech. 11. 16. who shall not v. those that be cut off
Acts 7. 23. it came into his heart to v. his brethren
15. 14. hath declared how God did v. the Gentiles
36. let us go again and v. our brethren in every
Jam. 1. 27. is this, to v. the fatherless and widows

VISITATION.

Num. 16. 29. if they be visited after the v. of all men
Job 10. 12. thy v. hath preserved my spirit
Isa. 10. 3. what will ye do in the day of v.?
Jer. 8. 12. in time of their v. shall be cast down
10. 15. in the time of v. they shall perish, 51. 18.
11. 23. I will bring evil on the men of Anathoth, even in the year of their v. 23. 12. | 48. 44.
46. 21. the time of their v. was come, 50. 27.
50. † 21. go up against the inhabitants of v.
Hos. 9. 7. the days of v. are come, Israel shall know
Mic. 7. 4. thy v. cometh, now shall be perplexity
Luke 19. 44. thou knewest not the time of thy v.
1 *Pet.* 2. 12. they may glorify God in the day of v.

VISITED.

Gen. 21. 1. and the Lord v. Sarah as he had said
Exod. 3. 16. saying, I have surely v. you
4. 31. they heard that the Lord had v. Israel
Num. 16. 29. if they be v. after visitation of all men
Judg. 15. 1. that Samson v. his wife with a kid
Ruth 1. 6. she heard how the Lord had v. his people
1 *Sam.* 2. 21. the Lord v. Hannah, she conceived
Job 35. 15. now it is not so, he hath v. in his anger
Psal. 17. 3. thou hast v. me, thou hast tried me
Prov. 19. 23. he shall not be v. with evil
Isa. 24. 22. after many days shall they be v.
26. 14. therefore hast thou v. and destroyed them
16. Lord, in trouble have they v. thee
29. 6. thou shalt be v. of the Lord with thunder
Jer. 6. 6. Jerusalem is the city to be v. oppression
23. 2. ye scattered my flock and have not v. them
Ezek. 38. 8. after many days thou shalt be v.
Zech. 10. 3. the Lord of hosts hath v. his flock
Mat. 25. 36. I was sick, ye v. me || 43. ye v. me not
Luke 1. 68. he hath v. and redeemed his people
78. the day-spring from on high hath v. us
7. 16. saying, that God hath v. his people

VISITEST.

Psal. 8. 4. son of man that thou v. him, *Heb.* 2. 6.
65. 9. thou v. the earth and waterest it, enrichest

VISITETH.

Job 31. 14. when he v. what shall I answer him?

VISITING.

Exod. 20. 5. v. the iniquity of the fathers upon the children, 34. 7. *Num.* 14. 18. *Deut.* 5. 9.

VOCATION.

Eph. 4. 1. I beseech that ye walk worthy of the v.

VOICE.

By this word is not only understood the voice of a man or beast, but all other sorts of sounds, noises, or cries. And even thunder has often the name of the voice of God given to it. Pharaoh begged of Moses to entreat the Lord that there might be no more mighty thunderings, in Hebrew, voices of God, Exod. 9. 28. Elihu says, Hear attentively the noise of his voice. And in Psal. 29. the voice of the Lord is frequently put for thunder. To hear or to hearken to any one's voice, is to obey him. Exod. 15. 26. If thou wilt diligently hearken to the voice of the Lord thy God, I will put none of these diseases upon thee, which I have brought upon the Egyptians. Our Saviour says, that his sheep hear his voice, and follow him; that is, they obey him, they depend upon his ministry, and imitate his example, John 10. 27. The spouse says, Cant. 2. 8. The voice of my beloved; I hear the voice of Christ, in the ministry of the word and motions of his Spirit.

To change the voice, Gal. 4. 20. I desire to change my voice. The apostle was forced to write somewhat roughly and sharply, as in chap. 3. ver. 1. Now he wishes to be present with the Galatians, and to order matters so, that if possible, he might have occasion to rejoice with them and comfort them, instead of complaining of them and reproving them.

The daughter of the voice, called in Hebrew, Bath-kol, was, as the Jewish writers say, a preternatural way in which God discovered his will to them, after the word of prophecy had ceased in Israel. The generality of their traditions, and the customs of their nation, are founded on this Bath-kol. They pretend that God revealed them to their elders, not by any articulate prophecy, but by some secret inspiration, or by some tradition which they call the daughter of the voice. They pretend, that the daughter of the voice, is a voice from heaven, heard in an articulate manner, much after the same way as the voice which called young Samuel, when God revealed to him what was to befall the high priest Eli and his family. God then called him three times with an articulate voice; and Samuel replied in the same manner as he would have answered a man, not knowing as yet how to distinguish the voice of God, 1 Sam. 3. 4, 5, &c. Or, the daughter of the voice, resembles that which was uttered from the sanctuary, when the Lord spake to Moses, or answered the high priest, who consulted him by the Urim and Thummim. These two sorts of voices were, as one may say, the mother of that other voice which succeeded them, and was called Bath-kol, daughter-voice, or daughter of the voice, because it was, as it were, the daughter of this first voice.

The Bath-kol, as Dr. Prideaux shews, was a fantastical way of divination, invented by the Jews, like the Sortes Virgilianæ among the heathens. For as with them the words first dipt at in the book of that poet, was the oracle whereby they prognosticated those future events which they desired to be informed of; so with the Jews, when they appealed to Bath-kol, the next words which they should hear from any one's mouth were the same oracle to them. It is said in the Talmud, that two Rabbins, desirous of visiting their friend Rabbi Samuel, Doctor of Babylon, said one to another, let us follow the direction of Bath-kol; as they were passing by a school, they heard a young lad reading this passage of the first book of Samuel, chap. 25. ver. 1. And Samuel died. From thence they concluded that Samuel was dead. The event justified what they had prognosticated, for they found that at that time Rabbi Samuel of Babylon had departed this life. These casual and odd oracles were esteemed as voices of God's appointment.

Gen. 4. 10. the v. of thy brother's blood crieth
27. 22. the v. is Jacob's v. but the hands are Esau's
29. 11. and Jacob lifted up his v. and wept
39. 15. when he heard that I lifted up my v.
Exod. 4. 8. they will believe the v. of the latter sign
19. 19. Moses spake, God answered him by a v.
23. 21. beware of him, obey his v. provoke not
24. 3. and all the people answered with one v.
32. 18. it is not the v. of them that shout
Lev. 5. 1. if a soul hear the v. of swearing
Num. 14. 1. the congregation lifted up their v.
Deut. 4. 30. if thou shalt be obedient to his v.
8. 20. because ye would not be obedient to his v.
Josh. 6. 10. nor make any noise with your v.
Judg. 18. 3. they knew the v. of the Levite
1 *Sam.* 24. 16. is this thy v. my son David? 26. 17.
2 *Sam.* 22. 14. and the Most High uttered his v.
1 *Kings* 18. 26. was no v. nor any that answered, 29.
† 27. at noon Elijah said, cry with a great v.
19. 12. and after the fire a still small v.
2 *Kings* 4. 31. there was neither v. nor hearing
7. 10. there was no v. of man, but horses tied
19. 22. against whom hast thou exalted thy v. and lifted up thine eyes on high? *Isa.* 37. 23.
1 *Chron.* 15. 16. by lifting up the v. with joy
2 *Chron.* 24. † 9. made a v. thro' Judah and Jerus.
Ezra 1. † 1. Cyrus caused a v. to pass thro' kingdom
Job 2. 12. Job's friends lifted up their v. and wept
3. 7. to be solitary, let no joyful v. come there
29. † 10. the v. of the nobles was hid
30. 31. my organ into the v. of them that weep
37. 4. a v. roareth, he thundereth with the v.
5. God thundereth marvellously with his v.
40. 9. or canst thou thunder with a v. like him?
Psal. 18. 13. and the Highest gave his v.
26. 7. I may publish with the v. of thanksgiving
31. 22. thou heardest the v. of my supplications
42. 4. I went to house of God with the v. of joy
44. 16. for the v. of him that reproacheth
46. 6. he uttered his v. the earth melted
47. 1. shout unto God with the v. of triumph
66. 19. he hath attended to the v. of my prayer
68. 33. he sendeth out his v. and that a mighty v.
74. 23. forget not the v. of thine enemies
77. 1. I cried unto the Lord with my v. 142. 1.
18. the v. of thy thunder was in heaven
86. 6. attend to the v. of my supplications
93. 3. O Lord, the floods have lifted up their v.
98. 5. sing unto the Lord with the v. of a psalm
102. 5. by reason of the v. of my groaning
103. 20. hearkening to the v. of his word
104. 7. at v. of thy thunder they hasted away
118. 15. v. of rejoicing in tabernacles of righteous
141. 1. give ear to my v. when I cry unto thee
Prov. 1. 20. she uttereth her v. in the streets
2. 3. if thou liftest up thy v. for understanding
5. 13. I have not obeyed the v. of my teachers
8. 1. doth not understanding put forth her v.
4. to you, O men, I call, my v. is to sons of men
26. † 25. when he maketh his v. gracious
Eccl. 5. 3. a fool's v. is known by multitude of words
6. wherefore should God be angry at thy v.?
10. 20. for a bird of the air shall carry the v.
12. 4. he shall rise up at the v. of the bird
Cant. 2. 8. the v. of my beloved, behold, he cometh
12. the v. of the turtle is heard in our land
5. 2. it is the v. of my beloved that knocketh
Isa. 6. 4. posts moved at the v. of him that cried
13. 2. exalt the v. unto them, shake the hand
29. 4. thy v. be as one that hath a familiar spirit
30. 19. be gracious to thee at the v. of thy cry
31. 4. the lion will not be afraid of their v.
40. 3. the v. of him that crieth in the wilderness, *Mat.* 3. 3. *Mark* 1. 3. *Luke* 3. 4.
6. v. said, cry || 48. 20. with the v. of singing
50. 10. that obeyeth the v. of his servant
51. 3. joy, thanksgiving, and the v. of melody
52. 8. with the v. together shall they sing
65. 19. I will joy in my people, the v. of weeping shall be no more heard in her, nor v. of crying
66. 6. a v. of noise, a v. from temple, a v. of Lord
Jer. 2. † 15. the young lions gave out their v.
4. 15. a v. declareth from Dan and publisheth
16. give out their v. against the cities of Judah
6. 23. their v. roareth like the sea, 50. 42.
7. 34. the v. of mirth, v. of gladness, v. of the bridegroom, v. of bride, 16. 9. | 25. 10. | 33. 11.
8. 19. v. of the cry of the daughter of my people
10. 13. when he uttereth his v. there is a multitude of waters in the heavens, 51. 16.
25. 36. a v. of the cry of shepherds and an howling
30. 19. and the v. of them that make merry
31. 15. a v. was heard in Ramah, lamentation
16. saith the Lord, refrain thy v. from weeping
46. 22. the v. thereof shall go like a serpent
48. 3. a v. of crying shall be from Horonaim
50. 28. the v. of them that flee and escape
51. 55. Lord hath destroyed out of her the great v.
Ezek. 1. 24. I heard as the v. of the Almighty
10. 5. as the v. of Almighty God when he speaketh
23. 42. and a v. of a multitude being at ease
33. 32. a lovely song of one that hath a pleasant v.
43. 2. and his v. was like the noise of many waters, and the earth shined with his glory, *Rev.* 1. 15.
Dan. 4. 31. there fell a v. from heaven, saying
6. 20. he cried with a lamentable v. to Daniel
10. 6. v. of his words like the v. of a multitude
Joel 2. 11. Lord shall utter his v. before his army
3. 16. shall utter his v. from Jerusalem, *Amos* 1. 2.
Jonah 2. 9. I will sacrifice with v. of thanksgiving
Nah. 2. 7. shall lead her as with the v. of doves
Mat. 3. 17. a v. from heaven, this is my beloved Son in whom I am well pleased, *Mark* 1. 11. *Luke* 3. 22.
17. 5. a v. out of the cloud, this is my beloved Son in whom I am well pleased, *Mark* 9. 7. *Luke* 9. 35. 36.
Luke 1. 44. as soon as v. of thy salutation sounded
John 1. 23. the v. of one crying in the wilderness
3. 29. rejoiceth because of the bridegroom's v.
10. 4. the sheep follow him, for they know his v.
5. for they know not the v. of strangers
12. 28. then came a v. saying, I have glorified it
30. this v. came not because of me, but for you
18. 37. he that is of the truth heareth my v.
Acts 9. 7. hearing a v. but seeing no man
10. 13. came a v. saying, rise, Peter, kill and eat
15. and the v. spake unto him again, 11. 9.
12. 14. when she knew Peter's v. she opened not
22. it is the v. of a god, and not of a man
19. 34. all with one v. cried, Great is Diana
24. 21. except it be for this one v. that I cried
26. 10. put to death, I gave my v. against them
1 *Cor.* 14. 11. if I know not the meaning of the v.
19. that by my v. I might teach others also
Gal. 4. 20. I desire now to change my v.
1 *Thess.* 4. 16. Lord descend with v. of the archangel
Heb. 12. 26. whose v. then shook the earth
2 *Pet.* 1. 17. there came a v. from the excellent glory
2. 16. the dumb ass speaking with man's v.
Rev. 1. 12. I turned to see the v. that spake
16. 17. there came a great v. saying, it is done

VOICE joined with hear.

Gen. 4. 23. hear my v. ye wives of Lamech
Deut. 4. 33. did ever people hear v. of God and live
36. out of heaven he made thee to hear his v.
5. 25. if we hear the v. of God, we shall die
33. 7. he said, hear, Lord, the v. of Judah
2 *Sam.* 19. 35. can I hear the v. of singing-men?
22. 7. and he did hear my v. out of his temple
Job 3. 18. they hear not the v. of the oppressor
37. 2. hear attentively the noise of his v.
Psal. 5. 3. my v. shalt thou hear in the morning
27. 7. hear, O Lord, when I cry with my v. 28. 2. | 64. 1. | 119. 149. | 130. 2. | 140. 6.
55. 3. hear me, because of the v. of the enemy
17. I will cry aloud and he shall hear my v.
95. 7. to-day if ye will hear his v. harden not your hearts as in the wilderness, *Heb.* 3. 7, 15. | 4. 7.
Cant. 2. 14. let me hear thy v. for sweet is thy v.
Isa. 32. 9. hear my v. ye careless daughters
Jer. 9. 10. nor can men hear the v. of the cattle
Mat. 12. 19. neither shall any man hear his v.
John 5. 25. the dead hear v. of Son of God, 28.
10. 3. porter opens, and sheep hear his v. 16. 27.
Acts 22. 14. and shouldest hear the v. of his mouth
Rev. 3. 20. if any man hear my v. and open door

See HEARD.

VOICE with hearken, hearkened.

Gen. 3. 17. because hast hearkened to v. of thy wife
16. 2. and Abram hearkened to the v. of Sarai
21. 12. in all Sarah hath said hearken to her v.
Exod. 3. 18. and they shall hearken to thy v.
4. 1. behold, they will not hearken unto my v.
8. nor hearken to the v. of the first sign
9. if thy will not hearken to thy v. shalt take
15. 26. if diligently hearken to the v. of the Lord
18. 19. hearken to my v. I will give thee counsel
24. and Moses hearkened to the v. of Jethro
Num. 14. 22. they have tempted me ten times and not hearkened to my v. *Deut.* 9. 23. | 28. 45.
21. 3. the Lord hearkened to the v. of Israel
Deut. 1. 45. the Lord would not hearken to your v.
13. 18. when thou shalt hearken to the v. of Lord
15. 5. only if thou carefully hearken to the v. of the Lord thy God, 26. 17. | 28. 1, 2. | 30. 10.
28. 15. if thou wilt not hearken to the v. of Lord
Josh. 10. 14. the Lord hearkened to the v. of a man
Judg. 2. 20. this people have not hearkened to my v.
13. 9. and God hearkened to the v. of Manoah
20. 13. Benjamin would not hearken to v. of Israel
1 *Sam.* 2. 25. they hearkened not to v. of their father
8. 7. hearken to the v. of the people, 9. 22.
12. 1. I have hearkened to your v. in all ye said
19. 6. Saul hearkened to the v. of Jonathan
25. 35. go in peace, see, I have hearkened to thy v.
28. 22. hearken thou to the v. of thy handmaid
2 *Sam.* 12. 18. he would not hearken to our v.
13. 14. howbeit, he would not hearken to her v.
1 *Kings* 20. 25. Ben-hadad hearkened to their v.
2 *Kings* 10. 6. if ye will hearken to my v.
Job 9. 16. not believe he had hearkened to my v.
34. 16. hearken to the v. of my words
Psal. 5. 2. hearken to the v. of my cry, my King
58. 5. will not hearken to the v. of charmers
81. 11. my people would not hearken to my v.

Cant. 8. 13. the companions *hearken* to thy *v.*
Jer. 18. 19. *hearken* to *v.* of them that contend
See LIFT, LORD, LOUD, OBEY, OBEYED.

VOICES.

Exod. 9. † 28. that there be no more *v.* of God
Luke 17. 13. the ten lepers lifted up their *v.*
23. 23. they were instant with loud *v.* that he might be crucified, the *v.* of them and priests prevailed
Acts 13. 27. because knew not the *v.* of the prophets
22. 22. they lift up their *v.* and said, away with
1 *Cor.* 14. 10. there are so many *v.* in the world
Rev. 4. 5. out of the throne proceeded *v.* 16. 18.
8. 5. angel cast censer into earth and there were *v.*
13. woe, by reason of the other *v.* of the trumpet
10. 3. the seven thunders uttered their *v.* 4.
11. 15. and there were great *v.* in heaven
19. the temple was opened, and there were *v.*

VOID.

Gen. 1. 2. the earth was without form and *v.*
Num. 30. 12. but if her husband made them *v.* 15.
Deut. 32. 28. they are a people *v.* of counsel
1 *Kings* 22. 10. kings sat in a *v.* place, 2 *Chr.* 18. 9.
Neh. 5. † 13. even thus be ye shaken out and *v.*
Job 15. † 4. makest *v.* fear and restrainest prayer
Psal. 89. 39. made *v.* the covenant of thy servant
107. † 40. causeth them to wander in a *v.* place
119. 126. for they have made *v.* thy law
Prov. 11. 12. *v.* of wisdom, despiseth his neighbour
15. † 21. folly is joy to him that is *v.* of heart
Isa. 55. 11. my word shall not return to me *v.*
Jer. 4. 23. the earth was without form and *v.*
19. 7. I will make *v.* the counsel of Judah
Nah. 2. 10. Nineveh is empty, *v.* and waste
Acts 24. 16. to have a conscience *v.* of offence
Rom. 1. † 28. gave them over to a mind *v.* of judgm.
3. 31. do we then make *v.* the law through faith?
4. 14. if they of the law be heirs, faith is made *v.*
1 *Cor.* 9. 15. lest any should make my glorying *v.*
Tit. 1. † 16. to every good work *v.* of judgment
See UNDERSTANDING.

VOLUME.

Psal. 40. 7. then said I, lo I come, in the *v.* of the book it is written of me, *Heb.* 10. 7.

VOLUNTARY.

Lev. 1. 3. he shall offer it of his own *v.* will
7. 16. a *v.* offering shall be eaten the same day,
Ezek. 46. 12. princes shall prepare a *v.* burnt-offering
Col. 2. 18. in a *v.* humility and worshipping angels

VOLUNTARILY.

Ezek. 46. 12. prepare offerings *v.* to the Lord

VOMIT.

Job 20. 15. he swallowed riches and shall *v.* them
Prov. 23. 8. the morsel eaten thou shalt *v.* up
25. 16. lest thou be filled with honey and *v.* it

VOMIT.

Prov. 26. 11. as the dog returneth to his *v.* so a fool
Isa. 19. 14. as a drunken man staggereth in his *v.*
28. 8. for all tables are full of *v.* and filthiness
Jer. 48. 26. Moab also shall wallow in his *v.*
2 *Pet.* 2. 22. the dog is turned to his own *v.* again

VOMITED.

Jonah 2. 10. the fish *v.* out Jonah on dry land

VOMITETH.

Lev. 18. 25. the land *v.* out her inhabitants

VOW

Is a promise made to God of doing some good thing hereafter. The use of vows is observable in many places of Scripture. When Jacob went into Mesopotamia he vowed to God the tenth of his estate, and promised to offer it at Beth-el to the honour and service of God, Gen. 28. 20, 22. *There are several laws for the regulation and due execution of* vows. *A man might devote himself, or his children, to the Lord. Samuel was vowed and consecrated to the service of the Lord, and was offered to him, to serve in the tabernacle,* 1 Sam. 1. 22, 28. *If a man or woman vowed themselves or their children to the Lord, they were obliged to adhere strictly to his service, according to the conditions of the* vow; *if not, they were to be redeemed. The price for redeeming persons of such and such an age is particularly limited,* Lev. 27. 2, 3, &c. *Only if the person was poor, and could not procure the sum limited, the priest imposed a ransom upon him according to his abilities.*

If any one had vowed an animal that was clean, he had not the liberty of redeeming it, or of exchanging it, but was obliged to sacrifice it to the Lord, or give it to the priest according to the manner of his vow. If it was an unclean animal, and such as was not allowed to be sacrificed, the priest made a valuation of it; and if the proprietor would redeem it, he added a fifth part to the value, by way of forfeit. They did the same in proportion, when the thing vowed was a house or a field. See Lev. 27. 9, 10, &c. *They could not devote the firstlings of beasts, because of their own nature they belonged to the Lord,* Lev. 27. 26. *Whatsoever was solemnly devoted to the Lord could not be redeemed, of whatever nature or quality it was,* Lev. 27. 28. *Concerning the* vows *of the* Nazarites, *See* NAZARITE.

The vows *and promises of children were void, except they were ratified, either by the express or tacit consent of their parents. And it was the same with the* vows *of married women; they were of no validity, except they were confirmed by the express or tacit consent of their husbands,* Num. 30. 1, 2, 3, &c.

Under the New Testament, a vow *is either general to all Christians, as that which is made at our baptism; or particular and special, as when we bind ourselves to a greater endeavour, to leave some sin, or perform some duty. A* vow, *as one observes, must be made deliberately and devoutly, for a sudden passion makes not a* vow; *and we ought to* vow *nothing but what is in our power to perform. Some* vows *are of evil things to an evil end; such* vows *ought neither to be made nor kept; of this kind was the* vow *or curse which the Jews bound themselves under, who conspired to murder* Paul, Acts 23. 12. *Some* vows *are of good things in an evil manner; such may be made, and ought to be kept in respect of the matter, but not in respect of the end; thus, we may vow to give alms, but not to be seen of men. Other* vows *are of good things in a good manner: and such may be made, and ought to be performed. St. Paul made a* vow *either of Nazariteship, or by way of gratitude for some particular mercy,* Acts 18. 18. *But commentators are not agreed whether this be spoken of Paul, or of Aquila, who is mentioned in the same verse.*

The performance of solemn vows *is strictly enjoined us in Scripture.* Eccl. 5. 4. When thou vowest a *vow* unto God, defer not to pay it: *Perform it while the sense of thy obligation is fresh and strong upon thee, lest either thou seem to repent of thy promises, or lest delays end in denials and resolutions of non-performance. Solomon adds,* For the Lord hath no pleasure in fools; *that is, in hypocritical and perfidious persons, who, when they are in distress, make liberal* vows, *and when the danger is past, neglect and break them, and so discover the highest folly, in thinking to mock and deceive the All-seeing and Almighty God. Moses speaks almost in the same words.* Deut. 23. 21. When thou shalt *vow a vow* unto the Lord thy God, thou shalt not slack to pay it; for the Lord will surely require it of thee. *The Psalmist in several places declares that* he would pay his *vows* to the Lord, *Psal.* 22. 25. | 66. 13.

Gen. 28. 20. Jacob vowed a *v.* saying, 31. 13.
Lev. 7. 16. if the sacrifice be a *v.* 22. 18, 21.
22. 23. but for a *v.* it shall not be accepted
27. 2. when a man shall make a singular *v.*
Num. 6. 2. when a man shall vow a *v.* of a Nazarite
5. the days of the *v.* ‖ 21. according to the *v.*
15. 3. or a sacrifice in performing a *v.* 8.
21. 2. Israel vowed a *v.* to the Lord, and said
30. 2. if a man vow a *v.* ‖ 3. if a woman vow a *v.*
4. and her father hear her *v.* and hold his peace
9. every *v.* of a widow shall stand against her
13. every *v.* her husband may estab. or make void
Deut. 23. 18. not bring the price of a dog for a *v.*
21. when thou shalt vow a *v.* not slack to pay it
Judg. 11. 30. Jephthah vowed a *v.* unto the Lord
39. who did with her according to his *v.*
1 *Sam.* 1. 11. Hannah vowed a *v.* and said, O Lord
21. Elkanah went up to offer to the Lord his *v.*
2 *Sam.* 15. 7. I pray thee let me go and pay my *v.*
8. for thy servant vowed a *v.* at Geshur in Syria
Psal. 65. 1. to thee shall the *v.* be performed
Eccl. 5. 4. when thou vowest a *v.* defer not to pay
Isa. 19. 21. they shall vow a *v.* unto the Lord
Acts 18. 18. having shorn his head, for he had a *v.*
21. 23. we have four men which have a *v.* on them

VOWS.

Lev. 22. 18. that will offer his oblation for all his *v.*
23. 38. beside your gifts and beside all your *v.*
Num. 29. 39. these ye shall do beside your *v.*
30. 4. then all her *v.* shall stand, 7, 9, 11.
5. not any of her *v.* or bonds shall stand, 8, 12.
14. then he establisheth all her *v.* or bonds
Deut. 12. 6. thither bring your *v.* 11, 17, 26.
Job 22. 27. and thou shalt pay thy *v.*
Psal. 22. 25. I will pay my *v.* 66. 13. | 116. 14, 18.
50. 14. pay thy *v.* ‖ 56. 12. thy *v.* are upon me, O G.
61. 5. for thou, O God, hast heard my *v.*
8. I will sing praise that I may daily perform my *v.*
Prov. 7. 14. this day have I paid my *v.*
20. 25. it is a snare after *v.* to make inquiry
31. 2. what my son? and what the son of my *v.*
Jer. 44. 25. we will surely perform our *v.*
Jonah 1. 16. the men feared the Lord and made *v.*
Nah. 1. 15. keep thy solemn feasts, perform thy *v.*

VOW.

Num. 6. 2. shall separate themselves to *v.* a vow
Deut. 23. 22. if forbear to *v.* shall be no sin in thee
Psal. 76. 11. *v.* and pay to the Lord your God
Eccl. 5. 5. better is it that thou shouldest not *v.*

VOWED.

Gen. 28. 20. Jacob *v.* a vow, saying, 31. 13.
Lev. 27. 8. according to his ability that *v.* shall priest
Num. 6. 21. the law of the Nazarites who hath *v.*
21. 2. Israel *v.* a vow to the Lord and said
30. 6. if she had at all an husband when she *v.*
10. and if she *v.* in her husband's house
Deut. 23. 23. shalt keep according as thou hast *v.*
Judg. 11. 30. Jephthah *v.* a vow unto the Lord
Psal. 132. 2. and *v.* to the mighty God of Jacob
Eccl. 5. 4. defer not, pay that which thou hast *v.*
Jonah 2. 9. I will pay that that I have *v.*

VOWEST.

Eccl. 5. 4. when thou *v.* a vow, defer not to pay it

VOWETH.

Mal. 1. 14. who *v.* to the Lord a corrupt thing

VOYAGE.

Acts 27. 10. I perceive this *v.* will be with hurt

VULTURE,

A bird of prey, which was declared unclean, Lev. 11. 14. *It is said that* vultures *feed upon human flesh; whence it was that the ancients placed them among birds of ill omen. In* Leviticus *the Hebrew word for* vulture *is* Doah, *of flying; but in* Deut. 14. 13. *it is* Roah, *of seeing, because the* vulture *sees and smells her prey from far; hence it is said, that in Hieroglyphics, the* vulture *signifies sharpness of sight. Job speaks of the* vulture *as having a very quick eye.* Job 28. 7. There is a path which the *vulture's* eye hath not seen.

Lev. 11. 14. the *v.* and the kite after his kind shall not be eaten, *Deut.* 14. 13.
Job 28. 7. a path which the *v.* eye hath not seen
Isa. 34. 15. there shall the *v.* also be gathered, every one with her mate

W.

WAFER.

Exod. 29. 23. one *w.* out of the basket of the unleavened bread that is before the Lord, *Lev.* 8. 26.
Num. 6. 19. one cake, one *w.* on hands of Nazarite

WAFERS.

Exod. 16. 31. manna, the taste of it was like *w.*
29. 2. and *w.* unleavened anointed with oil
Lev. 2. 4. *w.* anointed with oil, 7. 12. *Num.* 6. 15.

WAG.

Jer. 18. 16. every one that passeth by shall *w.* his head
Lam. 2. 15. *w.* their heads at daughter of Jerusalem
Zeph. 2. 15. every one that passeth shall *w.* his hand

WAGES.

Gen. 29. 15. tell me what shall thy *w.* be?
30. 28. appoint me thy *w.* and I will give it
31. 7. your father changed my *w.* ten times, 41.
8. the speckled shall be thy *w.* then the cattle
Exod. 2. 9. nurse this child, I will give thee *w.*
Lev. 19. 13. *w.* of hired not abide with thee all night
Jer. 22. 13. useth neighbour's service without *w.*
Ezek. 29. 18. yet had he no *w.* nor his army
19. her spoil shall be the *w.* for his army
Hag. 1. 6. earneth *w.* to put into a bag with holes
Mal. 3. 5. that oppress the hireling in his *w.*
Luke 3. 14. and be content with your *w.*
John 4. 36. and he that reapeth receiveth *w.*
Rom. 6. 23. for the *w.* of sin is death, but gift of God
2 *Cor.* 11. 8. taking *w.* of them to do you service
2 *Pet.* 2. 15. Balaam loved the *w.* of unrighteousn.

WAGGING.

Mat. 27. 39. and they that passed by reviled him, *w.* their heads, *Mark* 15. 29.

WAGGON.

Num. 7. 3. brought a *w.* for two of the princes

WAGGONS.

Gen. 45. 19. take you *w.* out of Egypt, 21.
27. when Jacob saw the *w.* Joseph had sent
Num. 7. 7. two *w.* four oxen to sons of Gershon
8. four *w.* and eight oxen to the sons of Merari
Ezek. 23. 24. they shall come against thee with *w.*

WAIL.

Ezek. 32. 18. *w.* for the multitude of Egypt
Mic. 1. 8. therefore I will *w.* and howl, go stript
Rev. 1. 7. all kindreds of the earth shall *w.* for him

WAILED.

Mark 5. 38. he seeth them that wept and *w.* greatly

WAILING.

Esth. 4. 3. whither his decree came there was *w.*
Jer. 9. 10. for the mountains will I take up *w.*
18. let them take up a *w.* for us that our eyes
19. for a voice of *w.* is heard out of Zion
20. O ye women, teach your daughters *w.*
Ezek. 7. 11. neither shall there be *w.* for them
27. 31. they shall weep for thee with bitter *w.*
Amos 5. 16. *w.* shall be in all streets, and say, alas, alas! such as are skilful of lamentation to *w.*
17. and in all vineyards shall be *w.* for I will pass
Mic. 1. 8. I will make a *w.* like the dragons
Mat. 13. 42. there shall be *w.* and gnashing teeth, 50.
Rev. 18. 15. the merchants stand afar off, *w.* 19.

WAIT, *Verb.*

Num. 35. 20. if he hurl at him by laying of *w.*
22. or cast on him any thing without laying *w.*
Jer. 9. 8. but in his heart he layeth his *w.*

WAIT.

Num. 3. 10. Aar. and sons shall *w.* on their priest's office, 8. 24. 1 *Chron.* 23. 28. 2 *Chron.* 5. 11. | 13. 10.
2 *Kings* 6. 33. should I *w.* for the Lord any longer?
Job 3. † 21. which *w.* for death, but it cometh not
14. 14. of my time I will *w.* till my change come
17. 13. if I *w.* the grave is my house
Ps. 25. 3. let none that *w.* on thee be ashamed, 69. 6.
5. art God of salvation, on thee do I *w.* all the day
21. let integrity preserve me, for I *w.* on thee
27. 14. *w.* on the Lord, 37. 34. *Prov.* 20. 22.
37. 7. *w.* patiently ‖ 52. 9. I will *w.* on thy name
9. that *w.* on the Lord shall inherit the earth
38. † 15. for in thee, O Lord, do I *w.* thou wilt
39. 7. Lord, what *w.* I for ‖ 62. 5. *w.* only on God
56. 6. they mark my steps when they *w.* for my soul
59. 9. because of his strength will I *w.* upon thee
69. 3. mine eyes fail while I *w.* for my God
104. 27. these all *w.* upon thee, 145. 15.
123. 2. so our eyes *w.* on the Lord our God
130. 5. I *w.* for the Lord, my soul doth *w.*
Isa. 8. 17. I will *w.* on the Lord who hideth his face
30. 18. therefore will the Lord *w.* to be gracious to you, blessed are all they that *w.* for him
40. 31. they that *w.* on L. shall renew their strength
42. 4. the isles shall *w.* for his law
49. 23. shall not be ashamed that *w.* for me
51. 5. and the isles shall *w.* upon me
59. 9. we *w.* for light, but behold obscurity
60. 9. surely the isles shall *w.* for me
Jer. 14. 22. therefore we will *w.* upon thee
Lam. 3. 25. Lord is good to them that *w.* for him
26. it is good that a man hope and quietly *w.*
Hos. 6. 9. as troops of robbers *w.* for a man
12. 6. keep mercy and *w.* on thy God continually
Mic. 7. 7. I will *w.* for the God of my salvation
Hab. 2. 3. though vision tarry, *w.* for it, it will come
Zeph. 3. 8. therefore *w.* ye upon me, saith the Lord
Mark 3. 9. that a small ship would *w.* on him
Luke 12. 36. like unto men that *w.* for their Lord
Acts 1. 4. but *w.* for the promise of the Father
Rom. 8. 25. then do we with patience *w.* for it
12. 7. or ministry, let us *w.* on our ministering
1 *Cor.* 9. 13. which *w.* at the altar are partakers
Gal. 5. 5. we through the Spirit *w.* for the hope
1 *Thess.* 1. 10. and to *w.* for his Son from heaven
See LAY, LAID, LIARS.

WAITED.

Gen. 49. 18. I have *w.* for thy salvation, O Lord
1 *Kings* 20. 38. the prophet *w.* for king by the way
2 *Kings* 5. 2. a little maid *w.* on Naaman's wife
1 *Chron.* 6. 32. and then they *w.* on their office, 33.
9. 18. porters that *w.* in king's gate, 2 *Chr.* 35. 15.
2 *Chron.* 7. 6. and the priests *w.* on their offices
Neh. 12. 44. for the priests and Levites that *w.*
Job 6. 19. the companies of Sheba *w.* for them
15. 22. and he is *w.* for of the sword
29. 21. to me men gave ear, *w.* and kept silence
23. and they *w.* for me as for the rain
30. 26. and when I *w.* for light darkness came
32. 4. now Elihu had *w.* till Job had spoken

Psal. 40. 1. I w. patiently for the Lord, he heard
106. 13. forget his works, they w. not for counsel
119. 95. the wicked have w. for me to destroy me
Isa. 25. 9. this is our God, we have w. for him
26. 8. in way of thy judgments have we w. for thee
33. 2. be gracious unto us, we have w. for thee
Ezek. 19. 5. she saw that she had w. and her hope lost
Mic. 1. 12. for the inhabitants of Maroth w. carefully
Zech. 11. 11. the poor of the flock that w. upon me
Mark 15.43. Joseph of Arimathea, who also w. for the kingdom of G. craved body of Jesus, Luke 23. 51.
Luke 1. 21. the people w. for Zacharias, marvelled
Acts 10. 7. Cornelius called a soldier that w. on him
24. Cornelius w. for Peter and certain brethren
17. 16. while Paul w. for them his spirit was stirred
1 Pet. 3.20. long-suffering of God w. in days of Noah

WAITETH.

Job 24.15 the eye of the adulterer w. for the twilight
Psal. 33.20. our soul w. for Lord our help and shield
62. 1. truly my soul w. upon God, 130. 6.
65. 1. praise w. for thee, O God, in Zion
Prov. 27. 18. he that w. on his master be honoured
Isa. 64. 4. he hath prepared for him that w. for him
Dan. 12. 12. blessed that w. and cometh to 1335 days
Mic. 5. 7. as showers that w. not for the sons of men
Rom. 8. 19. w. for manifestation of the sons of God
Jam. 5. 7. the husbandman w. for the precious fruit

WAITING.

Num. 8. 25. from the age of 50 years shall cease w.
Prov. 8. 34. w. at gates, w. at posts of my doors
Luke 2. 25. Simeon w. for the consolation of Israel
John 5. 3. folk w. for the moving of the water
Rom. 8. 23. we ourselves groan, w. for the adoption
1 Cor. 1. 7. w. for coming of our Lord Jesus Christ
2 Thess. 3. 5. and into the patient w. for Christ

WAKE.

Psal. 139. 18. when I w. I am still with thee
Jer. 51. 39. may sleep a perpetual sleep and not w.
Joel 3. 9. prepare war, w. up the mighty men
1 Thess. 5. 10. whether we w. or sleep live with him

WAKED.

Zech. 4. 1. the angel came again and w. me

WAKENED.

Joel 3. 12. let heathen be w. and come up to valley
Zech. 4. 1. as a man that is w. out of his sleep

WAKENETH.

Isa. 50. 4. to speak in season, he w. morning by morning, he w. mine ear to hear as the learned

WAKETH.

Psal. 127. 1. except Lord keep watchmen w. in vain
Cant. 5. 2. I sleep but my heart w. voice of beloved

WAKING.

Psal. 77. 4. thou holdest mine eyes w. I am troubled

WALK.

To walk *is one of the actions of the body that denotes motion from one place to another, and is often used in Scripture, for the conversation or manner of life,* Rom. 6. 4. Eph. 4. 1, 17. To *walk* in darkness, 1 John 1. 6, 7. *is to live in a course of ignorance, error, and sin; and to walk* in the light, *is to live in the ways of truth and holiness.* To *walk* by faith, 2 Cor. 5. 7. *is to rely upon Christ for salvation, and to live in the firm belief that the promises of the word will be fulfilled and accomplished.* To *walk* through the fire, Isa. 43. 2. *is to be exercised with many afflictions.* To *walk* after the flesh, Rom. 8. 1. *is to be guided by the sensual appetite, and the principles or dictates of corrupt nature.* To *walk* in the flesh, 2 Cor. 10. 3. *is to live a natural life, that is subject to many infirmities and calamities.* To *walk* with God, Gen. 5. 24. *is to live in sweet communion with God, having a lively sense of his presence, and endeavouring above all things to please him, and to be approved and accepted of him.* To *walk* after the Spirit, Rom. 8. 1. *is to be led and guided by his counsels and motions, to regulate and order our whole conversation according to the rule and direction of God's word and Spirit.*

Gen. 24. 40. the Lord before whom I w. will send
48. 15. God before whom my fathers did w. bless
Exod. 16. 4. whether they will w. in my law or no
18. 20. shew them the way wherein they must w.
21. 19. if he w. abroad, he that smote shall be quit
Lev. 18. 3. nor shall w. in their ordinances, 20. 23.
26. 3. if ye w. in my statutes and keep my command. 1 Kings 6. 12. Ezek. 33. 15. Zech. 3. 7.
12. I will w. among you, and will be your God
21. if ye w. contrary to me I will bring, 23, 27.
24. then will I w. contrary to you and punish, 28.
Deut. 5. 33. you shall w. in all the ways of the Lord that ye may live, 13. 4. | 28. 9. Ezek. 37. 24.
8. 19. if ye w. after other gods ye shall perish
29. 19. tho' I w. in the imagination of my heart
Josh. 22. 5. take diligent heed to w. in all his ways
Judg. 5. 10. speak, ye that w. by the way
1 Sam. 2. 30. thy house should w. before me for ever
35. he shall w. before mine anointed for ever
8. 5. thou art old, thy sons w. not in thy ways
1 Kings 3. 14. if thou wilt w. to keep my commandments as thy father David did w. 8. 25. | 9. 4. | 11. 38. 2 Chron. 7. 17.
8. 23. who keepest covenant with thy servants that w. before thee with all their heart, 2 Chron. 6. 14.
36. teach them the good way wherein they should w. and give rain on thy land, 2 Chron. 6. 27.
Psal. 12. 8. the wicked w. on every side when vilest
23. 4. tho' I w. thro' the valley of shadow of death
26. 11. but as for me, I will w. in mine integrity
56. 13. that I may w. before God in light of living
82. 5. they know not, they w. on in darkness
84. 11. withhold no good from them w. uprightly
86. 11. teach me, O Lord, I will w. in thy truth
89. 15. they shall w. in light of thy countenance
30. if his children w. not in my judgments
101. 2. I will w. in my house with a perfect heart
115. 7. feet have they, but they w. not
116. 9. I will w. before the Lord in land of living
119. 3. they do no iniquity, they w. in his ways
45. I will w. at liberty, for I seek thy precepts
138. 7. tho' I w. in midst of trouble, thou wilt revive
143. 8. cause me to know way wherein I should w.

Prov. 2. 7. he is a buckler to them that w. uprightly
20. that thou mayest w. in the way of good men
3. 23. then shalt thou w. in thy way safely
Isa. 2. 3. we will w. in his paths, Mic. 4. 2.
5. O Jacob, let us w. in the light of the Lord
3. 16. they w. with stretched-forth necks
8. 11. that I should not w. in the way of this people
35. 9. but the redeemed shall w. there
40. 31. they that wait on Ld. shall w. and not faint
42. 5. that giveth spirit to them that w. therein
24. for they would not w. in his ways nor obedient
59. 9. wait for brightness, but we w. in darkness
Jer. 3. 17. nor w. after imagination of their heart
18. the house of Judah shall w. with Israel
6. 16. but they said, we will not w. therein
7. 6. if ye w. not after other gods to your hurt
9. will ye w. after other gods whom ye know not?
9. 4. every neighbour will w. with slanders
13. 10. this evil people, which w. in imagination of their heart, and w. after other gods, 16. 12. | 18. 12.
23. 14. they commit adultery, and w. in lies
42. 3. God may shew us way wherein we may w.
Lam. 5. 18. Zion is desolate, the foxes w. upon it
Ezek. 11. 20. that they may w. in my statutes
37. 24. they shall w. in my judgments and statutes
Dan. 4. 37. those that w. in pride he is able to abase
Hos. 11. 10. shall w. after the Lord, roar like a lion
14. 9. ways of Lord right, the just shall w. in them
Joel 2. 8. they shall w. every one in his path
Amos 3. 3. can two w. together except they be agreed?
Mic. 4. 5. every one will w. in name of his God, and we will w. in the name of the Lord our God
6. 16. and ye w. in the counsels of Omri and Ahab
Hab. 3. 15. thou didst w. thro' the sea, with horses
Zeph. 1. 17. that they shall w. like blind men
Zech. 6. 7. they might w. to and fro through earth
10. 12. they shall w. up and down in his name
Mat. 11. 5. the lame w. lepers cleansed, Luke 7. 22.
Mark 7. 5. why w. not thy disciples according to
Luke 11. 44. men that w. over them, are not aware
13. 33. I must w. to-day and to-morrow and day
24. 17. what communications as ye w. and are sad?
John 7. 1. for Jesus would not w. in Jewry
8. 12. shall not w. in darkness but have light of life
11. 9. if any man w. in the day, he stumbleth not
10. if a man w. in the night, he stumbleth
Rom. 4. 12. who w. in steps of that faith of Abraham
6. 4. even so we should w. in newness of life
8. 1. who w. not after flesh, but after Spirit, 4.
2 Cor. 5. 7. for we w. by faith, not by sight
6. 16. I will dwell in them and w. in them
10. 3. tho' we w. in the flesh, not war after the flesh
Gal. 6. 16. as many as w. according to this rule
Eph. 2. 10. God hath ordained we should w. in them
4. 1. that ye w. worthy of the vocation wherewith
17. that ye w. not as other Gentiles in vanity
5. 15. see then that ye w. circumspectly, not as fools
Phil. 3. 17. brethren, mark them which w. so
18. many w. of whom I told you, and tell weep.
Col. 1. 10. that ye might w. worthy of the Lord unto all pleasing, being fruitful, 1 Thess. 2. 12.
1 Thess. 4. 12. ye may w. honestly to those without
2 Thess. 3. 11. some which w. among you disorderly
2 Pet. 2. 10. but chiefly them that w. after the flesh
1 John 1. 6. if we say we have fellowship and w. in dark.
7. but if we w. in the light as he is in the light
2 John 6. w. after his commandments, as ye have heard from the beginning ye should w. in it
3 John 4. to hear that my children w. in the truth
Jude 18. mockers should w. after their ungodly lusts
Rev. 3. 4. and they shall w. with me in white
9. 20. idols that cannot see, nor hear, nor w.
16. 15. blessed is he that watcheth, lest he w. naked
21. 24. the nations shall w. in the light of the city

WALK, *Imperatively.*

Gen. 13. 17. arise, w. through the land, Josh. 18. 8.
17. 1. Almighty God, w. before me, and be perfect
Psal. 48. 12. w. about Zion and go round about her
Prov. 1. 15. my son, w. not in the way with them
Eccl. 11. 9. w. in the ways of thy heart and eyes
Isa. 2. 5. O Jacob, let us w. in the sight of the Lord
30. 21. a voice saying, this is the way, w. in it
50. 11. w. in the light of your fire and in sparks
Jer. 6. 16. ask, where is the good way, w. therein
25. go not forth into fields, nor w. by the way
7. 23. w. ye in all the ways I commanded you
Ezek. 20. 18. w. ye not in statutes of your fathers
Zech. 6. 7. they might w. to and fro thro' the earth
Mat. 9. 5. or to say, rise and w. Mark 2. 9. Luke 5. 23. John 5. 8, 11, 12. Acts 3. 6.
John 12. 35. w. while ye have the light, lest darkness
Rom. 13. 13. let us w. honestly as in the day
1 Cor. 7. 17. as Lord called every one, so let him w.
Gal. 5. 16. w. in the Spirit, and not fulfil lusts, 25.
Eph. 5. 2. w. in love || 8. w. as children of light
Phil. 3. 16. let us w. by the same rule and mind same
Col. 2. 6. as ye have received Christ, so w. in him
4. 5. w. in wisdom toward them that are without

To WALK.

Lev. 18. 4. to w. in my ordinances, for I am the Lord
Deut. 8. 6. to w. in his ways, and fear him, 10. 12. | 11. 22. | 13. 5. | 19. 9. | 26. 17. | 30. 16. Josh. 22. 5. Judg. 2. 22. 1 Kings 2. 3. | 8. 58. 2 Chron. 6. 31.
1 Kings 2. 4. take heed to w. before me in truth
8. 61. heart perfect, to w. in his statutes, Ez. 36. 27.
16. 31. a light thing to w. in the sins of Jeroboam
2 Kings 10. 31. Jehu took no heed to w. in law of L.
23. 3. Josiah made a covenant to w. after the Lord to keep his commandments, 2 Chron. 34. 31.
2 Chron. 6. 16. that children take heed to w. in my law
Neh. 5. 9. ought ye not to w. in the fear of God?
10. 29. they entered into an oath to w. in God's law
Psal. 78. 10. they refused to w. in his law
Prov. 2. 13. leave right to w. in ways of darkness
Eccl. 6. 8. poor that knoweth to w. before the living
Jer. 18. 15. to w. in paths, in a way not cast up
26. 4. if ye will not hearken to w. in my law
31. 9. I will cause them to w. in a straight way
Ezek. 36. 12. I will cause men to w. upon you
Dan. 9. 10. nor have we obeyed to w. in his laws
Mic. 6. 8. and to w. humbly with thy God

Hab. 3. 19. he will make me to w. on high places
Zech. 1. 10. whom Lord hath sent to w. to and fro
3. 7. will give places to w. among these that stand by
Mat. 15. 31. saw the lame to w. they glorified God
Luke 20. 46. the scribes desire to w. in long robes
Acts 3. 12. as though we had made this man to w.
14. 16. suffered all nations to w. in their own ways
21. 21. to circumcise, nor to w. after their customs
1 Thess. 4. 1. how you ought to w. and to please G.
1 John 2. 6. ought himself so to w. as he walked

WALKED.

Gen. 5. 24. Enoch w. with God, and was not, 22.
6. 9. Noah was a just man, and w. with God
Exod. 14. 29. Israel w. upon the dry land in the sea
Lev. 26. 40. that also they have w. contrary to me
Josh. 5. 6. Israel w. forty years in the wilderness
Judg. 2. 17. turned out of the way their fathers w. in
5. 6. in days of Jael the travellers w. thro' by-paths
11. 16. when Israel w. through the wilderness
1 Sam. 8. 3. Samuel's sons w. not in his ways
2 Sam. 2. 29. Abner and his men w. all that night
11. 2. David w. on the roof of the king's house
1 Kings 8. 25. that they walk bef. me as thou hast w.
9. 4. as David thy father w. 2 Chron. 6. 16. | 7. 17.
11. 33. have not w. in my ways, to do right in my eyes, Ezek. 5. 6, 7. | 11. 12. | 20. 13, 16, 21.
15. 26. he w. in the way of his father, 22. 52.
34. Baasha did evil in sight of Lord and w. in way of Jeroboam, 16. 2. 2 Kings 13. 6. | 17. 22.
2 Kings 4. 35. he returned, and w. in house to and fro
17. 8. Hoshea w. in the statutes of the heathen
19. Judah kept not commands of Lord, but w. in statutes of Israel which they made, 2 Chr. 21. 13.
21. 22. Amon forsook the Lord, and w. not in way of Lord, Jer. 9. 13. | 32. 23. | 44. 10, 23.
22. 2. Josiah w. in the ways of David, 2 Chr. 34. 2.
2 Chr. 11. 17. for three years they w. in way of Dav.
17. 4. Jehoshaphat w. in God's commandments
21. 12. hast not w. in the ways of Jehoshaphat
Job 29. 3. when by his light I w. thro' darkness
31. 7. if mine heart w. after mine eyes, and any blot
Psal. 55. 14. we w. to the house of God in company
81. 12. to hearts' lusts, they w. in their own counsels
13. O that Israel had w. in my ways!
142. 3. in the way I w. have they laid a snare
Isa. 9. 2. people that w. in darkness seen great light
20. 3. as my servant Isaiah hath w. naked for a sign
Jer. 2. 5. that they have w. after vanity, 8.
7. 24. but w. in counsels of their evil heart, 11. 8.
8. 2. after whom they have w. 9. 14. | 16. 11.
Ezek. 16. 47. yet hast not thou w. after their ways
18. 9. hath w. in my statutes and judgments, 17.
23. 31. thou hast w. in the way of thy sister
28. 14. hast w. in the midst of the stones of fire
Amos 2. 4. after the way which their fathers w.
Nah. 2. 11. where the lion, even the old lion, w.
Zech. 1. 11. we have w. to and fro thro' earth, 6. 7.
Mal. 3. 14. what profit that we have w. mournfully?
Mark 5. 42. straightway the damsel arose and w.
16. 12. Jesus appeared to two of them as they w.
John 6. 66. many disciples w. no more with him
11. 54. Jesus w. no more openly among the Jews
Acts 3. 8. and he leaping up, stood and w. 14. 10.
14. 8. a cripple from the womb, who never had w.
2 Cor. 10. 2. who think as if we w. according to flesh
12. 18. did Titus make gain of you? w. we not in the same spirit? w. we not in the same steps?
Gal. 2. 14. but when I saw they w. not uprightly
Eph. 2. 2. wherein in time past ye w. Col. 3. 7.
1 Pet. 4. 3. when we w. in lasciviousness, in lusts

He WALKED.

1 Kings 3. 6. to David, as he w. before thee in truth
15. 3. Abijam w. in all the sins of his father, which he had done before him, 2 Kings 21. 21.
16. 26. for he w. in all the ways of Jeroboam
22. 43. he w. in all the ways of Asa, 2 Chr. 20. 32.
2 Kings 8. 18. and he w. in the ways of the kings of Israel, 16. 3. 2 Chron. 21. 6. | 28. 2.
27. and he w. in the way of the kings of Israel as did the house of Ahab, 2 Chron. 22. 3, 5.
2 Chron. 17. 3. he w. in the first ways of David
Dan. 4. 29. Nebuchad. w. in the palace of Babylon
Hos. 5. 11. he willingly w. after the commandment
Mal. 2. 6. he w. with me in peace and equity
Mat. 14. 29. Peter w. on the water to go to Jesus
1 John 2. 6. ought himself so to walk even as he w.

I have WALKED.

Lev. 26. 41. and that I have w. contrary to them
1 Sam. 12. 2. I have w. before you from childhood
2 Sam. 7. 6. I have w. in a tent and tabernacle
7. in all places wherein I have w. with Israel
2 Kings 20. 3. remember how I have w. before thee
Job 31. 5. if I have w. with vanity or foot hasted
Psal. 26. 1. judge me, for I have w. in my integrity
3. and I have w. in thy truth, Isa. 38. 3.

WALKEDST.

John 21. 18. when young, w. whither thou wouldest

WALKEST.

Deut. 6. 7. shalt talk of them when thou w. 11. 19.
1 Kings 2. 42. on the day thou w. abroad any whither
Isa. 43. 2. when thou w. thro' the fire not be burnt
Acts 21. 24. thou thyself w. orderly and keepest law
Rom. 14. 15. if brother grieved now w. not charitably
3 John 3. truth in thee even as thou w. in the truth

WALKETH.

Gen. 24. 65. what man is this that w. in the field?
Deut. 23. 14. Lord thy God w. in midst of the camp
1 Sam. 12. 2. behold, the king w. before you
Job 18. 8. he is cast into a net, and he w. on a snare
22. 14. he w. in the circuit of heaven
34. 8. goeth in company, and w. with wicked men
Psal. 1. 1. blessed that w. not in counsel of ungodly
15. 2. he that w. uprightly shall dwell in holy hill
39. 6. surely every man w. in a vain shew
73. 9. and their tongue w. through the earth
91. 6. nor for the pestilence that w. in darkness
101. 6. he that w. in a perfect way shall serve me
104. 3. who w. upon the wings of the wind
128. 1. blessed is every one that w. in his ways
Prov. 6. 12. a wicked man w. with a froward mouth
10. 9. he that w. uprightly w. surely, 28. 18.
13. 20. he that w. with wise men shall be wise

Prov. 14. 2. he that *w.* in uprightness feareth Lord
15. 21. a man of understanding *w.* uprightly
19. 1. better is poor that *w.* in integrity, 28. 6.
20. 7. just man *w.* in his integrity, children blessed
28. 26. whoso *w.* wisely, he shall be delivered
Eccl. 2. 14. but the fool *w.* in darkness, I perceived
10. 3. when he that is a fool *w.* by the way
Isa. 33. 15. he that *w.* righteously shall dwell on high
50. 10. that *w.* in darkness and hath no light
65. 2. which *w.* in a way that was not good
Jer. 10. 23. it is not in man that *w.* to direct his steps
23. 17. that *w.* after the imagination of his heart
Ezek. 11. 21. heart *w.* after their detestable things
Mic. 2. 7. my words do good to him that *w.* uprightly
Mat. 12. 43. when the unclean spirit is gone out, he *w.* thro' dry places, seeking rest, *Luke* 11. 24.
John 12. 35. he that *w.* in darkness knoweth not
2 Thess. 3. 6. withdr. from brother that *w.* disorderly
1 Pet. 5. 8. devil *w.* about seeking whom he may dev.
1 John 2. 11. who hateth his brother, *w.* in darkness
Rev. 2. 1. *w.* in midst of the seven golden candlesticks

WALKING.

Gen. 3. 8. they heard the voice of Lord *w.* in garden
Deut. 2. 7. Lord knoweth thy *w.* thro' wilderness
1 Kings 3. 3. Solomon loved the Lord, *w.* as David
16. 19. Zimri *w.* in the way of Jeroboam
Job 1. 7. from *w.* up and down in the earth, 2. 2.
31. 26. or beheld the moon *w.* in brightness
Eccl. 10. 7. I have seen princes *w.* as servants
Isa. 3. 16. haughty, *w.* and mincing as they go
20. 2. and he did so, *w.* naked and bare-foot
57. 2. shall rest, each one *w.* in his uprightness
Jer. 6. 28. all grievous revolters, *w.* with slanders
Dan. 3. 25. I see four men loose *w.* in the fire
Mic. 2. 11. if a man *w.* in spirit and falsehood do lie
Mat. 14. 25. Jesus went to them *w.* on the sea
26. saw him *w.* on sea were troubled, *Mark* 6. 48.
Mark 8. 24. blind man said, I see men as trees *w.*
Luke 1. 6. *w.* in all the commandments blameless
Acts 3. 8. lame man *w.* leaping, and praising God, 9.
9. 31. were edified, *w.* in the fear of the Lord
2 Cor. 4. 2. not *w.* in craftiness, nor handling word
2 Pet. 3. 3. scoffers *w.* after their lusts, *Jude* 16.
2 John 4. that I found thy children *w.* in truth

WALL.

Gen. 49. 6. in their self-will they digged down a *w.*
22. a bough whose branches run over the *w.*
Exod. 14. 22. and the waters were a *w.* to them
Lev. 14. 37. if plague in sight lower than the *w.*
Num. 22. 24. a *w.* being on this side, a *w.* on that side
25. the ass crushed Balaam's foot against the *w.*
Josh. 2. 15. for Rahab dwelt upon the town-*w.*
6. 5. the *w.* of the city shall fall down flat, 20.
1 Sam. 18. 11. I will smite David to the *w.* 19. 10.
20. 25. and the king sat upon his seat by the *w.*
25. 16. they were a *w.* to us both by night and day
22. if I leave by the morning light any that pisseth against the *w.* 34. *1 Kings* 14. 10. | 16. 11. | 21. 21. *2 Kings* 9. 8.
31. 10. and they fastened Saul's body to the *w.*
2 Sam. 11. 20. knew ye not they would shoot from *w.*
21. millstone from the *w.* why went ye nigh the *w.*
20. 15. the people battered the *w.* to throw it down
21. behold, his head shall be thrown over the *w.*
22. 30. by my G. have leaped over a *w.* *Psal.* 18. 29.
1 Kings 4. 33. to the hyssop that springs out of the *w.*
20. 30. a *w.* fell upon 27,000 of the men left
21. 23. the dogs shall eat Jezebel by *w.* of Jezreel
2 Kings 3. 27. offered him for burnt-offering on *w.*
4. 10. let us make a little chamber on the *w.*
6. 26. the king of Israel was passing by on the *w.*
9. 33. Jezebel's blood was sprinkled on the *w.*
18. 26. talk not in the Jews' language in ears of the people that are on the *w.* *Isa.* 36. 11.
20. 2. then Hezekiah turned his face to the *w.* and prayed to the Lord, saying, *Isa.* 38. 2.
2 Chron. 25. 23. Joash brake down the *w.* of Jerus.
36. 19. Nebuchadnezzar brake down the *w.*
Ezra 5. 3. who hath commanded you to make this *w.*?
9. 9. to give us a *w.* in Judah and Jerusalem
Neh. 1. 3. the *w.* of Jerusalem is broken down
2. 15. I viewed the *w.* || 17. let us build the *w.*
4. 3. a fox shall even break down their stone *w.*
6. so built we the *w.* all the *w.* was joined together
15. that we returned all of us to the *w.* every one
6. 6. for which cause thou buildest the *w.* to be
15. so the *w.* was finished in the month Elul
12. 27. at the dedication of the *w.* of Jerusalem
13. 21. I said to them, why lodge ye about the *w.*?
Psal. 62. 3. a bowing *w.* shall ye be, as a tottering
Prov. 18. 11. as an high *w.* in his own conceit
24. 31. the stone *w.* thereof was broken down
Cant. 2. 9. my beloved standeth behind our *w.*
8. 9. if she be a *w.* we will build || 10. I am a *w.*
Isa. 2. 15. the day of the Lord on every fenced *w.*
5. 5. I will break down the *w.* of my vineyard
25. 4. when the blast is as a storm against the *w.*
30. 13. as a breach swelling out in an high *w.*
59. 10. we grope for the *w.* like the blind
Jer. 15. 20. I will make thee a fenced brasen *w.*
49. 27. I will kindle a fire in the *w.* of Damascus
51. 44. yea the *w.* of Babylon shall fall
Lam. 2. 8. to destroy the *w.* of the daughter of Zion
18. their heart cried, O *w.* of the daughter of Zion
Ezek. 4. 3. for a *w.* of iron between thee and the city
8. 7. a hole in the *w.* || 8. dig in the *w.* 12. 5.
10. the idols of Israel pourtrayed on the *w.*
13. 12. *w.* is fallen, 15. || 38. 20. every *w.* shall fall
15. then I will accomplish my wrath on the *w.*
41. 5. after he measured the *w.* of the house
43. 8. in setting the *w.* between me and them
Dan. 5. 5. fingers wrote on the plaster of the *w.*
9. 25. street shall be built, and *w.* in troublous times
Hos. 2. 6. I will make a *w.* that shall not find
Joel 2. 7. they shall climb the *w.* like men of war
9. they shall run upon the *w.* and climb up
Amos 1. 7. I will send a fire on the *w.* of Gaza
10. on the *w.* of Tyrus || 14. in the *w.* of Rabbah
5. 19. leaned his hand on the *w.* a serpent bit him
7. 7. behold, the Lord stood upon a *w.* made by
Nah. 2. 5. they shall make haste to the *w.* thereof
Hab. 2. 11. for the stone shall cry out of the *w.*

Acts 9. 25. then the disciples by night let Saul down by the *w.* in a basket, *2 Cor.* 11. 33.
23. 3. God shall smite thee, thou whited *w.*
Eph. 2. 14. Christ hath broken down the middle *w.*
Rev. 21. 14. the *w.* of the city had twelve foundations
18. the building of the *w.* of it was of jasper
See BUILT.

WALLED.

Lev. 25. 29. if a man sell a dwelling house in *w.* city
30. the house in the *w.* city shall be established
Num. 13. 28. cities *w.* and very great, *Deut.* 1. 28.

WALLOW.

Jer. 6. 26. gird with sackcloth, *w.* thyself in ashes
25. 34. ye shepherds, cry, *w.* yourselves in ashes
48. 26. Moab shall *w.* in his vomit, be in derision
Ezek. 27. 30. they shall *w.* themselves in the ashes

WALLOWED.

2 Sam. 20. 12. Amasa *w.* in blood in the high way
Mark 9. 20. he fell on the ground, and *w.* foaming

WALLOWING.

2 Pet. 2. 22. and the sow washed to *w.* in the mire

WALLS.

Lev. 14. 37. if plague be in the *w.* of the house, 39.
25. 31. the villages having no *w.* counted as fields
Deut. 3. 5. these cities were fenced with high *w.*
28. 52. till thy high fenced *w.* come down
2 Kings 25. 4. the men of war fled between two *w.*
10. the army of the Chaldees brake down the *w.* of Jerusalem round about, *Jer.* 39. 8.
Ezra 4. 13. if this city be built, and *w.* set up, 16.
5. 8. timber is laid in the *w.* work goeth fast on
Neh. 4. 7. heard that the *w.* of Jerus. were made up
Job 24. 11. which make oil within their *w.*
Psal. 51. 18. build thou the *w.* of Jerusalem
55. 10. day and night they go about on *w.* thereof
122. 7. peace be within thy *w.* and prosperity
Prov. 25. 28. is like a city broken down, without *w.*
Cant. 5. 7. the keepers of the *w.* took away my vail
Isa. 22. 5. it is a day of breaking down the *w.*
25. 12. the fortress of thy *w.* shall he bring down
26. 1. salvat. will G. appoint for *w.* and bulwarks
49. 16. behold, thy *w.* are continually before me
56. 5. within my *w.* a place and a name better
60. 10. the sons of strangers shall build up thy *w.*
18. thou shalt call thy *w.* salvation, and gates
62. 6. I have set watchmen on thy *w.* O Jerusalem
Jer. 1. 15. set their thrones against the *w.* of Jerus.
5. 10. go ye up upon her *w.* and destroy, make not
50. 15. Babylon's *w.* are thrown down, 51. 58.
Ezek. 26. 4. they shall destroy the *w.* of Tyrus, 12.
27. 11. the men of Arvad were upon thy *w.*
33. 30. still are talking against thee by the *w.*
38. 11. all of them dwelling without *w.* or gates
Mic. 7. 11. in the day that thy *w.* are to be built
Zech. 2. 4. Jerusal. inhabited as towns without *w.*
Heb. 11. 30. by faith the *w.* of Jericho fell down

WANDER.

Gen. 20. 13. when God caused me to *w.* from my
Num. 14. 33. your children shall *w.* in the wilderness forty years, 32. 13. *Psal.* 107. 40.
Deut. 27. 18. cursed is he that causeth blind to *w.*
Job 12. 24. he causeth them to *w.* in a wilderness
38. 41. when his young ravens *w.* for lack of meat
Psal. 55. 7. then would I *w.* far off and remain
59. 15. let them *w.* up and down for meat
119. 10. O let me not *w.* from thy commandments
Isa. 47. 15. they shall *w.* every one to his quarter
Jer. 14. 10. Lord saith, thus have they loved to *w.*
48. 12. send wanderers that shall cause him to *w.*
Amos 8. 12. and they shall *w.* from sea to sea

WANDERERS.

Jer. 48. 12. days come that I will send to him *w.*
Hos. 9. 17. they shall be *w.* among the nations

WANDERED.

Gen. 21. 14. Hagar *w.* in the wildern. of Beer-sheba
Psal. 107. 4. they *w.* in the wilderness, *Isa.* 16. 8.
Lam. 4. 14. they have *w.* as blind men in the streets
Ezek. 34. 6. my sheep *w.* through all the mountains
Amos 4. 8. two or three cities *w.* to one city to drink
Heb. 11. 37. *w.* about in sheep-skins and goat-skins
38. they *w.* in deserts, in mountains, and in dens

WANDEREST.

Jer. 2. 20. when under every green tree thou *w.*

WANDERETH. [is it?

Job 15. 23. he *w.* abroad for bread, saying, where
Prov. 21. 16. that *w.* out of way of understanding
27. 8. as a bird that *w.* from her nest, so is a man that *w.* from his place
Isa. 16. 3. take counsel, bewray not him that *w.*
Jer. 49. 5. and none shall gather up him that *w.*

WANDERING.

Gen. 37. 15. behold, he was *w.* in the field
Prov. 26. 2. as the bird by *w.* as swallow by flying
Eccl. 6. 9. better is the sight of the eyes than the *w.*
Isa. 16. 2. it shall be as a *w.* bird cast out of the nest
1 Tim. 5. 13. to be idle, *w.* about from house to house
Jude 13. *w.* stars to whom is reserved darkness

WANDERINGS.

Psal. 56. 8. thou tellest my *w.* put thou my tears

WANT.

Deut. 28. 48. thou shalt serve thy enemies in *w.*
57. she shall eat them for *w.* of all things secretly
Judg. 18. 10. a place where is no *w.* 19. 19.
Job 24. 8. they embrace the rock for *w.* of shelter
30. 3. for *w.* and famine they were solitary
31. 19. if I have seen any perish for *w.* of clothing
Psal. 34. 9. there is no *w.* to them that fear him
Prov. 6. 11. and thy *w.* as an armed man, 24. 34.
10. 21. but fools die for *w.* of wisdom
13. 23. there is that is destroyed for *w.* of judgment
14. 28. in *w.* of people is destruction of the prince
21. 5. but of every one that is hasty only to *w.*
22. 16. that giveth to rich shall surely come to *w.*
Lam. 4. 9. stricken thro' for *w.* of the fruits of field
Amos 4. 6. I have giv. you *w.* of bread in your places
Mark 12. 44. she of her *w.* cast in all she had
Luke 15. 14. a famine arose, he began to be in *w.*
2 Cor. 8. 14. your abundance be supply for their *w.*
9. 12. not only supplieth the *w.* of the saints
Phil. 4. 11. not that I speak in respect of *w.*

WANTS.

Judg. 19. 20. howsoever, let all thy *w.* lie on me

Phil. 2. 25. Epaphroditus that ministered to my *w.*

WANT.

Psal. 23. 1. the Lord is my shepherd, I shall not *w.*
34. 10. they that seek Lord shall not *w.* any good
Prov. 13. 25. but the belly of the wicked shall *w.*
Isa. 34. 16. no one shall fail, none shall *w.* her mate
Jer. 33. 17. David not *w.* a man to sit on the throne
18. Levites not *w.* a man || 35. 19. Jonadab not *w.*
Ezek. 4. 17. that they may *w.* bread and water

WANTED.

Jer. 44. 18. we have *w.* all things, been consumed
John 2. 3. when they *w.* wine, mother of Jesus saith
2 Cor. 11. 9. when I *w.* I was chargeable to no man

WANTETH.

Deut. 15. 8. shall lend him for his need in that he *w.*
Prov. 9. 4. for him that *w.* understanding she saith to him, 16.
10. 19. in multitude of words there *w.* not sin
28. 16. prince that *w.* understanding is an oppressor
Eccl. 6. 2. so that he *w.* nothing for his soul
Cant. 7. 2. like a round goblet that *w.* not liquor

WANTING.

2 Kings 10. 19. call all prophets of Baal and all his priests, let none be *w.* whoso be *w.* shall not live
Prov. 19. 7. pursueth with words, yet they are *w.* to
Eccl. 1. 15. that which is *w.* cannot be numbered
Dan. 5. 27. thou art weighed in the balances and found *w.*
Tit. 1. 5. shouldest set in order the things that are *w*
3. 13. that nothing be *w.* unto them
Jam. 1. 4. ye may be perfect and entire, *w.* nothing

WANTON.

Isa. 3. 16. the daughters of Zion walk with *w.* eyes
1 Tim. 5. 11. to wax *w.* against Christ, they marry
Jam. 5. 5. ye have lived in pleasure and been *w.*

WANTONNESS.

Rom. 13. 13. walk honestly, not in chambering and *w.*
2 Pet. 2. 18. they allure through lusts and much *w.*

WAR.

When the Hebrews drew out their armies and went to war against their enemies, and the time of battle was at hand, the high priest presented himself at the head of the army, and spoke to the people in this manner: Hear, O Israel, and be not in fear of your enemies; for the Lord your God fights for you. *After which the officers proclaimed aloud at the head of every troop:* Is there any one here that hath built a new house, and has not yet inhabited it? let him depart and return to his house, for fear that another should come and live in it first, &c. *as in Deut.* 20. 2, 3, 4, &c.

The Hebrews were formerly a very warlike nation. The books that inform us of their wars *are neither flattering authors, nor ignorant, but were authors inspired by the Spirit of truth and wisdom. Their warriors were none of those fabulous heroes, or professed conquerors, whose business it was to ravage cities and provinces, and to reduce foreign nations under their dominion, merely for the sake of governing them, or for purchasing a name. They were commonly wise and valiant generals, raised up by* God *to fight the battles of the* Lord, *and to exterminate his enemies. These were such as* Joshua, Caleb, Gideon, Jephthah, Samson, David, *and* Josiah, *whose names alone are a sufficient encomium.*

Their wars were not undertaken upon slight occasions, nor performed with a small number of people. Under Joshua, the affair was of no less importance, than to make himself master of a large country, which God had given to the Israelites; to root out several powerful enemies, which God had devoted to destruction; and to vindicate an offended Deity, and human nature, which had been debased by a wicked and corrupt people, who had filled up the measure of their iniquities. Under the Judges, the matter was to assert the liberty of the Israelites, by shaking off the yoke of powerful kings, who kept them in subjection. Under Saul and David, the same motives prevailed to undertake war; *and to these were added a further motive, the making a conquest of such provinces as God had promised to his people; so far was it from their intention merely to reduce the power of the Philistines, the Ammonites, the Moabites, the Idumeans, the Arabians, the Syrians, and the several princes that were in possession of those countries.*

In the latter times of the kingdoms of Israel and Judah, we may observe their kings bearing the shock of the greatest kings in the world, namely, those of Asia, the kings of Assyria and Chaldea, Shalmaneser, Sennacherib, Esar-haddon, and Nebuchadnezzar who made the whole east tremble. Under the Maccabees, the chosen people, with an handful of men, opposed the whole power of the kings of Assyria, and against all their power upheld the religion of their fathers, and shook off the yoke of their authority, who had a design both against their religion and liberty. In the latter times of their nation, with what courage, with what intrepidity and constancy, did they sustain the wars *against the Romans, who were the masters of the world!*

But how great armies did they bring into the field? In the beginning, under Moses and Joshua, they were all soldiers, and men bearing arms. They came out of Egypt to the number of six hundred thousand fighting men. When Joshua entered into the land of Canaan, he fought sometimes with detachments of his troops, and sometimes with his whole army, according as exigencies required. God would often give the victory to very small armies, to signalize his omnipotence, and to humble the pride of man. For example, under Gideon, where God ordered this general to send away the greatest part of his army, and only to keep with him three hundred men, *with which he defeated an innumerable multitude of Midianites and Amalekites. Sometimes numerous armies were brought into the field, Abijah, king of Judah, with an army of four hundred thousand men, made war with Jeroboam, king of Israel, who had to the number of eight hundred thousand. And of these eight hundred thousand, there were five hundred thousand slain in one battle,* 2 Chron. 13. 3—17. *Pekah, son of Remaliah, king of Israel, in one day killed one hundred and twenty thousand men of the troops of Judah,* 2 Chron. 28. 6. *Asa king of Judah, having an army of five hundred and eighty thousand men, was attacked by Zerah, king of Cush, who had an army of a million of men: Zerah was entirely routed by the troops of Asa,* 2 Chron. 14. 9—13.

We may distinguish two *kinds of* wars *among the Hebrews. Some were of obligation as being expressly commanded by the Lord; but others were free and voluntary. The first were such as God appointed them to undertake: for example, against the Amalekites, and the Canaanites, which were nations devoted to destruction for their sins. The others were undertaken by the captains of the people, to revenge some injuries offered to the nation, to punish some insults or offences. Such was that which the Hebrews made against the city of Gibeah, and against the tribe of Benjamin, which would uphold them in their fault,* Judg. 20. 8. *And such was that which David made against the Ammonites, whose king had affronted his ambassadors,* 2 Sam. 10. 1—14. *Or to maintain and defend their allies; as that of Joshua against the kings of the Canaanites, to protect the Gibeonites,* Josh. 10. 6—11. *Lastly, whatever just reasons may authorize a nation or a prince to make* war *against another, seems to have obtained among the Hebrews.* War *is threatened by God in Scripture as one of the greatest judgments, and may justly be reckoned among the many dreadful miseries which sin has entailed on mankind.*

The common acceptation of war, *in Scripture, is a state of hostility between nations, states, provinces, or parties, as in* 1 Kings 14. 30. Luke 14. 31. *and many other places. But it is taken in a spiritual sense in* 2 Cor. 10. 3. *where the apostle says,* We *war* not after the flesh, *that is, " We do not use outward force and strength; but as the end of our warfare is spiritual, so are the means: the gospel we preach has its effects on the minds and inward part of men; and, through the power of divine grace, is made effectual for the subduing and sanctifying their corrupt and sinful natures."*

Exod. 1. 10. when there is *w.* they join our enemies
13. 17. lest the people repent when they see *w.*
17. 16. the Lord will have *w.* with Amalek
32. 17. there is a noise of *w.* in the camp
Num. 1. 3. from twenty years old, all that are able to go forth to *w.* 20. 22. | 26. 2. *Deut.* 3. 18.
10. 9. if ye go to *w.* ye shall blow an alarm
31. 3. Moses spake, arm some of yourselves to *w.*
4. of every tribe 1000 shall ye send to *w.*
32. 6. shall your brethren go to *w.* and ye sit there?
20. if ye will go armed before the Lord to *w.* 27.
Deut. 4. 34. hath God assayed by *w.* to take a nation
20. 12. but will make *w.* against thee, 19, 20.
21. 10. when thou goest forth to *w.* against enemies
24. 5. when hath taken a wife shall not go to *w.*
Josh. 11. 23. and the land rested from *w.* 14. 15.
14. 11. so is my strength now for *w.* to go out
Judg. 3. 2. that Israel might know to teach them *w.*
5. 8. chose new gods, then was *w.* in the gates
11. 27. but thou dost me wrong to *w.* against me
21. 22. we reserved not to each his wife in the *w.*
1 *Sam.* 14. 52. was sore *w.* against Philistines, 19. 8.
28. 15. for the Philistines make *w.* against me
2 *Sam.* 3. 1. long *w.* between house of Saul and Dav.
11. 7. David demanded how the *w.* prospered
1 *Kings* 2. 5. shed the blood of *w.* put the blood of *w.*
14. 30. *w.* between Rehoboam and Jeroboam, 15. 6.
15. 7. there was *w.* between Abijam and Jeroboam
16. there was *w.* between Asa and Baasha, 32.
20. 18. or be come out for *w.* take them alive
22. 1. they continued three years without *w.*
2 *Kings* 18. 20. I have counsel and strength for *w.*
1 *Chron.* 5. 10. they made *w.* with the Hagarites, 19.
22. many slain, because the *w.* was of God
2 *Chron.* 15. 19. no *w.* to the 35th year of Asa
35. 21. but against the house wherewith I have *w.*
Job 5. 20. in *w.* redeem from power of the sword
10. 17. changes and *w.* are against me
38. 23. which I have reserved against the day of *w.*
Psal. 27. 3. though *w.* should rise against me
55. 21. words smooth, but *w.* was in his heart
68. 30. scatter thou the people that delight in *w.*
120. 7. but when I speak, they are for *w.*
140. 2. continually are gathered together for *w.*
Prov. 20. 18. and with good advice make *w.*
24. 6. for by wise counsel thou shalt make thy *w.*
Eccl. 3. 8. a time of *w.* and a time of peace
8. 8. of death, there is no discharge in that *w.*
Isa. 2. 4. nor shall they learn *w.* any more, *Mic.* 4. 3.
3. 25. thy mighty shall fall in the *w.*
21. 15. they fled from the grievousness of *w.*
36. 5. I have counsel and strength for *w.*
Jer. 4. 19. because thou hast heard the alarm of *w.*
6. 4. prepare ye *w.* against her, arise, let us go up
23. set in array as men for *w.* against thee
21. 2. Nebuchadnezzar maketh *w.* against us
42. 14. will go to Egypt, where we shall see no *w.*
48. 14. how say ye, we are mighty men for *w.*?
49. 2. an alarm of *w.* to be heard in Rabbah
Ezek. 17. 17. nor Pharaoh make for him in *w.*
Dan. 7. 21. the same horn made *w.* with the saints
9. 26. to the end of the *w.* are desolations
Joel 3. 9. prepare *w.* wake up the mighty men
Mic. 2. 8. that pass by, as men averse from *w.*
3. 5. they even prepare *w.* against him
Luke 14. 31. or what king going to make *w.*?
Rev. 11. 7. the beast shall make *w.* against them
12. 7. there was *w.* in heaven against the dragon
17. to make *w.* with the remnant of her seed
13. 4. who is able to make *w.* with the beast?
7. given to him to make *w.* with saints, 17. 14.
19. 11. in righteousness doth he make *w.*
19. the beast and kings gathered to make *w.*

See EXPERT, MAN, MEN.

Weapons of WAR.

Deut. 1. 41. when ye had girded on *weapons of w.*
Judg. 18. 11. six hundred with *weapons of w.* 16, 17.
2 *Sam.* 1. 27. how are the *weapons of w.* perished
Eccl. 9. 18. wisdom is better than *weapons of w.*
Jer. 21. 4. I will turn back the *weapons of w.*
51. 20. thou art my battle-axe and *weapons of w.*
Ezek. 32. 27. gone down to hell with *weapons of w.*

WAR, *Verb.*

2 *Sam.* 22. 35. the Lord teacheth my hands to *w.* a bow of steel is broken by me, *Psal.* 18. 34. | 144. 1.
2 *Kings* 16. 5. the kings Rezin and Pekah came up to Jerusalem, to *w.* against it, *Isa.* 7. 1.
2 *Chron.* 6. 34. if thy people go to *w.* against enemy
Isa. 41. 12. they that *w.* against thee be as nothing
2 *Cor.* 10. 3. walk in flesh, do not *w.* after the flesh
1 *Tim.* 1. 18. that thou mightest *w.* a good warfare
Jam. 4. 1. of your lusts that *w.* in your members
2. ye fight and *w.* yet ye have not because ask not
1 *Pet.* 2. 11. from lusts which *w.* against the soul

WARRED.

Num. 31. 7. and they *w.* against the Midianites
Josh. 24. 9. Balak king of Moab *w.* against Israel
1 *Kings* 14. 19. Jeroboam, how he *w.* and reigned
22. 45. acts of Jehoshaphat, how he *w.* are written
2 *Kings* 6. 8. the king of Syria *w.* against Israel
2 *Chron.* 26. 6. Uzziah *w.* against the Philistines

WARRETH.

2 *Tim.* 2. 4. no man that *w.* entangleth himself with

WARRING.

2 *Kings* 19. 8. Rabshakeh returned and found the king of Assyria *w.* against Libnah, *Isa.* 37. 8.
Rom. 7. 23. but I see a law in my members *w.*

WARRIOR, S.

1 *Kings* 12. 21. chosen men who were *w.* 2 *Chr.* 11. 1.
Isa. 9. 5. battle of the *w.* is with confused noise

WARS.

Num. 21. 14. it is said in book of the *w.* of the Lord
Judg. 3. 1. as had not known all the *w.* of Canaan
2 *Sam.* 8. 10. Toi sent Joram to David, for Hadadezer had *w.* with Toi, 1 *Chron.* 18. 10.
1 *Chron.* 22. 8. hast made great *w.* shalt not build
2 *Chron.* 16. 9. from henceforth thou shalt have *w.*
Psal. 46. 9. he maketh *w.* to cease to ends of earth
Mat. 24. 6. ye shall hear of *w.* and rumours of *w.* see that ye be not troubled, *Mark* 13. 7. *Luke* 21. 9.
Jam. 4. 1. from whence come *w.* and fightings?

WARD.

Gen. 40. 3. Pharaoh put them in *w.* 4. 7.
41. 10. Pharaoh was wroth and put me in *w.*
42. 17. Joseph put his brethren in *w.* three days
Lev. 24. 12. they put the blasphemer in *w.*
Num. 15. 34. they put the gatherer of sticks in *w.*
2 *Sam.* 20. 3. David put the ten concubines in *w.*
1 *Chron.* 12. 29. had kept the *w.* of the house of Saul
25. 8. they cast lots, *w.* against *w.* small as great
26. 16. lot came by cause of *w.* going up *w.* against *w.*
Neh. 12. 24. to give thanks *w.* over-against *w.*
25. were porters keeping the *w.* at the gates
45. kept *w.* of their God and *w.* of purification
Isa. 21. 8. I am set in my *w.* whole nights
Jer. 37. 13. Irijah a captain of the *w.* was there
Ezek. 19. 9. they put Zedekiah in *w.* in chains
Acts 12. 10. when they were past first and second *w.*

WARDS.

1 *Chron.* 9. 23. kept the house of the tabernacle by *w.*
26. 12. having *w.* one against another to minister
Neh. 13. 30. I appointed the *w.* of the priests

WARDROBE.

2 *Kings* 22. 14. Huldah the prophetess, the wife of Shallum, the keeper of the *w.* 2 *Chron.* 34. 22.

WARE.

Luke 8. 27. *w.* no clothes nor abode in any house

WARE.

Mat. 24. 50. Ld. shall come in an hour he is not *w.* of
Acts 14. 6. they were *w.* of it and fled to Lystra
2 *Tim.* 4. 15. of the copper-smith be thou *w.* also

WARE, *Substantive.*

Neh. 10. 31. if people bring *w.* on sabbath to sell
13. 16. men of Tyre brought all manner of *w.*
20. merchants and sellers of all kind of *w.* lodged

WARES.

Jer. 10. 17. gather up thy *w.* out of the land
Ezek. 27. 16. by reason of the multitude of *w.* 18. 33.
Jonah 1. 5. the mariners cast forth *w.* into the sea

WARFARE.

1 *Sam.* 28. 1. the Philistines gathered armies for *w.*
Job 7. † 1. is there not a *w.* to man upon earth?
Isa. 40. 2. cry to her that her *w.* is accomplished
1 *Cor.* 9. 7. goeth a *w.* any time at his own charges?
2 *Cor.* 10. 4. the weapons of our *w.* are not carnal
1 *Tim.* 1. 18. that thou mightest war a good *w.*

WARM.

2 *Kings* 4. 34. and the flesh of the child waxed *w.*
Job 6. 17. what time they wax *w.* they vanish
37. 17. how thy garments are *w.* when quitteth
Eccl. 4. 11. two have heat, how can one be *w.* alone
Isa. 44. 15. he will take thereof and *w.* himself
16. warmeth himself, and saith, aha, I am *w.*
47. 14. there shall not be a coal to *w.* at nor fire
Hag. 1. 6. ye clothe you, but there is none *w.*

WARMED.

Job 31. 20. if were not *w.* with fleece of my sheep
Mark 14. 54. Peter *w.* himself, *John* 18. 18, 25.
Jam. 2. 16. depart in peace, be you *w.* and filled

WARMETH.

Job 39. 14. the ostrich that *w.* her eggs in the dust
Isa. 44. 16. he *w.* himself and saith, aha, I am warm

WARMING.

Mark 14. 67. when she saw Peter *w.* himself

WARN.

2 *Chron.* 19. 10. shall *w.* them that they trespass not
Ezek. 3. 18. nor speakest to *w.* the wicked, 33. 8.
19. yet if thou *w.* the wicked, 33. 9.
21. if thou *w.* righteous || 33. 3. *w.* the people, 7.
Acts 20. 31. I ceased not to *w.* every one with tears
1 *Cor.* 4. 14. but as my beloved sons I *w.* you
1 *Thess.* 5. 14. brethren, *w.* them that are unruly

WARNED.

2 *Kings* 6. 10. sent to the place man of God *w.* him
Psal. 19. 11. moreover by them is thy servant *w.*
Ezek. 3. 21. he shall surely live, because he is *w.*
33. 6. if watchman see and the people be not *w.*
Mat. 2. 12. Joseph being *w.* of God departed, 22.
3. 7. O generation of vipers, who hath *w.* you to flee from the wrath to come? *Luke* 3. 7.
Acts 10. 22. Cornelius *w.* from God by an angel
Heb. 11. 7. by faith Noah being *w.* prepared an ark

WARNING.

Jer. 6. 10. to whom shall I speak and give *w.*?
Ezek. 3. 17. hear the word and give them *w.*
18. thou givest him not *w.* nor speakest, 20.
33. 4. taketh not *w.* || 5. he heard and took not *w.*
Col. 1. 28. *w.* every man, and teaching every man

WARP.

Lev. 13. 48. plague in the *w.* or woof, 49, 51, 57, 59.
52. burn *w.* || 56. rend *w.* || 58. wash the *w.*

WAS.

Gen. 5. 24. Enoch walked with God and *w.* not
21. 20. God *w.* with the lad, he grew and became
26. 28. we saw certainly the Lord *w.* with thee
29. 12. Jacob told Rachel, he *w.* her father's brother
31. 40. thus I *w.* in the day, drought consumed me
37. 29. and behold, Joseph *w.* not in the pit
39. 2. Lord *w.* with Joseph, he was prosperous, 22.
Exod. 20. 21. and Moses drew near where God *w.*
Num. 27. 3. he *w.* not in the company of Korah
Josh. 1. 5. as I *w.* with Moses, so I will be with thee
17. Lord thy God be with thee as he *w.* with Moses
6. 27. the Ld. *w.* with Joshua, and his fame noised
14. 11. as yet I am as strong as I *w.* for war
Judg. 20. 3. tell us, how *w.* this wickedness?
1 *Sam.* 9. 10. they went where the man of God *w.*
2 *Sam.* 12. 3. the ewe-lamb *w.* unto him as a daugh.
16. 23. the counsel of Ahithophel *w.* as if a man
1 *Kings* 3. 26. woman spake whose living child *w.*
8. 57. God be with us as he *w.* with our fathers
19. 11. the Lord *w.* not in the wind, the Lord *w.* not in the earthquake || 12. *w.* not in the fire
20. 41. king discerned him that he *w.* of prophets
2 *Kings* 10. 30. done to Ahab all that *w.* in my heart
Esth. 8. 1. Esther had told what he *w.* to her
Job 3. 26. I *w.* not in safety, neither had I rest
29. 4. as I *w.* in the days of my youth when secret
Psal. 37. 36. he passed away and lo he *w.* not
38. 14. thus I *w.* as a man that heareth not
53. 5. they were in great fear, where no fear *w.*
Isa. 9. 1. the dimness shall not be such as *w.* in her
23. 13. this people *w.* not till Assyrian founded it
Jer. 48. 27. *w.* not Israel a derision unto thee? *w.* he found among thieves? thou skippedst for joy
Amos 7. 14. I *w.* no prophet, neither *w.* I a prophet's son, but I *w.* an herdman and a gatherer of fruit
Jonah 4. 2. I pray thee, Lord, *w.* not this my saying?
Mal. 1. 2. *w.* not Esau Jacob's brother? saith the L
Mat. 24. 21. such as *w.* not since the beginning of the world, or ever shall be, *Mark* 13. 19.
Mark 2. 4. they uncovered the roof where he *w.*
5. 5. always night and day he *w.* in the mountains
11. 30. the baptism of John, *w.* it from heaven, or of men? answer me, *Luke* 20. 4.
John 1. 1. the Word *w.* with God, and Word *w.* God
9. that *w.* the true light, that lighteth every man
15. John cried, saying, he *w.* before me, 30.
3. 26. he that *w.* with thee beyond Jordan
6. 62. Son of man ascend up where he *w.* before
8. 58. Jesus said, verily before Abraham *w.* I am
11. 15. I am glad for your sakes I *w.* not there
16. 4. these things I said, because I *w.* with you
17. 5. the glory I had with thee before the world *w.*
20. 24. Thomas one of the twelve *w.* not with them
21. 11. full of fishes, yet *w.* not the net broken
Acts 5. 4. after sold, *w.* it not in thy own power?
7. 9. with envy sold Joseph, but God *w.* with him
11. 17. what *w.* I that I could withstand God?
21. 33. the captain came near, demanded who he *w.*
2 *Cor.* 1. 18. our word *w.* not yea and nay, 19.
11. 5. I *w.* not a whit behind chiefest apostles
1 *Thess.* 2. 1. our entrance unto you *w.* not in vain
3. our exhortation *w.* not in deceit, nor in guile
2 *Tim.* 3. 9. folly shall be manifest as theirs also *w.*
Heb. 7. 4. now consider how great this man *w.*
11. 38. of whom the world *w.* not worthy
Jam. 1. 24. forgetteth what manner of man he *w.*
Rev. 1. 4. from him which is and which *w.* 8. | 4. 8.
17. 8. the beast thou sawest *w.* and is not, yet is, 11.

See So.

It WAS.

Gen. 41. 13. came to pass as he interpreted, so *it w.*
42. 6. he *it w.* sold to all the people of the land
45. 8. now *it w.* not you that sent me, but God
Exod. 16. 15. manna for they wist not what *it w.*
Josh. 11. 20. *it w.* of the Lord to harden their hearts
14. 7. I brought Moses word as *it w.* in my heart
Judg. 6. 3. so *it w.* when Isr. had sown, Midian came
2 *Sam.* 3. 37. *it w.* not of the king to slay Abner
18. 29. saw a tumult, but I knew not what *it w.*
1 *Kings* 2. 15. is my brother's for *it w.* his from Ld.
13. 6. Jeroboam, his hand became as *it w.* before
22. 33. perceived that *it w.* not the king of Israel
2 *Kings* 7. 7. left the camp as *it w.* and fled for life
Esth. 4. 5. Esther gave Hatach a command to Mordecai to know what *it w.* and why *it w.*
Eccl. 12. 7. then shall dust return to earth as *it w.*
Cant. 3. 4. *it w.* but a little that I passed from them
Isa. 11. 16. as *it w.* to Israel in the day he came up
48. 16. from the time that *it w.* there am I
Ezek. 16. 15. his *it w.* || 19. thus *it w.* saith the Lord
Mark 5. 14. went to see what *it w.* that was done
Luke 20. 7. they could not tell whence *it w.*
22. 23. they began to inquire which of them *it w.*
John 2. 9. the ruler tasted and knew not whence *it w.*
5. 13. he that was healed wist not who *it w.*
20. 14. and knew not that *it w.* Jesus, 21. 4.
21. 12. the disciples knowing that *it w.* the Lord
Rom. 5. 16. not as *it w.* by one that sinned, so gift

Behold it WAS.

Gen. 1. 31. God saw every thing, *behold it w.* good
6. 12. God looked on earth, *behold it w.* corrupt
29. 25. in the morning, *behold it w.* Leah
31. 2. *behold it w.* not toward Jacob as before
41. 7. Pharaoh awoke and *behold it w.* a dream
42. 27. for *behold it w.* in the sack's mouth
Lev. 10. 16. and *behold it w.* burnt, 1 *Sam.* 30. 3.

1 *Kings* 3. 21. *behold it w.* dead, *behold it w.* my son

There WAS.

Gen. 1. 3. let there be light, and *there w.* light
2. 5. and *there w.* not a man to till the ground
20. *there w.* not found an help meet for him
Exod. 12. 30. *there w.* a great cry in Egypt, for *there w.* not an house where *there w.* not one dead
Num. 26. 64. *there w.* not a man Moses numbered
Deut. 2. 36. *there w.* not one city too strong; 3. 4.
32. 12. *there w.* no strange god with him
Josh. 8. 17. *there w.* not a man left in Ai or Beth-el
35. *there w.* not a word Joshua read not before Isr.
11. 11. *there w.* not any left to breathe
19. *there w.* not a city that made peace with Israel
Judg. 4. 16. host of Sisera fell, *there w.* not a man left
1 *Sam.* 7. 17. for *there w.* his house, there he judged
2 *Kings* 10. 21. *there w.* not a man that came not
11. 16. laid hands on her, and *there w.* she slain
Psal. 106. 11. *there w.* not one of them left
Hab. 3. 4. and *there w.* the hiding of his power
2 *Cor.* 8. 11. that as *there w.* a readiness to will

See NONE.

Behold there WAS.

Exod. 9. 7. *behold th. w.* not one of cattle of Isr. dead
Judg. 7. 13. *behold there w.* a man told a dream
14. 8. *behold there w.* a swarm of bees in the lion
1 *Sam.* 19. 16. *behold there w.* an image in the bed
1 *Kings* 19. 6. *behold there w.* a cake baken on coals
2 *Kings* 7. 5. *behold there w.* no man there, 10.
Zech. 5. 7. *behold there w.* lift up a talent of lead
Mat. 28. 2. *behold there w.* a great earthquake

WASH.

The Orientals were used to wash *the feet of strangers who came off a journey, because they commonly walked with their legs naked, and their feet only defended with a sandal. Thus Abraham* washed *the feet of three angels,* Gen. 18. 4. *The feet of Eliezer, Abraham's steward, and those that accompanied him, were* washed, *when they arrived at the house of Laban,* Gen. 24. 32. *And likewise those of Joseph's brethren, their feet were* washed, *when they came into Egypt,* Gen. 43. 24. *This office was commonly performed by servants and slaves.*

Our Lord Jesus, to give his apostles an example of humility, washed *their feet,* John 13. 5. After that, he poured water into a bason, and began to *wash* the disciples' feet. *This* washing, *as it was a servile employment, denoted our Saviour's humility, which Christians ought to imitate him in; and as it was such a particular act, it denoted his* washing *away their sins by his blood, as he himself told* Peter *in verse* 8. If I *wash* thee not, thou hast no part with me. Washing, *in Scripture, is frequently taken in this sense, as in* Psal. 51. 2, 7. *Wash* me throughly from mine iniquity; *that is,* "*Cleanse me from the guilt and defilement of sin by thy grace, and by the virtue of the blood of Christ;*" *which was signified by the ceremonial* washings *under the law. And our Saviour, in the forecited passage,* John 13. 10. *tells Peter,* He that is *washed,* needeth not save to *wash* his feet, but is clean every whit; *that is,* "*Those souls that are* washed *with my blood, their state is not to be renewed; they need not be justified a second time; yet in regard of the remainder of sin and lust that is in them, and will be so while they are in the world, and the temptations which every where lie before them, as snares for their feet, they will have need of a daily* washing, *by repentance, and fresh applications of their souls to my blood, by the repeated exercises of faith, according to their renewed and repeated acts of sin.*" See *also* 1 Cor. 6. 11. Tit. 3. 5. Rev. 1. 5.

Wash, *to purify, cleanse, and whiten. There were divers sorts of* washing, [1] *Natural,* Gen. 18. 4. [2] *Ceremonial,* Heb. 9. 10. [3] *Miraculous,* 2 Kings 5. 10, 13. [4] *Moral,* Psal. 26. 6. | 73. 13. [5] *Spiritual,* Psal. 51. 2. Ezek. 16. 9. [6] *Superstitious,* Mat. 15. 2. [7] *Sacramental,* Acts 22. 16. *Put for,* [1] *Plenty,* Job 29. 6. [2] *Pardon and sanctification,* 1 Cor. 6. 11. Rev. 1. 5. | 7. 14. [3] *Repentance,* Isa. 1. 16. [4] *Reformation,* Prov. 30. 12. To *wash* one's feet in butter, *Job* 29. 6. To *wash* one's clothes in wine, *Gen.* 49. 11. To *wash* one's feet in the blood of the wicked, *Psal.* 58. 10. *These are figurative and hyperbolical expressions, to signify the great abundance of butter, or wine, and the vengeance that the just obtain over the wicked.* To wash *the hands was a token of innocency,* Mat. 27. 24.

Gen. 18. 4. I pray you *w.* your feet, 19. 2. | 24. 32.
Exod. 2. 5. the daughter of Pharaoh came to *w.*
29. 4. Aaron and his sons thou shalt bring and *w.* them with water, 30. 19, 20, 21. | 40. 12.
Lev. 6. 27. shalt *w.* that whereon it was sprinkled
13. 54. *w.* the thing wherein the plague is
58. whatever thing of skin it be thou shalt *w.* it
14. 8. shave and *w.* himself in water, *Deut.* 23. 11.
9. *w.* his flesh in water, 15. 16. | 16. 4, 24. | 22. 6.
17. 16. if he *w.* not, he shall bear his iniquity
Deut. 21. 6. shall *w.* their hands over the heifer
Ruth 3. 3. *w.* thyself therefore and anoint thee
1 *Sam.* 25. 41. let thy handmaid be a serv. to *w.* feet
2 *Sam.* 11. 8. David said, go down and *w.* thy feet
2 *Kings* 5. 10. Elisha said, go *w.* in Jordan seven times
12. may I not *w.* in them and be clean?
13. when he saith to thee, *w.* and be clean?
2 *Chron.* 4. 6. lavers to *w.* in, sea for the priests to *w.* in
Job 9. 30. if I *w.* myself with snow-water and make
Psal. 26. 6. I will *w.* my hands in innocency
51. 2. *w.* me throughly from mine iniquity
7. *w.* me and I shall be whiter than snow
58. 10. he shall *w.* his feet in the blood of the wicked
Isa. 1. 16. *w.* ye, make you clean, put away evil
Jer. 2. 22. though thou *w.* thee with nitre and soap
4. 14. O Jerusalem, *w.* thy heart from wickedness
Ezek. 23. 40. for whom thou didst *w.* thyself
Mat. 6. 17. but when thou fastest, *w.* thy face
15. 2. they *w.* not their hands when they eat
Mark 7. 3. except they *w.* oft they eat not, 4.

Luke 7. 38. a woman began to *w.* his feet with tears
John 9. 7. Jesus said, go *w.* in the pool of Siloam, 11.
13. 5. Jesus began to *w.* the disciples' feet
6. Peter saith, Lord, dost thou *w.* my feet?
8. thou shalt never *w.* my feet, if I *w.* thee not
14. ye also ought to *w.* one another's feet
Acts 22. 16. arise, be baptized, and *w.* away thy sins

See CLOTHES, FEET.

WASHED.

Gen. 43. 24. gave them water, they *w.* their feet
31. Joseph *w.* his face and went out and said
49. 11. Judah *w.* his garments in wine and clothes
Exod. 40. 32. *w.* as the Lord commanded Moses
Lev. 13. 55. priest shall look on plague after it is *w.*
58. then it shall be *w.* the second time and be clean
Judg. 19. 21. the Levite and concubine *w.* their feet
2 *Sam.* 12. 20. then David arose and *w.* himself
1 *Kings* 22. 38. one *w.* the chariot in pool of Samaria
Job 29. 6. when I *w.* my steps with butter
Psal. 73. 13. I have *w.* my hands in innocency
Prov. 30. 12. a generation not *w.* from filthiness
Cant. 5. 3. I have *w.* my feet, how shall I defile them?
12. his eyes are *w.* with milk and fitly set
Isa. 4. 4. *w.* away the filth of the daughters of Zion
Ezek. 16. 4. nor wast *w.* in water to supple thee
9. I throughly *w.* away thy blood from thee
Mat. 27. 24. Pilate took water and *w.* his hands
Luke 7. 44. she hath *w.* my feet with her tears
11. 38. the Pharisee marvelled he had not first *w.*
John 9. 7. he went and *w.* and came seeing, 11, 15.
13. 10. is *w.* needeth not save to wash his feet
14. if I your Lord and Master have *w.* your feet
Acts 9. 37. Dorcas died, whom when they had *w.*
16. 33. he took them, *w.* their stripes, was baptized
1 *Cor.* 6. 11. but ye are *w.* but ye are sanctified
1 *Tim.* 5. 10. if she have *w.* the saints' feet
Heb. 10. 22. having our bodies *w.* with pure water
2 *Pet.* 2. 22. sow that was *w.* to wallowing in the mire
Rev. 1. 5. that *w.* us from our sins in his blood
7. 14. have *w.* their robes and made them white

See CLOTHES.

WASHEST.

Job 14. 19. thou *w.* away the things which grow

WASHING.

2 *Sam.* 11. 2. David saw a woman *w.* herself
Luke 5. 2. but the fishermen were *w.* their nets

WASHING, S.

Lev. 13. 56. the plague be somewhat dark after *w.*
Neh. 4. 23. that every one put them off for *w.*
Cant. 4. 2. like sheep which came up from the *w.* 6. 6.
Mark 7. 4. as the *w.* of cups, pots, and tables, 8.
Eph. 5. 26. cleanse it with *w.* of water by word
Tit. 3. 5. he saved us by the *w.* of regeneration
Heb. 9. 10. which stood only in meats and divers *w.*

WASH-POT.

Ps. 60. 8. Moab is my *w.* over Edom cast shoe, 108. 9.

WAST.

Deut. 5. 15. thou *w.* a servant in land of Egypt
15. 15. *w.* a bondman in Egypt, 16. 12. | 24. 18, 22.
23. 7. because thou *w.* a stranger in his land
2 *Sam.* 5. 2. thou *w.* he that leddest out Israel
Job 38. 4. where *w.* when I laid foundations of earth?
Jer. 50. 24. thou art taken and *w.* not aware
Ezek. 16. 6. I said to thee, when thou *w.* in thy blood
Obad. 11. even thou *w.* as one of them
Mat. 26. 69. a damsel came to Peter, saying, thou also *w.* with Jesus of Galilee, *Mark* 14. 67.
John 1. 48. when thou *w.* under fig-tree, I saw thee
Rev. 11. 17. who art, and *w.* and art to come, 16. 5.

WASTE.

Jer. 49. 13. have sworn that Bozrah shall become *w.*
Mat. 26. 8. to what purpose is this *w.*? *Mark* 14. 4.

WASTE.

Deut. 32. 10. he found him in the *w.* wilderness
Job 30. 3. solitary, fleeing into the *w.* wilderness
38. 27. to satisfy the desolate *w.* ground and cause
Isa. 24. 1. behold, the Lord maketh the earth *w.*
42. 15. I will make *w.* mountains and hills
49. 17. they that made the *w.* shall go forth
Jer. 2. 15. young lions yelled and made his land *w.*
46. 19. for Noph shall be *w.* and desolate
Ezek. 5. 14. I will make Jerusalem *w.* and a reproach
29. 9. the land of Egypt shall be *w.* 10. | 30. 12.
38. 8. the mountains which have been always *w.*
Nah. 2. 10. Nineveh is empty, and void and *w.*
Zeph. 3. 6. I have made their streets *w.* none passeth
Hag. 1. 9. because of mine house that is *w.*

See CITIES, LAY, LAID, PLACES.

WASTE.

1 *Kings* 17. 14. the barrel of meal shall not *w.*
1 *Chron.* 17. 9. no children of wickedness *w.* them
Psal. 17. † 9. hide me from the wicked that *w.* me
80. 13. the boar out of the wood doth *w.* it
Jer. 50. 21. *w.* inhabitants of Pekod saith the Lord
Mic. 5. 6. they shall *w.* land of Assyria with sword

WASTED.

Num. 14. 33. till your carcases be *w.* in wilderness
24. 22. nevertheless the Kenite shall be *w.*
Deut. 2. 14. till all generat. of men of war were *w.*
1 *Kings* 17. 16. and the barrel of meal *w.* not
1 *Chron.* 20. 1. Joab *w.* the country of Ammon
Psal. 137. 3. they that *w.* us required of us mirth
† 8. O daughter of Babylon, who art to be *w.*
Isa. 6. 11. till the cities be *w.* without inhabitant
19. 5. and the river shall be *w.* and dried up
60. 12. yea, those nations shall be utterly *w.*
Jer. 44. 6. are *w.* and desolate as at this day
Joel 1. 10. field is *w.* corn is *w.* new wine dried up
Luke 15. 13. the prodigal son *w.* his substance
16. 1. was accused that he had *w.* his goods
Gal. 1. 13. how I persecuted the church and *w.* it

WASTENESS.

Zeph. 1. 15. a day of *w.* desolation and darkness

WASTER.

Prov. 18. 9. is brother to him that is a great *w.*
Isa. 54. 16. I have created the *w.* to destroy

WASTES.

Isa. 44. † 26. I will raise up the *w.* thereof
61. 4. they shall build the old *w.* and repair cities
Jer. 49. 13. the cities of Bozrah shall be perpetual *w.*
Ezek. 33. 24. they that inhabit those *w.* of Israel
27. surely they in the *w.* shall fall by the sword

Ezek. 36. 4. thus saith the Lord to the desolate *w.*
10. and the *w.* shall be builded, 33.

WASTETH.

Job 14. 10. man dieth and *w.* away, giveth up ghost
Ps. 91. 6. nor for destruction that *w.* at noon-day
Prov. 19. 26. he that *w.* father and chaseth mother

WASTING.

Isa. 59. 7. *w.* and destruction are in their paths
60. 18. not heard *w.* nor destruction in thy borders

WATCH.

Exod. 14. 24. in morning *w.* L. looked to Egyptians
Judg. 7. 19. middle *w.* they had but newly set the *w.*
1 *Sam.* 11. 11. Saul came in the morning-*w.*
2 *Kings* 11. 6. so shall ye keep the *w.* of the house, that it be not broken down, 7. 2 *Chron.* 23. 6.
Neh. 4. 9. prayed to God, and set a *w.* against them
7. 3. every one in his *w.* and over-against his house
Job 7. 12. am I a sea, that thou settest a *w.* over me?
Psal. 90. 4. a thousand years as a *w.* in the night
141. 3. set a *w.* O Lord, before my mouth
Jer. 51. 12. make the *w.* strong, set up watchmen
Hab. 2. 1. I will stand upon my *w.* and will watch
Mat. 14. 25. in the fourth *w.* of the night Jesus went to them walking on the sea, *Mark* 6. 48.
24. 43. had known what *w.* the thief would come
27. 65. ye have a *w.* || 66. sealing stone, setting a *w.*
28. 11. behold, some of the *w.* came into the city
Luke 2. 8. the shepherds keeping *w.* over their flock
12. 38. if he shall come in the second *w.* or third

WATCHES.

Neh. 12. 9. their brethren over-against them in *w.*
Ps. 63. 6. when I meditate on thee in the night-*w.*
119. 148. mine eyes prevent the night-*w.*
Lam. 2. 19. in beginning of the *w.* pour out thy heart

WATCH, *Verb.*

Gen. 31. 49. the Lord *w.* between me and thee
1 *Sam.* 19. 11. Saul sent to *w.* David, and slay him
Ezra 8. 29. *w.* ye, keep vessels till ye weigh them
Job 14. 16. dost thou not *w.* over my sin?
Ps. 102. 7. I *w.* and am as a sparrow on house-top
130. 6. more than they that *w.* for morning, 6.
Isa. 21. 5. *w.* in the watch-tower, eat, drink
29. 20. and all that *w.* for iniquity are cut off
Jer. 5. 6. a leopard shall *w.* over their cities
31. 28. so will I *w.* over them to build and plant
44. 27. I will *w.* over them for evil, not for good
Nah. 2. 1. keep the munition, *w.* the way
Hab. 2. 1. I will *w.* to see what he will say to me
Mat. 24. 42. *w.* therefore, ye know not the hour, 25. 13. *Mark* 13. 35. *Luke* 21. 36. *Acts* 20. 31.
26. 38. Jesus said, tarry ye here, and *w.* with me
40. could ye not *w.* with me? *Mark* 14. 34, 37.
41. *w.* and pray, *Mark* 13. 33. | 14. 38. *Col.* 4. 2.
Mark 13. 34. who commanded the porter to *w.*
37. and what I say unto you, I say unto all, *w.*
1 *Cor.* 16. 13. *w.* ye, stand fast in faith, be strong
1 *Thess.* 5. 6. let us *w.* and be sober, 1 *Pet.* 4. 7.
2 *Tim.* 4. 5. *w.* thou in all things, endure afflictions
Heb. 13. 17. obey them, for they *w.* for your souls

WATCHED.

Jer. 20. 10. all my familiars *w.* for my halting
31. 28. like as I have *w.* over them to pluck up
Lam. 4. 17. *w.* for a nation that could not save us
Dan. 9. 14. Lord *w.* on evil, and brought it on us
Mat. 24. 43. good-man would have *w.* *Luke* 12. 39.
27. 36. and sitting down they *w.* him there
Mark 3. 2. they *w.* him whether he would heal him the sabbath-day, to accuse him, *Luke* 6. 7. | 14. 1.
Luke 20. 20. they *w.* him and sent forth spies
Acts 9. 24. *w.* the gates day and night to kill him

WATCHER, S.

Jer. 4. 16. published that *w.* come from far country
Dan. 4. 13. a *w.* and an holy one came from heaven
17. by decree of the *w.* || 23. the king saw a *w.*

WATCHETH.

Ps. 37. 32. the wicked *w.* the righteous, and seeketh
Ezek. 7. 6. end is come, it *w.* for thee, it is come
Rev. 16. 15. blessed is he that *w.* and keepeth garm.

WATCHFUL.

Rev. 3. 2. be *w.* strengthen the things that remain

WATCHING.

1 *Sam.* 4. 13. Eli sat on a seat by the way-side *w.*
Prov. 8. 34. blessed heareth me, *w.* daily at my gates
Lam. 4. 17. in our *w.* we have watched for a nation
Mat. 27. 54. the centurion *w.* Jesus, saw earth-quake
Luke 12. 37. whom Lord when he cometh find *w.*
Eph. 6. 18. praying and *w.* with all perseverance

WATCHINGS.

2 *Cor.* 6. 5. in tumults, in labours, in *w.* in fastings
11. 27. in *w.* often, in hunger, thirst, fastings

WATCHMAN.

2 *Sam.* 18. 25. the *w.* cried, and told the king
26. the *w.* saw another man running alone
2 *Kings* 9. 18. the *w.* told, he cometh not again, 20.
Psal. 127. 1. keeps city, the *w.* waketh but in vain
Isa. 21. 6. go set a *w.* || 11. *w.* what of the night?
Jer. 51. 12. set up the *w.* prepare the ambushes
Ezek. 3. 17. son of man, I have made thee a *w.* 33. 7.
33. 2. if the people set him up for their *w.*
Hos. 9. 8. the *w.* of Ephraim was with my God

WATCHMEN.

Cant. 3. 3. *w.* that go about the city found me, 5. 7.
Isa. 52. 8. thy *w.* shall lift up the voice, shall sing
56. 10. his *w.* are blind, they are all ignorant
62. 6. I have set *w.* on thy walls, O Jerusalem
Jer. 6. 17. also I set *w.* over you, saying, hearken
31. 6. *w.* on mount Ephraim shall cry, arise ye
Mic. 7. 4. the day of thy *w.* and visitation cometh

WATCH-TOWER.

2 *Chron.* 20. 24. when Judah came toward the *w.*
Isa. 21. 5. watch in the *w.* eat, drink, arise
8. I stand continually on the *w.* in day time
32. † 14. the *w.* shall be for dens for ever

WATER.

Or waters, *in Scripture, is put,* (1) *For the element of* water, *Gen.* 1. 10. (2) *For troubles and afflictions.* Psal. 69. 1. Save me, O God, for the *waters* are come in unto my soul. *Often in the Psalms and elsewhere it is used in this sense: hence is the phrase in* Mat. 20. 22. *of being baptized with* Christ's baptism; *that is,* "*dipped and plunged in afflictions, as he was.*" (3) *In the language of the prophets,* waters *often denote a great multitude of people.* Isa. 8. 7. The Lord bringeth upon them the *waters* of the river; *that is, the Assyrian army. And in* Rev. 17. 15. The *waters* which thou sawest, where the whore sitteth, are peoples, and multitudes, and nations, and tongues. (4) *It is put for children or posterity.* Num. 24. 7. He shall pour the *water* out of his buckets. *And in* Isa. 48. 1. Which are come forth out of the *waters* of Judah. (5) *For the clouds.* Psal. 104. 3. Who layeth the beams of his chambers in the waters. "*Who founded, as it were, the heavens upon the clouds.*" (6) Waters *sometimes stand for* tears. *Jer.* 9. 1. O that my head were *waters,* and mine eyes a fountain of tears. (7) *For the doctrines of the gospel,* Deut. 32. 2. 1 Cor. 3. 6. (8) *For the ordinances of the gospel, where the graces and comforts of the Holy Spirit are dispensed.* Isa. 55. 1. Ho, every one that thirsteth, come to the *waters. Or by* waters *here may be understood the graces and comforts of the Spirit themselves, which are frequently compared to* waters, *as in* Isa. 12. 3. | 35. 6, 7. John 7. 37, 38. (9) *All kinds of drink,* Exod. 23. 25. (10) *Unlawful pleasures,* Prov. 9. 17.

As in Scripture, bread *is put for all sorts of food, or solid nourishment, so* water *is used for all sorts of drink. The Moabites and Ammonites are reproached for not meeting the Israelites with* bread *and* water, *that is, with proper refreshments,* Deut. 23. 4. *Nabal says, in an insulting manner, to David's messengers,* Shall I then take my bread and my *water,* and my flesh that I have killed for my shearers, and give it unto men whom I know not whence they be? 1 *Sam.* 25. 11. Stolen waters *denote unlawful pleasures with strange women,* Prov. 9. 17. *The Israelites are upbraided for having forsaken the fountain of* living waters, *and hewing out broken cisterns; that is, for having quitted the worship of God for the worship of idols and false gods,* Jer. 2. 13. *The Hebrews called urine,* the *waters* of the feet, that they may drink their own piss; *in Hebrew, the water of their feet,* 2 Kings 18. 27.

The *waters* of Meribah, *so called because of the quarrelling, the contention, and murmuring, of the Israelites against Moses and against God. Moses tells us, that when the Israelites came to Kadesh, and there happened to be in want of* water, *they raised a sedition against him and his brother Aaron; this is recorded in* Num. 20. 1, 2, 3, &c. *It was on this occasion that Moses committed that sin, with which God was so displeased, that he deprived him of the honour of introducing his people into the land of promise. The Psalmist, in* Psal. 106. 32, 33, *tells us, that Moses was soured, vexed, or troubled at these murmurs of the people, and expressed some distrust by his words. He shewed some doubt in the promises of the Lord. God had absolutely promised him, that he should bring* water *out of the rock. Moses made some scruple to believe it;* Must we fetch you *water* out of this rock? *He struck the rock twice: and God had bid him only speak to it. He was afraid, that upon this occasion, God being provoked with his people, should refuse to fulfil the promises he had made. Moses and Aaron did not* sanctify the Lord, *they did not pay that honour that was due to him, by a strict, punctual, and faithful obedience to his words. They did not* sanctify him before the people. *They gave the people occasion to conceive too low an idea of the power and goodness of God; they did an injury in some measure to his power, by shewing so little confidence in it.*

Gen. 16. 7. angel found Hagar by a fountain of *w.*
18. 4. let a little *w.* I pray you, be fetched
21. 14. Abraham took bottle of *w.* and gave Hagar
24. 32. Laban gave the man *w.* to wash his feet
43. give me, I pray thee, a little *w.* to drink
26. 20. the *w.* is ours || 32. we have found *w.*
43. 24. the steward of Joseph's house gave them *w.*
49. 4. unstable as *w.* thou shalt not excel
Exod. 12. 9. eat it not raw, nor sodden with *w.*
17. 6. and there shall come *w.* out of the rock
20. 4. any likeness that is in the *w.* under the earth
23. 25. the Lord shall bless thy bread and thy *w.*
29. 4. Aaron and his sons shall wash them with *w.* 30. 20. | 40. 12. *Lev.* 8. 6. | 16. 4, 24.
32. 20. burnt the calf and strawed it on the *w.*
Lev. 6. 28. shall be scoured and rinsed in *w.* 15. 12.
11. 32. whatever vessel, it must be put into *w.*
38. but if any *w.* be put upon the seed
Num. 5. 22. this *w.* that causeth the curse shall go
8. 7. sprinkle *w.* of purification upon them
19. 9. for a *w.* of separation, 13, 20, 21. | 31. 23.
20. 8. thou shalt bring forth to them *w.* out of the rock, 10, 11. *Neh.* 9. 15. *Psal.* 114. 8.
13. this is the *w.* of Meribah, 24. | 27. 14.
21. 5. there is no bread, nor is any *w.*
16. gather ye the people and I will give them *w.*
24. 7. he shall pour the *w.* out of his buckets
31. 23. ye shall make go through the *w.*
Deut. 8. 7. Lord brings thee to a land of brooks of *w.*
11. 11. the land drinketh *w.* of rain of heaven
12. 16. shalt pour it on earth as *w.* 24. | 15. 23.
23. 4. met you not with *w.* in way, *Neh.* 13. 2.
Josh. 7. 5. hearts of people melted and became as *w.*
Judg. 5. 25. he asked *w.* and she gave him milk
7. 4. bring them down to the *w.* and I will try, 5.
15. 19. *w.* came out of the jaw and Samson drank
1 *Sam.* 7. 6. they gathered to Mizpeh and drew *w.*
25. 11. shall I then take my bread and my *w.?*
26. 11. take now the cruse of *w.* and let us go
30. 12. nor drunk any *w.* three days and nights
2 *Sam.* 14. 14. we must die and are as *w.* on ground
17. 21. arise and pass quickly over the *w.*
21. 10. till *w.* dropped on them out of heaven
1 *Kings* 13. 19. he did eat bread and drank *w.*
22. hast eaten bread and drunk *w.* in the place
14. 15. smite Israel as a reed is shaken in the *w.*
17. 10. fetch me, I pray thee, a little *w.*
18. 4. Obadiah fed them with bread and *w.* 13.
1 *Kings* 18. 35. *w.* ran about altar, fill. trench with *w.*
38. the fire of the Lord fell and licked up the *w.*
22. 27. feed him with bread and *w.* of affliction till I return in peace, 2 *Chron.* 18. 26.
2 *Kings* 2. 19. the *w.* is naught, and ground barren
3. 11. Elisha who poured *w.* on Elijah's hands
17. yet that valley shall be filled with *w.*
22. then rose up early and the sun shone on the *w.*
6. 5. was felling a beam, the ax-head fell into *w.*
22. set bread and *w.* before them to eat and drink
8. 15. he dipt a thick cloth in *w.* and he died
20. 20. made a conduit, brought *w.* into the city
2 *Chron.* 32. 4. the king of Assyria find much *w.*
Neh. 4. † 23. every one went with weapon for *w.*
Job 8. 11. can the flag grow without *w.?*
14. 9. yet through the scent of *w.* it will bud
15. 16. is man who drinketh iniquity like *w.*
22. 7. thou hast not given *w.* to the weary to drink
34. 7. who like Job, who drinketh scorning like *w.*
Psal. 22. 14. I am poured out like *w.* my bones out
63. † 10. they shall make him run out like *w.*
65. 9. with the river of God that is full of *w.*
66. 12. we went through fire and through *w.*
79. 3. their blood have they shed like *w.*
88. 17. they came round about me daily like *w.*
109. 18. so let it come into his bowels like *w.*
Prov. 17. 14. strife is as when one letteth out *w.*
20. 5. counsel in the heart of man is like deep *w.*
27. 19. as in *w.* face answereth to face, so heart of
30. 16. the earth that is not filled with *w.*
Isa. 1. 22. silver is dross, thy wine mixed with *w.*
3. 1. Lord doth take away the whole stay of *w.*
21. 14. the land of Tema brought *w.* to the thirsty
30. 14. not found a sherd to take *w.* out of pit
20. though the Lord gave you the *w.* of affliction
41. 17. when the poor seek *w.* and there is none
44. 3. I will pour *w.* on him that is thirsty
63. 12. led them, dividing the *w.* before them
Jer. 13. 1. get a linen girdle and put it not in *w.*
23. 15. and make them drink the *w.* of gall
Lam. 1. 16. mine eyes run down with *w.* 3. 48.
2. 19. pour out thy heart like *w.* before Lord
5. 4. we have drunken our *w.* for money
Ezek. 4. 17. that they may want bread and *w.*
7. 17. all knees shall be weak as *w.* 21. 7.
16. 4. nor wast thou washed in *w.* to supple thee
9. then washed I thee with *w.* and anointed him
36. 25. then will I sprinkle clean *w.* upon you
Hos. 2. 5. I will go after my lov. that give me my *w.*
5. 10. I will pour my wrath upon them like *w.*
10. 7. her king is cut off as foam upon *w.*
Amos 8. 11. not a famine of bread nor thirst of *w.*
Nah. 2. 8. but Nineveh is of old like a pool of *w.*
Hab. 3. 10. the overflowing of the *w.* passed by
Mat. 3. 11. I indeed baptize you with *w.* unto repentance, *Mark* 1. 8. *Luke* 3. 16. *John* 1. 26.
16. Jesus went up out of the *w.* *Mark* 1. 10.
10. 42. whoso giveth a cup of cold *w.* *Mark* 9. 41.
14. 28. Peter said, bid me come to thee on the *w.*
17. 15. for he falleth oft into the fire and *w.*
27. 24. Pilate took *w.* and washed his hands
Mark 14. 13. there shall meet you a man bearing a pitcher of *w.* follow him, *Luke* 22. 10.
Luke 8. 23. ship was filled with *w.* were in jeopardy
24. rebuked the *w.* || 25. the *w.* obeyed him
16. 24. that he may dip the tip of his finger in *w.*
John 2. 7. Jesus saith, fill the water-pots with *w.*
3. 5. except a man be born of *w.* and of the Spirit
23. near to Salim, because there was much *w.* there
4. 10. given living *w.* 11. || 15. give me this *w.*
46. Jesus came again where he made *w.* wine
5. 3. halt, withered, waiting for moving of the *w.*
4. an angel went down and troubled the *w.*
7. 38. out of his belly shall flow living *w.*
13. 5. after that he poureth *w.* into a bason
19. 34. forthwith came thereout blood and *w.*
Acts 1. 5. for John truly baptized with *w.* 11. 16.
8. 36. here is *w.* || 38. they went down both into *w.*
10. 47. can any forbid *w.* these be not baptized?
Eph. 5. 26. might cleanse it with the washing of *w.*
Heb. 9. 19. he took the blood of calves with *w.*
10. 22. and our bodies washed with pure *w.*
Jam. 3. 12. no fountain can yield salt *w.* and fresh
1 *Pet.* 3. 20. few, that is eight souls were saved by *w.*
2 *Pet.* 2. 17. are wells without *w.* || *Jude* 12. clouds
3. 6. world being overflowed with *w.* perished
1 *John* 5. 6. this is he that came by *w.* and blood
5. 8. three bear witness, Spirit, *w.* and blood
Rev. 12. 15. and the serpent cast out of his mouth *w.*
16. 12. the sixth on Euphrates, and *w.* dried up
21. 6. I will give of the fountain of the *w.* of life
22. 1. and he shewed me a pure river of *w.* of life
17. whosoever will, let him take *w.* of life freely
See Bathe, Bitter, Draw, Drew, Drink, Well.

No WATER.

Gen. 37. 24. pit was empty, there was *no w.* in it
Exod. 15. 22. they went three days and found *no w.* 17. 1. *Num.* 20. 2. | 33. 14. *Deut.* 8. 15.
1 *Kings* 13. 22. L. said, eat no bread and drink *no w.*
2 *Kings* 3. 9. there was *no w.* for the host and cattle
Psal. 63. 1. in a dry and thirsty land where *no w.* is
Isa. 1. 30. ye shall be as a garden that hath *no w.*
44. 12. the smith drinketh *no w.* and is faint
50. 2. their fish stinketh because there is *no w.*
Jer. 2. 13. broken cisterns that can hold *no w.*
14. 3. they came to the pits and found *no w.*
38. 6. in the dungeon there was *no w.* but mire
Zech. 9. 11. sent prisoners out of pit wherein is *no w.*
Luke 7. 44. thou gavest me *no w.* for my feet

WATER.

Gen. 2. 10. a river went out of Eden to *w.* the garden
29. 7. *w.* ye the sheep and go and feed them, 8.
Psal. 6. 6. I *w.* my couch with my tears
72. 6. come down as showers that *w.* the earth
Prov. 5. † 19. let her breasts *w.* thee at all times
Eccl. 2. 6. I made me pools of water to *w.* the wood
Isa. 16. 9. I will *w.* thee with my tears, O Heshbon
27. 3. I will *w.* it every moment, lest any hurt it
Ezek. 17. 7. he might *w.* it by furrows of plantation
32. 6. I will *w.* with my blood the land wherein
Joel 3. 18. a fountain shall *w.* the valley of Shittim

WATERED.

Gen. 2. 6. a mist that *w.* the face of the ground
13. 10. the plain of Jordan, that it was well *w.*
29. 2. of that well they *w.* flocks, 3. || 10. Jacob *w.*
Exod. 2. 17. Moses helped and *w.* their flocks, 19.
Prov. 11. 25. he that watereth shall be *w.* himself
Isa. 58. 11. and thou shalt be like a *w.* garden
Jer. 31. 12. their soul shall be as a *w.* garden
1 *Cor.* 3. 6. I have planted, Apollos *w.* but God gave

WATEREDST.

Deut. 11. 10. *w.* it with thy foot as a garden of herbs

WATEREST.

Psal. 65. 9. thou visitest the earth and *w.* it
10. thou *w.* the ridges thereof abundantly

WATERETH.

Psal. 104. 13. he *w.* the hills from his chambers
Prov. 11. 25. he that *w.* shall be watered himself
Isa. 55. 10. rain returneth not, but *w.* the earth
1 *Cor.* 3. 7. nor he that planteth, nor *w.* any thing, 8.

WATERING.

Gen. 30. 38. Jacob laid rods in the *w.* troughs
Job 37. 11. by *w.* he wearieth the thick clouds
Prov. 3. † 8. it shall be *w.* to thy bones
Luke 13. 15. doth not each of you lead his ass to *w.?*

WATER-BROOKS.

Psal. 42. 1. as the hart panteth after the *w.*

WATER-COURSE.

2 *Chron.* 32. 30. Hezekiah stopped the upper *w.*
Job 38. 25. who hath divided a *w.* for overflowing

WATER-COURSES.

Isa. 44. 4. they shall spring as willows by the *w.*

WATER-FLOOD.

Psal. 69. 15. let not the *w.* overflow me, nor deep

WATER-POT, WATER-POTS.

John 2. 6. there were set there six *w.* of stone
7. Jesus saith, fill the *w.* with water, they filled
4. 28. the woman then left her *w.* and went to city

WATER-SPOUTS.

Psal. 42. 7. deep calls to deep at noise of thy *w.*

WATER-SPRINGS.

Psal. 107. 33. he turneth the *w.* into dry ground
35. he turneth dry ground into *w.*

WATERS.

Gen. 1. 2. the Spirit of God moved upon face of *w.*
6. let the firmament divide the *w.* from the *w.* 7.
9. let the *w.* be gathered || 20. *w.* bring forth
6. 17. I, even I, do bring a flood of *w.* on earth
7. 17. *w.* increased || 18. *w.* prevailed, 19, 20, 24.
8. 1. *w.* decreased, 3, 5. || 13. *w.* were dried up
9. 11. not be cut off any more by *w.* of a flood
Exod. 7. 17. behold, I will smite the *w.* || 20. *w.* blood
8. 6. Aaron stretched out his hand over the *w.*
14. 21. by a strong east-wind the *w.* were divided
22. *w.* were a wall, 29. || 28. *w.* returned, 15. 19.
15. 8. the *w.* were gathered together, flood stood
23. they could not drink of the *w.* of Marah
27. come to Elim, they encamped there by the *w.*
Num. 24. 6. as trees planted, as cedar trees beside *w.*
Deut. 10. 7. journeyed to Jotbath, land of rivers of *w.*
32. 51. ye trespassed at the *w.* of Meribah-kadesh
33. 8. with whom didst strive at the *w.* of Meribah
Josh. 3. 16. the *w.* which came down rose up
4. 7. the *w.* of Jordan were cut off before the ark
23. the Lord dried up the *w.* of Jordan, 5. 1.
11. 5. they came and pitched at the *w.* of Merom
Judg. 5. 19. the kings of Canaan by *w.* of Megiddo
7. 24. come down and take the *w.* before them
2 *Sam.* 5. 20. the Lord hath broken forth as a breach of *w.* upon mine enemies, 1 *Chron.* 14. 11.
12. 27. and Joab said, I have taken the city of *w.*
2 *Kings* 2. 8. and Elijah smote the *w.* || 14. Elisha
21. and he went forth unto the spring of the *w.* thus saith Lord, I have healed these *w.*
5. 12. are not rivers of Damasc. better than *w.* of Isr.
2 *Chron.* 32. 3. he took counsel to stop the *w.*
Job 3. 24. my roarings are poured out like the *w.*
5. 10. who sendeth *w.* upon the fields
11. 16. remember thy misery as *w.* that pass away
12. 15. he withholdeth the *w.* and they dry up
14. 11. as the *w.* fail from the sea, and the flood
19. the *w.* wear the stones, thou washest away
22. 11. and abundance of *w.* cover thee, 38. 34.
24. 18. he is swift as the *w.* thou washest away
26. 5. dead things are formed from under the *w.*
8. he bindeth up the *w.* in his thick clouds
10. he hath compassed the *w.* with clouds
27. 20. terrors take hold on him as *w.* a tempest
28. 4. even the *w.* forgotten of the foot
25. and he weigheth the *w.* by measure
29. 19. my root was spread out by the *w.*
30. 14. came upon me as a wide breaking in of *w.*
37. 10. and the breadth of the *w.* is straitened
38. 30. the *w.* are hid as with a stone
Psal. 23. 2. he leadeth me beside the still *w.*
33. 7. he gathereth the *w.* of the seas together
46. 3. though the *w.* thereof roar and be troubled
58. 7. let them melt away as *w.* which run
69. 1. for the *w.* are come in unto my soul
73. 10. *w.* of a full cup are wrung out to them
77. 16. the *w.* saw thee, O God, the *w.* saw thee
78. 13. he made the *w.* to stand as an heap
16. and caused *w.* to run down like rivers
20. he smote the rock that the *w.* gushed out and streams overflowed, 105. 41. | 114. 8. *Isa.* 48. 21.
81. 7. I proved thee at the *w.* of Meribah, 106. 32.
104. 6. the *w.* stood above the mountains
105. 29. he turned their *w.* into blood and slew
106. 11. and the *w.* covered their enemies
119. 136. rivers of *w.* run down mine eyes because
124. 4. then the *w.* had overwhelmed us
5. then the proud *w.* had gone over our soul
136. 6. him that stretched the earth above the *w.*
147. 18. he causeth the wind to blow and *w.* flow
148. 4. ye *w.* above the heavens, praise him
Prov. 5. 15. drink *w.* out of thine own cistern
16. let rivers of *w.* be dispersed in the streets
8. 29. that the *w.* should not pass his commandment
9. 17. stolen *w.* are sweet, and bread eaten in secret
25. 25. as cold *w.* to a thirsty soul, so is good news
30. 4. who hath bound the *w.* in a garment
Eccl. 11. 1. cast thy bread upon *w.* thou shalt find
Cant. 4. 15. a well of living *w.* and streams from Leb.

Isa. 8. 6. as this people refuseth the w. of Shiloah
7. the Lord bringeth on them w. of the river
11. 9. as the w. cover the seas, Hab. 2. 14.
15. 6. for the w. of Nimrim shall be desolate
9. for the w. of Dimon shall be full of blood
17. 12. a rushing like the rushing of mighty w.
19. 5. and the w. shall fail from the sea
22. 9. and ye gathered the w. of the lower pool
28. 17. the w. shall overflow the hiding-place
32. 20. blessed are ye that sow beside all w.
33. 16. bread be given him, his w. shall be sure
35. 6. for in the wilderness shall w. break forth
40. 12. who hath measured the w. in his hand
43. 2. if thou pass through w. I will be with thee
16. and maketh a path in the mighty w.
20. I give w. in the wilderness and rivers in desert
48. 1. and are come forth out of the w. of Judah
21. he caused the w. to flow out of the rock
51. 10. which hath dried the w. of the great deep
54. 9. this is as w. of Noah unto me, w. not return
55. 1. ho every one that thirsteth, come ye to the w.
57. 20. like the sea, whose w. cast up mire and dirt
58. 11. like a spring of water, whose w. fail not
Jer. 2. 13. have forsaken me the fountain of living w.
18. what hast thou to do, to drink the w. of Sihor?
6. 7. as a fountain casteth out her w. so casteth out
8. 14. God hath given us w. of gall to drink
9. 1. O that my head were w. and mine eyes tears
18. eyes run with tears, eye lids gush out with w.
10. 13. is a multitude of w. in the heavens, 51. 16.
14. 3. their nobles sent little ones to the w.
15. 18. wilt be to me as a liar and as w. that fail
17. 8. he shall be as a tree planted by the w.
13. have forsaken the Lord, fountain of living w.
18. 14. shall the cold flowing w. be forsaken?
46. 7. whose w. are moved as the rivers, 8.
47. 2. behold, w. rise up out of the north
48. 34. for the w. of Nimrim shall be desolate
50. 38. a drought is upon her w. and shall be dried
Lam. 3. 54. w. flowed over mine head, I am cut off
Ezek. 19. 10. thy mother is like a vine by the w.
31. 4. w. made him great, the deep set him on high
14. that none of the trees by w. exalt themselves
32. 2. and troublest the w. with thy feet
47. 1. behold, w. issued from under the threshold
3. brought me through w. the w. were to ancles, 4.
5. for the w. were risen, w. to swim in
8. these w. issue out toward the east country, 12.
19. even to the w. of strife in Kadesh, 48. 28.
Dan. 12. 6. one said to the man upon the w. 7.
Amos 5. 8. calleth for w. of sea, and poureth, 9. 6.
24. but let judgment run down as w. and righte.
Jonah 2. 5. the w. compassed me about to the soul
Mic. 1. 4. as w. that are poured down a steep place
Nah. 3. 8. No, that had the w. round about it
14. draw the w. for the siege, fortify thy holds
Zech. 14. 8. living w. shall go from Jerusalem
2 Cor. 11. 26. in perils of w. in perils of robbers
Rev. 7. 17. lead them unto living fountains of w.
8. 11. a third part of the w. became wormwood, and many died of the w. because bitter
11. 6. have power over w. to turn them to blood
14. 7. worship him that made the fountain of w.
16. 4. and the third angel poured his vial on the w.
5. I heard angel of the w. say, thou art righteous
17. 15. the w. where the whore sits, are peoples

See DEEP, GREAT.

In, or into WATERS.

Exod. 15. 10. they sank as lead in the mighty w.
25. a tree when cast into the w. they were sweet
Lev. 11. 9. these shall ye eat, of all that are in w.
what hath fins and scales in w. 10. 46. Deut. 14. 9.
12. hath no fins nor scales in the w. unclean
Deut. 4. 18. the likeness of any fish in the w. 5. 8.
Josh. 3. 13. as the feet of priests rest in the w.
Neh. 9. 11. threwest a stone into the mighty w.
Psal. 74. 13. breakest the heads of dragons in w.
104. 3. layeth the beams of his chambers in w.
Mat. 8. 32. the swine ran and perished in the w.
Mark 9. 22. oft it cast him into fire and into w.

Many WATERS.

Num. 24. 7. and his seed shall be in many w.
2 Sam. 22. 17. drew me out of many w. Psal. 18. 16.
Psal. 29. 3. the voice of the Lord is upon many w.
93. 4. Lord mightier than the noise of many w.
Cant. 8. 7. many w. cannot quench love, nor floods
Isa. 17. 13. nations like the rushing of many w.
Jer. 51. 13. O thou that dwellest upon many w.
Ezek. 19. 10. she was fruitful by reason of many w.
43. 2. his voice was like a noise of many w. earth shined with his glory, Rev. 1. 15. | 14. 2. | 19. 6.
Rev. 17. 1. the great whore that sitteth on many w.

WAVE.

Jam. 1. 6. he that wavereth is like a w. of the sea

WAVE, Verb.

Exod. 29. 24. thou shalt w. them for a wave offering before the Lord, Lev. 8. 27. | 23. 20. Num. 6. 20.
26. thou shalt w. the breast || 27. w. the shoulder, Lev. 7. 30. | 8. 29. | 9. 21. | 10. 15.
Lev. 23. 11. he shall w. the sheaf before the Lord, 12.
Num. 5. 25. the priest shall w. the jealousy-offering

WAVED.

Lev. 14. 21. then he shall take one lamb to be w.

See BREAST, LOAVES, OFFERING.

WAVERETH.

Jam. 1. 6. he that w. is like a wave of the sea

WAVERING.

Heb. 10. 23. hold fast profession of faith without w.
Jam. 1. 6. but let him ask in faith, nothing w.

WAVES.

Psal. 42. 7. all thy w. are gone over me, Jonah 2. 3.
65. 7. stilleth the noise of their w. 89. 9. | 107. 29.
88. 7. thou hast afflicted me with all thy w.
93. 3. floods lift up voice, floods lift up their w.
4. the Lord on high is mightier than mighty w.
107. 25. the stormy wind which lifteth up the w.
Isa. 48. 18. thy righteousness as the w. of the sea
51. 15. but I am the Lord thy God that divided the sea, whose w. roared, Jer. 31. 35.
Jer. 5. 22. tho' the w. toss, yet can they not prevail
51. 42. Babylon is covered with the multitude of w.
55. Lord hath spoiled Babylon when her w. roar

Ezek. 26. 3. nations come, as the sea causeth his w.
27. † 28. w. shall shake at cry of thy pilots
Zech. 10. 11. and shall smite the w. in the sea
Mat. 8. 24. that the ship was covered with the w.
14. 24. but the ship was tossed with w. Mark 4. 37.
Luke 21. 25. be signs, the sea and the w. roaring
Acts 27. 41. the hinder part was broken with the w.
Jude 13. raging w. of sea, foaming out their shame

WAX.

Psal. 22. 14. my heart is like w. it is melted
68. 2. as w. melteth, so the wicked perish
97. 5. the hills melted like w. at presence of Lord
Mic. 1. 4. the valleys cleft as w. before the fire

WAX.

Exod. 22. 24. my wrath shall w. hot, 32. 10.
32. 11. Lord, why doth thy wrath w. hot against
22. let not the anger of my lord w. hot
Lev. 25. 47. if a sojourner or a stranger w. rich by thee, and thy brother by him w. poor
1 Sam. 3. 2. Eli laid down, his eyes began to w. dim
Job 6. 17. what time they w. warm they vanish
14. 8. though the root thereof w. old in the earth
Psal. 102. 26. all of them shall w. old as a garment, and be changed, Isa. 50. 9. | 51. 6. Heb. 1. 11.
Isa. 17. 4. the fatness of his flesh shall w. lean
29. 22. neither shall his face now w. pale
Jer. 6. 24. our hands w. feeble, anguish hath taken
Mat. 24. 12. the love of many shall w. cold
Luke 12. 33. provide bags which w. not old
1 Tim. 5. 11. begun to w. wanton against Christ
2 Tim. 3. 13. seducers shall w. worse and worse

WAXED.

Gen. 26. 13. Isaac w. great || 41. 56. famine w. sore
Exod. 1. 7. Israel w. exceeding mighty, 20.
16. 21. and when the sun w. hot, it melted
19. 19. when the trumpet w. louder and louder
32. 19. Moses' anger w. hot, and he cast the tables
Num. 11. 23. is the Lord's hand w. short?
Deut. 8. 4. raiment w. not old, 29. 5. Neh. 9. 21.
32. 15. but Jeshurun w. fat and kicked
Josh. 23. 1. that Joshua w. old and stricken in age
1 Sam. 2. 5. she that hath many children is w. feeble
2 Sam. 3. 1. but David w. stronger, 1 Chron. 11. 9.
21. 15. and David went down, fought, and w. faint
2 Kings 4. 34. and the flesh of the child w. warm
2 Chron. 13. 21. Abijah w. mighty and married wives
17. 12. Jehoshaphat || 24. 15. Jehoiada w. old
Esth. 9. 4. Mordecai w. greater and greater
Psal. 32. 3. when I kept silence my bones w. old
Jer. 49. 24. Damascus is w. feeble and turneth
50. 43. the king of Babylon's hands w. feeble
Dan. 8. 8. the he-goat w. great || 9. little horn, 10.
Mat. 13. 15. this people's heart w. gross, Acts 28. 27.
Luke 1. 80. the child w. strong in spirit, 2. 40.
13. 19. a grain of mustard seed w. a great tree
Acts 13. 46. Paul and Barnabas w. bold and said
Heb. 11. 34. w. valiant in fight, turned to flight
Rev. 18. 3. the merchants of the earth are w. rich

WAXEN, WAXED.

Gen. 18. 12. after I am w. old shall I have pleasure?
19. 13. because the cry of Sodom was w. great
Lev. 25. 25. if thy brother be w. poor, 35, 39.
Deut. 31. 20. w. fat, then will they turn to other gods
Josh. 17. 13. the children of Israel were w. strong
Jer. 5. 27. therefore are become great and w. rich
28. they are w. fat, they shine, they overpass
Ezek. 16. 7. thou hast increased and w. great

WAXETH.

Psal. 6. 7. mine eye w. old because of mine enemies
Heb. 8. 13. what w. old, is ready to vanish away

WAXING.

Phil. 1. 14. many brethren w. confident by my bonds

WAY,

Or path, *is taken in a moral sense,* (1) *For* conduct. *Isa.* 59. 8. They have made them crooked paths. *Psal.* 1. 6. The Lord knoweth the *way* of the righteous. (2) Ways *are put for the laws of the Lord,* Gen. 18. 19. They shall keep the *way* of the Lord. *Psal.* 18. 21. I have kept the *ways* of the Lord. (3) Way *is put for custom, manners, and way of life,* Gen. 6. 12. All flesh had corrupted his *way* upon the earth. *And in* Jer. 10. 2. Learn not the *way* of the heathen. (4) *The* way *of the Lord expresses his conduct in respect of us,* Isa. 55. 8, 9. My thoughts are not your thoughts, neither are your *ways* my *ways,* saith the Lord. For as the heavens are higher than the earth, so are my *ways* higher than your *ways,* and my thoughts than your thoughts. *And in* Rom. 11. 33. His *ways* are past finding out. (5) *The* ways *of God are put for his works.* Job 40. 19. He is the chief of the *ways* of God. (6) *Divine Providence,* Psal. 107. 7. (7) *Death.* Josh. 23. 14. (8) *The method of salvation, or doctrine of the gospel,* Acts 19. 9.

To go the *way* of all the earth, *is put to signify* dying *and the* grave, *Josh.* 23. 14. *A* hard way, *is put to represent the* way *of sinners,* a way *of impiety.* Judg. 2. 19. They ceased not from their stubborn *way; in Hebrew,* hard way. *It is so called to signify, that although it seemed at first very soft, and easy, and pleasant, yet they would certainly find that it was hard and difficult, and troublesome to them, as an hard way is to the traveller. The course that leadeth to destruction is called* a broad way, *that is obvious to all, and in which many walk; on the contrary, that course of life which will bring a man to heaven, is named* strait, narrow, difficult *to find and to walk in. A course of holiness is unpleasing to flesh and blood, it does not at all gratify men's sensual appetites; it is a* narrow way, *wherein men will meet with many crosses and temptations,* Mat. 7. 13, 14.

Jesus Christ is called the way, *John* 14. 6. *because it is by him alone that believers obtain eternal life, and an entrance into heaven. He is the* way *to heaven, by the doctrine which he taught; by his death, by which he purchased this heavenly inheritance for the elect; by his holy life and conversation,* setting us an example, that we should follows his steps; *and by the influence of his Spirit, whereby believers are* sanctified, and made meet to be partakers of the inheritance of the saints in light. *The Psalmist says,* Thou wilt shew me the path of life, *Psal.* 16. 11. *that is, "thou wilt raise my body from death to life, and conduct me to the place and state of everlasting happiness."* In Mat. 22. 16. *the Pharisees tell our Saviour by their disciples,* Master, we know that thou art true, and teachest the *way* of God in truth; *that is, the true principles of religion. St. Peter says, that the* way of truth shall be evil spoken of by false teachers, 2 *Pet.* 2. 2. *that is, the doctrine of the gospel, and the Christian religion. In* Jude 11. *it is said,* they have gone in the *way* of Cain; *that is, they have followed his example, in hating and persecuting their brethren.*

Gen. 24. 42. if thou prosper my w. which I go
42. 25. to give them provision for the w. 45. 21.
Exod. 13. 17. led not thro' the w. of the Philistines
18. led the people thro' the w. of the wilderness
21. in a pillar of cloud to lead them the w.
18. 20. shew them the w. Neh. 9. 19. Psal. 107. 4.
Num. 21. 4. was much discouraged because of the w.
22. 26. there was no w. to turn to the right or left
Deut. 1. 22. by what w. we must go, Josh. 3. 4.
8. 2. remember the w. which the Lord led you
14. 24. if the w. be too long for thee
17. 16. shall henceforth return no more that w.
19. 3. thou shalt prepare thee a w. || 6. the w. is long
28. 25. thou shalt go out one w. against them
31. 29. ye will turn aside from w. I commanded
Josh. 23. 14. behold, I am going w. of all the earth
24. 17. Lord preserved us in all the w. we went
Judg. 2. 19. they ceased not from their stubborn w.
9. 25. they robbed all that came along that w.
18. 5. whether our w. we go shall be prosperous
6. before the Lord is your w. wherein ye go
19. 9. and to-morrow get you early on your w.
1 Sam. 6. 12. kine took straight w. to Beth-shemesh
9. 6. peradventure he can shew us our w. to go
8. I will give to the man of God to tell us our w.
12. 23. I will teach you the good and the right w.
15. 20. I have gone the w. which the Lord sent me
20. † 19. remain by the stone which sheweth the w.
2 Sam. 19. 36. servant will go little w. over Jordan
1 Kings 2. 2. I go the w. of all the earth, be strong
8. 36. that thou teach them the good w. to walk
† 44. pray to the Lord toward the w. of the city
13. 9. nor turn again by the same w. thou camest
10. he went another w. || 12. what w. went he?
18. 6. Ahab went one w. Obadiah another w.
22. 24. he said, which w. went the Spirit of Lord from me to speak to thee? 2 Chron. 18. 23.
2 Kings 3. 8. which w. shall we go? w. thro' wildern.
5. 19. so he departed from him a little w.
7. 15. all the w. full of garments and vessels
2 Chr. 6. 27. when thou hast taught them good w.
Ezra 8. 21. to seek of him a right w. for us
Job 3. 23. light given to a man whose w. is hid
12. 24. to wander where there is no w. Ps. 107. 40.
16. 22. I shall go the w. whence I shall not return
22. 15. hast thou marked the old w. which wicked
23. 10. but he knoweth the w. that I take
28. 23. God understands the w. thereof, and knows
31. † 32. but I opened my doors to the w.
38. 19. where is the w. where light dwelleth?
Psal. 1. 6. Lord knoweth the w. of the righteous
2. 12. kiss the Son, lest ye perish from the w.
36. 4. he setteth himself in a w. that is not good
37. † 14. bent their bow to slay the upright of w.
78. 50. he made a w. to his anger, he spared not
101. 2. I will behave wisely in a perfect w. 6.
119. 27. make me understand the w. of thy precepts
29. remove from me the w. of lying, and grant
30. I have chosen the w. of truth
32. I will run the w. of thy commandments
33. teach me, O Lord, w. of thy statutes, 143. 8.
104. therefore I hate every false w. 128.
139. 24. and see if there be any wicked w. in me
146. 9. the w. of the wicked he turns upside down
Prov. 2. 8. he preserveth the w. of his saints
12. to deliver thee from the w. of the evil man
4. 19. the w. of the wicked is as darkness
6. 23. are the w. of life, 15. 24. Jer. 21. 8.
7. 8. near her corner, he went the w. to her house
27. her house is the w. to hell going down to death
12. 15. the w. of a fool is right in his own eyes
26. the w. of the wicked seduceth them
13. 15. but the w. of the transgressors is hard
14. 12. there is a w. which seemeth right, 16. 25.
15. 9. the w. of the wicked is an abomination
10. is grievous to him that forsaketh the w.
19. the w. of the slothful man is an hedge of thorns, but the w. of the righteous is made plain
16. 29. leadeth him into the w. that is not good
21. 8. the w. of man is froward and strange
30. 19. the w. of an eagle, of a serpent, of a ship
20. such is the w. of an adulterous woman
Eccl. 11. 5. knowest not what is the w. of the Spirit
Isa. 3. 12. they cause thee to err and destroy the w.
26. 7. the w. of the just is uprightness
35. 8. an high-way and a w. called w. of holiness
40. 14. who shewed him the w. of understanding?
43. 16. Lord, who maketh a w. in the sea, 51. 10.
19. I will even make a w. in the wilderness
49. 11. I will make all my mountains a w.
57. 14. prepare a w. || 62. 10. cast up the high w.
59. 8. the w. of peace they know not, Rom. 3. 17.
Jer. 6. 16. where is the good w. and walk therein
10. 2. learn not the w. of heathen, be not dismayed
23. I know that the w. of man is not in himself
12. 1. wherefore doth the w. of the wicked prosper?
18. 15. to walk in paths, in a w. not cast up
32. 39. I will give them one heart and one w.
42. 3. that the Lord thy God may shew us the w.
50. 5. they shall ask the w. to Zion with faces
Ezek. 21. 20. appoint a w. that the sword may come
23. 13. then I saw that they took both one w.
43. 2. the glory of G. came from the w. of the east
Amos 2. 7. and turn aside the w. of the meek
Nah. 2. 1. keep the munition, watch the w.
Mal. 3. 1. he shall prepare the w. before me

Mat. 7. 13. broad is the w. that leads to destruction
14. and narrow is the w. which leadeth unto life
8. 28. so that no man might pass by that w.
10. 5. go not into the w. of the Gentiles
22. 16. we know thou art true, and teachest the w. of God in truth, Mark 12. 14. Luke 20. 21.
Luke 5. 19. by what w. they might bring him in
10. 31. there came down a certain priest that w.
15. 20. when he was yet a great w. off, father saw
19. 4. Zaccheus ran to see him, was to pass that w.
John 10. 1. but climbeth up some other w. is a thief
14. 4. the w. ye know ‖ 6. I am the w. the truth
5. Thomas saith, Lord, how can we know the w.?
Acts 16. 17. which shew to us the w. of salvation
18. 26. expounded to him w. of God more perfectly
19. 9. believeth not, but spake evil of that w.
23. there arose no small stir about that w.
24. 14. after the w. which they call heresy
Rom. 14. 13. or an occasion to fall in brother's w.
1 Cor. 10. 13. with temptation make a w. to escape
12. 31. yet shew I unto you a more excellent w.
1 Thess. 3. 11. our Lord Jesus direct our w. unto you
Heb. 9. 8. the w. into the holiest not yet manifest
10. 20. by a living w. which he hath consecrated
12. † 17. for he found no w. to change his mind
Jam. 2. 25. she had sent them out another w.
2 Pet. 2. 2. the w. of truth shall be evil spoken of
15. which have forsaken the right w. and are gone astray, following the w. of Balaam son of Bosor
21. better not known the w. of righteousness
Rev. 16. 12. that w. of kings of the east be prepared

By the WAY.

Gen. 42. 38. if mischief befall him *by the w.* ye go
45. 24. Joseph said, see that ye fall not out *by the w.*
49. 17. Dan shall be a serpent *by the w.* an adder
Exod. 4. 24. *by the w.* in the inn the Lord met him
Num. 14. 25. turn you, get you into the wildern. *by the w.* of the Red sea, 21. 4. Deut. 1. 2, 40. | 2. 1.
Deut. 6. 7. talk of them when walkest *by the w.* 11. 19.
25. 17. what Amalek did to thee *by the w.*
18. how he met thee *by the w.* 1 Sam. 15. 2.
28. 68. Lord shall bring thee *by the w.* I spake
Josh. 5. 4. even all the men of war died *by the w.*
7. because they had not circumc. them *by the w.*
1 Kings 13. 9. not turn aga. *by the w.* thou camest, 17.
24. a lion met him *by the w.* and slew him
20. 38. the prophet waited for the king *by the w.*
2 Kings 3. 20. there came water *by the w.* of Edom
19. 28. put my bridle in lips, I will turn thee back *by the w.* by which thou camest, Isa. 37. 29, 34.
Ezra 8. 31. and of such as lay in wait *by the w.*
Job 21. 29. have ye not asked them that go *by the w.*?
Psal. 80. 12. all they who pass *by the w.* plucked her
89. 41. all that pass *by the w.* spoil him
Eccl. 10. 3. when fools walk *by the w.* wisdom fails
Isa. 42. 16. bring blind *by the w.* they knew not
48. 17. the Lord God that leadeth thee *by the w.*
Jer. 2. 17. forsaken God when he led thee *by the w.*
6. 25. walk not *by the w.* for the sword of the enemy
Lam. 1. † 12. ye that pass *by the w.* behold and see
Ezek. 43. 4. glory of Lord came *by the w.* of gate
44. 3. prince shall enter *by the w.* of porch, 46. 2, 8.
46. 9. he that entereth *by the w.* of north gate
Hos. 13. 7. as a leopard *by the w.* will I observe
Mark 8. 3. if I send them fasting, they faint *by the w.*
27. *by the w.* he asked his disciples, saying
9. 33. what was it ye disputed *by the w.*? 34.
Luke 10. 4. carry no shoes, salute no man *by the w.*
24. 32. heart burn while he talked with us *by the w.*
1 Cor. 16. 7. for I will not see you now *by the w.*

Every WAY.

Gen. 3. 24. a flaming sword which turned *every w.*
Psal. 119. 101. refrained my feet from *every* evil *w.*
104. therefore I hate *every* false *w.* 128.
Prov. 21. 2. *every w.* of man right in his own eyes
Ezek. 16. 31. buildest eminent place in *every w.*
Rom. 3. 2. much *every w.* because to them committed
Phil. 1. 18. *every w.* whether in pretence or in truth
See Evil.

His WAY.

Gen. 6. 12. all flesh had corrupted *his w.* on earth
2 Sam. 22. 31. as for God *his w.* is perfect, Psal. 18. 30.
1 Kings 8. 32. condemning the wicked, to bring *his w.* on his own head, 2 Chron. 6. 23.
Job 8. 19. behold, this is the joy of *his w.*
17. 9. the righteous also shall hold on *his w.*
21. 31. who shall declare *his w.* to his face?
23. 11. *his w.* have I kept and not declined
36. 23. who hath enjoined him *his w.*?
Psal. 25. 9. the meek will he teach *his w.*
37. 7. because of him who prospereth in *his w.*
23. steps of good man, and he delighteth in *his w.*
34. wait on the Lord and keep *his w.* and he shall
119. 9. wherewith shall a young man cleanse *his w.*
Prov. 8. 22. Lord possessed me in beginning of *his w.*
11. 5. righteousness of the perfect direct *his w.*
14. 8. the wisdom of prudent is to understand *his w.*
16. 9. a man's heart deviseth *his w.* but L. directs
17. he that keepeth *his w.* preserveth his soul
19. 3. the foolishness of man perverteth *his w.*
20. 14. when he is gone *his w.* then he boasteth
21. 29. as for the upright, he directeth *his w.*
Isa. 48. 15. he shall make *his w.* prosperous
55. 7. let the wicked forsake *his w.* and his thoughts
Jer. 4. 7. the destroyer of the Gentiles is on *his w.*
Ezek. 3. 18. to warn the wicked from *his* wicked *w.*
19. and he turn not from *his* wicked *w.* 33. 8, 9.
13. 22. he should not return from *his* wicked *w.*
Nah. 1. 3. the Lord hath *his w.* in the whirlwind
Jam. 1. 24. he beholdeth himself and goeth *his w.*
5. 20. who converteth the sinner from error of *his w.*
See Went.

In the WAY.

Gen. 24. 27. I being *in the w.* the Lord led me
48. blessed be the Lord who led me *in the* right *w.*
35. 3. the Lord was with me *in the w.* I went
19. Rachel buried *in the w.* to Ephrath, 48. 7.
Exod. 5. 20. Moses and Aaron stood *in the w.*
23. 20. send angel before thee to keep thee *in the w.*
Deut. 1. 33. who went *in the w.* before you to search
23. 4. because they met you not with bread *in t. w.*
1 Kings 11. 29. Ahijah found Jeroboam *in the w.*
13. 24. his carcase was cast *in the w.* 25. 28.
15. 26. he walked *in the w.* of his father, 22. 52.
34. he did evil in sight of the Lord, and walked *in the w.* of Jeroboam, 16. 2, 19, 26. | 22. 52.
18. 7. as Obadiah was *in the w.* Elijah met him
2 Kings 8. 18. he walked *in the w.* of the kings of Israel, as the house of Ahab, 16. 3. 2 Chr. 21. 6, 13.
27. he walked *in the w.* of the house of Ahab
21. 22. and walked not *in the w.* of the Lord
2 Chron. 11. 17. three years walked *in the w.* of Dav.
20. 32. he walked *in the w.* of Asa his father
Ezra 8. 22. to help us against the enemy *in the w.*
Neh. 9. 12. to give them light *in the w.* they shall go
19. departed not by day to lead them *in the w.*
Job 18. 10. snare laid and a trap for him *in the w.*
Psal. 1. 1. blessed, nor standeth *in the w.* of sinners
25. 8. therefore will he teach sinners *in the w.*
12. him shall he teach *in the w.* 32. 8.
85. 13. and shall set us *in the w.* of his steps
102. 23. he weakened my strength *in the w.*
110. 7. he shall drink of the brook *in the w.*
119. 1. blessed are the undefiled *in the w.*
14. I have rejoiced *in the w.* of thy testimonies
139. 24. search me, and lead me *in the w.* everlasting
142. 3. *in the w.* have they privily laid a snare
Prov. 1. 15. walk not thou *in the w.* with them
2. 20. that thou mayest walk *in the w.* of good men
4. 11. I have taught thee *in the w.* of wisdom
14. and go not *in the w.* of evil men
8. 20. I lead *in the w.* of righteousness
9. 6. live, and go *in the w.* of understanding
10. 17. he is *in the w.* of life that keepeth instruction
12. 28. *in the w.* of righteousness is life
13. 6. right. keepeth him that is upright *in the w.*
16. 31. if it be found *in the w.* of righteousness
22. 5. thorns and snares are *in the w.* of the froward
6. train up a child *in the w.* he should go
23. 19. be wise, and guide thy heart *in the w.*
26. 13. the slothful man saith there is a lion *in the w.*
29. 27. upright *in the w.* is abomination to wicked
Eccl. 12. 5. be afraid, and fears shall be *in the w.*
Isa. 8. 11. should not walk *in the w.* of this people
26. 8. *in the w.* of thy judgments we waited for thee
57. 17. went on frowardly *in the w.* of his heart
65. 2. which walked *in the w.* that was not good
Jer. 2. 18. what hast thou to do *in the w.* of Egypt? or what hast thou to do *in the w.* of Assyria?
Ezek. 23. 31. thou hast walked *in the w.* of thy sister
Hos. 6. 9. so priests murder *in the w.* by consent
Amos 4. † 10. I sent pestilence *in the w.* of Egypt
Mat. 5. 25. agree quickly whiles thou art *in the w.*
21. 32. John came *in the w.* of righteousness
Mark 11. 8. many spread garments *in the w.* others strewed branches *in the w.* Mat. 21. 8. Luke 19. 36.
Luke 1. 79. to guide our feet *in the w.* of peace
12. 58. as thou art *in the w.* give diligence
Acts 9. 17. Jesus that appeared to thee *in the w.*
27. how he had seen the Lord *in the w.*
Jude 11. they have gone *in the w.* of Cain
See Lord.

My WAY.

Gen. 24. 56. seeing the Lord hath prospered *my w.*
2 Sam. 22. 33. he maketh *my w.* perfect, Psal. 18. 32.
Job 19. 8. fenced up *my w.* that I cannot pass
Isa. 40. 27. why sayest thou, *my w.* is hid from Lord?
Ezek. 18. 25. hear, O Israel, is not *my w.* equal?
John 8. 21. I go *my w.* ‖ Rom. 15. 24. brought on *my w.*
2 Cor. 1. 16. to be brought on *my w.* to Jerusalem

Out of the WAY.

Exod. 32. 8. they have turned aside quickly *out of the w.* I commanded them, Deut. 9. 12, 16. Judg. 2. 17.
Num. 22. 23. the ass turned aside *out of the w.*
Deut. 11. 28. cursed if ye turn aside *out of the w.*
13. 5. thrust thee *out of the w.* L. God commanded
27. 18. that maketh blind to wander *out of the w.*
Job 24. 4. they turn the needy *out of the w.*
24. they are taken *out of the w.* and cut off
31. 7. if my step hath turned *out of the w.*
Prov. 21. 16. wandereth *out of the w.* of understand.
Isa. 28. 7. and thro' strong drink are *out of the w.*
30. 11. get you *out of the w.* turn aside out of path
57. 14. take stumbling-block *out of the w.* of people
Mal. 2. 8. but ye are departed *out of the w.*
Rom. 3. 12. are all gone *out of the w.* none doth good
Col. 2. 14. he took the hand-writing *out of the w.*
2 Thess. 2. 7. will let, till he be taken *out of the w.*
Heb. 5. 2. compassion on them that are *out of the w.*
12. 13. lest that which is lame be turned *out of the w.*

Own WAY.

Prov. 1. 31. shall they eat the fruit of their *own w.*
20. 24. how can a man understand his *own w.*?
Isa. 53. 6. we have turned every one to his *own w.*
56. 11. greedy dogs, they all look to their *own w.*
Ezek. 22. 31. their *own w.* have I recompensed
36. 17. they defiled Israel by their *o. w.* and doings

WAY-*side*.

Gen. 38. 21. where is harlot that was by the *w.-side*?
1 Sam. 4. 13. Eli sat on a seat by *w.-side* watching
Psal. 140. 5. the proud have spread a net by *w.-side*
Mat. 13. 4. when he sowed, some seeds fell by the *w.-side*, fowls came, 19. Mark 4. 4, 15. Luke 8. 5, 12.
20. 30. two blind men sitting by the *w.-side*
Mark 10. 46. as he went out of Jericho, blind Bartimeus sat by the *w.-side* begging, Luke 18. 35.

Their WAY.

1 Kings 2. 4. if thy children take heed to *their w.* to walk before me in truth, 8. 25. 2 Chron. 6. 16.
Job 6. 18. the paths of *their w.* are turned aside
19. 12. his troops raise up *their w.* against me
29. 25. I chose out *their w.* sat chief and dwelt
Psal. 35. 6. let *their w.* be dark and slippery
49. 13. this *their w.* is their folly, yet posterity
Jer. 3. 21. they have perverted *their w.* and forgot
6. 27. that thou mayest know and try *their w.*
23. 12. *their w.* shall be to them as slippery ways
Ezek. 7. 27. I will do to them after *their w.* and judge according to their deserts, 9. 10. | 11. 21.
14. 22. ye shall see *their w.* and their doings
33. 17. as for them *their w.* is not equal
36. 17. *their w.* was before me as uncleanness of
19. according to *their w.* and doings I judged them
Acts 15. 3. being brought on *their w.* by the church
See Went.

This WAY.

Gen. 28. 20. if God will keep me in *this w.* I go
Exod. 2. 12. Moses looked *this w.* and that way
Josh. 8. 20. had no power to flee *this w.* or that
2 Kings 6. 19. Elisha said, *this* is not the *w.* follow me
Isa. 30. 21. saying, *this* is the *w.* walk ye in it
Acts 9. 2. if he found any of *this w.* might bring
22. 4. I persecuted *this w.* unto the death

Thy WAY.

Gen. 24. 40. the Lord will prosper *thy w.*
Exod. 33. 13. therefore, I pray, shew me *thy w.*
Num. 22. 32. because *thy w.* is perverse before me
Josh. 1. 8. then thou shalt make *thy w.* prosperous
1 Kings 19. 15. return on *thy w.* to the wilderness
Psal. 5. 8. make *thy w.* straight before my face
27. 11. teach me *thy w.* O Lord, lead me, 86. 11.
37. 5. commit *thy w.* unto the Lord, trust in him
44. 18. neither have our steps declined from *thy w.*
67. 2. that *thy w.* may be known upon earth
77. 13. *thy w.* O God, is in the sanctuary
19. *thy w.* is in the sea, thy path in great waters
119. 37. and quicken thou me in *thy w.*
Prov. 3. 23. then shalt thou walk in *thy w.* safely
5. 8. remove *thy w.* far from her, come not nigh
Isa. 57. 10. art wearied in the greatness of *thy w.*
Jer. 2. 23. see *thy w.* in the valley, what hast done
33. why trimmest thou *thy w.* to seek love
36. why gaddest thou about to change *thy w.*?
4. 18. *thy w.* have procured these things unto thee
Ezek. 16. 43. I also will recompense *thy w.*
Hos. 2. 6. I will hedge up *thy w.* with thorns
10. 13. because thou didst trust in *thy w.*
Mat. 11. 10. behold, I send my messenger, who shall prepare *thy w.* before thee, Mark 1. 2. Luke 7. 27.

WAYS.

Gen. 19. 2. ye shall rise early and go on your *w.*
Deut. 5. 33. walk in all the *w.* Lord commanded
1 Kings 22. 43. he walked in the *w.* of Asa his father
2 Kings 21. 21. he walked in all the *w.* of Manasseh
22. 2. he walked in *w.* of David, 2 Chr. 17. 3. | 34. 2.
2 Chron. 21. 12. walked not in *w.* of Jehoshaphat
22. 3. he walked in the *w.* of the house of Ahab
28. 2. he walked in the *w.* of the kings of Israel
Job 24. 13. they know not the *w.* of the light
30. 12. they raise up the *w.* of their destruction
34. 21. for his eyes are upon the *w.* of man
40. 19. Behemoth is the chief of the *w.* of God
Psal. 84. 5. in whose heart are the *w.* of them
Prov. 1. 19. so are the *w.* of every one greedy of gain
2. 13. to walk in the *w.* of darkness
15. whose *w.* are crooked, and they froward
3. 17. wisdom's *w.* are *w.* of pleasantness and paths
5. 6. her *w.* are moveable, canst not know them
21. the *w.* of man are before the eyes of the Lord
6. 6. go to the ant, consider her *w.* and be wise
7. 25. let not thine heart decline to her *w.*
14. 12. the end thereof are the *w.* of death, 16. 25.
16. 2. the *w.* of a man are clean in his own eyes
7. when a man's *w.* please the Lord, he makes
17. 23. taketh a gift to pervert the *w.* of judgment
31. 27. she looketh well to the *w.* of her household
Eccl. 11. 9. O young man, walk in the *w.* of thy heart
Isa. 49. 9. they shall feed in the *w.* and pastures
Jer. 2. 23. a swift dromedary traversing her *w.*
3. 2. in the *w.* hast thou sat for them as Arabian
6. 16. stand in the *w.* and see, ask for old paths
7. 3. amend your *w.* and your doings, 5. | 26. 13.
23. walk in all the *w.* I have commanded you
12. 16. if they diligently learn the *w.* of my people
18. 11. make your *w.* and your doings good
32. 19. thy eyes are open on the *w.* of sons of men
Lam. 1. 4. the *w.* of Zion do mourn, none come
3. 40. let us search and try our *w.* and turn to Lord
Ezek. 18. 25. are not your *w.* unequal? 29.
20. 43. there shall ye remember your *w.* and doings
44. not according to your wicked *w.* or doings
21. 19. son of man appoint thee two *w.* that sword
21. stood at head of the two *w.* to use divination
Hag. 1. 5. thus saith the Lord, consider your *w.* 7.
Zech. 1. 6. do to us according to our *w.* and doings
Luke 3. 5. and the rough *w.* shall be made smooth
Acts 2. 28. hast made known to me the *w.* of life

Any WAYS.

Lev. 20. 4. do *any w.* hide their eyes from the man
Num. 30. 15. if ye shall *any w.* make them void
2 Chron. 32. 13. *any w.* able to deliver their lands
See By-Ways, Evil, High.

His WAYS.

Deut. 8. 6. shalt keep commandments of Lord to walk in *his w.* and fear him, 26. 17. | 28. 9. | 30. 16. 1 Kings 2. 3.
10. 12. to walk in all *his w.* to love him and to serve the Lord, 11. 22. Josh. 22. 5. 1 Kings 8. 58.
19. 9. to love the Lord and walk ever in *his w.*
32. 4. all *his w.* are judgment, Dan. 4. 37.
1 Sam. 8. 3. Samuel's sons walked not in *his w.*
18. 14. David behaved wisely in *his w.* L. with him
1 Kings 8. 39. hear thou in heaven, forgive and give to every man according to *his w.* 2 Chron. 6. 30.
2 Chron. 13. 22. Abijah's acts and *his w.* are written
27. 6. Jotham prepared *his w.* before the Lord
7. *his w.* are written in book of the kings, 28. 26.
Job 26. 14. these are parts of *his w.* but how little
34. 11. cause every man find according to *his w.*
27. and would not consider any of *his w.*
Psal. 10. 5. *his w.* are always grievous
103. 7. he made known *his w.* unto Moses
119. 3. they do no iniquity, they walk in *his w.*
128. 1. blessed is every one that walketh in *his w.*
145. 17. the Lord is righteous in all *his w.*
Prov. 3. 31. envy not and choose none of *his w.*
10. 9. he that perverteth *his w.* shall be known
14. 2. he that is perverse in *his w.* despiseth the Ld
19. 16. he that despiseth *his w.* shall die
22. 25. lest thou learn *his w.* and get a snare
28. 6. is better than he that is perverse in *his w.*
18. he that is perverse in *his w.* shall fall at once
Isa. 2. 3. he will teach us of *his w.* Mic. 4. 2.
42. 24. for they would not walk in *his w.*
45. 13. I will direct all *his w.* saith the Lord

Isa. 57. 18. I have seen *his w.* and will heal him
Jer. 17. 10. give every man according to *his w.* 32.19.
Ezek. 18. 23. that he should return from *his w.*
30. I will judge Israel according to *his w.* 33. 20.
Hos. 9. 8. is a snare of a fowler in all *his w.*
12. 2. Lord will punish Jacob according to *his w.*
Joel 2. 7. they shall march on every one in *his w.*
Hab. 3. 6. the hills did bow, *his w.* are everlasting
Luke 1. 76. thou shalt go before L. to prepare *his w.*
Rom. 11. 33. and *his w.* are past finding out
Jam. 1. 8. double-minded man is unstable in all *his w.*
11. so shall the rich man fade away in *his w.*
See LORD.
My WAYS.
1 *Kings* 3. 14. if thou wilt walk in *my w.* as thy father David did walk, 11. 38. *Zech.* 3. 7.
11. 33. worshipped Milcom and not walked in *my w.*
Job. 31. 4. doth not he see *my w.* and count my steps
Psal. 39. 1. I will take heed to *my w.* that I sin not
81. 13. O that Israel had walked in *my w.*
95. 10. they have not known *my w.* *Heb.* 3. 10.
119. 5. O that *my w.* were direct. to keep thy statutes
26. I have declared *my w.* and thou heardest me
59. I thought on *my w.* and turned my feet to thy
168. kept testimonies, all *my w.* are before thee
139. 3. and art acquainted with all *my w.*
Prov. 8. 32. blessed are they that keep *my w.*
23. 26. my son, let thine eyes observe *my w.*
Isa. 55. 8. neither are your ways *my w.* saith the Ld.
9. so are *my w.* higher than your ways
58. 2. seek me daily and delight to know *my w.*
Lam. 3. 9. he hath inclosed *my w.* with hewn stone
11. he turned aside *my w.* and pulled me in pieces
Ezek. 18. 29. are not *my w.* equal, your *w.* unequal?
Zech. 3. 7. if thou wilt walk in *my w.* and keep
Mal. 2. 9. according as ye have not kept *my w.*
1 *Cor.* 4. 17. bring you into remembrance of *my w.*
Own WAYS.
Job 13. 15. I will maintain my *own w.* before him
Prov. 14. 14. the backslider be filled with his *own w.*
Isa. 58. 13. honour him, not doing thine *own w.*
66. 3. yea, they have chosen their *own w.*
Ezek. 36. 31. then remember your *own* evil *w.*
32. be ashamed for your *own w.* O house of Israel
Acts 14. 16. he suffered all nations to walk in *own w.*
See SEVEN.
Their WAYS.
2 *Chron.* 7. 14. pray and turn from *their* wicked *w.*
Job 24. 23. yet his eyes are upon *their w.*
Psal. 125. 5. for such as turn to *their* crooked *w.*
Prov. 9. 15. call passengers who go right on *their w.*
Jer. 15. 7. since they return not from *their w.*
16. 17. for mine eyes are upon all *their w.*
18. 15. they caused them to stumble in *their w.*
Ezek. 14. 23. comfort you when ye see *their w.*
16. 47. yet hast thou not walked after *their w.*
Hos. 4. 9. I will punish them for *their w.*
Rom. 3. 16. destruction and misery are in *their w.*
2 *Pet.* 2. 2. many shall follow *their* pernicious *w.*
Thy WAYS.
Deut. 28. 29. thou shalt not prosper in *thy w.*
1 *Sam.* 8. 5. art old, thy sons walk not in *thy w.*
2 *Chron.* 6. 31. may fear thee to walk in *thy w.*
Job 4. 6. thy hope and the uprightness of *thy w.*
21. 14. we desire not the knowledge of *thy w.*
22. 3. is it gain to him thou makest *thy w.* perfect?
28. and the light shall shine upon *thy w.*
Psal. 25. 4. shew me *thy w.* O Lord, teach me
51. 13. then will I teach transgressors *thy w.*
91. 11. charge his angels, to keep thee in all *thy w.*
119. 15. I will have respect unto *thy w.*
Prov. 3. 6. in all *thy w.* acknowledge him, he direct
4. 26. and let all *thy w.* be established
31. 3. nor *thy w.* to that which destroyeth kings
Isa. 63. 17. why hast thou made us err from *thy w.*
64. 5. those that remember thee in *thy w.*
Jer. 2. 33. thou hast taught the wicked *thy w.*
3. 13. thou hast scattered *thy w.* to the strangers
Ezek. 7. 3. judge thee according to *thy w.* 4, 8, 9.
16. 47. corrupted more than they in all *thy w.*
61. then remember *thy w.* and be ashamed
24. 14. according to *thy w.* shall they judge thee
28. 15. thou wast perfect in *thy w.* from the day
Dan. 5. 23. the God in whose hand are all *thy w.*
Rev. 15. 3. just and true are *t. w.* thou king of saints
WAY-FARING.
Judg. 19. 17. he saw a *w.* man in the street of city
2 *Sam.* 12. 4. take his own flock to dress for *w.* man
Isa. 33. 8. high-ways lie waste, the *w.* man ceaseth
35. 8. *w.* men, though fools, shall not err therein
Jer. 9. 2. oh that I had a lodging place of *w.* men
14. 8. why shouldest thou be as a *w.* man?
WAY-MARKS.
Jer. 31. 21. set thee up *w.* make thee high heaps
WE.
Gen. 46. 34. been about cattle, *we* and our fathers
Num. 13. 31. *we* not able, they are stronger than *we*
Deut. 1. 28. the people is greater and taller than *we*
1 *Sam.* 8. 20. that *we* may be like all the nations
Ezra 10. 4. *we* will be with thee, be of courage
Neh. 2. 20. *we* his servants will arise and build
5. 2. *we* our sons and our daughters are many
8. *we* after our ability have redeemed the Jews
Job 8. 9. *we* are but of yesterday, know nothing
Psal. 100. 3. *we* are his people, sheep of his pasture
Isa. 14. 10. art thou also become weak as *we*?
63. 19. *we* are thine ‖ *Mark* 5. 9. for *we* are many
Mark 9. 28. why could not *we* cast him out?
Luke 1. 74. that *we* being delivered from enemies
John 8. 33. *we* be Abraham's seed, never in bondage
9. 28. thou art his disciple, *we* are Moses' disciples
40. are *we* blind also? ‖ 17. 11. may be one as *we* 22.
Acts 5. 32. and *we* are his witnesses, 10. 39.
10. 47. who received the Holy Ghost as well as *we*
14. 15. *we* are men of like passions with you
23. 15. *we* or ever he come are ready to kill him
Rom. 12. 5. *we* being many are one body in Christ
15. 1. *we* that are strong ought to bear infirmities
1 *Cor.* 3. 9. *we* are labourers together with God
4. 10. *we* are fools, but ye are wise, *we* are weak
12. being reviled, *we* bless, persecuted, *we* suffer it
8. 6. one God, and *we* in him; one Ld. and *we* by him

1 *Cor.* 9. 12. are not *we* rather ‖ 10. 17. *we* are one bread
10. 22. do *we* provoke Lord, are *we* stronger than he?
2 *Cor.* 1. 14. that *we* are your rejoicing, as ye ours
9. 4. *we* that *we* say not ye, should be ashamed
10. 7. that as he is Christ's, so are *we* Christ's
11. 12. they may be found even as *we*
Gal. 1. 8. though *we* or an angel from heaven preach
4. 3. *we* when *we* were children, were in bondage
28. now *we* as Isaac, are the children of promise
Eph. 2. 10. for *we* are his workmanship in Christ Jes.
1 *Thess.* 4. 17. *we* which are alive shall be caught in the clouds, and so shall *we* ever be with the Lord
5. 5. *we* are not of the night nor of darkness
Heb. 3. 6. whose house are *we* if *we* hold fast confiden.
10. 39. *we* are not of them who draw back to perdition
1 *John* 4. 6. *we* are of G. hereby *we* know Spirit of truth
5. 19. *we* know that *we* are of God and world lieth
WEAK.
Num. 13. 18. and see whether they be strong or *w.*
Judg. 16. 7. then shall I be *w.* as other men, 11, 17.
2 *Sam.* 3. 39. I am this day *w.* though anointed king
2 *Chron.* 15. 7. be strong, let not your hands be *w.*
Job 4. 3. thou hast strengthened the *w.* hands
Psal. 6. 2. I am *w.* ‖ 109. 24. my knees are *w.*
Isa. 14. 10. art thou also become *w.* as we?
35. 3. strengthen ye the *w.* hands
Ezek. 7. 17. all knees shall be *w.* as water, 21. 7.
16. 30. how *w.* is thy heart, saith the Lord God
Joel 3. 10. let the *w.* say, I am strong
Mat. 26. 41. but the flesh is *w.* *Mark* 14. 38.
Acts 20. 35. so labouring ye ought to support the *w.*
Rom. 4. 19. being not *w.* in faith, he considered not
8. 3. for the law was *w.* thro' the flesh, God sending
14. 1. him that is *w.* in the faith receive ye
2. another who is *w.* eateth herbs
21. whereby thy brother stumbleth or is made *w.*
15. 1. we ought to bear the infirmities of the *w.*
1 *Cor.* 1. 27. *w.* things to confound the mighty
4. 10. we are *w.* ‖ 8. 7. conscience being *w.* 10.
8. 12. wound their *w.* conscience, sin against Christ
9. 22. to the *w.* I became as *w.* that I might gain the *w.* I am made all things to all men
11. 30. for this cause many are *w.* and sickly
2 *Cor.* 10. 10. his bodily presence is *w.* and speech
11. 21. I speak as though we had been *w.*
29. who is *w.* and I am not *w.*?
12. 10. for when I am *w.* then am I strong
13. 3. which to you-ward is not *w.* but is mighty
4. for we are *w.* in him, but shall live with him
9. are glad when we are *w.* and ye strong
Gal. 4. 9. how turn ye again to the *w.* elements?
1 *Thess.* 5. 14. support the *w.* be patient toward all
WEAK-HANDED.
2 *Sam.* 17. 2. I will come on him while he is *w.*
WEAKEN.
Isa. 14. 12. how cut down, which didst *w.* nations?
WEAKENED.
Ezra 4. 4. then the people of the land *w.* Judah
Neh. 6. 9. their hands shall be *w.* from the work
Job 14. † 10. but man dieth and is *w.*
Psal. 102. 23. he *w.* my strength in the way
WEAKENETH.
Job 12. 21. he *w.* the strength of the mighty
Jer. 38. 4. he *w.* the hands of the men of war
WEAKER.
2 *Sam.* 3. 1. David stronger, Saul's house *w.* and *w.*
1 *Pet.* 3. 7. give honour to the wife as the *w.* vessel
WEAKNESS.
Exod. 32. † 18. nor voice of them that cry for *w.*
1 *Cor.* 1. 25. the *w.* of God is stronger than men
2. 3. I was with you in *w.* and in fear
15. 43. it is sown in *w.* it is raised in power
2 *Cor.* 12. 9. my strength is made perfect in *w.*
13. 4. tho' crucified thro' *w.* yet he liveth by power
Heb. 7. 18. a disannulling going before for the *w.*
11. 34. out of *w.* were made strong, waxed valiant
WEALTH.
Gen. 34. 29. the sons of Jacob took all their *w.*
Deut. 8. 17. my power and my hand got me this *w.*
18. the Lord giveth thee power to get *w.*
Ruth 2. 1. Naomi had a kinsman, a man of *w.*
1 *Sam.* 2. 32. thou shalt see an enemy in all the *w.*
2 *Kings* 15. 20. Menahem exacted money of men of *w.*
2 *Chron.* 1. 11. thou hast not asked *w.* nor honour
12. I will give thee riches, and *w.* and honour
Ezra 9. 12. nor seek their peace or *w.* for ever
Esth. 10. 3. Mordecai seeking the *w.* of his people
Job 21. 13. they spend their days in *w.* and go down
31. 25. if I rejoiced because my *w.* was great
Psal. 44. 12. and dost not increase *w.* by their price
49. 6. they that trust in *w.* and boast in riches
10. wise men die and leave their *w.* to others
112. 3. *w.* and riches shall be in his house
Prov. 5. 10. lest strangers be filled with thy *w.*
10. 15. the rich man's *w.* is his strong city, 18. 11.
13. 11. *w.* gotten by vanity shall be diminished
22. the *w.* of the sinner is laid up for the just
19. 4. *w.* maketh many friends, the poor separated
Eccl. 5. 19. to whom God hath given *w.* 6. 2.
Isa. 60. † 5. *w.* of Gentiles shall come to thee, 11.
Zech. 14. 14. *w.* of all the heathen shall be gathered
Acts 19. 25. ye know that by this craft we have *w.*
1 *Cor.* 10. 24. but seek every man another's *w.*
Common-WEALTH.
Eph. 2. 12. being aliens from the *common-w.* of Isr.
WEALTHY.
Psal. 66. 12. thou broughtest us out into a *w.* place
Jer. 49. 31. arise, get you up unto the *w.* nation
WEANED.
Gen. 21. 8. Isaac grew and was *w.* Abr. made feast
1 *Sam.* 1. 22. I will not go up till the child be *w.*
1 *Kings* 11. 20. whom Tahpenes *w.* in Pharaoh's ho.
Psal. 131. 2. surely I behaved myself as a child that is *w.* of his mother, my soul is as a *w.* child
Isa. 11. 8. the *w.* child put his hand on cockatrice' den
28. 9. them that are *w.* from the milk and drawn
Hos. 1. 8. when she *w.* Lo-ruhama, she conceived
WEAPON.
Deut. 23. 13. thou shalt have a paddle upon thy *w.*
Neh. 4. 17. and with the other hand held a *w.*
Job 20. 24. he shall flee from the iron *w.*
Isa. 54. 17. no *w.* formed against thee shall prosper

Ezek. 9. 1. with his destroying *w.* in his hand, 2.
WEAPONS.
Gen. 27. 3. take, I pray, thy *w.* thy quiver, and bow
1 *Sam.* 21. 8. neither my sword nor *w.* with me
2 *Kings* 11. 8. compass the king round about, every man with his *w.* in his hand, 11. 2 *Chr.* 23. 7, 10.
2 *Chron.* 32. † 5. Hezekiah made *w.* in abundance
Isa. 13. 5. Lord cometh and the *w.* of his indignation to destroy the whole land, *Jer.* 50. 25.
Jer. 22. 7. prepare destroyers, every one with his *w.*
Ezek. 39. 9. they shall set on fire and burn *w.* 10.
John 18. 3. Judas cometh with lanterns and *w.*
Rom. 6. † 13. nor yield members as *w.* of unrighteous.
2 *Cor.* 10. 4. the *w.* of our warfare are not carnal
See WAR.
WEAR.
Exod. 18. 18. wilt surely *w.* away, thou and people
Deut. 22. 5. woman not *w.* what pertains to man
11. thou shalt not *w.* garment of divers sorts
1 *Sam.* 2. 28. burn incense to *w.* an ephod before me
22. 18. Doeg slew 85 persons that did *w.* an ephod
Esth. 6. 8. the royal apparel the king useth to *w.*
Job 14. 19. the waters *w.* the stones, washest away
Isa. 4. 1. we eat our own bread and *w.* our apparel
65. † 22. mine elect shall *w.* out the work of hands
Dan. 7. 25. shall *w.* out the saints of the Most High
Zech. 13. 4. nor shall they *w.* a rough garment
Mat. 11. 8. that *w.* soft clothing are in kings' houses
Luke 9. 12. and when the day began to *w.* away
WEARETH.
Jam. 2. 3. ye respect him that *w.* the gay clothing
WEARING.
1 *Sam.* 14. 3. the Lord's priest in Shiloh *w.* an ephod
John 19. 5. Jesus came forth *w.* the purple robe
1 *Pet.* 3. 3. whose adorning, let it not be *w.* of gold
WEARY.
Gen. 27. 46. Rebekah said, I am *w.* of my life
Deut. 25. 18. Amalek smote thee, when thou wast *w.*
Judg. 4. 21. Jael smote Sisera when fast asleep and *w.*
8. 15. we should give bread to thy men that are *w.*
2 *Sam.* 16. 14. the king and all the people came *w.*
17. 2. I will come upon him while he is *w.*
23. 10. he smote Philistines till his hand was *w.*
Job 3. 17. the wicked cease, and the *w.* be at rest
10. 1. my soul is *w.* of my life, leave my complaint
16. 7. now he hath made me *w.* made desolate
22. 7. thou hast not given water to *w.* to drink
Ps. 6. 6. I am *w.* with groaning, I make my bed swim
63. † 1. my flesh longeth for thee in a *w.* land
68. 9. thou didst confirm thy inheritance when *w.*
69. 3. I am *w.* of my crying, my throat is dried
Prov. 3. 11. my son, be not *w.* of Lord's correction
25. 17. lest he be *w.* of thee, and so hate thee
Isa. 1. 14. feasts are trouble, I am *w.* to bear them
5. 27. none shall be *w.* nor stumble among them
7. 13. hear, O house of David, is it a small thing for you to *w.* men, but will ye *w.* my God also?
16. 12. when it is seen that Moab is *w.* in high place
28. 12. wherewith ye may cause the *w.* to rest
32. 2. as the shadow of a great rock in a *w.* land
40. 28. God, the Lord, fainteth not, neither is *w.*
30. even the youths shall faint and be *w.*
31. that wait on the Lord shall run and not be *w.*
43. 22. but thou hast been *w.* of me, O Israel
46. 1. they are a burden to the *w.* beast
50. 4. to speak a word in season to him that is *w.*
Jer. 2. 24. all that seek her will not *w.* themselves
6. 11. I am *w.* with holding in, I will pour it out
9. 5. they *w.* themselves to commit iniquity
15. 6. will destroy thee, I am *w.* with repenting
20. 9. I was *w.* with forbearing, I could not stay
31. 25. for I have satiated the *w.* soul
51. 58. the folk shall labour in the fire and be *w.*
64. thus shall Babylon sink and they shall be *w.*
Hab. 2. 13. people shall *w.* themselves for vanity
Luke 18. 5. lest by her continual coming she *w.* me
Gal. 6. 9. let us not be *w.* in well-doing, 2 *Thess.* 3. 13.
WEARIED.
Gen. 19. 11. they *w.* themselves to find the door
Isa. 43. 23. nor have I *w.* thee with incense
24. thou hast *w.* me with thine iniquities
47. 13. thou art *w.* in the multitude of thy counsels
57. 10. thou art *w.* in the greatness of thy way
Jer. 4. 31. my soul is *w.* because of murderers
12. 5. if run with footmen and they *w.* thee, if in the land of peace wherein trustedst they *w.* thee
Ezek. 24. 12. she hath *w.* herself with lies
Mic. 6. 3. O my people, wherein have I *w.* thee?
Mal. 2. 17. ye have *w.* the Lord, yet ye say, wherein have we *w.* him? every one that doeth evil
John 4. 6. Jesus being *w.* sat thus on the well
Heb. 12. 3. lest ye be *w.* and faint in your minds
WEARIETH.
Job 37. 11. by watering he *w.* the thick cloud
Eccl. 10. 15. the labour of the foolish *w.* every one
WEARINESS.
Eccl. 12. 12. much study is a *w.* of the flesh
Mal. 1. 13. he said, what a *w.* is it! and he snuffed
2 *Cor.* 11. 27. in *w.* and painfulness, in watchings
WEARISOME.
Job 7. 3. and *w.* nights are appointed to me
WEASEL.
Lev. 11. 29. the *w.* and the mouse, unclean to you
WEATHER.
Job 37. 22. fair *w.* cometh out of the north
Prov. 25. 20. as he that taketh a garment in cold *w.*
Mat. 16. 2. it will be fair *w.* for the sky is red
3. in the morning it will be foul *w.* to-day
WEAVE.
Isa. 19. 9. they that *w.* net-works be confounded
59. 5. they hatch cockatrice' eggs and *w.* spider's web
WEAVER.
Exod. 35. 35. with wisdom to work the work of *w.*
1 *Sam.* 17. 7. the staff of Goliath's spear was like a *w.* beam, 2 *Sam.* 21. 19. 1 *Chron.* 11. 23. | 20. 5.
Job 7. 6. my days are swifter than a *w.* shuttle
Isa. 38. 12. I have cut off like a *w.* my life
WEAVEST.
Judg. 16. 13. if thou *w.* seven locks of my head
WEB.
Judg. 16. 13. if thou weavest seven locks with the *w.*
14. and went away with pin of beam and the *w.*

Job 8. 14. and whose trust shall be a spider's w.
Isa. 59. 5. they weave the spider's w.

WEBS.

Isa. 59. 6. their w. shall not become garments

WEDDING.

Mat. 22. 3. to call them that were bidden to w.
8. the w. is ready || 10. the w. is furnished
11. he saw a man that had not on a w. garment
Luke 12. 36. when he will return from the w.
14. 8. when thou art bidden of any man to a w.

WEDGE.

Josh. 7. 21. Achan saw a w. of gold of 50 shekels
24. Joshua took Achan and the w. of gold
Isa. 13. 12. more precious than golden w. of Ophir

WEDLOCK.

Ezek. 16. 38. I will judge thee as women that [break w.

WEEDS.

Job 31. † 40. let w. grow instead of barley
Jonah 2. 5. the w. were wrapped about my head

WEEDY.

Jer. 49. † 21. the noise was heard in the w. sea

WEEK.

The Hebrews had three sorts of weeks. (1) Weeks of days, *which were reckoned from one sabbath to another.* (2) Weeks of years, *which were reckoned from one sabbatical year to another, and which consisted of seven years.* (3) Weeks *of seven times seven years,* or of forty-nine years, *which are reckoned from one* jubilee *to another.*

The seventy weeks, *in* Dan. 9. 24. *It is agreed that these are* weeks of years, *and not of days. They consist of seven lunar or Hebrew years: by which reckoning the seventy weeks make up four hundred and ninety years. This way of reckoning years by days is not unusual in the sacred writings,* See Lev. 25. 8. Ezek. 4. 4, 5. Rev. 12. 6. | 13. 5. *There are many different hypotheses concerning the beginning and end of Daniel's* seventy weeks, *even among Christian writers, who believe this prophecy marks out the time of the birth and death of our Saviour Jesus Christ. Some begin them from the first year of Darius the Mede, which is the epocha of Daniel's prophecy, and make them to determine at the profanation of the temple, which happened under the persecution of Antiochus Epiphanes. Others begin them from the first year of Cyrus at Babylon, and place the end of them at the destruction of the temple by the Romans. Others fix the beginning at the first year of Darius the Mede, in which this revelation was made to Daniel, and put the end at the birth of Jesus Christ. Julius Africanus places the first year of the* seventy weeks *at the twentieth year of king Artaxerxes Longimanus, who gave a commission or decree to Nehemiah, to rebuild the walls of Jerusalem. From thence to the* last week, *in which the* Messiah *was put to death, are reckoned* seventy weeks, *or four hundred and ninety lunar years. This hypothesis or system seems to be the most rational of any that have been proposed by the ancients, and is adhered to, some small particulars excepted, by the greatest part of interpreters and chronologers.*

The greatest difference among chronologers in the calculation of these years, does not exceed nine or ten years. Petavius, who has treated of this matter in his twelfth book De Doctrina Temporum, *reconciles all these differences by showing that the words of the prophecy of Daniel,* From the going forth of the commandment to restore and to build Jerusalem, *ought to be understood of the complete execution of the order to rebuild Jerusalem, which was not performed but by Nehemiah. He shows also, that the twentieth year of Artaxerxes, mentioned* Neh. 2. 1. *ought to be explained, not of the twentieth year of the reign of Artaxerxes alone, but of his twentieth year beginning from the time that his father associated him with himself in the kingdom, ten years before his death. These ten years being deducted from the number of years that elapsed from the decree of Artaxerxes in favour of Nehemiah, to the death of Jesus Christ, deliver the chronologers out of their perplexities, and dispel the difficulties that arose from the ten supernumerary years, given by their calculation of the four hundred and ninety years, contained in the* seventy weeks *of Daniel.*

The modern Jews are not agreed among themselves, fearing to be convicted, from this prophecy, that the Messiah *is already come, and that their expectation of him is in vain. Some pronounce a curse against them that compute the time, saying, it is in vain to expect the* Messiah, *who hath been come a long while ago: others say, he is not yet come, but that he would have come a great while ago, if the sins of the Jews had not prevented him. Others place the beginning of the* seventy weeks *at the destruction of the first temple by Nebuchadnezzar, and the end at the destruction of the second temple by Titus. Between these two events they reckon but two hundred and ninety years, which is a proof of their great ignorance in matters of chronology.*

Gen. 29. 27. fulfil her w. || 28. and fulfilled her w.
Dan. 9. 27. shall confirm the covenant with many for one w. in the midst of the w. sacrifice cease
Mat. 28. 1. to dawn, toward the first day of the w. Mark 16. 2, 9. Luke 24. 1. John 20. 1, 19.
Luke 18. 12. I fast twice in the w. I give tithes
Acts 20. 7. the first day of the w. Paul preached
1 Cor. 16. 2. on the first day of the w. let every one

WEEKS.

Lev. 12. 5. if a maid child shall be unclean two w.
Num. 28. 26. bring new meat offering after your w.
Jer. 5. 24. reserveth the appointed w. of harvest
Dan. 9. 24. seventy w. are determined on thy people
25. know, after threescore and two w. 26.
10. 2. I Daniel was mourning three full w.
3. nor anoint myself till three w. were fulfilled
See FEAST, SEVEN.

WEEP.

The ancient Hebrews wept, and made their trouble to appear openly, in mourning and affliction. They were not of opinion, that courage and greatness of soul consisted in seeming to be insensible in adversity, or in restraining their tears. It was even looked upon as a great disrespect for any one not to be bewailed at his funeral. Job says of the wicked man, His widow shall not weep, *Job* 27. 15. *And the Psalmist, speaking of the death of Hophni and Phinehas, says,* Their priests fell by the sword, and their widows made no lamentation, *Psal.* 78. 64. *God forbids Ezekiel to* weep, *or to express any sorrow for the death of his wife, to shew that the Jews should be reduced to so great calamities, that they should not have the liberty even to mourn or bewail themselves,* Ezek. 24. 16.

Weeping men, *and* weeping women. *The ancient Hebrews used to hire men and women to weep at funerals,* Jer. 9. 17, 18. Thus saith the Lord of hosts, Consider ye, and call for the mourning women that they may come, and send for cunning women that they may come, &c. *And in* Amos 5. 16. Wailing shall be in all streets, and they shall say in all the highways, alas! alas! and they shall call the husbandmen to mourning, and such as are skilful of lamentation to wailing. *All the* weeping men *and* women *of Israel heretofore sung the* Lamentations *that Jeremiah composed for the death of the pious king Josiah,* 2 Chron. 35. 25.

Gen. 23. 2. Abraham came to mourn and w. for Sarah
43. 30. Joseph's bowels did yearn, sought where to w.
Num. 11. 10. Moses heard the people w. their families
13. they w. unto me, saying, give us to eat
1 Sam. 11. 5. what aileth the people that they w.?
34. until they had no more power to w.
2 Sam. 1. 24. ye daughters of Israel, w. over Saul
12. 21. thou didst w. for the child while alive
2 Chron. 34. 27. and didst rend thy clothes, and w.
Neh. 8. 9. this day is holy, mourn not, nor w.
Job 27. 15. and his widows shall not w.
30. 25. did not I w. for him that was in trouble?
31. and my organ into the voice of them that w.
31. † 38. if the furrows likewise thereof w.
Eccl. 3. 4. a time to w. and a time to laugh
Isa. 15. 2. he is gone up to the high places to w.
22. 4. I will w. bitterly, labour not to comfort me
30. 19. thou shalt w. no more, he will be gracious
33. 7. the ambassadors of peace shall w. bitterly
Jer. 9. 1. that I might w. day and night for slain
13. 17. but if ye will not hear it, my soul shall w. in secret places for your pride, mine eyes shall w. sore
22. 10. w. ye not for the dead, nor bemoan him, w. sore for him that goeth away, he shall not return
48. 32. O vine of Sibmah, I will w. for thee
Lam. 1. 16. for these things I w. my eye runneth
Ezek. 24. 16. nor shalt thou mourn nor w. 23.
27. 31. shall w. for thee with bitterness of heart
Joel 1. 5. awake, ye drunkards, w. and howl
2. 17. let the priests w. between the porch and altar
Mic. 1. 10. declare it not in Gath, w. not at all
Zech. 7. 3. should I w. in fifth month, as have done
Mark 5. 39. why make ye this ado, and w.?
14. † 72. when he thought thereon, he began to w.
Luke 6. 21. blessed are ye that w. now, for ye shall
25. woe to you that laugh now, ye shall w.
7. 13. Lord saw her and said, w. not, 8. 52. Rev. 5. 5.
23. 28. w. not for me, but w. for yourselves
John 11. 31. she goeth unto the grave to w. there
16. 20. ye shall w. but the world shall rejoice
Acts 21. 13. what mean ye to w. and break my heart
Rom. 12. 15. and w. with them that w.
1 Cor. 7. 30. they that w. as though they wept not
Jam. 4. 9. be afflicted, and mourn, and w.
5. 1. go to now, ye rich men, w. and howl
Rev. 18. 11. merchants of earth shall w. and mourn

WEEPERS.

Judg. 2. † 5. they called the name of that place, w.

WEEPEST.

1 Sam. 1. 8. Hannah, why w. thou? why eat. thou not?
John 20. 13. angels said, woman, why w. thou? 15.

WEEPETH.

2 Sam. 19. 1. it was told Joab, behold the king w.
2 Kings 8. 12. Hazael said, why w. my lord?
Psal. 126. 6. he that goeth forth and w. bearing
Lam. 1. 2. she w. sore in night her tears on her cheeks

WEEPING.

Gen. 35. † 8. name of it was called, the oak of w.
45. † 2. Joseph gave forth his voice in w.
Num. 25. 6. w. before the door of the tabernacle
Deut. 34. 8. so the days of w. for Moses were ended
2 Sam. 3. 16. her husband went along with her w.
13. † 36. king and servants wept with a w. greatly
15. 30. they went up, w. as they went up
2 Kings 20. † 3. remember how I have walked before thee, Hezekiah wept with a great w. Isa. 38. † 3.
Ezra 3. 13. not discern the noise of joy from w.
10. 1. when Ezra had prayed and confessed, w.
Esth. 4. 3. in every province was fasting and w.
Job 16. 16. my face is foul with w. and on my eyelids
28. † 11. he bindeth the floods from w.
Psal. 6. 8. the Lord hath heard the voice of my w.
30. 5. w. may endure for a night, but joy cometh
102. 9. I have mingled my drink with w.
Isa. 15. 3. in their streets howl, w. abundantly
16. 9. therefore I will bewail with the w. of Jazer, the vine of Sibmah, O Heshbon, Jer. 48. 32.
22. † 4. look away from me, I will be bitter in w.
12. in that day did the Lord of hosts call to w.
65. 19. the voice of w. shall be no more heard
Jer. 3. 21. the w. of Israel heard on high places
9. 10. for the mountains will I take up a w.
31. 9. they shall come with w. and supplications
15. voice heard in Ramah, lamentation and bitter w. Rachel w. for her children, Mat. 2. 18.
16. thus saith Lord, restrain thy voice from w.
41. 6. Ishmael went forth to meet them w.
48. 5. continual w. shall go up, a cry of destruction
50. 4. Judah going and w. to seek Lord their God
Ezek. 8. 14. there sat women w. for Tammuz
Joel 2. 12. turn ye to me with fasting and with w.
Mal. 2. 13. covering the altar of the Lord with w.
Mat. 8. 12. there shall be w. and gnashing of teeth, 22. 13. | 24. 51. | 25. 30. Luke 13. 28.
Luke 7. 38. a woman stood at his feet behind him w.
John 11. 33. when Jesus saw her w. and the Jews also w. which came with her, he groaned in spirit
20. 11. Mary stood without at the sepulchre, w.
Acts 9. 39. and all the widows stood by him w.
Phil. 3. 18. I have told you often, now tell you w.
Rev. 18. 15. the merchant shall stand afar off w.
19. every ship-master and sailors cried, w.

WEIGH.

Exod. 22. † 17. if father refuse he shall w. money
1 Kings 20. † 39. thou shalt w. a talent of silver
1 Chron. 20. 2. David found his crown to w. a talent
Ezra 8. 29. keep them until ye w. them before priests and the Levites
Esth. 3. † 9. I will w. 10,000 talents of silver
Job 31. † 6. let him w. me in balances of justice
Psal. 58. 2. you w. violence of your hand in earth
Isa. 26. 7. thou dost w. the path of the just
55. † 2. why w. ye money for what is not bread?

WEIGHED.

Gen. 23. 16. Abraham w. to Ephraim the silver
1 Sam. 2. 3. by the Lord actions are w.
17. 7. his spear's head w. 600 shekels, 2 Sam. 21. 16.
2 Sam. 14. 26. Absalom w. the hair of his head
Ezra 8. 25. priests w. to them the silver and gold
26. I w. into their hands the silver of vessels, 33.
Job 6. 2. oh that my grief were thoroughly w.
28. 15. nor shall silver be w. for the price of it
31. 6. let me be w. in an even balance
Psal. 78. † 50. he w. a path to his anger
Isa. 40. 12. who hath w. the mountains in scales
Jer. 32. 9. Jeremiah w. him the money, 17 shekels
Dan. 5. 27. Tekel, thou art w. in the balances
Zech. 11. 12. so they w. for my price thirty pieces

WEIGHER.

Isa. 33. † 18. where is the scribe? where is the w.?

WEIGHETH.

Job 28. 25. and he w. the waters by measure
Prov. 16. 2. but the Lord w. the spirits

WEIGHING.

Num. 7. 85. each charger w. || 86. golden spoons w.

WEIGHT.

As the Hebrews had not the use of coined money, which was of a certain determined weight, *they* weighed *all the gold and silver they used in trade. The general word they used to denote a* weight *was* a stone; *Deut.* 25. 13. Thou shalt not have in thy bag divers *weights; the Hebrew says,* a stone and a stone. *That is, they were forbid to keep two different* weights, *one too heavy, to buy with, and another too light, to sell with; but only* one stone, *or one true* weight. *And in* Prov. 20. 10. *God condemns fraud and injustice in traffic.* Divers weights, and divers measures, both of them are alike abomination to the Lord. *The shekel, the half shekel, and the talents, are not only denominations of money of a certain value, of gold and silver, but also of a certain* weight. *When Moses expresses the drugs which were to compose the perfume to be burnt upon the golden altar, he says, that they were to take the* weight *of* five hundred shekels of myrrh, &c. *Exod.* 30. 23. *And in* 2 Sam. 14. 26. *it is said, that* Absalom's hair *weighed* two hundred shekels.

The shekel, or weight of the sanctuary, *according to several interpreters, was double to the common shekel; but others think it was the same as the common shekel, and the words* of the sanctuary *are added, to express a just and exact* weight, *according to the standards that were kept in the temple, or tabernacle.*

The weight of glory, *of which St. Paul speaks,* 2 Cor. 4. 17. a far more exceeding and eternal *weight of* glory, *is opposed to the lightness of the evils of this life. The troubles and afflictions we endure are of no* weight *at all, if compared to the* weight *of that glory which is to be revealed.*

Weight *is put for the burden of sin,* Heb. 12. 1.

Gen. 43. 21. man's money in mouth of sack in full w.
Exod. 30. 34. of each shall there be a like w.
Lev. 19. 35. ye shall do no unrighteousness in w.
26. 26. they shall deliver you your bread by w.
Deut. 25. 15. thou shalt have a perfect and just w.
Judg. 8. 26. w. of golden ear-rings 1,700 shekels
2 Sam. 12. 30. w. of king's crown a talent of gold
1 Kings 7. 47. Solomon left vessels unweighed neither was the w. of the brass found out, 2 Kings 25. 16.
1 Chron. 28. 14. he gave gold by w. for things of gold, silver also by w. for instruments of silver
Job 28. 25. to make the w. for the winds
Prov. 11. 1. but a just w. is his delight
16. 11. a just w. and balance are the Lord's
Ezek. 4. 10. thy meat shall be by w. twenty shekels
16. and they shall eat bread by w. and with care
Zech. 5. 8. he cast the w. of lead on the mouth
2 Cor. 4. 17. worketh for us a more exceeding w.
Heb. 12. 1. let us lay aside every w. and sin that besets
Rev. 16. 21. every stone of hail the w. of a talent

WEIGHTS.

Lev. 19. 36. just w. shall ye have, I am the Lord
Deut. 25. 13. thou shalt not have in thy bag divers w.
Prov. 16. 11. all the w. of the bag are his work
20. 10. divers w. and measures are abomination, 23
Mic. 6. 11. and with the bag of deceitful w.

WEIGHTY.

Prov. 27. 3. a stone is heavy and the sand w.
Zech. 5. † 7. there was lift up a w. piece of lead
2 Cor. 10. 10. for his letters say they, are w.

WEIGHTIER.

Mat. 23. 23. scribes have omitted w. matters of law

WELFARE.

Gen. 43. 27. he asked them of their w. and said
Exod. 18. 7. they asked each other of their w.
1 Chr. 18. 10. Tou sent to David to inquire of his w.
Neh. 2. 10. was come a man to seek the w. of Israel
Job 30. 15. and my w. passeth away as a cloud
Psal. 69. 22. that which should have been for their w.
Jer. 38. 4. this man seeketh not the w. of this people

WELL, *Substantive.*

Gen. 21. 19. she saw a w. of water and she went
30. that they may witness I have digged this w.
24. 13. behold, I stand here by w. of water, 43.
49. 22. Joseph is a fruitful bough by a w.

Num. 21. 16. that is the *w.* whereof the Lord spake
17. spring up, O *w.* ‖ 18. princes digged the *w.*
2 *Sam.* 17. 18. a man that had a *w.* in his own court
23. 15. oh that one would give me drink of the water of the *w.* Bethlehem, 1 *Chron.* 11. 17, 18.
Psal. 84. 6. who passing through Baca make it a *w.*
Prov. 5. 15. drink waters out of thine own *w.*
10. 11. the mouth of a righteous man is *w.* of life
Cant. 4. 15. a *w.* of living waters from Lebanon
John 4. 6. now Jacob's *w.* was there, Jesus being wearied with his journey sat thus on the *w.*
11. the *w.* is deep ‖ 12. Jacob gave us the *w.*
14. shall be in him a *w.* of water springing up

WELLS.

Gen. 26. 15. all *w.* Abraham's servants had digged
18. and Isaac digged again the *w.* of water
Exod. 15. 27. came to Elim, where were twelve *w.*
Num. 20. 17. nor will we drink of the water of *w.*
Deut. 6. 11. and *w.* digged which thou diggedst not
2 *Kings* 3. 19. and ye shall stop all *w.* of water
25. they stopped all the *w.* of water, felled trees
2 *Chron.* 26. 10. Uzziah built towers and digged *w.*
Isa. 12. 3. shall draw water out of the *w.* of salvation
2 *Pet.* 2. 17. these are *w.* without water, clouds carried

WELL-*spring.*

Prov. 16. 22. understanding is a *w.-spring* of life
18. 4. the *w.-spring* of wisdom as a flowing brook

WELL, *Adverb.*

Gen. 4. 7. if thou dost not *w.* sin lieth at the door
12. 13. that it may be *w.* with me for thy sake
16. he entreated Abram *w.* for her sake
13. 10. Jordan was *w.* watered every where
18. 11. Abraham and Sarah *w.* stricken in age, 24. 1.
29. 6. Jacob said, is he *w.?* and they said, he is *w.*
40. 14. think of me, when it shall be *w.* with thee
43. 27. is your father *w.?* is he yet alive?
Exod. 1. 20. therefore God dealt *w.* with midwives
4. 14. I know that he can speak *w.*
Num. 11. 18. for it was *w.* with us in Egypt
13. 30. Caleb said, we are *w.* able to overcome it
36. 5. the tribe of the sons of Joseph hath said *w.*
Deut. 1. 23. and the saying pleased me *w.*
3. 20. given rest to your brethren, as *w.* as you
4. 40. that it may go *w.* with thee and thy children, 5. 16. | 6. 3, 18. | 12. 25, 28. | 19. 13. | 22. 7. *Ruth* 3. 1. *Eph.* 6. 3.
5. 14. thy maid-servant may rest as *w.* as thou
28. I heard words of peo. they have *w.* said, 18. 17.
29. that it might be *w.* with them and theirs
33. that it may be *w.* with you, *Jer.* 7. 23.
7. 18. but shalt *w.* remember what the Lord did
15. 16. wilt not go away because he is *w.* with thee
Judg. 9. 16. if thou hast dealt *w.* with Jerubbaal
14. 3. get her for me, for she pleaseth me *w.* 7.
20. 48. as *w.* the men of every city as the beast
Ruth 3. 13. *w.* let him do the kinsman's part
1 *Sam.* 16. 16. he shall play and thou shalt be *w.*
20. 7. if he say thus, it is *w.* thy servant hath peace
24. 20. I know *w.* thou shalt surely be king
2 *Sam.* 6. 19. he dealt bread as *w.* to women as men
18. 28. Ahimaaz called, and said, all is *w.*
1 *Kings* 8. 18. the Lord said to David, thou didst *w.* it was in thy heart to build an house, 2 *Chron.* 6. 8.
18. 24. all the people answered, it is *w.* spoken
2 *Kings* 4. 26. is it *w.* with thee? is it *w.* with thy husband? is it *w.* with the child? it is *w.*
5. 21. is all *w.* 9. 11. ‖ 7. 9. we do not *w.*
25. 24. dwell in land, serve king of Babylon, and it shall be *w.* with you, *Psal.* 128. 2. *Jer.* 40. 9.
2 *Chron.* 12. 12. also in Judah things went *w.*
Psal. 49. 18. men praise when thou dost *w.* to thyself
119. 65. thou hast dealt *w.* with thy servant, O L.
Prov. 11. 10. when it goeth *w.* with the righteous
14. 15. the prudent man looketh *w.* to his goings
24. 32. then I saw and considered it *w.* looked on it
30. 29. there be three things which go *w.* yea four
31. 27. she looketh *w.* to the ways of her household
Eccl. 8. 12. it shall be *w.* with them that fear God
13. but it shall not be *w.* with the wicked
Isa. 3. 10. say to righteous, it shall be *w.* with him
Jer. 1. 12. the Lord said to me, thou hast *w.* seen
15. 11. Lord said, it shall be *w.* with thy remnant
22. 15. it was *w.* with him, he judged needy, 16.
39. 12. take him, look *w.* to him, do him no harm
40. 4. come, and I will look *w.* to thee
42. 6. that it may be *w.* with us when we obey
44. 17. for then we were *w.* and saw no evil
Ezek. 24. 5. make it boil *w.* seethe the bones therein
10. spice it *w.* ‖ 44. 5. mark *w.* behold and hear
33. 32. of one that can play *w.* on an instrument
Jonah 4. 4. the Lord said, dost thou *w.* to be angry?
9. I do *w.* to be angry, even unto death
Mat. 15. 7. ye hypocrites, *w.* did Esaias prophesy of you, saying, *Mark* 7. 6. *Acts* 28. 25.
25. 21. *w.* done, thou good and faithful servant, enter into the joy of thy Lord, 23. *Luke* 19. 17.
Mark 7. 37. he hath done all things *w.* deaf to hear
12. 28. perceiving that he had answered them *w.*
Luke 1. 7. Zacharias and Elisab. *w.* stricken in years
6. 26. woe unto you when all men speak *w.* of you
13. 9. if it bear fruit, *w.* if not, cut it down
20. 39. Master, thou hast *w.* said, *John* 4. 17.
John 8. 48. say we not *w.* thou hast a devil
13. 13. ye call me Lord, ye say *w.* for so I am
18. 23. but if *w.* why smitest thou me?
1 *Cor.* 7. 37. he that will keep his virgin, doth *w.*
38. he that giveth her in marriage, doth *w.*
Gal. 4. 17. they zealously affect you, but not *w.*
5. 7. ye did run *w.* who did hinder you?
Phil. 4. 14. ye have done *w.* ye did communicate
1 *Tim.* 3. 4. one that ruleth *w.* his own house
5. 17. let the elders that rule *w.* be counted worthy
Tit. 2. 9. and to please them *w.* in all things
Jam. 2. 19. believest there is one God, thou dost *w.*
See As, Do, Doing, Favoured, Pleased.

WELL-BELOVED.

Cant. 1. 13. a bundle of myrrh is my *w.* unto me
Isa. 5. 1. now will I sing to *w.* a song of my beloved
Mark 12. 6. he sent his *w.* son also to them
Rom. 16. 5. salute *w.* Epenetus first-fruits of Achaia
3 *John* 1. the elder to the *w.* Gaius, I love in truth

Very WELL.

Acts 25. 10. done no wrong, as thou *very w.* knowest
2 *Tim.* 1. 18. he ministered to me, thou knowest *v. w.*

WELL-*nigh.*

Psal. 73. 2. as for me my steps had *w.-nigh* slipped

WEN.

Lev. 22. 22. maimed, or having a *w.* or scurvy

WENCH.

2 *Sam.* 17. 17. a *w.* told Jonathan and Ahimaaz

WENT.

Gen. 35. 3. the Lord was with me in the way I *w.*
Num. 10. 14. in the first place *w.* standard of Judah
14. 24. him will I bring into land whereto he *w.*
22. 22. God's anger was kindled because Balaam *w.*
24. 1. Balaam *w.* not to seek for enchantments
25. 8. Phinehas *w.* after the man of Israel
Deut. 1. 31. God bare thee in all the way ye *w.*
Josh. 24. 17. he preserved us in all the way we *w.*
Judg. 1. 3. so Simeon *w.* with Judah
17. and Judah *w.* with Simeon his brother
16. 19. Samson's strength *w.* from him
1 *Sam.* 10. 14. Saul's uncle said, whither *w.* ye?
26. there *w.* with Saul a band of men
17. 12. the man *w.* for an old man in days of Saul
15. but David *w.* to feed his father's sheep
23. 13. Dav. and his men *w.* wherever they could go
30. 22. because they *w.* not with us, will not give
2 *Sam.* 1. 4. how *w.* the matter? I pray thee tell me
8. 3. as he *w.* to recover his border, 1 *Chron.* 18. 3.
6. Syrians became servants, and Lord preserved David whithersoever he *w.* 14. 1 *Chr.* 18. 6, 13.
15. 11. *w.* in their simplicity and knew nothing
18. 33. as he *w.* thus he said, O my son Absalom
1 *Kings* 11. 6. Solomon *w.* not fully after the Lord
13. 12. and their father said, what way *w.* he?
14. he *w.* after the man of God and found him
22. 24. he said, which way *w.* the Spirit of the Ld. from me, to speak to thee? 2 *Chron.* 18. 23.
48. but they *w.* not ‖ 2 *Kings* 2. 6. they two *w.* on
2 *Kings* 5. 26. he said, *w.* not my heart with thee?
6. 4. so he *w.* with them, and they cut down wood
1 *Chron.* 7. 23. when he *w.* in to his wife, she concei.
16. 20. when they *w.* from nation to nation, from one kingdom to another people, *Psal.* 105. 13.
2 *Chron.* 10. 16. so all Israel *w.* to their tents
12. 12. and also in Judah things *w.* well
23. 17. people *w.* to house of Baal and brake
Neh. 2. 16. the rulers knew not whither I *w.*
Esth. 2. 14. in evening she *w.* on morrow returned
Psal. 42. 4. I *w.* with them to the house of God
106. 32. it *w.* ill with Moses for their sakes
Prov. 7. 8. a young man *w.* the way to her house
Isa. 57. 17. he *w.* on frowardly in the way of his heart
Ezek. 1. 9. they *w.* every one straight forward
12. they turned not when they *w.* 10. 11.
17. they *w.* on their four sides and returned not
21. when those *w.* these *w.* those stood, these stood
20. 16. for their heart *w.* after their idols
Hos. 2. 13. she *w.* after her lovers and forgat the Ld.
5. 13. then *w.* Ephraim to the Assyrian and sent
9. 10. they *w.* to Baal-peor and separated thems.
11. 2. as they called them, so they *w.* from them
Hab. 3. 5. before him *w.* the pestilence, burning coals
11. at the light of thine arrows, they *w.*
Mat. 21. 29. but afterward he repented and *w.*
30. he answered and said, I go, sir, but *w.* not
25. 10. while they *w.* to buy, the bridegroom came
Mark 1. 20. they left their father and *w.* after him
Luke 2. 3. all *w.* to be taxed, every one to his city
16. 30. but if one *w.* to them from the dead
17. 14. that as they *w.* they were cleansed
23. 52. Joseph *w.* to Pilate and begged body of Jesus
John 4. 45. the Galileans also *w.* to the feast
7. 53. every man *w.* to his own house
9. 11. I *w.* and washed and I received sight
13. 3. that he was come from God and *w.* to God
18. 6. they *w.* backward and fell to the ground
21. 23. then *w.* this saying among the brethren
Acts 8. 4. they *w.* every where preaching the word
9. 1. Saul threatening *w.* unto the high priest
10. 9. as they *w.* on their journey, Peter *w.* to pray
14. 1. they *w.* both into synagogue of the Jews
15. 38. and *w.* not with them to the work
16. 16. as we *w.* to prayer, a damsel met us
26. 12. as I *w.* to Damascus with authority
1 *Pet.* 3. 19. which he *w.* preach. to spirits in prison
See Along.

WENT *about.*

Num. 11. 8. the people *w. about* and gathered it
2 *Kings* 3. 25. the slingers *w. about* it and smote it
2 *Chron.* 17. 9. they *w. about* and taught the people
Eccl. 2. 20. I *w. about* to cause my heart despair
Cant. 5. 7. the watchmen that *w. about* found me
Mat. 4. 23. Jesus *w. about* teaching, 9. 35. *Mark* 6. 6.
Acts 9. 29. they *w. about* to slay him, 21. 31. | 26. 21.
10. 38. Jesus *w. about* doing good and healing
13. 11. he *w. about* seeking some to lead him
See Arose.

WENT *aside.*

Luke 9. 10. Jesus took them and *w. aside* privately
Acts 23. 19. the chief captain *w. aside* privately

WENT *astray.*

Psal. 119. 67. before I was afflicted I *w. astray*
Ezek. 44. 10. when Israel *w. astray* after idols, 15.
48. 11. it shall be for the priests which *w.* not *astray* when Israel *w. astray* as Levites *w. astray*
Mat. 18. 13. than of ninety-nine which *w.* not *astray*

WENT *away.*

Judg. 16. 3. Samson *w. away* with doors of the gates
14. and *w. away* with the pin of the beam
19. 2. and his concubine *w. away* from him
2 *Sam.* 18. 9. the mule that was under him *w. away*
2 *Kings* 5. 11. but Naaman was wroth, and *w. away*
2 *Chron.* 9. 12. queen of Sheba *w. away* to her land
Mat. 19. 22. he *w. away* sorrowful, *Mark* 10. 22.
26. 42. he *w. away* the second time and prayed
44. he *w. away* the third time, *Mark* 14. 39.
John 12. 11. by reason of him many *w. away*
20. 10. the disciples *w. away* to their own home
Acts 10. 23. on the morrow Peter *w. away*

WENT *back.*

1 *Kings* 13. 19. so he *w. back* and did eat and drink
2 *Kings* 8. 29. king Joram *w. back* to be healed
John 6. 66. from that time many disciples *w. back*

WENT *before.*

Exod. 13. 21. the Lord *w. before* them in a cloud
14. 19. the angel of God which *w. before* the camp
Num. 10. 33. the ark of covenant *w. before, Josh.* 3. 6.
Josh. 6. 9. the armed men *w. before* the priests, 13.
1 *Sam.* 17. 7. one bearing a shield *w. before* him, 41.
2 *Sam.* 6. 4. and Ahio *w. before* the ark
10. 16. and Shobach *w. before* them, 1 *Chron.* 19. 16.
20. 8. when at Gibeon, Amasa *w. before* them
Job 18. 20. as they that *w. before* were affrighted
Psal. 68. 25. the singers *w. before* the players
Mat. 2. 9. the star which they saw *w. before* them
21. 9. the multitudes that *w. before* them cried, Hosanna to the son of David, *Mark* 11. 9.
Luke 18. 39. they which *w. before* rebuked him
22. 47. Judas *w. before* and drew near to kiss him
1 *Tim.* 1. 18. according to the prophecies which *w. b.*

WENT *behind.*

Exod. 14. 19. the angel removed and *w. behind*

WENT *down.*

Gen. 12. 10. Abram *w. down* into Egypt to sojourn
15. 17. when sun *w. down*, a smoking furnace and burning lamp passed, *Judg.* 19. 14. 2 *Sam.* 2. 24.
42. 3. Jos. brethren *w. down* ‖ 43. 15. Benj. *w. down*
Exod. 19. 14. Moses *w. down* from the mount to the people, and sanctified the people, 25. | 32. 15.
Num. 16. 33. *w. down* alive into the pit
20. 15. how our fathers *w. down* into Eg. and dwelt a long time, *Deut.* 10. 22. | 26. 5. *Josh.* 24. 4.
Judg. 3. 27. Israel *w. down* after Ehud, 28.
4. 14. Barak *w. down* from mount Tabor
7. 11. Gideon *w. down* with Phurah his servant
14. 1. Samson *w. down* to Timnath and saw a woman of the daughters of the Philistines, 5. 7.
18. the men said to him before the sun *w. down*
19. Samson *w. down* to Ashkelon and slew 30 men
Ruth 3. 6. Ruth *w. down* unto the floor to Boaz
1 *Sam.* 13. 20. the Israelites *w. down* to sharpen
22. 1. David's father's house *w. down* to him
2 *Sam.* 5. 17. David heard, and *w. down* to the hold
11. 9. but Uriah *w.* not *down* to his house, 10, 13.
17. 18. a well in his court, whither they *w. down*
21. 15. David *w. down* against the Philistines
23. 13. three of the thirty chief *w. down* and came to David to cave of Adullam, 1 *Chron.* 11. 15.
20. Benaiah *w. down* and slew a lion in time of snow
21. Benaiah *w. down* to the Egyptian, and slew him with his own spear, 1 *Chron.* 11. 22, 23.
2 *Kings* 1. 15. Elijah *w. down* with him to the king
2. 2. Elijah and Elisha *w. down* to Beth-el
5. 14. Naaman *w. down* and dipped himself in Jord.
8. 29. Ahaziah *w. d.* to see Joram, 2 *Chron.* 22. 6.
2 *Chron.* 18. 2. Jehoshaphat *w. down* to see Ahab
Psal. 133. 2. the ointment that *w. down* to the skirts
Cant. 6. 11. I *w. down* into the garden of nuts
Isa. 52. 4. my people *w. down* aforetime into Egypt
Jer. 18. 3. then I *w. down* to the potter's house
Ezek. 31. 15. in the day when he *w. down* to the grave
31. 17. they also *w. down* to hell with him
Jonah 1. 3. Jonah *w. down* to Joppa and found
2. 6. I *w. down* to the bottoms of the mountains
Luke 18. 14. this man *w. down* justified rather
John 5. 4. an angel *w. down* and troubled the water
Acts 7. 15. so Jacob *w. down* into Egypt and died
8. 5. Philip *w. down* to Samaria, preached Christ
38. and they both *w. down* into the water
10. 21. then Peter *w. down* to the men, and said
12. 19. Herod *w. down* from Judea to Cesarea
20. 10. Paul *w. down* and embracing him, said

WENT *forth.*

Gen. 8. 7. a raven *w. forth* ‖ 11. 31. *w. forth* from Ur
18. Noah *w. forth*, his sons and all out of ark, 19.
10. 11. out of that land *w. forth* Ashur
12. 5. they *w. forth* to go into land of Canaan
Num. 11. 31. there *w. forth* a wind from the Lord
31. 13. the princes *w. forth* to meet them, 33. 1.
Judg. 9. 8. trees *w. forth* to anoint a king over them
2 *Sam.* 20. 8. as he *w. forth* it fell out
2 *Kings* 2. 21. Elisha *w. forth* into the waters
18. 7. he prospered whithersoever he *w. forth*
Esth. 5. 9. then *w.* Haman *forth* that day joyful
Job 1. 12. Satan *w. forth* from presence of Lord, 2. 7.
Isa. 37. 36. angel of Ld. *w. forth* and smote 185,000
48. 3. the former things *w. forth*, I shewed them
Jer. 22. 11. Shallum who *w. forth* out of this place
Ezek. 16. 14. thy renown *w. forth* among the heathen
24. 12. her great scum *w.* not *forth* out of her
Amos 5. 3. that which *w. forth* by an hundred
Hab. 3. 5. and burning coals *w. forth* at his feet
Mat. 13. 3. behold, a sower *w. forth* to sow
25. 1. ten virgins *w. forth* to meet bridegroom
Mark 2. 12. he arose and took up bed and *w. forth*
3 *John* 7. because for his name's sake they *w. forth*
Rev. 6. 2. he *w. forth* conquering and to conquer

WENT *her way.*

1 *Sam.* 1. 18. woman *w. her way* and was no more sad
John 4. 28. the woman of Samaria *w. her way*
11. 28. when Martha had so said she *w. her way*

WENT *his way.*

Gen. 18. 33. and the Lord *w. his way* as soon as had
24. 61. the servant took Rebekah and *w. his way*
25. 34. Esau did eat and drink and *w. his way*
Exod. 18. 27. Jethro *w. his way* into his own land
Num. 24. 25. Balak ‖ 1 *Sam.* 24. 7. Saul *w. his way*
1 *Sam.* 26. 25. David *w.* on *his way*, Saul returned
1 *Kings* 1. 49. every guest of Adonijah *w. his way*
Esth. 4. 17. so Mordecai *w. his way*, did as Esth. com.
Jer. 28. 11. the prophet Jeremiah *w. his way*
Mat. 13. 25. his enemy sowed tares and *w. his way*
Luke 4. 30. he passing thro' midst of them, *w. his w.*
8. 39. and *w. his way* and published great things
22. 4. Judas *w. his way* and communed with priests
John 4. 50. and the man believed, and *w. his way*
Acts 8. 39. the eunuch *w.* on *his way* rejoicing
9. 17. Ananias *w. his way* and entered the house
See Jesus, Went.

WENT *in*, or *into.*

Gen. 7. 7. Noah *w. into* the ark and his sons with him
9. *w. in* two and two ‖ 16. *w. in* male and female
39. 11. Joseph *w. into* the house to do business

Exod. 5. 1. Moses and Aaron w. in to Pharaoh, 7. 10.
14. 22. Israel w. into midst of the sea on dry ground
23. the Egyptians w. in after them, 15. 19.
34. 35. until Moses w. in to speak with him
Lev. 16. 23. when Aaron w. into the holy place
Josh. 6. 23. the young men that were spies w. in
Judg. 3. 22. the haft also w. in after the blade
17. 10. so the Levite w. in and dwelt with Micah
19. 15. when the Levite w. in to lodge in Gibeah
1 Sam. 24. 3. Saul w. in to cover his feet
2 Sam. 7. 18. then w. David in before the Lord
1 Kings 1. 15. Bath-sheba w. in unto the king
22. 30. king of Israel disguised w. into the battle
2 Kings 4. 33. Elisha w. in shut the door and prayed
37. then she w. in fell at his feet and took her son
5. 4. and one w. in and told his lord, thus and thus
25. Gehazi w. in and stood before his master
10. 24. when they w. in to offer sacrifices
2 Chron. 26. 16. Uzziah w. into the temple of Lord
17. Azariah the priest w. in after him
Neh. 9. 24. so the children w. in and possessed
Esth. 7. 7. the king w. into the palace-garden
Psal. 73. 17. until I w. into the sanctuary of God
Jer. 26. 21. Urijah fled and w. into Egypt
Ezek. 8. 10. so I w. in ‖ 9. 2. six men w. in
10. 2. the man clothed with linen w. in, 3, 6.
25. 3. when they w. into captivity
39. 23. Israel w. into captivity for their iniquity
Dan. 2. 16. Daniel w. in and desired of the king
24. to Arioch ‖ 6. 10. he w. into his house to pray
Mat. 8. 32. the devils w. into the herd of swine
21. 33. there was a certain householder w. into a far
country, Mark 12. 1. Luke 19. 12. | 20. 9.
25. 10. they that were ready w. in to the marriage
27. 53. w. into the holy city, and appeared to many
Mark 2. 26. how David w. into the house of God,
and did eat the shew-bread, Luke 6. 4.
15. 43. Joseph w. in boldly to Pilate, craved body
Luke 1. 9. Lot was to burn incense when he w. in
39. Mary arose and w. into the hill country
24. 29. and he w. in to tarry with them
John 18. 15. that disciple w. in with Jesus
20. 5. he saw linen clothes lying, yet w. not in
8. then w. in also that other disciple, and saw
Acts 1. 21. all the time the Lord w. in and out
10. 27. as Peter talked he w. in and found many
12. 17. he departed and w. into another place
13. 14. they w. into synagogue on the sabbath-day
17. 2. Paul w. into the synagogue, 10. | 19. 8.
Rom. 10. 18. their sound w. into all the earth

WENT *in*, as to a woman.

Gen. 16. 4. Abram w. in to Hagar, she conceived
19. 33. the first-born w. in and lay with her father
29. 23. Laban brought Leah to Jacob, he w. in to her
30. he w. in also unto Rach. ‖ 30. 4. w. in to Bilh.
38. 2. Judah saw Shuah and w. in to her
9. when Onan w. in to his brother's wife
Judg. 16. 1. Samson saw an harlot and w. in to her
Ruth 4. 13. Boaz w. in to Ruth, she conceived
2 Sam. 12. 24. David comforted Bath-sheba his wife,
and w. in unto her, she bare a son, Solomon
16. 22. Absalom w. in to his father's concubines
17. 25. Ithra w. in to Abigail, Nahash's daughter
20. 3. but David w. not in to them
1 Chron. 2. 21. Hezron w. in to daughter of Machir
7. 23. when Ephraim w. in to his wife, she conceived
Ezek. 23. 44. yet they w. in unto her as a harlot

WENT *over*.

2 Sam. 2. 15. there arose and w. over by number
19. 17. and they w. over Jordan before the king
31. Barzillai w. over Jordan with the king
2 Kings 2. 8. so they two w. over on dry ground
14. Elisha smote the waters and w. over
1 Chr. 12. 15. these w. over Jordan when overflown
29. 30. David's reign, and times that w. over him
Neh. 12. 38. other company w. over against them
Isa. 51. 23. thy body as a street to them that w. over

WENT *out*.

Gen. 4. 16. Cain w. out from presence of Lord
24. 63. Isaac w. out to meditate in the field
34. 1. Dinah w. out to see the daughters of the land
43. 31. Joseph washed his face and w. out
44. 28. one w. out from me I saw him not since
Exod. 2. 11. Moses w. out to his brethren, 13.
8. 12. Aaron w. out from Pharaoh, 30. | 9. 33.
12. 41. all the hosts of the Lord w. out, 14. 8.
15. 20. all the women w. out after Miriam
16. 27. there w. out some people on sabbath-day
18. 7. Moses w. out to meet his father-in-law
33. 7. every one w. out unto the tabernacle
Lev. 10. 2. there w. out fire from the Lord
Num. 10. 34. cloud was on them when they w. out
11. 26. two men w. out into the tabernacle
21. 23. Sihon w. out against Israel into wilderness
33. Og, the king of Bashan, w. out against them
22. 32. behold, I w. out to withstand thee
Josh. 6. 1. none w. out, and none came in
8. 14. the men of Ai w. out against Israel, 17.
11. 4. the Canaanite w. out and all their hosts
Judg. 2. 15. they w. out, the Lord was against them
3. 19. all that stood by him w. out from him
19. 23. the master of the house w. out unto them
Ruth 1. 21. I w. out full, and came home empty
1 Sam. 3. 3. ere the lamp of God w. out in the temple
17. 35. I w. out after the bear, and smote him
18. 5. Dav. w. o. where Saul sent him, 13. 16. | 19. 8.
2 Sam. 11. 13. at even he w. out to lie on his bed
13. 9. they w. out every man from him
19. 19. the day the king w. out of Jerusalem
1 Kings 20. 16. they w. out at noon ‖ 17. w. out first
21. the king of Israel w. out and smote the horses
2 Kings 4. 18. the child w. out to his father to reapers
37. she went in and took up her son, and w. out
5. 27. Gehazi w. out from his presence a leper
9. 21. they w. out each in his chariot and met him
24. and the arrow w. out of Jehoram's heart
1 Chron. 12. 17. David w. out to meet them and said
14. 8. David heard of it, and w. out against them
2 Chron. 15. 2. Azariah w. out to meet Asa
5. was no peace to him that w. out or came in
19. 2. Jehu w. out to meet Jehoshaphat
20. 21. he appointed singers to praise as they w. out
2 Chron. 35. 20. Josiah w. out against Pharaoh necho
Esth. 7. 8. as the word w. out of the king's mouth
Job 29. 7. when I w. out to the gate thro' the city
31. 34. did fear terrify me that I w. not out at door
Psal. 81. 5. when he w. out thro' the land of Egypt
Jer. 37. 4. Jeremiah came in and w. out among peop.
Ezek. 10. 7. took fire from the cherub and w. out
Amos 5. 3. the city that w. out by a thousand
Zech. 8. 10. neither any peace to him that w. out
Mat. 11. 7. Jesus said, what w. ye out into the wilderness to see? 8, 9. Luke 7. 24, 25, 26.
20. 1. a man who w. out early to hire labourers
3. he w. out at third hour ‖ 5. sixth ‖ 6. eleventh
22. 10. those servants w. out into the high-ways
Mark 3. 21. his friends w. out to lay hold on him,
he is beside himself
5. 13. the unclean spirits w. out and entered into
the swine, and ran down, Luke 8. 33. Acts 19. 12.
14. they that fed the swine told it, they w. out to
see what it was that was done, Luke 8. 35.
Luke 6. 19. for there w. virtue out of him
22. 62. Peter w. out and wept bitterly
John 8. 9. they which heard it, w. out one by one
59. Jesus hid himself and w. out of the temple
11. 31. Mary rose up hastily, and w. out
13. 30. Judas having received the sop w. out
18. 16. then w. out that other disciple known to
Acts 1. 21. all the time the Lord w. in and out
15. 24. certain w. out from us have troubled you
Heb. 11. 8. Abraham w. out, not knowing whither
1 John 2. 19. they w. out from us, but not of us, they
w. out to be manifest that they were not all of us

WENT *their way*.

Judg. 18. 26. the children of Dan w. their way
1 Sam. 30. 2. Amalekites burnt Ziklag and w. their way
Neh. 8. 12. all the people w. their way to eat
Zech. 10. 2. therefore they w. their way as a flock
Mat. 8. 33. that kept swine fled and w. their way
20. 4. right I will give you, and they w. their way
22. 5. they made light of it and w. their ways
22. they heard these words, they w. their way
Mark 11. 4. w. their way and found colt, Luke 19. 32.
John 11. 46. but some w. their ways to Pharisees
Acts 8. 36. as they w. on their way came to water

WENT *through*.

Neh. 9. 11. thou didst divide the sea, they w. thro'
the midst of the sea on dry land, Psal. 66. 6.
Psal. 66. 12. we w. thro' fire and through water
Isa. 60. 15. forsaken, so that no man w. thro' thee
Mark 2. 23. he w. through the corn fields on the sab-
bath day, disciples began to pluck ears, Luke 6. 1.

WENT *up*.

Gen. 17. 22. and God w. up from Abraham
35. 13. God w. up from Jacob in place he talked
49. 4. w. up to father's bed, he w. up to my couch
Exod. 17. 10. Moses, Aaron, & Hur w. up to top of hill
19. 3. Moses w. up to God, and the Lord called to
him, 20. | 24. 13, 15. | 34. 4. Deut. 10. 3.
Num. 13. 21. so they w. up, and searched the land
31. but the men that w. up with him said
20. 27. they w. up into mount Hor, 33. 38.
Deut. 1. 43. and w. up presumptuously into the hill
Josh. 6. 20. so that the people w. up into the city
14. 8. brethren that w. up with me made heart melt
Judg. 1. 4. Judah w. up and the Lord delivered
22. the house of Joseph also w. up against Bethel
4. 10. Barak and Deborah w. up with 10,000 men
8. 8. Gideon w. up thence to Penuel, 11.
1 Sam. 1. 3. Elkanah w. up out of his city, 7, 21.
22. Hannah w. not up until child be weaned
5. 12. the cry of the city w. up to heaven
2 Sam. 15. 30. David wept as he w. up barefoot
24. 19. David, according to the saying of Gad, w.
up as the Lord commanded, 1 Chron. 21. 19.
2 Kings 2. 11. Elijah w. up by a whirlwind to heav.
4. 34. Elisha w. up and lay on the child, 35.
19. 14. Hezekiah w. up into the house of the Lord,
and spread it before the Lord, Isa. 37. 14.
23. 2. Josiah w. up to house of Lord, 2 Chr. 34. 30.
1 Chron. 11. 6. Joab w. up first and was chief captain
Ezra 2. 1. these are the children of the province that
w. up out of the captivity, 59. Neh. 7. 6, 61.
4. 23. they w. up in haste to Jerusalem to the Jews
7. 6. Ezra w. up ‖ Neh. 12. 1. the priest that w. up
8. 1. this is the genealogy of them that w. up
Ezek. 1. 13. it w. up and down among living creatures
8. 11. and a thick cloud of incense w. up
10. 4. the glory of the Lord w. up, 11. 23, 24.
19. 6. he w. up and down among the lions
Mat. 3. 16. Jesus w. up straightway out of the water
5. 1. and seeing the multitudes he w. up into a
mountain, 14. 23. | 15. 29. Luke 9. 28.
Luke 18. 10. two men w. up into the temple to pray
John 7. 10. then w. he also up unto the feast
Acts 1. 10. as he w. up two men stood by him
3. 1. Peter and John w. up into the temple
10. 9. Peter w. up upon the house-top to pray
24. 11. Paul w. up to Jerusalem, Gal. 1. 18. | 2. 1, 2.
Gal. 1. 17. neither w. I up to Jerusalem with them
Rev. 20. 9. they w. up on the breadth of the earth

WENT *a whoring*.

Judg. 2. 17. Isr. w. a whoring after other gods, 8. 33.
Psal. 106. 39. w. a whoring with their inventions

WENTEST.

Gen. 49. 4. Reuben, thou w. up to thy father's bed
Judg. 5. 4. Lord when thou w. out of Seir
2 Sam. 7. 9. I was with thee whithersoever thou w.
16. 17. why w. thou not with thy friend?
19. 25. wherefore w. thou not with me
Psal. 68. 7. O God, when thou w. before thy people
Isa. 57. 7. even thither w. thou up to offer sacrifice
9. thou w. to the king with ointment and increase
Jer. 2. 2. when thou w. after me in the wilderness
31. 21. set thine heart toward the way thou w.
Hab. 3. 13. thou w. forth for salvation of thy people
Acts 11. 3. thou w. in to men uncircumcised

WEPT.

Gen. 21. 16. Hagar sat and w. ‖ 27. 38. Esau w.
29. 11. Jacob w. 33. 4. | 37. 35. Hos. 12. 4.
42. 24. Joseph turned from his brethren and w.
43. 30. | 45. 2, 14, 15. | 46. 29. | 50. 1, 17.
50. † 3. the Egyptians w. for Joseph seventy days
Exod. 2. 6. she saw the child, and behold, babe w.
Num. 11. 14. and the children of Isr. also w. again,
18, 20. | 14. 1. Deut. 1. 45. | 34. 8. Judg.
2. 4. | 20. 23, 26. | 21. 2.
Judg. 14. 16. Samson's wife w. before him
Ruth 1. 9. Naomi kissed her daughters, and w. 14.
1 Sam. 1. 7. Hannah w. and did not eat, 10.
11. 4. all the people w. 2 Sam. 3. 32, 34.
20. 41. Jonathan and David w. one with another
24. 16. Saul w. ‖ 30. 4. David w. 2 Sam. 1. 12.
2 Sam. 3. 32. David w. at the grave of Abner
12. 22. while child was yet alive, I fasted and w.
13. 36. the king and servants w. sore for Amnon
15. 23. he and all country w. ‖ 30. w. as he went
18. 33. king was much moved, and w. for Absalom
2 Kings 8. 11. and the man of God w.
13. 14. Joash w. over Elisha, and said, O my father
20. 3. remember, Ld. Hezekiah w. sore, Isa. 38. 3.
22. 19. because the king of Judah hath w. before me
Ezra 3. 12. priests that had seen the first house w.
10. 1. for the people w. very sore, Neh. 8. 9.
Neh. 1. 4. when I heard these words I w. before God
Job 2. 12. Job's friends lifted up their voice and w.
Psal. 69. 10. when I w. and chastened my soul
137. 1. by rivers of Babylon we sat down and w.
Mat. 26. 75. Peter w. Mark 14. 72. Luke 22. 62.
Mark 5. 38. Jesus seeth them that w. Luke 8. 52.
16. 10. Mary told them as they mourned and w.
Luke 7. 32. we mourned to you and ye have not w.
19. 41. he beheld the city and w. over it
John 11. 35. Jesus w. ‖ 20. 11. Mary w. at sepulchre
Acts 20. 37. they w. sore, and fell on Paul's neck
1 Cor. 7. 30. they that weep as though they w. not
Rev. 5. 4. I w. because no man was found worthy

WERE.

Gen. 34. 14. cannot do this, for that w. a reproach
25. on the third day, when they w. sore
35. 2. Jacob said to all that w. with him, put away
4. gave all the strange gods that w. in their hand
Exod. 5. 19. Israel saw they w. in evil case
10. 6. since day they w. on earth to this day
Num. 12. 8. w. ye not afraid to speak against Moses?
13. 33. there we saw the giants, we w. in our own
sight as grasshoppers, so we w. in their sight
14. 3. w. it not better for us to return into Egypt?
Deut. 5. 29. O that there w. such an heart in them
10. 19. for ye w. strangers in the land of Egypt
28. 62. whereas ye w. as the stars of heaven
32. 27. w. it not that I feared the wrath of enemy
29. O that they w. wise, that they understood
Josh. 2. 4. men came to me, I wist not whence they w.
Judg. 9. 36. thou seest mountains as if they w. men
1 Sam. 9. 4. passed Shalim, and there they w. not
2 Sam. 11. 16. where he knew that valiant men w.
1 Kings 3. 18. we w. togeth. there was no stranger
4. 28. straw brought they where the officers w.
16. 30. Ahab did evil above all w. before him, 33.
2 Kings 3. 14. w. it not that I regard Jehoshaphat
7. 10. but horses tied, and the tents as they w.
2 Chron. 29. 31. as many as w. of a free heart
Neh. 1. 9. though there w. of you cast out to utmost
5. 2. for there w. that said, we, our sons, 3. 4.
7. 61. nor their seed, whether they w. of Israel
Job 29. 2. oh that I w. as in months past, in the days
Psal. 39. 12. a sojourner, as all my fathers w.
Isa. 14. 2. take them captives whose captives they w.
37. 19. they w. no gods, but work of men's hands
Jer. 31. 15. Rachel weeping, because they w. not
Ezek. 14. 14. tho' Noah, Daniel, and Job w. in it
should deliver but their own souls, 16. 18, 20.
20. 9. before the heathen among whom they w.
Hag. 2. 16. there w. but ten, there w. but twenty
Mat. 5. 12. persecuted prophets which w. before you
12. 3. have ye not read what David did, and they
that w. with him? 4. Mark 2. 25, 26. Luke 6. 3, 4.
Luke 3. 15. all men mused whether he w. Christ
7. 39. this man, if he w. a prophet, would known
17. 17. w. not ten cleansed, where are the nine?
John 9. 33. if this man w. not of G. could do nothing
11. 57. that if any man knew where he w.
15. 19. if ye w. of the world, world would love
17. 6. thine they w. thou gavest them me
18. 30. they said, if he w. not a malefactor
Acts 20. 12. and w. not a little comforted
24. 9. Jews assented, saying, these things w. so
Rom. 4. 17. calleth things that be not as tho' they w.
9. 25. I will call them my people that w. not
1 Cor. 12. 17. if whole body w. an eye, where w. hearing? if whole w. hearing, where w. smelling?
Gal. 2. 6. what they w. it maketh no matter to me
Eph. 2. 3. w. by nature children of wrath, as others
2 Thess 3. 10. from even when we w. with you
2 Pet. 3. 4. all things continue as they w. from begin.
Rev. 6. 11. till brethren killed as they w. fulfilled.

As it WERE.

Lev. 14. 35. it seemeth there is as it w. a plague
Cant. 6. 13. as it w. the company of two armies
Isa. 5. 18. that draw sin as it w. with a cart-rope
10. 15. as if staff lift up itself as it w. no wood
26. 20. hide thyself as it w. for a little moment
53. 3. and we hid as it w. our faces from him
Luke 22. 44. his sweat as it w. great drops of blood
John 7. 10. went up not openly, but as it w. in secret
Rom. 9. 32. sought it as it w. by works of the law
1 Cor. 4. 9. apostles, as it w. men appointed to death
Rev. 10. 1. and his face was as it w. the sun
13. 3. I saw one of his heads as it w. wounded
14. 3. they sung as it w. a new song before throne
15. 2. I saw as it w. a sea of glass with fire

If it WERE.

Job 21. 4. if it w. so, why not my spirit be troubled?
Mat. 24. 24. if it w. possible to deceive the very elect
Mark 6. 56. they might touch if it w. the border
John 14. 2. if it w. not so, I would have told you
Acts 18. 14. if it w. a matter of wrong, O ye Jews

WERT.

Cant. 8. 1. O that thou w. as my brother that sucked
Rev. 3. 15. nor cold nor hot, I would thou w. cold or

WEST.

Gen. 28. 14. thou shalt spread abroad to the w.
Deut. 33. 23. possess thou the w. and the south
1 Kings 7. 25. three oxen looking towards the w.

1 Chron. 9. 24. in four quarters were porters toward the east, w. north and south, 2 Chron. 4. 4.
12. 15. they put to flight them toward east and w.
Psal. 75. 6. promotion cometh not from the w.
103. 12. as far as the east is from the w. so far
107. 3. gathered them from the east and w.
Isa. 11. 14. shall fly on the Philistines toward the w.
43. 5. and gather thee from the w.
45. 6. that they may know from the w.
49. 12. these shall come from the north and w.
59. 19. they shall fear the Lord from the w.
Ezek. 48. 1. for these are his sides east and w.
Dan. 8. 5. behold, an he-goat came from the w.
Hos. 11. 10. the children shall tremble from the w.
Zech. 8. 7. I will save my people from the w.
14.4. the mount of Olives shall cleave toward the w.
Mat. 8. 11. many shall come from east and w. and sit down with Abrah. Isaac, and Jacob, Luke 13. 29.
24. 27. as lightn. cometh from east and shineth to w.
Luke 12. 54. when ye see a cloud rise out of the w.
Rev. 21. 13. on south three gates, and w. three gates

WEST border.

Num. 34.6. great sea for border, this shall be w. bord.
Josh. 15. 12. the w. border was to the great sea
Ezek. 45. 7. to the w. border a portion for prince

WESTERN.

Num. 34. 6. as for the w. border, the great sea

WEST quarter.

Josh. 18. 14. at Kirjath-baal, this was the w. quarter

WEST side.

Exod. 27. 12. on w. side hanging 50 cubits, 38. 12.
Num. 2. 18. on the w. side the standard of Ephraim
35. 5. measure on the w. side of the Levites' cities
Ezek. 48. 3. from the east side even to the w. side a portion for Naphtali, 4, 5, 6, 7, 8, 23, 24.

WESTWARD.

Gen. 13. 14. Abram looked eastward and w.
Num. 3. 23. pitch behind the tabernacle w.
Deut. 3. 27. lift up thine eyes w. and behold it
Ezek. 48. 18. the residue shall be 10,000 w.
Dan. 8. 4. I saw the ram pushing w.

WEST wind.

Exod. 10. 19. a strong w. wind took away the locusts

WET.

Job 24. 8. they are w. with showers of the mountains
Dan. 4. 15. let it be w. with the dew of heaven, and his portion be with the beasts, 23. 25, 33. | 5. 21.

WHALE

Is the greatest of fishes that we know of. Profane authors have given extravagant accounts of the bigness of this creature; some say, that whales *have been seen of six hundred feet long, and three hundred and sixty feet thick. Others write, that there have been seen some of eight hundred feet long. Modern writers say, that in America some* whales *measure ninety or an hundred feet from head to tail: and it is owned, that the* whales *in the north seas are yet larger than those that are found upon the coast of Guinea, or in the Mediterranean.*

In Scripture there is mention made of the whale. *But the Hebrew word* Thannim *is generally used for all large fishes, whether of rivers or of the sea. The Leviathan mentioned in* Job 41. 1. *is thought by a great many interpreters to be the* whale, *though others think it is the crocodile.*

The whale *brings forth her young ones alive, as other perfect animals: but it brings but one, or two at most, and nourishes it by the breast, with great care.* Whales *have generally no teeth, but only beards or whiskers on the throat, of about a span in breadth, and fifteen feet long, which end in fringes, like hogs' bristles at the end, which at top are set in the palate, and ranged in order. These beards serve to extend or contract the cheeks of this creature.* Whales *are maintained by a water or froth which they suck from the sea; and by some littles fishes, as the sea-flea, the sea-spider, anchovies, sea-weed, &c. Yet some of them have teeth, and in their bellies have been found thirty or forty cod-fish. The* Whale *always keeps its young one under its fins, and never leaves it till it is weaned. It has no udder, but it has nipples and teats, which contain milk in such abundance, that sometimes there have been drawn from it to the quantity of two hogsheads.*

Job 7. 12. am I a sea, or a w. that thou settest a watch
41. † 1. canst thou draw out a w. with a hook?
Ezek. 32. 2. Pharaoh, thou art as a w. in the seas
Mat. 12. 40. Jonas was three days in the w. belly

WHALES.

Gen. 1. 21. God created great w. after their kind
Psal. 74. † 13. thou breakest the heads of the w.

WHAT.

Gen. 27. 37. w. shall I do now to thee, my son?
39. 8. my master wotteth not w. is with me
44.16. w. shall we say to my lord? w. shall we speak
Exod. 10. 26. know not with w. we must serve Lord
13. 14. when son ask. w. is this? ‖ 16. 7. w. are we?
16. 15. it is manna, for they wist not w. it was
Lev. 25. 20. if ye shall say, w. shall we eat?
Num. 13. 18. and see the land w. it is, and the people
19. w. the land is, and w. cities they be, 20.
15. 34. it was not declared w. should be done
16. 11. w. is Aaron? ‖ 23. 17. w. hath Lord spoken?
24. 13. but w. the Lord saith, that will I speak, 1 Kings 22. 14. 2 Chron. 18. 13.
Deut. 4. 3. w. the Lord did because of Baal-peor
7. 18. w. Lord did to Pharaoh ‖ 11. 6. to Dathan
10. 12. w. doth Lord require of Israel? Mic. 6. 8.
20. 5. w. man is there? 6, 7, 8.
Josh. 7. 8. O Lord, w. shall I say, when Israel
15. 18. and Caleb said to her, w. wouldest thou? Judg. 1. 14. 1 Kings 1. 16. Mat. 20. 21.
22. 24. w. have you to do with the Lord of Israel?
Judg. 7. 11. thou shalt hear w. they say, and after.
11. 12. w. hast thou to do with me to fight in my land
18. 8. w. say ye? ‖ 18. the priest said, w. do ye?
24. w. have I more? w. is this? w. aileth thee?
Ruth 3. 4. thou shalt mark the place, and he will tell thee w. thou shalt do, 1 Sam. 10. 8.

1 Sam. 3. 17. w. is the thing Ld. hath said unto thee?
4. 16. and he said, w. is there done, my son?
2 Sam. 16. 10. w. have I to do with you? 19. 22.
17. 5. Absalom said, let us hear likewise w. he saith
18. 29. I saw a tumult but I knew not w. it was
1 Kings 13. 12. their father said, w. way went he?
14. 14. who cut off house of Jeroboam: w. even now?
17. 18. w. have I to do with thee, O thou man of God? 2 Kings 3. 13. 2 Chron. 35. 21. John 2. 4.
2 Kings 4. 2. Elisha said, w. shall I do for thee? 2. 9.
9. 18. Jehu said, w. hast thou to do with peace? 19.
20. 14. w. said these men, from whence? Isa. 39. 3.
15. w. have they seen in thine house? Isa. 39. 4.
2 Chron. 19. 6. Jehoshaphat said, take heed w. ye do
20. 12. nor know w. to do, but our eyes are on thee
25. 9. w. shall we do for the hundred talents given?
Ezra 9. 10. w. shall we say after this? Job 37. 19.
Neh. 2. 4. king said, for w. dost thou make request?
19. they said, w. thing is this ye do? 13. 17.
Esth. 4. 5. to know w. it was, and why it was
5. 3. w. wilt thou, queen Esther? w. is thy request? it shall be given thee, 6. | 7. 2. | 9. 12.
Job 7. 17. w. is man, that thou shouldest magnify him? 15. 14. Psal. 8. 4. | 144. 3. Heb. 2. 6.
20. w. shall I do unto thee, O thou preserver of men
9. 12. who will say unto him, w. dost thou? Eccl. 8. 4. Ezek. 12. 9. Dan. 4. 35.
13. 13. let me speak, and let come on me w. will
31. 14. w. then shall I do? w. shall I answer him? Luke 10. 25. | 12. 17. | 16. 3.
34. 4. let us know w. is good? Mic. 6. 8.
35. 6. w. doest thou against him? w. doest to him?
7. if thou be righteous, w. givest thou to him?
Psal. 25. 12. w. man is he fears Ld.? 34. 12. | 89. 48.
85. 8. I will hear w. God the Lord will speak
120. 3. w. shall be given unto thee, w. done to thee
Prov. 23. 1. consider diligently w. is before thee
25. 8. lest thou know not w. to do in the end
30. 4. w. is his name? w. is his son's name?
31. 2. w. my son? and w. the son of my womb?
Eccl. 2. 2. I said of mirth, w. doeth it?
Isa. 21. 11. he calleth watchman, w. of the night?
22. 16. w. hast thou here? and whom hast thou here?
38. 15. w. shall I say? John 12. 27.
52. 5. therefore w. have I here, saith the Lord?
Jer. 4. 30. w. wilt thou do? ‖ 13. 21. w. wilt thou say?
8. 6. w. have I done? 48. 19. and say, w. is done?
Hos. 6. 4. O Ephraim, w. shall I do unto thee?
9. 14. give them, O Lord, w. wilt thou give them?
14. 8. w. have I to do any more with idols?
Joel 3. 4. yea, and w. have ye to do with me?
Amos 4. 13. and declare unto man w. is his thought
Zech. 1. 9. O my Lord, w. are these? 4. 4. | 6. 4.
19. I said, w. be these? 4. 5, 13. ‖ 5. 6. w. is it?
Mat. 5. 47. w. do you more than others?
6. 25. I say to you, take no thought w. ye shall eat, or w. ye shall drink, 31. Luke 12. 22, 29.
8. 29. w. have we to do with thee, Jesus thou Son of God? Mark 1. 24. | 5. 7. Luke 4. 34. | 8. 28.
12. 3. have ye not read w. David did, when he was an hungered? Mark 2. 25. Luke 6. 3.
19. 27. have forsaken all w. shall we have therefore?
27. 4. they said, w. is that to us? see thou to that
Mark 6. 30. told w. they had done, and w. they taught
9. 6. for he wist not w. to say, they were afraid
14. 36. this cup, not w. I will, but w. thou wilt
Luke 3. 10. people asked w. shall we do then? 12. 17.
7. 31. the Lord said, unto w. are they like?
12. 49. w. will I, if it be already kindled?
23. 34. forgive them, they know not w. they do
John 1. 21. w. then? ‖ 9. 26. w. did he to thee
12. 49. w. I should say, and w. I should speak
16. 18. w. is this that he saith, a little while?
21. 22. w. is that to thee? follow thou me, 23.
Acts 2. 37. brethren, w. shall we do? 4. 16.
9. 6. Lord, w. wilt thou have me to do? 22. 10.
10. 4. w. is it, Lord ‖ 11. 17. w. was I, that withstand
16. 30. w. must I do? ‖ 21. 22. w. is it therefore?
19. 3. he said to them, to w. then were ye baptized?
Rom. 3. 5. w. shall we say? 4. 1. | 6. 1. | 7. 7.
9. w. then? 6. 15. | 8. 31. | 9. 14, 30. | 11. 7. 1 Cor. 10. 19. | 14. 15. Phil. 1. 18.
7. 15. for that which I do I allow not, w. I would that do I not, but w. I hate, that do I
1 Cor. 4. 21. w. will ye? shall I come with a rod?
2 Cor. 11. 12. w. I do, that I will do, I cut off occasion
Phil. 1. 22. yet w. I shall choose I wot not
1 Tim. 1. 7. understanding neither w. they say
2 Tim. 2. 7. consider w. I say, the Lord give underst.
Heb. 11. 32. w. shall I more say? time would fail
Jam. 4. 14. ye know not w. shall be on the morrow, for w. is your life? it is even a vapour
1 Pet. 1. 11. searching w. or w. manner of time
1 John 3. 2. it doth not appear w. we shall be

See THINGS.

WHATSOEVER.

Gen. 31. 16. now w. God hath said unto thee, do
Lev. 27. 32. even of w. passeth under the rod
Num. 22. 17. I will do w. thou sayest unto me
Deut. 2. 37. nor w. the Lord our God forbad us
12. 32. w. I command you, observe to do it
Judg. 10. 15. do thou to us w. 1 Sam. 14. 36.
1 Kings 8. 37. w. plague, w. sickness there be
38. w. supplication be made. 2 Chron. 6. 28.
Job 41. 11. w. is under the whole heaven is mine
Psal. 1. 3. leaf not wither, w. he doth shall prosper
8. 8. w. passeth through the paths of the sea
115. 3. but our God is in the heavens, he hath done w. he pleased, 135. 6. Eccl. 8. 3.
Eccl. 3. 14. w. God doeth, it shall be for ever
Jer. 1. 7. w. I command thee, thou shalt speak
15. † 7. I will bereave them of w. is dear
44. 17. we will do w. goeth out of our own mouth
Mat. 5. 37. w. is more than these cometh of evil
7. 12. w. ye would that men should do to you
14. 7. whereupon Herod promised with an oath to give her w. she would ask, Mark 6. 22.
17. 12. have done to him w. they listed, Mark 9. 13.
20. 4. and w. is right I will give you, 7.
21. 22. all things w. ye shall ask in prayer, believing, ye shall receive, Mark 11. 23, 24. John 14. 13.
23. 3. w. they bid you observe that observe and do

Mat. 28. 20. observe all things w. I have command.
John 2. 5. his mother saith, w. he saith to you, do it
15. 14. ye are my friends, if do w. I command you
16. w. ye shall ask in my name, 16. 23.
Acts 3. 22. him hear in all things w. shall say to you
Rom. 14. 23. for w. is not of faith is sin
1 Cor. 10. 25. w. is sold in the shambles, that eat
27. w. is set before you, eat, asking no questions
31. or w. ye do, do all to the glory of God
Gal. 2. 6. w. they were, it maketh no matter to me
6. 7. w. a man soweth, that shall he also reap
Phil. 4. 8. w. things are true, w. things are pure
11. I have learned in w. state I am to be content
Col. 3. 17. w. ye do in word, &c. do all in name of Jes.
23. w. ye do, do it heartily as to the Lord
1 John 3. 22. w. we ask we receive of him, 5. 15.
3 John 5. thou doest faithfully w. thou doest

WHEAT.

Gen. 30. 14. Reuben found mandrakes in w. harvest
Exod. 9. 32. but the w. and rye were not smitten
34. 22. the first-fruits of w. harvest, Num. 18. 12.
Deut. 32. 14. goats, with the fat of kidneys of w.
Judg. 6. 11. and Gideon threshed w. to hide it
15. 1. time of w. harvest Samson visited his wife
Ruth 2. 23. to glean unto the end of w. harvest
1 Sam. 6. 13. they of Beth-shemesh reaping w.
12. 17. is it not w. harvest day? I will call to Lord
2 Sam. 4. 6. as tho' they would have fetched w.
1 Kings 5. 11. Solomon gave Hiram w. for food
1 Chron. 21. 23. I give the w. for the meat-offering
Ezra 6. 9. give what they have need of, w. salt, wine
7. 22. done speedily, to an hundred measures of w.
Job 31. 40. let thistles grow instead of w.
Psal. 81. 16. he should have fed them with finest of w.
147. 14. he filleth thee with the finest of w.
Prov. 27. 22. bray a fool in a mortar among w.
Cant. 7. 2. thy belly is like a heap of w. set about
Jer. 12. 13. they have sown w. but reap thorns
23. 28. what is the chaff to the w. saith the Lord
31. 12. flow together for w. for wine, and for oil
Ezek. 27. 17. Judah traded in w. of Minnith
Joel 2. 24. the floors shall be full of w. fats overflow
Amos 5. 11. ye take from him burdens of w.
8. 5. the sabbath gone, that we may set forth w.
6. may buy the poor, and sell refuse of w.
Mat. 3. 12. gather his w. into garner, Luke 3. 17.
13. 25. the enemy sowed tares among the w.
29. lest ye root up also the w. with them
30. to burn them, but gather the w. into my barn
Luke 16. 7. owest thou? he said 100 measures of w.
22. 31. desired to have you, that he may sift as w.
John 12. 24. except a corn of w. fall to the ground
Acts 27. 38. and cast out the w. into the sea
1 Cor. 15. 37. it may chance of w. or some other grain
Rev. 6. 6. I heard a voice, a measure of w. for a penny
18. 13. the merchandise of w. is departed from thee

See BARLEY.

WHEATEN.

Exod. 29. 2. cakes and wafers shalt make of w. flour

WHEEL.

Psal. 83. 13. O my God, make them like a w.
Prov. 20. 26. a wise king bringeth the w. over them
Eccl. 12. 6. or the w. broken at the cistern
Isa. 28. 28. nor break it with the w. of his cart
Ezek. 1. 15. behold, one w. upon the earth
16. was as it were a w. in the midst of a w. 10. 10.
10. 13. was cried to the wheels in my hearing, O w.

WHEELS.

Exod. 14. 25. and took off their chariot w.
Judg. 5. 28. why tarry the w. of his chariots
Prov. 25. † 11. a word spoken upon his w. is like
Isa. 5. 28. and their w. like a whirlwind
Jer. 18. 3. he wrought a work on the w.
47. 3. and at the rumbling of his w.
Ezek. 1. 16. the appearance of the w. their work
3. 13. at the noise of w. over-against them
10. 19. the w. also were beside them, 11, 22.
23. 24. the Babylonians come against thee with w.
26. 10. thy walls shake at the noise of the w.
Dan. 7. 9. throne like flames, and his w. a burning fire
Nah. 3. 2. the noise of the rattling of the w.

WHELP, S.

2 Sam. 17. 8. as a bear robbed of her w. in the field
Prov. 17. 12. let a bear robbed of her w. meet a man
Ezek. 19. 2. she nourished her w. among lions
3. she brought up one of her w. a young lion
5. she took another of her w. and made him
Hos. 13. 8. will meet them as a bear bereav. of her w.
Nah. 2. 12. the lion did tear enough for his w.

See LIONS.

WHEN.

Lev. 14. 57. to teach w. it is unclean and w. clean
Deut. 6. 7. talk of them w. thou sittest and w. thou walkest, w. thou liest down, and w. thou risest up, 11. 19.
1 Sam. 3. 12. w. I begin, I will also make an end
1 Kings 8. 30. hear in heaven w. thou hearest, forgive
Neh. 2. 6. the king said, w. wilt thou return?
Psal. 94. 8. and, ye fools, w. will ye be wise?
Eccl. 8. 7. for who can tell him w. it shall be?
Jer. 13. 27. Jerusalem made clean, w. shall it be
Zech. 7. 5. w. ye fasted ‖ 6. w. ye did eat, and w. drink
Mat. 24. 3. tell us w. shall these things be, what shall be sign of thy coming? Mark 13. 4. Luke 21. 7.
John 4. 25. w. he is come, he will tell us all things, 16. 8.
20. 20. w. he had so said, shewed them his hands
Acts 2. 37. w. they heard this, they said to Peter
2 Thess. 3. 10. w. we were with you, this we command
1 John 2. 28. w. he shall appear, we may have confid.

WHENCE.

Gen. 16. 8. the angel said, Hagar, w. camest thou?
42. 7. Joseph said to them, w. come ye? Josh. 9. 8.
Deut. 11. 10. is not like Egypt, from w. ye came out
Josh. 2. 4. men came, but I wist not w. they were
Judg. 13. 6. I asked him not w. he was, nor told he me
17. 9. Micah said, w. comest thou? 19. 17. 2 Sam. 1. 3. 2 Kings 5. 25. Job 1. 7. | 2. 2. Jonah 1. 8.
2 Kings 20. 14. Isaiah said, what said these men? from w. came these men unto thee? Isa. 39. 3.
Job 10. 21. before I go w. I shall not return, 16. 22.
Isa. 47. 11. thou shalt not know from w. it riseth
51. 1. look to the rock w. ye are hewn, and pit

Mat. 12. 44. I will return to my house *w.* I came out, he findeth it empty, and swept and garnished, *Luke* 11. 24.
13. 54. *w.* hath this man this wisdom and works?
56. *w.* hath this man all these things? *Mark* 6. 2.
Mark 12. 37. calleth him Lord, *w.* is he then his son?
Luke 1. 43. *w.* is this to me that the mother of Lord?
13. 25. shall answer, I know you not *w.* ye are, 27.
John 1. 48. Nathanael said, *w.* knowest thou me?
7. 28. ye both know me, and ye know *w.* I am
8. 14. ye cannot tell *w.* I come and whither I go
9. 29. we know not from *w.* he is, 30.
Phil. 3. 20. from *w.* we look for the Saviour, L. Jes.
Heb. 11. 19. from *w.* he received him in a figure
Jam. 4. 1. from *w.* come wars and fightings?
Rev. 2. 5. remember from *w.* thou art fallen
7. 13. what are these in white robes, *w.* came they

WHENSOEVER.

Mark 14. 7. *w.* ye will ye may do them good

WHERE.

Gen. 3. 9. *w.* art thou? ‖ *Job* 38. 4. *w.* wast thou?
Exod. 2. 20. *w.* is he? 2 *Sam.* 9. 4. *Job* 14. 10.
20. 24. in all places *w.* I record my name will come
29. 42. *w.* I will meet you to speak, 30. 6, 36.
Deut. 32. 37. he shall say, *w.* are their gods
Job 9. 24. if not, *w.* and who is he?
35. 10. none saith, *w.* is G. my maker who gives
Psal. 42. 3. while they say to me, *w.* is thy G.? 10.
79. 10. why say, *w.* is their God? 115. 2. *Joel* 2. 17.
Isa. 49. 21. was left alone, these, *w.* had they been?
Jer. 2. 6. neither said they, *w.* is the Lord? 8.
36. 19. go hide thee, let no man know *w.* ye be
Hos. 1. 10. *w.* it was said to them, ye are not my peo.
Zech. 1. 5. fathers, *w.* are they? do they live for ever?
Luke 17. 37. *w.* Lord? ‖ *John* 7. 11. *w.* is he? 9. 12.
John 7. 34. *w.* I am, 12. 26. | 14. 3. | 17. 24.

WHEREABOUT.

1 *Sam.* 21. 2. let no man know *w.* I send thee

WHEREAS.

1 *Sam.* 24. 17. *w.* I reward thee evil for good
1 *Kings* 8. 18. *w.* it was in thy heart to build a house
Ezek. 13. 7. *w.* ye say, the Lord saith it
35. 10. we will possess it, *w.* the Lord was there
Jam. 4. 14. *w.* ye know not what will be on morrow

WHEREBY.

Jer. 33. 8. iniquity *w.* they have sinned against me
Ezek. 18. 31. transgressions *w.* ye have transgressed
39. 26. trespasses *w.* they have trespassed ag. me
Luke 1. 18. *w.* shall I know this? for I am an old man
Acts 4. 12. no other name *w.* we must be saved
Rom. 8. 15. the Spirit *w.* we cry, Abba, Father
Eph. 4. 30. *w.* ye are sealed to the day of redemption

WHEREFORE.

2 *Sam.* 12. 23. *w.* should I fast, can I bring him again
16. 10. who shall then say, *w.* hast thou done so?
Mal. 2. 15. *w.* one? that he might seek a godly seed
Mat. 14. 31. O thou of little faith, *w.* didst thou doubt
26. 50. Jesus said, friend, *w.* art thou come?
Acts 10. 21. what is the cause *w.* ye are come?

WHERETO.

Isa. 55. 11. it shall prosper in things *w.* I sent it
Phil. 3. 16. *w.* ye have already attained, let us walk

WHEREWITH.

Judg. 6. 15. O my Lord, *w.* shall I save Israel?
1 *Kings* 22. 22. the Lord said to him, *w.* 2 *Chr.* 18. 20.
2 *Chron.* 35. 21. but against the house *w.* I have war
Psal. 119. 42. so shall I have *w.* to answer him
Mic. 6. 6. *w.* shall I come before the Lord?
Mat. 5. 13. are salt of earth, if salt lose its savour, *w.* shall it be salted? *Mark* 9. 5. *Luke* 14. 34.
John 17. 26. the love *w.* thou hast loved me
Eph. 2. 4. for this great love *w.* he hath loved us

WHEREWITHAL.

Mat. 6. 31. what shall we eat? or *w.* we be clothed?

WHET.

Deut. 6. † 7. thou shalt *w.* them unto thy children
32. 41. if I *w.* my glittering sword, I will reward
Psal. 7. 12. if he turn not, he will *w.* his sword
64. 3. who *w.* their tongue like a sword, and bend
Eccl. 10. 10. if iron blunt, and he *w.* not the edge

WHETHER.

1 *Kings* 20. 18. *w.* they be for peace, or *w.* for war
Ezra 2. 59. *w.* they were of Israel, *Neh.* 7. 61.
Ezek. 2. 5. *w.* they will hear or forbear, 7. | 3. 11.
Mat. 21. 31. *w.* of them did the will of his father?
23. 17. *w.* is greater, the gold or the temple?
John 7. 17. shall know of the doctrine, *w.* it be of G.
Rom. 14. 8. *w.* we live or die, we are the Lord's
1 *Cor.* 15. 11. *w.* it were I or they, so we preach
2 *Cor.* 12. 2. *w.* in the body, or *w.* out of the body, 3.
1 *John* 4. 1. but try the spirits *w.* they are of God

WHICH.

Gen. 3. 17. of the tree *w.* I commanded thee, saying
45. 6. in *w.* there shall be neither earing nor harvest
Num. 19. 2. a heifer upon *w.* never came yoke
Luke 21. 6. in *w.* there shall not be left one stone
John 8. 46. *w.* of you convinceth me of sin?
10. 32. for *w.* of those works do ye stone me?
Acts 26. 16. in the *w.* I will appear unto thee
Col. 3. 7. in the *w.* ye also walked some time
Heb. 7. 19. a better hope by *w.* we draw nigh to G.
9. 5. of *w.* we cannot now speak particularly
12. 14. follow peace with all men, and holiness, without *w.* no man shall see the Lord
Jam. 2. 7. that worthy name, by *w.* ye are called
1 *Pet.* 3. 19. by *w.* he preached to spirits in prison

WHILE.

Deut. 31. 27. *w.* I am yet alive with you this day
1 *Sam.* 20. 14. not only *w.* yet I live shew kindness
2 *Sam.* 12. 18. *w.* the child was yet alive, 21. 22.
2 *Chr.* 15. 2. Lord is with you *w.* ye be with him
34. 3. *w.* Josiah was yet young, he began to seek G.
Job 20. 23. God shall rain it on him *w.* he is eating
Psal. 7. 2. tear my soul *w.* there is none to deliver
49. 18. though *w.* he lived, he blessed his soul
63. 4. thus will I bless thee *w.* I live, 146. 2.
104. 33. will praise G. *w.* I have my being, 146. 2.
Isa. 55. 6. seek ye the Lord *w.* he may be found
Jer. 15. 9. her sun is gone down *w.* it was yet day
40. 5. now *w.* he was not yet gone back
Mat. 5. 25. agree *w.* thou art in the way with him
27. 63. that deceiver said, *w.* he was yet alive

Mark 2. 19. can the children of bride-chamber fast *w.* the bridegroom is with them? *Luke* 5. 34.
Luke 24. 44. I spake *w.* I was yet with you
John 9. 4. do work of him that sent me *w.* it is day
1 *Tim.* 5. 6. that liveth in pleasure is dead *w.* she liv.
Heb. 3. 15. *w.* it is said, to-day if ye will hear his voice

A WHILE.

Gen. 46. 29. Joseph wept on his neck *a* good *w.*
1 *Sam.* 9. 27. Samuel said to Saul, stand thou still *a w.*
2 *Sam.* 7. 19. thou hast spoken for *a* great *w.*
Mat. 13. 21. hath not root, but dureth for *a w.*
Luke 8. 13. which for *a w.* believe, in time fall away
18. 4. he would not for *a w.* but afterwards he said
1 *Pet.* 5. 10. after have suffered *a w.* make you perfect

All the WHILE.

1 *Sam.* 22. 4. *all the w.* David was in the hold
25. 7. none missing *all the w.* they were in Carm. 16.
27. 11. so will be his manner *all the w.* he dwelleth
Job 27. 3. *all the w.* my breath is in me and Spirit of [God
See LITTLE.

Long WHILE.

Acts 20. 11. had talked a *long w.* even till break of [day

WHIP.

Prov. 26. 3. a *w.* for the horse, a rod for a fool's back
Nah. 3. 2. the noise of a *w.* the noise of the wheels

WHIPS.

1 *Kings* 12. 11. my father chastised you with *w.* I will chastise you with scorpions, 14. 2 *Chr.* 10. 11, 14.

WHIRLETH.

Eccl. 1. 6. wind *w.* continually and returneth again

WHIRLWIND.

2 *Kings* 2. 1. Lord would take up Elijah by a *w.* 11.
Job 37. 9. out of the south cometh the *w.* and cold
38. 1. the Lord answered Job out of the *w.* 40. 6.
Psal. 58. 9. he shall take them away as in a *w.* both living and in wrath, *Prov.* 10. 25. *Hos.* 13. 3.
Prov. 1. 27. when your destruction cometh as a *w.*
Isa. 5. 28. counted like flint and their wheels like a *w.*
17. 13. chased like a rolling thing before the *w.*
40. 24. the *w.* shall take them away as stubble
41. 16. shalt fan them, the *w.* shall scatter them
66. 15. Lord come with chariots like a *w.* *Jer.* 4. 13.
Jer. 23. 19. a *w.* of the Lord is gone forth in fury
25. 32. a great *w.* shall be raised up from earth
30. 23. a continuing *w.* shall fall on the wicked
Ezek. 1. 4. behold, a *w.* came out of the north
Dan. 11. 40. king shall come against him like a *w.*
Hos. 8. 7. they have sown wind, they shall reap the *w.*
Amos 1. 14. devour palaces in the day of the *w.*
Nah. 1. 3. the Lord hath his way in the *w.*
Hab. 3. 14. they came out as a *w.* to scatter me
Zech. 7. 14. but I scattered them with a *w.*

WHIRLWINDS.

Isa. 21. 1. as *w.* in the south pass through
Zech. 9. 14. Lord shall go forth with *w.* in the south

WHISPER.

Psal. 41. 7. all that hate me *w.* together against me
Isa. 29. 4. thy speech shall *w.* out of the dust

WHISPERED.

2 *Sam.* 12. 19. when David saw that his servants *w.*

WHISPERER.

Prov. 16. 28. a *w.* separateth chief friends
26. † 20. where there is no *w.* strife ceaseth

WHISPERERS.

Rom. 1. 29. full of envy, murder, debate, deceit, *w.*

WHISPERINGS.

2 *Cor.* 12. 20. lest there be *w.* swellings, tumults

WHIT.

1 *Sam.* 3. 18. Samuel told Eli every *w.* hid nothing
John 7. 23. I have made a man every *w.* whole
13. 10. save to wash his feet, but is clean every *w.*
2 *Cor.* 11. 5. I was not a *w.* behind chiefest apostles

WHITE.

Gen. 30. 37. Jacob made the *w.* appear in the rods
49. 12. and his teeth shall be *w.* with milk
Exod. 16. 31. manna was like coriander-seed, *w.*
Lev. 13. 3. if the hair be turned *w.* 4, 20, 25.
4. if the bright spot be *w.* in the skin, 19, 24.
10. if the rising be *w.* in the skin, 19, 43.
21. but if there be no *w.* hairs therein, 26.
Num. 12. 10. Miriam became leprous, *w.* as snow
Judg. 5. 10. speak, ye that ride on *w.* asses
2 *Kings* 5. 27. Gehazi went out a leper *w.* as snow
2 *Chr.* 5. 12. the Levites being arrayed in *w.* linen
Esth. 8. 15. Mordecai went out in *w.* apparel
Job 6. 6. is there any taste in the *w.* of an egg?
Psal. 68. 14. it was *w.* as snow in Salmon
Eccl. 9. 8. let thy garments be always *w.*
Cant. 5. 10. my beloved is *w.* and ruddy, the chiefest
Isa. 1. 18. your sins as scarlet, they shall be *w.* as snow
Ezek. 27. 18. Damascus traded in *w.* wool
Dan. 7. 9. whose garment was *w.* as snow
11. 35. some of them shall fall to make them *w.*
12. 10. many shall be purified and made *w.*
Joel 1. 7. the branches thereof are made *w.*
Zech. 1. 8. there were red horses, speckled and *w.*
Mat. 5. 36. thou canst not make one hair *w.* or black
17. 2. his raiment was *w.* as the light, *Luke* 9. 29.
28. 3. the angel's raiment was *w.* *Acts* 1. 10.
Mark 16. 5. a man clothed in a long *w.* garment
John 4. 35. the fields are *w.* already to harvest
Rev. 1. 14. his head and his hairs were *w.* like wool
2. 17. will give him a *w.* stone and a new name
3. 4. they shall walk with me in *w.* they are worthy
5. he that overcometh shall be clothed in *w.* raiment, 4. 4. | 7. 9, 13. | 15. 6. | 19. 8, 14.
18. buy *w.* raiment, that thou mayest be clothed
6. 2. and I saw, and behold a *w.* horse, 19. 11.
7. 14. have made them *w.* in the blood of the Lamb
14. 14. a *w.* cloud ‖ 20. 11. I saw a *w.* throne

WHITE.

Mark 9. 3. so as no fuller on earth can *w.* them

WHITED.

Mat. 23. 27. the scribes were like to *w.* sepulchres
Acts 23. 3. God shall smite thee, thou *w.* wall

WHITER.

Psal. 51. 7. wash me, and I shall be *w.* than snow
Lam. 4. 7. her Nazarites are *w.* than milk

WHITHER.

Gen. 16. 8. Hagar, Sarai's maid, *w.* wilt thou go?
1 *Sam.* 10. 14. Saul's uncle said, *w.* went ye?
2 *Kings* 5. 25. and he said, thy servant went no *w.*

Cant. 6. 1. *w.* is thy beloved gone? O thou fairest
Zech. 5. 10. I said, *w.* do these bear the ephah?
Heb. 11. 8. Abrah. obeyed and went, not knowing *w.*
See GO, GOEST, GOETH.

WHITHERSOEVER.

2 *Sam.* 8. 6. the Lord preserved David *w.* he went, 14. 2 *Kings* 18. 7. 1 *Chron.* 18. 6, 13.
Prov. 17. 8. *w.* it turneth it prospereth, a gift precious
21. 1. he turneth the king's heart *w.* he will
Mat. 8. 19. I will follow thee *w.* thou goest, *Luke* 9. 57.
Rev. 14. 4. these follow the Lamb *w.* he goeth

WHO.

Gen. 27. 18. *w.* art thou, my son? 32. *Ruth* 3. 9, 16. *John* 1. 19, 22. | 8. 25. | 21. 12.
33. 5. Esau said, *w.* are those with thee? 48. 8.
Exod. 3. 11. *w.* am I? 1 *Sam.* 18. 18. 2 *Sam.* 7. 18.
5. 2. *w.* is the Lord? *Prov.* 30. 9. *John* 9. 36.
15. 11. *w.* is like thee, O Lord, among the gods? *Deut.* 33. 29. 1 *Sam.* 26. 15. *Psal.* 35. 10.
32. 26. Moses stood and said, *w.* is on Lord's side?
1 *Sam.* 25. 10. *w.* is David? and *w.* is son of Jesse?
2 *Kings* 9. 32. Jehu said, *w.* is on my side, *w.*?
10. 9. but *w.* slew all these ‖ 13. Jehu said, *w.* are ye?
Neh. 6. 11. *w.* would go into temple to save his life?
Esth. 7. 5. *w.* is he? and where is he? *Job* 9. 24. | 17. 3. | 42. 3. *Jer.* 9. 12. *Mat.* 26. 68.
Psal. 4. 6. many say, *w.* will shew us any good?
59. 7. they belch out, for *w.* say they, doth hear?
Prov. 23. 29. *w.* hath woe? *w.* hath sorrow? *w.* hath contentions and babbling? *w.* hath redness of eyes?
Isa. 6. 8. *w.* will go for us? ‖ 29. 15. *w.* seeth us?
Jer. 21. 13. *w.* shall come down against us?
49. 4. saying, *w.* shall come unto me?
19. *w.* is like me? *w.* will appoint me time? 50. 44.
Lam. 2. 13. O daughter of Zion, *w.* can heal thee?
3. 37. *w.* is he that saith, and it cometh to pass
Mat. 21. 10. say, *w.* is this? *Luke* 5. 21. | 7. 49. | 9. 9.
Luke 19. 3. Zaccheus sought to see Jesus *w.* he was
John 5. 13. he that was healed, wist not *w.* it was
13. 25. Lord, *w.* is it? ‖ *Acts* 19. 15. *w.* are ye
Acts 9. 5. he said, *w.* art thou, Lord? 22. 8. | 26. 15.
21. 33. capt. demanded *w.* he was, what he had done
1 *Cor.* 3. 5. *w.* then is Paul? and *w.* is Apollos?
2 *Cor.* 2. 16. and *w.* is sufficient for these things?
11. 29. *w.* is weak? *w.* is offended and I burn not?
Jam. 4. 12. *w.* art thou that judgest another?
1 *John* 2. 22. *w.* is a liar, but he that denieth Christ?
Rev. 6. 17. and *w.* shall be able to stand?
13. 4. saying, *w.* is like unto the beast? *w.* is able to
15. 4. *w.* shall not fear thee, O L. glorify thy name?

WHOLE.

Exod. 29. 18. shalt burn *w.* ram on altar, *Lev.* 8. 21.
Lev. 4. 12. even the *w.* bullock shall he carry forth
10. 6. let the *w.* house of Israel bewail the burning
Josh. 11. 23. so Joshua took the *w.* land and gave it
2 *Sam.* 1. 9. because my life is yet *w.* in me
2 *Chr.* 15. 15. Judah sought him with their *w.* desire
Psal. 51. 19. shalt be pleased with *w.* burnt offering
Prov. 1. 12. let us swallow them up alive, and *w.*
16. 33. the *w.* disposing thereof is of the Lord
Eccl. 12. 13. for this is the *w.* duty of man
Isa. 54. 5. thy Redeemer, the Holy One, the God of *w.* earth shall he be called, *Mic.* 4. 13. *Zech.* 4. 14.
Jer. 19. 11. a vessel that cannot be made *w.* again
45. 4. I will pluck up even this *w.* land
Ezek. 15. 5. when *w.* it was meet for no work
Mal. 3. 9. ye have robbed me, even this *w.* nation
Mat. 5. 29. not that thy *w.* body be cast into hell, 30.
8. 32. the *w.* herd of swine ran violently down
13. 33. till the *w.* was leavened, *Luke* 13. 21.
16. 26. what is a man profited if he gain *w.* world and lose his own soul? *Mark* 8. 36. *Luke* 9. 25.
Luke 23. 1. *w.* multitude of them arose and led him
John 4. 53. and himself believed, and his *w.* house
11. 50. is expedient that the *w.* nation perish not
Acts 13. 44. came almost the *w.* city to hear word
1 *Cor.* 12. 17. if *w.* body were an eye, where hearing
1 *Thess.* 5. 23. I pray your *w.* spirit and body preser.
Jam. 2. 10. whosoever shall keep the *w.* law
1 *John* 2. 2. but also for the sins of the *w.* world
5. 19. and the *w.* world lieth in wickedness
See CONGREGATION, HEART.

WHOLE *for sound.*

Josh. 5. 8. they abode in the camp till they were *w.*
Job 5. 18. he woundeth, and his hands make *w.*
Mat. 9. 12. they that be *w.* need not a physician, but they that are sick, *Mark* 2. 17. *Luke* 5. 31.
21. touch his garment, I shall be *w.* *Mark* 5. 28.
22. the woman was made *w.* from that hour
12. 13. his hand was made *w.* *Mark* 3. 5. *Luke* 6. 10.
15. 28. her daughter was made *w.* from that hour
31. wondered when they saw the maimed to be *w.*
Mark 5. 34. thy faith hath made thee *w.* go in peace and be *w.* of thy plague, *Luke* 8. 48. | 17. 19.
Luke 7. 10. found the servant *w.* that had been sick
John 5. 6. Jesus saith, wilt thou be made *w.*?
14. behold, thou art made *w.* sin no more
7. 23. because I have made a man every whit *w.*
Acts 4. 9. if examined by what means he is made *w.*
9. 34. Eneas, Jesus Christ maketh thee *w.*

WHOLLY.

Lev. 6. 22. it is a statute, it shall be *w.* burnt, 23.
19. 9. thou shalt not *w.* reap corners of thy field
Num. 3. 9. for they are *w.* given to him out of Israel
4. 6. a cloth *w.* of blue ‖ 8. 16. are *w.* given me
32. 11. because they have not *w.* followed me
Deut. 1. 36. to Caleb's children give the land, because he hath *w.* followed the Lord, *Josh.* 14. 8, 9, 14.
Judg. 17. 3. I had *w.* dedicated the silver to Lord
1 *Sam.* 7. 9. Samuel offered a sucking lamb *w.*
1 *Chron.* 28. 21. all the people *w.* at thy command
Job 21. 23. one dieth, being *w.* at ease and quiet
Isa. 22. 1. thou art *w.* gone up to the house-tops
Jer. 2. 21. yet I had planted thee *w.* a right seed
6. 6. she is *w.* oppression in the midst of her
13. 19. Judah shall be *w.* carried away captive
42. 15. if ye *w.* set your faces to enter Egypt
46. 28. yet will I not leave thee *w.* unpunished
50. 13. Babylon not be inhabited, but *w.* desolate
Ezek. 11. 15. all the house of Israel *w.* are they
Amos 8. 8. and it shall rise up *w.* as a flood, 9. 5.
Acts 17. 16. he saw the city *w.* given to idolatry

1 Thess. 5. 23. the God of peace sanctify you w.
1 Tim. 4. 15. meditate, give thyself w. to them

WHOLESOME.

Prov. 15. 4. a w. tongue is a tree of life, but perv.
1 Tim. 6. 3. if any man consent not to w. words

WHOM.

Gen. 22. 2. take thy only son Isaac w. thou lovest
30. 26. give me my wives, for w. I served thee
43. 27. the old man of w. ye spake, is he alive? 29.
Exod. 33.19. will be gracious to w. I will be gracious
Lev. 17. 7. after w. they have gone a whoring
Num. 11. 21. people, amongst w. I am, are 600,000
Deut. 32. 20. they are children in w. is no faith
37. where their gods? their rock in w. they trusted
Josh. 24. 15. choose you this day w. ye will serve
Judg. 7. 4. that of w. I say, this shall go with thee
1 Sam. 6. 20. and to w. shall he go up from us?
9. 20. and on w. is all the desire of Israel?
29. 5. David, of w. they sang one to another
30. 13. David said unto him, to w. belongest thou?
2 Sam. 16. 19. and again, w. should I serve?
1 Kings 20. 14. Ahab said, by w.? 22. 8. Ezra 10.
44. Rom. 1. 5. | 5. 2, 11. Gal. 6. 14.
2 Kings 19. 10. thy G. in w. thou trustest, Isa. 37. 10.
Psal. 16. 3. but to the saints, in w. is all my delight
18. 2. my God, my strength, in w. I will trust
73. 25. w. have I in heav. but thee? none on earth
146. 3. not trust in son of man, in w. there is no help
Prov. 3. 12. as a father the son, in w. he delighteth
27. withhold not good from them to w. it is due
30. 31. a king against w. there is no rising up
Eccl. 4. 8. neither saith he, for w. do I labour?
Cant. 3. 1. I sought him w. my soul loveth, 2, 3.
Isa. 6. 8. I heard a voice saying, w. shall I send?
10. 3. what in visitation? to w. will ye flee for help
22. 16. what hast thou here? w. hast thou here?
31. 6. turn to him from w. Israel hath revolted
40. 18. to w. then will ye liken God? 25. | 46. 5.
42. 1. behold mine elect, in w. my soul delighteth
49. 3. art my servant, O Isr. in w. I will be glorified
51. 19. famine and sword, by w. shall I comfort thee
57. 4. against w. do ye sport yourselves?
11. and of w. hast thou been afraid, or feared?
Jer. 8. 2. w. they have loved, w. they have served,
after w. they have walked, and w. they sought
Lam. 1. 14. from w. I am not able to rise up
4. 20. of w. we said, under his shadow we live
Ezek. 31. 2. son of man spake unto Pharaoh, &c.
w. art thou like in thy greatness?
18. to w. art thou like in glory and greatness?
Dan. 5. 19. w. he would he slew, w. he would he kept
alive, set up, and w. he would he pulled down
Amos 7. 2. O Lord, by w. shall Jacob arise? 5.
Nah. 3. 19. on w. hath not thy wickedness passed?
Mat. 3. 17. this is my beloved Son, in w. I am well
pleased, 17. 5. Mark 1. 11. 2 Pet. 2. 17.
11. 10. this is he of w. it is written, John 1. 15, 30.
16. 15. Jesus saith to them, but w. say ye that I
am? Mark 10. 29. Luke 9. 20.
John 5. 21. w. he will || 45. Moses in w. ye trust
6. 68. Lord, to w. shall we go? || 17. 3. w. thou sent
Acts 8. 34. of w. speaketh the prophet this?
27. 23. angel of God, whose I am, and w. I serve
Rom. 15. 21. to w. he was not spoken of, shall see
1 Cor. 1. 9. God is faithful, by w. ye are called
3. 5. who is Paul and Apollos, but ministers by w. ye
7. 39. she is at liberty to be married to w. she will
8. 6. one God, of w. are all things, Heb. 2. 10.
2 Cor. 1. 10. in w. we trust that he will deliver us
Eph. 1. 7. in w. we have redemption through his
blood, the forgiveness of sins, Col. 1. 14.
11. in w. also we have obtained an inheritance
13. in w. ye also trusted, in w. ye were sealed
2. 3. among w. also we all had our conversation
21. in w. the building groweth to a temple
22. in w. you also are builded together for habitat.
3. 12. in w. ye have boldness and access with confid.
Phil. 2. 15. among w. ye shine as lights in the world
3. 8. for w. I have suffered the loss of all things
Col. 1. 28. w. we preach || 2. 11. in w. ye are circumcised
2. 3. in w. are hid all the treasures of wisdom
2 Thess. 2. 8. that wicked, w. the Lord shall consume
1 Tim. 1. 15. to save sinners, of w. I am chief
20. of w. is Hymeneus and Alex. 2 Tim. 2. 17.
2 Tim. 1. 15. of w. are Phygellus and Hermogenes
4. 15. the copper-smith, of w. be thou ware also
18. preserve to his heavenly kingd. to w. be glory
for ever, amen, Gal. 1. 5. Heb. 13. 21.
1 Pet. 4. 11.
Heb. 3. 17. with w. was he grieved forty years?
18. to w. sware he they should not enter into rest
4. 13. to the eyes of him with w. we have to do
7. 2. to w. Abraham gave the tenth part of all
11. 38. of w. the world was not worthy
Jam. 1. 17. father of lights, with w. is no variableness
1 Pet. 1. 12. unto w. it was revealed, that did minister
2. 4. to w. coming, as unto a living stone
2 Pet. 2. 17. to w. darkness is reserved, Jude 13.
19. for of w. a man is overcome, of him brought
Rev. 7. 2. to w. it was given to hurt the earth
17. 2. with w. kings of earth committed fornication
See BEFORE.

WHOMSOEVER.

Gen. 31. 32. with w. thou findest thy gods, not live
Judg. 11. 24. w. the Lord our God shall drive out
Dan. 4. 17. he giveth it to w. he will, 25. 32. | 5. 21.
Mat. 11. 27. he to w. the Son will reveal him
21. 44. but on w. it shall fall, Luke 20. 18.
Luke 4. 6. the devil said, to w. I will I give it
12. 48. to w. much is given, much shall be required
Acts 8. 19. on w. I lay hands, may receive Holy Ghost
1 Cor. 16. 3. w. ye shall approve by your letters

WHORE.

Lev. 19. 29. do not cause her to be a w. lest the land
21. 7. they shall not take a wife that is a w.
9. if she profane herself by playing the w.
Deut. 22. 21. to play the w. in her father's house
23. 17. there shall be no w. of the daughters of Israel
18. thou shalt not bring the hire of a w. or price
Judg. 19. 2. his concubine played the w. against him
Prov. 23. 27. a w. is a deep ditch and a narrow pit
Isa. 57. 3. the seed of the adulterer and the w.
Jer. 3. 3. and thou hast a w. forehead, not ashamed
Ezek. 16. 28. thou hast played the w. also with Assyr.
Rev. 17. 1. will shew judgment of the great w. 19. 2.
15. the waters where the w. sitteth, are peoples
16. these shall hate the w. and make her desolate

WHORES.

Ezek. 16. 33. they give gifts to all w. thou hirest them
Hos. 4. 14. for themselves are separated with w.

WHOREDOM.

Gen. 38. 24. Tamar, behold, she is with child by w.
Lev. 19. 29. lest the land fall to w. and be wicked
Jer. 3. 9. through the lightness of her w. she defiled
13. 27. I have seen the lewdness of thy w.
Ezek. 16. 33. that they may come to thee for thy w.
23. 8. they poured their w. upon her
17. the Babylonians defiled her with their w.
43. 7. Isr. shall not defile my holy name by their w.
9. let them put away their w. far from me
Hos. 4. 11. w. and wine take away the heart
5. 3. O Ephraim, thou committest w. Isr. is defiled
6. 10. there is the w. of Ephraim, Israel is defiled

WHOREDOMS.

Num. 14. 33. your children shall wander and bear w.
2 Kings 9. 22. so long as the w. of thy mother Jezebel
2 Chron. 21. 13. like to the w. of the house of Ahab
Jer. 3. 2. thou hast polluted the land with thy w.
Ezek. 16. 20. is this of thy w. a small matter?
22. in all thy w. hast not remembered days of youth
25. hast multiplied thy w. || 26. hast increased thy w.
34. the contrary from other women in thy w.
23. 35. bear thou also thy lewdness and thy w.
Hos. 1. 2. go take thee a wife and children of w.
2. 2. let her put away her w. out of her sight
4. not have mercy, for they be the children of w.
4. 12. the spirit of w. hath caused them to err, 5. 4.
Nah. 3. 4. because of the multitude of w. that selleth
nations thro' her w. and families thro' witchcraft
See COMMIT.

WHOREMONGER.

Eph. 5. 5. no w. hath any inheritance in kingd. of Ch.

WHOREMONGERS.

1 Tim. 1. 10. the law made for w. for liars
Heb. 13. 4. but w. and adulterers God will judge
Rev. 21. 8. w. shall have their part in the lake
22. 15. for without are w. and murderers

WHORING, See GO, GONE, WENT.

WHORISH.

Prov. 6. 26. for by means of a w. woman a man is
Ezek. 6. 9. because I am broken with their w. heart
16. 30. the work of an imperious w. woman

WHOSE.

Gen. 32. 17. w. art thou? w. are these before thee?
1 Sam. 12. 3. w. ox, or w. ass have I taken?
2 Sam. 3. 12. w. is the land, make thy league
Jer. 44. 28. a remnant shall know w. word shall stand
48. 15. w. name is the Lord of hosts, 51. 57.
Dan. 5. 23. the God in w. hand are all thy ways
Amos 5. 27. saith Lord, w. name is the God of hosts
Mat. 22. 20. he saith to them, w. is this image and
superscription? Mark 12. 16. Luke 20. 24.
42. w. son is he? || John 19. 24. w. it shall be
Luke 12. 20. then w. shall those things be?
Acts 27. 23. angel of God, w. I am, and whom I serve
Heb. 3. 6. Christ over his house, w. house are we
See HEART.

WHOSESOEVER.

John 20. 23. w. sins ye remit, w. sins ye retain

WHOSOEVER.

1 Kings 13. 33. w. would he consecrated him a priest
Mat. 11. 6. blessed w. shall not be offended in me
13. 12. w. hath to him shall be given, w. hath not,
from him shall be taken he hath, Luke 8. 18.
Rom. 2. 1. O man, w. thou art that judgest
1 Cor. 11. 27. w. shall eat this bread unworthily
Gal. 5. 10. shall bear his judgment, w. he be
Rev. 22. 17. w. will, let him take of water of life

WHY.

Gen. 25. 22. Rebekah said, if it be so, w. am I thus?
Judg. 11. 7. w. are ye come to me now in distress?
15. 10. Judah said, w. are ye come up against us?
Ruth 1. 11. turn again, w. will ye go with me?
1 Sam. 2. 23. Eli said, w. do ye such things?
21. 1. w. art thou alone, and no man with thee?
2 Sam. 13. 26. king said, w. should he go with thee?
1 Kings 1. 6. in saying, w. hast thou done so?
2 Chron. 25. 16. forbear, w. shouldest thou be smitten?
Esth. 4. 5. to know what it was and w. it was
Isa. 40. 27. w. sayest thou, O Jacob, my way is hid?
Jer. 8. 14. w. do ye sit still? assemble yourselves
27. 13. w. will ye die? Ezek. 18. 31. | 33. 11.
Mat. 21. 25. he will say to us, w. did ye not then
believe him? Mark 11. 31. Luke 20. 5.
Mark 5. 39. he saith, w. make ye this ado, and weep?
Luke 2. 48. w. hast thou thus dealt with us?
John 7. 45. they said, w. have ye not brought him?
10. 20. many said, he is mad, and w. hear ye him?
Acts 9. 4. he fell to the earth and heard a voice, Saul,
Saul, w. persecutest thou me? 22. 7. | 26. 14.
14. 15. sirs, w. do ye these things? we are men
Rom. 9. 19. thou wilt say, w. doth he yet find fault?
20. thing formed say, w. hast thou made me thus?
1 Cor. 10. 30. w. am I evil spoken of for that?

WICKED.

Gen. 18. 23. wilt thou destroy righteous with w.? 25.
38. 7. Er was w. || Exod. 9. 27. I and my people w.
Exod. 23. 7. for I will not justify the w.
Lev. 20. 17. it is a w. thing, they shall be cut off
Deut. 15. 9. there be not a thought in thy w. heart
17. 5. who have committed that w. thing
23. 9. and keep thee from every w. thing
25. 1. and condemn the w. 1 Kings 8. 32.
1 Sam. 2. 9. the w. shall be silent in darkness
24. 13. wickedness proceedeth from the w.
2 Kings 17. 11. Israel wrought w. things to provoke
2 Chron. 6. 23. judge thy servant by requiting the w.
7. 14. if my people humble themselves and turn
from their w. ways, Ezek. 18. 21. | 33. 11, 19.
24. 7. the sons of Athaliah that w. woman
Neh. 9. 35. our kings have not served thee, nor turned
they from their w. ways, Ezek. 3. 19. | 13. 22.
Esth. 7. 6. the adversary is this w. Haman
9. 25. Haman's w. device shall return on his head
Job 3. 17. there the w. cease from troubling
9. 22. he destroyeth the perfect and the w.
29. if I be w. why then labour I in vain? 10. 15.
10. 7. thou knowest that I am not w.
21. 7. wherefore do the w. live, become old?
30. the w. is reserved to the day of destruction
27. 7. let mine enemy be as the w. and unrighteous
34. 18. is it fit to say to a king, thou art w.?
38. 13. that the w. might be shaken out of it
15. from the w. their light is withholden
40. 12. and tread down the w. in their place
Psal. 7. 11. God is angry with the w. every day
9. 5. thou hast destroyed the w. for ever
16. the w. is snared in the work of his hands
17. w. shall be turned into hell and the nations
10. 2. the w. in pride doth persecute the poor
3. the w. boasteth || 4. the w. will not seek God
13. wherefore doth the w. contemn God?
11. 2. w. bend their bow, make ready their arrow
5. but the w. and violence his soul hateth
6. upon the w. he shall rain snares, fire brimstone
12. 8. the w. walk on every side when vilest men
17. 9. keep me from the w. that oppress me
13. O Lord, deliver my soul from the w.
26. 5. and I will not sit with the w.
27. 2. when the w. came upon me to eat my flesh
28. 3. draw me not away with the w.
31. 17. let the w. be ashamed and silent in the grave
34. 21. evil shall slay w. they that hate righteous
37. 7. the man who bringeth w. devices to pass
10. yet a little, the w. shall not be, Prov. 10. 25.
12. the w. plotteth || 20. the w. shall perish
14. the w. have drawn out the sword, they bent
16. is better than the riches of many w.
21. the w. borroweth, and payeth not again
32. the w. watcheth the righteous to slay him
34. when the w. are cut off, thou shalt see it
35. I have seen the w. in great power, spreading
40. he shall deliver them from the w. and save them
39. 1. keep my mouth, while the w. is before me
58. 3. the w. are estranged from the womb
59. 5. be not merciful to any w. transgressors
68. 2. so let the w. perish at the presence of God
75. 8. the w. of the earth shall wring them out
92. 7. when the w. spring as the grass, and flourish
94. 3. Lord, how long shall the w. triumph?
13. until the pit be digged for the w.
101. 3. I will set no w. thing before mine eyes
4. I will not know a w. person
8. I will early destroy all the w. of the land
104. 35. sinners consumed and let the w. be no more
106. 18. the flame burnt up the w.
112. 10. the w. shall see it and be grieved
119. 95. the w. have waited for me to destroy me
110. the w. laid a snare for me, yet I erred not
119. thou puttest away all the w. like dross
155. salvation is far from the w. they seek not thy
139. 19. surely thou wilt slay the w. O God
24. and see if there be any w. way in me
140. 8. further not his w. device lest they exalt
141. 4. to practise w. works with men that work
10. let the w. fall into their own nets
145. 20. but all the w. will he destroy
147. 6. he casteth the w. down to the ground
Prov. 2. 22. the w. shall be cut off from the earth
5. 22. his own iniquities shall take the w. himself
6. 18. a heart that deviseth w. imaginations
10. 30. but the w. shall not inhabit the earth
11. 5. the w. shall fall by his own wickedness
7. when a w. man dieth, his expectation perisheth
8. righteous delivered, the w. cometh in his stead
10. and when the w. perish there is shouting
18. the w. worketh a deceitful work
21. the w. shall not be unpunished, 31.
12. 2. but a man of w. devices will he condemn
7. the w. are overthrown, and are not, 21. 12.
12. the w. desireth the net of evil men
13. the w. is snared by the transgression of his lips
21. but the w. shall be filled with mischief
13. 17. a w. messenger falleth into mischief
14. 17. and a man of w. devices is hated
19. the w. bow at the gates of the righteous
32. the w. is driven away in his wickedness
15. 29. the Lord is far from the w.
16. 4. yea, even the w. for the day of evil
17. 4. a w. doer giveth heed to false lips
15. he that justifieth w. is an abomination to Lord
18. 3. when the w. cometh, then cometh contempt
20. 26. a wise king scattereth the w. brings wheel
21. 18. the w. shall be ransom for the righteous
27. when he bringeth it with a w. mind
24. 16. but the w. shall fall into mischief
19. neither be thou envious at the w.
25. 5. take away the w. from before the king
26. a righteous man falling down before the w.
26. 23. a w. heart is like a potsherd covered
28. 1. the w. flee when no man pursueth
4. they that forsake the law praise the w.
12. when the w. rise, 28. || 15. so is a w. ruler
29. 2. when the w. beareth rule, the people mourn
7. but the w. regardeth not to know it
12. his servants are w. || 16. the w. are multiplied
Eccl. 3. 17. God shall judge the righteous and the w.
7. 17. be not overmuch w. neither be foolish
8. 10. I saw the w. buried, they were forgotten
13. but it shall not be well with the w.
Isa. 5. 23. which justify the w. for reward
11. 4. with the breath of his lips shall he slay the w.
13. 11. I will punish the w. for their iniquity
32. 7. he deviseth w. devices to destroy the poor
53. 9. he made his grave with the w. and with rich
55. 7. let the w. forsake his way, let him return
57. 20. the w. are like troub. sea which cannot rest
Jer. 2. 33. thou hast taught the w. ones thy ways
6. 29. for the w. are not plucked away
17. 9. the heart is deceitful and desperately w.
25. 31. he will give the w. to the sword
Ezek. 3. 18. to warn the w. 19. | 33. 8, 9.
8. 9. behold the w. abominations they do here
11. 2. these men give w. counsel in this city
18. 23. have I any pleasure that the w. should die
20. 44. not according to your w. ways nor doings

Ezek. 21. 3. cut off from thee the right. and the *w.* 4.
25. profane *w.* prince of Israel whose day is come
33. 15. if the *w.* restore the pledge, he shall live
Dan. 12. 10. but the *w.* shall do wickedly
Mic. 6. 11. shall I count them pure with *w.* balances?
Nah. 1. 3. the Lord shall not at all acquit the *w.*
11. there is one come out of thee a *w.* counsellor
15. for the *w.* shall no more pass through thee
Hab. 1. 4. the *w.* doth compass about the righteous
13. the *w.* devoureth the man more righteous
Zeph. 1. 3. consume stumbling-blocks with the *w.*
Mal. 3. 18. shall discern between righteous and *w.*
4. 3. and ye shall tread down the *w.* as ashes
Mat. 12. 45. more *w.* than himself, even so shall it be also to this *w.* generation, *Luke* 11. 26.
13. 49. the angels shall sever the *w.* from the just
16. 4. a *w.* generation seeketh after a sign
18. 32. thou *w.* servant, 25. 26. *Luke* 19. 22.
Acts 2. 23. and by *w.* hands have ye slain him
18. 14. if it were a matter of *w.* lewdness, O Jews
1 *Cor.* 5. 13. therefore put away that *w.* person
Col. 1. 21. were enemies in your mind by *w.* works
2 *Thess.* 2. 8. and then shall that *w.* be revealed
See MAN, MEN.

Of the WICKED.

Job 8. 22. the place *of the w.* shall come to nought
9. 24. the earth is given into the hand *of the w.*
10. 3. and shouldest shine upon the counsel *of the w.*
11. 20. but the eye *of the w.* shall fail, not escape
16. 11. God turned me into the hands *of the w.*
18. 5. the light *of the w.* shall be put out
21. surely such are the dwellings *of the w.*
20. 5. the triumphing *of the w.* is short
22. every hand *of the w.* shall come upon him
21. 16. the counsel *of the w.* is far from me, 22. 18.
17. how oft is candle *of the w.* put out, and cometh destruction on them? *Prov.* 13. 9. | 24. 20.
28. where are the dwelling-places *of the w.?*
24. 6. and they gathered the vintage *of the w.*
29. 17. and I brake the jaws *of the w.* and plucked
36. 6. he preserveth not the life *of the w.*
17. thou hast fulfilled the judgment *of the w.*
Psal. 1. † 1. walketh not in the counsel *of the w.*
7. 9. let the wickedness *of the w.* come to an end
10. 15. break thou the arm *of the w.* man
22. 16. the assembly *of the w.* have inclosed me
36. 1. the transgression *of the w.* saith in my heart
11. let not the hand *of the w.* remove me
37. 17. the arms *of the w.* shall be broken
28. but the seed *of the w.* shall be cut off
38. the end *of the w.* shall be cut off
55. 3. because of the oppression *of the w.*
58. 10. he shall wash his feet in the blood *of the w.*
64. 2. hide me from the counsel *of the w.*
71. 4. deliver me out of hand *of the w.* and unrighteous cruel man, 74. 19. | 82. 4. | 97. 10.
73. 3. when I saw the prosperity *of the w.*
75. 10. all the horns *of the w.* also will I cut off
82. 2. how long will ye accept the persons *of the w.?*
91. 8. behold, and see the reward *of the w.*
92. 11. mine ears shall hear my desire *of the w.*
109. 2. the mouth *of the w.* is opened against me
112. 10. desire *of the w.* shall perish, *Prov.* 10. 28.
119. 53. because *of the w.* that forsake thy law
61. the hands *of the w.* have robbed me
125. 3. the rod *of the w.* shall not rest on the just
129. 4. Lord hath cut asunder the cords *of the w.*
140. 4. keep me, O Lord, from the hands *of the w.*
8. grant not, O Lord, the desires *of the w.*
146. 9. the way *of the w.* he turns upside down
Prov. 2. 14. who delight in frowardness *of the w.*
3. 25. be not afraid of the desolation *of the w.*
33. the curse of the Lord is in the house *of the w.*
4. 14. enter not into the path *of the w.*
19. the way *of the w.* is as darkness, they know not
10. 3. he casteth away the substance *of the w.*
6. but violence covereth the mouth *of the w.* 11.
10. 7. but the name *of the w.* shall rot
16. the fruit *of the w.* tendeth to sin
20. the heart *of the w.* is little worth
24. the fear *of the w.* it shall come upon him
27. but the years *of the w.* shall be shortened
32. the mouth *of the w.* speaketh frowardness
11. 11. the city is overthrown by mouth *of the w.*
23. but the expectation *of the w.* is wrath
12. 5. but the counsels *of the w.* are deceit
6. the words *of the w.* are to lie in wait for blood
10. but the tender mercies *of the w.* are cruel
26. but the way *of the w.* seduceth them
13. 25. but the belly *of the w.* shall want
14. 11. the house *of the w.* shall be overthrown
15. 6. but in the revenues *of the w.* is trouble
8. sacrifice *of the w.* is an abomination, 21. 27.
9. the way *of the w.* is an abomination to the Lord
26. the thoughts *of the w.* are an abomination
28. the mouth *of the w.* poureth out evil things
18. 5. it is not good to accept the person *of the w.*
19. 28. the mouth *of the w.* devoureth iniquity
21. 4. and the plowing *of the w.* is sin
7. the robbery *of the w.* shall destroy them
10. the soul *of the w.* desireth evil
12. he wisely considereth the house *of the w.*
Isa. 14. 5. the Lord hath broken the staff *of the w.*
Jer. 5. 28. they overpass the deeds *of the w.*
12. 1. wherefore doth the way *of the w.* prosper?
15. 21. I will deliver thee out of hand *of the w.*
23. 19. whirlwind fall on head *of the w.* 30. 23.
Ezek. 13. 22. have strengthened the hands *of the w.*
18. 20. the wickedness *of the w.* shall be on him
21. 29. to bring thee upon the necks *of the w.*
30. 12. I will sell the land into the hand *of the w.*
33. 11. I have no pleasure in the death *of the w.*
12. as for the wickedness *of the w.*
Dan. 12. 10. none *of the w.* shall understand
Mic. 6. 10. treasures of wickedness in house *of t. w.*
Hab. 3. 13. woundest the head out of house *of the w.*
Eph. 6. 16. able to quench all the fiery darts *of t. w.*
2 *Pet.* 2. 7. vexed with the conversation *of the w.*
3. 17. lest ye be led away with the error *of the w.*
See ONE.

To or *unto the* WICKED.

Job 31. 3. is not destruction *to the w.?*
Psal. 32. 10. many sorrows shall be *to the w.*
50. 16. *unto the w.* G. saith, what hast thou to do?
Prov. 24. 24. he that saith *unto the w.* thou art right.
29. 27. the upright is abomination *to the w.*
Eccl. 9. 2. one event to the righteous and *to the w.*
Isa. 3. 11. woe *unto the w.* it shall be ill with him
26. 10. let favour be shewed *to w.* yet will not learn
48. 22. no peace, saith God, *unto the w.* 57. 21.
Ezek. 3. 18. when I say *unto the w.* 33. 8, 14.
7. 21. give it *to the w.* of the earth for a spoil

WICKEDLY.

Gen. 19. 7. Lot said, do not so *w.* *Judg.* 19. 23.
Deut. 9. 18. your sins which ye sinned in doing *w.*
1 *Sam.* 12. 25. but if ye shall still do *w.* be consumed
2 *Sam.* 22. 22. I have kept the ways of the Lord and have not *w.* departed from my God, *Ps.* 18. 21.
24. 17. lo, I have sinned and have done *w.*
2 *Kings* 21. 11. Manasseh done *w.* above Amorites
2 *Chr.* 6. 37. we have sinned, we have done amiss, dealt *w.* *Neh.* 9. 33. *Psal.* 106. 6. *Dan.* 9. 5, 15.
20. 35. Ahaziah king of Israel, did very *w.*
22. 3. his mother was his counsellor to do *w.*
Job 13. 7. will you speak *w.* for God?
34. 12. yea, surely God will not do *w.*
Psal. 73. 8. they speak *w.* concerning oppression
74. 3. the enemy hath done *w.* in the sanctuary
139. 20. for they speak against thee *w.*
Dan. 11. 32. such as do *w.* against the covenant
12. 10. many purified, but the wicked shall do *w.*
Mal. 4. 1. all that do *w.* shall be as stubble

WICKEDNESS.

Gen. 6. 5. God saw that the *w.* of men was great
39. 9. how can I do this great *w.* and sin ag. God?
Lev. 18. 17. it is *w.* 20. 14. ‖ 19. 29. land full of *w.*
20. 14. that there be no *w.* among you
Deut. 9. 4. for the *w.* of these nations, 5.
13. 11. Israel shall do no more any such *w.*
17. 2. if there be any that hath wrought *w.*
28. 20. because of the *w.* of thy doings
Judg. 9. 56. thus God rendered the *w.* of Abimelech
20. 3. Israel said, tell us, how was this *w.?*
12. what *w.* is this that is done among you?
1 *Sam.* 12. 17. you may see that your *w.* is great
20. ye have done all this *w.* yet turn not aside
24. 13. *w.* proceedeth from the wicked
25. 39. returned the *w.* of Nabal on his own head
2 *Sam.* 3. 39. reward doer of evil according to his *w.*
7. 10. neither shall the children of *w.* afflict them any more as before-time, *Psal.* 89. 22.
1 *Kings* 1. 52. but if *w.* be found in him, he shall die
2. 44. thou knowest all the *w.* thy heart is privy to
8. 47. repent, saying, we have committed *w.*
21. 25. Ahab sold himself to work *w.*
2 *Kings* 21. 6. Manasseh wrought much *w.*
1 *Chron.* 17. 9. nor the children of *w.* waste them
Job 4. 8. they that sow *w.* reap the same
11. 11. he seeth *w.* ‖ 24. 20. *w.* shall be broken
14. let not *w.* dwell in thy tabernacles
20. 12. tho' *w.* be sweet in his mouth, tho' he hide it
27. 4. my lips shall not speak *w.* nor tongue deceit
34. 10. far be it from God that he should do *w.*
Psal. 5. 4. art not a God that hath pleasure in *w.*
9. their inward part is very *w.* throat a sepulchre
7. 9. let the *w.* of the wicked come to an end
10. 15. seek out his *w.* ‖ 45. 7. thou hatest *w.*
28. 4. according to the *w.* of their endeavours
52. 7. he strengthened himself in his *w.*
55. 11. *w.* is in the midst thereof, deceit and guile
15. *w.* is in their dwellings and among them
58. 2. yea, in heart you work *w.* weigh violence
84. 10. than to dwell in the tents of *w.*
107. 34. he turns a fruitful land into barrenness for the *w.* of them that dwell therein, *Jer.* 12. 4.
Prov. 4. 17. for they eat the bread of *w.*
8. 7. and *w.* is an abomination to my lips
10. 2. treasures of *w.* profit nothing
11. 5. but the wicked shall fall by his own *w.*
12. 3. a man shall not be established by *w.*
13. 6. but *w.* overthroweth the sinner
14. 32. the wicked is driven away in his *w.*
16. 12. it is abomination to kings to commit *w.*
21. 12. God overthroweth the wicked for their *w.*
26. 26. his *w.* shall be shewed before congregation
30. 20. she eateth and saith, I have done no *w.*
Eccl. 3. 16. saw place of judgment, that *w.* was there
7. 15. a wicked man prolongeth his life in *w.*
25. I applied my heart to know the *w.* of folly
8. 8. nor shall *w.* deliver those that are given to it
Isa. 9. 18. for *w.* burneth as the fire
58. 4. behold, ye smite with the fist of *w.*
6. the fast I have chosen, to loose the bands of *w.*
Jer. 2. 19. thine own *w.* shall correct thee
4. 14. O Jerusalem, wash thine heart from *w.*
6. 7. so she casteth out her *w.* continually
7. 12. see what I did for the *w.* of my people
8. 6. no man repented of his *w.* what have I done
14. 20. we acknowledge, O L. our *w.* and iniquity
23. 14. that none doth return from his *w.*
33. 5. for from the city whose *w.* I hid my face
44. 9. have ye forgot the *w.* of your kings, their wives, your own *w.* and the *w.* of your wives?
Ezek. 3. 19. if he turn not from his *w.* he shall die
5. 6. she hath changed my judgment into *w.*
7. 11. violence is risen up into a rod of *w.*
18. 20. the *w.* of the wicked shall be on him
27. turneth from the *w.* he hath committed
31. 11. I have driven him out for his *w.*
33. 12. in the day he turneth from his *w.* 19.
Hos. 7. 1. the *w.* of Samaria was discovered
9. 15. for the *w.* of their doings I will drive out
10. 13. ye have ploughed *w.* and reaped iniquity
15. so shall Beth-el do to you because of your *w.*
Joel 3. 13. the fats overflow for their *w.* is great
Mic. 6. 10. are treasures of *w.* in house of wicked?
Zech. 5. 8. and he said, this is *w.* and he cast it
Mal. 1. 4. they shall call them the border of *w.*
3. 15. yea, they that work *w.* are set up
Mark 7. 22. out of the heart proceedeth *w.* deceit
Luke 11. 39. but your inward part is full of *w.*
Acts 25. 5. and accuse this man, if any *w.* in him
Rom. 1. 29. being filled with all *w.* envy, murder
1 *Cor.* 5. 8. nor with the leaven of malice and *w.*
Eph. 6. 12. against spiritual *w.* in high places
1 *John* 5. 19. we know the whole world lieth in *w.*

Their WICKEDNESS.

Deut. 9. 27. look not to *their w.* nor to their sin
Psal. 94. 23. God shall cut them off in *their* own *w.*
Prov. 21. 12. God overthrows the wicked for *their w.*
Jer. 1. 16. utter judgments, touching all *their w.*
14. 16. for I will pour *their w.* upon them
23. 11. yea, in my house have I found *their w.*
44. 3. they are a desolation, because of *their w.*
5. inclined not their ear to turn from *their w.*
Lam. 1. 22. let all *their w.* come before thee
Hos. 7. 2. consider not that I remember all *their w.*
3. they make king glad with *their w.* and princes
9. 15. all *their w.* is in Gilgal, there I hated them
Jonah 1. 2. cry against Nineveh, for *th. w.* is come up
Mat. 22. 18. but Jesus perceived their *w.* and said

Thy WICKEDNESS.

1 *Kings* 2. 44. the Ld. shall return *thy w.* upon thee
Job 22. 5. is not *thy w.* great? thine iniquities infinite?
35. 8. *thy w.* may hurt a man as thou art
Isa. 47. 10. for thou hast trusted in *thy w.*
Jer. 3. 2. thou hast polluted the land with *thy w*
4. 18. this is *thy w.* for it is bitter to thy heart
22. 22. thou shalt be confounded for all *thy w.*
Ezek. 16. 23. it came to pass after all *thy w.*
57. before *thy w.* was discovered, as at the time
Nah. 3. 19. upon whom hath not *thy w.* passed
Acts 8. 22. repent therefore of this *thy w.* and pray

WIDE.

Deut. 15. 8. but thou shalt open thy hand *w.* 11.
1 *Chron.* 4. 40. the land was *w.* quiet and peaceable
Job 29. 23. they opened their mouth *w.* as for rain
30. 14. came on me as a *w.* breaking in of waters
Psal. 35. 21. they opened their mouth *w.* against me
81. 10. open thy mouth *w.* and I will fill it
104. 25. so is this great and *w.* sea, wherein are
Prov. 13. 3. he that openeth *w.* his lips, have destruct.
21. 9. it is better to dwell in a corner, than to dwell with a brawling woman in a *w.* house, 25. 24.
Isa. 57. 4. against whom make ye a *w.* mouth?
Jer. 22. 14. that saith, I will build me a *w.* house
Nah. 3. 13. thy gates be set *w.* open to thine enemies
Mal. 7. 13. *w.* is the gate that leadeth to destruction

WIDENESS.

Ezek. 41. 10. between chambers the *w.* of 20 cubits

WIDOW.

Among the Hebrews, even before the law, a widow *who had no children by her husband, was allowed to marry the brother of her deceased spouse, in order to raise up children who might enjoy his inheritance and perpetuate his name and family. We find the practice of this custom before the law, in the person of Tamar, who married successively Er and Onan, the sons of Judah, and who was likewise to have married Shelah, the third son of this patriarch, after the two former were dead without issue,* Gen. 38. 6, 8, 9, 11. *The law that appoints these marriages is delivered in* Deut. 25. 5, 6, &c.

The motives that prevailed to the enacting of this law were, the continuation of estates in the same family, and to perpetuate a man's name in Israel. It was looked upon as a great unhappiness for a man to die without an heir, and to see his inheritance pass into another family. This law was not confined to brothers-in-law only, but was extended to more distant relations of the same line; as may be seen in the example of Ruth, who married Boaz, after she had been refused by a nearer kinsman. Widowhood, as well as barrenness, was a kind of shame and reproach in Israel. Isa. 54. 4. Thou shalt forget the shame of thy youth, *passed away in celibacy and barrenness,* and shalt not remember the reproach of thy widowhood any more. *It was presumed, that a woman of merit and reputation might have found a husband, either in the family of her deceased husband, if he died without children, or in some other family, if he had left children.*

The widows *of kings continued in their widowhood. Adonijah was punished with death, for asking in marriage Abishag the Shunamite, who had been married to David, though he had never consummated this marriage,* 1 Kings 2. 13, 14, &c. *They shut up in the palace all the concubines of king David, who had been defiled by Absalom, there to spend the remainder of their days,* 2 Sam. 20. 3.

God discovers a special regard for widows, *and frequently recommends to his people to be very careful in affording relief to the* widow *and orphan,* Exod. 22. 22. Deut. 10. 18. *St. Paul would have us to honour widows* that are *widows* indeed, *and desolate, that is, destitute of such as ought to help and relieve them, of their husbands or children,* 1 Tim. 5. 3, 4, 5. *There were* widows *in the Christian church, who, because of their poverty, were maintained at the charge of the faithful, and who were to attend upon the poor and sick. St. Paul did not allow any to be chosen into the number of these* widows, *unless they were threescore years old at least; they must be such as had not parted from their husbands and married again; they must produce ample testimony of their good works; that they had given good education to their children; that they had exercised hospitality; that they had* washed the feet of the saints; *that they had given succour to the miserable and afflicted,* 1 Tim. 5. 9, 10.

Gen. 38. 11. remain a *w.* in thy father's house
14. she put her *w.* garments off from her
Exod. 22. 22. ye shall not afflict any *w.* or child
Lev. 21. 14. a *w.* or an harlot shall he not take
22. 13. if the priest's daughter be a *w.* she shall eat
Num. 30. 9. every vow of a *w.* shall stand against her
Deut. 10. 18. he doth execute the judgment of a *w.*
14. 29. the stranger, fatherless, and *w.* shall come and eat, and be satisfied, 16. 11, 14. | 26. 12.
24. 17. nor take a *w.* raiment to pledge
19. the sheaf in the field shall be for the stranger, for the fatherless and the *w.* 20. 21. | 26. 13.

Deut. 27. 19. he that perverteth the judgment of *w.*
2 *Sam.* 14. 5. I am a *w.* woman, mine husb. is dead
1 *Kings* 7. 14. he was a *w.* son of tribe of Naphtali
11. 26. Jeroboam's mother Zeruah was a *w.* woman
17. 9. I have commanded a *w.* to sustain thee
Job 24. 3. they take the *w.* ox for a pledge
21. and doeth not good to the *w.*
29. 13. I caused the *w.* heart to sing for joy
31. 16. or have caused the eyes of the *w.* to fail
Psal. 94. 6. they slay the *w.* and the stranger
109. 9. let his children be fatherless, his wife a *w.*
146. 9. he relieveth fatherless and the *w.*
Prov. 15. 25. he will establish the border of the *w.*
Isa. 1. 17. judge the fatherless, plead for the *w.*
23. neither doth the cause of *w.* come unto them
47. 8. I shall not sit as a *w.* nor know loss of childr.
Jer. 7. 6. if ye oppress not the *w.* 22. 3. *Zech.* 7. 10.
Lam. 1. 1. how is she become as a *w.* that was great
Ezek. 22. 7. in thee have they vexed the *w.*
44. 22. but take a *w.* that had a priest before
Mal. 3. 5. against those that oppress the *w.*
Mark 12. 42. a certain poor *w.* threw in two mites
43. *w.* cast in more than all, *Luke* 21. 2, 3.
Luke 2. 37. Anna was a *w.* about 84 years old
7. 12. the only son of his mother, and she was a *w.*
18. 3. there was a *w.* in that city came unto him
5. because this *w.* troubleth me, I will avenge her
1 *Tim.* 5. 4. if any *w.* have children or nephews
5. she that is a *w.* indeed trusteth in God
9. let not a *w.* be taken into the number under 60
Rev. 18. 7. she saith, I sit as queen, and am no *w.*

WIDOWS.

Exod. 22. 24. and your wives shall be *w.*
Job 22. 9. thou hast sent *w.* away empty
27. 15. be buried in death, and *w.* shall not weep
Psal 68. 5. a judge of the fatherless and *w.* is God
78. 64. and their *w.* made no lamentation
Isa. 9. 17. neither shall he have mercy on their *w.*
10. 2. *w.* may be their prey, that they may rob
Jer. 15. 8. their *w.* are increased above the sand
18. 21. let their wives be *w.* and men put to death
49. 11. leave thy children, let thy *w.* trust in me
Lam. 5. 3. we are fatherless, our mothers are as *w.*
Ezek. 22. 25. they have made her many *w.*
Mat. 23. 14. woe unto you, ye devour *w.* houses, for pretence make long prayers, *Mark* 12. 40. *Luke* 20. 47.
Luke 4. 25. were many *w.* in Israel in days of Elias
Acts 6. 1. murmuring because their *w.* were neglected
9. 39. all the *w.* stood by him weeping and shewing
41. when he had called the saints and *w.*
1 *Cor.* 7. 8. I said to the *w.* it is good if they abide as I
1 *Tim.* 5. 3. honour *w.* that are *w.* indeed
11. but the younger *w.* refuse, they will marry
16. if any have *w.* let them relieve them
Jam. 1. 27. pure religion is to visit the *w.* in affliction

WIDOWHOOD.

Gen. 38. 19. Tamar put on the garments of her *w.*
2 *Sam.* 20. 3. David's concubines shut up, liv. in *w.*
Isa. 47. 9. in one day the loss of children, and *w.*
54. 4. shalt not remember the reproach of thy *w.*

WIFE.

Gen. 11. 29. the name of Abraham's *w.* was Sarai, 31. | 12. 17, 20. | 20. 18. | 24. 36.
20. 3. the woman thou hast taken is a man's *w.*
21. 21. Hagar took a *w.* for Ishmael out of Egypt
24. 4. thou shalt take a *w.* to my son Isaac, 38.
25. 1. Abraham took a *w.* her name was Keturah
27. 46. if Jacob take a *w.* of the daughters of Heth, what good shall my life do me? 28. 1, 6.
38. 6. Judah took a *w.* for Er his first-born
8. go in unto thy brother's *w.* and marry her
39. 7. his master's *w.* cast her eyes upon Joseph
Exod. 20. 17. thou shalt not covet thy neighbour's *w.* nor any thing is thy neighbour's, *Deut.* 5. 21.
21. 4. if his master have given him a *w.*
10. if he take him another *w.* her food, her raiment and duty of marriage shall he not diminish
Lev. 18. 8. the nakedness of thy father's *w.* shalt thou not uncover, 20. 11. *Deut.* 27. 20.
15. of thy son's *w.* || 16. thy brother's *w.* 20. 21.
18. neither shalt thou take a *w.* to her sister
20. shalt not lie with thy neighbour's *w.* 20. 10.
20. 14. if a man take a *w.* and her mother, it is sin
20. if a man lie with his uncle's *w.* he uncovereth
21. 7. priests shall not take a *w.* that is a whore
13. the high priest shall take a *w.* in her virginity
Num. 5. 12. if any man's *w.* go aside, 29.
36. 8. shall be a *w.* to one of the family of the tribe
Deut. 13. 6. or if the *w.* of thy bosom entice thee
20. 7. what man hath betrothed a *w.* not taken her
22. 13. if any man take a *w.* and hate her
24. because he humbleth his neighbour's *w.*
30. a man shall not take his father's *w.*
24. 1. a man hath taken a *w.* and find uncleanness
2. she may go and be another man's *w.*
5. hath taken a new *w.* he shall not go out to war
25. 5. the *w.* of the dead shall not marry a stranger
7. if he like not to take his brother's *w.*
9. then shall his brother's *w.* come unto him
11. the *w.* of the one draweth near to deliver
28. 30. betroth a *w.* and another lie with her
54. his eye be evil toward the *w.* of his bosom
Judg. 4. 4. Deborah, *w.* of Lapidoth, judged Israel
17. Jael the *w.* of Heber the Kenite, 21. | 5. 24.
14. 3. thou goest to take a *w.* of the uncircumcised
16. Samson's *w.* wept before him, and said
20. but his *w.* was given to his companion
21. 18. cursed be he that giveth a *w.* to Benjamin
Ruth 4. 5. buy it of Ruth the *w.* of the dead
2 *Sam.* 12. 10. thou hast taken the *w.* of Uriah
1 *Kings* 14. 2. be not known to be the *w.* of Jeroboam
6. Ahijah said, come in, thou *w.* of Jeroboam
2 *Kings* 5. 2. and she waited on Naaman's *w.*
2 *Chr.* 22. 11. *w.* of Jehoiada hid him from Athaliah
Prov. 5. 18. rejoice with the *w.* of thy youth
6. 29. so he that goeth in to his neighbour's *w.*
18. 22. whoso findeth a *w.* findeth a good thing
19. 13. contentions of a *w.* a continual dropping
14. and a prudent *w.* is from the Lord
Eccl. 9. 9. live joyfully with the *w.* of thy youth
Isa. 54. 1. more than children of the married *w.*
Isa. 54. 6. the Lord hath called thee as a *w.* of youth
Jer. 3. 20. surely as a *w.* treacherously departeth
5. 8. every one neighed after his neighbour's *w.*
6. 11. the husband and the *w.* shall be taken
16. 2. thou shalt not take thee a *w.* in this place
Ezek. 16. 32. as a *w.* that committeth adultery
18. 6. nor hath defiled his neighbour's *w.* 15.
11. and defiled his neighbour's *w.* 22. 11. | 33. 26.
Hos. 1. 2. take unto thee a *w.* of whoredoms
12. 12. Israel served for a *w.* and kept sheep
Mal. 2. 14. Lord hath been witness between thee and the *w.* of thy youth, the *w.* of thy covenant
15. let none deal treacherously against his *w.*
Mat. 1. 6. of her that had been the *w.* of Urias
14. 3. Herod bound John for sake of Philip's *w.*
19. 29. every one that hath forsaken *w.* or children for my name's sake, *Mark* 10. 29. *Luke* 18. 29.
22. 25. seven brethren, the first, when he had married a *w.* deceased, *Mark* 12. 20. *Luke* 20. 29.
Luke 14. 20. I have married a *w.* and cannot come
17. 32. remember Lot's *w.*
1 *Cor.* 5. 1. that one should have his father's *w.*
7. 3. let the husband render to the *w.* due benevolence, and likewise also the *w.* to the husband
4. the *w.* hath not power over her own body
10. let not the *w.* depart from her husband
12. if any brother hath a *w.* that believeth not
14. unbelieving *w.* is sanctified by the husband
16. what knowest thou, O *w.* if thou shalt save
27. art thou loosed from a *w.* seek not a *w.*
34. there is difference between a *w.* and a virgin
39. the *w.* is bound as long as her husband liveth
Eph. 5. 23. for the husband is the head of the *w.*
33. let every one love his *w.* even as himself, and the *w.* see that she reverence her husband
1 *Tim.* 3. 2. the husband of one *w.* 12. *Tit.* 1. 6.
5. 9. a widow, having been the *w.* of one man
1 *Pet.* 3. 7. giving honour to *w.* as the weaker vessel
Rev. 21. 9. I will shew thee the bride, the Lamb's *w.*

His WIFE.

Gen. 2. 24. a man shall leave father and mother, and shall cleave unto *his w.* *Mat.* 19. 5. *Mark* 10. 7.
25. they were both naked, the man and *his w.*
12. 12. they shall say, this is *his w.* and will kill me
19. 16. the men laid hold on the hand of *his w.*
26. but *his w.* looked back from behind him
20. 7. now therefore, restore the man *his w.*
24. 67. and she become *his w.* 1 *Sam.* 25. 42.
25. 21. and Isaac entreated the Lord for *his w.*
26. 7. the men of the place asked him of *his w.*
11. he that toucheth this man or *his w.* shall die
39. 9. kept back thee, because thou art *his w.*
Exod. 21. 3. then *his w.* shall go out with him
22. 16. he shall surely endow her to be *his w.*
Lev. 18. 14. thou shalt not approach to *his w.*
Num. 5. 14. and if he be jealous of *his w.* 30.
15. the man shall bring *his w.* to the priest
30. 16. the statutes between a man and *his w.*
Deut. 22. 19. she shall be *his w.* all his days, 29.
24. 5. he shall cheer up *his w.* that he hath taken
Judg. 13. 11. Manoah arose and went after *his w.*
15. 1. Samson visited *his w.* with a kid
21. 21. come out, and catch you every man *his w.*
1 *Sam.* 30. 22. save to every man *his w.* and children
2 *Sam.* 12. 9. thou hast taken *his w.* to be thy wife
1 *Kings* 21. 25. whom Jezebel *his w.* stirred up
2 *Kings* 8. 18. the daughter of Ahab was *his w.*
Esth. 5. 10. Haman called his friends and *his w.*
Psal. 109. 9. and let *his w.* be a widow
Jer. 3. 1. if a man put away *his w.* *Mat.* 5. 31, 32. | 19. 9. *Mark* 10. 11. *Luke* 16. 18.
Mat. 8. 14. he saw *his w.* mother sick of a fever
19. 3. the Pharisees said, is it lawful for a man to put away *his w.* for every cause? *Mark* 10. 2.
10. if the case of a man be so with *his w.*
22. 25. seven brethren, the first deceased, and left *his w.* to his brother, *Mark* 12. 19. *Luke* 20. 28.
Luke 14. 26. and hate not *his w.* and children
Acts 5. 2. *his w.* also being privy to it
7. *his w.* not knowing what was done, came in
18. 2. Paul found Aquila with *his w.* Priscilla
24. 24. when Felix came with *his w.* Drusilla
1 *Cor.* 7. 2. let every man have *his* own *w.*
11. and let not the husband put away *his w.*
33. he careth how he may please *his w.*
Eph. 5. 28. he that loveth *his w.* loveth himself
31. shall be joined to *his w.* || 33. so love *his w.*
Rev. 19. 7. and *his w.* hath made herself ready

My WIFE.

Gen. 20. 11. they will slay me for *my w.* sake
12. she became *my w.* || 26. 7. she is *my w.*
29. 21. give me *my w.* || *Exod.* 21. 5. I love *my w.*
Judg. 15. 1. Samson said, I will go in to *my w.*
2 *Sam.* 3. 14. saying, deliver me *my w.* Michal
11. 11. shall I go into my house to lie with *my w.?*
Job 19. 17. *my* breath is strange to *my w.*
31. 10. then let *my w.* grind unto another
Ezek. 24. 18. so I spake, and at even *my w.* died
Hos. 2. 2. she is not *my w.* nor am I her husband
Luke 1. 18. and *my w.* is well stricken in years

Thy WIFE.

Gen. 3. 17. hast hearkened to the voice of *thy w.*
12. 18. why didst thou not tell me she was *thy w.*
19. behold *thy w.* take her, and go thy way
17. 19. Sarah, *thy w.* shall bear thee a son, 18. 10.
19. 15. arise, take *thy w.* and thy two daughters
26. 9. Abimelech said, of a surety she is *thy w.*
10. one might lightly have lien with *thy w.*
Exod. 18. 6. I, Jethro, am come unto thee, and *thy w.*
Deut. 21. 11. that thou wouldest have her to *thy w.*
13. thou shalt go in to her, and she shall be *thy w.*
2 *Sam.* 12. 10. taken the wife of Uriah to be *thy w.*
Psal. 128. 3. *thy w.* shall be as a fruitful vine
Amos 7. 17. *thy w.* shall be an harlot in the city
1 *Cor.* 7. 16. whether thou shalt save *thy w.*

To WIFE.

Gen. 12. 19. I might have taken her to me *to w.*
34. 4. Shechem said, get me this damsel *to w.*
8. I pray you, give him her *to w.* 12.
38. 14. she was not given to Shelah *to w.*
41. 45. Pharaoh gave Joseph *to w.* Asenath
Lev. 21. 14. take a virgin of his own people *to w.*
Deut. 22. 16. I gave my daughter to this man *to w.*
Josh. 15. 16. Caleb said, to him will I give Achsah my daughter *to w.* 17. *Judg.* 1. 12, 13.
Judg. 14. 2. now therefore get her for me *to w.*
1 *Sam.* 18. 17. Merab, her will I give thee *to w.*
1 *Kings* 2. 17. give me Abishag the Shunamite, *to w.*
2 *Kings* 14. 9. the thistle said to the cedar, give thy daughter to my son *to w.* 2 *Chron.* 25. 18.
2 *Chron.* 21. 6. Jehoram had daughter of Ahab *to w.*
Mark 12. 23. the seven had her *to w.* *Luke* 20. 33.
Luke 20. 30. the second took her *to w.* and died

WILD.

Gen. 16. 12. Ishmael will be a *w.* man
Rom. 11. 24. the olive-tree, which is *w.* by nature

See Ass, Beast, Beasts.

WILDERNESS,

Or Desert, *in Hebrew,* Midbar. *The Hebrews give this name to all places that are not cultivated, but which are chiefly destined to the feeding of cattle, and on which trees grow wild. So when* wilderness *is mentioned in Scripture, we are not always to imagine it to be a place forsaken, abandoned, void of cities or inhabitants; as this word often represents the soil near a city or village which was appointed for pasture, and where the plough never came. Thus, in Scripture, there are few cities which had not their* wilderness, *that is, uncultivated places for woods and pastures.*

The desert *of Arabia, wherein the Israelites sojourned forty years after their departure out of Egypt, is called* wilderness, *by way of eminence,* Neh. 9. 19, 21. Psal. 78. 40, 52. | 107. 4. Jer. 2. 2.

The *wilderness of* Shur *lies towards the point of the Red sea. Hagar being driven from Abraham's house, wandered in this* wilderness, *Gen.* 16. 7. *The Israelites, after their march through the Red sea, went into the* wilderness of Shur, *Exod.* 15. 22. *It is thought there was a city of this name anciently in these parts.*

The *wilderness* of Paran *was in Arabia Petrea, in the neighbourhood of the city of Paran. Ishmael, the son of Abraham, dwelt in the borders of this* wilderness, *Gen.* 21. 21. *The Israelites having decamped from Sinai, retired into the* wilderness of Paran, *Num.* 10. 12. *It was from hence that Moses sent out spies, to bring intelligence concerning the land of promise,* Num. 13. 3. *Moses seems to place mount Sinai in the country of Paran, when he says, that* the Lord appeared to the Israelites upon the mount of Paran, *Deut.* 33. 2. *And Habakkuk seems to say the same thing,* Hab. 3. 3. The Holy One came from mount Paran.

The desert of Sin. *There are two deserts of this name in Scripture, the first is written purely* Sin, *with a* Samech, *and lies between* Elim *and mount* Sinai, *Exod.* 16. 1. *The second is written* Zin, *or* Tzin *with a* Tzade: *it is near* Kadesh-barnea, *where Miriam the sister of Moses died,* Num. 20. 1.

The desert of Sinai, *is that which lies about, and is adjacent to, mount* Sinai. *The people encamped there a long time, and received the greatest part of those laws which are written in the books of* Moses, Exod. 19. 2.

It is said in Isa. 41. 18. I will make the *wilderness* a pool of water; *that is, "these people that are like a dry and barren* wilderness, *I will abundantly water them with my blessing, and make them fruitful and beautiful." God asks his people in* Jer. 2. 31. Have I been a barren *wilderness* to Israel? *Have not I accommodated you with all necessaries at all times? Nay, in the* wilderness *itself I was not a* wilderness *to you, but provided plentifully for you.*

Exod. 14. 3. are entangled, the *w.* hath shut them in
Num. 14. 2. or would God we had died in this *w.*
29. your carcases shall fall in this *w.* 32. 35.
Deut. 1. 19. went through all that terrible *w.* 8. 15.
32. 10. he found him in the waste howling *w.*
1 *Kings* 19. 15. go return on thy way to *w.* of Dam.
Job 24. 5. the *w.* yieldeth food for them and children
Psal. 106. 9. so he led them through the depths as through the *w.* 136. 16. *Amos* 2. 10.
107. 35. he turneth the *w.* into a standing water
Cant. 3. 6. who is this cometh out of the *w.?* 8. 5.
Isa. 14. 17. is this the man that made world as a *w.?*
35. 1. *w.* and solitary place shall be glad for them
41. 18. I will make the *w.* a pool of water
42. 11. let the *w.* and cities lift up their voice
50. 2. at my rebuke I make the rivers a *w.*
51. 3. and he will make her *w.* like Eden
64. 10. thy holy cities are a *w.* Zion is a *w.*
Jer. 2. 31. have I been a *w.* unto Israel?
4. 26. and lo, the fruitful place was a *w.*
12. 10. have made my pleasant portion a desol. *w.*
22. 6. yet surely I will make thee a *w.* *Hos.* 2. 3.
Ezek. 6. 14. make the land more desolate than the *w.*
Joel 2. 3. and behind them a desolate *w.*
3. 19. and Edom shall be a desolate *w.*
Zeph. 2. 13. he will make Nineveh dry like a *w.*

In the WILDERNESS.

Num. 14. 22. my miracles which I did *in the w.*
32. 15. he will yet again leave them *in the w.* and ye shall destroy all this people, *Ezek.* 29. 5.
Deut. 8. 2. thou shalt remember the Lord led thee forty years *in the w.* 29. 5. *Josh.* 5. 6. | 14. 10.
16. who fed thee *in the w.* with manna
Neh. 9. 21. forty years didst thou sustain them *in w.*
Psal. 95. 8. as in the day of temptation *in the w.*
Prov. 21. 19. better dwell *in the w.* than with
Isa. 32. 16. then judgment shall dwell *in the w.*
35. 6. for *in the w.* shall waters break out
40. 3. the voice of him that crieth *in the w.* *Mat.* 3. 3. *Mark* 1. 3. *Luke* 3. 4. *John* 1. 23.
41. 19. I will plant *in the w.* the cedar and oil-tree
43. 19. I will even make a way *in the w.*
Jer. 2. 2. when thou wentest after me *in the w.*
9. 2. oh that I had *in the w.* a lodging-place
31. 2. people that were left found grace *in the w.*
48. 6. flee and be like the heath *in the w.*

Lam. 4. 19. they laid wait for us *in the w.*
Ezek. 19. 13. and now she is planted *in the w.*
20. 13. Israel rebelled against me *in the w.*
15. I lifted my hand to them *in the w.* 23.
34. 25. and they shall dwell safely *in the w.*
Hos. 9. 10. I found Israel like grapes *in the w.*
13. 5. I did know thee *in the w.* in the dry land
Mat. 3. 1. John came preaching *in the w.* of Judea
15. 33. whence should we have so much bread *in the w.* to fill so great a multitude? *Mark* 8. 4.
Luke 15. 4. leave the ninety and nine *in the w.*
Acts 7. 30. an angel appeared to him *in the w.* 38.
2 *Cor.* 11. 26. I have been in perils *in the w.*

Into the WILDERNESS.

Lev. 16. 21. shall send him by a fit man *into the w.*
22. and he shall let go the goat *into the w.*
Ezek. 20. 10. and I brought them *into the w.*
35. I will bring you *into the w.* of the people
Hos. 2. 14. I will allure her and bring her *into the w.*
Mat. 11. 7. what went ye out *into the w.* to see? a reed shaken with the wind? *Luke* 7. 24.
Luke 8. 29. he was driven of the devil *into the w.*
Acts 21. 38. which leddest *into the w.* 4000 men
Rev. 12. 6. and the woman fled *into the w.* 14.
17. 3. so he carried me in the spirit *into the w.*

WILES.

Num. 25. 18. for they vex you with their *w.*
Eph. 6. 11. able to stand against the *w.* of the devil

WILILY.

Josh. 9. 4. Gibeonites did work *w.* and took old sacks

WILL,

Is that faculty of the soul whereby we freely choose or refuse things. It is of the nature of the will, *to* will *freely whatsoever it* wills, *for the* will *cannot be compelled: but it is unable, till it be changed by grace, to move itself toward God, and to* will *any good thing pleasing to him,* Psal. 110. 3. *Simply to* will *any thing, is of nature; but to* will *what is good, is of grace: our* will *being free in respect of sinful acts, but bound in respect of good works, till it be made free by Christ.* John 8. 36. If the Son therefore shall make you free, ye shall be free indeed. *And in* John 15. 5. Without me ye can do nothing. *And* Phil. 2. 13. It is God who worketh in you, both to *will* and to do of his good pleasure. *And St. Austin says,* Voluntas libera, quia libertas; libera ad peccatum, serva ad justitiam. *That doctrine therefore which teaches, "that when grace is offered, we may refuse it, if we* will; *and if we* will, *we may receive it;" is to be looked upon as contrary to the Scriptures.*
The *will* of God *is taken,* (1) *For this absolute* will, *which nothing can withstand.* Rom. 9. 19. For who hath resisted his *will?* (2) *For his purpose and decree.* Eph. 1. 11. Who worketh all things after the counsel of his own *will*; *that is, as he has most wisely and freely decreed.* (3) *For his laws and commands.* Mat. 7. 21. He that doeth the *will* of my Father which is in heaven. *So in* Rom. 12. 2. That ye may prove what is that good and acceptable and perfect *will* of God. *This is his revealed* will *contained in his word, which is called good, because it enjoins only what is for our benefit: it is* acceptable, *by obedience thereunto we shall be accepted; and it is* perfect, *the observance thereof will make us perfect,* 2 Tim. 3. 17.
Deut. 33. 16. for good *w.* of him that dwelt in bush
Psal. 27. 12. deliver me not to *w.* of mine enemies
41. 2. wilt not deliver him to *w.* of his enemies
Ezek. 16. 27. delivered thee to *w.* of them that hate
Mal. 2. 13. or receiveth it with good *w.* at your hand
Mat. 7. 21. that doeth the *w.* of my Father, 12. 50.
18. 14. it is not the *w.* of your Father in heaven
21. 31. whether of them did the *w.* of his father?
Luke 2. 14. on earth peace, good *w.* toward men
23. 25. but he delivered Jesus to their *w.*
John 1. 13. were born, not of the *w.* of the flesh
4. 34. meat is to do the *w.* of him that sent me
5. 30. I seek the *w.* of my Father which sent me
6. 39. and this is the Father's *w.* who sent me, 40.
Acts 21. 14. saying, the *w.* of the Lord be done
Eph. 5. 17. understanding what the *w.* of the Lord is
6. 7. with good *w.* doing service, as to the Lord
Phil. 1. 15. some also preach Christ of good *w.*
Heb. 10. 10. by the which *w.* we are sanctified
1 *Pet.* 4. 3. suffice to have wrought the *w.* of Gentiles
2 *Pet.* 1. 21. the prophecy came not by the *w.* of man

WILL *of God.*

Ezra 7. 18. that do after the *w. of* your *God*
Mark 3. 35. who shall do the *w. of G.* is my brother
John 1. 13. born, not of the *w.* of man, but *of God*
Acts 13. 36. served his generation by the *w. of God*
Rom. 1. 10. have a prosperous journey by *w. of G.*
8. 27. makes intercession according to the *w. of G.*
12. 2. prove that acceptable and perfect *w. of God*
15. 32. I come to you with joy, by the *w. of God*
1 *Cor.* 1. 1. Paul an apostle of Jesus Christ by the *w. of G.* 2 *Cor.* 1. 1. *Eph.* 1. 1. *Col.* 1. 1. 2 *Tim.* 1. 1.
2 *Cor.* 8. 5. gave themselves to us by the *w. of God*
Gal. 1. 4. deliver us from evil world by the *w. of G.*
Eph. 6. 6. doing the *w. of God* from the heart
Col. 4. 12. may stand complete in all the *w. of God*
1 *Thess.* 4. 3. for this is the *w. of God,* 5. 18.
Heb. 10. 36. after ye have done the *w. of God*
1 *Pet.* 2. 15. so is the *w. of G.* that ye put to silence
3. 17. for it is better if the *w. of God* be so
4. 2. live, not to the lusts of men, but to *w. of God*
19. them that suffer according to the *w. of God*
1 *John* 2. 17. he that doth the *w. of God* abideth

His WILL.

Dan. 4. 35. and he doth according to *his w.*
8. 4. he did accord. to *his w.* ‖ 11. 3. do *his w.* 16, 36.
Luke 12. 47. neither did according to *his w.*
John 7. 17. if any man will do *his w.* he shall know
Acts 22. 14. that thou shouldest know *his w.*
Rom. 2. 18. knowest *his w.* ‖ 9. 19. resisted *his w.*
1 *Cor.* 7. 37. he that hath power over *his* own *w.*
16. 12. *his w.* was not at all to come at this time
Eph. 1. 5. according to the good pleasure of *his w.*
9. made known to us the mystery of *his w.*
Col. 1. 9. might be filled with knowledge of *his w.*
2 *Tim.* 2. 26. were taken captive by him at *his w.*
Heb. 13. 21. perfect in every good work to do *his w.*
1 *John* 5. 14. if we ask according to *his w.* he hears
Rev. 17. 17. God put in their hearts to fulfil *his w.*

My WILL.

Luke 22. 42. this cup, not *my w.* but thine be done
Acts 13. 22. found David, who shall fulfil all *my w.*
1 *Cor.* 9. 17. if I do this thing against *my w.*

Own WILL.

Lev. 1. 3. he shall offer it of his *own* voluntary *w.*
19. 5. ye shall offer it as your *own w.* 22. 19, 29.
Dan. 11. 16. he shall do according to his *own w.*
John 5. 30. because I seek not mine *own w.*
6. 38. I came from heaven, not to do mine *own w.*
Eph. 1. 11. who worketh after counsel of his *own w.*
Heb. 2. 4. gifts of Holy Ghost, according to his *own w.*
Jam. 1. 18. of his *own w.* begat he us by word of truth

See SELF.

Thy WILL.

Psal. 40. 8. I delight to do *thy w.* O my God
143. 10. teach me to do *thy w.* thou art my God
Mat. 6. 10. *thy w.* be done in earth, *Luke* 11. 2.
26. 42. if this cup may not pass, *thy w.* be done
Heb. 10. 7. lo, I come to do *thy w.* O God, 9.

WILLS.

Eph. 2. † 3. fulfilling the *w.* of the flesh and mind

WILL.

Deut. 21. 14. thou shalt let her go whither she *w.*
Job 13. 13. let me alone, let come on me what *w.*
Prov. 21. 1. he turneth the king's heart whither he *w.*
Dan. 4. 17. God ruleth in the kingdom of men and giveth it to whomsoever he *w.* 25, 32. | 5. 21.
Mat. 8. 3. I *w.* be thou clean, *Mark* 1. 41. *Luke* 5. 13.
20. 15. is it not lawful to do what I *w.* with my own?
32. what *w.* ye that I shall do unto you?
26. 39. not as I *w.* but as thou wilt, *Mark* 14. 36.
27. 17. whom *w.* ye that I release unto you, Barabbas or Jesus? 21. *Mark* 15. 9. *John* 18. 39.
Mark 6. 25. I *w.* that thou give me John Baptist's head
14. 7. whensoever ye *w.* ye may do them good
15. 12. what *w.* ye then that I should do to him?
Luke 4. 6. to whomsoever I *w.* I give it
12. 49. and what *w.* I, if it be already kindled?
John 5. 21. even so the Son quickeneth whom he *w.*
9. 27. why hear it again? *w.* ye also be his disciples?
15. 7. ye shall ask what ye *w.* it shall be done to you
17. 24. I *w.* that they be with me where I am
21. 22. if I *w.* that he tarry till I come, 23.
Acts 18. 21. I *w.* return again to you, if God will
Rom. 7. 18. for to *w.* is present with me, but to perform
9. 18. therefore hath he mercy on whom he *w.* have mercy, and whom he *w.* he hardeneth
1 *Cor.* 4. 19. I will come to you shortly, if the Ld. *w.*
21. what *w.* ye, shall I come to you with a rod?
7. 36. let him do what he *w.* he sinneth not
39. she is at liberty to be married to whom she *w.*
12. 11. dividing to every man severally as he *w.*
2 *Cor.* 8. 11. that as there was a readiness to *w.*
Phil. 2. 13. God worketh in you, both to *w.* and to do
1 *Tim.* 2. 8. I *w.* that men pray every where
5. 14. I *w.* that the younger women marry
Tit. 3. 8. these things I *w.* that thou affirm constantly
Jam. 4. 15. if the Lord *w.* we shall do this or that
Rev. 11. 6. to smite the earth as often as they *w.*
22. 17. whosoever *w.* let him take the water of life

WILL *not.*

2 *Sam.* 13. † 28. *w.* ye *not,* since I have commanded
Psal. 80. 18. so *w. not* we go back from thee
Ezek. 20. 3. I *w. not* be inquired of by you
Amos 6. † 10. *w. not* make mention of name of Lord
7. 8. I *w. not* again pass by them any more, 8. 2.
Mat. 21. 29. he answered and said, I *w. not*
26. 35. though I should die, yet *w.* I *not* deny thee
Mark 14. 29. tho' all shall be offended, yet *w. not* I
John 5. 40. ye *w. not* come to me that ye may have life

WILLETH.

Rom. 9. 16. so then it is not of him that *w.* nor runneth

WILFULLY.

Heb. 10. 26. if we sin *w.* after we have received truth

WILLING.

Gen. 24. 5. the woman will not be *w.* to follow me
8. if the woman will not be *w.* to follow thee
Exod. 35. 5. whosoever is of a *w.* heart, 21, 22, 29.
1 *Chron.* 28. 9. my son, serve God with a *w.* mind
29. 5. who is *w.* to consecrate his service to Lord
Job 39. 9. will the unicorn be *w.* to serve thee
Psal. 110. 3. thy people shall be *w.* in day of thy power
Isa. 1. 19. if ye be *w.* ye shall eat good of the land
Mat. 1. 19. not *w.* to make her a public example
26. 41. the spirit is *w.* but flesh is weak
Mark 15. 15. Pilate *w.* to content the people
Luke 10. 29. but he *w.* to justify himself, said
22. 42. if thou be *w.* remove this cup from me
23. 20. Pilate therefore *w.* to release Jesus
John 5. 35. ye were *w.* for a season to rejoice
Acts 24. 27. Felix *w.* to shew the Jews a pleasure
25. 9. but Festus *w.* to do the Jews a pleasure
27. 43. but the centurion, *w.* to save Paul, kept them
Rom. 9. 22. what if God *w.* to shew his wrath
2 *Cor.* 5. 8. *w.* rather to be absent from the body
8. 3. they were *w.* of themselves beyond their power
12. if there be first a *w.* mind it is accepted
1 *Thess.* 2. 8. we were *w.* to have imparted unto you
1 *Tim.* 6. 18. ready to distribute, *w.* to communicate
Heb. 6. 17. God, *w.* to shew to the heirs of promise
13. 18. *w.* to live honestly in all things
2 *Pet.* 3. 9. not *w.* that any should perish, but all come

WILLINGLY.

Exod. 25. 2. an offering of every man that gives *w.*
Judg. 5. 2. the people *w.* offered themselves, 9.
8. 25. we will *w.* give the ear-rings of our prey
1 *Chr.* 29. 6. the princes of Israel and rulers offered *w.* 9. 14, 17. 2 *Chr.* 35. 8. *Ezra* 1. 6. | 3. 5.
2 *Chr.* 17. 16. Amaziah *w.* offered himself to God
Neh. 11. 2. blessed the men that *w.* offered themselves
Prov. 31. 13. she worketh *w.* with her hands
Lam. 3. 33. he doth not afflict *w.* nor grieve
Hos. 5. 11. Ephraim *w.* walked after commandment
John 6. 21. they *w.* received him into the ship
Rom. 8. 20. the creature made subject to vanity not *w.*
1 *Cor.* 9. 17. if I do this thing *w.* I have a reward
Philem. 14. not as of necessity, but *w.* 1 *Pet.* 5. 2.
2 *Pet.* 3. 5. for this they *w.* are ignorant of

WILLOWS.

Lev. 23. 40. ye shall take *w.* of the brook and rejoice
Job 40. 22. the *w.* of the brook compass him about
Psal. 137. 2. we hanged our harps upon the *w.*
Isa. 15. 7. shall carry their riches to the brook of *w.*
44. 4. they shall spring up as *w.* by the water-courses

WILLOW *tree.*

Ezek. 17. 5. by great waters, and he set it as a *w. t.*

WILL-*worship.*

Col. 2. 23. have a shew of wisdom in *w.-worship*

WILT.

Judg. 1. 14. Caleb said to her, what *w.* thou? *Esth.* 5. 3. *Mat.* 20. 21. *Mark* 10. 51. *Luke* 18. 41.
1 *Sam.* 1. 11. if thou *w.* look on thine handmaid
Psal. 60. 10. *w.* not thou, O God? 108. 11.
85. 5. *w.* thou be angry with us for ever?
6. *w.* thou not revive us again to rejoice in thee?
Prov. 5. 20. why *w.* thou, my son, be ravished?
Jer. 3. 4. *w.* thou not from this time cry unto me?
13. 27. O Jerusalem, *w.* thou not be made clean?
Ezek. 20. 4. *w.* thou judge them, son of man? 22. 2.
24. 19. *w.* thou not tell us what these things are
28. 9. *w.* thou yet say before him that slayeth thee?
Mat. 8. 2. a leper worshipped, saying, Ld. if thou *w.* thou canst make me clean, *Mark* 1. 40. *Luke* 5. 12.
13. 28. *w.* thou then that we go and gather them up?
15. 28. O woman, be it unto thee even as thou *w.*
17. 4. if thou *w.* let us make three tabernacles
26. 17. the disciples said, where *w.* thou that we prepare the passover? *Mark* 14. 12. *Luke* 22. 9.
39. not as I will, but as thou *w.* *Mark* 14. 36.
Mark. 6. 22. king said, ask of me whatsoever thou *w.*
Luke 9. 54. *w.* thou that we command fire to come?
John 5. 6. Jesus said, *w.* thou be made whole?
Acts 1. 6. *w.* thou at this time restore the kingdom?

WIMPLES.

Isa. 3. 22. the Lord will take away mantles and *w.*

WIN.

2 *Chron.* 32. 1. he thought to *w.* them for himself
Phil. 3. 8. count them dung that I may *w.* Christ

WINNETH.

Prov. 11. 30. and he that *w.* souls is wise

WIND.

The Hebrews acknowledged four principal winds, as we do, Ezek. 42. 16, 17, 18. He measured the east side, *in Hebrew, the east* wind, &c. *The east* wind *is called in Hebrew,* Kadim; *the north* wind, Tzaphon; *the south* wind, Darom; *and the west* wind, *or from the Mediterranean sea,* Rouach-Hajam. *Solomon says, in* Prov. 25. 23. *That the* north *wind* disperses the clouds and the rain; *but other interpreters translate it,* It produces rain. *The wind* Euroclydon, *see* EUROCLYDON.
The powerful operations and motions of God's Spirit, quickening or reviving the heart toward God, are compared to the blowing of the wind, *John* 3. 8. *For as it is with the* wind, *man perceives, by the effects of it, that there is such a thing, and that it does blow, yet his power cannot restrain it, neither can his reason reach to know whence it rises, or from how far it comes, or how far it reaches; so is the spiritual change wrought in the soul; freely, where, in whom, when, and in what measure the Spirit pleases; and also powerfully, so as to make an evident sensible change, though the manner thereof be incomprehensible. Elsewhere the motions of the Spirit are set forth by* wind, *as in* Cant. 4. 16. *The judgments of God are compared to* wind, *as in* Isa. 27. 8. He stayeth his rough *wind* in the day of his east *wind. He assuages the fury of the storm, and mitigates the severity of the judgment.*
It is said in Isa. 26. 18. We have been with child, we have, as it were, brought forth *wind, that is,* "*We have been in expectation of help, and deliverance out of our troubles, but our hopes have proved empty and unsuccessful, and we have not been able to do any thing towards our own deliverance.*" *So in* Hos. 12. 1. Ephraim feedeth on *wind:* "*The ten tribes flatter themselves with vain deluding hopes of help from the Egyptians and Assyrians.*" *In* Mat. 7. 25. *all sorts of* temptations *are thus described,* The rain descended, the floods came, the *winds* blew. *And in* Jer. 4. 11, 12. the *coming in of an army swiftly and fiercely, destroying all before them, is expressed by a* dry wind, *a* full wind.
The apostle Paul compares vain and inconstant opinions and doctrines to wind. Eph. 4. 14. Carried about with every *wind* of doctrine. *As the* wind *is a subtile body, so these doctrines are subtile, but without substance of truth. The* wind *is uncertain, now blowing from one quarter, now from another, now loud, and presently silent; so false doctrines are uncertain, now making a great noise, and suddenly vanishing. The* wind *likewise carrieth chaff, stubble, and such like things, along with it, but houses well founded, stand still; so the doctrines of false teachers carry aside unstable persons; but he that is rooted in faith and humility, knowing his misery by sin, and the grace of God in Christ, will not be moved with them.*
Gen. 3. † 8. walking in garden in the *w.* of the day
8. 1. God made a *w.* to pass over the earth
Exod. 15. 10. thou didst blow with thy *w.*
Num. 11. 31. the *w.* brought quails from the sea
2 *Sam.* 22. 11. he rode upon a cherub, he was seen upon the wings of the *w.* *Psal.* 18. 10. | 104. 3.
1 *Kings* 18. 45. the heaven was black with *w.*
19. 11. Lord passed by, a great and strong *w.* rent the mountains, but the Lord was not in the *w.*
2 *Kings* 3. 17. ye shall not see *w.* nor shall see rain
Job 1. 19. there came a *w.* from the wilderness
6. 26. to reprove speeches which are as *w.*
7. 7. O remember that my life is *w.*
8. 2. the words of thy mouth be like a strong *w.*
21. 18. they are as stubble before the *w.*
30. 15. terrors pursue my soul as the *w.*
22. thou liftest me up to the *w.*
37. 21. men see not light in the clouds, but the *w.* passeth and cleanseth them, *Psal.* 103. 16.

Psal. 1. 4. like chaff which the *w.* drives away
78. 39. *w.* that passeth away and comes not again
135. 7. he bringeth the *w.* out of his treasuries
147. 18. he causeth his *w.* to blow, and waters flow
Prov. 11. 29. troubleth his house, he shall inherit *w.*
25. 14. is like clouds and *w.* without rain
23. the north *w.* driveth away rain
27. 16. whoso hideth her, hideth the *w.*
30. 4. who hath gathered the *w.* in his fists
Eccl. 1. 6. *w.* goeth toward the south, and turneth about to the north, and the *w.* returneth again
5. 16. what profit hath he that laboured for the *w.*
11. 4. he that observeth the *w.* shall not sow
Cant. 4. 16. awake, O north-*w.* come, thou south
Isa. 7. 2. as trees are moved with the *w.*
11. 15. with his *w.* shake his hand over the river
26. 18. we have as it were brought forth *w.*
27. 8. he stayeth his rough *w.* in day of his east *w.*
32. 2. a man shall be as a hiding-place from the *w.*
41. 16. the *w.* shall carry them away, 57. 13.
29. their molten images are *w.* and confusion
64. 6. our iniquities, like *w.* have taken us away
Jer. 4. 12. a full *w.* from those places shall come
5. 13. prophets shall become *w.* word not in them
10. 13. brings the *w.* out of his treasuries, 51. 16.
22. 22. the *w.* shall eat up all thy pastures
Ezek. 5. 2. a third part thou shalt scatter in the *w.*
12. 14. I will scatter toward every *w.* all about him
37. 9. prophesy to the *w.* son of man, say to the *w.*
Dan. 2. 35. and the *w.* carried them away
Hos. 4. 19. the *w.* hath bound her up in her wings
8. 7. they have sown *w.* and shall reap whirlwind
12. 1. Ephraim feedeth on *w.* he follows east *w.*
Amos 4. 13. for lo, he that createth the *w.*
Jonah 1. 4. Lord sent out a great *w.* into the sea
Mic. 2. † 11. if a man walk with the *w.* and lie
Zech. 5. 9. and the *w.* was in their wings
Mat. 11. 7. a reed shaken with the *w.* *Luke* 7. 24.
14. 24. *w.* was contrary, *Mark* 6. 48. *Acts* 27. 4.
32. the *w.* ceased, *Mark* 4. 39. | 6. 51.
John 3. 8. the *w.* bloweth where it listeth
Acts 2. 2. a sound from heaven, as of a mighty *w.*
Eph. 4. 14. carried about with every *w.* of doctrine
Jam. 1. 6. like a wave driven with the *w.* and tossed
Rev. 6. 13. when she is shaken of a mighty *w.*
7. 1. that the *w.* should not blow on the earth

WINDS.

Job 28. 25. to make the weight for the *w.*
Ezek. 37. 9. come from the four *w.* O breath
Mat. 7. 25. the *w.* blew, and beat on that house, 27.
8. 26. he arose and rebuked the *w.* *Luke* 8. 24.
27. what manner of man is this that even the *w.* and sea obey him? *Mark* 4. 41. *Luke* 8. 25.
Jam. 3. 4. ships, tho' great, are driven of fierce *w.*
Jude 12. they are clouds carried about of *w.*
See EAST, FOUR, SCATTER, STORMY.

WINDY.

Psal. 55. 8. I would hasten from the *w.* storm

WINDOW.

Gen. 6. 16. a *w.* shalt thou make to the ark
8. 6. Noah opened the *w.* of the ark which he made
26. 8. the king of Gerar looked out at a *w.*
Josh. 2. 15. Rahab let the spies down through a *w.*
21. she bound the scarlet line in the *w.*
Judg. 5. 28. Sisera's mother looked out at a *w.*
2 *Sam.* 6. 16. Michal looked through a *w.* saw David
2 *Kings* 9. 30. Jezebel painted, and looked out at a *w.*
13. 17. and he said, open the *w.* eastward
Prov. 7. 6. at the *w.* of my house I looked through
Acts 20. 9. there sat in a *w.* a certain young man
2 *Cor.* 11. 33. thro' a *w.* was I let down in a basket

WINDOWS.

Gen. 7. 11. and the *w.* of heaven were opened
8. 2. and the *w.* of heaven were stopped
2 *Kings* 7. 2. if the Lord make *w.* in heaven, 19.
Eccl. 12. 3. those that look out of the *w.* be darkened
Cant. 2. 9. my beloved looked forth at the *w.*
Isa. 24. 18. for the *w.* from on high are open
54. 12. I will make thy *w.* of agates
60. 8. who are these that flee as the doves to their *w.*
Jer. 9. 21. for death is come up into our *w.*
22. 14. woe to him that cutteth him out *w.*
Dan. 6. 10. his *w.* being open in his chamber
Joel 2. 9. they shall enter in at the *w.* like a thief
Zeph. 2. 14. their voice shall sing in the *w.*
Mal. 3. 10. if I will not open you the *w.* of heaven

WINE.

Several of the ancients were of opinion, that wine *was not in use before the deluge, and that Noah was the first who used this liquor. If* wine, *say they, had been known before the flood, Abel would not have failed to bring an offering of it to the Lord, and Noah would have been upon his guard, so as not to have drank of it to excess. But, on the other hand, it is maintained by others, that it is much more probable that the first men were not ignorant of the use of* wine, *which is a liquor so generally useful and agreeable, that it could scarcely be unknown even to Adam himself. And as to Noah, they say, that though he knew the intoxicating quality of* wine, *yet he might be deceived in the strength of it, and think, that the quantity he drank of it was not capable of causing the drunkenness in him that he afterwards found it did.*

There were many excellent vineyards in Palestine; and to shew how great a number there should be of these in the single inheritance of the tribe of Judah, the patriarch Jacob says of his son Judah, He washed his garments in *wine,* and his clothes in the blood of grapes, *Gen.* 49. 11. *The use of* wine *was forbidden to the priests during all the time they were in the tabernacle, and employed in the service of the altar,* Lev. 10. 9. *Drunkenness is so odious a sin in itself, especially in a minister, and most of all in the time of his administration of sacred things, that the use of* wine *was strictly forbidden on those occasions. This liquor was also forbidden to the Nazarites,* Num. 6. 3.

In Gen. 27. 28, 37. Corn and wine *denote all sorts of temporal good things, which were more frequently promised and bestowed under the Old Testament, but were types of spiritual blessings. In the style of the sacred penmen,* the wine, *or* the cup, *often represents the anger of God.* Psal. 60. 3. Thou hast made us to drink the *wine* of astonishment. *And in* Jer. 25. 15. Take the *wine* cup of this fury at my hand, and cause all the nations to whom I send thee to drink it. *They were used to administer* wine, *by way of medicine, to such as were in trouble and sorrow.* Prov. 31. 6. Give strong drink to him that is ready to perish, and *wine* to those that be of heavy hearts. *The Rabbins say, that they used to give* wine *and strong liquors to those that were condemned to die, at their execution, to stupify them, and take off some part of the fear and sense of their pains. There were certain charitable women at Jerusalem, as they tell us, who used to mix certain drugs with* wine, *to make it stronger, and more capable of extinguishing the sense of pain. Some think it was such a kind of mixture that was offered to our Saviour to drink, before he was fastened to the cross,* Mark 15. 23. And they gave him to drink *wine* mingled with myrrh, but he received it not.

The *wine* of Helbon. *Ezekiel speaks of this* wine *that was sold at the fairs of Tyre,* Ezek. 27. 18. *Some say that this* wine *was well known to the ancients; they called it* Chalibonium vinum. *It was made at Damascus, and the Persians had planted vineyards there, on purpose, as Posidonius affirms. Others make it a common name,* sweet or fat *wine; for Helbon comes from a word that signifies* fat.

The *wine* of Lebanon. *Hosea speaks of this* wine, *Hos.* 14. 7. The scent thereof shall be as the *wine* of Lebanon. *The* wines *of those sides of mount Lebanon that had a good exposition to the sun, were heretofore much esteemed. But some think, that the Hebrew text,* wine of Lebanon, *may signify a sweet-scented* wine; wine *in which perfumes are mixed, or other drugs, to make it more palatable, and of a better flavour. Odoriferous* wines *were not unknown to the Hebrews. In* Cant. 8. 2. *mention is made of a medicated* wine, spiced wine, wine *mixed with perfumes. The* wines *of Palestine being heady, they used to qualify them with water, that they might be drunk without any inconvenience.* Prov. 9. 2, 5. She hath mingled her *wine;* Come, drink of the *wine* which I have mingled.

The wicked eat the bread of wickedness, and drink the *wine* of violence, *Prov.* 4. 17. *that is, "they are maintained with ill-gotten goods, or they abuse the good things that God gives them; they offend him by the bad use they make of the necessaries of life." In* Amos 2. 8. *it is said,* They drink the *wine* of the condemned in the house of their god: "*They drink the* wine, *they make themselves merry at the expense of those they have unjustly condemned." The Septuagint say, "They drink* wine *earned by their slanders." The Chaldee,* the wine of rapine. *In* Mat. 9. 14, 17. *our Lord Jesus Christ tells the disciples of John the Baptist, who inquired the reason why they and the Pharisees did fast often, but his disciples did not fast, that* men do not put new *wine* into old bottles; else the bottles break, and the *wine* runneth out, and the bottles perish. *Our Saviour hereby tells us, that it was not fit for him to impose upon his disciples, who were as yet but weak in grace and spiritual strength, the severe exercise of frequent and extraordinary fasting, lest they should be discouraged thereby, and so fall off; or lest it should produce hatred and contempt instead of obedience:* But, *adds he,* they put new *wine* into new bottles, and both are preserved: "*My disciples must be fitted by degrees, and strengthened for such exercises, and then they will perform them readily and acceptably.*" Wine *is put for gospel provisions,* Isa. 25. 6. *For consolations,* Prov. 31. 6. *And for the blood of Christ,* Mark 14. 25.

Gen. 9. 24. Noah awoke from his *w.* and knew
14. 18. Melchisedek brought forth bread and *w.*
49. 11. he washed his garments in *w.* and clothes in
12. his eyes were red with *w.* his teeth white
Exod. 29. 40. with the fourth part of an hin of *w.* for a drink offering, *Lev.* 23. 13. *Num.* 15. 5.
Num. 6. 3. he shall separate himself from *w.*
15. 10. for a drink-offering half an hin of *w.* 28. 14.
28. 7. shalt cause the strong *w.* to be poured out
Deut. 32. 33. their *w.* is the poison of dragons
Judg. 9. 13. leave *w.* which cheereth God and man
19. 19. there is also bread and *w.* for me and handm.
1 *Sam.* 1. 14. Eli said, put away thy *w.* from thee
25. 37. when the *w.* was gone out of Nabal
2 *Sam.* 6. 19. to every one a cake of bread, a good piece of flesh, and a flagon of *w.* 1 *Chron.* 16. 3.
13. 28. when Amnon's heart is merry with *w.*
16. 2. the *w.* that such as be faint may drink
Neh. 2. 1. *w.* was before him, I took up the *w.*
5. 15. the other governors had taken bread and *w.*
18. and once in ten days store of all sorts of *w.*
13. 15. lading asses with *w.* and grapes and figs
Esth. 1. 7. they gave them royal *w.* in abundance
10. the heart of the king was merry with *w.*
5. 6. king said to Esther at the banquet of *w.* 7. 2.
7. 7. the king arising from the banquet of *w.*
Job 1. 13. drinking *w.* in eldest brother's house, 18.
32. 19. behold, my belly is as *w.* that hath no vent
Psal. 75. 8. the *w.* is red, it is full of mixture
78. 65. mighty man that shouteth by reason of *w.*
104. 15. *w.* that maketh glad the heart of man
Prov. 9. 2. killeth her beasts, she hath mingled her *w.*
20. 1. *w.* is a mocker, strong drink is raging
23. 30. who hath woe? who hath sorrow? they that tarry long at the *w.* they that go to seek mixt *w.*
31. look not thou on the *w.* when it is red
31. 6. give *w.* to those that be of heavy hearts
Eccl. 2. 3. I sought in my heart to give myself to *w.*
10. 19. *w.* maketh merry, but money answereth
Cant. 1. 2. for thy love is better than *w.* 4. 10.
5. 1. I have drunk my *w.* with my milk, eat
7. 9. and the roof of thy mouth like the best *w.*
Isa. 1. 22. thy silver dross, thy *w.* mixt with water
5. 11. that continue till night till *w.* inflame them
12. pipe and *w.* are in their feasts, but regard not
22. 13. eating flesh and drinking *w.* let us eat
24. 11. there is a crying for *w.* in the streets
27. 2. a vineyard of red *w.* || 55. 1. come, buy *w.*
28. 1. valleys of them that are overcome with *w.*
7. they have also erred thro' *w.* and thro' strong drink out of the way, they are swallowed up of *w.*
29. 9. they are drunken, but not with *w.* 51. 21.
56. 12. come ye, say they, I will fetch *w.*
Jer. 23. 9. like a man whom *w.* hath overcome
25. 15. take the *w.* cup of this fury at my hand
35. 5. pots full of *w.* || 40. 12. Jews gathered *w.*
48. 33. I have caused *w.* to fail from wine-presses
51. 7. nations have drunken of her *w.* are mad
Ezek. 27. 18. Damascus traded in *w.* of Helbon
Dan. 1. 5. the king gave of the *w.* which he drank
8. but purposed not to defile himself with the *w*
5. 1. Belshazzar drank *w.* before the thousand, 4.
2. whiles he tasted *w.* || 23. concubines drunk *w*
10. 3. neither came *w.* nor flesh in my mouth
Hos. 2. 9. take away my *w.* in the season thereof
3. 1. who look to other gods and love flagons of *w.*
14. 7. the scent shall be as the *w.* of Lebanon
Joel 1. 5. weep and howl, all ye drinkers of *w.*
Mic. 2. 11. saying, I will prophesy to thee of *w.*
Hab. 2. 5. yea also, because he transgresseth by *w*
Zech. 9. 15. drink and make a noise, as though *w.*
10. 7. their heart shall rejoice, as through *w.*
Luke 7. 33. for John came, neither drinking *w.*
John 2. 3. and when they wanted *w.* the mother of Jesus saith unto him, they have no *w.*
9. had tasted the water that was made *w.* 4. 46.
10. every man at the beginning doth set forth good *w.* but thou hast kept good *w.* till now
Eph. 5. 18. be not drunk with *w.* wherein is excess.
1 *Tim.* 3. 3. not given to *w.* 8. *Tit.* 1. 7. | 2. 3.
5. 23. use a little *w.* for thy stomach's sake
1 *Pet.* 4. 3. when we walked in excess of *w.*
Rev. 16. 19. give her the cup of the *w.* of wrath
17. 2. drunk with *w.* of her fornication, 18. 3.
See BOTTLE, CORN, DRINK, NEW, OFFERINGS, OIL, SWEET.

WINE-BIBBER, S.

Prov. 23. 20. be not with *w.-bibbers,* eaters of flesh
Mat. 11. 19. behold a man a *w.-bibber, Luke* 7. 34.

WINE-*bottles.*

Josh. 9. 4. Gibeonites took *w.-bottles* old and rent
13. these *bottles* of *w.* which we filled were new

WINE-*cellars.*

1 *Chron.* 27. 27. over the *w.-cellars* was Zabdi

WINE-*fat.*

Isa. 63. 2. like him that treadeth in the *w.-fat*
Mark 12. 1. he digged a place for the *w.-fat*

WINE-*press.*

Num. 18. 27. as the fulness of the *w.-press,* 30.
Deut. 15. 14. shalt furnish him out of thy *w.-press*
Judg. 6. 11. Gideon threshed wheat by the *w.-press*
7. 25. Zeeb they slew at the *w.-press* of Zeeb
2 *Kings* 6. 27. shall I help thee out of the *w.-press?*
Isa. 5. 2. a vineyard, he also made a *w.-press* therein
63. 3. I trodden the *w.-press* alone, none with me
Lam. 1. 15. trodden daughter of Judah as in a *w.-p.*
Hos. 9. 2. the floor and *w.-press* shall not feed them
Mat. 21. 33. digged a *w.-press* in it, and let it out
Rev. 14. 19. the angel cast it into the great *w.-press*
20. the *w.-p.* was trodden without the city, blood came out of the *w.-press* to the horse-bridles
19. 15. he treadeth *w.-press* of the wrath of God

WINE-*presses.*

Neh. 13. 15. I saw some treading *w.-p.* on sabbath
Job 24. 11. tread their *w.-presses* and suffer thirst
Jer. 48. 33. caused wine to fail from the *w.-presses*
Zech. 14. 10. inhabited upon the king's *w.-presses*

WINES.

Isa. 25. 6. make a feast of *w.* on the lees well refined

WING.

By the name wing, *the Hebrews understand not only the wings of birds, but also divers things which have some kind of resemblance to* wings, *as,* (1) *The lappet or skirt of a garment,* Ruth 3. 9. Spread thy skirt over thine handmaid, *in Hebrew,* thy wing. *And in* Jer. 2. 34. In thy skirts, *Heb.* wings, is found the blood of the souls of the poor innocents. (2) *The wings of an army. Isaiah speaking of the army of the king of Assyria, that was coming into the land of Judah, says,* The stretching out of his *wings* shall fill the breadth of thy land, O Immanuel, *Isa.* 8. 8. *See also* Jer. 48. 40. (3) Wing *is put for the extremity or utmost part of a country,* Job 38. 13. That it might take hold of the ends of the earth, *in Heb.* the *wings* of the earth. *So in* Isa. 24. 16. From the uttermost part of the earth have we heard songs: *the Hebrew says,* from *the* wing *of the earth.* (4) *It is put for the sails of a ship,* Isa. 18. 1. Woe to the land shadowing with *wings: meaning Egypt, which abounded with ships, whose sails are like* wings, *that shadow the sea.* (5) *The name of* wings *is given to the sun-beams.* Mal. 4. 2. The sun of righteousness shall arise with healing in his *wings. This being applied to Christ, denotes that he should appear in the flesh, and by his doctrine, merit, and Spirit, should bring a remedy for all spiritual sicknesses and diseases. Some have observed, that by the word* wings, *may be insinuated the healing virtue that went forth from Christ to such as by faith did but touch the hem of his garment,* Mat. 9. 20, 21, 22. (6) Wing *is put for the battlement of an house.* Mat. 4. 5. The devil set our Saviour on a pinnacle *or wing* of the temple. (7) Wings, *in a figurative and metaphorical sense, are put for protection or defence. God says in* Exod. 19. 4. *that* he bare his people on the *wings* of eagles; *that is, "that he had brought them safely out of Egypt, as an eagle carries its young ones under its wings." David begs of God to* hide him under his wings, *to protect and defend him, as a*

hen doth her chickens under her wings, *Psal.* 17. 8. *And in* Psal. 36. 7. *he says that* the children of men put their trust under the shadow of his *wings.*
Gen. 7. † 14. every bird of every *w.* went into ark
1 *Kings* 6. 24. five cubits was one *w.* of the cherub, five cubits the other *w.* 27. 2 *Chron.* 3. 11, 12.
Psal. 148. † 10. birds of *w.* praise the Lord
Isa. 10. 14. and there was none that moved the *w.*
24. † 16. from the *w.* of the earth we heard songs
Ezek. 17. 23. under it shall dwell fowl of every *w.*
39. † 17. speak to the fowl of every *w.*

WINGS.

Exod. 19. 4. ye have seen how I bare you on eagles' [*w.*
25. 20. cherubims stretch forth their *w.* covering the mercy-seat with their *w.* 37. 9. 1 *Kings* 8. 7.
Lev. 1. 17. he shall cleave it with the *w.* thereof
Deut. 22. † 12. make fringes upon the four *w.*
32. 11. as an eagle spreadeth abroad her *w.* taketh her young, beareth them on her *w.*
Ruth 2. 12. under whose *w.* thou art come to trust
2 *Sam.* 22. 11. he was seen upon the *w.* of the wind
Job 37. † 3. his lightning to the *w.* of the earth
38. † 13. it might take hold of the *w.* of the earth
39. 13. gavest thou the goodly *w.* to the peacock? or *w.* and feathers to the ostrich?
Psal. 17. 8. hide me under the shadow of thy *w.*
18. 10. he did fly on the *w.* of the wind, 104. 3.
36. 7. therefore men put their trust under the shadow of thy *w.* 57. 1. | 61. 4. | 91. 4.
55. 6. I said, O that I had *w.* like a dove
63. 7. in the shadow of thy *w.* will I rejoice
68. 13. yet shall ye be as the *w.* of a dove
139. 9. if I take the *w.* of the morning, and dwell
Prov. 23. 5. riches make themselves *w.* they fly
Eccl. 10. 20. that which hath *w.* shall tell matter
Isa. 6. 2. stood the seraphims, each one had six *w.*
8. 8. the stretching out of his *w.* shall fill thy land
11. † 12. gather Judah from the *w.* of the earth
18. 1. woe to the land shadowing with *w.*
40. 31. they shall mount up with *w.* as eagles
Jer. 48. 9. give *w.* to Moab, it may fly and get away
40. behold, he shall spread his *w.* over Moab
49. 22. behold, he shall spread his *w.* over Bozrah
Ezek. 1. 6. every one had four faces and four *w.*
9. their *w.* were joined ‖ 10. 12. *w.* full of eyes
24. I heard the noise of their *w.* 3. 13. | 10. 5. when they stood, they let down their *w.* 25.
17. 3. a great eagle with great *w.* long-winged
7. there was also another great eagle with great *w.*
Dan. 7. 4. the first was like a lion, and had eagles' *w.* I beheld till the *w.* thereof were plucked
6. another having on the back four *w.* of a fowl
Hos. 4. 19. the wind hath bound her up in her *w.*
Zech. 5. 9. two women, and the wind was in their *w.*
Mal. 4. 2. sun of right. arise with healing in his *w.*
Mat. 23. 37. how often would I have gathered as a hen gath. her chickens under her *w.* *Luke* 13. 34.
Rev. 9. 9. the sound of their *w.* as of many horses
12. 14. to the woman were given two *w.* of an eagle

WINGED.

Gen. 1. 21. God created every *w.* fowl after his kind
Deut. 4. 17. and make the likeness of any *w.* fowl
Ezek. 17. 3. great eagle with great wings, long-*w.* of divers colours, full of feathers, came to Lebanon

WINK.

Job 15. 12. and what do thine eyes *w.* at?
Psal. 35. 19. neither let them *w.* with the eye

WINKED.

Acts 17. 30. and times of this ignorance God *w.* at

WINKETH.

Prov. 6. 13. a wicked man *w.* with his eyes
10. 10. he that *w.* with the eye, causeth sorrow

WINNOWED.

Isa. 30. 24. which hath been *w.* with the shovel

WINNOWEST.

Psal. 139. † 2. thou *w.* my path and lying down

WINNOWETH.

Ruth 3. 2. behold, Boaz *w.* barley to-night in floor

WINTER.

Gen. 8. 22. summer and *w.* shall not cease
Psal. 74. 17. thou hast made summer and *w.*
Prov. 20. † 4. sluggard will not plow by reason of *w.*
Cant. 2. 11. for lo, the *w.* is past, the rain is over
Zech. 14. 8. in summer and in *w.* shall it be
Mat. 24. 20. pray ye that your flight be not in the *w.* nor on the sabbath-day, *Mark* 13. 18.
John 10. 22. the feast of dedication was in *w.*
2 *Tim.* 4. 21. do thy diligence to come before *w.*

WINTER-*house*.

Jer. 36. 22. now the king sat in the *w.-house*
Amos 3. 15. I will smite *w.-house* with summer-house

WINTER, *Verb.*

Isa. 18. 6. the beasts of the earth shall *w.* on them
Acts 27. 12. because the haven was not commodious to *w.* in, the more part advised to *w.* at Phenice
1 *Cor.* 16. 6. it may be I will abide and *w.* with you
Tit. 3. 12. for I have determined there to *w.*

WINTERED.

Acts 28. 11. in a ship which had *w.* in the isle

WIPE.

2 *Kings* 21. 13. I will *w.* Jerusalem as a dish
Neh. 13. 14. *w.* not out my good deeds I have done
Isa. 25. 8. he will swallow up death in victory, Lord will *w.* away tears from all faces, *Rev.* 7. 17. | 21. 4.
Luke 7. 38. a woman did *w.* them with hairs of her head, and kissed his feet, 44. *John* 11. 2. | 12. 3.
John 13. 5. he began to *w.* them with the towel

WIPED.

Prov. 6. 33. his reproach shall not be *w.* away

WIPETH.

2 *Kings* 21. 13. as a man *w.* a dish, turning it
Prov. 30. 20. she eateth, *w.* her mouth, and saith

WIPING.

2 *Kings* 21. 13. *w.* it, and turning it upside down

WIRES.

Exod. 39. 3. they cut gold plates into *w.* to work it

WISDOM,

In Greek, σοφια· *in Hebrew*, Chachemah. *It is put*, 1. *For that prudence and discretion, which enables men to perceive what is fit to be done, according to the circumstances of time, place, persons, manners, and end of doing*, Eccl. 2. 13, 14. I saw that *wisdom* excelleth folly, for the wise man's eyes are in his head. "*The wise man has the use of his eyes and reason, he sees his way, and orders all his affairs with discretion; he foresees, and so avoid, many dangers and mischiefs.*" *Knowledge directs a man what is to be done, and what is not to be done; but* wisdom *directs him how to do things duly, conveniently, and fitly. It was this sort of* wisdom *that Solomon entreated of God with so much earnestness, and which God granted him with great liberality,* 1 Kings 3. 9, 12, 28.

II. Wisdom *is taken for quickness of invention, and dexterity in the execution of several works, which require not so much strength of body, as industry and labour of the mind.* Wisdom *is the gift of God, who told Moses, that he had* filled with *wisdom*, and understanding, and knowledge, *Bezaleel and Aholiab, to invent and perform several sorts of work for completing the tabernacle,* Exod. 31. 2, 3.

III. Wisdom *is used for craft, cunning, and stratagem, and that whether good or evil.* Exod. 1. 10. Come on, *said Pharaoh*, let us deal wisely with the Israelites: "*Let us fall upon some stratagem, whereby we may exhaust both their wealth and their strength.*" *It is observed of Jonadab, the friend of Amnon, and nephew of David, that* he was very wise, *that is, very subtle and crafty,* 2 Sam. 13. 3. *And in* Job 5. 13. *it is said, that* God taketh the wise in their own craftiness.

IV. Wisdom *is taken for doctrine, learning, and experience.* Job 12. 12. With the ancient is *wisdom*. *And in* Acts 7. 22. *it is said of Moses, that* he was learned in all the *wisdom* of the Egyptians; "*He was instructed in the knowledge of those arts and sciences, for which, in those times, the Egyptians were famous.*"

V. *It is taken for true piety, or the fear of God, which is spiritual* wisdom. *Psal.* 90. 12. So teach us to number our days, that we may apply our hearts unto *wisdom*; "*That we may devote ourselves to the study and practice of true piety.*" *And in* Job 28. 28. The fear of the Lord, that is *wisdom.*

VI. Wisdom *is put for Jesus Christ, the eternal, essential* Wisdom, *the word, the Son of God. It was by* Wisdom *that God established the heavens, and founded the earth,* Prov. 3. 19. *It was this* Wisdom *that the Lord* possessed from everlasting, from the beginning, or ever the earth was, *Prov.* 8. 22, 23. *He was set up, he was anointed from everlasting, before all worlds, to be the person by whom the Father resolved to do all his works, first to create, and then to uphold, govern, and judge, and afterwards to redeem and save the world; all which works are in Scripture particularly ascribed to the Son of God. Solomon, in* Prov. 8. *discourses largely and profoundly of this* wisdom.

The Psalmist says, Psal. 37. 30. The mouth of the righteous speaketh *wisdom*. *When the discourses of other men are either wicked or vain, his are pious and profitable, they flow from, and are so many evidences of,* wisdom, *and have a tendency to make others spiritually wise. In* Job 28. 12. *having mentioned several hidden things which man's* wisdom *has found out, Job asks this question,* But where shall *wisdom* be found? *He means that sublime and eminent* wisdom, *which consists in the exact knowledge of all God's counsels and ways, and of the several manners and reasons of his governing the world, and dealing with good and bad men; this is far above man's reach, and is the prerogative of God alone. Job says to his three friends,* chap. 12. 2. No doubt but ye are the people, and *wisdom* shall die with you. *This is an ironical expression; that is to say,* "*You are the only people for eminency of* wisdom; *you have engrossed all the reason of mankind; and you think that all the* wisdom *and knowledge of divine things, which is in the world, lives in you, and will die and be utterly lost when you die.*"

Wisdom *is put for natural instinct and sagacity.* Job 39. 17. *The ostrich is hardened against her young ones,* because God hath deprived her of *wisdom*: "*Because God hath not implanted in her that natural instinct, care, and affection, which he hath put into other birds and beasts, towards their young.*" Wisdom *is likewise put for the doctrine of the gospel.* 1 Cor. 2. 6, 7. Howbeit we speak *wisdom* among them that are perfect: yet not the *wisdom* of this world, nor of the princes of this world, that come to nought: *that is,* "*The subject-matter of my preaching is the most wise contrivance and counsel of God, concerning the salvation of man by Christ crucified, and so it will be owned to be, though not by learned philosophers, yet by humble, sincere Christians, and such who have attained to some ripeness of understanding in the knowledge of the gospel: but this is not the* wisdom of the world, *which teaches how to manage our temporal affairs, only in order to a comfortable life here; neither is it the maxims of state-policy, which statesmen count the only* wisdom, *who yet by all their plots and policies cannot secure themselves from ruin;* But we speak the *wisdom* of God in a mystery, even hidden *wisdom*; *it is such as no creature could make any discovery of, and was hidden formerly under holy mysteries and Jewish types; it was but darkly spoken of by the prophets, and altogether unknown to the Gentiles.*"

Christ Jesus is said to be made of God unto us *wisdom*, 1 Cor. 1. 30. "*He reveals the will and knowledge of God to us, and makes us wise unto salvation.*" *In* Mat. 11. 19. *our Saviour speaking of the bad treatment that John the Baptist and himself met with from the Jews, says,* But *Wisdom* is justified of her children. *Some take the meaning to be this;* "I, who am the *wisdom* of God, am justified by you, *who truly believe on me: you know I am no glutton, no winebibber, no friend of publicans and sinners.*" *Others thus,* "*Religion, in all the branches and duties thereof, enjoined by God, or the various methods that God uses to reclaim sinners, is owned and acknowledged to be full of* wisdom, *holiness, and equity, and also vindicated from the cavils and unjust imputations of all ungodly persons, by those who have devoted themselves to the study and practice of religion.*"

St. James speaks of the wisdom that is from above, *which comes from God, and teaches us to be humble and holy in all our conversation,* Jam. 3. 17. *It is known and expressed by several properties: it is* pure, *it makes men careful to avoid any defilement by sin and error, and to adhere both to truth and holiness. It is* peaceable, *it disposeth men to peace, both as to the making and keeping it, so far as is consistent with purity, and may be done without sin. It is* gentle, *it disposes men to bear with the infirmities of others, to forgive injuries, to interpret all things for the best, to recede from their own right, for peace sake. It is* easy to be entreated, *it makes men yield to persuasions of the word, to good counsel, good reason. It is* full of mercy, *it makes us pity others that are afflicted, or that offend. It is* full of good fruits, *of beneficence, liberality, and all other offices of humanity, which proceed from mercy. It is* without partiality, *it does not make a difference between person and person, upon carnal accounts. It is also* without hypocrisy, *or* counterfeiting, *as they do that judge others, being guilty of the same things themselves; it is unfeigned and sincere.* Wisdom *is put for the holy scriptures,* Luke 11. 49.

Exod. 31. 3. I have filled him with the Spirit of God in *w.* and in understanding, 6. | 35. 31, 35.
35. 26. whose heart stirred them up in *w.* 36. 1, 2.
Deut. 4. 6. for this is your *w.* and understanding
2 *Sam.* 14. 20. according to *w.* of an angel of God
20. 22. the woman went to all the people in her *w.*
1 *Kings* 3. 28. they saw that the *w.* of G. was in him
4. 29. God gave Solomon *w.* 5. 12. 2 *Chron.* 1. 12.
30. Solomon's *w.* excelled *w.* of Egypt, 34. | 7. 14. | 10. 4, 23, 24. 2 *Chron.* 9. 3, 22, 23.
1 *Chron.* 22. 12. only Lord give thee *w.* and underst.
2 *Chron.* 1. 10. give me *w.* ‖ 11. but hast asked *w.*
Ezra 7. 25. thou Ezra, after the *w.* of thy God
Job 4. 21. they die, even without *w.*
12. 2. ye are the people, *w.* shall die with you
13. 5. hold your peace and it should be your *w.*
15. 8. and dost thou restrain *w.* to thyself?
26. 3. hast thou counselled him that hath no *w.*?
28. 12. but where shall *w.* be found?
20. whence cometh *w.* and where place of underst.
30. † 22. and thou dissolvest my *w.*
32. 7. multitude of years should teach *w.*
13. lest ye should say, we have found out *w.*
33. 33. hearken to me and I shall teach thee *w.*
34. 35. Job's words were without *w.*
36. 5. behold, God is mighty in strength and *w.*
38. 37. who can number the clouds in *w.*?
39. 17. because God hath deprived her of *w.*
Psal. 37. 30. the mouth of the righteous speaks *w.*
51. 6. thou shalt make me to know *w.*
90. 12. that we may apply our hearts unto *w.*
104. 24. in *w.* hast thou made all thy works
105. 22. and teach his senators *w.*
136. 5. to him that by *w.* made the heavens
Prov. 1. 2. to know *w.* ‖ 7. fools despise *w.* and instruction
20. *w.* crieth, 8. 1. ‖ 2. 2. incline thine ear to *w.*
2. 6. the Lord giveth *w.* ‖ 3. 21. keep sound *w.*
7. he layeth up sound *w.* for the righteous
10. when *w.* entereth into thine heart
3. 13. happy is the man that findeth *w.* and getteth
19. the Lord by *w.* hath founded the earth
4. 5. get *w.* 7. ‖ 5. 1. my son, attend to my *w.*
7. 4. say to *w.* thou art my sister, and call underst.
8. 5. understand *w.* ‖ 9. 1. *w.* builded her house
12. I *w.* dwell with prudence, and find knowledge
14. counsel is mine, and sound *w.* I am understanding
10. 23. but a man of understanding hath *w.*
31. the mouth of the just bringeth forth *w.*
12. 8. a man is commended according to his *w.*
14. 6. a scorner seeketh *w.* and findeth it not
8. the *w.* of the prudent is to understand his way
33. *w.* resteth in heart of him that hath underst.
16. 16. how much better is it to get *w.* than gold
17. 16. is there a price in hand of a fool to get *w.*
18. 1. thro' desire a man intermeddleth with all *w.*
19. 8. he that getteth *w.* loveth his own soul
21. 30. there is no *w.* against the Lord
23. 4. labour not to be rich, cease from thy own *w.*
9. for a fool will despise the *w.* of thy words
23. buy *w.* ‖ 24. 3. thro' *w.* is an house built
29. 3. whoso loveth *w.* rejoiceth his father
15. the rod and reproof give *w.* but a child left
30. 3. I neither learned *w.* nor have I knowledge
31. 26. she openeth her mouth with *w.*
Eccl. 1. 13. I gave my heart to search out by *w.*
16. I have gotten more *w.* than all before me
17. I gave my heart to know *w.* and folly
18. for in much *w.* is much grief, he that increases
2. 3. yet acquainting mine heart with *w.*
9. so I was great, and my *w.* remained with me
12. I turned myself to behold *w.* and madness
13. *w.* excels folly ‖ 21. whose labour is in *w.*
26. God giveth to a man *w.* ‖ 7. 12. *w.* giveth life
7. 19. *w.* strengtheneth the wise more than ten men
23. all this have I proved by *w.* I will be wise
25. I applied mine heart to know and seek out *w.*
8. 1. a man's *w.* maketh his face to shine
16. when I applied my heart to know *w.*
9. 10. there is no *w.* in the grave where thou goe
13. this *w.* have I seen also under the sun
15. poor man by his *w.* delivered the city
10. 1. a little folly him that is in reputation for *w.*

Eccl. 10. 3. his *w.* faileth him, and he saith he is fool
Isa. 10. 13. by my *w.* I have done it, for I am prudent
29. 14. for the *w.* of their wise men shall perish
33. 6. *w.* shall be the stability of thy times
Jer. 9. 23. let not the wise man glory in his *w.*
10. 12. he established the world by his *w.* 51. 15.
Dan. 1. 4. children who were skilful in all *w.* 17.
2. 14. Daniel answered with counsel and *w.*
20. blessed be God, for *w.* and might are his
21. he giveth *w.* to the wise, and knowledge
23. I thank thee, O God, who hast given me *w.*
30. this secret is not revealed for any *w.* I have
5. 11. *w.* like the *w.* of the gods was found in him
Mat. 12. 42. the queen of the south came from utmost parts to hear the *w.* of Solomon, *Luke* 11. 31.
13. 54. whence hath this man this *w.* and works?
Luke 1. 17. turn the disobedient to the *w.* of the just
2. 40. Jesus filled with *w.* ‖ 52. increased in *w.*
11. 49. therefore also said the *w.* of God, will send
21. 15. for I will give you a mouth and *w.*
Acts 6. 3. look out seven men full of *w.* and Holy G.
10. they were not able to resist the *w.* and spirit
7. 10. God gave Joseph *w.* in the sight of Pharaoh
22. was learned in all the *w.* of the Egyptians
1 *Cor.* 1. 17. to preach gospel not with *w.* of words
19. I will destroy the *w.* of the wise, and bring
20. God hath made foolish the *w.* of this world
21. after that in the *w.* of God the world by *w.* knew not God, it pleased God by preaching
22. require a sign, and Greeks seek after *w.*
24. Christ the power of God and the *w.* of God
30. who of God is made to us *w.* and righteousness
2. 4. my speech was not with words of man's *w.*
5. your faith should not stand in the *w.* of men
6. we speak *w.* ‖ 7. but we speak the *w.* of God
13. not in words which man's *w.* teacheth
3. 19. the *w.* of this world is foolishness with God
2 *Cor.* 1. 12. with sincerity, not with fleshly *w.*
Eph. 1. 8. he hath abounded towards us in all *w.*
3. 10. might be known the manifold *w.* of God
Col. 1. 9. that ye might be filled with all *w.*
28. warning and teaching every man in all *w.*
3. 16. let Christ's words dwell in you in all *w.*
4. 5. walk in *w.* toward them that are without
Jam. 1. 5. if any lack *w.* let him ask of God
3. 15. this *w.* descendeth not from above
2 *Pet.* 3. 15. according to the *w.* given unto him
Rev. 5. 12. worthy is the Lamb to receive *w.*
7. 12. blessing, and glory, and *w.* be to our God
17. 9. and here is the mind which hath *w.*

WISDOM, joined with *is.*

Job 6. 13. and *is w.* driven quite from me?
12. 12. with the ancient *is w.* 13. 16.
28. 18. the price of *w. is* above rubies, *Prov.* 8. 11.
28. fear of the Lord that *is w.* to depart from evil
Prov. 4. 7. *w. is* the principal thing, get *w.*
10. 13. with him that hath understanding *w. is* found
11. 2. but with the lowly *is w.*
13. 10. but with the well-advised *is w.*
14. 8. the *w.* of prudent *is* to understand his way
17. 24. *w. is* before him that hath understanding
24. 7. *w. is* too high for a fool, he opens not
Eccl. 1. 18. for in much *w.* is much grief
7. 11. *w. is* good with an inheritance, and by it
12. for *w. is* a defence, and money is a defence
9. 16. *w. is* better than strength; nevertheless, the poor man's *w. is* despised, his words not heard
18. *w. is* better than weapons of war, but one
10. 10. but *w. is* profitable to direct
Jer. 8. 9. they rejected the word, what *w. is* in them?
49. 7. thus saith the Lord of hosts, *is w.* no more in Teman? *is* their *w.* vanished?
Dan. 5. 14. that excellent *w. is* found in thee
Mat. 11. 19. a friend of publicans and sinners, but *w. is* justified of her children, *Luke* 7. 35.
Mark 6. 2. what *w. is* this which is given to him?
Jam. 3. 17. the *w.* that *is* from above is first pure
Rev. 13. 18. here *is w.* let him that understands

Of WISDOM.

Job 11. 6. that he would shew thee the secrets *of w.*
28. 18. for the price *of w.* is above rubies
Psal. 49. 3. my mouth shall speak *of w.* and meditat.
111. 10. the fear of the Lord is the beginning *of w.* his praise endureth for ever, *Prov.* 9. 10.
Prov. 1. 3. to receive the instruction *of w.* justice
4. 11. I have taught thee in the way *of w.* have led
10. 21. but fools die for want *of w.*
11. 12. he that is void *of w.* despiseth his neighbour
15. 21. folly is joy to him that is destitute *of w.*
33. the fear of the Lord is the instruction *of w.*
18. 4. the well-spring *of w.* as a flowing brook
24. 14. so shall the knowledge *of w.* be to thy soul
Eccl. 1. 16. my heart had great experience *of w.*
Ezek. 28. 12. thou sealest up the sum full *of w.*
Dan. 1. 20. in all matters *of w.* he found them better
Mic. 6. 9. the man *of w.* shall see thy name
Rom. 11. 33. O the depth *of* the *w.* of God!
1 *Cor.* 2. 1. not with excellency of speech or *of w.*
12. 8. to one is given by the Spirit the word *of w.*
Col. 2. 3. in whom are hid all the treasures *of w.*
23. which things have indeed a shew *of w.*
Jam. 3. 13. shew his works with meekness *of w.*
See SPIRIT.

Thy WISDOM.

1 *Kings* 2. 6. do therefore according to *thy w.*
10. 6. it was a true report that I heard of *thy w.*
7. *thy w.* and prosperity exceedeth the fame
8. happy are these thy servants that stand before thee continually and hear *thy w.* 2 *Chr.* 9. 5, 7.
2 *Chron.* 9. 6. the half of *thy w.* was not told me
Job 39. 26. doth the hawk fly by *thy w.?*
Isa. 47. 10. *thy w.* it hath perverted thee
Ezek. 28. 4. with *thy w.* hast gotten thee riches, 5.
17. thou hast corrupted *thy w.* by thy brightness

WISE.

Gen. 3. 6. and a tree to be desired to make one *w.*
41. 39. there is none so discreet and *w.* as thou
Exod. 23. 8. the gift blindeth the *w. Deut.* 16. 19.
Deut. 4. 6. surely this great nation is a *w.* people
32. 29. O that they were *w.* that they understood
Judg. 5. 29. her *w.* ladies answered her
2 *Sam.* 14. 20. my lord is *w.* according to the wisd.

1 *Kings* 3. 12. I have given thee a *w.* heart
5. 7. blessed be the Lord that hath given David a *w.* son over this great people, 2 *Chron.* 2. 12.
1 *Chron.* 26. 14. fell for Zachariah a *w.* counsellor
Job 5. 13. he taketh the *w.* in their own craftiness
9. 4. he is *w.* in heart and mighty in strength
11. 12. for vain man would be *w.* though born like
22. 2. he that is *w.* may be profitable to himself
32. 9. great men are not always *w.* nor the aged
37. 24. he respecteth not any that are *w.* of heart
Psal. 2. 10. be *w.* now, O ye kings, be instructed
19. 7. testimony of Ld. is sure, making *w.* the simple
36. 3. he hath left off to be *w.* and to do good
94. 8. and ye fools, when will ye be *w.?*
107. 43. whoso is *w.* and will observe those things
Prov. 1. 5. a *w.* man shall attain to *w.* counsels
6. to understand the words of the *w.* and sayings
3. 7. be not *w.* in thine own eyes, fear the Lord
35. the *w.* shall inherit glory, but shame shall be
6. 6. be *w.* 8. 33. | 23. 19. | 27. 11.
9. 12. if thou be *w.* thou shalt be *w.* for thyself
10. 1. a *w.* son maketh a glad father, 15. 20.
5. he that gathereth in summer is a *w.* son
8. the *w.* in heart will receive commandments
19. but he that refraineth his lips is *w.*
11. 29. the fool shall be servant to the *w.* in heart
30. and he that winneth souls is *w.*
12. 15. but he that hearkeneth to counsel is *w.*
18. but the tongue of the *w.* is health
13. 1. a *w.* son heareth his father's instruction
14. the law of the *w.* is a fountain of life
20. he that walketh with *w.* men shall be *w.*
14. 3. but the lips of the *w.* shall preserve them
24. the crown of the *w.* is their riches
35. the king's favour is toward a *w.* servant
15. 2. tongue of the *w.* useth knowledge aright
7. the lips of the *w.* disperse knowledge
12. a scorner will not go to the *w.*
24. the way of life is above to the *w.*
31. that heareth reproof abideth among the *w.*
16. 21. the *w.* in heart shall be called prudent
23. the heart of the *w.* teacheth his mouth
17. 2. a *w.* servant shall have rule over a son
28. a fool when he holdeth his peace is counted *w.*
18. 15. the ear of the *w.* seeketh knowledge
19. 20. that thou mayest be *w.* in thy latter end
20. 1. whosoever is deceived thereby, is not *w.*
26. a *w.* king scattereth the wicked, and brings
21. 11. scorner punished, simple is made *w.* when the *w.* is instructed he receiveth knowledge
20. there is oil in the dwelling of the *w.*
22. 17. bow thine ear, hear the words of the *w.*
23. 15. if thy heart be *w.* my heart shall rejoice
24. he that begetteth a *w.* son shall have joy
24. 6. for by *w.* counsel thou shalt make thy war
23. these things also belong to the *w.*
25. 12. so is a *w.* reprover upon an obedient ear
26. 5. answer a fool lest he be *w.* in his conceit
12. seest thou a man *w.* in his own conceit
28. 7. whoso keepeth the law is a *w.* son
11. the rich man is *w.* in his own conceit
30. 24. there be four things that are exceeding *w.*
Eccl. 2. 15. I said in my heart, why was I more *w.*
16. for there is no remembrance of the *w.*
19. my labour wherein I have shewed myself *w.*
4. 13. better is a *w.* child than a foolish king
6. 8. for what hath the *w.* more than the fool?
7. 4. the heart of the *w.* is in the house of mourning
5. it is better to hear the rebuke of the *w.*
16. be not right. overm. neither make thys. over *w.*
19. wisdom strengtheneth *w.* more than ten men
23. I said, I will be *w.* but it was far from me
9. 1. the *w.* and their works are in the hand of God
11. I saw that bread is not to the *w.* nor riches
12. 9. because the preacher was *w.* he taught
11. the words of the *w.* are as goads and as nails
Isa. 5. 21. woe to them that are *w.* in their own eyes
19. 11. how say ye, I am the son of the *w.?*
31. 2. yet he also is *w.* and will bring evil
Jer. 4. 22. my people is foolish, they are *w.* to do evil
8. 8. how do ye say, we are *w.* law of God with us
18. 18. nor shall counsel perish from the *w.*
Dan. 2. 21. God giveth wisdom to *w.* and knowledge
12. 3. they that be *w.* shall shine as the firmament
10. wicked shall not, but the *w.* shall understand
Hos. 14. 9. the *w.* shall understand these things
Zech. 9. 2. though Tyrus and Zidon be very *w.*
Mat. 10. 16. be ye therefore *w.* as serpents
11. 25. because thou hast hid these things from *w.* and prudent, and revealed to babes, *Luke* 10. 21.
24. 45. who then is a faithful and *w.* servant?
25. 2. five virgins were *w.* and five foolish
4. the *w.* took oil in their vessels with their lamps
Luke 12. 42. who then is that faithful and *w.* steward
Rom. 1. 14. I am debtor to the *w.* and unwise
22. professing themselves *w.* they became fools
11. 25. lest ye should be *w.* in your own conceits
12. 16. be not *w.* in your own conceits
16. 19. I would have you *w.* to that which is good
27. to God only *w.* 1 *Tim.* 1. 17. *Jude* 25.
1 *Cor.* 1. 19. I will destroy the wisdom of the *w.*
20. where is the *w.?* ‖ 27. to confound the *w.*
3. 10. as a *w.* master-builder, I laid the foundation
18. if any man seemeth to be *w.* in this world, let him become a fool that he may be *w.*
19. he taketh the *w.* in their own craftiness
20. the Lord knows the thoughts of the *w.*
4. 10. we are fools, but ye are *w.* in Christ
2 *Cor.* 10. 12. comparing themselves, are not *w.*
11. 19. ye suffer fools, seeing ye yourselves are *w.*
Eph. 5. 15. that ye walk not as fools, but as *w.*
2 *Tim.* 3. 15. the scriptures are able to make thee *w.*

Any WISE.

Exod. 22. 23. if thou afflict them in *any w.*
Lev. 19. 17. shall in *any w.* rebuke thy neighbour
27. 19. if he will in *any w.* redeem the field
Deut. 17. 15. shalt in *any w.* set him king over thee
21. 23. thou shalt in *any w.* bury him that day
22. 7. thou shalt in *any w.* let the dam go
Josh. 6. 18. in *any w.* keep from the accursed thing
23. 12. else if ye do in *any w.* go back and cleave
1 *Sam.* 6. 3. in *any w.* send a trespass-offering

1 *Kings* 11. 22. howbeit let me go in *any w.*
Psal. 37. 8. fret not thyself in *any w.* to do evil.
Mark 14. 31. I will not deny thee in *any w.*
See MAN, MEN.

WISE-*hearted.*

Exod. 28. 3. speak to all that are *w.-hearted*
31. 6. I have put wisdom in all that are *w.-hearted*
35. 10. every *w.-hearted* among you shall make all
25. all the women that were *w.-hearted* did spin
36. 1. then wrought every *w.-hearted* man
2. Moses called Aholiab and every *w.-hearted* man
8. every *w.-hearted* man made ten curtains

WISE *men.*

Gen. 41. 8. Pharaoh called for all the magicians of Egypt, and all the *w. men, Exod.* 7. 1..

In no WISE.

Lev. 7. 24. the fat of beasts torn, *in no w.* eat of it
1 *Kings* 3. 26. give the child, and *in no w.* slay it, 27.
Mat. 5. 18. one tittle shall *in no w.* pass from the law
10. 42. he shall *in no w.* lose his reward
Luke 13. 11. a woman could *in no w.* lift up herself
18. 17. shall *in no w.* enter therein, *Rev.* 21. 27.
John 6. 37. he that cometh to me, I will *in no w.* cast
Acts 13. 41. a work which ye shall *in no w.* believe
Rom. 3. 9. are we better than they? no, *in no w.*

On this WISE.

Num. 6. 23. *on this w.* ye shall bless Israel
Mat. 1. 18. the birth of Jesus Christ was *on this w.*
John 21. 1. and *on this w.* shewed he himself
Acts 7. 6. God spake *on this w.* that his seed
13. 34. he said *on this w.* I will give sure mercies
Rom. 10. 6. the righteousness speaketh *on this w.*
Heb. 4. 4. he spake of the seventh day *on this w.*

WISE *woman.*

2 *Sam.* 14. 2. and Joab fetched thence a *w. woman*
20. 16. then cried a *w. woman* out of the city, hear
Prov. 14. 1. every *w. woman* buildeth her house

WISELY.

Exod. 1. 10. come on, let us deal *w.* with them
1 *Sam.* 18. 5. David behaved himself *w.* 14. 15, 30.
2 *Chron.* 11. 23. Rehoboam dealt *w.* he dispersed
Psal. 58. 5. the charmers, charming never so *w.*
64. 9. for they shall *w.* consider of his doings
101. 2. I will behave myself *w.* in a perfect way
Prov. 16. 20. he that handleth a matter *w.*
21. 12. he *w.* considereth the house of the wicked
28. 26. whoso walketh *w.* shall be delivered
Eccl. 7. 10. thou dost not inquire *w.* concerning this
Luke 16. 8. commended, because he had done *w.*

WISER.

1 *Kings* 4. 31. for Solomon was *w.* than all men
Job 35. 11. maketh us *w.* than the fowls of heaven
Psal. 119. 98. thou hast made me *w.* than my enemies
Prov. 9. 9. give instruction, and he will be yet *w.*
26. 16. the sluggard is *w.* in his own conceit
Ezek. 28. 3. behold, thou art *w.* than Daniel
Luke 16. 8. the children are in their generation *w.*
1 *Cor.* 1. 25. the foolishness of God is *w.* than men

WISH.

Job 33. 6. I am according to thy *w.* in God's stead
Psal. 40. 14. let them be put to shame that *w.* evil
73. 7. they have more than heart could *w.*
Rom. 9. 3. I could *w.* myself accursed from Christ
2 *Cor.* 13. 9. this also we *w.* even your perfection
3 *John* 2. I *w.* above all things thou mayest prosper

WISHED.

Jonah 4. 8. Jonah fainted, and *w.* himself to die
Acts 27. 29. they cast anchor, and *w.* for the day

WISHING.

Job 31. 30. my mouth to sin, by *w.* a curse to his soul

WIST.

Exod. 16. 15. it is manna, for they *w.* not what it was
34. 29. Moses *w.* not that his face shone
Lev. 5. 17. though he *w.* not, yet is he guilty, 18.
Josh. 2. 4. but I *w.* not whence they were
8. 14. he *w.* not that there were liers in ambush
Judg. 16. 20. he *w.* not that the Lord was departed
Mark 9. 6. he *w.* not what to say, they were afraid
14. 40. neither *w.* they what to answer him
Luke 2. 49. *w.* ye not I must be about Father's busin.
John 5. 13. he that was healed *w.* not who it was
Acts 12. 9. *w.* not that it was true which was done
23. 5. said Paul, I *w.* not he was the high-priest

WITCH.

Exod. 22. 18. thou shalt not suffer a *w.* to live
Deut. 18. 10. there shall not be among you a *w.*

WITCHCRAFT.

1 *Sam.* 15. 23. for rebellion is as the sin of *w.*
2 *Chron.* 33. 6. Manasseh used *w.* and enchantments
Gal. 5. 20. the works of the flesh are idolatry, *w.*

WITCHCRAFTS.

2 *Kings* 9. 22. so long as Jezebel's *w.* are so many
Mic. 5. 12. I will cut off *w.* out of thine hand
Nah. 3. 4. the mistress of *w.* that selleth nations through her whoredoms, and families through her *w.*

WITHAL.

1 *Kings* 19. 1. *w.* how Elijah had slain all the proph.
Psal. 141. 10. the wicked fall whilst that I *w.* escape.
Acts 25. 27. and not *w.* to signify the crimes

WITHDRAW.

1 *Sam.* 14. 19. Saul said to the priest, *w.* thine hand
Job 9. 13. if God will not *w.* his anger, the proud
13. 21. *w.* thine hand far from me, let not thy dread
33. 17. that he may *w.* man from his purpose
Prov. 25. 17. *w.* thy foot from thy neighbour's house
Eccl. 7. 18. also from this *w.* not thine hand
Isa. 60. 20. neither shall thy moon *w.* itself
Joel 2. 10. the stars shall *w.* their shining, 3. 15.
2 *Thess.* 3. 6. *w.* yourselves from every brother
1 *Tim.* 6. 5. from men of corrupt minds *w.* thyself

WITHDRAWN.

Deut. 13. 13. have *w.* the inhabitants of their city
Cant. 5. 6. but my beloved had *w.* himself
Lam. 2. 8. he hath not *w.* his hand from destroying
Ezek. 18. 8. that hath *w.* his hand from iniquity
Hos. 5. 6. the Lord hath *w.* himself from them
Luke 22. 41. was *w.* from them about a stone's cast

WITHDRAWEST.

Psal. 74. 11. why *w.* thou thy right hand?

WITHDRAWETH.

Job 36. 7. he *w.* not his eyes from the righteous

WITHDRAWING.

Neh. 9. † 29. and they gave a w. shoulder

WITHDREW.

Neh. 9. 29. they w. the shoulder and would not hear
Ezek. 20. 22. nevertheless I w. mine hand
Mat. 12. 15. when Jesus knew it, he w. himself
Mark 3. 7. Jesus w. himself from thence, Luke 5. 16.
Gal. 2. 12. but when they were come, he w.

WITHER.

Psal. 1. 3. his leaf also shall not w. and whatsoever he doth shall prosper
37. 2. and they shall w. as the green herb
Isa. 19. 6. brooks be emptied, reeds and flags shall w.
7. every thing sown by the brooks shall w.
40. 24. he shall blow upon them, and they shall w.
Jer. 12. 4. how long shall the herbs of the field w.?
Ezek. 17. 9. shall he not cut off the fruit thereof that it w. it shall w. in all the leaves of her spring
10. shall it not utterly w.? it shall w. in furrows
Amos 1. 2. and the top of Carmel shall w.

WITHERED.

Gen. 41. 23. behold seven ears w. thin and blasted
Ps. 102. 4. my heart is smitten and w. ‖ 11. I am w.
Isa. 15. 6. the hay is w. away, the grass faileth
27. 11. when bows thereof are w. be broken off
Lam. 4. 8. the Nazarite's skin is w. like a stick
Ezek. 19. 12. her strong rods were w. and consumed
Joel 1. 12. the trees of the field are w. joy is w.
17. the barns are broken down, for the corn is w.
Amos 4. 7. the piece whereupon it rained not w.
Jonah 4. 7. and it smote the gourd that it w.
Mat. 12. 10. and behold there was a man which had his hand w. Mark 3. 1, 3. Luke 6. 6, 8.
13. 6. when the sun was up they were scorched, because having no root, they w. away, Mark 4. 6.
21. 19. presently the fig-tree w. 20. Mark 11. 21.
Luke 8. 6. it w. away because it lacked moisture
John 5. 3. of w. folk waiting for moving of the water
15. 6. he is cast forth as a branch and is w.

WITHERETH.

Job 8. 12. the flag w. before any other herb
Psal. 90. 6. in the evening it is cut down and w.
129. 6. like grass that w. before it groweth up
Isa. 40. 7. grass w. the flower fadeth, 8. 1 Pet. 1. 24.
Jam. 1. 11. the sun no sooner risen, but it w. the grass
Jude 12. trees whose fruit w. without fruit, twice dead

WITHHELD.

Gen. 20. 6. for I w. thee from sinning against me
22. 12. seeing thou hast not w. thy son from me
30. 2. who w. from thee the fruit of the womb?
Ezra 9. † 13. hast w. beneath our iniquities
Job 31. 16. if I have w. the poor from their desire
Eccl. 2. 10. I w. not my heart from any joy

WITHHELDEST.

Neh. 9. 20. w. not thy manna from their mouth

WITHHOLD.

Gen. 23. 6. none of us shall w. from thee his sepulch.
2 Sam. 13. 13. for he will not w. me from thee
Job 4. 2. but who can w. himself from speaking?
30. † 10. they w. not spittle from my face
Psal. 40. 11. w. not thy tender mercies from me
84. 11. no good thing will he w. from them that
Prov. 3. 27. w. not good from them to whom it is due
23. 13. w. not correction from the child
30. † 7. two things I required, w. not from me
Eccl. 11. 6. in the evening w. not thy hand
Jer. 2. 25. w. thy foot from being unshod and throat

WITHHOLDEN.

1 Sam. 25. 26. Lord hath w. thee from revenging
Job 22. 7. thou hast w. bread from the hungry
38. 15. from the wicked their light is w.
42. 2. that no thought can be w. from thee
Psal. 21. 2. thou hast not w. the request of his lips
Jer. 3. 3. therefore the showers have been w.
5. 25. your sins have w. good things from you
Ezek. 18. 16. hath not w. the pledge, nor spoiled
Joel 1. 13. the drink offering is w. from God
Amos 4. 7. also I have w. the rain from you

WITHHOLDETH.

Job 12. 15. behold, he w. the waters, they dry up
Prov. 11. 24. there is that w. more than is meet
26. he that w. corn, the people shall curse him
2 Thess. 2. 6. and now ye know what w. that he might

WITHIN.

Gen. 39. 11. none of the men of the house was w.
Lev. 25. 29. w. a full year he may redeem it
Josh. 19. 1. the inheritance of Simeon was w. Judah
Judg. 11. 26. why not recover them w. that time?
1 Sam. 13. 11. thou camest not w. the days appointed
1 Kings 6. 23. w. the oracle he made two cherubims
2 Kings 7. 11. they told it to the king's house w.
Ezra 10. 8. whoso would not come w. three days
Psal. 45. 13. the king's daughter is all glorious w.
101. 2. will walk w. my house with a perfect heart
Eccl. 9. 14. there was a little city, few men w. it
Ezek. 3. 24. spirit said, go shut thyself w. thy house
12. 24. shall be no more any vain vision w. Israel
44. 17. whiles they minister in the gates and w.
Zeph. 3. 3. her princes w. are roaring lions, her judges
Mat. 3. 9. think not to say w. yourselves, Luke 3. 8.
9. 21. she said w. herself, if I but touch his garment
23. 25. w. they are full of extortion and excess
26. cleanse first what is w. the cup and platter
27. are w. full of dead men's bones and unclean.
28. w. ye are full of hypocrisy and iniquity
Mark 7. 21. for from w. proceed evil thoughts
23. all these evil things come from w. and defile
Luke 11. 7. he from w. shall answer and say
12. 17. he thought w. himself, 16. 3. | 18. 4.
John 20. 26. after eight days his disciples were w.
Acts 5. 23. when we opened, we found no man w.
1 Cor. 5. 12. do not ye judge them that are w.?
2 Cor. 7. 5. without were fightings, w. were fears
Rev. 4. 8. and they were full of eyes w. rest not
5. 1. a book written w. on the back side sealed
See Gates, Him, Me, Thee, Them, Us, Without, You.

WITHOUT.

Gen. 24. 31. come in, wherefore standest thou w.?
Deut. 25. 5. the wife of the dead shall not marry w.
2 Kings 10. 24. Jehu appointed eighty men w.
11. 15. and he said, have her forth w. the ranges
2 Kings 18. 25. am I now come up w. the Lord against this place to destroy it? Isa. 36. 10.
2 Chr. 15. 3. Israel hath been long w. the true God
21. 20. Jehoram departed w. being desired
Psal. 31. 11. they that did see me w. fled from me
Prov. 1. 20. wisdom crieth w. she uttereth her voice
7. 12. now she is w. ‖ 22. 13. there is a lion w.
24. 27. prepare thy work w. make it fit for thee
Isa. 33. 7. behold, their valiant ones shall cry w.
52. 3. and ye shall be redeemed w. money
55. 1. buy wine and milk w. money and w. price
Jer. 9. 21. to cut off the children from w.
33. 10. w. man, w. beast, and w. inhabitant, 12.
Hos. 3. 4. Israel w. a king, w. a prince, w. a sacrifice, w. an image, w. an ephod, and w. a teraphim
Mat. 10. 29. a sparrow shall not fall w. your father
Mark 4. 11. to them that are w. all these are done
7. 18. whatsoever from w. entereth into the man
Luke 1. 10. the whole multitude were praying w.
1 Cor. 5. 12. what to do to judge them that are w.
13. but them that are w. God judgeth
Eph. 2. 12. having no hope, and w. G. in the world?
Col. 4. 5. walk in wisdom toward them that are w.
1 Thess. 4. 12. walk honestly toward them that are w.
1 Tim. 3. 7. have a good report of them that are w.
Heb. 7. 3. Melchised. w. father, w. moth. w. descent
13. 12. wherefore Jesus also suffered w. the gate
1 Pet. 3. 1. that they also may w. the word be won
Rev. 22. 15. for w. are dogs and sorcerers

WITHOUT, joined with within.

Gen. 6. 14. pitch the ark within and w. with pitch
Exod. 25. 11. overlay the ark within and w. 37. 2.
Lev. 13. 55. if the garment be bare within or w.
Deut. 32. 25. the sword w. and terror within
Ezek. 2. 10. and it was written within and w.
7. 15. the sword is w. and famine within
Luke 11. 40. ye fools, did not he that made that which is w. make that which is within also?
2 Cor. 7. 5. w. were fightings, within were fears
See Blemish, Camp, Cause, City, Fail, Fear, Him, Knowledge, Law, Me, Stand, Stood, Us, You.

WITHS.

Judg. 16. 7. if they bind me with seven green w.
8. the lords brought w. ‖ 9. he brake the w.

WITHSTAND.

Num. 22. 32. the angel went out to w. Balaam
2 Chr. 13. 7. Rehoboam was young could not w. them
8. now ye think to w. the kingdom of the Lord
20. 6. power, so that none is able to w. thee
Esth. 9. 2. and no man could w. the Jews
Eccl. 4. 12. if one prevail, two shall w. him
Dan. 11. 15. the arms of the south, nor his people shall not w. nor shall there be any strength to w.
Acts 11. 17. what was I that I could w. God?
Eph. 6. 13. that ye may be able to w. in the evil day

WITHSTOOD.

2 Chron. 26. 18. they w. Uzziah the king
Dan. 10. 13. prince of Persia w. me twenty-one days
Acts 13. 8. but Elymas the sorcerer w. them
Gal. 2. 11. at Antioch I w. Peter to the face
2 Tim. 3. 8. as Jannes and Jambres w. Moses
4. 15. beware, for he hath greatly w. our words

WITNESS

Is one that gives testimony to any thing. Thus it is said, you are *witness,* a faithful *witness,* a false *witness,* God *is witness,* &c.

Witness *in Greek is* μαρτυς, *or* μαρτυρ, *and signifies one that gives testimony to the truth at the expense of his life.* Jesus Christ is the faithful *witness,* Rev. 1. 5. *He is so called, because as the great Prophet of his church, he hath revealed the will of God faithfully, plainly, and fully, so far as is necessary to the salvation of men: this Isaiah prophesied of him.* Isa. 55. 4. I have given him for a *witness* to the people, *to be a Prophet and Teacher, to declare the counsel and will of God concerning the duty and salvation of men,* to bear *witness* unto the truth, *as Christ himself affirms before Pontius Pilate,* John 18. 37. *Wherefore Paul saith,* 1 Tim. 6. 13. *that Christ* witnessed a good confession before Pontius Pilate. *He is called* the faithful *witness, not only because he revealed all truth, and bare record to the truth before Pilate, but also because he sealed it with his blood; he died, and was a martyr to the truth, which proves him to be a* faithful, constant *witness.*

The law appoints, that two or three witnesses *should be sufficient in matters of judicature; but one* witness *only was not sufficient,* Deut. 17. 6. *When any one was condemned to die, the* witnesses *were the first that began the execution. They threw the first stone, for example, if the party was to be stoned,* Deut. 17. 7. *The law condemned a false witness to undergo the same punishment that he would have subjected his neighbour to,* Deut. 19. 16, 17, 18, 19. *When God is said to be a* witness *to sin, as in* Jer. 29. 23. *it signifies, that he not only knows it, but he will also punish it: he is both judge and* witness, *he does not stay for any one to accuse the wicked to him, he has no need of the testimony or accusation of men, to know the demerits of the guilty. He accuses them himself, he punishes them, he condemns them, he knows all their transgressions, by his wisdom, his justice, his infinite penetration.*

In Mal. 3. 5. *God threatens perjured persons, adulterers, and other wicked men, with vengeance,* I will be a swift *witness* against false swearers, &c. *This is spoken of Christ the* Messiah, *to whom the Father hath committed all judgment,* John 5. 22. *The prophets and Old Testament believers, by their doing and suffering for God, have given testimony to the truth of our holy religion. The apostle calls them* a cloud of *witnesses,* Heb. 12. 1. *The apostles also are still more* witnesses, *of the coming, the mission, the doctrine, the resurrection of Christ.* 1 Cor. 15. 14, 15. If Christ be not risen, then we are found false *witnesses* of God. *And St. Peter says,* We are *witnesses* of all things which he did in Judea and in Jerusalem, *Acts* 10. 39. *He chose a small number of persons to be* witnesses *to him, and when they took upon them to put another apostle in the place of Judas, they thought fit to appoint one who had been a* witness *of the resurrection along with them,* Acts 1. 22.

The apostle Paul, in Rom. 8. 16. *says, that* the Spirit itself beareth *witness* with our spirit, that we are the children of God. *The Spirit of God, by an inward and secret suggestion, speaks the same things, gives the same evidence, concerning the truth of grace, and our sonship, and so ratifies what our enlightened and renewed consciences say. In* Heb. 11. 4. *it is said, that* Abel obtained *witness* that he was righteous, God testifying of his gifts. *The Spirit of God testified to his spirit that he was justified by the righteousness of Christ; and God witnessed from heaven to the truth of his state, by accepting of his person and sacrifice, and by giving a visible sign of it, so as that Cain could observe it. It is thought that God sent fire from heaven and consumed Abel's sacrifice, as he did others afterwards.*

Job says, Thou renewest thy *witnesses* against me, Job 10. 17. *Thou bringest fresh plagues and judgments upon me, which are the* witnesses *and evidences both of my sins, and of thy displeasure against me. In* Psal. 89. 37. *it is said that the house and kingdom of David shall be* established for ever as the moon, and as a faithful *witness* in heaven *By* faithful witness, *some understand the moon, which is called a* witness *of God's covenant of the night,* Jer. 33. 20. *so the meaning is. And though the moon be subject to eclipses and manifold changes, yet it still abides in heaven, as a* witness *of my covenant of the night, so shall the house and kingdom of David, who was a type of the* Messiah, *continue for ever, notwithstanding the changes and calamities that shall befall it. Others understand by this the rainbow, which is God's faithful and perpetual* witness, Gen. 9. 12, 16. Witness *is put for the miracles of Christ, which gave testimony to his Deity and Mediatorship,* John 5. 36. | 10. 25.

Gen. 21. 30. they may be a w. that I digged this well
31. 44. let this covenant be a w. between us
48. this heap is a w. this pillar is w. 52.
50. God is w. between me and thee, 1 Thess. 2. 5.
Exod. 22. 13. if it be torn, let him bring it for a w.
23. 1. put not thine hand to be an unrighteous w.
Lev. 5. 1. if a soul sin, and is a w. of swearing
Num. 5. 13. if there be no w. against her
35. 30. one w. shall not testify against any person to cause him to die, Deut. 17. 6. | 19. 15.
Deut. 31. 19. this song may be a w. 21. 26.
Josh. 22. 27. the altar is a w. between us, 28. 34.
24. 27. behold this stone shall be a w. to us
Judg. 11. 10. Lord be w. between us, Jer. 42. 5.
1 Sam. 12. 5. the Lord is w. against you this day
Job 16. 8. my wrinkles which is a w. against me
19. behold, my w. is in heaven, my record on high
29. 11. when the eye saw me, it gave w. to me
Psal. 89. 37. established as a faithful w. in heaven
Prov. 14. 5. a faithful w. will not lie, but a false w.
25. a true w. delivereth souls, but a deceitful w.
19. 28. an ungodly w. scorneth judgment
24. 28. be not w. against thy neighb. without cause
Isa. 19. 20. it shall be for a w. to the Lord of hosts
55. 4. I have given him for a w. to the people
Jer. 29. 23. I know, and am a w. saith the Lord
42. 5. Lord be a true and faithful w. between us
Mic. 1. 2. let the Lord God be w. against you
Mal. 2. 14. Lord be w. between thee and wife
3. 5. I will be a swift w. against the sorcerers
Mat. 24. 14. be preached for a w. to all nations
Mark 14. 55. the council sought for w. against Jesus
56. but their w. agreed not together, 59.
Luke 22. 71. they said, what need we further w.?
John 1. 7. the same came for a w. to bear w.
3. 11. we speak that we know, ye receive not our w.
26. to whom thou bearest w. the same baptizeth
5. 31. if I bear w. of myself, my w. is not true
32. I know the w. he witnesseth of me is true
36. but I have greater w. than that of John
37. Father who sent me hath borne w. of me
Acts 1. 22. must one be ordained to be w. with us
4. 33. gave w. of the resurrection of the Lord
10. 43. to him give all prophets w. whoso believeth
14. 17. he left not himself without w. he did good
22. 15. for thou shalt be his w. to all men of what
26. 16. to make thee a minister and a w. of these
Rom. 1. 9. God is my w. whom I serve in the gospel
2. 15. their conscience also bearing w. 9. 1.
Tit. 1. 13. this w. is true, rebuke them sharply
Heb. 2. 4. God also bearing them w. with signs
10. 15. whereof the Holy Ghost is a w. to us
11. 4. by which Abel obtained w. was righteous
Jam. 5. 3. the rust of them shall be w. against you
1 Pet. 5. 1. Peter a w. of the sufferings of Christ
1 John 5. 9. if we receive the w. of men, the w. of God is greater, for this is the w. of God
10. he that believeth hath the w. in himself
3 John 6. which have borne w. of thy charity
Rev. 1. 5. Jesus Christ, who is the faithful w.
3. 14. write these things, saith the true w.
20. 4. that were beheaded for the w. of Jesus
See Bare, Bear, Beareth, False, Tabernacle.

WITNESSES.

Num. 35. 30. murderer put to death by mouth of w.
Deut. 17. 6. at the mouth of two or three w. shall he be put to death, 19. 15. 2 Cor. 13. 1.
7. the hands of the w. shall be first upon him
Josh. 24. 22. Joshua said, ye are w. against yoursel. that ye have chosen Lord, they said, we are w
Ruth 4. 9. ye are w. that I have bought, 10.
11. the people and the elders said, we are w.
Job 10. 17. thou renewest thy w. against me
Isa. 8. 2. I took to me faithful w. to record
43. 9. let all the nations bring forth their w.
10. ye are my w. saith the Lord, 12. | 44. 8.
44. 9. they are their own w. they see not, nor know
Jer. 32. 10. I sealed the evidence and took w. 12.

Jer. 32. 25. buy the field for money, and take *w*. 44.
Mat. 18. 16. in the mouth of two or three *w*.
23. 31. wherefore ye be *w*. to yourselves that ye
26. 65. what further need of *w*.? *Mark* 14. 63.
Luke 24. 48. and ye are *w*. of these things
Acts 1. 8. ye shall be *w*. to me in Jerusalem
2. 32. Jesus God raised up, whereof we are *w*. 3. 15.
5. 32. we are his *w*. of these things, 10. 39.
7. 58. *w*. laid down their clothes at Saul's feet
10. 41. but unto *w*. chosen before of God to us
13. 31. who are his *w*. unto the people
1 *Thess*. 2. 10. ye are *w*. and God also, how we
1 *Tim*. 5. 19. receive no accusation but before two *w*.
6. 12. professed a good profession before many *w*.
2 *Tim*. 2. 2. things heard of me among many *w*.
Heb. 10. 28. died without mercy under two or three *w*.
12. 1. are compassed about with so great cloud of *w*.
Rev. 11. 3. I will give power to my two *w*

See FALSE.

WITNESS, *Verb*.

Deut. 4. 26. I call heaven and earth to *w*. against you
1 *Sam*. 12. 3. behold, here I am, *w*. against me
Isa. 3. 9. their countenance doth *w*. against them
Lam. 2. 13. what thing shall I take to *w*. for thee?
Mat. 26. 62. answerest thou nothing? what is it that these *w*. against thee? *Mark* 14. 60.
27. 13. Pilate saith to him, hearest thou not how many things they *w*. against thee, *Mark* 15. 4.

WITNESSED.

1 *Kings* 21. 13. the men of Belial *w*. against Naboth
Rom. 3. 21. being *w*. by the law and the prophets
1 *Tim*. 6. 13. who before Pilate *w*. a good confession
Heb. 7. 8. of whom it is *w*. that he liveth

WITNESSETH.

John 5. 32. the witness that he *w*. of me is true
Acts 20. 23. save that Holy Ghost *w*. in every city

WITNESSING.

Acts 26. 22. *w*. both to small and great, saying

WITS.

Psal. 107. 27. they stagger and are at their *w*. end

WITTY.

Prov. 8. 12. I find out knowledge of *w*. inventions

WITTINGLY.

Gen. 48. 14. Isr. guided his hands *w*. for Manasseh

WIVES.

Gen. 4. 19. Lamech took unto him two *w*.
6. 2. they took them *w*. of all which they chose
30. 26. give me my *w*. and children and let me go
31. 50. if thou take other *w*. besides my daughters
Num. 14. 3. that our *w*. and children should be a prey
Deut. 17. 17. nor shall he multiply *w*. to himself
21. 15. if a man have two *w*. one beloved, another
Judg. 8. 30. Gideon had seventy sons, had many *w*.
21. 7. how shall we do for *w*. for them? 16.
18. we may not give them *w*. of our daughters
1 *Sam*. 1. 2. Elkanah had two *w*. Hannah and Peninn.
25. 43. they were also both of them David's *w*.
2 *Sam*. 5. 13. David took more *w*. out of Jerusalem
12. 8. I gave thee thy master's *w*. into thy bosom
1 *Kings* 11. 3. Solomon had 700 *w*. princesses
4. his . turned away his heart when he was old
20. 7. he sent unto me for my *w*. and children
1 *Chron*. 4. 5. Ashur had two *w*. Helah and Naarah
7. 4. the sons of Uzzi had many *w*. and sons
8. 8. Shaharaim had two *w*. Hushim and Baara
2 *Chron*. 11. 21. Reh. loved Maachah above all his *w*.
23. he gave them victuals; he desired many *w*.
24. 3. Jehoiada took for him two *w*. he begat sons
29. 9. and our *w*. are in captivity for this
Ezra 10. 3. a covenant to put away all the *w*. 44.
Neh. 12. 43. the *w*. also and children rejoiced
13. 23. I saw Jews that had married *w*. of Ashdod
Esth. 1. 20. the *w*. shall give to husbands honour
Jer. 29. 6. take ye *w*. and take *w*. for your sons
35. 8. to drink no wine, we, nor our *w*. nor sons
Dan. 5. 2. his *w*. and concubines drink therein, 3.
Luke 17. 27. they eat, drank, they married *w*.
Acts 21. 5. they brought us on our way with *w*.
1 *Cor*. 7. 29. that have *w*. be as tho' they had none
Eph. 5. 22. *w*. submit yourselves to your own husbands as unto the Lord, *Col*. 3. 18. 1 *Pet*. 3. 1.
24. so let the *w*. be to their own husbands
1 *Tim*. 4. 7. refuse profane and old *w*. fables
1 *Pet*. 3. 1. may be won by the conversation of *w*.

See STRANGE.

Their WIVES.

Gen. 34. 29. all their wealth, all their little ones, and *their w*. took they captive, 1 *Sam*. 30. 3.
Judg. 3. 6. they took their daughters to be *their w*.
2 *Chron*. 20. 13. all Judah with *their w*. stood
Ezra 10. 19. that they would put away *their w*.
Neh. 5. 1. a great cry of the people and of *their w*
10. 28. *their w*. and daughters entered into an oath
Isa. 13. 16. their houses spoiled, and their *w*. ravished
Jer. 6. 12. *their w*. shall be turned to others, 8. 10.
14. 16. they shall have none to bury *their w*.
18. 21. let *their w*. be bereaved of their children
44. 9. have ye forgotten the wickedness of *their w*.
15. men who knew *their w*. had burnt incense
Ezek. 44. 22. nor take for *their w*. a widow
Dan. 6. 24. cast them and *their w*. into den of lions
Zech. 12. 12. *their w*. shall mourn apart, 13, 14.
Eph. 5. 28. to love *their w*. as their own bodies
1 *Tim*. 3. 11. even so must *their w*. be grave, sober

Thy WIVES.

2 *Sam*. 12. 11. I will take *thy w*. before thine eyes, and he shall lie with *thy w*. in sight of the sun
19. 5. who saved this day the lives of *thy w*.
1 *Kings* 20. 3. thy silver and gold is mine, and *thy w*.
5. thou shalt deliver me, *thy w*. and children
2 *Chron*. 21. 14. Lord will smite thy people and *thy w*.
Jer. 38. 23. so they shall bring *thy w*. and children
Dan. 5. 23. *thy w*. and concubines have drunk wine

Your WIVES.

Gen. 45. 19. take waggons for *your w*. and come
Exod. 19. 15. said to people, come not at *your w*.
22. 24. *your w*. shall be widows, children fatherless
32. 2. break off the golden ear-rings of *your w*.
Deut. 3. 19. *your w*. and your little ones and your cattle shall remain in your cities, *Josh*. 1. 14.
29. 11. *your w*. shall enter into covenant with Lord
Neh. 4. 14. fight for *your w*. and your houses

Jer. 44. 9. have ye forgotten wickedness of *your w*.
25. Lord saying, ye and *your w*. have both spoken
Mat. 19. 8. Moses suffered you to put away *your w*.
Eph. 5. 25. husbands, love *your w*. *Col*. 3. 19.

WIZARD.

Lev. 20. 27. a *w*. shall surely be put to death
Deut. 18. 11. there shall not be found among you *w*.

WIZARDS.

Lev. 19. 31. nor seek after *w*. to be defiled by them
20. 6. the soul that turns after *w*. I will cut off
1 *Sam*. 28. 3. Saul had put *w*. out of the land, 9.
2 *Kings* 21. 6. Manasseh dealt with *w*. 2 *Chr*. 33. 6.
23. 24. Josiah put the *w*. and idols out of the land
Isa. 8. 19. when say, seek unto *w*. that peep and mut.
19. 3. and they shall seek to idols and *w*.

WOE.

Num. 21. 29. *w*. to thee, Moab, *Jer*. 48. 46.
1 *Sam*. 4. 7. *w*. unto us, for there hath not been such a thing heretofore, 8. *Jer*. 4. 13. | 6. 4. *Lam*. 5. 16.
Prov. 23. 29. who hath *w*.? who hath sorrow?
Eccl. 4. 10. *w*. to him that is alone when he falls
10. 16. *w*. to thee, O land, when thy king is a child
Isa. 3. 9. *w*. to their soul, for they rewarded evil
11. *w*. to the wicked, it shall be ill with him
17. 12. *w*. to the multitude of many people
18. 1. *w*. to the land shadowing with wings
28. 1. *w*. to the crown of pride, to the drunkards
29. 1. *w*. to Ariel || 33. 1. *w*. to thee that spoilest
30. 1. *w*. to the rebellious children, saith the Lord
45. 9. *w*. to him that striveth with his Maker
10. *w*. to him that saith to fath. what begettest thou
Jer. 13. 27. *w*. unto thee, O Jerusalem, wilt thou
22. 13. *w*. to him that builds by unrighteousness
23. 1. *w*. to the pastors that destroy the sheep
48. 1. *w*. to Nebo || *Ezek*. 16. 23. *w*. *w*. to thee
Ezek. 2. 10. there was written, mourning and *w*.
13. 3. *w*. to foolish prophets, that follow their spirit
18. *w*. to women that sew pillows to all armholes
24. 6. *w*. to the bloody city, 9. *Nah*. 3. 1.
30. 2. thus saith the Lord, howl, *w*. worth the day
34. 2. *w*. be to the shepherds that feed themselves
Amos 5. 18. *w*. to you that desire the day of the Lord
Hab. 2. 6. *w*. to him that increaseth that is not his
9. *w*. to him that coveteth an evil covetousness
12. *w*. to him that buildeth a town with blood
15. *w*. to him that giveth his neighbour drink
19. *w*. to him that saith to the wood, awake
Zeph. 2. 5. *w*. to the inhabitants of the sea-coasts
3. 1. *w*. to her that is filthy and polluted, to city
Zech. 11. 17. *w*. to the idol shepherd that leaveth
Mat. 11. 21. *w*. to thee Chorazin, *w*. to thee Bethsaida, for if the works had been done, *Luke* 10. 13.
18. 7. *w*. to the world because of offences, *w*. to that man by whom the offence cometh, *Luke* 17. 1.
Mat. 23. 13. *w*. unto you scribes and Pharisees, hypocrites, 14, 15, 23, 25, 27, 29. *Luke* 11. 44.
16. *w*. unto you, ye blind guides, which say
26. 24. but *w*. unto that man by whom the Son of man is betrayed, *Mark* 14. 21. *Luke* 22. 22.
Luke 6. 24. but *w*. unto you that are rich, for ye have
25. *w*. to you that are full, *w*. to you that laugh
26. *w*. to you when all men speak well of you
11. 42. but *w*. unto you, Pharisees, 43.
46. he said, *w*. to you also, ye lawyers, 47. 52.
Rev. 8. 13. I heard an angel flying, saying, *w*. *w*. *w*. to the inhabiters of the earth, 12. 12.
9. 12. one *w*. is past || 11. 14. the second *w*. is past

WOE *is me*.

Psal. 120. 5. *w*. *is me*, that I sojourn in Mesech
Isa. 6. 5. *w*. *is me*, I am undone, I am of unclean lips
Jer. 4. 31. *w*. *is me* now, for my soul is wearied
10. 19. *w*. *is me* for my hurt || 15. 10. *w*. *is me* my mot.
45. 3. *w*. *is me*, for the Lord hath added grief
Mic. 7. 1. *w*. *is me*, I am as when they gathered fruit

WOE *unto me*.

Job 10. 15. if I be wicked, *w*. *unto me*, if righteous
Isa. 24. 16. but I said, my leanness, *w*. *unto me*
1 *Cor*. 9. 16. *w*. *unto me* if I preach not the gospel

WOE *to them*.

Isa. 5. 8. *w*. *to them* that join house to house
11. *w*. *to them* that rise up early in the morning
18. *w*. *to them* that draw iniquity with cords
20. *w*. *to them* that call evil good and good evil
21. *w*. *to them* that are wise in their own eyes
22. *w*. *to them* that are mighty to drink wine
10. 1. *w*. *to them* that decree unrighteous decrees
29. 15. *w*. *to them* that seek deep to hide counsel
31. 1. *w*. *to them* that go down to Egypt for help
Jer. 50. 27. *w*. *to them* for their day is come
Hos. 7. 13. *w*. *to them*, for they have fled from me
9. 12. *w*. *to them* when I depart from them
Amos 6. 1. *w*. *to them* that are at ease in Zion
Mic. 2. 1. *w*. *to them* that devise iniquity
Mat. 24. 19. *w*. *to them* which are with child, and to them that give suck, *Mark* 13. 17. *Luke* 21. 23.
Jude 11. *w*. *to them*, they have gone in way of Cain

WOES.

Rev. 9. 12. behold, there come two *w*. more hereafter

WOEFUL.

Jer. 17. 16. neither have I desired the *w*. day

WOLF.

In Greek Λυκος; *in Hebrew* Zeeb; *it is a wild creature very well known. The Scripture takes notice of these remarkable things of the* wolf: *that it lives upon rapine: that it is violent, cruel, and bloody: that it is voracious and greedy: that it goes abroad by night to seek its prey: that it is the great enemy of flocks of sheep. that* Benjamin shall ravin as a *wolf: that false teachers are* wolves *in sheep's clothing: that the persecutors of the church, and false pastors, are also ravening* wolves.

The prophets Jeremiah, Habakkuk, and Zephaniah, speak of the wolves of the evening. *It hath been observed that towards evening* wolves *are most dangerous, as being then more hungry. Instead of the* wolves of the evening, *the Septuagint translate it*, The *wolves* of Arabia; *because the Hebrew word* Arab *signifies both the* evening *and* Arabia. Wolves *are common in Arabia, but they have nothing peculiar in that country; so that there can be no reason to have recourse to that translation.*

As to what is said in Gen. 49. 27. *that* Benjamin shall ravin as a *wolf; this denotes the warlike and fierce disposition and carriage of this tribe. The Chaldee interpreters explain it of the altar of burnt offerings, which was at Jerusalem in the tribe of Benjamin, and upon which they burnt the morning and evening sacrifices to the Lord. Others refer it to that violent seizure which was made by the children of Benjamin, of the young women that came to the tabernacle at Shiloh*, Judg. 21. 21, 23. *Others again refer it to Mordecai, or to Saul, or to Paul, who were of the tribe of Benjamin.*

Isaiah describing the tranquillity of the reign of the Messiah, *says*, The *wolf* shall dwell with the lamb, and the leopard shall lie down with the kid, &c. *Isa*. 11. 6. *This is to be understood spiritually, and metaphorically; that is to say, "Men of fierce, cruel, and ungovernable dispositions, shall be so transformed by the preaching of the gospel, and by the grace of Christ, that they shall become most humble, gentle, and tractable, and shall no more vex and persecute, but shall live and converse in the same church with other poor Christians quietly and harmlessly." Persecutors are elsewhere compared to* wolves, *Mat*. 10. 16. Behold, I send you forth as sheep in the midst of *wolves*. *Both Jews and Pagans were at first like ravenous and voracious* wolves, *let loose against the faithful. They persecuted and put to a violent death almost all the apostles and disciples of our Saviour. But at last some of these* wolves *themselves became converts, and grew to be lambs; St. Paul, one of the most eager persecutors of the church, was afterwards one of its most zealous defenders.*

The wolf, *as it is said, is a fierce creature, abiding in forests, an enemy to cattle, ravenous, greedy, crafty, of an exquisite quickness of smell, having an head something square, and his hair inclined to grey. It is commonly said, that what makes him so voracious is, that he has but one very large, short gut, in which his food stays but a little time: but this is a popular mistake: his guts are as long as any other animal's, or as a dog's, being himself a kind of wild dog.*

In times of great famine, when they can get no prey, wolves *are said to destroy one another; for when they meet together, bemoaning themselves one to another, as it were by consent, they run round in a circle, and the first which, through giddiness, falleth to the ground, is forthwith devoured by the rest. They are frightened at the throwing of stones, at fire, at the sound of bells, and at the singing of men or women. When they set upon sheep, they make choice of a dark, cloudy day, that they may escape the more safely; and they go against the wind, to prevent the dogs smelling them. It is said also, that the female bringeth forth one the first year, two the second, and so on till the ninth year. If the young one lap as a dog, she rejecteth it; if it suck the water as a swine, or bite as a bear, she nourishes it. Many other things are said of this animal.*

It is recorded that one Gelon of Syracuse, then a scholar at school, was thus preserved: a wolf *entering the school, seized on Gelon's writing table and hasted to be gone; Gelon pursued after his table: in the meantime the school-house fell down, whereby both masters and scholars were all killed, Gelon alone being preserved. Many other things are reported of them.*

Gen. 49. 27. Benjamin shall ravin as a *w*.
Isa. 11. 6. the *w*. shall dwell with the lamb
65. 25. the *w*. and the lamb shall feed together
Jer. 5. 6. a *w*. of the evenings shall spoil them
John 10. 12. but he that is an hireling seeth the *w*. coming, the *w*. catcheth and scattereth the sheep

WOLVES.

Ezek. 22. 27. her princes are like *w*. ravening
Hab. 1. 8. their horses fiercer than evening *w*.
Zeph. 3. 3. her princes lions, her judges evening *w*.
Mat. 7. 15. but inwardly they are ravening *w*.
10. 16. I send you forth as sheep in the midst of *w*.
Luke 10. 3. I send you forth as lambs among *w*.
Acts 20. 29. grievous *w*. shall enter in among you

WOMAN.

God having created all the animals in pairs, male and female, and having brought them to Adam, that he might give them names; in this review that Adam made of all living creatures, he could not observe that any one of them was like himself, or created for him, Gen. 2. 19, 20. *But God was pleased to give him a companion and assistant, as he had done to all the other creatures. He therefore cast Adam into a profound sleep, and when he was fast asleep, God took a rib out of his side, of which he formed the* woman. *When Adam awoke, he perceived it, and cried out*, This is bone of my bones, and flesh of my flesh; *she shall be called by a name derived from that of man, because she is taken out of man.* Wherefore a man shall forsake father and mother, and shall cleave to his wife, and they two shall be one flesh; *or*, "*they shall be but one in two different bodies, because of the production of children, which are the blood of both*," Gen. 2. 21, 22, &c.

Some writers have thought, that Adam was created of both sexes; because it is said in Gen. 1. 26, 27. Let us make man in our image, after our likeness, and let them have dominion over the fish of the sea: So God created man in his own image, in the image of God created he him; male and female created he them. *He speaks of the work of the sixth day. And in the following chapter he relates the formation of the woman in the manner before mentioned. It is therefore affirmed, that man was already formed male and female, before Eve was created. Others think, that the bodies of Adam and Eve were created even from the sixth day, but joined and fastened sidewise to each other; and that afterwards God sent a deep sleep on Adam, and then separated the* woman *from him. And thus they explain those words,* Gen. 2. 21. He took one of his ribs, and closed up the flesh instead thereof; *they translate the Hebrew thus,* He took one (*woman*) out of his side, and put flesh in its place. *The opinion that generally prevails is, that the man and* woman *were created on the sixth day, according to* Gen. 1. 27. *and that what is related* chap. 2. 20, &c. *is only a recapitulation, or a supplement, to what had been before mentioned in a concise manner.*

Woman *was created to be a companion and assistant to man. She was equal to him in that authority and jurisdiction that God gave them over all other animals. But after the fall, God made her subject to the government of man.* Gen. 3. 16. Thy desire shall be to thy husband, and he shall rule over thee. *Besides the duties prescribed by the law, common to men and* women, *there were certain regulations peculiar to this sex; as were those legal uncleannesses which they contracted during the times of their ordinary infirmities,* Lev. 15. 19. *and those that attended their lying-in,* Lev. 12. 2. *and those which proceeded from certain fluxes of humours, at those seasons appointed by nature,* Lev. 15. 25. *The law also made them liable to the trial of the* waters of jealousy, *if their husbands had entertained any well-grounded suspicions of their fidelity,* Num. 5. 14, &c. *and when the tokens of virginity could not be found in them, they were stoned to death,* Deut. 22. 20, 21.

If a married woman *made a vow, of whatever nature it was, she could not be obliged to keep it, if her husband was against it, and contradicted it the same day. But if he staid till the next day before he contradicted it, or knowing the thing, if he held his peace, he was then supposed to consent to it, and the* woman *was obliged to perform her vow,* Num. 30. 6, 7, 8. *See the epistles of St. Paul, for the duties of women towards their husbands,* 1 Cor. 7. 3, 4, &c. Eph. 5. 22, &c. *See also* Tit. 2. 4, 5. *and* 1 Pet. 3. 1, 2, 3. *where modesty is recommended to them, and a great care in avoiding all superfluous ornaments, and unnecessary finery of dress.*

The prophet Isaiah says, As for my people, *women* rule over them; *that is, weak and effeminate men,* Isa. 3. 12. *And in* chap. 19. 16. In that day shall Egypt be like unto *women; that is, feeble and fearful. The prophet Ezekiel represents the kingdoms of Israel and Judah, who both sprung from the same stock by* two women, the daughters of one mother, *Ezek.* 23. 2, 44. *And in* Rev. 12. 1. *the church is represented by a woman* clothed with the sun, and the moon under her feet. *The church is compared to a* woman, *as she is the spouse of Christ; and as the* woman *is the weaker sex, so the church hath always been the weakest part of the world. The antichristian church is also represented as a woman* sitting on a scarlet coloured beast, full of names of blasphemy, *Rev.* 17. 3.

Gen. 2. 22. and the rib of the man made he a *w.*
23. she shall be called *w.* she was taken out of man
3. 15. I will put enmity between thee and the *w.*
24. 5. peradventure the *w.* will not come, 39.
44. let the same be the *w.* the Lord hath appointed
Exod. 21. 22. if men strive and hurt a *w.* with child
Lev. 18. 23. nor shall a *w.* stand before a beast
20. 13. if a man lie with mankind as with a *w.*
Num. 5. 18. he shall set the *w.* before the Lord, 30.
27. the *w.* shall be a curse among her people
25. 6. brought a Midianitish *w.* in the sight of Moses
8. Phinehas thrust the *w.* through her belly
30. 3. if a *w.* vow a vow to Lord and bind herself
31. 17. now kill every *w.* that hath known man
Deut. 22. 14. I took this *w.* and found her not a maid
Josh. 2. 4. the *w.* took the two men and hid them
6. 22. go, and bring out thence the *w.* Rahab
Judg. 4. 9. Lord shall sell Sisera into the hand of *w.*
9. 53. a certain *w.* cast a piece of a millstone upon Abimelech's head, brake his scull, 2 *Sam.* 11. 21.
54. that men say not of me, a *w.* slew him
13. 11. art thou the man that spakest to the *w.?*
14. 3. is there never a *w.* among all my people?
16. 4. Samson loved a *w.* in the valley of Sorek
19. 26. then came the *w.* in the dawning of the day
Ruth 1. 5. the *w.* was left of her sons and husband
3. 11. for my people know thou art a virtuous *w.*
4. 11. the Lord make the *w.* like Rachel and Leah
1 *Sam.* 1. 15. Hannah said, I am *w.* of sorrowful spirit
26. I am *w.* that stood by thee here, praying
2. 20. Lord give thee seed of this *w.* for the loan
28. 7. seek me a *w.* that hath a familiar spirit
2 *Sam.* 3. 8. thou chargest me concerning this *w.*
11. 2. from the roof David saw a *w.* washing herself
13. 17. put now this *w.* out from me and bolt door
17. 19. the *w.* spread a covering over the well
20. 22. then *w.* went unto all people in her wisdom
1 *Kings* 3. 17. I and this *w.* dwell in one house
14. 5. she shall feign herself to be another *w.*
17. 17. the son of the *w.* fell sick and died
2 *Kings* 4. 8. went to Shunem, where was a great *w.*
6. 26. there cried a *w.* saying, help, my lord, O king
8. 5. this is the *w.* ‖ 9. 34. see this cursed *w.*
2 *Chron.* 24. 7. the sons of Athaliah that wicked *w.*
Job 31. 9. if my heart have been deceived by a *w.*
Psal. 48. 6. pain as of a *w.* in travail, *Isa.* 13. 8. | 21. 3. | 26. 17. *Jer.* 4. 31. | 6. 24. | 13. 21. | 22. 23. | 30. 6. | 31. 8. | 48. 41. | 49. 22, 24. | 50. 43.
Prov. 6. 24. to keep thee from the evil *w.*
7. 10. behold there met him a *w.* subtile of heart
9. 13. a foolish *w.* is clamorous, she is simple
12. 4. a virtuous *w.* is a crown to her husband, 31. 10.
14. 1. every wise *w.* buildeth her house but foolish
21. 9. than with a brawling *w.* in a wide house, 19.
31. 10. who can find a virtuous *w.?* price rubies
30. a *w.* that fears the Lord shall be praised
Eccl. 7. 26. the *w.* whose heart is snares and nets
28. but a *w.* among all those have I not found
Isa. 42. 14. now will I cry like a travailing *w.*
45. 10. or to the *w.* what hast thou brought forth?
49. 15. can a *w.* forget her sucking child?
54. 6. the Lord hath called thee as a *w.* forsaken
Jer. 6. 2. likened daughter of Zion to a delicate *w.*
31. 22. created a new thing, a *w.* compass a man
Lam. 1. 17. Jerusalem is a menstruous *w.* among them
Ezek. 16. 30. the work of an imperious whorish *w.*
23. 44. they went in unto her, as they go in to a *w.*
36. 17. their way as the uncleanness of a removed *w.*
Hos. 3. 1. go yet, love a *w.* beloved of her friend
13. 13. the sorrows of a travailing *w.* shall come upon him, he is an unwise son, *Mic.* 4. 9, 10.
Zech. 5. 7. this is a *w.* that sits in the ephah
Mat. 5. 28. whoso looketh on a *w.* to lust after her
9. 20. a *w.* which was diseased with an issue of blood twelve years, *Mark* 5. 25. *Luke* 8. 43.
13. 33. leaven, which a *w.* took and hid in meal
15. 28. O *w.* great is thy faith, be it to thee as thou
22. 27. unto the seventh, and last of all the *w.* died also, *Mark* 12. 22. *Luke* 20. 32.
26. 10. Jesus said, why trouble ye the *w.?*
13. this that this *w.* hath done shall be told
Mark 10. 12. if a *w.* shall put away her husband
Luke 7. 39. who and what manner of *w.* is this?
44. Jesus said unto Simon, seest thou this *w.?*
13. 16. ought not this *w.* being a daughter of Abrah.
John 2. 4. *w.* what have I to do with thee?
4. 9. askest drink of me who am a *w.* of Samaria?
39. many believed on him for the saying of the *w.*
8. 3. brought to him a *w.* taken in adultery, 4.
10. when Jesus saw none but the *w.* he said
19. 26. he saith to his mother, *w.* behold thy son
Acts 9. 36. Dorcas, this *w.* was full of good works
17. 34. and a *w.* named Damaris believed
Rom. 1. 27. men leaving the natural use of the *w.*
7. 2. the *w.* that hath an husband is bound
1 *Cor.* 7. 1. it is good for a man not to touch a *w.*
2. let every *w.* have her own husband
11. 5. but every *w.* that prayeth uncovered
6. if the *w.* be not covered, let her be shorn
7. but the *w.* is the glory of the man
8. man is not of the *w.* but the *w.* of the man
9. man not for the *w.* but the *w.* for the man
10. the *w.* ought to have power on her head
11. nevertheless, neither is the man without the *w.* nor the *w.* without the man in the Lord
12. as the *w.* is of the man, so is the man by the *w.*
13. is it comely for a *w.* to pray to God uncovered?
15. if a *w.* have long hair, it is a glory to her
Gal. 4. 4. God sent forth his Son made of a *w.*
1 *Thess.* 5. 3. then destruc. cometh as travail on a *w.*
1 *Tim.* 2. 12. I suffer not a *w.* to teach or usurp
14. the *w.* being deceived, was in the transgression
Rev. 2. 20. thou sufferest that *w.* Jezebel to teach
12. 1. there appeared *w.* clothed with the sun
6. the *w.* fled ‖ 16. the earth helped the *w.*
17. and the dragon was wroth with the *w.*
17. 3. I saw a *w.* sit on a scarlet-coloured beast
6. a *w.* drunken ‖ 7. I will tell mystery of the *w.*
See BORN, MAN, STRANGE.

Young WOMAN.

Ruth 4. 12. let thy house be like that of Pharez, of the seed which Ld. shall give thee of this *young w.*

WOMANKIND.

Lev. 18. 22. shalt not lie with mankind as with *w.*

WOMB.

Gen. 25. 23. Lord said, two nations are in thy *w.*
24. behold, there were twins in her *w.* 38. 27.
29. 31. Lord opened Leah's *w.* ‖ 30. 22. Rachel's *w.*
49. 25. bless with blessings of breasts, and of *w.*
Exod. 13. 2. whatsoever openeth the *w.* is mine
Num. 8. 16. the Levites are given me, instead of such as open every *w.* even of the first-born
Judg. 13. 5. he shall be a Nazarite from the *w.* 7.
Ruth 1. 11. are there yet any more sons in my *w.?*
1 *Sam.* 1. 5. but the Lord had shut up her *w.* 6.
Job 3. 11. why died I not from the *w.?*
10. 18. why hast thou brought me forth of the *w.?*
24. 20. the *w.* shall forget him, he shall be no more
31. 15. did not he that made thee in *w.* make him?
38. 8. brake forth as if it had issued out of the *w.*
29. out of whose *w.* came the ice?
Psal. 22. 9. but thou art he who took me out of the *w.*
10. I was cast upon thee from the *w.* art my God
58. 3. the wicked are estranged from the *w.*
71. 6. by thee have I been holden up from the *w.*
110. 3. thy people willing, from *w.* of the morning
Prov. 30. 16. the barren *w.* says not, it is enough
31. 2. what, my son? and what, the son of my *w.?*
Eccl. 11. 5. thou knowest not how bones grow in *w.*
Isa. 44. 2. Lord formed thee from the *w.* 24. | 49. 5.
46. 3. O Israel which are carried from the *w.*
48. 8. wast called a transgressor from the *w.*
49. 1. the Lord hath called me from the *w.*
15. she not have compassion on the son of her *w.*
66. 9. shall I cause to bring forth, and shut the *w.?*
Jer. 1. 5. before thou camest forth out of the *w.*
20. 17. because he slew me not from the *w.* or my mother's *w.* to be always great with me
18. why came I forth of the *w.* to see labour?
Ezek. 20. 26. pass thro' the fire all that openeth the *w.*
Hos. 9. 11. their glory shall flee from the birth and *w.*
14. give them a miscarrying *w.* and dry breasts
12. 3. he took his brother by the heel in the *w.*
Luke 1. 31. behold, thou shalt conceive in thy *w.*
41. the babe leaped in her *w.* for joy, 44.
2. 21. name Jesus, before he was conceived in the *w.*
23. every male that openeth the *w.* shall be holy
See FRUIT, MOTHER.

WOMBS.

Gen. 20. 18. the Lord had fast closed up all the *w.*
Luke 23. 29. blessed are the *w.* that never bare

WOMEN.

Gen. 24. 11. the time that *w.* go out to draw water
Exod. 15. 20. all the *w.* went out after Miriam
35. 25. all the *w.* that were wise-hearted did spin
26. all the *w.* whose heart stirred them up
Lev. 26. 26. ten *w.* shall bake your bread in one oven
Num. 31. 15. Moses said, have ye saved all *w.* alive?
Deut. 20. 14. the *w.* and little ones take captives
Josh. 8. 35. Joshua read the law before the *w.*
Judg. 5. 24. blessed above *w.* shall Jael wife of Heb.
21. 14. they saved alive of the *w.* of Jabesh-Gilead
1 *Sam.* 2. 22. Eli heard how they lay with the *w.*
15. 33. as thy sword hath made *w.* childless, so shall
18. 6. the *w.* came out of the cities of Israel
7. the *w.* answered one another as they played
21. 4. if the young men kept themselves from *w.*
5. of a truth *w.* have been kept from us three days
30. 2. the Amalekites had taken the *w.* captives
2 *Sam.* 1. 26. thy love to me passing the love of *w.*
15. 16. the king left ten *w.* to keep the house
1 *Kings* 3. 16. then came two *w.* that were harlots
2 *Kings* 8. 12. and rip up their *w.* with child, 15. 16.
23. 7. where the *w.* wove hangings for the grove
Neh. 13. 26. even him did outlandish *w.* cause to sin
Esth. 1. 9. Vashti the queen made a feast for the *w.*
2. 17. Ahasuerus loved Esther above all the *w.*
3. 13. to slay all Jews, little children and *w.* 8. 11
Job 42. 15. no *w.* found so fair as Job's daughters
Ps. 45. 9. king's daughters among thy honourab. *w.*
Prov. 31. 3. give not thy strength to *w.*
Cant. 1. 8. O thou fairest among *w.* 5. 9. | 6. 1.
Isa. 3. 12. as for my people, *w.* rule over them
4. 1. in that day seven *w.* shall take hold of one man
19. 16. in that day Egypt shall be like to *w.*
27. 11. the *w.* come, and set them on fire
32. 9. rise up, ye *w.* that are at ease, hear my
10. careless *w.* ‖ 11. tremble, ye *w.* be troubled
Jer. 7. 18. the *w.* knead their dough to make cakes
9. 17. call for the mourning and cunning *w.*
20. yet hear the word of the Lord, O ye *w.*
38. 22. all the *w.* left shall be brought to the king
44. 21. Jeremiah said to all the *w.* hear the word
50. 37. they shall become *w.* and shall be robbed
51. 30. the mighty men of Babylon became as *w.*
Lam. 2. 20. shall the *w.* eat children of a span long?
4. 10. the pitiful *w.* have sodden their children
5. 11. they ravished *w.* in Zion, and maids in Judah
Ezek. 8. 14. there sat *w.* weeping for Tammuz
9. 6. slay utterly maids, little children, and *w.*
13. 18. woe to *w.* that sew pillows to all arm-holes
16. 34. the contrary is in thee from other *w.*
38. I will judge thee as *w.* that break wedlock
23. 2. there were two *w.* daughters of one mother
45. judge after the manner of *w.* that shed blood
48. *w.* may be taught not to do after your lewdness
Dan. 11. 17. he shall give him the daughter of *w.*
37. nor shall he regard the desire of *w.* nor any god
Hos. 13. 16. their *w.* with child shall be ripped up
Amos 1. 13. bec. they have ripped up *w.* with child
Mic. 2. 9. the *w.* of my people have ye cast out
Nah. 3. 13. thy people in the midst of thee are *w.*
Zech. 5. 9. there came out two *w.* and had wings
8. 4. old *w.* shall dwell in the streets of Jerusalem
14. 2. the houses rifled, the *w.* shall be ravished
Mat. 11. 11. among them that are born of *w.* not risen a greater than John Baptist, *Luke* 7. 28.
14. 21. Jesus fed 5,000 men, besides *w.* 15. 38.
24. 41. two *w.* grinding at the mill, *Luke* 17. 35.
27. 55. and many *w.* were then beholding afar off
Luke 1. 28. blessed art thou among *w.* 42.
24. 22. certain *w.* also made us astonished
24. and found it even so as the *w.* had said
Acts 1. 14. these all continued in prayer with the *w.*
13. 50. but the Jews stirred up the devout *w.*
16. 13. we speak to the *w.* which resorted thither
17. 4. of the chief *w.* not a few believed, 12.
Rom. 1. 26. their *w.* did change the natural use
1 *Cor.* 14. 34. let your *w.* keep silence in churches
35. it is a shame for *w.* to speak in the church
Phil. 4. 3. help those *w.* which laboured with me
1 *Tim.* 2. 9. *w.* adorn themselves in modest apparel
10. which becometh *w.* professing godliness
11. let the *w.* learn in silence with all subjection
5. 2. entreat the elder *w.* as mothers, younger as
14. I will therefore that the younger *w.* marry
2 *Tim.* 3. 6. lead captive silly *w.* laden with sins
Tit. 2. 3. the aged *w.* behave as becometh holiness
4. they may teach the younger *w.* to be sober
Heb. 11. 35. *w.* received their dead raised to life aga
1 *Pet.* 3. 5. after this manner the holy *w.* adorned
Rev. 9. 8. they had hair as hair of *w.* their teeth as
14. 4. these are they that are not defiled with *w.*
See CHILDREN, MEN, SINGING, STRANGE.

WOMEN-*servants.*

Gen. 20. 14. Abimelech gave *w.-servants* to Abrah.
32. 5. Jacob had men servants and *w.-servants*

WON.

1 *Chron.* 26. 27. out of the spoils *w.* in battles
Prov. 18. 19. a brother offended is harder to be *w.*
1 *Pet.* 3. 1. may be *w.* by the conversation of wives

WONDER.

Deut. 13. 1. if a prophet give thee a sign or a *w.*
2. and the sign of the *w.* come to pass
28. 46. they shall be upon thee for a sign and a *w.*
2 *Chr.* 32. 31. who sent to him to inquire of the *w.*
Ps. 71. 7. I am as a *w.* to many, thou art my refuge
Isa. 20. 3. like as Isaiah walked barefoot for a *w.*
29. 14. I will do a marvellous work and a *w.*
Acts 3. 10. they were filled with *w.* and amazement
Rev. 12. 1. there appeared a great *w.* in heaven, 3.

WONDER, *Verb.*

Isa. 13. † 8. they shall *w.* one at another
29. 9. stay yourselves and *w.* cry ye out, and cry
Jer. 4. 9. the priests and the prophets shall *w.*
Hab. 1. 5. behold ye, regard and *w.* marvellously
Acts 13. 41. behold, ye despisers, *w.* and perish
Rev. 17. 8. they that dwell on the earth shall *w.*

WONDERFUL.

Deut. 28. 59. the Lord will make thy plagues *w.*
2 *Sam.* 1. 26. thy love to me was *w.* passing love of
2 *Chron.* 2. 9. house I am to build shall be *w.* great
Job 42. 3. I have uttered things too *w.* for me
Ps. 119. 129. thy testimonies *w.* my soul keep them
131. † 1. nor do I exercise myself in things too *w.*
139. 6. such knowledge is too *w.* for me
Prov. 30. 18. there be three things that are too *w.*
Isa. 9. 6. his name shall be called *W.* Counsellor
25. 1. O Ld. I will praise thee, hast done *w.* things
28. 29. from the Lord of hosts who is *w.* in counsel

Jer. 5. 30. a *w.* thing is committed in the land
Dan. 8. † 13. a saint said to the *w.* numberer
Mat. 21. 15. when they saw the *w.* things he did
See WORKS.

WONDERFULLY.

1 *Sam.* 6. 6. when he had wrought *w.* among them
Psal. 139. 14. I will praise thee for I am *w.* made
Lam. 1. 9. therefore Jerusalem came down *w.*
Dan. 8. 24. he shall destroy *w.* and shall prosper

WONDERS.

Exod. 3. 20. I will stretch out my hand and smite Egypt with all my *w.* 7. 3. | 11. 9. *Deut.* 6. 22. | 7. 19. | 26. 8. | 34. 11.
4. 21. see thou do those *w.* || 11. 10. did these *w.*
15. 11. the Lord is fearful in praises, doing *w.*
Deut. 4. 34. hath God assayed to take a nation by *w.*
Josh. 3. 5. to-morrow the Lord will do *w.* among you
1 *Chron.* 16. 12. remember his *w.* *Psal.* 105. 5.
Neh. 9. 10. thou shewedst *w.* upon Pharaoh
17. nor were mindful of thy *w.* *Psal.* 78. 11, 43.
Job 9. 10. God doth *w.* without number
Psal. 77. 11. surely I will remember thy *w.* of old
14. thou art the God that dost *w.*
88. 10. wilt thou shew *w.* to the dead?
12. shall thy *w.* be known in the dark?
89. 5. the heavens shall praise thy *w.* O Lord
96. 3. declare his *w.* among all people
105. 27. they shewed his *w.* in the land of Ham
106. 7. our fathers understood not thy *w.* in Egypt
107. 24. these see his works and his *w.* in the deep
135. 9. who sent *w.* into the midst of Egypt
136. 4. to him who alone doth great *w.*
Isa. 8. 18. I and the children are for *w.* in Israel
Jer. 32. 20. who hath set signs and *w.* in land of Eg.
21. and hast brought forth thy people with *w.*
Dan. 4. 2. I thought good to shew the signs and *w.*
3. how great are his signs! how mighty his *w.!*
6. 27. he worketh *w.* in heaven and in earth
12. 6. how long shall it be to the end of these *w.?*
Joel 2. 30. I will shew *w.* in heaven, *Acts* 2. 19.
Mat. 24. 24. there shall arise false Christs and false prophets, and shall shew great *w.* *Mark* 13. 22.
John 4. 48. Jesus said, except ye see signs and *w.*
Acts 2. 22. Jesus, a man approved of God by *w.*
43. fear came on every soul, many signs and *w.* were done by the apostles, 5. 12. | 14. 3. | 15. 12.
4. 30. that *w.* may be done by the name of Jesus
6. 8. Stephen did great *w.* among the people
7. 36. after he had shewed *w.* in the land of Egypt
Rom. 15. 19. to make Gentiles obedient through *w.*
2 *Cor.* 12. 12. the signs of an apostle wrought in *w.*
2 *Thess.* 2. 9. whose coming is with signs and lying *w.*
Heb. 2. 4. God also bearing witness with signs and *w.*
Rev. 13. 13. he doth great *w.* in the sight of men

WONDERED.

Isa. 59. 16. he *w.* there was no intercessor
63. 5. and I *w.* that there was none to uphold
Zech. 3. 8. hear now, for they are men *w.* at
Luke 2. 18. all they that heard it *w.* at things told
4. 22. they all *w.* at the gracious words
24. 41. while they believed not for joy, and *w.*
Acts 7. 31. Moses *w.* || 8. 13. Simon Magus *w.*
Rev. 13. 3. all the world *w.* after the beast
17. 6. when I saw her, I *w.* with great admiration

WONDERING.

Gen. 24. 21. the man *w.* at her, held his peace
Luke 24. 12. Peter *w.* at that which was come to pass
Acts 3. 11. all the people ran together greatly *w.*

WONDROUS.

1 *Chron.* 16. 9. sing psalms, talk you of all his *w.* works, *Psal.* 26. 7. | 105. 2. | 119. 27. | 145. 5.
Job 37. 14. consider the *w.* works of God
16. dost thou know the *w.* works of him?
Psal. 71. 17. hitherto have I declared thy *w.* works
72. 18. the God who only doth *w.* things, 86. 10.
75. 1. that thy name is near, thy *w.* works declare
78. 32. they believed not for his *w.* works
106. 22. who had done *w.* works in the land of Ham
119. 18. that I may behold *w.* things out of thy law
Jer. 21. 2. he will deal according to his *w.* works

WONDEROUSLY.

Judg. 13. 19. the angel did *w.* Manoah looked on
Joel 2. 26. the Lord hath dealt *w.* with you

WONT.

Exod. 21. 29. if the ox were *w.* to push with his horns
Num. 22. 30. was I ever *w.* to do so to thee?
1 *Sam.* 30. 31. where David and his men *w.* to haunt
2 *Sam.* 20. 18. they were *w.* to speak in old time
Dan. 3. 19. seven times more than *w.* to be heated
Mat. 27. 15. the governor was *w.* to release
Mark 10. 1. as he was *w.* he taught them again
Luke 22. 39. he went as he was *w.* to the mount
Acts 16. 13. went where prayer was *w.* to be made

WOOD.

Gen. 22. 6. Abraham took *w.* and put it on Isaac
7. Isaac said, behold the fire and the *w.*
Num. 13. 20. whether there be *w.* therein or not
31. 20. purify all things that are made of *w.*
Deut. 10. 1. come up, and make thee an ark of *w.*
19. 5. when a man goeth into the *w.* to hew *w.*
29. 11. from the hewer of thy *w.* unto the drawer of thy water, *Josh.* 9. 21, 23, 27. *Jer.* 46. 22.
Josh. 17. 18. the mountain is a *w.* cut it down
1 *Sam.* 6. 14. and they clave the *w.* of the cart
14. 25. all they of the land came to a *w.*
23. 16. Jonathan went to David into the *w.*
2 *Sam.* 18. 8. the *w.* devoured more people that day
1 *Kings* 18. 23. lay the bullock on *w.* and no fire und.
2 *Kings* 2. 24. there came two she-bears out of the *w.*
1 *Chron.* 29. 2. I have prepared *w.* for things of *w.*
Psal. 80. 13. the boar out of the *w.* doth waste it
132. 6. we found it in the fields of the *w.*
141. 7. as when one cleaveth *w.* upon the earth
Prov. 26. 20. where no *w.* is, there the fire goeth out
21. as *w.* to fire, so is a contentious man to kin. fire
Eccl. 10. 9. he that cleaveth *w.* shall be in danger
Isa. 10. 15. staff should lift up itself as if it were no *w.*
30. 33. the pile thereof is fire and much *w.*
45. 20. they that set up the *w.* of their image
60. 17. for iron I will bring silver, for *w.* brass
Jer. 5. 14. I will make my words fire, this people *w.*
7. 18. the children gather *w.* the fathers kindle fire

Jer. 28. 13. thou hast broken the yokes of *w.* but shalt
Ezek. 15. 3. shall *w.* be taken thereof to do any work?
24. 10. heap on *w.* || 39. 10. no *w.* out of the field
Mic. 7. 14. the flock which dwell solitary in the *w.*
Hab. 2. 19. woe to him that saith to the *w.* awake
Hag. 1. 8. go up, bring *w.* and build the house
Zech. 12. 6. like an hearth of fire among the *w.*
1 *Cor.* 3. 12. if any build on this foundation, *w.* hay
2 *Tim.* 2. 20. but also vessels of *w.* and earth
See OFFERING, STONE.

WOODS.

Ezek. 34. 25. they shall sleep safely in the *w.*

WOOF.

Lev. 13. 48. if the plague be in the warp or *w.*
51. if the plague be spread in the warp or the *w.*
52. burnt that garment, whether warp or *w.*
53 if the plague be not spread, wash the *w.* 58.
56 then he shall rend it out of the warp or *w.*
59. this is the law of leprosy in the warp or *w.*

WOOL.

Judg. 6. 37. I will put a fleece of *w.* in the floor
2 *Kings* 3. 4. Mesha rendered 100,000 rams with *w.*
Psal. 147. 16. the Lord giveth snow like *w.*
Prov. 31. 13. she seeketh *w.* and flax, and worketh
Isa. 1. 18. tho' your sins like crimson, shall be as *w.*
51. 8. worm shall eat them like *w.* but my right.
Ezek. 27. 18. Damascus was thy merchant in *w.*
34. 3. ye eat the fat, ye clothe you with the *w.*
44. 17. and no *w.* shall come upon them
Dan. 7. 9. the hair of his head like *w.* *Rev.* 1. 14.
Hos. 2. 5. will go after my lovers that give me my *w.*
9. I will recover my *w.* and my flax given to cover

WOOLLEN.

Lev. 13. 47. the garment, whether *w.* or linen, 59.
48. the leprosy be in the warp or woof of *w.* 52.
19. 19. nor shall a garment mingled of linen and *w.* come upon thee, *Deut.* 22. 11.

WORD,

In Hebrew, Dabar; *in Greek,* Ῥημα, *or* Λογος. *It signifies,* 1. *The eternal Son of God, the uncreated Wisdom, the second Person of the most holy Trinity, equal and consubstantial with the Father. The evangelist John,* chap. 1. 1. *more expressly than any other, has opened the mystery of this* WORD, *when he tells us,* In the beginning was the *Word,* and the *Word* was with God, and the *Word* was God. The same was in the beginning with God. All things were made by him, and without him was not any thing made that was made. *Christ Jesus is called the* WORD, (1) *In respect of his person, he being the express image of the Father, as we are told,* Heb. 1. 3. *as our words are of our thoughts.* (2) *In respect of his office, because the Father made known his will to the church in all ages by him, as we declare our minds one to another by our words,* John 3. 34. (3) *Because the* Messiah *was called* The Word of God *by the Jews. The Chaldee Paraphrasts, the most ancient Jewish writers extant, generally make use of the word MEMRA, which signifies the* Word, *in those places where Moses puts the name* Jehovah. *And it is generally thought, that under this term the Paraphrasts would intimate the Son of God, the second Person of the Trinity. Now their testimony is so much the more considerable, as having lived before Christ, or at the time of Christ, they are irrefragable witnesses of the sentiments of their nation concerning this article, since their* Targum, *or Explication, has always been, and still is, in universal esteem among the Jews. And as they ascribe to* Memra *all the attributes of the Deity, it is concluded from thence, that they believed the divinity of the WORD.*

They say, that it was MEMRA, or the WORD, which created the world; which appeared to Moses on mount Sinai; which gave him the law; which spoke to him face to face; which brought Israel out of Egypt; which marched before the people; which wrought all those miracles which are recorded in the book of Exodus. It was the same WORD that appeared to Abraham in the plain of Mamre; that was seen of Jacob at Beth-el, to whom Jacob made his vow, and acknowledged as God, Gen. 28. 20. If God will be with me, and will keep me in this way that I go, &c. then shall the Lord be my God.

II. The word *is taken for what is written in the sacred books of the Old and New Testament,* Luke 11. 28. Blessed are they that hear the *word* of God and keep it. *Jam.* 1. 22. Be ye doers of the *word. This is the inspired and created* word. III. *For the divine law, which teaches and commands good things, and forbids evil.* Psal. 119. 101. I have refrained my feet from every evil way, that I might keep thy *word. This is the word of precept or commandment.* IV. *For every promise of God, touching any good things, whether temporal or eternal.* Psal. 119. 25. Quicken thou me according to thy *word. So in* verses 38. 49. Stablish thy *word* unto thy servant, who is devoted to thy fear. Remember the *word* unto thy servant, upon which thou hast caused me to hope. *This is the* word *of promise.* V. *For prophecy, or vision.* Isa. 2. 1. The *word* that Isaiah saw. VI. Word *also signifies the command of God.* Psal. 147. 18. He sendeth out his *word* and melteth them; *speaking of the ice. One* word *shall dissolve them. So in* Luke 5. 5. Nevertheless at thy *word* I will let down the net. *It was thus the good Centurion said to Christ.* Wherefore neither thought I myself worthy to come unto thee; but say in a *word,* and my servant shall be healed, *Luke* 7. 7. *This is a* word *of authority, ordering things to be done effectually.*

In Mat. 4. 3, 4. *the devil putting our Saviour upon an unnecessary proof of his divinity, and a distrust of God's providence, by desiring him to* turn the stones into bread; *our Saviour answers him, that* man does not live by bread alone, but by every *word* that proceedeth out of the mouth of God; *that is, by whatsoever the providence of God shall afford, and bless for our support; yea, a man may live by his power and will only without any means at all, if God so please; or be fed by ravens, as Elijah was; and therefore no man should absolutely rest upon the means, and, without warrant, run to an extraordinary course for supply, but should trust in God, and wait on him to provide as he pleases.*

Gen. 37. 14. go and bring me *w.* again, *Mat.* 2. 8.
44. 18. O my lord, let me speak a *w.* 2 *Sam.* 14. 12.
Exod. 8. 13. Lord did according to the *w.* of Moses
12. 35. Israel did according to the *w.* of Moses
32. 28. Levi did according to the *w.* *Lev.* 10. 7.
Num. 13. 26. they brought back *w.* unto them
22. 8. lodge here, I will bring you *w.* *Deut.* 1. 22.
20. yet the *w.* I shall say to thee, that do
35. the *w.* I shall speak || 38. the *w.* God putteth
23. 5. the Lord put a *w.* in Balaam's mouth
Deut. 1. 25. they brought us *w.* again, and said
4. 2. ye shall not add unto the *w.* I command you
8. 3. but by every *w.* that proceedeth out of the mouth of God doth man live. *Mat.* 4. 4.
15. † 9. beware there be not a *w.* in thy heart
18. 20. the prophets that presume to speak a *w.*
21. how shall we know the *w.?* *Jer.* 28. 9.
21. 5. by their *w.* shall every controversy be tried
30. 14. the *w.* is nigh thee, *Rom.* 10. 8.
Josh. 1. 13. remember the *w.* Moses commanded
8. 35. there was not a *w.* which Joshua read not
14. 7. I brought him *w.* || 22. 32. brought them *w.*
1 *Sam.* 4. 1. the *w.* of Samuel came to all Israel
17. † 30. he turned, and spake after the same *w.*
2 *Sam.* 3. 11. he could not answer Abner a *w.*
7. 7. in all places spake I a *w.* 1 *Chron.* 17. 6.
25. the *w.* thou hast spoken concerning thy servant
15. 28. till there come *w.* from you to certify me
19. 10. speak ye not a *w.* of bringing the king
24. 4. the king's *w.* prevailed, 1 *Chron.* 21. 4.
1 *Kings* 2. 30. Benaiah brought the king *w.* again, 2 *Kings* 22. 9, 20. 2 *Chron.* 34. 16, 28
42. the *w.* that I have heard is good
8. 56. hath not failed one *w.* of all his promise
18. 21. the people answered not a *w.* *Isa.* 36. 21.
† 24. all the people answered, the *w.* is good
2 *Kings* 6. 18. he smote according to the *w.* of Elisha
18. 28. hear the *w.* of the great king of Assyria
1 *Chron.* 16. 15. mindful of the *w.* which he commanded to a thousand generations, *Psal.* 105. 8.
21. 12. advise what *w.* I shall bring to him
Neh. 1. 8. remember *w.* thou commandedst Moses
Esth. 1. 21. he did according to *w.* of Memucan
7. 8. as the *w.* went out of the king's mouth
Job 2. 13. they sat down, none spake a *w.* to Job
Psal. 17. 4. by *w.* of thy lips, I have kept me
68. 11. the Lord gave the *w.* many published it
119. 49. remember the *w.* to thy servant, on which
123. mine eyes fail for the *w.* of thy righteousness
139. 4. there is not a *w.* in my tongue, but thou
Prov. 12. 25. a good *w.* maketh the heart glad
13. 13. whoso despiseth the *w.* shall be destroyed
14. 15. simple believeth every *w.* but the prudent
15. 23. *w.* spoken in due season, how good is it
18. † 13. he that returneth a *w.* before he hear it
25. 11. a *w.* fitly spoken is like apples of gold in pictures of silver
Eccl. 5. † 2. be not hasty to utter any *w.* before God
8. 4. where the *w.* of a king is, there is power
Isa. 5. 24. they despised *w.* of the Holy One of Israel
8. 10. speak *w.* and it shall not stand, God with us
9. 8. the L. sent a *w.* to Jacob, it lighted on Israel
29. 21. that make a man an offender for a *w.*
30. 21. thine ears shall hear a *w.* behind thee
41. 28. there was no counsellor could answer a *w.*
44. 26. that confirmeth the *w.* of his servant
45. 23. the *w.* is gone out of my mouth
50. 4. I should know how to speak a *w.* in season
Jer. 5. 13. become wind, and the *w.* is not in them
9. 20. let your ear receive *w.* of his mouth, 10. 1.
18. 18. nor shall the *w.* perish from the prophet
23. 36. for every man's *w.* shall be his burden
26. 2. speak unto them, diminish not a *w.*
34. 5. for I have pronounced the *w.* saith the Lord
37. 17. king said, is there any *w.* from the Lord
44. 16. as for the *w.* thou hast spoken unto us
Ezek. 3. 17. therefore hear *w.* at my mouth, 33. 7.
12. 25. the *w.* that I shall speak shall come to pass
28. the *w.* that I have spoken shall be done
13. 6. that they would confirm the *w.*
33. 30. hear what is *w.* that cometh from the Lord
Dan. 3. 28. who have changed the king's *w.*
4. 17. the demand is by the *w.* of the holy ones
31. while the *w.* was in the king's mouth
Jonah 3. 6. for *w.* came to the king of Nineveh
Hag. 2. 5. according to the *w.* I covenanted with you
Mat. 8. 8. speak the *w.* only, he shall be healed
12. 32. whoso speaketh a *w.* against the Son of man, it shall be forgiven him, *Luke* 12. 10.
36. of every idle *w.* men shall give account
13. 19. when any one heareth the *w.* of the kingdom, 20. 22, 23. *Mark* 4. 16, 18, 20. *Luke* 8. 15.
21. for when tribulation or persecution ariseth, because of the *w.* he is offended, *Mark* 4. 17.
15. 23. Jesus answered Syrophenic. woman not a *w.*
18. 16. that every *w.* may be established, 2 *Cor.* 13. 1.
22. 46. no man was able to answer him a *w.*
27. 14. Jesus answered him to never a *w.*
28. 8. they did run to bring his disciples *w.*
Mark 4. 14. the sower soweth the *w.*
14. 72. Peter called to mind the *w.* that Jesus said
16. 20. the Lord confirming the *w.* with signs
Luke 4. 36. were all amazed, saying, what a *w.* is this!
7. 7. say in a *w.* and my servant shall be healed
24. 19. Jesus a prophet mighty in *w.* and deed
John 1. 1. in the beginning was the *W.* and the *W.* was with God, and the *W.* was God
14. the *W.* was made flesh, and dwelt among us
2. 22. they believed the *w.* that Jesus said, 4. 50.
12. 48. *w.* I have spoken shall judge him in last day
14. 24. the *w.* which you hear is not mine
15. 3. ye are clean through the *w.* I spake to you
20. remember the *w.* that I said unto you
25. that *w.* might be fulfilled, written in their law
17. 20. who shall believe on me through their *w.*

Acts 10. 36. the w. which God sent to Israel
13. 15. if ye have any w. of exhortation, say on
26. to you is the w. of this salvation sent
15. 7. that Gentiles, by my mouth, should hear w.
17. 11. they received the w. with all readiness
20. 32. I commend you to the w. of his grace
28. 25. after that Paul had spoken one w.
Rom. 10. 8. that is the w. of faith which we preach
15. 18. to make Gentiles obedient by w. and deed
1 Cor. 4. 20. kingdom of G. is not in w. but in power
12. 8. w. of wisdom, to another w. of knowledge
2 Cor. 1. 18. our w. toward you was not yea and nay
5. 19. God committed to us the w. of reconciliation
10. 11. such as we are in w. by letters when absent
Gal. 5. 14. all the law is fulfilled in one w.
6. 6. let him that is taught in the w. communicate
Eph. 5. 26. cleanse with washing of water by the w.
Phil. 1. 14. are bold to speak the w. without fear
2. 16. holding forth the w. of life to rejoice in day
Col. 1. 5. heard in the w. of the truth of the gospel
3. 16. let the w. of Christ dwell in you richly
17. whatsoever ye do in w. or deed, do in name
1 Thess. 1. 5. our gospel come not to you in w. only
6. having received the w. in much affliction
2. 13. ye received it not as w. of men, but as it is in truth w. of God working effectually in you
2 Thess. 2. 2. or be troubled, not by Spirit, nor by w.
15. have been taught, whether by w. or our epistle
17. G. comfort and stablish you in every good w.
3. 14. if any man obey not our w. by this epistle
1 Tim. 4. 12. be thou an example of believers in w.
5. 17. they who labour in the w. and doctrine
2 Tim. 2. 17. their w. will eat as doth a canker
4. 2. preach w. be instant in season out of season
Tit. 1. 9. holding fast the faithful w. as taught
Heb. 1. 3. upholding all things by the w. of his power
2. 2. if the w. spoken by angels was stedfast
4. 2. but the w. preached did not profit them
5. 13. is unskilful in the w. of righteousness
7. 28. but the w. of the oath, which was since the law
12. 19. entreated w. should not be spoken any more
13. 22. brethren, suffer the w. of exhortation
Jam. 1. 21. receive with meekness the ingrafted w.
22. be ye doers of the w. and not hearers only
23. if any be a hearer of the w. and not a doer
3. 2. if any man offend not in w. is a perfect man
1 Pet. 2. 2. as babes desire the sincere milk of the w.
8. even to them who stumble at the w. being
3. 1. if any obey not the w. may without the w.
2 Pet. 1. 19. we have a more sure w. of prophecy
3. 7. the heavens by the same w. are kept in store
1 John 1. 1. our hands have handled the w. of life
3. 18. let us not love in w. but in deed and truth
5. 7. the Father, the W. and the Holy Ghost are one
Rev. 3. 10. because thou hast kept w. of my patience
12. 11. they overcame by the w. of their testimony

WORD *of God.*

1 Sam. 9. 27. that I may shew thee the w. of God
1 Kings 12. 22. the w. of God came to Shemaiah
1 Chron. 17. 3. the w. of God came to Nathan
Prov. 30. 5. every w. of God is pure, he is a shield
Isa. 40. 8. the w. of our God shall stand for ever
Mark 7. 13. making the w. of God of none effect
Luke 3. 2. the w. of God came unto John in wildern.
4. 4. not by bread alone, but by every w. of God
5. 1. the people pressed on him to hear the w. of G.
8. 11. parable is this, the seed is the w. of God
21. my brethren are these that hear the w. of God
11. 28. blessed are they that hear the w. of God
John 10. 35. if he called them gods to whom w. of G.
Acts 4. 31. they spake the w. of God with boldness
6. 2. not reason that we should leave the w. of God
7. the w. of God increased in Jerusalem, 12. 24.
8. 14. that Samaria had received the w. of God
11. 1. the Gentiles had received the w. of God
13. 7. Sergius Paulus desired to hear the w. of God
44. the whole city came to hear the w. of God
46. w. of God should have been first spoken to you
19. 20. so mightily grew the w. of God and prevailed
Rom. 9. 6. not as tho' w. of G. hath taken none effect
10. 17. faith by hearing, hearing by the w. of God
1 Cor. 14. 36. came the w. of God out from you?
2 Cor. 2. 17. as many which corrupt the w. of God
4. 2. not handling the w. of God deceitfully
Eph. 6. 17. take the helmet of salvation, and the sword of the Spirit, which is the w. of God
Col. 1. 25. which is given me to fulfil the w. of God
1 Thess. 2. 13. when ye received the w. of God
1 Tim. 4. 5. it is sanctified by w. of God and prayer
2 Tim. 2. 9. but the w. of God is not bound
Tit. 2. 5. that the w. of God be not blasphemed
Heb. 4. 12. the w. of God is quick and powerful
6. 5. and have tasted the good w. of God
11. 3. the worlds were framed by the w. of God
13. 7. who have spoken to you the w. of God
1 Pet. 1. 23. being born again by the w. of God
2 Pet. 3. 5. by the w. of God the heavens were of old
1 John 2. 14. are strong, the w. of God abideth in you
Rev. 1. 2. who bare record of the w. of God
9. I was in the isle of Patmos for the w. of God
6. 9. the souls of them that were slain for w. of God
19. 13. his name is called the w. of God
20. 4. them that were beheaded for the w. of God

See HEARD.

His WORD.

Num. 27. 21. at his w. shall they go out, and at his w. they shall come in, both he and Israel
30. 2. if a man vow a vow, he shall not break his w.
1 Sam. 1. 23. only the Lord establish his w.
2 Sam. 23. 2. and his w. was in my tongue
1 Kings 2. 4. that the Lord may continue his w.
8. 20. Lord hath performed his w. that he spake, I am risen up in room of my father, 2 Chr. 6. 10.
2 Kings 1. 16. no God in Israel, to inquire of his w.
2 Chr. 10. 15. that the Lord might perform his w.
Psal. 56. 4. in God will I praise his w. in him trust, 10.
103. 20. hearkening unto the voice of his w.
105. 19. until the time that his w. came
28. and they rebelled not against his w.
106. 24. they believed not his w. but murmured
107. 20. he sent his w. and healed them
130. 5. I wait for the Lord and in his w. do I hope

Psal. 147. 15. his w. runneth very swiftly
18. he sendeth out his w. and melteth them
19. he sheweth his w. unto Jacob, his statutes
148. 8. snow, vapour, stormy wind fulfilling his w.
Isa. 66. 5. hear, ye that tremble at his w.
Jer. 20. 9. but his w. was in my heart as a fire
Lam. 2. 17. he hath fulfilled his w. he commanded
Joel 2. 11. he is strong that executeth his w.
Mat. 8. 16. he cast out the spirits with his w.
Luke 4. 32. astonished, for his w. was with power
John 4. 41. many believed because of his own w.
5. 38. ye have not his w. abiding in you
Acts 2. 41. they that gladly received his w.
Tit. 1. 3. but hath in due times manifested his w.
1 John 2. 5. whoso keepeth his w. in him is the love

See LORD.

My WORD.

Num. 11. 23. whether my w. shall come to pass
20. 24. because ye rebelled against my w.
1 Kings 6. 12. then will I perform my w. with thee
17. 1. no dew nor rain, but according to my w.
Isa. 55. 11. so shall my w. be that goeth out of mouth
66. 2. I will look to him that trembleth at my w.
Jer. 1. 12. I will hasten my w. to perform it
23. 28. he that hath my w. let him speak my w.
29. is not my w. like as a fire, saith the Lord?
30. I am against the prophets that steal my w.
29. 10. I will perform my good w. towards you
Mat. 24. 35. but my w. shall not pass away
John 5. 24. he that heareth my w. and believeth
8. 31. continue in my w. ye are my disciples indeed
37. to kill me bec. my w. hath no place in you
43. even because ye cannot hear my w.
Rev. 3. 8. thou hast kept my w. not denied my name

This WORD.

Exod. 14. 12. is not this the w. that we did tell thee?
Josh. 14. 10. since the Lord spake this w. to Moses
2 Sam. 19. 14. they sent this w. to the king
1 Kings 2. 23. hast not spoken this w. against his life
2 Kings 19. 21. this is the w. that the Lord hath spoken of him, Isa. 16. 13. | 24. 3. | 37. 22.
Ezra 6. 11. that whosoever shall alter this w.
10. 5. swear that they should do according to this w.
Isa. 8. 20. if they speak not according to this w.
30. 12. because ye despise this w. and trust in oppres.
Jer. 5. 14. because ye speak this w. 23. 38.
7. 2. proclaim there this w. and say, hear word
13. 12. thou shalt speak unto them this w.
14. 17. therefore shalt thou say this w. to them
22. 1. Lord said, go down, and speak there this w.
26. 1. in the reign of Jehoiakim this w. came from the Lord, saying, 27. 1. | 34. 8. | 36. 1.
28. 7. hear now this w. Amos 3. 1. | 4. 1. | 5. 1.
Dan. 10. 11. when he had spoken this w. to me
Zech. 4. 6. this is the w. of the Lord to Zerubbabel
Acts 22. 22. they gave him audience to this w.
Rom. 9. 9. for this is w. of promise, Sarah have a son
Heb. 12. 27. this w. yet once more signifieth
1 Pet. 1. 25. this is the w. which is preached to you

Thy WORD.

Gen. 30. 34. I would it might be according to thy w.
41. 40. according to thy w. shall my people be ruled
Exod. 8. 10. he said, be it according to thy w.
Num. 14. 20. I have pardoned, according to thy w.
Deut. 33. 9. have observed thy w. and kept covenant
1 Kings 3. 12. I have done according to thy w.
8. 26. let thy w. I pray thee, be verified
18. 36. I have done all these things at thy w.
22. 13. let thy w. I pray thee, be like the word of one of them and speak what is good, 2 Chr. 18. 12.
Psal. 119. 9. by taking heed according to thy w.
11. thy w. have I hid in mine heart, not to sin
16. will delight in statutes, I will not forget thy w.
17. that I may live, and keep thy w. 101.
25. quicken me according to thy w. 107. 154.
28. strengthen thou me according to thy w. 116.
38. stablish thy w. || 42. I trust in thy w.
41. even thy salvation according to thy w.
50. comfort in affliction, for thy w. quickened me
58. be merciful to me according to thy w. 65, 76.
67. I went astray, but now have I kept thy w.
74. because I have hoped in thy w. 147.
81. I hope in thy w. 114. || 140. thy w. is pure
82. mine eyes fail for thy w. || 105. thy w. is a lamp
89. for ever, O Lord, thy w. is settled in heaven
133. order my steps in thy w. let not iniquity
148. night-watches, that I might meditate in thy w.
158. I was grieved, because they kept not thy w.
160. thy w. is true || 162. I rejoice at thy w.
161. but my heart standeth in awe of thy w.
169. give me understanding according to thy w.
170. supplication, deliver me according to thy w.
172. my tongue shall speak of thy w. for thy com.
138. 2. thou hast magnified thy w. above thy name
Jer. 15. 16. thy w. was to me the joy of my heart
Ezek. 20. 46. drop thy w. toward the south, prophesy
21. 2. drop thy w. toward the holy places, prophesy
Amos 7. 16. drop not thy w. against house of Isaac
Hab. 3. 9. thy bow was made naked, even thy w.
Luke 1. 38. be it unto me according to thy w.
2. 29. servant depart in peace, according to thy w.
5. 5. nevertheless at thy w. I will let down the net
John 17. 6. thine they were, and they have kept thy w.
14. I have given them thy w. || 17. thy w. is truth
Acts 4. 29. with all boldness they may speak thy w.

See TRUTH.

WORDS.

Gen. 11. † 1. the whole earth was of one w.
Exod. 4. † 10. and Moses said, I am not a man of w.
15. and thou shalt put w. in his mouth
5. 9. more work, and let them not regard vain w.
19. 8. Moses returned the w. of the people
23. 8. gift perverteth w. of righteous, Deut. 16. 19.
34. 1. the w. which were in the first tables
28. Moses wrote the w. of the covenant, Deut. 10. 2.
Deut. 2. 26. I sent to Sihon with w. of peace
28. 14. thou shalt not go aside from any of the w.
29. 9. keep the w. of his covenant and do them, that ye may prosper, 2 Kings 23. 3, 24. 2 Chron. 34. 31.
32. 1. give ear, O heavens, hear, O earth, the w. of my mouth, Psal. 54. 2. | 78. 1. Prov. 7. 24.
1 Sam. 28. 20. Saul was afraid of the w. of Samuel

2 Sam. 19. 43. the w. of men of Judah were fiercer
1 Kings 22. 13. behold, the w. of prophets declare good to the king with one mouth, 2 Chr. 18. 12.
2 Kings 6. 12. Elisha telleth the w. thou speakest
18. 20. but they are but vain w. Isa. 36. 5.
2 Chron. 9. † 29. Solomon's acts written in w. of Nat.
12. † 15. in w. of Shemaiah || 20. † 34. in w. of Jehu
29. 30. to sing praises with the w. of David
32. 8. the people rested on the w. of Hezekiah
Esth. 9. 30. he sent letters with w. of peace and truth
Job 6. 26. do ye imagine to reprove w. and speeches
8. 2. shall the w. of thy mouth be like a strong wind?
12. 11. doth not the ear try w.? 34. 3.
15. 13. thou lettest such w. go out of thy mouth
16. 3. shall vain w. have an end, or what emboldens
4. I could heap up w. against you and shake my
18. 2. how long will it be ere ye make an end of w.?
19. 2. how long will ye break me in pieces with w.?
23. 5. I would know the w. he would answer me
12. I have esteemed the w. of his mouth more
35. 16. he multiplieth w. without knowledge
36. † 2. shew thee, that there are yet w. for God
38. 2. who is this that darkeneth counsel by w.?
Psal. 19. 14. let the w. of my mouth be acceptable
22. 1. why so far from the w. of my roaring?
36. 3. the w. of his mouth are iniquity and deceit
52. 4. thou lovest all devouring w. O deceitful tongue
55. 21. w. of his mouth were smoother than butter
59. 12. for w. of their lips, let them be taken
65. † 3. w. of iniquities prevail against me
137. † 3. they required of us the w. of a song
Prov. 1. 6. to understand the w. of the wise
4. 5. decline not from the w. of my mouth, 5. 7.
6. 2. thou art snared with the w. of thy mouth
10. 19. in multitude of w. there wanteth not sin
12. 6. w. of the wicked are to lie in wait for blood
15. 26. the w. of the pure are pleasant w.
18. 4. the w. of a man's mouth are as deep waters
8. the w. of a tale-bearer are as wounds, 26. 22.
19. 7. he pursueth them with w. they are wanting
27. he causeth thee to err from w. of knowledge
22. 12. he overthrows the w. of the transgressor
17. bow down thine ear, hear the w. of the wise
21. make thee know certainty of the w. of truth that thou mightest answer the w. of truth
23. 8. and thou shalt lose thy sweet w.
29. 19. a servant will not be corrected by w.
Eccl. 5. 3. fool's voice known by multitude of w. 10. 14.
10. 12. the w. of a wise man's mouth are gracious
12. 10. the preacher sought to find out acceptable w. what was written, even the w. of truth
11. the w. of the wise are as goads and as nails
Isa. 29. 11. is become as the w. of a book sealed
37. 4. it may be God will hear the w. of Rabshakeh
59. 13. uttering from the heart w. of falsehood
Jer. 11. 2. hear ye the w. of this covenant, 6.
23. 9. because of the Lord and w. of his holiness
35. 14. w. of Jonadab son of Rechab are performed
44. 28. remnant shall know whose w. shall stand
Ezek. 3. 6. whose w. thou canst not understand
Dan. 7. 25. shall speak great w. against most High
12. 4. shut up the w. || 9. the w. are closed up
Hos. 6. 5. I have slain them by the w. of my mouth
14. 2. take with you w. and turn to the Lord
Zech. 1. 13. answered with good and comfortable w.
7. 7. should ye not hear the w. the Lord hath cried
Mat. 26. 44. saying the same w. Mark 14. 39.
Luke 4. 22. all wondered at gracious w. which proc
John 6. 63. the w. I speak to you they are life
68. to whom we go? thou hast the w. of eternal life
17. 8. I have given to them the w. thou gavest me
Acts 2. 40. with many other w. did he testify
7. 22. Moses was mighty in w. and in deeds
10. 22. Cornelius was warned to hear w. of thee
11. 14. send for Peter, who shall tell thee w.
15. 15. to this agree the w. of the prophets
24. that certain have troubled you with w.
18. 15. but if it be a question of w. and names
20. 35. to remember the w. of the Lord Jesus
38. sorrowing most of all for the w. he spake
26. 25. but I speak forth w. of truth and soberness
Rom. 16. 18. by good w. deceive hearts of the simple
1 Cor. 1. 17. not with wisdom of w. 2. 4, 13.
14. 9. except ye utter w. easy to be understood
19. I had rather speak five w. with understanding
Eph. 5. 6. let no man deceive you with vain w.
1 Tim. 4. 6. nourished up in w. of faith and doctrine
2 Tim. 2. 14. that they strive not about w. to no profit
4. 15. for he hath greatly withstood our w.
2 Pet. 3. 2. be mindful of the w. spoken by prophets
Rev. 1. 3. hear the w. of this prophecy, 22. 18.
22. 19. take away from the w. of this prophecy

All the WORDS.

Gen. 45. 27. they told Jacob all the w. of Joseph
Exod. 4. 28. Moses told Aaron all the w. of the Lord
24. 3. Moses told the people all the w. Num. 11. 24.
4. Moses wrote all the w. of the Lord and rose
Deut. 9. 10. on the tables were written all the w.
17. 19. keep all the w. || 29. 29. may do all the w.
27. 3. write on stones all the w. of this law, 8.
26. cursed is he that confirmeth not all the w.
28. 58. if thou wilt not observe to do all the w.
31. 12. and observe to do all the w. of this law
32. 44. Moses spake all the w. of this song in ears
46. set your hearts to all the w. I testify
Josh. 8. 34. he read all the w. of the law, blessings
1 Sam. 8. 10. Samuel told all the w. of the Lord
2 Kings 19. 4. it may be the Lord will hear all the w. of Rabshakeh sent by king of Assyria, Isa. 37. 17.
23. 2. Josiah read all the w. of the covenant found in the house of the Lord, 2 Chron. 34. 30.
Prov. 8. 8. all the w. of my mouth are righteousness
Eccl. 7. 21. also take no heed unto all the w. spoken
Jer. 11. 8. bring on them all the w. of this covenant
26. 2. speak all the w. that I command thee
20. according to all the w. of Jeremiah
30. 2. write all the w. I have spoken, 36. 2.
36. 4. Baruch wrote all the w. of the Lord, 32.
43. 1. when Jeremiah had ended all the w. of Lord
Acts 5. 20. speak to the people all the w. of this life

WORDS *of God.*

Num. 24. 4. hath said, which heard the w. of God, 16.

1 *Chr.* 25. 5. Heman the king's seer in the *w. of God*
Ezra 9. 4. every one that trembleth at the *w. of God*
Psal. 107. 11. they rebelled against the *w. of God*
John 3. 34. he whom God sent speaketh *w. of God*
8. 47. he that is of God heareth the *w. of God*
Rev. 17. 17. until the *w. of God* be fulfilled
See HEARD.

His WORDS.

Gen. 37. 8. they hated him yet the more for *his w.*
Deut. 4. 36. thou heardest *his w.* out of the fire
Judg. 11. 11. Jephthah uttered all *his w.* before Ld.
1 *Sam.* 3. 19. he let none of *his w.* fall to the ground
2 *Chr.* 36. 16. but they despised *his w.* and misused
Job 22. 22. and lay up *his w.* in thine heart
32. 14. now he hath not directed *his w.* against me
34. 35. and *his w.* were without wisdom
37. for he multiplieth *his w.* against God
Ps. 55. 21. *his w.* softer than oil, yet drawn swords
106. 12. then believed they *his w.* sang his praise
Prov. 17. 27. he that hath knowledge spareth *his w.*
29. 20. seest thou a man that is hasty in *his w.*
30. 6. add thou not unto *his w.* lest he reprove thee
Isa. 31. 2. the Lord will not call back *his w.*
Jer. 18. 18. let us not give heed to any of *his w.*
Dan. 9. 12. he hath confirmed *his w.* he spake
Amos 7. 10. the land is not able to bear all *his w.*
Mark 10. 24. the disciples were astonished at *his w.*
12. 13. to catch him in *his w. Luke* 20. 20.
Luke 20. 26. they could not take hold of *his w.*
24. 8. they remembered *his w.* and returned
See LORD.

My WORDS.

Num. 12. 6. he said, hear now *my w. Job* 34. 2.
Deut. 4. 10. I will make them hear *my w.*
11. 18. therefore lay up *my w.* in your heart
18. 18. and I will put *my w.* in his mouth
19. whosoever will not hearken to *my w.* I will require it of him, *Jer.* 29. 19. | 35. 13.
Neh. 6. 19. and they uttered *my w.* to him
Job 6. 3. therefore *my w.* are swallowed up
19. 23. O that *my w.* were now written!
29. 22. after my *w.* they spake not again
33. 1. hearken to all *my w.* 34. 16. *Acts* 2. 14.
3. *my w.* shall be of uprightn. of my heart, 36. 4.
Psal. 5. 1. give ear to *my w.* O Lord, consider
50. 17. seeing thou castest *my w.* behind thee
56. 5. every day they wrest *my w.* thought for evil
141. 6. they shall hear *my w.* for they are sweet
Prov. 1. 23. I will make known *my w.* unto you
2. 1. my son, if thou wilt receive *my w.*
4. 4. let thine heart retain *my w.* and live
4. 20. attend to *my w.* ‖ 7. 1. keep *my w.*
Isa. 51. 16. I have put *my w.* in thy mouth, and say to Zion, thou art my people, *Jer.* 1. 9.
59. 21. *my w.* which I have put in thy mouth
Jer. 5. 14. I will make *my w.* in thy mouth fire
6. 19. they have not hearkened to *my w.* nor law
11. 10. which refused to hear *my w.* 13. 10.
18. 2. there I will cause thee to hear *my w.*
19. 15. that they might not hear *my w.*
23. 22. if they caused my people to hear *my w.*
25. 8. because ye have not heard *my w.*
13. I will bring upon that land all *my w.*
39. 16. I will bring *my w.* on this city for evil
44. 29. you may know *my w.* shall surely stand
Ezek. 2. 7. thou shalt speak *my w.* to them, 3. 4, 10.
12. 28. there shall none of *my w.* be prolonged
Mic. 2. 7. do not *my w.* do good to him that walketh?
Zech. 1. 6. *my w.* did they not take hold of your fath.?
Mark 8. 38. whosoever shall be ashamed of me and *my w.* of him Son of man be ashamed, *Luke* 9. 26.
13. 31. but *my w.* shall not pass away, *Luke* 21. 33.
Luke 1. 20. because thou believest not *my w.* which shall be fulfilled in their season
John 5. 47. how shall ye believe *my w.*?
12. 47. if any man hear *my w.* and believe not
48. he that receiveth not *my w.* one judgeth him
14. 23. will keep *my w.* ‖ 15. 7. *my w.* abide in you

Their WORDS.

Gen. 34. 18. *their w.* pleased Hamor and Shechem
2 *Chron.* 9. 6. I believed not their *w.* until I came
Ps. 19. 4. their line is gone out thro' all the earth, *their w.* to the end of the world, *Rom.* 10. 18.
Ezek. 2. 6. son of man, be not afraid of *their w.*
Luke 24. 11. *their w.* seemed to them as idle tales

These WORDS.

Gen. 39. 17. she spake to him according to *these w.*
43. 7. we told according to the tenor of *these w.*
Exod. 19. 6. *these* are the *w.* thou shalt speak, 7.
20. 1. God spake all *these w. Deut.* 5. 22.
34. 27. Lord said, write thou *these w. Jer.* 36. 17.
35. 1. *these* are the *w.* which the Lord hath commanded you to do them, *Deut.* 6 6. | 29. 1.
Num. 16. 31. as he had made an end of speaking all *these w.* ground clave, *Deut.* 32. 45. 1 *Sam.* 24. 16.
Deut. 12. 28. observe, hear all *these w. Zech.* 8. 9.
1 *Sam.* 21. 12. David laid up *these w.* in his heart
24. 7. David stayed his servants with *these w.*
2 *Sam.* 7. 17. according to all *these w.* and this vision so did Nathan speak to David, 1 *Chron.* 17. 15.
2 *Kings* 18. 27. hath my master sent me to thy master and to thee to speak *these w.*? *Isa.* 36. 12.
23. 16. the man of God proclaimed *these w.*
Jer. 3. 12. go proclaim *these w.* toward the north
7. 27. speak all *these w.* unto them, 26. 15.
16. 10. shew *these w.* ‖ 25. 30. prophesy all *these w.*
22. 5. but if ye will not hear *these w.* I swear
38. 24. Zedekiah said, let no man know of *these w.*
45. 1. when he had written *these w.* 51. 60.
51. 61. when thou shalt read all *these w.*
Luke 24. 44. *these* are the *w.* I spake unto you
John 9. 22. *these w.* spake his parents, feared Jews
10. 21. *these* are not *w.* of him that hath a devil
Acts 2. 22. ye men of Israel, hear *these w.* Jesus
10. 44. while Peter yet spake *these w.* Holy Ghost
13. 42. besought *these w.* might be preached to them
28. 29. when he had said *these w.* Jews departed
1 *Thess.* 4. 18. comfort one another with *these w.*
Rev. 21. 5. for *these w.* are true and faithful

Thy WORDS.

Deut. 33. 3. every one shall receive of *thy w.*
Josh. 1. 18. whosoever will not hearken to *thy w.*
Judg. 11. 10. if we do not according to *thy w.*
13. 12. Manoah said, now let *thy w.* come to pass
1 *Sam.* 15. 24. I have transgressed *thy w.*
28. 21. behold, I have hearkened to *thy w.*
2 *Sam.* 7. 21. *thy w.* sake hast thou done these things
28. thou art that God, and *thy w.* be true
1 *Kings* 1. 14. I will come in and confirm *thy w.*
Neh. 9. 8. for thou hast performed *thy w.*
Job 4. 4. *thy w.* upheld him that was falling
Psal. 119. 57. I said that I would keep *thy w.*
103. how sweet are *thy w.* to my taste!
130. the entrance of *thy w.* giveth light
139. mine enemies have forgotten *thy w.*
Prov. 23. 8. thou shalt lose *thy* sweet *w.*
9. he will despise the wisdom of *thy w.*
Eccl. 5. 2. be not rash, therefore let *thy w.* be few
Jer. 15. 16. *thy w.* were found, and I did eat them
Ezek. 33. 31. hear *thy w.* but do them not, 32.
Dan. 10. 12. fear not, Daniel, from the first day *thy w.* were heard, and I am come for *thy w.*
Mat. 12. 37. for by *thy w.* thou shalt be justified, and by *thy w.* thou shalt be condemned

Your WORDS.

Gen. 42. 16. kept in prison, that *your w.* be proved
20. bring Benjamin, so shall *your w.* be verified
44. 10. let it be according to *your w. Josh.* 2. 21.
Deut. 1. 34. the Lord heard the voice of *your w.* 5. 28.
Job 32. 11. behold, I waited for *your w.* I gave ear
Isa. 41. 26. there is none that heareth *your w.*
Jer. 42. 4. I will pray to God according to *your w.*
Ezek. 35. 13. ye have multiplied *your w.* against me
Mal. 2. 17. ye have wearied the Lord with *your w.*
3. 13. *your w.* have been stout against me, saith Ld.
Mat. 10. 14. shall not receive you nor hear *your w.*

WORK

Is taken, (1) *For such business as is proper to every man's calling, which may be done in six days.* Exod. 20. 9. Six days shalt thou labour and do all thy *work.* (2) *For any thought, word, or outward action, whether good or evil.* Eccl. 12. 14. God shall bring every *work* into judgment. (3) Work *is put for wages.* Lev. 19. 13. *The wages, in Hebrew,* the *work,* of him that is hired, shall not abide with thee all night. *So in* Job 7. 2. As an hireling looketh for the reward of his *work, Heb.* for his *work.* (4) Work *is put for vengeance or judgment.* Isa. 5. 19. Let him make speed and hasten his *work: " Let him begin to execute vengeance as soon as he pleases." And in* Isa. 28. 21. That he may do his *work,* his strange *work: " That he may execute his extraordinary and unusual judgment against Israel; a judgment contrary to the benignity of God's nature, and to his usual way of dealing with his people."* (5) Work *is put for miracle,* John 7. 21. I have done one *work,* and ye all marvel. *The miracle our Saviour speaks of, is his healing the man who lay at the pool of Bethesda.*

The *works* of God denote, (1) *His* work *of creation.* Gen. 2. 2. On the seventh day God ended his *work.* (2) *His* works *of providence in preserving and governing the world.* John 5. 17. My Father *worketh* hitherto. (3) The work *of redemption is called* God's work. *John* 9. 4. I must *work* the *works* of him that sent me. *And particularly the faith of true believers is called* the work of God. *John* 6. 29. This is the *work* of God, that ye believe on him whom he hath sent. *The* work *of redemption is attributed to the Three Persons of the Trinity, and their acts herein are of the same extent: The Father loves those that are given to Christ in the covenant of redemption, and Christ is the Saviour of those that are loved by the Father; and the Spirit sanctifies those that are justified through the merits of Christ's blood. Thus there is a chain in salvation, the beginning is from the Father, the dispensation through the Son, and the application by the Spirit. So in looking after the comfort of election, believers must first look inward to the* work *of the Spirit on their hearts, then outward to the* work *of Christ on the cross, then upward to the everlasting love of the Father in heaven,* 1 Pet. 1. 2.

By good works *are to be understood all manner of duties inward and outward, as well thoughts, as words and actions, toward God or man, which are commanded in the law of God, and proceed from a pure heart and faith unfeigned, and are referred unto God's glory; for it is necessary that* good works *proceed from right principles, and have right motives and ends, namely, a principle of love to God, the motive of obedience to God's law, and the glory of God as the chief end.* 1 Cor. 10. 31. Whether therefore ye eat or drink, or whatsoever ye do, do all to the glory of God. *Eph.* 2. 10. For we are his workmanship, created in Christ Jesus unto good works.

It is said, James 2. 24. You see that by *works* a man is justified. *The apostle does not there treat of our justification in the sight of God, but of the justification of our faith in the sight of man, and therefore asserts that justification is by* works, ver. 18. I will shew thee my faith by my *works, for* works *justify our faith, and declare us to be justified before men, who cannot see nor know our faith but by our* works. *St. Paul, in his Epistles to the Romans and Galatians, asserts, by many arguments, our justification by faith, that receives and relies upon the righteousness of Christ, that is,* his obedience and sufferings, *Rom.* 3. 24, 28. *And surely the apostles, being inspired by the same Spirit, cannot be supposed to contradict one another.*

Man, because he is depraved and weakened with original sin, is not able to fulfil the law, and cannot be justified or accepted before God, on account of his works, for by the works of the law shall no flesh be justified, *Rom.* 3. 20. *Gal.* 2. 16. *The righteousness of Christ is the sole meritorious cause of our justification; but those that are justified, are also sanctified, and will be careful to maintain good* works, for without holiness no man shall see the Lord, *Heb.* 12. 14. *Christ's righteousness received by faith, and imputed to true believers, is the cause of their justification, and gives them a gracious title to heaven, and sanctification makes them meet for it. Bernard says,* Bona opera sunt via ad regnum, non causa regnandi; " *Good* works *are the way to the kingdom, not the cause of entering the kingdom.*"

Exod. 5. 9. let there more *w.* be laid on the men
12. 16. no manner of *w.* shall be done in them, 20. 10. *Lev.* 16. 29. | 23. 3, 28, 31. *Num.* 29. 7.
18. 20. shew them the *w.* that they must do
31. 14. whoso doeth any *w.* therein shall be cut off from amongst the people, 15. *Lev.* 23. 30.
35. 2. six days shall *w.* be done, 20. 9.
36. 7. sufficient for all the *w.* and too much
Lev. 23. 7. in seventh day an holy convocation, ye shall do no servile *w.* therein, 8. 21, 25, 35, 36. *Num.* 28. 18, 25, 26. | 29. 1, 12, 35.
Deut. 4. 28. the *w.* of men's hands, 27. 15. 2 *Kings* 19. 18. 2 *Chron.* 32. 19. *Psal.* 115. 4. | 135. 15.
5. 14. the sabbath of the Lord thy God, in it thou shalt not do any *w.* 16. 8. *Jer.* 17. 22, 24.
14. 29. that the L. may bless thee in all *w.* of thy hand which thou doest, 24. 19. | 28. 12. | 30. 9.
15. 19. do no *w.* with the firstling of thy bullock
31. 29. to provoke him to anger through the *w.* of your hands, 1 *Kings* 16. 7. *Jer.* 32. 30.
33. 11. bless the L. and accept the *w.* of his hands
1 *Kings* 5. 16. chief of Solomon's officers which were over the *w.* 9. 23. 1 *Chr.* 29. 6. 2 *Chr.* 2. 18.
7. 8. his house had another court of the like *w.*
2 *Kings* 12. 11. into hands that did the *w.* 22. 5, 9.
1 *Chron.* 9. 33. employed in that *w.* day and night
16. 37. to minister as every day's *w.* required
29. 1. Solomon young, and the *w.* is great, *Neh.* 4. 19.
2 *Chron.* 31. 21. in every *w.* that he began, he did it
34. 12. the men did the *w.* faithfully
Ezra 4. 24. then ceased the *w.* of the house of God
5. 8. this *w.* goeth fast on, prospereth in their hands
6. 7. let the *w.* of this house of God alone
22. to strengthen their hands in the *w.* of house
10. 13. neither is it a *w.* of one day or two
Neh. 3. 5. but their nobles put not their necks to *w.*
4. 11. slay them, and cause the *w.* to cease
6. 3. why should the *w.* cease whilst I leave it?
16. they perceived this *w.* was wrought of God
7. 70. the chief of the fathers gave to the *w.*
Job 1. 10. thou hast blessed the *w.* of his hands
10. 3. thou shouldest despise the *w.* of thine hands
14. 15. thou wilt have a desire to *w.* of thy hands
24. 5. as wild asses go they forth to their *w.*
34. 11. for the *w.* of a man shall he render to him, cause to find according to his ways, 1 *Pet.* 1. 17.
19. for they are all the *w.* of his hands
36. 9. he sheweth them their *w.* and transgression
Psal. 8. 3. when I consider the *w.* of thy fingers, 6.
9. 16. the wicked is snared in the *w.* of his hands
19. 1. the firmament sheweth his handy *w.*
28. 4. give them after the *w.* of their hands
44. 1. we heard what *w.* thou didst in their days
90. 17. establish thou the *w.* of our hands upon us
95. 9. when your fathers proved me and saw my *w.*
101. 3. I hate the *w.* of them that turn aside
102. 25. the heavens are the *w.* of thy hands
143. 5. I muse on the *w.* of thy hands
Prov. 11. 18. the wicked worketh a deceitful *w.*
Eccl. 3. 17. there is a time there for every *w.*
5. 6. why should God destroy the *w.* of thine hands?
8. 9. I applied my heart to every *w.* under the sun
14. to whom it happeneth according to *w.* of the wicked, according to the *w.* of the righteous
9. 10. there is no *w.* in grave whither thou goest
12. 14. God will bring every *w.* into judgment
Cant. 7. 1. *w.* of the hands of a cunning workman
Isa. 2. 8. they worship the *w.* of their own hands, 37. 19. *Jer.* 1. 16. | 10. 3, 9, 15. | 51. 18.
17. 8. he shall not look to the *w.* of his hands
19. 15. neither shall there be any *w.* for Egypt
25. blessed be Assyria the *w.* of my hands
28. 21. that he may do his *w.* his strange *w.*
29. 16. shall the *w.* say of him that made it
23. he seeth his children, and the *w.* of my hands
32. 17. the *w.* of the righteousness shall be peace
45. 11. concerning the *w.* of my hands command me
49. 4. yet surely my *w.* is with my God
60. 21. they shall inherit the *w.* of my hands
61. 8. and I will direct their *w.* in truth
64. 8. and we all are the *w.* of thy hands
65. 22. mine elect shall long enjoy *w.* of their hands
Jer. 32. 19. great in counsel and mighty in *w.*
50. 29. recompense her according to *w. Lam.* 3. 64.
Ezek. 15. 3. shall wood be taken to do any *w.*?
4. is it meet for any *w.*? ‖ 5. it was meet for no *w.*
16. 30. the *w.* of an imperious whorish woman
Hos. 13. 2. all of it the *w.* of the craftsman
14. 3. will say no more to the *w.* of our hands
Mic. 5. 13. shalt no more worship *w.* of thine hands
Hab. 1. 5. for I will work a *w.* in your days
Hag. 2. 14. and so is every *w.* of their hands
Mark 6. 5. he could there do no mighty *w.*
John 7. 21. I have done one *w.* and ye marvel
17. 4. I have finished the *w.* thou gavest me to do
Acts 5. 38. if this *w.* be of men it will come to nought
13. 2. for the *w.* whereunto I have called them
41. behold, ye despisers, and wonder, for I work a *w.* in your days, a *w.* which ye will not believe
14. 26. for the *w.* which they fulfilled
15. 38. who went not with them to the *w.*
Rom. 2. 15. which shew the *w.* of the law written
9. 28. a short *w.* will the Lord make upon the earth
11. 6. no more grace, otherwise *w.* is no more *w.*
1 *Cor.* 3. 13. every man's *w.* shall be made manifest
14. if any man's *w.* abide ‖ 15. if *w.* be burnt
9. 1. are not ye my *w.* in the Lord?
Eph. 4. 12. he gave some for the *w.* of the ministry
Phil. 2. 30. for the *w.* of Christ he was nigh death
2 *Thess.* 1. 11. that God may fulfil the *w.* of faith
2. 17. establish you in every good word and *w.*
2 *Tim.* 4. 5. do the *w.* of an evangelist, make full

Jam. 1. 4. let patience have her perfect w.
25. but a doer of the w. shall be blessed
See Evil.

WORK of God, WORKS of God.

Exod. 32. 16. the tables were the w. of God
Job 37. 14. consider the wondrous w. of God
Psal. 64. 9. all men shall declare the w. of God
66. 5. come and see the w. of God, he is terrible
78. 7. that they might not forget the w. of God
Eccl. 7. 13. consider the w. of God who can make
8. 17. then I beheld all the w. of God
11. 5. even so thou knowest not the w. of God
John 6. 28. that we might work the w. of God
29. this is the w. of God that ye believe on me
9. 3. that w. of God might be made manifest
Acts 2. 11. we hear them speak the w. of God
Rom. 14. 20. for meat destroy not the w. of God
See Good, Great.

His WORK.

Gen. 2. 2. God ended his w. || 3. rested from his w.
Exod. 36. 4. they came every man from his w.
Deut. 32. 4. he is the rock, his w. is perfect
Judg. 19. 16. an old man came from his w. at even
1 Sam. 8. 16. he will take asses and put to his w.
1 Kings 7. 14. Hiram came and wrought all his w.
1 Chron. 4. 23. they dwelt with the king for his w.
2 Chron. 8. 9. of Israel he made no servants for his w.
16. 5. Baasha let his w. cease, he left off building
Neh. 4. 15. that we returned every man to his w.
Job 7. 2. an hireling looketh for the reward of his w.
36. 24. remember that thou magnify his w.
37. 7. that all men may know his w.
Psal. 62. 12. to thee mercy, for thou renderest to
every man according to his w. Prov. 24. 29.
104. 23. man goeth forth to his w. and labour
111. 3. his w. is honourable and glorious
Prov. 16. 11. all the weights of the bag are his w.
20. 11. whether his w. be pure or whether right
21. 8. but as for the pure his w. is right
Isa. 5. 19. let him hasten his w. that we may see it
10. 12. the Lord hath performed his whole w.
28. 21. that he may do his w. his strange w.
40. 10. behold, his w. is before him, 62. 11.
54. 16. that bringeth forth an instrument for his w.
Jer. 22. 13. that giveth him not for his w.
Hab. 2. 18. the maker of his w. trusteth therein
Mark 13. 34. who gave to every man his w.
John 4. 34. my meat is to finish his w.
Gal. 6. 4. let every man prove his own w.
Rev. 22. 12. to give every man as his w. shall be
See Lord, Needle.

Our WORK.

Gen. 5. 29. this shall comfort us concerning our w.

Thy WORK.

Exod. 20. 9. six days do all thy w. 23. 12. Deut. 5. 13.
Ruth 2. 12. the Lord recompense thy w.
Psal. 77. 12. I will meditate also of all thy w.
90. 16. let thy w. appear unto thy servants
92. 4. thou, Lord, hast made me glad thro' thy w.
Prov. 24. 27. prepare thy w. without and make it fit
Isa. 45. 9. or shall thy w. say he hath no hands?
Jer. 31. 16. for thy w. shall be rewarded, saith the L.
Hab. 3. 2. revive thy w. in the midst of the years

Your WORK.

Exod. 5. 11. not ought of your w. shall be diminished
2 Chron. 15. 7. for your w. shall be rewarded
Isa. 41. 24. ye are of nothing, your w. is of nought
1 Thess. 1. 3. remember. your w. faith, labour of love
Heb. 6. 10. God is not unrighteous to forget your w.

WORK-fellow.

Rom. 16. 21. Timothy my w.-fellow saluteth you

WORK, Verb.

Exod. 5. 18. go and w. || 34. 21. six days thou shalt w.
35. 2. whoso doeth w. therein shall be put to death
Josh. 9. 4. they did w. wilily and went and made
1 Sam. 14. 6. it may be that the Lord will w. for us
1 Kings 21. 20. thou hast sold thyself to w. evil, 25.
Neh. 4. 6. for the people had a mind to w.
Job 23. 9. on the left hand where he doth w.
Psal. 58. 2. yea, in heart you w. wickedness
119. 126. it is time for thee, Lord, to w.
Prov. 11. 18. the wicked w. a deceitful work
Isa. 19. 9. they that w. in flax, shall be confounded
43. 13. I will w. and who shall let it
Ezek. 33. 26. ye w. abomination and ye defile
Dan. 11. 23. and he shall w. deceitfully
Mic. 2. 1. woe to them that w. evil upon their beds
Hab. 1. 5. I will w. a work in your days, which ye
will not believe, tho' it be told you, Acts 13. 41.
Hag. 2. 4. w. for I am with you, saith the Lord
Mal. 3. 15. they that w. wickedness are set up
Mat. 21. 28. son, go w. to-day in my vineyard
Luke 13. 14. six days in which men ought to w.
John 5. 17. my Father worketh hitherto, and I w.
6. 28. that we might w. the works of God
30. they said unto him, what dost thou w.?
9. 4. I must w. the works of him that sent me while
it is day, the night cometh when no man can w.
Rom. 7. 5. sin by the law did w. in our members
8. 28. we know that all things w. together for good
Eph. 4. 19. to w. all uncleanness with greediness
Phil. 2. 12. w. out your own salvation with fear
1 Thess. 4. 11. study to w. with your own hands
2 Thess. 2. 7. the mystery of iniquity doth w.
3. 10. if any would not w. neither should he eat
12. we exhort that with quietness they w.
See Iniquity.

WORKER.

1 Kings 7. 14. Hiram of Naphtali was a w. in brass

WORKERS.

2 Kings 23. 24. w. with familiar spirits and wizards
2 Cor. 6. 1. we then as w. together with him
11. 13. for such are false apostles, deceitful w.
Phil. 3. 2. beware of dogs, beware of evil w.
See Iniquity.

WORKS.

Exod. 5. 13. fulfil your w. and your daily tasks
Num. 16. 28. the Lord hath sent me to do all these w.
Deut. 2. 7. the Lord blessed thee in all the w. 16. 15.
Judg. 2. 10. a generation which knew not the w.
1 Sam. 8. 8. according to all the w. they have done
1 Kings 13. 11. told him all the w. the man of G. did
2 Kings 22. 17. have forsaken me and provoked me to
anger with all the w. of their hands, 2 Chr. 34. 25.
Neh. 9. 35. nor turned they from their wicked w.
Psal. 14. 1. corrupt, they have done abominable w.
17. 4. concerning the w. of men by word of thy lips
92. 4. I will triumph in the w. of thy hands
111. 2. the w. of the Lord are great, sought out
7. the w. of his hands are verity and judgment
138. 8. forsake not the w. of thine own hands
141. 4. to practise wicked w. with men that
Prov. 31. 31. let her own w. praise her in the gates
Eccl. 1. 14. I have seen the w. that are done, 2. 11.
Isa. 26. 12. thou hast wrought all our w. in us
Jer. 7. 13. because ye have done all these w.
25. 6. provoke me not to anger with the w. of your
hands to your own hurt, 7. | 44. 8.
14. recompense them according to their deeds and
the w. of their hands, Rev. 2. 23.
Ezek. 6. 6. that your w. may be abolished
Dan. 4. 37. honour him whose w. are truth
Mic. 6. 16. the w. of the house of Ahab are kept
Mat. 11. 2. John heard in prison the w. of Christ
John 5. 20. he will shew him greater w. than these
36. the w. which the Father hath given me, the
same w. that I do bear witness of me
7. 3. thy disciples may see the w. that thou doest
7. because I testify that the w. thereof are evil
8. 39. if children, ye would do the w. of Abraham
9. 4. I must work the w. of him that sent me
10. 25. the w. that I do in my Father's name
32. for which of these w. do ye stone me?
37. if I do not the w. || 38. believe the w.
14. 10. he doeth the w. || 11. believe for the w.
12. the w. that I do, shall he do, and greater w.
15. 24. if I had not done among them the w.
Acts 7. 41. they rejoiced in the w. of their hands
26. 20. Gentiles should do w. meet for repentance
Rom. 3. 27. by what law? of w.? nay, but of faith
4. 2. for if Abraham were justified by w.
6. God imputeth righteousness without w.
9. 11. not of w. but of him that calleth
32. not by faith, but as it were by the w. of the law
11. 6. if by grace, then is it no more of w. but if it
be of w. is it no more of grace
13. 12. let us therefore cast off the w. of darkness
Gal. 2. 16. knowing a man is not justified by the w.
of the law, for by the w. of law no flesh is justified
3. 2. received ye the Spirit by the w. of the law?
5. doeth he it by the w. of the law, or by faith?
10. as many as are of w. of the law, under curse
5. 19. the w. of the flesh are manifest, adultery
Eph. 2. 9. not of w. lest any man should boast
5. 11. with the unfruitful w. of darkness
Col. 1. 21. and enemies in your mind by wicked w.
1 Thess. 5. 13. to esteem in love for their w. sake
2 Tim. 1. 9. saved us, not according to our w. Tit. 3. 5.
Tit. 1. 16. but in w. they deny God, abominable
Heb. 1. 10. the heavens are the w. of thy hands
2. 7. thou didst set him over the w. of thy hands
3. 9. your fathers saw my w. forty years in wildern.
4. 3. although the w. were finished from foundation
6. 1. the foundation of repentance from dead w.
9. 14. purge conscience from dead w. to serve God
Jam. 2. 14. if he have not w. can faith save him?
17. faith without w. is dead, being alone, 20. 26.
18. I have w. shew me thy faith without thy w.
2. 21. was not Abraham justified by w.?
22. and by w. was faith made perfect
24. ye see then that by w. a man is justified
25. was not Rahab the harlot justified by w.?
2 Pet. 3. 10. the earth and the w. therein burnt up
1 John 3. 8. that he might destroy the w. of devil
Rev. 2. 26. he that keepeth my w. to the end
9. 20. yet repented not of the w. of their hands
18. 6. double to her double, according to her w.
See Evil, Good, Work of God.

His WORKS.

1 Sam. 19. 4. his w. have been to thee very good
2 Chron. 32. 30. Hezekiah prospered in all his w.
Psal. 33. 4. and all his w. are done in truth
78. 11. forget his w. and his wonders, 106. 13.
103. 22. bless the Lord, all his w. in all places
104. 31. the Lord shall rejoice in his w.
107. 22. let them declare his w. with rejoicing
111. 6. he shewed his people the power of his w.
145. 9. his tender mercies are over all his w.
17. the Lord is holy in all his w.
Prov. 8. 22. the Lord possessed me before his w.
24. 12. shall not he render to every man according
to his w.? Mat. 16. 27. 2 Tim. 4. 14.
Eccl. 3. 22. a man should rejoice in his own w.
Dan. 9. 14. God is righteous in all his w.
Acts 15. 18. known to God are all his w.
Heb. 4. 4. rested the seventh day from all his w.
10. he also hath ceased from his own w.?
Jam. 2. 22. seest how faith wrought with his w.?
3. 13. shew out of a good conversation his w.
See Lord, Marvellous, Mighty.

Their WORKS.

Exod. 5. 4. why do ye let the people from their w.
23. 24. thou shalt not do after their w.
Neh. 6. 14. according to these their w.
Job 34. 25. therefore he knoweth their w.
Psal. 33. 15. he considereth all their w.
106. 35. and they learned their w.
39. thus were they defiled with their own w.
Eccl. 9. 1. and their w. are in the hand of God
Isa. 29. 15. their w. are in the dark, they say
41. 29. they are vanity, their w. are nothing
59. 6. nor shall they cover themselves with their w.
their w. are works of iniquity, wasting
66. 18. I know their w. and their thoughts
Amos 8. 7. I will never forget any of their w.
Jonah 3. 10. God saw their w. that they turned
Mat. 23. 3. but do not ye after their w.
5. all their w. they do to be seen of men
2 Cor. 11. 15. whose end be according to their w.
Rev. 14. 13. and their w. do follow them
20. 12. the dead judged according to their w. 13.

Thy WORKS.

Deut. 3. 24. who can do according to thy w.?
15. 10. the Lord shall bless thee in all thy w.
2 Chron. 20. 37. the Lord hath broken thy w.
Psal. 26. 7. tell of all thy wondrous w. 145. 4.
66. 3. say to God, how terrible art thou in thy w.
73. 28. trust in Lord, that I may declare all thy w.
86. 8. nor are there any works like unto thy w.
92. 5. O Lord, how great are thy w.
104. 13. earth is satisfied with fruit of thy w.
24. O Lord, how manifold are thy w.?
143. 5. I remember, I meditate on all thy w.
145. 10. all thy w. shall praise thee, O Lord
Prov. 16. 3. commit thy w. unto the Lord
Eccl. 9. 7. for now God accepteth thy w.
Isa. 57. 12. I will declare thy w. shall not profit
Jer. 48. 7. because thou hast trusted in thy w.
Jam. 2. 18. shew me thy faith without thy w.
Rev. 2. 2. I know thy w. 9, 13, 19. | 3. 1, 8, 15.
3. 2. I have not found thy w. perfect before God

Wonderful WORKS.

Psal. 40. 5. many, O Lord, are thy wonderful w.
78. 4. shewing his wonderful w. he hath done
107. 8. would praise the Lord for his wonderful w.
to the children of men, 15, 21, 31.
111. 4. made his wonderful w. to be remembered
Mat. 7. 22. in thy name have done wonderful w.
Acts 2. 11. Cretes and Arabians, we do hear them
speak in our tongues the wonderful w. of God
See Wondrous.

WORKETH.

Job 33. 29. lo, all these things w. God for man
Psal. 15. 2. he that walketh uprightly, and w.
righteousness shall dwell
101. 7. he that w. deceit shall not dwell in my ho.
Prov. 11. 18. the wicked w. a deceitful work
26. 28. a flattering mouth w. ruin
31. 13. she w. willingly with her hands
Eccl. 3. 9. what profit hath he that w.?
Isa. 44. 12. the smith with his tongs w. in the coals,
and he w. it with the strength of his arms
64. 5. thou meetest him that w. righteousness
Dan. 6. 27. he w. signs and wonders in heaven
John 5. 17. my Father w. hitherto, and I work
Acts 10. 35. he that w. righteousness is accepted
Rom. 2. 10. glory and peace to every one that w. good
4. 4. to him that w. is the reward not of grace
5. to him that w. not, but believeth on him
15. because the law w. wrath, for where no law
5. 3. knowing that tribulation w. patience
13. 10. love w. no ill to his neighbour, therefore
1 Cor. 12. 6. it is the same God that w. all in all
11. all these w. that one and the same Spirit
16. 10. for he w. the work of the Lord, as I also do
2 Cor. 4. 12. so then death w. in us, but life in you
17. w. for us a more exceeding weight of glory
7. 10. for godly sorrow w. repentance to salvation,
but the sorrow of the world w. death
Gal. 3. 5. he therefore that w. miracles among you
5. 6. but faith which w. by love
Eph. 1. 11. who w. all things after the counsel
2. 2. the spirit that now w. in the disobedient
3. 20. according to the power that w. in us
Phil. 2. 13. for it is G. that w. in you to will and do
Col. 1. 29. his working, which w. in me mightily
1 Thess. 2. 13. effectually w. in you that believe
Jam. 1. 3. that the trying of your faith w. patience
20. the wrath of man w. not righteousness of God
Rev. 21. 27. nor whatsoever w. abomination

WORKING, Participle.

Psal. 52. 2. like a sharp razor, w. deceitfully
74. 12. w. salvation in the midst of the earth
Ezek. 46. 1. the gate shall be shut the six w. days
Mark 16. 20. the Lord w. with them, with signs
Rom. 1. 27. men with men w. that which is unseemly
7. 13. sin w. death in me by that which is good
1 Cor. 4. 12. and labour, w. with our own hands
Eph. 4. 28. w. with his hands the thing that is good
2 Thess. 3. 11. w. not at all, but are busy-bodies
Heb. 13. 21. w. in you that which is well pleasing
Rev. 16. 14. they are the spirits of devils w. miracles

WORKING, Substantive.

Isa. 28. 29. from the Lord who is excellent in w.
1 Cor. 9. 6. have not we power to forbear w.?
12. 10. to another the w. of miracles
Eph. 1. 19. according to the w. of his mighty power
3. 7. given me by the effectual w. of his power
4. 16. according to the effectual w. in the measure
Phil. 3. 21. according to the w. whereby he is able
Col. 1. 29. his w. which worketh in me mightily
2 Thess. 2. 9. whose coming is after the w. of Satan

WORKMAN.

Exod. 26. † 1. cherubims, the work of a cunning w.
35. 35. Bezaleel and Aholiab with wisdom to work
all manner of work of the cunning w. 38. 23.
Cant. 7. 1. like jewels, the work of a cunning w.
Isa. 40. 19. the w. melteth a graven image
20. he seeketh to him a cunning w. to prepare
Jer. 10. 3. the work of the w. with the axe
Hos. 8. 6. the w. made it, therefore it is not God
Mat. 10. 10. the w. is worthy of his meat
2 Tim. 2. 15. a w. that needeth not be ashamed

WORKMANSHIP.

Exod. 31. 3. and in all manner of w. 5. | 35. 31.
2 Kings 16. 10. according to all the w. thereof
Ezek. 28. 13. the w. of tabrets was prepared in thee
Eph. 2. 10. for we are his w. created in Christ Jesus

WORKMEN.

2 Kings 12. 14. but they gave that to the w. to repair
the house of the Lord, 15. 2 Chron. 34. 10, 17.
1 Chron. 22. 15. there are w. with thee in abundance
25. 1. number of w. || 2 Chron. 24. 13. w. wrought
Ezra 3. 9. to set forward the w. in the house of God
Isa. 44. 11. behold, the w. they are of men
Acts 19. 25. called with the w. of like occupation

WORLD.

In Greek, Κοσμος; in Hebrew, Thebal. *It is taken for the whole universe; comprehending the heavens, earth, sea, the elements, the angels, men, animals, in a word, all created beings.* John 1. 10. The world was made by him. *It is also put for the race of mankind; sometimes in an extensive sense, for all the posterity of Adam.* Rom. 5. 12. By one man sin entered into the world. *"Sin came to be among mankind;" it is a* metonymy, the thing containing being put for the inhabitants contained. Sometimes it is taken in a more restricted sense, as in John 15. 18. it is put for the wicked in the world, for unregenerated, unrenewed persons. If the world hate you, ye know that it hated me before it hated you. The wicked are called the world, because they relish and savour nothing but worldly things, and pursue nothing but worldly designs. It is put likewise for God's chosen people, whether Jews or Gentiles. 2 Cor. 5. 19. God was in Christ, reconciling the world to himself. And in John 3. 16. God so loved the world, that he gave his only-begotten Son to die in their stead, and give satisfaction for them to his justice. Believers are called the world, both because they are taken from among Jews and Gentiles, and do participate in the corruption of the world. World is put for the Gentiles only. Rom. 11. 12. If the fall of them be the riches of the world. The Jews rejecting the gospel, and so falling from being God's people, was the occasion of God's manifesting his abundant grace in the conversion of the Gentiles. It is put for sensual lusts and pleasures, for the riches, honours, and dignities of the world. 1 John 2. 15. Love not the world, neither the things that are in the world. It also stands for the good things of this world. 1 Cor 7. 31. They that use this world, as not abusing it.

The children of this world, are such as live in the world, whether they be good or bad, Luke 20. 34. The devil is called the prince of this world, John 12. 31. and the god of this world, 2 Cor. 4. 4. He boasted to our Saviour that he was so, Mat. 4. 9. and he acteth in this world like a prince, powerfully working in the children of disobedience, Eph. 2. 2. In Heb. 2. 5. the apostle calls the gospel-state of the church the world to come. It is put for the Roman empire, Luke 2. 1.

Concerning the creation of the world, it is asked if the whole mass of matter was created all at once? and if all corporeal things were ranged in order at the same time; or only in the space of seven days, as Moses describes in the beginning of Genesis? Some interpreters are of opinion that God created all the matter of the universe out of nothing in an instant, by one simple act of his almighty will; but they are not agreed about the other question. Some maintain, that sensible beings were not brought to their full perfection, till after the space of seven days was completed. This opinion is founded upon Moses's narration, who expresses it very distinctly. Besides, it cannot be easily conceived, that the chaos should settle into any regular order, till after an infinite variety of different motions by which the parts of the matter separated from one another, which were of different and incompatible qualities; and till there should be an union and coalescence of those which were of the same form and nature; and that all those motions could not be performed till after a sufficient space of time.

Others, fearing that consequences contrary to the immutability and omnipotence of the Creator, might be drawn from the opinion of a successive creation, have thought, that nothing should be inferred from Moses's description, but a mental succession of order, and that he only represents the creation as performed in succession of time, to accommodate himself to the apprehensions of the vulgar, and to give a more intelligible account of it. Matter, always obedient to the commands of the Almighty, had no need of preparation. But the first opinion has the greatest number of followers.

It is also inquired, at what season of the year the world was created? The generality of the fathers think it was created in the spring. But a great number of others, among whom are the most learned chronologists, contend that the world was created in autumn. They urge, (1.) That the Hebrews, the Egyptians, and most of the Orientals, began their year at autumn; which custom they had received from their ancestors, and they from the first men, who would naturally commence their year from the time when the world began. (2) When God created Adam and Eve, and all other animals, he was to provide them with necessary nourishment. (3) There was fruit upon the trees in the garden of Eden, Gen. 3. 2, 3. It was therefore autumn, say they, in whatever place we suppose Adam to have been created.

1 Sam. 2. 8. he hath set the w. upon them
2 Sam. 22. 16. the channels of the sea appeared, the foundations of the w. were discovered, Psal. 18. 15.
1 Chron. 16. 30. the w. also shall not be moved
Job 18. 18. he shall be chased out of the w.
34. 13. or who hath disposed the whole w.?
37. 12. that they may do on the face of the w.
Psal. 9. 8. he shall judge the w. in righteousness, minister judgment to the people, 96. 13. | 98. 9.
17. 14. deliver my soul from the men of the w.
19. 4. their words to the end of the w. Rom. 10. 18.
22. 27. all the ends of the w. shall remember
24. 1. the earth and the w. is the Lord's, and they that dwell therein, 98. 7. Nah. 1. 5.
33. 8. let the inhabitants of the w. stand in awe
49. 1. give ear, all ye inhabitants of the w.
50. 12. for the w. is mine
77. 18. the lightnings lightened the w. 97. 4.
89. 11. thou hast founded the w. and its fulness
90. 2. hadst formed the earth and the w.
93. 1. the w. also is established, it cannot be moved
96. 10. w. also shall be established, not be moved
Prov. 8. 26. while he had not made dust of the w.
Eccl. 3. 11. also he hath set the w. in their heart
Isa. 13. 11. I will punish the w. for their evil
14. 17. is this he that made the w. as a wilderness?
21. nor fill the face of the w. with cities
24. 4. the w. languisheth and fadeth away
27. 6. Israel shall fill the face of the w. with fruit
34. 1. let the w. hear, and all that come forth
45. 17. ye shall not be confounded, w. without end

Mat. 4. 8. the devil sheweth him all the kingdoms of the w. and the glory of them, Luke 4. 5.
5. 14. ye are the light of the w. a city on a hill
13. 38. the field is the w. good seed are children
40. so shall it be in the end of this w. 49.
16. 26. what profited, if he shall gain the whole w. and lose his own soul? Mark 8. 36. Luke 9. 25.
18. 7. woe to the w. because of offences
24. 14. this gospel of the kingdom shall be preached in all the w. for a witness to all, Mark 14. 9.
Luke 1. 70. who have been since w. began, Acts 3. 21.
2. 1. a decree that all the w. should be taxed
20. 35. they that are worthy to obtain that w.
John 1. 10. he was in the w. the w. was made by him, and the w. knew him not, Acts 17. 24.
29. the Lamb of God that takes away the sin of w.
3. 16. God so loved the w. that he gave his Son
17. that the w. through him might be saved
4. 42. Christ, the Saviour of the w. 1 John 4. 14.
6. 33. bread of God is he that giveth life unto the w.
51. my flesh, which I give for the life of the w.
7. 4. if thou do these things, shew thyself to the w.
7. the w. cannot hate you, but me it hateth
8. 12. Jesus said, I am the light of the w. 9. 5.
12. 19. behold, the w. is gone after him
47. I came not to judge, but to save the w.
14. 17. the Spirit, whom the w. cannot receive
19. a little while and the w. seeth me no more
22. Lord, how is it that thou wilt manifest thyself unto us and not unto the w.?
27. my peace I give, not as the w. giveth, give I
14. 31. that the w. may know I love Father
15. 18. if the w. hate you, 1 John 3. 13.
19. if ye were of the w. the w. would love his own
16. 20. but the w. shall rejoice
28. I leave the w. and go to the Father
33. be of good cheer, I have overcome the w.
17. 5. the glory I had with thee before the w. was
6. thy name to men thou gavest me out of the w.
9. I pray not for w. but for them hast given me
14. w. hated them, because they are not of the w.
15. thou shouldest not take them out of the w.
16. they are not of the w. even as I am not of w.
21. that the w. may believe thou hast sent me, 23.
25. O Father, the w. hath not known thee
18. 20. Jesus answered, I spake openly to the w.
21. 25. I suppose w. could not contain the books
Acts 17. 6. these that turned the w. upside down
19. 27. Diana, whom Asia and the w. worshippeth
24. 5. a mover of sedition thro' the w. a ringleader
Rom. 1. 8. your faith is spoken of thro' the whole w.
3. 6. for then how shall God judge the w.
19. that all the w. may become guilty before God
4. 13. the promise that he should be heir of the w.
11. 12. if the fall of them be the riches of the w.
15. if casting away of them be reconciling of w.
1 Cor. 1. 21. the w. by wisdom knew not God
2. 7. the wisdom which God ordained before the w.
12. now we have received not the spirit of the w.
3. 22. or the w. of life, or death, all are yours
4. 9. for we are made a spectacle to w. to angels
13. we are made as the filth of w. and offscouring
5. 10. for then must ye needs go out of the w.
6. 2. do ye not know that saints shall judge the w.?
7. 33. careth for the things that are in the w. 34.
8. 13. I will eat no flesh while the w. standeth
11. 32. that we should not be condemned with w.
2 Cor. 5. 19. God in Christ reconciling w. to himself
Gal. 6. 14. glory in the cross of our Lord Jesus, by whom the w. is crucified to me, and I to the w.
2 Tim. 1. 9. in Christ before the w. began, Tit. 1. 2.
Heb. 2. 5. he put not in subjection the w. to come
6. 5. have tasted the powers of the w. to come
11. 38. of whom the w. was not worthy
Jam. 1. 27. to keep himself unspotted from the w.
3. 6. the tongue is a fire, a w. of iniquity
4. 4. the friendship of the w. is enmity with God, a friend of the w. is the enemy of God
2 Pet. 2. 5. God spared not the old w. bringing in the flood on the w. of the ungodly
3. 6. whereby the w. that then was, perished
1 John 2. 2. he is the propitiation for the sins of w.
15. love not the w. ‖ 16. but is of the w.
17. the w. passeth away, and the lusts thereof
3. 1. the w. knoweth us not, because it knew him not
4. 5. they are of the w. therefore speak of the w.
5. 4. what is born of God, overcometh the w. 5.
19. we are of God, whole w. lieth in wickedness
Rev. 3. 10. hour of temptation shall come on all w.
12. 9. called Satan, who deceiveth the whole w.
13. 3. and all the w. wondered after the beast

See FOUNDATION.

In, or into the WORLD.

Psal. 73. 12. the ungodly who prosper in the w.
Mat. 26. 13. this gospel be preached in the whole w.
Mark 10. 30. he shall receive an hundred-fold, and in the w. to come eternal life, Luke 18. 30.
John 1. 9. lighteth every man that comes into the w.
10. he was in the w. and the w. was made by him
3. 17. God sent not his Son into the w. to condemn w.
19. light is come into the w. men loved darkness
6. 14. prophet that should come into the w. 11. 27.
9. 5. as long as I am in the w. I am the light of w.
12. 46. I am come a light into the w. who. believeth
16. 33. in w. ye shall have tribulation, in me peace
17. 11. I am no more in the w. these are in the w.
12. while I was with them in the w. I kept them
18. 37. and for this cause came I into the w.
Rom. 5. 12. as by one man sin entered into the w.
13. for until the law, sin was in the w.
1 Cor. 8. 4. we know an idol is nothing in the w.
Eph. 2. 12. having no hope, without God in the w.
Col. 1. 6. gospel is come to you as it is in all the w.
1 Tim. 1. 15. Chr. Jesus came into w. to save sinners
3. 16. seen of angels and believed on in the w.
Heb. 10. 5. when he cometh into the w. he saith
1 Pet. 5. 9. the same afflictions that are in the w.
1 John 2. 15. love not the things that are in the w.
4. 1. many false prophets are gone out into the w.
3. antichrist, even now already is it in the w.
4. because he is greater than he that is in the w.
9. God sent his Son into the w. that we might live
2 John 7. many deceivers are entered into the w.

This WORLD.

Mat. 12. 32. it shall not be forgiven him in this w.
13. 22. cares of this w. choke word, Mark 4. 19.
Luke 16. 8. for the children of this w. are wiser than
20. 34. Jesus said, the children of this w. marry
John 8. 23. ye are of this w. I am not of this w.
9. 39. for judgment I am come into this w.
12. 25. he that hateth life in this w. shall keep it
31. Jesus said, now is the judgment of this w. now shall the prince of this w. be cast out
13. 1. he should depart out of this w. to the Father
14. 30. for prince of this w. cometh, nothing in me
16. 11. because the prince of this w. is judged
18. 36. Jesus answered, my kingdom is not of this w. if my kingdom were of this w.
Rom. 12. 2. be not conformed to t. w. but transformed
1 Cor. 1. 20. where is the disputer of this w.? hath not God made foolish the wisdom of this w.?
2. 6. yet we speak not the wisdom of this w.
3. 18. if any man seemeth to be wise in this w.
19. the wisdom of this w. is foolishness with God
5. 10. yet not with the fornicators of this w.
7. 31. they that use this w. as not abusing it
2 Cor. 4. 4. the god of this w. hath blinded the minds
Gal. 1. 4. he might deliver us from this pres. evil w.
Eph. 1. 21. not only in this w. but in that to come
2. 2. ye walked according to the course of this w.
6. 12. against the rulers of the darkness of this w.
1 Tim. 6. 7. for we brought nothing into this w.
17. charge them that are rich in this w.
2 Tim. 4. 10. Demas having loved this present w.
Tit. 2. 12. we should live godly in this present w.
Jam. 2. 5. God hath chosen the poor of this w.
1 John 3. 17. but whoso hath this w. good and seeth
4. 17. because as he is, so are we in this w.

WORLDLY.

Tit. 2. 12. denying ungodliness and w. lusts
Heb. 9. 1. the first covenant had a w. sanctuary

WORLDS.

Heb. 1. 2. by his Son, by whom also he made the w.
11. 3. the w. were framed by the word of God

WORM.

When the Scripture would represent to us a person that is weak, mean, and despised in the world, it compares him to a worm of the earth, because nothing is found to be more contemptible than this creature. Job 25. 6. How much less man that is a worm? And the Psalmist says, I am a worm, and no man, Psal. 22. 6. The worm of the damned dies not, and their fire shall never be quenched, Isa. 66. 24. "They will feel a worm of conscience that shall never die, and the fiery wrath of God upon their souls and bodies that shall never go out."

Exod. 16. 24. neither was there any w. therein
Job 17. 14. I said to the w. thou art my mother
24. 20. the w. shall feed sweetly on him
25. 6. much less man that is a w. and son of man
Psal. 22. 6. but I am a w. and no man, a reproach
Isa. 14. 11. the w. is spread under thee, and worms
41. 14. fear not, thou w. Jacob, and ye men of Israel
51. 8. and the w. shall eat them like wool
66. 24. for their w. shall not die, nor their fire be quenched, Mark 9. 44, 46, 48.
Jonah 4. 7. God prepared a w. it smote the gourd

WORMS.

Exod. 16. 20. their manna bred w. and stank
Deut. 28. 39. grapes, for the w. shall eat them
Job 7. 5. my flesh is clothed with w. and dust
19. 26. tho' w. destroy this body, yet shall I see G.
21. 26. they shall lie down, and w. shall cover them
Isa. 14. 11. worm under thee, and the w. cover thee
Mic. 7. 17. they move out of their holes like w.
Acts 12. 23. Herod was eaten of w. and gave up ghost

WORMWOOD.

Deut. 29. 18. lest there be a root that beareth w.
Prov. 5. 4. her end is bitter as w. sharp as a sword
Jer. 9. 15. I will feed them with w. 23. 15.
Lam. 3. 15. he hath made me drunken with w.
19. remembering my misery, the w. and the gall
Amos 5. 7. ye who turn judgment to w.
Rev. 8. 11. the name of the star is called w. and the third part of the waters became w.

WORSE.

Gen. 19. 9. we will deal w. with thee than them
2 Sam. 19. 7. that will be w. than all that befell thee
1 Kings 16. 25. Omri did w. than all before him
2 Kings 14. 12. Judah was put to the w. before Israel, and fled to their tents, 2 Chron. 25. 22.
1 Chron. 19. 16. the Syrians were put to the w. 19.
2 Chron. 6. 24. if thy people be put to the w.
33. 9. Manasseh made Jerusalem do w.
Isa. 41. † 24. w. than nothing, w. than a viper
Jer. 7. 26. they did w. than their fathers, 16. 12.
Dan. 1. 10. why should he see your faces w. liking?
Mat. 9. 16. the rent is made w. Mark 2. 21.
12. 45. wicked spirits dwell there, the last state of that man is w. than the first, Luke 11. 26.
27. 64. the last error shall be w. than the first
Mark 5. 26. she was nothing bettered, but grew w.
John 2. 10. men have drunk, then that which is w.
5. 14. sin no more, lest a w. thing come unto thee
1 Cor. 8. 8. neither if we eat not are we the w.
11. 17. you come not for the better, but for the w.
1 Tim. 5. 8. denied the faith, he is w. than an infidel
2 Tim. 3. 13. but seducers shall wax w. and w.
2 Pet. 2. 20. the latter end is w. with them

WORSHIP.

Gen. 22. 5. I and the lad will go yonder and w.
Exod. 24. 1. come up to the Lord, and w. ye afar off
34. 14. for thou shalt w. no other god, Lord jealous
Deut. 4. 19. lest thou shouldest be driven to w. them
8. 19. if thou w. other gods, 11. 16. | 30. 17.
26. 10. shalt set first-fruits before Lord, and w. before the Lord thy God, Psal. 22. 27, 29. | 86. 9.
1 Sam. 1. 3. this man went up yearly to w.
15. 25. turn again, that I may w. the Lord, 30.
1 Kings 12. 30. the people went to w. before the one
2 Kings 5. 18. to w. in the house of Rimmon
17. 36. the Lord shall ye fear, and him shall ye w.
18. 22. hath said to Judah, ye shall w. before this altar in Jerusalem, 2 Chron. 32. 12. Isa. 36. 7

1 Chron. 16. 29. w. Lord in the beauty of holiness,
Psal. 29. 2. | 66. 4. | 96. 9. Mat. 4. 10. Luke 4. 8.
Psal. 5. 7. I will w. toward thy temple, 138. 2.
45. 11. he is thy Lord, and w. thou him
81. 9. neither shalt thou w. any strange god
95. 6. O come, let us w. and bow down and kneel
97. 7. w. him, all ye gods; Sion heard, was glad
99. 5. w. at his footstool, for he is holy, 132. 7.
9. exalt the Lord, and w. at his holy hill
Isa. 2. 8. they w. the work of their hands, 20. | 46. 6.
27. 13. shall w. the L. in holy mount at Jerusalem
49. 7. princes also shall w. because of the Lord
66. 23. all flesh shall come to w. before me
Jer. 7. 2. that enter in at these gates to w. 26. 2.
13. 10. they that w. other gods, be as this girdle
25. 6. go not after other gods to w. them
44. 19. did we w. her without our men?
Ezek. 46. 2. he shall w. at the threshold of the gate
3. the people of the land shall w. at the door
9. he that entereth to w. by the north gate
Dan. 3. 5. ye fall down, w. the golden image, 10, 15.
12. not w. the image, 18. 28. || 15. if ye w.
14. do not ye w. the golden image I have set up?
Mic. 5. 13. no more w. the work of thine hands
Zeph. 1. 5. them that w. the host of heaven
2. 11. men shall w. him, every one from his place
Zech. 14. 16. to w. the King the Lord of hosts, 17.
Mat. 2. 2. we have seen his star, and come to w. him
8. that I may come and w. him also
4. 9. if thou wilt fall down and w. me, Luke 4. 7.
15. 9. but in vain they do w. me, teaching the comm.
John 4. 20. ye say that in Jerusalem is the place
where men ought to w. Mark 7. 7.
22. ye w. ye know not what, we know what we
w. for salvation is of the Jews
23. they shall w. the Father in spirit, 24.
12. 20. certain Greeks came to w. at the feast
Acts 7. 42. God gave them up to w. the host, 43.
8. 27. an eunuch came to Jerusalem to w.
17. 23. whom ye ignorantly w. him declare I
18. 13. persuaded men to w. God contrary to law
24. 11. Paul came up to Jerusalem to w. God
14. they call heresy, so w. I the God of my fathers
1 Cor. 14. 25. so falling down, he will w. God
Phil. 3. 3. which w. God in spirit, rejoice in Christ
Heb. 1. 6. let all the angels of God w. him
Rev. 3. 9. make them come and w. before thy feet
4. 10. and w. him that liveth for ever and ever
9. 20. that they should not w. devils nor idols
11. 1. measure temple of God, and them w. therein
13. 8. all on the earth shall w. the beast, 12.
15. they that would not w. the image of the beast
14. 7. w. him that made heaven, earth, and sea
9. if any man w. the beast and his image
11. who w. the beast, have no rest day and night
15. 4. all nations shall come and w. before thee
19. 10. I fell at his feet to w. 22. 8. || 22. 9. w. God

WORSHIPPED.

Gen. 24. 26. Abraham bowed and w. the Lord, 48.
52. Abraham's servant w. Lord, bowing to earth
Exod. 4. 31. Israel bowed and w. 12. 27. | 33. 10.
32. 8. they made a calf, and w. it, Psal. 106. 19.
34. 8. Moses w. || Judg. 7. 15. Gideon w.
Deut. 17. 3. hath gone and served other gods, and
w. 29. 26. 1 Kings 9. 9. 2 Kings 21. 21. 2 Chron.
7. 22. Jer. 1. 16. | 8. 2. | 16. 11. | 22. 9.
1 Sam. 1. 19. Elkanah and Hannah w. before Lord
28. Samuel w. || 15. 31. Saul w. the Lord
2 Sam. 12. 20. then David arose and w. 15. 32.
1 Kings 11. 33. have forsaken me, and w. Ashtaroth
16. 31. Ahab served Baal and w. him, 22. 53.
2 Kings 17. 16. they w. all the host of heaven and
served Baal, 21. 3. 2 Chron. 33. 3.
1 Chron. 29. 20. all the congregation bowed down
and w. the Lord, 2 Chron. 7. 3. | 29. 28, 29, 30.
Neh. 8. 6. all the people w. the Lord, 9. 3.
Job 1. 20. Job w. || Ezek. 8. 16. w. the sun
Dan. 2. 46. king w. Daniel || 3. 7. w. golden image
Mat. 2. 11. the wise men fell down and w. Christ
8. 2. a leper came and w. him || 9. 18. a ruler w.
14. 33. they that were in the ship w. him
15. 25. the woman of Canaan came and w. him
18. 26. the servant fell down and w. his lord
28. 9. they held him by the feet and w. him
17. his disciples w. him, Luke 24. 52.
Mark 5. 6. the man ran out of the tombs and w. him
15. 19. they spit upon him, and bowing, w. him
John 4. 20. our fathers w. in this mountain
9. 38. the blind man believed, and w. him
Acts 10. 25. Cornelius fell down and w. Peter
16. 14. Lydia w. God || 18. 7. Justus w. God
17. 25. neither is w. with men's hands, gives life
Rom. 1. 25. w. the creature more than the Creator
2 Thess. 2. 4. exalteth himself above all that is w.
Heb. 11. 21. Jacob w. || Rev. 7. 11. the angels w. G.
Rev. 5. 14. the twenty four elders w. 11. 16. | 19. 4.
13. 4. they w. the dragon, they w. the beast
16. 2. a sore fell on them which w. his image
19. 20. he deceived them that w. his image
20. 4. I saw the souls that had not w. the beast

WORSHIPPER.

John 9. 31. if any man be a w. of God, him he heareth
Acts 19. 35. the city of Ephesus is a w. of Diana

WORSHIPPERS.

2 Kings 10. 19. Jehu might destroy the w. of Baal
21. all the w. of Baal came, none was left
23. that there be none but the w. of Baal only
John 4. 23. when the true w. shall worship in spirit
Heb. 10. 2. because that the w. once purged

WORSHIPPETH.

Neh. 9. 6. and the host of heaven w. thee
Isa. 44. 15. yea, he maketh a god, and w. it, 17.
Dan. 3. 6. and whoso falleth not down and w. 11.
Acts 19. 27. whom all Asia and the world w.

WORSHIPPING.

2 Kings 19. 37. as he was w. in the house of Nisroch his god, his sons smote him, Isa. 37. 38.
2 Chron. 20. 18. all Judah fell down, w. the Lord
Mat. 20. 20. mother of Zebedee's children came w.
Col. 2. 18. let no man beguile you in w. of angels

WORST.

Ezek. 7. 24. I will bring the w. of the heathen

WORTH.

Gen. 23. 9. for as much money as it is w. give it me
15. the land is w. four hundred shekels of silver
Lev. 27. 23. priest shall reckon the w. of estimation
Deut. 15. 18. hath been w. a double hired servant
2 Sam. 18. 3. but thou art w. ten thousand of us
1 Kings 21. 2. give the w. of thy vineyard in money
Job 24. 25. who will make my speech nothing w.
Prov. 10. 20. the heart of the wicked is little w.
Ezek. 30. 2. prophesy and say, howl ye, woe w. day

WORTHY.

Gen. 32. 10. I am not w. of the least of thy mercies
Deut. 25. 2. if the wicked man be w. to be beaten
1 Sam. 1. 5. but to Hannah he gave a w. portion
26. 16. as the Lord liveth, ye are w. to die
2 Sam. 22. 4. who is w. to be praised, Psal. 18. 3.
1 Kings 1. 52. if he will shew himself a w. man
Jer. 26. 11. this man is w. to die || 16. he is not w.
Mat. 3. 11. whose shoes I am not w. to bear
8. 8. the centurion said, Lord, I am not w. that thou
shouldest come under my roof, Luke 7. 6.
10. 10. for the workman is w. of his meat
11. inquire who in it is w. and there abide
13. and if the house be w. but if it be not w.
37. loveth more than me, he is not w. of me, 38.
22. 8. but they which were bidden were not w.
Mark 1. 7. whose shoes I am not w. to unloose, Luke
3. 16. John 1. 27. Acts 13. 25.
Luke 3. 8. bring forth fruits w. of repentance
7. 4. that he was w. for whom he should do this
7. nor thought I myself w. to come to thee
10. 7. for the labourer is w. of his hire
12. 48. he that did commit things w. of stripes
15. 19. I am no more w. to be called thy son, 21.
20. 35. shall be accounted w. to obtain that world
21. 36. be accounted w. to escape these things
Acts 24. 2. very w. deeds are done to this nation
Rom. 8. 18. are not w. to be compared with the glory
Eph. 4. 1. that ye walk w. of the vocation
Col. 1. 10. that ye might walk w. of the Lord
1 Thess. 2. 12. that ye would walk w. of God
1 Tim. 1. 15. a saying w. of all acceptation, 4. 9.
5. 18. the labourer is w. of his reward
Heb. 10. 29. of how much sorer punishment, suppose
ye, shall he be thought w. who hath trodden
11. 38. of whom the world was not w.
Jam. 2. 7. do they not blaspheme that w. name?
Rev. 3. 4. they shall walk in white, for they are w.
4. 11. thou art w. to receive glory, and power, 5. 12.
5. 2. who is w. to open the book and loose the seals
4. because no man was found w. to open the book
9. thou art w. to take the book, and open the seals
16. 6. give them blood to drink, for they are w.
See COUNT, COUNTED, DEATH.

WORTHIES.

Nah. 2. 5. he shall recount his w. they shall stumble

WORTHILY.

Ruth 4. 11. do thou w. in Ephratah and be famous

WOT, TETH.

Gen. 21. 26. I w. not who hath done this thing
39. 8. my master w. not what is with me in house
44. 15. w. ye not that such a man as I can divine?
Exod. 32. 1. as for this Moses, we w. not what is be-
come of him, 23. Acts 7. 40.
Num. 22. 6. I w. he whom thou blessest is blessed
Josh. 2. 5. whither the men went I w. not
Acts 3. 17. I w. that through ignorance ye did it
Rom. 11. 2. w. ye not what Scripture saith?
Phil. 1. 22. yet what I shall choose I w. not

WOVE.

2 Kings 23. 7. the women w. hangings for the grove

WOVEN.

Exod. 28. 32. ephod have binding of w. work, 39. 22.
39. 27. made coats of fine linen w. work for Aaron
John 19. 23. the coat was without seam, w.

WOULD.

Gen. 30. 34. I w. it might be according to thy word
Num. 22. 29. I w. there were a sword in mine hand
1 Kings 13. 33. whosoever w. he consecrated him
Neh. 9. 24. they might do with them as they w.
Esth. 9. 5. Jews did what they w. to their enemies
Psal. 81. 11. not hearken, and Israel w. none of me
Prov. 1. 25. but ye w. none of my reproof
30. they w. none of my counsel, despised reproof
Dan. 5. 19. whom he w. he slew, and whom he w. he
kept alive, and whom he w. he set up, and w.
Mat. 7. 12. whatsoever ye w. that men should do to
you, do ye even so to them, Luke 6. 31.
27. 15. governor wont to release pris. whom they w.
Mark 3. 13. and he calleth to him whom he w. and
they came unto him
10. 35. w. thou shouldest do for us what we desire
36. what w. ye that I should do for you?
John 6. 11. he distributed fishes as much as they w.
Acts 18. 14. reason w. that I should bear with you
Rom. 7. 15. what I w. that I do not, but what I hate
19. for the good that I w. I do not, but the evil
1 Cor. 7. 7. I w. that all men were even as I myself
14. 5. I w. that ye all spake with tongues
2 Cor. 12. 20. I shall not find you such as I w.
Gal. 2. 10. they w. that we remember the poor
5. 12. I w. they were cut off which trouble you
17. so that ye cannot do the things that ye w.
Col. 2. 1. I w. ye knew what great conflict I have
3 John 10. forbiddeth them that w. cast them out
Rev. 3. 15. I know thy works, I w. wert cold or hot

WOULD God.

Exod. 16. 3. w. God we had died in Egypt, when
we sat by the flesh-pots, Num. 14. 2.
Num. 11. 29. w. God all Lord's people were prophets
20. 3. w. God we had died when our brethren died
Deut. 28. 67. w. G. it were even, w. G. it were morn.
Josh. 7. 7. w. G. we had dwelt on other side Jordan
Judg. 9. 29. w. G. this people were under my hand
2 Sam. 18. 33. w. God I had died for thee, O Absalom
2 Kings 5. 3. w. God my lord were with the prophet
Acts 26. 29. w. God that all were such as I am
1 Cor. 4. 8. and I w. to God ye did reign
2 Cor. 11. 1. w. to God ye could bear with me

WOULD not.

1 Sam. 20. 9. if I knew, then w. not I tell thee?
31. 4. his armour-bearer w. not, 1 Chr. 10. 4.
2 Sam. 12. 17. he w. not, nor did he eat with them
13. 16. but Amnon w. not hearken unto her
25. howbeit David w. not go, but blessed him
14. 29. but Joab w. not come to Absalom
1 Kings 22. 49. but Jehoshaphat w. not
2 Kings 24. 4. which the Lord w. not pardon
Neh. 9. 30. yet w. they not give ear, therefore gavest
Job 9. 16. yet w. I not believe he had hearkened
Isa. 30. 15. and ye w. not, Mat. 23. 37. Luke 13. 34.
Mat. 18. 30. besought him to have patience, he w. not
22. 3. they that were bidden w. not come
23. 30. we w. not have been partakers with them
24. 43. w. not have suffered his house to be broken
27. 34. when he had tasted, he w. not drink
Mark 9. 30. he w. not that any man should know it
Luke 15. 28. and he was angry, and w. not go in
18. 4. he w. not for a while, but afterwards said
13. he w. not lift up so much as his eyes to heaven
19. 27. who w. not that I should reign over them
John 7. 1. for he w. not walk in Jewry
Acts 9. 38. that he w. not delay to come to them
21. 14. and when he w. not be persuaded we ceased
Rom. 7. 16. if then I do that which I w. not
19. but the evil that I w. not that I do
11. 25. I w. not, brethren, that ye should be ignorant
of this mystery, 1 Cor. 10. 1.
1 Cor. 10. 20. I w. not ye should have fellowship
2 Cor. 12. 20. shall be found to you, such as ye w. not
1 Thess. 2. 9. because we w. not be chargeable to you
Heb. 4. 8. then w. he not afterward have spoken

WOULDEST.

Josh. 15. 18. Caleb said, what w. thou? 1 Kings 1. 16.
John 21. 18. thou walkedst whither thou w.

WOULDEST not.

John 21. 18. shall carry thee whither thou w. not
Heb. 10. 5. sacrifice and offering thou w. not, 8.

WOUND.

Exod. 21. 25. give w. for w. stripe for stripe
1 Kings 22. 35. and the blood ran out of the w.
Job 34. 6. my w. is incurable without transgression
Psal. 64. †7. suddenly their w. shall be
Prov. 6. 33. a w. and dishonour shall he get
20. 30. the blueness of a w. cleanseth away evil
Isa. 30. 26. he healeth the stroke of their w.
Jer. 10. 19. woe is me, for my w. is grievous
15. 18. and why is my w. incurable?
30. 12. and thy w. is grievous, Nah. 3. 19.
14. I wounded thee with w. of an enemy
Hos. 5. 13. Judah saw his w. could not cure your w.
Obad. 7. they that eat have laid a w. under thee
Mic. 1. 9. her w. is incurable, it is come to Judah
Rev. 13. 3. and his deadly w. was healed, 12, 14.

WOUNDS.

2 Kings 8. 29. king Joram went to be healed of the
w. the Syrians had given him, 9. 15. 2 Chr. 22. 6.
Job 9. 17. he multiplied my w. without cause
Psal. 38. 5. my w. stink, are corrupt because of folly
147. 3. he healeth and bindeth up their w.
Prov. 18. 8. words of a tale-bearer are as w. 26. 22.
23. 29. who hath woe? who hath w. without cause?
27. 6. faithful are w. of friend, but kisses of enemy
Isa. 1. 6. there is no soundness in it, but w. bruises
Jer. 6. 7. before me continually is grief and w.
30. 17. I will heal thee of thy w. saith the Lord
Zech. 13. 6. what are these w. in thy hands?
Luke 10. 34. the Samaritan bound up his w.

WOUND.

Deut. 32. 39. I kill, I make alive; I w. and I heal
Psal. 68. 21. God shall w. the head of his enemies
110. 6. he shall w. the heads over many countries
Amos 9. †1. and w. them in the head all of them
1 Cor. 8. 12. when ye w. their weak conscience

WOUND.

John 19. 40. they w. body of Jesus in linen clothes
Acts 5. 6. young men w. up Ananias, buried him

WOUNDED.

Deut. 23. 1. he that is w. in the stones, not enter
Judg. 20. †31. to smite of the people w. †39.
1 Sam. 17. 52. the w. of the Philistines fell down
31. 3. Saul was w. of the archers, 1 Chron. 10. 3.
2 Sam. 22. 39. I have w. mine enemies, Psal. 18. 38.
1 Kings 20. 37. so that in smiting he w. him
22. 34. carry me out, for I am w. 2 Chron. 18. 33.
2 Kings 8. 28. and the Syrians w. Joram
2 Chron. 35. 23. have me away, for I am sore w.
Job 24. 12. and the soul of the w. crieth out
Psal. 64. 7. shoot at them, suddenly shall they be w.
69. 26. to the grief of those whom thou hast w.
109. 22. I am poor, and my heart is w. within me
Prov. 7. 26. for she hath cast down many w.
18. 14. but a w. spirit who can bear?
Cant. 5. 7. the watchmen found me, they w. me
Isa. 51. 9. art thou not it that w. the dragon?
53. 5. but he was w. for our transgressions
Jer. 30. 14. I w. thee with the wound of an enemy
37. 10. there remained but w. men among them
51. 52. through all the land the w. shall groan
Lam. 2. 12. when they swooned as w. in the streets
Ezek. 26. 15. when the w. cry, shall not isles shake?
28. 23. the w. shall be judged in the midst of her
30. 24. with the groanings of a deadly w. man
Joel 2. 8. when they fall on the sword, shall not be w.
Zech. 13. 6. I was w. in the house of my friends
Mark 12. 4. he sent another servant, they cast stones
and they w. him in the head, Luke 20. 12.
Luke 10. 30. he fell amongst thieves, which w. him
Acts 19. 16. they fled out of that house naked and w.
Rev. 13. 3. I saw one of his heads, as it were w.

WOUNDEDST.

Hab. 3. 13. thou w. the head out of house of wicked

WOUNDETH.

Job 5. 18. he w. and his hands make whole
Ezek. 28. †9. no God, in the hand of him that w.

WOUNDING.

Gen. 4. 23. for I have slain a man to my w.

WRANGLING.

Jam. 3. †17. the wisdom from above is without w.

WRAP.

Isa. 28. 20. narrower than that he can w. himself in it
Mic. 7. 3. judge asketh for a reward; so they w. it up

WRAPPED, or WRAPT.

Gen. 38. 14. Tamar w. herself and sat in open place

1 Sam. 21. 9. Goliath's sword is w. in a cloth
1 Kings 19. 13. Elijah w. his face in his mantle
2 Kings 2. 8. Elijah took his mantle, and w. it togeth.
Job 8. 17. his roots are w. about the heap
40. 17. the sinews of his stones are w. together
Ezek. 21. 15. the sword is w. up for slaughter
Jonah 2. 5. the weeds were w. about my head
Mat. 27. 59. Joseph w. the body in a clean linen cloth, Mark 15. 46. Luke 23. 53.
Luke 2. 7. Mary w. him in swaddling clothes
12. ye shall find the babe w. in swaddling clothes
John 20. 7. napkin w. together in a place by itself

WRATH.

Gen. 49. 7. cursed be their w. for it was cruel
Lev. 10. 6. lest w. come upon all the people
Num. 1. 53. that no w. be on the congregation, 18. 5.
16. 46. for there is w. gone out from the Lord
Deut. 9. 7. how thou provokedst the Lord to w. 22.
29. 28. the Lord rooted them out in anger and w.
32. 27. were it not I feared the w. of the enemy
Josh. 9. 20. let them live, lest w. be upon us
22. 20. and w. fell on all the congregation
2 Sam. 11. 20. if so be that the king's w. arise
2 Kings 23. 26. the Lord turned not from great w.
1 Chr. 27. 24. he finished not, because there fell w.
2 Chr. 19. 2. therefore is w. upon thee from Lord
10. they trespass not, and so w. come upon you
24. 18. w. came upon Judah for this trespass
28. 13. and there is fierce w. against Israel
29. 10. that his fierce w. may turn away from us
32. 25. therefore there was w. upon him
Ezra 5. 12. our fathers had provoked God to w.
7. 23. why should there be w. against the realm?
Neh. 13. 18. yet ye bring more w. upon Israel
Esth. 1. 18. thus shall there arise too much w.
2. 1. when the w. of the king was appeased
3. 5. Mordecai bowed not, then Haman full of w.
7. 10. then was the king's w. pacified
Job 5. 2. for w. killeth foolish man, and envy slays
19. 29. for w. brings the punishments of the sword
21. 20. he shall drink of the w. of the Almighty
36. 13. but the hypocrites in heart heap up w.
18. because there is w. beware lest he take thee
Psal. 37. 8. forsake w. || 55. 3. in w. they hate me
76. 10. surely the w. of man shall praise thee, the remainder of w. shalt thou restrain
138. 7. shalt stretch thy hand against w. of enemies
Prov. 11. 23. the expectation of the wicked is w.
12. 16. fool's w. presently known, but prudent men
14. 29. that is slow to w. is of great understanding
15. 1. a soft answer turneth away w. but words
16. 14. the w. of a king is as messengers of death
19. 12. the king's w. is as the roaring of a lion
19. a man of great w. shall suffer punishment
21. 14. a reward in the bosom pacifieth strong w.
24. scorner is his name, who dealeth in proud w.
27. 3. but a fool's w. is heavier than them both
4. w. is cruel, and anger is outrageous, who is able
29. 8. city into a snare, but wise men turn away w.
30. 33. the forcing of w. bringeth forth strife
Eccl. 5. 17. he hath much w. with his sickness
Isa. 13. 9. the day of the Lord cometh with w.
14. 6. he who smote the people in w. with a stroke
54. 8. in a little w. I hid my face from thee
Jer. 21. 5. I myself will fight against you in w.
32. 37. whither I have driven them in great w.
44. 8. in that ye provoke me to w. with idols
Ezek. 7. 12. w. is on all the multitude thereof
Nah. 1. 2. and he reserveth w. for his enemies
Hab. 3. 2. O Lord, in w. remember mercy
Zeph. 1. 18. gold shall not deliver in the day of w.
Zech. 7. 12. therefore came a great w. from the Lord
8. 14. when your fathers provoked me to w.
Mat. 3. 7. to flee from w. to come, Luke 3. 7.
Luke 4. 28. they were filled with w. Acts 19. 28.
21. 23. for there shall be w. on this people
Rom. 2. 5. but treasurest up w. against the day of w.
8. but to them that obey unrighteousness, w.
4. 15. because the law worketh w. where no law is
5. 9. we shall be saved from w. through him
9. 22. endured the vessels of w. fitted to destruction
12. 19. avenge not, but rather give place to w.
13. 4. for he is the minister of God to execute w.
5. ye must needs be subject, not only for w.
Gal. 5. 20. the works of the flesh are w. strife
Eph. 2. 3. we were by nature the children of w.
4. 26. let not the sun go down upon your w.
31. let all w. anger, and clamour be put away
6. 4. fathers, provoke not your children to w.
Col. 3. 8. put off all these, w. malice, blasphemy
1 Thess. 1. 10. who delivered us from the w. to come
2. 16. for w. is come on them to the uttermost
5. 9. for God hath not appointed us to w.
1 Tim. 2. 8. lifting up holy hands without w.
Heb. 11. 27. Moses not fearing the w. of the king
Jam. 1. 19. let every man be slow to speak, slow to w.
20. w. of man worketh not righteousness of God
Rev. 6. 16. and hide us from the w. of the Lamb
12. 12. the devil is come down, having great w.
14. 8. she made all nations drink wine of w. 18. 3.

Day of WRATH.

Job 20. 28. his goods flow away in the day of his w.
21. 30. the wicked brought forth to the day of w.
Psal. 110. 5. Lord strike thro' kings in day of his w.
Prov. 11. 4. riches profit not in the day of w.
Zeph. 1. 15. that day is a day of w. and trouble
Rom. 2. 5. but treasurest up w. against the day of w.
Rev. 6. 17. for the great day of his w. is come

WRATH of God.

2 Chron. 28. 11. the fierce w. of God is upon you
Ezra 10. 14. till the w. of God be turned from us
Psal. 78. 31. the w. of God came upon them
John 3. 36. but the w. of God abideth on him
Rom. 1. 18. the w. of God is revealed from heaven
Eph. 5. 6. because of these things w. of God cometh on the children of disobedience, Col. 3. 6.
Rev. 14. 10. shall drink of the wine of the w. of God
19. and cast it into wine-press of the w. of God
15. 1. for in them is filled up the w. of God
7. seven golden vials full of the w. of God
16. 1. pour out the vials of the w. of God on earth
19. 15. he treadeth the wine-press of the w. of God

His WRATH.

Deut. 29. 23. which the Lord overthrew in his w.
1 Sam. 28. 18. nor executedst his w. upon Amalek
2 Kings 23. 26. the Lord turned not from his w.
2 Chron. 29. 10. his fierce w. may turn away, 30. 8.
Ezra 8. 22. his w. is against them that forsake him
Esth. 7. 7. king arising from the banquet in his w.
Job 16. 9. he teareth me in his w. who hateth me
20. 23. God shall cast the fury of his w. on him
Psal. 2. 5. then shall he speak to them in his w.
21. 9. the Lord shall swallow them up in his w.
58. 9. he shall take them away in his w.
78. 38. turned away anger, did not stir up all his w.
49. he cast on them the fierceness of his w.
106. 23. had not Moses stood to turn away his w.
Prov. 14. 35. his w. against him that causeth shame
24. 18. lest the Lord turn away his w. from him
Isa. 16. 6. we heard of Moab's pride and his w.
Jer. 7. 29. Lord hath forsaken generation of his w.
10. 10. at his w. the earth shall tremble
48. 30. I know his w. saith Lord, shall not be so
Lam. 2. 2. hath thrown down in his w. the holds
3. 1. I have seen affliction by the rod of his w.
Amos 1. 11. because he kept his w. for ever
Rom. 9. 22. what if God willing to shew his w.
Rev. 16. 19. the cup of wine of fierceness of his w.
See KINDLED; Wrath of the LORD.

My WRATH.

Exod. 22. 24. my w. shall wax hot, I will kill you
32. 10. let me alone, that my w. may wax hot
Num. 25. 11. Phinehas hath turned my w. away
2 Chr. 12. 7. my w. shall not be poured out on Jerus.
Psal. 95. 11. unto whom I sware in my w.
Isa. 10. 6. send him against the people of my w.
60. 10. for in my w. I smote thee, but had mercy
Ezek. 7. 14. for my w. is on all the multitude
13. 15. thus will I accomplish my w. on the wall
21. 31. blow against thee in fire of my w. 22. 21.
22. 31. I consumed them with the fire of my w.
38. 19. for in the fire of my w. have I spoken
Hos. 5. 10. I will pour out my w. on them like water
13. 11. I gave a king, and I took him away in my w.
Heb. 3. 11. so I sware in my w. they shall not enter
4. 3. as I have sworn in my w. if they shall enter

Thy WRATH.

Exod. 15. 7. thou sentest thy w. which consumed them
32. 11. why doth thy w. wax hot against thy people?
12. turn from thy fierce w. and repent of this
Job 14. 13. keep me secret until thy w. be past
40. 11. cast abroad the rage of thy w. behold proud
Psal. 38. 1. O Lord, rebuke me not in thy w.
79. 6. pour out thy w. on the heathen
85. 3. thou hast taken away all thy w.
88. 7. thy w. lieth hard on me, thou hast afflicted
16. thy fierce w. goeth over me, thy terrors
89. 46. how long shall thy w. burn like fire?
90. 7. and by thy w. are we troubled
9. for all our days are passed away in thy w.
11. even according to thy fear, so is thy w.
102. 10. because of thy indignation and thy w.
Jer. 18. 20. I stood to turn away thy w. from them
Hab. 3. 8. was thy w. against the sea, that didst ride
Rev. 11. 18. thy w. is come, and time of the dead

WRATHFUL.

Psal. 69. 24. let thy w. anger take hold of them
Prov. 15. 18. a w. man stirreth up strife

WRATHS.

2 Cor. 12. 20. I fear lest there be envyings, w. strifes

WREATH.

2 Chr. 4. 13. two rows of pomegranates on each w.

WREATHED.

Lam. 1. 14. my transgressions are w. and come up

WREATHEN.

Exod. 28. 14. two chains at the ends, of w. work shalt make them, 22, 24, 25. | 39. 15, 17, 18.
2 Kings 25. 17. pillar of w. work he carried away

WREATHS.

1 Kings 7. 17. w. of chain-work for the chapiters
2 Chron. 4. 12. two w. to cover the two pommels
13. four hundred pomegranates on the two w.

WREST.

Exod. 23. 2. not decline after many, to w. judgment
6. thou shalt not w. the judgment of thy poor
Deut. 16. 19. thou shalt not w. judgm. nor take gift
Ps. 56. 5. every day they w. my words, their thoughts
2 Pet. 3. 16. which they that are unstable w.

WRESTED.

Hab. 1. † 4. therefore w. judgment proceedeth

WRESTING.

Ezek. 9. † 9. the city is full of w. of judgment

WRESTLE.

Eph. 6. 12. for we w. not against flesh and blood

WRESTLED.

Gen. 30. 8. with great wrestlings have I w. with sister
32. 24. Jacob was alone, there w. a man with him
25. Jacob's thigh was out of joint as he w.

WRESTLING.

Gen. 30. † 8. and Rachel called his name w.

WRESTLINGS.

Gen. 30. 8. with great w. have I wrestled with sister

WRETCHED.

Rom. 7. 24. O w. man that I am, who shall deliver me
Rev. 3. 17. and knowest not that thou art w.

WRETCHEDNESS.

Num. 11. 15. kill me and let me not see my w.

WRING.

Lev. 1. 15. the priest shall w. off his head, 5. 8.
Psal. 75. 8. all the wicked shall w. them out

WRINGED.

Judg. 6. 38. Gideon w. the dew out of the fleece

WRINGER.

Isa. 16. † 4. for the w. is at an end, spoiler ceaseth

WRINGING.

Prov. 30. 33. the w. of the nose bringeth forth blood

WRINKLE.

Eph. 5. 27. a glorious church not having spot or w.

WRINKLES.

Job 16. 8. and thou hast filled me with w.

WRINKLING.

Nah. 3. † 19. there is no w. of thy bruise

WRITE.

Exod. 34. 1. I will w. on these tables, Deut. 10. 2.
Exod. 34. 27. the L. said to Mos. w. thou these words
Num. 17. 2. w. thou every man's name on his rod
3. thou shalt w. Aaron's name on the rod of Levi
Deut. 6. 9. w. them on posts of thy house, 11. 20.
24. 1. then let him w. her a bill of divorcement, and send her out of his house, 3. Mark 10. 4.
27. 3. w. on the stones the words of this law, 8.
31. 19. now therefore w. ye this song for you
2 Chron. 26. 22. the acts of Uzziah did Isaiah w.
Ezra 5. 10. that we might w. the names of the men
Neh. 9. 38. we make a sure covenant and w. it
Esth. 8. 8. w. ye also for the Jews as it liketh you
Prov. 3. 3. w. them on the table of thy heart, 7. 3.
Isa. 8. 1. w. in the great roll with a man's pen
10. 1. that w. grievousness which they prescribed
19. trees shall be few, that a child may w. them
30. 8. now go w. it before them in a table
Jer. 22. 30. saith the Lord w. ye this man childless
30. 2. w. the words I have spoken, 36. 2, 17, 28.
31. 33. I will w. it in their hearts, Heb. 8. 10.
Ezek. 24. 2. son of man, w. the name of the day
37. 16. w. upon the sticks for Judah and Israel
43. 11. w. it in their sight, that they may keep form
Hab. 2. 2. w. the vision, make it plain on tables
Luke 1. 3. it seemed good to me to w. to thee in order
16. 6. take thy bill and w. fifty || 7. w. fourscore
John 1. 45. of whom Moses and the prophets did w.
19. 21. w. not, king of the Jews, but that he said
Acts 15. 20. that we w. to them that they abstain from
25. 26. of whom I have no certain thing to w. to my lord, that I might have somewhat to w.
1 Cor. 4. 14. I w. not these things to shame you
14. 37. things I w. are the commandments of Lord
2 Cor. 1. 13. for we w. none other things to you
2. 9. to this end also did I w. that I might know
9. 1. it is superfluous for me to w. to you
13. 2. I w. to them which heretofore have sinned
10. therefore I w. these things being absent
Gal. 1. 20. now the things I w. unto you, I lie not
Phil. 3. 1. to w. the same things, for you it is safe
1 Thess. 4. 9. ye need not that I w. to you, 5. 1.
2 Thess. 3. 17. so I w. || 1 Tim. 3. 14. these things I w.
Heb. 10. 16. and in their minds will I w. them
2 Pet. 3. 1. I now w. unto you, 1 John 2. 1.
1 John 1. 4. these things w. we to you that your joy
2. 7. brethren, I w. no new commandment to you
8. again, a new commandment I w. unto you
12. I w. to you, little children, 13.
13. I w. to you, fathers, I w. to you, young men
2 John 12. having many things to w. unto you
3 John 13. I will not with ink and pen w. to you
Jude 3. when I gave all diligence to w. of common salvation, it was needful for me to w. to you
Rev. 1. 11. what thou seest w. in a book, 19.
2. 1. to the angel of the church of Ephesus, w.
8. in Smyrna || 12. in Pergamus || 18. Thyatira
3. 1. in Sardis || 7. Philadelphia || 14. Laodicea
12. I will w. on him the name of my God and city of my God, I will w. on him my new name
10. 4. as I was about to w. a voice said, w. not
14. 13. w. blessed are the dead that die in the Lord
19. 9. w. blessed are they which are called to supper
21. 5. w. for these words are true and faithful
See BOOK.

WRITER.

Judg. 5. 14. they that handle the pen of the w.
Psal. 45. 1. my tongue is the pen of a ready w.
Ezek. 9. 2. a man with a w. inkhorn by his side, 3.

WRITEST.

Job 13. 26. for thou w. bitter things against me
Ezek. 37. 20. the sticks whereon thou w. shall be

WRITETH.

Psal. 87. 6. the Lord shall count when he w. up

WRITING.

Exod. 32. 16. and the w. was the w. of God
39. 30. and wrote on plate of the holy crown a w.
Deut. 10. 4. he wrote according to the first w.
31. 24. when Moses had made an end of w. the law
1 Chron. 28. 19. the Lord made me understand in w.
2 Chron. 2. 11. Huram king of Tyre answered in w.
21. 12. there came a w. from Jehoram to Elijah
35. 4. prepare according to the w. of David king
36. 22. Cyrus put the proclamation in w. Ezra 1. 1.
Ezra 4. 7. the w. of letter was in the Syrian tongue
Esth. 1. 22. for he sent letters unto all provinces according to the w. thereof, 3. 12. | 8. 9. | 9. 27.
3. 14. the copy of the w. was published to all
4. 8. Mordecai gave to Hatach a copy of the w.
8. 8. the w. in the king's name may no man reverse
Isa. 38. 9. the w. of Hezekiah when he had been sick
Ezek. 13. 9. not written in the w. of house of Israel
Dan. 5. 7. the king said, whoso shall read this w.
8. could not read the w. || 15. should read this w.
16. if thou canst read the w. thou shalt be clothed
17. yet I will read the w. to the king and make
24. this is the w. that was written, 25.
6. 8. sign the w. || 9. king Darius signed the w.
10. when Daniel knew that the w. was signed
Mat. 5. 31. give her a w. of divorcement, 19. 7.
John 19. 19. the w. was, Jesus of Nazareth king

Hand-WRITING.

Col. 2. 14. blotting out the hand-w. of ordinances

WRITING-table.

Luke 1. 63. Zacharias asked for a w.-table

WRITINGS.

John 5. 47. if ye believe not his w. how believe?

WRITTEN.

Exod. 31. 18. w. with the finger of God, Deut. 9. 10.
1 Kings 21. 11. elders did as it was w. in the letters
1 Chron. 4. 41. these w. by name smote their tents
2 Chron. 30. 5. had not kept the passover as it was w.
Ezra 5. 7. they sent a letter, wherein was w. thus
6. 2. and therein was a record thus w.
8. 34. the weight of the vessels was w. at that time
Neh. 6. 6. sent an open letter, wherein was w.
8. 14. found w. in the law to dwell in booths
13. 1. was w. Ammonite not come into congregation
Esth. 1. 19. let it be w. among the laws of the Medes
3. 9. let it be w. that they may be destroyed
12. in the name of king Ahasuerus was it w.
6. 2. found w. that Mordecai told of Bigthana
8. 5. let it be w. to reverse Haman's letters

Psal. 69. 28. let them not be w. with the righteous
102. 18. this shall be w. for the generation to come
149. 9. to execute on them the judgment w.
Prov. 22. 20. have not I w. to thee excellent things?
Eccl. 12. 10. that which was w. was upright
Jer. 17. 13. that depart from me shall be w. in earth
36. 29. why hast w. the king of Babylon shall come
Ezek. 2. 10. the roll was w. within and without
13. 9. nor w. in the writing of house of Judah
Dan. 5. 24. this is the writing that was w. 25.
Mat. 27. 37. they set up his accusation w.
Mark 11. 17. is it not w. my house shall be called
15. 26. the superscription of his accusation was w.
the king of the Jews, Luke 23. 38. John 19. 20.
Luke 4. 17. he found the place where it was w.
10. 20. rejoice that your names are w. in heaven
18. 31. all things w. shall be accomplished, 21. 22.
John 2. 17. the disciples remembered that it was w.
10. 34. is it not w. in your law, I said, ye are gods
20. 31. but these are w. that ye might believe
21. 25. if they should be w. every one, the world
could not contain the books that should be w.
Acts 13. 29. they had fulfilled all that was w.
21. 25. as touching the Gentiles, we have w.
Rom. 2. 15. which shew the work of the law w.
4. 23. now it was not w. for his sake alone
1 Cor. 10. 11. they are w. for our admonition
2 Cor. 3. 2. ye are our epistle w. in our hearts
3. w. not with ink, but with the Spirit of God
7. if the ministration of death w. in stones
Philem. 19. I Paul have w. with mine own hand
Heb. 12. 23. the church of the first-born w. in heaven
Rev. 1. 3. keep those things which are w. therein
2. 17. and in the stone a new name w.
13. 8. whose names are not w. in the book of life
14. 1. having his Father's name w. in their foreheads
17. 5. upon her head was a name w. Mystery
19. 12. he had a name w. on his thigh, 16.
21. 12. names of the twelve tribes w. on the gates

Is WRITTEN.

Josh. 1. 8. observe to do all that *is* w. therein
2 Kings 22. 13. that which *is* w. concerning us
Esth. 8. 8. for writing which *is* w. in the king's name
Isa. 4. 3. every one that *is* w. among the living
Jer. 17. 1. sin of Judah *is* w. with a pen of iron
Dan. 9. 11. the curse and oath that *is* w. in the law
Luke 10. 26. what *is* w. in the law? how readest?
20. 17. he said, what is this then that *is* w.?
22. 37. this that *is* w. must be accomplished
John 15. 25. the word might be fulfilled that *is* w.
1 Cor. 4. 6. to think of men above that which *is* w.
9. 10. for our sakes, no doubt, this *is* w.
15. 54. he brought to pass the saying that *is* w.

It is WRITTEN.

Josh. 8. 31. as *it is* w. in the law of Moses, 1 Kings
2. 3. 2 Chron. 23. 18. | 25. 4. | 31. 3. | 35. 12.
Ezra 3. 2, 4. | 6. 18. Neh. 8. 15. | 10. 34, 36.
Dan. 9. 13.
Psal. 40. 7. in the volume *it is* w. of me, Heb. 10. 7.
Isa. 65. 6. *it is* w. before me, I will recompense
Mat. 2. 5. thus *it is* w. by the prophet, Luke 24. 46.
11. 10. this is he of whom *it is* w. Luke 7. 27.
26. 24. as *it is* w. of him, Mark 9. 13. | 14. 21.
31. *it is* w. Mark 14. 27. Luke 4. 8. Acts 23. 5.
Mark 9. 12. and how *it is* w. of the Son of man
Luke 2. 23. as *it is* w. in the law of the Lord
Rom. 11. 8. accord. as *it is* w. 1 Cor. 1. 31. 2 Cor. 4. 13.
12. 19. for *it is* w. 14. 11. Gal. 3. 10.
15. 3. Christ pleased not himself, but as *it is* w.
1 Cor. 15. 45. so *it is* w. the first man Adam
1 Pet. 1. 16. because *it is* w. be ye holy, I am holy

I have, or *have I* WRITTEN.

Exod. 24. 12. will give thee commandment, *I have* w.
Hos. 8. 12. *I have* w. to him great things of my law
John 19. 22. Pilate said, what *I have* w. *I have* w.
1 John 2. 14. *I have* w. to you fathers, young men
26. these things *have I* w. unto you, 5. 13.

Were WRITTEN.

Num. 11. 26. and they were of them that *were* w.
Job 19. 23. O that my words *were* now w.
Luke 24. 44. all things be fulfilled which *were* w.
John 12. 16. that these things *were* w. of him
Rom. 15. 4. whatsoever things *were* w. aforetime *were*
w. for our learning that we might have hope
See BOOK, CHRONICLE.

WRONG.

Gen. 16. 5. Sarai said, my w. be upon thee
Exod. 2. 13. Moses said to him that did the w.
Deut. 19. 16. to testify against him that what is w.
Judg. 11. 27. thou dost me w. to war against me
1 Chron. 12. 17. seeing there is no w. in my hands
16. 21. he suffered no man to do them w. he reproved kings for their sakes, Psal. 105. 14.
Esth. 1. 16. Vashti hath not done w. to the king only
Job 19. 7. behold, I cry out of w. but am not heard
Jer. 22. 3. do no w. do no violence to the stranger
13. woe to him that buildeth his chambers by w.
Lam. 3. 59. O Lord, thou hast seen my w. judge thou
Hab. 1. 4. therefore w. judgment proceedeth
Mat. 20. 13. he answered, friend, I do thee no w.
Acts 7. 24. and seeing one of them suffer w.
26. ye are brethren, why do ye w. one to another?
27. he that did his neighbour w. thrust him away
18. 14. if it were a matter of w. or lewdness
25. 10. Paul said, to the Jews have I done no w.
1 Cor. 6. 7. why do ye not rather take w.?
8. nay, ye do w. and defraud your brethren
2 Cor. 7. 12. I did it not for his cause that had done the w. nor for his cause that suffered w.
12. 13. I was not burdensome, forgive me this w.
Col. 3. 25. he that doth w. shall receive for the w.

WRONGED.

2 Cor. 7. 2. receive us, we have w. no man
Philem. 18. if he hath w. thee, or oweth ought

WRONGETH.

Prov. 8. 36. he that sinneth against me w. his own soul

WRONGFULLY.

Job 21. 27. the devices ye w. imagine against me
Psal. 35. 19. let not mine enemies w. rejoice
38. 19. they that hate me w. are multiplied
69. 4. would destroy me, being mine enemies w.
119. 86. they persecute me w. help thou me

Ezek. 22. 29. they have oppressed the stranger w.
1 Pet. 2. 19. if a man endure grief, suffering w.

WROTE.

Exod. 24. 4. Moses w. all the words of the Lord, and rose early in the morning, Deut. 31. 9.
34. 28. Lord w. upon the tables words of covenant, ten commandment Deut. 4. 13. | 5. 22. | 10. 4.
Num. 33. 2. and Moses w. their goings out
Deut. 31. 22. Moses w. this song the same day
Josh. 8. 32. Joshua w. upon the stones the law
1 Sam. 10. 25. Samuel w. the manner of the kingdom
2 Sam. 11. 14. David w. a letter to Joab, 15.
1 Kings 21. 8. Jezebel w. letters in Ahab's name, 9.
2 Kings 10. 1. Jehu w. 6. || 1 Chr. 24. 6. Shemaiah w.
2 Chron. 30. 1. Hezekiah w. letters to Ephraim
32. 17. Sennacherib w. to rail on the God of Israel
Ezra 4. 6. they w. an accusation against Judah
8. Rehum w. 9. || Esth. 8. 5. the letters Haman w.
Esth. 8. 10. Mordecai w. letters, 9, 20, 29.
Jer. 36. 4. Baruch w. from Jeremiah, 18, 27, 32.
51. 60. so Jeremiah w. in a book all the evil
Dan. 5. 5. fingers of a man's hand w. on the wall
6. 25. then king Darius w. unto all people
7. 1. Daniel had a dream, and he w. the dream
Mark 10. 5. for your hardn. Mos. w. you this precept
12. 19. Master, Moses w. to us, Luke 20. 28.
Luke 1. 63. Zacharias w. saying, his name is John
John 5. 46. have believed me, for Moses w. of me
8. 6. Jesus with his finger w. on the ground, 8.
19. 19. Pilate w. a title and put it on the cross
21. 24. John w. and testified of these things
Acts 15. 23. the apostles w. letters by them
18. 27. the brethren w. exhorting the disciples
23. 25. Lysias w. a letter after this manner
Rom. 16. 22. I Tertius, who w. this epistle, salute
1 Cor. 5. 9. Paul w. in an epistle. 2 Cor. 2. 3, 4. |
7. 12. Eph. 3. 3. Philem. 21.
7. 1. concerning the things whereof ye w. to me
2 John 5. not as though I w. a new commandment
3 John 9. I w. to the church, Diotr. receives us not

WROTH.

Gen. 4. 5. Cain was very w. || 6. why art thou w.?
31. 36. Jacob was w. || 34. 7. Jacob's sons were w.
40. 2. Pharaoh was w. with two officers, 41. 10.
Exod. 16. 20. Moses was w. Num. 16. 15. | 31. 14.
Num. 16. 22. wilt thou be w. with all congregation?
Deut. 1. 34. the Lord heard your words and was w.
3. 26. | 9. 19. 2 Sam. 22. 8. 2 Chron. 28. 9.
Psal. 18. 7. | 78. 21, 59, 62.
1 Sam. 18. 8. and Saul was very w. 20. 7.
29. 4. the princes of Philistines were w. with him
2 Sam. 3. 8. Abner was w. || 13. 21. David was w.
2 Kings 5. 11. but Naaman was w. and went away
13. 19. and the man of God was w. with him
2 Chron. 16. 10. Asa was w. || 26. 19. Uzziah was w.
Neh. 4. 1. Sanballat, 7. || Esth. 1. 12. Ahasuerus w.
Esth. 2. 21. Bigthan and Teresh were w.
Psal. 89. 38. thou hast been w. with thine anointed
Isa. 28. 21. he shall be w. as in the valley of Gibeon
47. 6. I was w. with my people, I have polluted
54. 9. I have sworn I would not be w. with thee
57. 16. I will not contend, nor will I be always w.
17. for the iniquity of his covetousness was I w.
and smote him, I hid me, and was w.
64. 5. behold thou art w. for we have sinned
9. be not w. very sore, O Lord; we are thy people
Jer. 37. 15. princes were w. || Mat. 2. 16. Herod was w.
Lam. 5. 22. rejected us, thou art very w. against us
Mat. 18. 34. his Lord was w. and delivered him
22. 7. king was w. || Rev. 12. 17. dragon was w.

WROUGHT.

Gen. 34. 7. Shechem had w. folly in Israel
Exod. 10. 2. what things I have w. in Egypt
36. 1. then w. Bezaleel and Aholiab, L. put wisd.
4. all the wise men w. the work, 8. | 39. 6.
Lev. 20. 12. put to death, they have w. confusion
Num. 23. 23. it shall be said, what hath God w.?
Deut. 17. 2. man or woman that hath w. wickedness
22. 21. w. folly in Israel, Josh. 7. 15. Judg. 20. 10.
31. 18. for the evils which they shall have w.
Ruth 2. 19. shewed with whom she had w. the man's name with whom I w. to-day, is Boaz
1 Sam. 6. 6. Lord had w. wonderfully among them
11. 13. Lord hath w. salvation in Israel, 19. 5.
14. 45. for Jonathan hath w. with God this day
2 Sam. 18. 13. otherwise I should have w. falsehood
23. 10. the Lord w. a great victory that day, 12.
1 Kings 5. 16. who ruled over the people that w. 9. 23.
16. 20. the acts of Zimri, and the treason he w.
25. but Omri w. evil in the eyes of the Lord
2 Kings 3. 2. Jehoram w. evil, 2 Chron. 21. 6.
17. 11. Israel w. wicked things, Neh. 9. 18.
21. 6. Manasseh w. much wickedness, 2 Chr. 33. 6.
1 Chron. 4. 21. the families that w. fine linen
2 Chron. 3. 14. and he w. cherubims thereon
24. 12. they hired such as w. iron and brass
13. so the workman w. the work, 34. 10, 13.
32. † 24. the Lord w. a miracle for Hezekiah
Neh. 4. 16. half of my servants w. in the work
17. every one with one of his hands w. in the work
Job 12. 9. the hand of the Lord hath w. this
36. 23. or who canst say, thou hast w. iniquity?
Psal. 31. 19. hast w. for them that trust in thee
68. 28. strengthen that which thou hast w. for us
78. 43. how he had w. his signs in Egypt
Eccl. 2. 11. I looked on all works my hands had w.
Isa. 26. 12. for thou hast w. all our works in us
18. we have not w. any deliverance in the earth
41. 4. who hath w. and done it? I the Lord, I am
Jer. 11. 15. seeing she hath w. lewdness with many
18. 3. and behold, he w. a work on the wheels
Ezek. 20. 9. I w. for my name's sake, 14, 22, 44.
29. 20. given him Egypt, because they w. for me
Dan. 4. 2. the wonders that God hath w. toward me
Jonah 1. 11. the sea w. and was tempestuous, 13.
Zeph. 2. 3. meek of earth who have w. his judgment
Mat. 20. 12. these last have w. but one hour
26. 10. she hath w. a good work on me, Mark 14. 6.
Acts 15. 12. what wonders God hath w. 21. 19.
18. 3. Paul of same trade, abode with Aquila and w.
19. 11. God w. special miracles by hands of Paul
Rom. 7. 8. w. in me all manner of concupiscence

Rom. 15. 18. things which Christ hath not w. by me
2 Cor. 5. 5. he that hath w. us for same thing, is God
7. 11. what carefulness it w. in you?
Gal. 2. 8. for he that w. effectually in Peter
Eph. 1. 20. which he w. in Christ, when he raised
2 Thess. 3. 8. but we w. with labour and travail
Heb. 11. 33. who, through faith, w. righteousness
Jam. 2. 22. seest thou how faith w. with his works?
1 Pet. 4. 3. to have w. the will of the Gentiles
2 John 8. lose not those things which we have w.
Rev. 19. 20. the false prophet that w. miracles

WROUGHT, *Passively*.

Num. 31. 51. Moses took of them all w. jewels
Deut. 13. 14. that such abomination is w. 17. 4.
21. 3. take an heifer which hath not been w.
1 Kings 7. 26. the brim of the sea was w. like
1 Chron. 22. 2. he set masons to hew w. stones
Neh. 6. 16. this work was w. of our God
Psal. 45. 13. her clothing was of w. gold
139. 15. when I was made in secret, curiously w.
Eccl. 2. 17. the works w. under the sun is grievous
Mat. 14. † 2. John the Baptist is risen, therefore mighty works are w. by him, Mark 6. 2.
John 3. 21. made manifest that they are w. of God
19. † 23. coat was without seam, w. from the top
Acts 5. 12. wonders were w. among the people
2 Cor. 1. † 6. which is w. in enduring sufferings
12. 12. the signs of an apostle were w. among you

WROUGHTEST.

Ruth 2. 19. Naomi said to her, where w. thou?

WRUNG.

Lev. 1. 15. the blood shall be w. out, 5. 9.
Psal. 73. 10. waters of a full cup are w. to them
Isa. 51. 17. thou hast w. out the dregs of the cup

Y.

YARN.

1 Kings 10. 28. Solomon had linen y. out of Egypt, the king's merchants received y. 2 Chron. 1. 16.

YCE, or rather ICE.

Job 6. 16. which are blackish by reason of y.
38. 29. out of whose womb came the y. and frost
Psal. 147. 17. he casteth forth his y. like morsels

YE.

Gen. 3. 5. *ye* shall be as gods knowing good and evil
Luke 16. 15. *ye* are they which justify yourselves
1 Cor. 6. 11. but *ye* are washed, *ye* are sanctified, *ye* are justified in the name of the Lord Jesus
20. *ye* are bought with a price, glorify God in body
2 Cor. 3. 2. *ye* are our epistle written in our hearts
6. 12. *ye* are not straitened in us but in your own
Gal. 4. 12. brethren, be as I am, for I am as *ye* are
6. 1. *ye* which are spiritual, restore such an one
Eph. 2. 13. *ye* who sometimes were far off are nigh
1 Thess. 2. 19. what is our joy, are not even *ye*?
20. *ye* are our glory || 3. 8. if *ye* stand fast in Lord
5. 4. but *ye*, brethren, are not in darkness
5. *ye* are all children of light and of the day
2 Thess. 3. 13. but *ye*, brethren, be not weary?
1 Pet. 2. 9. but *ye* are a chosen generation

YEA.

Gen. 3. 1. y. hath God said, ye shall not eat
Mat. 5. 37. let your conversation be y. y. Jam. 5. 12.
9. 28. they said unto him, y. Lord, 13. 51.
Acts 5. 8. Sapphira said, y. for so much
22. 27. tell me, art thou a Roman? he said, y.
2 Cor. 1. 17. there should be y. y. and nay, nay
18. our word toward you was not y. and nay
19. for the Son of God was not y. and nay
20. all the promises of God in him are y. and amen
Phil. 1. 18. I do rejoice, y. and will rejoice
3. 8. y. and I count all things but loss for excellency
2 Tim. 3. 12. y. and all that live godly in Christ Jesus
Philem. 20. y. brother, let me have joy of thee

YEAR.

Concerning the Jewish year, *see* MONTH. *It is said in* Gen. 15. 13. *and in* Acts 7. 6. *that* they should entreat them evil four hundred *years: but in* Exod. 12. 40. *it is said*, The sojourning of the children of Israel who dwelt in Egypt, was four hundred and thirty *years. This difference is reconciled by distinguishing the beginning of the account, which, if taken from Abraham's leaving of Chaldea, and receiving the first promise of Canaan, when his sojourning did begin; then from that time to the giving of the law, there will be four hundred and thirty* years, *as it is in Exodus. But if it be taken from Abraham's seed, that is, from the birth of Isaac, which was in the hundredth* year *of Abraham's age, and so thirty* years *after his departure from Chaldea, then it must consequently be thirty* years *less from thence to the giving of the law; and so that will agree exactly with the four hundred* years *mentioned in Genesis and in the Acts, which are assigned to his seed's sojourning in a strange land; by the* strange land *both Canaan and Egypt being to be understood; for the Chaldee Paraphrast, and the generality of the Jews, determine the space wherein they sojourned in Egypt, to be but two hundred and ten* years; *only Josephus calls them two hundred and fifteen.*
Gen. 17. 21. whom Sarah shall bear the next y.
26. 12. Isaac received the same y. an hundred-fold
47. 17. Joseph fed them with bread that y.
Exod. 12. 2. it shall be the first month of the y.
23. 14. keep a feast to me in the y. Lev. 23. 41.
17. three times in the y. all thy males shall appear before the Lord God, 34. 23, 24.
Deut. 16. 16.
29. I will not drive them out from thee in one y.
Lev. 16. 34. to make an atonement once a y.
25. 5. it is a y. of rest || 29. redeem it within a y.
Num. 9. 22. if it were a y. that the cloud tarried
14. 34. each day for a y. shall ye bear iniquities
Deut. 15. 9. saying, the y. of release is at hand
26. 12. the third y. which is the y. of tithing
Josh. 5. 12. they did eat the fruit of Canaan that y.
Judg. 10. 8. that y. the Ammonites vexed Israel
11. 40. they went to lament four days in a y.

Judg. 17. 10. I will give thee ten shekels by the y.
1 Sam. 27. 7. David dwelt a y. and four months
2 Sam. 11. 1. that after the y. was expired
14. 26. it was at every y. end that he polled it
1 Kings 9. 25. three times in a y. did Solomon offer
10. 14. now the weight of the gold that came to
Solomon in one y. 2 Chron. 9. 13.
2 Kings 19. 29. ye shall eat this y. such things as
grow of themselves in second and third y.
Isa. 37. 30.
2 Chron. 27. 5. Ammon gave him the same y.
Esth. 9. 27. they would keep two days every y.
Ps. 65. 11. thou crownest the y. with thy goodness
Isa. 6. 1. in the y. that king Uzziah died
14. 28. in the y. king Ahaz died was this burden
21. 16. in a y. all the glory of Kedar shall fail
61. 2. to proclaim the acceptable y. of the Lord,
and the day of vengeance of our God, Luke 4. 19.
63. 4. and the y. of my redeemed is come
Jer. 11. 23. bring evil on the men of Anathoth, even
the y. of their visitation, 23. 12. | 48. 44.
17. 8. shall not be careful in the y. of drought
28. 16. thus saith the Lord, this y. thou shalt die
17. so Hananiah the prophet died the same y.
51. 46. a rumour shall both come in one y.
Ezek. 4. 6. I have appointed each day for a y.
46. 17. it shall be his to the y. of liberty
Mic. 6. 6. shall I come with calves of a y. old?
Luke 2. 41. his parents went to Jerusalem every y.
13. 8. he said, Lord, let it alone this y. also
John 11. 49. Caiaphas being high priest that y. said
one man should die for the people, 51. | 18. 13.
Acts 11. 26. a whole y. they assembled themselves
18. 11. Paul continued a y. at Corinth, teaching
2 Cor. 8. 10. but also to be forward a y. ago
9. 2. that Achaia was ready a y. ago, your zeal
Heb. 9. 7. the high priest went in once a y. 25.
10. 3. there is a remembrance made of sins every y.
Jam. 4. 13. we will continue there a y. and buy
Rev. 9. 15. who were prepared for a month and a y.

YEAR *after* YEAR.

2 Sam. 21. 1. there was a famine three years y. after y.

YEAR *by* YEAR.

Deut. 14. 22. thou shalt tithe the increase of thy
seed that the field bringeth forth y. by y.
15. 20. thou shalt eat it before the Lord y. by y.
1 Sam. 1. 7. as he did so y. by y. so she provoked her
1 Kings 5. 11. thus Solomon gave to Hiram y. by y.
10. 25. they brought a rate y. by y. 2 Chron. 9. 24.
2 Kings 17. 4. no present as he had done y. by y.
Neh. 10. 34. to bring the wood offering y. by y.
35. bring the first-fruits of all trees y. by y.
Heb. 10. 1. those sacrifices which they offered y. by y.

YEAR *to* YEAR.

Exod. 13. 10. keep this ordinance from y. to y.
1 Sam. 2. 19. brought a coat to him from y. to y.
7. 16. Samuel went from y. to y. in circuit to Bethel
2 Chr. 24. 5. repair house of your God from y. to y.
Isa. 29. 1. add ye y. to y. let them kill sacrifices
Zech. 14. 16. shall go up from y. to y. to worship L.
See First, Second, Third, Fifth, Seventh.

YEARLY.

Lev. 25. 53. as a y. hired servant shall he be
Judg. 11. 40. daughters of Israel went y. to lament
21. 19. there is a feast of the Lord in Shiloh y.
1 Sam. 1. 3. Elkanah went up y. to worship
21. went up to offer the y. sacrifice, 2. 19.
20. 6. there is a y. sacrifice there for all the family
Esth. 9. 21. that they should keep the 14th day of
the month Adar, and fifteenth of the same y.

YEARS.

Gen. 1. 14. let them be for seasons, days, and y.
25. 7. these are the days of the y. of Abraham
8. Abraham died an old man and full of y.
17. Ishmael was an hundred thirty seven y.
47. 9. few and evil have the y. of my life been
Exod. 34. 22. the feast of in-gathering at the y. end
Lev. 25. 15. according to number of y. 16, 50, 52.
27. 18. the money according to the y. that remain
Deut. 32. 7. consider the y. of many generations
Josh. 13. 1. Joshua was old and stricken in y.
1 Sam. 29. 3. David who hath been with these y.
1 Kings 1. 1. David was old and stricken in y.
17. 1. there shall not be dew nor rain these y.
2 Chr. 14. 6. land had rest, Asa had no war in those y.
18. 2. after certain y. he went down to Ahab
Job 10. 5. are thy y. as man's days, that searchest sin
15. 20. the number of y. is hidden to the oppressor
16. 22. when a few y. are come, I shall go the way
32. 7. and multitude of y. should teach wisdom
36. 11. they shall spend their y. in pleasures
26. nor can number of his y. be searched out
Psal. 31. 10. and my y. are spent with sighing
61. 6. wilt prolong his y. as many generations
77. 5. I considered the y. of ancient times
10. I will remember the y. of the right-hand
78. 33. their y. did he consume in trouble
90. 4. for a thousand y. in thy sight are but as
yesterday when it is past, 2 Pet. 3. 8.
9. we spend our y. as a tale that is told
10. the days of our y. are threescore y. and ten
15. according to the y. wherein we have seen evil
102. 24. thy y. are throughout all generations
27. thou art the same, thy y. shall have no end
Prov. 4. 10. the y. of thy life shall be many, 9. 11.
5. 9. lest thou give thy y. unto the cruel
10. 27. the y. of the wicked shall be shortened
Eccl. 12. 1. while evil days come not, nor y. draw nigh
Isa. 21. 16. according to the y. of an hireling
38. 10. I am deprived of the residue of my y.
15. I shall go softly all my y. in bitterness of soul
Ezek. 4. 5. I have laid on thee the y. of their iniquity
22. 4. and thou art come even unto thy y.
38. 8. in latter y. thou shalt come into the land
Dan. 9. 2. I understood by books the number of y.
11. 6. in the end of y. they shall join together
8. continue more y. than the king of the north
13. the king of north shall come after certain y.
Joel 2. 2. even to the y. of many generations
25. I will restore the y. the locusts hath eaten
Hab. 3. 2. revive thy work in the midst of the y.
Mal. 3. 4. the offerings pleasant as in the former y.

Luke 1. 7. both were well stricken in y. 18.
Gal. 4. 10. ye observe days and months, and y.
Heb. 1. 12. thou art the same, thy y. shall not fail
11. 24. by faith Moses when come to y. refused
Rev. 20. 2. an angel bound Satan a thousand y.
3. till the thousand y. should be fulfilled
4. they lived and reigned with Christ a thous. y.
7. when the thousand y. are expired, Satan shall
See Numeral words in their places, as Hundred,
Many, Two, Three, Six, Old.

YELL.

Jer. 51. 38. like lions, they shall y. as lions' whelps

YELLED.

Jer. 2. 15. the young lions roared and y. on him

YELLOW.

Lev. 13. 30. behold, if there be in it a y. thin hair
32. behold, if there be in it no y. hair
36. priests shall not seek for y. hair, is unclean
Psal. 68. 13. her feathers covered with y. gold

YEARN.

Gen. 43. 30. for his bowels did y. on his brother

YEARNED.

1 Kings 3. 26. for her bowels y. upon her son

YESTERDAY.

Gen. 31. † 2. not toward him as y. and day before
Exod. 4. † 10. not eloquent since y. nor third day
5. 14. why have ye not fulfilled your task y.?
Deut. 19. † 4. hated not from y. the third day, 6.
Josh. 3. † 4. ye have not passed this way since y.?
1 Sam. 19. † 7. David was in Saul's presence as y.
20. 27. why came not the son of Jesse to meat y.?
2 Sam. 15. 20. whereas thou camest but y.
2 Kings 9. 26. I have seen y. the blood of Naboth
1 Chr. 11. † 2. y. and third day, when Saul was king
Job 8. 9. we are but of y. and know nothing
Ps. 90. 4. a thousand years in thy sight are but as y.
Isa. 30. † 33. Tophet is ordained from y.
Mic. 2. † 8. y. my people is risen up as an enemy
John 4. 52. y. at the seventh hour the fever left him
Acts 7. 28. kill me as thou didst the Egyptian y.?
Heb. 13. 8. Jesus Christ, the same y. and for ever

YESTERNIGHT.

Gen. 19. 34. behold, I lay y. with my father
31. 29. the God of your father spake to me y.
42. God hath seen affliction, and rebuked thee y.

YET.

Gen. 40. 23. y. did not the butler remember Joseph
Exod. 9. 17. as y. exaltest thyself against my people
10. 7. knowest thou not y. that Egypt is destroyed?
Lev. 26. 18. if ye will not y. hearken unto me
44. y. for all that, when they be in the land
Deut. 1. 32. y. in this thing ye did not believe
9. 29. y. they are thy people and inheritance
12. 9. ye are not as y. come to the inheritance
29. 4. y. the Lord hath not given you eyes to see
Josh. 14. 11. as y. I am as strong this day as I was
Judg. 7. 4. Lord said, the people are y. too many
10. 13. y. ye have forsaken me and served gods
1 Sam. 15. 30. y. honour me now before the elders
2 Sam. 23. 5. y. made with me everlasting covenant
1 Kings 14. 8. y. hast not been as my servant David
19. 18. y. I have left me seven thousand in Israel
22. 8. there is y. one by whom we may inquire
43. as y. the people did sacrifice, 2 Kings 14. 4.
2 Kings 8. 19. y. the Lord would not destroy Judah
13. 23. nor cast he them from his presence as y.
2 Chron. 20. 33. as y. the people had not prepared
27. 2. and the people did y. corruptly
30. 18. not cleansed, y. did they eat the passover
Ezra 3. 6. the foundation of temple was not y. laid
9. 9. y. our God hath not forsaken us, Neh. 9. 19.
Neh. 5. 18. y. required not I bread of the governor
13. 18. y. ye bring more wrath upon Israel
Esth. 5. 13. y. all this availeth me nothing so long as
Job 1. 16. while he was y. speaking, 17, 18.
6. 10. then should I y. have comfort
13. 15. though he slay me y. will I trust in him
20. 7. y. he shall perish for ever, like his dung
29. 5. when the Almighty was y. with me
35. 15. y. he knoweth it not in great extremity
Psal. 2. 6. y. have I set my king on my holy hill
37. 25. y. have I not seen the righteous forsaken
42. 5. I shall y. praise him, 11. | 43. 5. | 71. 14.
44. 17. this is come, y. have we not forgotten
119. 51. y. have I not declined from thy law, 157.
83. y. do I not forget thy statutes, 109, 141.
Prov. 27. 22. y. will not his foolishness depart from
30. 12. y. is not washed from their filthiness
Eccl. 4. 3. better is he which hath not y. been
Cant. 8. 1. kiss thee, y. I should not be despised
Isa. 10. 22. y. a remnant of them shall return
14. 1. for the Lord will y. choose Israel and set them
17. 6. y. gleaning grapes shall be left in it
28. 4. while it is y. in his hand, he eateth it up
12. this is the rest, y. they would not hear
31. 2. y. he also is wise, and will bring evil
49. 5. though Israel be not gathered, y. shall I be
15. they may forget, y. will I not forget thee
53. 7. he was oppressed, y. he opened not his mouth
Jer. 2. 9. I will y. plead with you, saith the Lord
3. 1. y. return to me || 5. 28. y. they prosper
15. 1. y. my mind could not be toward this people
23. 21. prophets y. they ran, y. they prophesied
36. 24. y. they were not afraid, nor rent garments
Ezek. 8. 18. tho' they cry, y. will I not hear them
11. 16. y. will I be to them as a little sanctuary
28. 2. said, I am a god, y. thou art a man, and not G.
36. 37. I will y. for this be inquired of by Israel
Dan. 9. 13. y. made we not our prayer before God
11. 35. because it is y. for a time appointed
45. y. he shall come to his end, none shall help him
Hos. 7. 9. grey hairs are on him, y. he knoweth not
13. 4. y. I am the Lord thy God from land of Egypt
Amos 4. 6. I have given you want of bread, y. have
ye not returned to me, 8, 9, 10, 11. Hag. 2. 17.
6. 10. he shall say, is there y. any with thee
Jonah 2. 4. y. I will look toward thy holy temple
3. 4. y. forty days and Nineveh shall be overthrown
4. 2. was my saying, when I was y. in my country
Mic. 6. 10. are there y. the treasures of wickedness
Nah. 3. 10. y. was she carried away into captivity
Hab. 3. 18. y. I will rejoice in the Lord, I will joy

Mal. 2. 14. y. is she thy companion, and the wife
Mat. 15. 17. do ye not y. understand that whatsoever
entereth in at the mouth, 16. 9. Mark 8. 17.
19. 20. these things have I kept, what lack I y.?
24. 6. but the end is not y. Mark 13. 7.
Mark 11. 13. for the time of figs was not y.
Luke 24. 44. the words I spake while y. with you
John 2. 4. Jesus saith unto her, my hour is not y.
come, 7. 6, 30. | 8. 20.
7. 39. for the Holy Ghost was not y. given
11. 25. though he were dead y. shall he live
20. 9. for as y. they knew not the scripture
Acts 8. 16. as y. H. Ghost was fallen on none of them
Rom. 4. 11. he had y. being uncircumcised, 12.
5. 6. we were y. without strength || 8. y. sinners
8. 24. what a man seeth, why doth he y. hope for?
9. 19. thou wilt say, why doth he y. find fault?
1 Cor. 3. 3, ye are y. carnal? || 15. y. so as by fire
7. 10. to the married I comm. y. not I, but the L.
14. 21. y. for all that will they not hear me
15. 10. y. not I, but the grace of God with me
17. your faith is vain, ye are y. in your sins
2 Cor. 1. 10. we trust that he will y. deliver
23. to spare you I came not as y. to Corinth
6. 8. as deceivers, y. true as unknown, y. known
Gal. 2. 20. y. not I, but Christ liveth in me
3. 4. have ye suffered in vain? if it be y. in vain
5. 11. I, brethren, if I y. preach circumcision
2 Thess. 2. 5. when I was y. with you, I told you
2 Tim. 2. 5. y. is he not crowned, except he strive
Heb. 2. 8. we see not y. all things put under him
4. 15. was tempted like as we are, y. without sin
7. 10. for he was y. in the loins of his father
11. 4. and by it he being dead, y. speaketh
7. Noah, being warned of things not seen as y.
Jam. 2. 10. keep the whole law, y. offend in one point
11. y. if thou kill || 4. 2. y. ye have not
1 John 3. 2. it doth not y. appear what we shall be
Rev. 17. 8. the beast that was, and is not, and y. is
10. and one is, and the other is not y. come
12. ten kings who have received no kingdom as y.
See Alive.

YIELD.

Gen. 4. 12. the earth not henceforth y. her strength
49. 20. Asher's bread be fat, shall y. royal dainties
Lev. 19. 25. that it may y. to you the increase
26. 4. the land shall y. her increase, trees y. fruit
20. for your land shall not y. her increase
2 Chron. 30. 8. but y. yourselves to the Lord
Psal. 67. 6. the land shall y. her increase, 85. 12.
107. 37. plant vineyards may y. fruits of increase
Prov. 7. 21. with much fair speech she caused him y.
Isa. 5. 10. ten acres of vineyard shall y. one bath,
and the seed of an homer shall y. an ephah
Hos. 8. 7. have sown the wind, the bud shall y.
no meal, if so be it y. the stranger shall
swallow it up
Joel 2. 22. the fig-tree and vine y. their strength
Hab. 3. 17. altho' fields shall y. no meat, joy in God
Acts 23. 21. but do not thou y. unto them
Rom. 6. 13. nor y. ye your members as instruments
of unrighteousness to sin, y. yourselves to God
16. that to whom ye y. yourselves servants
19. y. your members servants to righteousness
Jam. 3. 12. no fountain y. salt water and fresh

YIELDED.

Gen. 49. 33. Jacob after commanding his sons, y. up
Num. 17. 8. behold the rod of Aaron y. almonds
Dan. 3. 28. y. their bodies that they might not serve
Mat. 27. 50. Jesus cried again, and y. up the ghost
Acts 5. 10. then Sapphira y. up the ghost
Rom. 6. 19. as ye have y. your members servants

YIELDETH.

Neh. 9. 37. it y. much increase to the kings
Job 24. 5. the wilderness y. food for them
Heb. 12. 11. y. the peaceable fruit of righteousness

YIELDING.

Gen. 1. 11. bring forth herb y. seed, tree y. fruit, 12.
29. I have given you every tree y. seed
Eccl. 10. 4. for y. pacifieth great offences
See Fruit.

YOKE.

Besides the common acceptation of this term, for an instrument put about the necks of cattle, to couple them for drawing, the Scripture makes mention (1) *Of the* yoke *of bondage, or slavery.* Lev. 26. 13. I have broken the bands of your *yoke.* Deut. 28. 48. He shall put a *yoke* of iron upon thy neck. (2) *Of the* yoke *of afflictions and crosses.* Lam. 3. 27. It is good for a man that he bear the *yoke* in his youth. "*It is a man's duty, it is profitable to him, patiently to bear what afflictions God will please to lay upon him, and to restrain his wanton spirits when they are most prone to be too brisk and lascivious.*" (3) *Of the* yoke *of punishment for sin, which the prophet Jeremiah expresses thus,* The *yoke* of my transgressions is bound by his hand, Lam. 1. 14. "*The punishment and bondage I undergo for my sins is bound so fast that I cannot shake it off.*" (4) *Of the* yoke *of God's commandments,* Mat. 11. 29, 30. Take my *yoke* upon you; for my *yoke* is easy. *The service of God to flesh and blood is a* yoke, *because it grates upon the sensitive appetites, and restrains our natural motions and inclinations; yet it is easy, in comparison of the service of sin, the covenant of works, and the ceremonial law; it is easy to them that love God, and are regenerated, because the law is written in their hearts,* Psal. 37. 31. *They are endued with faith,* Mark 9. 23. *And they are strengthened by Christ,* Phil. 4. 13. (5) *There is the* yoke *of legal ceremonies,* Acts 15. 10. Gal. 5. 1. *They are called a* yoke *in respect of their variety, and the difficulty in performing them; in respect of their chargeableness, and inefficacy, being only* shadows of good things to come, Heb. 10. 1.

Gen. 27. 40. that thou shalt break his y. Jer. 30. 8.
Lev. 26. 13. I have broken the bands of your y. and
made you go upright, Ezek. 34. 27.
Num. 19. 2. bring a red heifer without blemish, on
which never came y. Deut. 21. 3. 1 Sam. 6. 7

Deut. 28. 48. he shall put a *y*. of iron upon thy neck, until he have destroyed thee, *Jer.* 28. 14.
1 *Sam.* 11. 7. Saul took a *y*. of oxen and hewed them
14. 14. an half acre, which a *y*. of oxen might plow
1 *Kings* 12. 4. thy father made our *y*. grievous, make his heavy *y*. lighter, 10, 11, 14. 2 *Chron.* 10. 4.
19. 19. Elisha plowing with twelve *y*. of oxen
21. he took a *y*. of oxen, and slew them
Job 1. 3. Job had five hundred *y*. of oxen
42. 12. he had a thousand *y*. of oxen
Isa. 9. 4. thou hast broken the *y*. of his burden, and the staff of his shoulder, 10. 27. | 14. 25.
47. 6. on ancient thou hast very heavily laid thy *y*.
58. 6. oppressed go free, and that ye break every *y*.
Jer. 2. 20. for of old time I have broken thy *y*.
5. 5. but these have altogether broken the *y*.
27. 8. that will not put their neck under the *y*.
11. that bring their neck under the *y*. 12.
28. 2. broken the *y*. of the king of Babylon, 4, 11.
12. Hananiah had broken the *y*. from Jeremiah
31. 18. as a bullock unaccustomed to the *y*.
51. 23. will I break the husbandman and his *y*.
Lam. 1. 14. the *y*. of my transgressions is bound
3. 27. it is good for man to bear the *y*. in his youth
Hos. 11. 4. I was as they that take off the *y*.
Nah. 1. 13. now will I break his *y*. from off thee
Mat. 11. 29. take my *y*. on you || 30. my *y*. is easy
Luke 14. 19. I have bought five *y*. of oxen
Acts 15. 10. to put a *y*. on the disciples' neck
Gal. 5. 1. be not entangled with the *y*. of bondage
1 *Tim.* 6. 1. let as many servants as are under the *y*.

YOKES.

Jer. 27. 2. make thee bonds and *y*. 28. 13.
28. 13. hast broken the *y*. of wood, make *y*. iron
Ezek. 30. 18. when I shall break the *y*. of Egypt

YOKED.

2 *Cor.* 6. 14. be not unequally *y*. with unbelievers

YOKE-FELLOW.

Phil 4. 3. I entreat thee also, true *y.-fellow*

YONDER.

Gen. 22. 5. I and the lad will go *y*. and worship
Num. 16. 37. and scatter thou the fire *y*.
23. 15. stand here, while I meet the Lord *y*.
2 *Kings* 4. 25. behold, *y*. is that Shunamite
Mat. 17. 20. ye shall say, remove hence to *y*. place
26. 36. Jesus saith, sit here, while I go and pray *y*.

YOU.

Josh. 3. 4. there shall be a space between *y*. and ark
Neh. 2. 20. but *y*. have no portion in Jerusalem
Job 16. 4. I could shake my head at *y*.
Isa. 59. 2. your iniquities separate betw. *y*. and G.
Ezek. 11. 19. will put a new spirit within *y*. 36. 26, 27.
36. 7. the heathen that are about *y*. bear shame, 36.
Amos 2. 13. behold, I am pressed under *y*.
3. 2. *y*. only have I known of all families of earth
Luke 10. 16. he that heareth *y*. heareth me, he that despiseth *y*. despiseth me and him that sent me
13. 28. and *y*. yourselves thrust out of the kingdom
Rom. 2. 24. the name of God is blasphemed thro' *y*.
2 *Cor.* 1. 11. *y*. also helping by prayer for us
8. 13. that other men be eased and *y*. burdened
9. 4. lest we, that we say not *y*. be ashamed
10. 16. to preach the gospel in the regions beyond *y*.
12. 14. for I seek not yours but *y*.
Eph. 2. 1. *y*. hath he quickened who were dead
22. in whom *y*. also are builded together
Col. 1. 21. *y*. that were some time alienated
2. 13. *y*. being dead in sins hath he quickened

After YOU.

Gen. 9. 9. establish covenant with you, and seed *a. y*.
Lev. 25. 46. ye shall take them as an inheritance for your children *after y*. 1 *Chron.* 28. 8.
26. 33. and I will draw out a sword *after y*.
Deut. 11. 4. to overflow them, as they pursued *aft. y*.
29. 22. the generation that shall rise up *after y*.
1 *Sam.* 25. 19. go on before, behold, I come *after y*.
Jer. 42. 16. the famine shall follow close *after y*.
2 *Cor.* 9. 14. which long *after y*. *Phil.* 1. 8.
Phil. 2. 26. Epaphroditus longed *after y*.

Against YOU.

Exod. 10. 16. he said, I have sinned *against y*.
Lev. 26. 17. I will set my face *ag. y*. *Jer.* 44. 11.
Num. 17. 5. whereby they murmur *against y*.
Deut. 1. 44. the Amorites came out *against y*.
4. 26. I call heaven and earth to witness *against y*. this day ye shall soon utterly perish, 30. 19.
8. 19. I testify *ag. y*. that ye shall surely perish
9. 19. I was afraid of the anger wherewith the Lord was wroth *against y*. 11. 17. *Josh.* 23. 16.
Josh. 24. 11. the men of Jericho fought *against y*.
1 *Sam.* 12. 5. the Lord is witness *ag. y*. *Mic.* 1. 2.
12. Nahash king of the Ammonites came *ag. y*.
15. the hand of the Lord shall be *against y*.
2 *Sam.* 17. 21. thus Ahithophel counselled *ag. y*.
2 *Chron.* 13. 12. to cry alarm *against y*. O Israel
Job 16. 4. I could heap up words *against y*.
Jer. 18. 11. behold, I devise a device *against y*.
21. 5. and I myself will fight *against y*. in anger
26. 13. Lord will repent of evil pronounced *ag. y*.
37. 10. army of the Chaldeans that fight *against y*.
19. the king of Babylon shall not come *against y*.
38. 5. the king cannot do any thing *against y*.
44. 29. that my words shall stand *against y*.
49. 30. Neb. hath conceived a purpose *against y*.
Ezek. 13. 8. I am *ag. y*. || 36. 2. enemy said *ag. y*.
Amos 3. 1. Lord hath spoken *ag. y*. 5. 1. *Zeph.* 2. 5.
6. 14. behold, I will raise up *against y*. a nation
Mic. 2. 4. one shall take up a parable *against y*.
Mat. 5. 11. shall say all manner of evil *against y*.
21. 2. go into the village over *against y*. and ye shall find an ass tied, *Mark* 11. 2. *Luke* 19. 30.
Luke 10. 11. the dust of your city we wipe off *ag. y*.
Jam. 5. 3. the rust shall be a witness *against y*.
1 *Pet.* 2. 12. whereas they speak *ag. y*. as evil doers

Among, or *amongst* YOU.

Gen. 35. 2. put away the strange gods that are *am. y*. and be clean, *Josh.* 24. 23. 1 *Sam.* 7. 3.
Lev. 26. 11. I will set my tabernacle *amongst y*.
12. I will walk *among y*. and will be your God
22. I will send wild beasts *am. y*. || 25. pestilence
Num. 11. 20. ye have despised the Lord who is *am. y*. 14. 42. *Deut.* 6. 15. | 7. 21. *Josh.* 3. 10.
2 *Chron.* 36. 23. who is there *among y*. *Ezra* 1. 3.
Isa. 42. 23. who *among y*. will give ear to this?
50. 10. who is *among y*. that feareth the Lord?
Ezek. 20. 38. purge out from *among y*. the rebels
Hag. 2. 3. who is left *among y*. that saw this house?
Mal. 1. 10. who is there *among y*. that would shut
Mat. 20. 26. it shall not be so *among y*. *Mark* 10. 43.
27. and whosoever will be chief *among y*. let him be your servant, 23. 11. *Luke* 22. 26.
Luke 9. 48. he that is least *among y*. shall be great
22. 27. but I am *among y*. as he that serveth
John 1. 26. but there standeth one *among y*.
8. 7. he that is without sin *among y*. let him cast
Acts 6. 3. brethren, look ye out *among y*. seven men
13. 26. and whosoever *among y*. feareth God
25. 5. let them who *among y*. are able, go down
Rom. 1. 13. that I might have some fruit *among y*.
12. 3. I say to every man that is *among y*.
1 *Cor.* 1. 10. that there be no divisions *among y*.
11. there are contentions *among y*. 11. 18.
2. 2. I determined not to know any thing *among y*.
3. 3. whereas there is *among y*. envying, strife
18. if any man *among y*. seemeth to be wise
5. 1. is reported that there is fornication *among y*.
2. that he might be taken away from *among y*.
15. 12. how say some *among y*. is no resurrection
2 *Cor.* 1. 19. Christ who was preached *among y*.
10. 1. I Paul, who in presence am base *among y*.
12. 21. lest my God will humble me *among y*.
Eph. 5. 3. let it not be once named *amongst y*.
1 *Thess.* 1. 5. what manner of men we were *am. y*.
Jam. 1. 26. if any man *among y*. seem religious
5. 13. is any *among y*. afflicted? || 14. is any sick?
1 *Pet.* 5. 2. feed the flock of God which is *among y*.
2 *Pet.* 2. 1. there shall be false teachers *among y*.
Rev. 2. 13. Antipas, who was slain *among y*.

See SOJOURNETH.

Before YOU.

Gen. 34. 10. and the land shall be *before y*. dwell
45. 5. God did send me *before y*. to preserve life, 7.
Exod. 10. 10. look to it, for evil is *before y*.
Lev. 18. 24. in all these the nations are defiled which I cast out *before y*. 20. 23. *Num.* 33. 52, 55. *Deut.* 11. 23. *Josh.* 3. 10. | 9. 24. | 23. 5, 9. | 24. 8, 12. *Judg.* 6. 9.
27. men of land done which were *before y*. 28, 30.
26. 7. your enemies shall fall *before y*. 8.
Num. 14. 43. the Canaanites are there *before y*.
32. 29. and the land shall be subdued *before y*.
Deut. 1. 8. behold, I have set the land *before y*.
30. Lord who goeth *before y*. shall fight for you
4. 8. which I set *before y*. this day, 11. 32.
11. 26. I set *before y*. a blessing and curse, 30. 19.
Josh. 4. 23. the Lord dried up Jordan *before y*.
24. 12. I sent the hornet *before y*. which drave
1 *Sam.* 9. 12. behold, he is *before y*. make haste
12. 2. and now behold the king walketh *before y*.
2 *Chron.* 7. 19. if ye forsake my statutes which I have set *before y*. *Jer.* 26. 4. | 44. 10.
Isa. 52. 12. for the Lord will go *before y*.
Jer. 21. 8. behold, I set *before y*. the way of life
Mat. 5. 12. so persecuted prophets that were *b. y*.
21. 31. go into the kingdom of God *before y*.
26. 32. but after I am risen again, I will go *before y*. into Galilee, 28. 7. *Mark* 14. 28. | 16. 7.
Luke 10. 8. into whatsoever city ye enter, eat such things as are set *before y*. 1 *Cor.* 10. 27.
Acts 4. 10. this man stands here *before y*. whole

By YOU.

Ezek. 20. 3. I will not be inquired of *by y*. 31.
Rom. 15. 24. I trust to be brought on my way *by y*.
1 *Cor.* 6. 2. if the world shall be judged *by y*.
2 *Cor.* 7. 13. his spirit was refreshed *by y*. all
10. 15. we hope that we shall be enlarged *by y*.

Concerning YOU.

Num. 9. 8. what Lord will command *concerning y*.
Josh. 23. 14. which the Lord spake *concerning y*.
Jer. 42. 19. the Lord hath said *concerning y*.
1 *Thess.* 5. 18. this is the will of God *concerning y*.

For YOU.

Gen. 44. 17. as *for y*. 50. 20. *Num.* 14. 32. *Deut.* 1. 40. *Josh.* 23. 9. *Job* 17. 10.
Num. 15. 15. one ordinance shall be *for y*. 16.
Deut. 1. 30. all that he did *for y*. 4. 34. 1 *Sam.* 12. 24.
Ezek. 20. 39. as *for y*. O house of Israel, 34. 17.
36. 9. behold I am *for y*. and I will turn to you
Dan. 2. 9. there is but one decree *for y*.
Amos 5. 18. the day of Lord, to what end is it *for y*.
Mic. 3. 1. is it not *for y*. to know judgment?
Hag. 1. 4. is it time *for y*. to dwell in ceiled houses?
Mal. 2. 1. O priests, this commandment is *for y*.
Mat. 11. 22. I say to you, it shall be more tolerable for Tyre and Sidon, than *for y*. *Luke* 10. 14.
25. 34. come, inherit the kingdom prepared *for y*.
Mark 10. 36. what would ye that I should do *for y*.
Luke 22. 19. this is my body which is given *for y*.
20. my blood which is shed *for y*. 1 *Cor.* 11. 24.
John 14. 2. I go to prepare a place *for y*. 3.
16. 26. I say, that I will pray the Father *for y*.
Acts 1. 7. is not *for y*. to know the times or seasons
28. 20. for this cause therefore have I called *for y*.
Rom. 1. 8. I thank my God through Christ *for y*. all
1 *Cor.* 1. 13. is Chr. divided? was Paul crucified *f. y*.
2 *Cor.* 7. 12. that our care *for y*. appear, 8. 16.
9. 14. by their prayer *for y*. which long after you, *Phil.* 1. 4. *Col.* 1. 3, 9. | 4. 12. 2 *Thess.* 1. 11.
12. 15. I will gladly spend and be spent *for y*.
Eph. 1. 16. wheref. I cease not to give thanks *for y*. 1 *Thess.* 1. 2. | 3. 9. 2 *Thess.* 1. 3. | 2. 13.
3. 13. at my tribulations *for y*. *Col.* 1. 24.
Phil. 3. 1. is not grievous, but *for y*. it is safe
Col. 1. 5. for the hope which is laid up *for y*.
25. the dispensation which is given to me *for y*.
2. 1. ye knew what great conflict I have *for y*.
4. 13. that he hath a great zeal *for y*. and for them
Heb. 13. 17. for that is unprofitable *for y*.
1 *Pet.* 1. 4. to an inheritance reserved in heaven *for y*.
5. 7. cast your care on him, for he careth *for y*.

From YOU.

Gen. 26. 27. seeing ye have sent me away *from y*.
Josh. 9. 22. saying we are very far *from y*.
1 *Sam.* 6. 3. why his hand is not removed *from y*.
2 *Sam.* 15. 28. until there come word *from y*.
2 *Chron.* 30. 8. his wrath may turn away *from y*.
9. the Lord will not turn away his face *from y*.
Isa. 1. 15. I will hide mine eyes *from y*.
59. 2. but your sins have hid his face *from y*.
Jer. 5. 25. have withholden good things *from y*.
34. 21. king's army which are gone up *from y*.
42. 4. I will keep nothing back *from y*.
Ezek. 18. 31. cast away *from y*. your transgressions
Joel 2. 20. remove far *from y*. the northern army
Amos 4. 7. I have withholden the rain *from y*.
Mat. 21. 43. kingdom of God shall be taken *from y*.
John 16. 22. and your joy no man taketh *from y*.
Acts 1. 11. who is taken up *from y*. into heaven
13. 46. but seeing you put it *from y*. lo, we turn
1 *Cor.* 14. 36. came the word of God out *from y*.
2 *Cor.* 3. 1. or letters of commendation *from y*.
Eph. 4. 31. let evil-speaking be put away *from y*.
1 *Thess.* 1. 8. for *from y*. sounded out the word
2. 17. but we being taken *from y*. a short time
Jam. 4. 7. resist the devil, and he will flee *from y*.

In YOU.

Gen. 42. 16. whether there be any truth *in y*.
Judg. 9. 19. and let him also rejoice *in y*.
Ezek. 20. 41. I will be sanctified *in y*. 36. 23.
37. 6. and I will put breath *in y*. 14.
Mal. 1. 10. I have no pleasure *in y*. saith the Lord
Mat. 10. 20. but the Spirit which speaketh *in y*.
11. 21. if the mighty works which were done *in y*.
John 5. 38. ye have not his word abiding *in y*.
42. that ye have not the love of God *in y*.
6. 53. except ye eat the flesh, ye have no life *in y*.
14. 17. he shall be *in y*. || 20. and I *in y*. 15. 4.
15. 7. if my words abide *in y*. 1 *John* 2. 14, 24.
Rom. 8. 9. the Spirit dwelleth *in y*. 1 *John* 2. 27.
10. and if Christ be *in y*. the body is dead
12. 18. as much as lieth *in y*. live peaceably
1 *Cor.* 1. 6. the testimony of Christ is confirmed *in y*.
6. 19. the temple of the Holy Ghost which is *in y*.
14. 25. will report that God is *in y*. of a truth
2 *Cor.* 2. 3. I wrote this to you, having confidence *in y*. all, 7. 16. | 8. 22. *Gal.* 5. 10.
4. 12. but life *in y*. || 7. 7. he was comforted *in y*.
8. 6. he would finish *in y*. the same grace also
9. 14. for the exceeding grace of God *in y*.
13. 3. which to you is not weak, but mighty *in y*.
5. know ye not that Jesus Christ is *in y*.
Gal. 4. 19. I travail, till Christ be formed *in y*.
Eph. 4. 6. one God, who is above all, and *in y*. all
Phil. 2. 5. let this mind be *in y*. which was in Christ
13. it is God which worketh *in y*. to will and do
Col. 1. 6. which bringeth fruit, as it doth also *in y*.
27. which is Christ *in y*. the hope of glory
3. 16. let the word of Christ dwell *in y*. richly
1 *Thess.* 2. 13. which effectually worketh *in y*.
2 *Thess.* 1. 4. so that we glory *in y*. in the churches
12. the name of Christ may be glorified *in y*.
Philem. 6. acknowledging every good thing *in y*.
Heb. 13. 21. working *in y*. what is well-pleasing
1 *Pet.* 3. 15. a reason of the hope that is *in y*.
2 *Pet.* 1. 8. if these things be *in y*. and abound
1 *John* 2. 8. which thing is true in him and *in y*.
4. 4. greater is he that is *in y*. than in the world

Of YOU.

Gen. 27. 45. why should I be deprived *of y*. both?
Exod. 12. 16. that only may be done *of y*.
Deut. 1. 22. ye came near unto me every one *of y*.
Josh. 2. 9. the inhabitants faint because *of y*.
23. 3. hath done to these nations because *of y*.
1 *Sam.* 22. 8. that all *of y*. have conspired against me
1 *Kings* 22. 28. hearken, O people, every one *of y*.
Ezra 7. 21. what Ezra requires *of y*. it be done
Neh. 1. 9. though there were *of y*. cast out to heaven
Psal. 62. 3. ye shall be slain all *of y*. a bowing wall
Ezek. 6. 9. they that escape *of y*. shall remember
Mic. 1. 11. he shall receive *of y*. his standing
Mat. 6. 27. which *of y*. by taking thought can add one cubit to his stature? *Luke* 12. 25.
Luke 13. 15. doth not each one *of y*. lead his ox
John 8. 46. which *of y*. convinceth me of sin?
13. 18. I speak not *of y*. all, I know whom I chose
Acts 2. 22. which God did by him in the midst *of y*.
3. 26. in turning every one *of y*. from his iniquit.
4. 11. which was set at nought *of y*. builders
Rom. 1. 12. by the mutual faith both *of y*. and me
1 *Cor.* 1. 11. it hath been declared to me *of y*.
6. 11. such were some *of y*. but ye are washed
12. 21. the head to the feet, I have no need *of y*.
14. 26. every one *of y*. hath a psalm, a doctrine
16. 2. let every one *of y*. lay by him in store
2 *Cor.* 1. 7. and our hope *of y*. is stedfast
7. 14. if I have boasted any thing to him *of y*.
11. 20. for ye suffer, if a man take *of y*.
12. 17. did I make a gain *of y*.? || 18. or did Titus?
Gal. 3. 2. this only would I learn *of y*. received ye
27. for as many *of y*. as have been baptized into
4. 20. to change my voice, for I stand in doubt *of y*.
Col. 4. 9. a beloved brother, who is one *of y*. 12.
1 *Thess.* 2. 6. neither *of y*. sought we glory
4. 4. every one *of y*. should know how to possess
Tit. 2. 8. having no evil thing to say *of y*.
Jam. 5. 4. the hire which is *of y*. kept back by fraud
1 *Pet.* 3. 16. whereas they speak evil *of y*. 4. 4.

Over YOU.

Lev. 26. 16. I will even appoint *over y*. terror
17. they that hate you shall reign *over y*.
Deut. 28. 63. as the Lord rejoiced *over y*. to do you good, he will rejoice *over y*. to destroy you
Judg. 8. 23. Gideon said, I will not rule *over y*. nor my son rule *over y*. Lord shall rule *over y*.
9. 2. is it better that seventy reign *over y*. or one?
15. if in truth ye anoint me king *over y*.
1 *Sam.* 8. 11. manner of king that shall reign *over y*.
12. 1. behold, I have made a king *over y*.
13. behold, the Lord hath set a king *over y*.
2 *Sam.* 3. 17. ye sought David to be king *over y*.
2 *Chron.* 19. 11. Amariah the chief priest is *over y*.
Jer. 6. 17. also I set the watchmen *over y*. saying
Ezek. 20. 33. with fury poured out will I rule *over y*.
Hag. 1. 10. the heaven *over y*. is stayed from dew
Luke 12. 14. man, who made me a divider *over y*.?
Rom. 6. 14. sin shall not have dominion *over y*.

1 Cor. 9. 12. be partakers of this power over y.
2 Cor. 11. 2. I am jealous over y. with godly zeal
1 Thess. 3. 7. we were comforted over y. in affliction
5. 12. know them which are over y. in the Lord
Heb. 13. 7. remember them that have rule over y.
17. obey them that have the rule over y.
24. salute them that have the rule over y.
See TELL.

To or unto YOU.

Gen. 1. 29. every herb to y. it shall be for meat
34. 9. and take our daughters unto y.
Exod. 6. 7. I will take you to me, and will be to y. a G.
12. 26. when your children shall say unto y.
20. 23. ye shall not make unto y. gods of gold
30. 36. it shall be unto y. most holy
Lev. 26. 16. I also will do this unto y. appoint terror
Num. 10. 8. they shall be to y. for an ordinance
10. be to y. a memorial || 15. 39. unto y. for a fringe
33. 56. I shall do unto y. as I thought to do to them
Josh. 23. 12. if ye go in to them, and they to y.
1 Sam. 4. 9. be not servants, as they have been to y.
Prov. 8. 4. unto y. O men, I call, and my voice is
Isa. 30. 13. this iniquity shall be to y. as a breach
Dan. 3. 4. to y. it is commanded, O people
Mal. 4. 2. but unto y. that fear my name shall sun
Mat. 7. 12. that men should do to y. Luke 6. 31.
9. 29. according to your faith be it unto y.
13. 11. because it is given unto y. to know the mysteries of the kingdom, Mark 4. 11. Luke 8. 10.
Mark 4. 24. unto y. that hear shall more be given
Luke 2. 11. unto y. is born this day a Saviour
6. 33. if ye do good to them which do good to y.
22. 29. and I appoint unto y. a kingdom as my Fath.
Acts 2. 39. for the promise is unto y. and children
3. 26. unto y. first, God having raised up his Son
10. 29. therefore came I unto y. without gainsaying
13. 26. to y. is the word of this salvation sent
1 Cor. 9. 2. if not to others, doubtless I am to y.
14. 36. or came the word of God unto y. only?
2 Cor. 10. 13. a measure to reach even unto y.
14. we are come as far as to y. in preaching
Phil. 1. 28. but is to y. a token of salvation
29. unto y. it is given not only to believe
1 Thess. 1. 5. our gospel came not unto y. in word
2 Thess. 1. 7. to y. who are troubled, rest with us
1 Pet. 2. 7. unto y. that believe, he is precious
Rev. 2. 24. but unto y. I say, and to the rest
See SAY, TOLD.

Towards YOU.

Jer. 29. 10. I will perform my good word towards y.
11. I know the thoughts I think towards y.
Hos. 5. 1. give ear, for judgment is towards y.
2 Cor. 1. 18. our word towards y. was not yea
7. 15. inward affection is more abundant towards y.
9. 8. able to make all grace abound towards y.
10. 1. but being absent am bold towards y.
13. 4. we shall live by the power of God towards y.
1 Thess. 3. 12. abound in love, as we do towards y.

To YOU-ward.

2 Cor. 13. 3. which to y.-ward is not weak
Eph. 3. 2. the grace of God given me to y.-ward

On, or upon YOU.

Exod. 12. 13. the plague shall not be upon y.
32. 29. that he may bestow upon y. a blessing
Lev. 10. 7. the anointing oil of the Lord is upon y.
Num. 16. 3. they said, ye take too much upon y. 7.
Deut. 7. 7. the Lord did not set his love upon y.
Josh. 23. 15. as all good things are come upon y.
Neh. 4. 12. from all places they will be upon y.
Psal. 129. 8. the blessing of the Lord be upon y.
Isa. 29. 10. Lord hath poured upon y. spirit of sleep
30. 18. he may have mercy upon y. Jer. 42. 12.
Jer. 23. 2. I will visit upon y. the evil of your doings
40. 3. therefore this thing is come upon y.
Ezek. 22. 21. I will blow upon y. in the fire of my wr.
Amos 4. 2. that lo, the days shall come upon y.
Zeph. 2. 2. before day of Lord's anger come upon y.
Mat. 23. 35. upon y. may come the righteous blood
Luke 11. 20. the kingdom of God is come upon y.
21. 34. and so that day come upon y. unawares
24. 49. I send the promise of my Father upon y.
John 12. 35. walk, lest darkness come upon y.
Acts 1. 8. after the Holy Ghost is come upon y.
1 Cor. 7. 35. not that I may cast a snare upon y.
Gal. 4. 11. lest I bestowed upon y. labour in vain
Jam. 5. 1. howl for miseries that shall come on y.
1 Pet. 4. 14. the Spirit of God resteth upon y.
Rev. 2. 24. I will put upon y. none other burden

With YOU.

Gen. 34. 16. then we will dwell with y. be one people
48. 21. behold, I die, but God shall be with y.
Exod. 13. 19. shall carry up my bones hence with y.
20. 22. ye have seen that I have talked with y.
24. 14. tarry ye here, Aaron and Hur are with y.
Num. 1. 4. with y. shall be a man of every tribe
17. 4. the testimony, where I will meet with y.
Deut. 5. 33. and that it may be well with y.
12. 12. no part with y. || 20. 4. God goeth with y.
29. 14. nor with y. only do I make this covenant
Josh. 7. 12. neither will I be with y. any more
Ruth 2. 4. and Boaz said, the Lord be with y.
1 Sam. 22. 3. let my father and mother be with y.
23. 23. come again to me, and I will go with y.
2 Sam. 16. 10. what have I to do with y.? 19. 22.
18. 2. I will surely go forth with y. myself
2 Kings 10. 2. seeing your master's sons are with y.
23. see there be with y. none of servants of Lord
25. 24. and it shall be well with y. Jer. 40. 9.
1 Chron. 22. 18. is not the Lord your God with y.?
2 Chron. 13. 8. there are with y. golden calves
15. 2. the Lord is with y. while ye be with him
19. 6. for the Lord, who is with y. in the judgment
20. 17. fear not, for the Lord will be with y.
28. 10. are there not with y. even with y. sins
Ezra 4. 2. let us build with y. we seek your God
Job 42. 8. lest I deal with y. after your folly
Jer. 18. 6. cannot I do with y. as this potter?
42. 11. for I am with y. Hag. 1. 13. | 2. 4.
Ezek. 20. 35. there will I plead with y. 36.
44. know I am Lord when I have wrought with y.
Amos 5. 14. the God of hosts shall be with y.
Zech. 8. 23. we will go with y. for God is with y.

Mat. 17. 17. O faithless perverse generat. how long shall I be with y.? Mark 9. 19. Luke 9. 41.
26. 11. for ye have the poor always with y. but me ye have not always, John 12. 8.
29. when I drink it new w. y. in my Father's king.
28. 20. I am with y. always to the end of the world
Luke 24. 44. I spake to you, while I was with y.
John 7. 33. yet a little while am I with y. then I go to him that sent me, 12. 35. | 13. 33.
14. 9. Jesus said, have I been so long with y.?
16. Comforter, that he may abide with y. for ever
17. he dwelleth with y. || 25. being present with y.
27. peace I leave with y. || 16. 4. I was with y.
Acts 18. 14. reason would I should bear with y.
20. 18. I have been with y. at all seasons
Rom. 1. 12. I may be comforted together with y.
15. 32. that I may with y. be refreshed
33. now the God of peace be with y. all. Amen, 2 Cor. 13. 11. Phil. 4. 9.
16. 20. the grace of our Lord Jesus Christ be with y.
24. 1 Cor. 16. 23. Phil. 4. 23. Col. 4. 18. 1 Thess. 5. 28. 2 Thess. 3. 18. 2 Tim. 4. 15. Tit. 3. 15. Heb. 13. 25. 2 John 3. Rev. 22. 21.
1 Cor. 2. 3. I was with y. in weakness and in fear
4. 8. that we also might reign with y.
16. 10. see that he may be with y. without fear
24. my love be with y. all in Christ Jesus
2 Cor. 1. 21. he that establisheth us with y. is God
4. 14. shall raise us up and present us with y.
7. 3. ye are in our hearts to die and live with y.
11. 9. when I was present with y. Gal. 4. 18, 20.
Phil. 2. 17. I joy and rejoice with y. all
Col. 2. 5. yet am I with y. in the spirit, joying
2 Thess. 3. 1. word may be glorified, as it is with y.
16. Lord of peace give peace, the Ld. be w. y. all
Heb. 12. 7. God dealeth with y. as with sons
1 Pet. 5. 14. peace be with y. all that are in Christ
2 Pet. 2. 13. spots and blemishes, while they feast w. y.

YOURS.

Gen. 45. 20. the good of the land of Egypt is y.
Deut. 11. 24. the soles of your feet tread shall be y.
Josh. 2. 14. the men answered our life for y.
2 Chron. 20. 15. the battle is not y. but God's
Jer. 5. 19. shall serve strangers in land that is not y.
Luke 6. 20. for y. is the kingdom of God
John 15. 20. if kept my saying, they will keep y. also
1 Cor. 3. 21. not glory in men, for all things are y. 22.
8. 9. lest this liberty of y. become a stumbling
16. 18. for they have refreshed my spirit and y.
2 Cor. 12. 14. for I seek not y. but you

YOUNG.

Gen. 31. 38. thy she-goats have not cast their y.
33. 13. the flocks and herds with y. are with me
Exod. 23. 26. there shall nothing cast their y.
Lev. 22. 28. shall not kill it and her y. both in one day
Deut. 22. 6. thou shalt not take the dam with the y.
7. let the dam go and take the y. to thee
28. 50. which will not shew favour to the y.
32. 11. as the eagle fluttereth over her y.
2 Sam. 9. 12. Mephibosheth had a y. son Micha
1 Chron. 22. 5. Solomon my son is y. 29. 1.
2 Chron. 13. 7. when Rehoboam was y. and tender
34. 3. Josiah, while he was yet y. began to seek God
Psal. 78. 71. from following ewes great with y.
84. 3. swallow a nest, where she may lay her y.
Isa. 40. 11. shall gently lead those that are with y.
Jer. 31. 12. shall flow together for the y. of the flock
Ezek. 17. 4. cropped off the top of his y. twigs, 22.
Mark 7. 25. whose y. daughter had an unclean spirit
John 21. 18. when y. thou girdedst thyself
See OLD.

YOUNG ass, or asses.

Isa. 30. 6. carry riches on the shoulders of y. asses
24. the y. asses shall eat clean provender
John 12. 14. when he found a y. ass sat thereon
See BULLOCK.

YOUNG bullocks.

Num. 28. 11. shall offer two y. bullocks, 19. 27.
Ezra 6. 9. give what they need, both y. bullocks

YOUNG calf.

Lev. 9. 2. take thee a y. calf for a sin offering
See CHILD, CHILDREN.

YOUNG cow.

Isa. 7. 21. that a man shall nourish a y. cow

YOUNG dromedaries.

Esth. 8. 10. he sent letters by riders on y. dromedaries

YOUNG eagles.

Prov. 30. 17. and the y. eagles shall eat it

YOUNG hart.

Cant. 2. 9. my beloved is like a y. hart, 17. | 8. 14.
See LION, LIONS, MAN, MEN.

YOUNG one.

Deut. 28. 57. her eye shall be evil toward her y. one
Zech. 11. 16. neither shall seek the y. one, nor heal

YOUNG ones.

Deut. 22. 6. whether they be y. ones or eggs
Job 38. 41. when his y. ones cry to God they wander
39. 3. they bow, they bring forth their y. ones
4. their y. ones are in good liking, they grow up
16. the ostrich is hardened against her y. ones
30. the eagles' y. ones also suck up blood
Isa. 11. 7. their y. ones shall lie down together
Lam. 4. 3. the sea monsters give suck to their y. ones

YOUNG pigeon.

Gen. 15. 9. take me a turtle-dove, and a y. pigeon
Lev. 12. 6. bring a y. pigeon for a sin-offering

YOUNG pigeons.

Lev. 1. 14. he shall bring his offering of y. pigeons
5. 7. if not able to bring a lamb he shall bring two y. pigeons, 12. 8. | 14. 22, 30. | 15. 14, 29. Num. 6. 10. Luke 2. 24.
11. if he be not able to bring two y. pigeons

YOUNG ravens.

Psal. 147. 9. he giveth food to y. ravens which cry

YOUNG roes.

Cant. 4. 5. thy breasts are like two y. roes, 7. 3.

YOUNG virgin.

1 Kings 1. 2. let there be sought for my lord a y. v.

YOUNG virgins.

Judg. 21. 12. there were found 400 y. virgins
Esth. 2. 2. let fair y. virgins be sought for the king
3. they may gather together all the y. virgins

YOUNG unicorn.

Psal. 29. 6. Lebanon and Sirion like a y. unicorn

YOUNG woman.

Ruth 4. 12. Lord shall give thee of this y. woman

YOUNG women.

Tit. 2. 4. they may teach y. women to be sober

YOUNGER.

Gen. 9. 24. Noah knew what this y. son had done
19. 31. and the first-born said to the y. 34.
38. and the y. she also bare a son Ben-ammi
25. 23. the elder shall serve the y. Rom. 9. 12.
27. 15. Rebekah put them on Jacob her y. son
42. she sent and called Jacob her y. son
29. 16. the name of the y. daughter was Rachel
18. I will serve thee seven years for the y.
26. it must not be so done to give the y. first
43. 29. is this your y. brother of whom ye spake
48. 14. Israel laid his right hand on the y.
19. his y. brother shall be greater than he
Judg. 1. 13. Caleb's y. brother took it, 3. 9.
15. 2. is not her y. sister fairer than she?
1 Sam. 14. 49. Saul's y. daughter was Michal
1 Chr. 24. 31. cast lots over-against their y. brethren
Job 30. 1. that are y. than I, have me in derision
Ezek. 16. 46. and thy y. sister is Sodom
61. shalt receive thy sisters, thine elder and y.
Luke 15. 12. the y. said, father, give me the portion
13. the y. gathered all, and took his journey
22. 26. he that is greatest, let him be as the y.
1 Tim. 5. 1. intreat the y. men as brethren
2. the y. women as sisters, with all purity
11. the y. widows refuse, for when they begin
14. I will therefore that the y. women marry
1 Pet. 5. 5. likewise ye y. submit to the elder

YOUNGEST.

Gen. 42. 13. the y. is this day with our father, 32.
15. except your y. brother come, 20, 34. | 44. 23, 26.
43. 33. they sat, the y. according to his youth
44. 2. put silver cup in the sack's mouth of the y.
12. he began at the eldest, and left off at the y.
Josh. 6. 26. in his y. son set up gates, 1 Kings 16. 34.
Judg. 9. 5. yet Jotham the y. son was left
1 Sam. 16. 11. he said, there remains yet the y.
17. 14. David was y. the eldest followed Saul
2 Chron. 21. 17. none left save Jehoahaz the y.
22. 1. made Ahaziah his y. son king in his stead

YOUTH.

Gen. 8. 21. the imagination is evil from his y.
43. 33. and the youngest according to his y.
46. 34. about cattle, from our y. even till now
Lev. 22. 13. in her father's house, as in her y.
Num. 30. 3. being in her father's house, in her y. 16.
Judg. 8. 20. the y. drew not a sword, because yet a y.
1 Sam. 17. 33. thou but a y. he a man of war from y.
42. for he was but a y. || 55. whose son is this y.?
2 Sam. 19. 7. the evil that befell thee from thy y.
1 Kings 18. 12. but I fear the Lord from my y.
Job 13. 26. to possess the iniquities of my y.
20. 11. his bones are full of the sin of his y.
29. 4. as I was in days of my y. when secret of God
30. 12. on my right hand rise the y. they push away
31. 18. from my y. he was brought up with me
33. 25. he shall return to the days of his y.
36. 14. hypocrites die in y. and their life is unclean
Psal. 25. 7. remember not the sins of my y.
71. 5. O Lord, thou art my trust from my y.
17. O God, thou hast taught me from my y.
88. 15. I am afflicted, and ready to die from my y.
89. 45. the days of his y. hast thou shortened
103. 5. so that thy y. is renewed like the eagle's
110. 3. from morning, thou hast the dew of thy y.
127. 4. as arrows, so are the children of thy y.
129. 1. they have afflicted me from my y.
144. 12. that our sons be as plants grown up in y.
Prov. 2. 17. which forsaketh the guide of her y.
5. 18. and rejoice with the wife of thy y.
Eccl. 11. 9. rejoice, O young man, in thy y.
10. for childhood and y. are vanity
12. 1. remember thy Creator in the days of thy y.
Isa. 47. 12. wherein thou hast laboured from thy y.
15. thy merchants from thy y. shall wander
54. 4. thou shalt forget the shame of thy y.
6. for the Lord hath called thee as a wife of y.
Jer. 2. 2. I remember the kindness of thy y.
3. 4. my Father, thou art the guide of my y.
24. devoured the labour of our fathers from our y.
25. we and our fathers from our y. have sinned
22. 21. this hath been thy manner from thy y.
31. 19. I did bear the reproach of my y.
32. 30. have only done evil before me from their y.
48. 11. Moab hath been at ease from his y.
Lam. 3. 27. it is good that he bear the yoke in his y.
Ezek. 4. 14. my soul not been polluted from my y.
16. 22. thou hast not remembered days of thy y. 43.
60. I will remember my covenant in days of thy y.
23. 3. they committed whoredoms in their y.
8. for in her y. they lay with her and bruised
19. call to remembrance the days of her y. 21.
Hos. 2. 15. she shall sing there as in the days of her y.
Joel 1. 8. lament as virgin for the husband of her y.
Zech. 13. 5. man taught me to keep cattle from my y.
Mal. 2. 14. between thee and the wife of thy y.
15. let none deal treacherously ag. wife of his y.
Mat. 19. 20. all these have I kept from my y. what lack I yet? Mark 10. 20. Luke 18. 21.
Acts 26. 4. my manner of life from my y. know all
1 Tim. 4. 12. let no man despise thy y. be an examp.

YOUTHS.

Prov. 7. 7. I discerned among the y. a young man void of understanding
Isa. 40. 30. even the y. shall faint and be weary

YOUTHFUL.

2 Tim. 2. 22. flee also y. lusts, but follow faith

Z.

ZEAL

Is a mixed passion, composed of grief and anger, fervent love and desire; for what a man loves earnestly, he is careful to see it honoured, and grieved when it is dishonoured. Phinehas is commended for having expressed much zeal *against those wicked persons that violated the law of the Lord*, Num. 25. 11, 13. *And in* Psal. 69. 9. *the Psalmist says*, The *zeal* of thine house hath eaten me up: "*My earnest desire to have all things duly ordered about thy worship, and my just displeasure and indignation at all abuses therein, have overcome me, have wasted my natural moisture and vital spirits.*"

Zeal *is taken either in good or ill part. There may be an eagerness in pursuing good things, when neither the end nor manner of doing it is good. Such was the* zeal *of Jehu*, 2 Kings 10. 16. *He was eager in executing the commands of God, but he did it* to be seen of men: Come, see my *zeal* for the Lord. *Such also was the* zeal *of those Jews whom St. Paul speaks of*, Rom. 10. 2. They have a *zeal* of God, but not according to knowledge. "*They have an earnest desire to maintain the law and worship of God instituted by Moses, thinking thereby to promote the glory of God, but though this be a warm, yet it is a blind* zeal: *they know not the will of God, or what that righteousness is whereby a person is justified before God.*"

2 *Sam.* 21. 2. Saul sought to slay them in his *z.*
2 *Kings* 10. 16. come and see my *z.* for the Lord
19. 31. the *z.* of the Lord shall do this, *Isa.* 37. 32.
Psal. 69. 9. the *z.* of thy house hath eaten me up, and reproaches are fallen on me, *John* 2. 17.
119. 139. my *z.* hath consumed me, because enemies
Isa. 9. 7. the *z.* of the Lord will perform this
59. 17. and he was clad with *z.* as a cloak
63. 15. where is thy *z.* and thy strength?
Ezek. 5. 13. that I the Lord have spoken it in my *z.*
Rom. 10. 2. I bear record, that they have *z.* of God
2 *Cor.* 7. 11. ye a what *z.* ‖ 9. 2. your *z.* provok. many
Phil. 3. 6. concerning *z.* persecuting the church
Col. 4. 13. that he hath a great *z.* for you

ZEALOUS.

Num. 25. 11. while he was *z.* for my sake
13. he was *z.* for his God and made atonement
Acts 21. 20. and they are all *z.* of the law
22. 3. Paul was *z.* towards God, *Gal.* 1. 14.
1 *Cor.* 14. 12. as ye are *z.* of spiritual gifts
Tit. 2. 14. purify a peculiar people, *z.* of good works
Rev. 3. 19. as many as I love, I rebuke and chasten; be *z.* therefore and repent

ZEALOUSLY.

Gal. 4. 17. they *z.* affect you, but not well
18. it is good to be *z.* affected in a good thing

A COLLECTION OF THE NAMES AND TITLES GIVEN TO JESUS CHRIST.

ADAM, 1 *Cor.* 15. 45.
Advocate, 1 *John* 2. 1.
Amen, *Rev.* 3. 14.
Angel, *Isa.* 63. 9. *Mal.* 3. 1.
Ancient of Days, *Dan.* 7. 22.
Anointed, *Psal.* 2. 2. | 45. 7.
Apostle, *Heb.* 3. 1.
Apple-tree, *Cant.* 2. 3.
Author and Finisher of faith, *Heb.* 12. 2.
Babe, *Luke* 2. 16.
Beginning of Creat. of God, *Rev.* 3. 14.
Begotten of the Father, *John* 1. 14.
Beloved, *Cant.* 1. 13. *Eph.* 1. 6.
Bishop, 1 *Pet.* 2. 25.
Blessed, 1 *Tim.* 6. 15.
Branch of Righteousness, *Zech.* 3. 8.
Brazen Serpent, *John* 3. 14.
Bread of Life, *John* 6. 48, 51.
Bridegroom, *Mat.* 9. 15.
Bright Morning Star, *Rev.* 22. 16.
Brightness of Father's Glory, *Heb.* 1. 3.
Bundle of Myrrh, *Cant.* 1. 13.
Camphire, *Cant.* 1. 14.
Captain, *Josh.* 5. 14. *Heb.* 2. 10.
Child, *Isa.* 9. 6.
Chosen, *Mat.* 12. 18. *Luke* 23. 35.
Christ, *Mat.* 1. 16. | 2. 4.
Consolation of Israel, *Luke* 2. 25.
Corner-Stone, *Eph.* 2. 20. 1 *Pet.* 2. 7.
Covenant, *Isa.* 42. 6.
Counsellor, *Isa.* 9. 6.
Covert, *Isa.* 32. 2.
Creator, *Isa.* 43. 15.
Creditor, *Luke* 7. 41.
Cyrus, *Isa.* 45. 1.
David, *Jer.* 30. 9. *Ez.* 37. 24, 25. *Hos.* 3. 5.
Days-Man, *Job* 9. 33.
Day-Star, 2 *Pet.* 1. 19.
Deliverer, *Rom.* 11. 26.
Desire of all Nations, *Hag.* 2. 7.
Dew, *Hos.* 14. 5.
Diadem, *Isa.* 62. 3.
Door of Sheep, *John* 10. 7.
Eagle, *Deut.* 32. 11.
Elect, *Isa.* 42. 1.
Emmanuel, *Isa.* 7. 14. *Mat.* 1. 23.
Ensign, *Isa.* 11. 10.
Eternal Life, 1 *John* 5. 20.
Everlasting Father, *Isa.* 9. 6.
Express Image, &c. *Heb.* 1. 3.
Faithful Witness, *Rev.* 1. 5. | 3. 14. | 19. 11.
Fatted Calf, *Luke* 15. 23.
Father of Eternity, *Isa.* 9. † 6.
Feeder, *Isa.* 40. 11.
Finisher of Faith, *Heb.* 12. 2.
Fir-tree, *Hos.* 14. 8.
First-Begotten, *Rev.* 1. 5.
First-Fruits, 1 *Cor.* 15. 23.
First and Last, *Rev.* 2. 8.
Flesh, *John* 1. 14.
Foundation, *Isa.* 28. 16.
Fountain, *Zech.* 13. 1.
Forerunner, *Heb.* 6. 20.
Friend of Sinners, *Matt.* 11. 19.
Gift of God, 2 *Cor.* 9. 15.
Glory of God, *Isa.* 40. 5.
Glorious Lord, *Isa.* 33. 21.
God, *John* 1. 1. *Rom.* 9. 5. 1 *Tim.* 3. 16. 1 *John* 5. 20.
Gold, *Cant.* 5. 11.
Golden Altar, *Rev.* 8. 3.
Governor, *Matt.* 2. 6.
Gracious, 1 *Pet.* 2. 3.
Guide, *Psal.* 48. 14.
Habitation, *Psal.* 91. 9.
Harmless, *Heb.* 7. 26.
Head of the Church, *Col.* 1. 18.
Heir of all Things, *Heb.* 1. 2.
Help, *Psal.* 33. 20. | 40. 17.
Heritage, *Isa.* 58. 14.
Highest, *Psal.* 18. 13. *Luke* 1. 32.
High Priest, *Heb.* 3. 1. | 7. 1.
Most High, *Luke* 8. 28.
Holy One of God, *Mark* 1. 24.
Holy One of Israel, *Isa.* 41. 14.
Holy Child, *Acts* 4. 30.
Honey-Comb, *Cant.* 4. 11.
Hope, *Acts* 28. 20. 1 *Tim.* 1. 1.
Horn of Salvation, *Psal.* 18. 2.
Husband, *Isa.* 54. 5. *Jer.* 31. 32.
I am, *Exod.* 3. 14. *John* 8. 58.
Jacob, *Isa.* 41. 8. | 44. 1. 5.
Jah, *Psal.* 68. 4.
Jehovah, *Isa.* 26. 4. | 40. † 3.
Jerusalem, *Cant.* 6. 4.
Jesus, *Matt.* 1. 21. 1 *Thess.* 1. 10.
Image of God, *Heb.* 1. 3.
Immanuel, *Isa.* 7. 14. *Mat.* 1. 23.
Immortal, 1 *Tim.* 1. 17.
Inheritance, *Ezek.* 44. 28.
Invisible, 1 *Tim.* 1. 17.
Israel, *Isa.* 44. 21. | 49. 3.
Judah, *Rev.* 5. 5.
Judge, *Mic.* 5. 1. *Acts* 10. 42.
King, *Mat.* 21. 5. | 25. 34.
Ladder, *Gen.* 28. 12.
Lamb, *John* 1. 29. *Rev.* 5. 6.
Lawgiver, *Isa.* 33. 22. *James* 4. 12.
Leader, *Isa.* 55. 4.
Light, *John* 1. 9. | 8. 12. | 12. 46.
Life, *John* 14. 6.
Lion of the Tribe of Judah, *Rev.* 5. 5.
Living God, 1 *Tim.* 3. 15.
Long-suffering, *Exod.* 34. 6.
Lord, *Rom.* 1. 3. *Rev.* 17. 14.
Lovely, *Cant.* 5. 16.
Man, *Acts* 17. 31. 1 *Tim.* 2. 5.
Master, *Mat.* 8. 19. | 23. 8.
Mediator, 1 *Tim.* 2. 5.
Melchisedek, *Heb.* 7. 1.
Merciful, *Heb.* 2. 17.
Messenger, *Mal.* 2. 7. | 3. 1.
Messiah, *Dan.* 9. 25. *John* 1. 41.
Michael, *Dan.* 12. 1. *Rev.* 12. 7.
Mighty God, *Isa.* 9. 6. | 63. 1.
Minister, *Heb.* 8. 2.
Morning-star, *Rev.* 2. 28. | 22. 16.
Moses, *Acts* 3. 22.
Nazarite. *Mat.* 1. 23.
Offspring of David, *Rev.* 22. 16.
Only-Begotten, *John* 1. 14.
Ointment, *Cant.* 1. 3.
Pass-over, 1 *Cor.* 5. 7.
Plant of Renown, *Ezek.* 34. 29.
Potentate, 1 *Tim.* 6. 15.
Prince, *Acts* 3. 15. | 5. 31.
Prophet, *Luke* 4. 19. *Acts* 3. 22.
Propitiation, 1 *John* 2. 2. | 4. 10.
Power of God, 1 *Cor.* 1. 24.
Purifier, *Mal.* 3. 3.
Physician, *Mat.* 9. 12.
Polished Shaft, *Isa.* 49. 2.
Priest, *Heb.* 4. 14. | 7. 26.
Ransom, 1 *Tim.* 2. 6.
Reaper, *Rev.* 14. 15.
Redeemer, *Isa.* 59. 20. | 60 16.
Resurrection, *John* 11. 25.
Refiner, *Mal.* 3. 3.
Refuge, *Isa.* 25. 4.
Righteousness, *Jer.* 23. 6.
Rock, *Deut.* 32. 15. 1 *Cor.* 10. 4.
Rod and Branch, *Isa.* 11. 1.
Root of David, *Rev.* 22. 16.
Roe and Hart, *Cant.* 2. 9.
Rose of Sharon, *Cant.* 2. 1.
Ruler in Israel, *Mic.* 5. 2.
Sacrifice, *Eph.* 5. 2.
Salvation, *Luke* 2. 30.
Samaritan, *Luke* 10. 33.
Sanctification, 1 *Cor.* 1. 30.
Sanctuary, *Isa.* 8. 14.
Seed of Abraham, *Gal.* 3. 29.
Seed of the Woman, *Gen.* 3. 15.
Seed of David, 2 *Tim.* 2. 8.
Second Man, 1 *Cor.* 15. 47.
Servant, *Isa.* 42. 1, 19. | 44. 21.
Shepherd, *John* 10. 11. *Heb.* 13. 20.
Shield, *Gen.* 15. 1. *Psal.* 18. 35.
Shiloh, *Gen.* 49. 10.
Solomon, *Cant.* 3. 7. | 8. 11, 12.
Son of God, *Mat.* 4. 3. | 8. 29.
Son of Man, *Mat.* 8. 20.
Sower, *Mat.* 13. 3.
Spirit, 1 *Cor.* 15. 45. *Heb.* 9. 14.
Stone Refused, *Mat.* 21. 42.
Strength of Israel, 1 *Sam.* 15. 29.
Strong God, *Psal.* 89. 8. *Rev.* 18. 8.
Substance, *Heb.* 10. 34.
Sun of Righteousness, *Mal.* 4. 2.
Surety, *Heb.* 7. 22.
Sharp Sword, *Isa.* 49. 2.
Tabernacle, *Heb.* 8. 2. | 9. 11.
Teacher, *John* 3. 2.
Temple, *Mark* 14. 58.
Testator, *Heb.* 9. 16, 17.
Treasure, *Luke* 12. 33.
Tree of Life, *Rev.* 2. 7.
Truth, *John* 14. 6.
Vine, *John* 15. 1.
Wall of Fire, *Zech.* 2. 5.
Way, *Isa.* 35. 8. *John* 14. 6.
Well of Living Water, *Cant.* 4. 15.
Wedding Garment, *Mat.* 22. 12.
Wisdom of God, 1 *Cor.* 1. 24.
Witness, *Rev.* 1. 5. | 3. 14.
Wonderful, *Isa.* 9. 6. | 28. 29.
Word of God, *Rev.* 19. 13.
Worthy, *Heb.* 3. 3. *Rev.* 5. 12.
Yesterday, To-day, Forever, *Heb.* 13. 8.

A COLLECTION OF THE APPELLATIONS GIVEN TO THE CHURCH OF GOD IN THE SCRIPTURES.

ADOPTED Sons, *Gal.* 4. 5.
Angels, *Luke* 20. 36.
Assembly of Saints, *Heb.* 10. 25.
Believers, *Acts* 5. 14.
Beloved of God, *Psal.* 60. 5. | 108. 6.
Blessed, *Psal.* 2. 12. | 32. 1.
Blameless, *Phil.* 2. 15.
Body of Christ, *Eph.* 1. 23.
Branches of Righteousness, *John* 15. 5.
Brethren, *Rom.* 8. 29. | 12. 1.
Bride, *Rev.* 21. 2, 9. | 22. 17.
Building of God, 1 *Cor.* 3. 9.
Called, *Isa.* 62. 12. *Rom.* 8. 28.
Candlestick, *Rev.* 1. 12. | 2. 5.
Cedars, *Psal.* 92. 12. *Ezek.* 31. 8.
Children of the Kingdom, *Mat.* 13. 38.
Christ, 1 *Cor.* 12. 12.
Christians, *Acts* 11. 26. 1 *Pet.* 4. 16.
Church of God, 1 *Cor.* 1. 2.
Circumcision, *Phil.* 3. 3.
City of God, *Heb.* 12. 22. *Rev.* 3. 12.
Citizens, *Eph.* 2. 19. | Comely, *Cant.* 1. 5.
Companions, *Psal.* 45. 14. *Cant.* 1. 7.
Complete, *Col.* 2. 10.
Congregation of Saints, *Psal.* 149. 1.
Contrite, *Isa.* 57. 15. | 66. 2.
Converts, *Isa.* 1. 27.
Corner Stones, *Psal.* 144. 12.
Daughter of the King, *Psal.* 45. 13.
Dead in Christ, 1 *Thess.* 4. 16.
Dearly Beloved, *Jer.* 12. 7.
Delights, *Cant.* 7. 6.
Dew, *Psal.* 110. 3. *Mic.* 5. 7.
Disciples, *Isa.* 8. 16. *Mat.* 5. 1.
Dove, *Cant.* 2. 14. | 5. 2.
Eagles, *Psal.* 103. 5. *Isa.* 40. 31.
Elect, *Isa.* 45. 4. *Mat.* 24. 22.
Election, *Rom.* 9. 11. | 11. 5, 7.
Escaped, *Isa.* 45. 20. 2 *Pet.* 1. 4
Excellent, *Psal.* 16. 3. *Prov.* 12. 26.
Fair, *Cant.* 1. 15. | 2. 10. | 4. 10.
Faithful, *Eph.* 1. 1. *Col.* 1. 2.
Family of God, *Eph.* 3. 15.
Fearful, *Isa.* 35. 4. | Fig-trees, *Cant.* 2. [13.
First-fruits, *Jam.* 1. 18.
Flock of God, *Acts* 20. 28.
First-born, *Heb.* 12. 23.
Fold of Christ, *John* 10. 16.
Followers of God, *Eph.* 5. 1.
Fountain, *Cant.* 4. 12.
Free men, 1 *Cor.* 7. 22.
Friends of God, *Jam.* 2. 23.
Fruitful, *Col.* 1. 10.
Fulness of Christ, *Eph.* 1. 23.
Garden enclosed, *Cant.* 4. 12.
Gathered, *Isa.* 56. 8.
General Assembly, *Heb.* 12. 23.
Generation of the Upright, *Psal.* 112. 2.
Glory of God, *Isa.* 46. 13.
Glorious, *Ps.* 45. 13. | Grapes, *Hos.* 9. [10.
Habitation of God, *Eph.* 2. 22.
Heirs of God, *Rom.* 8. 17.
Heritage of God, *Jer.* 12. 7.
Hidden Ones, *Psal.* 83. 3.
Holy, 1 *Cor.* 3. 17. *Eph.* 1. 4.
House of God, 1 *Tim.* 3. 15.
Humble, *Psal.* 9. 12. | 34. 2.
Husbandry of God, 1 *Cor.* 3. 9.
Jacob, *Psal.* 14. 7. | 147. 19.
Jerusalem above, *Gal.* 4. 29.—heavenly, *Heb.* 12. 22.—holy, *Rev.* 21. 10.
Jewels of the Lord, *Mal.* 3. 17.
Image of God, *Rom.* 8. 29.
Inhabitants of Zion, *Isa.* 12. 6.
Joy of the whole Earth, *Psal.* 48. 2.
Israel of God, *Gal.* 6. 16.
Justified, *Acts* 13. 39.
Kings, *Rev.* 1. 6. | 5. 10.
Kingdom of Heaven, *Mat.* 13. 38.
Lambs, *Isa.* 40. 11. *John* 21. 15.
Lamb's Wife, *Rev.* 21. 9.
Light of the World, *Mat.* 5. 14.
Lily among Thorns, *Cant.* 2. 2.
Little Ones, *Zech.* 13. 7.
Lively Stones, 1 *Pet.* 2. 5.
Lot of God's Inheritance, *Deut.* 32. 9.
Love, *or* his Love, *Cant.* 4. 7.
Lowly, *Psal.* 138. 6. *Prov.* 3. 34.
Members of Christ, *Eph.* 5. 30.
Merciful, *Mat.* 5. 7.
Mighty, *Psal.* 112. 2. *Acts* 18. 24.
Mount Zion, *Heb.* 12. 22.
Mourners, *Isa.* 57. 18.
Needy, *Psal.* 9. 18. *Isa.* 25. 4. | 41. 17.
Obedient, 1 *Pet.* 1. 14.
Palaces, *Psal.* 45. 15. | 48. 3, 13.
Palm-trees, *Psal.* 92. 12. *Cant.* 7. 8.
Peaceable, *Gen.* 34. 21.
Peculiar People, 1 *Pet.* 2. 9.
Perfect, 2 *Tim.* 3. 17. *Heb.* 12. 23.
Pilgrims, *Heb.* 11. 13.
Pillar of Truth, 1 *Tim.* 3. 15.
Plants, *Psal.* 144. 12. *Cant.* 4. 13.
Poor, *Mat.* 5. 3. | 11. 5.
Portion of the Lord, *Deut.* 32. 9.
Precious, *Psal.* 116. 15. *Isa.* 43. 4.
Princes, 1 *Sam.* 2. 8. *Psal.* 45. 16
Pure in Heart, *Mat.* 5. 8.
Ransomed, *Isa.* 45. 10. | 51. 11.
Redeemed, *Isa.* 51. 11. | 62. 12.
Sanctified, 1 *Cor.* 1. 2. | 6. 11.
Saved of the Lord, *Deut.* 33. 29.
Sheep, *John* 10. 3, 4. | 21. 16.
Sincere, *Phil.* 1. 10.
Stones, 1 *Pet.* 2. 5.
Sister, Spouse, *Cant.* 4. 12.
Sons of God, *Rom.* 8. 14.
Spiritual, *Gal.* 6. 1. 1 *Pet.* 2. 5.
Stars, *Psal.* 148. 3. *Rev.* 3. 1.
Strangers, *Psal.* 39. 12. | 119. 9.
Temple of God, 1 *Cor.* 3. 16.
Treasure of God, *Psal.* 135. 4.
Vessels of Mercy, *Rom.* 9. 23.
Vineyard, *Isa.* 5. 1. | 27. 2.
Virgins, *Jer.* 31. 4. *Rev.* 14. 4.
Undefiled, *Cant.* 5. 2. | 6. 9.
Upright, *Psal.* 11. 7. | 37. 37.
Watchman, *Isa.* 52. 8. | 62. 6.
Wayfaring-Men, *Isa.* 35. 8.
Wise Men, 1 *Cor.* 6. 5.
Woman, *Rev.* 12. 1.
Worshippers, *Heb.* 10. 2.
Worthy to walk with Christ, *Rev.* 3. 4.
Written in Heaven, *Heb.* 12. 23.
Zealous of good Works, *Tit.* 2. 14.
Zion, *Psal.* 69. 35. | 76. 2. | 87. 2.

Note.—*The † denotes that the reference is to a marginal Reading.*

AN ALPHABETICAL

TABLE OF THE PROPER NAMES

IN THE

OLD AND NEW TESTAMENT;

TOGETHER WITH THE

MEANING OR SIGNIFICATION OF THE WORDS IN THEIR ORIGINAL LANGUAGES.

NOTE,—*There are some* PROPER NAMES *in this* TABLE *which are not in the following Part of the* CONCORDANCE, *being seldom mentioned in Scripture. To these, a reference to the Place in which they are found is here annexed.*

AARON, *signifies* lofty, *or* mountainous; *or* mountain of strength; *or* a teacher, *or* teaching. *The first high priest of the Jews, the son of Amram, brother to Moses. He, at the desire of the people, made a calf, which they worshipped, and thereby committed a great sin. He was, with his sons, anointed and consecrated to the priest's office,* Lev. 8.

AARONITES.

ABADDON, the destroyer, *Rev.* 9. 11.

ABAGTHA, father of the wine-press.

ABANA, made of stone, *or* a building

ABARIM, passages, *or* passengers.

ABDA, a servant, *or* servitude.

ABDI, he is my servant.

ABDIEL, the servant of God; *or*, cloud of the abundance of God.

ABDON, a servant, *or* cloud of judgment.

ABED-NEGO, servant of light, *Dan.* 3. 23.

ABEL, *Adam's second son, signifies* vanity, *or* breath, *or* vapour, *Gen.* 4. 4.

ABEL, *a city, signifies,* mourning.

ABEL-BETH-MAACHAH, mourning to the house of Maachah.

ABEL-MAIM, the mourning of the waters; *or* the valley of waters.

ABEL-MEHOLAH, sorrow *or* mourning of weakness, *or* of sickness.

ABEL-MIZRAIM, the mourning of the Egyptians, *Gen.* 50. 11.

ABEL-SHITTIM, mourning of the thorns. *It was a city near the river Jordan in the wilderness,* Num. 33. 49.

ABEZ, an egg, *or* muddy. *A city in the tribe of Issachar,* Josh. 19. 20.

ABI, my father. *The mother of Hezekiah,* 2 Kings 18. 2.

ABIAH, the Lord is my father, *or* the father of the Lord.

ABI-ALBON, most intelligent father, *or* the father over the building; *or* father of injury.

ABIATHAR, excellent father, *or* father of him that survived, 1 *Sam.* 22. 20.

ABIB, green fruits, *or* ears of corn.

ABIDAH, the father of knowledge, *or* the knowledge of the father. *One of the sons of Midian,* Gen. 25. 4.

ABIDAN, father of judgment, *or* my father is judge.

ABIEL, God my father, *or* my God the father. *He was the father of Kish,* 1 Sam. 9. 1.

ABIEZER, father of help, *or* help of the father, *or* my father is my help.

ABI-EZRITE.

ABIGAIL, father of joy, *or* the joy of the father, 1 *Sam.* 25. 3.

ABIHAIL, the father of strength, *or* father of trouble.

ABIHU, he is my father, *or* his father.

ABIJAH, the will of the Lord, *or* the Lord is my father.

ABIJAM, father of the sea.

ABILENE, the father of the apartment, *or* of mourning. *A province between Libanus and Antilibanus, whereof Lysanias was tetrarch,* Luke 3. 1.

ABIMAEL, a father sent from God, *or* my father comes from God. *He was the son of Joktan,* Gen. 10. 28.

ABIMELECH, father of the king, *or* my father the king.

ABINADAB, father of willingness; *or* my father is a prince.

ABINOAM, father of beauty, *or* comeliness; *or* my father is beautiful.

ABIRAM, a high father, *or* father of fraud.

ABISHAG, ignorance of the father.

ABISHAI, the present of my father, *or* the father of the present; *otherwise,* the father of the sacrifice, *or* the sacrifice of my father.

ABISHALOM, the father of peace, *or* the peace of the father; *or* the recompence of the father, 1 *Kings* 15. 2.

ABISHUA, father of salvation, *or* of magnificence, *or* the salvation of my father, 1 *Chr.* 6. 4.

ABISHUR, the father of the wall, *or* of uprightness; *or* my father is upright, 1 *Chron.* 2. 28.

ABITAL, the father of the dew; *or* the father of the shadow, *according to the Syriac. One of David's wives,* 2 Sam. 3. 4.

ABITUB, father of goodness, *or* my father is good, 1 *Chron.* 8. 11.

ABIHUD, father of praise, *or* glory of my father.

ABNER, father of light, *or* the lamp of the father, *or* the son of the father.

ABRAM, a high father; the father of elevation.

ABRAHAM, the father of a great multitude. *At the command of God Abraham went out of Ur of the Chaldees, his native country, into Canaan, where the Lord promised to give that land to his seed.* The Messiah *was promised to be of his family, for in his seed* all the families of the earth *were to be blessed,* Gen. 12. 3. Acts 3. 25. Gal. 3. 8. *He was circumcised with all his household, and taught his family to keep the commands of God. His faith was tried in being commanded to offer up his son Isaac; but the angel of the Lord stayed him, and Isaac was exchanged with a ram. Isaac in this matter was an eminent type and figure of Christ, who in the time appointed by God, was to be offered up a sacrifice for the sins of those that believe in him. The spiritual children of faithful Abraham, are those that believe in Jesus Christ, and do the works of Abraham,* John 8. 39. Rom. 4. 16. *and* 9. 7. Gal. 3. 7, 29.

ABSALOM, father of peace, *or* the peace of the father.

ACCAD, a vessel, a pitcher; *or* a sparkle. *The city where Nimrod reigned,* Gen. 10. 10.

ACCHO, close, enclosed, pressed together.

ACELDAMA, the field of blood, *Acts* 1. 19.

ACHAIA, grief, *or* trouble.

ACHAICUS, a native of Achaia.

ACHAN, *or* ACHAR, he that troubles and bruises.

ACHBOR, a rat; *otherwise,* bruising *or* enclosing the well. *He was father of Baal-hanan, the seventh king of Edom,* Gen. 36. 38.

ACHIM, preparing, confirming, *or* revenging.

ACHISH, thus it is; *or* how is this?

ACHMETHA, *a city.*

ACHOR, trouble.

ACHSAH, adorned; *or* bursting of the veil.

ACHSHAPH, poison, tricks; *or* one that breaks; *or,* the lip *or* brim of any thing.

ACHZIB, liar, lying; *or* that runs; *or* that delays.

ADADAH, the witness *or* testimony of the assembly. *The name of a city,* Josh. 15. 22.

ADAH, an assembly. *The wife of Lamech,* Gen. 4. 19. *Also the wife of Esau,* Gen. 36. 2.

ADAIAH, the witness of the Lord. *The father of Jedidah mother of Josiah,* 2 Kings 22. 1.

ADALIAH, one that draws water; *or* poverty, *or* cloud, vapour, death. *One of Haman's sons,* Esth. 9. 8.

ADAM, earthy, taken out of red earth. *The name of the first man, who was made after the image of God, in a holy and happy estate, but by his fall and disobedience broke covenant with God, and thereby brought himself and all his posterity into an estate of sin and misery,* Rom. 5. 12. *But our Lord Jesus Christ, the second Adam, is the Saviour and Redeemer of all that truly believe in him,* Mark 16. 16. Acts 4. 12. *and* 16. 31.

ADAMAH, red earth. *A city,* Josh. 19. 36.

ADAMI, my man, red, earthy, human. *A city,* Josh. 19. 33.

ADAH, high, *or* eminent.

ADBEEL, a vapour, a cloud of God; *otherwise,* a vexer of God. *One of Ishmael's sons,* Gen. 25. 13.

ADDI, my witness, adorned, passage, prey.

ADDON, basis, foundation, the Lord. *The name of a place,* Neh. 7. 61.

ADIEL, the witness of the Lord. 1 *Chron.* 4. 36.

ADIN, adorned, *or* voluptuous, dainty. *Ezra* 8. 6.

ADITHAIM, assemblies, or testimonies. *Josh.* 15. 36.

ADLAI, my witness, my ornament. 1 *Chr.* 27. 29.

ADMAH, earthy, red earth.

ADMATHA, a cloud of death, a mortal vapour. *Esth.* 1. 14.

ADNAH, rest, *or* testimony eternal. 1 *Chr.* 12. 20.

ADONI-BEZEK, the lightning of the Lord, *or* the Lord of lightning; *or* the Lord of Bezek; *for he was king of this city.*

ADONIJAH, the Lord is my master.

ADONIKAM, the Lord is raised, *or* my Lord hath raised me.

ADONIRAM, my Lord is most high, *or* the Lord of might and elevation. 1 *Kings* 4. 6.

ADONI-ZEDEK, justice of the Lord, *or* the Lord of justice. *He was king of Jerusalem,* Josh. 10. 1.

ADORAM, their beauty, their power, *or* their praise. *He was David's tribute-gatherer,* 2 Sam. 20. 24.

ADORAIM, strength, *or* power of the sea. 2 *Chron.* 11. 9.

ADRAMMELECH, the cloak, glory, grandeur, *or* power of the king.

ADRAMYTTIUM, the court of death, the mansion of death.

ADRIA, *the name of a city, which gives name to the Adriatic sea, now the gulf of Venice.*

ADULLAM, their testimony, their prey, *or* their ornament.

AGABUS, a locust, *or* the feast of the father.

AGAG, roof, floor.

AGAGITE, *of the race of* Agag.

AGAR. *See* HAGAR.

AGRIPPA, *this word is Latin, and signifies* one who at his birth causes great pain, who is born with his feet foremost, *æger partus.*

AGUR, a stranger, *or* gathering, *or* gathered together.

AHAB, the brother of the father, uncle *or* father of the brother.

AHASUERUS, prince, head, *or* chief.

AHAVA, essence, *or* generation.

AHAZ, one that takes and possesses.

AHAZIAH, seizure, possession, *or* vision of the Lord.

AHIAH, brother of the Lord.

AHIEZER, brother of assistance. *A prince of the tribe of Dan,* Num. 1. 12.

AHIJAH, *the same with* AHIAH.

AHIKAM, a brother that raises up.

AHILUD, a brother born. *He was secretary to David,* 2 Sam. 8. 16.

AHIMAAZ, brother of the council, *or* my brother is counsellor.

AHIMAN, a brother prepared, *or* brother of the right hand.

AHIMELECH, my brother is a king, *or* the brother of my king.

AHIMOTH, brother of death, *or* my brother is dead. 1 *Chron.* 6. 25.

AHINOAM, the beauty and comeliness of the brother, *or* brother of motion.

AHIO, his brother, his brethren.

AHIRA, brother of iniquity; *otherwise*, brother or companion of the shepherd. *He was chief of the tribe of Naphtali*, Num. 1. 15.
AHISAMACH, brother of strength *or* support, *or* my brother supports me.
AHISHAR, brother of a prince, *or* brother of a song. *He was steward of Solomon's household*, 1 Kings 4. 6.
AHITHOPHEL, brother of ruin or folly.
AHITUB, brother of goodness, *or* my brother is good.
AHIHUD, brother of praise. *The prince of the tribe of Asher*, Num. 34. 27.
AHLAB, which is of milk, *or* which is fat; *otherwise*, brother of the heart. *The name of a city*, Judg. 1. 31.
AHOLAH, his tabernacle, his tent.
AHOLIAB, the tent *or* tabernacle of the father.
AHOLIBAH, my tent and my tabernacle in her
AHOLIBAMAH, my tabernacle is exalted.
AI, *or* HAI, mass, *or* heap.
AIOTH, *the same as* AI.
AJALON, a chain; *otherwise*, strength, *or* a stag.
ALAMMELECH, God is king. *A city*, Josh. 19. 26.
ALEXANDER, *is a Greek word, and signifies*, one that assists men, *or* one that helps stoutly; *or* one that turns away evil.
ALEXANDRIA, *a city in Egypt.*
ALLELUIA, praise the Lord, *or* praise to the Lord.
ALLON, an oak, *or* strong, 1 *Chron.* 4. 37.
ALLON-BACHUTH, the oak of weeping. *The place where Rebekah's nurse was buried*, Gen. 35. 8.
ALMODAD, measure of God, *Gen.* 10. 26.
ALPHA, *the first letter of the Greek alphabet, marked* A.
ALPHEUS, a thousand; *otherwise*, learned, *or* chief.
AMALEK, a people that licks up, *or* that takes away all; *otherwise*, a people that strikes, *or* that uses ill.
AMALEKITES, *people descended from Amalek.*
AMANA, integrity and truth.
AMARIAH, the Lord says, *or* the excellency of the Lord, *Zeph.* 1. 1.
AMASA, a forgiving people, *or* sparing the people; *otherwise*, the burden of the people.
AMAZIAH, the strength of the Lord.
AMMAH, my people.
AMMI, *the same with* AMMAH.
AMMI-NADAB, my people is liberal, *or* prince of the people, *or* a people that vows.
AMMIHUD, people of praise, *or* praise is with me, *Num.* 1. 10.
AMMISHADDAI, the people of the Almighty, *or* the Almighty is with me, *Num.* 1. 12.
AMMON, a people, *or* the son of my people.
AMMONITES, *a people that descended of* Ben-ammi, *son of Lot by his youngest daughter.*
AMNON, faithful and true; *otherwise*, foster-father, *or* tutor; *or*, son of the mother.
AMON, faithful, true.
AMORITE, bitter, a rebel; *otherwise*, a babbler *or* prater.
AMOS, loading, weighty.
AMOZ, strong, robust.
AMPHIPOLIS, a city encompassed by the sea.
AMPLIAS, large, extensive. *A Latin word.*
AMRAM, an exalted people; *or* their sheaves, *or* handfuls of corn.
AMRAPHEL, one that speaks of hidden things; *or* one that speaks of judgment, *or* of ruin.
ANAH, one who answers, *or* who sings; *otherwise*, poor, *or* afflicted.
ANAK, a collar, *or* ornament.
ANAKIMS.
ANAMMELECH, answer, *or* song of the king and council.
ANANIAS, the cloud of the Lord.
ANATHOTH, answer, song; *or*, affliction, poverty.
ANDREW, a stout and strong man. *A Greek word.*
ANDRONICUS, a man excelling others, a victorious man. *Greek.*
ANER, answer, song, affliction, of light.
ANNA, gracious, merciful.
ANNAS, one that answers, that afflicts and humbles, *or* gracious, merciful. *A high-priest who sent Christ bound to Caiaphas his father-in-law.*
ANTICHRIST, an adversary to Christ.
ANTIOCH, for *or* instead of a chariot; *or* equal in speed with a chariot.
ANTIPAS, for all, *or* against all. *One of the martyrs slain by the people of Pergamus*, Rev. 2. 13.
ANTIPATRIS, for, *or* against the father.
APELLES, *a Greek word, from the verb* απελλω, I exclude, I separate.
APHEK, a stream, a rapid torrent; *or* strength, vigour.
APPOLLONIA, perdition, destruction.
APOLLOS, one that destroys and lays waste.
APOLLYON, one that exterminates *or* destroys.
APPHIA, that produces, *or* is fruitful. *Philem.* 2.
APPII-FORUM, *a town so called from* Appius Claudius, *whose statue was erected there.*
AQUILA, an eagle. *Latin.*
AR, awaking, watching, evacuation, uncovering.
ARABIA, evening, *or* a place wild and desert; *or* hostages, ravens; *and also*, mixtures; *because this country was inhabited by different kinds of people.*
ARABIAN.
ARAM, highness, magnificence; *otherwise*, one that deceives, *or* their curse. ARAM *signifies* Syria *in* Gen. 22. 21. *and elsewhere.*
ARARAT, the curse of trembling.
ARAUNAH, ark, song, joyful cry, curse.
ARBA, the city of the four.
ARCHELAUS, the prince of the people. *Greek.*
ARCHIPPUS, a governor of horses, *or* master of the horse. *Greek.*
ARCTURUS, a gathering together.
ARD, one that commands, *or* he that descends. *A son of Benjamin*, Gen. 46. 21.
ARELI, the light *or* vision of God. *Gen.* 46. 16.
AREOPAGITE, belonging to the council called *Areopagus.*
AREOPAGUS, the hill of Mars; *a place where the magistrates of Athens held their supreme council; from* ἀρειος, Mars, *and* παγος, a hill.
ARETAS, one that is agreeable, that pleases, that is virtuous.
ARGOB, a turf of earth, *or* fat land, *or* curse of the well.
ARIEL, the altar, light, or lion of God.
ARIMATHEA, a lion dead to the Lord; *or* the light of the death of the Lord; *or simply* Ramath, *or* Ramah, *a city where Samuel dwelt*, 1 Sam. 1. 19.
ARIOCH, long, great, tall; *or* your drunkenness; *or* your lion.
ARISTARCHUS, a good prince, the best prince. *Greek.*
ARISTOBULUS, a good counsellor, good advice. *Greek.*
ARMAGEDDON, the mountain of *Megiddo*, *or* the mountain of the gospel; *otherwise*, the mountain of fruits, *or* of apples.
ARMENIA, *a province which is supposed to take its name from Aram.*
ARNON, rejoicing, or leaping for joy; *or* their chest or ark.
AROER, heath, tamarisk; *or* the nakedness of the skin; *or* nakedness of the watch, *or* of the enemy.
ARPAD, the light of redemption; *or* that lies down, that makes his bed.
ARPHAXAD, one that heals; *or* one that releases.
ARTAXERXES, *in Hebrew*, Artachsasta, *the* silence of light, *or* light that imposes silence; *otherwise* joy, that is in haste. *A Persian name.*
ARTEMAS, whole, sound, *or* without fault.
ASA, physician, *or* cure.
ASAHEL, the work *or* creature of God.
ASAIAH, the Lord hath wrought; *or* a creature of the Lord.
ASAPH, one that assembles together; *or* one that finishes and completes.
ASENATH, peril, *or* misfortune.
ASHDOD, inclination, leaning; *or* a wild open place; *or* pillage, theft.
ASHER, blessedness, *or* happiness.
ASHIMA, crime; *or* position; *or* fire of the sea. *The name of an idol*, 2 Kings 17. 30.
ASHKENAZ, a fire that distils or spreads. *One of the sons of* Gomer, *Gen.* 10. 3.
ASHTAROTH, flocks, the sheep, *or* riches.
ASHUR, one that is happy, that walks on prosperously.
ASIA, muddy, boggy.
ASKELON, weight, *or* balance; *or* fire of infamy.
ASNAPPER, unhappiness, misfortune of the bull *or* calf; *or* fruitless, *or* increase of danger.
ASSIR, prisoner, fettered, 1 *Chron.* 3. 17.
ASSOS, approaching, coming near to. *Acts* 20. 13.
ASSYRIA.
ASSYRIAN.
ASYNCRITUS, incomparable.
ATAD, a thorn.
ATHALIAH, the time of the Lord.
ATHENIANS, *inhabitants of* Athens.
ATHENS, *so called from* Athene, *or* Athenaia, Minerva.
ATTALIA, that increases *or* sends.
AVEN, iniquity, force, riches.
AUGUSTUS, increased, augmented; *or* royal, majestic.
AZARIAH, assistance, *or* help of the Lord; *or* he that hears the Lord, *or* whom the Lord hears.
AZEKAH, strength of walls.
AZGAD, a strong army, *or* the strength of a troop; *otherwise*, a gang of robbers, *or* a troop of soldiers. *Ezra* 2. 12.
AZNOTH-TABOR, the ears of *Tabor*; *or* the ears of choice, purity, contrition. *Josh.* 19. 34.
AZOTUS, *the same as* ASHDOD, pillage, theft. *Acts* 8. 40.
AZUR, he that assists, *or* he that is assisted. *Jer.* 28. 1.

B.

BAAL, he that rules and subdues; *or* master, lord, *or* husband.
BAALAH, her idol; *or* she that is governed or subdued, a spouse. *A city*, Josh. 15. 9.
BAAL-BERITH, idol of the covenant; *or* he that possesses, *or* subdues the covenant.
BAAL-GAD, the idol of the troop, of the army, *or* of felicity; *otherwise*, the Lord is master of the troop, *Josh.* 11. 17.
BAAL-HAMON, one that possesses *or* rules a multitude; a populous place.
BAAL-HERMON, the possessor of destruction; *or* of a thing cursed, devoted, *or* consecrated to God. *It is a mountain*, Judg. 3. 3.
BAALI, my idol, master, *or* lord over me.
BAALIM, idols, masters, false gods.
BAALIS, a rejoicing, *or* proud lord.
BAAL-MEON, the idol, the master of the house.
BAAL-PEOR, master of the opening.
BAAL-PERAZIM, master, *or* god of divisions, *or* he that possesses and enjoys divisions and dissipations.
BAAL-SHALISHA, the third idol, the third husband; *or* that governs *or* presides over three.
BAAL-TAMAR, master of the palm-tree.
BAAL-ZEBUB, the master of flies.
BAAL-ZEPHON, the idol, *or* possession of the north; *or* hidden, secret.
BAANAH, in the answer, in affliction.
BAASHAH, in the work, *or* in the compression; *or* he that seeks and demands, *or* who lays waste.
BABEL, confusion, *or* mixture.
BABYLON, *the same with* BABEL.
BABYLONIANS.
BABYLONISH.
BACA, mulberry-tree.
BAHURIM, choice, warlike, valiant.
BAJITH, a house.
BALAAM, the old age *or* ancient of the people, *or* their destruction; *or*, without the people.
BALAK, who lays waste and destroys; *or* who licks and laps.
BAMAH, an eminence, *or* high place.
BARABBAS, son of the father, *or* of the master, *or* the son of confusion and shame.
BARACHEL, who blesses God, who bends the knee before God. *The father of Elihu*, Job 32. 2.
BARACHIAS, *the same with* BARACHEL.
BARAK, thunder, *or* in vain.
BAR-JESUS, son of *Jesus*, or *Joshua*.
BAR-JONA, the son of *Jona*, *or* of a dove.
BARNABAS, the son of the prophet, *or* of consolation.
BARSABAS, son of return, *or* of conversion; *or* son of rest, *or* son of swearing.
BARTHOLOMEW, a son that suspends the waters.
BARTIMEUS, the son of *Timeus*, *or* of the perfect and honourable.
BARUCH, who is blessed, who bends the knee.
BARZILLAI, made of iron; *or* the son of contempt.
BASHAN, in the tooth, *or* in the ivory; *otherwise*, in the change, *or* the sleep.
BASHEMATH, perfumed; *or* confusion of death; *otherwise*, in desolation.
BATH-SHEBA, the seventh daughter, *or* the daughter of an oath.
BEDAD, alone, solitary; *or* in friendship, in the bosom, *or* the nipple. *He was father of Hadad*, Gen. 36. 35.
BEDAN, only; *or* in the judgment; *or* according to judgment.
BEEL-ZEBUB, *the same with* BAAL-ZEBUB.
BEER, a well. *The name of a city*, Num. 21. 16.
BEER-LAHAI-ROI, the well of him that liveth and seeth me. *Gen.* 16. 14.
BEER-SHEBA, the well, *or* fountain of an oath; *otherwise*, the seventh well, *or* the well of satiety.
BEKAH, *half a shekel.*
BEL, ancient; *or* nothing, vain, *or* what is subject to change. *The name of an idol.*
BELIAL, wicked, *or* the devil.
BELSHAZZAR, master of the treasure, *or* who lays up treasures in secret.
BELTESHAZZAR, who lays up treasures in secret; *or* he that secretly endures pain and pressure.
BENAIAH, son of the Lord; *or*, the understanding of the Lord; *or* the Lord's building.
BEN-AMMI, the son of my people.
BEN-HADAD, the son of *Hadad*, *or* of noise, clamour, cry.
BENJAMIN, the son of the right hand.
BENJAMITE.
BENONI, son of my grief, pain, sorrow.
BEOR, burning; *otherwise*, foolish, mad, beast.
BERACHAH, blessing, *or* bending of the knee.
BEREA, heavy, weighty; *from* βαρος, weight.
BERITH, covenant.
BERNICE, one that brings victory.
BESOR, glad news, *or* incarnation.
BETAH, confidence. *A city*, 2 Sam. 8. 8.
BETHABARA, the house of passage, *or* house of anger.
BETHANY, the house of song, *or* of affliction; *otherwise*, the house of obedience, *or* the house of the grace of the Lord.
BETH-AVEN, the house of vanity, of iniquity, of trouble, of strength.
BETH-BIREI, the house of my Creator; *or* the temple of my Creator. 1 *Chr.* 4. 31.
BETH-CAR, the house of the lamb, *or* the house of knowledge. *A city*, 1 Sam. 7. 11.
BETH-DAGON, the house of corn; *or* the habitation of the fish; *or* the temple of the god *Dagon*. Josh. 19. 27.
BETH-DIBLATHAIM, the house of dry figs.
BETH-EL, the house of God.
BETHELITE.
BETHER, division; *otherwise*, in the turtle, *or* in the trial, *or* perquisition.
BETHESDA, the house of effusion; *or* the house of pity, *or* mercy.
BETH-EZEL, a neighbour's house.
BETH-GAMUL, the house of recompence, *or* of the weaned; *or* the house of the camel.
BETH-HACCEREM, the house of the vineyard.
BETH-HORON, the house of wrath; *or* the house of the hole, *or* of the cave, *or* of liberty.
BETH-LEHEM, the house of bread, *or* the house of war.
BETH-LEHEM-EPHRATAH.
BETH-LEHEM-JUDAH.
BETH-LEHEMITE.
BETH-PEOR, the house of gaping *or* opening.
BETHPHAGE, the house of the mouth, *or* the drain of the valleys; *or*, the house of early figs.
BETHSAIDA, the house of fruits, *or* of food, *or* of hunters, *or* of snares.
BETH-SHAN, the house of the tooth, *or* of

ivory; *or* the house of change; *or* the dwelling of sleep.
BETH-SHEMESH, the house of the sun; *or* the house of service, *or* of ministry.
BETHUEL, filiation of God.
BEULAH, married.
BEZALEEL, in the shadow of God.
BEZEK, lightning; *or* in the chains *or* fetters.
BICHRI, first-born, *or* first-fruits; *otherwise*, in the ram, *or* the sheep.
BIDKAR, in compunction, *or* in sharp pain, in the wound.
BIGTHAN, giving meat, *Esth.* 2. 21. called also Bigthana, chap. 6. 2.
BILDAD, old friendship, *or* old love.
BILHAH, who is old, troubled, *or* confused; *or* which spreads itself.
BIRSHA, in evil; *or* son that beholds. *Gen.* 14. 2.
BITHIAH, daughter of the Lord. 1 *Chron.* 4. 18.
BITHRON, division; *or* in his examination; *or* daughter of the song; *or* the habitation of the song, *or* of anger, *or* of liberty.
BITHYNIA, violent precipitation, *from the Greek word* βια, violence, *and the verb* θυνω, I make haste.
BLASTUS, one that sprouts and brings forth.
BOANERGES, the sons of thunder, James and John the sons of Zebedee.
BOAZ, *or* BOOZ, in strength, *or* in the goat.
BOCHIM, the place of weeping, *or* of mourners, *or* of mulberry trees.
BOZEZ, mud, bog; *or* in him the flower. *The name of a rock*, 1 Sam. 14. 4.
BOZRAH, in tribulation *or* distress.
BUL, changeable, perishing. *The name of a month.*
BUZ, despised, *or* plundered.
BUZI, my contempt.
BUZITE, *a descendant from* Buz.

C.

CABUL, displeasing, *or* dirty.
CAIAPHAS, a searcher; *or* he that seeks with diligence.
CAIN, possession, *or* possessed.
CAINAN, possessor *or* purchaser; *or* one that laments; *or* the builder of a nest.
CALAH, favourable, opportunity; *or* as the verdure, *or* green fruit. *A city*, Gen. 10. 12.
CALEB, a dog, *or* a crow, *or* a basket; *or* as the heart.
CALEB-EPHRATAH, *a place so called by a conjunction of the names* Caleb *and his wife* Ephratah. *See* EPHRATAH.
CALNEH, our consummation, *or* all we; *or* as murmuring.
CALNO, our consummation: *according to others*, altogether himself.
CALVARY, the place of a scull.
CAMON, his resurrection.
CANA, zeal, *or* emulation; *otherwise*, possession, lamentation, the nest, cane, *or* staff.
CANAAN, a merchant, a trader. *He was the son of Ham, and gave name to the land of* Canaan. *The* Canaanites *were a wicked people, for they descended from a wicked father*, Gen. 13. 7.
CANAANITE.
CANDACE, who possesses contrition; *or* pure possession.
CAPERNAUM, the field of repentance, *or* city of comfort; *otherwise*, the propitiation of the penitent; *or* the town of pleasure, the handsome city.
CAPHTOR, a sphere, a buckle, a hand, a palm, doves, *or* those that seek and inquire.
CAPPADOCIA, *in Hebrew*, CAPHTOR, *which see.*
CARCAS, the covering of a lamb; *or* the lamb of the throne, *Esth.* 1. 10.
CARCHEMISH, a lamb, as taken away, withdrawn, *or* carried off.
CARMEL, a circumcised lamb; *otherwise*, harvest, full ears of corn, vineyard of God, excellent vineyard.
CARMELITE.
CARMI, my vineyard; *or* the knowledge of the waters; *or* the lamb of the waters.
CARPUS, fruit, *or* fruitful. *Greek.*
CASIPHIA, money, *or* covetousness.
CEDRON, black, *or* sad.
CENCHREA, millet, small pulse.
CEPHAS, a rock *or* stone.
CESAR, *a Latin name, from the word* cædo, I cut, *because he was cut out of his mother's womb*; or *from the word* Cæsaries, a head of hair, *which he is said to be born with.*
CESAREA, a bush of hair.
CHALCOL, who nourishes, consumes, and sustains the whole.
CHALDEA, as demons, *or* as robbers, *or* beasts, *or* fields.
CHALDEAN.
CHALDEES.
CHARRAN, a singing, *or* calling out, *or* the heat of wrath.
CHEBAR, strength, *or* power. *Ezek.* 10. 15, 20.
CHEDORLAOMER, as a generation of servitude; *otherwise*, the roundness of the sheaf, *Gen.* 14. 4.
CHEMARIMS, *the name of Baal's priests.*
CHEMOSH, as handling or stroking, *or* as withdrawing or taking away.
CHENANIA, preparation, *or* disposition *or* strength, *or* rectitude of the Lord.
CHERETHIMS, who cuts, who tears away and exterminates.
CHERETHITES. *See* CHERETHIMS.
CHERITH, cutting, piercing, slaying.
CHESED, as a devil, *or* as a destroyer, *or* as a breast *or* nipple, *Gen.* 22. 22.
CHILEAB, totality of the father, *or* the perfection of the father, 2 *Sam.* 3. 3.
CHILION, finished, complete, perfect.
CHILMAD, as teaching or learning.
CHIMHAM, as they, *or* like to them.
CHIOS, open, *or* opening.
CHISLEU, rashness, confidence, the flanks.
CHITTIM, those that bruise; *or* gold; *or* staining *or* dying.
CHIUN, *an Egyptian god, whom some think to be* Saturn.
CHLOE, green herb.
CHORAZIN, the secret, *or* here is a mystery.
CHUSHAN-RISHATHAIM, Ethiopian; *or* blackness of iniquities.
CHUZA, the seer, *or* prophet; *or* Ethiopian. *The husband of Joanna.*
CILICIA, which rolls *or* overturns.
CLAUDA, a broken voice, a lamentable voice. *It is an island.* Acts 27. 16.
CLAUDIA, lame, 2 *Tim.* 4. 21.
CLEMENT, mild, good, modest, merciful. *Phil.* 4. 3.
CLEOPHAS, the whole glory; *or* glory altogether.
COLOSSE, punishment, correction; *from the word* κολαζω, I punish.
CONIAH, the strength, *or* stability of the Lord.
CORINTH, which is satisfied, *or* ornament, *or* beauty.
CORINTHIANS.
CORNELIUS, of an horn. *Or* κερηλιος, *as if it were* κερας του ἡλιȣ, the beam of the sun. *Having a vision, he sent for Peter, who first preached the gospel to the Gentiles*, Acts 10.
COZBI, a liar; *or* as sliding away.
CRESCENS, growing, increasing.
CRETE, carnal, fleshly.
CRETES.
CRETIANS.
CRISPUS, curled.
CUSH, Ethiopians, *or* black.
CUSHAN, Ethiopia, black, blackness, heat.
CUSHI, *the same.*
CYPRUS, fair, *or* fairness.
CYRENE, a wall, *or* coldness, *or* meeting, *or* a floor.
CYRENIANS, *people of Cyrene.*
CYRENIUS, who governs.
CYRUS, as miserable, *or* as heir; *or* the belly.

D.

DABBASHETH, flowing with honey; *or* causing infamy.
DABERATH, word, thing; *or* a bee; *or* submissive and obedient.
DAGON, corn; *or* a fish.
DALMANUTHA, a bucket; *or* exhaustion, leanness, branch. *A country*, Mark 8. 10.
DALMATIA, deceitful lamps, *or* vain brightness.
DAMARIS, a little woman.
DAMASCUS, a sack full of blood; *or*, similitude of burning, *or* of the kiss, *or* of the pot.
DAN, judgment, *or* he that judges.
DANIEL, judgment of God; *or* God is my judge. *A prophet descended from the royal family of David, who was carried captive to Babylon when he was very young. He interpreted Nebuchadnezzar's dreams, was cast into the lions' den and saved, but his adversaries were devoured. He was favoured with the vision of the four beasts, and of the ram and he-goat; Gabriel informeth him of the* seventy weeks, *which is a famous prophecy of the time of the coming of the great* Messiah.
DARA, generation, *or* house of the shepherd, *or* of the companion; *or* race of wickedness, 1 *Chron.* 2. 6.
DARIUS, he that inquires and informs himself. *The king of the Medes*, Dan. 5. 31.
DATHAN, laws, *or* rites.
DAVID, beloved, dear. *The son of Jesse, the king of Judah and Israel, who was a great type of the* Messiah, *the king and spiritual head of his church. It is taken for Christ himself, who was descended of the family of David*, Jer. 30. 9. Ezek. 34. 23. *and* 37. 24, 25.
DEBORAH, a word, *or* a bee.
DECAPOLIS, *a Greek word compounded of two others, of* δεκα, ten, *and* πολις, a city, *because this country contained ten cities.*
DEDAN, their breasts, *or* their friendship, *or* their uncle; *or* a judge.
DEDANIM, *the descendants of* Dedan.
DELILAH, poor, small, *or* head of hair; *or* bucket.
DEMAS, popular.
DEMETRIUS, belonging to Ceres, *or* to corn.
DERBE, a sting. *The name of a city*, Acts 14. 6.
DEUEL, the knowledge, *or* science of God, *Num.* 1. 14.
DIANA, *the Latin word may signify* luminous. *The Greek word* ἀρτεμις *signifies* perfect.
DIBON, understanding, abundance of knowledge, *or* of building.
DIBON-GAD, abundance of sons happy and powerful; *or* happy, *or* great understanding, *or* edifice.
DIDYMUS, a twin.
DIMON, where it is red.
DINAH, judgment, *or* who judges.
DINHABAH, his judgment in her, *or* she gives judgment; *or* who gives judgment. *Gen.* 36. 32.
DIONYSIUS, divinely touched; *from* διος, divine, and νυω, I strike.
DIOTREPHES, nourished by Jupiter. *or* Jupiter's foster-child; *from* διος, of Jupiter, *and* τρεφος, a foster-child.
DOEG, who acts with uneasiness; *or* a fisherman.
DOR, generation, *or* habitation.
DORCAS, the female of a roe-buck. *Greek.*
DOTHAN, the law, *or* custom.
DRUSILLA, watered by the dew, *from* δροσος the dew.
DUMAH, silence, *or* resemblance.
DURAH, generation, or habitation.

E.

EASTER, the passover, *a feast of the Jews. This word is not properly translated, for in the original*, Acts 12. 4. *it is* το πασχα, *which signifies* the pass-over; *which was a yearly feast among the Jews, established in commemoration of the coming forth out of Egypt, and of the angel's passing by and sparing the houses of the Israelites sprinkled with blood, when the first-born of the Egyptians were slain.* Easter *was a goddess of the Saxons, in honour of which sacrifices were offered about that time of the year. The word* Easter *seems not to have been properly used in the English Bible or English Liturgy.*
EBAL, a heap, *or* collection of old age; *or* a mass that runs away and disperses.
EBED, a servant, or labourer.
EBED-MELECH, the king's servant.
EBEN-EZER, the stone of help.
EBER, one that passes, *or* a passage; or anger, wrath.
EBIASAPH, a father that gathers together, *or* adds; *or* my father who has added. 1 *Chron.* 6. 23.
ED, witness.
EDEN, pleasure, *or* delight.
EDOM, red, bloody, earthy, *or* red earth.
EDOMITE.
EDREI, a very great mass; *or* cloud, death of the wicked. *The city of Og*, Deut. 1. 4.
EGLAH, heifer, chariot, round.
EGLAIM, drops of the sea.
EGLON, *the same as* EGLAH.
EGYPT, *in Hebrew*, Mizraim; that binds or straitens; *or* that troubles, *or* oppresses.
EGYPTIAN.
EHUD, he that praises.
EKRON, barrenness, tore away.
EKRONITES.
ELAH, an oak, a curse, oath, imprecation.
ELAM, a young man, a virgin; *or* secret, *or* an age.
ELAMITES.
ELATH, a hind, *or* strength, *or* an oak.
EL-BETHEL, the God of Bethel.
ELDAD, loved of God, *or* favoured of God.
ELEALEH, ascension of God, *or* burnt-offering of GOD.
ELEAZAR, the help of God, *or* court of God.
EL-ELOHE-ISRAEL, God, the God of Israel.
ELHANAN, grace, gift, *or* mercy of God.
ELI, ELI, my God, my God.
ELI, the offering, *or* lifting up.
ELIAB, God my father, *or* my God father.
ELIADA, the knowledge of God.
ELIAKIM, the resurrection of God; *or* the God of the resurrection, *or* of strength; *or* God the revenger.
ELIAM, the people of God, *or* the God of the people.
ELIAS. *See* ELIJAH.
ELIASHIB, the God of conversion; *or* my God will bring back.
ELIATHAH, thou art my God; *or* my God comes. *The son of Heman*, 1 *Chron.* 25. 4.
ELIEZER, help, *or* court of my God.
ELIHOREPH, the God of winter; *or* the God of youth.
ELIHU, he is my God himself.
ELIJAH, God the Lord; *or* the strong Lord. *A famous prophet, who foretold a great famine, and was fed by the ravens*, 1 Kings 17. 6. *He was raised up by God to oppose idolatry, and particularly the worship of Baal, introduced into Israel by Jezebel and Ahab*, 1 Kings 18. *He was taken up into heaven in a whirlwind. Our Lord Jesus Christ interprets the* Elijah *promised in* Mal. 4. 5. *to be* John the Baptist, *Mat.* 11. 10, 14. *who came in the spirit and power of* Elijah.
ELIKA, pelican of God. 2 *Sam.* 23. 25.
ELIM, the rams; *or* the strong, *or* the stags, *or* the valleys.
ELIMELECH, my God is king.
ELIOENAI, towards him are my eyes; *or* towards him are my fountains; *or* towards him are my poverty and my misery. 1 *Chron.* 3. 23.
ELIPHALET, the God of deliverance; *or* my God who puts to flight.
ELIPHAZ, the endeavour of God.
ELISABETH, God hath sworn, the oath of God, *or* the fulness of God.
ELISHA, salvation of God, *or* God that saves. *The name of a prophet whom Elijah anointed in his room*, 1 Kings 19. 16.
ELISHAH, *son of Javan*, Gen. 10. 4. *Or the isles of* Elishah, *Ezek.* 27. 7. It is God; *or* the lamb of God; *otherwise*, God that gives help.
ELISHAMAH, God hearing.
ELISHEBA. *See* ELISABETH.
ELISHUA, God is my salvation.
ELIHUD, God is my praise, *or* the praise of my God.
ELIZUR, God is my strength, my rock; *or* stone, *or* rock of God. *Num.* 1. 5.

ELKANAH, God the zealous; *or* the possession, *or* the reed of God.
ELMODAM, the God of measure; *or* the God of the garment.
ELNATHAN, God has given, *or* the gift of God.
ELON, oak, *or* grove, *or* strong.
ELUL, cry, outcry. *The sixth month of the Hebrew year.*
ELUZAI, God is my strength. 1 *Chron.* 12. 5.
ELYMAS, *this name in Arabic signifies* a magician.
EMIMS, fears of terrors; *or* formidable, *or* people.
EMMAUS, people despised, *or* obscure.
EMMOR, an ass.
EN-DOR, fountain; *or* eye of generation, *or* habitation.
ENEAS, laudable, *from the Greek verb* αινεω, I praise.
EN-EGLAIM, the fountain, *or* the eye of the calves, *or* of the chariots, *or* of roundness.
EN-GEDI, fountain, *or* eye of the goat, *or* of happiness.
EN-MISHPAT, fountain of judgment, *Gen.* 14. 7.
ENOCH, dedicated, *or* disciplined, and well regulated. *The son of Jared, and father of Methuselah.* Enoch *and* Elijah *were translated to heaven without seeing death. It is said, that* Enoch walked with God, and he was not: for God took him. "*He lived in comfortable communion with God; God manifesting himself to him, and he having a lively sense of God's presence always upon his spirit, and seeking to approve himself to God in all things.*" Gen. 5. 24. Heb. 11. 5.
ENON, cloud *or* mass of darkness; *or* his fountain; *or* his eye.
ENOS, fallen man, subject to all kind of evil in soul and body.
EN-ROGEL, the fuller's fountain.
EN-SHEMESH, fountain, *or* eye of the sun, *Josh.* 18. 17.
EPAPHRAS, covered with foam. *Greek.*
EPAPHRODITUS, agreeable, handsome. *One whom Paul sent to the Philippians.*
EPENETUS, laudable, worthy of praise. *One that first embraced the gospel in Asia.*
EPHAH, weary, tired; *or* to fly in the air as a bird. *The son of Midian.*
EPHES-DAMMIM, the portion *or* effusion of blood, *or* drop of blood.
EPHESIANS, *the people of Ephesus.*
EPHESUS, desirable, *chief city of Asia Minor.*
EPHPHATHA, be opened.
EPHRAIM, that brings fruit, *or* that grows.
EPHRAIMITE.
EPHRATAH, abundance, *or* bearing fruit, *or* increasing. *It is believed that the city* Ephratah, *otherwise called* Beth-lehem, *took its name from* Ephratah, *Caleb's wife.*
EPHRATH. *See* EPHRATAH.
EPHRATHITE, *an inhabitant of* Ephratah, *or a descendant from* Ephraim.
EPHRON, dust.
EPICUREANS, who give assistance; *from the Greek word* επικηρεω, I help, I assist. *A sect of heathen philosophers.*
ER, watch, *or* enemy.
ERASTUS, lovely, *or* amiable.
ERECH, length, *or* which lengthens; *otherwise,* health, physic. *A city,* Gen. 10. 10.
ESAIAS. *See* ISAIAH.
ESAR-HADDON, that binds joy, *or* that closes the point.
ESAU, he that does, *or* acts, *or* finishes.
ESEK, contention.
ESHBAAL, the fire of the idol. 1 *Chron.* 8. 33.
ESHCOL, a bunch of grapes.
ESHTAOL, stout, strong woman. *Josh.* 15. 33.
ESHTEMOA, which is heard; *or* the bosom of a woman. *A city,* 1 Sam. 30. 28.
ESLI, near me; *otherwise,* he that separates.
ESROM, the dart of joy; *or* division of the song.
ESTHER, secret *or* hidden.
ETAM, their bird, *or* their covering, 1 *Chron.* 4. 3.
ETHAM, their strength, their sign.
ETHAN, strong; *or* the gift of the island.
ETHANIM, strong, *or* valiant. *The seventh month of the ecclesiastical year of the Hebrews.*
ETHBAAL, towards the idol, *or* with Baal; *or* he that rules and possesses, 1 *Kings* 16. 31.
ETHIOPIA, *in Hebrew,* Cush, blackness: *in Greek it signifies* heat, burning; *from* αιθω, I burn, *and* οψις, face.
ETHIOPIAN, ETHIOPIANS.
EUBULUS, a prudent, a good counsellor. *Gr.*
EVE, living, *or* enlivening.
EVIL-MERODACH, the fool of Merodach, *or* despising the wickedness of the fool; *or otherwise,* the fool grinds bitterly.
EUNICE, good victory.
EUODIAS, sweet scent, *or* that smells well.
EUPHRATES, that makes fruitful, *or* grows.
EUTYCHUS, happy, fortunate; *from* ευ, good, *and* τυχη, fortune.
EZEKIEL, the strength of God, *or* supported of God, *or* God is my strength.
EZEL, going abroad, walk; *or* distillation.
EZION-GEBER, the wood of the man, *or* of the strong; *or* counsel of the man. *A city,* 1 Kings 9. 26.
EZRA, a helper. *In his book we have the history of his return from Babylon to Jerusalem, after the seventy years' captivity. Zerubbabel restored the temple;* Ezra *the worship of God; Nehemiah the city of Jerusalem.*

F.

FELIX, happy, *or* prosperous.
FESTUS, festival, *or* joyful.
FORTUNATUS, happy, *or* prosperous.

G.

GAAL, contempt, *or* abomination.
GAASH, tempest, commotion, tumult, *or* overthrow. *A mountain,* Josh. 24. 30.
GABBATHA, high, *or* elevated. *In Greek lithostrotos,* paved with stones; *from* λιθος, a stone, *and* στρωτος, paved.
GABRIEL, God is my strength, *or,* man of God, *or* strength of God, *or* my strong God.
GAD, a band, *or* happy, *or* armed and prepared.
GADARENES, surrounded, walled.
GADDI, my happiness, my army, my troop; *otherwise,* a kid. *The son of Susi,* Num. 13. 12.
GADDIEL, goat of God; *or* the Lord is my happiness, *or* my army. *Num.* 13. 10.
GADITES.
GAIUS, Lord; *or* an earthy man.
GALATIA, white, of the colour of milk.
GALATIANS.
GALBANUM, *a sort of gum, or sweet spice.*
GALEED, the heap of witness.
GALILEE, wheel, revolution, *or* heap; *or* revolution of the wheel.
GALILEANS.
GALLIM, who heap up, who cover, who roll.
GALLIO, he that sucks, *or* lives upon milk.
GAMALIEL, recompence of God, *or* camel of God, *or* weaned of God.
GAMMADIMS, *soldiers placed in the towers of Tyrus. The word in Hebrew signifies a* cubit, *whence some call them* pigmies, *or* dwarfs. *Others think that the word is Syriac, and signifies* bold and courageous men. *Others say, they were men who came from* Gammade, *a town of Phenicia.*
GATAM, their lowing; *or,* their touch; *or,* the lowing of the perfect. *Grandson of Esau,* Gen. 36. 11.
GATH, a press.
GATH-RIMMON, the press of the granite; *or,* exalted press. *Josh.* 21. 25.
GAZA, strong, *or* a goat.
GEBA, a hill, *or* cup.
GEBAL, bound, *or* limit.
GEBIM, grasshoppers; *or* height.
GEDALIAH, God is my greatness; *or* fringe of the Lord.
GEHAZI, valley of sight, *or* vale of the breast.
GEMARIAH, completion, *or* accomplishment of the Lord.
GENNESARET, the garden of the prince; *otherwise,* protection of the prince, *or* of him that governs.
GENUBATH, theft, robbery; *or* garden, *or* protection of the daughter. 1 *Kings* 11. 20.
GERA, pilgrimage; *or* combat, dispute.
GERAH, *the twentieth part of a shekel.*
GERAR. *See* GERA.
GERGESENES, those who come from pilgrimage, *or from* fight. *A people beyond Galilee.*
GERIZIM, cutters.
GERSHOM, a stranger there; *or* a traveller of reputation.
GERSHON, his banishment; *or* the change of pilgrimage.
GESHUR, the sight of the valley; the vale of the ox; *or* the vale of the wall.
GESHURITES.
GETHER, the vale of trial, *or* of searching; *or* the press of inquiry, *or* of contemplation. *The son of Aram,* Gen. 10. 23.
GETHSEMANE, a very fat valley; *or* the valley of oil.
GIAH, to guide, draw out, produce; *or* a sigh or groan.
GIBEAH, a hill.
GIBEON, hill, *or* cup; *otherwise,* that which is without, *or* that which is lifted up; *or* the elevation of iniquity.
GIBEONITES, *people of* Gibeon.
GIDEON, he that bruises and breaks; *or* cutting off iniquity.
GIDEONI. *See* GIDEON.
GIHON, valley of grace; *or* breast, *or* impetuous.
GILBOA, revolution of inquiry; *or* collection of swelling and inflammation.
GILEAD, the heap *or* mass of testimony.
GILEADITES.
GILGAL, wheel, revolution, heap; *otherwise,* revolution of the wheel, *or* heap of heap.
GILOH, he that rejoices, that overturns, that passes, that reveals, *or* discovers. *A city,* Josh. 15. 51.
GILONITE.
GIRGASHITE, who arrives from pilgrimage.
GITTITE, a wine-press.
GOB, cistern, *or* grass-hopper, *or* eminence.
GOG, roof, covering.
GOLAN, passage, *or* revolution.
GOLGOTHA, an heap of skulls.
GOLIATH, passage, revolution, discovery, heap. *A giant slain by David.*
GOMER, to finish, complete, accomplish; *otherwise,* consuming, a consumer.
GOMORRAH, a rebellious people; *or* the people that fear.
GOSHEN, approaching, drawing near.
GOZAN, fleece, *or* pasture; *or* who nourishes the body.
GRECIA, *the country of the Greeks.*
GRECIANS.
GREECE.
GREEK.
GREEKS.
GUR, the young of a beast; *otherwise,* dwelling, assembly, *or* fear.

H.

HABAKKUK, he that embraces; *or* a wrestler *Hab.* 1. 1.
HACHALIAH, who waits for the Lord; *or* the hook of the Lord. *Neh.* 10. 1.
HACHILAH, my hope is in her; *or* hook in her.
HADAD, joy, noise, clamour, cry of mariners. *Gen.* 36. 35. 1 *Chron.* 1. 30.
HADADEZER, the beauty of assistance.
HADADRIMMON, the voice of height. Rimmon *was a god of the Syrians;* the invocation of the god *Rimmon.*
HADASSAH, a myrtle, *or* joy.
HADORAM, their beauty, their power, their cloak; *or* praise, *or* a cry lifted up.
HADRACH, point, *or* joy of tenderness; *or* your chamber.
HAGAR, a stranger, *or* that fears.
HAGARENES, *of the family of* Hagar.
HAGARITES, *the same.*
HAGGAI, feast, solemnity, turning round.
HAGGITH, rejoicing.
HALLELUIAH, praise the Lord, *or* praise to the Lord.
HAM, hot, heat, *or* brown.
HAMAN, noise, tumult; *or* he that prepares.
HAMATH, anger, heat, *or* a wall.
HAMMEDATHA, he that troubles the law; *or* measure.
HAMON-GOG, the multitude of *Gog.*
HAMOR, an ass, *or* clay, *or* wine.
HAMUTAL, the shadow of his heat; *or* the heat of the dew. 2 *Kings* 23. 31.
HANAMEEL, the grace that comes from God; *or* pity, *or* gift of God.
HANANEEL, grace, mercy, gift of God.
HANANI, my grace, my mercy; *or* he has shewed me mercy.
HANANIAH, grace, mercy; gift of the Lord.
HANNAH, gracious, merciful; *or* taking rest. *The wife of Elkanah, and mother of Samuel.*
HANOCH, dedicated.
HANUN, gracious, merciful: *or* he that rests.
HARAN, mountain, *or* mountainous country; *or* which is enclosed. *The son of Terah.*
HARAN, *a place. See* CHARRAN.
HARBONAH, his destruction, *or* his sword, *or* his dryness; *or* the anger of him that builds, *or* that understands.
HAROD, astonishment, fear.
HAROSHETH, agriculture, silence, deafness; *or* vessel of earth; *or* forest.
HASHMONAH, diligence, *or* enumeration; *or* embassy, *or* present. *Num.* 33. 29.
HATACH, he that strikes. *Esth.* 4. 5.
HAVILAH, that suffers pain; that brings forth; *or* that speaks, *or* declares to her. *Gen.* 10. 7.
HAVOTH-JAIR, the villages that enlighten, *or* that shew forth light. *Num.* 32. 41.
HAZAEL, that sees God.
HAZARMAVETH, court, *or* entry, *or* dwelling of death. *The son of Joktan,* Gen. 10. 26.
HAZELELPONI, shade, and sorrow of countenance; *or* submersion of the face.
HAZEROTH, villages, hamlets; court, *or* porch.
HAZOR, court, *or* hay.
HEBER, one that passes, *or* a passage; *otherwise,* anger, wrath.
HEBREWS, *descended from* Heber.
HEBRON, society, friendship, enchantment.
HEGAI, *or* HEGE, meditation, word, taking away, separation, groaning.
HELAM, their army, *or* their trouble, their strength; *or* expectation; *or* dream.
HELBON, milk, *or* fatness.
HELDAI, the world.
HELI, ascending, *or* climbing up.
HELKATH-HAZURIM, the field of strong men, *or* of rocks.
HEMAN, their trouble, their tumult. *The son of Lotan,* Gen. 36. 22.
HEMAN, much, *or* in great number; *otherwise,* tumult. 1 *Kings* 4. 31.
HEN, grace; *or* quiet, *or* rest.
HEPHZI-BAH, my pleasure, *or* delight in her. *The mother of Manasseh,* 2 Kings 21. 1. *The true church thus called,* Isa. 62. 4.
HERMES, Mercury, *or* gain, *or* refuge. *Greek.*
HERMOGENES, begotten of Mercury, *or* generation of lucre. *Greek.*
HERMON, anathema, destruction.
HERMONITES.
HEROD, the glory of the skin, *from* ηρος, favour, glory, *and* δερας, the skin; *or* son of the hero.
HERODIANS. *See* Appellatives.
HERODIAS, *the wife of* Herod.
HERODION, song of Juno; *from* Ηρα, Juno, *and* ωδη, a song; *or* the conqueror of heroes.
HESHBON, invention, industry, *or* thought; *or* he that hastens to understand, *or* to build.
HETH, trembling, *or* fear.
HETHLON, fearful dwelling; *or* his covering. *The name of a city,* Ezek. 47. 15.
HEZEKIAH, strong in the Lord; *or* taken and supported by the Lord.
HEZRON, the dart of joy; *or* division of the song.
HIDDEKEL, a sharp voice, *or* sound.
HIEL, God lives, *or* the life of God.
HIERAPOLIS, holy city; from ιερον, holy, *and* πολις, a city. *Col.* 4. 13.
HIGGAION, meditation, consideration.
HILKIAH, God is my portion; *according to others,* the Lord's gentleness.
HILLEL, he that praises; *or* folly; *or* Lucifer. *The father of Abdon,* Judg. 12. 13.
HINNOM, there they are; *or* their riches.
HIRAM, exaltation of life; *or* their whiteness, *or*

their liberty; *or* he that destroys, *or* anathematizes.
HITTITES, who is broken, *or* fears. *Descendants of* Heth *the son of Canaan*, Gen. 10. 15.
HIVITES, wicked, bad, *or* wickedness.
HOBAB, favoured and beloved.
HOBAH, love, friendship, *or* secrecy. *Gen.* 14. 15.
HOGLAH, his festival, *or* his dance.
HOPHNI, he that covers; *or* my fist.
HOR, who conceives, *or* shews.
HOREB, desert, solitude, destruction, dryness.
HOR-HAGIDGAD, the hill of felicity.
HORMAH, devoted *or* consecrated to God; utter destruction.
HORONAIM, anger, *or* raging.
HORONITE, anger, fury, *or* liberty.
HOSEA *and* HOSHEA, saviour, *or* salvation.
HUL, pain, infirmity, bringing forth children, sand, *or* expectation. *The son of Aram*, Gen. 10. 23.
HULDAH, the world. *A prophetess*, 2 Kings 22. 14.
HUR, liberty, whiteness, hole, cavern.
HUSHAI, their haste, *or* their sensuality, *or* their silence.
HUZZAB, molten.
HYMENEUS, nuptial, *or* marriage.

J.

JAALAM, who is hidden; *or* young man; *or* their kids. *Son of Esau*, Gen. 36. 5.
JAAZANIA, whom the Lord will hear, *or* who is attentive to the Lord; *or* the balances, the arms, the nourishment of the Lord.
JABAL, which glides away; *or* that brings, *or* that produces
JABBOK, evacuation, *or* dissipation.
JABESH, dryness, confusion, shame.
JABESH-GILEAD.
JABEZ, sorrow, *or* trouble.
JABIN, he that understands, he that builds.
JABNEEL, building of God; *or* understanding of God. *A city*, Josh. 19. 33.
JACHIN, he that strengthens and makes stedfast.
JACOB, he that supplants or undermines; *or* the heel. *The son of Isaac, and the father of the twelve patriarchs; he prevailed in prayer with God, and was called* Israel; *he went in the time of the famine with all his family into Egypt, and his son Joseph gave them habitation and maintenance.* Jacob *blessed his children before his death, and ordered them to bury him in Canaan.*
JAEL, he that ascends, *or* a kid.
JAH, the everlasting God.
JAHAZ, quarrel, dispute; *or* the going out of the Lord.
JAHAZA, *the same.*
JAIR, my light; *or* who diffuses light; *or* is enlightened.
JAIRUS, *the same.*
JAMBRES, the sea with poverty.
JAMES, *the same as* JACOB.
JANNA, who speaks, *or* who answers; *otherwise*, affliction, misery, *or* impoverished.
JANNES, *the same.*
JAPHETH, he that persuades, *or* extends, *or* handsome.
JAPHIA, which enlightens, appears, *or* shews; *or* which groans. *The son of David*, 2 Sam. 5. 15.
JAREB, a revenger.
JARED, he that descends; *or* he that rules *or* commands.
JASHER, righteous.
JASON, he that cures, *or* that gives medicines; *from* ιασις, health, *or* cure.
JAVAN, he that deceives, *or* makes sorrowful; *otherwise*, clay, dirt.
JAZER, assistance, *or* he that helps.
IBHAR, election, *or* he that is chosen.
ICHABOD, where is the glory? *or* woe to the glory.
ICONIUM, *a city, from* ικω, I come.
IDDO, his hand, his power, his praise, his witness, his ornament.
IDUMEA, red, earthy.
JEBUS, which treads under foot, *or* contemns. *A city, the same as* Jerusalem, *Judg.* 19. 10.
JEBUSITES, *inhabitants of* Jebus.
JECONIAH, preparation of the Lord, *or* stedfastness of the Lord.
JEDIDAH, well beloved, *or* amiable. *The mother of Josiah*, 2 Kings 22. 1.
JEDIDIAH, beloved of the Lord.
JEDUTHUN, his law; *or* who gives praise.
JEGAR-SAHADUTHA, the heap of witness.
JEHOAHAZ, the prize, *or* possession of the Lord; *or* the Lord that sees.
JEHOASH, the fire of the Lord; *or* the victim of the Lord.
JEHOIACHIN, preparation, *or* strength of the Lord.
JEHOIADA, the knowledge of the Lord.
JEHOIAKIM, the resurrection, *or* confirmation of the Lord.
JEHONADAB. *See* JONADAB.
JEHORAM, exaltation of the Lord; *or* rejected of the Lord.
JEHOSHAPHAT, God judges, *or* the judgment of the Lord.
JEHOVAH, *the incommunicable name of God.* Self-existing.
JEHOVAH-JIREH, the Lord will see *or* provide; the Lord will be manifested *or* seen.
JEHOVAH-NISSI, the Lord my banner.
JEHOVAH-SHALOM, the Lord send peace.
JEHOVAH-SHAMMAH, the Lord is there.
JEHOVAH-TSIDKENU, THE LORD OUR RIGHTEOUSNESS.
JEHU, he that is, *or* who exists.
JEHUDIJAH, the praise of the Lord. *The wife of Ezra.* 1 Chron. 4. 18.
JEMIMA, handsome as the day. *One of Job's daughters*, Job 42. 14.
JEPHTHAH, he that opens, *or* he will open.
JEPHUNNEH, he that beholds.
JERAH, the moon, *or* month; *otherwise*, to scent *or* smell. *Son of Joktan*, Gen. 10. 26.
JERAHMEEL, mercy of God, *or* the love of God.
JEREMIAH, exaltation *or* grandeur of the Lord; *or* who exalts, *or* gives glory to the Lord. *He was called to the extraordinary office of a prophet in his younger years, and continued in that office for at least forty years together. In his time iniquity did exceedingly abound in the land of Judah. He earnestly and frequently calls the people to repentance, both by his reproofs and threatenings for their sins. He denounces the captivity of the people by the Babylonians, for which he was put in prison; he lived to see this prophecy fulfilled. But for the comfort and support of the faithful, he foretells their return after* seventy years, *and the enlargement of the church by Christ. His style is generally the most plain of any of the prophets.*
JERICHO, his moon, *or* month; *or* his sweet smell.
JERIMOTH, eminences; *or* he that fears, that sees, that rejects death. 1 *Chron.* 7. 7.
JEROBOAM, fighting against, *or* increasing the people.
JERUBBAAL, he that disputes about Baal; *or* that revenges the idol; *or* let Baal defend his cause.
JERUBBESHETH, let the idol of confusion defend itself.
JERUSALEM, the vision, *or* possession of peace. *It was the chief city of Judea, and was first called* Salem, *where Melchizedek was king,* Gen. 14. 18. *It was also called* Jebus, *and was possessed by the* Jebusites, *who held therein the fort of Sion, till it was taken from them by David,* Judg. 10. 6. 1 Chron. 11. 4, 5, 7. *Here also was mount Moriah, near mount Sion, whereon Solomon built the temple, and where Abraham was commanded to offer his son Isaac; Abraham named the place* Jehovah-jireh, *because the providence of God was there eminently seen,* 2 Chron. 3. 1. Gen. 22. 2, 14. *which word* jireh *being put to the former name* Salem, *maketh it* Jerusalem, *where* peace is seen. *It is called* Salem, *by the first name*, Psal. 76. 2. *It is put for the church militant*, Isa. 62. 1. *and the church triumphant is called the* new Jerusalem, *Rev.* 3. 12.
JERUSHA, he that possesses the inheritance; *or* exiled, banished, rejected. 2 *Kings* 15. 33.
JESHIMON, solitude, desolation. *The name of a desert*, 1 Sam. 23. 24.
JESHUA, a saviour.
JESHURUN, upright *or* righteous. *Israel is so called.*
JESSE, to be, *or* who is; *or* my present.
JESUI, who is equal, proper, placed, *or* flat country. *The son of Asher*, Gen. 46. 17. Num. 26. 44.
JESUITES, *the posterity of Jesui.*
JESUS, *the holy name* Jesus; Saviour; who saveth his people from their sins, *Mat.* 1. 21. *The eternal Son of God, of one substance and equal with the Father, the mediator of the covenant of grace, who in the fulness of time became man, and so was and continues to be God and man in two distinct natures and one person for ever. The word* Jesus *is taken for the doctrine of* Jesus, *Acts* 8. 35. *and for* Joshua, *who brought God's people into the land of Canaan, and was therein an eminent type of our Lord* Jesus, *Heb.* 4. 8.
JETHER, he that excels *or* remains; *or* that examines, searches; *or* a line *or* string, *Judg.* 8. 20.
JETHRO, his excellence, his remains, his posterity.
JETUR, he that keeps; *otherwise*, order, succession; *or* mountainous. *Son of Ishmael*, Gen. 25. 15.
JEUSH, he that is devoured, gnawed by the moth; *otherwise*, assembled. *Son of Rehoboam*, 2 Chron. 11. 19.
JEW, JEWS, *so called from* Judah. *See* JUDAH.
JEWESS.
JEWISH.
JEWRY.
JEZEBEL, island of the habitation; *or* woe to the habitation; *or* isle of the dunghill, *or* woe to the dunghill.
JEZRAHIAH, the Lord is the east; *or* the Lord arises; *or* brightness of the Lord. *Chief of the singers*, Neh. 12. 42.
JEZREEL, seed of God; *or* God who spreads the evil; *or* dropping of the friendship of God.
JEZREELITE, *an inhabitant of the city* Jezreel.
IGDALIA, the greatness of the Lord; *or* the Lord shall exalt me, *or* make me great. *A man of God*, Jer. 35. 4.
JIDLAPH, he that distils, *or* drops water; *or* hands joined. *Son of Nahor and Milcah*, Gen. 22. 22.
IJON, look, eye, fountain. *A city*, 1 Kings 15. 20.
ILLYRICUM, joy, rejoicing.
IMLAH, plenitude, *or* repletion; *or* circumcision.
IMMANUEL, *a name given to our* Lord Jesus Christ, *Isa.* 7. 14. *It signifies*, God with us.
INDIA, praise, law. *A considerable country in the east*, Esth. 1. 1.
JOAB, paternity, *or* who has a father; *or* voluntary.
JOAH, fraternity, *or* who has a brother; *or* brother of the Lord.
JOANNA, the grace, the gift, *or* the mercy of the Lord.
JOASH, who despairs; *or* he that burns, who is on fire.
JOB, he that weeps, that cries; *or* that speaks out of an hollow place. *He dwelt in the land of Uz, and was an upright and just man, fearing God. Satan was permitted to bereave him of his children and substance, and to smite him with sore boils. He was visited by his friends in his affliction;* God blessed his latter end, and gave him twice as much as he had before. *Job's patience is recommended as an example to the godly in all ages*, Jam. 5. 11.
JOCHEBED, glorious, honourable, a person of merit; *or* the glory of the Lord. *The mother of Moses*, Exod. 6. 20.
JOEL, he that wills, commands, *or* swears.
JOEZER, he that aids and assists. 1 *Chron.* 12. 6.
JOHA, who enlivens and gives life. 1 *Chron.* 8. 16.
JOHANAN, who is liberal, merciful, pious and grants favour; *otherwise*, the grace of the Lord.
JOHN, the grace, gift, *or* mercy of the Lord.
JOKSHAN, hard, difficult, scandalous. *Gen.* 25. 2.
JOKTAN, small; *or* disgust, weariness; *or* dispute, contention. *The son of Heber*, Gen. 10. 25.
JONADAB, who acts in good earnest, gives and offers freely, liberally; *or* who acts as a prince.
JONAH, *or* JONAS, a dove; *or* he that oppresses.
JONATHAN, given of God; *or* the gift of the Lord.
JOPPA, beauty, comeliness.
JORAM, to cast; elevated.
JORDAN, the river of judgment; *or* he that shews, *or* rejects judgment, *or* descent.
JORIM, he that exalts the Lord, *or* the exaltation of the Lord.
JOSE, raised, *or* who exists; *or* who pardons, *or* saviour.
JOSEPH, increase, addition. *The eleventh son of Jacob, beloved by his father, but hated by his brethren. His two dreams foretold his advancement: he was cast into a pit by his brethren, and sold to the Ishmaelites. He interpreted Pharaoh's dreams, and was made ruler of Egypt. His brethren in the seven years' famine are sent to Egypt by Jacob for corn; and afterwards Jacob with his family come to Joseph in Egypt, who receives them kindly, and settles them in the land of Goshen. In the history of* Joseph *there are many wonderful steps of divine Providence relating to his afflicted and exalted state, which are recorded in the book of Genesis.* (2) Joseph *was also the name of a disciple of Christ, a rich man of Arimathea, who buried the body of our Lord Jesus in a tomb prepared for himself*, Mat. 27. 57. *and was likewise the name of several others*, Luke 3. 21, 26, 30. Acts 1. 23.
JOSES. *See* JOSE.
JOSHUA, the Lord, the Saviour.
JOSIAH, the Lord burns, *or* the fire of the Lord.
JOTHAM, perfection of the Lord.
IPHEDEIAH, the redemption of the Lord. 1 *Chron.* 8. 25.
IRA, city watch, spoil; *or* effusion, *or* heap of vision. *One of David's rulers*, 2 Sam. 20. 26.
IRAD, wild ass; *or* heap of descents, *or* of empire. *The son of Enoch*, Gen. 4. 18.
IRIJAH, the fear of the Lord, *or* vision of the Lord; *or* protection of the Lord, *Jer.* 37. 13.
ISAAC, laughter. *The son of Abraham and Sarah, being the seed promised to them by God. Abraham, for the trial of his faith, was commanded to offer up his son* Isaac, *and went to the place appointed, mount Moriah, where afterwards the temple was built; and binding* Isaac, *and taking the knife to kill him as a sacrifice, he was stayed by the angel of the Lord, and* Isaac *was exchanged for a ram caught in a thicket.* Isaac *taketh Rebekah to wife, by whom he had two sons, Esau and Jacob: he sends his eldest son Esau for venison, but Rebekah instructs Jacob the younger to obtain the blessing.*
ISAIAH, the salvation of the Lord. *The priests and Levites were the ordinary teachers of the Jewish church, so God sometimes raised up and sent extraordinary messengers, the prophets. Among these* Isaiah *is justly accounted the most eminent, both for the majesty of his style, and the excellency of his matter, wherein he so fully and clearly describes the person, offices, the sufferings, and kingdom of Christ, that he is commonly called the* Evangelical Prophet.
ISCAH, he that anoints; *or* that covers, *or* protects. *The daughter of Haran*, Gen. 11. 29.
ISCARIOT, *is thought to signify* a native of the town of Iscarioth. A man of murder; *from* איש ish, a man, *and* כרת careth, he that cuts off, *or* exterminates. *Others maintain, that the surname given to Judas, signifies that he was of the tribe of* Issachar, *a word signifying* recompence, restitution. *This traitor verified his nativity, by receiving the price of the blood of his Master Jesus Christ: from the word* שכר shachar, to receive a recompence.
ISHBAK, who is empty *or* exhausted; *or* who is

forsaken *or* abandoned. *One of Abraham's sons,* Gen. 25. 2.
ISHBI-BENOB, he that sits in the prophecy, *or* in the word, *or* in the prediction; *otherwise,* conversion, *or* blowing, *or* respiration in prophecy. *A giant,* 2 Sam. 21. 16.
ISH-BOSHETH, a man of shame; *or* the retarding of the man.
ISHMAEL, God who hears.
ISHMAELITES, *the posterity of* Ishmael.
ISRAEL, a prince with God, *or* prevailing with God; *or* one that wrestleth with God; *as if it had been written,* Ish-ra-el. *The name given by God to Jacob,* Gen. 32. 28. and 35. 10. Israel *is often in Scripture taken for the people of God,* Exod. 6. 6, 7.
ISRAELITES, *the posterity of* Israel.
ISSACHAR, price, reward, *or* recompence.
ITALIAN, *belonging to* Italy.
ITALY, *a Latin word, that has its original from* vitulus, or vitula, *because this country abounded in calves and heifers. According to others, it is taken from a king called* Italus.
ITHAMAR, island of the palm-tree; *or* of palms; *or* changing of the isle; *or* woe to the palm, *or* to the change.
ITHIEL, God with me; *or* sign, coming of God.
ITHREAM, excellence of the people. 2 *Sam.* 3. 5.
ITUREA, which is guarded; *or* a country of mountains.
IVAH, iniquity.
JUBAL, he that runs, *or* he that produces; *or* a trumpet.
JUBILEE, *a feast of the Jews, every fiftieth year; in Hebrew,* Jobel, *which, according to some, signifies* a ram's horn, *or* a trumpet, *by which the* Jubilee *year was proclaimed. Others derive the etymology of* Jobal *from the Hebrew* Jubal, *which formerly signified, as they say,* to play upon instruments; *and this year was celebrated with music and all expressions of joy. Others are of opinion, that it comes from the verb* Hobil, to bring or call back; *because then every thing was restored to its first possessor.*
JUDAH, the praise of the Lord.
JUDAS, *the same as* JUDAH.
JUDEA, *a country.*
JULIA, downy; *from* ιυλος, down, soft and tender hair. *A friend of St. Paul's,* Rom. 16. 15.
JULIUS, *from the same,* Acts 27. 1.
JUNIA, *from* Juno, *or from* Juventus, youth. *A kinsman of St. Paul's,* Rom. 16. 7.
JUPITER, *as if it were* juvans pater, the father that helpeth.
JUSTUS, just, upright.

K.

KABZEEL, the congregation of God, *Josh.* 15. 21.
KADESH, holy, *or* holiness.
KADESH-BARNEA, holiness of an inconstant son; *or* holiness of the corn, *or* of purity.
KEDAR, blackness, *or* sorrow.
KEDEMAH, oriental; *from* Kedem, the east, *Gen.* 25. 15.
KEDEMOTH, antiquity, old age; *or* orientals. *The name of a wilderness,* Deut. 2. 26.
KEILAH, she that divides *or* cuts.
KEMUEL, God is risen; *or* God has raised him. *The son of Nahor,* Gen. 22. 21.
KENAZ, this nest; *or* this lamentation, this possession, this purchase. *The father of Othniel,* Josh. 15. 17.
KENITES, possession, *or* purchase, *or* lamentation, *or* nest.
KEREN-HAPPUCH, the horn, *or* child of beauty. *Job's third daughter,* Job 42. 14.
KERIOTH, the cities, the callings.
KETURAH, he that burns, *or* makes the incense to fume; *otherwise,* perfumed, *or* odoriferous.
KEZIA, superficies, *or* angle; *or* cassia. *The daughter of Job,* Job 42. 14.
KEZIZ, end, extremity. *A valley,* Josh. 18. 21.
KIBROTH-HATTAAVAH, the graves of lust, *Num.* 11. 34.
KIDRON, obscurity, *or* obscure. 2 *Sam.* 15. 23.
KIR, a city, a wall, *or* meeting.
KIR-HARASETH, the city of the sun; the city with walls of burnt brick.
KIR-JATH, city, vocation, lesson, reading, *or* meeting. *A city,* Josh. 18. 28.
KIRIATHAIM, the two cities, the callings, the meetings.
KIRJATH-ARBA, the city of four.
KIRJATH-ARIM, city of cities; *or,* the city of those that watch. *Ezra* 2. 25.
KIRJATH-BAAL, the city of Baal, *or* of those that command, *or* that possess. *Josh.* 15. 60.
KIRJATH-JEARIM, the city of woods or forests.
KIRJATH-SANNAH, the city of the bush; *or* the city of enmity. *Josh.* 15. 49.
KIRJATH-SEPHER, the city of letters, *or* of the book. *Josh.* 15. 15.
KISH, hard, difficult; *otherwise,* straw, *or* forage.
KITTIM, they that bruise; *or* gold, *or* colouring.
KOHATH, congregation, wrinkle, obedience; *or* to make blunt.
KOHATHITES, *the posterity of* Kohath.
KORAH, bald, frozen, icy.

L.

LABAN, white, shining, gentle.
LACHISH, she walks, she goes; *or* who exists of himself.
LAHMI, my bread, *or* my war. *The brother of Goliath,* 1 Chron. 20. 5.
LAISH, a lion.
LAMECH, poor, made low; *or* who is struck.
LAODICEA, just people; *from* λαος, people, and δικαιος, just.
LAODICEANS, *inhabitants of* Laodicea.
LAPIDOTH, enlightened, *or* lamps. *The husband of Deborah,* Judg. 4. 4.
LAZARUS, the help of God.
LEAH, weary, tired.
LEBANON, white, *or* incense.
LEBBEUS, a man of heart.
LEGION.
LEHABIM, flames, *or* which are inflamed; *or* the points of a sword. *Gen.* 10. 13.
LEHI, jaw-bone. *The name of a place,* Judg. 15. 9.
LEMUEL, God with them.
LEVI, who is held and associated.
LEVITES, *of the posterity of* Levi.
LIBNAH, white, whiteness.
LIBNI, *the same. The son of Gershon,* Exod. 6. 17.
LIBYA, *in Hebrew,* Lubim, the heart of the sea; *or* a nation that has a heart.
LIBYANS, *the people of* Libya.
LINUS, nets. *A friend of St. Paul's,* 2 Tim. 4. 21.
LO-AMMI, not my people.
LOIS, better; *from the Greek word* λωιων, better.
LO-RUHAMAH, not having obtained mercy; not pitied.
LOT, wrapt up, hidden, covered; *otherwise,* myrrh, rosin.
LUCAS, luminous.
LUCIFER, bringing light.
LUCIUS. *See* LUCAS.
LUKE. *See* LUCAS.
LUZ, separation, departure.
LYCAONIA, she-wolf. *A province.*
LYDDA, *the name of a city.*
LYSANIAS, that destroys or drives away sorrow; *from* λυσις, solution, *and* ανια, sorrow.
LYSTRA, that dissolves, *or* disperses: *from* λυσις.

M.

MAACHAH, to squeeze.
MAASEIAH, the work of the Lord.
MACEDONIA, adoration, prostration, *according to the Hebrew; but* elevated, eminent, *according to the Greek; from* μακεδνος.
MACHIR, he that sells, *or* that knows.
MACHPELAH, double.
MAGDALA, tower, *or* greatness.
MAGDALENE, tower; *otherwise,* grand, elevated, magnificent. *Mat.* 27. 56.
MAGOG, roof, *or* that covers, *or* that dissolves.
MAGOR-MISSABIB, fear round about. *Jer.* 20. 3.
MAHALALEEL, he that praises God; *or* illumination of God. *The son of Cainan,* Gen. 5. 12.
MAHALATH, melodious song; *otherwise,* infirmity. *The wife of Rehoboam,* 2 Chron. 11. 18.
MAHANAIM, the two fields, *or* two armies.
MAHAR-SHALAL-HASH-BAZ, making speed to the spoil, he hasteneth the prey. *Marg.*
MAHLAH, *the same with* MAHALATH. *One of the daughters of Zelophehad,* Num. 26. 33.
MAHLON, song, *or* infirmity.
MAKKEDAH, adoration, *or* prostration, *according to the Hebrew; or* raised, eminent; *from the Greek word* μακεδνος. *A city,* Josh. 10. 10.
MALCHAM, their king.
MALCHISHUA, my king is a saviour; *or* magnificent king. *The son of Saul,* 1 Sam. 14. 49.
MALCHUS, king, *or* kingdom.
MAMMON, riches.
MAMRE, rebellious; *or* bitter; *or* that changes, that barters; *or* fat, *or* elevated.
MANAEN, a comforter; *or* he that conducts them; *or* preparation of heat.
MANASSEH, forgetfulness, *or* he that is forgotten.
MANEH, *a species of money.*
MANOAH, rest, *or* a present.
MAON, house, *or* habitation; *otherwise,* crime; *or* by sin. *A city,* Josh. 15. 55.
MARA, bitter, *or* bitterness.
MARAH, *the same.*
MARCUS, polite, shining.
MARK, *the same.*
MARS-HILL, *the place where the celebrated judges of Athens held their supreme council.*
MARTHA, who becomes bitter.
MARY, exalted, *or* bitterness of the sea, *or* myrrh of the sea; *or* lady or mistress of the sea.
MASREKAH, whistling, *or* hissing; *or* who touches vanity. *A city,* Gen. 36. 36.
MASSAH, temptation. *The name of a place,* Exod. 17. 7.
MATRI, rain, *or* prison. *One of the ancestors of Saul,* 1 Sam. 10. 21.
MATTAN, gift, *or* the reins; *or* the death of them.
MATTATHIAS, the gift of the Lord.
MATTHAT, gift, *or* he that gives. *Luke* 3. 24.
MATTHEW, given, *or* a reward.
MATTHIAS. *See* MATTATHIAS.
MAZZAROTH, the twelve signs. *Marg.*
MEDAD, he that measures; *or* the water of love *or* of paps.
MEDAN, judgment, process; *or* measure, habit, covering. *Son of Abraham,* Gen. 25. 2.
MEDES, *a people of the province of* Media.
MEDIA, measure, habit, covering, *or* abundance.
MEGIDDO, that declares; *or* his precious fruit; *or* that spoils.
MEGIDDON, *the same.*
MEHETABEL, how good is God? *or* has done good to us. *The wife of Hadar,* Gen. 36. 39.
MEHUJAEL, who proclaims God; *or* God that blots out; or *according to the Syriac and Hebrew,* who is smitten of God. *Gen.* 4. 18.
MELCHI, my king, *or* my counsel.
MELCHIZEDEK, king of righteousness.
MELITA, affording honey, from whence honey distils; *from* μελι, honey. *An island now called* Malta, *Acts* 28. 1.
MEMPHIS, by the mouth.
MEMUCAN, impoverished; *or* to prepare; *or* certain, true. *Esth.* 1. 16.
MENAHEM, comforter; *or* who conducts them, *or* preparation of heat.
MENE, *who* reckons, *or* who is counted.
MEPHIBOSHETH, out of my mouth proceeds reproach.
MERAB, he that fights, *or* disputes; *or* that multiplies.
MERARI, bitter; *or* to provoke.
MERCURIUS, *a false god, from the Latin word* mercari, to buy or sell, *because this god presided over merchandise. In Greek,* Hermes, *which signifies,* orator, *or* interpreter.
MERIBAH, dispute, quarrel.
MERIB-BAAL, rebellion; *or* he that resists *Baal,* and strives against the idol. 1 *Chron.* 8. 34.
MERODACH, bitter contrition; *or* bruised myrrh. *According to the Syriac, it signifies* the little lord. *This is the name of one of the Chaldean deities.*
MERODACH-BALADAN, who creates contrition; *or* the son of death, *or* of thy vapour.
MEROM, eminences, elevations.
MEROZ, secret, *or* leanness.
MESHACH, that draws with force; *or* that surrounds the waters.
MESHECH, who is drawn by force; *or* included, shut up, surrounded.
MESHELEMIAH, peace, *or* perfection, *or* retribution of the Lord; *or* the Lord is my recompence, *or* my happiness. *The father of Zechariah,* 1 Chron. 9. 21.
MESOPOTAMIA, *in Hebrew,* Aramnaharaim, *that is,* Syria of the two rivers. *The Greek word* Mesopotamia, *also signifies* between two rivers; *from* μεσος, middle, *and* ποταμος, river.
MESSIAH, anointed.
METHEG-AMMAH, the bridle of bondage.
METHUSAEL, who demands his death; *or* death is his hell *or* grave.
METHUSELAH, he has sent his death; *or* the arms of his death, *or* spoil of his death.
MICAH, poor, humble; *or* who strikes, *or* is struck; *or* who is there, *or* the waters here.
MICAIAH, who is like to God?
MICHAIAH, *the same.*
MICHAEL, *the same.*
MICHAL, who is it that has all? *or* who is perfect, *or* complete? *or* the whole is water.
MICHMASH, he that strikes; *or* poor who is taken away. *The name of a town,* 1 Sam. 13. 2.
MIDIAN, judgment; *or* measure, habit, covering.
MIDIANITES.
MIDIANITISH.
MIGRON, fear; *or* a farm, *or* throat, *Isa.* 10. 28.
MILCAH, queen.
MILCOM, their king.
MILETUM, red, *or* scarlet; *from the Greek word* μιλτος, vermilion, red.
MILLO, fulness, plenitude, repletion.
MINNI, disposed, reckoned, prepared. *Jer.* 51. 27.
MINNITH, counted, prepared. *A city,* Judg. 11. 33.
MIRIAM, exalted; *or* bitterness of the sea; *or* myrrh of the sea; *or* lady *or* mistress of the sea.
MISHAEL, who is asked for, *or* lent; *or* God takes away, *or* retires.
MISREPHOTH-MAIM, the burnings of the waters; *or* furnaces where metals are melted. *A place where there were salt pits,* Josh. 11. 8.
MITYLENE, *a Greek word, signifying* purity, cleansing, *or* press.
MIZAR, little. *Marg.*
MIZPAH, a sentinel, speculation, *or* that waits for.
MIZPEH, *the same.*
MISRAIM, tribulations; *or* who is straitened, *or* blocked up. *The son of Ham,* Gen. 10. 6.
MNASON, a diligent seeker, *or* betrothing, *or* remembering, *or* an exhorter.
MOAB, of the father.
MOABITES, *the posterity of* MOAB.
MOLADAH, birth, generation. *A city,* Josh 15. 26.
MOLECH, king.
MOLOCH, *the same.*
MORDECAI, contrition, *or* bitter bruising; *or* myrrh bruised; *or* who teaches to bruise.
MORIAH, bitterness of the Lord; *or* doctrine, *or* fear of the Lord.
MOSEROTH, erudition, discipline, bond. *Num.* 33. 30.

MOSES, taken out of the water. *He was of the house of Levi, born in Egypt, and miraculously preserved. God appeared to him in a burning bush, and sent him to deliver the Israelites out of Egypt. He was appointed by God to lead the Israelites through the wilderness to the land of Canaan. Being about to die, he blesseth all the tribes of Israel: He views the land of Canaan, dies, is buried by God, and Joshua made his successor. He was a very great man, and highly honoured by God in many respects.* The law was given by *Moses*, but grace and truth came by Jesus Christ, *John* 1. 17.

MUSHI, he that touches, that withdraws himself, that takes away. *Son of Merari*, Exod. 6. 19.

MYRA, *is derived from the Greek word* μυρω, I flow, pour out, weep.

MYSIA, criminal, *or* abominable; *from the Greek word* μυσος, crime.

N.

NAAMAN, beautiful, agreeable; *or* that prepares himself to motion.

NAAMATHITE, *who is of* Naamath.

NAASHON, that foretells, that conjectures; *or* serpent; *or* their auguries.

NABAL, a fool, *or* senseless.

NABOTH, words, *or* prophecies, *or* fruits.

NADAB, free and voluntary gift; *or* prince.

NAGGE, brightness.

NAHARAI, my nostrils, my nose; *or* hoarse, dry, hot, angry. *One of David's valiant captains*, 2 Sam. 23. 37.

NAHASH, snake, *or* serpent, *or* that foretells, *or* brass.

NAHOR, hoarse, dry, hot, angry.

NAHUM, comforter, penitent; *or* their guide. *The name of a prophet*, Nah. 1. 1.

NAIN, beauty, pleasantness.

NAIOTH, beauties; *or* habitations, abodes.

NAOMI, beautiful, agreeable.

NAPHISH, the soul; *or* he that rests *or* refreshes himself, that respires; *or according to the Syriac*, that multiplies. *The son of Ishmael*, Gen. 25. 15.

NAPHTALI, comparison, likeness; *or* that struggles, *or* fights.

NARCISSUS, astonishment, stupidity, surprise; *from the Greek word* ναρκησις. *Rom.* 16. 11.

NATHAN, who gives, *or* is given.

NATHANAEL, the gift of God.

NATHAN-MELECH, the gift of the king. 2 *Kings* 23. 11.

NAUM. *See* NAHUM.

NAZARENE, kept, *or* flower. *A native of* Nazareth.

NAZARETH, separated, sanctified.

NEAPOLIS, new city, *from* νεα, new, fresh, *and* πολις, a city.

NEBAIOTH, words, *or* prophecies, *or* fruits.

NEBAT, that beholds.

NEBO, that speaks, prophesies, *or* fructifies.

NEBUCHADNEZZAR, tears and groans of judgment; *or* trouble, *or* sorrow of judgment.

NEBUZAR-ADAN, fruits *or* prophecies of judgment; *or* winnowed, *or* spread.

NECHO, lame, *or* who was beaten. *The name of a king of Egypt*, 2 Kings 23. 29.

NEHELAMITE, dreamer, *or* dream; *or* vale, *or* brook, *or* inheritance of the waters.

NEHEMIAH, consolation, *or* repentance of the Lord; *or* **rest** of the Lord; *or* conduct of the Lord.

NEHUSHTA, snake, soothsayer, *or* of brass. *Mother of Jehoiakim*, 2 Kings 24. 8.

NEHUSHTAN, which is of brass *or* copper; *by derision*, a trifle of brass.

NER, lamp, brightness; *or* land new tilled.

NEREUS. *See* NER.

NERI, my light. *The father of Salathiel*, Luke 3. 27.

NERIAH, light, *and* lamp of the Lord; *or* the Lord is my light.

NETHANEEL. *See* NATHANAEL.

NETHANIA, the gift of the Lord.

NETHINIMS, given, *or* offered. *The Gibeonites, or those who succeeded them in their service.*

NIBHAZ, that fructifies, *or* that produces vision; *or* to prophesy, to foretell, *or* to speak. *An idol of the Avites*, 2 Kings 17. 31.

NICANOR, a conqueror, *or* victorious; *from the Greek word* νικαω, I conquer.

NICODEMUS, innocent blood: *or according to the Greek*, the victory of the people; *from* νικαω, I conquer, *and* δημος, the people.

NICOLAITANS, victory of the people; *from* νικαω, I overcome, *and* λαος, the people. *The followers of* Nicolas.

NICOLAS, *from the same. A deacon*, Acts 6. 5.

NICOPOLIS, the city of victory, *or* victorious city; *from* νικαω, I conquer, *and* πολις, a city.

NIGER, black.

NIMRIM, leopard, bitterness, rebellion, *or* change. *The name of a place*, Isa. 15. 6.

NIMROD, rebellious, *or* sleep of descent, *or* of him that rules.

NIMSHI, rescued from danger; *or* that touches.

NINEVEH, handsome, agreeable; *or* dwelling.

NINEVITES, *the people of* Nineveh.

NISAN, flight, *or* standard; *or* proof and temptation.

NISROCH, flight, *or* standard, *or* proof and temptation, tender, *or* delicate.

NO, stirring up, *or* a forbidding.

NOADIAH, witness; *or* assembly, *or* ornament of the Lord.

NOAH, repose, *or* rest, *or* consolation.

NOAH, that quavers, *or* totters. *Daughter of Zelophehad*, Num. 26. 33.

NOB, discourse, prophecy.

NOBAH, that barks *or* yelps. *A city*, Num. 32. 42.

NOD, vagabond. *A country*, Gen. 4. 16.

NOPH, honey-comb, a sieve, *or* that drops.

NUN, son, posterity, durable and eternal.

NYMPHAS, spouse, *or* bridegroom.

O.

OBADIAH, servant of the Lord.

OBAL, inconvenience of old age; *or* of the flux. *The son of Joktan*, Gen. 10. 28.

OBED, a servant.

OBED-EDOM, the servant of *Edom*, *or* the Idumean; *or* labourer of the man, of red, *or* earthy.

OBIL, that weeps, *or* deserves to be bewailed; *or* ancient; *or* who is brought. *One that had the care of David's camels*, 1 Chron. 27. 30.

OCRAN, disturber, *or* that disorders.

ODED, to sustain, to hold, to lift up.

OG, a cake, bread baked in the ashes.

OHEL, tent, tabernacle; *or* brightness. 1 *Chron.* 3. 20.

OLYMPAS, heavenly.

OMAR, he that speaks; *or* bitter. *Gen.* 36. 11.

OMEGA, *the last letter of the Greek alphabet.*

OMRI, a sheaf, *or* bundle of corn; *or* rebellion, *or* bitter.

ON, pain, force, iniquity.

ONAN, pain, strength, power, iniquity.

ONESIMUS, profitable, useful; *from* ονησις, usefulness.

ONESIPHORUS, who brings profit; *from the Greek word* ονησις, usefulness, *and* φορος, he that brings.

OPHEL, tower, *or* elevated place; *or* obscurity.

OPHIR, ashes.

OPHRAH, dust, fawn, lead. *A city*, Josh. 18. 23.

OREB, a raven, sweet, caution, *or* mixture, *or* evening.

ORION, *a constellation.*

ORNAN, that rejoices; their bow *or* ark; *or* light of the sun.

ORPAH, the neck, *or* the skull, nakedness of the mouth *or* face.

OTHNI, my time, my hour. *The son of Shemaiah*, 1 Chron. 26. 7.

OTHNIEL, the time, *or* the hour of God.

OZEM, that fasts; *or* their eagerness.

OZIAS, strength from the Lord.

P.

PAARAI, opening.

PADAN-ARAM, *Padan* of the field, and *Aram* Syria; *a city of Syria where Laban dwelt*, Gen. 25. 20.

PAGIEL, prevention of God, *or* prayer of God.

PALESTINA, which is covered, watered, *or* to bring *or* cause ruin.

PALTI, deliverance, *or* flight. *Son of Raphu*, Num. 13. 9.

PAMPHYLIA, *a nation made up of every tribe*, from πας, all, *and* φυλη, a tribe.

PAPHOS, which boils, *or* which is very hot; *from* παφλαζειν, to boil, *or* to be very hot.

PARAN, beauty, glory, ornament.

PARBAR, *a gate, or building belonging to the temple.*

PARMENAS, that abides and is permanent; *from the Greek word* παραμενω, I abide.

PAROSH, a flea; *or* the fruit of the moth. *Ezra* 2. 3.

PARSHANDATHA, revelation of corporeal impurities, *or* of his trouble; *or* dung of impurity. *The son of Haman*, Esth. 9. 7.

PARTHIANS, horsemen.

PARUAH, flourishing; *or according to the Syriac*, that flies away. *Father of Jehoshaphat*, 1 Kings 4. 17.

PASHUR, that extends, *or* multiplies the hole, *or* whiteness; *or* that multiplies *or* extends the liberty *or* the principality.

PATARA, which is trod under foot; *from the Greek word* πατεω, I tread under foot.

PATHROS, mouthful of dew; *or* persuasion, *or* dilatation of ruin.

PATMOS, mortal; *from* πατουμαι, I am squeezed to pieces.

PATROBAS, paternal, *or* that pursues the steps of his father; *from* πατηρ, a father, and βαινω, I go. *Rom.* 16. 14.

PAU, that cries aloud; *or* that appears. *A city*, Gen. 36. 39.

PAUL, a worker. *His former name was* Saul, a sepulchre, a destroyer.

PAULUS.

PEDAHZUR, saviour, strong and powerful; *or* stone of redemption; *or* the redemption of that which is placed *or* set up. *Num.* 1. 10.

PEDAIAH, redemption of the Lord. 2 *Kings* 23. 36.

PEKAH, he that opens; *or* that opens the eye, *or* that is at liberty.

PEKAHIAH, it is the Lord that opens.

PELATIAH, let the Lord deliver; *or* deliverance, *or* flight of the Lord.

PELEG, division. *The son of Eber*, Gen. 10. 25.

PELETHITES, judges, *or* destroyers. *These were troops or guards of king David*, 2 Sam. 8. 18.

PENIEL, face, *or* vision of God; *or*, that sees God.

PENINNAH, pearl, precious stone; *or* his face. *The wife of Elkanah*, 1 Sam. 1. 2.

PENUEL, *See* PENIEL.

PEOR, hole, *or* opening.

PERGA, very earthy; *from the preposition* περι, very, *and* γη, the earth.

PERGAMOS, height, elevation.

PERIZZITES, *the name of a people*, who dwell in villages, *or places not enclosed with walls.*

PERSIA, that cuts *or* divides; *or* nail, gryphon, horseman.

PERSIS, *the same.*

PETER, a rock, *or* stone.

PETHUEL, mouth of God; *or* dilatation, *or* persuasion of God. *Father of Joel*, Joel 1. 1.

PHALEC. *See* PELEG.

PHALLU, admirable, *or* hidden. *The son of Reuben*, Gen. 46. 9.

PHALTI, deliverance, *or* flight. *The son of Laish*, 1 Sam. 25. 44.

PHANUEL, face, *or* vision of God. *Luke* 2. 36.

PHARAOH, that disperses, that spoils, that discovers; *or according to the Syriac*, the revenger, the destroyer, the king, the crocodile.

PHAREZ, division, rupture; *or* that breaks forth violently.

PHARPAR, that produces fruits; *or* the fall of the bull.

PHEBE, shining, pure; *from* φοιβος.

PHENICE, red, *or* purple; *from the Greek word* φοινικις; *or* palm-tree; *from* φοινιξ.

PHICHOL, the mouth of all, *or* every tongue; *or* perfection, *or* completing of the mouth. *Gen.* 21. 22.

PHILADELPHIA, the love of a brother, *or* of fraternity; *from* φιλος, a friend, *and* αδελφος, a brother.

PHILEMON, that kisses, *or* is affectionate; *from* φιλημα, a kiss.

PHILETUS, amiable, *or* who is beloved; *from* φιληθεις.

PHILIP, warlike, *or* a lover of horses.

PHILIPPI, *the same.*

PHILISTIA, *the country of the* Philistines.

PHILISTINES, those that dwell in villages.

PHILOLOGUS, a lover of learning, *or* of the word; *from* φιλος, a lover, *and* λογος, the word.

PHINEHAS, a bold countenance, *or* face of trust, *or* protection.

PHLEGON, zealous, burning, *from* φλεγων.

PHRYGIA, dry, barren; *from* φρυγιος.

PHURAH, that bears fruit, *or* that grows.

PHYGELLUS, fugitive. *One who forsook St. Paul.*

PI-HAHIROTH, the mouth, the pass of Hiroth, *or* the opening of liberty; *or* mouth engraved.

PILATE, who is armed with a dart.

PINON, pearl, *or* gem; *or* that beholds. *One of the heads of Esau's posterity*, Gen. 36. 41.

PIRATHON, his dissipation, his deprivation; his rupture; *or according to the Syriac*, his vengeance. *A city*, Judg. 12. 15. *Whence* Pirathonite, *Judg.* 12. 13.

PISGAH, hill, eminence, fortress.

PISIDIA, pitch, *or* pitchy; *from* πισσωδης.

PISON, changing, *or* doubling, *or* extension of the mouth; *or* extended, *or* multitude. *One of the rivers of Paradise*, Gen. 2. 11.

PITHOM, their mouthful, *or* bit; *or* consummation, *or* dilatation of the mouth. *A city*, Exod. 1. 11.

PITHON, his mouth, *or* his persuasion, *or* gift of the mouth. *Son of Micah*, 1 Chron. 8. 35.

PONTIUS, marine, *or* belonging to the sea.

PONTUS, the sea; *from the Greek word* ποντος.

PORATHA, fruitful. *The son of Haman*, Esth. 9. 8.

PORCIUS.

POTIPHAR, the bull of Africa; *or* a fat bull.

POTI-PHERAH, that scatters, *or* demolishes the fat.

PRISCA, *a Latin word signifying* ancient. 2 *Tim.* 4. 19.

PRISCILLA, *from the same.*

PROCHORUS, he that presides over the choirs; *from* προ, before, *and* χορος, a company of singers. *Acts* 6. 5.

PUBLIUS, common.

PUDENS, shamefaced.

PUL, bean, *or* destruction.

PUNON, precious stone, *or* that beholds. *One of the stations of the Israelites*, Num. 33. 42.

PUR, lot. *See* Appellatives.

PUTEOLI, *a city in Campania.*

PUTIEL, God is my fatness. *The father-in law of Eleazar*, Exod. 6. 25.

Q.

QUARTUS, the fourth. *Rom.* 16. 23.

R.

RAAMAH, greatness, thunder; *or* some sort of evil, *or* bruising, *or* company, *Gen.* 10. 7.

RABBAH, great, powerful, contentious, *or* disputative.

RAB-MAG, who overthrows *or* destroys a multitude; *or* chief, *or* prince of dissolution; *or* chief of the magicians. *Jer.* 39. 3.

RAB-SARIS, grand master of the eunuchs 2 *Kings* 18. 17.

RAB-SHAKEH, cup-bearer of the prince, *or* chamberlain.

RACHAL, injurious; *or* perfumer, *or* trafficking. *A city*, 1 *Sam.* 30. 29.

RACHEL, a sheep.

RAGAU, a friend, a neighbour.

RAGUEL, shepherd of God, *or* friend of God; *or* rupture of God. *The father of Hobab*, Num. 10. 29.
RAHAB, proud, strong, quarrelsome. *Egypt, as most think, is called by this name*, Psal. 87. 4. | 89. 10.
RAHAB, which is large and extended, *or* public place. *The name of a woman.*
RAKKATH, empty, *or* spittle, *or* temple of the head. *A city*, Josh. 19. 35.
RAKKON, vain, void; *or* mountain of lamentations and tears; *or* mountain of enjoyment. *A city*, Josh. 19. 46.
RAM, elevated, sublime; *or* who rejects, *or* is rejected.
RAMAH, *from the same.*
RAMATH, raised, lofty. *A city*, Josh. 19. 8.
RAMATHAIM-ZOPHIM, *a city*, 1 Sam. 1. 1. *The same as* Ramah. *Literally*, Ramathaim *signifies the two* Ramathas, *probably because the city was divided into two parts. The city of* Ramah, *Samuel's birth-place, was also called* Zophim, *which signifies* watch-tower, *or* watchmen, *because the prophets, who are called* watchmen, *had a school or college there.*
RAMATH-LEHI, elevation of the jaw-bone. *The name of a place*, Judg. 15. 17.
RAMESES, thunder; *or* reproach of the moth; *or* he that destroys *or* dissolves evil. *Gen.* 47. 11. *Exod.* 1. 11.
RAMOTH, eminences, high places. *A city of this name was situate in Gilead, and called* Ramoth-gilead, 1 *Kings* 4. 13.
RAPHA, relaxation, *or* physic.
RAPHU, cured, comforted.
REBA, the fourth, *or* a square; *or* that stoops *or* lies down. *A king of Midian*, Num. 31. 8.
REBEKAH, fat, fattened; *or* quarrel appeased, *or* removed.
RECHAB, square, *or* chariot, *or* team of horses, *or* a rider.
RECHABITES, the posterity of *Rechab.*
REGEM, that stones, *or* is stoned, *or* purple. *The son of Jahdai*, 1 Chron. 2. 47.
REGEM-MELECH, he that stones the king; *or* the purple of the king, *or* of the council. *Zech.* 7. 2.
REHABIAH, breadth, *or* extent, *or* place of the Lord; *or* God is my extent, *he hath set me at liberty. The son of Eliezer*, 1 Chron. 23. 17.
REHOB, breadth, space, *or* extent. *A city*, Josh. 19. 28.
REHOBOAM, who sets the people at liberty; *or* space of the people; *or* that lets the people breathe, *or* blow.
REHOBOTH, spaces, *or* places.
REHUM, merciful, compassionate, *or* friendly.
REI, my shepherd, my companion, my friend; *or* my evil, *or* my breaking. 1 *Kings* 1. 8.
REMALIAH, the exaltation of the Lord; *or* who is rejected of the Lord.
REMMON, greatness, elevation; *or* a pomegranate tree. *A city*, Josh. 19. 7.
REMPHAN, *the name of an idol, which some think to be Saturn. See* STAR *in Appellatives.*
REPHAEL, the physic, *or* medicine of God. *The son of Shemaiah*, 1 Chron. 26. 7.
REPHAIM, giant, physician, *or* relaxed, *or* that relax, that weaken.
REPHAIMS, *from the same.*
REPHIDIM, beds, *or* places of rest.
RESIN, a bridle, *or* bit. *A city*, Gen. 10. 12.
REU, his friend, his shepherd. *The son of Peleg*, Gen. 11. 18.
REUBEN, who sees the son, *or* vision of the son. *Jacob's eldest son by Leah; he endeavoured to deliver Joseph from his brethren.*
REUBENITES, *the posterity of* Reuben.
REUEL, shepherd, *or* friend of God. *The son of Esau*, Gen. 36. 4.
REUMAH, lofty, sublime. *Nahor's concubine*, Gen. 22. 24.
REZIN, voluntary, *or* good will; *or* runner.
REZON, lean, *or* small, *or* secret, *or* prince. *The son of Eliadah*, 1 Kings 11. 23.
RHEGIUM, rupture, *or* fracture; *from the Greek word* ῥηγη.
RHESA, will, *or* course.
RHODA, a rose.
RHODES, a rose; from ῥοδη.
RIBLAH, quarrel, *or* greatness to him; *or* quarrel that increases, *or* that spreads. 2 *Kings* 23. 33.
RIMMON, exalted, pomegranate.
RIPHATH, remedy, *or* medicine, *or* release, *or* pardon. The son of Gomer, *Gen.* 10. 3.
RISSAH, watering, distillation, *or* dew. *One of the stations of the Israelites in the wilderness*, Num. 33. 21.
RIZPAH, bed, *or* extension, *or* coal, *or* fire-stone.
ROMAMTI-EZER, exaltation of help. *Son of Heman*, 1 Chron. 25. 4.
ROMAN, strong, powerful; *from the Greek word* ῥωμη, strength.
ROMANS.
ROME, strength, power; *from* ῥωμη.
ROSH, the head, *or* the top, *or* the beginning. *The son of Benjamin*, Gen. 46. 21.
RUFUS, red.
RUHAMAH, having obtained mercy. *Marg.*
RUMAH, exalted, sublime, *or* rejected. *A city*, 2 Kings 23. 36.
RUTH, filled, satisfied.

S.

SABEANS, captivity; *or* conversion, rest, old age.
SABTECHA, that surrounds, *or* causes wounding. *The son of Cush*, Gen. 10. 7.
SADOC, just, *or* justified. *The father of Achim*, Mat. 1. 14.
SALAH, mission, sending; *or* branches, *or* dart, *or, according to the Syriac*, that spoils, *or* is spoiled. *The son of Arphaxad*, Gen. 10. 24.
SALAMIS, shaken, tost, beaten; *from the Greek word* σαλευω, I beat, I toss. *An island*, Acts 13. 5.
SALATHIEL, I have asked of God; *or* loan of God.
SALEM, complete, perfect, *or* peace.
SALIM, *John* 3. 23. *See* SHALIM.
SALMON, peaceable, perfect, *or* that rewards.
SALMONE. *A city.*
SALOME. *See* SALMON.
SAMARIA, his lees, his prison, his guard, his throne, *or* his diamond. *In Heb.* Shomeron.
SAMARITANS, *people of* Samaria.
SAMLAH, raiment; *or* his left hand; *or* his name, his astonishment, or what has been put to him. *A king of Edom*, Gen. 36. 36.
SAMOS, full of gravel; *from* Αμμος, sand. *An island.*
SAMOTHRACIA, *an island, so called because it was peopled by* Samians *and* Thracians, Acts 16. 11.
SAMSON, his sun; *or, according to the Syriac*, his service, *or* his ministry; *or* here the second time.
SAMUEL, heard of God, *or* asked of God.
SANBALLAT, bush in secret; *or* the enemy in secret.
SAPH, rushes, *or* sea-moss, end, consummation; *or* vessel, flat, threshold. *A giant*, 2 Sam. 21. 18.
SAPHIR, *a city.*
SAPPHIRA, that relates *or* tells; *or* that writes *or* composes books; *or* handsome.
SARAH, lady, *or* princess; *or* the princess of the multitude.
SARAI, my lady, my princess.
SARDIS, prince of joy, *or* song of joy; *or* that which remains. *Syr.* a pot, a kettle.
SAREPTA, a goldsmith's ship, *where metals used to be melted and tried.*
SARGON, who takes away protection; *or* that takes away the garden; *or, according to the Syriac*, nets, snares. *A king of Assyria*, Isa. 20. 1.
SARON. *See* SHARON.
SARSECHIM, master of the wardrobe; *or* of the perfumes. *Jer.* 39. 3.
SARUCH, branch, layer; *or* twining.
SATAN, contrary, adversary, a party in a process, an enemy, an accuser.
SAUL, demanded, *or* lent, ditch, sepulchre, death, *or* hell.
SCEVA, disposed, prepared; *from* σκευαζω, I dispose, I prepare.
SCYTHIAN, tanner, *or* leather-dresser.
SEBA, drunkard; *or* that turns, *or* surrounds; *or* old man, *according to the Syriac.*
SEBAT, twig, sceptre, tribe. *Zech.* 1. 7.
SEGUB, fortified, *or* raised. 1 *Kings* 16. 34.
SEIR, hairy, goat, demon, tempest, *or* barley.
SELEUCIA, shaken *or* beaten by the waves, *or* that runs as a river.
SEMEI, hearing, *or* obeying.
SENEH, bush. *A rock*, 1 Sam. 14. 4.
SENNACHERIB, bush of the destruction of the sword, of solitude, of drought.
SEPHARVAIM, the two books, *or* the two scribes.
SERAH, lady of scent; *or* the song; *or* the morning, the morning star. *The daughter of Asher*, Gen. 46. 17.
SERAIAH, prince of the Lord, *or* the Lord is my prince; *or* song of the Lord.
SERGIUS PAULUS.
SERUG, branch, layer; *or* twining. *The father of Nahor*, Gen. 11. 22.
SETH, put, *or* who puts.
SHAALBIM, that beholds the heart; *or* fist, *or* hand, *or* fox of the sea. *Judg.* 1. 35.
SHAARAIM, gates, valuation, hairs, barley, tempests, goats, demons. *A city*, 1 Chron. 4. 31.
SHAASHGAZ, he that presses the fleece; *or* he that performs the shearing of the sheep. *Esth.* 2. 14.
SHADRACH, tender nipple; *or* field soft and tender. *Dan.* 1. 7.
SHALIM, fox, *or* fist, *or* path.
SHALISHA, three, *or* the third; *or* prince, *or* captain.
SHALLUM, perfect, *or* peaceable.
SHALMAN, peaceable, perfect; *or* that rewards. *Hos.* 10. 14.
SHALMANEZER, peace tied *or* chained, *or* perfection and retribution, *or* peace taken away.
SHAMGAR, named a stranger; *or* he is here a stranger; *or* surprise, astonishment of the stranger.
SHAMHUTH, desolation, destruction, astonishment; *or* desolation of iniquity. *One of David's captains*, 1 Chron. 27. 8.
SHAMIR, prison, bush, lees, thorn. *Josh.* 13. 48.
SHAMMAH, loss, desolation, astonishment.
SHAMMUAH, he that is heard, *or* obeyed.
SHAPHAN, a rabbit, *or* wild rat; *or* their brink, their lip, their breaking.
SHAPHAT, a judge, *or* judging.
SHARAI, my lord, my prince, *or* my song. *A man's name*, Ezra 10. 40.
SHAREZER, overseer of the treasury, *or* of the store-house; *or* the treasures of him that sings; *or* that sees the ambushes.
SHARON, his plain, field, his song.
SHASHAK, a bag of linen; *or* the sixth bag. 1 *Chron.* 8. 14.
SHAVEH, the plain; *or* that puts *or* makes equality. *Gen.* 14. 5.
SHEALTIEL, I have asked of God.
SHEARIAH, gate of the Lord; *or* tempest of the Lord. *The son of Azel*, 1 Chron. 8. 38.
SHEAR-JASHUB, the remnant shall return. *Marg.*
SHEBA, captivity, *or* compassing about, repose, old age.
SHEBANIAH, the Lord that converts, *or* that recalls from captivity, *or* that captivates; *or* that understands, that builds. *Neh.* 9. 4.
SHEBNA, who rests himself, *or* who is now captive.
SHECHEM, part, portion, the back, shoulders, early in the morning.
SHEDEUR, field, pap, all-mighty; *or* destroyer of fire, *or* of light. *Num.* 1. 5.
SHELAH, that breaks, that unties, that undresses.
SHELEMIAH, God is my perfection, my happiness, my peace; *or* the peace or perfection of the Lord.
SHELEPH, who draws out. *The son of Joktan*, Gen. 10. 26.
SHELOMITH, my peace, my happiness, my recompence. *Daughter of Zerubbabel*, 1 Chr. 3. 19.
SHELUMIEL, peace of God, *or* God is my happiness; *or* retribution *or* perfection of God. *The son of Zurishaddai*, Num. 1. 6.
SHEM, name, renown; *or* he that puts *or* places, *or* who is put *or* placed. *The son of Noah, from whom the* Messiah *was descended.*
SHEMAIAH, that hears, *or* that obeys the Lord.
SHEMARIAH, God is my guard, *or* the guard of the Lord; *or* diamond, dregs, thorn, *or* bush of the Lord. 1 *Chron.* 12. 5.
SHEMEBER, name of force, *or* fame, of the strong, *or* of the wing. *King of Zeboim*, Gen. 14. 2.
SHEMER, guardian, thorn. 1 *Kings* 16. 24.
SHEMIDA, name of knowledge, *or* that puts knowledge; *or* the knowledge of desolation, *or* of astonishment; *or* the science of the heavens. *Son of Gilead*, Num. 26. 32.
SHEMINITH, the eighth.
SHEMIRAMOTH, the height of the heavens; *or* the elevation of the name. 1 *Chron.* 15. 18.
SHEN, tooth, ivory, *or* change; *or* he that sleeps. *The name of a place*, 1 Sam. 7. 12.
SHENIR, lantern, *or* light that sleeps; *or* renewing of the lamp, *or* he that shews.
SHEPHATIAH, the Lord that judges; the judgment of the Lord; *or* God is my judge.
SHESHACH, bag of flax, *or* linen; *or* the sixth bag.
SHESHBAZZAR, joy in tribulation; *or* production, *or* defence of joy; *or* joy of the vintage.
SHETHER-BOZNAI, that makes to rot and corrupt; *or* that seeks and examines those who despise me. *Ezra* 5. 3.
SHEVA, vanity, elevation, fame, *or* tumult. *One of David's scribes*, 2 Sam. 20. 25.
SHIBBOLETH, burden, ear of corn, *or* current of water.
SHICRON, drunkenness; *or* his gift, *or* his wages. *A city*, Josh. 15. 11.
SHIGGAION, a song of trouble *or* comfort. *Psal.* 7. *Title.*
SHILOAH. *See* SILOAH.
SHILOH, sent. *See* Appellatives.
SHILOH, peace, *or* abundance. *A city.*
SHILONITE, *of the city of* Shiloh. 1 *Kings* 11. 29.
SHIMEAH, that hears, that obeys.
SHIMEI, that hears *or* obeys; *or* name of the heap; *or* that destroys the heap; *or* my reputation, my fame.
SHIMSHAI, my sun.
SHINAR, the watching of him that sleeps; *or* spoil of the tooth; *or* change of the city.
SHIPHRAH, handsome, *or* trumpet; *or* that does good. *An Egyptian midwife*, Exod. 1. 15.
SHISHAK, present of the bag, of the pot, of the thigh.
SHITTIM, that turn away, *or* divert; *otherwise*, scourge, rods, *or* thorns.
SHOBAB, returned, turned back. *The son of David*, 2 Sam. 5. 14.
SHOBACH, your bonds, your chains, your nets, your gins; *or* his captivity; *or* your conversion, your return; *or* a dove-house, *according to the Syriac. General of Hadarezer's army*, 2 Sam. 10. 16.
SHUAH, pit, *or* that swims; *or* humiliation, meditation, *or* word.
SHUAL, fox, hand, fist; *or* traces, way.
SHUHITE.
SHULAMITE, peaceable, perfect, that recompenses.
SHUNAMITE, *a native of.*
SHUNEM, their change, their repeating, their second, *or* their sleep. 1 *Sam.* 28. 4.
SHUR, wall, ox, *or* that beholds. *A wilderness*, Gen. 16. 7.
SHUSHAN, lily, rose, *or* joy.
SHUTHELAH, plant, *or* verdure; *or* moist pot, *or* drinking pot. *The son of Ephraim*, Num. 26. 35.
SIBMAH, conversion, return, captivity, old age, rest.
SIDON, hunting, fishing, venison.
SIGIONOTH, according to variable songs, *or* tunes. *Marg.*
SIHON, rooting out; *or* conclusion.
SIHOR, black, trouble; *or* early in the morning. *The river Nilus in Egypt*, Isa. 23. 3.

SILAS, three, *or* the third.
SILOAS *and* **SILOAM**, sent, *or* who sends ; *or* dart, branch, *or* whatever is sent.
SILOE, *the same.*
SILVANUS, who loves the woods, *or* forests ; *from the Latin word* silva, a wood.
SIMEON, that hears, that obeys, *or* is heard.
SIMON, that hears, *or* obeys.
SIN, bush.
SINAI, bush. *According to the Syriac*, enmity.
SION, noise, tumult. *A mountain of the country of the Amorites, the same as* Hermon, *Deut.* 4. 48.
SIRION, a breast-plate ; *or* deliverance, *or* a song of the dove.
SISERA, that sees a horse, *or* a swallow.
SIVAN, bush, *or* thorn. *This is the Babylonian name of the third month of the Hebrew year, which answers in part to our* May *and* June, *Esth.* 8. 9.
SMYRNA, myrrh.
SO, a measure for grain, *or* dry matters. *An Egyptian word.*
SOCOH, tents, *or* tabernacles. *A city*, Josh. 15. 48.
SODI, my secret. *Father of Gaddiel*, Num. 13. 10.
SODOM, their secret, their lime, their cement.
SODOMITES.
SOLOMON, peaceable, perfect, *or* who recompenses. *He was the son of David king of Israel. He prayed to God for wisdom, and obtained wisdom, riches, and honour. He built the temple at Jerusalem, where the sacrifices were to be offered to God. He married Pharaoh's daughter, and built for her an house. He loved many strange women, who turned away his heart after their gods. It is thought that the three books he wrote, namely,* Proverbs, Ecclesiastes, *and the* Canticles, *are an evidence of his repentance.*
SOPATER, who defends the father, *or* the health of the father ; *from* σωζω, I save, *and* πατηρ, father. *A disciple of St. Paul*, Acts 20. 4.
SOREK, vine, hissing, a colour inclining to yellow.
SOSIPATER. *See* SOPATER.
SOSTHENES, saviour, strong and powerful, *from* σωζω, I save, *and* θενος, strength, force.
SPAIN, *in Greek*, rare, *or* precious.
STACHYS, spike ; *from* ςαχυς.
STEPHANAS, a crown, *or* crowned ; *from* ςεφανη, a crown.
STEPHEN, *the same.*
SUCCOTH, tents, tabernacles.
SUCCOTH-BENOTH, the tabernacles of young women, *or* the tents of prostitutes. 2 *Kings* 17. 30.
SUR, that withdraws, *or* departs. *The name of one of the gates of Solomon's temple*, 2 Kings 11. 6.
SUSANNA, a lily, *or* a rose, *or* joy.
SUSI, horse, *or* swallow, *or* moth. *The father of Gaddi*, Num. 13. 11.
SYCHAR, *a city*, John 4. 5.
SYENE, bush ; *or* enmity, *according to the Syriac*, Ezek. 29. 10.
SYNTYCHE, that speaks *or* discourses, *from the Greek word*, συντυγχανω, to converse. *Phil.* 4. 2.
SYRACUSE, that draws violently.
SYRIA, *in Hebrew*, Aram, sublime, *or* that deceives.
SYRIAC.
SYRIAN, *who is of* Syria.
SYRIANS.
SYROPHENICIAN, red, *or* purple, drawn to ; *from* συρω, I draw, *and* φοινιξ, red, palm-tree, *or* of purple.

T.

TAANACH, who humbles thee, *or* answers thee, *or* afflicts thee. *A city*, 1 Kings 4. 12.
TABBATH, good, *or* goodness. *A place*, Judg. 7. 42.
TABEAL, good God.
TABEEL, *the same.* Ezra 4. 7.
TABERAH, burning.
TABITHA, *is a Syriac word, signifying* clear-sighted. *She is also called* Dorcas, *that is*, wild goat, *or* kid.
TABOR, choice, *or* purity. *Syr.* bruising, contrition.
TABRIMON, good pomegranate ; *or* goodness raised ; *or* the navel, *or* middle, prepared, reckoned, given. *The father of Ben-hadad*, 1 Kings 15. 18.
TADMOR, the palm, *or* palm-tree ; *or* bitterness, *or* change.
TAHAPANES, secret temptation, hidden flight, covered standard.
TAHPENES, standard, flight, temptation, secret.
TALITHA-CUMI, young woman, arise. *A Syriac and Hebrew expression*, Mark 5. 41.
TALMAI, my furrow ; *or* that suspends the waters ; *or* heap of waters. *The son of Anak*, Josh. 15. 14.
TAMAR, a palm, *or* palm-tree.
TAMMUZ, abstruse, concealed.
TANHUMETH, consolation, *or* repentance ; *or* bottle, *or* wall that is given, *or* of a gift. *The father of Seraiah*, 2 Kings 25. 23.
TAPHATH, little girl ; *from the Hebrew*, Taphah, *or* Taph, to take short steps, *like children ; otherwise*, distillation, drop. *The daughter of Solomon*, 1 Kings 4. 11.
TARPELITES, ravishers, *or* wearied ; *or* succession *or* order of miracles, *or* ruinous order, *or* rank. *The name of a people*, Ezra 4. 9.
TARSHISH, contemplation, *or* examination, of the marble, *or* of the joy ; *or* precious stone, the colour of marble.
TARSUS, winged, feathered.
TARTAK, chained, bound, shut up.
TARTAN, that searches and examines the gift of the turtle ; *or* their law. 2 *Kings* 18. 17.
TATNAI, that gives, *or* the overseer of the gifts, of the presents, of the tributes. *Ezra* 5. 3.
TEBAH, murder, butchery, *or* guarding of the body, a cook. *Son of Nahor and Reumah*, Gen. 22. 24.
TEBETH, *the Babylonish name of the tenth month of the Hebrews, that answers partly to* December, *and partly to* January.
TEKEL, weight.
TEKOA, trumpet, *or* sound of the trumpet ; *or* that is confirmed.
TEL-HARSA, heap, *or* suspension of the plough, *or* of deafness, of silence ; *or* suspension of the head. *A place*, Ezra 2. 59.
TEL-MELAH, heap of salt, *or* of mariners ; *or* suspension of the salt, *or* of the mariner. *Ezra* 2. 59.
TEMA, admiration, *or* perfection, consummation ; *or* the south.
TEMAN, the south, *or* Africa ; *or* perfect.
TEMANITE, *an inhabitant of* Teman.
TERAH, to breathe, to scent, to blow.
TERAPHIM, an image, an idol.
TERTIUS, the third. *Latin.*
TERTULLUS, a liar, an impostor ; *from* τερατολογος, a teller of stories, *or* monstrous things.
TETRARCH, governor of a fourth part of a kingdom.
THADDEUS, that praises and confesses. *Mark* 3. 18.
THAHASH, that makes haste, *or* that keeps silence ; *or* of the colour of hyacinth. *The son of Nahor*, Gen. 22. 24.
THAMAH, that blots out, *or* suppresses. *Ezra* 2. 53.
THEBEZ, muddy, *or* eggs ; *or* fine linen, *or* silk.
THELASAR, that unbinds and grants the suspension, *or* the heap. *A part of Syria*, 2 Kings 19. 12.
THEOPHILUS, a friend, *or* a lover of God ; *from* Θεος, God, *and* φιλος, a friend.
THESSALONICA, victory against the Thessalians.
THEUDAS, a false teacher.
THOMAS, a twin.
THYATIRA, a sweet savour of labour, *or* sacrifice of contrition ; *from* θυα, scent, perfume, *and* τειρω, I bruise, I disturb.
TIBERIAS, good vision, *or* the navel, *or* a breaking asunder.
TIBERIUS, son of *Tiber.* Luke 3. 1.
TIBNI, straw, *or* hay ; *otherwise*, understanding.
TIDAL, that breaks the yoke ; *or* the knowledge of elevation. *King of nations*, Gen. 14. 1.
TIGLATH-PILESER, that binds *or* takes away captivity, miraculous, *or* ruinous ; *or* that hinders *or* binds, and withholds the snow that falls.
TIMEUS, *in Greek may signify*, perfect, honourable ; *in Hebrew*, admirable.
TIMNATH, image, *or* figure, *or* enumeration.
TIMON, honourable ; *from* τιμη, Acts 6. 5.
TIMOTHEUS, honour of God, *or* valued of God ; *from* τιμη, honour, *and* Θεος, God.
TIPHSAH, passage, leap, *or* step ; *or* the passover. 1 *Kings* 4. 24.
TIRHAKAH, inquirer, examiner *or* dull observer : *or* law made dull. *King of Ethiopia*, 2 Kings 19. 9.
TIRSHATHA, that overturns the foundation ; *or* that beholds the time, *or* the year *according to the Syriac.*
TIRZAH, benevolent, pleasant, well-pleasing, *or* that runs.
TISHBITE, that makes captives ; *or* that turns back *or* recalls, that dwells. 1 *Kings* 17. 1.
TITUS, honourable, *from* τιω, I honour.
TOB, good, *or* goodness. *The name of a country*, Judg. 11. 5.
TOB-ADONIJAH, my good God ; *or* the goodness of the foundation of the Lord, 2 *Chron.* 17. 8.
TOBIAH, the Lord is good, *or* the goodness of the Lord.
TOGARMAH, which is all bone, *or* strong ; *or* breaking *or* gnawing of the bones.
TOHU, that lives, *or* that declares. 1 *Sam.* 1. 1.
TOI, who wanders, *King of Hamath*, 2 Sam. 8. 9.
TOLA, worm, *or* grub, *or* scarlet.
TOPHEL, ruin, folly, without understanding, insipid. *A desert place*, Deut. 1. 1.
TOPHET, a drum, *or* betraying. *See* Appellatives.
TROAS, penetrated ; from τιτρωσκω, I penetrate.
TROGYLLIUM, *a city in the isle of Samos.*
TROPHIMUS, well educated, *or* brought up ; *from* τρεφω, to bring up, *or* educate. *Acts* 20. 4.
TRYPHENA, delicious, delicate ; *from* τρεφω.
TRYPHOSA, thrice shining.
TUBAL, the earth, the world ; *or* that is carried, *or* led ; *or* confusion.
TUBAL-CAIN, worldly possession, *or* possessor of the world ; *or* who is jealous of confusion. *The son of Lamech*, Gen. 4. 22.
TYCHICUS, casual, happening ; *from* τυχη, fortune.
TYRANNUS, a prince, *or* that reigns.
TYRE, *in Hebrew*, Sor, *or* Tzur ; strength, rock, sharp.
TYRUS, *the same.*

U.

UCAL, power, *or* prevalency.
ULAI, strength ; *or* fool, senseless. *The name of a river*, Dan. 8. 2.
ULAM, the porch, the court ; *or* their strength, *or* their folly. 1 *Chron.* 7. 16.
ULLA, elevation, *or* holocaust, *or* leaf, *or* young child. 1 *Chron.* 7. 39.
UNNI, poor, *or* afflicted, *or* that answers. *The name of a porter or singer*, 1 Chron. 15. 18.
UPHAZ, gold of *Phasis*, *or* Pison, the finest gold.
UR, fire, *or* light.
URI, my light, *or* fire.
URIAH, *or* **URIJAH**, the Lord is my light, *or* fire ; the light of the Lord.
URIEL, God is my light *or* fire ; *or* the light of God. 1 *Chron.* 15. 5.
URIM *and* **THUMMIM**, lights and perfection.
UZ, counsel, *or* wood ; *or*, *according to the Syriac*, to fix, to fasten to.
UZZAH, strength, *or* a goat.
UZZEN-SHERAH, ear of the flesh, *or* of the parent ; *or* the ear of him that remains. *A city*, 1 Chron. 7. 24.
UZZI, my strength, *or* my kid. *Son of Bukki*, 1 Chron. 6. 5.
UZZIAH, the strength of the Lord ; *or* the kid of the Lord.
UZZIEL, the strength of God ; *or* kid of God. 1 *Chron.* 7. 7.
UZZIELITES, *the posterity of* Uzziel. *Num.* 3. 27.

V.

VASHNI, the second. *The son of Samuel*, 1 Chron. 6. 28.
VASHTI, that drinks ; *or* thread, *or* woof.
VOPHSI, fragment, *or* diminution. *Father of Nahbi*, Num. 13. 14.

Z.

ZABDI, portion, dowry. *The Father of Carmi*, Josh. 7. 1.
ZACCHEUS, pure, clean ; just, *or* justified.
ZACHARIAH, memory of the Lord, *or* man of the Lord.
ZADOK, just, *or* justified.
ZAHAM, crime, filthiness, impurity. *The son of Rehoboam*, 2 Chron. 11. 19.
ZAIR, little ; *or* afflicted, in tribulation. *A city*, 2 Kings 8. 21.
ZALMON, his shade, his obscurity, his image, *A mountain*, Judg. 9. 48.
ZALMONAH, the shade, *or* sound of the number ; *or*, your image, *or* picture. *One of the stations of the Israelites in the wilderness*, Num. 33. 41.
ZALMUNNA, shadow, image, *or* idol forbidden ; *or* noise of trouble.
ZAMZUMMIMS, thinking wickedness, *or* wickedness of wicked men. *Giants*, Deut. 2. 20.
ZANOAH, forgetfulness *or* desertion ; *or* this rest, this consolation. *A city*, Josh. 15. 34.
ZAPHNATH-PAANEAH, one that discovers hidden things ; *in the Egyptian tongue*, a Saviour of the world. *The name that Pharaoh gave to Joseph*, Gen. 41. 45.
ZARAH, east, brightness.
ZAREPHATH, ambush of the mouth ; *or* crucible, *in which metals are melted.*
ZEBADIAH, portion of the Lord, *or* the Lord is my portion. 1 *Chron.* 8. 15.
ZEBAH, victim, sacrifice, immolation.
ZEBEDEE, abundant portion.
ZEBOIM, deer, goats.
ZEBUL, an habitation.
ZEBULUN, dwelling, habitation.
ZECHARIAH. *See* ZACHARIAH.
ZEDEKIAH, the Lord is my justice, *or* the justice of the Lord.
ZEEB, wolf. *Judg.* 7. 25.
ZELEK, the shadow, *or* noise of him that licks, that laps, *or* strikes. *One of David's thirty valiant captains*, 2 Sam. 23. 37.
ZELOPHEHAD, the shade, *or* tingling of fear ; *or* the fear of submersion, *or* of being burnt.
ZELOTES, jealous, *or* full of zeal ; *from* ζηλος, zeal, jealousy. *The surname of Simon*, Luke 6. 15.
ZELZAH, noontide.
ZENAS, living ; *from* ζαω, I live.
ZEPHANIAH, the Lord is my secret ; *or* the secret of the Lord ; *or* the mouth of the Lord.
ZEPHATH, which beholds, that attends, that covers. *A city*, Judg. 1. 17.
ZEPHO, that sees and observes ; *or* that expects, *or* covers. *Son of Eliphaz*, Gen. 36. 11.
ZERAH. *See* ZARAH.
ZEREDAH, ambush, change of dominion, *or* descent ; *or* plan of power. *The country of Jeroboam*, 1 Kings 11. 26.
ZERESH, misery, stranger, strange *or* dispersed inheritance ; *otherwise*, crown of inheritance, *or* of misery.
ZEROR, root, *or* that straitens, that binds, that keeps tight ; *or* a stone. 1 *Sam.* 9. 1.
ZERUAH, leprous, *or* wasp, *or* hornet. *The mother of Jeroboam*, 1 Kings 11. 26.
ZERUBBABEL, banished, *or* a stranger at Babylon ; *or* dispersion of confusion.
ZERUIAH, pain, *or* tribulation, chains of the Lord.
ZETHAR, he that examines or beholds ; *or* olive of vision, *or* olive of the turtle. *Esth.* 1. 10.
ZIBA, army, fight, strength, stag.

ZIBEON, iniquity that dwells; *or* elevation, *or* swelling; *or* oath, *or* fulness, *or* the seventh.
ZIBIAH, deer, *or* goat, *or* honourable and fine; *or* the Lord dwells; *or* voluntary, *according to the Syriac. The mother of Joash*, 2 Kings 12. 1.
ZICHRI, that remembers, *or* that is a male, *Exod.* 6. 21.
ZIDON, hunting, fishing, venison.
ZIDONIANS, *the inhabitants of* Zidon.
ZIF, this, *or* that; *or, according to the Syriac*, brightness. *The second Hebrew month, which answers partly to* April *and* May.
ZIKLAG, measure pressed down.
ZILLAH, shadow; which is roasted; the tingling of the ear. *The wife of Lamech*, Gen. 4. 19.
ZILPAH, distillation; *or* contempt of the mouth.
ZIMRAN, song, singer, *or* vine. *The son of Abraham*, Gen. 25. 2.
ZIMRI, my field, *or* my vine, my branch.
ZIN, buckler, coldness.
ZION, a monument raised up, heap of stones set up, sepulchre, turret, dryness.
ZIOR, ship of him that watches, *or* is awake, *or* of him that is robbed, *or* of the enemy. *A city*, Josh. 15. 54.
ZIPH, this mouth, *or* mouthful. *A city*, Josh. 15. 24.
ZIPPOR, bird, *or* sparrow; *or* crown, *or* desert; *or, according to the Syriac*, early in the morning, *or* goat. *The father of Balak*, Num. 22. 2.
ZIPPORAH, beauty, trumpet.
ZITHRI, to hide; *or* demolished, *or* overturned; *or* my refuge. *Son of Uzziel*, Exod. 6. 22.
ZIZ, flower, branch, a lock of hair; *or, according to the Syriac*, wing, feather. *The side of a mountain or hill*, 2 Chron. 20. 16.
ZOAN, motion.
ZOAR, little, small.
ZOBAH, an army, *or* warring, *or* a commandment in that, *or* a swelling.
ZOHAR, white, shining, *or* dryness. *The father of Ephron*, Gen. 23. 8
ZOHELETH, that creeps, slides, *or* draws. *A rock*, 1 Kings 1. 9.
ZOPHAR, rising early, *or* crown; *or* sparrow, *or* little bird, *or* goat. *Syr.*
ZORAH, leprosy, *or* scab.
ZOROBABEL. *See* ZERUBBABEL.
ZUAR, small.
ZUPH, that beholds, *or* observes, *or* watches, *or* roof, covering; *or* honey-comb, *or* that floats. *The father of Tohu*, 1 Sam. 1. 1.
ZUR, stone, rock, that besieges, *or* preaches; *or* plan, form.
ZURISHADDAI, the Almighty is my rock, my strength; *otherwise*, splendour, beauty; *or, according to the Syriac*, revolters. *The father of Shelumiel*, Num. 1. 6.
ZUZIMS, the posts of a door; *or* splendour, beauty. *These were giants who dwelt beyond Jordan, and who were conquered by Chedorlaomer and his allies*, Gen. 14. 15.

A CONCORDANCE TO THE PROPER NAMES

OF THE

OLD AND NEW TESTAMENT.

AARON.
Exod. 4. 14. is not A. the Levite thy brother?
5. 20. they met Moses and A. who stood in way
6. 23. A. took Elisheba, sister of Naashon, to wife
7. 1. and A. thy brother shall be thy prophet
12. but A. rod swallowed up their rods
16. 34. A. laid up the pot of manna before testimony
17. 12. and A. and Hur stayed up his hands
19. 24. thou shalt come up, thou and A. with thee
24. 14. and behold A. and Hur are with you
28. 12. and A. shall bear their names, 29. 30.
30. 7. A. shall burn sweet incense every morning
8. when A. lighteth the lamps at even
10. A. shall make an atonement once in a year
32. 35. because they made calf, which A. made
40. 31. Moses and A. and his sons washed thereat
Lev. 8. 12. he poured oil on A. head to sanctify him
30. he sprinkled blood on A. and his sons
9. 22. A. blessed them ‖ 10. 3. A held his peace
16. 3. thus shall A. come into the holy place
8. A. shall cast lots ‖ 24. 3. A. shall order it
21. A. shall lay his hands on the head of the goat
Num. 1. 3. A shall number them by their armies
8. 11. A. shall offer the Levites before the Lord
16. 11. what is A. that ye murmur against him?
16. come thou, they, and A. to-morrow before L.
43. Moses and A. came before the tabernacle
17. 3. shalt write A. name upon the rod of Levi
10. bring A. rod again before the testimony
20. 8. thou and A. thy brother speak to the rock
28. A. died there in the top of the mount; Moses and Eleazar came down, 33. 38. *Deut.* 32. 50.
33. 39. A. was 120 years old when he died in Hor
Deut. 9. 20. the Lord was very angry with A.
Josh. 24. 5. I sent Moses and A. and I plagued Egypt and brought you out, 1 *Sam.* 12. 8. *Mic.* 6. 4.
1 *Sam.* 12. 6. the Lord that advanced Moses and A.
1 *Chron.* 6. 3. sons of Amram, A. and Moses, 23. 13.
Psal. 77. 20. thou leddest thy peop. by Moses and A.
99. 6. Moses and A. among his priests, and Samuel
106. 16. they envied A. the saint of the Lord
115. 10. O house of A. trust in the Lord
12. the Lord will bless the house of A.
118. 3. let house of A. say, his mercy endur. for ever
133. 2. ointment that ran down upon A. beard
135. 19. bless the Lord, O house of A.
Luke 1. 5. his wife was of the daughters of A.
Acts 7. 40. saying to A. make us gods to go before us
Heb. 5. 4. but he that is called of God, as was A.
7. 11. and not be called after the order of A.
9. 4. A. rod that budded, and tables of covenant
Sons of AARON. *See* Abihu *and* Nadab.

AARONITES.
1 *Chron.* 12. 27. Jehoiada was leader of the A.
27. 17. Zadok was the ruler of the A.

ABADDON.
Rev. 9. 11. the angel of the bottomless pit is A.

ABAGTHA.
Esth. 1. 10. A. was chamberlain to Ahasuerus

ABANA.
2 *Kings* 5. 12. are not rivers A. and Pharpar better

ABARIM. *See* Mount.

ABBA. *See* Father.

ABDA.
1 *Kings* 4. 6. Adoniram son of A. was over the tribu.
Neh. 11. 17. A. was for thanksgiving in prayer

ABDI.
2 *Chr.* 29. 12. of sons of Merari, Kish the son of A.
Ezra 10. 26. A. of them that married strange wives

ABDIEL.
1 *Chron.* 5. 15. Ahi son of A. chief of the house

ABDON.
Judg. 12. 13. A. judged Israel ‖ 15. A. died
2 *Chr.* 34. 20. commanded A. to inquire of the Lord

ABED-NEGO.
Dan. 1. 7. he gave to Azariah the name of A.
2. 49. the king set A. over the affairs, 3. 30.
3. 23. A. fell down bound into the fiery furnace

ABEL, *person*, or *place*.
Gen. 4. 4. Lord had respect to A. and his offering
1 *Sam.* 6. 18. stone of A. whereon they set the ark

2 *Sam.* 20. 18. they shall surely ask counsel at A.
Mat. 23. 35. from the blood of A. *Luke* 11. 51.
Heb. 11. 4. by faith A. offered a more excellent sacrifice
12. 24. speaks better things than the blood of A.

ABEL-BETH-MAACHAH.
1 *Kings* 15. 20. Ben-hadad's captains smote A.
2 *Kings* 15. 29. Tiglath-pileser came and took A.

ABEL-MAIM.
2 *Chron.* 16. 4. they smote Ijon, and Dan, and A.

ABEL-MEHOLAH.
Judg. 7. 22. the host fled to the border of A.
1 *Kings* 19. 16. Elisha the son of Shaphat of A.

ABEL-MIZRAIM.
Gen. 50. 11. mourning, name of it was called A.

ABIAH.
1 *Sam.* 8. 2. the name of Samuel's second son was A.
1 *Chr.* 2. 24. A. Hezron's wife ‖ 7. 8. son of Becher A.
3. 10. the son of Rehoboam was A. *Mat.* 1. 7.

ABI-ALBON.
2 *Sam.* 23. 31. A. was one of David's mighty men

ABIATHAR.
1 *Sam.* 22. 20. A. escaped and fled to David
23. 6. when A. son of Ahimelech fled to David
9. David said to A. bring hither the ephod, 30. 7.
2 *Sam.* 8. 17. Zadok and A. were the priests, and Seraiah was the scribe, 20. 25. 1 *Kings* 4. 4.
1 *Kings* 2. 22. ask the kingdom for him and A.
27. so Solomon thrust out A. from being priest
Mark 2. 26. how went into house of G. in days of A.

ABIB.
Exod. 13. 4. ye came out in the month A. 34. 18.
23. 15. thou shalt keep the feast of unleavened bread in the month A. 34. 18. *Deut.* 16. 1.

ABIDAN.
Num. 1. 11. of Benjamin, A. son of Gideoni, 2. 22.
7. 60. on the ninth day A. of Benjamin offered, 65.

ABIEZER.
Josh. 17. 2. there was a lot for the children of A.
Judg. 6. 34. and A. was gathered after him
8. 2. is it not better than the vintage of A.
2 *Sam.* 23. 27. A. was one of David's mighty men

ABI-EZRITE.
Judg. 6. 11. an oak that pertained to Joash the A.

ABIGAIL.
1 *Sam.* 25. 3. the name of Nabal's wife was A.
27. 3. David dwelt at Gath with his two wives, Ahinoam and A. 30. 5. 2 *Sam.* 2. 2.
1 *Chron.* 2. 16. whose sisters were Zeruiah and A.

ABIHAIL.
2 *Chr.* 11. 18. Rehoboam took A. daughter of Eliab
Esth. 2. 15. turn of Esther the daughter of A. 9. 29.

ABIHU.
Exod. 6. 23. Aaron's sons Nadab and A. 28. 1. *Lev.* 10. 1. *Num.* 3. 2. | 26. 60. 1 *Chron.* 6. 3. | 24. 1.
24. 1. come up, A. ‖ 9. then A. went up
Num. 3. 4. A. died before the Lord, 26. 61.

ABIJAH, ABIJAM.
1 *Kings* 14. 1. A. the son of Jeroboam fell sick
31. A. the son of Rehoboam reigned, 15. 1, 7.
1 *Chron.* 24. 10. the eighth lot came forth to A.
2 *Chron.* 29. 1. Hezekiah's mother's name was A.
Neh. 10. 7. those that sealed were A. Mijamin
12. 1. went up with Zerub. A. ‖ 17. of A. Zichri

ABIMELECH.
Gen. 20. 2. A. king of Gerar sent and took Sarah
21. 22. A. and Phichol spake to Abraham, saying
26. 1. Isaac went to A. ‖ 16. A. said, go from us
Judg. 8. 31. Gideon's concubine bare him A.
9. 1. A. the son of Jerubbaal went to Shechem
2 *Sam.* 11. 21. who smote A. son of Jerubbesheth
1 *Chron.* 18. 16. Zadok and A. were the priests

ABINADAB.
1 *Sam.* 7. 1. brought the ark into the house of A.
16. 8. Jesse called A. made him pass before Samuel
17. 13. A. followed Saul to the battle
31. 2. Philistines slew A. son of Saul, 1 *Chr.* 10. 2.
2 *Sam.* 6. 3. they set the ark on new cart, and brought it out of the house of A. 1 *Chron.* 13. 7.
1 *Kings* 4. 11. A. had Solomon's daughter to wife

ABINOAM. *See* Barak

ABIRAM.
Num. 16. 1. Dathan and A. the sons of Eliab, 26. 9.
12. and Moses sent to call Dathan and A.
Deut. 11. 6. and what he did to Dathan and A.
1 *Kings* 16. 34. he laid the foundation in A.
Psal. 106. 17. the earth covered the company of A.

ABISHAG.
1 *Kings* 1. 15. and A. ministered to king David
2. 22. and why dost thou ask A. for Adonijah?

ABISHAI.
1 *Sam.* 26. 6. A. said, I will go down with thee
2 *Sam.* 2. 18. and there were three sons of Zeruiah there, Joab, A. and Asahel, 1 *Chron.* 2. 16.
10. 14. the Ammonites fled also before A.
18. 12. the king charged thee, and A. and Ittai
21. 17. A. succoured him, and smote the Philistine
23. 18. A. was chief among three, 1 *Chron.* 11. 20.
1 *Chron.* 18. 12. A. slew of the Edomites 18,000.

ABIUD.
Mat. 1. 13. Zorobabel begat A. and A. beg. Eliakim

ABNER.
1 *Sam.* 14. 51. Ner father of A. was son of Abiel
17. 55. Saul said to A. whose son is this youth?
26. 7. but A. and the people lay round about him
14. David cried, answerest thou not, A.?
2 *Sam.* 2. 14. A. said, let young men play before us
3. 25. Jacob said, thou knowest A. the son of Ner
30. so Joab and Abishai his brother slew A.
32. they buried A. in Hebron, king wept at grave
33. the king said, died A. as a fool dieth?
37. that it was not of the king to slay A.
4. 1. when Saul's son heard that A. was dead
12. and buried Ish-bosheth's head in A. sepulchre
1 *Kings* 2. 5. thou knowest what Joab did to A.
1 *Chron.* 26. 28. all that A. had dedicated
27. 21. Jaasiel son of A. ruler of Benjamin

ABRAM, ABRAHAM.
Gen. 12. 1. Lord said to A. get out of thy country
10. A. went down into Egypt to sojourn there
13. 1. A. went up out of Egypt, he and his wife
12. A. dwelt in land of Canaan, and Lot in cities
18. A. came and dwelt in the plain of Mamre
14. 14. A. armed his trained servants, 318.
15. 1. fear not, A. I am thy exceeding great reward
18. that day the Lord made a covenant with A.
17. 5. thy name shall be A. 1 *Chr.* 1. 27. *Neh.* 9. 7.
18. 6. A. hastened into the tent unto Sarah
17. shall I hide from A. that thing which I do
22. but A. stood yet before the Lord
20. 2. A. said of Sarah his wife, she is my sister
21. 33. and A. planted a grove in Beer-sheba
22. 1. God did tempt A. and said, take thy son
11. the angel called out of heaven, and said, A. A.
23. 2. Sarah died, and A. came to mourn for her
17. A. bought the field of Ephron, 49. 30. | 50. 13.
24. 1. the Lord had blessed A. in all things
2. A. said, put thy hand under my thigh
34. Eliezer said, I am A. servant
42. O L. God of my master A. prosper my way
59. they sent away Rebekah and A. servant
25. 5. and A. gave all that he had unto Isaac
7. these are the days of the years of A. life
12. Ishmael, whom Hagar the Egyptian bare to A.
26. 1. besides famine that was in the days of A.
5. because A. obeyed my voice, kept my charge
24. I will multiply thy seed for A. sake
28. 4. and God give thee the blessing of A.
31. 42. except the God of A. had been with me
50. 24. bring to land which he sware to A. *Exod.* 33. 1. *Num.* 32. 11. *Deut.* 1. 8. | 6. 10. | 30. 20.
Exod. 3. 6. I am the God of A. 15, 16. | 4. 5. *Mat.* 22. 32. *Mark* 12. 26. *Luke* 20. 37. *Acts* 3. 13. | 7. 32.
32. 13. remember A. Isaac, and Israel, *Deut.* 9. 27.
Psal. 47. 9. even the people of the God of A.
105. 9. which covenant he made with A.
42. he remembered his promise, and A. his servant
Isa. 29. 22. thus saith the Lord, who redeemed A.
63. 16. art our father, though A. be ignorant of us
Ezek. 33. 24. A. was one, and he inherited the land
Mic. 7. 20. thou wilt perform the mercy to A.
Mat. 1. 1. Christ the son of David, the son of A.

Mat. 3. 9. G. able to raise up child. unto A. *Luke* 3. 8.
8. 11. shall sit down with A. in kingdom of heaven
Luke 3. 34. which was the son of A. son of Thara
13. 28. when ye shall see A. in the kingdom of God
16. 23. he lift up his eyes, and seeth A. afar off
19. 9. forasmuch as he also is the son of A.
John 8. 40. this did not A. ‖ 52. A. is dead
57. hast thou seen A.? ‖ 58. before A. was, I am
Acts 13. 26. children of the stock of A. word is sent
Rom. 4. 2. for if A. were justified by works, he hath
3. A. believed God, and it was counted to him
for righteousness, 9. *Gal.* 3. 6. *Jam.* 2. 23.
Gal. 3. 7. who are of faith are the children of A.
8. preached before the gospel to A. in thee shall
9. they of faith are blessed with faithful A.
18. God gave the inheritance to A. by promise
4. 22. A. had two sons, the one by a bond-maid
Heb. 6. 13. for when God made promise to A.
7. 1. who met A. returning from the slaughter
9. as I may so say, Levi paid tithes in A.
11. 8. A. obeyed ‖ 17. by faith A. offered up Isaac

ABRAHAM with *father*.

Gen. 26. 3. I will perform the oath to A. thy *father*
24. I am the God of A. thy *father*, 28. 13.
32. 9. O God of my *father* A. and God of Isaac
Josh. 24. 3. I took your *father* A. from the other side
Isa. 51. 2. look to A. your *father* and to Sarah
Mat. 3. 9. we have A. to our *father*, *Luke* 3. 8.
Luke 1. 73. the oath which he sware to our *father* A.
16. 24. he said, *father* A. have mercy on me
30. nay, *father* A. but if one went from the dead
John 8. 39. they said to him, A. is our *father*
53. art thou greater than our *father* A.?
56. your *father* A. rejoiced to see my day, was glad
Acts 7. 2. the God of glory appeared to our *father* A.
Rom. 4. 1. what say that A. our *father* hath found
12. in the steps of that faith of our *father* A.
16. the faith of A. who is the *father* of us all
Jam. 2. 21. was not A. our *father* justified by works?

ABRAHAM joined with *seed*.

2 *Chron.* 20. 7. and gavest it to *seed* of A. thy friend
Psal. 105. 6. O ye *seed* of A. his servant
Isa. 41. 8. thou Israel, the *seed* of A. my friend
Jer. 33. 26. to be rulers over the *seed* of A. Isaac
Luke 1. 55. as he spake to A. and his *seed* for ever
John 8. 33. we be A. *seed* and were never in bondage
37. I know ye are A. *seed* but ye seek to kill me
Rom. 4. 13. the promise was not to A. or to his *seed*
9. 7. neither because they are the *seed* of A.
11. 1. I also am of the *seed* of A. 2 *Cor.* 11. 22.
Gal. 3. 16. to A. and his *seed* were the promises made
29. if ye be Christ's, then are ye A. *seed* and heirs
Heb. 2. 16. he took on him the *seed* of A.

ABSALOM.

2 *Sam.* 3. 3. A. the son of Maacah, 1 *Chron.* 3. 2.
13. 22. A. spake to Amnon neither good nor bad
23. A. had sheep-shearers in Baal-hazor
30. saying, A. hath slain all the king's sons
39. the soul of king Dav. longed to go forth to A.
14. 23. so Joab arose and brought A. to Jerusalem
25. there was none to be so much praised as A.
15. 4. A. said, O that I were made a judge in land
6. so A. stole the hearts of the men of Israel
31. Ahithophel is among the conspirators with A.
16. 22. A. went in unto his father's concubines
17. 4. Ahithophel's counsel pleased A. well
14. that the Lord might bring evil upon A.
20. and when A. servants came to the woman
24. A. passed over Jordan ‖ 26. pitched in Gilead
18. 5. saying, deal gently for my sake with A.
10. behold, I saw A. hanged in an oak
14. he thrust three darts through the heart of A.
18. and it is called unto this day A. place
29. is young man A. safe? 32. ‖ 33. O my son A.
19. 6. if A. had lived, and all we had died this day
1 *Kings* 2. 7. when I fled because of A. thy brother
28. he turned after Adonijah, though not after A.
2 *Chron.* 11. 20. he took Maachah daughter of A.

ACCHO.

Judg. 1. 31. nor did Asher drive out inhabitants of A.

ACHAIA.

Acts 18. 12. when Gallio was the deputy of A.
27. Apollos was disposed to pass into A.
Rom. 15. 26. it pleased them of A. to make contrib.
16. 5. salute Epenetus, the first-fruits of A.
1 *Cor.* 16. 15. house of Stephanas, first-fruits of A.
2 *Cor.* 9. 2. that A. was ready a year ago
11. 10. no man shall stop me in the regions of A.
1 *Thess.* 1. 7. ye were ensamples to all in A.
8. from you the word sounded not only in A.

ACHAICUS.

1 *Cor.* 16. 17. I am glad of the coming of A.

ACHAN, *or* ACHAR.

Josh. 7. 18. A. of the tribe of Judah was taken
22. 20. did not A. son of Zerah commit a trespass
1 *Chr.* 2. 7. A. the troubler of Isr. who transgressed

ACHIM.

Mat. 1. 14. Sadoc begat A. and A. begat Eliud

ACHISH.

1 *Sam.* 21. 10. David fled and went to A. 27. 2.
12. was afraid of A. ‖ 27. 6. A. gave him Ziklag
29. 2. David passed on in the rereward with A.
9. A. said, I know thou art good in my sight
1 *Kings* 2. 40. and Shimei went to Gath to A.

ACHMETHA.

Ezra 6. 2. there was found at A. a roll

ACHOR.

Josh. 7. 26. was called the valley of A. to this day
Isa. 65. 10. the valley of A. a place for herds
Hos. 2. 15. give the valley of A. for a door of hope

ACHSAH.

Josh. 15. 16. to him I will give A. to wife, *Judg.* 1. 12.

ACHSHAPH.

Josh. 11. 1. king Jabin sent to the king of A.
12. 20. king of A. one ‖ 19. 25. their border A.

ACHZIB.

Josh. 19. 29. Asher's lot from the coast to A.
Mic. 1. 14. the houses of A. shall be a lie to Israel

ADAM.

Gen. 2. † 15. G. took A. and put him in the garden
20. A. gave names to all cattle and fowl of the air
5. 2. he blessed them, and called their name A.
Deut. 32. 8. when he separated the sons of A.
Job 31. 33. if I covered my transgressions as A.
Rom. 5. 14. death reigned from A. to Moses
1 *Cor.* 15. 22. for as in A. all die, even so shall
45. first man A. the last A. a quickening spirit
1 *Tim.* 2. 13. for A. was first formed, then Eve
14. and A. was not deceived, but the woman
Jude 14. Enoch the seventh from A. prophesied

ADAM.

Josh. 3. 16. the city A. that is beside Zaretan

ADAR.

Ezra 6. 15. this house was finished on third day of A.
Esth. 3. 7. they cast lot till the twelfth month A.
13. kill on 13th day of month A. 8. 12. ‖ 9. 1, 17.
9. 15. the Jews gathered on the 14th day of A.
19. Jews made 14th day of A. a day of gladness
21. to keep the 14th and 15th days of A. yearly

ADDI.

Luke 3. 28. which was the son of A. son of Cosam

ADMAH.

Gen. 14. 2. these made war with Shinab king of A.
Deut. 29. 23. like the overthrow of A. and Zeboim
Hos. 11. 8. how shall I make thee as A.!

ADONI-BEZEK.

Judg. 1. 5. and they found A. in Bezek and fought

ADONIJAH.

2 *Sam.* 3. 4. A. the son of Haggith, 1 *Chron.* 3. 2.
1 *Kings* 1. 5. then A. exalted himself, saying
11. hast thou not heard that A. doth reign?
24. God save king A. ‖ 50. A. feared, 51.
2. 21. she said, let Abishag be given to A. to wife
25. A. shall be put to death this day
28. Joab had turned after A. tho' not after Absal.
2 *Chr.* 17. 8. sent Levites to teach, A. and Tobijah
Neh. 10. 16. chief of the people sealed, A. and Adin

ADONIKAM.

Ezra 2. 13. the children of A. 666, *Neh.* 7. 18.

ADRAMMELECH.

2 *Kings* 17. 31. Sepharvites burnt children to A.
19. 37. A. and Sharezer smote him, *Isa.* 37. 38.

ADRAMYTTIUM.

Acts 27. 2. entering into a ship of A. we launched

ADRIA.

Acts 27. 27. as we were driven up and down in A.

ADULLAM.

1 *Sam.* 22. 1. David therefore departed thence, and
escaped to the cave A. 1 *Chron.* 11. 15.
2 *Sam.* 23. 13. three of the thirty came to Dav. to A.
Mic. 1. 15. he shall come to A. the glory of Israel

AGABUS.

Acts 11. 28. there stood up one of them, named A.
21. 10. there came down a prophet named A.

AGAG.

Num. 24. 7. his king shall be higher than A.
1 *Sam.* 15. 9. but Saul and the people spared A.
33. Samuel hewed A. in pieces before the Lord

AGAGITE. *See* HAMAN.

AGAR.

Gal. 4. 24. one gendereth to bondage, which is A.
25. for this A. is mount Sinai in Arabia

AGRIPPA.

Acts 25. 13. A. and Bernice came to Cesarea
22. A. said, I would also hear the man myself
26. and specially before thee, O king A.
26. 7. for which hope's sake, king A. I am accused
27. king A. believest thou the prophets?
28. A. said, almost thou persuadest me to be Chris.

AGUR.

Prov. 30. 1. the words of A. the son of Jakeh

AHAB.

1 *Kings* 16. 30. A. did evil above all before him
33. A. did more to provoke Lord than all kings
18. 1. Lord said to Elijah, go shew thyself to A.
6. A. went one way, and Obadiah went another
9. deliver me into the hand of A. to slay me
42. so A. went up to eat and to drink
46. Elijah ran before A. to the entrance of Jezreel
20. 13. behold there came a prophet to A.
21. 4. A. came to his house heavy and displeased
21. I will cut off from A. him that pisseth
25. there was none like A. who did sell himself
29. seest thou how A. humbleth himself before me
22. 20. who shall persuade A. that he may go
up and fall at Ramoth-Gilead? 2 *Chron.*
18. 19.
40. so A. slept with his fathers, Ahaziah reigned
2 *Kings* 1. 1. Moab rebelled after death of A. 3. 5.
8. 18. Jehoram walked as did the house of A. for
the daughter of A. was his wife, 27.
9. 7. thou shalt smite the house of A. thy master
8. for the whole house of A. shall perish
25. when I and thou rode after A. his father
10. 11. Jehu slew all that remained of A. in Jezreel
21. 3. Manasseh did as A. king of Israel
13. I will stretch the plummet of house of A.
2 *Chr.* 21. 13. like the whoredoms of the house of A.
Jer. 29. 21. saith the Lord of A. son of Kolaiah
22. a curse, saying, the Lord make thee like A.
Mic. 6. 16. the works of the house of A. are kept

AHASUERUS.

Ezra 4. 6. in the reign of A. wrote they to him
Esth. 1. 1. this is A. which reigned from India to
2. 16. so Esther was taken unto king A.
21. and sought to lay hand on the king A. 6. 2.
3. 12. in the name of A. was it written, 8. 10.
8. 1. A. gave to Esther the house of Haman
10. 3. Mordecai the Jew was next to king A.
Dan. 9. 1. in the first year of Darius son of A.

AHAVAH.

Ezra 8. 15. gathered to the river that runneth to A.
21. a fast at A. ‖ 31. then we departed from A.

AHAZ.

2 *Kings* 16. 2. A. was twenty years old when he began
to reign, did not what was right, 2 *Chron.* 28. 1.
11. Urijah made the altar against A. came
20. 11. had gone down in the dial of A. *Isa.* 38. 8.
23. 12. the altars of A. did Josiah beat down
1 *Chron.* 8. 35. the sons of Micah, Pithon, A. 9. 41.
2 *Ch.* 28. 19. Lord brought Judah low, because of A.
22. this is that king A. ‖ 24. A. gathered vessels
Isa. 1. 1. the vision in days of A. *Hos.* 1. 1. *Mic.* 1. 1.
7. 3. go forth to meet A. ‖ 10. the Lord spake to A.

AHAZIAH.

1 *Kings* 22. 40. A. reigned in his stead, 2 *Kings* 8. 24.
2 *Kings* 1. 2. A. fell through a lattice and was sick
8. 29. A. king of Judah went down to see Joram
9. 23. Joram said to A. there is treachery, O A.
27. A. fled, and Jehu followed after him
10. 13. they answered, we are the brethren of A.
2 *Chron.* 20. 35. Jehoshaphat did join with A.
22. 7. the destruction of A. was of God
9. house of A. had no power to keep the kingdom

AHIAH.

1 *Sam.* 14. 3. A. son of Ahitub, the Lord's priest
18. Saul said to A. bring hither the ark of God
1 *Kings* 4. 3. Elihoreph and A. were scribes

AHIJAH.

1 *Kings* 11. 29. the prophet A. found Jeroboam
12. 15. that he might perform his saying, which
the Lord spake by A. 2 *Chron.* 10. 15.
14. 2. there is A. that told me I should be king
4. Jeroboam's wife came to the house of A.
6. it was so, when A. heard the sound of her feet
15. 27. Baasha son of A. conspired against him
1 *Chron.* 2. 25. the sons of Jerahmeel, Hezron, A.
11. 36. David's valiant men, A. the Pelonite
26. 20. over treasury of Levites A. over treasures
2 *Chr.* 9. 29. the acts of Solomon in prophecy of A.
Neh. 10. 26. the Levites that sealed the covenant, A.

AHIKAM.

2 *Kings* 22. 12. Josiah commanded A. the son of
Shaphan to inquire of the Lord, 2 *Chr.* 34. 20.
25. 22. he made Gedaliah the son of A. ruler
Jer. 26. 24. the hand of A. was with Jeremiah
40. 6. Jeremiah went to Gedaliah the son of A.
See GEDALIAH.

AHIMAAZ.

1 *Sam.* 14. 50. Saul's wife was the daughter of A.
2 *Sam.* 17. 17. Jonathan and A. staid by En-rogel
18. 27. is like the running of A. son of Zadok
1 *Kings* 4. 15. A. was in Naphtali, he took Basmath
1 *Chron.* 6. 8. Ahitub begat Zadok, and Zadok A.

AHIMAN.

Num. 13. 22. A. was of the children of Anak
Judg. 1. 10. Judah slew A. ‖ 1 *Chr.* 9. 17. porters, A.

AHIMELECH.

1 *Sam.* 21. 1. A. was afraid at the meeting of David
22. 9. I saw the son of Jesse coming to A.
16. the king said, thou shalt surely die, A.
26. 6. Dav. said to A. who will go down with me?
2 *Sam.* 8. 17. Zadok and A. priests, 1 *Chron.* 18. 16.
1 *Chron.* 24. 3. A. of the sons of Ithamar according
6. Shemaiah the scribe wrote them before A.
31. these cast lots in the presence of David and A.

AHINOAM.

1 *Sam.* 14. 50. the name of Saul's wife was A.
25. 43. David also took A. of Jezreel his wife
See ABIGAIL.

AHIO.

2 *Sam.* 6. 3. Uzzah and A. drave the cart. 1 *Chr.* 13. 7.

AHISAMACH.

Exod. 35. 34. both he and the son of A. may teach

AHITHOPHEL.

2 *Sam.* 15. 12. Absalom sent for A. the Gilonite
31. Lord, turn the counsel of A. into foolishness
34. then mayest thou defeat the counsel of A.
16. 15. Absalom came to Jerusal. and A. with him
23. the counsel of A. was as if a man inquired
17. 7. the counsel of A. is not good at this time
15. thus and thus did A. counsel Absalom
23. A. saw that his counsel was not followed
1 *Chron.* 27. 33. A. was the king's counsellor

AHITUB.

1 *Sam.* 22. 12. Saul said, hear now, thou son of A.
2 *Sam.* 8. 17. Zadok the son of A. 1 *Chron.* 18. 16.

AHOLAH, AHOLIBAH.

Ezek. 23. 4. Samaria is A. Jerusalem Aholibah
36. son of man, wilt thou judge A. and Aholibah?

AHOLIAB.

Exod. 36. 1. then wrought Bezaleel and A.

AHOLIBAMAH.

Gen. 36. 2. Esau took to wife A. ‖ 5. A. bare Jeush

AI, or HAI.

Gen. 13. 3. Abram dwelt between Beth-el and A.
Josh. 7. 4. and they fled before the men of A.
8. 1. go up to A. ‖ 10. 2. Gibeon was greater than A.
Ezra 2. 28. the men of Beth-el and A. *Neh.* 7. 32.
Jer. 49. 3. howl, O Heshbon, for A. is spoiled

AIATH.

Isa. 10. 28. he is come to A. he is passed to Migron

AJALON.

Josh. 10. 12. stand, thou moon, in the valley of A.

ALEXANDER.

Mark 15. 21. Simon the father of A. and Rufus
Acts 4. 6. Annas, Caiaphas, A. were gathered
19. 33. they drew A. out of the multitude
1 *Tim.* 1. 20. of whom is Hymeneus and A.
2 *Tim.* 4. 14. A. the copper-smith did me much evil

ALEXANDRIA, ANS.

Acts 6. 9. the synagogue of the Libertines and A.
18. 24. a certain Jew named Apollos, born at A.
27. 6. centurion found a ship of A. sailing into Italy

ALPHEUS.

Mat. 10. 3. the names of the apostles, James the son
of A. *Mark* 3. 18. *Luke* 6. 15. *Acts* 1. 13.
Mark 2. 14. he saw Levi the son of A. sitting at

AMALEK.

Gen. 36. 12. Timna bare to Eliphaz Esau's son A.
Exod. 17. 8. then came A. and fought with Israel
14. I will utterly put out the remembrance of A.
16. Lord hath sworn he will have war with A.
Num. 24. 20. when he looked on A. he took up his
parable and said A. was the first of the nations
Deut. 25. 17. remember what A. did, 1 *Sam.* 15. 2.
19. thou shalt blot out the remembrance of A.
Judg. 5. 14. out of Ephraim was a root against A.
1 *Sam.* 15. 3. smite A. ‖ 5. Saul came to a city of A.
28. 18. thou didst not execute his wrath on A.
Psal. 83. 7. Gebal, Ammon, A. are confederate

AMALEKITE, S.

Num. 14. 45. the A. came down and smote Israel
Judg. 6. 3. when Israel had sown the A. came against
7. 12. Midianites and A. lay like grasshoppers
10. 12. the A. did oppress you, and ye cried to me

1 *Sam.* 14. 48. Saul smote the A. 15. 7.
15. 6. Saul said to Kenites, get you from among A.
20. yea, I have utterly destroyed the A.
27. 8. David and his men invaded the A.
30. 1. the A. had invaded the south and Ziklag
2 *Sam.* 1. 1. David returned from the slaughter of A.
8. and I answered him, I am an A. 13.
1 *Chron.* 4. 43. they smote the rest of the A.

AMANA.

Cant. 4. 8. look from the top of A. from Shenir

AMASA.

2 *Sam.* 17. 25. Absalom made A. captain of the host, which A. was the son of Ithra an Israelite
20. 9. Joab took A. by the beard to kiss him
12. A. wallowed in blood in the high-way
1 *Kings* 2. 5. thou knowest what Joab did to A. 32.
1 *Chr.* 2. 17. Abigail bare A. the father was Jether
2 *Chr.* 28. 12. A. son of Hadlai stood up against them

AMAZIAH.

2 *Kings* 12. 21. A. his son reigned, 2 *Chron.* 24. 27.
13. 12. wherewith he fought against A. 14. 15.
14. 11. but A. would not hear, therefore Jehoash
15. 3. as his father A. had done, 2 *Chron.* 26. 4.
1 *Chron.* 6. 45. of Merari, A. the son of Hilkiah
2 *Chron.* 25. 27. after A. did turn from the Lord
Amos 7. 10. A. priest of Beth-el, sent to Jeroboam

AMMAH.

2 *Sam.* 2. 24. when they were come to the hill A.

AMMI.

Hos. 2. 1. say ye unto your brethren, A. and sisters

AMMINADAB.

Exod. 6. 23. Aaron took Elisheba daughter of A.
Ruth 4. 20. and A. begat Nahshon, *Mat.* 1. 4.

AMMI-NADIB.

Cant. 6. 12. my soul made me like the chariots of A.

AMMON.

Gen. 19. 38. Ben-ammi, father of children of A.
Judg. 10. 11. did not I deliver you from A.?
11. 4. the children of A. made war against Israel
15. Israel took not the land of the children of A.
33. thus the children of A. were subdued
2 *Sam.* 10. 11. if the children of A. be too strong for thee, I will help thee, 1 *Chron.* 19. 12.
14. children of A. saw that the Syrians fled
12. 9. hast slain Uriah with sword of children of A.
31. thus did he to all children of A. 1 *Chr.* 20. 3.
1 *Kings* 11. 7. built an high place for Molech the abomination of the children of A. 2 *Kings* 23. 13.
33. Milcom the god of the children of A.
Neh. 13. 23. Jews that had married wives of A.
Psal. 83. 7. Gebal and A. confederate against thee
Isa. 11. 14. the children of A. shall obey them
Jer. 9. 26. I will punish the children of A.
25. 21. I made children of A. to drink of the cup
49. 6. I will bring again the captivity of A.
Dan. 11. 41. these shall escape, the chief of A.
Zeph. 2. 9. children of A. shall be as Gomorrah

AMMONITE, S.

Deut. 23. 3. A. not enter into congregat. *Neh.* 13. 1.
1 *Sam.* 11. 11. slew the A. till the heat of the day
1 *Kings* 11. 1. king Solomon loved women of the A.
2 *Chron.* 26. 8. and the A. gave gifts to Uzziah
Ezra 9. 1. do according to the abomination of A.
Jer. 27. 3. make yokes, and send to the king of A.
49. 2. an alarm of war to be heard in Rabbah of A.
Ezek. 25. 5. make A. a couching-place for flocks
10. that the A. may not be remembered

AMNON.

2 *Sam.* 3. 2. David's first-born was A. 1 *Chr.* 3. 1.
13. 2. A. vexed, fell sick for his sister Tamar
26. I pray thee, let my brother A. go with us
28. when I say, smite A. then kill him, fear not
1 *Chron.* 4. 20. the sons of Shimon, A. Rinnah

AMON.

1 *Kings* 22. 26. carry him back to A. 2 *Chr.* 18. 25.
2 *Kings* 21. 18. A. reigned ‖ 23. his servants slew A.
2 *Chron.* 33. 22. A. sacrificed to carved images
Neh. 7. 59. came out of captivity children of A.
Mat. 1. 10. Manasses begat A. and A. begat Josias

AMORITE, S.

Gen. 15. 16. the iniquity of the A. is not yet full
48. 22. which I took from A. with my sword
Deut. 20. 17. thou shalt utterly destroy the A.
Josh. 3. 10. God will without fail drive out the A.
10. 12. in the day when the Lord delivered up A.
24. 15. or gods of A. in whose land ye dwell
Judg. 6. 10. I said, fear not the gods of the A.
11. 23. the Lord God hath dispossessed the A.
1 *Sam.* 7. 14. was peace between Israel and the A.
2 *Sam.* 21. 2. the Gibeonites were of the A.
1 *Kings* 21. 26. Ahab did abominably as did the A.
2 *Kings* 21. 11. Manasseh did above all the A. did
Ezek. 16. 3. thy father an A. mother an Hittite, 45.
Amos 2. 9. yet destroyed I the A. before them

AMOS, *or* AMOZ.

2 *Kings* 19. 2. Isaiah the son of A. 20. | 20. 1. 2 *Chron.* 26. 22. | 32. 20, 32. *Isa.* 1. 1. | 2. 1. | 13. 1. | 20. 2. | 37. 2, 21. | 38. 1.
Amos 7. 14. then A. said, I was no prophet
Luke 3. 25. Mattathias, which was the son of A.

AMPHIPOLIS.

Acts 17. 1. now when they had passed through A.

AMPLIAS.

Rom. 16. 8. greet A. my beloved in the Lord

AMRAM.

Exod. 6. 18. the sons of Kohath, A. *Num.* 3. 19.
1 *Chron.* 1. 41. the sons of Dishon, A. and Eshban
6. 3. the children of A. Aaron, Moses, and Miriam
Ezra 10. 34. of the sons of Bani, Maadi, A.

ANAH.

Gen. 36. 24. this was that A. that found mules

ANAK.

Num. 13. 28. the cities are great, and moreover we saw the children of A. there, 33.
Deut. 9. 2. who can stand before the children of A.?
Josh. 15. 14. Caleb drove thence the three sons of A. Sheshai, Ahiman, and Talmai, *Judg.* 1. 20.

ANAKIMS.

Deut. 2. 10. the people great and tall as the A. 9. 2.
Josh. 11. 22. none of the A. were left but in Gaza
14. 15. which Arba was a great man among the A.

ANAMMELECH.

2 *Kin.* 17. 31. Adrammelech, A. gods of Sepharvaim

ANANIAS.

Acts 5. 5. A. hearing these words fell down
9. 12. he hath seen in a vision A. coming; 22. 12.
23. 2. the high priest A. commanded to smite
24. 1. A. the priest descended with the elders

ANATHOTH.

Josh. 21. 18. out of Benjamin, A. with her suburbs, Almon with her suburbs, 1 *Chron.* 6. 60.
1 *Kings* 2. 26. get thee to A. to thine own fields
1 *Chron.* 7. 8. the sons of Becher A. and Alameth
Neh. 10. 19. A. and Nebai sealed the covenant
Isa. 10. 30. lift up thy voice, O poor A.
Jer. 11. 23. I will bring evil on the men of A.
29. 27. why hast thou not reproved Jeremiah of A.
32. 7. saying, buy my field that is in A. 8.

ANDREW.

Mark 1. 29. they entered into the house of A.
13. 3. James, John, and A. asked him privately
John 1. 40. one of the two which heard was A.
44. Philip was of Bethsaida the city of A.
12. 22. Philip telleth A. and A. told Jesus
Acts 1. 13. where abode Peter, John, James, and A.

ANDRONICUS.

Rom. 16. 7. salute A. and Junia my kinsmen

ANER.

Gen. 14. 24. A. Eshcol, let them take their portion
1 *Chron.* 6. 70. out of the half tribe of Manasseh, A.

ANNA.

Luke 2. 36. was A. a prophetess daughter of Phanuel

ANNAS.

Luke 3. 2. A. and Caiaphas being high priests
John 18. 13. A. was father-in-law to Caiaphas
24. A. had sent Jesus bound to Caiaphas

ANTICHRIST, S.

1 *John* 2 18. A. will come, now there are many A.
22. he is A. that denieth the Father and Son
4. 3. this is that spirit of A. whereof ye heard
2 *John* 7. this is a deceiver and an A.

ANTIOCH.

Acts 11. 19. they travelled as far as A. 22.
20. some when come to A. spake to the Grecians
26. the disciples were called Christians first in A.
13. 14. they came to A. in Pisidia and taught
14. 26. and from Attalia they sailed to A.
15. 22. to send men of their own company to A.
35. Paul also and Barnabas continued in A.
Gal. 2. 11. when Peter was come to A. I withstood
2 *Tim.* 3. 11. persecutions which came to me at A.

ANTIPAS. *See* Martyr.

ANTIPATRIS.

Acts 23. 31. the soldiers brought Paul by night to A.

APELLES.

Rom. 16. 10. salute A. approved in Christ

APHEK.

1 *Sam.* 4. 1. the Philistines pitched in A. 29. 1.
1 *Kings* 20. 30. the rest fled to A. there a wall fell
2 *Kings* 13. 17. thou shalt smite the Syrians in A.

APOLLONIA.

Acts 17. 1. more when they had passed through A.

APOLLOS.

Acts 18. 24. certain Jew named A. came to Ephesus
1 *Cor.* 1. 12. I am of A. 3. 4. ‖ 3. 5. who is A.?
3. 6. I have planted, A. watered, God gave increase
4. 6. I have in a figure transferred to A.
Tit. 3. 13. bring Zenas and A. on their journey

APOLLYON.

Rev. 9. 11. in the Greek tongue, his name is A.

APPII-FORUM.

Acts 28. 15. they came to meet us as far as A.

AQUILA.

Acts 18. 2. Paul found a certain Jew named A.
26. when A. and Priscilla heard Apollos
Rom. 16. 3. greet A. and Priscilla, 2 *Tim.* 4. 19.
1 *Cor.* 16. 19. A. and Priscilla salute you in the Lord

AR.

Num. 21. 28. the fire hath consumed A. of Moab
Deut. 2. 9. I have given A. to the children of Lot
Isa. 15. 1. in the night A. of Moab is laid waste

ARABIA.

1 *Kings* 10. 15. besides what Solomon had of merchant-men and of kings of A. 2 *Chron.* 9. 14.
Isa. 21. 13. the burden upon A. shall lodge A.
Jer. 25. 24. give the cup to all the kings of A.
Gal. 1. 17. I went into A. and returned to Damascus
4. 25. for this Agar is mount Sinai in A.

ARABIAN, S.

2 *Chron.* 17. 11. the A. brought Jehoshaphat flocks
26. 7. God helped Uzziah against the A.
Isa. 13. 20. nor shall the A. pitch tent there
Jer. 3. 2. thou sattest for them as A. in wilderness
Acts 2. 11. Cretes and A. we do hear them speak

ARAM.

Gen. 10. 22. the sons of Shem, Lud, A. 1 *Chron.* 1. 17.
Num. 23. 7. Balak king of Moab brought me from A.
Mat. 1. 3. Esrom begat A. ‖ 4. A. begat Aminadab
Luke 3. 33. Aminadab which was the son of A.
See Padan.

ARARAT.

Gen. 8. 4. the ark rested on the mountains of A.
Jer. 51. 27. call against her the kingdoms of A.

ARAUNAH.

2 *Sam.* 24. 16. angel was by the threshing-place of A.
23. all these did A. as a king give to David

ARBA.

Josh. 14. 15. A. was a great man among the Anakims

ARBA.

Josh. 21. 11. gave them A. which city is Hebron

ARCHELAUS.

Mat. 2. 22. when Joseph heard that A. did reign

ARCHIPPUS.

Col. 4. 17. say to A. take heed to the ministry
Philem. 2. Paul to A. fellow-soldier and the church

ARCTURUS.

Job 9. 9. which maketh A. Orion, and Pleiades
38. 32. or canst thou guide A. with his sons?

AREOPAGITE.

Acts 17. 34. among which was Dionysius the A.

AREOPAGUS.

Acts 17. 19. they took Paul, and brought him to A.

ARETAS.

2 *Cor.* 11. 32. the governor under A. the king

ARGOB.

Deut. 3. 4. all the region of A. 13, 14. 1 *Kings* 4. 13.

ARIEL.

Ezra 8. 16. I sent for Eliezer and A. chief men
Isa. 29. 1. woe to A. the city where David dwelt
2. I will distress A. it shall be to me as A.
7. multitude of the nations that fight against A.

ARIMATHEA.

Mat. 27. 57. Joseph of A. who was Jesus' disciple, *Mark* 15. 43. *Luke* 23. 51. *John* 19. 38.

ARIOCH.

Gen. 14. 1. in the days of A. king of Ellasar
Dan. 2. 25. then A. brought in Daniel before king

ARISTARCHUS.

Acts 19. 29. and having caught Gaius and A.
20. 4. A. accompanied Paul into Asia
27. 2. one A. a Macedonian being with us
Col. 4. 10. A. fellow-prisoner saluteth you, *Phile.* 24

ARISTOBULUS.

Rom. 16. 10. salute them that are of A. household

ARMAGEDDON.

Rev. 16. 16. he gathered them together to A.

ARMENIA.

2 *Kings* 19. 37. they escaped into land of A. *Isa.* 37. 38.

ARNON.

Num. 21. 14. what he did in the brooks of A.
22. 36. Balak met Balaam in the border of A.
Deut. 2. 24. rise up, and pass over the river A.
Judg. 11. 26. while Israel dwelt by the coasts of A.
Isa. 16. 2. daughters of Moab shall be at fords of A.
Jer. 48. 20. tell ye it in A. that Moab is spoiled

AROER.

Num. 32. 34. the children of Gad built A.
1 *Sam.* 30. 28. David sent a present to them in A.
2 *Sam.* 24. 5. passed over Jordan and pitched in A.
1 *Chron.* 5. 8. Bela, who dwelt in A. even to Nebo
Isa. 17. 2. the cities of A. are forsaken
Jer. 48. 19. O inhabitant of A. stand by the way

ARPAD, ARPHAD.

2 *Kings* 18. 34. where are the gods of A. *Isa.* 36. 19.
19. 13. where is the king of A.? *Isa.* 37. 13
Isa. 10. 9. for he saith, is not Hamath as A.?
Jer. 49. 23. Hamath is confounded and A.

ARPHAXAD.

Gen. 10. 22. the son of Shem, A. 11. 10. 1 *Chr.* 1. 17.
Luke 3. 36. Cainan, who was the son of A.

ARTAXERXES.

Ezra 4. 7. in the days of A. wrote Bishlam
6. 14. according to the commandment of A.
7. 1. in the reign of A. Ezra went up, 8. 1.
11. the copy of the letter that A. gave to Ezra
21. I, even I A. the king do make a decree
Neh. 2. 1. in 20th year of A. wine was before him
5. 14. was governor from 20th to 32d year of A.

ARTEMAS.

Tit. 3. 12. when I shall send A. to thee or Tychicus

ASA.

1 *Kings* 15. 11. A. did what was right, 2 *Chr.* 14. 2.
14. A. his heart was perfect, 2 *Chron.* 15. 17.
18. A. took the silver and gold, 2 *Chron.* 16. 2.
1 *Chron.* 9. 16. Berechiah the son of A. a Levite
2 *Chron.* 14. 11. A. cried to the Lord his God
15. 2. Azariah went out to meet A. and said
19. there was no war to the 35th year of A.
16. 10. A. was wroth with the seer, and put him in prison, A. oppressed some of the people
Jer. 41. 9. the pit was it which A. had made
Mat. 1. 7. Abia begat A. ‖ 8. A. begat Josaphat

ASAHEL.

2 *Sam.* 2. 18. sons of Zeruiah, Joab, A. 1 *Chr.* 2. 16.
21. A. would not turn aside from following Abner
32. they took up A. and buried him in Beth-lehem
3. 27. Abner died for the blood of A. his brother
23. 24. A. was one of the thirty, 1 *Chron.* 11. 26.
2 *Chron.* 17. 8. he sent Levites, Zebadiah, A.
31. 13. Jehiel, Nahath, and A. were overseers
Ezra 10. 15. son of A. was employed about this

ASAIAH.

1 *Chron.* 4. 36. Jeshohaiah and A. were princes
6. 30. the sons of Merari, Haggiah, A.
9. 5. of the Shilonites, A. the first-born
2 *Chron.* 34. 20. king Josiah sent A. to Huldah

ASAPH.

2 *Kings* 18. 18. Shebna the scribe and Joah the son of A. the recorder, 37. *Isa.* 36. 3, 22.
1 *Chr.* 6. 39. A. son of Berechiah, 9. 15 | 15. 17.
16. 7. David delivered first this psalm to A.
25. 1. of the sons of A. 2. | 26. 1. 2 *Chron.* 5. 12. | 20. 14. | 29. 13. | 35. 15. *Ezra* 2. 41. | 3. 10. *Neh.* 7. 44. | 11. 17, 22. | 12. 35.
9. the first lot came forth for A. to Joseph
2 *Chr.* 29. 30. the Levites to sing with words of A.
35. 15. according to the commandment of A.
Neh. 2. 8. a letter to A. keeper of the forest
12. 46. in the days of A. were songs of praise

ASENATH.

Gen. 41. 45. A. daughter of Poti-pherah, 50. | 46. 20.

ASHDOD.

1 *Sam.* 5. 1. the Philistines brought the ark to A.
6. the hand of the Lord was heavy on them of A.
2 *Chr.* 26. 6. Uzziah warred against Philistines and brake down wall of A. and built cities about A.
Neh. 13. 23. Jews that had married wives of A.
24. their children spake half in the speech of A.
Isa. 20. 1. Tartan came and fought against A.
Jer. 25. 20. I made remnant of A. drink of the cup
Amos 1. 8. I will cut off the inhabitant from A.
3. 9. publish in the palaces at A. and of Egypt
Zeph. 2. 4. they shall drive out A. at noon-day
Zech. 9. 6. and a bastard shall dwell in A.

ASHER.

Gen. 30. 13. and Leah called his name A.
35. 26. the sons of Zilpah, Leah's maid, Gad, A.
46. 17. the children of A. *Num.* 1. 40. | 26. 44. 1 *Chron.* 7. 30, 40. | 12. 36.
49. 20. out of A. his bread shall be fat and yield
Num. 1. 13. prince of A. was Pagiel, 2. 27. | 7. 72.
26. 46. the name of the daughter of A. was Sarah
Deut. 27. 13. these on Ebal to curse; Gad and A.
33. 24. of A. he said, let A. be blessed with children

Judg. 5. 17. A. continued on the sea shore and abode
6. 35. Gideon sent messengers to A. and Zebulun
7. 23. men out of A. pursued the Midianites
1 Kings 4. 16. Baanah the son of Hushai was in A.
1 Chron. 12. 36. of A. expert in war 40,000
2 Chron. 30. 11. divers of A. humbled themselves
Ezek. 48. 2. a portion for A. || 34. one gate of A.

Tribe of ASHER.

Num. 1. 41. numbered of the tribe of A. 41,500
2. 27. the tribe of A. shall encamp by Dan
10. 26. over the host of tribe of A. was Pagiel
13. 13. of the tribe of A. to spy the land, Shetur
34. 27. prince of the tribe of A. to divide, Ahihud
Josh. 19. 24. the fifth lot for the tribe of A.
31. this is the inheritance of the tribe of A.
21. 6. the children of Gershom had cities out of the tribe of A. 30. | 1 Chron. 6. 62, 74.
Luke 2. 36. Anna daughter of Phanuel of tribe of A.
Rev. 7. 6. of the tribe of A. were sealed 12,000

ASHTAROTH.

Deut. 1. 4. Og, who dwelt at A. Josh. 9. 10. | 12. 4.
Judg. 2. 13. the children of Israel served A. 10. 6.
1 Sam. 7. 3. put away the strange gods and A. 4.
12. 10. we have sinned because we have served A.
31. 10. they put Saul's armour in the house of A.
1 Kings 11. 33. have worshipped A. goddess of Zidon
1 Chr. 6. 71. to children of Gershom was given A.

ASHUR, or ASSUR.

Gen. 10. 11. A. went forth and built Nineveh
22. children of Shem, Elam and A. 1 Chr. 1. 17.
Num. 24. 22. till A. shall carry thee away captive
24. ships shall come from Chittim and afflict A.
1 Chron. 2. 24. Hezron's wife bare him A.
4. 5. A. had two wives, Helah and Naarah
Ezra 4. 2. Esar-haddon king of A. which brought up
Psal. 83. 8. A. also is joined with them
Ezek. 27. 23. A. and Chilmad were thy merchants
32. 22. A. is there, and all her company
Hos. 14. 3. A. shall not save us, we will not ride

ASIA.

Acts 6. 9. them of A. disputing with Stephen
16. 6. they were forbidden to preach the word in A.
19. 10. all they that dwelt in A. heard the word
27. whom all A. and the world worshippeth
31. certain of the chief of A. sent unto him
20. 16. because he would not spend time in A.
18. ye know from the first day that I came into A.
27. 2. we launched, meaning to sail by coasts of A.
1 Cor. 16. 19. the churches of A. salute you
2 Cor. 1. 8. our trouble which came to us in A.
2 Tim. 1. 15. they that are in A. are turned away
1 Pet. 1. 1. to the strangers scattered in A.
See CHURCHES.

ASKELON, or ASHKELON.

Judg. 1. 18. Judah took Gaza and A. and Ekron
14. 19. Sams. went down to A. and slew thirty men
1 Sam. 6. 17. for A. one, for Gath one, for Ekron one
2 Sam. 1. 20. publish it not in the streets of A.
Jer. 25. 20. I made A. and Azzah to drink of cup
47. 5. A. is cut off with remnant of their valley
7. the Lord hath given it a charge against A.
Amos 1. 8. cut off him that holds sceptre from A.
Zeph. 2. 4. Gaza shall be forsaken, A. a desolation
7. in the houses of A. shall they lie down
Zech. 9. 5. A. shall see it, and fear; king shall perish from Gaza, and A. shall not be inhabited

ASNAPPAR.

Ezra 4. 10. whom the noble A. brought over

ASSYRIA.

Gen. 2. 14. Hiddekel goeth toward the east of A.
25. 18. Ishmael's sons dwelt as thou goest to A.
2 Kings 15. 29. carried captive to A. 17. 6. | 18. 11.
Isa. 7. 18. hiss for the bee that is in the land of A.
11. 11. to recover remnant of his people from A.
16. an high-way for his people left from A.
19. 23. shall be an high-way out of Egypt to A.
24. Israel shall be the third with Egypt and A.
25. blessed be A. the work of my hands
27. 13. shall come who were ready to perish in A.
Jer. 2. 18. what hast thou to do in the way of A.?
36. ashamed of Egypt, as wast ashamed of A.
Ezek. 23. 7. committed whoredoms with men of A.
Hos. 7. 11. they go to A. || 8. 9. they are gone up to A.
9. 3. they shall eat unclean things in A.
10. 6. it shall be carried to A. for a present
11. 11. shall tremble as a dove out of land of A.
Mic. 5. 6. and they shall waste the land of A.
7. 12. in that day he shall come to thee from A.
Zeph. 2. 13. and he will destroy A. and Nineveh
Zech. 10. 10. I will gather them out of A.
11. the pride of A. shall be brought down
See KING, KINGS.

ASSYRIAN.

Isa. 10. 5. O A. the rod of mine anger, and staff
24. O my people, be not afraid of the A.
14. 25. that I will break the A. in my land
23. 13. this people was not till the A. founded
30. 31. the A. shall be beaten down which smote
31. 8. then shall the A. fall with the sword
52. 4. the A. oppressed them without cause
Ezek. 31. 3. behold, the A. was a cedar in Lebanon
Hos. 5. 13. then went Ephraim to the A. and sent
11. 5. but the A. shall be his king, they refused
Mic. 5. 5. this man shall be the peace when A. come
6. thus shall he deliver us from the A. when comes

ASSYRIANS.

2 Kings 19. 35. the angel of the Lord smote in the camp of A. 185,000 men, Isa. 37. 36.
Lam. 5. 6. we have given the hand to the A.
Ezek. 16. 28. thou hast played the whore with the A.
23. 5. she doted on the A. her neighbours, 12.
9. I have delivered her into the hand of the A.
23. I will bring all the A. against thee
Hos. 12. 1. they make a covenant with the A.

ASYNCRITUS.

Rom. 16. 14. salute A. Phlegon, Hermas, Patrobas

ATAD.

Gen. 50. 10. they came to the threshing-floor of A.
11. when inhabitants saw mourning in floor of A.

ATHALIAH.

2 Kings 8. 26. Ahaziah's mother was A. 2 Chr. 22. 2.
11. 1. A. destroyed the seed royal, 2 Chron. 22. 10.
2 Kings 11. 2. Jehosheba hid Joash fr. A. 2 Ch. 22. 11.
20. they slew A. with the sword, 2 Chron. 23. 21.
1 Chron. 8. 26. of Benjamin, Sheariah and A.
2 Chron. 24. 7. the sons of A. that wicked woman
Ezra 8. 7. Jeshaiah son of A. with him 70 males

ATHENIANS.

Acts 17. 21. A. spent their time in telling or hearing

ATHENS.

Acts 17. 15. they conducted and brought Paul to A.
16. now while Paul waited for them at A.
22. ye men of A. I perceive ye are superstitious
18. 1. Paul departed from A. and came to Corinth
1 Thess. 3. 1. we thought it good to be left at A. alone

ATTALIA.

Acts 14. 25. from Perga they went down into A.

AVEN.

Ezek. 30. 17. the young men of A. shall fall by sword
Hos. 10. 8. the high places of A. the sin of Israel
Amos 1. 5. I will cut off the inhabitant from A.

AUGUSTUS.

Luke 2. 1. there went out a decree from Cesar A.
Acts 25. 21. when Paul had appealed to A. 25.
27. 1. to one Julius, a centurion of A. band

AZARIAH.

1 Kings 4. 2. A. was one of Solomon's princes
5. A. the son of Nathan was over the officers
2 Kings 14. 21. the people of Judah made A. king
1 Chron. 2. 8. A. son of Ethan || 38. Jehu begat A.
3. 12. Amaziah his son, A. his son
6. 9. Ahimaaz begat A. || 10. Johanan begat A.
13. Hilkiah begat A. || 36. Zephaniah begat A.
2 Chron. 15. 1. Spirit of God came on A. son of Oded
21. 2. A. son of Jehoshaphat || 22. 6. of Jehoram
23. 1. A. son of Jehoram, and A. son of Obed
26. 17. A. the priest went in after him, 20.
Ezra 7. 1. the son of A. the son of Hilkiah, 3.
Neh. 3. 23. A. the son of Maaseiah repaired
7. 7. Nehemiah, A. came up with Zerubbabel
8. 7. A. caused the people to understand the law
10. 2. those that sealed were A. Jeremiah
Jer. 43. 2. A. and all the proud men spake, saying
Dan. 1. 6. of the children of Judah were Daniel, A.
7. he gave to A. the name of Abed-nego
2. 17. then Daniel made the thing known to A.

AZEKAH.

Josh. 10. 11. Lord cast down stones on them to A.
Jer. 34. 7. the king of Babylon fought against A.

B.

BAAL.

Num. 22. 41. brought Balaam to high places of B.
Judg. 2. 13. Israel served B. and Ashtaroth
6. 25. the Lord said, throw down the altar of B.
31. will ye plead for B.? will ye save him?
1 Kings 16. 31. Ahab served B. and worshipped him
18. 21. but if B. be God, then follow him
26. called on name of B. saying, O B. hear us
40. take the prophets of B. let none escape
19. 18. yet I have left seven thousand in Israel, knees which have not bowed to B. Rom. 11. 4.
2 Kings 10. 19. I have a great sacrifice to do to B.
20. Jehu said, proclaim a solemn assembly for B.
28. thus Jehu destroyed B. out of Israel
11. 18. the people brake down the house of B.
17. 16. they worshipped host of heaven, served B.
21. 3. Manasseh reared up altars for B. made grove
23. 4. to bring forth all the vessels made for B.
5. he put down them that burnt incense to B.
Jer. 2. 8. and the prophets prophesied by B.
7. 9. will ye burn incense to B.? 11. 13, 17. | 32. 29.
12. 16. as they taught my people to swear by B.
19. 5. they have built the high places of B. to burn their sons with fire for burnt-offerings to B.
23. 13. they prophesied in B. and caused Israel err
27. as their fathers have forgotten my name for B.
Hos. 2. 8. silver and gold which they prepared for B.
13. 1. but when Ephraim offended in B. he died
Zeph. 1. 4. and I will cut off the remnant of B.

BAAL-BERITH.

Judg. 8. 33. the children of Israel made B. their god

BAAL-HAMON.

Cant. 8. 11. Solomon had a vineyard at B.

BAALI.

Hos. 2. 16. and thou shalt call me no more B.

BAALIM.

Judg. 2. 11. Israel served B. 3. 7. | 10. 6, 10.
8. 33. the children of Israel went a whoring after B.
1 Sam. 7. 4. the children of Israel put away B.
1 Kings 18. 18. and thou hast followed B.
2 Chron. 17. 3. Jehoshaphat sought not to B.
24. 7. all the dedicated things did they bestow on B.
28. 2. Ahaz made also molten images for B.
33. 3. Manasseh reared up altars for B.
34. 4. and they brake down the altars of B.
Jer. 2. 23. how canst say, I have not gone after B.
9. 14. have walked after B. which fathers taught
Hos. 2. 13. I will visit on her the days of B.
17. for I will take away the names of B.

BAALIS.

Jer. 40. 14. B. king of Ammonites hath sent Ishmael

BAAL-MEON.

Ezek. 25. 9. the glory of Beth-jeshimoth, B.

BAAL-PEOR.

Num. 25. 3. Israel joined himself to B. and the anger of the Lord was kindled, Psal. 106. 28. Hos. 9. 10.
5. slay the men that were joined unto B.
Deut. 4. 3. have seen what Lord did because of B.

BAAL-PERAZIM.

2 Sam. 5. 20. David called the place B. 1 Chr. 14. 11.

BAAL-SHALISHA.

2 Kings 4. 42. and there came a man from B.

BAAL-TAMAR.

Judg. 20. 33. Israel put themselves in array at B.

BAAL-ZEBUB.

2 Kings 1. 2. enquire of B. the God of Ekron, 16.

BAAL-ZEPHON.

Exod. 14. 2. and encamp over against B. Num. 33. 7.

BAANAH.

2 Sam. 4. 6. Rechab and B. his brother escaped
23. 29. Heleb the son of B. one of the mighty men
1 Kings 4. 16. B. the son of Hushai was in Ashe
Ezra 2. 2. B. came to Jerusalem, Neh. 7. 7.
Neh. 10. 27. Malluth, Harim, B. sealed the covenant

BAASHA. [32.

1 Kings 15. 16. there was war between Asa and B.
19. come, break thy league with B. 2 Chr. 16. 3.
27. B. son of Ahijah conspired against him
16. 1. the word of the L. came to Jehu against B.
6. B. slept with his fathers and was buried
11. Zimri slew all the house of B. 12.
21. 22. I will make Ahab's house like the house of B. the son of Ahijah, 2 Kings 9. 9.
Jer. 41. 9. the pit which Asa made for fear of B.

BABEL.

Gen. 10. 10. the beginning of his kingdom was B.
11. 9. therefore is the name of it called B.
Ezek. 23. † 17. the children of B. came to her into

BABYLON. [bed

Gen. 10. † 10. the beginning of his kingdom was B.
2 Kings 17. 30. the men of B. made Succoth-benoth
25. 28. above kings that were in B. Jer. 52. 32.
2 Chr. 32. 31. the ambassadors of the princes of B.
36. 7. he put the vessels in his temple at B.
Ezra 5. 14. those did Cyrus take out of temple of B.
6. 1. where the treasures were laid up in B.
Psal. 87. 4. I will make mention of Rahab and B.
137. 1. by the rivers of B. there we sat down
Isa. 13. 1. the burden of B. which Isaiah did see
19. B. shall be as when God overthrew Sodom
21. 9. B. is fallen, Jer. 51. 8. Rev. 14. 8. | 18. 2.
48. 14. the Lord will do his pleasure on B.
20. go ye forth of B. flee from the Chaldeans
Jer. 20. 4. he shall carry them captive into B.
28. 4. the captives of Judah that went into B.
29. 10. after seventy years be accomplished at B.
15. the Lord hath raised us up prophets in B.
40. 4. if it seem good to come with me into B.
50. 1. the word that the Lord spake against B.
8. remove out of the midst of B. and go forth
13. every one that goeth by B. shall hiss
23. how is B. become a desolation among nations!
29. call together the archers against B.
34. that he may disquiet the inhabitants of B.
45. hear the counsel of the Lord against B.
51. 6. flee out of the midst of B. and deliver
35. the violence done to me be upon B.
42. the sea is come up upon B. she is covered
48. the heaven and the earth shall sing for B.
49. at B. shall fall the slain of all the earth
53. though B. should mount up to heaven
55. because the Lord hath spoiled B.
58. the broad walls of B. shall be utterly broken
60. wrote all the evil that shall come on B.
64. thus shall B. sink, and shall not rise from evil
Ezek. 17. 16. with him in the midst of B. he shall die
Dan. 4. 30. is not this great B. that I have built?
Mat. 1. 17. from David till the carrying into B.
Acts 7. 43. I will carry you away beyond B.
1 Pet. 5. 13. the church at B. saluteth you
Rev. 16. 19. great B. came in remembrance bef. G.
17. 5. B. the great, the mother of harlots
18. 10. saying, alas, alas, that great city B.!
21. thus shall that great city B. be thrown down
See DAUGHTER, PROVINCE, Wise MEN.

From BABYLON.

2 Kings 20. 14. from a far country from B. Isa. 39. 3.
Ezra 7. 9. on first day began he to go up from B.
8. 1. of them that went up with me from B.
Isa. 14. 22. I will cut off from B. the name
Jer. 50. 16. cut off the sower from B. and him that
51. 54. a sound of a cry cometh from B.
Zech. 6. 10. take of them which are come from B.

King of BABYLON. [40. 9.

2 Kings 25. 24. serve the king of B. Jer. 27. 17. |
Ezra 5. 12. he gave them into the hand of the king of B. the Chaldean, Jer. 21. 7. | 22. 25.
Isa. 14. 4. take up this proverb against king of B.
Jer. 21. 4. wherewith ye fight against the king of B.
25. 11. nations shall serve the king of B. 70 years
12. after that I will punish the king of B.
27. 8. kingdoms which will not serve king of B. 13.
28. 11. I have broken the yoke of the king of B.
29. 22. whom the king of B. roasted in the fire
34. 3. thine eyes shall behold the eyes of king of B.
36. 29. king of B. shall certainly come and destroy
39. 11. king of B. gave charge concerning Jeremiah
42. 11. be not afraid of the king of B.
49. 30. king of B. hath taken counsel against you
50. 17. the king of B. hath broken his bones
Ezek. 21. 19. that sword of the king of B. may come
29. 18. the king of B. caused his army to serve
19. I will give Egypt unto the king of B.
30. 24. I will strengthen the arms of king of B. 25.
32. 11. sword of the king of B. shall come on thee

To or unto BABYLON.

2 Kings 20. 17. shall be carried to B. 24. 15. | 25. 7, 13. 1 Chron. 9. 1. 2 Chron. 36. 6, 7, 20. Ezra 5. 12. Isa. 39. 6. Jer. 27. 20. | 28. 3. | 29. 1, 4. | 40. 1, 7.
2 Chr. 33. 11. took Manasseh and carried him to B.
36. 18. the treasures, all these he brought to B.
Isa. 43. 14. for your sake I have sent to B.
Jer. 20. 6. Pashur, thou shalt come to B.
34. 3. Zedekiah, thou shalt go to B.
51. 24. I will render unto B. || 61. when comest to B.
Ezek. 17. 20. I will bring him to B. and plead with
Mic. 4. 10. the daughter of Zion shall go to B.
Mat. 1. 11. about the time they were carried to B.

BABYLONIANS.

Ezek. 23. 15. after the manner of the B. of Chaldea
17. the B. came to her into the bed of love

BABYLONISH.

Josh. 7. 21. Achan saw a goodly B. garment

BACA.

Psal. 84. 6. who passing through the valley of B.

BAHURIM.

2 Sam. 3. 16. went along weeping behind her to B.
16. 5. when David came to B. Shimei came out
17. 18. and they came to a man's house in B.
19. 16. Shimei a Benjamite of B. 1 Kings 2. 8.

BAJITH.

Isa. 15. 2. he is gone up to B. and to Dibon to weep

BALAAM.
Num. 22. 5. Balak sent messengers to B. son of Beor
9. God came to B. and said, what men are these?
14. they said, B. refuseth to come with us
25. the ass crushed B. foot against the wall
31. then the Lord opened the eyes of B.
35. so B. went with the princes of Balak
23. 4. God met B. and said unto him, 16.
30. Balak did as B. had said, and offered a bullock
24. 2. B. lifted up his eyes and saw Israel
3. B. the son of Beor hath said, 15.
25. B. rose up and returned to his place
31. 8. B. the son of Beor they slew, *Josh.* 13. 22.
16. through the counsel of B. to commit trespass
Deut. 23. 4. because they hired B. *Neh.* 13. 2.
5. the Lord thy God would not hearken to B.
Josh. 24. 9. Balak sent and called B. to curse you
Mic. 6. 5. remember what B. answered him
2 *Pet.* 2. 15. following the way of B. the son of Bosor
Jude 11. they ran greedily after the error of B.
Rev. 2. 14. them that hold the doctrine of B.

BALAK.
Num. 22. 4. B. was king of the Moabites at that time
16. thus saith B. let nothing hinder thee
23. 2. and B. did as Balaam had spoken, 30.
7. B. king of Moab hath brought me from Aram
18. rise up, B. and hear ‖ 24. 10. B. anger kindled
24. 13. if B. would give me his house full of gold
Josh. 24. 9. then B. arose and warred against Israel
Judg. 11. 25. art thou any thing better than B.?
Mic. 6. 5. remember what B. king of Moab consulted
Rev. 2. 14. who taught B. to cast a stumbling-block

BAMAH.
Ezek. 20. 29. the name thereof is called B.

BARABBAS.
Mat. 27. 17. release B. 21. *Mark* 15. 11. *Luke* 23. 18.
John 18. 40. then cried they all again, saying, not this man but B. now B. was a robber

BARACHIAS.
Mat. 23. 35. to the blood of Zacharias, son of B.

BARAK.
Judg. 4. 6. Deborah called B. the son of Abinoam
9. Deborah went with B. ‖ 16. B. pursued after
5. 1. then sang Deborah and B. son of Abinoam
12. arise B. and lead thy captivity captive
Heb. 11. 32. the time would fail me to tell of B.

BAR-JESUS.
Acts 13. 6. they found a sorcerer whose name was B.

BAR-JONA.
Mat. 16. 17. Jesus said, blessed art thou, Simon B.

BARNABAS.
Acts 4. 36. Joses who by apostles was surnamed B.
11. 22. that B. should go as far as Antioch
25. then departed B. to Tarsus to seek Saul
30. they sent it by the hands of B. and Saul
12. 25. B. and Saul returned from Jerusalem
13. 1. at Antioch were teachers, as B. and Saul
2. the Holy Ghost said, separate me B. and Saul
50. Jews raised persecution against Paul and B.
14. 12. they called B. Jupiter; Paul, Mercurius
15. 2. Paul and B. had no small dissension
12. the multitude gave audience to B. and Paul
37. B. determined to take with them John
1 *Cor.* 9. 6. or I only and B. have not we power
Gal. 2. 1. I went up again to Jerusalem with B.
9. gave to me and B. the right hands of fellowship
13. B. carried away with their dissimulation
Col. 4. 10. Marcus, sister's son to B. saluteth you
See Saul, Paul.

BARSABAS.
Acts 1. 23. Joseph called B. ‖ 15. 22. Judas B.

BARTHOLOMEW.
Mat. 10. 3. *Mark* 3. 18. *Luke* 6. 14. *Acts* 1. 13.

BARTIMEUS.
Mark 10. 46. blind B. sat by the way-side begging

BARUCH.
Neh. 3. 20. B. son of Zabbai earnestly repaired
10. 6. Ginnethon, B. sealed the covenant
11. 5. Maaseiah son of B. dwelt at Jerusalem
Jer. 32. 12. I gave the evidence to B. 16.
36. 4. then Jeremiah called B. and B. wrote
10. then read B. in the book in the house of Lord
14. B. took the roll in his hand and came
26. the king commanded to take B. the scribe
43. 3. but B. setteth thee on against us
6. Johanan took Jeremiah and B. into Egypt
45. 1. the word that Jeremiah spake to B.

BARZILLAI.
2 *Sam.* 17. 27. B. of Rogelim brought beds to David
19. 32. B. was a very aged man, even 80 years old
39. the king kissed B. and blessed him
21. 8. whom she brought up for Adriel son of B.
1 *Kings* 2. 7. but shew kindness to the sons of B.
Ezra 2. 61. the children of B. which took a wife of the daughters of B. the Gileadite, *Neh.* 7. 63.

BASHAN.
Num. 21. 33. they went up by the way of B. *Deut.* 3. 1.
32. 33. Og king of B. *Deut.* 1. 4. | 3. 1, 3, 11. | 4. 47. | 29. 7. *Josh.* 9. 10. | 12. 4. | 13. 30. 1 *Kings* 4. 19. *Neh.* 9. 22. *Psal.* 135. 11. | 136. 20.
Deut. 3. 4. kingd. of Og in B. 10. *Josh.* 13. 12, 30, 31.
4. 43. and Golan in B. *Josh.* 20. 8. | 21. 27.
32. 14. with rams of the breed of B. and goats
33. 22. of Dan he said, Dan shall leap from B.
Josh. 17. 1. therefore he had Gilead and B.
2 *Kings* 10. 33. even Gilead and B. Hazael smote
1 *Chron.* 6. 71. to the sons of Gershon, Golan in B.
Psal. 22. 12. strong bulls of B. have beset me round
68. 15. the hill of God is as the hill of B. an high hill as the hill of B. why leap ye, ye high hills?
22. the Lord said I will bring again from B.
Isa. 33. 9. B. and Carmel shake off their fruits
Jer. 22. 20. cry, lift up thy voice in B. and cry
50. 19. Israel shall feed on Carmel and B.
Ezek. 39. 18. all of them fatlings of B.
Amos 4. 1. hear this word, ye kine of B.
Mic. 7. 14. let them feed in B. as in the days of old
Nah. 1. 4. B. languished, Carmel and Lebanon
See Oaks.

BASHEMATH.
Gen. 26. 34. Esau took to wife B. the Hittite
Gen. 36. 3. B. Ishmael's daughter, sister of Nebajoth

BATH-SHEBA.
2 *Sam.* 11. 3. is not this B. daughter of Eliam?
12. 24. and David comforted B. his wife
1 *Kings* 1. 15. B. went to the king into the chamber
28. then the king said, call me B. ‖ 31. B. bowed
2. 13. Adonijah came to B. the mother of Solomon
1 *Chron.* 3. 5. Solomon of B. daughter of Ammiel

BEDAN.
1 *Sam.* 12. 11. the Lord sent B. and delivered you
1 *Chron.* 7. 17. and the sons of Ulam, B.

BEELZEBUB.
Mat. 10. 25. if they have called the master B.
12. 24. this fellow doth not cast out devils, but by B. prince of devils, *Mark* 3. 22. *Luke* 11. 15.
27. if I by B. cast out devils, *Luke* 11. 18, 19.

BEER-SHEBA.
Gen. 21. 14. Hagar wandered in wilderness of B.
33. and Abraham planted a grove in B.
22. 19. they went to B. Abraham dwelt at B.
26. 33. therefore the name of the city is B.
28. 10. Jacob went out from B. toward Haran
46. 1. Israel took his journey and came to B.
Josh. 19. 2. Simeon had in their inheritance B.
1 *Kings* 19. 3. Elijah went for his life and came to B.
Amos 5. 5. seek not to Beth-el, and pass not to B.
8. 14. they that say, the manner of B. liveth
See Dan.

BEKAH.
Exod. 38. 26. a B. for each, that is half a shekel

BEL.
Isa. 46. 1. B. boweth down, Nebo stoopeth
Jer. 50. 2. Babylon is taken, B. is confounded
51. 44. and I will punish B. in Babylon, will bring

BELIAL.
Deut. 13. 13. certain children of B. are gone out
Judg. 19. 22. certain sons of B. beset the house
20. 13. deliver us the man, the children of B.
1 *Sam.* 1. 16. count not thy handmaid a daughter of B.
2. 12. now the sons of Eli were sons of B.
10. 27. childr. of B. said, how shall this man save us?
25. 17. is such a son of B. man cannot speak to him
25. let not my lord regard this man of B.
30. 22. then answered the men of B. and said
2 *Sam.* 16. 7. come out, come out, thou man of B.
20. 1. there happened to be there a man of B. Sheba
23. 6. the sons of B. shall be as thorns thrust away
1 *Kings* 21. 10. set two sons of B. before Naboth, 13.
2 *Chron.* 13. 7. gathered to Jeroboam children of B.
2 *Cor.* 6. 15. what concord hath Christ with B.?

BELSHAZZAR.
Dan. 5. 22. thou, O B. hast not humbled thy heart
7. 1. in the first year of B. ‖ 8. 1. in third year of B.

BELTESHAZZAR.
Dan. 1. 7. for he gave to Daniel the name of B.
2. 26. name was B. 4. 8, 9, 19. | 5. 12. | 10. 1.

BENAIAH.
2 *Sam.* 23. 22. these things did B. 1 *Chron.* 11. 24.
1 *Kings* 1. 32. the king said, call me Zadok and B.
2. 35. the king put B. in Joab's room
4. 4. B. the son of Jehoiada was over the host
1 *Chron.* 4. 36. Jesimiel and B. sons of Simeon
11. 31. B. the Pirathonite, a mighty man
15. 18. brethren of second degree, B. 20. | 16. 5, 6.
27. 5. the third captain for the third month, B.
14. the captain for the eleventh month, B.
2 *Chron.* 31. 13. Mahath and B. were overseers
Ezra. 10. 25. B. son of Parosh ‖ 30. of Pahath-moab
35. B. the son of Bani ‖ 43. B. son of Nebo
Ezek. 11. 1. among whom I saw Pelatiah son of B.
13. when I prophesied, the son of B. died

BEN-AMMI.
Gen. 19. 38. the younger called his name B.

BEN-HADAD.
1 *Kings* 15. 18. Asa sent them to B. 2 *Chron.* 16. 2.
20. 2. thus saith B. thy silver and gold is mine
16. B. was drinking himself drunk in the pavilions
20. B. escaped on an horse, with the horsemen
32. thy servant B. saith, I pray thee, let me live
2 *Kings* 6. 24. B. went up and besieged Samaria
8. 7. B. was sick ‖ 9. thy son B. hath sent me
13. 3. he delivered Israel into the hand of B.
25. Jehoash took again out of the hand of B.
Jer. 49. 27. I will kindle a fire in the wall of Damascus, it shall consume the palaces of B. *Amos* 1. 4.

BENJAMIN.
Gen. 35. 18. but his father called him B.
24. the sons of Rachel, Joseph and B. 46. 19.
42. 36. Joseph is not, and ye will take B. also
43. 14. he may send away your brother and B.
16. and when Joseph saw B. with them, 29.
34. B. mess was five times so much as theirs
44. 12. and the cup was found in B. sack
45. 14. he fell on his brother B. neck and wept
46. 21. the sons of B. *Num.* 26. 38, 41. 1 *Chron.* 7. 6. | 8. 1, 40. | 9. 7. *Neh.* 11. 7.
49. 27. B. shall ravin as a wolf, devour the prey
Num. 1. 11. the prince of B. was Abidan
Deut. 27. 12. these shall stand to bless, Joseph, B.
33. 12. of B. Moses said, the beloved of the Lord
Judg. 5. 14. after thee, B. among thy people
19. 14. they were by Gibeah, which belongs to B.
20. 20. men of Israel went out to battle against B.
35. the Lord smote B. before Israel
46. all that fell that day of B. were 25,000 men
21. 1. not any of us give his daughter to B. 18.
16. seeing the women are destroyed out of B.
1 *Sam.* 4. 12. there ran a man of B. out of the army
9. 1. there was a man of B. whose name was Kish
10. 2. by Rachel's sepulchre, in the border of B.
13. 2. in Gibeah of B. 15. 16. | 14. 16.
2 *Sam.* 2. 15. there arose by number twelve of B.
3. 19. and Abner also spake in the ears of B.
19. 17. there were a thousand men of B. with him
21. 14. the bones of Saul buried they in B.
1 *Kings* 4. 18. Shimei son of Elah officer in B.
1 *Chron.* 7. 10. the sons of Bilhan, Jeush and B.
21. 6. Levi and B. counted he not among them
27. 21. over B. was Jaasiel the son of Abner
2 *Chron.* 17. 17. of B. Eliada a mighty man of valour
34. 32. caused all in Jerusalem and B. to stand
Neh. 3. 23. after him repaired B. and Hashub
Psal. 68. 27. there is little B. with their ruler
80. 2. before B. and Manasseh, stir up thy strength
Jer. 37. 13. when Jeremiah was in the gate of B.
38. 7. the king then sitting in the gate of B.
Ezek. 48. 23. B. have a portion ‖ 32. one gate of B.
Hos. 5. 8. cry aloud at Beth-aven, after thee, O B.
Obad. 19. possess Ephraim, B. shall possess Gilead
Zech. 14. 10. it shall be inhabited from B. gate
See Children.

BENJAMIN with *Judah*.
Judg. 10. 9. Ammon passed to fight *Judah* and B.
1 *Kings* 12. 23. sp. to house of *Jud.* B. 2. *Chr.* 11. 3.
1 *Chr.* 12. 16. there came of B. and *Judah* to David
2 *Chr.* 11. 12. Rehoboam having *Judah* and B.
15. 2. hear ye me, Asa, and all *Judah* and B.
8. put away the idols out of *Judah* and B.
25. 5. Amaziah made captains thro' *Judah* and B.
31. 1. threw down the altars out of *Judah* and B.
34. 9. money that was gathered of *Judah* and B.
Ezra 1. 5. rose up chief fathers of *Judah* and B.
4. 1. when the adversaries of *Judah* and B. heard
Neh. 11. 4. at Jerusalem dwelt of *Judah* and B.
12. 34. after them went *Judah*, B. and Jeremiah
Ezek. 48. 22. between the border of *Judah* and B.

***Land* of BENJAMIN.**
Judg. 21. 21. take his wife and go into the *land of* B.
1 *Sam.* 9. 16. send thee a man out of the *land of* B.
2 *Chron.* 15. 8. put away idols out of the *land of* B.
Jer. 17. 26. come from *land of* B. bringing offerings
32. 44. shall take witnesses in the *land of* B.
33. 13. in the *land of* B. shall flocks pass again
37. 12. Jeremiah went to go into the *land of* B.

***Tribe of* BENJAMIN.**
Num. 1. 37. of the *tribe of* B. were numbered 35,400
2. 22. captain of the *tribe of* B. Abidan, 10. 24.
13. 9. of the *tribe of* B. to spy the land, Palti
34. 21. of the *tribe of* B. to divide, Elidad
Josh. 18. 11. the lot of the *tribe of* B. came up
21. the cities of the *tribe of* B. were Jericho
21. 4. cities to the Levites out of the tribe of Judah and the *tribe of* B. 17. 1 *Chron.* 6. 60, 65.
Judg. 20. 12. Israel sent men thro' all the *tribe of* B.
1 *Sam.* 9. 21. I am least of families of the *tribe of* B.
10. 20. tribes come near, the *tribe of* B. was taken
Acts 13. 21. Saul a man of the *tribe of* B.
Rom. 11. 1. I am of the *tribe of* B. *Phil.* 3. 5.
Rev. 7. 8. of the *tribe of* B. were sealed 12,000

BENJAMITE.
Judg. 3. 15. Ehud a B. ‖ 1 *Sam.* 9. 1. Kish a B.
1 *Sam.* 9. 21. Saul answered and said, am not I a B.?
2 *Sam.* 16. 11. Shimei a B. 19. 16. 1 *Kings* 2. 8.
20. 1. Sheba a B. ‖ *Esth.* 2. 5. Mordecai a B.

BENJAMITES.
Judg. 19. 16. the men of the place were B.
20. 35. Israel destroyed of the B. 25,100
43. thus they enclosed the B. round about
1 *Sam.* 22. 7. then said Saul, hear now, ye B.
1 *Chron.* 27. 12. the ninth captain was Abiezer of B.

BENONI.
Gen. 35. 18. departing, she called his name B.

BEOR.
Gen. 36. 32. Bela the son of B. reigned, 1 *Chr.* 1. 43.
Num. 22. 5. Balaam the son of B. 24. 3, 15. | 31. 8. *Deut.* 23. 4. *Josh.* 13. 22. | 24. 9. *Mic.* 6. 5.

BERACHAH.
1 *Chron.* 12. 3. B. came to David to Ziklag
2 *Chron.* 20. 26. therefore called the valley of B.

BEREA.
Acts 17. 10. breth. sent Paul and Silas by night to B
13. the Jews heard that Paul preached at B.
20. 4. Sopater of B. accompanied Paul to Asia

BERITH.
Judg. 9. 46. an hold of the house of their God B.

BERNICE.
Acts 25. 13. Agrippa and B. came unto Cesarea, 23.
26. 30. the king rose up, the governor and B.

BESOR.
1 *Sam.* 30. 9. six hundred men came to the brook B.

BETHABARA.
John 1. 28. these things done in B. beyond Jordan

BETHANY.
Mat. 21. 17. Jesus went into B. 26. 6. *Mark* 11. 1, 11. | 14. 3. *Luke* 19. 29. *John* 12. 1.
Mark 11. 12. when come from B. he was hungry
Luke 24. 50. he led them out as far as to B.
John 11. 1. a man was sick named Lazarus of B.

BETH-AVEN.
Josh. 7. 2. sent men to Ai, which is beside B.
1 *Sam.* 14. 23. and the battle passed over to B.
Hos. 4. 15. come ye not to Gilgal, nor go ye up to B.
5. 8. cry aloud at B. after thee, O Benjamin
10. 5. shall fear, because of the calves of B.

BETH-DIBLATHAIM.
Jer. 48. 22. judgment is come upon B.

BETH-EL.
Gen. 28. 19. Jacob called the place B. 35. 15.
31. 13. I am God of B. where thou vowedst a vow
35. 1. go up to B. 3. ‖ 6. so Jacob came to B.
Josh. 16. 2. the lot of Joseph goeth from B. to Luz
Judg. 1. 22. the house of Joseph went up against B.
4. 5. Deborah dwelt between Ramah and B.
21. 19. in a place which is on the north side of B
1 *Sam.* 7. 16. he went from year to year to B.
10. 3. shall meet three men going up to God to B.
13. 2. two thousand were with Saul in mount B.
30. 27. a present to them which were in B.
1 *Kings* 12. 29. he set the one calf in B. 33.
13. 1. behold, there came a man of God to B.
4. which had cried against the altar in B. 32.
11. now there dwelt an old prophet in B.
2 *Kings* 2. 2. tarry here, the Lord hath sent me to B.
23. and he went up from thence unto B.
10. 29. Jehu departed not from the calves in B.
17. 28. one of the priests came and dwelt in B.
23. 4. he burnt them and carried the ashes to B.
15. the altar at B. Josiah brake down
17. who proclaimed against the altar of B.
19. according to all that he had done in B.
Ezra 2. 28. the men of B. and Ai 223, *Neh.* 7. 32.
Jer. 48. 13. as the house of Isr. was ashamed of B.
Hos. 10. 15. so shall B. do to you because of wicked.
12. 4. he found him in B. there he spake with us

Amos 3. 14. I will also visit the altars of B.
4. 4. come to B. and transgress, multiply transgres.
5. 5. seek not B. for B. shall come to nought
6. lest there be none to quench it in B.
7. 13. but prophesy not again any more at B.

BETH-ELITE.
1 *Kings* 16. 34. Hiel the B. did build Jericho

BETHER.
Cant. 2. 17. like a hart on the mountains of B.

BETHESDA.
John 5. 2. there is a pool called in Hebrew B.

BETH-EZEL.
Mic. 1. 11. came not forth in the mourning of B.

BETH-GAMUL.
Jer. 48. 23. judgment is come upon B.

BETH-HACCEREM.
Jer. 6. 1. O Benjamin, set up a sign of fire in B.

BETH-HORON.
Josh. 10. 11. going down to B. the Lord cast stones
21. 22. Ephraim gave Levites B. 1 *Chron.* 6. 68.
1 *Sam.* 13. 18. another company turned to B.
1 *Kings* 9. 17. and Solomon built B. 2 *Chron.* 8. 5.
1 *Chron.* 7. 24. his daughter Sherah built B.

BETH-LEHEM.
Gen. 35. 19. Rachel died in the way to B. 48. 7.
Josh. 19. 15. Idala and B. cities of Zebulun
Judg. 12. 8. after him Ibzan of B. judged Israel
Ruth 1. 19. they two went till they came to B.
2. 4. Boaz came from B. ‖ 4. 11. be famous in B.
1 *Sam.* 16. 4. Samuel came to B. elders trembled
20. 6. David asked leave of me to run to B. 28.
2 *Sam.* 23. 15. David said, O that one would give me drink of water of the well of B. 1 *Chron.* 11. 17.
1 *Chron.* 2. 51. Salma the father of B. 54.
4. 4. the first-born of Ephratah, the father of B.
2 *Chron.* 11. 6. Rehoboam built B. and Etam
Ezra 2. 21. the children of B. *Neh.* 7. 26.
Jer. 41. 17. dwelt in habitation of Chimham by B.
Mat. 2. 1. when Jesus was born in B. of Judea, 5.
6. thou B. in the land of Juda, art not the least
16. Herod slew all the children that were in B.
Luke 2. 4. Joseph went up from Galilee to B.
15. let us now go to B. and see this thing
John 7. 42. Christ cometh out of the town of B.

BETH-LEHEM-EPHRATAH.
Mic. 5. 2. thou B.-Ephratah, though thou be little

BETH-LEHEM-JUDAH.
Judg. 17. 7. a Levite of B. went to sojourn, 8, 9.
19. 1. a Levite took him a concubine out of B.
18. we are passing from B. and I went to B.
Ruth 1. 1. Elimelech of B. went to sojourn
1 *Sam.* 17. 12. David son of an Ephrathite of B.

BETH-LEHEMITE.
1 *Sam.* 16. 1. Jesse the B. 18. | 17. 58.
2 *Sam.* 21. 19. Elhanan the B. slew Goliath's brother

BETH-PEOR.
Deut. 3. 29. we abode in the valley over-against B.
4. 46. the statutes Moses spake over-against B.
34. 6. he buried Moses in a valley over-against B.

BETH-PHAGE.
Mat. 21. 1. when come to B. *Mark* 11. 1. *Luke* 19. 29.

BETHSAIDA.
Mat. 11. 21. woe unto thee, B. *Luke* 10. 13.
Mark 6. 45. he constrained his disciples to go to B.
8. 22. cometh to B. they bring a blind man to him
Luke 9. 10. he went into a desert belonging to B.
John 1. 44. now Philip was of B. 12. 21.

BETH-SHAN.
1 *Sam.* 31. 10. fastened Saul's body to the wall of B.

BETH-SHEMESH.
Josh. 15. 10. the border of Judah went down to B.
19. 22. Issachar's coast reacheth to B.
38. Beth-anath and B. cities of Naphtali
21. 16. Judah gave to Levites B. with her suburbs
Judg. 1. 33. did not drive out the inhabitants of B.
1 *Sam.* 6. 9. if he goeth up by the way of B.
12. the kine took the straight way to B.
19. he smote the men of B. because they looked
1 *Kings* 4. 9. the son of Dekar was in B. an officer
2 *Kings* 14. 11. kings of Judah and Israel looked one another in the face at B. 2 *Chron.* 25. 21.
2 *Chron.* 28. 18. the Philistines had taken B.
Jer. 43. 13. he shall break the images of B.

BETHUEL.
Gen. 22. 22. behold, Milcah bare to Nahor, B.
23. B. begat Rebekah, 24. 15. | 25. 20.
24. 24. she said, I am the daughter of B. 47.
28. 2. go to the house of B. thy mother's father

BEULAH.
Isa. 62. 4. call thy land B. for Lord delighteth in thee

BEZALEEL.
Exod. 31. 2. I have called by name B. son of Uri, of the tribe of Judah, 35. 30. 1 *Chron.* 2. 20.
36. 1. then wrought B. ‖ 37. 1. B. made the ark
38. 22. B. made all the Lord commanded Moses
2 *Chron.* 1. 5. the brazen altar that B. had made
Ezra 10. 30. the sons of Pahath-moab, B. Binnui

BEZEK.
Judg. 1. 4. they slew of them in B. 10,000 men, 5.
1 *Sam.* 11. 8. Saul numbered Israel in B. 300,000

BICHRI.
2 *Sam.* 20. 1. Sheba the son of B. a Benjamite
2. so every man followed Sheba the son of B.
6. now shall the son of B. do us more harm
22. they cut off the head of Sheba the son of B.

BIDKAR.
2 *Kings* 9. 25. Jehu said to B. his captain, take up

BIGTHAN.
Esth. 2. 21. B. sought to lay hand on king Ahasuerus
6. 2. that Mordecai had told of B. and Teresh

BILDAD.
Job 2. 11. B. the Shuhite, 8. 1. | 18. 1. | 25. 1. | 42. 9.

BILHAH.
Gen. 29. 29. Laban gave to Rachel B. to be her maid
30. 3. behold my maid B. go in unto her, 4.
5. B. conceived, 7. ‖ 35. 22. Reuben lay with B.
35. 25. the sons of B. 37. 2. | 46. 25. 1 *Chr.* 7. 13.
1 *Chron.* 4. 29. Shimei, his sons dwelt at B.

BITHYNIA.
Acts 16. 7. they assayed to go into B. but Spirit
1 *Pet.* 1. 1. to strangers scattered thro' Asia and B.

BLASTUS.
Acts 12. 20. and having made B. their friend

BOANERGES.
Mark 3. 17. surnamed them B. the sons of thunder

BOAZ.
1 *Kings* 7. 21. the left pillar called B. 2 *Chron.* 3. 17.

BOAZ.
Ruth 2. 1. Naomi had a kinsman, his name was B.
19. the man's name with whom I wrought, is B.
3. 2. is not B. of our kindred ‖ 7. when B. had eaten
4. 1. then went B. up to the gate, and sat down
13. so B. took Ruth, and she was his wife
21. B. begat Obed, 1 *Chron.* 2. 11, 12. *Mat.* 1. 5.
Luke 3. 32. Obed, which was the son of B.

BOCHIM.
Judg. 2. 1. an angel came up from Gilgal to B.
5. and they called the name of that place B.

BOSOR. *See* BALAAM.

BOZRAH.
Gen. 36. 33. Joab of B. reigned in his stead
Isa. 34. 6. for the Lord hath a sacrifice in B.
63. 1. that cometh with dyed garments from B.
Jer. 48. 24. and judgment is come upon B.
49. 13. have sworn that B. shall become desolation
22. and he shall spread his wings over B.
Amos 1. 12. which shall devour the palaces of B.
Mic. 2. 12. put them together as the sheep of B.

BUL.
1 *Kings* 6. 38. in month B. the house was finished

BUZ.
Gen. 22. 21. Milcah bare to Nahor B. and Kemuel
1 *Chr.* 5. 14. Jeshishai, son of Jahdo, the son of B.
Jer. 25. 23. I made Dedan and B. to drink the cup

BUZI.
Ezek. 1. 3. word came to Ezekiel the priest, son of B.

BUZITE.
Job 32. 2. Elihu the son of Barachel the B. 6.

C.

CABUL.
1 *Kings* 9. 13. Hiram called them the land of C.

CAIAPHAS.
Mat. 26. 3. the high-priest who was called C.
57. they led Jesus away to C. the high-priest
John 11. 49. C. said, ye know nothing at all
18. 14. C. was he that gave counsel to the Jews
28. led Jesus from C. to the hall of judgment
See ANNAS.

CAIN.
Josh. 15. 57. C. and Gibeah cities of Judah

CAIN.
Gen. 4. 2. but C. was a tiller of the ground
5. to C. and his offering he had not respect
15. the L. set a mark on C. lest any should kill him
25. another seed instead of Abel whom C. slew
Heb. 11. 4. a more excellent sacrifice than C.
1 *John* 3. 12. not as C. who was of that wicked one
Jude 11. they have gone in the way of C.

CAINAN.
Luke 3. 36. which was the son of C. 37.

CALDEA. *See* CHALDEA.

CALEB.
Num. 13. 6. of the tribe of Judah, C. to spy the land
30. and C. stilled the people before Moses
14. 24. but my servant C. having another spirit, will I bring into the land, 30. | 32. 12. *Deut.* 1. 36.
38. but Joshua and C. lived still, 26. 65.
34. 19. of the tribe of Judah, C. to divide the land
Josh. 14. 13. Joshua gave C. Hebron for inheritance
15. 14. C. drove thence the three sons of Anak
16. C. said, he that smiteth Kirjath-sepher
Judg. 1. 15. and C. gave her the upper springs
1 *Sam.* 25. 3. Nabal was of the house of C.
1 *Chron.* 2. 18. and C. begat children, 42. 50. | 4. 15.

CALEB.
1 *Sam.* 30. 14. on the south of C. we burnt Ziklag

CALEB-EPHRATAH.
1 *Chron.* 2. 24. after that Hezron was dead in C.

CALNEH.
Gen. 10. 10. Babel and C. in the land of Shinar
Amos 6. 2. pass ye unto C. from thence to Hamath

CALNO.
Isa. 10. 9. not C. as Carchemish? Hamath as Arpad?

CALVARY.
Luke 23. 33. when come to the place called C.

CAMON.
Judg. 10. 5. Jair died, and was buried in C.

CANA.
John 2. 1. there was a marriage in C. of Galilee
11. this beginning of miracles did Jesus in C.
4. 46. so Jesus came again into C. of Galilee
21. 2. there were Thomas and Nathanael of C.

CANAAN.
Gen. 9. 18. and Ham is the father of C.
22. Ham the father of C. saw the nakedness
25. cursed be C. ‖ 26. C. shall be his servant, 27.
10. 15. C. begat Sidon his first-born, 1 *Chr.* 1. 13.
28. 1. not take a wife of the daughters of C. 6.

CANAAN.
Exod. 15. 15. the inhabitants of C. shall melt
Judg. 3. 1. as had not known all the wars of C.
4. 2. the Lord sold them to Jabin king of C.
23. and God subdued Jabin the king of C. 24.
5. 19. then fought the kings of C. in Taanach
Psal. 106. 38. they sacrificed to the idols of C.
135. 11. who smote all the kingdoms of C.
Isa. 19. 18. five cities in Egypt speak language of C.
Zeph. 2. 5. O C. I will even destroy thee
Mat. 15. 22. a woman of C. cried to Jesus, saying

Land of CANAAN.
Gen. 12. 5. went forth to go into the *land of* C.
16. 3. Abraham dwelt ten years in the *land of* C.
17. 8. I will give thee the *land of* C. *Lev.* 25. 38. *Num.* 34. 2. *Deut.* 32. 49. 1 *Chron.* 16. 18. *Psal.* 105. 11.
37. 1. and Jacob dwelt in the *land of* C.
42. 5. for the famine was in the *land of* C.
7. whence come ye? they said, from *land of* C.
13. thy servants are sons of one man in *land of* C.
45. 17. and go, get ye up unto the *land of* C.
Gen. 50. 13. his sons carried him into the *land of* C.
Lev. 14. 34. when ye be come into the *land of* C. which I gave for a possession, *Num.* 34. 2.
18. 3. do not after the doings of the *land of* C.
Num. 13. 17. Moses sent them to spy the *land of* C.
32. 32. we will pass over armed into the *land of* C.
Josh. 5. 12. they did eat the fruit of the *land of* C.
22. 11. have built an altar over-against *land of* C.
24. 3. I led him through all the *land of* C.
Ezek. 16. 3. thy nativity is of the *land of* C.
Acts 7. 11. there came dearth over all the *land of* C.
13. 19. had destroyed seven nations in *land of* C.

CANAANITE, S.
Gen. 12. 6. and the C. was then in the land, 13. 7.
15. 21. the Amorites, C. Girgashites, and Jebusites, *Exod.* 3. 8, 17. | 23. 23. *Deut.* 7. 1. | 20. 17. *Josh.* 3. 10. | 12. 8. *Judg.* 3. 5. *Neh.* 9. 8.
24. 3. thou shalt not take a wife of the C.
34. 30. to make me to stink amongst the C.
38. 2. Judah saw the daughter of a certain C.
Exod. 23. 28. I will drive out the C. 33. 2. | 34. 11.
Num. 21. 3. the L. delivered up the C. *Neh.* 9. 24.
Josh. 17. 12. but C. would dwell in land, *Judg.* 1. 27.
18. shall drive out the C. tho' have iron chariots
Judg. 1. 1. who shall go up against the C. first?
9. Judah went down to fight against the C. 10.
29. neither did Ephraim drive out the C. in Gezer
33. but Naphtali dwelt among the C. of the land
1 *Kings* 9. 16. Pharaoh had slain the C. in Gezer
Ezra 9. 1. doing according to the abominations of C.
Obad. 20. captiv. of this host shall possess that of C.
Zech. 14. 21. no more C. in the house of the Lord
Mat. 10. 4. Simon the C. *Mark* 3. 18.

CANAANITESS.
1 *Chron.* 2. 3. were born to Judah of Shua the C.

CANDACE.
Acts 8. 27. an eunuch of great authority under C

CAPERNAUM.
Mat. 4. 13. Jesus leaving Nazareth, dwelt in C.
8. 5. when Jesus was entered into C. there came
11. 23. thou C. which art exalted, *Luke* 10. 15.
17. 24. when they were come to C. they that
Mark 1. 21. and they went into C. he taught, 2. 1.
Luke 4. 23. whatsoever we have heard done in C.
John 2. 12. they continued not many days in C.
4. 46. was a nobleman whose son was sick at C.
6. 17. the disciples went over the sea towards C.
24. the people came to C. seeking for Jesus
59. these things said he, as he taught in C.

CAPHTOR.
Jer. 47. 4. will spoil the remnant of the country of C.
Amos 9. 7. I brought the Philistines from C.

CAPPADOCIA.
Acts 2. 9. the dwellers in C. we hear them speak
1 *Pet.* 1. 1. to the strangers scattered thro' C. Asia

CARCHEMISH.
2 *Chron.* 35. 20. Necho came up to fight against C.
Isa. 10. 9. is not Calno as C.? Hamath as Arpad?
Jer. 46. 2. which was by the river Euphrates in C.

CARMEL.
Josh. 15. 55. C. and Ziph in the inheritance of Judah
1 *Sam.* 15. 12. it was told Samuel, Saul came to C.
25. 2. Nabal's possessions were in C. the man great
7. nothing missing all the while they were in C.
40. David's servants were come to Abigail to C.
1 *Kings* 18. 19. gather to me all Israel to mount C.
42. and Elijah went up to the top of C.
2 *Kings* 2. 25. Elisha went from thence to mount C.
4. 25. the woman of Shunem came to mount C.
19. 23. I will enter into forest of his C. *Isa.* 37. 24.
2 *Chron.* 26. 10. Uzziah had vine-dressers in C.
Cant. 7. 5. thine head upon thee is like C. hair purp.
Isa. 35. 2. the excellency of C. and Sharon
Jer. 46. 18. and as C. by the sea, so shall he come
Amos 1. 2. and the top of A. shall wither
9. 3. though they hide themselves in the top of C.
Mic. 7. 14. which dwell solitary in the midst of C.
See BAASHAN.

CARMELITE. [2. 2. | 3. 3.
1 *Sam.* 30. 5. Abigail wife of Nabal the C. 2 *Sam.*
2 *Sam.* 23. 35. Hezrai, C. one of David's worthies

CARMI.
Gen. 46. 9. the sons of Reuben, Hezron and C.
Josh. 7. 1. Achan the son of C. 18. 1 *Chron.* 2. 7.
1 *Chr.* 4. 1. the sons of Judah, Pharez, Hezron, C.

CARPUS.
2 *Tim.* 4. 13. the cloke that I left with C. bring

CASIPHIA.
Ezra 8. 17. to Iddo the chief at the place C.

CEDRON.
John 18. 1. he went with disciples over the brook C.

CENCHREA.
Acts 18. 18. Paul having shorn his head in C.
Rom. 16. 1. sister Phebe a servant of church at C.

CEPHAS.
John 1. 42. thou shalt be called C. a stone
1 *Cor.* 1. 12. every one of you saith, I am of C.
3. 22. whether Paul, or Apollos, or C. or life
9. 5. and as the brethren of the Lord, and C.
15. 5. that he was seen of C. then of the twelve
Gal. 2. 9. James, C. and John, who seemed pillars

CESAR.
Mat. 22. 17. tell us, is it lawful to give tribute to C. or not? *Mark* 12. 14. *Luke* 20. 22.
21. render to C. the things that are Cesar's, and to God the things that are God's, *Mark* 12. 17.
Luke 2. 1. there went out a decree from C. Augustus
3. 1. now in the fifteenth year of Tiberius C.
23. 2. and forbidding to give tribute to C. saying
John 19. 12. the Jews cried out, if thou let this man go, thou art not Cesar's friend; speaketh ag. C.
15. the priests answered, we have no king but C.
Acts 11. 28. came to pass in days of Claudius C.
17. 7. these all do contrary to the decrees of C.
25. 8. nor against C. have I offended any thing
11. I appeal unto C. ‖ 21. till I send him to C.
26. 32. set at liberty, if he had not appealed to C.
27. 24. fear not, thou must be brought before C.
28. 19. I was constrained to appeal to C.
Phil. 4. 22. chiefly they that are of C. household

CESAREA.
Mat. 16. 13. Jesus came into the coasts of C

Mark 8. 27. Jesus went out into the towns of C.
Acts 8. 40. Philip preached, till he came to C.
9. 30. the brethren brought Paul down to C.
10. 24. the morrow after they entered into C.
11. 11. Cornelius sent three men from C. to me
12. 19. Herod went down from Judea to C.
18. 22. when he had landed at C. and saluted
21. 16. there went with us of the disciples of C.
23. 23. make ready 200 soldiers to go to C.
25. 1. after 3 days he ascended from C. to Jerusal.
4. Festus answered, Paul should be kept at C.

CHALCOL.

1 *Kings* 4. 31. Solomon was wiser than C.
1 *Chron.* 2. 6. the sons of Zerah, Heman, C. and Dara

CHALDEA.

Jer. 50. 10. C. shall be a spoil, saith the Lord
51. 24. I will render to inhabitants of C. their evil
35. my blood be upon the inhabitants of C.
Ezek. 16. 29. hast multiplied thy fornication to C.
23. 16. she sent messengers to them into C.

CHALDEAN.

Ezra 5. 12. gave them into hand of Nebuchad. the C.
Dan. 2. 10. that asked such things at any C.

CHALDEANS.

Job 1. 17. C. made out three bands, fell on camels
Isa. 23. 13. the land of C. the Assyrian founded
43. 14. I have brought down all the C.
47. 1. there is no throne, O daughter of the C.
5. get thee into darkness, O daughter of the C.
48. 14. and his arm shall be on the C.
20. go ye forth of Babylon, flee ye from the C.
Jer. 21. 4. wherewith ye fight against the C.
9. he that falleth to the C. he shall live, 38. 2.
25. 12. I will punish the land of C. 50. 1, 45.
32. 5. tho' ye fight with the C. ye shall not prosper
24. the city is given into the hand of the C. 43.
29. the C. shall come and set fire on this city
33. 5. come to fight with the C. but to fill them
37. 8. the C. shall come again and fight against the city
9. saying, surely the C. shall depart from us
10. tho' ye had smitten the whole army of the C.
14. then said Jeremiah, I fall not away to the C.
38. 19. am afraid of Jews that are fallen to the C.
23. they shall bring out thy children to the C.
39. 8. C. burnt king's house, and houses of people
40. 9. Gedaliah said, fear not to serve the C.
10. I will dwell at Mizpah, to serve the C.
41. 3. Ishmael slew the C. that were at Mizpah
43. 3. Baruch setteth thee on to deliver us to C.
50. 35. a sword is upon the C. saith the Lord
45. the Lord hath purposed against the C.
51. 4. thus the slain shall fall in the land of the C.
52. 8. but the army of the C. pursued Zedekiah
Ezek. 12. 13. I will bring him to the land of the C.
23. 14. she saw the images of the C. portrayed
Dan. 1. 4. they might teach the tongue of the C.
2. 2. then the king commanded to call the C.
3. 8. at that time certain C. accused the Jews
4. 7. then came in the C. and the soothsayers
5. 7. the king cried aloud to bring in the C.
11. whom thy father made master of the C.
9. 1. Darius made king over the realm of the C.
Hab. 1. 6. lo, I raise up the C. that hasty nation
Acts 7. 4. Abram came out of the land of the C.

CHALDEES.

2 *Kings* 24. 2. Lord sent against him bands of the C.
25. 4. the C. were against the city round about
10. the army of the C. brake down the walls
26. came to Egypt, for they were afraid of the C.
2 *Chr.* 36. 17. he brought on them the king of the C.
Isa. 13. 19. Babylon the beauty of C. excellency
See Ur.

CHARRAN.

Acts 7. 2. God appeared bef. Abraham dwelt in C. 4.

CHEBAR.

Ezek. 1. 1. by river of C. 3. | 3. 15, 23. | 10. 15. 20.

CHEMARIMS.

Zeph. 1. 4. I will cut off the name of the C.

CHEMOSH.

Num. 21. 29. thou art undone, O people of C.
Judg. 11. 24. wilt not thou possess what C. giveth?
1 *Kings* 11. 7. Solomon built an high place for C. 33.
Jer. 48. 7. and C. shall go forth into captivity
13. and Moab shall be ashamed of C. as Israel
46. woe to thee, O Moab, people of C. perisheth

CHENANIAH.

1 *Chr.* 15. 22. C. chief of the Levites, was for song, 27.

CHERETHIMS.

Ezek. 25. 16. behold, I will cut off C. and destroy

CHERETHITES.

1 *Sam.* 30. 14. made an invasion on the south of C.
2 *Sam.* 8. 18. Benaiah the son of Jehoiada was over the C. and Pelethites, 20. 23. 1 *Chron.* 18. 17.
Zeph. 2. 5. woe unto the nation of the C. O Canaan

CHERITH.

1 *Kings* 17. 3. and hide thyself by the brook C.

CHILION. *See* Mahlon.

CHILMAD.

Ezek. 27. 23. Ashur and C. were thy merchants

CHIMHAM.

2 *Sam.* 19. 37. thy servant C. let him go over, 38, 40.
Jer. 41. 17. they dwelt in the habitation of C.

CHIOS.

Acts 20. 15. we came next day over-against C.

CHISLEU.

Neh. 1. 1. in the month C. || *Zech.* 7. 1. ninth month C.

CHITTIM.

Num. 24. 24. the ships shall come from coasts of C.
Isa. 23. 1. from the land of C. it is revealed to them
12. pass over to C. there shalt thou have no rest
Jer. 2. 10. for pass over the isles of C. and see
Ezek. 27. 6. benches of ivory brought out of isles C.
Dan. 11. 30. the ships of C. shall come against him

CHIUN.

Amos 5. 26. have born Moloch and C. your images

CHLOE.

1 *Cor.* 1. 11. by them which are of the house of C.

CHORAZIN.

Mat. 11. 21. woe unto thee, C. *Luke* 10. 13.

CHUSHAN-RISHATHAIM.

Judg. 3. 8. Lord sold Israel into the hand of C.

CHUZA.

Luke 8. 3. Joanna wife of C. ministered unto him

CILICIA.

Acts 6. 9. they of C. disputed with Stephen
15. 23. the brethren which are of the Gentiles in C.
41. he went through C. confirming the churches
21. 39. a man of Tarsus, a city in C. 22. 3. | 23. 34.
27. 5. when we had sailed over the sea of C.
Gal. 1. 21. I came into the regions of C.

CLEOPAS.

Luke 24. 18. one of them, whose name was C. said
John 19. 25. Mary the wife of C. stood by the cross

COLOSSE.

Col. 1. 2. Paul to the saints and brethren at C.

CONIAH.

Jer. 22. 24. though C. were the signet on my hand
28. is this man C. a despised, broken idol?
37. 1. king Zedekiah reigned instead of C.

CORINTH.

Acts 18. 1. after these things, Paul came to C.
19. 1. it came to pass that while Apollos was at C.
1 *Cor.* 1. 2. unto the church of God which is at C. to them sanctified in Christ Jesus, 2 *Cor.* 1. 1.
2 *Cor.* 1. 23. to spare you I came not as yet to C.
2 *Tim.* 4. 20. Erastus abode at C. Trophimus at [Miletum

CORINTHIANS.

Acts 18. 8. many of the C. hearing, believed
2 *Cor.* 6. 11. O ye C. our mouth is open unto you

CORNELIUS.

Acts 10. 1. there was a man in Cesarea, called C.
7. the angel which spake to C. was departed
25. C. met Peter, and fell down at his feet
31. the angel said, C. thy prayer is heard

COZBI.

Num. 25. 15. name of the Midianitish woman was C.
18. they have beguiled you in the matter of C.

CRESCENS.

2 *Tim.* 4. 10. C. is departed to Galatia, Titus to Dal- [matia

CRETE.

Acts 27. 7. we sailed under C. || 13. close by C.
12. attain to Phenice, which is an haven of C.
21. hearkened to me, and not have loosed from C.
Tit. 1. 5. for this cause left I thee in C. to set in order

CRETES.

Acts 2. 11. C. we hear them speak in our tongues

CRETIANS.

Tit. 1. 12. the C. are always liars, evil beasts

CRISPUS.

Acts 18. 8. C. chief ruler of the synagogue believed
1 *Cor.* 1. 14. that I baptized none of you but C.

CUSH.

Gen. 10. 6. sons of Ham, C. Mizraim, 1 *Chr.* 1. 8.
7. the sons of C. Sebah and Havilah, 1 *Chron.* 1. 9.
Isa. 11. 11. to recover the remnant left from C.

CUSHAN.

Hab. 3. 7. I saw the tents of C. in affliction

CUSHI.

2 *Sam.* 18. 21. C. tell the king what thou hast seen
23. Ahimaaz ran by the plain, and overran C.
Jer. 36. 14. all princes sent the son of C. to Baruch
Zeph. 1. 1. the word came to Zephaniah son of C.

CYPRUS.

Acts 4. 36. Joses was of the country of C.
11. 19. travelled as far as Phenice and C.
20. some of them were men of C. and Cyrene
13. 4. and from Seleucia they sailed to C.
15. 39. Barnabas took Mark and sailed to C.
21. 3. when we had discovered C. we left it
16. they brought with him one Mnason of C.
27. 4. when we launched, we sailed under C.

CYRENE.

Mat. 27. 32. found a man of C. Simon by name
Acts 2. 10. and in the parts of Libya about C.
11. 20. some of them were men of Cyprus and C.
13. 1. Lucius of C. was in the church at Antioch

CYRENIAN.

Mark 15. 21. compel Simon a C. to bear his cross

CYRENIANS.

Acts 6. 9. is called the synagogue of the C.

CYRENIUS.

Luke 2. 2. was made when C. was governor of Syria

CYRUS.

2 *Chron.* 36. 22. in the first year of C. king of Persia the Lord stirred up the spirit of C. *Ezra* 1. 1.
23. thus saith C. king of Persia, *Ezra* 1. 2.
Ezra 1. 7. C. brought forth the vessels, 8. | 5. 14.
3. 7. according to the grant they had of C.
4. 3. will build as C. the king hath commanded us
5. 13. C. made a decree to build this house, 17.
Isa. 44. 28. that saith of C. he is my shepherd
45. 1. thus saith the Lord to his anointed, to C.
Dan. 1. 21. Daniel continued to the first year of C.
6. 28. Daniel prospered in the reign of C.
10. 1. in the third year of C. a thing was revealed

D.

DABBASHETH.

Josh. 19. 11. their border toward sea reached to D.

DABERATH.

Josh. 19. 12. and then goeth out to D. up to Japhia
1 *Chron.* 6. 72. out of Issachar, D. with her suburbs

DAGON.

Judg. 16. 23. to offer a sacrifice to D. their god
1 *Sam.* 5. 2. brought the ark into the house of D.
3. D. was fallen || 4. the head of D. was cut off
7. his hand is sore on us, and on D. our god
1 *Chr.* 10. 10. fastened Saul's head in temple of D.

DALMATIA.

2 *Tim.* 4. 10. Titus is departed to D. only Luke is

DAMARIS.

Acts 17. 34. and a woman named D. believed

DAMASCUS.

Gen. 15. 2. the steward of my house is Eliezer of D.
2 *Sam.* 8. 6. David put garrisons in Syria of D. and Syrians became servants to David, 1 *Chron.* 18. 6.
1 *Kings* 11. 24. Rezon went to D. and reigned in D.
19. 15. return on thy way to the wilderness of D.
20. 34. thou shalt make streets for thee in D.
2 *Kings* 5. 12. are not Abana, Pharpar, rivers of D.?
8. 7. Elisha came to D. || 14. 28. Jerob. recovered D.
2 *Kings* 16. 9. the king of Assyria went up ag. D.
10. king Ahaz saw an altar that was at D.
1 *Chr.* 18. 5. Syrians of D. came to help Hadarezer
2 *Chr.* 24. 23. sent the spoil of them to the king of D.
28. 5. carried a great multitude of captives to D.
23. for Ahaz sacrificed to the gods of D.
Cant. 7. 4. Lebanon, which looketh toward D.
Isa. 7. 8. the head of Syria is D. head of D. Rezin
8. 4. the riches of D. shall be taken away
10. 9. for he saith, is not Samaria as D.?
17. 1. the burden of D. is taken, *Jer.* 49. 23.
3. and the kingdom shall cease from D.
Jer. 49. 24. D. is waxed feeble, and turneth to flee
27. I will kindle a fire in the wall of D.
Ezek. 27. 18. D. thy merchant in wine and wool
Amos 1. 3. for three transgressions of D. and for four
5. I will break also the bar of D. and cut off
3. 12. and that dwell in D. in a couch
5. 27. will cause you to go into captivity beyond D.
Zech. 9. 1. and D. shall be the rest thereof
Acts 9. 2. Saul desired of high priest letters to D.
10. there was a disciple at D. named Ananias
19. then was Saul with the disciples at D.
22. Saul confounded the Jews who dwelt at D.
27. declared how he had preached boldly at D.
22. 6. as I was come nigh to D. about noon, 26. 12.
10. the Lord said to me, arise, and go into D.
2 *Cor.* 11. 32. in D. governor desirous to apprehend me
Gal. 1. 17. but I returned again unto D.

DAN, *a person.*

Gen. 30. 6. therefore called she his name D.
35. 25. son of Bilhah, D. || 46. 23. of D. *Num.* 26. 42.
49. 16. D. shall judge his people, as one of the tribes
17. D. shall be a serpent by the way, an adder
Num. 1. 12. of D. Ahiezer the son of Ammi-shaddai
2. 25. the standard of the camp of D. on north side
31. all numbered in the camp of D. were 157,600
Deut. 33. 22. of D. he said, D. is a lion's whelp
Josh. 19. 47. after the name of D. *Judg.* 18. 29.
Judg. 5. 17. and why did D. remain in ships?
13. 25. the Spirit moved him in the camp of D.
Ezek. 48. 1. a portion for D. || 32. one gate of D.
See Children.

Tribe of DAN.

Exod. 31. 6. Aholiab of the *tribe of* D. 35. 34. | 38. 23.
Lev. 24. 11. daughter of Dibri, of the *tribe of* D.
Num. 1. 39. numbered of the *tribe of* D. 62,700
13. 12. of *tribe of* D. to spy the land, Ammiel
34. 22. of *tribe of* D. to divide the land, Bukki
Josh. 19. 40. lot came for the *tribe of* D. 48.
21. 5. out of the *tribe of* D. to the Levites, 23.
Judg. 18. 30. were priests to *tribe of* D. till captivity

DAN, *a place.*

Gen. 14. 14. Abraham pursued them unto D.
Deut. 34. 1. Lord shewed Moses all Gilead unto D.
Josh. 19. 47. they called Leshem, D. *Judg.* 18. 29.
Judg. 20. 1. from D. to Beer-sheba, 1 *Sam.* 3. 20.
2 *Sam.* 3. 10. | 17. 11. | 24. 2, 15. 1 *Kings* 4. 25. 1 *Chron.* 21. 2. 2 *Chron.* 30. 5.
1 *Kings* 12. 29. other calf put he in D. 2 *Kings* 10. 29.
15. 20. the king of Syria smote D. 2 *Chron.* 16. 4.
Jer. 4. 15. for a voice declareth from D.
8. 16. the snorting of horses was heard from D.
Ezek. 27. 19. D. and Javan occupied in thy fairs
Amos 8. 14. they that say, thy God, O D. liveth

DANIEL.

1 *Chr.* 3. 1. David had D. of Abigail the Carmelitess
Ezra 8. 2. of Ithamar, D. || *Neh.* 10. 6. D. sealed
Ezek. 14. 14. tho' Noah, D. and Job were in it, 20.
28. 3. behold, thou art wiser than D. no secret
Dan. 1. 6. D. of Judah || 19. none was found like D.
7. he gave to D. the name of Belteshazzar
17. D. had understanding in all visions and dreams
2. 13. sought D. to be slain || 16. then D. went in
19. the secret was revealed to D. in a vision
46. king Nebuchadnezzar worshipped D.
48. then the king made D. a great man
49. D. sat in the gate || 4. 8. at last D. came in
4. 19. then D. was astonied for one hour
5. 12. dissolving of doubts was found in D.
29. and they clothed D. with scarlet and put
6. 2. D. was first || 14. king set his heart on D.
5. we shall not find occasion against this D.
11. these men found D. praying before his God
13. D. regardeth not thee, O king, nor the decree
23. that they should take up D. out of the den
26. that men tremble before the God of D.
27. who hath delivered D. from power of the lions
28. so this D. prospered in the reign of Darius
7. 1. D. had a dream, and visions of his head
28. as for me D. || 10. 12. he said, fear not, D.
8. 1. a vision appeared to me, even unto me D.
12. 9. he said, go thy way, D. the words are closed
Mat. 24. 15. when shall see abomination of desolation, spoken of by D. the prophet, *Mark* 13. 14.

I DANIEL.

Dan. 7. 15. *I* D. was grieved || 8. 27. *I* D. fainted
8. 15. when *I*, even *I* D. had seen the vision
9. 2. *I* D. understood by books the number of years
10. 2. *I* D. was mourning three full weeks
7. *I* D. alone saw the vision. || 12. 5. *I* D. looked

O DANIEL.

Dan. 6. 20. *O* D. servant of the living God
9. 22. *O* D. I am now come to give thee skill
10. 11. he said to me, *O* D. a man greatly beloved
12. 4. *O* D. shut up the words and seal the book

DARIUS.

Ezra 4. 5. to frustrate, till the reign of D. 24.
5. 5. not to cease, till the matter came to D.
6. 1. then D. the king made a decree, 12.
15. this house was finished in sixth year of D.
Neh. 12. 22. also the priests to the reign of D.
Dan. 5. 31. D. the Median took the kingdom
6. 9. wherefore king D. signed the writing
25. king D. wrote to all people and nations
9. 1. in the first year of D. the Mede, 11. 1.
Hag. 1. 1. in second year of D. 15. | 2. 10. *Zech.* 1. 7.
Zech. 7. 1. in fourth year of D. the word came

DATHAN, *See* Abiram.

DAVID.

Ruth 4. 22. Jesse begat D. *Mat.* 1. 6. *Luke* 3. 31.
1 *Sam.* 16. 13. the Spirit of the Lord came upon D.

1 *Sam* 16. 19. send me D. thy son || 21. D. came to S.
23. D. played with his hand, 18. 10. | 19. 9.
17. 14. D. was youngest || 15. returned from Saul
23. and D. heard the words of Goliath
28. Eliab's anger was kindled against D.
38. Saul armed D. || 42. when Goliath saw D.
43. the Philistine cursed D. by his gods
50. D. prevailed over the Philistine with a sling
57. as D. returned from the slaughter of Philistin.
18. 1. the soul of Jonathan was knit to D.
3. then Jonathan and D. made a covenant
5. D. went out whithersoever Saul sent him
7. D. hath slain his ten thousands, 29. 5.
9. Saul eyed D. from that day and forward
14. D. behaved himself wisely in all his ways
16. but all Israel and Judah loved D.
24. the servants said, on this manner spake D.
28. Saul saw and knew that the Ld. was with D.
29. and Saul became D's enemy continually
19. 1. Saul spake to his servants to kill D.
5. wilt thou sin against innocent blood to slay D.?
10. Saul sought to smite D. but D. escaped, 18.
19. D. is at Naioth || 22. where are Samuel and D.
20. 6. D. ask. leave of me to run to Beth-lehem, 28.
17. and Jonathan caused D. to swear again
24. D. hid himself || 25. D. place was empty, 27.
34. Jonathan eat not, for he was grieved for D.
41. wept one with another, till D. exceeded
21. 1. Ahimelech was afraid at the meeting of D.
10. D. arose, and fled to Achish for fear of Saul
11. is not this D. the king of the land? 29. 3.
22. 1. D. departed and escap. to the cave Adullam
3. and D. went thence to Mispeh of Moab
5. D. departed and came into the forest of Hareth
14. who is so faithful among thy servants as D.?
17. because their hand also is with D.
23. 2. therefore D. inquired of the Lord, 4. | 30. 8. 2 *Sam.* 2. 1. | 3. 19, 22. | 21. 1.
5. so D. and his men went to Keilah and fought
9. D. knew that Saul practised mischief
15. D. was in the wilderness of Ziph in a wood
24. D. and his men were in wilderness of Maon
28. Saul return. from pursuing after D. and went
24. 1. D. is in the wilderness of En-gedi
5. D. heart smote him || 7. D. stayed his servants
16. Saul said, is this thy voice, my son D.? 26. 17.
22. D. sware unto Saul || 25. 1. D. went to Paran
25. 5. D. sent out ten young men to go to Nabal
22. so and more also do God to the enemies of D.
26. 1. doth not D. hide himself in hill Hachilah?
5. and D. beheld the place where Saul lay
12. D. took the spear and the cruse of water
17. Saul knew D. voice || 21. return, my son D.
27. 1. D. said, I shall perish by the hand of Saul
4. D. was fled to Gath || 8. D. invaded Geshurites
11. saying, so did D. and so will be his manner
28. 17. Lord given it to thy neighbour, even to D.
29. 3. is not this D. || 6. then Achish called D.
30. 1. when D. and his men were come to Ziklag
5. and D. two wives were taken captives
10. D. pursued || 17. smote them from twilight
18. D. recovered all, 19. || 20. D. took the flocks
2 *Sam.* 1. 11. D. took hold on his clothes, and rent
15. D. called one of the young men, and said
17. D. lamented over Saul and over Jonathan
2. 5. D. sent messengers to men of Jabesh-gilead
10. but the house of Judah followed D.
3. 1. but house of D. waxed stronger and stronger
2. unto D. were sons born in Hebron
9. except as Ld. hath sworn to D. so I do to him
17. ye sought for D. in times past to be king
28. D. said, I and my kingdom are guiltless
5. 1. then came all the tribes of Israel to D.
6. thinking D. cannot come in hither
7. nevertheless, D. took the strong-hold of Zion
10. D. grew great || 21. D. burnt their images
12. D. perceived the Lord had established him
17. D. heard of it, and went down to the hold
6. 2. D. went to bring up the ark of God
5. D. all Israel played before the Lord, and said
9. and D. was afraid of the Lord that day
14. D. danced || 15. so D. brought up the ark
7. 20. what can D. say more to thee? 1 *Chr.* 17. 18.
8. 1. D. smote the Philistines || 3. Hadadezer
6. Lord preserved D. whithersoever he went, 14.
7. D. took the shields of gold, 1 *Chron.* 18. 7.
13. D. gat him a name || 15. D. reign. 1 *Chr.* 18. 14.
15. D. reigned executed judgment to his people
10. 2. D. sent to comfort Hanun, 1 *Chron.* 19. 2.
3. thinkest thou that D. doth honour thy father, in sending comforters to thee? 1 *Chron.* 19. 3.
18. D. slew men of 700 chariots of the Syrians
11. 3. D. sent and inquired after the woman
6. D. sent for Uriah || 14. D. wrote a letter to Joab
27. the thing D. had done displeased the Lord
12. 5. D. anger was kindled against the man
13. D. said, I have sinned against the Lord
16. D. besought God for the child, D. fasted
19. D. perceived that the child was dead
24. and D. comforted Bath-sheba his wife
29. D. fought against Rabbah and took it
30. their king's crown was set on D. head
13. 7. D. sent to Tamar || 30. tidings came to D.
15. 30. D. went up by the ascent of mount Olivet
16. 6. Shimei cast stones at D. || 10. curse D.
17. 1. I will arise and pursue after D. this night
16. send quickly and tell D. || 22. then D. arose
27. D. was come to Mahanaim || 29. honey for D.
18. 1. D. numbered the people that were with him
24. D. sat between the two gates, the watchman
19. 43. we have also more right in D. than ye
20. 1. Sheba said, we have no part in D.
3. and D. came to his house at Jerusalem
11. he that is for D. let him go after Joab
21. 16. Ishbi-benob thought to have slain D.
22. 51. he shewed mercy unto D. *Psal.* 18. 50.
23. 1. the last words of D. || 15. D. longed and said
8. the mighty men whom D. had, 1 *Chron.* 11. 10.
24. 10. D. heart smote him after he had numbered
25. D. built there an altar unto the Lord
1 *Kings* 1. 11. and D. our lord knoweth it not
2. 10. D. slept with his fathers, and was buried

1 *Kings* 2. 32. slew them, my father D. not knowing
44. thou knowest what thou didst to D. my father
3. 14. if thou wilt walk as thy father D. did walk
5. 7. who hath given D. a wise son over this people
8. 16. I chose D. to be over my people Israel
20. I am risen up in the room of D. my father
9. 5. as I promised to D. || 11. 38. as I built for D.
11. 39. I will for this afflict the seed of D.
12. 16. what portion have we in D.? now see to thine own house, D. 2 *Chron.* 10. 16.
1 *Chron.* 10. 14. the Lord turned the kingdom to D.
11. 3. D. made a covenant with them in Hebron
12. 18. thine are we, D. then D. received them
21. they helped D. against the band of rovers
14. 17. the fame of D. went out into all lands
15. 27. D. was clothed with a robe of fine linen
16. 1. they set the ark in the tent D. had pitched
43. and D. returned to bless his house
21. 21. Arnan saw D. and bowed himself to D.
23. 1. so when D. was old and full of days
29. 10. D. blessed the Lord before the congregation
2 *Chron.* 1. 8. thou hast shewed great mercy unto D.
34. 3. he began to seek after the God of D.
Ezra 8. 2. of the sons of D. Hattush was the chief
Neh. 3. 16. to the place over against sepulchres of D.
12. 36. with musical instruments of D. man of God
Psal. 72. 20. prayers of D. the son of Jesse are ended
89. 35. I will not lie unto D. || 49. swarest to D.
132. 1. Lord, remember D. || 11. hath sworn to D.
17. there will I make the horn of D. to bud
Cant. 4. 4. thy neck is like the tower of D.
Isa. 9. 7. on the throne of D. and on his kingdom
29. 1. woe to Ariel, the city where D. dwelt
55. 3. even the sure mercies of D. *Acts* 13. 34.
Jer. 17. 25. kings and princes sitting on throne of D.
23. 5. I will raise to D. a righteous branch
33. 15. I will cause the branch to grow up unto D.
17. D. shall never want a man to sit on the throne
36. 30. he shall have none to sit on throne of D.
Amos 6. 5. invent instruments of music like D.
9. 11. in that day will I raise up the tabernacle of D. that is fallen, and will build it, *Acts* 15. 16.
Zech. 12. 8. the feeble shall be as D. and D. as God
Mat. 9. 27. thou Son of D. have mercy, 15. 22. | 20. 30, 31. *Mark* 10. 47, 48. *Luke* 18. 38, 39.
12. 3. have ye not read what D. did when he was an hungered? *Mark* 2. 25. *Luke* 6. 3.
23. the people said, is not this the Son of D.?
21. 9. saying, Hosanna to the Son of D. 15.
22. 42. Christ is the Son of D. *Mark* 12. 35.
45. if D. then call him Lord, how is he his son? *Mark* 12. 37. *Luke* 20. 41, 44.
Mark 11. 10. blessed be the kingdom of our father D.
John 7. 42. that Christ cometh of the seed of D.
Acts 2. 29. let me freely speak of the patriarch D.
34. for D. is not ascended into the heavens
13. 22. he raised up to them D. to be their king
36. for D. fell on sleep, and saw corruption
Rom. 1. 3. Christ, made of the seed of D. 2 *Tim.* 2. 8.
4. 6. even as D. also describeth the blessedness
Heb. 4. 7. he limiteth a certain day, saying, in D.
11. 32. the time would fail me to tell of D.
Rev. 3. 7. hath the key of D. || 5. 5. root of D. 22. 16.

See CITY, FATHER.

Days of DAVID.

2 *Sam.* 21. 1. there was a famine in the *days of* D.
1 *Kings* 2. 1. *days of* D. drew nigh that he should die
1 *Chron.* 7. 2. whose number was in the *days of* D.
Neh. 12. 46. in the *days of* D. were chief singers
Acts 7. 45. God drave out unto the *days of* D.

Hand of DAVID.

1 *Sam.* 20. 16. let Lord require it at *h. of* D. enemies
2 *Sam.* 3. 8. have not delivered thee into *hand of* D.
18. by *hand of* my servant D. I will save Israel
21. 22. fell by the *hand of* D. 1 *Chron.* 20. 8.

House of DAVID.

1 *Sam.* 20. 16. Jonathan made covenant with *h. of* D.
2 *Sam.* 3. 1. war between the *house of* Saul and D. 6.
7. 26. let *house of* thy servant D. be established
1 *Kings* 12. 19. so Israel rebelled against the *house of* D. unto this day, 2 *Chron.* 10. 19.
12. 20. none followed the *house of* D. but Judah
26. shall the kingdom return to the *house of* D.
13. 2. a child be born to the *house of* D. Josiah
14. 8. rent kingdom from *h. of* D. 2 *Kings* 17. 21.
2 *Chron.* 21. 7. Lord would not destroy the *h. of* D.
Psal. 122. 5. the thrones of the *house of* D.
Isa. 7. 2. it was told the *house of* D. saying, Syria
13. hear ye now, O *house of* D. *Jer.* 21. 12.
22. 22. key of *h. of* D. I will lay on his shoulders
Zech. 12. 7. that glory of *house of* D. do not magnify
8. feeble as D. and the *house of* D. shall be as God
10. I will pour on *house of* D. the spirit of grace
12. the family of the *house of* D. shall mourn apart
13. 1. shall be a fountain opened to the *house of* D.
Luke 1. 27. whose name was Joseph, of the *h. of* D.
69. raised up a horn of salvation in the *h. of* D.
2. 4. because he was of the *house* and lineage *of* D.

DAVID *joined with king.*

1 *Sam.* 21. 11. is not this D. the *king* of the land?
2 *Sam.* 2. 4. there they anointed D. *king* over Judah
11. time that D. was *king* in Hebron over Judah
3. 31. and *king* D. himself followed the bier
5. 3. *king* D. made a league with them, and they anointed D. *k.* over Israel, 1 *Chr.* 11. 3. | 12. 31, 38.
8. 11. which *king* D. did dedicate to the Lord with the silver and gold, 1 *Chron.* 26. 26.
20. 21. lifted up his hand against the *king*, even D.
1 *Kings* 1. 37. greater than throne of my lord *king* D.
47. the king's servants came to bless our lord *k.* D.
1 *Chron.* 29. 9. D. the *king* rejoiced with great joy
2 *Chron.* 2. 12. who hath given to D. the *k.* a wise son
29. 27. ordained by D. *king* of Israel, *Ezra* 3. 10.
Jer. 30. 9. shall serve the Lord and D. their *king*
Hos. 3. 5. shall seek the Lord and D. their *king*
Mat. 1. 6. Jesse begat D. the *king*, and D. the *king*
Acts 13. 22. he raised up D. to be their *king*

Servant DAVID.

2 *Sam.* 3. 18. by hand of my *servant* D. I will save
7. 5. go and tell my *servant* D. thus saith Lord, 8.
26. Lord is God of Israel, let the house of thy *s.* D. be established before thee? 1 *Chron.* 17. 24.

1 *Kings* 3. 6. hast shewed thy *servant* D. great mercy
8. 24. kept with thy *serv.* D. that thou promisedst
25. keep with thy *servant* D. 26. 2 *Chron.* 6. 16.
66. for all the goodness he had done for D. his *s.*
11. 13. for D. my *servant's* sake, and for Jerusalem's sake, 32, 34. *Psal.* 132. 10. *Isa.* 37. 35.
36. that D. my *servant* may have a light
38. to keep my statutes, as my *servant* D. did, 14. 8.
2 *Chron.* 6. 42. remember the mercies of D. thy *serv.*
Psal. 78. 70. he chose D. also his *servant* and took him
89. 3. I have sworn unto D. my *servant*
20. I have found D. my *servant*, I anointed him
144. 10. who delivered D. his *servant* from sword
Jer. 33. 21. my covenant broken with D. my *servant*
22. I will multiply the seed of D. my *servant*
26. then will I cast away the seed of D. my *serv.*
Ezek. 34. 23. even my *servant* D. shall feed them
24. my *servant* D. shall be a prince among them
37. 24. D. my *servant* shall be king over them
25. my *servant* D. shall be their prince for ever
Luke 1. 69. horn of salvation in house of his *s.* D.
Acts 4. 25. who by the mouth of thy *servant* D.

DEBORAH.

Gen. 35. 8. but D. Rebekah's nurse died, was buried
Judg. 4. 4. and D. a prophetess judged Israel
5. 7. until that I D. arose a mother in Israel
12. awake D. || 15. the princes were with D.

DECAPOLIS.

Mat. 4. 25. great multitudes followed him from D.
Mark 5. 20. and he began to publish in D.
7. 31. through the midst of the coasts of D.

DEDAN.

Gen. 10. 7. sons of Raamah, Sheba, D. 1 *Chron.* 1. 9.
1 *Chron.* 1. 32. the sons of Jokshan, Sheba and D.
Jer. 25. 23. I made D. and Tema, and Buz to drink
49. 8. flee ye, dwell deep, O inhabitants of D.
Ezek. 25. 13. they of D. shall fall by the sword
27. 20. D. was thy merchant in precious clothes

DEDANIM.

Isa. 21. 13. O ye travelling companies of D.

DELILAH.

Judg. 16. 4. a woman in the valley of Sorek, D.
12. D. therefore took new ropes and bound Sams.

DEMAS.

Col. 4. 14. Luke and D. greet you, *Philem.* 24.
2 *Tim.* 4. 10. D. hath forsaken me, having loved

DEMETRIUS.

Acts 19. 24. D. a silversmith, who made shrines
38. if D. have a matter against any man
3 *John* 12. D. hath good report of all men and of truth

DIANA.

Acts 19. 24. which made silver shrines for D.
27. the temple of the great goddess D.
28. they cried, great is D. of the Ephesians, 34.
35. Ephesus is a worshipper of the goddess D.

DIBON.

Num. 21. 30. Heshbon is perished even to D.
32. 34. the children of Gad built D. and Aroer
Josh. 13. 17. Moses gave D. to the children of Reuben
Neh. 11. 25. the children of Judah dwelt at D.
Isa. 15. 2. he is gone up to D. the high place
Jer. 48. 18. thou daughter, that dost inhabit D.
22. judgment is come upon D. and Nebo

DIBON-GAD.

Num. 33. 45. pitched in D. || 46. removed from D.

DIDYMUS.

John 11. 16. Thomas, who is called D. 20. 24. | 21. 2.

DIMON.

Isa. 15. 9. for the waters of D. shall be full of blood, for I will bring more upon D. lions upon him

DINAH.

Gen. 30. 21. Leah bare a daughter called her name D.
34. 5. Jacob heard that he had defiled D.

DIONYSIUS.

Acts 17. 34. among which was D. the Areopagite

DIOTREPHES.

3 *John* 9. D. who loveth to have the pre-eminence

DOEG.

1 *Sam.* 21. 7. and his name was D. an Edomite
22. 18. D. turned and slew the priests, 85 persons
22. I knew it that day when D. was there

DOR.

Judg. 1. 27. did Manasseh drive out inhabitants of D.
1 *Kings* 4. 11. the son of Abinadab in the region of D.

DORCAS.

Acts 9. 36. named Tabitha, by interpretation is D.
39. shewing coats and garments which D. made

DOTHAN.

Gen. 37. 17. let us go to D. he found them in D.
2 *Kings* 6. 13. saying, behold Elisha is in D.

DRUSILLA.

Acts 24. 24. when Felix came with his wife D.

DUMAH.

Gen. 25. 14. sons of Ishmael, D. Massa, 1 *Chr.* 1. 30.

DUMAH.

Josh. 15. 52. D. was in Judah's inheritance
Isa. 21. 11. the burden of D. he called to me.

DURA.

Dan. 3. 1. he set the image up in the plain of D.

E.

EASTER.

Acts 12. 4. intending after E. to bring him forth

EBAL.

Deut. 11. 29. thou shalt put the curse upon mount E.
27. 4. ye shall set up these stones in mount E.
13. these shall stand upon mount E. to curse
Josh. 8. 30. Joshua built an altar in mount E.
33. half of them stood over-against mount E.

EBED.

Judg. 9. 30. Zebul heard the words of Gaal son of E.
Ezra 8. 6. E. the son of Jonathan with 50 males

EBED-MELECH.

Jer. 38. 8. E. spake to the king for Jeremiah
39. 16. go and speak to E. the Ethiopian

EBEN-EZER.

1 *Sam.* 4. 1. Israel went out and pitched beside E.
5. 1. the Philistines brought the ark from E.
7. 12. Samuel called the name of the stone E.

EBER.
Gen. 10. 21. Shem the father of the children of E.
25. unto E. were born two sons, 1 *Chron.* 1. 19.
Num. 24. 24. ships from Chittim shall afflict E.
ED.
Josh. 22. 34. children of Gad called the altar E.
EDEN.
Gen. 2. 15. God put the man into the garden of E.
3. 23. God sent him forth from the garden of E.
Isa. 51. 3. make her wilderness like E. *Ezek.* 36. 35.
Ezek. 28. 13. thou hast been in E. the garden of God
31. 9. so that all the trees of E. envied him
16. all the trees of E. shall be comforted
18. thou shalt be brought down with the trees of E.
Joel 2. 3. the land is as the garden of E. before them
Amos 1. 5. and cut off him that holds sceptre from E.
EDOM.
Gen. 25. 30. therefore was his name called E.
36. 1. Esau is E. ‖ *Exod.* 15. 15. dukes of E. amazed
Num. 20. 14. Moses sent messengers from Kedesh to the king of E. *Judg.* 11. 17.
21. E. refused to give Isr. passage thro' his border
24. 18. E. shall be a possession for his enemies
Judg. 5. 4. thou marchedst out of the field of E.
1 *Sam.* 14. 47. Saul fought against Moab and E.
2 *Sam.* 8. 14. David put garrisons in E. 1 *Chr.* 18. 13.
1 *Kings* 11. 14. Hadad was of the king's seed in E.
16. Joab rem. till he had cut off every male in E.
22. 47. there was then no king in E.
2 *Kings* 3. 20. there came water by the way of E.
8. 20. in his days E. revolted from under Judah
14. 10. thou hast indeed smitten E. glory of this
2 *Chron.* 25. 20. they sought after the gods of E.
Psal. 60. 8. over E. will I cast out my shoe, 108. 9.
9. who will lead me into E.? 108. 10.
83. 6. the tabernacles of E. are confederate
137. 7. remember, O Lord, the children of E.
Isa. 11. 14. they shall lay their hand on E.
63. 1. who is this that cometh from E.?
Jer. 9. 26. Judah and E. I will punish, 25. 21.
27. 3. send bonds and yokes to the king of E.
49. 7. concerning E. saith the Lord, *Obad.* 1.
17. E. shall be a desolation, every one astonished
20. the counsel he hath taken against E.
Ezek. 25. 12. because E. hath dealt against Judah
14. and I will lay my vengeance upon E.
32. 29. there is E. her kings and all her princes
Dan. 11. 41. E. shall escape out of his hand
Joel 3. 19. E. shall be a desolate wilderness
Amos 1. 6. captivity to deliver them up to E. 9.
2. 1. he burnt the bones of the king of E.
9. 12. that they may possess the remnant of E.
Obad. 8. I will destroy the wise men out of E.
Mal. 1. 4. whereas E. saith, we are impoverished
See DAUGHTER.
EDOMITE, S
Gen. 36. 9. Esau father of the E. in mount Seir, 43.
Deut. 23. 7. shalt not abhor an E. he is thy brother
1 *Kings* 11. 14. the Lord stirred up Hadad the E.
2 *Kings* 8. 21. Joram smote the E. 2 *Chron.* 21. 9.
1 *Chron.* 18. 13. the E. became David's servants
2 *Chron.* 21. 10. the E. revolted from under Judah
25. 19. thou sayest, lo, thou hast smitten the E.
28. 17. the E. had come and smitten Judah
See DOEG.
EGLAH.
2 *Sam.* 3. 5. the sixth, Ithream, by E. David's wife
EGLAIM.
Isa. 15. 8. the howling thereof is gone unto E.
EGLON.
Judg. 3. 14. Israel served E. the king of Moab
17. brought presents to E. and E. was very fat man
EGYPT.
Gen. 15. 18. from the river of E. to Euphrates
45. 9. God hath made me lord of all E. come down
Exod. 3. 20. I will smite E. *Jer.* 9. 26. | 46. 25.
7. 4. not hearken, that I may lay my hand on E.
8. 6. Aaron stretched his hand over the waters of E.
9. 4. sever between the cattle of Israel and of E.
10. 7. knowest thou not that E. is destroyed
23. 15. for in it thou camest out of E. 34. 18.
Num. 14. 19. thou hast forgiven this people from E.
22. 5. behold, there is a people come out of E.
Deut. 6. 22. the Lord shewed great signs upon E.
7. 15. will put none of the diseases of E. on thee
11. 4. and what he did unto the army of E.
28. 27. Lord will smite thee with the botch of E.
60. he will bring on thee all the diseases of E.
Josh. 5. 9. I have rolled away the reproach of E.
24. 5. I sent Moses and Aaron, and I plagued E.
1 *Sam.* 30. 13. he said, I am a young man of E.
1 *Kings* 4. 30. Solomon's wisd. excelled wisd. of E.
2 *Kings* 18. 21. thou trustest on E. 24. *Isa.* 36. 6, 9.
Psal. 105. 38. E. was glad when they departed
135. 8. who smote the first-born of E. of man and
9. who sent wonders into the midst of thee, O E.
136. 10. to him that smote E. in their first-born
Prov. 7. 16. decked my bed with fine linen of E.
Isa. 10. 24. after the manner of E. *Amos* 4. 10.
11. 11. to recover the remnant of people from E.
19. 1. burden of E. the idols of E. shall be moved
3. the spirit of E. shall fail in midst thereof
16. in that day shall E. be like unto women
24. in that day shall Israel be the third with E.
25. shall bless, saying, blessed be ye E. my people
20. 5. they shall be ashamed of E. their glory
23. 5. as at the report concerning E. so of Tyre
27. 12. Lord shall beat off from the stream of E.
30. 3. the trust in the shadow of E. your confusion
43. 3. I gave E. for thy ransom, Seba for thee
45. 14. the labour of E. shall come over to thee
Jer. 2. 18. what hast thou to do in the way of E.?
36. thou shalt be ashamed of E. as of Assyria
46. 2. the word of the Lord which came against E.
20. E. is like a fair heifer, but destruction comes
Ezek. 20. 7. defile not yourselves with the idols of E.
23. 8. nor left she her idols brought from E.
27. thou shalt not remember E. any more
27. 7. fine linen with broidered work from E.
29. 2. prophesy against him and against all E.
14. I will bring again the captivity of E.
30. 6. they also that uphold E. shall fall

Ezek. 30. 9. pain shall come on them, as in day of E.
15. I will pour my fury on Sin the strength of E.
32. 12. they shall spoil the pomp of E. and all
16. they shall lament for her, even for E.
18. son of man, wail for the multitude of E.
Dan. 11. 43. have power over precious things of E.
Hos. 9. 6. they are gone, E. shall gather them up
Joel 3. 19. E. shall be a desolation, and Edom a wilder.
Amos 8. 8. be drowned, as by the flood of E. 9. 5.
Nah. 3. 9. Ethiopia and E. were her strength
Zech. 10. 11. the sceptre of E. shall depart away
14. 18. if family of E. go not up and come not
Acts 7. 10. he made him governor over E. and his
Heb. 11. 27. by faith he forsook E. not fearing
Rev. 11. 8. which spiritually is called Sodom and E.
See DAUGHTER.
In EGYPT.
Gen. 45. 13. tell my father of all my glory *in* E.
47. 29. Jacob said, bury me not, I pray thee, *in* E.
Exod. 3. 7. I have seen affliction of my people *in* E.
16. I have seen that which is done to you *in* E.
9. 18. grievous hail, such as hath not been *in* E.
10. 2. what things I wrought *in* E. *Josh.* 24. 7.
12. 30. a great cry *in* E. 14. 11. no graves *in* E.
Num. 11. 18. for it was well with us *in* E.
20. 15. and we have dwelt *in* E. a long time
Deut. 1. 30. all that he did for you *in* E. 4. 34.
Josh. 9. 9. we have heard all that he did *in* E.
Psal. 78. 43. how he had wrought his signs *in* E.
51. he smote all the first-born *in* E.
106. 7. they understood not thy wonders *in* E.
21. forgat God, who had done great things *in* E.
Jer. 42. 16. famine shall follow close after you *in* E.
46. 14. declare ye *in* E. and publish it in Migdol
Ezek. 23. 3. they committed whoredoms *in* E.
30. 8. shall know, when I have set a fire *in* E. 16.
19. thus will I execute judgments *in* E.
Mat. 2. 19. an angel appeared to Joseph *in* E.
Acts 2. 10. the dwellers *in* E. we do hear them speak
Heb. 11. 26. greater riches than the treasures *in* E.
Into EGYPT.
Gen. 41. 57. all countries came *into* E. to buy corn
46. 4. I will go down with thee *into* E.
26. all the souls that came with Jacob *into* E.
Num. 14. 3. better for us to return *into* E. 4.
Isa. 19. 1. behold, the Lord shall come *into* E.
30. 2. that walk to go down *into* E. to strengthen
Jer. 26. 21. Urijah afraid, fled and went *into* E.
41. 17. if ye set your faces to go *into* E. 42. 15.
42. 19. the Lord said, go ye not *into* E. 43. 2.
Ezek. 17. 15. sending his ambassadors *into* E.
Dan. 11. 8. he shall also carry captives *into* E.
Hos. 12. 1. with Assyrians, and oil is carried *into* E.
Mat. 2. 13. flee *into* E. ‖ 14. he departed *into* E.
Acts 7. 9. the patriarchs sold Joseph *into* E.
34. and now come, I will send thee *into* E.
39. in their hearts turned back again *into* E.
See KING.
Land of EGYPT.
Gen. 13. 10. Sodom was like the *land of* E.
21. 21. Ishmael's wife out of the *land of* E.
41. 19. such as I never saw in all the *land of* E.
29. seven years plenty, thro' all *land of* E. 30, 53.
41. set thee over all the *land of* E. 45. 8, 26.
54. but in all the *land of* E. was bread
45. 18. I will give you the good of the *land of* E. 20.
47. 6. the *land of* E. is before thee, in best of land
15. when money failed in the *land of* E.
20. Joseph bought all the *land of* E. for Pharaoh
26. Joseph made it a law over the *land of* E.
50. 7. all the elders of the *land of* E. went up
Exod. 7. 19. that there may be blood in all *land of* E.
8. 6. frogs covered the *land of* E. ‖ 16. lice ‖ 24. flies
9. 9. blains ‖ 22. hail ‖ 10. 14. locusts in *land of* E.
10. 21. may be darkness over all the *land of* E. 22.
11. 3. Moses was very great in the *land of* E.
12. 29. Lord smote first-born in *land of* E. 13. 15.
16. 3. would God we had died in *l. of* E. *Num.* 14. 2.
6. brought you out of *land of* E. 20. 2. | 29. 46.
22. 21. for ye were strangers in the *land of* E. 23. 9.
Lev. 19. 34. *Deut.* 10. 19. *Acts* 13. 17.
32. 4. these be thy gods which brought thee out of the *land of* E. 1 *Kings* 12. 28. *Neh.* 9. 18.
Lev. 18. 3. after doings of *land of* E. shall ye not do
19. 36. I am the Lord thy God, who brought you out of the *land of* E. 26. 13. *Num.* 15. 41. *Deut.* 5. 6. | 13. 5, 10. | 20. 1. *Judg.* 2. 12. 1 *Sam.* 12. 6.
Deut. 9. 7. from the day that thou didst depart out of the *land of* E. *Judg.* 19. 30. *Isa.* 11. 16. *Jer.* 7. 22. | 11. 7. | 34. 13. *Mic.* 7. 15.
11. 10. the land whither thou goest is not *land of* E.
16. 3. thou camest out of the *land of* E. in haste
Ps. 78. 12. marvellous things did he in the *land of* E.
81. 5. when he went out through the *land of* E.
Isa. 19. 18. shall in *l. of* E. speak language of Canaan
19. altar to Lord for a witness in *land of* E. 20.
27. 13. the outcasts in the *land of* E. shall come
Jer. 42. 14. no, but we will go into the *land of* E.
16. the sword shall overtake you in the *land of* E.
43. 7. so they came into the *land of* E.
12. he shall array himself with the *land of* E.
44. 28. shall return out of the *land of* E. into Judah
Ezek. 20. 5. myself known to them in *land of* E.
23. 19. she had played the harlot in the *land of* E.
27. thy whoredom brought from the *land of* E.
29. 9. the *land of* E. desolate, 12. ‖ 10. utterly waste
20. have given him the *land of* E. for his labour
30. 13. shall be no more a prince of the *land of* E.
Dan. 11. 42. and the *land of* E. shall not escape
Hos. 7. 16. this shall be their derision in *land of* E.
12. 9. the Lord thy God from the *land of* E. 13. 4.
Zech. 10. 10. I will bring them out of the *land of* E.
Heb. 8. 9. to lead them out of the *land of* E.
Jude 5. having saved the people out of the *land of* E.
Out of EGYPT.
Gen. 13. 1. Abraham *o. of* E. ‖ 47. 30. carry me *o. of* E.
Exod. 3. 11. that I should bring Israel *out of* E.
12. 39. because they were thrust *out of* E.
13. 9. it shall be for a sign, for with a strong hand hath the Lord brought thee *out of* E. 16.
Num. 11. 20. saying, why came we forth *out of* E.?
22. 11. behold there is a people come *out of* E.

Num. 32. 11. none of the men that came *out of* E.
Deut. 16. 6. at season thou camest forth *out of* E.
Josh. 2. 10. dried up Red Sea, when came *out of* E.
5. 6. till all that came *out of* E. were consumed
Judg. 2. 1. I made you go *out of* E. 1 *Sam.* 10. 18.
1 *Sam.* 15. 6. shewed kindness when Is. came *out of* E.
1 *Chr.* 17. 21. whom thou hast redeemed *out of* E.
2 *Chr.* 12. 3. the people that came with him *out of* E.
Psal. 68. 31. princes shall come *out of* E. Ethiopia
80. 8. thou hast brought a vine *out of* E.
114. 1. when Israel went *out of* E. house of Jacob
Isa. 19. 23. there shall be a high-way *out of* E.
Jer. 26. 23. they set forth Urijah *out of* E.
37. 5. then Pharaoh's army was come *out of* E.
Hos. 11. 1. I called my son *out of* E. *Mat.* 2. 15.
11. they shall tremble as a bird *out of* E.
12. 13. by a prophet Lord brought Israel *out of* E.
Hag. 2. 5. I covenanted, when ye came *out of* E.
Heb. 3. 16. howbeit not all that came *out of* E.
To EGYPT.
1 *Kings* 11. 18. Hadad and the Edomites came *to* E.
2 *Kings* 23. 34. Jehoahaz came *to* E. 2 *Chr.* 36. 4.
Isa. 19. 17. the land of Judah shall be a terror *to* E.
21. and the Lord shall be known *to* E.
31. 1. woe to them that go down *to* E. for help
Hos. 7. 11. they call *to* E. they go to Assyria
See RETURN.
EGYPTIAN.
Gen. 16. 1. Sarai had an hand-maid an E. 3. | 21. 9.
39. 1. an E. bought Joseph of the Ishmaelites
5. Lord blessed the E. house for Joseph's sake
Exod. 1. 19. the Hebrews are not as the E. women
2. 11. Moses spied an E. smiting an Hebrew
12. he slew the E. and hid him, *Acts* 7. 24.
19. an E. delivered us from the shepherds
Lev. 24. 10. whose father was an E. went out
Deut. 23. 7. thou shalt not abhor an E. because
1 *Sam.* 30. 11. they found an E. in the field
2 *Sam.* 23. 21. Benaiah slew an E. a goodly man, and the E. had a spear in his hand, 1 *Chron.* 11. 23.
1 *Chron.* 2. 34. Sheshan had a servant an E. Jarha
Isa. 11. 15. Lord shall destroy the tongue of E. sea
19. 23. and the E. shall come into Assyria
Acts 21. 38. art not thou that E. who madest uproar?
EGYPTIANS.
Gen. 41. 55. Pharaoh said to the E. go to Joseph
43. 32. that is abomination to the E. 46. 34.
50. 3. the E. mourned for Jacob seventy days
Exod. 3. 22. and ye shall spoil the E. 12. 36.
8. 26. shall we sacrifice the abomination of E.?
11. 7. Lord put a difference between E. and Israel
12. 35. they borrowed of the E. jewels of gold
14. 9. but the E. pursued after them, 10.
13. the E. whom ye have seen to day, see no more
25. the E. said, let us flee from the face of Israel, for the Lord fighteth for them against the E.
27. the Lord overthrew E. in the midst of the sea
19. 4. ye have seen what I did to the E. and how
32. 12. wherefore should the E. speak and say?
Num. 14. 13. Moses said, then the E. shall hear it
20. 15. and E. vexed us and our fathers
Deut. 26. 6. the E. evil entreated and afflicted us
Josh. 24. 7. he put darkness between you and the E.
Judg. 10. 11. did not I deliver you from the E.?
1 *Sam.* 4. 8. these are the gods that smote the E.
6. 6. why do you harden your hearts, as the E. did?
Ezra 9. 1. according to the abominations of the E.
Isa. 19. 2. I will set the E. against the E.
4. the E. will I give into the hand of a cruel lord
21. the E. shall know the Lord in that day
23. the E. shall serve with the Assyrians
20. 4. king of Assyria shall lead away E. prisoners
30. 7. the E. shall help in vain and to no purpose
31. 3. now E. are men and not God, their horses
Jer. 43. 13. houses of the gods of the E. shall he burn
Lam. 5. 6. we have given the hand to the E.
Ezek. 16. 26. hast committed fornication with the E.
23. 21. in bruising thy teats by E. for the paps
29. 12. and I will scatter the E. 30. 23, 26.
13. I will gather the E. from the people
Acts 7. 22. Mos. was learned in the wisdom of the E.
Heb. 11. 29. which E. assaying to do, were drowned
EHUD.
Judg. 3. 15. raised up E. the son of Gera a Benjamite
16. E. made him a dagger ‖ 23. E. went forth
26. and E. escaped while they tarried and passed
4. 1. Israel again did evil, when E. was dead
1 *Chr.* 7. 10. sons of Bilham, E. ‖ 8. 6. the sons of E.
EKRON.
1 *Sam.* 5. 10. it came to pass, as the ark came to E.
7. 14. cities were restored to Israel from E.
2 *Kings* 1. 2. Baal-zebub the god of E. 3. 6, 16.
Amos 1. 8. I will turn mine hand against the E.
Zeph. 2. 4. and E. shall be rooted up
Zech. 9. 5. E. very sorrowful ‖ 7. E. a Jebusite
EKRONITES.
Josh. 13. 3. the land of the E. not yet conquered
1 *Sam.* 5. 10. when ark came to Ekron, E. cried out
ELAH.
Gen. 36. 41. duke E. ‖ 1 *Kings* 4. 18. Shimei son of E.
1 *Kings* 16. 8. E. son of Baasha began to reign
2 *Kings* 15. 30. Hoshea the son of E. 17. 1. | 18. 1, 9.
1 *Chron.* 4. 15. the son of Caleb, E. the sons of E.
9. 8. E. the son of Uzzi, the son of Michri
ELAH.
1 *Sam.* 17. 2. Israel pitched by the valley of E.
21. 9. David slew Goliath in the valley of E.
ELAM.
Gen. 10. 22. the children of Shem, E. and Ashur
14. 1. in the days of Chedorlaomer king of E.
1 *Chron.* 8. 24. Hananiah and E. of Benjamin
26. 3. E. the fifth son of Meshelemiah
Ezra 2. 7. the children of E. ‖ 8. 7. *Neh.* 7. 12, 34.
10. 2. one of the sons of E. answered to Ezra
Neh. 10. 14. the chief of the people, E. Zatthu
12. 42. Jehohanan and E. and Ezer, priests
Isa. 11. 11. to recover his people from E.
21. 2. go up, O E. ‖ 22. 6. and E. bare the quiver
Jer. 25. 25. I made all the kings of E. to drink
49. 34. the word of the Lord that came against E.
36. upon E. will I bring the four winds
39. I will bring again the captivity of E. saith Ld.

Ezek. 32. 24. there is E. and all her multitude
Dan. 8. 2. Shushan which is in the province of E.

ELAMITES.

Ezra 4. 9. the E. wrote a letter to Artaxerxes
Acts 2. 9. Parthians, E. we hear them speak

ELATH.

2 *Kings* 14. 22. Azariah built E. and restored it
16. 6. at that time Rezin recovered E. to Syria

EL-BETHEL.

Gen. 35. 7. Jacob built an altar, and called it E.

ELDAD.

Num. 11. 26. the name of the one was E.
27. E. and Medad do prophesy in the camp

ELEALEH.

Num. 32. 37. the children of Reuben built E.
Isa. 15. 4. and Heshbon shall cry, and E. their voice
16. 9. I will water thee with my tears, O E.
Jer. 48. 34. from the cry of Heshbon even to E.

ELEAZAR.

Exod. 6. 25. Aaron's son E. 28. 1. *Num.* 3. 2. | 26. 60. 1 *Chron.* 6. 3. | 24. 1. *Ezra* 8. 33.
Lev. 10. 16. Moses was angry with E. and Ithamar
Num. 3. 4. E. ministered in the priest's office
32. E. son of Aaron shall be chief over the Levites
4. 16. to the office of E. pertaineth the oil
16. 39. E. the priest took the brasen censers
20. 26. and put his garments upon E. his son
28. Moses and E. came down from the mount
26. 63. that were numbered by Moses and E.
27. 22. he set Joshua before E. the priest
31. 12. they brought the spoil to Moses and E.
26. take the sum of prey thou and E. the priest
41. and Moses gave tribute unto E.
34. 17. E. and Joshua shall divide the land
Josh. 17. 4. came near before E. || 24. 33. E. died
1 *Sam.* 7. 1. they sanctified E. to keep the ark
2 *Sam.* 23. 9. after him E. son of Dodo, 1 *Chr.* 11. 12.
1 *Chron.* 9. 20. the son of E. was ruler over them
23. 21. the sons of Mahli, E. and Kish, 24. 28.
22. E. died, and had no sons, but daughters
24. 4. more chief men of sons of E. than Ithamar
5. the governors were of the sons of E.
Neh. 12. 42. Shemaiah and E. were priests
Mat. 1. 15. Eliud begat E. and E. begat Matthan

EL-ELOHE-*Israel.*

Gen. 33. 20. Jacob called the altar E.-*Israel*

ELHANAN.

2 *Sam.* 21. 19. E. slew brother of Goliath, 1 *Chr.* 20. 5.
23. 24. E. the son of Dodo, 1 *Chron.* 11. 26.

ELI.

1 *Sam.* 1. 25. they brought the child to E.
2. 11. the child did minister to the L. before E. 3. 1.
12. now the sons of E. were sons of Belial
27. there came a man of God to E. and said
3. 5. Samuel ran to E. and said, here am I, 6, 8.
12. in that day I will perform against E. all things
14. iniquity of E. house shall not be purged
4. 14. the man came in hastily and told E.
1 *Kings* 2. 27. which he spake concerning E.

ELI, ELI, *lama sabachthani.*

Mat. 27. 46. Jesus cried, E. E. *lama sab. Mark* 15. 34.

ELIAB.

Num. 1. 9. of the tribe of Zebulun, E. the son of Helon, 2. 7. | 24. 29. | 10. 16.
16. 1. Dathan and Abiram sons of E. 12. | 26. 9.
26. 8. sons of Pallu, E. || 1 *Sam.* 16. 6. looked on E.
Deut. 11. 6. what he did to the sons of E.
1 *Sam.* 17. 28. E. heard, and his anger was kindled
1 *Chron.* 2. 13. and Jesse begat his first-born E.
6. 27. E. the son of Nahath, the son of Zophai
12. 9. E. captain of the Gadites came to David
15. 18. E. porter, 20. || 16. 5. E. with a psaltery
2 *Chron.* 11. 18. Rehoboam took the daughter of E.

ELIADA.

2 *Sam.* 5. 16. E. a son of David, 1 *Chron.* 3. 8.
2 *Chron.* 17. 17. of Benjamin, E. a mighty man

ELIAKIM.

2 *Kings* 18. 18. there came out to Rab-shakeh E. the son of Hilkiah and Shebna the scribe, *Isa.* 36. 3.
19. 2. Hezekiah sent E. to Isaiah, *Isa.* 37. 2.
23. 34. made E. son of Josiah king, 2 *Chron.* 36. 4.
Neh. 12. 41. E. and Maaseiah the priests
Isa. 22. 20. that I will call my servant E.
Mat. 1. 13. Abiud begat E. and E. begat Azor
Luke 3. 30. Jonan, which was the son of E.

ELIAM.

2 *Sam.* 11. 3. Bath-sheba the daughter of E.
23. 34. E. the son of Ahithophel the Gilonite

ELIAS. *See* ELIJAH.

ELIASHIB.

1 *Chron.* 3. 24. E. and Pelaiah sons of Elioenai
24. 12. the eleventh lot came forth to E.
Ezra 10. 6. Johanan the son of E. *Neh.* 12. 23.
24. E. a singer || 27. E. the son of Zattu
36. E. son of Bani || *Neh.* 3. 1. E. the high-priest
Neh. 12. 10. Joiakim begat E. and E. begat Joiada
13. 4. E. was allied to Tobiah || 7. the evil E. did
28. one of the sons of Joiada, the son of E.

ELIEZER.

Gen. 15. 2. the steward of my house is this E.
Exod. 18. 4. name of Moses' son was E. 1 *Chr.* 23. 15.
1 *Chron.* 7. 8. the sons of Becher, E. and Elioenai
15. 24. Benaiah and E. the priests did blow
23. 17. the son of E. was Rehabiah the chief
27. 16. the ruler of the Reubenites was E.
2 *Chron.* 20. 37. E. prophesied against Jehoshaphat
Ezra 8. 16. then sent I for E. and Ariel, chief men
10. 18. E. had taken strange wives, 23, 31.
Luke 3. 29. Jose, which was the son of E.

ELIHOREPH.

1 *Kings* 4. 3. E. and Ahiah, sons of Shisha, scribes

ELIHU.

1 *Sam.* 1. 1. Elkanah, son of Jeroham, son of E.
1 *Chron.* 12. 20. E. fell to David out of Manasseh
26. 7. E. and Semachiah were strong men
27. 18. of Judah, E. one of the brethren of David
Job 32. 2. wrath of E. the Buzite was kindled
4. E. had waited || 6. answered, 34. 1. | 35. 1.

ELIJAH, or ELIAS.

1 *Kings* 17. 1. E. the Tishbite said unto Ahab
15. she went and did according to the saying of E.
22. and the Lord heard the voice of E.
1 *Kings* 17. 23. E. took the child and brought him down
18. 2. E. went to shew himself unto Ahab
7. art thou that my lord E.? || 8. E. is here
16. Ahab went to meet E. || 27. E. mocked them
40. E. slew all the prophets of Baal
46. and the hand of the Lord was on E.
19. 1. Ahab told Jezebel all that E. had done
9. the Lord said, what dost thou here E.? 13.
20. Elisha left the oxen and ran after E. 21.
21. 20. Ahab said to E. hast thou found me?
2 *Kings* 1. 8. Ahaziah said, it is E. the Tishbite
13. the third captain fell on his knees before E.
17. he died, according to the word E. had spoken
2. 1. when the Lord would take up E. into heaven
8. E. took his mantle, and wrapped it together
11. E. went up by a whirlwind into heaven
14. Elisha said, where is the Lord God of E.?
15. the spirit of E. doth rest on Elisha
3. 11. which poured water on the hands of E.
9. 36. done that which he spake by E. 10. 10, 17.
2 *Chron.* 21. 12. there came a writing from E.
Ezra 10. 21. Masseiah and E. the sons of Harim
Mal. 4. 5. behold, I will send you E. the prophet
Mat. 11. 14. this is *Elias* which was to come
16. 14. some say, *Elias, Mark* 6. 15. *Luke* 9. 8, 19.
17. 3. there appeared *Elias, Mark* 9. 4. *Luke* 9. 30.
4. three tabernacles, one for thee, one for Moses, one for *Elias, Mark* 9. 5. *Luke* 9. 33.
10. that *Elias* must first come, *Mark* 9. 11.
11. *Elias* shall come and restore things, *Mark* 9. 12.
12. I say to you, *Elias* is come already, *Mark* 9. 13.
27. 47. this man calleth for *Elias, Mark* 15. 35.
49. let us see whether *Elias* will come, *Mark* 15. 36.
Luke 1. 17. shall go before him in the power of *Elias*
4. 25. many widows were in the days of *Elias*
9. 54. commanded fire to consume them as *Elias* did
John 1. 21. art thou *Elias?* art thou that prophet?
25. if thou be not *Elias*, why baptizest thou?
Rom. 11. 2. what the scripture saith of *Elias*
Jam. 5. 17. *Elias* was a man subject to like passions

ELIM.

Exod. 15. 27. they came to E. *Num.* 33. 9.
16. 1. they took their journey from E. *Num.* 33. 10.

ELIMELECH.

Ruth 1. 2. the name of the man was E. || 3. E. died
2. 1. Boaz was a kinsman of the family of E.
4. 9. that I have bought all that was E. of Naomi

ELIPHALET.

2 *Sam.* 5. 16. Eliada and E. David's son, 1 *Chr.* 3. 6, 8.

ELIPHAZ.

Gen. 36. 4. Adah bare to Esau, E. 10. 1 *Chr.* 1. 35.
11. the sons of E. 12, 15. 1 *Chron.* 1. 36.
Job 2. 11. E. came from his place to mourn
4. 1. E. the Temanite answered, 15. 1. | 22. 1.
42. 9. E. did as the Lord commanded him

ELISABETH.

Luke 1. 5. Zacharias' wife E. || 7. E. was barren
24. E. conceived, 36. || 40. Mary saluted E.
57. E. full time came that she should be delivered

ELISHA, ELISEUS.

1 *Kings* 19. 16. thou shalt anoint E. to be prophet
17. that escaped from Jehu, shall E. slay
19. Elijah departed, and found E. plowing
2 *Kings* 2. 5. the prophets at Jericho came to E.
12. E. saw it, and cried, my father, my father
15. the spirit of Elijah doth rest on E.
3. 11. one said, here is E. the son of Shaphat
4. 1. now there cried a certain woman unto E.
8. E. passed to Shunem, where was a great woman
17. bare a son at that season that E. had said
32. when E. was come, behold the child was dead
5. 9. so Naaman came and stood at the door of E.
6. 12. E. telleth the words that thou speakest
18. E. prayed to the Lord, the Lord smote them with blindness according to the word of E.
20. E. said, Lord, open the eyes of these men
31. if the head of E. stand on him this day
8. 4. tell me the great things that E. hath done
5. the woman whose son E. restored to life
14. Ben-hadad said, what said E. to thee?
13. 14. E. was fallen sick || 17. E. said, shoot
16. and E. put his hands upon the king's hands
21. they cast the man into the sepulchre of E.
Luke 4. 27. many lepers in Israel in days of *Eliseus*

ELISHAH.

Ezek. 27. 7. blue and purple from isles of E. covered

ELISHAMA.

Num. 1. 10. E. the son of Ammihud, 2. 18. | 7. 48, 53. | 10. 22. 1 *Chron.* 7. 26.
2 *Sam.* 5. 16. E. David's son, 1 *Chr.* 3. 6, 8. | 14. 7.
1 *Chron.* 2. 41. and Jekamiah begat E.
2 *Chron.* 17. 8. he sent with them E. priest
Jer. 36. 12. E. scribe || 41. 1. E. of the seed royal

ELISHEBA.

Exod. 6. 23. Aaron took him E. to wife

ELISHUA.

2 *Sam.* 5. 15. Ibhar and E. David's sons, 1 *Chr.* 14. 5.

ELIUD.

Mat. 1. 14. Achim begat E. || 15. E. begat Eleazar

ELKANAH.

Exod. 6. 24. the sons of Korah, Assir, and E.
1 *Sam.* 1. 1. his name was E. the son of Jeroham
21. E. went up to offer the yearly sacrifice
2. 11. E. went to his house || 20. Eli blessed E.
1 *Chron.* 6. 23. the son of E. 27. 34, 35. | 9. 16.
25. the sons of E. 26. || 12. 6. E. the Korhite
15. 23. E. was door-keeper for the ark
2 *Chron.* 28. 7. E. that was next to the king

ELMODAM.

Luke 3. 28. Cosam, which was the son of E.

ELNATHAN.

2 *Kings* 24. 8. Nehushta the daughter of E.
Ezra 8. 16. I sent for E. and Jarib, chief men
Jer. 26. 22. Jehoiakim sent E. into Egypt
36. 12. E. the son of Achbor sat there
25. E. had made intercession to the king

ELON.

Gen. 26. 34. Esau took Bashemath daughter of E.
36. 2. Esau took Adah the daughter of E.
46. 14. the sons of Zebulun, Sered and E.
Judg. 12. 11. E. judged Israel || 12. E. died

ELUL.

Neh. 6. 15. wall finished the 25th day of the month E.

ELYMAS.

Acts 13. 8. but E. the sorcerer withstood them

EMIMS.

Gen. 14. 5. Chedorlaomer came and smote the E.
Deut. 2. 10. the E. dwelt therein in times past

EMMANUEL. See *Appellatives.*

EMMAUS.

Luke 24. 13. two of them went that same day to E.

EMMOR.

Acts 7. 16. Abraham bought of the sons of E.

EN-DOR.

Josh. 17. 11. Manasseh had E. and her towns
1 *Sam.* 28. 7. a woman at E. hath a familiar spirit
Psal. 83. 10. as to Jabin, which perished at E.

ENEAS.

Acts 9. 34. E. Jesus Christ maketh thee whole

EN-EGLAIM.

Ezek. 47. 10. fishers shall stand from En-gedi to E.

EN-GEDI.

Josh. 15. 62. in the wilderness of Judah, E.
1 *Sam.* 23. 29. David dwelt in holds at E. 24. 1.
2 *Chr.* 20. 2. cometh against Jehoshaphat are in E.
Cant. 1. 14. as camphire in the vineyards of E.
Ezek. 47. 10. the fishers shall stand from E.

ENOCH.

Gen. 4. 17. Cain's wife bare E. || 5. 18. Jared begat E.
5. 22. E. walked with God, and God took him, 24.
Luke 3. 37. Mathusala, which was the son of E.
Heb. 11. 5. by faith E. was translated, and was not
Jude 14. E. also prophesied of these, saying

ENON.

John 3. 23. John was baptizing in E. near to Salim

ENOS.

Gen. 4. 26. Seth called his son's name E.
Luke 3. 38. Cainan, which was the son of E.

EN-ROGEL.

2 *Sam.* 17. 17. Jonathan and Ahimaaz stayed by E.
1 *Kings* 1. 9. Adonijah slew sheep and oxen by E.

EPAPHRAS.

Col. 1. 7. as ye learned of E. our fellow-servant
4. 12. E. a serv. of Christ saluteth you, *Philem.* 23.

EPAPHRODITUS.

Phil. 2. 25. to send to you E. || 4. 18. received of E.

EPENETUS.

Rom. 16. 5. salute my well-beloved E. first-fruits

EPHAH.

Gen. 25. 4. E. the son of Midian, 1 *Chron.* 1. 33.
1 *Chron.* 2. 46. E. Caleb's concubine bare Haran
47. the sons Jahdai, Pelet, E. and Shaaph
Isa. 60. 6. the dromedaries of E. shall cover thee

EPHES-DAMMIM.

1 *Sam.* 17. 1. the Philistines pitched in E.

EPHESIANS.

Acts 19. 28. they cried out, great is Diana of E. 34.
35. the city of the E. is a worshipper of Diana

EPHESUS.

Acts 18. 19. Paul came to E. || 21. sailed from E.
24. a certain Jew named Apollos came to E.
19. 17. this was known to Jews and Greeks at E.
26. ye see, that not alone at E. but thro' all Asia
35. ye men of E. || 1 *Cor.* 16. 8. I will tarry at E.
20. 16. for Paul had determined to sail by E.
1 *Cor.* 15. 32. I have fought with beasts at E.
1 *Tim.* 1. 3. as I besought thee to abide still at E.
2 *Tim.* 1. 18. Onesiphorus ministered to me at E.
4. 12. and Tychicus have I sent to E.
Rev. 1. 11. send it to E. || 2. 1. to the angel at E.

EPHPHATHA.

Mark 7. 34. he saith to him, E. that is, be opened

EPHRAIM, *a place.*

2 *Sam.* 13. 23. Absalom had sheep-shearers beside E.
2 *Chron.* 13. 19. Abijah took E. and towns thereof
John 11. 54. Jesus went into a city called E.

Mount EPHRAIM.

Josh. 17. 15. if *mount* E. be too narrow for thee
20. 7. Shechem in *mount* E. a city of refuge, 21. 21.
Judg. 2. 9. they buried Joshua in the *mount* of E.
7. 24. Gideon sent messengers through *mount* E.
17. 1. Micah of *mount* E. || 8. Levite came to *m.* E.
18. 13. the Danites passed unto *mount* E.
19. 1. a Levite sojourning on the side of *mount* E.
1 *Sam.* 1. 1. Elkanah of *m.* E. || 2 *Sam.* 20. 21. Sheba
9. 4. Saul passed through *mount* E. and passed
2 *Kings* 5. 22. two men be come to me from *m.* E.
Jer. 4. 15. publisheth affliction from *mount* E.
31. 6. the watchman upon *mount* E. shall cry
50. 19. Israel shall be satisfied on *mount* E.

EPHRAIM, *a person*, or *people.*

Gen. 41. 52. the name of Joseph's second son was E.
48. 14. Israel laid his right hand on E. head
20. in thee shall Israel bless, saying, God make thee as E. and he set E. before Manasseh
Num. 1. 10. the prince of E. was Elishama, 7. 48.
2. 18. on the west side shall be the standard of E.
10. 22. the standard of the camp of E. set forward
26. 35. these are the sons of E. 1 *Chron.* 7. 20.
Deut. 33. 17. they are the ten thousands of E.
Josh. 16. 9. the cities for the children of E. 17. 9.
Judg. 1. 29. nor did E. drive out the Canaanites
5. 14. out of E. was there a root against Amalek
8. 2. is not the gleaning of the grapes of E. better
12. 4. then Jephthah fought with E. smote E.
2 *Sam.* 2. 9. Abner made Ish-bosheth king over E.
1 *Chron.* 7. 22. E. their father mourned many days
9. 3. in Jerusalem dwelt of the children of E.
2 *Chron.* 15. 9. the strangers out of E. fell to Asa
17. 2. Jehoshaphat set garrisons in the cities of E.
25. 10. Amasiah separated the army out of E.
28. 7. Zichri a mighty man of E. slew Maaseiah
30. 18. many of E. had not cleansed themselves
31. 1. all Israel brake images in E. and Manasseh
Psal. 78. 9. the children of E. being armed, turned
80. 2. before E. stir up thy strength and save us
Isa. 7. 2. saying, Syria is confederate with E.
5. E. hath taken evil counsel against thee
8. within sixty-five years shall E. be broken
9. the head of E. is Samaria, and head of Samaria
17. from the day that E. departed from Judah
9. 9. E. that say in the pride and stoutness of heart
21. Manasseh shall eat E. and E. Manasseh

Isa. 11. 13. the envy also of E. shall depart; E. shall not envy Judah, and Judah shall not vex E.
17. 3. the fortress also shall cease from E.
28. 1. woe to the drunkards of E. whose beauty
3. drunkards of E. shall be trodden under feet
Jer. 7. 15. as I have cast out the whole seed of E.
31. 18. I have heard E. bemoaning himself thus
Ezek. 37. 16. the stick of E. || 48. 5. a portion for E.
19. I will take stick of Joseph in the hand of E.
Hos. 5. 3. I know E. O E. thou committest whored.
5. Israel and E. shall fall in their iniquity
9. E. shall be desolate || 12. be to E. as a moth
13. when E. saw his sickness, E. went to Assyrian
14. E. as a lion || 6. 4. O E. what shall I do to thee?
6. 10. there is the whoredom of E. Israel is defiled
7. 1. then the iniquity of E. was discovered
8. E. hath mixed himself among the people
8. 9. E. hired lovers || 11. E. made altars to sin
9. 3. but E. shall eat unclean things in Assyria
8. the watchman of E. was with my God
11. as for E. their glory shall fly away
13. E. shall bring forth children to the murderer
10. 6. E. shall receive shame, Israel be ashamed
11. I will make E. to ride; Judah shall plow
11. 3. I taught E. to go || 8. how shall I give thee up E.
9. I will not return to destroy E. for I am God
12. E. compasseth me about with lies
12. 1. E. feedeth on wind || 8. E. said, I am rich
14. E. provoked him to anger most bitterly
13. 1. when E. spake trembling, he exalted himself
12. the iniquity of E. is bound up, his sin is hid
14. 8. E. shall say, what have I to do with idols?
Obad. 19. they shall possess the fields of E.
Zech. 9. 10. I will cut off the chariot from E.
13. when I have filled the bow with E. and raised
10. 7. they of E. shall be like a mighty man
See GATE.

EPHRAIM *is.*

Psal. 60. 7. E. *is* the strength of my head, 108. 8.
Jer. 31. 9. and a father to Israel, E. *is* my first born
20. *is* E. my dear son? is he a pleasant child?
Hos. 4. 17. E. *is* joined to idols, let him alone
5. 11. E. *is* oppressed || 7. 8. E. *is* a cake not turned
7. 11. E. *is* like a silly dove || 9. 16. E. *is* smitten
10. 11. E. *is* as an heifer that is taught and loveth

EPHRAIM with *tribe.*

Num. 1. 33. were numbered of the *tribe* of E. 40,500
13. 8. of the *tribe* of E. to spy the land, Oshea
34. 24. of *tribe* of E. to divide the land, Kemuel
Josh. 16. 8. the inheritance of the *tribe* of E.
21. 5. the Kohathites had cities out of the *tribe* of E. Dan and Manasseh, 20. 1 *Chr.* 6. 66.
Psal. 78. 67. and he chose not the *tribe* of E.

EPHRAIMITE, S.

Judg. 12. 5. the men of Gilead said, art thou an E.?
6. there fell at that time of the E. 42,000

EPHRATAH.

Ruth 4. 11. do thou worthily in E. and be famous
1 *Chron.* 2. 50. Hur, the first-born of E. 4. 4.
Psal. 132. 6. lo, we heard of it at E. we found it
Mic. 5. 2. but thou, Beth-lehem E. though little

EPHRATH.

Gen. 35. 16. there was a little way to come to E.
19. Rachel was buried in the way to E. 48. 7.
1 *Chron.* 2. 19. Caleb took to him E. who bare Hur

EPHRATHITE, S.

Ruth 1. 2. Mahlon, Chilion, E. of Beth-lehem-Judah
1 *Sam.* 1. 1. Elkanah was an E. 17. 12. Jesse an E.
1 *Kings* 11. 26. Jeroboam an E. of Zereda

EPHRON.

Gen. 23. 8. entreat for me to E. the son of Zoar
16. Abraham hearkened to E. weighed silver to E.
25. 9. Abraham was buried in the field of E.
49. 30. Abraham bought with the field of E. 50. 13.

EPICUREANS.

Acts 17. 18. certain of the E. encountered Paul

ER.

Gen. 38. 3. called his name E. || 6. took a wife for E.
7. E. Judah's first-born was wicked, 1 *Chron.* 2. 3.
1 *Chron.* 4. 21. E. the father of Lecah
Luke 3. 28. Elmodam, which was the son of E.

ERASTUS.

Acts 19. 22. Paul sent Timotheus and E. into Maced.
2 *Tim.* 4. 20. E. abode Corinth, Trophimus Miletum

ESAIAS. *See* ISAIAH.

ESAR-HADDON.

2 *Kings* 19. 37. E. reigned in his stead, *Isa.* 37. 38.
Ezra 4. 2. since the days of E. king of Assur

ESAU.

Gen. 25. 25. and they called his name E.
27. E. was a hunter || 29. E. came from field
34. thus E. despised his birthright
27. 11. behold, E. my brother is a hairy man
21. whether thou be my very son E. or not, 24.
41. E. hated Jacob because of the blessing
42. these words of E. were told to Rebekah
28. 9. then went E. to Ishmael, and took Mahalath
32. 3. Jacob sent messengers before him to E.
11. deliver me, I pray thee, from the hand of E.
18. it is a present sent unto my lord E.
33. 4. E. ran to meet him, and embraced him
9. and E. said, I have enough, my brother
35. 1. when thou fleddest from E. thy brother
36. 1. now these are the generations of E.
43. he is E. the father of the Edomites
Deut. 2. 5. have given mount Seir to E. 12. *Josh.* 24. 4.
22. as he did to the children of E. in Seir
Josh. 24. 4. unto Isaac, Jacob, and E. 1 *Chr.* 1. 34.
Jer. 49. 8. I will bring the calamity of E. on him
10. I have made E. bare, I have uncovered
Obad. 6. how are the things of E. searched out!
18. the house of E. shall be for stubble
21. saviours shall come to judge the mount of E.
Mal. 1. 2. was not E. Jacob's brother, saith the Lord?
3. I loved Jacob, and I hated E. *Rom.* 9. 13.
Heb. 11. 20. by faith Isaac blessed Jacob and E.
12. 16. lest there be any profane person, as E.

ESEK.

Gen. 26. 20. Isaac called the name of the well E.

ESHCOL.

Gen. 14. 13. Mamre the Amorite, brother of E.
24. Aner, E. Mamri, let them take their portion
Num. 13. 24. the place was called the brook E.
32. 9. when they went up unto the valley of E.

ESLI.

Luke 3. 25. Naum, which was the son of E.

ESROM.

Mat. 1. 3. and E. begat Aram, *Luke* 3. 33.

ESTHER.

Esth. 2. 7. he brought up Hadassah, that is E.
17. the king loved E. || 18. the king made E. feast
22. told it to E. || 5. 3. what wilt thou, queen E.?
4. 4. E. maids came, she sent raiment to clothe Mor.
12. and they told to Mordecai E. words
17. Mordecai did all that E. had commanded
5. 2. the king held out to E. the golden sceptre, 8. 4.
12. E. let no man come with the king but myself
7. 2. the king said, what is thy petition, queen E.?
7. Haman stood up to make request for life to E.
8. 3. and E. spake yet again before the king
7. behold, I have given E. the house of Haman
9. 29. E. the queen wrote with all authority
32. decree of E. confirmed these matters of Purim

ETAM.

Judg. 15. 8. Samson dwelt in top of the rock E.
11. then 3000 men went to top of the rock E.

ETHAM.

Exod. 13. 20. they encamped in E. *Num.* 33. 6.
Num. 33. 8. went three days' journey in wilder. of E.

ETHAN.

1 *Kings* 4. 31. for Solomon was wiser than E.
1 *Chron.* 2. 6. the sons of Zerah, Zimri, and E.

ETHANIM.

1 *Kings* 8. 2. all Israel assembled in the month E.

ETHIOPIA.

2 *Kings* 19. 9. when he heard say of Tirhakah king of E. behold, he is come out to fight, *Isa.* 37. 9.
Esth. 1. 1. Ahasuerus reigned from India to E. 8. 9.
Job 28. 19. the topaz of E. shall not equal it
Psal. 68. 31. E. shall stretch out her hands to God
87. 4. behold Philistia and Tyre with E. man born
Isa. 18. 1. which is beyond rivers of E. *Zeph.* 3. 10.
20. 3. Isaiah hath walked bare-foot for a sign on E.
5. they shall be ashamed of E. their expectation
43. 3. I gave Egypt for thy ransom, E. for thee
45. 14. the merchandise of E. shall come to thee
Ezek. 30. 4. great pain in E. || 5. E. shall fall, 38. 5.
Nah. 3. 9. E. and Egypt were the strength of No
Acts 8. 27. behold, a man of E. an eunuch of author.

ETHIOPIAN.

Num. 12. 1. because of the E. woman he married
2 *Chron.* 14. 9. Zerah the E. came out against Asa
Jer. 13. 23. can E. change his skin or leopard
38. 7. Ebed-melech the E. 10. 12. | 39. 16.

ETHIOPIANS.

2 *Chron.* 14. 12. the Lord smote the E. the E. fled
16. 8. were not the E. and Lubims a huge host?
21. 16. the Ld. stirred Arabians that were near E.
Isa. 20. 4. he shall lead the E. captives
Jer. 46. 9. the E. that handle the shield
Ezek. 30. 9. to make the careless E. afraid
Dan. 11. 43. the Libyans and E. shall be at his steps
Amos 9. 7. are ye not as the children of E. unto me?
Zeph. 2. 12. ye E. shall be slain by the sword
Acts 8. 27. an eunuch under Candace queen of E.

EUBULUS.

2 *Tim.* 4. 21. E. greeteth thee, Pudens and Linus

EVE.

Gen. 3. 20. Adam called his wife's name E.
4. 1. Adam knew E. his wife, and she conceived
2 *Cor.* 11. 3. lest as serpent beguiled E. thro' subtlety
1 *Tim.* 2. 13. for Adam was first formed, then E.

EVIL-MERODACH.

2 *Kings* 25. 27. E. king of Babylon did lift up the head of Jehoiachin out of prison, *Jer.* 52. 31.

EUNICE.

2 *Tim.* 1. 5. faith which dwelt in Lois and mother E.

EUODIAS.

Phil. 4. 2. I beseech E. and beseech Syntyche

EUPHRATES.

Gen. 2. 14. and the fourth river is E.
15. 18. unto the great river, the river E.
Deut. 1. 7. go to the great river E. *Josh.* 1. 4.
11. 24. shall be yours from the river E. to the sea
2 *Sam.* 8. 3. David smote Hadadezer as he went to recover his border at the river E. 1 *Chr.* 18. 3.
2 *Kings* 23. 29. Necho went up to E. 2 *Chr.* 35. 20.
24. 7. the king of Babylon took from Egypt to E.
1 *Chron.* 5. 9. Reuben inhabited from the river E.
Jer. 13. 4. arise, go to E. || 5. so I hid it by E.
7. I went to E. || 46. 10. hath a sacrifice by E.
46. 2. the word came against Pharaoh by E.
6. they shall stumble and fall by the river E.
51. 63. thou shalt cast it into the midst of E.
Rev. 9. 14. angels that are bound in the river E.
16. 12. sixth angel poured out his vial on E.

EUTYCHUS.

Acts 20. 9. there sat a young man named E. fallen

EZEKIEL.

Ezek. 24. 24. thus E. is unto you a sign

EZEL.

1 *Sam.* 20. 19. thou shalt remain by the stone E.

EZRA.

1 *Chron.* 4. 17. the sons of E. Jether and Mered
Ezra 7. 12. Artaxerxes king to E. the priest
25. thou, E. after the wisdom of thy God, set
10. 1. when E. had prayed and confessed, weeping
Neh. 8. 2. E. brought the law before congregation
6. and E. blessed the Lord the great God
12. 1. these are the priests, Seraiah, Jeremiah, E.
13. of E. Meshullam was priest
26. these were in days of E. the priest, the scribe
36. and E. the scribe before them

F.

FELIX.

Acts 23. 24. that they may bring Paul safe to F.
26. Lysias to the most excellent governor F.
24. 3. we accept it always, most noble F.
24. when F. came with his wife Drusilla
25. as Paul reasoned of judgment, F. trembled
25. 14. there is a certain man left in bonds by F.

FESTUS.

Acts 24. 27. Porcius F. came into Felix' room
25. 9. F. willing to do the Jews a pleasure
13. king Agrippa came to Cesarea to salute F.
14. F. declared Paul's cause unto the king
23. at F. commandment Paul was brought forth
26. 25. Paul said, I am not mad, most noble F.

FORTUNATUS.

1 *Cor.* 16. 17. I am glad of the coming of F.

G.

GAAL.

Judg. 9. 41. Zebul thrust out G. and his brethren

GABBATHA.

John 19. 13. called the pavement, in Hebrew, G

GABRIEL.

Dan. 8. 16. G. make this man understand the vision
9. 21. while I was praying, the man G. touched me
Luke 1. 19. I am G. that stand in presence of God
26. the angel G. was sent from God to Mary

GAD.

Gen. 30. 11. a troop comes, she called his name G.
35. 26. the sons of Zilpah, G. and Asher
46. 16. sons G. *Num.* 1. 24. | 26. 15, 18. 1 *Chr.* 12. 14.
49. 19. G. a troop shall overcome him
Num. 1. 14. the prince of G. Eliasaph, 2. 14. | 7. 42.
32. 1. children of G. had a multitude of cattle
2. the children of G. came and spake to Moses
29. if the children of G. will pass over Jordan
33. Moses gave to G. the kingdom of Sihon
34. 14. the tribe of the children of G. have received their inheritance, *Josh.* 13. 28. | 18. 7
Deut. 27. 13. on mount Ebal to curse G. and Asher
33. 20. and of G. blessed be he that enlargeth G.
Josh. 4. 12. the children of G. passed over armed
22. 9. the children of G. returned out of Shiloh
1 *Sam.* 13. 7. some Hebrews went to the land of G.
2 *Sam.* 24. 5. that lieth in the midst of the river of G.
11. the word of the Lord came to the prophet G. David's seer, saying, 1 *Chron.* 21. 9, 18.
14. David said unto G. I am in a great strait
19. David did according to the saying of G.
1 *Chron.* 29. 29. acts of David are in the book of G.
2 *Chr.* 29. 25. Levites according to command of G.
Jer. 49. 1. why then doth their king inherit G.?
Ezek. 48. 27. a portion for G. || 34. one gate of G.

Tribe of GAD.

Num. 1. 25. that were numbered of *tribe of* G. 45,650.
2. 14. then the *tribe of* G. shall set forward, the captain of G. shall be Eliasaph, 10. 20.
13. 15. of the *tribe of* G. to spy the land, Geuel
34. 14. the *tribe of* the children of G. have received their inheritance, *Josh.* 13. 24.
Josh. 20. 8. out of the *tribe of* G. assigned Ramoth-Gilead to the Levites, 21. 7, 38. 1 *Chr.* 6. 63, 80.
Rev. 7. 5. of the *tribe of* G. were sealed 12,000

GADARENES.

Mark 5. 1. they came over to the other side of the sea into the country of the G. *Luke* 8. 26.
Luke 8. 37. country of G. besought him to depart

GADITE, S.

Deut. 3. 12. this land gave I unto the G. 16.
Josh. 22. 1. Joshua called the Reubenites and G.
2 *Sam.* 23. 36. Bani G. one of David's mighty men
2 *Kings* 10. 33. Hazael smote the G. and Reubenites
1 *Chron.* 12. 8. of the G. there separated to David
26. 32. whom David made rulers over the G.

GAIUS.

Acts 19. 29. having caught G. a man of Macedonia
20. 4. G. of Derbe accompanied Paul into Asia
Rom. 16. 23. G. mine host saluteth you
1 *Cor.* 1. 14. I baptized none but Crispus and G.
3 *John* 1. the elder unto the well-beloved G.

GALATIA.

Acts 16. 6. had gone through the region of G. 18. 23.
1 *Cor.* 16. 1. have given order to the churches of G.
2 *Tim.* 4. 10. Crescens is departed to G.
1 *Pet.* 1. 1. to the saints scattered through Pontus, G.

GALATIANS.

Gal. 3. 1. O foolish G. who hath bewitched you?

GALBANUM.

Exod. 30. 34. take sweet spices, onycha, and G

GALEED.

Gen. 31. 47. but Jacob called the heap G.
48. therefore was the name of it called G.

GALILEE.

Josh. 20. 7. Kedesh in G. for a city of of refuge
21. 32. Kedesh in G. to the Levites, 1 *Chron.* 6. 76.
1 *Kings* 9. 11. Solomon gave Hiram 20 cities in G.
2 *Kings* 15. 29. Tiglath-pileser took Ijon and G.
Isa. 9. 1. did more grievously afflict her in G.
Mat. 2. 22. Joseph turned into the parts of G.
3. 13. then cometh Jesus from G. to John, *Mark* 1. 9.
4. 15. G. of the Gentiles || 21. 11. Jesus of G.
18. Jesus walking by the sea of G. *Mark* 1. 16.
25. there followed multitudes from G. *Mark* 3. 7.
15. 29. Jesus came nigh unto the sea of G.
26. 32. I will go before you into G. *Mark* 14. 28.
27. 55. many women beholding afar off which followed Jesus from G. *Mark* 15. 41. *Luke* 23. 49, 55.
28. 7. he goeth before you into G. *Mark* 16. 7.
Mark 1. 39. he preached throughout all G.
Luke 4. 14. Jesus returned in power of Spirit into G.
44. he preached in synagogues of G.
23. 5. beginning from G. to this place
6. when Pilate heard of G. he asked whether Gal.?
24. 6. how he spake to you when he was in G.
John 7. 41. some said, shall Christ come out of G.
52. art thou of G.? out of G. ariseth no prophet
12. 21. Philip who was of Bethsaida in G.
Acts 1. 11. ye men of G. || 5. 37. Judas of G. rose up
9. 31. then had the churches rest through all G.
10. 37. the word you know which began from G.
13. 31. he was seen of them that came from G.
See CANA.

GALILEAN, S.

Mark 14. 70. for thou art a G. *Luke* 22. 59.
Luke 13. 1. there were some told him of the G.
2. suppose ye these G. were sinners above all G.
23. 6. Pilate asked whether the man were a G.?

John 4. 45. when he was come, the G. received him
Acts 2. 7. are not all these that speak, G.?

GALLIM.

1 *Sam.* 25. 44. Saul gave Michal to Phalti of G.
Isa. 10. 30. lift up thy voice, O daughter of G.

GALLIO.

Acts 18. 12. when G. was the deputy of Achaia
17. and G. cared for none of those things

GAMALIEL.

Num. 1. 10. of Manasseh, G. son of Pedahzur, 2. 20. | 7. 54, 59. 10. 23.
Acts 5. 34. then stood up a Pharisee named G.
22. 3. yet I was brought up at the feet of G.

GAMMADIMS.

Ezek. 27. 11. and the G. were in thy towers

GATH.

1 *Sam.* 5. 8. let the ark be carried about to G.
6. 17 these are the golden emerods, for G. one
27. 4. it was told Saul, that David was fled to G.
2 *Sam.* 1. 20. tell it not in G. publish it not in Ashkelon
21. 22. these four were born to the giant in G. and fell by the hand of David and serv. 1 *Chr.* 20. 8.
1 *Kings* 2. 39. two servants of Shimei ran to G.
40. Shimei went to G. to seek his servants
2 *Kings* 12. 17. Hazael went and fought against G.
1 *Chr.* 8. 13. Beraiah drove away inhabitants of G.
18. 1. David took G. from the Philistines
2 *Chron.* 26. 6. Uzziah brake down the wall of G.
Amos 6. 2. then go down to G. of the Philistines
Mic. 1. 10. declare ye it not at G. weep not at all

GAZA.

Judg. 16. 1. Samson went to G. and saw an harlot
21. the Philistines brought Samson down to G.
Jer. 47. 1. before that Pharaoh smote G.
5. baldness is come upon G. Ashkelon is cut off
Amos 1. 6. for three transgressions of G. and for four
7. but I will send a fire on the wall of G.
Zeph. 2. 4. G. shall be forsaken and Ashkel. a desol.
Zech. 9. 5. G. shall see it, king shall perish from G.
Acts 8. 26. the way that goeth from Jerusalem to G.

GEBA.

Josh. 21. 17. given out of the tribe of Benjamin to the priests, G. with her suburbs, 1 *Chron.* 6. 60.
1 *Kings* 15. 22. king Asa built G. 2 *Chron.* 16. 6.
2 *Kings* 23. 8. Josiah defiled the high places from G.
Isa. 10. 29. they have taken up lodging at G.
Zech. 14. 10. the land shall be as a plain from G.

GEBAL.

Psal. 83. 7. G. and Ammon are confederate
Ezek. 27. 9. the ancients of G. were thy calkers

GEBIM.

Isa. 10. 31. the inhabitants of G. gather to flee

GEDALIAH.

2 *Kings* 25. 24. and G. sware to them, *Jer.* 40. 9.
1 *Chron.* 25. 3. the sons of Jeduthun, G. and Zeri
9. now the second lot came forth to G.
Ezra 10. 18. Jarib and G. had taken strange wives
Jer. 38. 1. G. the son of Pashur heard Jeremiah
40. 14. but G. son of Ahikam believed them not
41. 2. Ishmael smote G. with the sword
43. 6. Johanan took all that were left with G.
Zeph. 1. 1. Zephaniah the son of Cushi, son of G.
See AHIKAM.

GEHAZI.

2 *Kings* 4. 12. Elisha said to G. call Shunamite, 36.
27. but G. came near to thrust her away
5. 21. so G. followed after Naaman, said, is all well
25. Elisha said to him, whence comest thou, G.
8. 4. the king talked with G. servant of Elisha

GEMARIAH.

Jer. 29. 3. the words that Jeremiah sent by G.
36. 25. G. made intercession not to burn the roll

GENNESARET, ETH.

Mat. 14. 34. they came to the land of G. *Mark* 6. 53.
Luke 5. 1. people pressed, Jesus stood by lake of G.

GERA.

Judg. 3. 15. the Lord raised up Ehud the son of G.
2 *Sam.* 16. 5. Shimei son of G. 19. 16, 18. 1 *Kings* 2. 8.

GERAHS.

Exod. 30. 13. a shekel is twenty G. *Lev.* 27. 25. *Num.* 3. 47. | 18. 16. *Ezek.* 45. 12.

GERAR.

Gen. 20. 1. Abraham sojourned in G. || 26. 6. Isaac
2. Abimelech king of G. || 20. the herdman of G.

GERGESENES.

Mat. 8. 28. he was come into the country of the G.

GERIZIM.

Deut. 11. 29. thou shalt put the blessing on mount G.
27. 12. these shall stand on mount G. to bless
Josh. 8. 33. half of them over against mount G.
Judg. 9. 7. Jotham stood on the top of mount G.

GERSHOM, GERSHON.

Gen. 46. 11. the sons of Levi, G. Kohath and Merari, *Exod.* 6. 16. *Num.* 3. 17. 1 *Chron.* 6. 1, 16. | 23. 6.
Exod. 2. 22. the name of Moses' son was G.
6. 17. the sons of G. Libni, Shimei, *Num.* 3. 18.
Num. 3. 21. of G. was the family of the Libnites
25. charge of the sons of G. || 4. 22. their sum, 38.
4. 28. this is the service of the sons of G.
7. 7. two waggons and four oxen gave to sons of G.
10. 17. the sons of G. bearing the tabernacle
Josh. 21. 6. cities the children of G. had, 27.
Judg. 18. 30. Jonathan the son of G. was priest
Ezra 8. 2. of the sons of Phinehas, G. went up

GESHUR.

2 *Sam.* 13. 37. Absalom fled and went to G. 38.
14. 23. Joab went to G. || 32. why I come from G.
15. 8. thy servant vowed a vow at G. in Syria
1 *Chron.* 2. 23. Jair took G. and Aram from them

GESHURITES.

Josh. 13. 13. the G. dwell among the Israelites
1 *Sam.* 27. 8. David and his men invaded the G.

GETHSEMANE.

Mat. 26. 36. cometh to a place called G. *Mark* 14. 32.

GIAH.

2 *Sam.* 2. 24. the hill Ammah that lieth before G.

GIBEAH.

Judg. 19. 14. sun went down when they were by G.
16. an old man of mount Ephraim sojourned in G.
20. 9. this shall be the thing we will do to G.
13. deliver us the children of Belial in G.
30. they put themselves in array against G.

1 *Sam.* 10. 26. Saul also went home to G. 15. 34.
14. 2. Saul tarried in the uttermost part of G.
2 *Sam.* 21. 6. let seven men of his sons be delivered to us, we will hang them up to the Lord in G.
Isa. 10. 29. Ramah is afraid, G. of Saul is fled
Hos. 5. 8. blow ye the cornet in G. cry aloud
9. 9. have corrupted themselves as in the days of G.
10. 9. O Israel, thou hast sinned from the days of G. the battle in G. did not overtake them

GIBEON.

Josh. 10. 2. feared, because G. was a great city
4. come up and help me, that we may smite G.
12. Joshua said, sun, stand thou still upon G.
2 *Sam.* 2. 13. they met together by the pool of G.
3. 30. because he had slain Asahel at G. in battle
20. 8. when they were at the great stone in G.
1 *Kings* 3. 5. in G. the Lord appear. to Solomon, 9. 2.
1 *Chron.* 8. 29. at G. dwelt the father of G. 9. 35.
21. 29. the altar of burnt offering was at G.
Isa. 28. 21. he shall be wrath as in the valley of G.
Jer. 28. 1. Hananiah the son of Azur in G.
41. 12. they found Ishmael by the waters in G.

GIBEONITES.

2 *Sam.* 21. 1. a famine, because Saul slew the G.
9. he delivered them into the hands of the G.

GIDEON.

Judg. 6. 11. G. threshed wheat by the wine-press
24. G. built an altar there unto the Lord
34. but the Spirit of the Lord came upon G.
7. 1. then Jerubbaal, who is G. rose up early
14. there is nothing else, save the sword of G.
18. the sword of the Lord and of G. 20.
8. 21. G. slew Zeba || 27. G. made an ephod thereof
30. G. had 70 sons || 32. G. died in a good old age
35. nor shewed they kindness to the house of G.
Heb. 11. 32. the time would fail me to tell of G.

GIDEONI.

Num. 1. 11. the prince of Benjamin was Abidan the son of G. 2. 22. | 7. 60, 65

GIHON.

Gen. 2. 13. the name of the second river is G.
1 *Kings* 1. 33. and bring Solomon down to G. 38.
45. they have anointed him king in G.

GILBOA.

1 *Sam.* 28. 4. Saul and all Israel pitched in G.
31. 1. Israel and Saul fell down slain in mount G. 8. 2 *Sam.* 21. 12. 1 *Chron.* 10. 1, 8.
2 *Sam.* 1. 6. as I happened by chance on mount G.
21. ye mountains of G. let there be no dew

GILEAD.

Num. 32. 1. saw the land of G. was a place for cattle
40. Moses gave G. to Machir, *Deut.* 3. 15.
Deut. 34. 1. the Lord shewed him the land of G.
Josh. 17. 1. Machir, being a man of war, had G.
22. 13. Israel sent Phinehas into the land of G.
Judg. 10. 18. be head over the inhabitants of G.
11. 11. then Jephthah went with the elders of G.
2 *Sam.* 2. 9. Abner made Ishbosheth king over G.
17. 26. Israel and Absalom pitched in land of G.
1 *Kings* 17. 1. Elijah the Tishbite, who was of G.
Psal. 60. 7. G. is mine, Manasseh is mine, 108. 8.
Cant. 4. 1. thy hair as a flock of goats from G. 6. 5.
Jer. 8. 22. is there no balm in G.? no physician there?
22. 6. thou art G. to me || 46. 11. go up into G.
50. 19. his soul shall be satisfied on mount G.
Hos. 6. 8. G. is the city of them that work iniquity
12. 11. is there iniquity in G.? they are vanity
Amos 1. 3. they have threshed G. with instruments
13. they have ripped up women with child of G.
Obad. 19. and Benjamin shall possess G.
Mic. 7. 14. let them feed in Bashan and G.
Zech. 10. 10. I will bring them into the land of G.
See RAMOTH.

GILEADITE, S.

Judg. 10. 3. Jair G. judged Israel || 11. 1. Jephthah
12. 4. ye G. are fugitives of Ephraim
5. and the G. took the passages of Jordan
2 *Sam.* 17. 27. Barzillai the G. brought beds
See BARZILLAI.

GILGAL.

Josh. 4. 19. the people came up and encamped in G.
9. 6. they went to Joshua unto the camp at G.
10. 6. the men of G. sent to the camp at Gibeon
Judg. 2. 1. an angel came up from G. to Bochim
1 *Sam.* 7. 16. Samuel went in circuit to G.
10. 8. and thou shalt go down before me to G.
11. 14. let us go to G. and renew the kingdom
13. 7. Saul was in G. || 8. Samuel came not to G.
15. 33. Samuel hewed Agag in pieces in G.
Hos. 4. 15. come not ye to G. nor go to Beth-aven
9. 15. their wickedness is in G. there I hated them
12. 11. they sacrifice bullocks in G. their altars
Amos 4. 4. at G. multiply transgression and bring
5. 5. enter not into G. for G. shall go into captivity
Mic. 6. 5. Balaam answered him from Shittim to G.

GILONITE.

2 *Sam.* 15. 12. Ahithophel the G. 23. 34.

GIRGASHITE, S.

Gen. 10. 16. Canaan begat the G. 1 *Chron.* 1. 14.
15. 21. to thy seed have I given this land to Euphrates and the land of the G. *Neh.* 9. 8.
Deut. 7. 1. when the Lord hath cast out the G.
Josh. 3. 10. he will without fail drive out the G.

GITTITE.

2 *Sam.* 6. 10. the house of Obed-edom the G. 11.
15. 19. Ittai the G. 22. | 18. 2. || 21. 19. Goliath

GOB.

2 *Sam.* 21. 18. a battle with the Philistines at G.

GOG.

1 *Chron.* 5. 4. sons of Joel, G. his son, Shimei his son
Ezek. 38. 2. son of man, set thy face against G.
3. say, behold, I am against thee, O G. 39. 1.
16. when I shall be sanctified in thee, O G.
18. when G. shall come against the land of Israel
39. 11. I will give to G. a place of graves in Israel
Rev. 20. 8. G. and Magog, to gather them together

GOLAN, *See* BASHAN.

GOLGOTHA.

Mat. 27. 33. were come to a place called G. that is to say, a place of a skull, *Mark* 15. 22. *John* 19. 17.

GOLIATH.

1 *Sam.* 17. 4. G. of Gath a champion went out, 23.

1 *Sam.* 21. 9. the sword of G. the Philistine is here
22. 10. he gave him the sword of G. the Philistine
2 *Sam.* 21. 19. slew the brother of G. 1 *Chr.* 20. 5.

GOMER.

Gen. 10. 2. sons of Japheth, G. Magog, 1 *Chr.* 1. 5.
3. the sons of G. Ashkenaz, Riphath, 1 *Chr.* 1. 6.
Ezek. 38. 6. G. and all his bands, house of Togarmah
Hos. 1. 3. he took G. the daughter of Diblaim

GOMORRAH.

Gen. 13. 10. before the Lord destroyed Sodom and G.
14. 11. they took all the goods of Sodom and G.
18. 20. because the cry of Sodom and G. is great
19. 24. the Lord rained on G. fire from heaven
28. Abraham looked towards Sodom and G.
Deut. 29. 23. like the overthrow of Sodom and G. *Isa.* 1. 9. | 13. 19. *Jer.* 23. 14. | 49. 18. | 50. 40. *Amos* 4. 11. *Rom.* 9. 29. 2 *Pet.* 2. 6. *Jude* 7.
32. 32. for their vine is of the fields of G.
Isa. 1. 10. give ear to the law, ye people of G.
Zeph. 2. 9. the children of Ammon shall be as G.
Mat. 10. 15. be more tolerable for G. *Mark* 6. 11.

GOSHEN.

Gen. 45. 10. dwell in G. 46. 34. | 47. 4, 6, 27.
Exod. 8. 22. I will sever that day the land of G.
9. 26. only in the land of G. was there no hail
Josh. 10. 41. Joshua smote the country of G.
11. 16. so Joshua took all the land of G.
15. 51. the inheritance of Judah, G. Holon

GOZAN.

2 *Kings* 17. 6. the king of Assyria placed Israel by the river of G. 18. 11. 1 *Chron.* 5. 26.
19. 12. my fathers have destroyed, as G. *Isa.* 37. 12.

GRECIA.

Dan. 8. 21. the rough goat is the king of G.
10. 20. when I am gone the king of G. shall come
11. 2. he shall stir up all against the realm of G.

GRECIANS.

Joel 3. 6. the children of Judah have ye sold to the G.
Acts 6. 1. there arose a murmuring of the G.
9. 29. Paul spake boldly and disputed against the G.
11. 20. who spake to the G. preaching the L. Jesus

GREECE.

Zech. 9. 13. thy sons, O Zion, against thy sons, O G.
Acts 20. 2. Paul came to G. and there abode

GREEK.

Mark 7. 26. the woman was a G. a Syrophenician
Acts 16. 1. the father of Timotheus was a G. 3.
Rom. 1. 16. to Jew first, and also to G. 2. † 9, † 10.
10. 12. for there is no difference between the Jew and the G. the same Lord, *Gal.* 3. 28. *Col.* 3. 11.
Gal. 2. 3. nor Titus who was with me, being a G.
See APPELLATIVES.

GREEKS.

John 7. † 35. will he go to dispersed among the G.?
12. 20. certain G. came to worship at the feast
Acts 14. 1. a multitude of G. believed, 17. 4, 12.
18. 4. he persuaded the Jews and the G.
17. then the G. took Sosthenes and beat him
19. 10. the Jews and G. heard the word of the Lord
17. this was known to all the G. at Ephesus
20. 21. testifying to the Jews and G. repentance
21. 28. he brought the G. also into the temple
Rom. 1. 14. I am a debtor both to G. and Barbarians
1 *Cor.* 1. 22. and the G. seek after wisdom
23 we preach Christ crucified, to the G. foolishness
24. to called, Jews and G. Christ the power of God

GUR.

2 *Kings* 9. 27. smote Ahaziah at the going up to G.

H.

HACHILAH.

1 *Sam.* 23. 19. David hid in the hill of H. 26. 1.
26. 3. and Saul pitched in the hill of H.

HADADEZER, HADAREZER.

2 *Sam.* 8. 3. David smote H. 9, 10. 1 *Chron.* 18. 3.
5. when the Syrians came to succour H.
7. took shields on servants of H. || 8. cities of H.
10. H. had wars with Toi || 12. the spoil of H.
10. 16. H. sent and brought out the Syrians
1 *Kings* 11. 23. Rezon fled from lord H. king of Zob.

HADADRIMMON.

Zech. 12. 11. as the mourning of H. in the valley

HADASSAH.

Esth. 2. 7. brought up H. his uncle's daughter

HADORAM.

Gen. 10. 27. and Joktan begat H. 1 *Chron.* 1. 21.
1 *Chron.* 18. 10. Tou sent H. his son to king David
2 *Chr.* 10. 18. Rehoboam sent H. Israel stoned him

HADRACH.

Zech. 9. 1. the burden of the Lord in the land of H.

HAGAR.

Gen. 16. 1. H. an Egyptian was Sarai's maid, 3, 8.
15. H. bare Abram a son, 16. | 25. 12.
21. 9. Sarah saw son of H. the Egyptian mocking
14. Abraham gave H. bread, and sent her away
17. angel of God called to H. what aileth thee, H.?
See AGAR.

HAGARENES.

Psal. 83. 6. the H. are confederate against thee

HAGARITES.

1 *Chron.* 5. 10. they made war with the H. 19.
20. the H. were delivered into their hand

HAGGAI.

Gen. 46. 16. the sons of Gad, H. Shuni, and Ezbon
Ezra 5. 1. H. the prophet prophesied to the Jews
6. 14. prospered thro' prophesying of H. the prophet
Hag. 1. 1. word of the Lord by H. 3. | 2. 1, 10, 20.

HAGGITH.

2 *Sam.* 3. 4. and the fourth, Adonijah the son of H. 1 *Kings* 1. 5, 11. | 2. 13. 1 *Chron.* 3. 2.

HALLELUIAH.

Psal. 106. † 1. | 111. † 1. | 113. † 1. | 146. † 1. | 148. † 1. | 149. † 1. | 150. † 1.
See ALLELUIAH, *in Appellatives.*

HAM.

Gen. 5. 32. Noah begat Shem, H. and Japheth 6. 10. | 9. 18. | 10. 1. 1 *Chron.* 1. 4
7. 13. the self-same day H. entered into the ark
9. 18. and H. is the father of Canaan
10. 6. sons of H. Cush, Mizraim, 20. 1 *Chr.* 1. 8

Gen. 14. 5. Chedorlaomer smote the Zuzims in H.
1 *Chron.* 4. 40. they of H. had dwelt there of old
Psal. 78. 51. he smote in the tabernacles of H.
105. 23. Jacob sojourned in the land of H.
27. they shewed wonders in the land of H. 106. 22.

HAMAN.

Esth. 3. 1. king promoted H. ‖ 5. H. full of wrath
2. all the king's servants bowed and reverenced H.
6. wherefore H. sought to destroy all the Jews
7. cast the lot before H. ‖ 4. 7. H. promised to pay
15. and the king and H. sat down to drink
5. 4. the king and H. came to the banquet, 5. 8. | 7. 1.
9. then went H. forth that day joyful and glad
11. H. told them of the glory of his riches
14. the thing pleased H. ‖ 6. 5. H. stands in court
6. 6. H. thought ‖ 11. then H. took the apparel
12. but H. hasted to his house mourning
13. H. told Zeresh his wife ‖ 7. 6. this wicked H.
7. 7. H. made request ‖ 8. H. was fallen on the bed
10. hanged H. ‖ 8. 1. gave Esther the house of H.
9. 10. slew the sons of H. ‖ 14. they hanged them

HAMATH.

Num. 13. 21. Zin to Rehob, as men come to H.
34. 8. from mount Hor to the entrance of H. *Josh.* 13. 5. *Judg.* 3. 3. 1 *Kings* 8. 65. 2 *Kings* 14. 25. 2 *Chron.* 7. 8.
2 *Sam.* 8. 9. Toi king of H. 1 *Chron.* 18. 9.
2 *Kings* 14. 28. now Jeroboam recovered H.
17. 24. the king of Assyria brought men from H.
30. the men of H. made Ashima their god
18. 34. where are the gods of H.? *Isa.* 36. 19.
19. 13. where is the king of H.? *Isa.* 37. 13.
23. 33. put him in bands in the land of H. 25. 21.
1 *Chron.* 18. 3. David smote Hadarezer to H.
2 *Chron.* 8. 4. Solomon built store-cities in H.
Isa. 10. 9. is not H. as Arpad? Samaria as Damascus?
11. 11. Lord shall recover his people from H.
Jer. 39. 5. to H. where he gave judgment, 52. 9.
49. 23. about Damascus, H. is confounded, and Arpad
Ezek. 47. 16. the border on the north, H. 17.
20. from border till a man come over against H.
Zech. 9. 2. H. also shall border thereby, Tyre, Sidon

HAMMEDATHA.

Esth. 8. 5. Haman the son of H. 9. 10, 24.

HAMON-GOG.

Ezek. 39. 11. they shall call it the valley of H.
15. the buriers have buried it in the valley of H.

HAMOR.

Gen. 33. 19. Jacob bought a field of the children of H. Shechem's father, *Josh.* 24. 32.
34. 6. H. went out to commune with Jacob, 8.
24. to H. and Shechem hearkened all the citizens
26. they slew H. and Shechem, and took Dinah
Judg. 9. 28. serve the men of H. father of Shechem

HANAMEEL.

Jer. 32. 7. H. thine uncle's son shall come, 8.
9. I bought the field of H. my uncle's son
12. I gave the evidence to Baruch in sight of H.

HANANEEL.

Neh. 3. 1. tower of H. 12. 39. *Jer.* 31. 38. *Zech.* 14. 10.

HANANI.

1 *Kings* 16. 1. to Jehu son of H. the word came, 7.
1 *Chr.* 25. 4. H. son of Heman ‖ 25. 18th lot to H.
2 *Chr.* 16. 7. at that time H. the seer came to Asa
19. 2. Jehu son of H. went to meet Jehoshaphat
20. 34. his acts in the book of Jehu son of H.
Ezra 10. 20. of the sons of Immah, H. Zebadiah
Neh. 1. 2. that H. one of my brethren came
7. 2. I gave my brother H. charge over Jerusalem
12. 36. H. with the musical instruments of David

HANANIAH.

1 *Chr.* 3. 19. the sons of Zerubbabel; Meshullam, H.
21. the sons of H. ‖ 8. 24. H. a Benjamite
25. 4. H. son of Heman ‖ 23. sixteenth lot to H.
2 *Chron.* 26. 11. Uzziah had an host under H.
Ezra 10. 28. H. Zabbai had taken strange wives
Neh. 3. 8. H. the son of an apothecary repaired
7. 2. I gave H. ruler of palace charge over Jerus.
10. 23. H. sealed ‖ 12. 12. H. with trumpets, 41.
Jer. 28. 1. H. son of Azur a false prophet
11. H. spake in the presence of all the people
12. after that H. had broken Jeremiah's yoke
17. H. died that year in the seventh month
36. 12. Zedekiah son of H. sat in scribes' chamber
37. 13. Irijah the son of H. took Jeremiah
Dan. 1. 6. of the children of Judah, Daniel, H.
7. he gave to H. the name of Shadrach
11. Melzar was set over Daniel, H. Mishael
19. among all was found none like Daniel, H.
2. 17. then Daniel made thing known to H.

HANNAH.

1 *Sam.* 1. 2. Elkanah's wife H. had no children
8. H. why weepest thou? ‖ 9. so H. rose up
13. H. spake in her heart only her lips moved
19. Elkanah knew H. ‖ 20. after H. conceived
22. but H. went not up ‖ 2. 1. H. prayed, and said
2. 21. the Lord visited H. so that she conceived

HANOCK.

Gen. 25. 4. sons of Midian, Ephah, H. 1 *Chr.* 1. 33.
46. 9. H. son of Reuben, *Num.* 26. 5. 1 *Chr.* 5. 3.

HANUN.

2 *Sam.* 10. 1. H. his son reigned in his stead
2. I will shew kindness unto H. 1 *Chron.* 19. 2.
4. H. took David's servants, and shaved off the one half of their beards, 1 *Chron.* 19. 4.
Neh. 3. 13. H. repaired the valley gate
30. H. sixth son of Zalaph repaired another piece

HARAN, *a man.*

Gen. 11. 26. Terah begat H. 27. ‖ 28. H. died
29. Nahor's wife was Milcah daughter of H.
31. Terah took Lot the son of H. his son's son
1 *Chron.* 2. 46. Ephah, Caleb's concubine, bare H. and Moza and H. begat Gazez
23. 9. the sons of Shimei, H. Shelomith, Haziel

HARAN, *a place.*

Gen. 11. 31. Terah came to H. ‖ 32. Terah died in H.
12. 4. Abram was 75 years departed out of H.
5. he took the souls that they had gotten in H.
27. 43. flee to H. ‖ 29. 4. they said, of H. are we
28. 10. Jacob went from Beer-sheba toward H.
2 *Kings* 19. 12. my fathers destroyed H. *Isa.* 37. 12.

HARBONAH.

Esth. 1. 10. H. was one of the chamberlains, 7. 9.

HAROD.

Judg. 7. 1. Gideon pitched beside the well of H.

HAROSHETH. *See* GENTILES.

HAZAEL.

1 *Kings* 19. 15. anoint H. to be king over Syria
17. that escapeth the sword of H. shall Jehu slay
2 *Kings* 8. 9. H. went to meet Elisha, took a present
15. Ben-hadad died, and H. reigned in his stead
28. Ahaziah went with Joram against H.
9. 14. Joram kept Ramoth-gilead because of H.
10. 32. H. smote them in all the coasts of Israel
12. 17. H. set his face to go up to Jerusalem
18. Jehoash sent the hallowed things to H.
13. 3. Lord delivered Israel into the hand of H.
22. but H. oppressed Israel ‖ 24. so H. died
25. recovered from Ben-hadad son of H. cities
Amos 1. 4. I will send fire into the house of H.

HAZELELPONI.

1 *Chron.* 4. 3. the name of their sister was H.

HAZEROTH.

Num. 11. 35. the people abode at H. 33. 17.
12. 16. the people removed from H. 33. 18.

HAZOR.

Josh. 11. 10. Joshua took H. head of those kingdoms
11. and he burnt H. with fire, 13.
15. 23. Kedesh and H. cities of Judah, 25.
19. 36. Ramah and H. cities of Naphtali
Judg. 4. 2. sold them to Jabin who reigned in H.
1 *Kings* 9. 15. Solomon raised a levy to build H.
2 *Kings* 15. 29. the king of Syria took H.
Jer. 49. 28. concerning the kingdoms of H.
30. flee, dwell deep, O ye inhabitants of H.
33. and H. shall be a dwelling for dragons

HEBER.

Gen. 46. 17. the sons of Beriah, H. 1 *Chron.* 7. 31.
Judg. 4. 11. H. the Kenite, 17. | 5. 24.
Luke 3. 35. Phalec, which was the son of H.

HEBREW.

Gen. 14. 13. one came and told Abraham the H.
39. 14. see he hath brought in an H. to mock us
41. 12. there was there with us a young man, a H.
Exod. 2. 11. he spied an Egyptian smiting an H.
Jer. 34. 9. should let an H. or Hebrewess go free
Jonah 1. 9. he said unto them, I am an H.

HEBREWS.

Gen. 40. 15. I was stolen out of the land of the H.
43. 32. the Egyptians might not eat with the H.
Exod. 2. 6. she said, this is one of the H. children
13. behold, two men of the H. strove together
3. 18. God of the H. 5. 3. | 7. 16. | 9. 1, 13. | 10. 3.
1 *Sam.* 4. 6. this great shout in the camp of the H.
9. be strong, that ye be not servants to the H.
13. 3. let the H. hear ‖ 19. lest the H. make swords
14. 11. behold the H. come forth out of holes
21. the H. that were with the Philistines
29. 3. the princes said, what do these H. here?
Acts 6. 1. a murmuring of Grecians against the H.
2 *Cor.* 11. 22. are they H. or Israelites? so am I
Phil. 3. 5. I am of Benjamin, an Hebrew of the H.

HEBREW.

Luke 23. 38. written over him in H. *John* 19. 20.
John 5. 2. a pool called in the H. tongue, Bethesda
19. 13. called in H. Gabbatha ‖ 17. Golgotha
Acts 21. 40. Paul spake to them in H. 22. 2.
26. 14. a voice saying in the H. tongue, Saul, Saul
Rev. 9. 11. in H. Abaddon ‖ 16. 16. Armageddon

HEBREW *man.*

Deut. 15. 12. if thy brother, an H. *man,* be sold

HEBREW *servant.*

Gen. 39. 17. the H. *servant* came in to mock me
Exod. 21. 2. if thou buy an H. *servant*

HEBREW *woman, women.*

Exod. 1. 16. do the office of a midwife to H. *women*
19. H. *women* are not as the Egyptian women
2. 7. shall I call to thee a nurse of the H. *women?*
Deut. 15. 12. if any H. *woman* be sold unto thee

HEBREWESS.

Jer. 34. 9. every man should let an H. go free

HEBRON, *place.*

Gen. 23. 2. Sarah died in Kirjath-arba, the same is H. 35. 27. *Josh.* 14. 15. | 20. 7. *Judg.* 1. 10.
37. 14. Jacob sent Joseph out of the vale of H.
Num. 13. 22. H. was built seven years before Zoan
Josh. 10. 39. as he did to H. so he did to Debir
14. 13. Joshua gave to Caleb H. 14. *Judg.* 1. 20.
1 *Sam.* 30. 31. a present to them which were in H.
2 *Sam.* 2. 1. whither shall I go up? he said, unto H.
11. the time David was king in H. was seven years, 5. 5. 1 *Kings* 2. 11. 1 *Chron.* 29. 27.
32. Joab and his men came to H. at break of day
3. 2. to David were sons born in H. 5. 1 *Chr.* 3. 1, 4.
32. they buried Abner in H. and the king wept
4. 12. they buried the head of Ish-bosheth in H.
5. 3. the elders of Israel came to H. and David made a league with them in H. 1 *Chron.* 11. 3.
13. took more wives after he was come from H.
15. 7. which I have vowed to the Lord in H.
10. then ye shall say, Absalom reigneth in H.
1 *Chron.* 6. 57. cities of Judah H. a city of refuge
12. 38. all these came with a perfect heart to H.
2 *Chron.* 11. 10. Rehoboam built Zorah, H. in Judah

HEBRON, *person.*

Exod. 6. 18. the sons of Kohath, Amram, H. and Uzziel, *Num.* 3. 19. 1 *Chron.* 6. 2, 18. | 23. 12.
1 *Chron.* 2. 42. sons of Mareshah the father of H.
43. the sons of H. 15. 9. | 23. 19. | 24. 23.

HEGE.

Esth. 2. 3. unto the custody of H. the chamberlain

HELAM.

2 *Sam.* 10. 16. Syrians beyond the river came to H.

HELBON.

Ezek. 27. 18. was thy merchant in the wine of H.

HELDAI.

Zech. 6. 10. take of them of the captivity even of H.

HELI.

Luke 3. 23. Joseph, which was the son of H.

HELKATH-HAZZURIM.

2 *Sam.* 2. 16. wherefore that place was called H.

HEMAN.

1 *Kings* 4. 31. Solomon was wiser than Ethan, H.
1 *Chron.* 2. 6. the sons of Zerah, H. and Calcol
6. 33. sons of Kohathites, H. a singer, son of Joel, the son of Shemuel, 15. 17, 19. | 16. 42.
25. 1. David appointed of the sons of Asaph and of H. 4, 6. 2 *Chron.* 5. 12. | 29. 14. | 35. 15.
5. all these were sons of H. God gave H. 14 sons

HEN.

Zech. 6. 14. crown shall be for H. son of Zephaniah

HEPHZI-BAH.

2 *Kings* 21. 1. Manasseh's mother's name was H.
Isa. 62. 4. thou shalt be called H. and land Beulah

HERMAS, HERMES.

Rom. 16. 14. salute *Hermas,* Patrobas, *Hermes*

HERMOGENES.

2 *Tim.* 1. 15. from me, of whom are Phygellus and H.

HERMON.

Deut. 4. 48. from Aroer to mount Sion, which is H.
Josh. 13. 11. all mount H. Reuben and Gad had
Psal. 89. 12. Tabor and H. shall rejoice in thy name
133. 3. it is the dew of H. that descended on Zion
Cant. 4. 8. look from the top of Shenir and H.

HERMONITES.

Ps. 42. 6. I will remember thee from the land of H.

HEROD.

Mat. 2. 12. warned, that they should not return to H.
15. Joseph was there till the death of H.
16. H. slew all the children in Beth-lehem
14. 3. for H. had laid hold on John, *Mark* 6. 17.
6. but when H. birth-day was kept, *Mark* 6. 21.
Mark 6. 20. H. feared John, knowing he was a just
8. 15. take heed, beware of the leaven of H.
Luke 3. 1. and H. being tetrarch of Galilee
19. for all the evils which H. had done
9. 7. H. heard of all that was done by Jesus
13. 31. depart hence, for H. will kill thee
23. 7. Pilate sent Jesus to H. ‖ 8. H. was glad
11. H. with his men of war set him at nought
12. Pilate and H. were made friends together
15. I found no fault in this man, no, nor yet H.
Acts 4. 27. both H. and Pontius Pilate against Jesus
12. 1. H. vexed the church, and killed James
6. when H. would have brought forth Peter
11. hath delivered me out of the hand of H.
21. on a set day H. made an oration to them
13. 1. which had been brought up with H. and Sau.
23. 35. command. him to be kept in H. judgme.-hal.

HERODIANS. *See Appellatives.*

HERODIAS.

Mat. 14. 3. John in prison for H. sake, *Mark* 6. 17.
6. the daughter of H. danced, *Mark* 6. 22.
Mark 6. 19. H. had a quarrel against John
Luke 3. 19. Herod being reproved by John for H.

HERODION.

Rom. 16. 11. salute H. my kinsman, greet them

HESHBON.

Num. 21. 25. Israel dwelt in H. and its villages
26. H. was the city of Sihon ‖ 27. come into H.
28. a fire gone out of H. ‖ 30. H. is perished
32. 37. children of Reuben built H. and Elealeh
Deut. 2. 24. I have given thee Sihon king of H.
Judg. 11. 26. while Israel dwelt in H. and Aroer
Neh. 9. 22. they possessed the land of the king of H.
Cant. 7. 4. thine eyes like the fish-pools of H.
Isa. 15. 4. H. shall cry ‖ *Jer.* 49. 3. howl, O H.
16. 8. for field of H. languish, and vine of Sibmah
9. will water thee with my tears, O H. and Elealeh
Jer. 48. 2. in H. they have devised evil against it
34. from cry of H. even to Elealeh and Jahaz
45. that fled stood under the shadow of H. because of the force, but a fire shall come out of H.
See SIHON.

HETH.

Gen. 10. 15. Canaan begat Sidon and H. 1 *Chr.* 1. 13.
23. 7. Abraham bowed before the children of H.
25. 10. Abraham purchased of the sons of H. 49. 32.
27. 46. am weary of life because of daughters of H.

HEZEKIAH, *called* EZEKIAS.

2 *Kings* 16. 20. H. Ahaz's son reigned in his stead
18. 14. H. sent to the king of Assyria to Lachish
15. H. gave him all the silver in house of the Lord
22. whose altars H. hath taken away, *Isa.* 36. 7.
29. thus saith the king, let not H. deceive you, not able to deliver you, 2 *Chr.* 32. 15. *Isa.* 36. 14.
31. hearken not to H. 32. *Isa.* 36. 16.
19. 1. king H. heard it, he rent his clothes, *Isa.* 37. 1.
15. H. prayed, 2 *Chron.* 30. 18. *Isa.* 37. 15.
20. 1. H. was sick to death, 2 *Chr.* 32. 24. *Isa.* 38. 1.
3. H. wept sore, *Isa.* 38. 3. ‖ 5. turn again, tell H.
12. Berodach sent a present to H. *Isa.* 39. 1.
13. nothing, that H. shewed them not, *Isa.* 39. 2.
19. H. said, good is the word of the Lord, *Isa.* 39. 8.
21. H. slept with his fathers, 2 *Chron.* 32. 33.
21. 3. built what H. had destroyed, 2 *Chron.* 33. 3.
1 *Chr.* 3. 23. the sons of Neariah, H. and Azrikam
4. 41. came in days of H. and smote their tents
2 *Chr.* 29. 27. H. commanded to offer burnt-offerings
36. and H. rejoiced, and all the people that God
30. 20. the Lord hearkened to H. and healed them
22. H. spake comfortably to all the Levites
24. H. gave the congregation 1000 bullocks
31. 2. H. appointed the courses of the priests
11. then H. commanded to prepare chambers
32. 8. the people rested on the words of H.
17. so shall not the God of H. deliver his people
22. thus the Lord saved H. from Sennacherib
25. H. rendered not again according to the benefit
26. wrath came not on them in the days of H.
30. and H. prospered in all his works
Ezra 2. 16. the children of Ater of H. *Neh.* 7. 21.
Prov. 25. 1. which the men of H. copied out
Jer. 15. 4. because of Manasseh the son of H.
26. 18. Micah prophesied in days of H. *Mic.* 1. 1.
19. did H. and all Judah put Micah to death
Hos. 1. 1. the word that came to Hosea in days of H.
Mat. 1. 9. Achaz begat H. ‖ 10. H. begat Manasses

HEZRON.

Gen. 46. 9. sons of Reuben, H. Carmi, *Exod.* 6. 14.
12. son of Pharez, H. *Ruth* 4. 18. 1 *Chr.* 2. 5. | 4. 1.
Ruth 4. 19. H. begat Ram, Ram begat Amminadab
1 *Chr.* 2. 9. the sons of H. ‖ 18. Caleb the son of H.
21. H. begat Segub ‖ 24. after that H. was dead
25. the sons of Jerahmeel the first born of H.

HIDDEKEL.
Gen. 2. 14. the name of the third river is H.
Dan. 10. 4. as I was by the side of the river H.
HIEL.
1 *Kings* 16. 34. H. the Beth-elite built Jericho
HIGGAION.
Psal. 9. 16. the wicked snared in his work, H. Selah
HILKIAH.
2 *Kings* 18. 18. there came out Eliakim son of H.
37. then came Eliakim the son of H. to Hezekiah with his clothes rent, and told him, *Isa.* 36. 22.
22. 4. saying, go up to H. the high-priest
8. H. gave the book to Shaphan, 10. 2 *Chr.* 34. 15.
12. the king commanded H. to inquire of the Lord for him, 2 *Chron.* 34. 20.
14. so H. went to Huldah, 2 *Chron.* 34. 22.
23. 4. commanded H. to bring forth the vessels
1 *Chr.* 6. 13. Shallum begat H. and H. begat Azariah
45. H. son of Amaziah ‖ 9. 11. H. son of Meshullam
26. 11. H. the second son of Hosah, Tabaliah
Ezra 7. 1. H. the son of Shallum, son of Zadok
Neh. 8. 4. H. stood on Ezra's right hand
11. 11. Seraiah the son of H. dwelt at Jerusalem
12. 7. H. the priest went up with Zerubbabel
21. of H. Hashabiah was a priest, of Jedaiah
Isa. 22. 20. I will call my servant Eliakim son of H.
Jer. 1. 1. the words of Jeremiah the son of H.
29. 3. Gemariah son of H. was sent to Babylon
HINNOM.
Josh. 15. 8. the border went up by the valley of H.
2 *Kings* 23. 10. Tophet, which is in the valley of H.
2 *Chron.* 28. 3. he burnt incense in the valley of H.
33. 6. he caused his children to pass thro' fire in H.
Jer. 19. 2. go forth to the valley of the son of H.
32. 35. they built high places in the valley of H.
HIRAM.
2 *Sam.* 5. 11. H. king of Tyre sent messengers to David and cedar-trees and masons, 1 *Chr.* 14. 1.
1 *Kings* 5. 1. H. king of Tyre sent his servants to Solomon, for H. was ever a lover of David, 8.
10. H. gave Solomon cedar-trees and fir-trees
11. Solomon gave H. 20,000 measures of wheat
12. there was peace between H. and Solomon
7. 13. Solomon sent and fetched H. out of Tyre
40. H. made the lavers, H. made an end of doing
9. 12. H. came to see the cities Solomon had given
27. H. sent in the navy his servants, shipmen
10. 11. the navy of H. brought in almug-trees
22. king had at sea a navy, with the navy of H.
HITTITE.
Gen. 25. 9. buried him in the field of Ephron the H.
26. 34. daughter of Beri the H. Elon the H. 36. 2.
49. 30. Abraham bought of Ephron the H. 50. 13.
Exod. 23. 28. I will drive out the H. 33. 2. | 34. 11.
Josh. 9. 1. the H. and Amorite gathered, 11. 3.
1 *Sam.* 26. 6. David said to Ahimelech the H.
2 *Sam.* 11. 6. David said, send me Uriah the H.
21. thy servant Uriah the H. is dead also, 24.
12. 9. thou hast killed Uriah the H. with sword
10. taken the wife of Uriah the H. to be thy wife
23. 39. Uriah the H. thirty-seven worthies in all
1 *Kings* 15. 5. save only in matter of Uriah the H.
Ezek. 16. 3. and thy mother an H. 45.
HITTITES.
Gen. 15. 20. seed have I given land of H. *Josh.* 1. 4.
Exod. 3. 8. Canaanites, H. Amorites, 17. | 13. 5. | 23. 23. *Deut.* 7. 1. | 20. 17. *Josh.* 3. 10. | 12. 8. | 24. 11. *Judg.* 3. 5. 1 *Kings* 9. 20. *Neh.* 9. 8.
Judg. 1. 26. the man went into the land of the H.
3. 5. the children of Israel dwelt among the H.
1 *Kings* 11. 1. but Solomon loved women of the H.
2 *Kings* 7. 6. Israel hired the kings of the H.
2 *Chron.* 8. 7. of H. left Solomon made pay tribute
Ezra 9. 1. done after the abominations of the H.
HIVITE, much in HITTITE.
HOBAB.
Num. 10. 29. Moses said to H. come thou with us
Judg. 4. 11. Heber was of the children of H.
HOPHNI.
1 *Sam.* 1. 3. two sons of Eli, H. and Phinehas, 4. 4.
2. 34. H. and Phinehas shall both die in one day
4. 11. Eli's sons H. and Phinehas were slain, 17.
HOR. *See* MOUNT.
HOREB.
Exod. 3. 1. Moses led the flock and came to the mountain of God, even to H. 1 *Kings* 19. 8.
17. 6. I will stand before thee on the rock in H.
33. 6. Israel stripped of ornaments by mount H.
Deut. 1. 6. the Lord spake to us in H. 4. 15.
4. 10. when thou stoodest before the Lord in H.
5. 2. the Lord made a covenant with us in H. 29. 1.
9. 8. also in H. ye provoked the Lord to wrath
18. 16. all thou desiredst of the Lord in H.
1 *Kings* 8. 9. nothing in the ark save the two tables which Moses put in the ark at H. 2 *Chron.* 5. 10.
Psal. 106. 19. they made a calf in H. and worshipped
Mal. 4. 4. which I commanded unto Moses in H.
HOR-HAGIDGAD.
Num. 33. 32. encamped at H. ‖ 33. went from H.
HORMAH.
Num. 14. 45. the Canaanites discomfited them to H.
21. 3. and he called the name of the place H.
Deut. 1. 44. and destroyed you in Seir even to H.
Josh. 15. 30. the cities of Judah, Eltolad, H.
19. 4. Simeon had out of Judah, Bethul, H.
Judg. 1. 17. the name of the city was called H.
1 *Sam.* 30. 30. a present to them that were in H.
1 *Chron.* 4. 30. Shimei's sons dwelt at H. at Ziklag
HORONAIM.
Isa. 15. 5. in the way of H. they shall raise a cry
Jer. 48. 3. a voice of crying shall be from H.
5. in going down of H. the enemies heard a cry
34. from Zoar to H. they uttered their voice
HORONITE. *See* SANBALLAT.
HOSHEA.
Deut. 32. 44. he and H. son of Nun spake to people
2 *Kings* 15. 30. H. made a conspiracy against Pekah
17. 1. H. son of Elah began to reign in Samaria
3. H. became the king of Assyria's servant
6. in the ninth year of H. Samaria taken, 18. 10.
1 *Chron.* 27. 20. the ruler of Ephraim was H.
Neh. 10. 23. H. and Hananiah sealed the covenant

HUR.
Exod. 17. 10. Moses, Aaron, H. went up to top of h.
12. and Aaron and H. stayed up his hands
24. 14. behold, Aaron and H. are with you
31. 2. Lord hath called Bezaleel, the son of Uri, son of H. of the tribe of Judah, 35. 30. | 38. 22.
Num. 31. 8. they slew Evi, Rekem, Zur, H. and Reba, five kings of Midian, *Josh.* 13. 21.
1 *Kings* 4. 8. the son of H. in mount Ephraim
1 *Chron.* 2. 19. Caleb took Ephratah, which bare H.
20. H. begat Uri ‖ 4. 1. sons of Judah, H. Shobal
50. these were the sons of Caleb the son of H.
4. 4. these are the sons of H. Ephratah, Ashur
Neh. 3. 9. Rephaiah son of H. repaired next to them
HUSHAI.
2 *Sam.* 15. 32. H. the Archite came to meet David
37. so H. David's friend came into the city
16. 16. H. came to Absalom and said, G. save king
17. said to H. is this thy kindness to thy friend?
17. 5. call H. ‖ 8. for, said H. thou knowest thy fath.
14. the counsel of H. is better than of Ahithophel
15. then said H. to Zadok and to Abiathar
1 *Kings* 4. 16. Baanah the son of H. was in Ashur
1 *Chron.* 27. 33. and H. was the king's companion
HUZZAB.
Nah. 2. 7. H. shall be led away capt. be brought up
HYMENEUS.
1 *Tim.* 1. 20. of whom is H. and Alexander
2 *Tim.* 2. 17. of whom is H. and Philetus

J.

JAAZANIAH.
2 *Kings* 25. 23. J. came to Gedaliah, to Mizpeh
Jer. 35. 3. J. of the house of the Rechabites
Ezek. 8. 11. J. stood with his censer in his hand
11. 1. J. and Pelatiah princes of the people
JABAL.
Gen. 4. 20. J. was the father of such as dwell in tents
JABBOK.
Gen. 32. 22. and Jacob passed over the ford J.
Deut. 2. 37. thou camest not to any place of river J.
3. 16. I gave to Reuben and Gad the border to J.
Josh. 12. 2. Sihon ruled from Gilead to the river J.
JABESH.
1 *Sam.* 11. 5. they told Saul the tidings of men of J.
9. shewed to the men of J. and they were glad
31. 12. came to J. and burned the body of Saul
13. they buried their bones at J. 1 *Chron.* 10. 12.
2 *Kings* 15. 10. Shallum the son of J. conspired
13. Shallum the son of J. began to reign
14. Menahem smote Shallum the son of J.
JABESH-GILEAD.
Judg. 21. 8. there came none to the camp from J.
10. saying, go and smite the inhabitants of J.
12. they found 400 young virgins of J. not known
14. gave Benjamites wives of women of J.
1 *Sam.* 11. 1. Nahash came and encamped against J.
31. 11. the inhabitants of J. heard what the Philistines had done to Saul, 1 *Chron.* 10. 12.
2 *Sam.* 2. 4. men of J. were they that buried Saul
21. 12. David took bones of Saul from men of J.
JABEZ.
1 *Chron.* 2. 55. the families of scribes who dwelt at J.
JABEZ.
1 *Chron.* 4. 9. J. was more honourable than his brethren, and his mother called his name J.
10. J. called on God of Israel, saying, O bless me
JABIN.
Josh. 11. 1. when J. king of Hazor heard these things
Judg. 4. 2. the Lord sold them into the hand of J.
17. was peace between J. and the house of Heber
23. God subdued that day, J. king of Canaan
24. the hand of Israel prevailed against J.
Psal. 83. 9. do to them as unto J. at brook Kison
JACHIN.
1 *Kings* 7. 21. he set up pillars in temple, he called the pillar on the right hand J. 2 *Chron.* 3. 17.
JACOB.
Gen. 25. 26. he was called J. ‖ 27. J. was a plain man
29. J. sod pottage ‖ 34. J. gave Esau pottage
27. 22. the voice is J. ‖ 30. J. was scarce gone out
36. Esau said, is not he rightly named J.
41. Esau hated J. ‖ 46. if J. take a wife of Heth
28. 5. Isaac sent away J. ‖ 7. J. obeyed his father
16. J. awaked out of sleep ‖ 20. J. vowed a vow
29. 10. J. saw Rachel the daughter of Laban
20. and J. served seven years for Rachel
28. and J. did so, and fulfilled her week
30. 16. J. came out of the field in the evening
37. and J. took him rods of green poplar
42. the feebler were Laban's, the stronger J.
31. 1. J. hath taken all that was our father's
20. J. stole away unawares to Laban the Syrian
53. J. sware by the fear of his father Isaac
32. 3. J. sent messengers before him to Esau
4. J. saith thus ‖ 7. then J. was greatly afraid
18. then thou shalt say, they be thy servant J.
24. J. was left alone, and there wrestled a man
28. thy name shall be no more J. but Isr. 35. 10.
30. J. called the name of the place Peniel
33. 1. J. looked, and behold, Esau came
17. J. journeyed to Succoth ‖ 18. to Shalem
34. 5. J. held his peace until they were come
7. sons of J. 13, 25. | 35. 26. | 49. 1, 2. 1 *Kings* 18. 31.
35. 6. J. came to Luz ‖ 15. J. called the place Beth-el
37. 2. these are the generations of J.
34. J. rent his clothes, put sackcloth on his loins
45. 26. J. heart fainted, for he believed not
46. 6. J. and all his seed came into Egypt
26. all the souls that came with J. were sixty six
47. 10. J. blessed Pharaoh ‖ 28. the whole age of J.
49. 24. by hands of the mighty God of J. *Exod.* 3. 6, 15, 16. | 4. 5. 2 *Sam.* 23. 1. *Psal.* 20. 1.
Exod. 2. 24. rememb. his covenant with J. *Lev.* 26. 42.
Num. 23. 7. come, curse me J. and defy Israel
10. who can count dust of J. and number of Israel
23. there is no enchantment against J. it shall be said of J. and Israel, what hath God wrought
24. 17. there shall come a star out of J. and sceptre
19. out of J. come he that shall have dominion

Deut. 32. 9. J. is the lot of his inheritance
33. 10. they shall teach J. thy judgments and Isr.
28. fountain of J. shall be on land of corn, wine
1 *Chron.* 16. 13. O ye seed of Israel his servant, ye children of J. his chosen, *Psal.* 105. 6.
Psal. 14. 7. J. shall rejoice, Isr. shall be glad, 53. 6.
20. 1. the name of the God of J. defend thee
22. 23. all ye seed of J. glorify him and fear him
44. 4. my king, O G. command deliverances for J.
46. 7. the god of J. 11. | 75. 9. | 76. 6. | 81. 1, 4. | 84. 8. | 94. 7. | 114. 7. | 132. 2, 5. | 146. 5.
47. 4. the excellency of J. whom he loved, *Nah.* 2. 2.
78. 21. a fire was kindled ag. J. anger against Isr.
71. he brought him to feed J. his people
79. 7. for they have devoured J. and laid waste
85. 1. thou hast brought back the captivity of J.
87. 2. gates of Zion more than all the dwellings of J.
105. 23. and J. sojourned in the land of Ham
135. 4. the Lord hath chosen J. unto himself
Isa. 2. 3. the God of J. 41. 21. *Mic.* 4. 2. *Mat.* 22. 32. *Mark* 12. 26. *Luke* 20. 37. *Acts* 3. 13. | 7. 32, 46.
10. 21. the remnant of J. shall return to God
14. 1. for the Lord will have mercy on J.
17. 4. in that day the glory of J. shall be made thin
27. 6. shall cause them that come of J. to take root
9. by this shall the iniquity of J. be purged
29. 23. they shall sanctify the holy One of J.
41. 8. J. whom I have chosen, the seed of Abraham
14. fear not, thou worm J. and ye men of Israel
42. 24. who gave J. for a spoil? did not the Lord?
43. 28 therefore I have given J. to the curse
44. 5. another shall call himself by the name of J.
23. for the Lord hath redeemed J. *Jer.* 31. 11.
45. 4. for J. my servant's sake, I called thee
48. 20. the Lord hath redeemed his servant J.
49. 5. that formed me to bring J. again to him
6. be my servant to raise up the tribes of J.
26. thy Redeemer, the mighty One of J. 60. 16.
58. 14. I will feed thee with the heritage of J.
65. 9. I will bring forth a seed out of J. and Judah
Jer. 10. 16. the portion of J. not like them, 51. 19.
25. for they have eaten up J. and devoured him
30. 7. it is even the time of J. trouble, be saved
10. therefore fear thou not, O my servant J.
18. I will bring again the captivity of J. tents
31. 7. saith the Lord, sing with gladness for J.
33. 26. then will I cast away the seed of J.
46. 27. J. shall return to be in rest and ease
Lam. 1. 17. Lord hath commanded concerning J.
2. 3. he burned against J. like a flaming fire
Hos. 10. 11. Jud. shall plow, J. shall break his clods
12. 2. I will punish J. ‖ 12. J. fled into Syria
Amos 6. 8. I abhor the excellency of J. and hate
7. 2. by whom shall J. arise, for he is small? 5.
8. 7. the Lord hath sworn by the excellency of J.
Mic. 1. 5. for the transgression of J. is all this
3. 1. and I said, hear, I pray you, O heads of J.
5. 8. remnant of J. shall be among the Gentiles
Mal. 1. 2. was not Esau J. brother? yet I loved J.
3. 6. therefore, ye sons of J. are not consumed
Mat. 1. 2. Isaac begat J. ‖ 15. Matthan begat J.
8. 11. shall sit down with Abraham, Isaac, and J.
Luke 13. 28. when ye see J. in the kingdom of God
John 4. 6. now J. well was there, Jesus sat on the well
Acts 7. 14. Joseph called his father J. to him
Rom. 9. 13. J. have I loved, but Esau have I hated
11. 26. and shall turn away ungodliness from J.
Heb. 11. 9. Abraham dwelling in tabernacles with J.
20. by faith Isaac blessed J. ‖ 21. J. blessed sons
See HOUSE.
In JACOB.
Gen. 49. 7. I will divide them *in* J. and scatter them
Num. 23. 21. he hath not beheld iniquity *in* J.
Psal. 59. 13. let them know that God ruleth *in* J.
78. 5. for he established a testimony *in* J. and a law
99. 4. thou executest judgment and righteous. *in* J.
Isa. 59. 20. to them that turn from transgression *in* J.
O JACOB.
Num. 24. 5. how goodly are thy tents, *O* J.!
Psal. 24. 6. the generation that seek thy face, *O* J.
Isa. 40. 27. why sayest thou, *O* J. my way is hid?
43. 1. saith the Lord that created thee, *O* J.
22. but thou hast not called upon me, *O* J.
44. 1. yet hear, *O* J. ‖ 48. 12. hearken unto me, *O* J.
2. fear not, *O* J. my servant, *Jer.* 46. 27, 28.
21. remember these, *O* J. for thou art my servant
Mic. 2. 12. I will surely assemble, *O* J. all of thee
To or *unto* JACOB.
Gen. 31. 24. speak not *to* J. either good or bad, 29.
35. 9. God appeared unto J. and blessed him
50. 24. the land which he sware to give *to* J. *Exod.* 6. 8. | 33. 1. *Num.* 32. 11. *Deut.* 6. 10. | 29. 13. | 30. 20. | 34. 4. *Ezek.* 37. 25.
1 *Chr.* 16. 17. and hath confirmed the same *to* J. for a law, and to Israel for a covenant, *Ps.* 105. 10.
Psal. 147. 19. he shewed his word *unto* J. his statutes
Isa. 9. 8. the Lord sent a word *unto* J. it lighted on
Mic. 3. 8. to declare *unto* J. his transgression and Is.
7. 20. wilt perform truth *to* J. and mercy to Abrah.
JAEL.
Judg. 4. 17. Sisera fled away to the tent of J.
21. J. took a nail of the tent and an hammer
22. J. came out to meet Barak, and said
5. 6. in days of J. the high-ways were unoccupied
24. blessed above women shall J. wife of Heber be
JAH.
Psal. 68. 4. extol him by his name J. and rejoice
JAHAZ.
Num. 21. 23. Sihon gathered his people and came and fought at J. *Deut.* 2. 32. *Judg.* 11. 20.
Isa. 15. 4. their voice shall be heard even to J.
Jer. 48. 34. to J. have they uttered their voice
JAHAZAH.
Josh. 21. 36. out of Reuben J. given to the Levites
Jer. 48. 21. judgment is come upon Holon and J.
JAIR.
Num. 32. 41. J. took the small towns, *Deut.* 3. 14.
Judg. 10. 3. J. the Gileadite judged Israel 22 years
5. J. died ‖ 1 *Chron.* 2. 22. Segub begat J.
1 *Chron.* 20. 5. Elhanan the son of J. slew Lahmi
Esth. 2. 5. Mordecai the son of J. a Benjamite

JAIRUS.
Mark 5. 22. J. a ruler of the synagogue, *Luke* 8. 41.
JAKEH, *See* AGUR.
JAMBRES.
2 *Tim.* 3. 8. as Jannes and J. withstood Moses
JAMES.
Mat. 4. 21. saw two brethren J. and John, *Mark* 1. 19.
10. 2. J. the son of Zebedee, *Mark* 3. 17.
3. J. the son of Alpheus, *Mark* 3. 18. *Acts* 1. 13.
13. 55. and his brethren J. and Joses, *Mark* 6. 3.
17. 1. after six days Jesus taketh Peter, J. and
John, *Mark* 5. 37. | 9. 2. | 14. 33. *Luke* 8. 51.
27. 56. Mary Magdalene and Mary mother of J.
and Joses, *Mark* 15. 40. | 16. 1. *Luke* 24. 10.
Mark 10. 41. began to be much displeased with J.
13. 3. Peter, J. and John asked him privately
Luke 5. 10. J. was astonished at draught of fishes
Acts 1. 13. where abode both Peter, J. and John
12. 2. Herod killed J. brother of John with sword
17. Peter said, shew these things to J. and brethren
15. 13. J. answered, saying, hearken unto me
21. 18. Paul went in with us unto J. and elders
1 *Cor.* 15. 7. after that was seen of J. then of apostles
Gal. 1. 19. I saw none, save J. the Lord's brother
2. 9. when J. perceived the grace given to me
12. before certain came from J. did eat with Gent.
JANNA.
Luke 3. 24. Melchi who was the son of J. who was
JANNES. *See* JAMBRES.
JAPHETH.
Gen. 5. 32. Shem, Ham, J. the sons of Noah, 6. 10.
| 7. 13. | 9. 18. 1 *Chron.* 1. 4.
9. 23. Shem and J. took a garment and covered
27. God shall enlarge J. he shall dwell in tents
10. 1. unto J. were sons born, 2. 1 *Chron.* 1. 5.
21. Shem father of Eber, brother of J. the elder
JAREB.
Hos. 5. 13. then Ephraim saw, and sent to king J.
10. 6. shall be carried for a present to king J.
JARED.
Gen. 5. 15. Mahaleel begat J. *Luke* 3. 37.
JASHER.
Josh. 10. 13. written in the book of J. 2 *Sam.* 1. 18.
JASON.
Acts 17. 5. the Jews assaulted the house of J.
6. they drew J. || 7. whom J. hath received
9. and when they had taken security of J.
Rom. 16. 21. Lucius, J. and Sosipater salute you
JAVAN.
Gen. 10. 2. sons of Japheth, J. Tubal, 1 *Chron.* 1. 5.
Isa. 66. 19. I will send those that escape to J.
Ezek. 27. 13. J. and Tubal were thy merchants, 19.
JAZER.
Num. 32. 1. they saw J. was a land for cattle, 3.
Isa. 16. 8. they are come even unto J. they wandered
9. I will bewail with weeping of J. vine of Sibmah
IBHAR.
2 *Sam.* 5. 15. David's son I. 1 *Chron.* 3. 6. | 14. 5.
ICHABOD.
1 *Sam.* 4. 21. she named the child I. glory departed
14. 3. Ahiah the son of Ahitub, I. brother
ICONIUM.
Acts 13. 51. Paul and Barnabas came unto I.
14. 1. in I. they went both into the synagogue
19. there came thither certain Jews from I.
16. 2. well reported of by the brethren at I.
2 *Tim.* 3. 11. afflictions which came to me at I.
IDDO.
1 *Kings* 4. 14. Ahinadab son of I. had Mahanaim
1 *Chron.* 6. 21. of Gershom, Joash his son, I. his son
27. 21. of the half tribe of Manasseh I. was ruler
2 *Chr.* 9. 29. the rest of the acts of Solomon written
in the visions of I. the seer, 12. 15. | 13. 22.
Ezra 5. 1. Zech. son of I. prophesied, *Zech.* 1. 1, 7.
6. 14. through prophesying of Zechariah son of I.
8. 17. I sent them to I. the chief, and told them
what they should say to I. and his brethren
Neh. 12. 4. I. with priests went up with Zerubbabel
IDUMEA.
Isa. 34. 5. my sword shall come down on I. 6.
Ezek. 35. 15. and all I. shall be desolate
36. 5. in jealousy have I spoken against all I.
Mark 3. 8. a multitude followed him from I.
JEBUSITE.
Gen. 10. 16. Canaan begat the J. 1 *Chron.* 1. 14.
Exod. 33. 2. I will drive out the J. 34. 11.
2 *Sam.* 24. 16. angel of Lord was by the threshing-
place of Araunah the J. 18. 1 *Chron.* 21. 15.
Zech. 9. 7. a governor in Judah, and Ekron as a J.
JEBUSITES.
Num. 13. 29. the J. dwell in the mountains
Josh. 15. 63. the J. dwell with the children of Judah
Judg. 1. 21. drive the J. that inhabited Jerusalem
19. 11. let us turn into this city of the J. and dwell
2 *Sam.* 5. 8. whoso getteth up and smiteth the J.
See HITTITES.
JECONIAH.
1 *Chron.* 3. 16. the sons of Jehoiakim, J. Zedekiah
17. the sons of J. Assir and Salathiel
Jer. 24. 1. had carried away captive J. 27. 20.
28. 4. I will bring again to this place J. the son of
JEDIDIAH.
2 *Sam.* 12. 25. the Lord called Solomon J.
JEDUTHUN.
1 *Chron.* 16. 41. Heman and J. to give thanks to L.
42. the sons of J. 25. 3. 2 *Chron.* 29. 14.
25. 6. according to the king's order to J. and Heman
JEGAR-SAHADUTHA.
Gen. 31. 47. Laban called the heap J. but Jacob
JEHOAHAZ, *called* AHAZIAH.
2 *Kings* 10. 35. J. son of Jehu reigned in his stead
13. 1. J. son of Jehu began to reign over Israel
23. 30. the people of the land took J. the son of
Josiah, and anointed him, 2 *Chron.* 36. 1.
34. Pharaoh-necho took J. away, 2 *Chron.* 36. 4.
2 *Chron.* 21. 17. left Jehoram never a son save J.
JEHOASH, *or* JOASH.
2 *Kings* 11. 21. J. seven years old when began to reign
12. 2. J. did what was right in sight of the Lord
18. J. sent all the hallowed things to Hazael
20. his servant slew J. in the house of Millo
13. 10. J. the son of Jehoahaz began to reign
2 *Kings* 14. 8. then Amaziah sent messengers to J.
16. J. slept with his fathers and was buried
JEHOIACHIN.
2 *Kings* 24. 8. J. was 18 years old when he began
12. J. king of Judah went out to king of Babylon
25. 27. did lift up the head of J. *Jer.* 52. 31.
2 *Chr.* 36. 9. J. was eight years old when he began
JEHOIADA.
2 *Sam.* 8. 18. Benaiah the son of J. 20. 23. | 23. 20,
22. 1 *Chron.* 11. 22, 24. | 18. 17.
1 *Kings* 1. 44. sent with Solomon Benaiah son of J.
4. 4. Benaiah the son of J. was over the host
2 *Kings* 11. 17. J. made a covenant, 2 *Chr.* 23. 16.
12. 2. wherein J. the priest instructed him
1 *Chron.* 12. 27. J. was leader of the Aaronites
27. 34. after Ahithophel was J. a counsellor
2 *Chron.* 24. 2. Joash did right all the days of J.
17. after the death of J. came the princes of Judah
22. Joash remembered not the kindness J. had done
25. for the blood of the sons of J. the priest
Neh. 3. 6. the old gate repaired J. son of Paseah
Jer. 29. 26. hath made thee priest instead of J.
JEHOIAKIM.
2 *Kings* 23. 34. turned his name to J. 2 *Chr.* 36. 4.
35. J. gave the silver and gold to Pharaoh
24. 1. J. became his servant three years
Jer. 22. 18. thus saith the Lord concerning J.
26. 22. J. sent men after Urijah into Egypt
36. 28. the roll which J. the king hath burnt
30. thus saith the Lord of J. king of Judah
52. 2. Zedekiah did what was evil as J. had done
Dan. 1. 2. and the Lord gave J. into his hand
JEHONADAB.
2 *Kings* 10. 15. he lighted on J. the son of Rechab
23. Jehu and J. went into the house of Baal
JEHORAM.
1 *Kings* 22. 50. J. son of Jehoshaphat, 2 *Kings* 8. 16.
2 *Kings* 1. 17. J. the son of Ahab reigned over Israel
2 *Chron.* 17. 8. he sent Elishama and J. priests
21. 9. J. went forth and smote the Edomites
16. the Lord stirred up against J. the Philistines
22. 5. he went with J. to war against Hazael
7. Ahaziah went out with J. against Jehu
JEHOSHAPHAT.
2 *Sam.* 8. 16. J. the son of Ahilud was recorder, 20.
24. 1 *Kings* 4. 3. 1 *Chron.* 18. 15.
1 *Kings* 4. 17. J. son of Paruah was in Issachar
15. 24. J. the son of Asa reigned, 2 *Chron.* 17. 1.
22. 2. J. came down to Ahab king of Israel
10. Ahab and J. sat each on his throne, 2 *Chr.* 18. 9.
29. J. went up to Ramoth-Gilead, 2 *Chron.* 18. 28.
32. J. cried out || 50. J. slept with his fathers
49. let my servants go, but J. would not
2 *Kings* 3. 14. were it not that I regard presence of J.
9. 2. look out there Jehu the son of J. and go in
1 *Chron.* 15. 24. J. blew with the trumpet before ark
2 *Chron.* 17. 3. Lord was with J. because he walked
10. so that they made no war against J.
12. J. waxed great exceedingly and built castles
18. 1. J. had riches and honour in abundance
20. 3. J. feared and set himself to seek the Lord
27. they returned and J. in the fore-front of them
35. after this did J. join with Ahaziah king of Isr.
37. then Eliezer prophesied against J. because
21. 12. thou hast not walked in the ways of J.
22. 9. because, said they, he is the son of J.
Joel 3. 2. bring them down to the valley of J.
12. let the heathen come up to the valley of J.
JEHOSHUA.
Num. 13. 16. Moses called Oshea, son of Nun, J.
1 *Chron.* 7. 27. Non his son, J. his son
JEHOVAH.
Exod. 6. 3. by my name J. was I not known to them
Psal. 83. 18. that thou whose name alone is J.
Isa. 12. 2. the Lord J. is my strength and song
26. 4. for in the Lord J. is everlasting strength
JEHOVAH-JIREH.
Gen. 22. 14. Abraham called the name of the place J.
JEHOVAH-NISSI.
Exod. 17. 15. Moses called the name of the altar J.
JEHOVAH-SHALOM.
Judg. 6. 24. Gideon built and called the altar J.
JEHOVAH-SHAMMAH.
Ezek. 48. † 35. the name of the city shall be J.
JEHOVAH-TSIDKENU.
Jer. 23. † 6. this is his name, J. 33. † 16.
JEHU.
1 *Kings* 16. 1. word came to J. son of Hanani, 7, 12.
19. 16. J. son of Nimshi shalt thou anoint king
17. shall J. slay; that escapeth the sword of J.
2 *Kings* 9. 2. look out there J. || 13. J. is king
14. J. son of Nimshi conspired against Joram
17. a watchman spied company of J. as he came
20. the driving is like the driving of J. son of
24. J. drew a bow with his full strength, smote
10. 11. J. slew all that remained of house of Ahab
18. Ahab served Baal, J. shall serve Baal much
29. J. departed not from the sins of Jeroboam
31. J. took no heed to walk in the law of God
15. 12. this was the word which he spake to J.
1 *Chron.* 2. 38. Obed begat J. and J. begat Azariah
4. 35. J. son of Josibiah || 12. 3. J. son of Azmaveth
2 *Chron.* 19. 2. J. went out to meet Jehoshaphat
20. 34. written in the book of J. son of Hanani
22. 8. J. was executing judgment on Ahab
Hos. 1. 4. I will avenge the blood of Jezreel on J.
JEPHTHAH.
Judg. 11. 1. now J. the Gileadite was a mighty man
of valour, and Gilead begat J.
3. J. fled from his brethren, and dwelt in Tob
11. J. uttered all his words before the Lord
28. the king hearkened not to words of J.
29. the Spirit came on J. || 30. J. vowed a vow
40. went yearly to lament the daughter of J.
12. 7. J. judged Israel six years, then died J.
1 *Sam.* 12. 11. the Lord sent J. and delivered you
Heb. 11. 32. for the time would fail me to tell of J.
JEPHUNNEH.
Num. 13. 6. of the tribe of Judah, Caleb the
son of J.
1 *Chron.* 7. 38. the sons of Jether J. and Pispah
See CALEB.
JERAHMEEL.
1 *Chron.* 2. 9. the sons of Hezron, J. and Ram
33. the sons of J. || 24. 29. J. the son of Kish
Jer. 36. 26. the king commanded J. to take Baruch
JEREMIAH.
2 *Kings* 23. 31. his mother's name was Hamutal,
the daughter of J. of Libnah, 24. 18. *Jer.* 52. 1.
1 *Chron.* 5. 24. J. a mighty man, 12. 4, 10, 13.
2 *Chron.* 35. 25. and J. lamented for Josiah
36. 12. Zedekiah humbled not himself before J.
21. to fulfil the word of the Lord by the mouth of
J. till land enjoyed her sabbaths, 22. *Ezra* 1. 1.
Neh. 10. 2. Azariah, J. sealed the covenant
12. 1. Seraiah, J. went up with Zerubbabel
12. in days of Joiakim, of J. Hananiah was priest
34. J. and Shemaiah went after them
Jer. 1. 1. the words of J. the son of Hilkiah
7. 1. the word that came to J. 11. 1. | 14. 1. | 18. 1.
18. 18. come, let us devise devices against J.
20. 2. Pashur smote J. and put him in the stocks
24. 3. then said the Lord, what seest thou, J.?
26. 9. all the people were gathered against J.
24. the hand of Ahikam was with J. not to put
28. 10. took the yoke from the prophet J.'s neck
29. 27. why hast thou not reproved J. of Anathoth?
32. 2. J. was shut up in the court of the prison
34. 6. J. spake all these words to Zedekiah
35. 3. then I took Jaazaniah the son of J.
36. 19. the princes said, go hide thee, thou and J.
26. Lord hid Baruch the scribe and J. the prophet
37. 4. J. came in and went out among the people
14. so Irijah took J. and brought him to princes
15. wherefore the princes were wroth with J.
16. when J. was entered into the dungeon
21. to commit J. into the court of the prison
38. 6. then they cast J. into the dungeon
13. drew up J. with cords out of the dungeon
16. Zedekiah the king sware secretly to J.
39. 11. Nebuchadrezzar gave charge concerning J.
40. 6. then went J. to Gedaliah son of Ahikam
51. 60. so J. wrote in a book all the evil on Babylon
64. thus far are the words of J.
Mat. 2. 17. fulfilled that was spoken by J. 27. 9.
16. 14. others say thou art J. or one of prophets
JERICHO.
Josh. 2. 1. go view J. || 6. 1. J. was straitly shut up
3. 16. the people passed over right against J.
6. 2. Lord said, see, I have given into thine hand J.
26. cursed be the man that buildeth the city J.
7. 2. Joshua sent men from J. to view Ai
24. 11. ye came to J. and the men of J. fought
2 *Sam.* 10. 5. king said, tarry at J. till your beards
be grown, and then return, 1 *Chron.* 19. 5.
1 *Kings* 16. 34. in his days did Hiel build J.
2 *Kings* 2. 4. for the Lord hath sent me to J.
25. 5. the army of Chaldees pursued and overtook
him in the plains of J. *Jer.* 39. 5. | 52. 8.
2 *Chron.* 28. 15. they brought the captives to J.
Luke 10. 30. a certain man went down to J. and fell
Heb. 11. 30. by faith the walls of J. fell down
JEROBOAM.
1 *Kings* 11. 28. J. was a mighty man of valour
40. Solomon sought to kill J. and J. fled
12. 2. J. dwelt in Egypt || 20. J. was come again
25. J. built Shechem, and dwelt therein
32. J. ordained a feast in the eighth month
13. 1. J. stood by the altar to burn incense
33. after this J. returned not from his evil way
34. this thing became sin to the house of J.
14. 1. at that time Abijah the son of J. fell sick
6. Ahijah said, come in, thou wife of J.
10. behold, I will bring evil upon the house of J.
11. him that dieth of J. shall the dogs eat
13. for he only of J. shall come to the grave
16. because of the sins of J. 15. 30.
30. there was war between Rehoboam and J.
15. 29. Baasha left not to J. any that breathed
34. Baasha did evil, and walked in the way of J.
2 *Kings* 10. 31. | 13. 6. | 14. 24. | 17. 22.
2 *Kings* 13. 13. J. son of Joash sat on his throne
14. 27. the Lord saved Israel by the hand of J.
17. 21. J. drave Israel from following the Lord
1 *Chr.* 5. 17. reckoned by genealogies in days of J
2 *Chron.* 11. 14. J. had cast off the Levites from
13. 8. golden calf which J. made for your gods
15. God smote J. and all Israel before Abijah
20. neither did J. recover strength again in days
Hos. 1. 1. prophesied in the days of J. *Amos* 1. 1.
Amos 7. 9. rise against house of J. with the sword
11. thus Amos saith, J. shall die by the sword
JEROBOAM, joined with *Nebat.*
1 *Kings* 11. 26. J. son of *Nebat* lifted up his hand
12. 15. which the Lord spake by Ahijah the Shilonite to J. the son of *Nebat*, 2 *Chron.* 10. 15.
16. 3. I will make thy house like the house of J.
the son of *Nebat*, 21. 22. | 2 *Kings* 9. 9.
26. for he walked in all the way of J. the son of
Nebat, and his sin, 31. | 22. 52. 2 *Kings* 3. 3.
2 *Kings* 10. 29. Jehu departed not from the sins of J.
son of *Nebat*, 13. 2, 11. | 14. 24. | 15. 9, 18, 24, 28.
JERUBBAAL.
Judg. 6. 32. on that day he called him J. saying
7. 1. then J. (who is Gideon) rose up early
8. 29. and J. went and dwelt in his own house
35. nor shewed they kindness to the house of J.
9. 2. either that all sons of J. reign, or one reign
5. Abimelech slew his brethren the sons of J.
16. if ye dealt well with J. || 19. if sincerely with J.
28. who is Abimelech? is not he the son of J.?
1 *Sam.* 12. 11. the Lord sent J. and delivered you
JERUBBESHETH.
2 *Sam.* 11. 21. who smote Abimelech the son of J.
JERUSALEM, or **HIERUSALEM.**
Josh. 18. 28. Jebusi, which is J. *Judg.* 19. 10.
1 *Sam.* 17. 54. David brought Goliath's head to J.
2 *Sam.* 5. 6. king David and his men went to J.
8. 7. David brought the shields of gold to J.
12. 31. so David and all the people returned to J
15. 8. if the Lord shall bring me again to J. then
29. they carried the ark of God again to J.
19. 19. the day that my lord went out of J.
24. 8. they came to J. at the end of nine months

2 *Sam.* 24. 16. when the angel stretched out his hand
on J. to destroy it, Lord repented, 1 *Chron.* 21. 15.
1 *Kings* 3. 1. made an end of building the wall of J.
10. 2. she came to J. with a very great train
11. 13. for J. sake which I have chosen, 2 *Chr.* 6. 6.
15. 4. to set up his son after him and to establish J.
2 *Kings* 18. 35. delivered their country, that Lord
should deliver J. out of mine hand, *Isa.* 36. 20.
19. 31. out of J. shall go forth a remnant, and they
that escape out of mount Zion, *Isa.* 37. 32.
21. 12. behold, I will bring such evil upon J.
13. I will wipe J. as a man wipeth a dish, wiping
16. shed innocent blood till he had filled J. 24. 4.
23. 27. I will cast off J. which I have chosen
24. 14. he carried away all J. and the princes
25. 9. Nebuzar-adan burnt all the houses of J.
2 *Chron.* 12. 7. my wrath shall not be poured on J.
20. 28. they came to J. with psalteries, harps
24. 18. wrath was upon J. 29. 8. | 32. 25.
28. 24. Ahaz made altars in every corner of J.
32. 19. they spake against the God of J.
34. 3. Josiah began to purge J. from high places
Ezra 7. 14. thou art sent to inquire concerning J.
19. those deliver thou before the God of J.
Neh. 2. 11. so I came to J. 7. 6. | 13. 7.
13. 20. merchants lodged without J. once or twice
Ps. 51. 18. do good to Zion, build thou the walls of J.
79. 1. the heathens have laid J. on heaps
3. their blood have they shed round about J.
122. 3. J. is builded as a city compact together
6. pray for the peace of J. they shall prosper
125. 2. as the mountains are round about J.
128. 5. thou shalt see the good of J. all thy life
137. 6. if I prefer not J. above my chief joy
7. remember children of Edom in the day of J.
147. 2. the Lord doth build up J. he gathereth
Cant. 6. 4. thou art comely, O my love, as J.
Isa. 1. 1. the vision he saw concerning J. 2. 1.
3. 8. for J. is ruined ‖ 10. 11. so will I do to J.
4. 4. the Lord shall have purged the blood of J.
10. 12. Lord hath performed his whole work on J.
22. 10. and ye have numbered the houses of J.
31. 5. so will the Lord of hosts defend J.
33. 20. thine eyes see J. a quiet habitation
40. 2. speak ye comfortably to J. and cry to her
41. 27. give to J. one that bringeth good tidings
44. 26. that saith to J. thou shalt be inhabited
52. 9. sing together, ye waste places of J. for Lord
hath comforted his people, he hath redeemed J.
62. 1. for J. sake I will not rest till righteousness
7. give him no rest till he make J. a praise
64. 10. Zion is a wilderness, J. a desolation
65. 18. for behold, I create J. a rejoicing
66. 10. rejoice ye with J. and be glad with her
Jer. 2. 2. go, and cry in the ears of J. saying
3. 17. they shall call J. the throne of the Lord
5. 1. run ye to and fro through the streets of J.
6. 1. gather you to flee out of the midst of J.
8. 5. why then is this people of J. slidden back
9. 11. I will make J. heaps, and a den of dragons
11. 6. proclaim these words in the streets of J.
13. 9. I will mar the great pride of Judah and J.
14. 2. Judah mourneth, the cry of J. is gone up
17. 26. they shall come from the places about J.
19. 7. I will make void the counsel of J.
13. the houses of J. shall be defiled as Tophet
23. 14. have seen in prophets of J. an horrible thing
26. 18. J. shall become heaps, *Mic.* 3. 12.
33. 13. in the places about J. shall flocks pass
16. in those days J. shall dwell safely, this is
35. 11. let us go to J. for fear of the Chaldeans
38. 28. till day that J. was taken, there when taken
39. 8. the Chaldeans brake down the walls of J.
44. 2. ye have seen the evil I have brought on J.
6. mine anger was kindled in the streets of J.
51. 50. let J. come into your mind, remember Lord
Lam. 1. 8. J. hath grievously sinned, theref. remov.
17. J. is as a menstruous woman among them
Ezek. 5. 5. this is J. ‖ 9. 4. go through the midst of J.
16. 2. son of man cause J. to know her abominations
17. 12. the king of Babylon is come to J.
21. 20. that the sword may come to Judah in J.
22. at his right hand the divination for J.
22. 19. I will gather you into the midst of J.
33. 21. one that had escaped out of J. came to me
36. 38. as the flock of J. in her solemn feasts
Dan. 6. 10. his windows being open toward J.
9. 12. not been done, as hath been done upon J.
25. from going forth of the commandm. to build J.
Joel 3. 1. when I bring again the captivity of J.
17. then shall J. be holy ‖ 20. J. shall dwell
Obad. 11. foreigners entered and cast lots upon J.
Mic. 1. 5. are they not J.? ‖ *Zech.* 1. 14. jealous for J.
3. 10. build up Zion with blood, J. with iniquity
Zeph. 1. 12. I will search J. with candles and punish
Zech. 1. 12. how long wilt thou not have mercy on J.?
17. L. shall yet comfort Zion, and choose J. 2. 12.
19. these are the horns which have scattered J.
2. 2. whither goest thou? I go to measure J.
4. J. shall be inhabited as towns without walls
8. 3. I will dwell in the midst of J. and I shall
15. so again have I thought to do well to J.
12. 2. behold, I will make J. a cup of trembling
3. that day I will make J. a burdensome stone
14. 11. but J. shall be safely inhabited
Mal. 3. 4. the offering of J. shall be pleasant
Mat. 3. 5. then went out to him J. *Mark* 1. 5.
5. 35. neither swear by J. ‖ 21. 10. come into J.
16. 21. Jesus began to shew how he must go to J.
Luke 2. 22. his parents brought him to J.
45. they turned back again to J. seeking him
6. 17. a great multitude out of J. came to hear
9. 53. his face was as though he would go to J.
13. 33. it cannot be that a prophet perish out of J.
19. 11. spake a parable, because he was nigh to J.
21. 20. when ye shall see J. compassed with armies
24. J. shall be trodden down of the Gentiles
24. 49. tarry ye in J. till ye be endued with power
52. and they returned to J. with great joy
John 12. 12. when heard that Jesus was coming to J.
Acts 5. 28. ye have filled J. with your doctrine
9. 2. that he might bring them bound unto J.

Acts 20. 22. behold, I go bound in the Spirit to J.
21. 31. tidings came that all J. was in an uproar
22. 18. make haste, get thee quickly out of J.
25. 20. I asked him whether he would go to J.?
Rom. 15. 31. that my service for J. may be accepted
1 *Cor.* 16. 3. will send to bring your liberality unto J.
Gal. 4. 25. Agar answereth to J. which now is
26. but J. which is above is free, mother of us all
Rev. 3. 12. the new J. 21. 2. ‖ 21. 10. the holy J.
See DWELL.

Against JERUSALEM.

Judg. 1. 8. Judah hath fought *against* J. and taken it
1 *Kings* 14. 25. Shishak came *against* J. 2 *Chr.* 12. 9.
2 *Kings* 18. 17. Sennacherib *against* J. 2 *Chr.* 32. 2.
24. 10. the king of Babylon came *against* J. 25. 1.
Jer. 34. 1, 7. | 39. 1. | 52. 4. *Ezek.* 24. 2.
Ezra 4. 8. Rehum, Shimshai, wrote *against* J.
Neh. 4. 8. they conspired to come and fight *ag.* J.
Jer. 4. 16. publish *ag.* J. ‖ 6. 6. cast a mount *ag.* J.
Ezek. 26. 2. because that Tyrus hath said *against* J.
Zech. 12. 9. destroy nations that come *ag.* J. 14. 12.

At JERUSALEM.

Josh. 15. 63. the Jebusites dwelt with Judah *at* J.
2 *Sam.* 20. 3. David came to his house *at* J.
1 *Kings* 12. 27. go up to do sacrifice in the house of
the Lord *at* J. 2 *Chron.* 9. 25. *Isa.* 27. 13.
1 *Chron.* 9. 34. these chief fathers dwelt *at* J. 38.
2 *Chron.* 3. 1. Solomon began to build the house of
Lord *at* J. in mount Moriah, *Ezra* 1. 2. | 5. 2.
Neh. 11. 2. willingly offered themselves to dwell *at* J.
13. 6. but in all this time was not I *at* J.
Ps. 68. 29. because of thy temple *at* J. bring presents
135. 21. blessed be the Lord who dwelleth *at* J.
Isa. 30. 19. the people shall dwell in Zion *at* J.
Jer. 35. 11. let us go into J. so we dwell *at* J.
Zech. 14. 14. and Judah also shall fight *at* J.
Luke 9. 31. decease which he should accompl. *at* J.
23. 7. Herod himself was also *at* J. at that time
24. 47. preached among all nations, beginning *at* J.
John 4. 21. nor yet shall ye *at* J. worship the Father
45. having seen all things that he did *at* J.
Acts 1. 19. it was known to all the dwellers *at* J.
8. 1. a great persecution against the church *at* J.
9. 13. what evil he hath done to thy saints *at* J.
13. 27. they that dwell *at* J. have fulfilled them
20. 16. he hasted to be *at* J. the day of Pentecost
21. 11. so shall the Jews *at* J. bind the man
13. but also to die *at* J. for the name of Jesus
26. 20. but shewed first to them of Damascus *at* J.
Rom. 15. 26. contribution for the poor saints *at* J.
See DAUGHTER, TERS.

From JERUSALEM.

1 *Kings* 2. 41. told that Shimei had gone *from* J.
2 *Kings* 12. 18. Hazael went away *from* J.
24. 15. carried into captivity *from* J. to Babylon,
Esth. 2. 6. *Jer.* 24. 1. | 27. 20. | 29. 1. | 52. 29.
Isa. 2. 3. the word of the Lord *from* J. *Mic.* 4. 2.
3. 1. the Lord doth take away *from* J. the stay
Joel 3. 16. the Lord utter his voice *from* J. *Amos* 1. 2.
Zech. 9. 10. I will cut off the horse *from* J.
14. 8. that living waters shall go out *from* J.
Mat. 4. 25. multitudes followed him *from* J.
Luke 10. 30. a certain man went down *from* J.
24. 13. which was *from* J. about sixty furlongs
Acts 1. 4. that they should not depart *from* J.
8. 26. the way that goeth down *from* J. to Gaza
11. 27. there came prophets *from* J. to Antioch
Rom. 15. 19. *from* J. to Illyricum I have preached

In JERUSALEM.

Judg. 1. 21. Jebusites dwell with Benjamin *in* J.
2 *Sam.* 19. 33. I will feed thee with me *in* J.
1 *Kings* 2. 36. build thee an house *in* J. and dwell
11. 36. may have a light alway before me *in* J. 15. 4.
2 *Kings* 18. 22. ye shall worship before this altar *in* J.
21. 4. the Lord said, *in* J. will I put my name
22. 14. now Huldah dwelt *in* J. in the college
1 *Chron.* 8. 28. these dwelt *in* J. 32. | 9. 3.
23. 25. that they may dwell *in* J. for ever
2 *Chron.* 9. 27. the king made silver *in* J. as stones
30. 14. they took away the altars that were *in* J.
26. there was great joy *in* J. not the like *in* J.
Ezra 1. 3. the house of the Lord which is *in* J.
7. 15. God of Israel, whose habitation is *in* J.
9. 9. and to give us a wall in Judah and *in* J.
Neh. 2. 20. ye have no right nor memorial *in* J.
4. 22. I said, let every one lodge *in* J.
11. 1. cast lots, to bring one of ten to dwell *in* J.
Ps. 102. 21. to declare in Zion and his praises *in* J.
Eccl. 1. 16. that have been before me *in* J. 2. 7, 9.
Isa. 4. 3. that remaineth *in* J. be called holy
24. 23. when the Lord of hosts shall reign *in* J.
28. 14. hear, ye scornful men that rule *in* J.
31. 9. whose fire is in Zion, his furnace *in* J.
65. 19. I will rejoice *in* J. and joy in my people
66. 13. and ye shall be comforted *in* J.
Jer. 4. 5. publish *in* J. and say, blow the trumpet
15. 4. for that which Manasseh did *in* J.
Ezek. 4. 16. I will break the staff of bread *in* J.
Joel 2. 32. in mount Zion and J. shall be deliverance
Zech. 12. 6. J. be inhabited in her place, even *in* J.
14. 21. every pot *in* J. shall be Holiness to Lord
Mal. 2. 11. an abomination is committed *in* J.
Luke 2. 25. a man *in* J. whose name was Simeon
38. spake to all that looked for redemption *in* J.
43. the child Jesus tarried behind *in* J.
13. 4. they were sinners above all that dwelt *in* J.
24. 18. one said, art thou only a stranger *in* J.?
John 4. 20. *in* J. is the place where to worship
Acts 1. 8. shall be witnesses to me *in* J. 10. 39.
6. 7. the number of the disciples multiplied *in* J.
23. 11. for as thou hast testified of me *in* J.
26. 10. which thing I also did *in* J. many saints

Inhabitants of JERUSALEM.

2 *Chron.* 20. 15. ye *inhabitants of* J. be not afraid
32. 22. thus the Lord saved the *inhabitants of* J.
33. *inhabitants of* J. did him honour at his death
34. 32. *inhabit. of* J. did according to the covenant
Isa. 5. 3. O *inhab. of* J. judge betwixt me and viney.
8. 14. for a gin and snare to the *inhabitants of* J.
22. 21. he shall be a father to the *inhabitants of* J.
Jer. 17. 25. *inhabitants of* J. shall remain for ever
35. 13. go and tell Judah and the *inhabitants of* J.

Ezek. 11. 15. to whom *inhabitants of* J. have said
15. 6. so will I give the *inhabitants of* J. for fuel
Zech. 12. 5. the *inhabit. of* J. shall be my strength
7. the glory of the *inhabit. of* J. do not magnify
8. the Lord shall defend the *inhabitants of* J.
10. pour upon *inhabit. of* J. the Spirit of grace
13. 1. a fountain opened to the *inhabitants of* J.

O JERUSALEM.

Ps. 116. 19. I will pay my vows in midst of thee, O J.
122. 2. our feet shall stand within thy gates, O J.
137. 5. if I forget, O J. ‖ 147. 12. praise Lord, O J.
Isa. 40. 9. O J. that bringest good tidings, lift up
51. 17. stand up, O J. ‖ 52. 2. arise, and sit down, O J.
52. 1. put on thy beautiful garments, O J.
Jer. 4. 14. O J. wash thy heart from wickedness
6. 8. be thou instructed, O J. lest I depart from thee
7. 29. cut off thine hair, O J. and cast it away
13. 27. woe to thee, O J. wilt not be made clean
15. 5. for who shall have pity upon thee, O J.?
Mat. 23. 37. O J. J. thou that killest the prophets
and stonest them sent to thee, *Luke* 13. 34.

Up to JERUSALEM.

2 *Sam.* 19. 34. that I should go *up* with the king *to* J.
1 *Kings* 12. 28. it is too much for you to go *up to* J.
2 *Kings* 12. 17. Hazael set his face to go *up to* J.
16. 5. Rezin and Pekah came *up to* J. to war
Ezra 1. 3. and let him go *up to* J. 7. 13.
Mat. 20. 18. behold, we go *up to* J. Son of man shall
be betrayed, *Mark* 10. 33. *Luke* 18. 31.
Mark 10. 32. they were in the way going *up to* J.
Luke 19. 28. he went before, ascending *up to* J.
Acts 11. 2. and when Peter was come *up to* J.
15. 2. they should go *up to* J. to the apostles
21. 4. who said, that he should not go *up to* J. 12.
25. 9. wilt thou go *up to* J. and there be judged?
Gal. 1. 17. neither went I *up to* J. to them apostles
18. I went *up to* J. to see Peter and abode with him
2. 1. I went *up to* J. with Barnabas, took Titus

JESHUA.

Ezra 2. 2. those that came with Zerubbabel, J.
3. 2. then stood up J. son of Jozadak, and brethren

JESHURUN.

Deut. 32. 15. but J. waxed fat and kicked
33. 5. he was king in J. when Israel was gathered
26. there is none like to the God of J.
Isa. 44. 2. fear not, thou J. whom I have chosen

JESSE.

Ruth 4. 17. Obed, he is the father of J. *Mat.* 1. 5.
22. Obed begat J. and J. begat David, *Mat.* 1. 6.
1 *Sam.* 16. 1. I will send thee to J. the Beth-lehemite
9. he sanctified J. and his sons and called them
18. I have seen a son of J. that is cunning
19. wherefore Saul sent messengers unto J.
17. 58. David said, I am the son of thy servant J.
20. 30. I know thou hast chosen the son of J.
31. as long as the son of J. liveth on the ground
22. 7. will the son of J. give every one of you fields?
8. my son hath made a league with the son of J.
9. Doeg said, I saw the son of J. coming to Nob
25. 10. who is David? and who is the son of J.?
2 *Sam.* 20. 1. neither have we inheritance in the son
of J. 1 *Kings* 12. 16. 2 *Chron.* 10. 16.
1 *Chr.* 10. 14. turned kingdom to David the son of J.
12. 18. on thy side are we, thou son of J. peace
Isa. 11. 1. there shall come a rod out of the stem of J.
10. there shall be a root of J. *Rom.* 15. 12.
Acts 13. 22. I have found David the son of J.

JESUITES.

Num. 26. 44. of Jesus, the family of the J.

JESUS.

Mat. 1. 21. shalt call his name J. for he shall save
his people from their sins, 25. *Luke* 1. 31. | 2. 21.
4. 1. J. was led up of the Spirit into wilderness
17. from that time J. began to preach and say
8. 3. J. put forth his hand and touched him
10. when J. heard it, he marvelled, and said
29. what have we to do with thee, J. thou Son of
God? *Mark* 1. 24. | 5. 7. *Luke* 8. 28.
34. behold, the whole city came out to meet J.
9. 2. J. seeing their faith ‖ 10. as J. sat at meat
22. J. turned him about ‖ 27. J. departed thence
12. 25. J. knew their thoughts, and said to them
13. 34. these things spake J. to the multitude
14. 1. at that time Herod heard of the fame of J.
29. Peter walked on the water to go to J.
17. 8. they saw no man save J. only, *Mark* 9. 8.
18. J. rebuked the devil and he departed
25. when come into the house, J. prevented him
18. 2. J. called a little child to him, and set him
20. 30. two blind men heard that J. passed by
34. J. had compassion on them, touched their eyes
21. 11. this is J. the prophet of Nazareth of Galilee
22. 18. but J. perceived their wickedness and said
26. 4. they might take J. by subtilty and kill him
19. the disciples did as J. had appointed them
26. J. took bread and blessed it, *Mark* 14. 22.
69. thou also wast with J. 71. *Mark* 14. 67.
75. and Peter remembered the words of J.
27. 37. written, this is J. the king of the Jews
46. J. cried with a loud voice, *Mark* 15. 37.
57. Joseph, who also himself was J. disciple
28. 5. fear not ye, I know ye seek J. *Mark* 16. 6.
9. J. met them ‖ 18. J. came and spake to them
Mark 1. 45. J. could no more enter into the city
3. 7. J. withdrew himself with his disciples
5. 13. J. gave them leave ‖ 19. J. suffered him not
30. J. knowing that virtue had gone out of him
9. 4. Elias and Moses were talking with J.
10. 21. then J. beholding him, loved him
12. 34. when J. saw that he answered discreetly
15. 1. they bound J. and carried him away
Luke 5. 19. let him down in the midst before J.
6. 11. they communed what they might do to J.
10. 39. who sat at J. feet and heard his word
19. 3. Zaccheus sought to see J. who he was
23. 26. that he might bear the cross after J.
24. 15. J. himself drew near and went with them
John 6. 42. they said, is not this J. son of Joseph?
9. 11. a man, that is called J. made clay, anointed
11. 13. J. spake of his death ‖ 35. J. wept
12. 21. sir, we would see J. ‖ 13. 23. leaning on J.
13. 1. when J. knew that his hour was come

John. 18. 7. whom seek ye? they said, J. of Nazar.
22. one of the officers that stood by struck J.
19. 5. then came J. forth, wearing crown of thorns
25. now there stood by the cross of J. his mother
28. J. knowing that all things were accomplished
40. took the body of J. || 42. there laid they J.
20. 14. and she knew not that it was J. 21. 4.
Acts 1. 1. of all that J. began to do and teach
11. this same J. which is taken up from you
16. Judas, who was guide to them who took J.
2. 32. this J. hath God raised up, 3. 26. | 5. 30.
3. 13. God of Abraham hath glorified his Son J.
4. 2. preaching thro' J. resurrection from the dead
13. they took knowledge that they had been with J.
18. they commanded not to teach in the name of J.
27. for of a truth against thy holy child J.
30. signs done by the name of thy holy child J.
5. 40. they should not speak in the name of J.
6. 14. this J. shall destroy this place and change
7. 55. he saw J. standing on the right hand of God
8. 35. then Philip preached unto him J.
9. 5. I am J. whom thou persecutest, 22. 8. | 26. 15.
17. even J. that appeared to thee in the way
27. had preached at Damascus in the name of J.
10. 38. how God anointed J. with the Holy Ghost
13. 23. God hath raised to Israel a Saviour J.
17. 7. saying, that there is another king, one J.
18. because he preached J. and the resurrection
19. 13. we adjure you by J. whom Paul preacheth
15. J. I know, and Paul I know, but who are ye?
25. 19. had questions of one J. who was dead
28. 23. persuading concerning J. law and prophets
Rom. 3. 26. the justifier of him that believes in J.
8. 11. the Spirit of him that raised up J. from dead
1 Cor. 12. 3. no man speaking by Spirit calleth J.
2 Cor. 4. 5. and ourselves your servants for J. sake
10. that the life of J. might be made manifest
11. we are delivered to death for J. sake
14. that he who raised J. shall raise up us also by J.
11. 4. for if he that cometh, preach another J.
Eph. 4. 21. been taught by him as the truth is in J.
Phil. 2. 10. at the name of J. every knee should bow
1 Thess. 1. 10. even J. who delivered us from wrath
4. 14. so them that sleep in J. will God bring
Heb. 2. 9. we see J. who was made lower than angels
4. 14. we have a great high priest, J. son of G. 6. 20.
7. 22. by so much was J. made surety of better testa.
10. 19. to enter into the holiest by the blood of J.
12. 2. looking unto J. the author of our faith
24. to J. the Mediator of the new covenant
13. 12. wherefore J. suffered without the gate
1 John 4. 15. whoso shall confess J. is Son of God
5. 5. that believeth that J. is the Son of God
Rev. 14. 12. here are they that keep the faith of J.
17. 6. woman drunken with blood of martyrs of J.
20. 4. that were beheaded for the witness of J.
22. 16. I J. have sent mine angel to testify to you
See CHRIST.

JESUS joined with *Lord*.

Acts 1. 21. all the time the *Lord* J. went in and out
2. 36. God made that same J. both *Lord* and Christ
7. 59. Stephen saying, *Lord* J. receive my spirit
8. 16. were baptized in the name of the *Lord* J.
9. 29. he spake boldly in the name of the *Lord* J.
11. 20. spake to Grecians, preaching the *Lord* J.
16. 31. believe on the *Lord* J. Christ and be saved
19. 10. all in Asia heard the word of the *Lord* J.
17. and the name of the *Lord* J. was magnified
20. 35. and to remember the words of the *Lord* J.
1 Cor. 11. 23. *Lord* J. same night he was betrayed
12. 3. that no man can say that J. is the *Lord*
2 Cor. 1. 14. as ye are ours in the day of the *Lord* J.
4. 10. always bearing about the dying of *Lord* J.
Gal. 6. 17. I bear in my body the marks of *Lord* J.
1 Thess. 2. 15. who both killed *Lord* J. and prophets
4. 1. we beseech and exhort you by the *Lord* J.
2. what commandments we gave you by *Lord* J.
2 Thess. 1. 7. when the *Lord* J. shall be revealed
Heb. 13. 20. brought again from dead our *Lord* J.
2 Pet. 1. 2. through the knowledge of J. our *Lord*
Rev. 22. 20. I come quickly, even so, come *Lord* J.
See GRACE, NAME.

JESUS *said*.

Mark 14. 72. Peter called to mind the word J. *said*
John 2. 22. the disciples believed the word J. *said*
4. 53. it was at the same hour in which J. *said*
13. 21. when J. had thus *said*, he was troubled
21. 23. yet J. *said* not to him, he shall not die

JESUS, for *Joshua*.

Acts 7. 45. brought in with J. into possession of Gent.
Heb. 4. 8. for if J. had given them rest then would not

JESUS.

Col. 4. 11. J. who is called Justus of circumcision

JETHRO, called *Reuel*.

Exod. 3. 1. Moses kept the flock of J. his father
4. 18. Moses returned to J. his father-in-law
18. 1. when J. heard of all that God had done
5. J. came with his sons and his wife to Moses
6. I thy father-in-law J. am come unto thee
9. J. rejoiced for the goodness done to Israel, 10.
12. J. took a burnt offering and sacrifices for God

JEW.

Esth. 2. 5. a certain J. whose name was Mordecai
3. 4. for he told them that he was a J.
6. 10. make haste, do even so to Mordecai the J.
Jer. 34. 9. himself of them, to wit, of a J. his brother
Zech. 8. 23. ten men shall take hold of skirt of a J.
John 4. 9. how is it that thou being a J. askest drink
18. 35. Pilate ans. am I a J.? what hast thou done
Acts 10. 28. it is unlawful for a man that is a J.
13. 6. they found a sorcerer, a J. named Barjesus
18. 2. Paul found a certain J. named Aquila, born in
24. a J. named Apollos || 19. 14. sons of Sceva a J.
19. 34. Alexander a J. || 21. 39. Paul a J. 22. 3.
Rom. 1. 16. to the J. first, also to Gentile, 2. 9, 10.
2. 17. behold, thou called a J. and restest in law
28. he is not a J. || 29. he is a J. who is one inwardly
3. 1. what advantage then hath the J.? or what
10. 12. for there is no difference between the J.
and the Greek, Gal. 3. 28. Col. 3. 11.
1 Cor. 9. 20. to the J. I became as a J. to gain Jews
Gal. 2. 14. if thou being a J. livest as the Gentiles

JEWS.

2 Kings 16. 6. king Rezin drave the J. from Elath
Ezra 4. 12. the J. are come up to Jerusalem
Neh. 1. 2. I asked concerning the J. that escaped
4. 2. Sanballat said, what do these feeble J.?
5. 17. there were at my table one hundr. and fifty J.
6. 6. that thou and the J. think to rebel
13. 23. I saw J. that married wives of Ashdod
Esth. 4. 3. there was great mourning among the J.
14. then shall deliverance arise unto the J.
6. 13. they said, if Mordecai be of the seed of the J.
8. 7. because Haman laid his hand upon the J.
8. write ye in king's name for the J. as it liketh
16. the J. had light and gladness and joy, 17.
17. for the fear of the J. fell upon them
9. 3. the officers of the king helped the J.
28. days of Purim should not fail from among J.
10. 3. for Mordecai was great among the J.
Jer. 38. 19. Zedekiah said, I am afraid of the J.
52. 28. carried away captive 3023 of the J. 30.
Dan. 3. 8. Chaldeans came near and accused the J.
Mat. 28. 15. this saying is reported among the J.
John 3. 25. question between John's disciples and J.
4. 9. the J. have no dealings with the Samaritans
22. salvation is of the J. || 5. 1. feast of the J.
5. 16. and therefore did the J. persecute Jesus
18. therefore the J. sought the more to kill him
6. 52. the J. therefore strove among themselves
7. 13. no man spake openly of him, for fear of J.
9. 18. the J. did not believe that he had been blind
10. 31. the J. took up stones again to stone him
11. 8. master, the J. of late sought to stone thee
33. when Jesus saw her and the J. also weeping
12. 11. many of J. went away and believed on Jes.
18. 20. I taught in temple, whither J. always resort
36. that I should not be delivered to the J.
19. 40. body of Jesus as the manner of J. is to bury
Acts 11. 19. preaching to none, but the J. only
12. 3. because Herod saw it pleased the J.
16. 3. because of the J. that were in those parts
20. these men being J. do trouble our city
19. 10. J. and Greeks heard the word of the Lord
13. then certain of the vagabond J. exorcists
20. 3. and when the J. laid wait for him, 19.
21. 11. so shall the J. at Jerusalem bind the man
23. 12. certain of the J. banded together and bound
27. this man was taken of the J. had been killed
24. 18. certain J. from Asia found me purified
25. 10. to the J. have done no wrong, thou knowest
Rom. 3. 29. is he G. of J. only? is he not of Gentiles?
1 Cor. 1. 23. Christ, to the J. a stumbling-block
9. 20. to J. I became as a Jew, that I might gain J.
2 Cor. 11. 24. of J. five times received forty stripes
Gal. 2. 14. as the Gentiles, and not as do the J.
15. we who are J. by nature, and not sinners
1 Thess. 2. 14. even as they have suffered of the J.
Rev. 2. 9. which say they are J. and are not, 3. 9.

All the JEWS. [*See* GENTILES.

Esth. 3. 6. Haman sought to destroy *all the* J. 13.
4. 13. more than *all the* J. || 16. go, gather *all the* J.
Jer. 40. 11. when *all the* J. in Moab heard that
12. even *all the* J. returned out of all places
41. 3. Ishmael slew *all the* J. that were with him
44. 1. the word concerning *all the* J. in Egypt
Mark 7. 3. *all the* J. except they wash, they eat not
Acts 18. 2. command. *all the* J. to depart from Rome
19. 17. this was known to *all the* J. at Ephesus
21. 21. thou teachest *all the* J. to forsake Moses
22. 12. Ananias had a good report of *all the* J.
24. 5. and a mover of sedition among *all the* J.
26. 4. my manner of life at Jerus. know *all the* J.

King of the JEWS.

Mat. 2. 2. where is he that is born *King of the* J.?
27. 11. the governor asked Jesus, art thou *King of the* J.? Mark 15. 2. Luke 23. 3. John 18. 33.
29. hail, *King of the* J. Mark 15. 18. John 19. 3.
37. set up his accusation, this is the *King of the* J. Mark 15. 26. Luke 23. 38. John 19. 19.
Mark 15. 9. but Pilate answered them, will ye that I release to you the *King of the* J. John 18. 39.
12. do unto him whom you call the *King of the* J.
Luke 23. 37. if thou be the *King of the* J. save thyself
John 19. 21. the chief priests said, write not the *King of the* J. but that he said, I am *King of the* J.

JEWESS.

Acts 16. 1. Timotheus was son of a J. who believed
24. 24. Felix' wife Drusilla was a J. sent for Paul

JEWISH.

Tit. 1. 14. not giving heed to J. fables and comm.

JEWRY.

Dan. 5. 13. whom my father brought out of J.

JEZEBEL.

1 Kings 16. 31. Ahab took to wife J. and served Baal
18. 4. when J. cut off the prophets of the Lord
13. what I did when J. slew the prophets of Lord
19. the prophets of Baal which eat at J. table
19. 1. Ahab told J. all that Elijah had done
21. 11. the elders did as J. had sent unto them
15. when J. heard Naboth was stoned and dead
23. dogs shall eat J. by wall, 2 Kings 9. 10, 36.
25. none like Ahab, whom J. his wife stirred up
2 Kings 9. 7. that I may avenge at the hand of J.
22. so long as the whoredoms of thy mother J.
37. carcase of J. shall be as dung upon the face of the field, so that they shall not say, this is J.
Rev. 2. 20. because thou sufferest that woman J.

JEZREEL, name of place and person.

Judg. 6. 33. Amalek pitched in the valley of J.
1 Sam. 25. 43. David also took Ahinoam of J.
29. 1. Israel pitched by a fountain which is in J.
2 Sam. 2. 9. Abner made Ish-bosheth king over J.
1 Kings 18. 45. and Ahab rode and went to J.
46. Elijah ran before Ahab to entrance of J.
21. 1. Naboth had a vineyard which was in J.
23. dogs eat Jezebel by wall of J. 2 Kings 9. 10, 36.
2 Kings 8. 29. Joram went back to J. 2 Chr. 22. 6.
9. 16. so Jehu rode in a chariot, and went to J.
10. 6. come to me to J. by to-morrow this time
7. they sent the heads of the king's sons to J.
1 Chron. 4. 3. these were of the father of Etam, J.
Hos. 1. 4. Lord said to him, call his name J. for I will avenge the blood of J. on the house of Jehu

Hos. 1. 5. I will break the bow of Isr. in valley of J.
11. one head, for great shall be the day of J.
2. 22. the corn, wine, and oil shall hear J.

JEZREELITE. *See* NABOTH.

ILLYRICUM.

Rom. 15. 19. round about unto I. I have preached

IMLAH. *See* MICAIAH.

JOAB.

2 Sam. 2. 18. three sons of Zeruiah, J. Abishai
22. how should I hold up my face to J. thy brother?
24. J. also and Abishai pursued after Abner
3. 29. let the blood of Abner rest on the head of J.
30. so J. and Abishai his brother slew Abner
8. 16. J. the son of Zeruiah was over the host, 20. 23. 1 Chron. 11. 6. | 18. 15. | 27. 34.
11. 7. David demanded of Uriah how J. did
11. Isr. and Judah abide in tents, and my lord J.
14. in the morning David wrote a letter to J.
12. 26. J. fought against Rabbah of Ammon
14. 3. so J. put the words in the widow's mouth
19. is not the hand of J. with thee in all this?
29. Absalom sent for J. || 30. J. field is near
20. 9. J. killed Amasa || 17. woman said, art thou J.?
24. 4. notwithstanding the king's word prevailed against J. and captains of the host, 1 Chr. 21. 4.
1 Kin. 1. 7. Adonijah confer. with J. son of Zeruiah
2. 5. moreover thou knowest what J. did to me
28. J. fled to tabernacle of Lord and caught horns
11. 16. six months J. remain. every male in Edom
1 Chr. 4. 14. Seraiah begat J. || 20. 1. J. led the army
21. 6. for the king's word was abominable to J.
26. 28. all that Abner and J. had dedicated
Ezra 2. 6. of children of Jeshua and J. Neh. 7. 11.
8. 9. of the sons of J. Obadiah went with Ezra

JOAH.

2 Kings 18. 18. J. son of Asaph recorder, Isa. 36. 3.
1 Chr. 6. 21. J. son of Zimmah || 26. 4. of Obed-edom

JOANNA.

Luke 3. 27. Juda, which was the son of J.
8. 3. J. the wife of Chuza, Herod's steward

JOASH.

Judg. 6. 11. that pertaineth to J. the Abi-ezrite
7. 14. save the sword of Gideon the son of J.
1 Kings 22. 26. king of Israel said, carry him back to Amon and J. the king's son, 2 Chron. 18. 25.
2 Kings 11. 2. Jehosheba stole J. 2 Chron. 22. 11.
13. 9. J. the son of Jehoahaz reigned in his stead
14. J. the king of Israel wept over Elisha
25. J. beat Ben-hadad three times, and recovered
14. 27. by the hand of Jeroboam the son of J.
1 Chron. 7. 8. the sons of Becher, Zemira and J.
12. 3. J. the son of Shemaiah the Gibeathite
27. 28. and over the cellars of oil was J.
2 Chron. 24. 22. thus J. remembered not the kindness
24. so they executed judgment against J.

JOB.

Gen. 46. 13. the sons of Issachar J. and Shimron
Job 1. 1. a man in the land of Uz whose name was J.
8. hast thou considered my servant J.? 2. 3.
9. Satan said, doth J. fear God for nought?
22. in all this J. sinned not with his lips, 2. 10.
2. 7. Satan went and smote J. with sore boils
32. 1. so these three men ceased to answer J.
2. against J. was Elihu's wrath kindled
3. because they found no answer and condemned J.
12. there was none of you that convinced J.
33. 31. mark well, O J. hearken unto me
34. 7. what man is like J. who drinketh scorning?
35. J. hath spoken without knowledge
36. my desire is that J. may be tried to the end
35. 16. therefore doth J. open his mouth in vain
42. 7. ye have not spoken as my servant J. hath, 8.
8. take seven bullocks and go to my servant J.
9. did as Lord commanded, the L. also accepted J.
10. the Lord gave J. twice as much as he had
12. so the Lord blessed the latter end of J.
15. no women found so fair as the daughters of J.
16. after this lived J. 140 years and saw his sons
17. so J. died, being old and full of days
Ezek. 14. 14. tho' Noah, Daniel and J. were in it, 20.
Jam. 5. 11. ye have heard of the patience of J.

JOEL.

1 Sam. 8. 2. name of Samuel's first-born was J.
1 Chr. 4. 35. of the family of Simeon, J. and Jehu
5. 4. of the Reubenites, the sons of J. 8.
12. of the Gadites, J. the chief, and Shapham
6. 33. Heman, singer, son of J. son of Shemuel
36. Elkanah the son of J. a Kohathite
7. 3. the sons of Izrahiah, Michael, Obadiah, and J.
11. 38. J. and Mibhar were valiant men
15. 7. of the sons of Gershom, J. the chief
11. David called for Isaiah and J. the Levite
23. 8. the sons of Laadan, the chief was J.
26. 22. the sons of Jehuli, Zetham and J.
27. 20. of the half tribe of Manasseh, J. was captain
Ezra 10. 43. J. and Benaiah had taken strange wives
Neh. 11. 9. J. son of Zichri was their overseer
Joel 1. 1. the word came to J. the son of Pethuel
Acts 2. 16. which was spoken by the prophet J.

JOHANAN.

2 Kings 25. 23. J. came to Gedaliah, Jer. 40. 8, 13.
1 Chron. 3. 15. the sons of Josiah, the first-born J.
Ezra 10. 6. Ezra went into the chamber of J.
Jer. 41. 11. but when J. heard of all the evil
43. 4. so J. obeyed not the voice of the Lord

JOHN son of *Zacharias*.

Mat. 3. 4. J. had raiment of camel's hair, Mark 1. 6.
14. Jesus came to be baptized, but J. forbad him
4. 12. then J. was cast into prison, Mark 1. 14.
9. 14. then came to him the disciples of J. Mark 2. 18. Luke 5. 33. | 7. 18. | 11. 1. John 3. 25.
11. 2. J. had heard the works of Christ, Luke 7. 19.
4. go and shew J. these things, Luke 7. 22.
7. Jesus began to say concerning J. Luke 7. 24.
13. the law prophesied till J. Luke 16. 16.
14. 10. Herod beheaded J. Mark 6. 16. Luke 9. 9.
21. 26. all hold J. a prophet, Mark 11. 32. Luke 20. 6.
32. J. came in the way of righteousness
Mark 6. 20. Herod feared J. knowing he was just man
Luke 1. 13. bear a son, thou shalt call his name J. 60.
3. 15. all men mused in their hearts of J.
9. 7. it was said, that J. was risen from the dead

John 1. 6. a man sent from God, whose name was J.
19. and this is the record of J. 32.
29. next day J. seeth Jesus coming unto him
3. 23. J. also was baptizing in Enon near to Salim
24. for J. was not yet cast into prison
4. 1. that Jesus made more disciples than J.
5. 33. ye sent to J. and he bare witness to the truth
36. but I have greater witness than that of J.
10. 41. J. did no miracle; but all that J. spake
Acts 1. 5. for J. truly baptized with water, 11. 16.
13. 24. when J. had first preached before his coming
25. and as J. fulfilled his course, he said whom
See BAPTISM, BAPTIST.

JOHN, *the apostle.*

Mat. 4. 21. James and J. the sons of Zebedee, he called them, 10. 2. *Mark* 1. 19. | 3. 17.
Luke 22. 8. Jesus sent Peter and J. to prepare passover
Acts 3. 1. Peter and J. went up into the temple
11. and as the lame man held Peter and J.
4. 13. when they saw the boldness of Peter and J.
8. 14. the apostles sent to Samaria Peter and J.
12. 2. Herod killed James the brother of J.
Rev. 1. 1. signified it by his angel to his servant J.
4. J. to the seven churches which are in Asia
9. I J. who also am your brother and companion
21. 2. I J. saw the holy city new Jerusalem coming
See JAMES.

JOHN.

Acts 4. 6. J. and Alexander gathered together

JOHN, surnamed *Mark.*

Acts 12. 12. Peter came to house of J. surnamed M.
25. took with them J. whose surname was Mark
13. 5. and they had also J. to their minister
13. J. departing from them, returned to Jerusalem
15. 37. Barnabas determined to take with him J.

JONADAB, *called* JEHONADAB.

2 *Sam.* 13. 3. J. was Amnon's friend, a subtile man
2 *Kings* 10. 15. J. son of Rechab came to meet Jehu
Jer. 35. 6. J. our father commanded us, saying
8. thus have we obeyed the voice of J. 18.
19. J. shall not want a man to stand before me

JONAH, *or* JONAS.

2 *Kings* 14. 25. the word he spake by his servant J.
Jonah 1. 3. J. rose up to flee to Tarshish from Lord
7. so they cast lots, and the lot fell upon J.
15. they cast J. into the sea, the sea ceased raging
17. J. was in the belly of the fish 3 days and nights
2. 1. J. prayed || 10. the fish vomited out J.
3. 3. J. went to Nineveh || 4. 1. it displeased J.
4. 6. the Lord made the gourd to come up over J.
Mat. 12. 39. no sign be given to it, but the sign of the prophet J. 16. 4. *Luke* 11. 29, 30.
40. as J. was three days in the whale's belly
41. they repented at the preaching of J.
John 21. 15. Simon son of J. lovest thou me? 16, 17.

JONATHAN.

Judg. 18. 30. J. and his sons were priests to Dan
1 *Sam.* 13. 2. a thousand men were with J. in Gibeah
22. but with Saul and J. were swords found
14. 3. the people knew not that J. was gone
13. J. climbed up upon his hands and his feet
27. J. heard not when his father charged the people
39. though it be in J. my son, he shall surely die
40. I and J. my son will be on the other side
42. J. was taken || 44. thou shalt surely die, J.
45. so the people rescued J. that he died not
18. 1. the soul of J. was knit with the soul of David
19. 2. but J. Saul's son delighted much in David
4. J. spake good of David to Saul his father
20. 3. let not J. know this lest he be grieved
13. the Lord do so, and much more to J.
16. J. made a covenant with the house of David
30. then Saul's anger was kindled against J.
33. J. knew it was determined to slay David
37. J. cried after the lad || 39. J. and David knew
23. 16. J. arose and went to David into the wood
31. 2. the Philistines slew J. 1 *Chron.* 10. 2.
2 *Sam.* 1. 4. Saul and J. his son are dead also
22. the bow of J. turned not back, sword of Saul
23. Saul and J. were lovely in their lives
26. I am distressed for thee, my brother J.
4. 4. J. had a son that was lame of his feet, 9. 3.
9. 7. for I will shew thee kindness for J. sake
15. 27. J. the son of Abiathar, 36. 1 *Kings* 1. 42, 43.
17. 17. now J. and Ahimaaz stayed by En-rogel
21. 7. the king spared Mephibosheth the son of J.
12. David took the bones of Saul and J.
21. J. the son of Shimea slew him, 1 *Chron.* 20. 7.
23. 32. of the sons of Jashen, J. a valiant man
1 *Chron.* 2. 32. the sons of Jada, Jether and J.
11. 34. the sons of Hashem, J. Ahiham, and Eliphal
27. 32. also J. David's uncle was a counsellor
Ezra 8. 6. Ebed the son of J. went up with Ezra
10. 15. only J. and Jehaziah were employed
Neh. 12. 11. Joiada begat J. || 14. of Melicu, J.
35. Zechariah the son of J. with a trumpet
Jer. 37. 15. put Jeremiah in prison in the house of J.
20. not to return to the house of J. 38. 26.
40. 8. Johanan and J. came to Gedaliah to Mizpeh
See DAVID, SAUL.

JOPPA.

2 *Chr.* 2. 16. bring it by sea in floats to J. *Ezra* 3. 7.
Jonah 1. 3. Jonah went down to J. and found a ship
Acts 9. 36. was at J. a disciple named Tabitha
42. it was known throughout all J. many believed
43. Peter tarried many days in J. with Simon
10. 5. send men to J. and call for one Simon, 32.
23. certain brethren from J. accompanied him
11. 5. I was in the city of J. praying, saw a vision

JORAM, *called* JEHORAM.

2 *Sam.* 8. 10. Toi sent J. his son to king David
2 *Kings* 8. 16. J. of Ahab; J. son of Jehoshaphat
28. Syrians wounded J. || 29. J. went to Jezreel
9. 14. Jehu son of Jehoshaphat conspired against J.
24. drew a bow and smote J. between his arms
11. 2. Jehosheba the daughter of J. took Joash
1 *Chron.* 26. 25. of the Levites, J. over treasures
2 *Chr.* 22. 7. destruction of Ahaziah by coming to J.
Mat. 1. 8. Josaphat begat J. and J. begat Ozias

JORDAN.

Gen. 13. 11. Lot chose him all the plain of J.
Num. 34. 12. the border shall go down to J. and goings out at the salt sea, *Josh.* 13. 27. | 18. 12.
Josh. 3. 8. when ye are come to J. stand still in J.
11. the ark passeth over before you into J.
15. J. overfloweth all his banks in harvest
4. 3. take twelve stones out of the midst of J.
17. commanded the priests, come ye up out of J.
23. the Lord your God dried the waters of J.
22. 25. Lord hath made J. a border between us
Judg. 3. 28. they took the fords of J. 7. 24. | 12. 5.
12. 6. then they slew him at the passages of J.
2 *Sam.* 19. 15. the king returned and came to J.
1 *Kings* 2. 8. Shimei came down to meet me at J.
7. 46. in plain of J. did the king cast them in clay ground between Succoth and Zarthan, 2 *Chr.* 4. 17.
17. 3. Elijah by the brook Cherith before J. 5.
2 *Kings* 2. 6. tarry here, Lord hath sent me to J.
7. they two stood by J. || 13. Elisha stood by J.
5. 10. saying, go and wash in J. seven times
14. Naaman dipped himself seven times in J.
6. 2. let us go, we pray thee, to J. and take a beam
7. 15. and they went after the Syrians to J.
Job 40. 23. he trusteth that he can draw up J.
Psal. 42. 6. I will remember thee from the land of J.
114. 3. the sea fled, J. was driven back, 5.
Jer. 12. 5. how wilt thou do in the swelling of J.?
49. 19. like a lion from the swelling of J. 50. 44.
Zech. 11. 3. for the pride of J. is spoiled
Mat. 3. 6. were baptized of him in J. *Mark* 1. 5, 9.
13. then cometh Jesus from Galilee to J. to be bap.

Beyond JORDAN.

Gen. 50. 10. the floor of Atad which is *beyond* J.
11. called Abel-mizraim, which is *beyond* J.
Deut. 3. 25. see the good land that is *beyond* J.
Josh. 9. 10. did to the kings of Amorites *beyond* J.
13. 8. inheritance Moses gave them *beyond* J. 18. 7.
Judg. 5. 17. Gilead abode *beyond* J. Dan in ships
Isa. 9. 1. the land of Zebulun and land of Naphtali *beyond* J. in Galilee of the nations, *Mat.* 4. 15.
John 1. 28. these things done in Bethabara *beyond* J.
3. 26. he that was with thee *beyond* J. baptizeth

On the other side JORDAN.

Deut. 11. 30. Gerizim, Ebal, are they not *on o. s.* J.
Josh. 7. 7. been content and dwelt *on other side* J.
12. 1. Reuben, Gad, and half the tribe *on the other side* J. 13. 27, 32. | 14. 3. | 17. 5. | 22. 4.
20. 8. *on other side* J. Bezer, Ramoth, cities of ref.
24. 8. Amorites who dwelt *on the other side* J.
Judg. 7. 25. brought heads of Oreb, Zeeb *on o. s.* J.
10. 8. Israel *on o. s.* J. oppressed by the Amorites
1 *Sam.* 31. 7. they *on other s.* J. forsook their cities
1 *Chr.* 6. 78. to children of Merari cities *on other s.* J.
12. 37. *on the other side* J. were 120,000 men

On this side JORDAN.

Num. 32. 19. our inheritance is fallen *on this side* J. east-ward, 32. | 34. 15. *Josh.* 1. 14, 15. | 22. 7.
35. 14. give three cities *on this side* J. *Deut.* 4. 41.
Deut. 1. 5. *on t. s.* J. Moses began to declare this law
3. 8. we took the land *on this side* J. from Arnon
Josh. 9. 1. kings *on this side* J. gathered ag. Joshua
1 *Chr.* 26. 30. of Hebronites 1700 officers *this side* J.

Over JORDAN.

Gen. 32. 10. with my staff I passed *over* this J.
Num. 32. 5. give us this land, bring us not *over* J.
21. if ye will go all of you armed *over* J.
32. we will pass *over* J. armed before the Lord
33. 51. when ye are passed *over* J. into the land of Canaan, 35. 10. *Deut.* 12. 10. | 27. 4, 12.
Deut. 3. 27. thou shalt not go *over* J. 4. 21. | 31. 2.
4. 22. I must die in this land, I must not go *over* J.
9. 1. thou art to pass *over* J. this day, 11. 31.
Josh. 1. 2. go *over* this J. thou and all this people
11. within three days ye shall pass *over* J.
3. 17. the people were passed clean *over* J. 4. 1.
4. 22. Israel came *over* this J. on dry land
7. 7. brought this people *over* J. to deliver us
24. 11. ye went *over* J. and came unto Jericho
Judg. 10. 9. Ammon passed *over* J. to fight
1 *Sam.* 13. 7. some of the Hebrews went *over* J.
2 *Sam.* 2. 29. Abner and his men passed *over* J.
17. 22. David and the people passed *over* J.
24. Absalom and all Israel passed *over* J.
19. 15. Judah came to conduct the king *over* J. 31.
1 *Chron.* 12. 15. these are they that passed *over* J.
19. 17. David passed *over* J. against the Syrians

JORIM, JOSE.

Luke 3. 29. J. the son of Eliezer, the son of J.

JOSEDECH. *See* JOSHUA.

JOSEPH.

Gen. 30. 24. she called his name J. and said
33. 2. Jacob put Rachel and J. hindermost
35. 24. sons of Jacob twelve, the son of Rachel, J. and Benjamin, 46. 19. 1 *Chron.* 2. 2.
37. 2. J. brought to his father their evil report
3. Israel loved J. || 28. his brethren sold J.
5. J. dreamed a dream || 33. J. is rent in pieces
39. 2. but the Lord was with J. 21.
5. Lord blessed the Egyptian's house for J. sake
7. his master's wife cast her eyes upon J.
20. J. master took him and put him in prison
40. 9. the chief butler told his dream to J.
23. yet did not the chief butler remember J.
41. 14. they brought J. out of the dungeon
42. Pharaoh put his ring on J. hand, arrayed him
46. J. 30 years old when he stood before Pharaoh
49. J. gathered corn as the sand of the sea
55. go to J. || 42. 8. J. knew his brethren
42. 36. J. is not || 43. 17. the man did as J. bade
43. 30. J. made haste, for his bowels did yearn
45. 3. I am J. || 9. say, thus saith thy son J.
26. they told him, saying, J. is yet alive, 28.
46. 4. J. shall put his hand upon thine eyes
29. J. went up to meet Israel his father
47. 12. J. nourished his father and his brethren
15. money failed, all the Egyptians came to J.
29. Israel must die, and he called his son J.
48. 2. one told Jacob, thy son J. cometh to thee
12. J. brought them from between his knees
15. Jacob blessed J. and said, God bless the lads
49. 22. J. is a fruitful bough, even a bough by a well
26. blessings shall be on head of J. and on him
50. 7. and J. went up to bury his father
Gen. 50. 15. J. will peradventure hate us and requite
16. and they sent a messenger to J. saying
17. J. wept when they spake unto him
25. J. took an oath of the children of Israel
Exod. 1. 8. new king which knew not J. *Acts* 7. 18.
13. 19. Moses took the bones of J. with him
Num. 26. 28. sons of J. Manasseh, Ephraim, 37.
Deut. 27. 12. these on Gerizim to bless, Judah, J.
33. 13. of J. he said, blessed of the Lord be his land
16. let the blessing come upon the head of J.
1 *Chr.* 5. 2. the chief ruler, but the birth-right was J.
Psal. 77. 15. hast redeemed the sons of Jacob and J.
78. 67. moreover he refused the tabernacle of J.
80. 1. give ear, thou that leadest J. like a flock
81. 5. this he ordained in J. for a testimony
105. 17. even J. who was sold for a servant
Ezek. 37. 16. write for J. the stick of Ephraim, 19.
47. 13. tribes of Israel, J. shall have two portions
48. 32. one gate of J. one gate of Benjamin
Amos 5. 15. L. will be gracious to the remnant of J.
6. 6. but they are not grieved for the affliction of J.
John 4. 5. near the ground that Jacob gave to J.
Acts 7. 9. the patriarchs sold J. into Egypt
13. at the second time J. was made known
14. then J. called his father Jacob to him
Heb. 11. 21. by faith Jacob blessed the sons of J.
22. J. made mention of Israel's departing
See HOUSE.

JOSEPH with *tribe* and *children.*

Num. 1. 10. of the *children* of J. of Ephraim, 32.
13. 11. of the *tribe* of J. namely of Manasseh
34. 23. the princes of the *children* of J. Hanniel
36. 5. the *tribe* of the sons of J. hath said well
Josh. 14. 4. the *children* of J. two tribes, 16. 4.
16. 1. the lot of *children* of J. fell from Jordan
17. 14. the *children* of J. spake to Joshua, 16.
1 *Chron.* 7. 29. in these dwelt the *children* of J.
Rev. 7. 8. of the *tribe* of J. were sealed 12,000

JOSEPH, husband of *Mary.*

Mat. 1. 16. Jacob begat J. the husband of Mary
18. when as his mother Mary was espoused to J.
19. J. her husband being a just man was minded
24. J. did as angel of Lord had bidden him
2. 13. the angel of the Lord appeared to J. 19.
Luke 1. 27. his name was J. of the house of David
2. 4. J. also went up from Galilee to be taxed
16. the shepherds found Mary, J. and the babe
43. and J. and his mother knew not of it
3. 23. being as was supposed, the son of J.
4. 22. is not this J. son? *John* 1. 45. | 6. 42.

JOSEPH, the name of divers men.

Num. 13. 7. of the tribe of Issachar, Igal son of J.
1 *Chron.* 25. 2. of the sons of Asaph, Zaccur, J. 9.
Ezra 10. 42. Shallum, J. had taken strange wives
Neh. 12. 14. of Shebaniah, J. was a priest
Mat. 27. 57. Jesus' disciple, J. of Arimathea, 59. *Mark* 15. 43, 45. *Luke* 23. 50. *John* 19. 38.
Luke 3. 24. who was the son of J. 26, 30.
Acts 1. 23. they appointed two, J. called Barsabas

JOSES.

Mat. 13. 55. his brethren James and J. *Mark* 6. 3.
27. 56. Mary the mother of J. *Mark* 15. 40, 47.
Acts 4. 36. J. by apostles was surnamed Barnabas

JOSHUA, called JEHOSHUA, and OSHEA.

Exod. 17. 13. J. discomfited Amalek with the sword
14. write this, and rehearse it in the ears of J.
24. 13. and Moses rose up and his minister J.
32. 17. when J. heard the noise of the people
33. 11. J. departed not out of the tabernacle
Num. 13. 8. of tribe of Ephraim, *Oshea* son of Nun
16. Moses called *Oshea* the son of Nun, Jehoshua
14. 30. save Caleb and J. 38. | 26. 65. | 32. 12.
27. 18. take thee J. || 22. he set J. before Eleazar
34. 17. Eleazar and J. shall divide the land
Deut. 1. 38. but J. shall go in thither, 31. 3.
3. 28. charge J. and encourage him, 31. 23.
34. 9. J. was full of the spirit of wisdom
Josh. 1. 10. then J. commanded the officers
2. 1. J. sent two men to spy secretly the land
3. 7. L. said to J. 5. 9. | 6. 2. | 7. 10. | 8. 18. | 10. 8.
4. 8. the children of Israel did as J. commanded
14. on that day the Lord magnified J. in sight
5. 7. their children, them J. circumcised
14. J. fell on his face to the earth and did worship
15. and J. did so || 6. 27. so the Lord was with J.
7. 6. J. rent his clothes || 8. 16. pursued after J.
8. 30. then J. built an altar to the Lord
35. which J. read not before all the congregation
10. 12. then spake J. and said, sun, stand still
42. and their land did J. take at one time
11. 9. J. did unto them as the Lord bade him
13. 1. now J. was old and stricken in years, 23. 1.
14. 13. so J. blessed Caleb and gave him Hebron
18. 10. J. cast lots for them before the Lord
19. 49. Israel gave an inheritance to J.
22. 6. J. blessed the Reubenites and Gadites
24. 1. J. gathered the tribes of Israel to Shechem
25. so J. made a covenant with the people
29. J. the servant of the Lord died, *Judg.* 2. 8.
31. Israel served the Lord all the days of J. and of the elders that overlived J. *Judg.* 2. 7.
1 *Sam.* 6. 14. the cart came into the field of J. 18.
1 *Kings* 16. 34. which he spake by J. the son of Nun
2 *Kings* 23. 8. in the entering in of the gate of J.
Hag. 1. 1. J. son of Josedech, 12, 14. | 2. 2, 4.
Zech. 3. 1. and he shewed me J. the high-priest
3. now J. was clothed with filthy garments
9. behold, the stone that I have laid before J.
6. 11. make crowns, set them upon the head of J.

JOSIAH.

1 *Kings* 13. 2. a child shall be born, J. by name
2 *Kings* 21. 24. the people made J. king, 2 *Chr.* 33. 25.
22. 1. J. was eight years old when he began to reign
23. 19. did J. take away, 24. 2 *Chron.* 34. 33.
29. J. went against Pharaoh, 2 *Chron.* 35. 22.
1 *Chr.* 3. 15. the sons of J. were Johanan, Jehoiakim
2 *Chron.* 35. 1. J. kept a passover unto the Lord
18. nor did kings keep such a passover as J. kept
19. in the 18th year of J. was this passover
23. archers shot at king J. and wounded him
24. all Judah and Jerusalem mourned for J.
25. Jeremiah lamented for J. men spake of J

Jer. 1. 2. word of the Lord came in days of J. 3. 6.
Zeph. 1. 1. word came to Zephaniah in days of J.
Zech. 6. 10. go into the house of J. son of Zephaniah
Mat. 1. 10. Amon begat J. || 11. J. begat Jechonias

JOTHAM.

Judg. 9. 5. J. youngest son of Jerubbaal escaped, 21.
57. on them came the curse of J. son of Jerubbaal
2 *Kings* 15. 5. J. judged the people, 2 *Chron.* 26. 21.
1 *Chron.* 2. 47. the sons of Jahdai, Regem and J.
3. 12. Amaziah his son, Azariah his son, J. his son
5. 17. were reckoned by genealogies in the days of J.
2 *Chron.* 27. 6. J. became mighty, because prepared
Isa. 1. 1. in the days of J. Ahaz, *Hos.* 1. 1. *Mic.* 1. 1.
Mat. 1. 9. Ozias begat J. and J. begat Achaz

ISAAC.

Gen. 17. 19. thou shalt call his name I. 21. 3.
21. but my covenant will I establish with I.
21. 10. shall not be heir with my son, even I.
12. God said, hearken to Sarah's voice, for in I.
shall thy seed be called, *Rom.* 9. 7. *Heb.* 11. 18.
22. 2. take thine only son I. || 9. Abraham bound I.
24. 4. take a wife for I. || 14. appointed for I.
63. I. went out to meditate in the field
67. I. was comforted after his mother's death
25. 5. Abraham gave all that he had unto I.
9. his sons I. and Ishmael buried Abraham
11. God blessed I. || 28. I. loved Esau
20. I. forty years old when he took Rebekah
21. and I. entreated the Lord for his wife
26. I. was sixty years old when she bare Esau
26. 1. I. went to Abimelech king of Philistines
8. I. was sporting with Rebekah his wife
12. I. sowed and received an hundred-fold
19. I. servants digged in valley and found a well
35. which were a grief of mind to I. and Rebekah
27. 30. as I. had made an end of blessing Jacob
28. 1. I. called Jacob, blessed him, and charged him
5. I. sent Jacob away, he went to Padan-aram
31. 42. except the fear of I. had been with me
35. 27. Jacob came to I. || 29. I. gave up the ghost
46. 1. offered sacrifices to the God of his father I.
48. 15. God, before whom my father I. did walk
16. let the name of my father I. be on them
49. 31. there they buried I. || 50. 24. he sware to I.
Exod. 2. 24. God heard their groaning and remembered his covenant with A. with I. *Lev.* 26. 42.
3. 6. the God of I. 15, 16. | 4. 5. *Gen.* 32. 9. 1 *Kings* 18. 36. 1 *Chron.* 29. 18. 2 *Chron.* 30. 6. *Mat.* 22. 32. *Mark* 12. 26. *Luke* 20. 37. *Acts* 3. 13. | 7. 32.
Josh. 24. 3. I multiplied his seed and gave him I.
4. I gave unto I. Jacob and Esau, and to Esau
1 *Chron.* 16. 16. his oath unto I. *Psal.* 105. 9.
Jer. 33. 26. his seed to be rulers over the seed of I.
Amos 7. 9. and the high places of I. shall be desolate
16. drop not thy word against the house of I.
Mat. 1. 2. Abraham begat I. and I. begat Jacob, *Luke* 3. 34. *Acts* 7. 8.
8. 11. many shall sit down with I. in the kingdom
Luke 13. 28. when ye shall see I. in kingdom of God
Rom. 9. 10. Rebekah had conceived by our father I.
Gal. 4. 28. we, brethren, as I. was, are of the promise
Heb. 11. 9. dwelling in tabernacles with I. and Jac.
17. by faith Abraham offered up I. *Jam.* 2. 21.
20. by faith I. blessed Jacob, Esau, about things

ISAIAH or ESAIAS.

2 *Kings* 19. 2. Hezekiah sent Eliakim to I. *Isa.* 37. 2.
20. 1. Hezekiah was sick, I. came to him, *Isa.* 38. 1.
11. and I. cried unto the Lord, 2 *Chron.* 32. 20.
2 *Chron.* 26. 22. his acts did I. write, 32. 32.
Isa. 20. 3. as my servant I. hath walked naked
Mat. 3. 3. spoken by the prophet E. 4. 14. | 8. 17. | 12. 17. | 13. 14. *Luke* 3. 4. *John* 1. 23. | 12. 38.
15. 7. well did E. prophesy of you, *Mark* 7. 6.
Luke 4. 17. was delivered to him book of prophet E.
John 12. 39. because that E. said again, he blinded
41. these things said E. when he saw his glory
Acts 8. 28. the eunuch read E. the prophet, 30.
28. 25. well spake the Holy Ghost by E. the prophet
Rom. 9. 27. E. also crieth concerning Israel
29. as E. said before, except the Lord had left us
10. 16. E. saith, L. who hath believed our report?
20. E. is very bold, and saith, I was found
15. 12. again E. saith, there shall be a root of Jesse

ISCARIOT. *See* JUDAS.

ISH-BOSHETH.

2 *Sam.* 2. 8. Abner took I. and set him over Gilead
3. 8. Abner was very wroth for the words of I.
14. David sent messengers to I. Saul's son
4. 8. they brought the head of I. unto David
12. but they took the head of I. and buried it

ISHMAEL.

Gen. 16. 11. thou shalt call his name I. 15.
16. Abram was 86 years old when Hagar bare I.
17. 18. said to God, O that I. might live before thee
20. as for I. I have heard thee, I have blessed him
25. I. was 13 years old when he was circumcised
25. 9. his sons Isaac and I. buried Abraham
12. the generations of I. 13, 16. 1 *Chr.* 1. 29, 31.
17. these are the years of the life of I. 137.
28. 9. then went Esau unto I. and took Mahalath
2 *Kings* 25. 23. I. came to Gedaliah, *Jer.* 40. 8.
25. I. came and ten men with him, *Jer.* 41. 1.
1 *Chron.* 1. 28. the sons of Abraham, Isaac and I.
8. 38. Bocheru and I. were sons of Azel, 9. 44.
2 *Chron.* 19. 11. Zebadiah son of I. the ruler
23. 1. Jehoiada took I. into covenant with him
Ezra 10. 22. I. Elasah, had taken strange wives
Jer. 40. 14. king of the Ammonites hath sent I.
15. I will slay I. || 41. 2. I. smote Gedaliah
16. not do this thing, for thou speakest falsely of I.
41. 6. I. went forth to meet them, weeping
10. then I. carried away captive residue of people
12. then Johanan went to fight with I.
15. but I. escaped from Johanan with eight men

ISHMAELITES.

Gen. 37. 27. come, let us sell him to the I.
39. 1. Potiphar bought him of the hand of the I.
Judg. 8. 24. had ear-rings, because they were I.
Psal. 83. 6. Edomites and I. confederate against thee

ISRAEL.

Gen. 32. 28. thy name shall be no more Jacob but I.
Gen. 35. 10. but I. shall be thy name, 1 *Kings* 18. 31.
47. 27. I. dwelt in the land of Egypt, in Goshen
31. and I. bowed himself upon the bed's head
48. 20. in thee shall I. bless, saying, God make thee
49. 24. from thence is the shepherd, the stone of I.
Exod. 4. 22. I. is my son || 17. 11. I. prevailed
5. 2. that I should obey his voice to let I. go?
14. 5. that we have let I. go from serving us
25. let us flee from I. for Lord fighteth for them
30. the Lord saved I. that day from Egyptians
32. 13. remember Abraham, Isaac, and I. thy serv.
Lev. 24. 10. her son and a man of I. strove together
Num. 10. 29. Lord hath spoken good concerning I.
36. return, O Lord, to the many thousands of I.
20. 14. thus saith thy brother I. let us pass
21. 2. I. vowed a vow unto the Lord, and said
17. then I. sang this song, spring up, O well
23. 7. defy I. || 24. 17. a sceptre rise out of I.
23. shall be said of I. what hath God wrought?
24. 18. Edom a possession, and I. shall do valiantly
25. 8. Phinehas went after the man of I. and thrust
Deut. 25. 6. that his name be not put out of I.
33. 10. shall teach I. thy law, Jacob thy judg. and
28. I. then shall dwell in safety alone, fountain
Josh. 7. 8. when I. turned their backs before enemies
11. I. hath sinned || 22. 22. and I. he shall know
16. so Joshua took the mountain of I.
24. 31. I. served the Lord all the days of Joshua
Judg. 1. 28. it came to pass when I. was strong
2. 22. that through them I may prove I. 3. 1, 4.
5. 9. my heart is toward the governors of I.
6. 6. I. was greatly impoverished by Midianites
14. save I. 15, 36, 37. || 7. 2. lest I. vaunt themselves
10. 9. so that I. was sore distressed
16. his soul was grieved for the misery of I.
11. 13. because I. took away my land ev. to Jabbok
20. 35. the Lord smote Benjamin before I.
1 *Sam.* 4. 2. I. was smitten, 10. || 17. I. is fled
9. 20. on whom is the desire of I. is it not on thee?
13. 4. heard that I. also was had in abomination
15. 29. also the strength of I. will not lie
17. 45. in the name of the God of the armies of I.
2 *Sam.* 1. 19. the beauty of I. is slain on high places
7. 23. what one nation is like thy people I.?
11. 11. the ark, and I. and Judah abide in tents
19. 8. for I. had fled every man to his tent
1 *Kings* 4. 20. Judah and I. were many as the sand
25. Judah and I. dwelt safely, *Jer.* 23. 6
9. 7. I. shall be a proverb among all people
11. 25. he abhorred I. || 12. 19. so I. rebelled
14. 15. Lord shall smite I. as a reed is shaken
18. 17. Ahab said, art thou he that troubleth I.?
2 *Kings* 10. 32. the Lord began to cut I. short
14. 12. Judah was put to the worse before I.
27. not that he would blot out the name of I.
17. 6. carried I. away into Assyria, 23. | 23. 27.
34. the children of Jacob, whom he named I.
1 *Chron.* 11. 10. the word of the Lord concerning I.
21. 5. all they of I. were a thousand thousand
29. 18. the God of I. 1 *Kings* 18. 36. 2 *Chron.* 6. 16. | 30. 6. *Jer.* 31. 1.
2 *Chron.* 9. 8. because thy God loved I. to establish
Ezra 2. 59. whether they were of I. *Neh.* 7. 61.
3. 11. his mercy endureth for ever towards I.
10. 10. strange wives to increase the trespass of I.
Psal. 14. 7. Jacob shall rejo. I. shall be glad, 53. 6.
22. 23. glorify him, and fear him, all ye seed of I.
25. 22. redeem I. O God, out of all his troubles
68. 26. bless ye the Lord from the fountain of I.
78. 59. when God heard this, he abhorred I.
81. 11. would not hearken, I. would none of me
13. O that my people I. had walked in my ways
83. 4. that name of I. may be no more in remembr.
114. 2. Judah was his sanctuary, I. his dominion
121. 4. he that keepeth I. shall neither slumber
125. 5. but peace shall be upon I. 128. 6.
130. 7. let I. hope in the Lord, 131. 3.
135. 4. Lord hath chosen I. for his peculiar treasure
147. 2. he gathereth together the outcasts of I.
149. 2. let I. rejoice in him that made him
Isa. 1. 3. but I. doth not know nor consider
19. 25. blessed be I. mine inheritance
27. 6. I. shall blossom and bud, and fill the world
41. 8. but thou I. art my servant, seed of Abraham
42. 24. who gave I. to robbers? did not the Lord?
43. 28. and I have given I. to reproaches
44. 5. shall surname himself by the name of I.
45. 4. for I. mine elect's sake, I have called thee
17. I. shall be saved in Lord with everlasting salv.
25. in the Lord shall the seed of I. be justified
48. 1. which are called by the name of I.
49. 5. though I. be not gathered, I. shall be glorious
6. be my servant to restore the preserved of I.
56. 8. the Lord which gathereth the outcasts of I.
63. 16. and though I. acknowledge us not
Jer. 2. 3. I. was holiness to the Lord and first-fruits
14. is I. a servant? || 3. 23. the salvation of I.
10. 16. I. is the rod of his inheritance, 51. 19.
14. 8. O Lord, hope of I. Saviour in trouble, 17. 13.
48. 27. for was not I. a derision unto thee?
49. 1. hath I. no sons? hath he no heir?
2. I. shall be heir to them that were his heirs
50. 17. I. is a scattered sheep, lions have driven
19. I will bring I. again to his habitation
20. iniqu. of I. be sought for and shall be none
51. 5. I. hath not been forsaken of his God
Lam. 2. 5. the Lord hath swallowed up I.
Ezek. 11. 10. I will judge you in the border of I.
13. ah Lord God, wilt thou make a full end of I.?
37. 28. shall know that I, the Lord do sanctify I.
44. 10. are gone from me, when I. went astray
Hos. 4. 15. though thou I. play harlot, let not Judah
16. I. slideth back as a backsliding heifer
5. 3. I. is not hid from me, I. is defiled, 6. 10.
5. I. shall fall || 8. 2. I. shall cry to me, my God
8. 3. I. hath cast off the thing that is good
8. I. is swallowed up || 9. 7. I. shall know it
14. I. hath forgotten his Maker, and buildeth
9. 10. I found I. like grapes in the wilderness
10. 1. I. is an empty vine || 8. the sin of I. be destroy.
6. I. shall be ashamed of his own counsel
11. 1. when I. was a child, then I loved him
Hos. 11. 8. how shall I deliver thee, I.? my heart is turned
12. 12. I. served and kept sheep for a wife
Joel 3. 2. will plead with them for my heritage I.
Amos 7. 11. I. shall surely be led captive, 17.
Mic. 1. 15. shall come to Adullam the glory of I.
5. 1. they shall smite the judge of I. with a rod
Luke 1. 54. he hath holpen his servant I. in mercy
John 3. 10. art thou a master of I. and knowest not?
Acts 28. 20. that for the hope of I. I am bound
Rom. 9. 6. for they are not all I. which are of I.
27. Esaias crieth concerning I. tho' number of I.
31. I. which followed the law of righeousness
10. 19. but I say, did not I. know? Moses saith
11. 7. I. hath not obtained what he seeketh for
1 *Cor.* 10. 18. behold, I. after the flesh
Gal. 6. 16. peace and mercy on them, and on I. of G.
Phil. 3. 5. of the stock of I. of the tribe of Benjam.

Against ISRAEL.

Num. 21. 1. Arad fought *ag.* I. || 23. Sihon *against* I.
23. 23. is there any divination *against* I.?
25. 3. the anger of the Lord was kindled *against* I. 32. 13. *Judg.* 2. 14, 20. | 3. 8. | 10. 7. 2 *Sam.* 24. 1. 2 *Kings* 13. 3. 1 *Chron.* 27. 24. 2 *Chron.* 28. 13. *Psal.* 78. 21.
Josh. 8. 14. the kings of Canaan *against* I. 11. 5.
24. 9. Balak king of Moab warred *against* I.
Judg. 3. 12. Eglon *against* I. || 6. 2. Midian *against* I.
11. 4. childr. of Ammon made war *against* I. 5, 20.
25. Balak, did he ever strive *against* I.?
1 *Sam.* 4. 2. the Philistines put themselves in array *against* I. 7. 7, 10. | 31. 1. 1 *Chron.* 10. 1.
1 *Kings* 20. 26. Ben-hadad *against* I. 2 *Kings* 6. 8.
2 *Kings* 1. 1. then Moab rebelled *against* I.
3. 27. there was great indignation *against* I.
17. 13. yet the Lord testified *against* I. and Judah
1 *Chron.* 21. 1. and Satan stood up *against* I.
2 *Chron.* 11. 1. Rehoboam went out *against* I.
Jer. 36. 2. write the words I have spoken *against* I.
Amos 7. 16. thou sayest, prophesy not *against* I.
Rom. 11. 2. he maketh intercession *against* I.

All ISRAEL.

Exod. 18. 25. Moses chose able men out of *all* I.
Num. 16. 34. *all* I. round about fled at cry of them
Deut. 13. 11. *all* I. shall hear and fear, 21. 21.
Josh. 7. 25. *all* I. stoned Achan with stones
Judg. 8. 27. *all* I. went a whoring after the ephod
1 *Sam.* 2. 22. Eli heard all that his sons did to *all* I.
3. 20. *all* I. knew that Samuel was a prophet
4. 1. word of Samuel came to *all* I. now I. went
11. 2. that I may lay it for a reproach on *all* I.
18. 16. but *all* I. and Judah loved David
28. 3. *all* I. had lamented Samuel, and buried him
2 *Sam.* 3. 12. to bring about *all* I. unto thee
37. *all* I. understood that it was not of king David
12. 12. but I will do this thing before *all* I.
14. 25. in *all* I. none so much praised as Absalom
16. 21. *all* I. shall hear that thou art abhorred
17. 10. *all* I. know thy father is a mighty man
18. 17. and *all* I. fled every one to his tent
19. 11. seeing the speech of *all* I. is come to me
1 *Kings* 1. 20. the eyes of *all* I. are upon thee
2. 15. thou knowest that *all* I. set their faces on me
3. 28. *all* I. heard of the judgment of Solomon
8. 62. the king and *all* I. offered sacrifice before Ld.
12. 18. *all* I. ston. Adoram with stones that he died
14. 13. *all* I. shall mourn for him, and bury him
18. 19. gather to me *all* I. unto mount Carmel
22. 17. I saw *all* I. scattered, 2 *Chron.* 18. 16.
1 *Chron.* 11. 4. David and *all* I. went to Jerusalem
13. 8. David and *all* I. played before G. with might
15. 28. *all* I. brought up the ark of the covenant
17. 6. wheresoever I have walked with *all* I.
29. 23. *all* I. and the princes obeyed Solomon
2 *Chron.* 12. 1. *all* I. forsook the law of the Lord
13. 4. Abijah said, hear me, Jeroboam, and *all* I.
15. God smote Jeroboam and *all* I. before Judah
28. 23. they were the ruin of him and of *all* I.
29. 24. to make an atonement for *all* I. *Ezra* 6. 17.
31. 1. *all* I. went out and brake the images
Ezra 2. 70. *all* I. dwelt in their cities, *Neh.* 7. 73.
10. 5. he made *all* I. swear to do this thing
Neh. 12. 47. *all* I. gave the portions of the singers
Dan. 9. 7. confusion of faces belong. to us, to *all* I.
11. yea, *all* I. have transgressed thy law
Mal. 4. 4. remember ye the law of Moses for *all* I.
Rom. 9. 6. for they are not *all* I. which are of I.
11. 26. so *all* I. shall be saved, as it is written

See CHILDREN.

Camp of ISRAEL.

Exod. 14. 19. angel which went before the *camp of* I.
20. a cloud between Egyptians and the *camp of* I.
Josh. 6. 18. lest ye make the *camp of* I. a curse
23. they left them without the *camp of* I.
2 *Sam.* 1. 3. out of the *camp of* I. am I escaped
2 *Kings* 3. 24. when they came to the *camp of* I.

See CONGREGATION, ELDERS.

For ISRAEL.

Exod. 18. 1. all that God had done *for* I. 8. *Josh.* 24. 31. *Judg.* 2. 7, 10. 1 *Kings* 8. 66.
Josh. 10. 14. for the Lord fought *for* I. 42.
Judg. 6. 4. the Midianites left no sustenance *for* I.
1 *Sam.* 7. 9. Samuel cried unto the Lord *for* I.
30. 25. that David made it an ordinance *for* I.
2 *Kings* 14. 26. there was not any helper *for* I.
1 *Chron.* 6. 49. to make an atonement *for* I. as Moses had commanded, 22. 1. *Neh.* 10. 33.
Ps. 81. 4. this was statute *for* I. law of G. of Jacob
Isa. 46. 13. place salvation in Zion *for* I. my glory
Zech. 12. 1. the burden of the word of the Lord *for* I.
Rom. 10. 1. my prayer to G. *for* I. is, they be saved

From ISRAEL.

Exod. 12. 15. shalt be cut off *from* I. *Num.* 19. 13.
Num. 25. 4. that wrath may be turned away *from* I.
Deut. 17. 12. put evil *from* I. 22. 22. *Judg.* 20. 13.
Judg. 21. 6. there is one tribe cut off *from* I.
1 *Sam.* 4. 21. the glory is departed *from* I. 22.
7. 14. the cities taken *from* I. were restored
17. 26. that taketh away the reproach *from* I.
2 *Sam.* 24. 25. and the plague was stayed *from* I.
Neh. 13. 3. separated *from* I. the mixed multitude
Isa. 9. 14. Lord will cut off *from* I. head and tail

Hos. 8. 6. for *from* I. was it also, the workm. made it
See GOD, HOLY *One of Israel*, HOUSE.
In ISRAEL.
Gen. 34. 7. because he had wrought folly *in* I. *Deut.* 22. 21. *Josh.* 7. 15. *Judg.* 20. 6, 10.
49. 7. divide them in Jacob, scatter them *in* I.
Lev. 20. 2. strangers sojourn *in* I. 22. 18. *Ezek.* 14. 7.
Num. 1. 3. able to go forth to war *in* I. 45. | 26. 2.
16. these were heads of thousands *in* I. 10. 4.
3. 13. I hallowed to me all the first-born *in* I.
18. 14. every thing devoted *in* I. shall be thine
21. given all the tenth in I. for an inheritance
23. 21. nor hath he seen perverseness *in* I.
Deut. 17. 4. abomination is wrought *in* I. 22. 21.
25. 7. to raise up to his brother a name *in* I.
10. his name be called *in* I. the house of him that
34. 10. arose not a prophet since *in* I. like Moses
Josh. 6. 25. Rahab dwelleth *in* I. because hid spies
Judg. 5. 7. they ceased *in* I. till that I Deborah arose, that I arose a mother *in* I.
8. was there a spear seen among 40,000 *in* I.?
11. 39. custom *in* I. to lament Jephthah's daughter
17. 6. was no king *in* I. 18. 1. | 19. 1. | 21. 25.
18. 19. or that thou be priest to a family *in* I.
21. 3. come to pass *in* I. one tribe lacking *in* I.
Ruth 4. 7. this was the manner in former times *in* I. concerning redeeming, this was a testimony *in* I.
14. that his name may be famous *in* I.
1 *Sam.* 3. 11. behold, I will do a thing *in* I.
9. 9. beforetime *in* I. when a man went to inquire
11. 13. Lord hath wrought salvation *in* I. 14. 45.
17. 25. will make his father's house free *in* I.
46. the earth may know that there is a God *in* I.
18. 18. or what is my father's family *in* I.
26. 15. David said to Abner, who is like to thee *in* I.?
2 *Sam.* 3. 38. there is a great man fallen *in* I.
5. 2. thou broughtest *in* I. 1 *Chron.* 11. 2.
13. 12. no such thing ought to be done *in* I.
13. thou shalt be as one of the fools *in* I.
19. 22. shall any be put to death this day *in* I.?
20. 19. I am one that is faithful and peaceable *in* I. thou seekest to destroy a mother *in* I.
21. 4. nor for us shalt thou kill any man *in* I.
1 *Kings* 14. 10. behold, I will cut off him that is shut up and left *in* I. 21. 21. 2 *Kings* 9. 8.
18. 36. let it be known, that thou art God *in* I.
19. 18. yet I have left me seven thousand *in* I.
2 *Kings* 1. 3. because there is not a God *in* I. 6, 16.
5. 8. he shall know that there is a prophet *in* I.
15. there is no God in all the earth but *in* I.
6. 12. the prophet *in* I. telleth the king of Israel
1 *Chron.* 12. 40. for there was joy *in* I.
2 *Chron.* 7. 18. not fail thee a man to be ruler *in* I.
24. 16. buried him, because he had done good *in* I.
34. 21. inquire for them that are left *in* I.
33. Josiah made all present *in* I. to serve the Lord
35. 18. was no passover like to that kept *in* I.
25. singing-men made them an ordinance *in* I.
Ezra 10. 2. yet there is hope *in* I. concerning this
Psal. 76. 1. known in Judah, his name is great *in* I.
78. 5. testimony in Jacob, and he appointed law *in* I.
Isa. 8. 18. are for signs and for wonders *in* I.
44. 23. the Lord hath glorified himself *in* I.
Jer. 29. 23. they have committed villany *in* I.
32. 20. which hast set signs and wonders *in* I.
Ezek. 12. 23. no more use it as a proverb *in* I. 18. 3.
39. 7. shall know that I am the holy One *in* I.
11. will give to Gog a place of graves *in* I.
44. 28. ye shall give them no possession *in* I.
29. every dedicated thing *in* I. shall be theirs
45. 8. in the land shall be his possession *in* I.
16. shall give this oblation for the prince *in* I.
Hos. 13. 1. Ephraim spake, he exalted himself *in* I.
Mic. 5. 2. come out of thee, that is to be ruler *in* I.
Mal. 2. 11. an abomination is committed *in* I.
Mat. 8. 10. so great faith, no not *in* I. *Luke* 7. 9.
9. 33. marvelled, saying, it was never so seen *in* I.
Luke 2. 34. for the fall and rising of many *in* I.
4. 25. many widows were *in* I. || 27. lepers *in* I.
See KING, KINGS.
Land of ISRAEL.
1 *Sam.* 13. 19. no smith found in all the *land of* I.
2 *Kings* 5. 2. brought a little maid out of *land of* I.
6. 23. bands of Syria came no more into *land of* I.
1 *Chron.* 13. 2. send to brethren left in *land of* I.
22. 2. to gather together the strangers that were in the *land of* I. 2 *Chron.* 2. 17. | 30. 25.
2 *Chron.* 34. 7. cut down idols through the *land of* I.
Ezek. 7. 2. thus saith the Lord to the *land of* I.
11. 17. and I will give you the *land of* I.
12. 19. thus saith the Lord of the *land of* I.
13. 9. nor shall they enter into *land of* I. 20. 38.
20. 42. bring you into the *land of* I. 37. 12.
21. 2. and prophesy against the *land of* I.
25. 3. thou saidst, Aha, against the *land of* I.
6. rejoicedst with despite against the *land of* I.
27. 17. Judah and *land of* I. were thy merchants
38. 18. when Gog shall come against the *land of* I.
19. shall be a great shaking in the *land of* I.
40. 2. in visions he brought me into *land of* I.
Mat. 2. 20. go into the *land of* I. for they are dead
21. took the child and came into the *land of* I.
Made ISRAEL *sin.*
1 *Kings* 14. 16. Jeroboam *made* I. to *sin*, 15. 26, 30, 34. | 16. 19, 26. | 22. 52.
16. 2. Baasha *made* my people I. to *sin*, 13.
21. 22. Ahab provoked the Lord, and *made* I. to *sin*
2 *Kings* 3. 3. Jeroboam son of Nebat who *made* I. to *sin*, 10. 29, 31. | 13. 2, 6, 11. | 14. 24. | 15. 9, 18, 24, 28. | 23. 15.
Men of ISRAEL.
Josh. 10. 24. Joshua called for all the *men of* I.
Judg. 20. 11. *men of* I. gathered against the city
20. *men of* I. went out || 22. encouraged themselves
36. the *men of* I. gave place to the Benjamites
1 *Sam.* 14. 24. the *men of* I. were distressed that day
31. 1. the *men of* I. fled from the Philistines
2 *Sam.* 2. 17. Abner was beaten and the *men of* I.
15. 13. hearts of the *men of* I. are after Absalom
16. 18. whom the *men of* I. choose, his will I be
19. 43. words of Judah fiercer than of the *men of* I.
23. 9. and the *men of* I. were gone away

Psal. 78. 31. smote down the chosen *men of* I.
Isa. 41. 14. fear not, ye *men of* I. I will help you
Acts 2. 22. ye *men of* I. hear these words
3. 12. ye *men of* I. why marvel ye at this?
5. 35. ye *men of* I. take heed to yourselves
13. 16. Paul said, ye *men of* I. give audience
21. 28. Jews of Asia crying out, *men of* I. help
O ISRAEL.
Exod. 32. 4. they said, these be thy gods, *O* I.
Num. 24. 5. how goodly are thy tabernacles, *O* I.
Deut. 4. 1. hearken, *O* I. 27. 9. *Isa.* 48. 12.
5. 1. hear, *O* I. 6. 3, 4. | 9. 1. | 20. 3. *Psal.* 50. 7. | 81. 8. *Isa.* 44. 1. *Mark* 12. 29.
33. 29. happy art thou, *O* I. who is like to thee?
Josh. 7. 13. an accursed thing in the midst of thee, *O* I.
2 *Sam.* 20. 1. he said, every man to his tents, *O* I. 1 *Kings* 12. 16. 2 *Chron.* 10. 16.
1 *Kings* 12. 28. behold thy gods, *O* I. which brought
Psal. 115. 9. *O* I. trust thou in the Lord, their help
Isa. 40. 27. why speakest thou, *O* I. my way is hid
43. 1. *O* I. fear not, *Jer.* 30. 10. | 46. 27.
22. but thou hast been weary of me, *O* I.
44. 21. remember these, *O* I. for thou art my servant, *O* I. thou shalt not be forgotten, 49. 3.
Jer. 4. 1. if thou wilt return, *O* I. *Hos.* 14. 1.
Ezek. 13. 4. *O* I. thy prophets are like the foxes
Hos. 9. 1. rejoice not, *O* I. for joy, as other people
10. 9. *O* I. thou hast sinned from the days of Gibeah
13. 9. *O* I. thou hast destroyed thys. but in me help
Amos 4. 12. prepare to meet thy God, *O* I.
Zeph. 3. 14. shout, *O* I. be glad and rejoice with heart
Over ISRAEL.
Judg. 9. 22. Abimelech reigned three years *over* I.
14. 4. the Philistines had dominion *over* I.
1 *Sam.* 8. 1. Samuel made his sons judges *over* I.
13. 1. when Saul had reigned two years *over* I.
15. 26. Ld. hath rejected thee from being king *over* I.
2 *Sam.* 2. 10. Ish-bosheth Saul's son reigned *over* I.
3. 10. Dav. *over* I. 5. 2, 3, 12, 17. | 6. 21. 1 *Chr.* 11. 3.
7. 26. the Lord of hosts is the God *over* I.
1 *Kings* 1. 34. Solomon *over* I. || 11. 37. Jeroboam
14. 14. the Lord shall raise up a king *over* I.
15. 25. Nadab *over* I. || 16. 8. Elah || 16. Omri
16. 29. Ahab || 22. 51. Ahaziah reigned *over* I.
2 *Kin.* 3. 1. Jehoram *over* I. || 9. 3. Jehu, 6, 12. | 10. 36.
13. 1. Jehoahaz || 10. Jehoash || 15. 8. Zachariah
15. 17. Menahem || 23. Pekahiah || 17. 1. Hoshea
1 *Chr.* 26. 29. Chenaniah for outward business *over* I.
29. 30. times that went *over* I. are written
Psal. 68. 34. strength to God, his excellency is *over* I.
Eccl. 1. 12. I the preacher was king *over* I.
ISRAEL joined with *people*.
Num. 21. 6. much *people* of I. died by serpents
Deut. 21. 8. be merciful, O Lord, to thy *people* I.
26. 15. look down and bless thy *people* I.
Josh. 8. 33. that they should bless the *people* of I.
Judg. 11. 23. drave Amorites before his *people* I.
1 *Sam.* 2. 29. fat with the offerings of I. my *people*
9. 16. shall anoint Saul captain over my *people* I.
27. 12. hath made his *people* I. utterly to abhor him
2 *Sam.* 3. 18. by David I will save my *people* I.
5. 2. to feed my *people* I. 7. 7. 1 *Chron.* 11. 2.
12. exalted his kingdom for his *people* I. sake
7. 10. I will appoint a place for my *people* I. that they may dwell and move no more, 1 *Chr.* 17. 9.
24. thou hast confirmed to thyself thy *people* I.
1 *Kings* 6. 13. I will not forsake my *people* I.
8. 33. when thy *people* I. be smitten, 2 *Chr.* 6. 24.
38. what prayer shall be made by thy *people* I.
43. all people may fear thee, as do thy *people* I.
56. the Lord hath given rest to his *people* I.
1 *Chr.* 14. 2. was lifted up, because of his *people* I.
17. 7. be ruler over my *people* I. 2 *Chron.* 6. 5.
21. what one nation in earth is like thy *people* I.?
22. thy *people* I. didst thou make thine own
2 *Chr.* 7. 10. goodness of Lord shewed I. his *people*
31. 8. they blessed the Lord and his *people* I.
35. 3. serve now the Ld. your God and his *people* I.
Ezra 7. 13. all they of the *people* of I. minded to go up
9. 1. the *people* of I. have not separated themselves
Psal. 135. 12. gave for an heritage to I. his *people*
Isa. 10. 22. tho' thy people I. be as the sand, a remn.
Jer. 7. 12. for the wickedness of my *people* I.
12. 14. which I caused my *people* I. to inherit
23. 13. they have caused my *people* I. to err
30. 3. the days come that I will bring again the captivity of my *people* I. and Judah, *Amos* 9. 14.
Ezek. 25. 14. lay vengeance on Edom by my *people* I.
36. 8. ye shall yield your fruit to my *people* I.
12. I will cause my *people* I. to walk upon you
38. 14. when my *people* I. dwelleth safely
16. thou shalt come up against my *people* I.
Dan. 9. 20. was confessing the sin of my *people* I.
Amos 7. 15. Ld. said, go, prophesy unto my *people* I.
8. 2. the end is come upon my *people* I.
Mat. 2. 6. a Governor, that shall rule my *people* I.
Luke 2. 32. and the glory of thy *people* I.
Acts 4. 27. *people* of I. were gathered against Jesus
13. 17. God of this *people* I. chose our fathers
24. John preached repentance to all *people* of I.
Princes of ISRAEL.
Num. 1. 44. the *princes of* I. being twelve men
7. 2. the *princes of* I. heads and *princes of* the tribes offered at the setting up of the tabernacle, 84.
1 *Chr.* 22. 17. David commanded *princes of* I. to help
23. 2. David assembled the *princes of* I. 28. 1.
2 *Chron.* 12. 6. the *princes of* I. humbled themselves
21. 4. Jehoram slew divers of the *princes of* I.
Ezek. 19. 1. take up lamentation for the *princes of* I.
21. 12. a sword shall be upon all the *princes of* I.
22. 6. the *princes of* I. were on thee to shed blood
45. 9. Lord saith, let it suffice you, O *princes of* I.
To or *unto* ISRAEL.
Gen. 46. 2. God spake *unto* I. in the visions of night
49. 2. hear and hearken *unto* I. your father
Exod. 18. 9. goodness which the Lord hath done *to* I.
Josh. 11. 23. Joshua gave it for inheritance *to* I. 21. 43.
23. 1. Lord hath given rest *unto* I. from all enemies
Judg. 8. 35. the goodness he had shewed *unto* I.
1 *Sam.* 15. 2. remember what Amalek did *to* I.
2 *Sam.* 3. 19. Abner spake all that seemed good *to* I.
1 *Kings* 11. 25. Rezon was an adversary *to* I.

1 *Chron.* 16. 17. confirmed the same for a law, and *to* I. for an everlasting covenant, *Psal.* 105. 10.
21. 3. why will he be a cause of trespass *to* I.?
22. 9. I will give quietness *to* I. in his days
2 *Chron.* 2. 4. this is an ordinance for ever *to* I.
Ezra 7. 11. Ezra the priest, a scribe of his statutes *to* I.
Neh. 8. 1. law, which the Lord had commanded *to* I.
Psal. 73. 1. truly God is good *to* I. even to such
135. 12. even an heritage *unto* I. 136. 22.
147. 19. the Lord sheweth his judgments *to* I.
Isa. 11. 16. as it was *to* I. in the day that he came
Jer. 2. 31. have I been a wilderness *unto* I.?
31. 9. I am a father *to* I. Ephraim is my first-born
Hos. 14. 5. I will be as the dew *to* I. he shall grow
Mic. 3. 8. I am full of power to declare *to* I. his sin
Mal. 1. 1. the burden of the word of the Lord *to* I.
Luke 1. 80. till the day of his shewing *unto* I.
John 1. 31. that he should be made manifest *to* I.
Acts 1. 6. wilt thou restore the kingdom *to* I.?
5. 31. him hath God exalted to give repentance *to* I.
13. 23. God hath raised *unto* I. a Saviour Jesus
Rom. 10. 21. *to* I. he saith, all day long stretched out
11. 25. that blindness in part is happened *to* I.
Tribes of ISRAEL.
Gen. 49. 16. Dan shall judge as one of *tribes of* I.
28. all these are the twelve *tribes of* I.
Exod. 24. 4. twelve pillars according to 12 *tribes of* I.
Num. 31. 4. thousand through all *tribes of* I. to war
36. 3. if married to any of the other *tribes of* I.
9. every one of *tribes of* I. shall keep to his own.
Deut. 29. 21. separate him to evil out of *tribes of* I.
33. 5. when the *tribes of* I. were gathered together
Josh. 3. 12. take twelve men out of the *tribes of* I.
4. 5. stones according to number of *tribes of* I. 8.
7. 16. so Joshua brought I. by their *tribes*
12. 7. the land which Joshua gave to the *tribes of* I.
19. 51. which heads of fathers of *tribes of* I. divided
22. 14. princes through *tribes of* I. sent to Reuben
24. 1. Joshua gathered all *tribes of* I. to Shechem
Judg. 18. 1. inheritance of Dan not among *tribes of* I.
20. 2. the chief of *tribes of* I. presented before God
10. take ten men of an 100 out of all *tribes of* I.
21. 5. who among the *tribes of* I. came not up, 8.
15. Lord hath made a breach in the *tribes of* I.
1 *Sam.* 2. 28. did I choose him out of all *tribes of* I.?
9. 21. I am of the smallest of the *tribes of* I.
10. 20. Samuel caused all the *tribes of* I. to come
15. 17. wast thou not made head of the *tribes of* I.?
2 *Sam.* 5. 1. then came all the *tribes of* I. to David
7. 7. spake I a word with any of the *tribes of* I.?
15. 2. thy servant is of one of the *tribes of* I.
10. Absalom sent spies through all the *tribes of* I.
19. 9. people were at strife thro' the *tribes of* I.
24. 2. go through all the *tribes of* I. and number
1 *Kings* 8. 16. I chose no city out of all the *tribes of* I. to build an house in, 2 *Chron.* 6. 5.
11. 32. have chosen Jerusalem out of all the *tribes of* I. 14. 21. 2 *Kings* 21. 7. 2 *Chr.* 12. 13. | 33. 7.
2 *Chr.* 11. 16. after them out of all the *tribes of* I.
Ezra 6. 17. offered 12 goats according to *tribes of* I.
Psal. 78. 55. made *tribes of* I. to dwell in their tents
Ezek. 37. 19. I will take *tribes of* I. put with Judah
47. 13. according to the twelve *tribes of* I. 21. 22.
48. 19. serve the city out of all the *tribes of* I.
31. gates be after the names of the *tribes of* I.
Hos. 5. 9. among *tribes of* I. have I made known
Zech. 9. 1. the eyes of all *tribes of* I. be toward Ld.
Mat. 19. 28. judging the 12 *tribes of* I. *Luke* 22. 30.
Rev. 21. 12. gates with names of twelve *tribes of* I.
With ISRAEL.
Exod. 17. 8. Amalek fought *with* I. in Rephidim
34. 27. I have made a covenant *with* thee and I.
Deut. 18. 1. Levites shall have no inheritance *with* I.
33. 21. Gad executed his judgments *with* I.
Josh. 9. 2. the kings of Canaan fought *with* I.
10. 1. the inhabitants of Gibeon made peace *with* I.
1 *Sam.* 13. 5. the Philistines gathered themselves together to fight *with* I. 28. 1. 2 *Sam.* 21. 15.
2 *Sam.* 10. 19. the Syrians made peace *with* I.
2 *Kings* 17. 18. the Lord was very angry *with* I.
2 *Chr.* 25. 7. for Lord is not *with* I. with Ephraim
Mic. 6. 2. for the Lord will plead *with* I. O my people
ISRAELITE.
Num. 25. 14. the name of the I. that was slain, Zimri
2 *Sam.* 17. 25. Amasa was the son of Ithra, an I.
John 1. 47. behold an I. indeed, in whom is no guile
Rom. 11. 1. I also am an I. of the seed of Abraham
ISRAELITES.
Exod. 9. 7. was not one of the cattle of the I. dead
Lev. 23. 42. all that are I. born shall dwell in booths
Josh. 3. 17. all the I. passed over on dry ground
13. 6. only divide it by lot to the I. for inheritance
Judg. 20. 21. the Benjamites destroyed of the I.
1 *Sam.* 2. 14. so the priest's servant did to all I.
13. 20. I went to the Philistines to sharpen his axe
14. 21. the Hebrews turned to be with the I.
25. 1. all the I. lamented Samuel and buried him
29. 1. the I. pitched by a fountain in Jezreel
2 *Sam.* 4. 1. the I. were troubled at Abner's death
2 *Kings* 3. 24. the I. rose and smote the Moabites
7. 13. they are as all the multitude of the I.
1 *Chron.* 9. 2. the first inhabitants were the I.
Rom. 9. 4. who are I. to whom pertaineth adoption
2 *Cor.* 11. 22. are they Hebrews? are they I.? so am I
ISRAELITISH.
Lev. 24. 10. the son of an I. woman strove in camp
11. 1. woman's son blasphemed the name of Lord
ISSACHAR.
Gen. 30. 18. and Leah called his name I.
35. 23. Leah's son, I. || 46. 13. sons of I. 1 *Chr.* 7. 1.
49. 14. I. is a strong ass, couching down between
Exod. 1. 3. Israel's sons, I. Zebulun, 1 *Chron.* 2. 1.
Num. 1. 8. the princes of I. Nethaneel, 2. 5. | 7. 18.
Deut. 27. 12. I. and Joseph shall stand to bless
33. 18. rejoice, Zebulun and I. in thy tents
Josh. 17. 10. they met together in I. on the east
11. Manasseh had in I. and Asher, Beth-shean
Judg. 5. 15. the princes of I. were with Deborah, even I. and also Barak, he was sent into the valley
10. 1. Tola a man of I. arose to defend Israel
1 *Kings* 4. 17. Jehoshaphat was an officer in I.
15. 27. Baasha son of Ahijah of the house of I.

1 *Chr.* 12.40. they that were nigh to I. brought bread
26. 5. I. the seventh son of Obed-edom
27. 18. captain of I. Omri the son of Michael
2 *Chr.* 30. 18. many of I. had not cleansed themselv.
Ezek. 48. 25. by the border of Simeon, I. a portion
26. by the border of I. Zebulun a portion
33. south side, one gate of I. one gate of Zebulun

Tribe of ISSACHAR.

Num. 1. 29. that were numbered of the *tribe of* I.
2. 5. that pitch next Judah shall be the *tribe of* I.
10. 15. over the *tribe of* I. was Nethaneel
13. 7. of the *tribe of* I. to spy the land, Igal the son
34. 26. prince of the *tribe of* I. Paltiel son of Azzan
Josh. 19. 23. the inheritance of the *tribe of* I.
21. 6. Gershon had by lot out of the families of the *tribe of* I. and Asher, 28. 1 *Chron.* 6. 62, 72.
Rev. 7. 7. of the *tribe of* I. were sealed 12,000

ITALIAN.

Acts 10. 1. Cornelius a centurion of the I. band

ITALY.

Acts 18. 2. found a certain Jew lately come from I.
27. 1. it was determined that we should sail into I.
Heb. 13. 24. salute the saints, they of I. salute you

ITHAMAR.

Exod. 6. 23. Aaron's sons, Abihu and I. 1 *Chr.* 6. 3.
38. 21. as it was counted by the hand of I.
Num. 4. 28. their charge under the hand of I.
1 *Chron.* 24. 3. and Ahimelech of the sons of I.
4. were eight chief men among the sons of I.
Ezra 8. 2. of the sons of I. Daniel went up
See ELEAZAR.

ITHIEL.

Neh. 11. 7. I. son of Jesaiah dwelt at Jerusalem
Prov. 30. 1. the man spake to I. even to I. and Ucal

ITUREA.

Luke 3. 1. and his brother Philip tetrarch of I.

IVAH.

2 *Kings* 18. 34. where are the gods of Hena and I.?
19. 13. where is the king of I.? *Isa.* 37. 13.

JUBILEE.

Lev. 25. 9. cause the trumpet of the J. to sound
10. it shall be a J. it shall be holy to you, 12.
11. a J. shall that fiftieth year be to you
13. in the year of J. ye shall return to possession
28. a field shall go out in the year of J. 27. 21, 24.
30. then the house shall not go out in the J.
31. they shall go out in the year of J. 33, 54.
27. 17. if ye sanctify his field from year of J. 18.
Num. 36. 4. when J. then their inheritance be put

JUDAH.

Gen. 29. 35. therefore she called his name J.
35. 23. the sons of Leah, J. Issachar, Zebulun
38. 15. J. thought Tamar to be an harlot
26. J. acknowledged the signet and bracelets
46. 12. sons of J. *Num.* 26. 19. 1 *Chr.* 2. 3. | 4. 1.
28. Jacob sent J. before him to Joseph
49. 8. J. thou art he whom thy brethren shall praise
9. J. is a lion's whelp, he couched as a lion
10. sceptre shall not depart J. till Shiloh come
Exod. 1. 2. the sons of Israel, Levi, J. 1 *Chr.* 2. 1.
Num. 1. 7. J. Nashan son of Amminadab was prince
2. 3. the camp of J. shall pitch on the east-side
9. all that were numbered in the camp of J.
Deut. 27. 12. Simeon, Levi, J. shall stand to bless
33. 7. this is the blessing of J. the voice of J.
Josh. 7. 17. Joshua brought the family of J.
18. 5. J. shall abide in their coast on the south
Judg. 1. 2. the Lord said, J. shall go up first
19. the Lord was with J. || 10. 9. fight against J.
Ruth 4. 12. like Pharez, whom Tamar bare to J.
1 *Sam.* 23. 23. search him thro' all thousands of J.
2 *Sam.* 3. 8. which against J. do shew kindness
5. 5. David reigned over J. seven years, six months
11. 11. the ark, Israel, and J. abide in tents
19. 15. J. came to Gilgal to meet the king
24. 1. David said, go number Israel and J.
1 *Kings* 2. 32. Joab slew Amasa captain of host of J.
4. 20. J. and Israel were many as the sand by sea
25. J. and Israel dwelt safely under Solomon
13. 1. there came a man of God out of J. by the word of the Lord to Bethel, 2 *Kings* 23. 17.
14. 22. J. did evil in the sight of the Lord
15. 1. Abijam reigned over J. || 9. Asa over J.
17. Baasha went up against J. 2 *Chron.* 16. 1.
22. 41. Jehoshaphat began to reign over J.
2 *Kings* 8. 19. yet the Lord would not destroy J.
20. Edom revolted from J. 22. 2 *Chron.* 21. 8, 10.
9. 29. Ahaziah began to reign over J.
14. 10. to fall, thou and J. with thee, 2 *Chron.* 25. 19.
12. J. was put to the worse, 2 *Chron.* 25. 22.
22. Azariah restored Elath to J. 2 *Chron.* 26. 2.
15. 37. the Lord began to send against J. Rezin
17. 13. yet the Lord testified against Israel and J.
19. J. kept not the commandments of the Lord
21. 11. Manasseh made J. to sin, 16. 2 *Chron.* 33. 9.
12. behold, I am bringing such evil upon J.
23. 26. his anger kindled against J. 2 *Chron.* 25. 10.
27. I will remove J. also out of my sight
24. 2. the Lord sent bands of Chaldees against J.
3. at the command of the Lord came this on J.
25. 21. so J. was carried away, 1 *Chron.* 6. 15.
1 *Chron.* 5. 2. J. prevailed above his brethren
27. 18. of J. Elihu one of David's brethren was capt.
28. 4. for he hath chosen J. to be the ruler
2 *Chron.* 13. 13. so they were before J. and behind
16. the children of Israel fled before J.
14. 4. Asa commanded J. to seek the Lord
17. 6. Jehoshaphat took the groves out of J.
21. 11. Jehoram compelled J. to commit fornication
13. hast made J. and Jerusalem go a whoring
24. 18. wrath came upon J. 28. 9. | 29. 8. | 32. 25.
28. 19. the Lord brought J. low, made J. naked
29. 21. seven lambs for a sin-offering for J.
30. 25. all the congregation of J. rejoiced
33. 16. Manasseh commanded J. to serve the Lord
34. 3. in 12th year Josiah began to purge J. 5.
Ezra 3. 9. sons of J. to set forward the workmen
7. 14. thou art sent to inquire concerning J.
10. 23. J. and Eliezer had taken strange wives
Neh. 2. 5. that thou wouldst send me to J.
7. that they may convey me till I come into J.
6. 17. the nobles of J. sent letters to Tobiah
Neh. 11. 9. J. son of Senuah was second over city
12. 44. for J. rejoiced for the priests that waited
Psal. 60. 7. Gilead is mine, J. is my lawgiver, 108. 8.
114. 2. J. was his sanctuary, Israel his dominion
Isa. 1. 1. vision which he saw concerning J. 2. 1.
3. 1. Lord doth take from J. stay and staff of bread
8. J. is fallen || 7. 6. let us go up against J.
7. 17. from day that Ephraim departed from J.
8. 8. shall pass through J. shall overflow, go over
9. 21. and they together shall be against J.
11. 12. he shall gather together the dispersed of J.
13. the adversaries of J. shall be cut off; Ephraim shall not envy J. and J. not vex Ephraim
22. 8. he discovered the covering of J.
48. 1. and are come forth out of the waters of J.
65. 9. and out of J. an inheritor of my mountains
Jer. 2. 28. as number of cities are thy gods, O J.
3. 7. her sister J. saw it, and feared not, 8.
9. 26. Egypt, and J. and Edom are uncircumcised
13. 9. after this manner will I mar the pride of J.
19. J. shall be carried away captive all of it
14. 2. J. mourneth || 23. 6. J. shall be saved
19. hast thou utterly rejected J. and loathed Zion
17. 1. the sin of J. is written with a pen of iron
19. 7. I will void the counsel of J. and Jerusalem
32. 35. they should do this to cause J. to sin
33. 7. I will cause the captivity of J. to return
36. 2. the words that I have spoken against J.
42. 15. hear the word of the Lord, ye remnant of J.
44. 26. not named in mouth of any man of J.
50. 20. the sins of J. shall not be found
51. 5. J. hath not been forsaken of his God
52. 27. J. was carried away captive, *Lam.* 1. 3.
Ezek. 21. 20. that the sword may come to J. in Jerus.
27. 17. J. and Israel were thy merchants
37. 16. write upon it for J. and for Israel
48. 7. by the border of Reuben, a portion for J.
31. one gate of Reuben, one gate of J. one of Levi
Hos. 4. 15. tho' Israel play harlot, yet let not J. offe.
5. 5. J. shall fall || 13. when J. saw his wound
6. 4. O J. what shall I do unto thee? for your good
10. 11. J. shall plow, Jacob shall break his clods
11. 12. but J. ruleth yet with God, and is faithful
12. 2. the Lord hath also a controversy with J.
Joel 3. 20. but J. shall dwell for ever, and Jerusalem
Amos 2. 4. for three transgressions of J. and for four
5. but I will send a fire on J. it shall devour
Mic. 1. 9. her wound is incurable, it is come to J.
5. 2. though thou be little among the thousands of J.
Zeph. 1. 4. I will stretch out mine hand upon J.
Zech. 1. 19. the horns which have scattered J. 21.
2. 12. Lord shall inherit J. his portion in holy land
9. 13. when I have bent J. for me, filled the bow
12. 7. the Lord shall save the tents of J. first
14. 14. J. also shall fight at Jerusalem
Mal. 2. 11. J. hath dealt treacherously; J. hath profaned the holiness of the Lord which he loved
3. 4. then shall the offering of J. be pleasant
Mat. 1. 2. Jacob begat J. || 3. J. begat Phares
Luke 3. 33. Phares, which was the son of J.
Heb. 7. 14. for it is evident that our Lord sprang of J.

All JUDAH.

1 *Sam.* 18. 16. but all Israel and *all* J. loved David
2 *Sam.* 5. 5. David reigned 33 years over *all* J.
2 *Chron.* 15. 15. *all* J. rejoiced at the oath
20. 13. *all* J. stood before the Lord with their wives
32. 33. *all* J. did honour Hezekiah at his death
35. 24. *all* J. and Jerusalem mourned for Josiah
Neh. 13. 12. then *all* J. brought the tithe of the corn
Jer. 20. 4. I will give *all* J. to the king of Babylon
44. 11. I will set my face to cut off *all* J.
See BENJAMIN, BETH-LEHEM, CHILDREN, CITIES, DAUGHTER, DAUGHTERS, HOUSE.

In JUDAH.

1 *Sam.* 23. 3. behold, we be afraid here *in* J.
1 *Kings* 12. 32. like unto the feast that is *in* J.
2 *Kings* 24. 20. for through the anger of the Lord it came to pass *in* Jerusalem and J. *Jer.* 52. 3.
2 *Chron.* 2. 7. cunning men that are with me *in* J.
12. 12. and also *in* J. things went well
17. 9. they taught *in* J. and had book of law of Lord
28. 6. Pekah slew *in* J. 120,000 in one day
30. 12. *in* J. hand of God was to give one heart
34. 21. inquire for them that are left *in* J.
Ezra 5. 1. prophesied to the Jews that were *in* J.
9. 9. but hath extended mercy to give us a wall *in* J.
Neh. 6. 7. to preach, saying, there is a king *in* J.
13. 15. I saw *in* J. some treading wine presses
Psal. 76. 1. *in* J. is God known, his name is great
Jer. 4. 5. declare ye *in* J. publish in Jerusalem, 5. 20.
22. 30. none shall prosper, ruling any more *in* J.
Zech. 9. 7. he shall be as a governor *in* J.
14. 21. every pot *in* J. be holiness to the Lord
See KING, KINGS.

Land of JUDAH.

Deut. 34. 2. Lord shewed him all the *land of* J.
Ruth 1. 7. thus went to return into the *land of* J.
1 *Sam.* 22. 5. depart, get thee into the *land of* J.
2 *Kings* 25. 22. people that remained in *land of* J.
2 *Chr.* 17. 2. Jehoshaphat set garrisons in *land of* J.
Isa. 19. 17. the *land of* J. shall be a terror to Egypt
26. 1. this song shall be sung in the *land of* J.
Jer. 31. 23. use this speech in the *land of* J.
39. 10. the poor, who had nothing in the *land of* J.
44. 9. they have committed in the *land of* J.
14. that they should return into the *land of* J.
Amos 7. 12. flee, thou seer, into the *land of* J.
Zech. 1. 21. lift up their horn over the *land of* J.
Mat. 2. 6. thou, Bethlehem, in the *land of* J.

Men of JUDAH.

Judg. 15. 10. *men of* J. said, why are ye come ag. us?
2 *Sam.* 2. 4. the *men of* J. anointed David king
19. 14. he bowed the heart of all the *men of* J.
43. the words of the *men of* J. were fiercer
20. 2. but the *men of* J. clave to their king
4. assemble the *men of* J. within three days
24. 9. the *men of* J. were five hundred thousand
2 *Chron.* 13. 15. then the *men of* J. gave a shout
Ezra 10. 9. all the *men of* J. gathered together
Isa. 5. 7. the *men of* J. are his pleasant plant
Jer. 4. 4. circumcise your hearts, ye *men of* J.
11. 9. a conspiracy is found among the *men of* J.
Jer. 36. 31. bring upon the *men of* J. all the evil
43. 9. hide them in the sight of the *men of* J.
44. 27. all the *men of* J. shall be consumed
Dan. 9. 7. but confusion belongeth to the *men of* J.
See PRINCES.

Tribe of JUDAH.

Exod. 31. 2. Bezaleel of the *tribe of* J. 35. 30. | 38. 22.
Num. 1. 27. that were numbered of the *tribe of* J.
7. 12. Nahshon, the prince of the *tribe of* J.
13. 6. of the *tribe of* J. Caleb to spy, 34. 19.
Josh. 7. 1. Achan of *tribe of* J. took of accursed thing
16. and the *tribe of* J. was taken, 18.
15. 1. this was the lot of the *tribe of* J. 20.
21. 4. Levites out of the *tribe of* J. 9. 1 *Chron.* 6. 65.
1 *Kings* 12. 20. the *tribe of* J. only followed David
2 *Kings* 17. 18. none left but the *tribe of* J. only
Psal. 78. 68. but he chose the *tribe of* J. mount Sion
Rev. 5. 5. the Lion of the *tribe of* J. hath prevailed
7. 5. of the *tribe of* J. were sealed 12,000

JUDAS.

Mat. 13. 55. his brethren Joses, Simon, and J.
26. 47. J. one of the twelve came, and a great multitude, *Mark* 14. 43. *Luke* 22. 47. *John* 18. 3, 5.
27. 3. then J. repented himself and brought 30 pieces
John 13. 29. some thought because J. had the bag
14. 22. J. saith unto him, not Iscariot, how is it
Acts 1. 16. David spake before concerning J
25. from which J. by transgression, fell
5. 37. after this man rose up J. of Galilee
9. 11. inquire in the house of J. for one Saul
15. 22. they sent J. surnamed Barsabas, 27.
32. J. and Silas exhorted the brethren

JUDAS *Iscariot*.

Mat. 10. 4. J. *Iscariot*, who betrayed him, *Mark* 3. 19. *Luke* 6. 16. *John* 6. 71. | 13. 2.
26. 14. J. *Iscariot* went to chief priests, *Mark* 14. 10.
Luke 22. 3. then entered Satan into J. *Iscariot*
John 13. 26. he gave the sop to J. *Iscariot*

JUDEA.

Ezra 5. 8. that we went into the province of J.
Mat. 24. 16. then let them which be in J. flee into the mountains, *Mark* 13. 14. *Luke* 21. 21
John 4. 3. he left J. and departed to Galilee
7. 3. depart hence and go into J. again, 11. 7.
Acts 1. 8. in all J. ye shall be witnesses to me
2. 14. ye men of J. be this known unto you
9. 31. the churches had rest throughout J.
10. 37. that word which was published through J.
12. 19. he went down from J. to Cesarea
28. 21. we neither received letters out of J.
Rom. 15. 31. from them that do not believe in J.
2 *Cor.* 1. 16. to be brought on my way toward J.
1 *Thess.* 2. 14. churches which in J. are in Christ Jes.

JUPITER.

Acts 14. 12. and they called Barnabas, J.
13. then the priests of J. brought garlands
19. 35. of the image which fell down from J.

JUSTUS.

Acts 1. 23. Joseph, who was surnamed J. and Matthi.
18. 7. entered into a certain man's house, named J.
Col. 4. 11. Jesus who is called J. saluteth you

K.

KADESH.

Gen. 14. 7. they came to Enmishpat which is K.
Num. 13. 26. they came to wilderness of Paran to K.
20. 16. behold, we are in K. a city in thy border
27. 14. ye rebelled against me at water of Meribah, in K. *Deut.* 32. 51. *Ezek.* 47. 19. | 48. 28.
33. 36. pitched in wilderness of Zin, which is K.
Deut. 1. 46. so ye abode in K. many days
Psal. 29. 8. the Lord shaketh the wilderness of K.

KADESH-BARNEA.

Num. 32. 8. when I sent them from K. to see the land, *Deut.* 9. 23. *Josh.* 14. 7.
Josh. 10. 41. Joshua smote them from K. to Gaza
14. 6. what Lord said, concerning me and thee in K.

KAREAH. *See* JOHANAN.

KEDAR.

Gen. 25. 13. the son of Ishmael, K. 1 *Chron.* 1. 29.
Psal. 120. 5. woe is me that I dwell in the tents of K.
Cant. 1. 5. I am black but comely as the tents of K.
Isa. 21. 16. in a year all the glory of K. shall fail, 17.
42. 11. the villages that K. doth inhabit
60. 7. the flocks of K. shall be gathered to thee
Jer. 2. 10. see and send to K. and consider diligently
49. 28. concerning K. thus saith the L. go up to K.
Ezek. 27. 21. all the princes of K. occupied with thee

KEILAH.

Josh. 15. 44. K. and Achzib, cities of Judah
1 *Sam.* 23. 1. the Philistines fight against K.
4. arise, go down to K. || 5. David saved K.
6. when Abiathar son of Ahimelech fled to K.
11. will the men of K. deliver me to Saul? 12.
Neh. 3. 17. the ruler of half part of K. repaired, 18.

KENAZ. *See* OTHNIEL.

KENITES.

Gen. 15. 19. unto thy seed have I given the K.
Num. 24. 21. Balaam looked on the K. and said
1 *Sam.* 15. 6. Saul said to the K. depart lest I destroy
27. 10. I made a road against the south of the K.

KERIOTH.

Jer. 48. 24. judgment is come on K. || 41. K. is taken
Amos 2. 2. a fire shall devour the palaces of K.

KETURAH.

Gen. 25. 1. Abraham took a wife, her name was K.
4. all these were children of K. 1 *Chron.* 1. 32, 33.

KIDRON. *See* BROOK.

KIR.

2 *Kings* 16. 9. he carried the people captive to K.
Isa. 15. 1. in the night K. of Moab is laid waste
22. 6. Elam bare the quiver, K. uncovered shield
Amos 1. 5. the Syrians shall go into captivity to K.
9. 7. have not I brought the Assyrians from K.?

KIR-HARASETH.

2 *Kings* 3. 25. only in K. left they the stones
Isa. 16. 7. for the foundations of K. shall ye mourn
11. mine inward parts shall sound for K.

KIRIATHAIM.

Gen. 14. 5 Chedorlaomer smote Emims in Shaveh K.

Jer. 48. 1. thus saith Ld. K. is confounded and taken
23. judgment is come upon K. and Beth-gamul

KIRJATH-ARBA.

Gen. 23. 2. Sarah died in K. the same is Hebron in Canaan, *Josh.* 14. 15. | 20. 7. *Judg.* 1. 10.

KIRJATH-JEARIM.

Josh. 9. 17. K. a city of the Hivites made peace
15. 9. the border was to Baalah, which is K. 60.
18. 14. which is K. a city of Judah, 1 *Chron.* 13. 6.
1 *Sam.* 7. 1. the men of K. came and fetched the ark
1 *Chron.* 13. 5. to bring the ark of God from K.
2 *Chron.* 1. 4. David had brought the ark from K.

KISH.

1 *Sam.* 9. 1. a man of Benjamin whose name was K.
3. the asses of K. Saul's father were lost, 14. 51.
10. 11. what is this that is come to the son of K.?
21. and Saul the son of K. was taken
2 *Sam.* 21. 14. they buried Saul in sepulchre of K.
1 *Chr.* 8. 30. K. the son of Gibeon || 33. Ner begat K.
23. 21. K. son of Mahli || 2 *Chr.* 29. 12. son of Abdi
Esth. 2. 5. Mordecai, son of Jair, of Shimei, son of K.
Acts 13. 21. God gave them Saul the son of K.

KITTIM.

Gen. 10. 4. sons of Javan, Tarshish, K. 1 *Chr.* 1. 7. *See* CHITTIM.

KOHATH.

Gen. 46. 11. the sons of Levi, Gershon, K. and Merari, *Exod.* 6. 16. *Num.* 3. 17.
Exod. 6. 18. the sons of K. *Num.* 3. 19, 27, 29, 30. | 16. 1. 1 *Chron.* 6. 2, 22, 61.
the years of the life of K. were 133 years
Num. 4. 2. take the sum of the sons of K. of Levi
4. this be the service of the sons of K. 15. | 7. 9.
1 *Chron.* 15. 5. of the sons of K. Uriel the chief

KOHATHITES.

Num. 4. 18. cut ye not off the family of the K.
34. Moses and Aaron numbered the sons of K. 37.
10. 21. the K. set forward bearing the sanctuary
Josh. 21. 4. the lot came out for K. 1 *Chron.* 6. 54.
2 *Chron.* 29. 12. the sons of K. sanctified themselves
34. 12. the sons of the K. to set the work forward

KORAH.

Gen. 36. 5. Aholibamah bare K. || 16. duke K. 16.
Exod. 6. 21. sons of Izhar, K. Nepheg, *Num.* 16. 1.
Num. 16. 6. take censers, K. and all his company
19. K. gathered all the congregation against them
24. get you up from about the tabernacle of K.
40. that he be not as K. and as his company
26. 9. Dathan who strove in the company of K.
11. notwithstanding the children of K. died not
27. 3. our father was not in the company of K.
1 *Chron.* 1. 35. the sons of Esau, Joalam and K.
2. 43. son of Hebron, K. || 6. 22. of Amminadab
9. 19. son of K. and his brethren over the work
Jude 11. they perished in the gainsaying of K.

L.

LABAN.

Gen. 24. 29. Rebekah had a brother, his name was L.
27. 43. flee thou to L. my brother, to Haran
28. 2. take thee a wife of the daughters of L.
29. 5. know ye L. || 29. L. gave to Rachel, Bilhah
30. 36. and Jacob fed the rest of L. flocks
42. so the feebler were L. the stronger Jacob's
31. 2. Jacob beheld the countenance of L.
12. for I have seen all that L. doth to thee
20. Jacob stole away unawares to L. the Syrian
24. God came to L. in a dream by night
34. L. searched all the tent, but found them not
36. Jacob chode with L. || 55. L. kissed his sons
32. 4. I have sojourned with L. and stayed until now

LABAN.

Deut. 1. 1. words Moses spake between Paran and L.

LACHISH.

Josh. 10. 32. the Lord delivered L. to Israel
12. 11. the king of L. one || 15. 39. Judah had L.
2 *Kings* 14. 19. Amaziah fled to L. 2 *Chron.* 25. 27.
18. 14. Hezekiah sent to king of Assyria to L.
17. the king of Assyria sent Rab-shakeh from L. with a great host to Jerusalem, *Isa.* 36. 2.
2 *Chron.* 11. 9. Rehoboam built L. and Azekah
Jer. 34. 7. the king of Babylon fought against L.
Mic. 1. 13. O inhabitant of L. bind the chariot

LAISH.

Judg. 18. 14. that went to spy the country of L.
29. the name of the city was L. at the first
Isa. 10. 30. cause thy voice be heard to L. O Anathoth

LAISH.

1 *Sam.* 25. 44. Michal given to Phalti son of L.
2 *Sam.* 3. 15. Ish-bosheth took her from the son of L.

LAMECH.

Gen. 4. 18. Methusael begat L. || 19. L. took two wives
5. 25. Methuselah begat L. 1 *Chron.* 1. 3.
Luke 3. 36. Noe, which was the son of L.

LAODICEA.

Col. 2. 1. what great conflict I have for them at L.
4. 13. he hath a zeal for them that are in L.
15. salute brethren which are in L. and Nymphas
16. that ye likewise read the epistle from L.

LAODICEANS.

Col. 4. 16. that it be read in the church of the L.
Rev. 3. 14. to the angel of the church of the L.

LAZARUS.

Luke 16. 20. there was a certain beggar named L.
23. he seeth L. in Abraham's bosom || 24. send L.
25. and likewise L. received evil things, but now
John 11. 2. Mary whose brother L. was sick
5. Jesus loved L. || 11. our friend L. sleepeth
14. L. is dead || 43. he cried, L. come forth
12. 2. L. was one of them that sat at the table
9. much people came that they might see L.
17. when he called L. out of grave and raised him

LEAH.

Gen. 29. 16. the name of the elder daughter was L.
17. L. was tender-eyed, but Rachel was beautiful
25. in the morning, behold it was L.
31. when the Lord saw that L. was hated
32. L. conceived and bare a son, 30. 19.
30. 16. Jacob came out of the field, L. met him
31. 4. Jacob called Rachel and L. to his flock

Gen. 33. 2. Jacob put L. and her children after
34. 1. Dinah the daughter of L. went out to see
35. 23. the sons of L. Reuben, Simeon, 46. 15.
49. 31. they buried Abraham, there I buried L.
Ruth 4. 11. the Lord make this woman like L.

LEBANON.

Deut. 3. 25. let me see that goodly mountain and L.
Judg. 3. 3. the Hivites that dwelt in mount L.
1 *Kings* 5. 14. he sent ten thousand a month to L.
7. 2. the house of the forest of L. 10. 17, 21.
2 *Kings* 14. 9. the thistle that was in L. sent to cedar in L. give thy daughter to my son, 2 *Chron.* 25. 18.
19. 23. I am come up to the sides of L. *Isa.* 37. 24.
2 *Chr.* 2. 8. thy servants can skill to cut timber in L.
Psal. 29. 6. L. and Sirion like a young unicorn
72. 16. the fruit thereof shall shake like L.
92. 12. he shall grow like a cedar in L.
Cant. 3. 9. Solomon made a chariot of the wood of L.
4. 8. come with me from L. my spouse, from L.
11. smell of thy garments is like the smell of L.
15. a well of living waters, and streams from L.
5. 15. his countenance is as L. excellent as cedars
7. 4. thy nose is as tower of L. toward Damascus
Isa. 10. 34. L. shall fall || 33. 9. L. is ashamed
29. 17. L. shall be turned into a fruitful field
35. 2. the glory of L. shall be given unto it
40. 16. L. is not sufficient to burn for burnt-offering
60. 13. the glory of L. shall come to thee
Jer. 18. 14. will a man leave the snow of L.?
22. 6. thou art Gilead and the head of L. to me
20. go up to L. and cry, lift up thy voice in Bashan
Ezek. 17. 3. a great eagle, long-winged, came to L.
31. 15. and I caused L. to mourn for him
Hos. 14. 5. he shall cast forth his roots as L.
6. his smell as L. || 7. the scent as the wine of L.
Nah. 1. 4. Bashan and the flower of L. languisheth
Hab. 2. 17. the violence of L. shall cover thee
Zech. 10. 10. I will bring them into the land of L.
11. 1. open thy doors, O L. that fire may devour *See* CEDARS.

LEBBEUS.

Mat. 10. 3. L. whose surname was Thaddeus

LEGION.

Mark 5. 9. my name is L. for we are many, *Luke* 8. 30.

LEGIONS.

Mat. 26. 53. he shall give me more than twelve L.

LEMUEL.

Prov. 31. 1. the words of king L. the prophecy
4. it is not for kings, O L. to drink wine

LEVI.

Gen. 29. 34. therefore was his name called L.
46. 11. the sons of L. *Exod.* 6. 16. *Num.* 3. 17.
49. 5. Simeon, L. are brethren, instrum. of cruelty
Exod. 6. 16. the years of the life of L. were 137 years
Num. 16. 7. ye take too much upon you, ye sons of L.
26. 59. Amram's wife Jochebed, daughter of L.
Deut. 10. 9. L. hath no part with his brethren
21. 5. the priests the sons of L. shall come near
33. 8. of L. he said, let thy Thummim and Urim
1 *Kings* 12. 31. made priests which were not of L.
1 *Chron.* 21. 6. but L. and Benjamin counted he not
Ezra 8. 15. I found there none of the sons of L.
Psal. 135. 20. bless the Lord, O house of L.
Ezek. 40. 46. the sons of Zadok among the sons of L.
48. 31. one gate of Judah, one gate of L.
Zech. 12. 13. the family of the house of L. apart
Mal. 2. 4. that my covenant might be with L.
8. ye have corrupted the covenant of L.
3. 3. and he shall purify the sons of L.
Mark 2. 14. he saw L. the son of Alpheus sitting
Luke 3. 24. Matthat, which was the son of L. 29.
5. 27. he saw a publican named L. sitting at
29. L. made him a great feast in his own house
Heb. 7. 9. L. who receiv. tithes, payed tithes in Abr.

Tribe of LEVI.

Num. 1. 49. thou shalt not number the *tribe of* L.
3. 6. bring the *tribe of* L. near and present them
18. 2. *tr. of* L. bring, that they may minister to thee
Deut. 10. 8. the Lord separated the *tribe of* L.
18. 1. all the *tribe of* L. shall have no part nor inheritance with Israel, *Josh.* 13. 14, 33.
1 *Chr.* 23. 14. Moses' sons were named of the *tr. of* L.
Rev. 7. 7. of the *tribe of* L. were sealed 12,000

LEVITE, S. See *Appellatives.*

LIBNAH.

Num. 33. 20. pitched in L. || 21. removed from L.
Josh. 10. 29. passed to L. || 21. 13. gave L. to Levites
2 *Kings* 8. 22. then L. revolted, 2 *Chron.* 21. 10.
19. 8. Rab-shakeh returned, and found the king of Assyria warring against L. *Isa.* 37. 8.
23. 31. Jehoahaz mother's name Hammutal, daughter of Jeremiah of L. 24. 18. *Jer.* 52. 1.

LIBYA.

Ezek. 30. 5. L. shall fall with them by the sword
Acts 2. 10. in the parts of L. about Cyrene

LIBYANS.

Jer. 46. 9. and the L. that handled the shield
Dan. 11. 43. the L. and Ethiopians shall be at his steps

LO-AMMI.

Hos. 1. 9. call his name L. for ye are not my people

LOIS.

2 *Tim.* 1. 5. which dwelt in thy grandmother L.

LO-RUHAMAH.

Hos. 1. 6. God said unto him, call her name L.
8. when she had weaned L. she conceived and bare

LOT.

Gen. 11. 27. Haran begat L. || 31. Terah took L.
12. 4. Abram departed, L. went with him, 13. 1.
13. 5. L. had flocks || 14. 12. they took L. prisoner
7. was a strife between herdmen of Abram and L.
11. then L. chose him all the plain of Jordan
19. 1. L. sat in the gate of Sodom; L. seeing them
10. pulled L. into house || 15. the angels hastened L.
29. God sent L. out of the midst of the overthrow
36. both the daughters of L. were with child
Deut. 2. 9. I have given Ar to the children of L. 19.
Psal. 83. 8. they have holpen the children of L.
Luke 17. 28. likewise as it was in the days of L.
32. remember L. wife
2 *Pet.* 2. 7. deliv. just L. vexed with filthy convers.

LUCAS.

Philem. 24. Marcus, Demas, L. my fellow-labourers

LUCIFER.

Isa. 14. 12. how art thou fallen from heaven, O L.

LUCIUS.

Acts 13. 1. L. of Cyrene was a teacher at Antioch
Rom. 16. 21. L. Jason, and Sosipater salute you

LUKE.

Col. 4. 14. L. the beloved physician greeteth you
2 *Tim.* 4. 11. only L. is with me, bring Mark with thee

LUZ.

Gen. 28. 19. the city was called L. at first, *Judg.* 1. 23.
35. 6. Jacob came to L. in the land of Canaan
48. 3. G. Almighty appeared to me at L. in Canaan

LYCAONIA.

Acts 14. 6. they fled to Lystra and Derbe, cities of L.
11. lift up their voices, saying in the speech of L.

LYDDA.

Acts 9. 32. Peter came down to the saints at L.
35. all that dwelt at L. turned to the Lord
38. forasmuch as L. was nigh to Joppa

LYDIA.

Ezek. 30. 5. L. shall fall with them by the sword

LYDIA.

Acts 16. 14. L. worshipped God, heart Lord opened
40. they went out and entered into the house of L.

LYSANIAS.

Luke 3. 1. in reign of Tiberius, L. tetrarch of Abilene

LYSIAS.

Acts 23. 26. L. unto the most excellent Felix

LYSTRA.

Acts 14. 6. they were ware of it, and fled unto L.
8. a certain man at L. impotent in his feet
16. 1. Paul came to L. || 2. by the brethren at L.
2 *Tim.* 3. 11. afflictions which came unto me at L.

M.

MAACHAH.

Gen. 22. 24. Reumah Nahor's concubine bare M.
2 *Sam.* 3. 3. M. mother of Absalom, 1 *Chron.* 3. 2.
1 *Kings* 15. 2. M. the mother of Abijam, the daughter of Abishalom, 10. 2 *Chron.* 11. 22.
1 *Chron.* 2. 48. M. Caleb's concubine bare Sheber
7. 16. M. the wife of Machir bare Peresh
11. 43. Hanan the son of M. was a valiant man

MAASEIAH.

2 *Chron.* 28. 7. Zichri slew M. the king's son
Neh. 10. 25. Rehom and M. sealed the covenant
Jer. 21. 1. Zephaniah the son of M. 29. 25. | 37. 3.
29. 21. saith the Lord of Zedekiah son of M.
32. 12. to Baruch son of Neraiah son of M. 51. 59.
35. 4. above the chamber of M. son of Shallum

MAATH.

Luke 3. 26. Nagge, which was the son of M.

MACEDONIA.

Acts 16. 9. saying, come over into M. and help us
18. 5. Silas and Timotheus were come from M.
19. 21. Paul proposed, when passed through M.
Rom. 15. 26. for it hath pleased them of M.
2 *Cor.* 7. 5. when we were come into M.
8. 1. grace of God bestowed on the churches of M.
9. 2. for which I boast of you to them of M.
4. lest if they of M. find you unprepared
11. 9. brethren which came from M. supplied
1 *Thess.* 1. 7. ensamples to all that believe in M.
8. from you sounded out the word, not only in M.
4. 10. towards all the brethren that are in M.

MACHIR.

Gen. 50. 23. M. the son of Manasseh, *Num.* 32. 39.
Num. 26. 29. M. begat Gilead, 27. 1. | 36. 1. *Josh.* 17. 1.
32. 40. Moses gave Gilead unto M. *Deut.* 3. 15.
Judg. 5. 14. out of M. came down governors
2 *Sam.* 9. 4. M. the son of Ammiel, 5. | 17. 27.

MACHPELAH.

Gen. 23. 9. that he may give me the cave of M. 17.
19. Abraham buried Sarah in the cave of M.
25. 9. buried Abraham in M. || 49. 30. Jacob. 50. 13.

MAGDALA.

Mat. 15. 39. Jesus came into the coasts of M.

MAGOG.

Gen. 10. 2. the son of Japheth M. 1 *Chron.* 1. 5.
Ezek. 38. 2. set thy face against the land of M.
39. 6. I will send a fire on M. and in the isles
Rev. 20. 8. to gather Gog and M. to battle

MAHANAIM.

Gen. 32. 2. Jacob called the name of the place M.
Josh. 21. 38. out of Gad to Levites, M. 1 *Chr.* 6. 80.
2 *Sam.* 2. 8. Abner brought Ish-bosheth to M.
17. 24. then David came to M. 27.
19. 32. Barzillai provided sustenance at M.
1 *Kings* 2. 8. Shimei cursed me when I went to M.
4. 14. Abinadab the son of Iddo had M.

MAHER-SHALAL-HASH-BAZ.

Isa. 8. 1. write in the roll concerning M.
3. then said the Lord to me, call his name M.

MAHLON.

Ruth 1. 2. Elimelech's sons, M. and Chilion
5. M. and Chilion died also both of them
4. 9. that I have bought all that was M.
10. Ruth the wife of M. have I purchased

MALCHAM.

Zeph. 1. 5. that swear by the Lord and by M.

MALCHUS.

John 18. 10. the servant's name was M.

MAMMON.

Mat. 6. 24. no man can serve two masters, ye cannot serve God and M. *Luke* 16. 13.
Luke 16. 9. make friends of M. of unrighteousness
11. if not faithful in the unrighteous M. who will

MAMRE.

Gen. 13. 18. Abram dwelt in the plain of M. 14. 13.
14. 24. Eshcol, M. let them take their portion
18. 1. the Lord appeared to Abraham in M.
23. 17. Machpelah before M. 19. | 49. 30. | 50. 13.
35. 27. Jacob came to Isaac his father to M.

MANAEN.

Acts 13. 1. M. who had been brought up with H.

MANASSEH.

Gen. 41. 51. Joseph called the first-born M.

Gen. 48. 5. thy two sons M. and Ephraim are mine
20. in thee shall Israel bless, God make thee as Ephraim and M. and he set Ephraim before M.
Num. 1. 10. of M. Gamaliel was prince
7. 54. Gamaliel prince of M. offered on eighth day
26. 34. these are the families of M. 27. 1.
36. 12. they were married into the family of M.
Deut. 33. 17. they are the thousands of M.
Josh. 14. 4. of Joseph were two tribes, M. Ephraim
17. 2. these were the male children of M.
3. Zelophehad son of M. had no sons but daughters
5. there fell ten portions to M. beside Gilead
6. the daughters of M. had an inheritance
11. M. had in Issachar, Beth-shean and Ibleam
12. children of M. could not drive out inhabitants
Judg. 6. 15. behold, my family is poor in M.
18. 30. Jonathan son of Gershom, son of M. priest
2 *Kings* 20. 21. M. his son reigned, 2 *Chron.* 32. 33.
21. 9. and M. seduced them to do more evil
16. M. shed innocent blood, till he filled Jerusalem
23. 12. the altars M. made did Josiah beat down
26. provocations that M. had provoked him withal
24. 3. for the sins of M. this came upon Judah
1 *Chron.* 9. 3. in Jerusalem dwelt of the children of M.
12. 19. and there fell some of M. to David
2 *Chron.* 15. 9. the strangers out of M. fell to Asa
30. 1. Hezekiah wrote letters to Ephraim and M.
11. yet divers of M. humbled themselves
31. 1. all Israel cut down the groves in M.
33. 9. M. made Judah and Jerusalem to err
10. the Lord spake to M. he would not hearken
11. the captains took M. among the thorns
13. then M. knew that the Lord he was God
23. Amon humbled not himself, as M. had done
34. 6. so did Josiah in the cities of M. and Ephraim
Ezra 10. 30. M. had taken strange wives, 33.
Psal. 60. 7. Gilead is mine, M. is mine, 108. 8.
80. 2. before M. stir up thy strength, and save us
Isa. 9. 21. M. shall eat Ephraim, Ephraim M.
Jer. 15. 4. cause them to be removed, because of M.
Ezek. 48. 4. to the west side a portion for M.
Mat. 1. 10. Ezekias begat M. and M. begat Amon

Tribe of MANASSEH.

Num. 1. 35. numbered of the *tribe of* M. 32,200
2. 20. by Ephraim shall be the *tribe of* M. and the captain of the children of M. Gamaliel, 10. 23.
13. 11. of the *tribe of* M. Gaddi || 34. 23. Hanniel
32. 33. to half *tribe of* M. the kingdom of Og
34. 14. half *tribe of* M. have received inheritance
Josh. 4. 12. the half *tribe of* M. passed over armed
13. 7. divide to nine tribes and half *tribe of* M.
29. Moses gave inheritance to half *tribe of* M. this was possession of half *tribe of* M. 12. 6. | 18. 7.
17. 1. there was also a lot for the *tribe of* M.
20. 8. gave Golan out of the *tribe of* M. 21. 27.
22. 10. the half *tribe of* M. built there an altar
1 *Chr.* 5. 18. Reuben, Gad, and half *tribe of* M. vali.
6. 70. out of half *tribe of* M. to the Levites, 71.
12. 31. half *tribe of* M. 18,000 to make David king
26. 32. rulers over Gad half *tribe of* M. 27. 20, 21.
Rev. 7. 6. of the *tribe of* M. were sealed 12,000

MANEH.

Ezek. 45. 12. fifteen shekels shall be your M.

MANOAH.

Judg. 13. 8. then M. entreated the Lord, and said
9. and God hearkened to the voice of M.
11. M. arose and went after his wife and came
16. M. knew not that he was an angel of the Lord
19. M. took a kid, and offered it upon a rock
20. M. and his wife looked on it, and fell down
21. M. knew that he was an angel of the Lord
16. 31. buried Samson in the burying-place of M.

MARA.

Ruth 1. 20. Ruth said, call me not Naomi, call me M.

MARAH.

Exod. 15. 23. they could not drink of waters of M.
Num. 33. 8. went three days, and pitched in M.
9. they removed from M. and came unto Elim

MARCUS.

Col. 4. 10. M. sister's son to Barnabas, saluteth you
Philem. 24. M. saluteth you, 1 *Pet.* 5. 13.

MARK.

Acts 12. 12. Mary, mother of John, surnamed M.
25. took with them John, whose surname was M.
15. 39. Barnabas took M. and sailed to Cyprus
2 *Tim.* 4. 11. take M. and bring him with thee

MARS-HILL.

Acts 17. 22. Paul stood in the midst of M.

MARTHA.

Luke 10. 38. a woman named M. received him
40. M. was cumbered || 41. M. M. thou art careful
John 11. 1. the town of Mary and her sister M.
5. now Jesus loved M. Mary, and Lazarus
30. Jesus was in that place where M. met him
12. 2. they made him a supper, and M. served

MARY.

Mat. 1. 16. Jacob begat Joseph the husband of M.
18. when his mother M. was espoused to Joseph
20. fear not to take unto thee M. thy wife
2. 11. they saw the young child with M. his mother
13. 55. is not his mother called M. *Mark* 6. 3.
27. 56. among them was M. the mother of James and Joses, *Mark* 15. 40, 47. | 16. 1.
Luke 1. 27. house of David the virgin's name was M.
30. fear not, M. || 56. M. abode three months
41. when Elizabeth heard the salutation of M.
2. 5. Joseph went to be taxed with M. his wife
16. the shepherds found M. and the babe lying
19. but M. kept all these things in her heart
10. 39. she had a sister called M. which also sat
42. M. hath chosen that good part not to be taken
John 11. 1. the town of M. || 20. but M. sat still
2. it was that M. that anointed the Lord
28. she called M. her sister secretly, saying
12. 3. M. took a pound of ointment and anointed
19. 25. M. the wife of Cleophas stood by the cross
20. 11. M. stood without at the sepulchre, weeping
16. Jesus saith to her, M. she turned herself
Acts 1. 14. the apostles continued in prayer with M.
12. 12. Peter came to house of M. mother of John
Rom. 16. 6. greet M. who bestowed much labour

MARY *Magdalene.*

Mat. 27. 56. many women were there, among whom was M. *Magdalene, Mark* 15. 40. *John* 19. 25.
61. M. *Magdalene* sitting over-against sepulchre
28. 1. came M. *Mag.* to see sepulchre, *John* 20. 1.
Mark 16. 1. M. *Magdalene* and Mary the mother of James bought sweet spices, *Luke* 24. 10.
9. he appeared first to M. *Magdalene*, out of whom
John 20. 18. M. *Magdalene* told the disciples

MASSAH.

Exod. 17. 7. he called the name of the place M.
Deut. 6. 16. not tempt L. as tempted him in M. 9. 22.
33. 8. thy holy one, whom thou didst prove at M.

MATTAN.

2 *Kings* 11. 18. slew M. priest of Baal, 2 *Chr.* 23. 17.

MATTATHIAS.

Luke 3. 25. Joseph, which was the son of M.

MATTHEW.

Mat. 9. 9. saw man named M. and saith, follow me
10. 3. Philip, Thomas, and M. the publican, *Mark* 3. 18. *Luke* 6. 15. *Acts* 1. 13.

MATTHIAS.

Acts 1. 23. Joseph called Barsabas, and M.
26. the lot fell on M. and he was numbered

MAZZAROTH.

Job 38. 32. canst thou bring forth M. in season?

MEDAD.

Num. 11. 26. Spirit came on M. he prophesied, 27.

MEDE, S.

2 *Kings* 17. 6. placed them in cities of M. 18. 11.
Ezra 6. 2. was found in the province of the M. roll
Esth. 1. 19. let it be written among the laws of the M.
Isa. 13. 17. I will stir up M. ag. them, *Jer.* 51. 11.
Jer. 25. 25. I made all the kings of the M. to drink
Dan. 5. 28. Peres, thy kingdom is given to the M.
6. 8. according to the law of the M. 12, 15.
9. 1. Darius son of Ahasuerus, of the seed of M.
11. 1. in the first year of Darius the M.

MEDIA.

Esth. 1. 3. all the power of Persia and M.
14. seven princes of Persia and M. saw the king
18. the ladies of M. shall say this day to princes
10. 2. written in the book of the kings of M.
Isa. 21. 2. besiege, O M. all the sighing ceaseth
Dan. 8. 20. the two horns are kings of M. and Persia

MEGIDDO.

Judg. 1. 27. the Canaanites would dwell in M.
5. 19. kings of Canaan fought by the waters of M.
1 *Kings* 4. 12. to Baana pertained Taanach and M.
9. 15. Solomon raised a levy to build M.
2 *Kings* 9. 27. Ahaziah fled to M. and died there
23. 29. Josiah was slain at M. 30. 2 *Chron.* 35. 22.

MEGIDDON.

Zech. 12. 11. as the mourning in the valley of M.

MELCHI.

Luke 3. 24. Levi, which was the son of M.

MELCHISEDEK.

Gen. 14. 18. king M. brought forth bread and wine
Ps. 110. 4. thou art a priest for ever after the order of M. *Heb.* 5. 6, 10. | 6. 20. | 7. 17, 21.
Heb. 7. 1. this M. king of Salem, priest of God
10. in the loins of his father when M. met him
11. a priest should arise after the order of M.
15. after the similitude of M. ariseth a priest

MEMPHIS.

Hos. 9. 6. Egypt shall gather them, M. shall bury

MENAHEM.

2 *Kings* 15. 14. M. smote Shallum in Samaria
16. M. smote Tiphsah || 20. M. exacted money

MENE.

Dan. 5. 25. M. M. God hath numbered thy king. 26.

MEPHIBOSHETH.

2 *Sam.* 4. 4. Jonathan had a son, his name was M.
9. 10. but M. shall eat bread at my table, 11.
12. M. had a young son Micha; all that dwelt in the house of Ziba were servants to M.
16. 4. behold, thine are all that pertained unto M.
19. 25. wherefore wentest thou not with me, M.?
21. 7. but the king spared M. the son of Jonathan
8. king took two sons of Rizpah, Armoni and M.

MERAB.

1 *Sam.* 14. 49. Saul's eldest daughter M. 18. 17.
18. 19. when M. should have been given to David

MERARI.

Gen. 46. 11. the sons of Levi, Gershon, Kohath, M. *Exod.* 6. 16. *Num.* 3. 17. 1 *Chr.* 6. 1, 16. | 23. 6.
Exod. 6. 19. the sons of M. Mahali, Mushi, *Num.* 3. 20. 1 *Chron.* 6. 19, 29. | 23. 21. | 24. 26.
Num. 3. 36. under the charge of the sons of M.
4. 42. were numbered of M. || 10. 17. M. set forward
7. 8. waggons and oxen given to the sons of M.
Josh. 21. 7. cities given to M. 40. 1 *Chr.* 6. 63, 77.

MERCURIUS.

Acts 14. 12. Paul called M. because chief speaker

MERIBAH.

Exod. 17. 7. he called the name of the place M.
Num. 20. 13. this is the water of M. 27. 14.
24. rebelled at water of M. *Deut.* 32. 51. | 33. 8.
Psal. 81. 7. I proved thee at the waters of M.

MERODACH.

Jer. 50. 2. Babylon taken, M. is broken in pieces

MERODACH-BALADAN.

Isa. 39. 1. M. sent letters and present to Hezekiah

MEROM.

Josh. 11. 5. they pitched at the waters of M. 7.

MEROZ.

Judg. 5. 23. curse ye M. saith the angel of the Lord

MESHACH. *See* Abed-nego.

MESHECH.

Gen. 10. 2. M. the son of Japheth, 1 *Chron.* 1. 5.
1 *Chron.* 1. 17. the sons of Shem, Gether, and M.
Psal. 120. 5. woe is me, that I sojourn in M.
Ezek. 27. 13. Tubal and M. were thy merchants
32. 26. there is M. || 38. 2. chief prince of M. 3.
39. 1. I am against the chief prince of M. and Tubal

MESOPOTAMIA.

Gen. 24. 10. Eliezer went to M. to the city of Nahor
Deut. 23. 4. they hired Balaam of M. to curse thee
Judg. 3. 8. Chushan-rishathaim king of M.
10. Lord delivered the king of M. to Israel
1 *Chr.* 19. 6. Ammon sent to hire chariots out of M.
Acts 2. 9. the dwellers in M. we hear in our tongue
Acts 7. 2. the God of glory appeared to Abra. in M.

MESSIAH. See *Appellatives.*

METHEG-AMMAH.

2 *Sam.* 8. 1. David took M. from the Philistines

METHUSELAH.

Gen. 5. 21. Enoch begat M. || 25. M. begat Lamech
27. all the days of M. were 969 years
1 *Chron.* 1. 3. Henoch, M. Lamech
Luke 3. 37. Lamech, which was the son of M.

MICAH.

Judg. 17. 1. a man of mount Ephraim called M.
5. the man M. had an house of gods
12. M. consecrated the Levite for his priest
18. 4. thus dealeth M. || 31. they set up M. image
1 *Chron.* 5. 5. M. his son, Reaia his son, Baal his son
8. 34. Merib-baal of Benjamin begat M. 9. 40.
35. the sons of M. Pithon, and Melech, 9. 41.
9. 15. Mattaniah the son of M. son of Zichri
2 *Chron.* 34. 20. Josiah sent Abdon the son of M.
Neh. 10. 11. M. Rehob sealed the covenant
Jer. 26. 18. M. the Morasthite prophesied in the days of Hezekiah, Zion shall be plowed, *Mic.* 1. 1.

MICAIAH.

1 *Kings* 22. 8. M. the son of Imlah, 9. 2 *Chron.* 18. 8.
24. Zedekiah smote M. on the cheek
26. take M. carry him to Amon, 2 *Chr.* 18. 23, 25.

MICHAIAH.

Neh. 12. 35. son of M. to give thanks, 41.

MICHAIAH.

2 *Chron.* 13. 2. Abijah's mother was M. of Uriel
17. 7. Jehoshaphat sent M. to teach cities of Judah
Jer. 36. 11. M. heard what Baruch had read, 13.

MICHAEL.

Dan. 10. 13. M. one of the chief princes came
21. none holdeth with me but M. your prince
12. 1. at that time shall M. stand up for the people
Jude 9. yet M. the archangel, contending with dev.
Rev. 12. 7. M. and angels fought against the dragon

MICHAL.

1 *Sam.* 14. 49. Saul's younger daughter M.
18. 20. M. Saul's daughter loved David, 28.
19. 12. so M. let David down through a window
13. M. took an image and laid it in the bed
25. 44. Saul had given M. David's wife to Phalti
2 *Sam.* 3. 13. except thou first bring M.
14. deliver me my wife M. whom I espoused
6. 16. M. Saul's daughter looked through a window, and saw king David dancing, 1 *Chron.* 15. 29.
23. therefore M. had no child to her death
21. 8. king took five sons of M. brought up for Adriel

MIDIAN.

Exod. 2. 15. but Moses dwelt in the land of M.
18. 1. Jethro priest of M. heard all God had done
Num. 22. 4. Moab said to the elders of M.
25. 15. Cozbi daughter of Zur of a chief house in M.
31. 3. let them go and avenge the Lord of M.
8. they slew the kings of M. beside the rest
9. Israel took all the women of M. captives
Judg. 6. 1. the Lord delivered them to M. 2.
7. 14. for into his hand hath God delivered M.
8. 22. thou hast delivered us from M. 9. 17.
28. thus was M. subdued before Israel
1 *Kings* 11. 18. some Edomites arose out of M.
Isa. 9. 4. thou hast broken the yoke, as in day of M.
10. 26. according to the slaughter of M. at Oreb
60. 6. the dromedaries of M. shall cover thee
Hab. 3. 7. the curtains of the land of M. did tremble

MIDIANITES.

Gen. 37. 28. there passed by M. merchant-men
36. the M. sold him into Egypt to Potiphar
Num. 25. 17. vex the M. || 31. 2. avenge Isr. of the M.
Judg. 6. 7. Israel cried to the Lord because of M.
16. and thou shalt smite the M. as one man
7. 23. the men of Israel pursued after the M.
25. they took two princes of the M. Oreb, Zeeb
8. 1. when thou wentest to fight with the M.
Psal. 83. 9. do to them as to the M. as to Sisera

MIDIANITISH.

Num. 25. 6. behold, Zimri brought a M. woman
15. the name of the M. woman was Cozbi

MILCAH.

Gen. 11. 29. M. daughter of Haran, Nahor's wife
22. 20. M. also bare children to Nahor, 23.
24. 15. Bethuel son of M. the wife of Nahor
Num. 26. 33. Zelophehad's daughter's name was M.

MILCOM.

1 *Kings* 11. 5. Solomon went after M. god of Ammon
33. they have worshipped M. god of Ammon
2 *Kings* 23. 13. which Solomon had builded for M.

MILETUM.

2 *Tim.* 4. 20. Trophimus have I left at M. sick

MILETUS.

Acts 20. 15. and the next day we came to M.
17. from M. he sent to Ephesus to the elders

MILLO.

Judg. 9. 6. all the house of M. gathered together
20. but if not let fire devour the house of M.
2 *Sam.* 5. 9. David built round about from M.
1 *Kings* 9. 15. the reason of the levy to build M.
24. then did Solomon build M. 11. 27.
2 *Kings* 12. 20. they slew Joash in the house of M.

MIRIAM.

Exod. 15. 20. M. took a timbrel in her hand
Num. 12. 1. M. and Aaron spake against Moses
10. behold, M. became leprous white as snow
15. M. was shut out seven days || 20. 1. M. died there
26. 59. to Amram were born Aaron, Moses, M.
Deut. 24. 9. remember what G. did to M. by the way
Mic. 6. 4. I sent before thee Moses, Aaron, and M.

MISHAEL.

Exod. 6. 22. and the sons of Uzziel, M. Elzaphan and Zithri, *Lev.* 10. 4.
Neh. 8. 4. on Ezra's left hand stood M. and Hashum
Dan. 1. 6. of the children of Judah, M. and Azariah

MIZAR.

Psal. 42. 6. I will remember thee from the hill M.

MIZPAH.

Gen. 31. 49. the name of the heap was called M.
1 *Kings* 15. 22. king Asa built with those stones Geba of Benjamin and M. 2 *Chron.* 16. 6.
2 *Kings* 25. 23. Ishmael the son of Nethaniah came to Gedaliah to M. *Jer.* 41. 1.

Neh. 3. 7. the men of Gibeon and M. repaired
15. Shallum ruler of M. ‖ 19. Ezer ruler of M.
Jer. 40. 6. then Jeremiah went to Gedaliah to M.
10. as for me, behold, I will dwell at M.
41. 3. Ishmael slew all the Jews that were at M.
14. Ishmael had carried away captive from M.
Hos. 5. 1. because ye have been a snare on M.

MIZPEH.

Josh. 15. 38. Dilean and M. cities of Judah
18. 26. M. and Chephirah, cities of Benjamin
Judg. 10. 17. Israel assembled and encamped in M.
11. 11. Jephthah uttered all his words in M.
20. 1. Israel was gathered to the Lord in M.
21. 5. that came not up to the Lord to M. shall die
1 *Sam.* 7. 5. Samuel said, gather all Israel to M.
6. and Samuel judged Israel in M. 16.
10. 17. Samuel called the people to the Lord to M.
22. 3. David went thence to M. of Moab

MNASON.

Acts. 21. 16. they brought M. an old disciple

MOAB.

Gen. 19. 37. Lot's eldest daughter's son was M.
36. 35. smote Midian in field of M. 1 *Chr.* 1. 46.
Exod. 15. 15. trembling shall take hold on men of M.
Num. 21. 29. woe to thee, M. *Jer.* 48. 46.
22. 3. M. was sore afraid, and M. was distressed
24. 17. a sceptre shall smite the corners of M.
25. 1. people commit whoredom with daught. of M.
Deut. 2. 18. thou art to pass thro' the coast of M.
34. 5. so Moses died there in the land of M.
Judg. 3. 29. they slew of M. about 10,000 men
30. so M. was subdued under the hand of Israel
10. 6. Israel served the gods of Syria and M.
11. 15. Israel took not away the land of M.
Ruth 1. 2. Elimelech came into the country of M.
4. his sons took them wives of the women of M.
1 *Sam.* 14. 47. Saul fought against M. and Ammon
2 *Sam.* 8. 2. David smote M. and measured them
23. 20. Benaiah slew two lion-like men of M.
1 *Kings* 11. 7. for Chemosh the abomination of M.
2 *Kings* 1. 1. then M. rebelled against Israel
3. 7. wilt thou go with me against M. to battle?
23. the kings are slain, therefore M. to the spoil
1 *Chr.* 4. 22. Saraph, who had the dominion in M.
18. 11. the silver and gold he brought from M.
2 *Chron.* 20. 1. M. came against Jehoshaphat
10. behold, how the children of M. reward us
Neh. 13. 23. Jews that had married wives of M.
Psal. 60. 8. M. is my washpot, 108. 9.
83. 6. M. is confederate against thee
Isa. 11. 14. they shall lay their hand upon M.
15. 1. the burden of M. Ar of M. laid waste, 16.
13. *Jer.* 48. 1. *Ezek.* 25. 8. *Amos* 2. 2.
5. my heart shall cry out for M. his fugitives
16. 6. we have heard the pride of M. *Jer.* 48. 29.
11. my bowels shall sound like an harp for M.
14. and the glory of M. shall be contemned
25. 10. M. shall be trodden down under him
Jer. 9. 26. I will punish Egypt, Judah, and M.
25. 21. I made Edom and M. to drink of the cup
40. 11. all the Jews returned from M.
48. 2. there shall be no more praise of M.
9. give wings to M. that it may flee and get away
11. M. hath been at ease from his youth
20. tell ye it in Arnon, that M. is spoiled
26. M. shall wallow in his vomit, be in derision
33. joy and gladness is taken from the land of M.
39. how hath M. turned the back with shame!
47. yet will I bring again the captivity of M.
Amos 2. 2. but I will send a fire upon M. and devour
Zeph. 2. 9. saith the L. surely M. shall be as Sodom
See KING.

MOABITE.

Deut. 23. 3. a M. shall not enter into the congregation to tenth generation, *Neh.* 13. 1.
1 *Chron.* 11. 46. Ithmah the M. a valiant man

MOABITES.

Gen. 19. 37. the same is the father of the M.
Deut. 2. 9. the Lord said, distress not the M.
Judg. 3. 28. the Lord hath delivered the M. to you
2 *Sam.* 8. 2. so the M. became David's servants, and brought gifts, 1 *Chron.* 18. 2.
1 *Kings* 11. 1. Solomon loved women of the M.
33. they worshipped Chemosh god of the M.
2 *Kings* 3. 18. he will deliver the M. into your hand
24. the Israelites rose up and smote the M.
13. 20. the bands of the M. invaded the land
24. 2. the Lord sent against him bands of the M.
Ezra 9. 1. according to the abominations of the M.

MOABITESS. See RUTH.

MOLECH.

Lev. 18. 21. shalt not let thy seed pass thro' fire to M.
20. 2. whosoever he be that giveth of his seed to M. shall surely be put to death, 3, 4. *Jer.* 32. 35.
1 *Kings* 11. 7. Solomon built an high place for M.
2 *Kings* 23. 10. no man make his son pass thro' to M.

MOLOCH.

Amos 5. 26. have borne tabernacle of M. *Acts* 7. 43.

MORDECAI.

Ezra 2. 2. M. came up with Zerubbabel, *Neh.* 7. 7.
Esth. 2. 5. there was a Jew, whose name was M.
19. then M. sat in the king's gate, 21.
22. the thing was known to M. who told it
3. 5. when Haman saw that M. bowed not
6. for they had shewed him the people of M.
4. 1. M. rent his clothes, and put on sackcloth
9. Hatach came and told Esther the words of M.
15. Esther bade them return M. this answer
5. 13. so long as I see M. the Jew at the king's gate
14. gallows made, that M. may be hanged thereon
6. 3. what honour hath been done to M. for this?
10. make haste, and do even so to M. the Jew
7. 9. the gallows which Haman had made for M.
8. 2. the king took off his ring, and gave it to M. Esther set M. over the house of Haman.
15. M. went out from the king in royal apparel
9. 3. because the fear of M. fell upon them
10. 3. M. the Jew was next to king Ahasuerus

MORIAH.

Gen. 22. 2. and get thee into the land of M.
2 *Chr.* 3. 1. Solomon built the house of Lord in M.

MOSES.

Exod. 2. 10. Pharaoh's daughter called his name M.
14. M. feared, and said, this thing is known
15. Pharaoh sought to slay M. but M. fled
3. 4. the Lord called to him, and said, M. M.
6. M. hid his face, he was afraid to look on God
4. 14. the Lord's anger was kindled against M.
27. go to meet M. ‖ 11. 3. M. was very great
5. 22. M. returned unto the Lord and said
8. 13. accord. to word of M. 31. | 9. 12, 35. | 12. 35.
10. 22. M. stretched forth his hand toward heaven
14. 31. people believed the Lord and his servant M.
15. 24. the people murmured against M. 17. 3.
16. 20. notwithstanding they hearkened not to M.
17. 4. M. cried to the Lord ‖ 6. M. did so, *Num.* 17. 11.
12. M. hands were heavy ‖ 15. M. built an altar
18. 13. M. sat to judge ‖ 19. 3. M. went up unto G.
19. 8. M. returned the words of the people to Ld.
20. the Lord called M. up to mount Sinai
20. 21. M. drew near unto the thick darkness
24. 2. M. alone shall come near the Lord
4. M. wrote all the words of the Lord
18. and M. went into the midst of the cloud
32. 1. as for M. we wot not what become of him, 23.
11. M. besought the Lord ‖ 19. M. anger waxed hot
33. 9. the Lord talked with M. ‖ 34. 4. M. went up
34. 35. M. put the vail upon his face again
39. 43. M. did look on all work; M. blessed them
40. 35. M. was not able to enter into the tent
Lev. 10. 16. M. sought the goat of the sin-offering
24. 11. they brought the blasphemer to M.
Num. 5. 4. as the Lord spake to M. so did Israel
11. 2. the people cried to M. and M. prayed to Ld.
10. M. heard people weep through their families
12. 2. hath the Lord indeed spoken only by M.?
3. M. was very meek above all men upon the earth
7. M. is not so, who is faithful in all my house
14. 44. ark and M. departed not out of the camp
16. 4. when M. heard it, he fell upon his face
17. 7. M. laid up the rods before the Lord
20. 3. the people chode with M. and spake, saying
21. 5. people spake against God and against M.
9. M. made a serpent of brass and put it on a pole
25. 6. brought a Midianitish woman in sight of M.
31. 6. M. sent them to the war, them and Phinehas
14. M. was wroth with the officers of the host
33. 2. M. wrote their goings out by command of Ld.
Deut. 27. 11. M. charged the people the same day
31. 9. M. wrote this law and delivered it
22. M. wrote this song, and taught it Israel
33. 1. wherewith M. the man of God blessed Israel
34. 5. M. the servant of the Lord died there
10. not a prophet since in Israel like to M.
Josh. 1. 5. as I was with M. so I will be with thee, 3. 7.
17. as we hearkened to M. so will we to thee
4. 14. the people feared Joshua, as they feared M.
14. 10. ever since the Lord spake this word to M.
11. I am as strong as I was in the day M. sent me
1 *Kings* 2. 3. to keep his commandments, as it is written in the law of M. 2 *Kings* 23. 25. 2 *Chron.* 23. 18. *Ezra* 3. 2. *Dan.* 9. 11, 13. *Luke* 24. 44. 1 *Cor.* 9. 9.
8. 9. save the two tables which M. put there
1 *Chr.* 23. 14. now concerning M. the man of God
26. 24. the son of M. was ruler of the treasures
Psal. 103. 7. he made known his ways unto M.
105. 26. he sent M. his servant, and Aaron
106. 16. they envied M. also in the camp
23. had not M. stood before him in the breach
32. so that it went ill with M. for their sakes
Isa. 63. 12. that led them by the right hand of M.
Jer. 15. 1. though M. and Samuel stood before me
Mal. 4. 4. remember the law of M. my servant
Mat. 17. 3. behold there appeared M. and Elias talking with him, *Mark* 9. 4. *Luke* 9. 30.
4. let us make one tabernacle for M. *Mark* 9. 5.
19. 7. why did M. then command to give a writing?
8. M. suffered you to put away your wives, but
23. 2. the Scribes and Pharisees sit in M. seat
Mark 10. 3. he said, what did M. command you?
12. 19. M. wrote, if a man's brother die, *Luke* 20. 28.
Luke 16. 29. they have M. and the prophets
31. if they hear not M. and the prophets
20. 37. that dead are raised M. shewed at the bush
24. 27. beginning at M. and all the prophets
John 1. 17. law was given by M. grace by Jes. Christ
45. we have found him of whom M. did write
3. 14. as M. lifted up the serpent in the wilderness
5. 45. one accuseth you, even M. in whom ye trust
46. had ye believed M. ye had believed me
6. 32. M. gave you not that bread from heaven
7. 19. did not M. give you the law? none keepeth it
22. not because it is of M. but of the fathers
23. that the law of M. should not be broken
9. 28. thou art his disciple, we are M. disciples
29. we know that God spake unto M.
Acts 3. 22. for M. truly said unto the fathers
6. 11. heard him speak blasphemous words ag. M.
14. change the customs which M. delivered us
7. 20. in which time M. was born, and was fair
32. then M. trembled and durst not behold
35. this M. whom they refused did God send
37. this is that M. that said unto Israel
13. 39. ye could not be justified by the law of M.
15. 1. except ye be circumcised after manner of M.
5. to command them to keep the law of M.
21. M. hath in every city them that preach him
21. 21. thou teachest the Jews to forsake M.
26. 22. things which M. did say should come
28. 23. out of the law of M. and the prophets
Rom. 5. 14. death reigned from Adam to M.
10. 5. M. described the righteousness of the law
1 *Cor.* 10. 2. were all baptized to M. in the cloud
2 *Cor.* 3. 7. Israel could not behold the face of M.
13. not as M. who put a veil over his face
15. when M. is read, the veil is on their heart
2 *Tim.* 3. 8. as Jannes and Jambres withstood M.
Heb. 3. 2. M. was faithful in all his house, 5.
3. was counted worthy of more glory than M.
16. howbeit not all that came out of Egypt by M.
7. 14. which tribe M. spake nothing of priesthood
9. 19. for when M. had spoken every precept
Heb. 10. 28. despised M. law, died without mercy
11. 23. by faith M. was hid three months
24. M. refused be called son of Pharaoh's daught
12. 21. M. said, I exceedingly fear and quake
Jude 9. he disputed about the body of M.
Rev. 15. 3. they sing the song of M. and the Lamb
See AARON, BOOK, COMMANDED, LAW.

MYRA.

Acts 27. 5. we came to M. a city of Lycia

MYSIA.

Acts 16. 7. come to M. ‖ 8. they passing by M.

N.

NAAMAN.

Gen. 46. 21. the sons of Benjamin, N. and Rosh
Num. 26. 40. the son of Bela, N. 1 *Chron.* 8. 4.
2 *Kings* 5. 1. N. captain of Syria was a leper
11. but N. was wroth and went away, and said
20. my master hath spared N. the Syrian
27. the leprosy of N. shall cleave to thee
Luke 4. 27. and none was cleansed, saving N.

NAAMATHITE. See ZOPHAR.

NAASHON, or NAHSHON.

Exod. 6. 23. Aaron took Elisheba the sister of N
Num. 1. 7. of Judah, prince was N. 2. 3. | 10. 14.
7. 12. he that offered the first day was N.
17. this was the offering of N. son of Amminadab
Ruth 4. 20. Amminadab begat N. and N. begat Salmon, 1 *Chron.* 2. 10, 11. *Mat.* 1. 4.
Luke 3. 32. Salmon, which was the son of N.

NABAL.

1 *Sam.* 25. 3. now the name of the man was N.
4. N. did shear his sheep ‖ 5. go to N. and greet him
25. N. is his name, and folly is with him
38. that the Lord smote N. that he died
39. Lord hath returned the wickedness of N.
27. 3. Abigail N. wife, 30. 5. 2 *Sam.* 2. 2. | 3. 3.

NABOTH.

1 *Kings* 21. 1. N. the Jezreelite had a vineyard
7. I will give thee vineyard of N. the Jezreelite
9. set N. on high, 12. ‖ 14. heard N. was stoned
16. when Ahab heard that N. was dead
18. behold, Ahab is in the vineyard of N.
19. in the place where dogs licked the blood of N.
2 *Kings* 9. 21. they met him in the portion of N.
25. cast him in the portion of the field of N.
26. surely I have seen yesterday the blood of N

NADAB.

Exod. 6. 23. the sons of Aaron, N. Abihu, *Lev.* 10. 1.
24. 1. come up, N. and Abihu, seventy elders, 9.
Num. 3. 4. N. and Abihu died before Lord, 26. 61.
1 *Kings* 14. 20. N. son of Jeroboam reigned, 15. 25.
1 *Chr.* 2. 28. N. son of Shammai ‖ 30. the sons of N.
8. 30. Baal and N. the sons of Gibeon, 9. 36.

NAGGE.

Luke 3. 25. Esli, which was the son of N.

NAHASH.

1 *Sam.* 11. 1. N. came up against Jabesh, 12. 12.
2 *Sam.* 10. 2. then said David, I will shew kindness to Hanun the son of N. 1 *Chron.* 19. 2.
17. 25. went in to Abigail the daughter of N.
27. Shobi son of N. brought beds and basons

NAHOR.

Gen. 11. 22. Serug begat N. ‖ 29. N. wife Milcah
24. N. lived 29 years, begat Terah, 1 *Chr.* 1. 26.
26. Terah begat Abraham, N. and Haran, 27.
22. 20. behold Milcah, she hath borne children to thy brother N. 23. | 24. 15, 24.
24. 10. Abraham's servant went to the city of N.
31. 53. God of Abraham and N. judge betwixt us

NAIN.

Luke 7. 11. Jesus went into a city called N.

NAIOTH.

1 *Sam.* 19. 18. Samuel and David dwelt at N. 19. 22.
23. Saul went to N. ‖ 20. 1. David fled from N.

NAOMI.

Ruth 1. 2. the name of Elimelech's wife was N.
19. is this N.? ‖ 20. call me not N. call be Mara
2. 1. N. had a kinsman of her husband's, Boaz
4. 5. what day thou buyest the field of hand of N.
9. that I have bought all at the band of N.
17. the women said, there is a son born to N.

NAPHTALI.

Gen. 30. 8. and Rachel called his name N.
35. 25. sons of Bilhah Rachel's handmaid, Dan, N.
46. 24. sons of N. *Num.* 1. 42. | 26. 48. 1 *Chr.* 7. 13.
49. 21. N. is a hind let loose, he gives goodly words
Exod. 1. 4. the sons of Israel, N. Gad, and Asher
Num. 1. 15. of N. Ahira was prince, 2. 29. | 7. 78.
Deut. 27. 13. on mount Ebal to curse; Dan, N.
33. 23. of N. he said, O N. satisfied with favour
Josh. 19. 32. the sixth lot came out to N.
20. 7. appointed Kedesh in Galilee, in mount N.
Judg. 1. 33. nor did N. drive out the inhabitants
4. 10. Barak called Zebulun and N. to Kedesh
5. 18. Zebulun and N. jeoparded their lives
6. 35. Gideon sent messengers to N. and they came
7. 23. Israel gathered themselves together out of N.
1 *Kings* 4. 15. Ahimaaz was officer in N.
15. 20. Ben-hadad smote N. 2 *Chron.* 16. 4.
2 *Kings* 15. 29. carried N. captive to Assyria
1 *Chron.* 12. 40. N. brought bread on asses and mules
27. 19. the captain of N. was Jerimoth son of Azriel
2 *Chron.* 34. 6. Josiah in N. brake down the altars
Psal. 68. 27. there the princes of Zebulun and N.
Isa. 9. 1. he lightly afflicted the land of N.
Ezek. 48. 3. a portion for N. ‖ 34. one gate of N.
Mat. 4. 13. he dwelt in the borders of N.
15. the land of N. by the way of the sea

Tribe of NAPHTALI.

Num. 1. 43. numbered of the *tribe of* N. 53,400
10. 27. over the host of the *tribe of* N. Ahira
13. 14. of the *tribe of* N. Nahbi ‖ 34. 28. Pedahel
Josh. 19. 39. this the inheritance of the *tribe of* N.
21. 32. cities out of *tribe of* N. 1 *Chron.* 6. 62, 76.
1 *Kings* 7. 14. Hiram a widow's son of *tribe of* N.
Rev. 7. 6. of the *tribe of* N. were sealed 12,000

NATHAN.

2 *Sam.* 5. 14. son of David, N. ‖ 7. 2. N. the prophet

2 *Sam.* 7. 17. so did N. speak || 12. 1. Lord sent N. 25.
23. 36. Igal son of N. one of David's worthies
1 *Kings* 1. 10. but N. the prophet he called not
22. while she talked with David, N. came in
34. let Zadok and N. anoint him king over Israel
4. 5. Azariah son of N. was over the officers
1 *Chron.* 2. 36. Attai begat N. and N. begat Zabad
11. 38. Joel the brother of N. a valiant man
29. 29. David's acts written in the book of N.
2 *Chron.* 9. 29. acts of Solomon in the book of N.
Ezra 8. 16. I sent from Ahava for N. and Ariel
10. 39. Shelemiah, N. had taken strange wives
Zech. 12. 12. the family of the house of N. apart
Luke 3. 31. Mattatha, which was the son of N.

NATHANAEL.
John 1. 45. Philip findeth N. || 21. 2. N. of Cana

NAUM.
Luke 3. 25. Amos, which was the son of N.

NAZARENE.
Mat. 2. 23. by the prophet, he shall be called a N.

NAZARENES.
Acts 24. 5. a ring-leader of the sect of the N.

NAZARETH.
Mat. 2. 23. Joseph dwelt in a city called N.
21. 11. this is Jesus of N. *Mark* 1. 24. | 10. 47.
Luke 4. 34. | 18. 37. | 24. 19.
Mark 14. 67. thou wast also with Jesus of N.
16. 6. be not affrighted, ye seek Jesus of N.
Luke 1. 26. the angel Gabriel was sent to N.
2. 51. Jesus came to N. and was subject, 4. 16.
John 1. 45. Jesus of N. 18. 5, 7. | 19. 19. *Acts* 2. 22.
| 4. 10. | 6. 14. | 22. 8.
46. can there any good thing come out of N.?
Acts 3. 6. in the name of Jesus of N. rise up
10. 38. how God anointed Jesus of N. with power
26. 9. things contrary to the name of Jesus of N.

NEAPOLIS.
Acts 16. 11. and the next day we came to N.

NEBAIOTH.
Gen. 25. 13. the son of Ishmael, N. 1 *Chron.* 1. 29.
Isa. 60. 7. the rams of N. shall minister to thee

NEBAT. *See* JEROBOAM.

NEBO.
Num. 32. 3. Elealah and N. is a land for cattle
38. the children of Reuben built N.
Deut. 32. 49. get thee up unto mount N. 34. 1.
1 *Chron.* 5. 8. Bela dwelt in Aroer, even unto N.
Ezra 2. 29. the children of N. 10. 43.
Neh. 7. 33. the men of the other N. fifty-two
Isa. 15. 2. Moab shall howl over N. and Medeba
46. 1. N. stoopeth || *Jer.* 48. 1. woe unto N.
Jer. 48. 22. judgment is come upon Dibon and N.

NEBUCHADNEZZAR, NEBUCHADREZZAR.
2 *Kings* 24. 1. in his days N. came up against Jerusalem, 25. 1. 2 *Chron.* 36. 6. *Jer.* 39. 1. | 52. 4.
25. 22. as for the people whom N. had left
1 *Chron.* 6. 15. when the Lord carried away Judah
by N. *Jer.* 24. 1. | 29. 1. | 52. 28.
Ezra 1. 7. Cyrus brought forth the vessels which
N. had taken out of Jerusalem, 5. 14. | 6. 5.
Jer. 27. 8. the kingdom which will not serve N.
28. 11. even so will I break the yoke of N.
14. that they may serve N. king of Babylon
29. 21. I will deliver them into the hand of N.
32. 28. I will give this city into the hand of N.
39. 11. N. gave charge concerning Jeremiah
43. 10. behold, I will take N. my servant and set
49. 28. N. king of Babylon shall smite Kedar
50. 17. and last this N. hath broken his bones
51. 34. N. hath devoured me, he hath crushed me
Ezek. 26. 7. I will bring on Tyrus N. a king of kings
29. 19. I will give the land of Egypt to N. 30. 10.
Dan. 2. 1. N. dreamed || 4. 37. I N. praise and extol
3. 1. N. the king made an image of gold
19. N. was full of fury || 24. N. was astonished
4. 28. all this came upon the king N. 33.
31. at end of days I N. lift up mine eyes to heaven
5. 18. the most high God gave N. a kingdom

NEBUZAR-ADAN.
2 *Kings* 25. 8. N. captain of guard came to Jerusalem
Jer. 39. 10. N. left of the poor of the people

NEHELAMITE. *See* SHEMAIAH.

NEHEMIAH.
Ezra 2. 2. N. came with Zerubbabel, *Neh.* 7. 7.
Neh. 1. 1. the words of N. the son of Hachaliah
3. 16. N. son of Azbuk repaired after Shallum
8. 9. N. which is the Tirshatha, 10. 1.
12. 47. Israel in the days of N. gave portions

NEHUSHTAN.
2 *Kings* 18. 4. he called the brasen serpent N.

NER.
1 *Chron.* 8. 33. and N. begat Kish, 9. 36, 39.
See ABNER.

NEREUS.
Rom. 16. 15. salute Julia, N. and his sister

NERGAL.
2 *Kings* 17. 30. the men of Cuth made N. their god

NERAIAH. *See* BARUCH.

NETHANEEL.
Num. 1. 8. N. the son of Zuar was prince of Issachar, 2. 5. | 7. 18, 23. | 10. 15.
1 *Chron.* 2. 14. N. the fourth son of Jesse
15. 24. N. and Amasai blew with trumpets
24. 6. the son of N. the scribe, one of the Levites
26. 4. the sons of Obed-edom, Joah and N.
2 *Chron.* 17. 7. Jehoshaphat sent N. to teach
35. 9. N. gave to the Levites for passover-offerings
Ezra 10. 22. Ishmael, N. had taken strange wives
Neh. 12. 21. in days of Joiakim N. was priest
36. Maai and N. with the musical instruments

NETHANIAH.
2 *Kings* 25. 23. Ishmael son of N. 25. *Jer.* 40. 8. | 41. 1.
1 *Chron.* 25. 2. the sons of Asaph, Joseph and N.
12. fifth lot came forth to N. he, his sons twelve
2 *Chron.* 17. 8. he sent Levites to teach, even N.
Jer. 36. 14. princes sent the son of N. to Baruch
41. 2. Ishmael the son of N. slew Gedaliah
15. but Ishmael son of N. escaped from Johanan

NETHINIMS.
1 *Chron.* 9. 2. the first inhabitants were the N.
Ezra 2. 43. the N. went up with Zerubbabel
Ezra 2. 58. all the N. and the children of Solomon's servants were 392, *Neh.* 7. 60.
7. 7. some of the N. went to Jerusalem
24. it shall not be lawful to impose toll on the N.
8. 17. what to say to Iddo and brethren the N.
20. the N. whom David appointed for service
Neh. 3. 26. the N. dwelt in Ophel, 11. 21.
10. 28. the N. had separated from the people
11. 21. Ziha and Gispa were over the N.

NICANOR.
Acts 6. 5. they chose Stephen, Philip, and N.

NICODEMUS.
John 3. 1. N. a ruler of the Jews came to Jesus
7. 50. N. came to Jesus by night, 19. 39.

NICOLAITANS.
Rev. 2. 6. that thou hatest the deeds of the N.
15. hast them that hold the doctrine of the N.

NICOPOLIS.
Tit. 3. 12. be diligent to come unto me to N.

NIGER.
Acts 13. 1. at Antioch, Simeon who was called N.

NIMROD.
Gen. 10. 8. Cush begat N. 1 *Chron.* 1. 10.
9. as N. the mighty hunter before the Lord
Mic. 5. 6. they shall waste land of Assyria and N.

NIMSHI. *See* JEHU.

NINEVEH.
Gen. 10. 11. Asher went and builded N.
2 *Kings* 19. 36. Sennacherib dwelt at N. *Isa.* 37. 37.
Jon. 1. 2. go to N. 3. 2. || 4. 11. should not I spare N.?
3. 3. now N. was an exceeding great city
Nah. 1. 1. the burden of N. || 2. 8. N. is like a pool
3. 7. N. is laid waste, who will bemoan her?
Zeph. 2. 13. he will make N. a desolation, and dry
Mat. 12. 41. the men of N. shall rise up in judgment
and condemn this generation, *Luke* 11. 32.

NINEVITES.
Luke 11. 30. as Jonas was a sign unto the N.

NISAN.
Neh. 2. 1. in the month N. || *Esth.* 3. 7. first month N.

NISROCH.
2 *Kings* 19. 37. as he was worshipping in house of
N. his god, sons smote with the sword, *Isa.* 37. 38.

NO.
Jer. 46. 25. I will punish N. *Ezek.* 30. 14, 15, 16.
Nah. 3. 8. art thou better than populous N.

NOADIAH.
Ezra 8. 33. N. the son of Binnui, a Levite
Neh. 6. 14. my God, think on the prophetess N.

NOAH, NOE.
Gen. 5. 29. N. saying, this same shall comfort us
30. Lamech begat N. || 6. 8. N. found grace
6. 9. these are generat. of N. 10. 1, 32. 1 *Chr.* 1. 4.
7. 23. N. only remained alive, and they in the ark
8. 1. God remembered N. and every living thing
6. N. opened the window of the ark he had made
20. N. builded an altar to the Lord, and offered
9. 24. N. awoke from his wine || 29. the days of N.
Isa. 54. 9. this is as the waters of N. unto me
Ezek. 14. 14. tho' these three, N. Daniel, Job, 20.
Mat. 24. 37. as it was in the days of N. *Luke* 17. 26.
Luke 3. 36. Shem, which was the son of N.
Heb. 11. 7. by faith N. being warned of God
1 *Pet.* 3. 20. when God waited in the days of N.
2 *Pet.* 2. 5. God spared not old world, but saved N.

NOAH.
Num. 26. 33. the names of the daughters of Zelophehad were N. Tirzah, 27. 1. | 36. 11. *Josh.* 17. 3.

NOB.
1 *Sam.* 21. 1. David came to N. to Ahimelech
22. 9. Doeg said, I saw son of Jesse coming to N.
11. the king sent to call the priests in N.
19. Doeg smote N. the city of the priests
Neh. 11. 32. the children of Benjamin dwelt at N.
Isa. 10. 32. as yet shall he remain at N. that day

NOPH.
Isa. 19. 13. the princes of N. are deceived
Jer. 2. 16. the children of N. have broken the crown
46. 14. publish in N. || 19. for N. shall be waste
Ezek. 30. 13. will cause their images to cease out N.
16. and N. shall have distresses daily

NUN. *See* JOSHUA.

NYMPHAS.
Col. 4. 15. salute N. and the church in his house

O.

OBADIAH.
1 *Kings* 18. 3. Ahab called O. now O. feared the Ld.
4. O. took an hundred prophets, and hid them
7. as O. was in the way, behold Elijah met him
16. so O. went to meet Ahab, and told him
1 *Chr.* 3. 21. sons of O. || 27. 19. Ishmaiah son of O.
7. 3. son of Izrahiah, O. || 8. 38. O. s. of Azel, 9. 44.
9. 16. O. the son of Shemaiah, the son of Galal
12. 9. of Gadites men of might, O. the second
2 *Chr.* 17. 7. he sent to his princes, to O. to teach
34. 12. the overseers were Jahath and O.
Ezra 8. 9. O. son of Jehiel went up with Ezra
Neh. 10. 5. O. sealed || 12. 25. O. was a porter
Obad. 1. the vision of O. thus saith the Lord

OBED.
Ruth. 4. 17. and they called his name O.
21. Boaz begat O. 1 *Chron.* 2. 12. *Mat.* 1. 5.
1 *Chron.* 2. 37. Ephlal begat O. || 26. 7. Shemaiah
11. 47. O. one of David's valiant men
2 *Chr.* 23. 1. took Azariah son of O. into covenant
Luke 3. 32. Jesse, which was the son of O.

OBED-EDOM.
2 *Sam.* 6. 10. David carried the ark into the house
of O. 11. 1 *Chron.* 13. 13, 14.
11. Lord blessed the house of O. 12. 1 *Chr.* 13. 14.
12. David brought the ark from house of O. into
the city of David with gladness, 1 *Chr.* 15. 25.
1 *Chron.* 15. 18. O. a porter, 24. || 21. O. with harp
16. 5. O. and Jeiel with psalteries and harps
38. O. with their brethren, O. also son of Jeduthun, and Hosah, to be porters
26. 4. sons of O. 8. || 8. sons of O. fit for service
15. the lot southward fell to O. and his sons
2 *Chr.* 25. 24. Joash took the vessels found with O.

OCRAN. *See* PAGIEL.

ODED.
2 *Chron.* 15. 1. Spirit of G. came on Azariah son of O.
28. 9. a prophet of the Lord was there, called O.

OG.
Deut. 31. 4. the Lord shall do to them as he did to O.
Josh. 2. 10. for we have heard what you did to O.
13. 31. the cities of O. pertaining to Machir
1 *Kings* 4. 19. Geber was in the country of O.
See BASHAN.

OLYMPAS.
Rom. 16. 15. salute Julia, O. and all saints with them

OMEGA. *See* ALPHA, in *Appellatives.*

OMRI.
1 *Kings* 16. 16. wherefore all Israel made O. king
21. half followed O. || 25. but O. wrought evil
30. Ahab son of O. did evil in the sight of the Ld.
2 *Kings* 8. 26. Athaliah daughter of O. 2 *Chron.* 22. 2.
1 *Chron.* 7. 8. O. son of Becher || 9. 4. O. son of Imri
27. 18. O. son of Michael, ruler of Issachar
Mic. 6. 16. for statutes of O. are kept, works of Ahab

ON.
Gen. 41. 45. Poti pherah priest of O. 50. | 46. 20.
Num. 16. 1. O. the son of Peleth took men

ONAN.
Gen. 38. 4. she bare a son and called his name O.
9. O. knew that the seed should not be his
46. 12. sons of Judah, Er, O. *Num.* 26. 19. 1 *Ch.* 2. 3.
Er and O. died in the land of Canaan, *Num.* 26. 19.

ONESIMUS.
Col. 4. 9. O. a faithful and beloved brother
Philem. 10. I beseech thee for my son O.

ONESIPHORUS.
2 *Tim.* 1. 16. Lord give mercy to the house of O.
4. 19. salute Aquila and the household of O.

OPHEL.
2 *Chron.* 27. 3. Jotham built much on the wall of O.
33. 14. Manasseh compassed about O. and raised it
Neh. 3. 26. the Nethinims dwelt in O. 11. 21.
27. the Tekoites repaired to the wall of O.

OPHIR.
Gen. 10. 29. Joktan begat O. 1 *Chron.* 1. 23.
1 *Kings* 9. 28. they came to O. and fetch. from thence
gold, and brought to Solomon, 2 *Chr.* 8. 18. | 9. 10.
10. 11. brought from O. great plenty of almug-trees
22. 48. Jehoshaphat made ships to go to O. for gold
1 *Chron.* 29. 4. given 3000 talents of gold of O.
Job 22. 24. thou shalt lay up the gold of O. as stones
28. 16. wisdom not valued with the gold of O.
Psal. 45. 9. did stand the queen in gold of O.
Isa. 13. 12. a man more precious than wedge of O.

OREB.
Judg. 7. 25. they slew princes of Midian, Zeeb, O. 8. 3.
Psal. 83. 11. make their nobles like O. and Zeeb
Isa. 10. 26. slaughter of Midian at the rock of O.

ORION.
Job 9. 9. who maketh O. and Pleiades, *Amos* 5. 8.
38. 31. or canst thou loose the bands of O.?

ORNAN.
1 *Chron.* 21. 15. the threshing floor of O. 18. 28.
20. and O. turned back, and saw the angel
25. David gave to O. for the place 600 shekels

ORPAH.
Ruth 1. 4. the name of the one was O. other Ruth
14. O kissed Naomi, but Ruth clave to her

OSHEA. *See* JOSHUA.

OTHNIEL.
Josh. 15. 17. O. son of Kenaz took it, *Judg.* 1. 13.
Judg. 3. 9. Lord raised a deliverer, O. || 11. O. died
1 *Chron.* 4. 13. sons of Kenaz, O. Seraiah, sons of O
27. 15. the twelfth captain was Heldai of O.

OZEM.
1 *Chron.* 2. 15. O. was the sixth son of Jesse

OZIAS.
Mat. 1. 8. Joram begat O. || 9. O. begat Joatham

P.

PAARAI.
2 *Sam.* 23. 35. P. the Arbite, a mighty man

PADAN-ARAM.
Gen. 25. 20. Rebekah daughter of Bethuel of B.
28. 6. Isaac sent Jacob away to P. to take a wife
7. Jacob obeyed his father, and was gone to P.
31. 18. he carried away what he had gotten in P.
35. 9. G. appeared to Jacob when he came from P
26. sons which were born to him in P. 46. 15.

PAGIEL.
Num. 1. 13. P. son of Ocran, prince of Asher, 7. 72.

PALESTINA.
Exod. 15. 14. sorrow shall take hold on men of P.
Isa. 14. 29. rejoice not, thou whole P. because
31. cry, O city, thou whole P. art dissolved

PAMPHYLIA.
Acts 13. 13. Paul came from Paphos to Perga in P.
15. 38. John departed from them from P.
27. 5. when he had sailed over the sea of P.

PAPHOS.
Acts 13. 6. when they had gone thro' the isle to P.

PARAN.
Gen. 21. 21. Ishmael dwelt in the wilderness of P.
Num. 10. 12. | 12. 16. | 13. 3, 26. 1 *Sam.* 25. 1.
Deut. 33. 2. the Lord shined forth from mount P.
Hab. 3. 3. from Teman, the Holy One came from P

PARBAR.
1 *Chron.* 26. 18. porters, four at the causey, two at P

PARMENAS.
Acts 6. 5. they chose Timon, P. and Nicolas

PARTHIANS.
Acts 2. 9. P. we hear them speak in our tongues

PASHUR.
1 *Chr.* 9. 12. P. the son of Malchijah, *Neh.* 11. 12.
Ezra 2. 38. the children of P. 10. 22. *Neh.* 7. 41.
Neh. 10. 3. P. sealed || *Jer.* 20. 6. P. go into captivity
Jer. 20. 1. P. the son of Immer smote Jeremiah, 2.
3. L. called not thy name P. but Magor-missabib
21. 1. when king Zedekiah sent unto him P.
38. 1. Gedaliah the son of P. and P. the son of Malchiah heard the words Jeremiah had spoken

PATARA.
Acts 21. 1. and from Rhodes we came unto P.

PATHROS.
Isa. 11. 11. to recover remnant of his people from P.
Ezek. 29. 14. cause them return into the land of P.
30. 14. will make P. desolate, I will set fire in Zoan
PATMOS.
Rev. 1. 9. I was in the isle that is called P.
PAUL.
Acts 13. 9. then Saul, called P. filled with H. Gh.
43. many Jews and religious proselytes follow. P.
46. P. waxed bold ‖ 14. 9. the same heard P.
50. Jews raised persecution ag. P. and Barnabas
14. 12. called P. Mercurius, he was chief speaker
19. having stoned P. drew him out of the city
15. 38. P. thought not good to take him with them
40. P. chose Silas ‖ 17.10. brethr. sent P. away, 14.
16. 3. him would P. have to go forth with him
9. and a vision appeared to P. in the night
14. Lydia attended to the things spoken of P.
17. followed P. ‖ 18. but P. being grieved
25. P. and Silas prayed, and sang praises to God
28. but P. cried, saying, do thyself no harm
17. 2. P. as his manner was, went in unto them
4. some believed and consorted with P. and Silas
16. now while P. waited for them at Athens
18. 5. P. was pressed in spirit, and testified to Jews
9. the Lord spake to P. in the night by a vision
19. 11. God wrought miracles by the hands of P.
15. P. I know ‖ 23. 11. be of good cheer, P.
21. P. purposed in spirit to go to Jerusalem
26. this P. hath persuaded and turned away
20. 7. P. preached unto them, ready to depart
10. P. went down, and embracing him, said
37. they all wept sore, and fell on P. neck
21. 4. who said to P. through the Spirit, not go up
11. Agabus took P. girdle and bound his hands
18. the day following P. went in unto James
30. they took P. and drew him out of the temple
32. when they saw soldiers, they left beating P.
40. P. stood on the stairs ‖ 23. 1. P. beholding
23. 10. fearing lest P. should have been pulled
12. they would not eat till they had killed P. 14.
18. P. prayed me to bring this young man to thee
31. the soldiers brought P. to Antipatris
24. 1. who informed the governor against P.
26. that money should have been given him of P.
27. Felix left P. bound ‖ 27. 24. saying, fear not, P.
25. 19. one Jesus, whom P. affirmed to be alive
26. 24. Festus said, P. thou art beside thyself
27. 3. and Julius courteously entreated P.
33. P. besought them all to take meat, saying
43. the centurion, willing to save P. kept them
28. 16. but P. was suffered to dwell by himself
1 *Cor.* 1. 12. I am of P. 3. 4. ‖ 3. 5. who then is P.?
13. is Christ divided? was P. crucified for you?
3. 22. whether P. or Apollos, or Cephas, or world
16. 21. the salutation of me P. with mine own hand, *Col.* 4. 18. 2 *Thess.* 3. 17.
1 *Thess.* 2. 18. we would have come to you, even I P.
Philem. 9. being such a one as P. the aged
2 *Pet.* 3. 15. as our beloved brother P. wrote
PAULUS.
Acts 13. 7. a Jew Barjesus with the deputy Sergius P.
PEKAH.
2 *Kings* 15. 25. P. conspired against Pekahiah
29. in the days of P. came Tiglath-pileser
15. 30. Hoshea made a conspiracy against P.
37. against Judah came P. son of Remaliah, 16. 5.
2 *Chr.* 28. 6. P. slew in Judah 120,000 in one day
Isa. 7. 1. Rezin and P. went towards Jerusalem
PEKAHIAH.
2 *Kings* 15. 22. P. the son of Menahem reigned, 23.
PELATIAH.
1 *Chron.* 3. 21. the son of Hananiah P. of Judah
4. 42. of Simeon, having for their captain P.
Neh. 10. 22. P. and Hanan sealed the covenant
Ezek. 11. 13. that P. the son of Benaiah died
PENIEL.
Gen. 32. 30. Jacob called the name of the place P.
PENUEL.
Gen. 32. 31. as Jacob passed over P. he halted
Judg. 8. 8. Gideon went up thence to P. and spake
17. he beat down the tower of P. and slew men
1 *Kings* 12. 25. then Jeroboam went and built P.
1 *Chron.* 4. 4. P. the father of Gedor, and Ezer
8. 25. Iphedeiah and P. the sons of Shashak
PEOR.
Num. 23. 28. Balak brought Balaam to top of P.
25. 18. beguiled you in the matter of P. 31. 16.
Josh. 22. 17. is the iniquity of P. too little for us?
PERGA.
Acts 13. 13. Paul and his company came to P.
14. 25. when they had preached the word in P.
PERGAMOS.
Rev. 1. 11. send it to P. and Thyatira, and Sardis
2. 12. to the angel of the church in P. write
PERIZZITE.
Gen. 13. 7. the P. dwelled then in the land
Exod. 33. 2. and I will drive out the P. 34. 11.
Josh. 9. 1. when the P. and Hivite heard thereof
11. 3. Jabin sent to the P. and the Jebusite
PERIZZITES.
Gen. 15. 20. I have given to thy seed the land of the P. Lord made a covenant, *Exod.* 3. 8, 17. | 23. 23.
34. 30. to make me to stink among the P.
Josh. 17. 15. cut down the wood in the land of the P.
Judg. 1. 4. the Lord delivered the P. to Judah, 5.
3. 5. the children of Israel dwelt among the P.
2 *Chr.* 8. 7. Solomon made the P. to pay tribute
Ezra 9. 1. doing according to abominations of P.
PERSIA.
2 *Chron.* 36. 20. till the reign of the kingdom of P.
Esth. 1. 3. a feast to the power of P. and Media
14. the seven princes of P. which saw the king
18. the ladies of P. shall say to the king's princes
Ezek. 27. 10. they of P. and Lud were in thy army
38. 5. P. Ethiopia, and Libya with them, with shield
Dan. 8. 20. two horns are kings of Media and P.
10. 13. but the prince of P. withstood me twenty-one days; and I remained with the kings of P.
20. I will return to fight with the prince of P.
11. 2. there shall stand up yet three kings in P.
See KING.

PERSIANS. *See* MEDES.
PERSIS.
Rom. 16. 12. salute P. which laboured much in L.
PETER.
Mat. 14. 29. when P. was come down out of the ship
16. 18. I say also to thee that thou art P.
23. he said to P. get thee behind me, *Mark* 8. 33.
17. 1. he taketh P. James and John, 26. 37. *Mark* 5. 37. | 9. 2. | 14. 33. *Luke* 8. 51. | 9. 28.
24. they that received tribute-money came to P.
26. 58. P. followed him to the high priest's palace
75. P. remembered words of Jesus, *Mark* 14. 72.
Mark 16. 7. go your way, tell his disciples and P.
Luke 22. 61. the Lord turned and looked upon P.
John 1. 44. Bethsaida, the city of Andrew and P.
18. 26. being his kinsman, whose ear P. cut off
21. 17. P. was grieved because he said unto him
Acts 1. 15. in those days P. stood up in the midst
3. 3. seeing P. and John about to go into the temple
4. 8. P. filled with the Holy Ghost, said to them
13. when they saw the boldness of P. and John
5. 15. at least the shadow of P. might overshadow
8. 14. the apostles sent unto them P. and John
9. 38. the disciples had heard that P. was there
40. P. put them all forth, and kneeled down
10. 13. there came a voice, rise, P. kill and eat, 11. 7.
44. while P. spake these words, Holy Ghost fell
45. were astonished, as many as came with P.
12. 3. he proceeded further to take P. also
6. P. was sleeping between two soldiers in chains
7. the angel of the Lord smote P. on the side
13. as P. knocked at the door of the gate
18. there was no small stir what was become of P.
Gal. 1. 18. then I went up to Jerusalem to see P.
2. 7. the gospel of circumcision was committed to P.
8. for he that wrought effectually in P. to the ap.
14. I said unto P. before them all, if thou be a Jew
Simon PETER.
Mat. 4. 18. Jesus walking, saw *Simon* called P.
10. 2. the first *Simon*, who is called P. and Andrew
Mark 3. 16. to cast out devils, *Simon* he surnamed P.
Luke 5. 8. *Simon* P. fell down at Jesus' knees
6. 14. he chose *Simon*, whom he also named P.
John 13. 6. then cometh he to *Simon* P. he saith
20. 2. then she runneth and cometh to *Simon* P.
21. 15. Jesus saith to *Simon* P. *Simon* son of Jonas
Acts 10. 5. send men to Joppa, and call for one *Simon*, whose surname is P. 32. | 11. 13.
PHALEC.
Luke 3. 35. Ragau, which was the son of P.
PHARAOH.
Gen. 12. 15. princes commended Sarai before P.
17. the Lord plagued P. and his house
39. 1. Potiphar an officer of P. bought Joseph
40. 2. P. was wroth against two of his officers
13. P. shall lift up thine head and restore thee, 19.
14. make mention of me to P. and bring me out
41. 1. P. dreamed ‖ 4. so P. awoke, 7.
16. Joseph said, God shall give P. answer of peace
34. let P. do this ‖ 44. I am P. and without thee
55. people cried to P. ‖ 42. 15. by the life of P. 16.
44. 18. thou art as P. ‖ 45. 8. made me a father to P.
46. 31. Joseph said, I will go up and shew P.
47. 10. Jacob blessed P. and went out from P.
25. let us find grace, and we will be P. servants
26. only the land of the priests became not P.
50. 4. speak, I pray you, in the ears of P. saying
Exod. 2. 15. when P. heard, he sought to slay Moses
3. 10. come now, and I will send thee to P.
4. 21. see thou do all those wonders before P.
5. 2. P. said, who is the Lord that I should obey him?
15. then the officers came and cried unto P.
23. since I came to P. to speak in thy name
6. 1. now shalt thou see what I will do to P.
12. Moses spake, how then shall P. hear me? 30.
7. 1. Lord said, see, I have made thee a god to P.
3. I will harden P. heart, 13, 14, 22. | 8. 19. | 9. 12.
8. 20. stand before P. 9. 13. ‖ 9. 27. P. sent for Moses
11. 1. yet will I bring one plague more upon P.
10. Mos. and Aaron did all these wonders bef. P.
12. 29. from the first-born of P. on the throne
13. 17. when P. had let people go God led them not
14. 4. and I will be honoured upon P. 17.
28. the waters covered all the host of P.
1 *Kings* 3. 1. Solomon made affinity with P.
7. 8. Solomon made an house for P. daughter
11. 19. Hadad found favour in the sight of P.
2 *Kings* 17. 7. Lord, who brought them from under P.
18. 21. so is P. to all that trust in him, *Isa.* 36. 6.
23. 35. according to the commandment of P.
Neh. 9. 10. thou shewedst signs and wonders on P.
Psal. 135. 9. who sent tokens and wonders on P.
136. 15. but overthrew P. and his host in Red sea
Cant. 1. 9. to a company of horses in P. chariots
Isa. 19. 11. how say ye to P. I am the son of wise
30. 2. to strengthen themselves in strength of P.
3. the strength of P. shall be your shame
Jer. 25. 19. I made P. and his servants to drink
37. 11. army was broken up, for fear of P. army
46. 17. did cry, P. king of Egypt is but a noise
47. 1. word that came, before that P. smote Gaza
Ezek. 17. 17. P. with his army not make for him
29. 2. set thy face against P. king of Egypt
3. I am against thee, P. king of Egypt, 30. 22.
30. 21. I have broken the arm of P. 24. 25.
31. 18. this is P. and his multitude, saith the Lord
32. 2. son of man, take up a lamentation for P.
Acts 7. 13. Joseph's kindred made known to P.
21. P. daughter took him up and nourished him
Rom. 9. 17. for scripture saith to P. I raised thee up
Heb. 11. 24. to be called the son of P. daughter
PHARAOH-*Hophra.*
Jer. 44. 30. will give P.-*Hophra* into hand of enemies
PHARAOH-*Necho.*
2 *Kings* 23. 29. P.-*Necho* went against Assyria
33. P.-*Necho* put Jehoahaz in bands at Riblah
34. P.-*Necho* made Eliakim son of Josiah king
35. he taxed the land to give money to P.-*Necho*
Jer. 46. 2. word came to Jeremiah against P.-*Necho*
PHAREZ.
Gen. 38. 29. therefore his name was called P.

Gen. 46. 12. the sons of Judah, P. and Zerah, 1 *Chr.* 2. 4. *Mat.* 1. 3. *Luke* 3. 33. and the sons of P. were Hezron and Hamul, *Num.* 26. 20, 21. *Ruth* 4. 18. 1 *Chr.* 2. 5. | 9. 4.
Ruth 4. 12. let thy house be like the house of P.
PHARPAR. *See* ABANA.
PHEBE.
Rom. 16. 1. I commend unto you P. our sister
PHENICE.
Acts 11. 19. they travelled as far as P. and Cyprus
15. 3. Paul and Barnabas passed thro' P. and Sama.
21. 2. finding ship sailing over to P. we went aboard
27. 12. if by any means they might attain to P.
PHILADELPHIA.
Rev. 1. 11. write and send it unto P. and unto Laodic.
3. 7. to the angel of the church in P. write
PHILETUS. *See* HYMENEUS.
PHILIP.
Mat. 10. 3. P. and Bartholomew, Thomas and Matthew, *Mark* 3. 18. *Luke* 6. 14. *Acts* 1. 13.
14. 3. put John in prison for Herodias' sake his brother P. wife, *Mark* 6. 17. *Luke* 3. 19.
Luke 3. 1. his brother P. tetrarch of Iturea
John 1. 43. Jesus findeth P. and saith, follow me
44. now P. was of Bethsaida, the city of Andrew
45. P. findeth Nathanael, and saith to him
12. 21. the same came to P. and desired him
22. P. telleth Andrew, Andrew and P. told Jesus
14. 9. and yet hast thou not known me, P.?
Acts 6. 5. P. the deacon ‖ 8. 29. the Spirit said to P.
8. 5. P. went down to Samaria, and preached Christ
6. people gave heed to those things which P. spake
12. but when they believed P. preaching things
13. Simon continued with P. and wondered
30. P. ran to him, heard the eunuch read Esaias
39. the Spirit of the Lord caught away P.
21. 8. we entered into the house of P. the evangelist
PHILIPPI.
Acts 16. 12. from Neapolis we came to P. of Macedo.
20. 6. we sailed away from P. and came to Troas
1 *Thess.* 2. 2. we were shamefully entreated at P.
PHILISTIA.
Psal. 60. 8. P. triumph thou because of me
87. 4. behold P. and Tyre, this man was born there
108. 9. Moab my washpot, over P. will I triumph
PHILISTIM.
Gen. 10. 14. out of whom came P. 1 *Chron.* 1. 12.
PHILISTINE.
1 *Sam.* 17. 8. am not I a P.? ‖ 43. the P. cursed David
32. David said, thy serv. will go fight with this P.
49. David smote the P. in his forehead
21. 9. sword of Goliath the P. thou slewest is here
22. 10. he gave him the sword of Goliath the P.
2 *Sam.* 21. 17. Abishai succoured him and smote P.
PHILISTINES.
Gen. 21. 34. Abraham sojourned in the P. land
26. 14. Isaac had flocks, and the P. envied him
15. P. stopped the wells Abraham digged, 18.
Exod. 13. 17. God led them not thro' the land of P.
Josh. 13. 2. the borders of P. not yet conquered
3. from Sihor to Ekron, five lords of P. *Judg.* 3. 3.
Judg. 3. 31. Shamgar slew of the P. 600 men
10. 6. and Israel served the gods of the P.
7. he sold them into the hands of the P. 13. 1.
11. did not I deliver you from Egyptians and P.
14. 4. Samson sought an occasion against the P.
15. 3. now shall I be more blameless than the P.
6. the P. came up and burnt her and her father
11. knowest thou not that the P. are rulers over us?
20. Samson judged Israel in the days of the P.
16. 9. the P. be upon thee, Samson, 12, 14, 20.
21. the P. took Samson and put out his eyes
28. that I may be at once avenged of the P.
30. Samson said, let me die with the P. bowed him.
1 *Sam.* 4. 1. now Israel went out against the P.
3. why hath the Lord smitten us before the P.?
9. be strong, quit yourselves like men, O ye P.!
5. 1. the P. took the ark of God and brought it
6. 1. the ark was in the land of P. seven months
21. P. have brought again the ark of the Lord
7. 8. he will save us out of the hand of the P.
10. the P. drew near to battle against Israel
13. so the P. were subdued, and came no more
13. 12. the P. will come down upon me to Gilgal
20. Israelites went down to the P. to sharpen
14. 1. come, and let us go over to the P. garrison
19. noise that was in the host of the P. went on
52. was sore war against the P. all the days of Saul
17. 51. the P. saw their champion was dead
53. Israel returned from chasing after the P.
18. 17. but let the hand of the P. be on him, 21.
30. then the princes of the P. went forth
19. 8. David fought with the P. 23. 5. 2 *Sam.* 21. 15.
24. 1. Saul returned from following the P.
27. 1. than that I should escape into land of the P.
28. 15. for the P. make war against me, God depart.
29. 7. that thou displease not the lords of the P.
31. 2. P. followed hard upon Saul, 1 *Chron.* 10. 2.
9. sent into land of the P. round about to publish it
2 *Sam.* 5. 17. all the P. came up to seek David
19. shall I go up to the P.? wilt thou deliver
25. David smote the P. 8. 1. ‖ 8. 12. gold got fr. P.
23. 10. Eleazar smote the P. ‖ 12. Shammah slew P.
16. mighty men brake through the host of the P.
2 *Kings* 8. 2. the woman sojourned in land of the P.
2 *Chr.* 21. 16. stirred up against Jehoram spirit of P.
26. 7. God helped Uzziah ag. the P. and Arabians
28. 18. P. had invaded the cities of the low-country
Psal. 83. 7. the P. with the inhabitants of Tyre
Isa. 2. 6. they are soothsayers like the P.
9. 12. the Syrians before, and the P. behind
11. 14. they shall fly on the shoulders of the P.
Jer. 25. 20. the kings of the P. shall drink the cup
47. 1. the word of the Lord came against the P.
4. for the Lord will spoil the P. the remnant
Ezek. 16. 27. delivered thee to the daughters of P.
25. 15. because the P. have dealt by revenge
16. I will stretch out mine hand upon the P.
Amos 1. 8. the remnant of the P. shall perish
6. 2. then go down to Gath of the P.
9. 7. have not I brought the P. from Caphtor?
Obad. 19. they of the plain shall possess the P.

Zeph. 2. 5. O land of the P. I will destroy thee
Zech. 9. 6. I will cut off the pride of the P.
See DAUGHTERS.

PHILOLOGUS.
Rom. 16.15.salute P.Julia,and Nereus and his sister

PHINEHAS.
Exod. 6. 25. Eleazar's wife bare him P.
Num. 25. 11. P. hath turned my wrath from Israel
31. 6. Moses sent them and P. to the war
Josh. 22. 13. Israel sent P. to the Reubenites
24. 33. they buried in a hill that pertained to P.
Judg. 20. 28. P. stood before the ark in those days
1 *Sam.* 1. 3. Hophni and P. the priests were there
2. 31. Hophni and P. shall both die in one day
4. 17. thy two sons Hophni and P. are dead
19. P. wife was with child near to be delivered
14. 3. the son of P. the Lord's priest in Shiloh
1 *Chr.* 6. 4. Eleazar begat P. ‖ 50. P. begat Abishua
9. 20. P. son of Eleazar was ruler over them
Ezra 7. 5. Abishua son of P. the son of Eleazar
8. 2. of the sons of P. Gershom went up from Bab.
33. with Meremoth was Eleazar son of P.
Ps. 106. 30. then stood up P. and executed judgment

PHLEGON.
Rom. 16.14.salute Asyncritus, P.Hermas and breth.

PHRYGIA.
Acts 16. 6. when they had gone throughout P.
18. 23. Paul went over all the country of P.

PHURAH.
Judg. 7. 11. he went down with P. his servant

PHYGELLUS. *See* HERMOGENES.

PI-HAHIROTH. *See* BAAL-ZEPHON.

PILATE.
Mat. 27. 2.when they had bound him,they delivered him to Pontius P. the governor, *Mark* 15. 1.
24. when P. saw that he could prevail nothing
Mark 15. 5. so that P. marvelled, 44.
15. so P. willing to content the people released
Luke 3. 1. Pontius P. being governor of Judea
13. 1. whose blood P. had mingled with sacrifices
23. 12. same day P. and Herod were made friends
52. this man went to P. and begged the body
John 18. 29. P. then went out to them and said
33. then P. entered into the judgment-hall
19. 8. when P. heard that he was the more afraid
12. from thenceforth P. sought to release him
19. P. wrote a title, and put it on the cross
38. Joseph besought P. and P. gave him leave
Acts 3. 13. ye denied him in the presence of P.
4. 27. against Jesus Herod and P. were gathered
13. 28. yet desired they P. that he should be slain
1 *Tim.* 6.13.who before P. witnessed a good confess.

PISGAH.
Num. 23. 14. Balak brought Balaam to the top of P.
Deut. 3. 27. get thee up into the top of P. 34. 1.
4. 29. sea of the plain, under the springs of P.

PISIDIA.
Acts 13. 14. they came to Antioch in P.
14. 24. after they had passed throughout P.

PONTIUS. *See* PILATE.

PONTUS, *Acts* 2. 9.| 18. 2. 1 *Pet.* 1. 1.

PORCIUS.
Acts 24. 27. P. Festus came into Felix' room

POTIPHAR.
Gen. 37. 36. the Midianites sold Joseph to P. 39. 1.

POTI-PHERAH.
Gen. 41. 45. Asenath the daughter of P. 50.

PRISCILLA. *See* AQUILA.

PUBLIUS.
Acts 28. 8. the father of P. lay sick of a fever

PUDENS.
2 *Tim.* 4. 21. Eubulus greeteth thee and P.

PUL.
2 *Kings* 15. 19. P. king of Assyria came against Israel; Menahem gave P. 1000 talents of silver
1 *Chron.* 5. 26. God stirred up the spirit of P.
Isa. 66. 19. I will send those that escape to P.

PURPURIM. See *Appellatives.*

PUTEOLI.
Acts 28. 13. and we came the next day to P.

Q.

QUARTUS.
Rom. 16. 23. and Q. a brother saluteth you

R.

RABBAH, *or* RABBATH.
Deut. 3. 11. is it not in R. of the children of Ammon?
2 *Sam.* 11. 1. Joab and all Israel besieged R.
12. 26. Joab fought against R. and took the city
17. 27. Shobi of R. brought beds for David
1 *Chron.* 20. 1. Joab smote R. and destroyed it
Jer. 49. 2. I will cause an alarm to be heard in R.
3. cry, ye daughters of R. gird with sackcloth
Ezek. 21. 20. that the sword may come to R.
25. 5. I will make R. a stable for camels
Amos 1. 14. I will kindle a fire in the wall of R.

RAB-SHAKEH.
2 *Kings* 18. 17. the king of Assyria sent R. *Isa.* 36. 2.
37. they told him the words of R. *Isa.* 36. 22.
19. 4. God will hear the words of R. *Isa.* 37. 4.

RACHEL.
Gen. 29. 12. Jacob told R. that he was Rebekah's son
16. the name of the younger was R.
17. R. was beautiful and well-favoured
18. Jacob loved R. 30. ‖ 31. R. was barren
20. Jacob served seven years for R. 25.
28. Laban gave him R. his daughter to wife
30. 1. R. bare no children, R. envied her sister Leah
2. Jacob's anger was kindled against R. he said
22. God remembered R. and opened her womb
31. 19. R. had stolen her father's images, 34.
33. then Laban went into R. tent
33. 2. Jacob put R. and Joseph hindermost
35. 19. R. died, 48. 7. ‖ 35. 24. sons of R. 46. 19, 22.
Ruth 4. 11. the Lord make the woman like R.
1 *Sam.* 10. 2. thou shalt find two men by R. sepulchre
Jer. 31. 15. R. weeping for her children, *Mat.* 2. 18.

RAGAU.
Luke 3. 35. Saruch, which was the son of R.

RAHAB, *person, place.*
Josh. 2. 1. the spies entered into the house of R.
6. 17. only R. shall live ‖ 25. Joshua saved R.
Psal. 87. 4. I will make mention of R. and Babylon
89. 10. thou hast broken R. in pieces as one slain
Isa. 51. 9. art thou not it that hath cut R.?
Mat. 1. 5. Salmon begat Boaz of R.
Heb. 11. 31. by faith the harlot R. perished not
Jam. 2. 25. was not R. also justified by works?

RAM.
Ruth 4. 19. Pharez begat Hezron, Hezron begat R. and R. begat Amminadab, 1 *Chron.* 2. 9, 10.
1 *Chron.* 2. 25. the sons of Jerahmeel, R. Bunah
27. the sons of R. the first-born of Jerahmeel
Job 32. 2. Elihu the Buzite of the kindred of R.

RAMAH, RAMA.
Josh. 18. 25. R. a city of the tribe of Benjamin
Judg. 4. 5. Deborah dwelt between R. and Beth-el
1 *Sam.* 1. 19. Elkanah came to his house in R. 2. 11
7. 17. Samuel's return was to R. 15. 34. | 16. 13.
8. 4. all the elders came to Samuel unto R.
19. 18. so David fled, and came to Samuel to R.
22. Saul went to R. 23. ‖ 22. 6. Saul abode in R.
25. 1. Samuel was buried in his house at R. 28. 3.
1 *Kings* 15. 17. Baasha built R. 2 *Chron.* 16. 1.
21. Baasha left off building of R. 2 *Chron.* 16. 5.
2 *Kings* 8. 29. Joram went to be healed of wounds the Syrians had given him at R. 2 *Chron.* 22. 6.
Ezra 2. 26. the children of R. and Gaba six hundred and twenty-one, *Neh.* 7. 30.
Neh. 11. 33. the children of Benjamin dwelt at R.
Isa. 10. 29. R. is afraid, Gibeah of Saul is fled
Jer. 31. 15. a voice was heard in R. *Mat.* 2. 18.
Ezek. 27. 22. the merchants of R. were in Tyre
Hos. 5. 8. blow ye the trumpet in R. cry aloud

RAMOTH-GILEAD.
Deut. 4. 43. R. in Gilead of the Gadites, a city of refuge, Bezer and Golan, *Josh.* 20. 8. | 21. 38.
1 *Kings* 4. 13. the son of Geber was officer in R.
22. 3. know ye that R. is ours, and we be still
4. Ahab said to Jehoshaphat, wilt thou go with me to battle to R.? 2 *Chron.* 18. 3.
6. shall I go against R.? 15. 2 *Chron.* 18. 14.
12. saying, go up to R. and prosper, 2 *Chr.* 18. 11.
2 *Kings* 8. 28. Joram went against Hazael in R. and the Syrians wounded Joram, 2 *Chron.* 22. 5.
9. 1. Elisha said, take this box of oil, and go to R.
14. now Joram had kept R. because of Hazael
1 *Chr.* 6. 80. out of the tribe of Gad to the Levites, R.

RAPHA, and RAPHU.
Num. 13. 9. of the tribe of Benjamin, Palti son of R.
1 *Chr.* 8. 37. R. Eleasa, Azel, were the sons of Binea

REBEKAH.
Gen. 22. 23. Bethuel begat R. ‖ 24. 15. R. came out
24. 51. R. is before thee ‖ 67. Isaac took R. 25. 20.
59. they sent away R. ‖ 60. they blessed R.
25. 28. R. loved Jacob ‖ 26. 35. a grief of mind to R.
26. 7. lest men of the place should kill me for R.
27. 42. these words of Esau were told to R.
29. 12. that he was R. son ‖ 35. 8. R. nurse died
49. 31. there they buried Isaac and R. his wife
Rom. 9. 10. but when R. had conceived by Isaac

RECHAB.
2 *Sam.* 4. 2. R. the son of Rimmon, 5. ‖ 6. R. escaped
2 *Kings* 10. 15. Jehu lighted on Jehonadab son of R.
23. the son of R. went into the house of Baal
1 *Chron.* 2. 55. Hemath, father of the house of R.
Neh. 3. 14. Malchiah son of R. repaired dung-gate
Jer. 35. 6. Jonadab the son of R. commanded us
See JONADAB.

RECHABITES.
Jer. 35. 2. go to the house of the R. and speak

REHOBOAM.
1 *Kings* 11. 43. Solomon slept with his fathers, R. the son of Solomon reigned, 14. 21. 2 *Chr.* 9. 31.
12. 6. R. consulted with the old men, 2 *Chr.* 10. 6.
17. R. reigned over them, 2 *Chron.* 10. 17.
21. to bring the kingdom again to R. 2 *Chr.* 11. 1.
27. then their heart shall turn again to R.
14. 30. there was war between R. and Jerob. 15. 6.
1 *Chron.* 3 10. R. was Solomon's son, *Mat.* 1. 7.
2 *Chron.* 11. 17. they made R. strong three years
21. R. loved Maachah daughter of Absalom
22. R. made Abijah the son of Maachah the chief
13. 7. Jeroboam strengthened himself against R. when R. was young and tender-hearted

REHOBOTH.
Gen. 10. 11. Ashur went, builded Nineveh and R.
26. 22. Isaac called the name of the well R.
36. 37. Samlah died, Saul of R. reigned, 1 *Chr.* 1. 48.

REHUM.
Ezra 2. 2. R. came with Zerubbabel, *Neh.* 12. 3.
4. 8. R. the chancellor wrote against Jerusalem
17. the king sent an answer to R. and Shimshai
23. now when the letter was read before R.
Neh. 3. 17. R. the son of Bani repaired after him
10. 25. R. of chief of the people sealed the covenant

REMALIAH.
Isa. 7. 4. fear not, for the fierce anger of son of R.
5. the son of R. hath taken evil counsel
9. and the head of Samaria is R. son
8. 6. this people rejoice in Rezin and R. son

REMPHAN.
Acts 7. 43. ye took up the star of your god R.

REPHAIM.
2 *Sam.* 5. 18. the Philistines spread themselves in valley of R. 22. | 23. 13. 1 *Chr.* 11. 15. | 14. 9.
Isa. 17. 5. that gathereth ears in the valley of R.

REPHAIMS.
Gen. 14. 5. smote the R. in Ashteroth Karnaim
15. 20. to thy seed have I given the land of R.

REPHIDIM.
Exod. 17. 1. Israel pitched in R. *Num.* 33. 14.
8. Amalek came and fought with Israel in R.
19. 2. they were departed from R. *Num.* 33. 15.

REUBEN.
Gen. 29. 32. she bare a son, and called his name R.
30. 14. R. went in the days of wheat-harvest
35. 22. that R. went and lay with Bilhah
23. sons of Leah, R. Jacob's first born 46. 8. | 49. 3. *Num.* 26. 5. 1 *Chron.* 5. 1.
37. 22. R. said unto them, shed no blood
29. R. returned to the pit, Joseph was not in it
46. 9. the sons of R. *Exod.* 6. 14. *Num.* 16. 1. | 32. 1, 37. *Deut.* 11. 6. *Josh.* 4. 12. 1 *Chron.* 5. 3, 18.
48. 5. as R. and Simeon, they shall be mine
Num. 2. 10. the standard of the camp of R. 10. 18.
16. all that were numbered of the camp of R.
7. 30. Elizur prince of the children of R. did offer
32. 33. Moses gave to children of R. *Josh.* 13. 23.
Deut. 27. 13. these on mount Ebal to curse, R.
33. 6. let R. live, and let not his men be few
Josh. 15. 6. to the stone of Bohan the son of R. 18. 17.
22. 13. Israel sent to the children of R. and Gad
Judg. 5. 15. for divisions of R. great thoughts, 16.
Ezek. 48. 6. a portion for R. ‖ 31. one gate of R.

Tribe of REUBEN.
Num. 1. 5. of the *tribe of* R. Elizur was prince
21. of the *tribe of* R. were numbered 46,500
13. 4. of the *tribe of* R. Shammua to spy land
34. 14. the *tribe of* R. have received inheritance
Josh. 20. 8. out of the *tribe of* R. Gad and Manasseh the Levites had cities, 36. 1 *Chron.* 6. 63, 78.
Rev. 7. 5. of the *tribe of* R. were sealed 12,000

REUBENITES.
Num. 26. 7. these are the families of the R.
Deut. 3. 12. these cities gave I to the R. and to the Gadites, 16. | 29. 8. *Josh.* 12. 6. | 13. 8.
Josh. 1. 12. Joshua spake to the R. 22. 1.
2 *Kings* 10. 33. Hazael smote the R. and Manassites
1 *Chron.* 5. 6. Beerah was the prince of the R.
26. Tilgath-pilneser carried away R. and Gadites
11. 42. Adina a captain of the R. thirty with him
26. 32. Hashabiah and his brethren over the R.
27. 16. Eliezer son of Zichri was ruler of the R.

REZIN.
2 *Kings* 15. 37. the Lord began to send against Judah R. the king of Syria, 16. 5. *Isa.* 7. 1.
16. 6. at that time R. recovered Elath to Syria
9. the king of Assyria took Damascus and slew R.
Ezra 2. 48. the children of R. children of Nekoda and Gazzam came with Zerubbabel, *Neh.* 7. 50.
Isa. 7. 4. fear not for the fierce anger of R.
8. and the head of Damascus is R.
8. 6. forasmuch as this people rejoice in R.
9. 11. Lord shall set up the adversaries of R.

RHEGIUM.
Acts 28. 13. we set a compass and came to R.

RHESA.
Luke 3. 27. the son of Joanna, who was the son of R.

RHODA.
Acts 12. 13. a damsel came to hearken named R.

RHODES.
Acts 21. 1. the day following we came unto R.

RIMMON.
Josh. 15. 32. Shilhim, Ain, and R. cities of Judah
Judg. 20. 45. the Benjamites fled toward the wilderness, to the rock R. 47. | 21. 13.
2 *Sam.* 4. 2. Baanah and Rechab sons of R. 5, 9.
2 *Kings* 5. 18. my master goeth into the house of R.
1 *Chron.* 4. 32. the villages of Simeon were Ain, R.
6. 77. out of Zebulun was given to Merari, R.
Zech. 14. 10. the land shall be turned as a plain to R.

RIZPAH.
2 *Sam.* 3. 7. Saul had concubine whose name was R.
21. 8. David delivered two sons of R. to Gibeonites
10. R. spread sackcloth for her on the rock

ROMAN.
Acts 22. 25. is a R. 26. ‖ 27. tell me, art thou a R.?
29. after he knew that he was a R. 23. 27.

ROMANS.
John 11. 48. the R. shall come and take our place
Acts 16. 21. not lawful for us to observe, being R.
37. beaten us, being R. ‖ 38. heard they were R.
28. 17. delivered prisoner into the hands of the R.

ROME.
Acts 2. 10. strangers of R. we do hear them speak
18. 2. had commanded all Jews to depart from R.
19. 21. I must see R. ‖ 23. 11. bear witness at R.
28. 16. when we came to R. Paul dwelt by himself
Rom. 1. 7. to all that be in R. beloved of God
15. to preach the gospel to you that are at R.
2 *Tim.* 1. 17. when he was in R. he sought me out

RUFUS.
Mark 15. 21. Simon, father of Alexander and R.
Rom. 16. 13. salute R. chosen in the Ld. and mother

RUHAMAH.
Hos. 2. 1. say to your sisters, R. plead with mother

RUTH.
Ruth 1. 4. the name of the other was R.
14. R. clave to her ‖ 3. 9. who art thou? I am R.
4. 5. thou must buy it also of R. the Moabitess
10. moreover, R. have I purchased to be my wife
Mat. 1. 5. Boaz begat Obed of R. Obed begat Jesse

S.

SABEANS.
Job 1. 15. the S. fell on the oxen and asses of Job
Isa. 45. 14. merchandise of the S. shall come to thee
Ezek. 23. 42. with men of the common sort were S.
Joel 3. 8. and they shall sell them to the S.

SALATHIEL.
1 *Chron.* 3. 17. S. the son of Jechoniah, *Mat.* 1. 12.
Luke 3. 27. Zorobabel, which was the son of S.

SALEM.
Gen. 14. 18. Melchizedek king of S. brought wine
Ps. 76. 2. in S. also is his tabernacle, and in Zion
Heb. 7. 1. Melchizedek king of S. who blessed Abra.
2. being king of S. which is king of peace

SALMON.
Ruth 4. 20. Nahshon begat S. ‖ 21. S. begat Boaz, 1 *Chron.* 2. 11. *Mat.* 1. 4, 5.
Psal. 68. 14. it was white as snow in S.
Luke 3. 32. Boaz, which was the son of S.

SALMONE.
Acts 27. 7. we sailed under Crete, over-against S.

SALOME, *Mark* 15. 40. ‖ 16. 1.

SAMARIA.
1 *Kings* 13. 32. against high-places which are in S.

1 *Kings* 16. 24. Omri bought the hill S. of Shemer
20. 1. Ben-hadad besieged S. 2 *Kings* 6. 24.
10. if the dust of S. shall suffice for handfuls
17. told, saying, there are men come out of S.
22. 10. Ahab and Jehoshaphat sat on their throne in the entrance of the gate of S. 2 *Chron.* 18. 9.
38. one washed the chariot in the pool of S.
2 *Kings* 6. 20. behold, they were in the midst of S.
7. 1. barley for a shekel in the gate of S. 18.
17. 6. the king of Assyria took S. 18. 10.
18. 34. have they delivered S. out of mine hand? where are gods of Hamath and Arpad? *Isa.* 36. 19.
21. 13. I will stretch over Jerusalem the line of S.
23. 18. the bones of the prophet that came out of S.
2 *Chron.* 25. 13. soldiers fell on the cities from S.
Ezra 4. 10. the noble Asnapper set in the cities of S.
Neh. 4. 2. Sanballat spake before the army of S.
Isa. 7. 9. the head of Ephraim is S. and the head of S. is Remaliah's son, if not believe not established
8. 4. and the spoil of S. shall be taken away
9. 9. Ephraim and inhabitants of S. shall know
10. 9. is not Hamath as Arpad? S. as Damascus?
Jer. 23. 13. I have seen folly in the prophets of S.
31. 5. shall yet plant vines on the mountains of S.
41. 5. there came certain from Shechem and S.
Ezek. 16. 46. thine elder sister is S. she and daughters
51. nor hath S. committed half of thy sins
23. 4. S. is Aholah, and Jerusalem Aholibah
Hos. 7. 1. then the wickedness of S. was discovered
8. 5. thy calf, O S. hath cast thee off, anger kindled
6. but the calf of S. shall be broken in pieces
10. 5. the inhabitants of S. shall fear for the calves
7. as for S. her king is cut off as foam on water
13. 16. S. shall become desolate, she hath rebelled
Amos 3. 9. assemble yourselves on mountains of S.
4. 1. hear, ye kine of Bashan, in mountain of S.
6. 1. woe to them that trust in the mountain of S.
8. 14. they that swear by the sin of S. and say
Obad. 19. they shall possess the fields of S.
Mic. 1. 1. the word which he saw concerning S.
6. I will make S. as an heap of the field
Luke 17. 11. he passed through the midst of S.
John 4. 4. and he must needs go through S.
9. how askest drink of me, who am a woman of S.?
Acts 8. 1. were scattered through the regions of S.
5. Philip preached Christ to them of S.
14. the apostles heard that S. received the word

In SAMARIA.

1 *Kings* 16. 28. Omri buried *in* S. ‖ 22. 37. Ahab
29. Ahab reigned *in* S. ‖ 22. 51. Ahaziah *in* S.
18. 2. and there was a sore famine *in* S.
20. 34. streets in Damascus, as my father made *in* S.
21. 18. to meet Ahab king of Israel which is *in* S.
2 *Kings* 3. 1. now Jehoram began to reign *in* S.
5. 3. would God my lord were with the prophet *in* S.
6. 25. and there was a great famine *in* S.
10. 17. Jehu slew all that remained to Ahab *in* S.
13. 1. Jehoahaz reigned *in* S. ‖ 10. Jehoash
6. and there remained the grove also *in* S.
9. Jehoahaz buried *in* S. ‖ 13. Joash, 14. 16.
14. 23. Jeroboam the son of Joash reigned *in* S.
15. 8. Zechariah reigned over Israel *in* S. 13.
17. Menahem ‖ 27. Pekah ‖ 17. 1. Hoshea *in* S.
2 *Chron.* 22. 9. for Ahaziah was hid *in* S.
Amos 3. 12. so Israel be taken out that dwell *in* S.
Acts 1. 8. be witnesses to me in Judea and *in* S.
9. 31. then had the churches rest *in* S.

To or *unto* SAMARIA.

1 *Kings* 20. 43. Ahab being displeased came *to* S.
22. 37. so the king died and was brought *to* S.
2 *Kings* 2. 25. Elisha returned from Carmel *to* S.
6. 19. Elisha led them *to* S. open eyes of these men
10. 1. Jehu sent letters *to* S. ‖ 12. came *to* S. 17.
14. 14. Jehoash took all vessels in house of Lord, and took hostages, and returned *to* S. 2 *Chr.* 25. 24.
15. 14. Menahem came *to* S. and smote Shallum
17. 5. the king of Assyria went up *to* S.
2 *Chron.* 18. 2. Jehoshaphat went down *to* S.
28. 8. Israel brought the spoil of Judah *to* S.
Isa. 10. 11. as I have done *unto* S. and her idols

SAMARITAN, S.

Mat. 10. 5. into any city of the S. enter ye not
Luke 9. 52. they entered into a village of the S.
10. 33. but a certain S. came where he was
17. 16. one of them gave thanks, and he was a S.
John 4. 9. the Jews have no dealings with the S.
39. and many of the S. believed on him
8. 48. that thou art a S. and hast a devil

SAMSON.

Judg. 13. 24. the woman called his name S.
14. 1. S. went to Timnath ‖ 7. she pleased S. well
10. S. made there a feast ‖ 16. S. wife wept
15. 4. S. caught foxes ‖ 10. to bind S. are we come
16. 2. S. is come hither ‖ 3. S. lay till midnight
9. the Philistines be upon thee, S. 12, 14, 20.
23. our God hath delivered S. into our hand
25. call S. ‖ 30. S. said, let me die with Philistines
28. S. called unto the Lord ‖ 29. S. took hold
Heb. 11. 32. the time would fail me to tell of S.

SAMUEL.

1 *Sam.* 1. 20. Hannah bare a son, and called him S.
2. 18. S. ministered before the Lord ‖ 21. S. grew
3. 4. the Lord called S. he answered. 6, 8, 10.
15. and S. feared to shew Eli the vision
21. the Lord revealed himself to S. in Shiloh
4. 1. and the word of S. came to all Israel
7. 6. S. judged the children of Israel, 15.
9. S. cried to the Lord for Israel, the Lord heard
13. Lord was against Philistines all the days of S.
8. 6. displeased S. when they said, give us a king
19. the people refused to obey the voice of S.
21. and S. heard all the words of the people
9. 15. Lord told S. in his ear before Saul came
24. so Saul did eat with S. that day
26. S. called Saul to the top of the house
10. 1. S. took a vial of oil and anointed Saul
14. we came to S. ‖ 12. 11. the Lord sent S.
15. tell me, I pray thee, what S. said to you
25. then S. told the manner of the kingdom
11. 7. whosoever cometh not forth after Saul and S.
12. 18. all the people greatly feared the Lord and S.
13. 8. he tarried the set time that S. had appointed
1 *Sam.* 15. 11. it griev. S. ‖ 33. S. hewed Agag in pieces
27. as S. turned about to go away, S. mantle rent
35. nevertheless, S. mourned for Saul
16. 10. Jesse made seven of his sons to pass before S.
13. S. took the horn of oil and anointed David
19. 18. David fled and came to S. to Ramah
22. he said, where are S. and David? ‖ 25. 1. S. died
28. 11. Saul said to the woman, bring me up S.
14. Saul perceived that it was S. and bowed hims.
1 *Chr.* 6. 28. sons of S. ‖ 26. 28. all that S. had dedicat.
9. 22. whom David and S. the seer did ordain
11. 3. according to the word of the Lord by S.
2 *Chron.* 35. 18. was no passover like that from S.
Psal. 99. 6. S. among them that call on his name
Jer. 15. 1. though Moses and S. stood before me
Acts 3. 24. the prophets from S. have foretold
13. 20. gave them judges 450 years till S. prophet
Heb. 11. 32. the time would fail me to tell of S.

SANBALLAT.

Neh. 2. 10. when S. heard of it, it grieved him, 19.
4. 1. when S. heard we builded he was wroth, 7.
6. 2. S. sent to me, 5. ‖ 14. my God, think upon S.
12. for Tobiah and S. had hired him
13. 28. the son of Joiada was son-in-law to S.

SAPHIR.

Mic. 1. 11. pass ye away, thou inhabitant of S.

SAPPHIRA.

Acts 5. 1. Ananias, with S. his wife, sold a possession

SARAH.

Gen. 17. 15. not Sarai, but S. shall her name be
19. S. thy wife shall bear thee a son, 18. 14.
18. 9. where is S.? ‖ 20. 14. Abimelech restored S.
11. it ceased to be with S. after manner of women
12. S. laughed ‖ 13. wherefore did S. laugh?
20. 2. Abraham said of S. she is my sister
18. because of S. ‖ 23. 1. years of the life of S. 127
21. 1. the Lord did unto S. as he had spoken
7. that S. should have given children suck
12. in all that S. said to thee, hearken to her
23. 2. S. died ‖ 19. Abraham buried S. his wife
24. 67. Isaac brought her into his mother S. tent
25. 10. there was Abraham buried and S. 49. 31.
Num. 26. 46. name of the daughter of Asher was S.
Isa. 51. 2. look to Abraham and to S. that bare you
Rom. 4. 19. nor yet the deadness of S. womb
9. 9. at this time I will come, S. shall have a son
Heb. 11. 11. thro' faith S. received strength to concei.
1 *Pet.* 3. 6. as S. obeyed Abraham, calling him lord

SARAI.

Gen. 11. 29. the name of Abram's wife was S.
30. but S. was barren, she had no child, 16. 1.
12. 17. the Lord plagued Pharaoh because of S.
16. 6. when S. dealt hardly with Hagar, she fled
8. she said, I flee from the face of my mistress S.
17. 15. thou shalt not call her name S. but Sarah

SARDIS.

Rev. 1. 11. write and send it to S. and Philadelphia
3. 1. to the angel of the church in S. write
4. a few names in S. which have not defiled

SAREPTA.

Luke 4. 26. save to S. a city of Sidon, 1 *Kings* 17. 9.

SARON.

Acts 9. 35. and all that dwelt at S. saw him

SARUCH.

Luke 3. 35. Nachor, which was the son of S.

SATAN. See *Appellatives.*

SAUL, *called* SHAUL, 1 *Chron.* 1. 48.

Gen. 36. 37. S. of Rehoboth reigned ‖ 38. S. died
1 *Sam.* 9. 2. Kish had a son, whose name was S. 14. 51.
15. the Lord told Samuel a day before S. came
17. when Samuel saw S. ‖ 18. S. drew near to Sam.
24. set it before S. so S. did eat with Samuel
10. 11. is S. also among the prophets? 12. | 19. 24.
21. S. was taken ‖ 11. 12. shall S. reign over us?
11. 6. the Spirit of God came upon S. anger kindled
7. whosoever cometh not forth after S. and Samuel
15. people went to Gilgal, there they made S. king
13. 3. S. blew the trumpet through all the land
7. as for S. he was yet in Gilgal, and all the people
10. S. went out to meet Samuel ‖ 15. S. numbered
14. 24. for S. had injured the people, saying
35. S. built an altar ‖ 37. S. asked counsel of God
46. S. went up from following the Philistines
52. when S. saw any strong man he took him
15. 11. it repenteth me that I have set up S.
31. Samuel turned again after S. S. worshipped
35. and Samuel came no more to see S.
16. 1. Lord said, how long wilt thou mourn for S.?
2. if S. hear it ‖ 18. 6. came out to meet king S.
14. the Spirit of the Lord departed from S.
23. the evil Spir. from G. was on S. 18. 10. | 19. 9.
17. 8. am not I a Philistine, and you servants to S.?
12. Jesse went for an old man in the days of S.
19. S. and all Israel were in the valley of Elah
38. and S. armed David with his armour
18. 9. S. eyed David from that day and forward
12. S. afraid of David; Lord departed from S.
15. when S. saw that he behaved very wisely, 30.
29. S. became David's enemy continually
19. 4. Jonathan spake good of Dav. to S. his father
7. Jonathan brought David to S. he was as in times past
11. S. sent messengers to take David, 14, 15, 20.
20. 25. Abner sat by S. side ‖ 33. S. cast a javelin
21. 10. David arose and fled that day for fear of S.
11. saying, S. hath slain his thousands, 29. 5.
22. 22. I knew that he would surely tell S.
23. 11. will S. come down as thy serv. hath heard?
17. shall be king, and that S. my father knoweth
28. S. returned from pursuing after David
24. 4. David cut off the skirt of S. robe privily
7. David suffered them not to rise against S.
8. David cried after S. ‖ 22. David sware to S.
26. 4. David understood S. was come in very deed
5. and David beheld the place where S. lay
7. behold, S. lay sleeping within the trench
17. S. knew David's voice ‖ 25. S. returned
27. 1. I shall perish one day by the hand of S.
28. 9. behold, thou knowest what S. hath done
10. S. sware to her by Lord ‖ 12. for thou art S.
20. S. fell straightway all along on the earth
29. 3. is not this David servant of S. king of Israel?
1 *Sam.* 31. 2. the Philist. followed hard upon S. and his sons, and slew Jonathan, 1 *Chron.* 10. 2.
7. that S. and his sons were dead, 1 *Chron.* 10. 7.
31. 11. when inhabit. of Jabesh-gilead heard what the Philistines had done to S. 1 *Chron.* 10. 11.
2 *Sam.* 1. 6. S. leaned on his spear ‖ 21. the shield of S.
24. ye daughters of Israel, weep over S.
2. 7. be ye valiant, for your master S. is dead
3. 1. the house of S. waxed weaker and weaker
10. to translate the kingdom from house of S. and to set up the throne of David, 1 *Chron.* 12. 23.
2 *Sam.* 4. 10. one brought tidings saying, S. is dead
5. 2. in time past, when S. was king, 1 *Chron.* 11. 2.
7. 15. mercy shall not depart, as I took it from S.
9. 1. is there yet any left of the house of S.? 3.
7. I will restore thee all the land of S. thy father
12. 7. delivered thee out of the hand of S. 22. 1.
16. 8. on thee all the blood of the house of S.
21. 1. it is for S. and for his bloody house
4. will have no silver nor gold of S. nor his house
12. David took the bones of S. from men of Jabesh
1 *Chron.* 5. 10. in the days of S. they made war
10. 13. so S. died for his transgression ag. the Lord
12. 1. David kept himself close because of S.
13. 3. we inquired not at it in the days of S.
26. 28. all that Samuel and S. had dedicated
Isa. 10. 29. Ramah is afraid, Gibeah of S. is fled
Acts 7. 58. at a young man's feet whose name was S.
8. 1. and S. was consenting unto his death
3. as for S. he made havoc of the church
9. 4. S. S. why persecutest thou me? 22. 7. | 26. 14.
11. and inquire for one called S. of Tarsus
17. brother S. the Lord hath sent me, 22. 13.
22. but S. increased more in strength
24. but their laying wait was known of S.
26. when S. was come to Jerusalem, he assayed
11. 25. Barnabas went to Tarsus to seek S.
30. sent relief by the hands of Barnabas and S.
13. 1. at Antioch prophets brought up with S.
2. Holy Ghost said, separate me Barnabas and S.
7. Sergius Paulus called for Barnabas and S.
9. S. set his eyes on him, and said, O full of all
21. God gave unto them S. the son of Cis

See JONATHAN.

SCEVA.

Acts 19. 14. there were seven sons of one S. a Jew

SCYTHIAN.

Col. 3. 11. where there is neither barbarian, S.

SEBA.

Gen. 10. 7. the sons of Cush, S. and Havilah
Psal. 72. 10. the kings of Sheba and S. shall offer gifts
Isa. 43. 3. I gave Ethiopia and S. for thee

SEIR.

Gen. 32. 3. to the land of S. the country of Edom
33. 14. lead softly, till I come to my lord to S.
36. 20. these are sons of S. 21. 1 *Chron.* 1. 38.
Num. 24. 18. S. shall be a possession for enemies
Deut. 1. 44. the Amorites destroyed you in S.
33. 2. the Lord came from Sinai and rose up from S.
Judg. 5. 4. Lord, when thou wentest out of S.
2 *Chron.* 20. 23. made an end of the inhabitants of S.
25. 11. Amaziah smote of children of S. 10,000
14. he brought the gods of the children of S.
Isa. 21. 11. he calleth to me out of S. watchman
Ezek. 25. 8. because that Moab and S. do say

Mount SEIR.

Gen. 14. 6. and the Horites in their *mount* S.
36. 8. thus dwelt Esau in *mount* S. 9.
Deut. 2. 1. we compassed *mount* S. many days
5. I have given *mount* S. to Esau, *Josh.* 24. 4.
1 *Chr.* 4. 42. of sons of Simeon 500 went to *mount* S.
2 *Chr.* 20. 10. *mount* S. whom wouldst not let invade
22. the Lord set ambushments against *mount* S.
23. Ammon and Moab stood up against *mount* S.
Ezek. 35. 2. set thy face against *mount* S.
3. say to it, behold, O *mount* S. I am against thee
7. thus will I make *mount* S. most desolate, 15.

SELEUCIA.

Acts 13. 4. being sent forth, they departed unto S.

SEMEI.

Luke 3. 26. Mattathias which was the son of S.

SENNACHERIB.

2 *Kings* 18. 13. S. came up against Judah, *Isa.* 36. 1.
19. 16. see and hear the words of S. *Isa.* 37. 17.
20. thou hast prayed to me against S. *Isa.* 37. 21.
36. S. departed and dwelt at Nineveh, *Isa.* 37. 37.
2 *Chron.* 32. 22. the Lord saved Hezekiah from S.

SEPHARVAIM.

2 *Kings* 17. 24. king of Assyria brought men from S.
18. 34. where are the gods of S.? *Isa.* 36. 19.
19. 13. where is the king of S.? *Isa.* 37. 13.

SERAIAH.

2 *Sam.* 8. 17. Zadok the priest, and S. was the scribe
2 *Kings* 25. 18. the captain of the guard took S. the chief priest and Zephaniah, *Jer.* 52. 24.
23. there came to Gedaliah, S. *Jer.* 40. 8.
1 *Chron.* 4. 14. S. begat Joab ‖ 35. Josibiah son of S.
6. 14. Azariah begat S. and S. begat Jehozadak
Ezra 7. 1. Ezra the son of S. ‖ *Neh.* 10. 2. S. sealed
Neh. 11. 11. S. was ruler of the house of God
12. 1. S. the priest went up with Zerubbabel
12. the chief of the fathers of S. Meraiah
Jer. 36. 26. the king commanded S. to take Baruch
51. 59. the word which Jeremiah commanded S. the son of Neriah, this S. was a quiet prince
61. Jeremiah said to S. when comest to Babylon

SERGIUS PAULUS.

Acts 13. 7. S. Paulus a prudent man, the deputy

SETH.

Gen. 5. 3. a son after his image, and called him S.
6. S. begat Enos, 1 *Chron.* 1. 1. *Luke* 3. 38.

SHADRACH. *See* ABED-NEGO.

SHALIM.

1 *Sam.* 9. 4. S. then they passed thro' the land of S.

SHALISHA.

1 *Sam.* 9. 4. he passed through the land of S.

SHALLUM.

2 *Kings* 15. 10. S. son of Jabesh killed Zachariah
14. Menahem slew S. son of Jabesh in Samaria
22. 14. Hilkiah the priest went to Huldah the prophetess, the wife of S. 2 *Chron.* 34. 22.
1 *Chron.* 2. 40. of Judah, S. ‖ 4. 25. of Simeon, S.

1 *Chr.* 6. 12. of Levi, S. ‖ 7. 13. S. the son of Naphtali
9. 17. S. a porter, 19. ‖ 31. S. the Korahite
2 *Chron.* 28. 12. Jehizkiah the son of S. stood up
Ezra 2. 42. the children of the porters, the children of S. 10. 24. *Neh.* 7. 45. *Jer.* 35. 4.
7. 2. S. the son of Zadok, the son of Ahitub
10. 42. S. and Amariah had taken strange wives
Neh. 3. 12. next unto him repaired S. 15.
Jer. 22. 11. thus saith Lord touching S. son of Josiah
32. 7. Hanameel the son of S. thine uncle shall come

SHALMANESER.

2 *Kings* 17. 3. S. came up against Samaria, 18. 9.

SHAMGAR.

Judg. 3. 31. after him was S. the son of Anath
5. 6. in the days of S. high-ways were unoccupied

SHAMMAH.

Gen. 36. 13. the son of Reuel, S. 17. 1 *Chr.* 1. 37.
1 *Sam.* 16. 9. S. the son of Jesse, 17. 13. 1 *Chr.* 2. 13.
2 *Sam.* 23. 11. after him was S. the Hararite, 33.
25. S. the Harodite ‖ 1. *Chr.* 7. 37. son of Zophah, S.

SHAMMUAH.

Num. 13. 4. of Reuben to spy the land, S. son of Zaccur
2 *Sam.* 5. 14. S. the son of David, 1 *Chron.* 14. 4.
Neh. 11. 17. Abda son of S. dwelt at Jerusalem

SHAPHAN.

2 *Kings* 22. 3. king Josiah sent S. the scribe to repair the house of the Lord, 2 *Chron.* 34. 8.
8. Hilkiah gave the book to S. 2 *Chron.* 34. 15.
12. the king commanded Ahikam the son of S. and S. the scribe to inquire of the Lord
25. 22. Ahikam the son of S. *Jer.* 39. 14. | 40. 11.
Jer. 26. 24. the hand of son of S. was with Jeremiah
29. 3. the words Jeremiah sent by Elasah son of S.
36. 10. read in the chamber of Gemariah son of S.
Ezek. 8. 11. in the midst stood Jaazaniah son of S.

SHAPHAT.

Num. 13. 5. of the tribe of Simeon, S. to spy the land
1 *Kings* 19. 16. anoint Elisha son of S. to be prophet
2 *Kings* 6. 31. if the head of Elisha the son of S.
1 *Chron.* 3. 22. the sons of Shemaiah, Neariah, S.
5. 12. of the Gadites, S. in Bashan chief
27. 29. over the herds in valleys was S. son of Adlai

SHAREZER.

2 *Kings* 19. 37. S. his son smote him, *Isa.* 37. 38.

SHARON.

1 *Chron.* 5. 16. they dwelt in all the suburbs of S.
27. 29. over the herds that fed in S. was Shitrai
Cant. 2. 1. I am the rose of S. the lily of the valleys
Isa. 33. 9. S. is like a wilderness, Bashan and Carmel
35. 2. the excellency of Carmel and S. given thee
65. 10. S. shall be a fold of flocks and val. of Achor

SHEALTIEL. *See* ZERUBBABEL.

SHEAR-JASHUB.

Isa. 7. 3. go forth to meet Ahaz, thou and S.

SHEBA, SHEBAH.

Gen. 10. 7. son of Raamah S. ‖ 28. S. son of Joktan
25. 3. Jokshan begat S. and Dedan, 1 *Chr.* 1. 32.
26. 33. Isaac called the well S. city Beer-sheba
Josh. 19. 2. Simeon had in their inheritance S.
1 *Kings* 10. 1. when queen of S. heard of the fame of Solomon she came to prove him, 2 *Chron.* 9. 1.
1 *Chron.* 1. 9. the son of Raamah, S. ‖ 22. of Joktan
5. 13. of the children of Gad, S. and Jorai
Job 6. 19. the companies of S. waited for them
Psal. 72. 10. kings of S. and Seba shall offer gifts
15. to him shall be given of gold of S. *Isa.* 60. 6.
Jer. 6. 20. to what purpose is incense from S.?
Ezek. 27. 22. the merchants of S. thy merchants, 23.
38. 13. S. shall say, art thou come to take a spoil?
See BICHRI.

SHEBNA.

2 *Kings* 18. 18. when had called to the king there came to Rab-shakeh S. the scribe, 37. *Isa.* 36. 3.
19. 2. Hezekiah sent S. to Isaiah, *Isa.* 37. 2.
Isa. 22. 15. go, get thee to this treasurer, S.

SHECHEM.

Gen. 33. 18. Jacob came to Shalem a city of S.
19. he bought at the hand of Hamor S. father
34. 2. S. lay with Dinah ‖ 26. they slew S.
35. 4. Jacob hid them under an oak that was by S.
37. 12. went to feed their father's flock in S.
14. Joseph came from the vale of Hebron to S.
Num. 26. 31. of S. the family of the Shechemites
Josh. 17. 2. there was a lot for the children of S.
20. 7. S. in mount Ephraim, a city of refuge, and Hebron in Judah, 21. 21. 1 *Chron.* 6. 67.
24. 1. Joshua gathered all the tribes of Israel to S.
32. and the bones of Joseph buried they in S.
Judg. 8. 31. Gideon's concubine in S. bare a son
9. 1. Abimelech the son of Jerubbaal went to S.
7. Jotham cried, hearken to me, ye men of S.
20. let fire come out from the men of S.
28. who is S. ‖ 31. Gaal and brethren come to S.
41. thrust out, that they should not dwell in S.
57. the evil of the men of S. did God render
1 *Kings* 12. 1. Rehoboam went to S. 2 *Chron.* 10. 1.
25. Jeroboam built S. in mount Ephraim
1 *Chron.* 7. 19. the sons of Shemida, Ahian and S.
Psal. 60. 6. I will rejoice, I will divide S. 108. 7.
Jer. 41. 5. that there came certain from S.

SHELAH.

Gen. 38. 5. Judah's son S. ‖ 11. till S. be grown
26. because that I gave her not to S. my son
46. 12. the sons of Judah, Er, Onan, and S. *Num.* 26. 20. 1 *Chron.* 2. 3. | 4. 21.
1 *Chron.* 1. 18. Arphaxad begat S. and S. Eber, 24.

SHELEMIAH.

1 *Chron.* 26. 14. the lot eastward fell to S.
Ezra 10. 39. S. and Nathan had taken strange wives
Neh. 13. 13. I made S. the priest treasurer
Jer. 36. 14. S. son of Cushi ‖ 26. S. son of Abdeel

SHELUMIEL.

Num. 1. 6. the prince of Simeon, S. the son of Zurishaddai, 2. 12. | 7. 36. | 10. 19.

SHEM.

Gen. 5. 32. Noah begat S. 6. 10. | 10. 1. 1 *Chr.* 1. 4.
9. 23. S. took a garment and went backward
26. Noah said, blessed be the Lord God of S.
27. and he shall dwell in the tents of S.
10. 21. the children of S. 22. 31. | 11. 10. 1 *Chr.* 1. 17.
Luke 3. 36. Arphaxad, which was the son of S.

SHEMAIAH.

1 *Kings* 12. 22. the word of the Lord came to S. the man of God, 2 *Chron.* 11. 2. | 12. 7.
1 *Chron.* 4. 37. of Simeon, Shimri the son of S.
5. 4. of Reuben, S. the son of Joel
9. 14. of the Levites S. 16. | 15. 8, 11. | 24. 6. | 26. 4, 6, 7. 2 *Chron.* 17. 8. | 29. 14. | 31. 15. | 35. 9. *Ezra* 8. 16. | 10. 21, 31.
Ezra 8. 13. S. the son of Adonikam went up
Neh. 3. 29. S. keeper of the east gate, repaired
6. 10. I came to the house of S. son of Delaiah
10. 8. S. a priest sealed ‖ 12. 34. S. priest, 42.
11. 15. of the Levites, S. 12. 6, 18, 35, 36.
Jer. 26. 20. Urijah the son of S. who prophesied
29. 24. say to S. the Nehelamite, 31. 32.
36. 12. and Delaiah the son of S. a prince

SHEMINITH.

1 *Chron.* 15. 21. with harps on the S. to excel

SHENIR.

Deut. 3. 9. which Hermon the Amorites call S.
Cant. 4. 8. look from the top of S. and Hermon

SHEPHATIAH.

2 *Sam.* 3. 4. S. the fifth son of David, 1 *Chron.* 3. 3.
1 *Chron.* 9. 8. Meshullam son of S. dwelt in Jerus.
12. 5. S. the Haruphite came to David to Ziklag
27. 16. the ruler of the Simeonites was S.
Ezra 2. 4. the children of S. 372, *Neh.* 7. 9.
Jer. 38. 1. S. heard the words of Jeremiah to people

SHESHACH.

Jer. 25. 26. the king of S. shall drink after them
51. 41. how is S. taken! how is Babylon become

SHESHBAZZAR.

Ezra 1. 8. he numbered them to S. prince of Judah
11. all these did S. bring up from Babyl. to Jerus.
5. 14. delivered to S. whom he had made governor
16. S. laid the foundation of the house of God

SHIBBOLETH.

Judg. 12. 6. say now S. and he said Sibboleth

SHIGIONOTH.

Hab. 3. 1. a prayer of Habakkuk the prophet on S.

SHILOH for MESSIAH. See *Appellatives.*

SHILOH.

Josh. 18. 1. all Israel assembled together at S.
8. that I may here cast lots for you in S. 10.
22. 9. Reuben departed from Israel out of S.
Judg. 18. 31. the time that house of God was in S.
21. 12. they brought the young virgins to S.
19. there is a feast of the Lord in S. yearly
21. if the daughters of S. come out to dance
1 *Sam.* 1. 3. Elkanah went up to worship in S.
24. she brought Samuel to house of the Lord in S.
2. 14. so did the priests in S. to all the Israelites
3. 21. the Lord appeared again in S. Lord revealed
4. 3. let us fetch the ark of the Lord out of S.
12. a man came to S. with his clothes rent
14. 3. Ahiah son of Ahitub the Lord's priest in S.
1 *Kings* 2. 27. the word against the house of Eli in S.
14. 2. get thee to S. to Ahijah the prophet
4. Jeroboam's wife arose and went to S.
Psal. 78. 60. he forsook the tabernacle of S.
Jer. 7. 12. but go ye to my place which was in S.
14. I will do to this house as I have done to S.
26. 6. then will I make this house like S. 9.
41. 5. there came certain from S. and Samaria

SHILOAH.

Isa. 8. 6. this people refuseth the waters of S.

SHILONITE. *See* AHIJAH.

SHIMEAH.

2 *Sam.* 13. 3. Amnon had a friend, Jonadab son of S. David's brother, 32. | 21. 21. 1 *Chron.* 20. 7.
1 *Chron.* 3. 5. S. was born to David in Jerusalem
6. 39. Asaph son of Berachiah, the son of S.

SHIMEI.

2 *Sam.* 16. 5. S. son of Gera of Bahurim, 19. 16.
13. S. went along on the hill's side and cursed
1 *Kings* 2. 8. thou hast with thee S. who cursed me
39. that two of the servants of S. ran away
4. 18. S. the son of Elah, officer in Benjamin
1 *Chr.* 3. 19. S. son of Pedaiah ‖ 5. 4. S. son of Joel
4. 26. the sons of Mishma, Hamuel, Zaccur, S.
27. S. had sixteen sons and six daughters
6. 17. S. son of Gershom, 42. | 23. 7. ‖ 29. of Merari
23. 9. sons of S. 10. ‖ 25. 17. the tenth lot to S.
27. 27. over vineyards was S. the Ramathite
2 *Chron.* 29. 14. the sons of Heman, Jehiel and S.
31. 12. over the dedicated things was S. 13.
Ezra 10. 23. S. had taken a strange wife, 33. 38.
Esth. 2. 5. Mordecai son of Jair, the son of S.
Zech. 12. 13. the family of S. shall mourn apart

SHIMSHAI.

Ezra 4. 8. S. the scribe wrote a letter, 9.
17. the king sent an answer to S. the scribe

SHINAR.

Gen. 10. 10. Accad and Calneh in the land of S.
11. 2. that they found a plain in the land of S.
14. 1. in the days of Amraphel king of S.
Isa. 11. 11. recover remnant from S. and Hamath
Dan. 1. 2. which he carried into the land of S.
Zech. 5. 11. to build it an house in the land of S.

SHISHAK.

1 *Kings* 14. 25. in fifth year of Rehoboam S. king of Egypt came up against Jerusalem, 2 *Chr.* 12. 2.
2 *Chr.* 12. 5. to princes that were gathered together because of S. I left you in the hand of S.
7. wrath shall not be poured out on Jerus. by S.
9. S. took away the treasures of the house of Lord

SHITTIM.

Num. 25. 1. Israel abode in S. peo. began to commit
Josh. 2. 1. sent out of S. two men to spy the land
3. 1. they removed from S. and came to Jordan
Joel 3. 18. and shall water the valley of S.
Mic. 6. 5. Balaam answered him from S. to Gilgal

SHUAH.

Gen. 25. 2. Keturah bare Ishbak, S. 1 *Chron.* 1. 32.
38. 2. Judah married the daughter of a Canaanite named S. 12. 1 *Chron.* 2. 3.

SHUAL.

1 *Sam.* 13. 17. the spoilers turned to the land of S.

SHUHITE. *See* BILDAD.

SHULAMITE.

Cant. 6. 13. return, O S. what will ye see in the S.?

SHUNAMMITE.

1 *Kings* 1. 3. and they found a fair dams. Abishag a S
2. 17. that he gave me Abishag the S. to wife
22. why dost thou ask Abishag S. for Adonijah?
2 *Kings* 4. 12. call this S. 36. ‖ 25. yonder is that S.

SHUSHAN.

Neh. 1. 1. it came to pass as I was in S. the palace
Esth. 2. 8. many maidens were gathered to S.
3. 15. but the city S. was perplexed
4. 16. gather all the Jews in S. and fast for me
8. 15. the city of S. rejoiced and was glad
9. 11. number slain in S. was brought to the king
15. the Jews slew in S. three hundred men
See PALACE.

SIBMAH. *See* VINE.

SIDON, called ZIDON, 1 *Chron.* 1. 13.

Gen. 10. 15. Canaan begat S. his first-born
19. the border of the Canaanites was from S.
Judg. 18. 28. because Laish was far from S.
Mat. 11. 21. if works had been done in Tyre and S.
22. it shall be more tolerable for S. *Luke* 10. 13, 14.
15. 21. Jesus departed into the coasts of Tyre and S. behold, a woman of Canaan came, *Mark* 7. 24.
Mark 3. 8. they about Tyre and S. came, *Luke* 6. 17.
7. 31. departing from the coasts of Tyre and S.
Luke 4. 26. to none sent, save to Sarepta a city of S.
Acts 12. 20. Herod was displeased with them of S.
27. 3. and the next day we touched at S.

SIHON.

Num. 21. 23. S. would not suffer Isr. to pass thro' his border, but went out against Israel, *Judg.* 11. 20.
27. let the city of S. be built and prepared
28. a flame is gone out from the city of S.
34. do to him as thou didst to S. *Deut.* 3. 2, 6.
Deut. 2. 30. S. king of Heshbon would not let us pass
31. behold, I have begun to give S. and his land
32. S. came out against us, 29. 7. *Judg.* 11. 20.
31. 4. the Lord shall do to them as he did to S.
Josh. 9. 10. all that he did to S. king of Heshbon
Judg. 11. 21. God delivered S. into hand of Israel
Neh. 9. 22. so they possessed the land of S.
Jer. 48. 45. a flame shall come from the midst of S.

SIHON *king of the Amorites.*

Num. 21. 21. and Israel sent messengers to S. *king of the Amorites, Deut.* 2. 26. *Judg.* 11. 19.
26. Heshbon was a city of S. *king of A. Josh.* 12. 2.
29. his daughters into captivity to S. *king of Am.*
34. as thou didst to S. *king of Amorites, Deut.* 3. 2.
Deut. 1. 4. after he had slain S. *king of Amorites,* and king of Bashan, *Psal.* 135. 11. | 136. 19.
Josh. 13. 10. cities of S. *king of A.* ‖ 21. kingd. of S.
1 *Kings* 4. 19. Gebar officer in country of S. *k. of A.*

SIHOR.

Josh. 13. 3. from S. which is before Egypt to Ekron
Jer. 2. 18. in way of Egypt to drink the waters of S.

SILAS.

Acts 15. 22. sent S. chief among the brethren, 27.
34. it pleased S. to abide there still
40. Paul chose S. ‖ 16. 19. caught Paul and S.
16. 25. at midnight Paul and S. prayed and sang
29. the gaoler fell down before Paul and S.
17. 4. some of them consorted with Paul and S.
10. sent away S. by night ‖ 18. 5. when S. was come
15. receiving a commandment to S. to come

SILOAH, SILOAM.

Neh. 3. 15. Shallum repaired the wall of pool of S.
John 9. 7. Jesus said, go wash in the pool of S. 11.
Luke 13. 4. upon whom the tower in S. fell

SILVANUS.

2 *Cor.* 1. 19. was preached among you by me and S.
1 *Thess.* 1. 1. Paul, S. and Timotheus to the church of Thessalonians, grace be to you, 2 *Thess.* 1. 1.
1 *Pet.* 5. 12. by S. a faithful brother I have written

SIMEON.

Gen. 29. 33. Leah bare a son and called his name S.
34. 25. S. and Levi took each man his sword
35. 23. S. son of Leah ‖ *Exod.* 1. 2. S. son of Israel
42. 24. Joseph took from them S. ‖ 36. S. is not
43. 23. and he brought S. out unto them
46. 10. the sons of S. *Exod.* 6. 15. *Num.* 1. 22. | 26. 12. 1 *Chron.* 4. 24, 42. | 12. 25.
48. 5. as Reuben and S. they shall be mine
49. 5. S. and Levi, are brethren, they slew a man
Num. 1. 6. prince of S. was Shelumiel, 2. 12. | 7. 36.
Deut. 27. 12. S. Levi and Judah stand to bless
Josh. 19. 1. the second lot came forth to S.
9. S. had their inheritance within Judah
Judg. 1. 3. S. went with Judah ‖ 17. Judah with S.
2 *Chron.* 15. 9. the strangers out of S. fell to Asa
34. 6. so did Josiah in the cities of S. to Naphtali
Ezek. 48. 24. S. have a portion ‖ 33. one gate of S.
Luke 2. 25. a man in Jerusalem, whose name was S.
34. S. blessed Joseph and Mary, and said to Mary
3. 30. Levi, which was the son of S.
Acts 13. 1. at Antioch, S. that was called Niger
15. 14. S. hath declared how G. did visit Gentiles

Tribe of SIMEON.

Num. 1. 23. of the *tribe of* S. numbered 59,300
2. 12. the *tribe of* S. shall pitch by Reuben
10. 19. over the host of the *tribe of* S. Shelumiel
13. 5. of the *tribe of* S. Shaphat to spy the land
34. 20. of *tribe of* S. Shemuel to divide the land
Josh. 19. 1. second lot came out for the *tribe of* S.
8. this is the inheritance of the *tribe of* S.
21. 4. Levites had out of *tribe of* S. 9. 1 *Chr.* 6. 65.
Rev. 7. 7. of the *tribe of* S. were sealed 12,000

SIMON.

Mat. 10. 4. S. the Canaanite, *Mark* 3. 18.
13. 55. his brethren James, Joses, S. *Mark* 6. 3.
16. 17. Jesus said, blessed art thou, S. Bar-jona
17. 25. what thinkest thou, S. of whom do kings?
26. 6. in the house of S. the leper, *Mark* 14. 3.
27. 32. they found a man of Cyrene, S. by name, to bear the cross, *Mark* 15. 21. *Luke* 23. 26.
Mark 1. 29. they entered into house of S. *Luke* 4. 38.
14. 37. S. sleepest thou? couldest not thou watch.
Luke 5. 3. into one of the ships, which was S.
4. he said unto S. launch out into the deep
10. James and John who were partners with S.
6. 15. and S. called Zelotes, *Acts* 1. 13.
7. 40. S. I have somewhat to say unto thee
22. 31. S. S. Satan hath desired to have you

Luke 24. 34. the Lord is risen, and hath appea. to S.
John 1. 41. he first findeth his own brother S.
42. Jesus said, thou art S. the son of Jona
6. 71. Judas Iscariot the son of S. 12. 4. | 13. 2, 26.
21. 15. S. son of Jonas, lovest thou me? 16, 17.
Acts 8. 9. a man, S. who before time used sorcery
13. then S. himself believed also, when baptized
9. 43. it came to pass that Peter tarried many days at Joppa with one S. a tanner, 10. 6, 17, 32.
See PETER.

SIN.
Exod. 16. 1. they came unto the wilderness of S.
17. 1. Israel journeyed from S. *Num.* 33. 12.
Ezek. 30. 15. and I will pour my fury upon S.
16. S. shall have great pain, No shall be rent

SINAI.
Deut. 33. 2. the Lord came from S. unto them
Judg. 5. 5. the mountains melted, even that S.
Psal. 68. 8. S. was moved at the presence of God
17. the Lord is among them as in S. in holy place
See MOUNT.

SIRION.
Deut. 3. 9. which Hermon the Sidonians call S.
Psal. 29. 6. Lebanon and S. like a young unicorn

SISERA.
Judg. 4. 2. the captain of Jabin's host was S.
17. S. fled away on his feet || 22. S. lay dead
5. 20. the stars in their courses fought against S.
26. and with the hammer she smote S.
28. the mother of S. looked out at a window
1 *Sam.* 12. 9. he sold them into the hand of S.
Ezra 2. 53. the children of S. Nethinims went up with Zerubbabel, *Neh.* 7. 55.
Psal. 83. 9. do unto them, as to S. as to Jabin

SIVAN.
Esth. 8. 9. the third month, that is, the month S.

SMYRNA.
Rev. 1. 11. write and send to the church in S.
2. 8. to the angel of the church in S. write

SO.
2 *Kings* 17. 4. he sent messengers to S. king of Egypt

SODOM.
Gen. 13. 10. before Lord destroyed S. and Gomorrah
13. the men of S. were wicked exceedingly
14. 11. they took all the goods of S. and Gomorrah
12. they took Lot who dwelt in S. and his goods
17. the king of S. went out to meet Abram
18. 20. Lord said, because the cry of S. is great
26. if I find in S. fifty righteous, I will spare
19. 24. Lord rained upon S. fire out of heaven
Deut. 29. 23. like the overthrow of S. and Gomorrah, *Isa.* 13. 19. *Jer.* 49. 18. | 50. 40.
32. 32. their vine is of the vine of S. and Gomorrah
Isa. 1. 9. we should have been as S. like Gomorrah
10. hear the word of the Lord, ye rulers of S.
3. 9. and they shall declare their sin as S.
Jer. 23. 14. they are all of them unto me as S.
Lam. 4. 6. greater than the punishment of sin of S.
Ezek. 16. 46. thy younger sister is S. 48, 49, 55.
53. when I bring again the captivity of S.
Amos 4. 11. overthrown you, as God overthrew S.
Zeph. 2. 9. as I live, surely Moab shall be as S.
Mat. 10. 15. it shall be more tolerable for the land of S. 11. 24. *Mark* 6. 11. *Luke* 10. 12.
Luke 17. 29. the same day that Lot went out of S.
Rom. 9. 29. had left us a seed, we had been as S.
2 *Pet.* 2. 6. turning cities of S. and Gom. into ashes
Jude 7. even as S. and Gom. and cities about them
Rev. 11. 8. great city spiritually called S. and Egypt

SODOMITE.
Deut. 23. 17. there shall be no S. of the sons of Israel

SODOMITES.
1 *Kings* 14. 24. there were also S. in the land
15. 12. Asa took away the S. || 22. 46. Jehoshaphat
2 *Kings* 23. 7. Josiah brake down the houses of the S.

SOLOMON.
2 *Sam.* 5. 14. there was born to David in Jerusalem, S. 1 *Chron.* 3. 5. | 14. 4.
12. 24. he called his name S. and God loved him
1 *Kings* 1. 10. S. his brother he called not, 19, 26.
13. S. thy son shall reign after me, 17, 30.
21. I, and my son S. shall be counted offenders
34. God save king S. 39. || 43. hath made S. king
37. L. hath been with David even so be he with S.
47. God make the name of S. better than thine
51. let S. swear to me that he will not slay me
2. 1. David charged S. his son || 23. king S. sware
46. the kingdom was established in the hand of S.
3. 1. S. made affinity with Pharaoh king of Egypt
3. S. loved the Lord || 10. S. had asked this thing
5. the Lord appeared to S. 9. 2. 2 *Chron.* 1. 7. | 7. 12.
4. 22. S. provision for one day was thirty measures
29. God gave S. wisdom exceeding much, 5. 12.
34. came to hear the wisdom of S. from all kings of the earth, *Mat.* 12. 42. *Luke* 11. 31.
5. 1. Hiram king of Tyre sent his servants to S.
13. king S. raised a levy out of all Israel
6. 14. so S. built the house and finished it, 2 *Chron.* 7. 11. *Acts* 7. 47.
7. 51. so was ended all the work that S. made
8. 1. S. assembled the elders of Israel, 2 *Chron.* 5. 2.
22. S. spread forth his hands to heaven
54. when S. made an end of praying, 2 *Chron.* 7. 1.
65. S. held a feast || 9. 26. S. made a navy of ships
10. 1. when the queen of Sheba heard of the fame of S. she came to prove him, 2 *Chron.* 9. 1.
24. all the earth sought to S. 2 *Chron.* 9. 23.
11. 1. but king S. loved many strange women
2. S. clave to these in love || 4. when S. was old
5. S. went after Ashtoreth and after Milcom
6. S. did evil || 7. built for Chemosh and Molech
9. the Lord was angry with S. || 27. S. built Millo
14. Hadad the Edomite, an adversary to S.
28. S. made Jeroboam ruler over house of Joseph
40. S. sought therefore to kill Jeroboam
43. S. slept with his fathers, and was buried
12. 2. Jeroboam fled from the presence of S.
14. 26. shields of gold which S. made, 2 *Chron.* 12. 9.
2 *Kings* 21. 7. of which the Lord said to David and to S. I will put my name for ever, 2 *Chr.* 33. 7.
1 *Chron.* 22. 5. S. my son is young and tender
9. for his name shall be S. || 17. to help S.
1 *Chron.* 28. 6. S. thy son, he shall build my house
9. thou S. my son, know the God of thy fathers
11. David gave to S. the pattern of the house
29. 1. S. my son, whom God alone hath chosen
19. give to S. my son a perfect heart to keep
23. S. sat on the throne of the Lord as king
25. the Lord magnified S. exceedingly before Isr.
2 *Chr.* 2. 17. S. numbered all the strangers in Israel
3. 3. are the things wherein S. was instructed
30. 26. since time of S. not such joy in Jerusalem
Ezra 2. 55. the children of S. servants, 58. *Neh.* 7. 57, 60. | 11. 3.
Neh. 12. 45. according to the commandment of S.
13. 26. did not king S. sin by these things?
Prov. 1. 1. the proverbs of S. 10. 1. | 25. 1.
Cant. 1. 1. the song of songs which is S.
5. I am black, but comely, as the curtains of S.
3. 7. behold, his bed which is S. sixty men about it
11. behold king S. || 8. 12. S. must have a thousand
8. 11. S. had a vineyard at Baal-hamon
Jer. 52. 20. the sea S. made was carried away
Mat. 1. 6. David begat S. || 7. S. begat Roboam
6. 29. S. in all his glory, not arrayed, *Luke* 12. 27.
12. 42. a greater than S. is here, *Luke* 11. 31.
John 10. 23. and Jesus walked in S. porch
Acts 3. 11. the people ran to them to S. porch
5. 12. they were all with one accord in S. porch

SOREK.
Judg. 16. 4. Samson loved a woman in valley of S.

SOSIPATER.
Rom. 16. 21. Jason and S. my kinsmen salute you

SOSTHENES.
Acts 18. 17. the Greeks took S. and beat him
1 *Cor.* 1. 1. Paul and S. to the church at Corinth

SPAIN.
Rom. 15. 24. whensoever I take my journey into S.
28. I will come by you into S.

STACHYS.
Rom. 16. 9. salute Urbane, and S. my beloved

STEPHANAS.
1 *Cor.* 1. 16. I baptized also the household of S.
16. 15. the house of S. the first-fruits of Achaia
17. I am glad of the coming of S. and Fortunatus

STEPHEN.
Acts 6. 5. they chose S. a man full of faith, 8.
7. 59. they stoned S. calling on God, and saying
8. 2. devout men carried S. to his burial
11. 19. scattered abroad on the persecution about S.
22. 20. when the blood of thy martyr S. was shed

SUCCOTH.
Gen. 33. 17. Jacob journeyed to S. and made booths for his cattle, therefore it is called S.
Exod. 12. 37. Israel journeyed from Rameses to S.
13. 20. they took their journey from S. *Num.* 33. 5, 6.
Josh. 13. 27. Gad had in the valley, S. and Zaphon
Judg. 8. 5. Gideon said to the men of S. give bread
8. the men of Penuel answered as the men of S.
16. with them he taught the men of S.
1 *Kings* 7. 46. the king cast them in the clay-ground between S. and Zarthan, 2 *Chron.* 4. 17.
Psal. 60. 6. I will mete out the valley of S. 108. 7.

SUCCOTH-BENOTH.
2 *Kings* 17. 30. men of Babylon made S. their god

SUSANNA.
Luke 8. 3. Joanna and S. ministered to Christ

SYRIA.
Judg. 10. 6. Israel served the gods of S. and Zidon
2 *Sam.* 8. 6. David put garrisons in S. 1 *Chr.* 18. 6.
15. 8. vowed a vow while I abode at Geshur in S.
1 *Kings* 10. 29. for the kings of S. did they bring
11. 25. Rezon abhorred Israel and reigned over S.
19. 15. anoint Hazael to be king of S. 2 *Kings* 13. 3.
22. 1. continued without war between S. and Israel
2 *Kings* 5. 1. by Naaman deliverance given to S.
6. 23. the bands of S. came no more into the land
7. 5. behold, there was no man in the camp of S.
8. 13. Ld. shewed me that thou shalt be king of S.
13. 7. for the king of S. had destroyed them
17. he said, the arrow of deliverance from S.
19. but now thou shalt smite S. but thrice
16. 6. Rezin king of S. recovered Elath to S.
2 *Chron.* 18. 10. with these thou shalt push S.
24. 23. the host of S. came up against Joash
28. 23. because the gods of kings of S. help them
Isa. 7. 2. saying, S. is confederate with Ephraim
8. for head of S. is Damascus, and Rezin of Dam.
Ezek. 16. 57. reproach of the daughters of S.
27. 16. S. was thy merchant for thy wares
Hos. 12. 12. Jacob fled into the country of S.
Amos 1. 5. the people of S. shall go into captivity
Mat. 4. 24. his fame went throughout all S.
Luke 2. 2. when Cyrenius was governor of S.
Acts 15. 23. send greeting to the brethren in S.
41. he went through S. and Cilicia confirming
18. 18. sailed thence into S. 21. 3. *Gal.* 1. 21.
See KING.

SYRIAC.
Dan. 2. 4. the Chaldeans spake to the king in S.

SYRIAN.
Gen. 25. 20. Rebekah daughter of Bethuel the S. Laban the S. 28. 5. | 31. 20, 24.
Deut. 26. 5. a S. ready to perish was my father
2 *Kings* 5. 20. my master spared Naaman this S.
18. 26. speak in the S. language, *Isa.* 36. 11.
Ezra 4. 7. the writing of the letter was written in the S. tongue, and interpreted in the S. tongue
Luke 4. 27. none cleansed, saving Naaman the S.

SYRIANS.
2 *Sam.* 8. 5. when the S. of Damascus came to succour Hadadezer, David slew of S. 22,000 men
6. the S. became David's servants, 1 *Chr.* 18. 5, 6.
13. when he returned from smiting of the S.
10. 6. the Ammonites sent and hired the S.
11. if the S. be too strong for me, 1 *Chr.* 19. 12.
19. so the S. feared to help the children of Ammon any more, 1 *Chron.* 19. 19.
1 *Kings* 20. 20. the S. fled and Israel pursued them
27. Israel like little flocks, but S. filled country
29. Israel slew of the S. 100,000 in one day
22. 11. Lord saith, with these shalt thou push the S.
2 *Kings* 5. 2. the S. had taken a maid captive
6. 9. beware, for thither the S. are come down
2 *Kings* 7. 4. come, let us fall unto host of the S.
6. Lord made the host of the S. to hear a noise
10. we came to camp of the S. no man was there
8. 28. S. wounded Joram, 29. | 9. 15. 2 *Chr.* 22. 5.
13. 5. Israel went out from under the hand of S.
17. for thou shalt smite the S. in Aphek
16. 6. the S. came to Elath and dwelt there
Isa. 9. 12. the S. before, and the Philistines behind
Jer. 35. 11. to Jerusalem for fear of the army of S.
Amos 9. 7. have not I brought the S. from Kir?

SYROPHENICIAN.
Mark 7. 26. the woman was a Greek, a S. by nation

T.

TABEAL.
Isa. 7. 6. a king in midst of it, even the son of T.

TABERAH.
Num. 11. 3. he called the name of the place T.
Deut. 9. 22. at T. he provoked the Lord to wrath

TABITHA.
Acts 9. 36. was at Joppa a disciple named T.
40. Peter turning to the body, said, T. arise

TABOR.
Judg. 4. 6. Lord said, go and draw toward mount T.
12. shewed that Barak was gone up to mount T.
8. 18. what men were they whom ye slew at T.?
1 *Sam.* 10. 3. thou shalt come to the plain of T.
Ps. 89. 12. T. and Hermon shall rejoice in thy name
Jer. 46. 18. surely, as T. is among the mountains
Hos. 5. 1. because ye have been a net spread upon T.

TADMOR.
2 *Chron.* 8. 4. Solomon built T. in the wilderness

TAHAPANES, *or* TEHAPHNEHES.
Jer. 2. 16. the children of T. have broken the crown
43. 7. came to Egypt, thus came they even to T.
46. 14. publish in Noph and T. say, stand fast
Ezek. 30. 18. at T. also the day shall be darkened

TAHPENES.
1 *Kings* 11. 19. gave him the sister of T. the queen

TALITHA-CUMI.
Mark 5. 41. he said unto her, T. damsel, arise

TAMAR.
Gen. 38. 6. Judah took a wife for Er, whose name was T.
24. was told Judah, T. hath played the harlot
Ruth 4. 12. thy house like house of Pharez, whom T. bare to Judah, 1 *Chron.* 2. 4. *Mat.* 1. 3.
2 *Sam.* 13. 1. Absalom had a fair sister, named T.
2. Amnon fell sick for T. || 22. he forced T. 32.
14. 27. Absalom a daughter, whose name was T.
Ezek. 47. 19. south side southward from T.

TAMMUZ.
Ezek. 8. 14. there sat women weeping for T.

TARSHISH.
Gen. 10. 4. the sons of Javan, Elishah, T. 1 *Chr.* 1. 7.
1 *Kings* 10. 22. for the king had at sea a navy of T. with a navy of Hiram, 2 *Chron.* 9. 21.
2 *Chron.* 20. 36. joined to make ships to go to T.
37. the ships were broken and not able to go to T.
Ps. 48. 7. thou breakest ships of T. with east-wind
72. 10. the kings of T. shall bring presents
Isa. 2. 16. the day of the Lord on all the ships of T.
23. 1. howl, ye ships of T. it is laid waste, 14.
6. pass over to T. howl, ye inhabitants of the isle
10. pass through thy land, O daughter of T.
60. 9. the ships of T. shall wait for me
66. 19. I will send those that escape to T.
Jer. 10. 9. silv. spread into plates is brought from T.
Ezek. 27. 12. T. was thy merchant, with iron
25. the ships of T. did sing of thee in thy market
38. 13. the merchants of T. shall say to thee
Jonah 1. 3. Jonah rose up to flee unto T.
4. 2. therefore I fled before unto T. for I knew

TARSUS.
Acts 9. 11. inquire for one Saul of T. he prayeth
30. the brethren sent him forth to T.
11. 25. Barnabas departed to T. to seek Saul
21. 39. I am a man who am a Jew of T. 22. 3.

TARTAK.
2 *Kings* 17. 31. the Avites made T. their god

TEBETH.
Esth. 2. 16. in the tenth month, which is T.

TEKEL.
Dan. 5. 25. was written, Mene, Mene, T. Upharsin
27. T. thou art weighed in the balances

TEKOAH, *or* TEKOA.
2 *Sam.* 14. 2. Joab sent to T. to fetch a wise woman
4. when the woman of T. spake to the king, 9.
1 *Chron.* 2. 24. Abiah bare Asher the father of T.
4. 5. Asher the father of T. had two wives
2 *Chron.* 11. 6. Rehoboam built Etam and T.
20. 20. army went into the wilderness of T.
Jer. 6. 1. O Benjamin, blow the trumpet in T.
Amos 1. 1. Amos, who was among herdmen of T.

TEMA.
Gen. 25. 15. sons of Ishmael, Hadar, T. 1 *Chr.* 1. 30.
Job 6. 19. the troops of T. looked for them
Isa. 21. 14. the inhabitants of T. brought water
Jer. 25. 23. I made Dedan and T. to drink the cup

TEMAN.
Gen. 36. 11. the sons of Eliphaz were T. Omar
15. duke T. duke Kenaz, 42. 1 *Chron.* 1. 53.
Jer. 49. 7. is wisdom no more in T.? counsel perish.
20. that the Lord hath purposed against T.
Ezek. 25. 13. I will make it desolate from T.
Amos 1. 12. but I will send a fire upon T.
Obad. 9. thy mighty men O T. shall be dismayed
Hab. 3. 3. God came from T. Holy One from Paran

TEMANITE. *See* ELIPHAZ.

TERAH.
Gen. 11. 24. Nahor begat T. 1 *Chron.* 1. 26.
26. T. begat Abram, 27. *Josh.* 24. 2.
31. T. took Abram his son, and Lot, and went forth

TERAPHIM.
Judg. 17. 5. the man Micah made an ephod and T.
18. 14. in these houses is T. || 20. took the T.
Hos. 3. 4. Israel shall abide many days without T.

TERTIUS.
Rom. 16. 22. I T. who wrote this epistle, salute you

TERTULLUS.
Acts 24. 1. with a certain orator named T

Acts 24. 2. T. began to accuse Paul, saying
TETRARCH. See HEROD.
THEBEZ.
Judg. 9. 50. then went Abimelech to T. and took T.
2 Sam. 11. 21. smote Abimelech that he died in T.
THEOPHILUS.
Luke 1. 3. to write to thee, most excellent T.
Acts 1. 1. the former treatise have I made, O T.
THESSALONICA.
Acts 17. 1. at T. was a synagogue of the Jews
11. these were more noble than those of T.
27. 2. one Aristarchus of T. being with us
Phil. 4. 16. even in T. ye sent once and again
2 Tim. 4. 10. for Demas is departed unto T.
THEUDAS.
Acts 5. 36. before these days rose up T. boasting
THOMAS.
Mat. 10. 3. T. and Matthew the publican, apostles,
Mark 3. 18. Luke 6. 15. Acts 1. 13.
John 11. 16. T. said, let us go and die with him
20. 24. T. was not with them when Jesus came
26. T. was with them || 21. 2. Simon Peter and T.
27. he saith to T. reach hither thy finger
THUMMIM. See Appellatives.
THYATIRA.
Acts 16. 14. Lydia, of city of T. worshipped God
Rev. 1. 11. send it to T. || 2. 24. to you and to rest in T.
2. 18. to the angel of the church in T. write
TIBERIAS.
John 6. 1. sea of Galilee, which is the sea of T.
23. howbeit there came other boats from T.
TIBNI.
1 Kings 16. 21. half of the people followed T.
22. Omri prevailed against those that followed T.
TIGLATH-PILESER.
2 Kings 15. 29. T. came and took Ijon and Kedesh
16. 7. Ahaz sent messengers to T. king of Assyria
1 Chron. 5. 6. T. carried away Beerah captive
26. God of Israel stirred up the spirit of T.
2 Chron. 28. 20. T. came and distressed Ahaz
TIMNATH.
Gen. 38. 12. Judah went to his shearers in T.
Judg. 14. 1. Samson went down to T. saw a woman
TIMOTHEUS.
Acts 16. 1. a certain disciple there named T.
Rom. 16. 21. T. my workfellow saluteth you
1 Cor. 16. 10. if T. come || 2 Cor. 1. 1. T. our brother
2 Cor. 1. 19. who was preached even by me and T.
Phil. 2. 19. I trust in the Lord to send T. to you
1 Thess. 3. 2. we sent T. to establish and comfort you
1 Tim. 1. 2. to T. my own son, 18. 2 Tim. 1. 2.
Heb. 13. 23. our brother T. is set at liberty
TIRSHATHA.
Ezra 2. 63. T. said, they should not eat, Neh. 7. 65.
Neh. 7. 70. the T. gave gold to the treasure
10. 1. those that sealed were Nehemiah the T.
TIRZAH.
Num. 26. 33. Hoglah, Milcah, and T. daughters of
Zelophehad, 27. 1. | 36. 11. Josh. 17. 3.
Josh. 12. 24. Joshua smote the king of T.
1 Kings 14. 17. Jeroboam's wife came to T.
15. 21. Baasha dwelt and reigned in T. 33.
16. 8. Elah reigned in T. || 15. Zimri reigned in T.
17. Omri besieged T. || 23. Omri reigned in T.
2 Kings 15. 16. Menahem smote coasts from T.
Cant. 6. 4. thou art beautiful, O my love, as T.
TISHBITE. See ELIJAH.
TITUS.
2 Cor. 2. 13. I had no rest, because I found not T.
7. 6. God comforted us by the coming of T.
13. yea the more joyed we for joy of T.
14. even so our boasting which I made before T.
8. 6. we desired T. || Gal. 2. 1. I took T. with me
16. the same earnest care into the heart of T.
23. whether any inquire of T. he is my partner
12. 18. I desired T. did T. make a gain of you?
Gal. 2. 3. nor was T. compelled to be circumcised
2 Tim. 4. 10. T. is departed to Dalmatia
TOBIAH.
Ezra 2. 60. children of T. not shew father's house
Neh. 2. 10. Sanballat and T. heard, 19. | 4. 7. | 6. 1.
6. 12. T. had hired him || 14. my God, think of T.
19. and T. sent letters to put me in fear
13. 4. Eliashib the priest was allied to T.
8. I cast forth all the household-stuff of T.
TOGARMAH.
Gen. 10. 3. sons of Gomer, Riphath, T. 1 Chr. 1. 6.
Ezek. 27. 14. they of the house of T. traded
TOLA.
Gen. 46. 13. T. the son of Issachar, 1 Chron. 7. 1.
Judg. 10. 1. T. son of Puah arose to defend Israel
TOPHET. See Appellatives.
TROAS.
Acts 16. 8. passing by Mysia they came to T.
11. loosing from T. || 20. 5. tarried for us at T.
2 Cor. 2. 12. when I came to T. to preach Christ
2 Tim. 4. 13. the cloak I left at T. bring with thee
TRYPHENA, TRYPHOSA, Rom. 16. 12.
TUBAL.
Gen. 10. 2. sons of Japheth, Javan, T. 1 Chron. 1. 5.
Isa. 66. 19. I will send those that escape to T.
Ezek. 27. 13. Javan, T. they were thy merchants
32. 26. there is Meshech, T. and her multitude
38. 2. the chief prince of Meshech and T. 3. | 39. 1.
TYCHICUS.
Acts 20. 4. T. of Asia accompanied Paul
Eph. 6. 21. T. shall make known to you all things
Col. 4. 7. all my state shall T. declare unto you
2 Tim. 4. 12. and T. have I sent to Ephesus
Tit. 3. 12. when I shall send T. unto thee
TYRANNUS.
Acts 19. 9. disputing in the school of one T.
TYRE.
Josh. 19. 29. coast turneth to the strong city T.
2 Sam. 24. 7. they came to the strong hold of T.
1 Kings 7. 13. Solomon fetched Hiram out of T.
14. his father was a man of T. 2 Chron. 2. 14.
9. 12. Hiram came out from T. to see the cities
Ezra 3. 7. they gave meat and drink to them of T.
Neh. 13. 16. there dwelt men of T. also therein
Psal. 45. 12. the daughter of T. shall be there
83. 7. Philistines, with the inhabitants of T.
Ps. 87. 4. Philistia and T. || Isa. 23. 1. burden of T.
Isa. 23. 5. they shall be pained at the report of T.
8. who hath taken this counsel against T.?
15. T. shall be forgotten || 17. Lord will visit T.
Joel 3. 4. yea, what have ye to do with me, O T.?
Mat. 11. 21. works had been done in T. Luke 10. 13.
Acts 12. 20. Herod was displeased with them of T.
See KING, SIDON.
TYRUS.
Jer. 25. 22. I made all the kings of T. to drink
27. 3. send the yokes to the kings of T. and Zidon
47. 4. to cut off from T. and Zidon every helper
Ezek. 26. 2. because T. said against Jerusalem, aha
3. behold, I am against thee, O T.
27. 2. son of man, take up a lamentation for T.
32. what city like T. like the destroyed in the sea?
28. 2. son of man, say to the prince of T.
12. take up a lamentation on the king of T.
29. 18. to serve a great service against T.
Hos. 9. 13. Ephraim, as I saw T. is planted
Amos 1. 9. for three transgressions of T. and four
10. I will send a fire on the wall of T.
Zech. 9. 2. T. and Zidon, though it be very wise
3. T. build herself a strong hold, heaped up silver

U.

UCAL.
Prov. 30. 1. the man spoke to Ithiel and U.
UPHARSIN.
Dan. 5. 25. was written, Mene, Mene, Tekel, U.
UPHAZ.
Jer. 10. 9. and gold is brought from U.
Dan. 10. 5. his loins were girded with gold of U.
UR.
Gen. 11. 28. Haran died before his father in U.
15. 7. brought thee out of U. of Chaldees, Neh. 9. 7.
1 Chr. 11. 35. Eliphal the son of U. a mighty man
URI.
Exod. 31. 2. I called Bezaleel the son of U. 35. 30.
| 38. 22. 1 Chron. 2. 20. 2 Chron. 1. 5.
1 Kings 4. 19. Geber the son of U. was in Gilead
Ezra 10. 24. Shallum, Telem, and U. porters
URIAH, called URIJAH, Neh. 3. 21. | 8. 4.
2 Sam. 11. 3. is not this Bath-sheba the wife of U.?
6. send me U. || 14. sent it by U. || 21. U. is dead
12. 9. thou hast killed U. the Hittite with sword
23. 39. U. one of David's worthies, 1 Chr. 11. 41.
1 Kings 15. 5. save only in the matter of U.
Ezra 8. 33. vessels weighed by Meremoth son of U.
Neh. 3. 4. next repaired Meremoth the son of U.
Isa. 8. 2. I took faithful witnesses, U. the priest
Mat. 1. 6. David begat Solomon of the wife of U.
URIJAH.
2 Kings 16. 10. Ahaz sent U. the fashion of the altar
16. thus did U. as king Ahaz commanded
Jer. 26. 20. U. prophesied || 21. U. fled into Egypt
URIM. See Appellatives.
UZ.
Gen. 10. 23. the children of Aram; U. Hul, Gether
36. 28. children of Dishan; U. Aran, 1 Chr. 1. 42.
1 Chr. 1. 17. the sons of Shem; Lud, Aram, and U.
Job 1. 1. there was a man in land of U. named Job
Jer. 25. 20. I made the king of U. to drink the cup
Lam. 4. 21. rejoice, O daughter of Edom, in U.
UZZA, UZZAH.
2 Sam. 6. 3. U. and Ahio drave the cart, 1 Chr. 13. 7.
6. U. put forth his hand to the ark, 1 Chr. 13. 9.
8. because the Lord had made a breach upon U.
2 Kings 21. 18. Manasseh buried in garden of U.
26. Amon || 1 Chr. 6. 29. sons of Merari, Mahli, U.
1 Chron. 8. 7. he removed them, and begat U.
Ezra 2. 49. the children of U. Neh. 7. 51.
UZZIAH, called AZARIAH, OZIAS.
2 Kings 15. 13. Shallum to reign in 39th year of U.
34. Jotham did as his father U. had done
1 Chron. 6. 24. a son of Kohath, U. and Shaul
11. 44. U. the Ashterathite, a valiant man
27. 25. over the storehouses was the son of U.
2 Chron. 26. 1. all the people made U. king
8. the Ammonites gave gifts to U. and his name
18. it pertaineth not to thee, U. to burn incense
21. U. the king was a leper to the day of his death
Ezra 10. 21. U. son of Harim had taken strange wife
Neh. 11. 4. at Jerusalem dwelt Athaiah son of U.
Isa. 1. 1. saw in days of U. Hos. 1. 1. Amos 1. 1.
6. 1. in the year king U. died, I saw the Lord
Zech. 14. 5. before the earthquake in the days of U.
Mat. 1. 8. Joram begat Ozias || 9. Oz. begat Joatham
UZZIEL.
Exod. 6. 18. the sons of Kohath, Amram, Izhar, U.
Num. 3. 19. 1 Chron. 6. 2, 18. | 23. 12.
22. the sons of U. Lev. 10. 4. Num. 3. 30. 1 Chr.
15. 10. | 23. 20. | 24. 24.
1 Chron. 4. 42. of Simeon had U. for their captain
7. 7. U. son of Bela || 25. 4. U. the son of Heman
2 Chron. 29. 14. sons of Jeduthun; Shemaiah, U.
Neh. 3. 8. U. of the goldsmiths repaired next

V.

VASHTI.
Esth. 1. 9. V. the queen made a feast for women
12. queen V. refused to come at king's command
19. that V. come no more before king Ahasuerus
2. 17. the king made Esther queen instead of V.

Z.

ZACCHEUS.
Luke 19. 5. Z. make haste and come down
ZACHARIAH, ZECHARIAH.
2 Kings 14. 29. Z. son of Jeroboam reigned, 15. 8, 11.
18. 2. Abi the daughter of Z. 2 Chron. 29. 1.
1 Chron. 5. 7. chief of the Reubenites, Jeiel, Z.
9. 21. Z. of Levites, porter, 15. 18, 20, 24. | 26. 2.
37. Geder, Ahio, Z. and Mickloth
16. 5. next to Asaph, Z. || 24. 25. of Isshiah, Z.
26. 11. Z. the fourth son of Hosah
1 Chron. 26. 14. Z. son of Shelemiah, wise counsell.
27. 21. ruler in Gilead was Iddo the son of Z.
2 Chron. 17. 7. Jehoshaphat sent to Z. to teach
20. 14. on Jahaziel son of Z. came the Spirit
21. 2. Jehiel and Z. the sons of Jehoshaphat
24. 20. the Spirit of God came upon Z.
26. 5. Uzziah sought God in the days of Z.
29. 13. of the sons of Asaph, Z. sanctified himself
34. 12. Z. of the Kohathites was overseer
35. 8. Hilkiah, Z. rulers of the house of God
Ezra 5. 1. Z. the son of Iddo prophesied to the
Jews in Judah, 6. 14. Neh. 12. 16.
8. 3. of the sons of Pharosh, Z. || 11. of Bebai, Z.
10. 26. Elam, Z. || Neh. 11. 4. Z. son of Amariah
Neh. 8. 4. and on Ezra's left hand stood Z.
11. 5. Z. the son of Shiloni || 12. Z. son of Pashur
12. 35. Z. son of Jonathan || 41. Z. with trumpets
Isa. 8. 2. Z. the son of Jeberechiah and Uriah priest
Zech. 1. 1. Z. the son of Barachiah, the son of Iddo
the prophet, 7. 1. Mat. 23. 35. Luke 11. 51.
Luke 1. 5. Z. a priest of the course of Abia
13. fear not, Z. || 59. and they called him Z.
ZADOK.
2 Sam. 8. 17. Z. and Abimelech were the priests
15. 29. Z. and Abiathar carried the ark of God
35. hast thou not with thee Z. and Abiathar?
20. 25. Z. and Abiathar were priests, 1 Kings 4. 4.
1 Kings 1. 8. but Z. was not with Adonijah, 26.
45. Z. and Nathan have anointed him king
2. 35. and Z. the priest did the king put in the
room of Abiathar, 1 Chron. 29. 22.
4. 2. Azariah the son of Z. the priest
2 Kings 15. 33. Jerusha the daughter of Z. was
Jotham's mother, 2 Chron 27. 1.
1 Chron. 6. 8. Ahitub begat Z. 12. 53. | 9. 11. | 18. 16.
12. 28. Z. a young man, mighty man of valour
24. 3. both Z. of the sons of Eleazar, and Ahimelech
27. 17. of the Aaronites, Z. was captain
2 Chron. 31. 10. the chief priest of the house of Z.
Ezra 7. 2. the son of Shallum, the son of Z.
Neh. 3. 4. Z. repaired, 29. || 10. 21. Z. sealed
11. 11. of the priests, the son of Z. Meshullam
13. 13. I made Z. the scribe treasurer of treasuries
Ezek. 40. 46. these the sons of Z. 43. 19. | 44. 15.
48. 11. it shall be for priests sanctified of sons of Z.
ZALMUNNA.
Judg. 8. 5. I am pursuing after Zeba and Z.
6. the hands of Zeba and Z. in thy hand, 15.
21. and Gideon arose and slew Zeba and Z.
Psal. 83. 11. make all their princes as Zeba and Z.
ZARAH. See also ZERAH.
Gen. 38. 30. Judah's son was called Z. 46. 12.
1 Chron. 2. 4. Tamar bare Pharez and Z. Mat. 1. 3.
6. the sons of Z. Zimri, and Ethan, and Heman
ZAREPHATH.
1 Kings 17. 9. get thee to Z. || 10. he went to Z.
Obad. 20. the captivity of Israel shall possess to Z.
ZEBAH. See ZALMUNNA.
ZEBEDEE.
Mat. 4. 21. in a ship with Z. their father, mending
10. 2. now the names of the apostles, James and
John the sons of Z. 26. 37. Mark 1. 19. | 3. 17.
| 10. 35. Luke 5. 10. John 21. 2.
20. 20. came to him the mother of Z. childr. 27. 56.
Mark 1. 20. they left their father Z. in the ship
ZEBOIM.
Gen. 14. 2. king of Z. || Deut. 29. 23. overthrow of Z.
1 Sam. 13. 18. the valley of Z. to the wilderness
Neh. 11. 34. the children of Benjamin dwelt at Z.
Hos. 11. 8. Israel, how shall I set thee at Z.?
ZEBUL.
Judg. 9. 28. the son of Jerubbaal, and Z. his officer
41. Z. thrust out Gaal and his brethren
ZEBULUN.
Gen. 30. 20. Leah called his name Z.
35. 23. the sons of Leah, Reuben, Simeon, Judah, Z.
46. 14. the sons of Z. Num. 1. 30. | 26. 26.
49. 13. Z. shall dwell at the haven of the sea
Num. 1. 9. of Z. Eliab captain, 2. 7. | 7. 24. | 10. 16.
Deut. 27. 13. mount Ebal to curse; Reuben, Gad, Z.
33. 18. of Z. he said, rejoice Z. in thy going out
Josh. 19. 10. the third lot came up for Z.
Judg. 1. 30. nor did Z. drive out the inhabitants
4. 10. Barak called Z. and Naphtali to Kedesh
5. 14. and out of Z. they that handle the pen
18. Z. and Naphtali a people jeoparded their lives
6. 35. he sent messengers to Z. and they came
12. 12. Elon was buried in the country of Z.
1 Chron. 27. 19. of Z. Ishmaiah was the ruler
2 Chron. 30. 11. divers of Z. humbled themselves
Psal. 68. 27. the princes of Z. and Naphtali
Isa. 9. 1. at first he lightly afflicted the land of Z.
Ezek. 48. 26. Z. a portion || 33. one gate of Z.
Mat. 4. 13. in the borders of Z. and Nephthalim
15. the land of Z. and Nephthalim beyond Jordan
Tribe of ZEBULUN.
Num. 1. 31. numbered of the tribe of Z. 57,400
2. 7. then the tribe of Z. Eliab captain, 10. 16.
13. 10. of the tribe of Z. Gaddiel to spy the land
34. 25. prince of the tribe of Z. to divide the land
Josh. 21. 7. out of the tribe of Z. twelve cities were
given to the Levites, 34. 1 Chron. 6. 63, 77.
Rev. 7. 8. of the tribe of Z. were sealed 12,000
ZEDEKIAH.
1 Kings 22. 11. Z. made horns of iron, 2 Chr. 18. 10.
24. Z. smote Micaiah on cheek, 2 Chron. 18. 23.
2 Kings 24. 17. king of Babyl. changed his name to Z.
25. 7. they slew the sons of Z. and put out the
eyes of Z. Jer. 39. 6, 7. | 52. 10, 11.
1 Chron. 3. 15. son of Josiah, Z. || 16. Jehoiakim
2 Chron. 36. 10. he made Z. his brother king
Jer. 21. 7. I will deliver Z. and his people
29. 22. the Lord make thee like Z. and Ahab
32. 4. Z. shall not escape from the Chaldeans
5. he shall lead Z. to Babylon, there shall he be
39. 5. the army overtook Z. in the plains, 52. 8.
ZEEB. See OREB.
ZELOPHEHAD.
Num. 26. 33. Z. had no sons, but daughters, Josh. 17. 3.
27. 7. the daughters of Z. speak right, surely give
36. 11. the daughters of Z. were married
ZELOTES. See SIMON.

ZELZAH.
1 *Sam.* 10. 2. two men by Rachel's sepulchre at Z.

ZENAS.
Tit. 3. 13. bring Z. the lawyer on his journey

ZEPHANIAH.
2 *Kings* 25. 18. took Z. second priest, *Jer.* 52. 24.
1 *Chron.* 6. 36. Z. of the sons of the Kohathites
Jer. 21. 1. when Zedekiah sent Z. to Jeremiah
29. 25. thou hast sent letters in thy name to Z.
29. Z. read this letter in the ears of Jeremiah
37. 3. Z. the son of Maaseiah the priest
Zeph. 1. 1. the word came to Z. the son of Cushi
Zech. 6. 10. go into the house of Josiah son of Z.
14. the crowns shall be to Hen the son of Z.

ZERAH. *See also* ZARAH.
Gen. 36. 13. the son of Reuel, Z. 17. 1 *Chron.* 1. 37.
33. Jobab the son of Z. reigned, 1 *Chron.* 1. 44.
Num. 26. 13. of Z. the family of the Zarhites, 20.
Josh. 7. 1. the son of Zabdi, the son of Z.
22. 20. did not Achan son of Z. commit a trespass
1 *Chron.* 4. 24. sons of Simeon were Z. and Shaul
6. 21. Z. son of Iddo || 41. Ethni the son of Z.
9. 6. of the sons of Z. Jeuel dwelt in Jerusalem
2 *Chr.* 14. 9. Z. the Ethiopian came against Asa
Neh. 11. 24. Pethahiah of the children of Z.

ZERESH.
Esth. 5. 10. Haman called for Z. his wife

ZERUBBABEL.
1 *Chron.* 3. 19. the son of Pedaiah, Z. sons of Z.
Ezra 2. 2. which came up with Z. *Neh.* 12. 1.
3. 2. Z. the son of Shealtiel, 8. | 5. 2.
Neh. 12. 47. Israel in the days of Z. gave portions
Hag. 1. 1. the word of the Lord by Haggai to Z.
12. then Z. obeyed the voice of the Lord
14. the Lord stirred up the spirit of Z.
2. 4. yet now be strong, O Z. || 21. speak to Z.
Zech. 4. 6. this is the word of the Lord unto Z.
7. before Z. thou shalt become a plain
9. the hands of Z. have laid the foundation

ZERUIAH.
2 *Sam.* 2. 18. there were three sons of Z. there
3. 39. the sons of Z. be too hard for me
8. 16. Joab son of Z. over the host, 1 *Chr.* 18. 15.
16. 10. and the king said, what have I to do with you, ye sons of Z.? 19. 22.
1 *Chron.* 2. 16. whose sisters were Z. and Abigail

ZIBA.
2 *Sam.* 9. 2. art thou Z.? || 10. Z. had fifteen sons
16. 4. the king said to Z. thine are all that pertain
19. 29. I said, thou and Z. divide the land

ZIBEON.
Gen. 36. 2. Anah the daughter of Z. the Hivite, 14.
24 these are the children of Z. 1 *Chr.* 1. 40. as he fed the asses of Z. his father || 29. duke Z.

ZIDON.
Gen. 49. 13. Zebulun's border shall be to Z.
Josh. 11. 8. Israel chased them to great Z.
19. 28. Hammon and Kanah, even unto great Z.
Judg. 10. 6. Israel did evil, and served the gods of Z.
18. 28. no deliverer, because it was far from Z.
1 *Kings* 17. 9. Zarephath, which belongeth to Z.
Ezra 3. 7. they gave drink unto them of Z.
Isa. 23. 2. whom the merchants of Z. replenished
4. be thou ashamed, O Z. the sea hath spoken
12. O thou oppressed virgin, daughter of Z.
Jer. 25. 22. all the kings of Z. shall drink
27. 3. send bonds and yokes to the king of Z.
47. 4. to cut off from Tyre and Z. every helper
Ezek. 27. 8. the inhabitants of Z. thy mariners
28. 21. set thy face against Z. and prophesy against
22. and say, behold, I am against thee, O Z.
Joel 3. 4. what have ye to do with me, O Tyre and Z.
Zech. 9. 2. Tyrus and Z. though it be very wise

ZIDONIANS.
Judg. 10. 12. the Z. and Amalekites did oppress you
18. 7. they dwelt careless, after manner of the Z.
1 *Kings* 11. 1. but king Solomon loved women of Z.
33. they worshipped Ashtoreth, goddess of Z.
Ezek. 32. 30. Z. that are gone down with the slain

ZIF.
1 *Kings* 6. 1. the month Z. which is the second
37. the foundation was laid in the month Z.

ZIKLAG.
1 *Sam.* 27. 6. Achish gave Z. to David
30. 14. we burnt Z. || 2 *Sam.* 4. 10. I slew them in Z.
2 *Sam.* 1. 1. David had abode two days in Z.
1 *Chron.* 4. 30. they dwelt at Z. *Neh.* 11. 28.
12. 1. they that came to David to Z. 20.

ZILPAH.
Gen. 29. 24. Laban gave to Leah Z. for an handmaid
Gen. 30. 9. Leah gave Z. her maid to Jacob to wife
10. Z. Leah's maid bare Jacob a son, 12.
35. 26. the sons of Z. Gad and Asher, 46. 18.
37. 2. the lad was with the sons of Z.

ZIMRI.
Num. 25. 14. the Israelite that was slain was Z.
1 *Kings* 16. 9. Z. conspired against Elah, 16.
15. Z. reigned seven days in Tirzah
2 *Kings* 9. 31. had Z. peace, who slew his master?
1 *Chron.* 2. 6. the sons of Zerah Z. and Ethan
8. 36. Z. the son of Jehoadah || 9. 42. of Jarah
Jer. 25. 25. I made all the kings of Z. to drink

ZIN.
Num. 13. 21. they searched from wilderness of Z.
20. 1. congreg. came to the desert of Z. 33. 36.
27. 14. ye rebelled in the desert of Z. *Deut.* 32. 51.

ZION.
2 *Sam.* 5. 7. nevertheless, David took strong hold of Z. the same is the city of David, 1 *Chron.* 11. 5.
1 *Kings* 8. 1. the city of Dav. which is Z. 2 *Chr.* 5. 2.
Psal. 2. 6. I set my king on my holy hill of Z.
48. 12. walk about Z. and go round about her
51. 18. do good in thy good pleasure unto Z.
69. 35. for God will save Z. and build cities of Judah
87. 2. the Lord loveth the gates of Z. more than
5. be said of Z. this and that man was born there
97. 8. Z. heard and was glad, Judah rejoiced
102. 13. thou shalt arise and have mercy on Z.
16. when the Lord shall build up Z. he shall appear in his glory
126. 1. when the Lord turned the captivity of Z.
129. 5. let them be turned back that hate Z.
132. 13. the Lord hath chosen Z. he desired it
133. 3. as the dew on the mountains of Z.
137. 1. yea, we wept, when we remembered Z.
3. saying, sing us one of the songs of Z.
146. 10. the Lord shall reign, even thy God, O Z.
147. 12. praise the L. O Jerus. praise thy G. O Z.
149. 2. let the children of Z. be joyful in their King
Isa. 1. 27. Z. shall be redeemed with judgment
12. 6. cry out and shout, thou inhabitant of Z.
14. 32. that the Lord hath founded Z. and poor
33. 5. the Lord hath filled Z. with judgment
20. look on Z. || 35. 10. come to Z. with songs
34. 8. year of recompences for controversy of Z.
40. 9. O Z. that bringest good tidings, get up
41. 27. the first shall say to Z. behold them
49. 14. but Z. said, the Lord hath forsaken me
51. 3. for the Lord shall comfort Z. will comfort
11. the redeemed shall come with singing to Z.
16. and say unto Z. thou art my people
52. 1. awake, awake, put on thy strength, O Z.
7. that saith unto Z. thy God reigneth
8. when the Lord shall bring again Z.
59. 20. and the Redeemer shall come to Z.
60. 14. call thee the Z. of the holy One of Israel
62. 1. for Z. sake will I not hold my peace
64. 10. Z. is a wilderness, Jerusalem a desolation
66. 8. as soon as Z. travailed, she brought forth
Jer. 3. 14. turn, I will bring you to Z.
4. 6. set up the standard towards Z. stay not
14. 19. hast thou reject. Jud.; thy soul loathed Z.
26. 18. Z. shall be plowed like a field, *Mic.* 3. 12.
30. 17. this is Z. whom no man seeketh after
31. 6. arise ye, and let us go up to Z. to the Lord
12. they shall come and sing in the height of Z.
50. 5. they shall ask the way to Z. saying, come
51. 35. shall the inhabitant of Z. say, and my blood
Lam. 1. 4. the ways of Z. do mourn, because
17. Z. spreads forth her hands, none to comfort
4. 2. the precious sons of Z. comparable to gold
5. 18. because the mountain of Z. is desolate
Joel 2. 23. be glad, ye children of Z. and rejoice
Amos. 1. 2. he said, the Lord will roar from Z.
Mic. 3. 10. they build up Z. with blood, and Jerusalem
4. 2. for law shall go forth of Z. word from Jerusa.
11. nations that say, let our eye look upon Z.
Zech. 1. 14. I am jealous for Z. with great jealousy
17. cry, saying, the Lord shall yet comfort Z.
2. 7. deliver thyself O Z. || 8. 2. jealous for Z.
8. 3. thus saith the Lord, I am returned to Z.
9. 13. when I have raised up thy sons, O Z.
See DAUGHTER, DAUGHTERS.

In ZION.
Psal. 9. 11. sing praises to the Lord, who dwelleth *in* Z. 76. 2. *Joel* 3. 21.
65. 1. praise waiteth for thee, O God, *in* Z.
84. 7. every one *in* Z. appeareth before God
99. 2. Lord is great *in* Z. he is high above all people
102. 21. to declare the name of the Lord *in* Z.
Isa. 4. 3. that is left *in* Z. shall be called holy
10. 24. O my people that dwellest *in* Z.
28. 16. behold, I lay *in* Z. for a foundation stone, a tried stone, a precious corner-stone, 1 *Pet.* 2. 6.
30. 19. for the people shall dwell *in* Z. at Jerusalem
31. 9. saith the Lord, whose fire is *in* Z.
33. 14. the sinners *in* Z. are afraid, fearfulness hath
46. 13. I will place salvation *in* Z. for Israel
61. 3. to appoint unto them that mourn *in* Z.
Jer. 8. 19. is not Lord *in* Z.? is not her king in her?
50. 28. to declare *in* Z. the vengeance of the Lord
51. 10. let us declare *in* Z. the work of the Lord
24. all their evil that they have done *in* Z.
Lam. 2. 6. Lord caused sabbaths be forgotten *in* Z.
4. 11. the Lord hath kindled a fire *in* Z. and it hath devoured the foundations thereof
5. 11. they ravished the women *in* Z. and maids
Joel 2. 1. blow ye the trumpet *in* Z. and sound, 15.
3. 17. I am the Lord your God dwelling *in* Z.
Amos 6. 1. woe to them that are at ease *in* Z.
Rom. 9. 33. behold, I lay *in* Z. a stumbling stone

Mount ZION.
2 *Kings* 19. 31. out of Jerusalem shall go a remnant, they that escape out of *mount* Z. *Isa.* 37. 32.
Psal. 48. 2. the joy of the whole earth is *mount* Z.
11. let *mount* Z. rejoice || 78. 68. *mount* Z. he loved
74. 2. this *mount* Z. wherein thou hast dwelt
125. 1. as *mount* Z. which cannot be removed
Isa. 4. 5. on every dwelling-place of *mount* Z. a cloud
8. 18. Lord which dwelleth in *mount* Z. 18. 7.
10. 12. Lord performed his work upon *mount* Z.
24. 23. when the Lord shall reign in *mount* Z.
29. 8. fight ag. *mount* Z. || 31. 4. fight for *mount* Z.
Joel 2. 32. in *mount* Z. be deliverance, *Obad.* 17.
Obad. 21. saviours shall come up on *mount* Z.
Mic. 4. 7. Lord shall reign over them in *mount* Z.
Heb. 12. 22. but ye are come unto *mount* Z.
Rev. 14. 1. lo, a Lamb stood on the *mount* Z.

Out of ZION.
Psal. 14. 7. salvation were come *out of* Z. 53. 6.
20. 2. the Lord strengthen thee *out of* Z. 110. 2.
128. 5. the Lord shall bless thee *out of* Z. 134. 3.
135. 21. blessed be the Lord *out of* Z. who dwells
Isa. 2. 3. for *out of* Z. shall go forth the law
Jer. 9. 19. a voice of wailing is heard *out of* Z.
Joel 3. 16. the Lord also shall roar *out of* Z.
Rom. 11. 26. there shall come *out of* Z. the deliverer

ZIPPOR. *See* BALAK.

ZIPPORAH.
Exod. 2. 21. Jethro gave Moses Z. his daughter
4. 25. Z. took a sharp stone || 18. 2. Jethro took Z.

ZOAN.
Num. 13. 22. Hebron was built seven years before Z.
Psal. 78. 12. marvellous things did he in Z. 43.
Isa. 19. 11. surely the princes of Z. are fools, 13.
30. 4. for his princes were at Z. and his ambass.
Ezek. 30. 14. I will set fire in Z. and execute judgm.

ZOAR.
Gen. 14. 2. the king of Bela, which is Z. 8.
19. 22. the name of the city was called Z.
Deut. 34. 3. shewed him the city of palm-trees to Z.
Isa. 15. 5. his fugitives shall flee unto Z.
Jer. 48. 34. they uttered their voice from Z.

ZOBAH.
1 *Sam.* 14. 47. Saul fought against the kings of Z.
2 *Sam.* 8. 3. David smote Hadadezer the king of Z 1 *Kings* 11. 24. 1 *Chron.* 18. 3, 9.
23. 36. Igal son of Nathan of Z. David's worthy
1 *Kings* 11. 23. Rezon fled from the king of Z.

ZOPHAR.
Job 2. 11. Z. the Naamathite, 11. 1. | 20. 1. | 42. 9.

ZORAH.
Josh. 19. 41. coast of inheritance of Dan, was Z.
Judg. 13. 2. a certain man of Z. called Manoah
25. Spirit moved Samson between Z. and Eshtaol
16. 31. they buried Samson between Z. and Eshtaol
18. 2. the Danites sent from Z. to spy the land
8. they came unto their brethren to Z.
2 *Chron.* 11. 10. Rehoboam built Z. and Ajalon

ZOROBABEL.
Mat. 1. 12. Salathiel begat Z. || 13. Z. begat Abihud
Luke 3. 27. Rhesa, which was the son of Z.

ZUAR. *See* NATHANEEL.

ZUR.
Num. 25. 15. Cozbi the daughter of Z. was slain
31. 8. Z. a prince of Midian slain, *Josh.* 13. 21.
1 *Chron.* 8. 30. Z. the son of Gibeon, 9. 36.

ZURISHADDAI. *See* SHELUMIEL.

ZUZIMS.
Gen. 14. 5. the kings smote the Z. in Ham

A CONCORDANCE TO THE BOOKS CALLED APOCRYPHA.

AARON.
1 *Esd.* 1. 13. for their brethren the sons of A. 14.
5. 5. priests the sons of Phinees, the son of A.
2 *Esd.* 1. 3. Eleazar son of A. of the tribe of Levi
13. I gave Moses for a leader, and A. for a priest
Tob. 1. 6. I gave to the priests the children of A.
Eccl. 36. 17. hear, according to the blessing of A.
45. 6. he exalted A. an holy man like unto him
20. but he made A. more honourable, gave him
25. the inheritance of A. should be to his seed
50. 13. so were all the sons of A. in their glory
16. then shouted the sons of A. and sounded
1 *Mac.* 7. 14. a priest of the seed of A. is come
2 *Esd.* 1. 40. I will give for leaders, Nahum, A.
ABASEMENT.
Eccl. 20. 11. there is an *a.* because of glory
ABASHED.
Tob. 2. 14. I did not believe, and I was *a.* at her
Eccl. 4. 25. but be *a.* of the error of thy ignorance
ABATETH.
Wisd. 16. 24. and *a.* his strength for the benefit
Eccl. 25. 23. a wicked woman *a.* the courage
ABATED.
1 *Mac.* 5. 3. he *a.* their courage, and took spoils
11. 49. so when they saw, their courage was *a.*
ABDIAS.
2 *Esd.* 1. 39. I will give for leaders, Joel, A. Jonas
ABHOR.
Esth. 14. 15. I *a.* the bed of the uncircumcised
16. and that I *a.* it as a menstruous rag
Eccl. 11. 2. nor *a.* a man for outward appearance
13. 20. have humility, so doth the rich *a.* the poor
38. 4. he that is wise will not *a.* medicines
ABHORRED.
Jud. 9. 4. which *a.* the pollution of their blood
Eccl. 16. 8. but he *a.* them for their pride
20. 8. he that useth many words shall be *a.*
ABHORREST.
Wisd. 11. 24. thou *a.* nothing which thou hast made
ABHORRETH.
Eccl. 50. 25. there be two nations which my heart *a.*
ABIDE.
Sus. 57. she would not *a.* your wickedness
ABIDE.
2 *Esd.* 7. 42. the end where much glory doth *a.*
Jud. 15. 2. so that there was no man that durst *a.*
Wisd. 1. 5. will not *a.* when unrighteousness comes
3. 9. such as be faithful in love shall *a.* with him
Eccl. 2. 10. did any *a.* in his fear, and was forsaken?
6. 8. he will not *a.* in the day of thy trouble
11. 21. trust in the Lord, and *a.* in thy labour
12. 15. for a while, he will *a.* with thee
22. 23. *a.* stedfast to him in the time of trouble
24. 7. and in whose inheritance shall I *a.*?
28. 6. remember death, *a.* in the commandments
43. 3. and who can *a.* the burning heat thereof?
1 *Mac.* 7. 25. he was not able to *a.* their force
10. 73. thou shalt not be able to *a.* the horsemen
2 *Mac.* 7. 17. but *a.* a while, and behold his power
9. 12. when he could not *a.* his own smell
ABIDETH.
Eccl. 43. 20. it *a.* upon every gathering of water
ABILITY.
1 *Esd.* 5. 44. to set up the house, according to their *a.*
Wisd. 13. 19. for good success asketh *a.* to do
Eccl. 11. 12. wanting *a.* and full of poverty
14. 11. my son, according to thy *a.* do good
13. according to thy *a.* give to thy friend
44. 6. rich men furnished with *a.* living peaceably
ABIRON.
Eccl. 45. 18. that were on Dathan's and A. side
ABLE.
2 *Esd.* 2. 28. but they shall be *a.* to do nothing
4. 6. then I said, what man is *a.* to do that?
11. how should thy vessel be *a.* to comprehend?
7. 45. no man *a.* to save him that is destroyed
8. 47. be *a.* to love my creature more than I
9. 7. shall be *a.* to escape by his works and faith
10. 32. I have seen that I am not *a.* to express
55. as much as thine eyes be *a.* to see

2 *Esd.* 15. 17. desire to go into a city, shall not be *a.*
Jud. 6. 4. footsteps shall not be *a.* to stand before us
7. 4. the hills are not *a.* to bear their weight
Esth. 16. 3. but not being *a.* to bear abundance
Wisd. 12. 14. tyrant not *a.* to set his face against thee
13. 9. for if they were *a.* to know so much
16. 20. send bread *a.* to content every man's delight
Eccl. 7. 6. being not *a.* to take away iniquity
16. 20. and who is *a.* to conceive his ways?
41. 1. yea, to him that is yet *a.* to receive meat
43. 28. how shall we be *a.* to magnify him?
Bar. 6. 34. they are not *a.* to recompense it
41. may speak, as tho' he were *a.* to understand
64. seeing they are not *a.* to judge causes
1 *Mac.* 3. 17. how shall we be *a.* being few to fight
30. not be *a.* to bear the charges any longer
5. 40. we shall not be *a.* to withstand him
6. 3. he sought to take the city, but was not *a.*
27. neither shalt thou be *a.* to rule them
7. 25. that he was not *a.* to abide their force
10. 72. thy foot is not *a.* to stand before our face
73. shall not be *a.* to abide the horsemen
2 *Mac.* 15. 17. words *a.* to stir them up to valour
ABODE.
2 *Esd.* 3. 22. the good departed, the evil *a.* still
Jud. 10. 2. in which she *a.* in the sabbath-days
12. 7. thus she *a.* in the camp three days
2 *Mac.* 12. 27. a strong city wherein Lysias *a.*
14. 23. Nicanor *a.* in Jerusalem and did no hurt
ABOLISH.
Esth. 14. 9. they will *a.* the thing thou hast ordained
Eccl. 47. 22. he will not *a.* the posterity of his elect
1 *Mac.* 3. 42. given commandment utterly to *a.* them
ABOLISHED.
Eccl. 45. 26. that their good things be not *a.*
ABOMINABLE.
Eccl. 41. 5. the children of sinners are *a.* children
1 *Mac.* 1. 48. they should make their souls *a.*
2 *Mac.* 6. 25. get a stain to old age, and make it *a.*
ABOMINATION.
Wisd. 14. 11. because they are become an *a.*
Eccl. 1. 25. but godliness is an *a.* to a sinner
10. 13. he that hath pride shall pour out *a.*
17. 26. and hate thou *a.* vehemently
19. 23. there is a wickedness, and the same an *a.*
1 *Mac.* 1. 54. they set up the *a.* of desolation
6. 7. they pulled down the *a.* which he had set up
2 *Mac.* 5. 8. being had in *a.* as an open enemy
6. 19. than to live stained with such an *a.*
ABOMINATIONS.
1 *Esd.* 7. 13. had separated from the *a.* of the people
2 *Esd.* 11. 44. they are ended, and his *a.* are fulfilled
Wisd. 12. 23. tormented them with their own *a.*
Eccl. 27. 30. malice and wrath, even these are *a.*
49. 2. he took away the *a.* of iniquity
ABOVE.
2 *Esd.* 8. 20. O Lord, which beholdest from *a.*
Wisd. 9. 17. and send thy Holy Spirit from *a.*
Eccl. 16. 17. shall any remember me from *a.*?
ABOVE.
1 *Esd.* 1. 24. that did wickedly *a.* all people
3. 12. but *a.* all things truth beareth the victory
2 *Esd.* 4. 34. do not thou hasten *a.* the most Highest, for thy haste is in vain to be *a.* him
10. 57. for thou art blessed *a.* many other
Eccl. 3. 21. nor search things that are *a.* thy strength
13. 2. burden not thyself *a.* thy power
25. 10. none *a.* him that feareth the Lord
15. there is no head *a.* the head of a serpent
30. 16. there is no riches *a.* a sound body, and no joy *a.* the joy of the heart
40. 18. he that findeth a treasure is *a.* them both
20. but the love of wisdom is *a.* them both
21. but a pleasant tongue is *a.* them both
23. but *a.* both is a wife with her husband
26. but the fear of the Lord is *a.* them both
43. 28. for he is great *a.* all his works
Prayer of Manass. *a.* the number of the sands
ABOUND.
Eccl. 21. 13. knowledge of a wise man *a.* like a flood
23. 3. lest my sins *a.* to my destruction

Eccl. 24. 26. the understanding to *a.* like Euphrates
ABOUNDED.
1 *Mac.* 3. 30. he *a.* above the kings before him
2 *Mac.* 3. 19. the women *a.* in the streets
ABOUNDETH.
Eccl. 10. 27. that laboureth and *a.* in all things
ABRAHAM.
2 *Esd.* 1. 39. I will give for leaders, A. Isaac, Jacob
3. 13. whose name was A. ‖ 6. 8. from A. to Isaac
7. 36. A. prayed first for the Sodomites
Tob. 4. 12. we are children of the prophets, Noe, A
Jud. 8. 26. remember what things he did to A.
Esth. 14. 18. no joy, but in thee, O Lord God of A.
Eccl. 44. 19. A. was a great father of many people
Bar. 2. 34. which I promised to their father A.
Dan. 3. 12. not depart for thy beloved A. sake
1 *Mac.* 2. 52. was not A. found faithful in temptation?
12. 21. found that they are of the stock of A.
2 *Mac.* 1. 2. his covenant that he made with A.
ABRIDGE.
2 *Mac.* 2. 23. we will essay to *a.* in one volume
ABRIDGING.
2 *Mac.* 2. 26. have taken this painful labour of *a.*
ABRIDGMENT.
2 *Mac.* 2. 31. granted to him that will make an *a.*
ABSALOM.
1 *Mac.* 11. 70. except Mattathias son of A.
13. 11. he sent Jonathan the son of A. to Joppe
2 *Mac.* 11. 17. John and A. were sent from you
ABSENT.
Wisd. 11. 11. whether they were *a.* or present
14. 17. that they might flatter him that was *a.*
ABSTAIN.
Eccl. 28. 8. *a.* from strife, thou shalt diminish sins
ABSTAINETH.
Wisd. 2. 16. he *a.* from our ways as from filthiness
ABSTINENCE.
2 *Esd.* 7. 55. the faces of them which have used *a.*
ABUBUS.
1 *Mac.* 16. 11. Ptolemeus the son of A. made capt.
15. the son of A. receiving them deceitfully
ABUNDANCE.
1 *Esd.* 8. 20. they shall give other things in *a.*
2 *Esd.* 2. 27. but thou shalt be merry and have *a.*
6. 56. the *a.* of them to a drop that falleth
15. 41. may be full with the *a.* of great waters
Tob. 2. 2. when I saw *a.* of meat, I said to my son
4. 16. and according to thine *a.* give alms
Wisd. 11. 7. thou gavest unto them *a.* of water
Eccl. 27. 1. he that seeks for *a.* will turn his eyes
1 *Mac.* 16. 11. and he had *a.* of silver and gold
ABUNDANTLY.
Eccl. 24. 31. I will water *a.* my garden-bed
ABUSE.
Eccl. 26. 10. keep her in straitly, lest she *a.* herself
Bar. 6. 28. the priest *a.* things sacrificed
ABUSED.
2 *Esd.* 9. 9. which now have *a.* my ways
1 *Mac.* 7. 34. but he *a.* them shamefully
2 *Mac.* 14. 42. choosing rather to die than to be *a.*
ACCARON.
1 *Mac.* 10. 89. he also gave him A. in possession
ACCEPT.
Tob. 13. 6. turn, who can tell if he will *a.* you?
Eccl. 4. 22. *a.* no person, 27. | 35. 13. | 42. 1.
1 *Mac.* 8. 1. such as would *a.* all that joined them
ACCEPTABLE.
Wisd. 3. 14. an inheritance more *a.* to his mind
9. 9. and knew what was *a.* in thy sight
12. so shall my works be *a.* then shall I judge
Eccl. 2. 5. *a.* men tried in furnace of adversity
15. 15. if thou wilt, to keep the commandments, and to perform *a.* faithfulness
35. 7. the sacrifice of a just man is *a.*
41. 2. O death, *a.* is thy sentence to the needy
ACCEPTED.
Wisd. 18. 7. so of thy people was *a.* the salvation
Eccl. 19. 18. the fear of the L. is the first step to be *a.*
34. 18. the gifts of unjust men are not *a.*
35. 16. he that serveth the Lord shall be *a.*
Dan. 3. 16. in an humble spirit let us be *a*

1 Mac. 6. 60. to make peace, and they a. thereof
9. 71. which thing he a. and sware unto him
14. 47. then Simon a. hereof, and was pleased
2 Mac. 12. 4. who a. of it according to the decree
13. 24. a. well of Maccabeus, made him governor

ACCEPTING.

1 Esth. 4. 39. with her there is no a. of persons
Eccl. 20. 22. by a. persons, overthroweth himself

ACCESS.

2 Mac. 14. 3. nor have any more a. to the altar

ACCLAMATIONS.

1 Mac. 5. 64. the people assembled with joyful a.

ACCOMPANY.

Jud. 10. 17. an 100 men, to a. her and her maid

ACCOMPLISH.

2 Esd. 12. 25. for these shall a. his wickedness
Jud. 2. 13. but a. them fully, as I commanded
10. 8. the God of our fathers a. thy enterprises
9. that I may go forth to a. things you spake
2 Mac. 14. 29. he watched his time to a. this thing

ACCOMPLISHED.

1 Esd. 1. 17. the things belonging to sacrifices a.
2. 1. that the word of the Lord might be a.
1 Mac. 3. 49. Nazarites, who had a. their days

ACCORD.

1 Esd. 5. 58. all Levites with one a. labouring
9. 38. the multitude came together with one a.
Jud. 15. 9. they blessed her with one a. and said
Wisd. 10. 20. magnified with one a. thine hand

ACCOUNT.

Wisd. 5. 1. such as made no a. of his labours
1 Mac. 6. 9. and he made a. that he should die
2 Mac. 15. 18. was in least a. with them

ACCOUNTED.

Wisd. 5. 4. we fools a. his life madness
Bar. 3. 35. none be a. of in comparison of him

ACCOUNTS.

Tob. 1. 21. who appointed over his father's a.
22. Achiacharus was overseer of the a.
Wisd. 4. 20. when they cast up the a. of their sins
1 Mac. 10. 40. I give silver out of the king's a.
42. which they took out of the a. year by year
44. expenses shall be given of the king's a.

ACCUSATION.

Eccl. 26. 5. my heart feareth a false a.
51. 6. by an a. to the king from unrighteous tongue
2 Mac. 4. 43. an a. was laid against Menelaus

ACCUSATIONS.

2 Mac. 14. 27. with the a. of the wicked man

ACCUSE.

2 Esd. 16. 50. and shall a. her to her face
Wisd. 12. 12. who shall a. thee for the nations
Eccl. 46. 19. taken no goods, and no man did a. him
1 Mac. 10. 61. assembled themselves to a. him

ACCUSED.

Wisd. 10. 14. as for them that had a. him
1 Mac. 7. 6. and they a. the people to the king
2 Mac. 5. 8. being a. before Aretas the king
10. 13. being a. of the king's friends before Eupator
21. a. those men, that they had sold their brethren
14. 38. formerly Raziz had been a. of Judaism

ACCUSER.

2 Mac. 4. 5. not to be an a. of his countrymen

ACCUSERS.

2 Esd. 16. 65. your own sins shall be your a.
1 Mac. 10. 64. when his a. saw he was honoured

ACCUSTOM.

Eccl. 23. 9. a. not thy mouth to swearing

ACCUSTOMED.

Eccl. 20. 25. a thief is better than a man a. to lie
23. 15. the man that is a. to opprobrious words

ACHAN.

2 Esd. 7. 37. prayed for Israel in the time of A.

ACHIACHARUS.

Tob. 1. 21. A. my brother Anael's son, over affairs
22. A. entreating for me, I returned to Nineve
2. 10. A. did nourish me till I went to Elymais
11. 18. A. and Nasbas his brother's son came
14. 10. remember, how Aman handled A.

ACHIOR.

Jud. 5. 5. then said A. the captain of Ammon
22. when A. had finished these sayings
6. 2. who art thou, A.? ‖ 5. A. hireling of Ammon
10. then Olofernes commanded to take A.
13. they bound A. cast him down and left him
16. they set A. in the midst of all their people
11. 9. concerning the matter which A. did speak
14. 10. when A. had seen all that God had done

ACHITOB.

2 Esd. 1. 1. Sidamias son of Sadoc, the son of A.

ACKNOWLEDGE.

2 Esd. 1. 36. yet they shall a. their sins
10. 16. if thou shalt a. the determination of God
Jud. 9. 14. a. that thou art the God of all power
Wisd. 13. 1. nor did they a. the work-master
Eccl. 23. 11. if he a. not his sin, a double offence
Prayer of Manass. I a. mine iniquities

ACKNOWLEDGED.

Wisd. 12. 27. they a. him to be the true God
18. 13. they a. this people to be the sons of God
Eccl. 44. 23. he a. him in his blessing and gave
Sus. 14. they asked the cause, they a. their lust
2 Mac. 3. 28. manifestly they a. the power of God

ACQUAINTANCE.

Eccl. 30. 2. shall rejoice of his son among his a.
2 Mac. 6. 21. the old a. they had with the man

ACQUIT.

Wisd. 1. 6. will not a. a blasphemer of his words

ACT.

Jud. 8. 34. but inquire not you of mine a.

ACTION.

Eccl. 37. 16. let counsel go before every a.

ACTIONS.

2 Esd. 15. 16. their a. shall stand in their power

ACTIVE.

Wisd. 15. 11. that inspired into him an a. soul

ACTS.

1 Esd. 1. 25. now after all these a. of Josias
33. the a. that Josias did are reported
Eccl. 17. 9. gave them to glory in his marvellous a.
18. 4. and who shall find out his noble a.?
51, 8. then thought I upon thy a. of old

1 Mac. 2. 51. call to remembrance what a. our fathers did in their time to receive great honour
3. 4. in his a. he was like a lion roaring for his prey
7. he made Jacob glad with his a.
5. 56. heard of valiant a. and deeds they had done
8. 2. it was told him of their wars and noble a.
9. 22. his wars, and the noble a. which he did
14. 35. the people seeing the a. of Simon
2 Mac. 2. 13. gathered together the a. of king
10. 10. now will we declare the a. of Antiochus

ADAM.

2 Esd. 3. 5. thou gavest a body to A. without soul
10. as death was to A. so was the flood to these
21. the first A. bearing a wicked heart transgressed
26. in all things did even as A. had done
4. 30. evil seed hath been sown in the heart of A.
6. 54. A. whom thou madest lord of thy creatures
7. 11. when A. transgressed my statutes
46. been better not to have given the earth to A.
48. O thou A. what hast thou done?
Tob. 8. 6. thou madest A. and gavest him Eve
Eccl. 33. 10. and A. was created of the earth
40. 1. and an heavy yoke is upon the sons of A.
49. 16. so was A. above every living thing in crea.

ADAMANT.

Eccl. 16. 16. his light from the darkness with an a.

ADAR.

1 Esd. 7. 5. holy house was finished in the month A.
Esth. 13. 6. of the twelfth month A. 16. 20.
1 Mac. 7. 43. the thirteenth day of the month A.
2 Mac. 15. 36. in the Syrian tongue is called A.

ADASA.

1 Mac. 7. 40. Judas pitched in A. with 3000 men
45. they pursued after them from A. to Gazera

ADD.

Tob. 5. 15. I will a. something to thy wages
18. be not greedy to a. money to money
Eccl. 4. 3. a. not more trouble to an heart vexed
5. 5. be not without fear to a. sin to sin
21. 15. he will commend it, and a. unto it
1 Mac. 8. 30. shall think meet to a. or diminish any thing; and whatsoever they shall a. or take away

ADDED.

1 Esd. 7. 6. that were a. to them did according to
Eccl. 3. 14. instead of sins shall be a. to build thee up
42. 21. to him may nothing be a. nor diminished
1 Mac. 10. 30. governments which are a. thereto
38. the three that are a. to Judea, 11. 34.
14. 30. after that Jonathan was a. to his people

ADDING.

2 Mac. 2. 32. only a. thus much to what is said

ADDO.

1 Esd. 6. 1. Zacharias the son of A. prophesied

ADHERENTS.

1 Mac. 9. 60. he sent letters to his a. in Judea

ADIDA.

1 Mac. 12. 33. Simon also set up A. in Sephela
13. 13. but Simon pitched his tents at A.

ADJOINING.

1 Mac. 12. 33. Simon passed thro' the holds there a.
2 Mac. 12. 16. a lake near a. thereto, being filled

ADMIRABLE.

1 Esd. 4. 29. Apame, daughter of the a. Bartacus

ADMIRATION.

Eccl. 22. 23. nor the rich that is foolish to be had in a.
38. 3. in the sight of great men he shall be in a.

ADMIRE.

Eccl. 27. 23. he will speak sweetly and a. thy words

ADMIRED.

Jud. 10. 19. wondered at her beauty, and a. Israel
Wisd. 8. 11. I shall be a. in the sight of great men
11. 14. when they saw what came to pass they a.

ADMONISH.

Jud. 8. 27. that come near to them to a. them
Wisd. 11. 10. for these thou didst a. as a father
Eccl. 19. 13. a. a friend, may be not done it, 14, 15.
17. a. thy neighbour before thou threaten him

ADMONISHED.

Wisd. 16. 6. were troubled that they might be a.

ADORE.

Bel 4. the king worshipped it and went daily to a. it

ADORNED.

Esth. 15. 2. being gloriously a. she took maids

ADORNING.

2 Mac. 2. 29. must seek fit things for a. thereof

ADVANTAGE.

2 Mac. 8. 7. but especially took he a. of the night

ADVENTURE.

Wisd. 2. 2. for we are born at all a. be as not been

ADVERSARY.

Eccl. 36. 7. take away the a. destroyer, the enemy
1 Mac. 1. 36. it was an evil a. to Israel

ADVERSARIES.

1 Esd. 8. 51. conduct for safeguard against our a.
Wisd. 11. 3. they were avenged of their a.
8. declaring how thou hadst punished their a.
18. 8. for wherewith thou didst punish our a.
Eccl. 23. 3. lest my sins abound and I fall bef. mine a.
47. 7. he brought to nought the Philistines his a.
51. 2. thou hast been my helper against mine a.
1 Mac. 9. 29. against them that are a. to us

ADVERSITY.

Eccl. 2. 5. acceptable men in the furnace of a.
11. 14. prosperity and a. life and death come of God
12. 8. and an enemy cannot be hidden in a.
9. but in his a. even a friend will depart
17. if a. come upon thee, thou shalt find him there
2 Mac. 6. 16. though he punish with a. yet not forsake
12. 30. entreated them kindly in time of their a.

ADVERSITIES.

2 Esd. 10. 20. for how many are the a. of Sion!
2 Mac. 5. 20. partaker of the a. that happened

ADVICE.

Eccl. 32. 19. do nothing without a. done repent not

ADULTERER.

Eccl. 25. 2. my soul hateth an old a. that doteth

ADULTERERS.

Wisd. 3. 16. children of a. shall not come to perfection

ADULTERY.

Wisd. 14. 24. slew another, or grieved him by a.
Eccl. 23. 23. she hath played the whore in a.

AFAR off.

1 Esd. 5. 65. sounded, so that it was heard a. off
Eccl. 16. 22. for his covenant is a. off, trial in end

AFFAIRS.

1 Esd. 8. 12. that they may look to the a. of Judea
Tob. 1. 21. over father's accounts, and over all his a.
Esth. 13. 7. cause our a. to be well settled
16. 5. put in trust to manage their friends' a.
1 Mac. 3. 32. Lysias to oversee the a. of the king
6. 56. sought to take to him the ruling of the a.
57. and the a. of the kingdom lie upon us
10. 37. some set over the a. of the kingdom
2 Mac. 4. 21. not to be well affected to his a.
7. 24. that he would trust him with his a.
8. 8. wrote to yield more aid to the king's a.
9. 20. and if your a. be to your contentment
11. 1. Lysias, who managed a. took displeasure
23. that every one may attend upon his own a.
26. they may go cheerfully about their own a.
13. 2. Lysias, his protector and ruler of his a.
23. who was left over the a. in Antioch

AFFECT.

Eccl. 13. 11. a. not to be made equal to him in talk

AFFECTED.

Esth. 13. 5. this people is evil a. to our state
16. 23. be safety to us, and the well a. Persians
2 Mac. 4. 21. understanding him not to be well a.
13. 26. Lysias pacified, and made them well a.
14. 5. being called and asked how the Jews stood a.
26. Nicanor was not well a. toward the state

AFFECTION.

Wisd. 6. 11. therefore set your a. on my words

AFFLICT.

Eccl. 30. 21. a. not thyself in thine own counsel
49. 7. that he might root out, and a. and destroy

AFFLICTED.

2 Esd. 11. 42. for thou hast a. meek, hurt peaceable
Jud. 9. 11. for thou art a God of the a. an helper
16. 11. my a. shouted for joy, my weak ones cried
Wisd. 5. 1. before the face of such as have a. him
14. 15. a father a. with untimely mourning
18. 19. they should not know why they were a.
19. 16. but these very grievously a. them
Eccl. 4. 4. reject not the supplication of the a.
30. 14. than a rich man that is a. in his body
Bar. 4. 31. miserable are they that a. thee
1 Mac. 9. 68. and they a. Bacchides sore
10. 46. for he had a. them very sore

AFFLICTING.

Jud. 2. 2. and concluded the a. of the whole earth

AFFLICTION.

2 Esd. 6. 19. when the a. of Sion shall be fulfilled
Jud. 13. 20. not spared for the a. of our nation
Esth. 11. 8. a day of anguish a. and great uproar
14. 12. make thyself known in time of our a.
16. 20. who in time of their a. shall set upon them
Eccl. 2. 11. for the Lord saveth in time of a.
3. 15. in the day of a. it shall be remembered
6. 10. will not continue in the day of thine a.
11. 25. in prosperity there is a forgetfulness of a. and in the day of a. there is no remembrance
27. a. of an hour makes a man forget pleasure
25. 14. any a. but the a. from them that hate me
29. 12. and it shall deliver thee from all a.
35. 20. mercy is seasonable in the time of a.
38. 19. in a. also sorrow remaineth, life of the poor
Bar. 5. 1. the garment of thy mourning and a.
1 Mac. 9. 27. so was there a great a. in Israel

AFFLICTIONS.

2 Esd. 8. 27. of those that keep thy testimonies in a.
Jud. 4. 13. so God heard and looked upon their a.
Eccl. 51. 3. and from the manifold a. which I had
1 Mac. 2. 30. because a. increased sore on them

AFFRIGHTED.

2 Esd. 10. 55. fear not, let not thy heart be a.
12. 5. great fear wherewith I was a. this night

AFORE.

1 Esd. 6. 32. make light of any thing a. spoken

AFOREHAND.

Jud. 7. 1. to take a. the ascents of the hill-country

AFORETIME.

Sus. 52. sins committed a. are come to light
1 Mac. 3. 46. was the place where they prayed a.
9. 72. the prisoners taken a. out of land of Judea
11. 34. the king received of them yearly a.

AFRAID.

2 Esd. 6. 15. therefore when it speaks, be not a.
23. when they hear shall be suddenly a.
10. 25. I was a. of her, and mused what it might be
27. then was I a. and cried with a loud voice
38. I shall tell thee wherefore thou art a.
13. 8. they were sore a. and yet durst fight
11. dust and smoke, when I saw this, I was a.
15. 18. houses be destroyed, and men shall be a.
37. and they that see the wrath shall be a.
43. they shall go to Babylon, and make her a.
16. 10. he shall thunder, and who shall not be a.?
Tob. 2. 8. this man is not yet a. to be put to death
4. 8. be not a. to give according to that little
6. 14. and I am a. lest if I go in unto her, I die
Jud. 1. 11. for they were not a. of him
4. 2. therefore they were exceedingly a. of him
5. 23. we will not be a. of the face of Israel
10. 16. when before him be not a. in thy heart
16. 25. there was none made Israel any more a.
Wisd. 8. 15. horrible tyrants be a. when hear of me
18. 25. the destroyer gave place and was a.
Eccl. 26. 5. and for the fourth I was sore a.
30. 9. cocker thy child he shall make thee a.
34. 14. whoso feareth the Lord, shall not be a.
Bar. 6. 5. neither be ye a. when ye see multitude
1 Mac. 1. 18. but Ptolemee was a. of him and fled
3. 22. and as for you, be ye not a. of them
4. 8. fear not, neither be ye a. of their assault
21. perceived these things, they were sore a.
5. 41. but if he be a. and camp beyond the river
8. 12. all that heard of their name were a.
12. 40. he was a. Jonathan would not suffer him
52. they bewailed Jonathan, and were sore a.
16. 6. he saw that the people were a. to go over
2 Mac. 3. 24. all that came with him were sore a.

AFTERWARD.
Eccl. 19. 21. say, I will not do it, though a. he do it
AGAGITE.
Esth. 12. 6. howbeit, Aman the A. sought to molest
AGARENES.
Bar. 3. 23. the A. that seek wisdom upon earth
AGE.
2 Esd. 3. 18. thou troubledst the men of that a.
5. 50. for our mother draweth now nigh to a.
53. and they that are born in the time of a.
Tob. 1. 9. when I was come to the a. of a man
3. 10. shall bring old a. with sorrow to the grave
14. 5. till the time of that a. be fulfilled
Jud. 8. 18. there arose none in our a. that worship
Wisd. 3. 17. their last a. shall be without honour
4. 8. honourable a. is not in length of time
9. and an unspotted life is old a.
16. the many years and old a. of the unrighteous
Eccl. 3. 12. my son, help thy father in his a.
6. 18. so shalt thou find wisdom till thy old a.
8. 6. dishonour not a man in his old a.
26. 17. so is the beauty of the face in ripe a.
19. my son, keep the flower of thine a. sound
30. 24. carefulness brings a. before the time
41. 2. that is now in the last a. and is vexed
42. 9. lest she pass away the flower of her a.
46. 9. which remained with him till his old a.
1 Mac. 16. 3. I am old, and ye are of sufficient a.
2 Mac. 6. 24. for it becometh not our a. to dissemble
25. I get a stain to my old a. and abominable
27. shew myself such an one as my a. requireth
7. 27. nourished and brought thee up to this a.
AGED.
2 Esd. 5. 49. the things that belong to the a.
Tob. 8. 7. that we may become a. together
14. 3. for behold, I am a. and ready to depart
Wisd. 2. 10. the ancient gray hairs of the a.
Eccl. 25. 20. as climbing a sandy way is to feet of a.
42. 8. be not ashamed to inform the extreme a.
2 Mac. 6. 18. Eleazar the scribe, an a. man
8. 30. made the a. equal in spoils with themselves
AGES.
1 Esd. 4. 40. she is the strength and majesty of all a.
Wisd. 7. 27. and in all a. entering into holy souls
14. 6. and left to all a. a seed of generation
Eccl. 24. 33. I will leave it to all a. for ever
1 Mac. 2. 61. thus consider throughout all a.
AGGEUS.
1 Esd. 6. 1. A. and Zacharias prophesied to the Jews
7. 3. the holy works prospered when A. prophesied
2 Esd. 1. 40. A. Zachary and Malachi for leaders
AGO.
1 Esd. 6. 14. this house was builded many years a.
AGONY.
2 Mac. 3. 14. there was no small a. thro' the city
21. the fear of the high priest being in such an a.
AGREE.
Tob. 7. 11. I will eat nothing here till we a.
Eccl. 13. 2. how a. kettle and earthen pot together
25. 1. a man and a wife that a. together
2 Mac. 11. 14. he persuaded them to a. to conditions
AGREEABLE.
Wisd. 12. 15. thinking it not a. to condemn him
AGREEABLY.
1 Esd. 8. 12. a. to that which is in law of the Lord
AGREEING.
Wisd. 16. 20. didst send them bread a. to every taste
AGREEMENT.
Eccl. 13. 18. what a. between the hyena and a dog?
2 Mac. 12. 25. restore them according to the a.
AID.
Tob. 8. 6. let us make to him an a. like himself
Jud. 9. 4. thy children called upon thee for a.
Esth. 16. 20. ye shall a. them, that they be avenged
Wisd. 13. 18. for a. he beseecheth what hath least
1 Mac. 7. 7. punish them, with all that a. them
8. 26. nor shall they a. them with victuals
10. 24. promise them gifts, that I may have their a.
15. 19. nor yet a. their enemies against them
16. 18. that he should send him an host to a. him
2 Mac. 4. 11. who went to Rome for amity and a.
8. 8. to yield more a. to the king's affairs
15. 8. expect victory and a. from the Almighty
AILETH.
2 Esd. 9. 42. I said to her, what a. thee? tell me
10. 31. what a. thee? and why art thou disquieted?
AIM.
Wisd. 13. 9. to know that they could a. at the world
AIR.
2 Esd. 6. 4. or ever the heights of the a. were lifted
11. 2. all the winds of the a. blew on her
Jud. 11. 7. the fowls of the a. shall live by thy power
Wisd. 2. 3. our spirits shall vanish as the soft a.
5. 11. as when a bird hath flown through the a.
but the light a. being beaten with her wings
12. an arrow is shot at a mark, it parteth the a.
7. 3. when I was born, I drew in the common a.
17. 10. they died, denying that they saw the a.
Bar. 3. 17. had pastime with the fowls of the a.
Dan. 3. 58. O all ye fowls of the a. bless the Lord
2 Mac. 4. 46. taking aside, as it were to take the a.
5. 2. there were seen horsemen running in the a.
ALARM.
1 Mac. 7. 45. sounding an a. after them with trump.
ALCIMUS.
1 Mac. 7. 5. having A. who was desirous to be priest
9. and him he sent with that wicked A.
12. did there assemble to A. a company of scribes
to require justice, 20, 23, 25. | 9. 1, 57.
21. but A. contended for the high-priesthood
9. 54. A. commanded that the wall be pulled down
55. even at that time was A. plagued and hindered
56. A. died at that time with great torment
2 Mac. 14. 3. one A. who had been high priest
13. to make A. high priest of the great temple
26. A. perceiving the love that was betwixt them
ALEXANDER.
1 Mac. 1. 1. A. son of Philip the Macedonian, 6. 2.
7. A. reigned twelve years, and then died
10. 1. A. the son of Antiochus the Ptolemais
4. let us first make peace with him, before he
join with A. 15, 18, 47, 49, 59, 68, 88.

1 Mac. 10. 23. what have we done that A. prev. us?
51. A. sent ambassadors to Ptolemee king of Egypt
ALIENS.
1 Mac. 3. 45. sanctuary trodden, a. kept strong-hold
ALIKE.
Wisd. 6. 7. made small and great, he careth for all a.
11. 11. absent or present, they were vexed a.
14. 9. are both a. hateful unto God
ALIVE.
2 Esd. 12. 33. set them before him a. in judgment
Tob. 3. 15. nor any son of his a. to whom I may keep
7. 5. they said, he is both a. and in good health
8. 12. send and let her see whether he be a.
14. came forth, and told them that he was a.
1 Mac. 1. 6. and parted his kingdom while he was a.
8. 7. how they took him a. and covenanted
14. 2. he sent one of his princes to take him a.
2 Mac. 6. 26. not escape the Almighty a. nor dead
7. 5. commanded him, being yet a. to be brought
24. whilst the youngest was yet a. did exhort him
12. 35. he would have taken that cursed man a.
ALLEGING.
Wisd. 18. 22. a. the oaths made with the fathers
ALLIED.
Wisd. 8. 17. to be a. to wisdom is immortality
ALLOWANCE.
1 Esd. 1. 7. these things were given of the king's a.
2 Mac. 4. 14. to be partakers of the unlawful a.
ALLOWED.
2 Esd. 8. 52. to you rest is a. yea, perfect wisdom
ALLURE.
Jud. 10. 4. to a. the eyes of all that should see her
ALLURED.
Wisd. 14. 20. multitude a. by the grace of the work
ALMIGHTY.
1 Esd. 9. 46. Esdras blessed the God of hosts A.
2 Esd. 1. 15. thus saith the A. Lord, 22, 28, 33. |
2. 9, 31. Jud. 4. 13. | 16. 6, 17.
9. 45. and we gave great honour unto the A.
Jud. 8. 13. try the Lord A. but you shall never know
15. 10. blessed be thou of the A. Lord for ever
Esth. 13. 9. saying, O Lord, Lord, the King A.
16. 21. A. God hath turned to joy unto them
Wisd. 7. 25. flowing from the glory of the A.
11. 17. thy A. hand that made the world
18. 15. thine A. word leaped down from heaven
Eccl. 24. 24. for the Lord A. is God alone
42. 17. works which the A. Lord firmly settled
50. 14. the offering of the most high A.
17. worship their Lord God A. the Most High
Bar. 3. 4. O Lord A. thou God of Israel, hear now
Prayer of Manass. O Lord, A. God of our fathers
2 Mac. 1. 25. the only Just, A. and Everlasting
3. 22. they then called upon the A. Lord
30. when the A. Lord appeared, filled with joy
5. 20. it was forsaken in wrath of the A. 7. 38.
6. 26. I should not escape the hand of the A.
7. 35. thou hast not escaped the judgment of A. God
8. 11. that was to follow upon him from the A. God
18. but our confidence is in the A. God
24. by the help of the A. they slew above 9000
9. 5. Lord A. smote him with an incurable plague
11. 13. because the A. God helped them, he sent
12. 28. Judas and his company called on the A. G.
15. 8. which should come to them from the A.
29. praising the A. in their own language
32. stretched against the holy temple of the A.
ALMOST.
2 Esd. 10. 10. they walk a. into destruction
22. the name that is named on us is a. profaned
ALMS.
Tob. 1. 3. I did many a.-deeds to my brethren
16. I gave many a. to my brethren, I gave bread
2. 11. where are thine a. and righteous deeds?
4. 7. give a. of thy substance, and when thou
givest a. let not thine eye be envious, 16.
8. if thou hast abundance, give a. accordingly
10. because a. doth deliver from death, 12. 9.
11. for a. is a good gift to all that give it
12. 8. prayer is good with fasting, a. and righteousness, it is better to give a. than to lay up gold
14. 2. he gave a. and increased in the fear of God
10. Manasses gave a. and escaped the snares
11. wherefore, my son, consider what a. doth
Eccl. 3. 30. and a. maketh an atonement for sins
7. 10. not faint-hearted, and neglect not to give a.
12. 3. no good can come to him that giveth no a.
17. 22. the a. of a man is as a signet with him
29. 12. shut up a. in thy store-houses
31. 11. the congregation shall declare his a.
35. 2. he that giveth a. sacrificeth praise
ALOFT.
1 Esd. 8. 92. married strange wom. now is all Isr. a.
1 Mac. 13. 27. Simon raised it a. to the sight
ALONE.
1 Esd. 5. 71. we ourselves a. will build to the Lord
2 Esd. 3. 4. didst plant the earth, and that thyself a.
6. 6. they all were made thro' me a. and no other
7. 48. O Adam, thou art not fallen a. but we all
9. 41. Sir, let me a. that I may bewail myself
Tob. 1. 6. I a. went often to Jerusalem at feasts
8. 6. it is not good that man should be a.
Esth. 13. 5. that this people a. is in opposition to all
Wisd. 10. 1. father of the world that was created a.
Eccl. 6. 2. torn in pieces, as a bull straying a.
Bar. 4. 16. these have left her that was a.
Sus. 14. a time, when they might find her a.
36. the elders said, as we walked in the garden a.
1 Mac. 10. 70. thou a. liftest up thyself against us
12. 36. to separate it that so it might be a.
13. 4. my brethren are slain and I am left a.
2 Mac. 15. 39. hurtful to drink wine or water a.
ALREADY.
1 Esd. 6. 9. and the timber a. laid upon the walls
2 Esd. 2. 13. the kingdom is a. prepared for you
Tob. 3. 8. thou hast had a. seven husbands
15. my seven husbands a. dead, why should I live
Wisd. 19. 4. forget the things that had a. happened
16. were a. made partakers of the same laws
ALTAR.
1 Esd. 1. 18. offer sacrifices upon the a. of the Lord
4. 52. to maintain burnt offerings upon the a.

1 Esd. 5. 48. make ready the a. of the God of Israel
50. they erected the a. upon his own place
8. 15. may offer sacrifices on the a. of the Lord
2 Esd. 10. 21. thou seest that our a. is broken down
Tob. 1. 6. then I gave at the a. to the priests
Jud. 4. 3. the vessels and the a. were sanctified
11. also they put sackcloth about the a.
9. 8. to cast down with the sword the horn of thy a.
Esth. 14. 9. quench the glory of thy house and a.
Wisd. 9. 8. an a. in the city wherein thou dwellest
Eccl. 35. 6. offering of righteous maketh the a. fat
50. 11. when he went up to the holy a. he made
12. he himself stood by the hearth of the a.
14. and finishing the service at the a.
15. he poured out at the foot of the a. a savour
Bar. 1. 10. offer upon the a. of the Lord our God
1 Mac. 1. 21. Antiochus took away the golden a.
54. the abomination of desolation on the a.
59. did sacrifice, which was upon the a. of God
2. 23. sacrifice upon the a. which was at Modin
24. wherefore he ran and slew him upon the a.
25. he killed, and the a. he pulled down
4. 38. they saw the a. profaned, the gates burnt
44. what to do with the a. of burnt offerings
47. they took whole stones, and built a new a.
50. and upon the a. they burnt incense
56. so they kept the dedication of the a. eight days
6. 7. the abomination which he had set upon the a.
2 Mac. 1. 19. the priests took the fire of the a. privily
32. consumed by the light that shined from the a.
2. 5. where he laid the ark and the a. of incense
4. 14. the priests had no courage to serve at the a.
10. 3. they made another a. and offered sacrifice
14. 3. nor have any more access to the holy a.
33. I will break down the a. and erect a temple
15. 31. when he had set the priests before the a.
ALTARS.
1 Mac. 1. 47. set up a. and groves, and chapels
54. they builded idol-a. thro' the cities of Juda
2 Mac. 10. 2. the a. which the heathen had built
ALTERATIONS.
Wisd. 7. 18. the a. of the turning of the sun
ALTER.
Wisd. 4. 11. lest wickedness should a. his under- [standing
ALTERED.
Jud. 10. 7. they saw that her countenance was a.
Wisd. 16. 25. even then was it a. into all fashions
Eccl. 33. 8. and he a. seasons and feasts
ALTOGETHER.
2 Esd. 6. 20. books be opened, and they shall see a.
Jud. 15. 2. rushing out a. they fled to the plain
Wisd. 18. 12. so they a. had innumerable dead
Eccl. 41. 16. nor is it a. approved in every thing
ALWAY.
2 Esd. 15. 47. have a. desired to commit whoredom
16. 20. they shall not be a. mindful of scourges
AMADATHA.
Esth. 16. 10. Aman a Macedonian the son of A. 17.
AMADATHUS.
Esth. 12. 6. Aman the son of A. the Agagite
AMAN.
Tob. 14. 10. remember how A. handled Achiacha-
rus, but A. fell into the snare and perished
Esth. 10. 7. and the two dragons are I and A.
12. 6. howbeit A. was in great honour with king
13. 6. are signified in writing to you by A.
14. 17. thy handmaid hath not eaten at A. table
16. 10. for A. a Macedonian had obtained favour
17. not to execute the letters sent to you by A.
AMAIN.
2 Mac. 12. 22. the enemies being smitten, fled a.
AMATHIS.
1 Mac. 12. 25. Jonathan met them in the land of A.
AMAZED.
Wisd. 5. 2. shall be a. at strangeness of his salvation
AMBASSADOR.
1 Mac. 12. 8. Onias entreated the a. that was sent
2 Mac. 4. 11. who went a. to Rome for amity and aid
AMBASSADORS.
Jud. 3. 1. so they sent a. to him to treat of peace
1 Mac. 9. 70. he sent a. to him, to make peace
11. 9. Ptolemee sent a. to king Demetrius
12. 23. we do command our a. to make report
14. 21. the a. that were sent to our people
40. that they had entertained the a. of Simon
15. 17. the Jews a. our friends came unto us
2 Mac. 11. 34. a. of the Romans, send greeting
AMBASSAGE.
1 Mac. 14. 23. put the copy of their a. in records
AMBUSH.
1 Mac. 9. 40. from the place where they lay in a.
10. 79. had left a thousand horsemen in a.
11. 68. having laid men in a. in the mountains
69. when they that lay in a. arose out of places
AMBUSHMENT.
1 Mac. 10. 80. Jonathan knew that there was an a.
AMEN.
1 Esd. 9. 47. and all the people answered a.
Tob. 8. 8. she said with him a. they slept that night
Eccl. 50. 29. blessed be the Lord for ever, a. a.
AMEND.
Wisd. 11. 23. at sins of men, because they should a.
AMENDMENT.
2 Esd. 16. 19. and anguish are sent as scourges for a.
AMIABLE.
Esth. 15. 5. her countenance was cheerful and a.
AMISS.
2 Esd. 8. 35. there is none which hath not done a.
Eccl. 7. 36. remember the end, thou shalt never do a.
24. 22. they that work by me, shall not do a.
40. 23. a friend and companion never meet a.
AMITY.
1 Mac. 8. 1. such as would make a league of a.
12. with such as relied on them they kept a.
17. sent them to Rome to make a league of a.
10. 23. in making a. with the Jews to strengthen
54. now therefore let us make a league of a.
12. 16. to renew the a. that we had with them
2 Mac. 4. 11. who went to Rome for a. and aid
AMMON.
Jud. 5. 2. was angry, he called all the captains of A.
6. 5. thou Achior, an hireling of A. who hast spoken

Jud. 7. 17. the camp of the children of A. departed

AMMONITES.

2 *Mac.* 4. 26. to flee into the country of the A.

AMORITES.

2 *Esd.* 1. 22. when you were in the river of the A.
Jud. 5. 15. so they dwelt in the land of the A.

AMOS.

2 *Esd.* 1.39. I will give for leaders, A. and Micheus
Tob. 2.6. remembering that prophecy of A. as he said

ANANIAS.

Tob. 5. 12. I am Azarias, the son of A. the great
Dan. 3. 66. O A. Azarias, and Misael, 1 *Mac.* 2. 59.

ANCESTORS.

Jud. 5. 8. for they left the way of their *a.*
Eccl. 8. 4. jest not, lest thy *a.* be disgraced
1 *Mac.* 7. 2. he entered into the palace of his *a.*
2 *Mac.* 14. 7. I being deprived of mine *a.* honour

ANCIENT.

Esth. 16. 7. not so much by *a.* histories, as ye may
Wisd. 2. 10. nor reverence *a.* gray hairs of the aged
13. 10. or a stone, the work of an *a.* hand
Eccl. 25. 4. and for *a.* men to know counsel
32. 9. when *a.* men are in place, use not many words
39. 1. he will seek out the wisdom of all the *a.*
1 *Mac.* 14. 9. the *a.* men sat all in the streets
2 *Mac.* 6. 6. nor was it lawful to keep *a.* feasts
23. as became the excellency of his *a.* years

ANCIENTS.

1 *Esd.* 5. 63. the *a.* who had seen the former house
7. 2. assisting the *a.* of the Jews and governors
Jud. 6. 16. they called together all the *a.* of the city
8. 10. Chabris, and Charmis, *a.* of the city, 10. 6.
15. 8. the *a.* of the children of Israel came
Sus. 5. two of the *a.* of the people to be judges

ANDRONICUS.

2 *Mac.* 4. 31. leaving A. a man in authority
34. taking A. apart, prayed him to get Onias
38. forthwith he took away A. his purple and rent
5. 23. at Garizim he left A. governor

ANEW.

1 *Esd.* 2. 24. if the walls thereof be set up *a.*
Wisd. 19. 6. the creature was fashioned again *a.*

ANGEL.

2 *Esd.* 1. 40. who is called also an *a.* of the Lord
2. 44. I asked the *a.* and said, sir, what are these?
4. 1. the *a.* that was sent to me gave an answer
5. 15. the *a.* that was come to talk with me
20. I fasted, as Uriel the *a.* commanded me
31. the *a.* that came to me the night afore
7. 1. there was sent to me the *a.* who had been sent
12. 51. but I remained, as the *a.* commanded me
Tob. 5. 4. he found Raphael that was an *a.*
16. and the *a.* of God keep you company
21. for the good *a.* will keep him company
6. 5. the young man did as the *a.* commanded him
8. 3. the evil spirit fled and the *a.* bound him
12. 5. so he called the *a.* and said unto him
22. how the *a.* of the Lord had appeared to them
Esth. 15. 13. I saw thee, my lord, as an *a.* of God
Eccl. 48. 21. smote the host, his *a.* destroyed them
Bar. 6. 7. my *a.* is with you, and I caring your souls
Dan. 3. 26. but the *a.* of the Lord came down
Sus. 55. the *a.* of God hath received the sentence
59. the *a.* of God waiteth to cut thee in two
Bel. 34. but the *a.* of the Lord said to Habbacuc
36. the *a.* of the Lord took him by the crown
39. the *a.* of the Lord set Habbacuc in his place
1 *Mac.* 7. 41. the *a.* went out, and smote 185,000
2 *Mac.* 11. 6. would send a good *a.* to deliver Israel
15. 22. thou didst send thy *a.* in time of Ezekias
23. send a good *a.* before us for a dread to them

ANGELS.

2 *Esd.* 1. 19. I gave you manna, ye did eat *a.* bread
6. 3. before the *a.* were gathered together
8. 21. before whom the hosts of *a.* stand trembling
16. 66. how hide your sins before God and his *a.*?
Tob. 8. 15. let all thy *a.* and thine elect praise thee
11. 14. and blessed are all thine holy *a.*
12. 15. I am Raphael one of the seven holy *a.*
Wisd. 16. 20. thou feddest thy people with *a.* food
Dan. 3. 37. O ye *a.* of the Lord, bless ye the Lord

ANGER.

2 *Esd.* 10. 5. then I spake to her in *a.* saying
Jud. 8. 14. provoke not the Lord our God to *a.*
11. 11. they will provoke their God to *a.*
Wisd. 10. 3. unrighteous went away from her in *a.*
Eccl. 8. 11. rise not up in *a.* at the presence of an
10. 18. nor furious *a.* for them that are born
25. 22. a woman is full of *a.* and much reproach
26. 8. a drunken woman causeth great *a.*
28. 10. according to his riches, his *a.* riseth
40. 5. trouble, fear of death, and *a.* and strife
1 *Mac.* 2. 24. nor could he forbear to shew his *a.*
44. they smote sinful men in their *a.*
2 *Mac.* 4. 38. and being kindled with *a.* he took
9. 4. then swelling with *a.* he thought to avenge

ANGERETH.

Eccl. 3. 16. he that *a.* his mother is cursed of God
19. 21. a servant *a.* him that nourisheth him

ANGRY.

1 *Esd.* 8. 88. mightest not thou be *a.* with us?
2 *Esd.* 16. 48. the more will I be *a.* with them
Jud. 1. 12. Nabuchodonosor *a.* with all his country
5. 2. he was very *a.* and called the princes of Moab
Eccl. 8. 16. strive not with an *a.* man, go not with
20. 2. it is better to reprove than be *a.* secretly
26. 28. two things grieve, and the third maketh *a.*
Bel 20. I see footsteps, and then the king was *a.*
Prayer of Manass. be not *a.* with me for ever
1 *Mac.* 6. 28. when he heard this he was *a.* 11. 22.
2 *Mac.* 5. 17. he considered not that the Lord was *a.*
7. 33. though the living Lord be *a.* a little while

ANGUISH.

2 *Esd.* 16. 19. tribulation and *a.* sent for amendment
Esth. 11. 8. and lo, a day of tribulation and *a.*
14. 2. put on garments of *a.* and mourning
15. 5. but her heart was in *a.* for fear
Wisd. 5. 3. they groaning for *a.* of spirit, shall say
Eccl. 27. 29. *a.* shall consume them before they die
Bar. 3. 1. the soul in *a.* the troubled spirit crieth

ANNA.

Tob. 1. 9. I married A. of mine own kindred
Tob. 1. 20. not any thing left me, besides my wife A.
2. 1. my wife A. was restored to me with my son
11. my wife A. did take women's work to do
5. 17. A. his mother wept, and said to Tobit
11. 5. now A. sat looking about for her son
9. A. ran forth, and fell on the neck of her son
14. 12. when A. his mother was dead, he buried

ANNOYANCE.

1 *Esd.* 2. 29. proceed no further to the *a.* of kings

ANNOYED.

2 *Mac.* 8. 32. who had *a.* the Jews many ways

ANOINT.

Tob. 6. 8. it is good to *a.* a man that hath whiteness
11. 8. therefore *a.* thou his eyes with the gall

ANOINTED.

2 *Esd.* 12. 32. this is the *a.* which the Highest kept
Jud. 10. 3. washed, *a.* herself with precious ointment
16. 8. and she *a.* her face with ointment
Eccl. 45. 15. Moses *a.* him with holy oil
46. 19. in the sight of the Lord and his *a.*
48. 8. who *a.* kings to take revenge and prophets
2 *Mac.* 1. 10. who was of the stock of the *a.* priests

ANSWER.

1 *Esd.* 6. 6. signification was given, and an *a.* received
13. they gave us this *a.* we are the servants
2 *Esd.* 4. 1. the angel Uriel gave me an *a.*
9. yet canst thou give me no *a.* of them
Wisd. 6. 10. that have learned, shall find what to *a.*
Eccl. 4. 8. gave him a friendly *a.* with meekness
5. 11. be swift to hear, and with patience give *a.*
12. if thou hast understanding, *a.* thy neighbour
8. 9. of the elders thou shalt learn understanding, and to give *a.* as need requireth
11. 8. *a.* not before thou hast heard the cause
20. 6. holds his tongue, because he hath not to *a.*
33. 4. bind up instruction, and then make *a.*

ANSWERED.

1 *Esd.* 9. 47. and all the people *a.* amen
Jud. 14. 15. but because none *a.* he opened it
Sus. 54. who *a.* under a mastick-tree
58. who *a.* under an holm-tree
1 *Mac.* 2. 36. they *a.* them not, nor cast they a stone

ANSWERING.

2 *Mac.* 1. 23. the rest *a.* thereunto as Neemias did

ANTILIBANUS.

Jud. 1. 7. sent to all that dwelt in Libanus and A.

ANTIOCH.

1 *Mac.* 3. 37. he departed from A. his royal city
10. 68. king Alexander returned into A.
11. 13. then Ptolemee entered into A. where he set
44. Jonathan sent three thousand men unto A.
2 *Mac.* 8. 35. he came like a fugitive servant to A.
11. 36. for we are now going to A.
13. 23. who was left over the affairs in A.
26. made them well-affected, returned to A.

ANTIOCHIA.

1 *Mac.* 4. 35. he went to A. and gathered strangers
2 *Mac.* 5. 21. he departed in all haste into A.

ANTIOCHIANS.

2 *Mac.* 4. 9. to write them by the name of A
19. sent messengers from Jerusalem who were A.

ANTIOCHIS.

2 *Mac.* 4. 30. the king's concubine called A.

ANTIOCHUS.

1 *Mac.* 1. 10. A. surnamed Epiphanes, son of A. the king, who had been an hostage at Rome
16. the kingdom was established before A.
20. after A. had smitten Egypt, he returned again
41. king A. wrote to his whole kingdom
3. 27. when A. heard, he was full of indignation
33. he left Lysias to bring up his son A.
6. 1. A. heard say, that Elymais was city renowned
15. to the end he should bring up his son A.
16. so king A. died there in the 149th year
55. whom A. had appointed to bring up his son A.
7. 2. so it was, that his forces had taken A.
8. 6. A. the great king of Asia came in battle
11. 39. that brought up A. young son of Alexander
40. lay sore on him to deliver him this young A.
57. at that time young A. wrote to Jonathan
12. 16. we chose Numenius the son of A. 14. 22.
39. Tryphon went about to kill A. the king
13. 31. dealt deceitfully with the young king A.
15. 1. A. son of Demetrius the king, sent letters
2. king A. to Simon the high priest, greeting
10. A. went into the land of his fathers
11. being pursued by king A. he fled to Dora
13. then camped A. against Dora, 25.
2 *Mac.* 1. 14. A. as though he would marry her
15. they shut the temple as soon as A. was come
4. 7. A. called Epiphanes took the kingdom
21. A. understanding him not to be well affected
37. A. was heartily sorry and moved to pity
5. 1. A. prepared his second voyage into Egypt
5. gone forth a false rumour, as if A. been dead
17. haughty was A. in mind, he considered not
21. so when A. had carried out of the temple
9. 1. A. came with dishonour out of Persia
19. A. king and governor to the good Jews
25. I have appointed my son A. king
29. who fearing the son of A. went into Egypt
10. 9. this was the end of A. called Epiphanes
10. we will declare the acts of A. Eupator
11. 22. king A. unto his brother Lysias sendeth
27. king A. sendeth greeting to the council
13. 1. A. Eupator was coming with great power
3. Menelaus with great dissimulat. encouraged A.
4. but the King of kings moved A. mind
14. 2. had killed A. and Lysias his protector
See EPIPHANES.

ANVIL.

Eccl. 38. 28. the smith also sitting by the *a.* the noise of the hammer and *a.* is ever in his ears

APAME.

1 *Esd.* 4. 29. I did see A. the king's concubine

APART.

1 *Esd.* 4. 44. all the vessels which Cyrus set *a.* 57.
Tob. 12. 6. then he took them both *a.* and said
2 *Mac.* 13. 13. Judas being *a.* with the elders

APHEREMA.

1 *Mac.* 11. 34. governments of A. Lydda, Ramath

APOLLONIUS.

1 *Mac.* 3. 10. A. gathered the Gentiles together
12. Judas took their spoils, and A. sword also
10. 69. Demetrius made A. governor of Celosyria
74. when Jonathan heard these words of A.
75. because A. had a garrison there
77. A. took 3000 horsemen with a great host
79. A. had left a thousand horsemen in ambush
2 *Mac.* 3. 5. he gat him to A. the son of Thraseas
7. when A. came to the king, and had shewed
4. 4. that A. as being the governor, did rage
21. A. son of Menestheus was sent to Egypt
5. 24. he sent that detestable ringleader A.
12. 2. A. son of Genneus would not suffer them

APOTHECARY.

Eccl. 38. 8. of such doth the *a.* make a confection
49. 1. the composition made by the art of the *a.*

APPAREL.

Jud. 8. 5. she put on sackcloth, and wore widows' *a.*
10. 7. when her *a.* was changed, they wondered
12. 15. she arose, and decked herself with her *a.*
Esth. 14. 2. Esther laid away her glorious *a.*
1 *Mac.* 14. 9. the young men put on warlike *a.*
2 *Mac.* 3. 26. to other young men comely in *a.*

APPARITION.

2 *Mac.* 5. 4. prayed that that *a.* might turn to good

APPARITIONS.

Wisd. 17. 3. being troubled with strange *a.*
15. were partly vexed with monstrous *a.*

APPEAR.

2 *Esd.* 6. 40. a fair light, that thy work might *a.*
7. 26. the bride shall *a.* and she shall be seen
33. the Most High shall *a.* on the seat of judgment
11. 16. before thou beginnest to *a.* no more
45. and therefore *a.* no more, thou eagle
Tob. 12. 19. all these days did I *a.* unto you
Jud. 14. 2. so soon as the morning shall *a.*
Eccl. 19. 25. that turneth aside to make judgment *a.*
24. 27. he maketh the doctrine of knowledge *a.*
35. 4. thou shalt not *a.* empty before the Lord
37. 18. four manner of things *a.* good, evil, life
39. 4. and he shall *a.* before princes
Bar. 6. 51. it shall manifestly *a.* to all nations
2 *Mac.* 2. 8. and the glory of the Lord shall *a.*

APPEARANCE.

2 *Esd.* 15. 28. and the *a.* thereof from the east
Eccl. 11. 2. abhor not a man for his outward *a.*
2 *Mac.* 4. 24. for the glorious *a.* of his power
15. 27. for by the *a.* of God they were cheered

APPEARED.

2 *Esd.* 10. 27. behold, the woman *a.* to me no more
42. but there *a.* unto thee a city builded
11. 13. and the place thereof *a.* no more
14. so that it *a.* no more, 18, 19, 20, 26, 33. | 12. 3
26. 2 *Mac.* 3. 34.
Tob. 12. 22. how the angel of the Lord had *a.* to them
Wisd. 17. 4. visions *a.* to them with sad countenanc.
6. there *a.* to them a fire kindled of itself
19. 7. where water stood before, dry land *a.*
1 *Mac.* 4. 19. there *a.* a part of them looking out
2 *Mac.* 1. 33. where fire was hid, there *a.* water
3. 25. there *a.* to them a horse, with a rider
26. two other young men *a.* notable in strength
30. when the Almighty Lord *a.* temple was filled
33. the same young men, in the same clothing, *a.*
11. 8. there *a.* before them on horseback one white
14. 20. it *a.* that they were all of one mind
15. 13. this done, there *a.* a man with gray hairs

APPEARETH.

Eccl. 43. 2. the sun when it *a.* declaring at his rising
Bar. 2. 6. to us and father's shame, as *a.* this day, 11.

APPEARING.

2 *Mac.* 12. 22. the *a.* of him that seeth all things

APPEASE.

Eccl. 39. 28. *a.* the wrath of him that made them
2 *Mac.* 4. 31. the king came in all haste to *a.* matters

APPEASED.

Eccl. 46. 7. they *a.* the wicked murmuring
1 *Mac.* 13. 47. so Simon was *a.* towards them

APPEASETH.

Eccl. 43. 23. by his counsel he *a.* the deep

APPERTAIN.

1 *Esd.* 8. 95. for to thee doth this matter *a.*
Tob. 6. 11. for to thee doth the right of her *a.*
12. the right of inheritance doth rather *a.* to thee

APPERTAINED.

2 *Mac.* 4. 28. to him *a.* the gathering of customs

APPERTAINETH.

1 *Esd.* 1. 12. they roasted the passover with fire, [as *a.*
Bar. 2. 6. to the Lord our God *a.* righteousness
1 *Mac.* 10. 30. that which *a.* to me to receive

APPETITE, S.

Wisd. 16. 2. preparest even quails to stir up their *a.*
19. 11. being led with their *a.* asked meats
Eccl. 18. 30. but refrain thyself from thine *a.*

APPLE.

Eccl. 17. 22. keep good deeds as the *a.* of the eye

APPLY.

Eccl. 6. 32. my son, if thou wilt *a.* thy mind

APPLIETH.

Eccl. 38. 30. he *a.* himself to lead it over

APPOINTED.

1 *Esd.* 3. 9. to him the victory be given, as was *a.*
4. 42. ask more than is *a.* in the writing
5. 58. they *a.* the Levites from twenty years old
6. 27. which were *a.* rulers in Syria and Phenice
9. 12. let all of them come at the time *a.*
Tob. 1. 21. who *a.* over his father's accounts
22. and Sarchedonus *a.* him next unto him
6. 17. for she is *a.* unto thee from the beginning
Jud. 7. 16. he *a.* to do as they had spoken
Esth. 13. 9. O Lord, if thou hast *a.* to save Israel
Eccl. 36. 26. who will trust a thief well *a.*
45. 15. was *a.* to him by an everlasting covenant
Bar. 1. 20. the curse which the Lord *a.* by Moses
5. 7. God hath *a.* that every high hill be cast down
Sus. 5. the same year were *a.* two of the ancients
Prayer of Manass. hast not *a.* repentance to the just, but hast *a.* repentance to me a sinner
1 *Mac.* 1. 51. he *a.* overseers over all the people
4. 41. then Judas *a.* certain men to fight
5. 27. had *a.* to bring their host against forts

1 *Mac.* 6. 55. whom Antiochus had *a.* to bring up his son
8. 25. Jews shall help them, as time shall be *a.*
12. 26. *a.* to come upon them in the night season
2 *Mac.* 3. 14. at the day which he *a.* he entered
4. 20. this money was *a.* to Hercules' sacrifice
8. 23. also he *a.* Eleazar to read the holy book
9. 23. considering that my father *a.* a successor
25. I have *a.* my son Antiochus king
14. 21. *a.* a day to meet together by themselves

APPOINTEDST.

2 *Esd.* 3. 7. immediately thou *a.* death in him

APPOINTMENT.

1 *Esd.* 1. 15. singers according to the *a.* of David
6. 4. said, by whose *a.* do ye build this house?

APPREHENDED.

1 *Esd.* 1. 38. but Zaraces his brother he *a.*

APPROACH.

2 *Esd.* 12. 21. be kept until their end begin to *a.*

APPROACHED.

Jud. 13. 7. *a.* to his bed, and took hold of the hair

APPROACHING.

2 *Esd.* 12. 21. the middle time *a.* four shall be kept
2 *Mac.* 12. 31. came to Jerus. the feast of the weeks *a.*

APPROVED.

2 *Esd.* 5. 27. thou gavest a law that is *a.* of all
Eccl. 3. 17. shalt be beloved of him that is *a.*
39. 34. for in time they shall all be well *a.*
41. 16. nor is it altogether *a.* in every thing
42. 8. thus shalt thou be *a.* of all men living

APT.

Wisd. 19. 21. meat that was of nature *a.* to melt

ARABIA.

2 *Esd.* 15. 29. where the dragons of A. shall come
1 *Mac.* 11. 16. Alexander fled into A. to be defended
2 *Mac.* 12. 11. the Nomades of A. besought Judas

ARABIAN.

1 *Mac.* 11. 17. Zabdiel A. took off Alexander's head
39. one Tryphon went to Simalcue the A.

ARABIANS.

1 *Mac.* 12. 31. Jonathan turned to the A.
2 *Mac.* 5. 8. being accused before Aretas king of the A.
12. 10. horsemen of the A. set upon him

ARADUS.

1 *Mac.* 15. 23. the same thing wrote he to A.

ARRAY.

Jud. 1. 4. for the setting in *a.* his footmen
2 *Mac.* 5. 3. were seen troops of horsemen in *a.*
15. 20. now when the army was set in *a.*

ARRAYED.

1 *Esd.* 1. 2. being *a.* in long garments in the temple
7. 9. the Levites stood *a.* in their vestments

ARBATTIS.

1 *Mac.* 5. 23. those that were in A. took he away

ARBELA.

1 *Mac.* 9. 2. before Massaloth, which is in A.

ARBONAI.

Jud. 2. 24. he destroyed the cities on the river A.

ARCHANGEL.

2 *Esd.* 4. 36. Uriel the *a.* gave them answer

ARCHER, S.

2 *Esd.* 16. 7. arrow that is shot of a strong *a.* 16.
Jud. 2. 15. he mustered 12,000 *a.* on horseback
1 *Mac.* 9. 11. their slingers and *a.* going before

ARDATH.

2 *Esd.* 9. 26. in the field which is called A.

ARETAS. *See* ARABIANS.

ARIGHT.

2 *Esd.* 8. 37. some things hast thou spoken *a.*
Wisd. 2. 1. reasoning with themselves, but not *a.*
6. 4. you have not judged *a.* nor kept the law
9. 16. and hardly do we guess *a.* at things
Eccl. 2. 2. set thy heart *a.* and constantly endure
6. 17. who feareth L. shall direct his friendship *a.*
20. 17. for he knoweth not *a.* what it is to have
38. 10. order thy hands *a.* and cleanse thy heart

ARIOCH.

Jud. 1. 6. came all that dwelt in the plain of A.

ARISE.

2 *Esd.* 2. 38. *a.* up and stand, behold the number
15. 39. strong winds shall *a.* from the east
Eccl. 31. 21. hast been forced to eat, *a.* vomit
Bar. 5. 5. *a.* O Jerusalem, and stand on high
1 *Mac.* 14. 41. there should *a.* a faithful prophet

ARISETH.

Eccl. 26. 16. the sun when it *a.* in high heaven

ARISTOBULUS.

2 *Mac.* 1. 10. sent greeting and health unto A.

ARK.

1 *Esd.* 1. 3. to set the holy *a.* of the Lord in the house
4. shall no more bear the *a.* on your shoulders
54. they took the vessels of the *a.* of God
2 *Esd.* 10. 22. the *a.* of our covenant is spoiled
2 *Mac.* 2. 4. commanded the *a.* to go with him
5. where laid the *a.* and altar of incense

ARM.

2 *Esd.* 15. 11. bring them with a stretched out *a.*
Wisd. 5. 16. with his *a.* shall he protect them
11. 21. who may withstand the power of thy *a.*?
16. 16. were scourged by the strength of thy *a.*
Eccl. 21. 21. as a bracelet upon his right *a.*
36. 6. glorify thy hand and thy right *a.*
38. 30. he fashioneth the clay with his *a.*
Bar. 2. 11. hast brought thy people out with high *a.*
2 *Mac.* 15. 24. through the might of thine *a.*

ARMS.

Esth. 15. 8. the king took her in his *a.*
Eccl. 9. 9. nor sit down with her in thine *a.*

ARM.

1 *Mac.* 3. 58. *a.* yourselves, and be valiant men

ARMED.

1 *Mac.* 6. 35. a thousand men *a.* with coats of mail
43. one of the beasts *a.* with royal harness
14. 32. Simon *a.* the valiant men of his nation
2 *Mac.* 4. 40. Lysimachus *a.* about 3,000 men
5. 2. *a.* with lances like a band of soldiers
14. 22. Judas placed *a.* men in convenient places
15. 11. thus he *a.* every one of them

ARMS.

Wisd. 18. 22. not with strength, nor force of *a.*
1 *Mac.* 12. 27. he commanded his men to be in *a.*
2 *Mac.* 5. 11. he took the city by force of *a.*
15. 5. I command to take *a.* and do king's business

ARMY.

Jud. 1. 16. there he banqueted, both he and his *a.*
2. 7. I will cover the earth with the feet of my *a.*
14. Holofernes called the officers of the *a.* of Assur
16. ranged them, as a great *a.* is ordered for war
18. plenty of victual for every man of the *a.*
22. then he took all his *a.* footmen, horsemen
3. 10. might gather all the carriages of his *a.*
5. 1. captain of the *a.* of Assur, 10. 13. | 13. 15.
24. be a prey to be devoured of all thine *a.*
7. 1. next day Holofernes commanded all his *a.*
2. *a.* of the men of war was 170,000 footmen
9. that there be not an overthrow in thine *a.*
12. remain in camp, keep all the men of thy *a.*
18. and the rest of the *a.* camped in the plain
26. and deliver the whole city for a spoil to his *a.*
11. 18. thou shalt go forth with all thine *a.*
16. 4. Assur came with ten thousands of his *a.*
1 *Mac.* 3. 13. Seron, a prince of the *a.* of Syria
27. he gathered together a very strong *a.*
35. that he should send an *a.* against them
4. 3. that he might smite the king's *a.*
9. when Pharaoh pursued them with an *a.*
30. when he saw that mighty *a.* he prayed
31. shut up this *a.* in the hand of thy people Israel
35. when Lysias saw his *a.* put to flight
6. 28. he gathered together the captains of his *a.*
30. the number of his *a.* was 100,000 footmen
40. part of the *a.* being spread on high mountains
41. for the *a.* was very great and mighty
42. there were slain of the king's *a.* 600 men
7. 14. one that is a priest is come with this *a.*
8. 6. having a very great *a.* was discomfited
2 *Mac.* 1. 13. the *a.* with him that seemed invincible
5. 24. he sent Apollonius with an *a.* of 22,000
8. 12. imparted to him that the *a.* was at hand
9. 9. his smell was noisome to all his *a.*
23. what time he led an *a.* into the countries
12. 20. Maccabeus ranged his *a.* by bands
15. 20. and the *a.* was set in array, and the beasts

ARMIES.

1 *Esd.* 4. 10. all his people and his *a.* obey him
Jud. 1. 4. for the going forth of his mighty *a.*
Eccl. 43. 8. being an instrument of the *a.* above

ARMOUR.

Jud. 14. 3. then they shall take their *a.* and go
15. 13. the men of Israel followed in their *a.*
1 *Mac.* 1. 35. they stored with *a.* and victuals
4. 6. had neither *a.* nor swords to their minds
6. 6. that they were made strong by the *a.*
10. 21. gathered forces and provided much *a.*
14. 33. where the *a.* of the enemies had been
42. to set them over the *a.* and fortresses
15. 7. let all the *a.* thou hast made remain
2 *Mac.* 8. 27. so when they had gathered their *a.*
11. 8. one in white, shaking his *a.* of gold
15. 21. seeing the divers preparations of *a.*

ARMOUR-BEARER.

1 *Mac.* 4. 30. Jonathan the son of Saul, and his *a.*

AROSE.

1 *Esd.* 9. 7. so Esdras *a.* up and said unto them
Tob. 8. 4. Tobias *a.* out of the bed, and said, arise
Jud. 8. 18. *a.* none in our age which worship gods
12. 5. she *a.* when it was toward morning-watch
15. she *a.* and decked herself with her apparel
14. 11. as soon as the morning *a.* they hanged
Bel 16. betime the king *a.* and Daniel with him
39. so Daniel *a.* and did eat, angel set Habbacuc

ARPHAXAD.

Jud. 1. 1. in days of A. which reigned over Medes
5. Nabuchodonosor made war with king A. 13.
15. he took also A. in the mountains of Ragau

ARROW.

2 *Esd.* 16. 7. may one turn again the *a.* that is shot
16. like as an *a.* which is shot of a mighty archer
Wisd. 5. 12. or like as when an *a.* is shot at a mark
Eccl. 19. 12. as an *a.* that sticketh in the thigh
26. 12. she will open her quiver against every *a.*

ARROWS.

2 *Esd.* 16. 13. his *a.* that he shooteth are sharp

ARSACES.

1 *Mac.* 14. 2. A. king of Persia, 3. | 15. 22.

ART.

Wisd. 14. 4. though a man went to sea without *a.*
17. 7. as for the illusions of *a.* magic, were put down
Eccl. 49. 1. that is made by the *a.* of the apothecary

ARTAXERXES.

1 *Esd.* 2. 16. in time of A. king of the Persians
17. to king A. our lord || 7. 4. with consent of A.
8. 1. when A. the king reigned, 6. 28.
8. the commission which was written from A.
9. king A. unto Esdras the priest, greeting
19. I king A. have commanded the keepers
2 *Esd.* 1. 3. A. king of the Persians, *Esth.* 11. 2.
Esth. 12. 2. they were about to lay hands on A.
16. 1. greet king A. unto the princes and governors

ARTICLES.

1 *Mac.* 8. 29. according to these *a.* did the Romans
2 *Mac.* 14. 28. should make void the *a.* agreed on

ARTIFICER.

Wisd. 14. 18. the diligence of the A. did help
Eccl. 9. 17. for hand of *a.* the work be commended

ARTILLERY.

1 *Mac.* 6. 51. and he set there *a.* with engines

ASADIAS.

Bar. 1. 1. Sedecias, son of A. son of Chelcias

ASAEL.

Tob. 1. 1. of the seed of A. of tribe of Naphtali

ASANIAS.

1 *Esd.* 8. 54. separated Esabrias, and A. and ten men

ASAPH.

1 *Esd.* 1. 15. also the sons of A. were in their order,
to wit, A. Zacharias, and Jeduthun

ASPHARASUS.

1 *Esd.* 5. 8. Beelsarus, A. Reelius returned to Jerus

ASBAZARETH.

1 *Esd.* 5. 69. from days of A. the king of the Assyria.

ASCALON.

Jud. 2. 28. that dwelt in A. feared him greatly
1 *Mac.* 10. 86. Jonathan camped against A.
11. 60. he came to A. they of the city met him
12. 33. Simon passed through the country to A.

ASER.

Tob. 1. 2. called Naphtali in Galilee above A.

ASHAMED.

1 *Esd.* 8. 51. for I was *a.* to ask the king's footmen
74. I said, O Lord, I am *a.* before thy face
Wisd. 13. 17. is not *a.* to speak to what hath no life
Eccl. 4. 26. be not *a.* to confess thy sins
21. 22. but a man of experience is *a.* of him
22. 25. I will not be *a.* to defend a friend
41. 17. be *a.* of whoredom before father and mother
42. 1. of these things be not thou *a.*
8. be not *a.* to inform the unwise and foolish
11. lest she make thee *a.* before the multitude
Bar. 6. 27. they also that serve them are *a.*
Dan. 3. 20. let all that do thy servants hurt, be *a.*
Sus. 11. for they were *a.* to declare their lust
27. when elders declared, servants were greatly *a.*

ASHES.

2 *Esd.* 2. 9. in clods of pitch and heaps of *a.*
9. 38. and she had *a.* upon her head
Tob. 6. 16. thou shalt take thee *a.* of perfume
Jud. 4. 11. they cast *a.* upon their heads
15. had *a.* on their mitres, and cried to the Lord
9. 1. put *a.* on her head, and uncovered sackcloth
Esth. 14. 2. she covered her head with *a.* and dung
Wisd. 2. 3. our body shall be turned into *a.*
15. 10. his heart is *a.* his hope more vile than earth
Eccl. 10. 9. why is earth and *a.* proud?
17. 32. and all men are but earth and *a.*
40. 3. to him that is humbled in earth and *a.*
Bel 14. Daniel commanded his servants to bring *a.*
1 *Mac.* 3. 47. then they cast *a.* upon their heads
2 *Mac.* 13. 5. now there was a tower of fifty cubits
high full of *a.* instrument hanged down into *a.*
8. committed many sins about the altar, whose fire
and *a.* were holy, he received his death in *a.*

ASIA.

2 *Esd.* 15. 46. thou A. that art partaker of hope
16. 1. woe be unto thee Babylon and A.
1 *Mac.* 8. 6. Antiochus the great king of A.
12. 39. Tryphon went about to get kingdom of A.
13. 32. and he crowned himself king of A.
2 *Mac.* 3. 3. Seleucus king of A. bare all the costs

ASIDE.

Sus. 51. put these two *a.* one far from another
56. so he put him *a.* and commanded to bring

ASK.

1 *Esd.* 4. 42. then said the king, *a.* what thou wilt
2 *Esd.* 4. 6. that thou shouldest *a.* such things of me
7. if I should *a.* how great dwellings are in the sea
35. *a.* question of these things in their chambers
5. 11. one land also shall *a.* another, and say
46. he said unto me, *a.* the womb of a woman
51. *a.* a woman that beareth children
10. 9. *a.* the earth, and she shall tell thee
Tob. 4. 18. *a.* counsel of all that are wise, despise not
Eccl. 20. 15. and to-morrow will he *a.* it again
21. 1. but *a.* pardon for thy former sins
28. 4. and doth he *a.* forgiveness of his own sins?
1 *Mac.* 10. 72. *a.* and learn whom I am, and the rest
2 *Mac.* 7. 2. what wouldest thou *a.* or learn of us?

ASKED.

2 *Esd.* 2. 44. I *a.* the angel, and said, what are these?
4. 9. now have I *a.* thee but of the fire and wind
25. of these things have I *a.* then answered he me
5. 50. I *a.* and said, seeing thou hast given me
Tob. 7. 3. Raguel *a.* them, from whence are you
Jud. 6. 16. Ozias *a.* him of that which was done
10. 12. they *a.* her, of what people art thou
Esth. 13. 3. when I *a.* counsellors how this might be
Wisd. 19. 11. led by appetite, they *a.* delicate meats
Eccl. 32. 7. scarcely when thou art *a.* twice *a.*
Sus. 14. after they *a.* one another the cause
40. we *a.* who the man was, she would not tell
2 *Mac.* 14. 5. being *a.* how the Jews stood affected

ASKEST.

2 *Esd.* 4. 28. the things thou *a.* me, I will tell, 52.
8. 2. as when thou *a.* the earth, it shall say

ASKETH.

Wisd. 13. 18. he *a.* of that which cannot set a foot
19. for gaining and getting, *a.* ability to do

ASLEEP.

2 *Esd.* 7. 32. earth restore those that are *a.* in her
Tob. 8. 13. so the maid found them both *a.*

ASMODEUS.

Tob. 3. 8. whom A. the evil spirit, had killed, 17.

ASPHAR.

1 *Mac.* 9. 33. pitched their tents by the pool A.

ASS.

Eccl. 13. 19. as the wild *a.* is the lion's prey
33. 24. fodder, a wand and burdens are for the *a.*

ASSABIAS.

1 *Esd.* 1. 9. A. and Othiel gave to the Levites

ASSAULT.

1 *Mac.* 4. 8. neither be ye afraid of their *a.*
2 *Mac.* 5. 5. Jason made an *a.* upon the city
12. 15. Judas gave a fierce *a.* against the walls

ASSAULTED.

1 *Mac.* 5. 16. were in trouble, and *a.* of them, 30, 35, 50.
6. 31. Bethsura, which they *a.* many days

ASSAULTING.

1 *Mac.* 11. 50. let the Jews cease from *a.* us
15. 25. the second day *a.* it continually
2 *Mac.* 10. 17. *a.* them strongly, they won the holds

ASSAY.

2 *Mac.* 2. 23. we will *a.* to abridge in one volume

ASSEMBLED.

1 *Esd.* 8. 72. all that were then moved *a.* unto me
9. 55. the words for which they had been *a.*
Jud. 1. 6. many nations *a.* themselves to battle
7. 23. then all the people *a.* to Ozias
Sus. 28. when the people were *a.* to her husband
Joachim, 1 *Mac.* 3. 52, 58. | 4. 37. |
5. 9, 15, 16.
1 *Mac.* 10. 61. pestilent fellows *a.* themselves
2 *Mac.* 8. 1. they *a.* about six thousand men

ASSEMBLY.

Jud. 6. 16. and the women ran to the *a.*
21. Ozias took him out of the *a.* to his house
7. 29. then there was great weeping in the *a.*
14. 6. in the *a.* of the people he fell down
Sus. 60. all the *a.* cried out with a loud voice

1 *Mac.* 14. 41. or to gather an *a.* in the country
ASSIDEANS.
1 *Mac.* 2. 42. there came to him a company of A.
7. 13. the A. were the first that sought peace
2 *Mac.* 14. 6. these of the Jews that he called A.
ASSIGN.
2 *Mac.* 4. 9. he promised to *a.* an hundred and fifty
ASSIST.
Wisd. 19. 22. didst *a.* them in every time and place
ASSISTING.
1 *Esd.* 7. 2. *a.* the ancients of the Jews and governors
ASSUERUS.
Tob. 14. 15. Nineve, which was taken by A.
ASSUR.
2 *Esd.* 2. 8. woe be to thee, A. thou that hidest
Jud. 2. 14. Holofernes called the officers of the army of A. 5. 1. | 6. 1. | 13. 15. | 14. 3.
6. 17. spoken in the midst of the princes of A.
7. 20. the company of A. remained about them
15. 6. residue of Bethulia fell on the camp of A.
16. 4. A. came out of the mountains from the north
ASSURANCE.
Wisd. 6. 18. giving heed to laws is *a.* of incorruption
ASSURED.
Eccl. 49. 10. they delivered them by *a.* hope
2 *Mac.* 7. 24. but also *a.* him with oaths
12. 25. when he had *a.* them with many words
ASSUREDLY.
Wisd. 18. 6. *a.* knowing to what oaths they had
ASSUAGE.
Eccl. 18. 16. shall not the dew *a.* the heat?
ASSYRIA.
1 *Esd.* 7. 15. he had turned counsel of the king of A.
ASSYRIANS.
Tob. 1. 2. in time of Enemessar, king of the A.
3. who came with me into the land of the A.
Jud. 1. 7. Nabuchodonosor king of the A. 2. 1, 4.
7. 17. with them five thousand of A. departed
9. 7. behold, the A. are multiplied in their power
10. 11. the first watch of the A. met her
12. 13. be made as one of the daughters of the A.
14. 2. as though ye would go toward the watch of A.
12. when the A. saw them, they sent to leaders
19. when the captains of the A. army heard
Eccl. 48. 21. he smote the host of the A.
1 *Mac.* 7. 41. were sent from the king of the A.
ASTONISHED.
Jud. 11. 16. whereat all the earth shall be *a.*
13. 17. all the people were wonderfully *a.*
14. 7. which hearing thy name shall be *a.*
15. 1. they were *a.* at the thing that was done
Wisd. 13. 4. but if they were *a.* and their power
17. 3. being horribly *a.* and troubled by apparitions
Eccl. 43. 18. the heart is *a.* at the raining of it
1 *Mac.* 6. 8. the king was *a.* and sore moved
16. 22. hereof when he heard, he was sore *a.*
2 *Mac.* 3. 24. all were *a.* at the power of God
ASTONISHMENT.
2 *Esd.* 4. 24. and our life is *a.* and fear, not worthy
ASTRAY.
Wisd. 12. 24. they went *a.* in the ways of error
Bar. 4. 28. as it was your mind to go *a.* from God
ASTYAGES.
Bel 1. king A. was gathered to his fathers
ATARGATIS.
2 *Mac.* 12. 26. marched forth to the temple of A.
ATE.
Jud. 12. 19. then she *a.* and drank before him
ATHENOBIUS.
1 *Mac.* 15. 28. he sent to him A. one of his friends
ATHENS.
2 *Mac.* 6. 1. king sent an old man of A. compel Jews
9. 15. make them equals to the citizens of A.
ATONEMENT.
Eccl. 3. 3. honoureth father, makes *a.* for his sins
30. an alms maketh an *a.* for sins
2 *Mac.* 3. 33. as the high priest was making *a.*
ATTAIN.
Eccl. 15. 7. but foolish men shall not *a.* to her
2 *Mac.* 15. 38. it is that which I could *a.* unto
ATTALUS.
1 *Mac.* 15. 22. wrote to Demetrius the king and A.
ATTEMPT.
2 *Mac.* 4. 41. they seeing the *a.* of Lysimachus
ATTEMPTS.
Eccl. 9. 4. lest thou be taken with her *a.*
ATTEMPTED.
1 *Mac.* 12. 10. have nevertheless *a.* to send to you
ATTEND.
2 *Mac.* 11. 23. every one may *a.* on his own affairs
ATTENDANCE.
1 *Mac.* 15. 32. when Athenobius saw his great *a.*
ATTENDED.
Wisd. 10. 9. delivered from pain those that *a.* on her
ATTENDETH.
Eccl. 4. 15. he that *a.* to her shall dwell securely
ATTENTION.
Prol. of Jesus Sirach. to read it with favour and *a.*
ATTENTIVE.
Eccl. 3. 29. an *a.* ear is the desire of a wise man
ATTIRE.
Jud. 12. 15. decked herself with her woman's *a.*
Eccl. 19. 30. a man's *a.* and excessive laughter
AVAILETH.
Eccl. 34. 25. if he touch it, what *a.* his washing
AVENGE.
2 *Esd.* 15. 9. saith the Lord, I will surely *a.* them
Jud. 2. 1. he should *a.* himself on all earth
1 *Mac.* 2. 67. and *a.* ye the wrong of your people
6. 22. how long ere thou *a.* our brethren?
13. 6. doubtless I will *a.* my nation and our wives
2 *Mac.* 9. 4. he thought to *a.* upon the Jews the disgr.
AVENGED.
Jud. 1. 12. would surely be *a.* on all those coasts
Esth. 16. 20. that they may be *a.* on them
Wisd. 11. 3. they were *a.* of their adversaries
1 *Mac.* 3. 15. to be *a.* of the children of Israel
7. 38. be *a.* of this man and his host
9. 42. had *a.* fully the blood of their brother
15. 4. I may be *a.* of them that destroyed it
AVENGER.
Eccl. 30. 6. he left behind him an *a.*
AVENGERS.
2 *Mac.* 4. 16. he had them to be their enemies and *a.*
AUGMENTATION.
2 *Mac.* 5. 16. were dedicated by other kings to the *a.*
AVOID.
2 *Esd.* 7. 21. they should observe to *a.* punishment
Tob. 13. 2. neither is there any that can *a.* his hand
Wisd. 16. 4. penury which they could not *a.* 16.
2 *Mac.* 2. 31. to *a.* much labouring of the work
AVOIDED.
Wisd. 17. 10. which could of no side be *a.*
AURANUS.
2 *Mac.* 4. 40. began first to offer violence to one A.
AUTHOR.
Wisd. 13. 3. for first *a.* of beauty had created them
2 *Mac.* 2. 28. leaving to the *a.* the exact handling
30. belongeth to the first *a.* of the story
7. 31. thou that hast been the *a.* of all mischief
AUTHORS.
Bar. 3. 23. the *a.* of fables and searchers out of
1 *Mac.* 9. 61. that were *a.* of that mischief
AUTHORITY.
1 *Esd.* 8. 22. no man have *a.* to impose any thing
Esth. 13. 2. lifted up with presumption of my *a.*
16. 5. caused many that are in *a.* to be partakers
7. of them that are unworthily placed in *a.*
Wisd. 14. 19. for he willing to please one in *a.*
Eccl. 3. 2. Lord hath confirmed the *a.* of the mother
10. 3. through the prudence of them that are in *a.*
21. the fear of Lord goeth before the obtaining *a.*
20. 8. he that taketh to himself *a.* therein
45. 17. gave him *a.* in the statutes of judgments
1 *Mac.* 1. 58. thus did they by their *a.* 10. 6.
10. 32. as for the tower, I yield up my *a.* over it
35. no man shall have *a.* to meddle with them
2 *Mac.* 4. 50. Menelaus remained still in *a.*
AWE.
Wisd. 6. 7. nor stand in *a.* of any man's greatness
AWAKE.
Esth. 11. 12. when Mardocheus was *a.* he bare
Eccl. 13. 13. when hearest these things *a.* in thy sleep
AWAKED.
1 *Esd.* 3. 3. Darius slept, and soon after *a.*
2 *Esd.* 5. 14. I *a.* and fearfulness went thro' my body
11. 29. *a.* one of the heads that were at rest
12. 3. then *a.* I out of the trouble of my mind
13. 13. then was I sick through great fear, and I *a.*
Eccl. 33. 16. I *a.* up last of all, as one that gathers
AWAKETH.
2 *Esd.* 7. 31. the world that yet *a.* not be raised
Eccl. 40. 7. when all is safe, he *a.* and marvelleth
AWARE.
Eccl. 19. 27. do thee a mischief ere thou be *a.*
AXE.
Bar. 6. 15. he hath in his hand a dagger and an *a.*
AXLE-TREE.
Eccl. 33. 5. his thoughts are like a rolling *a.*
AZARIAS.
2 *Esd.* 1. 1. the son of A. the son of Helchias
Tob. 5. 12. he said, I am A. the son of Ananias
6. 6. brother A. to what use is the heart?
13. A. this maid hath been given to seven men
7. 8. Tobias said, brother A. speak of those things
9. 2. brother A. take with thee a servant
Dan. 3. 2. then A. stood up and prayed thus
26. angel came into the oven together with A.
66. O Ananias, A. and Misael, bless ye the Lord
1 *Mac.* 2. 59. A. by believing was saved out of fire
5. 18. so he left A. captain of the people
AZOTUS.
Jud. 2. 28. fear fell on them that dwelt in A.
1 *Mac.* 4. 15. to the plains of Idumea and A.
5. 68. Judas turned to A. in the land of Philistines
9. 15. who pursued them to the mount A.
10. 77. he went to A. as one that journeyed
83. the horsemen being scattered fled to A.
11. 4. when he came near to A. they shewed him the temple of Dagon that was burnt, and A.
14. 34. he fortified Gazara that bordereth upon A.
16. 10. they fled to the towers in the fields of A.

B.

BAAL.
Tob. 1. 5. Naphtali sacrificed to the heifer B.
BABES.
2 *Esd.* 1. 28. I prayed you as a nurse her young *b.*
Wisd. 15. 14. are more miserable than very *b.*
BABBLER.
Eccl. 20. 7. a *b.* and a fool will regard no time
BABBLING.
Eccl. 19. 6. he that hateth *b.* shall have less evil
20. 5. another by much *b.* becometh hateful
BABYLON.
1 *Esd.* 1. 40. and carried him into B. 54. 56.
41. he set them in his own temple at B.
2 *Esd.* 3. 1. I was in B. and lay troubled on my bed
28. are their deeds any better that inhabit B.?
31. are they of B. better than they of Sion?
15. 46. that art partaker of the hope of B.
16. 1. woe be to thee, B. and Asia, woe be to Egypt
Bar. 1. 1. the words which Baruch wrote in B.
Sus. 1. there dwelt a man in B. called Joacim
Bel. 34. carry the dinner that thou hast to B.
35. Lord, I never saw B. nor do I know the den
36. then the angel set him in B. over the den
BABYLONIANS.
Bel. 3. now the B. had an idol called Bel
BACCHUS.
2 *Mac.* 6. 7. when the feast of B. was kept, the Jews were compelled to go in procession to B.
BACCHIDES.
1 *Mac.* 7. 8. the king chose B. a friend of the king
9. 26. and they brought Judas' friends to B.
2 *Mac.* 8. 30. that were with Timotheus and B.
BACKBITING.
Wisd. 1. 11. and refrain your tongue from *b.*
Eccl. 28. 14. a *b.* tongue hath disquieted many
15. a *b.* tongue hath cast out virtuous women
BACKWARD.
2 *Esd.* 16. 16. like as an arrow returneth not *b.*
Eccl. 48. 23. in his time the sun went *b.*
BAG.
Jud. 10. 5. Judith filled a *b.* with parched corn
13. 10. she put his head in her *b.* of meat
15. so she took the head out of the *b.*
BAGS.
Tob. 9. 5. who brought forth *b.* sealed up
BAGGAGE.
Jud. 7. 2. beside the *b.* and other men afoot
2 *Mac.* 12. 21. he sent the other *b.* unto a fortress
BAGOAS.
Jud. 12. 11. then said he to B. the eunuch, 13. | 13. 3
15. soft skins, which she had received of B.
14. 14. then went B. and knocked at the door
BALANCE.
2 *Esd.* 3. 34. weigh thou our wickedness in the *b.*
Wisd. 11. 22. the world is as a little grain of the *b.*
Eccl. 21. 25. their words are weighed in the *b.*
28. 25. weigh thy words in a *b.* and make a door
BALTHASAR.
Bar. 1. 12. we shall live under the shadow of B.
BAND.
2 *Mac.* 5. 2. with lances like a *b.* of soldiers
8. 22. leaders of each *b.* to wit, Simon, Joseph
BANDS.
Jud. 14. 11. they went forth by *b.* to the straits
Eccl. 6. 30. and her *b.* are purple lace
28. 19. nor hath been bound in her *b.*
20. and the *b.* thereof are *b.* of brass
BANQUET.
Jud. 12. 10. called none of the officers to the *b.*
Eccl. 32. 5. a concert of music in a *b.* of wine
49. 1. it is as honey and music at a *b.* of wine
1 *Mac.* 16. 15. son of Abubus made them a great *b.*
2 *Mac.* 2. 27. no ease to him that prepareth a *b.*
BANQUETED.
Jud. 1. 16. and there he took his ease and *b.*
BANQUETING.
Eccl. 18. 33. be not made a beggar by *b.* or borrow.
1 *Mac.* 16. 16. came on Simon into the *b.* place
BAR.
Eccl. 28. 25. make a door and *b.* for thy mouth
BARS.
Wisd. 17. 16. shut up in prison, without iron *b.*
BARBAROUS.
2 *Mac.* 2. 21. so that a few chased *b.* multitudes
5. 22. for manners, more *b.* than he that set him
BARBAROUSLY.
2 *Mac.* 15. 2. O destroy not so cruelly and *b.*
BARE.
Eccl. 13. 5. he will make thee *b.* and not be sorry
BARE.
2 *Mac.* 7. 27. have pity on me that *b.* thee
BARK.
Wisd. 13. 11. and taken off all the *b.* skilfully
BARREN.
2 *Esd.* 9. 43. she said, I thy servant have been *b.*
Wisd. 3. 13. blessed is the *b.* that is undefiled
Eccl. 42. 10. when she is married, lest she should be *b.*
BARTACUS.
1 *Esd.* 4. 29. the daughter of the admirable B.
BARUCH.
Bar. 1. 1. the words of the book which B. wrote
3. B. did read the words of this book
BASENESS.
Eccl. 22. 9. they shall cover the *b.* of their parents
BASHFULNESS.
Eccl. 20. 23. there is that for *b.* promiseth to his friend
BASTARD.
Wisd. 4. 3. nor take deep rooting from *b.* slips
BATS.
Bar. 6. 22. on their bodies and heads sit *b.* and birds
BATTERED.
1 *Mac.* 13. 43. Simon *b.* a certain tower and took it
BATTLE.
1 *Esd.* 1. 29. but joined *b.* with him in the plain
30. carry me away out of *b.* for I am very weak, his servants took him away out of the *b.*
2 *Esd.* 7. 57. this is the condition of the *b.*
Jud. 1. 6. many assembled themselves to *b.*
13. then he marched in *b.* array with his power
5. 23. they have no power for a strong *b.*
7. 11. my lord, fight not against them in *b.*
14. 13. have been bold to come down against us to *b.*
Esth. 11. 7. all nations were prepared to *b.*
Wisd. 12. 9. under the hand of the righteous in *b.*
Eccl. 46. 6. he made the *b.* to fall on the nations
1 *Mac.* 2. 35. they gave them the *b.* with speed
41. whosoever shall come to make *b.* with us
4. 14. so they joined the *b.* and the heathen fled
6. 30. thirty-two elephants exercised in *b.*
2 *Mac.* 10. 28. making their rage leader of their *b.*
See Join.
BATTLES.
Jud. 5. 18. they were destroyed in many *b.* very sore
9. 7. thou art the Lord that breakest the *b.*
16. 3. God breaketh the *b.* for he delivered me
1 *Mac.* 3. 26. all nations talked of the *b.* of Judas
13. 9. they answered, saying, fight thou our *b.*
BATTLEMENTS.
Eccl. 9. 13. thou walkest on the *b.* of the city
BEAR.
1 *Esd.* 1. 4. Josias said, ye shall no more *b.* the ark
4. 15. all the people that *b.* rule by sea and land
Eccl. 1. 23. a patient man will *b.* for a time
6. 25. bow down thy shoulder and *b.* her
22. 15. a mass of iron is easier to *b.* than a man
BEARETH.
2 *Esd.* 5. 51. he said, ask a woman that *b.* children
BEARDS.
Bar. 6. 31. priests sit, and their heads and *b.* shaven
BEARS.
Wisd. 11. 17. to send a multitude of *b.* or fierce lions
Eccl. 47. 3. he played with *b.* as with lambs
BEAST.
Wisd. 13. 14. or made it like some vile *b.*
Eccl. 13. 15. every *b.* loveth his like, every man lov
1 *Mac.* 6. 36. wheresoever the *b.* was, they went
BEASTS.
2 *Esd.* 8. 29. them which have lived like *b.*
30. at them which are deemed worse than *b.*

Wisd. 11. 15. worshipped wild *b.* thou didst send a multitude of unreasonable *b.* for vengeance
12. 9. or to destroy them at once with cruel *b.*
15. 18. they worshipped those *b.* most hateful
16. 1. by the multitude of *b.* were tormented
3. for the ugly sight of the *b.* sent among them
5. the horrible fierceness of *b.* came on these
17. 9. yet being scared with *b.* that passed by
19. a terrible sound or a running of skipping *b.* or a roaring voice of most savage wild *b.*
1 *Mac.* 6. 37. on the *b.* were there strong towers
2 *Mac.* 15. 21. seeing the fierceness of the *b.*

BEAT.

Eccl. 30. 12. *b.* him on the sides while he is a child

BEATEN.

Eccl. 23. 10. as a servant that is continually *b.*
2 *Mac.* 6. 30. I endure pains in body by being *b.*

BEAUTY.

1 *Esd.* 4. 18. do they not love a woman comely in *b.?*
2 *Esd.* 10. 50. he shewed thee the comeliness of her *b.*
55. see the *b.* and greatness of the building
15. 63. and they shall mar the *b.* of thy face
Jud. 10. 7. they wondered greatly at her *b.* 14.
11. 21. both for *b.* of face and wisdom of words
16. 7. weakened him with the *b.* of her countenance
9. her *b.* ravished, took his mind prisoner
Esth. 15. 5. ruddy through the perfection of her *b.*
Wisd. 7. 10. I loved her above health and *b.*
8. 2. to wake my spouse, and I was a lover of her *b.*
13. 3. with whose *b.* they being delighted; for the first author of *b.* hath created them
5. by the greatness and *b.* of the creatures
Eccl. 9. 8. look not on another's *b.* many have been deceived by the *b.* of a woman, love kindled
11. 2. commend not a man for his *b.* nor abhor him
26. 16. so is *b.* of a good wife in ordering her house
17. so is the *b.* of the face in ripe age
36. 22. the *b.* of a woman cheereth the countenance
40. 22. thine eye desireth favour and *b.*
42. 12. behold not every body's *b.* and sit not
43. 1. pride of height, the *b.* of heaven, 9, 18.
Sus. 32. that they might be filled with her *b.*
1 *Mac.* 1. 26. so that the *b.* of women was changed

BEAUTIFIED.

Eccl. 25. 1. in three things I was *b.* and stood up
45. 7. he *b.* him with comely ornaments
47. 10. he *b.* their feasts and set in order the time
1 *Mac.* 14. 15. he *b.* the sanctuary, and multiplied

BEAUTIFUL.

Jud. 11. 23. *b.* in countenance and witty in words
Wisd. 5. 16. a *b.* crown from the Lord's hands
7. 29. for she is more *b.* than the sun
13. 7. because the things are but *b.* that are seen
15. 19. nor are they *b.* so much as to be desired
Eccl. 9. 8. turn away thine eye from a *b.* woman
25. 1. I stood up *b.* both before God and men
43. 11. very *b.* it is in the brightness thereof
45. 12. the desires of the eyes, goodly and *b.*
Bar. 6. 24. the gold about them to make them *b.*

BEAUTEOUS.

Sus. 31. was a delicate woman and *b.* to behold

BECOMETH.

2 *Esd.* 8. 49. thou hast humbled thyself, as it *b.* thee

BECTILETH.

Jud. 2. 21. they went forth of Nineve toward the plain of B. and pitched from B. near mountain

BED.

2 *Esd.* 12. 26. that one of them shall die on his *b.*
Tob. 8. 4. Tobias rose out of the *b.* and said
14. 11. he gave up the ghost in *b.* 158 years old
Jud. 9. 3. so that they dyed their *b.* in blood
10. 21. Holofernes rested on his *b.* under a canopy
13. 2. and Holofernes lying along on his *b.*
4. Judith standing by his *b.* said in her heart
6. then she came to the pillar of the *b.*
7. approached his *b.* and took the hair of his head
9. she tumbled his body down from the *b.*
Wisd. 3. 13. which hath not known the sinful *b.*
Eccl. 24. 31. and I will water my garden *b.*
31. 19. he fetcheth not his wind short on his *b.*
41. 22. and come not near his maid's *b.*
48. 6. broughtest honourable men from their *b.*

BED-CHAMBER.

Jud. 13. 3. her maid to stand without her *b.*
4. so all went forth, none was left in the *b.*
14. 15. he went into the *b.* and found him dead
16. 19. the canopy which he had taken out of his *b.*

BEDS.

Jud. 13. 1. they went to their *b.* they were weary
Wisd. 4. 6. for children begotten of unlawful *b.*

BEG.

Eccl. 40. 28. for better it is to die than to *b.*

BEGAN.

2 *Esd.* 3. 12. they that dwelt on earth *b.* to multiply

BEGAT.

Eccl. 22. 3. is the dishonour of his father that *b.* him

BEGET.

2 *Mac.* 14. 25. prayed him to take a wife and *b.* child.

BEGGAR, S.

Eccl. 18. 33. be not made a *b.* by banqueting
40. 28. lead not a *b.* life, for better to die than beg

BEGGING.

Eccl. 40. 30. *b.* is sweet in mouth of the shameless

BEGIN.

2 *Mac.* 2. 32. here then will we *b.* the story

BEGINNETH.

Eccl. 18. 7. when a man hath done then he *b.*
36. 24. he that getteth a wife, *b.* a possession

BEGINNING.

2 *Esd.* 1. 13. in the *b.* I gave you a safe passage
3. 4. O Lord, who bearest rule, thou spakest at the *b.*
4. 30. sown in the heart of Adam from the *b.*
9. 5. as all made in the world hath a *b.* and an end
16. 18. the *b.* of sorrows and great mournings, the *b.* of famine and great dearth, the *b.* of wars, the *b.* of evils, what shall I do?
Tob. 4. 12. that our fathers from the *b.* married
6. 17. for she is appointed to thee from the *b.*
Jud. 8. 29. from the *b.* people knew thy understand.
Esth. 13. 15. that hath been thine from the *b.*
Wisd. 6. 22. I will seek her out from the *b.*
7. 5. no king that had any other *b.* of birth
18. the *b.* ending, and midst of the times
9. 8. which thou hast prepared from the *b.*
12. 16. for thy power is the *b.* of righteousness
14. 12. devising of idols was the *b.* of fornication
13. for neither were they from the *b.*
27. for the worshipping of idols is the *b.* of evil
Eccl. 1. 14. to fear the Lord is the *b.* of wisdom, 25. 12.
10. 12. the *b.* of pride is when one departeth
11. 16. error and darkness had their *b.* with sinners
15. 14. he himself made man from the *b.*
24. 9. he created me from the *b.* before the world
25. 12. faith is the *b.* of cleaving unto him
36. 11. and inherit thou them as from the *b.*
39. 25. good things are created from the *b.*
Bar. 3. 26. there were the giants famous from the *b.*
2 *Mac.* 1. 23. Jonathan *b.* and the rest answering
7. 23. who found out the *b.* of all things
8. 27. which was the *b.* of mercy upon them

BEGOT.

Eccl. 7. 28. remember that thou wast *b.* of them

BEGOTTEN.

Tob. 8. 17. of two that were the only *b.* children
Wisd. 4. 6. childr. *b.* of unlawful beds are witnesses

BEGUILE.

Wisd. 4. 11. lest that wickedness should *b.* his soul

BEGUILING.

Esth. 16. 6. *b.* with falsehood of their lewd disposition

BEHAVED.

Eccl. 49. 2. he *b.* himself uprightly in the conversion
2 *Mac.* 2. 21. those that *b.* themselves manfully

BEHAVIOUR.

Esth. 16. 7. done through the pestilent *b.* of them
Wisd. 19. 13. they used a more hard and hateful *b.*

BEHIND.

Wisd. 8. 13. leave *b.* me an everlasting memorial
Eccl. 11. 11. that laboureth, and is so much more *b.*

BEHOLDER.

Esth. 15. 2. G. who is the *b.* and saviour of all things
Wisd. 1. 6. for God is a true *b.* of his heart

BEHOLDETH.

Eccl. 15. 18. mighty in power, and *b.* all things

BEL.

Bar. 6. 41. they entreat B. that he may speak
Bel 3. the Babylonians had an idol called B.
4. the king said, why dost not thou worship B.?
18. great art thou, O B. with thee is no deceit
22. the king delivered B. into Daniel's power

BELIEVE.

2 *Esd.* 1. 37. yet in spirit they *b.* the thing I say
16. 36. *b.* not the gods of whom the Lord spake
Tob. 2. 14. howbeit, I did not *b.* her, bade her render
14. 4. for I surely *b.* those things Jonas spake
Wisd. 12. 2. leaving wickedness, they may *b.* on thee
18. 13. and whereas they would not *b.* any thing
Eccl. 2. 6. *b.* in him, and he will help thee
13. 11. affect not to be equal, *b.* not his words
36. 26. so who will *b.* a man that hath no house?

BELIEVED.

2 *Esd.* 3. 32. or what generation hath so *b.* as Jacob?
5. 29. they which *b.* not thy covenants, 7. 60.
9. 7. and by faith, whereby ye have *b.*
Jud. 14. 10. he *b.* in God greatly, and was joined
Eccl. 31. 23. his good house-keeping will be *b.*
Sus. 41. then the assembly *b.* them as the elders
1 *Mac.* 7. 16. whereupon they *b.* him

BELIEVETH.

Eccl. 2. 13. woe to the faint hearted, for he *b.* not
32. 24. he that *b.* in the Lord taketh heed

BELIEVING.

1 *Mac.* 12. 46. so Jonathan *b.* him, did as he bade

BELLS.

Eccl. 45. 9. he compassed him with golden *b.*

BELLY.

Eccl. 23. 6. let not the greediness of the *b.* take hold
31. 20. pangs of *b.* are with an unsatiable man
36. 18. the *b.* devoureth all meats, yet one meat
37. 5. which helpeth his friend for the *b.*
40. 30. but in his *b.* there shall burn a fire
51. 5. delivered from the depth of the *b.* of hell

BELONGETH.

Tob. 3. 17. because she *b.* to Tobias by right

BELOVED.

2 *Esd.* 16. 74. hear, O ye my *b.* saith the Lord
Wisd. 4. 10. he pleased God, and was *b.* of him
Eccl. 7. 35. that shall make thee to be *b.* 20. 13.
24. 11. likewise in the *b.* city he gave me rest
45. 1. he brought out Moses *b.* of God and men
46. 13. Samuel the prophet of Lord, *b.* of his Lord
47. 16. and for thy peace thou wast *b.*
1 *Mac.* 6. 11. I was bountiful, and *b.* in my power

BENDED.

Eccl. 43. 12. the hands of the Most High have *b.* it

BENDETH.

2 *Esd.* 16. 13. his right hand that *b.* the bow

BENEFIT.

Wisd. 16. 24. for the *b.* of such as trust in thee
2 *Mac.* 2. 27. and that seeketh the *b.* of others

BENEFITS.

2 *Esd.* 9. 10. who in their life have received *b.*
Eccl. 12. 1. so shalt thou be thanked for thy *b.*
1 *Mac.* 11. 53. according to the *b.* which he received
2 *Mac.* 9. 26. I request you to remember the *b.*

BENEFITED.

Wisd. 11. 5. by the same they in their need were *b.*
13. when they heard the other to be *b.*

BERYL.

Tob. 13. 17. the streets shall be paved with *b.*

BESEECHETH.

Wisd. 13. 18. he humbly *b.* that which hath least

BESIEGE.

1 *Mac.* 6. 19. called the people together to *b.* them
24. for which they of our nation *b.* the tower

BESIEGED.

1 *Mac.* 6. 20. so they came together and *b.* them
21. howbeit, certain of them that were *b.* got forth

BESIEGING.

Eccl. 50. 4. he fortified the city against *b.*

BESOUGHT.

Jud. 12. 8. she *b.* Lord God of Isr. to direct her way
Wisd. 8. 21. I prayed to the Lord and *b.* him
18. 2. they thanked them, and *b.* them pardon

BESTOW.

Bar. 6. 10. the priests *b.* it upon themselves

BESTOWED.

2 *Mac.* 1. 35. the king took many gifts and *b.* on those

BETHORON.

Jud. 4. 4. sent to B. and Belmen, and Jericho
1 *Mac.* 7. 39. Nicanor pitched his tents in B.

BETHSHAN.

1 *Mac.* 5. 52. they went into the great plain before B.
12. 40. so he removed and came to B.

BETHSURA.

1 *Mac.* 4. 29. they pitched their tents at B. 6. 7, 31.
2 *Mac.* 13. 19. the king marched towards B.
22. the king treated with them in B. second time

BETHULIA.

Jud. 4. 6. Joacim wrote them that dwelt in B.
6. 14. the Israelites brought him into B. 10, 11.
8. 3. Manasses died in the city of B. they buried him
10. 6. but they went forth to the gate of B.
11. 9. for the men of B. saved Achior

BETIMES.

Eccl. 6. 36. get *b.* to him, and let thy foot wear
51. 30. work your work *b.* he will give reward
1 *Mac.* 4. 52. they rose up *b.* in the morning
See MORNING.

BETRAYING.

Wisd. 17. 12. for fear is nothing else but a *b.*

BETROTHED.

1 *Mac.* 3. 56. but as for such as had *b.* wives

BETTER.

2 *Esd.* 1. 18. it had been *b.* for us to have served
3. 31. are they of Babylon *b.* than they of Sion?
5. 33. lovest thou people *b.* than he that made them
7. 46. it had been *b.* not to have given the earth
12. 44. how much *b.* had it been for us
Tob. 12. 8. a little with righteousness is *b.* than much with unright. it is *b.* to give alms than to lay up
Wisd. 4. 1. *b.* it is to have no children and have virtue
15. 17. he himself is *b.* than things he worshipped
Eccl. 10. 27. *b.* is he that laboureth and aboundeth
16. 3. one that is just is *b.* than a thousand
18. 16. asswage the heat? so is a word *b.* than a gift
17. lo, is not a word *b.* than a gift?
19. 24. he that feareth God is *b.* than one that hath
20. 2. it is much *b.* to reprove than to be angry
18. it is *b.* than to slip with the tongue
25. a thief is *b.* than a man accustomed to lie
31. *b.* is he that hideth folly than wisdom
32. necessary patience in seeking the Ld. is *b.* than
28. 21. an evil death, the grave were *b.* than it
29. 13. *b.* than a mighty shield and strong spear
22. *b.* is the life of a poor man in a cottage
30. 14. *b.* is the poor being sound and strong
17. death is *b.* than a bitter life or sickness
36. 18. all meats, yet is one meat *b.* than another
22. and a man loveth nothing *b.*
40. 28. for *b.* it is to die than to beg
41. 15. is *b.* than a man that hideth his wisdom
42. 14. *b.* is the churlishness of a man than
Bar. 6. 59. *b.* be a king that sheweth his power
1 *Mac.* 3. 59. for it is *b.* for us to die in battle
13. 5. for I am no *b.* than my brethren

BEWAIL.

2 *Esd.* 16. 2. *b.* your children and be sorry
Tob. 10. 4. and she began to *b.* him and said
7. she ceased not whole nights to *b.* her son
Bel 40. on seventh day the king went to *b.* Daniel

BEWAILED.

Wisd. 18. 10. a noise for children that were *b.*
Eccl. 51. 19. I *b.* my ignorances of her
1 *Mac.* 12. 52. and there they *b.* Jonathan
13. 26. and all Israel *b.* him many days

BEWARE.

Tob. 4. 12. *b.* of all whoredom, my son
Wisd. 1. 11. *b.* of murmuring which is unprofitable
Eccl. 4. 20. *b.* of evil, and be not ashamed when
12. 11. though he humble himself, yet *b.* of him
13. 8. *b.* that thou be not deceived and brought down
17. 14. he said *b.* of all unrighteousness
18. 27. in the day of sinning he will *b.* of offence
22. 13. *b.* of him, lest thou have trouble
26. every one that heareth it, will *b.* of him
29. 20. *b.* thou thyself fall not into the same
32. 22. and *b.* of thine own children
37. 8. *b.* of a counsellor, know what need he hath
40. 29. but a wise man well nurtured will *b.*

BEWITCHING.

Wisd. 4. 12. the *b.* of naughtiness doth obscure

BEWRAYER.

2 *Mac.* 4. 1. having been a *b.* of the money

BEWRAYETH.

Eccl. 27. 21. he that *b.* secrets, is without hope

BIDDEN.

Tob. 7. 17. when she had done as he had *b.* her

BILL.

Eccl. 25. 26. give her a *b.* of divorce, let her go

BIND.

Jud. 8. 16. do not *b.* the counsels of the Lord
Eccl. 7. 8. *b.* not one sin upon another for in one
28. 24. and *b.* up thy silver and gold
30. 7. *b.* up his wounds, and his bowels be troubled

BIRD.

Wisd. 5. 11. or as when a *b.* has flown through the air
Eccl. 27. 19. as one that lets a *b.* go out of hand

BIRDS.

Wisd. 17. 18. melodious noise of *b.* among branches
Eccl. 27. 9. the *b.* will resort to their like
43. 17. as *b.* flying he scattereth the snow

BIRTH.

2 *Esd.* 4. 40. her womb may keep the *b.* any longer
16. 38. within two or three hours of her *b.*
Wisd. 7. 5. that had any other beginning of *b.*
2 *Mac.* 6. 7. in the day of the king's *b.* were brought

BITINGS.

Wisd. 16. 9. them *b.* of grasshoppers and flies killed

BITTEN.

Eccl. 12. 13. who will pity a charmer that is *b.?*

BITTER.

Esth. 14. 8. satisfieth not that we are in *b.* captivity
Eccl. 29. 25. moreover, thou shalt hear *b.* words
30. 17. death is better than a *b.* life or sickness
41. 1. O death, how *b.* is the remembrance of thee

2 *Mac.* 6. 7. they were brought by *b.* constraint
BITTERLY.
Eccl. 25. 18. when husband heareth it, shall sigh *b.*
38. 17. weep *b.* and make great moan
BITTERNESS.
Wisd. 8. 16. for her conversation hath no *b.*
Eccl. 4. 6. if he curse thee in the *b.* of his soul
7. 11. laugh no man to scorn in the *b.* of his soul
21. 12. there is a wisdom which multiplieth *b.*
31. 29. wine with excess maketh *b.* of the mind
BLACKER.
2 *Esd.* 7. 55. our faces shall be *b.* than darkness
BLAME.
Eccl. 11. 7. *b.* not before thou hast examined truth
31. in things worthy praise, will lay *b.* on thee
BLAMED.
Wisd. 13. 6. for this they are the less to be *b.*
2 *Mac.* 2. 7. when Jeremy perceived, he *b.* them
BLAMELESS.
Wisd. 2. 22. nor discerned a reward for *b.* souls
10. 5. she preserved him *b.* to God, and kept him
15. she delivered the righteous people and *b.* seed
18. 21. for then the *b.* man made haste to defend
BLASPHEME.
2 *Mac.* 15. 24. come against thy holy people to *b.*
BLASPHEMED.
1 *Mac.* 7. 41. they that were sent from Assyrians *b.*
2 *Mac.* 10. 34. they that were within *b.* exceedingly
BLASPHEMER.
Wisd. 1. 6. wisdom will not acquit a *b.* of his words
Eccl. 3. 16. that forsaketh his father, is as a *b.*
2 *Mac.* 9. 28. the *b.* died a miserable death
15. 32. he shewed them the hand of that *b.*
BLASPHEMIES.
2 *Esd.* 1. 23. I gave you not fire for your *b.*
1 *Mac.* 2. 6. when he saw the *b.* that were committed
7. 38. remember their *b.* and suffer them not
2 *Mac.* 8. 4. the *b.* committed against his name
BLASPHEMING.
2 *Mac.* 12. 14. they behaved themselves rudely, *b.*
BLASPHEMOUS.
2 *Mac.* 10. 4. might not be delivered to the *b.* nations
13. 11. to be in subjection to the *b.* nations
BLASPHEMOUSLY.
1 *Mac.* 7. 42. rest may know that he hath spoken *b.*
BLAST.
2 *Esd.* 4. 5. or measure me the *b.* of the wind
13. 27. out of his mouth came as a *b.* of wind
Wisd. 11. 20. they have fallen down with one *b.*
BLASTING.
2 *Esd.* 15. 13. for their seeds shall fail thro' the *b.*
BLEED.
Eccl. 42. 5. and to make side of an evil servant to *b.*
BLEMISH.
Eccl. 18. 15. my son, *b.* not thy good deeds
31. 8. blessed is the rich that is found without *b.*
BLESS.
Tob. 4. 19. *b.* the Lord thy God alway, and desire
8. 5. let the heavens *b.* thee, and all creatures
13. 13. they shall *b.* the Lord of the just
15. let my soul *b.* God the great King
Eccl. 4. 13. where she enters, the Lord will *b.*
32. 13. for these things *b.* him that made thee
39. 14. sing praise, *b.* the Lord in all his works
45. 15. they should *b.* the people in his name
50. 22. *b.* ye God of all who doth wondrous things
Dan. 3. 35. *b.* ye the Lord, 36, 37, 38, 39, 40, &c.
BLESSED.
1 *Esd.* 4. 40. *b.* be the God of truth
60. *b.* art thou who hast given me wisdom
9. 46. so Esdras *b.* the Lord God most high
2 *Esd.* 13. 24. are more *b.* than they that be dead
Tob. 3. 11. *b.* art thou, O Lord my God, thy holy
and glorious name is *b.* and honourable for
ever, 8. 5. | 11. 14. *Jud.* 13. 17.
4. 12. our fathers were *b.* in their children
7. 7. Raguel *b.* him, and said unto him, thou art
13. behold, take her and lead her, and he *b.* them
10. 11. he *b.* them, and sent them away, 11. 17.
13. 1. Tobit wrote prayer of rejoicing, and said, *b.*
be God that liveth for ever, and *b.* his kingdom
12. *b.* shall all be which love thee for ever
14. *b.* are they who love thee, *b.* are they who
have been sorrowful for all thy scourges
18. *b.* be God which hath extolled it for ever
Jud. 14. 7. *b.* art thou in the tabernacle of Juda
15. 9. they *b.* her with one accord, and said
10. *b.* be thou of the almighty Lord for ever
Wisd. 2. 16. he pronounceth the just to be *b.*
3. 13. *b.* is the barren that is undefiled
14. 7. *b.* is the word whereby righteousness comes
Eccl. 11. 28. judge none *b.* before his death
14. 1. *b.* is man that hath not slipped with mouth
2. *b.* is he whose conscience hath not condemned
20. *b.* is the man that doth meditate good things
26. 1. *b.* is the man that hath a virtuous wife
31. 8. *b.* is the rich that is found without blemish
9. who is he? and we will call him *b.*
33. 12. some of them hath he *b.* and exalted
34. 15. *b.* is the soul of him that feareth the Lord
45. 1. Moses beloved, whose memorial is *b.* 49. 10.
46. 11. the judges, let their memory be *b.*
48. 11. *b.* are they that saw thee, and slept in love
50. 28. *b.* is he shall be exercised in these things
29. *b.* be the Lord for ever, amen, amen
2 *Mac.* 1. 17. *b.* be our God in all things
15. 34. *b.* be he that hath kept his own place
BLESSETH.
1 *Esd.* 4. 36. calleth upon truth, and the heaven *b.* it
BLESSING.
Wisd. 15. 19. without the praise of God and his *b.*
Eccl. 3. 8. that a *b.* may come on thee from them
9. for *b.* of father establisheth houses of children
11. 22. *b.* of the Lord is the reward of the godly
33. 16. by the *b.* of the Lord I profited and filled
34. 17. he giveth health, life, and *b.*
36. 17. according to *b.* of Aaron over thy people
37. 24. a wise man shall be filled with *b.*
39. 22. his *b.* covered the dry land as a river
44. 22. with Isaac did he establish the *b.* of all men
23. he acknowledged him in his *b.* and gave him
50. 20. to give the *b.* of the Lord with his lips

Eccl. 50. 21. bowed down, that they might receive a *b.*
BLESSINGS.
Eccl. 16. 29. the Lord filled the earth with his *b.*
47. 6. the people praised him in the *b.* of the Lord
BLIND.
Eccl. 20. 29. presents and gifts *b.* the eyes of the wise
Bar. 6. 37. they cannot restore a *b.* man to sight
BLINDED.
Wisd. 2. 21. their own wickedness hath *b.* them
BLINDNESS.
Wisd. 19. 17. even with *b.* were these stricken
2 *Mac.* 10. 30. so that being confounded with *b.*
BLOOD.
2 *Esd.* 1. 26. for ye have defiled your hands with *b.*
32. whose *b.* I will require of your hands, saith L.
5. 5. and *b.* shall drop out of the wood, and stone
15. 8. behold, the innocent and righteous *b.* crieth
unto me, 9. 22. *Esth.* 16. 5. 2 *Mac.* 1. 8.
Jud. 6. 4. mountains shall be drunken with their *b.*
9. 3. so that they dyed their bed in *b.* being deceived
4. which abhorred the pollution of their *b.*
Esth. 16. 10. a stranger from the Persian *b.*
Wisd. 7. 2. being compacted in *b.* of the seed of man
11. 6. a running river, troubled with foul *b.*
12. 5. devourers of man's flesh, and the feasts of *b.*
14. 25. so that there reigned in all men, *b.* theft
Eccl. 8. 16. for *b.* is as nothing in his sight
11. 32. and a sinful man layeth wait for *b.*
12. 16. he will not be satisfied with *b.*
28. 11. and an hasty fighting sheddeth *b.*
34. 21. he that defraudeth him, is a man of *b.*
39. 26. the *b.* of the grape is for use of man's life
1 *Mac.* 6. 34. they shewed them the *b.* of grapes
7. 17. their *b.* have they shed about Jerusalem
10. 89. is to be given to such as are of the king's *b.*
2 *Mac.* 8. 3. and hear the *b.* that cried unto him
12. 16. a lake being filled was seen running with *b.*
14. 45. though his *b.* gushed out like spouts
46. when as his *b.* was now quite gone
See INNOCENT.
BLOOD-SHEDDER.
Eccl. 34. 22. he that defraudeth the labourer is a *b.*
BLOOD-SHEDDING.
Eccl. 27. 15. the strife of the proud is *b.*
BLOT.
Eccl. 11. 33. lest he bring upon thee a perpetual *b.*
20. 24. a lie is a foul *b.* in a man
46. 20. to *b.* out the wickedness of the people
BLOTTED.
Eccl. 23. 26. her reproach shall not be *b.* out
39. 9. so long as world endureth, shall not be *b.* out
41. 11. but an ill name of sinners shall be *b.* out
44. 13. and their glory shall not be *b.* out
BLOW.
Wisd. 5. 23. and like a storm shall *b.* them away
Eccl. 28. 12. if thou *b.* the spark it shall burn
BLOWN.
Wisd. 5. 14. like dust that is *b.* away with the wind
BLOWETH.
Eccl. 43. 16. and at his will the south-wind *b.*
BLUE.
Eccl. 23. 10. shall not be without a *b.* mark
BOARS.
2 *Esd.* 15. 30. shall go forth as wild *b.* of the wood
BOAST.
Wisd. 2. 16. he maketh his *b.* that God is his father
Eccl. 7. 5. *b.* not of thy wisdom before the king
11. 4. *b.* not of thy clothing and raiment
BOASTED.
Eccl. 48. 18. Sennacherib came ag. Sion *b.* proudly
BOASTETH.
Eccl. 10. 27. that *b.* himself, and wanteth bread
BOASTING.
Eccl. 47. 4. when he beat down the *b.* of Goliath
BOATS.
2 *Mac.* 12. 3. go with their wives and children into *b.*
6. Judas set the *b.* on fire and slew those that fled
BODY.
1 *Esd.* 3. 4. the guard that kept the king's *b.*
2 *Esd.* 3. 5. thou gavest a *b.* to Adam without soul
5. 14. extreme fearfulness went through all my *b.*
8. 10. commanded milk out of the parts of the *b.*
11. 45. appear not, thou eagle, nor thy vain *b.*
12. 3. the whole *b.* of the eagle was burnt
16. 61. he put his heart in the midst of the *b.*
Jud. 10. 3. she washed her *b.* all over with water
Wisd. 2. 3. our *b.* shall be turned into ashes
9. 15. the corruptible *b.* presseth down the soul
Eccl. 7. 24. hast daughters? have care of their *b.*
23. 16. a fornicator in the *b.* of his flesh not cease
18. the walls cover me, and no *b.* seeth me
30. 15. health and good state of *b.* are above gold
34. 25. washeth after the touching of a dead *b.*
38. 16. then cover his *b.* according to the custom
47. 19. by thy *b.* was brought into subjection
48. 13. and after his death his *b.* prophesied
51. 2. and hast preserved my *b.* from destruction
2 *Mac.* 7. 4. to cut off the utmost parts of his *b.*
7. be punished, through every member of thy *b.*
9. 7. the members of his *b.* were much pained
9. so that the worms rose up out of the *b.*
BODIES.
Jud. 6. 4. fields shall be filled with their dead *b.*
Eccl. 41. 11. the mourning of men is about their *b.*
Bar. 2. 17. whose souls are taken from their *b.*
6. 22. on their *b.* and heads sit bats and birds
BODILY.
2 *Esd.* 1. 37. they have not seen me with *b.* eyes
BOLD.
Jud. 14. 13. the slaves have been *b.* to come down
Eccl. 6. 11. he will be *b.* over thy servants
8. 15. travel not by the way with a *b.* fellow
19. 3. and a *b.* man shall be taken away
22. 5. she that is *b.* dishonoureth her father
2 *Mac.* 4. 2. thus was he *b.* to call him a traitor
BOLDLY.
1 *Mac.* 4. 18. after this you may *b.* take the spoils
2 *Mac.* 14. 43. he ran *b.* up the wall, and cast himself
BOLDNESS.
Jud. 16. 10. the Persians quaked at her *b.*
Wisd. 5. 1. the righteous shall stand in great *b.*
12. 17. thou makest their *b.* manifest

1 *Mac.* 4. 32. cause the *b.* of their strength to fall
2 *Mac.* 8. 18. they trust in their weapons and *b.*
BONDAGE.
1 *Esd.* 8. 80. when we were in *b.* we were not forsak.
2 *Esd.* 1. 7. I brought them from the house of *b.*
Jud. 8. 22. wheresoever we shall be in *b.*
Wisd. 19. 14. but these brought friends into *b.*
BOND-MAN.
1 *Esd.* 3. 19. mind of the *b.* and freeman to be one
BOND-SLAVE.
1 *Mac.* 2. 11. of a free-woman she is become a *b.*
BONDS.
Wisd. 10. 14. and she left him not in *b.*
17. 2. fettered with the *b.* of a long night, lay exiled
Eccl. 6. 25. and be not grieved with her *b.*
BONES.
Eccl. 28. 17. the stroke of the tongue breaks the *b.*
46. 12. let their *b.* flourish out of place, 49. 10.
Bar. 2. 24. that the *b.* of our kings, and the *b.* of
our fathers, should be taken out of their
places
BOOK.
1 *Esd.* 7. 6. things written in the *b.* of Moses, 9.
2 *Esd.* 12. 37. write these things in a *b.* *Tob.* 12. 20.
Tob. 1. 1. the *b.* of the words of Tobit, *Bar.* 1. 1.
Eccl. 24. 23. these things are the *b.* of the covenant
50. 27. hath written in this *b.* the instruction
Bar. 4. 1. this is the *b.* of the commandments of God
1 *Mac.* 1. 57. was found the *b.* of the testament
2 *Mac.* 6. 12. I beseech those that read this *b.*
BOOKS.
1 *Esd.* 2. 21. sought out in the *b.* of thy fathers
2 *Esd.* 6. 20. *b.* shall be opened before firmament
1 *Mac.* 1. 56. had rent in pieces the *b.* of the law
2 *Mac.* 2. 23. being declared by Jason in five *b.*
BOOTY.
2 *Mac.* 8. 20. and so they received a great *b.*
BORDERERS.
2 *Mac.* 9. 25. princes that are *b.* to my kingdom
BORN.
1 *Esd.* 4. 15. women have *b.* the king and all people
2 *Esd.* 3. 21. so be all they that are *b.* of him
14. 20. but they that shall be *b.* afterward
Jud. 12. 20. he had drunk in one day since he was *b.*
Wisd. 2. 2. for we are *b.* at all adventure
5. 13. as soon as we *b.* we began to draw to our end
7. 3. when I was *b.* I drew in the common air
Eccl. 10. 18. for them that are *b.* of a woman
14. 18. one cometh to an end and another is *b.*
23. 14. and wish that thou hadst not been *b.*
41. 9. and if you be *b.* you shall be *b.* to a curse
44. 9. perished, as though they had never been *b.*
49. 15. nor was there a man *b.* like unto Joseph?
1 *Mac.* 2. 7. wherefore was I *b.* to see this misery
BORNE.
Bar. 6. 4. ye shall see gods of gold *b.* upon shoulders
26. they are *b.* on shoulders having no feet
BORROWED.
Wisd. 15. 16. and he that *b.* his own spirit
BORROWING.
Eccl. 18. 33. not made a beggar by banqueting or *b.*
BOSOM.
2 *Esd.* 15. 21. I will recompense in their *b.*
BOTTLE.
Jud. 10. 5. then she gave her maid a *b.* of wine
BOTTOM.
Wisd. 10. 19. cast them out of the *b.* of the deep
Eccl. 24. 5. and I walked in the *b.* of the deep
BOTTOMS.
Wisd. 17. 14. came out of the *b.* of inevitable hell
BOUGHS.
2 *Mac.* 10. 7. they bear fair *b.* and palms also
14. 4. presenting unto him a crown, also of the *b.*
BOUGHT.
Jud. 4. 10. and their servants *b.* with money
Eccl. 33. 30. because thou hast *b.* him with a price
BOUND.
1 *Esd.* 1. 40. and *b.* him with a chain of brass
2 *Esd.* 13. 13. some sorry, some of them were *b.*
16. 77. woe to them that are *b.* with their sins
Tob. 8. 3. fled into Egypt, and the angel *b.* him
Jud. 6. 13. they *b.* Achior and cast him down
Wisd. 17. 17. all *b.* with one chain of darkness
Eccl. 27. 21. as for a wound, it may be *b.* up
28. 19. nor hath been *b.* in her bands
BOUNDS.
1 *Mac.* 14. 6. and enlarged the *b.* of his nation
BOUNTY.
Esth. 16. 2. are honoured with the great *b.* of princes
BOUNTIFUL.
2 *Esd.* 7. 65. that he is *b.* for he is ready to give
1 *Mac.* 6. 11. I was *b.* and beloved in my power
BOW.
2 *Esd.* 16. 13. his right hand that bendeth the *b.*
Jud. 9. 7. they trust in shield, and spear, and *b.*
Wisd. 5. 21. as from a well drawn *b.* shall they fly
BOW.
Esth. 13. 12. that I did not *b.* to proud Aman
Eccl. 4. 7. and *b.* thy head to a great man
8. let it not grieve thee to *b.* thine ear to poor
6. 25. *b.* down thy shoulder and bear her
33. if thou *b.* thine ear, thou shalt be wise
7. 23. *b.* down their neck from their youth, 30. 12.
33. 26. a yoke and a collar do *b.* the neck
47. 19. thou didst *b.* thy loins unto women
BOWED.
Eccl. 50. 21. they *b.* themselves down to worship
51. 16. I *b.* down mine ear, and received her
Bar. 6. 27. nor if they be *b.* down, can make straight
BOWETH.
Eccl. 38. 30. he *b.* down his strength before his feet
BOWING.
2 *Mac.* 7. 27. but she *b.* herself towards him
BOWELS.
Eccl. 10. 9. while he lives, he casteth away his *b.*
30. 7. his *b.* will be troubled at every cry
2 *Mac.* 9. 5. a pain of the *b.* that was remediless
6. for he had tormented other men's *b.*
BOWL.
Bel 33. Habbacuc a prophet had broken bread in a *b*
BOX-TREES.
2 *Esd.* 14. 24. but look thou prepare thee many *b.*

BRACELET.
Eccl. 21. 21. is like a *b.* upon his right hand
BRACELETS.
Jud. 10. 4. she put about her her *b.* and chains
BRAGGED.
Jud. 16. 5. he *b.* that he would burn my border
BRAGGING.
2 *Mac.* 9. 7. he nothing at all ceased from his *b.*
BRAIDED.
Jud. 10. 3. and *b.* the hair of her head
BRAN.
Bar. 6. 43. the women also burn *b.* for perfume
BRANCHES.
Wisd. 4. 4. though they flourish in *b.* for a time
5. the unperfect *b.* shall be broken off
Eccl. 1. 20. and the *b.* thereof are long life
14. 26. under her shelter, and lodge under her *b.*
23. 25. and her *b.* shall bring forth no fruit
24. 16. as the turpentine tree I stretched out my
b. and my *b.* are the *b.* of honour and grace
2 *Mac.* 10. 7. therefore they bare *b.* and boughs
BRASS.
1 *Esd.* 1. 40. came and bound him with a chain of *b.*
Wisd. 15. 9. to do like the workers in *b.*
Eccl. 28. 20. the bands thereof are bands of *b.*
1 *Mac.* 8. 22. wrote in tables of *b.* 14. 18, 27.
BRAVELY.
Jud. 10. 4. she decked herself *b.* to allure the eyes
BRAWLING.
Eccl. 31. 29. maketh bitterness of the mind with *b.*
BRAWLS.
Eccl. 27. 14. their *b.* make one stop his ears
BREAD.
1 *Esd.* 1. 19. held the feast of sweet *b.* seven days
2 *Esd.* 1. 19. gave you manna, so ye did eat angels' *b.*
Tob. 1. 16. I gave my *b.* to the hungry, 4. 16.
4. 17. pour out thy *b.* on the burial of the just
Jud. 10. 5. then she filled a bag with fine *b.*
Eccl. 10. 27. than he that boasteth and wanteth *b.*
12. 5. hold back thy *b.* and give it not unto him
14. 10. a wicked eye envieth his *b.*
15. 3. with the *b.* of understanding shall he feed
20. 16. they that eat my *b.* speak evil of me
23. 17. all *b.* is sweet to a whoremonger
29. 21. the chief thing for life is water and *b.*
33. 24. *b.* correction and work for a servant
34. 21. the *b.* of the needy is their life
45. 20. he prepared him *b.* in abundance
Bel 33. Habbacuc had broken *b.* in a bowl
BREADTH.
Eccl. 1. 3. who can find out the *b.* of the earth?
BREAK.
1 *Esd.* 4. 4. *b.* down mountains, walls, and towers
Jud. 9. 10. *b.* down their stateliness by a woman
BREAKEST.
Jud. 9. 7. thou art the Lord that *b.* the battles
BREAKETH.
Jud. 16. 3. for God *b.* the battles, he delivered
Eccl. 23. 18. a man that *b.* wedlock, saying, thus
BREAST.
2 *Esd.* 14. 40. when I drunk it, wisdom grew in my *b.*
BREAST-PLATE.
Wisd. 5. 18. he shall put on righteousness as a *b.*
Eccl. 43. 20. it clotheth the water as with a *b.*
45. 10. he compassed him with a *b.* of judgment
1 *Mac.* 3. 3. he put on a *b.* as a giant
BREASTS.
2 *Esd.* 8. 10. for thou hast commanded out of the *b.*
milk to be given, which is the fruit of the *b.*
2 *Mac.* 6. 10. the babes hanging at their *b.*
BREATH.
2 *Esd.* 3. 5. did breathe into him the *b.* of life
Wisd. 2. 2. the *b.* in our nostrils is as smoke
7. 25. for she is the *b.* of the power of God
15. 5. they desire a dead image that hath no *b.*
Eccl. 33. 20. as long as thou livest and hast *b.*
Bar. 6. 25. the things wherein there is no *b.*
2 *Mac.* 7. 22. for I neither gave you *b.* nor life
23. the Creator will give you life and *b.* again
14. 45. while there was yet *b.* within him
BREATHED.
Wisd. 15. 11. and that *b.* in him a living spirit
BREATHING.
Wisd. 11. 18. *b.* out a fiery vapour or smoke
2 *Mac.* 9. 7. *b.* out fire in his rage against the Jews
BRED.
Wisd. 12. 10. that their malice was *b.* in them
BREECHES.
Eccl. 45. 8. with *b.* with a long robe, and ephod
BRETHREN.
1 *Esd.* 3. 22. forget their love to friends and *b.*
4. 61. so he came to Babylon and told it to all his *b.*
5. 3. all their *b.* played, and he made them go up
Tob. 1. 3. and I did many alms-deeds to my *b.*
2. 2. what poor man thou shalt find out of our *b.*
4. 13. my son, love thy *b.* and despise not thy *b.*
5. 12. then he said, I am Azarias, of thy *b.*
13. were not seduced with the error of our *b.*
7. 3. Raguel asked them, from whence are you, *b.*?
11. 17. there was joy among all his *b.* at Nineve
14. 4. our *b.* shall be scattered in the earth
7. shall rejoice, shewing mercy to our *b.*
Jud. 7. 30. *b.* be of good courage, let us endure
8. 14. *b.* provoke not the Lord our God to anger
24. O *b.* let us shew an example to our *b.*
Eccl. 10. 20. among *b.* he that is chief is honourable
25. 1. the unity of *b.* the love of neighbours
40. 24. *b.* and help are against time of trouble
1 *Mac.* 3. 2. and all his *b.* helped him
5. 32. he said, fight this day for your *b.*
12. 11. as it becometh us to think on our *b.*
13. 4. all my *b.* are slain, for Israel's sake
5. for I am no better than my *b.*
2 *Mac.* 1. 1. the *b.* the Jews that be at Jerusalem
wish to the *b.* the Jews in Egypt health
7. 1. seven *b.* with their mother were taken
29. being worthy of thy *b.* take thy death, that I
may receive thee in mercy again with thy *b.*
36. our *b.* who have suffered a short pain
37. but I, as my *b.* offer up my body and life
10. 21. that they had sold their *b.* for money
15. 14. this is a lover of the *b.* who prayeth

BREVITY.
2 *Mac.* 2. 31. but to use *b.* and avoid labouring
BRIBERY.
Eccl. 40. 12. all *b.* and injustice shall be blotted out
BRIDE.
2 *Esd.* 7. 26. and the *b.* shall appear and be seen
Bar. 2. 23. the voice of bridegroom, and voice of *b.*
1 *Mac.* 9. 37. were bringing the *b.* from Nadabatha
BRIDEGROOM, S.
2 *Esd.* 16. 33. virgins shall mourn, having no *b.*
34. in the wars shall their *b.* be destroyed
1 *Mac.* 1. 27. every *b.* took up lamentation
9. 39. *b.* came forth, and his friends to meet them
BRIDGE.
2 *Mac.* 12. 13. he went also about to make a *b.*
BRIDLES.
1 *Esd.* 3. 6. and a chariot with *b.* of gold
2 *Mac.* 10. 29. five men on horses with *b.* of gold
BRIGHT. *See* FLAMES.
BRIGHTER.
Eccl. 17. 31. what is *b.* than the sun? yet light fails
23. 19. are ten thousand times *b.* than the sun
BRIGHTNESS.
2 *Esd.* 10. 50. he shewed thee the *b.* of her glory
Wisd. 7. 26. for she is the *b.* of the everlasting light
Eccl. 43. 11. very beautiful it is in the *b.* thereof
Bar. 5. 3. God will shew thy *b.* to every country
BRING.
1 *Esd.* 4. 5. get the victory, they *b.* all to the king
22. do ye not give, and *b.* all to the woman?
BRINGEST.
Wisd. 16. 13. leads to gates of hell, and *b.* up again
BRINGETH.
1 *Esd.* 4. 24. when he hath robbed, he *b.* it to his love
BRITTLE.
Wisd. 15. 13. of earthly matter maketh *b.* vessels
BROKEN.
Wisd. 4. 5. the unperfect branches shall be *b.* off
Eccl. 13. 2. if one smitten against other, it shall be *b.*
1 *Mac.* 7. 18. for they have *b.* the covenant and oath
BROOK.
Eccl. 24. 30. I also came out as a *b.* from a river
31. and lo, my *b.* became a river, my river a sea
39. 13. as a rose growing by the *b.* of the field
1 *Mac.* 5. 39. have pitched their tents beyond the *b.*
BROOKS.
Jud. 2. 8. their slain shall fill their valleys and *b.*
BROTHER.
2 *Esd.* 12. 11. seen in the vision of thy *b.* Daniel
Tob. 5. 6. I have lodged with our *b.* 10, 11, 13.
Jud. 8. 26. the sheep of Laban his mother's *b.*
Esth. 15. 9. I am thy *b.* be of good cheer
Wisd. 10. 3. in fury wherewith he murdered his *b.*
10. when the righteous fled from his *b.* wrath
Eccl. 7. 12. devise not a lie against thy *b.*
18. change not a faithful *b.* for the gold of Ophir
29. 10. lose thy money for thy *b.* and friend
27. give place my *b.* cometh to be lodged
33. 19. give not thy wife and *b.* power over thee
31. if thou have a servant, entreat him as a *b.*
1 *Mac.* 2. 65. your *b.* Simon is a man of counsel
BROTHERHOOD.
1 *Mac.* 12. 17. concerning the renewing of our *b.*
BUCKLE.
1 *Mac.* 10. 89. king Alexander sent him a *b.* of gold
11. 58. he gave him leave to wear a golden *b.*
BUCKLER.
Eccl. 37. 5. and taketh up the *b.* against the enemy
BUD.
Eccl. 39. 13. *b.* forth as a rose growing by the brook
BUDS.
Wisd. 2. 8. let us crown ourselves with rose *b.*
BUILD.
1 *Esd.* 2. 4. Lord commanded me to *b.* him an house
5. let him go up, and *b.* the house of the Lord
18. that the Jews do *b.* the market-places
4. 8. if he command to *b.* they *b.*
6. 2. Zorobabel and Jesus began to *b.* the house
4. by whose appointment do ye *b.* this house?
Tob. 14. 5. where they shall *b.* a temple; after their
captivity shall *b.* Jerusalem gloriously
Eccl. 3. 14. instead of sins it shall be added *b.* thee up
47. 13. that he might *b.* an house in his name
1 *Mac.* 15. 39. he commanded him to *b.* up Cedron
BUILDED.
1 *Esd.* 6. 14. this house was *b.* many years ago
2 *Esd.* 8. 52. to you a city is *b.* and rest allowed
Tob. 13. 10. that his tabernacle may be *b.* with joy
BUILDERS.
1 *Esd.* 2. 30. Rathumus began to hinder the *b.*
BUILDETH.
2 *Esd.* 16. 42. he that *b.* as he that shall not dwell
Eccl. 21. 8. *b.* his house with other men's money
34. 23. when one *b.* and another pulleth down
BUILDING.
1 *Esd.* 4. 51. twenty talents to the *b.* of the temple
5. 63. came to the *b.* of this with weeping and crying
6. 9. *b.* an house of the Lord of costly stones
2 *Esd.* 10. 54. there can no man's *b.* be able to stand
Tob. 14. 5. house of G. shall be built with a glorious *b.*
1 *Mac.* 16. 23. the *b.* of the walls which he made
BUILT.
1 *Esd.* 2. 24. that if this city be *b.* again and walls
4. 51. twenty talents till the time that it were *b.*
Tob. 13. 16. Jerusalem shall be *b.* with sapphires
14. 5. the house of God shall be *b.* in it for ever
BULL.
Eccl. 6. 2. that thy soul be not torn in pieces as a *b.*
BULLOCKS.
1 *Esd.* 6. 29. for sacrifices, for *b.* and rams and lambs
8. 14. silver and gold may be collected for *b.* rams
Eccl. 38. 25. in labours, and whose talk is of *b.*
BURDEN.
Eccl. 13. 2. *b.* not thyself above thy power
BURDENS.
Eccl. 33. 24. a wand and *b.* are for the ass
BURIAL.
Tob. 2. 9. the same night I returned from the *b.*
4. 17. pour out thy bread on the *b.* of the just
Eccl. 21. 8. that gathereth stones for the tomb of his *b.*
38. 16. then cover his body and neglect not his *b.*
2 *Mac.* 13. 7. not having so much as *b.* in the earth

BURIED.
Tob. 14. 11. he *b.* him honourably, 1. 17, 18. | 2. 7.
Eccl. 44. 14. their bodies are *b.* in peace, name liveth
2 *Mac.* 9. 15. he judged not worthy to be so much as *b*
BURIETH.
Tob. 2. 8. and yet lo, he *b.* the dead again
BURN.
Jud. 16. 5. he bragged he would *b.* up my borders
Wisd. 16. 18. that it might not *b.* up the beasts
Eccl. 28. 12. if thou blow the spark, it shall *b.*
23. it shall *b.* in them, and not be quenched
40. 30. but in his belly there shall *b.* a fire
BURNED.
Tob. 14. 4. and the house of God in it shall be *b.*
BURNETH.
Wisd. 16. 19. at another time it *b.* even in water
Eccl. 28. 10. as the matter of fire is, so it *b.*
BURNING.
Wisd. 16. 22. might know that fire *b.* in the hail
18. 3. thou gavest them a *b.* pillar of fire
Eccl. 23. 16. hot mind as a *b.* fire, not to be quenched
BURNT.
1 *Esd.* 6. 16. who pulled down the house and *b.* it
2 *Esd.* 13. 4. all they *b.* that heard his voice
11. the blast of fire *b.* them up every one
BURST.
Eccl. 19. 10. and be bold, it will not *b.* thee
BURY.
2 *Esd.* 2. 23. where thou findest the dead, *b.* them
Tob. 4. 3. he said, my son, when I am dead, *b.* me
4. when she is dead, *b.* her by me in one grave
6. 14. for they have no other son to *b.* them
12. 12. when thou didst *b.* the dead, I was with thee
14. 6. all nations shall turn and *b.* their idols
10. *b.* me decently, and thy mother with me
BURYING.
2 *Mac.* 9. 4. would make it a common *b.* place, 14.
BUSH.
2 *Esd.* 14. 1. there came a voice out of a *b.* and said
3. in the *b.* did manifestly reveal myself to Moses
BUSHES.
2 *Esd.* 16. 77. like as a field covered over with *b.*
BUSINESS.
1 *Esd.* 4. 11. neither may any one do his own *b.*
5. 58. Levites with one accord setters forward of *b.*
Tob. 7. 8. and let this *b.* be despatched
Eccl. 3. 17. my son, go on with thy *b.* in meekness
10. 26. be not over-wise in doing thy *b.* boast not
29. 19. he that followeth other men's *b.* for gain
37. 11. nor consult with an idle servant of much *b*
38. 24. he that hath little *b.* shall become wise
BUY.
Eccl. 51. 25. *b.* her for yourselves without money
1 *Mac.* 3. 41. came to the camp to *b.* children of Isr.
12. 36. that men might neither sell nor *b.* in it
13. 49. could not go into the country, nor *b.* nor sell
2 *Mac.* 8. 34. brought 1000 merchants to *b.* the Jews
BUYER.
Eccl. 37. 11. nor consult with a *b.* of selling
BUYETH.
Eccl. 20. 12. there is that *b.* much for a little
BUYING.
Eccl. 27. 2. so doth sin stick close betw. *b.* and selling

C.

CADES.
1 *Mac.* 11. 63. Demetrius' princes were come to C.
73. with him pursued them to C. to their tents
CALAMITY.
1 *Mac.* 13. 32. he brought a great *c.* on the land
2 *Mac.* 4. 16. by reason whereof *c.* came on them
CALAMITIES.
Eccl. 23. 11. but his house shall be full of *c.*
40. 9. strife, sword, *c.* famine, and tribulation
2 *Mac.* 6. 12. be not discouraged for these *c.*
10. 10. gathering briefly the *c.* of the wars
14. 14. thinking the *c.* of Jews to be their welfare
CALDRONS.
2 *Mac.* 7. 3. the king commanded *c.* to be made hot
CALEB.
Eccl. 46. 9. the Lord gave strength also to C.
1 *Mac.* 2. 56. C. received the heritage of the land
CALISTHENES.
2 *Mac.* 8. 33. they burnt C. that had set fire on gates
CALL.
1 *Esd.* 1. 50. sent by his messengers to *c.* them back
Eccl. 13. 14. and *c.* upon him for thy salvation
CALLED.
1 *Esd.* 3. 17. he shall be *c.* Darius his cousin
4. 42. thou shalt sit by me and be *c.* my cousin
2 *Esd.* 4. 25. unto his name whereby we are *c.*
Wisd. 1. 16. but ungodly men *c.* it to them
7. 7. I *c.* on God, and the Spirit of wisdom came
11. 25. or been preserved, if not *c.* by thee
Eccl. 46. 5. he *c.* on the most high Lord, 16. | 47. 5.
Bar. 2. 15. because Israel is *c.* by thy name
6. 30. for how can they be *c.* gods?
1 *Mac.* 6. 10. wherefore he *c.* for all his friends
14. then *c.* he for Philip one of his friends
7. 37. didst choose this house to be *c.* by thy name
10. 20. we ordain thee to be *c.* the king's friend
14. 40. the Romans *c.* the Jews their friends
2 *Mac.* 3. 15. the priests *c.* unto heaven upon him
4. 28. they were both *c.* before the king
7. 25. the king *c.* his mother, and exhorted her
8. 1. Judas and they *c.* their kinsfolks together
2. and they *c.* upon the Lord, 12. 36.
15. for his holy name's sake, by which they were *c*
10. 13. being accused and *c.* traitor at every word
14. 37. who for his kindness was *c.* a father
CALLETH.
1 *Esd.* 4. 36. all the earth *c.* on the truth
Wisd. 2. 13. he *c.* himself the child of the Lord
13. 18. for health, he *c.* on that which is weak
14. 1. one preparing to sail, *c.* on a piece of wood
Bar. 3. 33. that *c.* it again, and it obeyeth him
34. when he *c.* them, they say, here we be
CALLING.
1 *Mac.* 12. 35. *c.* the elders of the people together
2 *Mac.* 12. 6. and *c.* on God the righteous Judge

2 *Mac.* 12.15. Judas *c.* upon the great L. of the world
14. 46. and *c.* upon the Lord of life and spirit

CAMP.

1 *Mac.* 3. 41. they came into the *c.* to buy Israel
57. so the *c.* removed, and pitched near Emmaus
12. 28. and they kindled fires in their *c.*
2 *Mac.* 13. 15. he slew in the *c.* about 4,000 men
15. 17. not to pitch *c.* but courageously to set on

CAMPED.

1 *Mac.* 10. 86. Jonathan *c.* against Ascalon
11. 73. even to their own tents, and there they *c.*
13. 43. in those days Simon *c.* against Gaza
2 *Mac.* 13. 14. to fight manfully, Judas *c.* by Modin

CANAAN.

Jud. 5. 3. he said, tell me now, ye sons of C.
See CHANAAN.

CANDLES.

Bar. 6. 19. they light them *c.* more than for themselves

CANDLESTICK.

1 *Mac.* 1. 21. Antiochus took away the *c.* of light
4. 49. brought the *c.* and the altar into the temple

CANOPY.

Jud. 10. 21. Holofernes rested on his bed under a *c.*
13. 9. she pulled down the *c.* from the pillars
16. 19. gave the *c.* which she had taken to the Ld.

CAPHENATHA.

1 *Mac.* 12. 37. repaired that which was called C.

CAPTAIN.

1 *Mac.* 2. 66. let him be your *c.* and fight the battle
7. 5. there came, having Alcimus for their *c.*
11. 59. his brother Simon also he made *c.*
12. 53. they have no *c.* nor any to help them
13. 53. Simon made his son *c.* of all the host
2 *Mac.* 1. 16. and they struck down the *c.*
8. 9. with him he joined also Gorgias a *c.*

CAPTIVE.

2 *Mac.* 8. 10. make so much money of the *c.* Jews
11. he sent, proclaiming a sale of the *c.* Jews

CAPTIVES.

Bar. 6. 2. ye shall be led away *c.* unto Babylon
1 *Mac.* 14. 7. and gathered a great number of *c.*

CAPTIVITY.

1 *Esd.* 5. 7. these are they that came up from *c.*
6. 5. because the Lord had visited the *c.*
8. the ancients of the Jews that were of the *c.*
Bar. 3. 7. that we should praise thee in our *c.*
8. behold, we are yet this day in our *c.*

CARBUNCLE.

Tob. 13. 17. Jerus. shall be paved with beryl and *c.*
Eccl. 32. 5. is as a signet of *c.* set in gold

CARCASES.

Bel. 32. they had given them every day two *c.*

CARE.

Wisd. 3. 9. and he hath *c.* for his elect
6. 17. and the *c.* of discipline is love
7. 23. kind to man, stedfast, sure, free from *c.*
Eccl. 8. 13. if thou be surety, take *c.* to pay it
30. 25. a good heart will have *c.* of his meat
31. 2. watching *c.* will not let a man slumber
50. 4. he took *c.* of the temple, that it should not fall
1 *Mac.* 6. 10. and my heart faileth for very *c.*
9. 58. are at ease, and dwell without *c.*
16. 14. taking *c.* for the good ordering of them
2 *Mac.* 2. 29. must *c.* for the whole building
9. 21. to *c.* for the common safety of all
14. 8. for the unfeigned *c.* I have of things
15. 18. the *c.* they took for their wives
19. they in the city took not the least *c.*

CARED.

1 *Esd.* 1. 47. he *c.* not for the words spoken

CAREFUL.

2 *Mac.* 2. 25. we have been *c.* that they that read
11. 15. consented, being *c.* of the common good
14. 9. be *c.* for the country and our nation

CAREFULLY.

1 *Esd.* 7. 2. did very *c.* oversee the holy works
Wisd. 12. 22. we should *c.* think of thy goodness
Eccl. 38. 29. who is always *c.* set at his work
2 *Mac.* 8. 31. laid them up all *c.* in convenient places

CAREFULNESS.

Eccl. 30. 24. *c.* bringeth age before the time

CARES.

Wisd. 7. 4. I was nursed, and that with *c.*
8. 9. she would be a comfort in *c.* and grief

CARETH.

Wisd. 12. 13. nor is any God but thou that *c.* for all

CARNAIM.

1 *Mac.* 5. 43. fled unto the temple that was at C.
44. thus was C. subdued, nor could they stand

CARNION.

2 *Mac.* 12. 21. sent the baggage to a fortress called C.
26. then Maccabeus marched forth to C.

CARPENTER.

Wisd. 13. 11. now a *c.* that felleth timber
Eccl. 38. 27. so every *c.* that labours night and day

CARPENTERS.

1 *Esd.* 5. 54. gave unto the masons and *c.* money
Bar. 6. 45. they are made of *c.* and goldsmiths

CARRS.

1 *Esd.* 5. 55. unto them of Sidon they gave *c.*

CARRY.

Bel. 34. go *c.* the dinner that thou hast into Babylon
2 *Mac.* 9. 10. no man could endure to *c.* for stink

CARRIED.

2 *Mac.* 9. 8. was now *c.* in a horse litter
29. and Philip *c.* away his body

CARRIETH.

Wisd. 14. 1. more rotten than the vessel that *c.* him

CARRYING.

2 *Mac.* 6. 7. go in procession to Bacchus, *c.* ivy

CARTS.

Jud. 15. 11. she made ready her *c.* and laid them

CART-WHEEL.

Eccl. 33. 5. the heart of the foolish is like a *c.*

CARVED.

Wisd. 13. 13. a carpenter hath *c.* the wood diligently
1 *Mac.* 5. 68. Judas burnt their *c.* images with fire

CASLEU.

1 *Mac.* 4. 59. from the 25th day of the month C. with mirth and gladness, 2 *Mac.* 1. 18. | 10. 5.
2 *Mac.* 1. 9. keep the feast in the month C.

CASPIS.

2 *Mac.* 12. 13. and the name of it was C.

CAST.

1 *Mac.* 4. 33. *c.* them down with the sword
6. 51. he set artillery with instruments to *c.* fire and stones, and pieces to *c.* darts and slings
7. 17. the flesh of thy saints have they *c.* out
19. Bacchides *c.* them into the great pit
44. they *c.* away their weapons and fled, 11. 51.
10. 80. for they had *c.* darts at the people
2 *Mac.* 5. 8. as an enemy, he was *c.* out into Egypt
10. he that had *c.* out many unburied
9. 8. and thus he was now *c.* on the ground
15. but to be *c.* out with their children
14. 15. they *c.* earth upon their heads
43. he *c.* himself down manfully among them
46. he *c.* his bowels upon the throng, he thus died

CASTING.

1 *Mac.* 13. 11. who *c.* out them that were therein
2 *Mac.* 5. 3. drawing of swords and *c.* of darts

CASTING.

2 *Mac.* 11. 13. *c.* with himself what loss he had had

CASTLE.

2 *Mac.* 4. 27. though the ruler of the *c.* required it
5. 5. the city taken, Menelaus fled into the *c.*
10. 20. certain of those that were in the *c.*

CASTLES.

2 *Mac.* 10. 18. who fled into two very strong *c.*
22. so he immediately took the two *c.*

CATALOGUE.

1 *Esd.* 8. 49. the *c.* of whose names were shewed

CATTLE.

1 *Mac.* 12. 23. that your *c.* and goods are ours
2 *Mac.* 12. 11. to give him *c.* and to pleasure him

CAUGHT.

2 *Mac.* 4. 41. some of them *c.* stones, some clubs

CAUSE.

1 *Mac.* 6. 12. to destroy the inhabitants without *c.*
13. I perceive that for this *c.* these are come
2 *Mac.* 4. 44. three men pleaded the *c.* before him
47. who was *c.* of all the mischief; who if they had told their *c.* before the Scythians
7. 18. who said, be not deceived without *c.*
34. O godless man, be not lifted up without a *c.*
13. 4. that this man was the *c.* of all mischief

CEASE.

Eccl. 16. 27. nor do they *c.* from their works
28. 6. remember thy end, and let enmity *c.*
1 *Mac.* 11. 50. let the Jews *c.* from assaulting us
2 *Mac.* 7. 38. that the wrath of the Almighty may *c.*
9. 18. but for all this his pains would not *c.*

CEASED.

1 *Esd.* 1. 56. as for her glorious things, they never *c.*
Dan. 3. 23. *c.* not to make the oven hot with rosin
1 *Mac.* 9. 73. thus the sword *c.* from Israel

CEASING.

1 *Mac.* 12. 11. at all times without *c.* we remember
2 *Mac.* 9. 4. his chariot man to drive without *c.*

CEDAR.

Eccl. 24. 13. I was exalted like a *c.* in Libanus
50. 12. he stood as a young *c.* in Libanus

CEDRON.

1 *Mac.* 15. 39. also he commanded him to build C.
41. when he had built C. he set horsemen there
16. 9. John still followed, until he came to C.

CELEBRATE.

Tob. 6. 12. when we return, we will *c.* the marriage
2 *Mac.* 2. 16. we are about to *c.* the purification
15. 36. to *c.* the 13th day of the 12th month

CELEBRATING.

2 *Mac.* 5. 26. were gone to the *c.* of the sabbath

CELOSYRIA.

1 *Esd.* 2. 17. the judges in C. and Phenice
6. 29. out of the tribute of C. a portion given
7. 1. the governor of C. did oversee the works
2 *Mac.* 3. 8. visiting the cities of C. and Phenice
4. 4. being the governor of C. and Phenice, 10. 11.

CENDEBEUS.

1 *Mac.* 15. 38. then the king made C. captain
40. C. came to Jamnia || 16. 1. what C. had done
16. 4. with horsemen, who went out against C.
8. whereupon C. and his host were put to flight
9. till he came to Cedron which C. had built

CENSERS.

1 *Esd.* 2. 13. *c.* of silver twenty-nine, vials of gold
1 *Mac.* 1. 22. Antiochus took away the *c.* of gold

CEREMONIES.

Wisd. 14. 15. delivered to those under him, *c.*
23. for whilst they used secret *c.* or revellings

CERTIFY.

Bel 9. if ye can *c.* me that Bel devoureth them
2 *Mac.* 1. 18. we thought it necessary to *c.* you

CERTIFIED.

1 *Mac.* 14. 21. the ambassadors *c.* us of your glory
2 *Mac.* 11. 26. that when they are *c.* of our mind

CHAIN.

1 *Esd.* 1. 40. and bound him with a *c.* of brass
3. 6. Darius shall give him a *c.* about his neck
Wisd. 17. 17. were bound with one *c.* of darkness
Eccl. 6. 24. and put thy neck into her *c.*

CHAINS.

Jud. 10. 4. put about her her bracelets and her *c.*
Eccl. 6. 29. her *c.* shall be a robe of glory

CHAMBER.

1 *Esd.* 9. 1. Esdras went to the *c.* of Joanan
2 *Esd.* 5. 9. withdraw itself into his secret *c.*

CHAMBERS.

2 *Esd.* 4. 41. the *c.* of souls are like a woman's womb
1 *Mac.* 4. 38. they saw the priests' *c.* pulled down

CHANAAN.

Sus. 56. O thou seed of C. and not of Judah
1 *Mac.* 9. 37. of one of the great princes of C.
See CANAAN.

CHANGE.

Wisd. 7. 18. given me to know the *c.* of seasons
19. 18. in a psaltery notes *c.* the name of the tune
Eccl. 7. 18. *c.* not a friend for any good by no means
40. 5. anger, night-sleep do *c.* his knowledge
1 *Mac.* 1. 49. they might *c.* all the ordinances

CHANGED.

2 *Esd.* 6. 26. the heart of inhabitants shall be *c.*
Esth. 15. 8. then God *c.* the spirit of the king
Wisd. 19. 18. the elements were *c.* in themselves
Eccl. 2. 4. when thou art *c.* to a low estate
18. 26. from morning till the evening time is *c.*
1 *Mac.* 1. 26. the beauty of women was *c.*

CHANGETH.

Eccl. 13. 25. the heart of a man *c.* his countenance
25. 17. the wickedness of a woman *c.* her face
27. 11. but a fool *c.* as the moon

CHANGING.

Eccl. 37. 17. the countenance is a sign of *c.*
43. 8. increasing wonderfully in her *c.*
2 *Mac.* 3. 16. the *c.* of his colour declared agony
6. 27. manfully *c.* this life, I will shew myself
29. *c.* the good-will they bare him a little before

CHAPELS.

1 *Mac.* 1. 47. set up altars, groves, and *c.* of idols
2 *Mac.* 10. 2. also the *c.* they pulled down
11. 3. as of the other *c.* of the heathen

CHARGE.

2 *Esd.* 2. 33. Esdras received a *c.* of the Lord
6. 46. thou gavest them a *c.* to do service to man
1 *Mac.* 5. 19. saying, take ye the *c.* of this people
58. when they had given *c.* unto the garrison
12. 45. for I will give it to all that have any *c.*
14. 42. that he should take *c.* of the sanctuary
2 *Mac.* 15. 10. he gave them their *c.* shewing them

CHARGE.

2 *Mac.* 11. 11. and giving a *c.* on their enemies

CHARGED.

1 *Esd.* 4. 57. the same *c.* he also to be done
2 *Mac.* 2. 2. *c.* them not to forget the commands

CHARGES.

1 *Esd.* 4. 55. likewise for the *c.* of the Levites
1 *Mac.* 3. 30. he should not be able to bear the *c.*
2 *Mac.* 4. 19. but to be reserved for other *c.*
9. 16. defray the *c.* belonging to sacrifices

CHARIOT.

1 *Esd.* 1. 28. Josias did not turn back his *c.* from him
31. then gat he up upon his second *c.*
3. 6. a *c.* with bridles of gold and a chain about her
Eccl. 48. 9. was taken up in a *c.* of fiery horses
49. 8. shewed him upon the *c.* of the cherubims
2 *Mac.* 9. 7. he fell down from his *c.* carried violently

CHARIOTS.

1 *Mac.* 1. 17. he entered into Egypt with *c.*
2 *Mac.* 13. 2. three hundred *c.* armed with hooks

CHARIOT-MAN.

2 *Mac.* 9. 4. he commanded his *c.* to drive

CHARMER.

Eccl. 12. 13. who will pity a *c.* bitten with a serpent.

CHASED.

1 *Mac.* 14. 26. *c.* away their enemies from them

CHASTEN.

Wisd. 12. 22. whereas thou dost *c.* us, thou scourgest
2 *Mac.* 10. 4. that he would *c.* them with mercy

CHASTENEST.

Wisd. 12. 2. thou *c.* them by little and little

CHASTENING.

2 *Mac.* 6. 12. but for a *c.* of our nation
7. 33. angry with us for our *c.* and correction

CHASTISE.

Eccl. 30. 13. *c.* thy son and hold him to labour

CHASTISED.

2 *Esd.* 15. 51. be weakened, as one *c.* with wounds
Wisd. 3. 5. having been *c.* they shall be rewarded
11. 9. when they were tried, albeit in mercy *c.*

CHASTISETH.

Eccl. 30. 2. he that *c.* his son shall have joy

CHASTITY.

2 *Esd.* 6. 32. the mighty hath seen also thy *c.*

CHEEKS.

Eccl. 35. 15. doth not tears run down widows' *c.*?

CHEER.

1 *Esd.* 9. 54. then they went to make great *c.*
Eccl. 18. 32. take not pleasure in much good *c.*

CHEERED.

2 *Mac.* 15. 27. through the appearance they were *c.*

CHEERETH.

Eccl. 36. 22. beauty of a woman *c.* the countenance

CHEERFUL.

Eccl. 7. 24. shew not thyself *c.* toward them
13. 25. a merry heart maketh a *c.* countenance
26. a *c.* countenance is a token of prosperity
26. 4. he shall rejoice with a *c.* countenance
30. 25. a *c.* heart will have a care of his meat
35. 10. as thou hast gotten give with a *c.* eye
2 *Mac.* 15. 9. Maccabeus made them more *c.*

CHEERFULLY.

Eccl. 2. 4. what is brought upon thee, take *c.*
2 *Mac.* 11. 26. ever go *c.* about their own affairs

CHEERFULNESS.

Bar. 3. 34. so with *c.* they shewed light to him

CHEREAS.

2 *Mac.* 10. 32. strong-hold, where C. was governor
37. they killed Timotheus and C. his brother

CHERUBIMS.

Eccl. 49. 8. was shewed him on the chariot of the *c.*

CHETTIM.

1 *Mac.* 1. 1. Alexander came out of the land of C.

CHICKENS.

2 *Esd.* 1. 30. as a hen gathereth her *c.* under her wings

CHIEFLY.

Tob. 4. 12. *c.* take a wife of the seed of thy fathers

CHILD.

1 *Esd.* 1. 53. who spared neither old men nor *c.*
2 *Esd.* 4. 40. go thy way to a woman with *c.*
5. 49. like as a young *c.* may not bring forth thing
Wisd. 2. 13. he calleth himself the *c.* of the Lord
8. 19. for I was a witty *c.* and had a good spirit
14. 15. when he hath made an image of his *c.*
Eccl. 30. 8. a *c.* left to himself will be wilful
9. cocker thy *c.* and he shall make thee afraid
12. and beat him on the sides while he is a *c.*
2 *Mac.* 15. 12. exercised from a *c.* in all virtue

CHILDREN.

Esth. 16. 16. that they be *c.* of the Most High
Wisd. 3. 12. wives are foolish and their *c.* wicked
16. as for *c.* of adulterers they shall not come
4. 1. better it is to have no *c.* and to have virtue
6. for *c.* begotten of unlawful beds are witnesses
5. 5. how is he numbered among the *c.* of God?
9. 4. and reject me not from among thy *c.*

Eccl. 7. 23. hast thou c.? instruct them and bow down
11. 28. for a man shall be known in his c.
16. 1. desire not a multitude of unprofitable c.
3. better it is to die without c. than have ungodly
22. 9. if c. live honestly and have wherewithal
10. but c. being haughty through disdain do stain
22. 23. she hath brought c. by another man
24. 18. I therefore am given to all my c.
25. 7. a man that hath joy of his c.
32. 22. and beware of thine own c.
33. 21. better it is that thy c. should seek to thee
39. 13. hearken to me, ye holy c. and bud forth
40. 15. the c. of the ungodly shall not bring forth
19. c. and building a city continue a man's name
41. 5. the c. of sinners are abominable c.
6. the inheritance of sinners' c. shall perish
7. the c. will complain of an ungodly father
45. 13. before him none, nor did a stranger put them on, but his c. and his children's c. perpetually
Bel 20. I see the footsteps of men, women, and c.

CHILD-BED.
Bar. 6. 29. women in c. eat their sacrifices

CHIMNEYS.
2 Esd. 6. 4. or ever the c. in Zion were hot

CHOICE.
1 Mac. 4. 28. Lysias gathered 60,000 c. men of foot
2 Mac. 13. 15. with the valiant and c. young men

CHOLER.
Eccl. 37. 30. and surfeiting will turn into c.

CHOOSE.
2 Esd. 3. 13. thou didst c. thee a man among them
16. thou did c. him to thee, and put by Esau
Bar. 3. 27. those did not the Lord c. nor gave he
1 Mac. 5. 17. c. thee out men and deliver brethren
7. 37. thou, O Lord, didst c. this house to be called
10. 32. may set in it such men as he shall c. keep it
2 Mac. 1. 25. didst c. the fathers and sanctify them
5. 19. God did not c. the people for the place's sake

CHOOSING.
1 Mac. 10. 74. c. 10,000 men, he went out of Jerus.
2 Mac. 10. 12. c. rather to do justice to the Jews
14. 42. c. rather to die manfully than to come

CHOSE.
1 Esd. 9. 16. Esdras c. to him the principal men
Eccl. 45. 16. he c. him out of all men living
1 Mac. 4. 42. he c. priests of blameless conversation
9. 25. then Bacchides c. the wicked men
16. 4. so he c. out of the country 20,000 men
2 Mac. 3. 7. the king c. Heliodorus his treasurer

CHOSEN.
1 Esd. 5. 1. after this were the principal men c.
Wisd. 4. 15. that he hath respect unto his c.
9. 7. thou hast c. me to be a king of thy people
Eccl. 47. 2. so was David c. out of children of Israel
49. 6. they burnt the c. city of the sanctuary
1 Mac. 12. 41. went with men c. for the battle

CHRIST.
2 Esd. 7. 29. after these years shall my son C. die

CHRONICLES.
1 Esd. 2. 22. thou shalt find in the c. what is written
1 Mac. 16. 24. behold, these are written in the c.

CHURCH-ROBBER.
2 Mac. 4. 42. as for the c. himself, him they killed

CHURLISH.
2 Mac. 14. 30. Nicanor began to be c. unto him

CHURLISHLY.
Eccl. 18. 18. a fool will upbraid c. and a gift of

CHURLISHNESS.
Eccl. 42. 14. better is the c. of a man than a courteous

CILICIA.
Jud. 2. 21. which is at the left hand of upper C.
2 Mac. 4. 36. was come from the places about C.

CINNAMON.
Eccl. 24. 15. gave a sweet smell like c. and aspalathus

CIRCLE.
Wisd. 13. 2. deemed it either the c. of the stars

CIRCUIT.
Eccl. 24. 5. I alone compassed the c. of heaven
2 Mac. 6. 4. within the c. of the holy places

CIRCUMCISED.
Jud. 14. 10. Achior c. the foreskin of his flesh
1 Mac. 1. 60. women that caused their childr. to be c.
61. they slew them that had c. them

CIRCUMCISIONS.
2 Esd. 1. 31. for your c. have I forsaken

CIRCUMSPECT.
Tob. 4. 14. be c. my son, in all things thou dost

CIRCUMSPECTION.
Wisd. 12. 21. with how great c. didst judge thy sons

CISTERN.
Eccl. 50. 3. the c. was covered with plates of brass

CISTERNS.
Jud. 7. 21. the c. were emptied, they had no water

CITHERNS.
1 Mac. 4. 54. it was dedicated with songs and c.

CITY.
1 Esd. 2. 23. even this c. was made desolate
26. that that c. was practising against kings
5. 8. they returned every man to his own c.
Eccl. 26. 5. I was afraid of the slander of a c.
38. 32. without these cannot a c. be inhabited
40. 19. the building of a c. continues a man's name
49. 6. they burnt the chosen c. of the sanctuary
50. 4. and he fortified the c. against besieging
1 Mac. 1. 51. cities of Judah to sacrifice, c. by c.
5. 50. the soldiers assaulted the c. all that day
6. 3. he sought to take the c. and to spoil it
63. he found Philip to be master of the c. so he fought against him and took the c. by force
7. 1. Demetrius came unto a c. of the sea-coast
10. 75. but they of Joppe shut him out of the c.
12. 36. raising a great mount between the tower and the c. and to separate it from the c.
13. 47. fought no more, but put them out of the c.
2 Mac. 8. 17. and the cruel handling of the c.
15. 19. they that were in the c. took no care

CITIES.
Eccl. 46. 2. stretch out his sword against the c.
1 Mac. 5. 68. when he spoiled their c. he returned
10. 71. for with me is the power of the c.
2 Mac. 8. 11. he sent to the c. on the sea-coast

CITIZENS.
2 Mac. 4. 50. Menelaus being a great traitor to the c.
5. 6. but Jason slew his own c. without mercy
9. 15. would make them all equals to c. of Athens
19. to the good Jews his c. wisheth much joy

CLAY.
Wisd. 7. 9. silver shall be counted as c. before her
15. 7. yea, of the same c. he maketh both vessels
8. he maketh a vain god of the same c.
Eccl. 33. 13. as the c. is in the potter's hand
38. 30. he fashioneth the c. with his arm
Bel 7. for this is but c. within and brass without

CLEAN.
Eccl. 38. 30. is diligent to make c. the furnace

CLEANSE.
Eccl. 38. 10. c. thy heart from all wickedness
1 Mac. 4. 36. let us go up to c. and dedicate

CLEANSED.
1 Mac. 4. 41. until he had c. the sanctuary
43. who c. the sanctuary, and bare out the stones
13. 47. c. the houses wherein the idols were
50. Simon c. the tower from pollutions
2 Mac. 10. 5. on the very same day it was c. again
14. 36. keep this house undefil. which lately was c.

CLEANSING.
2 Mac. 1. 36. which is as much as to say a c.

CLEAR.
Sus. 46. I am c. from the blood of this woman

CLEAVE.
Eccl. 2. 3. c. unto him, and depart not away
6. 34. and c. unto him that is wise
24. 24. that he may confirm you, c. unto him
Bar. 3. 4. for which cause these plagues c. to us

CLEAVED.
Bar. 1. 20. the evils c. unto us, and the curse

CLEAVETH.
1 Esd. 4. 20. man leaveth his country, and c. to his wife
Eccl. 19. 2. that c. to harlots will become impudent

CLEAVING.
Eccl. 25. 12. faith is the beginning of c. to him

CLEMENCY.
2 Mac. 14. 9. according to the c. thou shewest

CLEOPATRA.
Esth. 11. 1. in the reign of Ptolemeus and C.
1 Mac. 10. 57. went out with his daughter C.

CLIMB.
2 Esd. 4. 8. neither did I ever c. up into heaven

CLIMBED.
2 Mac. 2. 4. the mountain where Moses c. up

CLIMBING.
Eccl. 25. 20. as the c. up a sandy way is to the feet

CLOSE.
Tob. 12. 11. I will keep c. nothing from you; I said it was good to keep c. the secrets of a king
Eccl. 27. 2. doth sin stick c. betw. buying and selling
1 Mac. 12. 50. went c. together prepared to fight

CLOSED.
1 Mac. 7. 46. c. them so that they were all slain

CLOTH.
2 Mac. 5. 2. men running in the air in c. of gold

CLOTHE.
2 Esd. 2. 20. give to the poor, c. the naked

CLOTHED.
1 Esd. 3. 6. as to be c. in purple, to drink in gold
Eccl. 50. 11. and was c. with the perfection of glory
1 Mac. 11. 58. to be c. in purple, 14. 43.

CLOTHES.
Bar. 6. 20. eat them and their c. they feel it not
1 Mac. 11. 71. then Jonathan rent his c. and prayed

CLOTHETH.
Eccl. 43. 20. and c. the water as with a breast-plate

CLOTHING.
Eccl. 29. 21. the chief thing for life is bread and c.
39. 26. the blood of the grape, and oil, and c.
2 Mac. 3. 33. the same young men in the same c.
11. 8. one in white c. shaking his armour of gold

CLOUD.
2 Esd. 15. 39. the c. which he raised up in wrath
Wisd. 2. 4. our life pass away as the trace of a c.
Eccl. 24. 3. and I covered the earth as a c.
50. 6. he was as the morning star in midst of a c.

CLOUDS.
2 Esd. 15. 40. great and mighty c. shall be lifted up
Wisd. 5. 21. from the c. as from a well-drawn bow
Eccl. 13. 23. what he saith, they extol it to the c.
35. 16. his prayer shall reach unto the c.
17. the prayer of the humble pierceth the c.
20. seasonable, as c. of rain in time of drought
43. 14. the treasures opened, c. fly forth as fowls
15. by his great power he maketh the c. firm
50. 7. as the rainbow, giving light in the bright c.
Dan. 3. 51. O ye lightnings and c. bless the Lord

CLOUDY.
Eccl. 24. 4. and my throne is in a c. pillar

CLUBS.
2 Mac. 4. 41. some of them caught stones, some c.

CLUSTER, S.
2 Esd. 9. 21. and I have kept me a grape of the c.
16. 30. there are left some c. of them that seek

CNIDUS.
1 Mac. 15. 23. the same thing wrote he to C.

COALS.
Eccl. 8. 10. kindle not the c. of a sinner, lest be burnt
11. 32. of a spark of fire a heap of c. is kindled

COAT.
2 Mac. 12. 35. taking hold of his c. drew him by force

COATS.
2 Mac. 12. 40. under the c. of every one slain

COCKER.
Eccl. 30. 9. c. thy child, he shall make thee afraid

COGITATIONS.
Eccl. 17. 5. an interpreter of the c. thereof

COLLECTION.
Bar. 1. 6. they made also a c. of money

COLLAR.
Eccl. 33. 26. a yoke and a c. do bow the neck

COLLECTOR.
1 Mac. 1. 29. the king sent his chief c. to Juda

COLONY.
Wisd. 12. 7. receive a worthy c. of God's children

COLOUR.
2 Mac. 3. 8. under a c. of visiting the cities
2 Mac. 3. 16. the chang. of his c. declared his agony

COLOURING.
Wisd. 13. 14. c. it red and covering every spot

COLOURS.
Wisd. 15. 4. any image spotted with divers c.

COME.
1 Mac. 6. 13. that these troubles are c. upon me
2 Mac. 6. 15. lest being c. to the height of sin
9. 18. the just judgment of God was c. upon them

COMEST, ETH.
Eccl. 21. 2. for if thou c. too near it, it will bite
5. and his judgment c. speedily

COMING.
1 Mac. 11. 44. the king was very glad of their c.
12. 45. for this is the cause of my c.
14. 21. wherefore we were glad of their c.
2 Mac. 6. 3. the c. in of this mischief was sore

COMELY.
1 Esd. 4. 18. love a woman, which is c. in favour
Eccl. 14. 3. riches are not c. for a niggard
20. 1. there is a reproof that is not c.
25. 4. O how c. a thing is judgment for grey hairs!
5. O how c. is the wisdom of old men!
2 Mac. 3. 26. excellent in beauty, c. in apparel
10. 29. there appeared five c. men upon horses

COMFORT.
2 Esd. 6. 33. and to say, be of good c. and fear not
14. 13. c. such of them as be in trouble
Wisd. 3. 18. nor have they c. in the day of trial
8. 9. that we should be a c. in cares and grief
Eccl. 3. 6. he shall be a c. to his mother
4. 18. she will c. him, and shew him her secrets
25. 23. a woman that will not c. her husband
30. 23. love thine own soul, and c. thy heart
36. 23. if there be meekness and c. in her tongue
38. 17. and then c. thyself for thy heaviness
Bar. 4. 27. be of good c. O my children, cry to God
30. he that gave thee that name will c. thee
1 Mac. 12. 9. the holy books of scripture to c. us
2 Mac. 7. 6. the Lord God in truth hath c. in us
11. 32. I have sent Menelaus that he may c. you

COMFORTED.
2 Esd. 5. 15. the angel c. me, and set me on my feet
Esth. 15. 8. the king c. her with loving words
16. and all the king's servants c. her
Eccl. 17. 24. he c. those that fail in patience
35. 17. till it come nigh, he will not be c.
38. 23. be c. for him, when spirit is departed
48. 24. he c. them that mourned in Sion
49. 10. for they c. Jacob, and delivered them
2 Mac. 7. 6. and he shall be c. in his servants
15. 17. thus being well c. by the words of Judas

COMFORTING.
2 Mac. 15. 9. so c. them out of the law and prophets

COMMAND.
2 Mac. 9. 8. he that thought he might c. the waves

COMMANDED.
Eccl. 15. 20. he hath c. no man to do wickedly
2 Mac. 7. 3. king c. pans and caldrons to be made hot
4. he c. to cut out the tongue of him that spake
5. he c. him, being yet alive, to be brought
15. 33. he c. that they should give it by pieces

COMMANDEDST.
2 Esd. 6. 45. upon the fourth day thou c. sun to shine

COMMANDMENT, S.
2 Esd. 6. 48. brought forth things at the c. of God
53. on the sixth day thou gavest c. to the earth
Eccl. 1. 26. if thou desire wisdom, keep the c.
2 Mac. 7. 30 I will not obey the king's c. but I will obey the c. of the law that was given by Moses

COMMENDABLE.
Eccl. 37. 22. understanding is c. in his mouth

COMMENDED.
1 Mac. 12. 43. but c. him to all his friends
2 Mac. 9. 25. whom I c. unto many of you often

COMMENTARIES.
2 Mac. 2. 13. were reported in the c. of Neemias

COMMISSIONER.
1 Mac. 2. 25. the king's c. who compelled men

COMMIT.
2 Mac. 2. 25. that are desirous to c. to memory

COMMITTED.
2 Esd. 4. 42. to deliver those things c. to them
5. 17. knowest thou not that Israel is c. to thee?
7. 32. shall deliver souls that were c. to them
1 Mac. 7. 20. then c. he the country to Alcimus
13. 39. as for any oversight or fault c. to this day
2 Mac. 3. 12. had c. it to the holiness of the place
22. to keep the things c. of trust safe and sure
9. 25. whom I often c. and commended to you
13. 6. or had c. any other grievous crime
8. as he had c. many sins about the altar
14. he had c. all to the Creator of the world

COMMODIOUS.
2 Mac. 10. 15. having gotten the most c. holds

COMMON.
Wisd. 7. 3. when I was born, I drew in the c. air
2 Mac. 4. 40. whereupon the c. people rising
8. 29. when they had made a c. supplication
9. 4. make it a c. burying place of the Jews, 14.
21. necessary to take care for the c. safety of all
10. 8. they ordained by a c. statute and decree
11. 15. consented, being careful of the c. good
12. 4. according to the c. decree of the city
13. 14. fight for the country and the c.-wealth

COMMOTIONS.
1 Esd. 5. 73. by persuasions and c. they hindered

COMMUNE.
1 Mac. 15. 28. he sent Athenobius to c. with him
2 Mac. 11. 20. I have given order to c. with you

COMMUNICATE.
Wisd. 7. 13. I do c. her liberally, I do not hide
2 Mac. 5. 20. c. in the benefits sent from the Lord

COMMUNICATETH.
Eccl. 26. 6. scourge of tongue which c. with all

COMMUNICATION.
Eccl. 9. 15. all thy c. in the law of the Most High
13. 11. for with much c. will he tempt thee

COMPACTED.
Wisd. 7. 2. being c. in blood of the seed of man

COMPANY.
Eccl. 9. 4. use not much the c. of a woman

1 *Mac.* 4. 35. he gathered a *c.* of strangers
6. 41. all that heard the marching of the *c.*
7. 12. assemble a *c.* of scribes to require justice
9. 44. Jonathan said to his *c.* let us go and fight
58. behold, Jonathan and his *c.* are at ease
12. 29. howbeit, Jonathan and his *c.* knew it not
49. sent an host to destroy all Jonathan's *c.*
13. 52. there he dwelt himself, with his *c.*
2 *Mac.* 5. 27. his *c.* fed on herbs continually

COMPANIED.

Sus. 57. and they for fear *c.* with you

COMPANIES.

1 *Mac.* 5. 33. went forth behind them in three *c.*

COMPANYING.

Sus. 54. under what tree sawest thou them *c.?*
58. under what tree didst thou take them *c.?*

COMPANION.

Eccl. 6. 10. some friend is a *c.* at the table
37. 4. there is a *c.* who rejoiceth, 5.
40. 23. a friend and *c.* never meet amiss

COMPANIONS.

1 *Esd.* 6. 3. Sathrabuzanes and his *c.* 7. 27.

COMPARABLE.

Eccl. 9. 10. for the new friend is not *c.* to him

COMPARED.

Wisd. 7. 9. nor *c.* I unto her any precious stone
15. 18. for being *c.* together, some are worse
Eccl. 22. 1. a slothful man is *c.* to a filthy stone, 2.

COMPASS.

1 *Mac.* 14. 48. within the *c.* of the sanctuary
2 *Mac.* 1. 15. was entered into the *c.* of the temple

COMPASSED.

Wisd. 19. 17. being *c.* with horrible darkness
Eccl. 23. 18. who seeth me? I am *c.* with darkness
24. 5. I alone *c.* the circuit of heaven
45. 9. and he *c.* him with pomegranates and bells
1 *Mac.* 4. 7. that it was *c.* about with horsemen
10. 80. for they had *c.* in his host and cast darts
15. 14. when he had *c.* the city round about
2 *Mac.* 3. 17. the man was so *c.* with fear and horror
27. Heliodorus was *c.* with great darkness

COMPASSETH.

1 *Esd.* 4. 34. the sun *c.* the heavens round about
Eccl. 43. 12. it *c.* the heaven with a glorious circle

COMPASSION.

Eccl. 17. 29. how great is his *c.* to such as turn to him
18. 12. therefore he multiplied his *c.*
Prayer of Manass. of great *c.* long-suffering
2 *Mac.* 8. 3. that he would have *c.* on the city

COMPEL.

1 *Esd.* 4. 6. they *c.* one another to pay tribute
2 *Mac.* 6. 1. to *c.* the Jews to depart from the laws

COMPELLED.

1 *Mac.* 2. 15. such as *c.* the people to revolt
25. the commissioner, who *c.* men to sacrifice
2 *Mac.* 4. 26. Jason was *c.* to flee into the country
6. 7. the Jews were *c.* to go in procession
7. 1. were *c.* by the king to taste swine's flesh
15. 2. the Jews that were *c.* to go with him

COMPLAIN.

Eccl. 29. 5. he will return words and *c.* of the time
41. 7. the children will *c.* of an ungodly father
1 *Mac.* 8. 32. if therefore they *c.* any more ag. thee

COMPLAINED.

2 *Mac.* 4. 36. the Jews *c.* because Onias was slain

COMPLAINT, S.

Eccl. 35. 14. when the widow poureth out her *c.*
1 *Mac.* 11. 25. some men had made *c.* against him

COMPLETE.

Wisd. 5. 17. take to him jealousy for *c.* armour
2 *Mac.* 3. 25. that he had *c.* harness of gold

COMPREHEND.

2 *Esd.* 4. 2. thinkest thou to *c.* the way of God?
11. how thy vessel be able to *c.* the way of Highest
5. 34. while I labour to *c.* way of the Most High

COMPREHENDED.

2 *Esd.* 8. 21. whose glory may not be *c.*

COMPREHENDING.

Eccl. 32. 8. thy speech be short, *c.* much in few words

CONCEIT.

Wisd. 8. 11. I shall be found of a quick *c.* in judg.
Eccl. 27. 6. so is the utterance of a *c.* in heart of man

CONCERT.

Eccl. 32. 5. a *c.* of music in a banquet of wine

CONCUBINE.

1 *Esd.* 4. 29. yet did I see Apame the king's *c.*
2 *Mac.* 4. 30. they were given to the king's *c.*

CONCUPISCENCE.

Wisd. 4. 12. the wandering of *c.* doth undermine
Eccl. 23. 5. turn away from me vain hopes and *c.*

CONDEMN.

2 *Esd.* 4. 18. if wert judge, whom wouldst thou *c.?*
Wisd. 2. 20. let us *c.* him with a shameful death
4. 16. the righteous that is dead shall *c.* the ungodly
Prayer of Manass. nor *c.* me into the lower parts

CONDEMNED.

Eccl. 14. 2. whose conscience hath not *c.* him
Sus. 41. the assembly *c.* Susanna to death
48. without knowledge have *c.* daughter of Israel
53. thou hast *c.* the innocent, and guilty go free
2 *Mac.* 4. 47. those poor men, them he *c.* to death
13. 6. whosoever was *c.* of sacrilege or committed

CONDITION.

2 *Esd.* 7. 57. he said, this is the *c.* of the battle
2 *Mac.* 9. 8. so proud was he beyond the *c.* of man
15. 12. Onias gentle in *c.* well spoken of

CONDITIONS.

2 *Mac.* 11. 14. persuaded to agree to all reasonable *c.*
13. 23. submitted himself and sware to all equal *c.*

CONDUCT.

1 *Esd.* 8. 51. was ashamed to ask king *c.* for safeguard
Jud. 10. 15. come to his tent and some of us will *c.* th.
2 *Mac.* 11. 30. that will depart shall have safe-*c.*

CONFECTION.

Eccl. 38. 8. of such the apothecary maketh a *c.*

CONFEDERATE.

1 *Mac.* 10. 16. we will make him our friend and *c.*

CONFEDERATES.

1 *Mac.* 8. 24. if there come war on any of their *c.*
31. yoke heavy on our friends and *c.* the Jews
14. 40. the Romans had called the Jews *c.*
15. 17. the Jews' ambassadors our friends and *c.*

CONFEDERACY.

1 *Mac.* 8. 17. sent them to Rome to make a *c.* 20.

CONFERENCE.

Wisd. 8. 18. in the exercise of *c.* with her prudence
2 *Mac.* 14. 22. so they made a peaceable *c.*

CONFESS.

Tob. 13. 6. therefore *c.* him with your whole mouth
14. 7. his people shall *c.* God, and Lord shall exalt
Wisd. 16. 8. in this thou madest thine enemies *c.*
Eccl. 4. 26. be not ashamed to *c.* thy sins
2 *Mac.* 7. 37. thou mayest *c.* that he alone is God

CONFESSED.

Tob. 12. 22. they *c.* the wonderful works of God

CONFESSETH.

Eccl. 20. 2. that *c.* his fault be preserved from hurt

CONFESSING.

1 *Esd.* 9. 8. now by *c.* give glory unto the Lord

CONFESSION.

1 *Esd.* 8. 91. in his prayer he made his *c.* weeping
Bar. 1. 14. to make *c.* in the house of the Lord

CONFIDENCE.

2 *Esd.* 8. 36. which have not the *c.* of good works
Jud. 13. 19. for this thy *c.* shall not depart
Eccl. 26. 21. having *c.* of their good descent
2 *Mac.* 8. 18. but our *c.* is in the Almighty God
15. 7. but Maccabeus had ever sure *c.* of Lord's help

CONFIDENT.

Eccl. 32. 21. be not *c.* in a plain way

CONFIRM.

Eccl. 24. 24. be strong in the L. that he may *c.* you
50. 24. that he would *c.* his mercy with us
1 *Mac.* 11. 57. I *c.* thee in the high-priesthood
12. 1. to *c.* and renew the friendship with them
13. 37. to *c.* the immunities we have granted
14. 24. sent Numenius to *c.* the league with them

CONFIRMED.

1 *Mac.* 11. 27. *c.* him in the high-priesthood and hon.
14. 26. he and his brethren *c.* their liberty
38. Demetrius *c.* him in the high-priesthood

CONFLICT.

Wisd. 10. 12. in a sore *c.* she gave him the victory
2 *Mac.* 5. 14. forty thousand were slain in the *c.*
15. 17. and manfully to try the matter by *c.*
19. took not the least care, being troubled for *c.*

CONFORM.

2 *Mac.* 6. 9. and whoso would not *c.* themselves

CONFOUNDED.

Eccl. 2. 10. did ever any trust in the L. and was *c.?*
24. 22. he that obeyeth me shall never be *c.*
Bar. 6. 39. they that worship them shall be *c.*
Dan. 3. 17. they shall not be *c.* that trust in thee
21. let them be *c.* in all their power and might
1 *Mac.* 4. 27. Lysias was *c.* and discouraged
31. let them be *c.* in their power and horsemen
2 *Mac.* 10. 30. so that being *c.* with blindness, and full of trouble, they were killed
13. 23. heard that Philip was desperately *c.*
14. 28. Nicanor was much *c.* in himself

CONFUSION.

2 *Esd.* 2. 6. that thou bring them to *c.*
5. 8. there shall be a *c.* also in many places
Bar. 1. 15. but to us belongeth the *c.* of faces
1 *Mac.* 1. 28. all house of Jacob was covered with *c.*

CONGEALED.

Eccl. 43. 19. being *c.* it lieth on the top of sharp stakes

CONGREGATION.

Eccl. 1. 30. cast thee down in midst of the *c.*
4. 7. get thyself the love of the *c.* and bow thy head
21. 9. the *c.* of the wicked is like tow wrapped
24. 2. in the *c.* of the Most High shall she open
23. the law for an heritage unto the *c.* of Jacob
31. 11. and the *c.* shall declare his alms
33. 18. hearken unto me, ye rulers of the *c.*
38. 33. they shall not sit high in the *c.*
45. 18. the *c.* of Core with fury and wrath
50. 13. oblations in their hands before all the *c.*
20. he lifted up his hands over the whole *c.*
1 *Mac.* 2. 56. for bearing witness before the *c.*
14. 19. which writings were read before the *c.*
28. at Saramel in the great *c.* of the priests

CONJECTURETH.

Wisd. 8. 8. she *c.* aright what is to come

CONQUERED.

1 *Mac.* 8. 2. it was told him how they had *c.* them
4. by their policy they had *c.* all that place

CONSCIENCE.

Wisd. 17. 11. being pressed with *c.* always forecasteth
Eccl. 14. 2. whose *c.* hath not condemned him
2 *Mac.* 6. 11. they made a *c.* to help themselves

CONSECRATED.

Tob. 1. 4. the temple was *c.* and built for all ages
Eccl. 45. 15. Moses *c.* and anointed him with oil
2 *Mac.* 12. 40. they found things *c.* to the idols

CONSENT.

1 *Esd.* 5. 47. they came altogether with one *c.*
6. 22. have been done with the *c.* of king Cyrus, 7. 4.
Jud. 7. 29. there was great weeping with one *c.*
2 *Mac.* 4. 39. committed with the *c.* of Menelaus
11. 24. that the Jews would not *c.* to our father

CONSENTED.

1 *Mac.* 1. 57. if any *c.* to the law, put him to death
11. 29. so the king *c.* and wrote letters to Jonathan
2 *Mac.* 11. 15. Maccabeus *c.* to all that Lysias desired
14. 20. all of one mind they *c.* to the covenants

CONSIDERATION.

1 *Mac.* 8. 17. in *c.* of these things Judas chose

CONSIDERATE.

Eccl. 32. 18. a man of council will be *c.*

CONSIDER.

Bar. 2. 16. O Lord, *c.* us, bow down thine ear
2 *Mac.* 7. 28. and *c.* that God made them of things

CONSIDERED.

2 *Esd.* 7. 16. why hast thou not *c.* to thy mind?
56. we *c.* not that we should begin to suffer
9. 20. so I *c.* the world, behold, there was peril
Wisd. 8. 17. when I *c.* these things in myself
2 *Mac.* 5. 17. he *c.* not that the Lord was angry

CONSIDERING.

2 *Mac.* 5. 6. not *c.* that to get the day of them
11. 4. not at all *c.* the power of God, but puffed up
13. *c.* that the Hebrews could not be overcome

CONSIST.

Eccl. 43. 26. and by his word all things *c.*

CONSORTETH.

Eccl. 13. 16. all flesh *c.* according to kind

CONSPICUOUS.

1 *Mac.* 11. 37. let it be set in a *c.* place, 14. 48.

CONSPIRED.

Eccl. 45. 18. strangers *c.* together against him
Bel. 28. they *c.* against the king, saying

CONSTRAINED.

Bel 30. being *c.* he delivered Daniel to them
2 *Mac.* 6. 18. Eleazar was *c.* to open his mouth

CONSTRAINT.

2 *Mac.* 6. 7. they were brought by bitter *c.* to eat

CONSUL.

1 *Mac.* 15. 16. Lucius *c.* of the Romans to Ptolemee

CONSULT.

Eccl. 8. 17. *c.* not with a fool ‖ 9. 14. *c.* with the wise
37. 10. *c.* not with one that suspecteth thee
1 *Mac.* 5. 16. assembled to *c.* what they should do

CONSULTED.

1 *Mac.* 4. 44. they *c.* what to do with the altar
12. 35. *c.* with them about building strong holds
16. 13. Ptolemeus *c.* deceitfully against Simon

CONSULTING.

1 *Mac.* 8. 15. *c.* alway for the people to be ordered

CONSUME.

Eccl. 27. 29. anguish shall *c.* them before death
45. 19. did wonders to *c.* them with the fiery flame
1 *Mac.* 5. 15. are assembled against us to *c.* us

CONSUMED.

2 *Esd.* 4. 16. for the fire came and *c.* the wood
Wisd. 5. 13. but were *c.* in our own wickedness
Eccl. 45. 14. their sacrifices shall be wholly *c.*
19. in his wrathful indignation were they *c.*
2 *Mac.* 1. 31. now when the sacrifice was *c.*
32. it was *c.* by light that shined from the altar
2. 10. *c.* the sacrifices, *c.* the burnt-offerings
11. sin-offering was not to be eaten, it was *c.*

CONSUMETH.

Eccl. 14. 19. every work rotteth and *c.* away
18. 18. a gift of the envious *c.* the eyes
31. 1. watching for riches *c.* the flesh
43. 21. the cold north-wind *c.* the grass as fire

CONSUMING.

Wisd. 6. 23. neither will I go with *c.* envy
2 *Mac.* 1. 23. priests prayed, whilst sacrifice was *c.*

CONTAINETH.

Wisd. 1. 7. that which *c.* all things hath knowledge

CONTEMNED.

Eccl. 22. 23. a mean estate is not alway to be *c.*

CONTEMNER.

1 *Mac.* 14. 14. every *c.* of the law he took away

CONTEMNETH.

Eccl. 19. 1. he that *c.* small things shall fall by little
26. 24. a dishonest woman *c.* shame, but an honest

CONTEMPT.

Esth. 13. 12. that it was neither in *c.* nor pride
2 *Mac.* 3. 18. the place was like to come into *c.*

CONTEND.

Eccl. 28. 10. the stronger they are which *c.*

CONTENT.

Esth. 13. 13. I could have been *c.* to kiss the soles
Tob. 11. 9. from henceforth I am *c.* to die
1 *Mac.* 6. 60. the king and the princes were *c.*
2 *Mac.* 5. 15. he was not *c.* with this, but presumed
6. 30. but in soul am well *c.* to suffer these things

CONTENTED.

Eccl. 29. 23. be it little or much, hold thee *c.*

CONTENTION.

Eccl. 28. 11. an hasty *c.* kindleth a fire
2 *Mac.* 4. 4. Onias seeing the danger of this *c.*

CONTENTMENT.

Wisd. 19. 12. quails came from the sea for their *c.*
2 *Mac.* 9. 20. if your affairs be to your *c.* I thank G.

CONTENTS.

1 *Mac.* 15. 2. the *c.* whereof were these
2 *Mac.* 11. 17. for the performance of the *c.* thereof

CONTINENT.

Eccl. 26. 15. and her *c.* mind cannot be valued

CONTINUALLY.

Eccl. 11. 19. and now I will eat *c.* of my goods
1 *Mac.* 15. 25. against Dora, assaulting it *c.*
2 *Mac.* 3. 26. who stood by him, and scourged him *c.*
5. 27. fed on herbs *c.* lest they should be polluted

CONTINUE.

Eccl. 6. 10. some friend will not *c.* in day of affliction
40. 19. children and building *c.* a man's name
41. 12. for that shall *c.* with thee above gold
1 *Mac.* 10. 27. *c.* ye still to be faithful unto us
2 *Mac.* 4. 6. that the state should *c.* quiet
10. 12. Ptolemeus endeavoured to *c.* peace

CONTINUED.

1 *Mac.* 6. 9. and there he *c.* many days
9. 13. the battle *c.* from morning till night
10. 26. whereas you have *c.* in our friendship
50. he *c.* the battle until the sun went down
2 *Mac.* 8. 1. took such as *c.* in the Jews' religion

CONTRACTS.

1 *Mac.* 13. 42. write in their instruments and *c.*

CONTRARY.

Wisd. 2. 12. because he is clean *c.* to our doings

CONTRITE.

Dan. 3. 16. in a *c.* heart let us be accepted

CONTROL.

Eccl. 5. 3. say not, who shall *c.* me for my works?

CONVEYED.

1 *Mac.* 9. 6. many *c.* themselves out of the host
2 *Mac.* 8. 13. they fled and *c.* themselves away

CONVENIENT.

Eccl. 10. 23. nor is it *c.* to magnify a sinful man
39. 17. at time *c.* they shall all be sought out
1 *Mac.* 4. 46. and laid up the stones in a *c.* place
12. 11. both in our feasts and other *c.* days
14. 34. he furnished them with all things *c.*
2 *Mac.* 4. 19. because it was not *c.* but to be reserved
32. Menelaus supposing he had gotten a *c.* time
8. 31. they laid them up carefully in *c.* places
10. 18. having all things *c.* to sustain the siege
11. 36. that we may declare as it is *c.* for you
14. 22. Judas placed armed men ready in *c.* places

CONVERSANT.
Wisd. 8. 3. in that she is *c.* with God she magnifies
13. 7. for being *c.* in his works, they search him
Eccl. 11. 20. in thy covenant, and be *c.* therein
39. 3. and he will be *c.* in dark parables
41. 5. they that are *c.* in the dwelling of the ungodly
CONVERSATION.
Tob. 4. 14. be circumspect and be wise in all thy *c.*
Wisd. 8. 16. for her *c.* hath no bitterness
1 *Mac.* 4. 42. so he choose priests of blameless *c.*
2 *Mac.* 15. 12. Onias reverend in *c.* prayed for Jews
CONVERSED.
Bar. 3. 37. shew himself on earth, and *c.* with men
CONVERSION.
Eccl. 49. 2. behaved uprightly in the *c.* of the people
CONVICTED.
2 *Mac.* 4. 45. Menelaus being now *c.* promised
CONVINCE.
Wisd. 4. 20. their own iniquities shall *c.* them
COPY.
Esth. 13. 1. the *c.* of the letters was this
16. 19. ye shall publish the *c.* of this letter
Bar. 6. 1. a *c.* of an epistle which Jeremy sent
1 *Mac.* 8. 22. this is the *c.* of the epistle
11. 31. we sent you here a *c.* of the letter
37. see that thou make a *c.* of these things
12. 5. this is the *c.* of the letters, 19. | 14, 20.
14. 23. and to put the *c.* of their ambassage
COPIES.
1 *Mac.* 14. 49. that the *c.* thereof should be laid up
CORE.
Eccl. 45. 18. the congregation of C. maligned him
CORES.
1 *Esd.* 8. 20. likewise of wheat, to an hundred *c.*
CORRECTION.
Wisd. 12. 26. that would not be reformed by that *c.*
Eccl. 16. 12. as his mercy is great, so is his *c.* also
22. 6. but stripes and *c.* are never out of time
42. 5. of much *c.* of children be not ashamed
2 *Mac.* 7. 33. be angry a little while for our *c.*
CORRUPTED.
2 *Esd.* 4. 11. the world being now outwardly *c.*
CORRUPTIBLE.
2 *Esd.* 7. 15. seeing thou art but a *c.* man
Wisd. 9. 15. the *c.* body presseth down the soul
14. 8. because being *c.* it was called god
19. 21. wasted not the flesh of the *c.* living things
2 *Mac.* 7. 16. thou art *c.* thou dost what thou wilt
CORRUPTION.
2 *Esd.* 7. 41. even so now seeing *c.* is grown up
43. beginning of immortality, wherein *c.* is past
Eccl. 28. 6. remember thy end, *c.* and death
CORS.
1 *Esd.* 8. 20. likewise of wheat, to an hundred *c.*
COS.
1 *Mac.* 15. 23. the same thing wrote he to C.
COSTLY.
1 *Esd.* 6. 9. building an house of hewn and *c.* stone
Wisd. 2. 7. let us fill ourselves with *c.* wine
COSTS.
2 *Mac.* 3. 3. Seleucus bare all *c.* belonging to sacrifice
COTTAGE.
Eccl. 29. 22. better is a poor man in a mean *c.*
COVENANT.
2 *Esd.* 2. 5. these childr. which would not keep my *c.*
7. be scattered, for they have despised my *c.*
3. 15. thou madest an everlasting *c.* with him
Wisd. 1. 16. and they made a *c.* with it
Eccl. 11. 20. be stedfast in thy *c.* and conversant
17. 12. he made an everlasting *c.* with them
45. 24. there was a *c.* of peace made with him
47. 11. he gave him a *c.* of kings, and a throne
1 *Mac.* 1. 15. they forsook the holy *c.* and joined
63. that they might not profane the holy *c.*
4. 10. and remember the *c.* of our fathers
7. 18. for they have broken the *c.* and oath
2 *Mac.* 1. 2. remember his *c.* he made with Abraham
7. 36. for our brethren are dead under God's *c.*
COVENANTS.
1 *Mac.* 15. 27. but brake all the *c.* he had made
2 *Mac.* 12. 1. when these *c.* were made, Lysias
13. 25. the people were grieved for the *c.* for they
stormed because they would make their *c.* void
14. 20. all of one mind, they consented to the *c.*
27. that he was much displeased with the *c.*
COVER.
Wisd. 5. 16. with his right hand shall he *c.* them
10. 17. she was to them for a *c.* by day
Eccl. 22. 9. they shall *c.* the baseness of their parents
23. 18. the walls *c.* me, and nobody seeth me
26. 8. and she will not *c.* her own shame
38. 16. then *c.* his body according to the custom
COVERED.
Eccl. 16. 30. with living things he hath *c.* face thereof
24. 3. and I *c.* the earth as a cloud
47. 15. thy soul *c.* the whole earth
Sus. 32. to uncover her face, for she was *c.*
2 *Mac.* 10. 30. *c.* him on every side with weapons
COVERETH.
Eccl. 40. 27. and *c.* him above all glory
COVERING.
2 *Mac.* 3. 25. a rider adorned with a very fair *c.*
COVETOUS.
Eccl. 10. 9. not a more wicked thing than a *c.* man
14. 9. a *c.* man's eye is not satisfied with his portion
COVETOUSNESS.
2 *Mac.* 4. 50. the *c.* of them that were in power
10. 20. they with Simon, being led with *c.*
COULD.
2 *Mac.* 15. 38. it is that which I *c.* attain unto
COUNCIL.
1 *Esd.* 2. 17. the rest of their *c.* and the judges
8. 55. vessels which the king and *c.* had given
1 *Mac.* 9. 58. then all the ungodly men held a *c.*
14. 22. register things they spake in *c.* of the people
COUNSEL.
1 *Esd.* 7. 15. had turned the *c.* of the king of Assyria
2 *Esd.* 4. 13. I went into a plain, the trees took *c.*
15. the floods of the sea also took *c.* and said, come
Tob. 4. 18. ask *c.* and desp. not any *c.* that is profitable
19. for every nation hath not *c.* but Lord himself
Wisd. 4. 17. what God in his *c.* decreed of him
Wisd. 6. 4. you have not walked after the *c.* of God
9. 13. what man is he that can know the *c.* of God
17. thy *c.* who hath known, except give wisdom
Eccl. 8. 17. consult not a fool, he cannot keep *c.*
15. 14. he left him in the hand of his *c.*
17. 6. *c.* a tongue and eyes and heart gave he them
21. 13. his *c.* is like a pure fountain of life
25. 4. and for ancient men to know *c.*
5. oh how comely is *c.* to men of honour!
30. 21. and afflict not thyself in thine own *c.*
32. 18. a man of *c.* will be considerate, but a proud
37. 8. for he will *c.* for himself
1 *Mac.* 2. 65. I know that Simon is a man of *c.*
7. 31. when he saw that his *c.* was discovered
9. 60. because their *c.* was known to them
2 *Mac.* 7. 25. she would *c.* the young man
26. that she would *c.* her son to save his life
COUNSELLOR.
Wisd. 8. 9. that she would be a *c.* of good things
Eccl. 6. 6. have but one *c.* of a thousand, nevertheless
37. 7. every *c.* extolleth counsel, but there is
8. beware of a *c.* and know what need he hath
42. 21. and he hath no need of any *c.*
COUNSELLORS.
1 *Esd.* 8. 11. to me and my seven friends the *c.*
COUNSELLETH.
Eccl. 37. 7. but there is some that *c.* for himself
COUNSELS.
2 *Esd.* 1. 7. but they have despised my *c.* 2. 1.
Tob. 4. 19. that all thy paths and *c.* may prosper
Wisd. 1. 9. for inquisition shall be made into the *c.*
of the ungodly, and sound of her words come
6. 3. from Highest, who shall search out your *c.*
Eccl. 23. 1. O Lord, leave me not to their *c.*
24. 29. her *c.* profounder than the great deep
COUNTENANCE.
Jud. 13. 16. my *c.* hath deceived him to destruction
Esth. 15. 14. and thy *c.* is full of grace
Eccl. 12. 18. he will whisper much and change his *c.*
13. 25. his *c.* and a merry heart maketh a cheerful *c.*
26. a cheerful *c.* is a token of a heart in prosperity
19. 29. one that hath understanding by his *c.*
25. 17. the wickedness of a woman darkeneth her *c.*
23. a wicked woman maketh a heavy *c.*
37. 17. the *c.* is a sign of changing of the heart
2 *Mac.* 3. 16. his *c.* declared the inward agony
6. 18. an aged man, and of a well-favoured *c.*
COUNTERFEIT, S.
Wisd. 2. 16. we are esteemed of him as *c.*
15. 9. and counteth it his glory to make *c.* things
COUNTERVAIL.
Eccl. 6. 15. nothing doth *c.* a faithful friend
COUNTRY.
2 *Esd.* 4. 15. that there we may make us another *c.*
1 *Mac.* 8. 8. and the *c.* of India, Media, and Lydia
16. to one man, who ruled over all their *c.*
9. 25. Bacchides made them lords of the *c.*
12. 25. he gave them no respite to enter his *c.*
14. 6. Simon enlarged bounds and recovered the *c.*
36. so that the heathen were taken out of their *c.*
37. he fortified it for the safety of the *c.*
2 *Mac.* 5. 8. as open enemy of his *c.* and countrymen
13. 14. to fight for the temple, the city, and *c.*
COUNTRYMEN.
2 *Mac.* 4. 5. he went, not to be an accuser of his *c.*
5. 6. thinking them his enemies and not his *c.*
8. as an open enemy of his country and *c.*
23. having a malicious mind against his *c.*
12. 5. when Judas heard of this cruelty done to his *c.*
14. 37. Razis a lover of his *c.* was accused
15. 30. who continued his love towards his *c.*
COUNTRIES.
Eccl. 10. 16. the Lord overthrew *c.* of the heathen
39. 4. he will travel through strange *c.* for he tried
47. 17. the *c.* marvelled at thee for thy songs
1 *Mac.* 1. 4. Alexander ruled over *c.* and nations
8. 8. and of the goodliest *c.* which they took of him
COURAGE.
Eccl. 45. 23. Phinees stood up with good *c.* of heart
1 *Mac.* 4. 32. make them to be of no *c.* and cause
5. 3. he abated their *c.* and took their spoils
11. 49. Jews had got the city, their *c.* was abated
2 *Mac.* 1. 3. and to do his will with a good *c.*
4. 14. the priests had no *c.* to serve at the altar
6. 31. his death for an example of a noble *c.*
7. 12. the king marvelled at the young man's *c.*
20. she bare it with a good *c.* because of hope
COURAGEOUS.
2 *Mac.* 7. 21. the mother filled with *c.* spirits said
COURAGEOUSLY.
1 *Mac.* 6. 45. wheref. he ran upon him *c.* thro' battle
2 *Mac.* 6. 28. an example to die willingly and *c.*
7. 11. he said *c.* these I had from heaven
10. 33. they laid siege against the fortress *c.*
15. 17. but *c.* to set upon them and try the matter
COURAGEOUSNESS.
2 *Mac.* 14. 18. and of the *c.* they had to fight
COURSE.
1 *Esd.* 4. 34. swift is the sun in his *c.* he fetcheth his
c. again to his own place in one day
COURT.
1 *Esd.* 9. 1. Esdras rising from the *c.* of the temple
1 *Mac.* 9. 54. the wall of inner *c.* to be pulled down
11. 46. wherefore the king fled into the *c.*
13. 40. who are meet among you to be in our *c.*
COURTS.
1 *Mac.* 4. 38. they saw shrubs growing in the *c.*
COURTEOUS.
Eccl. 42. 14. than a *c.* woman that brings shame
COURTEOUSLY.
2 *Mac.* 3. 9. when he had been *c.* received
COURTESY.
Eccl. 33. 21. that thou shouldst stand to their *c.*
COUSIN.
1 *Esd.* 3. 7. he shall be called Darius his *c.*
4. 42. thou shalt sit next me and be called my *c.*
Tob. 6. 10. we shall lodge with Raguel who is thy *c.*
2 *Mac.* 11. 1. Lysias the king's protector and *c.* 35.
CRAFT.
2 *Mac.* 12. 24. whom he besought with much *c.*
CRAFTY.
Eccl. 42. 18. he considereth their *c.* devices
CRATES.
2 *Mac.* 4. 29. Sostratus left C. who was governor
CREATED.
2 *Esd.* 5. 44. hold them that shall be *c.* therein
45. hast given life to the creature thou hast *c.*
49. so have I disposed the world which I *c.*
9. 13. but inquire for whom the world was *c.*
Wisd. 1. 14. he *c.* all things that they might have
10. 1. the first formed father that was *c.* alone
Eccl. 1. 4. Wisdom hath been *c.* before all things
14. it was *c.* with the faithful in the womb
17. 1. the Lord *c.* man of the earth, and turned
18. 1. he that liveth for ever *c.* all things
23. 20. he knew all things ere they were *c.*
24. 9. he *c.* me from the beginning before world
31. 13. what is *c.* more wicked than an eye?
38. 1. for the Lord hath *c.* the physician, 12.
4. the Lord hath *c.* medicines out of the earth
39. 25. for the good are good things *c.* from beginn.
28. there be spirits that are *c.* for vengeance
CREATION.
2 *Esd.* 6. 38. thou spakest from the beginning of the *c.*
Eccl. 49. 16. above every living thing in the *c.*
CREATOR.
Jud. 9. 12. C. of the waters, hear thou my prayer
Eccl. 24. 8. so the C. of all things gave command.
2 *Mac.* 1. 24. O Lord, C. of all things, who art fearful
7. 23. doubtless the C. of the world will give
13. 14. had committed all to the C. of the world
CREATURE.
2 *Esd.* 5. 44. the *c.* may not haste above the maker
56. shew thy servant by whom thou visitest thy *c.*
8. 8. thy *c.* is preserved in fire and water
13. thou shalt mortify it as thy *c.* and quicken it
45. for thou art merciful unto thy *c.*
Jud. 9. 12. King of every *c.* hear thou my prayer
Wisd. 5. 17. he shall make the *c.* his weapon
Eccl. 16. 16. his mercy is manifest to every *c.*
CREATURES.
2 *Esd.* 5. 55. as the *c.* which now begin to be old
6. 47. that it should bring forth living *c.*
49. then didst thou ordain two living *c.*
54. whom thou madest lord of all thy *c.*
Jud. 16. 14. let *c.* serve thee, thou spakest, they were
Wisd. 2. 6. let us use the *c.* like as in youth
7. 20. to know the natures of living *c.*
9. 2. that he should have dominion over the *c.*
CREDIT.
Eccl. 6. 7. prove him, and be not hasty to *c.* him
19. 4. he that is hasty to *c.* is light minded
1 *Mac.* 10. 46. they gave no *c.* unto them
CREPT.
1 *Mac.* 6. 46. he *c.* under the elephant, and thrust
CROOKED.
Wisd. 13. 13. being a *c.* piece of wood, full of knots
Eccl. 4. 17. he will walk with him by *c.* ways
CROUCHING.
Eccl. 12. 11. though he go *c.* yet take good heed
CROWN.
Bel 36. the angel of the Lord took him by the *c.*
CROWN.
Wisd. 2. 8. let us *c.* ourselves with rose-buds
4. 2. it weareth a *c.* and triumpheth for ever
5. 16. they shall receive a beautiful *c.* from the L.
Eccl. 1. 11. the fear of the Lord is a *c.* of rejoicing
18. the fear of the Lord is a *c.* of wisdom
32. 2. receive a *c.* for well-ordering the feas
45. 12. he set a *c.* of gold upon the mitre
47. 6. in that he gave him a *c.* of glory
1 *Mac.* 6. 15. he gave him the *c.* and his robe
8. 14. yet for all this, none of them wore a *c.*
10. 20. sent him a purple robe and a *c.* of gold
29. release from customs of salt and *c.* taxes
11. 35. the *c.* taxes, we discharge them of them
12. 39. that he might set the *c.* on his own head
13. 37. the golden *c.* and scarlet robe ye sent
39. we forgive the *c.* tax also which ye owe
2 *Mac.* 10. 11. when Antiochus was come to the *c.*
14. 4. came, presenting to him a *c.* of gold
CROWNS.
1 *Mac.* 1. 9. they all put *c.* upon themselves
4. 57. they decked the temple with *c.* of gold
CROWNETH.
Eccl. 19. 5. but he that resisteth pleasures *c.* his life
CROWS.
Bar. 6. 54. they are as *c.* between heaven and earth
CRUEL.
2 *Mac.* 4. 25. but having the fury of a *c.* tyrant
7. 27. she laughing the *c.* tyrant to scorn, spake
8. 17. and *c.* handling of the city
11. 9. not only to fight with men, but with *c.* beasts
CRUELLY.
Eccl. 13. 12. but *c.* he will lay up thy words
2 *Mac.* 15. 2. O destroy not so *c.* and barbarously
CRUELTY.
2 *Mac.* 12. 5. heard of this *c.* done to his countrymen
CRY.
1 *Mac.* 4. 10. now therefore let us *c.* unto heaven
CRIED.
1 *Esd.* 9. 10. then *c.* the whole multitude and said
Sus. 24. with that Susanna *c.* with a loud voice, and
the two elders *c.* out against her
Bel 37. Habbacuc *c.* saying, O Daniel, Daniel
1 *Mac.* 3. 50. then *c.* they with a loud voice, 54.
11. 49. they made supplication to the king and *c.*
13. 50. then *c.* they to Simon, beseeching him
2 *Mac.* 8. 3. and hear the blood that *c.* unto him
CRIER.
Eccl. 20. 15. he openeth his mouth like a *c.*
CRYING.
1 *Esd.* 5. 63. came with weeping and great *c.*
Wisd. 7. 3. the first voice which I uttered was *c.*
Eccl. 26. 27. a loud *c.* woman and a scold be sought
CUBITS.
2 *Mac* 13. 5. there was a tower of fifty *c.*
CUCUMBERS.
Bar. 6. 70. as a scare-crow in a garden of *c.*
CULTURE.
2 *Esd.* 8. 6. give us *c.* to our understanding
CUNNING.
Wisd. 8. 6. who is a more *c.* workman than she?
Eccl. 45. 11. the work of the *c.* workman

1 *Mac.* 13. 29. in these he made *c.* devices
CUP-BEARER.
Tob. 1. 22. now Achiacharus was *c.* and keeper
CUP-BOARD.
1 *Mac.* 15. 32. saw the *c.* of gold and silver plate
CUPS.
1 *Esd.* 2. 13. a thousand golden *c.* vials of gold
3. 22. when they are in their *c.* they forget their love
CURIOUS.
2 *Esd.* 4. 23. for it was not my mind to be *c.*
9. 13. be not *c.* how the ungodly shall be punished
Eccl. 3. 23. be not *c.* in unnecessary matters
2 *Mac.* 2. 30. to be *c.* in particulars belonging
CURSE.
Eccl. 4. 5. give him none occasion to *c.* thee
6. if he *c.* thee in the bitterness of his soul
23. 14. and so thou *c.* the day of thy nativity
28. 13. *c.* the whisperer and double-tongued
38. 19. the life of the poor is the *c.* of the heart
41. 9. if you be born, ye shall be born to a *c.* and if you die, a *c.* shall be your portion
10. so the ungodly shall go from a *c.* to destruction
Bar. 1. 20. and the *c.* which the Lord appointed
3. 8. we are in our captivity for a reproach and *c.*
CURSED.
Wisd. 3. 13. their offspring is *c.* blessed is the barren
12. 11. it was a *c.* seed from the beginning
14. 8. but that which is made with hands is *c.*
Eccl. 23. 26. she shall leave her memory to be *c.*
2 *Mac.* 4. 38. there slew he that *c.* murderer
12. 35. when he would have taken that *c.* man
CURSETH.
Eccl. 21. 27. when the ungodly *c.* Satan, he *c.* his own soul, a whisperer defileth his own soul
CUSTOM.
Wisd. 14. 16. in time an ungodly *c.* grown strong
Eccl. 7. 13. for the *c.* thereof is not good
23. 14. and so thou by thy *c.* become a fool
2 *Mac.* 4. 16. whose *c.* they followed so earnestly
11. 24. to be brought to the *c.* of the Gentiles
12. 38. they purified themselves as the *c.* was
CUSTOMS.
1 *Mac.* 10. 29. now I do free you from the *c.* of salt
11. 35. of the tithes and *c.* pertaining to us
2 *Mac.* 4. 28. appertained the gathering of the *c.*
11. 25. after the *c.* of their forefathers
CUT.
1 *Esd.* 4. 9. if he command. to *c.* down, they *c.* down
Eccl. 25. 26. *c.* her off from thy flesh, and let her go
2 *Mac.* 7. 4. he commanded to *c.* out the tongue of him that spake, and to *c.* off the utmost parts
CUTTING.
Jud. 13. 18. hath directed thee to the *c.* off of head
CYMBALS.
1 *Esd.* 5. 59. the Levites the sons of Asaph had *c.*
Jud. 16. 2. Judith said, sing to my Lord with *c.*
1 *Mac.* 4. 54. it was dedicated with harps and *c.*
CYPRESS.
Eccl. 24. 13. and as a *c.* tree on the mountains
50. 10. as a *c.* tree which groweth to the clouds
CYPRIANS.
2 *Mac.* 4. 29. Crates, who was governor of the C.
CYPRUS.
2 *Mac.* 10. 13. called traitor, because he had left C.
12. 2. Nicanor governor of C. would not suffer
CYRENE.
1 *Mac.* 15. 23. the same wrote he to Cyprus and C.
2 *Mac.* 2. 23. declared by Jason of C. in five books
CYRUS.
1 *Esd.* 2. 3. thus saith C. king of the Persians
4. 44. which C. set apart when he vowed to destroy
57. C. had set apart and all that C. had given
5. 71. we will build, as C. hath commanded us
73. they hindered all the time that king C. lived
6. 17. in the first year that king C. reigned in Babylon, C. the king wrote to build this house
21. search be made among the records of king C.

D.

DADDEUS.
1 *Esd.* 8. 46. that they should speak unto D.
DAGGER.
Bar. 6. 15. he hath also in his right hand a *d.*
DAGON.
1 *Mac.* 10. 84. took their spoils and the temple of D.
11. 4. they shewed him the temple of D. burned
DAINTY.
Eccl. 37. 29. be not unsatiable in any *d.* thing
DAINTIES.
Eccl. 14. 16. there is no seeking of *d.* in the grave
DALLIED.
Wisd. 12. 26. correction wherein he *d.* with them
DAMASCUS.
Jud. 15. 5. chased them until they were passed D.
1 *Mac.* 11. 62. passed through the country unto D.
12. 32. and removing thence he came to D.
DAMNATION.
Wisd. 12. 27. therefore came extreme *d.* on them
DANCE.
Jud. 15. 12. women made a *d.* among them for her
13. she went before the people in the *d.*
DANCES.
Jud. 3. 7. they received them with garlands and *d.*
DANGER.
Esth. 14. 4. for my *d.* is in my hand
Eccl. 3. 26. he that loveth *d.* shall perish therein
29. 17. will leave him in *d.* that delivered him
34. 12. I was ofttimes in *d.* of death, yet delivered
43. 24. they that sail on the sea, tell of the *d.*
2 *Mac.* 15. 1. resolved without any *d.* to set on them
DANGEROUS.
Eccl. 9. 18. a man of an ill tongue is *d.* in his city
DANGERS.
Tob. 4. 4. remember that she saw many *d.* for thee
DANIEL.
Sus. 45. a young youth whose name was D.
61. for D. had convicted them of false witness
64. from that day was D. in great reputation
Bel. 4. but D. worshipped his own God
10. the king went with D. into the temple of Bel

Bel 17. D. are the seals whole? and he said, yea
37. O D. D. take the dinner God hath sent thee
1 *Mac.* 2. 60. D. for his innocency was delivered
DAPHNE.
2 *Mac.* 4. 33. he withdrew into a sanctuary at D.
DAREST.
Eccl. 29. 24. thou *d.* not open thy mouth
DARIUS.
1 *Esd.* 2. 30. second year of the reign of D. 6. 1.
3. 1. now when D. reigned, he made a great feast
5. to him shall the king D. give great gifts
7. he shall sit next to D. because of his wisdom
8. sealed it, and laid it under D. his pillow
6. 7. wrote and sent to D. to king D. greeting
34. I D. the king have ordained that it be done
1 *Mac.* 12. 7. there were letters sent from D.
DARK.
Wisd. 8. 8. Wisdom can expound *d.* sentences
17. 3. they were under a *d.* vail of forgetfulness
Eccl. 45. 5. he brought him into the *d.* cloud
DARKNESS.
1 *Esd.* 4. 24. looketh on a lion and goeth in *d.*
2 *Esd.* 14. 20. thus the world is set in *d.*
Tob. 4. 10. alms suffereth not to come into *d.*
14. 10. how out of light he brought him into *d.* and rewarded him again, for he went down into *d.*
Esth. 11. 8. and lo, a day of *d.* and obscurity
Wisd. 18. 4. were worthy to be imprisoned in *d.*
Eccl. 11. 16. error and *d.* had their beginning
16. 16. he hath separated his light from *d.*
DARKENETH.
Eccl. 25. 17. her wickedness *d.* her countenance
DARTS.
Jud. 1. 15. he smote him through with his *d.*
DASH.
Jud. 16. 5. that he would *d.* the sucking children
DATHAN.
Eccl. 45. 18. the men that were of D.'s side
DAUGHTER.
Tob. 3. 10. I am the only *d.* of my father, 15.
6. 10. he hath also one only *d.* named Sara
7. 11. I have given my *d.* in marriage to seven men
13. then he called his *d.* Sara, and she came
10. 12. I commit my *d.* to thee of special trust
11. 17. blessed her, saying, thou art welcome, *d.*
Eccl. 7. 25. marry thy *d.* and so shalt thou have
22. 3. and a foolish *d.* is born to his loss
4. a wise *d.* shall bring an inheritance
26. 10. if thy *d.* be shameless, keep her in
36. 21. yet is one *d.* better than another
42. 9. father waketh for the *d.* when none knows
Sus. 48. ye have condemned a *d.* of Israel
1 *Mac.* 9. 37. as being the *d.* of a prince of Chanaan
10. 56. for I will marry my *d.* to thee
11. 12. wherefore he took his *d.* from him
DAUGHTERS.
1 *Esd.* 8. 84. ye shall not join your *d.* to their sons
2 *Esd.* 1. 28. I have prayed you as a mother her *d.*
Wisd. 9. 7. to be a judge of thy sons and *d.*
Eccl. 7. 24. hast thou *d.*? have a care of their body
DAVID.
1 *Esd.* 1. 3. that Solomon the son of D. had built
Eccl. 45. 25. to the covenant made with D.
47. 1. Nathan rose up to prophesy in the time of D.
2. so was D. chosen out of the children of Israel
22. and he gave out of him a root unto D.
48. 15. there remained a ruler in the house of D.
49. 4. all except D. and Ezekias were defective
DAUNTED.
Jud. 16. 10. the Medes were *d.* at her hardiness
Eccl. 32. 18. a proud man is not *d.* with fear
DAY.
1 *Esd.* 8. 89. thou art true, for we are left a root this *d.*
9. 11. and this is not a work of a *d.* or two
53. this *d.* is holy to the Lord, be not sorrowful
2 *Esd.* 1. 16. but ever to this *d.* do ye yet murmur
7. 43. *d.* of doom shall be the end of this time
Tob. 4. 9. thou layest up against the *d.* of necessity
5. 14. wilt thou a drachm a *d.* and things necessary?
10. 1. now Tobit his father counted every *d.*
7. she went out every *d.* into the way which they went, and did eat no meat on the *d.* time
Wisd. 3. 18. nor have they comfort in the *d.* of trial
Eccl. 10. 10. he that is a king to *d.* to-morrow dies
11. 25. in *d.* of prosperity, in the *d.* of affliction
26. it is easy in the *d.* of death to reward a man
20. 15. to *d.* he lendeth, to-morrow will he ask it
33. 7. why doth one *d.* excel another, when as all the light of every *d.* in the year is of the sun?
38. 22. yesterday for me, and to *d.* for thee
40. 1. from the *d.* they go out of their mother's womb, till the *d.* they return to mother of all
46. 4. sun go back, was not one *d.* as long as two?
Sus. 12. they watched from *d.* to *d.* to see her
1 *Mac.* 9. 44. it stands not with us to *d.* as before
2 *Mac.* 7. 20. seven slain within the space of one *d.*
DAYS.
Tob. 4. 3. but honour her all the *d.* of thy life
5. my son, be mindful of the Lord all thy *d.*
9. 4. but my father counteth the *d.* if I tarry long
10. 1. when the *d.* of the journey were expired
Jud. 12. 18. more than all the *d.* since I was born
Eccl. 17. 2. he gave them few *d.* and a short time
22. 12. seven *d.* do men mourn for the dead
33. 9. some of them hath he made high *d.* and some of them hath he made ordinary *d.*
41. 13. a good life hath few *d.* a good name endures
50. 3. in his *d.* the cistern to receive water
Bar. 1. 11. pray for the life of father and son, that their *d.* may be upon earth as the *d.* of heaven
DAILY.
1 *Esd.* 1. 2. having set priests according to *d.* courses
5. 51. they offered sacrifices *d.* as was meet
6. 30. as priests shall signify to be *d.* spent
Eccl. 47. 9. might *d.* sing praises in their songs
DAY-SPRING.
Wisd. 16. 28. that at the *d.* we pray to thee
DEAD.
2 *Esd.* 2. 16. those that be *d.* will I raise again
23. wherever thou findest the *d.* bury them
7. 39. prayed for the *d.* that he might live
10. 30. and lo, I lay as one that had been *d.*

2 *Esd.* 16. 23. the *d.* shall be cast out as dung
Tob. 3. 15. my seven husbands are already *d.*
4. 3. he said, my son, when I am *d.* bury me
8. 21. have the rest when I and my wife be *d.*
12. 12. when thou didst bury the *d.* I was with thee
13. leave thy dinner to go and cover the *d.*
Wisd. 4. 16. the righteous that is *d.* shall condemn
18. be a reproach among the *d.* for evermore
Eccl. 7. 33. and for the *d.* detain it not
8. 7. rejoice not over thy greatest enemy being *d.*
17. 28. thanksgiving perisheth from the *d.*
22. 11. weep for the *d.* for he hath lost the light, make little weeping for the *d.* he is at rest
30. 4. yet he is as though he were not *d.*
34. 25. he that washeth after touching of a *d.* body
38. 16. my son, let tears fall down over the *d.*
23. when the *d.* is at rest, be comforted for him
48. 5. who didst raise up a *d.* man from death, and his soul from the place of the *d.* by the word
2 *Mac.* 7. 36. are *d.* under God's covenant of life
12. 44. it had been vain to pray for the *d.*
45. he made a reconciliation for the *d.*
DEADLY.
1 *Mac.* 7. 26. a man that bare *d.* hate to Israel
DEAL.
Tob. 3. 6. *d.* with me as seemeth best to thee
4. 6. if thou *d.* truly, thy doings shall succeed
13. 6. if you *d.* uprightly before him
Dan. 3. 19. *d.* with us after thy loving-kindness
1 *Mac.* 13. 46. *d.* not with us according to our sin
DEALETH.
Eccl. 50. 22. *d.* with us according to his mercy
DEALING.
Wisd. 5. 23. ill *d.* shall overthrow the mighty
16. 2. *d.* graciously with thine own people
Eccl. 29. 7. refused to lend for other men's ill *d.*
40. 12. but true *d.* shall endure for ever
41. 18. ashamed of unjust *d.* before thy partner.
DEALT.
2 *Esd.* 8. 35. but he hath *d.* wickedly, and among the faithful there is none which hath not *d.* amiss
Tob. 8. 16. hast *d.* with us according to thy mercy
DEATH.
2 *Esd.* 3. 7. and thou appointedst *d.* in him
10. that as *d.* was to Adam, so was the flood
7. 47. after *d.* to look for punishment
49. we have done the works that bring *d.*
9. 12. the same must know it after *d.* by pain
Tob. 4. 2. I have wished for *d.* why do I not call
10. because that alms doth deliver from *d.*
14. 10. gave alms and escaped the snares of *d.*
Jud. 12. 14. it shall be my joy to the day of my *d.*
Wisd. 1. 12. seek not *d.* in the error of your life
13. for God made not *d.* nor hath he pleasure
2. 1. in the *d.* of a man there is no remedy
24. thro' envy of the devil came *d.* into the world
4. 7. though the righteous be prevented with *d.*
Eccl. 4. 28. strive for the truth unto *d.*
14. 12. remember *d.* will not be long in coming
18. 22. defer not till *d.* to be justified
22. 11. the life of the fool is worse than *d.*
28. 21. the *d.* thereof is an evil *d.*
33. 14. good is set against evil, and life against *d.*
37. 2. is it not a grief unto *d.* when a friend
38. 18. for of heaviness cometh *d.*
41. 1. O *d.* how bitter is the remembrance of thee!
2. O *d.* acceptable is thy sentence to the needy
3. fear not the sentence of *d.* remember them
46. 20. after his *d.* he prophesied, and shewed
48. 14. at his *d.* were his works marvellous
Bar. 6. 14. cannot put to *d.* one that offendeth him
36. they can save no man from *d.* nor deliver weak
2 *Mac.* 6. 30. I might have been delivered from *d.*
31. leaving his *d.* for an example of courage
7. 14. being put to *d.* by men to look for hope
9. 28. so died he a miserable *d.* in the mountains
13. 8. committed sins, he received his *d.* in ashes
DEBT.
1 *Esd.* 3. 20. a man remembereth not sorrow nor *d.*
DECAY.
Tob. 4. 13. in lewdness is *d.* and great want
DECEIT.
Jud. 9. 13. make my speech and *d.* to be their wound
Wisd. 1. 5. for the Holy Spirit of discipline will fly *d.*
14. 30. they unjustly swore in *d.* despising holiness
Eccl. 1. 30. but thy heart is full of *d.*
10. 8. because of riches got by *d.* the kingdom
Bel 18. O Bel, with thee is no *d.* at all
1 *Mac.* 11. 1. went about by *d.* to get the kingdom
DECEITFUL.
Eccl. 11. 29. for the *d.* man hath many trains
27. 25. and a *d.* stroke shall make wounds
DECEITFULLY.
1 *Mac.* 7. 27. sent unto Judas and his brethren *d.*
DECEIVABLE.
Eccl. 10. 19. they that transgress are a *d.* seed
DECEIVE.
Jud. 12. 16. for he waited a time to *d.* her
Wisd. 14. 21. this was an occasion to *d.* the world
15. 4. neither did the invention of men *d.* us
Eccl. 13. 6. if he have need of thee, he will *d.* thee
DECEIVED.
Jud. 13. 16. my countenance hath *d.* him
Eccl. 3. 24. many are *d.* by their own opinion
34. 7. dreams have *d.* many, and they have failed
2 *Mac.* 6. 25. and so they should be *d.* by me
7. 18. who said, be not *d.* without cause
DECKED.
Jud. 12. 15. she *d.* herself with her apparel
1 *Mac.* 4. 57. they *d.* the forefront of the temple
DECLARATION.
Eccl. 43. 6. for a *d.* of times, and a sign of the world
DECLARE.
2 *Esd.* 4. 4. whereof if thou canst *d.* me one
Tob. 13. 6. *d.* his might and majesty to a sinful nation
Jud. 8. 34. for I will not *d.* it unto you
10. 13. I am coming to *d.* words of truth
11. 5. I will *d.* no lie to my lord this night
Eccl. 14. 7. at the last he will *d.* his wickedness
16. 22. who can *d.* the works of his justice?
25. and I will *d.* his knowledge exactly
17. 9. that they might *d.* his works with understand

Eccl. 34. 9. he that hath experience will *d.* wisdom
39. 10. the congregation shall *d.* his praise
Sus. 11. they were ashamed to *d.* their lust
2 *Mac.* 3. 34. *d.* to all men the mighty power of God

DECLARED.

2 *Esd.* 8. 36. in this thy goodness shall be *d.*
Wisd. 16. 21. thy sustenance *d.* thy sweetness
Sus. 27. but when the elders had *d.* their matter

DECLARETH.

Eccl. 27. 6. the fruit *d.* if the tree have been dressed
42. 19. he *d.* the things that are past and for to come

DECLARING.

Eccl. 43. 2. the sun *d.* at his rising a marvellous
44. 3. men giving counsel and *d.* prophecies
2 *Mac.* 6. 17. we will come to the *d.* of the matter

DECREASETH.

Eccl. 43. 7. a light that *d.* in her perfection

DECREE.

2 *Mac.* 6. 8. went out a *d.* to the neighbouring cities

DECREED.

1 *Esd.* 8. 94. put away our wives, like as thou hast *d.*
Wisd. 4. 17. what God in his counsel hath *d.* of him
2 *Mac.* 3. 23. he executed that which was *d.*

DEDICATE.

Eccl. 35. 9. and *d.* thy tithes with gladness
1 *Mac.* 4. 36. let us go up to *d.* the sanctuary

DEDICATED.

Jud. 16. 19. Judith *d.* all the stuff of Holofernes
1 *Mac.* 4. 54. in that day was it *d.* with songs
2 *Mac.* 5. 16. pulled down the things that were *d.*

DEDICATION.

1 *Esd.* 7. 7. to the *d.* of the temple of the Lord
1 *Mac.* 4. 56. so they kept the *d.* of the altar
59. that the days of the *d.* should be kept
2 *Mac.* 2. 9. he offered the sacrifice of *d.*

DEEDS.

2 *Esd.* 3. 28. are their *d.* then any better?
7. 23. deceived themselves by their wicked *d.*
35. the reward shall be shewed, the good *d.* shall be of force, and the wicked *d.* shall bear no rule
8. 33. shall out of their own *d.* receive reward
Tob. 2. 14. where are thy alms and righteous *d.?*
Wisd. 1. 9. for manifestation of his wicked *d.*
Eccl. 4. 29. and in thy *d.* slack and remiss
17. 20. none of their unrighteous *d.* are hid
22. he will keep the good *d.* as the apple of the eye
48. 4. how wast thou honoured in wondrous *d.!*

DEEMED.

Wisd. 13. 2. but *d.* it either fire, or wind, or air

DEEP.

2 *Esd.* 4. 8. I never went down into the *d.*
7. 3. is set in a wide place that it might be *d.*
Wisd. 4. 3. nor take *d.* rooting from bastard slips
10. 19. cast them up out of the bottom of the *d.*
Eccl. 1. 3. who can find out the *d.* and wisdom?
16. 18. the *d.* shall be moved when he shall visit
24. 29. her counsels profounder than the great *d.*
42. 18. he seeketh out the *d.* and the heart
43. 23. by his counsel he appeaseth the *d.*

DEFECTIVE.

Eccl. 49. 4. all, except David and Josias, were *d.*

DEFENCE.

Eccl. 34. 16. he is a *d.* from heat, a cover from the sun
1 *Mac.* 4. 61. that the people might have a *d.*
2 *Mac.* 15. 11. not so much with *d.* of shields

DEFEND.

2 *Esd.* 2. 20. *d.* the orphan, clothe the naked
7. 52. to *d.* them which have led a wary life
Jud. 5. 21. pass by, lest their Lord *d.* them
6. 2. not war, because their God will *d.* them

DEFENDED.

Wisd. 10. 12. she *d.* him from his enemies
19. 8. the people that were *d.* with thy hand
Eccl. 2. 13. therefore shall he not be *d.*
28. 19. well is he that is *d.* from the tongue

DEFENDER.

Eccl. 51. 2. for thou art my *d.* and helper
2 *Mac.* 6. 2. temple of Jupiter the *d.* of strangers

DEFENDETH.

2 *Mac.* 3. 39. hath his eye on that place, and *d.* it

DEFER.

Jud. 2. 13. I have commanded thee, *d.* not to do them
Eccl. 4. 3. *d.* not give to him that is in need
18. 22. *d.* not till death to be justified

DEFILE.

Jud. 13. 16. he hath not committed sin to *d.* me

DEFILED.

1 *Esd.* 1. 49. the governors *d.* the temple of the Lord
2 *Esd.* 8. 60. *d.* the name of him that made them
Eccl. 13. 1. he that toucheth pitch shall be *d.*
22. 13. thou shalt never be *d.* with his fooleries
42. 10. in her virginity, lest she should be *d.*
Bar. 3. 10. that thou art *d.* with the dead
1 *Mac.* 1. 37. they shed blood, and *d.* the sanctuary
4. 45. to pull it down because the heathen had *d.* it

DEFILETH.

Eccl. 21. 28. a whisperer *d.* his own soul

DEFILING.

Wisd. 14. 26. there reigned in all men *d.* of souls

DEFLOWER.

Eccl. 20. 4. as the lust of an eunuch to *d.* a virgin

DEFRAUD.

Eccl. 4. 1. my son, *d.* not the poor of his living
7. 21. *d.* not a good servant of liberty
14. 14. *d.* not thyself of the good day

DEFRAUDED.

Eccl. 29. 7. many refused to lend, fearing to be *d.*

DEFRAUDING.

Eccl. 14. 4. he that gathereth by *d.* his own soul

DEFRAY.

2 *Mac.* 8. 10. so much as should *d.* the tribute
9. 16. out of his own revenue *d.* the charges

DEGREE.

Eccl. 11. 1. lifts up head of him that is of low *d.*

DELAY.

Tob. 12. 13. when thou didst not *d.* to rise up
Eccl. 29. 8. and *d.* not to shew him mercy

DELIBERATION.

Wisd. 12. 20. if thou didst punish with such *d.*

DELICATE.

Wisd. 19. 11. when they asked *d.* meats
Eccl. 29. 22. than *d.* fare in another man's house
Sus. 31. Susanna was a very *d.* woman

DELICATES.

Eccl. 30. 18. *d.* poured upon a mouth shut up
31. 3. the rich is filled with his *d.*

DELIGHT.

Jud. 12. 20. Holofernes took great *d.* in her
Wisd. 6. 21. if your *d.* be then in thrones
16. 20. bread able to content every man's *d.*
Eccl. 1. 27. and faith and meekness are his *d.*
9. 12. *d.* not in things the ungodly have
16. 1. neither *d.* in ungodly sons

DELIGHTED.

Wisd. 13. 3. if they being *d.* took them to be gods
Eccl. 51. 15. from the flower my heart hath *d.* in her

DELIGHTETH.

Eccl. 26. 13. the grace of a wife *d.* her husband
2 *Mac.* 15. 39. mingled wine is pleasant and *d.* the taste, so speech finely framed *d.* the ears

DELIVER.

1 *Esd.* 8. 59. till ye *d.* them to the chief of the priests
2 *Esd.* 7. 32. the secret places shall *d.* souls
Tob. 4. 10. because alms doth *d.* from death, 12. 9.
14. 11. consider how righteousness doth *d.*
Jud. 8. 9. had sworn to *d.* the city to the Assyrians
11. ye have promised to *d.* the city to our enemies
Esth. 14. 19. *d.* us out of the hands of mischievous
Eccl. 4. 9. *d.* him that suffereth wrong from oppression
29. 12. it shall *d.* thee from all affliction
33. 1. in temptation even again he will *d.* him
42. 7. *d.* all things in number and weight
50. 24. that he would *d.* us at this time
Bar. 6. 15. but cannot *d.* himself from war
36. nor can they *d.* the weak from the mighty
Dan. 3. 11. *d.* us not up wholly for thy name's sake
Bel. 29. *d.* us, Daniel, else we will destroy thee
1 *Mac.* 5. 12. come, and *d.* us from their hands

DELIVERANCE.

Eccl. 51. 9. I prayed for *d.* from death
1 *Mac.* 4. 25. thus Israel had a great *d.* that day
56. they sacrificed the sacrifice of *d.* and praise

DELIVERED.

1 *Esd.* 1. 53. for he *d.* all into their hands
3. 13. they *d.* their writings unto him
8. 56. I *d.* unto them 650 talents of silver
62. the gold and silver was *d.* into house of our L.
Tob. 3. 4. wherefore thou hast *d.* us for spoil
Wisd. 10. 6. she *d.* the righteous man who fled
9. Wisdom *d.* from pain those that attended on her
13. she forsook him not, but *d.* him from sin
Eccl. 29. 17. will leave him in danger that *d.* him
48. 20. Lord *d.* them by the ministry of Esay
2 *Mac.* 6. 26. I should be *d.* from punishment of men
30. whereas I might have been *d.* from death
12. 45. that they might be *d.* from sin

DELIVEREDST.

Eccl. 51. 12. thou *d.* me from the evil time

DELIVEREST.

Eccl. 51. 8. how thou *d.* such as wait for thee

DELIVERETH.

1 *Mac.* 4. 11. that there is One who *d.* Israel

DEMANDED.

1 *Esd.* 6. 12. we *d.* who were the chief doers
Wisd. 15. 8. life that was lent him shall be *d.*
2 *Mac.* 15. 3. he *d.* if there were a mighty one

DEMETRIUS.

1 *Mac.* 7. 1. D. son of Seleucus departed from Rome
8. 31. the evils that D. doth to the Jews
10. 52. I have overthrown D. ‖ 67. D. son of D.
11. 12. he took his daughter and gave her to D.
39. seeing all the host murmured against D.
14. 3. who went and smote the host of D.
2 *Mac.* 1. 7. what time as D. reigned in 169th year
14. 1. informed that D. had taken the country
4. came to king D. ‖ 11. did more incense D.

DEN.

Bel. 35. neither do I know where the *d.* is
36. the angel set him in Babylon over the *d.*

DENS.

2 *Mac.* 10. 6. they wandered in mountains and *d.*

DENIED.

Wisd. 12. 27. whom before they *d.* to know

DEPART.

1 *Esd.* 1. 27. *d.* from me, and be not against the Lord
4. 11. these keep watch, neither may any one *d.*
2 *Esd.* 4. 14. make war against the sea, that it may *d.*
Tob. 4. 21. if thou fear God and *d.* from all sin
14. 3. I am aged and am ready to *d.* out of this life
Jud. 13. 1. his servants made haste to *d.*
19. for this thy confidence shall not *d.* from men
Eccl. 7. 2. *d.* from unjust, and iniquity shall turn away
22. 13. *d.* from him, and thou shalt find rest
22. for these things every friend will *d.*
23. 11. the plague shall never *d.* from his house
27. 22. he that knoweth him, will *d.* from him
35. 3. to *d.* from wickedness pleases the Lord
17. and will not *d.* till the Most High behold
Dan. 3. 12. cause not thy mercy to *d.* from us
2 *Mac.* 2. 3. the law should not *d.* from their hearts
11. 30. they that will *d.* shall have safe conduct

DEPARTED.

1 *Esd.* 8. 61. from the river Theras we *d.*
2 *Esd.* 3. 22. the good *d.* away, the evil abode still
Eccl. 38. 23. when his spirit is *d.* from him
46. 11. whose heart *d.* not from the Lord
48. 15. neither *d.* they from their sins
Bar. 3. 8. which *d.* from the Lord our God
Sus. 7. now when the people *d.* away at noon

DEPARTURE.

Wisd. 3. 2. and their *d.* is taken for misery

DEPEND.

Jud. 8. 24. because their hearts *d.* upon us

DEPENDETH.

Eccl. 40. 29. the life of him that *d.* on another

DEPOSED.

1 *Esd.* 1. 35. then the king of Egypt *d.* him

DEPRIVE.

Esth. 16. 12. went about to *d.* us of our kingdom

DEPRIVED.

Wisd. 18. 4. they were worthy to be *d.* of light
Eccl. 28. 15. hath *d.* them of their labours
29. 6. he hath *d.* him of his money
37. 21. because he is *d.* of all wisdom
2 *Mac.* 14. 7. I being *d.* of my ancestor's honour

DEPTH, S.

2 *Esd.* 3. 18. and thou madest the *d.* to tremble
8. 23. whose look drieth up the *d.* mountains melt

DERISION.

1 *Esd.* 1. 51. but they had his messengers in *d.*
Wisd. 5. 3. this was he whom we had sometimes in *d.*

DESCENDED.

Jud. 5. 6. this people are *d.* of the Chaldeans
6. 14. but the Israelites *d.* from their city

DESCRIPTION.

1 *Esd.* 5. 39. when the *d.* of the kindred was sought

DESERTS.

Wisd. 5. 7. we have gone thro' *d.* where was no way

DESERTS.

Esth. 16. 18. rendering him according to his *d.*

DESERVED.

Wisd. 19. 14. friends that had well *d.* of them
2 *Mac.* 4. 2. that had *d.* well of the city
38. rewarded him his punishment as he had *d.*

DESIRE.

1 *Esd.* 4. 46. and now this is what I *d.* of thee, I *d.* therefore that thou make good the vow
2 *Esd.* 1. 25. when ye *d.* me to be gracious to you
8. 27. the *d.* of those that keep thy testimonies
32. for if thou hast a *d.* to have mercy upon us
Tob. 4. 19. *d.* that thy ways may be directed
Wisd. 4. 2. and when it is gone, they *d.* it
6. 11. *d.* my words, and ye shall be instructed
13. she preventeth them that *d.* her
17. the beginning of her is the *d.* of discipline
20. the *d.* of wisdom bringeth to a kingdom
8. 8. if a man *d.* much experience, she knoweth
14. 2. for verily *d.* of gain devised that
15. 5. so they *d.* the form of a dead image
6. they that *d.* them are lovers of evil things
16. 25. according to *d.* of them that had need
Eccl. 1. 26. if thou *d.* wisdom, keep commandments
3. 29. an attentive ear is the *d.* of a wise man
14. 14. let not the part of a good *d.* overpass thee
16. 1. *d.* not a multitude of unprofitable children
25. 21. and *d.* her not for pleasure
2 *Mac.* 6. 25. through my *d.* to live a little time
11. 28. if ye fare well, we have our *d.*
29. declared that your *d.* was to return home

DESIRABLE.

Eccl. 1. 17. she filleth all her house with things *d.*
42. 22. O how *d.* are all his works!

DESIRED.

Judg. 12. 16. Holofernes *d.* greatly her company
16. 22. many *d.* her but none knew her
Wisd. 8. 2. I *d.* to make her my spouse
15. 19. are not beautiful so much as to be *d.*
Sus. 11. that they *d.* to have to do with her
2 *Mac.* 15. 38. done well, it is that which I *d.*

DESIRES.

Eccl. 18. 31. if thou givest thy soul *d.* that please her
2 *Mac.* 9. 27. will graciously yield to your *d.*

DESIREST.

2 *Esd.* 4. 4. shew thee the way that thou *d.* to see
43. from beginning look what thou *d.* to see

DESIROUS.

Esth. 11. 12. he by all means was *d.* to know it
Wisd. 13. 6. they err, seeking God, and *d.* to find him
Eccl. 23. 5. that is *d.* always to serve thee
24. 19. come unto me, all ye that be *d.* of me
Sus. 15. she was *d.* to wash herself in the garden
1 *Mac.* 5. 67. certain priests *d.* to shew their valour

DESOLATE.

1 *Esd.* 4. 45. when Judah was made *d.* by Chaldees
8. 81. and they raised up the *d.* Sion
2 *Esd.* 1. 33. your house is *d.* I will cast you out
Tob. 14. 4. Jerusalem shall be *d.* the house of God in it shall be burned, shall be *d.* for a time
Esth. 14. 3. O my Ld. help me *d.* woman who have
14. help me that am *d.* have no helper but thee
Eccl. 21. 4. the house of proud men shall be made *d.*

DESOLATION.

1 *Esd.* 1. 58. the whole time of her *d.* shall she rest
2 *Esd.* 3. 2. for I saw *d.* of Sion and wealth at Babyl.

DESPAIR.

Eccl. 22. 21. yet *d.* not, there may be a returning

DESPAIRETH.

Eccl. 41. 2. to him that *d.* and hath lost patience

DESPAIRING.

2 *Mac.* 9. 18. therefore *d.* of his health, he wrote

DESPERATE.

2 *Mac.* 6. 29. the speeches proceeded from a *d.* mind

DESPERATELY.

2 *Mac.* 13. 23. heard that Philip was *d.* bent

DESPISE.

2 *Esd.* 7. 20. because they *d.* the law of God
Tob. 4. 3. bury me, and *d.* not thy mother
13. my son *d.* not in thy heart thy brethren
18. *d.* not any counsel that is profitable
Jud. 8. 20. we trust that he will not *d.* us
10. 19. every one said, who would *d.* this people?
Esth. 13. 16. *d.* not the portion thou hast delivered
Wisd. 4. 18. they shall see him and *d.* him
Eccl. 3. 13. *d.* him not when thou art in strength
10. 23. it is not meet to *d.* the poor man
31. 22. my son, hear me, and *d.* me not
31. and *d.* not thy neighbour in his mirth
35. 14. he will not *d.* the supplication of fatherless

DESPISED.

2 *Esd.* 1. 7. but they have *d.* my counsels
34. for they have *d.* my commandment, done evil
2. 33. they *d.* the commandment of the Lord
7. 24. his law have they *d.* and denied his covenant
8. 56. *d.* the Most High, and forsook his ways
Jud. 14. 5. know him that *d.* the house of Israel
Esth. 13. 4. that *d.* the commandments of kings
Wisd. 12. 24. among the beasts of enemies were *d.*
2 *Mac.* 7. 24. Antiochus thinking himself *d.*

DESPISETH.

Eccl. 14. 8. envious man hath a wicked eye and *d.* men

DESPISING.

Wisd. 14. 30. they swore in deceit, *d.* holiness

DESPITEFUL.

Eccl. 31. 31. give no *d.* words, press not on him

DESPITEFULNESS.

Wisd. 2. 19. let us examine him with *d.* and torture

DESTINY.
Wisd. 19. 4. the *d.* whereof they were worthy
DESTITUTE.
Wisd. 12. 6. the parents that killed souls *d.* of help
Eccl. 37. 20. and is hated, he shall be *d.* of all food
DESTROY.
1 Esd. 8. 88. mightest not thou be angry with us to *d.*?
Esth. 10. 8. were assembled to *d.* the name of Jews
Wisd. 11. 19. but the terrible sight utterly *d.* them
12. 8. didst send wasps to *d.* them by little and little
1 Mac. 5. 2. they thought to *d.* the generation of Jacob, they began to slay and *d.* the people
DESTROYED.
2 Esd. 1. 10. many kings have I *d.* for their sakes
11. all the nations have I *d.* before them
Jud. 5. 18. they were *d.* in many battles
13. 14. but hath *d.* our enemies by mine hands
Esth. 16. 24. every city shall be *d.* without mercy
Wisd. 16. 27. that which was not *d.* of the fire
Eccl. 8. 2. for gold hath *d.* many, and perverted
DESTROYEDST.
2 Esd. 3. 9. thou broughtest the flood and *d.* them
Wisd. 18. 5. *d.* them altogether in a mighty water
DESTROYER.
Wisd. 18. 22. he overcame the *d.* not with strength
25. to these the *d.* gave place, and was afraid
DESTROYETH.
Eccl. 20. 22. there is that *d.* his own soul
DESTRUCTION.
2 Esd. 1. 16. triumphed not for the *d.* of your enemi.
Tob. 4. 13. for in pride is *d.* and much trouble
Jud. 13. 5. execute my enterprises to *d.* of the enemies
16. my countenance hath deceived him to his *d.*
Esth. 16. 15. this wretch hath delivered to utter *d.*
23. that there may be a memorial of *d.*
Wisd. 1. 12. and pull not upon yourselves *d.*
3. 3. and their going from us to be utter *d.*
5. 7. we wearied ourselves in the way of *d.*
2 Mac. 6. 12. those punishments not to be for *d.*
DETAINED.
Tob. 10. 2. Tobit said, are they *d.* or is Gabael dead?
DETERMINED.
1 Esd. 8. 10. having *d.* to deal graciously
Jud. 5. 4. why have they *d.* not to come and meet me?
Esth. 11. 12. Mardocheus had seen what G. had *d.* to
Wisd. 18. 5. *d.* to slay the babes of the saints
2 Mac. 11. 25. we have *d.* to restore their temple
15. 6. Nicanor *d.* to set up a public monument
17. *d.* not to pitch camp, but to set upon them
DETESTABLE.
2 Mac. 5. 24. he sent also that *d.* ringleader
DEVICE.
Esth. 14. 11. but turn their *d.* upon themselves
1 Mac. 1. 12. so this *d.* pleased them well
DEVICES.
Wisd. 9. 14. and our *d.* are but uncertain
Eccl. 35. 19. the works of men according to their *d.*
42. 18. he considered their crafty *d.*
1 Mac. 6. 37. were girt fast unto them with *d.*
DEVIL.
Tob. 6. 7. if a *d.* or an evil spirit trouble any
17. and the *d.* shall smell it, and flee away
Wisd. 2. 24. through envy of the *d.* came death
DEVILS.
Bar. 4. 7. by sacrificing to *d.* and not to God
35. she shall be inhabited of *d.* a great time
DEVISE.
Eccl. 7. 12. *d.* not a lie against thy brother
DEVISED.
2 Esd. 4. 19. it is foolish that they both have *d.*
Wisd. 14. 2. for verily desire of gain *d.* that
DEVOUR.
2 Esd. 8. 4. swallow down, O my soul, and *d.* wisdom
Eccl. 28. 23. it shall *d.* them as a leopard
31. 16. and *d.* not, lest thou be hated
Bel 32. to the intent they might *d.* Daniel
DEVOURED.
2 Esd. 6. 52. kept him to be *d.* of whom thou wilt
Tob. 6. 2. a fish leaped out and would have *d.* him
Jud. 5. 24. they shall be a prey to be *d.* of all
Esth. 11. 11. lowly exalted, and *d.* the glorious
Bel 42. were *d.* in a moment before his face
DEVOURERS.
Wisd. 12. 5. those murderers, and *d.* of man's flesh
DEVOURETH.
Eccl. 36. 18. belly *d.* all meats, yet one meat better
Bel 8. who is this that *d.* these expenses?
9. but if ye can certify me that Bel *d.* them
DEW.
Wisd. 11. 22. the world is as a drop of morning *d.*
Eccl. 18. 16. shall not the *d.* assuage the heat?
DIADEM.
Wisd. 18. 24. thy majesty upon the *d.* of his head
Bar. 5. 2. and set a *d.* on thy head of the glory
DIE.
2 Esd. 1. 18. better than to *d.* in this wilderness
7. 29. after these years shall my son Christ *d.*
31. and that shall *d.* that is corrupt
8. 58. yea, and that knowing they must *d.*
Tob. 3. 15. if it please not thee that I should *d.*
10. 12. that I may see thy children before I *d.*
11. 9. from henceforth I am content to *d.*
Wisd. 3. 2. in sight of unwise they seemed to *d.*
18. or if they *d.* quickly, they have no hope
Eccl. 8. 7. but remember that we *d.* all
14. 13. do good to thy friend before thou *d.*
17. the covenant is, Thou shalt *d.* the death
19. 10. if thou hast heard a word, let it *d.* with thee
25. 24. and through the woman we all *d.*
30. 4. though his father *d.* yet he is as tho' he were
39. 11. if he *d.* he shall leave a greater name
40. 28. for better it is to *d.* than to beg
41. 9. and if you *d.* a curse shall be your portion
Bar. 4. 1. but such as leave the law shall *d.*
1 Mac. 1. 5. and he perceived that he should *d.*
2. 37. but said, let us *d.* all in our innocency
2 Mac. 7. 2. are ready to *d.* rather than transgress
5. they exhorted one another to *d.* manfully
14. so when he was ready to *d.* said thus
18. who being ready to *d.* said, be not deceived
14. 42. choosing rather to *d.* manfully, than to come

DIED.
Wisd. 17. 10. they *d.* for fear, denying they saw air
1 Mac. 1. 7. Alexander reigned 12 years, and then *d.*
2 Mac. 6. 31. thus this man *d.* leaving an example
7. 40. so this man *d.* undefiled, and put his trust
41. last of all, after the sons, the mother *d.*
9. 28. so *d.* he a miserable death in the mountains
12. 45. favour laid up for those that *d.* godly
14. 46. calling on the Lord of life, he thus *d.*
DIET.
Eccl. 30. 25. a good heart will have a care of his *d.*
DIGGED.
Eccl. 48. 17. he *d.* the hard rock with iron
DIGGETH.
Eccl. 27. 26. whoso *d.* a pit shall fall therein
DIGNITY.
Esth. 16. 12. but he not bearing his great *d.*
1 Mac. 10. 54. give gifts according to thy *d.*
DIGNITIES.
1 Esd. 1. 11. according to the several *d.* 8. 28.
DILIGENCE.
1 Esd. 6. 10. and with all glory and *d.* is it made
2 Esd. 3. 19. give *d.* to the generation of Israel
Wisd. 14. 18. the singular *d.* of the artificer
DILIGENT.
1 Esd. 2. 26. I commanded to make *d.* search
Eccl. 32. 1. take *d.* care for them, and so sit down
38. 26. he is *d.* to give the kine fodder
27. they are *d.* to make great variety
30. he is *d.* to make clean the furnace
DILIGENTLY.
1 Esd. 6. 28. that they look *d.* to help those that be
8. 24. whoso transgresseth, shall be punished *d.*
2 Esd. 9. 1. measure thou the time *d.* in itself
16. 30. clusters that *d.* seek through the vineyard
Wisd. 7. 13. I learned *d.* and do communicate her
13. 7. they search him *d.* and believe their sight
13. hath carved it *d.* when he had nothing to do
Eccl. 18. 14. that *d.* seek after his judgments
Sus. 12. yet they watched *d.* from day to day
DIMINISH.
Eccl. 28. 8. and thou shalt *d.* thy sins
35. 8. and *d.* not the first fruits of thy hands
DIMINISHED.
Bar. 2. 34. increase them, they shall not be *d.*
DIMINISHETH.
Eccl. 31. 30. drunkenness *d.* strength, maketh wounds
DIMMETH.
Eccl. 43. 4. sendeth bright beams, it *d.* the eyes
DINNER.
Tob. 12. 13. not delay to rise up and leave thy *d.*
Sus. 13. let us now go home, for it is *d.* time
Bel 34. carry the *d.* that thou hast into Babylon
37. take the *d.* which God hath sent thee
DIRECT.
Jud. 12. 8. she besought God of Israel do *d.* her way
Eccl. 6. 17. shall *d.* his friendship aright
37. 15. pray that he will *d.* thy way in truth
39. 7. he shall *d.* his counsel and knowledge
DIRECTED.
Tob. 4. 19. desire of him, that thy ways may be *d.*
Jud. 13. 18. which hath *d.* thee to the cutting off
Eccl. 49. 9. he *d.* them that went right
51. 20. I *d.* my soul unto her and found her
DIRECTETH.
Wisd. 7. 15. he leads to wisdom and *d.* the wise
DISANNUL.
Dan. 3. 11. neither *d.* thou thy covenant
DISAPPOINTED.
Jud. 16. 6. but the almighty Lord hath *d.* them
DISCERNED.
Wisd. 2. 22. nor *d.* a reward for blameless souls
DISCIPLINE.
Wisd. 1. 5. the holy Spirit of *d.* will flee deceit
6. 17. for the very true beginning of her is the desire of *d.* and the care of *d.* is love
Eccl. 4. 17. she will torment him with her *d.*
17. 18. being first-born, he nourished with *d.*
18. 14. he hath mercy on them that receive *d.*
23. 2. will set the *d.* of wisdom over my heart
7. hear, O ye children, the *d.* of the mouth
32. 14. whoso feareth the Lord will receive his *d.*
41. 14. my children keep *d.* in peace
Bar. 4. 13. nor trod they in the paths of *d.*
DISCLOSING.
Eccl. 22. 22. except for pride or *d.* of secrets
DISCOMFITED.
1 Mac. 4. 14. the heathen being *d.* fled into the plain
36. Judah said, behold, our enemies are *d.*
DISCOURAGED.
1 Mac. 4. 27. he was confounded and *d.*
2 Mac. 6. 12. that they be not *d.* for calamities
DISCOURSE.
Eccl. 6. 35. be willing to hear every godly *d.*
8. 9. miss not the *d.* of the elders, they learned
27. 11. the *d.* of a godly man is with wisdom
13. the *d.* of fools is irksome, and their sport
DISCOVER.
Eccl. 1. 30. so God *d.* thy secrets and cast down
DISCOVERED.
Jud. 9. 2. and who *d.* the thigh to her shame
Eccl. 11. 27. in his end his deeds shall be *d.*
1 Mac. 7. 31. when he saw that his counsel was *d.*
DISCOVERETH.
Eccl. 27. 16. whoso *d.* secrets loseth his credit
DISDAIN.
Eccl. 22. 10. but children being haughty through *d.*
DISEASE.
Eccl. 10. 10. the physician cutteth off a long *d.*
31. 2. as a sore *d.* breaketh sleep
DISEASES.
2 Esd. 8. 31. our fathers do languish of such *d.*
DISGRACE.
Wisd. 17. 7. their vaunting was reproved with *d.*
Eccl. 21. 24. but a wise man will be grieved with *d.*
22. 1. every one will hiss him out to his *d.*
29. 6. and for honour he will pay him *d.*
2 Mac. 9. 4. thought to avenge on the Jews the *d.*
DISGRACED.
Eccl. 8. 4. jest not lest thy ancestors be *d.*
11. 6. many mighty men have been greatly *d.*

DISHONEST.
Eccl. 26. 24. a *d.* woman contemneth shame
DISHONESTLY.
Eccl. 22. 4. she that lives *d.* is her father's heaviness
DISHONOUR.
Eccl. 1. 30. thou fall and bring *d.* on thy soul
3. 10. glory not in the *d.* of thy father
11. a mother in *d.* is a reproach to the children
8. 6. *d.* not a man in his old age, for we wax old
22. 3. an ill-nurtured son is the *d.* of his father
Bar. 6. 40. the Chaldeans themselves *d.* them
1 Mac. 1. 40. as glory, so was her *d.* increased
2 Mac. 8. 35. he came, having very great *d.*
9. 1. at that time came Antiochus with *d.*
DISHONOURABLE.
Eccl. 10. 19. they that regard not law, are a *d.* seed
31. he that is *d.* in riches, much more in poverty
20. 26. the disposition of liar is *d.* and shame
DISHONOURETH.
Eccl. 22. 5. she that is bold *d.* her father
26. 26. but she that *d.* him in her pride
DISMISSED.
Jud. 13. 1. he *d.* the waiters from the presence
DISOBEDIENT.
Bar. 1. 19. we have been *d.* to the Lord our God
DISOBEY.
Eccl. 2. 15. they that fear the Lord will not *d.*
16. 28. and they shall never *d.* his word
DISOBEYED.
Eccl. 23. 23. first she hath *d.* the law of the Lord
Bar. 1. 18. we have *d.* him and have not hearkened
DISORDER.
Wisd. 14. 26. there reigned *d.* in marriages
DISPATCH.
Wisd. 11. 19. the harm might *d.* them at once
2 Mac. 9. 4. he commanded him to *d.* the journey
DISPATCHED.
Tob. 7. 8. and let this business be *d.*
DISPERSED.
Tob. 3. 4. to all nations among whom we are *d.*
Jud. 7. 32. he *d.* the people every one to his charge
Wisd. 2. 4. our life shall be *d.* as a mist driven away
5. 14. as the smoke which is *d.* here and there
DISPLACE.
1 Mac. 8. 13. and whom again they would, they *d.*
DISPLEASED.
Eccl. 45. 19. this the Lord saw, and it *d.* him
1 Mac. 5. 1. the nations saw, it *d.* them very much
DISPLEASURE.
1 Esd. 4. 31. but if she took any *d.* at him
2 Esd. 8. 34. that thou shouldest take *d.* at him
DISPOSED.
2 Esd. 5. 49. even so have I *d.* the world
Eccl. 16. 26. he *d.* the parts thereof
DISPOSEST.
2 Esd. 8. 11. till thou *d.* it to thy mercy
DISPOSITION.
2 Esd. 8. 38. I will not think on the *d.* of them
39. I will rejoice over the *d.* of the righteous
Jud. 8. 29. because the *d.* of thy heart is good
Esth. 16. 6. with the deceit of their lewd *d.*
Eccl. 20. 26. the *d.* of a liar is dishonourable
DISQUIETED.
2 Esd. 10. 31. what aileth thee? why art thou *d.*?
Eccl. 22. 13. and never be *d.* with his madness
28. 14. a backbiting tongue hath *d.* many
DISQUIETETH.
Eccl. 28. 9. a sinful man *d.* friends
DISQUIETING.
Wisd. 14. 26. there reigned, *d.* of good men
DISSEMBLED.
1 Mac. 11. 53. he *d.* in all that ever he spake
DISSIMULATION.
Wisd. 14. 25. there reigned in all men *d.*
2 Mac. 13. 3. with great *d.* encouraged Antiochus
DISSOLVED.
Tob. 3. 6. that I may be *d.* and become earth
DISSOLUTELY.
Wisd. 12. 23. whereas men have lived *d.*
DISTANCE.
2 Esd. 5. 47. she cannot; but must do it by *d.* of time
DISTINGUISHED.
Eccl. 33. 8. by knowledge of Lord they were *d.*
DISTRESS.
2 Esd. 6. 37. my soul was in *d.* and I said
Tob. 3. 6. command theref. that I may be delivered out of this *d.* and go into the everlasting place
Eccl. 4. 2. neither provoke a man in his *d.*
10. 26. boast not thyself in the time of thy *d.*
25. 23. that will not comfort her husband in *d.*
Bar. 6. 37. they cannot help any man in his *d.*
1 Mac. 2. 53. Joseph in his *d.* kept commandment
DISTRIBUTE.
Jud. 16. 24. she did *d.* her goods to her kindred
Eccl. 33. 23. when finish life, *d.* thine inheritance
DISTRUST.
Wisd. 1. 2. shews himself to such as do not *d.* him
Eccl. 1. 28. *d.* not the fear of the Lord when poor
DISTRUSTING.
2 Mac. 9. 22. not *d.* my health, but having hope
DIVERS.
2 Esd. 6. 44. many and *d.* pleasures for the taste
Wisd. 15. 4. any image spotted with *d.* colours
Eccl. 33. 11. the Lord hath made their ways *d.*
DIVERSITIES.
Wisd. 7. 20. the *d.* of plants, and virtues of roots
DIVIDED.
Eccl. 14. 15. leave thy labours to be *d.* by lot
33. 11. in much knowledge the Lord hath *d.* them
44. 23. give him an heritage, and *d.* his portions
47. 21. so the kingdom was *d.* and out of Ephraim
DIVIDING.
Eccl. 18. 3. *d.* holy things among them from profane
DIVINATIONS.
Eccl. 34. 5. *d.* soothsayings and dreams are vain
DIVISION.
2 Esd. 6. 41. and to make a *d.* betwixt the waters
Eccl. 17. 17. in the *d.* of the nations of the earth
DIVORCE.
Eccl. 25. 26. give her a bill of *d.* and let her go
DO.
1 Esd. 9. 9. *d.* his will and separate yourselves

1 Esd. 9. 10. like as thou hast spoken, so will we d.
2 Esd. 1. 24. what shall I d. unto thee, O Jacob?
30. but now what shall I d. unto you?
Tob. 4. 15. d. that to no man which thou hatest
5. 1. father, I will d. all things thou hast commanded
Jud. 2. 12. whatever I have spoken, that will I d.
Wisd. 13. 19. for gaining and getting asketh ability to d. of him that is most unable to d. any thing
Eccl. 14. 11. according to thy ability d. good
21. 1. my son, hast thou sinned? d. so no more

DOCTRINE.
Eccl. 16. 25. I will shew forth d. in weight
24. 27. he maketh the d. of knowledge appear
32. I will yet make d. to shine as the morning
33. I will yet pour out d. as prophecy, and leave

DOERS.
1 Esd. 6. 12. demanded of them who were chief d.
2 Esd. 3. 30. how thou hast spared wicked d.
Esth. 16. 15. we find that the Jews are no evil d.

DOEST.
2 Mac. 7. 16. thou d. what thou wilt, yet think not

DOG.
Tob. 5. 16. and the young man's d. with them
11. 4. so they went, and the d. went after them
Eccl. 13. 8. what agreement between hyena and a d.?
26. 25. a shameless woman shall be counted as a d.

DOINGS.
Tob. 4. 6. thy d. shall prosperously succeed
Wisd. 2. 12. and he is clean contrary to our d.
9. 11. she shall lead me soberly in my d.
Eccl. 51. 19. my soul wrestled, in my d. I was exact

DOMINION.
1 Esd. 4. 3. but yet the king hath d. over them
22. you must know that women have d. over you
2 Esd. 3. 28. they should have the d. over Sion
12. 23. they shall have the d. of the earth
Esd. 13. 2. I had d. over the whole world
Wisd. 3. 8. they shall have d. over the people
9. 2. that he should have d. over the creatures
Eccl. 17. 4. the Lord gave him d. over beasts
1 Mac. 1. 16. he might have the d. of two realms

DONE.
1 Esd. 8. 86. all is d. to us for our wicked works
Esth. 10. 4. he said, God hath d. these things
Eccl. 16. 26. works of Lord are d. in judgment
18. 7. when a man hath d. then he beginneth
Bar. 2. 12. O Lord our God, we have d. ungodly
2 Mac. 7. 18. marvellous things are d. unto us
15. 5. he obtained not to have his wicked will d.

DOOM.
2 Esd. 7. 43. the day of d. shall be the end of time

DOOR.
Tob. 8. 13. so the maid opened the d. and went in
11. 10. Tobit also went forth toward the d.
Eccl. 21. 24. it is rudeness to hearken at the d.
28. 25. and make a d. and bar for thy mouth
Bar. 6. 59. or to be a d. in an house to keep safe
Sus. 26. the servants rushed in at the privy d.
2 Mac. 2. 5. he laid the ark, and so stopped the d.

DOORS.
Wisd. 6. 14. he shall find her sitting at his d.
Eccl. 14. 23. he shall also hearken at her d.
Bar. 6. 18. as the d. are made sure on every side
Sus. 20. the garden d. are shut, no man can see us
Bel 21. shewed the privy d. where they came in
1 Mac. 4. 57. and they hanged d. upon them

DORA.
1 Mac. 15. 13. then camped Antiochus against D.

DOSITHEUS.
Esth. 11. 1. D. who said he was a priest and Levite
2 Mac. 12. 35. D. one of Bacenor's company

DOTETH.
Eccl. 25. 2. I hate an old adulterer that d.

DOTHAIM.
Jud. 4. 6. toward the open country near to D.
7. 3. they spread themselves in breadth over D.

DOUBLE.
Eccl. 5. 9. the sinner that hath a d. tongue
14. an evil condemnation on the d. tongue
6. 1. so shall a sinner that hath a d. tongue
20. 10. there is a gift whose recompence is d.
26. 15. shamefaced and faithful woman is a d. grace
28. 13. curse the whisperer and d. tongued
42. 24. all things are d. one against another
50. 2. and by him was built the d. height

DOUBT.
Eccl. 9. 13. so shalt thou not d. the fear of death

DOUBTED.
Eccl. 31. 24. the testimonies shall not be d. of

DOUBTFUL.
Eccl. 18. 7. when he leaveth off, he shall be d.

DOUBTLESS.
2 Mac. 7. 23. but d. the Creator will give you life

DOWRY.
2 Mac. 1. 14. to receive money in name of a d.

DRACHM.
Tob. 5. 14. wilt thou a d. a day and things necessary

DRACHMS.
2 Mac. 4. 19. to carry three hundred d. of silver
12. 43. to the sum of two thousand d. of silver

DRAGON.
Eccl. 25. 16. I had rather dwell with a d.
Bel 23. in the same place was a great d.

DRAGONS.
2 Esd. 15. 29. where the d. of Arabia shall come
31. then shall the d. have the upper hand
Esth. 10. 7. and the two d. are I and Aman
11. 6. two great d. came forth ready to fight

DRANK.
Jud. 12. 20. d. much more wine than he had drunk

DRAW.
Wisd. 5. 13. even so we began to d. to our end
15. 15. idols that have not noses to d. breath
Eccl. 51. 23. d. near unto me, ye unlearned

DRAWN.
Eccl. 13. 7. until he have d. thee dry twice

DREAD.
Mac. 15. 23. send a good angel before us for a d.

DREADFUL.
Esth. 15. 6. all glittering, and he was very d.
Wisd. 10. 16. she withstood d. kings in wonders
17. 6. there appeared a fire kindled of itself, very d.

DREAM.
2 Esd. 10. 36. is sense deceived, or my soul in a d.
Esth. 10. 5. for I remember a d. which I saw
11. 4. Mardocheus who was a Jew, this was his d.
12. now when Mardocheus, who had seen this d. was awake, he bare this d. in mind
2 Mac. 15. 11. he told a d. worthy to be believed

DREAMS.
Wisd. 18. 19. the d. that troubled them foreshew
Eccl. 34. 1. hopes are vain, and d. lift up fools
2. whoso regardeth d. is like him that catcheth at
3. the vision of d. is the resemblance of one thing
5. divinations, soothsayings, and d. are vain
7. for d. have deceived many, they have failed

DRESSED.
Eccl. 27. 6. the fruit declareth if the tree have been d.

DRINK.
1 Esd. 3. 6. to d. on gold, and to sleep on gold
18. wine causeth all men to err that d. it
9. 54. then went they their way to eat and d.
Tob. 4. 15. d. not wine to make thee drunken
7. 9. Raguel said, eat and d. and make merry
Jud. 12. 1. that he should d. of his own wine
11. that she come unto us and eat and d. with us
13. fear not to d. wine and be merry with us
18. Judith said, I will d. now, my lord, because
Eccl. 9. 10. thou shalt d. it with pleasure
15. 3. shall she give him the water of wisdom to d.
24. 21. they that d. me shall yet be thirsty
26. 12. and d. of every water near her
31. 31. press not on him with urging him to d.
1 Mac. 11. 58. he gave him leave to d. in gold
2 Mac. 15. 39. for as it is hurtful to d. wine

DRIVE.
Jud. 11. 19. shall d. them as sheep have no shepherd
Eccl. 38. 20. take no heaviness to heart, d. it away
Bar. 2. 35. I will no more d. Israel out of the land

DRIVEN.
Eccl. 29. 18. mighty men hath it d. from houses
47. 24. that they were d. out of the land

DRIVETH.
Eccl. 1. 21. the fear of the Lord d. away sins
31. 1. the care thereof d. away sleep

DROP.
2 Esd. 6. 56. to a d. that falleth from a vessel
9. 16. like as a wave is greater than a d.
Wisd. 11. 22. the world is as a d. of morning dew
Eccl. 18. 10. as a d. of water unto the sea

DROPS.
2 Esd. 4. 49. the rain was past, the d. remained still
50. as the rain is more than the d. and fire greater than smoke, but the d. and the smoke remain
5. 36. gather me the d. that are scattered
Eccl. 1. 2. who can number the d. of rain?

DROUGHT.
Eccl. 35. 20. as clouds of rain in time of d.

DROWN.
Wisd. 5. 22. and the floods shall cruelly d. them

DROWNED.
Wisd. 10. 4. the earth being d. with the flood
19. but she d. their enemies and cast them up

DRUNK.
Esth. 14. 17. nor d. wine of the drink offerings
Eccl. 31. 27. wine is good, if it be d. moderately
28. wine measurably d. bringeth gladness of heart

DRUNKEN.
Tob. 4. 15. drink not wine to make thee d.
Jud. 6. 4. mountains shall be d. with their blood
Eccl. 26. 8. a d. woman causeth great anger
31. 29. wine d. with excess maketh bitterness

DRUNKENNESS.
Tob. 4. 15. nor let d. go with thee in thy journey
Jud. 13. 15. the canopy wherein he did lie in his d.
Eccl. 19. 1. a man given to d. shall not be rich
31. 26. wine proves the hearts of the proud by d.
30. d. increaseth the rage of a fool till he offend

DRY.
Wisd. 19. 7. where water stood d. land appeared
Eccl. 6. 3. thou shalt leave thyself as a d. tree
13. 7. till he have drawn thee d. twice or thrice
39. 22. his blessing covered the d. land

DRIED.
2 Esd. 6. 51. which was d. up the third day
15. 50. the glory of thy power shall be d. up

DRIETH.
2 Esd. 8. 23. whose look d. up the depths
Eccl. 14. 9. the iniquity of the wicked d. up his soul

DUE.
Eccl. 14. 11. give the Lord his d. offering
18. 22. let nothing hinder to pay thy vow in d. time
29. 2. pay thy neighbour again in d. season
38. 1. honour him with the honour d. to him
39. 33. he will give every thing in d. season

DUMB.
Wisd. 10. 21. wisdom opened the mouth of the d.
Bar. 6. 41. who if they shall see one d. cannot speak

DUNG.
1 Mac. 2. 62. for his glory shall be d. and worms

DUNGHILL.
Eccl. 22. 2. a slothful man is compared to filth of a d.

DURST.
Sus. 10. yet d. not one shew another his grief
1 Mac. 12. 42. he d. not stretch his hand against him

DUST.
2 Esd. 7. 32. so shall the d. those that dwell in silence
Eccl. 44. 21. he would multiply him as the d.

DWELL.
2 Esd. 6. 51. that he should d. in the same
7. 32. so shall the dust those that d. in silence
9. 18. even for them to d. in that now live
Wisd. 1. 4. nor d. in the body that is subject to sin
Eccl. 4. 15. attendeth to her shall d. securely
14. 27. and in her glory shall he d.
25. 16. I had rather d. with a lion and a dragon
38. 32. they shall not d. where they will
51. 23. draw near, and d. in the house of learning

DWELLEST.
2 Esd. 8. 20. O Lord, thou that d. in everlastingness
Wisd. 9. 8. an altar in the city wherein thou d.

DWELLETH.
1 Esd. 2. 5. he is the Lord that d. in Jerusalem
Tob. 5. 16. God which d. in heaven prosper you
Jud. 5. 3. this people that d. in the hill-country
Wisd. 7. 28. none but him that d. with wisdom
Eccl. 21. 28. and is hated wheresoever he d.
25. 8. well is him that d. with a wife of understanding
2 Mac. 3. 39. he that d. in heaven, hath his eye on

DWELLING.
1 Esd. 1. 21. that were found d. at Jerusalem
2 Esd. 5. 38. but he that hath not his d. with men

DWELLINGS.
2 Esd. 4. 7. how great d. are in the midst of the sea!
7. 51. are laid up for us d. of health and safety

DWELT.
Eccl. 47. 12. and for his sake he d. at large
Sus. 1. there d. a man in Babylon, called Joacim

E

EACH.
2 Esd. 8. 6. how shall e. man live that is corrupt?

EAGLE.
2 Esd. 11. 1. there came up from the sea an e.
12. 1. while the lion spake these words to the e.

EAR.
Wisd. 1. 10. the e. of jealousy heareth all things
8. 12. when I speak, they shall give good e.
Eccl. 3. 29. an attentive e. is the desire of a wise man
4. 8. grieve thee to bow down thine e. to the poor
15. whoso gives e. to her shall judge nations
6. 23. give e. my son, receive my advice
33. and if thou bow thine e. thou shalt be wise
16. 5. mine e. hath heard greater things than these
27. 15. their revilings are grievous to the e.
51. 16. I bowed down mine e. and received her
Bar. 3. 9. give e. to understand wisdom
1 Mac. 2. 65. he is a man of counsel, give e. to him
2 Mac. 5. 11. now when this came to the king's e.

EARS.
2 Esd. 10. 56. as much as thine e. may comprehend
Wisd. 15. 15. which have not eyes to see, nor e. to hear
Eccl. 17. 6. a tongue and eyes, and e. gave he them
13. and their e. heard his glorious voice
21. 5. a prayer reacheth to the e. of God
25. 9. that speaketh in the e. of him that will hear
27. 14. their brawls make one stop his e.
33. 18. and hearken with your e. ye rulers
38. 28. the noise of the anvil is ever in his e.
43. 24. when we hear it with our e. we marvel
Bar. 2. 31. I will give them an heart and e. to hear
2 Mac. 15. 39. delighteth the e. of them that read

EAR-RINGS.
Jud. 10. 4. put on her e. and all her ornaments

EARLY.
Tob. 9. 6. e. in the morning they went forth
Wisd. 6. 14. whoso seeketh her e. shall find her
Eccl. 4. 12. they that seek her e. shall be filled
31. 20. he riseth e. and his wits are with him
32. 14. they that seek him e. shall find favour
39. 5. will give his heart to resort e. to the Lord
1 Mac. 6. 33. the king rising very e. marched

EARNEST.
2 Mac. 12. 23. Judas was very e. in pursuing them

EARNESTLY.
Jud. 4. 12. all cried to God with one consent e.
Esth. 13. 18. all Israel cried most e. to the Lord
Eccl. 51. 18. and e. I followed that which is good
2 Mac. 4. 16. whose custom they followed so e.

EARTH.
1 Esd. 4. 36. all the e. calleth on the truth
6. 13. the Lord which made heaven and e.
2 Esd. 2. 14. take heaven and e. to witness, Jud. 7. 28.
3. 6. before ever the e. came forward
18. bowing heavens, thou didst set fast the e.
7. 32. the e. shall restore those that are asleep
46. been better not to have given the e. to Adam
8. 2. as when thou askest the e. it shall say
15. 22. that shed innocent blood upon the e.
Tob. 3. 6. that I may be dissolved and become e.
13. take me out of e. that I may hear no more
7. 18. the Lord of heaven and e. give thee joy
Jud. 2. 1. that he should avenge himself of all the e.
7. that they prepare for me e. and water; I will cover the face of the e. with feet of mine army
20. a great multitude like the sand of the e.
7. 4. these men will lick up the face of the e.
10. 19. being let go, might deceive the whole e.
11. 1. Nebuchodonosor king of all the e. 7.
8. it is reported in all the e. thou art mighty
16. whereat all the e. shall be astonished
21. not such a woman from one end of e. to other
13. 18. blessed art thou above all women on the e.
Esth. 11. 8. lo, a day of great uproar on the e.
Wisd. 1. 1. ye that be judges of the e. 6. 1.
5. 23. thus iniquity shall lay waste the whole e.
7. 1. offspring of him that was first made of the e.
3. when I was born, I fell upon the e.
9. 16. hardly guess aright at things that are on e.
10. 4. the e. being drowned with the flood
15. 8. he which a little before was made of e.
18. 16. touched the heaven, but it stood on the e.
Eccl. 1. 3. who can find out the breadth of the e.?
10. 4. the power of the e. is in the hand of the Lord
9. why is e. and ashes proud? not more wicked than
17. he made their memorial to cease from the e
16. 18. the e. and all therein shall be moved
29. after this the Lord looked on the e.
17. 32. and all men are but e. and ashes
33. 10. all men from ground, Adam was created of e.
38. 4. Lord hath created medicines out of the e.
8. and from him is peace over all the e.
40. 3. to him that is humbled in e. and ashes
11. all things that are of the e. shall turn to the e. again, and waters return to the sea
49. 14. but upon the e. was no man created like Enoch, for he was taken from the e.
Bar. 1. 11. that their days be on e. as days of heaven
2. 15. all the e. may know that thou art God
3. 23. the Agarenes that seek wisdom upon e.
6. 54. for they are crows between heaven and e.
Dan. 3. 54. all ye things that grow on e. bless Lord
Bel 5. who hath created the heaven and the e.
Prayer of Manass. who hast made heaven and e.

1 *Mac.* 1. 3. went through to the ends of the *e.* and took spoils, so that the *e.* was quiet before him
2. 37. let us die, heaven and *e.* shall testify for us
40. they will quickly root us out of the *e.*
3. 9. was renowned to the utmost parts of *e.* 8. 4.
9. 13. the *e.* shook at the noise of the armies
11. 71. Jonathan cast *e.* on his head, and prayed
14. 8. did till in peace, and the *e.* gave her increase
2 *Mac.* 7. 28. my son, look on the heaven and *e.*
10. 25. prayed, and sprinkled *e.* upon their heads
13. 7. not having so much as burial in the *e.*
14. 15. they cast *e.* on their heads, and prayed
15. 5. the other said, I also am mighty on *e.*

EARTHEN.

2 *Esd.* 8. 2. much mould whereof *e.* vessels are made
Eccl. 13. 2. how agree the kettle and *e.* pot together?

EARTHLY.

Wisd. 9. 15. the *e.* tabernacle weigheth down mind
15. 13. that of *e.* matter makes brittle vessels
19. 19. for *e.* things were turned into watery

EARTHQUAKES.

2 *Esd.* 9. 3. when there shall be seen *e.* and uproars
Esth. 11. 5. a noise of a tumult with thunder and *e.*

EASE.

Jud. 1. 16. there he took his *e.* and banqueted
Eccl. 38. 14. for *e.* and remedy to prolong life
1 *Mac.* 9. 58. Jonathan and his company are at *e.*
2 *Mac.* 2. 25. to commit to memory, might have *e.*
27. even as it is no *e.* to him that prepareth

EASED.

2 *Esd.* 7. 68. who committed iniquities, might be *e.*

EAST.

1 *Esd.* 9. 38. place of the holy porch toward the *e.*
2 *Esd.* 1. 38. the people that cometh from the *e.*
15. 20. from the south, from the *e.* and Libanus
34. behold, clouds from the *e.* and north to south
39. strong winds shall arise from the *e.* and open it
Bar. 4. 36. O Jerusalem, look toward the *e.* 5. 5.

EASY.

2 *Esd.* 8. 14. it is an *e.* thing to be ordained
Jud. 4. 7. it was *e.* to stop them that would come
7. 10. because it was not *e.* to come up to the tops
Eccl. 11. 21. an *e.* thing in the sight of the Lord
Bar. 6. 61. lightning breaking forth is *e.* to be seen
2 *Mac.* 2. 26. it was not *e.* but a matter of sweat

EASIER.

2 *Esd.* 13. 20. it is *e.* for him that is in danger
Eccl. 22. 15. salt and a mass of iron is *e.* to bear

EASILY.

Wisd. 6. 12. she is *e.* seen of them that love her
2 *Mac.* 8. 30. they very *e.* got high and strong holds

EAT.

1 *Esd.* 7. 13. that came out of the captivity did *e.*
8. 85. that ye may *e.* the good things of the land
9. 2. Esdras did *e.* no meat, nor drink water
51. go then and *e.* the fat, and drink the sweet
54. then went every one to *e.* and drink
2 *Esd.* 1. 19. had pity on your mournings, I gave you manna to *e.* so ye did *e.* angels' bread
5. 18. up, then, *e.* bread, and forsake us not
9. 24. *e.* only the flowers of the field, taste no flesh, drink no wine, but *e.* flowers only
26. I did *e.* of the herbs of the field
12. 51. I did *e.* only in those days of flowers
Tob. 1. 10. did *e.* of the bread of the Gentiles
2. 1. a good dinner, in the which I sat down to *e.*
13. it is not lawful to *e.* any thing stolen
6. 5. when they had roasted the flesh, they did *e.*
7. 9. Raguel said, *e.* and drink, and make merry
11. I will *e.* nothing here till we agree and swear
10. 7. she did *e.* no meat on the day-time
12. 19. but I did neither *e.* nor drink
Jud. 12. 2. I will not *e.* thereof, lest there be offence
15. that she might sit and *e.* upon them
Eccl. 6. 3. shalt *e.* up thy leaves and lose thy fruit
19. but thou shalt *e.* of her fruits right soon
9. 16. let just men *e.* and drink with thee
11. 19. now will I *e.* continually of my goods
20. 16. they that *e.* my bread speak evil of me
24. 21. they that *e.* me shall yet be hungry
30. 19. for neither can it *e.* nor smell
31. 16. *e.* as it becometh a man, and devour not
21. if thou hast been forced to *e.* arise, go forth
45. 21. they *e.* of the sacrifices of the Lord
Bar. 2. 3. a man should *e.* the flesh of his own son
6. 29. women in child-bed *e.* their sacrifices
Bel 7. this did never *e.* or drink any thing
15. the priests and wives did *e.* and drink up all
1 *Mac.* 1. 62. many resolved not *e.* any unclean thing
2 *Mac.* 6. 18. to open his mouth and *e.* swine's flesh
21. and make as if he did *e.* of the flesh
7. 7. wilt thou *e.* before thou be punished?

EATEN.

1 *Esd.* 3. 3. when they had *e.* and drunken
Esth. 14. 17. thy handmaid not *e.* at Aman's table
Bar. 6. 72. they themselves afterward shall be *e.*
Bel 12. if thou findest not that Bel hath *e.* up all
1 *Mac.* 6. 53. had *e.* up the residue of the store
2 *Mac.* 2. 11. the sin offering was not to be *e.*

EATETH.

1 *Esd.* 4. 10. he *e.* and drinketh, and taketh rest
Bel 24. lo, he liveth, he *e.* and drinketh

ECANUS.

2 *Esd.* 14. 24. E. and Asiel ready to write swiftly

ECBATANA.

1 *Esd.* 6. 23. to seek among the records at E.
Tob. 6. 5. they went on till they drew near to E.
7. 1. and when they were come to E.
14. 14. he died at E. in Media, being 127 years old
Jud. 1. 1. which reigned over the Medes in E.
2. built in E. walls round about, 14.
2 *Mac.* 9. 3. when he came to E. news was brought

ECHO.

Wisd. 17. 19. a rebounding *e.* from the mountains

EDGE.

Jud. 2. 27. smote young men with the *e.* of the sword
Eccl. 28. 18. many have fallen by the *e.* of the sword
31. 26. the furnace proveth the *e.* by dipping
1 *Mac.* 5. 28. slew all the males with the *e.* of sword

EDGED.

Eccl. 21. 3. all iniquity is as a two *e.* sword

EDNA.

Tob. 7. 2. then said Raguel to E. his wife, how like is this young man to Tobit? 8. 14, 16. | 11. 1.
10. 12. E. said to Tobias, the Lord restore thee

EDOMITES.

1 *Esd.* 8. 69. have not put away pollutions of the E.

EDUCATION.

Wisd. 2. 12. objecteth the transgressions of our *e.*
2 *Mac.* 6. 23. and his most honest *e.* from a child
7. 27. nourished thee and endured the troubles of *e.*

EFFECT.

2 *Esd.* 4. 23. written covenants come to none *e.*
Jud. 1. 11. without *e.* and without disgrace
1 *Mac.* 10. 25. he sent unto them to this *e.*

EFFECTS.

2 *Esd.* 9. 6. they have endings in *e.* and signs

EFFECTUALLY.

Tob. 6. 17. and his heart was *e.* joined to her

EGYPT.

1 *Esd.* 1. 26. the king of E. sent to him, saying
38. Zaraces his brother brought he out of E.
2 *Esd.* 1. 7. I brought them out of the land of E.
3. 17. when thou leddest his seed out of E. 14. 4.
9. 29. to our fathers when they came out of E.
14. 3. talked with him, when my people served in E.
29. our fathers were strangers in E. from whence
15. 11. I will smite E. with plagues as before
12. E. shall mourn, and the foundation of it smit.
Tob. 8. 3. he fled into the outmost parts of E.
Jud. 1. 9. sent unto all that were at the river of E.
6. 5. vengeance of this nation that came out of E.
Esth. 13. 16. which thou hast delivered out of E.
1 *Mac.* 1. 16. he thought to reign over E.
17. wherefore he entered into E. with a multitude
20. after that Antiochus had smitten E.
3. 32. from the river Euphrates unto borders of E.
11. 1. the king of E. gathered a great host
13. he set the crown of E. upon his head
2 *Mac.* 1. 1. to the Jews that are throughout E.
10. sent greeting to the Jews that were in E.
4. 21. when Apollonius was sent into E.
5. 1. Antiochus prepared his second voyage into E.
8. as an open enemy he was cast out into E.
9. 29. went into E. to Ptolemeus Philometor

EGYPTIANS.

2 *Esd.* 1. 18. been better for us to have served the E.
Jud. 5. 12. the E. cast them out of their sight

EIGHT.

2 *Esd.* 6. 36. in the *e.* night was my heart vexed
11. 11. and behold, there were *e.* of them
12. 20. that in him there shall arise *e.* kings
Tob. 14. 2. which was restored to him after *e.* years
1 *Mac.* 4. 56. they kept dedication of the altar *e.* days
59. kept from year to year by space of *e.* days
2 *Mac.* 2. 12. so Solomon kept those *e.* days
10. 6. they kept *e.* days with gladness as in feast

EIGHT *and fifty*.

Tob. 14. 2. was *e. and fifty* years old when lost sight

EIGHTEEN.

1 *Esd.* 1. 43. he was made king being *e.* years old
8. 47. his sons and his brethren who were *e.*

EIGHTEENTH.

1 *Esd.* 1. 22. in the *e.* year of the reign of Josias
Jud. 2. 1. in *e.* year, the 22nd day of first month
1 *Mac.* 14. 27. the *e.* day of the month Elul

EIGHTY.

2 *Mac.* 4. 8. and of another revenue *e.* talents

ELBOW.

Eccl. 41. 19. to lean with thine *e.* on the meat

ELDER, ELDER.

2 *Esd.* 7. 13. for the entrances of the *e.* world
Eccl. 32. 3. speak thou that art the *e.* it becometh thee

ELDERS.

1 *Esd.* 6. 5. the *e.* of the Jews obtained favour
11. then asked we those *e.* saying, by whose comm.
Jud. 6. 21. Ozias made a feast to the *e.*
13. 12. and they called the *e.* of the city
Wisd. 8. 10. I shall have honour with *e.* tho' young
Eccl. 6. 34. stand in the multitude of *e.*
7. 14. use not many words in a multitude of E.
8. 9. miss not the discourse of the *e.*
Sus. 8. the two *e.* saw her going in every day and walking, 18, 19, 34, 41, 50.
61. and they arose against the two *e.*
1 *Mac.* 1. 26. so that the princes and *e.* mourned
7. 33. there came out certain *e.* of the people
11. 23. he chose certain of the *e.* of Israel
12. 35. Jonathan calling the *e.* of the people together

ELDEST.

1 *Mac.* 16. 2. Simon called his two *e.* sons

ELEASA.

1 *Mac.* 9. 5. Judas had pitched his tents at E.

ELEAZAR.

1 *Esd.* 8. 43. then sent I to E. and Iduel and Masman
63. with him was E. the son of Phinees
1 *Mac.* 2. 5. E. called Avaran and Jonathan
6. 43. E. also surnamed Savaran, perceiving
8. 17. Jason the son of E. was sent to Rome
2 *Mac.* 6. 18. E. one of the principal scribes
24. E. being fourscore years old and ten
8. 23. he appointed E. to read the holy book

ELECT.

Tob. 8. 15. let thine angels and *e.* praise thee for ever
Eccl. 17. 10. the *e.* shall praise his holy name
46. 1. was made great for saving the *e.* of God
47. 22. nor will he abolish the posterity of his *e.*

ELEMENTS.

Wisd. 7. 17. to know the operation of the *e.*
19. 18. for the *e.* were changed in themselves

ELEPHANT.

1 *Mac.* 6. 35. for every *e.* they appointed 1000 men
46. which done, he crept under the *e.* and the *e.* fell down upon him, and there he died

ELEPHANTS.

1 *Mac.* 1. 17. he entered Egypt with chariots and *e.*
3. 34. delivered to him half of his forces and the *e.*
6. 34. that they might provoke the *e.* to fight
6. Antiochus king of Asia came, having an 120 *e.*
11. 56. Tryphon took the *e.* and won Antioch
2 *Mac.* 11. 4. but puffed up with his fourscore *e.*
13. 2. having either of them two and twenty *e.*
15. he slew in the camp the chiefest of the *e.*

ELEVEN.

2 *Mac.* 11. 11. they slew *e.* thousand footmen

ELEVENTH.

1 *Mac.* 16. 14. in the *e.* month called Sabat

ELEUTHERUS.

1 *Mac.* 11. 7. when he had gone to the river called E.
12. 30. for they were gone over the river E.

ELIAS.

Eccl. 48. 1. then stood up E. the prophet as fire
4. O E. how wast thou honoured in thy deeds?
1 *Mac.* 2. 58. E. being zealous and fervent for the law

ELIZEUS.

Eccl. 48. 12. and E. was filled with his spirit

ELOQUENT.

Esth. 14. 13. give *e.* speech in my mouth before him
Wisd. 10. 21. tongues of them that cannot speak *e.*
Eccl. 21. 7. an *e.* man is known far and near
44. 4. men wise and *e.* in their instructions

ELUL.

1 *Mac.* 14. 27. the eighteenth day of the month E.

ELYMAIS.

Tob. 2. 10. did nourish me until I went into E.
1 *Mac.* 6. 1. heard say E. was a city greatly renowned

EMBRACE.

2 *Esd.* 2. 15. mother *e.* thy children, bring them up

EMBRACED.

Esth. 15. 12. he *e.* her, and said, speak unto me

EMBRACETH.

Eccl. 30. 20. as an eunuch that *e.* a virgin and sigheth

EMBROIDERER.

Eccl. 45. 10. silk and purple, the work of the *e.*

EMERALD.

Eccl. 32. 6. as a signet of an *e.* set in a work of gold

EMERALDS.

Tob. 13. 16. Jerusalem shall be built with *e.*
Jud. 10. 21. Holofernes' bed was woven with *e.*

EMINENT.

2 *Esd.* 15. 40. pour out over every high and *e.* place

EMMAUS.

1 *Mac.* 3. 40. they pitched by E. in the plain
57. the camp pitched on the south side of E.
4. 3. might smite the king's army which was at E.
9. 50. he repaired the fort in Jericho and E.

EMPLOYED.

2 *Mac.* 4. 20. it was *e.* to the making of gallies

EMPLOYING.

Wisd. 15. 8. *e.* his labours lewdly, he makes a god

EMPTY.

2 *Esd.* 6. 22. the full store-houses suddenly be found *e.*
7. 25. therefore Esdras for the *e.* are *e.* things
Eccl. 35. 4. thou shalt not appear *e.* before the L.

EMPTIED.

Jud. 7. 21. the cisterns were *e.* they had no water

EMULATION.

1 *Mac.* 8. 16. was neither envy nor *e.* amongst them

ENCAMPED.

1 *Mac.* 5. 5. but shut them up and *e.* against them
37. and *e.* against Raphon beyond the brook
11. 65. then Simon *e.* against Bethsura and fought

ENCOURAGED.

1 *Mac.* 12. 50. they *e.* one another, and went close
2 *Mac.* 13. 3. Menelaus joined and also *e.* Antiochus

ENCOURAGEMENT.

1 *Mac.* 10. 24. I will write to them words of *e.*

ENCOUNTERED.

2 *Mac.* 15. 26. Judas and his company *e.* the enemies

END.

1 *Esd.* 9. 17. their cause was brought to an *e.*
2 *Esd.* 2. 34. that shall come in the *e.* of the world
3. 23. times passed the years were brought to an *e.*
5. 40. or in the *e.* the love that I have promised
41. nigh to them that be reserved till the *e.*
6. 9. for Esau is the *e.* of the world, and Jacob is
15. the word is of the *e.* ‖ 25. the *e.* of your world
16. the *e.* of these things must be changed
7. 33. the long-suffering shall have an *e.*
42. he said, this present life is not the *e.*
43. but the day of doom shall be the *e.* of time
44. intemperancy is at an *e.* infidelity is cut off
8. 54. in *e.* is shewed the treasure of immortality
9. 5. for like as all that is made in the world hath a beginning and an *e.* and the *e.* is manifest
10. 22. our song is put to silence, rejoicing is at an *e.*
28. *e.* is turned into corruption, prayer to rebuke
12. 6. that he will comfort me to the *e.*
Wisd. 2. 5. after our *e.* there is no returning
16. he pronounceth the *e.* of the just to be blessed
4. 17. for they shall see the *e.* of the wise
5. 4. we are accounted his *e.* to be without honour
13. soon as we were born, began to draw to our *e.*
8. 1. wisdom reacheth from one *e.* to another
14. 14. they shall come shortly to an *e.*
27. the beginning, the cause, and the *e.* of all evil
18. 21. and so brought the calamity to an *e.*
19. 1. came upon them without mercy to the *e.*
4. for the destiny drew them to this *e.*
Eccl. 7. 36. remember the *e.* thou shalt never do amiss
9. 11. for thou knowest not what shall be his *e.*
11. 27. in his *e.* his deeds shall be discovered
14. 18. one cometh to an *e.* and another is born
16. 22. the trial of all things is in the *e.*
18. 12. he saw and perceived their *e.* to be evil
24. think upon the wrath that shall be at the *e*
21. 9. the *e.* of them is a flame of fire to destroy
10. but the *e.* thereof is the pit of hell
28. 6. remember thy *e.* and let enmity cease
30. 1. that he may have joy of him in the *e.*
10. lest thou gnash thy teeth in the *e.*
33. 23. at the time when thou shalt *e.* thy days
38. 8. and of his works there is no *e.*
43. 26. by him the *e.* hath prosperous success
46. 20. he prophesied and shewed the king his *e.*
47. 10. he set in order the solemn times till the *e.*
51. 14. I will seek her out even to the *e.*
Bar. 3. 25. great is the house, and hath no *e.*
1 *Mac.* 2. 13. to what *e.* shall we live any longer?
14. 10. his name was renowned to *e.* of the world
2 *Mac.* 5. 8. in the *e.* he had an unhappy return
10. 9. this was the *e.* of Antiochus Epiphanes
15. 37. I will make an *e.* ‖ 39. here shall be an *e.*

ENDED.

1 *Esd.* 6. 20. the house of the Lord is not yet fully *e.*

2 *Esd.* 6. 6. by me they shall be *e.* and by none other
11. 44. the proud times, behold, they are *e.*
14. 9. thou shalt remain, until the times be *e.*
Jud. 2. 4. and when he had *e.* his counsel
Esth. 15. 1. on third day when she had *e.* her prayer
Eccl. 50. 19. till the solemnity of the Lord was *e.*
2 *Mac.* 15. 24. be stricken with terror, and he *e.* thus

ENDING.

Wisd. 7. 18. the beginning, *e.* and midst of times

ENDINGS.

2 *Esd.* 9. 6. the times have *e.* in effects and signs

ENDS.

2 *Esd.* 16. 13. begin to be shot into the *e.* of world
Wisd. 6. 1. ye that be judges of the *e.* of the earth
1 *Mac.* 1. 3. Alexander went thro' to *e.* of the earth

ENDAMAGE.

1 *Esd.* 6. 33. to hinder or *e.* the house of the Lord

ENDEAVOUR.

Esth. 16. 3. *e.* to hurt, not our subjects only
2 *Mac.* 11. 19. I will *e.* to be a means of your good

ENDUED.

Eccl. 17. 3. he *e.* them with strength by themselves

ENDURE.

Eccl. 2. 2. set thy heart aright, and constantly *e.*
16. 22. the works of his justice, who can *e.* them?
40. 12. but true dealing shall *e.* for ever
45. 26. and that their glory may *e.* for ever
2 *Mac.* 6. 30. I now *e.* sore pains in body being beaten
9. 10. no man could *e.* to carry for his stink

ENDURED.

Wisd. 11. 25. could any thing have *e.* if not thy will?
16. 5. they perished, thy wrath *e.* not for ever
17. 17. *e.* that necessity that could not be avoided
18. 20. but the wrath *e.* not long
1 *Mac.* 10. 15. told of the pains that they had *e.*
2 *Mac.* 7. 27. that *e.* the troubles of education

ENDUREST.

Bar. 3. 3. thou *e.* for ever and we perish utterly

ENEMESSAR.

Tob. 1. 13. the Most High gave me favour before E.
15. now when E. was dead, Sennacherib reigned
16. in the time of E. I gave many alms

ENEMY.

Eccl. 6. 1. instead of a friend become not an *e.*
8. 7. rejoice not over thy greatest *e.* being dead
12. 8. and an *e.* cannot be hidden in adversity
10. never trust thine *e.* for as iron rusteth so is
16. an *e.* speaketh sweetly with lips, but in heart
20. 23. that maketh him his *e.* for nothing
23. 3. lest mine *e.* rejoice over me
25. 7. and he that liveth to see the fall of his *e.*
15. there is no wrath above the wrath of an *e.*
27. 18. for as a man hath destroyed his *e.*
29. 6. he hath gotten him an *e.* without cause
30. 3. he that teacheth his son, grieveth the *e.*
36. 7. take away the adversary and destroy the *e.*
37. 2. when a companion and friend is turned to an *e.*
5. who taketh up the buckler against the *e.*
1 *Mac.* 2. 7. was delivered into the hand of the *e.*
9. her young men slain with the sword of the *e.*
8. 23. the sword and the *e.* be far from them
13. 51. there was destroyed a great *e.* out of Israel
2 *Mac.* 3. 38. if thou hast any *e.* or traitor send him
5. 8. as an open *e.* of his country and country-men
8. 16. not to be stricken with terror of the *e.*
10. 26. besought him to be an *e.* to their enemies

ENEMIES.

1 *Esd.* 4. 4. if he send them out against the *e.*
2 *Esd.* 1. 11. and I have slain all their *e.*
3. 27. thou gavest into hands of thine *e.* *Esth.* 14. 6.
30. I have seen how thou hast preserved thy *e.*
6. 24. friends shall fight one against another like *e.*
Tob. 12. 10. they that sin are *e.* to their own life
Jud. 8. 15. hath power to destroy us before our *e.*
19. our fathers had a great fall before our *e.*
35. Lord be before thee to take vengeance on our *e.*
13. 5. to the destruction of the *e.* that are risen
14. hath destroyed our *e.* by my hands, 17.
18. to the cutting off the head of the chief of our *e.*
15. 5. what things were done in camp of their *e.*
Esth. 13. 6. be destroyed by the sword of their *e.*
Wisd. 2. 18. deliver him from the hand of his *e.*
5. 17. his weapon for the revenge of his *e.*
10. 12. she defended him from his *e.* and kept him
19. but she drowned their *e.* and cast them up
11. 3. they stood against their *e.* and were avenged
5. for by what things their *e.* were punished
12. 20. if thou didst punish the *e.* of thy children
22. thou scourgest our *e.* a thousand times more
24. amongst the beasts of their *e.* were disposed
15. 14. all the *e.* of thy people are most foolish
16. 4. only he shewed how their *e.* were tormented
8. and in this thou madest thine *e.* confess
22. that fire did destroy the fruits of the *e.*
18. 2. they besought pardon, for that they had been *e.*
Eccl. 6. 4. be laughed to scorn of his *e.* 18. 31.
13. separate thyself from *e.* take heed of friends
12. 9. in prosperity of a man, *e.* will be grieved
25. 14. and any revenge, but the revenge of *e.*
26. 27. a scold shall be sought to drive away the *e.*
29. 13. it shall fight for thee against thine *e.*
42. 11. make thee a laughing-stock to thine *e.*
46. 1. taking vengeance of the *e.* that rose up
5. when the *e.* pressed on him on every side
47. 7. for he destroyed the *e.* on every side
51. 8. and savest them out of the hands of the *e.*
Bar. 3. 10. Israel, that thou art in thine *e.* land
4. 26. were taken as a flock caught of the *e.*
5. 6. for they were led away of their *e.*
6. 56. they cannot withstand any king or *e.*
Dan. 3. 9. didst deliver us into hands of lawless *e.*
1 *Mac.* 4. 18. but stand ye now against your *e.*
36. behold, our *e.* are discomfited, let us go up
7. 29. the *e.* were prepared to take away Judas
10. 26. nor joining yourselves with our *e.*
81. stood still, and so the *e.* horses were tired
15. 19. nor yet aid their *e.* against them
2 *Mac.* 10. 26. besought to be an enemy to their *e.*
29. there appeared to the *e.* from heaven
30. but they shot arrows and lightnings ag. the *e.*
11. 11. giving a charge on their *e.* like lions
12. 22. the *e.* being smitten with fear, fled amain
2 *Mac.* 12. 28. who breaketh the strength of his *e.*
13. 21. Rhodocus disclosed the secrets to the *e.*
14. 17. through the sudden silence of his *e.*
22. treachery should be suddenly practised by *e.*
15. 26. Judas and company encountered the *e.*

ENFORCETH.

1 *Esd.* 3. 24. is not wine strongest, that *e.* to do thus?

ENGADDI.

Eccl. 24. 14. I was exalted like a palm-tree in E.

ENGINE.

1 *Mac.* 13. 43. Simon made also an *e.* of war
44. they that were in the *e.* leaped into the city

ENGINES.

1 *Mac.* 5. 30. bearing ladders and other *e.* of war
6. 31. making *e.* for war, 9. 64. | 11. 20. | 15. 25.
51. and he set there artillery with *e.* and instrum.
52. they also made *e.* ag. their *e.* and held them
9. 67. Simon and his company burnt up the *e.* of war
2 *Mac.* 12. 15. without any *e.* of war did cast down
27. wherein was great provision of *e.* and darts

ENGRAVED.

Eccl. 45. 11. with a writing *e.* for a memorial
12. a crown of gold, wherein was *e.* holiness

ENJOY.

Wisd. 2. 6. let us *e.* the good things that are present

ENJOYED.

1 *Esd.* 1. 58. until the land had *e.* her sabbaths

ENLARGED.

1 *Mac.* 14. 6. Simon *e.* the bounds of his nation

ENMITY.

1 *Esd.* 5. 50. the nations were at *e.* with them
Eccl. 6. 9. there is a friend, who being turned to *e.*
28. 6. remember thy end, and let *e.* cease, rememb.
1 *Mac.* 11. 40. his men of war were at *e.* with him

ENOCH.

2 *Esd.* 6. 49. one thou calledst E. other Leviathan
51. to E. thou gavest one part, which was dried
Eccl. 44. 16. E. pleased Lord, and was translated
49. 14. on the earth was no man created like E.

ENOUGH.

Wisd. 14. 22. moreover, this was not *e.* for them
18. 25. it was *e.* that they only tasted of wrath
Eccl. 5. 1. and say not, I have *e.* for my life
11. 24. say not, I have *e.* and possess many things
18. 25. when hast *e.* remember the time of hunger
31. 5. he that followeth corruption shall have *e.* of
35. 1. that keeps the law bringeth offerings *e.*
43. 30. be not weary, for ye can never go far *e.*
2 *Mac.* 7. 42. let this be *e.* now to have spoken
10. 19. left them, who were *e.* to besiege them

ENQUIRE.

2 *Esd.* 9. 13. *e.* how the righteous shall be saved
Jud. 8. 34. but *e.* not you of mine act, not declare
Eccl. 21. 17. they *e.* at the mouth of the wise man

ENQUIRED.

Tob. 5. 13. I have *e.* to know thy tribe and family

ENQUIRY.

1 *Mac.* 9. 26. they made *e.* for Judas' friends

ENRICHED.

Eccl. 35. 10. give, according as he hath *e.* thee

ENROLLED.

1 *Mac.* 10. 36. there be *e.* amongst the king's forces

ENTER.

1 *Esd.* 8. 83. the land which ye *e.* into to possess
2 *Esd.* 7. 14. labour not to *e.* strait and vain things
Wisd. 1. 4. into a malicious soul wisdom shall not *e.*

ENTERPRISE.

Eccl. 37. 16. let reason go before every *e.* and counsel
2 *Mac.* 14. 5. opportunity to further his foolish *e.*

ENTERPRISES.

Jud. 10. 8. God accomplish thine *e.* to glory of Isr.
13. 5. to execute my *e.* to destruction of the enemies
1 *Mac.* 9. 55. was plagued, and his *e.* hindered

ENTERTAIN.

Wisd. 18. 3. an harmless sun to *e.* them honourably
Eccl. 29. 25. thou shalt *e.* and have no thanks
1 *Mac.* 14. 23. it pleased the people to *e.* the men

ENTERTAINED.

Tob. 7. 8. moreover, they *e.* them cheerfully

ENTICETH.

Wisd. 15. 5. the sight of which *e.* fools to lust

ENTRANCE.

2 *Esd.* 7. 4. but put the case, the *e.* were narrow
7. the *e.* thereof is narrow and is set to fall
Jud. 4. 7. by them there was an *e.* into Judea
Wisd. 7. 6. for all men have one *e.* into life
Bel 13. under the table they had made a privy *e.*
1 *Mac.* 14. 5. he made an *e.* to the isles of the sea

ENTRANCES.

2 *Esd.* 7. 12. then were *e.* of this world made narrow

ENTRAP.

Eccl. 8. 11. lest he lie in wait to *e.* thee in thy words

ENTREAT.

Tob. 10. 12. wherefore do not *e.* her evil
Jud. 10. 16. shew unto him, and he will *e.* thee well
Eccl. 7. 20. thy servant worketh truly, *e.* him not ev.

ENTREATED.

Eccl. 49. 7. for they *e.* him evil, who was a prophet
1 *Mac.* 11. 26. the king *e.* him as his predecessors
12. 8. Onias *e.* the ambassador honourably
2 *Mac.* 9. 28. as he *e.* others, so died he miserably
12. 30. *e.* them kindly in the time of adversity.

ENTERED.

2 *Esd.* 10. 1. it came to pass when my son was *e.* into his wedding chamber, he fell down and died
13. 43. they *e.* Euphrates by narrow passages
Tob. 3. 17. the same time came Tobit home and *e.*
Jud. 16. 18. as soon as they *e.* into Jerusalem
Wisd. 10. 16. she *e.* into the soul of the servant
14. 14. by vain-glory they *e.* into the world
Bel 13. entrance whereby they *e.* in continually
1 *Mac.* 12. 3. they *e.* into the senate and said
13. 47. so *e.* into it with songs and thanksgiving
51. he *e.* into it the 23d day of the second month
2 *Mac.* 14. 1. having *e.* by the haven of Tripolis

ENVY.

2 *Esd.* 2. 28. heathen shall *e.* thee but not be able
Wisd. 2. 24. through *e.* of the devil came death
Eccl. 9. 11. *e.* not the glory of a sinner
30. 24. *e.* and wrath shorten the life
37. 10. hide thy counsel from such as *e.* thee
40. 5. wrath and *e.* do change his knowledge
1 *Mac.* 8. 16. there was neither *e.* nor emulation

ENVIETH.

2 *Esd.* 16. 49. as an whore *e.* an honest woman
Eccl. 14. 6. none worse than he that *e.* himself
10. a wicked eye *e.* his bread, he is a niggard

ENVIOUS.

Tob. 4. 16. let not thine eye be *e.* when thou givest
Eccl. 14. 3. what should an *e.* man do with money?
8. the *e.* man hath a wicked eye, he despiseth men
18. 18. a gift of the *e.* consumeth the eyes
20. 14. nor yet of the *e.* for his necessity
37. 11. nor with an *e.* man of thankfulness

EPHOD.

Eccl. 45. 8. with breeches, a long robe, and the *e.*

EPHRAIM.

Jud. 6. 2. thou Achior, and the hirelings of E.
Eccl. 47. 21. out of E. ruled a rebellious kingdom
23. Jeroboam, who shewed E. the way of sin

EPHRON.

1 *Mac.* 5. 46 now when they came to E.
2 *Mac.* 12. 27. Judas removed the host towards E.

EPIPHANES.

1 *Mac.* 1. 10. came a wicked root, Antiochus surnamed E. 10. 1. 2 *Mac.* 2. 20. | 4. 7. | 10. 9.

EPISTLE, S.

Esth. 11. 1. they brought this *e.* of Phurim
Bar. 6. 1. a copy of an *e.* which Jeremy sent
1 *Mac.* 8. 22. this is the copy of the *e.* senate wrote
2 *Mac.* 2. 13. the *e.* of the kings about holy gifts

EQUAL.

Eccl. 13. 11. affect not to be made *e.* to him
32. 9. great men, make not thyself *e.* with them
2 *Mac.* 8. 30. they made the aged *e.* in spoils
13. 23. submitted and sware to all *e.* conditions

EQUALS.

2 *Mac.* 9. 15. make them all *e.* to the citizens

EQUITY.

Esth. 13. 2. but carrying myself alway with *e.*
Wisd. 9. 3. according to *e.* and righteousness
12. 18. thou judgest with *e.* and orderest us

ERECT.

2 *Mac.* 14. 33. I will *e.* a notable temple to Bacchus

ERECTED.

1 *Esd.* 5. 50. they *e.* the altar on his own place

ERR.

1 *Esd.* 3. 18. it causeth all men to *e.* that drink it
Wisd. 13. 6. they peradventure *e.* seeking God
Eccl. 15. 12. say not thou he hath caused me to *e.*
2 *Mac.* 2. 2. that they should not *e.* in their minds

ERRED.

1 *Esd.* 4. 27. many have *e.* and sinned for women
Wisd. 5. 6. we have *e.* from the way of truth
14. 22. that they *e.* in the knowledge of God
17. 1. therefore unnurtured souls have *e.*

ERROR.

Tob. 5. 13. not seduced with the *e.* of brethren
Jud. 5. 20. if there be any *e.* in this people
Wisd. 1. 12. seek not death in the *e.* of your life
12. 24. they went astray very far in the ways of *e.*
Eccl. 4. 25. be abashed of the *e.* of thy ignorance
11. 16. *e.* and darkness had their beginning

ERRORS.

1 *Esd.* 9. 20. to make reconcilement for their *e.*

ESAU.

2 *Esd.* 3. 16. thou didst choose Jacob, and put by E.
6. 8. he said to me, when Jacob and E. were born of him, Jacob's hand held fast the heel of E.
9. E. is the end of world, Jacob the beginning
Jud. 7. 8. all the chief of the children of E.
1 *Mac.* 5. 3. Judas fought against children of E. 65.

ESAY.

2 *Esd.* 2. 18. I will send my servants E. and Jeremy
Eccl. 48. 20. delivered them by the ministry of E.
22. as E. the prophet had commanded him

ESCAPE.

2 *Esd.* 6. 25. whoso shall *e.* and see my salvation
9. 7. that shall be able to *e.* by his works
16. 22. and the other that *e.* the hunger
Jud. 7. 19. there was no way to *e.* from among them
Esth. 16. 4. they think to *e.* the justice of God
Wisd. 16. 15. it is not possible to *e.* thine hand
Eccl. 6. 35. let not parables of understanding *e.* thee
11. 10. neither shalt thou *e.* by fleeing
16. 11. it is marvel if he *e.* unpunished
13. the sinner shall not *e.* with his spoils
20. 3. shew repentance, so shalt *e.* wilful sin
Bar. 6. 57. able to *e.* from thieves or robbers
Sus. 22. if I do it not, I cannot *e.* your hands
2 *Mac.* 3. 38. him well scourged, if he *e.* with life
6. 26. yet should I not *e.* the hand of the Almighty
7. 19. think not that thou shalt *e.* unpunished
9. 22. having great hope to *e.* this sickness
10. 20. they took money and let some of them *e.*

ESCAPED.

Wisd. 14. 6. hope of the world *e.* in a weak vessel
Eccl. 27. 20. he is as a roe *e.* out of the snare
40. 6. troubled, as if he were *e.* out of a battle
1 *Mac.* 14. 26. now all the strangers that had *e.* came
2 *Mac.* 7. 35. thou hast not yet *e.* judgment of God
11. 12. many of them also being wounded, *e.* naked, and Lysias fled away shamefully, and so *e.*

ESCAPETH.

Eccl. 36. 9. let him that *e.* be consumed by fire
42. 20. no thought *e.* him, nor is any word hidden

ESDRAS.

1 *Esd.* 8. 1. after this came E. the son of Seraias
3. this E. went up from Babylon as a scribe
7. for he had very great skill || 25. then said E.
9. 1. E. rising from the court of the temple
16. E. the priest chose the principal men
40. so E. the chief priest brought the law
45. then took E. the book of the law
2 *Esd.* 1. 1. the second book of the prophet E.
2. 33. I E. received a charge of the Lord
6. 10. other question, E. ask thou not
7. 2. up, E. and hear the words, 8. 2, 19. | 14. 1.

ESDRELON.

Jud. 1. 8. that were of the great plain of E.
3. 9. he came over against E. 4. 6. | 7. 3.

ESPY.

1 *Mac.* 5. 38. so Judas sent men to *e.* the host

ESPIED.
Tob. 11. 6. when she *e.* him coming, she said
ESTABLISH.
Eccl. 6. 37. he shall *e.* thy heart and give wisdom
ESTABLISHED.
Eccl. 24. 10. and so was I *e.* in Sion
31. 11. his goods shall be *e.* congregation declare
42. 17. whatsoever is, might be *e.* for his glory
44. 20. he *e.* the covenant in his flesh
49. 3. in time of ungodly Josias *e.* the worship of G.
1 *Mac.* 1. 16. now when the kingdom was *e.*
14. 26. for he and his brethren have *e.* Israel
2 *Mac.* 14. 15. to him that had *e.* his people
ESTABLISHETH.
Eccl. 3. 9. blessing of father *e.* the houses of childr.
42. 25. one thing *e.* the good of another
ESTATE.
Tob. 1. 15. whose *e.* was troubled that I could not go
Jud. 6. 19. O Lord, pity the low *e.* of our nation
Eccl. 2. 4. when thou art changed to a low *e.*
11. 12. yet the Lord set him up from his low *e.*
20. 11. that lifteth up his head from a low *e.*
22. 23. a mean *e.* is not always to be contemned
29. 8. yet have patience with a man in poor *e.*
16. a sinner will overthrow good *e.* of his surety
18. suretyship hath undone many of good *e.*
31. 4. the poor laboureth in his poor *e.*
1 *Mac.* 3. 43. let us restore decayed *e.* of our people
15. 3. that I may restore it to the old *e.*
ESTEEMED.
Esth. 14. 17. I have not greatly *e.* the king's feast
Wisd. 2. 16. we are *e.* of him as counterfeits
7. 8. I *e.* riches nothing in comparison of her
Eccl. 40. 25. but counsel is *e.* above them both
ESTEEMEDST.
Wisd. 12. 7. the land thou *e.* above all other
ESTHER.
Esth. 10. 6. this river is E. whom the king married
15. 9. E. what is the matter? I am thy brother
16. 13. the destruction also of blameless E.
ESTIMATION.
Wisd. 8. 10. for her sake I shall have *e.*
ESTRANGED.
1 *Mac.* 11. 53. and he *e.* himself from Jonathan
ETERNAL.
Wisd. 17. 2. lay there exiled from the *e.* Providence
Eccl. 24. 18. I being *e.* am given to my children
36. 17. know that thou art the Lord, the *e.* God
ETERNITY.
Wisd. 2. 23. made him to be an image of his own *e.*
Eccl. 1. 2. who can number the days of *e.?*
18. 10. so are a thousand years to the days of *e.*
ETHIOPIA.
1 *Esd.* 3. 2. from India to E. *Esth.* 13. 1. | 16. 1.
Jud. 1. 10. until ye come to the borders of E.
EVE.
Tob. 8. 6. thou gavest him E. his wife for an helper
EVEN.
Bar. 5. 7. to make *e.* the ground that Israel may go
EVENING.
1 *Esd.* 8. 72. I sat still until the *e.* sacrifice
Tob. 6. 1. they came in the *e.* to the river Tigris
Jud. 9. 1. the incense of that *e.* was offered
12. 9. she remained till she did eat her meat at *e.*
13. 1. when the *e.* was come, servants made haste
Eccl. 18. 26. from morning until *e.* 1 *Mac.* 10. 80.
EVENT.
2 *Mac.* 9. 25. princes expect what shall be the *e.*
EVENTS.
Wisd. 8. 8. foreseeth the *e.* of seasons and times
EVER.
1 *Esd.* 5. 61. his mercy is for *e.* in all Israel
2 *Esd.* 7. 53. a paradise, whose fruit endureth for *e.*
9. 31. ye shall be honoured in it for *e.*
16. 67. to meddle no more with them for *e.*
Tob. 3. 2. thou judgest truly and justly for *e.*
11. thy holy and glorious name is blessed and honourable for *e.* let all thy works praise thee for *e.*
8. 5. Tobias said, blessed is thy holy name for *e.*
15. and let thine elect praise thee for *e.*
11. 14. and blessed is thy name for *e.*
12. 18. by will of God came, wherefore praise for *e.*
13. 1. blessed be God that liveth for *e.*
10. love in thee for *e.* those that are miserable
12. blessed shall all be that love thee for *e.*
14. have seen all thy glory, and shall be glad for *e.*
18. blessed be God who hath extolled it for *e.*
14. 5. the house of God shall be built in it for *e.*
Jud. 13. 19. remember the power of God for *e.*
16. 17. they shall feel them and weep for *e.*
Esth. 14. 10. to magnify a fleshly king for *e.*
16. 24. hateful to wild beasts and fowls for *e.*
Wisd. 3. 8. and their Lord shall reign for *e.*
14. 13. for neither shall they be for *e.*
16. 5. thy wrath endureth not for *e.*
Eccl. 1. 1. all wisdom is with the Lord for *e.*
16. 27. he garnished his works for *e.*
17. 9. to glory in his marvellous acts for *e.*
15. their ways are *e.* before him and not hid
18. 1. he that liveth for *e.* created all things
24. 33. and I will leave it to all ages for *e.*
38. 28. the noise of the anvil is *e.* in his ears
40. 17. and mercifulness endureth for *e.*
42. 23. all these things live and remain for *e.*
44. 13. their seed shall remain for *e.* and glory
45. 24. the dignity of the priesthood for *e.*
26. and that their glory may endure for *e.*
47. 11. the Lord exalted his horn for *e.*
13. that he might prepare his sanctuary for *e.*
48. 25. he shewed what should come to pass for *e.* and secret things or *e.* they came
50. 23. that peace may be in Israel for *e.*
29. blessed be the Lord for *e.* amen, amen
Bar. 3. 3. for thou endurest for *e.* and we perish
13. thou shouldst have dwelt in peace for *e.*
4. 1. this is the law that endureth for *e.*
23. give you to me with joy and gladness for *e.*
5. 1. the glory that cometh from God for *e.*
Dan. 3. 29. blessed art thou, O Lord God, and to be praised and exalted above all for *e.* 30, 31, 32.
33. to be praised and glorified above all for *e.*
And so to the end of the chapter.

Prayer of Manass. I will praise thee for *e.* all the days of my life, thine is the glory for *e.* and *e.*
1 *Mac.* 3. 7. his memorial is blessed for *e.*
4. 24. because his mercy endureth for *e.*
8. 23. good success be to Jews by sea and land for *e.*
11. 36. be revoked from this time forth for *e.*
16. 2. we have *e.* fought against the enemies
2 *Mac.* 8. 29. reconciled with his servants for *e.*
11. 26. they may *e.* go cheerfully about affairs
14. 15. that had established his people for *e.*
EVERLASTING.
2 *Esd.* 2. 11. I will give these the *e.* tabernacles
34. he shall give you *e.* rest, for he is nigh
35. for the *e.* light shall shine upon you
3. 15. thou madest an *e.* covenant with him
7. 50. that there is promised us an *e.* hope
Tob. 1. 6. as it was ordained by an *e.* decree
3. 6. may be delivered, and go into the *e.* place
13. 6. praise the Lord, and extol the *e.* King
10. and praise the *e.* King, for he is good
Wisd. 7. 26. she is the brightness of the *e.* light
8. 13. I shall leave behind me an *e.* memorial
Eccl. 1. 4. the understanding of prudence from *e.*
5. and her ways are *e.* commandments
15. she hath built an *e.* foundation with men
2. 9. hope for good, and for *e.* joy and mercy
15. 6. she shall cause him to inherit an *e.* name
17. 12. he made an *e.* covenant with them
39. 20. he seeth from *e.* to *e.* ‖ 42. 21. he is fr. *e.* to *e.*
44. 18. an *e.* covenant was made with him
45. 7. an *e.* covenant he made with him
15. this was appointed to him by an *e.* covenant
49. 12. holy temple, which was prepar. for *e.* glory
Bar. 4. 10. which the E. brought upon them, 14.
20. I will cry to the E. in my days
22. my hope is in E. that he will save you, mercy shall come to you from the E. our Saviour
24. with great glory and brightness of the E.
29. shall bring you *e.* joy again and salvation
35. for fire shall come on her from the E.
5. 2. set a diadem of the glory of the E.
Sus. 42. O *e.* God, that knowest the secrets
1 *Mac.* 2. 51. so shall ye receive an *e.* name
54. obtained the covenant of an *e.* priesthood
57. David possessed the throne of an *e.* kingdom
2 *Mac.* 1. 25. the only Just, Almighty, and E.
7. 9. the King shall raise us up unto *e.* life
36. are dead unto God's covenant of *e.* life
EVERLASTINGNESS.
2 *Esd.* 8. 20. O Lord, thou that dwellest in *e.*
EVERMORE.
1 *Esd.* 8. 85. leave the land to your children for *e.*
2 *Esd.* 2. 35. light shall shine upon you for *e.*
Jud. 15. 10. blessed be thou of the Lord for *e.*
Wisd. 4. 18. be a reproach among the dead for *e.*
5. 15. but the righteous love for *e.* their reward is
6. 21. honour wisdom, that ye may reign for *e.*
Eccl. 44. 14. but their name liveth for *e.*
Bar. 3. 32. he that prepared the earth for *e.*
Dan. 3. 3. thy name is worthy to be praised for *e.*
1 *Mac.* 10. 30. from this day forth for *e.* 15. 8.
14. 4. as that *e.* his authority pleased them
EVIDENT.
2 *Esd.* 4. 11. the corruption that is *e.* in my sight
Esth. 16. 9. always judging things that are *e.*
2 *Mac.* 15. 35. and *e.* sign of the help of the Lord
EVIL.
1 *Esd.* 1. 44. and Joacim did *e.* before the Lord
47. he did *e.* also in the sight of the Lord
2 *Esd.* 2. 3. have done that which is *e.* before him
14. I have broken the *e.* in pieces and created good
3. 22. the good departed, and the *e.* abode still
29. then my soul saw many *e.* doers in 30th year
4. 28. the *e.* is sown, but destruction is not come
29. if place where the *e.* is sown pass not away
30. for the grain of *e.* seed hath been sown
31. the grain of *e.* seed hath brought forth
33. wherefore are our years few and *e.?*
6. 27. for *e.* shall be put out and deceit quenched
8. 53. the root of *e.* is sealed up from you
13. 38. shall lay before them their *e.* thoughts
Tob. 3. 8. whom Asmodeus the *e.* spirit killed
17. and to bind Asmodeus the *e.* spirit
6. 7. if a devil or an *e.* spirit trouble any
15. make thou no reckoning of the *e.* spirit
8. 3. which smell, when the *e.* spirit had smelled
10. 12. wherefore do not entreat her *e.*
12. 7. do what is good, and no *e.* shall touch thee
Jud. 7. 15. thou shalt render them an *e.* reward
8. 9. when she heard the *e.* words of the people
Esth. 13. 5. this people is *e.* affected to our state
16. 4. that seeth all things, and hateth *e.*
15. Jews are no *e.* doers, but live by most just laws
Wisd. 14. 27. idols the cause and the end of all *e.*
15. 6. but they are lovers of *e.* things
12. we must be getting, though it be by *e.* means
16. 8. that it is thou who deliverest from all *e.*
18. 9. saints be partakers of the same good and *e.*
Eccl. 3. 24. an *e.* suspicion hath overthrown judgm.
26. a stubborn heart shall fare *e.* at the last
4. 20. observe the opportunity, beware of *e.*
5. 14. an *e.* condemnation on the double tongue
7. 1. do none *e.* so shall no harm come to thee
20. thy servant worketh truly, entreat him not *e.*
9. 1. teach her not an *e.* lesson against thyself
11. 16. and *e.* shall wax old with them that glory
24. and what *e.* can come to me hereafter?
31. he lieth in wait, and turneth good into *e.*
18. 8. what is his good? and what is his *e?*
12. he saw and perceived their end to be *e.*
19. 6. he that hateth babbling shall have less *e.*
28. when he findeth opportunity he will do *e.*
20. 9. that hath good success in *e.* things
16. they that eat my bread speak *e.* of me
22. 26. if any *e.* happen unto me by him
26. 7. an *e.* wife is a yoke shaken to and fro
27. 22. he that winketh with the eyes worketh *e.*
28. 21. the death thereof is an *e.* death, grave better
31. 10. might have done *e.* and hath not done it
13. remember that a wicked eye is an *e.* thing
33. 26. so are tortures and torments for an *e.* servant
27. send to labour for idleness teacheth much *e.*

Eccl. 33. 31. if thou entreat him *e.* and he run from t.
37. 18. four manner of things appear, good and *e.*
27. prove thy soul, and see what is *e.* for it
38. 17. weep bitterly, lest thou be *e.* spoken of
39. 4. for he hath tried the good and the *e.*
42. 5. to make the side of an *e.* servant to bleed
6. sure keeping is good, where an *e.* wife is
51. 12. thou deliveredst me from the *e.* time
Prayer of Manass. be not angry with me for ever by reserving *e.* for me, nor condemn me
EVILS.
2 *Esd.* 7. 27. whoso is delivered from the foresaid *e.*
12. 43. are not *e.* which are come to us sufficient
14. 16. yet greater *e.* shall be done hereafter
17. so much the more shall *e.* increase on them
16. 18. the powers stand in fear, the beginning of *e.* what shall I do when these *e.* shall come
21. even then shall *e.* grow on earth, sword, fam.
40. in those *e.* be even as pilgrims upon earth
Esth. 10. 9. Lord hath delivered us from all those *e.*
11. 9. nation was troubled, fearing their own *e.*
Bar. 1. 20. wherefore the *e.* cleaved unto us
1 *Mac.* 1. 9. and *e.* were multiplied in the earth
6. 12. now I remember the *e.* I did at Jerusalem
8. 31. as touching the *e.* that Demetrius doth
10. 5. he will remember all the *e.* we have done
EUMENES.
1 *Mac.* 8. 8. which they took of him and gave king E.
EUNUCH.
Jud. 12. 11. then said he to Bagoas the *e.*
Wisd. 3. 14. blessed is the *e.* who wrought no iniquity
Eccl. 20. 4. as is the lust of an *e.* to deflower a virgin
30. 20. as an *e.* that embraceth a virgin and sigheth
EUNUCHS.
Esth. 12. 1. with the two *e.* of the king, 6.
3. king examined the two *e.* they were strangled
EUPATOR.
1 *Mac.* 6. 17. to reign, and his name he called E.
EUPHRATES.
1 *Esd.* 1. 25. to raise war at Carchamis upon E.
27. not sent against thee, for my war is upon E.
2 *Esd.* 13. 43. they entered E. by narrow passages
Jud. 1. 6. all that dwelt by E. came unto him
2. 24. he went over E. and went thro' Mesopotamia
Eccl. 24. 26. make understanding to abound like E.
1 *Mac.* 3. 32. from the river E. to borders of Egypt
37. and having passed the river E. he went thro'
EXACT.
Eccl. 51. 19. wrestled with her, and my doings was *e.*
EXACTED.
1 *Esd.* 2. 27. mighty kings who reigned and *e.* tribu.
EXACTLY.
2 *Esd.* 16. 64. L. hath *e.* searched out all your works
Eccl. 16. 25. I will declare his knowledge *e.*
EXACTNESS.
Eccl. 42. 4. of *e.* of weight be not thou ashamed
EXALT.
Tob. 12. 6. it is good to praise God and *e.* his name
Jud. 16. 2. *e.* him, and call upon his name
Eccl. 1. 30. *e.* not thyself, lest thou fall
11. 4. and *e.* not thyself, in the day of honour
15. 5. she shall *e.* him above his neighbours
43. 30. *e.* him as much as you can, for he will far exceed, when you *e.* him put forth your strength
44. 21. that he would *e.* his seed as the stars
Dan. 3. 35. praise and *e.* him above all for ever, 36, 37, 38, 39, 40, 41, 42, 43, 44, 45, 46, 47, 48, 49, 50, 51, 52, 53, 54, 55, 56, 57, 58, 59, 60, 61, 62, 63, 64, 65, 66.
1 *Mac.* 14. 35. he sought by all means to *e.* his people
EXALTATION.
Jud. 10. 8. thine enterprises to the *e.* of Jerusalem
13. 4. the works of my hands for the *e.* of Jerus.
15. 9. they said, thou art the *e.* of Jerusalem
16. 8. for *e.* of those that were oppressed in Israel
EXALTED.
2 *Esd.* 2. 43. a young man, and upon every one of their heads he set crowns and was more *e.*
Jud. 9. 7. behold, they are *e.* with horse and man
Esth. 11. 11. the sun rose, and the lowly were *e.*
Eccl. 24. 13. I was *e.* like a cedar in Libanus
14. I was *e.* like a palm-tree in Engaddi
33. 12. some of them hath he blessed and *e.*
45. 6. he *e.* Aaron an holy man like unto him
47. 11. Lord took away his sins, and *e.* his horn
Bar. 2. 5. thus we were cast down and not *e.*
5. 6. God bringeth them unto thee *e.* with glory
Dan. 3. 29. to be praised and *e.* above all, 30, 32.
1 *Mac.* 1. 3. he was *e.* and his heart was lifted up
8. 13. finally, that they were greatly *e.*
11. 16. Alexander fled, but king Ptolemee was *e.*
EXALTETH.
Eccl. 1. 19. wisdom *e.* them to honour that hold her
4. 11. wisdom *e.* her children and layeth hold
7. 11. for there is one which humbleth and *e.*
50. 22. which *e.* our days from the womb
EXALTING.
2 *Esd.* 15. 53. *e.* the stroke of thine hands
EXAMINE.
1 *Esd.* 9. 16. they sat together to *e.* the matter
Wisd. 2. 19. let us *e.* him with despitefulness
Eccl. 18. 20. before judgment *e.* thyself
Sus. 51. put these two aside, and I will *e.* them
EXAMINATION.
Jud. 8. 27. hath tried them, for the *e.* of their hearts
Sus. 48. that without *e.* ye have condemned her
EXAMINED.
Esth. 12. 3. then the king *e.* the two eunuchs
Eccl. 11. 7. blame not before thou hast *e.* truth
EXAMPLE.
Jud. 8. 24. let us shew an *e.* to our brethren
Esth. 14. 11. make him an *e.* that hath begun this
Wisd. 4. 2. when it is present, men take *e.* at it
Eccl. 44. 16. being an *e.* of repentance to all
2 *Mac.* 6. 28. leave a notable *e.* to such as be young
31. leaving his death for an *e.* of noble courage
EXCEED.
2 *Esd.* 4. 50. so the quantity which is past did more *e.*
EXCEEDED.
2 *Esd.* 4. 34. haste is in vain, for thou hast much *e.*
EXCEEDING.
1 *Esd.* 3. 18. O ye men, how *e.* strong is wine

Eccl. 39. 16. the works of the Lord are e. good
1 Mac. 3. 25. then an e. great dread began to fall
10. 2. king Demetrius gathered an e. great host
15. 36. whereupon the king was e. wroth
2 Mac. 8. 27. yielding e. praise and thanks to Lord
15. 6. so Nicanor in e. pride determined to set up
13. a man with gray hairs, and e. glorious

EXCEEDINGLY.

1 Esd. 1. 24. and how they grieved him e.
2 Esd. 10. 25. her face on a sudden shined e.
15. 6. wickedness hath e. polluted the earth
Jud. 4. 2. therefore they were e. afraid of him
Eccl. 47. 24. their sins were multiplied e.
2 Mac. 10. 34. and they within blasphemed e.

EXCEL.

1 Esd. 4. 2. O ye men, do not men e. in strength?
Wisd. 15. 9. but he striveth to e. goldsmiths
Eccl. 33. 7. why doth one day e. another?

EXCELLED.

Esth. 13. 3. Aman that e. in wisdom among us

EXCELLETH.

1 Esd. 4. 14. O ye men, neither is it wine that e.

EXCELLENCY.

Eccl. 6. 15. a faithful friend's e. is invaluable
1 Mac. 1. 40. her e. was turned into mourning
2 Mac. 6. 23. as becomes the e. of his ancient years

EXCELLENT.

Jud. 11. 8. it is reported that thou only art e.
Esth. 16. 16. ordered the kingd. in most e. manner
Eccl. 42. 21. he hath garnished the e. works
48. 24. he saw by an e. spirit what should come
2 Mac. 3. 26. e. in beauty, and comely in apparel
15. 13. who was of a wonderful and e. majesty

EXCEPTION.

Wisd. 14. 25. there reigned in all men, without e.

EXCESS.

Eccl. 31. 29. wine drunk with e. maketh bitterness
37. 30. for e. of meats bringeth sickness

EXCESSIVE.

Eccl. 19. 30. a man's attire and e. laughter shew
33. 29. be not e. toward any, and without discretion

EXCHANGE.

Eccl. 37. 11. nor with a merchant concerning e.
44. 17. Noah was taken in e. for the world

EXCUSE.

Eccl. 32. 17. but findeth an e. according to his will

EXECUTE.

1 Esd. 8. 46. send such men as might e. priest's office
Jud. 13. 5. to e. my enterprises to the destruction
Wisd. 9. 3. and e. judgment with an upright heart
Eccl. 35. 17. judge righteously and e. judgment
45. 15. should e. the office of the priesthood
1 Mac. 6. 22. how long will it be ere thou e. judgm.?

EXECUTED.

Dan. 3. 5. in all things thou hast e. true judgment
2 Mac. 3. 23. Heliodorus e. that which was decreed

EXECUTETH.

Eccl. 20. 4. he that e. judgment with violence

EXECUTING.

1 Esd. 5. 39. from e. the office of the priesthood
Wisd. 12. 10. but e. thy judgments upon them

EXECUTION.

1 Esd. 8. 95. arise, put in e. to thee doth this appertain
Esth. 16. 17. do well not to put in e. the letters

EXERCISE.

2 Esd. 15. 8. in which they wickedly e. themselves
Tob. 12. 9. those that e. alms and righteousness
Wisd. 8. 18. in the e. of conference with her
1 Mac. 1. 14. they built a place of e. at Jerusalem

EXERCISED.

Eccl. 50. 28. blessed is he that shall be e. in these
1 Mac. 6. 30. thirty-two elephants e. in battle
2 Mac. 15. 12. e. from a child in points of virtue

EXERCISING.

Wisd. 16. 4. on them, e. tyranny, should come penury

EXHORT.

2 Mac. 7. 24. Antiochus did not only e. by words

EXHORTATION.

1 Mac. 13. 3. Simon gave them e. saying

EXHORTED.

1 Mac. 5. 53. Judas e. the people all the way
2 Mac. 2. 3. with other such speeches e. he them
7. 5. they e. one another to die manfully
21. yea, she e. every one of them in her language
25. e. her that she would counsel the young man
26. and when he had e. her with many words
8. 16. he e. them not to be stricken with terror
12. 42. besides Judas e. the people, 13. 12.
15. 8. wherefore he e. his people not to fear

EXHORTING.

2 Mac. 11. 7. e. the other that they would jeopard

EXILED.

Wisd. 17. 2. lay e. from the eternal Providence

EXPECT.

2 Mac. 9. 25. princes e. what shall be the event
15. 8. now to e. the victory and aid that should come

EXPECTATION.

Wisd. 17. 13. the e. from within being less

EXPECTING.

2 Mac. 8. 11. not e. the vengeance that was to follow

EXPENSE.

Eccl. 18. 32. neither be tied to the e. thereof

EXPENSES.

1 Esd. 6. 25. the e. thereof to be given by Cyrus
Bel 8. tell me who this is that devoureth these e.?
1 Mac. 10. 39. for the necessary e. of the sanctuary
44. e. be given of the king's accounts, 45.

EXPERIENCE.

Wisd. 8. 8. if a man desire much e. she knoweth
Eccl. 1. 7. who hath understood her great e.?
21. 22. but a man of e. is ashamed of him
25. 6. much e. is the crown of old men
34. 9. he that hath much e. will declare wisdom
36. 20. but a man of e. will recompense him

EXPERT.

Bar. 3. 26. of so great stature, and so e. in war
1 Mac. 4. 7. with horsemen, these were e. in war

EXPIRED.

Tob. 10. 1. when the days of the journey were e.
1 Mac. 1. 29. after two years fully e. the king sent

EXPOUND.

2 Esd. 4. 47. I shall e. the similitude unto you
Wisd. 8. 8. and she can e. dark sentences

EXPOUNDED.

2 Esd. 12. 12. but it was not e. unto him, now I declare

EXPRESS.

2 Esd. 10. 32. and ye see that I am not able to e.
Wisd. 14. 17. they made an e. image of a king
Eccl. 34. 11. and I understand more than I can e.

EXPRESSED.

Wisd. 17. 1. great are thy judgments and cannot be e.

EXQUISITE.

Eccl. 18. 29. and poured forth e. parables
19. 25. there is an e. subtilty, the same unjust

EXTINGUISHED.

Wisd. 2. 3. which being e. our body shall be turned

EXTOL.

Tob. 13. 4. and e. him before all the living
6. praise the Lord, e. the everlasting King
7. I will e. my God, my soul shall praise the King
Eccl. 6. 2. e. not thyself in thine own heart
13. 23. they e. what a rich man saith to clouds

EXTOLLED.

Tob. 13. 18. blessed be God who hath e. it for ever

EXTOLLETH.

Eccl. 37. 7. every counsellor e. counsel, but there one

EXTREME.

2 Esd. 5. 14. an e. fearfulness went through my body
Wisd. 12. 27. therefore came e. damnation on them
Eccl. 42. 8. be not ashamed to inform the e. aged
2 Mac. 7. 42. to have spoken of the e. tortures

EXTREMITY.

2 Mac. 1. 7. we wrote to you in the e. of trouble

EYE.

Tob. 4. 16. let not thine e. be envious when givest
Jud. 2. 11. that rebel, let not thine e. spare them
Eccl. 4. 5. turn not away thine e. from the needy
7. 22. hast thou cattle? have an e. to them
9. 8. turn away thine e. from a beautiful woman
11. 12. yet the e. of the Lord looked upon him
14. 8. the envious man hath a wicked e.
9. a covetous man's e. not satisfied with his portion
10. a wicked e. envieth bread, he is a niggard
17. 8. he set his e. upon their hearts to shew them
22. will keep the deeds of man as apple of the e.
22. 19. he that pricketh the e. will make tears
26. 11. watch over an impudent e. marvel not
31. 13. remember that a wicked e. is an evil thing, and what is more wicked than an e.?
35. 8. give the Lord his honour with a good e.
10. give to the Most High with a cheerful e.
40. 22. thine e. desireth favour and beauty
43. 18. the e. marvelleth at the beauty of it
2 Mac. 5. 17. and his e. was not upon the place

EYE-LIDS.

Eccl. 26. 9. whoredom may be known in her e.

EYES.

1 Esd. 4. 19. they gape and fix their e. fast on her
2 Esd. 9. 38. I looked back with my e. and saw woman
10. 55. as much as thine e. be able to see
Tob. 2. 10. the sparrows muted warm dung into my e.
3. 12. I set mine e. and my face towards thee
17. scale away the whiteness of Tobit's e. 6. 8.
5. 20. he shall return, thine e. shall see him
10. 5. since I have let thee go, the light of mine e.
11. 7. I know that thy father will open his e.
8. therefore anoint his e. with the gall, 11.
12. when his e. began to smart, he rubbed them
13. whiteness pilled away from corners of his e.
Jud. 7. 27. the death of our infants before our e.
10. 4. decked herself to allure the e. of all men
16. 9. her sandals ravished his e. her beauty took
Esth. 13. 18. because death was before their e.
Wisd. 11. 18. shooting horrible sparks out of their e.
15. 15. which neither have the use of e. to see
Eccl. 3. 25. without e. thou shalt want light
4. 1. my son, make not the needy e. to wait long
12. 16. an enemy will weep with his e. but if find
15. 19. his e. are upon them that fear him
16. 5. many such things have I seen with mine e.
17. 6. a tongue, and e. and ears gave he them
13. and their e. saw the majesty of his glory
15. their ways shall not be hid from his e.
19. and his e. are continually on their ways
18. 18. a gift of the envious consumeth the e.
23. 19. only feareth the e. of man, and knoweth not that the e. of the Lord are brighter than the sun
27. 1. that seeks abundance will turn his e. away
22. he that winketh with his e. worketh evil
30. 20. he seeth with his e. and groaneth
34. 16. the e. of the Lord are on them that love him
17. he raiseth up the soul, and lighteneth the e.
20. that killeth the son before his father's e.
38. 28. and his e. look still upon the pattern
39. 19. and nothing can be hid from his e.
43. 4. sending bright beams it dimmeth the e.
45. 12. a costly work, the desires of the e.
51. 27. behold with your e. how I had little labour
Bar. 1. 12. will give us strength and lighten our e.
2. 18. the e. that fail will give thee praise
3. 14. where is the light of the e. and peace
6. 17. when they be set up, their e. be full of dust
Sus. 9. they perverted and turned away their e.
1 Mac. 4. 12. then the strangers lift up their e.
10. 55. sleep is gone from mine e. my heart fails
2 Mac. 3. 36. which he had seen with his e.

EZEKIEL.

Eccl. 49. 8. it was E. who saw the glorious vision

EZECHIAS, or EZEKIAS.

2 Esd. 7. 40. and e. for the people in the time of
Eccl. 48. 17. E. fortified his city, and brought water
22. E. had done the thing that pleased the Lord
49. 4. all, except David and E. were defective
2 Mac. 15. 22. didst send thy angel in time of E.

F.

FABLES.

Bar. 3. 23. merchants of Theman, authors of f.

FACE, FACE.

1 Esd. 8. 74. O Lord, I am ashamed before thy f.
2 Esd. 1. 30. I will cast you out from my f.
31. when you offer, I will turn my f. from you
10. 25. her f. on a sudden shined exceedingly
12. 7. if my prayer indeed be come before thy f.
15. 63. they shall mar the beauty of thy f.
Tob. 2. 9. I slept, and my f. was uncovered
3. 6. turn not thy f. away from me
12. O Lord, I set mine eyes and f. toward thee
4. 7. nor turn thy f. from any poor, and the f. of God shall not be turned away from thee
13. 6. and he will not hide his f. from you
Jud. 2. 7. cover the whole f. of the earth, 19.
4. 11. spread sackcloth before the f. of the Lord
6. 5. and thou Achior shalt see my f. no more
19. look on the f. of those that are sanctified
7. 4. these men will lick up the f. of the earth
9. 1. then Judith fell upon her f. 10. 23.
11. 13. that serve in Jerus. before the f. of our God
21. there is not such a woman for beauty of f.
14. 3. and they shall flee before your f.
6. he fell down on his f. and his spirit failed
Wisd. 4. 20. iniquities shall convince them to their f.
5. 1. before the f. of such as have afflicted him
12. 14. nor king or tyrant be able to set his f.
Eccl. 6. 12. he will hide himself from thy f.
17. 25. return, make thy prayer before his f.
18. 24. when he shall turn away his f.
21. 2. flee from sin as from the f. of a serpent
25. 17. the wickedness of a woman changeth her f.
26. 17. so is the beauty of the f. in ripe age
34. 3. even as the likeness of a f. to a f.
41. 21. to turn away thy f. from thy kinsman
Dan. 3. 18. now we fear thee, and seek thy f.
Sus. 32. these men commanded to uncover her f.
Bel 42. were devoured in a moment before his f.
1 Mac. 3. 22. overthrew them before our f. 4. 10.
7. 30. and he would see his f. no more
10. 72. thy foot is not able to stand before our f.
2 Mac. 3. 16. whoso had looked high priest in the f.

FACES.

2 Esd. 7. 55. whereas our f. shall be blacker than
Tob. 12. 16. they were troubled, and fell on their f.
Eccl. 50. 17. fell down to the earth on their f.
Bar. 1. 15. but to us belongeth confusion of f.
6. 13. they wipe their f. because of dust of temple
21. their f. are blacked thro' the smoke of temple
1 Mac. 4. 55. then all the people fell on their f.
7. 3. he said, let me not see their f.
2 Mac. 7. 6. which witnessed to their f. declared

FACT.

2 Mac. 4. 36. Greeks that abhorred the f. complained

FACTION.

2 Mac. 4. 3. by one of Simon's f. murders committed

FAIL.

2 Esd. 15. 13. their seeds shall f. through blasting
Jud. 11. 6. my lord shall not f. of his purposes
12. for their victuals f. them, and their water
12. 3. if thy provision should f. how should we give?
Eccl. 2. 8. believe him, your reward shall not f.
3. 13. if his understanding f. have patience
7. 34. f. not to be with them that weep
24. 9. he created me, and I shall never f.
37. 23. the fruits of his understanding f. not
Bar. 2. 18. the eyes that f. will give thee praise, O L.

FAILED.

2 Esd. 3. 29. saw evil-doers so that my heart f. me
Jud. 7. 19. Israel cried to Lord, because their heart f.
20. so that all their vessels of water f. Bethulia
14. 6. Achior fell down on his face, and his spirit f.
Esth. 10. 5. and nothing thereof hath f.
Eccl. 17. 24. he comforted those that f. in patience
34. 7. they have f. that put their trust in them
49. 4. forsook the law, even the kings of Judah f.
1 Mac. 3. 29. that the money of his treasures f.
2 Mac. 13. 19. he was put to flight, f. lost of his men

FAILETH.

2 Esd. 5. 53. born when the womb f. are otherwise
13. 4. as the earth f. when it feeleth the fire
Wisd. 7. 14. for wisdom is a treasure that never f.
Eccl. 17. 31. than the sun, yet the light thereof f.
41. 2. acceptable to him whose strength f.
1 Mac. 6. 10. and my heart f. for very care

FAILING.

Wisd. 17. 15. partly fainted, their heart f. them

FAIN.

1 Mac. 6. 54. they were f. to disperse themselves

FAINT.

Jud. 8. 31. send us rain, and we shall f. no more
Eccl. 2. 12. woe be to fearful hearts and f. hands
4. 9. be not f.-hearted when thou sittest in judgm.
7. 10. be not f.-hearted when makest thy prayer
24. 24. f. not to be strong in Lord, to confirm you
43. 10. they will never f. in their watches
1 Mac. 3. 17. we are ready to f. with fasting

FAINTED.

Jud. 7. 22. women and young men f. for thirst
8. 9. when she heard that they f. for lack of water
Esth. 15. 7. the queen fell down, was pale and f.
Wisd. 17. 15. vexed with apparitions, and partly f.
2 Mac. 3. 24. astonished at the power of God, and f.

FAINTNESS.

Esth. 15. 15. she was speaking, she fell down for f.

FAIR, FAIR.

Tob. 6. 12. the maid is f. and wise, now hear me
Jud. 12. 13. let not this f. damsel fear to come
Esth. 16. 5. the f. speech of those that are in trust
Eccl. 3. 15. as the ice in the f. warm weather
6. 5. a f. tongue will increase kind greetings
13. 6. will speak thee f. and say, what wantest thou?
22. 17. as f. plastering on the wall of a gallery
24. 14. as a f. olive-tree in a pleasant field
18. I am the mother of f. love, fear, and hope
26. 18. so are the f. feet with a constant heart
50. 10. as a f. olive-tree budding forth fruit
Sus. 2. a very f. woman, and one that feared the Ld.
4. Joacim had a f. garden joining to his house
2 Mac. 3. 25. an horse adorned with a very f. cover.

FAITH.

2 Esd. 5. 1. and the land shall be barren of f.
6. 5. that have gathered f. for a treasure
28. for f. it shall flourish, corruption be overcome
7. 34. truth shall stand, and f. shall wax strong
13. 23. such as have f. towards the Almighty
Wisd. 3. 14. to him shall be given special gift of f.

Eccl. 1. 27. *f.* and meekness are his delight
25. 12. *f.* is the beginning of cleaving to him
1 *Mac.* 14. 35. for the justice and *f.* that he kept

FAITHFUL.

2 *Esd.* 7. 24. in his statutes have they not been *f.*
8. 35. among *f.* there is none hath not done amiss
15. 2. cause them to be written, for they are *f.*
Esth. 16. 1. the king to all our *f.* subjects, greeting
Wisd. 3. 9. such as be *f.* in love shall abide with him
Eccl. 1. 14. it was created with the *f.* in the womb
6. 14. a *f.* friend is a strong defence and a treasure
15. nothing doth countervail a *f.* friend
16. a *f.* friend is the medicine of life
7. 18. nor a *f.* brother for the gold of Ophir
22. 23. be *f.* to thy neighbour in his poverty
26. 15. shamefaced and *f.* woman is a double grace
27. 17. love thy friend, and be *f.* to him
33. 3. the law is *f.* to him as an oracle
34. 8. wisdom is perfection to a *f.* mouth
36. 16. and let thy prophets be found *f.*
37. 13. for there is no man more *f.* to thee than it
44. 20. when he was proved, he was found *f.*
46. 15. by his word he was known to be *f.* in vision
48. 22. as Esay who was great and *f.* in vision
1 *Mac.* 2. 52. was not Abraham found *f.* in temptat.?
3. 13. Judas had gathered a company of the *f.*
7. 8. Bacchides was a great man and *f.* to the king
10. 27. now continue you still to be *f.* unto us
14. 41. till there should arise a *f.* prophet
2 *Mac.* 1. 2. Isaac and Jacob his *f.* servants
9. 26. that every man will be still *f.* to me

FAITHFULLY.

Eccl. 29. 3. keep thy word and deal *f.* with him

FAITHFULNESS.

Eccl. 15. 15. and to perform acceptable *f.*
45. 4. he sanctified him in his *f.* and meekness
46. 15. by his *f.* he was found a true prophet

FALL.

2 *Esd.* 7. 7. entrance is set in a dangerous place to *f.*
10. 9. that ought to mourn for the *f.* of so many
48. my son happened to have a *f.* and died
12. 18. it shall not then *f.* but be restored
28. but at the last shall he *f.* through the sword
13. 58. and such things as *f.* in their seasons
15. 57. and thou shalt *f.* through the sword
Tob. 11. 8. he shall rub, the whiteness shall *f.* away
Jud. 6. 6. and thou shalt *f.* among their slain
9. let not thy countenance *f.* I have spoken
8. 19. they had a great *f.* before our enemies
16. 7. the mighty one did not *f.* by young men
Esth. 14. 11. O Lord, let them not laugh at our *f.*
Wisd. 3. 15. the root of wisdom shall never *f.*
6. 9. that ye may learn wisdom, and not *f.* away
7. 25. therefore can no defiled thing *f.* into her
10. 1. and she brought him out of his *f.*
13. 16. he provided for it, that it might not *f.*
17. 18. or a pleasing *f.* of water running violently
Eccl. 1. 30. exalt not thyself, lest thou *f.*
2. 7. wait for mercy and go not aside, lest ye *f.*
18. we will *f.* into the hands of the Lord
5. 13. and the tongue of man is his *f.*
8. 1. strive not with a mighty man lest thou *f.*
9. 3. meet not an harlot lest thou *f.* into her snares
9. so through thy desire thou *f.* into destruction
12. 15. if thou begin to *f.* he will not tarry
13. 21. a rich man beginning to *f.* is held up
14. 18. as of the green leaves, some *f.* some grow
19. 1. small things, he shall *f.* by little and little
2. wine and women will make men to *f.* away
20. 18. the *f.* of the wicked shall come speedily
22. 19. that pricketh the eye will make tears *f.*
27. on my lips, that I *f.* not suddenly by them
23. 1. leave me not, and let me not *f.* by them
3. lest I *f.* before mine adversaries and my enemy
8. the evil speaker and proud shall *f.* thereby
25. 7. he that liveth to see the *f.* of his enemy
19. let the portion of a sinner *f.* upon her
27. 26. whoso diggeth a pit shall *f.* therein
27. he that worketh mischief it shall *f.* on him
29. they that rejoice at the *f.* of the righteous
28. 23. such as forsake the Lord shall *f.* into it
26. lest thou *f.* before him that lieth in wait
29. 19. a wicked man transgressing the commandm.
of L. shall *f.* into suretyship; shall *f.* into snares
20. beware that thou thyself *f.* not into the same
32. 20. go not in a way wherein thou mayest *f.*
35. 15. her cry against him that causeth them to *f.*
38. 15. let him *f.* into the hand of the physician
16. my son, let tears *f.* down over the dead
43. 13. by his commandm. he maketh snow to *f.*
46. 6. he made the battle to *f.* on the nations
47. 23. he took care of temple that it should not *f.*
Bar. 4. 31. miserable are they that rejoiced at thy *f.*
33. for as she rejoiced and was glad at thy *f.*
6. 27. for if they *f.* to the ground at any time
Sus. 23. it is better for me to *f.* into your hands
1 *Mac.* 2. 19. *f.* away every one from the religion
3. 25. an exceeding great dread to *f.* on the nations
4. 32. cause boldness of their strength to *f.* away
7. 38. be avenged, and let them *f.* by the sword
2 *Mac.* 9. 7. Antiochus fell, so that having a sore *f.*

FALLEN.

2 *Esd.* 7. 48. O Adam, thou art not *f.* alone, but we all
13. 23. that be *f.* into danger are such as have works
37. for their wicked life are *f.* into the tempest
Jud. 10. 2. Judith rose where she had *f.* down
11. 11. even death is now *f.* upon them and their sin
Wisd. 11. 20. they have *f.* down with one blast
18. 23. when the dead were now *f.* down by heaps
Eccl. 13. 22. when a rich man is *f.* he hath helpers
28. 18. many have *f.* by the edge of the sword, but
not so many as have *f.* by the tongue
49. 13. who raised up for us the walls that were *f.*?
1 *Mac.* 9. 21. how is the valiant man *f.* that delivered
12. 37. the wall on the east-side was *f.* down

FALLETH.

2 *Esd.* 6. 56. hast likened to a drop that *f.* from vessel
Wisd. 11. 22. as a drop of dew that *f.* on the earth
Eccl. 3. 31. when he *f.* he shall find a stay
Bar. 6. 55. when fire *f.* on house of gods of wood

FALLING.

2 *Esd.* 12. 18. great strivings, shall stand in peril of *f.*
Wisd. 16. 11. that not *f.* into deep forgetfulness
17. 4. noises as of waters *f.* sounded about them
Eccl. 34. 16. from stumbling, and he is a help from *f.*
43. 17. *f.* down thereof as lighting of grasshoppers
2 *Mac.* 3. 21. to see the *f.* down of the multitude

FALLS.

2 *Esd.* 8. 17. I see *f.* of us that dwell in the land

FALSE.

Eccl. 34. 1. the hopes of a man are vain and *f.*
4. from that which is *f.* what truth can come?
36. 19. so doth an heart of understanding *f.* speeches
Bar. 6. 8. yet are they but *f.* and cannot speak
44. whatsoever is done among them is *f.*
59. it is better to be a king than such *f.* gods
Sus. 43. knowest they have borne *f.* witness ag. me
49. for they have borne *f.* witness against her
61. for Daniel had convicted them of *f.* witness

FALSEHOOD.

Esth. 16. 6. beguiling with *f.* and deceit of disposition
2 *Mac.* 15. 10. shewing them the *f.* of the heathen

FALSELY.

Wisd. 14. 29. though they swear *f.* yet they look not
Bel 12. or else Daniel that speaketh *f.* against us

FAME.

1 *Mac.* 3. 26. insomuch as his *f.* came to the king
41. the merchants hearing the *f.* of them

FAMILY.

Tob. 5. 10. shew me of what tribe and *f.* thou art
11. dost thou seek a tribe or *f.* of an hired man?
13. I enquired to know thy tribe and thy *f.*
Jud. 8. 18. no *f.* who worship gods made with hands
Esth. 14. 5. I have heard in the tribe of my *f.*
16. 18. hanged at gates of Susa, with all his *f.*

FAMILIES.

1 *Esd.* 1. 4. prepare you after your *f.* and kindreds
5. the dignity of the *f.* of you the Levites
2. 8. then the chief of the *f.* of Judea stood up
5. 1. the principal men of the *f.* were chosen
4. the names of the men according to their *f.*
63. and of the chief of their *f.* the ancients
68. so they went to the chief of the *f.* and said
8. 28. the chief according to their *f.* and dignities
59. to the principal men of the *f.* of Israel
9. 16. Esdras chose the principal men of their *f.*

FAMINE.

2 *Esd.* 15. 5. I will bring *f.* death, and destruction
49. I will send poverty, *f.* sword, and pestilence
16. 18. the beginning of *f.* and great dearth
19. behold *f.* and plague are sent as scourges
21. sword, *f.* and great confusion shall grow
46. for in captivity and *f.* shall they get children
Tob. 4. 13. for lewdness is the mother of *f.*
Jud. 5. 10. a *f.* covered all the land of Chanaan
7. 14. they and children shall be consumed with *f.*
Eccl. 39. 29. *f.* and death created for vengeance
40. 9. calamities, *f.* were created for the wicked
48. 2. he brought a sore *f.* upon them
Bar. 2. 25. they died by *f.* sword, and by pestilence
1 *Mac.* 6. 54. the *f.* did so prevail against them
9. 24. in those days there was a very great *f.*
13. 49. a great number of them perished through *f.*

FAMOUS

Eccl. 44. 1. let us now praise *f.* men and fathers
Bar. 3. 26. the giants, *f.* from the beginning

FANCIETH.

Eccl. 34. 5. heart *f.* as a woman's heart in travail

FAR.

1 *Esd.* 9. 11. our sin in these things is spread *f.*
2 *Esd.* 4. 2. thy heart hath gone too *f.* in this world
Tob. 13. 11. many nations shall come from *f.*
Wisd. 12. 24. they went astray very *f.* in error
14. 17. because they dealt *f.* off; they took the
counterfeit of his visage from *f.*
Eccl. 9. 13. keep *f.* from the man that hath power
15. 8. for she is *f.* from pride, men that are liars
21. 7. an eloquent man is known *f.* and near
23. 3. whose hope is *f.* from thy mercy
12. all such things shall be *f.* from the godly
27. 20. he is too *f.* off, he is as a roe escaped
43. 30. exalt Lord, for even yet will he *f.* exceed
47. 16. thy name went *f.* unto the islands
Bar. 3. 21. their children were *f.* from that way
4. 15. he hath brought a nation on them from *f.*
6. 73. for the just man shall be *f.* from reproach
Sus. 51. put these two aside one *f.* from another
1 *Mac.* 8. 12. had conquered kingdoms *f.* and nigh
23. the sword also and enemy be *f.* from them
13. 5. be it *f.* from me that I should spare
2 *Mac.* 4. 40. a man *f.* gone in years, no less in folly
8. 25. they took their money and pursued them *f.*

FARE.

Eccl. 3. 26. a stubborn heart shall *f.* evil at last
32. 24. that trusteth shall *f.* never the worse

FARE *well.*

2 *Mac.* 9. 20. if ye and your children *f. well*
11. 21. *f.* ye *well*, 33. 38.
28. if ye *f. well* we have our desire, we are in health

FASHION.

2 *Esd.* 4. 35. how long shall I hope on this *f.*?
5. 53. that be born in strength of youth are of one *f.*
Wisd. 2. 15. not like others, his ways are of another *f.*
14. 19. to make the resemblance of the best *f.*

FASHIONED.

2 *Esd.* 8. 8. for when the body is *f.* in the womb
11. that the thing which is *f.* may be nourished
14. him who with so great labour was *f.*
Wisd. 7. 2. I was *f.* to be flesh in time of ten months
13. 13. formed it and *f.* it to the image of a man
15. 16. he that borrowed his own spirit *f.* them
19. 6. the whole creature was *f.* again anew

FASHIONETH.

Wisd. 15. 7. potter *f.* every vessel with much labour
Eccl. 38. 30. he *f.* the clay with his arm, boweth down

FASHIONS.

Wisd. 16. 25. even then was it altered into all *f.*
2 *Mac.* 4. 9. training up in the *f.* of the heathen
13. now such was the height of Greek *f.*
6. 8. that the Jews should observe the same *f.*

FAST.

2 *Esd.* 3. 18. thou didst set *f.* the earth
Wisd. 2. 5. it is *f.* sealed, no man cometh again
4. 4. yet standing not *f.* they shall be shaken
Wisd. 13. 15. set it in a wall, and made it *f.* with iron
Eccl. 4. 13. he that holds her *f.* shall inherit glory
44. 12. their seed stands *f.* children for their sakes
Bar. 6. 18. so the priests make *f.* their temples
Bel 11. shut the door *f.* and seal it with thy signet

FASTEN.

Eccl. 14. 24. he shall also *f.* a pin in her walls

FAST.

1 *Esd.* 8. 50. and there I vowed a *f.* to the young men
73. rising up from the *f.* with my clothes rent
2 *Esd.* 6. 31. if thou wilt *f.* seven days again
9. 23. seven days, but thou shalt not *f.* in them
10. 4. but I purpose to mourn and *f.* till I die

FASTED.

2 *Esd.* 5. 20. I *f.* seven days, mourning and weeping
6. 35. I wept and *f.* seven days in like manner
Jud. 4. 13. the people *f.* many days in all Judea
8. 6. she *f.* all the days of her widowhood
Bar. 1. 5. they wept, *f.* and prayed before the Lord
1 *Mac.* 3. 47. they *f.* that day, and put on sackcloth

FASTING.

Tob. 12. 8. prayer is good with *f.* alms and righteous.
1 *Mac.* 3. 17. ready to faint with *f.* all this day
2 *Mac.* 13. 12. they besought L. with weeping and *f.*

FAT.

1 *Esd.* 1. 14. the priests offered the *f.* until night
9. 51. go then, eat the *f.* and drink the sweet
Jud. 16. 16. and all the *f.* is not sufficient
Eccl. 26. 13. and her discretion will *f.* his bones
35. 6. the offering of righteous makes the altar *f.*
38. 11. and make a *f.* offering, as not being
47. 2. as the *f.* taken from the peace-offering
Dan. 3. 16. like as in ten thousands of *f.* lambs
Bel 27. Daniel took pitch, *f.* hair, and made lumps

FATHER.

1 *Esd.* 1. 34. made him king instead of Josias his *f.*
4. 20. a man leaveth his *f.* and cleaveth to his wife
21. remembereth neither *f.* mother, nor country
25. man loveth his wife better than *f.* and mother
2 *Esd.* 1. 28. have not I prayed you as a *f.* his sons
29. that ye should be my children, and I your *f.*
2. 5. as for me, O *f.* I call on thee for a witness
Tob. 3. 7. Sara was also reproached by her *f.* maids
5. 1. *f.* I will do all that thou hast commanded
6. 12. now hear me, and I will speak to her *f.*
15. the precepts which thy *f.* gave thee to marry
9. 4. but my *f.* counteth the days if I tarry long
10. 1. now Tobit his *f.* counted every day
12. honour thy *f.* and mother-in-law, thy parents
11. 2. thou knowest how thou didst leave thy *f.*
14. 13. he buried his *f.* and mother honourably
Jud. 9. 2. O L. God of my *f.* Simeon, to whom gavest
12. I pray thee, I pray thee, O God of my *f.*
Esth. 16. 11. as he was called our *f.* and honoured
Wisd. 10. 1. preserved the first formed *f.* of the world
11. 10. these thou didst admonish and try as a *f.*
14. 3. but thy providence, O *F.* governeth it
15. for a *f.* afflicted with untimely mourning
Eccl. 3. 1. hear me, your *f.* O children, and do
3. whoso honoureth his *f.* maketh an atonement
8. honour thy *f.* and mother in word and deed
9. for the blessing of the *f.* establisheth children
10. glory not in the dishonour of thy *f.*
11. for the glory of a man is from honour of his *f.*
12. my son, help thy *f.* in his age, grieve him not
4. 10. be a *f.* to fatherless, and husband to mother
7. 27. honour thy *f.* with thy whole heart
22. 3. an ill-nurtured son is the dishonour of his *f.*
4. she that lives dishonestly is her *f.* heaviness
5. she that is bold dishonoureth her *f.* and husband
23. 1. O Lord, *f.* and governor of all my life
4. O Lord, *f.* and God of my life, give me not
14. remember thy *f.* and thy mother
30. 4. though his *f.* die, yet he is as though not dead
34. 20. as one that killeth the son before his *f.* eyes
41. 17. be ashamed of whoredom before *f.* and mo.
42. 9. the *f.* waketh for the daughter, none knoweth
10. lest she should be got with child in her *f.* house
44. 19. Abraham was a great *f.* of many people
51. 10. I called on the Lord, the *f.* of my Lord
Sus. 30. so she came with her *f.* and mother
1 *Mac.* 2. 54. Phinees our *f.* obtained covenant
65. give ear to him, he shall be a *f.* unto you
3. 2. so did all they that held with his *f.*
6. 23. we have been willing to serve thy *f.*
11. 2. so to do because he was his *f.*-in-law
40. that he might reign in his *f.* stead
13. 3. what my *f.* house have done for the laws
27. a monument upon the sepulchre of his *f.*
28. he set up pyramids for his *f.* and mother
2 *Mac.* 9. 23. my *f.* at what time he led an army
11. 23. since our *f.* is translated to the gods
14. 37. who was called a *f.* of the Jews

FATHERLESS.

1 *Esd.* 3. 19. mind of king and *f.* child to be all one
2 *Esd.* 2. 20. judge for the *f.* give to the poor
Eccl. 4. 10. be as a father to the *f.* and a husband
35. 14. he will not despise the supplication of the *f.*
Bar. 6. 38. nor can they do good to the *f.*
2 *Mac.* 3. 10. for the relief of widows and *f.*

FATHERS.

1 *Esd.* 1. 11. according to the several dignities of *f.*
31. Josias died and was buried in his *f.* sepulchre
2. 21. it may be sought out in the books of thy *f.*
6. 15. but when our *f.* provoked God to wrath
Tob. 3. 3. punish me not for the sins of my *f.*
5. deal with me according to my sins and my *f.*
4. 12. take a wife of seed of thy *f.* not a strange woman who is not of thy *f.* tribe; our *f.* married
8. 5. blessed art thou, O God of our *f.*
Jud. 5. 7. they would not follow the gods of their *f.*
7. 28. take to witness our God and Lord of our *f.*
8. 25. who trieth us even as he did our *f.*
10. 8. the God, the God of our *f.* give thee favour
Wisd. 9. 1. O God of my *f.* and Lord of mercy
12. 21. to whose *f.* hast sworn and made covenant
18. 6. of that night were our *f.* certified afore
9. the *f.* now singing out the songs of praise
24. in stones was the glory of *f.* graven
Eccl. 8. 9. for they also learned of their *f.*
44. 1. let us now praise our *f.* that begat us
Bar. 2. 6. but to us and to our *f.* open shame

Bar. 2. 21. the land that I gave unto your *f.*
3. 8. according to all the iniquities of our *f.*
Dan. 3. 3. blessed art thou, O Lord God of our *f.*
Bel 1. king Astyages was gathered to his *f.*
Prayer of Manass. O Lord, almighty God of our *f.*
1 Mac. 2. 19. fall away from the religion of their *f.*
20. we will walk in the covenant of our *f.*
50. give your lives for the covenant of your *f.*
51. remember what acts our *f.* did in their time
69. he blessed them, and was gathered to his *f.*
4. 9. remember how our *f.* were delivered
2 Mac. 1. 25. thou that didst choose the *f.*
5. 10. nor had he sepulchre with his *f.*
6. 1. the Jews to depart from the laws of their *f.*
7. 2. rather than transgress the laws of our *f.*
24. if he would turn from the laws of his *f.*
30. the law that was given to our *f.* by Moses
37. I offer my body and life for laws of our *f.*
12. 39. to bury them in their *f.* graves
13. 9. worse than had been done in his *f.* time

FAUCHION.

Jud. 13. 6. she took down his *f.* from thence
16. 9. and the *f.* passed through his neck

FAULT.

Eccl. 9. 13. make no *f.* lest he take away thy life
1 Mac. 13. 39. as for any *f.* committed to this day
2 Mac. 14. 28. articles agreed on, man being in no *f.*

FAULTLESS.

Eccl. 23. 10. he that sweareth shall not be *f.*

FAVOUR.

1 Esd. 6. 5. the elders of the Jews obtained *f.*
2 Esd. 5. 56. if I have found *f.* in thy sight, 6. 11.
Tob. 1. 13. gave me grace and *f.* before Enemessar
12. 18. not of any *f.* of mine, but by the will of G.
Jud. 8. 23. our servitude shall not be directed to *f.*
10. 8. the God of our fathers give thee *f.*
Esth. 16. 11. had so far obtained the *f.* we shew
Wisd. 12. 18. thou orderest us with great *f.*
Eccl. 1. 13. he shall find *f.* in the day of death
3. 18. thou shalt find *f.* before the Lord
22. 21. for there may be a returning to *f.*
32. 10. before a shamefaced man goeth *f.*
14. they that seek him early shall find *f.*
40. 22. thine eye desireth *f.* and beauty
41. 24. so shalt thou find *f.* before all men
45. 1. which found *f.* in the sight of all flesh
Bar. 1. 12. we shall find *f.* in their sight
2. 14. give us *f.* in sight of them that led us captive
1 Mac. 10. 60. where he found *f.* in their sight
11. 24. to the king where he found *f.* in his sight
2 Mac. 2. 22. Lord being gracious to them with all *f.*
4. 11. privileges granted of special *f.* to the Jews
6. 22. and for the old friendship might find *f.*
12. 45. there was great *f.* laid up for those godly

FAVOURABLE.

1 Esd. 8. 53. we besought Lord and found him *f.* to us

FAVOURABLY.

Wisd. 6. 16. sheweth herself *f.* to them in the ways
2 Mac. 9. 27. he will *f.* yield to your desires

FAVOURED.

2 Mac. 6. 18. he was of a well *f.* countenance

FEAR.

2 Esd. 3. 3. I began to speak words full of *f.*
Tob. 1. 19. withdrew myself for *f.*
14. 2. he increased in the *f.* of the Lord God
Jud. 2. 28. the *f.* and dread of him fell upon all
14. 3. then *f.* shall fall upon them, they shall flee
15. 2. *f.* and trembling fell upon them
Esth. 14. 1. Esther in *f.* of death resorted to the Lord
19. O thou mighty God, deliver me out of my *f.*
15. 5. but her heart was in anguish for *f.*
8. the king, who in a *f.* leaped from his throne
13. my heart was troubled for *f.* of thy majesty
Wisd. 4. 20. they shall come with *f.* iniquities con- [vince
5. 2. they shall be troubled with terrible *f.*
6. 7. he who is Lord shall *f.* no man's person
12. 11. nor didst thou for *f.* give them pardon
17. 4. nor might the corner keep them from *f.*
10. they died for *f.* denying they saw the air
12. *f.* is nothing but a betraying of succours
15. for a sudden *f.* not looked for came upon them
19. these things made them to swoon for *f.*
Eccl. 1. 11. the *f.* of the Lord is honour and glory
12. the *f.* of the Lord maketh a merry heart
14. to *f.* the Lord is the beginning of wisdom
16. to *f.* the Lord is fulness of wisdom
18. the *f.* of the Lord is a crown of wisdom
20. the root of wisdom is to *f.* the Lord
21. the *f.* of the Lord driveth away sins
27. the *f.* of the Lord is wisdom and instruction
28. distrust not the *f.* of Lord when thou art poor
30. thou camest not in truth to the *f.* of the Lord
2. 7. ye that *f.* the Lord wait for his mercy
8. ye that *f.* the Lord, believe him
9. ye that *f.* the Lord, hope for good and joy
16. that *f.* the Lord will seek what is pleasing
4. 17. she will bring *f.* and dread upon him
5. 5. be not without *f.* to add sin unto sin
6. 16. and they that *f.* the Lord shall find him
9. 16. let thy glorying be in the *f.* of the Lord
10. 19. they that *f.* the Lord are a sure seed
21. the *f.* of the Lord goeth before authority
22. their glory is the *f.* of the Lord
15. 13. and they that *f.* God love it not
16. 2. except the *f.* of the Lord be with them
18. 27. a wise man will *f.* in every thing
19. 18. the *f.* of the Lord is the first step to be accepted
22. 18. a fearful heart cannot stand against any *f.*
23. 27. nothing better than the *f.* of the Lord
24. 18. I am the mother of fair love and *f.*
25. 6. the *f.* of God is the glory of old men
12. the *f.* of the Lord is beginning of his love
27. 3. hold himself diligently in the *f.* of the Lord
32. 16. they that *f.* the Lord shall find judgment
36. 2. send thy *f.* on all nations that seek not
40. 2. and cause *f.* of heart ‖ 5. *f.* of death
7. he marvelleth that the *f.* was nothing
26. but the *f.* of the Lord is above them both; there is no want in the *f.* of the Lord
27. the *f.* of the Lord is a fruitful garden
41. 3. *f.* not the sentence of death, remember
45. 23. Phinees had a zeal in the *f.* of the Lord

Bar. 3. 7. thou hast put thy *f.* in our hearts
33. calleth it again, and it obeyeth him with *f.*
Sus. 57. and they for *f.* companied with you
1 Mac. 2. 62. *f.* not then the words of a sinful man
3. 6. wherefore the wicked shrunk for *f.* of him
25. then began the *f.* of Judas to fall on nations
4. 8. *f.* ye not their multitude, nor be afraid
10. 76. they of the city let him in for *f.*
2 Mac. 3. 17. the man was so compassed with *f.*
21. the *f.* of the high priest being in an agony
30. the temple was full of *f.* and trouble
6. 30. I suffer these things, because I *f.* him
7. 29. *f.* not this tormentor, but take thy death
12. 22. the enemies being smitten with *f.* fled
13. 16. they filled the camp with *f.* and tumult
15. 18. but the principal *f.* was for the temple
23. send a good angel for a *f.* and dread to them

FEARED.

2 Esd. 12. 13. it shall be *f.* above all kingdoms
Tob. 12. 16. they fell on their faces, for they *f.*
Jud. 8. 8. none gave her an ill word, for she *f.* God
Eccl. 1. 8. there is one wise and greatly to be *f.*
Sus. 2. a fair woman and one that *f.* the Lord
1 Mac. 3. 30. *f.* he should not be able to bear charges
12. 28. they *f.* and trembled in their hearts

FEARETH.

Jud. 16. 16. but he that *f.* the Lord is great
Eccl. 1. 13. whoso *f.* the L. it shall go well with him
6. 17. whoso *f.* the Lord shall direct friendship
10. 24. none greater than he that *f.* the Lord
15. 1. he that *f.* the Lord, will do good
19. 24. that hath small understanding and *f.* God
21. 6. he that *f.* the L. will repent from his heart
23. 19. such a man only *f.* the eyes of men
25. 10. there is none above him that *f.* the Lord
26. 5. there be three things which my heart *f.*
23. but a godly woman given to him that *f.* the L.
32. 14. whoso *f.* the L. will receive his discipline
33. 1. no evil shall happen to him that *f.* the Lord
34. 14. whoso *f.* the L. shall not fear or be afraid
15. blessed is the soul of him that *f.* the Lord

FEARFUL.

2 Esd. 8. 22. word true, and whose ordinance is *f.*
12. shew me the plain difference of this *f.* vision
15. 13. their seeds shall fail with a *f.* constellation
Eccl. 2. 12. woe be to *f.* hearts and faint hands
22. 18. so a *f.* heart cannot stand against fear
1 Mac. 3. 56. such as were *f.* commanded to return
2 Mac. 1. 24. O Lord God, who art *f.* and strong
8. 13. they that were *f.* and distrusted, fled

FEARFULNESS.

2 Esd. 5. 14. an extreme *f.* went through my body
11. 40. had power over the world with great *f.*
15. 37. there shall be great *f.* and trembling

FEARING.

Esth. 11. 9. nation was troubled, *f.* their own evils
Eccl. 29. 7. refused to lend, *f.* to be defrauded
2 Mac. 9. 29. who also *f.* the son of Antiochus

FEAST.

1 Esd. 1. 1. Josias held the *f.* of the passover
19. Israel held the *f.* of sweet bread seven days
3. 1. Darius made a great *f.* to all his subjects
5. 51. also they held the *f.* of tabernacles
7. 14. they kept the *f.* of unleavened bread
2 Esd. 1. 31. your solemn *f.* days have I forsaken
2. 38. those that be sealed in the *f.* of the Lord
9. 47. the time he should have a wife, I made a *f.*
Tob. 2. 1. when I was come home in the *f.* of Pentecost, which is the holy *f.* of the seven weeks
8. 19. he kept the wedding *f.* fourteen days
Jud. 6. 21. Ozias made a *f.* to the elders
10. 2. in the sabbath-days, and in her *f.*-days
12. 10. Holofernes made a *f.* to his servants only
13. 1. were weary because the *f.* had been long
Esth. 14. 17. I have not greatly esteemed the king's *f.*
Eccl. 29. 25. shalt entertain and *f.* and have no thanks
32. 1. if thou be made the master of the *f.*
2. receive a crown for well-ordering the *f.*
Bar. 6. 32. as men do at the *f.* when one is dead
1 Mac. 10. 34. and the three days after the *f.*
2 Mac. 1. 9. see that ye keep the *f.* of tabernacles
6. 7. and when the *f.* of Bacchus was kept
21. they that had the charge of that wicked *f.*
8. 33. as they kept the *f.* for the victory
10. 6. with gladness, as in *f.* of tabernacles
12. 31. came to Jerus. the *f.* of weeks approaching
32. after the *f.* called Pentecost went forth

FEASTED.

1 Esd. 4. 63. they *f.* with instruments of music

FEASTING.

Jud. 16. 20. the people continued *f.* in Jerusalem
Esth. 16. 22. shall keep it an high day with all *f.*

FEASTINGS.

Wisd. 19. 16. whom they had received with *f.*

FEASTS.

Tob. 1. 6. I went often to Jerusalem at the *f.*
2. 6. your *f.* shall be turned into mourning
Jud. 8. 6. she fasted, save the *f.* and solemn days
Esth. 16. 22. among your solemn *f.* ye shall keep it
Eccl. 33. 8. and he altered seasons and *f.*
43. 7. from the moon is the sign of *f.* a light
47. 10. he beautified their *f.* and set in order
Bar. 1. 14. read this on the *f.* and solemn days
1 Mac. 1. 39. her *f.* were turned into mourning
10. 34. I will that all the *f.* and sabbaths
12. 11. in our *f.* and other convenient days
2 Mac. 6. 6. to keep sabbath and ancient *f.*
7. 42. have spoken concerning the idolatrous *f.*

FEATHER.

2 Esd. 11. 12. there arose one *f.* and reigned

FEATHERS.

2 Esd. 11. 3. out of her *f.* there grew other contrary *f.* and they became little *f.* and small
5. lo, the eagle flew with her *f.* and reigned
7. the eagle rose and spake to her *f.* saying
11. I numbered her contrary *f.* there were eight
20. the *f.* that followed stood up on the right side
22. after this I looked and behold, the twelve *f.* appeared no more, nor the two little *f.*
24. that two little *f.* divided themselves
25. the *f.* that were under the wing thought
31. the head eat up the two *f.* under the wing

2 Esd. 11. 45. appear no more, thou eagle, nor thy *f.*
12. 19. sawest the eight small under *f.* sticking
29. whereas thou sawest two *f.* under the wings

FEATHERED.

2 Esd. 11. 1. an eagle which had twelve *f.* wings

FEATS.

Jud. 11. 8. that thou art wonderful in *f.* of war

FED.

2 Mac. 5. 27. Judas who *f.* on herbs continually

FEDDEST.

Wisd. 16. 20. thou *f.* thy people with angels' food

FEEBLE.

Wisd. 2. 11. that which is *f.* is found nothing
9. 5. for I thy servant am a *f.* person
Eccl. 25. 23. maketh weak hands and *f.* knees
Bar. 2. 18. which goeth stooping, and *f.* eyes fail
1 Mac. 1. 26. virgins and young men were made *f.*

FEED.

2 Esd. 16. 68. *f.* you being idle with things offered

FEEL.

Jud. 16. 17. they shall *f.* them, and weep for ever
Eccl. 30. 1. causeth him oft to *f.* the rod
Bar. 6. 20. when they eat them, clothes *f.* it not
24. nor when they were molten, did they *f.* it

FEELETH.

2 Esd. 13. 4. as the earth faileth when it *f.* the fire

FEELING.

Wisd. 11. 13. they had some *f.* of the Lord

FEET.

2 Esd. 1. 26. *f.* are swift to commit man-slaughter
2. 15. make their *f.* as fast as a pillar
25. O thou good nurse, establish their *f.*
5. 15. so the angel set me up upon my *f.*
6. 13. stand up upon thy *f.* and hear a voice
10. 30. he set me upon my *f.* and said unto me
14. 2. I said, here am I, Lord, and stood on my *f.*
Jud. 2. 7. cover the earth with the *f.* of my army
10. 4. and she took sandals upon her *f.*
14. 7. he fell at Judith's *f.* and reverenced her
Esth. 13. 13. been content to kiss the soles of his *f.*
Wisd. 14. 11. a snare to the *f.* of the unwise
15. 15. as for their *f.* they are slow to go
Eccl. 6. 24. and put thy *f.* into her fetters
21. 19. doctrine to fools is as fetters on the *f.*
25. 20. as a sandy way is to the *f.* of the aged
26. 18. so are fair *f.* with a constant heart
38. 29. turning the wheel about with his *f.*
30. he boweth down his strength before his *f.*
Bar. 6. 17. through the *f.* of them that come in
26. they are borne on shoulders, having no *f.*

FEIGNEDLY.

2 Esd. 8. 28. think not on those that walk *f.*

FELL.

1 Esd. 9. 47. they *f.* to the ground, and worshipped
2 Esd. 10. 1. in his wedding-chamber he *f.* down
13. 11. and *f.* with violence on the multitude
Tob. 1. 4. Naphtali *f.* from the house of Jerusalem
11. 13. when he saw his son, he *f.* on his neck
14. 10. but Aman *f.* into the snare, and perished
Jud. 4. 11. *f.* before the temple, and cast ashes
6. 18. then the people *f.* down, and worshipped G.
7. 22. young men *f.* down in the streets of the city
8. 3. he *f.* on his bed, and died in Bethulia
9. 1. then Judith *f.* on her face, and put ashes
10. 23. she *f.* down on her face, and did reverence
14. 6. he *f.* down on his face, his spirit failed
7. he *f.* at Judith's feet, and reverenced her
15. 2. fear and trembling *f.* upon them
5. they all *f.* upon them with one consent
Esth. 15. 7. queen *f.* down, was pale, and fainted
15. as she was speaking, she *f.* down for faintness
Wisd. 10. 6. fire that *f.* down on the five cities
17. 16. so whosoever there *f.* down, was kept
Eccl. 15. 11. say not, it is thro' the Lord I *f.* away
16. 7. the old giants who *f.* away in foolishness
50. 17. the people *f.* to the earth on their faces
Sus. 15. it *f.* out as they watched a fit time
1 Mac. 1. 5. and after these things he *f.* sick
3. 11. many also *f.* down slain, the rest fled
4. 40. *f.* down flat to the ground on their faces
6. 8. laid him on his bed, and *f.* sick for grief
46. whereupon the elephant *f.* down on him
7. 18. the dread of them *f.* on all the people
9. 40. many *f.* down dead, and the remnant fled
13. 22. but there *f.* a very great snow
2 Mac. 3. 27. Heliodorus *f.* suddenly to the ground
40. and the things *f.* out on this sort
9. 7. it came to pass he *f.* down from his chariot
9. his flesh *f.* away, and his smell was noisome
24. if any thing *f.* out contrary to expectation
10. 4. they *f.* flat down, and besought the Lord
17. they slew all that *f.* into their hands
26. they *f.* down at the feet of the altar
12. 24. Timotheus *f.* into the hands of Dositheus
14. 41. being ready to be taken, *f.* on his sword

FELLOW.

Eccl. 8. 15. travel not by the way with a bold *f.*
13. 23. if poor speak, they say, what *f.* is this?
Bar. 6. 43. she reproacheth her *f.* that she was not

FELLOWS.

Dan. 3. 26. angel came with Azarias and his *f.*
1 Mac. 4. 5. for, said he, these *f.* flee from us
10. 61. certain pestilent *f.* of Israel assembled

FELLOWSHIP.

Wisd. 6. 23. such shall have no *f.* with wisdom
Eccl. 13. 1. he that hath *f.* with a proud man
2. have no *f.* with one that is mightier than thyself
17. what *f.* hath the wolf with the lamb?

FENCED.

2 Mac. 12. 13. which was *f.* about with walls

FERVENCY.

Jud. 4. 9. every man cried to God with great *f.*

FERVENT.

2 Esd. 6. 58. thy only begotten and thy *f.* lover
1 Mac. 2. 54. Phinees, in being zealous and *f.*
58. Elias, for being zealous and *f.* for the law

FESTIVAL.

1 Mac. 1. 45. profane the sabbaths and *f.* days

FETCH.

2 Mac. 2. 15. send some to *f.* them to you

FETCHETH.

1 Esd. 4. 34. sun *f.* his course to his own place

Eccl. 31. 19. he *f.* not his wind short on his bed

FETTERED.

Wisd. 17. 2. *f.* with the bonds of a long night

FETTERS.

Eccl. 6. 24. put thy feet into her *f.* neck into chain
29. then shall her *f.* be a strong defence to thee
21. 19. doctrine to fools is as *f.* on the feet

FEW.

2 *Esd.* 4. 33. wherefore are our years *f.* and evil?
7. 12. they are but *f.* and evil, full of perils
70. there should be very *f.* left in a multitude
8. 1. but he hath made the world to come for *f.*
3. there be many created, but *f.* shall be saved
62. but I have shewed to thee and a *f.* like thee
10. 57. called with the Highest, and so are but *f.*
Eccl. 17. 2. he gave them *f.* days, and a short time
41. 13. a good life hath but *f.* days, but a good name
43. 32. for we have seen but a *f.* of his works
Bar. 2. 13. we are but a *f.* among the heathen
1 *Mac.* 3. 17. how shall we be able being so *f.* to fight?
18. for many to be shut up in the hands of a *f.*
6. 54. there were but a *f.* left in the sanctuary
7. 1. Demetrius came up with a *f.* men to a city
28. I will come with a *f.* men, that I may see you
9. 9. let us now save our lives, for we are but *f.*
12. 45. and chose a *f.* men to wait on thee
15. 10. so that *f.* were left with Tryphon
2 *Mac.* 2. 21. so that being but a *f.* they overcame
6. 17. come to declaring of the matter in *f.* words
12. 34. in fighting, a *f.* of the Jews were slain
14. 30. he gathered together not a *f.* of his men

FEWER.

2 *Mac.* 5. 14. and no *f.* were sold than slain
10. 17. they killed no *f.* than twenty thousand
12. 10. no *f.* than 5000 men on foot, 500 horsemen

FIDELITY.

Esth. 13. 3. Aman was approved for his stedfast *f.*

FIELD.

2 *Esd.* 7. 6. a city is builded and set upon a broad *f.*
9. 17. like as the *f.* is, so is also the seed
24. go into a *f.* of flowers where no house is
26. there did I eat of the herbs of the *f.*
10. 3. then I came into this *f.* as thou seest
32. and I went into the *f.* and lo, I have seen
51. therefore I bade thee remain in the *f.*
12. 51. I remained still in the *f.* seven days and did eat only in those days of the flowers of the *f.*
13. 57. then went I forth into the *f.* giving
16. 28. two of the *f.* which shall hide themselves
77. like as a *f.* is covered over with bushes
Wisd. 17. 17. whether he were a labourer in the *f.*
19. 7. and out of the violent stream a green *f.*
Eccl. 24. 14. as an olive-tree in a pleasant *f.*
Bel 33. and who was going into the *f.* to bring it
1 *Mac.* 10. 71. come down to us into the plain *f.*
14. 8. the trees of the *f.* gave their fruit

FIELDS.

2 *Esd.* 15. 41. that all *f.* may be full and all rivers
16. 32. and *f.* thereof shall wax old, and her ways
Jud. 2. 27. he burnt up all their *f.* and destroyed
3. 3. all our *f.* of wheat lie before thy face
4. 5. for their *f.* were of late reaped
6. 4. their *f.* shall be filled with dead bodies
1 *Mac.* 16. 10. they fled to the towers in the *f.*

FIERCE.

1 *Esd.* 2. 27. mighty kings and *f.* were in Jerusalem
Wisd. 11. 17. a multitude of bears or *f.* lions
18. 15. as a *f.* man of war into the midst of a land
2 *Mac.* 10. 35. with a *f.* courage killed all they met
12. 15. who gave a *f.* assault against the walls

FIERCELY.

Esth. 15. 7. the king looked very *f.* upon her
1 *Mac.* 6. 33. the king marched *f.* with his host

FIERCENESS.

2 *Mac.* 15. 21. Maccabeus seeing the *f.* of the beasts

FIERY.

Wisd. 11. 18. breathing out either a *f.* vapour
Eccl. 43. 4. breathing out *f.* vapours and sending
45. 19. to consume them with the *f.* flame
48. 9. who was taken up in a chariot of *f.* horses

FIFTH.

2 *Esd.* 6. 47. on the *f.* day thou saidst to seventh part
2 *Mac.* 7. 15. afterward they brought the *f.* also

FIFTEENTH.

Esth. 10. 13. the 14th and *f.* day of the month
1 *Mac.* 1. 54. now the *f.* day of the month Casleu

FIFTY.

Jud. 1. 2. the breadth of the wall *f.* cubits
1 *Mac.* 9. 61. took about *f.* persons and slew them
2 *Mac.* 13. 5. there was a tower of *f.* cubits high

FIFTIES.

1 *Mac.* 3. 55. Judas ordained captains over *f.*

FIGS.

Jud. 10. 5. Judith filled a bag with lumps of *f.*

FIG-TREE.

1 *Mac.* 14. 12. every man sat under his vine and *f.*

FIGHT.

1 *Esd.* 1. 28. but undertook to *f.* with him
2 *Esd.* 6. 24. at that time shall friends *f.* like enemies
13. 8. all were sore afraid, and yet durst *f.*
11. the multitude which was prepared to *f.*
31. one shall undertake to *f.* against another
15. 15. shall stand up to *f.* one against another
Jud. 7. 11. *f.* not against them in battle-array
Esth. 11. 6. two great dragons came ready to *f.*
7. that they might *f.* against the righteous
Wisd. 5. 20. and the world shall *f.* with him
Eccl. 4. 28. strive for truth, the Lord shall *f.* for thee
29. 13. it shall *f.* for thee against thy enemies
1 *Mac.* 2. 40. if we *f.* not for our lives and laws
41. we will *f.* against him, nor will we die all
66. let him *f.* the battle of the people
3. 21. but we *f.* for our lives and our laws
43. let us *f.* for our people and the sanctuary
58. that ye may *f.* with these nations assembled
4. 21. the host of Judas in the plain, ready to *f.*
5. 32. he said, *f.* this day for your brethren
57. let us go and *f.* against the heathen
67. for that they went out to *f.* unadvisedly
6. 34. they might provoke the elephants to *f.*
8. 32. we will *f.* with thee by sea and by land
9. 8. peradventure we may be able to *f.* with them

1 *Mac.* 9. 30. that thou mayest *f.* our battles
44. let us go up now and *f.* for our lives
12. 50. they went close together prepared to *f.*
13. 9. *f.* our battles, which commandest, we will do
14. 13. nor was there any left to *f.* against them
26. have chased away in *f.* their enemies from them
16. 3. be instead of me, go and *f.* for our nation
2 *Mac.* 8. 16. not to fear, but to *f.* manfully
36. told that the Jews had God to *f.* for them
11. 9. they were ready, not only to *f.* with men
14. 18. that they had to *f.* for their country

FIGHTETH.

Esth. 14. 13. his heart to hate him that *f.* against us
Wisd. 16. 17. for the world *f.* for the righteous
Eccl. 38. 28. he *f.* with the heat of the furnace

FIGHTING.

2 *Esd.* 13. 34. and to overcome him by *f.*
Eccl. 28. 11. and an hasty *f.* sheddeth blood
1 *Mac.* 8. 10. *f.* with them, slew many of them
2 *Mac.* 12. 31. it happened that in their *f.* together
15. 27. *f.* with their hands, and praying to God

FIGURE.

Eccl. 49. 9. made mention under the *f.* of the rain

FILL.

2 *Esd.* 1. 20. and waters flowed out to your *f.*
4. 32. how great a floor shall they *f.*
Tob. 8. 18. Raguel bade his servants *f.* the grave
Jud. 2. 8. their slain shall *f.* their valleys
7. 21. they had no water to drink their *f.*
8. 31. the Lord will send rain to *f.* our cisterns
Wisd. 2. 7. let us *f.* ourselves with costly wine
Eccl. 24. 19. and *f.* yourselves with my fruits
36. 14. *f.* Sion with thy unspeakable oracles

FILLED.

2 *Esd.* 4. 36. when the number of seeds is *f.* in you
5. 25. of all depths of sea thou hast *f.* thee one river
Tob. 12. 9. that exercise alms shall be *f.* with life
Jud. 6. 4. their fields shall be *f.* with dead bodies
10. 5. she *f.* a bag with parched corn and figs
13. 2. Holofer. lying along, for he was *f.* with wine
Wisd. 13. 12. refuse to dress his meat, *f.* himself
18. 16. thy almighty word *f.* all things with death
Eccl. 2. 16. that love him shall be *f.* with the law
4. 12. that seek her early shall be *f.* with joy
16. 29. the Lord *f.* it with his blessings
17. 7. withal, he *f.* them with understanding
23. 11. a swearer shall be *f.* with iniquity
31. 3. when he resteth, he is *f.* with his delicates
32. 15. he that seeketh the law, be *f.* therewith
33. 16. I *f.* my wine-press like a gatherer of grapes
37. 24. a wise man shall be *f.* with blessings
39. 6. he shall be *f.* with the spirit of understanding
12. for I am *f.* as the moon at the full
42. 25. who shall be *f.* with beholding his glory
47. 14. and as a flood *f.* with understanding
48. 12. and Elizeus was *f.* with his spirit
Bar. 3. 32. he hath *f.* it with four-footed beasts
5. 7. God hath appointed that valleys be *f.* up
Sus. 32. that they might be *f.* with her beauty
2 *Mac.* 3. 30. the temple was *f.* with joy and gladness
4. 40. the common people being *f.* with rage
6. 4. the temple was *f.* with rioting and revelling
5. the altar was *f.* with profane things
7. 21. she exhorted, *f.* with courageous spirits
9. 7. but still was *f.* with pride, breathing out
12. 16. a lake, being *f.* full, was seen running
13. 16. at last they *f.* the camp with fear

FILLEDST.

Eccl. 47. 15. and thou *f.* it with dark parables

FILLETH.

Wisd. 1. 7. the Spirit of the Lord *f.* the world
Eccl. 1. 16. to fear the Lord, *f.* men with her fruits
24. 25. he *f.* all things with his wisdom

FILTH.

Eccl. 22. 2. is compared to the *f.* of a dunghill
27. 4. so the *f.* of a man in his talk remaineth

FILTHY.

Wisd. 11. 18. or *f.* scents of scattered smoke
Eccl. 22. 1. a slothful man is compared to a *f.* stone

FILTHINESS.

Wisd. 2. 16. he abstaineth from our ways as *f.*
2 *Mac.* 9. 9. and the *f.* of his smell was noisome

FIND.

1 *Esd.* 2. 22. thou shalt *f.* in the chronicles
2 *Esd.* 3. 36. shalt *f.* that Israel kept thy precepts
Tob. 2. 2. what poor man soever thou shalt *f.*
Jud. 8. 14. you cannot *f.* the depth of the heart
14. 3. run to the tent of Holofernes, but not *f.* him
Esth. 16. 15. we *f.* that the Jews are no evil-doers
Wisd. 2. 24. they that do hold of his side, do *f.* it
6. 10. that have learned shall *f.* what to answer
14. for he shall *f.* her sitting at his doors
9. 16. with labour do we *f.* the things before us
13. 6. seeking God and desirous to *f.* him
9. how did they not sooner *f.* out the Ld. thereof?
Eccl. 1. 13. he shall *f.* favour in the day of death
3. 18. thou shalt *f.* favour before the Lord
31. and when he falleth, he shall *f.* a stay
6. 16. they that fear the Lord shall *f.* him
18. so shalt thou *f.* wisdom till thine old age
28. for at the last thou shalt *f.* her rest
15. 6. he shall *f.* joy and a crown of gladness
16. 14. every man shall *f.* according to his works
18. 4. and who shall *f.* out his noble acts?
24. 28. no more shall the last *f.* her out
25. 3. how canst thou *f.* any thing in thine age?
27. 16. and shall never *f.* friend to his mind
28. 1. he that revengeth, shall *f.* vengeance
29. 3. thou shalt *f.* the thing that is necessary
31. 22. at the last thou shalt *f.* as I told thee
32. 14. they that seek him early shall *f.* favour
33. 25. if set thy servant to labour thou shalt *f.* rest
41. 24. thou shalt *f.* favour before all men
51. 26. instruction is hard at hand to *f.*
Bar. 1. 12. we shall *f.* favour in their sight
Dan. 3. 15. no place to sacrifice and *f.* mercy
Sus. 14. when they might *f.* Susannah alone
1 *Mac.* 10. 16. he said, shall we *f.* such another man?
2 *Mac.* 2. 6. mark the way but they could not *f.* it
24. the difficulty they *f.* which desire to look
5. 9. and thinking there to *f.* succour for his kindred
6. 22. the old friendship with them might *f.* favour

FINDEST.

2 *Esd.* 2. 23. wherever thou *f.* the dead bury them
Bel 12. if thou *f.* not that Bel hath eaten all

FINDETH.

Eccl. 19. 28. when he *f.* opportunity, he will do
25. 10. oh how great is he that *f.* wisdom!
32. 17. but *f.* an excuse according to his will
40. 18. he that *f.* a treasure is above them both

FINDING.

Esth. 16. 14. he thought, *f.* us destitute of friends
Eccl. 13. 26. the *f.* out of a parable is wearisome

FINE.

1 *Esd.* 3. 6. bridles of gold and an head-tire of *f.* linen
Jud. 10. 5. she filled a bag with figs and *f.* bread
Eccl. 35. 2. he that requiteth good, offers *f.* flour
38. 11. a sweet savour and a memorial of *f.* flour
Bel 3. were spent twelve great measures of *f.* flour
2 *Mac.* 1. 8. we offered sacrifices and *f.* flour

FINELY.

2 *Mac.* 15. 39. so speech *f.* framed delighteth the ears

FINGERS.

Wisd. 15. 15. idols nor have *f.* of hands to handle

FINISH.

Tob. 8. 17. grant mercy, O Ld. *f.* their life in health
Eccl. 38. 27. they that watch to *f.* a work
28. he setteth his mind to *f.* his work and watcheth

FINISHED.

1 *Esd.* 4. 55. till the day that the house was *f.*
6. 14. it was builded many years ago, and was *f.*
28. help them, till the house of the Lord be *f.*
7. 4. they *f.* these by the commandment of the Ld.
5. thus was the holy house *f.* in the month Adar
2 *Esd.* 6. 20. and when the world shall be *f.*
Tob. 8. 20. for before the days of the marriage were *f.*
Jud. 5. 22. when Achior had *f.* these sayings
8. 34. not declare it till the things be *f.* that I do
Eccl. 50. 19. besought Ld. till they had *f.* his service
1 *Mac.* 4. 51. they *f.* all the works they began to do

FINISHING.

1 *Esd.* 5. 73. they hindered the *f.* of the building
Eccl. 37. 11. with an hireling for a year of *f.* work
50. 14. *f.* the service at the altar to adorn offering
2 *Mac.* 2. 9. the sacrifice of the *f.* of the temple

FIRE.

1 *Esd.* 1. 12. they roasted the passover with *f.*
55. they broke walls and set *f.* upon her towers
6. 24. where they do sacrifice with continual *f.*
2 *Esd.* 1. 23. I gave you not *f.* for your blasphemies
3. 19. thy glory went through four gates of *f.*
4. 5. go thy way, weigh me the weight of the *f.*
9. I have asked thee but only of the *f.* and wind
16. for the *f.* came and consumed it
50. as the *f.* is greater than the smoke
6. 37. my spirit was greatly set on *f.* and in distress
7. 8. one only path between the *f.* and the water
8. 8. thy creature is preserved in *f.* and water
22. whose service is conversant in wind and *f.*
13. 4. the earth faileth when it feeleth the *f.*
10. only I saw as it had been a blast of *f.*
11. the blast of *f.* fell upon the multitude
27. there came as a blast of wind, and *f.* and storm
38. destroy them by the law, which is like to *f.*
14. 39. but the colour of the water was like *f.*
15. 23. the *f.* is gone forth from his wrath
41. *f.* hail, and flying swords, and many waters
61. thou as stubble, they shall be unto thee as *f.*
16. 4. a *f.* is sent among you, who may quench it?
6. or may any one quench the *f.* in the stubble?
9. *f.* shall go from his wrath, who may quench it?
15. the *f.* is kindled, and shall not be put out
53. for God shall burn coals of *f.* upon his head
73. they shall be tried as the gold in the *f.*
78. it is cast into the *f.* to be consumed therewith
Jud. 8. 27. for he hath not tried us in the *f.*
13. 13. they made a *f.* for a light, and stood round
16. 17. in putting *f.* and worms in their flesh
Esth. 16. 24. shall be destroyed with *f.* and sword
Wisd. 10. 6. who fled from the *f.* which fell down
13. 2. but deemed it either *f.* or wind, or swift air
16. 16. and through *f.* were they consumed
17. the *f.* had more force in the water that quench.
19. it burneth in water above the power of *f.*
22. but snow and ice endured the *f.* and melted not
27. that which was not destroyed of the *f.*
17. 5. no power of the *f.* might give them light
6. only there appeared a *f.* kindled of itself
18. 3. thou gavest them a burning pillar of *f.*
19. 20. the *f.* had power in the water forgetting
Eccl. 2. 5. for gold is tried in the *f.* men in adversity
3. 30. water will quench a flaming *f.*
7. 17. for the vengeance of ungodly is *f.* and worms
8. 3. and heap not wood upon his *f.*
10. lest thou be burnt with the flame of his *f.*
9. 8. for herewith love is kindled as a *f.*
11. 32. of a spark of *f.* an heap of coals is kindled
15. 16. he hath set *f.* and water before thee
16. 6. among the ungodly shall a *f.* be kindled
21. 9. the end is a flame of *f.* to destroy them
22. 24. as the vapour and smoke goeth before the *f.*
23. 16. a hot mind is a burning *f.* will not be quenched, never cease till he hath kindled a *f.*
28. 10. as the matter of the *f.* is, so it burneth
11. an hasty contention kindleth a *f.*
36. 9. let him be consumed by the rage of the *f.*
38. 28. the vapour of the *f.* wasteth his flesh
39. 26. water and *f.* are for the use of man's life
29. *f.* and death were created for vengeance
40. 30. but in his belly there shall burn a *f.*
43. 21. it burneth and consumeth the grass as *f.*
48. 1. then stood up Elias the prophet as *f.*
3. he also three times brought down *f.*
9. who was taken up in a whirlwind of *f.*
50. 9. as *f.* and incense in the censer, and as vessel
51. 4. from the choking of *f.* on every side; and from the midst of the *f.* which I kindled not
Bar. 4. 35. *f.* shall come on her from the Everlasting
6. 55. when *f.* falleth on the house of gods of wood
Dan. 3. 1. and they walked in the midst of the *f.*
2. opening his mouth in the midst of the *f.* said
26. the angel smote the flame of the *f.* out of oven
44. O ye *f.* and heat, bless ye the Lord
1 *Mac.* 1. 31. when taken spoils of city, he set it on *f.*

1 *Mac.* 1. 56. when rent books they burnt them with *f.*
5. 28. took all their spoils, and burnt city with *f.*
35. received spoils thereof, and burnt it with *f.*
68. Judas burnt their carved images with *f.*
6. 39. the mountains shined like lamps of *f.*
51. set their instruments to cast *f.* and stones
10. 84. the temple of Dagon he burnt with *f.*
16. 10. wherefore he burnt towers in Azotus with *f.*
2 *Mac.* 1. 18. keep it as the *f.* which was given us
19. the priests took the *f.* of the altar privily
20. did send of those priests that had hid it to the *f.* they told us they found no *f.* but thick water
22. this done, there was a great *f.* kindled
33. where the priests had hid *f.* water appeared
2. 1. to take the *f.* as it had been signified
10. the *f.* came down from heaven and consumed
7. 5. to be brought to the *f.* and fried in the pan
8. 33. Callisthenes that had set *f.* on the holy gates
9. 7. breathing out *f.* in his rage against the Jews
10. 3. striking stones, they took *f.* out of them
12. 6. burnt the haven, and set the boats on *f.*
9. set *f.* on the haven and navy, so that the light of the *f.* was seen at Jerusalem 240 furlongs off
13. 8. the altar whose *f.* and ashes were holy
14. 41. bade that *f.* should be brought to burn it

FIRES.

Jud. 7. 5. when they kindled *f.* on their towers
1 *Mac.* 12. 28. they kindled *f.* in their camp
2 *Mac.* 10. 36. and kindling *f.* burnt the blasphemers

FIRM.

Eccl. 43. 15. by his great power he maketh clouds *f.*

FIRMLY.

Esth. 13. 5. that our kingd. may not be *f.* established
Eccl. 42. 17. which the Almighty Lord *f.* settled

FIRMAMENT.

2 *Esd.* 4. 7. how many springs are above the *f.*
6. 4. before the measures of the *f.* were named
20. the books shall be opened before the *f.*
41. on second day thou madest the spirit of the *f.*
Eccl. 43. 1. the clear *f.* the beauty of heaven
Dan. 3. 34. blessed art thou in the *f.* of heaven

FIRST.

1 *Esd.* 1. 1. the fourteenth day of the *f.* month
2. 1. in the *f.* year of Cyrus king of the Persians
3. 10. the *f.* wrote, wine is the strongest
17. then began the *f.* who had spoken of wine
5. 53. from the *f.* day of the seventh month
57. in the *f.* day of the second month
6. 17. in the *f.* year that king Cyrus reigned
7. 10. Israel held the passover 14th day of *f.* month
9. 16. in the *f.* day of the tenth month they sat
17. was brought to an end the *f.* day of *f.* month
40. hear the law in the *f.* day of seventh month
45. for he sat honourably in the *f.* place in sight
2 *Esd.* 3. 12. they began to be more ungodly than *f.*
5. 42. even so there is no swiftness of the *f.*
6. 7. or when shall be the end of the *f.*?
8. Jacob's hand held *f.* the heel of Esau
38. O Lord, thou spakest the *f.* day and saidst thus
58. whom thou hast called thy *f.*-born
10. 10. for out of her came all at the *f.* others come
14. 45. the *f.* that thou hast written publish openly
Tob. 1. 6. with that which was *f.* shorn
7. the *f.* tenth of all increase I give to Aaron
5. 13. we offered the *f.*-born and the tenths
14. 5. they shall build a temple, but not like the *f.*
Jud. 2. 1. the two and twentieth day of the *f.* month
8. 29. this is not the *f.* day wherein thy wisdom
Esth. 11. 2. in the *f.* day of the month Nisan
Wisd. 6. 13. in making herself *f.* known to them
7. 1. offspring of him that was *f.* made of the earth
3. the *f.* voice which I uttered, was crying
10. 1. preserved the *f.* formed father of the world
13. 3. the *f.* author of beauty hath created them
18. 13. upon the destruction of the *f.*-born
Eccl. 4. 17. at the *f.* she will walk with him
6. 7. if thou wouldest get a friend, prove him *f.*
11. 7. blame not, understand *f.* and then rebuke
12. 17. thou shalt find him there *f.* tho' he pretend
17. 18. whom, being his *f.*-born, he nourisheth
19. 18. the fear of the Lord is the *f.* step
23. 23. *f.* she hath disobeyed the law of the Lord
31. 17. leave off *f.* for manners' sake, not unsatiable
18. reach not out thine hand *f.* of all
36. 12. Israel, whom thou hast named thy *f.*-born
1 *Mac.* 1. 1. he reigned in his stead, *f.* over Greece
2. 18. come thou *f.* and fulfil king's commandment
5. 40. if he pass over *f.* to us, we shall not be able
43. he went *f.* over to them, and people after him
7. 13. the Assideans were the *f.* that sought peace
43. Nicanor himself was *f.* slain in the battle
8. 24. if there come *f.* any war on the Romans
27. if war come *f.* on the nation of the Jews
10. 47. he was the *f.* that entreated of true peace
16. 6. he went *f.* over himself, and then the men
2 *Mac.* 2. 30. belonging to the *f.* author of the story
4. 40. began *f.* to offer violence, one Auranus leader
7. 2. but one of them that spake *f.* said thus
4. to cut out the tongue of him that spake *f.*
7. when the *f.* was dead, they brought the second
8. 23. himself leading the *f.* band, he joined battle

FIRST-FRUITS.

Tob. 1. 6. having the *f.* and tenths of increase
Jud. 11. 13. are resolved to spend the *f.* of the corn
Eccl. 7. 31. give priest the *f.* and trespass offering
35. 8. and diminish not the *f.* of thy hands
45. 20. he divided to him the *f.* of the increase
1 *Mac.* 3. 49. they brought the *f.* and the tithes

FISH.

2 *Esd.* 5. 7. the Sodomitish sea shall cast out *f.*
Tob. 6. 2. to wash himself, a *f.* leaped out of the river
3. the angel said to him, take the *f.* and the young man laid hold of the *f.* and drew it to land
4. open the *f.* and take the heart and the liver
5. when they had roasted the *f.* they did eat it
6. to what use is the heart, liver, and gall of the *f.*?
16. lay on them some of the heart and liver of the *f.*
8. 2. put the heart and the liver of the *f.* thereon
11. 4. take in thine hand the gall of the *f.*

FISHES.

2 *Esd.* 6. 47. that it should bring forth fowls and *f.*
16. 12. the *f.* thereof are troubled before the Lord

Wisd. 19. 10. how the river cast up frogs instead of *f.*

FIT.

Wisd. 13. 11. a vessel *f.* for the service of man's life
Eccl. 33. 28. set him to work as is *f.* for him
Sus. 15. it fell out as they watched a *f.* time
2 *Mac.* 2. 29. must seek *f.* things for adorning thereof
3. 37. who might be a *f.* man to be sent again
4. 19. thought *f.* not to bestow on the sacrifice

FITTING.

2 *Mac.* 15. 38. if done well, and as is *f.* the story

FIVE.

Jud. 7. 30. Ozias said, let us yet endure *f.* days
8. 9. had sworn to deliver the city after *f.* days
Eccl. 17. 5. the use of the *f.* operations of the Lord
2 *Mac.* 2. 23. being declared by Jason in *f.* books
10. 29. *f.* comely men upon horses appeared

FLAME.

2 *Esd.* 4. 48. when the *f.* was gone by, I looked
Wisd. 16. 18. sometimes the *f.* was mitigated
Eccl. 8. 10. lest thou be burnt with the *f.* of his fire
21. 9. the end of them is a *f.* of fire to destroy
28. 22. nor shall they be burnt with the *f.* thereof
45. 19. to consume them with the fiery *f.*
Dan. 3. 24. so that *f.* streamed forth above furnace
26. the angel smote the *f.* of fire out of the oven
66. out of midst of the burning *f.* delivered us
1 *Mac.* 2. 59. by believing were saved out of the *f.*
2 *Mac.* 1. 32. this done, there was kindled a *f.*

FLAMES.

Wisd. 17. 5. nor could the bright *f.* of the stars
19. 21. on the other side, the *f.* wasted not the flesh

FLAMING.

2 *Esd.* 13. 10. out of his lips he sent a *f.* breath
11. the *f.* breath fell with violence on multitude
Eccl. 3. 30. water will quench a *f.* fire

FLAT.

1 *Esd.* 8. 91. lying *f.* on the ground before the temple
1 *Mac.* 4. 40. they fell down *f.* to the ground
2 *Mac.* 10. 4. they fell *f.* and besought the Lord
13. 12. lying *f.* on the ground three days long

FLATTER.

1 *Esd.* 4. 31. the king was fain to *f.* to be reconciled
Wisd. 14. 17. they might *f.* him that was absent

FLED.

2 *Esd.* 8. 53. corruption is *f.* into hell to be forgotten
10. 3. I rose up by night and *f.* and came hither
14. 18. truth is *f.* far away, leasing is at hand
Tob. 1. 18. when he was come, and *f.* from Judea
21. they *f.* into the mountains of Ararath
2. 8. this man is not yet afraid who *f.* away
8. 3. he *f.* into the utmost parts of Egypt
Jud. 5. 8. they *f.* into Mesopotamia, and sojourned
10. 12. I am of the Hebrews, and am *f.* from them
11. 3. but tell me why art thou *f.* from them?
16. knowing this I am *f.* from their presence
15. 2. they *f.* into every way of the plain
Wisd. 10. 6. who *f.* from fire, which fell on cities
10. when righteous *f.* from his brother's wrath
1 *Mac.* 2. 28. he and his sons *f.* to the mountains
43. also all they that *f.* for persecution joined
4. 14. heathen being discomfited *f.* into the plain
5. 9. but they *f.* to the fortress of Dathema
7. 32. and the rest *f.* into the city of David
44. they cast away their weapons and *f.*
9. 18. Judas was killed, and the remnant *f.*
33. they *f.* into the wilderness of Thecoe
10. 49. Demetrius' host *f.* Alexander followed
64. when his accusers saw, they *f.* all away
83. the horsemen being scattered *f.* to Azotus
84. them that were *f.* into it he burnt with fire
11. 16. Alexander *f.* to Arabia, there to be defended
46. wherefore the king *f.* into the court
55. against Demetrius, who turned his back and *f.*
69. all that were of Jonathan's side *f.*
15. 11. he *f.* to Dora, which lieth by the sea side
21. fellows that have *f.* from their country to you
37. in the mean time *f.* Tryphon to Orthosias
16. 10. so they *f.* to the towers in the field
2 *Mac.* 5. 5. city taken, Menelaus *f.* into the castle
7. *f.* again into the country of the Ammonites
8. 13. they that were fearful *f.* away
33. Callisthenes, who was *f.* into a little house
10. 18. were *f.* together into two very strong castles
32. as for Timotheus, he *f.* into a strong hold
11. 12. Lysias *f.* away shamefully, and escaped
12. 6. and those that *f.* thither, he slew
22. the enemies *f.* amain, one running this way
35. smote his shoulder, so that Gorgias *f.* to Marisa
14. 14. the heathen that had *f.* out of Judea

FLEE.

2 *Esd.* 2. 36. *f.* the shadow of this world
14. 15. and haste thee to *f.* from these times
Tob. 6. 17. the devil shall smell it and *f.* away
Jud. 14. 3. they shall *f.* before your face
Wisd. 1. 5. for holy spirit of discipline will *f.* deceit
Eccl. 21. 2. *f.* from sin as from the face of a serpent
Bar. 6. 55. their priests will *f.* away and escape
1 *Mac.* 1. 53. wherever they could *f.* for succour
4. 5. for, said he, these fellows *f.* from us
9. 10. God forbid that I should *f.* from them
10. 43. that *f.* to the temple at Jerusalem
73. where there is not a place to *f.* unto
2 *Mac.* 4. 26. Jason was compelled to *f.* to Ammon.
42. and all of them they forced to *f.*
9. 4. disgrace done to him by those that made him *f.*

FLESH.

Jud. 2. 3. then they decreed to destroy all *f.*
14. 10. he circumcised the foreskin of his *f.*
16. 17. in putting fire and worms in their *f.*
Wisd. 7. 2. I was fashioned to be *f.* in ten months
12. 5. and those devourers of man's *f.*
19. 21. flames wasted not the *f.* of the living things
Eccl. 1. 10. she is with all *f.* according to his gift
13. 16. all *f.* consorteth according to kind
14. 17. all *f.* waxeth old as a garment
18. so is the generation of *f.* and blood
17. 4. he put the fear of man upon all *f.*
31. and *f.* and blood will imagine evil
18. 13. but the mercy of the Lord is upon all *f.*
23. 6. let not the lust of the *f.* take hold of me
16. a fornicator in the body of his *f.*

Eccl. 25. 26. cut her off from thy *f.* and give her bill
28. 5. if he that is *f.* nourish hatred, who will entreat
17. the stroke of the whip maketh marks in the *f.*
31. 1. watching for riches consumeth the *f.*
38. 28. the vapour of the fire wasteth his *f.*
39. 19. the works of all *f.* are before him
40. 8. such things happen to all *f.* man and beast
41. 3. the sentence of the Lord over all *f.*
44. 18. that all *f.* should perish no more by the flood
20. he established the covenant in his *f.*
45. 1. who found favour in the sight of all *f.*
Bar. 2. 3. that a man should eat the *f.* of his son
Bel 5. living God who hath sovereignty over all *f.*
1 *Mac.* 7. 17. *f.* of thy saints have they cast out
2 *Mac.* 6. 21. besought him to bring *f.* of his own provision, and make as if he did eat the *f.*
7. 1. compelled against law to taste swine's *f.*
9. 9. while he lived in pain, his *f.* fell away

FLESHLY.

Esth. 14. 10. and to magnify a *f.* king for ever

FLESHY.

Eccl. 17. 16. nor could they make *f.* hearts for stony

FLEW.

2 *Esd.* 11. 5. lo, the eagle *f.* with her feathers
13. 6. he had graved a mountain, and *f.* up upon it

FLIES.

Wisd. 16. 9. for them the bitings of *f.* killed
19. 10. how the ground brought forth *f.*

FLIGHT.

2 *Esd.* 5. 6. the fowls shall take their *f.* away
1 *Mac.* 4. 20. that the Jews had put their host to *f.*
35. now when Lysias saw his army put to *f.*
5. 60. that Joseph and Azarias were put to *f.*
6. 5. that the armies against Judea were put to *f.*
10. 72. thy fathers have been twice put to *f.*
11. 15. king Ptolemee met him, and put him to *f.*
72. he put them to *f.* and so they ran away
16. 8. Cendebeus and his host were put to *f.*
2 *Mac.* 8. 6. put to *f.* no small number of enemies
24. by help of the Almighty they put all to *f.*
9. 2. Antiochus being put to *f.* returned with shame
11. 11. and they put all the others to *f.*
12. 27. after he had put to *f.* and destroyed them
37. rushing unawares he put them to *f.*

FLINT.

1 *Mac.* 10. 73. where is neither stone nor *f.* nor place

FLINTY.

Wisd. 11. 4. water was given them out of *f.* rock

FLOCK.

2 *Esd.* 5. 18. leaveth his *f.* in the hands of wolves
15. 10. my people is led as a *f.* to the slaughter
Tob. 7. 8. after they had killed a ram of the *f.*
Bar. 4. 26. were taken away as *f.* caught of enemies

FLOCKS.

Jud. 2. 27. he destroyed their *f.* and herds
3. 3. our *f.* and herds lie before thy face
2 *Mac.* 14. 14. the heathen came to Nicanor by *f.*

FLOCKING.

2 *Mac.* 3. 18. others ran *f.* out of their houses
14. 23. sent away people that came *f.* to him

FLOOD.

2 *Esd.* 3. 9. thou broughtest the *f.* on those that dwelt
10. as death was to Adam, so the *f.* to these
13. 44. held still the *f.* till they were passed over
Esth. 11. 10. from a little fountain a great *f.*
Wisd. 10. 4. the earth being drowned with the *f.*
Eccl. 21. 13. knowledge shall abound like a *f.*
39. 22. his blessing watered the dry land as a *f.*
40. 10. and for their sakes came the *f.*
44. 17. therefore was he left when the *f.* came
18. that all flesh should perish no more by the *f.*
47. 14. and as a *f.* filled with understanding
1 *Mac.* 6. 11. how great a *f.* of misery wherein I am
7. 8. Bacchides, who ruled beyond the *f.*

FLOODS.

2 *Esd.* 4. 15. the *f.* of the sea also took counsel
17. the thought of the *f.* of the sea came to nought
19. the sea also hath his place to bear his *f.*
21. like as the sea is given to his *f.* even so
16. 60. that the *f.* might pour down from rocks
Wisd. 5. 22. and the *f.* shall cruelly drown them

FLOOR, S.

2 *Esd.* 4. 32. how great a *f.* shall they fill
35. when cometh the fruit of the *f.* of our reward?
39. that the *f.* of the righteous are not filled
Jud. 14. 15. he found him cast upon the *f.* dead

FLOTES.

1 *Esd.* 5. 55. should be brought by *f.* to hav. of Joppe

FLOUR.

Eccl. 35. 2. that requites good, offereth fine *f.*
38. 11. give sweet savour, a memorial of fine *f.*
39. 26. *f.* of wheat for the use of man's life
Bel 3. spent on him twelve great measures of fine *f.*
2 *Mac.* 1. 8. we offered sacrifices and fine *f.*

FLOURISH.

2 *Esd.* 6. 28. as for faith, it shall *f.* corrupt. overcome
Wisd. 4. 4. though they *f.* in branches for a time
Eccl. 1. 18. making peace and perfect health to *f.*
11. 22. suddenly he maketh his blessing to *f.*
39. 14. *f.* as a lily ‖ 46. 12. let their bones *f.* 49. 10.

FLOW.

2 *Esd.* 3. 33. and I see that they *f.* in wealth

FLOWED, ETH.

2 *Esd.* 1. 20. and waters *f.* out to your fill
Eccl. 46. 8. that *f.* with milk and honey, *Bar.* 1. 20.

FLOWING.

2 *Esd.* 2. 19. as many fountains *f.* with milk
Wisd. 7. 25. a pure influence *f.* from the glory

FLOWN.

Wisd. 5. 11. as when a bird hath *f.* through the air

FLOWER.

2 *Esd.* 15. 50. the glory shall be dried up as a *f.*
Wisd. 2. 7. let no *f.* of the spring pass by us
Eccl. 26. 19. keep the *f.* of thine age sound
42. 9. lest she pass away the *f.* of her age
50. 8. as the *f.* of roses in the spring of the year
51. 15. even from the *f.* till the grape was ripe

FLOWERS.

2 *Esd.* 5. 24. and of all the *f.* thereof, one lily
36. make me the withered *f.* green again
6. 3. he said to me, before the fair *f.* were seen
44. there were *f.* of unchangeable colour

2 *Esd.* 9. 17. as the *f.* be, such are the colours also
24. but go into a field of *f.* eat only *f.* of field, taste no flesh, drink no wine, but eat *f.* only
26. and there I sat among the *f.* and did eat
12. 51. I did eat only in those days of the *f.*

FLUTES.

1 *Esd.* 5. 2. musical instruments, tabrets and *f.*

FLY.

Wisd. 5. 21. as from a bow shall they *f.* to the mark
Eccl. 11. 3. the bee is little among such as *f.*
43. 14. through this the clouds *f.* forth as fowls

FLYING.

Eccl. 11. 10. neither shalt thou escape by *f.*

FODDER.

Eccl. 33. 24. *f.* a wand, and burdens are for the ass
38. 26. and he is diligent to give the kine *f.*

FOLDED.

Jud. 10. 5. so she *f.* all these things together

FOLLOW.

2 *Esd.* 7. 35. work shall *f.* and reward be shewed
Tob. 4. 5. *f.* not the ways of unrighteousness
Jud. 11. 6. if thou *f.* the words of thy handmaid
Eccl. 5. 2. *f.* not thine own mind and thy strength
11. 10. if thou *f.* after, thou shalt not obtain
23. 28. it is great glory to *f.* the L. to be received
27. 17. if bewrayest secrets, *f.* no more after him, 20.
46. 10. Israel might see that it is good to *f.* the L.
Dan. 3. 18. and now we *f.* thee with all our heart
1 *Mac.* 2. 27. is zealous of the law, let him *f.* me
2 *Mac.* 2. 28. to *f.* the rules of an abridgment
8. 11. the vengeance that was to *f.* on him
11. 29. to return home and to *f.* your own business

FOLLOWED.

Jud. 15. 13. the men of Israel *f.* in their army
Esth. 15. 4. the other *f.* bearing up her train
Eccl. 46. 6. because he *f.* the mighty One
51. 18. and earnestly I *f.* that which is good
2 *Mac.* 4. 16. whose custom they *f.* so earnestly
8. 36. because they *f.* the laws he gave them

FOLLOWEST.

Eccl. 27. 8. if thou *f.* righteousness, shalt obtain her

FOLLOWETH.

2 *Esd.* 6. 7. and the beginning of it that *f.* 9.
Eccl. 29. 19. and *f.* other men's business for gain
31. 5. he that *f.* corruption, shall have enough
34. 2. is like him that *f.* after the wind
2 *Mac.* 9. 25. to whom I have written as *f*

FOLLOWING.

1 *Esd.* 2. 16. wrote to him these letters *f.*
7. 1. *f.* the commandments of king Darius
2 *Esd.* 11. 13. so the next *f.* stood up and reigned
2 *Mac.* 4. 17. the time *f.* shall declare these things
9. 4. the judgment of God now *f.* him
12. 39. on the day *f.* as the use had been

FOLLY.

Eccl. 8. 15. thou shalt perish with him through *f.*
20. 31. better is he that hideth his *f.* than a man
47. 20. and thou wast grieved for thy *f.*
2 *Mac.* 4. 6. that Simon should leave his *f.*
40. a man far gone in years, and no less in *f.*

FOLLIES.

Eccl. 16. 23. a foolish man erring, imagineth *f.*
30. 11. give him no liberty, and wink not at his *f.*

FOOD.

1 *Esd.* 8. 79. to give us *f.* in the time of servitude
80. he made us gracious so that they gave us *f.*
Wisd. 16. 3. to the end that they desiring *f.*
20. thou feddest thy own people with angels' *f.*
Eccl. 37. 20. he shall be destitute of all *f.*

FOOL.

Eccl. 8. 17. consult not with a *f.* cannot keep counsel
18. 27. but a *f.* will not observe time
19. 11. a *f.* travaileth with a word, as a woman
12. as an arrow, so is a word within a *f.* belly
20. 7. a babbler and a *f.* will regard no time
14. the gift of a *f.* shall do thee no good
16. the *f.* saith, I have no friends, no thank for
20. rejected, when it cometh out of a *f.* mouth
21. 14. inner parts of a *f.* are like a broken vessel
16. talking of a *f.* is like a burden in the way
18. as a house destroyed, so is wisdom to a *f.*
23. a *f.* will peep in at the door into the house
22. 7. whoso teacheth a *f.* is as one that glueth
8. he that telleth a tale to a *f.* speaketh to one
11. weep for the *f.* he wants understanding, but the life of the *f.* is worse than death
12. but for a *f.* and an ungodly man, all his life
13. talk not much with a *f.* and go not to him
14. and what is the name thereof but a *f.*?
18. a fearful heart in the imagination of a *f.*
23. 14. so thou by thy custom become a *f.*
27. 11. but a *f.* changeth as the moon
31. 7. and every *f.* shall be taken therewith
30. drunkenness increaseth the rage of a *f.*

FOOLERIES.

Eccl. 22. 13. thou shalt never be defiled with his *f.*

FOOLISH.

2 *Esd.* 4. 19. it is a *f.* thought they have devised
10. 6. thou *f.* woman above all other, seest thou not?
Wisd. 3. 12. their wives are *f.* their children wicked
11. 15. for *f.* devices of their wickedness
15. 14. the enemies of thy people are more *f.*
19. 3. they added another *f.* device, pursued them
Eccl. 4. 27. be not an underling to a *f.* man
15. 7. but *f.* men shall not attain unto her
16. 23. a *f.* man erring, imagineth foolish follies
21. 22. a *f.* man's foot is soon in neighbour's house
22. 3. and a *f.* daughter is born to his loss
23. nor rich that is *f.* to be had in admiration
33. 5. the heart of the *f.* is like a cart wheel
50. 26. and that *f.* people that dwell in Sichem
2 *Mac.* 2. 32. it is *f.* to make a long prologue
14. 5. opportunity to further his *f.* enterprise

FOOLISHNESS.

Wisd. 10. 8. left behind them a memorial of their *f.*
Eccl. 16. 7. who fell in the strength of their *f.*
23. 8. the sinner shall be left in his *f.*
41. 15. a man that hideth his *f.* is better than
47. 23. Roboam, even the *f.* of the people
Bar. 3. 28. but they perished by their own *f.*

FOOLS.

Wisd. 5. 4. we *f.* accounted his life madness
15. 5. the sight enticeth *f.* to lust after it
Eccl. 20. 13. the graces of *f.* shall be poured out
21. 19. doctrine to *f.* is as fetters on the feet
26. the heart of *f.* is in their mouth
27. 13. the discourse of *f.* is irksome, their sport
34. 1. hopes vain and false, and dreams lift up *f.*
Sus. 48. are ye such *f.* ye sons of Israel?

FOOT.

2 *Esd.* 16. 69. consent to them, be trodden under *f.*
Jud. 6. 4. for we will tread them under *f.*
13. they left him at the *f.* of the hill
Wisd. 13. 18. which cannot set a *f.* forward
Eccl. 6. 36. let thy *f.* wear the steps of his door
9. 2. to a woman, to set her *f.* upon thy substance
21. 22. a foolish man's *f.* is soon in his neighb. house
40. 25. gold and silver make the *f.* stand sure
46. 8. of six hundred thousand people on *f.*
50. 15. he poured out at the *f.* of the altar
51. 15. my *f.* went the right way from my youth
Bar. 5. 6. for they departed from thee on *f.*
1 *Mac.* 4. 28. threescore thousand men of *f.*
5. 48. none do hurt, we will only pass through on *f.*
10. 72. that thy *f.* is not able to stand before us
2 *Mac.* 5. 21. to make the sea passable by *f.*
10. 26. and fell down at the *f.* of the altar

FOOTMEN.

1 *Esd.* 8. 51. I was ashamed to ask the king's *f.*
Jud. 1. 4. and for the setting in array of his *f.*
2. 5. of *f.* an hundred and twenty thousand
19. to cover the face of the earth with chosen *f.*
22. he took all his army, his horsemen, and *f.*
7. 20. both their *f.* chariots and horsemen
9. 7. they glory in the strength of their *f.*
1 *Mac.* 9. 4. they went to Berea with 20,000 *f.*
10. 82. Simon set his host against the *f.*
12. 49. then sent Tryphon an host of *f.* to Galilee
16. 5. a mighty great host of *f.* and horsemen
2 *Mac.* 11. 4. puffed up with his ten thousand *f.*
13. 2. having a Grecian power of *f.* 110,000

FOOTSTEPS.

Jud. 6. 4. their *f.* shall not be able to stand
Bel 19. and mark well whose *f.* are these
20. I see the *f.* of men, women, and children

FORBEAR.

2 *Esd.* 1. 9. how long shall *f.* them to whom done good
1 *Mac.* 2. 24. nor could he *f.* to shew his anger
2 *Mac.* 5. 25. did *f.* till the holy day of sabbath

FORBEARETH.

2 *Mac.* 6. 14. nations whom the Lord patiently *f.*

FORBID.

1 *Mac.* 2. 21. God *f.* that we should forsake the law
9. 10. God *f.* that I should do this thing

FORBIDDEN.

Jud. 11. 12. things that God hath *f.* them to eat
2 *Mac.* 12. 40. which is *f.* the Jews by the law

FORBIDDETH.

2 *Mac.* 6. 5. with profane things which the law *f.*

FORCE.

2 *Esd.* 7. 35. and the good deed shall be of *f.*
9. 37. the law perisheth not but remaineth in his *f.*
Jud. 9. 8. and bring down their *f.* in thy wrath
Wisd. 4. 4. through *f.* of wind shall be rooted out
16. 17. the fire had more *f.* in the water
18. 22. not with strength of body nor *f.* of arms
19. 13. with former signs by the *f.* of thunders
Eccl. 4. 26. and *f.* not the course of the river
39. 28. in destruction they pour out their *f.*
1 *Mac.* 6. 63. he fought, and took the city by *f.*
7. 25. that he was not able to abide their *f.*
27. Nicanor came to Jerusalem with great *f.*
12. 42. that Jonathan came with so great a *f.*
2 *Mac.* 5. 11. he took the city by *f.* of arms
10. 24. tho' as he would take Jewry by *f.* of arms
12. 35. taking hold of his coat, drew him by *f.*

FORCED.

Wisd. 14. 19. *f.* his skill to make the resemblance
Eccl. 31. 21. if thou hast been *f.* to eat, arise
2 *Mac.* 4. 42. and all of them they *f.* to flee

FORCES.

1 *Mac.* 2. 44. so they joined *f.* and smote sinful men
3. 27. he gathered all the *f.* of his realm
3. 34. he delivered to him the half of his *f.*
37. the king took half the *f.* that remained
42. saw that the *f.* did encamp themselves
4. 4. while the *f.* were dispersed from the camp
7. 2. that his *f.* had taken Antiochus and Lysias
9. 52. he put *f.* in them and provision of victuals
67. when he began to smite, and came up with *f.*
10. 36. enrolled amongst the king's *f.* about 30,000 of Jews as belongeth to all the king's *f.*
48. then gathered king Alexander great *f.*
11. 38. he sent away all his *f.* every one to his own place, wherefore the *f.* of his father hated him
43. to help me, for all my *f.* are gone from me
60. all the *f.* of Syria gathered themselves to him
12. 45. will give the rest of the strong holds and *f.*
14. 1. king Demetrius gathered his *f.* together
15. 10. at which time all the *f.* came together
12. he saw that his *f.* had forsaken him
2 *Mac.* 10. 24. a great multitude of foreign *f.*

FORCIBLY.

1 *Esd.* 4. 49. should *f.* enter into their doors
Tob. 1. 20. then all my goods were *f.* taken away

FORECASTETH.

Wisd. 17. 11. wickedness always *f.* grievous things

FOREFATHERS.

2 *Esd.* 4. 23. why law of *f.* is brought to nought?
Bar. 1. 19. brought our *f.* out of the land of Egypt
3. 5. remember not the iniquities of our *f.*
7. the iniquity of our *f.* that sinned before thee
2 *Mac.* 8. 19. what helps their *f.* had found

FOREFEET.

2 *Mac.* 3. 25. he smote at Heliodorus with his *f.*

FOREFRONT.

1 *Mac.* 4. 57. they decked also the *f.* of the temple

FOREIGN.

1 *Mac.* 15. 3. have gathered multitude of *f.* soldiers
2 *Mac.* 10. 24. had gathered multitude of *f.* forces

FOREKNOWLEDGE.

Jud. 9. 6. and thy judgments are in thy *f.*
11. 19. these were told me according to my *f.*

FORERUNNERS.

Wisd. 12. 8. didst send wasps, *f.* of thine host

FORESEETH.

Wisd. 8. 8. she *f.* signs and wonders, and events

FORESHEW.

Wisd. 18. 19. dreams that trouble them did *f.* this

FORE-SKIN.

Jud. 14. 10. Achior circumcised the *f.* of his flesh

FOREST.

2 *Esd.* 4. 13. I went into a *f.* the trees took counsel
1 *Mac.* 4. 38. shrubs growing in the courts as in a *f.*

FORE-WARD.

1 *Mac.* 9. 11. they that marched in the *f.* mighty men

FORGAT.

Wisd. 19. 20. the water *f.* his own quenching nature

FORGE.

Eccl. 51. 2. and from the lips that *f.* lies

FORGET.

1 *Esd.* 3. 22. they *f.* their love to friends and brethren
2 *Esd.* 16. 67. leave off sins, and *f.* your iniquities
Wisd. 16. 23. this did even *f.* his own strength
19. 4. made them *f.* things that had happened
Eccl. 7. 27. and *f.* not the sorrows of thy mother
11. 27. affliction of an hour make man *f.* pleasure
29. 15. *f.* not the friendship of thy surety
37. 6. *f.* not thy friend in thy mind, in thy riches
38. 21. *f.* it not for there is no turning again
1 *Mac.* 1. 49. to the end they might *f.* the law
2 *Mac.* 2. 2. charged them not to *f.* the commands

FORGETFUL.

Eccl. 23. 14. be not *f.* before them, and so become

FORGETFULNESS.

Wisd. 14. 26. *f.* of good turns reigned in all
16. 11. that not falling deep into *f.* be mindful
17. 3. were scattered under a dark vail of *f.*
Eccl. 11. 25. in prosperity there is a *f.* of affliction

FORGETTING.

Wisd. 19. 20. the fire *f.* his own virtue had power

FORGIVE.

2 *Esd.* 7. 69. being judge, if he should not *f.* them
Eccl. 16. 11. he is mighty to *f.* and pour out displeas.
28. 2. *f.* thy neighbour the hurt he hath done
Prayer of Manass. *f.* me, O Lord, *f.* me
1 *Mac.* 13. 39. as for any oversight, we *f.* it

FORGIVEN.

Eccl. 28. 2. so shall thy sins be *f.* when thou prayest
1 *Mac.* 15. 8. let it be *f.* thee from this time

FORGIVENESS.

Eccl. 28. 4. and doth he ask *f.* of his own sins?
Prayer of Manass. *f.* to them that have sinned

FOREGO.

Eccl. 7. 19. *f.* not a wise and good wom. is above gold

FORGOTTEN.

2 *Esd.* 1. 6. for they have *f.* me, and have offered
14. yet have you *f.* me, saith the Lord
8. 53. and corruption is fled into hell to be *f.*
12. 47. the mighty hath not *f.* you in temptation
Wisd. 2. 4. and our name shall be *f.* in time
Eccl. 13. 10. stand not far off, lest thou be *f.*
35. 7. the memorial thereof shall never be *f.*
44. 10. whose righteousness hath not been *f.*
Bar. 4. 8. ye have *f.* the everlasting God

FORLORN.

Jud. 9. 11. for thou art a protector of the *f.*
Esth. 14. 19. O mighty G. hear the voice of the *f.*

FORM.

Wisd. 11. 17. made the world of matter without *f.*
15. 5. so they desire the *f.* of a dead image

FORMED.

2 *Esd.* 6. 39. the sound of man's voice was not yet *f.*
Wisd. 10. 1. she preserved first *f.* father of world
13. 13. and *f.* it by the skill of his understanding
2 *Mac.* 7. 22. nor was it I that *f.* the members
23. the Creator, who *f.* the generation of man

FORMER.

1 *Esd.* 1. 24. they were written in *f.* times
Wisd. 19. 13. punishments came not without *f.* signs
Eccl. 21. 1. but ask pardon for thy *f.* sins
1 *Mac.* 4. 47. built a new altar according to the *f.*
10. 41. the officers payed not in, as in *f.* time
12. 3. ye should renew the league as in *f.* time
16. to renew the amity and the *f.* league
2 *Mac.* 7. 8. he received the next torment as *f.* did
14. 38. in the *f.* times when they mingled not
15. 8. help which in *f.* times they had received

FORMERLY.

2 *Mac.* 5. 18. had been *f.* wrapped in many sins

FORNICATION.

Wisd. 14. 12. was the beginning of spiritual *f.*

FORNICATOR.

Eccl. 23. 16. a *f.* in the body of his flesh, never ceases

FORSAKE.

2 *Esd.* 1. 25. ye have forsaken me, I will *f.* you also
3. 15. that thou wouldest never *f.* his seed
5. 18. *f.* us not as the shepherd that leaveth flock
10. 34. only *f.* me not, lest I die frustrate of my hope
12. 44. if thou *f.* us, how much better to be burnt
Jud. 7. 30. for he will not *f.* us utterly
Eccl. 4. 19. but if he go wrong she will *f.* him
7. 26. hast thou a wife after thy mind? *f.* her not
30. love him made thee, and *f.* not his ministers
9. 10. *f.* not an old friend, the new is not comparable
13. 4. if thou have nothing, he will *f.* thee
7. he will *f.* thee, and shake his head at thee
17. 18. giving him the light of love doth not *f.* him
25. return to the Lord, and *f.* thy sins
28. 23. such as *f.* the Lord shall fall into it
29. 14. but he that is impudent will *f.* him
35. 3. to *f.* unrighteousness, is a propitiation
1 *Mac.* 2. 21. God forbid we should *f.* the law
2 *Mac.* 1. 5. God never *f.* you in time of trouble
6. 16. tho' he punish, yet doth he never *f.* his people

FORSAKEN.

1 *Esd.* 8. 80. in bondage, we were not *f.* of our Lord
2 *Esd.* 1. 25. seeing you have *f.* me, I will forsake you
27. ye have not *f.* me, but your own selves
31. your new moons and circumcisions have I *f.*
2. 2. I am a widow and *f.* go your way, 4.
Wisd. 3. 10. the ungodly punished, have *f.* the Lord
Eccl. 2. 10. or did any abide in his fear, and was *f.*?
41. 8. woe to you ungodly men who have *f.* the law
51. 20. found in pureness, therefore shall I not be *f.*

Bar. 3. 12. thou hast *f.* the fountain of wisdom
4. 12. let none rejoice over me a widow, and *f.* of
Bel 38. nor hast thou *f.* them that seek thee
1 *Mac.* 7. 19. he took many of them that had *f.* him
10. 14. certain of those that had *f.* the law remained
15. 12. for he saw that his forces had *f.* him
2 *Mac.* 5. 20. as it was *f.* in wrath of the Almighty
7. 16. think not that our nation is *f.* of God

FORSAKER, S.

Dan. 3. 9. lawless enemies, most hateful *f.* of God
2 *Mac.* 5. 8. pursued, hated as a *f.* of the laws

FORSAKEST.

2 *Esd.* 12. 41. what have we done? that thou *f.* us

FORSAKETH.

Eccl. 3. 16. he that *f.* his father, is as a blasphemer

FORSOOK.

2 *Esd.* 3. 25. they that inhabited the city *f.* thee
8. 56. thought scorn of his law, and *f.* his ways
Wisd. 10. 13. when righteous was sold, she *f.* him not
Eccl. 17. 21. neither left, nor *f.* them, but spared
49. 4. for they *f.* the law of the Most High
1 *Mac.* 1. 15. and they *f.* the holy covenant
11. 12. and *f.* Alexander, so their hatred was known

FORSWEAR.

Wisd. 14. 28. or else lightly *f.* themselves

FORSWORE.

1 *Esd.* 1. 48. he *f.* himself and rebelled, hardening

FORTIFICATION.

1 *Mac.* 10. 11. to build with square stones for *f.*

FORTIFY.

1 *Mac.* 15. 39. commanded to *f.* the gates and tower

FORTIFIED.

Jud. 4. 5. they *f.* the villages that were in them
5. 1. Israel had *f.* all the tops of the high hills
Eccl. 48. 17. Ezekias *f.* his city and brought in
50. 1. and in his days *f.* the temple
4. took care of temple and *f.* city against besieging
1 *Mac.* 1. 34. they *f.* themselves therein
4. 61. they *f.* Bethsura to preserve it
5. 46. Ephron was a great city, very well *f.*
6. 26. the sanctuary and Bethsura have they *f.*
9. 52. he *f.* also the city of Bethsura and Gazara
13. 10. he *f.* Jerusalem round about
14. 33. *f.* the cities of Judea ‖ 34. he *f.* Joppa
37. he *f.* it for the safety of the country

FORTIFYING.

1 *Mac.* 10. 45. and for the *f.* thereof round about

FORTITUDE.

Wisd. 8. 7. she teacheth prudence, justice, and *f.*

FORTRESS.

Eccl. 50. 2. by him was built the high *f.* of the wall
1 *Mac.* 4. 41. to fight against those that were in the *f.*
5. 9. but they fled to the *f.* of Dathema
11. they are preparing to come and take the *f.*
29. and he went till he came to the *f.*
2 *Mac.* 10. 33. but they laid siege against the *f.*
12. 19. had left in the *f.* above 10,000 men
21. he sent baggage to a *f.* called Carnion

FORTRESSES.

1 *Mac.* 10. 12. the strangers that were in *f.* fled away
11. 41. those of the tower, and those in the *f.*
14. 42. to set them over the armour and the *f.*
15. 7. *f.* that thou hast built, let them remain

FORWARD.

1 *Esd.* 1. 27. the Lord is with me, hasting me *f.*
2 *Esd.* 3. 6. before ever the earth came *f.*
Esth. 13. 4. so as the unit. of kingdoms cannot go *f.*
Wisd. 13. 18. of that which cannot set a foot *f.*
14. 18. the artificer did help to set *f.* the ignorant
1 *Mac.* 1. 13. the people were so *f.* herein
2 *Mac.* 11. 10. thus they marched *f.* in armour
15. 25. then Nicanor came *f.* with trumpets

FORWARDNESS.

Wisd. 14. 17. by their *f.* they might flatter him

FOUGHT.

Wisd. 10. 20. magnified thy hand that *f.* for them
Eccl. 46. 6. because he *f.* in the sight of the Lord
1 *Mac.* 3. 2. they *f.* with cheerfulness the battle
12. and therewith he *f.* all his life long
5. 3. Judas *f.* against the children of Esau, 65.
7. so he *f.* many battles with them
21. where he *f.* many battles with the heathen
11. 41. cast them out, for they *f.* against Israel
55. the men of war *f.* against Demetrius
12. 13. the kings round about have *f.* against us
13. 47. so Simon *f.* no more against them
14. 32. Simon rose up, and *f.* for his nation
16. 2. we have *f.* against the enemies of Israel
2 *Mac.* 1. 12. he cast them out that *f.* within holy city
10. 17. they kept off all that *f.* on the wall
12. 36. when they had *f.* long, were weary
13. 22. the king *f.* with Judas, was overcome

FOUL.

1 *Esd.* 9. 6. because of the present *f.* weather
11. it is *f.* weather, so that we cannot stand
Wisd. 11. 6. a fountain troubled with *f.* blood
Eccl. 5. 14. for a *f.* shame is upon the thief
20. 24. a lie is a *f.* blot in a man

FOWLS.

2 *Esd.* 5. 6. the *f.* shall take their flight away
6. 47. that it should bring forth *f.* and fishes
Jud. 11. 7. *f.* of the air shall live by thy power
Esth. 16. 24. hateful to wild beasts and *f.* for ever
Wisd. 19. 11. they saw a new generation of *f.*
Eccl. 17. 4. and gave him dominion over beasts and *f.*
43. 14. treasures opened, and clouds fly forth as *f.*
Bar. 3. 17. they have had their pastime with *f.*
Dan. 3. 58. O all ye *f.* of the air, bless the Lord
2 *Mac.* 9. 15. to be devoured of *f.* and wild beasts
15. 33. they should give it by pieces to the *f.*

FOUND.

1 *Esd.* 1. 7. and to the people that was *f.* there
21. with Israel that were *f.* dwelling at Jerusalem
4. 42. we will give it, because thou art *f.* wisest
5. 39. was sought in the register, and was not *f.*
6. 22. if it be *f.* that the building was done
8. 4. he *f.* grace in his sight in all requests
42. when I had *f.* there none of the priests
53. and we *f.* him favourable unto us
2 *Esd.* 3. 34. thy name no where be *f.* but in Israel
4. 44. if I have *f.* favour in thy sight, and if it be
possible and I be meet therefore, 5. 56. | 6. 11.

2 *Esd.* 5. 10. shall be sought of many, and yet not be *f.*
6. 22. full store-houses shall suddenly be *f.* empty
8. 42. I said, if I have *f.* grace let me speak
12. 7. Lord, if I have *f.* grace before thy sight
14. 22. but I have *f.* grace before thee
Tob. 1. 18. he killed many, but the bodies were not *f.*
5. 4. he *f.* Raphael that was an angel
8. 13. the maid went in and *f.* them both asleep
Jud. 14. 15. *f.* Holofernes cast on the floor dead
Wisd. 1. 2. he will be *f.* of them that tempt him not
2. 11. what is feeble is *f.* to be nothing worth
3. 5. G. proved them and *f.* them worthy for himself
5. 10. as a ship, the trace thereof cannot be *f.*
11. when a bird hath flown no token of her way
to be *f.* no sign where she went is to be *f.*
6. 12. wisdom is glorious, *f.* of such as seek her
7. 29. compared with the light, she is *f.* before it
8. 11. I shall be *f.* of quick conceit in judgment
15. I shall be *f.* good among the multitude
10. 5. she *f.* out the righteous and preserved him
16. 9. nor was there *f.* any remedy for their life
Eccl. 6. 14. a faithful friend is a strong defence, he
that hath *f.* such an one hath *f.* a treasure
11. 19. whereas he saith, I have *f.* rest
18. 6. neither can the ground of them be *f.* out
28. he will give praise of him that *f.* her
21. 16. grace shall be *f.* in the lips of the wise
23. 12. God grant that it be not *f.* in Jacob
25. 9. well is him that hath *f.* prudence
29. 4. a thing lent them, reckoned it to be *f.*
6. and he will count as if he had *f.* it
31. 8. blessed is the rich that is *f.* without blemish
10. who hath been tried thereby and *f.* perfect
34. 8. the law shall be *f.* perfect without lies
36. 16. and let thy prophets be *f.* faithful
38. 33. shalt not be *f.* where parables are spoken
44. 5. such as *f.* out musical tunes, and recited
20. when he was proved, he was *f.* faithful
45. 1. who *f.* favour in the sight of all flesh
46. 15. by faithfulness he was *f.* a true prophet
51. 20. I directed my soul to her, *f.* her in pureness
Bar. 3. 15. who hath *f.* out her place?
30. who hath gone over the sea and *f.* her?
32. he hath *f.* her out with his understanding?
36. he hath *f.* out all the way of knowledge
Sus. 63. there was no dishonesty *f.* in her
1 *Mac.* 1. 23. he took the hidden treasures which he *f.*
56. they rent the books of the law which they *f.*
57. where was *f.* with any the book of testament
2. 46. what children soever they *f.* in Israel
52. was not Abraham *f.* faithful in temptation
63. and to-morrow he shall not be *f.*
4. 5. when he *f.* no man there, he sought him
5. 6. where he *f.* a mighty power with Timotheus
6. 63. where he *f.* Philip to be master of the city
10. 60. and he *f.* favour in their sight
11. 24. where he *f.* favour in his sight went to king
12. 21. it is *f.* in writing that the Lacedemonians
2 *Mac.* 1. 20. when they told us they *f.* no fire
2. 1. it is also *f.* in the records that Jeremy
7. 23. who *f.* out the beginning of all things
8. 19. what helps their forefathers had *f.*
10. 22. so he slew those that were *f.* traitors
12. 18. but as for Timotheus they *f.* him not
40. they *f.* things consecrated to idols of Jamnites

FOUNDATION.

1 *Esd.* 2. 18. the Jews do lay the *f.* of the temple
5. 57. they laid the *f.* of the house of God
2 *Esd.* 6. 15. the *f.* of the earth is understood
10. 53. where no *f.* of any building was
15. 12. the *f.* of it shall be smitten with plague
16. 15. till it consume the *f.* of the earth
Jud. 1. 3. the breadth thereof in the *f.* 60 cubits
Wisd. 4. 3. brood of ungodly shall not lay fast *f.*
19. and he shall shake them from the *f.*
Eccl. 1. 15. she hath built an everlasting *f.*
50. 2. by him was built from the *f.* the height

FOUNDATIONS.

1 *Esd.* 6. 11. and lay the *f.* of these works
20. laid the *f.* of the house of the Lord
2 *Esd.* 6. 2. or ever the *f.* of Paradise were laid
10. 27. a large place shewed itself from the *f.*
15. 23. fire hath consumed the *f.* of the earth
Jud. 16. 15. mountains shall be moved from their *f.*
Eccl. 10. 16. destroyed them to the *f.* of the earth
16. 19. the *f.* of the earth shall be shaken

FOUNDING.

2 *Mac.* 2. 13. how he *f.* a library gathered the acts

FOUNTAIN.

Jud. 7. 3. they camped in the valley by the *f.*
7. he came to the *f.* of their waters and took them
12. let thy servants get the *f.* of water
12. 7. she washed herself in a *f.* of water by camp
Esth. 10. 6. a little *f.* became a river, there was light
11. 10. as it were from a little *f.* was a flood
Wisd. 11. 6. instead of a *f.* of a running river
Eccl. 1. 5. the word of God is the *f.* of wisdom
21. 13. his counsel is like a pure *f.* of life
26. 12. as a traveller, when he hath found a *f.*
Bar. 3. 12. thou hast forsaken the *f.* of wisdom

FOUNTAINS.

2 *Esd.* 2. 19. as many *f.* flowing with milk and honey
6. 24. the springs of the *f.* shall stand still
14. 47. for in them is the *f.* of wisdom
Jud. 6. 11. they came to the *f.* under Bethulia
7. 17. and they took the *f.* of the waters
Dan. 3. 55. O ye *f.* praise ye the Lord, praise for ever

FOUR.

2 *Esd.* 3. 19. thy glory went through *f.* gates of fire
6. 21. untimely children of three or *f.* months old
11. 39. art thou not it that remainest of the *f.* beasts
12. 2. and the *f.* wings appeared no more
21. *f.* shall be kept till their end begin to approach
13. 5. from the *f.* winds of the heaven to subdue
16. 29. there are left three or *f.* olives, 31.
Wisd. 18. 24. in the *f.* rows of the stones was glory
1 *Mac.* 11. 57. thee ruler over the *f.* governments
13. 28. for his mother, and his *f.* brethren
2 *Mac.* 8. 21. he divided his army into *f.* parts

FOURTEEN.

Tob. 8. 19. he kept the wedding-feast *f.* days
20. till the *f.* days of the marriage expired

Tob. 10. 7. till *f.* days of the wedding were expired

FOURTEENTH.

1 *Esd.* 1. 1. the *f.* day of the first month, 7. 10.
Esth. 10. 13. the *f.* and fifteenth day of same month
13. 6. the *f.* day of the twelfth month Adar

FOURTH.

Jud. 12. 10. in the *f.* day Holofernes made a feast
Esth. 11. 1. in the *f.* year of the reign of Ptolemeus
Eccl. 26. 5. and for the *f.* I was sore afraid
2 *Mac.* 7. 13. they mangled the *f.* in like manner

FORTY.

2 *Esd.* 14. 23. that they seek thee not for *f.* days
36. let no man seek after me these *f.* days
42. they sat *f.* days, and they wrote in the day
44. in *f.* days they wrote 204 books
45. when the *f.* days were fulfilled
Bel 3. were spent on him every day *f.* sheep

FRAMED.

2 *Mac.* 15. 39. so speech finely *f.* delighteth

FRANKINCENSE.

Eccl. 24. 15. as the fume of *f.* in the tabernacle
39. 14. and give ye a sweet savour as *f.*
50. 8. as the branches of the *f.* tree in summer

FRANTIC.

Eccl. 4. 30. be not *f.* among thy servants

FRAYETH.

Eccl. 22. 20. casteth a stone at birds, *f.* them away

FREE.

1 *Esd.* 2. 9. with many *f.* gifts of a great number
4. 53. all that went should have *f.* liberty
Jud. 4. 14. with vows and *f.* gifts of the people
16. 18. they offered their *f.* offerings and gifts
23. she waxed old, and made her maid *f.*
Wisd. 7. 23. kind to man, stedfast, sure, *f.* from care
Eccl. 10. 25. they that are *f.* shall do service
Sus. 53. and thou hast let the guilty go *f.*
1 *Mac.* 10. 29. I *f.* you, and for your sakes I release
31. let Jerusalem also be holy and *f.*
39. I give it as a *f.* gift to the sanctuary
11. 28. that he would make Judea *f.* from tribute
15. 7. let them be *f.* and all the armour remain

FREED.

Eccl. 26. 29. an huckster shall not be *f.* from sin
2 *Mac.* 2. 22. they *f.* the city and upheld the laws

FREELY.

Esth. 16. 19. publish that the Jews may *f.* live
1 *Mac.* 10. 33. I *f.* set at liberty every one

FREEDOM.

1 *Esd.* 4. 49. he wrote concerning their *f.*
62. because he had given them *f.* and liberty
1 *Mac.* 10. 34. *f.* for all the Jews in my realm

FREE-*man.*

1 *Esd.* 3. 19. mind of bond-man and *f.-man* all one

FREE-*woman.*

1 *Mac.* 2. 11. of a *f-woman* she is become bond-slave

FRIED.

2 *Mac.* 7. 5. he commanded him to be *f.* in the pan

FRIEND.

Wisd. 1. 16. they thought to have it their *f.*
Eccl. 6. 1. instead of a *f.* become not an enemy
7. if thou wouldst get a *f.* prove him first
8. for some man is a *f.* for his own occasion
9. there is a *f.* who being turned to enmity
10. again, some *f.* is a companion at the table
14. a faithful *f.* is a strong defence
16. a faithful *f.* is the medicine of life
7. 12. devise not a lie, nor do the like to thy *f.*
18. change not a *f.* for any good by no means
9. 10. forsake not an old *f.* for the new is not comparable, a new *f.* is as new wine
12. 8. a *f.* cannot be known in prosperity
9. but in his adversity even a *f.* will depart
14. 13. do good unto thy *f.* before thou die
19. 8. whether to *f.* or foe, talk not of lives
13. admonish a *f.* it may be he hath not done it
14. admonish thy *f.* it may be he hath not said it
15. admonish a *f.* for many times it is a slander
20. 23. there is that promiseth to his *f.*
22. 20. he that upbraideth his *f.* breaks friendship
21. though thou drewest a sword at thy *f.*
22. if thou hast opened thy mouth against thy *f.*
for these things every *f.* will depart
25. I will not be ashamed to defend a *f.*
27. 16. and shall never find a *f.* to his mind
17. love thy *f.* and be faithful unto him
29. 10. lose money for thy brother and thy *f.*
37. 1. every *f.* saith, I am his *f.* also, but there is a
f. who is only a *f.* in name
2. when a companion and *f.* is turned an enemy
4. which rejoiceth in the prosperity of a *f.*
5. a companion which helpeth his *f.* for the belly
6. forget not thy *f.* in thy mind when in riches
40. 23. a *f.* and companion never meet amiss
41. 18. be ashamed before thy partner and *f.*
1 *Mac.* 7. 8. chose Bacchides a *f.* of the king
10. 16. we will make him our *f.* and confederate
19. a man of great power, and meet to be our *f.*
20. we ordain thee to be called the king's *f.*
13. 36. to Simon, high-priest and *f.* of king's
15. 32. Athenobius the king's *f.* came to Jerusalem
2 *Mac.* 7. 24. that he would take him for his *f.*
11. 14. that he must needs be a *f.* to them

FRIENDS.

1 *Esd.* 3. 22. they forget their love to *f.*
8. 13. the gifts which I and my *f.* have vowed
26. honoured me in sight of all his *f.* and nobles
2 *Esd.* 5. 9. and all *f.* shall destroy one another
6. 24. at that time *f.* shall fight one against another
Esth. 16. 5. put in trust to manage their *f.* affairs
14. he thought, finding us destitute of *f.*
Wisd. 7. 14. which they that use, become *f.* of God
27. she maketh them *f.* of God and prophets
19. 14. but these brought *f.* into bondage
Eccl. 6. 5. sweet language will multiply *f.*
13. separate from enemies, take heed of thy *f.*
13. 21. a rich man falling, is held up of his *f.*
20. 16. the fool saith, I have no *f.* I have no thank
28. 9. a sinful man disquieteth *f.* and makes debate
30. 3. and before his *f.* he shall rejoice of him
6. and one that shall requite kindness to his *f.*
41. 22. be ashamed of upbraiding speeches before *f.*
42. 3. be not ashamed of the gift of the heritage of *f.*

Sus. 33. therefore her f. and all that saw her wept
Bel 2. Daniel was honoured above all his f.
1 Mac. 2. 18. thou shalt be in number of king's f.
39. Mattathias and his f. understood thereof
45. Mattathias and his f. went round about
3.38. Nicanor, Gorgias, mighty men of the king's f.
6. 10. wherefore he called for all his f.
14. then called he for Philip one of his f.
28. the king gathered together all his f.
58. now therefore let us be f. with these men
7. 6. Judas and his brethren have slain all thy f.
15. we will not procure harm of you nor your f.
8. 12. with their f. and such as relied on them
20. we be registered your confederates and f.
31. why hast thou made thy yoke heavy on our f.
9. 26. they made inquiry and search for Judas' f.
28. for this cause all Judas' f. came together
35. had sent to pray his f. the Nabathites
39. the bridegroom came forth and his f.
10. 60. who gave them and their f. silver
65. so the king wrote him among his chief f.
11. 26. promoted him in the sight of all his f.
27. gave him pre-eminence among his chief f.
33. to do good to the Jews, who are our f.
57. appoint thee to be one of the king's f.
12. 14. our confederates and f. in these wars
43. Tryphon commended him to all his f.
14. 39. Demetrius made him one of his f.
40. the Romans had called the Jews their f.
15. 17. the Jews' ambassadors, our f. came to us
28. he sent to him Athenobius one of his f.
2 Mac. 1. 14. came and his f. that were with him
3. 31. certain of Heliodorus' f. prayed Onias
8. 9. choosing Nicanor one of his special f.
10. 13. whereupon being accused of the king's f.
14. 11. others of the king's f. being maliciously set

FRIENDLY.
Wisd. 19. 15. because they used strangers not f.
Eccl. 4. 8. and give him a f. answer with meekness
1 Mac. 7. 27. he sent deceitfully with f. words
2 Mac. 12. 31. desiring them to be f. still to them

FRIENDSHIP.
Wisd. 8. 18. great pleasure it is to have her f.
Eccl. 6.17. whoso feareth L. shall direct his f. aright
22. 20. he that upbraids his friend, breaks f.
29. 15. forget not the f. of thy surety
1 Mac. 10. 20. to take our part, and keep f. with us
26. whereas you have continued in our f.
12. 1. to confirm and renew the f. with them
3. sent us to the end you should renew the f.
8. declaration was made of the league and f.
10. to send for renewing of brotherhood and f.
14. 18. they wrote in tables of brass to renew f.
22. Jews came to renew f. they had with us
15. 17. the Jews came to us to renew the old f.
2 Mac. 6. 22. for the old f. with them find favour

FROCK.
Eccl. 40. 4. to him that is clothed with a linen f.

FROGS.
Wisd. 19. 10. a multitude of f. instead of fishes

FRONTIERS.
Jud. 3. 8. yet he did cast down their f. and groves

FROST.
Wisd. 16. 29. shall melt away as the winter's hoar f.
Bar. 2. 25. they are cast out to the f. of the night
Dan. 3. 50. O ye f. and snow, bless ye the Lord

FROTH.
Wisd. 5. 14. like a thin f. that is driven away

FROWARD.
Wisd. 1. 3. for f. thoughts separate from God
Eccl. 36. 20. a f. heart causeth heaviness

FRUIT.
2 Esd. 3. 20. thy law might bring forth f. in them
33. reward appeareth not, labour hath no f.
4. 31. ponder now how great f. of wickedness
35. when cometh the f. of the floor of our reward
6. 44. there was great and innumerable f.
8. 6. give us seed, that there may come f. of it
10. milk to be given, which is the f. of the breasts
9. 31. I sow my law in you, it shall bring forth f.
32. though the f. of thy law did not perish
10. 12. because I have lost the f. of my womb
14. even so the earth also hath given her f.
11. 42. the dwellings of them that brought forth f.
16.25. trees shall give f. and who shall gather them?
Wisd. 3. 13. she shall have f. in the visitation of souls
15. for glorious is the f. of good labours
4. 5. their f. unprofitable, not ripe to eat
10. 7. plants bearing f. that never come to ripeness
Eccl. 6. 3. lose thy f. and leave thyself a dry tree
11. 3. but her f. is the chief of sweet things
19. 19. shall receive f. of the tree of immortality
23. 25. her branches shall bring forth no f.
24. 17. my flowers are the f. of honour and riches
27. 6. the f. declares if the tree have been dressed
50. 10. as a fair olive-tree budding forth f.
1 Mac. 10. 30. the half of the f. of the trees
14. 8. and the trees of the field gave their f.

FRUITS.
2 Esd. 2. 18. twelve trees, laden with divers f.
16. 46. strangers shall reap their f. and spoil goods
Tob. 5. 13. we offered the tenths of the f.
Wisd. 16. 19. it might destroy the f. of an unjust land
22. fire did destroy the f. of the enemies
26. the growing of f. that nourisheth man
Eccl. 6. 19. come to her and wait for her good f. for thou shalt eat of her f. right soon
24. 19. come and fill yourselves with my f.
25. and as Tigris in the time of the new f.
37. 23. and the f. of his understanding fail not
1 Mac. 11. 34. king received out of the f. of the earth

FRUITFUL.
2 Esd. 1. 34. and your children shall not be f.
15. 62. thy f. trees shall they burn up with fire
Eccl. 26. 20. thou hast gotten a f. possession
40. 27. the fear of the Lord is a f. garden

FRUITLESS.
Wisd. 15. 4. nor an image the painter's f. labour

FRUSTRATE.
2 Esd. 10. 34. forsake me not, lest I die f. of hope
Jud. 11. 11. not defeated, and f. of his purpose

FUGITIVE.
2 Mac. 8. 35. he came like a f. servant to Antioch

FUGITIVES.
Jud. 16. 12. and have wounded them as f. children
Wisd. 19. 3. and they pursued them as f.

FULL.
1 Esd. 1. 23. with an heart f. of godliness
58. until the f. term of seventy years
2 Esd. 3. 3. I began to speak words f. of fear
4. 27. for this world is f. of unrighteousness
38. I said, even we all are f. of impiety
6. 22. f. store-houses suddenly be found empty
7. 6. a city is set on a field, f. of all good things
12. entrances of this world were f. of sorrow
25. and for the f. are the f. things
10. 7. how that Sion our mother is f. of heaviness
12. 2. their kingdom was small and f. of uproar
14. 39. and behold, he reached me a f. cup
15. 34. the clouds are f. of wrath and storm
40. the clouds shall be lifted up f. of wrath
41. and many waters, that all fields may be f.
16. 32. all her paths shall grow f. of thorns
Esth. 15. 14. and thy countenance is f. of grace
Wisd. 5. 22. hailstones f. of wrath shall be cast
11. 18. or unknown wild beasts f. of rage
12. 17. not believe that thou art of a f. power
13. 13. a crooked piece of wood, and f. of knots
Eccl. 1. 30. but thy heart is f. of deceit
2. 11. the Lord is f. of compassion and mercy
3. 13. when thou art in thy f. strength
8. 3. strive not with a man that is f. of tongue
19. 26. but inwardly he is f. of deceit
23. 11. but his house shall be f. of calamities
25. 20. so is a wife f. of words to a quiet man
34. 10. but he that hath travelled, is f. of prudence
39. 12. I am filled as the moon at the f. 50. 6.
42. 16. the work is f. of the glory of the Lord
Bar. 6. 17. when set up their eyes be f. of dust
1 Mac. 3. 27. Antiochus was f. of indignation
2 Mac. 3. 6. was f. of infinite sums of money
30. the temple which afore was f. of fear
12. 16. a lake filled f. seen running with blood

FULFIL.
1 Esd. 1. 57. to f. the word of the Lord, spoken by Jeremiah
2 Esd. 6. 35. that I may f. the three weeks
Wisd. 19. 4. that they might f. the punishment
Eccl. 26. 2. he shall f. the years of his life
1 Mac. 2. 18. come and f. the king's commandment
2 Mac. 3. 8. but indeed to f. the king's purpose

FULFILLED.
2 Esd. 2. 40. which have f. the law of the Lord
41. the number of thy children is f.
4. 37. doth not move till the said measure be f.
40. ask her when she hath f. her nine months
6. 19. when the affliction of Sion shall be f.
11. 44. and his abominations are f.
14. 45. when the forty days were f.
15. 6. and their hurtful works are f.
Tob. 14. 5. until the time of that age be f.
Wisd. 4. 13. he being made perfect f. a long time

FULFILLING.
1 Mac. 2. 55. Jesus, for f. the word, was made a judge

FULLY.
1 Esd. 6. 20. the house of Lord is not yet f. ended
Jud. 2. 13. but accomplish the commandments f.
1 Mac. 1. 29. after two years f. expired
62. many in Israel were f. resolved not to eat
2. 68. recompense f. the heathen, and take heed
9. 42. so when they had avenged f. the blood

FULNESS.
Eccl. 1. 16. to fear the Lord is f. of wisdom
2 Mac. 6. 14. till come to the f. of their sins

FUME.
Eccl. 24. 15. as the f. of frankincense in tabernacles

FUNERALS.
2 Mac. 5. 10. had none to mourn, nor any solemn f.

FURLONGS.
2 Mac. 11. 5. distant from Jerusalem about five f.
12. 9. was seen two hundred and forty f. off
16. a lake two f. broad being filled full
17. then departed they from thence 750 f.
29. Scythopolis lieth 600 f. from Jerusalem

FURNACE.
Wisd. 3. 6. as gold in the f. hath he tried them
Eccl. 2. 5. acceptable men in the f. of adversity
22. 24. as the vapour of a f. goeth before fire
27. 5. the f. proveth the potter's vessel
31. 26. the f. proveth the edge by dipping
38. 28. he fighteth with the heat of the f.
30. he is diligent to make clean the f.
43. 4. a man blowing a f. is in works of heat
Dan. 3. 24. the flame streameth forth above the f.
25. it burnt Chaldeans it found about the f.
27. made the midst of the f. as a moist wind
28. then the three blessed God in the f.
66. he hath delivered us out of midst of the f.

FURNISH.
Eccl. 29. 26. f. a table and feed me of that ready

FURNISHED.
Eccl. 44. 6. rich men f. with ability, living
1 Mac. 14. 34. and he f. them with all things

FURROWS.
Eccl. 7. 3. sow not on the f. of unrighteousness
38. 26. he giveth his mind to make f.

FURTHER.
1 Esd. 2. 29. those wicked workers proceed no f.
6. 30. and that every year without f. question
2 Esd. 13. 41. would go forth into a f. country

FURTHERMORE.
1 Esd. 4. 10. f. he lieth down, he eateth, drinketh
1 Mac. 9. 1. f. when Demetrius heard that Nicanor

FURY.
Wisd. 10. 3. he perished in the f. wherewith
Eccl. 1. 22. the sway of his f. be his destruction
45. 18. the congregation of Core with f. and wrath
48. 10. wrath, before it break forth into f.
Bar. 1. 13. to this day the f. of Lord is not turned
2 Mac. 4. 25. having the f. of a cruel tyrant
7. 9. thou like a f. takest us out of this life

FURIES.
Wisd. 7. 20. to know the f. of wild beasts

FURIOUS.
Eccl. 1. 22. a f. man cannot be justified
10. 18. nor f. anger for them that are born of wom.
28. 8. for a f. man will kindle strife
2 Mac. 5. 11. removing out of Egypt in a f. mind

G.

GABAEL.
Tob. 1. 1. Adael son of G. of the seed of Asael
14. I left in trust with G. ten talents of silver
4. 1. the money which he had committed to G.
20. I signify that I committed ten talents to G.
5. 6. for I have lodged with our brother G.
9. 2. go to Rages of Media, to G. and bring money
5. so Raphael went out and lodged with G.
10. 2. are they detained? or is G. dead?

GABATHA.
Esth. 12. 1. took his rest in the court with G.

GABRIAS.
Tob. 1. 14. I left with Gabael the brother of G.
4. 20. committed ten talents to Gabael son of G.

GAD.
Eccl. 25. 25. nor a wicked wom. liberty to g. abroad

GADDER.
Eccl. 26. 8. and, a g. abroad causeth great anger

GAIN.
Wisd. 14. 2. for verily desire of g. deviseth that
15. 12. they counted our time here a market for g.
Eccl. 20. 9. there is a g. that turneth to loss
29. 19. that followeth other men's business for g.
2 Mac. 11. 3. thinking to make a g. of the temple

GAINING.
Wisd. 13. 19. for g. and getting asketh ability to do

GAINSAY.
2 Esd. 5. 29. they who did g. thy promises
Jud. 8. 28. there is none that may g. thy words
12. 14. who am I that I should g. my lord?
Esth. 13. 9. there is no man that can g. thee
1 Mac. 14. 44. to break, or to g. his words

GAIT.
Eccl. 19. 30. man's laughter and g. shew what he is

GALAAD.
Jud. 1. 8. to those that were of Carmel and G.
15. 5. they in G. and Galilee chased them
1 Mac. 5. 9. the heathen that were at G. assembled
17. I and Jonathan will go to the country of G.
25. that had happened to their brethren in G.
27. shut up in cities of the country of G. 36.
45. Israelites that were in the country of G.
55. Judas and Jonathan were in the land of G.
13. 22. he came into the country of G.

GALBANUM.
Eccl. 24. 15. I yielded a pleasant odour as G.

GALLERY.
Eccl. 22. 17. as plastering on the wall of a g.

GALATIANS.
1 Mac. 8. 2. which they had done amongst the G.
2 Mac. 8. 20. battle they had in Babylon with G.

GALILEE.
Tob. 1. 2. which is called properly Nephthali in G.
Jud. 1. 8. those of higher G. and the great plain
15. 5. they that were in Galaad and in G.
1 Mac. 5. 14. there came other messengers from G.
15. and all G. of the Gentiles are assembled
17. go, and deliver thy brethren that are in G.
20. were given three thousand men to go into G.
21. then went Simon into G. where he fought
23. and those that were in G. took he away
55. and Simon his brother was in G.
10. 30. out of the country of Samaria and G.
11. 63. his princes were come to Cades in G.
12. 47. of whom he sent two thousand into G.
49. Tryphon sent an host of footmen into G.

GALL.
Tob. 6. 4. take the heart, the liver, and the g. 6.
8. as for the g. it is good to anoint a man
11. 4. take in thine hand the g. of the fish
8. therefore anoint thou his eyes with the g.
11. he strake off the g. on his father's eyes

GALLIES.
2 Mac. 4. 20. it was employed to the making of g.

GAME.
2 Mac. 4. 14. after the g. of Discus called them forth
18. now when the g. that was used was kept

GAPE.
1 Esd. 4. 19. do they not g. and with open mouth?

GAPED.
1 Esd. 4. 31. the king g. and gazed upon her

GARDEN.
Eccl. 24. 30. I came out as a conduit into a g.
31. I said, I will water my best g. and will water abundantly my g. bed, my brook became a river
40. 17. bountifulness is as a most fruitful g.
27. the fear of the Lord is a fruitful g.
Bar. 6. 70. as a scare-crow in a g. of cucumbers
Sus. 4. Joacim had a fair g. joining to his house
7. Susanna went into her husband's g. to walk
15. she was desirous to wash herself in the g.
17. and shut the g. doors that I may wash me
18. and they shut the g. doors and went out
25. then ran the one and opened the g. door
26. when the servants heard the cry in the g.
36. elders said, as we walked in the g. alone, this woman shut the g. doors, and sent maids away
38. we that stood in a corner of the g. ran to them

GARRISON.
1 Mac. 4. 61. they set there a g. to keep it
5. 58. when they had given charge to the g.
6. 50. the king set a g. there to keep it
9. 51. in them he set a g. that they might work
10. 75. because Apollonius had a g. there
11. 3. he set in every one of them a g. of soldiers
66. he took the city and set a g. in it
12. 34. wherefore he set a g. there to keep it
14. 33. but he set a g. of the Jews there
2 Mac. 12. 18. having left a strong g. in a hold

GARRISONS.
Jud. 3. 6. Holofernes set g. in the high cities
7. 7. Holofernes set g. of men of war over them
1 Mac. 5. 56. captains of the g. heard of the acts

GARIZIM.
2 Mac. 5. 23. and at G. he left Andronicus
6. 2. that in G. of Jupiter defender of strangers
GARLAND.
Jud. 15. 13. they put a g. of olive upon her
GARLANDS.
Jud. 3. 7. they received them with g. and dances
15. 13. men followed in their armour with g.
GARMENT.
1 Esd. 8. 71. I rent my clothes and the holy g. 73.
Jud. 16. 8. for she put off the g. of her widowhood,
and took a linen g. to deceive him
Wisd. 18. 24. in the long g. was the whole world
Eccl. 14. 17. all flesh waxeth old as a g.
45. 10. he compassed him with an holy g.
50. 11. he made the g. of holiness honourable
Bar. 5. 1. put off, O Jerusalem, the g. of mourning
2. cast about thee a double g. of righteousness
GARMENTS.
1 Esd. 1. 2. the priests being arrayed in long g.
4. 17. these make g. for men, these bring glory
2 Esd. 2. 39. have received glorious g. of the Lord
Tob. 4. 16. give of thy g. to them that are naked
Jud. 10. 3. she put off the g. of her widowhood,
washed her body, and put on her g. of gladness
Esth. 14. 2. put on the g. of anguish and mourning
15. 1. the third day she laid away her mourning g.
Eccl. 42. 13. for from g. cometh a moth
45. 8. he strengthened him with rich g.
Bar. 6. 11. they will deck them as men with g.
33. the priests also take off their g. and clothe
58. whose g. they that are strong do take away
1 Mac. 3. 49. they brought also the priests' g.
10. 62. the king commanded to take off his g.
GARNERS.
Eccl. 1. 17. she filleth the g. with her increase
GARNISH.
2 Mac. 9. 16. he would g. with goodly gifts
GARNISHED.
Eccl. 16. 27. he g. his works for ever
42. 21. he hath g. the excellent works of wisdom
GASP.
2 Mac. 7. 9. when he was at the last g. he said
GAT.
1 Esd. 1. 31. then g. he up on his second chariot
Wisd. 10. 8. they g. not only this hurt
Eccl. 46. 2. how great glory g. he when he did lift up
51. 16. I received her and g. much learning
1 Mac. 3. 3. so he g. his people great honour
9. 32. when Bacchides g. knowledge thereof
11. 67. they g. them to the plain of Nasor
GATE.
1 Esd. 1. 16. the porters were at every g. 7. 9.
Tob. 11. 16. went to meet his daughter at the g.
Jud. 8. 33. you shall stand this night in the g.
10. 6. thus they went forth to the g. of the city
13. 11. then said Judith to the watchmen at the g.
open, open now the g. our God is with us
12. they made haste to go down to the g.
13. so they opened the g. and received them
1 Mac. 5. 22. he pursued them to the g. of Ptolemais
GATES.
2 Esd. 3. 19. thy glory went thro' four g. of fire
Jud. 1. 4. he made the g. thereof; even g. that
were raised to the height of seventy cubits
7. 22. young men fell by the passages of the g.
10. 9. commanded the g. of the city to be opened
Esth. 16. 18. he is hanged at the g. of Susa
Eccl. 49. 13. who set up the g. and the bars
1 Mac. 4. 38. they saw altar profaned and g. burned
57. the g. and the chambers they renewed
5. 47. they stopped up the g. with stones
9. 50. these did he strengthen with g. and bars
12. 38. Simon made it strong with g. and bars
48. they of Ptolemais shut the g. and took him
13. 33. Simon fenced them with great walls and g.
15. 39. to build Cedron, and to fortify the g.
2 Mac. 3. 19. the virgins ran, some to the g.
10. 36. others broke open the g. and took city
GATHER.
2 Esd. 14. 23. go thy way, g. the people together
16. 25. trees give fruit, and who shall g. them?
Tob. 13. 5. he will g. us out of all nations
Eccl. 6. 18. g. instruction from thy youth up
36. 11. g. all the tribes of Jacob together
47. 18. thou didst g. gold as tin, and multiply
1 Mac. 3. 31. determined there to g. much money
9. 7. that he had no time to g. them together
10. 8. had given authority to g. together an host
14. 44. or to g. an assembly in the country
2 Mac. 1. 27. g. those together that are scattered
2. 7. till the time that God g. his people again
18. God will g. us together out of every land
GATHERED.
1 Esd. 4. 18. have g. together gold and silver
8. 41. these I g. to the river called Theras
91. there g. to him a very great multitude
9. 3. they should be g. together at Jerusalem
5. they of Judah and Benjamin were g. together
2 Esd. 1. 30. I g. you together as a hen gathereth
16. 30. when a vineyard is g. there are left
Jud. 16. 22. after Manasses was g. to his people
Eccl. 25. 3. if thou hast g. nothing in thy youth
Bel 1. Astyages was g. to his fathers, 1 Mac. 2. 69.
1 Mac. 1. 4. he g. a mighty strong host
15. 3. I have g. a multitude of foreign soldiers
2 Mac. 2. 13. he founding a library, g. the acts
8. 27. they had g. their armour together, 31.
10. 24. had g. a multitude of foreign forces
12. 38. so Judas g. his host, and came to Odollam
GATHERETH.
Eccl. 14. 4. he that g. by defrauding his own soul,
g. for others that shall spend his goods riotously
21. 8. that g. stones for the tomb of his burial
Eccl. 33. 16. as one that g. after grape-gatherers
GATHERING.
Eccl. 26. 5. the g. together of an unruly multitude
31. 3. the rich hath great labour in g. riches
43. 20. it abideth on every g. together of water
2 Mac. 4. 28. appertained the g. of the customs
10. 10. g. briefly the calamities of the wars
12. 43. when he had made a g. thro' the company

GAVE.
1 Esd. 6. 13. they g. us this answer, we are servants
15. he g. them over into the power of Nabuchod.
8. 80. made us gracious, so that they g. us food
9. 20. they g. their hands to put away their wives
41. and all the multitude g. heed to the law
2 Esd. 1. 13. I g. you a large and safe passage
14. I g. you light in a pillar of fire, and wonders
19. then I had pity, and g. you manna to eat
23. I g. you not fire for your blasphemies
2. 1. I g. them my commandments by the prophets
16. 61. he g. him breath, life, and understanding
Tob. 1. 6. them I g. at the altar to the priests
7. the first tenth part I g. to the sons of Aaron
8. the third I g. to them to whom it was meet
13. the Most High g. me grace and favour
16. in time of Enemesser, I g. many alms to my
brethren, and g. my bread to the hungry
2. 12. and they g. her also besides a kid
7. 13. and he g. her to be wife to Tobias
10. 10. then Raguel g. him Sara his wife
14. 2. he g. alms, and increased in the fear of Lord
11. he g. up the ghost in the bed, being 158 years
Jud. 8. 8. there was none that g. her an ill word
10. 5. then she g. her maid a bottle of wine
15. 11. they g. to Judith Holofernes his tent
12. she g. branches to the women with her
16. 19. g. the canopy she had taken for gift to Lord
Wisd. 10. 2. she g. him power to rule all things
10. she g. him knowledge of holy things
14. she showed them liars and g. him perpet. glory
18. 25. unto these the destroyer g. place, was afraid
Eccl. 17. 6. an heart he g. them to understand
9. he g. them to the glory in his marvellous acts
11. besides this he g. them knowledge
24. 8. so the Creator g. me a commandment
15. I g. a sweet smell like cinnamon and aspalathus
45. 3. he g. him a commandment for his people
7. he g. him the priesthood among the people
17. he g. unto him his commandments
20. he made Aaron honourable and g. him heritage
21. sacrifices, which he g. to him and his seed
46. 9. the Lord g. strength also to Caleb
47. 5. he g. him strength in his right hand to slay
6. in that he g. him a crown of glory
11. he g. him a covenant of kings, and a throne
22. wherefore he g. a remnant to Jacob
49. 5. therefore he g. their power to others
Bar. 1. 18. in commandments that he g. us openly
3. 27. nor g. he the way of knowledge to them
4. 30. he that g. thee that name will comfort thee
1 Mac. 1. 13. who g. them license to do after ordin.
3. 28. he g. his soldiers pay for a year
5. 3. he g. them a great overthrow and abated
7. 11. but they g. no heed to their words
8. 8. which they took of him and g. to king Eumenes
10. 46. these words, they g. no credit to them
58. he g. to him his daughter Cleopatra
60. he g. them and their friends silver and gold
89. he g. him Accaron with the borders thereof
11. 10. I repent that I g. my daughter to him
12. 43. he g. him gifts, and commanded his men
13. 3. Simon g. them exhortation, saying
14. 8. the earth g. her increase, trees their fruit
32. Simon armed valiant men and g. them wages
2 Mac. 2. 17. hope that g. them all an heritage
7. 22. for I neither g. you breath nor life
8. 36. they followed the laws that he g. them
12. 15. Judas g. a fierce assault against the wall
15. 15. Jeremias g. to Judas a sword of gold
GAVEST.
1 Esd. 8. 82. which thou g. by thy servants the proph.
2 Esd. 3. 5. thou g. a body to Adam without soul
16. to him thou g. Isaac, to Isaac thou g. Jacob
27. thou g. the city into hands of enemies
5. 27. thou g. a law that is approved by all
6. 46. thou g. them a charge to do service to man
51. to Enoch thou g. one part, which was dried
52. unto Leviathan thou g. the seventh part
53. on the sixth day thou g. commandment
Tob. 8. 6. thou madest Adam and g. him Eve
Jud. 9. 2. to whom thou g. a sword to take vengeance
3. wherefore thou g. their rulers to be slain
Wisd. 11. 7. thou g. to them abundance of water
12. 10. thou g. them place of repentance
18. 3. thou g. them a burning pillar of fire
1 Mac. 4. 30. and thou g. the host of strangers
GAY.
Bar. 6. 9. as it were for a virgin that loves to go g.
GAZA.
1 Mac. 11. 61. went to G. but they of G. shut him out
62. when they of G. made supplication to Jonathan
13. 43. in those days Simon encamped against G.
GAZARA.
1 Mac. 4. 15. for they pursued them unto G.
7. 45. pursued a day's journey from Adasa to G.
13. 53. captain of all the hosts, and dwelt at G.
14. 7. he had the dominion of G. and Bethsura
34. he fortified G. that bordereth on Azotus
15. 28. you withhold Joppe and G. with the tower
35. and whereas thou demandest Joppe and G.
16. 1. then came up John from G. and told Simon
19. he set others also to G. to kill John
21. one had run afore unto G. and told John
GAZE.
Eccl. 9. 5. g. not on a maid, that thou fall not
41. 21. or to g. upon another man's wife
GAZED.
1 Esd. 4. 31. yet the king gaped and g. on her
GEBA.
Jud. 3. 10. he pitched between G. and Scythopolis
GEDEON.
Jud. 8. 1. the son of G. the son of Raphaim
GENERAL.
2 Esd. 8. 15. touching man in g. thou knowest best
Esth. 15. 10. tho' our commandment be g. come near
Eccl. 18. 1. he that liveth for ever created all things g.
2 Mac. 3. 18. others ran to the g. supplication
GENERATION.
2 Esd. 3. 19. give diligence to the g. of Israel
32. or what g. hath so believed thy covenants?
8. 34. or what is a corruptible g. to be bitter?

Wisd. 3. 19. horrible is the end of the unrighteous g.
12. 10. not ignorant that they were a naughty g.
14. 6. and left to all ages a seed of g.
19. 11. afterwards they saw a new g. of fowls
Eccl. 4. 16. his g. shall hold her in possession
14. 18. so is the g. of flesh and blood
39. 9. and his name shall live from g. to g.
1 Mac. 5. 2. they thought to destroy the g. of Jacob
2 Mac. 7. 23. the Creator who formed the g. of man
8. 9. to root out the whole g. of the Jews
GENERATIONS.
2 Esd. 3. 7. appointedst death in him and his g.
26. they did as Adam and all his g. had done
Tob. 13. 11. all g. shall praise thee with joy
Jud. 8. 32. which shall go throughout all g.
Esth. 10. 13. according to the g. for ever
Wisd. 1. 14. the g. of the world were healthful
Eccl. 2. 10. look at the g. of old and see
16. 27. in his hand are the chief of them to all g.
44. 7. all these were honoured in their g.
16. being an example of repentance to all g.
Bar. 6. 3. ye shall remain at Babylon seven g.
GENTILES.
1 Esd. 8. 69. not put away the pollutions of the G.
Tob. 13. 3. confess him before the G. ye children
Jud. 8. 22. will he turn on our heads among the G.
Esth. 10. 9. which have not been done among the G.
10. he hath made another lot for all the G.
Wisd. 14. 11. a visitation upon the idols of the G.
1 Mac. 2. 12. our sanctuary, the G. have profaned it
48. recovered the law out of the hand of the G.
3. 10. then Apollonius gathered the G. together
4. 60. lest the G. should come and tread it down
5. 15. and all Galilee of the G. are assembled
6. 53. they that were delivered from the G.
2 Mac. 6. 4. temple was filled with revelling by G.
9. would not conform to the manners of the G.
11. 2. to make the city an habitation of the G.
24. to be brought unto the custom of G.
14. 3. the times of their mingling with the G.
GENTLE.
2 Mac. 15. 12. g. in condition, well spoken also
GEON.
Eccl. 24. 27. and as G. in the time of vintage
GERGESITES.
Jud. 5. 16. they cast forth before them the G.
GESEM.
Jud. 1. 9. the king sent unto all the land of G.
GET.
1 Esd. 4. 5. if they g. the victory they bring all
2 Esd. 7. 58. if he g. the victory he shall receive
16. 44. as they that shall g. no children
46. in captivity and famine shall g. children
Eccl. 4. 7. g. thyself the love of the congregation
13. 11. smiling on thee, he will g. thy secrets
27. 19. and thou shalt not g. him again
51. 28. g. learning with a great sum of money, and
g. much gold by her, rejoice in his mercy
1 Mac. 3. 14. I will g. me a name in the kingdom
6. 44. that he might g. him a perpetual name
2 Mac. 5. 6. that to g. the day of his own nation
GETTETH.
Eccl. 21. 11. g. the understanding thereof
36. 24. he that g. a wife, beginneth a possession
GETTING.
Wisd. 13. 19. for gaining and g. and good success
15. 12. for say they, we must be g. every way
Eccl. 42. 4. be not thou ashamed of g. much or little
Bar. 3. 17. they that made no end of their g.
GHOST.
2 Esd. 14. 22. send the Holy G. into me
Tob. 14. 11. he gave up the g. in the bed, 158 years
2 Mac. 3. 31. who lay ready to give up the g.
GIANT.
Eccl. 47. 4. slew he not a g. when he was yet young?
1 Mac. 3. 3. he put on a breastplate as a g.
GIANTS.
Jud. 16. 7. nor did the high g. set upon him
Wisd. 14. 6. in old time when the proud g. perished
Eccl. 16. 7. he was not pacified towards the old g.
Bar. 3. 26. there were g. famous from the beginning
GIFT.
2 Esd. 2. 37. O receive the g. that is given you
Tob. 2. 14. it was given for a g. more than wages
4. 11. for alms is a good g. to all that give it
Jud. 16. 19. she gave the canopy for a g. to the Ld.
Wisd. 3. 14. shall be given the special g. of faith
8. 21. a point of wisdom to know whose g. she was
Eccl. 1. 10. she is with all flesh according to his g.
7. 31. give him the g. of the shoulders
33. a g. hath grace in the sight of every man
11. 17. the g. of the Lord remaineth with the godly
18. 16. so is a word better than a g.
17. lo, is not a word better than a g.?
18. a g. of the envious consumeth the eyes
20. 10. there is a g. that shall not profit thee, and
there is a g. whose recompence is double
14. the g. of a fool shall do thee no good
26. 14. a silent and loving woman is a g. of the L.
41. 21. or to take away a portion or a g.
42. 3. or of the g. or the heritage of friends
1 Mac. 10. 39. I give it as a free g. to the sanctuary
2 Mac. 15. 16. take this holy sword, a g. from God
GIFTS.
1 Esd. 2. 7. help him with g. horses, and cattle
9. they helped them with very many free g.
3. 5. to him shall king Darius give great g.
8. 13. carry the g. to the Lord of Israel to Jerus.
Tob. 13. 11. many nations shall come with g. in
their hands, even g. to the King of heaven
Jud. 4. 14. with vows and free g. of the people
16. 18. offered their free offerings and their g.
Wisd. 7. 14. for the g. that come from learning
Eccl. 1. 18. both which are the g. of God
20. 29. presents and g. blind the eyes of the wise
34. 18. the g. of unjust men are not accepted
35. 9. in all thy g. shew a cheerful countenance
12. do not think to corrupt with g.
Bar. 6. 27. they set g. before them as to dead men
1 Mac. 3. 30. nor to have such g. to give so liberally
10. 24. I will promise them dignities and g.
12. 43. received him honourably, and gave him g.

1 *Mac.* 15. 5. and whatever *g.* besides they granted
2 *Mac.* 1. 35. the king took many *g.* and bestowed
2. 13. the epistles of kings concerning the holy *g.*
3. 2. kings did magnify the temple with their best *g.*
9. 16. holy temple he would garnish with goodly *g.*

GILDED.

Bar. 6. 8. they themselves are *g.* and laid over

GIRD.

2 *Esd.* 16. 2. *g.* up yourselves with clothes of sack

GIRDED.

2 *Mac.* 10. 25. and *g.* their loins with sackcloth

GIRDLE.

Jud. 9. 2. who loosened the *g.* of a maid to defile her

GIRT.

Jud. 4. 14. priests had their loins *g.* with sackcloth
Eccl. 22. 16. as timber *g.* and bound together
1 *Mac.* 3. 3. he *g.* his warlike harness about him
6. 37. and were *g.* fast unto them with devices
2 *Mac.* 3. 19. the women *g.* with sackcloth under

GIVE.

1 *Esd.* 2. 19. they will not only refuse to *g.* tribute
4. 60. for to thee I *g.* thanks, O Lord of our fathers
8. 19. they should *g.* it him with speed
79. and to *g.* us food in the time of servitude
9. 8. by confessing *g.* glory to the Lord God
54. and to *g.* part to them that had nothing
2 *Esd.* 2. 20. *g.* to the poor, defend the orphan
34. he shall *g.* you everlasting rest, he is nigh
3. 19. thou mightest *g.* the law to the seed of Jacob
5. 5. the stone shall *g.* his voice, people be troubled
6. 23. and the trumpet shall *g.* a sound
45. commandedst that moon should *g.* her light
7. 65. for he is ready to *g.* where it needeth
8. 6. and culture if thou *g.* us seed to our heart
24. *g.* ear to the petition of thy creature
Tob. 3. 17. to *g.* Sara for a wife to Tobias son of Tobit
4. 7. *g.* alms of thy substance, thy eye not envious
8. if thou hast abundance, *g.* alms accordingly; if little, be not afraid to *g.* according to that
11. for alms is a good gift to all that *g.* it
14. wages not tarry with thee, but *g.* it out of hand
16. *g.* of thy bread to the hungry, and of garments
17. but *g.* nothing to the wicked
5. 3. man may go with thee, and I will *g.* him wages
14. but tell me, what wages shall I *g.* thee?
7. 12. the merciful God *g.* you good success
18. the Lord *g.* thee joy for this thy sorrow
10. 11. God *g.* you a prosperous journey
12. 1. have his wages, and thou must *g.* him more
2. O Father, it is no harm to me to *g.* him half
8. it is better to *g.* alms than to lay up gold
20. now therefore *g.* God thanks
13. 10. *g.* praise to the Lord, for he is good
Jud. 4. 12. would not *g.* their children for a prey
Esth. 14. 12. *g.* me boldness, O king of nations
13. *g.* me eloquent speech in my mouth
Wisd. 6. 2. *g.* ear, ye that rule the people
8. 12. when I speak, they shall *g.* good ear to me
9. 4. *g.* me wisdom that sittest by thy throne
17. except thou *g.* wisdom, and send thy Spirit
16. 28. we must prevent the sun to *g.* thee thanks
Eccl. 1. 26. the Lord shall *g.* her unto thee
4. 3. and defer not to *g.* to him that is in need
5. and *g.* him none occasion to curse thee
8. *g.* him a friendly answer with meekness
19. she will forsake him, and *g.* him over to ruin
5. 11. be swift to hear, with patience *g.* answer
6. 23. *g.* ear, my son, receive my advice, refuse not
37. he shall *g.* thee wisdom at thine own desire
7. 10. be not faint-hearted, neglect not to *g.* alms
25. but *g.* her to a man of understanding
26. but *g.* not thyself over to a light woman
31. *g.* him his portion as it is commanded thee
8. 9. learn to *g.* answer as need requireth
9. 2. *g.* not thy soul to a woman, to set her foot
6. *g.* not thy soul unto harlots, that thou lose
10. 28. *g.* it honour according to the dignity thereof
12. 4. *g.* to the godly man, and help not a sinner
5. but *g.* not to the ungodly, *g.* it not to him
7. *g.* unto the good, and help not the sinner
14. 11. my son, *g.* the Lord his due offering
13. stretch out thy hand, and *g.* to him
16. *g.* and take, and sanctify thy soul
15. 3. she shall *g.* him the water of wisdom to drink
17. 22. *g.* repentance to his sons and daughters
27. instead of them which live and *g.* thanks
18. 28. and will *g.* praise to him that found her
23. 4. O God of my life, *g.* me not a proud look
6. and *g.* me not over into an impudent mind
25. 13. *g.* me any plague but the plague of heart
25. *g.* the waters no passage, nor a wicked woman
26. *g.* her a bill of divorce, and let her go
29. 27. *g.* place, stranger, to an honourable man
30. 11. *g.* him no liberty in his youth, wink not
21. *g.* not over thy mind to heaviness
33. 19. *g.* not thy son, wife, brother, and friend power over thee, *g.* not thy goods to another
20. while thou livest, *g.* not thyself over to any
35. 8. *g.* the Lord his honour with a good eye
10. *g.* to the Most High according as he hath enriched thee, *g.* with a cheerful eye
11. the Lord will *g.* thee seven times as much
36. 15. *g.* testimony to those thou hast possessed
37. 27. what is evil for it, *g.* not that unto it
38. 11. *g.* a sweet savour and memorial of flour
14. that he would prosper that which they *g.*
39. 5. he will *g.* his heart early to resort to the Lord
6. he shall *g.* thanks to the Lord in his prayer
14. *g.* ye a sweet savour as frankincense
33. he will *g.* every thing needful in season
41. 19. and of scorning to *g.* and take
45. 26. God *g.* you wisdom in your heart
50. 20. to *g.* the blessing of the Lord with his lips
51. 30. in his time he will *g.* you your reward
Bar. 1. 20. to *g.* us a land that flows with milk
2. 14. *g.* us favour in sight of them that led us
17. they will *g.* to the Lord neither praise nor
18. but the hungry soul shall *g.* thee praise
31. for I *g.* them an heart, and ears to hear
4. 3. *g.* not thine honour to another, nor things
6. 28. but to the poor they *g.* nothing of it
35. they can neither *g.* riches nor money

Bar. 6. 53. neither can they set up a king, nor *g.* rain
67. nor shine as the sun, nor *g.* light as the moon
Dan. 3. 20. deliver us, and *g.* glory to thy name
1 *Mac.* 2. 50. and *g.* your lives for the covenant
8. 4. the rest did *g.* them tribute every year
7. should pay a great tribute, and *g.* hostages
9. 55. he could not *g.* order concerning his house
10. 28. be faithful to us we will *g.* you rewards
54. and *g.* me now thy daughter to wife
11. 9. make a league, I will *g.* thee my daughter
15. 6. I *g.* thee leave also to coin money
2 *Mac.* 1. 3. God *g.* you all a heart to serve him
7. 23. will of his mercy *g.* you breath and life again
9. 20. if ye fare well, I *g.* great thanks to God
15. 33. they should *g.* it by pieces to the fowls

GIVEN.

1 *Esd.* 1. 6. the commandm. which was *g.* to Moses
7. these things were *g.* of the king's allowance
32. and this was *g.* out for an ordinance
2. 27. the men therein were *g.* to rebellion
4. 60. blessed art thou who hast *g.* me wisdom
62. because he had *g.* them freedom and liberty
6. 25. expenses *g.* out of the house of king Cyrus
2 *Esd.* 7. 46. better not to have *g.* the earth to Adam, or else when it was *g.* to have restrained him
8. 10. commanded out of the breasts milk to be *g.*
Tob. 5. 19. which the Lord hath *g.* us to live with
6. 10. that she may be *g.* thee for a wife
13. that this maid hath been *g.* to seven men
15. O my brother, she shall be *g.* thee to wife, for this night she shall be *g.* thee in marriage
7. 11. I have *g.* my daughter in marriage to 7 men
11. 1. that he had *g.* him a prosperous journey
Jud. 8. 19. our fathers were *g.* to the sword
9. 4. thou hast *g.* their wives for a prey
10. 12. for they shall be *g.* you to be consumed
Esth. 14. 6. hast *g.* us into the hands of our enemies
Wisd. 7. 7. I prayed, and understanding was *g.* me
15. to conceive for the things that are *g.*
17. he hath *g.* me certain knowledge of things
11. 4. water was *g.* them out of the flinty rock
18. 4. the law was to be *g.* to the world
6. knowing to what oaths they had *g.* credence
Eccl. 15. 17. and whether him liketh, shall be *g.* him
20. neither hath he *g.* any man licence to sin
17. 16. every man from his youth is *g.* to evil
19. 1. labouring man that is *g.* to drunkenness
24. 18. I am *g.* to all my children named of him
26. 3. which shall be *g.* in the portion of them
23. a wicked woman is *g.* to a wicked man, but a godly woman is *g.* to him that feareth Lord
29. 15. for he hath *g.* his life for thee
37. 21. for grace is not *g.* him from the Lord
38. 6. hath *g.* men skill that he might be honoured
41. 22. and after thou hast *g.* upbraid not
42. 17. the Lord hath not *g.* power to the saints
43. 33. and to the godly hath he *g.* wisdom
51. 22. Lord hath *g.* me a tongue for my reward
Sus. 50. God hath *g.* thee the honour of an elder
Bel 32. they had *g.* them every day two carcases, which then were not *g.* to devour Daniel
1 *Mac.* 4. 55. who had *g.* them good success
10. 8. they heard the king had *g.* him authority
45. expenses shall be *g.* out of the king's accounts
89. sent a buckle of gold, as the use is to be *g.*
2 *Mac.* 1. 18. of the fire which was *g.* us
8. 23. and when he had *g.* them this watch-word
28. they had *g.* part of the spoils to the maimed
10. 38. praised God, who had *g.* them the victory
13. 15. and having *g.* the watch-word to them

GIVEST.

2 *Esd.* 5. 45. that thou which *g.* life to all
Tob. 4. 7. when thou *g.* alms, let not thine eye, 16.
Wisd. 12. 19. that thou *g.* repentance for sins
Eccl. 18. 15. nor use words when thou *g.* any thing
31. if thou *g.* thy soul the desires that please her
42. 7. writing all that thou *g.* out or receivest in

GIVETH.

2 *Esd.* 2. 46. that *g.* them palms in their hands
8. 2. it shall say to thee, that it *g.* much mould
Tob. 4. 19. the Lord himself *g.* all good things
Eccl. 1. 12. the fear of the Lord *g.* gladness
4. 15. whoso *g.* ear to her shall judge nations
12. 3. no good can come to him that *g.* no alms
20. 15. he *g.* little, and upbraideth much
34. 17. he *g.* life, health, and blessing
35. 2. and he that *g.* alms sacrificeth praise
38. 26. he *g.* his mind to make furrows
39. 1. he that *g.* his mind to the law of the Lord
42. 16. the sun that *g.* light, looks on all things
50. 29. leadeth him, who *g.* wisdom to the godly
51. 17. ascribe glory to him that *g.* me wisdom
2 *Mac.* 15. 21. he *g.* it to such as are worthy

GIVING.

2 *Esd.* 2. 37. *g.* thanks to him that hath called you
13. 57. *g.* praise and thanks to the Most High
Wisd. 6. 18. *g.* heed to her law is the assurance of
Eccl. 17. 18. and *g.* him the light of his love
43. 9. an ornament *g.* light in highest places
44. 3. men *g.* counsel by their understanding
50. 7. the rainbow *g.* light in the bright clouds
1 *Mac.* 6. 38. horsemen *g.* them signs what to do
2 *Mac.* 8. 22. *g.* each one fifteen hundred men
11. 11. *g.* a charge on their enemies like lions
15. 15. gave him a sword, and in *g.* it, spake thus

GLAD.

2 *Esd.* 2. 37. receive gift that is given, and be *g.*
Tob. 13. 13. rejoice and be *g.* for the children of just
14. have seen thy glory, shall be *g.* for ever
Eccl. 31. 27. wine was made to make men *g.*
Bar. 4. 33. for as she was *g.* at thy fall
1 *Mac.* 3. 7. he made Jacob *g.* with his acts
10. 26. we have heard hereof and are *g.*
11. 44. the king was very *g.* of their coming
12. 12. and we are right *g.* of your honour
14. 21. wherefore we were *g.* of their coming

GLADLY.

2 *Mac.* 2. 27. we undertake *g.* this great pains
4. 12. for he built *g.* a place of exercise

GLADNESS.

1 *Esd.* 4. 63. they feasted with *g.* seven days
2 *Esd.* 1. 37. whose little ones rejoice in *g.*

2 *Esd.* 2. 3. I brought you up with *g.* with sorrow I lost
15. embrace children, bring them up with *g.*
Jud. 10. 3. she put on her garments of *g.*
Esth. 10. 13. those days shall be with *g.* before G.
Eccl. 1. 11. the fear of the Lord is glory and *g.*
12. it giveth joy, *g.* and a long life
15. 6. he shall find joy and a crown of *g.*
30. 22. the *g.* of the heart is the life of man
31. 28. wine measurably drunk bringeth *g.*
35. 9. and dedicate thy tithes with *g.*
Bar. 4. 23. God will give you to me again with *g.*
1 *Mac.* 4. 56. they offered burnt-offerings with *g.*
58. thus was there very great *g.* among people
59. the dedication kept with mirth and *g.*
5. 54. so they went up to mount Sion with *g.*
7. 48. they kept that day a day of great *g.*
10. 66. Jonathan returned with peace and *g.*
13. 52. that that day should be kept with *g.*
2 *Mac.* 3. 30. for the temple was filled with joy and *g.*
10. 6. and they kept eight days with *g.*

GLASS.

Eccl. 12. 11. if thou hadst wiped a looking *g.*

GLISTERED.

2 *Esd.* 10. 25. on a sudden her countenance *g.*
1 *Mac.* 6. 39. the mountains *g.* therewith

GLISTERING.

1 *Esd.* 8. 57. even of fine brass *g.* like gold
Esth. 15. 6. all *g.* with gold and precious stones
2 *Mac.* 5. 3. horsemen with *g.* of golden ornaments

GLORY.

1 *Esd.* 1. 33. his *g.* and understanding in the law
4. 17. make garments for men, bring *g.* to men
59. thine is the *g.* and I am thy servant
5. 61. his mercy and *g.* is for ever in all Israel
9. 8. and by confessing give *g.* to the Lord
2 *Esd.* 8. 21. whose *g.* may not be comprehended
Tob. 13. 14. when they have seen all thy *g.*
Jud. 9. 7. they *g.* in strength of their footmen
10. 8. accomplish thy enterprises to the *g.* of Israel
15. 9. they said to her, thou art the *g.* of Israel
Esth. 13. 12. it was not for any desire of *g.*
14. I did this, that I might not prefer the *g.* of man above the *g.* of God, nor worship any but
14. 9. they will quench the *g.* of thine house
15. that I hate the *g.* of the unrighteous
Wisd. 6. 2. and *g.* in the multitude of nations
7. 25. flowing from the *g.* of the Almighty
9. 10. O send her from the throne of thy *g.*
10. 14. and she gave him perpetual *g.*
14. 14. by vain *g.* of men they entered into the world
15. 9. counted it his *g.* to make counterfeit things
18. 24. in rows was the *g.* of the fathers graven
Eccl. 3. 10. *g.* not in the dishonour of thy father, for thy father's dishonour is no *g.* to thee
11. *g.* of a man is from the honour of his father
4. 21. there is a shame which is *g.* and grace
6. 29. and her chains shall be a robe of *g.*
9. 11. envy not *g.* of a sinner, knowest not his end
10. 22. their *g.* is the fear of the Lord
11. 16. shall wax old with them that *g.* therein
14. 27. and in her *g.* shall he dwell
17. 9. he gave them to *g.* in his marvellous acts
13. their eyes saw the majesty of his *g.*
20. 11. there is an abasement because of *g.*
23. 28. it is great *g.* to follow the Lord
24. 1. wisdom shall *g.* in midst of her people
25. 6. and the fear of God is their *g.*
31. 10. been found perfect, then let him *g.*
36. 14. and fill thy people with thy *g.*
37. 26. a wise man shall inherit *g.* among his people
39. 8. he shall *g.* in the law of his covenant
40. 3. from him that sitteth on a throne of *g.*
27. the fear of the Lord covereth him above all *g.*
42. 16. the work thereof is full of the *g.* of the Lord
17. whatever is might be established for his *g.*
25. who shall be filled with beholding his *g.*
43. 9. *g.* of the stars, an ornament giving light
44. 2. the Lord hath wrought great *g.* by them
7. all these were the *g.* of their times
13. and their *g.* shall not be blotted out
19. in *g.* was there none like unto him
45. 3. and he shewed him part of his *g.*
7. and he clothed him with a robe of *g.*
8. he put upon him perfect *g.* and strengthened
23. the third in *g.* is Phinees son of Eleazar
26. and that their *g.* may endure for ever
46. 2. how great *g.* gat he when he lift up his hands
47. 6. in that he gave him a crown of *g.*
8. he praised the Most High with words of *g.*
11. he gave him a throne of *g.* in Israel
48. 4. and who may *g.* like unto thee!
49. 5. he gave their *g.* to a strange nation
49. 12. which was prepared for everlasting *g.*
50. 11. and was clothed with the perfection of *g.*
13. so were all the sons of Aaron in their *g.*
51. 17. I ascribe the *g.* to him that giveth wisdom
Bar. 4. 24. which shall come on you with great *g.*
37. thy sons come, rejoicing in the *g.* of God
5. 1. the *g.* that cometh from God for ever
2. set a diadem on thy head the *g.* of Everlasting
4. thy name shall be called the *g.* of God's worship
6. God bringeth them to thee exalted with *g.*
7. that Israel may go safely in the *g.* of God
9. shall lead Israel with joy in the light of his *g.*
Dan. 3. 20. deliver us, and give *g.* to thy name
31. blessed art thou in the temple of thy holy *g.*
Prayer of Manass. the majesty of thy *g.* cannot be borne, thine is the *g.* for ever and ever
1 *Mac.* 1. 40. as had been her *g.* so her dishonour
2. 8. her temple is become as a man without *g.*
12. even our beauty and our *g.* is laid waste
62. for his *g.* shall be dung and worms
64. for by the law shall you obtain *g.*
10. 58. celebrated her marriage with great *g.*
14. 21. they certified us of your *g.* and honour
15. 32. and when he saw the *g.* of Simon
36. made report to him of the *g.* of Simon
2 *Mac.* 2. 8. and the *g.* of the Lord shall appear
5. 16. were dedicated to *g.* and honour of the place
20. so again it was set up with all *g.*

GLORIETH.

Eccl. 38. 25. that *g.* in the goad, that driveth oxen

GLORIFY.
1 Esd. 8. 25. to g. his house that is in Jerusalem
Wisd. 18. 8. by the same thou didst g. us
19. 22. didst magnify thy people and g. them
Eccl. 10. 28. my son, g. thyself in meekness
36. 6. shew signs, g. thy hand and thy right arm
43. 30. when you g. the Lord, exalt him as much

GLORIFIED.
2 Esd. 8. 49. not judged thyself worthy to be g.
Dan. 3. 28. the three praised g. and blessed God
30. blessed is thy glorious holy name, to be praised and g. above all for ever, 31, 32, 33, 34.

GLORIOUS.
1 Esd. 1. 56. as for her g. things, they never ceased
2 Esd. 2. 39. have received g. garments of the Ld.
Tob. 3. 11. and thy holy and g. name is blessed
3. 5. blessed is thy holy and g. name for ever
4. 5. house of God shall be built with a g. building
Jud. 9. 8. tabernacle, where thy g. name resteth
16. 13. O Lord, thou art great, g. and wonderful
Esth. 11. 11. the lowly exalted, and devoured the g.
14. 2. and she laid away her g. apparel
15. 1. on the third day she put on her g. apparel
16. 4. but also lifted up with the g. words
Wisd. 3. 15. for g. is the fruit of good labours
5. 16. they shall receive a g. kingdom
6. 12. wisdom is g. and never fadeth away
Eccl. 17. 13. and their ears heard his g. voice
27. 8. thou shalt put her on as a g. long robe
43. 1. the beauty of heaven, with his g. shew
12. it compasseth the heaven with a g. circle
45. 2. he made him like to the g. saints
3. he made him g. in the sight of kings
49. 8. it was Ezekiel who saw the g. vision
Dan. 3. 22. that thou art g. over the whole world
Prayer of Manass. by thy terrible and g. name
1 Mac. 2. 9. her g. vessels are carried away
14. 9. and the young men put on g. apparel
2 Mac. 4. 24. for the g. appearance of his power
8. 35. putting off g. apparel, he came to Antioch
15. 13. there appeared a man exceeding g.
34. so every man praised the g. Lord, saying

GLORIOUSLY.
Tob. 14. 5. return and build up Jerusalem g.
Esth. 15. 2. being g. adorned, she took two maids
2 Mac. 6. 19. rather to die g. than to live stained

GLORYING.
Eccl. 9. 16. let thy g. be in the fear of the Lord

GLUETH.
Eccl. 22. 7. as one that g. a potsherd together

GNASH.
Eccl. 30. 10. and lest thou g. thy teeth in the end

GNAWED.
Bar. 6. 20. their hearts are g. on by things creeping

GO.
1 Esd. 1. 16. it was not lawful to g. from service
2. 5. let him g. up to Jerusalem that is in Judea
4. 4. if he send them against the enemies, they g.
8. 10. the Jews should g. with thee to Jerusalem
27. I gathered men of Israel to g. up with me
45. that they should g. to Saddeus the captain
Tob. 1. 15. that I could not g. into Media
3. 6. that I may g. into the everlasting place
4. 15. neither let drunkenness g. with thee
5. 16. his father said, g. thou with this man
10. 7. let me g. for my father and mother look not
8. they shall declare how things g. with thee
9. Tobias said, no, but let me g. to my father
12. 17. fear not, for it shall g. well with you
14. 4. g. into Media, my son, for I believe
9. keep the law, that it may g. well with thee
Jud. 8. 35. g. in peace, the Lord be before thee
10. 9. that I may g. to accomplish the things
13. whereby he shall g. and win the hill country
11. 17. and thy servant will g. out by night
18. then thou shalt g. forth with thine army
12. 6. that thine handmaid may g. to prayer
11. g. now and persuade this Hebrew woman
12. will be a shame if we let such a woman g.
13. 12. they made haste to g. down to the gate
14. 2. g. forth every valiant man out of the city
Esth. 13. 7. may with violence g. into the grave
Wisd. 1. 11. word so secret shall g. for nought
2. 9. let none of us g. without his part
6. 23. neither will I g. with consuming envy
15. 15. as for their feet they are slow to g.
Eccl. 1. 13. it shall g. well with him at the last
2. 7. ye that fear the Lord, g. not aside lest you fall
3. 17. my son, g. on with thy business in meekness
5. 4. the Lord will in no wise let thee g.
9. g. not into every way, for so doth the sinner
6. 27. when thou hast got hold, let her not g.
8. 14. g. not to law with the judge, they will judge
16. g. not with him into a solitary place
9. 12. remember they shall not g. unpunished
12. 11. though he g. crouching, yet take good heed
14. 22. g. after her as one that traceth
18. 30. g. not after thy lusts, but refrain thyself
22. 13. g. not to him that hath no understanding
25. 26. if she g. not as thou wouldest have her
27. 19. as one that letteth a bird g. out of his hand
29. 24. a miserable life to g. from house to house
31. 21. if thou hast been forced to eat, g. vomit
32. 10. before a shamefaced man shall g. favour
20. g. not in a way wherein thou mayest fall
33. 25. but if thou let him g. idle, he shall seek
31. which way wilt thou g. to seek him?
38. 12. let him not g. for thou hast need of him
32. not dwell where they will, nor g. up and down
40. 1. from the day that they g. out of the womb
43. 30. not weary, for you can never g. far enough
Bar. 3. 11. with them that g. down into the grave
4. 19. g. your way, O my children, g. your way
5. 7. Israel may g. safely in the glory of God
6. 9. as it were for a virgin that loves to g. gay
58. they that are strong do take and g. away
Bel 11, so Baal's priests said, lo, we g. out
34. g. carry the dinner thou hast to Babylon
1 Mac. 1. 11. let us g. and make a covenant
2. 22. to the king's words to g. from our religion
3. 13. a multitude to g. out with him to war
14. I will get a name, for I will g. fight with Judas
5. 57. let us g. fight against the heathen
9. 8. let us arise and g. up against our enemies
13. 16. send hostages, and we will let them g.
19. neither would he let Jonathan g.
15. 14. neither suffered he any to g. out or in
25. Tryphon could neither g. out nor in
2 Mac. 2. 30. and to g. over things at large
5. 15. but presumed to g. into the holy temple
6. 7. the Jews were compelled to g. in procession
11. 26. ever g. cheerfully about their own affairs
12. 24. he besought to let him g. with his life
25. let him g. for saving of their brethren
15. 2. the Jews that were compelled to g. with him

GOEST.
Jud. 10. 12. whence comest thou? whither g. thou?
Eccl. 9. 13. that thou g. in the midst of snares

GOETH.
1 Esd. 4. 23. a man g. his way to rob and steal
24. a man looketh on a lion, and g. in darkness
6. 10. the work g. on prosperously in their hands
Wisd. 6. 16. she g. seeking such as are worthy of her
7. 10. light that cometh from her never g. out
12. I rejoiced, because wisdom g. before them
24. she passeth and g. through all things
Eccl. 2. 12. woe to the sinner that g. two ways
10. 21. the fear of the Lord g. before authority
12. 14. so one that g. to a sinner, and is defiled
22. 24. as the smoke of a furnace g. before the fire
32. 10. before the thunder g. lightning
Bar. 2. 18. the soul which g. stooping and feeble
3. 33. he that sendeth forth light, and it g.

GOING.
Tob. 2. 4. until the g. down of the sun
7. after the g. down of the sun I made a grave
5. 17. a staff of our hand in g. in and out before us
Jud. 1. 4. for the g. forth of his mighty armies
Wisd. 3. 3. their g. from us to be utter destruction
7. 6. have one entrance to life and the like g. out
23. and g. through all understanding, pure spirits
Sus. 8. the two elders saw her g. in every day
Bel 33. who was g. into the field to the reapers
1 Mac. 3. 16. came near to the g. up to Bethoron
24. pursued from the g. down of Bethoron
2 Mac. 2. 22. they upheld the laws that were g. down
9. 14. the city, to the which he was g. in haste
11. 36. for we are now g. to Antioch

GOADS.
Eccl. 38. 25. that glorieth in g. that driveth oxen

GOATS.
Jud. 2. 17. sheep, and oxen, and g. without number

GOD.
1 Esd. 4. 62. they praised the G. of their fathers
5. 53. all they that had made any vow to G.
6. 31. offerings may be made to the most high G.
8. 16. that do according to the will of thy G.
17. thou shalt set before thy G. in Jerusalem
19. the reader of the law of the most high G.
23. according to the wisdom of G. ordain judges
24. whosoever shall transgress the law of thy G.
9. 46. the Lord G. most high, the G. of hosts
2 Esd. 1. 29. ye my people, and I should be your G.
6. 42. some being planted of G. and tilled
7. 19. he said to me, there is no judge above G.
8. 58. said in their heart, that there is no G.
16. 67. so shall G. lead you forth and deliver you
75. fear not, neither doubt, for G. is your guide
Tob. 1. 12. I remembered G. with all my heart
3. 16. heard before the majesty of the great G.
4. 7. the face of G. shall not be turned away
14. for if thou serve G. he will repay thee
21. if thou fear G. and depart from all sin
5. 16. G. send you a good journey, and G. who dwelleth in heaven prosper your journey, and the angel of G. keep your company
6. 17. rise up and pray to G. who is merciful
7. 12. G. give you good success in all things
8. 5. blessed art thou, O G. of our fathers
15. then Raguel praised G. and said, O G. thou art worthy to be praised with all holy praise
10. 11. G. give you a prosperous journey
11. 14. he wept and said, blessed art thou, O G.
16. Tobit went out, rejoicing and praising G.
17. gave thanks, because G. had mercy on him; G. be blessed who hath brought thee to us
12. 6. bless G. praise and magnify him; it is good to praise and shew forth the works of G.
7. it is honourable to reveal the works of G.
11. it was honourable to reveal the works of G.
14. now G. hath sent me to heal thee and Sara
17. it shall go well with you, praise G. therefore
18. but by the will of our G. I came, praise him
20. now therefore give G. thanks, for I go up
13. 4. and he is the G. our Father for ever
15. let my soul bless G. the great King
18. blessed be G. who hath extolled it for ever
14. 5. again G. will have mercy on them, and the house of G. shall be built in it for ever
7. his people shall confess G. who love G. in truth
Jud. 3. 8. all tribes shall call upon him as G.
4. 13. so G. heard their prayers, and looked on
5. 8. they left way of ancestors and worshipped the G. of heaven, the G. whom they knew
12. then they cried to their G. he smote Egypt
13. and G. dried up the Red sea before them
17. whilst they sinned not before their G. because the G. that hateth iniquity was with them
19. but now are they returned to their G.
20. and if they sin against their G. let us consider
21. lest G. be for them, and we become a reproach
6. 2. and who is G. but Nabuchodonosor?
3. and their G. shall not deliver them
18. then the people fell down and worshipped G. and cried unto G. saying
19. O Lord G. of heaven, behold their pride
21. they called on the G. of Israel all night
7. 24. G. be a judge between us and you
25. but G. hath sold us into their hands
8. 8. none gave her an ill word, for she feared G.
12. who are you that have tempted G. this day, and stand instead of G. amongst children
14. can you search out G. who made all things
Jud. 8. 16. do not bind the counsels of the Lord our G. G. is not as man, that he may be threatened
20. we know none other G. therefore we trust
9. 4. O G. O my G. hear me also a widow
11. for thou art a G. of the afflicted, an helper
12. I pray thee, O G. of my father, and G. of the inheritance of Israel, Lord of heavens
14. acknowledge that thou art the G. of all power
10. 1. she had ceased to cry to the G. of Israel
8. the G. the G. of our fathers give thee favour
11. 10. nor sword prevail, except they sin against G.
12. consume all those things G. hath forbidden
13. for the priests that serve before face of our G.
16. G. hath sent me to work things with thee
17. thy servant serveth the G. of heaven day and night, I will pray to G. and he will tell me
23. thy G. shall be my G. and thou shalt dwell
13. 11. G. even our G. is with us to shew power
14. then said she to them, praise G. praise G.
19. which remember the power of G. for ever
14. 10. when Achior had seen all that the G. of Israel had done, he believed in G. greatly
16. 2. Judith said, begin to my G. with timbrels
3. G. breaketh the battles, for he delivered me
Esth. 10. 4. said, G. hath done these things
9. my nation is Israel, which cried to G. and were saved, G. hath wrought signs and wonders
10. he made two lots, one for the people of G.
11. lots came at the day of judgment before G.
12. so G. remembered his people and justified
11. 10. then they cried to G. and on their cry
12. and what G. had determined to do
13. 14. might not prefer glory of man above glory of G. nor will I worship any but thee, O G.
15. 2. after she had called upon G. who beholds
8. then G. changed the spirit of the king
13. I saw thee, my lord, as an angel of G.
16. 4. they think to escape the justice of G.
16. that they be children of the most high G.
18. G. who ruleth all things, rendering vengeance
Wisd. 1. 6. for G. is witness of his reins
13. for G. made not death, nor hath pleasure
2. 13. he professeth to have the knowledge of G.
16. he maketh his boast that G. is his father
18. if the just man be son of G. he will help him
23. for G. created man to be immortal
3. 1. the souls of righteous are in the hand of G.
5. for G. proved them, and found them worthy
14. nor imagined wicked things against G.
4. 1. because it is known with G. and with men
10. he pleased G. and was beloved of him
17. they shall not understand what G. decreed
18. but G. shall laugh them to scorn
6. 4. nor have walked after the counsel of G.
19. incorruption maketh us near unto G.
7. 14. which they that use, become the friends of G.
15. G. hath granted me to speak as I would
25. for she is the breath of the power of G.
26. the unspotted mirror of the power of G.
27. she maketh them friends of G. and prophets
28. G. loves none but him that dwells with wisdom
8. 3. she is conversant with G. she magnifieth
4. for she is privy to the mysteries of G.
21. I could not obtain her, except G. gave
9. 1. O G. of my fathers, and Lord of mercy
13. what man that can know the counsel of G.?
10. 5. she preserved him blameless unto G.
10. she shewed him the kingdom of G.
12. 7. might receive a worthy colony of G. child.
13. nor is there any G. but thou, that careth
26. they shall feel a judgment worthy of G.
13. 1. vain are all men, who are ignorant of G.
6. for they peradventure err, seeking G.
14. 8. because being corruptible, it was called G.
9. they are both alike hateful unto G.
11. in the creature of G. they are an abomination
20. the multitude allured, took him for a g.
22. that they erred in the knowledge of G.
30. both because they thought not well of G.
15. 1. but thou, O G. art gracious and true
8. he maketh a vain g. of the same clay
16. but no man can make a g. like to himself
19. but they went without the praise of G.
16. 18. were persecuted with the judgment of G.
18. 13. acknowledged this people to be sons of G.
Eccl. 1. 18. both which are the gifts of G.
30. so G. discover thy secrets and cast thee down
3. 16. that angereth his mother is cursed of G.
7. 9. say not, G. will look on my oblations, when I offer to the most high G. he will accept it
10. 5. in the hand of G. is the prosperity of man
7. pride is hateful before G. and man
12. pride is, when one departeth from G.
15. 13. and they that fear G. love it not
18. 11. therefore is G. patient with them
19. 24. that hath small understanding and fears G.
20. 15. such a one is to be hated of G. and man
21. 5. prayer of a poor man reacheth to ears of G.
23. 4. O G. of my life, give me not a proud look
10. he that swears and names G. continually
12. G. grant that it be not found in Jacob
24. 23. the book of the covenant of the most high G.
25. 1. I stood beautiful, both before G. and men
6. and the fear of G. is their glory
36. 5. that there is no G. but only thou, O G.
17. that thou art the Lord, the eternal G.
41. 8. have forsaken the law of the most high G.
19. in regard of truth of G. and his covenant
45. 1. even Moses beloved of G. and men
26. G. give you wisdom in your heart to judge
46. 1. was made great for saving the elect of G.
47. 13. for G. made all quiet round about him
48. 16. some did that which was pleasing to G.
49. 3. he established the worship of G.
50. 22. now therefore bless ye the G. of all
51. 1. I will praise thee, O G. my Saviour
Bar. 3. 35. this is our G. ‖ 4. 6. ye moved G. to wrath
4. 7. by sacrificing to devils and not to G.
8. ye have forgotten the everlasting G.
37. they come, rejoicing in the glory of G.
5. 1. the glory that cometh from G. for ever
2. the righteousness which cometh from G.

Bar.5.3.G.will shew thy brightness to every country
4. shall be called, the glory of G. worship
5. rejoicing in the remembrance of G.
6. G. bringeth them to thee exalted with glory
7. G. hath appointed every high hill be cast down
8. overshadow Israel by the commandment of G.
9. for G. shall lead Israel with joy
6.51. and that there is no work of G. in them
Dan. 3. 1. they walked in the fire, praising G.
22. let them know thou art Lord, the only G.
Sus. 42. G. everlasting G. that knowest the secrets
50. G. hath given thee the honour of an elder
55. Daniel said, even now the angel of G. hath received the sentence of G. to cut thee in two
59. the angel of G. waiteth with the sword
60. praised G. who saveth them that trust in him
63. they praised G. for their daughter Susanna
Bel 4. but Daniel worshipped his own G.
5. the living G. who created heaven and earth
37. take the dinner which G. hath sent thee
38. Daniel said, thou hast remembered me, O G.
Prayer of Manass. thou art the G. of the just, for thou art G. even the G. of them that repent
1 *Mac*. 2. 21. G. forbid we should forsake the law
3. 18. with the G. of heaven it is all one to deliver
53. able to stand, except thou, O G. help
60. as the will of G. is in heaven, so let him do
4. 55. worshipping and praising the G. of heaven
9. 10. G. forbid that I should do this thing
2 *Mac*. 1. 2. G. be gracious unto you and remember
27. let the heathen know that thou art G.
2. 4. that the prophet being warned of G.
7. till the time that G. gather his people together
17. we hope that the G. that delivered his people
3. 24. all were astonished at the power of G.
28. they acknowledged the power of G.
29. for he by the hand of G. was cast down
34. declare to all men the mighty power of G.
36. the works of the great G. which he had seen
38. no doubt there is an especial power of G.
4. 17. to do wickedly against the laws of G.
5. 19. G. did not choose people for the places' sake
6. 1. and not to live after the laws of G.
23. the holy law made and given by G.
7. 14. to look for hope from G. to be raised up
16. think not our nation is forsaken of G.
18. we suffer, having sinned against our G.
19. thou that takest in hand to strive against G.
28. G. made them of things that were not
31. thou shalt not escape the hands of G.
36. our brethren are dead under G. covenant
37. that thou mayest confess that he alone is G.
8. 23. given them this watch-word, the help of G.
36. that the Jews had G. to fight for them
9. 4. the judgment of G. now following him
5. the G. of Israel smote him with a plague
8. shewing forth the manifest power of G.
11. acknowledge of himself by the scourge of G.
12. it is meet to be subject to G. a mortal man should not think of himself as if he were G.
17. that he would declare the power of G.
18. the just judgment of G. was come on him
20. if ye fare well, I give great thanks to G.
10. 16. besought G. that he would be their helper
25. they turned themselves to pray to G.
11. 4. not at all considering the power of G.
9. then they praised the merciful G. together
13. because the almighty G. helped them
12. 6. calling on G. the righteous Judge
11. but Judas' side by the help of G. got victory
16. Judas took the city by the will of G.
13. 15. given the watch-word, victory is of G.
15. 14. to wit, Jeremias the prophet of G.
27. praying to G. with their hearts, for through the appearance of G. they were cheered

GODLY.

Jud. 8. 31. pray for us, because thou art a *g*. woman
Eccl. 6. 35. be willing to hear every *g*. discourse
11. 17. the gift of the Lord remaineth with the *g*.
22. the blessing of Lord is in the reward of the *g*.
12. 2. do good to the *g*. man, and thou shalt find
4. give to the *g*. man, and help not a sinner
13. 17. what fellowship hath the sinner with *g*.?
16. 13. the patience of *g*. shall not be frustrated
23. 12. all such things shall be far from the *g*.
26. 23. a *g*. woman is given to him that feareth Ld.
27.11. the discourse of the *g*. is always with wisdom
33. 14. life against death, so is the *g*. set against the sinner, and the sinner against the *g*.
37. 12. but be continually with a *g*. man
39. 27. all these things are for good to the *g*.
43. 33. and to the *g*. hath he given wisdom
50. 29. who giveth wisdom to the *g*.
2 *Mac*. 12. 45. favour laid up for those that died *g*.

GODLESS.

2 *Mac*. 7. 34. but thou, O *g*. man and most wicked

GODLINESS.

1 *Esd*. 1. 23. upright with an heart full of *g*.
Wisd. 10. 12. might know *g*. is stronger than all
Eccl. 1. 25. but *g*. is an abomination to a sinner
2 *Mac*. 3. 1. because of the *g*. of Onias the priest

GODS.

2 *Esd*. 1. 6. they have offered to strange *g*.
16. 36. believe not *g*. of whom the Lord spake
Jud. 3. 8. decreed to destroy all the *g*. of the land
5. 7. they would not follow the *g*. of their fathers
8. they cast them out from the face of their *g*.
8. 18. which worship *g*. made with hands
Esth. 14. 7. because we worshipped their *g*.
Wisd. 12. 27. them whom they thought to be *g*.
13. 2. to be the *g*. which govern the world
3. if they being delighted, took them to be *g*.
10. called them *g*. which are the works of men
15. 15. counted the idols of the heathen to be *g*.
Bar. 6. 4. ye shall see in Babylon *g*. of silver
9. they make crowns for the heads of their *g*.
10. the priests convey from their *g*. gold and silv.
11. being *g*. of silver, and *g*. of gold and wood
12. yet cannot these *g*. save themselves from rust
16. whereby they are known not to be *g*.
17. even so it is with their *g*. when they be set up
18 lest their *g*. be spoiled with robbers

Bar. 6. 23. by this ye may know they are not *g*. 29.
30. how can they be called *g*.? set meat before *g*.
32. they roar and cry before their *g*. as men do
39. their *g*. of wood, and which are overlaid
40. how should a man think and say, they are *g*.?
44. how may it be thought or said they are *g*.?
46. how should the things that are made be *g*.?
49. how cannot men perceive that they be no *g*.?
51. that they are no *g*. but works of men's hands
52. who then may not know that they be no *g*.?
55. when fire falleth on the house of *g*. of wood
56. how can it be thought or said, that they be *g*.?
57. nor are those *g*. of wood able to escape
Bel 27. Daniel said, lo, these are *g*. you worship

GOLD.

1 *Esd*. 1. 36. a tax on the land of one talent of *g*.
2. 6. his neighbours help him with *g*. and silver
13. vials of g. 30, of silver 2410, and other vessels
3. 6. to drink in *g*. to sleep on *g*. and a chariot with bridles of *g*. and an head tire of fine linen
2 *Esd*. 8. 2. but little dust that *g*. cometh of
16. 73. they shall be tried as *g*. in the fire
Tob. 12. 8. better to give alms, than lay up *g*.
13. 16. and thy battlements with pure *g*.
Jud. 2. 18. very much *g*. out of the king's house
5. 9. they were increased with *g*. and silver
8. 7. Manasses had left her *g*. and silver
10. 21. which was woven with purple and *g*.
Esth. 15. 6. before the king all glittering with *g*.
Wisd. 3. 6. as *g*. in furnace hath he tried them
7. 9. all *g*. in respect of her is as a little sand
13. 10. gods that are *g*. and silver, to shew art in
Eccl. 2. 5. for *g*. is tried in the fire, men in adversity
7. 18. nor a faithful brother for *g*. of Ophir
19. forego not a good woman, her grace is above *g*.
8. 2. for *g*. hath destroyed many, and perverted
21. 21. learning to a man is as an ornament of *g*.
28. 24. look that thou bind up thy silver and *g*.
29. 11. it shall bring thee more profit than *g*.
30. 15. health and a good state of body is above *g*.
31. 5. he that loveth *g*. shall not be justified
6. *g*. hath been ruin of many and their destruction
8. blessed is the rich that hath not gone after *g*.
32. 5. is as a signet of carbuncle set in *g*.
6. as a signet of an emerald set in a work of *g*.
40. 25. *g*. and silver make the foot stand sure
41. 12. above a thousand great treasures of *g*.
45. 11. and set in *g*. the work of the jeweller
12. he set a crown of *g*. upon the mitre
47. 18. thou didst gather *g*. as tin and multiply
50. 9. as a vessel of beaten *g*. set with stones
51. 28. get learning, and get much *g*. by her
Bar. 3. 17. they that hoarded up silver and *g*.
30. who found her, and will bring her for pure *g*.
6. 4. shall ye see in Babylon gods of silver and *g*.
9. and taking *g*. as it were for a virgin to go gay
30. set meat before gods of silver, *g*. and wood
1 *Mac*. 1. 22. censers of *g*. and the vail and crowns
23. he took also the silver and the *g*. and vessels
2. 18. children shall be honoured with silver and *g*.
3. 41. the merchants took silver and *g*. very much
4. 23. where they got much *g*. and silver and silk
57. they decked the temple with crowns of *g*.
6. 1. was a city renowned for riches, silver and *g*.
2. a temple, wherein were coverings of *g*.
12. and I took all the vessels of *g*. and silver
39. when the sun shone on the shields of *g*.
8. 3. winning the mines of the silver and *g*.
10. 60. who gave them and friend silver and *g*.
89. he sent him a buckle of *g*. as the use is
14. 24. Simon sent to Rome with a great shield of *g*.
43. should be clothed in purple, wear *g*.
44. clothed in purple, or wear a buckle of *g*.
15. 18. they brought a shield of *g*. of 1000 pound
26. sent him silver, and *g*. and much armour
32. saw the glory of Simon, and cupboard of *g*.
16. 11. he had abundance of silver and *g*.
19. might give them silver and *g*. and rewards
2 *Mac*. 2. 2. when they see images of silver and *g*.
3. 25. it seemed that he had complete harness of *g*.
4. 32. stole certain vessels of *g*. out of the temple
5. 2. horsemen running in the air in cloth of *g*.
10. 29. appeared five men with bridles of *g*.
11. 8. one in white, shaking his armour of *g*.
15. 15. Jeremias gave to Judas a sword of *g*.

GOLDEN.

1 *Esd*. 8. 57. twenty *g*. vessels, twelve of brass
Esth. 15. 11. so he held up his *g*. sceptre
Eccl. 6. 30. there is a *g*. ornament upon her
26. 18. as *g*. pillars are on sockets of silver
45. 9. with many *g*. bells round about
1 *Mac*. 1. 21. and took away the *g*. altar
22. and the *g*. ornaments before the temple
11. 58. on this he sent him *g*. vessels to be served in, and gave him leave to wear a *g*. buckle
13. 37. the *g*. crown and scarlet robe ye sent
2 *Mac*. 5. 3. and glittering of *g*. ornaments

GOLDSMITHS.

Wisd. 15. 9. he striveth to excel *g*. and silversmiths
Bar. 6. 45. they are made of carpenters and *g*.

GOLIATH.

Eccl. 47. 4. he beat down the boasting of G.

GOMORRAH.

2 *Esd*. 2. 8. remember what I did to Sodom and G.

GONE.

2 *Esd*. 10. 22. our Levites are *g*. into captivity
14. 11. the ten parts of it are *g*. already
Jud. 10. 10. till she was *g*. down the mountain
Wisd. 4. 2. and when it is *g*. they desire it
5. 10. when *g*. by the trace cannot be found
16. 14. the spirit when it is *g*. forth returneth not
19. 3. whom they had entreated to be *g*.
Eccl. 31. 8. the rich that hath not *g*. after gold
Bar. 3. 19. they are *g*. down to the grave
30. who hath *g*. over the sea and found her?
4. 26. my delicate ones have *g*. rough ways
Sus. 19. now when the maids were *g*. forth
Bel 14. when *g*. forth, king set meats before Bel
1 *Mac*. 6. 10. the sleep is *g*. from mine eyes
11. 43. for all my forces are *g*. from me
12. 30. they were *g*. over the river Eleutherus
2 *Mac*. 4. 40. a man far *g*. in years, no less in folly

2 *Mac*. 6. 24. were now *g*. to another religion
12. 4. when they were *g*. forth into the deep
10. when they were *g*. from thence nine furlongs

GOOD.

1 *Esd*. 4. 46. I desire that thou make *g*. the vow
6. 21. if it seem *g*. to the king, let search be made
8. 11. as it hath seemed *g*. to me and my friends
85. that ye may eat the *g*. things of the land
2 *Esd*. 1. 9. to whom I have done so much *g*.
2. 14. I have broken the evil, and created the *g*.
25. nourish thy children, O thou *g*. nurse
3. 22. the *g*. departed away, the evil abode still
6. 33. sent me to say, be of *g*. comfort, fear not
7. 6. a city builded, and full of all *g*. things
35. and the *g*. deeds shall be of force
16. 21. victuals shall be so *g*. cheap on earth
Tob. 2. 1. there was a *g*. dinner prepared me
4. 9. thou layest up a *g*. treasure for thyself
11. for alms is a *g*. gift to all that give it
19. the Lord himself giveth all *g*. things
5. 13. for thou art my brother, of an honest and *g* stock; my brother, thou art of a *g*. stock
21. for the *g*. angel will keep him company
7. 4. then said he, is he in *g*. health?
5. he is both alive and in *g*. health
12. God give you *g*. success in all things
18. be of *g*. comfort, my daughter
8. 6. it is not *g*. that man should be alone
10. 12. that I may hear *g*. report of thee
11. 11. saying, be of *g*. hope, my father
12. 6. it is *g*. to praise God and exalt his name
7. it is *g*. to keep close the secret of a king, 11. do that which is *g*. and no evil shall touch you
8. prayer is *g*. with fasting and alms
13. thy *g*. deed was not hid from me
13. 10. give praise to the Lord, for he is *g*.
Jud. 3. 2. use us as shall be *g*. in thy sight
4. and deal with them as seemeth *g*. to thee
7. 30. Ozias said, brethren, be of *g*. courage
8. 28. thou hast spoken all with a *g*. heart
29. because the disposition of thy heart is *g*.
10. 19. it is not *g*. that one man of them be left
11. 1. wom. be of *g*. comfort, fear not in thy heart, 3.
13. 20. for a praise, to visit thee in *g*. things
15. 8. *g*. things that God hath shewed to Israel
10. thou hast done much *g*. to Israel
Esth. 13. 3. was approved for his constant *g*. will
13. for I could have been content with *g*. will
15. 9. Esther, I am thy brother, be of *g*. cheer
16. 3. to practise against these that do them *g*.
4. words of lewd persons, that were never *g*.
13. who continually procured our *g*.
Wisd. 2. 6. let us enjoy the *g*. things present
3. 15. for glorious is the fruit of *g*. labours
5. 8. what *g*. hath riches with vaunting brought?
6. 25. receive instruction, it shall do you *g*.
7. 11. all *g*. things together came to me with her
22. clear, undefiled, plain, loving the thing that is *g*. that cannot be letted, ready to do *g*.
8. 9. she would be a counsellor of *g*. things
12. when I speak, they shall give *g*. ear unto me
15. I shall be found *g*. among the multitude
18. and in talking with her is a *g*. report
20. being *g*. I came into a body undefiled
10. 8. they knew not the things which were *g*.
12. 19. hast made thy children to be of a *g*. hope
21. thou hast made covenants of *g*. promises
13. 1. could not, out of the *g*. things that are seen
10. to shew art in a stone *g*. for nothing
14.26. disquieting of *g*. men, forgetfuln. of *g*. turns, defiling souls, disorder in marriages, adultery
18. 6. they might afterwards be of *g*. cheer
9. the children of *g*. men did sacrifice secretly; should be alike partakers of the same *g*. and evil
Eccl. 1. 29. take *g*. heed what thou speakest
2. 9. ye that fear the Lord, hope for *g*.
6. 19. come to her, and wait for her *g*. fruits
7. 13. for the custom thereof is not *g*.
18. change not a friend for any *g*. by no means
21. love a *g*. servant, defraud him not of liberty
11. 12. the eye of the Lord looked on him for *g*.
15. love, and the way of *g*. works, are from him
23. what *g*. things shall I have hereafter?
31. he lieth in wait, and turneth *g*. into evil
12. 1. when thou wilt do *g*. know to whom dost it
2. do *g*. to the godly man, and thou shalt find
3. there can no *g*. come to one occupied in evil
5. shalt receive twice as much evil for all the *g*.
7. give to the *g*. and help not the sinner
13. 24. riches are *g*. to him that hath no sin
25. his countenance, whether it be for *g*. or evil
14. 5. is evil to himself, to whom will he be *g*.?
7. and if he doth *g*. he doth it unwillingly
11. my son, according to thy ability, do *g*. to thys.
13. do *g*. to thy friend before thou die
14. defraud not thyself of the *g*. day, and let not the part of a *g*. desire overpass thee
20. the man that doth meditate *g*. things
25. lodge in a lodging where *g*. things are
15. 1. he that feareth the Lord, will do *g*.
17. 7. withal, he shewed them *g*. and evil
22. he will keep the *g*. deeds of man as the apple
18. 8. what is man? what is his *g*.? what is his evil?
15. my son, blemish not thy *g*. deeds
32. take not pleasure in much *g*. cheer
20. 3. how *g*. is it when reproved to shew repentan.
9. there is a sinner that hath *g*. success in evil
14. the gift of a fool shall do thee no *g*.
16. I have no thank for all my *g*. deeds
26. 4. if he have a *g*. heart toward the Lord
16. so is the beauty of a *g*. wife in her house
21. having the confidence of their *g*. descent
29. 16. will overthrow the *g*. estate of his surety
18. suretyship hath undone many of *g*. estate
30. 15. health and *g*. state of body are above gold
19. what *g*. doth the offering to an idol?
25. a *g*. heart will have a care of his meat
31. 23. the report of his *g*. house-keeping
27. wine drunk moderately is as *g*. as life to a man
32. 13. and hath replenished thee with *g*. things
23. in every *g*. work trust thine own soul
33. 14. *g*. is set against evil, life against death

Eccl. 35. 2. he that requiteth *g.* offereth fine flour
8. give the Lord his honour with a *g.* eye
37. 9. he will say unto thee, thy way is *g.*
18. four things appear, *g.* and evil, life and death
38. 13. when in their hands there is *g.* success
21. thou shalt not do him *g.* but hurt thyself
39. 4. for he hath tried the *g.* and evil among men
16. all the works of the Lord are exceeding *g.*
25. for the *g.* are *g.* things created from beginning
27. all these things are for *g.* to the godly
33. all the works of the Lord are *g.*
41.13. a *g.* life hath but few days, a *g.* name endures
16. it is not *g.* to retain all shamefacedness
42. 6. sure keeping is *g.* where an evil wife is
25. one thing establisheth the *g.* of another
45. 23. he stood up with *g.* courage of heart
26. that their *g.* things be not abolished
46. 10. might see that it is *g.* to follow the Lord
51. 18. earnestly I followed that which is *g.*
21. therefore have I gotten a *g.* possession
Bar. 2. 1. the Lord hath made *g.* his word
4. 5. be of *g.* cheer, my people, memorial of Israel
30. take a *g.* heart, O Jerusalem, he will comfort
6. 34. whether evil or *g.* they cannot recompense
38. nor can they do *g.* to the fatherless
64. seeing they are not able to do *g.* to men
1 *Mac.* 4. 24. they praised the Lord, because it is *g.*
55. praising God, who had given them *g.* success
8. 53. *g.* success be to the Romans and Jews
11. 33. determined to do *g.* to people of the Jews our friends, because of their *g.* will towards us
14. 4. he sought the *g.* of his nation in such wise
9. they sat communing together of *g.* things
16. 14. taking care for the *g.* ordering of them
17. great treachery, he recompensed evil for *g.*
2 *Mac.* 1. 3. to do his will with a *g.* courage
4. 5. not to be accuser but seeking the *g.* of all
5. 4. that that apparition might turn to *g.*
6. 29. changing the *g.* will they bare him before
7. 5. the vapour was for a *g.* space dispersed
14. it is *g.* being put to death by men, to look
8. 36. to make *g.* to the Romans their tribute
9. 19. Antiochus, to the *g.* Jews his citizens
21. would have remembered kindly your *g.* will
10. 23. having *g.* success with his weapons
11. 6. would send a *g.* angel to deliver Israel
15. consented, being careful of the common *g.*
19. I will endeavour to be a means of your *g.*
26. when certified that they may be of *g.* comfort
28. we have our desire, we are also in *g.* health
12. 45. it was an holy and *g.* thought
13. 16. at last they departed with *g.* success
14. 8. I intend the *g.* of mine own countrymen
30. that such sour behaviour came not of *g.*
37. Razis a man of very *g.* report was accused
15. 12. Onias, a virtuous and *g.* man, prayed
17. by the words of Judas, which were very *g.*
23. O Lord of heaven, send a *g.* angel before us

GOODLY.

1 *Esd.* 4. 18. gold, silver, or any other *g.* thing
Jud. 8. 7. she was also of a *g.* countenance
2 *Mac.* 9. 16. he would garnish with *g.* gifts

GOODLIEST.

1 *Mac.* 8. 8. of the *g.* countries which they took

GOODNESS.

2 *Esd.* 7. 68. he pardons, if he did not so of his *g.*
8. 52. rest allowed, yea, perfect *g.* and wisdom
Esth. 16. 6. the innocency and *g.* of princes
10. and far distant from our *g.* and as a stranger
Wisd. 7. 26. and she is the image of his *g.*
12. 22. we should carefully think of thy *g.*
16. 11. they might be continually mindful of thy *g.*
Eccl. 26. 20. trusting in the *g.* of thy stock
Bar. 2. 27. thou hast dealt with us after all thy *g.*
Prayer of Manass. in me thou wilt shew all thy *g.*
2 *Mac.* 6. 13. for it is a token of his great *g.*

GOODS.

1 *Esd.* 6. 32. and all his *g.* seized for the king
2 *Esd.* 15. 19. destroy their house, and spoil their *g.*
Tob. 1. 20. all my *g.* were forcibly taken away
8. 21. then he should take the half of his *g.*
10. 10. gave him Sara his wife, and half his *g.*
Jud. 16. 24. she did distribute her *g.* to them
Wisd. 13. 17. then maketh he prayer for his *g.*
Eccl. 5. 1. set not thy heart upon thy *g.*
11. 19. now I will eat continually of thy *g.*
14. 4. others that shall spend his *g.* riotously
5. he shall not take pleasure in his *g.*
31. 11. his *g.* shall be established, congregation
33. 19. give not thy *g.* to another, lest it repent
34. 20. brings an offering of the *g.* of the poor
40. 13. the *g.* of the unjust shall be dried up
46. 19. I have not taken any man's *g.* not a shoe
1 *Mac.* 12. 23. that your cattle and *g.* are ours

GORGIAS.

1 *Mac.* 3. 38. chose Nicanor and G. mighty men
4. 1. then took G. five thousand footmen
5. in the mean season came G. by night
18. G. and his host are here in the mountain
5. 59. then came G. and his men out of the city
2 *Mac.* 8. 9. and with him he joined G. a captain
10. 14. but when *g.* was governor of the holds
12. 32. they went forth against *g.* the governor
35. was still upon G. so that G. fled into Marisa
36. when they that were with G. had fought long
37. rushing unawares on G. men, he put to flight

GOT.

Eccl. 6. 27. when hast *g.* hold of her, let her not go
24. 6. and in every nation I *g.* a possession
1 *Mac.* 4. 23. where they *g.* much gold and silver
11. 49. the Jews had *g.* the city as they would
2 *Mac.* 4. 24. he *g.* the priesthood to himself
27. so Menelaus *g.* the principality

GOTTEN.

2 *Esd.* 3. 12. when they had *g.* them many children
Wisd. 4. 2. having *g.* victory striving for rewards
Eccl. 5. 8. set not thy heart on goods unjustly *g.*
26. 20. when thou hast *g.* a fruitful possession
29. 6. he hath *g.* him an enemy without cause
34. 18. he that sacrificeth of a thing wrongfully *g.*
35. 10. as thou hast *g.* give with a cheerful eye
42. 10. lest should *g.* with child in her father's house

Eccl. 51. 21. therefore have I *g.* a good possession
27. and I have *g.* unto me much rest
Bar. 2. 11. O Lord, that hast *g.* thyself a name
1 *Mac.* 2. 10. what nation hath not *g.* of her spoils
49. now hath pride and rebuke *g.* strength
2 *Mac.* 13. 21. they had *g.* him, they put him in prison

GOVERN.

Wisd. 13. 2. to be the gods which *g.* the world
Sus. 5. to be judges, who seemed to *g.* the people
1 *Mac.* 9. 73. Jonathan began to *g.* the people

GOVERNANCE.

2 *Esd.* 11. 32. and it had the *g.* of the world
1 *Mac.* 9. 31. Jonathan took the *g.* upon him

GOVERNED.

Wisd. 14. 6. the hope of the world *g.* by thy hand

GOVERNETH.

2 *Esd.* 13. 58. and because he *g.* the same
Wisd. 14. 3. but thy providence, O Father, *g.* it
Eccl. 18. 3. who *g.* the world with palm of his hand

GOVERNMENT.

Jud. 8. 10. that had the *g.* of all things she had
Eccl. 10. 1. the *g.* of a prudent man is well ordered
1 *Mac.* 6. 16. they committed their *g.* to one man
2 *Mac.* 8. 17. taking away the *g.* of forefathers

GOVERNMENTS.

1 *Mac.* 10. 30. nor of the three *g.* that are added
38. concerning the three *g.* that are added
11. 28. as also the three *g.* with Samaria
34. the borders of Judea, with the three *g.*
57. I appoint thee ruler over the four *g.*
2 *Mac.* 4. 11. putting down the *g.* which were by law

GOVERNOR.

1 *Esd.* 2. 12. to Sanabassar the *g.* of Judea
3. 21. a man remembereth neither king nor *g.*
6. 3. Sisinnes *g.* of Syria and Phenice, 7, 21.
29. a portion to be given to Zorobabel the *g.*
7. 1. Sisinnes the *g.* of Celosyria did oversee
Jud. 5. 20. my lord and *g.* if there be any error
8. 9. the words of the people against the *g.*
11. 10. O Lord and *g.* reject not his word
Eccl. 23. 1. O Lord, Father and *g.* of all my life
49. 15. a *g.* of his brethren, a stay of the people
1 *Mac.* 13. 42. Simon the *g.* and leader of the Jews
14. 35. people made him their *g.* and chief priest
41. were well pleased that Simon should be *g.*
47. Simon was well pleased to be *g.* of the Jews
2 *Mac.* 3. 4. Simon was made *g.* of the temple
4. 29. left Crates who was *g.* of the Cyprians
9. 19. Antiochus king and *g.* to the good Jews
10. 14. but when Gorgias was *g.* of the holds
32. he fled to Gazara, where Chereas was *g.*
12. 2. Nicanor *g.* of Cyprus would not suffer them
32. they went against Gorgias *g.* of Idumea
13. 3. because he thought to have been made *g.*
24. made him principal *g.* from Ptolemais
14. 12. making him *g.* over Judea, he sent him forth

GOVERNORS.

1 *Esd.* 1. 8. *g.* of the temple gave to the priests
49. the *g.* also of the people and of the priests
3. 2. and to all the *g.* and captains, 14.
4. 47. Darius wrote letters to captains and *g.*
7. 2. assisting the ancients and *g.* of the temple
Jud. 2. 14. Holofernes called all the *g.* and captains
5. 2. he called all the *g.* of the sea coast
6. 14. they presented him to the *g.* of the city
7. 8. and all the *g.* of the people of Moab
8. 11. hear me, O ye *g.* of inhabitants of Bethulia
Esth. 13. 1. the princes and *g.* that are under him
16. 1. unto the princes and *g.* of 127 provinces
1 *Mac.* 10. 37. their overseers and *g.* be of themselves
12. 4. Romans gave letters to *g.* of every place
2 *Mac.* 5. 22. he left *g.* to vex the nation
10. 21. he called the *g.* of the people together
12. 2. but of the *g.* of several places

GRACE.

1 *Esd.* 8. 4. he found *g.* in his sight in his requests
2 *Esd.* 1. 37. I take to witness the *g.* of the people
2. 32. my wells run over, and my *g.* shall not fail
8. 42. I said, if I have found *g.* let me speak
12. 7. if I have found *g.* before thy sight
14. 22. but if I have found *g.* before thee
Tob. 1. 13. the Most High gave me *g.* and favour
Esth. 15. 14. and thy countenance is full of *g.*
Wisd. 3. 9. *g.* and mercy is to his saints, 4. 15.
14. 20. the multitude allured by the *g.* of the work
16. 25. it was obedient to thy *g.* that nourisheth
Eccl. 4. 21. there is a shame which is glory and *g.*
7. 19. a wise and good woman her *g.* is above gold
33. a gift hath *g.* in the sight of every man
21. 16. but *g.* shall be found in the lips of the wise
24. 16. my branches are branches of honour and *g.*
26. 13. the *g.* of a wife delighteth her husband
15. a shamefaced woman is a double *g.*
37. 21. for *g.* is not given him from the Lord
Prayer of Manass. I bow knee, beseeching thee of *g.*

GRACES.

Eccl. 20. 13. the *g.* of fools shall be poured out

GRACIOUS.

1 *Esd.* 8. 80. he made us *g.* before the kings
2 *Esd.* 1. 25. when ye desire me to be *g.* unto you
Esth. 16. 2. with the great bounty of their *g.* princes
Wisd. 12. 16. it maketh thee to be *g.* to all
15. 1. but thou, O God, art *g.* and true
Eccl. 17. 21. the Lord being *g.* forsook them not
18. 17. but both are with a *g.* man
Dan. 3. 67. give thanks to the Lord because he is *g.*
2 *Mac.* 1. 2. God be *g.* unto you, and remember
24. O Lord God, who art the only and *g.* king
2. 22. the Lord being *g.* unto them with favour

GRACIOUSLY.

Wisd. 16. 2. dealing *g.* with thine own people
2 *Mac.* 9. 27. he will *g.* yield to your desires

GRAIN.

2 *Esd.* 4. 30. the *g.* of evil seed hath been sown
31. the *g.* of evil seed hath brought forth
Wisd. 11. 22. is as a little *g.* of the balance

GRANT.

2 *Esd.* 5. 4. but if the Most High *g.* thee to live
Tob. 10. 12. Lord *g.* that I may see thy children
Eccl. 23. 12. God *g.* that it be not found in Jacob
50. 23. he *g.* us joyfulness of heart and peace
1 *Mac.* 11. 50. *g.* us peace, and let the Jews cease

1 *Mac.* 13. 45. beseeching Simon to *g.* them peace
2 *Mac.* 3. 31. call on the Most High, to *g.* him his life
11. 26. to send unto them, and *g.* them peace

GRANTED.

Wisd. 7. 15. God hath *g.* me to speak as I would
Eccl. 17. 24. to them that repent he *g.* return
1 *Mac.* 11. 66. to have peace with him, which he *g.*
13. 37. confirm the immunities which we have *g.*
50. to be at one with them, which thing he *g.*
15. 5. I confirm all the oblations the kings before me *g.* thee, and whatsoever gifts besides they *g.*
2 *Mac.* 2. 31. *g.* to him that will make abridgment
3. 33. Lord *g.* thee life ‖ 4. 10. when the king had *g.*
4. 11. and the royal privileges *g.* to the Jews
11. 15. whatever Maccabeus wrote, the king *g.*
18. and he hath *g.* as much as might be
35. whatsoever Lysias the king's cousin *g.*
12. 12. *g.* them peace, whereon they shook hands

GRAPE.

2 *Esd.* 9. 21. I have kept me a *g.* of the cluster
Eccl. 33. 16. that gathereth after the *g.* gatherers
39. 26. honey, milk, and the blood of the *g.*
50. 15. he poured of the blood of the *g.*
51. 15. from the flower, till the *g.* was ripe

GRAPES.

2 *Esd.* 16. 26. the *g.* shall ripen, who shall tread them?
43. as he that shall not gather the *g.*
Eccl. 33. 16. my wine-press, like a gatherer of *g.*
1 *Mac.* 6. 34. they shewed them the blood of the *g.*

GRASS.

2 *Esd.* 9. 27. after seven days I sat on the *g.*
15. 42. shall break down the *g.* of the meadows
Eccl. 40. 16. shall be pulled up before all *g.*
43. 21. and it consumeth the *g.* as fire

GRASSHOPPERS.

2 *Esd.* 4. 24. we pass away out of the world as *g.*
Wisd. 16. 9. for them the bitings of *g.* and flies killed
Eccl. 43. 17. falling of snow is as the lighting of *g.*

GRATIFY.

2 *Mac.* 1. 35. bestowed on those whom he would *g.*

GRAVE.

Eccl. 39. 3. he will seek out the secrets of *g.* sentences

GRAVE.

2 *Esd.* 4. 41. in the *g.* the chambers of souls are like
Tob. 2. 7. I went and made a *g.* and buried him, 8. 9.
3. 10. I shall bring his old age with sorrow to the *g.*
4. 4. when she is dead bury her by me in one *g.*
6. 14. bring my father's and mother's life to the *g.*
Esth. 13. 7. may in one day with violence go into *g.*
Eccl. 9. 12. they shall not go unpunished to their *g.*
14. 12. the covenant of the *g.* is not shewed to thee
16. there is no seeking of dainties in the *g.*
17. 27. who shall praise the Most High in the *g.*
28. 21. an evil death, the *g.* were better than it
30. 18. delicates are as messes of meat set on a *g.*
41. 4. there is no inquisition in the *g.*
Bar. 3. 11. with them that go down into the *g.*
2 *Mac.* 6. 23. and willed them to send him to the *g.*

GRAVES.

Wisd. 19. 3. making lamentation at the *g.* of the dead
2 *Mac.* 12. 39. to bury them in their father's *g.*

GRAVE.

Eccl. 38. 27. and they that cut and *g.* seals

GRAVED.

2 *Esd.* 13. 6. lo, he had *g.* himself a great mountain

GRAVEL.

Eccl. 18. 10. and a *g.* stone in comparison of sand

GRAVEN.

2 *Esd.* 13. 7. have seen the place whereout hill was *g.*
36. as thou sawest the hill *g.* without hands
Wisd. 14. 16. and *g.* images were worshipped
15. 13. maketh brittle vessels and *g.* images
18. 24. in rows was the glory of the fathers *g.*

GRAY.

Wisd. 2. 10. nor reverence the ancient *g.* hairs
4. 9. but wisdom is the *g.* hair unto men
Eccl. 25. 4. how comely is judgment for *g.* hairs
2 *Mac.* 6. 23. as became the honour of his *g.* head
15. 13. there appeared a man with *g.* hairs

GREAT.

1 *Esd.* 3. 5. to him shall king Darius give *g.* gifts
4. 14. O ye men, it is not the *g.* king that excelleth
34. O ye men, *g.* is the earth, high is the heaven
35. is he not *g.* that maketh these things? therefore *g.* is the truth, stronger than all things
41. *g.* is truth, and mighty above all things
8. 76. we have been and are in *g.* sin to this day
86. done to us for wicked works and *g.* sins
2 *Esd.* 7. 66. and that he is of *g.* mercy he multiplies
8. 50. many *g.* miseries shall be done to them in latter time, because they have walked in *g.* pride
Tob. 3. 16. before the majesty of the *g.* God
4. 13. and in lewdness his decay and *g.* want
5. 12. I am Azarias the son of Ananias the *g.*
13. Ananias and Jonathan sons of *g.* Samaias
8. 16. hast dealt with us according to thy *g.* mercy
13. 15. let my soul bless God the *g.* King
Jud. 1. 1. who reigned in Nineve the *g.* city
5. made war with king Arphaxad in the *g.* plain
8. nations that were of the *g.* plain of Esdrelon
2. 5. thus saith the *g.* king, lord of the earth
3. 2. the servants of Nabuchodonosor the *g.* king
9. he came over-against the *g.* strait of Judea
8. 19. they had a *g.* fall before our enemies
15. 9. thou art the exaltation of Jerus. the *g.* glory of Israel, thou art the *g.* rejoicing of our nation
16. 13. O Lord, thou art *g.* and glorious
16. he that feareth the Lord is *g.* at all times
Esth. 11. 6. and behold, two *g.* dragons came forth ready to fight and their cry was *g.*
10. a little fountain was made a *g.* flood
12. 6. Aman, who was in *g.* honour with the king
16. 1. the *g.* king Artaxerxes to the princes
12. but he not bearing his *g.* dignity, went
Wisd. 6. 14. whoso seeketh early shall have no *g.* tra.
8. 11. I shall be admired in the sight of *g.* men
11. 21. thou canst shew thy *g.* strength at all times
12. 18. and thou orderest us with *g.* favour
14. 22. they lived in the *g.* war of ignorance
17. 1. *g.* are thy judgments, and cannot be expressed
18. 1. nevertheless thy saints had a very *g.* light
Eccl. 1. 7. who hath understood her *g.* experience?

Eccl. 3.20. for the power of the Ld. is g. he is honour.
4. 7. and bow thy head to a g. man
5. 6. say not, his mercy is g. he will be pacified
8. 8. shalt learn how to serve g. men with ease
10. 24. g. men and judges shall be honoured
11. 1. wisdom maketh him to sit among g. men
15. 18. for the wisdom of the Lord is g.
16. 12. as his mercy is g. so is his correction also
17. 29. how g. is the loving-kindness of the Lord
20. 28. he that pleaseth g. men shall get pardon
24. 29. her counsels profounder than the g. deep
25. 10. oh how g. is he that findeth wisdom!
28. 14. hath overthrown the houses of g. men
32. 9. if thou be among g. men make not thyself
33. 18. hear ye, O ye g. men of the people
38. 16. as if thou hadst suffered g. harm thyself
17. weep bitterly, and make g. moan, use lament.
27. they are diligent to make g. variety
39. 4. he shall serve among g. men, and appear
6. when the g. Lord will, he shall be filled
40. 1. g. travel is created for every man
43. 5. g. is the Lord that made it
15. by his g. power he maketh the clouds firm
28. magnify him, for he is g. above all his works
29. Lord is terrible, and very g. and marvellous
44. 2. the Lord hath wrought g. glory by them
through his g. power from the beginning
19. Abraham was a g. father of many people
46. 1. who according to his name was made g.
2. how g. glory gat he, when he lift up his hands
5. he called on Lord, and the g. Lord heard him
48. 22. who was g. and faithful in his vision
49. 13. Neemias whose renown is g. raised up
16. Sem and Seth were in g. honour among men
50. 16. sons of Aaron made a g. noise to be heard
51. 28. get learning with a g. sum of money
Bar. 3. 24. O Israel, how g. is the house of God
25. g. and hath no end, high and unmeasurable
Bel 18. g. art thou, O Bel, with thee is no deceit
41. saying, g. art thou, O Lord God of Daniel
1 Mac. 1. 17. he entered into Egypt with a g. navy
33. they builded the city of David with a g. wall
64. and there was very g. wrath on Israel
7. 19. when slain, he cast them into the g. pit

GREATER.

2 Esd. 5. 13. thou shalt hear yet g. things
6. 31. if thou pray, I shall tell thee g. things
9. 16. like as a wave is g. than a drop
14. 16. for yet g. evils shall be done hereafter
Eccl. 3. 18. the g. thou art, the more humble thyself
10. 24. none g. than he that feareth the Lord
16. 5. mine ear hath heard g. things than these
39. 11. if he die, he shall leave a g. name than
43. 32. there are yet hid g. things than these
1 Mac. 6. 27. they will do g. things than these
12. 24. to fight ag. him with a g. host than before

GREATEST.

Eccl. 8. 7. rejoice not over thy g. enemy being dead

GREATLY.

Wisd. 3.5. a little chastised they shall be g. rewarded
Eccl. 1. 8. there is one wise, and g. to be feared
7. 17. humble thy soul g. for the vengeance is fire
11. 6. many mighty men have been g. disgraced
25. 2. and I am g. offended at their life
1 Mac. 3. 31. being g. perplexed in mind
5. 63. Judas and his brethren were g. renowned
6. 1. Elimais was a city g. renowned for riches
11. 42. I will g. honour thee and thy nation

GREATNESS.

2 Esd. 10. 55. the beauty and g. of the building
Tob. 13. 4. there declare his g. and extol him
Wisd. 6. 7. nor shall he stand in awe of a man's g.
13. 5. for by the g. and beauty of the creatures
Eccl. 17. 8. might shew them the g. of his works
51. 3. delivered me according to the g. of thy name
1 Mac. 9. 22. the noble acts he did and his g.

GRECIAN.

2 Mac. 13. 2. having either of them a G. power

GRECIANS.

1 Mac. 6. 2. who reigned first among the G.
8. 9. how the G. had determined to destroy them
2 Mac. 4. 15. but liking the glory of the G. best

GREECE.

1 Mac. 1. 1. he reigned in his stead the first over G.

GREEDY.

Tob. 5. 18. be not g. to add money to money
Eccl. 37. 29. nor be too g. upon meats
1 Mac. 4. 17. Judas said, be not g. of the spoils

GREEDINESS.

Eccl. 23. 6. let not the g. of the belly take hold on me

GREEK, S.

1 Mac. 1. 10. the 137th year of the kingdom of the G.
2 Mac. 4. 13. such was the height of G. fashions
36. certain G. which abhorred the fact also

GREEKISH.

2 Mac. 4. 10. brought his own nation to G. fashions

GREEN.

Wisd. 19. 7. out of the violent stream, a g. field
Eccl. 14. 18. as of g. leaves on a thick tree
40. 22. but more than both, corn while it is g.

GREETING.

1 Esd. 6. 7. the copy of letters to king Darius g.
8. 9. king Artaxerxes to Esdras sendeth g.
Esth. 16. 1. to all our faithful subjects, g.
1 Mac. 10. 18. Alexander to Jonathan sendeth g.
25. Demetrius unto the Jews sendeth g. 11. 30.
11. 32. Demetrius unto Lasthenes, sendeth g.
12. 20. Areus king, to Onias the high-priest, g.
13. 36. king Demetrius unto Simon sendeth g.
14. 20. rulers of Lacedemonians to Simon, send g.
15. 2. Antiochus to the people of the Jews, g.
16. Lucius consul to king Ptolemee, g.
2 Mac. 1. 10. Judas sent g. and health to Aristobulus
11. 16. Lysias to the people of the Jews, sendeth g.
22. Antiochus to his brother Lysias sends g.
27. king Antiochus sends g. to the council
34. ambassadors of Romans send g. to the Jews

GREETINGS.

Eccl. 6. 5. a fair tongue will increase kind g.

GREW.

2 Esd. 8. 9. delivereth up the things that g. in it
9. 47. so when he g. up, and came to the time

2 Esd. 11. 3. out of her feathers g. other feathers
14. 40. when I had drunk, wisdom g. in my breast

GRIEF.

Wisd. 8. 9. she would be a comfort in cares and g.
11. 12. for a double g. came upon them
Eccl. 26. 6. but a g. of heart and sorrow is a woman
29. 5. return words of g. and complain of the time
37. 2. is it not a g. when a companion is turned
Sus. 10. yet durst not one shew another his g.
1 Mac. 6. 8. the king laid him down and fell sick for g.
9. for his g. was ever more and more
13. I perish through great g. in a strange land

GRIEVE.

Tob. 4. 3. which shall please her and g. her not
Eccl. 3. 12. g. him not as long as he liveth
4. 8. let it not g. thee to bow down thine ear

GRIEVED.

1 Esd. 1. 24. and how they g. him exceedingly
2 Esd. 9. 38. and she was much g. in heart
40. I said, why art thou so g. in thy mind?
10. 8. we all mourn, art thou g. for one son?
50. God seeth that thou art g. unfeignedly
Tob. 3. 1. then I being g. did weep and prayed
Wisd. 14. 24. slew him, or g. him by adultery
Eccl. 6. 25. bear her, and be not g. with her bonds
12. 9. in the prosperity of a man, enemies will be g.
21. 24. a wise man will be g. with the disgrace
47. 20. and thou wast g. for thy folly
Bar. 4. 8. ye have g. Jerusalem that nursed you
33. so shall she be g. for her own desolation
1 Mac. 3. 7. he g. many kings and made Jacob glad
2 Mac. 4. 35. were much g. for the unjust murder
13. 25. the people there were g. for the covenants

GRIEVETH.

Eccl. 30. 3. he that teacheth his son, g. the enemy

GRIEVOUS.

2 Esd. 5. 21. the thoughts of my heart were g.
Wisd. 2. 15. he is g. to us even to behold
17. 11. wickedness always forecasteth g. things
21. were to themselves more g. than darkness
Eccl. 8. 15. travel not, lest he become g. to thee
27. 15. and their revilings are g. to the ears
29. 28. these things are g. to a man of understanding
2 Mac. 6. 3. this mischief was g. to the people
9. 21. and being taken with a g. disease thought
24. if any tidings were brought that were g.
13. 6. or had committed any other g. crime
14. 45. and though his wounds were g. yet he ran

GRIEVOUSLY.

Wisd. 19. 16. but these very g. afflicted them
2 Mac. 7. 39. and took it g. that he was mocked
9. 28. the murderer having suffered most g.
14. 28. took it g. that he should make void articles

GROANED.

2 Mac. 6. 30. when ready to die with stripes he g.

GROANETH.

Eccl. 30. 20. he g. as an eunuch that embraceth

GROANING.

Wisd. 5. 3. g. for anguish of spirit, they shall say
11. 12. a g. for the remembrance of things past

GROVES.

2 Esd. 16. 28. who shall hide themselves in thick g.
Jud. 3. 8. yet he did cut down their frontiers and g.
1 Mac. 1. 47. set up altars, and g. and chapels of idols

GROUND.

1 Esd. 8. 91. lying flat on the g. before the temple
9. 47. they fell to the g. and worshipped the Lord
2 Esd. 4. 19. for the g. is given to the wood
21. for like as the g. is given to the wood
8. 41. as husbandman soweth much seed on the g.
9. 34. when the g. hath received seed or the sea a ship
10. 22. psaltery is laid on the g. our song to silence
15. 13. they that till the g. shall mourn
Jud. 12. 15. her maid laid soft skins on the g.
14. 18. Holofernes lieth on the g. without a head
16. 5. dash the sucking children against the g.
Wisd. 19. 10. how the g. brought forth flies
19. things that before swam, now went on the g.
Eccl. 11. 5. many kings have sat down on the g.
18. 6. neither can the g. of them be found out
33. 10. all men from the g. Adam of the earth
Bar. 5. 7. to make even the g. that Israel may go
6. 27. for if they fall to the g. at any time
1 Mac. 14. 8. then did they till their g. in peace
2 Mac. 3. 27. Heliodorus fell suddenly to the g.
4. 42. and some they struck to the g.
8. 3. defaced and ready to be made even with the g.
9. 8. he was now cast on the g. and carried
14. was going to lay the holy city even with the g.
14. 33. lay this temple of God even with the g.

GROW.

2 Esd. 2. 19. whereon there g. roses and lilies
10. 9. for the fall of so many that g. upon her
16. 21. even then shall evils g. upon earth, sword
32. and all her paths shall g. full of thorns
Eccl. 14. 18. green leaves, some fall and some g.
Dan. 3. 54. O all ye things that g. bless ye the Lord

GROWETH.

Eccl. 50. 10. a cypress which g. up to the clouds

GROWING.

Wisd. 16. 26. that it is not the g. of fruits
Eccl. 39. 13. and bud forth as a rose g. by the brook
40. 16. the weed g. on every water and bank
1 Mac. 4. 38. they saw shrubs g. in the courts

GROWN.

2 Esd. 4. 10. and such as are g. up with thee
7. 41. even so now seeing corruption is g. up
Wisd. 14. 16. an ungodly custom g. strong

GRUDGE.

Eccl. 10. 25. he will not g. when he is reformed

GRUDGED.

Wisd. 12. 27. what things they g. when punished

GUARD.

1 Esd. 3. 4. three young men that were of the g.
Jud. 12. 7. then Holofernes commanded his g.
2 Mac. 3. 24. he was present himself with his g.
28. lately came with all his g. into the treasury

GUESS.

Wisd. 9. 16. hardly do we g. aright at things
Eccl. 9. 14. as near as thou canst g. at thy neighbour

GUEST.

Wisd. 5. 14. remembrance of a g. tarrieth but a day

GUIDE.

2 Esd. 16. 75. neither doubt, for God is your g.
76. the g. of them who keep my commandments
Wisd. 18. 3. to be a g. of the unknown journey
Eccl. 20. 32. that leadeth his life without a g.
2 Mac. 5. 15. Menelaus that traitor being his g.

GUIDED.

Wisd. 10. 10. she g. him in right paths, shewed him
17. she g. him in a marvellous way, and was

GUIDING.

2 Mac. 10. 1. the Lord g. them, recovered the temple

GUILTY.

Tob. 6. 12. but he shall be g. of death because
Sus. 53. and thou hast let the g. go free

GUSHED.

2 Mac. 14. 45. though his blood g. out like spouts

H.

HABBACUC.

Bel 33. there was in Jewry a prophet called H.
34. but the angel of the Lord said unto H.
35. and H. said, Lord, I never saw Babylon
37. and H. cried, saying, O Daniel, Daniel
39. the angel of the Lord set H. in his own place

HABITATION.

Tob. 1. 4. the temple of the h. of the Most High
2 Mac. 11. 2. to make the city an h. of Gentiles
14. 35. the temple of thy h. should be among us

HABITATIONS.

1 Esd. 9. 12. and let all them of our h. come
Eccl. 44. 6. rich men living peaceably in their h.

HAIL.

2 Esd. 15. 13. seeds shall fail through blasting and h.
41. fire and h. and flying swords, and waters
Wisd. 16. 22. fire burning in the h. did destroy
Eccl. 39. 29. fire and h. created for vengeance

HAILS.

Wisd. 16. 16. with strange h. were they persecuted

HAILSTONES.

Wisd. 5. 22. and h. full of wrath shall be cast
Eccl. 43. 15. by his power the h. are broken small
46. 6. with h. of mighty power he made the battle

HAIR.

1 Esd. 8. 71. I pulled the h. from off my head
2 Esd. 1. 8. pull thou off the h. of thy head
16. 2. gird yourselves with clothes of sack and h.
Jud. 10. 3. she braided the h. of her head
13. 7. she took hold of the h. of his head
16. 8. she bound her h. in a tire and took
Esth. 14. 2. the places of joy she filled with torn h.
Eccl. 27. 14. maketh the h. stand upright
Bel 27. then Daniel took pitch, fat, and h.
36. the angel bare him by the h. of his head
2 Mac. 7. 7. they pulled off the skin with the h.
Gray HAIRS. See GRAY.

HALF.

2 Esd. 11. 17. none after thee attain to h. thy time
13. 45. a great way to go, of a year and an h.
14. 11. ten parts are gone, and h. of a tenth part
12. that which is after the h. of a tenth part
Tob. 8. 21. then he should take the h. of his goods
12. 2. it is no harm to me to give him h. of those
5. take h. of all that ye have brought and go
Wisd. 18. 18. and another thrown there h. dead
Eccl. 29. 6. if prevail, he shall hardly receive the h.
1 Mac. 3. 37. the king took the h. of the forces
10. 30. and the h. of the fruit of the trees

HALLELUIA.

Tob. 13. 18. and all her streets shall say h.

HALLOW.

1 Esd. 1. 3. the Levites should h. themselves to Lord

HALLOWED.

2 Esd. 2. 41. that thy people may be h.
5. 25. of all cities thou hast h. Sion to thyself
Jud. 9. 13. against thy covenant and thy h. house
Eccl. 33. 9. he hath made high days and h. them
1 Mac. 4. 48. made up the sanctuary h. the courts

HAMMER.

Eccl. 38. 28. the noise of h. and anvil is in his ears

HAND.

1 Esd. 6. 33. that stretcheth out his h. to endamage
2 Esd. 3. 6. which thy right h. had planted
6. 8. Jacob's h. held the first heel of Esau
10. the h. of man is betwixt the heel and the h.
Tob. 4. 14. but give him his wages out of h.
5. 17. is he not the staff of our h. in going in and out?
7. 13. he took her by the h. and gave her to Tobias
11. 4. take in thine h. the gall of the fish
13. 2. nor is there any that can avoid his h.
Jud. 2. 12. that will I do by mine h.
8. 33. the Lord will visit Israel by mine h.
9. 9. give it into mine h. who am a widow
10. break their stateliness by the h. of a woman
12. 4. before the Lord work by mine h.
13. 15. Ld. hath smitten him by the h. of a woman
15. 10. hath done all these things by thine h.
16. 6. hath disappointed them by the h. of a woman
Esth. 14. 4. for my danger is in mine h.
14. but deliver us from thine h. and help me
Wisd. 2. 18. deliver him from the h. of his enemies
3. 1. the souls of the righteous are in the h. of God
7. 16. for in his h. are both we and our words
10. 20. magnified thine h. that fought for them
11. 1. she prospered in the h. of the holy prophet
17. thy almighty h. that made the world
13. 10. a stone, the work of an ancient h.
14. 6. the hope of the world governed by thy h.
16. 15. it is not possible to escape thine h.
19. 8. all the people that were defended with thy h.
Eccl. 4. 9. deliver him from the h. of the oppressor
5. 12. if not, lay thy h. upon thy mouth
7. 32. and stretch thy h. unto the poor
36. whatever thou takest in h. remember the end
9. 17. for h. of artificer the work shall be commended
10. 4. the power of the earth is in the h. of Lord
5. in the h. of God is the prosperity of man
12. 12. neither let him sit at thy right h.
14. 13. stretch out thine h. and give to him

Eccl. 15. 14. and left him in the *h.* of his counsel
16. stretch forth thy *h.* unto whither thou wilt
16. 27. and in his *h.* are the chief of them
18. 3. governs the world with the palm of his *h.*
21. 19. and like manacles on the right *h.*
22. 2. every man that takes it up, will shake his *h.*
27. 19. as one that letteth a bird go out of his *h.*
29.1. he that strengtheneth his *h.* keepeth command
5. till he hath received, he will kiss a man's *h.*
31. 14. stretch out thine *h.* whither it looketh
18. reach not thy *h.* out first of all
33. 13. as clay is in the potter's *h.* to fashion it
36. 3. lift up thy *h.* against strange nations
6. shew signs, glorify thy *h.* and thy right arm
38. 15. let him fall into the *h.* of the physician
40. 14. while he openeth his *h.* he shall rejoice
47. 4. when he lifted up his *h.* with the stone
5. he gave him strength in his right *h.* to slay
48. 18. Sennacherib lift up his *h.* against Sion
49. 11. even he was as a signet on the right *h.*
50. 15. he stretched out his *h.* to the cup
51. 26. receive instruction, she is hard at *h.* to find
Bar. 6. 15. he hath also in his right *h.* a dagger
Dan. 3. 66. hath saved us from the *h.* of death
2 *Mac.* 3. 29. he by the *h.* of God was cast down
5. 23. Menelaus bare an heavy *h.* over the citizens
6. 26. I should not escape the *h.* of the Almighty
7. 19. that takest in *h.* to strive against God
34. lifting up thy *h.* against the servants of God
13. 22. gave his *h.* took theirs, departed, fought
15. 15. Jeremias holding forth right *h.* gave Judas
30. commanded to strike off Nicanor's head and *h.*
32. he shewed them the *h.* of that blasphemer
HANDFULS.
2 *Mac.* 4. 41. others taking *h.* of dust, cast them
HANDLE.
Wisd. 15. 15. nor have fingers of hands to *h.*
HANDLED.
2 *Mac.* 7. 39. the king *h.* him worse than all the rest
HANDLING.
2 *Mac.* 2. 28. the exact *h.* of every particular
8. 17. injury to holy place, the cruel *h.* of the city
HANDMAID.
2 *Esd.* 9. 45. after thirty years God heard me thy *h.*
Jud. 11. 5. suffer thy *h.* to speak in thy presence
6. if thou wilt follow the words of thine *h.*
16. I thine *h.* knowing all this, am fled
12. 4. thine *h.* shall not spend these things
6. command that thine *h.* may go forth to prayer
Esth. 14. 17. thine *h.* hath not eaten at Aman's table
18. nor hath thine *h.* any joy since the day
Wisd. 9. 5. I thy servant and son of thine *h.*
HANDS.
1 *Esd.* 1. 53. for he delivered all into their *h.*
7. 15. to strengthen their *h.* in the works of Lord
8. 73. stretching forth my *h.* unto the Lord
9. 20. they gave their *h.* to put away their wives
47. lifting up their *h.* they fell to the ground
2 *Esd.* 1. 26. ye have defiled your *h.* with blood
32. whose blood I will require of your *h.*
3. 5. which was the workmanship of thine *h.*
5. 30. yet shouldst punish them with thine own *h.*
8. 7. we are all one workmanship of thine *h.*
Jud. 7. 25. but God hath sold us into their *h.*
Esth. 12. 2. were about to lay *h.* upon Artaxerxes
Wisd. 1. 12. destruction with the works of your *h.*
3. 14. who with his *h.* hath wrought no iniquity
8. 12. they shall lay their *h.* on their mouth
18. in the works of her *h.* are infinite riches
12. 3. thy will to destroy by the *h.* of our fathers
6. the parents that killed with their own *h.*
13. 10. gods which are the works of men's *h.*
19. for good success of his *h.* asketh ability to do
14. 8. but that which is made with *h.* is cursed
15. 15. which have not fingers of *h.* to handle
17. he worketh a dead thing with wicked *h.*
Eccl. 2. 12. woe be to the fearful hearts and faint *h.*
18. saying, we will fall into the *h.* of the Lord
8. 1. strive not with a mighty man, lest fall in his *h.*
11. 6. the honourable delivered into other men's *h.*
12. 18. he will shake his head and clap his *h.*
25. 23. she maketh weak *h.* and feeble knees
35. 8. diminish not the first-fruits of thy *h.*
38. 10. leave off sin, and order thy *h.* aright
13. a time when in their *h.* there is good success
31. all these trust to their *h.* every one is wise
42. 6. and shut up where many *h.* are
46. 2. when he did lift up his *h.* against cities
48. 19. then trembled their hearts and *h.*
20. they stretched out their *h.* towards him
50. 12. when he took the portions out of priests' *h.*
13. the oblations of the Lord in their *h.*
20. he lifted up his *h.* over the congregation
51. 3. out of the *h.* of such as sought my life
8. thou savest them out of the *h.* of the enemies
19. I stretched forth my *h.* to the heavens above
Bar. 6. 51. no gods but the works of men's *h.*
Dan. 3. 9. deliver us into *h.* of lawless enemies
Sus. 22. if I do it not, I cannot escape your *h.*
23. it is better for me to fall into your *h.*
34. the two elders laid their *h.* upon her head
Bel 5. I may not worship idols made with *h.*
1 *Mac.* 3. 18. to be shut up in the *h.* of a few
12. 9. we have holy books of scripture in our *h.*
14. 31. that they might lay *h.* on the sanctuary
2 *Mac.* 2. 25. that all into whose *h.* it comes
3. 20. all holding their *h.* towards heaven
5. 16. taking the holy vessels with polluted *h.* and
with profane *h.* pulling down things dedicated
7. 10. holding forth his *h.* manfully
31. thou shalt not escape the *h.* of God
12. 12. whereupon they shook *h.* and departed
14. 34. then the priests lift up their *h.* to heaven
46. and taking his bowels in both his *h.*
15. 12. holding up his *h.* prayed for the Jews
HANDSOMELY.
Wisd. 13. 11. the carpenter hath wrought it *h.*
HAND-WRITING.
Tob. 5. 3. then he gave him the *h.* and said
9. 5. Raphael went out and gave Gabael the *h.*
HANG.
Jud. 14. 1. take his head, and *h.* it on your walls

2 *Mac.* 15. 33. *h.* up the reward of his madness
HANGED.
1 *Esd.* 6. 32. a tree taken, and he thereon be *h.*
2 *Esd.* 16. 58. he hath *h.* the earth on the waters
Jud. 14. 11. they *h.* the head of Holofernes
Esth. 16. 18. the worker of these things is *h.*
1 *Mac.* 1. 61. they *h.* infants about their necks
4. 57. chambers they renewed and *h.* doors on them
7. 47. they *h.* them up towards Jerusalem
2 *Mac.* 13. 5. on every side *h.* down into the ashes
15. 35. he *h.* also Nicanor's head on the tower
HANGETH, ING.
Eccl. 19. 26. a wicked man that *h.* down his head
2 *Mac.* 6. 10. the babes *h.* at their breasts
HAPPEN.
2 *Esd.* 4. 51. or what shall *h.* in those days
13. 18. which shall *h.* to them and to those left
20. pass away, and not see the things that *h.*
32. the signs shall *h.* which I shewed thee
14. 16. than those which thou hast seen *h.*
Wisd. 2. 17. let us prove what shall *h.* in the end
Eccl. 22. 26. and if any evil *h.* to me by him
33. 1. no evil shall *h.* to him that feareth the Lord
40. 8. such things *h.* to all flesh, man and beast
HAPPENED.
2 *Esd.* 9. 35. but with us it hath not *h.* so
10. 48. that my son *h.* to have a fall and died
Tob. 11. 15. things that had *h.* to him in Media
Jud. 8. 26. and what *h.* to Jacob in Mesopotamia
Wisd. 19. 4. the things that had already *h.*
Eccl. 5. 4. and what harm *h.* unto me?
Bar. 2. 2. bring great plagues, such as never *h.*
1 *Mac.* 1. 1. it *h.* after that Alexander had smitten
4. 26. the strangers told Lysias what had *h.*
5. 25. Nabathites told them every thing that *h.*
2 *Mac.* 9. 3. what had *h.* to Nicanor and Timotheus
13. 7. such a death it *h.* that wicked man to die
HAPPENETH.
2 *Esd.* 10. 6. seest thou not what *h.* unto us?
Bar. 3. 10. how *h.* it thou art in thine enemies' land?
HAPPY.
Wisd. 18. 1. had not suffered, they counted them *h.*
Eccl. 25. 7. nine things which I judged to be *h.*
37. 24. all they that see him shall count him *h.*
Bar. 4. 4. O Israel, *h.* are we, things are made known
1 *Mac.* 10. 55. *h.* day wherein thou didst return
2 *Mac.* 7. 24. would make him both a rich and *h.* man
HARD.
Wisd. 11. 4. thirst was quenched out of the *h.* stone
19. 13. they used a more *h.* and hateful behaviour
Eccl. 3. 21. the things that are too *h.* for thee
40. 15. are as unclean roots upon a *h.* rock
48. 17. he digged the *h.* rock with iron
1 *Mac.* 3. 18. it is no *h.* matter for many to be shut up
2 *Mac.* 12. 21. for the town was *h.* to besiege
HARDENED.
Eccl. 16. 15. Lord *h.* Pharaoh that he should not
HARDENING.
1 *Esd.* 1. 48. *h.* his heart, he transgressed the laws
HARDINESS.
Jud. 16. 10. the Medes were daunted at her *h.*
HARDLY.
Wisd. 9. 16. and *h.* do we guess aright at things
Eccl. 26. 29. a merchant shall *h.* keep himself
29. 6. if he prevail, he shall *h.* receive the half
HARDNESS.
Eccl. 16. 10. were gathered in the *h.* of their hearts
HARDY.
1 *Mac.* 9. 14. he took with him all the *h.* men
HARLOT.
Eccl. 9. 3. meet not with an *h.* lest thou fall
26. 22. an *h.* shall be accounted as spittle
41. 20. be ashamed to look upon an *h.*
HARLOTS.
Eccl. 9. 6. give not thy soul unto *h.*
19. 2. he that cleaveth to *h.* will become impudent
Bar. 6. 11. they will give thereof to common *h.*
2 *Mac.* 6. 4. the Gentiles who dallied with *h.*
HARM.
Tob. 12. 2. O father, it is no *h.* to me to give him half
Wisd. 11. 19. the *h.* might despatch them at once
Eccl. 5. 4. say not I sinned, what *h.* hath happened
7. 1. do no evil, so shall no *h.* come unto thee
38. 16. thou hadst suffered great *h.* thyself
1 *Mac.* 7. 15. we will procure the *h.* neither of you
9. 71. he sware that he would never do them *h.*
15. 19. to write that they should do them no *h.*
31. give me for the *h.* that you have done
35. albeit they did great *h.* to the people
2 *Mac.* 14. 14. the *h.* of the Jews to be their welfare
HARMLESS.
Wisd. 18 3. thou gavest an *h.* sun to entertain them
2 *Mac.* 8 4. the wicked slaughter of *h.* infants
HARMONY.
Wisd. 19. 18. the elements changed by a kind of *h.*
HARNESS.
1 *Mac.* 3. 3. he girt his warlike *h.* about him
6. 41. all that heard the rattling of *h.* were moved
43. one of the beasts armed with royal *h.*
2 *Mac.* 3. 25. that he had complete *h.* of gold
5. 3. were seen ornaments and *h.* of all sorts
15. 28. they knew that Nicanor lay dead in his *h.*
HARNESSED.
1 *Mac.* 4. 7. they saw that it was strong and well *h.*
6. 38. and being *h.* all over amidst the ranks
HARP.
1 *Mac.* 3. 45. joy taken the pipe with the *h.* ceased
HARPS.
Eccl. 39. 15. and shew forth his praise with *h.*
1 *Mac.* 4. 54. it was dedicated with *h.* and cymbals
13. 51. he entered into it with *h.* and cymbals
HARVEST.
Eccl. 24. 26. to abound as Jordan in time of *h.*
HASTE.
1 *Esd.* 2. 30. removing in *h.* towards Jerusalem
2 *Esd.* 4. 34. thy *h.* is in vain to be above him
42. a woman maketh *h.* to escape the necessity
5. 44. the creature may not *h.* above the Maker
14. 15. and *h.* thee to flee from these times
Tob. 11. 3. let us *h.* before thy wife and prepare
Jud. 13. 1. his servants made *h.* to depart
12. they made *h.* to go down to the gate

Wisd. 18. 21. then the blameless man made *h.*
Eccl. 2. 2. and make not *h.* in time of trouble
Sus. 50. all the people turned again in *h.*
1 *Mac.* 6. 57. he went in all *h.* and said to the king
63. afterward departed he in all *h.* and returned
11. 22. but come and speak with him in great *h.*
13. 10. he made *h.* to finish the walls of Jerusalem
2 *Mac.* 4. 31. the king came in all *h.* to appease
5. 21. he departed in all *h.* into Antiochia
9. 7. and commanding to *h.* the journey
14. the holy city, to which he was going in *h.* to
lay even with ground, and make a burying
14. 43. but missing his stroke through *h.*
HASTED.
Jud. 10. 15. in that thou hast *h.* to come to our lord
Wisd. 4. 14. therefore *h.* he to take him away
5. 9. those things passed away as a post that *h.* by
Eccl. 50. 17. then all the people *h.* and fell down
HASTEN.
2 *Esd.* 4. 34. do not thou *h.* above the Most Highest
6. 34. *h.* not with the times that are past
1 *Mac.* 13. 21. that he should *h.* his coming to them
HASTETH.
2 *Esd.* 4. 26. for the world *h.* fast to pass away
14. 18. now *h.* vision to come which thou sawest
HASTENED.
2 *Mac.* 4. 14. *h.* to be partakers of unlawful allow.
HASTY.
Eccl. 4. 29. be not *h.* in thy tongue, in deeds slack
6. 7. prove him first, and be not *h.* to credit him
19. 4. he that is *h.* to give credit, is light-minded
28. 11. an *h.* contention kindleth a fire, and an *h.*
fighting sheddeth blood
HASTILY.
Wisd. 19. 2. and having sent them *h.* away
Eccl. 43. 5. at his commandment it runneth *h.*
HAT.
2 *Mac.* 4. 12. made the chief young men wear a *h.*
HATE.
2 *Esd.* 5. 30. if thou didst so much *h.* thy people
10. 23. delivered into the hands of them that *h.* us
16. 50. so shall righteousness *h.* iniquity
Tob. 13. 12. cursed are all they which *h.* thee
Esth. 14. 13. turn his heart to *h.* him that fights
15. thou knowest I *h.* the glory of the unrighteous
Eccl. 7. 15. *h.* not laborious work nor husbandry
13. 20. as proud *h.* humility, so doth rich the poor
19. 9. and when time cometh, he will *h.* thee
25. 14. but the affliction from them that *h.* me
1 *Mac.* 7. 26. a man that bare deadly *h.* to Israel
2 *Mac.* 14. 39. willing to declare the *h.* he bare
HATED.
2 *Esd.* 15. 48. *h.* in all her works and inventions
Wisd. 11. 24. made any thing, if thou hadst *h.* it
Eccl. 9. 18. he that is rash in his talk shall be *h.*
20. 8. that taketh to himself authority shall be *h.*
15. such a one is to be *h.* of God and man
21. 28. a whisperer is *h.* wheresoever he dwelleth
27. 24. I have *h.* many things, nothing like him
31. 16. eat as becomes, devour not lest thou be *h.*
37. 20. one sheweth wisdom in words, and is *h.*
42. 9. and being married, lest she should be *h.*
1 *Mac.* 11. 21. ungodly persons *h.* their own people
38. wherefore all the forces of his father *h.* him
2 *Mac.* 5. 8. *h.* as a forsaker of the laws
HATEFUL.
Wisd. 14. 9. ungodly and ungodliness are *h.* to God
15. 18. those beasts also that are most *h.*
19. 13. they used a more hard and *h.* behaviour
Eccl. 10. 7. pride is *h.* before God and man
20. 5. another by much babbling becometh *h.*
Dan. 3. 9. lawless enemies, most *h.* forsakers of G.
HATEST.
Tob. 4. 15. do that to no man which thou *h.*
Wisd. 12. 4. whom thou *h.* for doing odious works
HATETH.
Jud. 5. 17. God that *h.* iniquity was with them
Esth. 16. 4. God that seeth all things, and *h.* evil
Eccl. 12. 6. for the Most High *h.* sinners
15. 11. thou oughtest not to do the things that he *h.*
13. the Lord *h.* all abomination
19. 6. he that *h.* babbling, shall have less evil
21. 6. he that *h.* to be reproved, is in way of sinners
25. 2. three sorts of men my soul *h.* and am offended
33. 2. a wise man *h.* not the law
HATRED.
Eccl. 10. 6. bear not *h.* to thy neighbour
28. 3. one man beareth *h.* against another
5. if he that is but flesh nourish *h.*
1 *Mac.* 11. 12. so that their *h.* was openly known
13. 17. he should procure to himself great *h.*
2 *Mac.* 3. 1. because of his *h.* of wickedness
4. 3. but when their *h.* went so far
49. moved with *h.* of that wicked deed
6. 29. changing the good will they bare into *h.*
HAVEN.
1 *Esd.* 5. 55. brought by floats to the *h.* of Joppe
2 *Esd.* 12. 42. as a *h.* or ship preserved from tempest
1 *Mac.* 14. 5. in this, that he took Joppe for an *h.*
2 *Mac.* 12. 6. and he burnt the *h.* by night
9. he set fire on the *h.* and the navy
14. 1. having entered by the *h.* of Tripolis
HAUGHTY.
Eccl. 22. 10. but children being *h.* through disdain
23. 4. but turn away from thy servant a *h.* mind
26. 9. the whoredom may be known in her *h.* looks
2 *Mac.* 5. 17. so *h.* was Antiochus in mind
13. 9. the king came with a barbarous and *h.* mind
HAUGHTINESS.
2 *Mac.* 5. 21. such was the *h.* of his mind
15. 6. Nicanor in exceeding pride and *h.* determin.
HAVOCK.
1 *Mac.* 7. 7. see what *h.* he hath made amongst us
HEAD.
1 *Esd.* 4. 30. taking the crown from the king's *h.*
and setting it on her own *h.* she struck the king
8. 71. I pulled the hair from off my *h.*
2 *Esd.* 1. 8. pull thou off then the hair of thy *h.*
9. 38. clothes were rent, she had ashes on her *h.*
16. 53. God shall burn coals of fire on his *h.*
Jud. 8. 3. as he stood, the heat came upon his *h.*
9. 1. Judith fell on her face, and put ashes on her *h.*

Jud. 13. 8. and she took away his *h.* from him
9. she gave Holofernes his *h.* to her maid
15. she took the *h.* out of the bag and shewed it
18. hath directed thee to the cutting off of the *h.*
14. 1. take this *h.* and hang it on your walls
6. he saw the *h.* of Holofernes in a man's hand
11. they hanged the *h.* of Holofernes on the wall
15. and his *h.* was taken from him
18. Holofernes lieth on the ground without a *h.*
Esth. 14. 2. she covered her *h.* with ashes
16. abhor sign of my high estate which is on my *h.*
Wisd. 18. 24. thy majesty on the diadem of his *h.*
Eccl. 4. 7. and bow thy *h.* to a great man
11. 1. wisdom lifteth up the *h.* of him that is low
13. the Lord lifted up his *h.* from misery
12. 18. he will shake his *h.* and clap his hands
19. 26. a wicked man that hangeth down his *h.*
20. 11. that lifteth up his *h.* from a low estate
25. 15. there is no *h.* above the *h.* of a servant
27. 25. casteth a stone, casteth it on his own *h.*
38. 3. the skill of the physician shall lift up his *h.*
44. 23. and made it rest on *h.* of Jacob
Bar. 5. 2. and set a diamond on thy *h.* of glory
Sus. 34. the elders laid their hands on her *h.*
55. thou hast lied against thine own *h.* 59.
Bel 36. the angel bare him by the hair of his *h.*
Prayer of Manass. that I cannot lift up mine *h.*
1 *Mac.* 7. 47. they smote off Nicanor's *h.*
11. 13. where he set two crowns upon his *h.*
71. Jonathan cast earth on his *h.* and prayed
2 *Mac.* 7. 7. they had pulled off the skin of his *h.*
15. 30. commanded to strike off Nicanor's *h.*
32. and he shewed them vile Nicanor's *h.*
35. he hanged also Nicanor's *h.* on the tower

HEADLONG.

Wisd. 4. 19. for he shall cast them down *h.*
2 *Mac.* 6. 10. they cast them down *h.* from the wall

HEADS.

1 *Esd.* 8. 75. our sins are multiplied above our *h.*
2 *Esd.* 2. 43. upon every one of their *h.* he set crowns
Jud. 4. 11. they cast ashes upon their *h.*
8. 22. the desolation will he turn on our *h.*
9. 9. and send thy wrath upon their *h.*
Eccl. 17. 23. render their recompence on their *h.*
36. 10. smite in sunder the *h.* of the rulers
Bar. 6. 9. they make crowns for the *h.* of their gods
22. upon their bodies and *h.* sit bats, birds
31. priests sit in their temples, their clothes rent, their *h.* and beards shaven, nothing on their *h.*
1 *Mac.* 3. 47. they cast ashes on their *h.* 4. 39.
6. 35. with helmets of brass on their *h.*
9. 23. the wicked began to put forth their *h.*
2 *Mac.* 1. 16. they smote off their *h.* and cast them out
10. 25. and they sprinkled earth on their *h.*
14. 15. they cast earth on their *h.* and prayed

HEADSTRONG.

Eccl. 30. 8. an horse not broken becometh *h.*

HEAD-TIRE.

1 *Esd.* 3. 6. and an *h.* of fine linen, and a chain

HEAL.

2 *Esd.* 2. 21. *h.* the broken and the weak
Tob. 3. 17. Raphael was sent to *h.* them both
12. 14. now God hath sent me to *h.* thee
Eccl. 38. 7. with such doth he *h.* men

HEALED.

Tob. 6. 8. it is good to anoint a man, and he shall be *h.*
12. 3. he brought me money, and likewise *h.* thee
Wisd. 16. 10. thy mercy was ever by them and *h.* them
Eccl. 21. 3. the wounds whereof cannot be *h.*

HEALETH.

Wisd. 16. 12. thy word, O Lord, which *h.* all things

HEALING.

Eccl. 38. 2. for of the Most High cometh *h.*

HEALTH.

2 *Esd.* 7. 51. laid up for us dwellings of *h.* and safety
Tob. 7. 4. then said he, is he in good *h.?*
5. they said, he is both alive and in good *h.*
8. 17. finish their life in *h.* with joy and mercy
Wisd. 7. 10. I loved her above *h.* and beauty
13. 18. for *h.* he calleth on that which is weak
16. 12. no herb nor plaister that restored them to *h.*
Eccl. 1. 18. making peace and perfect *h.* to flourish
17. 26. will lead out of darkness into the light of *h.*
30. 15. *h.* and good state of body are above all gold
34. 17. he giveth *h.* life, and blessing
2 *Mac.* 1. 10. sent greeting and *h.* to Aristobulus
3. 32. offered a sacrifice for the *h.* of the man
9. 18. therefore despairing of his *h.* he wrote
19. wisheth much joy, *h.* and prosperity to the Jews
22. not distrusting my *h.* but having hope
11. 28. if ye fare well, we are also in good *h.*

HEALTHFUL.

Wisd. 1. 14. the generations of the world were *h.*

HEAP.

Eccl. 3. 27. the wicked man shall *h.* sin upon sin
20. 28. that tilleth his land shall increase his *h.*
39. 17. at his command the waters stood as an *h.*

HEAPS.

2 *Esd.* 2. 9. lieth in clods of pitch and *h.* of ashes
Wisd. 18. 23. the dead were fallen down by *h.*
1 *Mac.* 11. 4. they had made *h.* of them by the way

HEAR.

1 *Esd.* 9. 40. to *h.* the law the first day of the month
2 *Esd.* 1. 26. when you call on me, I will not *h.* you
2. 1. by the prophets, whom they would not *h.*
9. even so will I do to them that *h.* me not
Tob. 3. 13. that I may *h.* no more reproach, 15.
6. 15. wherefore *h.* me, O my brother
10. 12. that I may *h.* good report of thee
Jud. 8. 17. he will *h.* our voice, if it please him
32. *h.* me, and I will do a thing which shall go
9. 4. O God, O my God, *h.* me also a widow
12. Lord of heavens and earth, *h.* thou my prayer
14. 1. *h.* me now, my brethren, and hang it up
Esth. 13. 17. *h.* my prayer, turn our sorrow into joy
14. 19. O mighty God, *h.* the voice of the forlorn
Wisd. 6. 1. *h.* therefore, O ye kings, and understand
8. 15. shall be afraid when they do but *h.* of me
15. 15. nor noses to draw breath, nor ears to *h.*
Eccl. 3. 1. *h.* me your father, O children, and do
5. 11. be swift to *h.* and let thy life be sincere
6. 33. if thou love to *h.* shalt receive understanding
35. be willing to *h.* every godly discourse
21. 15. if a skilful man *h.* a wise word will commend
23. 7. *h.* O ye children, the discipline of the mouth
25. 9. that speaketh in the ears of him that will *h.*
29. 25. moreover, thou shalt *h.* bitter words
31. 22. my son, *h.* me, and despise me not
33. 18. *h.* me, O ye great men of the people
34. 24. whose voice will the Lord *h.?*
26. that doth the same, who will *h.* his prayer?

HEARD.

1 *Esd.* 5. 65. that the trumpets might not be *h.* yet the multitude sounded so that it was *h.* afar off
9. 50. for they all wept when they *h.* the law
Tob. 3. 16. the prayers of them both were *h.*
Jud. 4. 13. so God *h.* their prayers, and looked
Esth. 12. 2. he *h.* their devices, and searched out
Eccl. 3. 5. when he maketh his prayer, he shall be *h.*
4. 6. his prayer shall be *h.* of him that made him
11. 8. answer not before thou hast *h.* the cause
16. 5. mine ear hath *h.* greater things than these
17. 13. and their ears *h.* his glorious voice
19. 9. he *h.* and observed thee, and will hate thee
10. if thou hast *h.* a word, let it die with thee
27. down his countenance, making as if he *h.* not
33. 4. prepare what to say, and so thou shalt be *h.*
41. 23. or speaking again what thou hast *h.*
45. 9. a noise that might be *h.* in the temple
46. 5. he called, and the great Lord *h.* him
48. 20. and immediately the holy One *h.* them
50. 16. sons of Aaron made a great noise to be *h.*
51. 11. I will praise, and so my prayer was *h.*

HEARDEST.

Eccl. 48. 7. who *h.* the rebuke of the Lord in Sinai

HEARER.

Wisd. 1. 6. for God is witness and a *h.* of his tongue

HEAREST.

Eccl. 13. 13. when thou *h.* these things, awake
27. 7. praise no man before thou *h.* him speak

HEARETH.

Wisd. 1. 10. for the ear of jealousy *h.* all things
Eccl. 21. 15. when one of no understanding *h.* it
22. 26. every one that *h.* it will beware of him
25. 18. and when he *h.* it, shall sigh bitterly

HEARING.

Wisd. 18. 1. whose voice they *h.* and not seeing
Bar. 1. 4. in the *h.* of nobles, in the *h.* of elders

HEARKEN.

Eccl. 14. 23. he shall also *h.* at her doors
16. 24. my son, *h.* to me, and learn knowledge
21. 24. it is the rudeness of a man to *h.* at the door
33. 18. *h.* with your ears, ye rulers of congregation
37. 11. *h.* not to these in any matter of counsel
39. 13. *h.* to me, ye holy children, and bud forth
Bar. 2. 24. but we would not *h.* to thy voice
1 *Mac.* 2. 22. we will not *h.* to the king's words
2 *Mac.* 7. 25. the young man would in no case *h.*

HEARKENED.

Bar. 3. 4. have not *h.* to the voice of thee their God

HEART.

1 *Esd.* 1. 23. with an *h.* full of godliness
48. hardening his *h.* he transgressed the laws
3. 21. and it maketh every *h.* rich so that a man
8. 25. who hath put these things into *h.* of the king
2 *Esd.* 3. 21. the first Adam bearing a wicked *h.*
26. did even as Adam, they also had a wicked *h.*
4. 30. evil seed hath been sown in the *h.* of Adam
8. 58. and said in their *h.* that there is no God
Tob. 1. 12. because I remember God with all my *h.*
4. 13. my son, despise not in thy *h.* thy brethren
6. 4. and take the *h.* and the liver and the gall
6. brother, to what use is the *h.* and the liver?
7. he said to him, touching the *h.* and the liver
17. and his *h.* was effectually joined to her
8. 2. put the *h.* and the liver of the fish thereon
Jud. 8. 14. you cannot find the depth of the *h.*
Esth. 14. 13. turn his *h.* to hate him that fighteth
15. 5. but her *h.* was in anguish for fear
Wisd. 1. 6. for God is a true beholder of his *h.*
2. 2. as a little spark in the moving of our *h.*
8. 17. when I pondered these things in my *h.*
21. besought him, and with my whole *h.* I said
15. 10. his *h.* is ashes, his hope more vile than earth
Eccl. 1. 12. the fear of the Lord maketh a merry *h.*
28. and come not to him with a double *h.*
30. camest not in truth, but thy *h.* is full of deceit
2. 2. set thy *h.* aright, and constantly endure
3. 26. a stubborn *h.* shall fare evil at the last
27. an obstinate *h.* shall be laden with sorrows
29. the *h.* of the prudent will understand
5. 1. set not thy *h.* on thy goods, and say not
2. thy strength to walk in the ways of thy *h.*
6. 26. come unto her with thy whole *h.* and keep
37. he shall establish thy *h.* and give wisdom
7. 27. honour thy father with thy whole *h.*
8. 19. open not thine *h.* to every man lest he
9. 9. lest thy *h.* incline unto her, and thou fall
10. 12. his *h.* is turned away from his Maker
11. 30. kept in a cage, so is the *h.* of the proud
13. 25. the *h.* of a man changeth his countenance, a merry *h.* maketh a cheerful countenance
26. is a token of a *h.* that is in prosperity
14. 21. he that considereth her ways in his *h.*
16. 20. no *h.* can think on these things worthily
24. my son, mark my words with thy *h.*
17. 6. an *h.* gave he them to understand
28. the living and sound in *h.* shall praise the Lord
19. 16. that slippeth in speech, but not from his *h.*
21. 6. that fears the Lord, will repent from his *h.*
17. they shall ponder his words in their *h.*
26. the *h.* of fools is in their mouth
22. 16. the *h.* that is established by advised counsel
17. a *h.* settled on a thought of understanding
18. so a fearful *h.* in the imagination of a fool
11. he that pricketh the *h.* maketh it to shew
23. 2. set the discipline of wisdom over my *h.*
18. saying thus in his *h.* who seeth me?
25. 7. which I have judged in my *h.* to be happy
13. give me any plague, but the plague of the *h.*
26. 4. if he have a good *h.* toward the Lord
5. there be three things that my *h.* feareth
18. so are the fair feet with a constant *h.*
28. there be two things that grieve my *h.*
27. 6. so is the utterance of a conceit in the *h.*
30. 16. there is no joy above the joy of the *h.*
23. love thine own soul, and comfort thine *h.*
25. a good *h.* will have a care of his meat and diet
31. 28. wine in season brings gladness of the *h.*
33. 5. the *h.* of the foolish is like a cart-wheel
34. 5. the *h.* fancieth as a woman's *h.* in travail
36. 20. a froward *h.* causeth heaviness
37. 17. the countenance is a sign of changing the *h.*
38. 10. and cleanse thy *h.* from all wickedness
18. the heaviness of the *h.* breaketh strength
20. take no heaviness to *h.* drive it away
40. 20. wine and music rejoice the *h.* but wisdom
42. 18. he seeketh out the deep and the *h.*
43. 18. the *h.* is astonished at the raining of it
45. 26. God give you wisdom in your *h.* to judge
46. 11. every one whose *h.* went not a whoring
49. 3. he directed his *h.* unto the Lord
50. 23. he grant us joyfulness of *h.* and that peace
25. two manner of nations my *h.* abhorreth
27. who out of his *h.* poured forth wisdom
28. he that layeth them up in his *h.* shall be wise
Bar. 2. 8. from the imaginations of his wicked *h.*
Dan. 2. 16. in a contrite *h.* let us be accepted
65. O ye holy and humble men of *h.* bless Lord
Sus. 35. for her *h.* trusted in the Lord
Prayer of Manass. now I bow the knee of my *h.*
1 *Mac.* 6. 10. sleep gone, my *h.* faileth for very care
2 *Mac.* 3. 17. what sorrow he had now in his *h.*

HEARTH.

Eccl. 50. 12. he stood by the *h.* of the altar

HEARTILY.

2 *Mac.* 4. 37. therefore Antiochus was *h.* sorry

HEARTS.

2 *Esd.* 14. 34. if so be ye will reform your *h.*
16. 54. the Lord knoweth their thoughts and *h.*
63. he knoweth what you think in your *h.*
Jud. 8. 24. because their *h.* depend upon us
Eccl. 2. 12. woe be to fearful *h.* and faint hands
17. that fear the Lord will prepare their *h.*
8. 2. for gold hath perverted the *h.* of kings
16. 10. were gathered in the hardness of their *h.*
17. 8. he set his eye upon their *h.* to shew them
16. could not make to themsel. fleshly *h.* for stony
31. 26. so doth wine prove the *h.* of the proud
48. 19. then trembled their *h.* and hands
Bar. 3. 7. thou hast put thy fear in our *h.*
6. 6. say ye in your *h.* O Lord, we must worship
20. their *h.* are gnawed upon by things creeping
1 *Mac.* 12. 28. they feared and trembled in their *h.*
2 *Mac.* 1. 4. open your *h.* in his law and commands
2. 3. the law should not depart from their *h.*
15. 17. able to encourage the *h.* of the young men
27. fighting with hands, praying with their *h.*

HEAT.

2 *Esd.* 1. 20. for the *h.* I covered you with leaves
Jud. 8. 3. *h.* came on his head, and he fell on his bed
Wisd. 2. 4. that is overcome with the *h.* thereof
Eccl. 14. 27. by her he shall be covered from *h.*
18. 16. shall not the dew assuage *h.?* so is a word
34. 16. a defence from *h.* a cover from the sun
38. 28. he fighteth with the *h.* of the furnace
43. 3. who can abide the burning *h.* thereof?
22. a dew coming after *h.* refresheth
Bar. 2. 25. they are cast out to the *h.* of the day
Dan. 3. 41. O ye fire and *h.* bless ye the Lord

HEATED.

2 *Mac.* 7. 4. the caldrons forthwith being *h.*

HEATHEN.

1 *Esd.* 5. 72. the *h.* of the land lying heavy
8. 93. wives which we have taken of the *h.*
9. 9. and separate yourselves from the *h.*
2 *Esd.* 3. 36. Israel kept thy precepts, not the *h.*
Esth. 14. 15. I abhor the bed of all the *h.*
Wisd. 15. 15. they counted idols of the *h.* to be gods
Eccl. 35. 18. and repaid vengeance to the *h.*
36. 10. smite in sunder the heads of the *h.*
39. 23. so shall the *h.* inherit his wrath
Bar. 2. 13. for we are but a few left among the *h.*
1 *Mac.* 1. 11. let us make a covenant with the *h.*
13. give licence to do after the ordinances of *h.*
14. according to the customs of the *h.*
15. they joined themselves to the *h.* and were sold
42. so all the *h.* agreed to command of the king
2. 18. like as all the *h.* and Judea have done
68. recompense fully the *h.* and take heed
4. 11. that so all the *h.* may know there is One
45. pull it down, because *h.* had defiled it
54. look at what day the *h.* had profaned it
58. that the reproach of the *h.* was put away
5. 57. let us go fight against the *h.* round us
13. 41. thus the yoke of the *h.* was taken away
2 *Mac.* 1. 27. deliver them that serve among the *h.* look on them, let the *h.* know that thou art God
4. 9. training up of youth in the fashions of the *h.*
6. 8. decree to the neighbour cities of the *h.*
10. 2. but the altars which the *h.* had built
11. 3. as of the other chapels of the *h.* and to set
15. 10. shewing them the falsehood of the *h.*

HEATHENISH.

2 *Mac.* 4. 13. such was the increase of *h.* manners

HEAVEN.

1 *Esd.* 4. 36. the earth calleth on truth, the *h.* blesseth
46. thou hast vowed to the King of *h.*
58. he lifted up his face to *h.* praised King of *h.*
6. 13. servants of the Lord who made *h.* and earth
8. 75. our ignorances have reached up unto *h.*
2 *Esd.* 2. 14. take *h.* and earth to witness
4. 8. neither did I ever climb up into *h.*
6. 38. thou saidst, let *h.* and earth be made
8. 20. who beholdest things in the *h.* and in the air
13. 3. waxed strong with the thousands of *h.*
5. was gathered from the four winds of the *h.*
16. 55. let the *h.* be made, and it was created
Tob. 5. 16. God which dwelleth in *h.* prosper you
7. 18. the Lord of *h.* and earth give thee joy
10. 11. God of *h.* give you a prosperous journey
12. the Lord of *h.* restore thee, dear brother
13. 11. many nations come with gifts to King of *h.*
Jud. 5. 8. they worshipped the God of *h.*
11. 17. thy servant serveth God of *h.* day and night
Esth. 13. 10. for thou hast made *h.* and earth

Wisd. 9. 16. things in h. who hath searched out?
13. 2. they deemed the lights of h. to be the gods
16. 20. thou didst send them from h. bread
18. 15. thine almighty word leaped down from h.
16. and it touched h. but stood on the earth
Eccl. 1. 3. who can find out the height of h.!
16. 18. behold, the h. and the h. of heavens
17. 32. he vieweth the power of the height of h.
24. 5. I alone compassed the circuit of h.
26. 16. the sun when it ariseth in the high h.
43. 1. the beauty of h. with his glorious shew
8. shining in the firmament of h.
12. it compasseth the h. about with a circle
46. 17. and the Lord thundered from h.
48. 3. by the word of the Lord he shut up the h.
20. and the holy One heard them out of h.
51. 19. I stretched forth my hands to h. above
Bar. 1. 11. days may be on earth as the days of h.
2. 2. such as never happened under the whole h.
3. 29. who hath gone up into h. and taken her
5. 3. will shew it unto every country under h.
6. 54. they are as crows between h. and earth
Sus. 9. that they might not look unto h.
35. and she weeping, looked up towards h.
Bel 5. who hath created the h. and the earth
Prayer of Manass. who hast made h. and earth, I am not worthy to behold and see the height of h.
1 Mac. 2. 37. h. and earth shall testify for us
58. Elias, for his zeal, was taken up into h.
3. 18. with the God of h. it is all one to deliver
19. but strength cometh from h.
60. as the will of God is in h. so let him do
4. 10. now therefore let us cry unto h.
24. sung a song, and praised the Lord in h.
40. cried towards the h. ‖ 55. praising God of h.
5. 31. the cry of the city went up to h.
9. 46. wherefore cry ye now to h. to be delivered?
12. 15. we have help from h. that succoureth us
16. 3. ye fight, and the help from h. be with you
2 Mac. 2. 10. fire came down from h. and consumed
21. the manifest signs that came from h. to those
3. 15. the priests called to h. on him that made a law
20. all holding their hands towards h. made suppl.
34. seeing thou hast been scourged from h.
39. for he that dwelleth in h. hath his eye
7. 11. these I had from h. and for his laws
28. my son, look upon the h. and the earth
8. 20. because of the help that they had from h.
9. 10. that thought he could reach to the stars of h.
20. I give thanks to God, having my hope in h.
10. 29. there appeared to the enemies from h.
11. 10. they marched, having an helper from h.
14. 34. the priests lift up their hands towards h.
15. 3. demanded if there were a mighty One in h.
8. the help which they had received from h.
34. so every man praised towards the h.

HEAVENLY.

2 Esd. 2. 37. hath called you to the h. kingdom
Wisd. 19. 21. nor melted the icy kind of h. meat

HEAVENS.

1 Esd. 4. 34. he compasseth the h. round about
2 Esd. 3. 18. bowing the h. thou didst set fast the earth
4. 21. he that dwelleth above the h. may understand the things that are above the height of h.
16. 59. he spreadeth out the h. like a vault
Tob. 8. 5. let h. bless thee and all thy creatures
Jud. 9. 12. Lord of h. and earth, hear my prayer
Wisd. 9. 10. O send her out of thy holy h.
Eccl. 16. 18. the heaven of h. shall be moved
45. 15. to his seed so long as the h. should remain
Bar. 6. 67. nor can they shew signs in the h.

HEAVY.

1 Esd. 5. 72. the heathen lying h. on the inhabitants
2 Esd. 5. 16. and why is thy countenance so h.?
12. 46. and be not h. thou house of Jacob
Wisd. 17. 4. appeared to them with h. countenances
Eccl. 25. 23. a wicked woman makes h. countenance
33. 28. if not obedient, put on more h. fetters
40. 1. an h. yoke is upon the sons of Adam
1 Mac. 8. 31. why hast thou made thy yoke h.?
2 Mac. 5. 23. bare an h. hand over the citizens

HEAVIER.

Eccl. 22. 14. what is h. than lead? the name is a fool

HEAVINESS.

2 Esd. 10. 7. Sion is full of h. ‖ 8. we are all in h.
24. therefore shake off thy great h. put away
Tob. 2. 5. I washed myself and eat my meat in h.
Eccl. 22. 4. that liveth dishonestly, is her father's h.
30. 9. play with him, and he will bring thee to h.
21. give not over thy mind to h. afflict not thyself
36. 20. a froward heart causeth h. but a man
38. 17. then comfort thyself for thy h.
18. for of h. cometh death, and the h. of the heart breaketh strength, in affliction sorrow remains
20. take no h. to heart, drive it away, remember
1 Mac. 1. 27. she in the marriage-chamber was in h.
3. 51. thy priests are in h. and brought low
6. 4. he fled, and departed thence with great h.

HEBREW.

Jud. 12. 11. persuade this H. woman to come to us

HEBREWS.

Jud. 10. 12. and she said, I am a woman of the H.
14. 18. one woman of the H. hath brought shame
2 Mac. 7. 31. author of all mischief against the H.
11. 13. considering the H. could not be overcome
15. 37. the H. had the city in their power

HEBRON.

1 Mac. 5. 65. where he smote H. and towns thereof

HEDGE.

Eccl. 26. 12. by every h. will she sit down
28. 24. look that thou h. thy possession about
36. 25. where no h. is, the possession is spoiled

HEIFER.

Tob. 1. 5. the tribes sacrificed unto the h. Baal

HEIGHT.

1 Esd. 6. 25. whose h. shall be sixty cubits
Jud. 1. 2. the h. of the wall seventy cubits
7. 10. but they trust in the h. of the mountains
Eccl. 1. 3. who can find out the h. of heaven?
43. 1. the pride of the h. the clear firmament
50. 2. and by him was built the double h.
Prayer of Manass. to behold the h. of heaven

2 Mac. 4. 13 such was the h. of Greek fashions
6. 15. lest that being come to the h. of sin

HEIR.

Tob. 3. 15. nor hath he any child to be his h.
Eccl. 22. 23. that thou mayest be h. with him
23. 22. that bringeth in an h. by another

HELD.

1 Esd. 1. 21. kings of Israel h. not such pass. as Josias
3. 24. when he had so spoken, he h. his peace
4. 12. he h. his tongue ‖ 41. he h. his peace
50. the villages of the Jews which they h.
5. 51. also they h. the feast of tabernacles
2 Esd. 5. 15. so the angel h. me, comforted me
6. 8. Jacob's hand h. the first heel of Esau
13. 9. nor h. sword nor any instrument of war
28. he h. neither sword nor any instrument
44. h. still the flood, till they were passed over
Esth. 15. 11. and so he h. up his golden sceptre
Wisd. 12. 24. h. them for gods, being deceived
17. 4. nor might the corner that h. them keep
Eccl. 13. 21. a rich man is h. up of friends
26. 7. hath hold of her, as though he h. a scorpion
Bel 19. Daniel h. the king that he should not go in
1 Mac. 3. 2. so did all they that h. with his father
6. 52. they h. them battle a long season
11. 5. might blame him, but the king h. his peace
2 Mac. 10. 6. they had h. the feast of tabernacles
14. 4. and so that day he h. his peace

HELIODORUS.

2 Mac. 3. 7. the king chose out H. his treasurer
8. so forthwith H. took his journey
25. he ran and smote at H. with his fore-feet
27. and H. fell suddenly to the ground
31. then certain of H. friends prayed Onias
32. treachery had been done to H. by the Jews
33. the same young men stood by H. saying
35. H. after he had offered sacrifice, returned
37. when the king asked H. who might be a fit
40. the things concerning H. fell out thus
4. 1. slandered Onias, as if he had terrified H.

HELL.

2 Esd. 2. 29. that thy children shall not see h.
4. 8. never went into the deep, nor as yet into h.
8. 53. corruption is fled into h. to be forgotten
Tob. 13. 2. he leadeth down to h. and bringeth up
Wisd. 17. 14. out of the bottoms of inevitable h.
Eccl. 21. 10. at the end thereof is the pit of h.
51. 5. from the depth of the belly of h.
6. my life was near to the h. beneath
Dan. 3. 66. for he hath delivered us from h.

HELMET.

Wisd. 5. 18. and true judgment instead of an h.

HELMETS.

1 Mac. 6. 35. with h. of brass on their heads

HELP.

1 Esd. 2. 6. dwell in places about, let them h. him
6. 28. to h. those that be of the captivity of Jews
8. 27. I was encouraged by the h. of the Lord
Jud. 6. 21. they called all that night for h.
7. 31. if these days pass, and there come no h. to us
8. 11. unless in these days the Lord h. you
15. if he will not h. us within these five days
17. therefore let us call upon him to h. us
13. 5. now is the time to h. thine inheritance
Esth. 14. 3. O my Lord, h. me desolate woman
14. deliver us, and h. me that am desolate
Wisd. 2. 18. he will h. him and deliver him
12. 6. the parents killed souls destitute of h.
13. 16. knowing that it was unable to h. itself, for it is an image, and hath need of h.
18. that which hath least means to h.
14. 18. did h. to set forward the ignorant
Eccl. 2. 6. believe in him, and he will h. thee
3. 12. my son, h. thy father in his age
8. 16. where there is no h. he will overthrow
11. 12. another that is slow and hath need of h.
12. 4. give to the godly man, and h. not a sinner
7. give to the good, and h. not the sinner
17. and though he pretend to h. thee, yet shall he
13. 23. stumble, they will h. to overthrow him
29. 9. h. the poor for the commandment's sake
20. h. thy neighbour according to thy power
34. 16. and he is an h. from falling
36. 24. a h. like himself, and a pillar of rest
40. 24. brethren and h. are against trouble
26. the fear of the Lord needeth not to seek h.
51. 7. they compassed me, there was no man to h.
10. in time of the proud, when there was no h.
Bar. 4. 17. but what can I h. you?
6. 37. nor can they h. any man in his distress
58. neither are they able to h. themselves
68. they can get under a covert and h. themselves
1 Mac. 3. 15. a mighty host of ungodly to h. him
53. able to stand, except thou, O God, be our h.
5. 39. he hath hired the Arabians to h. them
8. 13. also whom they would h. to a kingdom
25. the people of the Jews shall h. them
27. the Romans shall h. with all their heart
10. 74. Simon his brother met him to h. him
11. 43. shalt do well if thou send me men to h. me
60. the forces gathered unto him for to h. him
12. 15. we have h. from heaven that succoureth
53. they have no captain, nor any to h. them
14. 1. to get him h. to fight against Tryphon
16. 3. and the h. from heaven be with you
2 Mac. 3. 28. being unable to h. himself with weapons
6. 11. they made conscience to h. themselves
8. 20. because of the h. they had from heaven
23. had given them this watch-word, The h. of G.
24. by the h. of the Almighty they slew 9000
35. he was through the h. of the L. brought down
10. 19. unto places which more needed his h.
11. 7. jeopard themselves to h. their brethren
12. 11. Judah's side, by the h. of God, got victory
13. 10. if at any other time, he would now h. them
13. try the matter in fight, by the h. of the Lord
17. the protection of the Lord did h. them
15. 7. confidence that the Lord would h. him
8. to remember the h. received in former times
35. a manifest sign to all of the h. of the Lord

HELPED.

1 Esd. 2. 9. h. them in all things with silver and gold

Tob. 2. 10. I went to physicians, but they h. me not
Eccl. 29. 4. and put them to trouble that h. them
1 Mac. 3. 2. all his brethren h. Maccabeus
2 Mac. 11. 13. because the almighty God h. them

HELPER.

Tob. 8. 6. thou gavest him Eve his wife for an h.
Jud. 7. 25. now we have no h. but God hath sold us
Esth. 14. 3. help me, who have no h. but thee, 14.
Eccl. 51. 2. for thou art my defender and h. and hast been my h. against mine adversaries
2 Mac. 10. 16. besought G. that he would be their h.
11. 10. they marched, having an h. from heaven
12. 36. that he would shew himself to be their h.

HELPERS.

2 Esd. 16. 33. daughters shall mourn having no h.
Eccl. 13. 22. a rich man is fallen, he hath many h.

HELPETH.

Eccl. 37. 5. a companion which h. his friend
2 Mac. 14. 15. and who always h. his portion

HELPING.

1 Esd. 6. 2. prophets being with them, and h. them

HELPS.

2 Mac. 8. 19. what h. their forefathers found

HEN.

2 Esd. 1. 30. as a h. gathereth her chickens under her

HERB.

Wisd. 16. 12. it was neither h. that restored them

HERBS.

2 Esd. 9. 26. and I did eat of the h. of the field
12. 51. and I had my meat of the h.
2 Mac. 5. 27. his company who fed on h. continually

HERCULES.

2 Mac. 4. 19. to carry silver to the sacrifice of H.
20. this money was appointed to H. sacrifice

HERDS.

Jud. 2. 27. he destroyed their flocks and h.
3. 3. our flocks and h. lie before thy face

HERITAGE.

1 Esd. 8. 83. the land ye enter into to possess as an h.
Eccl. 17. 11. he gave them the law of life for an h.
19. 3. moths and worms shall have him to h.
20. 25. but both shall have destruction to h.
22. 23. thou mayest be heir with him in his h.
44. 23. and he gave him an h. 45. 20.
46. 8. were preserved to bring them into the h.
9. and his seed obtained it for an h.
1 Mac. 2. 56. Caleb received the h. of the land
2 Mac. 2. 4. Moses climbed up, and saw the h. of G.
17. God delivered his people, and gave them an h.

HERMON.

Eccl. 24. 13. as a cypress on the mountains of H.

HEWED.

2 Mac. 1. 16. h. them in pieces, smote off their heads

HEWN.

Jud. 1. 2. and built walls round about of stones h.
Bar. 6. 39. like stones h. out of the mountain
1 Mac. 13. 27. built a monument with h. stone

HID.

2 Esd. 8. 53. weakness and the moth is h. from you
Tob. 1. 19. that I buried them and h. myself
12. 13. thy good deed was not h. from me
Wisd. 1. 8. speaketh unrighteous things cannot be h.
10. the noise of murmurings is not h.
10. 8. they could not so much as be h.
17. 3. they supposed to lie h. in their secret sins
Eccl. 16. 21. the most part of his works are h.
17. 15. their ways shall not be h. from his eyes
20. none of their unrighteous deeds are h.
20. 30. wisdom that is h. and treasure, 41. 14.
39. 19. and nothing can be h. from his eyes
43. 32. there are h. greater things than these
Sus. 16. the two elders that had h. themselves
18. saw not the elders, because they were h.
37. a young man who was there h. came to her
1 Mac. 2. 36. nor stopped places where they lay h
9. 38. they h. themselves under the covert
2 Mac. 1. 19. they h. it in an hollow place of a pit
20. the posterity of those priests that h. it
22. the sun shone, which afore was h. in the cloud
33. the priests that were led away had h. the fire
10. 37. killed Timotheus, that was h. in a pit
12. 41. who had opened the things that were h.

HIDDEN.

2 Esd. 5. 1. and the way of truth shall be h.
16. 62. the Spirit searcheth out all h. things
Eccl. 11. 4. and his works among men are h.
12. 8. and an enemy cannot be h. in adversity
42. 19. he revealeth the steps of h. things
20. neither any word is h. from him
Bar. 6. 48. consult where they may be h. with them
1 Mac. 1. 23. also he took the h. treasures he found

HIDE.

2 Esd. 5. 9. then shall wit h. itself and understanding
12. 37. write all these things and h. them
14. 6. these declare, and these shalt thou h.
16. 63. even them that sin, and would h. their sin
66. or how will you h. your sins before God?
Tob. 13. 6. he will not h. his face from you
Wisd. 6. 22. I will not h. mysteries from you
7. 13. I do communicate, I do not h. her riches
Eccl. 1. 24. he will h. his words for a time
4. 23. and h. not thy wisdom in her beauty
6. 12. and he will h. himself from thy face
16. 17. say not thou, I will h. myself from the Lord
22. 25. neither will I h. my face from him
37. 10. h. thy counsel from such as envy thee

HIDETH.

Eccl. 20. 31. wisdom said, better is he that h. his folly, than a man that h. his wisdom, 41. 15.

HIGH.

1 Esd. 2. 3. the most h. Lord hath made me king
4. 34. h. is the heaven, swift is the sun in his course
5. 40. till there arose up an h. priest clothed
6. 31. their offerings may be made to most h. God
9. 46. Esdras blessed the Lord God most h.
Tob. 1. 4. the temple of the habitation of the Most H.
13. the Most H. gave me grace and favour
4. 11. that give it in the sight of the Most H.
Jud. 3. 6. he set garrisons in the h. cities
4. 6. Joacim the h. priest wrote to them in Bethulia
8. did as Joacim the h. priest had commanded
14. Joacim the h. priest and all the priests

Jud. 13. 18. blessed art thou of the most *h.* God
15. 8. then Joacim the *h.* priest came to behold
16. 7. nor did *h.* giants set upon him
Esth. 14. 16. I abhor the sign of my *h.* estate
16. 22. shall keep it an *h.* day with all feasting
Wisd. 5. 15. the care of them is with the Most H.
6. 5. judgment be to them that be in *h.* places
Eccl. 1. 5. the word of God most *h.* is the fountain
3. 19. many are in *h.* place and of renown
4. 10. so shalt thou be as the son of the Most H.
7. 9. when I offer to the most *h.* God, he will accept
15. husbandry, which the Most H. hath ordained
9. 15. thy communication in the law of the M. H.
12. 2. and if not from him, yet from Most H.
6. for the Most H. hateth sinners, and will repay
17. 26. turn to the Most H. turn from iniquity
27. who shall praise the Most H. in the grave?
19. 17. give place to the law of the Most H.
24. and transgresseth the law of the Most H.
22. 18. pales set on an *h.* place will never stand
23. 18. the Most H. will not remember my sins
23. she hath disobeyed the law of the Most H.
26. 16. the sun when it ariseth in the *h.* heaven
33. 9. some of them hath he made *h.* days
15. so look on all the works of the Most H.
34. 6. if they be not sent from the Most H.
19. the Most H. is not pleased with the offerings
35. 6. the savour thereof is before the Most H.
10. give to the Most H. according as he enriched
17. till the Most H. shall behold to judge
37. 14. watchmen that sit above in an *h.* tower
15. and above all this pray to the Most H.
38. 2. for of the Most H. cometh healing
33. not sought for, nor sit *h.* in the congregation
39. 1. giveth his mind to the law of the Most H.
5. and he will pray before the Most H.
41. 4. why against the pleasure of the Most H.?
8. who have forsaken the law of the most *h.* God
42. 2. be not ashamed of the law of the Most H.
43. 2. the sun declareth the work of the Most H.
12. the hands of the Most H. have bended it
44. 20. Abraham kept the law of the Most H.
46. 5. he called upon the most *h.* Lord, 47. 5.
9. he entered upon the *h.* places of the land
47. 8. in all he praised the holy One most *h.*
48. 5. didst raise a dead man by word of Most H.
49. 4. for they forsook the law of the Most H.
50. 1. Simon the *h.* priest repaired the house
2. the *h.* fortress of the wall about the temple
7. sun shining upon the temple of the Most H.
14. adorn the offering of the most *h.* Almighty
15. a savour to the most *h.* King of all
16. for a remembrance before the Most H.
17. their Lord God almighty the Most H.
19. besought the Lord the Most H. by prayer
21. might receive a blessing from the Most H.
Bar. 1. 7. they sent collection to Joachim *h.* priest
2. 11. brought with a mighty hand and *h.* arm
3. 25. and hath no end, *h.* and unmeasurable
6. 25. things are bought for a most *h.* price
Prayer of Manass. thou art the most *h.* Lord
1 *Mac.* 4. 60. builded mount Sion with *h.* walls
6. 7. compassed about the sanctuary with *h.* walls
7. 5. Alcimus who was desirous to be *h.* priest
9. the wicked Alcimus, whom he made *h.* priest
21. Alcimus contended for the *h.* priesthood
10. 20. we ordain thee to be *h.* priest of thy nation
32. as for the tower, I give it to the *h.* priest
38. to obey other authority than *h.* priest's
69. sent unto Jonathan the *h.* priest, saying
11. 27. confirmed him in the *h.* priesthood, 14. 38.
57. I confirm thee in the *h.* priesthood
12. 3. Jonathan the *h.* priest sent us unto you
6. Jonathan the *h.* priest to the Lacedemonians
7. there were letters sent to Onias the *h.* priest
20. Areus to Onias the *h.* priest, greeting
13. 36. king Demetrius to Simon the *h.* priest
42. in the first year of Simon the *h.* priest
14. 17. his brother Simon was made *h.* priest
20. the Lacedemonians, to Simon the *h.* priest
23. written a copy thereof to Simon the *h.* priest
27. the third year of Simon the *h.* priest
41. should be governor and *h.* priest for ever
47. Simon was well pleased to be *h.* priest
15. 17. being sent from Simon the *h.* priest
21. deliver them to Simon the *h.* priest
24. the copy they wrote to Simon the *h.* priest
16. 12. for he was the *h.* priest's son-in-law
2 *Mac.* 3. 1. the godliness of Onias the *h.* priest
4. but one Simon fell out with the *h.* priest
9. had been courteously received of the *h.* priest
10. then the *h.* priest told him there was money
16. whoso had looked the *h.* priest in the face
21. the fear of the *h.* priest being in an agony
31. prayed that he would call upon the Most H.
32. the *h.* priest suspecting lest the king
33. as the *h.* priest was making an atonement
4. 7. Jason laboured under-hand to be *h.* priest
13. Jason that ungodly wretch and no *h.* priest
25. bringing nothing worthy *h.* priesthood
8. 30. they very easily got *h.* and strong holds
9. 8. and weigh the *h.* mountains in a balance
23. when he led an army into the *h.* countries
25. when I went up into *h.* provinces
11. 3. and to set the *h.* priesthood to sale
14. 3. one Alcimus, who had been *h.* priest
7. ancestors' honour, I mean the *h.* priesthood
15. 12. Onias who had been *h.* priest, a good man

HIGHEST.

2 *Esd.* 4. 11. able to comprehend the way of the H.
34. do not thou hasten above the Most H.
Jud. 14. 1. hang it on the *h.* place of your walls
Wisd. 6. 3. power and sovereignty from the H.
Eccl. 28. 7. remember the covenant of the H.
43. 9. an ornament giving light in the *h.* places
Bar. 1. 4. the people from the lowest to the *h.*

HIGHLY.

2 *Mac.* 1. 11. God hath delivered, we thank him *h.*

HILL.

2 *Esd.* 13. 7. the place, whereout the *h.* was graven
36. thou sawest the *h.* graven without hands
Jud. 1. 6. all they that dwelt in the *h.* country
Jud. 2. 22. he went from thence into the *h.* country
4. 7. charging them to keep the passages of *h.* count.
5. 1. had shut up the passages of the *h.* country
6. 7. shall bring thee back into the *h.* country
11. they went from the plain into the *h.* country
12. they went out of the city to the top of the *h.*
13. having gotten privily under the *h.*
1 *Mac.* 13. 52. the *h.* of the temple he made stronger

HILLS.

2 *Esd.* 6. 51. in same part wherein are a thousand *h.*
Jud. 5. 1. had fortified the tops of the high *h.*
7. 4. nor are the *h.* able to bear their weight
16. 4. and their horsemen have covered the *h.*
Bar. 6. 63. fire sent from above to consume the *h.*
Dan. 3. 53. O ye mountains and little *h.* bless the L.

HIMSELF.

Eccl. 37. 7. but there is some that counselleth for *h.*

HINDER.

1 *Esd.* 2. 28. commanded *h.* those men from building
30. they began to *h.* the builders of the temple
6. 33. that stretcheth out his hand to *h.* that house
Eccl. 18. 22. let nothing *h.* thee to pay thy vow
32. 3. speak with sound judgment, *h.* not music
39. 18. and none can *h.* when he will save

HINDMOST.

1 *Mac.* 4. 15. howbeit, all the *h.* of them were slain

HINDERED.

1 *Esd.* 5. 72. but the heathen *h.* their building
73. they *h.* the finishing of the building, so they were *h.* from building till the reign of Darius
6. 6. they were not *h.* from building until such time
Wisd. 17. 20. and none were *h.* in their labour
Eccl. 19. 28. if for want of power he be *h.* from sinn.
20. 21. there is that is *h.* from sinning for want
1 *Mac.* 9. 55. was plagued, and his enterprises *h.*

HINDERETH.

Eccl. 16. 28. none of them *h.* another, not disobey

HIRCANUS.

2 *Mac.* 3. 11. some of it belong. to H. son of Tobias

HIRE.

Eccl. 34. 22. that defraudeth the labourer of his *h.*

HIRED.

Tob. 5. 11. to whom he said, dost thou seek for a tribe or family, or an *h.* man to go with thy son?
1 *Mac.* 5. 39. he hath *h.* the Arabians to help them
6. 29. there came to him bands of *h.* soldiers
2 *Mac.* 10. 14. he *h.* soldiers, and nourished war

HIRELING.

Jud. 4. 10. every stranger and *h.* put on sackcloth
6. 5. thou Achior, an *h.* of Ammon, shalt see my face

HIRELINGS.

Jud. 6. 2. who art thou, Achior, and *h.* of Ephraim?

HISS.

Eccl. 22. 1. every one will *h.* him to his disgrace

HISSING.

Wisd. 17. 9. scared with beasts and *h.* of serpents

HISTORIES.

Esth. 16. 7. have declared, not so much by ancient *h.*
See STORY.

HITTITES.

1 *Esd.* 8. 69. the pollutions of the Canaanites, H.

HOAR.

Wisd. 16. 29. shall melt away as winter's *h.* frost
Eccl. 43. 19. the *h.* frost as salt he poureth on earth

HOARDED.

Eccl. 20. 30. treasure that is *h.* up, what profit?
Bar. 3. 17. they that *h.* up silver and gold

HOLD.

1 *Mac.* 1. 33. and made it a strong *h.* for them
3. 45. and aliens kept the strong *h.*
6. 61. whereupon they went out of the strong *h.*
12. 34. he heard that they would deliver the *h.*
16. 8. the remnant gat them to the strong *h.*
15. receiving them into a little *h.* called Docus
2 *Mac.* 10. 32. he fled into a very strong *h.*
13. 19. which was a strong *h.* of the Jews

HOLDS.

1 *Mac.* 1. 2. made many wars, and many strong *h.*
8. 10. and pulled down their strong *h.* and brought
10. 37. some shall be placed in the king's strong *h.*
11. 18. they that were in the strong *h.* were slain
12. 35. consulted about building strong *h.* in Judea
13. 33. Simon built up the strong *h.* in Judea
38. the strong *h.* which ye have builded
2 *Mac.* 8. 30. and very easily got high and strong *h.*
10. 15. having gotten the most commodious *h.*
16. they ran on the strong *h.* of the Idumeans
17. they won the *h.* and kept off all that fought
23. he slew in the two *h.* more than 20,000
11. 6. when they heard that he besieged the *h.*
13. 18. he went about to take the *h.* by policy

HOLD.

1 *Esd.* 1. 17. that they might *h.* the passover
Tob. 10. 6. *h.* thy peace, take no care, he is safe
7. she said, *h.* thy peace, and deceive me not
11. 11. took *h.* of his father, and strake the gall
Wisd. 2. 24. they that *h.* of his side do find it
8. 12. when I *h.* my tongue they shall bide my leisure
15. 14. the enemies that *h.* them in subjection
Eccl. 1. 19. exalteth them to honour that *h.* her fast
4. 11. wisdom layeth *h.* of them that seek her
6. 27. when thou hast got *h.* of her, let her not go
12. 5. back thy bread, and give it not to him
20. 7. a wise man will *h.* his tongue till he see
21. 14. he will *h.* no knowledge while he liveth
23. 5. thou shalt *h.* him up that is desirous to serve
6. let not the lust of the flesh take *h.* of me
26. 7. he that hath *h.* of her, is as though he held
27. 3. unless a man *h.* himself diligently in fear of L.
29. 23. be it little or much, *h.* thee contented
30. 13. chastise thy son, and *h.* him to labour
Bar. 3. 21. nor understood paths, nor laid *h.* of it
Sus. 39. the man we could not *h.* he was stronger
1 *Mac.* 15. 34. we *h.* the inheritance of our fathers
2 *Mac.* 12. 35. and taking *h.* of his coat, drew him

HOLDETH.

Eccl. 4. 13. he that *h.* her fast shall inherit glory
13. 23. when rich speaketh, every man *h.* his tongue
20. 1. some man *h.* his tongue, and he is wise, 6.
25. 11. he that *h.* it, whereto shall he be likened?
32. 8. as one that knoweth, and yet *h.* his tongue
38. 25. how can he get wisdom that *h.* the plough?
Bar. 6. 14. *h.* a sceptre, as though he were a judg

HOLDING.

2 *Mac.* 3. 20. all *h.* their hands towards heaven
7. 10. the third *h.* forth his hands manfully
15. 12. *h.* up his hands, prayed for the Jews
15. Jeremias *h.* forth his right hand, gave Judas

HOLM-TREE.

Sus. 58. under what tree? who answered, under a *h.*

HOLOFERNES, *or* OLOFERNES.

Jud. 2. 4. H. the chief captain of his army
14. then H. went from the presence of his lord
10. 13. I am coming before H. the chief captain
17. and they brought her to the tent of H.
21. H. rested upon his bed under a canopy
11. 1. then said H. unto her, 22. | 12. 3. 17.
12. 10. H. made a feast to his own servants only
16. H. his heart was ravished with her
20. H. took great delight in her, and drank
13. 2. H. lying along on his bed in the tent
6. the pillar of the bed which was at H. head
9. she went forth and gave H. his head to her maid
15. she said unto them, behold the head of H.
14. 3. then they shall run to the tent of H. 13
18. H. lieth upon the ground without a head

HOLY.

1 *Esd.* 1. 3. Levites, the ministers of Israel, should hallow themselves to set the *h.* ark of the Lord
15. the *h.* singers also the sons of Asaph
45. brought with the *h.* vessels of the Lord
53. within the compass of their *h.* temple
2. 10. king Cyrus brought forth the *h.* vessels
5. 45. to give into the *h.* treasury 1000 pounds
52. of the new moons, and of all *h.* feasts
6. 18. *h.* vessels of gold and of silver carried away
7. 2. did very carefully oversee the *h.* works
3. and so the *h.* works prospered when Aggeus
5. and thus was the *h.* house finished in Adar
8. 5. went up of the Levites, of the *h.* singers
58. you are *h.* to the Lord, and the vessels are *h.*
70. the *h.* seed is mixed with the strange people
71. I rent my clothes and the *h.* garments
73. with my clothes and the *h.* garment rent
9. 38. came into the broad place of the *h.* porch
41. he read in the broad court before the *h.* porch
50. this day is *h.* to the Lord, 52, 53.
2 *Esd.* 10. 22. our *h.* things are defiled, and wives
14. 22. if I found grace, send the *h.* Ghost into me
Tob. 2. 1. which is the *h.* feast of the seven weeks
3. 11. thy *h.* and glorious name is blessed
8. 5. blessed is thy *h.* and glorious name for ever
15. to be praised with all pure and *h.* praise
11. 14. and blessed are all thine *h.* angels
12. 12. bring your prayers before the *h.* One
15. I am Raphael, one of the seven *h.* angels, who go in and out before the glory of the *h.* One
13. 9. O Jerusalem, the *h.* city, he will scourge
Wisd. 1. 5. the *h.* spirit of discipline will flee
6. 10. they that keep holiness, shall be judged *h.*
7. 22. in her is an understanding spirit, *h.* lively
27. and in all ages entering into *h.* souls
9. 8. to build a temple on thy *h.* mount, an altar in the city, a resemblance of the *h.* tabernacle
10. O send her out of thy *h.* heavens, from throne
17. except thou send thy *h.* Spirit from above
10. 10. she gave him knowledge of *h.* things
20. the righteous praised thy *h.* name, O Lord
11. 1. she prospered in the hand of the *h.* prophet
12. 3. both those old inhabitants of thy *h.* land
17. 2. men thought to oppress the *h.* nation
18. 9. and with one consent made an *h.* law
Eccl. 4. 14. they shall minister to the *h.* One
7. 31. give him the first-fruits of the *h.* things
14. 20. the man that reasoneth of *h.* things
17. 10. and the elect shall praise his *h.* name
18. 3. by power dividing *h.* things among them
23. 9. nor use thyself to naming of the *h.* One
24. 10. in the *h.* tabernacle I served before him
18. am mother of fear, and knowledge, and *h.* hope
26. 17. as clear light is on the *h.* candlestick
36. 13. be merciful to Jerusalem thy *h.* city
39. 13. hearken to me, ye *h.* children, and bud
24. as his ways are clean and plain unto the *h.*
43. 10. at the commandment of the *h.* One
45. 10. with an *h.* garment, with gold and blue
15. Moses anointed him with *h.* oil
47. 8. in all his works he praised the *h.* One
49. 12. who set up an *h.* temple to the Lord
50. 11. when he went up to the *h.* altar
Bar. 2. 16. O Lord, look down from thy *h.* house
4. 22. and joy is come unto me from the *h.* One
37. by the word of the *h.* One, 5. 5.
Dan. 3. 5. hast brought on the *h.* city of our fathers
12. mercy not depart, for thy *h.* Israel's sake
65. O ye *h.* and humble men of heart, bless Lord
Sus. 45. Lord raised the *h.* spirit of a young youth
1 *Mac.* 1. 46. and pollute the sanctuary and *h.* peop
63. they might not profane the *h.* covenant
2. 7. the misery of my people and of the *h.* city
4. 49. they made also new *h.* vessels
10. 21. at the feast Jonathan put on the *h.* robe
31. let Jerusalem also be *h.* and free
11. 37. let it be set upon the *h.* mount
12. 9. that we have the *h.* books of scripture
14. 36. and did much hurt in the *h.* place
16. 8. then sounded they with the *h.* trumpets
2 *Mac.* 1. 7. his company revolted from the *h.* land
12. he cast them out that fought within the *h.* city
29. plant thy people again in thy *h.* place
34. the king enclosing the place, made it *h.*
2. 13. the epistles concerning the *h.* gifts
18. God will gather us into the *h.* place
3. 1. when the *h.* city was inhabited with peace
4. 48. that followed the matter for the *h.* vessels
5. 15. but presumed to go into the most *h.* temple
16. taking the *h.* vessels with polluted hands
25. did forbear till the *h.* day of the sabbath
6. 4. within the circuit of the *h.* places
23. or rather the *h.* law made and given by God
28. to die for the honourable and *h.* laws
30. to the Lord, that hath the *h.* knowledge
8. 15. for his *h.* and glorious name's sake
17. the injury unjustly done to the *h.* place

2 *Mac.* 8. 23. he appointed Eleazar to read *h.* book
33. Callisthenes that set fire upon the *h.* gates
9. 14. that the *h.* city he would set at liberty
16. *h.* temple, which before he had spoiled, he would garnish with gifts and restore *h.* vessels.
12. 45. it was an *h.* and good thought
13. 8. the altar, whose fire and ashes were *h.*
10. at the point to be put from the *h.* temple
14. 3. nor have any more access to the *h.* altar
31. the other came into the great and *h.* temple
36. O *h.* Lord of all holiness, keep this house
15. 16. take this *h.* sword, a gift from God

HOLILY.

Wisd. 6. 10. for they that keep holiness *h.* be holy

HOLINESS.

Wisd. 5. 19. take *h.* for an invincible shield
6. 10. they that keep *h.* holily shall be judged holy
14. 30. they swore in deceit, despising *h.*
Eccl. 17. 29. to such as turn to him in *h.*
45. 12. a crown, wherein was engraved *h.*
50. 11. he made the garment of *h.* honourable
2 *Mac.* 3. 12. had committed it to the *h.* of the place
14. 36. O holy Lord of all *h.* keep this house
15. 2. that day which he hath honoured with *h.*

HOLLOW.

Wisd. 17. 19. an echo from the *h.* mountains
2 *Mac.* 1. 19. and hid it in a *h.* place of a pit
2. 5. Jeremy found an *h.* cave where he laid the ark

HOME.

1 *Esd.* 3. 3. and being satisfied, were gone *h.*
2 *Esd.* 12. 49. now go your way *h.* every man
Tob. 3. 17. the self-same time came Tobit *h.*
Eccl. 32. 11. but get thee *h.* without delay
Sus. 13. one said to the other, let us now go *h.*
1 *Mac.* 4. 24. after this they went *h.* and sung
12. 35. after this came Jonathan *h.* again
45. therefore send them now *h.* again, and choose
2 *Mac.* 11. 29. that your desire was to return *h.*

HONEST.

2 *Esd.* 16. 49. as a whore envieth an *h.* woman
Tob. 5. 13. thou art of an *h.* and good stock
7. 7. thou art the son of an *h.* and good man
Wisd. 4. 12. doth obscure things that are *h.*
Eccl. 26. 24. but an *h.* woman will reverence husb.
29. 14. an *h.* man is surety for his neighbour
2 *Mac.* 6. 23. his most *h.* education from a child

HONESTLY.

Eccl. 22. 9. if children live *h.* have wherewithal
2 *Mac.* 12. 43. doing therein very well and *h.*

HONOUR.

1 *Esd.* 8. 4. the king did him *h.* for he found grace
9. 52. for the Lord will bring you to *h.*
2 *Esd.* 9. 45. we give great *h.* to the Almighty
10. 23. the seal of Sion hath now lost her *h.*
Tob. 4. 3. but *h.* her all the days of thy life
10. 12. *h.* thy father and thy mother-in-law
14. 13. where he became old with *h.*
Jud. 16. 23. she increaseth more and more in *h.*
Esth. 12. 6. Haman was in great *h.* with the king
13. 3. had the *h.* of the second place in the kingdom
Wisd. 3. 17. their last age shall be without *h.*
5. 4. we accounted his end to be without *h.*
6. 21. O ye kings of the people, *h.* wisdom
8. 10. I shall have *h.* with the elders, tho' young
14. 17. whom men could not *h.* in presence
Eccl. 1. 11. the fear of the Lord is *h.* and glory
19. wisdom exalteth them to *h.* that hold her
3. 2. given the father *h.* over the children
7. he that feareth the Lord will *h.* his father
8. *h.* thy father and mother both in word and deed
11. the glory of a man is from the *h.* of his father
5. 13. *h.* and shame is in talk, the tongue is his fall
6. 31. thou shalt put her on as a robe of *h.*
7. 4. nor seek of the king the seat of *h.*
27. *h.* thy father with thy whole heart
31. fear the Lord and *h.* the priest
8. 14. they will judge for him according to his *h.*
10. 5. on the person of the scribe shall he lay his *h.*
28. give it *h.* according to the dignity thereof
29. who will *h.* him that dishonoureth his life
11. 4. exalt not thyself in the day of *h.*
24. 16. my branches are the branches of *h.*
17. my flowers are the fruit of *h.* and riches
25. 5. how comely is counsel to men of *h.!*
29. 6. for *h.* he will pay him disgrace
33. 22. leave not a stain in thine *h.*
35. 8. give the Lord his *h.* with a good eye
38. 1. *h.* a physician with the *h.* due to him
2. and he shall receive *h.* of the king
45. 12. holiness an ornament of *h.* a costly work
47. 20. thou didst stain thy *h.* and pollute thy seed
49. 16. Sem and Seth were in great *h.* among men
50. 11. when he put on the robe of *h.* was clothed
Bar. 4. 3. give not thine *h.* to another, nor the things
Sus. 50. God hath given thee the *h.* of an elder
1 *Mac.* 1. 39. her *h.* was turned into contempt
2. 51. so shall ye receive great *h.* and a name
3. 3. he gat his people great *h.* put on breast-plate
14. I will get me a name and *h.* in the kingdom
9. 10. let us die, and let us not stain our *h.*
11. 42. but I will greatly *h.* thee and thy nation
12. 12. and we are right glad of your *h.*
14. 4. his authority and *h.* pleased them well
21. the ambassadors certified us of your *h.*
29. they did their nation great *h.*
39. Demetrius honoured him with great *h.*
15. 9. we will *h.* thee and thy nation and temple with great *h.* so that your *h.* shall be known
2 *Mac.* 2. 21. those behaved to their *h.* for Judaism
3. 2. the kings themselves did *h.* the place
5. 16. dedicated to the glory and *h.* of the place
6. 11. to help for the *h.* of the most sacred day
23. as became the *h.* of his gray head
9. 21. I would have remembered kindly your *h.*
14. 7. I being deprived of mine ancestors' *h.*
15. 2. give *h.* to that day which he hath honoured

HONOURABLE.

Tob. 3. 11. thy glorious name is *h.* for ever
12. 7. it is *h.* to reveal the works of God, 11.
Jud. 16. 21. was in her time *h.* in the country
Wisd. 4. 8. for *h.* age is not in length of time
Eccl. 10. 19. that love the Lord, are an *h.* plant
20. among brethren, he that is chief is *h.*
11. 6. the *h.* delivered into other men's hands
24. 12. I took root in an *h.* people
29. 27. give place, thou stranger, to an *h.* man
45. 20. but he made Aaron more *h.*
48. 6. who broughtest *h.* men from their bed
50. 11. he made the garment of holiness *h.*
Sus. 4. because he was more *h.* than all others
1 *Mac.* 1. 6. he called his servants such as were *h.*
2. 17. thou art an *h.* and great man in this city
7. 26. the king sent Nicanor one of his *h.* princes
14. 5. as he was *h.* in all his acts, so in this
10. so that his *h.* name was renowned
2 *Mac.* 6. 28. to die for the *h.* and holy laws
7. 20. the mother was worthy of *h.* memory
10. 13. seeing that he was in no *h.* place

HONOURABLY.

1 *Esd.* 9. 45. for he sat *h.* in the first place
Tob. 12. 6. *h.* to shew forth the works of God
14. 11. he gave up the ghost, and he buried him *h.*
13. he buried his father and mother-in-law *h.*
Esth. 13. 4. so as the uniting of our kingdoms *h.*
Wisd. 18. 3. an harmless sun to entertain them *h.*
1 *Mac.* 10. 60. went *h.* to Ptolemais, where he met
11. 60. at Ascalon, they of city met him *h.*
12. 8. Onias entreated the ambassador *h.*
43. but received him *h.* and commended him
14. 23. it pleased the people to entertain the men *h.*
40. that they had entertained the ambassadors *h.*
2 *Mac.* 2. 8. that the place might be *h.* sanctified
4. 22. where he was *h.* received of Jason
49. they of Tyrus caused them to be *h.* buried

HONOURED.

1 *Esd.* 8. 26. hath *h.* me in the sight of the king
67. and they *h.* the people and the temple of God
81. yea, and they *h.* the temple of our Lord
2 *Esd.* 9. 31. and ye shall be *h.* in it for ever
Jud. 12. 13. to be *h.* in his presence, and drink wine
Esth. 16. 2. the more often they are *h.* with bounty
11. that he was continually *h.* of all men
Wisd. 14. 15. now *h.* him as a god, then a dead man
17. an express image of a king whom they *h.*
20. which a little before was but *h.* as a man
Eccl. 3. 20. power great, and Lord is *h.* of the lowly
10. 24. judges and potentates shall be *h.*
30. the poor man is *h.* for his skill, and the rich man is *h.* for his riches
31. he that is *h.* in poverty, is much more in riches
38. 6. he might be *h.* in his marvellous works
44. 7. all these were *h.* in their generations
46. 12. let the name of them that were *h.*
47. 6. so the people *h.* him with ten thousands
13. Solom. reigned in a peaceable time, and was *h.*
48. 4. O Elias, how wast thou *h.* in thy deeds!
50. 5. how was he *h.* in the midst of the people!
Bel 2. Daniel was *h.* above all his friends
1 *Mac.* 2. 18. thy children shall be *h.* with silver
10. 64. when his accusers saw that he was *h.*
65. so the king *h.* him, and made him a duke
88. king Alexander *h.* Jonathan yet more
11. 51. the Jews were *h.* in the sight of the king
14. 39. Demetrius *h.* him with great honour
2 *Mac.* 3. 12. the temple *h.* over all the world
30. that had miraculously *h.* his own place
13. 23. *h.* the temple, and dealt kindly with place
15. 2. hath *h.* with holiness above other days

HONOURETH.

Eccl. 3. 3. who *h.* his father, maketh an atonement
4. *h.* his mother is as one that layeth up treasure
5. whoso *h.* his father, shall have joy of children
6. he that *h.* father shall have long life
26. 26. a woman that *h.* her husband be judged wise

HONOURS.

1 *Mac.* 11. 27. in all the *h.* that he had before
2 *Mac.* 4. 15. not setting by the *h.* of their fathers

HONEY.

2 *Esd.* 2. 19. many fountains flowing with milk and *h.*
Eccl. 24. 20. my memorial is sweeter than *h.*
39. 26. *h.* and milk are for the use of man's life
46. 8. land that floweth with milk and *h.* *Bar.* 1. 20.
49. 1. it is sweet as *h.* in all mouths, and as music

HOOKS.

2 *Mac.* 13. 2. three hundred chariots armed with *h.*

HOPE.

2 *Esd.* 4. 35. how long shall I *h.* on this fashion?
5. 12. at the same time shall men *h.* but not obtain
7. 50. there is promised us an everlasting *h.*
10. 34. forsake me not, lest I die frustrate of *h.*
11. 46. that she may *h.* for the judgment of him
15. 46. that art partaker of the *h.* of Babylon
Tob. 11. 11. saying, be of good *h.* my father
Jud. 9. 11. a Saviour of them that are without *h.*
Wisd. 3. 4. yet is their *h.* full of immortality
11. he is miserable, and their *h.* is vain
18. they have no *h.* nor comfort in the day of trial
5. 14. the *h.* of the ungodly is like dust
12. 19. hast made thy children to be of good *h.*
13. 10. and in dead things is there *h.*
14. 6. the *h.* of the world governed by thy hand
15. 10. his *h.* is more vile than earth
16. 29. the *h.* of the unfaithful shall melt away
Eccl. 2. 9. ye that fear the Lord, *h.* for good
13. 6. he will smile on thee, and put thee in *h.*
14. 2. who is not fallen from his *h.* in the Lord
23. 3. whose *h.* is far from thy mercy
24. 18. I am the mother of fair love, and holy *h.*
27. 21. but he that bewrayeth secrets is without *h.*
34. 13. for their *h.* is in him that saveth them
14. not fear, nor be afraid, for he is his *h.*
49. 10. they delivered them by assured *h.*
Bar. 4. 22. for my *h.* is in the Everlasting
2 *Mac.* 2. 17. we *h.* also that the God that delivered
3. 29. he lay speechless, without all *h.* of life
7. 11. from him I *h.* to receive them again
14. it is good to look for *h.* from God
20. because of the *h.* that she had in the Lord
9. 20. I give thanks to God having *h.* in heaven
22. having great *h.* to escape this sickness

HOPED.

Wisd. 2. 22. neither *h.* they for wages of righteousn.
11. 7. gavest them water, by means they *h.* not for
2 *Mac.* 12. 44. if he had not *h.* they should rise

HOPES.

Eccl. 23. 5. turn away from me vain *h.*
34. 1. the *h.* of a man void of understanding
2 *Mac.* 7. 34. nor puffed up with uncertain *h.*

HOREB.

Eccl. 48. 7. and in H. the judgment of vengeance

HORN.

Jud. 9. 8. to cast down with sword the *h.* of thy altar
Eccl. 47. 5. and set up the *h.* of his people
7. he brake their *h.* in sunder to this day
11. the Lord exalted his *h.* for ever

HORRIBLE.

2 *Esd.* 11. 45. appear no more, nor thy *h.* wings
15. 28. behold, an *h.* vision from the east
34. they are very *h.* to look on, full of wrath
Wisd. 3. 19. *h.* is the end of the unrighteous
8. 15. *h.* tyrants shall be afraid when they hear
11. 18. shooting *h.* sparkles out of their eyes
16. 5. when the *h.* fierceness of beasts came
17. 5. nor stars endure to lighten that *h.* night
18. 17. visions of *h.* dreams troubled them sore
19. 17. being compassed with *h.* great darkness

HORRIBLY.

Wisd. 6. 5. *h.* and speedily shall he come on you

HORROR.

2 *Mac.* 3. 17. the man was so compassed with *h.*

HORSE.

Jud. 9. 7. they are exalted with *h.* and man
Eccl. 30. 8. an *h.* not broken becomes headstrong
33. 6. a stallion *h.* is as a mocking friend
1 *Mac.* 6. 28. those that had charge of the *h.*
2 *Mac.* 3. 25. there appeared to them a *h.* with a terrible rider, and it seemed that he that sat on the *h.*

HORSES.

1 *Esd.* 2. 7. with gifts, with *h.* and with cattle
9. they helped them with *h.* and cattle
Jud. 2. 5. *h.* with their riders twelve thousand
6. 3. not able to sustain the power of our *h.*
Wisd. 19. 9. for they went at large like *h.*
Eccl. 48. 9. wast taken up in a chariot of fiery *h.*
1 *Mac.* 10. 81. and so the enemies' *h.* were tired
2 *Mac.* 10. 29. there appeared five comely men on *h.*

HORSEBACK.

Jud. 2. 15. and twelve thousand archers on *h.*
2 *Mac.* 11. 8. there appeared before them on *h.*
12. 35. Dositheus who was on *h.* and a strong man

HORSE-LITTER.

2 *Mac.* 9. 8. he was now carried in a *h.*

HORSEMAN.

2 *Mac.* 12. 35. an *h.* of Thracia coming on him

HORSEMEN.

1 *Esd.* 5. 2. Darius sent with them a thousand *h.*
8. 51. for I was ashamed to ask of the king *h.*
Jud. 1. 13. he overthrew all his *h.* and chariots
2. 19. to cover the earth with chariots and *h.*
7. 6. Holofernes brought forth all his *h.*
1 *Mac.* 1. 17. he entered Egypt with chariots and *h.*
4. 1. Gorgias took a thousand of the best *h.*
7. the camp compassed round about with *h.*

HOST.

2 *Esd.* 15. 33. in their *h.* shall be fear and dread
Wisd. 12. 8. didst send wasps forerunners of thy *h*
Eccl. 48. 21. he smote the *h.* of the Assyrians
1 *Mac.* 1. 4. he gathered a mighty strong *h.*
2. 31. the *h.* that was at Jerusalem in the city
3. 3. protecting the *h.* with his sword
4. 10. destroy this *h.* before our face this day
5. 11. Timotheus being captain of their *h.*

HOSTS.

2 *Esd.* 8. 21. before whom the *h.* of angels stand
1 *Mac.* 7. 43. the 13th day the *h.* joined battle
13. 53. he made him captain of all the *h.* and dwelt

HOSTAGE.

1 *Mac.* 1. 10. Antiochus, who had been an *h.*

HOSTAGES.

1 *Mac.* 8. 7. should pay a great tribute, and give *h.*
9. 53. he took the chief men's sons for *h.* 11. 62.
10. 6. that the *h.* in tower should be delivered him
9. they of the tower delivered their *h.* to Jonathan
13. 16. wherefore send two of his sons for *h.*

HOT.

2 *Esd.* 4. 48. behold, an *h.* burning oven passed by
6. 4. or ever the chimneys in Sion were *h.*
Dan. 3. 23. to make the oven *h.* with rosin
2 *Mac.* 7. 3. comm. pans and caldrons to be made *h.*

HOUGH.

2 *Esd.* 15. 36. dung of men unto the camels' *h.*

HOUR.

1 *Esd.* 8. 64. the weight was written up the same *h.*
2 *Esd.* 5. 34. for my reins pain me every *h.*
9. 44. every *h.* I did nothing else but pray
14. 26. to-morrow this *h.* shalt thou begin
Jud. 14. 8. until that *h.* she spake to them
Esth. 10. 11. these two lots came at the *h.* and time
Eccl. 11. 27. the affliction of an *h.* makes a man

HOURS.

2 *Esd.* 16. 38. within two or three *h.* of her birth

HOUSE.

1 *Esd.* 1. 3. in the *h.* that king Solomon built
55. as for the *h.* of the Lord, they burnt it
2. 4. commanded me to build him an *h.* at Jerusalem
5. and build the *h.* of the Lord of Israel
8. to build an *h.* for the Lord at Jerusalem
5. 57. they laid the foundation of the *h.* of God
6. 32. out of his own *h.* should a tree be taken
8. 25. to glorify his *h.* that is in Jerusalem
2 *Esd.* 1. 7. brought them from the *h.* of bondage
33. your *h.* is desolate, I will cast you out
9. 24. a field, where no *h.* is builded, 10. 51.
12. 46. and be not heavy, thou *h.* of Jacob
14. 13. now therefore set thine *h.* in order
Tob. 2. 13. when it was in my *h.* and began to cry
3. 17. Tobit came home, and entered into his *h.*
7. 1. they came to the *h.* of Raguel, and Sara
8. 11. but when Raguel was come into his *h.*
14. 4. the *h.* of God in it shall be burned
5. the *h.* of God shall be built in it for ever
Jud. 2. 1. there was talk in the *h.* of Nabuchodonosor
18. much gold and silver out of the king's *h.*
4. 3. the altar and the *h.* were sanctified
15. look on all the *h.* of Israel graciously

Jud. 6. 17. had spoken proudly against *h.* of Israel
8. 5. she made her a tent on the top of her *h.*
6. save the solemn days of the *h.* of Israel
9. 13. have purposed evil against thy hallowed *h.*
13. 14. nor taken his mercy from the *h.* of Israel
14. 5. know him that despised the *h.* of Israel
10. Achior was joined unto the *h.* of Israel
Esth. 14. 9. they will quench the glory of thy *h.*
Wisd. 8. 16. after I am come into my *h.*
Eccl. 1. 17. she fills her *h.* with things desirable
4. 30. be not as a lion in thy *h.* nor frantic
11. 34. receive a stranger into thy *h.* will disturb
14. 24. he that doth lodge near her *h.* shall fasten
21. 4. thus the *h.* of proud men shall be desolate
8. he that buildeth his *h.* with other men's money
18. as is an *h.* that is destroyed, so is wisdom
22. foolish man's foot is soon in his neighbour's *h.*
23. a fool will peep in at the door into the *h.*
23. 11. the plague shall never depart from his *h.* if he swear in vain, his *h.* shall be full of calamity
25. 16. than to keep *h.* with a wicked woman
26. 16. so is a good wife in ordering of her *h.*
27. 3. his *h.* shall be soon overthrown
29. 21. water, bread, and an *h.* to cover shame
22. than delicate fare in another man's *h.*
23. that thou hear not the reproach of thy *h.*
24. it is a miserable life to go from *h.* to *h.*
27. my brother comes, and I have need of my *h.*
36. 26. who will believe a man that hath no *h.*?
42. 10. and gotten with child in her father's *h.*
47. 13. that he might build an *h.* in his name
48. 15. there remained a ruler in the *h.* of David
49. 12. who in their time builded the *h.* and set up
50. 1. who in his life repaired the *h.* again
51. 23. and dwell in the *h.* of learning
Bar. 1. 14. to make confession in the *h.* of the Lord
2. 16. O Lord, look down from thy holy *h.*
26. the *h.* which is called by thy name
3. 24. O Israel, how great is the *h.* of God!
6. 55. when fire falleth on the *h.* of gods of wood
59. it is better to be a profitable vessel in a *h.* than such false gods, or to be a door in an *h.*
Sus. 4. Joacim had a fair garden joining to his *h.*
6. these kept much at Joacim's *h.*
Bel. 29. else we will destroy thee and thy *h.*
1 *Mac.* 1. 28. *h.* of Jacob was covered with confusion
2. 18. so shalt thou and thy *h.* be in the number
3. 56. should return every man to his own *h.*
7. 35. if I come again, I will burn this *h.*
37. thou, O Lord, didst choose this *h.* to be called by thy name, and a *h.* of prayer for thy people
9. 55. he could not give order concerning his *h.*
13. 3. great things my father's *h.* have done
1 *Mac.* 14. 26. the *h.* of his father established Israel
16. 2. I and my brethren, and my father's *h.*
2 *Mac.* 2. 29. as the master-builder of a new *h.*
8. 33. Callisthenes, who was fled into a little *h.*
14. 36. O Lord, keep this *h.* ever undefiled

HOUSEHOLD.

1 *Esd.* 3. 1. Darius made a great feast to his *h.*
2 *Esd.* 3. 11. one thou leftest, Noah with his *h.*

HOUSE-KEEPING.

Eccl. 31. 23. report of his good *h.* will be believed

HOUSE-ROOM.

Eccl. 29. 23. the upbraiding of *h.* is grievous

HOUSES.

2 *Esd.* 1. 35. your *h.* will I give to a people
15. 18. for pride, the *h.* shall be destroyed
49. to waste thy *h.* with destruction and death
16. 31. by them that search their *h.* with the sword
72. that shall cast them out of their *h.*
Wisd. 17. 2. they being shut up in their *h.*
Eccl. 3. 9. establish the *h.* of children
28. 14. it hath overthrown the *h.* of great men
29. 18. mighty men hath suretiship driven from *h.*
1 *Mac.* 1. 31. he pulled down the *h.* and walls
61. they hanged infants and rifled their *h.*
13. 47. cleansed the *h.* wherein the idols were
2 *Mac.* 3. 18. others ran flocking out of their *h.*
5. 12. to slay such as went up upon the *h.*

HUCKSTER.

Eccl. 26. 29. an *h.* shall not be freed from sin

HUMBLE.

Jud. 4. 9. with vehemency did they *h.* their souls
Eccl. 2. 17. they will *h.* their souls in his sight
7. 17. *h.* thy soul greatly, for vengeance is fire
12. 11. though he *h.* himself, and go crouching
18. 21. *h.* thyself before thou be sick
35. 17. the prayer of the *h.* pierceth the clouds

HUMBLED.

2 *Esd.* 8. 49. in that thou hast *h.* thyself as becometh
10. 7. Sion is much *h.* mourning very sore
Esth. 14. 2. Esther *h.* her body greatly
Eccl. 40. 3. to him that is *h.* in earth and ashes

HUMBLETH.

Tob. 4. 19. the Lord *h.* whom he will
Eccl. 7. 11. there is one which *h.* and exalteth

HUMBLING.

Eccl. 34. 26. or what doth his *h.* profit him?

HUMBLY.

Wisd. 13. 18. *h.* beseecheth that which hath least
Prayer of Manass. wherefore I *h.* beseech thee

HUMILITY.

Eccl. 13. 20. as proud hate *h.* so doth the rich

HUNDRED.

1 *Esd.* 1. 36. he set a tax on land of an *h.* talents
7. 7. they offered an *h.* bullocks, two *h.* rams
8. 20. the sum of an *h.* talents of silver, of wheat to an *h.* cors, an *h.* pieces of wine, and other things
Jud. 1. 3. set the towers on gates an *h.* cubits high
Eccl. 18. 9. man's days at the most are an *h.* years
41. 4. whether thou hast lived ten or an *h.* years
1 *Mac.* 15. 35. will we give an *h.* talents for them

HUNDREDS.

1 *Mac.* 3. 55. ordained captains over thous. and *h.*

HUNGER.

2 *Esd.* 15. 57. thy children shall die of *h.*
58. they in the mountain shall die of *h.*
16. 22. the other that escape the *h.* sword destroy
Eccl. 18. 25. when enough, remember the time of *h.*

HUNGRY.

2 *Esd.* 1. 17. when you were *h.* and thirsty in wilder.

2 *Esd.* 16. 6. may any drive away a *h.* lion in wood?
Tob. 1. 16. and I gave my bread to the *h.*
4. 16. give of thy bread to the *h.* and garments

HURT.

2 *Esd.* 6. 19. what they be that have *h.* unjustly
11. 42. thou hast *h.* the peaceable, loved liars
Wisd. 10. 8. they gat not only this *h.*
14. 29. swear falsely, yet they look not to be *h.*
18. 2. but for that they did not *h.* them now
19. 6. thy children might be kept without *h.*
Eccl. 13. 12. and he will not spare to do thee *h.*
28. 2. forgive thy neighbour the *h.* he hath done
38. 21. thou shalt not do him good but *h.* thyself
Dan. 3. 27. the fire neither *h.* nor troubled them
1 *Mac.* 5. 48. let us pass thro', none shall do you *h.*
6. 18. they in tower sought always their *h.*
7. 22. Juda in their power did much *h.* in Israel
14. 36. and did much *h.* in the holy place
15. 29. ye have done great *h.* in the land
2 *Mac.* 3. 39. he destroyeth them that come to *h.* it
8. 36. and therefore they could not be *h.*
12. 3. as though they had meant them no *h.*
22. that they were often *h.* of their own men
25. that he would restore them without *h.*

HURTFUL.

2 *Esd.* 11. 45. appear no more, nor thy *h.* claws
15. 6. and their *h.* works are fulfilled

HUSBAND.

2 *Esd.* 9. 43. barren, though I had an *h.* thirty years
10. 17. go thy way then into the city to thy *h.*
Jud. 8. 2. Manasses was her *h.* of her kindred
7. her *h.* Manasses had left her gold and silver
10. 3. was clad during the life of Manasses her *h.*
16. 22. but none knew her after her *h.* was dead
24. were nearest of kindred to Manasses her *h.*
Eccl. 4. 10. be instead of an *h.* to their mother
22. 4. shall bring an inheritance to her *h.*
5. dishonoureth both her father and her *h.*
23. 22. thus with the wife that leaveth her *h.*
23. she hath trespassed against her own *h.*
25. 18. her *h.* shall sit among his neighbours
22. a woman, if she maintain her *h.* is full of anger
23. a woman that will not comfort her *h.* in distress
26. 2. a virtuous woman rejoiceth her *h.*
13. the grace of a wife delighteth her *h.*
22. is a tower against death to her *h.*
24. but an honest woman will reverence her *h.*
26. a woman that honoureth her *h.* judged wise
36. 23. then is not her *h.* like other men
40. 23. but above both is a wife with her *h.*
42. 10. having an *h.* lest she should misbehave
Sus. 28. people were assembled to her *h.* Joacim
63. Susanna with her *h.* praised God

HUSBANDS.

2 *Esd.* 16. 33. women shall mourn, having no *h.*
34. and their *h.* shall perish of famine
Tob. 3. 8. dost thou not know that thou hast strangled thy *h.*? thou hast had already seven *h.*
15. my seven *h.* are dead, why should I live?

HYDASPES.

Jud. 1. 6. there came to him all that dwelt by H.

HYÆNA.

Eccl. 13. 18. what agreement between *h.* and a dog?

HYMNS.

1 *Mac.* 13. 51. entered with viols, and *h.* and songs

HYPOCRISY.

2 *Mac.* 6. 25. they through my *h.* should be deceived

HYPOCRITE.

Eccl. 1. 29. be not an *h.* in the sight of men
32. 15. but the *h.* will be offended thereat
33. 2. he that is an *h.* therein, is as a ship in a storm

J.

JACOB.

2 *Esd.* 1. 24. what shall I do to thee, O J.?
3. 16. thou gavest Isaac, to Isaac also thou gavest J. and Esau, so J. became a great multitude
19. mightest give the law unto the seed of J.
5. 35. I might not have seen the travel of J.
6. 8. J. hand held the first heel of Esau
9. J. is the beginning of it that followeth
9. 30. thou saidst, mark my words thou seed of J.
12. 46. and be not heavy, thou house of J.
Jud. 8. 26. what happened to J. in Mesopotamia
Eccl. 23. 12. be not found in the heritage of J.
24. 8. Creator said, let thy dwelling be in J.
36. 11. gather all the tribes of J. together
44. 23. he made it rest upon the head of J.
45. 5. that he might teach J. his covenant
14. and the Lord had respect unto J.
47. 22. wherefore he gave a remnant to J.
48. 10. and to restore the tribes of J.
49. 10. for they comforted J. and delivered them
Bar. 3. 36. and hath given it to J. his servant
4. 2. turn thee, O J., and take hold of it
1 *Mac.* 1. 28. house of J. was covered with confusion
3. 7. and he made J. glad with his acts
45. joy was taken from J. the pipe ceased
5. 2. they thought to destroy the generation of J.

JAMBRI.

1 *Mac.* 9. 36. but the children of J. came out
37. the children of J. made a great marriage

JAMNIA.

1 *Mac.* 4. 15. they pursued them to the plains of J.
5. 58. they had given charge, they went toward J.
10. 69. who gathered a great host and camped in J.
15. 40. Cendebeus came to J. and began to provoke

JAMNITES.

2 *Mac.* 12. 8. the J. were minded to do in like manner
9. he came upon the J. by night, and set fire
40. found things consecrated to the idols of the J.

JAPHETH.

Jud. 2. 25. and he came to the borders of J.

JAZAR.

1 *Mac.* 5. 8. when he had taken J. with the towns

ICE.

Wisd. 16. 22. but snow and *i.* endured the fire
Eccl. 3. 15. thy sins shall melt away as the *i.*
43. 20. and the water is congealed into *i.*
Dan. 3. 49. O ye *i.* and cold, bless ye the Lord

ICY.

Wisd. 19. 21. nor melted the *i.* kind of heavenly meat

IDLE.

2 *Esd.* 15. 60. they shall rush on the *i.* city
16. 68. they shall take and feed you being *i.*
Wisd. 14. 5. the works of thy wisdom should be *i.*
Eccl. 37. 11. nor with an *i.* servant of business

IDOL.

Eccl. 30. 19. what good doth the offering to an *i.*
Bel 3. the Babylonians had an *i.* called Bel

IDOLS.

1 *Esd.* 2. 10. Nabuch. had set up in his temple of *i.*
Tob. 14. 6. all nations shall turn and bury their *i.*
Esth. 14. 10. to set forth the praises of the *i.*
Wisd. 14. 11. on the *i.* of Gentiles be a visitation
12. the devising of *i.* was beginning of fornication
27. the worshipping of *i.* not to be named
29. as their trust is in *i.* which have no life
30. giving heed to *i.* and also unjustly swore
15. 15. they counted the *i.* of the heathen to be gods
Bar. 6. 73. better is the just man that hath no *i.*
Bel 5. who said, because I may not worship *i.*
1 *Mac.* 1. 43. many Israelites sacrificed to *i.*
47. set up altars, groves, and chapels of *i.*
10. 83. went to Beth-dagon their *i.* temple
13. 47. and cleansed the houses wherein the *i.* were
2 *Mac.* 12. 40. things consecrated to *i.* of Jamnites

IDOL-*altar.*

1 *Mac.* 1. 59. they did sacrifice on the *i.-altar*

IDOL-*altars.*

1 *Mac.* 1. 54. they builded *i.-alt.* thro' cities of Juda

IDOLATROUS.

Wisd. 12. 6. out of the midst of their *i.* crew
2 *Mac.* 7. 42. have spoken concerning the *i.* feast

IDUMEA.

1 *Mac.* 4. 15. they pursued them to the plains of I
29. so they came into I. and pitched their tents
61. the people might have a defence against I.
5. 3. Judas fought against the children of Esau in I.
6. 31. these went thro' I. and pitched ag. Bethsura
2 *Mac.* 12. 32. against Gorgias the governor of I.

IDUMEANS.

2 *Mac.* 10. 15. the I. have gotten into their hands

JEALOUS.

Eccl. 9. 1. be not *j.* over the wife of thy bosom
26. 6. a woman that is *j.* over another woman
37. 11. not consult, touching her of whom she is *j.*

JEALOUSY.

2 *Esd.* 15. 52. would I with *j.* have so proceeded
Wisd. 1. 10. the ear of *j.* heareth all things
5. 17. he shall take to him his *j.* for armour

JEBUSITE.

Jud. 5. 16. they cast forth before them the *j.*

JEDUTHUN.

1 *Esd.* 1. 15. Zacharias and J. of the king's retinue

JEOPARD.

2 *Mac.* 11. 7. that they would *j.* themselves to help

JEOPARDY.

1 *Mac.* 6. 44. put himself in *j.* to deliver his people

JEPHUNNETH. *See* CALEB.

JEREMIAS, JEREMY.

1 *Esd.* 1. 28. not regarding the words of prophet J.
32. yea, J. the prophet lamented for Josias
47. the words spoken to him by the prophet J.
57. to fulfil the words spoken by the mouth of J.
2. 1. that he had promised by the mouth of J.
2 *Esd.* 2. 18. I will send my servants Esay and J.
Eccl. 49. 6. according to the prophecy of J.
Bar. 6. 1. a copy of an epistle which J. sent
2 *Mac.* 2. 1. that J. the prophet commanded them
5. when J. came there, he found an hollow cave
7. which when J. perceived, he blamed them
15. 15. J. holding forth his right hand

JERICHO.

Eccl. 24. 14. I was exalted as a rose-plant in J.
1 *Mac.* 9. 50. repaired the fort in J. and Emmaus
16. 11. in the plain of J. was Ptolemeus
14. he came down himself to J. with his sons
2 *Mac.* 12. 15. did cast down J. in the time of Joshua

JEROBOAM.

Eccl. 47. 23. there was also J. the son of Nebat

JERUSALEM.

1 *Esd.* 1. 21. Israel that were found dwelling at J.
49. the temple which was sanctified in J.
55. they brake down the walls of J.
2. 4. to build him an house at J. in Jewry
5. if there be any of his people, let him go up to J.
4. 43. thy vow which thou hast vowed to build J.
Tob. 1. 6. I alone went often to J. at the feasts
7. another tenth part I spent every year at J.
13. 9. O J. the holy city, he will scourge thee
16. for J. shalt be built up with sapphires
17. the streets of J. shall be paved with beryl
14. 4. J. shall be desolate, and house of God burnt
5. they shall return and build up J. gloriously
Jud. 4. 2. they were troubled for J. and the temple
Eccl. 24. 11. gave me rest, and in J. was my power
36. 13. O be merciful to J. thy holy city
50. 27. Jesus the son of Sirach of J. wrote
Bar. 4. 8. ye have grieved J. that nursed you
30. take a good heart, O J. he will comfort thee
5. 1. put off, O J. the garment of thy mourning
5. arise, O J. and stand on high, and look about
1 *Mac.* 6. 12. I remember the evils I did at J.
7. 17. their blood have they shed about J.
39. so Nicanor went out of J. and pitched tents
9. 53. put them in the tower at J. to be kept
10. 31. let J. also be holy and free, with borders
11. 41. would cast those of the tower out of J.
14. 36. that were in the city of David in J.
2 *Mac.* 1. 1. the brethren the Jews that be at J.
9. 4. spoken proudly, that he would come to J
10. 15. those that were banished from J.
11. 5. but distant from J. about five furlongs
12. 9. that the light of the fire was seen at J.
29. Scythopolis lieth 600 furlongs from J.
15. 30. to bring Nicanor's head and hand to J.

JESSE.

Eccl. 45. 25. the covenant made with David son of J

JEST.

Eccl. 8. 4. *j.* not with a rude man, lest ancestors

JESU.
1 *Esd.* 8. 63. with them was Josabad son of J.
JESUS.
1 *Esd.* 5. 5. J. the son of Josedec son of Saraias
8. with J. Nehemias, and Zacharias, their guides
48. then stood up J. the son of Josedec,
58. then stood up J. and his sons and brethren
70. Zorobabel and J. chief of the families
6. 2. J. the son of Josedec began to build the house
2 *Esd.* 7. 28. for my son J. shall be revealed
37. J. after him for Israel in the time of Achan
Eccl. 46. 1. J. the son of Nave was valiant in wars
49. 12. so was J. the son of Josedec, who builded
50. 27. J. the son of Sirach of Jerusalem
51. 1. a prayer of J. the son of Sirach
1 *Mac.* 2. 55. J. for fulfilling word was made a judge
JEW.
Esth. 11. 3. who was J. and dwelt in the city of Susa
2 *Mac.* 6. 6. or profess himself at all to be a J.
9. 17. that also he would become a J. himself
JEWELLER.
Eccl. 45. 11. like seals set in gold, work of the *j.*
JEWRY.
1 *Esd.* 1. 32. in all J. they mourned for Josias
4. 49. the Jews that went out of his realm up to J.
5. 8. they returned to the other parts of J.
57. in the second year after they were come to J.
6. 1. the prophets prophesied to the Jews in J.
8. 81. they have given us a sure abiding in J.
9. 3. there was a proclamation in all J. and Jerus.
Bel 33. there was in J. the prophet Habbacuc
2 *Mac.* 10. 24. came as though would take J. by force
JEWS.
1 *Esd.* 1. 21. and the J. held with all Israel
2. 18. that the J. do build the market-places
23. and that the J. were rebellious, and raised
4. 49. he wrote for all the J. that went out
50. Edomites should give over the villages of the J.
6. 1. the prophets prophesied to the J. in Jewry
8. the ancients of the J. that were of the captivity
27. the elders of the J. to build the house of Lord
7. 2. assisting the ancients of the J. and governors
8. 10. I have given orders that such of the J.
Esth. 10. 8. assembled to destroy the name of the J.
16. 15. we find that the J. are no evil-doers
19. the J. may freely live after their own laws
Sus. 4. to him resorted the J. because he was more
1 *Mac.* 2. 23. came one of the J. in sight of all
4. 2. that he might rush in on the camp of the J.
6. 6. that Lysias was driven away of the J.
8. 31. on our friends and confederates the J.
10. 23. prevented us, in making amity with the J.
29. now I release all the J. from tributes
11. 30. and to the nation of the J. 13. 36.
33. determined to do good to the people of the J.
47. then the king called to the J. for help
14. 22. the J. ambassadors came to us, 15. 17.
33. but he set a garrison of J. there
34. but he placed J. there, and furnished them
15. 1. to Simon the priest and prince of the J.
17. being sent from Simon and people of the J.
2 *Mac.* 1. 1. the brethren the J. that be at Jerusalem
7. we the J. wrote unto you in trouble
3. 32. had been done to Heliodorus by the J.
4. 11. the royal privileges granted to the J.
5. 23. a mind against his countrymen the J.
25. when taking the J. keeping holy-day
6. 1. to compel the J. to depart from the laws
8. 1. took such as continued in the J. religion
10. to make so much money of the captive J.
9. 4. he thought to avenge on the J. the disgrace,
make it a common burying-place of the J.
7. breathing out fire in his rage against the J.
19. Antiochus to the good J. his citizens
10. 29. five men, and two of them led the J.
11. 16. there were letters written to the J.
12. 1. the J. were about their husbandry
13. 9. to do far worse to the J. than had been done
18. had taken a taste of the manliness of the J.
19. Beth-sura, which was a strong-hold of the J.
14. 5. being asked how the J. stood affected
6. those of the J. that be called Assideans
14. thinking the harm of the J. to be their welfare
37. who for kindness was called a father of the J.
38. did jeopard his life for the religion of the J.
39. to declare the hate that he bare to the J.
40. by taking him, to do the J. much hurt
15. 2. the J. that were compelled to go with him
12. Onias prayed for the whole body of the J.
IGNORANCE.
Wisd. 14. 22. they lived in the great war of *i.*
17. 13. counteth the *i.* more than the cause
Eccl. 4. 25. but be abashed of the error of thine *i.*
28. 7. remember the covenant, and wink at *i.*
IGNORANCES.
1 *Esd.* 8. 75. our *i.* have reached up to heaven
Tob. 3. 3. punish me not for my sins and *i.*
Eccl. 23. 2. that they spare me not for mine *i.*
3. lest mine *i.* increase and my sins abound
51. 19. and I bewailed mine *i.* of her
IGNORANT.
Wisd. 13. 1. vain are all men, who are *i.* of God
14. 18. set forward the *i.* to more superstition
Eccl. 5. 15. be not *i.* of any thing in a great manner
IGNORANTLY.
2 *Mac.* 11. 31. shall be molested for things *i.* done
ILL.
Jud. 8. 8. there was none that gave her an *i.* word
Wisd. 5. 23. *i.* dealing shall overthrow the thrones
Eccl. 9. 18. a man of an *i.* tongue is dangerous
29. 7. many have refused to lend for others *i.* dealing
41. 11. an *i.* name of sinners shall be blotted out
ILL-*according.*
Wisd. 18. 10. sounded an *i.-according* cry of enemies
ILLUMINATED.
Bar. 4. 2. walk in light that thou mayest be *i.*
ILLUMINATION.
Eccl. 25. 11. love of the Lord passeth all things for *i.*
ILLUSIONS.
Wisd. 17. 7. as for the *i.* of magic, were put down
IMAGE.
2 *Esd.* 5. 37. shew me the *i.* of a voice, and declare
2 *Esd.* 8. 44. so perish. man, who is called thy own *i.*
Wisd. 2. 23. made him to be an *i.* of his eternity
7. 26. and she is the *i.* of his goodness
13. 13. and fashioned it to the *i.* of a man
16. for it is an *i.* and hath need of help
14. 15. when he hath made an *i.* of his child
17. they made an express *i.* of a king
15. 4. nor any *i.* spotted with divers colours
5. and so they desire the form of a dead *i.*
17. 21. an *i.* of that darkness spread over them
IMAGERY.
Eccl. 38. 27. and give themselves to counterfeit *i.*
IMAGES.
Wisd. 15. 13. maketh brittle vessels and graven *i.*
1 *Mac.* 3. 48. sought to paint the likeness of their *i.*
5. 68. when he burnt their carved *i.* with fire
2 *Mac.* 2. 2. when they see *i.* of silver and gold
IMAGINATION.
Eccl. 22. 18. a fearful heart in the *i.* of a fool
37. 3. O wicked *i.* whence camest thou in to cover
40. 2. their *i.* of things to some causeth fear
Bar. 1. 22. the *i.* of his own wicked heart
IMAGINATIONS.
2 *Esd.* 15. 3. fear not the *i.* against thee
16. 54. behold the Lord knoweth their *i.*
Wisd. 3. 10. shall be punished accord. to their own *i.*
Bar. 2. 8. turn from the *i.* of his wicked heart
Sus. 28. full of mischievous *i.* against Susanna
IMAGINE.
Eccl. 17. 31. flesh and blood will *i.* evil
1 *Mac.* 3. 52. what they *i.* against us, thou knowest
IMAGINED.
2 *Esd.* 7. 22. spake against him, and *i.* vain things
Wisd. 3. 14. nor *i.* wicked things against God
1 *Mac.* 11. 8. *i.* wicked counsels against Alexander
IMAGINETH.
Eccl. 12. 16. in his heart he *i.* how to throw thee
16. 23. and a foolish man erring *i.* follies
IMMORTAL.
2 *Esd.* 7. 13. for the entrances brought *i.* fruit
49. if there be promised us an *i.* time
Wisd. 1. 15. for righteousness is *i.*
2. 23. for God created man to be *i.* and made him
4. 1. for the memorial thereof is *i.*
Eccl. 17. 30. because the son of man is not *i.*
IMMORTALITY.
2 *Esd.* 7. 43. the beginning of the *i.* for to come
8. 54. in the end is shewed the treasure of *i.*
Wisd. 3. 4. yet is their hope full of *i.*
8. 13. by the means of her I shall obtain *i.*
17. how that to be allied unto wisdom is *i.*
15. 3. yea, to know thy power, is the root of *i.*
Eccl. 19. 19. receive the fruit of the tree of *i.*
IMMUNITY.
1 *Mac.* 10. 34. shall be all the days of *i.* and freedom
13. 34. to the end he shall give the land an *i.*
IMMUNITIES.
1 *Mac.* 10. 28. we will grant you many *i.* and give
13. 37. to confirm the *i.* which we have granted
IMPARTED.
Eccl. 17. 5. in sixth place he *i.* them understanding
2 *Mac.* 8. 12. he had *i.* to those that were with him
IMPEDIMENT.
Wisd. 19. 7. out of the Red sea, a way without *i.*
IMPEDIMENTS.
Jud. 5. 1. and had laid *i.* in the campaign countries
IMPIETY.
1 *Esd.* 1. 42. recorded of his uncleanness and *i.*
2 *Esd.* 4. 38. O Lord, even we all are full of *i.*
2 *Mac.* 4. 38. the place where he had committed *i.*
IMPIETIES.
2 *Esd.* 3. 29. when I had seen *i.* without number
IMPORTABLE.
Prayer of Manass. threatening towards sinners is *i.*
IMPOSITION.
1 *Esd.* 8. 22. nor any other *i.* of any of the priests
IMPOSSIBLE.
2 *Mac.* 3. 12. that it was altogether *i.* such wrongs
4. 6. he saw it *i.* that the state should continue
IMPOTENT.
Bar. 6. 28. but to poor and *i.* they give nothing
IMPRISONED.
Wisd. 18. 4. they were worthy to be *i.* in darkness
IMPRISONMENT.
1 *Esd.* 8. 24. by penalty of money, or by *i.*
IMPUDENCE.
Eccl. 25. 22. is full of *i.* and much reproach
IMPUDENT.
Eccl. 19. 2. he that cleaveth to harlots will become *i.*
23. 6. give not over me thy servant into an *i.* mind
26. 11. watch over an *i.* eye, and marvel not
29. 14. but he that is *i.* will forsake him
IMPUTED.
1 *Mac.* 2. 52. it was *i.* to him for righteousness
INCOMMUNICABLE.
Wisd. 14. 21. did ascribe to stocks the *i.* name
INCENSE.
2 *Esd.* 3. 24. to offer *i.* and oblations to thee
Jud. 9. 1. about time *i.* of that evening was offered
Wisd. 18. 21. bringing the propitiation of *i.*
Eccl. 45. 16. *i.* and a sweet savour for a memorial
50. 9. as fire and *i.* in the censer, and a vessel
Bar. 1. 10. sent money to buy sin-offerings and *i.*
Dan. 3. 15. nor is their oblation, or *i.* or place
1 *Mac.* 1. 55. and burnt *i.* at the doors of their houses
4. 49. they brought the altar of *i.* and the table
50. and upon the altar they burnt *i.*
INCHANTMENTS.
Wisd. 18. 13. not believe any thing by reason of *i.*
INCLOSING.
2 *Mac.* 1. 34. the king *i.* the place, made it holy
INCONTINENCY.
2 *Esd.* 5. 10. *i.* shall be multiplied upon earth
INCORRUPTIBLE.
Wisd. 12. 1. for thine *i.* spirit is in all things
18. † 4. by whom the *i.* light was to be given
INCORRUPTION.
2 *Esd.* 4. † 11. to understand the *i.* that is evident
Wisd. 6. 18. keeping laws is the assurance of *i.*
INCREASE.
1 *Esd.* 9. 7. thereby to *i.* the sins of Israel
Tob. 1. 7. the first tenth part of all *i.* I gave
Eccl. 6. 5. a fair tongue will *i.* kind greetings
20. 28. that tilleth his lands, shall *i.* his heap
23. 3. lest mine ignorances *i.* and sins abound
39. 11. and if he live he shall *i.* it
45. 20. divided to him the first-fruits of the *i.*
Bar. 2. 34. I will *i.* them, they shall not be diminish.
1 *Mac.* 14. 8. the earth gave her *i.* and trees fruit
2 *Mac.* 4. 4. did rage, and *i.* Simon's malice
13. such was the *i.* of heathenish manners
INCREASED.
2 *Esd.* 1. 6. the sins of their fathers are *i.*
5. 2. iniquity shall be *i.* above that thou seest
7. 41. even so now seeing wickedness is *i.*
Tob. 14. 2. he *i.* in the fear of the Lord
Jud. 5. 9. they were *i.* with gold and silver
16. 23. but she *i.* more and more in honour
Eccl. 2. 3. that thou mayest be *i.* at thy last end
1 *Mac.* 1. 40. as had her glory, so was her dishonour *i.*
2. 30. because afflictions *i.* sore upon them
2 *Mac.* 8. 8. so when Philip saw that this man *i.*
INCREASETH.
Wisd. 16. 24. *i.* his strength against the unrighteous
Eccl. 31. 30. drunkenness *i.* the rage of a fool
INCREASING.
Eccl. 43. 8. *i.* wonderfully in her changing
2 *Mac.* 4. 50. *i.* in malice, and being a traitor
INCREDULITY.
2 *Esd.* 15. 3. let not the *i.* of them trouble thee
INCURABLE.
Jud. 5. 12. he smote all Egypt with *i.* plagues
INDEBTED.
1 *Mac.* 10. 43. flee to temple, being *i.* to the king
INDIA.
Esth. 13. 1. to the princes from I. to Ethiopia
1 *Mac.* 8. 8. the country of I. and Media, and Lydia
INDIAN.
1 *Mac.* 6. 37. besides the I. that ruled him
INDIFFERENT.
Eccl. 42. 5. and of merchants *i.* selling
INDIGNATION.
2 *Esd.* 8. 30. take thou no *i.* at them which are
Eccl. 5. 6. and his *i.* resteth upon sinners
36. 7. rise up *i.* and pour out wrath
45. 19. in his wrathful *i.* were they consumed
Bar. 2. 20. thou hast sent out thy wrath and *i.*
Bel 28. they took great *i.* and conspired against king
1 *Mac.* 2. 49. pride got strength, and the wrath of *i.*
3. 27. king Antiochus was full of *i.*
2 *Mac.* 4. 35. many other nations took great *i.*
INESTIMABLE.
2 *Esd.* 8. 21. whose throne is *i.* whose glory
INEVITABLE.
Wisd. 17. 14. came out of the bottoms of *i.* hell
INFAMY.
Wisd. 2. 12. he objecteth to our *i.* the transgressings
INFANTS.
Jud. 7. 27. not see the death of our *i.* before our eyes
16. 5. make my *i.* as a prey, my virgins a spoil
Wisd. 11. 7. commandment whereby *i.* were slain
1 *Mac.* 2. 9. her *i.* are slain in the streets
2 *Mac.* 5. 13. there was slaying of virgins and *i.*
8. 4. remember the wicked slaughter of harmless *i.*
INFIDELITY.
2 *Esd.* 7. 44. *i.* is cut off, righteousness is grown
INFINITE.
Wisd. 8. 18. in works of her hands are *i.* riches
Eccl. 16. 17. such an *i.* number of creatures
30. 15. and a strong body above *i.* wealth
Prayer of Manass. of thy *i.* mercies hast appointed
2 *Mac.* 2. 24. for considering the *i.* number
3. 6. treasury was full of *i.* sums of money
INFIRMITY.
2 *Esd.* 3. 22. thus *i.* was made permanent
INFIRMITIES.
2 *Esd.* 4. 27. this world is full of unrighteousn. and *i.*
INFLAMED.
Eccl. 28. 10. the more they will be *i.*
Sus. 8. so that their lust was *i.* towards her
1 *Mac.* 2. 24. Mattathias was *i.* with zeal
INFLUENCE.
Wisd. 7. 25. a pure *i.* from the glory of Almighty
INFORMED.
2 *Mac.* 13. 4. Lysias *i.* king that this man was cause
14. 1. Judas was *i.* that Demetrius had taken
INHABIT.
2 *Esd.* 3. 28. are their deeds better that *i.* Babylon?
Jud. 5. 3. what are the cities that they *i.*?
14. 4. you and all that *i.* the coast of Israel
INHABITANTS.
2 *Esd.* 6. 26. the heart of the *i.* shall be changed
Jud. 1. 10. till you come to all the *i.* of Egypt
11. the *i.* of the land made light of the command
12. he would slay all the *i.* of the land of Moab
2. 28. fear fell on all the *i.* of the sea-coasts
4. 11. the *i.* of Jerusalem fell before the temple
5. 4. more than all the *i.* of the west
7. 13. the *i.* of Bethulia have their water thence
20. vessels of water failed all the *i.* of Bethulia
8. 11. O ye governors of the *i.* of Bethulia
Wisd. 12. 3. to destroy those old *i.* of thy holy land
Bar. 1. 15. to Juda and to the *i.* of Jerusalem
1 *Mac.* 1. 28. the land also was moved for the *i.*
38. the *i.* of Jerusalem fled because of them
6. 12. that I sent to destroy the *i.* of Judea
2 *Mac.* 9. 2. that being put to flight of the *i.*
INHABITED.
2 *Esd.* 3. 25. they that *i.* the city forsook thee
Wisd. 11. 2. through the wilderness that was not *i.*
Eccl. 10. 3. through prudence the city shall be *i.*
38. 32. without these cannot a city be *i.*
Bar. 4. 35. she shall be *i.* of devils for a time
2 *Mac.* 3. 1. when the holy city was *i.* with peace
9. 17. would go through all the world that was *i.*
12. 13. city was *i.* by people of divers countries
INHERIT.
2 *Esd.* 7. 17. the righteous should *i.* these things
67. the world not continue with them that *i.*
Tob. 4. 12. and their seed shall *i.* the land
Eccl. 4. 13. he that holdeth her fast, shall *i.* glory
16. he shall *i.* her, and his generation shall hold
6. 1. for thereby thou shalt *i.* an ill name
10. 11. he shall *i.* creeping things, beasts, worms

Eccl. 15. 6. she shall cause him *i.* an everlast. name
39. 23. so shall the heathen *i.* his wrath
44. 21. would cause them to *i.* from sea to sea

INHERITANCE.

1 *Esd.* 8. 85. that ye may leave the *i.* of the land?
2 *Esd.* 6. 59. why do we not possess an *i.* with world?
7. 9. were given for *i.* how shall we receive this *i.*
8. 45. and have mercy upon thine own *i.*
Tob. 3. 17. she belongeth to Tobias by right of *i.*
6. 12. because the right of *i.* doth appertain to thee
Jud. 9. 12. I pray thee, O God of the *i.* of Israel
13. 5. for now is the time to help thine *i.*
16. 21. every one returned to his own *i.*
Esth. 10. 12. so God remembered and justified his *i.*
13. 15. yea, they desire to destroy the *i.*
17. hear my prayer, and be merciful to thine *i.*
14. 5. thou tookest Israel for a perpetual *i.*
Wisd. 3. 14. an *i.* in the temple of the Lord
Eccl. 9. 6. not to harlots that thou lose not thine *i.*
24. 7. I sought rest, and in whose *i.* shall I abide?
12. I took root in the portion of the Lord's *i.*
20. and mine *i.* is sweeter than the honey-comb
45. 22. howbeit in the land of the people he had no
i. for the Lord himself is his portion and *i.*
25. that the *i.* of the king be to his posterity alone,
so the *i.* of Aaron should also be to his seed
46. 1. that he might set Israel in their *i.*
1 *Mac.* 6. 24. they slew, and spoiled our *i.*
See FATHERS.

INHERITED.

Tob. 14. 13. he *i.* their substance and his father Tobit's

INIQUITY.

1 *Esd.* 8. 70. great men have been partakers of this *i.*
72. assembled to me, whilst I mourned for the *i.*
2 *Esd.* 5. 2. *i.* shall be increased above that thou seest
7. 56. for while we lived and committed *i.*
16. 52. *i.* shall be taken away out of the earth
Jud. 5. 17. the God that hateth *i.* was with them
21. but if there be no *i.* in their nation
6. 5. hast spoken these words in the day of thine *i.*
Wisd. 5. 23. thus *i.* shall lay waste the earth
Eccl. 7. 2. and *i.* shall turn away from thee
6. seek not to be judge, not able to take away *i.*
10. 7. and by both doth one commit *i.*
17. 26. turn to Most High, and turn away from *i.*
20. 28. that pleaseth great men, get pardon for *i.*
21. 3. all *i.* is as a two edged sword, wounds whereof
23. 11. that useth swearing, shall be filled with *i.*
27. 10. as lion for prey, so sin for them that work *i.*
41. 18. of *i.* before a congregation and people
49. 2. he took away the abomination of *i.*
Bar. 3. 7. for we have called to mind all the *i.*
Dan. 3. 6. for we have sinned and committed *i.*
Prayer of Manass. for the multitude of mine *i.*
1 *Mac.* 3. 6. all the workers of *i.* were troubled
20. they come against us in much pride and *i.*
9. 23. and there arose all such as wrought *i.*

INIQUITIES.

1 *Esd.* 8. 90. now are we before thee in our *i.*
9. 2. mourning for the great *i.* of the multitude
2 *Esd.* 7. 68. that they which have committed *i.*
16. 67. leave off your sins, and forget your *i.*
76. and let not your *i.* lift up themselves
77. woe to them that are covered with their *i.*
Prayer of Manass. I have sinned, I acknow. mine
i. forgive me and destroy me not with mine *i.*

INJURY.

2 *Mac.* 8. 17. set before their eyes the *i.* they had done

INJURIES.

Eccl. 10. 8. because of *i.* and riches got by deceit

INJURIOUS.

Eccl. 8. 11. rise not up in anger at pres. of an *i.* person

INJUSTICE.

Eccl. 40. 12. all bribery and *i.* shall be blotted out

INNER.

Eccl. 21. 14. *i.* parts of a fool like a broken vessel
1 *Mac.* 9. 54. the wall of *i.* court of the sanctuary
2 *Mac.* 9. 5. and sore torments of the *i.* parts

INNOCENCY.

Esth. 16. 6. the *i.* and goodness of princes
1 *Mac.* 2. 37. but said, let us die all in our *i.*
60. Daniel for his *i.* was delivered from lions

INNOCENT.

2 *Esd.* 15. 8. the *i.* and righteous blood crieth
9. I will receive the *i.* blood from among them
22. my hand shall not spare them that shed *i.* blood
Esth. 16. 5. caused many to be partakers of *i.* blood
Eccl. 11. 10. if thou meddle much, thou shalt not be *i.*
23. 11. if he swear in vain, he shall not be *i.*
Sus. 53. for thou hast condemned the *i.* albeit the L.
saith, the *i.* and righteous shalt thou not slay
62. thus the *i.* blood was saved the same day
1 *Mac.* 1. 37. thus they shed *i.* blood on every side
2 *Mac.* 4. 47. they should have been judged *i.*

INNUMERABLE.

2 *Esd.* 6. 3. before the *i.* multitude of angels
44. immediately there was great and *i.* fruit
Wisd. 7. 11. all good things and *i.* riches in her hands
18. 12. so they altogether had *i.* dead with one death
Eccl. 37. 25. but the days of Israel are *i.*
2 *Mac.* 3. 6. the multitude of their riches was *i.*

INQUISITION.

2 *Esd.* 6. 19. and I will begin to make *i.* of them
Eccl. 23. 24. and *i.* shall be made of her children
41. 4. there is no *i.* in the grave

INSPIRED.

Wisd. 15. 11. him that *i.* into him an active soul

INSTRUCT.

2 *Esd.* 5. 32. angel said, hear me, and I will *i.* thee
Eccl. 7. 23. hast thou children? *i.* them, and bow down
10. 1. a wise judge will *i.* his people

INSTRUCTED.

Wisd. 6. 11. desire my word, and ye shall be *i.*
Eccl. 26. 14. nothing so much worth as a mind well *i.*

INSTRUCTETH.

Eccl. 37. 23. a wise man *i.* his people and fruits

INSTRUCTION.

Eccl. 1. 27. the fear of the Lord is wisdom and *i.*
6. 18. my son, gather *i.* from thy youth up
8. 8. for of them thou shalt learn *i.* and to serve
33. 4. and bind up *i.* and then make answer
51. 26. let your soul receive *i.* she is at hand

INSTRUCTIONS.

Eccl. 44. 4. wise and eloquent in their *i.*

INSTRUMENT.

2 *Esd.* 13. 9. nor held sword, nor any *i.* of war, 28.
Tob. 7. 14. and did write an *i.* of covenants
Eccl. 43. 2. declaring at his rising a marvellous *i.*
8. being an *i.* of the armies above, shining in
2 *Mac.* 13. 5. it had a round *i.* which hanged down

INSTRUMENTS.

1 *Esd.* 4. 63. they feasted with the *i.* of music
5. 2. and with musical *i.* and tabrets, 59.
1 *Mac.* 6. 51. engines and *i.* to cast fire and stones
9. 39. with drums and *i.* of music, and weapons
13. 42. the people began to write in their *i.*

INSURRECTION.

2 *Esd.* 16. 70. a great *i.* on those that fear the Lord
2 *Mac.* 4. 30. they of Tharsus and Mallos made *i.*

INTELLIGENCE.

2 *Mac.* 3. 9. he told him what *i.* was given of money

INTEMPERANCE.

2 *Esd.* 7. 44. *i.* is at an end, infidelity is cut off

INTEMPERATE.

Eccl. 23. 13. use not thy mouth to *i.* swearing

INTEND.

2 *Mac.* 14. 8. I *i.* the good of my own countrymen

INTENDED.

Esth. 13. 4. the uniting of kingdoms honourably *i.*
Sus. 62. they did in such sort as they maliciously *i.*
2 *Mac.* 14. 5. Jews stood affected, and what they *i.*

INTENT.

Wisd. 12. 22. to the *i.* that when we judge
Bel 32. to the *i.* they might devour Daniel

INTERPRETATION.

2 *Esd.* 12. 8. shew me thy servant the *i.* of vision
10. he said to me, this is the *i.* of the vision
17. this is the *i.* 19. 22. | 13. 22, 28.
13. 15. shew me now yet the *i.* of this dream
21. the *i.* of the vision shall I shew thee
53. this is the *i.* of the dream thou sawest

INTERPRETATIONS.

2 *Esd.* 12. 35. this is the dream, and these are the *i.*
Eccl. 47. 17. they marvelled at thee for thy *i.*

INTERPRETED.

Esth. 11. 1. the same, and that Lysimachus had *i.* it

INTERPRETER.

Eccl. 17. 5. speech, an *i.* of the cogitations thereof

INTERRUPT.

Eccl. 11. 8. nor *i.* men in the midst of their talk

INTOLERABLE.

Wisd. 17. 14. sleeping the same sleep, which was *i.*
2 *Mac.* 9. 10. no man could carry for his *i.* stink

INTREAT.

Eccl. 13. 3. the poor is wronged, and he must *i.* also
28. 5. who will *i.* for pardon of his sins?
Bar. 6. 41. they *i.* Bel that he may speak
1 *Mac.* 8. 18. to *i.* them they would take the yoke

INTREATED.

Wisd. 19. 3. whom they had *i.* to be gone
2 *Mac.* 13. 23. *i.* the Jews submitting himself

INTREATING.

Tob. 1. 22. Achiacharus *i.* for me, I returned

INVADE.

1 *Mac.* 13. 12. removed to *i.* the land of Judea
20. after this came Tryphon to *i.* the land
14. 31. their enemies purposed to *i.* their country
15. 40. to provoke the people, and to *i.* Judea

INVADING.

2 *Esd.* 15. 16. sedition among men, and *i.* one anoth.

INVENTED.

Sus. 43. as these men have maliciously *i.* against me

INVENTION.

Wisd. 14. 12. and *i.* of them the corruption of life
15. 4. nor did the mischievous *i.* of men deceive

INVENTIONS.

2 *Esd.* 6. 5. or ever the *i.* of them that now sin
8. 27. regard not the wicked *i.* of the heathen
13. 37. rebuke the wicked *i.* of those nations
15. 48. hast followed her that is hated in all her *i.*
16. 63. he knoweth your *i.* and what you think

INVINCIBLE.

Jud. 16. 13. thou art wonderful in strength and *i.*
Wisd. 5. 19. he shall take holiness for an *i.* shield
2 *Mac.* 1. 13. the army with him that seemed *i.*

INVIOLABLE.

2 *Mac.* 3. 12. and the *i.* sanctity of the temple

INVISIBLE.

2 *Mac.* 9. 5. the Lord smote him with an *i.* plague

INVITE.

Eccl. 13. 9. so much the more will he *i.* thee

INVITED.

Eccl. 13. 9. if thou be *i.* of a mighty man, withdr.

INVOCATION.

2 *Mac.* 15. 26. encountered enemies with *i.* and pra.

INWARD.

2 *Mac.* 3. 16. declared the *i.* agony of his mind

INWARDLY.

Eccl. 19. 26. but *i.* he is full of deceit

JOACIM.

1 *Esd.* 1. 37. the king made J. his brother king of Jud.
38. and he bound J. and the nobles, but Zaraces
39. five and twenty years old was J. when king
43. and J. his son reigned in his stead
5. 5. and J. the son of Zorobabel, a priest, went up
Jud. 4. 6. also J. the high priest in Jerusalem
8. did as J. the high priest had commanded
14. J. had his loins girt with sackcloth, and offered
15. 8. then J. the high priest came to behold
Sus. 1. there dwelt a man in Babylon called J.
4. J. was a great rich man and had a fair garden
28. when people were assembled to her husband J.
29. Susanna, daughter of Chelchias, J. wife
63. Susanna, with J. her husband, praised God

JOEL.

2 *Esd.* 1. 39. I will give for leaders, Amos, J.

JOHN.

1 *Mac.* 2. 1. then arose Mattathias, the son of J.
8. 17. Judas chose Eupolemus the son of J.
9. 35. now Jonathan had sent his brother J.
36. the children of Jambri came and took J.
38. they remembered J. their brother and went up
13. 53. when Simon saw that J. was a valiant man
16. 1. then came up J. from Gazara and told Simon
16. 2. called his two eldest sons Judas and J.
9. but J. still followed after them to Cedron
19. he sent others also to Gazara to kill J.
21. one had run afore to Gazara, and told J.
23. as concerning the rest of the acts of J.
2 *Mac.* 4. 11. by J. the father of Eupolemus
11. 17. J. and Absalom who were sent from you

JOIN.

1 *Esd.* 8. 84. ye shall not *j.* your daughters to sons
2 *Esd.* 15. 30. with great power come and *j.* battle
1 *Mac.* 10. 4. before he *j.* with Alexander against us
11. 1. to get his kingdom, and *j.* it to his own
13. 14. that Simon meant to *j.* battle with him

JOINED.

1 *Esd.* 1. 29. but *j.* battle with him in the plain
Tob. 6. 17. his heart was effectually *j.* to her
Jud. 14. 10. Achior was *j.* to the house of Israel
Eccl. 51. 20. I have had my heart *j.* with her
1 *Mac.* 1. 15. they *j.* themselves to the heathen
4. 14. so they *j.* battle, and the heathen fled, 34.
| 7. 43. | 9. 47. | 10. 49, 53, 78. | 11. 69.
2 *Mac.* 8. 23.
6. 21. to whom some ungodly men *j.* themselves
8. 1. accept all that *j.* themselves to them
15. 14. when he had *j.* ships close to the town
2 *Mac.* 8. 22. and *j.* with himself his own brethren

JOINING.

Sus. 4. Joacim had a fair garden *j.* unto his house
1 *Mac.* 10. 26. now *j.* yourselves with our enemies

JOININGS.

Eccl. 27. 2. as a nail sticketh fast between the *j.*

JOLLITY.

1 *Esd.* 3. 20. it turneth every thought into *j.*
Eccl. 13. 8. thou be not brought down in thy *j.*

JONAS.

2 *Esd.* 1. 39. I will give for leaders, Abdias and J.
Tob. 14. 4. those things which J. spake of Nineve
8. those things which the prophet J. spake

JONATHAN.

1 *Mac.* 2. 5. called J. whose surname was Apphus
4. 30. into the hands of J. the son of Saul
5. 17. I and J. my brother will go into Galaad
9. 19. J. and Simon took Judas their brother
31. upon this J. took the governance upon him
33. then J. and Simon fled into the wilderness
35. J. had sent his brother John to pray his friends
37. after this came word to J. and Simon
44. then J. said to his company, let us go up
48. then J. and they that were with him leaped
58. behold, J. and his company are at ease
10. 3. moreover Demetrius sent letters to J.
21. J. put on the holy robe and gathered forces
11. 6. J. met the king with great pomp at Joppa
20. J. gathered together them that were in Judah
41. in the mean time J. sent to king Demetrius
44. on this J. sent him three thousand strong men
67. as for J. and his host they pitched at Genesar
69. men in ambush, all that were of J. side fled
12. 1. now when J. saw that the time served him
3. J. the high priest and the people sent us
52. there they bewailed J. and them with him
13. 11. also he sent J. the son of Absalom
19. Tryphon dissembled, nor would he let J. go
23. at Bascama he slew J. who was buried there
25. Simon took the bones of J. his brother
14. 16. when it was heard that J. was dead
18. they made with Judas and J. his brethren
30. after that J. having gathered his nation
2 *Mac.* 1. 23. J. beginning, and the rest answering
8. 22. he joined Simon, and Joseph, and J.

JOPPA, JOPPE.

1 *Esd.* 5. 55. bring cedar-trees by floats to haven of J.
1 *Mac.* 10. 75. and he pitched his tents against J.
but they of J. shut him out of the city
76. they let him in, and so Jonathan won J.
11. 6. Jonathan met the king with great pomp at J.
12. 33. whence he turned aside to J. and won it
13. 11. he sent Jonathan with a great power to J.
14. 5. so in this that he took J. for an haven
34. moreover, he fortified J. and Gazara
15. 28. you withhold J. and Gazara, and the tower
35. whereas thou demandest J. and Gazara
2 *Mac.* 4. 21. he came to J. from thence to Jerusalem
12. 3. men of J. also did such an ungodly deed
7. root out all them of the city of J.

JORAM.

1 *Esd.* 1. 9. Assabias, and Ochiel, and J. captains

JORDAN.

Jud. 5. 15. and passing over J. they possessed all
Eccl. 24. 26. abound as J. in the time of harvest
1 *Mac.* 5. 24. Judas and Jonathan went over J.
52. after this went they over J. into the plain
9. 34. he came near to J. with all his host
42. they turned aside to the marish of J.
43. he came to the banks of J. with a great power
45. the water of J. on this side and that side
48. they leapt into J. and swam over to the farther
bank, the other passed not over J. unto them

JOSABAD.

1 *Esd.* 8. 63. with them were J. and Moeth, Levites

JOSEDEC.

1 *Esd.* 5. 5. Jesus the son of J. son of Saraias, 48.
See JESUS.

JOSEPH.

Eccl. 49. 15. nor was there a man born like to J.
1 *Mac.* 2. 53. J. in time of distress kept commandm.
5. 18. so he left J. son of Zacharias, and Azarias
56. J. son of Zacharias, and Azarias, captains
60. it was, that J. and Azarias were put to flight
2 *Mac.* 8. 22. to wit, Simon, and J. and Jonathan
10. 19. Maccabeus left Simon, and J. and Zaccheus

JOSHUA.

2 *Mac.* 12. 15. who did cast down Jericho in time of J.

JOSIAS.

1 *Esd.* 1. 1. J. held the feast of the passover
7. J. gave thirty thousand lambs and kids
25. Pharaoh came, and J. went out against him
26. howbeit, J. did not turn back his chariot
32. Jeremy the prophet lamented for J.
33. and every one of the acts that J. did
34. the people made Joachaz the son of J. king
Eccl. 49. 1. the remembrance of J. is like perfume

Eccl. 49. 4. all except David, Ezekias, and J. were [defective

JOURNEY.

1 *Esd.* 8. 50. to desire of him a prosperous *j.*
Tob. 4. 15. nor let drunkenness go with thee in *j.*
5. 16. God send you a good *j.* God prosper your *j.*
21. his *j.* shall be prosperous, he shall return
6. 1. as they went on their *j.* they came to Tigris
10. 1. and when the days of the *j.* were expired
11. the God of heaven give you a prosperous *j.*
11. 1. that he had given him a prosperous *j.*
Wisd. 13. 18. and for a good *j.* he asketh of that
18. 3. to be a guide of the unknown *j.* and a sun
1 *Mac.* 7. 45. they pursued after them a day's *j.*
11. 2. whereupon he took his *j.* into Syria
2 *Mac.* 9. 4. his chariot-man to despatch the *j.*
7. filled with pride, commanding to haste the *j.*
12. 10. were gone in their *j.* towards Timotheus

JOURNEYED.

1 *Mac.* 10. 77. he went to Azotus as one that *j.*

JOY.

2 *Esd.* 2. 19. I will fill thy children with *j.*
7. 61. as shall be *j.* over them that are persuaded
Tob. 7. 18. Lord give thee *j.* for this thy sorrow
8. 17. finish their life in health with *j.* and mercy
11. 17. there was *j.* amongst all his brethren
13. 10. his tabernacle built in thee again with *j.*
11. all generations shall praise thee with great *j.*
Jud. 12. 14. it shall be my *j.* to the day of my death
16. 11. then my afflicted shouted for *j.*
Esth 10. 13. with an asembly, and *j.* and gladness
13. 17. turn our sorrow into *j.* that we may live
14. 2. all places of her *j.* she filled with her torn hair
18. nor had thine handmaid any *j.* since the day
16. 21. God hath turned the day to *j.* unto them
Wisd. 8. 16. hath no sorrow, but mirth and *j.*
Eccl. 1. 12. giveth *j.* and gladness, and a long life
23. and afterwards *j.* shall spring up to him
2. 9. that fear L. hope for everlasting *j.* and mercy
3. 5. he shall have *j.* of his own children
4. 12. that seek to her early shall be filled with *j.*
6. 28. and that shall be turned to thy *j.*
31. shall put her about thee as a crown of *j.*
15. 6. he shall find *j.* and a crown of gladness
25. 7. a man that hath *j.* of his children
30. 1. that he may have *j.* of him in the end
2. that chastiseth his son, shall have *j.* in him
16. there is no *j.* above the *j.* of the heart
Bar. 2. 23. the voice of mirth and the voice of *j.*
4. 11. with *j.* did I nourish them but sent them away
22. and *j.* is come to me from the Holy One
23. but God will give you to me again with *j.*
29. he shall bring you everlasting *j.* again
36. behold the *j.* that cometh to thee from God
5. 9. God shall lead Israel with *j.* in light of glory
1 *Mac.* 3. 45. *j.* was taken from Jacob, pipe ceased
5. 23. he brought them to Judea with great *j.*
54. so they went up to mount Sion with *j.*
14. 11. and Israel rejoiced with great *j.*
2 *Mac.* 3. 30. for the temple was filled with *j.*
9. 19. wisheth much *j.* health, and prosperity
15. 28. returning again with *j.* they knew

JOYFUL.

2 *Esd.* 2. 30. be *j.* O thou mother with children
12. 34. he shall make them *j.* till the coming
Tob. 8. 16. to be praised, for thou hast made me *j.*
13. 10. let him make *j.* those that are captives
Jud. 14. 9. the people made a *j.* noise in their city

JOYFULNESS.

2 *Esd.* 2. 36. receive the *j.* of your glory
Wisd. 2. 9. let us leave tokens of our *j.* in every place
Eccl. 30. 22. the *j.* of a man prolongeth his days

IRKSOME.

Eccl. 27. 13. the discourse of fools is *i.* and their part

IRON.

Eccl. 12. 10. like as *i.* rusteth, so is his wickedness
22. 15. sand and a mass of *i.* is easier to bear
28. 20. for the yoke thereof is a yoke of *i.* and made
38. 28. the smith considering the *i.* work
39. 26. fire, *i.* and salt for the use of man's life
48. 17. he digged the hard rock with *i.*
Prayer of Manass. I am bowed down with *i.* bands
2 *Mac.* 11. 9. were ready to pierce thro' walls of *i.*

ISAAC.

2 *Esd.* 3. 16. and unto him thou gavest I. and unto I. also thou gavest Jacob and Esau
Jud. 8. 26. and how he tried I. and what happened
Eccl. 44. 22. with I. did he establish the blessing
Dan. 3. 12. mercy not depart, for thy servant I. sake

ISLANDS.

Eccl. 43. 23. by counsel he planteth *i.* therein
47. 16. thy name went far unto the *i.* for thy peace

ISLES.

1 *Mac.* 6. 29. came to him from *i.* of the sea, bands
11. 38. whom he gathered from *i.* of the heathen
14. 5. he made an entrance to the *i.* of the sea
15. 1. Antiochus sent letters from *i.* of the sea

ISMAEL.

Jud. 2. 23. they spoiled all the children of I.

ISRAEL.

1 *Esd.* 1. 3. the Levites, the holy ministers of I.
4. serve the Lord, and minister unto his people I.
2. 3. Lord of I. the most high Lord made me king
5. 61. because his glory is for ever in all I.
7. 8. they offered twelve goats for the sin of all I.
8. 7. but taught I. the ordinances and judgments
27. I gathered together men of I. to go with me
9. 7. in marrying, thereby to increase the sins of I.
2 *Esd.* 2. 16. for I have known my name in I.
3. 36. that I. by name hath kept thy precepts
4. 23. wherefore I. is given up a reproach
5. 34. that I might not have seen the toil of I.
9. 30. hear me, O I. and mark my words, 14. 28.
12. 46. be of good comfort, O I. be not heavy
Jud. 8. 33. the Lord will visit I. by mine hand
10. 1. after she ceased to cry to the God of I.
16. 1. Judas began to sing this thanksgiving in all I.
Esth. 10. 9. my nation is this I. which crieth to God
13. 9. if thou hast appointed to save I.
14. 5. thou, O Ld. tookest I. from among all people
Eccl. 17. 17. but I. is the Lord's portion
24. 8. and let thine inheritance be in I.
36. 12. on I. whom thou hast named thy first-born
Eccl. 37. 25. but the days of I. are innumerable
45. 5. that he might teach I. his judgments
11. after the number of the tribes of I.
17. that should inform I. in his laws
46. 1. that he might set I. in their inheritance
47. 11. he gave him a throne of glory in I.
50. 13. before all the congregation of I.
Bar. 2. 1. pronounced agst. our judges that judged I.
3. 1. O God of I. the soul in anguish crieth
36. and he hath given it to I. his beloved
4. 4. O I. happy are we, for things are made known
5. be of cheer, my people, the memorial of I.
5. 7. that I. may go safely in the glory of God
Dan. 3. 12. mercy not depart for thy holy I. sake
Sus. 48. are ye such fools, ye sons of I. that without knowledge have condemned a daughter of I.
1 *Mac.* 3. 2. they fought with cheerfulness the battle of I.
4. 11. there is One who delivereth and saveth I.
5. 3. ag. Esau in Idumea, because they besieged I.
7. 5. all the wicked and ungodly men of I.
22. Judah into their power, did much hurt in I.
26. sent Nicanor that bare deadly hate unto I.
8. 18. the Grecians did oppress I. with servitude
9. 21. the valiant man fallen that delivered I.
51. that they might work malice upon I.
10. 46. remembered the great evil he had done in I.
11. 23. he chose certain of the elders of I.
12. 52. wherefore all I. made great lamentation
13. 4. all my brethren are slain for I. sake
41. thus the yoke was taken away from I.
14. 11. he made peace and I. rejoiced with great joy
16. 2. that we have delivered I. oftentimes
2 *Mac.* 1. 25. thou that deliverest I. from trouble
26. receive the sacrifice for thy whole people I.
9. 5. but the God of I. smote them with a plague
10. 38. Lord who had done such great things for I.
11. 6. he would send a good angel to deliver I.

ISRAELITES.

Jud. 6. 14. the I. descended from their city
Bar. 3. 4. hear now the prayers of the dead I.
1 *Mac.* 1. 43. many I. consented to his religion
53. and drove the I. into secret places
58. thus did they to the I. every month
3. 46. the I. assembled themselves together
6. 18. they shut up the I. round about the sanctuary
7. 23. the mischief Alcimus had done among the I.

ISSUED.

1 *Mac.* 14. 36. made a tower out of which they *i.*

ITERATING.

Eccl. 41. 23. or of *i.* and speaking again that

JUDA.

2 *Esd.* 1. 24. thou J. wouldst not obey me
Jud. 14. 7. blessed art thou in the tabernacle of J.
Eccl. 49. 4. even the kings of J. failed
Sus. 56. O thou seed of Chanaan, and not of J.
57. but the daughter of J. would not abide
1 *Mac.* 2. 6. blasphemies that were committed in J.
7. 22. had gotten the land of J. into their power
50. the land of J. was in rest a little while

JUDAISM.

2 *Mac.* 2. 21. that behaved to their honour for J.

JUDAS.

1 *Mac.* 3. 12. J. took their spoils, Apollonius' sword
25. the fear of J. began to fall on nations round
42. when J. saw that miseries were multiplied
4. 5. Gorgias came by night into the camp of J.
16. J. returned with his host from pursuing
21. the host of J. in the plain ready to fight
23. then J. returned to spoil the tents
41. J. appointed men to fight against those
5. 28. J. turned by the way of the wilderness
38. J. sent men to espy ‖ 39. J. went to meet
44. nor could they stand any longer before J.
48. J. sent unto them in peaceable manner
61. because they were not obedient unto J.
65. afterward went J. forth with his brethren
6. 19. J. purposing to destroy them, called people
42. then J. and his host entered into battle
7. 6. J. and his brethren have slain thy friends
10. they sent messengers to J. and his brethren
23. J. went out into all the coasts of Judea
40. but J. pitched in Adasa with 3000 men
8. 1. J. had heard of the fame of the Romans
9. 7. J. therefore saw that his host slipped away
13. they of J. side sounded their trumpets also
18. J. also was killed, and the remnant fled
28. for this cause J. friends came together
31. Jonathan rose up instead of his brother J.
11. 70. J. the son of Calphi, a captain was left
2 *Mac.* 12. 5. when J. heard of his cruelty done
28. when J. had called upon Almighty God
39. J. came to take up the bodies of the slain
42. J. exhorted the people to keep from sin
13. 1. it was told J. that Antiochus was coming
12. J. commanded they should be in readiness
20. J. conveyed such things as were necessary
22. the king fought with J. and was overcome
14. 1. J. was informed ‖ 10. as long as J. liveth
22. J. placed armed men in convenient places
15. 26. but J. encountered the enemies with prayer

See MACCABEUS.

JUDEA.

1 *Esd.* 1. 26. what to do with thee, O king of J.
4. 45. when J. was made desolate by the Chaldees
Tob. 1. 18. when he fled from J. I buried them
Jud. 3. 9. over-against Esdraelon, near unto J.
4. 7. by them there was an entrance into J.
8. 21. if we be taken so, all J. shall lie waste
11. 19. I will lead thee through the midst of J.
1 *Mac.* 6. 5. that went against the land of J. 48.
9. 1. sent them into the land of J. the second time
10. 30. they shall not be taken of the land of J.
11. 28. that he would make J. free from tribute
12. 35. about building strong holds in J. 13. 33.
13. 1. a great host to invade the land of J. 12.
14. 33. Simon fortified the cities of J.
15. 30. of the places without the borders of J.
40. came to invade J. ‖ 41. on the ways of J.
16. 10. he returned into the land of J. in peace
2 *Mac.* 5. 11. he thought that J. had revolted
11. 5. he came to J. and drew near to Bethsura
2 *Mac.* 13. 1. was coming with great power into J.

JUDGE.

2 *Esd.* 4. 18. if thou wert *j.* betwixt these two
7. 19. he said to me, there is no *j.* above God
8. 18. the swiftness of the *j.* that is to come
14. 32. forasmuch as he is a righteous *j.*
16. 67. behold, God himself is the *j.* fear him
Jud. 7. 24. God be *j.* between us and you
Wisd. 9. 7. to be *j.* of thy sons and daughters
15. 7. of either sort, the potter himself is the *j.*
Eccl. 7. 6. seek not to be *j.* being not able to take
8. 14. go not to law with a *j.* for they will judge
10. 1. a wise *j.* will instruct his people
2. as the *j.* of the people is himself, so are officers
35. 12. for the Lord is *j.* with him is no respect
41. 18. of an offence before a *j.* and ruler
Bar. 6. 14. as though he were a *j.* of the country
1 *Mac.* 2. 55. Jesus was made a *j.* in Israel
2 *Mac.* 12. 6. calling on God the righteous *j.* 41.

JUDGE, *Verb.*

1 *Esd.* 3. 9. the three princes of Persia shall *j.*
8. 23. they may *j.* in all Syria and Phenice
2 *Esd.* 2. 20. *j.* for the fatherless, give to the poor
Wisd. 3. 8. they shall *j.* the nations have dominion
9. 12. then shall I *j.* thy people righteously
12. 21. with circumspection didst thou *j.* thy sons
22. that when we *j.* we should carefully think
Eccl. 4. 15. who gives ear to her shall *j.* the nations
8. 14. they will *j.* for him according to his honour
11. 28. *j.* none blessed before his death
31. 15. *j.* of thy neighbour by thyself, be discreet
35. 17. the Most High shall behold to *j.* righteously
45. 26. wisdom to *j.* his people in righteousness
Bar. 6. 54. neither can they *j.* their own cause
64. are able neither to *j.* causes, nor do good to men
1 *Mac.* 7. 42. *j.* him according to his wickedness
2 *Mac.* 6. 12. but that they *j.* those punishments

JUDGED.

2 *Esd.* 8. 49. hast not *j.* thyself worthy to be much
11. 41. the earth hast thou not *j.* with truth
12. 9. thou hast *j.* me worthy to shew me last times
Wisd. 6. 4. you have not *j.* aright nor kept law
10. that keep holiness holily shall be *j.* holy
11. 9. knew how the ungodly were *j.* in wrath
12. 22. when we ourselves are *j.* look for mercy
Eccl. 25. 7. nine things which I have *j.* to be happy
26. 26. that honoureth, shall be *j.* wise of all
35. 19. till he have *j.* the cause of his people
Bar. 2. 1. pronounced against our judges that *j* Isr.
2 *Mac.* 4. 47. should have been *j.* innocent
9. 15. *j.* not worthy so much as to be buried
11. 36. such things as he *j.* to be referred to kings

JUDGES.

1 *Esd.* 2. 17. the *j.* that are in Celosyria and Phenice
8. 23. and thou, Esdras, ordain *j.* and justices
9. 13. with them rulers and *j.* of every place
Wisd. 1. 1. love righteousness, ye that be *j.* of earth
6. 1. learn, ye that be *j.* of the ends of the earth
Eccl. 10. 24. great men and *j.* shall be honoured
38. 33. they shall not sit on the *j.* seat nor unders.
Bar. 2. 1. pronounced against our *j.* that judged Isr.
Sus. 5. two of the ancients of the people to be *j.* from ancient *j.* who seemed to govern the people
41. as those that were elders and *j.* of the people

JUDGEST.

2 *Esd.* 4. 20. but why *j.* thou not thyself also?
Tob. 3. 2. and thou *j.* truly and justly for ever
Wisd. 12. 18. thou mastering thy power *j.* with

JUDGETH.

Eccl. 16. 12. he *j.* a man according to his works

JUDGING.

Esth. 16. 9. and always *j.* things that are evident

JUDGMENT.

1 *Esd.* 3. 15. sat him down on the royal seat of *j.*
4. 40. nor in her *j.* is any unrighteousness
2 *Esd.* 4. 20. he said, thou hast given a right *j.*
5. 34. while I labour to seek out part of his *j.*
40. even so canst thou not find out my *j.*
42. he said to me, I will liken my *j.* to a ring
43. that thou mightest shew thy *j.* the sooner
7. 33. the Most High shall appear on the seat of *j.*
34. *j.* only shall remain, truth shall stand and faith
8. 12. and thou reformedst it with thy *j.*
38. not think on them that sinned before *j.*
61. and therefore is my *j.* now at hand
11. 46. may hope for the *j.* of him that made her
12. 33. he shall set them before him alive in *j.*
34. make joyful until the coming of the day of *j.*
14. 35. after death shall *j.* come, when live again
Jud. 16. 17. the Lord will take vengeance in day of *j.*
Esth. 10. 11. two lots came at the day of *j.* before God
Wisd. 5. 18. put on true *j.* instead of an helmet
6. 5. a sharp *j.* shall be to them in high places
8. 11. I shall be found of quick conceit in *j.*
9. 3. and execute *j.* with an upright heart
5. too young for the understanding of *j.* and laws
12. 12. or who shall withstand thy *j.*?
13. thou mightest shew that thy *j.* is not unrighte.
25. to them didst send a *j.* to mock them
26. they shall feel a *j.* worthy of God
16. 18. they were persecuted with the *j.* of God
Eccl. 3. 24. an evil suspicion hath overthrown their *j.*
4. 9. be not faint-hearted when thou sittest in *j.*
11. 9. and sit not in *j.* with sinners
16. 26. the works of the Lord are done in *j.*
18. 20. before *j.* examine thyself, and find mercy
19. 25. there is one that turns aside to make *j.* appear, there is a wise man that justifieth in *j.*
20. 4. so is he that executeth *j.* with violence
21. 5. and his *j.* cometh speedily
25. 4. O how comely a thing is *j.* for gray hairs!
32. 3. speak, thou elder, but with sound *j.*
16. they that fear the Lord shall find *j.*
35. 17. not depart, till the Most High execute *j.*
38. 22. remember my *j.* for thine also shall be so
33. shall not sit in judge's seat, nor understand sentence of *j.* they cannot declare justice and *j.*
42. 2. and of *j.* to justify the ungodly
43. 13. and sends swiftly the lightnings of his *j.*
45. 10. with a breastplate of *j.* and with Urim
48. 7. who heardest in Horeb the *j.* of vengeance
10. to pacify the wrath of the Lord's *j.*

Dan. 3. 5. thou hast executed true *j.* accord. to truth and *j.* didst thou bring these things on us
8. every thing thou hast done, hast done in true *j.*
Sus. 49. return again to the place of *j.*
53. for thou hast pronounced false *j.*
1 *Mac.* 2. 24. to shew his anger according to *j.*
29. many that sought after justice and *j.*
6. 22. how long will it be ere thou execute *j.*
2 *Mac.* 7. 35. thou hast not escaped *j.* of almighty G.
36. but thou thro' the *j.* of God shalt receive just
9. 4. to despatch the *j.* of God now following him
18. for the just *j.* of God was come upon him
13. 26. Lysias went up to the *j.* seat, said as much

JUDGMENTS.

2 *Esd.* 7. 30. into silence, like as in the former *j.*
Tob. 3. 5. and now thy *j.* are many and true
Jud. 9. 6. and thy *j.* are in thy foreknowledge
Wisd. 12. 10. but executing thy *j.* on them by little
17. 1. great are thy *j.* and cannot be expressed
Eccl. 17. 12. and he shewed them his *j.*
18. 14. and that diligently seek after his *j.*
45. 5. teach Jacob his covenants, Israel his *j.*
17. he gave him authority in the statutes of *j.*
Dan. 3. 4. thy ways are right, and all thy *j.* truth
Sus. 9. not look to heaven, nor remember just *j.*

JUDITH.

Jud. 8. 1. at that time J. heard thereof, 9.
4. so J. was a widow in her house three years
32. then said J. unto them, hear me, and I will do
9. 1. then J. fell upon her face and put ashes on her head, J. cried with a loud voice, and said
10. 10. J. went out, she and her maid with her
23. when J. was come before him and servants
11. 5. J. said, receive the words of thy servant
12. 2. J. said, I will not eat thereof, lest offence
4. then said J. to him, as thy soul liveth
14. then said J. to him, who am I now, that I
16. now when J. came in and sat down, Holofernes
18. so J. said, I will drink now, my lord
13. 3. J. had commanded her maid to stand within
4. J. standing by his bed, said in her heart, O Lord
11. then said J. afar off to watchmen at the gate
14. 1. then said J. to them, hear me, my brethren
7. Achior fell at J. feet and reverenced her
8. J. declared unto him all that she had done
14. for he thought that he had slept with J.
17. he went into the tent where J. lodged
15. 8. Joacim came to see J. and to salute her
11. they gave unto J. Holofernes his tent
16. 1. then J. began to sing this thanksgiving
2. J. said, begin unto my God with timbrels
7. but J. the daughter of Merari weakened him
19. J. also dedicated all the stuff of Holofernes
20. and J remained with them three months
21. and J. went to Bethulia, and remained in her
25. none made Israel afraid in the days of J.

JUPITER.

2 *Mac.* 6. 2. and to call it the temple of J. Olympias and in Garizim of J. the defender of strangers

JURY. *See* JEWRY.

JUST.

1 *Esd.* 4. 39. but she doeth the things that are *j.*
2 *Esd.* 8. 33. the *j.* who have many good works
10. 16. the determination of God to be *j.*
Tob. 3. 2. O Lord, thou art *j.* and all thy works
13. 13. rejoice and be glad for the children of the *j.* shall be gathered and bless the Lord of the *j.*
14. 9. and shew thyself merciful and *j.*
Esth. 16. 15. the Jews live by most *j.* laws
Wisd. 2. 16. pronounceth the end of *j.* to be blessed
18. if the *j.* man be son of God, he will help him
11. 9. thirsting in another manner than the *j.*
12. 19. that the *j.* man should be merciful
14. 31. but it is the *j.* vengeance of sinners
Eccl. 9. 16. let *j.* men eat and drink with thee
16. 3. for one that is *j.* is better than a thousand
35. 7. the sacrifice of a *j.* man is acceptable
Bar. 6. 73. better is the *j.* man that hath no idols
Sus. 9. they might not remember *j.* judgments
Prayer of Manass. thou, O Lord, that art the God of the *j.* hast not appointed repentance to the *j.*
2 *Mac.* 7. 36. shalt receive *j.* punishment for thy pride
9. 18. the *j.* judgment of God was come on him

JUSTICE.

Tob. 1. 3. I walked in the way of truth and *j.*
13. 6. O ye sinners, turn and do *j.* before him
14. 7. all those who love God in truth and *j.*
Esth. 16. 4. they think to escape the *j.* of God
Wisd. 8. 7. she teacheth prudence, *j.* and fortitude
Eccl. 16. 22. who can declare the works of his *j.?*
32. 16. that fear the Lord shall kindle *j.* as a light
38. 33. they cannot declare *j.* and judgment
1 *Mac.* 2. 29. many that sought after *j.* and judgment went down into the wilderness to dwell
7. 12. assemble a company of Scribes to require *j.*
8. 32. if they complain, we will do them *j.*
14. 35. for the *j.* and faith he kept to his nation
2 *Mac.* 8. 13. they that distrusted the *j.* of God
10. 12. choosing rather to do *j.* to the Jews

JUSTICES.

1 *Esd.* 8. 23. thou Esdras, ordain judges and *j.*

JUSTIFY.

2 *Esd.* 4. 18. whom wouldst thou begin to *j?*
Eccl. 7. 5. *j.* not thyself before the Lord, boast not
10. 29. who will *j.* him that sinneth ag. his soul?
13. 22. things not be spoken, yet men *j.* him
42. 2. and of judgment to *j.* the ungodly

JUSTIFIED.

2 *Esd.* 12. 7. if I am *j.* with thee before others
Esth. 10. 12. so God *j.* his inheritance
Eccl. 1. 22. a furious man cannot be *j.*
18. 22. and defer not until death to be *j.*
31. 5. he that loveth gold shall not be *j.*

JUSTIFIETH.

Eccl. 19. 25. there is a wise man that *j.* in judgment

JUSTLY.

Tob. 3. 2. thou judgest truly and *j.* for ever
4. 6. doings shall succeed to all them that live *j.*
Wisd. 14. 30. for both shall they be *j.* punished
19. 13. they suffered *j.* accord. to their wickedness
2 *Mac.* 7. 38. that is *j.* brought on all our nation
9. 6. and that most *j.* for he had tormented other

2 *Mac.* 13. 7. hav. no burial in earth, and that most *j.*

IVY.

2 *Mac.* 6. 7. go in procession to Bacchus, carrying *i.*

K.

KADES.

Jud. 1. 9. Chellus, and K. and the river of Egypt

KEEL.

Wisd. 5. 10. the path-way of the *k.* in the waves

KEEP.

1 *Esd.* 4. 11. these *k.* watch round about him
2 *Esd.* 1. 24. that they may *k.* my statutes
2. 22. *k.* the old and young within thy walls
4. 40. ask of her, if her womb may *k.* the birth
8. 27. those that *k.* thy testimonies in affliction
10. 15. therefore *k.* thy sorrow to thyself
12. 38. whose hearts may *k.* these secrets
13. 42. they might here *k.* their statutes
14. 30. received the law of life, which they *k.* not
15. 24. woe to them that *k.* not my commandments
32. these shall be troubled and *k.* in silence
Tob. 3. 15. to whom I may *k.* myself for a wife
5. 21. the good angel will *k.* him company
14. 9. but *k.* thou the law and commandments
Jud. 4. 7. to *k.* the passages of the hill-country
7. 12. remain in camp, *k.* all the men of thy army
Wisd. 6. 10. for they that *k.* holiness holily
17. 4. nor might the corner *k.* them from fear
Eccl. 1. 26. if thou desire wisdom *k.* commandments
2. 15. and they that love him will *k.* his ways
6. 26. and *k.* her ways with all thy power
7. 22. if they be for thy profit, *k.* them with thee
8. 17. consult not a fool, he cannot *k.* counsel
9. 13. *k.* far from the man that hath power to kill
15. 15. to *k.* the commandments and to perform
17. 22. he will *k.* the good deeds of man as apple
25. 16. than to *k.* house with a wicked woman
26. 10. *k.* her in straitly, lest she abuse herself
19. my son, *k.* the flower of thine age sound
28. 1. he will surely *k.* his sins in remembrance
29. 3. *k.* thy word, and deal faithfully with him
37. 12. whom thou knowest to *k.* the commandm.
39. 2. he will *k.* the sayings of the renowned men
41. 14. my children *k.* my discipline in peace
42. 11. *k.* sure watch over a shameless daughter
Bar. 4. 1. all they that *k.* it shall come to life
6. 35. tho' a man make a vow to them and *k.* it not
59. to *k.* such things safe as be therein
1 *Mac.* 4. 61. they set there a garrison to *k.* it, and fortified Bethsura, 6. 50. | 11. 3. | 12. 34.
7. 49. they ordained to *k.* yearly this day
8. 26. but they shall *k.* their covenant
10. 20. take our part, and *k.* friendship with us
13. 48. but such men there, as would *k.* the law
2 *Mac.* 1. 9. see ye *k.* the feast of tabernacles
18. we are purposed to *k.* the purification of the temple, might *k.* it as the feast of tabernacles
3. 22. to *k.* the things committed of trust safe
6. 6. for a man to *k.* the sabbath-days, 11.
11. 19. if then you will *k.* yourselves loyal
24. had rather *k.* their own manner of living
12. 42. the people to *k.* themselves from sin

KEEPERS.

1 *Esd.* 8. 19. commanded the *k.* of the treasures
Esth. 12. 1. two eunuchs of the king and *k.* of palace

KEEPEST.

1 *Mac.* 15. 7. the fortresses thou *k.* in thy hands

KEEPETH.

2 *Esd.* 8. 9. that which *k.* and is kept, shall both
Eccl. 12. 6. *k.* them against the day of punishment
20. 5. there is one that *k.* silence, and is wise
6. and some *k.* silence, knowing his time
21. 11. he that *k.* the law of the Lord, 35. 1.
23. 7. he that *k.* it, shall never be taken in his lips
29. 1. strengtheneth his hand, *k.* commandments
Bar. 6. 70. as a scarecrow in a garden *k.* nothing

KEEPING.

Wisd. 6. 18. love is the *k.* of her laws
Eccl. 32. 23. for this is *k.* of the commandments
40. 6. he is in his sleep, as in a day of *k.* watch
42. 6. sure *k.* is good where an evil wife is
2 *Mac.* 3. 40. concerning the *k.* of the treasury
5. 25. when taking the Jews *k.* holy-day

KEPT.

1 *Esd.* 1. 20. such passover was not *k.* in Israel since
3. 4. men of the guard that *k.* the king's body
4. 56. to give to all that *k.* the city, pensions
7. 14. they *k.* the feast of unleavened bread
2 *Esd.* 3. 35. who hath so *k.* thy commandments
36. that Israel by name hath *k.* thy precepts
8. 9. but that which keepeth and is *k.* be preserved
9. 21. I have *k.* me a grape of the cluster
22. and let my grape be *k.* and my plant
32. our fathers who received the law, *k.* it not
33. they *k.* not the thing that was sown in them
12. 21. four shall be *k.* until their end begin to approach, but two shall be *k.* unto the end
30. they whom the Highest hath *k.* to their end
32. the anointed which Highest hath *k.* for them
13. 23. he that shall endure hath *k.* himself
26. the same whom God hath *k.* a great season
42. which they never *k.* in their own land
14. 31. ye have not *k.* ways God commanded you
34. if ye reform your hearts, ye shall be *k.* alive
Tob. 11. 19. Tobias' wedding was *k.* seven days
Jud. 6. 12. *k.* them from coming up, by casting
8. 26. to Jacob when he *k.* the sheep of Laban
13. 16. who hath *k.* me in my way that I went
Wisd. 6. 4. have not judged aright, nor *k.* the law
10. 5. *k.* him strong against his tender compassion
12. she *k.* him safe from those that lay in wait
14. 16. an ungodly custom was *k.* as a law
24. they *k.* neither lives nor marriages undefiled
17. 16. whosoever fell down, was straitly *k.*
19. 6. thy children might be *k.* without hurt
Eccl. 11. 30. like as a partridge *k.* in a cage
44. 20. who *k.* the law of the Most High
Dan. 3. 7. not obeyed commandments, nor *k.* them
14. we be *k.* under this day in all the world
Prayer of Manass. nor I thy commandments

1 *Mac.* 3. 45. and aliens *k.* the strong hold
4. 56. so they *k.* the dedication of the altar
59. the days should be *k.* in their season
7. 48. they *k.* that day, a day of great gladness
8. 12. but with their friends they *k.* amity
10. 26. whereas you have *k.* covenants with us
11. 46. but they of the city *k.* the passages
13. 52. that that day should be *k.* every year
14. 35. for the faith which he *k.* to his nation
2 *Mac.* 1. 19. the priests hid it where they *k.* it sur
2. 12. so Solomon *k.* those eight days
3. 1. and the laws were *k.* very well
15. things given to be *k.* that they should be preserved for such as committed them to be *k.*
19. virgins that were *k.* in ran to the gates
6. 7. and when the feast of Bacchus was *k.*
8. 33. at such time as they *k.* the feast for victory
10. 6. and they *k.* eight days with gladness
15. the Idumeans *k.* the Jews occupied
17. they *k.* off all that fought on the wall
27. drew near to enemies, they *k.* by themselves
15. 3. who commanded the sabbath-day to be *k.*
4. who commanded the seventh day to be *k.*

KID.

Tob. 2. 12. they gave her also besides a *k.*
13. I said unto her, from whence is this *k.?*

KIDS.

Eccl. 47. 3. David played with lions as with *k.*

KILL.

1 *Esd.* 4. 7. if he commanded to *k.* they *k.*
2 *Esd.* 1. 18. why brought into this wildern. to *k.* us?
Jud. 5. 22. the people spake that he should *k.* him
7. 13. so shall thirst *k.* them, and they give up
16. 5. he would *k.* my young men with the sword
Eccl. 9. 13. from the man that hath power to *k.*
1 *Mac.* 12. 40. take Jonathan, that he might *k.* him
16. 19. he sent others to Gazara to *k.* John

KILLED.

Tob. 1. 18. Sennacherib in his wrath *k.* many
21. two of his sons *k.* him, and they fled
3. 8. whom Asmodeus the evil spirit had *k.*
7. 8. and after they had *k.* a ram of the flock
Jud. 2. 25. Holofernes he *k.* all that resisted him
Wisd. 12. 6. parents that *k.* with their own hands
16. 9. for them the bitings of grasshoppers *k.*
Eccl. 30. 23. for sorrow hath *k.* many, no profit
1 *Mac.* 2. 25. also the king's commissioner he *k.*
5. 34. there were *k.* of them that day about 8000
9. 18. Judas also was *k.* and the remnant fled
2 *Mac.* 4. 42. him they *k.* beside the treasury
10. 17. they *k.* no fewer than twenty thousand
30. so that being full of trouble, they were *k.*
35. with fierce courage *k.* al. they met withal
37. and *k.* Timotheus that was hid in a pit
14. 2. Demetrius had *k.* Antiochus and Lysias

KILLETH.

Wisd. 16. 14. a man indeed *k.* through his malice
Eccl. 34. 20. as one that *k.* the son before his father

KILLING.

2 *Mac.* 5. 13. thus there was *k.* of young and old
12. 23. Judas also *k.* those wicked wretches

KIND.

Wisd. 7. 23. *k.* to man, stedfast, sure, free from care
Eccl. 6. 5. fair tongue will increase *k.* greetings

KINDNESS.

Eccl. 30. 6. one that shall requite *k.* to friends
36. 23. if there be *k.* and comfort in her tongue
37. 11. nor with an unmerciful man touching *k.*
Dan. 3. 19. but deal with us after thy loving *k.*

KIND.

Wisd. 14. 26. changing of *k.* disorder in marriages
18. 12. innumerable dead with one *k.* of death
19. 6. the creature in his proper *k.* was fashioned
18. elements were changed by a *k.* of harmony
21. nor melted the icy *k.* of heavenly meat
Eccl. 13. 16. all flesh consorteth according to *k.*
2 *Mac.* 11. 31. Jews shall use their own *k.* of meats

KINDS.

Eccl. 36. 19. the palate tasteth divers *k.* of venison
43. 25. therein be variety of all *k.* of beasts

KINDLE.

Eccl. 8. 10. *k.* not the coals of a sinner lest be burnt
28. 8. for a furious man will *k.* strife
32. 16. and they shall *k.* justice as a light

KINDLED.

2 *Esd.* 15. 23. consumed sinners like straw that is *k.*
16. 15. the fire is *k.* and shall not be put out
68. the wrath of a great multitude is *k.*
Jud. 7. 5. when they had *k.* fires on their towers
Wisd. 17. 6. a fire *k.* of itself, very dreadful
Eccl. 9. 8. for herewith love is *k.* as a fire
11. 32. of a spark of fire a heap of coals is *k.*
2 *Mac.* 1. 32. this done, there was *k.* a flame
4. 38. Antiochus being *k.* with anger
See FIRE, and FLAME.

KINDLETH.

Eccl. 28. 11. an hasty contention *k.* a fire

KINDLING.

2 *Mac.* 10. 36. *k.* fires, burnt the blasphemers alive

KINDLY.

2 *Mac.* 9. 21. would have remembered *k.* your hon.
13. 23. honoured the temple, and dealt *k.* with place

KINDRED.

1 *Esd.* 5. 5. out of the *k.* of Phares of tribe of Juda
Tob. 1. 9. I married Anna of mine own *k.*
10. my *k.* did eat of the bread of the Gentiles
4. 12. that they all married wives of their own *k.*
5. 11. I would know, brother, thy *k.* and name
6. 11. seeing thou only art of her *k.*
15. the precepts which thy father gave thee, that thou shouldst marry a wife of thine own *k.*
Jud. 8. 2. Manasses was of her tribe and *k.*
16. 17. woe to the nations that rise against my *k.*
24. gave goods to the nearest of *k.* Manasses, and to them that were nearest of her *k.*
Eccl. 16. 4. the *k.* of the wicked shall become desol
22. 10. children do stain the nobility of their *k.*
Sus. 30. she came with her children and all her *k.*
63. with Joacim her husband and all the *k.*

KING.

1 *Esd.* 1. 7. these were given of the *k.* allowance
26. what have I to do with thee, O *k.* of Jude

Esd. 1. 34. the people made *k.* instead of Josias
39. Joacim, when he was made *k.* 43.
2. 24. now we do declare to thee, O lord the *k.*
3. 8. and laid it under *k.* Darius his pillow
9. when the *k.* is risen, some will give him
11. the second wrote, the *k.* is the strongest
13. now when the *k.* was risen up, they took
19. it maketh the mind of *k.* and fatherless all one
21. a man remembereth neither *k.* nor governor
4. 1. that had spoken of the strength of the *k.*
3. the *k.* is more mighty, for he is lord of all
12. O ye men, how should not the *k.* be mightiest!
14. O ye men, it is not the great *k.* that excelleth
15. women have born the *k.* and all the people
30. taking the crown from the *k.* head and setting
31. for all this the *k.* gaped and gazed upon her
37. wine is wicked, the *k.* is wicked, women
wicked, all the children of men are wicked
6. 14. this house was builded by a *k.* of Israel
8. 4. the *k.* did him honour for he found grace
21. that wrath come not on the kingdom of the *k.*
51. for I was ashamed to ask the *k.* footmen
52. we had said to the *k.* that the power of God
Tob. 1. 19. Ninevites complained of me to the *k.*
12. 7. good to keep close the secret of a *k.* 11.
13. 6. and extol the everlasting K. 10.
7. my soul shall praise the K. of heaven
15. let my soul bless God the great K.
Jud. 2. 5. thus saith the great *k.* lord of the earth
3. 2. the servants of Nabuchodonosor the great *k.*
5. 11. the *k.* of Egypt rose up against them
9. 12. K. of every creature, hear thou my prayer
11. 1. Nabuchodonosor the *k.* of all the earth
Esth. 10. 6. this river is Esther, whom the *k.* married
12. 1. Gabatha and Tharra, two eunuchs of the *k.*
2. they were about to lay hands on Artaxerxes
the *k.* and so he certified the *k.* of them, 3, 4, 5.
6. A man who was in great honour with the *k.*
13. 9. saying, O Lord, Lord, the K. Almighty
14. 3. saying, O my Lord, thou only art our K.
10. and to magnify a fleshly *k.* for ever
12. give me boldness, O K. of nations, Lord of all
15. 6. she stood before the *k.* who sat on his throne
8. then God changed the spirit of the *k.*
16. she fell down, then the *k.* was troubled
16. 11. was honoured as the next person to the *k.*
Wisd. 6. 24. a wise *k.* is the upholding of people
7. 5. there is no *k.* had any other beginning
9. 7. thou hast chosen me to be a *k.* of thy people
11. 10. the other as a severe *k.* thou didst punish
12. 14. neither shall *k.* nor tyrant be able
14. 17. they made an express image of a *k.*
18. 11. like as the *k.* so suffered the common person
Eccl. 7. 4. nor seek of the *k.* the seat of honour
5. boast not of thy wisdom before the *k.*
10. 3. an unwise *k.* destroyeth his people
10. he that is to-day a *k.* to-morrow shall die
18. 3. all obey his will, for he is the K. of all
38. 2. and he shall receive honour of the *k.*
45. 25. the inheritance of the *k.* be to his posterity
50. 15. a sweet savour to the most high K. of all
51. 6. by an accusation to the *k.* from a tongue
Bar. 2. 21. to serve the *k.* of Babylon, 22. 24.
6. 53. neither can they set up a *k.* in the land
56. they cannot withstand any *k.* or enemies
59. better to be a *k.* that sheweth his power
Dan. 3. 9. thou didst deliver us to an unjust *k.*
Bel 2. and Daniel conversed with the *k.*
7. then Daniel said, O *k.* be not deceived
8. so the *k.* was wroth, and called for his priests,
king is mentioned in verses 10, 11, 14, 16, 17,
18, 19, 20, 22, 24, 25, 26, 20, 29, 30, 40.
1 *Mac.* 8. 5. had discomfited Perseus *k.* of Citims
15. 32. Athenobius the *k.* friend to Jerusalem
2 *Mac.* 1. 11. having been in battle against a *k.*
24. who art merciful, the only and gracious *k.*
35. and the *k.* took many gifts, and bestowed
3. 37. and when the *k.* asked Heliodorus
6. 1. the *k.* sent an old man of Athens to compel
7. 3. the *k.* being in a rage commanded, 39.
9. but the K. of the world shall raise us up
8. 10. which the *k.* was to pay to the Romans
11. 15. concerning the Jews, the *k.* granted it
18. what things were meet to be reported to the *k.*
13. 4. but the K. of kings moved Antiochus' mind
14. 4. came to *k.* Demetrius in the 151st year
9. wherefore O *k.* seeing thou knowest these things
26. he had ordained Judas to be the *k.* successor
27. then the *k.* being in a rage, wrote to Nicanor
29. because there was no dealing against the *k.*
15. 5. I command to do the *k.* business

KINGS.

1 *Esd.* 2. 27. mighty *k.* and fierce were in Jerusalem
29. proceed no further to the annoyance of *k.*
2 *Esd.* 12. 20. in him there shall arise eight *k.*
15. 20. I will call together all the *k.* of the earth
33. shall be fear, dread, and strife among their *k.*
Esth. 13. 4. that despised the commandments of *k.*
Wisd. 6. 1. hear therefore, O ye *k.* and understand
21. if your delight be then in thrones, O ye *k.*
10. 16. she withstood dreadful *k.* in wonders and
signs
14. 16. were worshipped by the commandments of *k.*
Eccl. 8. 2. gold hath perverted the hearts of *k.*
11. 5. many *k.* had sat down upon the ground
45. 3. he made him glorious in the sight of *k.*
47. 11. he gave him a covenant of *k.* and a throne
48. 6. who broughtest *k.* to destruction and men
8. who anointedst *k.* to take revenge, and prophets
49. 4. even the *k.* of Juda failed
Bar. 1. 16. confusion of face belongs to our *k.*
2. 19. the righteousness of our fathers and *k.*
24. that the bones of our *k.* shall be taken
6. 51. it shall appear to all nations and *k.*
Dan. 3. 23. the *k.* servants that put them in
1 *Mac.* 1. 2. Alexander slew the *k.* of the earth
3. 7. he grieved many *k.* and made Jacob glad
30. he had abounded above the *k.* before him
10. 60. to Ptolemais, where he met the two *k.*
13. 36. to Simon the high priest and friend of *k.*
14. 13. the *k.* themselves were overthrown
15. 5. which the *k.* before me granted thee

2 *Mac.* 2. 13. gathered the acts of the *k.* and prophets, and the epistles of *k.* concerning holy gifts
3. 2. even *k.* themselves did honour the place
6. it was possible to bring all into the *k.* hand
8. but indeed to fulfil the *k.* purpose
5. 16. things that were dedicated by other *k.*
13. 4. but the King of *k.* moved Antiochus' mind
13. before the *k.* host should enter into Judea
15. he went into the *k.* tent by night and slew him
26. thus it went touching the *k.* coming

KINGDOM.

1 *Esd.* 4. 40. truth is the strength and *k.* of all ages
43. in the day when thou camest to the *k.*
8. 21. that wrath come not on the *k.* of the king
2 *Esd.* 2. 37. that called you to the heavenly *k.*
12. 30. this is the small *k.* and full of trouble
Tob. 13. 1. blessed be God, and blessed be his *k.*
Jud. 1. 12. Nabuchod. sware by his throne and *k.*
2. 12. as I live, and by the power of my *k.*
11. 8. thou only art excellent in all the *k.*
Esth. 13. 2. and making my *k.* peaceable
3. Aman had the honour of second place in the *k.*
5. that our *k.* may not be firmly established
16. 8. we must take care that our *k.* may be quiet
12. he went about to deprive us of our *k.* and life
13. also blameless Esther, partaker of our *k.*
14. to have translated this *k.* to the Persians
16. who hath ordered the *k.* both unto us
Wisd. 1. 14. nor the *k.* of death upon the earth
5. 16. therefore they shall receive a glorious *k.*
6. 4. because being ministers of his *k.*
20. the desire of wisdom bringeth to a *k.*
10. 10. she shewed him the *k.* of God
14. till she brought him the sceptre of the *k.*
Eccl. 10. 8. the *k.* is translated to another people
46. 13. Samuel the prophet established a *k.*
47. 21. so the *k.* was divided ; a rebellious *k.*
Bar. 5. 6. exalted with glory, as children of the *k.*
1 *Mac.* 1. 6. and parted his *k.* among them
10. in the 137th year of the *k.* of the Greeks
51. in the same manner wrote he to his whole *k.*
2. 10. what nation hath not had a part in her *k.*?
57. David possessed the throne of everlasting *k.*
3. 14. I will get me a name and honour in the *k*
6. 15. his son, and nourish him up for the *k.*
10. 33. were carried captives into any part of my *k.*
11. 1. king of Egypt went about to get Alexand. *k.*
9. and thou shalt reign in thy father's *k.*
11. did slander, because he was desirous of his *k.*
15. 39. Tryphon went about to get the *k.* of Asia
15. 3. pestilent men have usurped *k.* of our fathers
2 *Mac.* 2. 17. gave them the *k.* and the priesthood
4. 7. Antiochus called Epiphanes, took the *k.*

KINGDOMS.

1 *Esd.* 1. 24. did wickedly above all people and *k.*
2 *Esd.* 12. 23. the Most High shall raise up three *k.*
Esth. 13. 4. so as the uniting of our *k.* cannot go
Eccl. 44. 3. such as did bear rule in their *k.*

KINSFOLKS.

2 *Mac.* 8. 1. they went and called their *k.* together

KINSMAN.

Tob. 3. 15. neither hath he any near *k.* nor son
7. 4. he said to them, do you know Tobit our *k.*?
Eccl. 41. 21. to turn away thy face from thy *k.*

KINSMEN.

2 *Mac.* 12. 39. they came to bury them with their *k.*

KISS.

Esth. 13. 13. been content to *k.* the soles of his feet
Eccl. 29. 5. till he hath received, will *k.* man's hand

KISSED.

1 *Esd.* 4. 47. Darius the king stood up and *k.* him
Tob. 7. 6. Raguel leaped up and *k.* him, and wept
10. 12. may hear good report of thee, and he *k.* her

KNEE.

Prayer of Manass. now I bow the *k.* of my heart

KNEW.

2 *Esd.* 7. 23. that he is not and *k.* not his ways
10. 35. for I have seen that I *k.* not, and hear
Tob. 2. 10. I *k.* not that there were sparrows
5. 5. Raphael that was an angel, but he *k.* not
Jud. 16. 22. none *k.* her all the days of her life
Wisd. 2. 22. the mysteries of God, they *k.* them not
9. 9. and *k.* what was acceptable in thy sight
10. 8. they *k.* not the things which were good
11. 9. they *k.* how the ungodly were judged
15. 11. forasmuch as he *k.* not his Maker
19. 1. for he *k.* before what they would do
14. those whom they *k.* not when they came
Eccl. 23. 20. he *k.* all things ere ever they were
24. 28. the first man *k.* her not perfectly
Bar. 2. 30. for I *k.* that they would not hear me
4. 13. they *k.* not his statutes, nor walked in comm.

KNOCKED.

Jud. 14. 14. Bagoas *k.* at the door of the tent

KNOTS.

Wisd. 13. 13. a crooked piece of wood, and full of *k.*

KNOW.

1 *Esd.* 4. 22. you must *k.* that women have dominion
5. 66. they came to *k.* what the noise should mean
8. 23. all those that *k.* the law of thy God
2 *Esd.* 4. 46. shew me then, what is past I *k.* but
what is for to come, I *k.* not
52. I am not sent to shew thee, for I do not *k.* it
9. 12. the same must *k.* it after death by pain
12. 36. thou only hast been meet to *k.* this secret
13. 52. nor *k.* the thing in the deep of the sea
Tob. 3. 8. dost thou not *k.* that thou hast strangled
11. 7. I *k.* Tobias, thy father, will open his eyes
Jud. 8. 20. but we *k.* none other God, therefore
9. 7. they *k.* not that thou art the Lord
14. 5. that he may *k.* him that despised Israel
Esth. 11. 12. by all means was desirous to *k.* it
Wisd. 2. 19. examine, that we may *k.* his meekness
7. 17. namely, to *k.* how the world was made
21. things either secret or manifest, them I *k.*
8. 21. a point of wisdom to *k.* whose gift she was
9. 10. that I may *k.* what is pleasing to thee
13. what man is he that can *k.* the counsel of God?
10. 12. might *k.* that goodness is stronger than all
12. 17. and among them that *k.* it, makest manifest
27. the true God, whom before they denied to *k.*
13. 1. not out of good things seen *k.* him that is

Wisd. 13. 3. let him *k.* how much better L. of them is
15. 3. to *k.* thee is perfect righteousness, yea to *k.*
thy power is the root of immortality
16. 16. the ungodly that denied to *k.* thee
22. they might *k.* that fire burning did destroy
26. might *k.* that it is not the growing of fruits
18. 19. and not *k.* why they were afflicted
Eccl. 12. 11. thou shalt *k.* his rust hath not been wiped
16. 15. hardened Pharaoh that he should not *k.* him
23. 27. *k.* there is nothing better than fear of Lord
25. 4. and for ancient men to *k.* counsel
27. 27. he shall not *k.* whence it cometh
36. 5. let them *k.* thee as we have known thee
17. that all may *k.* that thou art the Lord
37. 8. and *k.* before what need he hath
46. 6. that nations might *k.* all their strength
Bar. 2. 15. that all the earth may *k.* thou art Lord
31. shall *k.* that I am the Lord their God
3. 14. that thou mayest *k.* where is length of days
6. 29. ye may *k.* that they are no gods, 52. 72.
Dan. 3. 22. let them *k.* that thou art Lord, only God
Bel 35. neither do I *k.* where the den is
1 *Mac.* 2. 65. I *k.* that Simon is a man of counsel
4. 11. that all the heathen may *k.* there is One
33. let all those that *k.* thy name praise thee
2 *Mac.* 1. 27. let heathen *k.* that thou art our God
11. 37. that we may *k.* what is your mind

KNOWEST.

2 *Esd.* 5. 17. *k.* thou not Israel is committed to thee?
12. 38. whose hearts thou *k.* may comprehend
Tob. 3. 14. thou *k.* Lord, I am pure from sin with man
11. 2. thou *k.* brother, how didst leave thy father
Esth. 13. 12. thou *k.* all things, and thou *k.* Lord,
that it was not in contempt or pride, 14. 15.
14. 16. thou *k.* my necessity, for I abhor the sign
Eccl. 8. 18. thou *k.* not what he will bring forth
9. 11. for thou *k.* not what shall be his end
37. 12. whom thou *k.* to keep the commandments
Sus. 42. Susanna cried and said, O everlasting God,
thou *k.* the secrets, and *k.* all things before
43. thou *k.* that they have borne false witness
1 *Mac.* 3. 52. what things they imagine thou *k.*
2 *Mac.* 14. 9. O king, seeing thou *k.* all these things

KNOWETH.

2 *Esd.* 3. 32. or any other people that *k.* thee
15. 26. the Lord *k.* all them that sin, 16. 54.
16. 56. the stars, he *k.* the number of them
63. he *k.* your inventions, and what you think
Wisd. 8. 8. she *k.* the things of old, she *k.* the subtilties of speeches, and can expound dark
9. 9. wisdom, which *k.* thy works, and was present
11. she *k.* and understandeth all things
15. 13. he *k.* himself to offend above all others
Eccl. 11. 19. he *k.* not what time shall come on him
15. 19. his eyes on them, he *k.* every work of man
18. 28. every man of understanding *k.* wisdom
20. 17. he *k.* not aright what it is to have
21. 7. a man of understanding *k.* when he slips
23. 19. *k.* not the eyes of the Lord are brighter
27. 22. he that *k.* him will depart from him
32. 8. be as one that *k.* yet holdeth his tongue
34. 9. a man that hath travelled, *k.* many things
10. he that hath no experience *k.* little
42. 9. father waketh for daughter, when no man *k.*
18. for the Lord *k.* all that may be known
Bar. 3. 31. no man *k.* her way, nor thinketh of path
32. but he that *k.* all things, *k.* her, and found her

KNOWING.

2 *Esd.* 8. 58. yea, and that *k.* they must die
Jud. 11. 16. I thy handmaid *k.* all this, am fled
Wisd. 8. 9. *k.* that she would be a counsellor of good
13. 16. *k.* that it was unable to help itself
15. 2. for if we sin, we are thine, *k.* thy power, but
we will not sin, *k.* we are counted thine
18. 6. *k.* to what oaths they had given credence
Eccl. 20. 6. some keepeth silence, *k.* his time
Bar. 6. 65. *k.* that they are no gods, fear them not
1 *Mac.* 5. 34. the host *k.* that it was Maccabeus fled
2 *Mac.* 9. 24. *k.* to whom the state was left
15. 21. *k.* that victory cometh not by arms

KNOWLEDGE.

1 *Esd.* 6. 12. to the intent we might give *k.* to thee
2 *Esd.* 14. 47. for in them is the stream of *k.*
Jud. 11. 8. that thou only art mighty in *k.*
Wisd. 1. 7. containeth all things, hath *k.* of the voice
2. 13. he professeth to have the *k.* of God
7. 16. in his hand is the *k.* of workmanship
17. for he hath given me certain *k.* of things
8. 4. she is privy to the mysteries of the *k.* of God
10. 10. she gave him *k.* of holy things
14. 22. not enough that they erred in *k.* of God
Eccl. 1. 7. to whom hath *k.* of wisdom been manifest
25. the parables of *k.* are in treasures of wisdom
3. 25. profess not the *k.* that thou hast not
10. 25. and he that hath *k.* will not grudge
11. 15. wisdom and *k.* are of the Lord
15. 1. he that hath *k.* of the law shall obtain her
16. 24. my son, hearken to me, and learn *k.*
25. and I will declare his *k.* exactly
17. 7. he filled them with the *k.* of understanding
11. besides this he gave them *k.* and the law
19. 19. the *k.* of the commandments of the Lord
20. and the *k.* of his omnipotency
22. and the *k.* of wickedness is not wisdom
21. 13. the *k.* of a wise man shall abound
14. he will hold no *k.* as long as he liveth
18. *k.* of the unwise, is as talk without sense
22. 19. pricketh the heart, makes it show her *k.*
24. 18. I am the mother of fair love, fear and *k.*
27. he makes the doctrine of *k.* appear as light
33. 8. by *k.* of the Lord they were distinguished
11. in much *k.* the Lord hath divided them
39. 7. he shall direct his counsel and *k.*
40. 5. in time of rest his night-sleep changes his *k*
44. 4. leaders by their *k.* meet for the people
45. 5. he gave him the law of life and *k.*
50. 27. the instruction of understanding and *k.*
Bar. 3. 20. but the way of *k.* have they not known
27. neither gave he the way of *k.* to them
36. he hath found out all the way of *k.*
6. 42. they cannot understand, they have no *k.*
Sus. 48. without examination or *k.* of truth

2 Mac. 6. 30. to the Lord that hath the holy *k.*
9. 11. come to *k.* of himself by scourge of God
KNOWN.
1 *Esd.* 6. 8. let all things be *k.* to our lord the king
2 Esd. 5. 7. make a noise, which many have not *k.*
16. 73. then shall they be *k.* who are my chosen
Jud. 8. 29. thy people have *k.* thy understanding
Esth. 14. 12. make thyself *k.* in our affliction
Wisd. 2. 1. nor *k.* to have returned from the grave
3. 13. which hath not *k.* the sinful bed
4. 1. because it is *k.* with God and with men
6. 13. in making herself first *k.* to them
9. 17. thy counsel who hath *k.* except thou give
16. 28. that it might be *k.* we must prevent the sun
Eccl. 1. 6. or who hath *k.* her wise counsels?
4. 24. for by speech wisdom shall be *k.*
6. 27. search, and she shall be made *k.* to thee
11. 28. for a man shall be *k.* in his children
12. 8. a friend cannot be *k.* in prosperity
16. 15. that his works might be *k.* to the world
19. 27. where he is not *k.* he will do a mischief
29. a man may be *k.* by his look
21. 7. an eloquent man is *k.* far and near
26. 9. whoredom of a woman be *k.* in her looks
36. 5. let them know thee, as we have *k.* thee
38. 5. that the virtue thereof might be *k.*
42. 18. the Lord knoweth all that may be *k.*
46. 15. and by his word he was *k.* to be faithful
Bar. 4. 4. things pleasing to God are made *k.* to us
6. 16. whereby they are *k.* not to be gods
50. it shall be *k.* hereafter that they are false

L.

LABAN.
Jud. 8. 26. kept the sheep of L. his mother's brother
LABOUR.
1 *Esd.* 4. 22. do ye not *l.* and bring all to the woman
2 Esd. 3. 33. and yet their *l.* hath no fruit
5. 12. they shall *l.* but their ways shall not prosper
34. while I *l.* to comprehend the way of God
7. 14. if they that live *l.* not to enter these things
8. 14. which with so great *l.* was fashioned
39. 22. for with great *l.* have I made it perfect
10. 14. like as thou hast brought forth with *l.*
24. the Highest shall give rest and ease from thy *l.*
47. told thee that she nourished him with *l.*
13. 38. and he shall destroy them without *l.*
Wisd. 9. 10. that being present, she may *l.* with me
16. with *l.* do we find the things before us
15. 4. an image spotted, the painter's fruitless *l.*
7. the potter fashioneth every vessel with much *l.*
9. his care is, not that he shall have much *l.*
16. 20. didst send bread prepared without their *l.*
17. 20. and none were hindered in their *l.*
Eccl. 11. 21. trust in the Lord, and abide in thy *l.*
13. 26. it is a wearisome *l.* of the mind
16. 27. they neither *l.* nor are weary, nor cease
19. 11. as a woman in *l.* of a child
30. 13. chastise thy son, and hold him to *l.*
31. 3. the rich hath great *l.* in gathering riches
34. 23. what profit have they then but *l.*?
40. 18. to *l.* and be content with that a man hath
51. 27. behold, how that I have had but little *l.*
2 Mac. 2. 26. taken on us this painful *l.* of abridging
LABOURED.
Eccl. 24. 34. that I have not *l.* for myself only
33. 17. consider that I *l.* not for myself only
2 Mac. 4. 7. Onias *l.* under hand to be high priest
LABOURER.
Wisd. 17. 17. whether he were a *l.* in the field
LABOUREST.
2 Esd. 5. 37. declare the thing that thou *l.* to know
LABOURETH.
Eccl. 10. 27. better is he that *l.* and aboundeth
11. 11. there is one that *l.* and taketh pains
31. 4. the poor *l.* in his poor estate, and is needy
38. 27. every work-master that *l.* night and day
LABOURING.
1 *Esd.* 5. 58. *l.* to advance the works in the house
Jud. 5. 11. brought them low with *l.* in brick
Eccl. 19. 1. a *l.* man that is given to drunkenness
2 Mac. 2. 28. *l.* to follow the rules of abridgment
31. to use brevity and avoid much *l.* of work
LABORIOUS.
Eccl. 7. 15. hate not *l.* work, neither husbandry
LABOURS.
Wisd. 3. 11. their *l.* unfruitful, works unprofitable
15. for glorious is the fruit of good *l.*
5. 1. afflicted him, and made no account of his *l.*
10. 10. she multiplied the fruit of his *l.*
17. rendered to the righteous a reward of their *l.*
15. 8. employing his *l.* lewdly, he makes a god
Eccl. 14. 15. leave thy *l.* to be divided by lot
28. 15. and hath deprived them of their *l.*
38. 25. he that is occupied in their *l.*
LACE.
Eccl. 6. 30. ornament, and her bands are purple *l.*
LACEDEMONIANS.
1 *Mac.* 12. 2. sent letters to the L. and other places
5. sent letters which Jonathan wrote to the L. 6
20. Areus king of the L. to Onias high priest
21. found that the L. and Jews are brethren
14. 20. the copy of the letters that the L. sent
23. the people of the L. might have a memorial
15. 23. he wrote to Sampsanes and the L.
2 Mac. 5. 9. he retiring to the L. to find succour
LACKING.
2 Mac. 8. 25. but *l.* time they returned
LADDERS.
1 *Mac.* 5. 30. was an innumerable people bearing *l.*
LADEN.
Eccl 3. 27. obstinate heart shall be *l.* with sorrows
LAID.
1 *Esd.* 3. 8. and *l.* it under king Darius his pillow
Esth. 14. 2. she *l.* away her glorious apparel
15. 1. she *l.* away her mourning garments
11. held up his sceptre, and *l.* it upon her neck
Wisd. 4. 15. nor *l.* they up this in their minds
2 Mac. 3. 10. money *l.* up for the relief of widows

LAKE.
2 Mac. 12. 16. a *l.* was seen running with blood
LAMB, S.
Wisd. 19. 9. they went at large and leaped like *l.*
Eccl. 13. 17. what fellowship hath wolf with the *l.*?
46. 16. when he offered the sucking *l.*
LAME.
2 Esd. 2. 21. laugh not a *l.* man to scorn, defend
LAMENT, ED.
Jud. 16. 24. the house of Israel *l.* her seven days
Eccl. 38. 16. begin to *l.* as if thou hadst suffered
LAMENTATION.
Tob. 2. 6. your mirth shall be turned into *l.*
Wisd. 19. 3. making *l.* at the graves of the dead
Eccl. 38. 17. weep, and use *l.* as he is worthy
1 *Mac.* 1. 27. every bridegroom took up *l.*
2. 70. and all Israel made great *l.* for him
4. 39. they rent their clothes and made great *l.*
9. 20. all Israel made great *l.* 12. 52. | 13. 26.
41. and the noise of their melody into *l.*
2 Mac. 11. 6. people with *l.* and tears besought Lord
LAMP, S.
Eccl. 48. 1. Elias, his word burnt like a *l.*
1 *Mac.* 4. 50. the *l.* that were on the candlestick
6. 39. the mountains shined like *l.* of fire
LANCES.
2 Mac. 5. 2. armed with *l.* like a band of soldiers
LAND.
Wisd. 10. 7. waste *l.* that smoketh is a testimony
12. 3. to destroy those old inhabitants of thy holy *l.*
16. 19. might destroy the fruits of an unjust *l.*
18. 15. into the midst of a *l.* of destruction
19. 7. where water stood before, dry *l.* appeared
10. while they sojourned in the strange *l.*
Eccl. 20. 28. he that tilleth his *l.* shall increase
39. 22. his blessing covered the dry *l.* as a river
46. 8. even unto the *l.* that floweth with milk
47. 24. that they were driven out of the *l.*
48. 15. till they were carried out of their *l.*
2 Mac. 5. 21. weening to make the *l.* navigable
LANGUAGE.
Eccl. 6. 5. sweet *l.* will multiply friends
Bar. 4. 15. a shameless nation of a strange *l.*
2 Mac. 7. 8. but he answered in his own *l.* and said
21. she exhorted every one of them in her own *l.*
27. she spake in her country *l.* on this manner
12. 37. he began in his own *l.* and sung psalms
15. 29. praising the Almighty in their own *l.*
LANGUISH.
2 Esd. 8. 31. we and our fathers do *l.* of such diseases
LARGE.
2 Esd. 1. 13. I gave you a *l.* and safe passage
Wisd. 19. 9. for they went at *l.* like horses
Eccl. 47. 12. and for his sake he dwelt at *l.*
Bar. 3. 24. how *l.* is the place of his possession
2 Mac. 2. 30. to go over things at *l.* and be curious
LARGELY.
1 *Mac.* 16. 16. when Simon and sons had drunk *l.*
LAST.
Wisd. 3. 17. their *l.* age shall be without honour
Eccl. 1. 13. it shall go well with him at the *l.*
2. 3. that thou mayest be increased at thy *l.* end
3. 26. a stubborn heart will fare evil at the *l.*
6. 28. for at the *l.* thou shalt find her rest
12. 12. and thou at the *l.* remember my words
14. 7. at the *l.* he will declare his wickedness
24. 28. no more shall the *l.* find her out
27. 23. but at the *l.* he will writhe his mouth
31. 22. at the *l.* thou shalt find as I told thee
32. 11. rise up betimes, be not *l.* but get home
33. 16. I awaked up *l.* of all as one that gathers
38. 20. drive it away, and remember the *l.* end
41. 2. unto him that is now in the *l.* age
48. 24. he saw what should come to pass at *l.*
LAUGH.
2 Esd. 2. 21. *l.* not a lame man to scorn, defend
Jud. 12. 12. if we draw her not, she will *l.* us to scorn
Esth. 14. 11. and let them not *l.* at our fall
Wisd. 4. 18. but God shall *l.* them to scorn
Eccl. 7. 11. *l.* no man to scorn in bitterness of his soul
13. 7. and at the last he will *l.* thee to scorn
30. 10. *l.* not with him, lest thou have sorrow
LAUGHED.
1 *Esd.* 4. 31. if she *l.* upon him, he *l.* also
Wisd. 17. 8. were sick of fear worthy to be *l.* at
Eccl. 6. 4. made him be *l.* to scorn of his enemies
20. 17. of how many shall he be *l.* to scorn!
Bel 19. then *l.* Daniel, and held the king
1 *Mac.* 7. 34. he mocked them and *l.* at them
10. 70. and I am *l.* to scorn for thy sake
LAUGHING.
Eccl. 18. 31. she will make thee a *l.*-stock, 42. 11.
2 Mac. 7. 27. she *l.* the cruel tyrant to scorn
LAUGHTER.
Eccl. 19. 30. a man's excessive *l.* shews what he is
21. 20. a fool lifteth up his voice with *l.*
LAW.
1 *Esd.* 8. 3. being very ready in the *l.* of Moses
7. he omitted nothing of the *l.* of the Lord
8. to Esdras reader of the *l.* of the Lord, 9.
19. and the reader of the *l.* of the most high God
9. 42. Esdras the priest and leader of the *l.*
46. and when he opened the *l.* they stood up
Tob. 6. 12. not to another, according to *l.* of Moses
7. 13. saying, take her after the *l.* of Moses
14. 9. but keep thou the *l.* and commandments
Wisd. 2. 11. let our strength be the *l.* of justice
Eccl. 2. 16. that love him shall be filled with the *l.*
9. 15. communication in the *l.* of the Most High
10. 19. they that regard not *l.* are dishonourable
11. 15. understanding of the *l.* is of the Lord
15. 1. he that hath knowledge of the *l.*
17. 11. he gave the *l.* of life for an heritage
19. 17. gave place to the *l.* of the Most High
20. in wisdom is the performance of the *l.*
23. 23. she hath disobeyed the *l.* of the Most High
24. 23. even the *l.* which Moses commanded
32. 15. he that seeketh the *l.* shall be filled
33. 2. a wise man hateth not the *l.*
34. 8. the *l.* shall be found perfect without lies
39. 1. giveth his mind to the *l.* of the Most High
8. he shall glory in the *l.* of the covenant

Eccl. 41. 8. woe be to you who have forsaken the *l.*
42. 2. be not ashamed of the *l.* of the Most High
45. 5. even the *l.* of life and knowledge
46. 14. by *l.* of the Ld. he judged the congregation
Bar. 2. 2. that were written in the *l.* of Moses
Sus. 6. all that had any suits in the *l.* came to them
1 *Mac.* 1. 49. to the end they might forget the *l.*
52. to wit, every one that forsook the *l.*
56. they rent in pieces the books of the *l.*
57. or if any consented to the *l.* put him to death
2. 26. thus dealt he zealously for the *l.* of God
27. whosoever is zealous of the *l.* follow me
42. all such as were voluntarily devoted to the *l.*
50. be zealous for the *l.* and give your lives
3. 48. they laid open the book of the *l.*
4. 42. priests, such as had pleasure in the *l.*
14. 14. the *l.* he searched out, and every contemner of the *l.* and wicked person he took away
2 Mac. 1. 4. and open your hearts in his *l.*
2. 3. the *l.* should not depart from their hearts
18. as he promised in *l.* will shortly have mercy
4. 11. he brought up new customs against the *l.*
6. 23. or rather the holy *l.* made and given by God
7. 1. compelled against the *l.* to taste swine's flesh
30. the commandment of the *l.* that was given
12. 40. which is forbidden the Jews by the *l.*
13. 10. being at the point to be put from their *l.*
15. 9. and so comforting them out of the *l.*
LAWS.
Jud. 11. 12. God hath forbidden them to eat by his *l.*
Esth. 16. 15. that the Jews live by the most just *l.*
19. the Jews may freely live after their own *l.*
Wisd. 6. 18. love is the keeping of her *l.*
Eccl. 4. 17. trust his soul, and try him by her *l.*
45. 17. that he should inform Israel in his *l.*
1 *Mac.* 1. 42. that every one should leave his *l.*
2. 40. if we fight not for our lives and *l.*
6. 59. and covenant with them that they shall live after their *l.* because we abolished their *l.*
13. 3. have done for the *l.* and the sanctuary
2 Mac. 3. 1. and the *l.* were kept very well
4. 2. that was so zealous of the *l.*
5. 8. being hated as a forsaker of the *l.*
6. 1. and not to live after the *l.* of God
28. to die for the honourable and holy *l.*
7. 9. shall raise us up, who have died for his *l.*
11. and for his *l.* I despise them
23. as you regard not yourselves for his *l.* sake
37. offer up my body and life for *l.* of our fathers
8. 21. he had made them ready to die for the *l.*
36. because they followed the *l.* he gave them
11. 24. should suffer them to live after their own *l.*
31. the Jews shall use their own kind of *l.*
LAWFUL.
1 *Esd.* 1. 16. it was not *l.* for any to go from service
Tob. 2. 13. it is not *l.* to eat any thing stolen
Jud. 11. 13. which it is not *l.* to be tasted
2 Mac. 6. 4. brought in things that were not *l.*
20. such things as are not *l.* to be tasted
21. to bring flesh, such as was *l.* for him to use
LAWLESS.
Dan. 3. 9. deliver us into the hands of *l.* enemies
LAY.
Tob. 12. 8. better to give alms, than *l.* up gold
Esth. 12. 2. they were to *l.* hands on Artaxerxes
Wisd. 5. 7. through deserts where there *l.* no way
23. thus iniquity shall *l.* waste the whole earth
11. 2. they pitched tents where there *l.* no way
Eccl. 5. 12. if not *l.* thy hand upon thy mouth
7. 6. *l.* a stumbling-block in the way of uprightness
13. 12. but cruelly he will *l.* up thy words
29. 11. *l.* up treasure according to commandments
LEAD.
Wisd. 9. 11. she shall *l.* me soberly in my doings
Eccl. 17. 26. he will *l.* thee out of darkness
40. 28. *l.* not a beggar's life, better die than beg
LEAD.
Eccl. 22. 14. what is heavier than *l.*?
38. 30. he applieth himself to *l.* it over
47. 18. thou didst multiply silver as *l.*
LEAN.
Eccl. 41. 19. and to *l.* with thy elbow on meat
LEAPED.
Tob. 6. 2. a fish *l.* out of river, would have devoured
7. 6. then Raguel *l.* up, and kissed him, and wept
Jud. 14. 17. he *l.* out to the people and cried
Esth. 15. 8. who in a fear *l.* from his throne
Wisd. 18. 15. thy almighty word *l.* down from heav.
19. 9. they *l.* like lambs, praising thee, O Lord
LEAGUE.
1 *Mac.* 11. 9. come, let us make a *l.* betwixt us
12. 3. renew the *l.* as in the former time
8. wherein declaration was made of the *l.*
16. renew the amity we had, and the former *l.*
14. 18. to renew the friendship and *l.* they had
24. sent to Rome to confirm the *l.* with them
15. 17. came to renew the old friendship and *l.*
See AMITY.
LEARN.
Wisd. 6. 1. *l.* ye that be judges of ends of the earth
9. that ye may *l.* wisdom, and not fall away
Eccl. 8. 8. for of them thou shalt *l.* instruction
9. and of them thou shalt *l.* understanding
16. 24. my son, hearken to me, and *l.* knowledge
1 *Mac.* 10. 72. ask and *l.* who I am, and the rest
2 Mac. 7. 2. what wouldest thou ask or *l.* of us?
LEARNED.
Esth. 12. 2. *l.* that they were about to lay hands
Wisd. 6. 10. they that have *l.* such things, shall find
7. 13. I *l.* diligently and communicate her liberally
Eccl. 8. 9. for they also *l.* of their fathers
38. 24. the wisdom of a *l.* man comes by opportunity
39. 8. he shall shew forth that which he hath *l.*
42. 8. thus shalt thou be truly *l.* and approved
LEARNING.
Wisd. 7. 14. for the gifts that come from *l.*
Eccl. 4. 24. *l.* known by the word of the tongue
21. 21. *l.* is to a wise man as an ornament of gold
33. 17. I laboured for all them that seek *l.*
44. 4. by their knowledge of *l.* meet for the people
51. 16. I received her and gat much *l.*
23. draw near and dwell in the house of *l.*

Eccl. 51. 28. get *l.* with a great sum of money
LEAVE.
1 *Esd.* 8. 85. may *l.* the inheritance to your children
Tob. 11. 2. knowest how thou didst *l.* thy father
12. 13. *l.* thy dinner to go and cover the dead
Wisd. 2. 9. let us *l.* tokens of our joyfulness
Eccl. 6. 3. thou shalt *l.* thyself as a dry tree
11. 19. he must *l.* those things to others
14. 15. shalt thou not *l.* thy travels to another?
23. 1. O Lord, *l.* me not to their counsels
17. a whoremonger will not *l.* off till he die
26. she shall *l.* her memory to be cursed
24. 33. I will *l.* it to all ages for ever
29. 17. will *l.* him in danger that delivered him
31. 17. *l.* off first for manners' sake
33. 22. *l.* not a stain in thine honour
38. 10. *l.* off sin, and order thy hands aright
39. 11. he shall *l.* a greater name than a thousand
47. 22. but the Lord will never *l.* off his mercy
51. 10. he would not *l.* me in days of my trouble
LEAVE.
1 *Mac.* 11. 58. he gave him *l.* to drink in gold
15. 6. I give thee *l.* to coin money for thy country
LEAVES.
Eccl. 6. 3. thou shalt eat up thy *l.* and lose fruit
14. 18. as for the green *l.* on a thick tree, some fall
LED.
Tob. 1. 2. who was *l.* captive out of Thisbe
Wisd. 10. 18. and *l.* them through much water
19. 11. being *l.* with their appetite, they asked
LEFT.
Tob. 1. 8. I was *l.* an orphan by my father
20. nor any thing *l.* me besides my wife Anna
Wisd. 10. 14. *l.* him not in bonds, till she brought
14. 6. and *l.* to all ages a seed of generation
Eccl. 15. 14. he *l.* him in the hand of his counsel
17. 21. neither *l.* nor forsook them, but spared
23. 8. the sinner shall be *l.* in his foolishness
30. 8. and a child *l.* to himself will be wilful
44. 8. of them that have *l.* a name behind them
LENGTH.
Wisd. 4. 8. age is not what standeth in *l.* of time
LENGTHENED.
Eccl. 48. 23. and he *l.* the king's life
LENT.
Wisd. 15. 8. his life *l.* him shall be demanded
Eccl. 29. 4. many, when a thing was *l.* them
LEOPARD.
Eccl. 28. 23. it shall devour them as a *l.*
LESS.
Wisd. 15. 10. his life is of *l.* value than clay
LESSON.
Eccl. 9. 1. teach her not an evil *l.* against thyself
LET.
Eccl. 27. 19. so hast thou *l.* thy neighbour go
LETTED.
Wisd. 7. 22. wisdom quick, which cannot be *l.*
LETTETH.
Eccl. 27. 19. as one that *l.* a bird go out of hand
LETTER.
Esth. 16. 19. shall publish copy of this *l.* in all places
LETTERS.
1 *Mac.* 12. 2. he sent *l.* to the Lacedemonians, 5.
See also 7, 8, 17, 19. | 14. 20. | 15. 1, 15. 2 *Mac.* 11. 16.
2 *Mac.* 9. 18. he wrote the *l.* underwritten
LEVITE.
Esth. 11. 1. who said he was a priest and *l.*
LEWD.
Esth. 16. 4. but lifted up with words of *l.* persons
6. with falsehood and deceit of their *l.* disposition
Eccl. 30. 13. lest his *l.* behaviour be an offence
LEWDLY.
Wisd. 15. 8. employing his labours *l.* he maketh
LEWDNESS.
Tob. 4. 13. in *l.* is decay and great want
LIAR.
Eccl. 20. 26. the disposition of a *l.* is dishonourable
25. 2. a poor man proud, a rich man that is a *l.*
LIARS.
2 *Esd.* 11. 42. hast hurt the peaceable, hast loved *l.*
Wisd. 10. 14. she shewed them to be *l.* and gave
Eccl. 15. 8. men that are *l.* cannot remember her
LIBANUS.
1 *Esd.* 4. 48. he wrote letters also to them in L.
2 *Esd.* 15. 20. from the south, from the east, and L.
Eccl. 24. 13. I was exalted like a cedar in L. 50. 12.
LIBERAL.
Eccl. 31. 23. whoso is *l.* of his meat, men speak well
LIBERALLY.
Wisd. 7. 13. and I do communicate her *l.*
1 *Mac.* 3. 30. nor have such gifts to give so *l.*
LIBERALITY.
1 *Esd.* 4. 46. princely *l.* proceeding from thyself
LIBERTY.
1 *Esd.* 4. 53. that they should have free *l.*
62. because he had given them freedom and *l.*
2 *Esd.* 8. 56. when they had taken *l.* they despised
Eccl. 7. 21. a good servant, defraud him not of *l.*
25. 25. nor a wicked woman *l.* to gad abroad
26. 10. lest she abuse herself through over-much *l.*
30. 11. give him no *l.* in his youth, and wink not
1 *Mac.* 13. 16. when he is at *l.* he may not revolt
14. 26. chased away enemies, and confirmed their *l.*
2 *Mac.* 9. 14. the holy city, he would set at *l.*
LIBRARY.
2 *Mac.* 2. 13. how he founded a *l.* gathered acts
LICENCE.
Jud. 11. 14. to bring them a *l.* from the senate
Eccl. 15. 20. nor hath he given any man *l.* to sin
1 *Mac.* 1. 13. gave them *l.* to do after the heathen
2 *Mac.* 4. 9. if he might have *l.* to set up a place
LIE.
Wisd. 2. 12. let us *l.* in wait for the righteous
Eccl. 5. 14. and *l.* not in wait with thy tongue
6. 21. she will *l.* upon him as a mighty stone
8. 11. lest he *l.* in wait to entrap thee in thy words
14. 22. go after her, and *l.* in wait in her ways
27. 28. but vengeance shall *l.* in wait for them
LIETH.
Eccl. 11. 31. for he *l.* in wait, and turneth good
27. 10. as the lion *l.* in wait for the prey

Eccl. 28. 26. lest thou fall before him that *l.* in wait
LIFE.
1 *Esd.* 4. 21. he sticks not to spend his *l.* with his
2 *Esd.* 2. 12. they shall have the tree of *l.*
3. 5. thou didst breathe into him the breath of *l.*
7. 59. this is the *l.* whereof Moses spake to the people, choose the *l.* that thou mayest live
14. 30. received the law of *l.* which they kept not
16. 61. he gave them breath, *l.* and understanding
Tob. 8. 17. finish their *l.* in health, with joy and mer.
12. 9. that exercise alms, shall be filled with *l.*
10. they that sin are enemies to their own *l.*
Jud. 10. 13. without losing the *l.* of any man
15. thou hast saved thy *l.* in that thou hast hasted
12. 18. because my *l.* is magnified in me this day
13. 20. because thou hast not spared thy *l.*
Esth. 13. 2. to settle my subjects in a quiet *l.*
16. 12. went to deprive us of our kingdom and *l.*
13. as well of Mardocheus, who saved our *l.*
Wisd. 1. 12. seek not death in the error of your *l.*
4. 9. and an unspotted *l.* is old age
5. 4. we fools accounted his *l.* madness
7. 6. for all men have one entrance to *l.*
8. 5. if riches be to be desired in this *l.*
7. men can have nothing more profitable in *l.*
13. 11. a vessel fit for the service of man's *l.*
17. not ashamed to speak to that which hath no *l.*
18. for *l.* he prayeth to that which is dead
14. 12. the invention of them the corruption of *l.*
29. their trust is in idols which have no *l.*
15. 8. when his *l.* which was lent him shall be
10. and his *l.* is of less value than clay
12. but they counted our *l.* a pastime
16. 9. nor was there found any remedy for *l.*
13. for thou hast power of *l.* and death
Eccl. 1. 12. the fear of the Lord giveth long *l.*
20. and the branches thereof are long *l.*
3. 6. that honoureth his father, shall have a long *l.*
4. 12. he that loveth her, loveth *l.*
5. 1. and say not I have enough for my *l.*
11. be swift to hear, and let thy *l.* be sincere
6. 16. a faithful friend is the medicine of *l.*
9. 13. lest he take away thy *l.* presently
10. 29. him that dishonoureth his own *l.*
11. 14. *l.* and death, poverty and riches come of L.
13. 14. love the Lord all thy *l.* and call on him
15. 17. before man is *l.* and death
16. 3. trust not thou in their *l.* nor respect
17. 11. he gave them the law of *l.* for an heritage
18. 33. thou shalt lie in wait for thy own *l.*
19. 5. he that resisteth pleasures, crowneth his *l.*
19. the knowledge of commandm. is doctrine of *l.*
20. 32. he that leadeth his *l.* without a guide
21. 13. his counsel is like a pure fountain of *l.*
22. 11. the *l.* of the fool is worse than death
12. for an ungodly man all the days of his *l.*
23. 1. Father and Governor of all my whole *l.*
4. O Fa. and G. of my *l.* give me not a proud look
25. 2. and I am greatly offended at their *l.*
26. 2. he shall fulfil the years of his *l.* in peace
29. 15. for he hath given his *l.* for thee
22. better is the *l.* of a poor man in a cottage
24. it is a miserable *l.* to go from house to house
31. 27. wine is as good as *l.* to a man if drunk moderately, what *l.* is to a man that is without wine
33. 14. good is set against evil, *l.* against death.
23. at the time when thou shalt finish thy *l.*
34. 21. the bread of the needy is their *l.*
37. 18. four things, good and evil, *l.* and death
27. my son, prove thy soul in thy *l.* and see
31. he that taketh heed, prolongeth his *l.*
38. 14. for ease and remedy to prolong *l.*
39. 26. the principal things for the use of man's *l.*
40. 29. the *l.* of him that dependeth on another man's table, is not to be counted for a *l.*
41. 13. a good *l.* hath but few days, but good name
45. 5. he gave him the law of *l.* and knowledge
48. 14. he did wonders in his *l.* and at his death
23. sun went back, he lengthened the king's *l.*
50. 1. who in his *l.* repaired the house again
51. 3. out of the hands of such as sought my *l.*
6. my *l.* was near to the hell beneath
Bar. 1. 11. pray for the *l.* of Nabuchodonosor king of Babylon, and for the *l.* of Balthasar his son
4. 1. all they that keep it shall come to *l.*
1 *Mac.* 3. 12. therewith he fought all his *l.* long
10. 61. men of a wicked *l.* assembled against him
13. 5. that I should spare my own *l.* in trouble
2 *Mac.* 3. 29. he lay speechless, without hope of *l.*
31. call upon the Most High, to grant him his *l.*
33. for his sake the Lord hath granted thee *l.*
35. made vows unto him that hath saved his *l.*
38. him well scourged, if he escape with his *l.*
6. 20. are not lawful for love of *l.* to be tasted
27. manfully changing this *l.* I will shew myself
7. 9. the king shall raise us up unto everlasting *l.*
14. thou shalt have no resurrection to *l.*
23. will also give you breath and *l.* again
25. she would counsel the young man to save his *l.*
36. dead under God's covenant of everlasting *l.*
37. I offer up my body and *l.* for the laws
12. 24. he besought to let him go with his *l.*
14. 25. was quiet, and took part of this *l.*
38. he did boldly jeopard his body and *l.*
46. and calling on the Lord of *l.* and spirit
LIFT.
Eccl. 32. 1. *l.* not thyself up, but be as the rest
38. 3. the skill of the physicians shall *l.* his head
40. 26. riches and strength *l.* up the heart
46. 2. when he did *l.* up his hands against cities
LIFTED.
Eccl. 11. 13. and *l.* up his head from misery
47. 4. when he *l.* up his hand with the stone
50. 20. he *l.* up his hands over the congregation
51. 9. then *l.* I up my supplication from earth
LIGHT.
1 *Esd.* 8. 79. to discover to us a *l.* in the house
Tob. 10. 5. I have let thee go, the *l.* of mine eyes
Wisd. 5. 6. the *l.* of righteousness not shined to us
7. 10. I chose to have her, instead of *l.* for the *l.* that cometh from her never goeth out

Wisd. 7. 26. she is the brightness of everlasting *l.*
29. being compared with *l.* she is found before it
10. 17. and a *l.* of stars in the night season
18. 1. but thy saints had a very great *l.*
4. they were worthy to be deprived of *l.* by whom uncorrupt *l.* of the law was to be given
Eccl. 16. 16. he hath separated his *l.* from darkness
17. 26. he will lead thee out of darkness into *l.*
31. what brighter than sun, yet *l.* thereof faileth
22. 11. weep for the dead, for he hath lost the *l.*
26. 17. as the clear *l.* is on the holy candlestick
32. 16. they that fear L. shall kindle justice as a *l.*
33. 7. when all the *l.* of every day is of the sun
42. 16. the sun that giveth *l.* looketh on all
43. 7. a *l.* that decreaseth in her perfection
9. ornament giving *l.* in the highest places of Lord
50. 7. as the rainbow giving *l.* in the clouds
29. for the *l.* of the Lord leadeth him
Bar. 3. 14. where is the *l.* of the eyes, and peace
20. young men have seen *l.* and dwelt on earth
33. he that sendeth forth *l.* and it goeth
34. they shewed *l.* to him that made them
5. 9. God shall lead Israel in the *l.* of his glory
6. 19. they *l.* them candles more than for themselves
67. nor shine as the sun, nor give *l.* as the moon
Dan. 3. 48. O ye *l.* and darkness, bless ye the Lord
LIGHT.
1 *Esd.* 8. 86. thou, O Lord, didst make our sins *l.*
Eccl. 7. 26. give not thyself over to a *l.* woman
19. 4. he that is hasty to give credit is *l.*-minded
2 *Mac.* 4. 17. for it is not a *l.* thing to do wickedly
LIGHTEN.
Wisd. 17. 5. the stars endure to *l.* that horrible night
LIGHTENED.
2 *Esd.* 6. 2. he said to me before it thundered and *l.*
13. 53. whereby thou only art here *l.*
LIGHTNINGS.
Eccl. 43. 13. he sendeth the *l.* of his judgment
Dan. 3. 51. O ye *l.* and clouds, bless ye the Lord
LIGHTS.
Wisd. 13. 2. deemed the *l.* of heaven to be the gods
LIKE.
Tob. 7. 2. how *l.* is this young man to Tobit
8. 6. let us make to him an aid *l.* to himself
14. 5. shall build a temple, but not *l.* to the first
Wisd. 5. 14. for the hope of the ungodly is *l.* dust
13. 14. or made it *l.* some vile beast, laying it
15. 16. but no man can make a god *l.* to himself
16. 1. by the *l.* were they punished worthily
Eccl. 13. 1. with a proud man, shall be *l.* to him
15. every beast loveth his *l.* and every man
21. 9. the wicked is *l.* tow wrapped together
27. 9. the birds will resort to their *l.* so will truth
30. 4. he hath left one behind him *l.* himself
33. 5. the heart of the foolish is *l.* a cart-wheel, and his thoughts are *l.* a rolling axle-tree
34. 2. is *l.* him that catcheth at a shadow
36. 23. then is not her husband *l.* other men
44. 19. in glory was there none *l.* to him
49. 14. but on earth was no man created *l.* Enoch
LIKENED.
Eccl. 25. 11. holdeth it, whereto shall he be *l.*?
LIKENESS.
Eccl. 34. 3. even as the *l.* of a face to a face
LIKING.
Wisd. 16. 21. tempered itself to every man's *l.*
LION.
2 *Esd.* 11. 37. lo as it were a roaring *l.* chased
12. 1. while the *l.* spake these words to the eagle
31. and the *l.* whom thou sawest rising up
16. 6. may any man drive away a hungry *l.*?
Esth. 14. 13. give eloquent speech before the *l.*
Eccl. 4. 30. be not as a *l.* in thine house
21. 2. the teeth thereof are as the teeth of a *l.*
25. 16. I had rather dwell with a *l.* and a dragon, than to keep house with a wicked woman
27. 10. as the *l.* lieth in wait for the prey
28. but vengeance as a *l.* shall lie in wait for them
28. 23. it shall be sent upon them as a *l.*
1 *Mac.* 3. 4. Judas Maccabeus in his acts was like a *l.* and like a *l.* whelp roaring for prey
LIONS.
Wisd. 11. 17. a multitude of bears or fierce *l.*
Eccl. 13. 19. as the wild ass is *l.* prey in wilderness
47. 3. he played with *l.* as with kids, and with bears
Bel 31. who cast him into the *l.* den where he was
32. and in the den there were seven *l.*
34. carry it to Daniel who is in the *l.* den
1 *Mac.* 2. 60. Daniel was delivered from mouth of *l.*
2 *Mac.* 11. 11. giving a charge on enemies like *l.*
LIPS.
Jud. 9. 10. smite by the deceit of my *l.* the servant
Eccl. 1. 24. *l.* of many shall declare his wisdom
12. 16. an enemy speaketh sweetly with his *l.*
21. 16. grace shall be found in the *l.* of the wise
25. the *l.* of talkers will be telling such things
22. 27. who shall set a seal of wisdom on my *l.*
23. 7. that keeps it, shall not be taken in his *l.*
39. 15. shew forth his praise with songs of your *l.*
50. 20. give the blessing of the Lord with his *l.*
51. 2. hast preserved from the *l.* that forge lies
LITTLE.
Tob. 4. 8. if abundance give accordingly, if thou have but *l.* be not afraid to give according to that *l.*
Jud. 16. 16. all sacrifice is too *l.* for a sweet savour
Wisd. 3. 5. and having been a *l.* chastised
7. 9. all gold in respect of her is as a *l.* sand
12. 2. therefore chastenest thou them by *l.* and *l.*
8. didst send wasps to destroy them by *l.* and *l.*
10. executing judgments on them by *l.* and *l.*
14. 20. who a *l.* before was but honoured as a man
15. 8. he which a *l.* before was made of earth
16. 27. being warmed with a *l.* sun-beam, melted
Eccl. 11. 3. the bee is *l.* among such as fly
19. 1. contemns small things, shall fall by *l.* and *l.*
20. 12. there is that buyeth much for a *l.*
15. he giveth *l.* and upbraideth much
21. 20. but a wise man doth scarce smile a *l.*
22. 11. make a *l.* weeping for the dead, he is at rest
25. 19. all wickedness is *l.* to wickedness of woman
29. 23. be it *l.* or much, hold thee contented
31. 19. a *l.* is sufficient for a man well nurtured

Eccl. 34. 10. he that hath no experience, knoweth *l.*
38. 24. he that hath *l.* business, shall become wise
40. 6. a *l.* or nothing is his rest, he is in his sleep
42. 4. be not ashamed of getting much or *l.*
51. 27. how that I have had but *l.* labour
Dan. 3. 53. O ye mountains and *l.* hills bless Lord
1 *Mac.* 7. 50. the land of Juda was in rest a *l.* while
2 *Mac.* 6. 25. through my desire to live a *l.* time
7. 33. though the Lord be angry with us a *l.* while

LIVE.

2 *Esd.* 2. 14. for I *l.* saith the Lord
Tob. 4. 6. succeed to thee and all them that *l.* justly
5. 3. which may go with thee while I yet *l.*
Jud. 7. 27. be his servants, that our souls may *l.*
Esth. 16. 15. that the Jews *l.* by most just laws
19. publish this, that the Jews may freely *l.*
Wisd. 3. 17. for though they *l.* long, yet not regarded
5. 15. but the righteous *l.* for evermore
8. 9. I purposed to take her to me to *l.* with me
16. to *l.* with her hath no sorrow, but joy
14. 28. they prophesy lies, or *l.* unjustly
Eccl. 13. 5. if have any thing, he will *l.* with thee
19. 6. that can rule his tongue, shall *l.* without strife
34. 13. the spirit of those that fear the Lord shall *l.*
39. 9. his memorial shall not depart away, and his name shall *l.* from generation to generation
42. 23. all these things *l.* and remain for ever
48. 11. that slept in love, for we shall surely *l.*
1 *Mac.* 2. 13. to what end shall we *l.* any longer?
33. do the command of the king, and you shall *l.*
6. 59. covenant that they shall *l.* after their laws
2 *Mac.* 6. 1. and not to *l.* after the laws of God
19. than to *l.* stained with such an abomination
25. through my desire to *l.* a little time
11. 23. they that are in our realm *l.* quietly
24. should suffer them to *l.* after their own laws
25. that they may *l.* according to the customs

LIVED.

Wisd. 15. 17. whereas he *l.* once, but they never
Eccl. 30. 5. while he *l.* he saw and rejoiced in him
41. 4. whether thou have *l.* ten or an hundred years
48. 12. whilst he *l.* he was not moved with presence
2 *Mac.* 5. 27. Maccabeus *l.* in the mountains
9. 9. while he *l.* in sorrow his flesh fell away

LIVETH.

Tob. 13. 1. blessed be God that *l.* for ever
Jud. 12. 4. Judith said, as thy soul *l.* my Lord
13. 16. as the Lord *l.* who hath kept me in my way
Eccl. 3. 12. and grieve him not as long as he *l.*
18. 1. he that *l.* for ever created all things
22. 4. but she that *l.* dishonestly is father's heaviness
25. 7. he that *l.* to see the fall of his enemy
41. 1. O death, how bitter to a man that *l.* at rest!
44. 14. but their name *l.* for evermore

LIVING, LIVING.

Tob. 13. 4. and extol him before all the *l.*
Wisd. 1. 13. not pleasure in the destruction of the *l.*
4. 10. so *l.* among sinners, he was translated
16. shall condemn the ungodly which are *l.*
7. 20. to know the natures of *l.* creatures
15. 11. he knew not him that breathed in a *l.* spirit
18. 12. nor were the *l.* sufficient to bury them
23. he stayed wrath, and parted the way to the *l.*
Eccl. 4. 1. my son, defraud not the poor of his *l.*
17. 28. the *l.* and sound in heart shall praise Lord
45. 16. he chose him out of all men *l.*
49. 16. so was Adam above every *l.* thing
Bel 5. I may not worship idols, but the *l.* God
6. thinkest thou not that Bel is a *l.* god?
24. thou canst not say that he is no *l.* god
2 *Mac.* 7. 33. though the *l.* Lord be angry with us
11. 24. had rather keep their own manner of *l.*
15. 4. there is in heaven a *l.* Lord, and mighty

LOAVES.

1 *Mac.* 4. 51. they set the *l.* upon the table
2 *Mac.* 1. 8. we lighted lamps, and set forth the *l.*

LODGE.

Tob. 6. 10. brother, to-day we shall *l.* with Raguel
Eccl. 14. 24. he that doth *l.* near her house
25. shall *l.* in a lodging where good things are
26. and he shall *l.* under her branches

LODGED.

Tob. 6. 1. they came to river Tigris, and *l.* there
9. 5. Raphael went out and *l.* with Gabael
Eccl. 29. 27. my brother cometh to be *l.*
1 *Mac.* 11. 6. they saluted one another and *l.*

LOINS.

Jud. 4. 10. put sackcloth upon their *l.* 8. 5.
14. their *l.* girt with sackcloth, 2 *Mac.* 10. 25.
Eccl. 35. 18. he hath smitten in sunder the *l.*
47. 19. thou didst bow thy *l.* unto women

LONG.

Tob. 9. 4. if I tarry *l.* he will be very sorry
10. 4. my son is dead, seeing he stayeth *l.*
Wisd. 3. 17. though they live *l.* yet not regarded
4. 13. perfect in a short time, fulfilled a *l.* time
17. 2. fettered with the bonds of a *l.* night
18. 20. but the wrath endured not *l.*
24. in the *l.* garment was the whole world
Eccl. 1. 12. the fear of the Lord giveth a *l.* life
20. and the branches thereof are *l.* life
3. 6. that honoureth his father shall have a *l.* life
4. 1. make not the needy eyes to wait *l.*
7. 16. remember that wrath will not tarry *l.*
10. 10. the physician cutteth off a *l.* disease
14. 12. remember death will not be *l.* in coming
23. 28. and to be received of him is *l.* life
46. 4. and was not one day as *l.* as two?

LONG-SUFFERING.

Wisd. 15. 1. *l.* and in mercy ordering all things
Eccl. 2. 11. the Lord is full of compassion and *l.*
5. 4. the Lord is *l.* he will in no wise let thee go

LOOK, S.

Eccl. 19. 29. a man may be known by his *l.*
23. 4. O Lord, give me not a proud *l.*
26. 9. whoredom may be known in her haughty *l.*

LOOK.

Wisd. 12. 22. when judged, we should *l.* for mercy
Eccl. 9. 8. and *l.* not upon another's beauty
33. 15. so *l.* on all the works of the Most High
34. 15. to whom doth he *l.*? who is his strength?
38. 28. his eyes *l.* still upon the pattern of the thing
Eccl. 41. 20. be ashamed to *l.* upon an harlot
43. 11. *l.* on the rainbow, praise him that made it

LOOKED.

Eccl. 16. 29. the Lord *l.* upon the earth
23. 20. after they were perfected, *l.* upon them all
51. 7. I *l.* for the succour of men, there was none

LOOKETH.

Eccl. 16. 19. shaken, when the Lord *l.* upon them
20. 14. he *l.* to receive many things for one
42. 16. the sun that gives light, *l.* on all things
2 *Mac.* 7. 6. the Lord God *l.* upon us, and in truth

LOOKING.

Tob. 11. 5. Anna sat *l.* towards the way for her son
Eccl. 12. 11. shalt be to him, as if wiped a *l.* glass
2 *Mac.* 7. 4. his brethren and his mother *l.* on

LOOSED.

Jud. 6. 14. the Israelites came to him and *l.* him
Eccl. 22. 16. timber cannot be *l.* with shaking

LOOSENED.

Jud. 9. 2. who *l.* the girdle of a maid to defile her

LORD.

Tob. 2. 2. a poor man who is mindful of the L.
3. 12. now, O L. I set mine eyes towards thee
4. 19. bless the L. thy God alway, and desire
5. 19. that which the L. hath given us to live
7. 18. the L. of heaven and earth give thee joy
10. 12. the L. of heaven restore thee, my brother
13. 10. give praise to the L. for he is good
Wisd. 1. 1. think of the L. with a good heart
3. 8. and their L. shall reign for ever
4. 14. for his soul pleased the L. therefore
5. 7. as for the way of the L. we have not known it
15. their reward also is with the L.
6. 7. he which is L. over all, shall fear no man
8. 3. the L. of all things, himself loved her
21. I prayed to the L. and besought him
9. 1. O God of my fathers, and L. of mercy
13. who can think what the will of the L. is?
10. 20. the righteous praised thy holy name, O L.
11. 13. they had some feeling of the L.
26. they are thine, O L. thou lover of souls
12. 2. that they may believe on thee, O L.
16. and because thou art the L. of all
Eccl. 1. 1. all wisdom cometh from the L.
2. 1. if thou come to serve the L. prepare
11. the L. is full of compassion and mercy
3. 20. the power of the L. is great, he is honoured
4. 28. and the L. shall fight for thee
5. 7. make no tarrying to turn to the L. for suddenly shall the wrath of the L. come forth
11. 4. for the works of the L. are wonderful
12. the eye of the L. looked on him for good
14. poverty and riches come of the L.
15. wisdom, understanding the law are of the L.
17. the gift of the L. remaineth with the godly
26. for it is an easy thing unto the L.
13. 14. love the L. all thy life, and call on him
14. 2. who is not fallen from his hope in the L.
11. do good, and give the L. his due offering
15. 9. for it was not sent him of the L.
11. say not, it is through the L. that I fell away
16. 17. say not, I will hide myself from the L.
17. 1. the L. created man of the earth, and turned
5. the use of the five operations of the L.
20. but all their sins are before the L.
21. but the L. being gracious, spared them
18. 2. the L. only is righteous, and there is none
13. but the mercy of the L. is on all flesh
23. and be not as one that tempteth the L.
26. all things are soon done before the L.
23. 1. O L. Father and God of my life, 4.
28. it is great glory to follow the L.
24. 24. faint not to be strong in the L.
25. 11. the love of the L. passeth all things
26. 4. if he have a good heart towards the L.
14. a silent and loving woman is a gift of the L.
28. 23. such as forsake the L. shall fall into it
42. 18. the L. knoweth all that may be known
43. 5. great is the L. that made it
29. the L. is terrible and very great
30. when you glorify the L. exalt him as much
33. for the L. hath made all things
44. 16. Enoch pleased the L. and was translated
45. 19. this the L. saw, and it displeased him
22. for the L. himself is his portion and inherit.
46. 10. see that it is good to follow the L.
13. the prophet of the L. beloved of his L.
Dan. 3. 1. they walked in the fire, blessing the L.

LOSE.

Eccl. 9. 6. that thou *l.* not thine inheritance
29. 10. *l.* thy money for thy brother and friend

LOSETH.

Eccl. 27. 16. whoso discovereth secrets, *l.* his credit

LOSING.

Eccl. 10. 21. but roughness and pride is the *l.* thereof

LOSS.

Eccl. 22. 3. a foolish daughter is born to his *l.*

LOST.

Tob. 14. 2. Tobit was 58 years old when he *l.* his sight
Eccl. 2. 14. woe unto you that have *l.* patience
8. 12. for if thou lendest him, count it but *l.*
22. 11. weep for the dead, for he hath *l.* the light
27. 18. so hast thou *l.* the love of thy neighbour
29. 10. let it not rust under a stone to be *l.*
41. 2. to him that despaireth and hath *l.* patience

LOT.

Eccl. 16. 8. nor spared the place where L. sojourned

LOT.

Wisd. 2. 9. this is our portion, and our *l.* is this
Eccl. 14. 15. and thy labours to be divided by *l.*
37. 8. beware, lest he cast the *l.* upon thee
1 *Mac.* 3. 36. he should divide their land by *l.*

LOTS.

Esth. 10. 10. therefore hath he made two *l.*
11. these two *l.* came at the hour and time

LOVE.

1 *Esd.* 3. 22. forget their *l.* to friends and brethren
4. 18. do they not *l.* a woman who is comely?
24. when he hath robbed, he brings it to his *l.*
Tob. 4. 13. therefore, my son, *l.* thy brethren
13. 14. O blessed are they that *l.* thee
Wisd. 1. 1. *l.* righteousness, ye that be judges of earth
Wisd. 3. 9. such as be faithful in *l.* shall abide with him
6. 12. she is easily seen of them that *l.* her
17. and the care of discipline is *l.*
18. and *l.* is the keeping of her laws
8. 7. if man *l.* righteousness, her labours are virtues
Eccl. 1. 18. it enlargeth their rejoicing that *l.* him
2. 15. and they that *l.* him will keep his ways
16. they that *l.* him, shall be filled with the law
4. 7. get thyself the *l.* of the congregation
10. he shall *l.* thee more than thy mother doth
14. and them that *l.* her, the Lord doth *l.*
6. 33. if thou *l.* to hear, thou shalt receive understanding
7. 21. let thy soul *l.* a good servant, defraud him not
30. *l.* him that made thee with all thy strength
10. 19. they that *l.* him are an honourable plant
13. 14. *l.* the Lord all thy life, and call on him
15. 13. they that fear God *l.* not abomination
17. 18. and giving him the light of his *l.*
19. 18. and wisdom obtaineth his *l.*
24. 18. I am the mother of fair *l.* and fear
25. 1. the unity of brethren, the *l.* of neighbours
11. but the *l.* of the Lord passeth all things
12. the fear of the Lord is the beginning of his *l.*
27. 17. *l.* thy friend, and be faithful to him
18. so hast thou lost the *l.* of thy neighbour
30. 23. *l.* thine own soul, and comfort thy heart
34. 16. the eyes of the Lord are on them that *l.* him
40. 20. but the *l.* of wisdom is above them both
48. 11. blessed are they that saw thee and slept in *l.*
Sus. 10. they both were wounded with her *l.*
20. the doors are shut and we are in *l.* with thee
Bel 38. nor hast thou forsaken them that *l.* thee
2 *Mac.* 6. 20. not lawful for *l.* of life to be tasted
14. 26. perceiving the *l.* that was betwixt them

LOVED.

Wisd. 7. 10. I *l.* her above health and beauty
8. 2. I *l.* her and sought her out from my youth
3. yea, the Lord of all things himself *l.* her
Eccl. 47. 8. he sung songs, and *l.* him that made him

LOVEST.

Wisd. 11. 24. for thou *l.* all the things that are
16. 26. thy children, O Lord, whom thou *l.*

LOVETH.

1 *Esd.* 4. 25. a man *l.* his wife better than father
Tob. 6. 14. lest I die, for a wicked spirit *l.* her
Wisd. 7. 28. God *l.* none but him that dwelleth
Eccl. 4. 12. he that *l.* her *l.* life, that seek her early
13. 15. call on the Ld. for his salvation, every beast *l.* his like, and every man *l.* his neighbour
31. 5. he that *l.* gold shall not be justified
36. 22. a man *l.* nothing better than beauty
Bar. 6. 9. as it were for a virgin that *l.* to go gay

LOVER.

Wisd. 8. 2. I sought her, and I was a *l.* of her beauty
4. for she is a *l.* of God's works

LOVERS.

Wisd. 15. 6. that worship them are *l.* of evil things

LOVING.

Esth. 15. 8. he comforted her with *l.* words
Wisd. 1. 6. for wisdom is a *l.* spirit, will not acquit
Eccl 17. 29. how great is the *l.* kindness of the Lord!
26. 14. a *l.* woman is a gift of the Lord
Dan. 3. 19. deal with us after thy *l.* kindness

LOVINGLY.

1 *Mac.* 8. 1. such as would *l.* accept all that joined
2 *Mac.* 12. 30. the Scythopolitans dealt *l.* with them

LOW.

2 *Esd.* 9. 41. let me alone, for I am brought very *l.*
12. 48. seek mercy for the *l.* estate of your sanctuary
Jud. 6. 19. and pity the *l.* estate of our nation
7. 32. and they were very *l.* brought in the city
Eccl. 2. 4. be patient when art changed to a *l.* estate
11. 1. wisdom lifteth up the head of him of *l.* degree
12. the Lord set him up from his *l.* estate
20. 11. there is that lifteth his head from a *l.* estate
33. 12. but some he hath cursed and brought *l.*
1 *Mac.* 3. 51. priests are in heaviness and brought *l.*
14. 14. he strengthened all his people brought *l.*

LOWLY.

Eccl. 3. 20. the Lord is honoured of the *l.*
10. 15. and hath planted the *l.* in their place
12. 5. do well unto him that is *l.* but give not to

LOYAL.

2 *Mac.* 14. 19. if you will keep yourselves *l.* to state

LUCIUS.

1 *Mac.* 15. 16. L. consul of the Romans, to Ptolemee

LUD.

Jud. 2. 23. he destroyed Phud and L. and spoiled

LUMPS.

Jud. 10. 5. she filled a bag with corn and *l.* of figs

LUST.

Tob. 8. 7. I take not this my sister for *l.* but uprightly
Wisd. 15. 5. the sight enticeth fools to *l.* after it
Sus. 8. that their *l.* was inflamed towards her
11. for they were ashamed to declare their *l.*
14. turning back, they acknowledged their *l.*

LYAR. *See* LIAR.

LYING.

Eccl. 51. 5. from an unclean tongue, from *l.* words

LYSIAS.

1 *Mac.* 3. 32. he left L. to oversee affairs of the king
38. then L. chose Ptolemee son of Dorymenes
7. 2. his forces had taken Antiochus and L.
2 *Mac.* 10. 11. he set one L. over affairs of the realm
11. 1. L. the king's protector and cousin, took sore
12. and L. himself fled away shamefully
15. Maccabeus wrote unto L. concerning Jews
16. letters to the Jews from L. to this effect
22. Antiochus to his brother L. greeting
35. what L. the king's cousin hath granted
12. 1. these being made, L. went unto the king
27. Ephron a strong city wherein L. abode
13. 2. L. his protector and ruler of his affairs
14. 2. had killed Antiochus and L. his protector

LYSIMACHUS.

Esth. 11. 1. L. the son of Ptolemeus interpreted it
2 *Mac.* 4. 29. Menelaus le his brother L. in his stead
39. many gathered themselves together against L.
40. L. armed about 3000 men, and began first
41. they seeing the attempt of L. caught stones

M.

MACCABEUS.
Mac. 2. 4. Judas who was called M.
3. 1. his son Judas called M. rose in his stead
5. 24. Judas M. and Jonathan went over Jordan
34. the host, knowing it was M. fled from him
2 *Mac.* 5. 27. Judas M. with nine others withdrew
8. 16. M. called his men together about 6000
10. 19. M. left Simon, and Joseph, and Zaccheus
30. they took M. betwixt them and covered him
11. 7. then M. himself first of all took weapons
12. 19. Dositheus and Sosipater of M. captains
26. then M. marched forth to Carnion
13. 24. accepted well of M. made him governor
14. 6. the Assideans, whose captain is Judas M.
27. that he should send M. prisoner to Antioch
30. M. saw that Nicanor began to be churlish
15. 7. M. had confidence that Lord would help him
21. M. seeing the coming of the multitude
MACEDONIAN.
Esth. 16. 10. Aman a M. the son of Amadatha
1 *Mac.* 1. 1. Alexander son of Philip the M. 6. 2.
MACEDONIANS.
Esth. 16. 14. the kingdom of the Persians to the M.
2 *Mac.* 8. 20. the battle in Babylon, with four thousand M. and that the M. being perplexed
MAD.
Wisd. 14. 28. for either they are *m.* when merry
MAD-*men.*
2 *Esd.* 16. 71. shall be like *m.-men,* sparing none
MADNESS.
Wisd. 5. 4. we fools accounted his life *m.*
Eccl. 22. 13. thou shalt never be disquieted with *m.*
2 *Mac.* 15. 33. and hang up the reward of his *m.*
MADE.
Wisd. 1. 13. for G. *m.* not death, nor hath pleasure
6. 7. for he hath *m.* the small and the great
11. 24. thou abhorrest nothing which thou hast *m.* for never wouldest thou have *m.* any thing if thou
13. 15. set it in a wall, and *m.* it fast with iron
14. 3. thou hast *m.* a way in the sea, a safe path
8. is cursed, as well it as he that *m.* it
10. for that which is *m.* shall be punished
17. they *m.* an express image of a king
15. 8. who a little before was *m.* of earth himself
Eccl. 24. 8. he that *m.* me caused my tabernacle rest
32. 13. for these things bless him that *m.* thee
39. 21. he hath *m.* all things for their uses
43. 6. he *m.* the moon also to serve in her season
33. for the Lord hath *m.* all things
MAGIC.
Wisd. 17. 7. as for the illusions of art *m.* put down
MAGNIFICENCE.
1 *Esd.* 1. 5. according to the *m.* of Solomon
MAGNIFY.
Tob. 12. 6. bless God, praise him and *m.* him
Esth. 14. 10. heathen to *m.* a fleshly king for ever
Wisd. 19. 22. O Lord, thou didst *m.* thy people
Eccl. 39. 15. *m.* his name, shew forth his praise
43. 28. how shall we be able to *m.* him?
31. who hath seen him? who can *m.* him as he is?
49. 11. how shall we *m.* Zorobabel?
MAGNIFIED.
Jud. 12. 18. because my life is *m.* in me this day
Wisd. 10. 20. they *m.* with one accord thy hand
MAGNIFIETH.
Wisd. 8. 3. conversant with God, she *m.* her nobility
MAID.
Tob. 6. 12. the *m.* is fair and wise, therefore hear me
13. that this *m.* hath been given to seven men
8. 13. so the *m.* opened the door and went in
Jud. 9. 2. who loosened the girdle of a *m.*
10. 2. she called her *m.* and went into the house
5. then she gave her *m.* a bottle of wine
10. Judith went out, she and her *m.* with her
12. 19. then she took what her *m.* had prepared
13. 9. she gave Holofernes his head to her *m.*
15. 13. they put a garland of olive on her and her *m.*
16. 23. being 105 years, and made her *m.* free
Esth. 15. 7. bowed herself on the head of the *m.*
Eccl. 41. 22. or to be over-busy with his *m.*
MAIDS.
Tob. 3. 7. Sara was reproached by her father's *m.*
8. 12. he said, send one of the *m.* and let her see
Sus. 15. she went in as before with two *m.* only
19. now when the *m.* were gone forth the elders
36. shut the garden-doors, and sent the *m.* away
MAJESTY.
1 *Esd.* 4. 40. she is the strength and *m.* of all ages
Tob. 3. 16. prayers heard before the *m.* of great God
13. 6. and I do declare his might and *m.*
Esth. 15. 6. and was clothed with all his robes of *m.*
7. lifting up his countenance that shone with *m.*
13. my heart was troubled for fear of thy *m.*
Wisd. 18. 24. thy *m.* on the diadem of his head
Eccl. 2. 18. for as is his *m.* so is his mercy
MAINTAIN.
1 *Esd.* 4. 52. to *m.* burnt-offerings on the altar
Eccl. 25. 22. a woman if she *m.* her husband is full
38. 34. but they will *m.* the state of the world
MAINTENANCE.
1 *Mac.* 14. 29. for the *m.* of their sanctuary
MAKE.
1 *Esd.* 2. 26. I commanded to *m.* diligent search
8. 86. thou, O Lord, didst *m.* our sins light
Wisd. 15. 6. they that *m.* them are lovers of evil
9. counteth it his glory to *m.* counterfeit things
MAKETH.
Wisd. 15. 8. he *m.* a vain god of the same clay
Eccl. 43. 13. he *m.* the snow to fall apace
15. by his great power he *m.* the clouds firm
17. the noise of thunder *m.* the earth to tremble
MALES.
1 *Mac.* 5. 28. he slew all the *m.* with the sword, 51.
MALICE.
Wisd. 12. 10. and that their *m.* was bred in them
20. whereby they might be delivered from their *m.*
16. 14. a man indeed killeth through his *m.*
Eccl. 27. 30. *m.* and wrath, these are abominations
Eccl. 28. 7. and bear no *m.* to thy neighbour
1 *Mac.* 9. 51. that they might work *m.* on Israel
13. 6. heathen are gathered to destroy us of very *m.*
2 *Mac.* 4. 50. still in authority, increasing in *m.*
MALICIOUS.
Esth. 13. 4. there was scattered a certain *m.* people
7. they who of old and now also are *m.*
Wisd. 1. 4. into a *m.* soul wisdom shall not enter
2 *Mac.* 5. 23. a *m.* mind against his countrymen
MALICIOUSLY.
Sus. 43. these men have *m.* invented against me
62. as they *m.* intended to do to their neighbour
2 *Mac.* 14. 11. others being *m.* set against Judas
MALIGNED.
Eccl. 45. 18. strangers *m.* him in the wilderness
MAN.
Esth. 13. 9. there is no *m.* that can gainsay thee
11. there is no *m.* that can resist thee the Lord
14. not prefer the glory of *m.* above glory of God
Wisd. 2. 1. nor was any *m.* known to have returned
5. it is fast sealed, so that no *m.* cometh again
7. 2. being compacted in blood, of the seed of *m.*
23. kind to *m.* stedfast, sure, free from care
9. 13. what *m.* is he that can know counsel of God?
11. 16. might know that wherewithal a *m.* sinneth
15. 16. *m.* made them, but no *m.* can make a god
16. 20. bread, able to content every *m.* delight
21. tempered itself to every *m.* liking
26. the growing of fruits that nourisheth *m.*
Eccl. 8. 4. jest not with a rude *m.* lest be disgraced
MANFULLY.
1 *Mac.* 9. 10. let us die *m.* for our brethren
2 *Mac.* 2. 21. to those that behaved themselves *m.*
6. 27. *m.* changing this life, I will shew myself
7. 5. they exhorted one another to die *m.*
10. the third holding forth his hands *m.*
8. 16. Maccabeus exhorted them to fight *m.*
14. 42. choosing rather to die *m.* than to come
MANGLED.
2 *Mac.* 7. 15. they brought the fifth also and *m.* him
MANIFEST.
Wisd. 12. 17. thou makest their boldness *m.*
Eccl. 6. 22. and she is not *m.* to many
16. 16. his mercy is *m.* to every creature
MANIFESTATION.
Wisd. 1. 9. for the *m.* of his wicked deeds
MANIFOLD.
Wisd. 7. 22. a Sp. one only, *m.* subtile, lively, clear
Eccl. 51. 3. from the *m.* afflictions which I had
MANLY.
2 *Mac.* 7. 21. with a *m.* stomach she said to them
MANLINESS.
2 *Mac.* 8. 7. that the bruit of his *m.* was spread
14. 18. Nicanor hearing of the *m.* of them
MANNA.
2 *Esd.* 1. 19. and I gave you *m.* to eat
Bar. 1. 10. prepare ye *m.* and offer on the altar
MANNER.
Tob. 7. 12. then take her according to the *m.*
Esth. 13. 5. in the strange *m.* of their laws
Wisd. 11. 9. thirsting in another *m.* than the just
18. 11. master servant were punished after one *m.*
Eccl. 37. 18. four *m.* of things appear; good, evil
1 *Mac.* 10. 58. with great glory, as the *m.* of kings is
MANNERS.
Eccl. 31. 17. leave off first for *m.* sake, not unsatiable
2 *Mac.* 4. 13. such was the increase of heathenish *m.*
5. 22. for *m.* more barbarous than he that set him
6. 9. would not conform to *m.* of the Gentiles
MANSLAUGHTER.
2 *Esd.* 1. 26. your feet are swift to commit *m.*
Wisd. 14. 25. there reigned in all men, blood, *m.*
MANY.
Eccl. 34. 7. for dreams have deceived *m.* they failed
42. 6. and shut up where *m.* hands are
MARCHED.
Jud. 1. 13. he *m.* in battle-array against Arphaxad
1 *Mac.* 6. 33. the king *m.* fiercely with his host
40. they *m.* on safely and in order
2 *Mac.* 11. 10. they *m.* forward in their armour
12. 26. then Maccabeus *m.* forth to Carnion
13. 19. *m.* to Bethsura a strong hold of the Jews
MARCHING.
1 *Mac.* 6. 41. that heard the *m.* of the company
MARDOCHEUS.
1 *Esd.* 5. 8. came with Enenius, M. Beelsarus
Esth. 10. 4. M. said, God hath done these things
11. 2. M. of the tribe of Benjamin had a dream
MARKET.
Wisd. 15. 12. they counted our time here *m.* for gain
MARKET-*place,* and *places.*
1 *Esd.* 2. 18. the Jews do build the *m.-places*
Tob. 2. 3. one of our nation is cast in the *m.-place*
MARK.
Wisd. 5. 12. like as when an arrow is shot at a *m.*
21. the thunderbolts shall fly to the *m.*
Eccl. 23. 10. shall not be without a blue *m.*
MARKS.
Eccl. 28. 17. the whip maketh *m.* in she flesh
MARRIAGE.
1 *Mac.* 9. 37. the children of Jambri made a great *m.*
41. thus was their *m.* turned into mourning
10. 58. and celebrated her *m.* at Ptolemais
MARRIAGES.
Wisd. 14. 24. they kept not lives nor *m.* undefiled
26. changing of kind, disorder in *m.* adultery
MARRIAGE-CHAMBER.
Tob. 6. 16. when thou shalt come into the *m.*
1 *Mac.* 1. 27. she that sat in *m.* was in heaviness
MARRY.
Eccl. 7. 25. *m.* thy daught. so shalt have performed
1 *Mac.* 10. 56. I will *m.* my daughter to thee
2 *Mac.* 1. 14. Antiochus as though he would *m.* her
MARRIED.
1 *Esd.* 5. 38. who *m.* Augia one of the daughters
8. 70. they and sons have *m.* with their daughters
92. O Esdras, we have *m.* strange women
Tob. 1. 9. I *m.* Anna of mine own kindred
3. 8. she had been *m.* to seven husbands
4. 12. they all *m.* wives of their own kindred
Esth. 10. 6. whom the kings *m.* and made queen
Eccl. 15. 2. receive him as a wife *m.* of a virgin
26. 22. a *m.* woman is a tower against death
42. 9. and being *m.* lest she should be hated
10. and when she is *m.* lest she should be barren
2 *Mac.* 14. 25. so he *m.* was quiet, and took part
MARSH.
1 *Mac.* 9. 42. they turned again to the *m.* of Jordan
45. the water on this and that side the *m.*
MARVEL.
Eccl. 11. 21. *m.* not at the works of sinners, but trust
16. 11. it is *m.* if he escape unpunished
26. 11. *m.* not if she trespass against thee
43. 24. and when we hear it, we *m.* thereat
MARVELLED.
Eccl. 11. 13. so that many that saw it, *m.* at him
47. 17. the countries *m.* at thee for thy songs
2 *Mac.* 1. 22. a fire kindled, so that every man *m.*
7. 12. the king *m.* at the young man's courage
MARVELLETH.
Eccl. 40. 7. when all is safe, he awaketh and *m.*
43. 18. eye *m.* at the beauty of the whiteness
MARVELLOUS.
Wisd. 10. 17. guided the righteous in a *m.* way
19. 8. seeing the *m.* strange wonders
Eccl. 17. 9. he gave them to glory in his *m.* acts
38. 6. he might be honoured in his *m.* works
42. 17. not given power to declare all his *m.* works
43. 2. declaring at his rising a *m.* instrument
29. the Lord is great and *m.* in his power
48. 14. and at his death were his works *m.*
2 *Mac.* 7. 18. therefore *m.* things are done to us
20. but the mother was *m.* above all
MASS. *See* IRON.
MASSACRE.
1 *Mac.* 1. 24. having made a great *m.* and spoken
MASTER.
Wisd. 18. 11. *m.* and servant punished one manner
Eccl. 19. 21. if a servant say to his *m.* I will not do
32. 1. if thou be made a *m.* of the feast
2 *Mac.* 1. 10. to Aristobulus, king Ptolemeus' *m.*
2. 29. as the *m.* builder of a new house must care
14. 12. Nicanor, who had been *m.* of the elephants
MASTERS.
Eccl. 3. 7. do service unto his parents, as to his *m.*
MASTICK.
Sus. 54. who answered, under a *m.* tree
MATTATHIAS.
1 *Mac.* 2. 14. M. and his sons rent their clothes
16. M. also and his sons came together
17. the king's officers said to M. on this wise
19. M. answered and spake with a loud voice
24. which thing when M. saw, he was inflamed
27. M. cried throughout the city, saying
39. when M. and his friends understood hereof
45. M. and his friends went round about
49. when the time drew near that M. should die
11. 70. none left, except M. the son of Absalom
14. 29. Simon son of M. with his brethren
16. 14. Simon came with his sons M. and Judas
2 *Mac.* 14. 19. wherefore he sent M. to make peace
MATTER.
Wisd. 11. 17. that made world of M. without form
15. 13. that of earthly *m.* makes brittle vessels
Eccl. 5. 15. be not ignorant in a great *m.* or small
7. 25. so shalt thou have performed a weighty *m.*
11. 9. strive not in a *m.* that concerns thee not
22. 8. when he hath told, he will say, what is the *m.*
27. 1. many have sinned for a small *m.*
28. 10. as the *m.* of the fire, so it burneth
37. 11. hearken not to these in any *m.* of counsel
MATTERS.
Eccl. 3. 23. be not curious in unnecessary *m.*
11. 10. my son, meddle not with many *m.*
37. 11. neither with a coward in *m.* of war
2 *Mac.* 4. 23. to put him in mind of necessary *m.*
31. then came the king in haste to appease *m.*
8. 9. who in *m.* of war had great experience
MEANLY.
2 *Mac.* 15. 38. but if I have done slenderly and *m.*
MEANS.
Eccl. 46. 4. did not the sun go back by his *m.*?
MEASURABLY.
Eccl. 31. 28. wine *m.* drunk bringeth gladness
MEASURE.
Wisd. 11. 20. thou hast ordered all things in *m.*
MEASURED.
Wisd. 4. 8. nor that is *m.* by number of years
MEAT.
Tob. 2. 2. when I saw abundance of *m.* I said
4. then before I had tasted of any *m.* I started up
7. 8. they set store of *m.* on the table
10. 7. and she did eat no *m.* on the day-time
Jud. 12. 9. until she did eat her *m.* at evening
13. 10. and she put it in her bag of *m.*
Wisd. 13. 12. the refuse of his work to dress his *m.*
16. 2. preparedst for them *m.* of a strange taste
19. 21. nor melted the icy kind of heavenly *m.*
Eccl. 30. 18. are as messes of *m.* set on a grave
25. a good heart will have a care of his *m.*
31. 23. whoso is liberal of his *m.* men speak well
24. but against him that is a niggard of his *m.*
36. 18. yet is one *m.* better than another
40. 29. he polluteth himself with other men's *m.*
41. 1. to him that is yet able to receive *m.*
19. be ashamed to lean thy elbow on the *m.*
Bel 11. set on the *m.* and make ready the wine
MEATS.
Wisd. 19. 11. when they asked delicate *m.*
Eccl. 13. 7. and he will shame thee by his *m.*
36. 18. the belly devoureth all *m.* yet is one meat
37. 29. be not unsatiable, nor too greedy upon *m.*
30. for excess of *m.* bringeth sickness
Bel 14. when gone out, the king set *m.* before Bel
1 *Mac.* 1. 63. they might not be defiled with *m.*
2 *Mac.* 11. 31. Jews shall use their own kind of *m.*
MEDDLE.
1 *Esd.* 6. 27. be careful not to *m.* with the place
2 *Esd.* 16. 67. to *m.* no more with them for ever
Eccl. 11. 10. my son, *m.* not with many matters, for if thou *m.* much, thou shalt not be innocent
1 *Mac.* 10. 35. no man have authority to *m.* with them
MEDES.
2 *Esd.* 1. 3. who was captive in the land of the M

Jud. 1. 1. which reigned over the M. in Ecbatane
16. 10. the M. were daunted at her hardiness
1 *Mac.* 1. 1. Darius king of the Persians and M.

MEDIA.

1 *Esd.* 3. 1. a feast to all the princes of M. and Persia
Tob. 1. 14. I went into M. and left in trust with Gabael at Rages, a city of M. ten talents of silver
15. was troubled that I could not go into M.
4. 1. had committed to Gabael in Rages of M. 20.
9. 2. take two camels, and go to Rages of M.
11. 15. told great things had happened to him in M.
14. 4. go into M. my son, for I surely believe that for a time peace shall rather be in M.
14. he died at Ecbatane in M. being 127 years

MEDICINE.

Eccl. 6. 16. a faithful friend is the *m.* of life

MEDICINES.

Eccl. 38. 4. the L. hath created *m.* out of the earth

MEDITATE.

Eccl. 14. 20. blessed is the man that doth *m.* good

MEDITATION.

Eccl. 39. 1. he that is occupied in the *m.* thereof

MEDITATIONS.

2 *Esd.* 10. 5. then left I the *m.* wherein I was

MEEK.

Eccl. 3. 19. but mysteries are revealed unto the *m.*
10. 14. the Lord hath set up the *m.* in their stead

MEEKNESS.

Wisd. 2. 19. examine that we may know his *m.*
Eccl. 1. 27. and faith and *m.* are his delight
3. 17. my son, go on with thy business in *m.*
4. 8. give him a friendly answer with *m.*
10. 28. my son, glorify thy soul in *m.* and give it
36. 23. if there be kindness and *m.* in her tongue

MEET.

Tob. 11. 16. Tobit went out to *m.* his daughter
Eccl. 9. 3. *m.* not with an harlot lest thou fall
15. 2. as a mother shall she *m.* him, and receive
40. 23. a friend and companion never *m.* amiss
1 *Mac.* 3. 11. Judas went forth to *m.* him, 16.
17. when they saw the host coming to *m.* them
5. 39. upon this Judas went to *m.* them
10. 56. *m.* me therefore at Ptolemais, that we
59. that Jonathan should come and *m.* him
11. 64. he went to *m.* them and left Simon
12. 41. then Jonathan went out to *m.* him
2 *Mac.* 14. 21. appointed a day to *m.* in together

MEET.

1 *Esd.* 2. 20. we think it *m.* not to neglect such matter
5. 51. they offered sacrifices daily as was *m.*
2 *Esd.* 4. 44. and if I be *m.* therefore, shew me
12. 36. thou only hast been *m.* to know this
Tob. 1. 8. the third I gave to them to whom it was *m.*
7. 10. it is *m.* that thou shouldst marry my daughter
Wisd. 4. 5. not ripe to eat, yea, *m.* for nothing
7. 15. to conceive as is *m.* for things given me
13. 11. he hath sawn a tree *m.* for the purpose
Eccl. 10. 23. it is not *m.* to despise the poor man
1 *Mac.* 8. 30. shall think *m.* to add or diminish
10. 19. thou art a man *m.* to be our friend
13. 40. look who are *m.* among you to be in court
2 *Mac.* 8. 33. he received a reward *m.* for wickedness
9. 12. he said, it is *m.* to be subject to God

MELODY.

Eccl. 32. 6. so is the *m.* of music with wine
40. 21. the pipe and psaltery make sweet *m.*
47. 9. that the singers might make sweet *m.*
50. 18. with variety of sounds was made sweet *m.*

MELODIOUS.

Wisd. 17. 18. or a *m.* noise of birds among branches

MELT.

Jud. 16. 15. the rocks shall *m.* as wax at thy presence
Wisd. 16. 29. the hope of the unfaithful shall *m.* away
19. 21. kind of meat that was of nature apt to *m.*

MELTED.

Wisd. 16. 22. snow endured the fire and *m.* not
19. 21. neither *m.* they the icy kind of meat

MEMBER.

2 *Mac.* 7. 7. punish. throughout every *m.* of thy body

MEMORIAL.

Esth. 16. 23. conspire against us, a *m.* of destruction
Wisd. 4. 1. for the *m.* thereof is immortal
19. shall be in sorrow, and their *m.* shall perish
8. 13. shall leave behind me an everlasting *m.*
10. 8. left behind them a *m.* of their foolishness
Eccl. 10. 17. he hath made their *m.* to cease
24. 20. my *m.* is sweeter than honey, and inheritance
35. 7. the *m.* thereof shall never be forgotten
38. 11. give a sweet savour and a *m.* of fine flour
39. 9. his *m.* shall not depart away
44. 9. some there be which have no *m.*
45. 1. even Moses beloved, whose *m.* is blessed
9. for a *m.* to the children of his people
11. with a writing engraved for a *m.*
16. a *m.* to make reconciliation for his people
49. 10. of the twelve prophets, let the *m.* be blessed
Bar. 4. 5. be of good cheer, my people, *m.* of Israel
1 *Mac.* 3. 7. and his *m.* is blessed for ever
35. and to take away their *m.* from that place
8. 22. that they might have by them a *m.* of peace
12. 53. take away their *m.* from amongst men
2 *Mac.* 6. 31. leaving his death for a *m.* of virtue

MEMORY.

Eccl. 23. 26. she shall leave her *m.* to be cursed
46. 11. concerning the judges, let their *m.* be blessed
1 *Mac.* 13. 29. he made armour for a perpetual *m.*
2 *Mac.* 2. 25. that are desirous to commit to *m.*
7. 20. the mother was worthy of honourable *m.*

MEN.

Wisd. 3. 4. though they be punished in sight of *m.*
4. 2. when it is present *m.* take example at it
8. 11. I shall be admired in sight of great *m.*
11. 23. for thou winkest at the sins of *m.*
12. 17. when *m.* will not believe that thou art
13. 1. vain are all *m.* by nature, ignorant of God
14. 11. and stumbling-blocks to the souls of *m.*
14. by the vain-glory of *m.* they entered the world
17. whom *m.* could not honour in presence
25. there reigned in all *m.* without exception
Eccl. 1. 16. and filleth *m.* with her fruits
2. 5. acceptable *m.* in the furnace of adversity
18. into hands of Lord and not into hands of *m.*
21. 2. as teeth of a lion, slaying souls of *m.*
33. 10. and all *m.* are from the ground
37. 28. all things are not profitable for all *m.*
38. 6. he hath given *m.* skill that he might be
44. 3. let us praise *m.* renowned for their power
45. 16. he chose him out of all the *m.* living
49. 16. Sem and Seth in great honour among *m.*
Prayer of Manass. whom all *m.* fear and tremble

MENELAUS.

2 *Mac.* 4. 23. Jason sent M. Simon's brother
27. so *m.* got the principality
29. M. left his brother Lysimachus in his stead
32. M. supposing he had gotten convenient time
34. M. taking Andronicus apart, prayed him
43. there was an accusation laid against M.
45. but M. being now convicted, promised
47. he discharged M. from the accusations
50. M. remained still in authority, increasing
5. 5. the city taken M. fled into the castle
15. M. that traitor to the laws being his guide
23. besides M. who bear an heavy hand over
11. 29. M. declared to us, that your desire was
32. I have sent also M. that he may comfort you
13. 3. M. also joined himself with them

MENSTRUOUS.

2 *Esd.* 5. 8. and *m.* women shall bring forth monsters
Esth. 14. 16. that I abhor it as a *m.* rag
Bar. 6. 29. *m.* women eat their sacrifices

MERCHANT.

Eccl. 26. 29. a *m.* shall hardly keep from wrong
37. 11. nor consult with a *m.* concerning exchange

MERCHANTS.

Eccl. 42. 5. and of *m.* indifferent selling
Bar. 3. 23. the *m.* of Merran and Theman
1 *Mac.* 3. 41. the *m.* of the country hearing the fame
2 *Mac.* 8. 34. Nicanor brought *m.* to buy the Jews

MERCY.

1 *Esd.* 5. 61. because his *m.* and glory is for ever
8. 78. *m.* hath been shewed to us from thee
2 *Esd.* 1. 25. I shall have no *m.* upon you
2. 4. go, O my children, and ask *m.* of the Lord
31. I shall shew *m.* to them, for I am merciful
32. until I come and shew *m.* unto them
4. 24. and we are not worthy to obtain *m.*
7. 66. I know that he is of great *m.*
8. 11. nourished, till thou disposest it to thy *m.*
32. if thou hast a desire to have *m.* on us
45. and have *m.* upon thine own inheritance
Tob. 3. 2. and all thy ways are *m.* and truth
8. 17. because thou hast had *m.* grant them *m.* O Lord, finish their life in health with joy and *m.*
13. 2. for he doth scourge and hath *m.*
5. he will scourge, and will have *m.* again, 9.
14. 7. shall rejoice, shewing *m.* to our brethren
Jud. 13. 14. he hath not taken away his *m.*
Wisd. 3. 9. for grace and *m.* is to his saints
4. 15. that his grace and *m.* is with his saints
6. 6. for *m.* will soon pardon the meanest
9. 1. God of my fathers and Lord of *m.* who hast
11. 9. when tried, albeit but in *m.* chastised
23. thou hast *m.* upon all, thou canst do all things
12. 22. when we are judged, we should look for *m.*
15. 1. gracious, and in *m.* ordering all things
16. 10. thy *m.* was ever by them and healed them
19. 1. wrath came on them without *m.* to the end
Eccl. 2. 7. wait for his *m.* and go not aside
9. hope for good, and for everlasting joy and *m.*
11. for the Lord is full of compassion and *m.*
18. for as his majesty is, so is his *m.*
5. 6. say not, his *m.* is great, he will be pacified
16. 11. *m.* and wrath are with him, he is mighty
12. as his *m.* is great, so is his correction also
14. make way for every work of *m.*
16. his *m.* is manifest to every creature
18. 11. God poureth forth his *m.* upon them
13. the *m.* of man is toward his neighbour, but the *m.* of the Lord is upon all flesh
14. he hath *m.* on them that receive discipline
23. 3. whose hope is far from thy *m.*
28. 4. he sheweth no *m.* to a man like himself
29. 8. with a poor man, delay not to shew him *m.*
35. 19. and made them to rejoice in his *m.*
20. *m.* is seasonable in time of affliction
36. 1. have *m.* upon us, O Lord, and behold us
12. O Lord, have *m.* on the people that is called
46. 7. in the time of Moses he did a work of *m.*
47. 22. but the Lord will never leave off his *m.*
50. 24. that he would confirm his *m.* with us
51. 8. then thought I upon thy *m.* O Lord
29. let your soul rejoice in his *m.*
Bar. 6. 38. they can shew no *m.* to the widow
Dan. 3. 12. cause not thy *m.* to depart from us
67. his *m.* endureth for ever, 68. 1 *Mac.* 4. 24.
1 *Mac.* 3. 44. they might ask *m.* and compassion
4. 10. if peradventure the Lord will have *m.* on us
2 *Mac.* 2. 7. till God receive them unto *m.*
18. he will shortly have *m.* upon us
6. 16. he never withdraweth his *m.* from us
7. 29. that I may receive thee again in *m.*
8. 5. the wrath of the Lord was turned into *m.*
27. which was beginning of *m.* unto them
9. 13. who now no more would have *m.* on him
10. 4. that he would chasten them with *m.*

MERCIES.

Eccl. 18. 5. and who shall also tell out his *m.*?
51. 3. to the multitude of thy *m.* *Dan.* 3. 19.
Prayer of Manass. thou of thine infinite *m.* hast

MERCIFUL.

2 *Esd.* 2. 31. I am *m.* saith Lord almighty
7. 62. I know that the Most High is called *m.*
8. 31. because of us thou shalt be called *m.* 32.
Tob. 6. 17. rise up, and pray to God who is *m.*
7. 12. the *m.* God give you good success in all
14. 9. shew thyself *m.* that it may go well with thee
Jud. 16. 15. thou art *m.* to them that fear thee
Esth. 13. 17. be *m.* to thine inheritance
Wisd. 12. 19. that the just man should be *m.*
Eccl. 29. 1. he that is *m.* will lend to his neighbour
36. 13. O be *m.* to Jerusalem thy holy city
44. 10. these were *m.* men, whose righteousness
45. 1. he brought not of him a *m.* man, even Moses
48. 20. they called on the Lord who is *m.*
50. 19. besought L. by prayer bef. him that is *m*
Bar. 3. 2. O Lord, have mercy, for thou art *m.*
Prayer of Manass. but thy *m.* promise is unmeasurable and unsearchable, for thou art very *m.*
1 *Mac.* 2. 57. David for being *m.* possessed the throne
2 *Mac.* 1. 24. who art strong, and righteous, and *m.*
7. 37. that he would speedily be *m.* to our nation
8. 29. besought the *m.* L. to be reconciled, 13. 12.
10. 26. they besought him to be *m.* to them
11. 9. they praised the *m.* God, and took heart
10. having an helper, for the Ld. was *m.* to them

MERCIFULLY.

Tob. 8. 7. *m.* ordain that we may become aged

MERCIFULNESS.

Eccl. 40. 17. and *m.* endureth for ever

MERCILESS.

Wisd. 12. 5. and also those *m.* murderers of children

MERRY.

1 *Esd.* 7. 14. they kept feast making *m.* before Lord
9. 54. they went to eat, and drink, and make *m.*
2 *Esd.* 2. 27. thou shalt be *m.* and have abundance
Tob. 7. 9. Raguel said, eat, and drink, and make *m*
Jud. 12. 13. drink wine, and be *m.* with us, 17.
Wisd. 14. 28. for either they are mad when *m.*
Eccl. 1. 12. the fear of the Lord maketh a *m.* heart
13. 25. a *m.* heart makes a cheerful countenance
32. 2. that thou mayest be *m.* with them

MESOPOTAMIA.

Jud. 2. 24. he went through M. and destroyed cities

MESSAGE.

1 *Mac.* 10. 51. Alexander sent a *m.* to this effect
15. 32. Athenobius told him the king's *m.*

MESSENGER.

1 *Esd.* 1. 50. God sent by his *m.* to call them back

MESSENGERS.

1 *Mac.* 1. 44. the king had sent letters by *m.*
5. 14. behold, there came other *m.* from Galilee
7. 10. came to Judea, where they sent *m.* to Judas
13. 14. Tryphon sent *m.* unto Simon, saying
21. they in the tower sent *m.* to Tryphon
2 *Mac.* 4. 19. Jason sent special *m.* from Jerusalem

MESSES.

Eccl. 30. 18. are as *m.* of meat set on a grave

MET.

1 *Esd.* 9. 4. whosoever *m.* not there in two or three
Tob. 7. 1. they came to the house, and Sara *m.* them
Jud. 10. 11. the first watch of Assyrians *m.* her
1 *Mac.* 4. 29. Judas *m.* them with ten thousand men
10. 60. to Ptolemais, where he *m.* the two kings
74. where Simon his brother *m.* him to help him
11. 2. they opened unto him, and *m.* him
6. then Jonathan *m.* the king with great pomp
2 *Mac.* 5. 12. commanded not to spare such as they *m.*
8. 14. being sold before they *m.* together
10. 35. they killed all that they *m.* withal

MID-DAY.

1 *Esd.* 9. 41. he read from morning to *m.*

MIDNIGHT.

Jud. 12. 5. and she slept till *m.* and she arose

MID-LAND.

2 *Mac.* 8. 35. he came through the *m.* to Antioch

MIDST.

Jud. 6. 11. they went from the *m.* of the plain
11. 19. I will lead thee through the *m.* of Judea, and I will set thy throne in the *m.* thereof
Wisd. 7. 18. the ending and *m.* of the times
Eccl. 9. 13. remember thou goest in the *m.* of snares
11. 8. nor interrupt men in the *m.* of their talk
42. 12. and sit not in the *m.* of women
Dan. 3. 1. and they walked in the *m.* of the fire
2. opening his mouth in the *m.* of the fire, said
27. and made the *m.* of the furnace moist
66. he hath delivered us out of the *m.* of furnace
Sus. 34. two elders stood in the *m.* of the people
48. so he standing in the *m.* of them, said
2 *Mac.* 14. 44. he fell in the *m.* of the void place
45. yet he ran through the *m.* of the throng

MIGHT.

Tob. 13. 6. praise the Lord of *m.* declare his *m.*
Jud. 9. 11. nor standeth thy *m.* in strong men
14. thou art the God of all power and *m.*
13. 8. she smote twice on his neck with all her *m.*

MIGHTY.

1 *Esd.* 4. 41. great is truth, and *m.* above all things
8. 47. by the *m.* hand of our Lord, 61.
2 *Esd.* 6. 32. the M. hath seen thy righteous dealing
10. 24. that the M. may be merciful unto thee
Esth. 14. 19. O thou *m.* God above all, hear us
16. 16. they be children of the most *m.* living God
Wisd. 5. 23. a *m.* wind shall stand up against them; ill dealing shall overthrow the thrones of the *m.*
6. 6. but *m.* men shall be mightily tormented
Eccl. 4. 27. neither accept the person of the *m.*
7. 6. lest at any time thou fear the person of the *m.*
11. 6. many *m.* men have been greatly disgraced
12. 6. against the *m.* day of their punishment
15. 18. he is *m.* in power, and beholdeth all things
29. 13. it shall fight for thee better than a *m.* shield
18. suretiship hath driven *m.* men from houses
34. 16. he is their *m.* protection and strong stay
46. 6. and he followed the *m.* One
16. he called upon the *m.* Lord, when his enemies
47. 5. he gave strength to slay that *m.* warrior

MIGHTIER.

Wisd. 13. 4. how much *m.* is he that made him
Eccl. 8. 12. lend not to him that is *m.* than thyself
13. 2. have no fellowship with one that is *m.*

MIGHTIEST.

1 *Esd.* 4. 12. O men, how should not the king be *m.*?

MIGHTILY.

Wisd. 6. 6. but mighty men shall be *m.* tormented

MILDNESS.

Esth. 13. 2. carrying myself with equity and *m.*
15. 8. God changed the spirit of the king into *m.*

MILK.

2 *Esd.* 8. 10. out of the breasts *m.* to be given
See HONEY.

MIND.

1 *Esd.* 2. 8. all they whose *m.* the Lord had moved
3. 17. declare your *m.* concerning the writings
19. it maketh the *m.* of the king and child all one
8. 11. as many therefore as have a *m.* thereunto

2 *Esd.* 4. 23. for it was not my *m.* to be curious
5. 14. my *m.* was troubled, so that it fainted
33. thou art sore troubled in *m.* for Israel
9. 40. I said, why art thou so grieved in thy *m.?*
41. let me alone, for I am vexed in my *m.*
12. 3. out of the trouble and trance of my *m.*
5. lo, yet am I weary in my *m.* and very weak
Tob. 4. 19. neither let them be put out of thy *m.*
13. 6. if you turn to him with your whole *m.*
Jud. 12. 16. his *m.* was moved, and he desired her
Esth. 11. 12. Mardocheus bare this dream in *m.*
Wisd. 3.14. an inheritance more acceptable to his *m.*
4. 12. the wandering of concupiscence doth undermine the simple *m.*
9. 15. the earthly tabernacle weigheth down the *m.*
Eccl. 5. 2. follow not thine own *m.* and strength
6.32. if thou wilt apply thy *m.* thou shalt be prudent
37. let thy *m.* be upon the ordinances of the Lord
7. 26. hast thou a wife after thy *m.* forsake her not
13. 26. is a wearisome labour of the *m.*
23. 4. turn away from thy servants a haughty *m.*
6. give not over thy servant to an impudent *m.*
26. 14. so much worth, as a *m.* well instructed
15. and her continent *m.* cannot be valued
27. 16. and shall never find friend to his *m.*
29. 17. he that is of an unthankful *m.*
30. 21. give not over thy *m.* to heaviness
31. 28. wine bringeth cheerfulness of the *m.*
29. wine to excess maketh bitterness of the *m.*
37. 6. forget not thy friend in thy *m.*
12. a godly man, whose *m.* is according to thy *m.*
14. a man's *m.* is sometime wont to tell him more than seven watchmen that sit in a tower
38. 26. he giveth his *m.* to make furrows
28. he setteth his *m.* to finish his work
39. 1. he that giveth his *m.* to the law of God
Bar. 4. 28. as it was your *m.* to go astray from God
Sus. 9. they perverted their own *m.* and turned away
1 *Mac.* 10. 74. Jonathan was moved in his *m.*
2 *Mac.* 1. 3. to do his will with a willing *m.*
3. 16. declared the inward agony of his *m.*
4. 46. Ptolemee brought him to be of another *m.*
5. 11. removing out of Egypt in a furious *m.*
17. and so haughty was Antiochus in *m.*
21. such was the haughtiness of his *m.*
6. 29. the speeches proceeded from a desperate *m.*
9. 27. that he understanding my *m.* will yield
11. 7. so they went forth with a willing *m.*
25. our *m.* is that this nation shall be in rest
37. send that we may know what is your *m.*
13. 4. the King of kings moved Antiochus' *m.*
9. king came with a barbarous and haughty *m.*
14. 20. it appeared that they were all of one *m.*
15. 30. Judas the chief defender in body and *m.*

MINDED.

Esth. 14. 13. of all that are like *m.* to him
Eccl. 19. 4. that is hasty to give credit, is light *m.*
2 *Mac.* 12. 8. heard that the Jamnites were *m.* to do

MINDS.

1 *Esd.* 2. 9. whose *m.* were stirred up thereto
Wisd. 4. 15. nor laid they up this in their *m.*
2 *Mac.* 2. 2. that they should not err in their *m.*
15. 10. when he stirred up their *m.* he gave them

MINDFUL.

2 *Esd.* 16. 20. nor be alway *m.* of the scourges
Tob. 2. 2. bring what poor man is *m.* of the Lord
4. 5. my son, be *m.* of the Lord all thy days
Wisd. 16. 11. they might be *m.* of thy goodness
19. 10. for they were yet *m.* of the things done
Eccl. 3. 31. is *m.* of that which may come after
2 *Mac.* 12. 43. that he was *m.* of the resurrection

MINGLE.

1 *Esd.* 8. 87. to *m.* ourselves with the uncleanness

MINGLED.

2 *Mac.* 14. 38. when they *m.* not themselves
15. 39. as wine *m.* with water is pleasant

MINGLING.

2 *Mac.* 14. 3. in the times of their *m.* with Gentiles

MINISTER.

1 *Esd.* 1. 4. and *m.* unto his people Israel
5. who *m.* in the presence of your brethren
4. 54. the priests' vestments wherein they *m.*
Eccl. 4. 14. serve her, shall *m.* to the holy One
45. 15. that they should *m.* to him, and bless
1 *Mac.* 10. 42. appertain to the priests that *m.*

MINISTERS.

1 *Esd.* 1. 3. the Levites, the holy *m.* of Israel
5. 35. all the *m.* of the temple, 8. 5, 22.
Wisd. 6. 4. because being *m.* of his kingdom

MINISTERED.

Tob. 1. 7. the sons of Aaron who *m.* at Jerusalem
Jud. 4. 14. they that *m.* to the Lord had sackcloth

MINISTRY.

Wisd. 18. 21. bringing the shield of his proper *m.*
Eccl. 48. 20. delivered them by the *m.* of Esay

MIRACULOUSLY.

2 *Mac.* 3. 30. that had *m.* honoured his own place

MIRROR.

Wisd. 7. 26. the unspotted *m.* of the power of God

MIRTH.

1 *Esd.* 3. 20. it turneth every thought into *m.*
Tob. 2. 6. all your *m.* be turned into lamentation
Wisd. 8. 16. hath no sorrow, but *m.* and joy
Eccl. 31. 31. despise not thy neighbour in his *m.*
Bar. 2. 23. the voice of *m.* and the voice of joy
1 *Mac.* 4. 59. the dedication of altar be kept with *m.*

MISCHIEF.

2 *Esd.* 15. 56. so shall God deliver thee into *m.*
Esth. 13. 5. this people working all the *m.* they can
Eccl. 19. 27. will do thee a *m.* before thou be aware
27. 27. he that worketh *m.* it shall fall on him
1 *Mac.* 1. 15. joined to heathen and sold to do *m.*
7. 23. now when Judas saw all the *m.*
9. 61. they took men that were authors of that *m.*
2 *Mac.* 4. 47. who was the cause of all the *m.* 13. 4.
6. 3. the coming in of this *m.* was sore
7. 31. thou that hast been the author of all *m.*

MISCHIEVOUS.

Esth. 14. 19. deliver us out of the hands of the *m.*
Wisd. 15. 4. nor did the *m.* invention of men
Eccl. 11. 33. take heed of a *m.* man lest he bring
Sus. 28. the two elders came full of *m.* imagination

MISCONCEIVE.

2 *Mac.* 3. 32. suspecting lest the king should *m.*

MISERABLE.

Tob. 13. 10. love in thee for ever those that are *m.*
Wisd. 3. 11. whoso despiseth nurture, he is *m.*
9. 14. for the thoughts of mortal men are *m.*
13. 10. but *m.* are they, and in dead things hope
15. 14. and are more *m.* than very babes
Eccl. 29. 24. it is a *m.* life to go from house to house
Bar. 4. 31. *m.* are they that afflicted thee
32. *m.* are the cities which thy children served
2 *Mac.* 9. 28. so died he a *m.* death in strange country

MISERY.

2 *Esd.* 7. 33. *m.* shall pass away, and long suffering
9. 45. God heard me, looked upon my *m.*
Wisd. 3. 2. and their departure is taken for *m.*
Eccl. 11. 13. and lifted up his head from *m.*
1 *Mac.* 2. 7. woe is me, to see this *m.* of my people
6. 11. how great a flood of *m.* it is wherein now I am
2 *Mac.* 6. 9. then might a man have seen present *m.*
14. 8. for all our nation is in no small *m.*

MISERIES.

2 *Esd.* 8. 50. many great *m.* shall be done to them
Bar. 2. 25. and they died in great *m.* by famine
1 *Mac.* 3. 42. Judas saw that *m.* were multiplied

MISINFORMED.

2 *Mac.* 3. 11. and not as that wicked Simon had *m.*

MISS.

2 *Esd.* 16. 13. arrows are sharp and shall not *m.*
Eccl. 8. 9. *m.* not the discourse of the elders

MISSING.

2 *Mac.* 14. 43. but *m.* his stroke through haste

MIST.

Wisd. 2. 4. and our life shall be dispersed as a *m.*
Eccl. 43. 22. a present remedy of all is a *m.* coming

MITHRIDATES.

1 *Esd.* 2. 11. he delivered them to M. his treasurer
16. in time of Belemus, and M. and Tabellius

MITIGATED.

Wisd. 16. 18. for some time the flame was *m.*

MITRE.

Eccl. 45. 12. he set a crown of gold upon the *m.*

MIXED.

1 *Esd.* 8. 70. holy seed is *m.* with the strange people
2 *Esd.* 13. 11. and they were all *m.* together

MOAB.

Jud. 1. 12. slay all the inhabitants of the land of M.
5. 2. and called all the princes of M.
22. all that dwelt by the sea-side and in M.

MOABITES.

1 *Esd.* 8. 69. the M. Egyptians, and Edomites
Jud. 6. 1. Holofernes said to Achior and all the M.

MOAN.

Eccl. 38. 17. weep bitterly, and make great *m.*

MOCK.

Wisd. 12. 25. thou didst send a judgment to *m.* them

MOCKED.

Tob. 2. 8. but my neighbours *m.* me and said
1 *Mac.* 7. 34. but he *m.* them and laughed at them
2 *Mac.* 7. 39. king took it grievously that he was *m.*

MOCKERY.

Eccl. 27. 28. *m.* and reproach are from the proud
2 *Mac.* 8. 17. injury, whereof they made a *m.*

MOCKING.

Eccl. 33. 6. a stallion horse is as a *m.* friend
2 *Mac.* 7. 7. brought second to make him a *m.*-stock

MODERATE.

Eccl. 31. 20. sound sleep cometh of *m.* eating

MODERATELY.

Eccl. 31. 27. wine is good, if it be drunk *m.*

MODEST.

2 *Mac.* 4. 37. the *m.* behaviour of him that was dead

MODIN.

1 *Mac.* 2. 1. then arose Mattathias and dwelt in M.
15. came into city of M. to make them a sacrifice
23. to sacrifice on the altar which was at M.
70. in sepulchre of his fathers at M. 9. 19.
13. 25. buried them in M. the city of his fathers
30. this is the sepulchre which he made at M.
16. 4. who went out and rested that night at M.
2 *Mac.* 13. 14. so Judas camped by M.

MOIST.

Dan. 3. 27. as it had been a *m.* whistling wind

MOLEST.

Esth. 12. 6. Aman sought to *m.* Mardocheus
1 *Mac.* 10. 35. or to *m.* any of them in any matter

MOLLIFYING.

Wisd. 16. 12. nor *m.* plaister that restored them

MOMENT.

2 *Esd.* 16. 38. which pains slack not a *m.*
Wisd. 18. 12. in one *m.* noblest offspring destroyed
2 *Mac.* 6. 25. through my desire to live a *m.* longer
9. 11. his pain increasing every *m.*

MONTH.

1 *Esd.* 5. 6. in the *m.* Nisan, the first *m.* *Esth.* 11. 2.
47. but when the seventh *m.* was at hand
53. began from the first day of the seventh *m.*
7. 5. the three and twentieth day of the *m.* Adar
10. passover, the fourteenth day of the first *m.*
9. 5. the twentieth day of the ninth *m.*
16. in the first day of the tenth *m.* they sat
2 *Esd.* 16. 38. a woman in the ninth *m.* bringeth forth
Esth. 10. 13. and the fifteenth day of the same *m.*
13. 6. the fourteenth day of the twelfth *m.* Adar
16. 20. the thirteenth day of the twelfth *m.*
Eccl. 43. 8. the *m.* is called after her name
1 *Mac.* 1. 54. the fifteenth day of the *m.* Casleu
4. 52. on the five and twentieth day of the ninth *m.*
59. from the five and twentieth day of the *m.*
14. 27. the eighteenth day of the *m.* Elul
16. 14. in the eleventh *m.* called Sabat
2 *Mac.* 1. 9. see that ye keep the feast in *m.* Casleu
18. upon the five and twentieth day of the *m.*
11. 21. the twenty-fourth day of *m.* Dioscorinthius
33. in the fifteenth day of the *m.* Xanthicus, 38.
15. 36. the thirteenth day of the twelfth *m.*

MONTHS.

1 *Esd.* 1. 44. Joacim reigned but three *m.* and ten days
2 *Esd.* 4. 40. when she hath fulfilled her nine *m.*
8. 8. and nine *m.* doth thy workmanship endure
Wisd. 7. 2. to be flesh in the time of ten *m.*
2 *Mac.* 7. 27. have pity on me that bare thee nine *m.*

MONEY.

1 *Esd.* 5. 54. they gave the masons and carpenters *m.*
8. 24. by penalty of *m.* or by imprisonment
Tob. 4. 1. in that day Tobit remembered the *m.*
2. I may signify to him of the *m.* before I die
5. 2. how can I receive *m.* seeing I know him not
3. seek thee a man, and go and receive the *m.*
18. be not greedy to add *m.* to *m.*
9. 2. go to Gabael and bring me the *m.*
10. 2. and there is no man to give him the *m.*
10. Raguel gave him servants, cattle, and *m.*
12. 3. he hath brought me the *m.* and healed thee
Jud. 4. 10. servants bought with *m.* put sackcloth
Eccl. 9. 9. spend not thy *m.* with her at the wine
14. 3. what should an envious man do with *m.*
21. 8. that builds his house with other men's *m.*
29. 5. for his neighbour's *m.* he will speak submissly
10. lose thy *m.* for thy brother and thy friend
51. 25. buy her for yourselves without *m.*
28. get learning with a great sum of *m.*
Bar. 1. 6. they made also a collection of *m.*
10. we have sent you *m.* to buy you offerings
6. 35. they can neither give riches nor *m.*
1 *Mac.* 3. 31. to go into Persia to gather much *m.*
8. 26. nor aid them with victuals or *m.* 28.
13. 15. it is for *m.* he is owing to the king's treasure
17. yet sent he the *m.* and the children, 18.
15. 6. I give thee leave also to coin *m.*
2 *Mac.* 1. 14. to receive *m.* in name of a dowry
3. 6. the treasury was full of infinite sums of *m.*
7. Apollonius came and had shewed him of the *m.* and sent him to bring the foresaid *m.*
9. that intelligence was given him of the *m.*
10. there was *m.* laid up for the relief of widows
4. 1. having been a bewrayer of the *m.*
20. this *m.* was appointed to Hercules' sacrifice
23. sent Menelaus to bear the *m.* unto the king
27. but as for the *m.* that he had promised
45. to give him *m.* if he would pacify the king
8. 10. to make so much *m.* of the captive Jews
25. took their *m.* that came to buy them
10. 21. they had sold their brethren for *m.*

MONUMENT.

Wisd. 10. 7. a standing pillar of salt is a *m.*
1 *Mac.* 13. 27. Simon built a *m.* on the sepulchre
2 *Mac.* 15. 6. determined to set up a public *m.*

MOON.

2 *Esd.* 5. 4. the *m.* shall shine thrice in the day
6. 45. thou commandedst the *m.* to give her light
Eccl. 27. 11. but a fool changeth as the *m.*
39. 12. for I am filled as the *m.* at the full
43. 6. he made the *m.* also to serve in her season
7. from the *m.* is the sign of feasts
50. 6. he was as the *m.* at the full
Bar. 6. 60. for sun, *m.* and stars are obedient
67. nor shine as the sun, nor give light as the *m.*
Dan. 3. 40. O ye sun and *m.* bless ye the Lord

MORDOCHEUS. *See* MARDOCHEUS.

MORNING.

1 *Esd.* 1. 11. and thus did they in the *m.*
5. 50. they offered to the Lord *m.* and evening
9. 41. he read in the court from *m.* unto mid-day
Tob. 9. 6. early in the *m.* they both went forth
Jud. 12. 5. when it was towards the *m.*-watch
14. 11. as soon as *m.* arose, they hanged the head
Wisd. 11. 22. yea as a drop of *m.* dew that falleth
Eccl. 18. 26. from *m.* till evening time is changed
24. 32. I will yet make doctrine to shine as the *m.*
47. 10. that the temple might sound from *m.*
50. 6. he was as the *m.*-star in the midst of a cloud
Bel 16. in the *m.* betime the king arose
1 *Mac.* 4. 52. they rose up betimes in the *m.*
5. 30. betimes in the *m.* they looked up
9. 13. the battle continued from *m.* till night
10. 80. cast darts at the people from *m.* till evening
11. 67. betimes in the *m.* they gat to the plain

MOSES.

1 *Esd.* 1. 6. commandment which was given to M.
11. to offer as it is written in the book of M.
5. 49. as it is commanded in the book of M.
7. 6. did the things written in the book of M.
9. stood arrayed, according to the book of M.
8. 3. as a scribe, being very ready in the law of M.
9. 39. that he would bring the law of M.
2 *Esd.* 1. 13. I gave you M. for a leader
7. 36. M. prayed for the fathers that sinned
59. for this is the life whereof M. spake
14. 3. I did manifestly reveal myself to M.
Eccl. 45. 1. even M. beloved of God and men
15. M. consecrated and anointed him with oil
46. 1. Jesus was successor of M. in prophecies
7. in the time of M. he did a work of mercy
Bar. 1. 20. curse which the Lord appointed by M.
2. 28. as thou spakest by thy servant M.
Sus. 3. taught according to the law of M. 62.
2 *Mac.* 1. 29. plant thy people as M. hath spoken
2. 4. where M. climbed up and saw the heritage
8. the cloud also as it was shewed under M.
10. as when M. prayed to the Lord, fire came
11. M. said, because the sin offering was not
7. 6. as M. in his song declared, saying
30. law that was given unto our fathers by M.

MOTHER.

2 *Esd.* 1. 28. I prayed you as a *m.* her daughters
10. 7. how that Sion our *m.* is full of heaviness
13. 55. thou hast called understanding thy *m.*
Tob. 1. 8. as Debora my father's *m.* commanded me
4. 3. and despise not thy *m.* but honour her
13. for lewdness is the *m.* of famine
5. 17. but Anna his *m.* wept, and said to Tobit
10. 12. honour thy father and thy *m.*-in-law
11. 17. and blessed be thy father and thy *m.*
14. 10. bury me decently, and thy *m.* with me
12. when Anna his *m.* was dead, he buried her
13. he buried his father and his *m.* honourably
Wisd. 7. 2. in my *m.* womb I was fashioned
12. I knew not that she was the *m.* of them
Eccl. 3. 2. the authority of the *m.* over the sons
4. he that honoureth his *m.* is as one that layeth up
6. the obedient shall be a comfort to his *m.*
9. curse of the *m.* rooteth out foundations
11. a *m.* in dishonour is a reproach to children

Eccl. 3. 16. he that angereth his m. is cursed of God
4. 10. be instead of a husband to their m.
7. 27. and forget not the sorrows of thy m.
15. 2. as a m. shall she meet him and receive him
24. 18. I am the m. of fair love and fear
40. 1. from the day they go out of their m. womb, till the day they return to the m. of all things
49. 7. was a prophet sanctified in his m. womb
1 Mac. 13. 28. for his m. and his four brethren
2 Mac. 7. 1. seven brethren with their m. taken
4. the rest of his brethren and m. looking on
5. they exhorted one another with the m. to die
20. but the m. was marvellous above all
25. the king called his m. and exhorted her
41. last of all after the sons the m. died

MOTH, S.

Eccl. 19. 3. m. and worms shall have him to heritage
42. 13. for from garments cometh a m.
Bar. 6. 12. gods cannot save themselves from m.

MOTION.

2 Esd. 6. 14. it shall be as it were a great m.
Wisd. 7. 24. wisdom is more moving than any m.

MOVE.

2 Esd. 4. 37. he doth not m. nor stir them
Bar. 6. 27. neither can they m. of themselves
Dan. 3. 57. whales and all that m. in the waters

MOVED.

1 Esd. 2. 8. all they whose mind the Lord had m.
8. 72. all that were m. at the word of the Lord
2 Esd. 3. 3. my spirit was sore m. and I spake
6. 14. the place where thou standest shall not be m.
7. 15. why art thou m. whereas thou art mortal
13. 2. that the wind m. all the waves thereof
Jud. 9. 4. children, which were m. with thy zeal
12. 16. his heart was ravished, his mind was m.
16. 15. for the mountains shall be m. from foundat.
Eccl. 16. 18. shall be m. when he shall visit
48. 12. he was not m. with the presence of any prince
Bar. 4. 6. but because you m. God to wrath
1 Mac. 10. 74. Jonathan was m. in his mind
2 Mac. 4. 37. Antiochus was sorry, and m. to pity
49. they of Tyrus m. with hatred of that deed
13. 4. the King of kings m. Antiochus' mind

MOVEDST.

2 Esd. 3. 18. thou m. the whole world, and madest

MOVING.

Wisd. 2. 2. as a little spark in m. of our heart
7. 24. for wisdom is more m. than any motion

MOUNT.

2 Esd. 2. 33. a charge of the Lord on m. Horeb
42. I Esdras saw on m. Sion a great people
13. 35. he shall stand upon the top of m. Sion
Wisd. 9. 8. to build a temple on thy holy m.
1 Mac. 4. 37. all the host went up into m. Sion
60. they builded the m. Sion with high walls
5. 54. so they went up to m. Sion with joy
6. 48. the king pitched his tents against m. Sion
62. then the king entered into m. Sion
9. 15. who pursued them to the m. Azotus
11. 37. set on the holy m. in a conspicuous place
12. 36. raising a m. between the tower and the city

MOUNTAIN.

2 Esd. 13. 6. he had graved himself a great m.
12. I saw the same man come down from the m.
Jud. 2. 21. pitched from Bectileth near the m.
10. 10. looked, until she was gone down the m.
13. 10. they went up the m. of Bethulia
Eccl. 50. 26. that sit upon the m. of Samaria
Bar. 6. 39. like stones that be hewn out of the m.
1 Mac. 16. 20. he sent to take the m. of the temple
2 Mac. 2. 4. as he went forth into the m.

MOUNTAINS.

1 Esd. 4. 4. they go and break down m. and towers
2 Esd. 8. 23. whose indignation makes the m. melt
15. 42. they shall break down the m. and hills
16. 60. hath made pools on the tops of the m.
Tob. 1. 21. they fled into the m. of Ararath
Jud. 1. 15. he took also Arphaxad in the m.
Eccl. 24. 13. as a cypress upon the m. of Hermon
43. 4. the sun burneth the m. three times more
16. at his sight the m. are shaken, the wind bloweth
21. it devoureth the m. and burneth the wilderness

MOURN.

2 Esd. 8. 16. thy inheritance, for whose cause I m.
10. 4. but continually to m. and to fast until I die
8. now seeing we all m. art thou griev. for one son?
9. tell thee that it is she which ought to m.
15. 12. Egypt shall m. and foundation be smitten
13. they that till the ground shall m.
16. 33. the women shall m. having no husbands
39. world shall m. and sorrows shall come
2 Mac. 5. 10. he had none to m. for him

MOURNED.

1 Esd. 1. 32. in all Jewry they m. for Josias
8. 72. assembled, whilst I m. for the iniquity
2 Esd. 9. 38. she m. and wept with a loud voice
10. 49. because she m. for her son thou beganuest
Eccl. 48. 24. he comforted them that m. in Sion
1 Mac. 1. 26. so that the princes and elders m.
2. 14. Mattathias and his sons m. very sore
9. 20. and all Israel m. many days, saying

MOURNING.

1 Esd. 9. 2. m. for the great iniquities of multitude
2 Esd. 5. 20. so I fasted seven days, m. and weeping
10. 6. seest thou not our m. and what happeneth
11. who then should make more m. than she?
41. thou sawest a woman m. and beganuest
Tob. 2. 6. your feasts shall be turned into m.
Esth. 14. 2. put on garments of anguish and m.
15. 1. third day she laid away her m. garments
Wisd. 14. 15. for a father afflicted with untimely m.
19. 3. for whilst they were yet m. at the graves

MOURNINGS.

2 Esd. 1. 19. I had pity on your m. and gave manna
16. 18. the beginnings of sorrows and great m.

MOUTH.

1 Esd. 1. 28. words spoken by the m. of the Lord
47. words spoken to him from the m. of the Lord
57. word of the Lord spoken by the m. of Jeremy
2. 1. that he had promised by the m. of Jeremy
4. 19. with open m. fix their eyes fast on her
31. the king gazed upon her with open m.
2 Esd. 14. 38. open thy m. and drink that I gave thee
41. and my m. was opened, and shut no more
Tob. 13. 6. therefore confess him with your m.
Jud. 11. 19. a dog shall not open his m. at thee
Wisd. 1. 11. the m. that belieth slayeth the soul
8. 12. they shall lay their hands on their m.
10. 21. wisdom openeth the m. of the dumb
Eccl. 5. 12. if not, lay thy hand upon thy m.
14. 1. blessed man that hath not slipt with his m.
15. 9. praise is not seemly in the m. of a sinner
20. 19. will always be in the m. of the unwise
20. rejected when it comes out of a fool's m.
21. 5. a prayer out of a poor man's m. reacheth to
17. they inquire at the m. of the wise man
22. 22. if thou hast opened thy m. against thy friend
23. 7. hear, O ye children, the discipline of the m.
9. accustom not thy m. to swearing
13. use not thy m. to untemperate swearing
24. 2. in the congregation shall she open her m.
3. I came out of the m. of the Most High
26. 12. she will open her m. as a thirsty traveller
27. 23. at last he will writhe his m. and slander
28. 12. and both these come out of thy m.
29. 24. art a stranger, thou darest not open thy m.
30. 18. delicates poured upon a m. shut up
34. 8. wisdom is perfection to a faithful m.
37. 22. the fruits are commendable in his m.
39. 5. and he will open his m. in prayer
40. 30. begging is sweet in the m. of the shameless
Dan. 3. 2. opening his m. in the midst of the fire
28. then the three, as out of one m. praised God
Sus. 61. Daniel had convicted them by their own m.
Bel 27. this he put in the dragon's m.
1 Mac. 2. 60. Daniel was delivered from the m. of
9. 55. for his m. stopped, he could not speak
2 Mac. 6. 18. Eleazar was constrained to open his m.

MOUTHS.

Jud. 15. 13. Israel followed with songs in their m.
Esth. 13. 17. destroy not the m. of them that praise
14. 10. open the m. of the heathen to set forth
Eccl. 49. 1. it is sweet as honey in all m.
Dan. 3. 10. and now we cannot open our m.

MUCH.

Tob. 12. 8. a little with righteousness is better than m.
Wisd. 8. 12. if I talk m. they shall lay their hands
10. 18. and led them through m. water
Eccl. 37. 11. with an idle servant of m. business
43. 27. we may speak m. and yet come short
30. when ye glorify God exalt him as m. as you can
51. 16. I received her, and gat m. learning
27. how that I have gotten unto me m. rest
28. get learning, and get m. gold by her
2 Mac. 15. 14. who prayeth m. for the people

MULBERRIES.

1 Mac. 6. 34. they shewed the blood of grapes and m.

MULE.

Jud. 15. 11. she took it and laid it on her m.

MULES.

1 Esd. 5. 43. two hundred forty and five m.

MULTIPLY.

2 Esd. 3. 12. when they on the earth began to m.
7. 67. for if he shall not m. his mercies
Eccl. 6. 5. sweet language will m. friends
16. 2. though they m. rejoice not in them
23. 16. two sorts of men m. sin, a hot mind
44. 21. he would m. him as the dust of the earth
47. 18. and thou didst m. silver as lead
Dan. 3. 13. that thou wouldst m. their seed as stars

MULTIPLIED.

1 Esd. 8. 75. for our sins are m. above our heads
2 Esd. 5. 10. incontinency shall be m. on earth
Wisd. 10. 10. she m. the fruits of his labours
Eccl. 18. 12. therefore he m. his compassion
48. 16. some pleasing to God, and some m. sins
Prayer of Manass. my transgressions are m. and m.
1 Mac. 1. 9. and evils were m. in the earth
3. 42. when Judas saw that miseries were m.
14. 15. he m. the vessels of the temple

MULTIPLIETH.

Eccl. 21. 12. as wisdom which m. bitterness

MULTIPLYING.

Wisd. 4. 3. the m. brood of the ungodly not thrive

MULTITUDE.

1 Esd. 4. 14. it is not the great king, nor m. of men
5. 65. yet the m. sounded marvellously
9. 6. all the m. sat trembling in the court
2 Esd. 3. 16. and so Jacob became a great m.
6. 3. before the innumerable m. of angels
Wisd. 6. 2. you that glory in the m. of nations
24. the m. of the wise is the welfare of the world
Eccl. 5. 6. he will be pacified for the m. of my sins
6. 34. stand in the m. of the elders, and cleave
7. 7. offend not against the m. of a city
9. God will look upon the m. of my oblations
14. 1. that is not pricked with the m. of sins
16. 1. desire not a m. of unprofitable children
3. trust not in their life, nor respect their m.
26. 5. the gathering together of an unruly m.
34. 19. nor is he pacified for sin by m. of sacrifices
35. 18. till he have taken away the m. of the proud
42. 11. lest she make thee ashamed before the m.
51. 3. according to the m. of thy mercies
Prayer of Manass. for the m. of mine iniquity

MUNITION.

1 Mac. 14. 10. he set in them all manner of m.

MURDER, S.

2 Mac. 4. 3. by Simon's faction m. were committed
35. were much grieved for the unjust m. of the man

MURDERED.

Wisd. 10. 3. the fury wherewith he m. his brother
1 Mac. 2. 41. as our brethren that were m.

MURDERER.

2 Mac. 4. 38. there slew he the cursed m.
9. 28. thus the m. and blasphemer died

MURDERERS.

Wisd. 12. 5. also those merciless m. of children
2 Mac. 12. 6. he came against those m. of his brethren

MURMUR.

2 Esd. 1. 16. but even to this day do ye yet m.
Eccl. 31. 24. against a niggard the whole city m.

MURMURED.

2 Esd. 1. 15. nevertheless you m. there
Jud. 5. 22. the people standing about the tent m.
1 Mac. 11. 39. all the host m. against Demetrius

MURMURING.

Wisd. 1. 11. beware of m. which is unprofitable
Eccl. 46. 7. and they appeased the wicked m.

MURMURINGS.

Wisd. 1. 10. and the noise of m. is not hid

MUSED.

2 Esd. 10. 25. I was afraid, and m. what it might be

MUSETH.

Wisd. 9. 15. the mind that m. upon many things

MUSIC.

Eccl. 22. 6. a tale out of season is as m. in mourning
32. 3. with sound judgment, and hinder not m.
5. concert of m. in a banquet of wine
6. so is the melody of m. with pleasant wine
40. 20. wine and m. rejoice the heart
49. 1. it is as m. at a banquet of wine
1 Mac. 9. 39. to meet them with the instruments of m.

MUSICAL.

1 Esd. 5. 2. brought them back with m. instruments
59. priests in vestments with m. instruments
Eccl. 44. 5. such as found out m. tunes, and recited

MUSICIAN.

Eccl. 32. 4. pour not out words where there is a m.

MUSTERED.

Jud. 2. 15. he m. the chosen men for the battle

MUTED.

Tob. 2. 10. the sparrows m. dung into mine eyes

MYRRH.

Eccl. 24. 15. a pleasant odour like the best m.

MYSTERIES.

Wisd. 2. 22. as for the m. of God they knew them not
6. 22. and I will not hide m. from you
8. 4. she is privy to the m. of the knowledge of God
Eccl. 3. 19. but m. are revealed unto the meek

N.

NABATHITES.

1 Mac. 5. 25. where they met with the N.

NABUCHODONOSOR.

1 Esd. 1. 41. N. also took of the holy vessels
Tob. 14. 15. of Nineve which was taken by N.
Jud. 1. 1. in the twelfth year of the reign of N.
2. 19. to go before king N. in the voyage
3. 8. that all nations should worship N. only
6. 4. saith king N. lord of all the earth
11. 1. I never hurt any that was willing to serve N.
4. entreat thee well, as they do the servants of N.
7. as N. king of all the earth liveth
12. 13. which serve in the house of N.
Esth. 11. 4. one of the captives which N. carried
Bar. 1. 9. N. king of Babylon, 6. 2.
11. pray for the life of N. king of Babylon
12. we shall live under the shadow of N.

NAHUM.

2 Esd. 1. 40. I give for leaders, N. and Abacuc

NAIL.

Eccl. 27. 2. as a n. sticks between the joinings

NAKED.

Tob. 1. 17. and I gave my clothes to the n.
4. 16. give of thy garments to them that are n.
2 Mac. 11. 12. many being wounded, escaped n.

NAME.

1 Esd. 1. 48. made him swear by the n. of the Lord
4. 63. the temple which is called by his n.
6. 33. the Lord, whose n. is there called upon
8. 78. be left us a n. in the place of thy sanctuary
88. till thou hadst left us neither root, seed, nor n.
2 Esd. 4. 1. the angel, whose n. was Uriel, gave me
Tob. 3. 15. and that I never polluted my n. nor the n. of my father, in the land of my captivity
5. 11. I would know, brother, thy kindred and n.
11. 14. he said, blessed is thy n. for ever
13. 11. shall come from far to the n. of the Ld. God
Jud. 9. 7. breakest the battle, the Lord is thy n.
Esth. 10. 8. assembled to destroy the n. of the Jews
Wisd. 2. 4. and our n. shall be forgotten in time
14. 21. ascribe to stocks the incommunicable n.
19. 18. in a psaltery, notes change n. of the tune
Eccl. 6. 1. thereby thou shalt inherit an ill n.
22. for wisdom is according to her n.
15. 6. shall cause him to inherit an everlasting n.
17. 10. and the elect shall praise his holy n.
22. 14. what is the n. thereof but a fool?
37. 1. a friend which is only a friend in n.
26. and his n. shall be perpetual
39. 9. his n. shall live from generation to generat.
11. he shall leave a greater n. than a thousand
15. magnify his n. and shew forth his praise
40. 19. building of a city continueth a man's n.
41. 11. an ill n. of sinners shall be blotted out
12. have regard to thy n. for that shall continue
13. but a good n. endureth for ever
43. 8. the month is called after her n.
44. 8. there be that have left a n. behind them
14. bodies buried, but their n. liveth for ever
45. 15. they should bless the people in his n.
47. 16. thy n. went far unto the islands
50. 20. to give blessing, and to rejoice in his n.
Bar. 2. 11. and thou hast gotten thyself a n.
32. they shall praise me, and think on my n.
3. 5. but think upon thy power and thy n.
4. 30. he that gave thee that n. will comfort thee
1 Mac. 3. 14. he said, I will get me a n. and honour
4. 33. let all those that know thy n. praise thee
5. 57. let us also get us a n. and go fight ag. heathen
63. renowned, wheresoever their n. was heard of
6. 44. that he might get him a perpetual n.
14. 10. that his honourable n. was renowned
2 Mac. 12. 13. strong city, the n. of it was Caspis

NAMED.

2 Esd. 5. 26. of fowls thou hast n. thee one dove
Tob. 3. 8. neither wast thou n. after any of them
Wisd. 14. 27. for worshipping of idols not to be n.
Eccl. 24. 18. all my children, which are n. of him
36. 12. people, whom thou hast n. thy first-born

NAMES.

1 Esd. 6. 12. and we required the n. in writing
8. 49. the catalogue of whose n. were shewed

NAMETH.
Eccl. 23. 10. who sweareth and *n.* God continually
NAMING.
Eccl. 23. 9. nor use thyself to the *n.* of the holy One
NANEA.
2 *Mac.* 1. 13. when the leader came, they were slain in the temple of N. by the deceit of N. priests
NARRATIONS.
2 *Mac.* 2. 24. desire to look into the *n.* of the story
NARROW.
2 *Esd.* 7. 4. but put the case, the entrance were *n.* 7.
13. 43. they entered by the *n.* passages of the river
NATHAN.
Eccl. 47. 1. after him rose up N. to prophesy
NATION.
1 *Esd.* 6. 33. the Lord destroy every king and *n.*
Tob. 1. 17. if I saw any of my *n.* dead, I buried him
2. 3. one of our *n.* is strangled and cast out
4. 19. for every *n.* hath not counsel, but Lord giveth
Jud. 5. 10. that one could not number their *n.*
21. but if there be no iniquity in their *n.*
6. 5. vengeance of this *n.* that came out of Egypt
19. O Lord God, pity the low estate of our *n.*
15. 9. thou art the great rejoicing of our *n.*
Esth. 10. 9. my *n.* is this Israel, which cried to God
Wisd. 10. 15. from the *n.* that oppressed them
17. 2. unrighteous thought to oppress the holy *n.*
Eccl. 16. 6. in a rebellious *n.* wrath is on fire
28. 14. hath driven them from *n.* to *n.*
49. 5. he gave their glory to a strange *n.*
50. 25. and the third is no *n.*
Bar. 4. 15. a shameless *n.* and of a strange language
Dan. 3. 14. for we are become less than any *n.*
1 *Mac.* 1. 34. they put therein a sinful *n.*
2. 10. what *n.* hath not had a part in her kingdom?
11. 42. I will greatly honour thee and thy *n.*
13. 6. I will avenge my *n.* and the sanctuary
14. 4. he sought the good of his *n.* in such wise
6. and he enlarged the bounds of his *n.*
29. put themselves in jeopardy, and resisting the enemies of their *n.* did their *n.* great honour
16. 3. now I am old, go out and fight for our *n.*
2 *Mac.* 4. 2. that had tendered his own *n.*
10. brought his own *n.* to the Greekish fashion
6. 12. not for destruct. but for a chastening of our *n.*
31. not only to young men, but to all his *n.*
7. 16. think not that our *n.* is forsaken of God
37. he would speedily be merciful to our *n.*
38. the wrath justly brought on all our *n.*
10. 8. should be kept of the whole *n.* of the Jews
11. 25. our mind is, that this *n.* shall be in rest
14. 9. be careful for the country and our *n.*
34. him that was ever a defender of their *n.*
NATIONS.
1 *Esd.* 1. 49. passed all the pollutions of all *n.*
2 *Esd.* 3. 7. of whom came *n.* tribes, people
Tob. 3. 4. for a proverb of reproach to all *n.*
13. 5. and he will gather us out of all *n.*
11. many *n.* shall come from far to the Lord
14. 6. and all *n.* shall turn and fear the Lord
7. so shall all *n.* praise the Lord, and his people
Jud. 16. 17. wo to the *n.* that rise up ag. my kindred
Esth. 13. 4. that had laws contrary to all *n.*
14. 12. O king of the *n.* and Lord of all power
Wisd. 3. 8. they shall judge the *n.* and have dominion
6. 2. you that glory in the multitude of *n.*
8. 14. and the *n.* shall be subject to me
10. 5. the *n.* in their wicked conspiracy
12. 12. shall accuse thee for the *n.* that perish
Eccl. 4. 15. whoso gives ear to her, shall judge *n.*
10. 15. Lord hath plucked up the roots of proud *n.*
17. 17. in the division of the *n.* he set a ruler
29. 18. so that they wandered among strange *n.*
36. 2. send thy fear upon all *n.* that seek not thee
39. 10. *n.* shall shew forth his wisdom
44. 21. that he would bless the *n.* in his seed
46. 6. he made the battle to fall upon the *n.*
50. 25. there be two manner of *n.* which I abhor
Bar. 4. 6. ye were sold to *n.* not for destruction
6. 4. see gods of gold, which cause *n.* to fear
51. it shall manifestly appear to *n.* and kings
1 *Mac.* 1. 3. Alexander took spoils of many *n.*
4. he ruled over countries, and *n.* and kings
NATIVITY.
Wisd. 6. 22. seek out from the beginning of her *n.*
Eccl. 23. 14. and so thou curse the day of thy *n.*
NATURE.
Wisd. 13. 1. surely vain are all men by *n.*
19. 20. the water forgat his own quenching *n.*
21. the icy meat, that was of *n.* apt to melt
NATURES.
Wisd. 7. 20. to know the *n.* of living creatures
NAVE.
Eccl. 46. 1. Jesus son of N. was valiant in wars
NAUGHTY.
Wisd. 12. 10. that they were a *n.* generation
NAUGHTINESS.
Wisd. 4. 12. the bewitching of *n.* doth obscure
NAVIGABLE.
2 *Mac.* 5. 21. in his pride to make the land *n.*
NAVY.
1 *Mac.* 1. 17. he entered into Egypt with a great *n.*
2 *Mac.* 12. 9. he set fire on the haven and the *n.*
14. 1. Demetrius with a great power and *n.*
NAZARITES.
1 *Mac.* 3. 49. and the N. they stirred up
NEBAT.
Eccl. 47. 23. there was also Jeroboam the son of N.
NECESSARY.
Tob. 5. 14. wilt thou a drachm a day, and things *n.*
Eccl. 20. 32. *n.* patience in seeking the Lord
29. 3. shalt find the thing that is *n.* for thee
1 *Mac.* 10. 39. for the *n.* expences of the sanctuary
2 *Mac.* 1. 18. we thought it *n.* to certify you
4. 23. to put him in mind of certain *n.* matters
9. 21. I thought it *n.* to care for the safety of all
13. 20. Judas conveyed such things as were *n.*
NECESSITY.
2 *Esd.* 4. 42. to escape the *n.* of the travail
Tob. 4. 9. a good treasure against the day of *n.*
Esth. 14. 16. thou knowest my *n.* for I abhor
Wisd. 17. 17. endured *n.* that could not be avoided

Eccl. 20. 14. nor yet the envious for his *n.*
NECESSITIES.
2 *Esd.* 13. 19. come into great perils, and many *n.*
NECK.
1 *Esd.* 1. 48. he rebelled, and hardened his *n.*
3. 6. and head-tire, and chain about his *n.*
Tob. 11. 9. Anna fell on the *n.* of her son, 13.
Jud. 13. 8. and she smote twice upon his *n.*
16. 9. and the fauchion passed through his *n.*
Esth. 15. 11. his sceptre, and laid it upon her *n.*
Eccl. 6. 24. and put thy *n.* into her chain
7. 23. and bow down their *n.* from their youth
30. 12. bow down his *n.* while he is young
33. 26. a yoke and collar do bow the *n.*
51. 26. put your *n.* under the yoke
Bar. 2. 33. they shall return from their stiff *n.*
4. 25. but shortly thou shalt tread upon his *n.*
NECKS.
1 *Mac.* 1. 61. they hanged infants about their *n.*
NEED.
Wisd. 11. 5. they in their *n.* were benefited
13. 16. for it is an image, and hath *n.* of help
16. 25. according to the desire of them that had *n.*
Eccl. 4. 3. defer not to give him that is in *n.*
8. 9. learn to give answer as *n.* requireth
11. 12. another that is slow and hath *n.* of help
13. 6. if he have *n.* of thee he will deceive thee
18. 25. when rich, think on poverty and *n.*
23. 18. no body seeth me, what *n.* I to fear?
29. 2. lend to thy neighbour in time of his *n.*
27. my brother cometh, I have *n.* of my house
32. 7. speak, young man, if there be *n.* of thee
33. 31. thou hast *n.* of him, as of thine own soul
37. 8. and know before what *n.* he hath
38. 12. let him not go from thee, thou hast *n.* of him
39. 21. a man *n.* not to say, what is this?
31. they shall be ready on earth when *n.* is
42. 21. and he hath no *n.* of any counsellor
1 *Mac.* 3. 28. be ready whenever he should *n.* them
12. 9. albeit we *n.* none of these things
2 *Mac.* 2. 15. if ye have *n.* thereof, send to fetch
14. 35. thou, O Lord of all, who hast *n.* of nothing
NEEDETH.
Eccl. 40. 26. the fear of the Lord *n.* not to seek help
NEEDFUL.
Eccl. 39. 33. he will give every *n.* thing in season
NEEDY.
Eccl. 4. 1. make not the *n.* eyes to wait long
5. turn not away thine eyes from the *n.*
31. 4. and when he leaveth off, he is still *n.*
34. 21. the bread of the *n.* is their life
41. 2. acceptable is thy sentence to the *n.*
NEGLECT.
Eccl. 7. 10. and *n.* not to give alms
38. 16. cover his body, and *n.* not his burial
NEGLECTED, ING.
Wisd. 3. 10. ungodly which have *n.* the righteous
2 *Mac.* 4. 14. despising the temple, and *n.* sacrifices
NEGLIGENT.
Eccl. 38. 9. my son, in thy sickness be not *n.*
Bar. 1. 19. we have been *n.* in not hearing him
NEHEMIAS, *or* NEEMIAS.
1 *Esd.* 5. 8. with Jesus, N. and Zacharias
40. for unto them said N. and Atharias
Eccl. 49. 13. among the elect was N. who raised up
2 *Mac.* 1. 18. given when N. offered sacrifice
20. N. being sent from the king of Persia
21. N. commanded the priests to sprinkle wood
23. the rest answering thereunto as N. did
31. N. commanded water to be poured on stones
33. that N. had purified the sacrifices therewith
36. N. called this thing Naphthar, a cleansing
2. 13. in the writings and commentaries of N.
NEIGHBOUR.
2 *Esd.* 15. 19. a man shall have no pity on his *n.*
Jud. 7. 4. they said every one to his *n.* 10. 19.
15. 2. no man that durst abide in sight of his *n.*
Eccl. 5. 12. if thou hast understanding, answer thy *n.*
6. 17. for as he is, so shall his *n.* be also
9. 14. as near as thou canst, guess at thy *n.*
10. 6. bear not hatred to thy *n.* for every wrong
13. 15. and every man loveth his *n.*
17. 14. he gave commandment concerning his *n.*
18. 13. the mercy of man is towards his *n.*
19. 17. admonish thy *n.* before thou threaten him
22. 23. be faithful to thy *n.* in his poverty
27. 18. so hast thou lost the love of thy *n.*
19. so hast thou let thy *n.* go, and shalt not get him
28. 2. forgive thy *n.* the hurt he hath done thee
7. remember commands, bear no malice to thy *n.*
29. 1. he that is merciful will lend to his *n.*
2. lend to thy *n.* in time of his need, and pay thou thy *n.* again in due season
14. an honest man is surety for his *n.*
20. help thy *n.* according to thy power
31. 15. judge of thy *n.* by thyself, be discreet
31. rebuke not thy *n.* at wine, despise him not
Sus. 62. as they intended to do to their *n.*
2 *Mac.* 6. 8. there went a decree to the *n.* cities
NEIGHBOURS.
1 *Esd.* 2. 6. those, I say, that are his *n.* let them help
2 *Esd.* 9. 45. I was glad of him, so were all my *n.*
10. 2. all my *n.* rose up to comfort me
Tob. 2. 8. but my *n.* mocked me, and said
Eccl. 15. 5. she shall exalt him above his *n.*
21. 22. a foolish man's foot is soon in his *n.* house
25. 1. the unity of brethren the love of *n.*
18. her husband shall sit among his *n.*
29. 5. for his *n.* money he will speak submissly
34. 22. he that taketh away his *n.* living
Bar. 4. 24. as *n.* of Sion have seen your captivity
2 *Mac.* 9. 25. the princes that are borderers and *n.*
NEPHTHALI.
Tob. 1. 1. of the seed of Asael, of the tribe of N.
2. which is called properly N. in Galilee
4. all the tribe of N. fell from Jerusalem
5. the house of my father N. sacrificed to Baal
7. 3. to whom they said, we are of the sons of N.
NEVER.
Wisd. 2. 2. we shall be as though we had *n.* been
3. 15. the root of wisdom shall *n.* fall away
6. 12. wisdom is glorious, and *n.* fadeth away

Wisd. 7. 10. light that cometh from her *n.* goeth out
14. she is a treasure to men that *n.* faileth
15. 17. whereas he lived once, but they *n.*
Eccl. 7. 36. remember the end, thou shalt *n.* do amiss
12. 10. *n.* trust thine enemy, for as iron rusteth
22. 6. stripes and correction of wisdom are *n.* out of
23. 7. keepeth it, shall *n.* be taken in his lips
11. the plague shall *n.* depart from his house
40. 23. a friend and companion *n.* meet amiss
44. 9. who are perished as tho' they had *n.* been
NEW.
1 *Esd.* 5. 52. of the *n.* moons, and of all holy feasts
6. 9. building an house to the Lord, great and *n.*
25. one row of *n.* wood of that country
2 *Esd.* 1. 31. for your *n.* moons have I forsaken
Jud. 8. 6. save the eves of the *n.* moons, and the *n.* moons, and the feasts and solemn days of Israel
16. 2. tune to him a *n.* psalm, exalt him
13. I will sing unto the Lord a *n.* song
Wisd. 7. 27. remaining, she maketh all things *n.*
Eccl. 9. 10. forsake not an old friend, for the *n.* is not comparable to him, a *n.* friend is as *n.* wine
24. 25. as Tygris in the time of the *n.* fruit
36. 6. shew *n.* signs and make strange wonders
1 *Mac.* 4. 47. they built a *n.* altar as the former
49. they made also *n.* holy vessels, and brought
53. offered on the *n.* altar of burnt offering
2 *Mac.* 2. 29. as the master-builder of a *n.* house
4. 11. he brought up *n.* customs against the law
NEWLY.
Jud. 4. 3. were *n.* returned from the captivity
Wisd. 11. 18. O beasts full of rage, *n.* created
2 *Mac.* 10. 28. the sun being *n.* risen, they joined
NEWS.
2 *Mac.* 9. 3. *n.* was brought what had happened
NEXT.
1 *Esd.* 3. 7. he shall sit *n.* to Darius for his wisdom
Tob. 1. 22. Sarchedonus appointed him *n.* to him
Jud. 2. 4. called Holofernes, who was *n.* to him
Esth. 13. 6. who is over the affairs, and is *n.* to us
16. 11. honoured as the *n.* person unto the king
2 *Mac.* 4. 41. taking handfuls of dust that was *n.*
NICANOR.
1 *Mac.* 3. 38. chose N. and Gorgias, mighty men
7. 26. then the king sent N. one of his princes
27. so N. came to Jerusalem with a great force
44. when N. host saw that he was slain, they fled
2 *Mac.* 8. 9. then choosing N. son of Patroclus
14. being sold by the wicked N. before they met
34. as for that most ungracious N. who brought
12. 2. N. governor of Cyprus would not suffer them
14. 12. calling N. who had been master of elephants
14. then the heathen came to N. by flocks
30. when Maccabeus saw that N. began to be churlish to him, he withdrew himself from N.
15. 6. so N. determined to set up a monument
28. they knew that N. lay dead in his harness
30. Judas comanded to strike off N. head
32. he shewed them vile N. head and the hand
33. he had cut out the tongue of ungodly N.
35. he hanged also N. head on the tower
37. thus went it with N. and from that time
NIGGARD.
Eccl. 14. 3. riches are not comely for a *n.*
10. a wicked eye is a *n.* at his table
31. 24. against a *n.* the city shall murmur
NIGGARDNESS.
Eccl. 31. 24. testimonies of his *n.* not be doubted
NIGH.
Eccl. 12. 13. or any such as come *n.* wild beasts
14. 25. he shall pitch his tent *n.* to her
35. 17. till it come *n.* he will not be comforted
NIGHT.
1 *Esd.* 1. 14. the priests offered fat until *n.*
Tob. 8. 9. so they slept both that *n.*
Jud. 6. 21. called on the God of Israel all that *n*
7. 5. they remained and watched all that *n.*
8. 33. you shall stand this *n.* in the gate
11. 3. thou shalt live this *n.* and hereafter
5. I will declare no lie to my lord this *n.*
17. is religious, and serveth G. of heaven day and *n.* thy servant will go out by *n.* to the valley
13. 14. destroyed our enemies by my hands this *n.*
Wisd. 7. 30. for after this cometh *n.*
10. 17. and a light of stars in the *n.* season
17. 2. and fettered with the bonds of a long *n.*
5. nor stars endure to lighten that horrible *n.*
14. but they sleeping the same sleep that *n.*
21. over them only was spread an heavy *n.*
18. 6. of that *n.* were our fathers certified
14. that *n.* was in the midst of her swift course
Eccl. 36. 26. lodges wherever the *n.* taketh him
38. 27. every carpenter that laboureth *n.* and day
40. 5. his *n.* sleep doth change his knowledge
Bar. 2. 25. they are cast out to the frosts of the *n.*
Bel 15. in the *n.* came the priests with wives
1 *Mac.* 4. 5. in the mean season came Gorgias by *n.*
5. 29. from whence he removed by *n.* and went
9. 13. the battle continued from morning till *n.*
58. Bacchides, who shall take them all in one *n.*
16. 4. who went out and rested that *n.* in Modin
2 *Mac.* 8. 7. specially took he advantage of the *n.*
12. 6. he came and burnt the haven by *n.*
13. 10. commanded to call on the Lord *n.* and day
15. he went into the king's tent by *n.* and slew
NIGHTS.
Tob. 10. 7. she ceased not whole *n.* to bewail
Dan. 3. 47. O ye *n.* and days, bless ye the Lord
NINE.
2 *Esd.* 4. 40. she hath fulfilled her *n.* months
8. 8. *n.* months doth thy workmanship endure
Eccl. 25. 7. there be *n.* things I have judged happy
2 *Mac.* 5. 27. but Judas with *n.* others withdrew
7. 27. that bare thee *n.* months in my womb
12. 10. when gone from thence *n.* furlongs
NINEVE.
Tob. 1. 3. my brethren, who came with me to N.
10. when we were carried away captives to N.
17. or if I saw any cast about the walls of N.
22. Achiacharus entreating, I returned to N.
7. 3. of Nephthali, which are captives in N.
11. 1. went on his way till they drew near to N.

Tob. 14. 4. which Jonas the prophet spake of N.
8. now, my son, depart not out of N. because
10. bury me decently, but tarry no longer at N.
15. but he heard of the destruction of N.
Jud. 1. 1. who reigned in N. the great city
16. so he returned afterward to N.

NOAH.

2 Esd. 3. 11. thou leftest N. with his household
Eccl. 44. 17. N. was found perfect and righteous

NOBILITY.

Wisd. 8. 3. she magnified her n. the Lord loved her
Eccl. 22. 10. children do stain the n. of her kindred

NOBLE.

Eccl. 10. 22. whether he be rich, n. or poor
18. 4. and who shall find out his n. acts?
1 Mac. 3. 32. so he left Lysias a n. man to oversee
8. 2. their wars and n. acts which they had done
2 Mac. 6. 31. death for an example of n. courage
12. 42. besides, n. Judas exhorted the people
14. 42. otherwise than beseemed his n. birth

NOBLES.

1 Esd. 1. 38. and he bound Joacim and the n.
8. 26. hath honoured me in the sight of king, and n.
Jud. 2. 2. so he called unto him all his n.
Bar. 1. 4. in the hearing of the n. and elders

NOBLEST.

Wisd. 18. 12. the n. offspring was destroyed

NOE.

Tob. 4. 12. we are the children of N. Abraham

NOISE.

1 Esd. 5. 66. came to know what the n. should mean
2 Esd. 5. 7. the sea shall make a n. in the night
Jud. 14. 9. the people made a joyful n. in their city
19. there was a great n. throughout their camp
Esth. 11. 5. behold, a n. of tumult with thunder
Wisd. 1. 10. the n. of murmurings is not hid
5. 11. parted with the violent n. and motion
17. 18. or a melodious n. of birds among branches
18. 10. a lamentable n. was carried abroad
Eccl. 38. 28. the n. of the hammer is ever in his ears
40. 13. the goods of the unjust shall vanish with n.
43. 17. the n. of thunder makes the earth tremble
45. 9. there might be a sound and a n. made, that might be heard in the temple for a memorial
46. 17. with a great n. made his voice to be heard
50. 16. the sons of A. made a great n. to be heard
1 Mac. 9. 13. the earth shook at the n. of the armies
41. the n. of their melody into lamentation

NOISED.

Jud. 10. 18. her coming was n. among the tents

NOISES.

Wisd. 17. 4. but n. as of waters falling down, sounded

NOISOME.

2 Mac. 9. 9. his smell was n. to all his army

NONE.

Jud. 6. 4. n. of my words shall be in vain, 9.
9. 14. there is n. other that protecteth Israel
16. 14. there is n. that can resist thy voice
Eccl. 11. 28. judge n. blessed before his death
36. 10. that say, that there is n. other but me
39. 17. n. may say, what is this? why is that?
18. and n. can hinder when he will save
44. 19. in glory was there n. like unto him
45. 13. before him there was n. such
51. 7. I looked for succour, but there was n.
Bar. 3. 23. n. of these have known way of wisdom
25. great, and hath n. end, high, unmeasurable
6. 73. better is the just man that hath n. idols
Bel 41. and there is n. other besides thee
1 Mac. 3. 45. n. of her children went in or out
7. 17. bloodshed, and there was n. to bury them
8. 14. yet for all this n. of them wore a crown
14. 12. sat under his vine, there was n. to fray them
2 Mac. 5. 10. he had n. to mourn for him

NORTH.

2 Esd. 15. 34. clouds from the n. to the south
Jud. 16. 4. out of the mountains from the n.

NORTHERN.

Eccl. 43. 17. so doth the n. storm and whirlwind

NOSES.

Wisd. 15. 15. which have not n. to draw breath

NOSTRILS.

Wisd. 2. 2. for the breath in our n. is as smoke

NOTABLE.

2 Mac. 3. 26. two other young men n. in strength
6. 28. leave a n. example to such as be young
14. 33. and I will erect a n. temple to Bacchus

NOTABLY.

2 Mac. 14. 31. he was n. prevented by Judas' policy

NOTES.

Wisd. 19. 18. as n. change the name of the tune

NOMADES.

2 Mac. 12. 11. the N. of Arabia being overcome

NOTHING.

1 Esd. 8. 7. he omitted n. of the law of the Lord
9. 51. and send part to them that have n.
54. they went to give part to them that had n.
2 Esd. 5. 12. then shall men hope, but n. obtain
Tob. 4. 17. but give n. to the wicked
10. 5. now I care for n. my son, since I let thee go
12. 11. surely I will keep close n. from you
Esth. 10. 5. a dream, and n. thereof hath failed
14. 11. give not thy sceptre to them that be n.
Wisd. 2. 11. what feeble is found to be n. worth
4. 5. the fruit not ripe to eat, yea, meet for n.
7. 8. I esteemed riches n. in comparison of her
8. 7. men can have n. more profitable in their lives
9. 6. without wisdom he shall be n. regarded
11. 24. thou abhorrest n. which thou hast made
13. 10. resemblances of beasts, or a stone good for n.
17. 12. fear is n. but a betraying of succours
Eccl. 6. 15. n. doth countervail a faithful friend
8. 16. for blood is as n. in his sight
10. 6. do n. at all by injurious practices
13. 4. but if thou have n. he will forsake thee
18. 6. works of L. there may be n. taken from them
22. let n. hinder thee to pay thy vow in time
20. 23. and maketh him his enemy for n.
23. 27. n. better than the fear of the Lord, and n. is sweeter than to take heed to commandments
26. 14 n. so much worth as a mind well instructed
32. 19. do n. without advice, then repent not

Eccl. 33. 29. and without discretion do n.
39. 19. and n. can be hid from his eyes
20. and there is n. wonderful before him
40. 6. a little or n. is his rest, and he is in sleep
7. awaketh, and marvelleth that the fear was n.
41. 1. unto the man that hath n. to vex him
42. 21. to him may n. be added, nor diminished
24. and he hath made n. imperfect
Bar. 6. 17. a vessel is n. worth when it is broken
26. they declare to men that they be n. worth
28. but to the poor they give n. of it
70. for as a scarecrow in a garden keepeth n.
1 Mac. 2. 63. and his thought is come to n.
2 Mac. 4. 25. bringing n. worthy the priesthood
7. 12. so that he n. regarded the pains
9. 7. howbeit, he n. ceased from his bragging
12. 4. to live in peace, and suspecting n.
14. 35. O Lord of all things, who hast need of n.

NOUGHT.

1 Esd. 1. 56. till they had brought them all to n.
2 Esd. 2. 33. when I came to them, they set me at n.
8. 59. it was not his will men should come to n.
Jud. 4. 1. spoiled temples, and brought them to n.
13. 17. brought to n. the enemies of thy people
Esth. 13. 15. their eyes are on us to bring us to n.
Wisd. 1. 11. no word so secret that shall go for n.
16. they consumed to n. and made a covenant
Eccl. 40. 14. so shall transgressors come to n.
47. 7. he brought to n. the Philistines his adversaries

NOURISH.

2 Esd. 2. 25. n. thy children, O thou good nurse
Tob. 2. 10. moreover Achiacharus did n. me
Eccl. 28. 5. if he that is but flesh n. hatred
Bar. 4. 11. with joy did I n. them, but sent them
1 Mac. 6. 15. he should n. him up for the kingdom
2 Mac. 10. 15. they went about to n. war

NOURISHED.

1 Esd. 4. 16. they n. them that planted vineyards
2 Esd. 8. 11 that the thing fashioned may be n.
9. 46. and I n. him with a great travel
Jud. 5. 10. while they were n. and became a multitude
Wisd. 16. 23. that the righteous might be n.
2 Mac. 7. 27. gave thee suck three years, and n. thee
10. 14. he n. war continually with the Jews

NOURISHETH.

Wisd. 16. 25. was obedient to thy grace that n.
26. it is not the growing of fruits that n. a man
Eccl. 17. 18. his first-born he n. with discipline

NUMBER.

1 Esd. 2. 9. with many free gifts of a great n.
13. this was the n. of them, 1000 golden cups
8. 63. all was delivered them by n. and weight
2 Esd. 2. 38. behold the n. of those that be sealed
3. 7. came tribes, people, and kindreds, out of n.
29. when I had seen impieties without n.
4. 37. by n. hath he numbered the times
16. 56. and he knoweth the n. of them
Jud. 2. 20. for the multitude was without n.
5. 10. so that one could not n. their nation
Wisd. 4. 8. nor that is measured by n. of years
11. 20. all things in measure, and n. and weight
Eccl. 1. 2. who can n. the sand of the sea?
7. 16. n. not thyself among the multitude of sinners
16. 17. among such an infinite n. of creatures
18. 5. who shall n. the strength of his majesty?
9. the n. of a man's days at most are 100 years
38. 29. who maketh all his work by n.
42. 7. deliver all things in n. and weight
45. 11. after the n. of the tribes of Israel
48. 2. and by his zeal he diminished their n.
Bar. 2. 29. multitude shall be turned into a small n.
Prayer of Manass. seemed above n. of sands of sea

NUMBERED.

Wisd. 5. 5. how is he n. among the children of God!
Eccl. 1. 9. he created her, and saw her, and n. her
37. 25. the days of the life of man may be n.

NUMENIUS.

1 Mac. 12. 16. we chose N. the son of Antiochus

NURSE.

2 Esd. 1. 28. prayed you, as a n. her young babes
2. 25. O thou good n. stablish their feet

NURSED.

Wisd. 7. 4. I was n. in swaddling clothes
Bar. 4. 8. ye have grieved Jerusalem that n. you

NURTURE.

Wisd. 3. 11. whoso despiseth n. he is miserable
Eccl. 22. 10. haughty through disdain an. I want of n.

NURTURED.

Eccl. 21. 23. he that is well n. will stand without
22. 3. an evil n. son is the dishonour of his father
31. 19. a little is sufficient for a man well n.
40. 29. a wise man well n. will beware thereof

NURTUREDST.

2 Esd. 8. 12. thou n. it in thy law, and reformedst it

NURTURETH.

Eccl. 18. 13. he reproveth, and n. and teacheth

O.

OATH.

1 Esd. 8. 93. let us make an o. to the Lord
96. Esdras took an o. of the chief of the priests
Tob. 8. 20. Raguel had said to him by an o.
Jud. 8. 11. touching this o. which ye made
30. compelled us to bring an o. on ourselves
Eccl. 44. 21. therefore he assured him by an o.
Bar. 2. 34. the land which I promised with an o.
1 Mac. 6. 61. the princes made an o. to them
62. but he brake his o. that he had made
7. 18. for they have broken the covenant and o.
2 Mac. 14. 33. and he made an o. in this manner

OATHS.

Wisd. 18. 6. to what o. they had given credence
22. alleging o. and covenants made with fathers
2 Mac. 4. 34. who gave him his right hand with o.
7. 24. but also he assured him with o.
15. 10. shewing him the breach of o.

OBEDIENT.

2 Esd. 1. 8. for they have not been o. to my law
Wisd. 16 25. it was o. to thy grace that nourisheth
Eccl. 3. 6. he that is o. unto the Lord shall be

Eccl. 33. 28. if he be not o. put on more heavy fetters
42. 23. for all uses, and they are all o.
Bar. 2. 5. we have not been o. to his voice
6. 60. being sent to do their offices, are o.

OBEY.

1 Esd. 4. 10. all his people and armies o. him
5. 69. for we likewise, as you do, o. your Lord
8. 94. as many as do o. the law of the Lord
2 Esd. 1. 24. thou Judah wouldst not o. me
Jud. 2. 3. all that did not o. the commandment
Eccl. 18. 3. gov. the world, and all things o. his will
2 Mac. 7. 30. I will not o. the king's commandment

OBEYED.

1 Esd. 4. 12. be mightiest, when in such sort he is o.

OBEYETH.

Eccl. 24. 22. that o. me shall never be confounded
Bar. 3. 33. calleth it, and it o. him with fear

OBJECTETH.

Wisd. 2. 12. o. to our infamy the transgressings

OBLATION.

Dan. 3. 15. nor is there at this time o. or incense

OBLATIONS.

1 Esd. 5. 52. and after that the continual o.
Eccl. 7. 9. God will look on the multitude of my o.
50. 13. and the o. of the Lord in their hands
1 Mac. 15. 5. how I confirm to thee all the o.

OBSCURE.

Wisd. 4. 12. doth o. things that are honest

OBSCURITY.

Esth. 11. 8. and lo, a day of darkness and o.

OBSERVE.

2 Esd. 7. 21. they should o. to avoid punishment
Eccl. 4. 20. o. the opportunity and beware of evil
13. 13. o. and take heed, for thou walkest in peril
18. 27. a wise man will fear, but a fool will not o.
27. 12. if among the indiscreet, o. the time
1 Mac. 2. 67. take all those that o. the law
2 Mac. 6. 8. that they should o. the same fashions

OBSERVED.

2 Esd. 9. 32. our fathers o. not thy ordinances
Eccl. 19. 9. he heard and o. thee and will hate

OBTAIN.

2 Esd. 4. 24. and we are not worthy to o. mercy
5. 12. then shall men hope, but nothing o.
14. 34. and after death ye shall o. mercy
Wisd. 8. 13. by means of her o. immortality
21. perceived that I could not o. her
Eccl. 11. 10. thou shalt not o. nor escape by fleeing
15. 1. that hath knowledge of the law shall o. her
1 Mac. 2. 64. for by it shall you o. glory

OBTAINED.

1 Esd. 6. 5. the elders of the Jews o. favour
Esth. 16. 11. Aman had so far forth o. favour
Eccl. 46. 9. and his seed o. it for an heritage
1 Mac. 2. 54. o. the covenant of everlasting priesthood
15. 9. when we have o. our kingdom we will honour
2 Mac. 5. 7. howbeit he o. not the principality
15. 5. he o. not to have his wicked will done

OBTAINETH.

Eccl. 19. 18. and wisdom o. the love of God

OBTAINING.

Eccl. 10. 21. fear of Lord goeth before o. of authority

OCCASION.

Wisd. 14. 21. this was an o. to deceive the world
Eccl. 4. 5. and give him none o. to curse thee
23. refrain not when there is o. to do good

OCCUPIED.

Eccl. 12. 3. no good to him that is always o. in evil
38. 25. and that is o. in their labours
39. 1. he that is o. in the meditation of the law of the Most High, will be o. in prophecies
2 Mac. 8. 27. they o. themselves about the sabbath
10. 15. the Idumeans kept the Jews o.

OCCUPIETH.

2 Esd. 16. 42. he that o. merchandise hath no profit

ODIOUS.

Wisd. 12. 4. thou hatedst it for doing most o. works

ODOLLAM.

2 Mac. 12. 38. so Judas came into the city O.

ODOUR.

Eccl. 24. 15. I yielded a pleasant o. like myrrh

ODOURS.

2 Esd. 6. 44. there were o. of wonderful smell

OFFENCE.

Jud. 12. 2. I will not eat thereof, lest there be o.
Wisd. 14. 31. that punisheth the o. of the ungodly
Eccl. 18. 27. a wise man will beware of o.
19. 8. if thou canst without o. reveal them not
23. 11. acknowledge not, he maketh a double o.
30. 13. lest his lewd behaviour be an o. to thee
41. 18. of an o. before a judge and ruler
1 Mac. 5. 4. who had been an o. unto the people

OFFENCES.

Prayer of Manass. and I have multiplied o.

OFFEND.

Wisd. 12. 2. therefore chastenest thou them that o.
15. 13. knoweth himself to o. above all others
Eccl. 7. 7. o. not against the multitude of a city
17. 25. make thy prayer before his face, and o. less
19. 4. that sinneth shall o. against his own soul
23. 11. if he shall o. his sin shall be upon him
31. 10. who might o. and hath not offended
17. leave off, and be not unsatiable lest thou o.
30. drunkenness increaseth rage of a fool till he o.

OFFENDED.

2 Esd. 12. 41. what have we o. that thou forsakest us?
Wisd. 10. 8. that in the things wherein they o.
12. 2. putting in remembrance wherein they o.
Eccl. 19. 16. who hath not o. with his tongue?
25. 2. and I am greatly o. at their life
31. 10. who might offend and hath not o.?
32. 15. but the hypocrite will be o. thereat

OFFENDETH.

Bar. 6. 14. that cannot put to death one that o. him

OFFENDING.

Wisd. 2. 12. he upbraideth us with our o. the law

OFFER.

1 Esd. 1. 6. o. the passover in order and make ready
9. 20. and to o. rams to make reconcilement
Eccl. 7. 9. when I o. to God, he will accept it
Bar. 1. 10. prepare ye manna, and o. on the altar
2 Mac. 4. 40. he began first to o. violence

2 *Mac.* 7. 37. but I *o.* up my body and life for the laws
12. 43. he sent it to Jerusalem to *o.* a sin-offering

OFFERED.

Tob. 5. 13. we *o.* the first-born and tenths of fruits
Eccl. 46. 16. when he *o.* the sucking lamb
2 *Mac.* 1. 18. given us when Neemias *o.* sacrifice
3. 32. *o.* a sacrifice for the health of the man
10. 3. they *o.* a sacrifice after two years

OFFERETH.

Wisd. 17. 12. fear betraying the succours reason *o.*
Eccl. 35. 1. he that taketh heed *o.* a peace-offering
2. he that requiteth a good turn *o.* fine flour

OFFERING.

2 *Esd.* 10. 45. wherein there was no *o.* made in her
Eccl. 14. 11. my son, give the Lord his due *o.*
30. 19. what good doeth the *o.* to an idol!
34. 18. a thing wrongfully gotten, his *o.* is ridiculous
20. whoso brings an *o.* of the goods of the poor
35. 6. *o.* of the righteous maketh the altar fat
50. 14. that he might adorn the *o.* of Most High
2 *Mac.* 4. 24. *o.* more than Jason by 300 talents
14. 31. the priests that were *o.* usual sacrifices

OFFERINGS.

1 *Esd.* 6. 31. that *o.* may be made to the most high G.
2 *Esd.* 10. 46. Solomon builded the city, and offered *o.*
Jud. 16. 18. they offered their burnt-*o.* and gifts
Eccl. 34. 19. is not pleased with the *o.* of the wicked
35. 1. he that keepeth the law, brings *o.* enough

OFFICE.

1 *Esd.* 5. 38. priests that usurped *o.* of the priesthood
Eccl. 32. 2. when done all thy *o.* take thy place
45. 15. should execute the *o.* of the priesthood

OFFICES.

Bar. 6. 60. being sent to do their *o.* are obedient

OFFICERS.

Eccl. 10. 2. as the judge is himself, so are his *o.*
1 *Mac.* 10. 33. I will that all my *o.* remit tributes
41. all the overplus which the *o.* paid not in
13. 37. to write to our *o.* to confirm immunities

OIL.

1 *Esd.* 6. 30. and also corn, salt, wine, and *o.*
Jud. 10. 5. then she gave her maid a cruse of *o.*
11. 13. resolved to spend the tenths of wine and *o.*
Eccl. 39. 26. the blood of the grape, *o.* and clothing
45. 15. Moses anointed him with holy *o.*
Sus. 17. she said, bring me *o.* and washing-balls

OINTMENT, S.

2 *Esd.* 2. 12. they shall have the tree of life for an *o.*
Jud. 10. 3. she anointed herself with precious *o.*
Wisd. 2. 7. let us fill ourselves with costly wine and *o.*

OLD.

Tob. 3. 10. I shall bring his *o.* age with sorrow to gr.
14. 13. where he became *o.* with honour
Jud. 16. 23. she waxed *o.* in her husband's house
Esth. 13. 7. who of *o.* and now are malicious
Wisd. 4. 16. the years and *o.* age of the unrighteous
8. 8. she knoweth things of *o.* and conjectureth
12. 3. those *o.* inhabitants of the holy land
14. 6. for in *o.* time when proud giants perished
Eccl. 2. 10. look at the generations of *o.* and see
6. 18. so shalt thou find wisdom till thine *o.* age
8. 6. dishonour not a man in his *o.* age, for even some of us wax *o.* rejoice not over thy enemy
9. 10. forsake not an *o.* friend, for new is not comparable, when wine is *o.* shalt drink with pleas.
11. 16. evil shall wax *o.* with them that glory in it
20. be stedfast in covenant, and wax *o.* in thy work
14. 17. all flesh waxeth *o.* as a garment
16. 7. he was no. pacified towards the *o.* giants
25. 2. I hate an *o.* adulterer that doeth
51. 8. then thought I upon thy acts of *o.*
Bar. 3. 10. that thou art waxen *o.* in a strange country
Sus. 52. O thou that art waxen *o.* in wickedness
1 *Mac.* 3. 29. the laws which had been of *o.* time
15. 3. that I may restore it to the *o.* estate
17. to renew the *o.* friendship and league
16. 3. but now I am *o.* and ye are of a sufficient age
2 *Mac.* 5. 13. there was killing of young and *o.*
6. 21. for the *o.* acquaintance they had with the man
22. for the *o.* friendship with them, find favour

OLIVE.

Jud. 15. 13. they put a garland of *o.* upon her

OLIVE-TREE.

Eccl. 50. 10. as a fair *o.-tree* budding forth fruit

OLIVES.

2 *Esd.* 16. 29. as in an orchard of *o.* on every tree are left three or four *o.* when vineyard gathered

ONE.

Tob. 4. 4. when dead, bury her by me in *o.* grave
6. 10. he also hath *o.* only daughter, named Sara
Esth. 15. 3. upon the *o.* she leaned, as carrying
Wisd. 7. 22. a spirit, holy, *o.* only manifold
11. 20. they have fallen down with *o.* blast
Eccl. 1. 8. there is O. wise and greatly to be feared
6. 6. have but *o.* counsellor of a thousand
7. 8. bind not *o.* sin upon another, for in *o.* thou shalt not be unpunished
16. 3. *o.* that is just is better than a thousand
46. 4. and was not *o.* day as long as two?
Dan. 3. 28. the three, as out of *o.* mouth, praised G.
Sus. 52. he called *o.* of them and said unto him
1 *Mac.* 3. 32. he left *o.* of the blood royal to oversee
4. 11. may know that there is O. that delivereth
8. 16. they committed their government to *o.* man every year, and all were obedient to that *o.*
9. 58. who shall take them all in *o.* night
2 *Mac.* 1. 5. hear prayers, and be at *o.* with you
7. 2. but *o.* of them that spake first, said thus
20. saw her seven sons slain in the space of *o.* day
21. yea, she exhorted every *o.* of them

ONIAS.

2 *Mac.* 3. 1. laws kept because of the godliness of O.
5. when he could not overcome O.
4. 1. Simon slandered O. as if he terrified Heliod.
4. O. seeing the danger of this contention
34. he prayed him to get O. into his hands
36. because O. was slain without cause
15. 14. then O. answered, saying, this is a lover

ONYX.

Eccl. 24. 15. I yielded a pleasant odour like *o.*

OPEN.

1 *Esd.* 4. 31. the king gaped on her with *o.* mouth
Tob. 2. 10. my eyes being *o.* the sparrows muted
6. 4. *o.* the fish, and take the heart and the liver
11. 7. I know that thy father will *o.* his eyes
Jud. 4. 6. toward the *o.* country near Dothaim
10. 9. they commanded the young men to *o.* to her
11. 19. a dog shall not so much as *o.* his mouth
13. 11. *o. o.* now the gate, our God is with us
Esth. 14. 10. *o.* the mouths of the heathen
Eccl. 8. 19. and *o.* not thine heart to every man
15. 5. in the midst of congreg. shall she *o.* his mouth
29. 24. a stranger, thou darest not *o.* thy mouth
39. 5. and he will *o.* his mouth in prayer
Bar. 2. 6. but to us and our fathers *o.* shame
17. *o.* thine eyes and behold; for the dead
Dan. 3. 10. and now we cannot *o.* our mouths
1 *Mac.* 3. 48. and they laid *o.* the book of the law
5. 48. howbeit they could not *o.* unto him
2 *Mac.* 1. 4. God *o.* your hearts in his law
6. 18. Eleazar was constrained to *o.* his mouth

OPENED.

1 *Esd.* 9. 46. when he *o.* the law they stood all up
2 *Esd.* 6. 20. books shall be *o.* before the firmament
8. 52. for unto you is paradise *o.* tree of life planted
9. 28. I *o.* my mouth, and began to talk before God
Tob. 8. 13. so the maid *o.* the door and went in
Jud. 10. 9. the gates of the city to be *o.* to me
Eccl. 43. 14. through this the treasures are *o.*
51. 25. I *o.* my mouth and said, buy her for yours.
Sus. 25. then ran the one and *o.* the garden door
2 *Mac.* 12. 41. who had *o.* the things that were hid

OPENETH.

Eccl. 20. 15. he *o.* his mouth like a crier
40. 14. while he *o.* his hand he shall rejoice

OPENLY.

Eccl. 51. 13. I desired wisdom *o.* in my prayer

OPERATION.

Wisd. 7. 17. to know the *o.* of the elements

OPERATIONS.

Eccl. 17. 5. they received the use of the five *o.*

OPHIR. *See* GOLD.

OPINION.

Eccl. 3. 24. are deceived by their own vain *o.*

OPPORTUNITY.

Eccl. 4. 20. observe the *o.* and beware of evil
12. 16. if he find *o.* he will not be satisfied
19. 28. yet when he findeth *o.* he will do evil
20. 7. a wise man will hold his tongue till he see *o.*
38. 24. the wisdom of a learned man cometh by *o.*
1 *Mac.* 11. 42. I will honour thy nation, if *o.* serve
15. 34. we having *o.* hold the inheritance

OPPRESS.

Wisd. 2. 10. let us *o.* the poor righteous man
17. 2. unrighteous thought to *o.* the holy nation
Eccl. 36. 9. let them perish that *o.* the people
1 *Mac.* 8. 18. they saw that the Grecians did *o.* Israel
2 *Mac.* 1. 28. punish them that *o.* and do us wrong

OPPRESSED.

Jud. 9. 11. an helper of the *o.* and upholder of weak
16. 8. for the exaltation of those that were *o.*
Wisd. 10. 11. the covetousness of such as *o.* him
Eccl. 35. 13. he will hear the prayer of the *o.*

OPPRESSOR.

Eccl. 4. 9. him that suffereth wrong from the *o.*

OPPROBRIOUS.

Eccl. 23. 15. the man that is accustomed to *o.* words

ORACLE.

Eccl. 33. 3. the law is faithful to him as an *o.*

ORACLES.

Eccl. 36. 14. fill Sion with thine unspeakable *o.*

ORCHARD.

2 *Esd.* 16. 29. as in an *o.* of olives, on every tree

ORDAIN.

1 *Esd.* 8. 23. *o.* judges and justices in all Syria
2 *Esd.* 6. 49. thou didst *o.* two living creatures
Tob. 8. 7. mercifully *o.* that we may become aged
1 *Mac.* 10. 20. this day we *o.* thee to be high priest

ORDAINED.

1 *Esd.* 6. 34. I Darius the king have *o.* it be done
8. 49. the servants of the temple whom David *o.*
2 *Esd.* 7. 17. O Lord, thou hast *o.* in thy law
8. 14. it is an easy thing to be *o.* by commandment
Tob. 1. 6. as it was *o.* to all the people of Israel
Esth. 13. 6. by Aman who is *o.* over the affairs
14. 9. they will abolish the thing thou hast *o.*
Wisd. 9. 2. *o.* man thro' thy wisdom to have dominion
Eccl. 7. 15. husbandry which the Most High hath *o.*
48. 10. who wast *o.* for reproofs in their times
1 *Mac.* 3. 55. Judas *o.* captains over the people
4. 59. *o.* that the days of the dedication be kept
7. 49. moreover, they *o.* to keep yearly this day

ORDER.

1 *Esd.* 1. 6. offer the passover in *o.* and make ready
10. the priests and Levites stood in comely *o.*
15. the sons of Asaph were in their *o.*
8. 10. I have given *o.* that such of the nation
2 *Esd.* 6. 45. and the stars should be in *o.*
13. 26. he shall *o.* them that are left behind
14. 13. now therefore set thine house in *o.*
Wisd. 7. 29. she is above all the *o.* of stars
8. 14. I shall set the people in *o.* and nations
9. 3. *o.* the world according to equity and righteous.
Eccl. 2. 6. *o.* thy way aright, and trust in him
38. 10. *o.* thy hands aright, and cleanse thy heart
43. 10. they will stand in their *o.* and never faint
47. 10. and he set in *o.* the solemn times
1 *Mac.* 6. 40. they marched on safely and in *o.*
9. 55. nor could give *o.* concerning his house
2 *Mac.* 3. 14. he entered in to *o.* this matter
4. 27. as for the money he took no good *o.* for it
7. 8. he received also the next torment in *o.*

ORDERED.

Wisd. 11. 20. but thou hast *o.* all things in measure
Eccl. 10. 1. government of a prudent man is well *o.*

ORDEREST.

Wisd. 12. 15. thou *o.* all things righteously

ORDERING.

Wisd. 15. 1. gracious, and in mercy *o.* all things
Eccl. 26. 16. a good wife in the *o.* of her house
32. 2. receive thy crown for thy well *o.* of the feast
1 *Mac.* 16. 14. taking care for the good *o.* of them

ORDINANCES.

Eccl. 6. 37. let thy mind be upon the *o.* of the Lord
Bar. 2. 12. we have dealt unrighteously in all thy *o.*
1 *Mac.* 1. 13. gave them licence to do after the *o.*
2. 21. God forbid that we should forsake the *o.*

ORDINARY.

1 *Esd.* 1. 16. not lawful for any to go from his *o.* serv.
Eccl. 33. 9. some of them hath he made *o.* days

OREB.

2 *Esd.* 2. 33. a charge of the Lord on mount O.

ORNAMENT.

Eccl. 6. 30. for there is a golden *o.* upon her
21. 21. learning is to a wise man as an *o.* of gold
43. 9. an *o.* giving light in the highest places
45. 12. an *o.* of honour, a costly work
Prayer of Manass. made earth with all *o.* thereof

ORNAMENTS.

Jud. 10. 4. and she put about her all her *o.*
Eccl. 45. 7. he beautified him with comely *o.*
1 *Mac.* 1. 22. the golden *o.* before the temple
2. 11. all her *o.* are taken away, is a bond-slave
2 *Mac.* 2. 2. images of silver and gold with their *o.*
5. 3. there was seen glittering of golden *o.*

ORPHAN.

2 *Esd.* 2. 20. defend the *o.* clothe the naked
Tob. 1. 8. because I was left an *o.* by my father

ORPHANS.

2 *Mac.* 8. 28. had given spoils to the maimed and *o.*

OSEA.

2 *Esd.* 13. 40. carried in the time of O. the king

OSEAS.

2 *Esd.* 1. 39. I will give for leaders, O. Amoz

OVEN.

2 *Esd.* 4. 48. behold, an hot burning *o.* passed by
Dan. 3. 23. servants ceased not to make the *o.* hot
26. the angel of the Lord came down into the *o.* and smote the flame of the fire out of the *o.*

OVERCAME.

2 *Esd.* 11. 40. the fourth came and *o.* all beasts
Wisd. 16. 10. not the teeth of venomous dragons *o.*
18. 22. so he *o.* the destroyer, not with strength
2 *Mac.* 2. 21. being few they *o.* the whole country

OVERCOME.

1 *Esd.* 3. 5. let every one speak, he that shall *o.*
2 *Esd.* 3. 21. the first Adam was *o.* and so be all
6. 28. corruption shall be *o.* and truth be declared
7. 58. if he be *o.* he shall suffer as thou hast said
13. 34. willing to come and *o.* him by fighting
Jud. 5. 20. let us go up, and we shall *o.* them
Wisd. 2. 4. and *o.* with the heat thereof
Eccl. 48. 13. no word could *o.* him
1 *Mac.* 2. 61. none that trust in him shall be *o.*
2 *Mac.* 11. 13. that the Hebrews could not be *o.*
12. 11. so that the Nomades of Arabia being *o.*

OVERFLOW.

Jud. 2. 8. be filled with their dead till it *o.*

OVERLAID.

Bar. 6. 39. their gods of wood, which are *o.* 50.

OVERMASTER.

Eccl. 12. 5. give it not, lest he *o.* thee thereby

OVERMUCH.

Eccl. 26. 10. lest she abuse herself through *o.* liberty

OVERPASS.

Eccl. 14. 14. let not part of a good desire *o.* thee

OVERPLUS.

1 *Mac.* 10. 41. all the *o.* which officers paid not

OVERSEE.

1 *Esd.* 7. 2. did very carefully *o.* the holy works
1 *Mac.* 3. 32. he left Lysias to *o.* the affairs

OVERSEEING.

Jud. 8. 3. as he stood *o.* them that bound sheaves
Wisd. 7. 23. having all power, *o.* all things

OVERSEER.

Tob. 1. 22. Achiacharus was *o.* of the accounts

OVERSEERS.

1 *Mac.* 1. 51. he appointed *o.* over the people
10. 37. I will that their *o.* be of themselves

OVERSHADOW.

Bar. 5. 8. every sweet smelling tree shall *o.* Israel

OVERSIGHT.

1 *Mac.* 13. 39. as for any *o.* or fault committed

OVERTAKEN.

Jud. 11. 11. and their sin hath *o.* them

OVERTHREW.

Eccl. 10. 16. the Lord *o.* countries of the heathen

OVERTHROW.

Wisd. 5. 23. ill dealings shall *o.* the thrones
Eccl. 8. 16. where there is no help he will *o.* thee
13. 23. if he stumble, they will help to *o.* him
29. 16. a sinner will *o.* the good estate of his surety
1 *Mac.* 3. 22. the Lord himself will *o.* them
5. 3. Judas gave them a great *o.* and abated courage

OVERTHROWING.

Eccl. 13. 13. for thou walkest in peril of thy *o.*

OVERTHROWN.

Tob. 14. 4. Jonah spake of Nineve, that it should be *o.*
Jud. 7. 14. they shall be *o.* in the streets
16. 11. these lifted their voice, but they were *o.*
Eccl. 3. 24. evil suspicion has *o.* their judgment
12. 12. lest when he hath *o.* thee, he stand up
27. 3. his house shall soon be *o.*
28. 14. hath *o.* the houses of great men

OVERTOOK.

1 *Mac.* 12. 30. pursued after them, but *o.* them not

OVERWEIGH.

Eccl. 8. 2. be not at variance with rich, lest he *o.*

OVERWISE.

Eccl. 10. 26. be not *o.* in doing thy business

OUGHTEST.

Eccl. 15. 11. thou *o.* not to do the things he hateth

OURS.

1 *Mac.* 12. 23. we do write back again to you, that your cattle and goods are *o.* and *o.* are yours

OUT-GOINGS.

2 *Esd.* 4. 7. or which are the *o.* of paradise

OUT-ROADS.

1 *Mac.* 15. 41. might make *o.* on the ways of Judea

OUTWARD.

Eccl. 11. 2. nor abhor a man for his *o.* appearance

OWE.

1 *Mac.* 13. 39. the crown-tax also which ye *o.* us

OWING.

1 *Mac.* 13. 15. it is for money he is *o.* to the king
15. 8. if any thing be or shall be *o.* to the king

OWNERS.
Tob. 2. 12. when she had sent them home to the o.
13. is it not stolen? render it to the o.
OX.
Jud. 8. 1. the daughter of Merari, the son of O.

P.

PACIFY.
Eccl. 48. 10. to p. the wrath of the Lord's judgment
2 Mac. 4. 45. if he would p. the king towards him
PACIFIED.
Eccl. 5. 6. he will be p. for multitude of my sins
16. 7. he was not p. towards the old giants
34. 19. neither is he p. for sin by sacrifices
2 Mac. 13. 26. Lysias p. made them well affected
PAIN.
2 Esd. 8. 59. thirst and p. are prepared for them
9. 12. the same must know it after death by p.
12. 26. one shall die on his bed, and yet with p.
Wisd. 10. 9. but wisdom delivered from p. those
Eccl. 31. 20. but the p. of watching and choler
48. 19. they were in p. as women in travail
2 Mac. 7. 36. who have suffered a short p.
9. 5. a p. of the bowels that was remediless
9. whilst he lived in p. his flesh fell away
11. his p. increasing every moment
PAINED.
2 Mac. 9. 7. the members of his body were much p.
PAINS.
Eccl. 11. 11. one that laboureth and taketh p.
38. 7. with such he taketh away their p.
1 Mac. 10. 15. of the p. that they had endured
2 Mac. 2. 27. we will undertake this great p.
6. 30. I endure sore p. in body by being beaten
7. 12. for that he nothing regarded the p.
9. 18. but for all this his p. would not cease
PAINFUL.
2 Esd. 7. 12. they are full of perils and very p.
2 Mac. 2. 26. that have taken upon us this p. labour
PAINT.
1 Mac. 3. 48. to p. the likeness of their images
2 Mac. 2. 29. undertaketh to set it out and p. it
PAINTERS.
Wisd. 15. 4. image spotted, the p. fruitless labour
PALACE.
Esth. 12. 1. two eunuchs, and keepers of the p.
Bar. 6. 59. better be a pillar of wood in a p.
PALATE.
Eccl. 36. 19. as the p. tasteth divers kinds of venison
PALES.
Eccl. 22. 18. p. will never stand against the wind
PALSY.
1 Mac. 9. 55. Alcimus was taken with a p.
PAMPHYLIA.
1 Mac. 15. 23. the same things wrote he to P.
PANGS.
Eccl. 31. 20. p. of the belly with an unsatiable man
PAN.
2 Mac. 7. 5. to be brought and fried in the p.
PANS.
1 Esd. 1. 12. sod in pots and p. with a good savour
2 Mac. 7. 3. the king commanded p. to be made hot
PAPER.
2 Esd. 15. 2. and cause them to be written in p.
Tob. 7. 14. took p. and did write an instrument
PARABLES.
Eccl. 1. 25. the p. of knowledge are in wisdom
6. 35. let not p. of understanding escape thee
13. 26. finding out of p. is a wearisome labour
18. 29. and they poured forth exquisite p.
38. 33. shall not be found where p. are spoken
39. 2. and where subtil p. are, he will be there
3. and he will be conversant in dark p.
47. 15. and thou filledst it with dark p.
17. marvelled at thee for thy songs and p.
PARCHED.
Jud. 10. 5. she filled a bag with p. corn and figs
PARCHETH.
Eccl. 43. 3. at noon it p. the country, who can abide
PARDON.
Wisd. 6. 6. for mercy will soon p. the meanest
12. 11. nor didst for fear of any give them p.
18. 2. they thanked them and besought them p.
Prol. of Jes. to p. us wherein we come short
Eccl. 20. 28. that pleaseth, shall get p. for iniquity
21. 1. do so no more, ask p. for thy former sins
28. 3. and doth he seek p. from the Lord?
5. who will entreat for p. for his sins?
PARDONED.
Wisd. 13. 8. howbeit, neither are they to be p.
PARDONETH.
2 Esd. 7. 68. he p. for if he did not so of goodness
PARENTS.
Wisd. 4. 6. witnesses of wickedness against their p.
12. 6. the p. that killed with their own hands
Eccl. 3. 7. he will do service to his p. as to masters
22. 9. they shall cover the baseness of their p.
Sus. 3. her p. also were righteous, and taught her
1 Mac. 10. 9. he delivered them to their p.
2 Mac. 12. 24. because he had many of the Jews' p.
PART.
Jud. 7. 1. and all his people come to take his p.
Wisd. 1. 16. they are worthy to take p. with it
2. 9. none go without his p. of voluptuousness
Eccl. 44. 23. among the twelve tribes did he p. them
Bar. 6. 28. their wives lay up p. thereof in salt
1 Mac. 2. 10. what nation hath not had a p. in her?
10. 20. we require thee to take our p.
2 Mac. 8. 28. had given p. of spoils to the maimed
PARTAKERS.
Esth. 16. 5. caused many to be p. of innocent blood
Wisd. 16. 3. might be made p. of a strange taste
18. 9. should be p. of the same good and evil
2 Mac. 4. 14. to be p. of the unlawful allowance
5. 27. lest they should be p. of the pollution
PARTED, ETH.
Wisd. 5. 12. or like as when an arrow p. the air
1 Mac. 1. 6. and p. his kingdom among them
PARTS.
Eccl. 16. 26. he disposed the p. thereof
2 Mac. 7. 4. to cut off the utmost p. of his body
9. 5. sore torments of the inner p. came on him
PARTICULARS.
2 Mac. 2. 30. to go over things, and to be curious in p.
11. 20. but of the p. I have given order
PARTLY.
Wisd. 17. 15. were p. vexed with monstrous apparitions, and were p. fainted, their heart failing them
PARTNERS.
Eccl. 42. 3. of reckoning with p. and travellers
PARTRIDGE.
Eccl. 11. 30. as a p. taken and kept in a cage
PASS.
Wisd. 1. 8. neither shall vengeance p. by him
2. 4. our life shall p. as the trace of a cloud
7. and let no flower of the spring p. by us
6. 22. and I will not p. over the truth
Eccl. 23. 2. spare me not, and it p. not by my sins
42. 9. lest she p. away the flower of her age
1 Mac. 5. 40. if Judas p. over first unto us
2 Mac. 15. 36. in no case to let that day p.
PASSABLE.
2 Mac. 5. 21. to make the sea p. by foot
PASSED.
Jud. 16. 9. and the fauchion p. through his neck
Esth. 15. 6. then having p. through all the doors
Wisd. 5. 9. those things are p. away as a shadow
Eccl. 28. hath not p. through the venom thereof
1 Mac. 3. 37. and having p. the river Euphrates
PASSETH.
Wisd. 2. 5. our time is a very shadow that p. away
5. 10. as a ship that p. over the waves of water
14. p. away as the remembrance of a guest
7. 24. wisdom p. and goeth through all things
Eccl. 25. 11. the love of the Lord p. all things
PASSING.
Wisd. 14. 5. and p. the rough sea in a weak vessel
PASSOVER.
1 Esd. 1. 1. Josias held the feast of the p. in Jerusalem, and offered the p. the fourteenth day
12. they roasted the p. with fire, as appertaineth
20. such a p. was not kept in Israel since Samuel
PAST.
2 Esd. 4. 5. or call me again the day that is p.
45. shew me then whether there be more to come than is p. or more p. than is to come
46. what is p. I know, what is to come I know not
9. 1. when thou seest part of the signs p.
Wisd. 11. 12. for the remembrance of things p.
Eccl. 42. 19. he declareth the things that are p.
PASTIME.
Wisd. 15. 12. but they counted our life a p.
Eccl. 32. 12. take thy p. and do what thou wilt
Bar. 3. 17. had their p. with the fowls of the air
PATH.
2 Esd. 14. 22. that men may find thy p. and live
Bar. 3. 31. no man knoweth or thinketh of her p.
PATHS.
Tob. 4. 19. that all thy p. and counsels may prosper
Bar. 3. 21. nor understood they the p. thereof
PATHWAY.
Wisd. 5. 10. nor the p. of the keel in the waves
PATIENCE.
Wisd. 2. 19. examine him with torture and despitefulness, to know his meekness, and prove his p.
Eccl. 2. 14. woe unto you that have lost p.
3. 13. have p. with him, and despise him not
5: 11. be swift to hear, with p. give answer
16. 13. the p. of the godly shall not be frustrate
17. 24. he comforted those that fail in p.
20. 32. necessary p. in seeking the Lord is better
29. 8. have thou p. with a man in poor estate
41. 2. to him that despaireth and hath lost p.
PATIENT.
2 Esd. 7. 64. that he is p. and long suffereth those
Eccl. 1. 23. a p. man will bear for a time
2. 4. be p. when thou art changed to low estate
18. 11. therefore is God p. with them
35. 18. nor will the mighty be p. towards them
PATIENTLY.
Bar. 4. 25. suffer p. the wrath that is come from God
2 Mac. 6. 14. whom the Lord p. forbeareth to punish
PATTERN.
Eccl. 38. 28. his eyes look still upon the p. of thing
PAVEMENT.
Eccl. 20. 18. to slip on a p. is better than to slip with
Bel 19. behold now the p. and mark well
PAY.
Eccl. 18. 22. let nothing hinder thee to p. thy vow
29. 2. p. thou thy neighbour again in season
6. and for honour he will p. him disgrace
1 Mac. 3. 28. he gave his soldiers p. for a year
10. 36. of the Jews, to whom p. shall be given
2 Mac. 8. 10. which the king was to p. to the Romans
PAID.
Tob. 2. 12. they p. her wages, and gave her a kid
1 Mac. 10. 41. all the overplus which officers p. not in
PAYETH.
Eccl. 29. 6. he p. him with cursings and railings
PAYMENTS.
Bar. 3. 8. in our captivity, to be subject to p.
1 Mac. 11. 34. instead of p. which the king received
PEACE.
Tob. 13. 14. for they shall rejoice in thy p.
Jud. 3. 1. they sent ambassadors to treat of p.
7. 24. in that you have not required p. of Assur
Wisd. 3. 3. utter destruction; but they are in p.
14. 22. those so great plagues called they p.
Eccl. 1. 18. making p. and perfect health flourish
13. 18. what p. between the rich and the poor
26. 2. he shall fulfil the years of his life in p.
28. 9. maketh debate among them that be at p.
13. such have destroyed many that were at p.
38. 8. from him is p. over all the earth
41. 14. my children keep discipline in p.
44. 14. their bodies are buried in p. but name lives
47. 16. and for thy p. thou wast beloved
50. 23. that p. may be in our days in Israel
Bar. 3. 13. thou shouldst have dwelt in p. for ever
14. where is the light of the eyes and p.
4. 20. I have put off the clothing of p.
5. 4. for thy name be called the p. of righteousness
1 Mac. 5. 54. until they had returned in p.
6. 49. but with them in Bethsura he made p.
7. 13. the Assideans were the first that sought p.
8. 20. to make a confederacy and p. with you
22. might have a memorial of p. and confederacy
9. 70. to the end he should make p. with him
10. 47. he was the first that entreated of true p.
66. Jonathan returned to Jerusalem with p.
11. 50. grant us p. and let the Jews cease
51. they cast away their weapons and made p.
13. 37. we are ready to make a stedfast p. with you
40. and let there be p. betwixt us
14. 8. then did they till their ground in p.
11. he made p. in the land, and Israel rejoiced
16. 10. he returned into the land of Judea in p.
2 Mac. 3. 1. the city was inhabited with all p.
5. 25. coming to Jerusalem, and pretending p.
10. 12. endeavoured to continue p. with them
12. 2. would not suffer them to live in p.
4. accepted it, as being desirous to live in p.
11. being overcome, besought Judas for p.
14. 6. Assideans will not let the realm be in p.
PEACEABLE.
2 Esd. 11. 42. thou hast hurt the p. and loved liars
Esth. 16. 8. that our kingdom may be quiet and p.
Eccl. 47. 13. Solomon reigned in a p. time
1 Mac. 1. 30. and spake p. words to them
5. 25. Nabathites came unto them in p. manner
2 Mac. 14. 22. so they made a p. conference
PEACEABLY.
Jud. 7. 15. because they met not thy person p.
Eccl. 44. 6. living p. in their habitations
Bar. 6. 3. I will bring you away p. from thence
1 Mac. 7. 15. so he spake unto them p. and sware
29. came to Judas, they saluted one another p.
12. 4. they should bring them into the land p.
PEACE-OFFERING.
Eccl. 35. 1. that taketh heed offereth a p.-offering
47. 2. as is the fat taken from the p.-offering
PEEP.
Eccl. 21. 23. a fool will p. in at the door into house
PENALTY.
1 Esd. 8. 24. by p. of money, or by imprisonment
PENSIONS.
1 Esd. 4. 56. to give to all that kept the city p.
PENTECOST.
Tob. 2. 1. in the feast of p. which is the holy feast
2 Mac. 12. 32. after the feast called p. they went
PENURY.
Wisd. 16. 3. these sufferings p. in a short space
4. it was necessary that on them should come p
PEOPLE.
Jud. 5. 3. he said to them, tell me now who this p. is
6. 18. then the p. fell down and worshipped God
14. 17. he leaped out to the p. and cried
Esth. 10. 12. so God remembered his p. and justified
Wisd. 6. 2. give ear, you that rule the p.
21. O ye kings of the p. honour wisdom
24. a wise king is the upholding of the p.
9. 7. thou hast chosen me to be a king of thy p.
12. and then shall I judge thy p. righteously
16. 2. dealing graciously with thine own p.
20. feedest thine own p. with angels' food
18. 7. so of thy p. was accepted both the salvation
19. 5. that thy p. might pass a wonderful way
Eccl. 9. 17. the wise ruler of p. for his speech
10. 2. as the judge of the p. is himself, so are
8. the kingdom is translated from one p. to another
16. 11. if there be one stiff-necked among the p.
17. 17. he set a ruler over every p.
24. 1. wisdom shall glory in the midst of her p.
6. in every p. and nation I got a possession
12. and I took root in an honourable p.
31. 9. wonderful things hath he done among his p.
33. 18. hear me, O ye great men of the p.
35. 19. till he have judged the cause of his p.
36. 9. and let them perish that oppress the p.
14. fill Sion with oracles, thy p. with glory
37. 23. a wise man instructeth his p.
41. 18. of iniquity before a congregation and p.
42. 11. lest she make thee a reproach among the p.
44. 4. leaders of the p. by their counsels
15. the p. will tell of their wisdom
45. 3. he gave him a commandment for his p.
15. that they should bless the p. in his name
16. to make reconciliation for his p.
22. neither had he any portion among the p.
46. 7. in that they withheld the p. from sin
8. of six hundred thousand p. they two preserved
13. Samuel anointed princes over his p.
20. to blot out the wickedness of the p.
47. 4. did he not take away reproach from the p.?
5. and to set up the horn of his p.
6. so the p. honoured him with ten thousands
23. even the foolishness of the p. and one who turned away the p. through his counsel
49. 2. he behaved in the conversion of the p.
15. not a man like unto Joseph, a stay of the p.
50. 5. how was he honoured in the midst of the p.?
17. then all the p. together hasted, and fell
19. and the p. besought the Lord by prayer
Bar. 2. 30. because it is a stiff-necked p.
35. and they shall be my p. and I will no more drive my p. of Israel out of the land given them
4. 5. be of good cheer, my p. the memorial of Israel
Sus. 7. now when the p. departed away at noon
47. then all the p. turned them towards him
50. wherefore all the p. turned again in haste
1 Mac. 1. 41. wrote, that all should be one p.
3. 43. let us restore the decayed estate of our p. and let us fight for our p. and sanctuary
8. 15. in council consulting alway for the p.
11. 21. ungodly persons who hated their own p.
33. determined to do good to the p. of the Jews
42. I will not only do this for thee and thy p.
14. 23. it pleased the p. to entertain the men
15. 40. Cendebeus began to provoke the p.
2 Mac. 4. 48. that followed for the city and the p.
5. 19. God did not choose the p. for the place's sake, but the place for the p. sake
6. 3. this mischief was grievous to the p.
16. though he punish, yet doth he not forsake his p.

2 *Mac.* 10. 21. he called the governors of the *p.*
12. 13. and inhabited by *p.* of divers countries
42. exhorted the *p.* to keep themselves from sin
13. 25. the *p.* there were grieved for the covenants
15. 14. who prayeth much for the *p.* and city
24. that come against thy holy *p.* to blaspheme

PERADVENTURE.

Wisd. 13. 6. for they *p.* err, seeking God
1 *Mac.* 4. 10. if *p.* the Lord will have mercy on us
9. 8. if *p.* we may be able to fight with them

PERCEIVE.

Wisd. 16. 18. but themselves might see and *p.*
Bar. 6. 49. how cannot men *p.* that they be no gods?

PERCEIVED.

Wisd. 19. 18. which may well be *p.* by the sight
Eccl. 18. 12. he saw and *p.* their end to be evil
2 *Mac.* 2. 7. which when Jeremy *p.* he blamed them

PERDITION.

Eccl. 16. 9. he pitied not the people of *p.*

PERFECT.

Wisd. 4. 13. he being made *p.* in a short time
15. 3. for to know thee is *p.* righteousness
Eccl. 1. 18. making peace and *p.* health flourish
31. 10. who hath been tried, and found *p.*
34. 8. the law shall be found *p.* without lies
44. 17. Noah was found *p.* in the time of wrath
45. 8. he put on him *p.* glory, and strengthened

PERFECTED.

Wisd. 4. 16. and youth that is soon *p.*
Eccl. 7. 32. that thy blessing may be *p.*
23. 20. so after they were *p.* he looked on them

PERFECTION.

Esth. 15. 5. she was ruddy through the *p.* of beauty
Wisd. 3. 16. they shall not come to their *p.*
6. 15. to think therefore on her is *p.* of wisdom
Eccl. 21. 11. the *p.* of the fear of the Lord is wisdom
34. 8. and wisdom is *p.* to a faithful mouth
43. 7. a light that decreaseth in her *p.*
50. 11. when he was clothed with the *p.* of glory

PERFECTLY.

Jud. 11. 6. God will bring the thing *p.* to pass
Eccl. 24. 28. the first man knew her not *p.*
38. 28. and he watcheth to polish it *p.*

PERFORMANCE.

Eccl. 19. 20. in all wisdom is the *p.* of the law
2 *Mac.* 11. 17. made request for *p.* of the contents

PERFORMED.

1 *Esd.* 8. 21. let all things be *p.* after the law
2 *Esd.* 7. 24. and they have not *p.* his works
14. 25. till things be *p.* which thou shalt write
Eccl. 7. 25. so shalt thou have *p.* a weighty matter

PERFUME.

Tob. 6. 16. thou shalt take the ashes of *p.*
Eccl. 49. 1. is like the composition of the *p.*
Bar. 6. 43. women sitting in ways, burn bran for *p.*

PERIL.

Eccl. 13. 13. walkest in *p.* of thy overthrowing
1 *Mac.* 11. 23. Jonathan put himself in *p.*

PERISH.

Jud. 6. 8. thou shalt not *p.* till thou be destroyed
7. 11. shall not so much as one of thy people *p.*
Esth. 11. 9. the righteous nation were ready to *p.*
Wisd. 4. 19. and their memorial shall *p.*
12. 12. will accuse thee for the nations that *p.*
18. 19. did foreshew this, lest they should *p.*
Eccl. 3. 26. that loveth danger, shall *p.* therein
5. 7. thou shalt *p.* in the day of vengeance
8. 15. thou shalt *p.* with him through his folly
36. 9. let them *p.* that oppress the people
41. 6. the inheritance of sinners' children shall *p.*
44. 18. all flesh should *p.* no more by the flood
47. 22. neither shall any of his works *p.*
Bar. 3. 3. for thou endurest, and we *p.* utterly
1 *Mac.* 3. 9. he received such as were ready to *p.*
6. 13. behold, I *p.* thro' great grief in a strange land

PERISHED.

1 *Esd.* 4. 27. many also have *p.* and erred for women
Tob. 14. 10. Aman fell into the snare and *p.*
Esth. 16. 21. the chosen people should have *p.*
Wisd. 10. 3. he *p.* in fury wherewith he murdered
6. when ungodly *p.* she delivered the righteous
14. 6. in the old time, when the proud giants *p.*
16. 5. they *p.* with the stings of crooked serpents
Eccl. 37. 31. by surfeiting have many *p.*
44. 9. who are *p.* as though they had never been
Bar. 3. 28. they *p.* through their own foolishness
1 *Mac.* 13. 49. a number of them *p.* through famine
2 *Mac.* 5. 9. thus he *p.* in a strange land
8. 19. an hundred fourscore five thousand *p.*

PERISHETH.

2 *Esd.* 9. 37. notwithstanding, the law *p.* not
Eccl. 17. 28. thanksgiving *p.* from the dead

PERJURY.

Wisd. 14. 25. so that there reigned tumults, *p.*

PERMANENT.

2 *Esd.* 3. 22. thus infirmity was made *p.*

PERPETUAL.

2 *Esd.* 9. 19. manners are corrupted by a *p.* seed
Jud. 13. 20. God turn these to thee for a *p.* praise
Esth. 14. 5. thou tookest Israel for a *p.* inheritance
Wisd. 10. 14. them to be liars, and gave him *p.* glory
11. 6. instead of a fountain of a *p.* running river
Eccl. 11. 33. lest he bring upon thee a *p.* blot
37. 26. a wise man's name shall be *p.*
41. 6. their posterity shall have a *p.* reproach
1 *Mac.* 6. 44. that he might get him a *p.* name
13. 29. made all their armour for a *p.* memory

PERPETUALLY.

Eccl. 45. 13. but his children's children *p.*

PERPLEXED.

1 *Mac.* 3. 31. being greatly *p.* in his mind

PERSECUTE.

2 *Esd.* 15. 31. conspiring in great power to *p.* them

PERSECUTED.

Jud. 16. 3. out of the hands of them that *p.* me
Wisd. 11. 20. fallen down, being *p.* of vengeance
16. 16. the ungodly, with showers were they *p.*
Eccl. 30. 19. so is he that is *p.* of the Lord
Bar. 4. 25. for thine enemy hath *p.* thee

PERSECUTION.

Mac. 2. 43. they that fled for *p.* joined them

PERSEPOLIS.

2 *Mac.* 9. 2. he had entered the city called P.

PERSIA.

1 *Esd.* 3. 9. the three princes of P. shall judge
8. 80. made us gracious before the kings of P.
1 *Mac.* 3. 31. he determined to go into P.
6. 1. heard that Elymais, in the country of P.
5. there came one who brought tidings into P.
56. Philip was returned out of P. and Media
14. 2. but when Arsaces the king of P. heard
2 *Mac.* 1. 13. for when the leader was come into P.
19. for when our fathers were led into P.
33. this matter was told to the king of P.

PERSIANS.

1 *Esd.* 1. 57. became servants, till the P. reigned
Jud. 16. 10. the P. quaked at her boldness
Esth. 16. 23. safety to us, and the well-affected P.
1 *Mac.* 1. 1. had smitten Darius king of the P.

PERSON.

Jud. 7. 15. because they met not thy *p.* peaceably
12. 12. for lo, it will be a shame for our *p.*
Esth. 16. 11. honoured as the next *p.* to the king
Wisd. 6. 7. is Lord over all, shall fear no man's *p.*
Eccl. 4. 22. accept no *p.* against thy soul
27. neither accept the *p.* of the mighty
7. 6. lest thou fear the *p.* of the mighty
10. 5. on *p.* of the scribe shall he lay his honour
35. 13. will not accept any *p.* against a poor man
42. 1. and accept no *p.* to sin thereby
1 *Mac.* 14. 14. and every wicked *p.* he took away

PERSONS.

Esth. 16. 4. with the glorious words of lewd *p.*
Eccl. 20. 22. by accepting of *p.* overthrows himself
35. 12. and with him is no respect of *p.*

PERSUADE.

2 *Mac.* 11. 14. promised that he would *p.* the king

PERSUADED.

2 *Esd.* 7. 61. joy over them that are *p.* to salvation
2 *Mac.* 10. 20. they with Simon were *p.* for money
11. 14. and *p.* them to agree to all conditions
13. 26. Lysias *p.* pacified, and made well-affected

PERSUASIONS.

1 *Esd.* 5. 73. by popular *p.* they hindered the building

PERTAIN.

Eccl. 21. 25. telling such things as *p.* not to them
2 *Mac.* 3. 6. which did not *p.* to the sacrifices

PERTAINING.

2 *Mac.* 14. 8. care I have of things *p.* to the king

PERVERTED.

Sus. 9. they *p.* their own mind, and turned away

PESTILENCE.

2 *Esd.* 15. 49. I will send famine, sword, and *p.*

PESTILENT.

Esth. 16. 7. done through the *p.* behaviour of them
1 *Mac.* 10. 61. certain *p.* fellows of Israel assembled

PETITION.

2 *Esd.* 8. 24. give ear to the *p.* of thy creature
1 *Mac.* 7. 37. house of prayer and *p.* for thy people

PHENICE.

2 *Mac.* 4. 22. afterward he went with his host to P.

PHILIP.

1 *Mac.* 6. 2. shields which Alexander son of P. left
14. then called he for P. one of his friends
63. where he found P. to be master of the city
8. 5. how they had discomfited in battle P.
2 *Mac.* 5. 22. he left governor, at Jerusalem, P.
6. 11. being discovered to P. were all burned

PHILOMETOR.

2 *Mac.* 4. 21. the coronation of Ptolemeus P.
10. 13. left Cyprus, that P. had committed to him

PHINEES, PHINEAS.

2 *Esd.* 1. 2. the son of P. the son of Eleazar
1 *Mac.* 2. 26. as P. did to Zambri the son of Salom
54. P. our father, in being zealous, obtained

PHRYGIAN.

2 *Mac.* 5. 22. at Jerus. Philip for his country a P.

PHYSICIAN.

Eccl. 10. 10. the *p.* cutteth off a long disease
38. 1. honour a *p.* with honour due to him
3. the skill of the *p.* shall lift up his head
12. then give place to the *p.* the Lord created him
15. let him fall into the hand of the *p.*

PHYSICIANS.

Tob. 2. 10. I went to the *p.* but they helped me not

PHYSIC.

Eccl. 18. 19. and use *p.* or ever thou be sick

PIECES.

2 *Esd.* 1. 32. ye have slain, and torn their bodies in *p.*
2. 14. for I have broken the evil in *p.* and created
2 *Mac.* 15. 33. they should give it by *p.* to the fowls

PIERCE.

2 *Mac.* 11. 9. were ready to *p.* thro' walls of iron

PIERCED.

Jud. 16. 12. the sons of damsels have *p.* them thro'

PIERCETH.

Eccl. 35. 17. the prayer of the humble *p.* the clouds

PIKES.

2 *Mac.* 5. 3. shaking of shields and a multitude of *p.*

PILGRIMAGE.

2 *Esd.* 8. 39. I will remember their *p.* and salvation

PILGRIMS.

2 *Esd.* 16. 40. be even as *p.* upon the earth

PILLED.

Tob. 11. 13. the whiteness *p.* away from his eyes

PILLOW.

1 *Esd.* 3. 8. and laid it under king Darius his *p.*

PINCHING.

Eccl. 11. 18. waxeth rich by his wariness and *p.*

PIN.

Eccl. 14. 24. shall also fasten a *p.* in her walls

PIPE.

Eccl. 40. 21. the *p.* and psaltery make sweet melody

PIT.

Wisd. 10. 13. she went down with him into the *p.*
Eccl. 12. 16. imagineth how to throw thee into a *p.*
21. 10. but at the end thereof is the *p.* of hell
27. 26. whoso diggeth a *p.* shall fall therein
1 *Mac.* 7. 19. he cast them into the great *p.*
2 *Mac.* 1. 19. and hid it in a hollow place of a *p.*

PITCH.

Eccl. 13. 1. he that toucheth *p.* shall be defiled
Dan. 3. 23. to make oven hot with rosin, *p.*
Bel 27. then Daniel took *p.* fat, and hair

PITCH.

Eccl. 14. 25. he shall *p.* his tent nigh unto her
1 *Mac.* 5. 49. every man *p.* his tent where he was
2 *Mac.* 15. 17. they determined not to *p.* camp

PITCHED.

Wisd. 11. 2. they *p.* tents where there lay no way
1 *Mac.* 3. 40. so they came and *p.* by Emmaus

PITY.

2 *Esd.* 1. 19. then had I *p.* on your mournings
15. 19. a man shall have no *p.* on his neighbour
Tob. 3. 15. *p.* taken of me that hear no more reproach
6. 17. who will have *p.* on you and save you?
8. 4. let us pray that God would have *p.* on us
11. 15. for thou hast scourged and taken *p.* on me
Jud. 6. 19. and *p.* the low estate of our nation
Eccl. 12. 13. who will *p.* a charmer that is bitten?
14. so one that goeth to a sinner who will *p.*
Bar. 3. 2. have *p.* on us, because we have sinned
2 *Mac.* 4. 37. Antiochus was moved to *p.* and wept
7. 27. have *p.* on me that bare thee nine months

PITIED.

Eccl. 16. 9. he *p.* not the people of perdition
Bar. 4. 15. nor reverenced old man, nor *p.* child
2 *Mac.* 3. 21. then it would have *p.* a man to see

PITIFUL.

Eccl. 2. 11. Lord is long-suffering and very *p.*

PLACE.

Esth. 13. 3. had the second *p.* in the kingdom
Wisd. 12. 20. giving them time and *p.* whereby
19. 22. but didst assist them in every time and *p.*
Eccl. 8. 16. go not with him into a solitary *p.*
10. 15. the Lord planted the lowly in their *p.*
12. 12. set him not by, lest he stand up in thy *p.*
16. 8. nor spared he the *p.* where Lot sojourned
19. 17. give *p.* to the law of the Most High
29. 27. give *p.* thou stranger, to an honourable man
32. 2. take thy *p.* that thou mayest be merry
41. 19. of theft in regard of *p.* where thou sojournest
48. 5. didst raise his soul from the *p.* of the dead
Bar. 3. 15. who hath found out her *p.*?
24. and how large is the *p.* of his possession
Sus. 49. return again to the *p.* of judgment
1 *Mac.* 10. 14. for it was their *p.* of refuge
14. 36. they did much hurt in the holy *p.*
16. 16. came on Simon into the banqueting *p.*
2 *Mac.* 1. 19. so that the *p.* was unknown to all men

PLACED.

2 *Mac.* 15. 20. the beasts were conveniently *p.*

PLACES.

Tob. 5. 5. and knowest thou those *p.* well?
Eccl. 9. 7. nor wander in the solitary *p.* thereof
24. 4. I dwelt in high *p.* my throne is in a pillar
33. 12. some of them he turned out of their *p.*
46. 9. so that he entered on the high *p.* of the land

PLAGUE.

2 *Esd.* 15. 12. Egypt shall be smitten with the *p.*
16. 19. behold famine and *p.* tribulat. and anguish
Eccl. 23. 11. *p.* shall never depart from his house
25. 13. give me any *p.* but the *p.* of the heart
Bar. 6. 48. when there cometh any war or *p.*
49. neither save themselves from war nor *p.*
1 *Mac.* 3. 29. because of *p.* he had brought on land
2 *Mac.* 9. 5. with an incurable and invisible *p.*

PLAGUED.

1 *Mac.* 9. 55. even at that time was Alcimus *p.*
2 *Mac.* 9. 11. being *p.* he began to leave off his pride

PLAGUES.

Wisd. 14. 22. those so great *p.* called they peace
Bar. 2. 2. to bring upon us great *p.* such as never
7. all *p.* are come upon us the Lord pronounced
3. 4. for the which cause these *p.* cleave to us
2 *Mac.* 7. 37. by torments and *p.* thou mayest confess

PLAIN.

Wisd. 7. 22. undefiled, *p.* not subject to hurt
Eccl. 21. 10. way of sinners is made *p.* with stone
32. 21. be not confident in a *p.* way
1 *Mac.* 5. 52. into the great *p.* before Bethsan
16. 11. in the *p.* of Jericho was Ptolemeus

PLAISTER.

Wisd. 16. 12. nor mollifying *p.* that restored health

PLAISTERING.

Eccl. 22. 17. as a fair *p.* on the wall of a gallery

PLANT.

Eccl. 10. 19. that love him, an honourable *p.*
49. 7. and that he might build up also and *p.*
2 *Mac.* 1. 29. *p.* thy people in thy holy place

PLANTED.

Eccl. 10. 15. the Lord *p.* the lowly in their place

PLANTS.

Wisd. 7. 20. to know the diversities of *p.*
10. 7. *p.* bearing fruit, that never come to ripeness

PLATE.

Jud. 12. 1. to bring her in where his *p.* was set
15. 11. they gave to Judith all his *p.* and beds
1 *Mac.* 15. 32. the cupboard of gold and silver *p.*

PLATES.

Eccl. 50. 3. cistern was covered with *p.* of brass

PLAY.

Eccl. 30. 9. *p.* with him, he will bring to heaviness

PLAYED.

Eccl. 23. 23. she hath *p.* the whore in adultery
47. 3. he *p.* with lions as with kids, and with bears

PLEADED.

2 *Mac.* 4. 44. three men *p.* the cause before him

PLEASANT.

Eccl. 32. 6. so is melody of music with *p.* wine
40. 21. but a *p.* tongue is above them both
2 *Mac.* 15. 39. as wine mingled with water is *p.*

PLEASE.

Tob. 3. 15. if it *p.* not thee that I should die
4. 3. do that which shall *p.* her, grieve her not
Wisd. 14. 19. be willing to *p.* one in authority
Eccl. 18. 31. if givest thy soul desires that *p.* her
19. 19. and they that do things that *p.* him
20. 27. hath understanding, will *p.* great men

PLEASED.

Tob. 5. 16. so they were well *p.* then said he
Jud. 7. 16. these words *p.* Holofernes and his servan.
15. 10. done much good, and God is *p.* therewith
Wisd. 4. 10. he *p.* God, and was beloved of him
14. for his soul *p.* the Lord, therefore he hasted

Eccl. 34. 19. the Most High is not *p.* with offerings
44. 16. Enoch *p.* the Lord, and was translated
48. 22. Ezekias did the thing that *p.* the Lord
1 *Mac.* 1. 12. so this device *p.* them well
8. 21. so that matter *p.* the Romans well
10. 47. but with Alexander they were well *p.*
14. 4. his authority and honour *p.* them well
47. then Simon was well *p.* to be high priest
2 *Mac.* 1. 20. when it *p.* God, Neemias being sent
11. 35. hath granted, therewith we are well *p.*
14. 35. wast *p.* that the temple should be among us

PLEASETH.

Jud. 3. 3. our flocks and herds, use them as *p.* thee
Eccl. 19. 21. master, I will not do as it *p.* thee
20. 28. he that *p.* great men shall get pardon
39. 18. at his command is done whatever *p.* him

PLEASING.

Tob. 4. 21. do that which is *p.* in his sight
Wisd. 9. 10. that I may know what is *p.* to thee
17. 18. a *p.* fall of water running violently
Eccl. 48. 16. some did that which was *p.* to God

PLEASURE.

Wisd. 1. 13. nor hath he *p.* in the destruction
7. 2. and the *p.* that came with sleep
8. 18. great *p.* it is to have her friendship
Eccl. 9. 10. when old thou shalt drink it with *p.*
12. in the thing that the ungodly have *p.* in
11. 27. affliction maketh a man forget *p.*
14. 5. he shall not take *p.* in his goods
18. 32. take not *p.* in much good cheer
19. 5. whoso taketh *p.* in wickedness, be condemned
25. 21. and desire her not for *p.*
33. 13. as the clay is in the potter's hand to fashion it
at *p.* so man is in hand of him that made him
37. 28. nor hath every soul *p.* in every thing
41. 4. why art thou against the *p.* of the Most High?
1 *Mac.* 4. 42. priests, such as had *p.* in the law
2 *Mac.* 12. 11. promising to *p.* him otherwise

PLEASURES.

Eccl. 19. 5. he that resisteth *p.* crowneth life
1 *Mac.* 8. 30. think meet, they may do it at their *p.*

PLENTY.

Jud. 2. 18. *p.* of victual for every man of the army

PLOTS.

1 *Esd.* 5. 73. by secret *p.* and popular persuasions

PLOUGH.

Eccl. 38. 25. how can he get wisdom that holdeth *p.*?

PLOWETH.

Eccl. 6. 19. come to her, as one that *p.* and soweth

POINT.

Eccl. 31. 15. judge, and be discreet in every *p.*
2 *Mac.* 2. 30. to stand on every *p.* and go over things
13. 10. being at the *p.* to be put from their law

POINTS, POINTS.

2 *Mac.* 12. 22. wounded with *p.* of their own swords
15. 12. and exercised in all *p.* of virtue

POISONED.

2 *Mac.* 10. 13. that he *p.* himself, and died

POLICY.

1 *Mac.* 8. 4. that by their *p.* they had conquered
2 *Mac.* 13. 18. went about to take the holds by *p.*
14. 29. watched to accomplish this thing by *p.*
31. he was notably prevented by Judas' *p.*

POLICIES.

Jud. 11. 8. we have heard of thy wisdom and *p.*

POLISH.

Eccl. 38. 28. and watcheth to *p.* it perfectly

POLISHED.

Bar. 6. 8. his tongue is *p.* by the workman

POLLUTE.

1 *Mac.* 1. 46. *p.* the sanctuary and holy people
2 *Mac.* 6. 2. to *p.* also the temple in Jerusalem

POLLUTED.

1 *Esd.* 8. 83. is a land *p.* with the pollutions
2 *Esd.* 15. 6. wickedness hath *p.* the whole earth
Tob. 2. 9. being *p.* and my face was uncovered
3. 15. that I never *p.* my name nor name of my
Jud. 9. 2. and *p.* her virginity to her reproach
1 *Mac.* 14. 36. they *p.* all about the sanctuary
2 *Mac.* 5. 16. taking the holy vessels with *p.* hands

POLLUTETH.

Eccl. 40. 29. he *p.* himself with other men's meat

POLLUTION, S.

Jud. 9. 4. which abhorred the *p.* of their blood
1 *Mac.* 13. 50. he cleansed the tower from *p.*
2 *Mac.* 5. 27. lest they should be partakers of the *p.*

POMEGRANATES.

Eccl. 45. 9. he compassed him with *p.* and bells

POMP.

1 *Mac.* 10. 86. men of city met him with great *p.*

PONDER.

2 *Esd.* 4. 31. *p.* now by thyself, how great fruit
Eccl. 21. 17. they shall *p.* his words in their hearts

PONDERED.

Wisd. 8. 17. when I *p.* them in my heart

POOLS.

2 *Esd.* 16. 60. *p.* upon the tops of the mountains

POOR.

1 *Esd.* 3. 19. the mind of the *p.* man and of the rich
2 *Esd.* 15. 51. thou shalt be weakened as a *p.* woman
Tob. 2. 2. bring what *p.* man soever thou findest
4. 7. neither turn thy face from any *p.*
21. fear not, my son, that we are made *p.*
Wisd. 2. 10. let us oppress the *p.* righteous man
Eccl. 1. 28. distrust not the Lord when thou art *p.*
4. 1. my son, defraud not the *p.* of his living
4. neither turn away thy face from a *p.* man
8. not grieve to bow down thine ear to the *p.*
7. 32. and stretch thine hand unto the *p.*
10. 22. whether he be rich, noble, or *p.*
23. it is not meet to despise the *p.* man
30. the *p.* man is honoured for his skill
11. 21. easy on the sudden to make a *p.* man rich
13. 3. the *p.* is wronged, and must entreat also
18. what peace between the rich and the *p.*?
19. rich eat up the *p.* ‖ 20. rich abhor the *p.*
21. but a *p.* man is thrust away by his friends
22. the *p.* man slept, and yet they rebuked him
23. if *p.* man speak, they say, what fellow is this?
21. 5. a prayer out of a *p.* man's mouth reacheth
25. 2. my soul hates a *p.* man that is proud
26. 4. a man be rich or *p.* if he have a good heart

Eccl. 29. 8. have thou patience with a man in *p.* estate
9. help the *p.* for the commandment's sake
22. better is the life of a *p.* man in a cottage
30. 14. better is the *p.* being sound and strong
31. 4. the *p.* laboureth in his *p.* estate, and is needy
34. 20. brings an offering of the goods of the *p.*
35. 13. will not accept any person against a *p.* man
38. 19. the life of the *p.* is the curse of the heart
Bar. 6. 28. but to the *p.* they give nothing of it
2 *Mac.* 4. 47. and those *p.* men he condemned

POPULAR.

1 *Esd.* 5. 73. by their secret plots and *p.* persuasions

PORCH.

1 *Esd.* 9. 41. the broad court before the holy *p.*
2 *Mac.* 1. 8. burnt the *p.* and shed innocent blood

PORTERS.

1 *Esd.* 1. 16. moreover the *p.* were at every gate

PORTION.

Esth. 13. 16. despise not the *p.* thou deliveredst
Wisd. 2. 9. for this is our *p.* and our lot is this
Eccl. 7. 31. give him his *p.* as it is commanded
11. 18. and this is the *p.* of his reward
14. 9. the covetous is not satisfied with his *p.*
17. 17. but Israel is the Lord's *p.*
24. 12. in the *p.* of the Lord's inheritance
25. 19. let the *p.* of a sinner fall upon her
26. 3. a good wife is a good *p.* which shall be given
in the *p.* of them that fear the Lord
23. a wicked woman given as a *p.* to wicked man
41. 9. and if you die, a curse shall be your *p.*
21. be ashamed to take away a *p.* or a gift
45. 22. nor had he any *p.* among the people, for
the Lord himself is his *p.* and inheritance
2 *Mac.* 1. 26. preserve thy own *p.* and sanctify it
14. 15. and who always helpeth his *p.*

PORTIONS.

Eccl. 44. 23. gave him an heritage, and divided his *p.*
50. 12. when he took *p.* out of the priests' hands

POSSESS.

Jud. 8. 22. a reproach to all them that *p.* us
Eccl. 11. 24. I have enough, and *p.* many things

POSSESSED.

Eccl. 36. 15. thou hast *p.* from the beginning

POSSESSION.

Jud. 16. 21. Judith remained in her own *p.*
Wisd. 8. 5. if riches be a *p.* to be desired in life
Eccl. 4. 16. his generation shall hold her in *p.*
24. 6. in every people and nation I got a *p.*
28. 24. look that thou hedge thy *p.* with thorns
51. 21. therefore have I gotten a good *p.*

POSSESSIONS.

Eccl. 41. 1. to a man that liveth at rest in his *p.*

POSSIBLE.

Wisd. 16. 15. it is not *p.* to escape thine hand
2 *Mac.* 3. 6. it was *p.* to bring all into the king's hand
14. 10. it is not *p.* that the state should be quiet

POST.

Wisd. 5. 9. passed away as a *p.* that hasted by

POSTERITY.

1 *Esd.* 4. 53. have free liberty, as well they as their *p.*
Eccl. 45. 24. he and *p.* should have the dignity
25. the inheritance should be to his *p.* alone
47. 22. nor will he abolish the *p.* of his elect
Bar. 2. 15. Israel and his *p.* is called by thy name
2 *Mac.* 1. 20. did send of the *p.* of those priests

POTENTATES.

Eccl. 10. 24. judges and *p.* shall be honoured

POTS.

1 *Esd.* 1. 12. the sacrifices, they sod them in brass *p.*

POTTAGE.

Bel 33. a prophet Habbacuc, who had made *p.*

POTTER.

Wisd. 15. 7. the *p.* tempering soft earth; but what is
the use of either sort, the *p.* himself is the judge
Eccl. 27. 5. the furnace proveth the *p.* vessels
33. 13. as the clay is in the *p.* hand to fashion it
38. 29. so doth the *p.* sitting at his work

POVERTY.

Eccl. 10. 31. honoured in *p.* how much more in riches
dishonourable in riches, how much more in *p.*
11. 12. is slow, wanting ability, and full of *p.*
14. life, death, *p.* and riches come of the Lord
13. 24. *p.* is evil in the mouth of the ungodly
18. 25. when thou art rich, think on *p.* and need
22. 23. be faithful to thy neighbour in his *p.*
26. 28. a man of war that suffereth *p.*
29. 9. turn him not away because of his *p.*

POWER.

2 *Esd.* 1. 10. all his *p.* have I smitten down
Jud. 2. 12. as I live, and by the *p.* of my kingdom
9. 11. for thy *p.* standeth not in multitude
14. that thou art the God of all *p.* and might
11. 7. as his *p.* liveth, who hath sent thee, and the
fowls of the air shall live by thy *p.*
13. 4. O Lord God of all *p.* look at this present
11. God is with us to shew his *p.* in Jerusalem
19. which remember the *p.* of God for ever
Wisd. 1. 3. his *p.* when it is tried reproveth unwise
6. 3. *p.* is given you of the Lord, and sovereignty
7. 23. stedfast, free from care, having all *p.*
25. for she is the breath of the *p.* of God
26. the unspotted mirror of the *p.* of God
9. 11. and she shall preserve me in her *p.*
10. 2. and gave him *p.* to rule all things
11. 20. being scattered through the breath of thy *p.*
21. who may withstand the *p.* of thine arm?
12. 15. thinking it not agreeable with thy *p.*
16. thy *p.* is the beginning of righteousness
17. men will not believe thou art of a full *p.*
18. but thou mastering thy *p.* judgest with equity;
for thou mayest use *p.* when thou wilt
14. 31. it is not the *p.* of them by whom they swear
15. 2. if we sin we are thine, knowing thy *p.*
3. to know thy *p.* is the root of immortality
16. 13. for thou hast *p.* of life and death
19. it burneth in water above the *p.* of fire
Eccl. 3. 20. for the *p.* of the Lord is great
6. 26. and keep her ways with all thy *p.*
8. 13. be not surety above thy *p.* for if thou be
9. 13. keep far from the man that hath *p.* to kill
10. 4. the *p.* of the earth is in the hand of the Lord
13. 2. burden not thyself above thy *p.* while livest

Eccl. 15. 18. he is mighty in *p.* and behold. all things
18. 4. to whom he hath given *p.* to declare works
46. 6. and with hailstones of mighty *p.*
49. 5. therefore he gave their *p.* to others
Bar. 1. 6. collection, according to every man's *p.*
3. 5. think on thy *p.* and thy name at this time
6. 59. better to be a king that sheweth his *p.*
63. these like to them neither in shew nor *p.*
Prayer of Manass. fear and tremble before thy *p.*
2 *Mac.* 3. 24. the Lord of spirits, and the prince of
all *p.* all were astonished at the *p.* of God
28. manifestly they acknowledged the *p.* of God
9. 8. shewing forth to all the manifest *p.* of God
11. 4. not at all considering the *p.* of God
12. 28. who with his *p.* breaks strength of enemies

POWERS.

Dan. 3. 39. O all ye *p.* of the Lord, bless ye the Lord
Prayer of Manass. all the *p.* of heavens praise thee

POWERFUL.

Eccl. 16. 15. that his *p.* works might be known

POUR.

Tob. 4. 17. *p.* out thy bread on burial of the just
Eccl. 10. 13. he that hath it, shall *p.* out abominat.
16. 11. he is mighty to *p.* out displeasure
24. 33. I will yet *p.* out doctrine as prophecy
36. 7. raise up indignation, and *p.* out wrath
39. 6. he shall *p.* out wise sentences and give thanks
28. they *p.* out their force, and appease wrath

POURED.

Eccl. 18. 29. they *p.* forth exquisite parables
50. 15. he *p.* of the blood of the grape, he *p.* out at
the foot of the altar a sweet-smelling savour
27. who out of his heart *p.* forth wisdom
2 *Mac.* 1. 31. water to be *p.* on the great stones

POURETH.

Eccl. 18. 11. God *p.* forth mercy on them
35. 14. the widow, when she *p.* out her complaint
43. 19. the hoar-frost as salt he *p.* on the earth

PRACTICE, S.

Eccl. 10. 6. do nothing at all by injurious *p.*
27. 9. truth will return to them that *p.* in her

PRACTISED.

2 *Mac.* 14. 22. lest treachery be suddenly *p.*

PRACTISING.

1 *Esd.* 2. 26. that city was *p.* against kings

PRAISE.

2 *Esd.* 13. 57. giving *p.* greatly to the Most High
Tob. 3. 11. let all thy works *p.* thee for ever
8. 15. thou art worthy to be praised with all pure
and holy *p.* therefore let thy saints *p.* thee
12. 6. bless God, *p.* him, *p.* him, it is good to *p.* and
exalt God, therefore be not slack to *p.* him
13. 6. *p.* the Lord of might, and extol the King
7. my soul shall *p.* the king of heaven and rejoice
14. 7. so shall all nations *p.* Lord and confess God
Jud. 13. 14. then said she, *p.* *p.* God, *p.* God I say
20. God turn these to thee for a perpetual *p.*
16. 1. the people sang after her this song of *p.*
Esth. 13. 17. we may live, O Lord, and *p.* thy name,
destroy not the mouths of them that *p.* thee
Wisd. 15. 19. nor are they to be desired, but they
went without the *p.* of God and his blessing
Eccl. 11. 31. in things worthy *p.* will lay blame
15. 9. *p.* is not seemly in the mouth of a sinner
10. for *p.* shall be uttered in wisdom
17. 27. who shall *p.* the Most High in the grave?
28. the sound in heart shall *p.* the Lord
18. 28. and will give *p.* to him that found her
24. 1. wisdom shall *p.* herself, and shall glory
27. 7. *p.* no man before thou hearest him speak
35. 2. he that giveth alms, sacrificeth *p.*
39. 10. the congregation shall declare his *p.*
14. sing a song of *p.* and bless the Lord
15. shew forth his *p.* with the songs of your lips
35. *p.* ye the Lord with the whole heart
43. 11. look on the rainbow, and *p.* him that made it
44. 1. let us now *p.* famous men, and our fathers
51. 1. I will thank thee, I do give *p.* to thy name
29. rejoice in his mercy, be not ashamed of his *p.*
Bar. 3. 6. thou art our God, thee, O Lord, will we *p.*
7. that we should *p.* thee in our captivity
Dan. 3. 35. *p.* and exalt him above all for ever
And so to the end of the chapter.
Prayer of Manass. I will *p.* thee for ever all days
of my life, all the powers of heaven do *p.* thee
1 *Mac.* 4. 33. let all *p.* thee with thanksgiving

PRAISED.

1 *Esd.* 4. 62. they *p.* the God of their fathers
2 *Esd.* 2. 42. they all *p.* the Lord with songs
Tob. 8. 15. then Raguel *p.* God, and said, O God,
thou art worthy to be *p.* with all holy praise
Jud. 6. 20. comforted Achior, and *p.* him greatly
Wisd. 10. 20. the righteous *p.* thy holy name
Eccl. 47. 6. people *p.* him in the blessings of the Lord
Dan. 3. 29. blessed art thou, O Lord God, to be *p.*
and exalted above all for ever, 30, 31, 32,
33, 34.
Sus. 63. they *p.* God for their daughter Susanna
1 *Mac.* 4. 24. went home, and *p.* the Lord in heaven
2 *Mac.* 11. 9. then they *p.* the merciful God

PRAISES.

Esth. 14. 10. heathen to set forth the *p.* of the idols

PRAISING.

Tob. 11. 1. after this, Tobias went his way *p.* God
16. Tobit went out, rejoicing and *p.* God
14. 1. so Tobit made an end of *p.* God
Wisd. 19. 9. *p.* thee, O Ld. who hadst delivered them
Eccl. 39. 15. and in *p.* him you shall say thus
Dan. 3. 1. and they walked in the fire, *p.* God
1 *Mac.* 4. 55. worshipping and *p.* the God of heaven
2 *Mac.* 12. 41. *p.* the Lord, the righteous judge
15. 29. *p.* the Almighty in their own language

PRAY.

Tob. 6. 17. rise up and *p.* to God, who is merciful
8. 4. let us *p.* that God would have mercy on us
12. 12. when thou didst *p.* and bury the dead
Jud. 8. 31. therefore now *p.* thou for us, because
9. 12. I *p.* thee, I *p.* thee, O God of my father
11. 17. I will *p.* to God, and he will tell me
Wisd. 16. 28. and at the day-spring *p.* to thee
Eccl. 37. 15. above all this, *p.* to the Most High
39. 5. and he will *p.* before the Most High

PRAYED.
Tob. 3. 1. I did weep, and in sorrow *p.* saying
11. then she *p.* towards the window and said
Esth. 14. 3. she *p.* unto the Lord God of Israel
Wisd. 7. 7. I *p.* and understanding was given me
1 *Mac.* 11. 71. he cast earth on his head and *p.*
2 *Mac.* 1. 8. then we *p.* to the Lord and were heard
2. 10. as when Moses *p.* to the Lord, the fire came down from heaven, even so *p.* Solomon also
5. 4. every one *p.* that that apparition might turn
15. 12. Onias *p.* for the whole body of the Jews

PRAYER.
Tob. 12. 8. *p.* is good with fasting and alms
13. 1. then Tobit wrote a *p.* of rejoicing, and said
Jud. 9. 12. King of every creature, hear thou my *p.*
13. 10. they went according to their custom to *p.*
Esth. 13. 8. Mardocheus made his *p.* to the Lord
Wisd. 13. 17. then maketh he *p.* for his goods
Eccl. 4. 6. his *p.* be heard of him that made him
7. 10. be not faint-hearted when thou makest thy *p.*
17. 25. return, and make thy *p.* before his face
21. 5. a *p.* out of a poor man's mouth reacheth to the ears of God, and his judgment cometh
34. 26. and doth the same, who will hear his *p.*
35. 13. he will hear the *p.* of the oppressed
16. his *p.* shall reach unto the clouds
17. the *p.* of the humble pierceth the clouds
36. 17. O Lord, hear the *p.* of thy servants
39. 5. and he will open his mouth in *p.*
6. he shall give thanks to the Lord in his *p.*
50. 19. the people besought the Lord by *p.*
51. 11. I called on the Lord, and so my *p.* was heard
13. when young, I desired wisdom openly in *p.*
1 *Mac.* 5. 33. who sounded trumpets and cried with *p.*
7. 37. be an house of *p.* and petition for thy people
2 *Mac.* 1. 23. the priests made a *p.* whilst sacrifice
24. *p.* was after this manner, O Lord, Lord God
10. 27. after the *p.* they took their weapons
12. 42. betook themselves to *p.* and besought him
15. 22. in his *p.* he said after this manner
26. encountered enemies with invocation and *p.*

PRAYERS.
Tob. 3. 16. so the *p.* of them both were heard
12. 15. which present the *p.* of the saints
Jud. 4. 13. so God heard their *p.* and looked on their
13. 3. for she said she would go forth to her *p.*
Bar. 2. 14. hear our *p.* O Lord, and our petitions
1 *Mac.* 12. 11. in our *p.* to think on our brethren
2 *Mac.* 1. 5. God hear your *p.* and be at one with you

PRAYEST.
Eccl. 7. 14. make not much babbling when thou *p.*
18. 23. before thou *p.* prepare thyself
28. 2. so thy sins shall be forgiven when thou *p.*

PRAYETH.
Eccl. 34. 24. when one *p.* and another curseth

PREACH.
2 *Esd.* 2. † 32. till I come and *p.* mercy unto them

PRECEPTS.
2 *Esd.* 16. 76. the guide of them who keep my *p.*
Tob. 6. 15. dost thou not remember the *p.*?

PRECIOUS.
Tob. 13. 16. for Jerusalem he built up with *p.* stones
Jud. 10. 3. she anointed herself with *p.* ointment
Esth. 14. 2. instead of *p.* ointments covered her head
15. 6. robes all glittering with gold and *p.* stones
Wisd. 7. 9. nor compared I to her any *p.* stones
Eccl. 9. 5. fall not by those things that are *p.* in her

PREDECESSORS.
Esth. 14. 5. thou tookest our fathers from all their *p.*

PRE-EMINENCE.
Eccl. 33. 22. in thy works keep to thyself the *p.*
1 *Mac.* 11. 27. and gave him *p.* among his friends

PREFERRED.
Wisd. 7. 8. I *p.* her before sceptres and thrones

PREPARE.
1 *Esd.* 1. 4. *p.* you after your families and kindreds
2 *Esd.* 14. 24 look thou *p.* thee many box-trees
Tob. 5. 16. he said *p.* thyself for the journey
11. 3. let us haste before, and *p.* the house
Jud. 2. 7. that they *p.* for me earth and water
12. 1. that they should *p.* for her of his meats
Eccl. 2. 1. my son, *p.* thy soul for temptation
17. they that fear the Lord will *p.* their hearts
18. 23. before thou prayest *p.* thyself
33. 4. *p.* what to say, so shalt thou be heard

PREPARED.
1 *Esd.* 1. 13. they *p.* for themselves and priests
14. the Levites *p.* for themselves and priests
Tob. 2. 1. there was a good dinner *p.* for me
5. 16. when his son had *p.* all things for journey
Jud. 9. 6. we are here, for all thy ways are *p.*
12. 19. she ate and drank what her maid had *p.*
Esth. 11. 7. at their cry all nations were *p.* to battle
Wisd. 9. 8. which thou hast *p.* from the beginning
16. 20. didst send bread *p.* without their labour
Eccl. 49. 12. which was *p.* for everlasting glory

PREPAREDST.
Wisd. 16. 2. thou *p.* for them meat of a strange taste

PREPARETH.
Eccl. 26. 28. Lord *p.* such an one for the sword

PREPARING.
Wisd. 14. 1. again, one *p.* to sail, calleth on wood

PRESCRIBED.
1 *Esd.* 1. 5. according as David the king of Israel *p.*

PRESENCE.
Wisd. 14. 17. whom men could not honour in *p.*
Eccl. 8. 11. rise not in anger at *p.* of injurious persons

PRESENT.
Wisd. 2. 6. let us enjoy the good things that are *p.*
4. 2. when it is *p.* men take example at it
9. 9. Wisdom was *p.* when thou madest the world
10. that being *p.* she may labour with me
11. 11. whether absent or *p.* they were vexed
14. 17. might flatter him absent as if he were *p.*
Eccl. 1. 21. where it is *p.* it turneth away wrath
27. 23. when thou art *p.* he will speak sweetly
31. 6. gold ruin of many, their destruction was *p.*

PRESENT.
Tob. 12. 15. which *p.* the prayers of the saints

PRESENTS.
Eccl. 20. 29. *p.* and gifts blind the eyes of the wise

PRESERVATION.
Eccl. 34. 16. he is a *p.* from stumbling and help

PRESERVE.
Tob. 6. 17. thou shalt *p.* her, and she shall go
Wisd. 9. 11. and she shall *p.* me in her power

PRESERVED, ETH.
Wisd. 10. 1. she *p.* the first formed father of world
4. wisdom again *p.* it, and directed the course
5. and she *p.* him blameless unto God
11. 25. or have been *p.* if not called by thee
16. 26. but that it is thy word which *p.* them
Eccl. 20. 2. he that confesseth shall be *p.* from hurt

PRESS.
Eccl. 13. 10. *p.* not on him, lest thou be put back
31. 31. *p.* not on him with urging him to drink

PRESSED.
Wisd. 17. 11. wickedness being *p.* with conscience
Eccl. 46. 5. when the enemies *p.* upon him
Bel 30. when the king saw that they *p.* him sore
2 *Mac.* 14. 9. our nation, which is *p.* on every side

PRESUMED.
2 *Mac.* 3. 24. all that *p.* to come in were astonished
5. 15. but *p.* to go into the most holy temple

PRESUMPTION.
Esth. 13. 2. not lifted up with *p.* of my authority
2 *Mac.* 5. 18. this man had been put back from *p.*

PRETEND.
Eccl. 12. 17. though he *p.* to help thee, yet undermine

PREVAIL.
Eccl. 29. 6. if he *p.* he shall hardly receive the half

PREVENT.
Wisd. 16. 28. we must *p.* the sun to give thanks

PREVENTETH.
Wisd. 6. 13. she *p.* them that desire her

PREY.
1 *Esd.* 8. 77. for our sins, we were given up for a *p.*
Jud. 5. 24. they shall be a *p.* to be devoured of all
9. 4. thou hast given their wives for a *p.*
16. 5. that he would make my infants as a *p.*
Eccl. 27. 10. as the lion lieth in wait for the *p.*
1 *Mac.* 7. 47. they took the spoils and the *p.*

PRICE.
Eccl. 33. 30. because thou hast bought him with a *p.*
Bar. 6. 25. the things are bought for a most high *p.*

PRICKED.
Wisd. 16. 11. they were *p.* that they should rememb.
Eccl. 12. 12. lest thou remember my words and be *p.*
14. 1. who is not *p.* with the multitude of sins

PRICKETH.
Eccl. 22. 19. he that *p.* the eye, will make tears

PRIDE.
Tob. 4. 13. for in *p.* is destruction and much trouble
Jud. 9. 9. behold their *p.* and send thy wrath
Esth. 13. 12. it was not in *p.* that I did not bow
14. not worship any but thee, nor will I do it in *p.*
Wisd. 5. 8. what hath *p.* profited us? or riches
Eccl. 10. 7. *p.* is hateful before God and man
13. *p.* is the beginning of sin, he that hath it
18. *p.* was not made for man, nor furious anger
21. roughness and *p.* is the losing thereof
15. 8. she is far from *p.* liars cannot remember
16. 8. but he abhorred them for their *p.*
26. 26. she that dishonoureth him in her *p.*
43. 1. the *p.* of the height, the clear firmament
Bar. 4. 34. her *p.* shall be turned into mourning
1 *Mac.* 2. 49. now hath *p.* and rebuke gotten strength
3. 20. they come against us in *p.* and iniquity
2 *Mac.* 1. 28. punish them that with *p.* do us wrong
5. 21. weening in his *p.* to make the land navigable
7. 36. shalt receive just punishment for thy *p.*
9. 7. but still was filled with *p.* breathing out
11. he began to leave off his great *p.*
15. 6. Nicanor in exceeding *p.* determined

PRIEST.
Eccl. 7. 31. fear the Lord, and honour the *p.*
50. 1. Simon high *p.* son of Onias, who repaired
1 *Mac.* 2. 1. Mattathias a *p.* of the sons of Joarib
7. 14. one that is a *p.* of the seed of Aaron
15. 1. to Simon the *p.* and prince of the Jews
See HIGH.

PRIESTS.
1 *Esd.* 1. 2. having set the *p.* according to courses
4. 53. the *p.* that went away should have liberty
54. the *p.* vestments wherein they minister
5. 59. the *p.* stood arrayed in their vestments
8. 77. we with our *p.* were given up to the sword
Jud. 11. 13. which they had reserved for the *p.*
Wisd. 12. 6. with their *p.* out of their idolatrous crew
Eccl. 7. 29. fear the Lord, and reverence his *p.*
50. 12. he took the portions out of the *p.* hands
Bar. 1. 7. to the *p.* and all the people at Jerusalem
1. 16. confusion of faces belongeth to our *p.*
6. 10. the *p.* convey from their gods, gold, silver
18. even so the *p.* make fast their temples
28. things sacrificed, their *p.* sell and abuse
31. the *p.* sit in their temples, their clothes rent
33. the *p.* also take off their garments
48. the *p.* consult with themselves where may be
55. when fire falleth their *p.* will flee away
Dan. 3. 62. O ye *p.* of the Lord, bless ye the Lord
Bel 8. the king was wroth, and called for his *p.*
10. now the *p.* of Bel were threescore and ten
15. in the night came the *p.* with their wives
28. the king hath put the *p.* to death
1 *Mac.* 3. 49. they brought also the *p.* garments
51. thy *p.* are in heaviness and brought low
4. 38. they saw the *p.* chambers pulled down
42. so he chose *p.* of blameless conversation
5. 67. certain *p.* desirous to shew their valour, slain
7. 36. the *p.* entered in, and stood before the altar
10. 42. because they appertain to the *p.* that minister
2 *Mac.* 1. 10. who was of the stock of the anointed *p.*
13. they were slain by the deceit of Nanea's *p.*
19. the *p.* that were then devout, took the fire
20. Neemias did send of the posterity of those *p.*
23. the *p.* made a prayer while sacrifice
30. the *p.* sung psalms of thanksgiving
3. 15. the *p.* prostrating themselves before the altar
4. 14. the *p.* had no courage to serve any more
14. 34. then the *p.* lift up their hands to heaven
15. 31. when he had set the *p.* before the altar

PRIESTHOOD.
Eccl. 45. 7. he gave him the *p.* among the people
15. they should execute the office of the *p.*
24. should have the dignity of the *p.* for ever
1 *Mac.* 2. 54. the covenant of an everlasting *p.*
7. 21. but Alcimus contended for the high *p.*
11. 27. the king confirmed him in the high *p.*
16. 24. are written in the chronicles of his *p.*
2 *Mac.* 2. 17. that gave them the *p.* and the sanctuary
4. 24. he got the *p.* to himself, offering more
11. 3. to set the high *p.* to sale every year
14. 7. of my ancestor's honour, I mean the high *p.*

PRIETH.
Eccl. 14. 23. he that *p.* in at her windows shall also

PRINCE.
Jud. 9. 10. the servant with the *p.* and the *p.* with
Eccl. 41. 17. be ashamed of a lie before a *p.*
48. 12. he was not moved with presence of any *p.*
Dan. 3. 15. nor is there at this time *p.* or prophet
1 *Mac.* 3. 13. when Seron a *p.* of the army heard
9. 30. we have chosen thee this day to be our *p.*
15. 1. unto Simon the priest and *p.* of the Jews
2. to Simon high priest and *p.* of his nation
2 *Mac.* 3. 24. the P. of all power caused an apparition

PRINCES.
Eccl. 10. 14. hath cast down the thrones of proud *p.*
39. 4. he shall appear before *p.* he will travail
46. 18. he destroyed all the *p.* of the Philistines
Bar. 2. 1. against our *p.* and the men of Israel
3. 16. where are the *p.* of the heathen become
1 *Mac.* 6. 60. the king and the *p.* were content
7. 26. the king sent Nicanor one of his honourable *p.*
9. 37. daughter of one of the great *p.* of Chanaan

PRINCELY.
1 *Esd.* 4. 46. this is the *p.* liberality from thee

PRINCIPALITY.
2 *Mac.* 4. 27. so Menelaus got the *p.*
5. 7. howbeit, for all this he obtained not the *p.*

PRISON.
Eccl. 13. 12. he will not spare to put thee in *p.*
2 *Mac.* 13. 21. when had gotten him, put him in *p.*

PRISONER.
Jud. 16. 9. her beauty took his mind *p.*
2 *Mac.* 14. 27. that he should send Maccabeus *p.*
33. if you will not deliver me Judas as a *p.*

PRISONERS.
2 *Esd.* 13. 40. ten tribes which were carried away *p.*
Wisd. 17. 2. *p.* of darkness, and fettered with night
1 *Mac.* 9. 70. that he should deliver them the *p.*
72. when he had restored unto him the *p.*
15. 40. Cendebeus began to take the people *p.*

PRIVATE.
Esth. 14. 16. I wear it not when I am *p.* by myself
2 *Mac.* 4. 5. the good of all, both public and *p.*

PRIVY.
Wisd. 8. 4. she is *p.* to the mysteries of knowledge
Sus. 18. they went out themselves at *p.* doors
Bel 13. under table they had made a *p.* entrance
21. who shewed him *p.* doors where they came
2 *Mac.* 1. 16. and opening a *p.* door of the roof
8. 7. took advantage of night for such *p.* attempts

PRIVILY.
1 *Mac.* 9. 60. he sent letters *p.* to his adherents
2 *Mac.* 1. 19. the priests took the fire of the altar *p.*
8. 1. they went *p.* into the towns and called

PROCEED.
1 *Esd.* 2. 29. those wicked workers *p.* no further

PROCEEDED.
2 *Esd.* 10. 19. so I *p.* to speak further unto her
2 *Mac.* 6. 29. the speeches *p.* from a desperate mind

PROCESS.
2 *Esd.* 11. 20. in *p.* of time the feathers stood up

PROCESSION.
2 *Mac.* 6. 7. were compelled to go in *p.* to Bacchus

PROCLAMATION.
1 *Esd.* 2. 2. he made *p.* through all his kingdom
1 *Mac.* 5. 49. Judas commanded a *p.* to be made

PROCLAIMING.
2 *Mac.* 8. 11. *p.* a sale of the captive Jews

PROCURE.
1 *Mac.* 7. 15. we will *p.* the harm neither of you
13. 17. he should *p.* to himself great hatred

PROCURED.
Esth. 16. 13. who continually *p.* our good

PROFANATION.
1 *Mac.* 1. 48. with all manner of uncleanness and *p.*

PROFANE.
1 *Mac.* 1. 45. that they should *p.* the sabbaths
63. that they might not *p.* the holy covenant
2. 34. neither will we *p.* the sabbath-day
2 *Mac.* 5. 16. with *p.* hands pulling down things
6. 5. the altar also was filled with *p.* things

PROFANED.
2 *Esd.* 10. 22. the name named on us is almost *p.*
1 *Mac.* 1. 43. many of the Israelites *p.* the sabbath
3. 51. thy sanctuary is trodden down and *p.*
4. 38. when they saw altar *p.* they rent their clothes
54. and what day the heathen had *p.* it
2 *Mac.* 8. 2. pity the temple *p.* of wicked men
10. 5. the same day that the strangers *p.* the temple

PROFANELY.
2 *Esd.* 15. 8. their wickedness they *p.* commit

PROFANENESS.
2 *Mac.* 4. 13. through the exceeding *p.* of Jason

PROFESS.
Eccl. 3. 25. *p.* not the knowledge thou hast not

PROFIT.
2 *Esd.* 7. 47. for what *p.* for men to live in heaviness?
49. what *p.* is it to us if there be promised us
Eccl. 5. 8. they shall not *p.* thee in the day of calamity
11. 23. say not, what *p.* is there of my service?
13. 4. if thou be for his *p.* he will use thee
20. 10. there is a gift that shall not *p.* thee
30. wisdom that is hid, and treasure that is hoarded up, what *p.* is in them both?
29. 11. it shall bring thee more *p.* than gold
30. 23. sorrow hath killed, and there is no *p.* therein
34. 23. what *p.* have they then but labour?
26. or what doth his humbling *p.* him?
2 *Mac.* 2. 25. been careful that all might have *p.*

PROFITABLE.
Tob. 3. 6. it is *p.* for me to die rather than live

Tob. 4. 18. and despise not any counsel that is *p.*
Wisd. 8. 7. can have nothing more *p.* in their life
Eccl. 10. 4. he will set over it one that is *p.*
37. 28. for all things are not *p.* for all men
2 *Mac.* 12. 12. that they would be *p.* in many things

PROFITED.

Wisd. 5. 8. what hath pride *p.* us, or riches
Eccl. 33. 16. by the blessing of Lord I *p.* and filled
51. 17. I *p.* therein, therefore will I ascribe glory

PROFOUNDER.

Eccl. 24. 29. her counsels *p.* than the great deep

PROGENITORS.

Esth. 16. 16. who ordered the kingdom to our *p.*

PROLOGUE.

2 *Mac.* 2. 32. it is a foolish thing to make a long *p.*

PROLONG.

Eccl. 29. 5. he will *p.* the time, and return words
38. 14. they give for ease and remedy to *p.* life

PROLONGETH.

Eccl. 30. 22. the joyfulness of a man *p.* his days
37. 31. but he that taketh heed *p.* his life

PROMISED.

Bar. 2. 34. which I *p.* with an oath to their fathers
1 *Mac.* 11. 28. he *p.* him three hundred talents
2 *Mac.* 2. 18. he *p.* in the law, will have mercy on us
4. 9. besides this he *p.* to assign 150 more
7. 26. she *p.* him that she would counsel her son

PROMISES.

2 *Esd.* 5. 29. and they which did gainsay thy *p.*
Wisd. 12. 21. hast sworn and made coven. of good *p.*
1 *Mac.* 10. 15. had heard what *p.* Demetrius had sent

PROMISETH.

Eccl. 20. 23. that for bashfulness *p.* to his friend

PROMISING.

2 *Esd.* 3. 15. *p.* that thou wouldst never forsake
2 *Mac.* 4. 8. *p.* to the king by intercession talents

PROMOTE.

Eccl. 20. 27. a wise man shall *p.* himself to honour

PROMOTED.

1 *Mac.* 11. 26. king *p.* him in sight of all his friends

PRONOUNCED.

Jud. 8. 11. this oath which ye *p.* between G. and you
Bar. 2. 1. L. made good his word which he *p.* ag. us
7. plagues which the Lord hath *p.* against us
Sus. 53. for thou hast *p.* false judgment

PRONOUNCETH.

Wisd. 2. 16. he *p.* the end of the just to be blessed

PROPER.

Wisd. 18. 21. bringeth the shield of his *p.* ministry
19. 6. for the whole creature in his *p.* kind

PROPERLY.

Tob. 1. 2. Thisbe, which is called *p.* Naphtali

PROPHECY.

2 *Esd.* 15. 1. behold, speak thou the words of *p.*
Tob. 2. 6. remembering that *p.* of Amos, as he said
Eccl. 49. 6. according to the *p.* of Jeremias

PROPHECIES.

Eccl. 39. 1. he will be occupied in *p.*
44. 3. giving counsel and declaring *p.*

PROPHESY.

2 *Esd.* 8. 5. agreed to give ear, and art willing to *p.*
Wisd. 14. 28. either mad when merry, or *p.* lies
Eccl. 47. 1. and after him rose up Nathan to *p.*

PROPHESIED.

1 *Esd.* 6. 1. Aggeus and Zacharias *p.* to the Jews
Jud. 6. 2. that thou hast *p.* among us to-day
Eccl. 46. 20. and after his death he *p.* and shewed

PROPHET.

1 *Esd.* 1. 20. since the time of the *p.* Samuel
28. not regarding the words of the *p.* Jeremy
2 *Esd.* 1. 1. the second book of the *p.* Esdras
Tob. 14. 4. which Jonas the *p.* spake of Nineve
Wisd. 11. 1. she prospered in the hand of the holy *p.*
Eccl. 46. 13. Samuel the *p.* of the Lord, beloved
15. by his faithfulness he was found a true *p.*
48. 1. then stood up Elias the *p.* as fire
49. 7. Jeremias, who nevertheless was *p.* sanctified
Bel 33. there was in Jewry a *p.* called Habbacuc
1 *Mac.* 4. 46. till there should come a *p.* to shew
9. 27. since the time that a *p.* was not seen
14. 41. until there should arise a faithful *p.*
2 *Mac.* 2. 1. that Jeremy the *p.* commanded them
2. how that the *p.* having given them the law
4. the *p.* being warned of God, commanded
15. 14. this is Jeremias the *p.* of God

PROPHETS.

1 *Esd.* 1. 51. they made a sport of his *p.*
6. 1. the *p.* prophesied unto the Jews
Tob. 4. 12. for we are the children of the *p.*
14. 5. as the *p.* have spoken thereof
Wisd. 7. 27. she maketh them friends of God, and *p.*
Eccl. 36. 15. raise up *p.* that have been in thy name
16. and let thy *p.* be found faithful

PROPITIATION.

Wisd. 18. 21. even prayer and *p.* of incense
Eccl. 5. 5. concerning *p.* be not without fear
35. 3. and to forsake unrighteousness is a *p.*

PROPORTIONABLY.

Wisd. 13. 5. *p.* the maker of them is seen

PROSPER.

2 *Esd.* 5. 12. shall labour, but their ways shall not *p.*
Tob. 4. 19. that all thy paths and counsels may *p.*
5. 16. his father said, God *p.* your journey
Eccl. 15. 10. and the Lord will *p.* it
38. 14. that he would *p.* that which they give

PROSPERED.

Wisd. 11. 1. she *p.* their works in hand of prophet
1 *Mac.* 2. 47. and the work *p.* in their hand
3. 6. because salvation *p.* in his hand
14. 36. for in his time things *p.* in his hands
16. 2. things have *p.* so well in our hands
2 *Mac.* 8. 8. that things *p.* with him still more

PROSPERITY.

Eccl. 6. 11. but in thy *p.* he will be as thyself
10. 5. in the hand of God is the *p.* of man
11. 14. *p.* and adversity, life and death come of Ld.
17. and his favour bringeth *p.* for ever
25. in day of *p.* is a forgetfulness of affliction
12. 8. a friend cannot be known in *p.*
9. in the *p.* of a man enemies will be grieved
13. 26. is a token of a heart that is in *p.*
22. 23. that thou mayest rejoice in his *p.*

Eccl. 37. 4. which rejoiceth in the *p.* of a friend
41. 1. to the man that hath *p.* in all things
1 *Mac.* 12. 22. do well to write to us of your *p.*
2 *Mac.* 9. 19. wisheth much joy, health, and *p.*

PROSPEROUS.

1 *Esd.* 8. 50. to desire of him a *p.* journey for us
Tob. 5. 21. and his journey shall be *p.*
10. 11. the God of heaven give you a *p.* journey
Eccl. 43. 26. the end of them hath *p.* success

PROSPEROUSLY.

1 *Esd.* 6. 10. the work goeth on *p.* in their hands
Tob. 4. 6. thy doings shall *p.* succeed to thee

PROSTRATING.

2 *Mac.* 3. 15. but priests *p.* themselves before altar

PROTECT.

Wisd. 5. 16. and with his arm shall he *p.* them

PROTECTETH.

Jud. 9. 14. no other that *p.* the people of Israel

PROTECTING.

1 *Mac.* 3. 3. he made battles *p.* the host with the sword

PROTECTION.

Eccl. 34. 16. he is their mighty *p.* and strong stay
2 *Mac.* 13. 17. the *p.* of the Lord did help him

PROTECTOR.

Jud. 9. 11. for thou art a *p.* of the forlorn
2 *Mac.* 11. 1. Lysias the king's *p.* and cousin
13. 2. Lysias his *p.* and ruler of his affairs

PROTESTATIONS.

Eccl. 46. 19. he made *p.* in the sight of the Lord

PROUD.

2 *Esd.* 11. 44. Highest hath looked on the *p.* times
Esth. 13. 12. that I did not bow down to *p.* Aman
Wisd. 14. 6. in old time when the *p.* giants perished
Eccl. 3. 28. in the punishment of the *p.* no remedy
10. 9. why is earth and ashes *p.*?
14. the Lord cast down the thrones of *p.* princes
15. the Ld. hath plucked up roots of the *p.* nations
11. 30. as a partridge, so is the heart of the *p.*
13. 1. he that hath fellowship with a *p.* man
20. as the *p.* hate humility, so doth the rich
21. 4. the house of *p.* men shall be made desolate
23. 4. O God of my life, give me not a *p.* look
8. the evil-speaker and *p.* shall fall thereby
25. 2. my soul hateth a poor man that is *p.*
27. 15. the strife of the *p.* is blood-shedding
28. mockery and reproach are from the *p.*
31. 26. so wine the hearts of the *p.* by drunkenness
32. 12. do what thou wilt, but sin not by *p.* speech
18. but a *p.* man is not daunted with fear
35. 18. he have taken away the multitude of the *p.*
51. 10. he would not leave me in the time of the *p.*
1 *Mac.* 2. 47. they pursued also after the *p.* men
2 *Mac.* 9. 6. so *p.* was he beyond the condition
15. 32. the hand that with *p.* brags he had stretched

PROUDLY.

Jud. 6. 17. spoken *p.* against the house of Israel
Eccl. 48. 18. his hand against Sion and boasted *p.*
1 *Mac.* 1. 21. he entered *p.* into the sanctuary
24. having made great massacre and spoken *p.*
7. 34. but he mocked them and spake *p.*
47. his hand which he stretched out so *p.*
2 *Mac.* 9. 4. for he had spoken *p.* in this sort
12. that a man should not *p.* think of himself

PROVE.

Wisd. 2. 17. let us *p.* what shall happen in the end
19. we may know his meekness, and *p.* patience
Eccl. 6. 7. if thou wouldest get a friend, *p.* him first
37. 27. my son, *p.* thy soul in thy life

PROVED.

Wisd. 3. 5. for God *p.* and found them worthy
Eccl. 44. 20. when he was *p.* he was found faithful

PROVETH.

Eccl. 27. 5. the furnace *p.* the potter's vessel
31. 26. the furnace *p.* the edge by dipping

PROVERB.

Tob. 3. 4. and for a *p.* of reproach to all nations

PROVERBS.

Eccl. 8. 8. but acquaint thyself with their *p.*
47. 17. the countries marvelled at thee for thy *p.*

PROVIDE.

1 *Mac.* 10. 6. to *p.* weapons that he might aid him

PROVIDED.

Wisd. 13. 16. he *p.* for it, that it might not fall
1 *Mac.* 10. 21. gathered forces, and *p.* much armour
14. 10. he *p.* victuals for the cities, and set in them
2 *Mac.* 4. 21. Antiochus *p.* for his own safety

PROVIDENCE.

Wisd. 14. 3. but thy *p.* O Father, governeth it
17. 2. they lay exiled from the eternal *p.*

PROVISION.

Jud. 2. 17. and goats without number for their *p.*
4. 5. they laid up victuals for the *p.* of war
12. 3. if *p.* fail, how should we give thee the like?
2 *Mac.* 6. 21. to bring flesh of his own *p.*
12. 27. wherein was great *p.* of engines and darts

PROVOKE.

Jud. 8. 14. *p.* not the Lord our God to anger
11. 11. wherefore they will *p.* their God to anger
Eccl. 4. 2. neither *p.* a man in his distress
1 *Mac.* 6. 34. they might *p.* elephants to fight
15. 40. Cendebeus began to *p.* the people

PROVOKED.

1 *Esd.* 6. 15. but when our fathers *p.* God to wrath
2 *Esd.* 1. 7. they have *p.* me to wrath, and despised
Bar. 4. 7. for ye *p.* him that made you

PRUDENCE.

Wisd. 8. 6. if *p.* work, who more cunning than she?
7. teacheth temperance, *p.* justice, and fortitude
18. in the exercise of conference with her *p.*
Eccl. 1. 4. the understanding of *p.* from everlasting
10. 3. through the *p.* of them that are in authority
19. 22. nor at any time is the counsel of sinners *p.*
25. 9. well is him that hath found *p.*
34. 10. but he that hath travelled, is full of *p.*

PRUDENT.

Eccl. 3. 29. the heart of the *p.* will understand
6. 32. if thou apply thy mind, thou shalt be *p.*
10. 1. the government of a *p.* man is well ordered

PSALM.

Jud. 16. 2. tune unto him a new *p.* exalt him

PSALMS.

2 *Mac.* 1. 30. the priests sung *p.* of thanksgiving

2 *Mac.* 10. 7. they sang *p.* to him that had given success
38. this done, they praised the Lord with *p.*
12. 37. he sung *p.* with a loud voice

PSALTERY.

2 *Esd.* 10. 22. our *p.* is laid on the ground, our song
Wisd. 19. 18. like as in a *p.* notes change the tune
Eccl. 40. 21. the pipe and *p.* make sweet melody

PTOLEMAIS.

1 *Mac.* 5. 15. they of P. and of Tyrus are assembled
55. Simon his brother in Galilee before P.
10. 1. Alexander went up and took P.
58. Alexander celebrated her marriage at P.
60. who thereupon went honourably to P.
12. 48. they of P. shut the gates and took him

PTOLEMEE.

1 *Mac.* 1. 18. but P. was afraid of him and fled
3. 38. then Lysias chose P. son of Dorymenes
10. 51. sent ambassadors to P. king of Egypt
11. 3. now as P. entered into the cities
15. king P. brought forth his host and met him
16. Alexander fled, but king P. was exalted
18. king P. also dying the third day after
15. 16. Lucius consul, unto king P. greeting
16. 16. P. and his men rose up and took weapons
18. then P. wrote these things, and sent to king
21. and, quoth he, P. hath sent to slay thee also
2 *Mac.* 4. 45. promised P. the son of Dorymenes
46. P. taking the king aside into a gallery
6. 8. there went out a decree by the suggestion of P.

PTOLEMEUS.

Esth. 11. 1. P. his son brought this epistle
1 *Mac.* 16. 11. P. the son of Abubus made captain
2 *Mac.* 1. 10. to Aristobulus king P. master
4. 21. the coronation of king P. Philometor
8. 8. he wrote unto P. the governor of Celosyria
10. 12. P. that was called Macron endeavoured

PUBLIC.

Eccl. 38. 33. they shall not be sought for in *p.* counsel
1 *Mac.* 14. 23. to put copy of ambassage in *p.* records
2 *Mac.* 4. 5. seeking the good of all, *p.* and private
15. 6. to set up a *p.* monument of his victory

PUBLISH.

2 *Esd.* 14. 26. some things shalt thou *p.*
Esth. 16. 19. ye shall *p.* the copy of this letter

PUBLISHED.

1 *Esd.* 9. 53. the Levites *p.* all things to the people

PUFFED.

2 *Mac.* 7. 34. be not *p.* up with uncertain hopes
11. 4. but *p.* up with his ten thousand footmen

PULL.

2 *Esd.* 1. 8. *p.* thou off then the hair of thy head
Wisd. 1. 12. and *p.* not on yourselves destruction
1 *Mac.* 4. 45. they thought it best to *p.* it down
6. 62. he gave commandment to *p.* down the wall
9. 55. as he began to *p.* down, Alcimus was plagued

PULLED.

1 *Esd.* 6. 16. who *p.* down the house and burned it
8. 71. I *p.* off the hair from off my head
Jud. 10. 3. *p.* off the sackcloth which he had on
Eccl. 28. 14. strong cities hath it *p.* down
40. 16. the weed shall be *p.* up before all grass
1 *Mac.* 1. 22. the ornaments, all which he *p.* off
31. he *p.* down the houses and walls thereof
2. 25. commissioner he killed, the altar he *p.* down
45. then Mattathias *p.* down the altars
4. 38. they saw the priests' chambers *p.* down
5. 65. he *p.* down the fortress of it, and burnt towers
6. 7. they *p.* down the abomination he set up
2 *Mac.* 7. 7. they had *p.* off the skin of his head
10. 2. the altars and the chapels they *p.* down

PULLETH.

Eccl. 34. 23. one buildeth, and another *p.* down

PULLING.

2 *Mac.* 5. 16. with profane hands *p.* down things

PULPIT.

1 *Esd.* 9. 42. Esdras stood upon a *p.* of wood

PUNISH.

Tob. 3. 3. *p.* me not for my sins and ignorances
Wisd. 11. 10. the other thou didst condemn and *p.*
12. 20. if thou didst *p.* the enemies of children
18. 8. wherewith thou didst *p.* our adversaries
1 *Mac.* 7. 7. let him *p.* them with all that aid them
2 *Mac.* 1. 28. *p.* them that oppress us and do wrong
6. 14. whom the Lord patiently forbears to *p.*
16. tho' he *p.* with adversity, yet doth not forsake

PUNISHED.

2 *Esd.* 9. 13. how the ungodly shall be *p.* and when
Jud. 11. 10. for our nation shall not be *p.*
Wisd. 3. 4. for though they be *p.* in sight of men
10. but the ungodly shall be *p.* according to
11. 5. by what things their enemies were *p.*
8. how thou hadst *p.* their adversaries
16. by the same also shall he be *p.*
12. 14. for any of whom thou hadst *p.*
15. condemn him that hath not deserved to be *p.*
27. look for what things they grudged when they were *p.* now being *p.* in them when they saw it
14. 10. shall be *p.* together with him that made it
30. for both causes shall they be justly *p.*
16. 1. by the like were they *p.* worthily
9. for they were worthy to be *p.* by such
18. 11. the master and the servant were *p.*
22. but with a word subdued him that *p.*
Eccl. 23. 21. this man shall be *p.* in the streets
1 *Mac.* 14. 45. or break these things should be *p.*
2 *Mac.* 6. 13. not suffered long, but forthwith *p.*
7. 7. they asked, wilt thou eat before thou be *p.*?

PUNISHETH.

Jud. 7. 28. which *p.* us according to our sins
Wisd. 1. 8. nor vengeance when it *p.* pass by him
14. 31. that *p.* always the offence of the ungodly

PUNISHING.

Eccl. 39. 30. *p.* the wicked to destruction

PUNISHMENT.

2 *Esd.* 7. 21. what they should observe to avoid *p.*
47. what profit for men after death to look for *p.*
15. 12. Egypt smitten with the plague and *p.*
Wisd. 16. 2. instead of which *p.* dealing graciously
24. against the unrighteous for their *p.*
19. 4. they might fulfil the *p.* which was wanting
Eccl. 3. 28. in *p.* of the proud there is no remedy
8. 5. remember that we are all worthy of *p.*

Eccl. 12. 6. keep. against the mighty day of their *p.*
2 *Mac.* 4. 38. thus the Lord rewarded him his *p.*
48. thus they did soon suffer unjust *p.*
6. 26. tho' I should be delivered from the *p.* of men
7. 36. thou shalt receive just *p.* for thy pride

PUNISHMENTS.

Wisd. 11. 13. when they heard by their own *p.*
19. 13. and *p.* came upon the sinners
2 *Mac.* 6. 12. judge those *p.* not to be for destruction

PURE.

Tob. 3. 14. that I am *p.* from all sin with man
13. 16. thy towers and battlements with *p.* gold
Wisd. 7. 23. *p.* and most subtile spirits
Eccl. 21. 13. his counsel is like a *p.* fountain of life
Bar. 3. 30. who will bring her for *p.* gold ?

PURENESS.

Wisd. 7. 24. she goeth thro' all by reason of her *p.*
Eccl. 51. 20. and I found her in *p.*

PURGE.

Tob. 12. 9. for alms shall *p.* away all sin

PURIFICATION.

2 *Mac.* 1. 18. purposed to keep the *p.* of the temple

PURIFIED.

2 *Mac.* 1. 33. Neemias had *p.* sacrifices therewith
2. 18. he delivered us and hath *p.* the place
12. 38. they *p.* themselves as the custom was

PURPLE.

Eccl. 40. 4. from him that weareth *p.* and a crown
45. 10. with gold, and blue silk and *p.*
Bar. 6. 12. though they be covered with *p.* raiment
72. by the bright *p.* that rotteth upon them
1 *Mac.* 4. 23. where they got gold and *p.* of the sea
8. 14. none was clothed in *p.* to be magnified
10. 20. he sent him a *p.* robe and a crown of gold
62. the king commanded to clothe him in *p.*
2 *Mac.* 4. 38. he took away Andronicus's *p.*

PURPOSE.

Jud. 8. 14. can ye search God, or comprehend his *p.*
11. 11. he not defeated and frustrate of his *p.*
13. 3. spake to Bagoas according to the same *p.*
1 *Mac.* 15. 3. my *p.* is to challenge it again
2 *Mac.* 3. 8. but indeed to fulfil the king's *p.*

PURPOSED.

Jud. 9. 8. they have *p.* to defile thy sanctuary
13. who have *p.* cruel things against thy covenant
11. 12. they *p.* to consume all those things
Wisd. 8. 9. I *p.* to take her to me to live with me
Eccl. 51. 18. I *p.* to do after her, and I followed
1 *Mac.* 14. 31. enemies *p.* to invade their country
2 *Mac.* 1. 18. we are *p.* to keep the purification

PURPOSES.

Jud. 11. 6. my lord shall not fail of his *p.*
Esth. 12. 2. he searched out their *p.* and learned
16. 9. both by changing our *p.* and judging

PURSUE.

Jud. 14. 4. ye shall *p.* them, and overthrow them
2 *Mac.* 8. 26. they would no longer *p.* them

PURSUED.

Wisd. 19. 3. and they *p.* them as fugitives
1 *Mac.* 2. 47. they *p.* also after the proud men
3. 5. for he *p.* the wicked, and sought them out
4. 9. when Pharaoh *p.* them with an army
15. for they *p.* them unto Gazara and Idumea
5. 22. he *p.* them to the gate of Ptolemais
60. and *p.* them to the borders of Judea
9. 15. who *p.* them unto the mount Azotus
15. 11. being *p.* by king Antiochus, he fled
2 *Mac.* 5. 8. fleeing from city to city, *p.* of all men

PURSUING.

1 *Mac.* 4. 16. Judas returned again from *p.* them
2 *Mac.* 12. 23. Judas was very earnest in *p.* them

PURVEYOR.

Tob. 1. 13. before Enemessar, so that I was his *p.*

PUT.

2 *Esd.* 3. 16. didst choose him to thee, and *p.* by Esau
Wisd. 3. 9. that *p.* trust in him, shall understand
Eccl. 13. 6. smile on thee, and *p.* thee in hope
Sus. 51. *p.* these two aside one from another
56. so he *p.* him aside and commanded to bring
2 *Mac.* 13. 10. at the point to be *p.* from their law

PUTTING.

Jud. 16. 17. in *p.* fire and worms in their flesh
2 *Mac.* 4. 11. and *p.* down the governments

PYRAMIDS.

1 *Mac.* 13. 28. he set up seven *p.* one against another

Q.

QUAILS.

2 *Esd.* 1. 15. the *q.* were as a token for you
Wisd. 16. 2. even *q.* to stir up their appetite
19. 12. for *q.* came up to them from the sea

QUAKE.

1 *Mac.* 4. 32. let them *q.* at their destruction

QUAKED.

Jud. 16. 10. the Persians *q.* at her boldness

QUAKETH.

2 *Esd.* 16. 12. the earth *q.* and foundations thereof

QUANTITY.

2 *Esd.* 4. 50. the *q.* which is past did more exceed

QUARRELLING.

Eccl. 31. 29. excess maketh brawling and *q.*

QUARTERS.

1 *Mac.* 3. 36. should place strangers in all their *q.*
5. 9. the Israelites that were in their *q.*

QUELL.

1 *Mac.* 4. 30. who didst *q.* the violence of the mighty

QUENCH.

2 *Esd.* 16. 4. a fire is sent, and who may *q.* it ?
Esth. 14. 9. they will *q.* the glory of thy house

QUENCHED.

Wisd. 11. 4. their thirst was *q.* out of the hard stone
Eccl. 28. 12. if thou spit on it, it shall be *q.*
23. and it shall burn in them, and not be *q.*

QUENCHETH.

Wisd. 16. 17. had force in water that *q.* all things

QUENCHING.

Wisd. 19. 20. the water forgat his own *q.* nature

QUESTION.

1 *Esd.* 6. 30. every year, without further *q.*

QUESTIONS.

2 *Esd.* 8. 55. therefore ask thou no more *q.*

QUICK.

Wisd. 7. 22. loving the thing that is good, *q.*
8. 11. I shall be found of a *q.* conceit in judgment
Eccl. 31. 22. my son, in all thy works be *q.*

QUICKEN.

2 *Esd.* 8. 13. and thou shalt *q.* it as thy work

QUICKLY.

Wisd. 3. 18. or if they die *q.* they have no hope
6. 15. whoso watcheth, shall *q.* be without care
1 *Mac.* 2. 40, they will *q.* root us out of the earth
6. 27. wherefore if thou dost not prevent them *q.*
2 *Mac.* 14. 44. but they *q.* giving back, he fell

QUIET.

2 *Esd.* 10. 3. when they had all left off to comfort me, to the end I might be *q.* then I rose and fled
Esth. 16. 8. we must take care that our kingdom for time to come may be *q.* and peaceable for all men
Wisd. 18. 14. while all things were in *q.* silence
Eccl. 25. 20. so is a wife full of words to a *q.* man
47. 13. Solomon reigned in a peaceable time, was honoured, for God made all *q.* round about him
1 *Mac.* 1. 3. that the earth was *q.* before him
2 *Mac.* 12. 2. Nicanor would not suffer them to be *q.*
14. 10. not possible that the state should be *q.*
25. so he married, was *q.* and took part of life

QUIETLY.

Eccl. 28. 16. never find rest, and never dwell *q.*
2 *Mac.* 11. 23. they that are in our realm live *q.*

QUIETNESS.

2 *Esd.* 2. 24. abide, take rest, for thy *q.* shall come

QUIVER.

Eccl. 26. 12. by every hedge she will sit down, and open her *q.* against every arrow

R.

RABSACES.

Eccl. 48. 18. Sennacherib came up and sent R.

RACE.

Eccl. 26. 21. thy *r.* thou leavest shall be magnified

RAGE.

Wisd. 11. 18. or unknown wild beasts full of *r.*
Eccl. 31. 30. drunkenness increaseth the *r.*
36. 9. let him be consumed by the *r.* of the fire
1 *Mac.* 7. 35. with that he went out in a great *r.*
15. 36. but returned in a *r.* to the king
2 *Mac.* 4. 25. having the *r.* of a savage beast
40. the common people being filled with *r.*
7. 3. then the king being in a *r.* commanded
10. 28. making their *r.* leader of their battle

RAGES.

Tob. 1. 14. I left at R. a city of Media, ten talents
5. 5. he said to him, canst thou go with me to R. ?
6. 9. and when they were come near to R.

RAGUEL.

Tob. 3. 7. Sara the daughter of R. was reproached
6. 10. to-day we shall lodge with R. thy cousin
7. 6. then R. leaped up, and kissed him, and wept
9. he communicated the matter with R. and R. said to Tobias, eat, drink, and make merry
8. 9. R. arose, and went and made a grave
15. R. praised God, and said, thou art worthy
9. 3. R. hath sworn that I shall not depart

RAILINGS.

Eccl. 29. 6. he payeth him with cursings and *r.*

RAIN.

2 *Esd.* 4. 50. as the *r.* is more than the drops
8. 43. the seed perisheth if it receive not thy *r.* in due season, or if there come too much *r.*
Jud. 8. 31. pray for us, the Lord will send us *r.*
Wisd. 16. 22. fire sparkling in the *r.* destroyeth fruits
Eccl. 1. 2. who can number the drops of *r.* ?
35. 20. as clouds of *r.* in the time of drought
40. 13. goods shall vanish like a great thunder in *r.*
49. 9. of the enemies under the figure of the *r.*
Bar. 6. 53. nor can they give *r.* unto men

RAINBOW.

Eccl. 43. 11. look on *r.* and praise him that made it
50. 7. as *r.* giving light in the bright clouds

RAINS.

Wisd. 16. 16. with strange *r.* were persecuted

RAINETH.

Eccl. 1. 19. wisdom *r.* down skill and knowledge

RAINING.

Eccl. 43. 18. the heart is astonished at the *r.* of it

RAISE.

2 *Esd.* 2. 16. those that be dead will I *r.* again
12. 23. the Most High shall *r.* up three kingdoms
Eccl. 36. 7. *r.* up indignation, and pour out wrath
48. 5. who didst *r.* up a dead man from death
2 *Mac.* 7. 9. the King of the world shall *r.* us up

RAISED.

1 *Esd.* 2. 2. the Lord *r.* up the spirit of Cyrus
23. Jews were rebellious, and *r.* always wars
8. 81. honoured the temple and *r.* up desolate Sion
2 *Esd.* 6. 21. and they shall live and be *r.* up
7. 31. the world that awaketh shall not be *r.*
Eccl. 49. 13. Neemias who *r.* up for us the walls that were fallen, and *r.* up our ruins again
Sus. 45. Lord *r.* up the spirit of a young youth
1 *Mac.* 14. 37. he *r.* up the walls of Jerusalem

RAISETH.

Eccl. 34. 17. he *r.* up the soul, and lighteneth the eyes

RAM.

Tob. 7. 8. after they had killed a *r.* of the flock

RAMS.

1 *Esd.* 6. 29. for bullocks, and *r.* and lambs
7. 7. they offered two hundred *r.* 400 lambs
2 *Mac.* 12. 15. without any *r.* or engines of war

RAN.

Tob. 11. 9. Anna *r.* forth, and fell on neck of her son
10. Tobit stumbled, but his son *r.* to him
Jud. 6. 16. and all their youth *r.* together
Sus. 19. the two elders rose up, and *r.* to her
1 *Mac.* 2. 24. he *r.* and slew him upon the altar
11. 72. put them to flight, and so they *r.* away
2 *Mac.* 3. 18. others *r.* flocking out of their houses
19. the virgins kept in *r.* some to the gates
2 *Mac.* 10. 16. so they *r.* with violence on the holds
14. 43. he *r.* boldly up to the wall, cast himself down
45. yet he *r.* through the midst of the throng

RANGED.

Jud. 2. 16. he *r.* them as a great army is ordered
2 *Mac.* 12. 20. Maccabeus *r.* his army by bands

RANKS.

1 *Mac.* 6. 38. being harnessed all over amidst the *r*

RAPHAEL.

Tob. 3. 17. and R. was sent to heal them both
5. 4. he found R. that was an angel
8. 2. as he went, he remembered the words of R.
9. 1. then Tobias called R. and said to him
5. so R. went out and lodged with Gabael
12. 15. I am R. one of the seven holy angels

RAPHAN.

1 *Mac.* 5. 37. Timotheus encamped against R.

RASH.

Eccl. 9. 18. he that is *r.* in his talk shall be hated

RATIFIED.

1 *Mac.* 8. 30. what they add or take away shall be *r.*
11. 34. we have *r.* to them the borders of Judea

RATTLING.

1 *Mac.* 6. 41. all that heard the *r.* of the harness

RAVISHED.

2 *Esd.* 10. 22. our virgins defiled and our wives *r.*
Jud. 12. 16. Holofernes his heart was *r.* with her
16. 9. her sandals *r.* his eyes, her beauty took

RAZIS.

2 *Mac.* 14. 37. R. one of the elders of Jerusalem

REACH.

Eccl. 31. 18. *r.* not thy hand out first of all
35. 16. and his prayer shall *r.* unto the clouds
2 *Mac.* 9. 10. that he could *r.* to the stars of heaven

REACHED.

2 *Esd.* 14. 39. and behold he *r.* me a full cup

REACHETH.

Wisd. 8. 1. wisdom *r.* from one end to another
Eccl. 21. 5. a prayer *r.* to the ears of God

READ.

1 *Esd.* 2. 30. king Artaxerxes his letters being *r.*
3. 13. they delivered them to him, so he *r.* them
15. and the writings were *r.* before them
9. 41. he *r.* in the broad court before the porch
2 *Esd.* 14. 45. the worthy and unworthy may *r.* it
Bar. 1. 3. Baruch did *r.* the words of this book
14. ye shall *r.* this book which we have sent
1 *Mac.* 14. 19. which writings were *r.* before congre.
2 *Mac.* 2. 25. they that will *r.* might have delight
6. 12. now I beseech those that *r.* this book
8. 23. he appointed Eleazar to *r.* the holy book
15. 39. delighteth the ears of them that *r.* the story

READER.

1 *Esd.* 8. 8. Esdras priest and *r.* of the law, 9. 19.

READING.

1 *Mac.* 5. 14. while these letters were yet *r.* behold

READY.

Tob. 14. 3. for I am *r.* to depart out of this life
Esth. 11. 9. nation troubled, and were *r.* to perish
Wisd. 7. 22. which cannot be letted, *r.* to do good
Eccl. 29. 26. and feed me of that thou hast *r.*
39. 31. they shall be *r.* on earth when need is
51. 3. teeth of them that were *r.* to devour me
1 *Mac.* 3. 9. he received such as were *r.* to perish
17. we are *r.* to faint with fasting all day
2 *Mac.* 3. 31. who lay *r.* to give up the ghost
6. 30. when he was *r.* to die with stripes
7. 2. we are *r.* to die, rather than to transgress
14. so when he was *r.* to die, he said thus
8. 21. when he made them *r.* to die for the laws

READILY.

2 *Mac.* 14. 9. the clemency thou *r.* shewest to all

READINESS.

2 *Mac.* 13. 12. Judas commanded they should be in *r.*

REALM.

1 *Esd.* 4. 49. he wrote for Jews that went out of his *r.*
8. 10. the priests and Levites being within our *r.*
2 *Esd.* 13. 31. one *r.* shall fight against another
1 *Mac.* 3. 27. he gathered all the forces of his *r.*
6. 14. Philip, whom he made ruler over all his *r.*
10. 34. days of freedom for all Jews in my *r.*
52. forasmuch as I am come again to my *r.*
15. 28. Joppe and Gazara, cities of my *r.*
2 *Mac.* 10. 11. he set Lysias over the affairs of his *r.*
11. 23. they that are in our *r.* live quietly
14. 6. Assideans will not let the *r.* be in peace
26. Judas, a traitor to his *r.* to be successor

REALMS.

1 *Mac.* 1. 16. might have the dominion of two *r*

REAP.

2 *Esd.* 16. 43. he that soweth, as if he should not *r.*
46. strangers shall *r.* their fruits, spoil their goods
Eccl. 7. 3. and thou shalt not *r.* them seven-fold

REAPED.

1 *Esd.* 4. 6. when they *r.* that which they had sown
Jud. 4. 5. for their fields were of late *r.*

REAPERS.

Bel 33. he was going into field to bring it to the *r.*

REARING.

1 *Esd.* 5. 62. for *r.* up the house of the Lord

REASON.

Wisd. 11. 15. they worshipped serpents void of *r.*
17. 12. but a betraying of the succours *r.* offereth
Eccl. 37. 16. let *r.* go before every enterprise
1 *Mac.* 12. 11. we remember you in prayer, as *r.* is

REASONABLE.

2 *Mac.* 11. 14. them to agree to all *r.* conditions

REASONETH.

Eccl. 14. 20. blessed is the man that *r.* of holy things

REASONING.

Wisd. 2. 1. the ungodly said, *r.* with themselves
Eccl. 27. 5. so the trial of a man is in his *r.*

REASONINGS.

Wisd. 7. 20. the violence of winds, and *r.* of men

REBEL.

1 *Esd.* 2. 19. but they will also *r.* against kings
Jud. 2. 11. but concerning them that *r.* spare not

REBELLED.

1 *Esd.* 1. 48. he forswore himself and *r.*
Jud. 7. 15. because they *r.* and met not thy person

REBELLION.

1 *Esd.* 2. 27. the men therein were given to *r.*

REBELLIOUS.
1 *Esd.* 2. 18. Jerusalem, that *r.* and wicked city
22. thou shalt understand that city was *r.*
2 *Esd.* 1. 8. not obedient, but it is a *r.* people
Eccl. 16. 6. in a *r.* nation wrath is set on fire
47. 21. out of Ephraim ruled a *r.* kingdom

REBOUNDING.
Wisd. 17. 19. or a *r.* echo from hollow mountains

REBUKE.
2 *Esd.* 10. 28. and my prayer is turned into *r.*
Eccl. 11. 7. understand first, and then *r.*
31. 31. *r.* not thy neighbour at the wine
48. 7. who heardest the *r.* of the Lord in Sinai
1 *Mac.* 2. 49. now hath pride and *r.* gotten strength

REBUKED.
Eccl. 13. 22. poor man slipt, and yet they *r.* him too

RECEIVE.
Tob. 5. 2. how can I *r.* the money? I know him not
Jud. 11. 5. Judith said, *r.* the words of thy servant
Wisd. 6. 25. *r.* instruction through my words
12. 7. that the land might *r.* a worthy colony
17. 21. which should afterwards *r.* them
Eccl. 4. 31. let not thy hand be stretched to *r.*
6. 23. give ear, my son, *r.* my advice
33. love to hear, thou shalt *r.* understanding
11. 34. *r.* a stranger into thy house, and he will disturb thee
12. 5. else thou shalt *r.* twice as much evil
15. 2. *r.* him as a wife married of a virgin
18. 14. hath mercy on them that *r.* discipline
19. 19. shall *r.* fruit of the tree of immortality
29. 6. if he prevail, he shall hardly *r.* the half
32. 2. *r.* a crown for thy well-ordering the feast
35. 12. not with gifts, for such he will not *r.*
36. 21. a woman will *r.* every man
38. 2. and he shall *r.* honour of the king
41. 1. yea, unto him that is yet able to *r.* meat
50. 3. the cistern to *r.* water was covered with brass
21. they might *r.* a blessing from the Most High
51. 26. and let your soul *r.* instruction
2 *Mac.* 7. 11. from him I hope to *r.* them again
29. that I may *r.* thee again in mercy
36. thou shalt *r.* just punishment for thy pride

RECEIVED.
1 *Esd.* 6. 6. until such time as an answer was *r.*
Tob. 7. 17. she wept and *r.* the tears of her daughter
11. 16. they marvelled because he had *r.* his sight
Jud. 3. 7. the country about *r.* them with dances
Esth. 16. 10. and as a stranger *r.* of us
Wisd. 3. 6. he *r.* them as a burnt offering
16. 14. neither the soul *r.* up, cometh again
19. 16. whom they had *r.* with feastings
Eccl. 17. 5. they *r.* the use of the five operations
23. 28. and to be *r.* of him is long life
29. 5. till he hath *r.* he will kiss a man's hand
51. 16. I *r.* her, and gat much learning
2 *Mac.* 7. 8. he *r.* the next torment in order

RECEIVEST.
Eccl. 42. 7. all that thou gavest out, or *r.* in

RECEIVING.
1 *Mac.* 16. 15. the son of Abubus *r.* them deceitfully
2 *Mac.* 10. 15. *r.* those that were banished from Jeru.

RECEPTACLES.
Eccl. 39. 17. at the words of his mouth *r.* of waters

RECITED.
Eccl. 44. 5. such as *r.* verses in writing

RECKONED.
Eccl. 29. 4. many *r.* it found and put them to trouble
1 *Mac.* 10. 38. that they may be *r.* to be under one

RECKONING.
Tob. 6. 15. make thou no *r.* of the evil spirit
Eccl. 42. 3. of *r.* with partners and travellers

RECOMPENSE.
2 *Esd.* 15. 21. so will I do and *r.* in their bosom
55. therefore shalt thou receive *r.*
Eccl. 7. 28. how canst thou *r.* them the things
12. 2. do good to the godly, thou shalt find a *r.*
14. 6. and there is a *r.* of his wickedness
17. 23. it will render their *r.* on their heads
20. 10. there is a gift whose *r.* is double
36. 20. but a man of experience will *r.* him
Bar. 6. 34. evil or good, they are not able to *r.* it
1 *Mac.* 2. 68. *r.* fully the heathen, and take heed
10. 27. we will *r.* you for all the things ye do

RECOMPENSED.
1 *Mac.* 16. 17. in which doing he *r.* evil for good

RECOMPENSETH.
Eccl. 35. 11. for the Lord *r.* and will give thee

RECONCILED.
1 *Esd.* 4. 31. that she might be *r.* to him again
2 *Mac.* 5. 20. the great Lord being *r.* it was set up
8. 29. they besought the merciful Lord to be *r.*

RECONCILEMENT.
Eccl. 27. 21. and after reviling, there may be *r.*

RECONCILIATION.
Eccl. 22. 22. fear not, for there may be a *r.*
45. 16. he chose him to make *r.* for his people
23. Phinees stood up and made *r.* for Israel
2 *Mac.* 12. 45. whereupon he made a *r.* for the dead

RECORD.
Esth. 12. 4. the king made a *r.* of these things

RECORDED.
1 *Esd.* 1. 42. those things that are *r.* of him

RECORDS.
1 *Mac.* 14. 23. a copy of their ambassage in public *r.*
2 *Mac.* 2. 1. it is also found in the *r.* that Jeremy

RECOVERED.
Jud. 14. 7. but when they had *r.* him, he fell
1 *Mac.* 2. 48. they *r.* the law out of the hand of the Gentiles
10. 52. as I am come again, and have *r.* our country
2 *Mac.* 2. 22. *r.* again the temple and freed city

RECOUNTED.
2 *Mac.* 8. 19. he *r.* what helps their fathers found

RED.
Wisd. 10. 18. she brought them through the R. sea

REDRESS.
Bar. 6. 54. nor can *r.* a wrong, being unable

REFERRED.
2 *Mac.* 11. 36. touching things to be *r.* to the king

REFORM.
2 *Esd.* 14. 34. *r.* your hearts, ye shall be kept alive

REFORMED.
Wisd. 9. 18. for so the ways of them which lived on the earth were *r.* and men were taught the things
12. 26. they that would not be *r.* by correction
Eccl. 10. 25. he will not grudge when he is *r.*
23. 15. will never be *r.* all the days of his life

REFORMEDST.
2 *Esd.* 8. 12. and thou *r.* it with thy judgment

REFRAIN.
Wisd. 1. 11. and *r.* your tongue from backbiting
Eccl. 4. 23. *r.* not to speak when there is occasion
18. 30. but *r.* thyself from thine appetites

REFRESHED.
2 *Esd.* 11. 46. that all the earth may be *r.* and return

REFRESHETH.
Eccl. 43. 22. a dew coming after heat, *r.*

REFUGE.
1 *Mac.* 10. 14. for it was their place of *r.*
2 *Mac.* 10. 28. having their *r.* also unto the Lord

REFUSE.
1 *Esd.* 2. 19. they will not only *r.* to give tribute
Eccl. 6. 23. receive advice, and *r.* not my counsel

REFUSED.
Eccl. 29. 7. many have *r.* to lend for others' ill dealing

REFUSE.
Tob. 5. 18. let it be as *r.* in respect of our child
Wisd. 13. 12. after spending the *r.* of his work
13. taking the very *r.* which served to no use
Eccl. 27. 4. sifteth with a sieve, the *r.* remaineth

REGARD.
2 *Esd.* 8. 27. *r.* not wicked inventions of the heathen
15. 16. they shall not *r.* their kings or princes
Tob. 3. 15. command some *r.* to be had of me
Eccl. 10. 19. that *r.* not the law are dishonourable
20. 7. but a babbler and a fool will *r.* no time
41. 12. *r.* thy name, for that shall continue

REGARDED.
Wisd. 3. 17. yet shall they be nothing *r.*
2 *Mac.* 7. 12. for that he nothing *r.* the pains

REGARDETH.
Eccl. 34. 2. whoso *r.* dreams, is like him that

REGARDING.
Wisd. 10. 8. *r.* not wisdom, they gat this hurt

REGIONS.
1 *Esd.* 4. 28. do not all *r.* fear to touch him?

REGISTER.
1 *Mac.* 14. 22. did *r.* the things that they spake

REGISTERED.
1 *Mac.* 8. 20. we might be *r.* your confederates

REHEARSE.
Eccl. 19. 7. *r.* not to another what is told thee

REJECT, ED.
Jud. 11. 10. *r.* not his word, but lay it up in thy heart
Wisd. 9. 4. *r.* me not from among thy children
Eccl. 4. 4. *r.* not the supplication of the afflicted
20. 20. a wise sentence shall be *r.* when it comes

REIGN.
Wisd. 3. 8. and their Lord shall *r.* for ever
6. 21. honour wisdom, that ye may *r.* for evermore

REIGNED.
Wisd. 14. 25. there *r.* in all men without exception
Eccl. 47. 13. Solomon *r.* in a peaceable time
1 *Mac.* 1. 1. he *r.* in his stead, the first over Greece
7. Alexander *r.* twelve years, and then died
10. Antiochus *r.* in the 137th year of the kingdom
6. 2. Alexander who *r.* first among the Grecians
10. 1. by means whereof he *r.* there
11. 19. by this Demetrius *r.* in the 167th year
54. young Antiochus, who *r.* and was crowned
12. 7. letters from Darius, who *r.* among you

REINS.
1 *Mac.* 2. 24. when Mattathias saw, his *r.* trembled

REJOICE.
Tob. 13. 7. my soul shall *r.* in his greatness
14. love thee, for they shall *r.* in thy peace
14. 7. those who love the Lord in truth shall *r.*
Jud. 4. 12. the sanctuary for the nations to *r.* at
Eccl. 8. 7. *r.* not over thy greatest enemy
16. 2. though they multiply, *r.* not in them
22. 23. that thou mayest *r.* in his prosperity
26. 4. rich or poor, he shall at all times *r.*
30. 2. shall *r.* of him among his acquaintance
3. and before his friends he shall *r.* of him
35. 19. till he have made them to *r.* in his mercy
39. 31. they shall *r.* in his commandment
40. 20. wine and music *r.* the heart
50. 20. to give the blessing and *r.* in his name
51. 29. let your soul *r.* in his mercy
Bar. 4. 12. let no man *r.* over me a widow
2 *Mac.* 15. 11. which did not a little *r.* them

REJOICED.
Tob. 14. 15. before his death he *r.* over Nineve
Wisd. 7. 12. I *r.* in them all for wisdom goeth before
Eccl. 30. 5. while he lived, he saw and *r.* in him
Bar. 3. 34. the stars shined in their watches and *r.*
4. 31. miserable are they that *r.* at thy fall
33. for as she *r.* at thy ruin and was glad
1 *Mac.* 7. 48. for this the people *r.* greatly
14. 11. made peace, and Israel *r.* with great joy

REJOICETH.
Eccl. 26. 2. a virtuous woman *r.* her husband
37. 4. which *r.* in the prosperity of a friend

REJOICING.
2 *Esd.* 10. 22. our *r.* is at an end
Tob. 11. 15. his son went in *r.* and told his father
Eccl. 1. 11. the fear of the Lord is a crown of *r.*
18. and it enlargeth their *r.* that love him
Bar. 4. 34. I will take away the *r.* of her multitude
37. lo, thy sons come *r.* in the glory of God
5. 5. *r.* in the remembrance of God

RELEASE, ED.
Prayer of Manass. cannot lift my head, nor have *r.*
1 *Mac.* 10. 29. for your sakes I *r.* all the Jews
30. I *r.* it from this day forth
42. even those things shall be *r.* they appertain

RELIEF.
1 *Mac.* 11. 35. we discharge them of all for their *r.*
2 *Mac.* 3. 10. for the *r.* of widows and fatherless

RELIEVING.
Eccl. 3. 14. *r.* thy father shall not be forgotten

RELIGION.
1 *Mac.* 1. 43. the Israelites consented to his *r.*
2. 19. and fall away from the *r.* of their fathers
22. to go from our *r.* either on right hand or left
2 *Mac.* 6. 24. were now gone to a strange *r.*
8. 1. took all such as continued in the Jews' *r.*
14. 38. jeopard his body for the *r.* of the Jews

RELIGIOUS.
Jud. 11. 17. thy servant is *r.* and serveth God

RELY.
Eccl. 15. 4. he shall *r.* on her and not be confounded

RELIED.
1 *Mac.* 8. 12. with such as *r.* on them kept amity

REMAIN.
2 *Esd.* 13. 49. he shall defend his people that *r.*
Jud. 11. 17. therefore, my lord, I will *r.* with thee
Eccl. 23. 27. they that *r.* shall know there is
42. 23. all these things live and *r.* for ever
44. 11. shall continually *r.* a good inheritance
13. their seed shall *r.* for ever, and their glory
45. 15. to his seed so long as the heavens should *r.*
Bar. 2. 21. so shall ye *r.* in the land that I gave
6. 3. ye shall *r.* in Babylon many years, a long

REMAINED.
Eccl. 48. 15. there *r.* a small people and a ruler

REMAINETH.
Eccl. 38. 19. in affliction also sorrow *r.*

REMEDY.
Wisd. 2. 1. in the death of a man there is no *r.*
16. 9. nor was there found any *r.* for their life
Eccl. 3. 28. in punishment of proud there is no *r.*
43. 22. a present *r.* of all is a mist coming speedily

REMEDILESS.
Esth. 16. 5. hath enwrapped them in *r.* calamities

REMEMBER.
1 *Esd.* 3. 23. they *r.* not what they have done
4. 43. *r.* thy vow which thou hast vowed to build
2 *Esd.* 2. 31. *r.* thy children that sleep
8. 39. and I will *r.* also their pilgrimage
Tob. 3. 3. *r.* me, and look on me, punish me not
4. 4. *r.* that she saw many dangers for thee
19. therefore, my son, *r.* my commandments
6. 15. dost thou not *r.* precepts thy father gave thee?
14. 10. *r.* how Aman handled Achiacharus
Jud. 8. 26. *r.* what things he did to Abraham
13. 19. which *r.* the power of God for ever
Esth. 10. 5. for I *r.* a dream which I saw
14. 12. *r.* O Lord, make thyself known in affliction
Wisd. 16. 11. that they should *r.* thy words
Eccl. 7. 16. but *r.* that wrath will not tarry long
28. *r.* that thou wast begot of them
36. *r.* the end and thou shalt never do amiss
8. 5. *r.* that we are all worthy of punishment
7. rejoice not over enemy, but *r.* that we die all
9. 12. *r.* shall not go unpunished to their grave
13. *r.* that thou goest in the midst of snares
12. 12. and thou at last *r.* my words
14. 12. *r.* that death will not be long in coming
15. 8. and men that are liars cannot *r.* her
18. 25. thou hast enough, *r.* the time of hunger
23. 14. *r.* thy father and thy mother
18. the Most High will not *r.* my sins
28. 6. *r.* thy end, and let enmity cease, *r.* corruption and death, abide in the commandments
7. *r.* the commandments and bear no malice
31. 13. *r.* that a wicked eye is an evil thing
36. 8. make the time short, *r.* the covenant
38. 20. drive it away, and *r.* the last end
41. 3. *r.* them that have been before thee
42. 15. I will now *r.* the works of the Lord
Bar. 2. 30. in captivity they shall *r.* themselves
33. they shall *r.* the way of their fathers
3. 5. *r.* not the iniquities of our forefathers
4. 14. *r.* ye the captivity of my sons and daughters
Sus. 9. that they might not *r.* just judgments
1 *Mac.* 4. 9. *r.* how our fathers were delivered
6. 12. I *r.* the evils that I did at Jerusalem
7. 38. *r.* their blasphemies, and suffer them not
12. 11. we *r.* you in sacrifices we offer
2 *Mac.* 8. 4. *r.* the wicked slaughter of infants
15. 8. but to *r.* the help which they had received

REMEMBRANCE.
2 *Esd.* 1. 36. yet they shall call their sins to *r.*
12. 47. for the Highest hath you in *r.*
Tob. 12. 12. I did bring the *r.* of your prayers
Wisd. 2. 4. no man shall have our works in *r.*
11. 12. a groaning for the *r.* of things past
16. 6. to put them in *r.* of the commandment
Eccl. 11. 25. in affliction there is no *r.* of prosperity
28. 1. he will surely keep his sins in *r.*
38. 23. when the dead is at rest, let his *r.* rest
41. 1. O death, how bitter is the *r.* of thee!
49. 1. the *r.* of Josias is like the composition
50. 16. for a *r.* before the Most High
Bar. 5. 5. rejoicing in the *r.* of God
1 *Mac.* 2. 51. call to *r.* what acts our fathers did
2 *Mac.* 12. 42. the sin might wholly be put out of *r*

REMEMBERED.
Tob. 1. 12. because I *r.* God with all my heart
4. 1. in that day Tobit *r.* the money
8. 2. as he went he *r.* the words of Raphael
Esth. 10. 12. so God *r.* his people and justified
Eccl. 3. 15. in the day of affliction shall be *r.*
Bar. 3. 23. none of these have *r.* the paths of wisdom
4. 27. shall be *r.* of him that brought these things
Bel. 38. Daniel said, thou hast *r.* me, O God
1 *Mac.* 5. 4. he *r.* the injury of the children of Bean

REMEMBERETH.
1 *Esd.* 4. 21. he *r.* neither father nor mother

REMEMBERING.
Tob. 2. 6. *r.* that prophecy of Amos, as he said

REMISS.
Eccl. 4. 29. and in thy deeds be not slack and *r.*

REMOVE.
Wisd. 1. 5. *r.* from thoughts without understanding
Eccl. 30. 23. *r.* sorrow far from thee, for sorrow

REND.
Wisd. 4. 19. he shall *r.* them, and cast them down

RENDER.
Tob. 2. 13. is it not stolen? *r.* it to the owners
Eccl. 17. 23. I will *r.* recompence on their heads
33. 13. to *r.* to them as liketh him best

RENDERED.
Wisd. 10. 17. she *r.* to the righteous a reward

RENDERING.
Esth. 16. 18. *r.* to him according to his deserts
RENEW.
1 *Mac.* 12. 3. that you should *r.* the friendship
16. to *r.* the amity that we had with them
RENEWED.
1 *Mac.* 4. 57. the gates and the chambers they *r.*
5. 1. the nations heard that the sanctuary was *r.*
RENEWING.
1 *Mac.* 12. 10. to send for the *r.* of brotherhood
RENOUNCE.
2 *Esd.* 14. 13. therefore now *r.* corruption
RENOWN.
Eccl. 3. 19. many are in high place and of *r.*
RENOWNED.
Jud. 11. 23. thou shalt be *r.* through the whole earth
Eccl. 39. 2. he will keep the sayings of *r.* men
44. 3. men *r.* for their power giving counsel
1 *Mac.* 3. 9. was *r.* to the utmost part of the earth
5. 63. Judas and his brethren were greatly *r.*
6. 1. Elymais was a city greatly *r.* for riches
14. 10. so that his honourable name was *r.*
2 *Mac.* 2. 22. the temple *r.* all the world over
RENT.
1 *Esd.* 8. 71. as I heard these things, I *r.* my clothes
Jud. 14. 16. therefore he cried and *r.* his garments
19. when heard these words, they *r.* their coats
Bar. 6. 31. having their clothes *r.* and heads shaven
1 *Mac.* 1. 56. had *r.* in pieces the books of the law
2 *Mac.* 4. 38. took his purple, and *r.* off his clothes
REPAIR.
1 *Esd.* 2. 18. *r.* the walls of it, and lay foundation
REPAIRED.
Eccl. 50. 1. who in his life *r.* the house again
1 *Mac.* 9. 50. he *r.* the strong cities in Judea
62. they *r.* the decays thereof, and made it strong
12. 37. they *r.* that which was called Caphenatha
REPAIRING.
1 *Mac.* 10. 44. for *r.* the works of the sanctuary
REPARATION.
1 *Mac.* 14. 34. all things convenient for the *r.* thereof
REPAY.
2 *Esd.* 15. 20. to *r.* things that they have done
Tob. 4. 14. if thou serve God, he will also *r.* thee
Eccl. 4. 31. and shut when thou shouldest *r.*
12. 6. Most High will *r.* vengeance to the ungodly
29. 5. when he should *r.* he will prolong the time
REPAYED.
Eccl. 35. 18. he *r.* vengeance to the heathen
REPAYETH.
Eccl. 20. 12. much for little, and *r.* it seven-fold
REPENT.
Wisd. 19. 2. they would *r.* and pursue them
Eccl. 17. 24. to them that *r.* he granted them return
21. 6. but he that feareth the Lord will *r.*
32. 19. do nothing without advice, and when thou hast once done, *r.* not
33. 19. give not thy goods to another, lest it *r.* thee
Prayer of Manass. thou art the God of them that *r.*
REPENTANCE.
2 *Esd.* 9. 11. when place of *r.* was open to them
Wisd. 12. 10. thou gavest them place of *r.*
Eccl. 17. 22. give *r.* to his sons and daughters
18. 21. and in the time of sins shew *r.*
20. 3. how good is it when art reproved to shew *r.?*
44. 16. an example of *r.* to all generations
Pray. of Manass. thou hast promised *r.* and forgiveness, thou hast appointed *r.* to me that am a sinner
REPENTED.
Eccl. 48. 15. for all this the people *r.* not nor departed
REPENTEST.
Prayer of Manass. thou *r.* of the evils of men
REPENTING.
Wisd. 5. 3. they *r.* and groaning for anguish of spirit
REPLENISHED.
Eccl. 16. 4. by one of understanding shall city be *r.*
32. 13. who hath *r.* thee with his good things
REPLIED.
Tob. 2. 14. but she *r.* upon me, it was given as a gift
REPORT.
Wisd. 8. 18. in talking with her is a good *r.*
Eccl. 31. 23. the *r.* of his good housekeeping
Sus. 27. was never such a *r.* made of Susanna
1 *Mac.* 12. 23. to make *r.* to you on this wise
15. 36. and made *r.* to him of these speeches
2 *Mac.* 14. 37. Razis, a man of very good *r.*
REPORTED.
1 *Esd.* 1. 33. are *r.* in the books of the kings
Jud. 11. 8. it is *r.* in all the earth, that thou only
Eccl. 44. 8. that their praises might be *r.*
1 *Mac.* 5. 14. other messengers, who *r.* on this wise
2 *Mac.* 2. 13. the same things were *r.* in the writings
11. 18. what things were meet to be *r.* to the king
REPOSE.
Wisd. 8. 16. I am come, I will *r.* myself with her
REPROOF.
Wisd. 11. 7. for a manifest *r.* of that commandment
Eccl. 20. 1. there is a *r.* that is not comely
REPROOFS.
Eccl. 48. 10. who wast ordained for *r.* in their times
REPROACH.
Tob. 3. 4. for a proverb of *r.* to all nations
10. if I do this, it shall be a *r.* unto him
13. take me out that I may hear no more the *r.*
Jud. 4. 12. and the sanctuary to profanation and *r.*
5. 21. we become a *r.* before all the world
8. 22. we shall be a *r.* to all them that possess us
9. 2. who polluted her virginity to her *r.*
Wisd. 4. 18. a *r.* among the dead for evermore
5. 3. this was he whom we had a proverb of *r.*
Eccl. 3. 11. a mother in dishonour is a *r.* to children
6. 1. thou shalt inherit an ill name, shame and *r.*
9. being turned to enmity will discover thy *r.*
23. 26. and her *r.* shall not be blotted out
27. 28. mockery and *r.* are from the proud
29. 23. that thou hear not the *r.* of thy house
41. 6. their posterity shall have a perpetual *r.*
42. 11. lest she make thee a *r.* among the people
14. than a woman which bringeth shame and *r.*
47. 4. did he not take away *r.* from the people?
Bar. 2. 4. to be as a *r.* and desolation among all
Bar. 3. 8. thou hast scattered us for a *r.* and a curse
6. 72. they shall be a *r.* in the country
73. better is the just man, he shall be far from *r.*
Dan. 3. 10. become a shame and *r.* to thy servants
1 *Mac.* 1. 39. her sabbaths were turned into *r.*
4. 45. pull it down lest it should be a *r.* to them
58. for the *r.* of the heathen was put away
REPROACH.
Eccl. 8. 5. *r.* not a man that turneth from sin
REPROACHED.
Tob. 3. 7. Sara was *r.* by her father's maids
Eccl. 41. 7. the children shall be *r.* for his sake
REPROACHES.
Tob. 3. 6. because I have heard false *r.* have sorrow
REPROACHFUL.
2 *Mac.* 7. 24. Antiochus suspecting it to be a *r.* speech
REPROACHING.
Eccl. 29. 28. *r.* of the lender is grievous to a man
REPROVE.
2 *Esd.* 12. 32. he shall *r.* and upbraid them
14. 13. set thy house in order, and *r.* thy people
Wisd. 2. 14. he was made to *r.* our thoughts
18. 5. to *r.* them, thou tookest away their children
Eccl. 20. 2. it is much better to *r.* than be angry
29. gifts stop up his mouth, that he cannot *r.*
REPROVED.
Wisd. 17. 7. their vaunting was *r.* with disgrace
Eccl. 20. 3. when thou art *r.* to shew repentance
21. 6. he that hateth to be *r.* is in way of sinners
32. 17. a sinful man will not be *r.* but finds excuse
2 *Mac.* 4. 33. he *r.* him and withdrew himself
REPROVETH.
Wisd. 1. 3. his power when tried, *r.* the unwise
Eccl. 18. 13. he *r.* and nurtureth, and teacheth
REPUTATION.
Sus. 64. Daniel had in great *r.* in sight of the people
REQUEST.
2 *Mac.* 9. 26. I *r.* you to remember the benefits
11. 17. they made *r.* for the performance
REQUIRE.
1 *Esd.* 4. 46. O king, this is that which I *r.*
8. 22. that you *r.* no tax, nor any imposition
2 *Esd.* 1. 32. whose blood I will *r.* of your hands
Bar. 6. 35. though he keep it not, they will not *r.* it
1 *Mac.* 7. 12. a company of scribes to *r.* justice
2 *Mac.* 11. 24. they *r.* that we should suffer them
REQUIRED.
1 *Esd.* 6. 12. we *r.* of them the names in writing
2 *Esd.* 13. 21. I will open the thing that thou hast *r.*
Jud. 7. 24. in that you have not *r.* peace of Assur
2 *Mac.* 7. 10. when he was *r.* he put out his tongue
REQUIRETH.
Eccl. 8. 9. learn to give answer as need *r.*
2 *Mac.* 6. 27. shew myself such an one as mine age *r.*
REQUISITE.
Wisd. 16. 4. it was *r.* on them should come poverty
REQUITE.
Eccl. 8. 19. lest he *r.* thee with a shrewd turn
30. 6. one that shall *r.* kindness to his friends
REQUITETH.
Eccl. 3. 31. he that *r.* good turns is mindful of that
35. 2. he that *r.* a good turn, offereth fine flour
RESEMBLANCE.
Wisd. 14. 19. to make the *r.* of the best fashion
Eccl. 34. 3. dreams is the *r.* of one thing to another
RESERVE.
Jud. 2. 10. if they yield, thou shalt *r.* them for me
RESERVED.
Jud. 11. 13. to spend first-fruits *r.* for the priests
2 *Mac.* 4. 19. but to be *r.* for other charges
RESIDUE.
2 *Esd.* 11. 4. was greater, yet rested it with the *r.*
19. so went it with all the *r.* one after another
Jud. 15. 6. the *r.* that dwelt at Bethulia, spoiled
1 *Mac.* 3. 24. the *r.* fled into land of Philistines
2 *Mac.* 8. 28. the *r.* they divided among themselves
RESIST.
Jud. 11. 18. none of them that shall *r.* thee
Esth. 13. 11. there is no man that can *r.* thee
RESISTANCE.
1 *Mac.* 11. 38. saw that no *r.* was made against him
RESISTED.
Jud. 2. 25. and he killed all that *r.* him
1 *Mac.* 14. 7. neither was there any that *r.* him
RESISTETH.
Eccl. 19. 5. but he that *r.* pleasures, crowneth life
RESOLVED.
Jud. 11. 13. are *r.* to spend the first-fruits of corn
Eccl. 39. 32. I was *r.* and thought on these things
1 *Mac.* 1. 62. many *r.* not to eat any unclean thing
2 *Mac.* 15. 1. *r.* to set upon them on the sabbath-day
RESOLUTE.
2 *Mac.* 6. 20. are *r.* to stand against such things
RESORT.
Eccl. 27. 9. the birds will *r.* unto their like
39. 5. will give his heart to *r.* early to the Lord
RESORTED.
Esth. 14. 1. queen Esther *r.* unto the Lord
Sus. 4. Joacim was rich, and to him *r.* the Jews
RESPECT.
Tob. 5. 18. let it be as refuse in *r.* of our child
Wisd. 4. 15. that he hath *r.* unto his chosen
7. 9. all gold in *r.* of her is as a little sand
19. 15. but some *r.* shall be had of those
Eccl. 16. 3. trust not their life, nor *r.* their multitude
35. 12. and with him is no *r.* of persons
46. 14. and the Lord had *r.* unto Jacob
RESPECTED.
Wisd. 2. 20. for by his own saying he shall be *r.*
RESPITE.
1 *Mac.* 12. 25. he gave them no *r.* to enter his country
REST.
1 *Esd.* 1. 58. the time of her desolation shall she *r.*
Wisd. 4. 7. prevented with death, yet shall he be in *r.*
Eccl. 6. 28. at the last thou shalt find her *r.*
11. 19. he saith, I have found *r.* and now will eat
20. 21. when he taketh *r.* he shall not be troubled
22. 11. make little weeping for the dead, he is at *r.*
13. depart from him, and thou shalt find *r.*
24. 7. with all these I sought *r.* and in whose
8. he that made me caused my tabernacle to *r.*
11. likewise in the beloved city he gave me *r.*
Eccl. 28. 16. whoso hearken. to it, shall never find *r.*
33. 25. if set servant to labour, thou shalt find *r.*
36. 24. a help like himself, and a pillar of *r.*
38. 23. when dead is at *r.* let his remembrance *r.*
40. 5. and in the time of *r.* upon his bed
6. a little or nothing is his *r.* and afterward
41. 1. to a man that liveth at *r.* in his possessions
44. 23. and made it *r.* on the head of Jacob
51. 27. how I have gotten to me much *r.*
1 *Mac.* 7. 50. the land of Juda was in *r.* a while
9. 57. the land of Judea was in *r.* two years
2 *Mac.* 11. 25. that this nation shall be in *r.*
RESTED.
Jud. 10. 21. Holofernes *r.* on his bed under a canopy
Eccl. 47. 23. thus *r.* Solomon with his fathers
1 *Mac.* 16. 4. who *r.* that night at Modin
RESTETH.
Eccl. 5. 6. his indignation *r.* upon sinners
31. 3. when he *r.* he is filled with his delicates
RESTORE.
2 *Esd.* 7. 32. the earth shall *r.* those asleep in her
Tob. 10. 12. the Lord of heaven *r.* thee, my brother
Eccl. 48. 10. wast ordained to *r.* the tribes of Jacob
Bar. 6. 37. they cannot *r.* a blind man to sight
1 *Mac.* 3. 43. let us *r.* the decayed estate of people
15. 3. that I may *r.* it to the old estate
2 *Mac.* 9. 16. he would *r.* all the holy vessels
11. 25. we have determined to *r.* their temple
12. 25. that he would *r.* them without hurt
14. 46. calling on the Lord to *r.* him those again
RESTORED.
1 *Esd.* 6. 26. should be *r.* to the house at Jerusalem
2 *Esd.* 12. 18. but shall be *r.* to his beginning
Tob. 2. 1. my wife Anna was *r.* to me with my son
14. 2. his sight, which was *r.* to him after eight years
Wisd. 16. 12. was not herb that *r.* them to health
RESURRECTION.
2 *Esd.* 2. 23. I will give thee the first place in my *r.*
2 *Mac.* 7. 14. as for thee, thou shalt have no *r.* to life
12. 43. in that he was mindful of the *r.*
RETAIN.
Eccl. 41. 16. it is not good to *r.* all shamefacedness
RETIRING.
2 *Mac.* 5. 9. he perished, *r.* to the Lacedemonians
RETURN.
2 *Esd.* 16. 16. so the plagues shall not *r.* again
Tob. 5. 15. if ye *r.* safe, I will add something
20. he shall *r.* in safety, thy eyes shall see him
14. 5. they shall *r.* from all places of their captivity
Eccl. 4. 18. then will she *r.* the straight way to him
16. 30. and they shall *r.* into it again
17. 24. but to them that repent, he granted them *r.*
25. *r.* to the Lord, and forsake thy sins
27. 9. so will truth *r.* to them that practise in her
29. 5. *r.* words of grief, and complain of time
40. 1. till the day they *r.* to the mother of all
1 *Mac.* 3. 56. should *r.* every man to his own house
10. 55. thou didst *r.* into the land of thy fathers
2 *Mac.* 5. 8. in the end he had an unhappy *r.*
11. 29. declared, that your desire was to *r.* home
RETURNED.
Tob. 2. 5. then I *r.* and washed myself
9. the same night also I *r.* from the burial
Jud. 5. 19. but now are they *r.* to their God
Wisd. 2. 1. any man known to have *r.* from the grave
Bar. 4. 28. so being *r.* seek him ten times more
1 *Mac.* 2. 63. because he is *r.* into his dust
5. 54. not one slain, until they had *r.* in peace
RETURNETH.
2 *Esd.* 16. 16. as an arrow *r.* not backward
Wisd. 15. 8. within a little while *r.* to the same
16. 14. the spirit when it is gone forth, *r.* not
Eccl. 26. 28. one that *r.* from righteousness to sin
REVEAL.
2 *Esd.* 10. 38. the Highest will *r.* many secret things
14. 3. I did manifestly *r.* myself to Moses
Tob. 12. 11. honourable to *r.* the works of God
Eccl. 19. 8. if thou canst without offence, *r.* them not
REVEALED.
Eccl. 1. 6. to whom hath the root of wisdom been *r.?*
3. 19. but mysteries are *r.* to the meek
REVEALETH.
Eccl. 42. 19. he *r.* the steps of hidden things
REVEALING.
Eccl. 41. 23. be ashamed of *r.* of secrets
REVELLING.
2 *Mac.* 6. 4. the temple was filled with riot and *r.*
REVELLINGS.
Wisd. 14. 23. while they made *r.* of strange rites
REVENGE.
Wisd. 5. 17. his weapon for the *r.* of his enemies
Eccl. 5. 3. for the Lord will surely *r.* thy pride
25. 14. and any *r.* but the *r.* of enemies
48. 8. who anointed kings to take *r.* and prophets
REVENGED.
Jud. 13. 20. but thou hast *r.* our ruin
Wisd. 12. 12. to be *r.* for the unrighteous man
REVENGETH.
Eccl. 28. 1. he that *r.* shall find vengeance from L.
REVENUE.
2 *Mac.* 4. 8. and of another *r.* eighty talents
9. 16. would out of his own *r.* defray the charges
REVENUES.
2 *Mac.* 3. 3. Seleucus of his own *r.* bare the costs
REVERENCE.
2 *Esd.* 15. 20. call the kings of the earth to *r.* me
Jud. 10. 23. she fell down and did *r.* to him
Wisd. 2. 10. let us not *r.* the ancient gray hairs
Eccl. 4. 22. let not the *r.* of any man cause thee fall
7. 29. fear the Lord with thy soul, and *r.* his priests
26. 24. an honest woman will *r.* her husband
REVERENCED.
Jud. 14. 7. he fell at Judith's feet and *r.* her
Bar. 4. 15. who neither *r.* old man, nor pitied child
REVEREND.
2 *Mac.* 15. 12. a good man *r.* in conversation
REVILING.
Eccl. 22. 24. as smoke before fire, so *r.* before blood
27. 21. and after *r.* there may be reconcilement
REVILINGS.
Eccl. 27. 15. their *r.* are grievous to the ear

REVIVED.
1 Mac. 13. 7. people heard these words, their spirit r.
REVOKED.
1 Mac. 11. 36. and nothing hereof shall be r.
REVOLT.
1 Mac. 2. 15. such as compelled the people to r.
13. 16. that when he is at liberty he may not r.
REVOLTED.
Tob. 1. 5. all the tribes which together r.
1 Mac. 7. 24. he took vengeance of them that had r.
2 Mac. 1. 7. r. from the holy land and kingdom
5. 11. the king thought that Judea had r.
REWARD.
2 Esd. 2. 35. be ready to the r. of the kingdom
3. 33. and yet their r. appeareth not
4. 35. when cometh the fruit of the floor of our r.?
7. 35. the work shall follow, the r. shall be shewed
8. 33. the just shall out of their own deeds receive r.
39. I will remember the r. that they shall have
Jud. 7. 15. thus shalt thou render them an evil r.
Wisd. 5. 15. their r. also is with the Lord
10. 17. to the righteous a r. of their labours
Eccl. 2. 8. believe him, and your r. shall not fail
11. 18. and this is the portion of his r.
22. the blessing of the L. is in the r. of the godly
26. to r. a man according to his ways
17. 23. afterward he will rise up and r. them
36. 16. r. them that wait for thee, let thy prophets
51. 22. the Lord hath given me a tongue for my r.
30. in his time he will give you your r.
2 Mac. 5. 7. received shame for the r. of his treason
8. 33. so he received a r. for his wickedness
15. 33. they should hang up the r. of his madness
REWARDED.
Tob. 14. 10. remember how he r. him again
Esth. 12. 5. to serve in court, and for this he r. him
Wisd. 3. 5. a little chastised, they shall be greatly r.
1 Mac. 11. 53. nor r. him according to the benefits
2 Mac. 4. 38. thus the Lord r. him as he deserved
REWARDS.
1 Esd. 4. 39. there is no accepting of persons or r.
1 Mac. 2. 18. with silver and gold, and many r.
10. 28. will grant you immunities, and give you r.
16. 19. he might give them silver, gold, and r.
RICH.
1 Esd. 3. 19. mind of the poor man and r. to be one
21. and it maketh every heart r.
Eccl. 8. 2. be not at variance with a r. man
10. 22. whether he be r. noble, or poor
30. and the r. man is honoured for his riches
11. 18. there is that waxeth r. by his wariness
21. it is easy on a sudden to make a poor man r.
13. 3. the r. man hath done wrong, yet threateneth
22. when a r. man hath fallen, hath many helpers
23. when a r. man speaketh, every man holdeth
30. 14. than a r. man that is afflicted in body
31. 3. the r. hath great labour in gathering
8. blessed is the r. that is without blemish
44. 6. r. men furnished with ability, living peaceab.
45. 8. he strengthened him with r. garments
Sus. 4. now Joacim was a great r. man
1 Mac. 6. 2. that there was in it a very r. temple
2 Mac. 7. 24. make him both a r. and happy man
RICHER.
Wisd. 8. 5. what is r. than wisdom that worketh
Eccl. 13. 2. with one mightier and r. than thyself
RICHES.
Wisd. 5. 8. or what good hath r. brought us?
8. 5. if r. be a possession to be desired in life
18. in the works of her hands are infinite r.
Eccl. 10. 8. because of injuries, and r. got by deceit
30. the rich man is honoured for his r.
31. honoured in poverty, how much more in r.!
he that is dishonoured in r. how much in poverty!
11. 14. poverty and r. come of the Lord
13. 24. r. are good to him that hath no sin
14. 3. r. are not comely for a niggard
21. 4. to terrify and do wrong will waste r.
24. 17. my flowers are the fruit of honour and r.
28. 10. according to his r. his anger riseth
30. 16. there is no r. above a sound body
31. 1. watching for r. consumeth the flesh
3. the rich hath great labour in gathering r.
37. 6. be not unmindful of him in thy r.
40. 26. r. and strength lift up the heart
Bar. 6. 35. they can neither give r. nor money
1 Mac. 4. 23. to spoil tents, where they got great r.
6. 1. that Elymais was a city renowned for r.
2 Mac. 3. 6. multitude of their r. was innumerable
RIDER.
2 Mac. 3. 25. a horse with a terrible r. upon him
RIDERS.
Jud. 2. 5. horses with their r. twelve thousand
RIDICULOUS.
Eccl. 34. 18. he sacrificeth, his offering is r.
RIFLED.
1 Mac. 1. 61. they r. their houses, and slew them
RIGHT.
2 Esd. 10. 39. he hath seen that thy way is r.
Tob. 3. 17. belonged to Tobias by r. of inheritance
6. 11. for to thee doth the r. of her appertain
Jud. 8. 11. your words you have spoken are not r.
Wisd. 9. 9. knew what was r. in thy commandments
10. 10. she guided him in r. paths, shewed him
Eccl. 49. 9. and directed them that went r.
Dan. 3. 4. thy ways are r. all thy judgments truth
1 Mac. 9. 15. who discomfited the r. wing
RIGHT-AIMING.
Wisd. 5. 21. r. thunderbolts shall go abroad
RIGHT-hand.
1 Esd. 4. 29. sitting at the r.-hand of the king
2 Esd. 3. 6. which thy r.-hand had planted
16. 13. strong is his r.-hand that bendeth
Wisd. 5. 16. with his r.-hand shall he cover them
Eccl. 12. 12. neither let him sit at thy r.-hand
21. 19. doctrine to fools, like manacles on r.-hand
49. 11. Zorobabel was as a signet on the r.-hand
Bar. 6. 15. he hath also in his r.-hand a dagger
2 Mac. 4. 34. gave him his r.-hand with oaths
14. 33. he stretched out his r.-hand to the temple
15. 15. Jeremias holding forth his r.-hand

RIGHTEOUS.
2 Esd. 3. 11. Noah, of whom came all r. men
Tob. 2. 14. where are thy alms and thy r. deeds?
13. 9. he will have mercy on the sons of the r.
Esth. 11. 7. they might fight against the r. people
9. the whole r. nation was troubled
14. 7. worshipped their gods, O Lord, thou art r.
Wisd. 2. 12. let us lie in wait for the r.
3. 1. the souls of the r. are in the hand of God
10. the ungodly, which have neglected the r.
4. 7. but though the r. be prevented with death
16. the r. that is dead shall condemn the ungodly
5. 15. but the r. live for evermore
10. 4. wisdom directed the course of the r.
5. she found out the r. and preserved him
6. she delivered the r. man who fled from fire
10. when the r. fled from his brother's wrath
13. when the r. was sold, she forsook him not
17. rendered to the r. a reward of their labours
20. therefore the r. spoiled the ungodly
12. 9. to bring the ungodly under the hand of r.
15. as thou art r. thyself, thou orderest all
16. 17. for the world fighteth for the r.
23. that the r. might be nourished
18. 9. the r. children of good men did sacrifice
20. the tasting of death toucheth the r. also
19. 17. as those were at the doors of the r. man
Eccl. 18. 2. the Lord only is r. and none other
27. 29. that rejoice at the fall of the r. be taken
35. 6. the offering of the r. makes the altar fat
44. 17. Noah was found r. in the time of wrath
Bar. 2. 9. for the Lord is r. in all his works
Dan. 3. 64. O ye spirits and souls of the r. bless the Lord
Sus. 3. her parents also were r. and taught her
Prayer of Manass. G. of our fathers and their r. seed
2 Mac. 1. 24. who art strong and r. and merciful
12. 6. and calling upon God the r. judge
RIGHTEOUSNESS.
2 Esd. 5. 11. is r. that maketh a man righteous gone
7. 44. r. is grown, and truth is sprung up
8. 30. love them that put their trust in thy r.
32. to us, namely, that have no works of r.
Tob. 12. 8. a little with r. is better than much
13. 8. and let all praise him for his r.
14. 11. what alms doth, and how r. doth deliver
Wisd. 1. 1. love r. ye that be judges of the earth
15. for r. is immortal, but ungodly men called
2. 22. neither hoped they for the wages of r.
5. 6. we have erred, and the light of r. hath not shined on us, the sun of r. rose not upon us
18. he shall put on r. as a breast-plate
8. 7. if a man love r. her labours are virtues
9. 3. order the world according to equity and r.
12. 16. for thy power is the beginning of r.
14. 7. for blessed is the wood whereby r. cometh
15. 3. for to know thee is perfect r.
Eccl. 26. 28. one that turneth from r. to sin
27. 8. if thou followest r. thou shalt obtain her
44. 10. whose r. hath not been forgotten
45. 26. give wisdom, to judge his people in r.
Bar. 1. 15. to the Lord our God belongeth r.
2. 17. the dead will give neither praise nor r.
5. 4. thy name shall be called the Peace of r.
1 Mac. 2. 52. and it was imputed to him for r.
7. 18. there is neither truth nor r. in them
RING.
2 Esd. 5. 42. I will liken my judgment to a r.
RINGS.
Jud. 10. 4. her chains, and her r. and ear-rings
RISE.
Tob. 6. 17. r. up both of you, and pray to God
12. 13. when thou didst not delay to r. up
Jud. 16. 17. woe to nations that r. ag. my kindred
Eccl. 8. 11. r. not up in anger at the presence
17. 23. afterward he will r. up and reward them
32. 11. r. up betimes, and be not the last
RISEN.
1 Esd. 3. 9. when the king is r. some will give him
Jud. 13. 5. the enemies which are r. against us
2 Mac. 12. 44. they that were slain should have r.
RISETH.
Eccl. 31. 20. he r. early, and his wits are with him
RISING.
1 Esd. 8. 73. r. from the fast with my clothes rent
9. 1. Esdras r. from the court of the temple
2 Esd. 15. 20. which are from the r. of the sun
Eccl. 43. 2. declaring at r. a marvellous instrument
1 Mac. 6. 33. then the king r. very early, marched
2 Mac. 4. 40. whereupon the common people r.
RIOT.
2 Mac. 6. 4. for the temple was filled with r.
RIOTOUSLY.
Eccl. 14. 4. others that shall spend his goods r.
RIPE.
Wisd. 4. 5. the fruit unprofitable, not r. to eat
Eccl. 26. 17. so is the beauty of the face in r. age
RIVER.
2 Esd. 1. 23. tree in water, and made the r. sweet
5. 25. of all depths thou hast filled thee one r.
Tob. 6. 1. they came in the evening to the r. Tigris
Esth. 10. 6. a little fountain became a r.
Wisd. 11. 6. a fountain of a perpetual running r.
19. 10. how the r. cast up a multitude of frogs
Eccl. 4. 26. and force not the course of the r.
24. 30. I also came out as a brook from a r.
31. my brook became a r. and my r. became a sea
39. 22. his blessing covered the dry land as a r.
40. 13. the goods of unjust shall be dried up as a r.
16. growing on every water and bank of a r.
44. 21. from the r. to the utmost part of land
1 Mac. 11. 7. gone to the r. called Eleutherus
RIVERS.
1 Esd. 4. 23. goeth to sail on the sea, and upon r.
2 Esd. 15. 41. many waters, that all fields may be full, and all r. with abundance of great waters
Eccl. 50. 8. as lilies by the r. of waters
Dan. 3. 56. O ye seas and r. bless ye the Lord
ROB.
1 Esd. 4. 23. he goeth his way to r. and to steal
ROBBED.
1 Esd. 4. 24. when he hath stolen, spoiled, and r.

ROBBERS.
Bar. 6. 18. lest their gods be spoiled with r.
57. nor able to escape either from thieves or r.
ROBE.
Eccl. 6. 29. and her chains shall be a r. of glory
31. thou shalt put her on as a r. of honour
27. 8. thou shalt put her on as a glorious long r.
45. 7. and he clothed him with a r. of glory
8. with breeches, with a long r. and the ephod
50. 11. when he put on the r. of honour
1 Mac. 6. 15. he gave him the crown and his r.
10. 20. therewithal he sent him a purple r.
21. at the feast Jonathan put on the holy r.
13. 37. the scarlet r. which ye sent to us
ROBOAM.
Eccl. 47. 23. of his seed, he left behind him R.
ROCK.
Wisd. 11. 4. water given them out of the flinty r.
Eccl. 40. 15. are as unclean roots on a hard r.
48. 17. he digged the hard r. with iron
2 Mac. 14. 45. and standing upon a steep r.
ROCKS.
2 Esd. 16. 28. hide themselves in the clefts of r.
Jud. 16. 15. r. shall melt as wax at thy presence
ROD.
Eccl. 30. 1. he causeth him oft to feel the r.
ROE.
Eccl. 27. 20. he is as r. escaped out of the snare
ROLLING.
Eccl. 33. 5. his thoughts are like a r. axle-tree
ROMANS.
1 Mac. 8. 1. Judas had heard of the fame of the R.
21. so that matter pleased the R. well
23. good success be to the R. and to the Jews
29. according to these articles did the R.
12. 4. upon this the R. gave them letters
16. sent them to the R. to renew the amity
14. 40. the R. had called the Jews their friends
15. 16. Lucius consul of the R. to king Ptolemee
2 Mac. 8. 10. which the king was to pay to the R.
36. to make good to the R. their tribute
11. 34. the R. also sent unto them a letter; the ambassadors of the r. send greeting to the Jews
ROME.
1 Mac. 1. 10. who had been an hostage at R.
8. 17. send them to R. to make a league of amity
19. they went to R. a very great journey
12. 3. so they went to R. and entered the senate
14. 16. when it was heard at R. Jonathan was dead
24. after this Simon sent Numenius to R.
2 Mac. 4. 11. who went ambassador to R.
ROOF.
1 Esd. 6. 4. by whose appointment build ye this r.?
2 Mac. 1. 16. and opening a privy door of the r.
ROOM.
Tob. 2. 4. I started up, and took him up into a r.
Wisd. 13. 15. when he had made a convenient r.
ROOT.
1 Esd. 8. 78. that there should be left us a r.
87. and didst give unto us such a r.
88. till thou hadst left us neither r. nor name
2 Esd. 3. 22. with the malignity of the r.
5. 3. the land that thou seest now to have r.
28. on the one r. hast thou prepared others
8. 41. neither doth all that is planted take r.
53. the r. of evil is sealed up from you
Wisd. 3. 15. the r. of wisdom shall never fall away
15. 3. to know thy power is the r. of immortality
Eccl. 1. 6. hath the r. of wisdom been revealed?
20. the r. of wisdom is to fear the Lord
3. 28. the plant of wickedness hath taken r.
23. 25. her children shall not take r.
24. 12. I took r. in an honourable people
47. 22. wherefore he gave a remnant unto Jacob, and out of him he gave a r. unto David
1 Mac. 1. 10. there came out of them a wicked r.
ROOTS.
Wisd. 7. 20. diversities of plants and virtues of r.
Eccl. 10. 15. Lord plucked up the r. of the proud
40. 15. but are as unclean r. on a hard rock
ROOT.
Eccl. 49. 7. that he might r. out, afflict, and destroy
1 Mac. 2. 40. they will now r. us out of the earth
3. 35. to destroy and r. out the strength of Israel
2 Mac. 8. 9. to r. out the whole generation of the Jews
12. 7. to r. out all them of the city of Joppe
ROOTED.
Wisd. 4. 4. by force of winds they shall be r. out
ROOTETH.
Eccl. 3. 9. the curse of the mother r. out foundations
ROOTING.
Wisd. 4. 3. nor take deep r. from bastard slips
ROAR.
Bar. 6. 32. they r. and cry before their gods
ROARING.
2 Esd. 11. 37. as a r. lion chased out of the wood
12. 31. the lion thou sawest r. and speaking
Wisd. 17. 19. or a r. voice of most savage beasts
1 Mac. 3. 4. like a lion's whelp r. for his prey
ROSE.
Eccl. 39. 13. bud forth as a r. growing by the brook
ROSE-BUDS.
Wisd. 2. 8. let us crown ourselves with r.-buds
ROSE-PLANT.
Eccl. 24. 14. I was exalted as a r.-plant in Jericho
ROSE.
Wisd. 5. 6. the sun of righteousness r. not on us
ROSES.
2 Esd. 2. 19. mountains whereon grew r. and lilies
ROSIN.
Dan. 3. 23. make the oven hot with r. and pitch
ROASTED.
Tob. 6. 5. when they had r. the fish, they did eat it
ROUGH.
Wisd. 12. 9. or to destroy them with one r. word
ROUGHLY.
2 Mac. 14. 30. he intreated him more r. than wont
ROUGHNESS.
Eccl. 10. 21. r. and pride is the losing thereof
ROYAL.
1 Esd. 3. 15. sat down in the r. seat of judgment
Wisd. 18. 15. leaped down out of thy r. throne

1 *Mac.* 3. 32. he left Lysias, one of the blood *r.*
37. the king departed from Antioch his *r.* city
6. 43. one of the beasts armed with *r.* harness
2 *Mac.* 4. 11. the *r.* privileges granted to the Jews

RUB.

Tob. 11. 8. being pricked therewith, he shall *r.*

RUBBED.

Tob. 11. 12. when his eyes began to smart, he *r.* them

RUDDY.

Esth. 15. 5. she was *r.* through perfection of beauty

RUDE.

Eccl. 8. 4. jest not with a *r.* man, lest be disgraced

RUDELY.

2 *Mac.* 12. 14. that they behaved themselves *r.*

RUDENESS.

Eccl. 21. 24. it is the *r.* of a man to hearken at door

RUIN.

2 *Esd.* 3. 1. after *r.* of the city, I was in Babylon
Jud. 5. 20. consider, that this shall be their *r.*
13. 20. hast not spared, but hast revenged our *r.*
Eccl. 4. 19. she will give him over to his own *r.*
31. 6. gold hath been the *r.* of many

RUINS.

Eccl. 49. 13. Neemias, who raised up our *r.* again

RULE.

1 *Esd.* 4. 2. that bear *r.* over sea and land
15. all the people that bear *r.* by sea and land
9. 4. as the elders that bear *r.* appointed
Wisd. 6. 2. give ear, ye that *r.* the people
Eccl. 19. 6. he that can *r.* his tongue, shall live
28. 22. it shall not have *r.* over them that fear God
44. 3. such as did bear *r.* in their kingdoms
1 *Mac.* 1. 8. his servants bear *r.* every one in place
6. 27. neither shalt thou be able to *r.* them

RULETH.

1 *Esd.* 4. 14. who is it then that *r.* them?

RULER.

Eccl. 9. 17. the wise *r.* of the people, for his speech
10. 2. as the *r.* of the city is, such are all they
17. 17. he set a *r.* over every people, but Israel
41. 18. of an offence before a judge and *r.*
1 *Mac.* 2. 17. thou art a *r.* and an honourable man
6. 14. whom he made *r.* over all his realm
11. 57. I appoint thee *r.* over four governments
2 *Mac.* 4. 27. Sostratus *r.* of the castle required
13. 2. Lysias his protector, and *r.* of his affairs

RULERS.

Eccl. 33. 18. hearken ye *r.* of the congregation
46. 18. he destroyed the *r.* of the Tyrians
1 *Mac.* 14. 20. the *r.* of the Lacedemonians

RULES.

2 *Mac.* 2. 28. to follow the *r.* of an abridgment

RULING.

1 *Mac.* 6. 56. to take to him the *r.* of the affairs

RUMOUR.

2 *Mac.* 5. 5. when there was gone forth a false *r.*

RUN.

1 *Esd.* 4. 26. many have *r.* out of their wits for women
Wisd. 3. 7. they shall shine and *r.* to and fro
16. 29. and shall *r.* away as unprofitable water
Eccl. 33. 31. if entreat him evil, and he *r.* from thee
35. 15. do not tears *r.* down the widow's cheeks?
2 *Mac.* 6. 11. others that had *r.* together into caves

RUNNETH.

Eccl. 43. 5. at his commandment it *r.* hastily

RUNNING.

Wisd. 17. 18. or a fall of water *r.* violently
19. or a *r.* that could not be seen of beasts
2 *Mac.* 5. 2. there were seen horsemen *r.* in the air
3. encountering and *r.* one against another
26. *r.* thro' the city with weapons, slew multitudes
9. 2. the multitude *r.* to defend themselves
12. 16. a lake adjoining, was seen *r.* with blood

RUSH.

2 *Esd.* 15. 60. they shall *r.* on the idle city
Jud. 15. 4. that all should *r.* on their enemies
1 *Mac.* 4. 2. might *r.* in upon the camp of the Jews

RUSHED.

Jud. 15. 3. the children of Israel *r.* out upon them
Sus. 26. the servants *r.* in at a privy door to see

RUSHING.

Jud. 15. 2. but *r.* out all together they fled
2 *Mac.* 12. 37. and *r.* unawares upon Gorgias
14. 43. the multitude also *r.* within the doors

RUST.

Eccl. 12. 11. his *r.* not being altogether wiped away
29. 10. let it not *r.* under a stone to be lost
Bar. 6. 12. cannot these gods save themselves from *r.*

RUSTETH.

Eccl. 12. 10. for as iron *r.* so is his wickedness

S.

SABBATH.

1 *Mac.* 1. 43. sacrifice to idols, and profane the *s.*
2. 38. they rose against them in battle on the *s.*
2 *Mac.* 5. 25. did forbear till holy day of the *s.*
26. that were gone to the celebrating of the *s.*
8. 26. for it was the day before the *s.*
28. after *s.* when they had given of the spoils
12. 38. they kept the *s.* in the same place

SABBATH-*day.*

1 *Mac.* 2. 32. made war against them on the *s.-day*
34. nor do commandment to profane the *s.-day*
41. whoso will make battle with us on the *s.-day*
2 *Mac.* 6. 11. had run to keep the *s.-day* secretly
15. 1. resolved to set upon them on the *s.-day*
3. that had commanded the *s.-day* to be kept

SABBATH-*days.*

Jud. 10. 2. house in which she abode in the *s.-days*
2 *Mac.* 6. 6. nor was it lawful to keep *s.-days*

SABBATHS.

1 *Esd.* 1. 58. till the land had enjoyed her *s.*
5. 52. the sacrifice of the *s.* and new moons
Jud. 8. 6. save the *s.* and eves of the new moons
1 *Mac.* 1. 39. her *s.* were turned into reproach
45. and that they should profane the *s.*

SACKCLOTH.

Jud. 4. 10. and their servants put *s.* on their loins
11. cast ashes on their heads, spread out their *s.* before the Ld. also they put *s.* about the altar
Jud. 4. 14. the priests had their loins girt with *s.*
9. 1. uncovered the *s.* wherewith she was clothed
10. 3. she pulled off the *s.* which she had on
Eccl. 25. 17. and darkeneth her countenance like *s.*
Bar. 4. 20. I have put on me the *s.* of my prayer
1 *Mac.* 2. 14. put on *s.* and mourned very sore
3. 47. then they fasted that day and put on *s.*
2 *Mac.* 3. 19. the women girt with *s.* abounded
10. 25. and girded their loins with *s.*

SACRED.

2 *Mac.* 6. 11. for the honour of the most *s.* day

SACRIFICE.

Tob. 1. 4. that all the tribes should *s.* there
Jud. 16. 16. all *s.* is too little for a sweet savour
Wisd. 18. 9. the children of good men did *s.* secretly
Eccl. 7. 31. and the *s.* of sanctification
31. 7. a stumbling-block to them that *s.* to it
35. 7. the *s.* of a just man is acceptable
Dan. 3. 15. nor is there prince, or *s.* or oblation
1 *Mac.* 1. 47. and *s.* swine's flesh and unclean beasts
51. commanding the cities of Juda to *s.*
59. they did *s.* upon the idol altar
4. 53. and offered *s.* according to the law
56. sacrificed the *s.* of deliverance and praise
2 *Mac.* 1. 18. was given when Neemias offered *s.*
23. made a prayer whilst the *s.* was consuming
2. 9. he being wise offered the *s.* of dedication
3. 32. offered a *s.* for the health of the man
4. 19. to carry silver to the *s.* of Hercules; which the bearers thought fit not to bestow upon the *s.*
20. this money was appointed to Hercules' *s.*
6. 21. as if he did eat of flesh from the *s.*
10. 3. they offered a *s.* after two years
13. 23. Philip offered *s.* honoured the temple

SACRIFICED.

Tob. 1. 5. house of Nephthali *s.* to the heifer Baal
Bar. 6. 28. for the things that are *s.* unto them
1 *Mac.* 1. 43. many of the Israelites *s.* to idols
4. 56. they *s.* the sacrifice of deliverance and praise

SACRIFICES.

1 *Esd.* 1. 12. the *s.* they sod them in brass pots
5. 53. had made any vow, began to offer *s.* to God
Wisd. 12. 4. works of witchcrafts and wicked *s.*
14. 15. to those under him, ceremonies and *s.*
23. whilst they slew their children in *s.*
Eccl. 35. 12. and trust not to unrighteous *s.*
45. 14. their *s.* shall be wholly consumed
16. he chose him to offer *s.* to the Lord
Bar. 6. 29. women in childbed eat their *s.*
1 *Mac.* 12. 11. we remember you in the *s.* we offer
2 *Mac.* 1. 8. we offered also *s.* and fine flour
33. Neemias had purified the *s.* therewith
2. 10. the fire came down and consumed the *s.*
3. 3. Seleucus bare all the costs belonging to the *s.*
6. which did not pertain to the account of the *s.*
4. 14. neglecting the *s.* hastened to be partakers
6. 7. were brought by constraint to eat of the *s.*
8. that they should be partakers of their *s.*
9. 16. and defray the charges belonging to the *s.*
14. 31. the priests that were offering their usual *s.*

SACRIFICETH.

Eccl. 34. 18. he that *s.* of a thing wrongfully got
35. 2. and he that giveth alms, *s.* praise

SACRILEGES.

2 *Mac.* 4. 39. when many *s.* had been committed

SAD.

1 *Esd.* 8. 71. I sat me down *s.* and very heavy
2 *Esd.* 10. 8. now seeing we all mourn and are *s.*
Wisd. 17. 4. and *s.* visions appeared to them

SADLY.

Eccl. 19. 26. that hangeth down his head *s.*

SAFE.

2 *Esd.* 1. 13. I gave you a large and *s.* passage
Tob. 5. 15. if ye return *s.* I will add something
21. journey prosperous, and he shall return *s.*
10. 6. hold thy peace, take no care, for he is *s.*
2 *Mac.* 3. 22. to keep things committed of trust *s.*

SAFEGUARD.

1 *Esd.* 8. 51. for *s.* against our adversaries
Jud. 11. 3. be of good comfort, thou art come for *s.*
2 *Mac.* 13. 3. not for the *s.* of the country

SAFELY.

1 *Esd.* 4. 47. they should *s.* convey on their way
Tob. 6. 4. heart, liver, and gall, and put them up *s.*
1 *Mac.* 6. 40. they marched on *s.* and in order
2 *Mac.* 3. 15. that they should *s.* be preserved

SAFETY.

Tob. 5. 20. take no care, he shall return in *s.*
8. 21. half of his goods, and go in *s.* to his father
12. 3. he hath brought me again to thee in *s.*
5. take half of all ye brought, and go away in *s.*
Esth. 16. 23. hereafter there may be *s.* to us
Wisd. 4. 17. to what end the Lord hath set him in *s.*
1 *Mac.* 7. 35. if ever I come in *s.* I will burn house
10. 83. the horsemen scattered in the field fled to Azotus, and went into their idol's temple for *s.*
14. 37. he fortified it for the *s.* of the country
2 *Mac.* 4. 21. Antiochus provided for his own *s.*
9. 21. I thought to care for the common *s.* of all

SAIL.

1 *Esd.* 4. 23. a man goeth his way to *s.* on the sea
Wisd. 14. 1. again, one preparing himself to *s.*
Eccl. 43. 24. they that *s.* on the sea tell of danger
1 *Mac.* 13. 29. be seen of all that *s.* on the sea

SAINTS.

Tob. 8. 15. therefore let thy *s.* praise thee
12. 15. which present the prayers of the *s.*
Wisd. 3. 9. for grace and mercy is to his *s.*
4. 15. that his grace and mercy is with his *s.*
5. 5. and his lot is among the *s.*
18. 1. thy *s.* had a very great light
5. had determined to slay the babes of the *s.*
9. the *s.* shall be like partakers of good and evil
Eccl. 42. 17. Lord hath not given power to the *s.*
45. 2. he made him like to the glorious *s.*

SAKE.

Eccl. 47. 12. and for his *s.* he dwelt at large
Bar. 2. 14. and deliver us for thine own *s.*
Dan. 3. 12. thy mercy not depart for thy beloved Abraham's *s.* for servant Isaac's *s.* and Israel's *s.*
2 *Mac.* 5. 19. God did not choose the people for the place's *s.* but the place for the people's *s.*

SAKES.

Eccl. 40. 10. and for their *s.* came the flood
Eccl. 44. 12. and their children for their *s.*

SALE.

2 *Mac.* 8. 11. proclaiming a *s.* of the captive Jews
11. 3. set the high priesthood to *s.* every year

SALT.

1 *Esd.* 6. 30. also corn, *s.* wine and oil to be given
2 *Esd.* 5. 9. *s.* water shall be found in the sweet
Wisd. 10. 7. a standing pillar of *s.* is a monument
Eccl. 22. 15. sand, and *s.* and a mass of iron
39. 26. *s.* flour of wheat, for the use of man's life
43. 19. hoar-frost also as *s.* he poureth on earth
Bar. 6. 28. their wives lay up part thereof in *s.*

SALTNESS.

Eccl. 39. 23. he hath turned the waters into *s.*

SALT-PITS.

1 *Mac.* 11. 35. the *s.* and crown taxes we discharge

SALVATION.

2 *Esd.* 6. 25. shall escape, and see my *s.*
7. 61. be joy over them that are persuaded to *s.*
Esth. 13. 13. for the *s.* of Israel, to kiss the soles
Wisd. 5. 2. amazed at the strangeness of his *s.*
16. 6. having a sign of *s.* to put them in remembr
18. 7. was accepted both the *s.* of the righteous and destruction of the enemies
Eccl. 13. 14. and call upon him for thy *s.*
Bar. 4. 24. they shall see your *s.* from our God
1 *Mac.* 3. 6. because *s.* prospered in his hand

SALUTE.

Jud. 15. 8. came to see Judith, and to *s.* her
1 *Mac.* 7. 33. came priests and elders to *s.* peaceably
12. 17. commanded to go unto you, and to *s.* you

SALUTED.

Tob. 5. 9. he came in, and they *s.* one another
1 *Mac.* 7. 29. they *s.* one another peaceably
11. 6. where they *s.* one another, and lodged

SAMARIA.

1 *Esd.* 2. 16. dwelling in S. and other places
Jud. 1. 9. to all that were in S. and cities thereof
Eccl. 50. 26. that sit upon the mountains of S.
1 *Mac.* 3. 10. gathered a great host out of S.
5. 66. thence he removed, and passed through S.
10. 30. out of the country of S. and Galilee
2 *Mac.* 15. 1. were in the strong places about S.

SAMUEL.

1 *Esd.* 1. 20. since the time of the prophet S.
2 *Esd.* 7. 38. S. and David for the destruction

SANCTIFICATION.

Eccl. 7. 31. give the priest the sacrifice of *s.*

SANCTIFY.

2 *Mac.* 1. 25. didst choose the fathers and *s.* them
26. and preserve thine own portion and *s.* it

SANCTIFIED.

2 *Mac.* 2. 8. that the place might be honourably *s.*

SANCTITY.

2 *Mac.* 3. 12. to the inviolable *s.* of the temple

SANCTUARY.

1 *Esd.* 8. 78. be left us a name in the place of thy *s.*
2 *Esd.* 7. 38. for them that should come to the *s.*
10. 21. for thou seest that our *s.* is laid waste
12. 48. seek mercy for the low estate of your *s.*
15. 25. go your way, defile not my *s.*
Jud. 4. 12. the *s.* to profanation and reproach
13. before the *s.* of the Lord Almighty
Eccl. 47. 13. he might prepare his *s.* for ever
49. 6. they burned the chosen city of the *s.*
50. 5. how was he honoured in coming out of *s.*!
1 *Mac.* 1. 21. Antiochus entered proudly into the *s*
36. it was a place to lie in wait against the *s.*
3. 45. the *s.* also was trodden down, aliens kept
58. that are assembled to destroy us and our *s.*
4. 36. let us go cleanse and dedicate the *s.*
41. to fight, until he had cleansed the *s.*
48. made up the *s.* and things within the temple
5. 1. heard that the *s.* was renewed as before
10. 39. I give it as a free gift to the *s.* at Jerusalem for the necessary expenses of the *s.*
13. 3. what I have done for the laws and the *s.*
14. 15. he beautified the *s.* and multiplied
48. should be set up within the compass of the *s.*
2 *Mac.* 4. 33. he withdrew himself into a *s.*
34. he persuaded him to come forth of the *s.*

SAND.

Wisd. 7. 9. gold in respect to her is as a little *s.*
Eccl. 1. 2. who can number the *s.* of the sea?
18. 10. a gravel stone in comparison of the *s.*
22. 15. *s.* and salt, and a mass of iron is easier
Dan. 3. 13. as the *s.* that lieth on the sea-shore

SANDS.

Prayer of Manass. sinned above number of *s.* of sea

SANDALS.

Jud. 10. 4. and she took *s.* upon her feet
16. 9. her *s.* ravished his eyes, her beauty took

SANDY.

Eccl. 25. 20. as climbing up a *s.* way is to feet of aged

SAPPHIRES.

Tob. 13. 16. Jerusalem shall be built up with *s.*

SARA.

Tob. 3. 7. S. daughter of Raguel was reproached
17. to give S. the daughter of Raguel to Tobias
6. 10. he also hath one only daughter, named S.
11. 17. when he came near to S. his daughter
12. 12. when thou didst pray, and S. thy daughter

SARCHEDONUS.

Tob. 1. 21. S. his son reigned in his stead
22. and S. appointed him near unto him

SAT.

1 *Esd.* 3. 15. he *s.* him down in the royal seat
8. 72. but I *s.* still full of heaviness till sacrifice
9. 45. he *s.* honourably in the first place of all
Tob. 2. 1. in the which I *s.* down to eat
11. 5. now Anna *s.* looking about for her son
Esth. 15. 6. who *s.* upon his royal throne
Eccl. 11. 5. many kings have *s.* on the ground
1 *Mac.* 1. 27. she that *s.* in the marriage-chamber
8. 15. wherein 320 men *s.* in council daily
14. 12. every man *s.* under his vine and fig-tree
2 *Mac.* 3. 25. he that *s.* on the horse had harness

SATISFIED.

1 *Esd.* 3. 3. and being *s.* were gone home
Eccl. 12. 16. an enemy will not be *s.* with blood

SATISFIETH.
Esth. 14. 8. it *s.* not that we are in captivity
SAVAGE.
Wisd. 17. 19. or a voice of most *s.* wild beasts
2 *Mac.* 4. 25. but having the rage of a *s.* beast
SAVE.
Tob. 6. 17. who will have pity on you and *s.* you
Esth. 13. 9. if thou hast appointed to *s.* Israel
Bar. 4. 22. my hope is in God, that he will *s.* you
6. 36. they can *s.* no man from death, nor deliver
49. which can neither *s.* them from war
Prayer of Manass. wilt *s.* me that am unworthy
2 *Mac.* 7. 25. counsel the young man to *s.* his life
14. 3. seeing by no means he could *s.* himself
SAVED.
2 *Esd.* 8. 3. many be created, but few shall be *s.*
41. sown in the world, they shall not all be *s.*
Tob. 14. 10. yet Achiacharus was *s.*
Jud. 10. 15. thou hast *s.* thy life, in that thou hastedst
Esth. 10. 9. my nation is Israel, which cried to God and were *s.* for the Lord hath *s.* his people
16. 13. as well of Mardocheus who *s.* our life
Wisd. 14. 5. passing thro' sea in a weak vessel are *s.*
16. 7. he was not *s.* by the thing that he saw
11. were quickly *s.* that they might be mindful
Sus. 62. the innocent blood was *s.* the same day
Prayer of Manass. to sinners, that they may be *s.*
1 *Mac.* 2. 59. by believing were *s.* out of the flame
2 *Mac.* 3. 35. vows unto him that had *s.* his life
SAVEDST.
Eccl. 51. 12. for thou *s.* me from destruction
SAVEST.
Eccl. 51. 8. and *s.* them out of the hands of enemies
SAVETH.
Eccl. 2. 11. the Lord is full of compassion and mercy, forgiveth sins, and *s.* in time of affliction
34. 13. for their hope is in him that *s.* them
Sus. 60. praised God, who *s.* them that trust in him
1 *Mac.* 4. 11. one who delivereth and *s.* Israel
SAVING.
Eccl. 46. 1. his name great for *s.* the elect of God
SAVIOUR.
2 *Esd.* 2. 36. I testify my S. openly
Jud. 9. 11. a S. of them that are without hope
Esth. 15. 2. the beholder and *s.* of all things
Wisd. 16. 7. but by thee that art the S. of all
Eccl. 24. 24. besides him there is no other S.
51. 1. and I will praise thee, O God of my S.
Bar. 4. 22. shall come from the Everlasting, our S.
1 *Mac.* 4. 30. blessed art thou, O S. of Israel
SAVOUR.
1 *Esd.* 1. 12. they sod them in pans with a good *s.*
2 *Esd.* 2. 12. tree of life for an ointment of sweet *s.*
Eccl. 35. 6. the sweet *s.* is before the Most High
38. 11. give a sweet *s.* memorial of fine flour
39. 14. and give ye a sweet *s.* as frankincense
50. 15. a sweet-smelling *s.* to the most high King
SAW.
Tob. 1. 17. if I *s.* any of my nation dead or cast about
2. 2. when I *s.* abundance of meat, I said to my son
4. 4. remember that she *s.* many dangers for thee
12. 21. when they arose, they *s.* him no more
Jud. 10. 7. when they *s.* her countenance altered
14. 6. he *s.* the head of Holofernes in a man's hand
Esth. 15. 13. I *s.* thee, my lord, as an angel of God
Wisd. 16. 7. was not saved by the thing that he *s.*
17. 6. to be worse than the sight they *s.* not
10. they died for fear, denying that they *s.* the air
Eccl. 1. 9. he created her, *s.* her, and numbered her
18. 12. he *s.* and perceived their end to be evil
30. 5. while he lived, he *s.* and rejoiced in him
45. 19. this the Lord *s.* and it displeased him
48. 11. blessed are they that *s.* thee, and slept
Bar. 4. 9. for when she *s.* the wrath of God coming
10. I *s.* the captivity of my sons and daughters
Sus. 8. the two elders *s.* her going in every day
33. her friends, and all that *s.* her, wept
Bel 30. when the king *s.* that, they pressed him
35. Lord, I never *s.* Babylon, nor do I know
SAWEST.
Sus. 54. tell me, under what tree *s.* thou them?
SAWN.
Wisd. 13. 11. after he hath *s.* down a tree meet
SCALE.
Tob. 3. 17. to *s.* away the whiteness of Tobit's eyes
SCANT.
Jud. 11. 12. victuals fail, and all their water is *s.*
SCARLET.
Eccl. 45. 11. with twisted *s.* the work of the workman
SCATTER.
Bar. 2. 29. among the nations, where I will *s.* them
SCATTERED.
Tob. 13. 3. for he hath *s.* us among them
Wisd. 17. 3. they were *s.* under a dark vail
SCATTERETH.
Eccl. 43. 17. as birds flying he *s.* the snow
SCENTS.
Wisd. 11. 18. or filthy *s.* of scattered smoke
SCEPTRE.
Esth. 14. 11. O Lord, give not thy *s.* unto them
15. 11. held up his golden *s.* and laid it on her neck
Wisd. 10. 14. she brought him the *s.* of the kingdom
Eccl. 35. 18. and broken the *s.* of the unrighteous
Bar. 6. 14. holdeth a *s.* as though he were a judge
SCEPTRES.
Wisd. 6. 21. if your delight be in thrones and *s.*
7. 8. I preferred her before *s.* and thrones
SCOLD.
Eccl. 26. 27. a *s.* shall be sought out to drive away
SCORN.
2 *Esd.* 8. 56. thought *s.* of his law, forsook his ways
Jud. 12. 12. if draw her not, she will laugh us to *s.*
Wisd. 4. 18. but God shall laugh them to *s.*
Eccl. 6. 4. shall make him to be laughed to *s.*
7. 11. laugh no man to *s.* in the bitterness of soul
20. 17. of how many shall he be laughed to *s.*
SCORNING.
Eccl. 41. 19. be ashamed of *s.* to give and take
SCORPION, S.
Eccl. 26. 7. hath hold of her, is as tho' he held a *s.*
39. 30. teeth of wild beasts and *s.* punishing wicked

SCOURGE.
Tob. 13. 2. for he doth *s.* and hath mercy
5. and he will *s.* us for our iniquities
Jud. 8. 27. the Lord doth *s.* them that come near
Eccl. 26. 6. a *s.* of the tongue which communicateth
40. 9. famine, tribulation, and the *s.* happen to all
SCOURGED.
Tob. 11. 15. thou hast *s.* and hast taken pity on me
Wisd. 16. 16. were *s.* by the strength of thine arm
2 *Mac.* 3. 34. seeing thou hast been *s.* from heaven
5. 18. this man had forthwith been *s.*
SCOURGES.
2 *Esd.* 16. 19. are sent as *s.* for amendment
20. they shall not be alway mindful of the *s.*
Tob. 13. 14. having been sorrowful for all thy *s.*
Eccl. 23. 2. who will set *s.* over my thoughts
2 *Mac.* 7. 1. were tormented with *s.* and whips
SCOURGEST.
Wisd. 12. 22. thou *s.* our enemies a thousand times
SCRIBE.
1 *Esd.* 2. 25. to Semellius the *s.* and to the rest
Eccl. 10. 5. on person of the *s.* shall lay his honour
SCRIBES.
1 *Mac.* 5. 42. he caused the *s.* remain by the brook
7. 12. a company of *s.* to require justice
2 *Mac.* 6. 18. Eleazar, one of the principal *s.*
SCRIPTURE.
1 *Mac.* 12. 9. we have holy books of *s.* to comfort us
SCYTHIANS.
2 *Mac.* 4. 47. before S. have been judged innocent
SCYTHOPOLIS.
2 *Mac.* 12. 29. from thence they departed to S.
SCYTHOPOLITANS.
2 *Mac.* 12. 30. the S. dealt lovingly with them
SEA.
2 *Esd.* 1. 13. I led you through the *s.* gave a passage
16. 57. he measured the *s.* and what it contains
Jud. 2. 24. river Arbonai, till you come to the *s.*
Wisd. 5. 22. the water of the *s.* shall rage ag. them
14. 3. for thou hast made a way in the *s.*
4. yea, though a man went to *s.* without art
5. passing the rough *s.* in a weak vessel, are saved
19. 7. out of the Red *s.* a way without impediment
Eccl. 1. 2. who can number the sand of the *s.*?
18. 10. as a drop of water unto the *s.*
24. 29. for her thoughts are more than the *s.*
31. my brook became a river, and my river a *s.*
29. 18. and shaken them as a wave of the *s.*
40. 11. that of waters doth return into the *s.*
44. 21. would cause them to inherit from *s.* to *s.*
50. 3. the cistern, being in compass as the *s.*
Bar. 3. 30. who hath gone over *s.* and found her?
Dan. 3. 13. as sand that lieth on the *s.* shore
Prayer of Manass. above the sands of the *s.*
1 *Mac.* 4. 23. got blue silk, and purple of the *s.*
6. 29. there came from the isles of the *s.* bands
7. 1. Demetrius came to a city of the *s.*-coast
8. 23. good success to Jews by *s.* and by land
32. we will fight with thee by *s.* and by land
11. 1. like sand that lieth upon the *s.* shore
8. Ptolemee having the dominion of the cities by the *s.* unto Seleucia upon the *s.* coast
14. 5. he made an entrance to the isles of the *s.*
15. 38. made Cendebeus captain of the *s.* coast
2 *Mac.* 5. 21. to make the *s.* passable by foot
9. 8. thought he might command waves of the *s.*
SEAS.
Dan. 3. 56. O ye *s.* and rivers, bless ye the Lord
SEAL.
Bel 11. shut the door, and *s.* it with thy signet
SEALED.
1 *Esd.* 3. 8. every one wrote his sentence and *s.* it
2 *Esd.* 2. 38. those that be *s.* in the feast of the Lord
8. 53. the root of evil is *s.* up from you
Tob. 7. 14. an instrument of covenants, and *s.* it
9. 5. Gabael brought forth bags which were *s.*
Wisd. 2. 5. it is fast *s.* that no man cometh again
Bel 14. they *s.* the door with the king's signet
Prayer of Manass. hath shut up the deep, and *s.* it
SEALS.
Eccl. 38. 27. and they that cut and grave *s.*
45. 11. with precious stones graven like *s.* set in gold
SEARCH.
1 *Esd.* 2. 26. I commanded to make diligent *s.*
6. 21. let *s.* be made among the records of Cyrus
2 *Esd.* 16. 31. that *s.* their houses with the sword
Jud. 8. 14. then how can you *s.* out God?
Esth. 16. 7. if ye *s.* what hath been wickedly done
Wisd. 6. 3. try works and *s.* out your counsels
13. 7. they *s.* him diligently, and believe their sight
Eccl. 3. 21. neither *s.* the things that are above
6. 27. *s.* and seek, and she shall be made known
SEARCHED.
Esth. 12. 2. heard devices, and *s.* their purposes
Wisd. 9. 16. the things in heaven, who hath *s.* out?
1 *Mac.* 14. 14. law he *s.* out, and every contemner
SEARCHERS.
Bar. 3. 23. authors of fables, and *s.* out of underst.
SEARCHEST.
2 *Esd.* 4. 26. the more thou *s.* the more marvel
SEASONABLE.
Eccl. 35. 20. mercy is *s.* in time of affliction
SEASON.
2 *Esd.* 8. 41. the thing that is sown good in his *s.*
14. 4. where I held him by me a long *s.*
Wisd. 16. 6. they were troubled for a small *s.*
Eccl. 20. 20. for he will not speak it in due *s.*
29. 2. pay thou thy neighbour again in due *s.*
31. 28. wine measurably drunk and in *s.* brings
39. 16. shall be accomplished in due *s.*
33. he will give every needful thing in due *s.*
43. 6. he made the moon also to serve in her *s.*
SEASONS.
Wisd. 7. 18. turning of the sun, and change of *s.*
8. 8. she foreseeth the events of *s.* and times
Eccl. 33. 8. and he altered *s.* and feasts
SEAT.
1 *Esd.* 3. 15. he sat him down in the royal *s.*
Wisd. 9. 12. and be worthy to sit in my father's *s.*
Eccl. 7. 4. seek not of the king the *s.* of honour
12. 12. set him not by, lest he seek to take thy *s.*
38. 33. they shall not sit on the judge's *s.*

SECOND.
1 *Esd.* 1. 31. then he gat upon his *s.* chariot
2. 30. ceased till the *s.* year of the reign of Darius
3. 11. the *s.* wrote, the king is strongest
5. 56. in the *s.* year, and *s.* month after coming
57. in the first day of the *s.* month, in the *s.* year after they were come to Jerusalem
Esth. 13. 3. had honour of *s.* place in the kingdom
2 *Mac.* 5. 1. prepared his *s.* voyage into Egypt
7. 7. brought the *s.* to make a mocking-stock
SECONDLY.
Eccl. 23. 23. *s.* she hath trespassed against her husb.
SECRET.
1 *Esd.* 5. 73. by *s.* plots and popular persuasions
2 *Esd.* 10. 38. the Highest will reveal many *s.* things
Jud. 2. 2. nobles, and communicated his *s.* counsel
Wisd. 1. 11. no word so *s.* that shall go for nought
7. 21. such things as are either *s.* or manifest
14. 23. or used *s.* ceremonies, or made revellings
17. 3. they supposed to lie hid in their *s.* sins
Eccl. 3. 22. to see the things that are in *s.*
48. 25. he shewed *s.* things or ever they came
1 *Mac.* 1. 53. and drove the Israelites into *s.* places
2. 31. gone down into *s.* places in the wilderness
41. that were murdered in the *s.* places
SECRETLY.
Wisd. 18. 9. children of good men did sacrifice *s.*
Eccl. 20. 2. better to reprove, than to be angry *s.*
2 *Mac.* 6. 11. to keep the sabbath-day *s.*
SECRETS.
Tob. 12. 7. it is good to keep close the *s.* of a king, 11.
Eccl. 1. 30. and so God discover thy *s.*
4. 18. she will comfort him, and shew him her *s.*
13. 11. and smiling on thee, will get out thy *s.*
14. 21. he shall have understanding in her *s.*
22. 22. except for pride, or disclosing of *s.*
27. 17. if thou bewrayest his *s.* follow no more
39. 3. he will seek out the *s.* of grave sentences
7. and in his *s.* shall he meditate
Sus. 42. O everlasting God, that knowest the *s.*
2 *Mac.* 13. 21. disclosed the *s.* to the enemies
SECURELY.
Eccl. 4. 15. that attendeth to her, shall dwell *s.*
SECURITY.
2 *Esd.* 7. 53. paradise, wherein is *s.* and medicine
Eccl. 5. 7. in thy *s.* thou shalt be destroyed
SEDECIAS.
Bar. 1. 8. S. the son of Josias king of Juda had made
SEDITION.
2 *Esd.* 15. 16. for there shall be *s.* amongst men
SEDITIOUS.
2 *Mac.* 14. 16. Assideans nourish war, and are *s.*
SEE.
Eccl. 15. 7. and sinners shall not *s.* her
20. 7. will hold his tongue till he *s.* opportunity
37. 9. on other side, to *s.* what shall befall thee
27. prove thy soul, and *s.* what is evil for it
42. 22. that a man may *s.* even to a spark
Bar. 1. 20. floweth with milk, as it is to *s.* this day
4. 24. so shall they *s.* shortly your salvation
25. but shortly thou shalt *s.* his destruction
Sus. 20. the doors are shut that no man can *s.* us
SEED.
1 *Esd.* 8. 70. the holy *s.* is mixed with strange people
88. hadst left us neither root, *s.* nor name
2 *Esd.* 3. 15. thou wouldest never forsake his *s.*
8. 6. and thou give us *s.* to our heart and culture
Wisd. 3. 16. the *s.* of unrighteous bed be rooted out
7. 2. being compacted in blood of the *s.* of man
10. 15. she delivered the blameless *s.* from nation
12. 11. it was a cursed *s.* from the beginning
14. 6. left to all ages a *s.* of generation
Eccl. 1. 15. she shall continue with their *s.*
10. 19. regard not the law, are a dishonourable *s.*
44. 11. with their *s.* shall continually remain
12. their *s.* stands fast, and their children
21. that he would bless the nations in his *s.*
45. 15. to his *s.* so long as the heavens remain
21. sacrifices, which he gave to him and his *s.*
46. 9. his *s.* obtained it for an heritage
47. 20. didst stain thy honour, and pollute thy *s.*
22. not take away the *s.* of him that loveth him
23. of his *s.* he left behind him Roboam
Dan. 3. 13. wouldest multiply their *s.* as the star
Sus. 56. O thou *s.* of Chanaan, and not Juda
Prayer of Manass. and of their righteous *s.*
2 *Mac.* 7. 17. how he will torment thee and thy *s.*
SEEK.
1 *Esd.* 6. 23. to *s.* among the records at Babylon
8. 85. she shall never *s.* to have peace with them
2 *Esd.* 12. 48. that I might *s.* mercy for low estate
14. 23. that they *s.* thee not for forty days
Tob. 5. 3. *s.* thee a man which may go with thee
11. he said, dost thou *s.* for a tribe or family?
Wisd. 1. 1. and in simplicity of heart *s.* him
12. *s.* not death in the error of your life
6. 12. wisdom is easily found of such as *s.* her
22. but I will *s.* her out from the beginning
Eccl. 3. 21. *s.* not the things that are too hard for thee
4. 11. wisdom layeth hold on them that *s.* her
12. they that *s.* to her early, shall be filled
6. 27. *s.* and she shall be made known to thee
7. 4. *s.* not of the Lord pre-eminence
6. *s.* not to be judge, being not able to take
12. 12. set him not by, lest he *s.* to take thy seat
24. 34. I laboured for all them that *s.* wisdom
28. 3. and doth he *s.* pardon from the Lord?
32. 14. they that *s.* him early, shall find favour
33. 17. but for all them that *s.* learning
21. that thy children should *s.* to thee
25. if let him go idle, he shall *s.* liberty
31. which way wilt thou go to *s.* him?
36. 2. upon all nations that *s.* not after thee
39. 1. he will *s.* out the wisdom of all the ancient
3. he will *s.* out secrets of grave sentences
40. 26. the fear of the Lord needeth not to *s.* help
51. 14. I will *s.* her out even to the end
Bel 38. nor hast thou forsaken them that *s.* thee
SEEKETH.
Wisd. 6. 14. who *s.* her early, have no great travel
Eccl. 27. 1. he that *s.* for abundance will turn
32. 15. he that *s.* the law shall be filled

2 Mac. 2. 27. and s. the benefit of others
SEEKING.
Wisd. 6. 16. she goeth about s. such as are worthy
8. 18. I went about s. how to take her to me
13. 6. for they peradventure err, s. God
Eccl. 14. 16. no s. of dainties in the grave
20. 32. necessary patience in s. the Lord
51. 21. my heart was troubled in s. her
SEEMED.
Wisd. 3. 2. in sight of the unwise they s. to die
2 Mac. 1. 13. the army with him that s. invincible
SEEN.
Wisd. 13. 1. out of the good things that are s.
17. 19. that could not be s. of skipping beasts
Eccl. 16. 5. many things have I s. with my eyes
42. 15. I will declare the things that I have s.
43. 31. who hath s. him that he might tell us
Bar. 2. 26. laid waste, as it is to be s. this day
6. 61. the lightning breaking forth is easy to be s.
Sus. 54. if thou hast s. her, tell me, under what
1 Mac. 4. 20. for the smoke that was s. declared
13. 29. might be s. of all that sail on the sea
2 Mac. 3. 36. works, which he had s. with his eyes
6. 9. then might a man have s. present misery
SELEUCIA.
1 Mac. 11. 8. unto S. upon the sea-coast
SELEUCUS.
1 Mac. 7. 1. Demetrius the son of S. departed
2 Mac. 3. 3. S. king of Asia bare all the costs
4. 7. but after the death of S. Jason laboured
5. 18. whom S. the king sent to view the treasury
SELL.
Bar. 6. 28. the things sacrificed, their priests s.
1 Mac. 13. 49. they could neither buy nor s.
2 Mac. 5. 24. to s. the women and younger sort
SELLING.
Eccl. 27. 2. sin stick close between buying and s.
37. 11. consult not with a buyer of s.
42. 5. and of merchants indifferent s.
SENATE.
2 Mac. 4. 44. three men that were sent from the s.
SENATE-house.
1 Mac. 8. 15. had made for themselves a s.-house
SEND.
Tob. 8. 12. s. one of the maids, and let her see
10. 8. I will s. to thy father, and declare to him
Jud. 6. 3. he will s. his power and destroy them
9. 9. and s. thy wrath upon their heads
11. 22. God hath done well to s. thee before
Wisd. 9. 10. O s. her out of thy holy heavens
11. 17. wanted not means to s. among them bears
12. 8. did s. wasps forerunners of thy host
25. thou didst s. a judgment to mock them
16. 20. thou didst s. them from heaven bread
Eccl. 24. 32. I will s. forth her light afar off
33. 27. s. him to labour, that he be not idle
36. 2. and s. thy fear upon all the nations
Sus. 21. thou didst s. away thy maids from thee
29. s. for Susanna the daughter of Chelcias
1 Mac. 11. 43. if thou s. me men to help me
16. 18. that he should s. him an host to aid him
2 Mac. 1. 4. open your hearts, and s. you peace
6. 23. he willed them to s. him to the grave
11. 34. ambassadors of the Romans s. greeting
14. 27. commanded that he should s. Maccabeus
SENNACHERIB.
2 Mac. 8. 19. they were delivered when under S.
15. 22. and didst slay in the host of S. 185,000
SENSE.
2 Esd. 10. 36. is my s. received, or my soul in a dream
Eccl. 21. 18. knowledge of unwise, as talk without s.
SENT.
Tob. 2. 12. when she had s. them home to the owners
12. 20. for I go up to him that s. me
Eccl. 28. 23. it shall be s. on them as a lion
34. 6. if they be not s. from the Most High
SENTENCE.
Eccl. 20. 20. a wise s. shall be rejected when it cometh
41. 2. O death, acceptable is thy s. to the needy
Sus. 55. the angel of God hath received the s.
SENTENCES.
1 Esd. 3. 16. they shall declare their own s.
Eccl. 39. 6. he shall pour out wise s. and give thanks
SEPARATE.
Wisd. 1. 3. for froward thoughts s. from God
Eccl. 6. 13. s. thyself from thine enemies, take heed
SEPARATED.
1 Esd. 7. 13. all they that had s. themselves
8. 54. then I s. 12 of the chief of the priests
Eccl. 16. 16. he hath s. his light from darkness
SEPULCHRE.
1 Mac. 9. 19. buried him in the s. of his fathers
13. 30. this is the s. which he made at Modin
2 Mac. 5. 10. he had no s. with his fathers
SERPENT.
Eccl. 12. 13. a charmer that is bitten with a s.
21. 2. flee from sin as from the face of a s.
25. 15. there is no head above the head of a s.
SERPENTS.
Wisd. 11. 15. they worshipped s. void of reason
16. 5. they perished with the stings of crooked s.
17. 9. being scared with hissing of s. they died
Eccl. 39. 30. teeth of wild beasts, scorpions, and s.
SERVANT.
1 Esd. 4. 59. thine is the glory, and I am thy s.
Jud. 5. 5. no lie shall come out of the mouth of thy s.
9. 10. smite by the deceit of my lips the s. with
the prince, and the prince with the s.
11. 5. Judith said, receive the words of thy s.
17. for thy s. is religious and serveth God
Wisd. 9. 5. I thy s. and the son of thy handmaid
10. 16. she entered into the soul of the s. of the Lord
18. 11. the master and the s. were punished
21. declaring that he was thy s.
Eccl. 7. 20. thy s. worketh truly, entreat him
21. let thy soul love a good s. defraud him not
10. 25. unto the s. that is wise, shall they do service
19. 21. if a s. say to his master, I will not do
23. 6. give not over me thy s. to an impudent mind
10. for as a s. that is continually beaten
33. 24. bread, correction, and work for a s.
25. if thou set thy s. to labour shalt find rest
26. so are tortures and torments for an evil s.
30. if thou have a s. let him be as thyself
31. if thou have a s. entreat him as a brother
37. 11. consult not with an idle s. of business
42. 5. to make the side of an evil s. to bleed
2 Mac. 8. 35. he came like a fugitive s. to Antioch
SERVANTS.
1 Esd. 6. 13. we are the s. of the L. who made heaven
Tob. 10. 10. Raguel gave s. and cattle and money
Jud. 10. 23. she did reverence, and his s. took her up
Esth. 15. 16. and all his s. comforted her
Eccl. 4. 30. be not frantic among thy s.
6. 11. in prosperity he will be bold over thy s.
23. 4. but turn away from thy s. a haughty mind
36. 17. O Lord, hear the prayer of thy s.
Bar. 2. 20. as thou hast spoken by thy s.
Dan. 3. 10. we are become a reproach to thy s.
63. O ye s. of the Lord, bless ye the Lord
Sus. 27. the s. were greatly ashamed
1 Mac. 1. 6. wherefore he called his s.
8. his s. bare rule every one in his place
2 Mac. 7. 6. and he shall be comforted in his s.
33. yet shall he be at one again with his s.
34. lifting up thy hand against the s. of God
8. 29. to be reconciled with his s. for ever
SERVE.
1 Esd. 1. 4. now therefore s. the Lord your God
Jud. 11. 1. never hurt any that was willing to s.
Esth. 12. 5. command Mardocheus to s. in the court
Wisd. 15. 7. the vessels that s. for clean uses
Eccl. 2. 1. if thou come to s. the Lord, prepare
23. 5. hold him up that is desirous always to s. thee
39. 4. he shall s. among great men, and appear
43. 6. he made the moon also to s. in her season
2 Mac. 1. 3. God give you all an heart to s. him
4. 14. had no courage to s. any more at the altar
SERVED.
Wisd. 13. 13. the refuse among those that s. to no [use
Eccl. 25. 8. that hath not s. a man more unworthy
SERVETH.
Wisd. 16. 24. for the creature that s. thee
Eccl. 35. 16. he that s. the Lord shall be accepted
SERVICE.
Wisd. 15. 7. potter fashioneth every vessel for our s.
Eccl. 3. 7. and he will do s. unto his parents
10. 25. to servant shall they that are free do s.
11. 23. say not, what profit is there of my s.?
50. 14. and finishing the s. at the altar
2 Mac. 3. 3. belonging to the s. of the sacrifices
SERVING.
Wisd. 14. 21. for men s. either calamity or tyranny
19. 6. s. the peculiar commandments given to them
SERVITUDE.
Jud. 8. 23. our s. shall not be directed to favour
SET.
1 Esd. 1. 3. to s. the ark in the house Solomon built
2. 24. and if the walls thereof be s. up anew
2 Esd. 3. 18. thou didst s. fast the earth
Wisd. 13. 18. which cannot s. a foot forward
Eccl. 2. 2. s. thy heart aright and constantly endure
9. 2. to s. her foot upon thy substance
15. 16. he hath s. fire and water before thee
17. 17. he s. a ruler over every people
22. 27. who shall s. a watch before my mouth?
31. 16. eat those things which are s. before thee
33. 25. if thou s. thy servant to labour, find rest
28. s. him to work as is fit for him
34. 6. if not sent, s. not thy heart upon them
38. 29. who is alway carefully s. at his work
1 Mac. 1. 54. they s. up the abomination on altar
2 Mac. 5. 20. it was s. up with all glory
SETTETH.
Eccl. 10. 9. for such a one s. his own soul to sale
38. 28. he s. his mind to finish his work
SETTING.
1 Esd. 4. 30. the crown, and s. it upon her own head
SETTLED.
Esth. 13. 7. so cause our affairs to be well s.
Eccl. 22. 17. a heart s. on a thought of understanding
42. 17. declare works, which the Lord firmly s.
SEVEN.
1 Esd. 4. 63. and they feasted with gladness s. days
8. 11. and to my s. friends the counsellors
Tob. 2. 1. which is the holy feast of the s. weeks
3. 8. thou hast had already s. husbands
15. my s. husbands are already dead
6. 13. that this maid hath been given to s. men
11. 19. Tobias' wedding was kept s. days with joy
12. 15. I am Raphael, one of the s. holy angels
Jud. 16. 24. and Israel lamented her s. days
Eccl. 7. 3. thou shalt not reap them s.-fold
20. 12. buyeth for little, and repayeth it s.-fold
22. 12. s. days do men mourn for him that is dead
35. 11. give with a cheerful eye, for the Lord recompenseth and will give thee s. times as much
37. 14. wont to tell him more than s. watchmen
40. 8. and that is s.-fold more on sinners
Bar. 6. 3. for long season, namely, s. generations
Bel 32. and in the den there were s. lions
1 Mac. 13. 28. moreover, he set up s. pyramids
2 Mac. 7. 1. s. brethren with their mother taken
SEVENTH.
1 Esd. 5. 53. from the first day of the s. month
Eccl. 17. 5. in the s. place he imparted speech
1 Mac. 6. 53. for it was s. year, and they in Judea
2 Mac. 12. 38. when the s. day came, they purified
15. 4. who commanded the s. day to be kept
SEVENTY.
1 Esd. 1. 58. until the full term of s. years
2 Esd. 14. 46. keep the s. last, that mayest deliver
Jud. 1. 2. made the height of the wall s. cubits
SEVERAL.
1 Esd. 1. 11. according to the s. dignities of fathers
2 Mac. 12. 2. but of the governors of s. places
SEVERE.
Wisd. 5. 20. s. wrath shall he sharpen for a sword
11. 10. but the other as a s. king thou didst condemn
SHADOW.
Wisd. 2. 5. for our time is a very s. that passeth
5. 9. all these things are passed away as a s.
Eccl. 34. 2. is like him that catcheth at a s.
Bar. 1. 12. we shall live under the s. of Nabuchodon.
SHADOWING.
Wisd. 19. 7. namely, a cloud s. the camp
SHAKE.
Eccl. 13. 7. forsake thee, and s. his head at thee
SHAKEN.
Wisd. 4. 4. yet they shall be s. with the wind
Eccl. 16. 19. and foundations of the earth shall be s.
26. 7. an evil wife is a yoke s. to and fro
29. 18. hath s. them as a wave of the sea
43. 16. at his sight the mountains are s.
SHAKING.
Eccl. 22. 16. timber cannot be loosed with s.
2 Mac. 5. 3. horsemen in array with s. of shields
11. 8. one in white clothing s. his armour
SHAME.
2 Esd. 10. 22. our children are put to s. priests burnt
Jud. 12. 12. for lo, it will be a s. for our person
13. 16. hath not committed sin with me to s. me
14. 18. woman brought s. on house of Nabuchodon.
Eccl. 4. 21. for there is a s. that bringeth sin
5. 13. s. is in talk, the tongue of a man is his fall
14. for a foul s. is upon the thief
6. 1. thou shalt inherit an ill name, s. reproach
13. 7. he will s. thee by his meats, and laugh
20. 26. the s. of a liar is ever with him
26. 8. and she will not cover her own s.
24. a dishonest woman contemneth s.
42. 14. a woman which bringeth s. and reproach
Bar. 2. 6. to us and to our fathers open s.
Dan. 3. 10. we are become a s. and reproach
19. put us not to s. but deal with us after thy
2 Mac. 5. 7. at last received s. for his treason
9. 2. he being put to flight, returned with s.
SHAMEFACED.
Eccl. 26. 15. a s. woman is a double grace
25. but she that is s. will fear the Lord
32. 10. and before a s. man shall go favour
41. 16. therefore be s. according to thy word
24. so shalt thou be truly s. and find favour
SHAMEFACEDNESS.
Eccl. 41. 16. for it is not good to retain all s.
SHAMEFUL.
Wisd. 2. 20. let us condemn him with a s. death
SHAMEFULLY.
1 Mac. 7. 34. he abused them s. and spake proudly
2 Mac. 11. 12. and Lysias himself fled away s.
SHAMELESS.
Eccl. 26. 10. if thy daughter be s. keep her in
25. a s. woman shall be accounted as a dog
40. 30. begging is sweet in the mouth of the s.
42. 11. keep a sure watch over a s. daughter
Bar. 4. 15. a s. nation, and of strange language
SHAPE.
Wisd. 18. 1. hearing voice, and not seeing their s.
SHARP.
Wisd. 6. 5. for a s. judgment shall be to them
18. 16. unfeigned commandment as a s. sword
Eccl. 43. 19. it lieth on the top of s. stakes
SHARPEN.
Wisd. 5. 20. his wrath shall he s. for a sword
SHAVEN.
Bar. 6. 31. priests, having heads and beards s.
SHED.
1 Mac. 1. 37. thus they s. innocent blood
SHEDDETH.
Eccl. 28. 11. and an hasty fighting s. blood
SHEEP.
1 Esd. 1. 8. gave two thousand and six hundred s.
9. they gave to the Levites five thousand s.
SHEKELS.
1 Mac. 10. 42. the five thousand s. of silver
SHELTER.
Eccl. 14. 26. shall set his children under her s.
SHEPHERD.
Wisd. 17. 17. a s. or a labourer in the field
Eccl. 18. 13. he bringeth again, as a s. his flock
SHEW.
1 Esd. 5. 37. nor could they s. their families
2 Esd. 1. 5. s. my people their sinful deeds
Tob. 14. 9. s. thyself merciful and just that it may
Wisd. 5. 13. and we had no sign of virtue to s.
12. 13. s. that thy judgment is not unright
13. 10. which are gold and silver, to s. art in
Eccl. 4. 18. comfort him, and s. him her secrets
7. 24. s. not thy face cheerful toward him
16. 25. I will s. forth doctrine in weight
18. 21. and in the time of sins s. repentance
22. 19. maketh the heart to s. her knowledge
36. 6. s. new signs, and make strange wonders
39. 8. he shall s. forth what he hath learned
15. s. forth his praise with songs of your lips
43. 1. the beauty of heaven with his glorious s.
44. 15. the congregation will s. forth their praise
Bar. 3. 37. afterward did he s. himself on earth
6. 38. they can s. no mercy to the widow
Sus. 50. come sit down among us, and s. it us
Prayer of Manass. in me thou wilt s. thy goodness
2 Mac. 6. 27. I will s. myself such an one
8. 4. he would s. his hatred against the wicked
12. 36. that he would s. himself their helper
SHEWED.
1 Esd. 8. 78. now hath mercy been s. unto us
Wisd. 10. 10. she s. him the kingdom of God
18. 18. one and another s. the cause of his death
Eccl. 3. 23. for more things are s. unto thee
14. 12. covenant of the grave is not s. unto thee
45. 3. and he s. him part of his glory
46. 20. he prophesied, and s. the king his end
47. 23. Jeroboam, who s. Ephraim the way of sin
48. 25. he s. what should come to pass for ever
49. 8. which was s. him on chariot of cherubims
Bar. 3. 34. they s. light to him that made them
Bel 21. the priests, who s. him the privy doors
2 Mac. 2. 8. the cloud, as it was s. under Moses
3. 7. when Apollonius had s. him of the money
15. 32. and s. them vile Nicanor's head
SHEWETH.
Wisd. 1. 2. he s. himself to such as do not distrust
6. 16. s. herself favourably to them in the ways
Eccl. 28. 4. he s. no mercy to a man like himself
37. 20. there is one that s. wisdom in words
Bar. 6. 59. better to be a king that s. his power

SHIELD.
Jud. 9. 7. they trust in *s.* and spear, and bow
Eccl. 29. 13. than a mighty *s.* and strong spear
1 *Mac.* 15. 18. and they brought a *s.* of gold
20. it seemed good to receive the *s.* of them

SHIELDS.
1 *Mac.* 6. 2. in it a rich temple wherein were *s.*
2 *Mac.* 5. 3. with shaking of *s.* and drawing of swords
15. 11. not so much with defence of *s.* and spears

SHINE.
Wisd. 3. 7. they shall *s.* and run to and fro
Eccl. 24. 32. I will yet make doctrine to *s.* as morning

SHINED.
Wisd. 5. 6. the light of righteousness not *s.* to us
17. 20. the whole world *s.* with clear light
Bar. 3. 34. the stars *s.* in their watches
1 *Mac.* 6. 39. the mountains *s.* like lamps of fire
2 *Mac.* 1. 32. the light that *s.* from the altar

SHINING.
Eccl. 43. 8. *s.* in the firmament of heaven
50. 7. as the sun *s.* upon temple of most High

SHIP, S.
Wisd. 5. 10. as a *s.* that passeth over the waves
Eccl. 33. 2. an hypocrite is as a *s.* in a storm
1 *Mac.* 8. 26. that aid them with money or *s.*
15. 3. gathered soldiers, and prepared *s.* of war

SHOE.
Eccl. 46. 19. I have not taken so much as a *s.*

SHOOK.
2 *Esd.* 10. 26. so that the earth *s.* at the noise
2 *Mac.* 12. 12. whereupon they *s.* hands

SHOOTING.
Wisd. 11. 18. *s.* horrible sparks out of their eyes

SHORN.
Tob. 1. 6. having that which was first *s.*

SHORT.
Wisd. 2. 1. they said, our life is *s.* and tedious
4. 13. he being made perfect in a *s.* time
9. 5. of a *s.* time, and too young for understanding
15. 9. his care is not that his life is *s.*
16. 3. these suffering penury for a *s.* space
Eccl. 17. 2. he gave them few days, and a *s.* time
31. 19. he fetcheth not his wind *s.* on his bed
32. 8. let thy speech be *s.* comprehending much
36. 8. make the time *s.* remember the covenant
43. 27. we may speak much, and yet come *s.*
2 *Mac.* 2. 32. and to be *s.* in the story itself
7. 36. our brethren who have suffered a *s.* pain

SHORTEN.
Eccl. 30. 24. envy and wrath *s.* the life

SHORTLY.
Wisd. 14. 14. they shall come *s.* to an end
Bar. 4. 24. so shall they see *s.* your salvation
25. but *s.* thou shalt see his destruction

SHOULDER.
Eccl. 6. 25. bow down thy *s.* and bear her
2 *Mac.* 12. 35. horseman of Thracia smote off his *s.*
15. 30. strike off Nicanor's head with his *s.*

SHOULDERS.
1 *Esd.* 1. 4. ye shall no more bear the ark on your *s.*
Eccl. 7. 31. trespass-offering, and gift of the *s.*
Bar. 2. 21. bow down your *s.* to serve the king
6. 26. they are borne upon *s.* having no feet

SHOUTED.
Eccl. 50. 16. then *s.* the sons of Aaron and sounded

SHOWER.
Dan. 3. 42. O every *s.* and dew, bless ye the Lord

SHOWERS.
Wisd. 16. 16. with strange *s.* were they persecuted

SHREWD.
Eccl. 8. 19. lest he requite thee with a *s.* turn

SHRUBS.
1 *Mac.* 4. 38. they saw *s.* growing in the courts

SHRUNK.
1 *Mac.* 3. 6. the wicked *s.* for fear of him

SHUT.
Tob. 8. 4. after they were both *s.* in together
Jud. 13. 1. and Bagoas *s.* his tent without
Wisd. 18. 4. who had kept thy sons *s.* up
Eccl. 4. 31. and *s.* when thou shouldst repay
29. 12. *s.* up alms in thy store-houses
30. 18. delicates poured upon a mouth *s.* up
48. 3. by the word of the Lord he *s.* up heaven
1 *Mac.* 3. 18. for many to be *s.* up in hands of few
4. 31. *s.* up this army in the hand of thy people
6. 18. they *s.* up the Israelites round about
2 *Mac.* 1. 15. *s.* temple as soon as Antiochus came
4. 34. whom he *s.* up without regard of justice

SICHEM.
Eccl. 50. 26. that foolish people that dwell in S.

SICK.
Wisd. 17. 8. they that promised to drive troubles from a *s.* soul, were *s.* themselves of fear
Eccl. 7. 35. be not slow to visit the *s.*
18. 19. and use physic or ever thou be *s.*
21. humble thyself before thou be *s.*
1 *Mac.* 1. 5. and after these things he fell *s.*
6. 8. lay down on his bed, and fell *s.* for grief

SICKNESS.
Eccl. 30. 17. death is better than continual *s.*
31. 22. be quick, so shall there no *s.* come to thee
37. 30. for excess of meats bringeth *s.*
38. 9. my son, in thy *s.* be not negligent
2 *Mac.* 9. 22. having great hope to escape this *s.*

SIDE, S.
1 *Esd.* 3. 9. of whose *s.* the king shall judge
Wisd. 2. 24. they that do hold of his *s.* do find it
17. 10. which could of no *s.* be avoided
Eccl. 30. 12. beat him on the *s.* while he is a child
42. 5. to make the *s.* of an evil servant to bleed
1 *Mac.* 6. 38. they set them on this *s.* and that *s.*

SIEGE.
1 *Mac.* 6. 49. no victuals there to endure the *s.*
9. 64. then went he and laid *s.* against Bethbasi
2 *Mac.* 10. 18. things convenient to sustain the *s.*
33. they laid *s.* against the fortress four days
11. 5. he drew near to Bethsura, and laid *s.* to it

SIEVE.
Eccl. 27. 4. when one sifteth with a *s.* refuse remains

SIGH.
Eccl. 25. 18. when he heareth it shall *s.* bitterly

SIGHED.
Sus. 22. then Susanna *s.* and said, I am straitened

SIGHETH.
Eccl. 30. 20. a eunuch embraceth a virgin, and *s.*

SIGHING.
Jud. 14. 16. Bagoas cried with weeping and *s.*

SIGHT.
Tob. 4. 11. that give it in the *s.* of the Most High
21. and do that which is pleasing in his *s.*
11. 16. marvelled, because he had received his *s.*
12. 6. hath done unto you in *s.* of all that live
14. 2. fifty-eight years old when he lost his *s.*
Jud. 5. 12. Egyptians cast them out of their *s.*
15. 2. none durst abide in *s.* of his neighbour
Wisd. 3. 2. in *s.* of the unwise, they seemed to die
4. for though they be punished in the *s.* of men
8. 11. I shall be admired in the *s.* of great men
9. 9. wisdom knew what was acceptable in thy *s.*
13. 7. search him diligently, and believe their *s.*
15. 5. the *s.* whereof enticeth fools to lust after it
16. 3. the ugly *s.* of the beasts sent among them
17. 6. to be worse than the *s.* they saw not
Eccl. 1. 29. be not a hypocrite in the *s.* of men
2. 17. they will humble their souls in his *s.*
7. 33. a gift hath grace in the *s.* of every man
8. 16. for blood is as nothing in his *s.*
11. 21. it is an easy thing in the *s.* of the Lord
38. 3. in *s.* of great men he shall be in admiration
43. 16. at his *s.* the mountains are shaken
45. 1. which found favour in the *s.* of all flesh
3. he made him glorious in the *s.* of kings
46. 6. because he fought in the *s.* of the Lord
Bar. 1. 22. to do evil in the *s.* of the Lord our God
Sus. 23. than to sin in the *s.* of the Lord

SIGN, S.
Esth. 14. 16. I abhor the *s.* of my high estate
Wisd. 5. 11. no *s.* where she went is to be found
16. 6. be admonished, having a *s.* of salvation
Eccl. 37. 17. the countenance is a *s.* of changing
43. 6. a declaration of times, and a *s.* of world
7. from the moon is the *s.* of feasts, a light
Bar. 2. 11. out of Egypt with *s.* and with wonders
6. 67. neither can they shew *s.* in the heavens

SIGNET.
Tob. 1. 22. Achiacharus was keeper of the *s.*
Eccl. 17. 22. the alms of a man is as a *s.* with him
32. 6. as *s.* of an emerald set in a work of gold
49. 11. even he was as a *s.* on the right hand
Bel 11. and seal it with thine own *s.*
1 *Mac.* 6. 15. gave him the crown, his robe, and *s.*

SILENCE.
Eccl. 20. 5. there is one that keepeth *s.* found wise
6. and some keep *s.* knowing his time
41. 20. of *s.* before them that salute thee
2 *Mac.* 14. 17. through the sudden *s.* of his enemies

SILENT.
Eccl. 26. 14. a *s.* and loving woman is a gift of Lord

SILK.
1 *Mac.* 4. 23. got much gold, and silver, and blue *s.*

SILVER.
Jud. 5. 9. they were increased with gold and *s.*
Wisd. 7. 9. *s.* shall be counted as clay before her
13. 10. the works of men's hands, gold and *s.*
Eccl. 26. 18. pillars are upon the sockets of *s.*
28. 24. look that thou bind up thy *s.* and gold
40. 25. gold and *s.* make the foot stand sure
47. 18. and thou didst multiply *s.* as lead
50. 16. the sons of Aaron sounded the *s.* trumpets
Bar. 3. 17. they that hoarded up *s.* and gold
18. they that wrought in *s.* and were careful
6. 4. ye shall see in Babylon gods of *s.* and gold
39. their gods which are overlaid with gold and *s.*
2 *Mac.* 2. 2. when they see images of *s.* and gold

SILVER-SMITHS.
Wisd. 15. 9. but striveth to excel gold-smiths and *s.*

SIMEON.
Jud. 9. 2. O Lord God of my Father S. to whom
1 *Mac.* 2. 1. son of S. a priest of the sons of Joarib

SIMON.
1 *Mac.* 15. 24. the copy hereof they wrote to S.
32. when he saw the glory of S. he was astonished
33. then answered S. and said unto him
16. 2. S. called his eldest sons, Judas and John
13. Ptolemeus consulted against S. and his sons
14. S. was visiting the cities in the country
16. when S. and his sons had drunk largely, they came upon S. in banqueting-place and slew him
2 *Mac.* 3. 4. one S. of the tribe of Benjamin
11. not as that wicked S. had misinformed
4. 3. by one of S. faction murders were committed
4. Apollonius did rage, and increase S. malice
6. the state continue quiet, and S. leave his folly
8. 22. he joined S. and Joseph and Jonathan
10. 20. they that were with S. being led with

SIMPLICITY.
Wisd. 1. 1. and in *s.* of heart seek him

SIN.
1 *Esd.* 8. 76. we have been in great *s.* to this day
9. 11. seeing our *s.* in these things is spread far
2 *Esd.* 9. 36. we that received the law, perish by *s.*
15. 24. woe to them that *s.* and keep not my comm.
26. Lord knoweth all them that *s.* against him
16. 63. knoweth them that *s.* and would hide *s.*
Tob. 3. 14. that I am pure from all *s.* with man
4. 5. let not thy will be set to *s.* or transgress
21. if thou fear God and depart from all *s.*
12. 9. for alms shall purge away all *s.*
10. they that *s.* are enemies to their own life
Jud. 5. 20. and they *s.* against their God, 11. 10.
Wisd. 1. 4. nor dwell in the body that is subject to *s.*
10. 13. forsook not, but delivered him from *s.*
15. 2. if we *s.* we are thine, knowing thy power, but we will not *s.* knowing that we are thine
Eccl. 3. 27. the wicked man shall heap *s.* upon *s.*
4. 21. for there is a shame that bringeth *s.*
5. 5. be not without fear to add *s.* unto *s.*
7. 8. bind not one *s.* upon another
10. 13. for pride is the beginning of *s.*
13. 24. riches are good to him that hath no *s.*
15. 20. nor hath he given any man license to *s.*
20. 3. for so shalt thou escape wilful *s.*
21. 2. flee from *s.* as from the face of a serpent
Eccl. 23. 11. if he offend, his *s.* shall be upon him, if he acknowledge not his *s.* a double offence
13. to swearing, for therein is the word of *s.*
16. two sorts of men multiply *s.* and the third
25. 24. of the woman came the beginning of *s.*
26. 28. that returneth from righteousness to *s.*
29. an huckster shall not be freed from *s.*
27. 2. so *s.* sticks close between buying and selling
10. so *s.* for them that work iniquity
13. and their sport is the wantonness of *s.*
32. 12. take pastime, but *s.* not by proud speech
34. 19. nor is he pacified for *s.* by sacrifices
38. 10. leave off *s.* and order thy hands aright
42. 1. and accept no person to *s.* thereby
46. 7. and they withheld the people from *s.*
47. 23. there was also Jeroboam, who caused Israel to *s.* and shewed Ephraim the way of *s.*
2 *Mac.* 6. 15. lest being come to the height of *s.*
12. 42. that the *s.* committed might be put out of remembrance Judas exhorted to keep from *s.*

SINS.
1 *Esd.* 8. 75. our *s.* are multiplied above our heads
86. for thou, O Lord, didst make our *s.* light
9. 7. thereby to increase the *s.* of Israel
Wisd. 4. 20. they cast up the accounts of their *s.*
11. 23. and thou winkest at the *s.* of men
12. 19. of hope that thou givest repentance for *s.*
17. 3. they supposed to lie hid in their secret *s.*
Eccl. 1. 21. the fear of the Lord driveth away *s.*
2. 11. the Lord forgiveth *s.* and saveth in affliction
3. 3. maketh an atonement for his *s.*
14. instead of *s.* it shall be added to build thee
15. thy *s.* shall melt away as ice in fair weather
5. 6. he will be pacified for the multitude of my *s.*
12. 14. one that is defiled with him in his *s.*
14. 1. and is not pricked with the multitude of *s.*
16. 9. people, that were taken away in their *s.*
17. 20. but all their *s.* are before the Lord
25. return to the Lord, and forsake thy *s.*
18. 21. and in the time of *s.* shew repentance
21. 1. do so no more, ask pardon for thy former *s.*
23. 2. they spare me not, and it pass not by my *s.*
3. lest my *s.* abound to my destruction
12. and they shall not wallow in their *s.*
18. the Most High will not remember my *s.*
28. 2. forgive, so shall thy *s.* also be forgiven
4. and doth he ask forgiveness of his own *s.*
5. who will treat for pardon of his *s.*?
8. abstain from strife, thou shalt diminish thy *s.*
34. 26. so it is with a man that fasteth for his *s.*
47. 11. the Lord took away his *s.* and exalted
24. and their *s.* were multiplied exceedingly
48. 15. neither departed they from their *s.*
16. was pleasing to God, and some multiplied *s.*
Dan. 3. 5. bring these on us because of our *s.*
2 *Mac.* 5. 17. Lord was angry for awhile for the *s*
18. had been formerly wrapped in many *s.*
6. 14. till they be come to the fulness of their *s.*
7. 32. for we suffer because of our *s.*
12. 42. for the *s.* of those that were slain
13. 8. as he committed many *s.* about the altar

SINFUL.
Tob. 13. 6. declare his majesty to a *s.* nation
Wisd. 3. 13. which hath not known the *s.* bed
Eccl. 10. 23. nor convenient to magnify a *s.* man
11. 32. and a *s.* man layeth wait for blood
15. 12. for he hath no need of the *s.* man
27. 30. and the *s.* man shall have them both
32. 17. a *s.* man will not be reproved, but findeth
1 *Mac.* 1. 34. and they put therein a *s.* nation
2. 44. and they smote *s.* men in their anger

SINNED.
1 *Esd.* 1. 24. concerning those that *s.* and did wicked.
4. 27. many also have erred, and *s.* for women
Tob. 3. 3. my fathers, who have *s.* before thee
Jud. 5. 17. whilst they *s.* not before their God
Esth. 14. 6. and now we have *s.* before thee
Wisd. 12. 11. for those things wherein they *s.*
Eccl. 5. 4. say not I have *s.* and what harm happened
21. 1. my son, hast thou *s.*? do so no more
27. 1. many have *s.* for a small matter
Bar. 1. 13. we have *s.* against the Lord our God
Prayer of Manass. thou hast promised repentance to them that have *s.* thou hast not appointed repentance to the just, which have not *s.* but to me, for I have *s.* above the number of the sands of the sea; I have *s.* O Lord, I have *s.*
2 *Mac.* 7. 18. we suffer, having *s.* against our God

SINNER.
Eccl. 1. 25. godliness is an abomination to a *s.*
2. 12. woe to the *s.* that goeth two ways
5. 9. so doth the *s.* that hath a double tongue
6. 1. even so shall a *s.* that hath a double tongue
8. 10. kindle not the coals of a *s.* lest thou be burned
9. 11. envy not the glory of a *s.* knowest not his end
12. 4. give to the godly and help not the *s.* 7.
14. so one that goeth to a *s.* and is defiled
13. 17. what fellowship hath the wolf with the lamb? so the *s.* with the godly
15. 9. praise is not seemly in the mouth of a *s.*
16. 13. the *s.* shall not escape with his spoils
20. 9. there is a *s.* that hath good success in evil
23. 8. the *s.* shall be left in his foolishness
25. 19. let the portion of *s.* fall upon her
29. 16. a *s.* will overthrow the estate of his surety
33. 14. good is set against evil, so is the godly set against the *s.* and the *s.* against the godly
Prayer of Manass. repentance to me that am a *s.*
1 *Mac.* 2. 48. nor suffered they the *s.* to triumph

SINNERS.
Wisd. 4. 10. so that living among *s.* he was translated
19. 13. and punishments came upon the *s.*
Eccl. 5. 6. his indignation resteth upon *s.*
7. 16. number not thyself among the multitude of *s.*
11. 9. and sit not in judgment with *s.*
16. had their beginning together with *s.*
21. marvel not at the works of *s.* trust in the Lord
12. 6. for the Most High hateth *s.* and will repay
15. 7. not attain to her, and *s.* shall not see her
19. 22. nor at any time is the counsel of *s.* prudence
21. 6. hateth to be reproved, is in the way of *s.*
10. the way of *s.* is made plain with stones

Eccl. 39. 25. so evil things are created for *s.*
27. so to the *s.* they are turned into evil
40. 8. and that is seven-fold more upon *s.*
41. 5. the children of *s.* are abominable children
6. the inheritance of *s.* children shall perish
11. but an ill name of *s.* shall be blotted out
Prayer of Manass. thy angry threatening toward *s.* is unportable; hast appointed repentance to *s.*

SINNETH.

Wisd. 11. 16. might know wherewithal a man *s.*
Eccl. 10. 29. who will justify him that *s.* ag. his soul
19. 4. he that *s.* shall offend against his soul
38. 15. he that *s.* before his Maker, let him fall

SINNING.

Eccl. 18. 27. and in the day of *s.* he will beware
19. 28. if for want of power he be hindered from *s.*
20. 21. there is that is hindered from *s.* thro' want

SINAI.

Eccl. 48. 7. who heardest rebuke of the Lord in S.

SINCERE.

Eccl. 5. 11. be swift to hear, and let thy life be *s.*

SING.

Jud. 16. 1. Judith began to *s.* this thanksgiving
13. I will *s.* to the Lord a new song
Eccl. 47. 9. and daily *s.* praises in their songs
51. 11. and I will *s.* praises with thanksgiving

SINGER.

Eccl. 9. 4. use not company of a woman that is a *s.*

SINGERS.

1 *Esd.* 1. 15. the holy *s.* also were in their order
Eccl. 47. 9. he set *s.* also before the altar
50. 18. the *s.* also sang praises with their voices

SINGING.

1 *Esd.* 5. 62. *s.* songs of thanksgiving to the Lord
Wisd. 18. 9. fathers now *s.* out the songs of praise

SINGULAR.

Wisd. 14. 18. the *s.* diligence of the artificer

SION.

2 *Esd.* 3. 2. for I saw the desolation of S.
5. 25. thou hast hallowed S. to thyself
6. 4. or ever the chimneys in S. were hot
10. 7. that S. our mother is full of heaviness
Jud. 9. 13. purposed cruel things against top of S.
Eccl. 24. 10. and so was I established in S.
48. 18. Sennacherib lift up his hand against S.
24. he comforted them that mourned in S.

SIRNAME.

1 *Mac.* 2. 5. Jonathan whose *s.* was Apphus

SIRNAMED.

1 *Mac.* 1. 10. Antiochus *s.* Epiphanes, who had
6. 43. Eleazar also *s.* Savaran, perceiving

SISTER.

Tob. 8. 4. Tobias said, *s.* arise, and let us pray
7. O Lord, I take not this my *s.* for lust

SIT.

1 *Esd.* 3. 7. and he shall *s.* next to Darius
4. 42. art found wisest, thou shalt *s.* next to me
Jud. 12. 15. that she might *s.* and eat upon them
Wisd. 9. 12. be worthy to *s.* in my father's seat
Eccl. 9. 9. *s.* not at all with another man's wife, nor *s.* down with her in thine arms
11. 1. wisdom maketh him to *s.* among great men
9. and *s.* not in judgment with sinners
12. 12. neither let him *s.* at thy right hand
25. 18. her husband shall *s.* among his neighbours
26. 12. by every hedge will she *s.* down
31. 12. if thou *s.* at a bountiful table, be not greedy
32. 1. take diligent care for them, so *s.* down
38. 33. they shall not *s.* high in the congregation, they shall not *s.* on the judges' seat
42. 12. and *s.* not in the midst of women
Sus. 50. the elders said, come *s.* down among us

SITTEST.

Eccl. 4. 9. deliver from the hand of the oppressor, be not faint-hearted when thou *s.* in judgment
23. 14. remember when thou *s.* among great men
31. 18. when thou *s.* among many, reach not

SITTETH.

Wisd. 9. 4. give me wisdom that *s.* by thy throne
Eccl. 33. 6. neigheth under every one that *s.* on him
40. 3. from him that *s.* on a throne of glory
Bar. 6. 71. like a white thorn, that every bird *s.* on

SITTING.

1 *Esd.* 4. 29. Apame *s.* at the right hand of the king
Wisd. 6. 14. he shall find her *s.* at his doors
Eccl. 1. 8. there is one wise, *s.* on his throne
38. 28. the smith also *s.* by the anvil
29. so doth the potter *s.* at his work, and turning
Bar. 6. 43. the women also *s.* in the ways
Bel 40. he looked in, and behold Daniel was *s.*

SIX.

Tob. 14. 3. called his son, and *s.* sons of his son
Bel. 31. into the lions' den, where he was *s.* days

SIXTH.

1 *Esd.* 7. 5. in *s.* year of Darius king of the Persians
2 *Esd.* 6. 53. on the *s.* thou gavest commandment
Eccl. 17. 5. in *s.* place he imparted understanding
2 *Mac.* 7. 18. after him also they brought the *s.*

SKILL.

Wisd. 13. 13. formed it by the *s.* of his understanding
14. 2. and the workman built it by his *s.*
19. he forced all his *s.* to make the resemblance
Eccl. 1. 19. wisdom raineth down *s.* and knowledge
10. 30. the poor man is honoured for his *s.*
38. 3. the *s.* of the physician shall lift up his head
6. he hath given me *s.* that he might be honoured

SKILFUL.

Eccl. 21. 15. if a *s.* man hear wise word, will comm.

SKILFULLY.

Wisd. 13. 11. he hath taken off all the bark *s.*

SKIN.

2 *Mac.* 7. 7. and when they had pulled off the *s.*

SKIPPETH.

Eccl. 36. 26. a thief that *s.* from city to city

SKIPPING.

Wisd. 17. 19. sound of stones, or running of *s.* beasts

SLACK.

2 *Esd.* 16. 37. the plagues draw nigh, and are not *s.*
38. when the child cometh forth, they *s.* not
39. even so shall not the plagues be *s.* to come
Tob. 12. 6. therefore be not *s.* to praise him
Eccl. 4. 29. in thy deeds be not *s.* and remiss
Eccl. 35. 18. Lord will not be *s.* till he hath smitten

SLACKNESS.

2 *Esd.* 5. 42. like as there is no *s.* of the last

SLAIN.

1 *Esd.* 1. 56. people that were not *s.* with the sword
4. 5. they slay, and are *s.* and transgress not
2 *Esd.* 1. 32. whom ye have taken and *s.* and torn
Tob. 1. 18. if the king Sennacherib had *s.* any
Jud. 9. 3. wherefore thou gavest their rulers to be *s.*
Wisd. 11. 7. whereby the infants were *s.*
Bel 28. he hath *s.* the dragon, and put priests
1 *Mac.* 2. 9. her infants are *s.* in the streets
3. 11. many also fell down *s.* but the rest fled
5. 12. come and deliver us, for many of us are *s.*
16. 21. told that his father and brethren were *s.*
2 *Mac.* 1. 13. they were *s.* in the temple of Nanea
4. 36. because Onias was *s.* without cause
7. 20. when she saw her seven sons *s.* in one day

SLANDER.

Eccl. 19. 15. admonish, for many times it is a *s.*
26. 5. mine heart feareth the *s.* of a city
27. 23. he will writhe his mouth and *s.* thy sayings
1 *Mac.* 11. 11. thus did he *s.* him, because he was

SLANDEROUS.

Eccl. 51. 2. and from the snare of the *s.* tongue

SLAVES.

Jud. 5. 11. brought them low, and made them *s.*
14. 13. for the *s.* have been bold to come down
18. these *s.* have dealt treacherously
1 *Mac.* 3. 41. to buy the children of Israel for *s.*

SLAUGHTER.

2 *Mac.* 8. 4. remember the wicked *s.* of infants

SLAY.

1 *Esd.* 4. 5. they *s.* and are slain, and transgress not
Wisd. 18. 5. determined to *s.* the babes of the saints
Eccl. 47. 5. gave strength to *s.* that mighty warrior
Sus. 53. the righteous shalt thou not *s.*
Bel 26. I shall *s.* this dragon without sword or staff
1 *Mac.* 5. 2. began to *s.* and destroy the people
9. 32. but Bacchides sought for to *s.* him
11. 10. daughter to him, for he sought to *s.* me
16. 21. Ptolemee hath sent to *s.* thee also

SLAYETH.

Wisd. 1. 11. the mouth that belieth *s.* the soul
Eccl. 34. 22. that taketh neighbour's living *s.* him

SLAYING.

Eccl. 21. 2. as the teeth of a lion, *s.* souls of men
1 *Mac.* 6. 45. *s.* on the right hand, and on the left
2 *Mac.* 5. 13. there was *s.* of virgins and infants

SLEEP.

1 *Esd.* 3. 6. to drink in gold, and to *s.* upon gold
2 *Esd.* 2. 31. remember thy children that *s.*
Wisd. 7. 2. and the pleasure that came with *s.*
17. 14. but they sleeping the same *s.* that night
Eccl. 13. 13. hearest these things, awake in thy *s.*
22. 7. as he that waketh one from a sound *s.*
31. 1. and the care thereof driveth away *s.*
2. watching care, as a sore disease breaketh *s.*
20. sound *s.* cometh of moderate eating
40. 6. he is in his *s.* as in a day of keeping watch
42. 9. and the care for her taketh away *s.*
46. 19. before his long *s.* he made protestations
1 *Mac.* 6. 10. the *s.* is gone from mine eyes

SLEEPING.

Wisd. 17. 14. they *s.* the same sleep that night

SLENDERLY.

2 *Mac.* 15. 38. but if I have done *s.* and meanly

SLEPT.

2 *Esd.* 10. 59. so I *s.* that night and another
Tob. 8. 9. so they *s.* both that night
Jud. 12. 5. and she *s.* till midnight and arose
Eccl. 48. 11. they that saw thee and *s.* in love

SLEW.

Eccl. 47. 4. *s.* he not a giant when he was but young
1 *Mac.* 1. 2. Alexander *s.* the kings of the earth
61. they *s.* them that had circumcised them
2. 24. he ran and *s.* him upon the altar
38. they rose up and *s.* them with their wives
5. 51. who then *s.* all the males with the sword
16. 16. Ptolemee *s.* him and his two sons
2 *Mac.* 4. 38. there *s.* he the cursed murderer
5. 6. Jason *s.* his own citizens without mercy

SLIDE.

Eccl. 28. 26. beware thou *s.* not by it, lest thou fall

SLING.

Jud. 9. 7. they trust in spear, and bow, and *s.*
Eccl. 47. 4. lifted his hand with the stone in the *s.*

SLINGS.

1 *Mac.* 6. 51. and pieces to cast darts and *s.*

SLIP.

Eccl. 20. 18. to *s.* on a pavement is better than to *s.* with the tongue, so fall of wicked shall come

SLIPPED.

Eccl. 25. 8. he that hath not *s.* with his tongue

SLIPPETH.

Eccl. 19. 16. there is one that *s.* in his speech
21. 7. a man of understanding knows when he *s.*

SLIPPED.

Eccl. 14. 1. the man that hath not *s.* with his mouth
1 *Mac.* 9. 7. when Judas saw that his host *s.* away

SLOTHFUL.

Eccl. 22. 2. a *s.* man is compared to filth of dunghill
37. 11. consult not with the *s.* for any work

SLOW.

Wisd. 15. 15. as for their feet, they are *s.* to go
Eccl. 7. 35. be not *s.* to visit the sick
51. 24. wherefore are you *s.*? and what say you

SLUMBER.

Eccl. 22. 8. a tale to a fool speaketh to one in a *s.*
31. 2. watching care will not let a man *s.*

SMALL.

1 *Esd.* 1. 54. the vessels of the Lord, great and *s.*
Wisd. 6. 7. for he hath made the *s.* and great
14. 5. men commit their lives to a *s.* piece of wood
16. 6. they were troubled for a *s.* season
Eccl. 5. 15. ignorant in a great matter or a *s.*
19. 1. he that contemneth *s.* things shall fall
27. 1. many have sinned for a *s.* matter
43. 15. by his power the hailstones are broken *s.*
48. 15. there remained a *s.* people and a ruler
Bar. 2. 29. great multitude turned into a *s.* number
Dan. 3. 23. not with rosin, pitch, tow, and *s.* wood
1 *Mac.* 3. 16. went to meet him with a *s.* company
18. with a great multitude, or a *s.* company
2 *Mac.* 1. 15. he was entered with a *s.* company
3. 14. wherefore there was no *s.* agony through city
14. 8. for all our nation is in no *s.* misery

SMART.

Tob. 11. 12. when his eyes began to *s.* he rubbed

SMELL.

Tob. 8. 3. which *s.* when the evil spirit smelled
Eccl. 30. 19. for neither can it eat nor *s.*
2 *Mac.* 9. 9. the filthiness of his *s.* was noisome
12. when himself could not abide his own *s.*

SMELLED.

Tob. 8. 3. when evil spirit had *s.* he fled to Egypt

SMELLING.

Eccl. 50. 15. a sweet *s.* savour to the Most High

SMILE.

Eccl. 21. 20. a wise man doth scarce *s.* a little

SMILED.

Bel 7. then Daniel *s.* and said, be not deceived

SMILING.

Eccl. 13. 11. and *s.* on thee, will get out thy secrets

SMITE.

1 *Esd.* 4. 8. if he command to *s.* they *s.*
2 *Esd.* 15. 11. and I will *s.* Egypt with plagues
Jud. 9. 10. *s.* by the deceit of my lips the prince
Eccl. 36. 10. *s.* in sunder the heads of the rulers

SMITH.

Eccl. 38. 28. the *s.* also sitting by the anvil

SMITTEN.

Jud. 13. 15. Lord hath *s.* him by the hand of a woman
Eccl. 13. 2. if the one be *s.* against the other
35. 18. till he hath *s.* in sunder the loins
1 *Mac.* 1. 1. had *s.* Darius king of the Persians
2 *Mac.* 12. 22. being *s.* with fear and terror

SMOKE.

Tob. 6. 7. we must make a *s.* thereof before the man
16. the liver thou shalt make a *s.* with it
8. 2. the heart and liver he made a *s.* therewith
Wisd. 2. 2. the breath in our nostrils is as *s.*
Eccl. 22. 24. as the vapour and *s.* of a furnace
Bar. 6. 21. their faces are black through the *s.*
1 *Mac.* 4. 20. for the *s.* that was seen declared

SMOTE.

Jud. 5. 12. he *s.* the land of Egypt with plagues
13. 8. she *s.* twice upon his neck with all her might
Dan. 3. 26. and *s.* the flame of fire out of the oven
1 *Mac.* 2. 44. they *s.* sinful men in their anger
2 *Mac.* 3. 25. *s.* at Heliodorus with his fore feet
9. 5. God *s.* him with an incurable plague
12. 35. a horseman coming on him *s.* off his shoulder

SMOTEST.

Jud. 9. 3. thou *s.* the servants with their lords

SNARE.

Wisd. 14. 11. and a *s.* to the feet of the unwise
Eccl. 27. 29. they shall be taken in the *s.*
51. 2. and from the *s.* of the slanderous tongue
1 *Mac.* 1. 35. and so they became a sore *s.*
5. 4. who had been a *s.* and an offence to people

SNARES.

Tob. 14. 10. Manasses escaped the *s.* of death

SNOW.

Dan. 3. 46. O ye dews and storms of *s.* bless the Ld.
50. O ye frost and *s.* bless ye the Lord
1 *Mac.* 13. 22. but there fell a very great *s.*

SOBERLY.

Wisd. 9. 11. she shall lead me *s.* in my doings

SOCKETS.

Eccl. 26. 18. as golden pillars are on *s.* of silver

SODOM.

2 *Esd.* 2. 8. remember what I did to S. and Gomorrah

SODOMITES.

2 *Esd.* 7. 36. Abraham prayed first for the S.
Wisd. 19. 14. for the S. did not receive those

SODOMITISH.

2 *Esd.* 5. 7. the S. sea shall cast out fish

SOFT.

Jud. 12. 15. her maid laid *s.* skins on the ground
Wisd. 2. 3. our spirit shall vanish as the *s.* air
15. 7. for the potter tempering the *s.* earth

SOJOURNED.

Jud. 5. 7. they *s.* heretofore in Mesopotamia
Wisd. 19. 10. while they *s.* in the strange land
Eccl. 16. 8. nor spared he the place where Lot *s.*

SOJOURNEST.

Eccl. 41. 19. In regard of the place where thou *s.*

SOLD.

Tob. 1. 7. another tenth part I *s.* away and spent it
Jud. 7. 25. but God hath *s.* us into their hands
Wisd. 10. 13. when righteous was *s.* she forsook not
Bar. 4. 6. ye were *s.* to the nations not for destruction
1 *Mac.* 1. 15. and were *s.* to do mischief
2 *Mac.* 4. 32. and some of them he *s.* into Tyrus
5. 14. and no fewer *s.* than slain
8. 14. others *s.* all they had left and withal besought the Lord, being *s.* by the wicked Nicanor

SOLDIERS.

1 *Esd.* 4. 6. likewise for those that are no *s.*
1 *Mac.* 3. 28. and he gave his *s.* pay for a year
5. 50. so the *s.* pitched, and assaulted the city
6. 29. there came unto him bands of hired *s.*
11. 3. he left in every one a garrison of *s.* to keep it

SOLEMN.

2 *Esd.* 1. 31. your *s.* feast-days have I forsaken
Jud. 8. 6. and *s.* days of the house of Israel
Esth. 16. 22. among your *s.* feasts keep it a high day
Eccl. 47. 10. and he set in order the *s.* times
Bar. 1. 14. read this book upon the *s.* days

SOLEMNLY.

2 *Mac.* 14. 4. which were used *s.* in the temple

SOLEMNITY.

Eccl. 50. 19. till the *s.* of the Lord was ended
2 *Mac.* 15. 36. not to let that day pass without *s.*

SOLES.

Esth. 13. 13. have been content to kiss the *s.* of his feet

SOLITARY.

Eccl. 8. 16. go not with him into a *s.* place
9. 7. nor wander thou in the *s.* places thereof

SOLOMON.

2 *Esd.* 7. 38. S. for them that come to the sanctuary
Eccl. 47. 13. S. reigned in a peaceable time

Eccl. 47. 23. thus rested S. with his fathers
2 Mac. 2. 8. when S. desired the place might be
10. even so prayed S. also, and fire came down
12. so S. kept those eight days
SOLUTION.
2 Esd. 10. 43. of death of her son, this is the *s.*
SONG.
2 Esd. 10. 22. our *s.* is put to silence, joy at an end
Jud. 16. 1. all people sang after her this *s.* of praise
13. I will sing unto the Lord a new *s.* O Lord
Eccl. 39. 14. sing a *s.* of praise, bless the Lord
SONGS.
1 Esd. 5. 60. singing *s.* of thanksgiving, praising Lord
61. they sung with loud voices *s.* to the Lord
Eccl. 39. 15. shew forth his praise with *s.* of your lips
47. 8. with his whole heart he sung *s.* loved him
9. they might daily sing praises in their *s.*
17. the countries marvelled at thee for thy *s.*
SON.
Tob. 1. 22. and he was my brother's *s.*
3. 15. nor any *s.* of his alive to whom I may keep
4. 3. he said, my *s.* when I am dead bury me
4. remember, my *s.* she saw many dangers for thee
5. my *s.* be mindful of Lord our God all thy days
12. beware of all whoredom, my *s.* take a wife
14. be circumspect, my *s.* in all things thou dost
19. therefore, my *s.* remember my commandment
21. fear not, my *s.* that we are made poor
5. 11. dost thou seek an hired man to go with thy *s.*
14. and things necessary as to mine own *s.*
17. Anna said, why hast thou sent away our *s.*?
6. 14. I am the only *s.* of my father, I fear lest I
die, for they have no other *s.* to bury them
7. 7. thou art the *s.* of an honest and good man
10. 4. my *s.* is dead, seeing he stayeth long
5. I care for nothing, my *s.* is the light of mine eyes
7. my *s.* is dead, she ceaseth not to bewail her *s.*
11. 9. Anna fell on the neck of her *s.* and said, seeing I have seen thee, my *s.* I am content to die
10. Tobit stumbled but his *s.* ran unto him
13. when he saw his *s.* he fell upon his neck
15. taken pity, for behold, I see my *s.* Tobias
14. 3. he called his *s.* and the six sons of his *s.* and said to him, my *s.* take thy children
Wisd. 2. 18. for if the just man be the *s.* of God
10. 5. his tender compassion towards his *s.*
Eccl. 2. 1. my *s.* if thou come to serve the Lord
3. 12. my *s.* help thy father in his age
6. 23. give ear, my *s.* receive my advice
32. my *s.* if thou wilt, thou shalt be taught
7. 3. my *s.* sow not on the furrows of unrighteousness
10. 28. my *s.* glorify thy soul in meekness
11. 10. my *s.* meddle not with many matters
16. 24. my *s.* hearken to me, and learn knowledge
18. 15. my *s.* blemish not thy good deeds
21. 1. my *s.* hast thou sinned? do so no more
26. 19. my *s.* keep the flower of thine age sound
30. 2. he that chastiseth his *s.* shall have joy
3. he that teacheth his *s.* grieveth the enemy
7. he that maketh too much of his *s.* shall bind up
13. chastise thy *s.* and hold him to labour
31. 22. my *s.* hear me, and despise me not
33. 19. give not thy *s.* and wife power over thee
34. 20. as one that killeth the *s.* before his father
40. 28. my *s.* lead not a beggar's life, better to die
48. 10. to turn the heart of the father to the *s.*
Bar. 2. 3. a man should eat the flesh of his own *s.*
1 Mac. 1. 10. Epiphanes, *s.* of Antiochus the king
3. 33. he left Lysias to bring up his *s.* Antiochus
10. 54. I will be thy *s.* in law, and give gifts
13. 53. saw that John his *s.* was a valiant man
16. 11. Ptolemeus the son of Abubus made captain
2 Mac. 7. 26. promised that she would counsel her *s.*
27. O my *s.* have pity upon me that bare thee
28. I beseech thee, my *s.* look upon the heaven
10. 10. who was the *s.* of this wicked man
SONS.
1 Esd. 5. 35. the *s.* of the servants of Solomon
8. 21. upon the kingdom of the king and his *s.*
70. their *s.* have married with their daughters
84. ye shall not join your daughters to their *s.*
nor shall ye take their daughters to your *s.*
2 Esd. 1. 28. have I not prayed you as a father his *s.*
Tob. 1. 7. the first tenth I gave to the *s.* of Aaron
21. not 55 days before two of his *s.* killed him
Jud. 5. 3. he said, tell me now, ye *s.* of Canaan
Wisd. 9. 7. to be a judge of thy *s.* and daughters
12. 21. with circumspection didst thou judge thy *s.*
16. 10. thy *s.* not the teeth of dragons overcame
4. to be imprisoned who kept thy *s.* shut up
13. acknowledged this people to be the *s.* of God
Eccl. 3. 2. confirmed authority of the mother over *s.*
16. 1. neither delight in ungodly *s.*
40. 1. a heavy yoke is upon the *s.* of Adam
50. 13. so were all the *s.* of Aaron in their glory
Sus. 48. are ye such fools, ye *s.* of Israel, to condemn
1 Mac. 1. 9. so did their *s.* after them many years
2. 20. yet will I and my *s.* walk in the covenant
64. wherefore you, my *s.* be valiant, and shew
70. and his *s.* buried him in the sepulchre
13. 16. and send two of his *s.* for hostages
2 Mac. 7. 20. when she saw her seven *s.* slain
41. last of all, after the *s.* the mother died
SOOTHSAYINGS.
Eccl. 34. 5. divinations and *s.* and dreams are vain
SORE.
Wisd. 10. 12. in a *s.* conflict she gave him victory
Eccl. 31. 2. care as a *s.* disease breaketh sleep
39. 28. which in their fury lay on *s.* strokes
1 Mac. 2. 14. put on sackcloth, and mourned very *s.*
2 Mac. 3. 26. who gave him many *s.* stripes
9. 5. *s.* torments of the inner parts came upon him
SORROW.
1 Esd. 3. 20. a man remembereth neither *s.* nor debt
Tob. 3. 1. I did weep, and in my *s.* prayed, saying
6. 14. and bring my father's life to the grave with *s.*
Esth. 13. 17. turn our *s.* into joy, that we may live
Eccl. 26. 6. a grief of heart, and *s.* is a woman that
30. 12. be stubborn, and so bring *s.* to thy heart
23. remove *s.* far from thee, for *s.* hath killed
37. 12. who will *s.* with thee if thou shalt miscarry
38. 19. in affliction also *s.* remaineth

1 Mac. 1. 11. since departed, we have had much *s.*
2 Mac. 3. 17. what *s.* he had now in his heart
9. 9. while he lived in *s.* his flesh fell away
SORROWS.
Eccl. 3. 27. an obstinate heart be laden with *s.*
7. 27. and forget not the *s.* of thy mother
SORROWFUL.
1 Esd. 9. 52. this day is holy to Lord, be not *s.* 53.
Tob. 3. 10. when she heard these, she was very *s.*
7. 7. when he heard Tobit was blind he was *s.*
13. 14. who have been *s.* for all thy scourges
Eccl. 4. 2. make not an hungry soul *s.* nor provoke
30. 5. and when he died, he was not *s.*
SORRY.
2 Esd. 8. 15. thy people, for whose sake I am *s.*
Tob. 9. 4. and if I tarry long, he will be very *s.*
Eccl. 13. 5. he will make thee bare, and not be *s.*
SOVEREIGNTY.
Wisd. 6. 3. and *s.* is given from the Highest
SOUGHT.
1 Esd. 2. 21. that it may be *s.* out in the books
5. 39. was *s.* in the register, and was not found
Tob. 1. 19. that I was *s.* for to be put to death
Wisd. 8. 2. I loved her and *s.* her out from my youth
Eccl. 26. 27. a scold shall be *s.* out to drive away
38. 33. they shall not be *s.* for in counsel
39. 17. at a time convenient they shall all be *s.* out
47. 25. they *s.* out all wickedness, till vengeance
51. 3. out of the hand of such as *s.* after my life
15. from my youth up *s.* I after her
1 Mac. 7. 13. Assideans were the first that *s.* peace
SOUL.
Wisd. 1. 4. into a malicious *s.* wisdom shall not enter
11. the mouth that belieth, slayeth the *s.*
4. 11. was he taken away, lest deceit beguile his *s.*
14. his *s.* pleased the Lord, therefore he hasted
9. 15. the corruptible body presseth down the *s.*
10. 16. she entered into the *s.* of servant of the Lord
15. 11. his maker that inspired into him an active *s.*
16. 14. nor the *s.* received up, cometh again
17. 8. promised to drive away troubles from sick *s.*
Eccl. 1. 30. lest thou bring dishonour on thy *s.*
2. 1. my son, prepare thy *s.* for temptation
4. 2. make not an hungry *s.* sorrowful
6. if he curse thee in the bitterness of his *s.*
17. until she may trust his *s.* and try him by laws
20. be not ashamed when it concerneth thy *s.*
22. accept no person against thy *s.*
6. 2. that thy *s.* be not torn in pieces as a bull
7. 11. laugh no man to scorn in bitterness of his *s.*
17. humble thy *s.* greatly, for vengeance is fire
21. let thy *s.* love a good servant, defraud him not
9. 2. give not thy *s.* unto a woman, to set her foot
6. give not thy *s.* to harlots, that thou lose not
10. 28. my son, glorify thy *s.* in meekness
29. will justify him that sinneth against his own *s.*
14. 4. he that gathereth by defrauding his own *s.*
16. give and take, and sanctify thy *s.*
16. 17. for what is my *s.* among such a number?
19. 4. that sinneth, shall offend against his own *s.*
20. 22. there is that destroyeth his own *s.*
21. 27. curseth Satan, he curseth his own *s.*
28. a whisperer defileth his *s.* and is hated
30. 23. love thine own *s.* and comfort thy heart
32. 23. in every good work trust thine own *s.*
33. 31. thou hast need of him, as of thine own *s.*
34. 15. blessed is the *s.* of him that feareth the Lord
17. he raiseth up the *s.* and lighteneth the eyes
37. 27. prove thy *s.* and see what is evil for it
28. nor hath every *s.* pleasure in every thing
48. 5. raise his *s.* from the place of the dead
51. 19. my *s.* hath wrestled with her, I was exact
20. I directed my *s.* to her, and I found her
26. and let your *s.* receive instruction
29. let your *s.* rejoice in his mercy
Bar. 2. 18. but the *s.* that is greatly vexed
3. 1. O Lord, the *s.* in anguish crieth to thee
2 Mac. 6. 30. but in *s.* am well content to suffer
SOULS.
Wisd. 3. 1. the *s.* of righteous are in hand of God
13. she shall have fruit in the visitation of *s.*
7. 27. and in all ages entering into holy *s.*
11. 26. they are thine, O Lord, thou lover of *s.*
12. 6. the parents that killed *s.* destitute of help
14. 11. are stumbling-blocks to the *s.* of men
26. defiling of *s.* changing of kind, disorder
17. 1. therefore unnurtured *s.* have erred
Eccl. 2. 17. will humble their *s.* in his sight
21. 2. as the teeth of a lion, slaying *s.* of men
51. 24. what say you, seeing your *s.* are thirsty?
Bar. 2. 17. whose *s.* are taken from their bodies
6. 7. my angel with you, I myself caring for your *s.*
Dan. 3. 64. O ye spirits and *s.* of the righteous
1 Mac. 1. 48. should make their *s.* abominable
SOUND.
Wisd. 1. 9. the *s.* of his words come to the Lord
17. 19. or a terrible *s.* of stones cast down
Eccl. 45. 9. that there might be a *s.* and noise made
47. 10. that the temple might *s.* from morning
SOUNDED.
1 Esd. 5. 62. and all the people *s.* trumpets
65. yet the multitude *s.* marvellously, was heard
Wisd. 17. 4. noises, as of waters, *s.* about them
18. 10. there *s.* an ill-according cry of enemies
Eccl. 50. 16. sons of Aaron *s.* the silver trumpets
SOUNDS.
Wisd. 19. 18. notes change the tune, and yet are *s.*
Eccl. 50. 18. with great variety of *s.* made melody
SOUNDING.
1 Mac. 7. 45. *s.* an alarm after them with trumpets
SOUND.
Eccl. 17. 28. the *s.* in heart shall praise the Lord
22. 7. as he that waketh one from a *s.* sleep
26. 19. my son, keep the flower of thine age *s.*
30. 14. being *s.* and strong of constitution
16. there is no riches above a *s.* body, and no joy
SOUR.
2 Mac. 14. 30. such *s.* behaviour came not of good
SOUTH-SIDE.
1 Mac. 3. 57. the camp pitched on *s.* of Emmaus
SOW.
2 Esd. 9. 31. for behold, I *s.* my law in you

2 Esd. 16. 24. no man left to till earth, and *s.* it
Eccl. 7. 3. *s.* not on furrows of unrighteousness
26. 20. *s.* it with thine own seed, trusting in
SOWN.
1 Esd. 4. 6. when they reaped that which they had *s.*
SOWETH.
2 Esd. 8. 41. as the husbandman *s.* much seed
16. 43. he that *s.* as if he should not reap
SPACE.
Wisd. 16. 3. these suffering penury for a short *s.*
2 Mac. 14. 44. and a *s.* being made, he fell down
SPAIN.
1 Mac. 8. 3. what they had done in the country of S.
SPAKE.
1 Esd. 1. 51. and look when the Lord *s.* unto them
3. 4. young men of the guard *s.* one to another
Tob. 14. 8. things which the prophet Jonas *s.*
Eccl. 13. 22. he *s.* wisely, and could have no place
SPAKEST.
Jud. 16. 14. for thou *s.* and they were made
SPARE.
1 Esd. 4. 7. if he command to *s.* they *s.*
Wisd. 2. 10. ungodly said, let us not *s.* the widow
Eccl. 13. 12. and he will not *s.* to do thee hurt
23. 2. that they *s.* me not for mine ignorances
1 Mac. 13. 5. that I should *s.* mine own life
SPARED.
1 Esd. 1. 50. because he *s.* them and his tabernacle
53. who *s.* neither young man nor maid
Jud. 13. 20. because thou hast not *s.* thyself
Eccl. 16. 8. nor *s.* he the place where Lot sojourned
17. 21. neither left nor forsook them, but *s.* them
SPAREDST.
Wisd. 12. 8. nevertheless those thou *s.* as men
SPAREST.
Wisd. 11. 26. but thou *s.* all, for they are thine
SPARTA.
1 Mac. 14. 16. when heard at Rome, and as far as S.
SPEAK.
1 Esd. 3. 5. let every one of us *s.* a sentence
21. and it maketh to *s.* all things by talents
4. 13. the third, this was Zorobabel, began to *s.*
33. king looked, so he began to *s.* of the truth
Tob. 6. 10. I will *s.* for her that she may be given thee
12. now hear me, and I will *s.* to her father
7. 8. *s.* of those things thou didst talk in the way
Jud. 11. 5. suffer thy handmaid to *s.* in thy presence
Esth. 15. 12. he embraced her, and said, *s.* to me
Wisd. 6. 9. to you therefore, O kings, do I *s.*
7. 15. God hath granted me to *s.* as I would
8. 12. when I *s.* they shall give good ear to me
10. 21. made the tongues that cannot *s.* eloquent
13. 17. ashamed to *s.* to that which hath no life
Eccl. 4. 23. refrain not to *s.* when occasion to do good
25. in no wise *s.* against the truth
13. 6. he will *s.* thee fair, and say, what want. thou?
23. but if poor man *s.* they say, what fellow is this?
18. 19. learn before thou *s.* and use physic or ever
19. 14. and if he have, that he *s.* it not again
20. 16. they that eat my bread *s.* evil of me
20. for he will not *s.* it in due season
27. 7. praise no man before thou hearest him *s.*
32. 3. *s.* thou that art the elder, it becometh thee
43. 27. we may *s.* much, and yet come short
1 Mac. 9. 55. so that he could no more *s.* any thing
SPEAKER.
Eccl. 23. 8. the evil *s.* and proud shall fall thereby
SPEAKETH.
Wisd. 1. 8. that *s.* unrighteous things cannot be hid
Eccl. 12. 16. an enemy *s.* sweetly with his lips
13. 22. rich man *s.* things not to be spoken, yet men
23. when rich man *s.* every man holds his tongue
22. 8. that telleth tale to a fool, *s.* to one in slumber
25. 9. he that *s.* in ears of them that will hear
SPEAKING.
Eccl. 6. 5. a fair *s.* tongue will increase greetings
41. 23. or of *s.* again what thou hast heard
SPEAR.
Jud. 11. 2. I would not have lifted up my *s.*
See SHIELD.
SPECIAL.
Tob. 10. 12. I commit my daughter to thee of *s.* trust
Wisd. 3. 14. to him shall be given the *s.* gift of faith
SPEECH.
Jud. 9. 13. make my *s.* and deceit to be their wound
Esth. 14. 13. give me eloquent *s.* in my mouth
16. 5. oftentimes the fair *s.* of those put in trust
Eccl. 4. 24. for by *s.* wisdom shall be known
9. 17. and the wise ruler of the people for his *s.*
17. 5. *s.* an interpreter of the cogitations thereof
19. 16. there is one that slippeth in his *s.*
32. 8. let thy *s.* be short, comprehending much
12. take thy pastime, but sin not by proud *s.*
2 Mac. 15. 39. so *s.* finely framed delighteth the ears
SPEECHES.
Wisd. 8. 8. she knoweth the subtilties of *s.*
Eccl. 36. 19. so an heart of understanding, false *s.*
SPEECHLESS.
Wisd. 4. 19. he shall rend them, that they be *s.*
2 Mac. 3. 29. he lay *s.* without all hope of life
SPEED.
1 Esd. 6. 10. those works are done with great *s.*
8. 19. that they should give it him with *s.*
SPEEDILY.
Jud. 12. 14. whatever pleaseth him, I will do *s.*
Esth. 16. 18. God *s.* rendering vengeance to him
Wisd. 2. 6. let us *s.* use the creatures as in youth
4. 11. yea, *s.* was he taken away, lest wickedness
6. 5. horribly and *s.* shall he come upon you
Eccl. 16. 4. kindred of wicked shall *s.* become desol.
21. 5. and his judgment cometh *s.*
43. 22. a present remedy of all is a mist coming *s.*
2 Mac. 7. 37. he would *s.* be merciful to our nation
SPEND.
1 Esd. 4. 21. he sticks not to *s.* his life with his wife
Tob. 10. 7. which Raguel had sworn he should *s.* there
Jud. 11. 13. are resolved to *s.* the first-fruits of corn
12. 4. I shall not *s.* those things that I have before
Eccl. 9. 9. *s.* not thy money with her at the wine
14. 4. for others that shall *s.* his goods riotously
SPENDING.
Wisd. 13. 12. and after *s.* the refuse of his work

SPENT.
1 *Esd.* 6. 30. as priests in Jerus. signify to be daily *s.*
1 *Mac.* 14. 32. Simon *s.* much of his own substance
SPIRIT.
1 *Esd.* 2. 2. the Lord raised up the *s.* of Cyrus
Tob. 3. 6. and command my *s.* to be taken from me
6. 7. if a devil or an evil *s.* trouble any make smoke
14. lest I die, for a wicked *s.* loveth her
15. and make thou no reckoning of the evil *s.*
8. 3. which smell when the evil *s.* had smelled
Jud. 14. 6. Achior fell down, and his *s.* failed
16. 14. thou didst send forth thy *s.* it created them
Esth. 15. 8. then God changed the *s.* of the king
Wisd. 1. 5. the holy *s.* of discipline will flee deceit
6. wisdom is a loving *s.* and will not acquit
7. for the *s.* of the Lord filleth the world
2. 3. and our *s.* shall vanish as the soft air
5. 3. they repenting and groaning for anguish of *s.*
7. 7. I called on God, the *s.* of wisdom came to me
22. for in her is an understanding *s.* holy
9. 17. except thou send thy Holy S. from above
12. 1. for thine incorruptible *s.* in all things
15. 11. he knew not him that breathed in a living *s.*
16. he that borrowed his own *s.* fashioned them
16. 14. the *s.* when gone forth, returneth not
Eccl. 34. 13. the *s.* of those that fear the Lord
38. 23. when his *s.* is departed from him
39. 6. shall be filled with the *s.* of understanding
48. 12. and Eliseus was filled with his *s.*
24. he saw by an excellent *s.* what should come
Bar. 3. 1. O Lord, the troubled *s.* crieth unto thee
Sus. 45. raised up the holy *s.* of a young youth
Bel 36. through the vehemency of his *s.* set him
1 *Mac.* 13. 7. the people heard, their *s.* revived
SPIRITS.
Wisd. 7. 23. free from care, pure and most subtile *s.*
SPIRITUAL.
Wisd. 14. 12. idols was beginning of *s.* fornication
SPIT.
Eccl. 28. 12. if thou *s.* on it, it shall be quenched
2 *Mac.* 6. 19. he *s.* it forth, and came to torment
SPITTLE.
Eccl. 26. 22. an harlot shall be accounted as *s.*
SPOIL.
1 *Esd.* 4. 5. as well the *s.* as all the things else
Tob. 3. 4. thou hast delivered us for a *s.*
1 *Mac.* 3. 20. to destroy us and our wives and to *s.* us
SPOILED.
1 *Esd.* 4. 24. when he hath stolen, *s.* and robbed
Wisd. 10. 20. the righteous *s.* the ungodly
Eccl. 36. 25. where no hedge is, the possession is *s.*
48. 15. till they were *s.* and carried out of their land
Bar. 6. 18. lest their gods be *s.* with robbers
1 *Mac.* 6. 24. they slew, and *s.* our inheritance
2 *Mac.* 9. 16. holy temple, which before he had *s.*
SPOILS.
1 *Mac.* 1. 3. Alexander took *s.* of many nations
2 *Mac.* 8. 28. had given part of *s.* to the maimed
30. divided among themselves many *s.* more, and made the widows and the aged also equal in *s.*
SPOKEN.
1 *Esd.* 1. 28. the words *s.* by the mouth of the Lord
3. 17. who had *s.* of the strength of wine
4. 13. then the third, who had *s.* of women
9. 10. like as thou hast *s.* so will we do
Eccl. 13. 22. he speaketh things not to be *s.*
38. 17. weep a day or two, lest thou be evil *s.* of
33. they shall not be found where parables are *s.*
Bar. 2. 20. as thou hast *s.* by thy servants
Sus. 47. what mean these words that thou hast *s.*?
Bel 9. for he hath *s.* blasphemy against Bel
1 *Mac.* 1. 24. a great massacre, and *s.* very proudly
2 *Mac.* 1. 29. plant thy people, as Moses hath *s.*
3. 34. when they had *s.* these words, they appeared
6. 17. let this we have *s.* be for a warning to us
9. 5. as soon as he had *s.* these words a pain came on
SPORT.
1 *Esd.* 1. 51. they made a *s.* of his prophets
Eccl. 27. 13. their *s.* is in the wantonness of sin
SPOT.
Wisd. 13. 14. and covering every *s.* therein
SPOTTED.
Wisd. 15. 4. nor any image *s.* with divers colours
SPOUSE.
Wisd. 8. 2. I loved her, I desired to make her my *s.*
SPOUTS.
2 *Mac.* 14. 45. his blood gushed out like *s.* of water
SPREAD.
1 *Esd.* 9. 11. seeing our sin in these things is *s.* far
Jud. 4. 11. *s.* out their sackcloth before the Lord
Wisd. 17. 21. over them was *s.* an heavy night
1 *Mac.* 4. 51. they *s.* out the vails, and finished works
2 *Mac.* 8. 7. his manliness was *s.* every where
SPREADING.
Wisd. 17. 18. a noise of birds among *s.* branches
SPRING.
Wisd. 2. 7. and let no flower of the *s.* pass by us
SPRINGS.
2 *Esd.* 4. 7. how many *s.* are in the beginning of the deep, or how many *s.* are above the firmament
13. 47. the Highest shall stay the *s.* of the stream
SPRINKLE.
2 *Mac.* 1. 21. he commanded the priests to *s.* the wood
SPRINKLED.
2 *Mac.* 10. 25. they *s.* earth upon their heads
SPY.
Eccl. 11. 30. like as a *s.* watcheth he for thy fall
SPIES.
1 *Mac.* 12. 26. he sent *s.* also to their tents
SQUARE.
1 *Mac.* 10. 11. to build the walls with *s.* stones
STABLISHED.
Eccl. 22. 16. so the heart that is *s.* by counsel
STAFF.
Tob. 5. 17. is he not the *s.* of our hand in going?
Bel 26. I will slay the dragon without sword or *s.*
STAIN.
Eccl. 22. 10. do *s.* the nobility of their kindred
33. 22. leave not a *s.* in thine honour
47. 20. thou didst *s.* thy honour and pollute thy seed
2 *Mac.* 6. 25. and I shall get a *s.* to my old age

STAINED.
2 *Mac.* 6. 19. to live *s.* with such abomination
STAKES.
Eccl. 43. 19. it lieth on the top of sharp *s.*
STALLION.
Eccl. 33. 6. a *s.* horse is as a mocking friend
STAMP.
1 *Mac.* 15. 6. also to coin money with thine own *s.*
STAND.
1 *Esd.* 8. 90. we cannot *s.* any longer before thee
Jud. 6. 4. footsteps shall not be able to *s.* before us
8. 12. that *s.* instead of God amongst men
33. you shall *s.* this night in the gate
Wisd. 5. 23. a mighty wind shall *s.* up against them
6. 7. nor shall he *s.* in awe of any man's greatness
12. 12. or who shall come to *s.* against thee?
Eccl. 12. 12. set him not by, lest he *s.* in thy place
21. 23. he that is well nurtured will *s.* without
22. 18. pales on an high place will never *s.* against the wind, so a fearful heart cannot *s.* against fear
37. 13. let the counsel of thine own heart *s.*
40. 25. gold and silver make the foot *s.* sure
43. 10. they will *s.* in their order, and not faint
44. 12. their seed *s.* fast, and their children
1 *Mac.* 3. 53. how shall we be able to *s.* against them?
10. 72. thy foot is not able to *s.* before our face?
2 *Mac.* 2. 30. to *s.* on every point and go over things
STANDETH.
Jud. 9. 11. for thy power *s.* not in multitude
Wisd. 4. 8. is not that which *s.* in length of time
1 *Mac.* 9. 44. it *s.* not with us to-day, as in time past
STANDING.
1 *Esd.* 1. 5. *s.* in the temple according to dignity
Jud. 13. 4. then Judith *s.* by his bed, said in heart
Wisd. 4. 4. yet *s.* not fast, they shall be shaken
10. 7. and a *s.* pillar of salt is a monument
18. 16. and *s.* up, filled all things with death
23. *s.* between, he stayed the wrath and parted
Sus. 48. so he *s.* in the midst of them, said
2 *Mac.* 14. 45. he ran through and *s.* on a steep rock
STAR.
Eccl. 50. 6. he was as the morning *s.* in a cloud
STARS.
Wisd. 7. 19. the circuits of years and positions of *s.*
29. she is above all the order of *s.*
10. 17. and a light of *s.* in the night season
13. 2. but deemed it swift air, or the circle of the *s.*
17. 5. nor bright flames of *s.* endure to lighten
Eccl. 43. 9. the beauty of heaven, the glory of the *s.*
44. 21. that he would exalt his seed as the *s.*
Bar. 3. 34. the *s.* shined in their watches and rejoiced
6. 60. for the sun, moon, and *s.* are obedient
Dan. 3. 13. multiply their seed as the *s.* of heaven
41. O ye *s.* of heaven, bless ye the Lord
2 *Mac.* 9. 10. thought he could reach to the *s.*
STATE.
2 *Mac.* 4. 6. was impossible *s.* should continue quiet
9. 24. they knowing to whom the *s.* was left
11. 19. if you keep yourselves loyal to the *s.*
14. 26. was not well-affected towards the *s.*
STATELINESS.
Jud. 9. 10. break down their *s.* by hand of a woman
STATURE.
Bar. 3. 26. the giants, that were of so great *s.*
STATUTE.
2 *Mac.* 10. 8. they ordained also by a common *s.*
STATUTES.
2 *Esd.* 1. 24. will give my name that they may keep *s.*
7. 11. and when Adam transgressed my *s.*
13. 42. that they might there keep their *s.*
Eccl. 45. 17. he gave authority in *s.* of judgments
STAY.
1 *Mac.* 2. 43. joined and were a *s.* unto them
STAYED.
Wisd. 18. 23. standing between, he *s.* the wrath
Eccl. 15. 4. he shall be *s.* upon her, and not moved
STAYETH.
Tob. 10. 4. my son is dead seeing he *s.* long
STEAD.
1 *Esd.* 1. 34. people made him king in *s.* of Josias
Tob. 1. 21. Sarchedonus his son reigned in his *s.*
Jud. 8. 12. that stand in *s.* of God among men
Esth. 14. 2. in *s.* of precious ointments, ashes
Wisd. 5. 18. put on true judgment in *s.* of an helmet
7. 10. and I choose to have her in *s.* of light
11. 6. in *s.* of a fountain of a perpetual running
18. 3. in *s.* whereof thou gavest them a pillar
Eccl. 4. 10. be in *s.* of a husband to their mother
6. 1. in *s.* of a friend become not an enemy
17. 27. in *s.* of them which live and give thanks
Bar. 3. 19. and others are come up in their *s.*
1 *Mac.* 3. 1. then Maccabeus rose up in his *s.*
11. 34. in *s.* of payments the king received
14. 17. that Simon was made high priest in his *s.*
STEAL.
1 *Esd.* 4. 23. a man goeth his way to rob and to *s.*
STEDFAST.
Esth. 13. 3. for his constant good will and *s.* fidelity
Wisd. 7. 23. kind to man, *s.* sure, free from care
Eccl. 5. 10. be *s.* in thy understanding and thy word
11. 20. be *s.* in thy covenant, and be conversant
22. 23. abide *s.* to him in time of his trouble
1 *Mac.* 13. 37. we are ready to make a *s.* peace
STEEP.
2 *Mac.* 14. 45. he ran, and standing upon a *s.* rock
STEP.
Eccl. 19. 18. the fear of Lord is first *s.* to be accepted
STEPS.
Eccl. 6. 36. let thy foot wear the *s.* of his door
42. 19. he revealeth the *s.* of hidden things
STEWARDS.
1 *Esd.* 8. 67. the commandments to the king's *s.*
STICKETH.
Eccl. 19. 12. as an arrow that *s.* in a man's thigh
27. 2. as a nail *s.* fast between the joining of stones
STICKS.
1 *Esd.* 4. 21. he *s.* not to spend his life with his wife
STIFF.
Bar. 2. 30. not hear, because it is a *s.*-necked people
33. and they shall return from their *s.* neck
STIFFLY.
2 *Esd.* 2. 47. stood so *s.* for the name of the Lord

STINGS.
Wisd. 16. 5. perished with the *s.* of crooked serpents
STINK.
2 *Mac.* 9. 10. no man could endure to carry for his *s.*
STIR.
2 *Mac.* 15. 17. were able to *s.* them up to valour
STIRRED.
1 *Esd.* 2. 9. whose minds were *s.* up thereto
1 *Mac.* 3. 49. and the Nazarites they *s.* up
2 *Mac.* 15. 10. when he had *s.* up their minds
STIRRING.
2 *Mac.* 7. 21. *s.* up her womanish thoughts
STOCK.
1 *Esd.* 5. 37. neither could they shew their *s.*
Tob. 5. 13. then Tobit said, thou art of an honest and good *s.* my brother, thou art of a good *s.*
1 *Mac.* 12. 21. that they are of the *s.* of Abraham
2 *Mac.* 1. 10. was of the *s.* of the anointed priests
STOCKS.
Wisd. 14. 21. men did ascribe unto stones and *s.*
STOLE.
2 *Mac.* 4. 32. Menelaus *s.* certain vessels of gold
STOLEN.
1 *Esd.* 4. 24. when he hath *s.* spoiled, and robbed
Tob. 2. 13. I said to her, is it not *s.*? render it to the owners, for it is not lawful to eat any thing *s.*
STOMACH.
1 *Mac.* 7. 21. with a manly *s.* she said unto them
STONE.
Wisd. 11. 4. thirst was quenched out of the hard *s.*
Eccl. 6. 21. she will lie upon him as a mighty *s.*
22. 1. a slothful man is compared to a filthy *s.* and every one will hiss him out to his disgrace
20. whoso casteth a *s.* at the birds, frayeth them
29. 10. and let it not rust under a *s.* to be lost
47. 4. he lifted up his hand with the *s.* in the sling
1 *Mac.* 2. 36. neither cast they a *s.* at them
10. 73. where is neither *s.* nor flint, nor place
STONE-BOW.
Wisd. 5. 22. hail-stones shall be cast as out of a *s.*
STONES.
1 *Esd.* 6. 9. building an house of hewn and costly *s*
Tob. 13. 17. streets shall be paved with *s.* of Ophir
Jud. 1. 2. built walls round about of *s.* hewn
6. 12. from coming up by casting of *s.* against them
Wisd. 17. 19. or a terrible sound of *s.* cast down
Eccl. 21. 10. the way of sinners is made plain with *s.*
27. 2. as a nail sticketh between joinings of *s.*
32. 20. and stumble not among the *s.*
1 *Mac.* 4. 43. who bare out the defiled *s.*
5. 47. they stopped up the gates with *s.*
6. 51. with instruments to cast fire and *s.*
10. 11. to build Sion round about with square *s.*
2 *Mac.* 1. 16. they threw *s.* like thunderbolts
31. the water to be poured on the great *s.*
4. 41. some of them caught *s.* some clubs
10. 3. striking *s.* they took fire out of them
STOOD.
1 *Esd.* 5. 59. the priests *s.* arrayed in vestments
9. 46. he opened the law, they *s.* all straight up
Esth. 15. 6. she *s.* before the king who sat on his throne
Wisd. 10. 11. she *s.* by him, and made him rich
11. 3. they *s.* against their enemies, were avenged
18. 16. it touched heaven, but *s.* upon the earth
21. the blameless man *s.* forth to defend them
19. 7. where water *s.* before, dry land appeared
Eccl. 39. 17. at his commandment the waters *s.*
45. 2. so that his enemies *s.* in fear of him
23. Phinees *s.* up with good courage of heart
46. 3. who before him so *s.* to it? the Lord brought
48. 1. then *s.* up Elias the prophet as fire
50. 12. he himself *s.* by the hearth of the altar
Dan. 3. 2. then Azarias *s.* up and prayed thus
Sus. 34. two elders *s.* up in the midst of the people
1 *Mac.* 7. 36. the priests entered and *s.* before altar
2 *Mac.* 3. 26. two young men *s.* by him on either side
STOOLS.
2 *Mac.* 14. 21. when *s.* were set for either of them
STOOPING.
Bar. 2. 18. the soul that is vexed and goeth *s.*
STOP.
Jud. 4. 7. it was easy to *s.* them that would come up
Esth. 14. 9. *s.* the mouth of them that praise thee
Eccl. 20. 29. *s.* his mouth that he cannot reprove
27. 14. their brawls make one *s.* his ears
2 *Mac.* 14. 36. and *s.* every unrighteous mouth
STOPPED.
Jud. 16. 4. the multitude whereof *s.* the torrents
1 *Mac.* 2. 36. nor *s.* the places where they lay hid
9. 55. Alcimus was plagued, his mouth was *s.*
2 *Mac.* 2. 5. he laid altar of incense and *s.* the door
STORAX.
Eccl. 24. 15. a pleasant odour like sweet *s.*
STORE.
Tob. 7. 8. they set *s.* of meat on the table
1 *Mac.* 6. 6. *s.* of spoils which they had gotten
53. they had eaten up the residue of the *s.*
STORE-HOUSES.
Eccl. 29. 12. shut up alms in thy *s.* it shall deliver
STORM, S.
Wisd. 5. 14. like froth driven away with the *s.*
23. a wind like a *s.* shall blow them away
Dan. 3. 46. O ye dews and *s.* of snow, bless ye the Ld.
STORMED.
2 *Mac.* 13. 25. they *s.* because they would make
STORY.
2 *Mac.* 2. 24. to look into the narrations of the *s.*
30. belongeth to the first author of the *s.*
32. here then will we begin the *s.* foolish to make a long prologue, and to be short in the *s.* itself
15. 38. have done well, and as is fitting the *s.*
39. delighteth the ears of them that read the *s.*
STORIES.
1 *Esd.* 1. 33. in the book of the *s.* of the kings
STORY-WRITER.
1 *Esd.* 2. 17. thy servant Rathumus the *s.*
STRAIGHT.
Jud. 13. 20. walking a *s.* way before our God
Bar. 6. 27. nor can they make themselves *s.*
STRAIT.
Jud. 4. 7. because the passage was *s.* for two men

STRAITLY
Wisd. 17. 16. whosoever fell down was *s.* kept
Eccl. 26. 10. keep her in *s.* lest she abuse herself
STRAITNESS.
2 *Mac.* 12. 21. by reason of the *s.* of all the places
STRAITS.
Jud. 14. 11. went forth to the *s.* of the mountain
STRAKE.
Tob. 11. 11. he *s.* off the gall on his father's eyes
STRANGE.
1 *Esd.* 8.69. have not put away *s.* people of the land
9. 9. separate yourselves from the *s.* women
12. let all that have *s.* wives come at the time
36. these had taken *s.* wives, and put them away
2 *Esd.* 1. 6. and they have offered unto *s.* gods
Tob. 4. 12. and take not a *s.* woman to wife
Wisd. 14. 23. or made revellings of *s.* rites
16. 2. thou preparedst for them meat of a *s.* taste
3. might be made partakers of a *s.* taste
16. with *s.* showers were they persecuted
17. 3. they were troubled with *s.* apparitions
19. 5. but they might find a *s.* death
8. seeing thy marvellous *s.* wonders
10. while they sojourned in the *s.* land
Eccl. 10. 13. Lord brought on them *s.* calamities
29. 18. so that they wandered among *s.* nations
36. 3. lift up thy hand against the *s.* nations
39. 4. he will travel through *s.* countries
43. 25. for therein be *s.* and wondrous works
Bar. 1. 22. to serve *s.* gods, and to do evil before L.
3. 10. that thou art waxen old in a *s.* country
4. 15. a shameless nation, and of a *s.* language
1 *Mac.* 1. 38. and became *s.* to those born in her
44. that they should follow the *s.* laws
6. 13. I perish through great grief in a *s.* land
15. 27. brake covenants and became *s.* unto him
2 *Mac.* 5. 9. thus he perished in a *s.* land
6. 24. that he were now gone to a *s.* religion
9. 6. tormented men's bowels with *s.* torments
28. he died a miserable death in a *s.* country
STRANGER.
Esth. 16. 10. Aman as a *s.* received of us
Eccl. 8. 18. do not secret things before a *s.*
11. 34. receive a *s.* into thy house, he will turn
29. 26. come, thou *s.* furnish a table and feed me
27. give place, thou *s.* to an honourable man
STRANGERS.
1 *Esd.* 8. 83. a land polluted with the pollutions of *s.*
Wisd. 19. 13. used a hateful behaviour towards *s.*
15. because they used *s.* not friendly
Eccl. 26. 19. and give not thy strength to *s.*
45. 18. *s.* conspired together against him
Bar. 6. 5. that ye in no wise be like to *s.*
1 *Mac.* 1. 38. the city was made an habitation of *s.*
2. 7. the sanctuary delivered into the hand of *s.*
3. 36. he should place *s.* in all their quarters
4. 12. then the *s.* lift up their eyes and saw them
22. they fled every one into the land of *s.*
26. all the *s.* that had escaped came and told
30. gavest hosts of *s.* into the hands of Jonathan
2 *Mac.* 10. 5. the day that *s.* profaned the temple
STRANGENESS.
Wisd. 5. 2. shall be amazed at the *s.* of his salvation
STRANGLED.
Tob. 2. 3. he said, father, one of our nation is *s.*
3. 8. dost not know that thou hast *s.* thy husbands?
10. so that she thought to have *s.* herself
Esth. 12. 3. having confessed it they were *s.*
STRAYING.
Eccl. 6. 2. soul not torn in pieces, as a bull *s.* alone
STREAM.
Wisd. 19. 7. and out of the violent *s.* a green field
STREAMED.
Dan. 3. 24. so that the flame *s.* forth above
STREET.
2 *Mac.* 10. 2. the altars had built in the open *s.*
STREETS.
Eccl. 9. 7. look not round about thee in the *s.*
23. 21. this man shall be punished in the *s.*
49. 6. they burnt chosen city and made *s.* desolate
1 *Mac.* 1. 55. and they burnt incense in the *s.*
2. 9. her infants are slain in the *s.*
14. 9. the ancient men sat all in the *s.*
2 *Mac.* 3. 19. the women abounded in the *s.*
STRENGTH.
1 *Esd.* 3. 17. who had spoken of the *s.* of wine
4. 1. that had spoken of the *s.* of the king
2. O ye men, do not men excel in *s.*?
40. and she is the *s.* and majesty of all ages
Wisd. 2. 11. let our *s.* be the law of justice
11. 21. thou canst shew thy great *s.* at all times
12. 17. men will not believe thou shewedst thy *s.*
16. 16. were scourged by the *s.* of thine arm
23. but this again did even forget his own *s.*
24. increaseth his *s.* against the unrighteous, and abateth his *s.* for benefit of them that trust in thee
18. 22. so he overcame, not with *s.* of body
Eccl. 3. 13. when thou art in thy full *s.*
21. nor search things that are above thy *s.*
5. 2. follow not thine own mind, and thy *s.*
7. 30. love him that made thee with all thy *s.*
16. 7. who fell away in *s.* of their foolishness
17. 3. he endued them with *s.* by themselves
18. 5. who shall number the *s.* of his majesty?
26. 19. my son, give not thy *s.* to strangers
28. 10. and as a man's *s.* is, so is his wrath
31. 30. drunkenness diminisheth *s.* maketh wounds
34. 15. to whom doth he look? and who is his *s.*?
38. 18. the heaviness of the heart breaketh *s.*
30. he boweth down his *s.* before his feet
40. 26. riches and *s.* lift up the heart, but the fear
41. 2. death is acceptable to him whose *s.* faileth
43. 30. when you exalt him, put forth all your *s.*
46. 6. that the nations might know all their *s.*
9. the Lord gave *s.* also to Caleb, which remained
Bar. 1. 12. the Lord will give us *s.* and lighten our eyes, and we shall live under Nabuchodonosor
3. 14. learn where is wisdom, where is *s.*
Dan. 3. 21. and let their *s.* be broken
1 *Mac.* 2. 49. now hath pride and rebuke gotten *s.*
3. 19. but *s.* cometh from heaven
35. to destroy and root out the *s.* of Israel

1 *Mac.* 4. 32. cause boldness of their *s.* to fall away
6. 62. but when he saw the *s.* of the place
2 *Mac.* 12. 28. who breaketh the *s.* of his enemies
STRENGTHEN.
1 *Esd.* 7. 15. to *s.* their hands in works of the Lord
Jud. 13. 7. *s.* me, O Lord God of Israel, this day
1 *Mac.* 9. 50. these did he *s.* with high walls
10. 23. in making amity with Jews to *s.* himself
STRENGTHENED.
Eccl. 45. 8. he *s.* him with rich garments
1 *Mac.* 2. 17. thou art *s.* with sons and brethren
14. 14. he *s.* all those of his people brought low
STRENGTHENING.
1 *Mac.* 6. 18. he sought the *s.* of the heathen
STRETCH.
Eccl. 7. 32. and *s.* thine hand to the poor
31. 14. *s.* not thy hand whithersoever it looketh
STRETCHED.
Eccl. 4. 31. let not thy hand be *s.* out to receive
24. 16. as the turpentine tree I *s.* out branches
46. 2. he *s.* out his sword against the cities
48. 20. they *s.* out their hands toward him
50. 15. he *s.* out his hand to the cup, and poured
51. 19. I *s.* forth my hands to the heaven above
STRETCHETH.
1 *Esd.* 6. 33. that *s.* out his hand to hinder house
STRETCHING.
1 *Esd.* 8. 73. then *s.* forth my hands to the Lord
STREWED.
Bel 14. to bring ashes, those they *s.* thro' the temple
STRICKEN.
Esth. 14. 8. they have *s.* hands with their idols
Wisd. 19. 17. even with blindness were these *s.*
2 *Mac.* 15. 24. let those be *s.* with terror that come
STRIFE.
Eccl. 19. 6. that can rule his tongue, live without *s.*
27. 15. the *s.* of the proud is blood-shedding
28. 8. abstain from *s.* and thou shalt diminish thy sins, for a furious man will kindle *s.*
40. 5. anger and *s.* do change his knowledge
9. death and blood, *s.* and sword happen to all
STRIKING.
2 *Mac.* 10. 3. *s.* stones, they took fire out of them
STRIPE.
Jud. 9. 13. make my deceit to be their wound and *s.*
STRIPES.
Eccl. 22. 6. *s.* and correction are never out of time
2 *Mac.* 3. 26. who gave him many sore *s.*
6. 30. but when he was ready to die with *s.*
STRIVE.
Eccl. 4. 28. *s.* for the truth unto death, the Lord
8. 1. *s.* not with a mighty man lest thou fall
3. *s.* not with a man that is full of tongue
11. 9. *s.* not in a matter that concerneth thee not
2 *Mac.* 7. 19. that takest in hand to *s.* against God
STRIVING.
Wisd. 4. 2. got victory, *s.* for undefiled rewards
STROKE, S.
Wisd. 5. 11. light air beaten with the *s.* of her wings
Eccl. 27. 25. a deceitful *s.* shall make wounds
28. 17. the *s.* of the whip, the *s.* of the tongue
39. 28. spirits in their fury lay on sore *s.*
2 *Mac.* 14. 43. but missing his *s.* through haste
STRONG.
1 *Esd.* 3. 18. O ye men, how exceeding *s.* is wine!
4. 32. how can it be but women should be *s.*?
34. O ye men, are not women *s.*? great is the earth
38. as for truth, it endureth and is always *s.*
6. 14. was builded by a king of Israel great and *s.*
8. 85. that ye may be *s.* and eat the good things
Wisd. 14. 16. an ungodly custom grown *s.*
Eccl. 6. 14. a faithful friend is a *s.* defence
24. 24. faint not to be *s.* in the Lord
28. 14. *s.* cities hath it pulled down
29. 13. better than a mighty shield and *s.* spear
30. 14. being sound and *s.* of constitution
15. and a *s.* body is above infinite wealth
Bar. 6. 58. they that are *s.* do take and go away
1 *Mac.* 1. 2. made many wars, and won many *s.* holds
19. thus they got the *s.* cities in land of Egypt
33. then builded they the city of David with a great and *s.* wall, and made it a *s.* hold for them
3. 45. sanctuary trodden, and aliens kept *s.* hold
2 *Mac.* 1. 24. O Lord God, who art fearful and *s.*
11. 5. drew near to Bethsura, which was a *s.* town
12. 27. Ephron, a *s.* city, wherein Lysias abode
STRONGER.
1 *Esd.* 4. 35. great is the truth, and *s.* than all
Wisd. 10. 12. know that godliness is *s.* than all
Eccl. 28. 10. and the *s.* they are which contend
Sus. 39. for he was *s.* than we and leaped out
STRONGEST.
1 *Esd.* 3. 10. wine is the *s.* ‖ 11. the king is *s.*
12. women are *s.* ‖ 24. O ye men, is not wine the *s.*?
STRONGLY.
2 *Mac.* 10. 17. assaulting them *s.* they won holds
STRUCK.
1 *Esd.* 4. 30. she *s.* the king with her left hand
2 *Mac.* 1. 16. they threw stones and *s.* the captain
STUBBLE.
Wisd. 3. 7. they shall shine as sparks among *s.*
STUBBORN.
Eccl. 3. 26. a *s.* heart shall fare evil at last
30. 12. lest he wax *s.* and be disobedient to thee
STUFF.
Jud. 15. 11. plate, beds, vessels, and all his *s.*
STUMBLE.
Eccl. 13. 23. if he *s.* they will help to overthrow
25. 21. *s.* not at the beauty of a woman
32. 20. and *s.* not among the stones
STUMBLED.
Tob. 11 10. Tobit went toward the door and *s.*
STUMBLING.
Wisd. 14. 11. and *s.* blocks to the souls of men
Eccl. 7. 6. lay a *s.* block in way of thy uprightness
31. 7. it is a *s.* block to them that sacrifice
34. 16. he is a preservation from *s.* and a help
39. 24. so are they *s.* blocks to the wicked
SUBDUED.
Wisd. 18. 22. with a word *s.* he him that punished
SUBJECT.
Wisd. 1. 4. nor dwell in the body that is *s.* to sin

Wisd. 8. 14. and the nations shall be *s.* unto me
SUBJECTION.
Eccl. 47. 19. by thy body thou wast brought into *s.*
48. 12. neither could any bring him into *s.*
SUBJECTS.
1 *Esd.* 3. 1. Darius made a great feast to all his *s.*
Esth. 13. 2. I purposed to settle my *s.* in quiet
SUBMISSLY.
Eccl. 29. 5. for neighbour's money he will speak *s.*
SUBMITTED.
2 *Mac.* 13. 23. *s.* and sware to all equal conditions
SUBSTANCE.
Tob. 4. 7. give alms of thy *s.* and when thou givest
14. 13. he inherited their *s.* and his fathers
Eccl. 9. 2. to a woman, to set her foot on thy *s.*
SUBTILE.
Wisd. 7. 23. kind to man, pure and most *s.* spirits
Eccl. 39. 2. where *s.* parables are, he will be there
SUBTILLY.
Jud. 5. 11. the king of Egypt dealt *s.* with them
SUBTILTY.
Eccl. 19. 25. there is an exquisite *s.* and is unjust
SUBTILTIES.
Wisd. 8. 8. she knoweth the *s.* of speeches
SUBURBS.
1 *Mac.* 11. 4. they shewed him Azotus and *s.* thereof
61. he burned the *s.* thereof with fire and spoiled
SUCCEED.
Tob. 4. 6. thy doings shall prosperously *s.* to thee
Eccl. 48. 8. who anointed prophets to *s.* after him
SUCCESS.
Tob. 7. 12. God give you good *s.* in all things
Wisd. 13. 19. and for good *s.* of his hands, asketh
Eccl. 20. 9. a sinner that hath good *s.* in evil
38. 13. when in their hands there is good *s.*
43. 26. by him the hand of them hath prosperous *s.*
1 *Mac.* 4. 55. praising God, who had given good *s.*
8. 23. good *s.* be to the Romans and Jews by sea
2 *Mac.* 10. 23. having good *s.* with his weapons
28. for a pledge of their *s.* and victory
13. 16. at last they departed with good *s.*
SUCCESSOR.
Eccl. 46. 1. Jesus son of Nave was the *s.* of Moses
2 *Mac.* 9. 23. when he led an army he appointed *s.*
14. 26. he had ordained Judas to be the king's *s.*
SUCCOUR.
Eccl. 51. 7. I looked for *s.* of men, there was none
1 *Mac.* 1. 53. wheresoever they could flee for *s.*
2. 44. but the rest fled to the heathen for *s.*
2 *Mac.* 5. 9. and thinking there to find *s.*
SUCCOURS.
Wisd. 17. 12. for fear is a betraying of the *s.*
SUCCOURETH.
1 *Mac.* 12. 15. we have help from heaven that *s.* us
SUCK.
2 *Mac.* 7. 27. have pity on me that gave *s.* 3 years
SUCKING.
Eccl. 46. 16. when he offered the *s.* lamb
SUDDEN.
Wisd. 17. 15. for a *s.* fear came upon them
Eccl. 11. 21. on the *s.* to make a poor man rich
2 *Mac.* 14. 17. through the *s.* silence of his enemies
SUDDENLY.
Wisd. 18. 17. then *s.* visions of horrible dreams
Eccl. 5. 7. *s.* shall the wrath of the Lord come
11. 22. *s.* he maketh his blessing to flourish
22. 27. upon my lips, that I fall not *s.* by them
1 *Mac.* 1. 30. he fell *s.* on the city, and smote it
3. 23. had left off speaking, he leapt *s.* upon them
4. 2. might rush in on the Jews, and smite them *s.*
2 *Mac.* 3. 27. Heliodorus fell *s.* to the ground
14. 22. lest treachery should be *s.* practised
SUFFER.
Jud. 11. 5. *s.* thy handmaid to speak in thy presence
Bar. 4. 25. *s.* patiently the wrath that is come
6. 18. made sure as being committed to *s.* death
Bel 12. we will *s.* death, or else Daniel that speaks
2 *Mac.* 4. 48. they did soon *s.* unjust punishment
6. 30. but in soul am content to *s.* these things
7. 18. for we *s.* these things for ourselves
32. for we *s.* because of our sins
SUFFERED.
Wisd. 18. 1. they had not *s.* the same things
11. like as the king so *s.* the common person
Eccl. 38. 16. as if thou hadst *s.* great harm
1 *Mac.* 2. 48. nor *s.* they the sinner to triumph
15. 14. neither *s.* he any to go out or in
2 *Mac.* 7. 36. our brethren who now have *s.* pain
9. 28. the murderer having *s.* most grievously
SUFFERETH.
Tob. 4. 10. alms *s.* not to come into darkness
Eccl. 4. 9. deliver him that *s.* wrong from oppressor
26. 28. a man of war that *s.* poverty
SUFFERING.
Wisd. 16. 3. but these *s.* penury for a short space
SUFFICE.
Tob. 5. 19 what the Lord hath given us doth *s.* us
1 *Mac.* 2. 33. let that you have done hitherto *s.*
SUFFICIENT.
Wisd. 18. 12. nor were the living *s.* to bury them
Eccl. 31. 19. little is *s.* for a man well nurtured
SUGGESTION.
2 *Mac.* 6. 8. went a degree by the *s.* of Ptolemee
SUITS.
Eccl. 29. 19. business for gain shall fall into *s.*
Sus. 6. all that had any *s.* in law came to them
SUM.
Eccl. 43 27. come short, wherefore in *s.* he is all
51. 28. get learning with a great *s.* of money
2 *Mac.* 3. 11. the *s.* in all was 400 talents of silver
12. 43. to the *s.* of two thousand drachms
SUMS.
2 *Mac.* 3. 6. treasury was full of infinite *s.* of money
SUMMER.
Eccl. 50. 8. the frankincense-tree in time of *s.*
Dan. 3. 45. O ye winter and *s.* bless ye the Lord
SUN.
1 *Esd.* 4. 34. O men, swift is the *s.* in his course
2 *Esd.* 6. 45. commandest that the *s.* should shine
15. 20. kings which are from the rising of the *s.*
Tob. 2. 4. took him, till the going down of the *s.*
7. after the going down of the *s.* I made a grave

Jud. 14. 2. the s. shall come forth on the earth
Wisd. 2. 4. as mist that is driven away with the s.
5. 6. the s. of righteousness rose not on us
7. 29. for she is more beautiful than the s.
16. 28. we must prevent the s. to give thee thanks
18. 3. and an harmless s. to entertain them
Eccl. 17. 19. their works are as the s. before him
31. what is brighter than the s.? yet the light
26. 16. as the s. when it ariseth in the heaven
33. 7. all the light of every day is of the s.
34. 16. he is a cover from the s. at noon
43. 2. the s. when it appeareth, declaring
4. but the s. burneth the mountains more
46. 4. did not the s. go back by his means?
48. 23. in his time the s. went backward
50. 7. as the s. shining on the temple of Most High
Bar. 6. 60. for s. moon and stars are obedient
Dan. 3. 40. O ye s. and moon, bless ye the Lord

SUN-BEAM.
Wisd. 16. 27. being warmed with a little s. melted

SUNG.
Eccl. 47. 8. with his whole heart he s. songs
1 Mac. 4. 24. they s. a song of thanksgiving
2 Mac. 1. 30. the priests s. psalms of thanksgiving
12. 37. he s. psalms with a loud voice

SUPERSTITION.
Wisd. 14. 18. set forward the ignorant to more s.

SUPPED.
Tob. 8. 1. when they had s. they brought Tobias in

SUPPLICATION.
Eccl. 4. 4. reject not the s. of the afflicted
35. 14. he will not despise the s. of the fatherless
39. 5. and he will make s. for his sins
51. 9. then lifted I up my s. from the earth
Bar. 2. 19. we do not make our humble s. before thee for the righteousness of our fathers and kings
1 Mac. 11. 49. they made s. to the king and cried
2 Mac. 3. 18. others ran flocking to the general s.
8. 29. when they had made a common s.
9. 18. containing the form of a s. after this manner
14. 15. they made . to him that had established

SUPPORT.
1 Esd. 8. 52. power of Lord to s. them in all ways

SUPPOSE.
Tob. 6. 17. I s. that she shall bear thee children

SUPPOSED.
Wisd. 17. 3. they s. to lie hid in their secret sins
Bar. 6. 64. not to be s. nor said that they are gods

SUPPOSING.
2 Mac. 4. 32. Menelaus s. he had got convenient time

SURE.
Eccl. 10. 19. they that fear the Lord are a s. seed
40. 25. gold and silver make the foot stand s.
42. 6. s. keeping is good where an evil wife is
11. keep a s. watch over a shameless daughter
Bar. 6. 18. as the doors are made s. on every side
2 Mac. 3. 22. to keep things safe and s. for those

SURELY.
Wisd. 13. 1. s. vain are all men by nature
Eccl. 5. 3. the Lord will s. revenge thy pride
28. 1. he will s. keep his sins in remembrance
48. 11. and slept in love, for we shall s. live

SURNAME. See SIRNAME.

SURETY.
Eccl. 8. 13. not s. above thy power, if thou be s. pay it
29. 14. an honest man is s. for his neighbour
15. forget not the friendship of thy s.
16. will overthrow the good estate of his s.

SURETISHIP.
Eccl. 29. 18. s. hath undone many of good estate
19. a wicked man shall fall into s.

SURFEITING.
Eccl. 37. 30. and s. will turn into choler
31. by s. have many perished, but he that taketh

SUSA.
Esth. 11. 3. was a Jew, and dwelt in the city of S.
16. 18. is hanged at the gates of S. with his family

SUSANNA.
Sus. 7. S. went into her husband's garden to walk
22. then S. sighed, and said, I am straitened
24. with that S. cried with a loud voice
27. there was never such a report made of S.
31. S. was a very delicate woman and beauteous

SUSPECTED.
Tob. 8. 16. that is not come to me which I s.
2 Mac. 4. 34. tho' he were s. yet persuaded he him

SUSPECTETH.
Eccl. 23. 21. where he s. not, he shall be taken
37. 10. consult not with one that s. thee

SUSPECTING.
2 Mac. 3. 32. the high priest s. lest the king should
7. 24. and s. it to be a reproachful speech
12. 4. desirous to live in peace, and s. nothing

SUSPICION.
Eccl. 3. 24. evil s. hath overthrown their judgment

SUSTAIN.
2 Mac. 10. 18. things convenient to s. the siege

SUSTENANCE.
Wisd. 16. 21. for thy s. declared thy sweetness

SWADDLING-CLOTHES.
Wisd. 7. 4. I was nursed in s. and that with cares

SWALLOWS.
Bar. 6. 22. upon their bodies and heads sit s.

SWAM.
Wisd. 19. 19. the things that before s. in water
1 Mac. 9. 48. they s. over to the further bank

SWARE.
1 Esd. 8. 96. to do these things, and so they s.
2 Mac. 13. 23. and s. to all equal conditions
14. 32. s. they could not tell where the man was

SWAY.
Eccl. 1. 22. the s. of his fury shall be his destruction

SWEAR.
1 Esd. 1. 48. made him s. by the name of the Lord
Tob. 7. 11. till we agree and s. one to another
Wisd. 14. 29. tho' s. falsely, yet look not to be hurt
31. it is not the power of them by whom they s.
Eccl. 23. 11. if he s. in vain, shall not be innocent

SWEARETH.
Eccl. 23. 10. he that s. and nameth God continually
27. 14. the talk of him that s. much, maketh

SWEARING.
Eccl. 23. 9. accustom not thy mouth to s.
11. a man that useth much s. shall be filled
13. use not thy mouth to intemperate s.

SWEAT.
2 Mac. 2. 26. it was a matter of s. and watching

SWEET.
1 Esd. 9. 51. go eat the fat, and drink the s.
2 Esd. 1. 23. tree in water, and made the river s.
Eccl. 6. 5. s. language will multiply friends
11. 3. but her fruit is the chief of s. things
23. 17. all bread is s. to a whoremonger
24. 15. I gave a s. smell like cinnamon, I yielded a pleasant odour as myrrh, onyx, and s. storax
35. 6. s. savour thereof is before the Most High
38. 5. was not the water made s. with wood?
11. give a s. savour and memorial of fine flour
40. 18. to labour and to be content is a s. life
21. the pipe and the psaltery make s. melody
30. begging is s. in the mouth of the shameless
49. 1. it is s. as honey in all mouths
Bar. 5. 8. every s.-smelling tree shall overshadow

SWEETER.
Eccl. 23. 27. there is nothing s. than to take heed
24. 20. for my memorial is s. than honey

SWEETLY.
Wisd. 8. 1. and s. doth she order all things
Eccl. 12. 16. an enemy speaketh s. with his lips
27. 23. when thou art present, he will speak s.

SWEETNESS.
Wisd. 16. 21. for thy sustenance declared thy s.

SWIFT.
1 Esd. 4. 34. high is heaven, s. is the sun in his course
Wisd. 13. 2. or the s. air, or the circle of the stars
18. 14. that night was in midst of her s. course
Eccl. 5. 11. be s. to hear, and let thy life be sincere

SWIFTLY.
Eccl. 43. 13. sendeth s. the lightnings of judgment

SWIFTNESS.
2 Esd. 8. 18. the s. of the judge which is to come

SWINE'S.
1 Mac. 1. 47. sacrifice s. flesh and unclean beasts
2 Mac. 6. 18. Eleazar was constrained to eat s. flesh

SWOON.
Wisd. 17. 19. these things made them s. for fear

SWORD.
1 Esd. 1. 53. who slew their young men with the s.
4. 23. a man taketh his s. and goeth his way
8. 77. we were given up to the s. and to captivity
Eccl. 21. 3. all iniquity is as a two-edged s.
22. 21. though thou drewest a s. at thy friend
26. 28. the Lord prepared such a one for the s.
28. 18. many have fallen by the edge of the s.
39. 30. the s. punishing the wicked to destruction
40. 9. strife and s. happen unto all flesh
46. 2. and stretched out his s. against the cities
Bar. 2. 25. they died by famine, by s. and pestilence
1 Mac. 2. 9. young men are slain with s. of enemy
3. 3. made battles, protecting the host with his s.
12. Judas took their spoils and Apollonius' s.
4. 33. cast them down with the s. of them that love
7. 38. be avenged, and let them fall by the s.
8. 23. the s. also and enemy be far from them
9. 73. thus the s. ceased from Israel, but Jonathan
10. 85. burnt and slain with the s. 8000 men
2 Mac. 14. 18. durst not try the matter by the s.
41. he being ready to be taken, fell on his s.
15. 15. Jeremias gave to Judas a s. of gold
16. take this holy s. a gift from God

SWORDS.
1 Esd. 3. 22. and a little after they draw out s.
1 Mac. 4. 6. who had neither armour nor s.
2 Mac. 5. 3. drawing of s. and casting of darts
12. 22. and wounded with the points of their own s.

SWORE.
Wisd. 14. 30. and also they unjustly s. in deceit
1 Mac. 7. 35. Nicanor s. in his wrath, saying

SWORN.
Wisd. 12. 21. unto whose fathers thou hast s.

SYRIA.
1 Mac. 3. 13. Seron, a prince of the army of S.
41. a power also of S. and of the Philistines
7. 39. where an host out of S. met him
11. 2. took his journey into S. in peaceable manner
60. and all the forces of S. gathered themselves

SYRIAN.
2 Mac. 15. 36. in the S. tongue is called Adar

T.

TABERNACLE.
Jud. 9. 8. to pollute the t. where thy name resteth
14. 7. blessed art thou in all the t. of Juda
Wisd. 9. 8. a temple, a resemblance of the holy t.
15. the earthly t. weigheth down the mind
Eccl. 24. 10. in the holy t. I served before him
15. as the fume of frankincense in the t.
2 Mac. 2. 5. an hollow cave, wherein he laid the t.

TABERNACLES.
1 Esd. 5. 51. also they held the feast of t.
2 Esd. 2. 11. I will give these the everlasting t.
Jud. 2. 26. burnt their t. and spoiled sheep-cotes

TABLE.
Tob. 7. 8. they set store of meat on the t.
Eccl. 6. 10. some friend is a companion at the t.
31. 12. if thou sit at a bountiful t. be not greedy
40. 29. life that dependeth on another man's t.
Bel 21. consumed such things as were on the t.
1 Mac. 1. 22. the t. of the shew-bread and vials
4. 49. the altar of burnt offerings and the t.
51. they set loaves on the t. and spread vails

TABLES.
1 Mac. 14. 18. they wrote to him in t. of brass

TAKE.
Tob. 4. 12. my son, chiefly t. a wife of the seed of thy fathers, and t. not a strange woman to wife
5. 20. t. no care, my sister, he shall return in safety
6. 3. then the angel said to him, t. the fish
7. 13. saying, t. her after the law of Moses
8. 7. I t. not this my sister for lust, but uprightly
9. 2. t. with thee a servant and two camels
12. 5. t. half of all ye have brought, and go away
Wisd. 8. 18. I went about seeking how to t. her to me
Eccl. 8. 13. for if thou be surety, t. care to pay it
12. 12. set him not by, lest he seek to t. thy seat
14. 5. he shall not t. pleasure in his goods
16. give and t. and sanctify thy soul, there is no
23. 25. her children shall not t. root, and branches
41. 19. be ashamed of scorning to give and t.
47. 4. did he not t. away reproach from the people?
48. 8. who anointed kings to t. revenge
Bar. 4. 30. t. a good heart, O Jerusalem
Bel 37. O Daniel, t. the dinner God hath sent
1 Mac. 3. 35. and to t. away their memorial
5. 19. t. ye the charge of this people, and see
6. 26. besieging the tower at Jerusalem to t. it
8. 18. that they would t. the yoke from them
2 Mac. 14. 39. sent above 500 men of war to t. him
15. 5. I command to t. arms, and to do business

TAKE heed.
Eccl. 6. 13. separate from enemies, t. heed of friends
11. 33. t. heed of a mischievous man, lest bring a blot
13. 13. t. good heed, for thou walkest in peril
23. 27. t. heed to the commandment of the Lord

TAKEN.
1 Esd. 2. 28. heed to be t. that there be no more done
9. 36. all these t. strange wives, put them away
Tob. 11. 15. hast scourged, and hast t. pity on me
Wisd. 3. 2. and their departure is t. for misery
4. 11. speedily was he t. lest wickedness should alter
14. 15. made an image of his child soon t. away
15. 8. returns to the same out of which he was t.
Eccl. 9. 4. lest thou be t. with her attempts
11. 30. like as a partridge t. and kept in a cage
16. 9. people who were t. away in their sins
19. 3. and a bold man shall be t. away
23. 7. keepeth it, shall never be t. in his lips
21. where he suspecteth not, he shall be t.
27. 26. he that setteth a trap, shall be t. therein
31. 7. and every fool shall be t. therewith
44. 17. he was t. in exchange for the world
46. 19. I have not t. any man's goods, not a shoe
47. 2. as is the fat t. away from the peace-offering
48. 9. who was t. up in a whirlwind of fire
49. 14. Enoch, he was t. from the earth
Bar. 2. 17. whose souls are t. from their bodies
24. the bones shall be t. out of their places
3. 29. who hath gone up into heaven and t. her?
4. 26. they were t. as a flock caught of enemies
1 Mac. 2. 58. Elias was t. up into heaven
3. 45. joy was t. from Jacob, the pipe ceased
9. 55. Alcimus plagued, he was t. with a palsy
13. 41. thus the yoke was t. away from Israel
15. 33. we have neither t. other men's lands
2 Mac. 9. 21. being t. with a grievous disease
12. 35. he would have t. that cursed man alive

TAKEST.
Eccl. 7. 36. whatsoever thou t. in hand, remember

TAKETH.
Eccl. 11. 11. one that laboureth, and t. pains
19. 5. whoso t. pleasure in wickedness, condemned
20. 8. he that t. to himself authority therein
34. 22. he that t. away his neighbour's living
36. 26. and lodgeth wheresoever the night t. him
42. 9. and the care for her t. away sleep

TAKETH heed.
Eccl. 37. 31. he that t. heed prolongeth his life

TAKING.
1 Esd. 4. 30. t. the crown from the king's head
Tob. 4. 13. despise not, in not t. a wife of them
Wisd. 13. 13. and t. the very refuse among those
2 Mac. 5. 25. when t. the Jews keeping holy-day
12. 35. t. hold of his coat, drew him by force

TALE.
Eccl. 19. 15. admonish, and believe not every t.
22. 6. a t. out of season, is as music in mourning
8. he that telleth a t. to a fool, speaketh to one

TALENT.
1 Esd. 1. 36. set a tax on the land of one t. of gold

TALENTS.
1 Esd. 3. 21. it maketh to speak all things by t.
4. 51. should be yearly given twenty t. to building
52. other ten t. yearly to maintain offerings

TALK.
Wisd. 8. 12. if I t. much, they shall lay their hands
Eccl. 5. 13. honour and shame is in t.
9. 18. and he that is rash in his t. shall be hated
11. 8. nor interrupt men in the midst of their t.
13. 11. affect not to be made equal to him in t.
19. 8. to friend or foe, t. not of other men's lives
22. 13. t. not much with a fool, and go not to him
27. 14. the t. of him that sweareth much
38. 25. driveth oxen, whose t. is of bullocks

TALKED.
1 Mac. 3. 26. all nations t. of the battles of Judas

TALKING.
Wisd. 8. 18. and in t. with her, a good report
Eccl. 21. 16. the t. of a fool is like a burden

TAPHNES.
Jud. 1. 9. the river of Egypt, and T. and Ramesse

TARRY.
Tob. 2. 2. bring what poor man, and lo, I t. for thee
4. 14. let not the wages of any man t. with thee
5. 7. Tobias said, t. for me till I tell my father
9. 4. if I t. long, he will be very sorry
10. 8. t. with me, and I will send to thy father
14. 10. bury me, but t. no longer at Nineve
Eccl. 7. 16. remember that wrath will not t. long
12. 15. if thou begin to fall he will not t.

TARRIETH.
Wisd. 5. 14. passeth as a guest that t. but a day

TARRYING.
Eccl. 5. 7. make no t. to turn to the Lord

TASTE.
Wisd. 16. 2. thou preparest meat of a strange t.
20. able to content, and agreeing to every t.
2 Mac. 7. 1. were compelled to t. swine's flesh
15. 39. as wine with water delighteth the t.

TASTED.
Tob. 2. 4. before I had t. of any meat, I started up
Wisd. 18. 25. it was enough they only t. of wrath
2 Mac. 6. 20. not lawful for love of life to be t

TASTETH.
Eccl. 36. 19. as the palate *t.* divers kinds of venison
TASTING.
Wisd. 18. 20. the *t.* of death touched the righteous
TAUGHT.
1 *Esd.* 8. 7. but *t.* all Israel the ordinances
9. 49. to the Levites that *t.* the multitude
2 *Esd.* 8. 29. them that have clearly *t.* the law
Wisd. 9. 18. men were *t.* things pleasing to thee
Eccl. 6. 32. my son, if thou wilt, thou shalt be *t.*
21. 12. he that is not wise will not be *t.*
Sus. 3. *t.* their daughter according to law of Moses
TAX.
1 *Esd.* 1. 36. he set a *t.* on the land of 100 talents
8. 22. that ye require no *t.* nor imposition
See CROWN.
TEACH.
1 *Esd.* 8. 23. those that know it not, thou shalt *t.*
2 *Esd.* 12. 38. and *t.* them to the wise of the people
Eccl. 9. 1. *t.* her not an evil lesson against thyself
45. 5. that he might *t.* Jacob his covenants
TEACHETH.
Wisd. 8. 7. for she *t.* temperance and prudence
Eccl. 18. 13. he reproveth, nurtureth, and *t.*
22. 7. whoso *t.* a fool, is as one that glueth
30. 3. he that *t.* his son, grieveth the enemy
33. 27. send him to labour, for idleness *t.* evil
37. 19. there is one that is wise, and *t.* many
TEARS.
Eccl. 35. 15. do not *t.* run down widows' cheeks?
38. 16. my son, let *t.* fall down over the dead
2 *Mac.* 11. 6. with lamentation and *t.* he sought
TEDIOUS.
Wisd. 2. 1. ungodly said, our life is short and *t.*
TEETH.
Wisd. 16. 10. not the *t.* of venomous dragons
Eccl. 21. 2. the *t.* thereof are the *t.* of a lion
30. 10. lest thou gnash thy *t.* in the end
39. 30. *t.* of wild beasts punishing the wicked
51. 3. from *t.* of them that were ready to devour
TELL.
Tob. 5. 7. tarry for me till I *t.* my father
14. but *t.* me, what wages shall I give thee?
Jud. 11. 17. he will *t.* me when they have committed
Wisd. 6. 22. as for wisdom, what is she, I will *t.* you
Eccl. 18. 5. who shall also *t.* out his mercies?
37. 14. is wont to *t.* him more than seven watchmen
43. 24. that sail on the sea, *t.* of the danger
44. 15. the people will *t.* of their wisdom
Sus. 54. *t.* me, under what tree sawest thou them?
2 *Mac.* 7. 22. I cannot *t.* how ye came into my womb
TELLETH.
Eccl. 22. 8. he that *t.* a tale to a fool, speaketh
TELLING.
Eccl. 21. 25. the lips of talkers will be *t.* such things
TEMPERED.
Wisd. 16. 21. *t.* itself to every man's liking
TEMPERING.
Wisd. 15. 7. the potter *t.* soft earth, fashioneth
TEMPEST.
Wisd. 5. 14. dispersed here and there with a *t.*
Eccl. 16. 21. it is a *t.* which no man can see
TEMPLE.
1 *Esd.* 1. 41. he set them in his own *t.* of Babylon
49. the governors defiled the *t.* of the Lord
6. 19. put them in the *t.* at Jerusalem, and that the *t.* of the Lord should be built in his place
8. 18. vessels for the use of the *t.* of thy God
81. yea, and honoured the *t.* of our Lord
Tob. 14. 5. the land, where they shall build a *t.*
Jud. 4. 11. every man and woman fell before the *t.*
5. 18. the *t.* of their God was cast to the ground
Wisd. 3. 14. an inheritance in the *t.* of the Lord
9. 8. thou hast commanded me to build a *t.*
Eccl. 45. 9. a noise that might be heard in the *t.*
49. 12. who set up an holy *t.* to the Lord
50. 1. Simon in his days fortified the *t.*
4. he took care of the *t.* that it should not fall
51. 14. I prayed for her before the *t.* and will seek
Bar. 6. 20. they are as one of the beams of the *t.*
Bel 10. the king went with Daniel into the *t.* of Bel
1 *Mac.* 2. 8. her *t.* is become as a man without glory
4. 50. that the lamps might give light in the *t.*
5. 43. and fled to the *t.* that was at Carnaim
6. 2. and that there was in it a very rich *t.*
16. 20. he sent to take the mountain of the *t.*
2 *Mac.* 1. 13. they were slain in the *t.* of Nanea
2. 22. they recovered again the *t.* renowned
3. 12. to majesty and inviolable sanctity of the *t.*
4. 14. despising the *t.* and neglecting sacrifices
32. Menelaus stole vessels of gold out of the *t.*
5. 15. to go into the most holy *t.* of all the world
6. 2. and to call it the *t.* of Jupiter Olympius
4. the *t.* was filled with riot and revelling
8. 2. would pity the *t.* profaned of ungodly men
9. 2. entered city, and went about to rob the *t.*
10. 1. Maccabeus recovered the *t.* and the city
TEMPLES.
Jud. 4. 1. heard how he had spoiled all their *t.*
Bar. 6. 18. even so the priests make fast their *t.*
TEMPT.
Wisd. 1. 2. he will be found of them that *t.* him not
Eccl. 13. 11. with communication will he *t.* thee
TEMPTATION.
Eccl. 2. 1. if thou come, prepare thy soul for *t.*
33. 1. but in *t.* even again he will deliver him
1 *Mac.* 2. 52. Abraham was found faithful in *t.*
TEMPTED.
Jud. 8. 12. who are you that have *t.* God this day?
TEMPTETH.
Eccl. 18. 23. and be not as one that *t.* the Lord
TEN.
Eccl. 23. 19. are *t.* thousand times brighter
47. 6. the people honoured him with *t.* thousands
Dan. 3. 17. like as in *t.* thousands of fat lambs
TENDERED.
2 *Mac.* 4. 2. had *t.* his own nation, and was zealous
TENT.
Jud. 8. 5. she made her *t.* on the top of her house
10. 15. now therefore come to his *t.* some conduct
17. they brought her to the *t.* of Holofernes
14. 14. Bagoas knocked at the door of the *t.*
Eccl. 14. 25. he shall pitch his *t.* nigh to her
TENTS.
Wisd. 11. 2. they pitched *t.* where lay no way
TENTH.
Eccl. 25. 7. the *t.* I will utter with my tongue
TENTHS.
Tob. 5. 13. the first-born, and the *t.* of the fruits
1 *Mac.* 10. 31. free both from the *t.* and tributes
TERRIBLE.
Wisd. 5. 2. they shall be troubled with *t.* fear
11. 19. but also the *t.* sight utterly destroy them
17. 9. for though no *t.* thing did fear them
19. or a *t.* sound of stones cast down, or a running
Eccl. 43. 29. the Lord is *t.* and very great
Prayer of Manass. by thy *t.* and glorious name
2 *Mac.* 3. 25. a horse with a *t.* rider upon him
TERRIFY.
Eccl. 21. 4. to *t.* and do wrong will waste riches
TERRIFIED.
Wisd. 17. 6. for being much *t.* they thought things
2 *Mac.* 4. 1. as if he had *t.* Heliodorus, been worker
TERROR.
2 *Mac.* 8. 16. not to be stricken with *t.* of enemy
12. 22. enemies being smitten with fear and *t.*
TERRORS.
Wisd. 17. 8. they that promised to drive away *t.*
18. 17. and *t.* came upon them unlooked for
TESTAMENT.
1 *Mac.* 1. 57. was found with any the book of the *t.*
TESTIFY.
1 *Mac.* 2. 37. heaven and earth shall *t.* for us
TESTIFIED.
2 *Mac.* 3. 36. then *t.* he to all men the works of God
TESTIMONY.
Wisd. 10. 7. the waste land that smoketh is a *t.*
TESTIMONIES.
Eccl. 31. 24. the *t.* of his niggardness not be doubted
45. 17. that he should teach Jacob the *t.*
THANK.
Eccl. 20. 16. I have no *t.* for all my good deeds
THANKS.
1 *Esd.* 4. 60. blessed art thou who hast given me wisdom, for to thee I give *t.* O Lord of our fathers
Tob. 12. 20. give God *t.* I go up to him that sent me
Wisd. 16. 28. we must prevent the sun to give *t.*
Eccl. 17. 27. instead of them who live and give *t.*
29. 25. thou shalt entertain and have no *t.*
39. 6. he shall give *t.* to the Lord in his prayer
Dan. 3. 67. O give *t.* to Lord, because he is gracious
68. all ye that worship the Lord, give him *t.*
1 *Mac.* 14. 25. what *t.* shall we give to Simon?
2 *Mac.* 3. 33. give Onias the high-priest great *t.*
8. 27. yielding exceeding praise and *t.* to the Lord
9. 20. if ye fare well, I give very great *t.* to God
THANKED.
Eccl. 12. 1. so shalt thou be *t.* for thy benefits
THANKFULNESS.
Esth. 16. 4. and take not only *t.* away from men
Eccl. 37. 11. nor consult with an envious man of *t.*
THANKSGIVING.
1 *Esd.* 5. 60. singing songs of *t.* and praising the Lord
Eccl. 17. 28. *t.* perisheth from the dead, as one is not
51. 11. praise contin. and I will sing praise with *t.*
2 *Mac.* 10. 38. praised the Lord with psalms and *t.*
THARSUS.
2 *Mac.* 4. 30. they of T. and Mallos made insurrect.
THEFT.
Wisd. 14. 25. manslaughter, *t.* and dissimulation
THEMAN.
Bar. 3. 22. neither hath it been seen in T.
THICK.
Eccl. 14. 18. as of the green leaves a *t.* tree
2 *Mac.* 1. 20. they found no fire, but *t.* water
THICKEST.
2 *Mac.* 14. 43. cast himself down among *t.* of them
THIEF.
Eccl. 5. 14. for a foul shame is upon the *t.*
20. 25. a *t.* is better than a man that is a liar
36. 26. who will trust a *t.* well appointed?
THIEVES.
Bar. 6. 15. cannot deliver himself from war and *t.*
THIGH.
Jud. 9. 2. who discovered the *t.* to her shame
Eccl. 19. 12. as an arrow that sticketh in a man's *t.*
THIN.
Wisd. 5. 14. like a *t.* froth that is driven away
THINK.
Wisd. 1. 1. *t.* of the Lord with a good heart
6. 15. to *t.* upon her is perfection of wisdom
9. 13. or who can *t.* what the will of the Lord is?
Eccl. 3. 22. *t.* thereupon with reverence
18. 24. *t.* on the wrath that shall be at the end
25. when thou art rich, *t.* on poverty and need
Bar. 2. 32. and they shall *t.* upon my name
3. 5. but *t.* on thy power and name at this time
6. 40. how should a man then *t.* they are gods?
2 *Mac.* 2. 29. even so I *t.* it is with us
6. 24. whereby many young persons might *t.*
7. 16. yet *t.* not our nation is forsaken of God
19. *t.* not that thou shalt escape unpunished
9. 12. a man should not proudly *t.* of himself
THIRD.
1 *Esd.* 3. 12. the *t.* wrote, women are strongest
4. 13. then the *t.* who had spoken of women
Eccl. 23. 16. and the *t.* will bring wrath
26. 28. and the *t.* maketh me angry
50. 25. two I abhor, and the *t.* is no nation
1 *Mac.* 14. 27. the *t.* year of Simon the high-priest
2 *Mac.* 7. 10. after was the *t.* made a mocking-stock
THIRDLY.
Eccl. 23. 23. *t.* she hath played whore in adultery
THIRST.
Jud. 7. 13. so shall *t.* kill them, and they shall give
22. their women and young men fainted for *t.*
Wisd. 11. 4. their *t.* was quenched out of the stone
8. declaring by that *t.* how thou hadst punished
THIRSTY.
Wisd. 11. 4. when they were *t.* they called on thee
Eccl. 26. 12. open her mouth as a *t.* traveller
51. 24. what say ye, seeing your souls are very *t.*?
THIRSTING.
Wisd. 11. 9. *t.* in another manner than the just
THOUGHT.
Wisd. 1. 16. they *t.* to have had it their friend
6. 16. and she meeteth them in every *t.*
Eccl. 11. 5. one that was never *t.* on hath worn
22. 17. a heart settled upon a *t.* of understanding
42. 20. no *t.* escapeth him, nor any word hidden
51. 8. then *t.* I upon thy mercy, O Lord
Bar. 6. 56. how can it be then *t.* that they are gods?
THOUGHTS.
Wisd. 1. 3. for froward *t.* separate from God
5. remove from *t.* without understanding
2. 14. he was made to reprove our *t.*
9. 14. for the *t.* of mortal men are miserable
Eccl. 23. 2. who will set scourges over my *t.*?
33. 5. and his *t.* are like a rolling axle-tree
THOUSAND.
Wisd. 12. 22. scourgest our enemies a *t.* times more
Eccl. 6. 6. but have one counsellor of a *t.*
16. 3. for one that is just is better than a *t.*
18. 10. so are a *t.* years to the days of eternity
39. 11. he shall leave a greater name than a *t.*
41. 4. ten, or a hundred, or a *t.* years
12. continue above a *t.* great treasures of gold
1 *Mac.* 2. 38. slew to the number of a *t.* people
THRACIA.
2 *Mac.* 12. 35. an horsemen of T. coming upon him
THREATENED.
Jud. 8. 16. for God is not as man, that he may be *t.*
THREATENETH.
Eccl. 13. 3. rich man hath done wrong, and yet he *t.*
THREATENING.
Prayer of Manass. thine angry *t.* toward sinners
THREE.
1 *Esd.* 3. 4. *t.* young men that were of the guard
Eccl. 25. 1. in *t.* things I was beautified
2. *t.* sorts of men my soul hateth
26. 5. there be *t.* things that my heart feareth
48. 3. and also *t.* times brought down fire
Dan. 3. 28. then the *t.* as out of one mouth praised
THRICE.
Eccl. 13. 7. he have drawn thee dry twice or *t.*
THRIVE.
Wisd. 4. 3. the brood of the ungodly shall not *t.*
THRONE.
Esth. 15. 6. the king, who sat on his royal *t.*
Wisd. 9. 10. O send her from the *t.* of thy glory
18. 15. out of thy royal *t.* as a fierce man of war
Eccl. 1. 8. is one wise, the Lord sitting upon his *t.*
40. 3. from him that sitteth on a *t.* of glory
47. 11. the Lord gave him a *t.* of glory in Israel
1 *Mac.* 2. 57. possessed *t.* of an everlasting kingdom
7. 4. Demetrius was set on the *t.* of his kingdom
THRONES.
Wisd. 5. 23. ill-dealing shall overthrow *t.* of mighty
6. 21. if your delight be then in *t.* and sceptres
7. 8. I preferred her before sceptres and *t.*
Eccl. 10. 14. hath cast down the *t.* of proud princes
THRONG.
2 *Mac.* 14. 45. yet he ran through the midst of the *t.*
46. plucked out his bowels, and cast them on the *t.*
THROWN.
Wisd. 11. 14. when he was long before *t.* out
18. 18. one *t.* here, another there half dead
THRUST.
Eccl. 13. 21. a poor man is *t.* away by his friends
THUMMIM.
Eccl. 45. 10. a breast-plate, and with Urim and T.
THUNDER.
Esth. 11. 5. behold a noise of tumult with *t.*
Eccl. 32. 10. before the *t.* goeth lightning
40. 13. shall vanish with a noise like great *t.* in rain
43. 17. the noise of *t.* makes the earth tremble
THUNDER-BOLTS.
Wisd. 5. 21. the right-aiming *t.* shall go abroad
2 *Mac.* 1. 16. they threw stones like *t.* and struck
THUNDERED.
Eccl. 46. 17. and the Lord *t.* from heaven
TIDINGS.
2 *Mac.* 9. 24. or if any grievous *t.* were brought
TIGRIS.
Tob. 6. 1. they came in the evening to the river T.
Jud. 1. 6. there came to him all that dwelt by T.
Eccl. 24. 25. as T. in the times of the new fruits
TILLETH.
Eccl. 20. 28. he that *t.* his land shall increase
TIMBER.
Wisd. 13. 11. now a carpenter that felleth *t.*
Eccl. 22. 16. as *t.* girt and bound together in building
TIMBRELS.
Jud. 3. 7. they received them with dances and *t.*
TIME.
1 *Esd.* 1. 19. Israel held the passover at that *t.*
5. 73. hindered, all the *t.* that king Cyrus lived
Tob. 14. 4. the house shall be desolate for a *t.*
Esth. 16. 20. in the *t.* of affliction set on them
Wisd. 2. 4. our name shall be forgotten in *t.*
5. our *t.* is a very shadow that passeth away
4. 4. though they flourish in branches for a *t.*
8. age is not that which standeth in length of *t.*
13. made perfect in a short *t.* fulfilled a long *t.*
9. 5. I thy servant am of a short *t.* and too young
15. 12. counted our *t.* here a market for gain
19. 22. didst assist them in every *t.* and place
Eccl. 1. 24. he will hide his words for a *t.*
2. 2. and make not haste in *t.* of trouble
11. for the Lord saveth in *t.* of affliction
16. 26. from the *t.* he made them, he disposed
18. 21. and in the *t.* of sins shew repentance
22. let nothing hinder to pay thy vow in due *t.*
24. *t.* of vengeance when he shall turn his face
25. when thou hast enough, remember *t.* of hunge.
19. 9. and when *t.* cometh he will hate thee
22. nor at any *t.* the counsel of sinners prudence
20. 6. and some keepeth silence knowing his *t.*
7. but a babbler and fool will regard no *t.*
22. 16. so the heart established shall fear at no *t.*
23. abide stedfast to him in the *t.* of trouble
24. 26. and as Jordan in the *t.* of the harvest
27. to appear as Geon in the *t.* of vintage
27. 12. if among the undiscreet observe the *t.*
29. 2. lend thy neighbour in the *t.* of his need

Eccl. 29. 5. when he should repay, he will prolong *t.* and return words of grief, and complain of the *t.*
30. 24. carefulness bringeth age before the *t.*
32. 4. and shew not forth wisdom out of *t.*
33. 23. at the *t.* when thou shalt end thy days
35. 20. mercy is seasonable in *t.* of affliction
36. 8. make the *t.* short, remember the covenant
37. 4. but in *t.* of trouble will be against him
38. 13. there is a *t.* when in their hands there is
39. 28. in *t.* of destruction they pour out force
31. when their *t.* is come they shall not transgress
34. for in *t.* they shall all be well approved
40. 24. brethren are against the *t.* of trouble
44. 17. Noah was found perfect in the *t.* of wrath
46. 7. in the *t.* of Moses he did a work of mercy
48. 23. in his *t.* the sun went backward
49. 3. in *t.* of ungodly he established the worship
50. 24. and that he would deliver us at his *t.*
51. 10. in *t.* of the proud, when there was no help
12. and thou deliveredst me from the evil *t.*
30. in his *t.* he will give you your reward
Bar. 3. 5. but think on thy name now at this *t.*
Dan. 3. 15. nor is there at this *t.* prince or prophet
Sus. 15. it fell out as they watched a fit *t.*
2 *Mac.* 1. 22. when the *t.* came that the sun shone

TIMES.

Wisd. 7. 18. beginning, ending, and midst of the *t.*
8. 8. she foreseeth the events of seasons and *t.*
11. 21. thou canst shew thy great strength at all *t.*
Eccl. 19. 15. admonish, for many *t.* it is a slander
26. 4. have a good heart, he shall at all *t.* rejoice
43. 6. he made the moon for a declaration of *t.*
44. 7. all these were the glory of their *t.*
47. 10. he set in order the solemn *t.* till the end
48. 10. who wast ordained for reproofs in their *t.*
Bar. 4. 28. being returned seek him ten *t.* more

TIMOROUS.

Wisd. 17. 11. wickedness condemned is very *t.*

TIMOTHEUS.

1 *Mac.* 5. 11. T. being captain of their host
2 *Mac.* 8. 30. of those that were with T. they slew
9. 3. what had happened unto Nicanor and T.
10. 24. T. whom the Jews had overcome before
32. as for T. himself, he fled into a strong hold
37. and killed T. that was hid in a certain pit
12. 18. as for T. they found him not in the places
19. slew those that T. had left in the fortress
20. went against T. who had about him 120,000
21. when T. had knowledge of Judas coming
24. T. himself fell into the hands of Dositheus

TIN.

Eccl. 47. 18. didst gather gold as *t.* and multiply

TIRE.

Jud. 10. 3. braided her hair, and put a *t.* upon it
16. 8. bound her hair in a *t.* and took linen

TITHES.

Eccl. 35. 9. and dedicate thy *t.* with gladness
1 *Mac.* 11. 35. of the *t.* and customs pertaining

TOBIAS.

Tob. 1. 9. I married Anna, and of her I begat T.
3. 17. give Sara, daughter of Raguel, for wife to T. the son of Tobit, she belongeth to T. by right
4. 2. wherefore do I not call for my son T.?
7. 11. but T. said, I will eat nothing here, till
13. and he gave her to be wife to T. saying
8. 1. they supplied, and brought T. in unto her
4. T. rose out of the bed, and said, sister, arise
5. then began T. to say, blessed art thou, O God
9. 6. came to the wedding, and T. blessed his wife
11. 1. after this, T. went his way, praising God
7. I know, T. that thy father will open his eyes
19. T. wedding was kept seven days with joy
12. 1. then Tobit called his son T. and said
14. 12. but T. departed with his wife and children
2 *Mac.* 3. 11. some belonged to Hircanus son of T.

TOBIE.

1 *Mac.* 5. 13. our brethren that were in places of T.

TOBIEL.

Tob. 1. 1. the book of the words of Tobit son of T.

TOBIT.

Tob. 1. 3. I T. have walked in the way of truth
3. 17. the whiteness of T. eyes, then came T. home
4. 1. in that day T. remembered the money
7. 2. how like is this young man to T. my cousin!
4. he said to them, do you know T. our kinsman?
7. but when he heard that T. was blind, he wept
10. 1. now T. his father counted every day
11. 10. T. went toward the door and stumbled
16. T. went out to meet his daughter-in-law
17. but T. gave thanks before them, because
12. 1. T. called his son Tobias, and said to him
13. 1. then T. wrote a prayer of rejoicing
14. 1. so T. made an end of praising God
13. inherited their substance, and his father T.

TOIL.

1 *Esd.* 4. 22. do ye not *t.* and bring all to the woman?

TOKEN, S.

1 *Esd.* 3. 5. give great things in *t.* of victory
2 *Esd.* 1. 15. the quails were as a *t.* for victory
Wisd. 2. 9. let us leave *t.* of our joyfulness
5. 11. there is no *t.* of her way to be found
Eccl. 13. 26. is a *t.* of a heart in prosperity
2 *Mac.* 6. 13. for it is a *t.* of his great goodness

TOLD.

Tob. 8. 14. maid came and *t.* them that he was alive
Jud. 10. 18. came about her, till they *t.* him of her
Eccl. 19. 7. rehearse not that which is *t.* thee
31. 22. at the last thou shalt find as I *t.* thee

TOMB.

Eccl. 21. 8. gathers stones for the *t.* of his burial

TONGUE.

Wisd. 1. 6. for God is a hearer of his *t.*
11. and refrain your *t.* from backbiting
8. 12. when I hold my *t.* they shall bide my leisure
Eccl. 4. 24. and learning by the word of the *t.*
29. be not hasty in thy *t.* and in thy deeds slack
5. 9. so doth the sinner that hath a double *t.*
13. and the *t.* of man is his fall
14. not a whisperer, and lie not in wait with thy *t.*
8. 3. strive not with a man that is full of *t.*
9. 18. a man of an ill *t.* is dangerous in his city
17. 6. counsel and a *t.* eyes and ears gave he them

Eccl. 19. 6. he that can rule his *t.* shall live with. strife
16. who is he that hath not offended with his *t.*?
20. 1. some man holdeth his *t.* and he is wise
7. wise man will hold his *t.* till he see opportunity
18. is better than to slip with the *t.*
22. 27. who shall set a watch and a seal of wisdom upon my lips, that my *t.* destroy me not?
25. 7. and the tenth I will utter with my *t.*
8. well is him that hath not slipped with his *t.*
26. 6. a scourge of the *t.* which communicates
28. 14. a backbiting *t.* hath disquieted many
17. the stroke of the *t.* breaketh the bones
18. but not so many as have fallen by the *t.*
32. 8. one that knoweth and yet holdeth his *t.*
36. 23. if there be meekness and comfort in her *t.*
37. 18. but the *t.* ruleth over them continually
51. 2. preserved from the snare of the slanderous *t.*
5. from an unclean *t.* and from lying words
6. by an accusation from an unrighteous *t.*
Bar. 6. 8. as for their *t.* it is polished by workmen
2 *Mac.* 7. 4. to cut out *t.* of him that spake first
10. when he was required he put out his *t.*
15. 33. when he had cut out the *t.* of Nicanor

TONGUED.

Eccl. 28. 13. curse the whisperer and double-*t.*

TONGUES.

Wisd. 10. 21. made the *t.* that cannot speak, eloquent

TOOK.

1 *Esd.* 1. 41. Nabuchodonosor *t.* of the holy vessels
8. 96. Esdras arose, and *t.* an oath of the priests
Tob. 2. 4. I started up, and *t.* him up into a room
7. 13. *t.* her by the hand and gave her to Tobias
14. he *t.* paper and did write an instrument
8. 2. he *t.* the ashes of perfumes, and made smoke
12. 6. he *t.* them both apart, and said unto them
Esth. 15. 2. had called on God, she *t.* two maids with
Wisd. 13. 3. being delighted, *t.* them to be gods
Eccl. 47. 11. the Lord *t.* away his sins, and exalted

TOOKEST.

Esth. 14. 5. thou *t.* Israel from among all people

TOP.

Jud. 9. 13. who purposed evil against the *t.* of Sion

TOPS.

Jud. 4. 5. of all the *t.* of the high mountains

TORCH-LIGHT.

2 *Mac.* 4. 22. he was brought in with *t.* and shoutings

TORMENT.

Wisd. 3. 1. and there shall no *t.* touch them
17. 13. more than the cause which brings the *t.*
1 *Mac.* 9. 56. Alcimus died at that time with *t.*
2 *Mac.* 6. 19. he came of his own accord to the *t.*
28. had said this, immediately he went to the *t.*
7. 8. he also received the next *t.* in order
17. behold, how will he *t.* thee and thy seed

TORMENTED.

2 *Esd.* 13. 38. wherewith they shall begin to be *t.*
Wisd. 6. 6. but mighty men shall be mightily *t.*
11. 9. the ungodly were judged in wrath and *t.*
12. 23. hast *t.* them with their own abominations
16. 1. by multitude of beasts were they *t.*
4. should be shewed how their enemies were *t.*
2 *Mac.* 7. 1. and were *t.* with scourges and whips
13. they *t.* and mangled the fourth in like manner
9. 6. he had *t.* other men's bowels with torments

TORMENTOR.

2 *Mac.* 7. 29. fear not this *t.* but take thy death

TORMENTS.

2 *Esd.* 9. 9. have cast them away, shall dwell in *t.*
Wisd. 19. 4. the punishment wanting to their *t.*
Eccl. 33. 26. so are tortures and *t.* for an evil servant
2 *Mac.* 7. 37. that thou by *t.* mayest confess he is G.
9. 5. sore *t.* of the inner parts came upon him
6. he had tormented others with many *t.*

TORN.

Eccl. 6. 2. that thy soul be not *t.* in pieces

TORTURE.

Wisd. 2. 19. examine him with despitefulness and *t.*

TORTURES.

2 *Mac.* 7. 42. idolatrous feasts and extreme *t.*

TOUCH.

Tob. 12. 7. do good, and no evil shall *t.* you
Jud. 11. 13. it is not lawful for any so much as to *t.*
Wisd. 3. 1. and there shall no torment *t.* them
Eccl. 34. 25. if he *t.* it again, what availeth washing?

TOUCHED.

Wisd. 18. 16. and it *t.* heaven, but stood on earth
20. the tasting of death *t.* the righteous also
Dan. 3. 27. so that the fire *t.* them not at all

TOUCHETH.

Eccl. 13. 1. he that *t.* pitch shall be defiled therewith

TOWER.

Eccl. 26. 22. a married woman is a *t.* against death
37. 14. watchmen that sit above in an high *t.*
1 *Mac.* 6. 24. they of our nation besiege the *t.*
9. 53. and he put them in the *t.* at Jerusalem
13. 50. he cleansed the *t.* from pollutions
52. the hill of the temple that was by the *t.*
2 *Mac.* 4. 12. he built a place of exercise under the *t.*
13. 5. a *t.* of fifty cubits high full of ashes
15. 35. he hanged also Nicanor's head on the *t.*

TOWERS.

1 *Esd.* 1. 55. Jerusalem, they set fire on her *t.*
4. 4. they break down mountains, walls, and *t.*
Tob. 13. 16. thy walls, *t.* and battlements with gold
Jud. 1. 3. set the *t.* thereof on the gates of it
1 *Mac.* 1. 33. they builded city of Dav. with mighty *t.*
5. 65. and burned the *t.* thereof round about
16. 10. so they fled even to the *t.* in the fields

TOWN.

2 *Mac.* 11. 5. to Bethsura, which was a strong *t.*
12. 21. for the *t.* was hard to besiege, and uneasy

TOWNS.

1 *Mac.* 5. 65. he smote Hebron and the *t.* thereof
2 *Mac.* 8. 1. they with him went privily into *t.*
6. he came unawares and burnt up *t.* and cities

TRACE.

Wisd. 2. 4. shall pass away as the *t.* of a cloud
5. 10. the *t.* thereof cannot be found, nor path

TRACETH.

Eccl. 14. 22. go after her as one that *t.* and lie in wait

TRAINING.

2 *Mac.* 4. 9. for the *t.* up of youth in the fashions

TRAINS.

Eccl. 11. 29. for the deceitful man hath many *t.*

TRANCE.

2 *Esd.* 12. 3. I awaked out of trouble and *t.* of mind

TRANSGRESSED.

1 *Esd.* 1. 48. he *t.* the laws of the Lord God of Israel
8. 82. for we have *t.* thy commandments

TRANSGRESSETH.

Eccl. 19. 24. that *t.* the law of the Most High

TRANSGRESSING, S.

Wisd. 2. 12. he objecteth the *t.* of our education
Eccl. 29. 19. a wicked man *t.* the commandments

TRANSGRESSIONS. See *Prayer of Manass.*

TRANSGRESSORS.

Eccl. 40. 14. so shall *t.* come to nought

TRANSLATED.

Esth. 16. 14. to have *t.* the kingdom of the Persians
Wisd. 4. 10. so that living among sinners, he was *t.*
Eccl. 10. 8. kingdom is *t.* from one people to another
2 *Mac.* 11. 23. since our father is *t.* unto the gods

TRAVEL.

Wisd. 6. 14. seeketh her early, shall have no great *t.*
Eccl. 8. 15. *t.* not by the way with a bold fellow
34. 5. the heart fancieth as a woman's heart in *t.*
40. 1. great *t.* is created for every man
1 *Mac.* 9. 68. for his counsel and *t.* was in vain

TRAVELS.

Wisd. 10. 10. made him rich in his *t.* and multiplied

TRAVELLED.

Eccl. 34. 9. a man that hath *t.* knoweth things

TRAVELLER.

Eccl. 26. 12. she will open her mouth as a thirsty *t.*

TRAVELLERS.

Eccl. 42. 3. of reckoning with thy partners and *t.*

TRAVELLETH.

Eccl. 19. 11. a fool *t.* with a word, as a woman

TREACHERY.

1 *Mac.* 16. 17. in doing he committed great *t.*
2 *Mac.* 3. 32. some *t.* had been done to Heliodorus

TREACHEROUS.

Eccl. 22. 22. disclosing of secrets, or a *t.* wound

TREAD.

Jud. 6. 4. with them we will *t.* them under foot
Bar. 4. 25. see his destruction, and *t.* on his neck
1 *Mac.* 4. 60. *t.* it down as they had done before

TREASURE.

Tob. 4. 9. thou layest up a good *t.* for thyself
Wisd. 7. 14. for she is a *t.* that never faileth
Eccl. 3. 4. he is as one that layeth up *t.*
6. 14. that hath found such a one hath found a *t.*
20. 30. *t.* that is hoarded up, what profit is in it?
29. 11. lay up thy *t.* according to thy commandm.
40. 18. he that findeth a *t.* is above them both
41. 14. a *t.* that is not seen, what profit is in it?
1 *Mac.* 3. 28. he opened his *t.* and gave soldiers pay
13. 15. for money he is owing to the king's *t.*

TREASURER.

1 *Esd.* 2. 11. he delivered to Mithridates his *t.*
4. 49. no *t.* should forcibly enter their doors
2 *Mac.* 3. 7. the king chose out Heliodorus his *t.*

TREASURERS.

1 *Esd.* 4. 47. Darius wrote letters for him to all the *t.*

TREASURES.

1 *Esd.* 1. 54. they took holy vessels and the king's *t.*
8. 19. I commanded the keepers of the *t.* in Syria
Eccl. 1. 25. the parables are in the *t.* of wisdom
41. 12. thy name above a thousand great *t.* of gold
43. 14. through this the *t.* are opened, the clouds fly
Bar. 3. 15. or who hath come into her *t.*?
1 *Mac.* 1. 23. he took the hidden *t.* which he found
3. 29. when he saw the money of his *t.* failed

TREASURY.

1 *Esd.* 5. 45. give into the holy *t.* of the works
6. 10. thou shalt give it out of the king's *t.*
1 *Mac.* 14. 49. the copies should be laid up in the *t.*
2 *Mac.* 3. 6. and told that the *t.* in Jerusalem was full
13. that it must be brought into the king's *t.*
24. as he was there with his guard about the *t.*
40. the keeping of the *t.* fell out on this sort
4. 42. the robber, him they killed beside the *t.*
5. 18. whom Seleucus the king sent to view the *t.*

TREAT.

Jud. 3. 1. they sent ambassadors to him to *t.* of peace

TREATED.

2 *Mac.* 13. 22. the king *t.* with them in Bethsura

TREE.

1 *Esd.* 6. 32. out of his own house a *t.* be taken
Wisd. 13. 11. after he hath sawn down a *t.* meet
Eccl. 14. 18. as of the green leaves on a thick *t.*
27. 6. the fruit declareth if the *t.* have been dressed
Bar. 5. 8. every sweet-smelling *t.* shall overshadow
Sus. 54. tell me under what *t.* sawest thou them?

TREES.

1 *Mac.* 10. 30. half of the fruit of the *t.* I release
14. 8. and the *t.* of the field gave their fruit

TREMBLE.

1 *Esd.* 4. 36. all works shake and *t.* at it
Eccl. 43. 17. thunder maketh the earth to *t.*
Prayer of Manass. all men *t.* before thy power

TREMBLED.

Eccl. 48. 19. then *t.* their hearts and hands
1 *Mac.* 2. 24. inflamed with zeal, and his reins *t.*
12. 28. they feared and *t.* in their hearts

TREMBLING.

Jud. 15. 2. and fear and *t.* fell upon them

TRESPASS.

Eccl. 26. 11. marvel not if she *t.* against thee

TRESPASSED.

Eccl. 23. 23. she hath *t.* against her own husband

TRIAL.

Wisd. 3. 18. nor have they comfort in the day of *t.*
4. 6. are witnesses against parents in their *t.*
6. 8. but a sore *t.* shall come on the mighty
Eccl. 6. 21. will lie on him as a mighty stone of *t.*
16. 22. and the *t.* of all things is in the end
27. 5. so the *t.* of a man is in his reasoning
7. before hearest him speak, for this is *t.* of men

TRIBE.

Tob. 4. 12. a woman who is not of thy father's *t.*
5. 8. call him, that I may know of what *t.* he is
10. shew me of what *t.* and family thou art
11. he said, dost thou seek for a *t.* or family?

Tob. 5. 13. I inquired to know thy *t.* and thy family
Jud. 8. 2. was her husband of her *t.* and kindred
Esth. 14. 5. I have heard in the *t.* of my family

TRIBES.

Tob. 1. 4. which was chosen out of all the *t.* of Israel, that all the *t.* should sacrifice there
Eccl. 36. 11. gather all the *t.* of Jacob together
44. 23. among the twelve *t.* did he part them

TRIBULATION.

Esth. 11. 8. a day of darkness and *t.* and anguish
Eccl. 40. 9. calamities, famine, *t.* and scourge
1 *Mac.* 6. 11. I thought, into what *t.* am I come

TRIBUNES.

Jud. 14. 12. their leaders came to their captains and *t.*
1 *Mac.* 16. 19. to the *t.* he sent letters to come

TRIBUTARIES.

1 *Mac.* 1. 4. kings who became *t.* unto him

TRIBUTE.

1 *Esd.* 2. 19. they will not only refuse to give *t.*
4. 6. and compel one another to pay *t.* to the king
50. that the country should be free without *t.*
1 *Mac.* 8. 7. such as reigned after him pay great *t.*
11. 28. that he would make Judea free from *t.*
13. 39. if any other *t.* were paid in Jerusalem
2 *Mac.* 8. 10. the *t.* of two thousand talents
36. to make good to the Romans their *t.*

TRIBUTES.

1 *Mac.* 3. 29. that *t.* in the country were small
31. there to take the *t.* of the countries
10. 29. and now I release all the Jews from *t.*
31. let Jerusalem be free from tenths and *t.*
15. 30. deliver *t.* of the places ye have gotten
31. give for *t.* of the cities other 500 talents

TRIPOLIS.

2 *Mac.* 14. 1. having entered by the haven of T.

TRIUMPH.

Eccl. 24. 2. she shall *t.* before his power
1 *Mac.* 2. 48. nor suffered they the sinner to *t.*

TRIUMPHETH.

Wisd. 4. 2. it weareth a crown, and *t.* for ever

TRODDEN.

1 *Mac.* 3. 45. the sanctuary also was *t.* down
2 *Mac.* 8. 2. the people that was *t.* down of all

TROOPS.

2 *Mac.* 5. 3. there were seen *t.* of horsemen in array

TROUBLE.

Tob. 4. 13. in pride is destruction and much *t.*
6. 7. if a devil or an evil spirit *t.* any
Esth. 13. 7. to be well settled, and without *t.*
Eccl. 2. 2. and make not haste in time of *t.*
4. 3. add not more *t.* to an heart that is vexed
6. 8. for some man will not abide in the day of *t.*
22. 13. beware of him, lest thou have *t.*
23. abide stedfast to him in the time of his *t.*
29. 4. many put them to *t.* that helped them
37. 4. but in the time of *t.* will be against him
40. 5. *t.* and unquietness, fear of death, anger
51. 10. he would not leave me in the days of my *t.*
2 *Mac.* 1. 25. thou that deliveredst Israel from *t.*
3. 30. which a little before was full of fear and *t.*

TROUBLED.

Tob. 12. 16. they were both *t.* and fell on their faces
Esth. 15. 16. she fell down, then the king was *t.*
Wisd. 5. 2. they shall be *t.* with terrible fear
11. 6. a running river, *t.* with foul blood
17. 3. astonished, being *t.* with strange apparitions
Eccl. 20. 21. when he takes rest, he shall not be *t.*
30. 7. and his bowels will be *t.* with every cry
40. 6. *t.* in the vision of his heart, as if escaped
51. 21. my heart was *t.* in seeking her
Bar. 3. 1. the *t.* spirit crieth unto thee
Dan. 3. 27. the fire neither hurt nor *t.* them
1 *Mac.* 3. 6. all the workers of iniquity were *t.*
7. 22. to him resorted all such as *t.* the people
9. 7. Judas was sore *t.* in mind, and distressed
11. 53. nor rewarded him, but *t.* him very sore

TRUE.

1 *Esd.* 8. 89. O Lord of Israel, thou art *t.*
Jud. 11. 10. but lay it up in thy heart, for it is *t.*
Wisd. 1. 6. for God is a *t.* beholder of his heart
2. 17. let us see if his words be *t.* and let us prove
6. 17. the very *t.* beginning of her is the desire
12. 27. they acknowledged him to be the *t.* God
Eccl. 46. 15. Samuel was found a *t.* prophet
Dan. 3. 8. thou hast done in *t.* judgment

TRULY.

Tob. 3. 2. and thou judgest *t.* and justly for ever
14. 6. nations shall turn and fear the Lord God *t.*
Eccl. 41. 24. so shalt thou be *t.* shamefaced
42. 8. thus shalt thou be *t.* learned and approved

TRUMPETS.

1 *Esd.* 5. 62. and all the people sounded *t.*
64. many with *t.* and joy shouted with loud voice
65. the *t.* might not be heard for the weeping
66. to know what that noise of *t.* should mean
Eccl. 50. 16. the sons of Aaron sounded the silver *t.*

TRUST.

Tob. 10. 12. I commit my daugh. to thee of special *t.*
Jud. 2. 5. take men that *t.* in their own strength
7. 10. the children of Israel do not *t.* in spears
8. 20. therefore we *t.* that he will not despise us
Wisd. 3. 9. they that put their *t.* in him understand
14. 29. for insomuch as their *t.* is in idols
Eccl. 2. 6. order thy way aright, and *t.* in him
10. did ever any *t.* in Lord and was confounded?
4. 17. until she may *t.* his soul, and try him by laws
11. 21. *t.* in the lord, and abide in thy labour
12. 10. never *t.* thine enemy, for as iron rusteth
16. 3. *t.* not thou in their life, neither respect
32. 23. in every good work *t.* thine own soul
34. 7. they have failed that put their *t.* in them
35. 12. and *t.* not to unrighteous sacrifices
36. 26. who will *t.* a thief well appointed
38. 31. these *t.* to their hands, every one is wise
Bar. 3. 17. hoard. up silver and gold, wherein men *t.*
Dan. 3. 17. not confounded that put their *t.* in thee
Sus. 60. God who saveth them that *t.* in him
1 *Mac.* 2. 61. none that *t.* in him shall be overcome
2 *Mac.* 3. 22. to keep the things committed of *t.*
7. 24. that he also would *t.* him with affairs
40. so this man put his whole *t.* in the Lord
8. 18. for they, saith he, *t.* in their weapons

TRUSTING.

Eccl. 26. 20. *t.* in the goodness of thy stock
2 *Mac.* 10. 34. *t.* to the strength of the place

TRUSTY.

Tob. 5. 8. whether he be a *t.* man to go with thee

TRUTH.

1 *Esd.* 4. 13. who had spoken of women and the *t.*
33. the king looked, so he began to speak of the *t.*
35. great is the *t.* and stronger than all things
38. as for the *t.* it endureth and is strong
40. blessed be the God of *t.*
Tob. 14. 7. all those who love the Lord God in *t.*
Jud. 10. 13. I am coming to declare the words of *t.*
Wisd. 3. 9. they that trust in him shall understand *t.*
5. 6. therefore have we erred from the way of *t.*
6. 22. and I will not pass over the *t.*
Eccl. 1. 30. because thou camest not in *t.* to fear L.
4. 25. in no wise speak against the *t.* but be abashed
28. strive for the *t.* unto death, Ld. fight for thee
11. 7. blame not before thou hast examined the *t.*
27. 9. so will *t.* return to them that practise in her
34. 4. from that which is false, what *t.* can come?
37. 15. pray that he will direct thy way in *t.*
41. 19. in regard of the *t.* of God and his covenant
Dan. 3. 4. thy ways right, all thy judgments are *t.*
Sus. 48. that without examination of the *t.*

TRY.

Jud. 8. 13. and now *t.* the Lord Almighty
Wisd. 11. 10. these thou didst admonish and *t.*
2 *Mac.* 14. 18. durst not *t.* the matter by the sword

TRIED.

Jud. 8. 26. how he *t.* Isaac, and what happened
27. he hath not *t.* us in the fire, as he did them
Wisd. 1. 3. and his power when it is *t.* reproveth
3. 6. as gold in the furnace hath he *t.* them
11. 9. for when they were *t.* albeit but in mercy
Eccl. 2. 5. gold is *t.* in the fire, men in the furnace
31. 10. who hath been *t.* and found perfect
2 *Mac.* 1. 34. made it holy, after he had *t.* the matter

TRIETH.

Jud. 8. 25. who *t.* us even as he did our fathers

TRYPHON.

1 *Mac.* 11. 39. there was one T. that had been
56. T. took the elephants and won Antioch
12. 39. T. went about to get the kingdom of Asia
42. then sent T. an host of footmen into Galilee
13. 1. when Simon heard that T. had gathered
14. now when T. knew that Simon was risen
19. howbeit T. dissembled, nor would let him go
34. because all that T. did was to spoil
15. 10. came to him, so that few were left with T.
25. he shut up T. that he could not go out
37. in the mean time fled T. by ship to Orthosias
39. as for the king himself, he pursued T.

TUMBLED.

Jud. 13. 9. and she *t.* his body down from the bed

TUMULT.

Esth. 11. 5. behold, the noise of a *t.* with thunder
2 *Mac.* 13. 16. at last they filled the camp with *t.*

TUMULTS.

Wisd. 14. 25. corruption, unfaithfulness, *t.* perjury

TURN.

Esth. 13. 17. *t.* our sorrow into joy, that we may live
14. 11. but *t.* their device upon themselves
Wisd. 2. 12. because he is not for our *t.*
Eccl. 4. 4. not *t.* away thy face from a poor man
5. not away thine eye from the needy
5. 7. make no tarrying to *t.* to the Lord
7. 2. and iniquity shall *t.* away from thee
9. 8. *t.* away thine eye from a beautiful woman
11. 34. the stranger will *t.* thee out of thine own
17. 26. *t.* to the Most High, and *t.* away from iniquity, for he will lead thee out of darkness
18. 24. the time when he shall *t.* away his face
23. 4. *t.* away from thy servants a haughty mind
5. *t.* away from me vain hopes and concupiscence
27. 1. that seeketh abundance will *t.* his eyes away
35. 2. he that requiteth a good *t.* offereth flour
40. 11. things of earth shall *t.* to the earth again
41. 21. to *t.* away thy face from thy kinsman
48. 10. to *t.* the heart of the father to the son
Bar. 2. 8. might *t.* every one from imaginations
13. let thy wrath *t.* from us, for we are but a few
4. 2. *t.* thee, O Jacob, and take hold of it
2 *Mac.* 5. 4. that apparition might *t.* to good
7. 24. if he would *t.* from the laws of his fathers

TURNED.

1 *Esd.* 7. 15. the Lord had *t.* the counsel of the king
8. 87. we have *t.* again to transgress thy law
Wisd. 19. 19. earthly things were *t.* into watery
Eccl. 6. 9. there is a friend, who being *t.* to enmity
28. find her rest, and that shall be *t.* to thy joy
10. 12. his heart is *t.* away from his Maker
37. 2. when companion and friend is *t.* to an enemy
39. 27. so to the sinners they are *t.* into evil
45. 23. he stood up when the people were *t.* back
47. 23. who *t.* away the people through his counsel
Bar. 1. 13. and his wrath is not *t.* from us
2. 29. this multitude be *t.* into a small number
4. 34. and her pride shall be *t.* into mourning
Sus. 9. *t.* away their eyes, that they might not
47. then all the people *t.* them towards him
1 *Mac.* 5. 28. Judas and his host *t.* suddenly by
35. this done, Judas *t.* aside to Maspha
68. Judas *t.* to Azotus in the land of the Philistines
9. 41. thus was the marriage *t.* into mourning
11. 55. Demetrius, who *t.* his back and fled
12. 31. wherefore Jonathan *t.* to the Arabians
33. from whence he *t.* aside to Joppe, and won it
2 *Mac.* 8. 5. the wrath of the Lord was *t.* into mercy
10. 25. they *t.* themselves to pray to God

TURNING.

Wisd. 7. 18. the alterations of the *t.* of the sun
Eccl. 38. 21. forget not, for there is no *t.* again
1 *Mac.* 3. 8. and *t.* away wrath from Israel

TURNS.

Eccl. 3. 31. he that requiteth good *t.* is mindful

TURPENTINE.

Eccl. 24. 16. as the *t.* tree I stretched out my branches

TWELVE.

1 *Esd.* 5. 41. from them of *t.* years old and upward
7. 8. and *t.* goats for the sin of all Israel
1 *Esd.* 8. 54. then I separated *t.* of the chief of priests
Eccl. 49. 10. of *t.* prophets, let memorial be blessed
1 *Mac.* 1. 7. Alexander reigned *t.* years, and died

TWICE.

Jud. 13. 8. she smote *t.* upon his neck with might
Eccl. 12. 5. thou shalt receive *t.* as much evil
13. 7. till he have drawn thee dry *t.* or thrice
32. 7. and yet scarcely when thou art *t.* asked
45. 14. their sacrifice shall be consumed every day *t.*

TWISTED.

Eccl. 45. 11. with *t.* scarlet work of the cunning

TWO.

1 *Esd.* 5. 73. were hindered for the space of *t.* years
Eccl. 2. 12. woe to the sinner that goeth *t.* ways
26. 28. there be *t.* things that grieve my heart
33. 15. there be *t.* and *t.* one against another
50. 25. there be *t.* manner of nations I abhor
Sus. 5. *t.* of the ancients of the people to be judges
8. the *t.* elders saw her going in every day
1 *Mac.* 1. 16. might have the dominion of *t.* realms
9. 57. the land of Judea was in rest *t.* years
11. 13. Ptolemee set *t.* crowns on his head
13. 16. send *t.* of his sons for hostages
2 *Mac.* 6. 10. *t.* women brought, who circumcised

TYRANNY.

Wisd. 14. 21. for men serving either calamity or *t.*
16. 4. on them exercising *t.* should come penury

TYRANT.

Wisd. 12. 14. nor shall *t.* be able to set his face
2 *Mac.* 4. 25. but having the fury of a cruel *t.*

TYRANTS.

Wisd. 8. 15. horrible *t.* shall be afraid when hear

TYRE.

1 *Esd.* 5. 55. unto them of T. they gave cars

TYRIANS.

Eccl. 46. 18. he destroyed the rules of the T.

TYRUS.

1 *Mac.* 11. 59. the place called the ladder of T.
2 *Mac.* 4. 18. now when the game was kept at T.
32. and some he sold unto T. and cities about
44. when the king came to T. three men pleaded
49. they of T. moved with hatred of that deed

U.

UGLY.

Wisd. 16. 3. for the *u.* sight of the beasts sent

UNABLE.

Wisd. 12. 9. not that thou wast *u.* to bring ungodly
13. 16. knowing that it was *u.* to help itself
19. of him that is most *u.* to do any thing

UNADVISEDLY.

1 *Mac.* 5. 67. for that they went out to fight *u.*

UNAWARES.

2 *Mac.* 8. 6. he came at *u.* burnt up towns and cities
12. 37. and rushing *u.* upon Gorgias' men

UNBELIEVING.

Wisd. 10. 7. pillar of salt is monument of an *u.* soul

UNBURIED.

2 *Mac.* 5. 10. he that had cast out many *u.* had none

UNCERTAIN.

Wisd. 9. 14. and our devices are but *u.*
2 *Mac.* 7. 34. nor be puffed up with *u.* hopes

UNCHANGEABLE.

2 *Esd.* 6. 44. there were flowers of *u.* colour

UNCIRCUMCISED.

Esth. 14. 15. knowest that I abhor the bed of the *u.*
1 *Mac.* 1. 15. and they made themselves *u.*
48. they should also leave their children *u.*
2. 46. what children soever they found *u.*

UNCLEAN.

Eccl. 34. 4. of an *u.* thing what can be cleansed?
40. 15. but are as *u.* roots upon a hard rock
51. 5. delivered from an *u.* tongue and lying words
1 *Mac.* 1. 47. sacrifice swine's flesh and *u.* beasts
62. many confirmed not to eat any *u.* thing
4. 43. bear out the defiled stones into an *u.* place

UNCLEANNESS.

1 *Esd.* 1. 42. things recorded of his *u.* and impiety
8. 83. and they have filled it with their *u.*
87. to mingle ourselves with the *u.* of the nations
Wisd. 14. 26. defiling of souls, adultery, shameless *u.*
1 *Mac.* 1. 48. their souls abominable with all *u.*
13. 48. yea, he put all *u.* out of it, and placed men

UNCOMFORTABLE.

Eccl. 18. 15. nor use *u.* words when thou givest

UNCOVERED.

Jud. 9. 1. *u.* the sackcloth wherewith was clothed

UNDEFILED.

Wisd. 3. 13. blessed is the barren that is *u.*
4. 2. having gotten victory, striving for *u.* rewards
7. 22. holy, subtile, lively, clear, *u.* plain
8. 20. rather being good, I came into a body *u.*
14. 24. they keep neither lives nor marriages *u.*
2 *Mac.* 7. 40. this man died *u.* and put his trust in L.
14. 36. O holy Lord, keep this house ever *u.*
15. 34. he that hath kept his own place *u.*

UNDERMINE.

Wisd. 4. 12. wandering doth *u.* the simple mind
Eccl. 12. 17. pretend to help, yet shall he *u.* thee

UNDERMINED.

2 *Mac.* 4. 26. then Jason, who had *u.* his own brother, being *u.* by another, was compelled to flee

UNDERSTAND.

Wisd. 3. 9. they that trust in him shall *u.* truth
4. 17. they shall not *u.* what God hath decreed
6. 1. hear therefore, O ye kings and *u.*
13. 4. let them *u.* how much mightier he is
Eccl. 3. 23. more things are shewed than men *u.*
29. the heart of the prudent will *u.* a parable
11. 7. blame not, *u.* first, and then rebuke
17. 6. and a heart gave he them to *u.*
34. 11. and I *u.* more than I can express
Bar. 3. 9. hear, Israel, give ear to *u.* wisdom
6. 41. they intreat Bel as though he were able to *u.*

UNDERSTANDETH.

Wisd. 9. 11. for she knoweth and *u.* all things

UNDERSTANDING.

Wisd. 1. 5. from thoughts that are without *u.*
4. 11. lest that wickedness should alter his *u.*
7. 7. wherefore I prayed, and *u.* was given me

Wisd. 7. 22. wisdom taught me, for in her is an *u.* spi.
23. overseeing all things, and going through all *u.*
9. 5. for I am too young for the *u.* of judgment
12. 24. being deceived as children of no *u.*
13. 13. and formed it by the skill of his *u.*
Eccl. 1. 4. and the *u.* of prudence from everlasting
19. wisdom raineth down the knowledge of *u.*
3. 13. and if his *u.* fail, have patience with him
5. 10. be stedfast in thy *u.* and let thy word be same
12. if thou hast *u.* answer thy neighbour
6. 20. he that is without *u.* will not remain
33. if thou love to hear, thou shalt receive *u.*
35. and let not the parables of *u.* escape thee
36. if thou seest a man of *u.* get betimes to him
7. 25. marry daughter, but give her to a man of *u.*
8. 9. the elders, of them thou shalt learn *u.*
10. 23. to despise the poor man that hath *u.*
11. 15. knowledge and *u.* of the law are of Lord
14. 20. that reasoneth of holy things by his *u.*
21. shall also have *u.* in her secrets
15. 3. with the bread of *u.* shall she feed him
16. 4. by one that hath *u.* shall city be replenished
23. he that wanteth *u.* will think on vain things
17. 5. in the sixth place he imparted them *u.*
7. he filled them with the knowledge of *u.*
9. that they might declare his works with *u.*
18. 28. every man of *u.* knoweth wisdom
29. they that were of *u.* in sayings became wise
19. 2. wine will make men of *u.* to fall away
24. he that hath small *u.* and feareth God
29. one that hath *u.* knoweth by his countenance
21. 11. that keepeth the law, getteth the *u.* thereof
25. the words of such as have *u.* are weighed
22. 11. and weep for the fool, for he wanteth *u.*
13. go not to him that hath no *u.* beware of him
15. sand is easier to bear, than a man without *u.*
17. a heart settled on a thought of *u.* is as a fair
24. 26. he maketh the *u.* to abound like Euphrates
25. 5. O! how comely is *u.* to men of honour
8. well is him that dwelleth with a wife of *u.*
26. 28. and men of *u.* that are not set by
27. 12. but be continually among men of *u.*
33. 3. a man of *u.* trusteth in the law, and the law
34. 1. the hopes of a man void of *u.* are vain
36. 19. so doth an heart of *u.* false speeches
37. 22. and the fruits of *u.* are commendable
39. 6. he shall be filled with the spirit of *u.*
9. many shall commend his *u.* his name shall live
44. 3. men renowned, giving counsel by their *u.*
47. 14. and as a flood thou wast filled with *u.*
23. he left behind him Roboam, one that had no *u.*
50. 27. written in this book the instruction of *u.*
Bar. 3. 14. learn where is strength, where is *u.*
32. and he hath found her out with his *u.*
2 *Mac.* 9. 27. he *u.* my mind, will graciously yield
11. 13. who, as he was a man of *u.* sent to them
UNDERSTOOD.
1 *Esd.* 9. 55. because they *u.* the words wherein
Wisd. 4. 15. this the people saw, and *u.* it not
Eccl. 1. 7. who hath *u.* her great experience?
Bar. 3. 21. they have not *u.* the paths thereof
UNDERTAKE.
2 *Mac.* 2. 27. we will *u.* gladly this great pains
UNDERTAKETH.
Eccl. 29. 19. he that *u.* other men's business
2 *Mac.* 2. 29. he that *u.* to set it out and paint it
UNDERTOOK.
1 *Esd.* 1. 28. did not turn, but *u.* to fight with him
2 *Mac.* 8. 10. so Nicanor *u.* to make money of Jews
UNDERWRITTEN.
2 *Mac.* 9. 18. he wrote to the Jews the letters *u.*
UNDISCREET.
Eccl. 27. 12. if thou be among the *u.* observe time
UNDRESSED.
2 *Esd.* 16. 78. it is left *u.* and cast into the fire
UNFAITHFUL.
2 *Esd.* 15. 4. *u.* shall die in their unfaithfulness
Wisd. 16. 29. the hope of the *u.* shall melt away
UNFAITHFULNESS.
2 *Esd.* 15. 4. the unfaithful shall die in their *u.*
UNFEIGNED.
Wisd. 18. 16. brought thine *u.* commandment
2 *Mac.* 14. 8. for the *u.* care I have of things
UNFRUITFUL.
Wisd. 3. 11. their labours *u.* works unprofitable
UNGODLY.
Wisd. 1. 9. shall be made into the counsels of the *u.*
16. but *u.* men with the works called it to them
3. 10. the *u.* shall be punished accord. to their imag.
4. 3. multiplying brood of the *u.* shall not thrive
16. righteous shall condemn the *u.* who are living
5. 14. the hope of the *u.* is like dust blown away
10. 6. when *u.* perished, she delivered righteous
11. 9. they knew how the *u.* were judged in wrath
12. 9. unable to bring *u.* under the righteous
14. 9. the *u.* and his ungodliness are both alike
16. an *u.* custom grown strong was kept as a law
31. that punisheth the offence of the *u.*
16. 16. for the *u.* that denied to know thee
19. 1. as for the *u.* wrath came upon them
Eccl. 7. 17. for the vengeance of the *u.* is fire
9. 12. delight not in what *u.* have pleasure in
12. 5. do well to lowly, but give not to the *u.*
6. Most High will repay vengeance to the *u.*
13. 24. poverty is evil in the mouth of the *u.*
16. 1. not a multit. of childr. nor delight in *u.* sons
3. die without, than to have them that are *u.*
6. in congregation of *u.* shall a fire be kindled
21. 27. when the *u.* curseth Satan, he curseth
22. 12. but for an *u.* man all the days of his life
26. 26. dishonoureth him, shall be counted *u.* of all
41. 5. they that are conversant in dwelling of the *u.*
8. woe to you *u.* men who have forsaken the law
10. so the *u.* shall go from a curse to destruction
42. 2. and of judgment to justify the *u.*
49. 3. in time of *u.* he established the worship of G.
Bar. 2. 12. O Lord, we have sinned, we have done *u.*
1 *Mac.* 3. 8. destroying the *u.* out of them
15. there went a mighty host of *u.* to help him
6. 21. to whom some *u.* men of Israel joined
7. 5. there came to him all the *u.* men of Israel
9. 58. then all the *u.* men held a council

1 *Mac.* 9. 73. he destroyed the *u.* men out of Israel
11. 21. certain *u.* persons who hated their people
2 *Mac.* 1. 17. who hath delivered up the *u.*
4. 13. the profaneness of Jason, that *u.* wretch
8. 2. would pity the temple profaned of *u.* men
UNGODLINESS.
1 *Esd.* 1. 52. being wroth with his people for *u.*
Wisd. 14. 9. ungodly and his *u.* are alike hateful
UNGRACIOUS.
2 *Mac.* 4. 19. this *u.* Jason sent messengers from Jer.
8. 34. as that most *u.* Nicanor, brought merchants
15. 3. then this most *u.* wretch demanded
UNHAPPY.
2 *Mac.* 5. 6. that it would be a most *u.* day for him
8. in the end therefore he had an *u.* return
UNITY.
Eccl. 25. 1. *u.* of brethren, the love of neighbours
UNJUST.
1 *Esd.* 4. 39. she refraineth from all *u.* things
Wisd. 16. 19. might destroy fruits of an *u.* land
Eccl. 7. 2. depart from *u.* and iniquity shall turn
19. 25. there is subtilty, and the same is *u.*
40. 13. the goods of the *u.* shall be dried up
41. 18. of *u.* dealing before thy partner and friend
Dan. 3. 9. thou didst deliver us to an *u.* king
2 *Mac.* 4. 48. they did soon suffer *u.* punishment
UNJUSTLY.
Wisd. 14. 28. or they prophesy lies, or live *u.*
30. they *u.* swore in deceit, despising holiness
Eccl. 5. 8. set not thy heart on goods *u.* gotten
2 *Mac.* 8. 17. the injury that they had *u.* done
UNKNOWN.
Wisd. 11. 18. or *u.* wild beasts full of rage
18. 3. both to be a guide to the *u.* journey
2 *Mac.* 1. 19. so that the place was *u.* to all men
UNLAWFUL.
Wisd. 4. 6. for children begotten of *u.* beds
UNLEARNED.
Eccl. 6. 20. she is very unpleasant to the *u.*
51. 23. draw near to me, you *u.* and dwell in house
UNLOOKED.
Wisd. 18. 17. and terrors came upon them *u.* for
UNMEASURABLE.
Bar. 3. 25. great, and hath no end, high and *u.*
Prayer of Manass. thy merciful promises is *u.*
UNMERCIFUL.
Eccl. 37. 11. nor with an *u.* man touching kindness
UNMINDFUL.
Eccl. 37. 6. be not *u.* of him in thy riches
UNNECESSARY.
Eccl. 3. 23. be not curious in *u.* matters
UNPASSABLE.
Esth. 16. 24. shall be made not only *u.* for men
UNPERFECT.
Wisd. 4. 5. the *u.* branches shall be broken off
Eccl. 42. 24. and he hath made nothing *u.*
UNPLEASANT.
Eccl. 6. 20. she is very *u.* to the unlearned
UNPROFITABLE.
Wisd. 1. 11. beware of murmuring which is *u.*
4. 5. fruit *u.* not ripe to eat, meet for nothing
16. 29. for the hope of the unfaithful shall melt
away as hoar frost and run away as *u.* water
Eccl. 16. 1. desire not a multitude of *u.* children
37. 19. one is wise, and yet is *u.* to himself
UNPUNISHED.
Eccl. 7. 8. for in one sin thou shalt not be *u.*
UNREASONABLE.
Wisd. 11. 15. didst send a multitude of *u.* beasts
UNRIGHT.
Wisd. 12. 13. shew that thy judgment is not *u.*
UNRIGHTEOUS.
1 *Esd.* 4. 36. and with it is no *u.* thing
Esth. 14. 15. knowest that I hate the glory of the *u.*
Wisd. 1. 8. that speaketh *u.* things cannot be hid
3. 16. the seed of an *u.* bed shall be rooted out
19. horrible is the end of the *u.* generation
10. 3. but when the *u.* went from her in his anger
12. 12. to be revenged for the *u.* men
Eccl. 17. 20. none of their *u.* deeds are hid from him
35. 12. and trust not to *u.* sacrifices, the L. is judge
18. till he hath broken the sceptre of the *u.*
51. 6. by an accusation to king from an *u.* tongue
2 *Mac.* 14. 36. O holy Lord, stop every *u.* mouth
UNRIGHTEOUSLY.
Wisd. 12. 23. whereas men have lived *u.*
Bar. 2. 12. we have dealt *u.* in thy ordinances
UNRIGHTEOUSNESS.
1 *Esd.* 4. 37. in their *u.* also they shall perish
Tob. 4. 5. my son, follow not the ways of *u.*
12. 8. a little is better than much with *u.*
Wisd. 1. 5. and will not abide when *u.* cometh in
Eccl. 7. 3. my son, sow not upon the furrows of *u.*
17. 14. he said to them, beware of all *u.*
35. 3. and to forsake *u.* is a propitiation
UNRULY.
Eccl. 26. 5. the gathering together of an *u.* multitude
UNSATIABLE.
Eccl. 31. 17. and be not *u.* lest thou offend
20. but pangs of the belly are with an *u.* man
37. 29. be not *u.* in any dainty thing, nor greedy
UNSEARCHABLE.
2 *Esd.* 9. 19. are corrupted by a law which is *u.*
Bar. 3. 18. so careful, and whose works are *u.*
Prayer of Manass. thy merciful promise is *u.*
UNSEASONABLE.
Eccl. 20. 19. an *u.* tale will be in the mouth of unwise
UNSPEAKABLE.
Eccl. 36. 14. fill Sion with thine *u.* oracles
2 *Mac.* 12. 16. took city, and made *u.* slaughters
UNSPOTTED.
Wisd. 4. 9. and an *u.* life is old age
7. 26. *u.* mirror of the power of God and image
UNTAUGHT.
Eccl. 20. 24. continually in the mouth of the *u.*
UNTEMPERATE.
Eccl. 23. 13. use not thy mouth to *u.* swearing
UNTHANKFUL.
2 *Esd.* 8. 60. were *u.* to him who prepared life
Eccl. 29. 17. he that is of an *u.* mind will leave him
UNTIMELY.
2 *Esd.* 6. 21. women shall bring forth *u.* children

Wisd. 14. 15. for a father afflicted with *u.* mourning
UNWISE.
2 *Esd.* 5. 39. as for me, I am *u.* how may I speak?
Wisd. 1. 3. his power when tried reproveth the *u.*
5. 20. the world shall fight with him against the *u.*
14. 11. the idols of Gentiles are become a stumbling-
block to souls of men and a snare to feet of *u.*
Eccl. 10. 3. an *u.* king destroyeth his people
20. 19. an unseasonable tale will be in mouth of *u.*
21. 18. knowledge of *u.* is as talk without sense
42. 8. be not ashamed to inform the *u.* and foolish
UNWORTHY.
2 *Esd.* 14. 45. that the worthy and *u.* may read it
Eccl. 25. 8. not served a man more *u.* than himself
UNWORTHILY.
Esth. 16. 7. behaviour of them that are *u.* placed
UPBRAID.
Eccl. 18. 18. a fool will *u.* churlishly, and a gift
41. 22. and after thou hast given, *u.* not
UPBRAIDETH.
Wisd. 2. 12. he *u.* us with our offending the law
Eccl. 20. 15. he giveth little, and *u.* much
22. 20. he that *u.* his friend breaketh friendship
UPBRAIDING.
Eccl. 22. 22. there may be a reconciliation, except *u.*
29. 28. the *u.* of house-room, and reproaching lender
41. 22. be ashamed of *u.* speeches before friends
UPHOLDER.
Jud. 9. 11. an helper of oppressed, an *u.* of the weak
UPHOLDING.
Jud. 11. 7. for the *u.* of every thing living
UPRIGHT.
Wisd. 9. 3. execute judgment with an *u.* heart
Eccl. 27. 14. that sweareth, maketh the hair stand *u.*
Bar. 6. 27. nor if one set them *u.* they can move
UPRIGHTLY.
Tob. 4. 5. do *u.* all thy life long, and follow not
8. 7. I take not this my sister for lust, but *u.*
Eccl. 49. 2. he behaved himself *u.* in conversion
UPRIGHTNESS.
Eccl. 7. 6. a stumbling-block in the way of thy *u.*
UPWARD.
1 *Esd.* 5. 41. so of Israel from twelve years old and *u.*
URIM.
Eccl. 45. 10. a breast-plate with U. and Thummim
USE.
1 *Esd.* 8. 17. are given for the *u.* of the temple
Tob. 6. 6. to what *u.* is the heart and the liver?
Jud. 12. 15. had received of Bagoas for her daily *u.*
Wisd. 12. 18. thou mayest *u.* power when thou wilt
25. as to children without the *u.* of reason
13. 13. among those which served to no *u.*
15. 7. but what is the *u.* of either sort
Eccl. 7. 13. *u.* not to make any manner of lie
14. *u.* not many words in a multitude of elders
23. 9. nor *u.* thyself to the naming of the Holy One
13. *u.* not thy mouth to intemperate swearing
32. 9. when ancient men in place, *u.* not many words
39. 26. the things for the whole *u.* of man's life
2 *Mac.* 6. 21. flesh, such as was unlawful for him
to *u.*
11. 31. the Jews shall *u.* their own kind of meats
12. 39. as *u.* had been, Judas came to take bodies
USED.
Wisd. 14. 23. whilst they *u.* secret ceremonies
19. 13. as they *u.* a more hard behaviour
15. because they *u.* strangers not friendly
USES.
Wisd. 15. 7. the vessels that serve for clean *u.*
Eccl. 38. 1. for the *u.* which you may have of him
39. 21. for he hath made all things for their *u.*
USETH.
Eccl. 20. 8. he that *u.* many words shall be abhorred
23. 11. a man that *u.* much swearing filled with iniq.
USUAL.
2 *Mac.* 14. 31. priests were offering their *u.* sacrifices
USURPED.
1 *Esd.* 5. 38. of the priests that *u.* the office
1 *Mac.* 15. 3. pestilent men have *u.* the kingdom
UTMOST.
1 *Mac.* 3. 9. was renowned to the *u.* part of the earth
2 *Mac.* 7. 4. to cut off the *u.* parts of his body
UTTER.
Eccl. 25. 7. the tenth I will *u.* with my tongue
UTTERANCE.
Eccl. 27. 6. so is the *u.* of a conceit in the heart
UTTERED.
Wisd. 7. 3. the first voice which I *u.* was crying
Eccl. 15. 10. for praise shall be *u.* in wisdom
2 *Mac.* 10. 34. blasphemed and *u.* wicked words

V.

VAIL.
Wisd. 17. 3. under a dark *v.* of forgetfulness
1 *Mac.* 1. 22. censers of gold, the *v.* and crowns
VAIN.
Jud. 6. 9. and none of my words shall be in *v.*
Wisd. 3. 11. he is miserable, their hope is *v.*
13. 1. surely *v.* are all men by nature, ignorant of G.
14. 14. by *v.* glory of men they entered the world
15. 8. he maketh a *v.* god of the same clay
Eccl. 3. 24. many are deceived by their own *v.* opin.
23. 11. if he swear in *v.* he shall not be innocent
34. 1. the hopes of a man void of understand. are *v.*
5. divinations, soothsayings, and dreams are *v.*
VALIANT.
1 *Mac.* 2. 64. wherefore, ye my sons, be *v.* and shew
3. 58. Judas said, arm yourselves, and be *v.* men
4. 3. he himself removed and the *v.* men with
5. 56. heard of the *v.* acts which they had done
9. 21. how is the *v.* man fallen that delivered
13. 53. Simon saw that John his son was a *v.* man
14. 32. Simon armed the *v.* men of his nation
2 *Mac.* 13. 15. with the most *v.* young men he went
VALIANTLY.
1 *Mac.* 2. 46. those they circumcised *v.*
4. 35. how they were ready either to live or die *v.*
6. 31. they burned them with fire, and fought *v.*
VALIANTNESS.
Eccl. 31. 25. shew not thy *v.* in wine, hath destroyed

VALLEY.
Jud. 4. 4. they sent to Esora, and to the v. of Salem
7. 3. they camped in the v. near to Bethulia
10. 10. they looked until Judith had passed the v.
VALOUR.
1 *Mac.* 5. 67. certain priests desirous to shew their v.
8. 2. that the Romans were men of great v.
2 *Mac.* 15. 17. good and able to stir them up to v.
VALUE.
Wisd. 15. 10. and his life of less v. than clay
VALUED.
Eccl. 26. 15. her continent mind cannot be v.
VANISH.
Wisd. 2. 3. and our spirit shall v. as soft air
Eccl. 40. 13. and shall v. with noise as great thunder
VANISHED.
Bar. 3. 19. they are v. and gone down to the grave
VAPOUR.
Wisd. 11. 18. beasts breathing out either a fiery v.
Eccl. 22. 24. as the v. and smoke of a furnace
38. 28. the v. of the fire wasteth his flesh
2 *Mac.* 7. 5. as the v. of the pan was dispersed
VAPOURS.
Eccl. 43. 4. breathing out fiery v. and sending beams
VARIANCE.
Eccl. 8. 2. be not at v. with a rich man
VARIETY.
Eccl. 38. 27. and are diligent to make great v.
50. 18. with great v. of sounds was there melody
VAULT.
2 *Esd.* 16. 59. he spreadeth out the heavens like a v.
VAUNT.
1 *Mac.* 10. 70. why dost thou v. thy power ag. us?
VAUNTING.
Wisd. 5. 8. what good hath riches with v. brought?
17. 7. and their v. in wisdom was reproved
VEHEMENCY.
2 *Mac.* 14. 38. jeopard his body and life with all v.
VEHEMENTLY.
Eccl. 17. 26. and hate thou abomination v.
VENGEANCE.
Jud. 6. 5. till I take v. this nation come out of Egypt
8. 27. neither hath he taken v. on us
9. 2. thou gavest a sword to take v. of the strangers
16. 17. Lord will take v. of them in judgment
Esth. 16. 18. God speedily rendering v. to him
Wisd. 1. 8. nor v. when it punisheth shall pass by him
11. 15. unreasonable beasts upon them for v.
Eccl. 5. 7. thou shalt perish in the day of v.
7. 17. for the v. of ungodly is fire and worms
12. 6. and will repay v. unto the ungodly
18. 24. and the time of v. when he shall turn away
27. 28. v. as a lion shall lie in wait for them
28. 1. he that revengeth shall find v. from the Lord
35. 18. till he hath repayed v. to the heathen
39. 28. there be spirits that are created for v.
47. 25. they sought wickedness till v. came on
1 *Mac.* 7. 9. that he should take v. of Israel
24. and took v. of them that had revolted from
2 *Mac.* 6. 15. afterwards he should take v. of us
VENOM.
Eccl. 28. 19. hath not passed through the v. thereof
VENOMOUS.
Wisd. 16. 10. the very teeth of v. dragons overcame
VERMILION.
Wisd. 13. 14. laying it over with v. and paint
VERSES.
Eccl. 44. 5. such as recited v. in writing
VESSEL.
Wisd. 13. 11. hath made a v. thereof fit for service
14. 1. more rotten than the v. that carrieth him
5. passing the rough sea in a weak v. are saved
6. hope of the world, escaped in a weak v.
Eccl. 21. 14. inner parts of a fool like a broken v.
50. 9. as a v. of beaten gold with precious stones
Bar. 6. 17. for like as a v. that a man useth
59. or else a profitable v. in an house
VESSELS.
1 *Esd.* 1. 45. brought with the holy v. of the Lord
4. 44. to send away all the v. that were taken
Wisd. 15. 7. both the v. that serve for clean uses
13. maketh brittle v. and graven images
Eccl. 27. 5. the furnace proveth the potter's v.
Bar. 1. 8. when he received v. of the house of Lord
1 *Mac.* 1. 21. and took away all the v. thereof
23. he took silver and gold and precious v.
2. 9. her glorious v. are carried into captivity
6. 12. I took all the v. of gold and silver
11. 58. upon this he sent him golden v. to be served
14. 15. he multiplied the v. of the temple
2 *Mac.* 4. 32. Menelaus stole certain v. of gold
48. they that followed the matter for holy v.
5. 16. taking the holy v. with polluted hands
9. 16. restore all the holy v. with many more
VESTMENTS.
1 *Esd.* 4. 54. and priests' v. wherein they minister
5. 59. the priests stood arrayed in their v.
2 *Mac.* 3. 15. prostrating themselves in their v.
VEX.
2 *Mac.* 5. 22. he left governors to v. the nation
VEXED.
Tob. 6. 7. and the party shall be no more v.
Wisd. 11. 11. absent or present, they were v. alike
17. 15. they were v. with monstrous apparitions
Eccl. 4. 3. add not more trouble to a heart that is v.
41. 2. death unto him that is v. with all things
Bar. 2. 18. but the soul that is greatly v.
1 *Mac.* 3. 5. and burn up those that v. his people
VIALS.
1 *Esd.* 2. 13. v. of gold thirty, and of silver 2410
VICE.
Wisd. 7. 30. but v. shall not prevail against wisdom
VICTORY.
1 *Esd.* 3. 5. give great gifts and things in token of v.
9. to him shall the v. be given, as was appointed
12. above all things truth beareth away the v.
4. 5. if they get v. they bring all to the king
59. and said, from thee cometh v. and wisdom
Wisd. 4. 2. having got the v. striving for rewards
10. 12. in a sore conflict she gave him the v.
1 *Mac.* 3. 19. for v. standeth not in the multitude
2 *Mac.* 8. 33. at such times as they kept feast for v.
2 *Mac.* 10. 38. had done so great things given them v.
12. 11. Judas' side by the help of God got the v.
13. 15. given watch-word to them, v. is of God
15. 6. to set up a public monument of his v.
8. now to expect the v. and aid from the Almighty
21. knowing that v. cometh not by arms
VICTUALS.
Jud. 4. 5. and laid up v. for the provision of war
11. 12. for their v. fail them and water is scant
1 *Mac.* 1. 35. they stored it also with armour and v.
6. 49. because they had no v. to endure the siege
57. we decay daily, and our v. are but small
8. 26. that make war on them or aid them with v.
28. neither shall v. be given to them against
9. 52. and put forces in them and provision of v.
13. 21. should hasten his coming, and send them v.
33. Simon built up the strong holds and laid up v.
14. 10. he provided v. for the cities and set munition
VIEW.
2 *Mac.* 5. 18. king Seleucus sent to v. the treasury
VIEWED.
Jud. 7. 7. and v. the passages up to the city
VILE.
Wisd. 4. 18. they shall hereafter be a v. carcase
11. 15. they worshipped serpents and v. beasts
13. 14. or made it like some v. beast
2 *Mac.* 15. 32. and shewed them v. Nicanor's head
VINE.
2 *Esd.* 5. 23. O Ld. thou hast chosen thee one only v.
VINEYARD.
2 *Esd.* 16. 30. or as when a v. is gathered
43. so also he that planteth the v.
VINEYARDS.
1 *Esd.* 4. 16. they nourished them up that planted v.
VINTAGE.
Eccl. 24. 27. and as Geon in the time of v.
VIOLENCE.
Wisd. 7. 20. the v. of winds and reasonings of men
Eccl. 20. 4. he that executeth judgment with v.
1 *Mac.* 4. 30. who didst quell the v. of the mighty man
6. 47. Jews seeing v. of his forces turned away
7. 29. were prepared to take away Judas by v.
2 *Mac.* 4. 40. Lysimachus began first to offer v.
VIOLENT.
Wisd. 13. 2. or the v. water or the lights of heaven
19. 7. and out of the v. stream a green field
VIOLENTLY.
Wisd. 17. 18. a pleasant fall of water running v.
Eccl. 46. 6. made the battle to fall v. on the nations
2 *Mac.* 9. 7. carried v. so that having a sore fall
14. 41. and v. broken into the outer door
VIRGIN.
Eccl. 20. 4. as is lust of a eunuch to deflower a v.
30. 20. groaneth as a eunuch that embraceth a v.
VIRGINS.
2 *Esd.* 16. 33. v. shall mourn having no bridegrooms
Jud. 16. 5. make my infants a prey, my v. a spoil
1 *Mac.* 1. 26. the v. and young men were made feeble
2 *Mac.* 3. 19. and the v. that were kept in, ran
5. 13. thus there was slaying of v. and infants
VIRTUE.
Wisd. 4. 1. better to have v. for the memorial
13. 4. they were astonished at their power and v.
19. 20. the fire had power, forgetting his own v.
Eccl. 38. 5. that the v. thereof might be known
2 *Mac.* 6. 31. leaving his death for a memorial of v.
15. 12. exercised from a child in all points of v.
VIRTUES.
Wisd. 7. 20. the diversities of plants and v. of roots
VIRTUOUS.
2 *Esd.* 16. 49. like as a whore envieth a v. woman
Eccl. 26. 1. blessed is the man that hath a v. wife
2. a v. woman rejoiceth her husband
28. 15. a backbiting tongue hath cast out v. women
2 *Mac.* 15. 12. Onias a v. and good man, reverend
VISION.
2 *Esd.* 10. 37. thou wilt shew thy servant of this v.
Eccl. 34. 3. the v. of dreams is the resemblance
40. 6. troubled in the v. of his heart
46. 15. he was known to be faithful in v.
49. 8. it was Ezekiel who saw the glorious v.
2 *Mac.* 15. 12. and this was his v. that Onias
VISIONS.
Wisd. 17. 4. and sad v. appeared unto them
VISIT.
2 *Esd.* 6. 18. to v. them that dwell on the earth
9. 2. the Highest will begin to v. the world
Jud. 8. 33. the Lord will v. Israel by my hand
13. 20. to v. thee in good, because hast not spared
Eccl. 2. 14. what will ye do when Lord shall v. you?
7. 35. be not slow to v. the sick, make thee beloved
16. 18. all therein shall be moved when he shall v.
VISITATION.
Wisd. 3. 7. in the time of their v. they shall shine
13. she shall have fruit in the v. of souls
14. 11. on the idols of the Gentiles shall there be a v.
Eccl. 18. 20. in day of v. thou shalt find mercy
34. 6. if not sent from the Most High in the v.
VISITED.
1 *Esd.* 6. 5. because the Lord had v. the captivity
VISITING.
1 *Mac.* 16. 14. v. the cities that were in the country
2 *Mac.* 3. 8. Heliodorus under a colour of v. the cities
VOICE.
Wisd. 1. 7. containeth all, hath knowledge of the v.
7. 3. the first v. which I uttered, was crying
17. 19. or a roaring v. of most savage beasts
18. 1. whose v. they hearing, and not seeing
Eccl. 21. 20. a fool lifteth up his v. with laughter
34. 24. whose v. will the Lord hear?
45. 5. he made him to hear his v. and brought him
46. 17. with a great noise made his v. to be heard
Bar. 1. 18. have not hearkened to the v. of the Lord
19. we have been negligent in not hearing his v.
2. 5. we have not been obedient unto his v.
22. but if ye will not hear the v. of the Lord
23. I will cause to cease the v. of mirth, the v. of
joy, the v. of the bridegroom, and v. of the bride
Sus. 44. and the Lord heard her v.
2 *Mac.* 12. 37. and sung psalms with a loud v.
VOICES.
1 *Esd.* 5. 61. and they sung with loud v. songs
Eccl. 50. 18. the singers sang praises with their v.
VOID.
Wisd. 11. 15. they worshipped serpents v. of reason
Eccl. 34. 1. the hopes of a man v. of understanding
1 *Mac.* 3. 45. now Jerusalem lay v. as a wilderness
2 *Mac.* 13. 25. because they would make covenants v.
14. 28. that he should make v. the articles
44. he fell down into the midst of the v. place
VOLUNTARILY.
1 *Mac.* 2. 42. such as were v. devoted to the law
VOLUPTUOUSNESS.
Wisd. 2. 9. none of us without his part in our v.
VOMIT.
Eccl. 31. 21. go forth, v. and thou shalt have rest
VOW.
1 *Esd.* 2. 7. which have been set forth by v. for temple
4. 43. remember thy v. which thou vowed
46. I desire that thou make good the v.
5. 53. all they that had made any v. to God
8. 58. the gold and the silver is a v. to the Lord
VOWED.
1 *Esd.* 4. 43. remember thy vow which thou hast v.
44. Cyrus set apart, when he v. to destroy Babylon
45. thou hast also v. to build up the temple
46. the vow thou hast v. to the king of heaven
8. 13. the gifts which I and my friends have v.
50. there I v. a fast to the young men before Lord
2 *Mac.* 9. 13. this wicked person v. also to the Lord
VOWS.
Jud. 4. 14. with the v. and free gifts of the people
2 *Mac.* 3. 35. Heliodorus made great v. unto him
VOYAGE.
Jud. 2. 19. and his power to go before the king in v.
2 *Mac.* 5. 1. prepared his second v. into Egypt

W.

WAGES.
1 *Esd.* 4. 56. he commanded to give pensions and w.
Tob. 2. 12. they paid her w. and gave her also a kid
14. it was given for a gift more than the w.
4. 14. let not the w. of any man tarry with thee
5. 3. seek thee a man and I will give him w.
14. but tell me what w. shall I give thee?
15. moreover I will add something to thy w.
12. 1. my son, see that the man have his w.
1 *Mac.* 14. 32. armed the valiant men and gave w.
WAIT.
Jud. 8. 17. let us w. for salvation of him
13. 3. to stand and to w. for her coming forth
Wisd. 2. 12. let us lie in w. for the righteous
10. 12. and keep him safe from those that lie in w.
Eccl. 8. 11. lest he lie in w. to entrap thee
27. 28. vengeance as a lion shall lie in w. for them
36. 16. reward them that w. for thee
51. 8. how thou deliverest such as w. for thee
1 *Mac.* 1. 36. for it was a place to lie in w.
2 *Mac.* 7. 30. said, whom w. ye for? I will not obey
9. 25. w. for opportunities and expect the event
WAITED.
Jud. 6. 10. commanded his servant that w. in his tent
12. 16. for we w. a time to deceive Judith
WAITERS.
Jud. 13. 1. dismissed the w. from presence of his lord
WAITING.
Jud. 8. 33. I will go forth with my w. woman
WAKETH.
Eccl. 22. 7. as he that w. one from a sound sleep
42. 9. the father w. for the daughter, no man knows
WALK.
Eccl. 5. 2. to w. in the ways of thy heart
Bar. 4. 2. w. in the presence of the light thereof
Sus. 7. Susanna went into her husband's garden to w.
1 *Mac.* 2. 20. w. in the covenant of our fathers
WALKED.
Tob. 1. 3. I Tobit have w. all the days of my life
Wisd. 6. 4. nor w. after the counsel of God
19. 21. flames wasted not, though they w. therein
Bar. 3. 13. if thou hadst w. in the way of God
Dan. 3. 1. and they w. in the midst of the fire
Sus. 36. the elders said, as we w. in the garden
WALKEST.
Eccl. 9. 13. that thou w. on battlements of the city
WALKING.
Sus. 8. the elders saw her going in every day and w.
WALL.
Tob. 2. 9. and slept by the w. of my court yard
10. I knew not there were sparrows in the w.
Wisd. 13. 15. set it in a w. and made it fast with iron
Eccl. 50. 2. the fortress of the w. about the temple
1 *Mac.* 6. 62. to pull down the w. round about
9. 54. the w. of the inner court be pulled down
12. 37. as part of the w. toward the brook fallen
2 *Mac.* 6. 10. they cast them down from the w.
10. 17. they kept off all that fought on the w.
35. twenty young men assaulted the w. manly
14. 43. he ran boldly up to the w. cast himself down
WALLS.
1 *Esd.* 2. 24. and the w. thereof set up anew
4. 4. they break down mountains, w. and towers
6. 9. the timber already laid upon the w.
Tob. 1. 17. or cast about w. of Nineveh, I buried him
13. 16. w. and towers and battlements with gold
Eccl. 49. 13. Neemias raised up for us the w.
1 *Mac.* 1. 31. he pulled down houses and w. thereo
6. 7. compassed about the sanctuary with high w.
10. 11. the workmen to build the w. and Sion
45. for building the w. of Jerusalem and Judea
13. 45. people climbed on the w. with their wives
2 *Mac.* 3. 19. ran, some to the gates, and some to w.
5. 5. they that were on the w. being put back
11. 9. were ready to pierce through w. of iron
12. 13. a bridge to a strong city fenced with w.
WALLOW.
Eccl. 23. 12. and they shall not w. in their sins
WAND.
Eccl. 33. 24. fodder, a w. and burdens for the ass
WANDER.
Eccl. 36. 25. he that hath no wife will w. mourning
WANDERED.
Eccl. 29. 18. so that they w. among strange nations

2 *Mac.* 10. 6. when as they *w.* in the mountains

WANDERING.

Wisd. 4. 12. the *w.* of concupiscence doth undermine

WANT.

Eccl. 3. 25. without eyes thou shalt *w.* light
19. 28. if for *w.* of power he be hindered from sinning
20. 21. there is that is hindered from sinning thro' *w.*
40. 26. there is no *w.* in the fear of the Lord
1 *Mac.* 13. 49. in great distress for *w.* of victuals

WANTED.

Wisd. 11. 17. *w.* not means to send among them

WANTETH.

Eccl. 10. 27. than he that boasteth and *w.* bread
16. 23. he that *w.* understanding will think

WANTING.

Wisd. 19. 4. the punishment *w.* to their torments
Eccl. 11. 12. another *w.* ability and full of poverty
19. 23. and there is a fool *w.* in wisdom

WANTONNESS.

Eccl. 27. 13. the sport of fools is in the *w.* of sin

WAR.

Wisd. 8. 15. I shall be found good and valiant in *w.*
18. 15. as a fierce man of *w.* into the midst of land
Eccl. 26. 28. a man of *w.* that suffereth poverty
37. 11. nor consult with a coward in matters of *w.*
Bar. 3. 26. of so great stature, and so expert in *w.*
6. 15. cannot deliver himself from *w.* and thieves
1 *Mac.* 2. 32. made *w.* against them on sabbath day
3. 13. the faithful to go out with him to *w.*
8. 27. if *w.* come first on the nation of the Jews
2 *Mac.* 8. 9. who in matt. of *w.* had great experience
10. 15. the Idumeans went about to nourish *w.*

WARS.

1 *Esd.* 2. 23. the Jews raised always *w.* therein
4. 6. for those that have not to do with *w.*
Eccl. 46. 1. Jesus son of Nave was valiant in *w.*
1 *Mac.* 1. 2. made many *w.* and won many str.-holds
12. 13. we have had great troubles and *w.*
16. 23. the rest of the acts of John and his *w.*
2 *Mac.* 2. 20. the *w.* against Antiochus Epiphanes
10. 10. gathering briefly the calamities of the *w.*

WARD.

1 *Mac.* 14. 3. Arsaces by whom he was put into *w.*

WARINESS.

Eccl. 11. 18. there is that waxeth rich by his *w.*

WARLIKE.

1 *Mac.* 5. 56. valiant acts and *w.* deeds they had done

WARNING.

1 *Mac.* 6. 3. they of the city having had *w.* thereof
2 *Mac.* 6. 17. but let this be for a *w.* to us

WARRIOR.

Jud. 15. 3. every one that was a *w.* rushed out
Eccl. 47. 5. he gave strength to slay that mighty *w.*

WASH.

Sus. 15. she was desirous to *w.* herself in the garden
17. shut the garden doors that I may *w.* me

WASHED.

Jud. 10. 3. and *w.* her body all over with water

WASHETH.

Eccl. 31. 25. that *w.* after touching of a dead body

WASHING.

Eccl. 34. 25. if he touch again, what availeth his *w.*?
Sus. 17. said to her maids, bring me oil and *w.* balls

WASPS.

Wisd. 12. 8. didst send *w.* forerunners of thy host

WASTE.

Jud. 8. 21. if we be taken so, all Judea shall lie *w.*
Wisd. 5. 23. this iniquity shall lay *w.* the whole earth
Eccl. 21. 4. to terrify and do wrong will *w.* riches
Bar. 2. 26. the house hast thou laid *w.*
1 *Mac.* 1. 39. her sanctuary laid *w.* like a wilderness
2. 12. even our beauty and our glory is laid *w.*

WASTED.

Wisd. 19. 21. on other side the flames *w.* not the flesh

WATCH.

2 *Esd.* 2. 13. the kingdom is already prepared, *w.*
11. 8. *w.* not all at once, *w.* by course
Jud. 7. 13. to *w.* that none go out of the city
10. 11. the first *w.* of the Assyrians met her
Eccl. 22. 27. who shall set a *w.* before my mouth?
26. 11. *w.* over an impudent eye, and marvel not
40. 6. he is in sleep, as in a day of keeping *w.*
42. 11. keep a sure *w.* over a shameless daughter
1 *Mac.* 12. 27. Jonathan commanded his men to *w.*

WATCHED.

Jud. 7. 5. they remained and *w.* all that night
Sus. 12. they *w.* diligently from day to day to see her
15. and it fell out as they *w.* a fit time
16. the two elders hid themselves and *w.* her
2 *Mac.* 14. 29. he *w.* his time to accomplish by policy

WATCHES.

Eccl. 43. 10. they will stand, never faint in their *w.*
Bar. 3. 34. the stars shined in their *w.* and rejoiced

WATCHETH.

Wisd. 6. 15. whoso *w.* for her shall be without care
Eccl. 11. 30. and like as a spy *w.* he for thy fall
38. 28. he *w.* to polish his work perfectly

WATCHING.

Eccl. 31. 2. *w.* care will not let a man slumber
20. but the pain of *w.* and choler, and pangs
2 *Mac.* 2. 26. not easy, but a matter of sweat and *w.*

WATCHMEN.

Eccl. 37. 14. man's mind tell him more than seven *w.*

WATER.

Wisd. 5. 10. as a ship passeth over the waves of *w.*
22. the *w.* of the sea shall rage against them
10. 18. she led them through much *w.*
11. 4. *w.* was given them out of the flinty rock
13. 2. or the violent *w.* or the lights of heaven
16. 17. the fire had more force in the *w.*
19. it burneth even in the midst of *w.*
29. and shall run away as unprofitable *w.*
17. 18. *w.* | 19. 7, 19, 20. *w.*
Eccl. 3. 30. *w.* will quench a flaming fire
24. 31. I will *w.* my best garden, and will *w.*
25. 25. give the *w.* no passage, nor a wicked woman
26. 12. *w.* | 29. 21. *w.* | 38. 5. *w.* | 40. 16. *w.* | 43. 20. *w.* | 48. 17. *w.*
1 *Mac.* 9. 33. pitched by the *w.* of the pool Asphar
45. the *w.* of Jordan on this side and that side
11. 60. passed through the cities beyond *w.*

1 *Mac.* 16. 5. there was a *w.* brook between them
2 *Mac.* 1. 19. in a hollow place of a pit without *w.*
20. told us they found no fire but thick *w.*
14. 45. tho' his blood gushed out like spouts of *w.*
15. 39. as it is hurtful to drink wine or *w.* alone, as wine mingled with *w.* is pleasant and delights

WATERS.

2 *Esd.* 1. 20. and *w.* flowed out to your fill
6. 41. and to make a division betwixt the *w.*
13. 40. he carried them over the *w.*
16. 58. in midst of *w.* hanged the earth upon the *w.*
Jud. 7. 17. they took the *w.* and fountain of the *w.*
Wisd. 17. 4. but noises as of *w.* falling down
Eccl. 39. 17. at his command the *w.* stood as an heap, at the words of his mouth the receptacles of *w.*
23. as he that turned the *w.* into saltness
40. 11. what is of the *w.* do return into the sea
48. 17. he digged the rock and made wells for *w.*
50. 8. as lilies by the rivers of *w.* and as branches
Dan. 3. 38. O all ye *w.* above the heavens

WATERY.

2 *Esd.* 4. 49. there passed by before me a *w.* cloud
Wisd. 19. 19. for earthly things were turned into *w.*

WAY.

2 *Esd.* 3. 7. thou gavest commandment to love thy *w.*
13. 45. through country there was a great *w.* to go
Tob. 1. 3. I have walked in the *w.* of truth and justice
Wisd. 5. 6. we erred from the *w.* of truth
7. we wearied ourselves in the *w.* of wickedness
14. 3. for thou hast made a *w.* in the sea
15. 12. say they, we must be getting every *w.*
18. 23. and parted the *w.* to the living
Eccl. 2. 6. order thy *w.* aright and trust in him
4. 18. then will she return the straight *w.*
5. 9. *w.* | 8. 15. *w.* | 16. 14. *w.* | 21. 6, 10, 16. *w.* | 32. 20, 21. *w.* | 37. 9, 15. *w.* | 51. 15. *w.*

WAYS.

1 *Esd.* 8. 52. to support them in all their *w.*
Tob. 4. 5. follow not the *w.* of unrighteousness
Wisd. 2. 16. he abstaineth from our *w.* as filthiness
6. 16. she sheweth herself to them in the *w.*
9. 18. for so the *w.* of them that lived on the earth
Eccl. 1. 5. her *w.* are everlasting commandments
2. 12, 15. *w.* | 4. 17. *w.* | 5. 2. *w.* | 6. 26. *w.* | 14. 21. *w.* | 16. 20. *w.* | 17. 15. *w.* | 33. 11. *w.* | 39. 24. *w.* | 48. 22. *w.*
1 *Mac.* 5. 4. they lay in wait for them in the *w.*

WAVES.

2 *Esd.* 13. 2. that it moved all the *w.* thereof
Wisd. 5. 10. as a ship that passeth over the *w.* trace not found, the path-way of the keel in the *w.*
14. 3. thou hast made a safe path in the *w.*
Eccl. 24. 6. in the *w.* of the sea, and in all the earth
2 *Mac.* 9. 8. though he might command the *w.*

WEAK.

1 *Esd.* 1. 30. carry me out of battle, for I am very *w.*
2 *Esd.* 2. 21. heal the broken and the *w.*
7. 42. therefore have they prayed for the *w.*
Wisd. 13. 18. for health he called on what is *w.*
14. 5. passing the rough sea in a *w.* vessel are saved
6. the hope of the world escaped in a *w.* vessel
Eccl. 25. 23. maketh *w.* hands and feeble knees
Bar. 6. 36. nor deliver the *w.* from the mighty
2 *Mac.* 9. 21. as for me I was *w.* or else I could

WEAKENED.

Jud. 16. 7. but Judith *w.* him with her beauty

WEAKNESS.

2 *Esd.* 8. 53. *w.* and the moth is hid from you

WEALTH.

Tob. 4. 21. thou hast much *w.* if thou fear God
Eccl. 30. 15. and a strong body above infinite *w.*

WEAPON.

Wisd. 5. 17. make the creature his *w.* for revenge

WEAPONS.

1 *Mac.* 5. 43. the brethren cast away their *w.* and fled
10. 6. and to provide *w.* that he might aid him
2 *Mac.* 3. 28. being unable to help himself with his *w.*
10. 23. having good success with his *w.* in all things
27. they took their *w.* and went on further
11. 7. Maccabeus himself first of all took *w.*

WEAR.

Esth. 14. 16. that I *w.* it not when I am private
Eccl. 6. 36. let thy foot *w.* the steps of his door
1 *Mac.* 11. 58. gave him leave to *w.* a golden buckle
14. 43. be clothed in purple, and *w.* a golden girdle
2 *Mac.* 4. 12. chief young men, made them *w.* a hat

WEARETH.

Eccl. 40. 4. from him that *w.* purple, and a crown

WEARIED.

Wisd. 5. 7. we *w.* ourselves in way of wickedness

WEARISOME.

Eccl. 13. 26. finding out is a *w.* labour of the mind

WEARY.

Jud. 13. 1. they went to their beds, they were all *w.*
Eccl. 16. 27. they neither labour nor are *w.*
43. 30. put forth all your strength, and be not *w.*
2 *Mac.* 12. 36. with Gorgias, fought long and were *w.*

WEATHER.

Eccl. 3. 15. thy sins melt, as ice in the fair warm *w.*

WEDDING.

2 *Esd.* 10. 1. was entered into his *w.* chamber, he died
Tob. 8. 19. and he kept the *w.* feast fourteen days

WEED.

Eccl. 40. 16. the *w.* growing upon every water

WEEKS.

2 *Mac.* 12. 31. the feast of the *w.* approaching

WEENING.

2 *Mac.* 5. 21. *w.* in his pride to make land navigable

WEEP.

2 *Esd.* 2. 27. others shall *w.* and be sorrowful
Tob. 3. 1. then I being grieved, did *w.* and prayed
Jud. 16. 17. they shall feel them and *w.* for ever
Eccl. 7. 34. fail not to be with them that *w.*
12. 16. he will *w.* but if he find opportunity
22. 11. *w.* for the fool, for he wants understanding
38. 17. *w.* bitterly, and make great moan

WEEPING.

1 *Esd.* 5. 63. came with *w.* and great crying
65. trumpets might not be heard for *w.* of people
8. 91. there was great *w.* among the multitude
Tob. 5. 22. then she made an end of *w.*
Eccl. 22. 11. make little *w.* for the dead, he is at rest

Bar. 4. 11. but sent them away with *w.* and mourning
Sus. 35. and she *w.* looked up towards heaven
2 *Mac.* 13. 12. besought the Lord with *w.* and fasting

WEIGH.

2 *Esd.* 4. 5. then said, *w.* me the weight of the fire
16. 76. let not your sins *w.* you down
Eccl. 28. 25. *w.* thy words in a balance, make a door

WEIGHED.

1 *Esd.* 8. 55. I *w.* them the gold and the silver
56. and when I had *w.* it, delivered to them silver
2 *Esd.* 4. 36. he hath *w.* the world in the balance
Eccl. 21. 25. but the words are *w.* in the balance

WEIGHETH.

Wisd. 9. 15. earthly tabernacle *w.* down the mind

WEIGHT.

1 *Esd.* 8. 64. all the *w.* of them was written up
2 *Esd.* 4. 5. then said he, weigh me the *w.* of the fire
Eccl. 16. 25. I will shew forth doctrine in *w.*
42. 7. deliver all things in number and *w.*

WEIGHTY.

Eccl. 7. 25. and so shall have performed a *w.* matter

WELL.

Eccl. 28. 19. *w.* is he that is defended from it
1 *Mac.* 8. 15. to the end they might be *w.* ordered
2 *Mac.* 11. 35. therewith we also are *w.* pleased
12. 43. doing therein very *w.* and honestly
15. 38. if I have done *w.* and as is fitting the story

WELFARE.

Wisd. 6. 24. multitude of the wise is *w.* of the world
2 *Mac.* 14. 14. calamities of the Jews to be their *w.*

WELLS.

2 *Esd.* 2. 32. for my *w.* run over, and my grace
Eccl. 48. 17. he digged the hard rock, and made *w.*

WENT.

Wisd. 5. 11. no sign where she *w.* is to be found
Eccl. 49. 9. for he directed them that *w.* right

WEPT.

Tob. 7. 6. Raguel leaped up, and kissed him, and *w.*
7. Tobit was blind, he was sorrowful and *w.*
8. Edna his wife and Sara his daughter *w.*
11. 9. I am content to die, and they *w.* both
14. and he *w.* and said, blessed art thou, O God
Sus. 33. her friends and all that saw her *w.*
2 *Mac.* 4. 37. therefore Antiochus was heartily sorry, and moved to pity, and *w.* for him that was dead

WESTWARD.

Jud. 2. 19. to cover all the face of the earth *w.*

WHALES.

Eccl. 43. 25. all kinds of beasts and *w.* created
Dan. 3. 57. O ye *w.* and all that move in the waters

WHEAT.

Jud. 3. 3. all our fields of *w.* lie before thy face
Eccl. 39. 26. iron and salt, flour of *w.* honey, milk

WHELP.

1 *Mac.* 3. 4. was like a lion's *w.* roaring for his prey

WHIP.

Eccl. 28. 17. the stroke of the *w.* maketh marks

WHIRLWIND.

Eccl. 43. 17. so doth the northern storm and the *w.*
48. 9. who was taken up in a *w.* of fire and chariot

WHISPER.

Eccl. 12. 18. he will clap his hands and *w.* much

WHISPERER.

Eccl. 5. 14. be not called a *w.* and lie not in wait
21. 28. a *w.* defileth his own soul, and is hated
28. 13. curse the *w.* and double-tongued

WHISTLING.

Wisd. 17. 18. whether it were a *w.* wind or noise
Dan. 3. 27. as it had been a moist *w.* wind

WHITE.

Bar. 6. 71. are like a *w.* thorn in an orchard
2 *Mac.* 11. 8. appeared before them one in *w.* cloth.

WHITENESS.

Tob. 2. 10. a *w.* came in mine eyes and I went
3. 17. to scale away the *w.* of Tobit's eyes
6. 8. to anoint a man that hath *w.* in his eyes
11. 8. he shall rub, and the *w.* shall fall away
13. and the *w.* pilled away from his eyes
Eccl. 43. 18. the eye marvelleth at beauty of the *w.*

WHOLE.

Tob. 12. 3. he made *w.* my wife, brought me money
Eccl. 38. 9. pray to the L. and he will make thee *w.*

WHORE.

Eccl. 23. 23. she hath played the *w.* in adultery

WHOREDOM.

Eccl. 26. 9. the *w.* of a woman may be known
41. 17. be ashamed of *w.* before father or mother

WHOREMONGER.

Eccl. 23. 17. all bread is sweet to *w.* will not leave off

WHORING.

Eccl. 46. 11. judges, whose heart went not a *w.*

WICKED.

1 *Esd.* 8. 86. is done to us for our *w.* works and sins
Tob. 4. 17. but give nothing to the *w.*
6. 14. I am afraid, for a *w.* spirit loveth her
Esth. 16. 15. whom this *w.* wretch hath delivered
Wisd. 3. 12. their wives are foolish, and children *w.*
Eccl. 10. 9. a more *w.* thing than a covetous man
14. 8. envious man hath a *w.* eye, he turns away
10. a *w.* eye envieth his bread, he is a niggard
16. 4. the kindred of *w.* shall speedily be desolate
19. 26. there is a *w.* man, that hangeth his head
20. 18. so the fall of the *w.* shall come speedily
21. 9. *w.* | 25. 16, 25. *w.* | 31. 13. *w.* | 39. 24, 30. *w.* | 40. 10. *w.* | 46. 7. *w.* murmuring
Bar. 1. 22. the imagination of his own *w.* heart
2. 33. return from their stiff neck and *w.* deeds
1 *Mac.* 1. 10. there came out of them *w.* root
11. went out of Israel *w.* men who persuaded
34. they put *w.* men, who fortified themselves
3. 6. *w.* shrunk for fear of him and were troubled
9. 23. *w.* began to put forth their heads in Israel
14. 14. every contemner of the law and *w.* person
2 *Mac.* 3. 11. not as that *w.* Simon had misinformed
4. 49. they of Tyrus moved with hatr. of that *w.* deed
6. 13, 21. *w.* | 7. 34. *w.* | 8. 4, 32. *w.* | 9. 9, 13. *w.* | 10. 10, 34. *w.* | 12. 23. *w.* | 13. 7. *w.* | 14. 27, 42. *w.* | 15. 5. his *w.* will not done

WICKEDLY.

Esth. 16. 7. ye search what hath been *w.* done of late
Eccl. 15. 20. he hath commanded no man to do *w.*
2 *Mac.* 4. 17. for it is not a light thing to do *w.*

WICKEDNESS.

Wisd. 2. 21. for their own *w.* hath blinded them
4. 6, 11. *w.* | 5. 7, 13. *w.* | 10. 7. *w.* | 11. 15. *w.* | 17. 11. *w.* | 19. 13. suffered according to their *w.*
Eccl. 3. 28. for the plant of *w.* hath taken root in him
12. 10. for like as iron rusteth, so is his *w.*
14. 7. and at the last he will declare his *w.*
19. 23. there is a *w.* and the same an abomination
25. 13. and any *w.* but the *w.* of a woman
19. all *w.* is but little to the *w.* of a woman
46. 20. to blot out the *w.* of the people
Bar. 2. 26. for the *w.* of the house of Israel
Sus. 52. art waxen old in *w.* ‖ 57. not abide your *w.*
1 *Mac.* 13. 46. deal not with us according to our *w.*
2 *Mac.* 3. 1. because of Onias his hatred of *w.*
8. 33. he received a reward meet for his *w.*

WIDOW.

Jud. 8. 4. so Judith was a *w.* in her house
9. 9. give it into mine hand, who am a *w.*
Wisd. 2. 10. let us not spare the *w.* nor reverence
Eccl. 35. 14. nor *w.* when she poureth out complaint
Bar. 6. 38. they can shew no mercy to the *w.*

WIDOWS.

Jud. 8. 5. she put on sackcloth, wore her *w.* apparel
Eccl. 35. 15. do not tears run down the *w.* cheeks?
2 *Mac.* 3. 10. was money laid up for the relief of *w.*
8. 28. given part of spoils to the maimed and *w.*

WIDOWERS.

2 *Esd.* 16. 44. and they that marry not as the *w.*

WIDOWHOOD.

2 *Esd.* 15. 49. I will send plagues, *w.* poverty
Jud. 10. 3. she put off the garments of her *w.*

WIFE.

1 *Esd.* 4. 20. leaveth his father, and cleaveth to *w.*
25. wherefore a man loveth his *w.* better than
Tob. 1. 20. any thing left me besides my *w.* Anna
2. 11. my *w.* Anna did take women's work
3. 15, 17, *w.* | 4. 12. *w.* | 6. 15. *w.* | 7. 13. *w.* | 8. 6, 21. *w.* | 9. 6. *w.* | 10. 10. *w.* | 11. 3. *w.*
Wisd. 13. 17. prays for his goods, *w.* and children
Eccl. 9. 1. be not jealous over the *w.* of thy bosom
15. 2. receive him as a *w.* married of a virgin
23. 22. thus shall it go also with the *w.* that leaveth
25. 8. that dwelleth with a *w.* of understanding
20. so is a *w.* full of words to a quiet man
26. 1. blessed is a man that hath a virtuous *w.*
7. an evil *w.* is a yoke shaken to and fro
13. the grace of a *w.* delights her husband
16. is beauty of a good *w.* in ordering her house
33. 19. give not thy *w.* power over thee
36. 24. he that gets a *w.* beginneth a possession
40. 23. but above both is a *w.* with her husband
41. 21. be ashamed to gaze on another man's *w.*
42. 6. sure keeping is good where an evil *w.* is
Mac. 14. 25. he prayed him also to take a *w.*

WILD.

Esth. 16. 24. but also most hateful to *w.* beasts
Wisd. 7. 20. and the furies of *w.* beasts
Eccl. 12. 13. or any such as come nigh *w.* beasts
13. 19. the *w.* ass is the lion's prey in the wilderness
39. 30. teeth of *w.* beasts and scorpions and sword

WILL.

1 *Esd.* 9. 9. do his *w.* and separate yourselves
Wisd. 9. 13. who can think what the *w.* of the L. is?
Eccl. 8. 15. for he will do according to his own *w.*
38. 32. they shall not dwell where they *w.*
39. 18. none can hinder when he *w.* save
43. 16. at his *w.* the south wind bloweth
1 *Mac.* 2. 22. *w.* | 3. 60. *w.* | 2 *Mac.* 11. 23, 30. *w.* | 14. 33. *w.* | 15. 5. not to have his *w.* done

WILFUL.

Eccl. 30. 8. a child left to himself will be *w.*

WILLED.

2 *Mac.* 6. 23. *w.* them straightways to send to grave

WILLING.

Wisd. 14. 19. for he *w.* to please one in authority
Eccl. 6. 35. be *w.* to hear every godly discourse
2 *Mac.* 11. 7. they went together with a *w.* mind

WILLINGLY.

2 *Mac.* 14. 24. would not *w.* have Judas out of sight

WILT.

Wisd. 12. 18. thou mayest use power when thou *w.*
2 *Mac.* 7. 16. thou hast power, thou dost what thou *w.*

WIND.

Wisd. 4. 4. they shall be shaken with the *w.*
5. 14. is like dust blown away with the *w.*
23. a mighty *w.* shall stand up against them
13. 2. but deemed either fire, or *w.* or swift air
17. 18. whether it were a whistling *w.* or noise
Eccl. 5. 9. winnow not with every *w.* and go not
22. 18. pales will never stand against the *w.*
31. 19. he fetched not his *w.* short upon his bed
Dan. 3. 27. as it had been a moist whistling *w.*

WINDS.

Dan. 3. 43. O all ye *w.* bless ye the Lord, praise him

WINDOW.

Tob. 3. 11. then she prayed toward the *w.* and said

WINDOWS.

Eccl. 14. 23. he that prieth in at her *w.* shall hearken

WINE.

Jud. 12. 20. and drank more *w.* than he had drunk
Esth. 14. 17. nor drunk the *w.* of the drink offerings
Wisd. 2. 7. let us fill ourselves with costly *w.*
Eccl. 9. 9. spend not thy money with her at *w.*
10. forsake not a friend, a new friend is as new *w.*
19. 2. *w.* and women will make men to fall
31. 25. shew not thy valiantness in *w.* for *w.* hath
26. so doth *w.* the hearts of proud by drunkenness
27. *w.* is as good as life to man if it be moderately
28. *w.* measurably drunk and in season bringeth
29. but *w.* drunken in excess makes bitterness
32. 5. a concert of music in a banquet of *w.*
6. so is the melody of music with pleasant *w.*
40. 20. *w.* and music rejoice the heart
49. 1. and as music at a banquet of *w.*

WING.

1 *Mac.* 9. 12. as for Bacchides he was in the right *w.*

WINGS.

2 *Esd.* 1. 30. gathereth her chickens under her *w.*
11. 1. an eagle which had twelve feathered *w.*
Wisd. 5. 11. air being beaten with the stroke of her *w.*
2 *Mac.* 15. 20. and the horsemen set in *w.*

WINK.

Eccl. 30. 11. give no liberty and *w.* not at his follies

WINNING.

1 *Mac.* 8. 3. for the *w.* the mines of silver and gold

WINNOW.

Eccl. 5. 9. *w.* not with every wind and go not into

WINTER.

Wisd. 16. 29. shall melt away as the *w.* hoar-frost
Dan. 3. 45. O ye *w.* and summer, bless ye the Lord

WIPED.

Eccl. 12. 11. thou shalt be to him as if thou hadst *w.* a looking-glass, his rust not altogether *w.* away

WISDOM.

1 *Esd.* 4. 59. from thee cometh *w.* and thine is glory
60. blessed art thou who hast given me *w.*
Esth. 13. 3. Aman that excelled in *w.* among us
Wisd. 1. 6. for *w.* is a loving spirit and will not acqu.
3. 11. whoso despiseth *w.* and nurture is miserable
15. and the root of *w.* shall never fall away
4. 9. but *w.* is the gray hair unto men
6. 9. that ye may learn *w.* and not fall away
12. *w.* is glorious and never fadeth away
15. to think therefore on her is perfection of *w.*
20, 21, 22, 23. *w.* | 7. 7, 12, 15, 16, 22, 24, 28, 30. *w.* | 8. 5, 17, 21. *w.* | 9. 4, 6, 17, 18. *w.* | 10. 4, 8, 9, 21. *w.* | 14. 5. *w.* | 17. 7. *w.*
Eccl. 1. 1. all *w.* cometh from the Lord, is with him
4. *w.* hath been created before all things
5. the word of God most High is the fountain of *w.*
6. to whom hath the root of *w.* been revealed
14. to fear the Lord is the beginning of *w.*
16. to fear the Lord is fulness of *w.* and fills men
19. *w.* raineth down skill and knowledge
24. and the lips of many shall declare his *w.*
25. parables of knowledge are in the treasures of *w.*
26. if thou desire *w.* keep the commandments
4. 11. *w.* exalteth her children, and layeth hold
23. and hide not thy *w.* in her beauty
24. for by speech *w.* shall be known and learning
6. 18. so shalt thou find *w.* till thine old age
22. for *w.* is according to her name, not manifest
37. he shall give thee *w.* at thy own desire
7. 5. boast not of thy *w.* before the king
14. 20. that doth meditate good things in *w.*
15. 10. praise shall be uttered in *w.* and L. prosper
18. for the *w.* of the Lord is great, he is mighty
18. 28. every man of understanding knows *w.*
19. 18. and *w.* obtaineth his love
20. the fear of the Lord is all *w.* and in all *w.* is the performance of the law and knowledge of him
22. the knowledge of wickedness is not *w.*
23. and there is a fool wanting in *w.*
24. is better than one that hath much *w.*
20. 30. *w.* that is hid and treasure that is hoarded
31. that hides folly, than a man that hideth his *w.*
21. 12. there is a *w.* which multiplieth bitterness
18. as is a house destroyed, so is *w.* to a fool
22. 6. stripes and correction of *w.* never out of time
24. 1. *w.* shall praise herself and shall glory in midst
25. he filleth all things with his *w.* as Phison
34. but laboured for all them that seek *w.*
25. 5. O how comely is the *w.* of old men!
10. O how great is he that findeth *w.*!
27. 11. the discourse of a godly man is with *w.*
32. 4. and shew not forth *w.* out of time
34. 8, 9. *w.* | 37. 20, 21. *w.* | 38. 24, 25. *w.* | 39. 1, 10. *w.* | 40. 20. *w.* | 41. 14. *w.* | 43. 33. *w.* | 44. 15. *w.* | 50. 27, 29. *w.* | 51. 13, 17. *w.*
Bar. 3. 9. hear, Israel, give ear to understand *w.*
14. learn where is *w.* where is strength
23. the Agarens that seek *w.* on earth none of these have known the ways of *w.* or her paths

WISE.

Wisd. 4. 17. for they shall see the end of the *w.*
6. 24. the multitude of the *w.* is the welfare of the world, and a *w.* king the upholding of the people
Eccl. 1. 6. who hath known her *w.* counsels?
8. there is one *w.* and greatly to be feared
3. 29. an attentive ear is the desire of a *w.* man
6. 34. and cleave unto him that is *w.*
7. 19. forego not a *w.* good woman, grace above gold
8. 8. despise not the discourse of the *w.* but acquaint
9. 14. guess at thy neighbour and consult with the *w.*
15. let thy talk be with the *w.* and communication
10. 1. a *w.* judge will instruct his people
18. 27. a *w.* man will fear in every thing
29. became also *w.* themselves, and poured forth
21. 12. he that is not *w.* will not be taught
15. if a skilful man hear a *w.* word, will commend
16. but grace shall be found in the lips of the *w.*
26. but the mouth of the *w.* is in their heart
26. 26. her husband, she shall be judged *w.* of all
33. 2. a *w.* man hateth not the law
37. 19, 22. *w.* | 38. 4, 24, 31. *w.* | 47. 12, 14. *w.*

WISELY.

Eccl. 13. 22. he spake *w.* and could have no place

WISE *man.*

Eccl. 21. 17. they inquire at the mouth of the *w. man*
20. but a *w. man* doth scarce smile a little
24. a *w. man* will be grieved with the disgrace
37. 23. a *w. man* instructeth his people
24. a *w. man* shall be filled with blessing
26. a *w. man* shall inherit glory among his people
40. 29. a *w. man* well-nurtured will beware thereof

WISEST.

1 *Esd.* 3. 9. shall judge that his sentence is the *w.*
4. 42. will give it thee because thou art found *w.*

WISHETH.

2 *Mac.* 9. 19. *w.* much joy, health and prosperity

WITCHCRAFTS.

Wisd. 12. 4. thou hatedst for doing odious works of *w.*

WITHDRAW.

Eccl. 13. 9. if be invited of a mighty man, *w.* thyself

WITHDREW.

Tob. 1. 19. to be put to death, I *w.* myself for fear

WITHERED.

Wisd. 2. 8. crown with rose-buds before they be *w.*

WITHHELD.

Eccl. 46. 7. and *w.* the people from sin and appeased

WITHSTAND.

Wisd. 11. 21. who may *w.* the power of thy arm?
Wisd. 12. 12. who shall say, what hast thou done? or who shall *w.* thy judgment, or shall accuse thee
Bar. 6. 56. they cannot *w.* any king or enemies
1 *Mac.* 5. 40. we shall not be able to *w.* him

WITHSTOOD.

Wisd. 10. 16. *w.* dreadful kings in wonders and signs
Eccl. 46. 7. in that they *w.* the congregation
2 *Mac.* 8. 5. he could not be *w.* by the heathen

WITNESS.

Jud. 7. 28. we take to *w.* against you heaven and earth
Wisd. 1. 6. for God is *w.* of his reins, and a beholder
Sus. 21. if thou wilt not, we will bear *w.* against thee
43. knowest they have borne false *w.* against me
49. for they have borne false *w.* against her
61. for Daniel had convicted them of false *w.*
1 *Mac.* 2. 56. Caleb for bearing *w.* before congregat.

WITS.

Eccl. 31. 20. he riseth early, and his *w.* are with him

WITTY.

Jud. 11. 23. thou art beautiful and *w.* in thy words
Wisd. 8. 19. for I was a *w.* child, and had good spirit

WIVES.

1 *Esd.* 5. 1. to go up with their *w.* sons and daughters
9. 12. let all them that have strange *w.* come at time
17. cause that held strange *w.* was brought to end
Tob. 4. 12. they all married *w.* of their kindred
Jud. 4. 12. he would not give their *w.* for a spoil
7. 27. nor our *w.* nor our children to die
Esth. 13. 6. shall with *w.* and children be destroyed
Wisd. 3. 12. their *w.* are foolish and children wicked

WOE.

Eccl. 2. 12. *w.* be to fearful hearts, and faint hands
41. 8. *w.* be to you ungodly who have forsaken law
1 *Mac.* 2. 7. *w.* is me, wherefore was I born to see

WOLF.

Eccl. 13. 17. what fellowship hath the *w.* with lamb?

WOMAN.

1 *Esd.* 4. 18. do they not love a *w.* who is comely?
9. 40. to the whole multitude from man to *w.*
Tob. 4. 12. take not a strange *w.* to wife who is not
Eccl. 7. 19. forego not wise good *w.* grace above gold
26. but give not thyself over to a light *w.*
9. 2. give not thy soul to a *w.* to set her foot on
4. use not the company of a *w.* that is a singer
8. turn thy eye from beautiful *w.* for many have been deceived by the beauty of a *w.*
10. 18. nor anger for them that are born of a *w.*
19. 11. a fool travails as a *w.* in labour of a child
25. 13. any wickedness but the wickedness of a *w.*
26. 2, 6, 8, 9, 14, 15, 22, 23, 24, 25, 26, 27. *w.* | 36. 21, 22. *w.* | 42. 14. a *w.* who brings shame
Sus. 46. I am clear from the blood of this *w.*

WOMANISH.

2 *Mac.* 7. 21. stirring up her *w.* thoughts, she said

WOMB.

Tob. 4. 4. she saw dangers when thou wast in her *w.*
Eccl. 1. 14. it was created with the faithful in the *w.*
40. 1. from the day they go out of their mother's *w.*
49. 7. was a prophet, sanctified in his mother's *w.*
50. 22. who exalteth our days from the *w.*
2 *Mac.* 7. 22. I cannot tell how you came into my *w.*
27. that bare thee nine months in my *w.*

WOMEN.

Tob. 2. 11. my wife Anna did take *w.* works to do
Eccl. 19. 2. wine and *w.* will make men fall away
28. 15. backbiting tongue hath cast out virtuous *w.*
42. 12. and sit not in the midst of *w.*
13. and from *w.* cometh wickedness
47. 19. thou didst bow down thy loins to *w.*

WON.

1 *Mac.* 1. 2. he *w.* many strong holds and slew kings

WONDERFUL.

Tob. 12. 22. confessed the great and *w.* works of God
Jud. 11. 8. reported thou art *w.* in feats of war
16. 13. Lord is *w.* in strength and invincible
Esth. 15. 14. for *w.* art thou, Lord, and full of grace
Wisd. 19. 5. that thy people might pass a *w.* way
Eccl. 11. 4. for the works of the Lord are *w.*
31. 9. *w.* things hath he done among his people
36. 8. and let them declare thy *w.* works
39. 20. and there is nothing *w.* before him
2 *Mac.* 15. 13. was of a *w.* and excellent majesty

WONDERFULLY.

Jud. 14. 19. and their minds were *w.* troubled
Eccl. 43. 8. the moon increasing *w.* in her changing

WONDERS.

Wisd. 8. 8. she foreseeth signs and *w.* and events
10. 16. she withstood dreadful kings in *w.* and signs
19. 8. seeing thy marvellous strange *w.*
Eccl. 45. 3. by his words he caused the *w.* to cease
19. he did *w.* upon them to consume them
48. 14. he did *w.* in his life and at his death
2 *Mac.* 15. 21. called on the Lord that worketh *w.*

WONDERED.

Jud. 10. 19. they *w.* at her beauty and admired

WONDROUS.

Eccl. 18. 6. as for the *w.* works of the Lord, there may nothing be taken from them, nor put to them
36. 6. that they may set forth thy *w.* deeds
43. 25. for therein be strange and *w.* works
48. 4. O Elias, thou wast honoured in thy *w.* works
50. 22. bless ye God, who only doth *w.* things

WONT.

Eccl. 37. 14. a man's mind is *w.* to tell him more

WOOD.

1 *Esd.* 6. 25. one row of new *w.* of that country
Wisd. 10. 4. in a piece of *w.* of small value
13. 13. being a crooked piece of *w.* full of knots
14. 1. calleth upon a piece of *w.* more rotten
5. men commit their lives to a small piece of *w.*
7. blessed is the *w.* whereby righteousness cometh
Eccl. 8. 3. and heap not *w.* upon his fire
Bar. 6. 30. set meat before the gods of gold and *w.*
39. their gods of *w.* which are overlaid with gold
50. for seeing they be but of *w.* and overlaid
1 *Mac.* 6. 37. there were strong towers of *w.*
9. 45. and that side, the marish likewise and *w.*
2 *Mac.* 1. 21. command. the priests to sprinkle the *w*

WORD.

Jud. 5. 5. let my lord now hear a *w.* from mouth
Wisd. 1. 11. no *w.* so secret shall go for nought
16. 26. thy *w.* preserveth them that trust in thee

Wisd. 18. 15. thy almighty w. leaped down from hea.
Eccl. 1. 5. the w. of God is the fountain of wisdom
2. 15. they that fear the Lord will not disobey his w.
5. 10. be stedfast, and let thy w. be the same
16. 28. and they shall never disobey his w.
18. 16. so is a w. better than a gift, 17.
19. 10, 11, 12. w. | 21. 15. w. | 23. 12, 13. w. | 29. 3. w. | 39. 31. w. | 41. 16. w. | 43. 26. w. | 48. ', 13. no w. could overcome him
Bar. 2. 1. therefore the Lord hath made good his w.
5. 5. gathered from west to east by w. of Holy One
1 Mac. 2. 55. Jesus for fulfilling the w. made a judge
2 Mac. 10. 13. accused and called traitor at every w.

WORDS.

Esth. 15. 8. the king comforted her with loving w.
16. 4. lifted up with glorious w. of lewd persons
Wisd. 1. 6. will not acquit a blasphemer of his w.
9. the sound of his w. shall come to the Lord
2. 17. let us see if his w. be true, and let us prove
6. 25. receive therefore instructions through my w.
Eccl. 1. 24. he will hide his w. for a time
13. 11. not equal in talk, believe not his many w.
12. but cruelly he will lay up thy w.
20. 8. he that useth many w. shall be abhorred
13. a wise man by his w. makes himself beloved
21. 17. they shall ponder his w. in their heart
25. the w. of such as have understanding
23. 15. the man accustomed to opprobrious w.
25. 20. so a wife full of w. to a quiet man
32. 4, 9. w. | 37. 20. w. | 39. 17. w. | 42. 15. w. | 45. 3. w. | 51. 5. w. delivered from lying w.
2 Mac. 7. 30. while she was yet speaking these w.

WORK.

1 Esd. 9. 11. this is not a w. of a day or two
Wisd. 8. 6. and if prudence w. who of all that are
13. 10. good for nothing, the w. of an ancient hand
12. after spending the refuse of his w. to dress meat
14. 20. multitude allured by the grace of his w.
Eccl. 7. 15. hate not laborious w. nor husbandry
9. 17. for the artificer, the w. shall be commended
11. 20. be conversant therein and wax old in thy w.
14. 19. every w. rotteth and consumeth away
15. 19. and he knoweth every w. of man
16. 14. make way for every w. of mercy
27. 10. so sin for them that w. iniquity
32. 23. in every good w. trust thine own soul
33. 24. bread, correction, and w. for a servant
28. set him to w. as is fit for him, put fetters
37. 11. nor with an hireling of finishing w.
38. 27, 28, 29, 31, 34. w. | 42. 16. w. | 43. 2. w. | 45. 10, 11, 12. w. | 51. 30. w.
Bar. 6. 51. that there is no w. of God in them
1 Mac. 2. 47. and the w. prospered in their hand

WORKS.

1 Esd. 6. 10. these w. are done with great speed
8. 86. is done to us for our wicked w. and great sins
Tob. 3. 2. O Lord, thou art just in all thy w.
11. let all thy w. praise thee for ever
12. 6. honourably to shew forth the w. of God
Wisd. 1. 12. destruction, with the w. of your hands
2. 4. no man shall have our w. in remembrance
3. 11. their hope vain, and their w. unprofitable
6. 3. shall try your w. and search out your counsels
8. 18. and in w. of her hands are infinite riches
9. 9, 12. w. | 11. 1. w. | 12. 4, 19. w. | 13. 1, 7, 10. w. | 14. 5. the w. of wisdom should be idle
Eccl. 5. 3. say not, who shall control me for my w.?
11. 4. w. wonderful, his w. among men are hidden
21. marvel not at the w. of sinners but trust in Ld.
16. 15. that his powerful w. might be known
21. for the most part of his w. are hid
22. who can declare the w. of his justice?
27. he garnished his w. for ever, they neither labour, nor are weary, nor cease from their w.
17. 9. that they might declare his w. with underst.
19. all thy w. are as the sun before him
31. 22. in all thy w. be quick, so no sickness come
33. 22. in all thy w. keep to thyself the pre-eminence
35. 19. to w. of men according to their devices
38. 6. he might be honoured in his marvellous w.
8. of his w. there is no end, from him is peace
39. 16, 19. w. | 42. 15, 21, 22. w. | 43. 4, 28, 32. w. | 47. 8. in his w. he praised the Holy One
Bar. 3. 18. whose w. are unsearchable, are vanished
6. 51. they are no gods, but the w. of men's hands
Dan. 3. 35. O all ye w. of the L. bless ye the Lord
1 Mac. 4. 51. finished all the w. they began to make
9. 54. he pulled down the w. of the prophets
10. 44. for the repairing the w. of the sanctuary
14. 42. their captain, to set them over their w.
2 Mac. 3. 36. he testified the w. of the great God

WORKER.

Esth. 16. 18. for he that was the w. of these things
Eccl. 14. 19. and the w. thereof shall go withal
2 Mac. 4. 1. as if he had been the w. of these evils

WORKERS.

Wisd. 15. 9. endeavoureth to do like the w. in brass
1 Mac. 3. 6. all the w. of iniquity were troubled

WORKETH.

Wisd. 8. 5. what is richer than wisdom that w. things?
Eccl. 7. 20. whereas thy servant w. truly
27. 22. he that winketh his eyes, w. evil
27. he that w. mischief, it shall fall on him
2 Mac. 15. 21. called on the Lord that w. wonders

WORKING.

Esth. 13. 5. this people w. all the mischief they can

WORKMAN.

Wisd. 8. 6. who is a more cunning w. than she?
14. 2. and the w. built it by his skill
Eccl. 45. 11. the work of the cunning w. stones
Bar. 6. 8. as for their tongue, it is polished by the w.
45. can be nothing else than w. will have them be

WORKMANSHIP.

Wisd. 7. 16. all wisdom also and knowledge of w.

WORK-MASTER.

Eccl. 38. 27. every w. that laboureth night and day

WORLD.

2 Esd. 2. 34. he is nigh that shall come in end of w.
3. 9. broughtest flood on those that dwelt in the w.
4. 24. we pass away out of the w. as grasshoppers
27. for this w. is full of unrighteousness
5. 24. of all lands of the w. hast chosen one pit
2 Esd. 14. 11. for the w. is divided into twelve parts
Wisd. 1. 14. the generations of the w. were healthful
2. 24. through envy of devil came death into the w.
6. 24. the multitude of wise is the welfare of the w.
7. 17. namely, to know how the w. was made
10. 1. preserved the first-formed father of the w.
8. he left behind them to the w. a memorial
11. 22. the w. before thee is as a little grain
13. 2. to be the gods which govern the w.
9. to know so much that they could aim at the w.
14. 14. for by vain-glory they entered into the w.
21. this was an occasion to deceive the w.
18. 24. for in the long garment was the whole w.
Eccl. 18. 3. who governeth the w. with the palm
24. 9. he created me from beginning before the w.
38. 34. but they will maintain the state of the w.
42. 18. and he beholdeth the signs of the w.
Bar. 6. 62. when God commands clouds to go over w.
Dan. 3. 9. and to the most wicked in all the w.
14. be kept under this day in all w. for our sins
22. thou art Lord, glorious over the whole w.
2 Mac. 2. 22. the temple renowned all the w. over
3. 12. the temple honoured over all the w.
7. 23. doubtless the Creator of the w. who formed
9. 17. and go through all the w. that was inhabited

WORMS.

Eccl. 10. 11. shall inherit creep. things, beasts and w.
19. 3. moths and w. shall have him to heritage
1 Mac. 2. 62. for his glory shall be dung and w.
2 Mac. 9. 9. w. rose out of the body of this wicked man

WORN.

Eccl. 11. 5. one never thought of, hath w. the crown

WORSE.

Wisd. 15. 18. being compared, some w. than others
Eccl. 19. 7. thou shalt fare never the w.
22. 11. the life of the fool is w. than death
39. 34. a man cannot say, this is w. than that
2 Mac. 7. 39. the king handled him w. than the rest
13. 9. to do far w. to Jews than had been done

WORSHIP.

Tob. 5. 13. as we went together to Jerusalem to w.
Jud. 3. 8. that all nations should w. Nabuchodonosor
8. 18. nor people which w. gods made with hands
Esth. 13. 14. nor will I w. any but thee, O God
Wisd. 15. 6. they that w. them, are lovers of evil
Eccl. 49. 3. he established the w. of God
50. 17. the people fell on their faces to w. their Lord
21. they bowed down to w. the second time
Bar. 6. 6. but say ye, O Lord, we must w. thee
39. if they that w. them shall be confounded
Dan. 3. 10. become a reproach to them that w. thee
68. O all ye that w. the Lord, praise him
Bel 4. the king said, why dost not thou w. Bel?
5. Daniel said, because I may not w. idols made
25. Daniel said, I will w. the Lord my God
27. Daniel said, lo, these are the gods you w.

WORSHIPPED.

Jud. 5. 8. and w. the God of heaven whom they knew
Wisd. 11. 15. they w. serpents void of reason
14. 16. images were w. by the command of kings
15. 18. they w. those beasts that are most hateful
Bel. 4. the king w. it, but Daniel w. his own God

WORSHIPPETH.

Wisd. 15. 17. he is better than the things he w.

WORSHIPPING.

Wisd. 14. 27. for the w. of idols not to be named

WORTH.

Wisd. 2. 11. feeble is found to be nothing w.
Eccl. 26. 14. nothing so much w. as a mind instructed
Bar. 6. 17. a vessel is nothing w. when it is broken
26. they declare to men that they be nothing w.

WORTHY.

Wisd. 1. 16. they are w. to take part with it
3. 5. God proved them, found them w. for himself
6. 16. she goeth, seeking such as are w. of her
9. 12. w. | 12, 7. w. | 15. 6. w. | 16. 9. w. | 17. 8. w. | 18. 4. were w. to be deprived of light
Eccl. 8. 5. remember we are all w. of punishment
11. 31. in things w. praise, will lay blame on thee
38. 17. weep bitterly and use lamentation as he is w.
1 Mac. 16. 23. his wars and w. deeds which he did
2 Mac. 4. 25. bringing nothing w. the high priesth.
7. 20. the mother was w. of honourable memory
15. 11. he told them a dream w. to be believed
21. he giveth victory to such as are w.

WORTHILY.

Eccl. 16. 20. no heart can think on these things w.

WOVEN.

Jud. 10. 21. Holofernes' bed w. with purple and gold

WOULD.

Wisd. 7. 15. God hath granted me to speak as I w.

WOULDEST.

2 Mac. 7. 2. what w. thou ask or learn of us?

WOUND.

Eccl. 22. 22. except for pride, or a treacherous w.
27. 21. as for a w. it may be bound up
2 Mac. 15. 16. with which thou shalt w. adversaries

WOUNDED.

Jud. 16. 12. and w. them as fugitives' children
Eccl. 25. 23. a wicked woman maketh a w. heart
2 Mac. 3. 16. it would have w. his heart
12. 22. and w. with the points of their own swords

WOUNDS.

Eccl. 27. 25. a deceitful stroke shall make w.
30. 7. maketh too much of his son shall bind his w.
31. 30. it diminisheth strength, and maketh w.

WRAPPED.

Eccl. 21. 9. the wicked is like two w. together
2 Mac. 5. 18. had they not been w. in many sins

WRATH.

Tob. 1. 18. Sennacherib in his w. killed many
Jud. 2. 7. I will go forth in my w. against them
Wisd. 5. 22. and hailstones full of w. shall be cast
10. 10. the righteous fled from his brother's w.
11. 9. w. | 18. 21, 23, 25. w. | 19. 1. w. on them
Eccl. 7. 16. remember that w. will not tarry long
16. 11. for mercy and w. are with him
18. 24. think on the w. that shall be at the end
25. 15. there is no w. above the w. of an enemy
27. 30. malice and w. even these are abomination
28. 10. and as a man's strength is, so is his w.
30. 24. envy and w. shorten the life, and carefulness
Eccl. 39. 23. so shall the heathen inherit his w.
28. appease the w. of him that made them
40. 5. w. and envy, trouble and unquietness
44. 17. Noah was found righteous in time of w.
45. 18. the congregation of Core with fury and w.
47. 20. thou broughtest w. on thy children
Bar. 1. 13. and his w. is not turned from us
2. 13. let thy w. turn from us, we are but few
20. for thou hast sent out thy w. upon us
4. 9. when she saw the w. of God coming upon you
1 Mac. 3. 8. and turning away w. from Israel
2 Mac. 8. 5. the w. of the Lord was turned to mercy

WRATHFUL.

Eccl. 45. 19. in his w. indignation were consumed

WRESTLED.

Eccl. 51. 19. my soul hath w. with her, I was exact

WRETCH.

2 Mac. 4. 13. profaneness of Jason that ungodly w.
15. 3. then the most ungracious w. demanded

WRETCHES.

2 Mac. 12. 23. was earnest in killing those wicked w.

WRITE.

Tob. 7. 14. and did w. in an instrument of covenants
Bar. 2. 28. thou didst command him to w. thy law

WRITHE.

Eccl. 27. 23. but at the last he will w. his mouth

WRITING.

1 Esd. 2. 2. through all his kingdom, and also by w.
6. 12. we might give knowledge to thee by w. we required the names in w. of the principal men
Esth. 13. 6. that are signified in w. to you by Aman
Eccl. 42. 7. and put all in w. that thou givest out
45. 11. with a w. engraved for a memorial
2 Mac. 2. 4. it was also contained in the same w.

WRITINGS.

1 Esd. 3. 13. took their w. and delivered them to him
15. and the w. were read before them
2 Mac. 2. 13. the same things were reported in the w.

WRITTEN.

1 Esd. 1. 33. these things are w. in the book of stories
2. 22. thou shalt find in the chronicles what is w.
8. 64. the weight of them was w. that same hour
Eccl. 50. 27. Jesus the son of Sirach w. in this book
1 Mac. 9. 22. his acts and greatness, they are not w.
14. 23. we have w. a copy thereof to Simon
15. 15. letters wherein were w. these things

WRONG.

Eccl. 4. 19. but if he go w. she will forsake him
10. 6. bear not hatred to thy neighbour for every w.
13. 3. the rich man hath done w. yet threateneth
21. 4. to terrify and do w. will waste riches
1 Mac. 7. 14. for, said they, he will do us no w.
2 Mac. 1. 28. punish them that with pride do us w.
3. 12. was impossible such w. should be done them
10. 12. for the w. that had been done to them

WRONGFULLY.

1 Mac. 2. 37. testify that you put us to death w.
15. 33. which our enemies had w. in possession
2 Mac. 8. 16. the heathen who came w. against them

WROTE.

1 Esd. 4. 47. and w. letters for him to the treasurers
49. he w. for all the Jews that went to Jewry
6. 17. Cyrus the king w. to build up this house
Tob. 13. 1. then Tobit w. a prayer of rejoicing
Jud. 4. 6. Joacim w. to them that dwelt in Bethulia
1 Mac. 10. 65. and w. him among his chief friends
13. 35. to him king Demetrius w. after this manner
14. 18. they w. to him in tables of brass to renew

WROTH.

Bel 8. so the king was w. and called for his priests

WROUGHT.

Tob. 4. 14. the wages of any man that hath w. for thee
Jud. 9. 5. for thou hast w. not only those things
Esth. 10. 9. God hath w. signs and great wonders
Wisd. 3. 14. who with his hands w. no iniquity
13. 11. a carpenter that hath w. it handsomely
Eccl. 44. 2. the Lord hath w. great glory by them
Bar. 3. 18. for they w. in silver and were careful
1 Mac. 9. 23. there rose up all such as w. iniquity

Y.

YEAR.

1 Esd. 5. 57. in second y. after they come to Jewry
Eccl. 33. 7. light of every day of the y. is of the sun
37. 11. nor with a hireling for a y. of finishing
50. 8. as the flower of roses in the spring of the y.
Sus. 5. the same y. were appointed two ancients
1 Mac. 3. 28. and gave his soldiers pay for a y.
37. the king departed from Antioch the 147th y.
6. 49. no victuals, it being a y. of rest to the land
8. 16. their government to one man every y.
9. 54. in the 153d y. in the second month
10. 40. I give every y. 15,000 shekels of silver
42. silver they took out of the accounts y. by y.
11. 19. Demetrius reigned in the 167th y.
13. 42. in the first y. of Simon the high priest
51. entered into it in 171st y. with thanksgiving
52. that that day be kept every y. with gladness
14. 27. being the third y. of Simon the high priest
2 Mac. 10. 8. that every y. those days should be kept

YEARS.

1 Esd. 6. 14. this house, it was builded many y. ago
Wisd. 4. 8. nor that is measured by number of y.
16. the many y. and old age of the unrighteous
Eccl. 26. 2. he shall fulfil the y. of his life in peace
1 Mac. 1. 7. Alexander reigned twelve y. and died
9. so did their sons after them many y.
2 Mac. 1. 20. after many y. when it pleased God
4. 40. a man far gone in y. and no less in folly
6. 23. as became the excellency of his ancient y.
7. 27. gave thee suck three y. and nourished thee

YEARLY.

1 Mac. 7. 49. they ordained to keep y. this day
11. 34. the payments the king received of them y.

YESTERDAY.

Eccl. 38. 22. y. for me, and to day for thee

YIELD.

Jud. 2. 10. if they will y. themselves to thee
1 Mac. 10. 32. I y. up my authority over it
2 Mac. 8. 8. wrote to y. more aid to the king's affairs

2 *Mac.* 9. 27. will favourably and graciously *y.* to your desires

YOKE.

Eccl. 28. 20. for the *y.* thereof is *y.* of iron and bands
33. 26. a *y.* and a collar do bow the neck
51. 26. put your neck under the *y.* let your soul
1 *Mac.* 8. 18. that they would take the *y.* from them
13. 41. the *y.* of the heathen was taken away

YOUNG.

1 *Esd.* 1. 53. who slew their *y.* men with the sword
3. 4. the three *y.* men that were of the guard
4. 58. now when this *y.* man was gone forth
8. 50. I vowed a fast to the *y.* men before our Lord
2 *Esd.* 1. 28. have prayed you as a nurse her *y.* babes
Tob. 1. 4. when I was in my own country being but *y.*
6. 2. when the *y.* man went down to wash himself
3. the *y.* man laid hold of the fish and drew it
5. the *y.* man did as the angel commanded him
Jud. 2. 27. smote all their *y.* men with edge of sword
Wisd. 9. 5. and too *y.* for understanding of judgment
Eccl. 30. 12. bow down his neck while he is *y.*
32. 7. speak, *y.* man, if there be need of thee
42. 9. the care of her taketh away sleep, when *y.*
47. 4. slew he not a giant when he was yet but *y.*?
50. 12. he himself stood as a *y.* cedar in Libanus
51. 13. when I was *y.* or ever I went abroad
Bar. 3. 20. *y.* men have seen light and dwelt on earth
Sus. 21. will witness that a *y.* man was with thee
37. a *y.* man who was there hid, came unto her
40. we asked who the *y.* man was, would not tell
45. the Lord raised up the holy spirit of a *y.* youth
1 *Mac.* 2. 9. her *y.* men with the sword of the enemy
6. 17. whom he had brought up being *y.* to reign
11. 39. brought up Antiochus *y.* son of Alexander
40. to deliver him this *y.* Antiochus to reign
54. with him the *y.* child Antiochus who reigned
57. at that time *y.* Antiochus wrote to Jonathan
13. 31. Tryphon dealt deceitfully with *y.* Antiochus
14. 9. *y.* men put on glorious and warlike apparel
2 *Mac.* 3. 33. the same *y.* men, in the same clothing
4. 12. brought the chief *y.* men under his subjection
5. 13. thus there was killing of *y.* and old
6. 24. many *y.* persons might think that Eleazar
28. leave a notable example to such as be *y.*
31. not only to *y.* men but to all his nation
7. 12. the king marvelled at the *y.* man's courage
25. when the *y.* man would in no case hearken
30. the *y.* man said, whom wait ye for?
12. 27. strong *y.* men kept the walls and defended
13. 15. with the most valiant and choice *y.* men

YOUNGER.

2 *Mac.* 5. 24. to sell the women and the *y.* sort

YOUNGEST.

2 *Mac.* 7. 24. whilst the *y.* was yet alive did exhort

YOUTH.

Jud. 6. 16. all their *y.* ran together and women
Eccl. 6. 18. my son, gather instruction from thy *y.* up
30. 11. give him no liberty in his *y.* and wink not
51. 15. from my *y.* up sought I after her
Sus. 45. the Lord raised the holy spirit of a young *y.*
1 *Mac.* 1. 6. had been brought up with him from his *y.*
2. 66. Judas hath been mighty and strong from his *y.*
16. 2. from our *y.* fought against the enemies of Israel

Z.

ZABDEUS.

1 *Esd.* 9. 21. sons of Emmer, Ananias, Z. and Eanes

ZACHARIAS.

1 *Esd.* 1. 8. Helkias, Z. and Seclus the governors
15. the holy singers, Asaph, Z. and Jeduthun
5. 8. Nehemias, and Z. Reesaias, Enenius
7. 3. when Aggeus and Z. the prophets prophesied
8. 37. Z. the son of Bebai, with him 28 men
1 *Mac.* 5. 18. so he left Joseph the son of Z. 56.

ZAMBRI.

1 *Mac.* 2. 26. like as Phinehas did to Z. son of Salom

ZEDECHIAS.

1 *Esd.* 1. 46. and made Z. king of Judea and Jerusa

ZEAL.

Eccl. 48. 2. by his *z.* he diminished their number
1 *Mac.* 2. 24. was inflamed with *z.* and reins trembled

ZEALOUS.

1 *Mac.* 2. 27. whosoever is *z.* of the law of God
54. Phinehas our father, being *z.* and fervent
58. Elias for being *z.* and fervent for the law

ZEALOUSLY.

1 *Mac.* 2. 26. thus dealt he *z.* for the law of God

ZOROBABEL.

1 *Esd.* 5. 8. who came with Z. with Jesus, Nehemias
56. began Z. the son of Salathiel and Jesus
70. then Z. and Jesus, and the chief of the families
6. 2. then stood up Z. the son of Salathiel and Jesus
18. delivered to Z. and Sanabassarus the ruler
27. but suffer Z. servant of the Lord and governor
29. to Z. the governor, for bullocks rams and lambs

A

COMPENDIUM OF THE HOLY BIBLE:

WHEREIN

THE CONTENTS OF EACH CHAPTER ARE GIVEN:

DESIGNED FOR MAKING THE READING AND STUDY OF THE HOLY SCRIPTURES MORE EASY, PARTICULARLY TO THOSE THAT ARE IN THEIR YOUNGER YEARS.

TO WHICH IS PREFIXED,

A BRIEF ACCOUNT OF THE HISTORY AND EXCELLENCY OF THE SCRIPTURES

BY ALEXANDER CRUDEN, A. M.

AUTHOR OF THE CONCORDANCE TO THE BIBLE.

JOHN V. 39. SEARCH THE SCRIPTURES.

ADVERTISEMENT.

The chief design of publishing this COMPENDIUM *is to give the reader a Summary View of the Holy Scriptures, which are not only above all commendation, and far excelling all other books in the world, but also contain a most entertaining history of the most remarkable events that can be contained in any history whatsoever.*

Any disregard shown to this inspired Book by any persons that profess the Christian religion, is greatly to be lamented: but surely those that are true Christians, and have experienced the grace of God in truth, will esteem it as their only treasure, as being the rule of faith and practice, and a revelation of the grace of God to fallen sinful creatures, and containing the charter for their hopes of eternal salvation through Jesus Christ.

I pray, reader, that the Blessed Spirit who indited the Scriptures, may make gracious impressions upon your heart in reading and searching them, that thereby you may be made wise unto salvation, through faith which is in Christ Jesus. Amen.

OF THE HOLY SCRIPTURES.

THE word SCRIPTURE signifies Writing, and generally stands for the sacred books of the Old and New Testament, written by holy men, as they were inspired, instructed, and enabled by the Holy Ghost. They are called *The Scriptures*, by way of eminency and distinction, because they far excel all other writings, 2 Tim. iii. 16. "All Scripture is given by inspiration of God, and is profitable for doctrine," to declare and confirm the truth; "for reproof," to convince of sin and confute errors; "for correction," to reform the life; "and for instruction in righteousness;" that is, to teach us to make a further progress in the way to holiness and happiness in heaven; or to instruct in the true righteousness of Jesus Christ, in which we may appear with comfort before God.

The Scriptures are often called, *The Bible*, that is, *The Book*, by way of eminency, as being the best book in the world, and far excelling all other books. For the Scriptures are a revelation from God, and contain his whole will necessary to be known for our salvation: and they will be held in the highest esteem, and be read and studied by all the true members of the church of God, whose faith, hope, and comfort, are taken from these divine Oracles. No book but this brings such glory to God, or hath such an efficacy in converting the soul. Psalm xix. 7.

The holy Scripture is divided into two books, which are commonly called, The Old and New Testament, or The Old and New Covenant. The Old Testament was the old dispensation of the covenant of grace by types and sacrifices, which represented the coming of the Messiah, who was the promised seed of the woman, and afterwards foretold to be of the family of Abraham, and of the tribe of Judah, and of the seed of David.

The New Testament, or the Gospel, is the new dispensation of the covenant of grace, which fully shews the promised Messiah to be come, and to have published his gospel, to have died, and to have risen again, and to have ascended up into heaven, to plead that his atonement may be accepted as a propitiation for all true believers.

There is no history in the world so ancient as the Bible, nor is there any that gives so early an account of things. The OLD TESTAMENT begins at the creation of the world, and acquaints us that Adam and Eve were the first man and woman God made, and that he created them both in his own likeness, in a holy and happy state, which is called, The state of innocence. It informs us of their sin against God in eating the forbidden fruit, and of their being driven out of Paradise, and of the miserable state that sin brought man into, he having broken covenant with God, and being exposed to that dreadful threatening, "In the day thou eatest thereof thou shalt surely die."

The Scripture informs us, that after the fall or sin of Adam, God was pleased to give him a gracious promise of a Messiah or Redeemer, "That the seed of the woman should bruise the serpent's head," that is, that Jesus Christ, who was to assume the human nature in the fulness of time, should destroy the power and wicked works of the devil.

The religion of man, after the fall, was all the duties of the light of nature, which were required before: and besides these he was now called to repentance, faith or trust in the mercy of God, and expectation of the promised Saviour, and offering of sacrifices. This is called the Adamitical dispensation, and it reached to Noah's flood, which was about 1656 years after the creation of the world.

The Scripture tells us, that mankind had provoked God by their sins, which were exceeding great, and that the world was destroyed by a flood for their multiplied iniquities. Noah was saved in an ark, or great ship, or vessel, which God taught him to build; and all his family were with him, and some living creatures of every kind.

The religion of Noah was the same with that of Adam after his fall, with some few additions. The offering of sacrifices was to be continued. Flesh was given to man for food, as herbs were before. Blood was forbidden to be eaten, the blood of man was expressly forbidden to be shed, and murder was to be punished with death, Gen. ix. 2, 3, 4, 5, 6. And this was the Noahical dispensation of the covenant of grace.

After the flood, mankind did not freely divide themselves into several nations; but being all of one language, they built a chief city with a tower, that all men might be joined in one nation or kingdom. But God scattered them abroad into different nations, by making them speak different languages; and then they ceased to build their tower, which was called Babel or Confusion. It is supposed that the true religion was chiefly preserved in the family of Shem, for God is called "the Lord God of Shem," Gen. ix. 26.

The most religious and most famous man o Shem's posterity in these early ages, was Abraham the son of Terah, of the posterity of Eber. He left his own native country, to go wheresoever God pleased. He came first from Chaldea, and then to Haran, and by the command of God went to dwell among strangers in the land of Canaan.

Sodom became very wicked, and it was destroyed by fire and brimstone from heaven, together with Gomorrah and other cities, because of the abominable wickedness of their inhabitants. Abraham pleaded with God to spare Sodom, and he would have done it, had there been ten righteous men in all the city. Lot was grieved for the wicked conversation of Sodom, and he and his two daughters were saved. But his wife looking back, and hankering after Sodom, was struck dead immediately, and she stood like a pillar of salt.

Abraham had two sons, Ishmael by Hagar, and Isaac by Sarah his wife. Isaac was born, according to the promise of God, when they were both grown old. Isaac feared the God of his father Abraham; and his father sent afar, and took a wife for him, even Rebecca, out of his own family in Mesopotamia, because he was unwilling he should marry among the wicked Canaanites, whom God had doomed to destruction. Abraham's death was in the year of the world 2123.

Isaac had by Rebecca two sons, Esau and Jacob Esau sold his birthright for a mess of pottage when he was faint with hunting: and Jacob, by his mother's contrivance, obtained his father's blessing. Jacob was called Israel, because he prayed and prevailed with God for a blessing. Jacob had twelve sons, and the most famous of them in sacred history were Levi, Judah, and Joseph. The priesthood in the following times was committed to Levi's family. The kingdom and government in future ages were promised chiefly to Judah's family.

Joseph's brethren hated him, and he was sold for a slave into Egypt, where he became a ruler of the land. His brethren envied him, because his father loved him and made him a coat of many colours, and because Joseph dreamed that they should bow down to him. By a false accusation, Joseph was cast into prison, and interpreted the dreams of some of his fellow-prisoners; and when the interpretation proved true, then he was sent for to court, to interpret the king's dream about the seven years of plenty and seven years of famine.

In the famine, Joseph's brethren came to buy corn in Egypt, and bowed down to him according to his dreams; but he treated them roughly at first, as a great lord and a stranger, till their conscience smote them for their former cruelty to him: but afterwards he made himself known to them with much affection and tenderness. And he manifested his forgiveness of them; for he sent for his father, and bid his children bring all their families into Egypt, and he maintained them all during the famine. Jacob and Joseph died in Egypt; but according to their desire their bodies were carried up and buried in the land of Canaan, in faith of the promise that their seed should possess that land.

The Israelites were afterwards made slaves in Egypt, and a new king, who knew not Joseph, sorely oppressed them, and endeavoured to destroy them: but God heard their cry, and delivered them by the hand of Moses and Aaron. Upon Pharaoh's refusal to let the people of Israel go, they brought ten plagues upon the king and upon all the land, by the authority and power of God.

At last Pharaoh released the Israelites; and the number of them that went out of Egypt were six hundred thousand men, besides children, and all went on foot. When they were in distress, with the Red sea before them, and Pharaoh's army behind them, they cried unto God; whereon Moses bid them "stand still, and see the salvation of the Lord." Then at the command of God, Moses struck the sea with his rod, and divided the waters asunder; and the children of Israel went through upon dry land. And the Egyptians following, the waters returned upon them, and they were drowned. This was about the year of the world 2453.

The Israelites went wheresoever God guided them by the pillar of cloud and the pillar of fire. At every new difficulty, when they wanted meat or water, or met with enemies, they fell a murmuring against God and Moses: and they wandered forty years in the wilderness for their sins, before they came to the place God promised them.

While in the wilderness, about three months after their coming out of Egypt, God wrote with his own hand the ten commandments in two tables of stone, and gave them to Moses. The four first commandments contained their duty to God, and the six last their duty towards men. These ten commandments are called the Moral Law, and relate to their behaviour as men: and almost every thing contained in them is taught by the light of nature, and obliges all mankind. But the great end of the Jewish Ceremonies was to be emblems or types of Christ and his gospel.

The Scripture gives an account of God's bringing the Israelites into the land of Canaan, under the ministration of Joshua, and of their government by Judges several hundred years; and after that there is a narrative of their first four kings, namely, Saul, David, Solomon, and Rehoboam. In Rehoboam's days the nation was divided into two kingdoms, which were called the kingdom of Israel and the kingdom of Judah. There are also particular records of the government of these two distinct kingdoms, under a long succession of their own kings, till they were both carried into captivity by the kings of Assyria.

After this, the sacred history relates the return of many of them into their own land, and the rebuilding of the city of Jerusalem and the temple of God, and the settlement of the affairs of church and state by Ezra and Nehemiah, which is the end of the historical part of the Old Testament.

There is also a large and particular narrative of the lives or transactions of some extraordinary persons, several of which are much interwoven with the series of the history. But there are others which seem to stand separate and distinct, such as the affairs relating to *Job*, a rich man in the east; *Jonah*, a prophet in Israel; and *Esther*, the queen of Persia.

We have an account of the several prophets and messengers which were sent from God, on special occasions to reveal his mind and will to men. We have the writings of sixteen prophets, that is, of four greater and twelve lesser prophets. The four great prophets are Isaiah, Jeremiah, Ezekiel, and Daniel. The twelve lesser prophets are, Hosea, Joel, Amos, Obadiah, Jonah, Micah, Nahum, Habakkuk, Zephaniah, Haggai, Zechariah, and Malachi the last prophet. Malachi prophesied about 409 years before the coming of Christ, who assumed our nature about 4000 years after the creation of the world. God himself and his prophets, throughout all ages, foretold his coming as some great Deliverer, as the Messiah or anointed of God.

THE chief subjects of the history of the NEW TESTAMENT are, our Lord Jesus Christ, the great Redeemer and glorious Saviour; John the Baptist, who was his forerunner; and the Apostles, who were his followers.

The great Messiah was born at Bethlehem of the tribe of Judah, according to the predictions and prophecies of him in the Old Testament. John the Baptist was his forerunner, who preached the doctrine of repentance and forgiveness of sins, and directed the people to Jesus Christ the Messiah and Saviour, "the Lamb of God, who taketh away the sin of the world."

Jesus Christ, the eternal Son of God, veiled his divine glory, became man, and was born of Mary, who was a virgin, according to the prophecy of Isaiah. Jesus, being about thirty years of age, began his ministry, and appeared with the marks of a divine commission, and the characters of the Messiah upon him. He healed the sick, he raised the dead, he preached the glad tidings of forgiveness of sin, and of salvation to the poor, and received several testimonies from heaven. After he had preached his gospel about three years and a half, he was betrayed by Judas, and suffered the death of the cross, and rose again according to the Scriptures.

Jesus, after his resurrection, appeared to his apostles, continued on earth about forty days, and gave further instructions in the great things of the gospel. He appointed his disciples to meet him in Galilee; he told them that all power in heaven and in earth was given into his hands; he gave them their commission to preach the gospel to all nations; and promised his presence with them, and a power to work miracles for the vindication of their doctrine. He commanded his apostles to tarry at Jerusalem till the promised Spirit should fall upon them. And on the day of Pentecost which was ten days after the ascension of Christ the Spirit of God was sent down upon them; and upon their preaching of the resurrection and exaltation of Christ, three thousand souls believed, and were added to the disciples of Christ, and baptized on that day.

This was the proper beginning of the Christian or Gospel dispensation, the kingdom of Christ being set up in the world in its glory at the pouring down of the Spirit, after his resurrection, and his exaltation to the government of the world and the church. The dispensation, during the life of Christ, was a medium between the Jewish and Christian dispensations.

The apostles, after Christ's ascension, published the gospel he had preached, namely, pardon of sin and everlasting life to those that repent and believe in him, whether Jews or Gentiles, and pronounced the punishments of hell upon the impenitent and unbelieving. The apostles, in their epistles to the Christian churches, often mention the great article of the gospel, the redemption by Christ's death, and the atonement made for sin by his sufferings, and it shines every where through the epistles of St. Paul.

In the gospels, as well as epistles, faith, or believing in Jesus Christ, is required, as the way and method of being a partaker of the blessings of salvation; for without faith there is no salvation, according to the gospel. This faith unites the soul to Christ, and makes the believer a member of Christ's mystical body. Faith is wrought in the soul by the Spirit of God, who convinces him of the evil and danger of sin, which makes him obnoxious to the law of God; and seeing no other way of help, he applies to Christ to be his prophet, priest, and king; receives him as proposed in the gospel, and trusts and relies upon him and his righteousness for pardon and salvation. And where this faith is, it is attended with repentance and holiness, which give a meetness for heaven; and a true faith in Jesus Christ and his righteousness may be said to entitle the believer to the heavenly kingdom. "If any man be in Christ, he is a new creature." Justification and sanctification are blessings connected together, and graciously bestowed upon one and the same person.

The New Testament is the last dispensation of the Covenant of Grace: and it may be called New, because it is never to wax old or be abolished; and this is evident, because it concludes with a promise of Christ's second coming at the end of the world. Rev. xxii. 20. "Surely I come quickly: Amen. Even so, come, Lord Jesus. The grace of our Lord Jesus Christ be with you all." Amen.

A. C.

LONDON,
December 18, 1749.

THE

CONTENTS

OF ALL

THE HOLY BIBLE.

GENESIS.

I THE creation of heaven and earth, 5 of the light, 6. of the firmament, 9 of the earth separated from the waters, 11 and made fruitful; 14 of the sun, moon, and stars; 20 of fish and fowl; 24 of beasts and cattle; 26 of man in the image of God. 29 Also the appointment of food.

II. 1 The first sabbath. 4 The manner of the creation. 8 The planting of the garden of Eden, 10 and the river thereof. 17 The tree of knowledge only forbidden. 19, 20 The naming of the creatures. 21 The making of woman, and institution of marriage.

III. 1 The serpent deceiveth Eve. 6 Man's shameful fall. 9 God arraigns them. 14 The serpent is cursed. 15 The promised Seed. 16 The punishment of mankind. 21. Their first clothing. 22 Their casting out of paradise.

IV. 1 The birth, trade, and religion of Cain and Abel. 8 The murder of Abel. 9 The curse of Cain. 17. Enoch the first city. 19 Lamech and his two wives. 25 The birth of Seth, 26 and Enos.

V. 1 The genealogy, age, and death of the patriarchs from Adam to Noah. 24 The godliness and translation of Enoch.

VI. 1 The wickedness of the world, which provoked God's wrath, and caused the flood. 8 Noah finds grace. 13 The order, form, and end of the ark.

VII. 1 Noah, with his family, and the living creatures, enter into the ark. 17 The beginning, increase, and continuance of the flood.

VIII. 1 The waters assuage. 4 The ark resteth on Ararat. 7 The raven and the dove. 15 Noah, being commanded, 18 goeth forth of the ark. 20 He buildeth an altar, and offereth sacrifice, 21 which God accepteth, and promiseth to curse the earth no more.

IX. 1 God blesseth Noah. 4 Blood and murder are forbidden. 9 God's covenant, 13 signified by the rainbow. 18 Noah replenishes the world, 20 plants a vineyard, 21 is drunken, and mocked of his son: 25 Curseth Canaan, 26 blesseth Shem, 27 prayeth for Japhet, 28 and dieth.

X. 1 The generations of Noah. 2 The sons of Japhet, 6 the sons of Ham. 8 Nimrod the first monarch. 21 The sons of Shem.

XI. 1 One language in the world. 3 The building of Babel. 5 The confusion of tongues. 10 The generations of Shem. 27 The generations of Terah the father of Abram. 31 Terah goeth from Ur to Haran.

XII. 1 God calls Abram, and blesses him with a promise of Christ. 4 He departs with Lot from Haran. 6 He travels through Canaan, 7 which is promised him in a vision. 10 He is driven by a famine into Egypt. 11 Fear makes him feign his wife to be his sister. 14 Pharaoh having taken her from him, by plagues is compelled to restore her.

XIII. 1 Abram and Lot return out of Egypt. 7 By disagreement they part asunder. 10 Lot goes to wicked Sodom. 14 God renews the promise to Abram. 18 He removes to Hebron, and there builds an altar.

XIV. 1 The battle of four kings against five. 11 Lot is taken prisoner. 14 Abram rescues him. 18 Melchisedek blesses Abram. 20 Abram gives him tithe. 22 The rest of the spoil, his partners having had their portions, he restores to the king of Sodom.

XV. 1 God encourages Abram. 2 Abram complains for want of an heir. 4 God promises him a son, and a multiplying of his seed. 6 Abram is justified by faith. 7 Canaan is promised again, and confirmed by a sign, 12 and a vision.

XVI. 1 Sarai, being barren, gives Hagar to Abram. 4 Hagar being afflicted for despising her mistress, runneth away. 7 An angel sends her back to submit herself, 11 and tells her of her child. 15 Ishmael is born.

XVII. 1 God renews the covenant. 5 Abram's name is changed, in token of a greater blessing. 10 Circumcision is instituted. 15 Sarai's name is changed, and she blessed. 17 Isaac is promised. 23 Abraham and Ishmael are circumcised.

XVIII. 1 Abraham entertains three angels. 9 Sarah is reproved for laughing at the strange promise. 17 The destruction of Sodom is revealed to Abraham. 23 Abraham makes intercession for the men thereof.

XIX. 1 Lot entertains two angels. 4 The vicious Sodomites are stricken with blindness. 12 Lot is sent for safety into the mountains. 18 He obtains leave to go to Zoar. 24 Sodom and Gomorrah are destroyed. 26 Lot's wife is a pillar of salt. 30 Lot dwells in a cave. 31 The incestuous original of Moab and Ammon.

XX. 1 Abraham sojourns at Gerar, 2 denies his wife, and loses her. 3 Abimelech is reproved for her in a dream. 9 He rebukes Abraham, 14 restoreth Sarah, 16 and reproves her. 17 He is healed by Abraham's prayer.

XXI. 1 Isaac is born. 4 He is circumcised. 6 Sarah's joy. 9 Hagar and Ishmael are cast forth. 15 Hagar in distress. 17 The angel comforts her. 22 Abimelech's covenant with Abraham at Beersheba.

XXII. 1 Abraham is tempted to offer Isaac. 3 He gives proof of his faith and obedience. 11 The angel stayeth him. 13 Isaac is exchanged with a ram. 14 The place is called Jehovah jireh. 15 Abraham is blessed again. 20 The generation of Nahor unto Rebekah.

XXIII. 1 The age and death of Sarah. 3 The purchase of Machpelah, 19 where Sarah was buried.

XXIV. 1 Abraham swears his servant. 10 The servant's journey. 12 His prayer. 14 His sign. 15 Rebekah meets him, 18 fulfils his sign, 22 receives jewels, 23 shews her kindred, 25 and invites him home. 26 The servant blesses God. 28 Laban entertains him. 34 The servant shews his message. 50 Laban and Bethuel approve it. 58 Rebekah consents to go. 62 Isaac meets her.

XXV. 1 The sons of Abraham by Keturah. 5 The division of his goods. 7 His age and death. 9 His burial. 12 The generations of Ishmael. 17 His age and death. 19 Isaac prays for Rebekah, being barren. 22 The children strive in her womb. 24 The birth of Esau and Jacob. 27 Their difference. 29 Esau sells his birthright.

XXVI. 1 Isaac because of famine went to Gerar. 2 God instructs and blesses him. 7 He is reproved by Abimelech for denying his wife. 12 He grows rich. 18 He digs Esek, Sitnah, and Rehoboth. 23 Abimelech makes a covenant with him at Beersheba. 34 Esau's wives.

XXVII. 1 Isaac sends Esau for venison. 5 Rebekah instructeth Jacob to obtain the blessing. 15 Jacob, under the person of Esau, obtains it. 30 Esau brings venison. 33 Isaac trembles. 34 Esau complains, and by importunity obtains a blessing. 41 He threatens Jacob. 42 Rebekah disappoints it.

XXVIII. 1 Isaac blesses Jacob, and sends him to Padan-Aram. 9 Esau marries Mahalath the daughter of Ishmael. 10 The vision of Jacob's ladder. 18 The stone of Bethel. 20 Jacob's vow.

XXIX. 1 Jacob comes to the well of Haran. 9 He takes acquaintance of Rachel. 13 Laban entertains him. 18 Jacob covenants for Rachel. 23 He is deceived with Leah. 28 He marrieth also Rachel, and serves for her seven years more. 32 Leah bears Reuben, 33 Simeon, 34 Levi, 35 and Judah.

XXX. 1 Rachel, in grief for her barrenness, gives Bilhah, her maid, unto Jacob. 5 She bears Dan and Naphtali. 9 Leah gives Zilpah, her maid, who bears Gad and Asher. 14 Reuben finds mandrakes, with which Leah buyeth her husband of Rachel. 17 Leah bears Issachar, Zebulun, and Dinah. 22 Rachel bears Joseph. 25 Jacob desires to depart. 27. Laban stays him on a new covenant. 37 Jacob's policy, whereby he became rich.

XXXI. 1 Jacob upon displeasure departeth secretly. 19 Rachel steals her father's images. 22 Laban pursues him, 26 and complains of the wrong. 34 Rachel's policy to hide the images. 36 Jacob's complaint of Laban. 43 The covenant of Laban and Jacob at Galeed.

XXXII. 1 Jacob's vision at Mahanaim. 3 His message to Esau. 6 He is afraid of Esau's coming. 9 He prays for deliverance. 13 He sends a present to Esau. 24 He wrestles with an angel at Peniel, where he is called Israel. 31 He halteth.

XXXIII. 1 The kindness of Jacob and Esau at their meeting. 17 Jacob comes to Succoth. 18 He buys a field at Salem, and builds an altar called Elohe-Israel.

XXXIV. 1 Dinah is ravished by Shechem. 4 He sues to marry her. 13 The sons of Jacob offer the condition of circumcision to the Shechemites. 20 Hamor and Shechem persuade them to accept it. 25 The sons of Jacob, upon that advantage, slay them, 27 and spoil their city. 30 Jacob reproves Simeon and Levi.

XXXV. 1 God sends Jacob to Bethel. 2 He purgeth his house of idols. 6 He builds an altar at Bethel. 8 Deborah dies at Allon-Bachuth. 9 God blesses Jacob at Bethel. 16 Rachel travails of Benjamin, and dies in the way to Edar. 22 Reuben lies with Bilhah. 23 The sons of Jacob. 27 Jacob comes to Isaac at Hebron. 28 The age, death, and burial of Isaac.

XXXVI. 1 Esau's three wives. 6 His removing to mount Seir. 9 His sons. 15 The dukes which descended of his sons. 20 The sons and dukes of Seir. 24 Anah finds mules. 31 The kings of Edom. 40 The dukes that descended of Esau.

XXXVII. 2 Joseph is hated of his brethren. 5 His two dreams. 13 Jacob sends him to visit his brethren. 18 His brethren conspire his death. 21 Reuben saves him. 26 They sell him to the Ishmaelites. 31 His father, deceived by the bloody coat, mourns for him. 36 He is sold to Potiphar in Egypt.

XXXVIII. 1 Judah begets Er, Onan, and Shelah. 6 Er marries Tamar. 8 The trespass of Onan. 11 Tamar stays for Shelah. 13 She deceives Judah. 27 She bears twins, Pharez and Zarah.

XXXIX. 1 Joseph advanced in Potiphar's house. 7 He resisteth his mistress's temptation. 13 He is falsely accused. 19 He is cast into prison. 21 God is with him there.

XL. 1 The butler and baker of Pharaoh in prison. 4 Joseph hath charge of them. 5 He interprets their dreams. 20 They come to pass according to his interpretation. 23 The ingratitude of the butler.

XLI. 1 Pharaoh's two dreams. 9 Joseph interprets them. 33 He gives Pharaoh counsel. 38 Joseph is advanced. 50 He begets Manasseh and Ephraim. 54 The famine begins.

XLII. 1 Jacob sends his ten sons to buy corn in Egypt. 6 They are imprisoned by Joseph for spies. 18 They are set at liberty, on condition to bring Benjamin. 21 They have remorse for Joseph. 24 Simeon is kept for a pledge. 25 They return with corn, and their money. 29 Their relation to Jacob. 36 Jacob refuseth to send Benjamin.

XLIII. 1 Jacob is hardly persuaded to send Benjamin. 15 Joseph entertains his brethren. 31 He makes them a feast.

XLIV. 1 Joseph's policy to stay his brethren. 14 Judah's humble supplication to Joseph.

XLV. 1 Joseph makes himself known to his brethren. 5 He comforts them in God's providence. 9 He sends for his father. 16 Pharaoh confirms it. 21 Joseph furnishes them for their journey, and exhorts them to unity. 25 Jacob is revived with the news.

XLVI. 1 Jacob is comforted by God at Beersheba. 5 Thence he with his company goes into Egypt. 8 The number of his family that went into Egypt.

28. Joseph meets Jacob. 31 He instructs his brethren how to answer to Pharaoh.

XLVII. 1 Joseph presents five of his brethren, 7 and his father, before Pharaoh. 11 He gives them habitation and maintenance. 13 He gets all the Egyptians' money, 16 their cattle, 18 their lands, to Pharaoh. 22 The priests' land was not bought. 23 He lets the land to them for a fifth part. 28 Jacob's age. 29 He swears Joseph to bury him with his fathers.

XLVIII. 1 Joseph with his sons visit his sick father. 2 Jacob strengthens himself to bless them. 3 He repeats the promise. 5 He takes Ephraim and Manasseh as his own. 7 He tells him of his mother's grave. 9 He blesses Ephraim and Manasseh. 17 He prefers the younger before the elder. 21 He prophesies of their return to Canaan.

XLIX. 1 Jacob calls his sons to bless them. 3 Their blessing in particular. 29 He charges them about his burial. 33 He dies.

L. 1 The mourning for Jacob. 4 Joseph gets leave of Pharaoh to go to bury him. 7 The funeral. 15 Joseph comforts his brethren, who craved his pardon. 22 His age. 23 He sees the third generation of his sons. 24 He prophesies to his brethren of their return. 25 He takes an oath of them for his bones. 26 He dies, and is chested.

EXODUS.

I. The children of Israel, after Joseph's death do multiply. 8 The more they are oppressed by a new king, the more they multiply. 15 The godliness of the midwives in saving the men children alive. 22 Pharaoh commands the male children to be cast into the river.

II. 1 Moses is born, 3 and in an ark cast into the flags. 5 He is found, and brought up by Pharaoh's daughter. 11 He kills an Egyptian. 13 He reproves an Hebrew. 15 He flees into Midian. 21 He marries Zipporah. 22 Gershon is born. 23 God respects the Israelites' cry.

III. 1 Moses keeps Jethro's flock. 2 God appears to him in a burning bush. 9 He sends him to deliver Israel. 14 The name of God. 15 His message to Israel.

IV. 1 Moses's rod is turned into a serpent. 6 His hand is leprous. 10 He is loth to be sent. 14 Aaron is appointed to assist him. 18 Moses departs from Jethro. 21 God's message to Pharaoh. 24 Zipporah circumciseth her son. 27 Aaron is sent to meet Moses. 31 The people believe them.

V. 1 Pharaoh chides Moses and Aaron for their message. 5 He increases the Israelites' task. 15 He checks their complaints. 19 They cry out against Moses and Aaron. 22 Moses complains to God.

VI. 1 God renews his promise by his name JEHOVAH. 14 The genealogy of Reuben, 15 of Simeon, 16 of Levi, of whom came Moses and Aaron.

VII. 1 Moses is encouraged to go to Pharaoh. 7 His age. 8 His rod is turned into a serpent. 11 The sorcerers do the like. 13 Pharaoh's heart is hardened. 14 God's message to Pharaoh. 19 The river is turned into blood.

VIII. 1 Frogs are sent. 8 Pharaoh applies to Moses. 12 Moses by prayer removes them away. 16 The dust is turned into lice, which the magicians could by no means do. 20 The swarms of flies. 25 Pharaoh inclines to let the people go, 32 but yet is hardened.

IX. 1 The murrain of beasts. 8 The plague of boils and blains. 13 His message about the hail. 22 The plague of hail. 27 Pharaoh sues to Moses, 35 but yet is hardened.

X. 1 God threatens to send locusts. 7 Pharaoh, moved by his servants, inclines to let the Israelites go. 12 The plague of the locusts. 16 Pharaoh petitions Moses. 21 The plague of darkness. 24 Pharaoh sues unto Moses, but still is hardened.

XI. 1 God's message to the Israelites to borrow jewels of their neighbours. 4 Moses threatens Pharaoh with the death of the first-born.

XII. 1 The beginning of the year is changed. 3 The passover is instituted. 11 The rite of the passover. 15 Unleavened bread. 29 The first-born are slain. 31 The Israelites are driven out of the land. 37 They come to Succoth. 43 The ordinance of the passover.

XIII. 1 The first-born are sanctified to God. 3 The memorial of the passover is commanded. 11 The firstlings of beasts are now set apart. 17 The Israelites go out of Egypt, and carry Joseph's bones with them. 20 They come to Etham. 21 God guides them by a pillar of a cloud, and a pillar of fire.

XIV. 1 God instructs the Israelites in their journey. 5 Pharaoh pursues them. 10 The Israelites murmur. 13 Moses comforts them. 15 God instructs Moses. 19 The cloud removes behind the camp. 21 The Israelites pass through the Red sea, 23 which drowns the Egyptians.

XV. 1 Moses's song. 22 The people want water. 23 The waters of Marah are bitter. 25 A tree sweetens them. 27 At Elim are twelve wells, and seventy palm-trees.

XVI. 1 The Israelites come to Sin. 2 They murmur for want of bread. 4 God promises them bread from heaven. 11 Quails are sent, 14 and manna. 16 The ordering of manna. 25 It was not to be found on the sabbath. 32 An omer of it is preserved.

XVII. 1 The people murmur for water at Rephidim. 5 God sends him for water to the rock in Horeb. 8 Amalek is overcome by the holding up of Moses's hands. 15 Moses builds the altar JEHOVAH-Nissi.

XVIII. 1 Jethro bringeth to Moses his wife and two sons. 7 Moses entertains him. 13 Jethro's counsel is accepted. 27 Jethro departeth.

XIX. 1 The people come to Sinai. 3 God's message by Moses to the people out of the mount. 8 The people's answer returned again. 10 The people are prepared against the third day. 12 The mountain must not be touched. 16 The fearful presence of God upon the mount.

XX. 1 The ten commandments. 18 The people are afraid. 20 Moses comforts them. 22 Idolatry is forbidden. 24 Of what sort the altar should be.

XXI. 1 Laws for men-servants. 5 For the servant whose ear is bored. 7 For women-servants. 12 For man-slaughter. 16 For stealers of men. 17 For cursers of parents. 18 For smiters. 22 For a hurt by chance. 28 For an ox that goreth. 33 For him that is an occasion of harm.

XXII. 1 Of theft. 5 Of damage. 7 Of trespasses. 14 Of borrowing. 16 Of fornication. 18 Of witchcraft. 19 Of bestiality. 20 Of idolatry. 21 Of strangers, widows, and fatherless. 25 Of usury. 26 Of pledges. 28 Of reverence to magistrates. 29 Of the first-fruits.

XXIII. 1 Of slander and false witness. 3, 6 Of justice. 4 Of charitableness. 10 Of the year of rest. 12 Of the sabbath. 13 Of idolatry. 14 Of the three feasts. 18 Of the blood and the fat of the sacrifice. 20 An angel is promised, with a blessing, if they obey him.

XXIV. 1 Moses is called up into the mountain. 3 The people promise obedience. 4 Moses builds an altar, and twelve pillars. 6 He sprinkles the blood of the covenant. 9 The glory of God appeareth. 14 Aaron and Hur have the charge of the people. 15 Moses goeth into the mountain, where he continueth forty days and forty nights.

XXV. 1 What the Israelites must offer for the making of the tabernacle. 10 The form of the ark. 17 The mercy-seat, with the cherubims. 23 The table, with the furniture thereof. 31 The candlestick, with the instruments thereof.

XXVI. 1 The ten curtains of the tabernacle. 7 The eleven curtains of goats' hair. 14 The covering of rams' skins. 15 The board of the tabernacle, with their sockets and bars. 31 The vail for the ark. 36 The hanging for the door.

XXVII. 1 The altar of burnt offering with the vessels thereof. 9 The court of the tabernacle enclosed with hangings and pillars. 18 The measure of the court. 20 The oil for the lamp.

XXVIII. 1 Aaron and his sons are set apart for the priest's office. 2 Holy garments are appointed. 6 The ephod. 15 The breast-plate, with twelve precious stones. 30 The Urim and Thummim. 31 The robe of the ephod, with pomegranates and bells. 36 The plate of the mitre. 39 The embroidered coat. 40 The garments for Aaron's sons.

XXIX. 1 The sacrifice and ceremonies of consecrating the priests. 38 The continual burnt offering. 45 God's promise to dwell among the children of Israel.

XXX. 1 The altar of incense. 11 The ransom of souls. 17 The brazen laver. 22 The holy anointing oil. 34 The composition of the perfume.

XXXI. 1 Bezaleel and Aholiab are called and made meet for the work of the tabernacle. 12 The observation of the sabbath is again commanded. 18 Moses receives the two tables.

XXXII. 1 The people, in the absence of Moses, cause Aaron to make a calf. 7 God is displeased therewith. 11 By the intercession of Moses he is appeased. 15 Moses cometh down with the tables. 19 He breaks them. 20 He destroys the calf. 22 Aaron's excuse for himself. 25 Moses causes the idolaters to be slain. 30 He prays for the people.

XXXIII. 1 The Lord refuseth to go as he had promised with the people. 4 The people murmur thereat. 7 The tabernacle is removed out of the camp. 9 The Lord talketh familiarly with Moses. 12 Moses desires to see the glory of God.

XXXIV. 1 The tables are renewed. 5 The name of the Lord proclaimed. 8 Moses entreateth God to go with them. 10 God makes a covenant with them, repeating certain duties of the first table. 28 Moses, after forty days in the Mount, comes down with the tables. 29 His face shines, and he covers it with a vail.

XXXV. 1 The sabbath. 4 The free gifts for the tabernacle. 20 The readiness of the people to offer. 30 Bezaleel and Aholiab are called to the work.

XXXVI. 1 The offerings are delivered to the workmen. 5 The liberality of the people restrained. 8 The curtains of cherubims. 14 The curtains of goats' hair. 19 The covering of skins. 20 The boards with their sockets. 31 The bars. 35 The vail. 37 The hanging for the door.

XXXVII. 1 The ark. 6 The mercy-seat with cherubims. 10 The table with his vessels. 17 The candlestick with his lamps and instruments. 25 The altar of incense. 29 The anointing oil, and sweet incense.

XXXVIII. 1 The altar of burnt offerings. 8 The laver of brass. 9 The court. 21 The sum of what the people offered.

XXXIX. 1 The clothes of service and holy garments. 2 The ephod. 8 The breast-plate. 22 The robe of the ephod. 27 The coats, mitre, and girdle of fine linen. 30 The plate of the holy crown. 32 All is viewed and approved by Moses.

XL. The tabernacle is commanded to be reared, 9 and anointed. 13 Aaron and his sons to be sanctified. 16 Moses performs all things accordingly. 34 A cloud covers the tabernacle.

LEVITICUS.

I. Of the burnt offerings. 3 Of the herd, 10 of the flock, 13 of the fowls.

II. 1 The meat offering of flour with oil and incense, 4 either baked in the oven, 5 or on a plate, 7 or in a frying-pan, 12 or of the first-fruits in the ear. 13 The salt of the meat offering.

III. 1 The meat offering of the herd, 6 of the flock, 7 either a lamb, 12 or a goat.

IV. 1 The sin offering of ignorance, 3 for the priest, 13 for the congregation, 22 for the ruler. 27 for any of the people.

V. 1 He that sinneth in concealing his knowledge, 2 in touching an unclean thing, 4 or in making an oath. 6 His trespass offering, of the flock, 7 of fowls, 11 or of flour. 14 The trespass offering in sacrilege, 17 and in sins of ignorance.

VI. 1 The trespass offering for sins done wittingly. 8 The law of the burnt offering, 14 and of the meat offering. 19 The offering at the consecration of a priest. 24 The law of the sin offering.

VII. 1 The law of the trespass offering, 11 and of peace offerings, 12 whether it be for a thanksgiving, 16 or a vow, or a free-will offering. 22 The fat, 26 and the blood, are forbidden. 28 The priest's portion in the peace offerings.

VIII. 1 Moses consecrates Aaron and his sons. 14 Their sin offering. 18 Their burnt offering. 22 The ram of consecrations. 31 The place and time of their consecration.

IX. 1 The first offering of Aaron for himself and the people. 8 The sin offering, 12 and the burnt-offering for himself. 15 The offerings for the people. 23 Moses and Aaron bless the people. 24 Fire comes from the Lord upon the altar.

X. 1 Nadab and Abihu, for offering strange fire, are burnt by fire. 6 Aaron and his sons are forbidden to mourn for them. 8 The priests are forbidden wine when they are to go into the tabernacle. 12 The law of eating the holy things. 16 Aaron's excuse for transgressing thereof.

XI. 1 What beasts may, 4 and what may not, be eaten. 9 What fishes. 13 What fowls. 29 The creeping things which are unclean.

XII. 1 The purification of a woman after childbirth. 6. Her offerings for purifying.

XIII. 1 The laws and tokens whereby the priest is to be guided in discerning the leprosy.

XIV. 1 The rites and sacrifices in cleansing of the leper. 33 The signs of leprosy in a house. 43 The cleansing of that house.

XV. 1 The uncleanness of men in their issues. 13 The cleansing of them. 19 The uncleanness of women in their issues. 28 Their cleansing.

XVI. 1 How the high-priest must enter into the holy place. 11 The sin offering for himself. 15 The sin offering for the people. 20 The scape-goat. 29 The yearly feast of expiations.

XVII. 1 The blood of all slain beasts must be offered to the Lord at the door of the tabernacle. 7 They must not offer to devils. 10 All eating of blood is forbidden, 15 and all that dieth alone, or is torn.

XVIII. 1 Unlawful marriages. 19 Unlawful lusts.

XIX. 1 A repetition of divers laws.

XX. 1 Of him that giveth of his seed to Moloch. 4 Of him that favoureth such an one. 6 Of going to wizards. 7 Of sanctification. 9 Of him that curseth his parents. 10 Of adultery. 11, 14, 17, 19 Of incest. 13 Of sodomy. 15 Of bestiality. 18 Of uncleanness. 22 Obedience is required with holiness. 27 Wizards must be put to death.

XXI. 1 Of the priests' mourning. 6 Of their holiness. 8 Of their estimation. 7, 13 Of their marriages. 16 The priests that have blemishes must not minister in the sanctuary.

XXII. 1 The priests in their uncleanness must abstain from holy things. 6 How they shall be cleansed. 10 Who of the priest's house may eat of the holy things. 17 The sacrifices must be without blemish. 26 The age of the sacrifice. 29 The law of eating the sacrifice of thanksgiving.

XXIII. 1 The feasts of the Lord. 3 The sabbath. 4 The passover. 9 The sheaf of first-fruits. 15 The feast of pentecost. 22 Gleanings to be left for the poor. 23 The feast of trumpets. 26 The day of atonement. 33 The feast of tabernacles.

XXIV. 1 The oil for the lamps. 5 The shew-bread. 10 Shelomith's son blasphemeth. 13 The law of blasphemy. 17 Of murder. 18 Of damage. 23 The blasphemer is stoned.

XXV. 1 The sabbath of the seventh year. 8 The jubilee in the fiftieth year. 14 Of oppression. 18 A blessing of obedience. 23 Redemption of land; 29 of houses. 35 Compassion of the poor. 39 The usage of bondmen. 47 The redemption of servants.

XXVI. 1 Of idolatry. 2 Religiousness. A blessing to them that keep the commandments. 14 A curse to those that break them. 40 God promises to remember them that repent.

XXVII. 1 He that maketh a singular vow must be the Lord's. 2 The estimation of the person. 9 Of a beast given by vow. 14 Of a house. 16 Of a field, and the redemption thereof. 28 No devoted thing may be redeemed. 32 The tithe may not be changed.

NUMBERS.

I. God commandeth Moses to number the people. 5. the princes of the tribes. 17 The number of every tribe. 47 The Levites are exempted for the service of the Lord.

II. 1 The order of the tribes in their tents.

III. 1 The sons of Aaron. 5 The Levites are given to the priests for the service of the tabernacle, 11 instead of the first-born. 14 The Levites are numbered by their families. 21 The families, number, and charge of the Gershonites. 27 Of the Kohathites. 33 Of the Merarites. 38 The place and charge of Moses and Aaron. 40 The first-born are freed by the Levites. 44 The overplus are redeemed.

IV. 1 The age and time of the Levites' service. 4 The carriage of the Kohathites when the priests have taken down the tabernacle. 16 The charge of Eleazar. 17 The office of the priests. 21 The carriage of the Gershonites. 29 The carriage of the Merarites. 34 The number of the Kohathites, 38 of the Gershonites, 42 and of the Merarites.

V. 1 The unclean are removed out of the camp. 5 Restitution is to be made in trespasses. 11 The trial of jealousy.

VI. 1 The law of the Nazarites. 22 The form of blessing the people.

VII. 1 The offering of the princes at the dedication of the tabernacle. 10 Their several offerings at the dedication of the altar. 89 God speaks to Moses from the mercy-seat.

VIII. 1 How the lamps are to be lighted. 5 The consecration of the Levites. 23 The age and time of their service.

IX. 1 The passover is commanded again. 6 A second passover allowed for them that were unclean or absent. 15 The cloud guides the removings and encampings of the Israelites.

X. 1 The use of the silver trumpets. 11 The Israelites remove from Sinai to Paran. 14 The order of their march. 29 Hobab is entreated by Moses not to leave them. 35 The blessing of Moses at the removing and resting of the ark.

XI. 1 The burning at Taberah quenched by Moses's prayer. 4 The people lust for flesh, and loathe manna. 10 Moses complains of his charge. 16 God divides his burden unto seventy elders. 31 Quails are given in wrath at Kibroth-hattaavah.

XII. 1 God rebukes the sedition of Miriam and Aaron. 10 Miriam's leprosy is healed at the prayer of Moses. 14 God commands her to be shut out of the host.

XIII. 1 The names of the men who are sent to search the land. 17 Their instructions. 21 Their acts. 26 Their relation.

XIV. 1 The people murmur at the news. 6 Joshua and Caleb labour to still them. 11 God threatens them. 13 Moses persuades God, and obtains pardon. 26 The murmurers are deprived of entering into the land. 36 The men who raised the evil report, die by plague. 40 The people that would invade the land against the will of God, are smitten.

XV. 1 The law of the meat-offering and the drink-offering. 13, 29 The stranger is under the same law. 17 The law of the first of the dough for a heave-offering. 22 The sacrifice for sins of ignorance. 30 The punishment of presumption. 32 He that violates the sabbath is stoned. 37 The law of fringes.

XVI. 1 The rebellion of Korah, Dathan, and Abiram. 23 Moses separates the people from the rebels' tents. 31 The earth swallows up Korah, and a fire consumes the others. 36 The censers are reserved to holy use. 41 Fourteen thousand and seven hundred are slain by a plague for murmuring against Moses and Aaron. 46 Aaron by incense stays the plague.

XVII. 1 Aaron's rod among all the rods of the tribes only flourisheth. 10 It is left for a monument against the rebels.

XVIII. 1 The charge of the priests and Levites. 9 The priests' portion. 21 The Levites' portion. 25 The heave-offering to the priests out of the Levites' portion.

XIX. 1 The water of separation made of the ashes of a red heifer. 11 The law for the use of it in purification of the unclean.

XX. 1 The children of Israel come to Zin, where Miriam dies. 2 They murmur for want of water. 7 Moses smiting the rock brings forth water at Meribah. 14 Moses at Kadesh desires passage through Edom, which is denied him. 22 At mount Hor Aaron resigns his place to Eleazar, and dies.

XXI. 1 Israel, with some loss, destroy the Canaanites at Hormah. 4 The people murmuring are plagued with fiery serpents. 7 They repenting are healed by a brazen serpent. 10 Sundry journeys of the Israelites. 21 Sihon is overcome, 33 and Og.

XXII. 1 Balak's first message for Balaam is refused. 15 His second message obtains him. 22 An angel would have slain him, if his ass had not saved him. 36 Balak entertains him.

XXIII. 1, 13, 28 Balak's sacrifice. 7, 18 Balaam's parable.

XXIV. 1 Balaam leaving divinations, prophesies the happiness of Israel. 10 Balak in anger dismisses him. 15 He prophesies of the star of Jacob, and the destruction of some nations.

XXV. 1 Israel at Shittim commit whoredom and idolatry. 6 Phinehas killeth Zimri and Cozbi. 10 God therefore gives him an everlasting priesthood. 15 The Midianites are to be vexed.

XXVI. 1 The sum of all Israel is taken in the plains of Moab. 52 The law of dividing among them the inheritance of the land. 57 The families and number of Levites. 63 None were left of them which were numbered at Sinai, but Caleb and Joshua.

XXVII. 1 The daughters of Zelophehad sue for an inheritance. 6 The law of inheritance. 12 Moses being told of his death, sues for a successor. 18 Joshua is appointed to succeed him.

XXVIII. 1 Offerings are to be observed. 3 The continual burnt-offering. 9 The offering on the sabbath, 11 on the new moons, 16 at the passover, 26 in the day of first-fruits.

XXIX. 1 The offering at the feast of trumpets, 7 at the day of afflicting their souls, 13 and on the eight days of the feast of tabernacles.

XXX. 1 Vows are not to be broken. 3 The exception of a maid's vow. 6 Of a wife's. 9 Of a widow's, or her that is divorced.

XXXI. 1 The Midianites are spoiled, and Balaam slain. 13 Moses is wroth with the officers, for saving the women alive. 19 How the soldiers, with their captives and spoil, are to be purified. 25 The proportion whereby the prey is to be divided. 48 The voluntary oblation unto the treasury of the Lord.

XXXII. 1 The Reubenites and Gadites sue for their inheritance on that side Jordan. 6 Moses reproves them. 16 They offer him conditions to his content. 33 Moses assigns them the land. 39 They conquer it.

XXXIII. 1 Two and forty journeys of the Israelites. 50 The Canaanites are to be destroyed.

XXXIV. 1 The borders of the land. 16 The names of the men which shall divide it.

XXXV. 1 Eight and forty cities for the Levites, with their suburbs, and measure thereof. 6 Six of them are to be cities of refuge. 9 The laws of murder. 31 No satisfaction for murder.

XXXVI. 1 The inconvenience of the inheritance of daughters, 5 is remedied by marrying in their own tribes, 7 lest the inheritance should be removed from the tribe. 10 The daughters of Zelophehad marry their father's brother's sons.

DEUTERONOMY.

I. Moses's speech in the end of the fortieth year, briefly rehearsing the story, 6 of God's promise, 9 of giving them officers, 19 of sending the spies to search the land, 34 of God's anger for their incredulity, 41 and disobedience.

II. 1 The story is continued, that they were not to meddle with the Edomites, 9 nor with the Moabites, 17 nor with the Ammonites, 24 but Sihon the Amorite was subdued by them.

III. 1 The story of the conquest of Og king of Bashan. 11 The bigness of his bed. 12 The distribution of those lands to the two tribes and half. 23 Moses's prayer to enter into the land. 26 He is permitted to see it.

IV. 1 An exhortation to obedience. 41 Moses appoints the three cities of refuge on that side Jordan.

V. 1 The covenant in Horeb. 6 The ten commandments. 22 At the people's request Moses receives the law from God.

VI. 1 The end of the law is obedience. 3 An exhortation thereto.

VII. 1 Communion with the nations is forbidden, 4 for fear of idolatry, 6 for the holiness of the people, 9 for the nature of God in his mercy and justice, 17 for the assuredness of victory which God will give over them.

VIII. 1 An exhortation to obedience in regard of God's dealing with them.

IX. 1 Moses dissuades them from the opinion of their own righteousness, by rehearsing their several rebellions.

X. 1 God's mercy in restoring the two tables, 6 in continuing the priesthood, 8 in separating the tribe of Levi, 10 in hearkening to Moses's suit for the people. 12 An exhortation to obedience.

XI. 1 An exhortation to obedience, 2 by their own experience of God's great works, 8 by promise of God's great blessings, 16 and by threatenings. 18 A careful study is required in God's word. 26 The blessing and curse is set before them.

XII. 1 Monuments of idolatry are to be destroyed. 5 The place of God's service is to be kept. 16, 23 Blood is forbidden. 17, 20, 26 Holy things must be eaten in the holy place. 19 The Levite is not to be forsaken. 29 Idolatry is not to be inquired after.

XIII. 1 Enticers to idolatry, 6 though near of kin to the magistrate, 9 are to be stoned to death. 12 Idolatrous cities are not to spared.

XIV. 1 God's children are not to disfigure themselves in mourning. 3 What may and what may not be eaten, 4 of beasts, 9 of fishes, 11 of fowls. 21 That which dies of itself may not be eaten. 22 Tithes of divine service. 23 Tithes and first-lings of rejoicing before the Lord. 28 The third year's tithe of alms and charity.

XV. 1 The seventh year a year of release for the poor. 7 It must be no let of lending or giving. 12 An Hebrew servant, 16 except he will not depart, must in the seventh year go free and well furnished. 19 All firstling males of the cattle are to be sanctified unto the Lord.

XVI. 1 The feast of the passover, 9 of weeks, 13 of tabernacles. 16 Every male must offer, as he is able, at these three feasts. 18 Of judges and justice. 22 Groves and images are forbidden.

XVII. 1 The things sacrificed must be sound. 2 Idolaters must be slain. 8 Hard controversies are to be determined by the priests and judges. 12 The contemner of that determination must die. 14 The election, 16 and duty, of a king.

XVIII. 1 The Lord is the priests' and Levites' inheritance. 3 The priests' due. 6 The Levites' portion. 9 The abominations of the nations are to be avoided. 15 Christ the prophet is to be heard. 20 The presumptuous prophet is to die.

XIX. 1 The cities of refuge. 4 The privilege thereof for the manslayer. 14 The landmark is not to be removed. 15 Two witnesses at the least. 16 The punishment of a false witness.

XX. 1 The priests' exhortation to encourage the people to battle. 5 The officers' proclamation who are to be dismissed from the war. 10 How to use the cities that accept or refuse the proclamation of peace. 16 What cities must be devoted. 19 Trees of man's meat must not be destroyed in the siege.

XXI. 1 The expiation of an uncertain murder. 10 The usage of a captive taken to wife. 15 The first-born is not to be disinherited upon private affection. 18 A stubborn son is to be stoned to death. 22 The malefactor must not hang all night upon a tree.

XXII. 1 Of humanity toward brethren. 5 The sex is to be distinguished by apparel. 6 The dam is not to be taken with her young ones. 8 The house must have battlements. 9 Confusion is to be avoided. 12 Fringes upon the vesture. 13 The punishment of him that slanders his wife, 20, 22 of adultery, 25 of rape, 28 and of fornication, 30 incest.

XXIII. 1 Who may or may not enter into the congregation. 9 Uncleanness to be avoided in the host. 15 Of the fugitive servant. 17 Of filthiness. 18 Of abominable sacrifices. 19 Of usury. 21 Of vows. 24 Of trespasses.

XXIV. 1 Of divorce. 5 A new married man goeth not to war. 6, 10 Of pledges. 7 Of man-stealers. 8 Of leprosy. 14 The hire is to be given. 16 Of justice. 19 Of charity.

XXV. 1 Stripes must not exceed forty. 4 The ox is not to be muzzled. 5 Of raising seed unto a brother. 11 Of the immodest woman. 13 Of unjust weights. 17 The memory of Amalek is to be blotted out.

XXVI. 1 The confession of him that offers the basket of first fruits. 12 The prayer of him that gives his third year's tithes. 16 The covenant between God and the people.

XXVII. 1 The people are commanded to write the law upon stones, 5 and to build an altar of whole stones. 11 The tribes divided on Gerizzim and Ebal. 14 The curses pronounced on mount Ebal.

XXVIII. 1 The blessings for obedience. 15 The curses for disobedience.

XXIX. 1 Moses exhorts them to obedience, by the memory of the works they have seen. 10 All are presented before the Lord to enter into his covenant. 18 The great wrath on him that flatters himself in his wickedness. 29 Secret things belong to God.

XXX. 1 Great mercies promised to the penitent. 11 The commandment is manifest. 15 Death and life are set before them.

XXXI. 1 Moses encourages the people. 7 He encourages Joshua. 9 He delivers the law to the priests to read it in the seventh year to the people. 14 God gives a charge to Joshua, 19 and a song to testify against the people. 24 Moses delivers the book of the law to the Levites to keep. 28 He makes a protestation to the elders.

XXXII. 1 Moses's song, which displays God's mercy and vengeance. 46 He exhorts them to set their hearts upon it. 48 God sends him up to mount Nebo, to see the land and die.

XXXIII. 1 The majesty of God. 6 The blessings of the twelve tribes. 26 The excellency of Israel

XXXIV. 1 Moses from mount Nebo views the land. 5 He dies there. 6 His burial. 7 His age. 8 Thirty days' mourning for him. 9 Joshua succeeds him. 10 The praise of Moses.

JOSHUA.

I. The Lord appoints Joshua to succeed Moses. 3 The borders of the promised land. 5, 9 God promises to assist Joshua. 8 He gives him instructions. 10 He prepares the people to pass over Jordan. 12 Joshua puts the two tribes and a half in mind of their promise to Moses. 16 They promise him fealty.

II. 1 Rahab receives and conceals the two spies sent from Shittim. 8 The covenant between her and them. 23 Their return and relation.

III. 1 Joshua comes to Jordan. 2 The officers instruct the people for the passage. 7 The Lord encourages Joshua. 9 Joshua encourages the people. 14 The waters of Jordan are divided.

IV. 1 Twelve men are appointed to take twelve stones for a memorial out of Jordan. 9 Twelve other stones are set up in the midst of Jordan. 10, 19 The people pass over. 14 God magnifies Joshua. 20 The twelve stones are pitched in Gilgal.

V. 1 The Canaanites are afraid. 2 Joshua renews circumcision. 10 The passover is kept at Gilgal. 12 Manna ceases. 13 An angel appears to Joshua.

VI. 1 Jericho is shut up. 2 God instructs Joshua how to besiege it. 12 The city is compassed. 17 It must be accursed. 20 The walls fall down. 22 Rahab is saved. 26 The builder of Jericho is cursed.

VII. 1 The Israelites are smitten at Ai. 6 Joshua's complaint. 10 God instructs him what to do. 16 Achan is taken by lot. 19 His confession. 22 Both himself, and all he had, are destroyed in the valley of Achor.

VIII. 1 God encourages Joshua. 3 The stratagem whereby Ai was taken. 29 The king thereof is hanged. 30 Joshua builds an altar, 32 writes the law on stones, 33 propounds blessings and cursings.

IX. 1 The kings combine against Israel. 3 The Gibeonites by craft obtain a league: 16 for which they are condemned to perpetual bondage.

X. 1 Five kings war against Gibeon. 6 Joshua rescues it. 10 God fights against them with hailstones. 12 The sun and moon stand still at the word of Joshua. 16 The five kings are mured in a cave. 21 They are brought forth, 24 scornfully used, 26 and hanged. 40 Seven kings more are conquered. 43 Joshua returns to Gilgal.

XI. 1 Divers kings overcome at the waters of Merom. 10 Hazor is taken and burnt. 16 All the country taken by Joshua. 21 The Anakims cut off.

XII. 1 The two kings whose countries Moses took and disposed of. 7 The one and thirty kings on the other side of Jordan which Joshua smote.

XIII. 1 The bounds of the land not yet conquered. 8 The inheritance of the two tribes and half. 14, 33 The Lord, and his sacrifices, are the inheritance of Levi. 15 The bounds of the inheritance of Reuben. 22 Balaam slain. 24 The bounds of the inheritance of Gad, 29 and the half tribe of Manasseh.

XIV. 1 The nine tribes and a half are to have their inheritance by lot. 6 Caleb by privilege obtains Hebron.

XV. 1 The borders of the lot of Judah. 13 Caleb's portion and conquest. 16 Othniel for his valour hath Achsah, Caleb's daughter, to wife. 18 She obtains a blessing of her father. 21 The cities of Judah. 63 The Jebusites not conquered.

XVI. 1 The general borders of the sons of Joseph. 5 The border of the inheritance of Ephraim. 10 The Canaanites not conquered.

XVII. 1 The lot of Manasseh. 8 His coast. 12 The Canaanites not driven out. 14 The children of Joseph obtain another lot.

XVIII. 1 The tabernacle is set up at Shiloh. 2 The remainder of the land is described, and divided into seven parts. 10 Joshua divides it by lot. 11 The lot and border of Benjamin. 21 Their cities.

XIX. 1 The lot of Simeon, 10 of Zebulun, 17 of Issachar, 24 of Asher, 32 of Naphtali, 40 of Dan.

46 The children of Israel give an inheritance to Joshua.

XX. 1 God commands, 7 and the children of Israel appoint the six cities of refuge.

XXI. 1 Eight and forty cities given by lot, out of the other tribes, to the Levites. 43 God gave the land, and rest unto the Israelites, according to his promise.

XXII. 1 The two tribes and half with a blessing are sent home. 9 They build the altar of testimony, in their journey. 11 The Israelites are offended thereat. 21 They give them good satisfaction.

XXIII. 1 Joshua's exhortation before his death, 3 by former benefits, 5 by promises, 11 and by threats.

XXIV. 1 Joshua assembles the tribes at Shechem. 2 A brief history of God's benefits from Terah. 14 He renews a covenant between them and God. 26 A stone the witness of the covenant. 29 Joshua's age, death, and burial. 32 Joseph's bones are buried. 33 Eleazar dies.

JUDGES.

I. The acts of Judah and Simeon. 4 Adonibezek justly requited. 8 Jerusalem taken. 10 Hebron taken. 11 Othniel hath Achsah to wife for taking of Debir. 16 The Kenites dwell in Judah. 17 Hormah, Gaza, Askelon, and Ekron taken. 21 The acts of Benjamin. 22 Of the house of Joseph, who take Bethel. 30 Of Zebulun. 31 Of Asher. 33 Of Naphtali. 34 Of Dan.

II. 1 An angel rebukes the people at Bochim. 6 The wickedness of the new generation after Joshua. 14 God's anger and pity towards them. 20 The Canaanites are left to prove Israel.

III. 1 The nations which were left to prove Israel. 6 By communion with them they commit idolatry. 8 Othniel delivers them from Chushan-Rishathaim, 12 Ehud from Eglon, 31 Shamgar from the Philistines.

IV. 1 Deborah and Barak deliver them from Jabin and Sisera.

V. 1 The song of Deborah and Barak.

VI. 1 The Israelites for their sin are oppressed by Midian. 8 A prophet rebukes them. 11 An angel sends Gideon for their deliverance. 17 Gideon's present is consumed with fire. 24 Gideon destroys Baal's altar, and offers a sacrifice upon the altar Jehovah-shalom. 30 Joash defends his son, and calls him Jerubbaal. 33 Gideon's army. 36 Gideon's signs.

VII. 1 Gideon's army of two and thirty thousand is brought to three hundred. 9 He is encouraged by the dream and interpretation of the barley cake. 16 His stratagem of trumpets and lamps in pitchers. 24 The Ephraimites take Oreb and Zeeb.

VIII. 1 Gideon pacifies the Ephraimites. 4 Succoth and Penuel refuse to relieve Gideon's army. 10 Zebah and Zalmunna are taken. 13 Succoth and Penuel are destroyed. 17 Gideon revenges his brethren's death on Zebah and Zalmunna. 22 He refuses government. 24 His ephod cause of idolatry. 28 Midian subdued. 29 Gideon's children, and death. 33 The Israelites' idolatry and ingratitude.

IX. 1 Abimelech, by conspiracy with the Shechemites, and murder of his brethren, is made king. 7 Jotham by a parable rebukes them, and foretells their ruin. 22 Gaal conspires with the Shechemites against him. 30 Zebul reveals it. 34 Abimelech overcomes them, and sows the city with salt. 46 He burns the hold of the god Berith. 50 At Thebez he is slain by a piece of a millstone. 56 Jotham's curse is fulfilled.

X. 1 Tola judges Israel in Shamir. 3 Jair, whose thirty sons had thirty cities. 6 The Philistines and Ammonites oppress Israel. 10 In their misery, God sends them to their false gods. 15 Upon their repentance, he pities them.

XI. 1 The covenant between Jephthah and the Gileadites, that he should be their head. 12 The treaty of peace between him and the Ammonites is in vain. 29 Jephthah's vow. 32 His conquests of the Ammonites. 34 He performs his vow on his daughter.

XII. 1 The Ephraimites quarrelling with Jephthah, and discerned by Shibboleth, are slain by the Gileadites. 7 Jephthah dies. 8 Ibzan, who had thirty sons and thirty daughters, 12 and Elon, 13 and Abdon, who had forty sons and thirty nephews, judged Israel.

XIII. 1 Israel is in the hand of the Philistines. 2 An angel appears to Manoah's wife. 8 The angel appears to Manoah. 15 Manoah's sacrifice, whereby the angel is discovered. 24 Samson is born.

XIV. 1 Samson desires a wife of the Philistines. 6 In his journey he kills a lion. 8 In a second journey he finds honey in the carcase. 10 Samson's marriage feast. 12 His riddle by his wife is made known. 19 He spoils thirty Philistines. 20 His wife is married to another.

XV. 1 Samson is denied his wife. 3 He burns the Philistines' corn with foxes and firebrands. 6 His wife and her father are burnt by the Philistines. 7 Samson smites them hip and thigh. 9 He is bound by the men of Judah, and delivered to the Philistines. 14 He kills them with a jawbone. 18 God makes the fountain En-hakkore for him in Lehi.

XVI. 1 Samson at Gaza escapes, and carries away the gates of the city. 4 Delilah, corrupted by the Philistines, enticeth Samson. 6 She is deceived thrice. 15 At last she overcomes him. 21 The Philistines take him and put out his eyes. 22 His strength renewing, he pulls down the house upon the Philistines, and dies.

XVII. 1 Of the money that Micah first stole, then restored, his mother makes images, 5 and the ornaments for them. 6 He hires a Levite to be his priest.

XVIII. 1 The Danites send five men to seek out an inheritance. 3 At the house of Micah they consult with Jonathan, and are encouraged in their way. 7 They search Laish, and bring back news of good hope. 11 Six hundred men are sent to surprise it. 14 In the way they rob Micah of his priest and his consecrated things. 27 They win Laish, and call it Dan. 30 They set up idolatry, wherein Jonathan inherited the priesthood.

XIX. 1 A Levite goes to Bethlehem to fetch home his wife. 16 An old man entertains him at Gibeah. 22 The Gibeonites abuse his concubine to death. 29 He divides her into twelve pieces to send them to the twelve tribes.

XX. 1 The Levite in a general assembly declares his wrong. 8 The decree of the assembly. 12 The Benjamites being cited, make head against the Israelites. 18 The Israelites in two battles lose forty thousand. 26 They destroy by stratagem all the Benjamites, except six hundred.

XXI. 1 The people bewail the desolation of Benjamin. 8 By the destruction of Jabesh Gilead they provide them four hundred wives. 16 They advise them to surprise the virgins that danced at Shiloh.

RUTH.

I. Elimelech, driven by famine into Moab, dies there. 4 Mahlon and Chilion, having married wives of Moab, die also. 6 Naomi returning homeward, 8 dissuades her two daughters-in-law from going with her. 14 Orpah leaves her, but Ruth with great constancy accompanies her. 19 They two come to Bethlehem, where they are gladly received.

II. 1 Ruth gleans in the fields of Boaz. 4 Boaz taking knowledge of her, 8 shews her great favour. 18 What she got she carried to Naomi.

III. 1 By Naomi's instruction, 5 Ruth lies at Boaz's feet. 8 Boaz acknowledges the right of a kinsman. 14 He sends her away with six measures of barley.

IV. 1 Boaz calls into judgment the next kinsman. 6 He refuses the redemption according to the manner in Israel. 9 Boaz buys the inheritance. 11 He marries Ruth. 13 She bears Obed the grandfather of David. 18 The generation of Pharez.

I SAMUEL.

I. Elkanah, a Levite, having two wives, worships yearly at Shiloh. 4 He cherishes Hannah, though barren, and provoked by Peninnah. 9 Hannah in grief prays for a child. 12 Eli first rebuking her, afterwards blesses her. 19 Hannah having born Samuel, stays at home till he is weaned. 24 She presents him, according to her vow, to the Lord.

II. 1 Hannah's song in thankfulness. 12 The sin of Eli's sons. 18 Samuel's ministry. 20 By Eli's blessing, Hannah is more fruitful. 22 Eli reproves his sons. 27 A prophecy against Eli's house.

III. 1 How the word of the Lord was first revealed to Samuel. 11 God tells Samuel the destruction of Eli's house. 15 Samuel, though loth, tells Eli the vision. 19 Samuel grows in credit.

IV. 1 The Israelites are overcome by the Philistines at Eben-ezer. 3 They fetch the ark, to the terror of the Philistines. 10 They are smitten again, the ark taken, Hophni and Phinehas are slain. 12 Eli, at the news, falling backward, breaks his neck. 19 Phinehas's wife, discouraged in her travail with Ichabod, dies.

V. 1 The Philistines having brought the ark into Ashdod, set it in the house of Dagon. 3 Dagon falls down, and is cut in pieces, and they of Ashdod smitten with emerods. 8 So God deals with them of Gath, when it was brought thither. 10 And so with them of Ekron, when it was brought thither.

VI. 1 After seven months the Philistines take counsel how to send back the ark. 10 They bring it on a new cart with an offering unto Beth-shemesh. 19 The people are smitten for looking into the ark. 21 They send to them of Kirjath-jearim to fetch it.

VII. 1 They of Kirjath-jearim bring the ark into the house of Abinadab, and sanctify Eleazar's son to keep it. 2 After twenty years, 3 the Israelites, by Samuel's means, solemnly repent at Mizpeh. 7 While Samuel prays and sacrifices, the Lord discomfits the Philistines by thunder, at Ebenezer. 13 The Philistines are subdued. 15 Samuel peaceably and religiously judges Israel.

VIII. 1 By occasion of the evil government of Samuel's sons, the Israelites ask a king. 6 Samuel praying in grief, is comforted by God. 10 He tells the manner of a king. 19 God willeth Samuel to yield unto the importunity of the people.

IX. 1 Saul despairing to find his father's asses, 6 by the counsel of his servant, 11 and direction of young maidens, 15 according to God's revelation, 18 comes to Samuel. 19 Samuel entertains Saul at the feast. 25 Samuel, after secret communication, brings Saul on his way.

X. 1 Samuel anoints Saul. 2 He confirms him by prediction of three signs. 9 Saul's heart is changed, and he prophesies. 14 He conceals the matter of the kingdom from his uncle. 17 Saul is chosen at Mizpeh by lot. 26 The different affections of his subjects.

XI. 1 Nahash offers them of Jabesh Gilead a reproachful condition. 4 They send messengers, and are delivered by Saul. 12 Saul thereby is confirmed and his kingdom renewed

XII. 1 Samuel testifies his integrity. 6 He reproves the people of ingratitude. 16 He terrifies them with thunder in harvest time. 20 He comforts them in God's mercy.

XIII. 1 Saul's selected band. 3 He calls the Hebrews to Gilgal against the Philistines whose garrison Jonathan had smitten. 5 The Philistines' great host. 6 The distress of the Israelites. 8 Saul, weary of staying for Samuel, sacrificeth. 11 Samuel reproves him. 17 The three spoiling bands of the Philistines. 19 The policy of the Philistines, to suffer no smith in Israel.

XIV. 1 Jonathan, unknown to his father, the priest, or the people, goes and miraculously smites the Philistines' garrison. 15 A divine terror makes them beat themselves. 19 Saul not staying the priest's answer, sets on them. 21 The captivated Hebrews, and the hidden Israelites, join against them. 24 Saul's unadvised adjuration hinders the victory. 32 He restrains the people from eating blood. 35 He builds an altar. 36 Jonathan taken by lot, is saved by the people. 47 Saul's strength and family.

XV. 1 Samuel sends Saul to destroy Amalek. 6 Saul favours the Kenites. 8 He spares Agag and the best of the spoil. 16 Samuel denounces unto Saul, commending and excusing himself, God's rejection of him for his disobedience. 24 Saul's humiliation. 32 Samuel kills Agag. 34 Samuel and Saul part.

XVI. 1 Samuel sent by God, under pretence of a sacrifice, comes to Bethlehem. 6 His human judgment is reproved. 11 He anoints David. 15 Saul sends for David to quiet his evil spirit.

XVII. 1 The armies of the Israelites and Philistines being ready to battle, 4 Goliath comes proudly forth to challenge a combat. 12 David, sent by his father to visit his brethren, accepts the challenge. 28 Eliab chides him. 30 He is brought to Saul. 32 He shews the reason of his confidence. 38 Without armour, armed by faith, he kills the giant. 55 Saul takes notice of David.

XVIII. 1 Jonathan loves David. 5 Saul envies his praise, 10 seeks to kill him in his fury, 12 fears him for his good success, 17 offers him his daughters for a snare. 22 David persuaded to be the king's son-in-law, gives two hundred foreskins of the Philistines for Michal's dowry. 28 Saul's hatred, and David's glory, increases.

XIX. 1 Jonathan discovers his father's purpose to kill David. 4 He persuades his father to reconciliation. 8 By reason of David's good success in a new war, Saul's malicious rage breaks out against him. 12 Michal deceives her father with an image in David's bed. 18 David comes to Samuel in Naioth. 20 Saul's messengers, sent to take David, 22 and Saul himself, prophesy.

XX. 1 David consults with Jonathan for his safety. 11 Jonathan and David renew their covenant by oath. 18 Jonathan's token to David. 24 Saul, missing David, seeks to kill Jonathan. 35 Jonathan lovingly takes his leave of David.

XXI. 1 David at Nob obtains of Ahimelech hallowed bread. 7 Doeg was present. 8 David takes Goliath's sword. 10 David at Gath feigns himself mad.

XXII. 1 Companies resort unto David at Adullam. 3 At Mizpeh he commends his parents unto the king of Moab. 5 Admonished by Gad, he comes to Hareth. 6 Saul going to pursue him, complains of his servants' unfaithfulness. 9 Doeg accuses Ahimelech. 11 Saul commands to kill the priests. 17 The footmen refusing, Doeg executes it. 20 Abiathar escaping, brings David the news.

XXIII. 1 David inquiring of the Lord by Abiathar, rescues Keilah. 7 God shewing him the coming of Saul, and the treachery of the Keilites, he escapes from Keilah. 14 In Ziph Jonathan comes and comforts him. 19 The Ziphites discover him to Saul. 25 At Maon he is rescued from Saul by the invasion of the Philistines. 29 He dwells at Engedi.

XXIV. 1 David in a cave at Engedi, having cut off Saul's skirt, spares his life. 8 He shews thereby his innocency. 16 Saul acknowledging his fault, takes an oath of David, and departs.

XXV. 1 Samuel dies. 2 David in Paran sends to Nabal. 10 Provoked by Nabal's churlishness, he intends to destroy him. 14 Abigail discovering it, 18 takes a present, 23 and by her wisdom, 32 pacifies David. 36 Nabal hearing thereof, dies. 39 David takes Abigail and Ahinoam to be his wives. 44 Michal is given to Phalti.

XXVI. 1 Saul, by the discovery of the Ziphites, comes to Hachilah against David. 4 David coming into the trench, stays Abishai from killing Saul, but takes his spear and cruse. 13 David reproves Abner, 18 and exhorts Saul. 21 Saul acknowledges his sin.

XXVII. 1 Saul hearing David to be in Gath, seeks no more for him. 5 David begs Ziklag of Achish. 8 He, invading other countries, persuades Achish he fought against Judah.

XXVIII. 1 Achish puts confidence in David. 3 Saul having destroyed the witches, 4 and now in his fear forsaken of God, 7 seeks to a witch. 9 The witch, encouraged by Saul, raises up Samuel. 15 Saul hearing his ruin, faints. 21 The woman, with his servants, refresh him with meat.

XXIX. 1 David marching with the Philistines, 3 is disallowed by their princes. 6 Achish dismisses him with commendations of his fidelity.

XXX. 1 The Amalekites spoil Ziklag. 4 David asking counsel, is encouraged by God to pursue them. 11 By means of a revived Egyptian, he is brought to the enemies, and recovers all the spoil. 22 David's law to divide the spoil equally between them that fight and them that keep the stuff. 26 He sends presents to his friends.

XXXI. 1 Saul having lost his army, and his sons slain, he and his armour-bearer kill themselves. 7 The Philistines possess the forsaken towns of the Israelites. 8 They triumph over the dead carcases. 11 They of Jabesh Gilead, recovering the bodies by night, burn them at Jabesh, and mournfully bury their bones.

II SAMUEL.

I. The Amalekite, who brought tidings of the overthrow, and accused himself of Saul's death, is slain. 17 David lamenteth Saul and Jonathan with a song.

II. 1 David, by God's direction, with his company goes up to Hebron, where he is made king of Ju dah. 5 He commends them of Jabesh Gilead for their kindness to Saul. 8 Abner makes Ishbosheth king of Israel. 12 A mortal skirmish between twelve of Abner's and twelve of Joab's men. 18 Asahel is slain. 25 At Abner's motion Joab sounds a retreat. 32 Asahel's burial.

III. 1 During the war David grows yet stronger. 2 Six sons were born to him in Hebron. 6 Abner displeased with Ishbosheth, 12 revolts to David. 13 David requires a condition to bring him his wife Michal. 17 Abner having communed with the Israelites, is feasted by David, and dismissed. 22 Joab returning from battle, is displeased with the king, and kills Abner. 28 David curses Joab, 31 and mourns for Abner.

IV. 1 The Israelites being troubled at the death of Abner, 2 Baana and Rechab slay Ishbosheth, and bring his head to Hebron. 9 David causes them to be slain, and Ishbosheth's head to be buried.

V. 1 The tribes come to Hebron to anoint David over Israel. 4 David's age. 6 He taking Zion from the Jebusites, dwells in it. 11 Hiram sends to David. 13 Eleven sons are born to him in Jerusalem. 17 David directed by God, smites the Philistines at Baal Perazim, 22 and again at the mulberry-trees.

VI. 1 David fetches the ark from Kirjath-jearim on a new cart. 6 Uzzah is smitten at Perez-Uzzah. 9 God blesses Obed-Edom for the ark. 12 David brings the ark into Zion with sacrifices, dances before it, for which Michal despiseth him. 17 He places it in the tabernacle with great joy and feasting. 20 Michal reproving David for his religious joy, is childless to her death.

VII. 1 Nathan first approving the purpose of David to build God a house, 4 after by the word of God forbids him. 12 He promises him benefits and blessings in his seed. 18 David's prayer and thanksgiving.

VIII. 1 David subdues the Philistines and Moabites. 3 He smites Hadadezer, and the Syrians. 9 Toi sends Joram with presents to bless him. 11 The presents and the spoil David dedicates to God. 14 He puts garrisons in Edom. 16 David's officers.

IX. 1 David by Ziba sends for Mephibosheth. For Jonathan's sake he entertains him at his table, and restores him all that was Saul's. 9 He makes Ziba his farmer.

X. David's messengers sent to comfort Hanun the son of Nahash, are treated cruelly by him. 6 The Ammonites, strengthened by the Syrians, are overcome by Joab and Abishai. 15 Shobach making a new supply of the Syrians at Helam, is slain by David.

XI. 1 While Joab besiegeth Rabbah, David commits adultery with Bath-sheba. 6 Uriah sent for by David to cover the adultery, would not go home either sober or drunken. 14 He carries to Joab the order for his death. 18 Joab sends the report thereof to David. 26 David takes Bath-sheba to wife.

XII. 1 Nathan's parable of the ewe-lamb, causes David to be his own judge. 7 David reproved by Nathan, confesses his sin, and is pardoned. 15 David mourns and prays for the child while it lives. 24 Solomon is born, and named Jedidiah. 26 David takes Rabbah, and tortures the people thereof.

XIII. 1 Amnon loving Tamar, by Jonadab's counsel feigning himself sick, ravishes her. 15 He hates her, and shamefully turns her away. 19 Absalom entertains her, and conceals his purpose. 23 At a sheep-shearing among all the king's sons, he kills Amnon. 30 David grieving at the news, is comforted by Jonadab. 37 Absalom flies to Talmai at Geshur.

XIV. 1 Joab, suborning a widow of Tekoah, by a parable to incline the king's heart to fetch home Absalom, brings him to Jerusalem. 25 Absalom's beauty, hair, and children. 28 After two years, Absalom by Joab is brought into the king's presence.

XV. 1 Absalom, by fair speeches and courtesies, steals the hearts of Israel. 7 Under pretence of a vow, he obtains leave to go to Hebron. 10 He makes there a great conspiracy. 13 David, upon the news, flees from Jerusalem. 19 Ittai would not leave him. 24 Zadok and Abiathar are sent back with the ark. 30 David and his company go up mount Olivet weeping. 31 He curses Ahithophel's counsel. 32 Hushai is sent back with instructions.

XVI. 1 Ziba, by presents and false suggestions, obtains his master's inheritance. 5 At Bahurim Shimei curseth David. 9 David with patience abstains, and restrains others, from revenge. 15 Hushai insinuates himself into Absalom's counsel. 20 Ahithophel's counsel.

XVII. 1 Ahithophel's counsel is overthrown by Hushai's, according to God's appointment. 15 Secret intelligence is sent unto David. 23 Ahithophel hangs himself. 25 Amasa is made captain. 27 David at Mahanaim is furnished with provision.

XVIII. 1 David viewing the armies in their march, gives them charge of Absalom. 6 The Israelites are sorely smitten in the wood of Ephraim. 9 Absalom hanging in an oak, is slain by Joab, and cast into a pit. 18 Absalom's place. 19 Ahimaaz and Cushi bring tidings to David. 33 David mourns for Absalom.

XIX. 1 Joab causes the king to cease his mourning. 9 The Israelites are earnest to bring the king back. 11 David sends to the priests to incite them of Judah. 18 Shimei is pardoned. 24 Mephibosheth excused. 32 Barzillai dismissed. Chimham his son is taken into the king's family. 41 The Israelites expostulate with Judah for bringing home the king without them.

XX. 1 By occasion of the quarrel, Sheba makes a party in Israel. 3 David's ten concubines are shut up in perpetual prison. 4 Amasa made captain over Judah, is slain by Joab. 14 Joab pursueth Sheba unto Abel. 16 A wise woman saves the city by Sheba's head. 23 David's officers.

XXI. 1 The three years' famine for the Gibeonites cease, by hanging seven of Saul's sons. 10 Rizpah's kindness unto the dead. 12 David buries the bones of Saul and Jonathan in his father's sepulchre. 15 Four battles against the Philistines, wherein four valiants of David slay four giants.

XXII. 1 A psalm of thanksgiving for God's powerful deliverance, and manifold blessings.

XXIII. 1 David in his last words professes his faith in God's promises to be beyond sense or experience. 6 The different state of the wicked. 8 A catalogue of David's mighty men.

XXIV. 1 David, tempted by Satan, forces Joab to number the people. 5 The captains, in nine months and twenty days, bring the muster of thirteen hundred thousand fighting men. 10 David having three plagues propounded by Gad, repents, and chooses the three days' pestilence. 15 After the death of threescore and ten thousand, David, by repentance, prevents the destruction of Jerusalem. 18 David, by Gad's direction, purchases Araunah's threshing-floor, where having sacrificed, the plague is stayed.

I KINGS.

I. Abishag cherishes David in his extreme age. 5 Adonijah, David's favourite, usurps the kingdom. 11 By the counsel of Nathan, 15 Bath-sheba moves the king, 22 and Nathan seconds her. 28 David renews his oath to Bath-sheba. 32 Solomon, by David's appointment, being anointed king by Zadok and Nathan, the people triumph. 41 Jonathan, bringing the news, Adonijah's guests fly. 50 Adonijah fleeing to the horns of the altar, upon his good behaviour is dismissed by Solomon.

II. 1 David having given a charge to Solomon, 3 of religiousness, 5 of Joab, 7 of Barzillai, 8 of Shimei, 10 dies. 12 Solomon succeeds. 13 Adonijah, moving Bath-sheba to sue unto Solomon for Abishag, is put to death. 26 Abiathar having his life given him, is deprived of the priesthood. 28 Joab fleeing to the horns of the altar, is there slain. 35 Benaiah is put in Joab's room, and Zadok in Abiathar's. 36 Shimei confined to Jerusalem, by occasion of going thence to Gath, is put to death.

III. 1 Solomon marries Pharaoh's daughter. 2 High places being in use, Solomon sacrifices at Gibeon. 5 Solomon at Gibeon, in the choice which God gave him, preferring wisdom, obtains wisdom, riches, and honour. 16 Solomon's judgment between the two harlots, makes him renowned.

IV. 1 Solomon's princes. 7 His twelve officers for provision. 20, 24 The peace and largeness of his kingdom. 22 His daily provision. 26 His stables. 29 His wisdom.

V. 1 Hiram sending to congratulate Solomon, is certified of his purpose to build the temple, and desired to furnish him with timber thereto. 7 Hiram blessing God for Solomon, and requesting food for his family, furnishes him with trees. 13 The number of Solomon's workmen and labourers.

VI. 1 The building of Solomon's temple. 5 The chambers thereof. 11 God's promise to it. 15 The ceiling and adorning of it. 23 The cherubims. 31 The doors. 36 The court. 37 The time of building it.

VII. 1 The building of Solomon's house. 2 Of the house of Lebanon. 6 Of the porch of pillars. 7 Of the porch of judgment. 8 Of the house for Pharaoh's daughter. 13 Hiram's work of the two pillars. 23 Of the molten sea. 27 Of the ten bases. 38 Of the ten lavers, 40 and all the vessels.

VIII. 1 The feast of the dedication of the temple, 12 and 54 Solomon's blessing. 22 Solomon's prayer. 62 His sacrifice of peace offerings.

IX. 1 God's covenant in a vision, with Solomon. 10 The mutual presents of Solomon and Hiram. 15 In Solomon's works the Gentiles were his bondmen, the Israelites honourable servants. 24 Pharaoh's daughter removes to her house. 25 Solomon's yearly solemn sacrifices. 26 His navy fetches gold from Ophir.

X. 1 The queen of Sheba admires the wisdom of Solomon. 14 Solomon's gold. 16 His targets. 18 The throne of ivory. 21 His vessels. 24 His presents. 26 His chariots and horses. 28 His tribute.

XI. 1 Solomon's wives and concubines. 4 In his old age they drew him to idolatry. 9 God threatens him. 14 Solomon's adversaries were Hadad, who was entertained in Egypt, 23 Rezon, who reigned in Damascus, 26 and Jeroboam, to whom Ahijah prophesied. 41 Solomon's acts, reign, and death: Rehoboam succeeds him.

XII. 1 The Israelites assembled at Shechem to crown Rehoboam, by Jeroboam make a suit of relaxation unto him. 6 Rehoboam refusing the old men's counsel, by the advice of young men, answers them roughly. 16 Ten tribes revolting, kill Adoram, and make Rehoboam to flee. 21 Rehoboam raising an army, is forbidden by Shemaiah. 25 Jeroboam strengthens himself by cities, 26 and by the idolatry of the two calves.

XIII. 1 Jeroboam's hand, that offered violence to him who prophesied against his altar at Bethel, withers, 6 and at the prayer of the prophet is restored. 7 The prophet, refusing the king's entertainment, departs from Bethel. 11 An old prophet seducing him, brings him back. 20 He is reproved by God, 23 slain by a lion, 26 buried by the old prophet, 31 who confirms his prophecy. 33 Jeroboam's obstinacy.

XIV. 1 Abijah being sick, Jeroboam sends his wife disguised with presents to the prophet Ahijah at Shiloh. 5 Abijah, forewarned by God, denounces God's judgment. 17 Abijah dies and is buried. 19 Nadab succeeds Jeroboam. 21 Rehoboam's wicked reign. 25 Shishak spoils Jerusalem. 29 Abijam succeeds Rehoboam.

XV. 1 Abijam's wicked reign. 7 Asa succeeds him. 9 Asa's good reign. 16 The war between Baasha and him, causes him to make a league with Benhadad. 23 Jehoshaphat succeeds Asa. 25 Nadab's wicked reign. 27 Baasha conspiring against him, executes Ahijah's prophecy. 31 Nadab's acts and death. 33 Baasha's wicked reign.

XVI. 1, 7 Jehu's prophecy against Baasha. 5 Elah succeeds him. 8 Zimri conspiring against Elah succeeds him. 11 Zimri executes Jehu's prophecy. 15 Omri made king by the soldiers, forceth Zimri desperately to burn himself. 21 The kingdom being divided, Omri prevails against Tibni. 23 Omri buildeth Samaria. 25 His wicked reign. 27 Ahab succeeds him. 29 Ahab's most wicked reign. 34 Joshua's curse upon Hiel the builder of Jericho.

XVII. 1 Elijah having prophesied against Ahab, is sent to Cherith, where the ravens feed him. 8 He is sent to the widow of Zarephath. 17 He raises the widow's son. 24 The woman believes him.

XVIII. 1 In the extremity of famine, Elijah sent to Ahab, meets good Obadiah. 9 Obadiah brings Ahab to Elijah. 17 Elijah reproving Ahab, by fire from heaven convinces Baal's prophets. 41 Elijah by prayer obtaining rain, follows Ahab to Jezreel.

XIX. 1 Elijah threatened by Jezebel, flees to Beer-sheba. 4 In the wilderness, being weary of his life, is comforted by an angel. 9 At Horeb God appears unto him, sending him to anoint Hazael, Jehu, and Elisha. 19 Elisha taking leave of his friends, follows Elijah.

XX. 1 Benhadad not content with Ahab's homage, besiegeth Samaria. 13 By the direction of a prophet, the Syrians are slain. 22 As the prophet forewarned Ahab, the Syrians trusting in the valleys, come against him in Aphek. 28 By the word of the prophet, and God's judgment, the Syrians are smitten again. 31 The Syrians submitting themselves, Ahab sends Benhadad away with a covenant. 35 The prophet, under the parable of a prisoner, making Ahab to judge himself, denounces God's judgment against him.

XXI. 1 Ahab being denied Naboth's vineyard, is grieved. 5 Jezebel writing letters against Naboth, he is condemned of blasphemy. 15 Ahab takes possession of the vineyard. 17 Elijah denounces judgments against Ahab and Jezebel. 25 Wicked Ahab repenting, God defers the judgment.

XXII. 1 Ahab seduced by false prophets, according to the word of Micaiah, is slain at Ramoth-Gilead. 37 The dogs lick up his blood, and Ahaziah succeeds him. 41 Jehoshaphat's good reign, 45 his acts. 50 Jehoram succeeds him. 51 Ahaziah's evil reign.

II KINGS.

I. Moab rebels. 2 Ahaziah, sending to Baalzebub, hath his judgment by Elijah. 5 Elijah twice brings fire from heaven upon those whom Ahaziah sent to apprehend him. He pities the third captain, and encouraged by an angel, tells the king of his death. 17 Jehoram succeeds Ahaziah.

II. 1 Elijah, taking his leave of Elisha, with his mantle divides Jordan, 9 and granting Elisha his request, is taken up by a fiery chariot into heaven. 12 Elisha, dividing Jordan with Elijah's mantle, is acknowledged his successor. 16 The young prophets, hardly obtaining leave to seek Elijah, could not find him. 19 Elisha with salt heals the unwholesome waters. 23 Bears destroy the children that mocked Elisha.

III. 1 Jehoram's reign. 4 Mesha rebelleth. 6 Jehoram, with Jehoshaphat, and the king of Edom, being distressed for want of water, by Elisha obtains water, and promise of victory. 21 The Moabites deceived by the colour of the water, coming to spoil, are overcome. 26 The king of Moab, by sacrificing the king of Edom's son, raises the siege.

IV. 1 Elisha multiplies the widow's oil. 8 He gives a son to the good Shunammite. 18 He raises again her dead son. 38 At Gilgal he heals the deadly pottage. 42 He satisfies an hundred men with twenty loaves.

V. 1 Naaman, by the report of a captive maid, is sent to Samaria to be cured of his leprosy. 8 Elisha, sending him to Jordan, cures him. 15 He refusing Naaman's gifts, grants him some of the earth. 20 Gehazi, abusing his master's name unto Naaman, is smitten with leprosy.

VI. 1 Elisha giving leave to the young prophets to enlarge their dwellings, causeth iron to swim. 8 He discloses the king of Syria's counsel. 13 The army which was sent to Dothan to apprehend Elisha, is smitten with blindness: 19 Being brought into Samaria, they are dismissed in peace. 24 The famine in Samaria causeth women to eat their own children. 30 The king sends to slay Elisha.

VII. 1 Elisha prophesies incredible plenty in Samaria. 3 Four lepers venturing on the host of the Syrians, bring tidings of their flight. 12 The king finding by spies the news to be true, spoils the tents of the Syrians. 17 The lord, who would not believe the prophecy of plenty, having the charge of the gate, is trodden to death in the multitude.

VIII. 1 The Shunammite having left her country seven years, to avoid the forewarned famine, for Elisha's miracle's sake, hath her land restored by the king. 7 Hazael being sent with a present by Benhadad to Elisha at Damascus, after he had heard the prophecy, kills his master, and succeeds him. 16 Jehoram's wicked reign in Judah. 20 Edom and Libnah revolt. 24 Ahaziah succeeds Jehoram. 25 Ahaziah's wicked reign. 28 He visits Jehoram, wounded, at Jezreel.

IX. 1 Elisha sends a young prophet instructions to anoint Jehu at Ramoth-gilead. 4 The prophet having done his message, fleeth. 11 Jehu being made king by the soldiers, kills Joram in the field of Naboth. 27 Ahaziah is slain at Gur, and buried at Jerusalem. 30 Proud Jezebel is thrown down out of a window, and eaten by dogs.

X. 1. Jehu, by his letters, causes seventy of Ahab's children to be beheaded. 8 He excuses the fact by the prophecy of Elijah. 12 At the shearing-house he slays two and forty of Ahaziah's brethren. 15 He takes Jehonadab into his company. 18 By subtilty he destroys all the worshippers of Baal. 29 Jehu follows Jeroboam's sins. 32 Hazael oppresses Irsael. 34 Jehoahaz succeeds Jehu.

XI. 1 Jehoash being saved by his aunt Jehosheba, from Athaliah's massacre of the seed royal, is hid six years in the house of God. 4 Jehoiada giving order to the captains, in the seventh year anoints him king. 13 Athaliah is slain. 17 Jehoiada restores the worship of God.

XII. 1 Jehoash reigns well all the days of Jehoiada. 4 He gives order for the repair of the temple. 17 Hazael is diverted from Jerusalem by a present of their hallowed treasures. 19 Joash being slain by his servants, Amaziah succeeds him.

XIII. 1 Jehoahaz's wicked reign. 3 Jehoahaz oppressed by Hazael, is relieved by prayer. 8 Joash succeeds him. 10 His wicked reign. 12 Jeroboam succeeds him. 14 Elisha dying, prophesies to Joash three victories over the Syrians. 20 The Moabites invading the land, Elisha's bones raise up a dead man. 22 Hazael dying, Joash gets three victories over Benhadad.

XIV. 1 Amaziah's good reign. 5 His justice on the murderers of his father. 7 His victory over Edom. 8 Amaziah, provoking Jehoash, is overcome and spoiled. 15 Jeroboam succeeds Jehoash. 17 Amaziah slain by a conspiracy. 21 Azariah succeeds him. 23 Jeroboam's wicked reign. 28 Zachariah succeeds him.

XV. 1 Azariah's good reign. 5 He dying a leper, Jotham succeeds. 8 Zachariah, the last of Jehu's generation, reigning ill, is slain by Shallum. 13 Shallum reigning a month, is slain by Menahem. 16 Menahem strengthens himself by Pul. 21 Pekahiah succeeds him. 23 Pekahiah is slain by Pekah. 27 Pekah is oppressed by Tiglath-pileser, and slain by Hoshea. 32 Jotham's good reign. 36 Ahaz succeeds him.

XVI. 1 Ahaz's wicked reign. 5 Ahaz assailed by Rezin and Pekah, hires Tiglath-pileser against them. 10 Ahaz sending a pattern of an altar from Damascus to Urijah, diverts the brasen altar to his own devotion. 17 He spoils the temple. 19 Hezekiah succeeds him.

XVII. 1 Hoshea's wicked reign. 3 Being subdued by Shalmaneser, he conspires against him with So, king of Egypt. 5 Samaria, for their sins, is captivated. 24 The strange nations, which were transplanted to Samaria, being plagued with lions, make a mixture of religions.

XVIII. 1 Hezekiah's good reign. 4 He destroys idolatry, and prospers. 9 Samaria is carried captive for their sins. 13 Sennacherib invading Judah, is pacified by a tribute. 17 Rabshakeh sent by Sennacherib again, reviles Hezekiah, and by blasphemous persuasion solicits the people to revolt.

XIX. 1 Hezekiah mourning, sends to Isaiah to pray for them. 6 Isaiah comforts them. 8 Sennacherib going to encounter Tirhakah, sends a blasphemous letter to Hezekiah. 14 Hezekiah's prayer. 20 Isaiah's prophecy of the pride and destruction of Sennacherib, and the good of Zion. 35 An angel slays the Assyrians. 36 Sennacherib is slain at Nineveh by his own sons.

XX. 1 Hezekiah having received a message of death, by prayer has his life lengthened. 8 The sun goes ten degrees backward, for a sign of that promise. 12 Berodach-baladan sending to visit Hezekiah, because of the wonder, hath notice of his treasures. 14 Isaiah understanding thereof, foretells the Babylonian captivity. 20 Manasseh succeeds Hezekiah.

XXI. 1 Manasseh's reign. 3 His great idolatry. 10 His wickedness causes prophecies against Judah. 17 Amon succeeds him. 19 Amon's wicked reign. 23 He being slain by his servants, and those murderers slain by the people, Josiah is made king.

XXII. 1 Josiah's good reign. 3 He takes care for the repair of the temple. 8 Hilkiah having found a book of the law, Josiah sends to Huldah to inquire of the Lord. 15 Huldah prophesies the destruction of Jerusalem, but the respite thereof in Josiah's time.

XXIII. 1 Josiah causes the book to be read in a solemn assembly. 3 He renews the covenant of the Lord. 4 He destroys idolatry. 15 He burnt dead men's bones upon the altar of Bethel, as was prophesied. 21 He kept a solemn passover. 24 He puts away witches, and all abomination. 26 God's final wrath against Judah. 29 Josiah provoking Pharaoh-nechoh, is slain at Megiddo. 31 Jehoahaz succeeding him, is imprisoned by Pharaoh-nechoh, who made Jehoiakim king. 36 Jehoiakim's wicked reign.

XXIV. 1 Jehoiakim, first subdued by Nebuchadnezzar, then rebelling against him, procured his own ruin. 5 Jehoiachin succeeds him. 7 The king of Egypt is vanquished by the king of Babylon. 8 Jehoiachin's evil reign. 10 Jerusalem is taken and carried captive into Babylon. 17 Zedekiah is made king, and reigns ill, unto the utter destruction of Judah.

XXV. 1 Jerusalem is beseiged. 4 Zedekiah taken his sons slain, his eyes put out. 8 Nebuzar-adan defaces the city, carries the remnant, except a few poor labourers, into captivity, 13 spoils and carries away the treasures. 18 The nobles are slain at Riblah. 22 Gedaliah, who was set over them that remained, being slain, the rest flee into Egypt. 27 Evil-merodach advances Jehoiachin in his court.

I CHRONICLES.

I. Adam's line to Noah. 5 The sons of Japheth. 8 The sons of Ham. 17 The sons of Shem. 24 Shem's line to Abraham. 29 Ishmael's sons. 32 The sons of Keturah. 34 The posterity of Abraham by Esau. 43 The kings of Edom. 51 The dukes of Edom.

II. 1 The sons of Israel. 3 The posterity of Judah by Tamar. 13 The children of Jesse. 18 The posterity of Caleb the son of Hezron. 21 Hezron's posterity by the daughter of Machir. 25 Jerahmeel's posterity. 34 Sheshan's posterity. 42 Another branch of Caleb's posterity. 50 The posterity of Caleb the son of Hur.

III. 1 The sons of David. 10 His line to Zedekiah. 17 The successors of Jeconiah.

IV. 1, 11 The posterity of Judah by Caleb the son of Hur. 5 Of Ashur the posthumous son of Hezron. 9 Of Jabez, and his prayer. 21 The posterity of Shelah. 24 The posterity and cities of Simeon. 39 Their conquest of Gedor, and of the Amalekites in mount Seir.

V. 1 The line of Reuben (who lost his birth-right) unto the captivity. 9 Their habitation and conquest of the Hagarites. 11 The chief men and habitations of Gad. 18 The number and conquest of Reuben, Gad, and the half of Manasseh. 23 The habitations and chief men of that half tribe. 25 Their captivity for their sins.

VI. 1 The sons of Levi. 4 The line of the priests unto the captivity. 16 The families of Gershom, Merari, and Kohath. 49 The office of Aaron and his line unto Ahimaaz. 54 The cities of the priests and Levites.

VII. 1 The sons of Issachar, 6 of Benjamin, 13 of Naphtali, 14 of Manasseh, 20, 24 and of Ephraim. 21 The calamity of Ephraim by the men of Gath. 23 Beriah is born. 28 Ephraim's habitations. 30 The sons of Asher.

VIII. 1 The sons and chief men of Benjamin. 33 The stock of Saul and Jonathan.

IX. 1 The original of Israel's and Judah's genealogies. 2 The Israelites, 10 the priests, 14 and the Levites with Nethinims that dwelt in Jerusalem. 27 The charge of certain Levites. 35 The stock of Saul and Jonathan.

X. 1 Saul's overthrow and death. 8 The Philistines triumph over Saul. 11 The kindness of Jabesh-gilead towards Saul and his sons. 13 Saul's sin, for which the kingdom was translated from him to David.

XI. 1 David, by a general consent, is made king at Hebron. 4 He wins the castle of Sion from the Jebusites, by Joab's valour. 10 A catalogue of David's mighty men.

XII. 1 The companies that came to David at Ziklag. 23 The armies that came to him at Hebron.

XIII. 1 David fetches the ark with great solemnity from Kirjath-jearim. 9 Uzza being smitten the ark is left at the house of Obed-edom.

XIV. 1 Hiram's kindness to David. 2 David's felicity in people, wives, and children. 8 His two victories against the Philistines.

XV. 1 David having prepared a place for the ark, orders the priests and Levites to bring it from Obed-edom. 25 He performs the solemnity thereof with great joy. 29 Michal despises him.

XVI. 1 David's festival sacrifice. 4 He orders a choir to sing thanksgiving. 7 The psalm of thanksgiving. 37 He appoints ministers, porters, priests, and musicians, to attend continually on the ark.

XVII. 1 Nathan first approving the purpose of David to build God a house, 3 after by the word of God forbids him. 11 He promises him blessings and benefits in his seed. 16 David's prayer and thanksgiving.

XVIII. 1 David subdues the Philistines and the Moabites. 3 He smites Hadadezer and the Syrians. 9 Tou sends Hadoram with presents to bless David. 11 The presents and the spoil David dedicates to God. 13 He puts garrisons in Edom. 14 David's officers.

XIX. 1 David's messengers, sent to comfort Hanun the son of Nahash, are basely treated. 6 The Ammonites strengthened by the Syrians, are overcome by Joab and Abishai. 16 Shophach making a new supply of the Syrians, is slain by David.

XX. 1 Rabbah is besieged by Joab, spoiled by David, and the people thereof tortured. 4 Three giants are slain in three several overthrows of the Philistines.

XXI. 1 David tempted by Satan, forces Joab to number the people. 5 The number of the people being brought, David repents of it. 9 David having three plagues propounded by Gad, chooses the pestilence. 14 After the death of 70,000, David by repentance prevents the destruction of Jerusalem. 18 David, by Gad's direction, purchases Ornan's threshing-floor, where having built an altar, God gives a sign of his favour by fire, and stays the plague. 28 David sacrifices there, being restrained from Gibeon by fear of the angel.

XXII. 1 David, foreknowing the place of the temple, prepares abundance for the building of it. 6 He instructeth Solomon in God's promises, and his duty in building the temple. 17 He charges the princes to assist his son.

XXIII. 1 David in his old age maketh Solomon king. 2 The number and distribution of the Levites. 7 The families of the Gershonites. 12 The sons of Kohath. 21 The sons of Merari. 24 The office of the Levites.

XXIV. 1 The divisions of the sons of Aaron by lot into four and twenty orders. 20 The Kohathites, 27 and the Merarites, divided by lot.

XXV. 1 The number and offices of the singers. 8 Their division by lot into four and twenty orders.

XXVI. 1 The divisions of the porters. 13 The gates assigned by lot. 20 The Levites that had charge of the treasures. 29 Officers and judges.

XXVII. 1 The twelve captains for every several month. 16 The princes of the twelve tribes. 23 The numbering of the people is hindered. 25 David's several officers.

XXVIII. 1 David in a solemn assembly, having declared God's favour to him, and promise to his son Solomon, exhorts them to fear God. 9, 20 He encourageth Solomon to build the temple. 11 He gives him patterns for the form and gold and silver for the materials.

XXIX. 1 David by his example and entreaty, 6 causes the princes and people to offer willingly. 10 David's thanksgiving and prayer. 20 The people having blessed God and sacrificed, make Solomon king. 26 David's reign and death.

II CHRONICLES.

I. The solemn offering of Solomon at Gibeon. 7 Solomon's choice of wisdom is blessed by God. 13 Solomon's strength and wealth.

II. 1 and 17 Solomon's labourers for the building of the temple. 3 His embassage to Huram for workmen and provision of stuff. 11 Huram sends him a kind answer.

III. 1 The place and time of building the temple. 3 The measure and ornaments of the house. 11 The cherubims. 14 The vail and pillars.

IV. 1 The altar of brass. 2 The molten sea upon twelve oxen. 6 The ten lavers, candlesticks, and tables. 9 The courts and the instruments of brass. 19 The instruments of gold.

V. 1 The dedicated treasures. 2 The solemn induction of the ark into the oracle. 11 God being praised, gives a visible sign of his favour.

VI. 1 Solomon having blessed the people, blesses God. 12 Solomon's prayer at the consecration of the temple, upon the brasen scaffold.

VII. 1 God having given testimony to Solomon's prayer, by fire from heaven, and glory in the temple, the people worship him. 4 Solomon's solemn sacrifice. 8 Solomon having kept the feast of tabernacles, and the feast of the dedication of the altar, dismisses the people. 12 God appearing to Solomon, gives him promises upon condition.

VIII. 1 Solomon's buildings. 7 The Gentiles which were left, Solomon makes tributaries, but the Israelites, rulers. 11 Pharaoh's daughter removes to her house. 12 Solomon's yearly solemn sacrifice. 14 He appoints the priests and Levites to their places. 17 The navy fetches gold from Ophir.

IX. 1 The queen of Sheba admires the wisdom of Solomon. 13 Solomon's gold. 15 His targets. 17 The throne of ivory. 20 His vessels. 23 His presents. 25 His chariots and horses. 26 His tributes. 29 His reign and death.

X. 1 The Israelites assembled at Shechem to crown Rehoboam, by Jeroboam make a suit of relaxation unto him. 6 Rehoboam, refusing the old men's counsel, by the advice of young men, answers them roughly. 16 Ten tribes revolting, kill Hadoram, and make Rehoboam to flee.

XI. 1 Rehoboam raising an army to subdue Israel, is forbidden by Shemaiah. 5 He strengthens his kingdom with forts and provision. 13 The priests and Levites, and such as feared God, forsaken by Jeroboam, strengthen the kingdom of Judah. 18 The wives and children of Rehoboam.

XII. 1 Rehoboam forsaking the Lord, is punished by Shishak. 5 He and the princes repenting at the preaching of Shemaiah, are delivered from destruction, but not from spoil. 13 The reign and death of Rehoboam.

XIII. 1 Abijah succeeding, makes war against Jeroboam. 4 He declares the right of his cause. 13 Trusting in God, he overcomes Jeroboam. 21 The wives and children of Abijah.

XIV. 1 Asa succeeding, destroys idolatry. 6 Having peace, he strengthens his kingdom with forts and armies. 9 Calling on God, he overthrows Zerah, and spoils the Ethiopians.

XV. 1 Asa, with Judah and many of Israel, moved by the prophecy of Azariah the son of Oded, make a solemn covenant with God. 16 He puts down Maachah his mother, for her idolatry. 18 He brings dedicated things into the house of God, and enjoys a long peace.

XVI. 1 Asa, by the aid of the Syrians, diverts Baasha from building of Ramah. 7 Being reproved thereof by Hanani, he puts him in prison. 11 Among his other acts, in his disease he seeks not to God, but to the physicians. 13 His death and burial.

XVII. 1 Jehoshaphat succeeding Asa, reigns well, and prospers. 7 He sends Levites to the princes to teach Judah. 10 His enemies being terrified by God, some of them bring him presents and tribute. 12 His greatness, captains, and armies.

XVIII. 1 Jehoshaphat, joined in affinity with Ahab, is persuaded to go with him against Ramoth-gilead. 4 Ahab, seduced by false prophets, according to the word of Micaiah, is slain there.

XIX. 1 Jehoshaphat, reproved by Jehu, visits his kingdom. 5 His instructions to the judges, 8 to the priests and Levites.

XX. 1 Jehoshaphat, in his fear, proclaims a fast. 5 His prayer. 14 The prophecy of Jahaziel. 20 Jehoshaphat exhorts the people, and setteth singers to praise the Lord. 22 The great overthrow of the enemies. 26 The people having blessed God at Berachah, return in triumph. 31 Jehoshaphat's reign. 35 His convoy of ships which he made with Ahaziah, according to the prophecy of Eliezer, unhappily perished.

XXI. 1 Jehoram succeeding Jehoshaphat, slays his brethren. 5 His wicked reign. 8 Edom and Libnah revolt. 12 The prophecy of Elijah against him in writing. 16 The Philistines and Arabians oppress him. 18 His incurable disease, infamous death, and burial.

XXII. 1 Ahaziah succeeding, reigns wickedly. 5 In his confederacy with Joram the son of Ahab, he is slain by Jehu. 10 Athaliah, destroying all the seed royal save Joash, whom Jehoshabeath his aunt hid, usurps the kingdom.

XXIII. 1 Jehoiada having set things in order, makes Joash king. 12 Athaliah is slain. 16 Jehoiada restores the worship of God.

XXIV. 1 Joash reigns well all the days of Jehoiada. 4 He gives order for the repair of the temple. 15 Jehoiada's death and honourable burial. 17 Joash falling to idolatry, slayeth Zechariah the son of Jehoiada. 23 Joash is spoiled by the Syrians, and slain by Zabad and Jehozabad. 27 Amaziah succeeds him.

XXV. 1 Amaziah begins to reign well. 3 He executes justice on the traitors. 5 Having hired an army of Israelites against the Edomites, at the word of a prophet he loses the hundred talents, and dismisses them. 11 He overthrows the Edomites. 10, 13 The Israelites, discontented with their dismission, spoil as they return home. 14 Amaziah, proud of his victory, serves the gods of Edom, and despises the admonition of the prophet. 17 He provokes Joash to his overthrow. 25 His reign. 27 He is slain by conspiracy.

XXVI. 1 Uzziah succeeding, and reigning well in the days of Zechariah, prospers. 16 Waxing proud, he invades the priest's office, and is smitten with leprosy. 22 He dies, and Jotham succeeds him.

XXVII. 1 Jotham reigning well, prospers. 5 He subdues the Ammonites. 7 His reign. 9 Ahaz succeeds him.

XXVIII. 1 Ahaz reigning very wickedly, is greatly afflicted by the Syrians. 6 Judah being captivated by the Israelites, is sent home by the counsel of Oded the prophet. 16 Ahaz sending for aid to Assyria, is not helped thereby. 22 In his distress he grows more idolatrous. 26 He dying, Hezekiah succeeds him.

XXIX. 1 Hezekiah's good reign. 3 He restores religion. 5 He exhorts the Levites. 12 They sanctify themselves, and cleanse the house of God. 20 Hezekiah offereth solemn sacrifices, wherein the Levites were more forward than the priests.

XXX. 1 Hezekiah proclaims a solemn passover on the second month, for Judah and Israel. 13 The assembly having destroyed the altars of idolatry, keep the feast fourteen days. 27 The priests and Levites bless the people.

XXXI. 1 The people are forward in destroying idolatry. 2 Hezekiah orders the courses of the priests and Levites, and provides for their work and maintenance. 5 The people's forwardness in offerings and tithes. 11 Hezekiah appoints officers to dispose of the tithes. 20 The sincerity of Hezekiah.

XXXII. 1 Sennacherib invading Judah, Hezekiah fortifies himself, and encourages his people. 9 Against the blasphemies of Sennacherib by message and letters, Hezekiah and Isaiah pray. 21 An angel destroys the host of the Assyrians, to the glory of Hezekiah. 24 Hezekiah praying in his sickness, God gives him a sign of recovery. 25 He growing proud, is humbled by God. 27 His wealth and works. 31 His error in the embassage of Babylon. 32 He dying, Manasseh succeeds him.

XXXIII. 1 Manasseh's wicked reign. 3 He sets up idolatry, and would not be admonished. 11 He is carried into Babylon. 12 Upon his prayer to God he is released, and puts down idolatry. 18 His acts. 20 He dying, Amon succeeds him. 21 Amon reigning wickedly, is slain by his servants. 25 The murderers being slain, Josiah succeeds him.

XXXIV. 1 Josiah's good reign. 3 He destroys idolatry. 8 He takes order for the repair of the temple. 14 Hilkiah having found a book of the law, Josiah sends to Huldah to inquire of the Lord. 23 Huldah prophesies the destruction of Jerusalem, but respite thereof in Josiah's time. 29 Josiah causing it to be read in a solemn assembly, renews the covenant with God.

XXXV. 1 Josiah keeps a most solemn passover. 20 He provoking Pharaoh-nechoh, is slain at Megiddo. 25 Lamentations for Josiah.

XXXVI. 1 Jehoahaz succeeding, is deposed by Pharaoh, and carried into Egypt. 5 Jehoiakim reigning ill, is carried bound into Babylon. 9 Jehoiachin succeeding, reigns ill; and is brought into Babylon. 11 Zedekiah succeeding, reigns ill, and despises the prophets, and rebels against Nebuchadnezzar. 14 Jerusalem, for the sins of the priests and people, is wholly destroyed. 22 The proclamation of Cyrus.

EZRA.

I. The proclamation of Cyrus for the building of the temple. 5 The people provide for the return. 7 Cyrus restores the vessels of the temple to Sheshbazzar.

II. 1 The number that return, of the people, 36 of the priests, 40 of the Levites, 43 of the Nethinims, 55 of Solomon's servants, 62 of the priests who could not shew their pedigree. 64 The whole number of them with their substance. 68 Their oblations.

III. 1 The altar is set up. 4 Offerings frequented. 7 Workmen prepared. 8 The foundations of the temple are laid in great joy and mourning.

IV. 1 The adversaries, being not accepted in the building of the temple with the Jews, endeavour to hinder it. 7 Their letter to Artaxerxes. 17 The decree of Artaxerxes. 23 The building is hindered.

V. 1 Zerubbabel and Jeshua, incited by Haggai and Zechariah, set forward the building of the temple. 3 Tatnai and Shethar-Boznai could not hinder the Jews. 6 Their letter to Darius against the Jews.

VI. 1 Darius finding the decree of Cyrus, makes a new decree for the advancement of the building. 13 By the help of the enemies, and the directions of the prophets, the temple is finished. 16 The feast of the dedication is kept. 19 And the passover.

VII. 1 Ezra goes up to Jerusalem. 11 The gracious commission of Artaxerxes to Ezra. 27 Ezra blesses God for his favour.

VIII. 1 The companions of Ezra, who returned from Babylon. 15 He sends to Iddo for ministers for the temple. 21 He keeps a fast. 24 He commits the treasures to the custody of the priests. 31 From Ahava they come to Jerusalem. 33 The treasure is weighed in the temple. 36 The commission is delivered.

IX. 1 Ezra mourns for the affinity of the people with strangers. 5 He prays unto God with confession of sins.

X. 1 Shechaniah encourages Ezra to reform the strange marriages. 6 Ezra mourning, assembles the people. 9 The people, at the exhortation of Ezra, repent and promise amendment. 15 The care to perform it. 18 The names of those who had married strange wives.

NEHEMIAH.

I. 1 Nehemiah, understanding by Hanani, the misery of Jerusalem, mourneth, fasteth, and prayeth. 5 His prayer.

II. 1 Artaxerxes understanding the cause of Nehemiah's sadness, sends him with letters and commission to Jerusalem. 9 Nehemiah, to the grief of the enemies, comes to Jerusalem. 12 He vieweth secretly the ruins of the walls. 17 He incites the Jews to build in despite of the enemies.

III. 1 The names and order of those who built the wall.

IV. 1 While the enemies scoff, Nehemiah prays and continues the work. 7 Understanding the wrath and secrets of the enemy, he sets a watch. 13 He arms the labourers, 19 and gives military precepts.

V. 1 The Jews complain of their debt, mortgage, and bondage. 6 Nehemiah rebukes the usurers, and causes them to make a covenant of restitution. 14 He forbears his own allowance, and keeps hospitality.

VI. 1 Sanballat practiseth by craft, by rumours, by hired prophecies, to terrify Nehemiah. 15 The work is finished to the terror of the enemies. 17 Secret intelligence passes between the enemies and the nobles of Judah.

VII. 1 Nehemiah commits the charge of Jerusalem to Hanani and Hananiah. 5 A register of the genealogy of them which at first came out of Babylon: 9 Of the people. 39 Of the priests. 43 Of the Levites. 46 Of the Nethinims. 57 Of Solomon's servants. 63 And of the priests which could not shew their pedigree. 66 The whole number of them, with their substance. 70 Their oblations.

VIII. 1 The religious manner of reading and hearing the law. 9 They comfort the people. 13 The forwardness of them to hear and be instructed. 16 They keep the feast of tabernacles.

IX. 1 A solemn fast, and repentance of the people. 4 The Levites make a religious confession of God's goodness, and their wickedness.

X. 1 The names of them that sealed the covenant. 29 The points of the covenant.

XI. 1 The rulers, voluntary men, and the tenth man chosen by lot, dwell at Jerusalem. 3 A catalogue of their names. 20 The residue dwell in other cities.

XII. 1 The priests and the Levites which came up with Zerubbabel. 10 The succession of high priests. 22 Certain chief Levites. 27 The solemnity of the dedication of the walls. 44 The offices of priests and Levites appointed in the temple.

XIII. 1 Upon the reading of the law, separation is made from the mixed multitude. 4 Nehemiah at his return causes the chambers to be cleansed. 10 He reforms the offices in the house of God. 15 The violation of the sabbath, 23 and the marriages with strange wives.

ESTHER.

I. 1 Ahasuerus makes royal feasts. 10 Vashti, sent for, refuses to come. 1 Ahasuerus, by the counsel of Memucan, makes the decree of men's sovereignty.

II. 1 Out of the choice of virgins, a queen is to be chosen. 5 Mordecai, the nursing father of Esther. 8 Esther is preferred by Hegai before the rest. 12 The manner of purification, and going in to the king. 15 Esther best pleasing the king, is made queen. 21 Mordecai discovering a treason, is recorded in the chronicles.

III. 1 Haman advanced by the king, and despised by Mordecai, seeks revenge upon all the Jews. 7 He casts lots. 8 He obtains, by calumniation, a decree of the king to put all the Jews to death.

IV. 1 The great mourning of Mordecai and the Jews. 4 Esther understanding it, sends to Mordecai, who shews the cause, and advises her to undertake the suit. 10 She excusing herself, is threatened by Mordecai. 15 She appointing a fast, undertakes the suit.

V. 1 Esther adventuring on the king's favour, obtains the grace of the golden sceptre, and invites the king and Haman to a banquet. 6 She being encouraged by the king in her suit, invites them to another banquet the next day. 9 Haman, proud of his advancement, repines at the contempt of Mordecai. 14 By the counsel of Zeresh he builds for him a pair of gallows.

VI. 1 Ahasuerus reading in the chronicles of the good service done by Mordecai, takes care for his reward. 4 Haman coming to sue that Mordecai might be hanged, unawares gives counsel that he might do him honour. 12 Complaining of his misfortune, his friends tell of his final destiny.

VII. 1 Esther entertaining the king and Haman, maketh suit for her own life, and her people's. 5 She accuses Haman. 7 The king, in his anger, understanding of the gallows that Haman had made for Mordecai, causes him to be hanged thereon.

VIII. 1 Mordecai is advanced. 3 Esther maketh suit to reverse Haman's letters. 7 Ahasuerus gives the Jews liberty to defend themselves. 15 Mordecai's honour and the Jews' joy.

IX. 1 The Jews (the rulers, for fear of Mordecai, helping them) slay their enemies, with the ten sons of Haman. 12 Ahasuerus, at the request of Esther, grants another day of slaughter, and Haman's sons to be hanged. 20 The two days of Purim are made festival.

X. 1 Ahasuerus's greatness. 3 Mordecai's advancement.

JOB.

I. The holiness, riches, and religious care of Job for his children. 6 Satan appearing before God, by calumniation obtains leave to tempt Job. 13 Understanding of the loss of his goods and children, in his mourning he blesses God.

II. 1 Satan appearing again before God, obtains further leave to tempt Job. 7 He smites him with sore boils. 9 Job reproves his wife, moving him to curse God. 11 His three friends condole with him in silence.

III. 1 Job curses the day and services of his birth. 13 The ease of death. 20 He complains of life because of his anguish.

IV. 1 Eliphaz reproves Job for want of religion. 7 He teaches God's judgments to be not for the righteous, but for the wicked. 12 His fearful vision, to humble the excellences of creatures before God.

V. 1 The harm of inconsideration. 3 The end of the wicked is misery. 6 God is to be regarded in affliction. 17 The happy end of God's correction.

VI. 1 Job shews that his complaints are not causeless. He wishes for death, wherein he is assured of comfort. 14 He reproves his friends of unkindness.

VII. 1 Job excuses his desire of death. 12 He complains of his own restlessness, 17 and God's watchfulness.

VIII. 1 Bildad shews God's justice, in dealing with men according to their works. 8 He alleges antiquity to prove the certain destruction of the hypocrite. 20 He applies God's just dealing with Job.

IX. 1 Job acknowledging God's justice, shews there is no contending with him. 22 Man's innocency is not to be condemned by afflictions.

X. 1 Job, taking liberty of complaint, expostulates with God about his afflictions. 18 He complains of life, and craves a little ease before death.

XI. 1 Zophar reproves Job for justifying himself. 5 God's wisdom is unsearchable. 13 The assured blessing of repentance.

XII. 1 Job maintains himself against his friends that reprove him. 7 He acknowledges the general doctrine of God's omnipotency.

XIII. 1 Job reproves his friends of partiality. 14 He professes his confidence in God: 20 and entreats to know his own sins, and God's purpose in afflicting him.

XIV. 1 Job entreats God for favour, by the shortness of life, and certainty of death. 7 Though life once lost be irrecoverable, yet he waits for his change. 16 By sin the creature is subject to corruption.

XV. 1 Eliphaz reproves Job of impiety in justifying himself. 17 He proves by tradition the unquietness of wicked men.

XVI. 1 Job reproves his friends of unmercifulness. 7 He shews the pitifulness of his case. 17 He maintains his innocency.

XVII. 1 Job appeals from men to God. 6 The unmerciful dealing of men with the afflicted, may astonish, but not discourage, the righteous. 11 His hope is not in life, but in death.

XVIII. 1 Bildad reproves Job of presumption and impatience. 5 The calamities of the wicked.

XIX. 1 Job complaining of his friends' cruelty, shews there is misery enough in him to feed their cruelty. 21, 28 He craves pity. 25 He believes the resurrection.

XX. 1. Zophar shews the state and portion of the wicked.

XXI. 1 Job shews that even in the judgment of man, he has reason to be grieved. 7 Sometimes the wicked do so prosper, as they despise God. 16 Sometimes their destruction is manifest. 22 The happy and unhappy are alike in death. 27 The judgment of the wicked is in another world.

XXII. 1 Eliphaz shews that man's goodness profits not God. 5 He accuses Job of divers sins. 21 He exhorts him to repentance, with promises of mercy.

XXIII. 1 Job longs to appear before God, 6 in confidence of his mercy. 8 God, who is invisible, observes our ways. 11 Job's innocency. 13 God's decree is immutable.

XXIV. Wickedness often goes unpunished. 17 There is a secret judgment for the wicked.

XXV. Bildad shews that man cannot be justified before God.

XXVI. 1 Job reproving the uncharitable spirit of Bildad, 5 acknowledges the power of God to be infinite and unsearchable.

XXVII. 1 Job declares his sincerity. 8 The hypocrite is without hope. 11 The seeming blessings that the wicked have, are turned into curses.

XXVIII. 1 There is a knowledge of natural things. 12 But true wisdom is the gift of God.

XXIX. 1 Job bemoans himself of his former prosperity and honour.
XXX. 1 Job's honour is turned into extreme contempt. 15 His prosperity into calamity.
XXXI. Job makes a solemn protestation of his integrity in several duties.
XXXII. 1 Elihu is angry with Job and his three friends. 6 Because wisdom comes not from age, he excuses the boldness of his youth. 11 He reproves them for not satisfying of Job. 16 His zeal to speak.
XXXIII. 1 Elihu offers himself instead of God, with sincerity and meekness to reason with Job. 8 He excuses God from giving man an account of his ways, by his greatness. 14 God calls man to repentance by visions, 19 by afflictions, 23 and by his ministry. 31 He incites Job to attention.
XXXIV. 1 Elihu accuses Job for charging God with injustice. 10 God omnipotent cannot be unjust. 31 Man must humble himself unto God. 34 Elihu reproves Job.
XXXV. 1 Comparison is not to be made with God, because our good or evil cannot extend unto him. 9 Many cry in their afflictions, but are not heard for want of faith.
XXXVI. 1 Elihu shews how God is just in his ways. 16 How Job's sins hinder God's blessings. 24 God's works are to be magnified.
XXXVII. 1 God is to be feared because of his great works. 15 His wisdom is unsearchable in them.
XXXVIII. 1 God challenges Job to answer. 4 God, by his mighty works, convinces Job of ignorance, 31 and of imbecility.
XXXIX. 1 Of the wild goats and hinds. 5 Of the wild ass. 9 The unicorn. 13 The peacock, stork, and ostrich. 19 The horse. 26 The hawk. 27 The eagle.
XL. 1 Job humbles himself to God. 6 God stirs him up to shew his righteousness, power, and wisdom. 15 Of the Behemoth.
XLI. 1 Of God's great power in Leviathan.
XLII. 1 Job submits himself unto God. 7 God preferring Job's cause, makes his friends submit themselves, and accepts him. 10 He magnifies and blesses Job. 16 Job's age and death.

PSALMS.

I. The happiness of the godly. 4 The unhappiness of the ungodly.
II. 1 The kingdom of Christ. 10 Kings are exhorted to accept it.
III. The security of God's protection.
IV. 1 David prays for audience. 2 He reproves and exhorts his enemies. 6 Man's happiness is in God's favour.
V. 1 David prays, and professes his study in prayer. 4 God favours not the wicked. 7 David professing his faith, prays unto God to guide him, 10 to destroy his enemies, and to preserve the godly.
VI. 1 David's complaint in his sickness. 8 By faith he triumphs over his enemies.
VII. 1 David prays against the malice of his enemies, professing his innocency. 10 By faith he sees his defence and the destruction of his enemies.
VIII. 1 God's glory is manifested by his works, and by his love to man.
IX. 1 David praises God for executing of judgment. 11 He incites others to praise him. 13 He prays that he may have cause to praise him.
X. 1 David complains to God of the outrage of the wicked. 12 He prays for remedy. 16 He professes his confidence.
XI. 1 David encourages himself in God, against his enemies. 4 The providence and justice of God.
XII. 1 David, destitute of human comfort, craves help of God. 3 He comforts himself with God's judgments on the wicked, and confidence in God's experienced promises.
XIII. 1 David complains of delay in help. 3 He prays for preventing grace. 5 He boasteth of divine mercy.
XIV. 1 David describes the corruptions of a natural man. 4 He convinces the wicked by the light of their conscience. 7 He glories in the salvation of God.
XV. David describes a citizen of Sion.
XVI. 1 David in distrust of merits, and hatred of idolatry, flies to God for preservation. 5 He shews the hope of his calling, of the resurrection, and life everlasting.
XVII. 1 David in confidence of his integrity, craves defence of God against his enemies. 10 He shews their pride, craft, and eagerness. 12 He prays against them in confidence of his hope.
XVIII. David praises God for his manifold and marvellous blessings.
XIX. 1 The creatures shew God's glory. 7 The word his grace. 32 David prays for grace.
XX. 1 The church blesses the king in his exploits. 7 Her confidence in God's succour.
XXI. 1 A thanksgiving for victory. 7 Confidence of further success.
XXII. 1 David complains in great discouragements. 9 He prays in great distress. 23 He praises God.
XXIII. David's confidence in God's grace.
XXIV. 1 God's lordship in the world. 3 The citizens of his spiritual kingdom. 7 An exhortation to receive him.
XXV. 1 David's confidence in prayer. 7 He prays for remission of sins, 16 and for help in affliction.
XXVI. David resorts to God in confidence of his integrity.
XXVII. 1 David sustains his faith, by the power of God, 4 by his love to the service of God, 9 and by prayer.
XXVIII. 1 David prays earnestly against his enemies. 6 He blesses God. 9 He prays for the people.
XXIX. 1 David exhorts princes to give glory to God, 3 by reason of his power, 11 and protection of his people.
XXX. 1 David praises God for his deliverance. 4 He exhorts others to praise him by example of God's dealing with him.
XXXI. 1 David shewing his confidence in God, craves his help. 7 He rejoices in his mercy. 9 He prays in his calamity. 19 He praises God for his goodness.
XXXII. 1 Blessedness consisteth in the remission of sins. 3 Confession of sins giveth ease to the conscience. 8 God's promises bring joy.
XXXIII. 1 God is to be praised for his goodness, 6 for his power, 12 and for his providence. 20 Confidence is to be placed in God.
XXXIV. 1 David praises God, and exhorts others thereto by his experience. 8 They are blessed that trust in God. 11 He exhorts to the fear of God. 15 The privileges of the righteous.
XXXV. 1 David prays for his safety and his enemies' confusion. 11 He complains of their wrongful dealing. 22 Thereby he incites God against them.
XXXVI. 1 The grievous estate of the wicked. 5 The excellency of God's mercy. 10 David prays for favour to God's children.
XXXVII. David persuades to patience, and confidence in God, by the different state of the godly and the wicked.
XXXVIII. David moves God to take compassion of his pitiful case.
XXXIX. 1 David's care of his thoughts, 4 the consideration of the brevity and vanity of life, 7 the reverence of God's judgments, 10 and prayer, are his bridles of impatience.
XL. 1 The benefit of confidence in God. 6 Obedience is the best sacrifice. 11 The sense of David's evils inflames his prayer.
XLI. 1 God's care of the poor. 4 David complains of his enemies' treachery. 10 He flees to God for succour.
XLII. 1 David's zeal to serve God in the temple. 5 He encourages his soul to trust in God.
XLIII. 1 David praying to be restored to the temple, promises to serve God joyfully. 5 He encourageth his soul to trust in God.
XLIV. 1 The church, in memory of former favours, 7 complains of their present evils. 17 Professing her integrity, 24 she fervently prays for succour.
XLV. 1 The majesty and grace of Christ's kingdom. 10 The duty of the church, and the benefits thereof.
XLVI. 1 The confidence which the church hath in God. 8 An exhortation to behold it.
XLVII. 1 The nations are exhorted cheerfully to entertain the kingdom of Christ.
XLVIII. 1 The ornaments and privileges of the church.
XLIX. 1 An earnest persuasion to build the faith of the resurrection, not on worldly power, but on God. 16 Worldly prosperity is not to be admired.
L. 1 The majesty of God in the church. 5 His order to gather saints. 7 The pleasure of God is not in ceremonies, 14 but in sincerity of obedience.
LI. 1 David prays for remission of sins, whereof he makes a deep confession. 6 He prays for sanctification. 16 God delights not in sacrifice, but in sincerity. 18. He prays for the church.
LII. 1 David condemning the spitefulness of Doeg, prophesies his destruction. 6 The righteous shall rejoice at it. 8 David, upon his confidence in God's mercy, gives thanks.
LIII. 1 David describes the corruptions of a natural man. 4 He convinces the wicked by the light of their own conscience. 6 He glories in the salvation of God.
LIV. 1 David complains of the Ziphims, prays for salvation. 4 Upon his confidence in God's help, he promises sacrifice.
LV. 1 David in his prayer complains of his fearful case. 9 He prays against his enemies, of whose wickedness and treachery he complains. 6 He comforts himself in God's preservation of him, and confusion of his enemies.
LVI. 1 David praying to God in confidence of his word, complains of his enemies. 9 He professes his confidence in God's word, and promises to praise him.
LVII. 1 David in prayer flying unto God, complains of his dangerous case. 7 He encourages him to praise God.
LVIII. 1 David reproves wicked judges, 3 describes the nature of the wicked, 6 devotes them to God's judgments, 10 whereat the righteous shall rejoice.
LIX. 1 David prays to be delivered from his enemies. 6 He complains of their cruelty. 8 He trusts in God. 11 He prays against them. 16 He praises God.
LX. 1 David complaining to God of former judgment, 4 now upon better hope prayeth for deliverance. 6 Comforting himself in God's promises, he craves that help whereon he trusteth.
LXI. 1 David flees to God upon his former experience. 4 He vows perpetual service to him because of his promises.
LXII. 1 David professing his confidence in God, discourages his enemies. 5 In the same confidence he encourages the godly. 9 No trust is to be put in worldly things. 11 Power and mercy belong to God.
LXIII. 1 David's thirst for God. 4 His manner of blessing God. 9 His confidence of his enemies' destruction, and his own safety.
LXIV. 1 David prays for deliverance, complaining of his enemies. 7 He promises himself to see such an evident destruction of his enemies, as the righteous shall rejoice at it.
LXV. 1 David praises God for his grace. 4 The blessedness of God's chosen, by reason of benefits.
LXVI. 1 David exhorts to praise God, 5 to observe his great works, 8 to bless him for his gracious benefits. 12 He vows for himself religious service to God. 16 Declares God's special goodness to himself.
LXVII. 1 A prayer for the enlargement of God's kingdom, 3 to the joy of the people, 6 and the increase of God's blessings.
LXVIII. 1 A prayer at the removing of the ark. 4 An exhortation to praise God for his mercies, 7 for his care of the church, 19 for his great works.
LXIX. 1 David complains of his affliction. 13 He prays for deliverance. 22 He devotes his enemies to destruction. 30 He praises God with thanksgiving.
LXX. David solicits God to the speedy destruction of the wicked, and preservation of the godly.
LXXI. 1 David in confidence of faith and experience of God's favour, prays both for himself and against the enemies of his soul. 14 He promises constancy. 17 He prays for perseverance. 19 He praises God, and promises to do it cheerfully.
LXXII. 1 David praying for Solomon, shews the goodness and glory of his, in type, and in truth, of Christ's kingdom. 18 He blesses God.
LXXIII. 1 The prophet prevailing in a temptation, 2 shews the occasion thereof, the prosperity of the wicked. 13 The wound given thereby, diffidence. 15 The victory over it, knowledge of God's purpose, in destroying of the wicked, and sustaining the righteous.
LXXIV. 1 The prophet complaineth of the desolation of the sanctuary. 10 He moveth God to help, in consideration of his power. 18 Of his reproachful enemies, of his children, and of his covenant.
LXXV. 1 The prophet praises God. 2 He promises to judge uprightly. 4 He rebukes the proud by consideration of God's providence. 9 He praises God, and promises to execute justice.
LXXVI. 1 A declaration of God's majesty in the church. 11 An exhortation to serve him reverently.
LXXVII. 1 The psalmist shews what fierce combat he had with diffidence. 10 The victory which he had by consideration of God's great and gracious works.
LXXVIII. 1 An exhortation both to learn and to preach the law of God. 9 The story of God's wrath against the incredulous and disobedient. 67 The Israelites being rejected, God chose Judah, Sion, and David.
LXXIX. 1 The psalmist complains of the desolation of Jerusalem. 8 He prays for deliverance, 13 and promises thankfulness.
LXXX. 1 The psalmist in his prayer complains of the miseries of the church. 8 God's former favours are turned into judgments. 14 He prays for deliverance.
LXXXI. 1 An exhortation to a solemn praising of God. 4 God challenges that duty by reason of his benefits. 8 God exhorting to obedience, complains of their disobedience, which proves their own hurt.
LXXXII. 1 The psalmist having exhorted the judges, 5 and reproved their negligence, 8 prays God to judge.
LXXXIII. 1 A complaint to God of the enemies conspiracies. 9 A prayer against them that oppress the church.
LXXXIV. 1 The prophet longing for the communion of the sanctuary, 4 shews how blessed they are that dwell therein. 8 He prays to be restored unto it.
LXXXV. 1 The psalmist, out of the experience of former mercies, prays for the continuance thereof. 8 He promises to wait thereon, out of confidence of God's goodness.
LXXXVI. 1 David strengthens his prayer by the conscience of his religion, 5 by the goodness and power of God. 11 He desires the continuance of former grace. 14 Complaining of the proud, he craves some token of God's goodness.
LXXXVII. 1 The nature and glory of the church. 4 The increase, honour, and comfort of the members thereof.
LXXXVIII. 1 A prayer containing a grievous complaint.
LXXXIX. 1 The psalmist praises God for his covenant, 5 for his wonderful power, 15 for the care of his church, 19 for his favour to the kingdom of David. 38 Then complaining of the contrary events, 46 he expostulates, prays, and blesses God.
XC. 1 Moses setting forth God's providence, 3 complains of human fragility, 7 divine chastisements, 10 and brevity of life. 12 He prays for the knowledge and sensible experience of God's good providence.
XCI. 1 The state of the godly. 3 Their safety. 9 Their habitation. 11 Their servants. 14 Their friends, with the effects of them all.
XCII. 1 The prophet exhorts to praise God, 4 for his great works, 6 for his judgments on the wicked, 10 and for his goodness to the godly.
XCIII. 1 The majesty, power, and holiness of Christ's kingdom.
XCIV. 1 The prophet calling for justice, complains of tyranny and impiety. 8 He teaches God's providence. 12 He shews the blessedness of affliction. 16 God is the defender of the afflicted.
XCV. 1 An exhortation to praise God, 3 for his greatness, 6 and for his goodness; 8 and not to tempt him.
XCVI. 1 An exhortation to praise God, 4 for his greatness, 8 for his kingdom, 11 for his general judgment.

XCVII. 1 The majesty of God's kingdom. 7 The church rejoices at God's judgments upon idolaters. 10 An exhortation to godliness and gladness.
XCVIII. 1 The psalmist exhorts the Jews, 4 the Gentiles, 7 and all the creatures, to praise God.
XCIX. 1 The prophet setting forth the kingdom of God in Zion, 5 exhorts all, by the example of forefathers, to worship God at his holy hill.
C. 1 An exhortation to praise God cheerfully, 3 for his greatness, 4 and for his power.
CI. 1 David makes a vow and profession of godliness.
CII. 1 The prophet in his prayer makes a grievous complaint. 12 He takes comfort in the eternity and mercy of God. 18 The mercies of God are to be recorded. 23 He sustains his weakness by the unchangeableness of God.
CIII. 1 An exhortation to bless God for his mercy, 15 and for the constancy thereof.
CIV. 1 A meditation upon the mighty power, 7 and wonderful providence of God. 31 God's glory is eternal. 33 The prophet vows perpetually to praise God.
CV. 1 An exhortation to praise God, and to seek out his works. 7 The story of God's providence over Abraham, 16 over Joseph, 23 over Jacob in Egypt, 26 over Moses delivering the Israelites, 37 over the Israelites brought out of Egypt, fed in the wilderness, and planted in Canaan.
CVI. 1 The psalmist exhorts to praise God. 4 He prays for pardon of sin, as God did with the fathers. 7 The story of the people's rebellion, and God's mercy. 47 He concludes with prayer and praise.
CVII. 1 The psalmist exhorts the redeemed, in praising God, to observe his manifold providence, 4 over travellers, 10 over captives, 17 over sick men, 23 over seamen, 33 and in divers varieties of life.
CVIII. 1 David encourages himself to praise God. 5 He prays for God's assistance according to his promise. 11 His confidence in God's help.
CIX. 1 David complaining of his slanderous enemies, under the person of Judas, devotes them. 16 He shews their sin. 21 Complaining of his own misery, he prays for help. 30 He promises thankfulness.
CX. 1 The kingdom, 4 the priesthood, 5 the conquest, 7 and the passion of Christ.
CXI. 1 The psalmist by his example incites others to praise God, for his glorious, 5 and gracious works. 10 The fear of God breeds true wisdom.
CXII. 1 Godliness has the promises of this life, 4 and of the life to come. 10 The prosperity of the godly shall be an eye-sore to the wicked.
CXIII. 1 An exhortation to praise God for his excellency, 6 and for his mercy.
CXIV. 1 An exhortation, by the example of the dumb creatures, to fear God in his church.
CXV. 1 Because God is truly gracious, 4 and idols are vanity, 9 he exhorts to confidence in God. 12 God is to be blessed for his blessings.
CXVI. 1 The psalmist professes his love and duty to God for his deliverance. 12 He studies to be thankful.
CXVII. 1 An exhortation to praise God for his mercy and truth.
CXVIII. 1 An exhortation to praise God for his mercy. 5 The psalmist by his experience shows how good it is to trust in God. 19 Under the type of the psalmist, the coming of Christ in his kingdom is expressed.
CXIX. This psalm containeth sundry prayers, praises, and professions of obedience.
CXX. 1 David prays against Doeg. 3 reproves his tongue, 5 and complains of his necessary conversation with the wicked.
CXXI. 1 The great safety of the godly, who put their trust in God's protection.
CXXII. 1 David professes his joy for the church, 6 and prays for the peace thereof.
CXXIII. 1 The godly profess their confidence in God, 3 and pray to be delivered from contempt.
CXXIV. The church blesseth God for a miraculous deliverance.
CXXV. 1 The safety of such as trust in God. 4 A prayer for the godly, and against the wicked.
CXXVI. 1 The church celebrating her incredible return out of captivity, 4 prays for, and prophesies, the good success thereof.
CXXVII. 1 The virtue of God's blessing. 3 Good children are his gift.
CXXVIII. The sundry blessings which follow them that fear God.
CXXIX. 1 An exhortation to praise God for saving Israel in their great afflictions. 5 The haters of the church are cursed.
CXXX. 1 The psalmist professes his hope in prayer, 5 and his patience in hope. 7 He exhorts Israel to hope in God.
CXXXI. 1 David professing his humility, 3 exhorts Israel to hope in God.
CXXXII. 1 David in his prayer recommends unto God the religious care he had for the ark. 8 His prayer at the removing of the ark, 11 with a repetition of God's promises.
CXXXIII. The benefit of the communion of saints.
CXXXIV. An exhortation to bless God.
CXXXV. 1 An exhortation to praise God for his mercy, 5 for his power, 8 for his judgments. 15 The vanity of idols. 19 An exhortation to bless God.
CXXXVI. An exhortation to give thanks to God for particular mercies.
CXXXVII. 1 The constancy of the Jews in captivity. 7 The prophet curseth Edom and Babel.
CXXXVIII. 1 David praiseth God for the truth of his word. 4 He prophesies that the kings of the earth shall praise God. 7 He professeth his confidence in God.
CXXXIX. 1 David praiseth God for his all-seeing providence, 17 and for his infinite mercies. 19 He defies the wicked. 23 He prays for sincerity.
CXL. 1 David prays to be delivered from Saul and Doeg. 8 He prays against them. 12 He comforts himself by confidence in God.
CXLI. 1 David prays that his suit may be acceptable, 3 his conscience sincere, 7 and his life safe from snares.
CXLII. David shews that in his trouble, all his comfort was in prayer to God.
CXLIII. 1 David prays for favour in judgment, 3 He complains of his grief. 5 He strengtheneth his faith by meditation and prayer. 7 He prays for grace, 9 for deliverance, 10 for sanctification, 12 for destruction of his enemies.
CXLIV. 1 David blesseth God for his mercy both to him and to man. 5 He prays that God would powerfully deliver him from his enemies. 9 He promises to praise God. 11 He prays for the happy state of the kingdom.
CXLV. 1 David praiseth God for his fame, 8 for his goodness, 11 for his kingdom, 14 for his providence, 17 for his saving mercy.
CXLVI. 1 The psalmist vows perpetual praises to God. 3 He exhorts not to trust in man. 5 God for his power, justice, mercy, and kingdom, is only worthy to be trusted.
CXLVII. 1 The prophet exhorts to praise God, for his care of the church, 4 his power, 6 and his mercy: 7 to praise him for his providence: 12 to praise him for his blessings upon the kingdom, 15 for his power over the meteors, 19 and for his ordinances in the church.
CXLVIII. 1 The psalmist exhorts the celestial, 7 the terrestrial, 11 and the rational creatures, to praise God.
CXLIX. 1 The prophet exhorts to praise God for his love to the church, 5 and for the power he gave the church.
CL. 1 An exhortation to praise God, 3 with all sorts of instruments.

PROVERBS.

I. The use of the proverbs. 7 An exhortation to fear God and believe in his word. 10 To avoid the enticings of sinners. 20 Wisdom complains of her contempt. 24 She threatens her contemners.
II. 1 Wisdom promiseth godliness to her children, 10 and safety from evil company, 20 and direction in good ways.
III. 1 An exhortation to obedience, 5 to faith, 7 to mortification, 9 to devotion, 11 to patience. 13 The happy gain of wisdom. 19 The power, 21 and the benefits of wisdom. 27 An exhortation to charitableness, 30 peaceableness, 31 and contentedness. 33 The cursed state of the wicked.
IV. 1 Solomon, to persuade to obedience, 3 shews what instructions he had of his parents, 5 to study wisdom, 14 and to shun the path of the wicked. 20 He exhorts to faith, 23 and sanctification.
V. 1 Solomon exhorts to the study of wisdom. 3 He shews the mischief of whoredom and riot. 15 He exhorts to contentedness, liberality, and chastity. 22 The wicked are overtaken with their own sins.
VI. 1 Against suretiship, 6 idleness, 12 and mischievousness. 16 Seven things hateful to God. 20 The blessings of obedience. 25 The mischiefs of whoredom.
VII. 1 Solomon persuades to a sincere and kind familiarity with wisdom. 6 In an example of his own experience, he shews, 10 the cunning of a whore, 22 and the desperate simplicity of a young wanton. 24 He dehorteth from such wickedness.
VIII. 1 The fame, 6 and evidence of wisdom. 10 The excellency, 12 the nature, 15 the power, 18 the riches, 22 and the eternity of wisdom. 32 Wisdom is to be desired for the blessedness it bringeth.
IX. 1 The discipline, 4 and doctrine of wisdom. 13 The custom, 16 and error of folly.
X. *** From this chapter to the twenty-fifth, are sundry observations of moral virtues, and their contrary vices.
XXV. 1 Observations about kings, 8 and about avoiding of quarrels, and sundry causes thereof.
XXVI. 1 Observations about fools, 13 sluggards, 17 and contentious busy-bodies.
XXVII. 1 Observations of self-love, 5 of true love, 11 of care to avoid offences, 23 and of household care.
XXVIII. General observations of impiety, and religious integrity.
XXIX. 1 Observations of public government, 15 and of private. 22 Of anger, pride, thievery, cowardice, and corruption.
XXX. 1 Agur's confession of his faith. 7 The two points of his prayer. 10 The meanest are not to be wronged. 11 Four wicked generations. 15 Four things insatiable. 17 Parents are not to be despised. 18 Four things hard to be known. 21 Four things intolerable. 24 Four things exceeding wise. 29 Four things stately. 32 Wrath is to be prevented.
XXXI. 1 Lemuel's lesson of chastity and temperance. 6 The afflicted are to be comforted and defended. 10 The praise and properties of a good wife.

ECCLESIASTES.

I. The preacher shews that all human courses are vain: 4 Because the creatures are restless in their courses. 9 They bring forth nothing new, and all old things are forgotten. 12 and because he hath found it so in the studies of wisdom.
II. 1 The vanity of human courses in the works of pleasure. 12 Though the wise be better than the fool, yet both have one event. 18 The vanity of human labour, in leaving it they know not to whom. 24 Nothing better than joy in our labour, but that is God's gift.
III. 1 By the necessary change of times, vanity is added to human travail. 11 There is an excellency in God's works. 16 But as for man, God shall judge his works there, and here he shall be like a beast.
IV. 1 Vanity is increased unto men by oppression, 4 by envy, 5 by idleness, 7 by covetousness, 9 by solitariness, 13 by wilfulness.
V. 1 Vanities in divine service, 8 in murmuring against oppression, 9 and in riches. 18 Joy in riches is the gift of God.
VI. 1 The vanity of riches without use. 3 Of children, 6 and old age without riches. 9 The vanity of sight and wandering desires. 11 The conclusion of vanities.
VII. 1 Remedies against vanity are a good name, 2 mortification, 7 patience, 11 wisdom. 23 The difficulty of wisdom.
VIII. 1 Kings are greatly to be respected. 6 The divine providence is to be observed. 12 It is better with the godly in adversity, than with the wicked in prosperity. 16 The work of God is unsearchable.
IX. 1 Like things happen to good and bad. 4 There is a necessity of death unto men. 7 Comfort is all their portion in this life. 11 God's providence rules over all. 13 Wisdom is better than strength.
X. 1 Observations of wisdom and folly. 16 Of riot, 18 slothfulness, 19 and money. 20 Men's thoughts of kings ought to be reverent.
XI. 1 Directions for charity. 7 Death in life, 9 and the day of judgment in the days of youth, are to be thought on.
XII. 1 The Creator is to be remembered in due time. 8 The preacher's care to edify. 13 The fear of God is the chief antidote of vanity.

SOLOMON'S SONG.

I. The church's love to Christ. 5 She owns her deformity, 7 and prays to be directed to his flock. 8 Christ directs her to the shepherds' tents. 9 And shewing his love to her, 11 gives her gracious promises. 12 The church and Christ congratulate each other.
II. 1 The mutual love of Christ and his church. 8 The hope, 10 and calling of the church. 14 Christ's care of the church. 16 The profession of the church, her faith and hope.
III. 1 The church's fight and victory in temptation. 6 The church glorieth in Christ.
IV. 1 Christ sets forth the graces of the church. 8 He shews his love to her. 16 The church prays to be made fit for his presence.
V. 1 Christ awakes the church with his calling. 2 The church having a taste of Christ's love, is sick of love. 9 A description of Christ by his graces.
VI. 1 The church professeth her faith in Christ. 4 Christ shews the graces of the church, 10 and his love towards her.
VII. 1 A further description of the church's graces. 10 The church professes her faith and desire.
VIII. 1 The love of the church of Christ. 6 The force of love. 8 The calling of the Gentiles. 14 The church prays for Christ's coming.

ISAIAH.

I. Isaiah complains of Judah for her rebellion. 5 He laments her judgments. 10 He upbraids their whole service. 16 He exhorts to repentance, with promises and threatenings. 21 Bewailing their wickedness, he denounces God's judgments. 25 He promises grace, 28 and threatens destruction to the wicked.
II. 1 Isaiah prophesieth of the coming of Christ's kingdom. 6 Wickedness is the cause of God's forsaking. 10 He exhorts to fear, because of the powerful effects of God's majesty.
III. 1 The great confusion which comes by sin. 9 The impudence of the people. 12 The oppression and covetousness of the rulers. 16 The judgments which shall be for the pride of the women.
IV. In the extremity of evils Christ's kingdom shall be a sanctuary.
V. 1 Under the parable of a vineyard, God excuseth his severe judgment. 8 His judgments upon covetousness, 11 upon lasciviousness, 13 upon impiety, 20 and upon injustice. 26 The executioners of God's judgments.
VI. 1 Isaiah in a vision of the Lord in his glory, 5 being terrified, is confirmed for his message. 9 He shews the obstinacy of the people, to their desolation. 13 A remnant shall be saved.
VII. 1 Ahaz, being troubled with fear of Rezin and Pekah, is comforted by Isaiah. 10 Ahaz having liberty to choose a sign, and refusing it, hath for a sign Christ promised. 17 His judgment is prophesied to come by Assyria.
VIII. 1 In Maher-shalal hash baz, he prophesies that Syria and Israel shall be subdued by Assyria; 5 Judah likewise for their infidelity. 9 God's judgments are irresistible. 11 Comfort to them that fear God. 19 Great afflictions to idolaters.
IX. 1 What joy shall be in the midst of afflictions, by the kingdom and birth of Christ. 8 The judgments upon Israel for their pride, 13 for their hypocrisy, 18 and for their impenitence.
X. 1 The woe of tyrants. 5 Assyria, the rod of hypocrites, for his pride shall be broken. 20 A remnant of Israel shall be saved. 24 Israel is comforted with promise of deliverance from Assyria.
XI. 1 The peaceable kingdom of the Branch out of the root of Jesse. 10 The victorious restoration of Israel, and vocation of the Gentiles.
XII. A joyful thanksgiving of the faithful for the mercies of God.
XIII. 1 God musters the armies of his wrath. 6 He threatens to destroy Babylon by the Medes. 19 The desolation of Babylon.
XIV. 1 God's merciful restoration of Israel. 4 Their triumphant exultation over Babel. 24 God's

purpose against Assyria. 29 Palestina is threatened.

XV. The lamentable state of Moab.

XVI. 1 Moab is exhorted to yield obedience to Christ's kingdom. 6 Moab is threatened for her pride. 9 The prophet bewails her. 12 The judgment of Moab.

XVII. 1 Syria and Israel are threatened. 6 A remnant shall forsake idolatry. 9 The rest shall be plagued for their impiety. 12 The woe of Israel's enemies.

XVIII. 1 God, in care of his people, will destroy the Ethiopians. 7 An access thereby shall grow unto the church.

XIX. 1 The confusion of Egypt. 11 The foolishness of their princes. 18 The calling of Egypt to the church. 23 The covenant of Egypt, Assyria, and Israel.

XX. A type prefiguring the shameful captivity of Egypt and Ethiopia.

XXI. 1 The prophet bewailing the captivity of his people, seeth in a vision the fall of Babylon by the Medes and Persians. 11 Edom scorning the prophet, is moved to repentance. 13 The set-time of Arabia's calamity.

XXII. 1 The prophet laments the invasion of Jewry by the Persians. 8 He reproves their human wisdom and worldly joy. 15 He prophesieth Sheba's deprivation, 20 and Eliakim prefiguring the kingdom of Christ, his substitution.

XXIII. 1 The miserable overthrow of Tyre. 17 Their unhappy return.

XXIV. 1 The doleful judgments of God upon the land. 13 A remnant shall joyfully praise him. 16 God in his judgments shall advance his kingdom.

XXV. 1 The prophet praiseth God, for his judgments, 6 for his saving benefits, 9 and for his victorious salvation.

XXVI. 1 A song inciting to confidence in God, 5 for his judgments, 12 and for his favour to his people. 20 An exhortation to wait on God.

XXVII. 1 The care of God over his vineyard. 7 His chastisements differ from judgments. 12 The church of Jews and Gentiles.

XXVIII. 1 The prophet threatens Ephraim for their pride and drunkenness. 5 The residue shall be advanced in the kingdom of Christ. 7 He rebukes their error. 9 Their untowardness to learn, 14 and their security. 16 Christ the sure foundation is promised. 18 Their security shall be tried. 23 They are incited to the consideration of God's discreet providence.

XXIX. 1 God's heavy judgment upon Jerusalem. 7 The unsatiableness of her enemies. 9 The senselessness, 13 and deep hypocrisy of the Jews. 18 A promise of sanctification to the godly.

XXX. 1 The prophet threatens the people, for their confidence in Egypt, 8 and contempt of God's word. 18 God's mercies to his church. 27 God's wrath, and the people's joy in the destruction of Assyria.

XXXI. 1 The prophet shews their cursed folly, in trusting to Egypt, and forsaking of God. 6 He exhorts to conversion. 8 He shews the fall of Assyria.

XXXII. 1 The blessings of Christ's kingdom. 9 Desolation is foreshewn. 15 Restoration is promised to succeed.

XXXIII. 1 God's judgments against the enemies of the church. 13 The privileges of the godly.

XXXIV. 1 The judgments wherewith God revengeth his church. 11 The desolation of her enemies. 16 The certainty of the prophecy.

XXXV. 1 The joyful flourishing of Christ's kingdom. 3 The weak are encouraged by the virtues and privileges of the gospel.

XXXVI. 1 Sennacherib invades Judah. 4 Rabshakeh sent by Sennacherib, by blasphemous persuasions solicits the people to revolt. 22 His words are told to Hezekiah.

XXXVII. 1 Hezekiah mourning, sends to Isaiah to pray for them. 6 Isaiah comforts them. 8 Sennacherib going to encounter Tirhakah, sends a blasphemous letter to Hezekiah. 14 Hezekiah's prayer. 21 Isaiah's prophecy of the pride and destruction of Sennacherib, and the good of Zion. 36 An angel slays the Assyrians. 37 Sennacherib is slain at Nineveh by his own sons.

XXXVIII. 1 Hezekiah receiving a message of death, by prayer his life is lengthened. 8 The sun goes ten degrees backward, for a sign of that promise. 9 His song of thanksgiving.

XXXIX. 1 Merodach-baladan sending to visit Hezekiah because of the wonder, hath notice of his treasures. 3 Isaiah understanding thereof, foretells the Babylonian captivity.

XL. 1 The promulgation of the gospel. 3 The preaching of John the Baptist. 9 The preaching of the apostles. 12 The prophet by the omnipotence of God, 18 and his incomparableness, 26 comforts the people.

XLI. 1 God expostulates with the people, about his mercies to the church, 10 about his promises, 21 and about the vanity of idols.

XLII. 1 The office of Christ, graced with meekness and constancy. 5 God's promise unto him. 10 An exhortation to praise God for his gospel. 17 He reproves the people of incredulity.

XLIII. 1 The Lord comforts the church with his promises. 8 He appeals to the people for witness of his omnipotence. 14 He foretells them the destruction of Babylon, 18 and his wonderful deliverance of his people. 22 He reproves the people as inexcusable.

XLIV. 1 God comforts the church with his promises. 7 The vanity of idols, 9 and folly of idolmakers. 21 He exhorts to praise God for his redemption and omnipotence.

XLV. 1 God calleth Cyrus for his church's sake. 5 By his omnipotence he challengeth obedience. 20 He convinces the idols of vanity, by his saving power.

XLVI. 1 The idols of Babylon could not save themselves. 3 God saves his people to the end. 5 Idols are not comparable to God for power, 12 or present salvation.

XLVII. 1 God's judgments upon Babylon and Chaldea, 6 for their unmercifulness, 7 pride, 10 and overboldness, 11 shall be irresistible.

XLVIII. 1 God, to convince the people of their foreknown obstinacy, revealed his prophecies. 9 He saves them for his own sake. 12 He exhorts them to obedience, because of his power and providence. 16 He laments their backwardness. 20 He powerfully delivers his out of Babylon.

XLIX. 1 Christ being sent to the Jews, complains of them. 5 He is sent to the Gentiles, with gracious promises. 13 God's love is perpetual to his church. 18 The ample restoration of the church. 24 The powerful deliverance out of the captivity.

L. 1 Christ shews that the dereliction of the Jews is not to be imputed to him, by his ability to save, 5 by his obedience in that work, 7 and by his confidence in that assistance. 10 An exhortation to trust in God and not in ourselves.

LI. 1 An exhortation after the pattern of Abraham, to trust in Christ, 3 by reason of his comfortable promises, 4 of his righteous salvation, 7 and man's mortality. 9 Christ, by his sanctified arm, defendeth his from the fear of man. 17 He bewails the afflictions of Jerusalem, 21 and promises deliverance.

LII. 1 Christ persuades the church to believe his free redemption, 7 to receive the ministers thereof, 9 to joy in the power thereof, 11 and to free themselves from bondage. 13 Christ's kingdom shall be exalted.

LIII. 1 The prophet complaining of their incredulity, excuses the scandal of the cross, 4 by the benefit of his passion, 10 and the good success thereof.

LIV. 1 The prophet, for the comfort of the Gentiles, prophesies the amplitude of their church, 4 their safety, 6 their certain deliverance out of affliction, 11 their fair edification, 15 and sure preservation.

LV. 1 The prophet, with the promises of Christ, calls to faith, 6 and to repentance. 8 The happy success of them that believe.

LVI. 1 The prophet exhorts to sanctification. 3 He promises it shall be general without respect of persons. 9 He inveighs against blind watchmen.

LVII. 1 The blessed death of the righteous. 3 God reproves the Jews for their whorish idolatry. 13 He gives evangelical promises to the penitent.

LVIII. 1 The prophet being sent to reprove hypocrisy, 3 expresses a counterfeit fast and a true. 8 He declares what promises are due to godliness, 13 and to the keeping of the sabbath.

LIX. 1 The damnable nature of sin. 3 The sins of the Jews. 9 Calamity is for sin. 16 Salvation is only of God. 20 The covenant of the Redeemer.

LX. 1 The glory of the church, in the abundant access of the Gentiles, 15 and the great blessings after a short affliction.

LXI. 1 The office of Christ. 4 The forwardness, 7 and blessings of the faithful.

LXII. 1 The fervent desire of the prophet, to confirm the church in God's promises. 5 The office of the ministers (unto which they are incited) in preaching the gospel, 10 and preparing the people thereto.

LXIII. 1 Christ sheweth who he is, what his victory over his enemies, 7 and what his mercy towards his church. 10 In his just wrath he remembers his free mercy. 15 The church in her prayer, 17 and complaint, professes her faith.

LXIV. 1 The church prays for the illustration of God's power. 5 Celebrating God's mercy, she makes confession of her natural corruptions, 9 and complains of her affliction.

LXV. 1 The calling of the Gentiles. 2 The Jews, for their incredulity, idolatry, and hypocrisy, are rejected. 8 A remnant shall be saved. 11 Judgments on the wicked, and blessings on the godly. 17 The blessed state of the new Jerusalem.

LXVI. 1 The glorious God will be served in humble sincerity. 5 He comforts the humble with the marvellous generation, 10 and with the gracious benefits of the church. 15 God's severe judgments against the wicked. 19 The Gentiles shall have an holy church, 24 and see the damnation of the wicked.

JEREMIAH.

I. The time, 3 and the calling of Jeremiah. 11 His prophetical visions of an almond-rod, and a seething-pot. 15 His heavy message against Judah. 17 God encourages him with his promise of assistance.

II. 1 God having shewn his former kindness, expostulates with the Jews their causeless revolt, 9 beyond any example. 14 They are the causes of their own calamities. 20 The sins of Judah. 31 Her confidence is rejected.

III. 1 God's great mercy in Judah's vile whoredom. 6 Judah is worse than Israel. 12 The promises of the gospel to the penitent. 20 Israel, reproved and called by God, make a solemn confession of their sins.

IV. 1 God calls Israel by his promise. 3 He exhorts Judah to repentance by fearful judgments. 19 A grievous lamentation for the miseries of Judah.

V. 1 The judgments of God upon the Jews, for their perverseness, 7 for their adultery, 10 for their impiety, 19 contempt of God, 25 and for their great corruption in the civil state, 30 and ecclesiastical.

VI. 1 The enemies sent against Judah, 4 encourage themselves. 6 God sets them on work, because of their sins. 9 The prophet laments the judgments of God because of their sins. 18 He proclaims God's wrath. 26 He calls the people to mourn for the judgment on their sins.

VII. 1 Jeremiah is sent to call for true repentance, to prevent the Jews' captivity. 8 He rejects their vain confidence, 12 by the example of Shiloh. 17 He threatens them for their idolatry. 21 He rejects the sacrifices of the disobedient. 29 He exhorts to mourn for their abominations in Tophet, 32 and the judgments for the same.

VIII. 1 The calamity of the Jews, both dead and alive. 4 He upbraids their foolish and shameless impenitence. 13 He shews their grievous judgment, 18 and bewails their desperate estate.

IX. 1 Jeremiah laments the Jews for their sins, 9 and judgment. 12 Disobedience is the cause of their calamity. 17 He exhorts to mourn for their destruction, 23 and to trust, not in themselves, but in God. 25 He threatens both Jews and Gentiles.

X. 1 The unequal comparison of God and idols. 17 The prophet exhorts to fly from the calamity to come. 19 He laments the spoil of the tabernacle by foolish pastors. 23 He makes an humble supplication.

XI. 1 Jeremiah proclaims God's covenant: 8 rebukes the Jews' disobeying thereof: 11 prophesieth evils to come upon them, 18 and upon the men of Anathoth, for conspiring to kill Jeremiah.

XII. 1 Jeremiah complaining of the prosperity of the wicked, by faith sees their ruin. 5 God admonishes him of his brethren's treachery against him, 7 and laments his heritage. 14 He promises to the penitent return from captivity.

XIII. 1 In the type of a linen girdle, hidden at Euphrates, God prefigures the destruction of his people. 12 Under the parable of the bottles filled with wine, he foretells their drunkenness in misery. 15 He exhorts to prevent their future judgments. 22 He shews their abominations are the cause thereof.

XIV. 1 The grievous famine, 7 causes Jeremiah to pray. 10 The Lord will not be entreated for the people. 13 Lying prophets are no excuse for them. 17 Jeremiah is moved to complain for them.

XV. 1 The utter rejection, and manifold judgments of the Jews. 20 Jeremiah complaining of their spite, receives a promise for himself, 12 and a threatening for them. 15 He prays, 19 and receives a gracious promise.

XVI. 1 The prophet, under the types of abstaining from marriage, from houses of mourning and feasting, foreshews the utter ruin of the Jews, 10 because they were worse than their fathers. 14 Their return from captivity shall be stranger than their deliverance out of Egypt. 16 God will doubly recompense their idolatry.

XVII. 1 The captivity of Judah for her sin. 5 Trust in man is cursed, 7 in God is blessed. 10 The deceitful heart cannot deceive God. 12 The salvation of God. 15 The prophet complains of the mockers of his prophecy. 19 He is sent to renew the covenant in hallowing the sabbath.

XVIII. 1 Under the type of a potter is shewn God's absolute power in disposing of nations. 11 Judgments threatened to Judah for her strange revolt. 18 Jeremiah prays against his conspirators.

XIX. 1 Under the type of breaking a potter's vessel is foreshewn the desolation of the Jews for their sins.

XX. 1 Pashur smiting Jeremiah, receives a new name, and a fearful doom. 7 Jeremiah complains of contempt, 10 of treachery, 14 and of his birth.

XXI. 1 Zedekiah sends to Jeremiah to inquire the event of Nebuchadrezzar's war. 3 Jeremiah foretells a hard siege and miserable captivity. 8 He counsels the people to fall to the Chaldeans, 11 and upbraids the king's house.

XXII. 1 He exhorts to repentance, with promises and threats. 10 The judgment of Shallum, 13 of Jehoiakim, 20 and of Coniah.

XXIII. 1 He prophesies a restoration of the scattered flock. 5 Christ shall rule and save them. 9 Against false prophets, 33 and mockers of the true prophets.

XXIV. 1 Under the type of good and bad figs, 4 he foreshews the restoration of them that were in captivity, 8 and the desolation of Zedekiah and the rest.

XXV. 1 Jeremiah reproving the Jews' disobedience to the prophets, 8 foretells the seventy years' captivity, 12 and after that the destruction of Babylon. 15 Under the type of a cup of wine he foreshews the destruction of all nations. 34 The howling of the shepherds.

XXVI. 1 Jeremiah, by promises and threatenings, exhorts to repentance. 8 He is therefore apprehended, 10 and arraigned. 11 His apology. 16 He is quit in judgment, by the example of Micah, 20 and of Urijah, 24 and by the care of Ahikam.

XXVII. 1 Under the type of bonds and yokes, he prophesies the subduing of the neighbour kings unto Nebuchadnezzar. 8 He exhorts them to yield, and not to believe the false prophets. 12 The like he doth to Zedekiah. 19 He foretells the remnant of the vessels shall be carried into Babylon, and there continue until the day of visitation.

XXVIII. 1 Hananiah prophesies falsely the return of the vessels and of Jeconiah. 5 Jeremiah wishing it to be true, shews that the event will declare who are true prophets. 10 Hananiah breaks Jeremiah's yoke. 12 Jeremiah tells of an iron yoke, 15 and foretells Hananiah's death.

XXIX. 1 Jeremiah sends a letter to the captives in Babylon, to be quiet there, 8 and not to believe the dreams of the prophets, 10 and that they shall return with grace, after seventy years. 15 He foretells the destruction of the rest for their disobedience. 29 He shews the fearful end of Ahab and Zedekiah, two lying prophets. 24 Shemaiah writes a letter against Jeremiah. 30 Jeremiah reads his doom.

XXX. 1 God shews Jeremiah the return of the Jews. 4 After their trouble, they shall have deliverance. 10 He comforts Jacob. 18 Their return shall be gracious. 20 Wrath shall fall on the wicked.

XXXI. 1 The restoration of Israel. 10 The publication thereof. 15 Rachel mourning, is comforted. 18 Ephraim repenting, is brought home again. 22 Christ is promised. 27 His care over the church. 31 His new covenant. 35 The stability, 38 and amplitude of the church.

XXXII. 1 Jeremiah being imprisoned by Zedekiah for his prophecy, 6 buys Hanameel's field. 13 Baruch must preserve the evidence, as tokens of the people's return. 16 Jeremiah in his prayer complains to God. 26 God confirms the captivity for their sins, 36 and promises a gracious return.

XXXIII. 1 God promises to the captivity, a gracious return, 9 a joyful state, 12 a settled government, 15 Christ, the branch of righteousness, 17 a continuance of kingdom and priesthood, 20 and a stability of a blessed seed.

XXXIV. 1 Jeremiah prophesies the captivity of Zedekiah, and the city. 8 The princes and the people having dismissed their bond-servants, contrary to the covenant of God, reassume them. 12 Jeremiah for their disobedience, gives them and Zedekiah into the hands of their enemies.

XXXV. 1 By the obedience of the Rechabites, 12 Jeremiah condemns the disobedience of the Jews. 18 God blesses the Rechabites for their obedience.

XXXVI. 1 Jeremiah causes Baruch to write his prophecy, 5 and publicly to read it. 11 The princes having knowledge of it by Micaiah, send Jehudi to fetch the roll and read it. 19 They will Baruch to hide himself and Jeremiah. 20 The king Jehoiakim being certified thereof, hears part of it, and burns the roll. 27 Jeremiah denounceth his judgment. 32 Baruch writes a new copy.

XXXVII. 1 The Egyptians having raised the siege of the Chaldeans, king Zedekiah sends to Jeremiah to pray for the people. 6 Jeremiah prophesies the Chaldeans' certain return and victory. 11 He is taken for a fugitive, beaten, and put in prison. 16 He assures Zedekiah of the captivity. 18 Entreating for his liberty, he obtaineth some favour.

XXXVIII. 1 Jeremiah by a false suggestion is put into the dungeon of Malchiah. 7 Ebed-melech, by suit, gets him some enlargement. 14 Upon secret conference, he counsels the king by yielding to save his life. 24 By the king's instructions he conceals the conference from the princes.

XXXIX. 1 Jerusalem is taken. 4 Zedekiah is made blind, and sent to Babylon. 8 The city ruinated, 9 the people captivated. 11 Nebuchadrezzar's charge for the good usage of Jeremiah. 15 God's promise to Ebed-melech.

XL. 1 Jeremiah being set free by Nebuzar-adan, goes to Gedaliah. 7 The dispersed Jews repair unto him. 13 Johanan revealing Ishmael's conspiracy, is not believed.

XLI. 1 Ishmael, treacherously killing Gedaliah and others, purposes with the residue to flee unto the Ammonites. 11 Johanan recovers the captives, and intends to flee into Egypt.

XLII. 1 Johanan desires Jeremiah to inquire of God, promising obedience to his will. 7 Jeremiah assures him of safety in Judea, 13 and destruction in Egypt. 19 He reproves their hypocrisy in requiring of the Lord that which they meant not.

XLIII. 1 Johanna discrediting Jeremiah's prophecy, carries Jeremiah and others into Egypt. 8 Jeremiah prophesies by a type the conquest of Egypt by the Babylonians.

XLIV. 1 Jeremiah expresses the desolation of Judah for their idolatry. 11 He prophesies their destruction, who commit idolatry in Egypt. 15 The obstinacy of the Jews. 20 Jeremiah threatens them for the same, 29 and for a sign prophesies the destruction of Egypt.

XLV. 1 Baruch being dismayed, 4 Jeremiah instructs and comforts him.

XLVI. 1 Jeremiah prophesies the overthrow of Pharaoh's army at Euphrates, 13 and the conquest of Egypt, by Nebuchadrezzar. 27 He comforts Jacob in their chastisement.

XLVII. The destruction of the Philistines.

XLVIII. 1 The judgment of Moab, 7 for their pride, 11 for their security, 14 for their carnal confidence, 26 and for their contempt of God and his people. 47 The restoration of Moab.

XLIX. 1 The judgment of the Ammonites. 6 Their restoration. 7 The judgment of Edom, 23 of Damascus, 28 of Kedar, 30 of Hazor, 34 and of Elam. 39 The restoration of Elam.

L. 1, 9, 21, 35 The judgment of Babylon. 4, 17, 33 The redemption of Israel.

LI. 1 The severe judgment of God against Babylon, in revenge of Israel. 59 Jeremiah delivers the book of this prophecy to Seraiah, to be cast into Euphrates, in token of the perpetual sinking of Babylon.

LII. 1 Zedekiah rebels. 4 Jerusalem is besieged and taken. 8 Zedekiah's sons killed, and his own eyes put out. 12 Nebuzaradan burns and spoils the city. 24 He carries away the captives. 32 Evil-merodach advanceth Jehoiakim.

LAMENTATIONS.

I. The miserable state of Jerusalem by reason of her sin. 12 She complains of her grief, 18 and confesses God's judgment to be righteous.

II. 1 Jeremiah laments the misery of Jerusalem. 20 He complains of it to God.

III. 1 The faithful bewail their calamities. 22 By the mercies of God they nourish their hope. 37 They acknowledge God's justice. 55 They pray for deliverance, 64 and vengeance on their enemies.

IV. 1 Zion bewails her pitiful condition. 13 She confesses her sins. 21 Edom is threatened. 22 Zion is comforted.

V. A pitiful complaint of Zion, in prayer to God.

EZEKIEL.

I. The time of Ezekiel's prophecy at Chebar. 4 His vision of the four cherubims, 15 of the four wheels, 26 and of the glory of God.

II. 1 Ezekiel's commission. 6 His instruction. 9 The roll of his heavy prophecy.

III. 1 Ezekiel eats the roll. 4 God encourages him. 15 God shews him the rule of prophecy. 22 God shuts and opens the prophet's mouth.

IV. 1 Under the type of a siege, is shewn the time from the defection of Jeroboam to the captivity. 9 By the provision of the siege, is shewn the hardness of the famine.

V. 1 Under the type of hair, 5 is shewn the judgment of Jerusalem for their rebellion, 12 by famine, sword, and dispersion.

VI. 1 The judgment of Israel for their idolatry. 8 A remnant shall be blessed. 11 The faithful are exhorted to lament their calamities.

VII. 1 The final desolation of Israel. 16 The mournful repentance of them that escape. 20 The enemies defile the sanctuary, because of the Israelites' abominations. 23 Under the type of a chain is shewn their miserable captivity.

VIII. 1 Ezekiel in a vision of God, at Jerusalem, 5 is shewn the image of jealousy. 7 The chambers of imagery. 13 The mourners for Tammuz. 15 The worshippers toward the sun. 18 God's wrath for their idolatry.

IX. 1 A vision whereby is shewn the preservation of some, 5 and the destruction of the rest. 8 God cannot be entreated for them.

X. 1 The vision of the coals of fire, to be scattered over the city. 8 The vision of the cherubims.

XI. 1 The presumption of the princes. 4 Their sin and judgment. 13 Ezekiel complaining, God shews him his purpose in saving a remnant, 21 and punishing the wicked. 22 The glory of God leaves the city. 24 Ezekiel is returned to the captivity.

XII. 1 The type of Ezekiel's removing. 8 It shewed the captivity of Zedekiah. 17 Ezekiel's trembling shews the Jews' desolation. 21 The Jews' presumptuous proverb is reproved. 26 The speediness of the vision.

XIII. 1 The reproof of lying prophets, 10 and their untempered mortar. 17 Of prophetesses and their pillows.

XIV. 1 God answers idolaters according to their own heart. 6 They are exhorted to repent, for fear of judgments, by means of seduced prophets. 17 God's irrevocable sentence of famine, 15 of some noisome beasts, 17 of the sword, 19 and of pestilence. 22 A remnant shall be reserved for the example of others.

XV. 1 By the unfitness of the vine-branch for any work, 16 is shewn the rejection of Jerusalem.

XVI. 1 Under the similitude of a wretched infant, is shewn the natural state of Jerusalem. 6 God's extraordinary love towards her. 15 Her monstrous whoredom. 35 Her grievous judgment. 44 Her sin, matching her mother, and exceeding her sisters, Sodom and Samaria, calls for judgments. 60 Mercy is promised her in the end.

XVII. 1 Under the parable of two eagles and a vine, 11 is shewn God's judgment upon Jerusalem for revolting from Babylon to Egypt. 22 God promiseth to plant the cedar of the gospel.

XVIII. 1 God reproves the unjust parable of sour grapes. 5 He shews how he deals with a just father: 10 with a wicked son of a just father: 14 with a just son of a wicked father: 19 With a wicked man repenting: 24 with a just man revolting. 25 He defends his justice, 31 and exhorts to repentance.

XIX. 1 A lamentation for the princes of Israel, under the parable of lion's whelps taken in a pit, 10 and for Jerusalem, under the parable of a wasted vine.

XX. 1 God refuses to be consulted by the elders of Israel. 5 He shews the story of their rebellions in Egypt, 10 in the wilderness, 27 and in the land. 33 He promises to gather them by the gospel. 45 Under the name of a forest, he shews the destruction of Jerusalem.

XXI. 1 Ezekiel prophesies against Jerusalem, with a sign of sighing. 8 The sharp and bright sword, 18 against Jerusalem, 25 against the kingdom, 28 and against the Ammonites.

XXII. 1 A catalogue of sins in Jerusalem. 13 God will burn them as dross in his furnace. 23 The general corruption of prophets, priests, princes, and people.

XXIII. 1 The whoredoms of Aholah and Aholibah. 22 Aholibah is to be plagued by her lovers. 36 The prophet reproves the adulteries of them both, 45 and shews their judgments.

XXIV. 1 Under the parable of a boiling pot, 6 is shewn the irrevocable destruction of Jerusalem. 15 By the sign of Ezekiel not mourning for the death of his wife, 19 is shewn the calamity of the Jews to be beyond all sorrow.

XXV. 1 God's vengeance for their insolence against the Jews, upon the Ammonites. 8 Upon Moab and Seir, 12 Upon Edom. 15 And upon the Philistines.

XXVI. 1 Tyrus, for insulting against Jerusalem, is threatened. 7 The power of Nebuchadrezzar against her. 15 The mourning and astonishment of the sea at her fall.

XXVII. 1 The rich supply of Tyrus. 26 The great and irrecoverable fall thereof.

XXVIII. 1 God's judgment upon the prince of Tyrus, for his sacrilegious pride. 11 A lamentation, of his great glory corrupted by sin. 20 The judgment of Zidon. 24 The restoration of Israel.

XXIX. The judgment of Pharaoh, for his treachery to Israel. 8 The desolation of Egypt. 12 The restoration thereof, after forty years. 17 Egypt the reward of Nebuchadrezzar. 21 Israel shall be restored.

XXX. 1 The desolation of Egypt and her helpers. 20 The arm of Babylon shall be strengthened to break the arm of Egypt.

XXXI. 1 A relation unto Pharaoh, 3 of the glory of Assyria, 10 and the fall thereof, for pride. 18 The like destruction of Egypt.

XXXII. 1 A lamentation for the fearful fall of Egypt. 11 The sword of Babylon shall destroy it. 17 It shall be brought down to hell, among all the uncircumcised nations.

XXXIII. 1 According to the duty of a watchman, in warning the people, 7 Ezekiel is admonished of his duty. 20 God shews the justice of his ways towards the penitent, and revolters. 17 He maintains his justice. 21 Upon the news of the taking of Jerusalem, he prophesies the desolation of the land. 30 God's judgment upon the mockers of the prophets.

XXXIV. 1 A reproof of the shepherds. 7 God's judgment against them. 11 His providence for his flock. 20 The kingdom of Christ.

XXXV. 1 The judgment of mount Seir, for their hatred of Israel.

XXXVI. 1 The land of Israel is comforted, both by destruction of the heathen, who spitefully used it, 8 and by the blessings of God promised unto it. 16 Israel was rejected for their sin, 11 and shall be restored without their desert. 25 The blessings of Christ's kingdom.

XXXVII. 1 By the resurrection of dry bones, 11 the dead hope of Israel revived. 15 By the uniting of two sticks, 18 is shewn the incorporation of Israel into Judah. 20 The promises of Christ's kingdom.

XXXVIII. 1 The army, 8 and malice of Gog. 14 God's judgment against him.

XXXIX. 1 God's judgment upon Gog. 8 Israel's victory. 11 Gog's burial in Hamon-gog. 17 The feast of the fowls. 23 Israel having been plagued for their sins, shall be gathered again with eternal favour.

XL. 1 The time, manner, and end of the vision. 6 The description of the east gate, 20 of the north gate, 24 of the south gate, 32 of the east gate, 35 and of the north gate. 39 Eight tables. 44 The chambers. 48 The porch of the house.

XLI. The measures, parts, chambers, and ornaments of the temple.

XLII. 1 The chambers for the priests. 13 The use thereof. 19 The measures of the outward court.

XLIII. 1 The returning of the glory of God into the temple. 7 The sin of Israel hindered God's presence. 10 The prophet exhorts them to repentance, and observation of the law of the house. 13 The measures, 18 and the ordinances of the altar.

XLIV. 1 The east gate assigned only to the prince. 4 The priests reproved for polluting of the sanctuary. 9 Idolaters incapable of the priest's office. 15 The sons of Zadok are accepted thereto. 17 Ordinances for the priests.

XLV. 1 The portion of land for the sanctuary, 6 for the city, 7 and for the prince. 9 Ordinances for the prince.

XLVI. 1 Ordinances for the prince in his worship, 9 and for the people. 16 An order for the prince's inheritance. 19 The courts for boiling and baking.

XLVII. 1 The vision of the holy waters. 6 The virtue of them. 13 The borders of the land. 22 The division of it by lot.

XLVIII. 1, 23 The portions of the twelve tribes, 8 of the sanctuary, 15 of the city and suburbs, 21 and of the prince. 30 The dimensions and gates of the city.

DANIEL.

I. Jehoiakim's captivity. 3 Ashpenaz takes Daniel, Hananiah, Mishael, and Azariah. 8 They refusing the king's portion, do prosper with pulse and water. 17 Their excellency in wisdom.

II. 1 Nebuchadnezzar forgetting his dream, requires it of the Chaldeans, by promises and threatenings. 10 They owning their inability, are judged to die. 14 Daniel obtaining some respite, finds the dream. 19 He blesses God. 24 He staying the decree, is brought to the king. 31 The dream. 36 The interpretation. 46 Daniel's advancement.

III. 1 Nebuchadnezzar dedicates a golden image in Dura. 8 Shadrach, Meshach, and Abed-nego are accused for not worshipping the image. 13 They being threatened, make a good confession. 19 God delivers them out of the furnace. 26 Nebuchadnezzar, seeing the miracle, blesses God.

IV. 1 Nebuchadnezzar confesses God's kingdom, 4 relates his dream, which the magicians could not interpret. 8 Daniel hears the dream. 19 He interprets it. 28 The story of the event.

V. Belshazzar's impious feast. 5 A hand-writing, unknown to the magicians, troubles the king. 10 By advice of the queen, Daniel is brought. 17 He reproving the king of pride and idolatry, 25 reads and interprets the writing. 30 The monarchy is translated to the Medes.

VI. 1 Daniel is made chief of the presidents. 4 They conspiring against him, obtain an idolatrous decree. 10 Daniel accused of the breach thereof, is cast into the lions' den. 18 Daniel is saved, 24 his adversaries devoured, 25 and God magnified by a decree.

VII. 1 Daniel's vision of four beasts. 9 Of God's kingdom. 15 The interpretation thereof.

VIII. 1 Daniel's vision of the ram and he-goat. 13 The two thousand three hundred days of sacrifice. 15 Gabriel comforts Daniel, and interprets the vision.

IX. 1 Daniel considering the time of the captivity, 3 makes confession of sins, 16 and prays for the restoration of Jerusalem. 20 Gabriel informs him of the seventy weeks.

X. 1 Daniel having humbled himself, sees a vision. 10 Being troubled with fear, he is comforted by the angel.
XI. 1 The overthrow of Persia by the king of Grecia. 5 Leagues and conflicts between the kings of the south and of the north. 30 The invasion and tyranny of the Romans.
XII. 1 Michael shall deliver Israel from their troubles. 5 Daniel is informed of the times.

HOSEA.

I. Hosea, to shew God's judgment for spiritual whoredom, takes Gomer, 4 and hath by her Jezreel, 6 Lo-ruhamah, 8 and Lo-ammi. 10 The restoration of Judah and Israel.
II. 1 The idolatry of the people. 6 God's judgments against them. 14 His promises of reconciliation with them.
III. 1 By the expiation of an adulteress, 4 is shewn the desolation of Israel before their restoration.
IV. 1 God's judgments against the sins of the people, 6 and of the priests, 12 and against their idolatry. 15 Judah is exhorted to take warning by Israel's calamity.
V. 1 God's judgments against the priests, the people, and the princes of Israel, for their manifold sins, 15 until they repent.
VI. 1 An exhortation to repentance. 4 A complaint of their untowardness and iniquity.
VII. 1 A reproof of manifold sins. 11 God's wrath against them for their hypocrisy.
VIII. 1, 12 Destruction is threatened for their impiety and idolatry.
IX. 1 The distress and captivity of Israel for their sins and idolatry.
X. Israel is reproved and threatened for their impiety and idolatry.
XI. 1 The ingratitude of Israel unto God for his benefits. 5 His judgment. 8 God's mercy to them.
XII. 1 A reproof of Ephraim, Judah, and Jacob. 3 By former favours he exhorts to repentance. 7 Ephraim's sins provoke God.
XIII. 1 Ephraim's glory, by reason of idolatry, vanisheth. 5 God's anger for their unkindness. 9 A promise of God's mercy. 15 A judgment for rebellion.
XIV. 1 An exhortation to repentance. 4 A promise of God's blessing.

JOEL.

I. Joel declaring sundry judgments of God, exhorts to observe them, 8 and to mourn. 14 He prescribes a fast for complaint.
II. 1 He shews unto Zion the terribleness of God's judgment. 12 He exhorts to repentance, 15 prescribes a fast, 18 promises a blessing thereon. 21 He comforteth Zion with present, 28 and future blessings.
III. 1 God's judgments against the enemies of his people. 9 God will be known in his judgment. 18 His blessing upon the church.

AMOS.

I. Amos shews God's judgment upon Syria, 6 upon the Philistines, 9 upon Tyrus, 11 upon Edom, 13 upon Ammon.
II. 1 God's wrath against Moab, 4 upon Judah, 6 and upon Israel. 9 God complains of their unthankfulness.
III. 1 The necessity of God's judgment against Israel. 9 The publication of it, with the causes thereof.
IV. 1 He reproves Israel for oppression, 4 for idolatry, 6 and for their incorrigibleness.
V. 1 A lamentation for Israel. 4 An exhortation to repentance. 21 God rejects their hypocritical service.
VI. 1 The wantonness of Israel, 7 shall be plagued with desolation, 12 and their incorrigibleness.
VII. 1 The judgments of the grasshoppers, 4 and of the fire, are diverted by the prayer of Amos. 7 By the wall of a plumb-line, is signified the rejection of Israel. 10 Amaziah complains of Amos. 14 Amos shews his calling, 16 and Amaziah's judgment.
VIII. 1 By a basket of summer fruit, is shewn the propinquity of Israel's end. 4 Oppression is reproved. 11 A famine of the word threatened.
IX. 1 The certainty of the desolation. 11 The restoring of the tabernacle of David.

OBADIAH.

1 The destruction of Edom, 3 for their pride, 10 and for their wrong unto Jacob. 17 The salvation and victory of Jacob.

JONAH.

I. Jonah sent to Nineveh, flees to Tarshish. 4 He is bewrayed by a tempest, 11 thrown into the sea, 17 and swallowed by a fish.
II. 1 The prayer of Jonah. 10 He is delivered from the fish.
III. 1 Jonah sent again, preaches to the Ninevites. 5 Upon their repentance, 10 God repents.
IV. 1 Jonah repining at God's mercy, 4 is reproved by the type of a gourd.

MICAH.

I. Micah shews the wrath of God against Jacob for idolatry. 10 He exhorts to mourning.
II. 1 Against oppression. 4 A lamentation. 7 A reproof of injustice and idolatry. 12 A promise of restoring Jacob.
III. 1 The cruelty of the princes. 5 The falsehood of the prophets. 8 The security of them both.
IV. 1 The glory, 3 peace, 8 kingdom, 11 and victory of the church.
V. 1 The birth of Christ. 4 His kingdom. 8 His conquest.
VI. 1 God's controversy for unkindness, 6 for ignorance, 10 for injustice, 16 and for idolatry.
VII. 1 The church complaining of her small number, 3 and the general corruption, 5 puts her confidence not in man, but in God. 8 She triumphs over her enemies. 14 God comforts her by promises, 16 by confusion of the enemies, 18 and by his mercies.

NAHUM.

I. God's majesty, in goodness to his people, and severity against his enemies.
II. 1 The fearful and victorious armies of God against Nineveh.
III. 1 The miserable ruin of Nineveh.

HABAKKUK.

I. Unto Habakkuk, complaining of the iniquity of the land, 5 is shewn the fearful vengeance by the Chaldeans. 12 He complains, that vengeance should be executed by them who are far worse.
II. 1 To Habakkuk, waiting for an answer, is shewn that he must wait in faith. 5 The judgment upon the Chaldeans for unsatiableness, 9 for covetousness, 12 for cruelty, 15 for drunkenness, 18 and for idolatry.
III. 1 Habakkuk, in his prayer, trembles at God's majesty. 17 The confidence of faith.

ZEPHANIAH.

I. God's severe judgment against Judah for divers sins.
II. 1 An exhortation to repentance. 4 The judgment of the Philistines, 8 of Moab and Ammon, 12 Ethiopia and Assyria.
III. 1 A sharp reproof of Jerusalem for divers sins. 8 An exhortation to wait for the restoration of Israel, 14 and to rejoice for their salvation by God.

HAGGAI.

I. Haggai reproves the people for neglecting the building of the house. 7 He incites them to the building. 12 He promises God's assistance to them being forward.
II. 1 He encourages the people to the work, by promise of greater glory to the second temple, than was in the first. 10 In the type of the holy things and unclean, he shews their sins hindered the work. 20 God's promise to Zerubbabel.

ZECHARIAH.

I. Zechariah exhorts to repentance. 7 The vision of the horses. 12 At the prayer of the angel, comfortable promises are made to Jerusalem. 18 The vision of the four horns, and the four carpenters.
II. 1 God in the care of Jerusalem sends to measure it. 6 The redemption of Zion. 10 The promise of God's presence.
III. 1 Under the type of Joshua, the restoration of the church is promised. 18 Christ the Branch foretold.
IV. 1 By the golden candlestick is foreshewn the good success of Zerubbabel's foundation. 11 By the two olive-trees, the two anointed ones.
V. 1 By the flying roll, is shewn the curse of thieves and swearers. 5 By a woman pressed in an ephah, the final damnation of Babylon.
VI. 1 The vision of the four chariots. 9 By the crowns of Joshua is shewn the temple and kingdom of Christ the Branch.
VII. 1 The captives inquire of fasting. 4 Zechariah reproves their fasting. 8 Sin the cause of their captivity.
VIII. 1 The restoration of Jerusalem. 9 They are encouraged to the building by God's favour to them. 16 Good works are required of them. 18 Joy and enlargement are promised.
IX. 1 God defends his church. 9 Zion is exhorted to rejoice for the coming of Christ, and his peaceable kingdom. 12 God's promises of victory and defence.
X. 1 God is to be sought unto, and not idols. 5 As he visited his flock for sin, so he will save and restore them.
XI. 1 The destruction of Jerusalem. 3 The elect being cared for, the rest are rejected. 10 The staves of Beauty and Bands broken by the rejection of Christ. 15 The type and curse of a foolish shepherd.
XII. 1 Jerusalem a cup of trembling to herself, and a burdensome stone to her adversaries. 6 The victorious restoring of Judah. 9 The repentance of Jerusalem.
XIII. 1 The fountain of purgation for Jerusalem, 2 from idolatry, and false prophecy. 7 The death of Christ, and the trial of a third part.
XIV. 1 The destroyers of Jerusalem destroyed. 4 The coming of Christ, and the graces of his kingdom. 12 The plague of Jerusalem's enemies. 16 The remnant shall turn to the Lord, 20 and their spoils shall be holy.

MALACHI.

I. Malachi complains of Israel's unkindness, 6 of their irreligiousness, 12 and profaneness.
II. 1 He sharply reproves the priests for neglecting their covenant, 11 and the people for idolatry, 14 for adultery, 17 and for infidelity.
III. 1 Of the messenger, majesty, and grace of Christ. 7 Of the rebellion, 8 sacrilege, 13 and infidelity of the people. 16 The promise of blessing to them that fear God.
IV. 1 God's judgment on the wicked, 2 and his blessing on the good. 4 He exhorts to the study of the law, 5 and tells of Elijah's coming, and office.

A COMPLETE

SUMMARY OF THE NEW TESTAMENT;

OR,

THE CONTENTS OF ALL THE CHAPTERS;

TAKEN FROM THE FIRST EDITION OF THE LAST TRANSLATION OF THE HOLY BIBLE

CAREFULLY COMPARED WITH, AND CORRECTED BY, THE SACRED TEXT

COL. II. 16. LET THE WORD OF CHRIST DWELL IN YOU RICHLY.

ST. MATTHEW.

I GENEALOGY of Christ from Abraham to Joseph. 18 He was conceived by the Holy Ghost, and born of the Virgin Mary, when she was espoused to Joseph. 19 The angel satisfieth the misdeeming thoughts of Joseph, and interpreteth the names of Christ.

II. 1 The wise men from the east are directed to Christ by a star: 11 they worship him, and offer their presents. 14 Joseph fleeth into Egypt, with Jesus and his mother. 16 Herod slayeth the children. 20 Himself dieth. 23 Christ is brought back again into Galilee to Nazareth.

III. 1 John preacheth: his office, life, and baptism. 7 He reprehendeth the Pharisees, 13 and baptizeth Christ in Jordan.

IV. 1 Christ fasteth, and is tempted. 11 The angels minister unto him. 13 He dwelleth in Capernaum, 17 beginneth to preach, 18 calleth Peter and Andrew, 21 James and John, 23 and healeth all the diseased.

V. 1 Christ beginneth his sermon in the mount: 3 declaring who are blessed, 13 who are the salt of the earth, 14 the light of the world, the city on an hill: 15 the candle: 17 that he came to fulfil the law. 21 What it is to kill, 27 to commit adultery, 33 to swear: 38 exhorteth to suffer wrong, 44 to love our enemies, 48 and to labour after perfectness.

VI. 1 Christ continueth his sermon in the mount, speaking of alms, 5 prayer, 14 forgiving our brethren, 16 fasting, 19 where our treasure is to be laid up, 24 of serving God and mammon: 25 exhorteth not to be careful for worldly things; 33 but to seek God's kingdom.

VII. 1 Christ endeth his sermon in the mount, reproveth rash judgment, 6 forbiddeth to cast holy things to dogs, 7 exhorteth to prayer, 13 to enter in at the strait gate, 15 to beware of false prophets, 21 not to be hearers, but doers of the word: 24 like houses built on a rock, 26 and not on the sand.

VIII. 2 Christ cleanseth the leper. 5 healeth the centurion's servant, 14 Peter's mother-in-law, 16 and many other diseased: 18 shews how he is to be followed: 23 stilleth the tempest at sea, 28 driveth the devils out of two men possessed, 31 and suffereth them to go into the swine.

IX. 2 Christ curing one sick of the palsy, 9 calls Matthew from the receipt of custom, 10 eats with publicans and sinners, 14 defends his disciples for not fasting, 20 cureth the bloody issue, 23 raiseth Jairus's daughter, 27 giveth sight to two blind men, 32 heals a dumb man possessed of a devil, 36 and hath compassion on the multitude.

X. 1 Christ sends out his twelve apostles with power to do miracles, 5 giveth them their charge, teaches, 16 and comforts them against persecutions, 40 and promises a blessing to those that receive them.

XI. 2 John sends his disciples to Christ. 7 Christ's testimony concerning John. 18 The opinion of the people, both concerning John and Christ. 20 Christ upbraids the ingratitude and impenitence of Chorazin, Bethsaida, and Capernaum: 25 and praising his Father's wisdom in revealing the gospel to the simple, 28 he calls to him all such as feel the burden of their sins.

XII. 1 Christ reproves the blindness of the Pharisees concerning the breach of the sabbath, 3 by Scripture, 10 by reason, 13 and by a miracle. 22 He healeth the man possessed that was blind and dumb. 13 Blasphemy against the Holy Ghost shall never be forgiven. 36 Account shall be made of idle words. 38 He rebuketh the unfaithful, who seek after a sign, 49 and shews who is his brother, sister, and mother.

XIII. 3 The parable of the sower and the seed: 18 the exposition of it. 24 The parable of the tares, 31 of the mustard-seed, 33 of the leaven, 44 of the hidden treasure, 45 of the pearl, 47 of the draw-net cast into the sea: 53 and how Christ is contemned of his own countrymen.

XIV. 1 Herod's opinion of Christ. 3 Wherefore John Baptist was beheaded. 13 Jesus departeth into a desert place: 15 where he feedeth five thousand men with five loaves and two fishes. 22 He walketh on the sea to his disciples: 34 and landing at Gennesaret, healeth the sick by the touch of the hem of his garment.

XV. 3 Christ reproves the scribes and Pharisees for transgressing God's commandments through their own traditions; 11 teaches how that which goeth into the mouth doth not defile a man. 21 He healeth the daughter of the woman of Canaan, 30 and other great multitudes: 32 and with seven loaves and a few little fishes feedeth four thousand men, besides women and children.

XVI. 1 The Pharisees require a sign. 6 Jesus warns his disciples of the leaven of the Pharisees and Sadducees. 13 The people's opinion of Christ, 16 and Peter's confession of him. 21 Jesus foresheweth his death, 23 reproving Peter for dissuading him from it, 24 and admonishes those that will follow him to bear the cross.

XVII. 1 The transfiguration of Christ. 14 He heals the lunatic, 22 foretells his own passion, 24 and pays tribute.

XVIII. 1 Christ warns his disciples to be humble and harmless, 7 to avoid offences, and not to despise the little ones: 15 teaches how we are to deal with our brethren when they offend us, 21 and how oft to forgive them; 23 which he sets forth by a parable of the king, that took account of his servants, 32 and punished him who shewed no mercy to his fellow.

XIX. 2 Christ heals the sick: 3 answers the Pharisees concerning divorcement: 10 shews when marriage is necessary: 13 receives little children: 16 instructs the young man how to attain eternal life, 20 and how to be perfect: 23 telleth his disciples how hard it is for a rich man to enter into the kingdom of God: 27 and promises reward to those that forsake any thing to follow him.

XX. 1 Christ by the similitude of the labourers in the vineyard, shews that God is debtor to no man: 17 foretells his passion: 20 by answering the mother of Zebedee's children, teaches his disciples to be lowly: 30 and giveth two blind men their sight.

XXI. 1 Christ rides into Jerusalem upon an ass: 12 drives the buyers and sellers out of the temple: 17 curses the fig-tree: 23 silences the priests and elders, 28 and rebuketh them by the similitude of the two sons, 33 and the husbandmen who slew such as were sent unto them.

XXII. 1 The parable of the marriage of the king's son. 9 The vocation of the Gentiles. 12 The punishment of him that wanted the wedding garment. 15 Tribute ought to be paid to Cæsar. 23 Christ confutes the Sadducees concerning the resurrection: 34 answers the lawyer, which is the great commandment: 41 and poseth the Pharisees about the Messias.

XXIII. 1 Christ admonishes the people to follow the good doctrine, not the evil examples, of the Scribes and Pharisees: 5 his disciples must beware of their ambition. 13 He denounces eight woes against their hypocrisy and blindness; 34 and foretells the destruction of Jerusalem.

XXIV. 1 Christ foretells the destruction of the temple. 3 What and how great calamities shall be before it. 29 The signs of his coming to judgment: 36 and because that day and hour is unknown, 42 we ought to watch, like good servants, expecting every moment our master's coming.

XXV. 1 The parable of the ten virgins, 14 and of the talents. 31 Also the description of the last judgment.

XXVI. 1 The rulers conspire against Christ. 7 The woman anoints his head. 14 Judas sells him. 17 Christ eats the passover: 26 institutes his holy supper: 36 prays in the garden: 47 and, being betrayed with a kiss, 57 is carried to Caiaphas, 69 and denied of Peter.

XXVII. 1 Christ is delivered bound to Pilate. 5 Judas hangs himself. 19 Pilate admonished of his wife, 24 washeth his hands, 26 and looseth Barabbas. 29 Christ is crowned with thorns, 35 crucified, 40 reviled, 50 dieth, and is buried. 66 His sepulchre is sealed, and watched.

XXVIII. 1 Christ's resurrection is declared by an angel to the women. 9 He himself appears to them. 11 The high priests give the soldiers money to say that he was stolen out of his sepulchre. 16 Christ appears to his disciples; 19 and sends them to baptize and teach all nations.

ST. MARK.

I. Office of John Baptist. 9 Jesus is baptized, 12 tempted: 14 he preacheth: 16 calls Peter, Andrew, James, and John: 23 heals one that had a devil, 29 Peter's mother-in-law, 32 many diseased persons, 41 and cleanseth a leper.

II. 3 Christ heals one sick of the palsy, 14 calls Matthew from the receipt of custom, 15 eats with publicans and sinners, 18 excuses his disciples for not fasting, 23 and for plucking the ears of corn on the sabbath-day.

III. 1 Christ heals the withered hand, 10 and many other infirmities: 11 rebukes the unclean spirits: 13 chooses his twelve apostles: 22 convinces the blasphemy of casting out devils by Beelzebub: 31 and shews who are his brother, sister, and mother.

IV. 1 The parable of the sower, 14 and the meaning thereof. 21 We must communicate the light of our knowledge to others. 26 The parable of the seed growing secretly, 30 and of the mustard seed. 35 Christ stills the tempest on the sea.

V. 1 Christ delivering the possessed of the legion of devils, 13 they enter into the swine. 25 He heals the woman of a bloody issue, 35 and raiseth from death Jairus's daughter.

VI. 1 Christ is contemned of his countrymen. 7 He gives the twelve power over unclean spirits. 14 Divers opinions of Christ. 18 John Baptist is beheaded, 29 and buried. 30 The apostles return from preaching. 34 The miracle of five loaves and two fishes. 48 Christ walks on the sea: 53 and heals all that touch him.

VII. 1 The Pharisees find fault at the disciples for eating with unwashen hands. 8 They break the commandment of God by the traditions of men. 14 Meat defileth not the man. 24 He healeth the Syrophœnician woman's daughter of an unclean spirit, 31 and one that was deaf, and stammered in his speech.

VIII. 1 Christ feeds the people miraculously: 10 refuseth to give a sign to the Pharisees: 14 admonishes his disciples to beware of the leaven of the Pharisees, and of the leaven of Herod: 22 gives a blind man his sight: 17 acknowledgeth that he is the Christ, who should suffer and rise again: 34 and exhorts to patience in persecution, for the profession of the gospel.

IX. 2 Jesus is transfigured. 11 He instructeth his disciples concerning the coming of Elias: 13 casteth forth a dumb and deaf spirit: 30 foretelleth his death and resurrection: 33 exhorts his disciples to humility: 38 bids them not to prohibit such as be not against them, nor to give offence to any of the faithful.

X. 2 Christ disputes with the Pharisees touching divorcement: 13 blesseth the children that are brought to him: 17 resolveth a rich man how he may inherit life everlasting: 23 tells his disciples of the danger of riches: 28 promises rewards to them that forsake any thing for the gospel: 32 foretells his death and resurrection: 35 bids the two ambitious suitors to think rather of suffering with him: 46 and restores to Bartimeus his sight.

XI. Christ rides with triumph into Jerusalem: 12 curses the fruitless fig-tree: 15 purges the temple; 20 exhorts his disciples to stedfastness of faith, and to forgive their enemies; 27 and defends the lawfulness of his actions, by the witness of John, who was a man sent of God.

XII. 1 In a parable of the vineyard let out to unthankful husbandmen, Christ foretelleth the reprobation of the Jews, and the calling of the Gentiles. 13 He avoids the snare of the Pharisees and Herodians about paying tribute to Cæsar: 18 convinces the error of the Sadducees, who denied the resurrection: 28 resolves the scribe who questioned of the first commandment: 35 refutes the opinion that the scribes held of Christ: 38 bidding the people to beware of their ambition and hypocrisy: 41 and commends the poor widow for her two mites, above all.

XIII. 1 Christ foretells the destruction of the temple: 9 the persecutions for the gospel: 10 that the gospel must be preached to all nations: 14 that great calamities shall happen to the Jews: 24 and the manner of his coming to judgment. 32 The hour whereof being known to none, every man is to watch and pray, that we be not found unprovided, when he cometh to each one particularly by death.

XIV. 1 A conspiracy against Christ. 3 Precious ointment is poured on his head by a woman. 10 Judas sells his master for money. 12 Christ himself foretells how he shall be betrayed of one of his disciples: 22 after the passover prepared, and eaten, institutes his supper: 26 foretells the flight of all his disciples, and Peter's denial. 43 Judas betrayeth him with a kiss. 46 He is apprehended in the garden, 55 falsely accused, and impiously condemned of the Jews' council, 65 shamefully abused by them, 66 and thrice denied of Peter.

XV. 1 Jesus brought bound, and accused before Pilate. 15 Upon the clamour of the common people, the murderer Barabbas is loosed, and Jesus delivered up to be crucified. 17 He is crowned with thorns, 19 spit on, and mocked: 21 fainteth in bearing his cross: 27 hangeth between two thieves: 29 suffereth the triumphing reproaches of the Jews: 39 but confessed by the centurion to be the Son of God: 43 and is honourably buried by Joseph.

XVI. 1 An angel declares the resurrection of Christ to three women. 9 Christ himself appears to Mary Magdalene: 12 to two going into the country: 14 then to the apostles, 15 whom he sendeth forth to preach the gospel: 19 and ascends into heaven.

ST. LUKE.

I. The preface of Luke to his whole gospel. 5 The conception of John Baptist, 26 and of Christ. 39 The prophecy of Elisabeth, and of Mary, concerning Christ. 57 The nativity and circumcision of John. 67 The prophecy of Zacharias, both of Christ, 76 and of John.

II. 1 Augustus taxeth all the Roman empire. 6 The nativity of Christ. 8 One angel relateth it to the shepherds: 13 many sing praises to God for it. 21 Christ is circumcised. 22 Mary purified. 28 Simeon and Anna prophesy of Christ: 40 who increaseth in wisdom, 46 questioneth in the temple with the doctors, 51 and is obedient to his parents.

III. 1 The preaching and baptism of John. 15 His testimony of Christ. 20 Herod imprisoneth John. 21 Christ baptized, receives testimony from heaven. 23 The age and genealogy of Christ, from Joseph upwards.

IV. 1 The temptation and fasting of Christ. 13 He overcomes the devil: 14 begins to preach. 16 The people of Nazareth admire his gracious words. 33 He cures one possessed of a devil, 38 Peter's mother-in-law, 40 and divers other sick persons. 41 The devils acknowledge Christ, and are reproved for it. 43 He preaches through the cities.

V. 1 Christ teaches the people out of Peter's ship: 4 in a miraculous taking of fishes, shews how he will make him and his partners fishers of men: 12 cleanseth the leper: 16 prays in the wilderness: 18 heals one sick of the palsy: 27 calls Matthew the publican: 29 eats with sinners, as being the physician of souls; 34 foretells the fastings and afflictions of the apostles after his ascension: 36 and likens faint-hearted and weak disciples to worn garments and old bottles.

VI. 1 Christ reproves the Pharisees' blindness about the observation of the sabbath, by scripture, reason, and miracle: 13 chooseth twelve apostles: 17 heals the diseased: 20 preacheth to his disciples before the people, of blessings and curses; 27 how we must love our enemies; 46 and join the obedience of good works to the hearing of the word, lest in the evil day of temptation we fall like an house built upon the face of the earth without any foundation.

VII. 1 Christ finds a greater faith in the centurion, a Gentile, than in any of the Jews: 10 heals his servant being absent: 11 raiseth from death the widow's son at Nain: 19 answers John's messengers with the declaration of his miracles: 24 testifies to the people what opinion he held of John: 30 inveighs against the Jews, who with neither the manners of John nor of Jesus could be won: 36 and shews by occasion of Mary Magdalene how he is a friend of sinners, not to maintain them in sins, but to forgive them their sins upon their faith and repentance.

VIII. 1 Women minister to Christ of their substance. 4 Christ, after he had preached from place to place, attended with his apostles, propounds the parable of the sower, 16 and of the candle: 21 declares who are his mother and brethren: 22 rebukes the wind: 26 casteth the legion of devils out of the man, into the herd of swine: 37 is rejected of the Gadarenes: 43 heals the woman of her bloody issue: 49 and raises from death Jairus's daughter.

IX. 1 Christ sends his apostles to work miracles, and to preach. 7 Herod desireth to see Christ. 17 Christ feeds five thousand: 18 inquireth what opinion the world had of him: 21 foretells his passion: 23 proposes to all the pattern of his patience. 28 The transfiguration. 37 He heals the lunatic: 43 again forewarns his disciples of his passion: 46 commends humility: 51 bids them to shew mildness towards all, without desire of revenge. 57 Divers would follow him but upon conditions.

X. 1 Christ sends out at once seventy disciples to work miracles, and to preach: 17 admonishes them to be humble, and wherein to rejoice: 21 thanks his Father for his grace: 23 magnifies the happy estate of his church: 25 teaches the lawyer what the law requires to attain eternal life, and to take every one for his neighbour, that needeth his mercy. 41 Reprehends Martha, and commends Mary her sister.

XI. 1 Christ teaches to pray, and that instantly: 11 assuring that God so will give us good things. 14 He casting out a dumb devil, rebukes the blasphemous Pharisees: 28 shews who are blessed: 29 preaches to the people, 37 and reprehends the outward shew of holiness in the Pharisees, scribes, and lawyers.

XII. 1 Christ preaches to his disciples to avoid hypocrisy, and fearfulness in publishing his doctrine: 13 warns the people to beware of covetousness, by the parable of the rich man, who set up greater barns. 22 Take no thought for your life; 31 but seek the kingdom of God, 33 give alms, 36 be ready at a knock to open to our Lord, whensoever he cometh. 41 Christ's ministers are to see to their charge, 49 and look for persecution. 54 Take this time of grace, 58 because it is a fearful thing to die without reconciliation.

XIII. 1 Christ preacheth repentance upon the punishment of the Galileans, and others. 6 The fruitless fig-tree may not stand. 11 He healeth the crooked woman: 18 shews the powerful working of the word in the hearts of his chosen, by the parable of the grain of mustard-seed, and of leaven: 24 exhorts to enter in at the strait gate, 31 and reproveth Herod and Jerusalem.

XIV. 2 Christ heals the dropsy on the sabbath: 7 teaches humility: 12 to feast the poor: 16 Under the parable of the great supper, sheweth how worldly-minded men, who contemn the word of God, shall be shut out of heaven. 25 Those who will be his disciples, to bear their cross, are advised to count the cost, lest with shame they revolt from him afterward, 34 and become altogether unprofitable, like salt that has lost its savour.

XV. 1 The parable of the lost sheep; 8 of the piece of silver; 11 of the prodigal son.

XVI. 1 The parable of the unjust steward. 14 Christ reproves the hypocrisy of the covetous Pharisees. 19 Dives and Lazarus.

XVII. 1 Christ teaches to avoid occasion of offence. 3 One to forgive another. 6 The power of faith. 7 How we are bound to God, and not he to us. 11 He heals ten lepers. 22 Of the kingdom of God, and the coming of the Son of man.

XVIII. 1 Of the importunate widow: 9 of the Pharisee and publican. 15 Children brought to Christ. 18 A ruler that would follow Christ, but is hindered by his riches. 28 The reward of them that leave all for his sake. 31 He foretells his death, 35 and restores a blind man to his sight.

XIX. 1 Of Zaccheus a publican. 11 The ten pieces of money. 28 Christ rides into Jerusalem with triumph: 41 weeps over it: 45 drives the buyers and sellers out of the temple: 47 teaching daily in it. The rulers would have destroyed him, but for fear of the people.

XX. 1 Christ asserts his authority by a question of John's baptism. 9 The parable of the vineyard. 19 Of giving tribute to Cæsar. 27 He convinces the Sadducees that denied the resurrection. 41 How Christ is the son of David: 45 He warns his disciples to beware of the scribes.

XXI. 1 Christ commends the poor widow. 5 He foretells the destruction of the temple and city of Jerusalem: 25 the signs also that shall be before the last day. 34 He exhorts them to be watchful.

XXII. 1 The Jews conspire against Christ. 3 Satan prepares Judas to betray him. 7 The apostles sent to prepare the passover. 19 Christ institutes his holy supper: 21 covertly foretells of the traitor: 24 dehorts the rest of his apostles from ambition: 32 assures Peter his faith should not fail, 34 and yet he should deny him thrice. 39 He prays on the mount, and sweats blood: 47 is betrayed with a kiss. 50 He heals Malchus's ear. 54 He is thrice denied of Peter, 63 shamefully abused, 66 and confesses himself to be the Son of God.

XXIII. 1 Jesus is accused before Pilate, and sent to Herod. 8 Herod mocks him. 12 Herod and Pilate are made friends. 18 Barabbas is desired of the people, and is loosed by Pilate, and Jesus given to be crucified. 27 He tells the women that lament him, the destruction of Jerusalem: 34 Prayeth for his enemies. 39 Two thieves are crucified with him. 46 His death. 50 His burial.

XXIV. 1 Christ's resurrection is declared by two angels, to the women that came to the sepulchre. 9 These report it to others. 13 Christ himself appears to the two disciples that went to Emmaus. 36 Afterwards he appears to the apostles, and reproves their unbelief: 47 gives them a charge: 49 promises the Holy Ghost: 51 and so ascends into heaven.

ST. JOHN.

I. The divinity, humanity, and office of Christ. 15 The testimony of John. 38 The calling of Andrew, Peter, &c.

II. 1 Christ turns water into wine, 12 departs into Capernaum, and to Jerusalem, 14 where he purges the temple of buyers and sellers. 19 He foretells his death and resurrection. 23 Many believed because of his miracles, but he would not trust himself with them.

III. 1 Christ teaches Nicodemus the necessity of regeneration: 14 of faith in his death. 16 The great love of God towards the world. 18 Condemnation for unbelief. 23 The baptism, witness, and doctrine of John concerning Christ.

IV. 1 Christ talks with a woman of Samaria, and reveals himself unto her. 27 His disciples marvel. 31 He declares to them his zeal to God's glory. 39 Many Samaritans believe on him. 43 He departs into Galilee, and heals the ruler's son that lay sick at Capernaum.

V. 1 Jesus on the sabbath-day cures him that was diseased eight-and-thirty years. 10 The Jews therefore cavil and persecute him for it. 17 He answers for himself, and reproves them, shewing by the testimony of his Father, 32 of John, 36 of his works, 39 and of the Scriptures, who he is.

VI. 1 Christ feedeth five thousand men with five loaves and two fishes. 15 Thereupon the people would have made him king. 16 But withdrawing himself, he walked on the sea to his disciples: 26 reproves the people flocking after him, and all the fleshly hearers of his word: 32 declares himself to be the bread of life to believers. 66 Many disciples depart from him. 68 Peter confesseth him. 70 Judas is a devil.

VII. 1 Jesus reproved the ambition and boldness of his kinsmen: 10 goes up from Galilee to the feast of tabernacles: 14 teaches in the temple. 40 Divers opinions of him among the people. 45 The Pharisees are angry that their officers took him not, and chide Nicodemus for taking his part.

VIII. 1 Christ delivers the woman taken in adultery: 12 he preaches himself the light of the world, and justifieth his doctrine; 33 answers the Jews that boasted of Abraham, 59 and conveys himself from their cruelty.

IX. 1 The man that was born blind restored to sight. 8 He is brought to the Pharisees. 16 They are offended at it, and 34 excommunicate him: 35 but he is received of Jesus, and confesseth him. 39 Who they are whom Christ enlighteneth.

X. 1 Christ is the door and the good shepherd: 19 divers opinions of him: 25 he proves, by his works, that he is Christ the Son of God: 39 escapes the Jews, 40 and went again beyond Jordan, where many believed on him.

XI. 1 Christ raises Lazarus four days buried. 45 Many Jews believe. 47 The chief priests and Pharisees gather a council against Christ. 49 Caiaphas prophesies. 54 Jesus hid himself. 55 At the passover they inquire after him, and lay wait for him.

XII. 1 Jesus excuses Mary anointing his feet. 9 The people flock to see Lazarus. 10 The chief priests consult to kill him. 12 Christ rideth into Jerusalem. 20 Greeks desire to see Jesus. 23 He foretells his death. 37 The Jews are generally blinded: 42 yet many chief rulers believe, but not confess him: 44 therefore Jesus calls earnestly for confession of faith.

XIII. 1 Jesus washes the disciples' feet: 14 exhorts them to humility and charity. 18 He foretells and discovers to John by a token, that Judas should betray him: 31 commands them to love one another, 36 and forewarns Peter of his denial.

XIV. 1 Christ comforts his disciples with the hope of heaven: 6 professes himself the way, the truth, and the life; and one with the Father: 13 assures their prayers in his name to be effectual: 15 requests love and obedience: 16 promises the Holy Ghost the Comforter: 27 and leaves his peace with them.

XV. 1 The consolation and mutual love between Christ and his members, under the parable of the vine. 18 A comfort in the hatred and persecution of the world. 26 The office of the Holy Ghost, and of the apostles.

XVI. 1 Christ comforts his disciples against tribulation, by the promise of the Holy Ghost, and by his resurrection and ascension; 23 assures their prayers made in his name to be acceptable to his Father. 33 Peace in Christ, and in the world affliction.

XVII. 1 Christ prays to his Father to glorify him: 6 to preserve his apostles, 11 in unity, 17 and truth: 20 to glorify them, and all other believers with him, in heaven.

XVIII. 1 Judas betrays Jesus. 6 The officers fall to the ground. 10 Peter smites off Malchus's ear. 12 Jesus is taken and led unto Annas and Caiaphas. 15 Peter's denial. 19 Jesus examined before Caiaphas. 28 His arraignment before Pilate. 36 His kingdom. 40 The Jews ask Barabbas to be set loose.

XIX. 1 Christ is scourged, crowned with thorns, and beaten. 4 Pilate is desirous to release him, but being overcome with the outrage of the Jews, he delivered him to be crucified. 23 They cast lots for his garments. 26 He commendeth his mother to John. 28 He dieth. 31 His side is pierced. 38 He is buried by Joseph and Nicodemus.

XX. 1 Mary comes to the sepulchre: 3 so do Peter and John, ignorant of the resurrection. 11 Jesus appears to Mary Magdalene, 19 and to his disciples. 24 The incredulity and confession of Thomas. 30 The Scripture is sufficient to salvation.

XXI. 1 Christ appearing again to his disciples, was known of them by the great draught of fishes. 12 He dineth with them; 15 earnestly commandeth Peter to feed his lambs and sheep; 18 foretells him of his death; 22 rebukes his curiosity touching John. 25 The conclusion.

ACTS.

I. Christ preparing his apostles to behold his ascension, gathers them together into the mount Olivet, commands them to expect in Jerusalem the sending down of the Holy Ghost, promises after few days to send it; by virtue whereof they should be witnesses unto him, even to the utmost parts of the earth. 9 After his ascension they are warned by two angels to depart, and to set their minds upon his second coming. 12 They accordingly return, and giving themselves to prayer, choose Matthias apostle in the place of Judas.

II. 1 The apostles filled with the Holy Ghost, and speaking divers languages, are admired by some, and derided by others. 14 Whom Peter disproving, and shewing that the apostles spake by the power of the Holy Ghost, that Jesus was risen from the dead, ascended into heaven, had poured down the same Holy Ghost, and was the Messias, a man known to them to be approved of God, by his miracles, wonders, and signs, and not crucified without his determinate counsel and foreknowledge: 37 he baptizeth a great number that were converted, 41 who afterwards devoutly and charitably converse together: the apostles working many miracles, and God daily increasing his church.

III. 1 Peter preacheth to the people that came to see a lame man restored to his feet, 12 and professes the cure not to have been wrought by his or John's own power, or holiness, but by God, and his Son Jesus, and through faith in his name: 13 withal reprehending them for crucifying Jesus. 17 Which because they did it through ignorance, and that thereby were fulfilled God's determinate counsel, and the Scriptures, 19 he exhorts them by repentance and faith to seek remission of their sins, and salvation in the same Jesus.

IV. 1 The rulers of the Jews, offended with Peter's sermon, 4 (though thousands of the people were converted that heard the word,) imprison him and John. 5 After, upon examination, Peter boldly avouching the lame man to be healed by the name of Jesus, and that by the same Jesus only we must be eternally saved, 13 they commanded him and John to preach no more in that name, adding threatenings also. 23 Whereupon the church goes to prayer: 31 and God, by moving the place where they were assembled, testified that he heard their prayer, confirming the church with the gift of the Holy Ghost, and with mutual love and charity.

V. 1 After that Ananias and Sapphira his wife, for their hypocrisy, at Peter's rebuke, had fallen down dead, 12 and that the rest of the apostles had wrought many miracles; 14 to the increase of the faith: 17 the apostles are again imprisoned, 19 but delivered by an angel, bidding them to preach openly to all. 21 When, after their teaching accordingly in the temple, 29 and before the council, 33 they are in danger to be killed; through the advice of Gamaliel, a great counsellor among the Jews, they are kept alive, 40 and only beaten: for which they glorify God, and cease no day from preaching.

VI. 1 The apostles, desirous to have the poor regarded for their bodily sustenance, as also careful themselves to dispense the word of God, the food of the soul, 3 appoint the office of deaconship to seven chosen men: 38 of whom Stephen, a man full of faith and of the Holy Ghost, is one: 12 who is taken of those whom he confounded in disputing, 13 and falsely accused of blasphemy against the law and the temple.

VII. 1 Stephen permitted to answer to the accusation of blasphemy, 2 shews that Abraham worshipped God rightly, and how God chose the fathers, 20 before Moses was born, and before the tabernacle and temple were built: 37 that Moses himself witnessed of Christ: 44 and that all outward ceremonies were ordained according to the heavenly pattern, to last but for a time: 51 reprehending their rebellion, and murdering of Christ, the Just One, whom the prophets foretold should come into the world: 54 whereupon they stone him to death; who commends his soul to Jesus, and humbly prays for them.

VIII. 1 Stephen's burial. 5 The church planted in Samaria, by Philip the deacon, who preached, did miracles, and baptized many, among the rest Simon the sorcerer, a great seducer of the people. 14 Peter and John come to confirm and enlarge the church: where by prayer and imposition of hands giving the Holy Ghost, 18 when Simon would have bought the like power of them, 20 Peter sharply reproves his hypocrisy and covetousness, and exhorts him to repentance: Peter and John, preaching the word, return to ' salem. 26 The angel sends Philip to teac baptize the Ethiopian eunuch.

IX. 1 Saul going towards Damascus, 4 is struck down to the earth, 10 is called to the apostleship, 18 and is baptized by Ananias. 20 He preaches Christ boldly. 23 The Jews lay wait to kill him; 29 so do the Grecians; but he escapes both. 31 The church having rest, Peter heals Æneas of the palsy, 36 and restores Tabitha to life.

X. 1 Cornelius, a devout man, 5 being commanded by an angel, sends for Peter: 11 who by a vision, 15, 20 is taught not to despise the Gentiles. 34 As he preaches Christ to Cornelius and his company, 44 the Holy Ghost falls on them, 48 and they are baptized.

XI. 1 Peter, being accused for going in to the Gentiles, 5 makes his defence, 18 which is accepted. 19 The gospel being spread into Phenice, and Cyprus, and Antioch, Barnabas is sent to confirm them. 26 The disciples there are first called Christians. 27 They send relief to the brethren in Judea in time of famine.

XII. 1 King Herod persecutes the Christians, kills James, and imprisons Peter, whom an angel delivers upon the prayers of the church. 20 In his pride, taking to himself the honour due to God, he is struck by an angel, and dies miserably. 24 After his death the word of God prospers.

XIII. 1 Paul and Barnabas are chosen to go to the Gentiles. 7 Of Sergius Paulus, and Elymas the sorcerer. 14 Paul preaches at Antioch, that Jesus is Christ. 42 The Gentiles believe; 45 but the Jews gainsay and blaspheme; 46 whereupon they turn to the Gentiles. 48 As many as were ordained to life believed.

XIV. 1 Paul and Barnabas are persecuted from Iconium. 7 At Lystra Paul heals a cripple; whereupon they are reputed as gods. 19 Paul is stoned. 21 They pass through divers churches, confirming the disciples in faith and patience: 26 returning to Antioch, they report what God had done with them.

XV. 1 Great dissension arises about circumcision. 6 The apostles consult about it, 22 and send their determination by letters to the churches. 36 Paul and Barnabas, thinking to visit the brethren together, fall at strife, and depart asunder.

XVI. 1 Paul having circumcised Timothy, 7 and being called by the Spirit from one country to another, 14 converteth Lydia, 16 casteth out a spirit of divination: 19 for which cause he and Silas are whipped and imprisoned. 25 The prison doors are opened. 31 The jailor is converted, 37 and they are delivered.

XVII. 1 Paul preaches at Thessalonica: 4 where some believe, and others persecute him: 10 he is sent to Berea, and preacheth there. 13 Being persecuted at Thessalonica, 15 he cometh to Athens, and disputes, and preaches the living God to them unknown, 34 whereby many are converted unto Christ.

XVIII. 3 Paul labours with his hands, and preaches at Corinth to the Gentiles: 9 the Lord encourages him in a vision: 12 he is accused before Gallio the deputy, but is dismissed. 18 Afterwards, passing from city to city, he strengthens the disciples. 24 Apollos, being more perfectly instructed by Aquila and Priscilla, 28 preaches Christ with great efficacy.

XIX. 6 The Holy Ghost is given by Paul's hands. 9 The Jews blaspheme his doctrine, which is confirmed by miracles. 13 The Jewish exorcists, 16 are beaten by the devil. 19 Conjuring-books are burnt. 24 Demetrius, for love of gain, raiseth an uproar against Paul, 35 which is appeased by the town-clerk.

XX. 1 Paul goes to Macedonia. 7 He celebrates the Lord's supper, and preaches. 9 Eutychus being killed by a fall, 10 is raised to life. 17 At Miletus Paul calls the elders together, tells them what shall befall to himself, 28 commits God's flock to them, 29 warns them of false teachers, 32 commends them to God, 36 prays with them, and goes his way.

XXI. 1 Paul will not by any means be dissuaded from going to Jerusalem. 9 Philip's daughters prophetesses. 17 Paul comes to Jerusalem: 27 where he is apprehended, and in great danger, 31 but by the chief captain is rescued, and permitted to speak to the people.

XXII. 1 Paul declares at large, how he was converted to the faith, 17 and called to his apostleship. 22 At the very mentioning of the Gentiles, the people exclaim on him. 24 He should have been scourged; 25 but claiming the privilege of a Roman, he escapes.

XXIII. 1 As Paul pleads his cause, 2 Ananias commands them to smite him. 7 Dissension among his accusers. 11 God encourages him. 14 The Jews' lying in wait for Paul, 20 is declared unto the chief captain. 27 He sends him to Felix the governor.

XXIV. 2 Paul being accused by Tertullus the orator, 10 answers for his life and doctrine. 24 He preaches Christ to the governor and his wife. 26 The governor hopes for a bribe, but in vain; 27 at last going out of his office, he leaves Paul in prison.

XXV. 1 The Jews accuse Paul before Festus. 8 He answers for himself, 11 and appeals to Cæsar. 14 Afterwards Festus opens his matter to king Agrippa, 23 and he is brought forth. 25 Festus declares him to have done nothing worthy of death.

XXVI. 2 Paul, in the presence of Agrippa, declares his life from his childhood, 12 and how miraculously he was converted and called to his apostleship. 24 Festus charges him to be mad, whereunto he answers modestly. 28 Agrippa is almost persuaded to be a christian. 31 The whole company pronounce him innocent.

XXVII. 1 Paul shipping towards Rome, 10 foretells the danger of the voyage, 11 but is not believed. 14 They are tossed to and fro with tempest, 41 and suffer shipwreck, 22, 34, 44 yet all come safe to land.

XXVIII. 1 Paul, after his shipwreck, is kindly entertained by the Barbarians. 5 The viper on his hand hurts him not. 8 He heals many diseases in the island. 11 They depart towards Rome. 17 He declares to the Jews the cause of his coming. 24 After his preaching some were persuaded, and some believed not: 30 yet he preaches there two years.

ROMANS.

I. Paul commends his calling to the Romans, 9 and his desire to come to them. 16 What his gospel is, and the righteousness which it shews. 18 God is angry with all manner of sin. 21 What were the sins of the Gentiles.

II. 1 They that sin, though they condemn it in others, cannot excuse themselves, 6 and much less escape the judgment of God, 9 whether they be Jews or Gentiles. 14 The Gentiles cannot escape, 17 nor yet the Jews, 25 whom their circumcision shall not profit, if they keep not the law.

III. 1 The Jews' prerogative; 3 which they have not lost; 9 howbeit the law convinces them also of sin. 20 Therefore no flesh is justified by the law, 28 but all, without difference, by faith only: 31 and yet the law is not abolished.

IV. 1 Abraham's faith was imputed to him for righteousness, 10 before he was circumcised. 13 By faith only he and his seed received the promise. 16 Abraham is the father of all that believe. 24 Our faith also shall be imputed to us for righteousness.

V. 1 Being justified by faith, we have peace with God, 2 and joy in our hope; 8 that since we were reconciled by his blood, when we were enemies, 10 we shall much more be saved, being reconciled. 12 As sin and death came by Adam, 17 so much more righteousness and life by Jesus Christ. 20 Where sin abounded, grace did superabound.

VI. 1 We may not live in sin, 2 for we are dead unto it, 3 as appears by our baptism. 12 Let not sin reign any more, 18 because we have yielded ourselves to the service of righteousness, 23 and for that death is the wages of sin.

VII. 1 No law hath power over a man longer than he liveth. 4 But we are dead to the law. 7 Yet is not the law sin, 12 but holy, just, and good, 16 as I acknowledge who am grieved because I cannot keep it.

VIII. 1 They that are in Christ, and live according to the Spirit, are free from condemnation. 5, 13 What harm comes of the flesh, 6, 14 and what good of the Spirit: 17 and what of being God's children, 19 whose glorious deliverance all things long for. 29 It was beforehand decreed from God. 38 What can sever us from his love?

IX. 1 Paul is sorry for the Jews. 7 All the seed of Abraham were not the children of the promise. 18 God hath mercy upon whom he will. 21 The potter may do with his clay what he list. 25 The calling of the Gentiles, and rejecting of the Jews, were foretold. 32 The cause why so few Jews embraced the righteousness of faith.

X. 5 The Scripture sheweth the difference betwixt the righteousness of the law, and that of faith, 11 and that all, both Jew and Gentile, that believe, shall not be confounded, 18 and that the Gentiles shall receive the word, and believe. 19 Israel was not ignorant of these things.

XI. 1 God hath not cast off all Israel. 7 Some were elected, though the rest were hardened. 16 There is hope of their conversion. 18 The Gentiles may not insult upon them: 26 for there is a promise of their salvation. 33 God's judgments are unsearchable.

XII. 1 God's mercies must move us to please God. 3 Not to think highly of oneself, 6 but attend every one on that calling wherein he is placed. 9 Love without dissimulation. 19 Revenge is especially forbidden.

XIII. 1 Subjection, and many other duties, we owe to the magistrates. 8 Love is the fulfilling of the law. 11 Gluttony and drunkenness, and the works of darkness, are out of season in the time of the gospel.

XIV. 3 Men may not contemn nor condemn each other for things indifferent; 13 but take heed that they give no offence in them: 15 for that the apostle proves unlawful by many reasons.

XV. 1 The strong must bear with the weak. 2 We may not please ourselves, 3 for Christ did not so, 7 but receive one another, as Christ did us all, 8 both Jews, 9 and Gentiles. 15 Paul excuseth his writing, 28 and promises to see them, 33 and desires their prayers.

XVI. 3 Paul wills the brethren to greet many, 17 and advises them to take heed of those which cause dissension and offences, 21 and after sundry salutations, ends with praise and thanks to God.

I CORINTHIANS.

I. After his salutation and thanksgiving, 10 he exhorts them to unity, 12 and reproves their dissensions. 18 God destroys the wisdom of the wise, 21 by the foolishness of preaching, 26 and calls not the wise, mighty, and noble, 27, 28 but the foolish, weak, and men of no account.

II. 1 He declares that his preaching, though it bring not excellency of speech, or of 4 human wisdom; yet consists in the 4, 5 power of God; and so far excels 6 the wisdom of this world, and 9 human sense, as that 14 the natural man cannot understand it.

III. 2 Milk is fit for children. 3 Strife and division are arguments of a fleshly mind. 7 He that plants, and he that waters, is nothing. 9 The ministers are God's fellow-workmen. 11 Christ the only foundation. 16 Men the temples of God, 17 which must be kept holy. 19 The wisdom of this world is foolishness with God.

IV. 1. In what account the ministers ought to be had. 7 We have nothing which we have not received. 9 The apostles spectacles to the world, angels, and men, 13 the filth and off-scouring of the world; 15 yet our fathers in Christ, 16 whom we ought to follow.

V. 1 The incestuous person, 6 is cause rather of shame unto them, than of rejoicing. 7 The old leaven is to be purged out. 10 Heinous offenders are to be shunned and avoided.

VI. 1 The Corinthians must not vex their brethren, in going to law with them; 6 especially under infidels. 9 The unrighteous shall not inherit the kingdom of God. 15 Our bodies are the members of Christ, 19 and temples of the Holy Ghost: 16, 17 they must not therefore be defiled.

VII. 2 Of marriage, 4 shewing it to be a remedy against fornication; 10 and that the bond thereof ought not lightly to be dissolved. 18, 20 Every man must be content with his vocation. 25 Virginity wherefore to be embraced, 35 and for what respects we may either marry, or abstain from marrying.

VIII. 1 To abstain from meats offered to idols: 8, 9 not to abuse our Christian liberty, to the offence of our brethren: 11 but must bridle our knowledge with charity.

IX. 1 He shews his liberty, 7 and that the minister ought to live by the gospel: 15 yet that himself hath of his own accord abstained 18 to be either chargeable to them, 22 or offensive to any in matters indifferent. 24 Our life is like a race.

X. 1 The sacraments of the Jews, 6 are types of ours, 7 and their punishments, 11 examples for us. 14 We must flee from idolatry, 21 and not make the Lord's table the table of devils: 24 and in things indifferent we should have regard to the weak brethren.

XI. 1 He reproves them, because in holy assemblies 4 their men prayed with their heads covered, and 6 their women with heads uncovered: 17 and because generally their meetings were not for the better, but for the worse; as, 21 namely, in profaning with their own feasts the Lord's supper. 23 Lastly, he calls them to the first institution thereof.

XII. 1 Spiritual gifts 4 are divers, 7 yet all to profit withal; 8 and to that end are diversely bestowed: 12 that by the like proportion, as the members of a natural body tend all to the 16 mutual decency, 22 service, and 26 succour of the same body; 27 so we should do one for another, to make up the mystical body of Christ.

XIII. 1 All gifts, 2, 3 how excellent soever, are nothing worth without charity. 4 The praises thereof, and 13 prelation before hope and faith.

XIV. 1 Prophecy is commended, 2, 3, 4 and preferred before speaking with tongues, 6 by a comparison drawn from musical instruments. 12 Both must be referred to edification, 22 as to their true and proper end. 26 The true use of each is taught, 29 and the abuse taxed. 34 Women are forbidden to speak in the church.

XV. 3 By Christ's resurrection, 12 he proves the necessity of ours, against all such as deny the resurrection of the body. 21 The fruit 35 and manner thereof, 51 and of the changing them that shall be found alive at the last day.

XVI. 1 He exhorts them to relieve the want of the brethren at Jerusalem; 10 commends Timothy; 13 and after friendly admonitions, 16 shuts up his epistle with divers salutations.

II CORINTHIANS.

I. The apostle encourages them against troubles, by the comforts and deliverances which God had given him, as in all his afflictions, 8 so particularly in his late danger in Asia: 12 and calling both his own conscience, and theirs, to witness, of his sincere manner of preaching the immutable truth of the gospel, 15 he excuseth his not coming to them, as proceeding not of lightness, but of his lenity towards them.

II. 1 Having shewed the reason why he came not to them, 6 he requires them to forgive and to comfort that excommunicated person, 10 even as himself also, upon his true repentance, had forgiven him: 12 declaring withal why he departed from Troas to Macedonia, 14 and the happy success which God gave to his preaching in all places.

III. 1 Lest their false teachers should charge him with vain glory, he shews the faith and graces of the Corinthians, to be a sufficient commendation of his ministry. 6 Whereupon entering a comparison between the ministers of the law and of the gospel, 12 he proves that his ministry is so far the more excellent, as the gospel of life and liberty is more glorious than the law of condemnation.

IV. 1 He declares how he hath used all sincerity and faithful diligence in preaching the gospel; 7 and how the troubles and persecutions which he daily endured for the same, did redound to the praise of God's power, 12 to the benefit of the church, 16 and to the apostle's own eternal glory.

V. 1 That in his assured hope of immortal glory, 9 and in expectation of it, and of the general judgment, he labours to keep a good conscience, 12 not that he may herein boast of himself, 14 but as one that having received life from Christ, lives as a new creature to Christ only, 18 and by his ministry of reconciliation, to reconcile others also in Christ to God.

VI. 1 That he hath approved himself a faithful minister of Christ, both by his exhortations, 3 and by integrity of life, 4 and by patient enduring all kinds of affliction and disgraces for the gospel. 10 Of which he speaks the more boldly amongst them, because his heart is open to them, 13 and he expects the like affection from them again: 14 exhorts them to flee the society and pollutions of idolaters, as being themselves temples of the living God.

VII. 1 He proceeds in exhorting them to purity of life, 2 and to bear him like affection as he doth to them. 3 Whereof, lest they might seem to doubt, he declares what comfort he took in his afflictions, by the report which Titus gave of their godly sorrow, which his former epistle had wrought in them, 13 and of their loving kindness and obedience towards Titus, answerable to his former boastings of them.

VIII. 1 He stirs them up to a liberal contribution for the poor saints at Jerusalem, by the example of the Macedonians, by commendation of their former forwardness, 9 by the example of Christ, 14 and by the spiritual profit that should redound to themselves thereby: 16 commending to them the integrity and willingness of Titus, and those other brethren, who, upon his request, exhortation, and commendation, were purposely come to them for this business.

IX. 1 He yields the reason why, though he knew their forwardness, yet he sent Titus and his brethren beforehand: 6 and he proceeds in stirring them up to bountiful alms, as being but a kind of sowing of seed, 10 which shall return a great increase to them, 13 and occasion a great sacrifice of thanksgiving unto God.

X. 1 Against the false apostles, who disgraced the weakness of his person and bodily presence, he sets out the spiritual might and authority, with which he is armed against all adverse powers; 7 assuring them that at his coming he will be found as mighty in word, as he is now in writing, being absent. 12 And withal taxing them for extending themselves beyond their compass, and vaunting themselves of other men's labours.

XI. 1 Out of his jealousy over the Corinthians, who seemed to make more account of the false apostles than of him, he entereth into a forced commendation of himself, 5 of his equality with the chief apostles, 7 of his preaching the gospel to them freely, and without their charge: 13 shewing that he was not inferior to those deceitful workers in any legal prerogative; 23 and in the service of Christ, and in all kind of sufferings for his ministry, far superior.

XII. 1 For commending of his apostleship, though he might glory of his wonderful revelations, 9 yet he rather chooses to glory of his infirmities, 11 blaming them for forcing him to this vain boasting. 14 He promises to come to them again; but yet altogether in the affection of a father, 20 although he fears he shall, to his grief, find many offenders and public disorders there.

XIII. 1 He threateneth severity, and the power of his apostleship, against obstinate sinners: 5 and advising them to a trial of their faith, 7 and to reformation of their sins before his coming, 11 he concludeth his epistle with a general exhortation and a prayer.

GALATIANS.

I. He wonders that they have so soon left him, and the gospel; 8 and accurses those that preach another gospel than he did. 11 He learned the gospel not of men, but of God: 13 and shews what he was before his calling, 17 and what he did presently after it.

II. 1 He shews when he went up again to Jerusalem, and for what purpose: 3 and that Titus was not circumcised: 11 and that he resisted Peter, and told him the reason 14 why he and others, being Jews, do believe in Christ to be justified by faith, and not by works: 20 and that they live not in sin, who are so justified.

III. 1 He asks what moved them to leave the faith, and hang upon the law. 6 They that believe are justified, 9 and blessed with Abraham. 10 And this he shews by many reasons.

IV. 1 We were under the law till Christ came, as the heir is under his guardian till he be of age; 5 but Christ freed us from the law; 7 therefore we are servants no longer to it. 14 He remembers their good-will to him, and his to them; 22 and shews that we are the sons of Abraham by the free-woman.

V. 1 He moves them to stand in their liberty, 3 and not observe circumcision; but rather love, which is the sum of the law: 19 he reckoneth up the works of the flesh, 22 and the fruits of the Spirit; 25 and exhorts to walk in the Spirit.

VI. 1 He moves them to deal mildly with a brother that hath slipped, 2 and to bear one another's burdens; 6 to be liberal to their teachers; 9 and not weary of well-doing: 12 he shews what they intend that preach circumcision: 14 he glories in nothing, save the cross of Christ.

EPHESIANS.

I. After the salutation, 3 and thanksgiving for the Ephesians, 4 he treats of our election, 6 and adoption by grace, 11 which is the true and proper fountain of man's salvation; 13 and because the height of this mystery cannot easily be attained unto by man's power, 16 he prays that they may come 18 to the full knowledge and 20 possession thereof in Christ.

II. 1 By comparing what we were 3 by nature, with what we are by grace; 10 he declares, that we are made for good works: and 13 being brought near by Christ, should not live as 11 Gentiles, and 12 foreigners in time past, but as 19 citizens with the saints, and the family of God.

III. 5 The hidden mystery, 6 that the Gentiles should be saved, was made known to Paul by revelation; 8 and to him was that grace given, that 9 he should preach it. 13 He desires them not to faint for his tribulation, 14 and prays 19 that they may perceive the great love of Christ toward them.

IV. 1 He exhorts to unity; 7 and declares that God therefore gives divers 11 gifts to men, that his church might be 13 edified, and 15 grow up in Christ. 18 He calls them from the impurity of the Gentiles, 24 to put on the new man; 25 to cast off lying, and 29 corrupt communication.

V. 2 After general exhortations to love, 3 to flee fornication, 4 and all uncleanness, 7 not to converse with the wicked, 15 to walk warily, and to be 18 filled with the Spirit, 22 he descends to the particular duties, how wives ought to obey their husbands, 25 and husbands ought to love their wives, 32 even as Christ doth his church.

VI. 1 The duty of children to parents, 5 and servants to masters. 10 Our life is a warfare, 12 not only against flesh and blood, but also spiritual enemies. 13 The complete armour of a christian, 18 and how it ought to be used. 21 Tychicus is commended.

PHILIPPIANS.

I. Paul testifieth his thankfulness to God, and his love towards them, for the fruits of their faith, and fellowship in his sufferings, 9 daily praying to him for their increase in grace; 12 he shews what good the faith of Christ had received by his troubles at Rome, 21 and how ready he is to glorify Christ either by his life or death: 27 exhorting them to unity, 28 and to fortitude in persecution.

II. 1 He exhorts them to unity, and to all humbleness of mind, by the example of Christ's humility and exaltation: 12 to a careful proceeding in the way of salvation, that they be as lights to the wicked world, 16 and comforts to him their apostle, who is now ready to be offered up to God. 15 He hopes to send Timothy to them, whom he greatly commends, 25 as Epaphroditus also, whom he presently sends to them.

III. 1 He warns them to beware of the false teachers of the circumcision, 4 shewing that himself hath greater cause than they to trust in the righteousness of the law; 7 which notwithstanding he counts as dung and loss to gain Christ and his righteousness, 12 therein acknowledging his own imperfection. 15 He exhorts them to be thus minded, 17 to imitate him, 18 and to decline the ways of carnal men.

IV. 1 From particular admonitions, 4 he proceeds to general exhortations, 10 shewing how he rejoiced at their liberality towards him lying in prison, not so much for the supply of his own wants, as for the grace of God in them: 19 and concludes with prayer and salutations.

COLOSSIANS.

I. After salutation, Paul thanks God for their faith, 7 confirms the doctrine of Epaphras, 9 prays further for their increase in grace, 14 describes the true Christ, 21 encourageth them to receive Jesus Christ, and commends his own ministry.

II. 1 He still exhorts them to be constant in Christ, 8 to beware of philosophy and vain traditions, 18 worshipping of angels, 20 and legal ceremonies, which are ended in Christ.

III. 1 He shews where we should seek Christ. 5 He exhorts to mortification, to put off the old man, and to put on Christ; 12 exhorting to charity, humility, and other several duties.

IV. 1 He exhorts them to be fervent in prayer, 5 to walk wisely toward them that are not yet come to the true knowledge of Christ. 10 He salutes them, and wishes them all prosperity.

I THESSALONIANS.

I. The Thessalonians are given to understand both how mindful of them Paul was at all times in thanksgiving and prayer; 5 and also how well he was persuaded of the truth and sincerity of their faith and conversion to God.

II. 1 In what manner the gospel was brought and preached to the Thessalonians, and in what sort also they received it. 18 A reason is rendered both why Paul was so long absent from them, and also why he was so desirous to see them.

III. 1 Paul testifies his great love to the Thessalonians; partly by sending Timothy unto them to strengthen and comfort them; partly by rejoicing in their well-doing; 10 and partly by praying for them, and desiring a safe coming unto them.

IV. 1 He exhorts them to walk in all manner of godliness, 6 to live holy and justly, 9 to love one another, 11 and quietly to follow their own business; 13 and last of all to sorrow moderately for the dead: 15 and to his last exhortation is annexed a brief description of the resurrection, and second coming of Christ to judgment.

V. 1 He proceeds in the former description of Christ's coming to judgment, 14 and gives divers precepts, 23 and so concludes the epistle.

II THESSALONIANS.

I. Paul certifies them of the good opinion which he had of their faith, love, and patience; 11 and therewithal useth divers reasons for the comforting of them in persecution, whereof the chief is taken from the righteous judgment of God.

II. 1 He wills them to continue stedfast in the truth received; 3 shews that there shall be a departure from the faith, 8 and a discovery of antichrist, before the day of the Lord come: 15 and thereupon repeats his former exhortation, and prays for them.

III. 1 He begs their prayers for himself, 3 and testifies what confidence he has in them, 5 makes request to God in their behalf, 6 gives them divers precepts, especially to shun idleness and ill company, 16 and last of all concludes with prayer and salutation.

I TIMOTHY.

I. Timothy is put in mind of the charge which was given unto him by Paul at his going to Macedonia, 5 of the right use and end of the law, 11 of Paul's calling to be an apostle, 20 and Hymeneus and Alexander.

II. 1 That it is meet to pray and give thanks for all men, and the reason why. 9 How women should be attired. 12 They are not permitted to teach. 15 They shall be saved, notwithstanding the testimonies of God's wrath, in childbirth, if they continue in faith.

III. How bishops, deacons, and their wives, should be qualified; 14 and to what end Paul wrote to Timothy of these things. 15 Of the church, and the blessed truth therein taught and professed.

IV. 1 He foretells that in the latter times there shall be a departure from the faith. 6 And to the end that Timothy might not fail in doing his duty, he furnishes him with divers precepts relating thereto.

V. 1 Rules to be observed in reproving. 3 Of widows. 17 Of elders. 23 A precept for Timothy's health. 24 Some men's sins go before unto judgment, and some men's do follow after.

VI. 1 Of the duty of servants. 3 Not to have fellowship with new-fangled teachers. 6 Godliness is great gain, 10 and love of money the root of all evil. 11 What Timothy is to flee, and what to follow, 17 and whereof to admonish the rich. 20 To keep the purity of true doctrine, and to avoid profane janglings.

II TIMOTHY.

I. Paul's love to Timothy, and the unfeigned faith which was in Timothy himself, his mother, and grandmother. 5 He is exhorted to stir up the gift of God which was in him, 8 to be stedfast and patient in persecution, 13 and to persist in the form and truth of that doctrine which he had learned of him. 15 Phygellus and Hermogenes, and such like, are noted, and Onesiphorus is highly commended.

II. He is exhorted again to constancy and perseverance, and to do the duty of a faithful servant of the Lord in dividing the word aright, and shunning profane and vain babblings. 17 Of Hymeneus and Philetus. 19 The foundation of the Lord is sure. 22 He is taught whereof to beware, and what to follow after, and in what sort the servant of the Lord ought to behave himself.

III. 1 He advertises him of the times to come, 6 describes the enemies of the truth, 10 propounds unto him his own example, 16 and commends the holy Scriptures.

IV. 1 He exhorts him to do his duty with all care and diligence, 6 certifies him of the nearness of his death, 9 wills him to come speedily unto him, and 11 to bring Mark with him, and certain other things which he wrote for, 14 warns him to beware of Alexander the smith, 16 informs him what had befallen him at his first answering, 19 and soon after he concludes.

TITUS.

I. For what end Titus was left in Crete. 6 How they that are to be chosen ministers ought to be qualified. 11 The mouths of evil teachers to be stopped: 12 and what manner of men they be.

II. 1 Directions given unto Titus, both for his doctrine and life. 9 Of the duty of servants, and, in general, of all Christians.

III. 1 Titus is yet further directed by Paul both concerning the things he should teach, and not teach. 10 He is willed also to reject obstinate heretics: 12 which done, he appoints him both time and place, wherein he should come unto him, and so concludes.

PHILEMON.

Paul rejoices to hear of the faith and love of Philemon; 9 whom he desires to forgive his servant Onesimus, and lovingly to receive him again.

HEBREWS.

I. Christ in these last times coming to us from the Father, 4 is preferred above the angels, both in person and office.

II. 1 We ought to be obedient to Christ Jesus, 5 and that because he vouchsafed to take our nature upon him, 14 as it was necessary.

III. 1 Christ is more worthy than Moses: 7 therefore if we believe not in him, we shall be more worthy of punishment than hard-hearted Israel.

IV. 1 The rest of Christians is attained by faith. 12 The power of God's word. 14 By our High-priest, Jesus the Son of God, subject to infirmities, but not to sin, 16 we must and may go boldly to the throne of grace.

V. 1 The authority and honour of our Saviour's priesthood. 11 Negligence in the knowledge thereof is reproved.

VI. 1 He exhorts not to fall back from the faith, 11 but to be stedfast, 12 diligent, and patient to wait upon God, 13 because God is most sure in his promise.

VII. 1 Christ Jesus is a priest after the order of Melchisedec, 11 and so far more excellent than the priests of Aaron's order.

VIII. 1 By the eternal priesthood of Christ, the Levitical priesthood of Aaron is abolished, 7 and the temporal covenant with the fathers, by the eternal covenant of the gospel.

IX. 1 The description of the rights and bloody sacrifices of the law, 11 far inferior to the dignity and perfection of the blood and sacrifice of Christ.

X. 1 The weakness of the law sacrifices. 10 The sacrifice of Christ's body once offered, 14 for ever hath taken away sins. 19 An exhortation to hold fast the faith, with patience and thanksgiving.

XI. 1 What faith is. 6 Without faith we cannot please God. 7 The worthy fruits thereof in the fathers of old time.

XII. 1 An exhortation to constant faith, patience, and godliness. 22 A commendation of the New Testament above the Old.

XIII. 1 Divers admonitions, as to charity, 4 to honest life, 5 to avoid covetousness, 7 to regard God's preachers, 9 to take heed of strange doctrines, 10 to confess Christ, 16 to give alms, 17 to obey governors, 18 to pray for the apostle. 20 The conclusion.

JAMES.

I. We are to rejoice under the cross, 5 to ask wisdom of God, 13 and in our trials not to impute our weakness or sins unto him, 22 but rather to hearken to the word, to meditate in it, and do thereafter: 26 otherwise men may seem, but never be, truly religious.

II. 1 It is not agreeable to Christian profession to regard the rich, and to despise the poor brethren: 13 rather we are to be loving and merciful; 14 and not to boast of faith where no fruits are, 17 which is but a dead faith, 19 the faith of devils, 21 and not of Abraham, 25 and Rahab.

III. 1 We are not rashly or arrogantly to reprove others, 5 but rather to bridle the tongue, a little member, but a powerful instrument of much good, and great harm. 13 They who be truly wise, be mild and peaceable without envying and strife.

IV. 1 We are to strive against covetousness, 4 intemperance, 5 pride, 11 detraction, and rash judgment of others: 13 and not to be confident in the good success of worldly business; but mindful ever of the uncertainty of this life, to commit ourselves and all our affairs to God's providence.

V. 1 Wicked rich men are to fear God's vengeance. 7 We ought to be patient in afflictions, after the example of the prophets and Job; 12 to forbear swearing; 13 to pray in adversity, to sing in prosperity; 16 to acknowledge mutually our several faults, to pray for each other; 19 and to restore a straying brother to the truth.

I PETER.

I. Peter blesses God for his manifold spiritual graces, 10 shewing that the salvation of Christ is no news, but a thing prophesied of old: 13 and exhorts them accordingly, to a godly conversation, forasmuch as they are now born anew by the word of God.

II. 1 He dehorts them from the breach of charity; 4 shewing that Christ is the foundation whereon they are built. 11 He beseeches them also to abstain from fleshly lusts, 13 to be obedient to magistrates, 18 and teaches servants how to obey their masters, 20 patiently suffering for well-doing, after the example of Christ.

III. 1 He teaches the duty of wives and husbands to each other, 8 exhorting all men to unity and love, 14 and to suffer persecution. 19 He declares also the benefits of Christ towards the old world.

IV. 1 He exhorts them to cease from sin by the example of Christ, and the consideration of the general end that now approaches: 12 and comforts them against persecution.

V. 1 He exhorts the elders to feed their flocks; 5 the younger to obey; 8 and all to be sober, watchful, and constant in the faith, 9 to resist the cruel adversary the devil.

II PETER.

I. Confirming them in hope of the increase of God's graces, 5 he exhorts them by faith and good works to make their calling and election sure: 12 whereof he is careful to remember them, knowing that his death is at hand: 16 and warns them to be constant in the faith of Christ, who is the true Son of God, by the eye-witness of the apostles' beholding his majesty, and by the testimony of the Father and the prophets.

II. 1 He foretells them of false teachers, shewing the impiety and punishment both of them and their followers; 7 from which the godly shall be delivered, as Lot was out of Sodom: 10 and more fully describes the manners of those profane and blasphemous seducers, whereby they may be the better known and avoided.

III. 1 He assures them of the certainty of Christ's coming to judgment, against those scorners who dispute against it: 8 warning the godly for the long patience of God, to hasten their repentance. 10 He describes also the manner how the world shall be destroyed: 11 exhorting them from the expectation thereof, to all holiness of life: 15 and again to think the patience of God to tend to their salvation, as Paul wrote to them in his epistles.

I JOHN.

I. He describes the person of Christ, in whom we have eternal life by a communion with God. 5 Holiness of life will testify the truth of that our communion. Faith assures us of the forgiveness of our sins by Christ's death.

II. 1 He comforts them against the sins of infirmity. 3 Rightly to know God, is to keep his commandments, 9 to love our brethren, 15 and not to love the world. 18 We must beware of seducers: 20 from whose deceits the godly are safely preserved by perseverance through faith.

III. 1 He declares the singular love of God towards us, in making us his sons; 3 who therefore ought obediently to keep his commandments, 11 as also brotherly to love one another.

IV. 1 He warns them not to believe all teachers who boast of the Spirit, but to try them by the rules of the Christian faith: 7 and by many reasons exhorts to brotherly love.

V. 1 He that loves God, loves his children, and keeps his commandments; 3 which to the faithful are light, and not grievous. 9 Jesus is the Son of God, able to save us, 14 and to hear our prayers, which we make for ourselves, and for others.

II JOHN.

He exhorts a certain honourable matron, with her children, to persevere in Christian love and belief, 8 lest they love the reward of their former profession; 10 and to have nothing to do with those seducers that bring not the true doctrine of Christ Jesus.

III JOHN.

He commends Gaius for his piety, 5 and hospitality, 7 to true preachers; 9 complaining of the unkind dealing of ambitious Diotrephes on the contrary side, 11 whose evil example is not to be followed; 12 and gives special testimony to the good report of Demetrius.

JUDE.

He exhorts them to be constant in the profession of the faith. 4 False teachers are crept in to seduce them; for whose damnable doctrine and manners, horrible punishment is prepared: 20 whereas the godly, by the assistance of the Holy Spirit, and prayers to God, may persevere, and grow in grace, and keep themselves, and recover others out of the snares of those deceivers.

REVELATION.

I. John writes his Revelation to the seven churches of Asia, signified by the seven golden candlesticks. 7 The coming of Christ. 14 His glorious power and majesty.

II. 1 What is commanded to be written to the angels (that is, the ministers) of the churches of 1 Ephesus, 8 Smyrna, 12 Pergamos, 18 Thyatira: and what is commended, or found wanting, in them.

III. 1 The angel of the church of Sardis is reproved, 3 exhorted to repent, and threatened if he do not repent. 8 The angel of the church of Philadelphia 10 is approved for his diligence and patience. 15 The angel of Laodicea is rebuked, for being neither hot nor cold, 19 and admonished to be more zealous. 20 Christ stands at the door and knocks.

IV. 2 John sees the throne of God in heaven. 4 The four-and-twenty elders. 6 The four beasts full of eyes before and behind. 10 The elders lay down their crowns, and worship him that sat on the throne.

V. 1 The book sealed with seven seals: 9 which only the Lamb that was slain is worthy to open. 12 Therefore the elders praise him, 9 and confess that he redeemed them with his blood.

VI. 1 The opening of the seals in order, and what followed thereupon; containing a prophecy to the end of the world.

VII. 3 An angel seals the servants of God in their foreheads. 4 The number of them that were sealed: of the tribes of Israel a certain number, 9 of all other nations an innumerable multitude, which stand before the throne, clad in white robes, and palms in their hands. 14 Their robes were washed in the blood of the Lamb.

VIII. 1 At the opening of the seventh seal, 2 seven angels had seven trumpets given them. 6 Four of them sound their trumpets, and great plagues follow. 3 Another angel puts incense to the prayers of the saints on the golden altar.

IX. 1 A star falls from heaven at the sounding of the fifth angel, to whom is given the key of the bottomless pit. 2 He opens the pit, 3 and there come forth locusts like scorpions. 12 The first woe past. 13 The sixth trumpet sounds. 14 Four angels are let loose that were bound.

X. 1 A mighty strong angel appears with a book open in his hand. 6 He swears by him that lives for ever, that there shall be no more time. 9 John is commanded to take and eat the book.

XI. 3 The two witnesses prophesy. 6 They have power to shut heaven, that it rain not. 7 The beast shall fight against them, and kill them. 8 They lie unburied, 11 and after three days and an half rise again. 14 The second woe is past. 15 The seventh trumpet sounds.

XII. 1 A woman clothed with the sun travails. 4 The great red dragon stands before her, ready to devour her child. 6 When she was delivered she fled into the wilderness. 7 Michael and his angels fight with the dragon, and prevail. 13 The dragon being cast down unto the earth, persecutes the woman.

XIII. 1 A beast rises out of the sea, with seven heads and ten horns, to whom the dragon gives his power. 11 Another beast comes up out of the earth; 14 causes an image to be made of the former beast, 15 and that men should worship it, 16 and receive his mark.

XIV. 1 The Lamb, standing on mount Sion, with his company; 6 an angel preaches the gospel. 8 The fall of Babylon. 15 The harvest of the world, and putting in of the sickle. 20 The vintage and wine-press of the wrath of God.

XV. 1 The seven angels with the seven last plagues. 3 The song of them that overcome the beast. 7 The seven vials full of the wrath of God.

XVI. 2 The angels pour out the vials full of wrath: 6 The plagues that follow thereupon. 15 Christ comes as a thief. Blessed are they that watch.

XVII. 3, 4 A woman arrayed in purple and scarlet, with a golden cup in her hand, sits upon the beast, 5 which is great Babylon, the mother of all abominations. 9 The interpretation of the seven heads, 12 and the ten horns. 14 The victory of the Lamb. 16 The punishment of the whore.

XVIII. 2 Babylon is fallen. 4 The people of God commanded to depart out of her. 9 The kings of the earth, 11 with the merchants and mariners, lament over her. 20 The saints rejoice for the judgments of God upon her.

XIX. 1 God is praised in heaven for judging the great whore, and avenging the blood of his saints. 7 The marriage of the Lamb. 10 The angel will not be worshipped. 17 The fowls called to the great slaughter.

XX. 2 Satan bound for a thousand years. 5 The first resurrection: 6 they are blessed that have part therein. 7 Satan let loose again. 8 Gog and Magog. 10 The devil cast into the lake of fire and brimstone. 12 The last and general resurrection.

XXI. 1 A new heaven and a new earth. 10 The heavenly Jerusalem, with a full description thereof. 23 She needeth no sun, the glory of God is her light. 24 The kings of the earth bring their riches unto her.

XXII. 1 The river of the water of life. 2 The tree of life. 5 The light of the city of God is himself. 9 The angel will not be worshipped. 18 Nothing may be added to the word of God, nor taken therefrom.

PRINTED FOR THE PUBLISHERS

BY

WILLIAM CLOWES AND SONS, LIMITED

LONDON AND BECCLES

1292. 165

PRINTED IN GREAT BRITAIN